THE MOTION PICTURE GUIDE

THE MOTION PICTURE GUIDE

INDEX
A - J

with
Alternate Title Index
Series Index
Awards Index

Jay Robert Nash
Stanley Ralph Ross

CINEBOOKS, INC.
Chicago, 1987
Publishers of THE COMPLETE FILM RESOURCE CENTER

Publishers: Jay Robert Nash, Stanley Ralph Ross; **Editor-in-Chief:** Jay Robert Nash; **Executive Editor:** Stanley Ralph Ross; **Associate Publisher:** Kenneth H. Petchenik; **Senior Editor-in-Charge:** Jim McCormick; **Senior Editors:** David Tardy, Robert B. Connelly; **Production Editor:** William Leahy; **Associate Editors:** Oksana Lydia Creighton, Jeffrey H. Wallenfeldt, Edie McCormick, Michaela Touhy, Jeannette Hori; **Senior Staff Writer:** James J. Mulay; **Staff Writers:** Daniel Curran, Michael Theobald, Arnie Bernstein, Phil Pantone, Brian Brock; **Contributing Editors:** Andrew S. Ross, Dan Harrison, James Gibson, Marshall Hyman, Marla Brooks; **Art Production and Book Design:** Cathy Anetsberger; **Research Staff:** Shelby Payne, William C. Clogston.

Editorial and Sales Offices: CINEBOOKS, 990 Grove, Evanston, Illinois 60201.

Library of Congress Catalog Number: 85-71145
ISBN: 0-933997-00-0 THE MOTION PICTURE GUIDE (10 Vols.)
0-933997-11-6 THE MOTION PICTURE GUIDE (2 Vols.)
0-933997-12-4 THE MOTION PICTURE GUIDE (Vol. XI-Index)

Printed in the United States
First Edition

1 2 3 4 5 6 7 8 9 10

Table of Contents

Alternate Title Index

Since many films are known by more than one title, and films are often released in Great Britain under titles other than those used in the United States, the Motion Picture Guide offers extensive cross referencing of titles. This index provides a listing of alternate titles (shown as AKA's in the MPG) and Great Britain titles (shown as GB's in the MPG), divided into four sections to aid users in locating films which they may know by titles other than the main ones used in these volumes.

The first section is a listing of MPG titles followed by the alternate title(s) under which the films may have been released. The second section is an alphabetical listing of alternate titles followed by the title under which the film is listed in the MPG. Section three is a listing of MPG titles followed by the title which was used for the release of the film in Great Britain. The last section offers an alphabetical listing of Great Britain titles followed by the title under which the film is listed in the MPG.

MPG TITLE TO ALTERNATE TITLE (AKA)

Below is an alphabetical listing of MPG titles, followed by the alternate title(s) (AKA's) under which the film may have been released.

* Denotes films which appear in the Miscellaneous Talkie section, Volume IX.
** Denotes films which appear in the 1984 film section, Volume IX.

A Nous Amours (1984, Fr.)**
 To Our Lovers
Abraham our Patriarch (1933)*
 Eternal Jew, The
Abandoned (1949)
 Abandoned Woman
Abdulla the Great (1956, Brit./Egypt)
 Abdulla's Harem
Abominable Snowman of the Himalayas, The (1957, Brit.)
 Abominable Snowman
Accused, The (1949)
 Strange Deception
Acid Eaters, The (1968)*
 Acid People, The
Act of Murder, An (1948)
 Live Today for Tomorrow
Actor's Revenge, An (1963, Jap.)
 Revenge of Yuki-No-Jo, The
Adalen 31 (1969, Swed.)
 Adalen Riots
Adam and Evelyne (1950, Brit.)
 Adam and Evalyn
Adam's Woman (1972, Aus.)
 Return of the Boomerang
Adele Hasn't Had Her Supper Yet (1978, Czech.)
 Dinner for Adele
 Nick Carter in Prague
Admirable Crichton, The (1957, Brit.)
 Paradise Lagoon
Adventurers, The (1951, Brit.)
 Great Adventure, The
 Fortune in Diamonds
Adventures of a Young Man (1962)
 Hemingway's Adventures of a Young Man
Adventures of Pinocchio, The (1978)*
 Pinocchio
Adventures of Rabbi Jacob, The (1973, Fr.)
 Mad Adventures of "Rabbi" Jacob, The
Adventures of Tartu (1943, Brit.)
 Tartu
Affairs of Adelaide (1949, U.S./Brit.)
 Forbidden Street
Affairs of Robin Hood, The (1981)*
 Ribald Tales of Robin Hood, The
 Gosh!
 Starlet, The
Affairs of Dr. Holl (1954, Ger.)
 Angelika
Age of Infidelity (1958)
 Death of a Cyclist
Albert, R.N. (1953, Brit.)
 Break to Freedom
Albuquerque (1948)
 Silver City
Alice of Wonderland in Paris (1966)*
 Alice in Wonderland in Paris
 Alice of Wonderland in New Adventures
 Alice of Wonderland
Alice, Sweet Alice (1978)
 Communion
 Holy Terror
Alien Thunder (1975)
 Dan Candy's Law
Alien Zone (1978)*
 House of the Dead, The
Aliki—My Love (1963, U.S./Gr.)*
 Aliki

All Screwed Up (1976, Ital.)
 All in Place
 Nothing in Order
All the Young Wives (1975)*
 You All Come
 Race, The
 Naked Rider
All These Women (1964, Swed.)
 Now About All These Women
All Things Bright and Beautiful (1979, Brit.)
 It Shouldn't Happen to a Vet
Allotment Wives, Inc. (1945)
 Woman in the Case
Alone on the Pacific (1964, Jap.)
 My Enemy the Sea
American Empire (1942)
 My Son Alone
American Raspberry (1980)*
 Prime Time
Amorous Adventures of Don Quixote and Sancho Panza (1976)*
 Erotic Adventures of Super Knight, The
Amorous Mr. Prawn, The (1965, Brit.)
 Playgirl and the War Minister, The
Amos 'n' Andy (1930)
 Check and Double Check
Anatahan (1953, Jap.)
 Saga of Anatahan
And God Created Woman (1957, Fr,)
 And Woman...Was Created
Andrea (1979)*
 Sex & Violence
Andy Warhol's Dracula (1974)*
 Blood for Dracula
 Young Dracula
Andy Warhol's Frankenstein (1974)*
 Flesh for Frankenstein
Angel, Angel Down We Go (1969)
 Cult of the Damned
Angels' Wild Women (1972)*
 Wild Women
 Angels' Dirty Women
 Screaming Angels
Anything Goes (1936)
 Tops is the Limit
Apache Gold (1965, Ger.)
 Winnetou the Warrior
 Winnetou
Ape Creature, The (1968)*
 Gorilla of Soho, The
 Gorilla Gang, The
April Blossoms (1937)
 April Romance
Ariane (1931)
 Loves of Ariane, The
Arousers, The (1973)
 Sweet Kill
 Kiss from Eddie, A
Arson Gang Busters (1938)
 Arson Racket Squad
Assault (1971, Brit.)
 In the Devil's Garden
Assignment Outer Space (1960, Ital.)
 Space Men
Assignment Terror (1970, Ger./Span./Ital.)
 Dracula vs. Frankenstein
Asylum (1972, Brit.)
 House of Crazies
Asylum of Satan (1972)*
 Satan's Spectrum

Atlantic City (1981, U.S./Can.)
 Atlantic City, U.S.A.
Atlas Against the Czar (1964, Ital.)
 Maciste Against the Czar
Atomic Brain, The (1964)
 Monstrosity
Ator (1982)*
 Ator, the Fighting Eagle
 Ator L'Invincible
Atragon (1965, Jap.)
 Atoragon
 Ataragon, the Flying Supersub
Attack at Noon, Sunday (1971)*
 Noon Sunday
Attack of the Giant Horny Gorilla (1976, US/Korea)
 A*P*E
Attack of the Giant Leeches (1959)
 Giant Leeches, The
Attack of the Mushroom People (1964, Jap.)
 Matango, Fungus of Terror
 Curse of the Mushroom People
Au Hasard, Balthazar (1970, Fr.)
 Balthazar
Au Pair Girls (1973, Brit.)*
 Young Playmates, The
Austerlitz (1960, Fr./Ital./Yugo.)
 Battle of Austerlitz, The
Avenger, The (1962, Fr./Ital.)
 Last Glory of Troy, The
Awful Dr. Orloff, The (1964, Span./Fr.)
 Cries of the Night
Axe (1977)*
 Lisa, Lisa
 California Axe Murder
Aztec Mummy, The (1957, Mex.)
 Aztec Mummy vs. the Human Robot, The

Babes in Toyland (1934)
 March of the Wooden Soldiers
Baby Needs a New Pair of Shoes*
 Niggerich
Back at the Front (1952)
 Willie and Joe Back at the Front
Background (1953, Brit.)
 Edge of Divorce
Bad Boy (1938, Brit.)
 Branded
Bad Georgia Road (1977)*
 Out of Control
Bad Manners (1984)**
 Growing Pains
Bambole! (1965, Ital.)
 Dolls, The
 Four Kinds of Love
Band of Outsiders (1966, Fr.)
 Outsiders, The
Bandits in Rome (1967)*
 Rome Like Chicago
Bang, Bang, You're Dead (1966)
 Bang, Bang!
Bang! You're Dead (1954, Brit.)
 Game of Danger
Banished (1978, Jap.)
 Melody in Gray
Bank Holiday (1938, Brit.)
 Three on a Weekend
Barbarella (1968, Fr./Ital.)
 Barbarella, Queen of the Galaxy

Bargain with Bullets*
  Gangsters on the Loose
Barn of the Naked Dead (1976)
  Terror Circus
Baron Munchausen (1962, Czech.)
  Baron Prasil
Barracuda (1978)
  Lucifer Project, The
Barrets of Wimpole Street (1934)
  Forbidden Alliance
Bat People, The (1974)
  It Lives By Night
Battle, The (1934, Brit./Fr.)
  Thunder in the East
  Hara-Kiri
Battle in Outer Space (1960, Jap.)
  World of Space, The
Battle of the Villa Fiorita, The (1965, Brit.)
  Affair of the Villa Fiorita
Battle of the Worlds (1965, Ital.)
  Planet of the Lifeless Men
Battletruck (1982)
  Warlords of the 21st Century
Bay of Saint Michel, The (1963, Brit.)
  Operation Mermaid
Beachcomber, The (1938, Brit.)
  Vessels of Wrath
Beast in the Cellar, The (1971, Brit.)
  Are You Dying Young Man?
Beast of the City, The (1932)
  City Sentinel
Beast of Blood (1970, U.S./Phil.)
  Return of the Horrors of Blood Island
  Beast of the Dead
Beasts of Berlin (1939)
  Hitler—Beast of Berlin
Beat Generation, The (1959)
  This Rebel Age
"Beat" Girl (1962, Brit.)
  Wild for Kicks
Best Friends (1975)*
  Couples
Beautiful Stranger (1954, Brit.)
  Twist of Fate
Beautiful Swindlers, The (1967, Fr./Ital./Jap./Neth.)
  World's Greatest Swindles
Beauty and the Body (1963)*
  Beast and the Body
Beauty Jungle, The (1966, Brit.)
  Contest Girl
Behemoth, The Sea Monster (1959, Brit.)
  Giant Behemoth, The
Behind the Mask (1946)
  Shadow Behind the Mask, The
Bela Lugosi Meets a Brooklyn Gorilla (1952)
  Boys from Brooklyn, The
Bells (1981, (1981, Can.)
  Murder by Phone
  Calling, The
Beloved, The (1972)
  Restless
Beware the Black Widow (1968)*
  Black Widow
  Beware the Widow Spider
Beyond Control (1971)*
  What a Way to Die
Beyond the Door II (1979, Ital.)
  Shock
Beyond the Fog (1981, Brit.)
  Tower of Evil
  Horror of Snape Island
Beyond This Place (1959, Brit.)
  Web of Evidence
Big Carnival, The (1951)
  Ace in the Hole
  Human Interest Story, The
Big Operator, The (1959)
  Anatomy of a Syndicate
Big Show, The (1937)
  Home in Oklahoma
Big Town After Dark (1947)
  Underworld After Dark
Bill of Divorcement (1940
  Never to Love
Billy Two Hats (1973, Brit.)
  Lady and the Outlaw, The
Bird with the Crystal Plumage, The (1970, Ital./Ger.)
  Phantom of Terror, The
Birds Come to Die in Peru (1968, Fr.)
  Birds in Peru
Bizarre (1969)*
  Secrets of Sex
  Tales of the Bizarre
Bizet's Carmen (1984)**
  Carmen
Black Book, The (1949, Brit.)
  Reign of Terror

Black Godfather, The (1974)*
  Power to Spare
Black Heat (1976)*
  Girls' Hotel
Black Hooker (1974)*
  Don't Leave Go My Hand
Black Jack (1973)
  Wild in the Sky
Black Lolita (1975)*
  Busting Out
Black Roses (1936, Ger.)
  Did I Betray?
Blackenstein (1973)
  Black Frankenstein
Blazing Stewardesses (1975)*
  Jet Set, The
  Smoking Saddles
Blind Dead, The (1972, Span.)
  Tombs of the Blind Dead
Blood Bath (1966)
  Track of the Vampire
Blood Beast from Outer Space (1965, Brit.)
  Night Caller, The
Blood Beast Terror, The (1967, Brit.)
  Vampire-Beast Craves Blood, The
Blood Demon (1967, Ger.)
  Torture Chamber of Dr. Sadism, The
Blood Drinkers, The (1966, U.S./Phil.)
  Vampire People, The
Blood Feast (1976, Ital.)
  Feast of Flesh
Blood Feud (1979, Ital.)
  Revenge
Blood in the Streets (1975, Ital./Fr.)
  Revolver, The
Blood Kin (1969)*
  Last of the Mobile Hotshots, The
Blood of Dracula's Castle (1967)
  Dracula's Castle
Blood of Fu Manchu, The (1968, Brit.)
  Kiss and Kill
Blood on Satan's Claw, The (1970, Brit.)
  Satan's Claw
Blood Shack (1971)*
  Chooper, The
Blood Song (1982)*
  Bloodsong
Blood Thirst (1965)*
  Blood Thurst
Blood Tide (1982)
  Red Tide, The
Blood Waters of Doctor Z
  Zaat
Bloodeaters (1980)
  Forest of Fear
Bloodline (1979)
  Sidney Sheldon's Bloodline
Bloodsucking Freaks (1982)
  Incredible Torture Show, The
Bloody Birthday (1980)*
  Creeps
  Hide and Go Kill
Bloody Pit of Horror, the (1965, Ital.)
  Crimson Executioner
  Red Hangman, The
Bloomfield (1971, Brit./Israel)
  Hero, The
Blue Demon vs. the Infernal Brains (1967, Mex.)
  Cerebro Infernal
  Blue Demon vs. El Crimen
Blues for Lovers (1966, Brit.)
  Ballad in Blue
Body and Soul (1947)
  Affair of the Heart, An
Bombshell (1933)
  Blonde Bombshell
Bone (1972)
  Housewife
  Dial Rat for Terror
  Beverly Hills Nightmare
  Funny Bone
Bootleggers (1974)
  Bootlegger's Angel
Boots Turner (1973)*
  Brother on the Run
Bop Girl Goes Calypso (1957)
  Bop Girl
Born for Glory (1935)
  Forever England
Born to Kill (1975)
  Cockfighter
Boss Lady (1982)*
  Champagne for Breakfast
Boy of Two Worlds (1970)*
  Lure of the Jungle
Boy Ten Feet Tall, A (1965)
  Sammy Going South
Brady's Escape (1984, U.S./Hung.)**
  Long Ride, The

Brain of Blood (1971, Phil.)
  Creature's Revenge, The
Brass Ring, The (1975)*
  Frank Challenge—Manhunter
Breakers Ahead (1938, Brit.)
  As We Forgive
Breakthrough (1978, Ger.)
  Sergeant Steiner
Bride, The (1973)
  House that Cried Murder, The
Bride and the Beast, The (1958)
  Queen of the Gorillas
Bride of the Atom (1955)
  Bride of the Monster
Brides of Blood (1968)
  Blood Brides
  Grave Desires
  Island of Living Horror
Brighton Rock (1947, Brit.)
  Young Scarface
Broken Melody, The (1934, Brit.)
  Vagabond Violinist
Bubble, The (1967)
  Fantastic Invasion of Planet Earth
Burn! (1970
  Queimada!
Bus Stop (1956)
  Wrong Kind of Girl, The
Bushido Blade, The (1982, Brit./Aus.)
  Bloody Bushido Blade, The
Buster and Billie (1974)*
  Black Creek Billie
Butcher, Baker (Nightmare Maker) (1982)
  Night Warning
  Nightmare Maker

Cafe Colette (1937, Brit.)
  Danger In Paris
Cafe Hostess (1940)
  Streets of Missing Women
Caged Virgins (1972)*
  Crazed Vampire
  Virgins and the Vampires, The
Cain's Way (1969)
  Cain's Cutthroats
  Blood Seekers, The
Californian, The (1937)
  Gentleman from California, The
Call Him Mr. Shatter (1976, Hong Kong)
  Shatter
Call Northside 777 (1948)
  Calling Northside 777
Call of the Flesh (1930)
  Singer from Seville, The
Calliope (1971)*
  Love Is Catching
Camper John (1973)*
  I Spit on Your Grave
  Up Yours
  Pilgrim
  Once Upon a Tribe
Canaris (1955, Ger.)
  Canaris, Master Spy
Cannibals in the Streets (1982, Ital./Span.)
  Savage Apocalypse
  Slaughterers, The
  Cannibals in the City
  Virus
  Invasion of the Flesh Hunters
Cannon for Cordoba (1970)
  Dragon Master
Captain from Koepenick (1933, Ger.)
  Hauptmann Von Koepenick
Captive Women (1952)
  1,000 Years from Now
  3,000 A.D.
Carhops, The (1980)*
  Kitty Can't Help It
Carnival (1931, Brit.)
  Venetian Nights
Carry On Admiral (1957, Brit.)
  Ship Was Loaded, The
Carry on Jack (1963, Brit.)
  Carry On Venus
Cars That Ate Paris, The (1974, Aus.)
  Cars That Eat People, The
Cartouche (1962, Fr./Ital.)
  Swords of Blood
Casanova (1976, Ital.)
  Fellini's Casanova
Case of Clara Deane, The (1932)
  Strange Case of Clara Deane, The
Case of the Frightenend Lady, The (1940, Brit.)
  Frighteneed Lady, The
Case of the Red Monkey (1955, Brit.)
  Little Red Monkey

Casque D'Or (1956, Fr.)
 Golden Marie
Castillian, The (1963, Span./U.S.)
 Valley of the Swords
Castle of Fu Manchu, The (1968, Ger./Span./Ital./Brit.)
 Assignment Istanbul
Cat and Mouse (1958, Brit.)
 Desperate Men, The
Cat Women of the Moon (1953)
 Rocket to the Moon
Catch as Catch Can (1937, Brit.)
 Atlantic Episode
Catch My Soul (1974)
 To Catch a Spy
 Santa Fe Satan
Cathy's Curse (1977, Can.)
 Cauchemares
Castle of Blood (1964, Fr./Ital.)
 Danza Macabra
 Castle of Terror
 Coffin of Terror
Cattle Queen (1951)
 Queen of the West
Cauldron of Blood (1971, Span.)
 Blind Man's Bluff
Cavalry Command (1963, U.S./Phil.)
 Cavalleria Commandos
Centurion, The (1962, Fr./Ital.)
 Conqueror of Corinth
Cerebros Diabolicos (1966, Mex.)
 Aranas Infernales
Chain Gang Women (1972)*
 Chain, The
Challenge To Be Free (1976)
 Mad Trapper of the Yukon
Charlie Chan in the Secret Service (1937)
 Secret Service, The
Chasing Rainbows (1930)
 Road Show
Chastity Belt, The (1968, Ital.)
 On My Way to the Crusades I Met a Girl Who...
Che? (1973, Ital./Fr./Ger.)
 Diary of Forbidden Dreams
 What?
Cheaters, The (1961, Fr.)
 Peccatori in Blue Jeans
Cherokee Strip (1937)
 Strange Laws
Chesty Anderson, US Navy (1976)
 Anderson's Angels
Cheyenne (1947)
 Wyoming Kid, The
Child, The (1977)
 Kill and Go Hide!
Chilly Scenes of Winter (1982)
 Head Over Heels
Chimes at Midnight (1967, Span./Switz.)
 Falstaff
Chino (1976, Ital./Span./Fr,)
 Valdez, the Halfbreed
Christine Keeler Affair, The (1964, Brit.)
 Keeler Affair, The
 Scandal '64
Cheaters, The (1945)
 Castaway, The
Christmas Eve (1947)
 Sinner's Holiday
Chushingura (1963, Jap.)
 47 Samurai
 Loyal 47 Ronin
Circle, The (1959, Brit.)
 Vicious Circle, The
Circle of Deceit (1982, Fr./Ger.)
 False Witness
Circle of Iron (1979, Brit.)
 Silent Flute, The
Citizens Band (1977)
 Handle with Care
City of Secrets (1963, Ger.)
 Secrets of the City
City of the Walking Dead (1983, Span./Ital.)
 Nightmare City
 Nightmare
City Under the Sea (1965, Brit.)
 War Gods of the Deep
Clairvoyant, The (1935, Brit.)
 Evil Mind
Claws (1977)*
 Devil Bear
Cleopatra's Daughter (1963, Fr./Ital.)
 Daughter of Cleopatra
Climax, The (1967, Fr./Ital.)
 Too Much for One Man
Clones, The (1973)
 Clones
Clonus Horror, The (1979)
 Parts: The Clonus Horror
Closet Casanova, The (1979)*
 Paul, Lisa, & Caroline

Love Times Three
Code of Silence (1960)
 Killers' Cage
Colossus: The Forbin Project (1969)
 Forbin Project, The
 Colossus 1980
Colt .45 (1950)
 Thundercloud
Come and Get It (1936)
 Roaring Timbers
Comeback, The (1982, Brit.)
 Day the Screaming Stopped, The
Committee, The (1968, Brit.)
 Session with the Committee
Con Artists, The (1981, Ital.)
 Con Man, The
Concorde, The—Airport '79 (1979)
 Airport '79
Condemned Men (1946)*
 Four Shall Die
Confessional, The (1977, Brit.)
 House of Mortal Sin
Confessions of an Opium Eater (1962)
 Souls for Sale
 Secrets of a Soul
Confidentially Yours (1983, Fr.)
 Finally Sunday
Conquered City (1966, Ital.)
 Captive City, The
Conqueror Worm, The (1968, Brit.)
 Edgar Allan Poe's Conqueror Worm
Conquerors, The (1932)
 Pioneer Builders
Conspiracy in Teheran (1948, Brit.)
 Plot to Kill Roosevelt, The
Convicted (1950)
 One Way Out
Convicts Four (1962)
 Reprieve
Cool Sound from Hell, A (1959)*
 Young and the Beat, The
Corky (1972)
 Lookin' Good
Corpse of Beverly Hills, The (1965, Ger.)
 That Girl From Beverly Hills
Corridors of Blood (1962, Brit.)
 Doctor From Seven Dials, The
Corrupt (1984, Ital.)
 Order of Death
Corrupt Ones, The (1967, Ger.)
 Peking Medallion, The
 Hell to Macao
Corruption of Chris Miller, The (1979, Span.)
 Behind the Shutters
Cosmo Jones, Crime Smasher (1943)*
 Crime Smasher, The
Cotton Queen (1937, Brit.)
 Crying Out Loud
Count Dracula (1971, Ital./Span./Ger./Brit.)
 Bram Stoker's Count Dracula
Count Dracula and His Vampire Bride (1978, Brit.)
 Satanic Rites of Dracula
Count Your Bullets (1972)
 Cry for Me Billy
 Face to the Wind
 Naked Revenge
Counterfeit Commandos (1981, Ital.)
 Inglorious Bastards
Counterfeiters of Paris, The (1961, Fr./Ital.)
 Money, Money, Money
Country Boy (1966)
 Here Comes That Nashville Sound
Country Bride (1938, USSR)
 Rich Bride, The
Courage of Lassie (1946)
 Blue Sierra
Courageous Mr. Penn, The (1941, Brit.)
 Penn of Pennsylvania
Covergirl (1984, Can.)**
 Dreamworld
Craze (1974, Brit.)
 Infernal Idol, The
Crazies, The (1973)
 Code Name: Trixie
Crazy Knights (1944)
 Ghost Crazy
Crazy World of Julius Vrooder, The (1974)
 Vrooder's Hooch
Creature Wasn't Nice, The (1983)
 Spaceship
Creeper, The (1980, Can.)
 Rituals
Creeping Terror, The (1964)
 Crawling Monster, The
 Dangerous Charter
Creeping Unknown, The (1956, Brit.)
 Quartermass Experiment, The
Crest of the Wave (1954, Brit.)
 Seagulls Over Sorrento

Crime Does Not Pay (1962, Fr.)
 Gentle Art of Murder, The
Criminal at Large (1932, Brit.)
 Frightened Lady, The
Criminal Life of Archibaldo de la Cruz, The (1962, Mex.)
 Rehearsal for a Crime
Crimson Blade, The (1964, Brit.)
 Scarlet Blade, The
Crimson Cult, The (1970, Brit.)
 Curse of the Crimson Altar
 Crimson Altar, The
Cross My Heart (1937, Brit.)
 Loaded Dice
Crossroads (1942)
 Man Who Lost His Way, The
Cross-Up (1958)
 Tiger by the Tail
Crosswinds (1951)
 Jungle Attack
Crucible of Horror (1971, Brit.)
 Velvet House
Cry of the Battle (1963)
 To Be a Man
Cry of the Penguins (1972, Brit.)
 Mr. Forbush and the Penguins
Cry, The Beloved Country (1952, Brit.)
 African Fury
Cuba Crossing (1980)
 Kill Castro
 Assignment: Kill Castro
Cuban Rebel Girls (1960)
 Assault of the Rebel Girls
Curse of the Blood Ghouls (1969, Ital.)
 Slaughter of the Vampires, The
 Curses of the Ghouls
Curse of the Demon (1958)
 Night of the Demon
Curse of the Vampires (1970, U.S./Phil.)
 Creatures of Evil
Curse of the Voodoo (1965, Brit.)
 Curse of Simba
Curtain at Eight (1934)
 Backstage Mystery
Cutter and Bone (1981)
 Cutter's Way
Cycles South (1971)*
 Great American Escape, The
Cyclotrode X (1946)
 Crimson Ghost, The
Cynara (1932)
 I Was Faithless

D-Day, the Sixth of June (1956)
 Sixth of June, The
Daddy-O (1959)
 Out On Probation
Daddy's Deadly Darling (1984)**
 Daddy's Girl
 Pigs, The
Dagora the Space Monster (1964, Jap.)
 Dagora
 Space Monster Dagora
Daleks—Invasion Earth 2150 A.D. (1966, Brit.)
 Invasion Earth 2150 A.D.
Damon and Pythias (1962)
 Tyrant of Syracuse, The
Dan Matthews (1936)
 Calling of Dan Matthews, The
Dance of the Dwarfs (1983)*
 Jungle Heat
Danger: Diabolik (1968, Ital./Fr.)
 Diabolik
 Danger Diabolik
Daredevil in the Castle (1969, Jap.)
 Devil in the Castle
Daring Young Man, The (1942)
 Brownie
Dark August (1975)*
 Hant, The
Dark Delusion (1947)
 Cynthia's Secret
Dark Eyes of London (1961, Ger.)
 Dead Eyes of London, The
Dark Journey (1937, Brit.)
 Anxious Years, The
Dark Odyssey (1961)
 Passionate Sunday
Dark Sands (1938, Brit.)
 Jericho
Darkened Skies (1930)
 Dark Skies
Darkest Africa (1936)
 Batmen of Africa
 King of the Jungleland
Darktown Strutters (1975)
 Get Down and Boogie

Das Boot (1982, Ger.)
  Boat, The
Dawn Express, The (1942)
  Nazi Spy Ring
Day After Halloween, The (1961, Aus.)
  Snapshot
Day and the Hour, The (1963, Fr./Ital.)
  Today We Live
Day of the Animals (1977)
  Something Is Out There
Day the Hotline Got Hot, The (1968, Fr./Span.)
  Hot Line, The
Day the Lord Got Busted, The (1976)*
  Soul Hustler
  Loving Man, The
Day the Sky Exploded, The (1958, Fr./Ital.)
  Death from Outer Space
Day the War Ended (1961, USSR)
  First Day of Peace, The
Day Time Ended, The (1980, Span.)
  Vortex
Daydreamer, The (1975, Fr.)
  Absent-Minded
Dead Cert (1974)*
  Dead Certain
Dead End (1937)
  Cradle of Crime
Dead End Kids on Dress Parade (1939)
  Dead End Kids at Military School
Dead Kids (1981, Aus./New Zealand)
  Strange Behavior
Dead People (1974)
  Messiah of Evil
  Return of the Living Dead
  Revenge of the Screaming Dead
  Second Coming, The
Deadly Eyes (1974)
  Rats, The
Deadly Mantis, The (1957)
  Incredible Praying Mantis, The
Deadly Spawn, The (1983)
  Return of the Aliens: The Deadly Spawn
Dear Detective (1978, Fr.)
  Dear Inspector
Death at a Broadcast (1934, Brit.)
  Death at Broadcasting House
Death Collector (1976)
  Family Enforcer
Death in the Garden (1977, Fr./Mex.)
  Evil Eden
Death in the Sky (1937)
  Pilot X
Death is Called Engelchen (1963, Czech.)
  For We Too Do Not Forgive
Death Rage (1978)*
  Shadow of a Killer
Deathdream (1972, Can.)
  Death of Night
  Night Walk
  Veteran, The
Deathline (1973, Brit.)
  Raw Meat
Deathwatch (1980, Ger./Fr.)
  Death in Full View
Decline and Fall...of A Bird Watcher (1966, Brit.)
  Decline and Fall
Decoy for Terror (1970, Can.)
  Playgirl Killer
Dedee (1949, Fr.)
  Woman of Antwerp
Deep in the Heart (1983)
  Handgun
Deep Red (1976, Ital.)
  Hatchet Murders, The
  Dripping Deep Red
  Deep Red Hatchet Murders
Defeat of Hannibal, The (1937, Ital.)
  Scipio, the African
Defense of Volotchayevsk, The (1938, USSR)
  Volochayesk Days
Deliver Us from Evil (1975)*
  Joey
Dementia (1955)
  Daughter of Horror
Demoniaque (1958, Fr.)
  She Wolves, The
Demonoid (1981)
  Macabra
Department Store (1935, Brit.)
  Bargain Basement
Designing Women (1934, Brit.)
  House of Cards
Destiny of a Man (1961, USSR)
  Fate of a Man
Destructors, The (1974, Brit.)
  Marseilles Contract, The
Devil, The (1963, Ital.)
  To Bed or Not to Bed
  Amore in Stockholm

Devil Bat, The (1941)
  Killer Bats
Devil is a Sissy, The (1936)
  Devil Takes the Count, The
Devil and Daniel Webster, The (1941)
  All that Money Can Buy
  Here is a Man
  Certain Mr. Scratch, A
  Daniel and the Devil
Devil is an Empress, The (1939, Fr.)
  Checker Player, The
  Chess Player, The
Devil Made a Woman, The (1962, Span.)
  Girl Against Napoleon, A
Devil Strikes at Night, The (1959, Ger.)
  Nazi Terror at Night
  Nights When the Devil Came
Devil Times Five (1974)
  Peopletoys
  People Toys
  Horrible House on the Hill, The
Devil Within Her, The (1976, Brit.)
  I Don't Want to be Born
Devil's Commandment, The (1956, Ital.)
  Lust of the Vampires
Devil's Express (1975)
  Gang Wars
Devil's Hand, The (1961)
  Devil's Doll
  Naked Goddess, The
  Live to Love
Devil's Man, The (1967, Ital.)
  Devilman Story
Devil's Nightmare, The (1971, Bel./Ital.)
  Vampire Playgirls
Devil's Wanton, The (1962, Swed.)
  Prison
Diabolic Wedding (1972)*
  Diabolique Wedding
Diamond Horseshoe (1945)
  Billy Rose's Diamond Horseshoe
Dick Deadeye (1977)*
  Dick Deadeye, or Duty Done
Dick Tracy (1945)
  Dick Tracy, Detective
Dick Tracy Meets Gruesome (1947)
  Dick Tracy Meets Karloff
Dictator, The (1935, Brit./Ger.)
  For Love of a Queen
  Loves of a Dictator, The
Die, Monster, Die (1965, Brit.)
  Monster of Terror
Diplomatic Lover, The (1934, Brit.)
  How's Chances
Dirty Knight's Work (1976, Brit.)
  Trial by Combat
  Choice of Arms
Dirty Mouth (1971)*
  Dirtymouth
  Story of Lenny Bruce—Dirtymouth, The
Disobedient (1953, Brit.)
  Intimate Relations
Divine Nymph, The (1979, Ital.)
  Divine Creature
Do You Love Me? (1946)
  Kitten on the Keys
Dobbin, The (1939)*
  Light Ahead, The
Dr. Black and Mr. Hyde (1976)
  Watts Monster, The
Dr. Butcher, M.D. (1982, Ital.)
  Queen of the Cannibals
Dr. Ehrlich's Magic Bullet (1940)
  Story of Dr. Ehrlich's Magic Bullet, The
Dr. Frankenstein on Campus (1970, Can.)
  Flick
Dr. Kildare's Wedding Day (1941)
  Mary Names the Day
Dr. Terror's Gallery of Horrors (1967)
  Blood Suckers
  Return from the Past
Dodeska-Den (1970, Jap.)
  Clickety-Clack
Dogpound Shuffle (1975, Can.)
  Spot
Doll, The (1962, Fr.)
  He, She or It
Doll Squad, The (1973)
  Hustler Squad
Dollars for a Fast Gun (1969, Ital./Span.)
  100,000 Dollars for Lassiter
Don is Dead, The (1973)
  Beautiful but Deadly
Don't Answer the Phone (1980)
  Hollywood Strangler, The
Don't Open the Window (1974, Ital.)
  Breakfast at Manchester Morgue
  Living Dead at Manchester Morgue, The
Don't Say Die (1950, Brit.)
  Never Say Die

Don't Trust Your Husband (1948)
  Innocent Affair, An
Doolins of Oklahoma, The (1949)
  Great Manhunt, The
Dorian Gray (1970, Ital./Brit./Ger./Liechtenstein)
  Secret of Dorian Gray, The
Double Dynamite (1951)
  It's Only Money
Double Exposures (1937, Brit.)
  Alibi Breaker
Down Our Alley (1939, Brit.)
  Gang Show
Down to the Sea (1936)
  Down Under the Sea
Dracula A.D. 1972 (1972, Brit.)
  Dracula Today
Dracula and the Seven Golden Vampires (1978, Brit./Chin.)
  Legend of the Seven Golden Vampires
  Seven Brothers Meet Dracula
Dracula's Great Love (1972, Span.)
  Count Dracula's Great Love
  Vampire Playgirls
Dracula Sucks (1979)*
  Dracula's Bride
  Dracula Ssucks
Drake the Pirate (1935, Brit.)
  Elizabeth of England
Dream of a Cossack (1982, USSR)
  Cavalier of the Golden Star
Dream One (1984, Brit./Fr.)**
  Nemo
Dream Town (1973, Ger.)
  City of Dreams
Dressed to Kill (1946)
  Sherlock Holmes in Dressed to Kill
Dreyfus Case, The (1940, Ger.)
  Dreyfus
Drift Fence (1936)
  Texas Desperadoes
Drifter (1975)
  Two-Way Drifter
Driver's Seat, The (1975, Ital.)
  Identikit
Drums O' Voodoo (1934)
  She Devil
Drums of Jeopardy (1931)
  Mark of Terror
Duck, You Sucker (1972, Ital.)
  Fistful of Dynamite
Dulcimer Street (1948)
  London Belongs to Me
Dungeons of Harrow (1964)
  Dungeons of Horror
Dynamite Johnson (1978, Phil.)
  12 Million Dollar Boy, The
  New Adventures of the Bionic Boy, The

Eagle and the Hawk, The (1950)
  Spread Eagle
Eagle Over London (1973, Ital.)
  Eagles Over London
Early Autumn (1962, Jap.)
  Last of Summer
  End of Summer, The
Earth vs. the Flying Saucers (1956)
  Invasion of the Flying Saucers
Earth vs. the Spider (1958)
  Spider, The
Eaten Alive (1976)
  Death Trap
  Starlight Slaughter
  Horror Hotel Massacre
  Legend of the Bayou
Eboli (1980, Ital.)
  Christ Stopped at Eboli
Ebony, Ivory & Jade (1977)*
  Olympians
Echoes of a Summer (1976)
  Last Castle, The
Ecstasy (1940, Czech.)
  Symphony of Love
Eden Cried (1967)
  In the Fall of '55 Eden Cried
Edge of the City (1957)
  Man is Ten Feet Tall, A
Effects (1980)
  Manipulator, The
Effi Briest (1974, Ger.)
  Fontane Effi Briest
8 1/2 (1963, Ital.)
  Federico Fellini's 8 1/2
Eighteen and Anxious (1957)
  No Greater Sin
Eighteen in the Sun (1964, Ital.)
  Beach Party Italian Style

1812 (1944, USSR)
  Kutuzov
El (1955, Mex.)
  El, This Strange Passion Torments
Electronic Monster, The (1960, Brit.)
  Electric Monster, The
11 Harrow House (1974, Brit.)
  Anything for Love
Eliza Fraser (1976)
  Rollicking Adventures of Eliza Fraser, The
Embracers, The (1966)
  Great Dream The
  Now
Enemy of Women (1944)
  Private Life of Paul Joseph Goebbels
Endless Night (1971, Brit.)
  Agatha Christie's Endless Night
End of the Game (1976, Ger./Ital.)
  Getting Away with Murder
End of Desire (1962, Fr./Ital.)
  One Life
Emperor of the North Pole (1973)
  Emperor of the North
Enjo (1959, Jap.)
  Flame of Torment
  Conflagration
Enough Rope (1966, Fr./Ital./Ger.)
  Murderer, The
Eric Soya's "17" (1967, Den.)
  Seventeen
Erik the Conqueror (1963, Fr./Ital.)
  Fury of the Vikings
Eroica (1966, Pol.)
  Heroism
Erotique (1969, Fr.)
  Traquenards
  Traquenards Erotiques
Escape (1940)
  When the Door Opened
Escape from East Berlin (1962)
  Tunnel 28
Escape to Berlin (1962, U.S./Switz./Ger.)
  Captives, The
Escape to Glory (1940)
  Submarine Zone
Escape 2000 (1983, Aus.)
  Turkey Shoot
Eva (1962, Fr./Ital.)
  Eva the Devil's Woman
Every Bastard a King (1968, Israel)
  Every Man a King
Every Man for Himself (1980, Fr.)
  Slow Motion
Every Man for Himself and God Against All (1975,
Ger.)
  Mystery of Kaspar Hauser
  Enigma of Kaspar Hauser, The
Exorcism at Night (1966, Brit.)
  Naked Evil
Exorcism's Daughter (1974, Span.)
  House of Insane Women
Experiment in Terror (1962)
  Grip of Fear
Explosion (1969, Can.)
  Blast, The
Exterminators, The (1965, Fr.)
  FX-Superspy
Extreme Close-Up (1973)*
  Sex Through a Window

Fable, A (1971)
  Slave, The
Face of Terror (1964, Span.)
  Face of Fear
Face the Screaming Werewolf (1959, Mex.)
  House of Terror
Fallen Idol, The (1949, Brit.)
  Lost Illusion, The
Fallguy (1962)
  Fall Guy, The
False Rapture (1941)
  Secrets of Sin
Fame Street (1932)
  Police Court
Fanfan the Tulip (1952, Fr.)
  Soldier in Love
Fangs of the Wild (1954)
  Follow the Hunter
Fantasies (1981)
  And Once Upon A Love
Fantastic Voyage (1966)
  Microscopia
  Strange Journey
Far Horizons, The (1955)
  Untamed West, The
Farmer's Other Daughter, The (1965)
  Farm Girl

Fashions of 1934 (1934)
  Fashions
Fast Charlie...The Moonbeam Rider (1979)
  Fast Charlie and the Moonbeam
Fast Company (1938)
  Rare Book Murder, The
Fatal Desire (1953, Ital.)
  Cavalleria Rusticana
Father of a Soldier (1966, USSR)
  Soldier's Father, A
Fear (1946)
  Suspense
Fear Eats the Soul (1974, Ger.)
  Ali—Fear Eats the Soul
Fearless Frank (1967)
  Frank's Greatest Adventure
Fellini Satyricon (1969, Fr./Ital.)
  Satyricon
Female, The (1960, Fr.)
  Woman and the Puppet, The
Female Bunch, The (1969)
  Time to Run, A
Female Butcher, The (1972, Ital./Span.)
  Legend of Blood Castle
  Blood Ceremony
Female Jungle, The (1955)
  Hangover, The
Ffolkes (1980, Brit.)
  Assault Force
Fickle Finger of Fate, the (1967, Span./U.S.)
  Cups of San Sebastian, The
50,000 B.C. (Before Clothing) (1963)
  Nudes on the Rocks
Fighter, The (1952)
  First Time, The
Fighting Caravans (1931)
  Blazing Arrows
Fighting O'Flynn, The (1949)
  O'Flynn, The
Fighting Thru (1931)
  California in 1878
File on Thelma Jordan, The (1950)
  Thelma Jordan
Final Chord, The (1936, Ger.)
  Ninth Symphony
Final Comedown, The (1972)*
  Blast
  Hollywood
Final Terror, The (1983)
  Bump in the Night
  Forest Primeval, The
Final War, The (1960, Jap.)
  World War III Breaks Out
Fingerman, The (1963, Fr.)
  Stoolie, The
Finnegans Wake (1965)
  Passages from "Finnegans Wake"
  Passages from James Joyce's "Finnegans Wake"
Fino A Farti Male (1969, Fr./Ital.)
  Adelaide
Fire Maidens from Outer Space (1956, Brit.)
  Fire Maidens of Outer Space
Fireball Jungle (1968)
  Jungle Terror
Firebrand Jordan (1930)
  Firebrand Johnson
First Man Into Space (1959, Brit.)
  Satellite of Blood
First Offence (1936, Brit.)
  Bad Blood
First Time, The (1952)
  Beginners Three, The
  Beginners, The
  They Don't Wear Pajamas at Rosie's
Fist in his Pocket (1968, Ital.)
  Fists in the Pocket
Fists of Fury (1973, Chi.)
  Big Boss, The
Five and Ten (1931)
  Daughter of Luxury
Five Fingers (1952)
  Operation Cicero
Five Fingers of Death (1973, Hong Kong)
  Hand of Death
Five Minutes to Live (1961)
  Door-to-Door Maniac
Five Sinners (1961, Ger.)
  Sinners, The
Five Star Final (1931)
  One Fatal Hour
Five the Hard Way (1969)
  Sidehackers, The
Five Wild Girls (1966, Fr.)
  Five Wild Kids
Flame Barrier, The (1958)
  It Fell From the Flame Barrier
Flame of the West (1945)
  Flaming Frontier
Flame Over India (1960, Brit.)
  North West Frontier

Flamingo Affair, The (1948, Brit.)
  Blonde for Danger
Flap (1970)
  Nobody Loves a Drunken Indian
  Nobody Loves a Flapping Eagle
Flesh and Blood Show, The (1974, Brit.)
  Asylum of the Insane
Flesh and the Woman (1954, Fr./Ital.)
  Big Game, The
Flight that Disappeared, The (1961)
  Flight that Vanished, The
Flight to Fury (1966, US/Phil.)
  Cordillera
Flipper's New Adventure (1964)
  Flipper and the Pirates
Floating Weeds (1970, Jap.)
  Duckweed Story, The
  Drifting Weeds
Fly-Away Baby (1937)
  Adventures of Torchy Blane, The
Follow the Band (1943)
  Trombone from Heaven
Flash Gordon (1936)
  Rocket Ship
  Spaceship to the Unknown
  Space Soldiers
  Atomic Rocketship
Flareup (1969)
  Flare Up
  Flare-Up
Follow the Leader (1944)
  East of the Bowery
Fool Killer, The (1965)
  Violent Journey
For Better, For Worse (1954, Brit.)
  Cocktails in the Kitchen
For Love and Money (1967)
  For Love of Money
For Members Only (1960)*
  Nudist Story, The
For Men Only (1952)
  Tall Lie, The
For Pete's Sake (1977)
  July Pork Bellies
Forbidden World (1982)
  Mutant
Force of Arms (1951)
  Girl for Joe, A
Forced Entry (1975)
  Last Victim, The
Forest, The (1983)
  Terror in the Forest
Forever Young, Forever Free (1976, South Afr.)
  Lollipop
  E Lollipop
Fortune Teller, The (1961, Gr.)
  Coffee Fortune Teller, The
48 Hours to Live (1960, Brit./Swed.)
  Man in the Middle
Forty Guns (1957)
  Woman with a Whip
4D Man (1959)
  Master of Terror, The
Four Faces West (1948)
  They Passed this Way
Four Musketeers, The (1975)
  Revenge of Milady, The
Fox and His Friends (1976, Ger.)
  Fist-Right of Freedom
  Fox
Fox Movietone Follies of 1930 (1930)
  New Movietone Follies of 1930, The
Fox Style (1977)*
  Fox Style Killer
Foxtrot (1977, Mex./Switz.)
  Other Side of Paradise, The
Frankenstein Conquers the World (1964, Jap./US)
  Frankenstein vs. the Giant Devilfish
  Frankenstein and the Giant Lizard
Frankenstein Meets the Space Monster (1965)
  Mars Invades Puerto Rico
  Frankenstein Meets the Spacemen
Frankenstein's Daughter (1958)
  She Monster of the Night
Fraternity Row (1977)
  Oh Brotherhood
Freaks (1932)
  Nature's Mistakes
  Forbidden Love
  Monster Show, The
Free and Easy (1930)
  Easy Go
Free Grass (1969)
  Scream Free
Freeze Bomb (1978)*
  Death Dimension
French Cancan (1956, Fr.)
  Only the French Can
French They Are a Funny Race, The (1956, Fr.)
  French Are a Funny Race

Notebooks of Major Thompson
  Diary of Major Thompson
French Way, The (1975, Fr.)
  Love at the Top
Fresh from Paris (1955)
  Paris Follies of 1956
Freud (1962)
  Secret Passion, The
Friday the 13th...The Orphan (1979)
  Killer Orphan
Friend of the Family (1965, Fr./Ital.)
  Patate
Fright (1971, Brit.)
  Night Legs
Frightmare (1983)
  Horror Star, The
Frisco Kid, The (1979)
  No Knife
Frisky (1955, Ital.)
  Bread, Love, and Jealousy
From a Roman Balcony (1961, Fr./Ital.)
  Crazy Day, A
  Love is a Day's Work
  Pickup in Rome
From Beyond the Grave (1974, Brit.)
  Creatures from Beyond the Grave, The
  Creatures
From the Mixed-Up Files of Mrs. Basil E. Frankweiler (1973)
  Hideaways, The
Frontier Hellcat (1966, Fr./Ital./Ger./Yugo.)
  Among Vultures
Frustrations (1967, Fr./Ital.)
  Hot Frustrations
Full Circle (1977, Brit./Can.)
  Haunting of Julia, The
Funeral Home (1982, Can.)
  Two Cries in the Night
Further Adventures of the Wilderness Family (1978)
  Wilderness Family, Part 2
Fury of Hercules, The (1961, Ital.)
  Fury of Samson

Galaxy Express (1982, Jap.)
  Galaxy Express 999
Galaxy of Terror (1981)
  Mindwarp
  Infinity of Terror, An
  Planet of Horrors
  Mindwarp: An Infinity of Terror
Galia (1966, Fr./Ital.)
  I and My Lovers
  I and My Love
Game for Six Lovers, A (1962, Fr.)
  Games for Six Lovers
Game of Death, The (1979)
  Goodbye Bruce Lee: His Last Game of Death
Gamera the Invincible (1966, Jap.)
  Gamera
  Gammera
  Gammera the Invincible
Gamera Versus Barugon (1966, Jap./US)
  Gambara Versus Barugon
  War of the Monsters, The
Gamera Versus Gaos (1967, Jap.)
  Gamera Versus Gyaos
  Return of the Giant Monsters, The
  Boyichi and the Supermonster
Gamera Versus Guiron (1969, Jap.)
  Attack of the Monsters
Gamera Versus Monster X (1970, Jap.)
  Gamera Versus Jiger
  Monsters Invade Expo '70
Gamera Versus Viras (1968, Jap.)
  Gamera Versus Outer Space Monster Viras
  Destroy All Planets
Gamera Versus Zigra (1971, Jap.)
  Gamera Versus the Deep Sea Monster Zigra
Games Men Play, The (1968, Arg.)
  Hotel, The
  Cicada Is Not an Insect, The
Ganja and Hess (1973)
  Double Possession
  Blood Couple
Gappa the Trifibian Monster (1967, Jap.)
  Monster from a Prehistoric Planet
Garbage Man, The (1963)
  Garbage Man Cometh, The
Gaslight (1940)
  Angel Street
Gas-s-s-s! (1970)
  Gas-s-s-s, or It Became Necessary to Destroy the World in Order to Save It
Gates of Hell (1983, Ital./US)
  City of the Living Dead
  Fear, The

Twilight of the Dead
  Fear in the City of the Living Dead
Gavilan (1968)
  Ballad of Gavilan
Gawain and the Green Knight (1973, Brit.)
  Sir Gawain and the Green Knight
Gay Adventure, The (1953, Brit.)
  Three Men and a Girl
Gay Blades (1946)*
  Tournament Tempo
Geek Maggot Bingo (1983)
  Freak from Suckweasel Mountain, The
Geisha, A (1978, Jap.)
  Gion Music
Gentle Peple and the Quiet Land, The (1972)
  Gentle People, The
Get Outta Twn (1960)
  Get Out of Town
  Day Kelly Came Home, The
  Gangster's Revenge
Get Yourself a College Girl (1964)
  Go-Go Set
Getting It On (1983)*
  American Voyeur
Ghidrah, the Three-Headed Monster (1965, Jap.)
  Battle of the Monsters
  Ghidora, the Three-Headed Monster
  Ghidrah
  Greatest Battle on Earth, The
  Biggest Fight on Earth, The
  Monster of Monsters
Ghosts, Italian Style (1969, Ital./Fr.)
  Three Ghosts
Ghosts on the Loose (1943)
  East Side Kids Meet Bela Lugosi, The
Giant of Metropolis, The (1963, Ital.)
  Giant of Metropolis
Gigantis (1959, Jap./US)
  Return of Godzilla, The
  Fire Monster, The
  Volcano Monster, The
  Godzilla Raids Again
  Godzilla's Counterattack
  Counterattack of the Monster
Gina (1961, Fr./Mex.)
  Evil Eden
Girara (1967, Jap.)
  X From Outer Space, The
Girl Crazy (1943)
  When the Girls Meet the Boys
Girl from Poltava (1937)
  Natalka Poltavka
Girl Game (1968, Braz./Fr./Ital.)
  Copacabana Palace
  Saga of the Flying Hostesses, The
Girl in White, The (1952)
  So Bright the Flame
Girl on a Motorcycle, The (1968, Fr./Brit.)
  Naked Under Leather
Girl, the Body, and the Pill, The (1967)
  Pill, The
Girl Who Couldn't Say No, The (1969, Ital.)
  Tenderly
Girl with a Suitcase (1961, Fr./Ital.)
  Pleasure Girl
Girls Can Play (1937)
  Fielder's Field
Girls Next Door, The (1979)*
  Teen Lust
Girls Night Out (1984)**
  Scaremaker, The
Girls on the Beach (1965)
  Summer of '64
Girls' Town (1959)
  Innocent and the Damned, The
Giro City (1982, Brit.)
  And Nothing But the Truth
Give Me Your Heart (1936)
  I Give My Heart
Gladiators, The (1970, Swed.)
  Peace Game, The
Glass Cage, The (1964)
  Den of Doom
  Don't Touch My Sister
  Bed of Fire
Glass Tomb, The (1955, Brit.)
  Glass Cage, The
Glen or Glenda (1953)
  I Led Two Lives
  I Changed My Sex
  He or She
  Transvestite, The
Glory Boy (1971)
  My Old Man's Place
  Old Man's Place, The
Glory Trail, The (1937)
  Glorious Sacrifice
God Told Me To (1976)
  Demon

God's Country and the Man (1931)
  God's Country
  Rose of the Rio Grande
Godzilla Versus the Cosmic Monster (1974, Jap.)
  Godzilla Versus the Bionic Monster
Godzilla Versus the Sea Monster (1966, Jap.)
  Ebirah, Terror of the Deep
  Big Duel in the North
Godzilla Versus the Smog Monster (1972, Jap.)
  Godzilla Vs. Hedora
Godzilla Vs. the Thing (1964, Jap.)
  Godzilla Vs. Mothra
  Godzilla Vs. the Giant Moth
  Mothra Vs. Godzilla
  Godzilla Fights the Giant Moth
Goke, Body Snatcher from Hell (1968, Jap.)
  Goke the Vampire
  Body Snatchers from Hell
Gone with the West (1976)*
  Little Moon and Jud McGraw
Good Luck, Miss Wyckoff (1979)
  Sin, The
Grand Slam (1968, Ital./Span./Ger.)
  Top Job
Gone Are the Days (1963)
  Man from C.O.T.T.O.N., The
  Purlie Victorious
Goldbergs, The (1950)
  Molly
Golden Horde, The (1951)
  Golden Horde of Genghis Khan
Golden Needles (1974)
  Chase for the Golden Needles
Goliath Against the Giants (1963, Ital./Span.)
  Goliath and the Giants
Goliath and the Vampires (1964, Ital.)
  Vampires, The
Goliathon (1979, Hong Kong)
  Mighty Peking Man, The
Grand Illusion, The (1939, Fr.)
  La Grande Illusion
Grave of the Vampire (1972)
  Seed of Terror
Graveyard of Horror (1971, Span.)
  Necrophagus
Gravy Train, The (1974)
  Dion Brothers, The
Great American Bugs Bunny—Road Runner Chase (1979)
  Bugs Bunny—Road Runner Movie, The
Great Bank Hoax, The (1977)
  Great Georgia Bank Hoax, The
  Shenanigans
Great Lester Boggs, The (1975)*
  Hardheads, The
Great Locomotive Chase, The (1956)
  Andrews' Raiders
Great Plane Robbery, The (1940)
  Keep Him Alive
Great Scout and Cathouse Thursday, The (1976)
  Wildcat
Great Sioux Massacre, The (1965)
  Custer Massacre
  Massacre at the Rosebud, The
Great Skycopter Rescue, The (1982)*
  Skycopter Summer
Great Smokey Roadblock, The (1978)
  Last of the Cowboys, The
Great Texas Dynamite Chase, The (1976)
  Dynamite Women
Greatest Love, The (1954, Ital.)
  Europe '51
Greed of William Hart, The (1948, Brit.)
  Horror Maniacs
Greeks Had a Word for Them (1932)
  Three Broadway Girls
Green Buddha, The (1954, Brit.)
  Green Carnation, The
  Man with the Green Carnation, The
Green Cockatoo, The (1947, Brit.)
  Four Dark Hours
  Race Gang
Green Grow the Rushes (1951, Brit.)
  Brandy Ashore
Green Mare, The (1961, Fr./Ital.)
  Bedroom Vendetta
Green Slime, The (1969)
  Battle Beyond the Stars
  Death and the Green Slime
Greenwich Village Story (1963)
  Birthplace of the Hootenanny
  They Love as They Please
Greh (1962, Ger./Yugo.)
  Beginning Was Sin, The
Greystoke, the Legend of Tarzan (1984)**
  Greystoke: The Legend of Tarzan, Lord of the Apes
Grim Reaper, The (1981, Ital.)
  Anthropophagus

Gringo (1963, Ital./Span.)
  Gunfight at Red Sands
Grizzly (1976)
  Killer Grizzly
Groove Room, The (1974, Brit.)*
  What the Swedish Butler Saw
Grouch, The (1961, Gr.)
  Old Grouchy, The
Grumpy (1930)
  Cascarrabias
Guest at Steenkampskraal, The (1977, South Africa)
  Guest, The
Guide, The (1965, US/India)
  Survival
Guilt (1967, Swed.)
  With Gunilla Monday Evening and Tuesday
Gun Crazy (1949)
  Deadly is the Female
Gun Duel in Durango (1957)
  Duel in Durango
Gun Man from Bodie, The (1941)
  Gunman from Bodie
Gun Moll (1938)*
  Gang Smashers
Gun Play (1936)
  Lucky Boots
Gun Riders, The (1969)
  Five Bloody Graves
  Lonely Man
  Five Bloody Days to Tombstone
Gun Runner (1969)
  Gunrunners, The
Gun Runners, The (1958)
  Gunrunners
Gun the Man Down (1957)
  Arizona Mission
Guns in the Heather (1968, Brit.)
  Spy Busters
Guns of Hate (1948)
  Guns of Wrath
Guns of the Timberland (1960)
  Stampede
Gunsmoke (1947)*
  Gunsmoke Killers
Guru, the Mad Monk (1971)
  Garu, the Mad Monk
Guyana, Cult of the Damned (1980, Mex./Span./Panama)
  Guyana, Crime of the Century
Gutter Girls (1964, Brit.)
  Thrill Seekers
Gypsy Fury (1950, Fr,)
  Singoalla
  Saga of Singoalla, The
  Wind is My Lover, The

Hagbard and Signe (1968, Den./Iceland/Swed.)
  Red Mantle, The
Hail (1973)
  Hail to the Chief
  Washington B.C.
Hallelujah, I'm a Bum (1933)
  New York
  Heart of New York, The
  Happy Go Lucky
  Optimist, The
  Lazy Bones
Hand of Death (1962)
  Five Fingers of Death
Hand of Night, The (1968, Brit.)
  Beast of Morocco
Hands of Orlac, The (1964, Brit./Fr.)
  Hands of a Strangler
Hangar 18 (1980)
  Invasion Force
Hangmen Also Die (1943)
  Lest We Forget
Hangup (1974)
  Superdude
Hannah Lee (1953)
  Outlaw Territory
Happiness Cage, The (1972)
  Mind Snatchers, The
Happy Birthday, Davy (1970)
  I Am Curious Gay
Happy Days Are Here Again (1936, Brit.)
  Happy Days Revue
Happy Mother's Day...Love, George (1973)
  Run, Stranger, Run
Happy Thieves, The (1962)
  Once a Thief
Hard Steel (1941, Brit.)
  What Shall it Profit
Hard Times (1975)
  Streetfighter, The
Hard Trail (1969)
  Hard on the Trail

Harem Bunch; Or War and Piece, The (1969)
  Harem Bunch; Or War and Peace, The
  Desert Odyssey
Harlem on the Prairie (1938)
  Bad Man of Harlem
Harp of Burma (1967, Jap.)
  Burmese Harp, The
Harry Tracy—Desperado (1982, Can.)
  Harry Tracy
Harvest (1939, Fr.)
  Regain
Hatari! (1962)
  African Story, The
Hatchet for a Honeymoon (1969, Span./Ital.)
  Blood Brides
Haunts (177)
  Veil, The
He Loved an Actress (1938, Brit.)
  Mad About Money
  Stardust
Head, The (1961, Ger.)
  Head for the Devil, A
  Screaming Head, The
Head of a Tyrant (1960, Fr./Ital.)
  Judith and Holophernes
Head Over Heels in Love (1937, Brit.)
  Head Over Heels
Healer, The (1935)
  Little Pal
Health (1980)
  H.E.A.L.T.H.
Heart Song (1933, Brit.)
  Only Girl, The
Hearts of Humanity (1936, Brit.)
  Crypt, The
Hearts of the West (1975)
  Hollywood Cowboy
Heat of Midnight (1966, Fr.)
  Heat at Midnight
Heatwave (1954, Brit.)
  House Across the Lake, The
Heaven Only Knows (1947)
  Montana Mike
Hell on Earth (1934, Ger.)
  No Man's Land
Hell on Frisco Bay (1956)
  Darkest Hour, The
Helldorado (1946)
  Heldorado
Hello Down There (1969)
  Sub A-Dub Dub
Hello, Elephant (1954, Ital.)
  Pardon My Trunk
Hello London (1958, Brit.)
  London Calling
Hello Sister! (1933)
  Walking Down Broadway
Hell's Belles (1969)
  Girl in the Leather Suit
Hell's Bloody Devils (1970)
  Operation M
  Fakers, The
  Smashing the Crime Syndicate
Hell's Island (1955)
  Ruby Virgin, The
  Love is a Weapon
  South Seas Fury
Hell's Playground (1967)
  Riot at Lauderdale
Help I'm Invisible (1952, Ger.)
  Alas I'm Invisible
Hentai (1966, Jap.)
  Abnormal
Her First Romance (1940)
  Right Man, The
Hercules and the Captive Women (1963, Fr./Ital.)
  Hercules and the Conquest of Atlantis
  Hercules and the Haunted Women
Here Come the Nelsons (1952)
  Meet the Nelsons
Here Come the Tigers (1978)
  Manny's Orphans
Here Comes the Navy (1934)
  Hey Sailor
Hero Of Babylon (1963, Ital.)
  Beast of Babylon Against the Son of Hercules
Hero's Island (1962)
  Land We Love, The
Hi Diddle Diddle (1943)
  Diamonds and Crime
  Try and Find It
Hidden Fortress, The (1959, Jap.)
  Three Rascals in the Hidden Fortress
  Three Bad Men in the Hidden Fortress
Hideous Sun Demon, The (1959)
  Blood on His Lips
  Terror from the Sun
  Sun Demon, The
High and Dry (1954, Brit.)
  Maggie, The

High Country, The (1981, Can.)
  First Hello, The
High Rolling (1977, Aus.)
  High Rolling in a Hot Corvette
High School Confidential (1958)
  Young Hellions
Hiken Yaburi (1969, Jap.)
  Broken Swords
Hillbilly Blitzkrieg (1942)
  Enemy Roundup
Hills of Home (1948)
  Master of Lassie
Hills Run Red, The (1967, Ital.)
  River of Dollars, A
Hindu, The (1953, Brit.)
  Sabaka
Hired Gun (1952)*
  Hired Guns
His Majesty, King Ballyhoo (1931, Ger.)
  We Need No Money
Hit Parade of 1943 (1943)
  Change of Heart
Hit Parade of 1951 (1950)*
  Song Parade
Hit the Ice (1943)
  Oh Doctor
Hitler (1962)
  Women of Nazi Germany
Hitler's Madman (1943)
  Hitler's Hangman
Hold That Ghost (1941)
  Oh, Charlie
Hollow Triumph (1948)
  Scar, The
Hollywood Cowboy (1937)
  Wings Over Wyoming
Hollywood Mystery (1934)
  Hollywood Hoodlum
Hollywood 90028*
  Hollywood Hillside Strangler
Holocaust 2000 (1978, Ital./Brit.)
  Chosen, The
Honey Pot, The (1967, Brit.)
  It Comes Up Murder
  Anyone for Venice?
  Mr. Fox of Venice
Honeymoon Hotel (1946, Brit.)
  Under New Management
Honeymoon in Bali (1939)
  My Love for Yours
Honeymoon Killers, The (1969)
  Lonely Hearts Killers, The
Honeymoon Merry-Go-Round (1939, Brit.)
  Olympic Honeymoon
Honeymoon of Horror (1964)
  Deadly Circle, The
  Golden Nymphs, The
  Orgy of the Golden Nudes
Honeymoon of Terror (1961)
  Ecstasy on Lovers Island
  Ecstasy of Lovers
Honeysuckle Rose (1980)
  On the Road Again
Hong Kong (1951)
  Bombs Over China
Hopalong Cassidy (1935)
  Hopalong Cassidy Enters
Hope of His Side (1935, Brit.)
  Where's George?
Horror Castle (1965, Ital.)
  Terror Castle
  Castle of Terror
  Castle of the Living Dead
  Virgin of Nuremburg, The
Horror Chamber of Dr. Faustus, The (1962, Fr./Ital.)
  Eyes Without a Face
Horror Express (1972, Span./Brit.)
  Panic on the Trans-Siberian Express
Horror High (1974)
  Twisted Brain
Horror Hospital (1973, Brit.)
  Computer Killers
Horror of the Blood Monsters (1970, US/Phil.)
  Creatures of the Prehistoric Planet
Horror of the Blood Monsters (1970, US/Phil.)
  Horror Creatures of the Prehistoric Planet
  Space Mission of the Lost Planet
  Vampire Men of the Lost Planet
  Creatures of the Red Planet
  Flesh Creatures of the Red Planet
  Flesh Creatures, The
Horror Planet (1982, Brit.)
  Inseminoid
Horse, The (1984, Turkey)**
  Horse, My Horse
Hospital Massacre (1982)
  Be My Valentine...Or Else
  Ward 13

Hot and Deadly (1984)**
   Retrievers, The
Hot Lead (1951)
   Taste of Hot Lead, A
Hot Rod Gang (1958)
   Fury Unleashed
Hot Rod Girl (1956)
   Hot Car Girl
Hot Rods to Hell (1967)
   52 Miles to Midnight
   52 Miles to Terror
Hot Spur (1968)
   Naked Spur, The
   Fiery Spur
   Longest Spur, The
Hotel for Women (1939)
   Elsa Maxwell's Hotel for Women
Hound of the Baskervilles, The (1939)
   Sherlock Holmes in the Hound of the Baskervilles
House by the Lake, The (1977, Can.)
   Death Weekend
House of Exorcism, The (1976, Ital.)
   Lisa and the Devil
House of Fear (1945)
   Sherlock Holmes in House of Fear
House of Freaks (1973, Ital.)
   Frankenstein's Castle of Freaks
House of Fright (1961)
   Jekyll's Inferno
House of the Black Death (1965)
   Blood of the Man Devil
   Night of the Beast
House of the Living Dead (1973, S. Afr.)
   Doctor Maniac
House of Usher (1960)
   Fall of the House of Usher
House of Women (1962)
   Ladies of the Mob
House on Sorority Row, The (1983)
   Seven Sisters
House on the Square, The (1951, Brit.)
   I'll Never Forget You
House that Vanished, The (1974, Brit.)
   Scream and Die
House Where Death Lives, The (1984)**
   Delusion
How to Score with Girls (1980)*
   Cry Your Purple Heart Out
How to Save a Marriage—And Ruin Your Life (1968)
   Band of Gold
Huckleberry Finn (1939)
   Adventures of Huckleberry Finn, The
Human Condition, The (1959, Jap.)
   No Greater Love
Human Experiments (1980)
   Beyond the Gate
Hungry Wives (1973)
   Jack's Wife
   Season of the Witch
Hunted Men (1938)
   Crime Gives Orders
Hurricane (1979)
   Forbidden Paradise
Hyperboloid of Engineer Garin, The (1965, USSR)
   Engineer Garin's Death Ray

I Am Frigid...Why? (1973)*
   Let Me Love You
I Became a Criminal (1947)
   They Made Me Criminal
I Bombed Pearl Harbor (1961, Jap.)
   Storm Over the Pacific, The
I Can Get It For You Wholesale (1951)
   Only The Best
I Cover the Big Town (1947)
   I Cover the Underworld
I Dismember Mama (1974)
   Poor Albert and Little Annie
I Eat Your Skin (1971)
   Voodoo Blood Bath
   Zombie
   Zombies
I Escaped from the Gestapo (1943)
   No Escape
I Even Met Happy Gypsies (1968, Yugo.)
   Happy Gypsies
I Live in Fear (1967, Jap.)
   Record of a Living Being
I Love You, Alice B. Toklas! (1968)
   Kiss My Butterfly
I Spit on Your Grave (1983)
   Day of the Woman
I Was a Male War Bride (1949)
   You Can't Sleep Here

I've Gotta Horse (1965, Brit.)
   Wonderful Day
Ice House, The (1969)
   Cold Blood
   Passion Pit, The
   Love in Cold Blood
Ikiru (1960, Jap.)
   Doomed
   Living
Il Grido (1962, US/Ital.)
   Outcry, The
Illicit Interlude (1954, Swed.)
   Summerplay
Immoral Charge (1962, Brit.)
   Touch of Hell, A
Impossible Object (1973, Fr.)
   Story of a Love Story
Imposter, The (1944)
   Strange Confession
Impulse (1975)
   Want a Ride, Little Girl?
In Old Los Angeles (1948)*
   California Outpost
In Old Oklahoma (1943)
   War of the Wildcats
In Old Sacramento (1946)
   Flame of Sacramento
In the Year 2889 (1966)
   Year 2889
In Trouble with Eve (1964, Brit.)
   In Walked Eve
Incense for the Damned (1970, Brit.)
   Doctors Wear Scarlet
   Bloodsuckers, The
Incredibly Strange Creatures Who Stopped Living and Became Crazy Mixed-UpZombies, The (1965)
   Incredibly Strange Creatures, The
   Teenage Psycho Meets Bloody Mary
Indecent (1962, Ger.)
   All Bad
   Waylaid Women
Indiscretion of an American Wife (1954, US/Ital.)
   Terminal Station
   Indiscretion
Infra-Man (1975, Hong Kong)
   Super Inframan, The
   Infra Superman, The
Inside Moves (1980)
   Guys from Max's Bar, The
Insect Woman, The (1964, Jap.)
   Insect, The
Inspector General, The (1949)
   Happy Times
Intermezzo (1937, Swed.)
   Interlude
Intermezzo: A Love Story (1939)
   Intermezzo
Interplay (1970)*
   Part-Time Virgins
Intimacy (1966)
   Deceivers, The
Intimate Playmates, The (1976)*
   Naughty Freshmen
Intruder, The (1962)
   I Hate Your Guts
   Shame
Inside Out (1975, Brit.)
   Hitler's Gold
   Golden Heist, The
Invasion of the Animal People (1962, US/Swed.)
   Terror in the Midnight Sun
   Space Invasion from Lapland
   Space Invasion of Lapland
   Horror in the Midnight Sun
Invasion of the Bee Girls (1973)
   Graveyard
Invasion of the Saucer Men (1957)
   Invasion of the Hell Creatures
   Hell Creatures, The
   Spacemen Saturday Night
Invasion 1700 (1965, Fr./Ital./Yugo.)
   With Fire and Sword
   Daggers of Blood
Invisible Avenger, The (1958)
   Bourbon St. Shadows
Invisible Dr. Mabuse, The (1965, Ger.)
   Invisible Horror, The
Iron Curtain, The (1948)
   Behind the Iron Curtain
Iroquois Trail, The (1950)
   Tomahawk Trail, The
Is This Trip Really Necessary? (1970)
   Trip to Terror
   Blood of the Iron Maiden
Isadora (1968, Brit.)
   Loves of Isadora, The
Island, The (1962, Jap.)
   Naked Island
Island Claws (1981)
   Night of the Claw, The

Island of Love (1963)
   Not on Your Life
Island of Terror (1967, Brit.)
   Night of the Silicates
   Creepers, The
Island of the Burning Damned (1971, Brit.)
   Island of the Burning Doomed
Island of the Damned (1976, Span.)
   Who Can Kill a Child?
   Who Would Kill a Child?
   Man Eater of Hydra
Island Women (1958)
   Island Woman
Isle of Fury (1936)
   Three in Eden
It! (1967, Brit.)
   Curse of the Golem
It Couldn't Have Happened—But It Did (1936)
   It Couldn't Have Happened
It Fell from the Sky (1980)
   Alien Dead
It Happened in Gibraltar (1943, Fr.)
   Gibraltar
It Happened to Jane (1959)
   Twinkle and Shine
It Lives Again (1978)
   It's Alive II
It Takes a Thief (1960, Brit.)
   Challenge, The
It! The Terror from Beyond Space (1958)
   It! The Vampire from Beyond Space
It's a 2' 6" Above the Ground World (1972, Brit.)
   Love Ban, The
It's Hot in Paradise (1962, Ger./Yugo.)
   Body in the Web
   Spider's Web, The
   Girls of Spider Island
   Horrors of Spider Island
   Hot in Paradise
It's in the Air (1940, Brit.)
   George Takes the Air
It's Not the Size that Counts (1979, Brit.)
   Percy's Progress
Italian Connection, The (1973, US/Ital./Ger.)
   Manhunt
Italiano Brava Gente (1965, Ital./USSR)
   Attack and Retreat
Ivory Hunter (1952, Brit.)
   Ivory Hunters, The

J.C. (1972)*
   J.C. and the Boys
J.D.'s Revenger (1976)
   Revenge of J.D. Walker, The
J'Accuse (1939, Fr.)
   That They May Live
   I Accuse
Jail Bait (1954)
   Hidden Face
Jail Bait (1977, Ger.)
   Wild Game
   Game Pass
Jason and the Argonauts (1963, Brit.)
   Jason and the Golden Fleece
Jaws of Satan (1980)
   King Cobra
Jaws of the Jungle (1936)
   Jungle Virgin
Je T'Aime (1974, Can.)
   I Love You
Jennie, Wife-Child (1968)*
   Tender Grass
Jennifer (1978)
   Jennifer (The Snake Goddess)
Jenny (1969)
   And Jenny Makes Three
Jessie's Girls (1976)
   Wanted Women
Jet Attack (1958)
   Jet Squad
Jet Storm (1961, Brit.)
   Killing Urge
Jewish Daughter (1933)*
   Daughter of Her People
Jewish Father (1934)*
   Youth of Russia
Jigsaw (1949)
   Gun Moll
Jim, the World's Greatest (1976)
   Story of a Teenager
Joan of the Angels (1962, Pol.)
   Mother Joan of the Angels
Joe Palooka in Humphrey Takes a Chance (1950)
   Humphrey Takes a Chance
Joey (1977)*
   Deliver Us from Evil

Johnny Doesn't Live Here Any More (1944)
  And So They Were Married
Joke of Destiny Lying in Wait Around the Corner
Like a Street Bandit, A (1984,Ital.)**
  Joke of Destiny, A
Joker Is Wild, The (1957)
  All the Way
Jolly Bad Fellow, A (1964, Brit.)
  They All Died Laughing
Jonas—Who Will Be 25 in the Year 2000 (1976,
Swed.)
  Jonah—Who Will Be 25 in the Year 2000
Joniko and the Kush Ta Ka (1969)
  Joniko
  Alaska Boy
  Frontier Alaska
Jour de Fete (1952, Fr.)
  Holdiay
Journey into Fear (1976, Can.)
  Burn Out
Journey into Nowhere (1963, Brit.)
  Murder by Agreement
Journey to the Beginning of Time (1966, Czech.)
  Voyage to Prehistory
Joy House (1964, Fr.)
  Love Cage, The
Joysticks (1983)
  Video Madness
Judy's Little No-No (1969)
  Let's Do It
Jumbo (1962)
  Billy Rose's Jumbo
Jungle Book (1942)
  Rudyard Kipling's Jungle Book
Jungle Captive (1945)
  Wild Jungle Captive
Jungle of Chang (1951)
  Handful of Rice
Juno and the Paycock (1930, Brit.)
  Shame of Mary Boyle, The
Just Be There (1977)*
  Stranger at Home
  Comin' Home
  Swingin' Teacher
Just Me (1950, Fr.)
  My Apple
Just Once More (1963, Swed.)
  Just One More
Justine (1969, Ital./Span.)
  Marquis de Sade: Justine

Kagemusha (1980, Jap.)
  Double, The
  Shadow Warrior, The
Kamilla (1984, Norway)**
  Betrayal
  Betrayal, The
  Story of Kamilla, The
Kanal (1961, Pol.)
  They Loved Life
Karamazov (1931, Ger.)
  Murderer Dmitri Karamazov, The
  Brothers Karamazov, The
Karen, the Lovemaker (1970)
  Africa Erotica
  Happening in Africa
Keep Off! Keep Off! (1975)*
  Keep Off My Grass
Kenner (1969)
  Year of the Cricket
Key Man, The (1957, Brit.)
  Life at Stake
Kid Dynamite (1943)
  Queen of Broadway
Kid Galahad (1937)
  Battling Bellhop, The
Kiev Comedy, A (1963, USSR)
  Chasing Two Hares
Kill (1968, Jap.)
  Kiru
Kill Baby Kill (1966, Ital.)
  Curse of the Living Dead
Kill! Kill! Kill! (1972, Fr.)
  Kill!
Killer Fish (1979, Ital./Braz.)
  Treasure of the Piranha
  Deadly Treasure of the Piranha
Killer Force (1975, Switz./Ireland)
  Diamond Mercenaries, The
Killers of the Wild (1940)
  Children of the Wild
Killing Game, The (1968, Fr.)
  All Weekend Lovers
Kind Lady (1935)
  House of Menace
Kind Stepmother (1936, Hung.)
  Sweet Stepmother

Kinfolk (1970)
  Kin Folk
  Closest of Kin, The
  All the Lovin' Kinfolk
King Kong Escapes (1968, Jap.)
  Revenge of King Kong, The
  King Kong's Counterattack
King of the Gamblers (1937)
  Czar of the Slot Machines
King of Hearts (1936, Brit.)
  Little Gel
Kingfish Caper, The (1976, S. Afr.)
  Kingfisher Caper, The
Kino, Padre on Horseback (1977)*
  Father Kino Story
  Padre on Horseback
Kipperbang (1984)**
  P'Tang, Yang, Kipperbang
Kirlian Witness, the (1978)
  Plants are Watching, The
Kismet (1944)
  Oriental Dream
Kiss for Corliss, A (1949)
  Almost a Bride
Kiss My Grits (1982)*
  Texas Legend
  Summer Heat
Kiss the Girls and See Them Die! (1968)*
  Kiss The Girls; Make Them Die
Kiss the Other Sheik (1968, Fr./Ital.)
  Blonde Wife, The
Kisses for My President (1964)
  Kisses for the President
Klondike Fever (1980)
  Jack London's Klondike Fever
Knack...and How to Get it, The (1965, Brit.)
  Knack, The
Knife for the Ladies, A (1974)*
  Silent Sentence
Knight Without Armor (1937, Brit.)
  Knight Without Armour
Knights of the Teutonic Order, The (1962, Pol.)
  Knights of the Black Cross
Knock (1955, Fr.)
  Dr. Knock
Kolberg (1945, Ger.)
  Burning Hearts
Krakatoa, East of Java (1969)
  Volcano
Kuragejima—Legends from a Southern Island
(1970, Jap.)
  Deep Desire of Gods
Kuroenko (1968, Jap.)
  Black Cat, The

La Baby Sitter (1975, Fr./Ital./Ger.)
  Babysitter
La Balance (1983, Fr.)
  Nark, The
La Belle Americaine (1961, Fr.)
  American Beauty, The
La Bete Humaine (1938, Fr.)
  Human Beast, The
La Bonne Soupe (1964, Fr./Ital.)
  Careless Love
  Good Soup, The
La Cage Aux Folles (1979, Fr./Ital.)
  Mad Cage, The
  Birds of a Feather
La Chienne (1975, Fr.)
  Isn't Life a Bitch?
  Bitch, The
La Cucaracha (1961, Mex.)
  Soldiers of Pancho Villa, The
La Femme Infidele (1969, Fr./Ital.)
  Unfaithful Wife, The
La Ferme du Pendu (1946, Fr.)
  Hanged Man's Farm
La Grande Bouffe (1973, Fr.)
  Big Feast, The
  Great Feed, The
  Grande Bouffe, The
La Grande Bourgeoise (1977, Ital.)
  Murri Affair, The
La Guerre Est Finie (1967, Fr./Swed.)
  War Is Over, The
La Marie du Port (1951, Fr.)
  Marie du Port
La Maternelle (1933, Fr.)
  Children of Montmarte
La Notte (1961, Fr./Ital.)
  Night, The
La Notte Brava (1962, Fr./Ital.)
  On Nay Street
  Bad Girls Don't Cry
La Prisonniere (1969, Fr./Ital.)
  Female Prisoner, The

La Strada (1956, Ital.)
  Road, The
La Terra Trema (1947, Ital.)
  Earth Will Tremble, The
La Viaccia (1962, Fr./Ital.)
  Love Makers, The
La Vie de Chateau (1967, Fr.)
  Matter of Resistance, A
Ladies Must Live (1940)
  Hometowners
Ladies They Talk About (1933)
  Women in Prison
Lady and the Monster, The (1944)
  Tiger Man
Lady Cocoa (1975)*
  Pop Goes the Weasel
Lady Dracula, The (1974)
  Legendary Curse of Lemora, The
  Lemora, Lady Dracula
Lady Frankenstein (1971, Ital.)
  Daughter of Frankenstein, The
  Madame Frankenstein
Lady From the Sea, The (1929, Brit.)
  Goodwin Sands
Lady General, The (1965, Hong Kong)
  Hua Mu-Lan
Lady Hamilton (1969, Ger./Ital./Fr.)
  Making of a Lady, The
Lady in Question, The (1940)
  It Happened in Paris
Lady in Red, The (1979)
  Guns, Sin and Bathtub Gin
Lady Jane Grey (1936, Brit.)
  Nine Days a Queen
Lady of Monza, The (1970, Ital.)
  Nun of Monza, The
Lady with a Lamp, The (1951, Brit.)
  Lady with the Lamp, The
Lady without Camellias, The (1981, Ital.)
  Camille Without Camillias
Ladykillers, The (1956, Brit.)
  Lady Killers, The
L'Age D'Or (1979, Fr.)
  Age of Gold
Lake of Dracula (1973, Jap.)
  Bloodthirsty Eyes
  Dracula's Lust for Blood
Lancelot of the Lake (1975, Fr.)
  Grail, The
  Lancelot du Lac
  Le Graal
Land of No Return, The (1981)
  Challenge to Survive
  Snowman
Land of the Minotaur (1976, Gr.)
  Devil's Men, The
  Devil's People, The
  Minotaur
Land Raiders (1969)
  Day of the Landgrabbers
Landru (1963, Fr.)
  Bluebeard
L'Armee des Ombres (1969, Fr./Ital.)
  Army of Shadows, The
Las Vegas Hillbillies (1966)
  Country Music, U.S.A.
Last Adventurers, The (1937, Brit.)
  Down to the Sea in Ships
Last American Hero, The (1973)
  Hard Driver
Last Days of Dolwyn, The (1949, Brit.)
  Dolwyn
  Woman of Dolwyn
Last Days of Man on Earth (1975, Brit.)
  Final Programme, The
Last Days of Mussolini (1974, Ital.)
  Last Four Days, The
Last Frontier, The (1955)
  Savage Wilderness
Last Gunfighter, The (1961, Can.)
  Hired Gun
  Devil's Spawn, The
Last Horror Film, The (1984)**
  Fanatic, The
Last House on Dead End Street (1977)
  Fun House
Last Hunter, The (1984, Ital.)**
  Hunter of the Apocalypse
Last Movie, The (1971)
  Chinchero
Last of the Comanches (1952)
  Sabre and the Arrow, The
Last Porno Flick, The (1974)
  Mad, Mad Moviemakers, The
Last Rites (1980)
  Dracula's Last Rites
Last Stop, The (1949, Pol.)
  Last Stage, The
Last Stop on the Night Train (1976)*
  Night Train Murders

Malaga (1962, Brit.)
   Moment of Danger
Male and Female Since Adam and Eve (1961, Arg.)
   Male and Female
   Souls of Sin
Malenka, the Vampire (1972, Span./Ital.)
   Fangs of the Living Dead
Malicious (1974, Ital.)
   Malice
Maltese Falcon, The (1931)
   Dangerous Female
Man, a Woman, and a Bank, A (1979, Can.)
   Very Big Withdrawal, A
Man and the Beast, The (1951, Arg.)
   Strange Case of the Man and the Beast, The
Man Betrayed, A (1941)
   Wheel of Fortune
Man Called Flintstone, The (1966)
   That Man Flintstone
Man Could Get Killed, A (1966)
   Welcome, Mr. Beddoes
Man Eater (1958)*
   African Hunter
Man Escaped, A (1957, Fr.)
   Wind Bloweth Where It Listeth, The
Man from Dakota, The (1940)
   Arouse and Beware
Man from Hong Kong (1975, Aus./Chi.)
   Dragon Flies, The
Man from O.R.G.Y., The (1970)
   Real Gone Girls, The
Man from the First Century, The (1961, Czech.)
   Man from the Past, The
   Man in Outer Space
Man I Married, The (1940)
   I Married a Nazi
Man in the Middle (1964, U.S./Brit.)
   Winston Affair, The
Man in the Moonlight Mask, The (1958, Jap.)
   Moonbeam Man, The
Man in the Water, The (1963)
   Escape from Hell Island
Man Made Monster (1941)
   Atomic Monster, The
Man of Violence (1970, Brit.)
   Sex Racketeers, The
Man Who Changed His Name, The (1934, Brit.)
   Man Who Changed, The
Man Who Lived Again, The (1936, Brit.)
   Brainsnatchers, The
   Dr. Maniac
Man Who Wagged His Tail, The (1961, Ital./Span.)
   Angel Passed over Brooklyn, An
Man Who Walked Through the Wall, The (1964, Ger.)
   Man Goes Through the Wall, A
Man Who Would Not Die, The (1975)
   Target in the Sun
Man with Bogart's Face, The (1980)
   Sam Marlow, Private Eye
Man with the Gun (1955)
   Man without a Gun
Mandabi (1970, Fr.)
   Money Order, The
Mandragola (1966, Fr./Ital.)
   Mandragola—The Love Root
   Love Root, The
Manhandlers, The (1975)*
   Soft Touch
Mania (1961, Brit.)
   Psycho Killers
   Fiendish Ghouls, The
Maniac! (1977)
   Ransom
   Assault on Paradise
   Town that Cried Terror, The
Maniac Mansion (1978, Ital.)
   Amuck
   Maniac
   Replica of a Crime
Mansion of the Doomed (1976)
   Terror of Dr. Chaney, The
Manson Massacre, The (1976)*
   Together Girls
Manster, The (1962, Jap.)
   Manster—Half Man, Half Monster
   Split, The
Mantis in Lace (1968)
   Lila
Mara of the Wilderness (1966)
   Valley of the White Wolves
March of the Spring Hare (1969)
   Roommates
Marco Polo (1962, Fr./Ital.)
   Grand Khan
Mardi Gras Massacre (1978)
   Crypt of Dark Secrets
Marilyn (1953, Brit.)
   Roadhouse Girl

Marizinia (1962, U.S./Braz.)
   Marizinia, the Witch Beneath the Sea
   Witch Beneath the Sea, The
Mark of the Devil (1970, Ger./Brit.)
   Burn, Witch, Burn
Mark of the Devil II (1975, Ger./Brit.)
   Witches—Violated and Tortured To Death
Mark Twain, American (1976)*
   Mountain Man
Married Too Young (1962)
   I Married Too Young
Mask, the (1961, Can.)
   Eyes of Hell
   Spooky Movie Show, The
Mask of Korea (1950, Fr.)
   Gambling Hell
Masquerade (1965, Brit.)
   Operation Masquerade
   Shabby Tiger, The
Master of Horror (1965, Arg.)
   Masterworks of Terror
Master of the World (1935, Ger.)
   Ruler of the World
Master Touch, The (1974, Ital./Ger.)
   Hearts and Minds
Mata-Hari (1965, Fr./Ital.)
   Mata Hari Agent H-21
Mata Hari's Daughter (1954, Fr./Ital.)
   Daughter of Mata Hari
McMasters, The (1970)
   Blood Crowd, The
   McMasters...Tougher Than the West Itself, The
Me (1970, Fr.)
   Naked Childhood
Meat Cleaver Massacre (1977)
   Hollywood Meat Cleaver Massacre, The
Mechanic, The (1972)
   Killer of Killers
Medico of Painted Springs, The (1941)
   Doctor's Alibi
Meet Me at Dawn (1947, Brit.)
   Gay Duelist, The
Melody (1971, Brit.)
   S.W.A.L.K.
Memoirs of Prison (1984, Braz.)**
   Memories of Prison
Memory of Love (1949)*
   Long Search, The
Men, The (1950)
   Battle Stripe
Merry Widow, The (1934)
   Lady Dances, The
Mesa of Lost Women, The (1956)
   Lost Women
   Lost Women of Zarpa
Michelle (1970, Fr.)
   Sexy Gang
Mid-Day Mistress (1968)
   Businessman's Lunch, The
   Mid-Day Miss
Midas Run (1969)
   Run on Gold, A
Midnight (1934)
   Call It Murder
Midnight Angel (1941)
   Pacific Blackout
Mighty Ursus (1962, Ital./Span.)
   Ursus
Military Academy with that Tenth Avenue Gang (1950)
   Military Academy
Mill of the Stone Women (1963, Fr./Ital.)
   Horror of the Stone Women
   Horrible Mill Women, The
Million Eyes of Su-Muru, The (1967, Brit.)
   1,000,000 of Su-Muru, The
Minotaur, The 1961, Ital.)
   Minotaur—The Wild Beast of Crete
   Theseus Against the Minotuar
   Warlord of Crete, The
Minute to Pray, a Second to Die, A (1968, Ital.)
   Dead Or Alive
Miracle of Santa's White Reindeer, The (1963)
   Miracle of the White Reindeer, The
Miracle of the White Stallions (1963)
   Flight of the White Stallions, The
Mirrors (1984)**
   Marianne
Miss Fane's Baby Is Stolen (1934)
   Miss Fane's Baby
Miss Jessica Is Pregnant (1970)
   Spring Night, Summer Night
   Jessica
Miss V from Moscow (1942)
   Intrigue in Paris
Missile from Hell (1960, Brit.)
   Unseen Heroes
   Battle of the V1
   V1

Missing Lady, The (1946)
   Shadow and the Missing Lady, The
Mr. Bug Goes To Town (1941)
   Hoppity Goes To Town
Mr. Hulot's Holiday (1954, Fr.)
   Monsieur Hulot's Holiday
Mr. Moto in Danger Island (1939)
   Danger Island
Mr. Quilp (1975, Brit.)
   Old Curiosity Shop, the
Mr. Sardonicus (1961)
   Sardonicus
Mr. Stringfellow Says No (1937, Brit.)
   Accidental Spy
Mr. Superinvisible (1974, Ital./Span./Ger.)
   Mr. Invisible
Mistress For the Summer, A (1964, Fr./Ital.)
   Lover For the Summer, A
Mistress of Atlantis, The (1932, Ger.)
   Lost Atlantis
Modern Marriage, A (1962)
   Frigid Wife
Modigliani of Montparnasse (1961, Fr./Ital.)
   Lovers of Montparnasse, The
Mohammad, Messenger of God (1976, Lebanon/Brit.)
   Message, The
Money Jungle, The (1968)
   Silken Trap, The
   Billion Dollar Caper, The
Monkey in Winter, A (1962, Fr.)
   It's Hot in Hell
Monster a Go-Go (1965)
   Terror at Halfday
Monster from the Ocean Floor, The (1954)
   It Stalked the Ocean Floor
   Monster Maker
Monster Island (1981, Span./U.S.)
   Mystery on Monster Island
Monster Zero (1970, Jap.)
   Battle of the Astros
   Invasion of the Astro-Monsters
   Invasion of The Astros
   Invasion of Planet X
Monsters from the Unknown Planet (1975, Jap.)
   Terror of Mechagodzilla
   Escape of Megagodzilla, The
Montana Incident (1952)*
   Gun Smoke Range
Montenegro (1981, Brit./Swed.)
   Montenegro—Or Pigs and Pearls
Monty Python's Life of Brian (1979, Brit.)
   Life of Brian
Moonchild (1972)
   Full Moon
Moonshine Mountain (1964)
   White Trash on Moonshine Mountain
More Than a Miracle (1967, Ital./Fr.)
   Cinderella, Italian Style
   Happily Ever After
   Once Upon a Time
Morituri (1965)
   Saboteur: Code Name Morituri, The
Mother Goose a Go-Go (1966)
   Unkissed Bride, The
Mother Lode (1982)
   Search For The Mother Lode
   Last Great Treasure, The
Mountain Justice (1930)
   Kettle Creek
Movie Stuntmen (1953)
   Hollywood Thrillmakers
   Hollywood Stunt Man
Ms.45 (1981)
   Angel of Vengeance
Mumsy, Nanny, Sonny and Girly (1970, Brit.)
   Girly
Murder by Television (1935)
   Houghland Murder Case, The
Murder Clinic, The (1967, Ital./Fr.)
   Murder Society, The
   Revenge of the Living Dead
   Knife in the Body, The
   Night of Terrors, The
Murder in Mississippi (1965)
   Murder Mississippi
Murder in the Big House (1942)
   Born For Trouble
Murder in the Music Hall (1946)
   Midnight Melody
Murder She Said (1961, Brit.)
   Meet Miss Marple
Muriel (1963, Fr./Ital.)
   Time of Return, The
   Muriel, Or the Time of Return
Murieta (1965, Span.)
   Joaquin Murrieta
Murph the Surf (1974)
   Live a Little, Steal a Lot
   You Can't Steal Love

Mutations, The (1974, Brit.)
 Mutations
 Mutation, The
Mutineers, The (1949)
 Pirate Ship
Mutiny in Outer Space (1965)
 Invasion from The Moon
 Space Station X-14
 Space Station X
My Brother, the Outlaw (1951)
 My Outlaw Brother
My Father's Mistress (1970, Swed.)
 Bamse
 Teddy Bear, The
My Margo (1969, Israel)
 Love in Jerusalem
My Name Is Ivan (1963, USSR)
 Ivan's Childhood
 Youngest Spy, The
My Night at Maud's 1970, Fr.)
 My Night with Maud
My Old Duchess (1933, Brit.)
 Oh What a Duchess!
My Seven Little Sins (1956, Fr./Ital.)
 I Have Seven Daughters
My Son the Vampire (1963, Brit.)
 Vampire and the Robot, The
 Old Mother Riley Meets the Vampire
 Vampire over London
 Mother Riley Meets the Vampire
My Third Wife George (1968)
 My Third Wife by George
My Way (1974, S. Africa)
 Winner, The
Mysterians, The (1959, Jap.)
 Earth Defence Forces
Mysterious Island of Captain Nemo, The (1973,
Fr./Ital./Span./Cameroon)
 Mysterious Island, The
Mysterious Rider, The (1933)
 Fighting Phantom, The
 Mark of the Avenger
Mysterious Satellite, The (1956, Jap.)
 Cosmic Man Appears in Tokyo, The
 Space Men Appear in Tokyo
 Warning from Space
 Unknown Satellite over Tokyo
Mystery at the Burlesque (1950, Brit.)
 Murder at the Burlesque
Mystery of Marie Roget, The (1942)
 Phantom of Paris
Mystery of the Black Jungle (1955)
 Black Devils of Kali, The
Mystery of the Golden Eye, The (1948)
 Golden Eye, The
Mystery Ranch (1932)
 Killer, The
Mystery Submarine (1963, Brit.)
 Decoy
Mystic Circle Murder (1939)
 Religious Racketeers
Mystique (1981)
 Circle of Power
Myth, The (1965, Ital.)
 Pushover, The

N.P. (1971, Ital.)
 N.P.—the Secret
Nabonga (1944)
 Gorilla
Nada Gang, The (1964, Fr./Ital.)
 Nada
Naked Heart, The (1955, Brit.)
 Maria Chapdelaine
Naked Kiss, The (1964)
 Iron Kiss, The
Naked Night, The (1956, Swed.)
 Sunset of a Clown
Naked Paradise (1957)
 Thunder Over Hawaii
Naked Set (1962)*
 Naked Road
Naked Witch, The (1964)
 Naked Temptress, The
Naked World of Harrison Marks, The (1967, Brit.)
 Dream World of Harrison Marks, The
Naked Youth (1961, Jap.)
 Cruel Story of Youth
 Story of the Cruelties of Youth, A
Naked Zoo, The (1970)
 Hallucinators, The
 Grove, The
 Naked Lovers, The
Name of the Game Is Kill, The (1968)
 Lovers in Limbo
 Female Trap, The

Narcotic, The (1937)*
 Dope Dens of the Orient
 Peddler
Narcotics Story, The (1958)
 Dreaded Persuasion, The
Nasty Rabbit, The (1964)
 Spies-A-Go-Go
Nathalie (1958, Fr.)
 Foxiest Girl in Paris
Nathalie, Agent Secret (1960, Fr.)
 Atomic Agent
National Lampoon's Animal House (1978)
 Animal House
Naughty Stewardesses, The (1973)*
 Dear Debbie
Naughty Wives (1974)*
 Secrets of a Door-To-Door Salesman
Navy vs. the Night Monsters, The (1966)
 Night Crawlers, The
Nazi Agent (1942)
 Salute to Courage
Neapolitan Carousel (1961, Ital.)
 Neapolitan Carousel
Necromancy (1972)
 Witching, The
Neptune Factor, The (1973, Can.)
 Underwater Odyssey, An
 Neptune Disaster, The
Nero's Mistress (1962, Ital.)
 Nero's Big Weekend
 My Son Nero
Nesting, The (1981)
 Phobia
Never Fear (1950)
 Young Lovers, The
Never Take Candy from a Stranger (1961, Brit.)
 Molester, The
New Adventures of Tarzan, The (1935)
 Tarzan and the Green Goddess
New Frontier (1939)
 Frontier Horizon
New Girl in Town (1977)
 Nashville Girl
 Country Music Daughter
New House on the Left, The (1978, Brit.)
 Second House from the Left
New Land, The (1971, Swed.)
 Settlers, The
 Unto a Good Land
New Life Style, The (1970, Ger.)
 Just to Be Loved
Newly Rich (1931)
 Forbidden Adventure
Next! (1971, Ital./Span.)
 Next Victim! The
Night Child (1975, Brit./Ital.)
 Cursed Medallion, The
Night Comes Too Soon (1948, Brit.)
 Ghost of Rashmon Hall, The
Night Creature (1979)
 Out of the Darkness
 Fear
Night Digger, The (1971, Brit.)
 Road Builder, The
Night Encounter (1963, Fr./Ital.)
 Double Agents, The
Night God Screamed, The (1975)
 Scream
Night Hair Child (1971, Brit.)
 Child of the Night
Night Monster (1942)
 House of Mystery
Night of Dark Shadows (1971)
 Curse of Dark Shadows
Night of Lust (1965, Fr.)
 Night of Love
Night of Terror (1933)
 He Lived to Kill
Night of the Askari (1978, Ger./S. Africa)
 Whispering Death
Night of the Assassin (1972)*
 Incredible Challenge, The
 Naked Choice, The
Night of the Bloody Apes (1968, Mex.)
 Gomar—The Human Gorilla
Night of the Ghouls (1959)
 Revenge of the Dead
Night of the Living Dead (1968)
 Night of the Flesh Eaters
Night of the Quarter Moon (1959)
 Flesh and Fame
Night of the Witches (1970)
 Night of Witches
Night of the Zombies (1981)
 Night of the Wehrmacht Zombies
 Gamma 693
 Hell of the Living Dead
 Zombie Creeping Flesh
Night School (1981)
 Terror Eyes

Night Shadows (1984)**
 Mutant
 November Children
Night They Killed Rasputin, The (1962, Fr./Ital)
 Giant Monster
 Nights of Rasputin, The
Night to Dismember, A (1983)*
 Satan's Axe
Night Train (1940)
 Gestapo
Nightmare Castle (1966, Ital.)
 Faceless Monsters, The
 Lovers from Beyond the Tomb
Nightmare County (1977)*
 Nightmare of Death
Nightmare in Wax (1969)
 Crimes in the Wax Museum
Nights of Cabiria (1957, Ital.)
 Cabiria
Nights of Prague, The (1968, Czech.)
 Prague Nights
Nine Lives Are Not Enough (1941)
 Nine Loves Are Not Enough
1914 (1932, Ger.)
 1914: The Last Days Before the War
1990: Bronx Warriors (1983, Ital.)
 Bronx Warriors
Ninth Configuration, The (1980)
 Twinkle, Twinkle, Killer Kane
99 Women (1969)*
 Isle of Lost Women
 99 Mujeres
 99 Donne
 Der Heisse Tod
 Prostitutes in Prison
No Deposit, No Return (1976)
 Double Trouble
No Escape (1936, Brit.)
 No Escape—No Exit
No Escape (1953)
 City on a Hunt
No Exit (1962, US/Arg.)
 Sinners Go to Hell
 Stateless
No Greater Sin (1941)
 Social Enemy No. 1
No Highway in the Sky (1951, Brit.)
 No Highway
No Man's Range (1935)
 No Man's Land
No Mercy Man, The (1975)
 Trained to Kill
No Place to Hide (1975)
 Rebel
No Ransom (1935)
 Bonds of Honour
No Roses for OSS 117 (1968, Fr.)
 OSS 117: Double Agent
No Survivors, Please (1963, Ger.)
 Chief Wants No Survivors, The
No Time for Comedy (1940)
 Guy with a Grin
No Way Out (1975, Ital./Fr.)
 Tony Arzenta
 Big Guns
Nocturna (1979)
 Nocturna, Granddaughter of Dracula
North Star, The (1943)
 Armored Attack
Northville Cemetery Massacre, The (1976)
 Northville Cemetery Massacre, The
Nosferatu, the Vampire (1979, Fr./Ger.)
 Nosferatu, the Vampyre
Not Mine to Love (1969, Israel)
 Three Days and a Child
Not My Daughter (1975)*
 Like it Is
Not Reconciled or "Only Violence Helps Where It
Rules" (1968, Ger.)
 Unreconciled
 Not Reconciled
Not Wanted (1949)
 Streets of Sin
Nothing but the Night (1975, Brit.)
 Resurrection Syndicate, The
Notorious Sophie Lang, The (1934)
 Sophie Lang
Novel Affair, A (1957, Brit.)
 Passionate Stranger, The
Now Barabbas Was a Robber (1949, Brit.)
 Now Barabbas
Now I'll Tell (1934)
 While New York Sleeps
Nude Bomb, The (1980)
 Return of Maxwell Smart, The
Nude in a White Car (1960, Fr.)
 Blonde in a White Car
Nude in His Pocket (1962, Fr.)
 Girl in His Pocket

Nude Odyssey (1962, Fr./Ital.)
  Love—Tahiti Style
  Diary of a Voyage in the South Pacific
Nuisance, The (1933)
  Chaser, The
  Accidents Wanted
  Ambulance Chaser
  Never Give a Sucker a Break
Nun at the Crossroads, A (1970, Ital./Span.)
  Crossroads for a Nun
Nurse Sherri (1978)
  Beyond the Living
Nymph (1974)*
  Hot Child

O, My Darling Clementine (1943)
  Oh My Darling Clementine
Oblong Box, The (1969, Brit.)
  Edgar Allan Poe's "The Oblong Box"
Obsession (1968, Swed.)
  Royal Track, The
Ocean Breakers (1949, Swed.)
  Surf, The
Octaman (1971)
  Octoman
Odd Man Out (1947, Brit.)
  Gang War
Odyssey of the Pacific (1983, Can./Fr.)
  Emperor of Peru, The
Oedipus Rex (1957, Can.)
  King Oedipus
Offbeat (1961, Brit.)
  Devil Inside, The
Offense, The (1973, Brit.)
  Something Like the Truth
Office Girl (1932, Brit.)
  Sunshine Susie
Oh! Susanna (1951)
  Oh, Susanna
Ohayo (1962, Jap.)
  Good Morning
Okay Bill (1971)
  Sweed Dreams
Old Louisiana (1938)
  Louisiana Gal
Old Mother Riley (1937, Brit.)
  Return of Old Mother Riley, The
  Original Old Mother Riley, The
Old Mother Riley in Paris (1938, Brit.)
  Old Mother Riley Catches a Quisling
Old Shatterhand (1968, Ger./Yugo./Fr./Ital.)
  Apaches Last Battle
  Shatterhand
Olly, Olly, Oxen Free (1978)
  Great Balloon Adventure, The
Olsen's Big Moment (1934)
  Olsen's Night Out
Omen, The (1976)
  Birthmark
Omoo Omoo, the Shark God (1969)
  Omoo-Omoo
On His Own (1939, USSR)
  Among People
On Our Merry Way (1948)
  Miracle Can Happen, A
On Our Selection (1930, Aus.)
  On Our Little Place
On the Air Live with Captain Midnight (1970)
  Captain Midnight
On the Great White Trail (1938)
  Renfrew of the Royal Mounted on the Great
  White Trail
  Renfrew on the Great White Trail
Once Is Not Enough (1975)
  Jacqueline Susann's Once Is Not Enough
Once Upon a Horse (1958)
  Hot Horse
One April 2000 (1952, Aust.)
  April 1st 2000
One Is a Lonely Number (1972)
  Two Is a Happy Number
One Million BC (1940)
  Cave Dwellers, The
  Cave Man
$1,000,000 Duck (1971)
  Million Dollar Duck
One New York Night (1935)
  Trunk Mystery, The
One Plus One (1961, Can.)
  1ǂ1 (Exploring the Kinsey Reports)
One Plus One (1969, Brit.)
  Sympathy for the Devil
One Russian Summer (1973)*
  Fury
One Step to Hell (1969, US/Ital./Span.)
  King of Africa

One Summer Love (1976)
  Dragonfly
One Russian Summer (1973)*
  Fury
Outside Chance (1978)*
  Return to Jackson County Jail
1000 Convicts and a Woman (1971, Brit.)
  Fun and Games
1,000 Shapes of a Female (1963)
  1,000 Female Shapes
One Too Many (1950)
  Killer with a Label
One Way Wahini (1965)
  One Way Wahine
Onibaba (1965, Jap.)
  Demon, The
  Devil Woman, The
  Hole, The
Operation CIA (1965)
  Last Message from Saigon
Operation Crossbow (1965, US/Ital.)
  Great Spy Mission, The
  Code Name: Operation Crossbow
Operation Daybreak (1976, US/Brit./Czech.)
  Price of Freedom
Opeation Snafu (1965, Brit.)
  War Head
  Operation War Head
Operation Thunderbolt (1978, Israel)
  Entebbe: Operation Thunderbolt
Opiate '67 (1967, Fr./Ital.)
  15 from Rome
Orca (1977)
  Orca—Killer Whale
Ordet (1957, Den.)
  Word, The
Organizer, The (1964, Fr./Ital./Yugo.)
  Strikers, The
Other Love, The (1947)
  Man-Killer
Other Men's Women (1931)
  Steel Highway, The
Ouanga (1936, Brit.)
  Crime of Voodoo
Our Hitler, a Film from Germany (1980, Ger.)
  Our Hitler
  Hitler, a Film from Germany
Out of Season (1975, Brit.)
  Winter Rates
Out of Singapore (1932)
  Gangsters of the Sea
Out of the Fog (1962, Brit.)
  Fog for a Killer
Outcry (1949, Ital.)
  Sun Always Rises, The
  Sun Rises Again, The
Outfit, The (1973)
  Good Guys Always Win, The
Outlaws Is Coming, The (1965)
  Three Stooges Meet the Gunslingers
Outside Chance (1978)*
  Return to Jackson County Jail
Outside In (1972)
  Red, White and Busted
Overland Stagecoach (1942)
  Overland Stage Coach

Pack, The (1977)
  Long Dark Night, The
Paddy (1970, Ireland)
  Goodbye to the Hill
Padre, Padrone (1977, Ital.)
  Father Master
  My Father, My Master
Paid to Dance (1937)
  Hard to Handle
Palace of Nudes (1961, Fr./Ital.)
  Palace of Shame
Palooka (1934)
  Joe Palooka
Pandemonium (1982)
  Thursday the 12th
Panic in Year Zero! (1962)
  End of the World
Panique (1947, Fr.)
  Panic
Paper Bullets (1941)
  Gangs, Inc.
Parades (1972)*
  Break Loose
Paradise Alley (1962)
  Stars in Your Backyard
Paradise in Harlem (1939)*
  Othello in Harlem
Pardon Us (1931)
  Jail Birds

Paris Belongs to Us (1962, Fr.)
  Paris Is Ours
Paris Follies of 1956 (1955)
  Showtime
  Fresh from Paris
Partings (1962, Pol.)
  Lydia Ate the Apple
Passenger, The (1975, Ital.)
  Profession: Reporter
Passion for Life (1951, Fr.)
  I Have a New Master
Passion Holiday (1963)
  Miami Rendezvous
Passion in the Sun (1964)
  Passion of the Sun
Passion of Slow Fire, The (1962, Fr.)
  End of Belle, The
Passion Street, U.S.A. (1964)
  Passion Street
  Passion Streets
  Bourbon Street
Passport to Alcatraz (1940)
  Passport to Hell
Passport to Destiny (1944)
  Passport to Adventure
Pather Panchali (1958, India)
  Song of the Road, The
  Saga of the Road, The
  Lament of the Path, The
Patient Vanishes, The (1947, Brit.)
  This Man is Dangerous
Payroll (1962, Brit.)
  I Promise to Pay
Peace to Him Who Enters (1963, USSR)
  Peace to Him
Pearl of Death, The (1944)
  Sherlock Holmes and the Pearl of Death
Peeper (1975)
  Fat Chance
Peeping Tom (1960, Brit.)
  Face of Fear
Pelvis (1977)*
  Toga Party
  Disco Madness
  Disco Girls
Penitente Murder Case, The (1936)
  Lash of the Penitentes
Pennywhistle Blues, The (1952, S. Africa)
  Magic Garden, The
Perfect Strangers (1984)**
  Blind Alley
Persecution (1974, Brit.)
  Terror of Sheba
  Sheba
Persona (1967, Swed,)
  Masks
Petersen (1974, Aus.)
  "Jock" Petersen
Petty Story, The (1974)*
  Smash-Up Alley
  43—The Petty Story
Phantom of Liberty, The (1974, Fr.)
  Specter of Freedom, The
Phantom Ship, The (1937, Brit.)
  Mystery of the Marie Celeste, The
  Secrets of the Mary Celeste
Phenix City Story, The (1955)
  Phoenix City Story, The
Picadilly Incident (1948, Brit.)
  They Met at Midnight
Pick a Star (1937)
  Movie Struck
Pickup Alley (1957)
  International Police
Pick-Up Summer (1981)
  Pinball Summer
  Pinball Pick-Up
Pie in the Sky (1964)
  Terror in the City
Pimpernel Smith (1941)
  Mister V
  Fighting Pimpernel, The
Pink Motel (1983)
  Motel
Pinocchio in Outer Space (1965, US/Bel.)
  Pinocchio's Adventure in Outer Space
Pioneers of the Frontier (1940)
  Anchor, The
Piranha II: The Spawning (1981, Neth.)
  Piranha II: Flying Killers
Pirates of Capri, The (1949)
  Captain Sirocco
Pit, The (1980)*
  Teddy
Pizza Triangle, The (1970, Ital./Span.)
  Drama of Jealousy (and Other Things)
  Jealousy Italian Style
Place Without Parents, A (1974)*
  Pigeon
  Truckin'

Rovin' Tumbleweeds (1939)
  Washington Cowboy
Royal Affair, A (1950)
  King, The
Royal Affairs in Versailles (1957, Fr.)
  Affairs in Versailles
Ruckus (1981)
  Loner, The
Rugged O'Riordans, The (1949, Aus.)
  Sons of Matthew
Ruling Voice, The (1931)
  Upper Underworld
Run for the Roses (1978)
  Thoroughbred
Runaround, The (1931)
  Lovable and Sweet
  Waiting at the Church
Running Hot (1984)**
  Lucky 13
Rustler's Roundup (1946)
  Rustler's Hideout
Ruthless Four, The (1969, Ital./Ger.)
  Sam Cooper's Gold
  Each Man for Himself
  Every Man for Himself
  Each One for Himself
RX Murder (1958, Brit.)
  Prescription Murder
  Prescription for Murder

Sabotage (1936, Brit.)
  Woman Alone, The
Sabra (1970, Fr./Ital./Israel)
  Death of a Jew
Sacred Knives of Vengeance, The (1974, Hong Kong)
  Killer, The
Sadist, The (1963)
  Profile of Terror, The
Saga of the Viking Women and Their Voyage to the Waters of the Great SeaSerpent, The (1957)
  Viking Women and the Sea Serpent, The
Sailor of the King (1953, Brit.)
  Able Seaman Brown
Sam Small Leaves Town (1937, Brit.)
  It's Sam Small Again
Sammy Stops the World (1978)
  Stop the World—I Want to Get Off
Sam's Song (1971)
  Swap, The
Samson and the Seven Miracles of the World (1963, Fr./Ital.)
  Maciste at the Court of the Great Khan
  Goliath and the Golden City
Samson and the Slave Queen (1963, Ital.)
  Zorro Against Maciste
Samurai (Part III) (1967, Jap.)
  Duel at Ganryu Island
Sand (1949)
  Will James' Sand
Sanders (1963, Brit.)
  Death Drums Along the River
Sanders of the River (1935, Brit.)
  Bosambo
  Coast of Skeletons
Sandokan the Great (1964, Fr./Ital./Span.)
  Sandokan, the Tiger of Mompracem
Sandu Follows the Sun (1965, USSR)
  Man Following the Sun
Saragossa Manuscript, The (1972, Pol.)
  Adventures of a Nobleman
  Manuscript Found in Saragossa
Satan Never Sleeps (1962)
  Flight from Terror
Sasquatch (1978)
  Sasquatch, the Legend of Bigfoot
Satanist, The (1968)*
  Succubus
Satan's Mistress (1982)
  Fury of the Succubus
  Demon Rage
  Dark Eyes
Satan's Satellites (1958)
  Zombies of the Stratosphere
Satin Mushroom, The (1969)
  Soft Warm Experience, A
Savage! (1962)
  Mission to Hell
Savage, The (1975, Fr.)
  Lovers Like Us
Savage Weekend (1983)
  Killer Behind the Mask, The
  Upstate Murders, The
Savages from Hell (1968)
  Big Enough and Old Enough
Scalpel (1976)
  False Face

Scared Stiff (1945)
  Treasure of Fear
Scared to Death (1981)
  Terror Factor, The
Scarface, a Shame of a Nation (1932)
  Scarface
Scarlet Claw, The (1944)
  Sherlock Holmes and the Scarlet Claw
Scarred (1984)**
  Red on Red
  Street Love
Scavengers, The (1959)
  City of Sin
Scavengers, The (1969)
  Grabbers, The
Scent of Mystery (1960)
  Holiday in Spain
Schizo (1977, Brit.)
  Amok, Blood of the Dead
Schizoid (1980)
  Murder by Mail
Schlock (1973)
  Banana Monster, The
School for Secrets (1946, Brit.)
  Secret Flight
School for Sex (1966, Jap.)
  School of Love
School for Unclaimed Girls (1973, Brit.)
  House of Unclaimed Women
Schweik's New Adventure (1943, Brit.)
  It Started at Midnight
Scream in the Night (1943)
  Murder in Morocco
Scream of the Butterfly (1965)
  Passion Pit, The
Screamers (1979, Ital.)
  Something Waits in the Dark
  Island of the Fishmen, The
Scum of the Earth (1963)
  Devil's Camera
Scum of the Earth (1976)
  Poor White Trash II
Seabo (1978)
  Buckstone County Prison
Season of Passion (1961, Aus./Brit.)
  Summer of the Seventeenth Doll
Second-Hand Hearts (1981)
  Hamsters of Happiness
Second Woman, The (1951)
  Here Lies Love
  Ellen
  Twelve Miles Out
Secret Agent (1933, Brit.)
  Spy 77
Secret Agent Fireball (1965, Fr./Ital.)
  Killers are Challenged
Secret Agent Super Dragon (1966, Fr./Ital./Ger./Monaco)
  Super Dragon
Secret File: Hollywood (1962)
  Secret File of Hollywood
Secret Honor (1984)**
  Secret Honor: The Last Testament of Richard M. Nixon
  Secret Honor: A Political Myth
Secret of Magic Island, The (1964, Fr./Ital.)
  Secret of Outer Space Island
Secret of Stamboul, The (1936, Brit.)
  Spy in White, The
Secret of the Telegian, The (1961, Jap.)
  Telegian, The
Secret Partner, The (1961, Brit.)
  Street Partner, The
Secret Witness, The (1931)
  Terror By Night
Secretary, The (1971)*
  Three Girls in Hot Pants
  Girl in Hot Pants, The
Secrets of Women (1961, Swed.)
  Waiting Women
Seed of Innocence (1980)
  Teen Mothers
Seeds of Evil (1981)
  Gardener, The
Sellers of Girls (1967, Fr.)
  Girl Merchants
Sensations of 1945 (1944)
  Sensations
Senso (1968, Ital.)
  Wanton Contessa, The
Sensualita (1954, Ital.)
  Barefoot Savage
Sequoia (1934)
  Malibu
Sergeant Deadhead (1965)
  Sergeant Deadhead the Astronut
Sergeant Jim (1962, Yugo.)
  Mr. Jim American, Soldier and Gentleman
Serpent, The (1973, Fr./Ital./Ger.)
  Night Flight from Moscow

Seven Alone (1975)
  House without Windows
Seven Beauties (1976, Ital.)
  Pasqualino; Seven Beauties
Seven Samurai, The (1956, Jap.)
  Magnificent Seven, The
Sex Du Jour (1976)*
  Soup Du Jour
Sex Kittens Go to College (1960)
  Beauty and the Robot
  Beauty and the Brain
Sex Madness (1937)
  They Should Be Told
  They Must Be Told
Shadow of the Werewolf (1970, Span./Ger.)
  Werewolf vs. the Vampire Woman, The
Shadowman (1974, Fr./Ital.)
  Man without a Face, The
Shadows Grow Longer, The (1962, Switz./Ger.)
  Defiant Daughters
Shadows of Forgotten Ancestors (1967, USSR)
  Shadows of Our Ancestors
  Shadows of Our Forgotten Ancestors
Shame of the Sabine Women, The (1962, Mex.)
  Mating of the Sabine Women, The
  Rape of the Sabine Women, The
Shangri-La (1972)*
  Xanadu
Shark (1970, US/Mex.)
  Maneater
She Devil (1940)*
  Louisiana
She-Devil Island (1936, Mex.)
  Maria Elena
She Freak (1967)
  Alley of Nightmare
She-Wolf, The (1931)
  Mother's Millions
She'll Follow You Anywhere (1971)*
  Passion Potion
Shepherd of the Hills, The (1964)
  Thunder Mountain
Sheriff of Sage Valley (1942)
  Billy the Kid, Sheriff of Sage Valley
Sherlock Holmes and the Deadly Necklace (1962, Ger.)
  Valley of Fear
Sherlock Holmes and the Spider Woman (1944)
  Spider Woman
Ship that Died of Shame, The (1956, Brit.)
  PT Raiders
Shivers (1984, Pol.)**
  Creeps
Shock Waves (1977)
  Death Corps
  Almost Human
Shoeshine (1947, Ital.)
  Sciusia
Shop on Main Street, The (1966, Czech)
  Shop on High Street, The
Short Eyes (1977)
  Slammer
Sidelong Glances of a Pigeon Kicker, The (1970)
  Pigeons
Siege of Sidney Street, The (1960, Brit)
  Siege of Hell Street, The
Sign of Aquarius (1970)
  Love Commune
  Ghetto Freaks
Silence (1974)
  Crazy Jack and the Boy
Silent Night, Bloody Night (1974)
  Night of the Dark Full Moon
  Death House
Silver Lining (1932)
  Silver Lining, The
  Thirty Days
Sin of Mona Kent, The (1961)
  Sins of Mona Kent, The
Sin of Nora Moran (1933)
  Voice from the Grave
Sin on the Beach (1964, Fr.)
  Romance on the Beach
Sing as You Swing (1937, Brit.)
  Let the People Laugh
Sing, Dance, Plenty Hot (1940)
  Mania for Melody
Singapore, Singapore (1969, Fr./Ital.)
  Five Ashore for Singapore
Singing Hill, The (1941)
  Singing Hills, The
  Hellborn
Singleton's Pluck (1984, Brit.)**
  Laughter House
Sinister Urge, The (1961)
  Young and the Immoral, The
Sinner's Holiday, 1930
  Women in Love
Sins of Rachel Cade (1960)
  Rachel Cade

Sins of the Children (1930)
Father's Day
Sir, You Are a Widower (1971, Czech.)
Mister, You Are a Widower
Siren of Atlantis (1948)
Atlantis
Queen of Atlantis
Sisters, The (1969, Ger.)
Make Me a Woman
Sixty Glorious Years (1938, Brit)
Queen of Destiny
Skeleton on Horseback (1949, Czech.)
White Sickness, The
Skin Game, The (1965, Brit.)
Skin Games
Skipalong Rosenbloom (1951)
Square Shooter, The
Sky Above Heaven (1964, Fr./Ital.)
Skies Above Heaven
Sky Beyond Heaven
Sky Pirate (1939)*
Mystery Plane
Skyjacked (1941)
Sky Terror
Slasher, The (1975)
Bad Girls
Slaughter Hotel (1971, Ital.)
Asylum Erotica
Slave, The (1963, Ital.)
Son of Spartacus
Slave of The Cannibal God (1979, Ital.)
Mountain of Cannibal Gods
Slayer, The (1982)
Nightmare Island
Slithis (1977)
Spawn of the Slithis
Small Hours, The (1962)
Flaming Desire
Small Town Girl (1936)
One Horse Town
Smallest Show on Earth (1957, Brit.)
Big Time Operators
Smell of Honey, a Swallow of Brine! A (1966)
Smell of Honey, The!
Taste of Honey, a Swallow of Brine, A!
Smokey and the Goodtime Outlaws (1978)*
Made It On My Own
J.D. and the Salt Flat Kid
Snake People, The (1968, Mex./U.S.)
Isle of the Snake People
Isle of the Dead, The
Living Dead, The
Snow Devils, The (1965, Ital.)
Space Devils
Snow Demons
Devils from Space, The
Devil Men from Space
Snuffy Smith, Yard Bird (1942)
Private Snuffy Smith
Society Doctor (1935)
Only Eight Hours
Sod Sisters (1969)
Head for the Hills
Sodom and Gomorrah (1962, US/Fr./Ital.)
Last Days of Sodom and Gomorrah, The
Sol Madrid (1968)
Heroin Gang, The
Some Like it Cool (1979, Ger./Aust./Ital./Fr.)
Casanova and Co.
Some Like it Hot (1939)
Rhythm Romance
Some of My Best Friends Are...(1971)
Bar, The
Something For Everyone (1970)
Rook, The
Something to Hide (1972, Brit.)
Shattered
Something to Sing About (1937)
Battling Hoofer
Sometimes a Great Notion (1971)
Never Give an Inch
Son of Dracula (1974, Brit.)
Young Dracula
Son of Sinbad (1955)
Nights in a Harem
Sons of New Mexico (1949)
Brat, The
Sons of The Desert (1933)
Sons of the Legion
Convention City
Fraternally Yours
Sorority Girl (1957)
Confessions of a Sorority Girl
Sound of Horror (1966, Span.)
Sound from a Million Years Ago
Prehistoric Sound, The
Sound of Trumpets, The (1963, Ital.)
Il Posto
Southern Yankee, A (1948)
My Hero!

Space Amoeba, The (1970, Jap.)
Yog—Monster from Space
Space Cruiser (1977, Jap)
Space Cruiser Yamato
Space Firebird 2772 (1979, Jap.)
Phoenix 2772
Space Master X/7 (1958)
Mutiny in Outer Space
Space Monster (1965)
First Woman into Space
Voyage Beyond the Sun
Space Raiders (1983)
Star Child
Spaced Out (1981, Brit.)
Outer Touch
Spacehunter: Adventures in the Forbidden Zone
(1983)
Road Gangs
Adventures in the Creep Zone
Spaceship, The (1935, USSR)
Cosmic Voyage, The
Special Day, A (1977, Ital./Can.)
Great Day, The
Specialist, The (1975)
Special Touch, The
Hand of the Godfather
Spell of the Hypnotist (1956)
Fright
Spider, The (1958)
Earth Vs. the Spider
Spider Baby (1968)
Liver Eaters, The
Spider Baby or the Strangest Story Ever Told
Cannibal Orgy or the Maddest Story Ever Told
Spies of the Air (1940, Brit.)
Spies in the Air
Spirits of the Dead, The (1969, Fr./Ital.)
Histoires Extraordinaires
Spiritualist, The (1948)
Amazing Mr. X, The
Spoiled Rotten (1968, Ger.)
Prized as a Mate!
Sputnik (1960, Fr.)
Dog, a Mouse and a Sputnik, A
Spy in Your Eye (1966, Ital.)
Berlin, Appointment For the Spies
Spy Ring, The (1938)
International Spy
Square Root of Zero (1964)
This Immoral Age
Squares (1972)
Riding Tall
Sssssss (1973)
Sssssnake
Stacey (1973)
Stacey and Her Gangbusters
Stacey's Knights (1983)
Double Down
Stage to Blue River (1951)
Stage from Blue River
Star! (1968)
Those Were the Happy Times
Star Pilot (1977, Ital.)
2¢5 Missione Hydra
Starcrash (1979)
Stella Star
Starship Invasion (1978, Can.)
Alien Encounter
War of the Aliens
Winged Serpent
Stateline Motel (1976, Ital.)
Last Chance For a Born Loser
Steel (1980)
Look Down and Die
Men of Steel
Stepchildren (1962, USSR)
Somebody Else's Children
Stepmother, The (1973)*
Impulsion
Stick Up, The (1978, Brit.)
Mud
Stoker, The (1935, Brit.)
Shovel Up a Bit More Coal
Stolen Dirigible, The (1966, Czech.)
Two Years Holiday
Stony Island (1978)
My Main Man from Stony Island
Storm in a Water Glass (1963, Aust.)
Flower Woman of Lindenau, The
Storm Planet (1962, USSR)
Planet of Storms
Cosmonauts on Venus
Stormy Crossing (1958, Brit.)
Black Tide
Story of Adele H. (1975, Fr.)
L'Histoire d'Adele H.
Story of Cinderella, The (1976, Brit.)
Slipper and the Rose, The
Story of Esther Costello, The (1957, Brit.)
Golden Virgin

Story of Joseph and His Brethren (1962, Ital.)
Joseph and His Brethren
Joseph Sold By His Brothers
Story of Robin Hood, The (1952, Brit.)
Story of Robin Hood and His Merry Men
Story of the Count of Monte Cristo (1962, Fr./Ital.)
Count of Monte Cristo, The
Story of Monte Cristo, The
Stowaway in the Sky (1962, Fr.)
Voyage in a Balloon
Strange Adventure (1933)
Wayne Murder Case
Strange Fetishes, The (1967)
Strange Fetishes of the Go-Go Girls, The
Strange Holiday (1945)
Day After Tomorrow, The
Strange Illusion (1945)
Out of the Night
Strange Love of Molly Louvain, The (1932)
Molly Louvain
Strange Shadows in An Empty Room (1977, Can./
Ital.)
Shadows in An Empty Room
Blazing Magnum
Stranger from Venus, The (1954, Brit.)
Immediate Disaster
Venusian, The
Stranger in Town, A (1968, US/Ital.)
Dollar Between the Teeth, A
Strangers, The (1955, Ital.)
Journey to Italy
Lonely Lady, The
Trip to Italy, A
Lonely Woman, The
Stranger's Gundown, The (1974, Ital.)
Django the Bastard
Strangers of the Evening (1932)
Hidden Corpse
Strategy of Terror (1969)
In Darkness Waiting
Street Girls (1975)*
Crackers
Strictly Illegal (1935, Brit.)
Here Comes a Policeman
Strictly Unconventional (1930)
Circle, The
Study in Terror, A (1966, Brit./Ger.)
Fog
Such Is Life (1936, Brit.)
Music and Millions
Sucker, The (1966, Fr./Ital.)
Sucker...Or How to Be Glad When You've Been
Had, The
Sudden Terror (1970, Brit.)
Eyewitness
Sugar Hill (1974)
Voodoo Girl
Zombies of Sugar Hill
Sugarfoot (1951)
Swirl of Glory
Summer Run (1974)*
Back Pack Girls
Good Times
Sundance Cassidy and Butch the Kid (1975)*
Sundance and the Kid
Go for Broke
Sunshine Run (1979)*
Catch the Black Sunshine
Super Fuzz (1981)
Supersnooper
Super Soul Brother (1978)*
Six Thousand Dollar Nigger
Supreme Secret, The (1958, Brit.)
God Speaks Today
Surabaya Conspiracy (1975)*
Goldseekers
Surf II (1984)**
Surf II—The End of the Trilogy
Surftide 77 (1962)
Call Surftide 77
Call Girl 77
Surftide 777
Swamp Women (1956)
Swamp Diamonds
Cruel Swamp
Sweater Girls (1978)*
Super Flirts
Sweet Beat (1962, Brit.)
Amorous Sex, The
Sweet Body of Deborah, The (1969, Fr./Ital.)
Soft Body of Deborah, The
Sweet Body, The
Sweet Ecstasy (1962, Fr.)
Sweet Violence
Sweet Light in a Dark Room (1966, Czech.)
Romeo, Juliet and Darkness
Sweet Love, Bitter (1967)
It Won't Rub Off, Baby!
Black Love—White Love

Sweet Savior (1971)*
    Love Thrill Murders
Sweet Skin (1965, Fr./Ital.)
    Strip Tease
Sweet Substitute (1964, Can.)
    Caressed
Sweet Suzy (1973)
    Blacksnake
Swindler, The (1962, Fr./Ital.)
    Il Bidone
Swing, Cowboy, Swing (1944)*
    Bad Man from Big Bend
Swingin' Affair, A (1963)
    Rebel in the Ring
Swingin' Along (1962)
    Double Trouble
Swinging Barmaids, The (1976)
    Eager Beaver
Swinging Cheerleaders, The (1974)*
    Locker Room Girls
Switchblade Sisters (1975)
    Jezebelles, The
    Jezebels, The
    Playgirl Gang
Sylvie and the Phantom (1950, Fr.)
    Sylvie Et Le Fantome
    Sylvia and the Ghost
Symphony of a Massacre (1965, Fr./Ital.)
    Mystifiers, The

T-Bird Gang (1959)
    Pay-Off, The
Take Her by Surprise (1967, Can.)
    Taken by Surprise
    Violent Love
Take It from the Top (1982)*
    "Go Mama Go!"
Tales of a Salesman (1965)
    Tales of a Traveling Salesman
Tales of Paris (1962, Fr./Ital.)
    Of Beds and Broads
    Les Parisiennes
Tales of Terror (1962)
    Poe's Tales of Terror
Talisman, The (1966)
    Savage American, The
Talk About a Lady (1946)
    Duchess of Broadway
Target: Harry (1980)
    How to Make It
    What's in It for Harry?
Tarzan's Deadly Silence (1970)
    Deadly Silence, The
Taste of Blood, A (1967)
    Secret of Dr. Alucard, The
Taxi to Heaven (1944, USSR)
    Air-Chauffeur
Tea and Rice (1964, Jap.)
    Flavor of Green Tea Over Rice, The
Teacher, The (1974)
    Seductress, The
Teenage Bad Girl (1959, Brit.)
    Bad Girl
Teenage Caveman (1958)
    Out of the Darkness
    Prehistoric World
Teenage Doll (1957)
    Young Rebels, The
Teenage Monster (1958)
    Meteor Monster
Teenager (1975)*
    Real Thing, The
Tell-Tale Heart, The (1962, Brit.)
    Hidden Room of 1,000 Horrors, The
Temptress and the Monk, The (1963, Jap.)
    Temptress, The
Ten Little Indians (1975, Ital./Fr./Span./Ger.)
    And Then There Were None
Tender Flesh (1976)
    Welcome to Arrow Beach
Teorema (1968, Ital.)
    Theorem
Terrace, The (1964, Arg.)
    Roof Garden, The
Terror, The (1963)
    Lady of the Shadows
Terror Beneath the Sea (1966, Jap.)
    Water Cyborgs
Terror by Night (1946)
    Sherlock Holmes in Terror by Night
Terror from the Year 5,000 (1958)
    Terror from 5,000 A.D.
    Girl from 5,000 A.D., The
Terror from Under the House
    Inn of the Frightened People
    After Jenny Died

Terror House (1972)
    Terror at Red Wolf Inn
    Folks at Red Wolf Inn, The
Terror Is a Man (1959, US/Phil.)
    Blood Creatures
Terror of Dr. Mabuse, The (1965, Ger.)
    Testament of Dr. Mabuse, The
    Terror of the Mad Doctor, The
Test of Pilot Pirx, The (1978, Pol./USSR)
    Test Pilot Pirx
Testament of Dr. Mabuse, The (1933, Ger.)
    Last Will of Dr. Mabuse, The
Texas Justice (1942)*
    Lone Rider in Texas Justice
Texas Lawman (1952)
    Lone Star Lawmen
Thank Heaven for Small Favors (1965, Fr.)
    Funny Parishioner, The
    Heaven Sent
Thank You Aunt (1969, Ital.)
    Come Play with Me
That Kind of Girl (1963, Brit.)
    Teen Age Tramp
That Man George (1967, Fr./Ital./Span.)
    Our Man in Marrakesh
That Tennessee Beat (1966)
    Tennessee Beat, The
That's the Way of the World (1975)
    Shining Star
Theatre of Death (1967, Brit.)
    Blood Fiend
Their Only Chance (1978)*
    To Speak As Brothers
    Spirits of the Wild
There Is Still Room in Hell (1963, Ger.)
    Still Room in Hell
There Was an Old Couple (1967, USSR)
    Couple, The
There's Always Vanilla (1972)*
    Affair, The
There's Magic in Music (1941)
    Hard-Boiled Canary, The
Therese (1963, Fr.)
    Therese Desqueyroux
They Call Me Bruce (1982)
    Fistful of Chopsticks, A
They Call Me Robert (1967, USSR)
    His Name Is Robert
    He Was Called Robert
    Call Me Robert
They Came from Within (1976, Can.)
    Parasite Murders, The
    Frissons
    Shivers
They Live by Night, (1948)
    Your Red Wagon
They Saved Hitler's Brain (1964)
    Madmen of Mandoras
    Return of Mr. H., The
They're Coming to Get You (1976)*
    All the Colors of the Dark
Think Dirty (1970, Brit.)
    Every Home Should Have One
Third Man on the Mountain (1959)
    Banner in the Sky
This Angry Age (1958, Ital./Fr.)
    Sea Wall, The
This England (1941, Brit.)
    Our Heritage
This Is Spinal Tap (1984)**
    Spinal Tap
This Rebel Breed (1960)
    Three Shades of Love
    Lola's Mistake
This Was Paris (1942, Brit.)
    So This Was Paris
Those Fantastic Flying Fools (1967, Brit.)
    Blast-Off
Those Were the Days (1940)
    At Good Old Siwash
Thousand Eyes of Dr. Mabuse, The (1960, Fr./Ital./Ger.)
    Eye of Evil
    Shadow Versus the Thousand Eyes of Dr. Mabuse, The
Three Faces of Sin (1963, Fr./Ital.)
    Three Sinners
Three Faces West (1940)
    Refugee, The
Three Godfathers (1936)
    Miracle in the Sand
300 Spartans, The (1962)
    Lion of Sparta
Three Moves to Freedom (1960, Ger.)
    Royal Game, The
Three Rogues (1931)
    Not Exactly Gentlemen
Three Worlds of Gulliver, The (1960, Brit.)
    Worlds of Gulliver, The

Thrill Killers, The (1965)
    Monsters Are Loose, The
    Maniacs Are Loose, The
Throne of Blood (1961, Jap.)
    Cobweb Castle
    Castle of the Spider's Web, The
Thunder in the Blood (1962, Fr.)
    Warm Body, The
Thunder Trail (1937)
    Thunder Pass
Thundering Herd, The (1934)
    In the Days of the Thundering Herd
Tidal Wave (1975, US/Jap.)
    Submersion of Japan, The
    Japan Sinks
Tight Little Island (1949, Brit.)
    Mad Little Island
Tight Skirts, Loose Pleasures (1966, Fr.)
    Tight Skirts
    Chainwork Love
    Loose Pleasures
Till Marriage Do Us Part (1979, Ital.)
    How Low Can You Fall?
Time in the Sun, A (1970, Swed.)
    Princess, The
Time of Their Lives, The (1946)
    Ghost Steps Out, The
Time to Die, A (1983)
    Seven Graves for Rogan
Timerider (1983)
    Adventure of Lyle Swann
Tin Girl, The (1970, Ital.)
    Girl of Tin, The
Tintorera...Bloody Waters (1977, Brit./Mex.)
    Tintorera...Tiger Shark
To Find a Man (1972)
    Boy Next Door, The
    Sex and the Teenager
To Hell You Preach (1972)*
    Vengeance of a Gunfighter
Tobo, the Happy Clown (1965)*
    Happy Clown, The
Todd Killings, The (1970)
    Dangerous Friend, A
    Skipper
Together for Days (1972)*
    Black Cream
Tomb of Ligeia, The (1965, Brit.)
    Tomb of the Cat
Tombstone, the Town Too Tough to Die (1942)
    Tombstone
Tonight's the Night (1932, Brit.)
    Tonight's the Night—Pass It On
Tonight's the Night (1954, Brit.)
    O'Leary Night
Tonka (1958)
    Horse Named Comanche, A
Too Hot to Handle (1961, Brit.)
    Playgirl After Dark
Too Soon to Love (1960)
    High School Honeymoon
Too Young to Marry (1931)
    Broken Dishes
Tormented, The (1978, Ital.)
    Eerie Midnight Horror Show
    Sexorcists, The
Touch of Her Flesh, The (1967)
    Way Out Love
    Touch of Her Life, The
Touch of Satan, The (1971)
    Touch of Melissa, The
    Night of the Demon
    Curse of Melissa
Touched by Love (1980)
    To Elvis with Love
Town Called Hell, A (1971, Span.)
    Town Called Bastard, A
Town Like Alice (1959, Brit.)
    Rape of Malaya
Toy Wife, The (1938)
    Frou-Frou
Trails of Danger (1930)
    Trails of Peril
Train Goes to Kiev, The (1961, USSR)
    Age of Youth
Trapped by G-Men (1937)
    River of Missing Men, The
Treasure of Jamaica Reef, The (1976)
    Evil in the Deep
Triple Echo (1973, Brit.)*
    Soldiers in Skirts
Triple Irons (1973, Hong Kong)
    New One-Armed Swordsman, The
Tristan and Isolt (1981)
    Lovespell
Trojan Horse, The (1962, Fr./Ital.)
    Trojan War, The
    Mighty Warrior, The
Trojan Brothers, The (1946)
    Murder in the Footlights

Truckin' Man (1974)*
   Trucker's Woman
Try and Get Me, (1950)
   Sound of Fury, The
Turkish Cucumber, The (1963, Ger.)
   Wedding Present
   Daddy's Delectable Dozen
Turned Out Nice Again (1941, Brit.)
   It's Turned Out Nice Again
20th Century Oz (1977, Aus.)
   Oz
24 Hour Lover (1970, Ger.)
   Crunch
Twenty-One Days Together (1939, Brit.)
   Twenty-One Days
Twenty Questions Murder Mystery, The (1950, Brit.)
   Murder in the Air
Twice Told Tales (1963)
   Nathaniel Hawthorne's "Twice Told Tales"
Twilight Path (1965, Jap.)
   Radishes and Carrots
   Mr. Radish and Mr. Carrot
Twist, The (1976, Fr.)
   Folies Bourgeoises
   Continental Twist, The
   Young and the Cool,The
Twitch of the Death Nerve (1973, Ital.)
   Last House On the Left, Part II
Two and Two Make Six (1962, Brit.)
   Change of Heart, A
   Girl Swappers, The
Two Are Guilty (1964, Fr.)
   Sword and the Balance, The
Two Girls on Broadway (1940)
   Choose Your Partners
Two Loves (1961)
   Spinster, The
Two of Us, The (1968, Fr.)
   Claude
   Old Man and the Boy

Ugetsu (1954, Jap.)
   Ugetsu Monogatari
Ultimate Solution of Grace Quigley, The (1984)**
   Grace Quigley
Ultimate Thrill, The (1974)
   Ultimate Chase, The
Un Carnet de Bal (1938, Fr.)
   Life Dances On
   Christine
Und Immer Ruft das Herz (1966, Ger.)
   Moonlight
Under California Stars (1948)
   Under California Skies
Under Mexicali Stars (1950)
   Under Mexicali Skies
Under the Banner of Samurai (1969, Jap.)
   Samurai Banners
Underground Guerrillas (1944, Brit.)
   Chetnik
Uneasy Virtue (1931, Brit.)
   Flirting Wives
Unidentified Flying Oddball,The (1979, Brit.)
   UFO
University of Life (1941, USSR)
   Mu University
Up for Murder (1931)
   Fires of Youth
Up in the Cellar (1970)
   Three in the Cellar
Up the Academy (1980)
   Mad Magazine's Up the Academy
Up Your Teddy Bear (1970)
   Toy Grabbers, The
   Mother
Upper Hand, The (1967, Fr./Ital./Ger.)
   Rififi in Paris
Upper World (1934)
   Upperworld
Utilities (1983, Can.)
   Getting Even

V.D. (1961)
   Damaged Goods

Valachi Papers, The (1972, Ital.)
   Valachi Papers or Costra Nostra
Vampire, The (1957)
   Mark of the Vampire
Vampire Hookers (1979, Phil.)
   Sensuous Vampires
   Cemetery Girls
Vampires, The (1969, Mex.)
   Vampire Girls, The
Vampyr (1932, Fr./Ger.)
   Strange Adventure of David Gray, The
   Castle of Doom
   Vampire, The
   Not Against the Flesh
Varan the Unbelievable (1962, US/Jap.)
   Monster Varan
Vault of Horror, The (1973, Brit.)
   Tales from the Crypt II
Very Happy Alexander, A (1969, Fr.)
   Happy Alexander
   Alexander
Very Curious Girl, A (1970, Fr.)
   Dirty Mary
   Pirate's Fiancee
Vicious Circle, The (1948)
   Circle, The
Victor Frankenstein (1975, Brit.)
   Terror of Frankenstein
Vienna, City of Songs (1931, Ger.)
   City of Songs
Vigilante (1983)
   Street Gang
Villain, The (1979)
   Cactus Jack
Violent Midnight (1963)
   Psychomania
Violent Road (1958)
   Hell's Highway
Violent Years (1956)
   Female
Virgin Island (1960, Brit.)
   Our Virgin Island
Virgin Witch, The (1973, Brit.)
   Lesbian Twins
Vitelloni (1956, Ital.)
   I Vitelloni
   Young and the Passionate, The
Vixens, The (1969)
   Friends and Lovers
   Women, The
Viva Italia (1978, Ital.)
   New Monsters, The
Voyage, The (1974, Ital.)
   The Trip
   The Journey
Voyage to the End of the Universe (1963, Czech.)
   Icarus XB-1
Voyage to the Planet of Prehistoric Women (1966)
   Gill Woman
   Gill Women of Venus
Voodoo Island 1957)
   Silent Death

W (1974)
   I Want Her Dead
Wagon Wheels (1934)
   Caravans West
Waitress (1982)
   Soup to Nuts
Wall of Death (1952, Brit.)
   There Is Another Sun
Wallet, The (1952, Brit.)
   Blueprint for Danger
Waltz of the Toreadors (1962, Brit.)
   Amorous General, The
Wanderlove (1970)
   Wander Love Story
Wanted for Murder (1946, Brit.)
   Voice in the Night, A
War Between the Planets (1971, Ital.)
   Planet on the Prowl
War Dogs (1942)
   Unsung Heroes
War of the Gargantuas, The (1970, Jap.)
   Duel of the Gargantuas
War of the Monsters (1972, Jap.)
   Godzilla on Monster Island
   Godzilla Vs. Gigan
War of the Planets (1977, Jap.)
   War in Space
War of the Wizards (1983, Taiwan)
   Phoenix, The
War of the Zombies (1965, Ital.)
   Night Star
   Goddess of Electra
Warhead (1974)*
   Prisoner in the Middle

Warlords of Atlantis (1978)
   7 Cities to Atlantis
Way Ahead, The (1945, Brit.)
   Immortal Battalion, The
Way Back Home (1932)
   Other People's Business
We Joined the Navy (1962, Brit.)
   We Are in the Navy Now
Web of Passion (1961, Fr.)
   Leda
   Double Tour, A
Web of the Spider (1972, Ital./Fr./Ger.)
   In the Grip of the Spider
   Dracula in the Castle of Blood
   And Comes the Dawn...But Colored Red
Wedding Night (1970, Ireland)
   I Can't...I Can't
Weekend, Italian Style (1967, Fr./Ital./Span.)
   Weekend Wives
Week-End Marriage (1932)
   Working Wives
Weekend with the Babysitter (1970)
   Weekend Babysitter
Weird Love Makers, The (1963, Jap.)
   Wild Love-Makers
Welcome to Hard Times (1967)
   Killer on a Horse
Werewolf in a Girl's Dormitory (1961, Ital.)
   Ghoul in School, The
   Lycanthropus
West Is Still Wild (1977)
   Mule Feathers
West of Shanghai (1937)
   Warlord, The
West of Texas (1943)
   Shootin' Irons
Westerner, The (1936)
   Fighting Westerner, The
What (1965, Fr./Brit./Ital.)
   Night is the Phantom
What a Carve Up (1962, Brit.)
   No Place Like Homicide
What Changed Charley Farthing (1976, Brit.)
   Bananas Boat
What Do I Tell the Boys at the Station? (1972)*
   Broad Coalition
   That Man Is Pregnant
   For Women Only
What Would You Say to Some Spinach (1976, Czech.)
   Nice Plate of Spinach, A
What's Up Front (1964)
   Fall Guy, The
Wheeler Dealers, The (1963)
   Separate Beds
When Ladies Meet (1933)
   Truth Is Stranger
When London Sleeps (1934, Brit.)
   Menace
   While London Sleeps
When the Boys Meet the Girls (1965)
   Girl Crazy
When the Clock Strikes (1961)
   Clock Strikes Three, The
When the North Wind Blows (1974)*
   Snow Tigers, The
When Time Ran Out (1980)*
   Day the World Ended, The
Where Is This Lady? (1932, Brit.)
   Where Is This Girl?
Where the Hot Wind Blows (1960, Fr./Ital.)
   Law, The
While I Live (1947, Brit.)
   Dream of Olwen, The
While Thousands Cheer (1940)*
   Crooked Money
   Gridiron Graft
Whipped, The (1950)
   Underworld Story, The
Whirlpool of Women (1966, Jap.)
   Whirlpool of Flesh
White Buffalo, The (1977)
   Hunt to Kill
White Dog (1982)
   Trained to Kill
White Nights (1961, Ital./Fr.)
   Le Notti Blanche
   Nuits Blanches
White Sister (1973, Ital./Fr./Span.)
   Sin, The
White Slave Ship (1962, Fr./Ital.)
   Mutiny, The
White Stallion (1947)
   Harmony Trail
White Tie And Tails (1946)
   Swindlers, The
White Voices (1964, Fr./Ital.)
   Under Cover Rogue
Who Fears the Devil (1972)
   Legend of Hillbilly John, The

Who Killed "Doc" Robbin? (1948)
　Curley and His Gang in the Haunted Mansion
Who Killed Fen Markham (1937, Brit.)
　Angelus, The
Who Killed Jessie? (1965, Czech.)
　Who Would Kill Jessie?
　Who Wants to Kill Jessie?
Who's that Knocking at My Door? (1968)
　J.R.
　I Call First
Wife of General Ling, The (1938, Brit.)
　Revenge of General Ling
Wife Wanted (1946)*
　Shadow of Blackmail
Wifemistress (1979, Ital.)
　Lover, Wife
　Mogliamante
Wild Child, The (1970, Fr.)
　L'Enfant Sauvage
Wild Horse (1931)
　Silver Devil
Wild McCullochs, The (1975)
　McCullochs, The
Wild North, The (1952)
　Big North, The
Wild One, The (1953)
　Hot Blood
Wild Ones on Wheels (1967)
　Drivers to Hell
Wild Pack, The (1972)
　Sandpit Generals, The
Wild Strawberries (1959, Swed.)
　Smultronstallet
Wild Weed (1949)
　She Should'a Said No
　Devil's Weed
Wild West (1946)
　Prairie Outlaws
Wild World of Batwoman, The (1966)
　She Was a Hippy Vampire
Wild Youth (1961)
　Naked Youth
Wildflowers (1968)
　Wildflowers: The Story of a Draft Dodger
William Comes to Town (1948, Brit.)
　William at the Circus
Win, Place or Steal (1975)
　Three for the Money
Wind From the East (1970, Fr./Ital./Ger.)
　East Wind
　Le Vent D'Est
Wise Age (1962, Jap.)
　Woman's Place, A
Wise Girls (1930)
　Kempy
Wishbone Cutter (1978)
　Shadow Mountain
　Shadow of Chikara

Witches, The (1969, Fr./Ital.)
　Le Streghe
　Les Sorcieres
Witchmaker, The (1969)
　Legend of Witch Hollow
Without Warning (1952)
　Story Without a Name, The
Witness, The (1982, Hung.)
　Without a Trace
Wolf Lake (1979)*
　Honor Guard, The
Wolf Larson (1975, Ital.)
　Legend of Sea Wolf, The
Woman and Temptation (1967, Arg.)
　Naked Temptation
Woman for All Men, A (1975)*
　Part Time Wife
Woman in Chains (1932, Brit.)
　Woman in Bondage
Woman in Green, The (1945)
　Sherlock Holmes in the Woman in Green
Woman in Hiding (1953, Brit.)
　Man in Hiding
Woman Is a Woman, A (1961, Fr.)
　Une Femme Est Une Femme
Woman on Pier 13, The (1950)
　I Married a Communist
Woman's Devotion, A (1956)
　Battleshock
Women and Bloody Terror (1970)
　His Wife's Habit
Women and War (1965, Fr.)
　Women in War
Women for Sale (1973)*
　Intrigue in the Orient
Women in Bondage (1943)
　Hitler's Women
Women in Cages (1972)*
　Women in Prison
Women in the Night (1948)
　When Men Are Beasts
Wonder Boy (1951, Brit.)
　Wonder Kid
Won't Write Home Mom...I'm Dead (1975)*
　Terror from Within
Working Man, The (1933)
　Adopted Father, The
World Gone Mad, The (1933)
　Public Be Damned
World in My Pocket, The (1962, Fr./Ital./Ger.)
　On Friday at Eleven
World of Apu, The (1960, India)
　Apur Sansar
Wyoming (1940)
　Bad Man of Wyoming

Yank in Viet-Nam, A (1964)
　Year of the Tiger, The
Yankee Don (1931)
　Daredevil Dick
Year One (1974, Ital.)
　Anno Uno
Yellow Passport, The (1931)
　Yellow Ticket, The
Yongkari Monster From The Deep (1967, S.K.)
　Monster Yongkari
　Great Monster Yongkari
Yor, The Hunter from the Future (1983, Ital.)
　World of Yor, The
You Are the World for Me (1964, Aust.)
　Richard Tauber Story, The
You Better Watch Out (1980)
　Christmas Evil
You Can't Fool An Irishman (1950, Ireland)
　Strangers Came, The
You Have to Run Fast (1961)
　Man Missing
You May Be Next (1936)
　Calling All G-Men
　Trapped by Wireless
Young and Evil (1962, Mex.)
　Yambao
　Cry of the Bewitched
Young and Innocent (1937, Brit.)
　Girl Was Young, A
Young Bride (1932)
　Love Starved
Young Nurses, The (1973)
　Nightingale
Young Rebel, The (1969, Fr./Ital./Span.)
　Cervantes
Young Sinner, The (1965)
　Among the Thorns
You're in the Navy Now (1951)
　U.S.S. Teakettle

Z.P.G. (1972)
　Zero Population Growth
Zatoichi (1968, Jap.)
　Zatoichi and the Scoundrels
Zazie (1961, Fr.)
　Zazie in the Underground
　Zazie in the Subway
Zenobia (1939)
　Elephants Never Forget
Zero to Sixty (1978)
　Repo
00-2 Most Secret Agents (1965, Ital.)
　Oh! Those Most Secret Agents
　Worst Secret Agents
Zombie (1980, Ital.)
　Zombie 2
　Zombie Flesh Eaters

ALTERNATE TITLE (AKA) TO MPG TITLE

Below is an alphabetical listing of Alternate Titles (AKA's), followed by the main title under which the film is listed in the MPG.

* Denotes films which appear in the Miscellaneous Talkie section, Volume IX.
** Denotes films which appear in the 1984 film section, Volume IX.

Abandoned Woman
    Abandoned (1949)
Abdulla's Harem
    Abdulla the Great (1956, Brit./Egypt)
Able Seaman Brown
    Sailor of the King (1953, Brit.)
Abnormal
    Hentai (1966, Jap.)
Abominable Snowman
    Abominable Snowman of the Himalayas, The (1957, Brit.)
Absent-Minded
    Daydreamer, The (1975, Fr.)
Absinthe
    Madame X (1929)
Accidental Spy
    Mr. Stringfellow Says No (1937, Brit.)
Accidents Wanted
    Nuisance, The (1933)
Ace in the Hole
    Big Carnival, The (1951)
Acid People, The
    Acid Eaters, The (1968)*
Action Man
    Leather and Nylon (1969, Fr./Ital.)
Adalen Riots
    Adalen 31 (1969, Swed.)
Adam and Evalyn
    Adam and Evelyne (1950, Brit.)
Adelaide
    Fino A Farti Male (1969, Fr./Ital.)
Adopted Father, The
    Working Man, The (1933)
Adorable Idiot
    Ravishing Idiot, A (1966, Ital./Fr.)
Adua and Her Companions
    Love a la Carte (1965, Ital.)
Adua and Her Friends
    Love a la Carte (1965, Ital.)
Adventure of Lyle Swann
    Timerider (1983)
Adventurer, The
    Rover, The (1967, Ital.)
Adventures in the Creep Zone
    Spacehunter: Adventures in the Forbidden Zone (1983)
Adventures of a Nobleman
    Saragossa Manuscript, The (1972, Pol.)
Adventures of Huckleberry Finn, The
    Huckleberry Finn (1939)
Adventures of Quentin Durward
    Quentin Durward (1955)
Adventures of the Prince and the Pauper, The
    Prince and the Pauper, The (1969)
Adventures of Torchy Blane, The
    Fly-Away Baby (1937)
Affair, The
    There's Always Vanilla (1972)
Affair of the Heart, An
    Body and Soul (1947)
Affair of the Heart, An
    Love Affair; or the Case of the Missing Switchboard Operator (1968, Yugo.)
Affair of the Villa Fiorita
    Battle of the Villa Fiorita, The (1965, Brit.)
Affairs in Versailles
    Royal Affairs in Versailles (1957, Fr.)
Africa Erotica
    Karen, the Lovemaker (1970)
African Fury
    Cry, The Beloved Country (1952, Brit.)
African Hunter
    Man Eater (1958)*
African Story, The
    Hatari! (1962)
After Jenny Died
    Terror from Under the House
Again a Love Story
    Love Is a Funny Thing (1970, Fr./Ital.)
Agatha Christie's Endless Night
    Endless Night (1971, Brit.)
Age of Gold
    L'Age D'Or (1979, Fr.)
Age of Youth
    Train Goes to Kiev, The (1961, USSR)
Agent 38-24-36
    Ravishing Idiot, A (1966, Ital./Fr.)

Air-Chauffeur
    Taxi to Heaven (1944, USSR)
Airport '79
    Concorde, The—Airport '79 (1979)
Alas I'm Invisible
    Help I'm Invisible (1952, Ger.)
Alaska Boy
    Joniko and the Kush Ta Ka (1969)
Alexander
    Very Happy Alexander, A (1969, Fr.)
Ali—Fear Eats the Soul
    Fear Eats the Soul (1974, Ger.)
Alibi Breaker
    Double Exposures (1937, Brit.)
Alice in Wonderland in Paris
    Alice of Wonderland in Paris (1966)*
Alice of Wonderland in New Adventures
    Alice of Wonderland in Paris (1966)*
Alice of Wonderland
    Alice of Wonderland in Paris (1966)*
Alien Dead
    It Fell from the Sky (1980)
Alien Encounter
    Starship Invasion (1978, Can.)
Aliki
    Aliki—My Love (1963, U.S./Gr.)*
All Bad
    Indecent (1962, Ger.)
All in Place
    All Screwed Up (1976, Ital.)
All that Money Can Buy
    Devil and Daniel Webster, The (1941)
All the Colors of the Dark
    They're Coming to Get You (1976)*
All the Lovin' Kinfolk
    Kinfolk (1970)
All the Way
    Joker Is Wild, The (1957)
All Weekend Lovers
    Killing Game, The (1968, Fr.)
Alley of Nightmare
    She Freak (1967)
Almost a Bride
    Kiss for Corliss, A (1949)
Almost Human
    Shock Waves (1977)
Amazing Mr. X, The
    Spiritualist, The (1948)
Ambulance Chaser
    Nuisance, The (1933)
American Beauty, The
    La Bèlle Americaine (1961, Fr.)
American Voyeur
    Getting It On (1983)*
Amok
    Rape, The (1965, Gr.)
Amok, Blood of the Dead
    Schizo (1977, Brit.)
Among People
    On His Own (1939, USSR)
Among the Thorns
    Young Sinner, The (1965)
Among Vultures
    Frontier Hellcat (1966, Fr./Ital./Ger./Yugo.)
Amore in Stockholm
    Devil, The (1963, Ital.)
Amorous Adventures of Don Quixote and Sancho Panza (1976)*
    Erotic Adventures of Super Knight, The
Amorous General, The
    Waltz of the Toreadors (1962, Brit.)
Amorous Sex, The
    Sweet Beat (1962, Brit.)
Amuck
    Maniac Mansion (1978, Ital.)
Anatomy of a Syndicate
    Big Operator, The (1959)
Anchor, The
    Pioneers of the Frontier (1940)
And Comes the Dawn...But Colored Red
    Web of the Spider (1972, Ital./Fr./Ger.)
And Jenny Makes Three
    Jenny (1969)
And Nothing But the Truth
    Giro City (1982, Brit.)
And Once Upon A Love
    Fantasies (1981)
And So They Were Married
    Johnny Doesn't Live Here Any More (1944)
And Then There Were None
    Ten Little Indians (1975, Ital./Fr./Span./Ger.)

And Woman...Was Created
    And God Created Woman (1957, Fr,)
Anderson's Angels
    Chesty Anderson, US Navy (1976)
Andrews' Raiders
    Great Locomotive Chase, The (1956)
Angel of H.E.A.T.
    Protectors, Book 1, The (1981)
Angel of Vengeance
    Ms. 45 (1981)
Angel Passed over Brooklyn, An
    Man Who Wagged His Tail, The (1961, Ital./Span.)
Angel Street
    Gaslight (1940)
Angelika
    Affairs of Dr. Holl (1954, Ger.)
Angels' Dirty Women
    Angels' Wild Women (1972)*
Angelus, The
    Who Killed Fen Markham (1937, Brit.)
Animal House
    National Lampoon's Animal House (1978)
Anno Uno
    Year One (1974, Ital.)
Another Woman, Another Day
    Love Merchant, The (1966)
Anthropophagous
    Grim Reaper, The (1981, Ital.)
Anxious Years, The
    Dark Journey (1937, Brit.)
Anyone for Venice?
    Honey Pot, The (1967, Brit.)
Anything for Love
    11 Harrow House (1974, Brit.)
Apaches Last Battle
    Old Shatterhand (1968, Ger./Yugo./Fr./Ital.)
April 1st 2000
    One April 2000 (1952, Aust.)
April Romance
    April Blossoms (1937)
Apur Sansar
    World of Apu, The (1960, India)
Aranas Infernales
    Cerebros Diabolicos (1966, Mex.)
Are You Dying Young Man?
    Beast in the Cellar, The (1971, Brit.)
Arizona Mission
    Gun the Man Down (1957)
Armored Attack
    North Star, The (1943)
Army of Shadows, The
    L'Armee des Ombres (1969, Fr./Ital.)
Arouse and Beware
    Man from Dakota, The (1940)
Arson Racket Squad
    Arson Gang Busters (1938)
As We Forgive
    Breakers Ahead (1938, Brit.)
Assault Force
    Ffolkes (1980, Brit.)
Assault of the Rebel Girls
    Cuban Rebel Girls (1960)
Assault on Paradise
    Maniac! (1977)
Assignment Istanbul
    Castle of Fu Manchu, The (1968, Ger./Span./Ital./Brit.)
Assignment: Kill Castro
    Cuba Crossing (1980)
Asylum Erotica
    Slaughter Hotel (1971, Ital.)
Asylum of the Insane
    Flesh and Blood Show, The (1974, Brit.)
At Good Old Siwash
    Those Were the Days (1940)
Ataragon, the Flying Supersub
    Atragon (1965, Jap.)
Atlantic City, U.S.A.
    Atlantic City (1981, U.S./Can.)
Atlantic Episode
    Catch as Catch Can (1937, Brit.)
Atlantis
    Siren of Atlantis (1948)
Atomic Agent
    Nathalie, Agent Secret (1960, Fr.)
Atomic Monster, The
    Man Made Monster (1941)
Atomic Rocketship
    Flash Gordon (1936)

Bootlegger's Angel
  Bootleggers (1974)
Bop Girl
  Bop Girl Goes Calypso (1957)
Born For Trouble
  Murder in the Big House (1942)
Bosambo
  Sanders of the River (1935, Brit.)
Bourbon St. Shadows
  Invisible Avenger, The (1958)
Bourbon Street
  Passion Street, U.S.A. (1964)
Boxer, The
  Ripped-Off (1971, Ital.)
Boy Next Door, The
  To Find a Man (1972)
Boy of Two Worlds
  Lure of the Jungle, The (1970, Den.)
Boyichi and the Supermonster
  Gamera Versus Gaos (1967, Jap.)
Boys from Brooklyn, The
  Bela Lugosi Meets a Brooklyn Gorilla (1952)
Brainsnatchers, The
  Man Who Lived Again, The (1936, Brit.)
Bram Stoker's Count Dracula
  Count Dracula (1971, Ital./Span./Ger./Brit.)
Branded
  Bad Boy (1938, Brit.)
Brandy Ashore
  Green Grow the Rushes (1951, Brit.)
Brass Monkey, The
  Lucky Mascot, The (1951, Brit.)
Brat, The
  Sons of New Mexico (1949)
Bread, Love, and Jealousy
  Frisky (1955, Ital.)
Break Loose
  Parades (1972)
Break to Freedom
  Albert, R.N. (1953, Brit.)
Breakfast at Manchester Morgue
  Don't Open the Window (1974, Ital.)
Bride of the Monster
  Bride of the Atom (1955)
Broad Coalition
  What Do I Tell the Boys at the Station? (1972)*
Broken Dishes
  Too Young to Marry (1931)
Broken Swords
  Hiken Yaburi (1969, Jap.)
Bronx Warriors
  1990: Bronx Warriors (1983, Ital.)
Brother on the Run
  Boots Turner (1973)*
Brothers Karamazov, The
  Karamazov (1931, Ger.)
Brownie
  Daring Young Man, The (1942)
Buckstone County Prison
  Seabo (1978)
Bugs Bunny—Road Runner Movie, The
  Great American Bugs Bunny-Road Runner
  Chase, The (1979)
Bump in the Night
  Final Terror, The (1983)
Burmese Harp, The
  Harp of Burma (1967, Jap.)
Burn Out
  Journey into Fear (1976, Can.)
Burn, Witch, Burn
  Mark of the Devil (1970, Ger./Brit.)
Burning Hearts
  Kolberg (1945, Ger.)
Burning Question, The
  Reefer Madness (1936)
Businessman's Lunch, The
  Mid-Day Mistress (1968)
Busting Out
  Black Lolita (1975)*
Butcher, The
  Le Boucher (1971, Fr./Ital.)
Butterfly Affair, The
  Popsy Pop (1971, Fr.)

Cabiria
  Nights of Cabiria (1957, Ital.)
Cactus Jack
  Villain, The (1979)
Caged Heat
  Renegade Girls (1974)
Cain's Cutthroats
  Cain's Way (1969)
California in 1878
  Fighting Thru (1931)
California Axe Murder
  Axe (1977)*

California Outpost
  In Old Los Angeles (1948)*
Call Girl 77
  Surftide 77 (1962)
Call It Murder
  Midnight (1934)
Call Me Robert
  They Call Me Robert (1967, USSR)
Call Surftide 77
  Surftide 77 (1962)
Calling All G-Men
  You May Be Next (1936)
Calling Northside 777
  Call Northside 777 (1948)
Calling of Dan Matthews, The
  Dan Matthews (1936)
Calling, The
  Bells (1981, (1981, Can.))
Camille Without Camillias
  Lady without Camellias, The (1981, Ital.)
Canaris, Master Spy
  Canaris (1955, Ger.)
Cannibal Orgy or the Maddest Story Ever Told
  Spider Baby (1968)
Cannibals in the City
  Cannibals in the Streets (1982, Ital./Span.)
Captain Midnight
  On the Air Live with Captain Midnight (1970)
Captain Sirocco
  Pirates of Capri, The (1949)
Captive City, The
  Conquered City (1966, Ital.)
Captives, The
  Escape to Berlin (1962, U.S./Switz./Ger.)
Caravans West
  Wagon Wheels (1934)
Careless Love
  La Bonne Soupe (1964, Fr./Ital.)
Caressed
  Sweet Substitute (1964, Can.)
Carmen
  Bizet's Carmen (1984)** Carry On Venus
  Carry on Jack (1963, Brit.)
Cars That Eat People, The
  Cars That Ate Paris, The (1974, Aus.)
Casanova and Co.
  Some Like it Cool (1979, Ger./Aust./Ital./Fr.)
Cascarrabias
  Grumpy (1930)
Case of Mrs. Loring, The
  Question of Adultery, A (1959, Brit.)
Castaway, The
  Cheaters, The (1945)
Castle of Doom
  Vampyr (1932, Fr./Ger.)
Castle of Terror
  Horror Castle (1965, Ital.)
Castle of Terror
  Castle of Blood (1964, Fr./Ital.)
Castle of the Living Dead
  Horror Castle (1965, Ital.)
Castle of the Spider's Web, The
  Throne of Blood (1961, Jap.)
Catastrophe 1999
  Prophecies of Nostradamus (1974, Jap.)
Catch the Black Sunshine
  Sunshine Run (1979)*
Cauchemares
  Cathy's Curse (1977, Can.)
Cavalier of the Golden Star
  Dream of a Cossack (1982, USSR)
Cavalleria Commandos
  Cavalry Command (1963, U.S./Phil.)
Cavalleria Rusticana
  Fatal Desire (1953, Ital.)
Cave Dwellers, The
  One Million BC (1940)
Cave Man
  One Million BC (1940)
Cemetery Girls
  Vampire Hookers (1979, Phil.)
Cerebro Infernal
  Blue Demon vs. the Infernal Brains (1967, Mex.)
Certain Mr. Scratch, A
  Devil and Daniel Webster, The (1941)
Cervantes
  Young Rebel, The (1969, Fr./Ital./Span.)
Chain, The
  Chain Gang Women (1972)*
Chained to Yesterday
  Limbo (1972)
Chainwork Love
  Tight Skirts, Loose Pleasures (1966, Fr.)
Challenge, The
  It Takes a Thief (1960, Brit.)
Challenge to Survive
  Land of No Return, The (1981)
Champagne for Breakfast
  Boss Lady (1982)*

Change of Heart
  Hit Parade of 1943 (1943)
Change of Heart, A
  Two and Two Make Six (1962, Brit.)
Chase for the Golden Needles
  Golden Needles (1974)
Chaser, The
  Nuisance, The (1933)
Chasing Two Hares
  Kiev Comedy, A (1963, USSR)
Cheat, The
  Lone Hand Texan, The (1947)
Check and Double Check
  Amos 'n' Andy (1930)
Checker Player, The
  Devil is an Empress, The (1939, Fr.)
Chess Player, The
  Devil is an Empress, The (1939, Fr.)
Chetnik
  Underground Guerrillas (1944, Brit.)
Chief Wants No Survivors, The
  No Survivors, Please (1963, Ger.)
Child of the Night
  Night Hair Child (1971, Brit.)
Children Are Watching Us, The
  Little Martyr, The (1947, Ital.)
Children of Montmarte
  La Maternelle (1933, Fr.)
Children of the Wild
  Killers of the Wild (1940)
Chinchero
  Last Movie, The (1971)
Chips Are Down, The
  Les Jeux Sont Faits (1947, Fr.)
Chiuato
  Rebellion in Cuba (1961)
Choice of Arms
  Dirty Knight's Work (1976, Brit.)
Chooper, The
  Blood Shack (1971)*
Choose Your Partners
  Two Girls on Broadway (1940)
Chosen, The
  Holocaust 2000 (1978, Ital./Brit.)
Christ Stopped at Eboli
  Eboli (1980, Ital.)
Christine
  Un Carnet de Bal (1938, Fr.)
Christmas Evil
  You Better Watch Out (1980)
Cicada Is Not an Insect, The
  Games Men Play, The (1968, Arg.)
Cinderella, Italian Style
  More Than a Miracle (1967, Ital./Fr.)
Circle of Power
  Mystique (1981)
Circle, The
  Vicious Circle, The (1948)
Circle, The
  Strictly Unconventional (1930)
City of Dreams
  Dream Town (1973, Ger.)
City of Sin
  Scavengers, The (1959)
City of Songs
  Vienna, City of Songs (1931, Ger.)
City of the Living Dead
  Gates of Hell, The (1983, Ital./US)
City on a Hunt
  No Escape (1953)
City Sentinel
  Beast of the City, The (1932)
Claude
  Two of Us, The (1968, Fr.)
Clickety-Clack
  Dodeska-Den (1970, Jap.)
Clock Strikes Three, The
  When the Clock Strikes (1961)
Clones
  Clones, The (1973)
Closest of Kin, The
  Kinfolk (1970)
Clown Ferdinand and the Rocket
  Rocket to Nowhere (1962, Czech.)
Coast of Skeletons
  Sanders of the River (1935, Brit.)
Cobweb Castle
  Throne of Blood (1961, Jap.)
Cockfighter
  Born to Kill (1975)
Cocktails in the Kitchen
  For Better, For Worse (1954, Brit.)
Code Name: Operation Crossbow
  Operation Crossbow (1965, US/Ital.)
Code Name: Trixie
  Crazies, The (1973)
Coffee Fortune Teller, The
  Fortune Teller, The (1961, Gr.)
Coffin of Terror
  Castle of Blood (1964, Fr./Ital.)

Cold Blood
  Ice House, The (1969)
Colossus 1980
  Colossus: The Forbin Project (1969)
Come 'n Get It
  Lunch Wagon (1981)
Come Play with Me
  Thank You Aunt (1969, Ital.)
Comin' Home
  Just Be There (1977)*
Coming Attractions
  Loose Shoes (1980)
Communion
  Alice, Sweet Alice (1978)
Computer Killers
  Horror Hospital (1973, Brit.)
Con Man, The
  Con Artists, The (1981, Ital.)
Confession, The
  Quick, Let's Get Married (1965)
Confessions of a Sorority Girl
  Sorority Girl (1957)
Confessions of a Vahine
  Maeva (1961)
Conflagration
  Enjo (1959, Jap.)
Conqueror of Corinth
  Centurion, The (1962, Fr./Ital.)
Contest Girl
  Beauty Jungle, The (1966, Brit.)
Continental Twist, The
  Twist All Night (1961)
Convention City
  Sons of The Desert (1933)
Copacabana Palace
  Girl Game (1968, Braz./Fr./Ital.)
Cordillera
  Flight to Fury (1966, US/Phil.)
Cosmic Man Appears in Tokyo, The
  Mysterious Satellite, The (1956, Jap.)
Cosmic Voyage, The
  Spaceship, The (1935, USSR)
Cosmonauts on Venus
  Storm Planet (1962, USSR)
Count Dracula's Great Love
  Dracula's Great Love (1972, Span.)
Count of Monte Cristo, The
  Story of the Count of Monte Cristo (1962, Fr./
  Ital.)
Counterattack of the Monster
  Gigantis (1959, Jap./US)
Country Doctor
  Life of a Country Doctor (1961, Jap.)
Country Music Daughter
  New Girl in Town (1977)
Country Music, U.S.A.
  Las Vegas Hillbillies (1966)
Couple, The
  There Was an Old Couple (1967, USSR)
Couples
  Best Friends (1975)*
Courage
  Raw Courage (1984)**
Cowboy Roundup
  Ride 'Em Cowboy
Crackers
  Street Girls (1975)*
Cradle of Crime
  Dead End (1937)
Crawling Monster, The
  Creeping Terror, The (1964)
Crazed Vampire
  Caged Virgins (1972)*
Crazy Day, A
  From a Roman Balcony (1961, Fr./Ital.)
Crazy Jack and the Boy
  Silence (1974)
Creature's Revenge, The
  Brain of Blood (1971, Phil.)
Creatures
  From Beyond the Grave (1974, Brit.)
Creatures from Beyond the Grave, The
  From Beyond the Grave (1974, Brit.)
Creatures of Evil
  Curse of the Vampires (1970, U.S./Phil.)
Creatures of the Prehistoric Planet
  Horror of the Blood Monsters (1970, US/Phil.)
Creatures of the Red Planet
  Horror of the Blood Monsters (1970, US/Phil.)
Creepers, The
  Island of Terror (1967, Brit.)
Creeps
  Bloody Birthday (1980)*
Creeps
  Shivers (1984, Pol.)** Cries of the Night
  Awful Dr. Orloff. The (1964, Span./Fr.)
Crime Gives Orders
  Hunted Men (1938)
Crime of Voodoo
  Ouanga (1936, Brit.)

Crime Smasher, The
  Cosmo Jones, Crime Smasher (1943)*
Crimes in the Wax Museum
  Nightmare in Wax (1969)
Crimson Altar, The
  Crimson Cult, The (1970, Brit.)
Crimson Executioner
  Bloody Pit of Horror, the (1965, Ital.)
Crimson Ghost, The
  Cyclotrode X (1946)
Crooked Money
  While Thousands Cheer (1940)*
Crossroads for a Nun
  Nun at the Crossroads, A (1970, Ital./Span.)
Crowd for Lisette, A
  Lisette (1961)
Cruel Story of Youth
  Naked Youth (1961, Jap.)
Cruel Swamp
  Swamp Women (1956)
Crunch
  24 Hour Lover (1970, Ger.)
Cry for Me Billy
  Count Your Bullets (1972)
Cry of the Bewitched
  Young and Evil (1962, Mex.)
Cry Your Purple Heart Out
  How to Score with Girls (1980)*
Crying Out Loud
  Cotton Queen (1937, Brit.)
Crypt of Dark Secrets
  Mardi Gras Massacre (1978)
Crypt, The
  Hearts of Humanity (1936, Brit.)
Cult of the Damned
  Angel, Angel Down We Go (1969)
Cups of San Sebastian, The
  Fickle Finger of Fate, the (1967, Span./U.S.)
Curley and His Gang in the Haunted Mansion
  Who Killed "Doc" Robbin? (1948)
Curse of Dark Shadows
  Night of Dark Shadows (1971)
Curse of Melissa
  Touch of Satan, The (1971)
Curse of Simba
  Curse of the Voodoo (1965, Brit.)
Curse of the Crimson Altar
  Crimson Cult, The (1970, Brit.)
Curse of the Golem
  It! (1967, Brit.)
Curse of the Living Dead
  Kill Baby Kill (1966, Ital.)
Curse of the Mushroom People
  Attack of the Mushroom People (1964, Jap.)
Curse of the Vampire
  Playgirls and the Vampire (1964, Ital.)
Cursed Medallion, The
  Night Child (1975, Brit./Ital.)
Curses of the Ghouls
  Curse of the Blood Ghouls (1969, Ital.)
Custer Massacre
  Great Sioux Massacre, The (1965)
Cutter's Way
  Cutter and Bone (1981)
Cynthia's Secret
  Dark Delusion (1947)
Czar of the Slot Machines
  King of the Gamblers (1937)

Daddy's Delectable Dozen
  Turkish Cucumber, The (1963, Ger.)
Daddy's Girl
  Daddy's Deadly Darling (1984)** Daggers of
  Blood
  Invasion 1700 (1965, Fr./Ital./Yugo.)
Dagora
  Dagora the Space Monster (1964, Jap.)
Damaged Goods
  V.D. (1961)
Dan Candy's Law
  Alien Thunder (1975)
Danger Diabolik
  Danger: Diabolik (1968, Ital./Fr.)
Danger In Paris
  Cafe Colette (1937, Brit.)
Danger Island
  Mr. Moto in Danger Island (1939)
Dangerous Charter
  Creeping Terror, The (1964)
Dangerous Female
  Maltese Falcon, The (1931)
Dangerous Friend, A
  Todd Killings, The (1970)
Dangerous Love Affair
  Les Liaisons Dangereuses (1961, Fr./Ital.)
Daniel and the Devil
  Devil and Daniel Webster, The (1941)

Danny Travis
  Last Word, The (1979)
Danza Macabra
  Castle of Blood (1964, Fr./Ital.)
Daredevil Dick
  Yankee Don (1931)
Dark Eyes
  Satan's Mistress (1982)
Dark Skies
  Darkened Skies (1930)
Darkest Hour, The
  Hell on Frisco Bay (1956)
Daughter of Cleopatra
  Cleopatra's Daughter (1963, Fr./Ital.)
Daughter of Frankenstein, The
  Lady Frankenstein (1971, Ital.)
Daughter of Her People
  Jewish Daughter (1933)*
Daughter of Horror
  Dementia (1955)
Daughter of Luxury
  Five and Ten (1931)
Daughter of Mata Hari
  Mata Hari's Daughter (1954, Fr./Ital.)
Day After Tomorrow, The
  Strange Holiday (1945)
Day Kelly Came Home, The
  Get Outta Town (1960)
Day of the Landgrabbers
  Land Raiders (1969)
Day of the Woman
  I Spit on Your Grave (1983)
Day the Screaming Stopped, The
  Comeback, The (1982, Brit.)
Day the World Ended, The
  When Time Ran Out (1980)*
Dead Certain
  Dead Cert (1974)*
Dead Eyes of London, The
  Dark Eyes of London (1961, Ger.)
Dead Or Alive
  Minute to Pray, a Second to Die, A (1968, Ital.)
Deadly Circle, The
  Honeymoon of Horror (1964)
Deadly is the Female
  Gun Crazy (1949)
Deadly Silence, The
  Tarzan's Deadly Silence (1970)
Deadly Treasure of the Piranha
  Killer Fish (1979, Ital./Braz.)
Dear Debbie
  Naughty Stewardesses, The (1973)*
Dear Inspector
  Dear Detective (1978, Fr.)
Death and the Green Slime
  Green Slime, The (1969)
Death at Broadcasting House
  Death at a Broadcast (1934, Brit.)
Death Corps
  Shock Waves (1977)
Death Dimension
  Freeze Bomb (1978)*
Dead End Kids at Military School
  Dead End Kids on Dress Parade (1939)
Death Drums Along the River
  Sanders (1963, Brit.)
Death from Outer Space
  Day the Sky Exploded, The (1958, Fr./Ital.)
Death House
  Silent Night, Bloody Night (1974)
Death in Full View
  Deathwatch (1980, Ger./Fr.)
Death is a Woman
  Love Is a Woman (1967, Brit.)
Death of a Cyclist
  Age of Infidelity (1958)
Death of a Jew
  Sabra (1970, Fr./Ital./Israel)
Death of Night
  Deathdream (1972, Can.)
Death Trap
  Eaten Alive (1976)
Death Weekend
  House by the Lake, The (1977, Can.)
Death Wheelers, The
  Psychomania (1974, Brit.)
Deceivers, The
  Intimacy (1966)
Decline and Fall
  Decline and Fall...of A Bird Watcher (1966, Brit.)
Decoy
  Mystery Submarine (1963, Brit.)
Deep Desire of Gods
  Kuragejima—Legends from a Southern Island
  (1970, Jap.)
Deep Red Hatchet Murders
  Deep Red (1976, Ital.)
Defiant Daughters
  Shadows Grow Longer, The (1962, Switz./Ger.)

Deliver Us from Evil
  Joey (1977)*
Delusion
  House Where Death Lives, The (1984)**
Demon
  God Told Me To (1976)
Demon, The
  Onibaba (1965, Jap.)
Demon Planet
  Planet of the Vampires (1965, US/Ital./Span.)
Demon Rage
  Satan's Mistress (1982)
Den of Doom
  Glass Cage, The (1964)
Der Heisse Tod
  99 Women (1969)*
Desert Odyssey
  Harem Bunch; Or War and Piece, The (1969)
Desperate Men, The
  Cat and Mouse (1958, Brit.)
Desperate Siege
  Rawhide (1951)
Destroy All Planets
  Gamera Versus Viras (1968, Jap.)
Detective Geronimo
  Mad Bomber, The (1970)
Devil Bear
  Claws (1977)*
Devil Got Angry, The
  Majin (1968, Jap.)
Devil in the Castle
  Daredevil in the Castle (1969, Jap.)
Devil Inside, The
  Offbeat (1961, Brit.)
Devil Men from Space
  Snow Devils, The (1965, Ital.)
Devil Takes the Count, The
  Devil is a Sissy, The (1936)
Devil Woman, The
  Onibaba (1965, Jap.)
Devil's Camera
  Scum of the Earth (1963)
Devil's Daughter, The
  Pocomania (1939)
Devil's Doll
  Devil's Hand, The (1961)
Devil's Men, The
  Land of the Minotaur (1976, Gr.)
Devil's People, The
  Land of the Minotaur (1976, Gr.)
Devil's Spawn, The
  Last Gunfighter, The (1961, Can.)
Devil's Weed
  Wild Weed (1949)
Devilman Story
  Devil's Man, The (1967, Ital.)
Devils from Space, The
  Snow Devils, The (1965, Ital.)
Diabolik
  Danger: Diabolik (1968, Ital./Fr.)
Diabolique Wedding
  Diabolic Wedding (1972)*
Dial Rat for Terror
  Bone (1972)*
Diamond Mercenaries, The
  Killer Force (1975, Switz./Ireland)
Diamonds and Crime
  Hi Diddle Diddle (1943)
Diary of a Voyage in the South Pacific
  Nude Odyssey (1962, Fr./Ital.)
Diary of Forbidden Dreams
  Che? (1973, Ital./Fr./Ger.)
Diary of Major Thompson
  French They Are a Funny Race, The (1956, Fr.)
Diary of Oharu
  Life of Oharu (1964, Jap.)
Dick Deadeye, or Duty Done
  Dick Deadeye (1977)*
Dick Tracy, Detective
  Dick Tracy (1945)
Dick Tracy Meets Karloff
  Dick Tracy Meets Gruesome (1947)
Did I Betray?
  Black Roses (1936, Ger.)
Dig that Juliet
  Romanoff and Juliet (1961)
Dinner for Adele
  Adele Hasn't Had Her Supper Yet (1978, Czech.)
Dion Brothers, The
  Gravy Train, The (1974)
Dirty Hands
  Les Mains Sales (1954, Fr.)
Dirty Mary
  Very Curious Girl, A (1970, Fr.)
Dirtymouth
  Dirty Mouth (1971)*
Disco Girls
  Pelvis (1977)*
Disco Madness
  Pelvis (1977)*

Divine Creature
  Divine Nymph, The (1979, Ital.)
Django the Bastard
  Stranger's Gundown, The (1974, Ital.)
Doctor From Seven Dials, The
  Corridors of Blood (1962, Brit.)
Dr. Knock
  Knock (1955, Fr.)
Dr. Maniac
  Man Who Lived Again, The (1936, Brit.)
Doctor Maniac
  House of the Living Dead (1973, S. Afr.)
Doctor's Alibi
  Medico of Painted Springs, The (1941)
Doctors Wear Scarlet
  Incense for the Damned (1970, Brit.)
Dog, a Mouse and a Sputnik, A
  Sputnik (1960, Fr.)
Dollar Between the Teeth, A
  Stranger in Town, A (1968, US/Ital.)
Dolls, The
  Bambole! (1965, Ital.)
Dolwyn
  Last Days of Dolwyn, The (1949, Brit.)
Don Juan
  Private Life of Don Juan, The (1934, Brit.)
Don't Leave Go My Hand
  Black Hooker (1974)*
Don't Touch My Sister
  Glass Cage, The (1964)
Doomed
  Ikiru (1960, Jap.)
Door-to-Door Maniac
  Five Minutes to Live (1961)
Dope Addict
  Reefer Madness (1936)
Dope Dens of the Orient
  Narcotic, The (1937)*
Doped Youth
  Reefer Madness (1936)
Double Agents, The
  Night Encounter (1963, Fr./Ital.)
Double Down
  Stacey's Knights (1983)
Double Possession
  Ganja and Hess (1973)
Double, The
  Kagemusha (1980, Jap.)
Double Tour, A
  Web of Passion (1961, Fr.)
Double Trouble
  Swingin' Along (1962)
Double Trouble
  No Deposit, No Return (1976)
Down to the Sea in Ships
  Last Adventurers, The (1937, Brit.)
Down Under the Sea
  Down to the Sea (1936)
Dracula and the Seven Golden Vampires (1978, Brit./Chin.)
  Legend of the Seven Golden Vampires
Dracula in the Castle of Blood
  Web of the Spider (1972, Ital./Fr./Ger.)
Dracula Ssucks
  Dracula Sucks (1979)*
Dracula Today
  Dracula A.D. 1972 (1972, Brit.)
Dracula vs. Frankenstein
  Assignment Terror (1970, Ger./Span./Ital.)
Dracula's Bride
  Dracula Sucks (1979)*
Dracula's Castle
  Blood of Dracula's Castle (1967)
Dracula's Last Rites
  Last Rites (1980)
Dracula's Lust for Blood
  Lake of Dracula (1973, Jap.)
Dragon Flies, The
  Man from Hong Kong (1975, Aus./Chi.)
Dragon Master
  Cannon for Cordoba (1970)
Dragonfly
  One Summer Love (1976)
Drama of Jealousy (and Other Things)
  Pizza Triangle, The (1970, Ital./Span.)
Dreaded Persuasion, The
  Narcotics Story, The (1958)
Dream of Olwen, The
  While I Live (1947, Brit.)
Dream World of Harrison Marks, The
  Naked World of Harrison Marks, The (1967, Brit.)
Dreamworld
  Covergirl (1984, Can.)**
Dreyfus
  Dreyfus Case, The (1940, Ger.)
Drifting Weeds
  Floating Weeds (1970, Jap.)
Dripping Deep Red
  Deep Red (1976, Ital.)

Drivers to Hell
  Wild Ones on Wheels (1967)
Duchess of Broadway
  Talk About a Lady (1946)
Duckweed Story, The
  Floating Weeds (1970, Jap.)
Duel at Ganryu Island
  Samurai (Part III) (1967, Jap.)
Duel in Durango
  Gun Duel in Durango (1957)
Duel of the Gargantuas
  War of the Gargantuas, The (1970, Jap.)
Dungeons of Horror
  Dungeons of Harrow (1964)
Dynamite Women
  Great Texas Dynamite Chase, The (1976)

E Lollipop
  Forever Young, Forever Free (1976, South Afr.)
Each Man for Himself
  Ruthless Four, The (1969, Ital./Ger.)
Each One for Himself
  Ruthless Four, The (1969, Ital./Ger.)
Eager Beaver
  Swinging Barmaids, The (1976)
Eagles Over London
  Eagle Over London (1973, Ital.)
Earth Defence Forces
  Mysterians, The (1959, Jap.)
Earth Vs. the Spider
  Spider, The (1958)
Earth Will Tremble, The
  La Terra Trema (1947, Ital.)
East End Chant
  Limehouse Blues (1934)
East of Shanghai
  Rich and Strange (1932, Brit.)
East of the Bowery
  Follow the Leader (1944)
East Side Kids Meet Bela Lugosi, The
  Ghosts on the Loose (1943)
East Wind
  Wind From the East (1970, Fr./Ital./Ger.)
Easy Go
  Free and Easy (1930)
Ebirah, Terror of the Deep
  Godzilla Versus the Sea Monster (1966, Jap.)
Ecstasy of Lovers
  Honeymoon of Terror (1961)
Ecstasy on Lovers Island
  Honeymoon of Terror (1961)
Edgar Allan Poe's "The Oblong Box"
  Oblong Box, The (1969, Brit.)
Edgar Allan Poe's Conqueror Worm
  Conqueror Worm, The (1968, Brit.)
Edge of Divorce
  Background (1953, Brit.)
Eerie Midnight Horror Show
  Tormented, The (1978, Ital.)
El, This Strange Passion Torments
  El (1955, Mex.)
Electric Monster, The
  Electronic Monster, The (1960, Brit.)
Elephants Never Forget
  Zenobia (1939)
Elizabeth of England
  Drake the Pirate (1935, Brit.)
Ellen
  Second Woman, The (1951)
Elsa Maxwell's Hotel for Women
  Hotel for Women (1939)
Emperor of Peru, The
  Odyssey of the Pacific (1983, Can./Fr.)
Emperor of the North
  Emperor of the North Pole (1973)
End of Belle, The
  Passion of Slow Fire, The (1962, Fr.)
End of Summer, The
  Early Autumn (1962, Jap.)
End of the World
  Panic in Year Zero! (1962)
Enemy Roundup
  Hillbilly Blitzkrieg (1942)
Engineer Garin's Death Ray
  Hyperboloid of Engineer Garin, The (1965, USSR)
Enigma of Kaspar Hauser, The
  Every Man for Himself and God Against All (1975, Ger.)
Entebbe: Operation Thunderbolt
  Operation Thunderbolt (1978, Israel)
Escape from Hell Island
  Man in the Water, The (1963)
Escape of Megagodzilla, The
  Monsters from the Unknown Planet (1975, Jap.)
Escape of Princess Charming, The
  Princess Charming (1935, Brit.)

Eternal Jew, The
  Abraham our Patriarch (1933)*
Eternal Woman
  Loves of Three Queens, The (1954, Ital.)
Europe '51
  Greatest Love, The (1954, Ital.)
Eva the Devil's Woman
  Eva (1962, Fr./Ital.)
Every Home Should Have One
  Think Dirty (1970, Brit.)
Every Man a King
  Every Bastard a King (1968, Israel)
Every Man for Himself
  Ruthless Four, The (1969, Ital./Ger.)
Every Man's Woman
  Rose for Everyone, A (1967, Ital.)
Everyman's Woman
  Rose for Everyone, A (1967, Ital.)
Evil Eden
  Gina (1961, Fr./Mex.)
Evil Eden
  Death in the Garden (1977, Fr./Mex.)
Evil in the Deep
  Treasure of Jamaica Reef, The (1976)
Evil Mind
  Clairvoyant, The (1935, Brit.)
Excuse Me, My Name Is Rocco Papaleo
  Rocco Papaleo (1974, Ital./Fr.)
Expedition Moon
  Rocketship X-M (1950)
Eye for an Eye, An
  Psychopath, The (1973)
Eye of Evil
  Thousand Eyes of Dr. Mabuse, The (1960, Fr./
  Ital./Ger.)
Eyes of Hell
  Mask, the (1961, Can.)
Eyes Without a Face
  Horror Chamber of Dr. Faustus, The (1962,
  Fr./Ital.)
Eyewitness
  Sudden Terror (1970, Brit.)

Face of Fear
  Face of Terror (1964, Span.)
Face of Fear
  Peeping Tom (1960, Brit.)
Face That Launched a Thousand Ships, The
  Loves of Three Queens, The (1954, Ital.)
Face, The
  Magician, The (1959, Swed.)
Face to the Wind
  Count Your Bullets (1972)
Faceless Monsters, The
  Nightmare Castle (1966, Ital.)
Fakers, The
  Hell's Bloody Devils (1970)
Fall Girl
  Lisette (1961)
Fall Guy, The
  What's Up Front (1964)
Fall Guy, The
  Fallguy (1962)
Fall of the House of Usher
  House of Usher (1960)
False Face
  Scalpel (1976)
Falstaff
  Chimes at Midnight (1967, Span./Switz.)
Family Enforcer
  Death Collector (1976)
Fanatic, The
  Last Horror Film, The (1984)**
Fangs of the Living Dead
  Malenka, the Vampire (1972, Span./Ital.)
Fantastic Disappearing Man, The
  Return of Dracula (1958)
Fantastic Invasion of Planet Earth
  Bubble, The (1967)
Farm Girl
  Farmer's Other Daughter, The (1965)
Fashions
  Fashions of 1934 (1934)
Fast Charlie and the Moonbeam
  Fast Charlie...The Moonbeam Rider (1979)
Fat Chance
  Peeper (1975)
Fate of a Man
  Destiny of a Man (1961, USSR)
Father Kino Story
  Kino, Padre on Horseback (1977)*
Father Master
  Padre, Padrone (1977, Ital.)
Father's Day
  Sins of the Children (1930)
Fear
  Night Creature (1979)

Fear, The
  Gates of Hell, The (1983, Ital./US)
Fear in the City of the Living Dead
  Gates of Hell, The (1983, Ital./US)
Feast of Flesh
  Blood Feast (1976, Ital.)
Federico Fellini's 8 1/2
  8 1/2 (1963, Ital.)
Fellini's Casanova
  Casanova (1976, Ital.)
Fellini's Roma
  Roma (1972, Ital./Fr.)
Female
  Violent Years (1956)
Female and the Flesh, The
  Light Across the Street, The (1957, Fr.)
Female Prisoner, The
  La Prisonniere (1969, Fr./Ital.)
Female Trap, The
  Name of the Game Is Kill, The (1968)
Fielder's Field
  Girls Can Play (1937)
Fiend with the Electronic Brain
  Psycho a Go-Go (1965)
Fiendish Ghouls, The
  Mania (1961, Brit.)
Fiery Spur
  Hot Spur (1968)
Fighting Phantom, The
  Mysterious Rider, The (1933)
Fighting Pimpernel, The
  Pimpernel Smith (1941)
Fighting Westerner, The
  Westerner, The (1936)
Fighting Westerner, The
  Rocky Mountain Mystery (1935)
Final Programme, The
  Last Days of Man on Earth (1975, Brit.)
Final War, The
  Last War, The (1962, Jap.)
Finally Sunday
  Confidentially Yours (1983, Fr.)
Fire Maidens of Outer Space
  Fire Maidens from Outer Space (1956, Brit.)
Fire Monster, The
  Gigantis (1959, Jap./US)
Firebrand Johnson
  Firebrand Jordan (1930)
Fires of Youth
  Up for Murder (1931)
First Day of Peace, The
  Day the War Ended (1961, USSR)
First Hello, The
  High Country, The (1981, Can.)
First Time, The
  Fighter, The (1952)
First Woman into Space
  Space Monster (1965)
Fist-Right of Freedom
  Fox and His Friends (1976, Ger.)
Fistful of Chopsticks, A
  They Call Me Bruce (1982)
Fistful of Dynamite
  Duck, You Sucker (1972, Ital.)
Fists in the Pocket
  Fist in his Pocket (1968, Ital.)
Five Ashore for Singapore
  Singapore, Singapore (1969, Fr./Ital.)
Five Bloody Days to Tombstone
  Gun Riders, The (1969)
Five Bloody Graves
  Gun Riders, The (1969)
Five Fingers of Death
  Hand of Death (1962)
Five Wild Kids
  Five Wild Girls (1966, Fr.)
Flame of Sacramento
  In Old Sacramento (1946)
Flame of Torment
  Enjo (1959, Jap.)
Flaming Desire
  Small Hours, The (1962)
Flaming Frontier
  Flame of the West (1945)
Flare Up
  Flareup (1969)
Flare-Up
  Flareup (1969)
Flavor of Green Tea Over Rice, The
  Tea and Rice (1964, Jap.)
Flesh and Fame
  Night of the Quarter Moon (1959)
Flesh Creatures of the Red Planet
  Horror of the Blood Monsters (1970, US/Phil.)
Flesh Creatures, The
  Horror of the Blood Monsters (1970, US/Phil.)
Flesh for Frankenstein
  Any Warhol's Frankenstein (1974)*
Flick
  Dr. Frankenstein on Campus (1970, Can.)

Flight from Terror
  Satan Never Sleeps (1962)
Flight of the White Stallions, The
  Miracle of the White Stallions (1963)
Flight that Vanished, The
  Flight that Disappeared, The (1961)
Flipper and the Pirates
  Flipper's New Adventure (1964)
Flirting Wives
  Uneasy Virtue (1931, Brit.)
Flower Woman of Lindenau, The
  Storm in a Water Glass (1963, Aust.)
Fog
  Study in Terror, A (1966, Brit./Ger.)
Fog for a Killer
  Out of the Fog (1962, Brit.)
Folies Bourgeoises
  Twist, The (1976, Fr.)
Folks at Red Wolf Inn, The
  Terror House (1972)
Follow the Hunter
  Fangs of the Wild (1954)
Fontane Effi Briest
  Effi Briest (1974, Ger.)
For Love of a Queen
  Dictator, The (1935, Brit./Ger.)
For Love of Money
  For Love and Money (1967)
For We Too Do Not Forgive
  Death is Called Engelchen (1963, Czech.)
For Women Only
  What Do I Tell the Boys at the Station @ 1 (1972)*
Forbidden Adventure
  Newly Rich (1931)
Forbidden Alliance
  Barrets of Wimpole Street (1934)
Forbidden Love
  Freaks (1932)
Forbidden Love Affair
  Lollipop (1966, Braz.)
Forbidden Paradise
  Hurricane (1979)
Forbidden Street
  Affairs of Adelaide (1949, U.S./Brit.)
Forbin Project, The
  Colossus: The Forbin Project (1969)
Forest of Fear
  Bloodeaters (1980)
Forest Primeval, The
  Final Terror, The (1983)
Forever England
  Born for Glory (1935)
Forgotten Women
  Mad Parade, The (1931)
Fortune in Diamonds
  Adventurers, The (1951, Brit.)
43—The Petty Story
  Petty Story, The (1974)*
47 Samurai
  Chushingura (1963, Jap.)
Four Dark Hours
  Green Cockatoo, The (1947, Brit.)
Four Kinds of Love
  Bambole! (1965, Ital.)
Four Shall Die
  Condemned Men (1946)*
Fox
  Fox and His Friends (1976, Ger.)
Fox Style Killer
  Fox Style (1977)*
Foxiest Girl in Paris
  Nathalie (1958, Fr.)
Frank Challenge—Manhunter
  Brass Ring, The (1975)*
Frank's Greatest Adventure
  Fearless Frank (1967)
Frankenstein and the Giant Lizard
  Frankenstein Conquers the World (1964, Jap./
  US)
Frankenstein Meets the Spacemen
  Frankenstein Meets the Space Monster (1965)
Frankenstein vs. the Giant Devilfish
  Frankenstein Conquers the World (1964, Jap./
  US)
Frankenstein's Castle of Freaks
  House of Freaks (1973, Ital.)
Fraternally Yours
  Sons of The Desert (1933)
Freak from Suckweasel Mountain, The
  Geek Maggot Bingo (1983)
Freeze Bomb
  Death Dimension (1978)*
French Are a Funny Race
  French They Are a Funny Race, The (1956, Fr.)
Fresh from Paris
  Paris Follies of 1956 (1955)
Friends and Lovers
  Vixens, The (1969)
Fright
  Spell of the Hypnotist (1956)

Frightened Lady, The
  Criminal at Large (1932, Brit.)
Frightenened Lady, The
  Case of the Frightenend Lady, The (1940, Brit.)
Frigid Wife
  Modern Marriage, A (1962)
Frissons
  They Came from Within (1976, Can.)
Frontier Alaska
  Joniko and the Kush Ta Ka (1969)
Frontier Horizon
  New Frontier (1939)
Frou-Frou
  Toy Wife, The (1938)
Full Moon
  Moonchild (1972)
Fun and Games
  1000 Convicts and a Woman (1971, Brit.)
Fun House
  Last House on Dead End Street (1977)
Fun Loving
  Quackser Fortune Has a Cousin in the Bronx
  (1970)
Funny Bone
  Bone (1972)*
Funny Parishioner, The
  Thank Heaven for Small Favors (1965, Fr.)
Fury
  One Russian Summer (1973)*
Fury of Samson
  Fury of Hercules, The (1961, Ital.)
Fury of the Succubus
  Satan's Mistress (1982)
Fury of the Vikings
  Erik the Conqueror (1963, Fr./Ital.)
Fury Unleashed
  Hot Rod Gang (1958)
Future Women
  Rio 70 (1970, US/Ger./Span)
FX-Superspy
  Exterminators, The (1965, Fr.)

Galaxy Express 999
  Galaxy Express (1982, Jap.)
Gambara Versus Barugon
  Gamera Versus Barugon (1966, Jap./US)
Gambling Hell
  Mask of Korea (1950, Fr.)
Game of Danger
  Bang! You're Dead (1954, Brit.)
Game Pass
  Jail Bait (1977, Ger.)
Gamera
  Gamera the Invincible (1966, Jap.)
Gamera Versus Gyaos
  Gamera Versus Gaos (1967, Jap.)
Gamera Versus Jiger
  Gamera Versus Monster X (1970, Jap.)
Gamera Versus Outer Space Monster Viras
  Gamera Versus Viras (1968, Jap.)
Gamera Versus the Deep Sea Monster Zigra
  Gamera Versus Zigra (1971, Jap.)
Games for Six Lovers
  Game for Six Lovers, A (1962, Fr.)
Gamma 693
  Night of the Zombies (1981)
Gammera
  Gamera the Invincible (1966, Jap.)
Gammera the Invincible
  Gamera the Invincible (1966, Jap.)
Gang Show
  Down Our Alley (1939, Brit.)
Gang Smashers
  Gun Moll (1938)*
Gang War
  Odd Man Out (1947, Brit.)
Gang Wars
  Devil's Express (1975)
Gangs, Inc.
  Paper Bullets (1941)
Gangsters on the Loose
  Bargain with Bullets*
Gangster's Revenge
  Get Outta Town (1960)
Gangsters of the Sea
  Out of Singapore (1932)
Garbage Man Cometh, The
  Garbage Man, The (1963)
Gardener, The
  Seeds of Evil (1981)
Garu, the Mad Monk
  Guru, the Mad Monk (1971)
Gas-s-s-s, or It Became Necessary to Destroy the
  World in Order to Save It
  Gas-s-s-s (1970)
Gaunt Stranger, The
  Ringer, The (1932, Brit.)

Gay Duelist, The
  Meet Me at Dawn (1947, Brit.)
Gentle Art of Murder, The
  Crime Does Not Pay (1962, Fr.)
Gentle People, The
  Gentle People and the Quiet Land, The (1972)
Gentleman from California, The
  Californian, The (1937)
George Takes the Air
  It's in the Air (1940, Brit.)
Gestapo
  Night Train (1940)
Get Down and Boogie
  Darktown Strutters (1975)
Get Out of Town
  Get Outta Town (1960)
Getting Away with Murder
  End of the Game (1976, Ger./Ital.)
Getting Even
  Utilities (1983, Can.)
Ghetto Freaks
  Sign of Aquarius (1970)
Ghidora, the Three-Headed Monster
  Ghidrah, the Three-Headed Monster (1965, Jap.)
Ghidrah
  Ghidrah, the Three-Headed Monster (1965, Jap.)
Ghost Crazy
  Crazy Knights (1944)
Ghost of Rashmon Hall, The
  Night Comes Too Soon (1948, Brit.)
Ghost Steps Out, The
  Time of Their Lives, The (1946)
Ghoul in School, The
  Werewolf in a Girl's Dormitory (1961, Ital.)
Giant Behemoth, The
  Behemoth, The Sea Monster (1959, Brit.)
Giant Leeches, The
  Attack of the Giant Leeches (1959)
Giant Monster
  Night They Killed Rasputin, The (1962, Fr./Ital)
Giant of Metropolis
  Giant of Metropolis, The (1963, Ital.)
Gibraltar
  It Happened in Gibraltar (1943, Fr.)
Gill Woman
  Voyage to the Planet of Prehistoric Women
  (1966)
Gill Women of Venus
  Voyage to the Planet of Prehistoric Women
  (1966)
Gion Music
  Geisha, A (1978, Jap.)
Girl Against Napoleon, A
  Devil Made a Woman, The (1962, Span.)
Girl Crazy
  When the Boys Meet the Girls (1965)
Girl for Joe, A
  Force of Arms (1951)
Girl Friends, The
  Le Amiche (1962, Ital.)
Girl from 5,000 A.D., The
  Terror from the Year 5,000 (1958)
Girl from Hamburg, The
  Port of Desire (1960, Fr.)
Girl I Made, The
  Made on Broadway (1933)
Girl in His Pocket
  Nude in His Pocket (1962, Fr.)
Girl in Hot Pants, The
  Secretary, The (1971)*
Girl in the Leather Suit
  Hell's Belles (1969)
Girl Merchants
  Sellers of Girls (1967, Fr.)
Girl of Tin, The
  Tin Girl, The (1970, Ital.)
Girl Swappers, The
  Two and Two Make Six (1962, Brit.)
Girl Was Young, A
  Young and Innocent (1937, Brit.)
Girls' Hotel
  Black Heat (1976)*
Girls in Uniform
  Maedchen in Uniform (1932, Ger.)
Girls of Spider Island
  It's Hot in Paradise (1962, Ger./Yugo.)
Girly
  Mumsy, Nanny, Sonny and Girly (1970, Brit.)
Give Me Your Hand My Love
  Life and Loves of Mozart, The (1959, Ger.)
Glass Cage, The
  Glass Tomb, The (1955, Brit.)
Glorious Sacrifice
  Glory Trail, The (1937)
Go for Broke
  Sundance Cassidy and Butch the Kid (1975)*
Go Mama Go!
  Take It from the Top (1982)*
Go-Go Set
  Get Yourself a College Girl (1964)

God Speaks Today
  Supreme Secret, The (1958, Brit.)
God's Country
  God's Country and the Man (1931)
Goddess of Electra
  War of the Zombies (1965, Ital.)
Godzilla Fights the Giant Moth
  Godzilla Vs. the Thing (1964, Jap.)
Godzilla on Monster Island
  War of the Monsters (1972, Jap.)
Godzilla Raids Again
  Gigantis (1959, Jap./US)
Godzilla Versus the Bionic Monster
  Godzilla Versus the Cosmic Monster (1974, Jap.)
Godzilla Vs. Gigan
  War of the Monsters (1972, Jap.)
Godzilla Vs. Hedora
  Godzilla Versus the Smog Monster (1972, Jap.)
Godzilla Vs. Mothra
  Godzilla Vs. the Thing (1964, Jap.)
Godzilla Vs. the Giant Moth
  Godzilla Vs. the Thing (1964, Jap.)
Godzilla's Counterattack
  Gigantis (1959, Jap./US)
Goke the Vampire
  Goke, Body Snatcher from Hell (1968, Jap.)
Golden Eye, The
  Mystery of the Golden Eye, The (1948)
Golden Heist, The
  Inside Out (1975, Brit.)
Golden Horde of Genghis Khan
  Golden Horde, The (1951)
Golden Marie
  Casque D'Or (1956, Fr.)
Golden Nymphs, The
  Honeymoon of Horror (1964)
Golden Virgin
  Story of Esther Costello, The (1957, Brit.)
Goldseekers
  Surabaya Conspiracy (1975)*
Goliath and the Giants
  Goliath Against the Giants (1963, Ital./Span.)
Goliath and the Golden City
  Samson and the Seven Miracles of the World
  (1963, Fr./Ital.)
Gomar—The Human Gorilla
  Night of the Bloody Apes (1968, Mex.)
Good Guys Always Win, The
  Outfit, The (1973)
Good Marriage, A
  Le Beau Marriage (1982, Fr.)
Good Morning
  Ohayo (1962, Jap.)
Good Soup, The
  La Bonne Soupe (1964, Fr./Ital.)
Good Times
  Summer Run (1974)*
Goodbye Bruce Lee: His Last Game of Death
  Game of Death, The (1979)
Goodbye to the Hill
  Paddy (1970, Ireland)
Goodwin Sands
  Lady From the Sea, The (1929, Brit.)
Gorilla
  Nabonga (1944)
Gorilla Gang, The
  Ape Creature, The (1968)*
Gorilla of Soho, The
  Ape Creature, The (1968)*
Gosh!
  Alice Goodbody (1974)*
Grabbers, The
  Scavengers, The (1969)
Grace Quigley
  Ultimate Solution of Grace Quigley, The (1984)**
Grail, The
  Lancelot of the Lake (1975, Fr.)
Grand Khan
  Marco Polo (1962, Fr./Ital.)
Grande Bouffe, The
  La Grande Bouffe (1973, Fr.)
Grave Desires
  Brides of Blood (1968)
Grave Robbers from Outer Space
  Plan 9 from Outer Space (1959)
Graveyard
  Invasion of the Bee Girls (1973)
Great Adventure, The
  Adventurers, The (1951, Brit.)
Great American Escape, The
  Cycles South (1971)*
Great Balloon Adventure, The
  Olly, Olly, Oxen Free (1978)
Great Day, The
  Special Day, A (1977, Ital./Can.)
Great Dream The
  Embracers, The (1966)
Great Feed, The
  La Grande Bouffe (1973, Fr.)

Great Georgia Bank Hoax, The
   Great Bank Hoax, The (1977)
Great Manhunt, The
   Doolins of Oklahoma, The (1949)
Great Monster Yongkari
   Yongkari Monster From the Deep (1967, S.K.)
Great Spy Mission, The
   Operation Crossbow (1965, US/Ital.)
Greatest Battle on Earth, The
   Ghidrah, the Three-Headed Monster (1965, Jap.)
Green Carnation, The
   Green Buddha, The (1954, Brit.)
Greystoke: The Legend of Tarzan, Lord of the Apes
   Greystoke, the Legend of Tarzan (1984)**
Gridiron Graft
   While Thousands Cheer (1940)*
Grip of Fear
   Experiment in Terror (1962)
Grove, The
   Naked Zoo, The (1970)
Growing Pains
   Bad Manners (1984)**
Guest, The
   Guest at Steenkampskraal, The (1977, South
   Africa)
Gun Moll
   Jigsaw (1949)
Gun Smoke Range
   Montana Incident (1952)*
Gunfight at Red Sands
   Gringo (1963, Ital./Span.)
Gunman from Bodie
   Gun Man from Bodie, The (1941)
Gunrunners
   Gun Runners, The (1958)
Gunrunners, The
   Gun Runner (1969)
Gunsmoke Killers
   Gunsmoke (1947)*
Guns A' Blazing
   Law and Order (1932)
Guns in the Afternoon
   Ride the High Country (1962)
Guns of Wrath
   Guns of Hate (1948)
Guns, Sin and Bathtub Gin
   Lady in Red, The (1979)
Guy with a Grin
   No Time for Comedy (1940)
Guyana, Crime of the Century
   Guyana, Cult of the Damned (1980 Mex./Span./
   Panama)
Guys from Max's Bar, The
   Inside Moves (1980)

H.E.A.L.T.H.
   Health (1980)
H.R. Pufnstuff
   Pufnstuf (1970)
Hail to the Chief
   Hail (1973)
Hallucinators, The
   Naked Zoo, The (1970)
Hamsters of Happiness
   Second-Hand Hearts (1981)
Hand of Death
   Five Fingers of Death (1973, Hong Kong)
Hand of the Godfather
   Specialist, The (1975)
Handful of Rice
   Jungle of Chang (1951)
Handgun
   Deep in the Heart (1983)
Handle with Care
   Citizens Band (1977)
Hands of a Strangler
   Hands of Orlac, The (1964, Brit./Fr.)
Hands of the Killer
   Planets Against Us, The (1961, Ital./Fr.)
Handsome Serge
   Le Beau Serge (1959, Fr.)
Hanged Man's Farm
   La Ferme du Pendu (1946, Fr.)
Hangover, The
   Female Jungle, The (1955)
Hant, The
   Dark August (1975)*
Happening in Africa
   Karen, the Lovemaker (1970)
Happily Ever After
   More Than a Miracle (1967, Ital./Fr.)
Happiness
   Le Bonheur (1966, Fr.)
Happy Alexander
   Very Happy Alexander, A (1969, Fr.)
Happy Clown, The
   Tobo, the Happy Clown (1965)*

Happy Days Revue
   Happy Days Are Here Again (1936, Brit.)
Happy Go Lucky
   Hallelujah, I'm a Bum (1933)
Happy Gypsies
   I Even Met Happy Gypsies (1968, Yugo.)
Happy Knowledge
   Le Gai Savior (1968, Fr.)
Happy Times
   Inspector General, The (1949)
Hara-Kiri
   Battle, The (1934, Brit./Fr.)
Hard Driver
   Last American Hero, The (1973)
Hard on the Trail
   Hard Trail (1969)
Hard to Handle
   Paid to Dance (1937)
Hard-Boiled Canary, The
   There's Magic in Music (1941)
Hardheads, The
   Great Lester Boggs, The (1975)*
Harem Bunch; Or War and Peace, The
   Harem Bunch; Or War and Piece, The (1969)
Harmony Trail
   White Stallion (1947)
Harry Tracy
   Harry Tracy—Desperado (1982, Can.)
Hatchet Murders, The
   Deep Red (1976, Ital.)
Haunting of Julia, The
   Full Circle (1977, Brit./Can.)
Hauptmann Von Koepenick
   Captain from Koepenick (1933, Ger.)
He Lived to Kill
   Night of Terror (1933)
He or She
   Glen or Glenda (1953)
He, She or It
   Doll, The (1962, Fr.)
He Was Called Robert
   They Call Me Robert (1967, USSR)
Head for the Devil, A
   Head, The (1961, Ger.)
Head for the Hills
   Sod Sisters (1969)
Head Over Heels
   Head Over Heels in Love (1937, Brit.)
Head Over Heels
   Chilly Scenes of Winter (1982)
Heart of New York, The
   Hallelujah, I'm a Bum (1933)
Hearts and Minds
   Master Touch, The (1974, Ital./Ger.)
Heat at Midnight
   Heat of Midnight (1966, Fr.)
Heaven Sent
   Thank Heaven for Small Favors (1965, Fr.)
Heldorado
   Helldorado (1946)
Hell Creatures, The
   Invasion of the Saucer Men (1957)
Hell of the Living Dead
   Night of the Zombies (1983, Span./Ital.)
Hell to Macao
   Corrupt Ones, The (1967, Ger.)
Hell's Highway
   Violent Road (1958)
Hellborn
   Singing Hill, The (1941)
Hemingway's Adventures of a Young Man
   Adventures of a Young Man (1962)
Her Enlisted Man
   Red Salute (1935)
Hercules and the Conquest of Atlantis
   Hercules and the Captive Women (1963, Fr./Ital.)
Hercules and the Hydra
   Loves of Hercules, The (1960, Ital./Fr.)
Hercules and the Haunted Women
   Hercules and the Captive Women (1963, Fr./Ital.)
Hercules: The Movie
   Hercules in New York (1970)
Here Comes a Policeman
   Strictly Illegal (1935, Brit.)
Here Comes That Nashville Sound
   Country Boy (1966)
Here is a Man
   Devil and Daniel Webster, The (1941)
Here Lies Love
   Second Woman, The (1951)
Hero, The
   Bloomfield (1971, Brit./Israel)
Heroin Gang, The
   Sol Madrid (1968)
Heroism
   Eroica (1966, Pol.)
Heterosexuals, The
   Les Biches (1968, Fr.)
Hey Sailor
   Here Comes the Navy (1934)

Hide and Go Kill
   Bloody Birthday (1980)*
Hidden Corpse
   Strangers of the Evening (1932)
Hidden Face
   Jail Bait (1954)
Hidden Room of 1,000 Horrors, The
   Tell-Tale Heart, The (1962, Brit.)
Hideaways, The
   From the Mixed-Up Files of Mrs. Basil E. Frank-
   weiler (1973)
High Rolling in a Hot Corvette
   High Rolling (1977, Aus.)
High School Honeymoon
   Too Soon to Love (1960)
Hired Gun
   Last Gunfighter, The (1961, Can.)
Hired Guns
   Hired Gun (1952)*
His Name Is Robert
   They Call Me Robert (1967, USSR)
His Wife's Habit
   Women and Bloody Terror (1970)
Histoires Extraordinaires
   Spirits of the Dead, The (1969, Fr./Ital.)
Hitler, a Film from Germany
   Our Hitler, a Film from Germany (1980, Ger.)
Hitler's Gold
   Inside Out (1975, Brit.)
Hitler's Hangman
   Hitler's Madman (1943)
Hitler's Women
   Women in Bondage (1943)
Hitler—Beast of Berlin
   Beasts of Berlin (1939)
Holdiay
   Jour de Fete (1952, Fr.)
Hole, The
   Onibaba (1965, Jap.)
Holiday in Spain
   Scent of Mystery (1960)
Hollywood
   Final Comedown, The (1972)*
Hollywood Cowboy
   Hearts of the West (1975)
Hollywood Hillside Strangler
   Hollywood 90028*
Hollywood Hoodlum
   Hollywood Mystery (1934)
Hollywood Meat Cleaver Massacre, The
   Meat Cleaver Massacre (1977)
Hollywood Strangler, The
   Don't Answer the Phone (1980)
Hollywood Stunt Man
   Movie Stuntmen (1953)
Hollywood Thrillmakers
   Movie Stuntmen (1953)
Holy Terror
   Alice, Sweet Alice (1978)
Home in Oklahoma
   Big Show, The (1937)
Hometowners
   Ladies Must Live (1940)
Hopalong Cassidy Enters
   Hopalong Cassidy (1935)
Hopeless Ones, The
   Round Up, the (1969, Hung.)
Hoppity Goes To Town
   Mr. Bug Goes To Town (1941)
Horrible House on the Hill, The
   Devil Times Five (1974)
Horrible Mill Women, The
   Mill of the Stone Women (1963, Fr./Ital.)
Horror Creatures of the Prehistoric Planet
   Horror of the Blood Monsters (1970, US/Phil.)
Horror Hotel Massacre
   Eaten Alive (1976)
Horror in the Midnight Sun
   Invasion of the Animal People (1962, US/Swed.)
Horror Maniacs
   Greed of William Hart, The (1948, Brit.)
Horror of Snape Island
   Beyond the Fog (1981, Brit.)
Horror of the Stone Women
   Mill of the Stone Women (1963, Fr./Ital.)
Horror Star, The
   Frightmare (1983)
Horrors of Spider Island
   It's Hot in Paradise (1962, Ger./Yugo.)
Horse, My Horse
   Horse, The (1984, Turkey)**
Horse Named Comanche, A
   Tonka (1958)
Horsie
   Queen for a Day (1951)
Hot Blood
   Wild One, The (1953)
Hot Car Girl
   Hot Rod Girl (1956)

Hot Child
　Nymph (1974)*
Hot Frustrations
　Frustrations (1967, Fr./Ital.)
Hot Horse
　Once Upon a Horse (1958)
Hot in Paradise
　It's Hot in Paradise (1962, Ger./Yugo.)
Hot Line, The
　Day the Hotline Got Hot, The (1968, Fr./Span.)
Hotel, The
　Games Men Play, The (1968, Arg.)
Houghland Murder Case, The
　Murder by Television (1935)
House Across the Lake, The
　Heatwave (1954, Brit.)
House of Cards
　Designing Women (1934, Brit.)
House of Crazies
　Asylum (1972, Brit.)
House of Insane Women
　Exorcism's Daughter (1974, Span.)
House of Menace
　Kind Lady (1935)
House of Mortal Sin
　Confessional, The (1977, Brit.)
House of Mystery
　Night Monster (1942)
House of Pleasure
　Le Plaisir (1954, Fr.)
House of Terror
　Face the Screaming Werewolf (1959, Mex.)
House of the Dead, The
　Alien Zone (1978)*
House of Unclaimed Women
　School for Unclaimed Girls (1973, Brit.)
House that Cried Murder, The
　Bride, The (1973)
House without Windows
　Seven Alone (1975)
Housewife
　Bone (1972)
How Low Can You Fall?
　Till Marriage Do Us Part (1979, Ital.)
How to Make It
　Target: Harry (1980)
How's Chances
　Diplomatic Lover, The (1934, Brit.)
Hua Mu-Lan
　Lady General, The (1965, Hong Kong)
Human Beast, The
　La Bete Humaine (1938, Fr.)
Human Interest Story, The
　Big Carnival, The (1951)
Humphrey Takes a Chance
　Joe Palooka in Humphrey Takes a Chance (1950)
Hunt to Kill
　White Buffalo, The (1977)
Hunter of the Apocalypse
　Last Hunter, The (1984, Ital.)** Hustler Squad
Doll Squad, The (1973)

I Accuse
　J'Accuse (1939, Fr.)
I Am Curious Gay
　Happy Birthday, Davy (1970)
I and My Love
　Galia (1966, Fr./Ital.)
I and My Lovers
　Galia (1966, Fr./Ital.)
I Call First
　Who's that Knocking at My Door? (1968)
I Can't...I Can't
　Wedding Night (1970, Ireland)
I Changed My Sex
　Glen or Glenda (1953)
I Cover the Underworld
　I Cover the Big Town (1947)
I Don't Want to be Born
　Devil Within Her, The (1976, Brit.)
I Give My Heart
　Give Me Your Heart (1936)
I Hate Your Guts
　Intruder, The (1962)
I Have a New Master
　Passion for Life (1951, Fr.)
I Have Seven Daughters
　My Seven Little Sins (1956, Fr./Ital.)
I Led Two Lives
　Glen or Glenda (1953)
I Love You
　Je T'Aime (1974, Can.)
I Married a Communist
　Woman on Pier 13, The (1950)
I Married a Nazi
　Man I Married, The (1940)

I Married Too Young
　Married Too Young (1962)
I Promise to Pay
　Payroll (1962, Brit.)
I Spit on Your Grave
　Camper John (1973)*
I Vitelloni
　Vitelloni (1956, Ital.)
I Want Her Dead
　W (1974)
I Was Faithless
　Cynara (1932)
I'll Never Forget You
　House on the Square, The (1951, Brit.)
Icarus XB-l
　Voyage to the End of the Universe (1963, Czech.)
Identikit
　Driver's Seat, The (1975, Ital.)
Il Bidone
　Swindler, The (1962, Fr./Ital.)
Il Posto
　Sound of Trumpets, The (1963, Ital.)
Immediate Disaster
　Stranger from Venus, The (1954, Brit.)
Immortal Battalion, The
　Way Ahead, The (1945, Brit.)
Impulsion
　Stepmother, The (1973)*
In Darkness Waiting
　Strategy of Terror (1969)
In the Days of the Thundering Herd
　Thundering Herd, The (1934)
In the Devil's Garden
　Assault (1971, Brit.)
In the Fall of '55 Eden Cried
　Eden Cried (1967)
In the Grip of the Spider
　Web of the Spider (1972, Ital./Fr./Ger.)
In the Woods
　Rashomon (1951, Jap.)
In Walked Eve
　In Trouble with Eve (1964, Brit.)
Incredible Challenge, The
　Night of the Assassin (1972)*
Incredible Praying Mantis, The
　Deadly Mantis, The (1957)
Incredible Torture Show, The
　Bloodsucking Freaks (1982)
Incredibly Strange Creatures, The
　Incredibly Strange Creatures Who Stopped Liv-
　ing and Became Crazy Mixed-Up Zombies, The
　(1965)
Indian Love Call
　Rose Marie (1936)
Indiscretion
　Indiscretion of an American Wife (1954, US/Ital.)
Infernal Idol, The
　Craze (1974, Brit.)
Infinity of Terror, An
　Galaxy of Terror (1981)
Infra Superman, The
　Infra-Man (1975, Hong Kong)
Inglorious Bastards
　Counterfeit Commandos (1981, Ital.)
Inisde Out
　Life Upside Down (1965, Fr.)
Inn of the Frightened People
　Terror from Under the House
Innocent Affair, An
　Don't Trust Your Husband (1948)
Innocent and the Damned, The
　Girls' Town (1959)
Insect, The
　Insect Woman, The (1964, Jap.)
Inseminoid
　Horror Planet (1982, Brit.)
Inspector Maigret
　Maigret Lays a Trap (1958, Fr.)
Interlude
　Intermezzo (1937, Swed.)
Intermezzo
　Intermezzo: A Love Story (1939)
International Police
　Pickup Alley (1957)
International Spy
　Spy Ring, The (1938)
Intimate Relations
　Disobedient (1953, Brit.)
Intrigue in Paris
　Miss V from Moscow (1942)
Intrigue in the Orient
　Women for Sale (1973)*
Invasion Earth 2150 A.D.
　Daleks—Invasion Earth 2150 A.D. (1966, Brit.)
Invasion Force
　Hangar 18 (1980)
Invasion from The Moon
　Mutiny in Outer Space (1965)
Invasion of Planet X
　Monster Zero (1970, Jap.)

Invasion of the Astro-Monsters
　Monster Zero (1970, Jap.)
Invasion of The Astros
　Monster Zero (1970, Jap.)
Invasion of the Flying Saucers
　Earth vs. the Flying Saucers (1956)
Invasion of the Flesh Hunters
　Cannibals in the Streets (1982, Ital./Span.)
Invasion of the Hell Creatures
　Invasion of the Saucer Men (1957)
Invisible Horror, The
　Invisible Dr. Mabuse, The (1965, Ger.)
Iron Kiss, The
　Naked Kiss, The (1964)
Island of Living Horror
　Brides of Blood (1968)
Island of the Burning Doomed
　Island of the Burning Damned (1971, Brit.)
Island of the Fishmen, The
　Screamers (1979, Ital.)
Island Woman
　Island Women (1958)
Isle of Lost Women
　99 Women (1969)*
Isle of the Dead, The
　Snake People, The (1968, Mex./U.S.)
Isle of the Snake People
　Snake People, The (1968, Mex./U.S.)
Isn't Life a Bitch?
　La Chienne (1975, Fr.)
It Comes Up Murder
　Honey Pot, The (1967, Brit.)
It Couldn't Have Happened
　It Couldn't Have Happened—But It Did (1936)
It Fell From the Flame Barrier
　Flame Barrier, The (1958)
It Happened in Paris
　Lady in Question, The (1940)
It Lives By Night
　Bat People, The (1974)
It Only Takes 5 Minutes
　Rotten Apple, The (1963)
It Shouldn't Happen to a Vet
　All Things Bright and Beautiful (1979, Brit.)
It Stalked the Ocean Floor
　Monster from the Ocean Floor, The (1954)
It Started at Midnight
　Schweik's New Adventure (1943, Brit.)
It Won't Rub Off, Baby!
　Sweet Love, Bitter (1967)
It! The Vampire from Beyond Space
　It! The Terror from Beyond Space (1958)
It's Alive II
　It Lives Again (1978)
It's Hot in Hell
　Monkey in Winter, A (1962, Fr.)
It's Only Money
　Double Dynamite (1951)
It's Sam Small Again
　Sam Small Leaves Town (1937, Brit.)
It's Turned Out Nice Again
　Turned Out Nice Again (1941, Brit.)
Italian Mouse, The
　Magic World of Topo Gigio, The (1961, Ital.)
Ivan's Childhood
　My Name Is Ivan (1963, USSR)
Ivory Hunters, The
　Ivory Hunter (1952, Brit.)

J.C. and the Boys
　J.C. (1972)*
J.D. and the Salt Flat Kid
　Smokey and the Goodtime Outlaws (1978)*
J.R.
　Who's that Knocking at My Door? (1968)
Jack London's Klondike Fever
　Klondike Fever (1980)
Jack's Wife
　Hungry Wives (1973)
Jacqueline Susann's Once Is Not Enough
　Once Is Not Enough (1975)
Jail Birds
　Pardon Us (1931)
Japan Sinks
　Tidal Wave (1975, US/Jap.)
Jason and the Golden Fleece
　Jason and the Argonauts (1963, Brit.)
Jaws of Death, The
　Mako: the Jaws of Death (1976)
Jealousy Italian Style
　Pizza Triangle, The (1970, Ital./Span.)
Jekyll's Inferno
　House of Fright (1961)
Jericho
　Dark Sands (1938, Brit.)
Jessica
　Miss Jessica Is Pregnant (1970)

Jet Set, The
  Blazing Stewardesses (1975)*
Jet Squad
  Jet Attack (1958)
Jezebelles, The
  Switchblade Sisters (1975)
Jezebels, The
  Switchblade Sisters (1975)
Jimmy Valentine
  Return of Jimmy Valentine, The (1936)
Joaquin Murrieta
  Murieta (1965, Span.)
Jock
  Petersen (1974, Aus.)
Joe Palooka
  Palooka (1934)
Joey
  Deliver Us from Evil (1975)*
Johnny Oro
  Ringo and his Golden Pistol (1966, Ital.)
Joke of Destiny Lying in Wait Around the Corner
  Like a Street Bandit, A (1984, Ital.)**
  Joke of Destiny, A
Jonah—Who Will Be 25 in the Year 2000
  Jonas—Who Will Be 25 in the Year 2000 (1976,
  Swed.)
Joniko
  Joniko and the Kush Ta Ka (1969)
Joseph and His Brethren
  Story of Joseph and His Brethren (1962, Ital.)
Joseph Desa
  Reluctant Saint, The (1962, US/Ital.)
Joseph Sold By His Brothers
  Story of Joseph and His Brethren (1962, Ital.)
Journey to Italy
  Strangers, The (1955, Ital.)
Joy of Learning
  Le Gai Savior (1968, Fr.)
Juarez and Maximillian
  Mad Empress, The (1940)
Judith and Holophernes
  Head of a Tyrant (1960, Fr./Ital.)
July Pork Bellies
  For Pete's Sake (1977)
Jungle Attack
  Crosswinds (1951)
Jungle Fighters
  Long and the Short and the Tall, The (1961, Brit.)
Jungle Heat
  Dance of the Dwarfs (1983)*
Jungle Terror
  Fireball Jungle (1968)
Jungle Virgin
  Jaws of the Jungle (1936)
Just One More
  Just Once More (1963, Swed.)
Just to Be Loved
  New Life Style, The (1970, Ger.)

Keeler Affair, The
  Christine Keeler Affair, The (1964, Brit.)
Keep Him Alive
  Great Plane Robbery, The (1940)
Keep Off My Grass
  Keep Off! Keep Off! (1975)*
Kempy
  Wise Girls (1930)
Kettle Creek
  Mountain Justice (1930)
Kill and Go Hide!
  Child, The (1977)
Kill Castro
  Cuba Crossing (1980)
Kill!
  Kill! Kill! Kill! (1972, Fr.)
Killer Bats
  Devil Bat, The (1941)
Killer Behind the Mask, The
  Savage Weekend (1983)
Killer Grizzly
  Grizzly (1976)
Killer of Killers
  Mechanic, The (1972)
Killer on a Horse
  Welcome to Hard Times (1967)
Killer Orphan
  Friday the 13th...The Orphan (1979)
Killer, The
  Sacred Knives of Vengeance, The (1974, Hong
  Kong)
Killer, The
  Mystery Ranch (1932)
Killer with a Label
  One Too Many (1950)
Killers are Challenged
  Secret Agent Fireball (1965, Fr./Ital.)

Killers' Cage
  Code of Silence (1960)
Killing Urge
  Jet Storm (1961, Brit.)
Kin Folk
  Kinfolk (1970)
King Cobra
  Jaws of Satan (1980)
King Kong's Counterattack
  King Kong Escapes (1968, Jap.)
King Oedipus
  Oedipus Rex (1957, Can.)
King of Africa
  One Step to Hell (1969, US/Ital./Span.)
King of the Jungleland
  Darkest Africa (1936)
King, The
  Royal Affair, A (1950)
Kingfisher Caper, The
  Kingfish Caper, The (1976, S. Afr.)
Kiru
  Kill (1968, Jap.)
Kiss and Kill
  Blood of Fu Manchu, The (1968, Brit.)
Kiss from Eddie, A
  Arousers, The (1973)
Kiss My Butterfly
  I Love You, Alice B. Toklas! (1968)
Kiss the Girls; Make Them Die
  Kiss the Girls and See Them Die! (1968)*
Kisses for the President
  Kisses for My President (1964)
Kitten on the Keys
  Do You Love Me? (1946)
Kitty Can't Help It
  Carhops, The (1980)*
Knack, The
  Knack...and How to Get it, The (1965, Brit.)
Knife in the Body, The
  Murder Clinic, The (1967, Ital./Fr.)
Knight Without Armour
  Knight Without Armor, The (1937, Brit.)
Knights of the Black Cross
  Knights of the Teutonic Order, The (1962, Pol.)
Konska Opera
  Lemonade Joe (1966, Czech.)
Kuni Lemel in Tel Aviv
  Rabbi and the Shikse, The (1976, Israel)
Kutuzov
  1812 (1944, USSR)

L'Enfant Sauvage
  Wild Child, The (1970, Fr.)
L'Histoire d'Adele H.
  Story of Adele H. (1975, Fr.)
La Grande Illusion
  Grand Illusion, The (1939, Fr.)
La Revolte des Vivants
  Le Monde Tremblera (1939, Fr.)
Labyrinth
  Reflection of Fear, A (1973)
Ladies of the Mob
  House of Women (1962)
Lady and the Outlaw, The
  Billy Two Hats (1973, Brit.)
Lady Dances, The
  Merry Widow, The (1934)
Lady Killers, The
  Ladykillers, The (1956, Brit.)
Lady of the Shadows
  Terror, The (1963)
Lady with the Lamp, The
  Lady with a Lamp, The (1951, Brit.)
Lancelot du Lac
  Lancelot of the Lake (1975, Fr.)
Land We Love, The
  Hero's Island (1962)
Last Castle, The
  Echoes of a Summer (1976)
Last Chance For a Born Loser
  Stateline Motel (1976, Ital.)
Last Days of Sodom and Gomorrah, The
  Sodom and Gomorrah (1962, US/Fr./Ital.)
Last Four Days, The
  Last Days of Mussolini (1974, Ital.)
Last Glory of Troy, The
  Avenger, The (1962, Fr./Ital.)
Last Great Treasure, The
  Mother Lode (1982)
Last House On the Left, Part II
  Twitch of the Death Nerve (1973, Ital.)
Last Message from Saigon
  Operation CIA (1965)
Last of Summer
  Early Autumn (1962, Jap.)
Last of the Cowboys, The
  Great Smokey Roadblock, The (1978)

Last of the Mobile Hotshots, The
  Blood Kin (1969)*
Last Stage, The
  Last Stop, The (1949, Pol.)
Last Ten Days of Adolf Hitler
  Last Ten Days, The (1956, Ger.)
Last Victim, The
  Forced Entry (1975)
Last Will of Dr. Mabuse, The
  Testament of Dr. Mabuse, The (1933, Ger.)
Laughter House
  Singleton's Pluck (1984, Brit.)**
Law, The
  Law and Order (1932)
Law, The
  Where the Hot Wind Blows (1960, Fr./Ital.)
Law of the Wild
  Law of the Wolf (1941)*
Lawless Clan
  Lawless Breed, The (1946)
Lazy Bones
  Hallelujah, I'm a Bum (1933)
Le Graal
  Lancelot of the Lake (1975, Fr.)
Le Notti Blanche
  White Nights (1961, Ital./Fr.)
Le Streghe
  Witches, The (1969, Fr./Ital.)
Le Vent D'Est
  Wind From the East (1970, Fr./Ital./Ger.)
Learn, Baby, Learn
  Learning Tree, The (1969)
Leda
  Web of Passion (1961, Fr.)
Legacy of Maggie Walsh, The
  Legacy, The (1979, Brit.)
Legend in Leotards
  Return of Captain Invincible, The (1983, U.S./
  Aus.)
Legend of Blood Castle
  Female Butcher, The (1972, Ital./Span.)
Legend of Hillbilly John, The
  Who Fears the Devil (1972)
Legend of Sea Wolf, The
  Wolf Larson (1975, Ital.)
Legend of the Bayou
  Eaten Alive (1976)
Legend of Witch Hollow
  Witchmaker, The (1969)
Legendary Curse of Lemora, The
  Lady Dracula, The (1974)
Lemora, Lady Dracula
  Lady Dracula, The (1974)
Les Parisiennes
  Tales of Paris (1962, Fr./Ital.)
Les Sorcieres
  Witches, The (1969, Fr./Ital.)
Lesbian Twins
  Virgin Witch, The (1973, Brit.)
Lest We Forget
  Hangmen Also Die (1943)
Let Me Love You
  I Am Frigid...Why? (1973)*
Let the People Laugh
  Sing as You Swing (1937, Brit.)
Let's Do It
  Judy's Little No-No (1969)
Let's Go Wakadaisho
  Let's Go, Young Guy! (1967, Jap.)
Let's Have Fun
  Laugh Your Blues Away (1943)
Letter from a Novice
  Rita (1963, Fr./Ital.)
Letter That Was Not Sent, The
  Letter That Never Was Sent, The (1962, USSR)
Life at Stake
  Key Man, The (1957, Brit.)
Life Dances On
  Un Carnet de Bal (1938, Fr.)
Life of Brian
  Monty Python's Life of Brian (1979, Brit.)
Light Ahead, The
  Dobbin, The (1939)*
Lightnin' Smith's Return
  Lightnin' Smith Returns (1931)*
Like it Is
  Not My Daughter (1975)*
Lisa, Lisa
  Axe (1977)*
Little Moon and Jud McGraw
  Gone with the West (1976)*
Lila
  Mantis in Lace (1968)
Lila: Love Under the Midnight Sun
  Make Way For Lila (1962, Swed./Ger.)
Limbo
  Rebel Rousers (1970)
Lion of Sparta
  300 Spartans, The (1962)

Lisa and the Devil
   House of Exorcism, The (1976, Ital.)
Lisa, the Greek Tosca
   Lisa, Tosca of Athens (1961, Gr.)
Little Gel
   King of Hearts (1936, Brit.)
Little Pal
   Healer, The (1935)
Little Red Monkey
   Case of the Red Monkey (1955, Brit.)
Little Red Riding Hood and Her Three Friends
   Little Red Riding Hood and Her Friends (1964,
   Mex.)
Live a Little, Steal a Lot
   Murph the Surf (1974)
Live to Love
   Devil's Hand, The (1961)
Live Today for Tomorrow
   Act of Murder, An (1948)
Liver Eaters, The
   Spider Baby (1968)
Living
   Ikiru (1960, Jap.)
Living Dead at Manchester Morgue, The
   Don't Open the Window (1974, Ital.)
Living Dead, The
   Snake People, The (1968, Mex./U.S.)
Loaded Dice
   Cross My Heart (1937, Brit.)
Locker Room Girls
   Swinging Cheerleaders, The (1974)*
Lola's Mistake
   This Rebel Breed (1960)
Lollipop
   Forever Young, Forever Free (1976, South Afr.)
Lolly Madonna War, The
   Lolly-Madonna XXX (1973)
London Belongs to Me
   Dulcimer Street (1948)
London Calling
   Hello London (1958, Brit.)
Lone Rider in Texas Justice
   Texas Justice (1942)*
Lone Star Lawmen
   Texas Lawman (1952)
Lonely Heart Bandits
   Lonely Hearts Bandits (1950)
Lonely Hearts Killers, The
   Honeymoon Killers, The (1969)
Lonely Lady, The
   Strangers, The (1955, Ital.)
Lonely Man
   Gun Riders, The (1969)
Lonely Woman, The
   Strangers, The (1955, Ital.)
Loner, The
   Ruckus (1981)
Long John Silver Returns to Treasure Island
   Long John Silver (1954, Aus.)
Long Ride, The
   Brady's Escape (1984, U.S./Hung.)**
Long Search, The
   Memory of Love (1949)*
Longest Spur, The
   Hot Spur (1968)
Look Before You Laugh
   Make Mine a Million (1965, Brit.)
Look Down and Die
   Steel (1980)
Lookin' Good
   Corky (1972)
Loose Pleasures
   Tight Skirts, Loose Pleasures (1966, Fr.)
Lost Atlantis
   Mistress of Atlantis, The (1932, Ger.)
Lost Illusion
   Fallen Idol, The (1949, Brit.)
Lost Women
   Mesa of Lost Women, The (1956)
Lost Women of Zarpa
   Mesa of Lost Women, The (1956)
Louisiana
   She Devil (1940)*
Louisiana Gal
   Old Louisiana (1938)
Lovable and Sweet
   Runaround, The (1931)
Love at the Top
   French Way, The (1975, Fr.)
Love Ban, The
   It's a 2' 6" Above the Ground World (1972, Brit.)
Love Cage, The
   Joy House (1964, Fr.)
Love Commune
   Sign of Aquarius (1970)
Love in Cold Blood
   Ice House, The (1969)
Love in Jerusalem
   My Margo (1969, Israel)

Love is a Day's Work
   From a Roman Balcony (1961, Fr./Ital.)
Love is a Weapon
   Hell's Island (1955)
Love Is Catching
   Calliope (1971)*
Love Italian Style
   Love, the Italian Way (1964, Ital.)
Love Madness
   Reefer Madness (1936)
Love Makers, The
   La Viaccia (1962, Fr./Ital.)
Love Mates, The
   Madly (1970, Fr.)
Love Merchants
   Love Merchant, The (1966)
Love of Three Queens
   Loves of Three Queens, The (1954, Ital.)
Love Root, The
   Mandragola (1966, Fr./Ital.)
Love Starved
   Young Bride (1932)
Love—Tahiti Style
   Nude Odyssey (1962, Fr./Ital.)
Love Thrill Murders
   Sweet Savior (1971)*
Love Times Three
   Closet Casanova, The (1979)*
Loving Man, The
   Day The Lord Got Busted, The (1976)*
Loving Touch, The
   Psycho Lover (1969, Brit.)*
Lovemaker, The
   Main Street (1956, Span.)
Lover Boy
   Lovers, Happy Lovers (1955, Brit.)
Lover For the Summer, A
   Mistress For the Summer, A (1964, Fr./Ital.)
Lover, Wife
   Wifemistress (1979, Ital.)
Lovers from Beyond the Tomb
   Nightmare Castle (1966, Ital.)
Lovers in Limbo
   Name of the Game Is Kill, The (1968)
Lovers Like Us
   Savage, The (1975, Fr.)
Lovers of Montparnasse, The
   Modigliani of Montparnasse (1961, Fr./Ital.)
Loves of a Dictator, The
   Dictator, The (1935, Brit./Ger.)
Loves of Ariane, The
   Ariane (1931)
Loves of Isadora, The
   Isadora (1968, Brit.)
Lovespell
   Tristan and Isolt (1981)
Loyal 47 Ronin
   Chushingura (1963, Jap.)
Lucifer Project, The
   Barracuda (1978)
Lucky Boots
   Gun Play (1936)
Lucky Luciano
   Re: Lucky Luciano (1974, Fr./Ital.)
Lucky 13
   Running Hot (1984)** Lucretia Borgia
   Lucrece Borgia (1953, Ital./Fr.)
Lunch Wagon Girls
   Lunch Wagon (1981)
Lure of the Jungle
   Boy of Two Worlds (1970)*
Lust of the Vampires
   Devil's Commandment, The (1956, Ital.)
Lycanthropus
   Werewolf in a Girl's Dormitory (1961, Ital.)

M3: The Gemini Strain
   Plague (1978, Can.)
Macabra
   Demonoid (1981)
Maciste Against the Czar
   Atlas Against the Czar (1964, Ital.)
Maciste at the Court of the Great Khan
   Samson and the Seven Miracles of the World
   (1963, Fr./Ital.)
Mad About Money
   He Loved an Actress (1938, Brit.)
Mad Adventures of "Rabbi" Jacob, The
   Adventures of Rabbi Jacob, The (1973, Fr.)
Mad Cage, The
   La Cage Aux Folles (1979, Fr./Ital.)
Mad Dog
   Mad Dog Morgan (1976, Aus.)
Mad Little Island
   Tight Little Island (1949, Brit.)
Mad, Mad Moviemakers, The
   Last Porno Flick, The (1974)

Mad Magazine's Up the Academy
   Up the Academy (1980)
Mad Max II
   Road Warrior, The (1982, Aus.)
Mad Trapper of the Yukon
   Challenge To Be Free (1976)
Madame Frankenstein
   Lady Frankenstein (1971, Ital.)
Madame Sans-Gene
   Madame (1963, Fr./Ital./Span.)
Made It On My Own
   Smokey and the Goodtime Outlaws (1978)*
Mademoiselle Striptease
   Please! Mr. Balzac (1957, Fr.)
Madmen of Mandoras
   They Saved Hitler's Brain (1964)
Maeva—Portrait of a Tahitian Girl
   Maeva (1961)
Maggie, The
   High and Dry (1954, Brit.)
Magic Garden, The
   Pennywhistle Blues, The (1952, S. Africa)
Magical Spectacle
   Magic Spectacles (1961)
Magnificent Seven, The
   Seven Samurai, The (1956, Jap.)
Maiden for the Prince, A
   Maiden for a Prince, A (1967, Fr./Ital.)
Majin, the Hideous Idol
   Majin (1968, Jap.)
Majin, the Monster of Terror
   Majin (1968, Jap.)
Make Me a Woman
   Sisters, The (1969, Ger.)
Making of a Lady, The
   Lady Hamilton (1969, Ger./Ital./Fr.)
Male and Female
   Male and Female Since Adam and Eve (1961,
   Arg.)
Malibu
   Sequoia (1934)
Malice
   Malicious (1974, Ital.)
Man Eater of Hydra
   Island of the Doomed (1968, Span./Ger.)
Man Following the Sun
   Sandu Follows the Sun (1965, USSR)
Man from C.O.T.T.O.N., The
   Gone Are the Days (1963)
Man from the Past, The
   Man from the First Century, The (1961, Czech.)
Man Goes Through the Wall, A
   Man Who Walked Through the Wall, The (1964,
   Ger.)
Man in Hiding
   Woman in Hiding (1953, Brit.)
Man in Outer Space
   Man from the First Century, The (1961, Czech.)
Man in the Middle
   48 Hours to Live (1960, Brit./Swed.)
Man is Ten Feet Tall, A
   Edge of the City (1957)
Man Missing
   You Have to Run Fast (1961)
Man of Iron
   Railroad Man, The (1965, Ital.)
Man Who Changed, The
   Man Who Changed His Name, The (1934, Brit.)
Man Who Lost His Way, The
   Crossroads (1942)
Man with the Green Carnation, The
   Green Buddha, The (1954, Brit.)
Man with the Synthetic Brain
   Psycho a Go-Go (1965)
Man With the X-Ray Eyes, The
   X—The Man with the X-Ray Eyes (1963)
Man with the Yellow Eyes, The
   Planets Against Us, The (1961, Ital./Fr.)
Man without a Face, The
   Shadowman (1974, Fr./Ital.)
Man without a Gun
   Man with the Gun (1955)
Man-Killer
   Other Love, The (1947)
Mandragola—The Love Root
   Mandragola (1966, Fr./Ital.)
Maneater
   Shark (1970, US/Mex.)
Manhunt
   Italian Connection, The (1973, US/Ital./Ger.)
Mania for Melody
   Sing, Dance, Plenty Hot (1940)
Maniac
   Maniac Mansion (1978, Ital.)
Maniacs Are Loose, The
   Thrill Killers, The (1965)
Manipulator, The
   Effects (1980)
Manny's Orphans
   Here Come the Tigers (1978)

Manster—Half Man, Half Monster
  Manster, The (1962, Jap.)
Manuscript Found in Saragossa
  Saragossa Manuscript, The (1972, Pol.)
March of the Wooden Soldiers
  Babes in Toyland (1934)
Maria Candelaria
  Portrait of Maria (1946, Mex.)
Maria Chapdelaine
  Naked Heart, The (1955, Brit.)
Maria Elena
  She-Devil Island (1936, Mex.)
Maria, the Wonderful Weaver
  Magic Weaver, The (1965, USSR)
Marianne
  Mirrors (1984)**
Marie du Port
  La Marie du Port (1951, Fr.)
Marizinia, the Witch Beneath the Sea
  Marizinia (1962, U.S./Braz.)
Mark of Terror
  Drums of Jeopardy (1931)
Mark of the Avenger
  Mysterious Rider, The (1933)
Mark of the Vampire
  Vampire, The (1957)
Marquis de Sade: Justine
  Justine (1969, Ital./Span.)
Mars Invades Puerto Rico
  Frankenstein Meets the Space Monster (1965)
Marseilles Contract, The
  Destructors, The (1974, Brit.)
Mary Names the Day
  Dr. Kildare's Wedding Day (1941)
Masks
  Persona (1967, Swed.)
Massacre at Fort Holman
  Reason to Live, a Reason to Die, A (1974, Ital./Fr./Ger./Span.)
Massacre at the Rosebud, The
  Great Sioux Massacre, The (1965)
Master of Lassie
  Hills of Home (1948)
Master of Terror, The
  4D Man (1959)
Masterworks of Terror
  Master of Horror (1965, Arg.)
Mata Hari Agent H-21
  Mata-Hari (1965, Fr./Ital.)
Matango, Fungus of Terror
  Attack of the Mushroom People (1964, Jap.)
Mating of the Sabine Women, The
  Shame of the Sabine Women, The (1962, Mex.)
Matter of Resistance, A
  La Vie de Chateau (1967, Fr.)
McCullochs, The
  Wild McCullochs, The (1975)
McMasters...Tougher Than the West Itself, The
  McMasters, The (1970)
Meat Is Meat
  Mad Butcher, The (1972)
Meet Miss Marple
  Murder She Said (1961, Brit.)
Meet the Nelsons
  Here Come the Nelsons (1952)
Melody in Gray
  Banished (1978, Jap.)
Memories of Prison
  Memoirs of Prison (1984, Braz.)**
Men of Steel
  Steel (1980)
Men of the Tenth
  Red, White and Black, The (1970)
Menace
  When London Sleeps (1934, Brit.)
Merry Wisdom
  Le Gai Savior (1968, Fr.)
Message, The
  Mohammad, Messenger of God (1976, Lebanon/Brit.)
Messiah of Evil
  Dead People (1974)
Meteor Monster
  Teenage Monster (1958)
Miami Rendezvous
  Passion Holiday (1963)
Microscopia
  Fantastic Voyage (1966)
Mid-Day Miss
  Mid-Day Mistress (1968)
Midnight Melody
  Murder in the Music Hall (1946)
Mighty Peking Man, The
  Goliathon (1979, Hong Kong)
Mighty Warrior, The
  Trojan Horse, The (1962, Fr./Ital.)
Military Academy
  Military Academy with that Tenth Avenue Gang (1950)

Million Dollar Duck
  $1,000,000 Duck (1971)
Millionaire Merry-Go-Round
  Playboy, The (1942, Brit.)
Mind Snatchers, The
  Happiness Cage, The (1972)
Mindwarp
  Galaxy of Terror (1981)
Mindwarp: An Infinity of Terror
  Galaxy of Terror (1981)
Minotaur
  Land of the Minotaur (1976, Gr.)
Minotaur—The Wild Beast of Crete
  Minotaur, The 1961, Ital.)
Miracle Can Happen, A
  On Our Merry Way (1948)
Miracle in the Sand
  Three Godfathers (1936)
Miracle of the White Reindeer, The
  Miracle of Santa's White Reindeer, The (1963)
Miss Fane's Baby
  Miss Fane's Baby Is Stolen (1934)
Missing Witness, The
  Love's Old Sweet Song (1933, Brit.)
Mission to Hell
  Savage! (1962)
Mr. Forbush and the Penguins
  Cry of the Penguins (1972, Brit.)
Mr. Fox of Venice
  Honey Pot, The (1967, Brit.)
Mr. Invisible
  Mr. Superinvisible (1974, Ital./Span./Ger.)
Mr. Jim American, Soldier and Gentleman
  Sergeant Jim (1962, Yugo.)
Mr. Radish and Mr. Carrot
  Twilight Path (1965, Jap.)
Mister V
  Pimpernel Smith (1941)
Mister, You Are a Widower
  Sir, You Are a Widower (1971, Czech.)
Mogliamante
  Wifemistress (1979, Ital.)
Molester, The
  Never Take Candy from a Stranger (1961, Brit.)
Molly
  Goldbergs, The (1950)
Molly Louvain
  Strange Love of Molly Louvain, The (1932)
Moment of Danger
  Malaga (1962, Brit.)
Momman, Little Jungle Boy
  Little Jungle Boy (1969, Aus.)
Money, Money, Money
  Counterfeiters of Paris, The (1961, Fr./Ital.)
Money Order, The
  Mandabi (1970, Fr.)
Monsieur Hulot's Holiday
  Mr. Hulot's Holiday (1954, Fr.)
Monster from a Prehistoric Planet
  Gappa the Trifibian Monster (1967, Jap.)
Monster Maker
  Monster from the Ocean Floor, The (1954)
Monster of Monsters
  Ghidrah, the Three-Headed Monster (1965, Jap.)
Monster of Terror
  Die, Monster, Die (1965, Brit.)
Monster Show, The
  Freaks (1932)
Monster Varan
  Varan the Unbelievable (1962, US/Jap.)
Monster Yongkari
  Yongkari Monster From the Deep (1967, S.K.)
Monsters Are Loose, The
  Thrill Killers, The (1965)
Monsters from the Moon
  Robot Monster (1953)
Monsters Invade Expo '70
  Gamera Versus Monster X (1970, Jap.)
Monstrosity
  Atomic Brain, The (1964)
Montana Mike
  Heaven Only Knows (1947)
Montenegro—Or Pigs and Pearls
  Montenegro (1981, Brit./Swed.)
Moonbeam Man, The
  Man in the Moonlight Mask, The (1958, Jap.)
Moonlight
  Und Immer Ruft das Herz (1966, Ger.)
Motel
  Pink Motel (1983)
Mother
  Up Your Teddy Bear (1970)
Mother Joan of the Angels
  Joan of the Angels (1962, Pol.)
Mother Riley Meets the Vampire
  My Son the Vampire (1963, Brit.)
Mother's Millions
  She-Wolf, The (1931)
Mothra Vs. Godzilla
  Godzilla Vs. the Thing (1964, Jap.)

Mountain Man
  Mark Twain, American (1976)*
Mountain of Cannibal Gods
  Slave of The Cannibal God (1979, Ital.)
Movie Struck
  Pick a Star (1937)
Mozart
  Life and Loves of Mozart, The (1959, Ger.)
Mu University
  University of Life (1941, USSR)
Mud
  Stick Up, The (1978, Brit.)
Mud Honey
  Rope of Flesh (1965)
Mudhoney
  Rope of Flesh (1965)
Mule Feathers
  West Is Still Wild (1977)
Murder at the Burlesque
  Mystery at the Burlesque (1950, Brit.)
Murder by Agreement
  Journey into Nowhere (1963, Brit.)
Murder by Mail
  Schizoid (1980)
Murder by Phone
  Bells (1981, (1981, Can.)
Murder in Morocco
  Scream in the Night (1943)
Murder in the Air
  Twenty Questions Murder Mystery, The (1950, Brit.)
Murder in the Footlights
  Trojan Brothers, The (1946)
Murder Mississippi
  Murder in Mississippi (1965)
Murder Society, The
  Murder Clinic, The (1967, Ital./Fr.)
Murderer Dmitri Karamazov, The
  Karamazov (1931, Ger.)
Murderer, The
  Enough Rope (1966, Fr./Ital./Ger.)
Muriel, Or the Time of Return
  Muriel (1963, Fr./Ital.)
Murri Affair, The
  La Grande Bourgeoise (1977, Ital.)
Music and Millions
  Such Is Life (1936, Brit.)
Mutant
  Forbidden World (1982)
Mutant
  Night Shadows (1984)**
Mutation, The
  Mutations, The (1974, Brit.)
Mutations
  Mutations, The (1974, Brit.)
Mutiny in Outer Space
  Space Master X-7 (1958)
Mutiny, The
  White Slave Ship (1962, Fr./Ital.)
My Apple
  Just Me (1950, Fr.)
My Enemy the Sea
  Alone on the Pacific (1964, Jap.)
My Father, My Master
  Padre, Padrone (1977, Ital.)
My Hero!
  Southern Yankee, A (1948)
My Love for Yours
  Honeymoon in Bali (1939)
My Love Letters
  Love Letters (1983)
My Main Man from Stony Island
  Stony Island (1978)
My Night with Maud
  My Night at Maud's 1970, Fr.)
My Old Man's Place
  Glory Boy (1971)
My Outlaw Brother
  My Brother, the Outlaw (1951)
My Sister, My Love
  Mafu Cage, The (1978)
My Son
  Living Orphan, The (1939)*
My Son Alone
  American Empire (1942)
My Son Nero
  Nero's Mistress (1962, Ital.)
My Soul Runs Naked
  Rat Fink (1965)
My Third Wife by George
  My Third Wife George (1968)
Mysterious Island, The
  Mysterious Island of Captain Nemo, The (1973, Fr./Ital./Span./Cameroon)
Mystery of Kaspar Hauser
  Every Man for Himself and God Against All (1975, Ger.)
Mystery of the Marie Celeste, The
  Phantom Ship, The (1937, Brit.)

Mystery on Monster Island
  Monster Island (1981, Span./U.S.)
Mystery Plane
  Sky Pirate (1939)*
Mystifiers, The
  Symphony of a Massacre (1965, Fr./Ital.)

N.P.—the Secret
  N.P. (1971, Ital.)
Nada
  Nada Gang, The (1964, Fr./Ital.)
Naked Childhood
  Me (1970, Fr.)
Naked Choice, The
  Night of the Assassin (1972)*
Naked Evil
  Exorcism at Night (1966, Brit.)
Naked Goddess, The
  Devil's Hand, The (1961)
Naked Island
  Island, The (1962, Jap.)
Naked Lovers, The
  Naked Zoo, The (1970)
Naked Revenge
  Count Your Bullets (1972)
Naked Rider
  All the Young Wives (1975)*
Naked Road
  Naked Set (1962)*
Naked Spur, The
  Hot Spur (1968)
Naked Temptation
  Woman and Temptation (1967, Arg.)
Naked Temptress, The
  Naked Witch, The (1964)
Naked Under Leather
  Girl on a Motorcycle, The (1968, Fr./Brit.)
Naked Youth
  Wild Youth (1961)
Nark, The
  La Balance (1983, Fr.)
Nashville Girl
  New Girl in Town (1977)
Natalka Poltavka
  Girl from Poltava (1937)
Nathaniel Hawthorne's "Twice Told Tales"
  Twice Told Tales (1963)
Nature's Mistakes
  Freaks (1932)
Naughty Freshmen
  Intimate Playmates, The (1976)*
Nazi Spy Ring
  Dawn Express, The (1942)
Nazi Terror at Night
  Devil Strikes at Night, The (1959, Ger.)
Necrophagus
  Graveyard of Horror (1971, Span.)
Nemo
  Dream One (1984, Brit./Fr.)**
Neopolitan Carousel
  Neapolitan Carousel (1961, Ital.)
Neptune Disaster, The
  Neptune Factor, The (1973, Can.)
Nero's Big Weekend
  Nero's Mistress (1962, Ital.)
Never Give a Sucker a Break
  Nuisance, The (1933)
Never Give an Inch
  Sometimes a Great Notion (1971)
Never Say Die
  Don't Say Die (1950, Brit.)
Never to Love
  Bill of Divorcement (1940)
New Adventures of Dr. Fu Manchu, The
  Return of Dr. Fu Manchu, The (1930)
New Adventures of the Bionic Boy, The
  Dracula's Great Love (1972, Span.)
New Monsters, The
  Viva Italia (1978, Ital.)
New Movietone Follies of 1930, The
  Fox Movietone Follies of 1930 (1930)
New One-Armed Swordsman, The
  Triple Irons (1973, Hong Kong)
New York
  Hallelujah, I'm a Bum (1933)
Next Victim! The
  Next! (1971, Ital./Span.)
Nice Plate of Spinach, A
  What Would You Say to Some Spinach (1976,
  Czech.)
Nick Carter in Prague
  Adele Hasn't Had Her Supper Yet (1978, Czech.)
Niggerich
  Baby Needs a New Pair of Shoes*
Night, The
  La Notte (1961, Fr./Ital.)

Night Caller, The
  Blood Beast from Outer Space (1965, Brit.)
Night Crawlers, The
  Navy vs. the Night Monsters, The (1966)
Night Flight from Moscow
  Serpent, The (1973, Fr./Ital./Ger.)
Night is the Phantom
  What (1965, Fr./Brit./Ital.)
Night Legs
  Fright (1971, Brit.)
Night of Love
  Night of Lust (1965, Fr.)
Night of Terrors, The
  Murder Clinic, The (1967, Ital./Fr.)
Night of the Beast
  House of the Black Death (1965)
Night of the Claw, The
  Island Claws (1981)
Night of the Dark Full Moon
  Silent Night, Bloody Night (1974)
Night of the Demon
  Touch of Satan, The (1971)
Night of the Demon
  Curse of the Demon (1958)
Night of the Flesh Eaters
  Night of the Living Dead (1968)
Night of the Silicates
  Island of Terror (1967, Brit.)
Night of the Tiger
  Ride Beyond Vengeance (1966)
Night of the Wehrmacht Zombies
  Night of the Zombies (1981)
Night of Witches
  Night of the Witches (1970)
Night Star
  War of the Zombies (1965, Ital.)
Night Train Murders
  Last Stop on the Night Train (1976)*
Night Walk
  Deathdream (1972, Can.)
Night Warning
  Butcher, Baker (Nightmare Maker)
Nightingale
  Young Nurses, The (1973)
Nightmare
  City of the Walking Dead (1983, Span./Ital.)
Nightmare City
  City of the Walking Dead (1983, Span./Ital.)
Nightmare Island
  Slayer, The (1982)
Nightmare Maker
  Butcher, Baker (Nightmare Maker)
Nightmare of Death
  Nightmare County (1977)*
Nights in a Harem
  Son of Sinbad (1955)
Nights of Rasputin, The
  Night They Killed Rasputin, The (1962, Fr./Ital)
Nights When the Devil Came
  Devil Strikes at Night, The (1959, Ger.)
Nine Days a Queen
  Lady Jane Grey (1936, Brit.)
Nine Loves Are Not Enough
  Nine Lives Are Not Enough (1941)
Ninth Symphony
  Final Chord, The (1936, Ger.)
99 Mujeres
  99 Women (1969)*
99 Donne
  99 Women (1969)*
No Escape
  I Escaped from the Gestapo (1943)
No Escape—No Exit
  No Escape (1936, Brit.)
No Greater Love
  Human Condition, The (1959, Jap.)
No Greater Sin
  Eighteen and Anxious (1957)
No Highway
  No Highway in the Sky (1951, Brit.)
No Knife
  Frisco Kid, The (1979)
No Man's Land
  No Man's Range (1935)
No Man's Land
  Hell on Earth (1934, Ger.)
No Place Like Homicide
  What a Carve Up (1962, Brit.)
Nobody Loves a Drunken Indian
  Flap (1970)
Nobody Loves a Flapping Eagle
  Flap (1970)
Nocturna, Granddaughter of Dracula
  (1979)
Noon Sunday
  Attack at Noon, Sunday (1971)* (1979)
North West Frontier
  Flame Over India (1960, Brit.)
Northville Cemetery Massacre, The
  Northville Cemetery Massacre, The (1976)

Nosferatu, the Vampyre
  Nosferatu, the Vampire (1979, Fr./Ger.)
Not Against the Flesh
  Vampyr (1932, Fr./Ger.)
Not Exactly Gentlemen
  Three Rogues (1931)
Not on Your Life
  Island of Love (1963)
Not Reconciled
  Not Reconciled or "Only Violence Helps Where It
  Rules" (1968, Ger.)
Notebooks of Major Thompson
  French They Are a Funny Race, The (1956, Fr.)
Nothing in Order
  All Screwed Up (1976, Ital.)
November Children
  Nightmare County (1977)*
Now
  Embracers, The (1966)
Now About All These Women
  All These Women (1964, Swed.)
Now Barabbas
  Now Barabbas Was a Robber (1949, Brit.)
Nudes on Credit
  Love Now...Pay Later (1966, Ital.)
Nudes on the Rocks
  50,000 B.C. (Before Clothing) (1963)
Nudist Story, The
  For Members Only (1960)*
Nuits Blanches
  White Nights (1961, Ital./Fr.)
Nun of Monza, The
  Lady of Monza, The (1970, Ital.)

O'Flynn, The
  Fighting O'Flynn, The (1949)
O'Leary Night
  Tonight's the Night (1954, Brit.)
Octoman
  Octaman (1971)
Of Beds and Broads
  Tales of Paris (1962, Fr./Ital.)
Oh Brotherhood
  Fraternity Row (1977)
Oh, Charlie
  Hold That Ghost (1941)
Oh Doctor
  Hit the Ice (1943)
Oh My Darling Clementine
  O, My Darling Clementine (1943)
Oh, Susanna
  Oh! Susanna (1951)
Oh What a Duchess!
  My Old Duchess (1933, Brit.)
Oh! Those Most Secret Agents
  00-2 Most Secret Agents (1965, Ital.)
Oil Girls, The
  Legend of Frenchie King, The (1971, Fr./Ital./
  Span./Brit.)
Oil Town
  Lucy Gallant (1955)
Old Curiosity Shop, the
  Mr. Quilp (1975, Brit.)
Old Grouchy, The
  Grouch, The (1961, Gr.)
Old Man and the Boy
  Two of Us, The (1968, Fr.)
Old Man's Place, The
  Glory Boy (1971)
Old Mother Riley Catches a Quisling
  Old Mother Riley in Paris (1938, Brit.)
Old Mother Riley Meets the Vampire
  My Son the Vampire (1963, Brit.)
Olsen's Night Out
  Olsen's Big Moment (1934)
Olympians
  Ebony, Ivory & Jade (1977)*
Olympic Honeymoon
  Honeymoon Merry-Go-Round (1939, Brit.)
Omar Mukhtar
  Lion of the Desert (1981, Libya/Brit.)
Omoo-Omoo
  Omoo Omoo, the Shark God (1969)
On Friday at Eleven
  World in My Pocket, The (1962, Fr./Ital./Ger.)
On My Way to the Crusades I Met a Girl Who...
  Chastity Belt, The (1968, Ital.)
On Nay Street
  La Notte Brava (1962, Fr./Ital.)
On Our Little Place
  On Our Selection (1930, Aus.)
On the Road Again
  Honeysuckle Rose (1980)
Once a Thief
  Happy Thieves, The (1962)
Once Upon a Time
  More Than a Miracle (1967, Ital./Fr.)

Once Upon a Tribe
  Camper John (1973)*
One Fatal Hour
  Five Star Final (1931)
One Horse Town
  Small Town Girl (1936)
100,000 Dollars for Lassiter
  Dollars for a Fast Gun (1969, Ital./Span.)
One Life
  End of Desire (1962, Fr./Ital.)
1,000 Years from Now
  Captive Women (1952)
One Way Out
  Convicted (1950)
One Way Wahine
  One Way Wahini (1965)
Only Eight Hours
  Society Doctor (1935)
Only Girl, The
  Heart Song (1933, Brit.)
Only The Best
  I Can Get It For You Wholesale (1951)
Only the French Can
  French Cancan (1956, Fr.)
Operation Cicero
  Five Fingers (1952)
Operation M
  Hell's Bloody Devils (1970)
Operation Masquerade
  Masquerade (1965, Brit.)
Operation Mermaid
  Bay of Saint Michel, The (1963, Brit.)
Operation War Head
  Opeation Snafu (1965, Brit.)
Optimist, The
  Hallelujah, I'm a Bum (1933)
Orca—Killer Whale
  Orca (1977)
Order of Death
  Corrupt (1984, Ital.)
Orgy of the Golden Nudes
  Honeymoon of Horror (1964)
Oriental Dream
  Kismet (1944)
Original Old Mother Riley, The
  Old Mother Riley (1937, Brit.)
OSS 117: Double Agent
  No Roses for OSS 117 (1968, Fr.)
Othello in Harlem
  Paradise in Harlem (1939)*
Other People's Business
  Way Back Home (1932)
Other Side of Paradise, The
  Foxtrot (1977, Mex./Switz.)
Our Heritage
  This England (1941, Brit.)
Our Hitler
  Our Hitler, a Film from Germany (1980, Ger.)
Our Man in Marrakesh
  That Man George (1967, Fr./Ital./Span.)
Our Virgin Island
  Virgin Island (1960, Brit.)
Out of Control
  Bad Georgia Road (1977)*
Out of the Darkness
  Teenage Caveman (1958)
Out of the Darkness
  Night Creature (1979)
Out of the Night
  Strange Illusion (1945)
Out on Probation
  Daddy-O (1959)
Outcry, The
  Il Girdo (1962, US/Ital.)
Outer Touch
  Spaced Out (1981, Brit.)
Outlaw Territory
  Hannah Lee (1953)
Outsiders, The
  Band of Outsiders (1966, Fr.)
Overland Stage Coach
  Overland Stagecoach (1942)
Oz
  20th Century Oz (1977, Aus.)

Pacific Blackout
  Midnight Angel (1941)
Padre on Horseback
  Kino, Padre on Horseback (1977)*
Pagan Hellcat
  Maeva (1961)
Palace of Shame
  Palace of Nudes (1961, Fr./Ital.)
Panic
  Panique (1947, Fr.)
Panic on the Trans-Siberian Express
  Horror Express (1972, Span./Brit.)

Paradise Lagoon
  Admirable Crichton, The (1957, Brit.)
Parasite Murders, The
  They Came from Within (1976, Can.)
Pardon My Trunk
  Hello, Elephant (1954, Ital.)
Paris Follies of 1956
  Fresh from Paris (1955)
Paris Is Ours
  Paris Belongs to Us (1962, Fr.)
Part Time Wife
  Woman for All Men, A (1975)*
Part-Time Virgins
  Interplay (1970)*
Parts: The Clonus Horror
  Clonus Horror, The (1979)
Pasqualino; Seven Beauties
  Seven Beauties (1976, Ital.)
Passages from "Finnegans Wake"
  Finnegans Wake (1965)
Passages from James Joyce's "Finnegans Wake"
  Finnegans Wake (1965)
Passion of the Sun
  Passion in the Sun (1964)
Passion Pit, The
  Scream of the Butterfly (1965)
Passion Pit, The
  Ice House, The (1969)
Passion Potion
  She'll Follow You Anywhere (1971)*
Passion Street
  Passion Street, U.S.A. (1964)
Passion Streets
  Passion Street, U.S.A. (1964)
Passionate Stranger, The
  Novel Affair, A (1957, Brit.)
Passionate Sunday
  Dark Odyssey (1961)
Passport to Adventure
  Passport to Destiny (1944)
Passport to Hell
  Passport to Alcatraz (1940)
Patate
  Friend of the Family (1965, Fr./Ital.)
Paul, Lisa, & Caroline
  Closet Casanova, The (1979)*
Pay-Off, The
  T-Bird Gang (1959)
Peace Game, The
  Gladiators, The (1970, Swed.)
Peace to Him
  Peace to Him Who Enters (1963, USSR)
Peccatori in Blue Jeans
  Cheaters, The (1961, Fr.)
Peddler
  Narcotic, The (1937)*
Peking Medallion, The
  Corrupt Ones, The (1967, Ger.)
Penn of Pennsylvania
  Courageous Mr. Penn, The (1941, Brit.)
People Toys
  Devil Times Five (1974)
Peopletoys
  Devil Times Five (1974)
Percy's Progress
  It's Not the Size that Counts (1979, Brit.)
Petroleum Girls, The
  Legend of Frenchie King, The (1971, Fr./Ital./Span./Brit.)
Phantom Fiend
  Return of Dr. Mabuse, The (1961, Ger./Fr./Ital.)
Phantom of Paris
  Mystery of Marie Roget, The (1942)
Phantom of Terror, The
  Bird with the Crystal Plummage, The (1970, Ital./Ger.)
Philly
  Private Lessons (1981)
Phobia
  Nesting, The (1981)
Phoenix 2772
  Space Firebird 2772 (1979, Jap.)
Phoenix City Story, The
  Phenix City Story, The (1955)
Phoenix, The
  War of the Wizards (1983, Taiwan)
Pickup in Rome
  From a Roman Balcony (1961, Fr./Ital.)
Pigeon
  Place Without Parents, A (1974)*
Pigeons
  Sidelong Glances of a Pigeon Kicker, The (1970)
Pigs, The
  Daddy's Deadly Darling (1984)**
Pilgrim
  Camper John (1973)*
Pill, The
  Girl, the Body, and the Pill, The (1967)
Pilot X
  Death in the Sky (1937)

Pinball Pick-Up
  Pick-Up Summer (1981)
Pinball Summer
  Pick-Up Summer (1981)
Pinocchio
  Adventures of Pinocchio, The (1978)*
Pinocchio's Adventure in Outer Space
  Pinocchio in Outer Space (1965, US/Bel.)
Pioneer Builders
  Conquerors, The (1932)
Piranha II: Flying Killers
  Piranha II: The Spawning (1981, Neth.)
Pirate Ship
  Mutineers, The (1949)
Pirate's Fiancee
  Very Curious Girl, A (1970, Fr.)
Plague—M3: The Gemini Strain
  Plague (1978, Can.)
Plainsman, The
  Raiders, The (1964)
Planet of Blood
  Planet of the Vampires (1965, US/Ital./Span.)
Planet of Blood
  Queen of Blood (1966)
Planet of Horrors
  Galaxy of Terror (1981)
Planet of Storms
  Storm Planet (1962, USSR)
Planet of the Lifeless Men
  Battle of the Worlds (1965, Ital.)
Planet on the Prowl
  War Between the Planets (1971, Ital.)
Plants are Watching, The
  Kirlian Witness, the (1978)
Playgirl After Dark
  Too Hot to Handle (1961, Brit.)
Playgirl and the War Minister, The
  Amorous Mr. Prawn, The (1965, Brit.)
Playgirl Gang
  Switchblade Sisters (1975)
Playgirl Killer
  Decoy for Terror (1970, Can.)
Pleasure Girl
  Girl with a Suitcase (1961, Fr./Ital.)
Pleasure Lover
  Pleasure Lovers, The (1964, Brit.)
Plot to Kill Roosevelt, The
  Conspiracy in Teheran (1948, Brit.)
Poe's Tales of Terror
  Tales of Terror (1962)
Police Connection
  Mad Bomber, The (1970)
Police Court
  Fame Street (1932)
Poncomania
  Pocomania (1939)
Poor Albert and Little Annie
  I Dismember Mama (1974)
Poor Outlaws, The
  Round Up, The (1969, Hung.)
Poor White Trash II
  Scum of the Earth (1976)
Pop Goes the Weasel
  Lady Cocoa (1975)*
Power to Spare
  Black Godfather, The (1974)*
Port of Shame
  Lover's Net (1957, Fr.)
Positions of Love
  Put Up or Shut Up (1968, Arg.)
Prague Nights
  Nights of Prague, The (1968, Czech.)
Prairie Outlaws
  Wild West (1946)
Prehistoric Sound, The
  Sound of Horror (1966, Span.)
Prehistoric World
  Teenage Caveman (1958)
Preppies
  Making the Grade (1984)**
Prescription for Murder
  RX Murder (1958, Brit.)
Prescription Murder
  RX Murder (1958, Brit.)
Price of Freedom
  Operation Daybreak (1976, US/Brit./Czech.)
Prime Time
  American Raspberry (1980)*
Princess, The
  Time in the Sun, A (1970, Swed.)
Prison
  Devil's Wanton, The (1962, Swed.)
Prisoner in the Middle
  Warhead (1974)*
Private Life of Paul Joseph Goebbels
  Enemy of Women (1944)
Private Snuffy Smith
  Snuffy Smith, Yard Bird (1942)
Prized as a Mate!
  Spoiled Rotten (1968, Ger.)

Profession: Reporter
  Passenger, The (1975, Ital.)
Profile of Terror, The
  Sadist, The (1963)
Promise Her Anything
  Promises, Promises (1963)
Prostitutes in Prison
  99 Women (1969)*
Proud, the Damned and the Dead, The
  Proud and the Damned, The (1972)
Psycho Killers
  Mania (1961, Brit.)
Psychomania
  Violent Midnight (1963)
PT Raiders
  Ship that Died of Shame, The (1956, Brit.)
P'Tang, Yang, Kipperbang
  Kipperbang (1984)**
Public Be Damned
  World Gone Mad, The (1933)
Purlie Victorious
  Gone Are the Days (1963)
Pushover, The
  Myth, The (1965, Ital.)
Put Out or Shut Up
  Put Up or Shut Up (1968, Arg.)
Pyro—Man without a Face
  Pyro (1964, U.S./Span.)
Pyro—The Thing without a Face
  Pyro (1964, U.S./Span.)

Quartermass Experiment, The
  Creeping Unknown, The (1956, Brit.)
Queen of Atlantis
  Siren of Atlantis (1948)
Queen of Broadway
  Kid Dynamite (1943)
Queen of Clubs
  Love Cycles (1969, Gr.)
Queen of Destiny
  Sixty Glorious Years (1938, Brit)
Queen of the Cannibals
  Dr. Butcher, M.D. (1982, Ital.)
Queen of the Gorillas
  Bride and the Beast, The (1958)
Queen of the West
  Cattle Queen (1951)
Queimada!
  Burn! (1970)
Quitter, The
  Quitters, The (1934)

R.P.M. Revolutions per Minute
  R.P.M. (1970)
Race, The
  All the Young Wives (1975)*
Race Gang
  Green Cockatoo, The (1947, Brit.)
Rachel Cade
  Sins of Rachel Cade(1960)
Radishes and Carrots
  Twilight Path (1965, Jap.)
Radon
  Rodan (1958, Jap.)
Radon the Flying Monster
  Rodan (1958, Jap.)
Rafferty and the Highway Hustlers
  Rafferty and the Gold Dust Twins (1975)
Rage
  Rabid (1976, Can.)
Rage Within, The
  Rage, The (1963, U.S./Ital.)
Rainbow Gang, The
  Rainbow Boys, The (1973, Can.)
Ramrodders
  Ramrodder, The (1969)
Ransom
  Maniac! (1977)
Rape of Malaya
  Town Like Alice (1959, Brit.)
Rape of the Sabine Women, The
  Shame of the Sabine Women, The (1962, Mex.)
Rape, The
  Le Viol (1968, Fr./Swed.)
Rare Book Murder, The
  Fast Company (1938)
Rasputin
  Rasputin the Mad Monk (1932)
Rats, The
  Deadly Eyes (1974)
Ravishing Idiots, The
  Ravishing Idiot, A (1966, Ital./Fr.)
Raw Meat
  Deathline (1973, Brit.)
Real Gone Girls, The
  Man from O.R.G.Y., The (1970)
Real Thing, The
  Teenager (1975)*

Rebel
  No Place to Hide (1975)
Rebel
  Lions of St. Petersburg (1971)*
Rebel in the Ring
  Swingin' Affair, A (1963)
Rebel with a Cause
  Loneliness of the Long Distance Runner, The
  (1962, Brit.)
Record of a Living Being
  I Live in Fear (1967, Jap.)
Red Hangman, The
  Bloody Pit of Horror, the (1965, Ital.)
Red Head, The
  Poil de Carotte (1932, Fr.)
Red Mantle, The
  Hagbard and Signe (1968, Den./Iceland/Swed.)
Red on Red
  Scarred (1984)** Red Tide, The
  Blood Tide (1982)
Red, White and Busted
  Outside In (1972)
Redeemer, The
  Rat Saviour, The (1977, Yugo.)
Redneck County
  Poor Pretty Eddie (1975)*
Refugee, The
  Three Faces West (1940)
Regain
  Harvest (1939, Fr.)
Rehearsal for a Crime
  Criminal Life of Archibaldo de la Cruz, The (1962,
  Mex.)
Reign of Terror
  Black Book, The (1949, Brit.)
Religious Racketeers
  Mystic Circle Murder (1939)
Remember When
  Riding High (1937, Brit.)
Renfrew of the Royal Mounted on the Great White
Trail
  On the Great White Trail (1938)
Renfrew on the Great White Trail
  On the Great White Trail (1938)
Rented
  Rent-A-Girl (1965)
Replica of a Crime
  Maniac Mansion (1978, Ital.)
Repo
  Zero to Sixty (1978)
Reprieve
  Convicts Four (1962)
Resurrection Syndicate, The
  Nothing but the Night (1975, Brit.)
Restless
  Beloved, The (1972)
Retrievers, The
  Hot and Deadly (1984)**
Return from the Past
  Dr. Terror's Gallery of Horrors (1967)
Return of Godzilla, The
  Gigantis (1959, Jap./US)
Return of Maxwell Smart, The
  Nude Bomb, The (1980)
Return of Mr. H., The
  They Saved Hitler's Brain (1964)
Return of Old Mother Riley, The
  Old Mother Riley (1937, Brit.)
Return of the Aliens: The Deadly Spawn
  Deadly Spawn, The (1983)
Return of the Bad Men
  Return of the Badmen (1948)
Return of the Boomerang
  Adam's Woman (1972, Aus.)
Return of the Giant Monsters, The
  Gamera Versus Gaos (1967, Jap.)
Return of the Horrors of Blood Island
  Beast of Blood (1970, U.S./Phil.)
Return of the Living Dead
  Dead People (1974)
Return to Jackson County Jail
  Outside Chance (1978)*
Revenge
  Blood Feud (1979, Ital.)
Revenge of General Ling
  Wife of General Ling, The (1938, Brit.)
Revenge of J.D. Walker, The
  J.D.'s Revenger (1976)
Revenge of King Kong, The
  King Kong Escapes (1968, Jap.)
Revenge of Milady, The
  Four Musketeers, The (1975)
Revenge of the Dead
  Night of the Ghouls (1959)
Revenge of the Living Dead
  Murder Clinic, The (1967, Ital./Fr.)
Revenge of the Screaming Dead
  Dead People (1974)
Revenge of Yuki-No-Jo, The
  Actor's Revenge, An (1963, Jap.)

Revolver, The
  Blood in the Streets (1975, Ital./Fr.)
Rhythm Romance
  Some Like it Hot (1939)
Ribald Tales of Robin Hood, The
  Affairs of Robin Hood, The (1981)*
Rich Bride, The
  Country Bride (1938, USSR)
Rich, Young and Deadly
  Platinum High School (1960)
Richard Tauber Story, The
  You Are the World for Me (1964, Aust.)
Riders in the Sky
  Riders of the Sky (1949)
Riders of Vengeance
  Raiders, The (1952)
Riding Tall
  Squares (1972)
Rififi for Girls
  Riff Raff Girls (1962, Fr./Ital.)
Rififi in Paris
  Upper Hand, The (1967, Fr./Ital./Ger.)
Right Man, The
  Her First Romance (1940)
Riot at Lauderdale
  Hell's Playground (1967)
Rituals
  Creeper, The (1980, Can.)
River 70
  Rio 70 (1970, US/Ger./Span)
River of Dollars, A
  Hills Run Red, The (1967, Ital.)
River of Missing Men, The
  Trapped by G-Men (1937)
Road, The
  La Strada (1956, Ital.)
Road Builder, The
  Night Digger, The (1971, Brit.)
Road Gangs
  Spacehunter: Adventures in the Forbidden Zone
  (1983)
Road Show
  Chasing Rainbows (1930)
Roadhouse Girl
  Marilyn (1953, Brit.)
Roaring Timbers
  Come and Get It (1936)
Rob Roy
  Rob Roy, The Highland Rogue (1954, Brit.)
Robinson Crusoe
  Robinson Crusoe and the Tiger (1972)*
Rocket Ship
  Flash Gordon (1936)
Rocket to the Moon
  Cat Women of the Moon (1953)
Rockets Galore
  Mad Little Island (1958, Brit.)
Rollicking Adventures of Eliza Fraser, The
  Eliza Fraser (1976)
Romance on the Beach
  Sin on the Beach (1964, Fr.)
Rome Like Chicago
  Bandits in Rome (1967)*
Romeo, Juliet and Darkness
  Sweet Light in a Dark Room (1966, Czech.)
Roof Garden, The
  Terrace, The (1964, Arg.)
Rook, The
  Something For Everyone (1970)
Roommates
  March of the Spring Hare (1969)
Rope
  Rope of Flesh (1965)
Rose of the Rio Grande
  God's Country and the Man (1931)
Rosemary's Killer
  Prowler, The (1981)
Rosie the Riveter
  Room for Two (1944)
Roundtrip
  Round Trip (1967)
Royal Game, The
  Three Moves to Freedom (1960, Ger.)
Royal Track, The
  Obsession (1968, Swed.)
Ruby Virgin, The
  Hell's Island (1955)
Rudyard Kipling's Jungle Book
  Jungle Book (1942)
Ruler of the World
  Master of the World (1935, Ger.)
Run Like a Thief
  Make Like a Thief (1966, Fin.)
Run on Gold, A
  Midas Run (1969)
Run, Stranger, Run
  Happy Mother's Day...Love, George (1973)
Runaway Daughter
  Red Salute (1935)

Runaway Daughters
   Prowl Girls (1968)
Rustler's Hideout
   Rustler's Roundup (1946)

S.W.A.L.K.
   Melody (1971, Brit.)
Sabaka
   Hindu, The (1953, Brit.)
Saboteur: Code Name Morituri, The
   Morituri (1965)
Sabre and the Arrow, The
   Last of the Comanches (1952)
Saga of Anatahan
   Anatahan (1953, Jap.)
Saga of Singoalla, The
   Gypsy Fury (1950, Fr,)
Saga of the Flying Hostesses, The
   Girl Game (1968, Braz./Fr./Ital.)
Saga of the Road, The
   Pather Panchali (1958, India)
Salute to Courage
   Nazi Agent (1942)
Sam Cooper's Gold
   Ruthless Four, The (1969, Ital./Ger.)
Sam Marlow, Private Eye
   Man with Bogart's Face, The (1980)
Sammy Going South
   Boy Ten Feet Tall, A (1965)
Samurai Banners
   Under the Banner of Samurai (1969, Jap.)
Samurai Pirate
   Lost World of Sinbad, The (1965, Jap.)
Sandokan, the Tiger of Mompracem
   Sandokan the Great (1964, Fr./Ital./Span.)
Sandpit Generals, The
   Wild Pack, The (1972)
Sands of Beersheba
   Rebels Against the Light (1964)
Santa Fe Satan
   Catch My Soul (1974)
Sardonicus
   Mr. Sardonicus (1961)
Sasquatch, the Legend of Bigfoot
   Sasquatch (1978)
Satan's Axe
   Night to Dismember, A (1983)*
Satan's Claw
   Blood on Satan's Claw, The (1970, Brit.)
Satan's Spectrum
   Asylum of Satan (1972)*
Satanic Rites of Dracula
   Count Dracula and His Vampire Bride (1978,
   Brit.)
Satellite of Blood
   First Man Into Space (1959, Brit.)
Satyricon
   Fellini Satyricon (1969, Fr./Ital.)
Savage American, The
   Talisman, The (1966)
Savage Apocalypse
   Cannibals in the Streets (1982, Ital./Span.)
Savage Wilderness
   Last Frontier, The (1955)
Scandal '64
   Christine Keeler Affair, The (1964, Brit.)
Scar, The
   Hollow Triumph (1948)
Scaremaker, The
   Girls Night Out (1984)**
Scarface
   Scarface, a Shame of a Nation (1932)
Scarlet Blade, The
   Crimson Blade, The (1964, Brit.)
School of Love
   School for Sex (1966, Jap.)
Scipio, the African
   Defeat of Hannibal, The (1937, Ital.)
Sciusia
   Shoeshine (1947, Ital.)
Scream
   Night God Screamed, The (1975)
Scream and Die
   House that Vanished, The (1974, Brit.)
Scream Free
   Free Grass (1969)
Screaming Angels
   Angels' Wild Women (1972)*
Screaming Head, The
   Head, The (1961, Ger.)
Sea Wall, The
   This Angry Age (1958, Ital./Fr.)
Seagulls Over Sorrento
   Crest of the Wave (1954, Brit.)
Search For The Mother Lode
   Mother Lode (1982)

Season of the Witch
   Hungry Wives (1973)
Seaweed Children, The
   Malachi's Cove (1973, Brit.)
Second Coming, The
   Dead People (1974)
Second House from the Left
   New House on the Left, The (1978, Brit.)
Secret File of Hollywood
   Secret File: Hollywood (1962)
Secret Flight
   School for Secrets (1946, Brit.)
Secret Honor: A Political Myth
   Secret Honor(1984)**
Secret Honor: The Last Testament of Richard M.
Nixon
   Secret Honor (1984)**
Secret of Dorian Gray, The
   Dorian Gray (1970, Ital./Brit./Ger./Liechten-
   stein)
Secret of Dr. Alucard, The
   Taste of Blood, A (1967)
Secret of Outer Space Island
   Secret of Magic Island, The (1964, Fr./Ital.)
Secret Passion, The
   Freud (1962)
Secret Service, The
   Charlie Chan in the Secret Service (1937)
Secrets of a Door-To-Door Salesman
   Naughty Wives (1974)*
Secrets of a Soul
   Confessions of an Opium Eater (1962)
Secrets of Sex
   Bizarre (1969)*
Secrets of Sin
   False Rapture (1941)
Secrets of Su Maru
   Rio 70 (1970, US/Ger./Span)
Secrets of the City
   City of Secrets (1963, Ger.)
Secrets of the Mary Celeste
   Phantom Ship, The (1937, Brit.)
Seductress, The
   Teacher, The (1974)
Seed of Terror
   Grave of the Vampire (1972)
Sensations
   Sensations of 1945 (1944)
Sensuous Vampires
   Vampire Hookers (1979, Phil.)
Separate Beds
   Wheeler Dealers, The (1963)
Sergeant Deadhead the Astronut
   Sergeant Deadhead (1965)
Sergeant Steiner
   Breakthrough (1978, Ger.)
Session with the Committee
   Committee, The (1968, Brit.)
Settlers, The
   New Land, The (1971, Swed.)
Seven Bad Men
   Rage at Dawn (1955)
Seven Brothers Meet Dracula
   Dracula and the Seven Golden Vampires (1978,
   Brit./Chin.)
Seven Cities to Atlantis
   Warlords of Atlantis (1978, Brit.)
Seven Different Ways
   Quick, Let's Get Married (1965)
Seven Graves for Rogan
   Time to Die, A (1983)
Seven Sisters
   House on Sorority Row, The (1983)
Seventeen
   Eric Soya's "17" (1967, Den.)
Sex and the Teenager
   To Find a Man (1972)
Sex & Violence
   Andrea (1979)*
Sex at Night
   Love at Night (1961, Fr.)
Sex is a Woman
   Love Is a Woman (1967, Brit.)
Sex Racketeers, The
   Man of Violence (1970, Brit.)
Sex Through a Window
   Extreme Close-Up (1973)*
Sexorcists, The
   Tormented, The (1978, Ital.)
Sexy Gang
   Michelle (1970, Fr.)
Shabby Tiger, The
   Masquerade (1965, Brit.)
Shadow and the Missing Lady, The
   Missing Lady, The (1946)
Shadow Behind the Mask, The
   Behind the Mask (1946)
Shadow Mountain
   Wishbone Cutter (1978)

Shadow of a Killer
   Death Rage (1978)*
Shadow of Blackmail
   Wife Wanted (1946)
Shadow of Chikara
   Wishbone Cutter (1978)
Shadow Versus the Thousand Eyes of Dr. Mabuse,
The
   Thousand Eyes of Dr. Mabuse, The (1960, Fr./
   Ital./Ger.)
Shadow Warrior, The
   Kagemusha (1980, Jap.)
Shadows in An Empty Room
   Strange Shadows in An Empty Room (1977,
   Can./Ital.)
Shadows of Our Ancestors
   Shadows of Forgotten Ancestors (1967, USSR)
Shadows of Our Forgotten Ancestors
   Shadows of Forgotten Ancestors (1967, USSR)
Shame
   Intruder, The (1962)
Shame of Mary Boyle, The
   Juno and the Paycock (1930, Brit.)
Shatter
   Call Him Mr. Shatter (1976, Hong Kong)
Shattered
   Something to Hide (1972, Brit.)
Shatterhand
   Old Shatterhand (1968, Ger./Yugo./Fr./Ital.)
She Devil
   Drums O' Voodoo (1934)
She Monster of the Night
   Frankenstein's Daughter (1958)
She Should'a Said No
   Wild Weed (1949)
She Was a Hippy Vampire
   Wild World of Batwoman, The (1966)
She Wolves, The
   Demoniaque (1958, Fr.)
Sheba
   Persecution (1974, Brit.)
Shenanigans
   Great Bank Hoax, The (1977)
Sherlock Holmes and the Scarlet Claw
   Scarlet Claw, The (1944)
Sherlock Holmes and the Pearl of Death
   Pearl of Death, The (1944)
Sherlock Holmes in the Woman in Green
   Woman in Green, The (1945)
Sherlock Holmes in Terror by Night
   Terror by Night (1946)
Sherlock Holmes in Pursuit to Algiers
   Pursuit to Algiers (1945)
Sherlock Holmes in the Hound of the Baskervilles
   Hound of the Baskervilles, The (1939)
Sherlock Holmes in House of Fear
   House of Fear (1945)
Sherlock Holmes in Dressed to Kill
   Dressed to Kill (1946)
Shining Star
   That's the Way of the World (1975)
Ship Was Loaded, The
   Carry On Admiral (1957, Brit.)
Shivers
   They Came from Within (1976, Can.)
Shock
   Beyond the Door II (1979, Ital.)
Shogun Island
   Raw Force (1982)
Shootin' Irons
   West of Texas (1943)
Shop on High Street, The
   Shop on Main Street, The (1966, Czech)
Shovel Up a Bit More Coal
   Stoker, The (1935, Brit.)
Showtime
   Paris Follies of 1956 (1955)
Sidehackers, The
   Five the Hard Way (1969)
Sidney Sheldon's Bloodline
   Bloodline (1979)
Siege of Hell Street, The
   Siege of Sidney Street, The (1960, Brit)
Silent Death
   Voodoo Island (1957)
Silent Flute, The
   Circle of Iron (1979, Brit.)
Silent Sentence
   Knife for the Ladies, A (1974)*
Silken Trap, The
   Money Jungle, The (1968)
Silver City
   Albuquerque (1948)
Silver Devil
   Wild Horse (1931)
Silver Lining, The
   Silver Lining (1932)
Sin Now...Pay Later
   Love Now...Pay Later (1966, Ital.)

Sin of Harold Diddlebock, The
  Mad Wednesday (1950)
Sin, The
  White Sister (1973, Ital./Fr./Span.)
Sin, The
  Good Luck, Miss Wyckoff (1979)
Singer from Seville, The
  Call of the Flesh (1930)
Singing Hills, The
  Singing Hill, The (1941)
Singoalla
  Gypsy Fury (1950, Fr.)
Sinner's Holiday
  Christmas Eve (1947)
Sinners Go to Hell
  No Exit (1962, US/Arg.)
Sinners, The
  Five Sinners (1961, Ger.)
Sins of Lola Montes, The
  Lola Montes (1955, Fr./Ger.)
Sins of Mona Kent, The
  Sin of Mona Kent, The (1961)
Sir Gawain and the Green Knight
  Gawain and the Green Knight (1973, Brit.)
Six Thousand Dollar Nigger
  Super Soul Brother (1978)*
Sixteen
  Like a Crow on a June Bug (1972)
Sixth of June, The
  D-Day, the Sixth of June (1956)
Skies Above Heaven
  Sky Above Heaven (1964, Fr./Ital.)
Skin Games
  Skin Game, The (1965, Brit.)
Skipper
  Todd Killings, The (1970)
Sky Beyond Heaven
  Sky Above Heaven (1964, Fr./Ital.)
Sky Is Yours, The
  Le Ciel Est a Vous (1957, Fr.)
Sky Terror
  Skyjacked (1941)
Skycopter Summer
  Great Skycopter Rescue, The (1982)*
Slammer
  Short Eyes (1977)
Slaughter of the Vampires, The
  Curse of the Blood Ghouls (1969, Ital.)
Slaughterers, The
  Cannibals in the Streets (1982, Ital./Span.)
Slave, The
  Fable, A (1971)
Slipper and the Rose, The
  Story of Cinderella, The (1976, Brit.)
Slow Motion
  Every Man for Himself (1980, Fr.)
Smashing the Crime Syndicate
  Hell's Bloody Devils (1970)
Smash-Up Alley
  Petty Story, The (1974)*
Smell of Honey, The!
  Smell of Honey, a Swallow of Brine! A (1966)
Smoke Jumpers
  Red Skies of Montana (1952)
Smoking Saddles
  Blazing Stewardesses (1975)*
Smultronstallet
  Wild Strawberries (1959, Swed.)
Snapshot
  Day After Halloween, The (1961, Aus.)
Snow Demons
  Snow Devils, The (1965, Ital.)
Snow Tigers, The
  When the North Wind Blows (1974)*
Snowman
  Land of No Return, The (1981)
So Bright the Flame
  Girl in White, The (1952)
So Evil, My Sister
  Psycho Sisters (1972)*
So This Was Paris
  This Was Paris (1942, Brit.)
Social Enemy No. 1
  No Greater Sin (1941)
Soft Body of Deborah, The
  Sweet Body of Deborah, The (1969, Fr./Ital.)
Soft Touch
  Manhandlers, The (1975)*
Soft Warm Experience, A
  Satin Mushroom, The (1969)
Soldier in Love
  Fanfan the Tulip (1952, Fr.)
Soldier's Father, A
  Father of a Soldier (1966, USSR)
Soldiers in Skirts
  Triple Echo, The (1973, Brit.)
Soldiers of Pancho Villa, The
  La Cucaracha (1961, Mex.)
Soldiers, The
  Les Carabiniers (1968, Fr.)

Somebody Else's Children
  Stepchildren (1962, USSR)
Something Is Out There
  Day of the Animals (1977)
Something Like the Truth
  Offense, The (1973, Brit.)
Something Waits in the Dark
  Screamers (1979, Ital.)
Son of Spartacus
  Slave, The (1963, Ital.)
Song of the Road, The
  Pather Panchali (1958, India)
Song Parade
  Hit Parade of 1951 (1950)*
Sons of Matthew
  Rugged O'Riordans, The (1949, Aus.)
Sons of the Legion
  Sons of The Desert (1933)
Sophie Lang
  Notorious Sophie Lang, The (1934)
Sorry You've Been Troubled
  Life Goes On (1932, Brit.)
Soul Hustler
  Day the Lord Got Busted, The (1976)*
Soul Soldier
  Red, White and Black, The (1970)
Soul Soldiers
  Red, White and Black, The (1970)
Souls for Sale
  Confessions of an Opium Eater (1962)
Souls of Sin
  Male and Female Since Adam and Eve (1961, Arg.)
Sound from a Million Years Ago
  Sound of Horror (1966, Span.)
Sound of Fury, The
  Try and Get Me, (1950)
Soup Du Jour
  Sex Du Jour (1976)*
Soup to Nuts
  Waitress (1982)
South Seas Fury
  Hell's Island (1955)
Southerner, The
  Prodigal, The (1931)
Space Cruiser Yamato
  Space Cruiser (1977, Jap)
Space Devils
  Snow Devils, The (1965, Ital.)
Space Invasion from Lapland
  Invasion of the Animal People (1962, US/Swed.)
Space Invasion of Lapland
  Invasion of the Animal People (1962, US/Swed.)
Space Men
  Assignment Outer Space (1960, Ital.)
Space Men Appear in Tokyo
  Mysterious Satellite, The (1956, Jap.)
Space Mission of the Lost Planet
  Horror of the Blood Monsters (1970, US/Phil.)
Space Monster Dagora
  Dagora the Space Monster (1964, Jap.)
Space Soldiers
  Flash Gordon (1936)
Space Station X
  Mutiny in Outer Space (1965)
Space Station X-14
  Mutiny in Outer Space (1965)
Spacemen Saturday Night
  Invasion of the Saucer Men (1957)
Spaceship
  Creature Wasn't Nice, The (1981)
Spaceship to the Unknown
  Flash Gordon (1936)
Spawn of the Slithis
  Slithis (1978)
Special Touch, The
  Specialist, The (1975)
Specter of Freedom, The
  Phantom of Liberty, The (1974, Fr.)
Speed Limit: 65
  Limit, The (1972)
Spider Baby or the Strangest Story Ever Told
  Spider Baby (1968)
Spider, The
  Earth vs. the Spider (1958)
Spider Woman
  Sherlock Holmes and the Spider Woman (1944)
Spider's Web, The
  It's Hot in Paradise (1962, Ger./Yugo.)
Spies in the Air
  Spies of the Air (1940, Brit.)
Spies-A-Go-Go
  Nasty Rabbit, The (1964)
Spinal Tap
  This Is Spinal Tap (1984)**
Spinster, The
  Two Loves (1961)
Spirits of the Wild
  Their Only Chance (1978)*

Split, The
  Manster, The (1962, Jap.)
Spooky Movie Show, The
  Mask, the (1961, Can.)
Spot
  Dogpound Shuffle (1975, Can.)
Spread Eagle
  Eagle and the Hawk, The (1950)
Spring Night, Summer Night
  Miss Jessica Is Pregnant (1970)
Spy 77
  Secret Agent (1933, Brit.)
Spy Busters
  Guns in the Heather (1968, Brit.)
Spy in White, The
  Secret of Stamboul, The (1936, Brit.)
Square Shooter, The
  Skipalong Rosenbloom (1951)
Ssssnake
  Ssssssss (1973)
Stacey and Her Gangbusters
  Stacey (1973)
Stage from Blue River
  Stage to Blue River (1951)
Stampede
  Guns of the Timberland (1960)
Star Child
  Space Raiders (1983)
Stardust
  He Loved an Actress (1938, Brit.)
Starlet, The
  Alice Goodbody (1974)*
Starlight Slaughter
  Eaten Alive (1976)
Stars in Your Backyard
  Paradise Alley (1962)
Stateless
  No Exit (1962, US/Arg.)
Steel Highway, The
  Other Men's Women (1931)
Stella Star
  Starcrash (1979)
Still Room in Hell
  There Is Still Room in Hell (1963, Ger.)
Stoolie, The
  Fingerman, The (1963, Fr.)
Stop the World—I Want to Get Off
  Sammy Stops the World (1978)
Storm Over the Pacific, The
  I Bombed Pearl Harbor (1961, Jap.)
Storm Within, The
  Les Parents Terribles (1950, Fr.)
Story of a Love Story
  Impossible Object (1973, Fr.)
Story of a Teenager
  Jim, the World's Greatest (1976)
Story of Dr. Ehrlich's Magic Bullet, The
  Dr. Ehrlich's Magic Bullet (1940)
Story of Kamilla, The
  Kamilla (1984, Norway)**
Story of Lenny Bruce—Dirtymouth, The
  Dirty Mouth (1971)*
Story of Monte Cristo, The
  Story of the Count of Monte Cristo (1962, Fr./Ital.)
Story of Robin Hood and His Merry Men
  Story of Robin Hood, The (1952, Brit.)
Story of the Cruelties of Youth, A
  Naked Youth (1961, Jap.)
Story Without a Name, The
  Without Warning (1952)
Strange Adventure of David Gray, The
  Vampyr (1932, Fr./Ger.)
Strange Behavior
  Dead Kids (1981, Aus./New Zealand)
Strange Case of Clara Deane, The
  Case of Clara Deane, The (1932)
Strange Case of Madeleine
  Madeleine (1949, Brit.)
Strange Case of the Man and the Beast, The
  Man and the Beast, The (1951, Arg.)
Strange Confession
  Imposter, The (1944)
Strange Deception
  Accused, The (1949)
Strange Fetishes of the Go-Go Girls, The
  Strange Fetishes, The (1967)
Strange Journey
  Fantastic Voyage (1966)
Strange Laws
  Cherokee Strip (1937)
Strange Love
  Room of Chains (1972)*
Strange Ones, The
  Les Enfants Terribles (1952, Fr.)
Stranger at Home
  Just Be There (1977)*
Strangers Came, The
  You Can't Fool An Irishman (1950, Ireland)

Street Gang
    Vigilante (1983)
Street Love
    Scarred (1984)**
Street Partner, The
    Secret Partner, The (1961, Brit.)
Streetfighter, The
    Hard Times (1975)
Streets of Missing Women
    Cafe Hostess (1940)
Streets of Sin
    Not Wanted (1949)
Strikers, The
    Organizer, The (1964, Fr./Ital./Yugo.)
Strip Tease
    Sweet Skin (1965, Fr./Ital.)
Sub A-Dub Dub
    Hello Down There (1969)
Submarine Zone
    Escape to Glory (1940)
Submersion of Japan, The
    Tidal Wave (1975, US/Jap.)
Succubus
    Satanist, The (1968)*
Sucker...Or How to Be Glad When You've Been
Had, The
    Sucker, The (1966, Fr./Ital.)
Summer Heat
    Kiss My Grits (1982)*
Summer of '64
    Girls on the Beach (1965)
Summer of the Seventeenth Doll
    Season of Passion (1961, Aus./Brit.)
Summer School
    Mag Wheels (1978)*
Summer Tales
    Love on the Riviera (1964, Fr./Ital.)
Summerplay
    Illicit Interlude (1954, Swed.)
Sun Always Rises, The
    Outcry (1949, Ital.)
Sun Demon, The
    Hideous Sun Demon, The (1959)
Sun Rises Again, The
    Outcry (1949, Ital.)
Sundance and the Kid
    Sundance Cassidy and Butch the Kid (1975)*
Sunset of a Clown
    Naked Night, The (1956, Swed.)
Sunshine Susie
    Office Girl (1932, Brit.)
Super Dragon
    Secret Agent Super Dragon (1966, Fr./Ital./Ger./
    Monaco)
Super Flirts
    Sweater Girls (1978)*
Super Inframan, The
    Infra-Man (1975, Hong Kong)
Superdude
    Hangup (1974)
Supersnooper
    Super Fuzz (1981)
Surf, The
    Ocean Breakers (1949, Swed.)
Surf II—The End of the Trilogy
    Surf II (1984)**
Surftide 777
    Surftide 77 (1962)
Survival
    Guide, The (1965, US/India)
Suspense
    Fear (1946)
Swamp Diamonds
    Swamp Women (1956)
Swap, The
    Sam's Song (1971)
Sweed Dreams
    Okay Bill (1971)
Sweet Body, The
    Sweet Body of Deborah, The (1969, Fr./Ital.)
Sweet Kill
    Arousers, The (1973)
Sweet Stepmother
    Kind Stepmother (1936, Hung.)
Sweet Violence
    Sweet Ecstasy (1962, Fr.)
Swindlers, The
    White Tie And Tails (1946)
Swingin' Teacher
    Just Be There (1977)*
Swinging Fink, The
    Rat Fink (1965)
Swirl of Glory
    Sugarfoot (1951)
Sword and the Balance, The
    Two Are Guilty (1964, Fr.)
Swords of Blood
    Cartouche (1962, Fr./Ital.)
Sylvia and the Ghost
    Sylvie and the Phantom (1950, Fr.)

Sylvie Et Le Fantome
    Sylvie and the Phantom (1950, Fr.)
Sympathy for the Devil
    One Plus One (1969, Brit.)
Symphony of Love
    Ecstasy (1940, Czech.)

Taken by Surprise
    Take Her by Surprise (1967, Can.)
Taking Sides
    Lightning Guns (1950)
Tales from the Crypt II
    Vault of Horror, The (1973, Brit.)
Tales of a Traveling Salesman
    Tales of a Salesman (1965)
Tales of the Bizarre
    Bizarre (1969)*
Tall Lie, The
    For Men Only (1952)
Target in the Sun
    Man Who Would Not Die, The (1975)
Tartu
    Adventures of Tartu (1943, Brit.)
Tarzan and the Green Goddess
    New Adventures of Tarzan, The (1935)
Taste of Honey, a Swallow of Brine, A!
    Smell of Honey, a Swallow of Brine! A (1966)
Taste of Hot Lead, A
    Hot Lead (1951)
Teddy
    Pit, The (1980)*
Teddy Bear, The
    My Fathers's Mistress (1970, Swed.)
Teen Age Tramp
    That Kind of Girl (1963, Brit.)
Teen Lust
    Girls Next Door, The (1979)*
Teen Mothers
    Seed of Innocence (1980)
Teenage Innocence
    Little Miss Innocence (1973)*
Teenage Psycho Meets Bloody Mary
    Incredibly Strange Creatures Who Stopped Liv-
    ing and Became Crazy Mixed-Up Zombies, The
    (1965)
Telegian, The
    Secret of the Telegian, The (1961, Jap.)
Tell Your Children
    Reefer Madness (1936)
Temptress, The
    Temptress and the Monk, The (1963, Jap.)
Tender Grass
    Jennie, Wife-Child (1968)*
Tenderly
    Girl Who Couldn't Say No, The (1969, Ital.)
Tennessee Beat, The
    That Tennessee Beat (1966)
Terminal Station
    Indiscretion of an American Wife (1954, US/Ital.)
Terror at Halfday
    Monster a Go-Go (1965)
Terror at Red Wolf Inn
    Terror House (1972)
Terror By Night
    Secret Witness, The (1931)
Terror Castle
    Horror Castle (1965, Ital.)
Terror Circus
    Barn of the Naked Dead (1976)
Terror Eyes
    Night School (1981)
Terror Factor, The
    Scared to Death (1981)
Terror from 5,000 A.D.
    Terror from the Year 5,000 (1958)
Terror from the Sun
    Hideous Sun Demon, The (1959)
Terror from Within
    Won't Write Home Mom...I'm Dead (1975)*
Terror in the City
    Pie in the Sky (1964)
Terror in the Forest
    Forest, The (1983)
Terror in the Midnight Sun
    Invasion of the Animal People (1962, US/Swed.)
Terror of Dr. Chaney, The
    Mansion of the Doomed (1976)
Terror of Frankenstein
    Victor Frankenstein (1975, Brit.)
Terror of Mechagodzilla
    Monsters from the Unknown Planet (1975, Jap.)
Terror of Sheba
    Persecution (1974, Brit.)
Terror of the Mad Doctor, The
    Terror of Dr. Mabuse, The (1965, Ger.)
Test Pilot Pirx
    Test of Pilot Pirx, The (1978, Pol./USSR)

Testament of Dr. Mabuse, The
    Terror of Dr. Mabuse, The (1965, Ger.)
Texas Desperadoes
    Drift Fence (1936)
Texas Legend
    Kiss My Grits (1982)*
Texas Road Agent
    Road Agent (1941)
That Girl From Beverly Hills
    Corpse of Beverly Hills, The (1965, Ger.)
That Man Flintstone
    Man Called Flintstone, The (1966)
That Man Is Pregnant
    What Do I Tell the Boys at the Station? (1972)*
That They May Live
    J'Accuse (1939, Fr.)
The Journey
    Voyage, The (1974, Ital.)
Thelma Jordan
    File on Thelma Jordan, The (1950)
Theorem
    Teorema (1968, Ital.)
There Is Another Sun
    Wall of Death (1952, Brit.)
Therese Desqueyroux
    Therese (1963, Fr.)
Theseus Against the Minotuar
    Minotaur, The 1961, Ital.)
They All Died Laughing
    Jolly Bad Fellow, A (1964, Brit.)
They Don't Wear Pajamas at Rosie's
    First Time, The (1952)
They Love as They Please
    Greenwich Village Story (1963)
They Loved Life
    Kanal (1961, Pol.)
They Made Me Criminal
    I Became a Criminal (1947)
They Met at Midnight
    Picadilly Incident (1948, Brit.)
They Must Be Told
    Sex Madness (1937)
They Passed this Way
    Four Faces West (1948)
They Should Be Told
    Sex Madness (1937)
Thirty Days
    Silver Lining (1932)
This Immoral Age
    Square Root of Zero (1964)
This Man is Dangerous
    Patient Vanishes, The (1947, Brit.)
This Rebel Age
    Beat Generation, The (1959)
Thoroughbred
    Run for the Roses (1978)
Those Were the Happy Times
    Star! (1968)
Three Bad Men in the Hidden Fortress
    Hidden Fortress, The (1959, Jap.)
Three Broadway Girls
    Greeks Had a Word for Them (1932)
Three Days and a Child
    Not Mine to Love (1969, Israel)
Three for the Money
    Win, Place or Steal (1975)
Three Ghosts
    Ghosts, Italian Style (1969, Ital./Fr.)
Three Girls in Hot Pants
    Secretary, The (1971)*
Three in Eden
    Isle of Fury (1936)
Three in the Cellar
    Up in the Cellar (1970)
Three Men and a Girl
    Gay Adventure, The (1953, Brit.)
Three on a Weekend
    Bank Holiday (1938, Brit.)
Three Rascals in the Hidden Fortress
    Hidden Fortress, The (1959, Jap.)
Three Shades of Love
    This Rebel Breed (1960)
Three Sinners
    Three Faces of Sin (1963, Fr./Ital.)
Three Stooges Meet the Gunslingers
    Outlaws Is Coming, The (1965)
3,000 A.D.
    Captive Women (1952)
Thrill Seekers
    Gutter Girls (1964, Brit.)
Thunder in the East
    Battle, The (1934, Brit./Fr.)
Thunder Mountain
    Shepherd of the Hills, The (1964)
Thunder Over Hawaii
    Naked Paradise (1957)
Thunder Pass
    Thunder Trail (1937)
Thundercloud
    Colt .45 (1950)

Thursday the 12th
   Pandemonium (1982)
Tickled Pink
   Magic Spectacles (1961)
Tiger by the Tail
   Cross-Up (1958)
Tiger Man
   Lady and the Monster, The (1944)
Tight Skirts
   Tight Skirts, Loose Pleasures (1966, Fr.)
Time of Return, The
   Muriel (1963, Fr./Ital.)
Time to Run, A
   Female Bunch, The (1969)
Tintorera...Tiger Shark
   Tintorera...Bloody Waters (1977, Brit./Mex.)
To Be a Man
   Cry of the Battle (1963)
To Bed or Not to Bed
   Devil, The (1963, Ital.)
To Catch a Spy
   Catch My Soul (1974)
To Elvis with Love
   Touched by Love (1980)
To Love a Vampire
   Lust for a Vampire (1971, Brit.)
To New Shores
   Life Begins Anew (1938, Ger.)
To Our Lovers
   A Nous Amours (1984, Fr.)**
To Speak As Brothers
   Their Only Chance (1978)*
Today We Live
   Day and the Hour, The (1963, Fr./Ital.)
Toga Party
   Pelvis (1977)*
Together Girls
   Manson Massacre, The (1976)*
Tomahawk Trail, The
   Iroquois Trail, The (1950)
Tomb of the Cat
   Tomb of Ligeia, The (1965, Brit.)
Tomb of the Living Dead
   Mad Doctor of Blood Island, The (1969, U.S./
   Phil.)
Tombs of the Blind Dead
   Blind Dead, The (1972, Span.)
Tombstone
   Tombstone, the Town Too Tough to Die (1942)
Tonight's the Night—Pass It On
   Tonight's the Night (1932, Brit.)
Tony Arzenta
   No Way Out (1975, Ital./Fr.)
Too Much for One Man
   Climax, The (1967, Fr./Ital.)
Top Job
   Grand Slam (1968, Ital./Span./Ger.)
Tops is the Limit
   Anything Goes (1936)
Torture Chamber of Dr. Sadism, The
   Blood Demon (1967, Ger.)
Touch of Hell, A
   Immoral Charge (1962, Brit.)
Touch of Her Life, The
   Touch of Her Flesh, The (1967)
Touch of Melissa, The
   Touch of Satan, The (1971)
Tournament Tempo
   Gay Blades (1946)*
Tower of Evil
   Beyond the Fog (1981, Brit.)
Town Called Bastard, A
   Town Called Hell, A (1971, Span.)
Town that Cried Terror, The
   Maniac! (1977)
Toy Grabbers, The
   Up Your Teddy Bear (1970)
Track of the Vampire
   Blood Bath (1966)
Trails of Peril
   Trails of Danger (1930)
Trained to Kill
   White Dog (1982)
Trained to Kill
   No Mercy Man, The (1975)
Transvestite, The
   Glen or Glenda (1953)
Trapped by Wireless
   You May Be Next (1936)
Traquenards
   Erotique (1969, Fr.)
Traquenards Erotiques
   Erotique (1969, Fr.)
Travels with Anita
   Lovers and Liars (1981, Ital.)
Treasure of Fear
   Scared Stiff (1945)
Treasure of the Piranha
   Killer Fish (1979, Ital./Braz.)

Trial by Combat
   Dirty Knight's Work (1976, Brit.)
Trip, The
   Voyage, The (1974, Ital.)
Trip to Italy, A
   Strangers, The (1955, Ital.)
Trip to Terror
   Is This Trip Really Necessary? (1970)
Trip with Anita, A
   Lovers and Liars (1981, Ital.)
Trojan War, The
   Trojan Horse, The (1962, Fr./Ital.)
Trombone from Heaven
   Follow the Band (1943)
Trouble at 16
   Platinum High School (1960)
Trucker's Woman
   Truckin' Man (1974)*
Truckin'
   Place Without Parents, A (1974)*
True Diary of a Wahine
   Maeva (1961)
True Diary of Avahine
   Maeva (1961)
True Story of a Whine
   Maeva (1961)
Trunk Mystery, The
   One New York Night (1935)
Truth Is Stranger
   When Ladies Meet (1933)
Try and Find It
   Hi Diddle Diddle (1943)
Tunnel 28
   Escape from East Berlin (1962)
Turkey Shoot
   Escape 2000 (1983, Aus.)
Twelve Miles Out
   Second Woman, The (1951)
12 Million Dollar Boy, The
   Dynamite Johnson (1978, Phil.)
Twenty-One Days
   Twenty-One Days Together (1939, Brit.)
Twilight of the Dead
   Gates of Hell, The (1983, Ital./US)
Twinkle and Shine
   It Happened to Jane (1959)
Twinkle, Twinkle, Killer Kane
   Ninth Configuration, The (1980)
Twist of Fate
   Beautiful Stranger (1954, Brit.)
Twisted Brain
   Horror High (1974)
Twisted Lives
   Liars, The (1964, Fr.)
Two Cries in the Night
   Funeral Home (1982, Can.)
Two Is a Happy Number
   One Is a Lonely Number (1972)
Two Years Holiday
   Stolen Dirigible, The (1966, Czech.)
Two-Way Drifter
   Drifter (1975)
Tyrant of Syracuse, The
   Damon and Pythias (1962)

U.S.S. Teakettle
   You're in the Navy Now (1951)
UFO
   Unidentified Flying Oddball, The (1979, Brit.)
Ugetsu Monogatari
   Ugetsu (1954, Jap.)
Ultimate Chase, The
   Ultimate Thrill, The (1974)
Under California Skies
   Under California Stars (1948)
Under Cover Rogue
   White Voices (1964, Fr./Ital.)
Under Mexicali Skies
   Under Mexicali Stars (1950)
Under New Management
   Honeymoon Hotel (1946, Brit.)
Underwater Odyssey, An
   Neptune Factor, The (1973, Can.)
Underworld After Dark
   Big Town After Dark (1947)
Underworld After Dark
   Big Town After Dark (1947)
Underworld Story, The
   Whipped, The (1950)
Une Femme Est Une Femme
   Woman Is a Woman, A (1961, Fr.)
Unfaithful Wife, The
   La Femme Infidele (1969, Fr./Ital.)
Unkissed Bride, The
   Mother Goose a Go-Go (1966)
Unknown Satellite over Tokyo
   Mysterious Satellite, The (1956, Jap.)

Unreconciled
   Not Reconciled or "Only Violence Helps Where It
   Rules" (1968, Ger.)
Unsatisfied Love
   Love After Death (1968)*
Unseen Heroes
   Missile from Hell (1960, Brit.)
Unsent Letter, The
   Letter That Never Was Sent, The (1962, USSR)
Unsung Heroes
   War Dogs (1942)
Untamed West, The
   Far Horizons, The (1955)
Unto a Good Land
   New Land, The (1971, Swed.)
Up Yours
   Camper John (1973)*
Upper Underworld
   Ruling Voice, The (1931)
Upperworld
   Upper World (1934)
Upstate Murders, The
   Savage Weekend (1983)
Ursus
   Mighty Ursus (1962, Ital./Span.)

V1
   Missile from Hell (1960, Brit.)
Vagabond Violinist
   Broken Melody, The (1934, Brit.)
Valachi Papers or Costra Nostra
   Valachi Papers, The (1972, Ital.)
Valdez, the Halfbreed
   Chino (1976, Ital./Span./Fr.)
Valley of Fear
   Sherlock Holmes and the Deadly Necklace (1962,
   Ger.)
Valley of the Bad Men
   Lightnin' Smith Returns (1931)*
Valley of the Swords
   Castillian, The (1963, Span./U.S.)
Valley of the White Wolves
   Mara of the Wilderness (1966)
Vampire and the Robot, The
   My Son the Vampire (1963, Brit.)
Vampire Girls, The
   Vampires, The (1969, Mex.)
Vampire Men of the Lost Planet
   Horror of the Blood Monsters (1970, U.S./Phil.)
Vampire over London
   My Son the Vampire (1963, Brit.)
Vampire People, The
   Blood Drinkers, The (1966, U.S./Phil.)
Vampire Playgirls
   Devil's Nightmare, The (1971, Bel./Ital.)
Vampire Playgirls
   Dracula's Great Love (1972, Span.)
Vampire, The
   Vampyr (1932, Fr./Ger.)
Vampire-Beast Craves Blood, The
   Blood Beast Terror, The (1967, Brit.)
Vampires, The
   Goliath and the Vampires (1964, Ital.)
Veil, The
   Haunts (1977)
Velvet House
   Crucible of Horror (1971, Brit.)
Venetian Nights
   Carnival (1931, Brit.)
Vengeance of a Gunfighter
   To Hell You Preach (1972)*
Venom
   Legend of Spider Forest, The (1976, Brit.)
Venusian, The
   Stranger from Venus, The (1954, Brit.)
Very Big Withdrawal, A
   Man, a Woman, and a Bank, A (1979, Can.)
Vessels of Wrath
   Beachcomber, The (1938, Brit.)
Veteran, The
   Deathdream (1972, Can.)
Vicious Circle, The
   Circle, The (1959, Brit.)
Video Madness
   Joysticks (1983)
Viking Women and the Sea Serpent, The
   Saga of the Viking Women and Their Voyage to
   the Waters of the Great Sea Serpent, The (1957)
Violent Journey
   Fool Killer, The (1965)
Violent Love
   Take Her by Surprise (1967, Can.)
Violent Midnight
   Psychomania (1964)
Virgin of Nuremburg, The
   Horror Castle (1965, Ital.)

Virgins and the Vampires, The
  Caged Virgins (1972)*
Virus
  Cannibals in the Streets (1982, Ital./Span.)
Voice from the Grave
  Sin of Nora Moran (1933)
Voice in the Night, A
  Wanted for Murder (1946, Brit.)
Volcano
  Krakatoa, East of Java (1969)
Volcano Monster, The
  Gigantis (1959, Jap./U.S.)
Volochayesk Days
  Defense of Volotchayevsk, The (1938, USSR)
Voodoo Blood Bath
  I Eat Your Skin (1971)
Voodoo Girl
  Sugar Hill (1974)
Vortex
  Day Time Ended, The (1980, Span.)
Voyage Beyond the Sun
  Space Monster (1965)
Voyage in a Balloon
  Stowaway in the Sky (1962, Fr.)
Voyage to Prehistory
  Journey to the Beginning of Time (1966, Czech.)
Vrooder's Hooch
  Crazy World of Julius Vrooder, The (1974)

Wahine
  Maeva (1961)
Waiting at the Church
  Runaround, The (1931)
Waiting Women
  Secrets of Women (1961, Swed.)
Walking Down Broadway
  Hello Sister! (1933)
Wander Love Story
  Wanderlove (1970)
Want a Ride, Little Girl?
  Impulse (1975)
Wanted Women
  Jessie's Girls (1976)
Wanton Contessa, The
  Senso (1968, Ital.)
War
  Rat (1960, Yugo.)
War Dogs
  Pride of the Army (1942)
War Gods of the Deep
  City Under the Sea (1965, Brit.)
War Head
  Opeation Snafu (1965, Brit.)
War in Space
  War of the Planets (1977, Jap.)
War Is Over, The
  La Guerre Est Finie (1967, Fr./Swed.)
War of the Aliens
  Starship Invasion (1978, Can.)
War of the Monsters, The
  Gamera Versus Barugon (1966, Jap./U.S.)
War of the Wildcats
  In Old Oklahoma (1943)
Ward 13
  Hospital Massacre (1982)
Warlord of Crete, The
  Minotaur, The 1961, Ital.)
Warlord, The
  West of Shanghai (1937)
Warlords of the 21st Century
  Battletruck (1982)
Warm Body, The
  Thunder in the Blood (1962, Fr.)
Warm-Blooded Spy, The
  Ravishing Idiot, A (1966, Ital./Fr.)
Warning from Space
  Mysterious Satellite, The (1956, Jap.)
Warrior's Rest
  Love on a Pillow (1963, Fr./Ital.)
Washington B.C.
  Hail (1973)
Washington Cowboy
  Rovin' Tumbleweeds (1939)
Water Cyborgs
  Terror Beneath the Sea (1966, Jap.)
Watts Monster, The
  Dr. Black and Mr. Hyde (1976)
Way Out Love
  Touch of Her Flesh, The (1967)
Waylaid Women
  Indecent (1962, Ger.)
Wayne Murder Case
  Strange Adventure (1933)
We Are in the Navy Now
  We Joined the Navy (1962, Brit.)
We Need No Money
  His Majesty, King Ballyhoo (1931, Ger.)

Web of Evidence
  Beyond This Place (1959, Brit.)
Wedding Present
  Turkish Cucumber, The (1963, Ger.)
Weekend Babysitter
  Weekend with the Babysitter (1970)
Weekend Wives
  Weekend, Italian Style (1967, Fr./Ital./Span.)
Welcome, Mr. Beddoes
  Man Could Get Killed, A (1966)
Welcome to Arrow Beach
  Tender Flesh (1976)
Well-Made Marriage, The
  Le Beau Marriage (1982, Fr.)
Werewolf vs. the Vampire Woman, The
  Shadow of the Werewolf (1970, Span./Ger.)
What?
  Che? (1973, Ital./Fr./Ger.)
What a Way to Die
  Beyond Control (1971)*
What Shall it Profit
  Hard Steel (1941, Brit.)
What the Swedish Butler Saw
  Groove Room, The (1974, Brit.)*
What's in It for Harry?
  Target: Harry (1980)
Wheel of Fate
  Road House Girl (1955)
Wheel of Fortune
  Man Betrayed, A (1941)
When Lovers Meet
  Lover Come Back (1946)
When Men Are Beasts
  Women in the Night (1948)
When the Door Opened
  Escape (1940)
When the Girls Meet the Boys
  Girl Crazy (1943)
Where Is This Girl?
  Where Is This Lady? (1932, Brit.)
Where's George?
  Hope of His Side (1935, Brit.)
While London Sleeps
  When London Sleeps (1934, Brit.)
While New York Sleeps
  Now I'll Tell (1934)
While Plucking Daisies
  Please! Mr. Balzac (1957, Fr.)
Whirlpool of Flesh
  Whirlpool of Women (1966, Jap.)
Whispering Death
  Night of the Askari (1978, Ger./S. Africa)
White, Red, Yellow, and Pink
  Love Factory (1969, Ital.)
White Sickness, The
  Skeleton on Horseback (1949, Czech.)
White Trash on Moonshine Mountain
  Moonshine Mountain (1964)
Who Can Kill a Child?
  Island of the Damned (1976, Span.)
Who Wants to Kill Jessie?
  Who Killed Jessie? (1965, Czech.)
Who Would Kill a Child?
  Island of the Damned (1976, Span.)
Who Would Kill Jessie?
  Who Killed Jessie? (1965, Czech.)
Why Not!
  Pourquoi Pas! (1979, Fr.)
Wild and the Sweet, The
  Lovin' Molly (1974)
Wild and Willing
  Rat Fink (1965)
Wild for Kicks
  Beat
Wild Game
  Jail Bait (1977, Ger.)
Wild in the Sky
  Black Jack (1973)
Wild Jungle Captive
  Jungle Captive (1945)
Wild Love-Makers
  Weird Love Makers, The (1963, Jap.)
Wild Women
  Angels' Wild Women (1972)*
Wildcat
  Great Scout and Cathouse Thursday, The (1976)
Wilderness Family, Part 2
  Further Adventures of the Wilderness Family (1978)
Wildflowers: The Story of a Draft Dodger
  Wildflowers (1968)
Will James' Sand
  Sand (1949)
William at the Circus
  William Comes to Town (1948, Brit.)
Willie and Joe Back at the Front
  Back at the Front (1952)
Wind Bloweth Where It Listeth, The
  Man Escaped, A (1957, Fr.)

Wind is My Lover, The
  Gypsy Fury (1950, Fr,)
Winged Serpent
  Starship Invasion (1978, Can.)
Winged Serpent, The
  Q (1982)
Wings Over Wyoming
  Hollywood Cowboy (1937)
Winner, The
  My Way (1974, S. Africa)
Winnetou
  Apache Gold (1965, Ger.)
Winnetou the Warrior
  Apache Gold (1965, Ger.)
Winston Affair, The
  Man in the Middle (1964, U.S./Brit.)
Winter Rates
  Out of Season (1975, Brit.)
Witch Beneath the Sea, The
  Marizinia (1962, U.S./Braz.)
Witches—Violated and Tortured To Death
  Mark of the Devil II (1975, Ger./Brit.)
Witching, The
  Necromancy (1972)
With Fire and Sword
  Invasion 1700 (1965, Fr./Ital./Yugo.)
With Gunilla Monday Evening and Tuesday
  Guilt (1967, Swed.)
Without a Trace
  Witness, The (1982, Hung.)
Woman Alone, The
  Sabotage (1936, Brit.)
Woman and the Puppet, The
  Female, The (1960, Fr.)
Woman in Bondage
  Woman in Chains (1932, Brit.)
Woman in the Case
  Allotment Wives, Inc. (1945)
Woman of Antwerp
  Dedee (1949, Fr.)
Woman of Dolwyn
  Last Days of Dolwyn, The (1949, Brit.)
Woman with a Whip
  Forty Guns (1957)
Woman's Place, A
  Wise Age (1962, Jap.)
Women in Limbo
  Limbo (1972)
Women in Love
  Sinner's Holiday (1930)
Women in Prison
  Ladies They Talk About (1933)
Women in Prison
  Women in Cages (1972)*
Women in War
  Women and War (1965, Fr.)
Women of Nazi Germany
  Hitler (1962)
Women, The
  Vixens, The (1969)
Wonder Kid
  Wonder Boy (1951, Brit.)
Wonderful Day
  I've Gotta Horse (1965, Brit.)
Wooden Crosses
  Road to Glory (1936)
Word, The
  Ordet (1957, Den.)
Working Wives
  Week-End Marriage (1932)
World of Space, The
  Battle in Outer Space (1960, Jap.)
World of Yor, The
  Yor, the Hunter from the Future (1983, Ital.)
World War III Breaks Out
  Final War, The (1960, Jap.)
World's Greatest Swindles
  Beautiful Swindlers, The (1967, Fr./Ital./Jap./Neth.)
Worlds of Gulliver, The
  Three Worlds of Gulliver, The (1960, Brit.)
Worst Secret Agents
  00-2 Most Secret Agents (1965, Ital.)
Written on the Sand
  Play Dirty (1969, Brit.)
Wrong Kind of Girl, The
  Bus Stop (1956)
Wyoming Kid, The
  Cheyenne (1947)

X From Outer Space, The
  Girara (1967, Jap.)
Xanadu
  Shangri-La (1972)*
Xica Da Silva
  Xica (1982, Brazil)

Yambao
  Young and Evil (1962, Mex.)
Year 2889
  In the Year 2889 (1966)
Year of the Cricket
  Kenner (1969)
Year of the Tiger, The
  Yank in Viet-Nam, A (1964)
Yellow Ticket, The
  Yellow Passport, The (1931)
Yog—Monster from Space
  Space Amoeba, The (1970, Jap.)
You All Come
  All the Young Wives (1975)*
You Can't Sleep Here
  I Was a Male War Bride (1949)
You Can't Steal Love
  Murph the Surf (1974)
Young and the Beat, The
  Cool Sound from Hell, A (1959)*
Young and the Cool, The
  Twist All Night (1961)
Young and the Damned, The
  Los Olvidados (1950, Mex.)
Young and the Immoral, The
  Sinister Urge, The (1961)

Young and the Passionate, The
  Vitelloni (1956, Ital.)
Young Dracula
  Son of Dracula (1974, Brit.)
Young Dracula
  Andy Warhol's Dracula (1974)*
Young Hellions, The
  High School Confidential (1958)
Young Lovers, The
  Never Fear (1950)
Young Playmates, The
  Au Pair Girls (1973, Brit.)*
Young Rebels, The
  Teenage Doll (1957)
Young Scarface
  Brighton Rock (1947, Brit.)
Youngest Spy, The
  My Name Is Ivan (1963, USSR)
Your Red Wagon
  They Live by Night, (1948)
Youth of Russia
  Jewish Father (1934)*

Zaat
  Blood Waters of Doctor Z
Zatoichi and the Scoundrels
  Zatoichi (1968, Jap.)
Zazie in the Subway
  Zazie (1961, Fr.)
Zazie in the Underground
  Zazie (1961, Fr.)
Zero Hour
  Road to Glory (1936)
Zero Population Growth
  Z.P.G. (1972)
Zombie
  I Eat Your Skin (1971)
Zombie 2
  Zombie (1980, Ital.)
Zombie Creeping Flesh
  Night of the Zombies (1983, Span./Ital.)
Zombie Flesh Eaters
  Zombie (1980, Ital.)
Zombies
  I Eat Your Skin (1971)
Zombies of Sugar Hill
  Sugar Hill (1974)
Zombies of the Stratosphere
  Satan's Satellites (1958)
Zorro Against Maciste
  Samson and the Slave Queen (1963, Ital.)

MPG TITLE TO GREAT BRITAIN TITLE (GB)

Below is a listing of main titles used in the MPG followed by titles used for the release of the film in Great Britain (GB).

Aaron Slick from Punkin Crick (1952)
  Marshmallow Moon
Abandon Ship (1957, Brit.)
  Seven Waves Away
Abbott and Costello Meet Frankenstein (1948)
  Abbott and Costello Meet the Ghosts
Abe Lincoln in Illinois, (1940)
  Spirit of the People
Above the Clouds (1933)
  Winged Devils
Accursed, The (1958, Brit.)
  Traitors, The
Across the Badlands (1950)
  Challenge, The
Across the Sierras (1941)
  Welcome Stranger
Advance to the Rear (1964)
  Company of Cowards
Adventure for Two (1945)
  Demi-Paradise, The
Adventure in Baltimore (1949)
  Bachelor Bait
Adventure in Blackmail (1943, Brit.)
  Breach of Promise
Adventure in Manhattan (1936)
  Manhattan Madness
Adventure in Washington (1941)
  Female Correspondent
Adventures in Silverado (1948)
  Above All Laws
Adventures of Don Juan (1949)
  New Adventures of Don Juan, The
Adventures of Sadie, The (1955, Brit.)
  Our Girl Friday
Adventures of Sherlock Holmes, The (1939)
  Sherlock Holmes
Affair in Monte Carlo (1953, Brit.)
  24 Hours of a Woman's Life
Affairs of a Rogue, The (1949, Brit.)
  First Gentleman, The
Affairs of Adelaide (1949, U.S./Brit.)
  Britannia Mews
Affairs of Martha, The (1942)
  Once Upon a Thursday
African Treasure (1952)
  Bomba and the African Treasure
After Midnight with Boston Blackie (1943)
  After Midnight
After Tonight (1933)
  Sealed Lips
Against the Law (1934)
  Urgent Call
Age of Consent (1932)
  Are These Our Children?
Agent 8-3/4 (1963, Brit.)
  Hot Enough for June
Aggie Appleby, Maker of Men (1933)
  Cupid in the Rough
Air Cadet (1951)
  Jet Men of the
Air Air Police (1931)
  Air Patrol, The
Albuquerque (1948)
  Silver City
Alias Bulldog Drummond (1935, Brit.)
  Bulldog Jack
Alias French Gertie (1930)
  Love Finds a Way
Alias Nick Beal (1949)
  Contact Man, The
All American, The (1932)
  Sport of a Nation
All American, The (1953)
  Winning Way, The
All American Chump (1936)
  Country Bumpkin
All at Sea (1958, Brit.)
  Barnacle Bill (1957)
All Mine to Give (1957)
  Day They Gave Babies Away, The
...All the Marbles (1981)
  California Dolls, The
Allegheny Uprising (1939)
  First Rebel, The
Allotment Wives (1945)
  Woman in the Case
Almost a Gentleman (1939)
  Magnificent Outcast
Aloha (1931)
  No Greater Love

Alphabet Murders, The (1966)
  ABC Murders, The
Amateur Crook (1937)
  Crooked but Dumb
Amazon Quest (1949)
  Amazon
America, America (1963)
  Anatolian Smile, The
American Dream, An (1966)
  See You in Hell, Darling
American Empire (1942)
  My Son Alone
American Guerrilla in the Philippines, An (1950)
  I Shall Return
And Then There Were None (1945)
  Ten Little Niggers
Angel on the Amazon (1948)
  Drums Along the Amazon
Angels in the Outfield (1951)
  Angels and the Pirates
Animal Kingdom, The (1932)
  Women in His House, The
Annapolis Farewell (1935)
  Gentlemen of the Navy
Annapolis Salute (1937)
  Salute to Romance
Annapolis Story, An (1955)
  Blue and the Gold, The
Anne of Windy Poplars (1940)
  Anne of Windy Willows
Another Face (1935)
  It Happened in Hollywood
Any Wednesday (1966)
  Bachelor Girl Apartment
Anybody's Blonde (1931)
  When Blonde Meets Blonde
Anzio (1968, Ital.)
  Battle for Anzio, The
Aparajito (1959, India)
  Unvanquished, The
Ape Man, The (1943)
  Lock Your Doors
Appaloosa, The (1966)
  Southwest to Sonora
Appointment With a Shadow (1958)
  Big Story, The
Aqua Sex, The (1962)
  Mermaids of Tiburon, The
Are These Our Parents? (1944)
  They Are Guilty
Arkansas Judge (1941)
  False Witness
Army Girl (1938)
  Last of the Cavalry, The
Arson Racket Squad (1938)
  Fire Fighters
Artists and Models Abroad (1938)
  Stranded in Paris
Astounding She-Monster, The (1958)
  Mysterious Invader
At Gunpoint (1955)
  Gunpoint
At Sword's Point (1951)
  Sons of the Musketeers
Atlantic Ferry (1941, Brit.)
  Sons of the Sea
Atomic Man, The (1955, Brit.)
  Timeslip
Attack of the Giant Leeches (1958)
  Demons of the Swamp
Attack of the Puppet People (1958)
  Six Inches Tall
August Week-End (1936)
  Week-End Madness
Avengers, The (1942, Brit.)
  Day Will Dawn, The
Awakening of Jim Burke (1935)
  Iron Fist

B.F.'s Daughter (1948)
  Polly Fulton
Bachelor and the Bobby-Soxer, The (1947)
  Bachelor Knight
Bachelor's Daughters, The (1946)
  Bachelor Girls
Bachelor's Folly (1931, Brit.)
  Calendar, The

Bad Boy (1939)
  Perilous Journey
Bad Man, The (1941)
  Two-Gun Cupid
Bad Men of the Hills (1942)
  Wrongly Accused
Bail Out at 43,000 (1957)
  Bale Out at 43,000
Bandits of Corsica, The (1953)
  Return of the Corsican Brothers
Bandits of El Dorado (1949)
  Tricked
Bank Dick, The (1940)
  Bank Detective, The
Bar Sinister, The (1955)
  It's a Dog's Life
Barbarian, The (1933)
  Night in Cairo, A
Barbed Wire (1952)
  False News
Basketball Fix, The (1951)
  Big Decision, The
Battle of Bloody Beach (1961)
  Battle on the Beach
Battling Buckaroo (1934)
  His Last Adventure
Beasts of Marseilles, The (1959, Brit.)
  Seven Thunders
Beautiful Cheat, The (1946)
  What a Woman!
Beauty for Sale (1933)
  Beauty
Behind Prison Walls (1943)
  Youth Takes a Hand
Behind the Eight Ball (1942)
  Off the Beaten Track
Bela Lugosi Meets a Brooklyn Gorilla (1952)
  Monster Meets the Gorilla
Beloved Brat (1938)
  Dangerous Age, A
Bend of the River (1952)
  Where the River Bends
Bengal Brigade (1954)
  Bengal Rifles
Betrayed (1944)
  When Strangers Marry
Betty Co-Ed (1946)
  Melting Pot, The
Beware of Children (1961, Brit.)
  No Kidding
Beyond the Limit (1983)
  Honorary Consul, The
Beyond the Pecos (1944)
  Beyond the Seven Seas
Beyond the Sacramento (1940)
  Power of Justice
Big Bluff, The (1933)
  Worthy Deceiver
Big Boodle, The (1957)
  Night in Havana
Big Brain, The (1933)
  Enemies of Society
Big Carnival, The (1951)
  Ace in the Hole
Big Hand for the Little Lady, A (1966)
  Big Deal at Dodge City
Big Land, The (1957)
  Stampeded
Big Money (1930)
  Easy Money
Big Noise, The (1936)
  Modern Madness
Big Race, The (1933)
  Raising the Wind
Big Shot, The (1931)
  Optimist, The
Big Switch, The (1970, Brit.)
  Strip Poker
Big Time or Bust (1933)
  Heaven Bound
Bill Cracks Down (1937)
  Men of Steel
Biscuit Eater, The (1940)
  God Gave Him a Dog
Bishop Misbehaves, The (1935)
  Bishop's Misadventures, The
Biter Bit, The (1937, Brit.)
  Calling All Ma's
Black Arrow, The (1948)
  Black Arrow Strikes, The

Black Bart (1948)
  Black Bart, Highwayman
Black Cat, The (1934)
  House of Doom, The
Black Glove, The (1954, Brit.)
  Face the Music
Black Market Rustlers (1943)
  Land and the Law
Black Watch, The (1929)
  King of the Khyber Rifles
Blackout (1940, Brit.)
  Contraband
Blackout (1954)
  Murder by Proxy
Blame the Woman (1932, Brit.)
  Diamond Cut Diamond
Blarney Kiss, The (1933, Brit.)
  Blarney Stone, The
Blazing Six Shooters (1940)
  Stolen Wealth
Blazing Trail, The (1949)
  Forged Will, The
Blind Date (1934)
  Her Sacrifice
Blockade (1928, Brit.)
  Q-Ships
Blonde Blackmailer (1955, Brit.)
  Stolen Time
Blonde Crazy (1931)
  Larceny Lane
Blonde from Singapore, The (1941)
  Hot Pearls
Blondie for Victory (1942)
  Troubles Through Billets
Blondie Goes Latin (1941)
  Conga Swing
Blondie Goes to College (1942)
  Boss Said 'No', The
Blondie Hits the Jackpot (1949)
  Hitting the Jackpot
Blondie in Society (1941)
  Henpecked
Blondie's Big Deal (1949)
  Big Deal, The
Blondie's Blessed Event (1942)
  Bundle of Trouble, A
Blood of Dracula (1957)
  Blood Is My Heritage
Blood on Satan's Claws, The (1970, Brit.)
  Satan's Skin
Blue Denim (1959)
  Blue Jeans
Boat from Shanghai (1931, Brit.)
  Chin Chin Chinaman
Bob Mathias Story, The (1954)
  Flaming Torch, The
Bold Caballero, The (1937)
  Bold Cavalier, The
Bombers B-52 (1957)
  No Sleep Till Dawn
Bombs Over London (1937, Brit.)
  Midnight Menace
Bombshell (1933)
  Blonde Bombshell
Bombsight Stolen (1941, Brit.)
  Cottage to Let
Bonanza Town (1951)
  Two Fisted Agent
Border Outlaws (1950)
  Phantom Horseman, The
Born for Glory (1935, Brit.)
  Brown on Resolution
Born for Glory (1935, Brit.)
  Forever England
Born to Kill (1947)
  Lady of Deceit
Boston Blackie and the Law (1946)
  Blackie and the Law
Boston Blackie Booked on Suspicion (1945)
  Booked on Suspicion
Boston Blackie Goes Hollywood (1942)
  Blackie Goes Hollywood
Boston Blackie's Chinese Venture (1949)
  Chinese Adventure
Boston Blackie's Rendezvous (1945)
  Blackie's Rendezvous
Both Sides of the Law (1953, Brit.)
  Street Corner
Bottom of the Bottle, The (1956)
  Beyond the River
Bowery Blitzkreig (1941)
  Stand and Deliver
Boy, a Girl, and a Dog, A (1946)

Lucky Boy from Indiana (1950)
  Blaze of Glory

Brasher Doubloon, The (1947)
  High Window, The
Brat, The (1930, Brit.)
  Nipper, The
Breakfast in Hollywood (1946)
  Mad Hatter
Breakout (1960, Brit.)
  Danger Within
Breed of the Border (1933)
  Speed Brent Wins
Bride of the Lake (1934, Brit.)
  Lily of Killarney
Bride of the Regiment (1930)
  Lady of the Rose
Bridegroom for Two (1932, Brit.)
  Let's Love and Laugh
Brigham Young—Frontiersman (1940)
  Brigham Young
Bright Lights (1935)
  Funny Face
Bright Victory (1951)
  Lights Out
British Intelligence (1940)
  Enemy Agent
Broadway Bad (1933)
  Her Reputation
Broadway Bill (1934)
  Strictly Confidential
Broadway Hoofer, The (1929)
  Dancing Feet
Broadway Limited (1941)
  Baby Vanishes, The
Broadway to Hollywood (1933)
  Ring up the Curtain
Broken Lullaby (1932)
  Man I Killed, The
Brother Rat and a Baby (1940)
  Baby Be Good
Brotherly Love (1970)
  Country Dance
Brothers (1930)
  Blood Brothers
Buck Privates (1941)
  Rookies
Buck Privates Come Home (1947)
  Rookies Come Home
Bucket of Blood (1934, Brit.)
  Tell-Tale Heart, The
Buckskin Frontier (1943)
  Iron Road, The
Bulldog Edition (1936)
  Lady Reporter
Bullets for Rustlers (1940)
  On Special Duty
Bunker Bean (1936)
  His Majesty Bunker Bean
Burn-'Em-Up Barnes (1934)
  Devils on Wheels
Burn, Witch, Burn (1962, Brit.)
  Night of the Eagle
Bushwhackers, The (1952)
  Rebel, The
Busman's Honeymoon (1940, Brit.)
  Haunted Honeymoon

Californian, The (1937)
  Beyond the Law
Call Me Genius (1961, Brit.)
  Rebel, The
Call the Mesquiteers (1938)
  Outlaws of the West
Callaway Went Thataway (1951)
  Star Said No, The
Campus Confessions (1938)
  Fast Play
Cannonball (1976, Hong Kong, U.S,)
  Carquake
Caper of the Golden Bulls, The (1967)
  Carnival of Thieves
Captain Black Jack (1951)
  Black Jack
Captain Carey, U.S.A. (1950)
  After Midnight
Captain Horatio Hornblower (1951, Brit.)
  Captain Horatio Hornblower, R.N.
Captain John Smith and Pocahontas (1953)
  Burning Arrows
Captain Pirate (1952)
  Captain Blood, Fugitive
Captive Women (1952)
  3000 A.D.
Caretakers, The (1963)
  Borderlines
Caretaker's Daughter, The (1952, Brit.)
  Love's a Luxury
Caribbean (1952)
  Caribbean Gold

Carmen (1931, Brit.)
  Gipsy Blood
Carnaby, M.D. (1967, Brit.)
  Doctor in Clover
Carnival (1935)
  Carnival Nights
Carolina (1934)
  House of Connelly
Carry on Cabbie (1963, Brit.)
  Call Me a Cab
Carry on Henry VIII (1970, Brit.)
  Carry on Henry
Caryl of the Mountains (1936)
  Get that Girl
Cash on Delivery (1956, Brit.)
  To Dorothy, A Son
Castle of Crimes (1941, Brit.)
  House of the Arrow
Castle on the Hudson (1940)
  Years without Days
Catered Affair, The (1956)
  Wedding Breakfast
Catherine the Great (1934, Brit.)
  Rise of Catherine the Great, The
Cattle King (1963)
  Guns of Wyoming
Cattle Queen (1950)
  Queen of the West
Challenge of the Range (1949)
  Moonlight Raid
Chamber of Horrors (1941, Brit.)
  Door with Seven Locks, The
Chance Meeting (1954, Brit.)
  Young Lovers, The
Charley's Aunt (1941)
  Charley's American Aunt
Charming Deceiver, The (1933, Brit.)
  Heads We Go
Cheating Blondes (1933)
  House of Chance
Cherokee Strip, The (1937)
  Strange Laws
Cherokee Strip (1940)
  Fighting Marshal
Cheyenne Cyclone (1932)
  Smashing Through
Cheyenne Kid, The (1931)
  Fighting Test, The
Chief, The (1933)
  My Old Man's a Fireman
Chief Crazy Horse (1955)
  Valley of Fury
Children's Hour, The (1961)
  Loudest Whisper, The
Chinese Den, The (1940, Brit.)
  Chinese Bungalow, The
Christmas in Connecticut (1945)
  Indiscretion
Circus World (1964)
  Magnificent Showman, The
Citadel of Crime (1941)
  Outside the Law
City After Midnight (1957, Brit.)
  That Woman Opposite
City Beneath the Sea (1953)
  One Hour to Doom's Day
Claudelle Inglish (1961)
  Young and Eager
Clock, The (1945)
  Under the Clock
Close Call for Boston Blackie, A (1946)
  Lady of Mystery
Close Call for Ellery Queen, A (1942)
  Close Call, A
Clouds Over Europe (1939, Brit.)
  Q Planes
Clown Must Laugh, A (1936, Brit.)
  Pagliacci
Clue of the Missing Ape, The (1953, Brit.)
  Gibraltar Adventure
Cockeyed Miracle, The (1946)
  Mr. Griggs Returns
Code of the Lawless (1945)
  Mysterious Stranger, The
College Coach (1933)
  Football Coach
College Scandal (1935)
  Clock Strikes Eight, The
College Swing (1938)
  Swing, Teacher, Swing
Collegiate (1936)
  Charm School, The
Colonel Blimp (1945, Brit.)
  Life and Death of Colonel Blimp, The
Colonel Effingham's Raid (1945)
  Man of the Hour
Coming-Out Party, A (1962, Brit.)
  Very Important Person, A
Compromised! (1931)
  We Three

Compromised (1931, Brit.)
 Compromising Daphne
Concorde—Airport '79, The (1979)
 Airport '80: The Concorde
Concrete Jungle, The (1962, Brit.)
 Criminal, The
Confessions of a Co-Ed (1931)
 Her Dilemna
Confessions of an Opium Eater (1962)
 Evils of Chinatown
Confessions of Boston Blackie (1942)
 Confessions
Connecticut Yankee, A (1931)
 Yankee in King Arthur's Court, The
Conqueror Worm, The (1968, Brit.)
 Witchfinder General
Conquest (1937)
 Marie Walewska
Consolation Marriage (1931)
 Married in Haste
Continental Express (1939, Brit.)
 Silent Battle, The
Convention Girl (1934)
 Atlantic City Romance
Cop-Out (1967, Brit.)
 Stranger in the House
Corky of Gasoline Alley (1951)
 Corky
Corpse in the Morgue (1938)
 Lady in the Morgue
Corpse Vanishes, The (1942)
 Case of the Missing Brides, The
Corruption (1933)
 Double Exposure
Corvette K-225 (1943)
 Nelson Touch, The
Corvette Summer (1978)
 Hot One, The
Cosmo Jones—Crime Smasher (1943)
 Crime Smasher
Costello Case, The (1930)
 Costello Murder Case, The
Cougar, The King Killer (1933)
 Cougar
Count the Hours (1953)
 Every Minute Counts
Counter-Attack (1945)
 One Against Seven
County Fair (1933, Brit.)
 Song of the Plough
Coup de Torchon (1981, Fr.)
 Clean Slate
Court Martial (1954, Brit.)
 Carrington V.C.
Court Martial of Billy Mitchell, The (1955)
 One Man Mutiny
Courtney Affair, The (1947, Brit.)
 Courtneys of Curzon Street, The
Cowboy Blues (1946)
 Beneath the Starry Skies
Cowboy Canteen (1944)
 Close Harmony
Cowboy from Brooklyn (1938)
 Romance and Rhythm
Cowboy from Lonesome River (1944)
 Signed Judgment
Cowboy Serenade (1942)
 Serenade of the West
Crash of Silence (1952, Brit.)
 Mandy
Crawling Eye, The (1958, Brit.)
 Trollenberg Terror, The
Crazy Over Horses (1951)
 Win, Place and Show
Crime Doctor's Courage, The (1945)
 Doctor's Courage, The
Crime Doctor's Gamble, The (1947)
 Doctor's Gamble, The
Crime Doctor's Strangest Case, The (1943)
 Strangest Case, The
Crime Doctor's Warning, The (1945)
 Doctor's Warning, The
Crime of Peter Frame, The (1938, Brit.)
 Second Thoughts
Crime Wave (1954)
 City is Dark, The
Crooked Trail (1936)
 Lead Law
Crosby Case, The (1934)
 Crosby Murder Case, The
Crossed Swords (1978)
 Prince and the Pauper, The
Crucible of Horror (1971, Brit.)
 Corpse, The
Cuban Pete (1946)
 Down Cuban Way
Curtain Call at Cactus Creek (1950)
 Take the Stage
Cutter and Bone (1981)
 Cutter's Way

Cynthia (1947)
 Rich, Full Life, The

Daddy O (1959)
 Downbeat
Damaged Goods (1937)
 Marriage Forbidden
Damn the Defiant (1962, Brit.)
 HMS Defiant
Damn Yankees (1958)
 What Lola Wants
Dancing Co-Ed (1939)
 Every Other Inch a Lady
Dandy, the All American Girl (1976)
 Sweet Revenge
Danger Flight (1939)
 Scouts of the Air
Dangerous Cargo (1939, Brit.)
 Hell's Cargo
Dangerous Millions (1946)
 House of Tao Ling, The
Dangerous Youth (1958, Brit.)
 These Dangerous Years
Darby's Rangers (1958)
 Young Invaders
Daring Daughters (1933)
 Behind the Counter
Dark Delusion (1947)
 Cynthia's Secret
Dark of the Sun (1968, Brit.)
 Mercenaries, The
Darling, How Could You? (1951)
 Rendezvous
Daughter of Shanghai (1937)
 Daughter of the Orient
Davy Crockett, Indian Scout (1950)
 Indian Scout
Dawn Over Ireland (1938, Irish)
 Dawn, The
Dead Ringer (1964)
 Dead Image
Deadliest Sin, The (1956, Brit.)
 Confession
Deadline U.S.A. (1952)
 Deadline
Deadly Game, The (1955, Brit.)
 Third Party Risk
Decision Against Time (1957, Brit.)
 Man in the Sky, The
Delinquent Daughters (1944)
 Accent on Crime
Dementia 13 (1963)
 Haunted and the Hunted, The
Demon Barber of Fleet Street, The (1939, Brit.)
 Sweeney Todd, the Demon Barber of Fleet Street
Desert Attack (1958, Brit.)
 Ice Cold in Alex Desert
Desperados (1959)
 Sinner,

The Desert Fox, The (1951)
 Rommel—Desert Fox

Desert Horseman, The (1946)
 Checkmate
Desert Justice (1936)
 Crime's Highway
Desert Patrol (1962, Brit.)
 Sea of Sand
Design for Murder (1940, Brit.)
 Trunk Crime
Desk Set (1957)
 His Other Woman
Desperate Adventure, A (1938)
 It Happened in Paris
Desperate Chance for Ellery Queen, A (1942)
 Desperate Chance, A
Detective, The (1954, Brit.)
 Father Brown
Devil is a Sissy, The (1936)
 Devil Takes the Count, The
Devil's Bride, The (1968, Brit.)
 Devil Rides Out, The
Devil's Brother, The (1933)
 Fra Diavolo
Devil's Brother, The (1933)
 Virtuous Tramps, The
Devil's Harbor (1954, Brit.)
 Devil's Point
Devil's Mate (1933)
 He Knew Too Much

Devil's Own, The (1967, Brit.)
 Witches, The
Devil's Plot, The (1948, Brit.)
 Counterblast
Devil's Trail, The (1942)
 Rogues' Gallery
Devil's Widow, The (1972, Brit.)
 Tamlin
Dial 1119 (1950)
 Violent Hour, The
Diamond Wizard, The (1954, Brit.)
 Diamond, The
Dick Tracy (1945)
 Splitface
Dick Tracy Meets Gruesome (1947)
 Dick Tracy's Amazing Adventure
Dick Tracy's Dilemma (1947)
 Mark of the Claw
Die, Die My Darling (1965, Brit.)
 Fanatic
Ding Dong Williams (1946)
 Melody Maker
Dino (1957)
 Killer
Dino Dispatch From Reuters, A (1940)
 This Man Reuter
Docteur Popaul (1972, Fr.)
 Scoundrel in White
Dr. Ehrlich's Magic Bullet (1940)
 Story of Dr. Ehrlich's Magic Bullet
Dr. Gillespie's Criminal Case (1943)
 Crazy to Kill
Dr. Kildare's Victory (1941)
 Doctor and the Debutante, The
Dr. Kildare's Wedding Day (1941)
 Mary Names the Day
Doing Time (1979, Brit.)
 Porridge
Doll Face (1945)
 Come Back to Me
$ (Dollars) (1971)
 Heist, The
Domino Principle, The (1977)
 Domino Killings, The
Doolins of Oklahoma, The (1949)
 Great Manhunt, The
Doomed Cargo (1936, Brit.)
 Seven Sinners
Doomed to Die (1940)
 Mystery of Wentworth Castle, The
Doorway to Hell (1930)
 Handful of Clouds, A
Double Jeopardy (1955)
 Crooked Ring
Dough Boys (1930)
 Forward March
Doughnuts and Society (1936)
 Stepping into Society
Down Rio Grande Way (1942)
 Double Punch, The
Down to Their Last Yacht (1934)
 Hawaiian Nights
Dracula's Dog (1978)
 Zoltan, Hound of Dracula
Draegerman Courage (1936)
 Cave In, The
Dragnet Patrol (1932)
 Love Redeemed
Dragstrip Riot (1958)
 Reckless Age, The
Drake the Pirate (1935, Brit.)
 Drake of England
Dream Maker, The (1963, Brit.)
 It's All Happening
Dressed to Kill (1946)
 Sherlock Holmes and the Secret Code
Dreyfus Case, The (1931, Brit.)
 Dreyfus
Drums (1938, Brit.)
 Drum, The
Du Barry, Woman of Passion (1930)
 Du Barry
Dude Wrangler, The (1930)
 Feminine Touch
Duffy of San Quentin (1954)
 Men Behind Bars
Duke Comes Back, The (1937)
 Call of the Ring, The
Dulcimer Street (1948, Brit.)
 London Belongs to Me
Durango Kid, The (1940)
 Masked Stranger, The
Dynamite Delany (1938)
 Fighting Chump, The
Dynamite Denny (1932)
 Denny of the Railroad

Earl Carroll Sketchbook (1946)
  Hats Off to Rhythm
Earl of Puddlestone (1940)
  Jolly Old Higgins
Earthworm Tractors (1936)
  Natural Born Salesman, A
East of Fifth Avenue (1933)
  Two in a Million
East of Java (1935)
  Java Seas
East of Kilimanjaro (1962, Brit./Ital.)
  Big Search, The
Edge of Doom (1950)
  Stronger than Fear
Edge of the City (1956)
  Man Is Ten Feet Tall, A
Eight on the Lam (1967)
  Eight on the Run
El Alamein (1953)
  Desert Patrol
El Dorado Pass (1948)
  Desperate Men
Electronic Monster, The (1960, Brit.)
  Escapement
Elephant Stampede (1951)
  Bomba and the Elephant Stampede
Ellery Queen and the Murder Ring (1941)
  Murder Ring, The
Emergency Wedding (1950)
  Jealousy
Emil (1938, Brit.)
  Emil and the Detectives
End of the Trail (1936)
  Revenge
Enemy Agent (1940)
  Secret Enemy
Enemy Agents Meet Ellery Queen (1942)
  Lido Mystery, The
Enemy from Space (1957, Brit.)
  Quatermass II
Enforcer, The (1951)
  Murder, Inc.
Escapade (1932)
  Dangerous Ground
Escape by Night (1965, Brit.)
  Clash by Night
Escape to Victory (1981)
  Victory
Escaped from Dartmoor (1930, Brit.)
  Cottage on Dartmoor, A
Eternal Return, The (1943, Fr.)
  Love
Eternal Eve (1968, Brit./Span.)
  Face of Eve, The
Everything Okay (1936, Brit.)
  On Top of the World
Ex-Champ (1939)
  Golden Gloves
Exposed (1932)
  Strange Roads
Eyes of the Jungle (1953)
  Destiny Danger
Eyewitness (1981)
  Janitor, The

Face Behind the Scar, The (1940, Brit.)
  Return of a Stranger
Facts of Love (1949, Brit.)
  29 Acacia Avenue
Faithful Hearts (1933, Brit.)
  Faithful Heart, The
Fall Guy, The (1930)
  Trust Your Wife
False Faces (1943)
  Attorney's Dilemma, The
False Madonna, The (1931)
  False Idol, The
Family, The (1974, Fr./Ital.)
  Violent City
Family Affair (1954, Brit.)
  Life with the Lyons
Family Life (1971, Brit.)
  Wednesday's Child
Fan, The (1949)
  Lady Windermere's Fan
Fanny Foley Herself (1931)
  Top of the Bill
Farewell to Love (1931, Brit.)
  City of Song
Fast Bullets (1936)
  Law and Order
Fatal Hour (1940)
  Mr. Wong at Headquarters
Fearless Vampire Killers, or Pardon Me but Your
Teeth are in my Neck, The (1967)
  Dance of the Vampires

Federal Man Hunt (1938)
  Flight from Justice
Female Fiends (1958, Brit.)
  Strange Awakening, The
Female Fugitive (1938)
  Fugitive Lady
Ferocious Pal, The (1934)
  His Ferocious Pal
Feud of the West (1936)
  Vengeance of Gregory Walters, The
Feudin' Rhythm (1949)
  Ace Lucky
Ffolkes (1980, Brit.)
  North Sea Hijack
Fighting Frontiersman, The (1946)
  Golden Lady
Fighting Mad (1948)
  Joe Palooka in Fighting Mad
Fighting Pimpernel, The (1950, Brit.)
  Elusive Pimpernel, The
Fighting Rookie, The (1934)
  Dangerous Enemy
Fighting Texans (1933)
  Randy Strikes Oil
Fighting Trooper, The (1935)
  Trooper, The
Fighting Wildcats, The (1957, Brit.)
  West of Suez
Final Edition, The (1932)
  Determination
Final Option, The (1983, Brit.)
  Who Dares Wins
Final Terror, The (1983)
  Campsite Massacre
Finger of Guilt (1956, Brit.)
  Intimate Stranger, The
Fire Over Africa (1954, Brit.)
  Malaga
First Aid (1931)
  In Strange Company
First Time, The (1969)
  You Don't Need Pajamas at Rosie's
First Yank into Tokyo (1945)
  Mask of Fury
Fitzwilly (1967)
  Fitzwilly Strikes Back
Five and Ten (1931)
  Daughter of Luxury
Five Angles on Murder (1950, Brit.)
  Woman in Question, The
Five Million Miles to Earth (1968, Brit.)
  Quatermass and the Pit
Fixer Dugan (1939)
  Double Daring
Flaming Guns (1932)
  Rough Riding Romeo
Flap (1970)
  Last Warrior, The
Flat Top (1952)
  Eagles of the Fleet
Flim-Flam Man, The (1967)
  One Born Every Minute
Flood Tide (1957)
  Above All Things
Floradora Girl, The (1930)
  Gay Nineties, The
Fly By Night (1942)
  Secrets of G32
Fly-Away Baby (1937)
  Crime in the Clouds
Flying Devils (1933)
  Flying Circus, The
Flying High (1931)
  Happy Landing
Folies Bergere (1935)
  Man from the Folies Bergere, The
Fools' Parade (1971)
  Dynamite Man from Glory Jail
Footsteps in the Night (1932, Brit.)
  Honeymoon Adventure, A
For Love or Money (1939)
  Tomorrow at Midnight
For Me and My Gal (1942)
  For Me and My Girl
For the Love of Mike (1960)
  None but the Brave
For Them that Trespass (1949, Brit.)
  Mr. Drew
Forbidden Music (1936, Brit.)
  Land Without Music
Force of Arms (1951)
  Girl for Joe, A
Forever Yours (1937, Brit.)
  Foget Me Not
Forever Yours (1945)
  Right to Live, The
Fortune Cookie, The (1966)
  Meet Whiplash Willie
48 Hours (1944, Brit.)
  Went the Day Well?

Four Against Fate (1952, Brit.)
  Derby Day
4D Man (1959)
  Evil Force, The
Four Desperate Men (1960, Brit.)
  Siege of Pinchgut, The
Four Faces West (1948)
  They Passed This Way
Four Friends (1981)
  Georgia's Friends
Fox Movietone Follies (1929)
  Movietone Follies of 1929
Fox Movietone Follies of 1930 (1930)
  Movietone Follies of 1930
Framed (1947)
  Paula
French Leave (1948)
  Kilroy on Deck
Frenzy (1946, Brit.)
  Latin Quarter
Freshman Love (1936)
  Rhythm on the River
Frightened Bride, The (1952, Brit.)
  Tall Headlines
Frisco Waterfront (1935)
  When We Look Back
From Hell to Texas (1958)
  Manhunt
Frontier Gal (1945)
  Bride Wasn't Willing, The
Fugitive, The (1940, Brit.)
  On the Night of the Fire
Fugitive Sheriff, The (1936)
  Law and Order
Fuller Brush Gal, The (1950)
  Affairs of Sally, The
Fuller Brush Girl, The (1950)
  Affairs of Sally, The
Fuller Brush Man, The (1948)
  That Mad Mr. Jones
Fury of the Jungle (1934)
  Jury of the Jungle
Fuss Over Feathers (1954, Brit.)
  Conflict of Wings

Gables Mystery, The (1931, Brit.)
  Man at Six, The
Gaiety Girls, The (1938, Brit.)
  Paradise for Two
Gaily, Gaily (1969)
  Chicago, Chicago
Gang, The (1938, Brit.)
  Gang Show, The
Gang Bullets (1938)
  Crooked Way, The
Gang's All Here, The (1941)
  In the Night
Gang's All Here, The (1943)
  Girls He Left Behind, The
Gaslight (1944)
  Murder in Thornton Square, The
Gay Adventure, The (1953, Brit.)
  Golden Arrow
Gay Divorcee, The (1934)
  Gay Divorce, The
Gay Lady, The (1949, Brit.)
  Trottie True
Gene Krupa Story, The (1959)
  Drum Crazy
Generation (1969)
  Time for Giving, A
Gentle Touch (1956, Brit.)
  Feminine Touch, The
George Raft Story, The (1961)
  Spin of a Coin
Get Hep to Love (1942)
  It Comes Up Love
Get Hep to Love (1942)
  She's My Lovely
Get On with It (1963, Brit.)
  Dentist on the Job
Ghosts on the Loose (1943)
  Ghosts in the Night
Gideon of Scotland Yard (1959, Brit.)
  Gideon's Day
Gigolette (1935)
  Night Club Girl, A
Guy, and A Gob, A (1941)
  Navy Steps Out, The
Girl from Missouri, The (1934)
  One Hundred Percent Pure
Girl from Tenth Avenue, The (1935)
  Men on Her Mind
Girl in Distress (1941, Brit.)
  Jeannie
Girl in the Bikini, The (1958, Fr.)
  Lighthouse Keeper's Daughter, The

Girl in the Case (1944)
  Silver Key, The
Girl in the Painting, The (1948, Brit.)
  Portrait from Life
Girl in the Street (1938, Brit.)
  London Melody
Girl in White, The (1952)
  So Bright the Flame
Girl O' My Dreams (1934)
  Love Race, The
Girl of the Rio (1932)
  Dove, The
Girl on the Canal, The (1947, Brit.)
  Painted Boats
Girl Overboard (1929)
  Port O' Dreams
Girl Thief, The (1938)
  Love at Second Sight
Girls in the Night (1953)
  Life After Dark
Girls' School (1950)
  Dangerous Inheritance
Git Along Little Dogies (1937)
  Serenade of the West
Give Me Your Heart (1936)
  Sweet Aloes
Glamour Boy (1941)
  Hearts in Springtime
Glamour Girl (1947)
  Night Club Girl
Glory at Sea (1952, Brit.)
  Gift Horse, The
Glory Trail, The (1936)
  Glorious Sacrifice, The
Go into Your Dance (1935)
  Casino De Paree
Go West (1940)
  Marx Brothers Go West, The
Gobs and Gals (1952)
  Cruising Casanovas
God's Country and the Man (1937)
  Avenging Stranger, The
God's Gift to Women (1931)
  Too Many Women
Godzilla, King of the Monsters (1956, Jap.)
  Godzilla
Gold (1932)
  Valley of Gold, The
Gold Diggers in Paris (1938)
  Gay Imposters
Gold Dust Gertie (1931)
  Why Change Your Husband?
Gold Raiders (1952)
  Stooges Go West
Golden Mask, The (1954, Brit.)
  South of Algiers
Great Gilbert and Sullivan, The (1953, Brit.)
  Story of Gilbert and Sullivan, The
Great Guy (1936)
  Pluck of the Irish
Great John L., The (1945)
  Man Called Sullivan, A
Great Manhunt, The (1951, Brit.)
  State Secret
Great McGinty, The (1940)
  Down Went McGinty
Great Train Robbery, The (1979, Brit.)
  First Great Train Robbery, The
Green Promise, The (1949)
  Raging Waters
Gridiron Flash (1935)
  Luck of the Game, The
Grief Street (1931)
  Stage Whispers
Guest, The (1963, Brit.)
  Caretaker, The
Guilty as Hell (1932)
  Guilty as Charged
Guilty of Treason (1950)
  Treason
Gun Play (1936)
  Invisible Message, The
Gunfighters (1947)
  Assassin, The
Gunfire (1950)
  Frank James Rides Again
Gutter Girls (1964, Brit.)
  Yellow Teddybears, The
Gypsy Girl (1966, Brit.)
  Sky West and Crooked

Hallelujah, I'm a Bum (1933)
  Hallelujah, I'm a Tramp
Hallelujah, I'm a Bum (1933)
  Lazy Bones
Happy Landing (1934)
  Air Patrol

Hard Guy (1941)
  Professional Bride
Hardcore (1979)
  Hardcore Life, The
Harold Teen (1934)
  Dancing Fool, The
Harper (1966)
  Moving Target, The
Harry Black and the Tiger (1958, Brit.)
  Harry Black
Harem Scarum (1965)
  Harem Holiday
Harvard, Here I Come (1941)
  Here I Come
Hat Check Girl (1932)
  Embassy Girl
Hatchet Man, The (1932)
  Honorable Mr. Wong, The
Hatchet Man, The (1932)
  Honourable Mr. Wong, The
Hate in Paradise (1938, Brit.)
  Tea Leaves in the Wind
Haunted House (1940)
  Blake Murder Mystery, The
Haunted Strangler, The (1958, Brit.)
  Grip of the Strangler
Having a Wild Weekend (1965, Brit.)
  Catch Us If You Can
Hawaiians, The (1970)
  Master of the Islands
He Couldn't Take It (1933)
  One of the Many
Heading West (1946)
  Cheat's Last Throw, The
Headleys At Home, The (1938)
  Among Those Present
Headline Shooter (1933)
  Evidence in Camera
Headline Woman, The (1935)
  Woman in the Case, The
Heat's On, The (1943)
  Tropicana
Heatwave (1954, Brit.)
  House Across the Lake, The
Helen Morgan Story, The (1959)
  Both Ends of the Candle
Hell and High Water (1933)
  Cap'n Jericho
Hell Canyon Outlaws (1957)
  Tall Trouble, The
Hell, Heaven or Hoboken (1958, Brit.)
  I Was Monty's Double
Hell in Korea (1956, Brit.)
  Hill in Korea, A
Hello Annapolis (1942)
  Personal Honour
Hello Sister (1930)
  Clipped Wings
Hell's Cargo (1935, Brit.)
  McGlusky the Sea Rover
Henry Aldrich, Boy Scout (1944)
  Henry—Boy Scout
Henry Aldrich Gets Glamour (1943)
  Henry Gets Glamour
Henry Aldrich Haunts a House (1943)
  Henry Haunts a House
Henry Aldrich Plays Cupid (1943)
  Henry Plays Cupid
Henry Aldrich Swings It (1943)
  Henry Swings It
Henry Aldrich's Little Secret (1944)
  Henry's Little Secret
Henry Goes to Arizona (1939)
  Spats to Spurs
Her First Romance (1951)
  Girls Never Tell
Her Mad Night (1932)
  Held for Murder
Her Man Gilbey (1949, Brit.)
  English without Tears
Her Panelled Door (1951, Brit.)
  Woman with No Name, The
Her Strange Desire (1931, Brit.)
  Potiphar's Wife
Her Unborn Child (1929)
  Her Child
Here Come the Marines (1952)
  Tell It to the Marines
Here Comes Carter (1936)
  Voice of Scandal
Here Comes Cookie (1935)
  Plot Thickens, The
Hi Beautiful (1944)
  Pass to Romance
Hidden Menace, The (1940, Brit.)
  Star of the Circus
Hidden Room, The (1949, Brit.)
  Obsession
Hideout (1948, Brit.)
  Small Voice, The

Hideout in the Alps (1938, Brit.)
  Dusty Ermine
High Commissioner, The (1968, U.S./Brit.)
  Nobody Runs Forever
High Fury (1947, Brit.)
  White Cradle Inn
High Gear (1933)
  Big Thrill, The
High School Hellcats (1958)
  School for Violence
High Treason (1937, Brit.)
  Rocks of Valpre, The
High Voltage (1929)
  Wanted
Hills of Home (1948)
  Master of Lassie
Hired Wife (1934)
  Marriage of Convenience
His Glorious Night (1929)
  Breath of Scandal
Hitch Hike Lady (1936)
  Eventful Journey
Hitch Hike to Heaven (1935)
  Footlights and Shadows
Hi'Ya, Chum (1943)
  Everything Happens to Us
Hold 'Em Navy (1937)
  That Navy Spirit
Hold 'Em Yale (1935)
  Uniform Lovers
Hold That Co-ed (1938)
  Hold That Girl
Holiday (1938)
  Free to Live
Holiday (1938)
  Unconventional Linda
Holiday Week (1952, Brit.)
  Hindle Wakes
Hollow Triumph (1948)
  Scar, The
Hollywood and Vine (1945)
  Daisy Goes Hollywood
Homicide for Three (1948)
  Interrupted Honeymoon, An
Homicide Squad, The (1931)
  Lost Men
Honeymoon (1947)
  Two Men and a Girl
Honeymoon in Bali (1939)
  Husbands or Lovers
Honor of the Mounted (1932)
  Beyond the Border
Honor of the Press (1932)
  Scoop, The
Hoosier Holiday (1943)
  Farmyard Follies
Hoosier Schoolboy, The (1937)
  Yesterday's Hero
Hoosier Schoolmaster, The (1935)
  Schoolmaster, The
Horror Hotel (1960, Brit.)
  City of the Dead, The
Horror House (1970, Brit.)
  Dark, The
Horror House (1970, Brit.)
  Haunted House of Horror, The
Horror of Dracula, The (1958, Brit.)
  Dracula
Horsemen of the Sierras (1950)
  Remember Me
Horse's Mouth, The (1953, Brit.)
  Oracle, The
Hospital Massacre (1982)
  X-Ray
Hot Money Girl (1962, Brit./Ger.)
  Long Distance
Hot Money Girl (1962, Brit./Ger.)
  Treasure of San Teresa, The
Hot Rock, The (1972)
  How to Steal a Diamond in Four Easy Lessons
Hot Rod Gang (1958)
  Fury Unleashed
Hotel Variety (1933)
  Passing Show, The
Hour of Glory (1949, Brit.)
  Small Back Room, The
House of Fright (1961)
  Two Faces of Dr. Jekyll
House of Horrors (1946)
  Joan Medford is Missing
House of Mystery (1941, Brit.)
  At the Villa Rose
House on Sorority Row, The (1983)
  House of Evil
Howards of Virginia, The (1940)
  Tree of Liberty, The
Huddle (1932)
  Impossible Lover
Human Monster, The (1940, Brit.)
  Dark Eyes of London

Humanoids from the Deep (1980)
    Monster
Hundred Hour Hunt (1953, Brit.)
    Emergency Call
Hurricane Horseman (1931)
    Mexican, The

I Am a Fugitive from a Chain Gang (1932)
    I Am a Fugitive from the Chain Gang
I Can Get It for You Wholesale (1951)
    This is My Affair
I Dood It (1943)
    By Hook or by Crook
I, Jane Doe (1948)
    Diary of a Bride
I Like Money (1962, Brit.)
    Mr. Topaze
I Live for Love (1945)
    I Live for You
I Love a Bandleader (1935)
    Memory for Two
I Married a Spy (1938)
    Secret Lives
I Stand Condemned (1936, Brit.)
    Moscow Nights
I Wake Up Screaming (1942)
    Hot Spot
I Was a Male War Bride (1949)
    You Can't Sleep Here
I Was a Teenage Frankenstein (1958)
    Teenage Frankenstein
Ice-Capades Revue (1942)
    Rhythm Hits the Ice
Iceland (1942)
    Katina
If I Were Free (1933)
    Behold We Live
If This Be Sin (1950, Brit.)
    That Dangerous Age
I'll Never Forget You (1951)
    House in the Square, The
Illicit Interlude (1954, Swed.)
    Summer Interlude
Immoral Charge (1962, Brit.)
    Serious Charge
Imperfect Lady, The (1947)
    Mrs. Loring's Secret
Inbetween Age, The (1958, Brit.)
    Golden Disc, The
In Love With Life (1934)
    Re-Union
In Old Cheyenne (1931)
    Guest House, The
In Old New Mexico (1945)
    Cisco Kid in Old New Mexico, The
In Trouble with Eve (1964, Brit.)
    Trouble with Eve
Indianapolis Speedway (1939)
    Devil on Wheels
Inheritance, The (1951, Brit.)
    Uncle Silas
Intermezzo (1939)
    Escape to Happiness
Internes Can't Take Money (1937)
    You Can't Take Money
Intruder, The (1962)
    Stranger, The
Invasion of the Saucermen (1957)
    Invasion of the Hell Creatures, The
Ireland's Border Line (1939, Ireland)
    Blarney
Irish Luck (1939)
    Amateur Detective
Iroquois Trail (1950)
    Tomahawk Trail, The
Island of the Burning Damned (1971, Brit.)
    Night of the Big Heat
Island Rescue (1952, Brit.)
    Appointment with Venus
It Ain't Hay (1943)
    Money for Jam
It Comes Up Love (1942)
    Date with an Angel, A
It Happened in Hollywood (1937)
    Once a Hero
It Happened Out West (1937)
    Man from the Big City, The
It Happened to One Man (1941, Brit.)
    Gentleman of Venture
It's in the Bag (1945)
    Fifth Chair, The
I've Always Loved You (1946)
    Concerto
Ivory Hunter (1952, Brit.)
    Where No Vultures Fly

Jack Slade (1953)
    Slade
Jailbreak (1936)
    Murder in the Big House
Jamboree (1957)
    Disc Jockey
Jamboree Jazz Boat (1960, Brit.)
    Jazzboat
Jazz Cinderella (1930)
    Love is Like That
Jeepers Creepers (1939)
    Money Isn't Everything
Jet Attack (1958)
    Through Hell to Glory
Jim Thorpe—All American (1951)
    Man of Bronze
Jivaro (1954)
    Lost Treasure of the Amazon
Jive Junction (1944)
    Swing High
Joan of Ozark (1942)
    Queen of Spies
Joe Palooka in Humphrey Takes a Chance (1950)
    Humphrey Takes a Chance
Joe Palooka in the Squared Circle (1950)
    Squared Circle, The
Joe Palooka in Triple Cross (1951)
    Triple Cross, The
Joe Palooka in Winner Take All (1948)
    Winner Take All
Joe Smith, American (1942)
    Highway to Freedom
Johnny Allegro (1949)
    Hounded
Johnny Come Lately (1943)
    Johnny Vagabond
Johnny in the Clouds (1945, Brit.)
    Way to the Stars, The
Journey to the Far Side of the Sun (1969, Brit.)
    Doppelganger
Journey to the Lost City (1960, Ger./Fr./Ital.)
    Tiger of Bengal
Judge, The (1948)
    Gamblers, The
Judge Steps Out, The (1949)
    Indian Summer
Jungle Street Girls (1963, Brit.)
    Jungle Street
Just a Gigolo (1931)
    Dancing Partner, The

Kansas City Confidential (1952)
    Secret Four, The
Kathleen Mavourneen (1930)
    Girl From Ireland, The
Keep Smiling (1938)
    Miss Fix-It
Kentucky Blue Streak (1935)
    Blue Streak, The
Kentucky Kernels (1935)
    Triple Trouble
Kentucky Moonshine (1938)
    Three Men and a Girl
Key Man (1955)
    Life at Stake, A
Kibitzer, The (1929)
    Busybody, The
Kid Comes Back, The (1937)
    Don't Pull Your Punches
Kid From Amarillo, The (1951)
    Silver Chains
Kid From Kokomo, The (1939)
    Orphan of the Ring, The
Kid From Texas, The (1950)
    Texas Kid, Outlaw
Kid Monk Baroni (1952)
    Young Paul Baroni
Killer That Stalked New York, The (1950)
    Frightened City
King and the Chorus Girl, The (1937)
    Romance is Sacred
King of Alcatraz (1938)
    King of the Alcatraz
King of Hockey (1936)
    King of the Ice Rink
King of the Roaring Twenties—The Story of Arnold
    Rothstein (1961)
    Big Bankroll, The
King of the Sierras (1938)
    Killers on the Prairie
King of the Wild Horses (1933)
    King of the Wild
Kisenga, Man of Africa (1952, Brit.)
    Men of Two Worlds
Kiss Me Again (1931)
    Toast of the Legion

Kiss Me Goodbye (1935, Brit.)
    Going Gay
Kiss of Evil (1963, Brit.)
    Kiss of the Vampire
Kiss the Blood Off My Hands (1948)
    Blood on My Hands
Klondike (1932)
    Doctor's Sacrifice, The
Knute Rockne—All American (1940)
    Modern Hero, A
Konga, the Wild Stallion (1939)
    Konga

Ladies in Love (1930)
    Wings of Song
Lady and the Bandit, The (1951)
    Dick Turpin's Ride
Lady and the Monster, The (1944)
    Lady and the Doctor, The
Lady Godiva (1955)
    Lady Godiva of Coventry
Lady in Distress (1942, Brit.)
    Window in London, A
Lady in the Morgue (1938)
    Case of the Missing Blonde, The
Lady Jane Grey (1936, Brit.)
    Tudor Rose
Lady of Burlesque (1943)
    Strip-Tease Lady
Lady of Scandal, The (1930)
    High Road, The
Lady of the Pavements (1929)
    Lady of the Night
Lady Surrenders, A (1930)
    Blind Wives
Lady Surrenders, A (1947)
    Love Story
Lady Tubbs (1935)
    Gay Lady, The
Lady With a Past (1932)
    Reputation
Lady's Morals, A (1930)
    Jenny Lind
Lafayette Escadrille (1957)
    Hell Bent for Glory
Land of Fury (1955, Brit.)
    Seekers, The
Landrush (1946)
    Claw Strikes, The
Laramie Mountains (1952)
    Mountain Desperadoes
Larceny Street (1941, Brit.)
    Smash and Grab
Lariats and Six Shooters (1931)
    Fearless Deputy, The
Las Vegas Nights (1941)
    Gay City, The
Last of the Comanches (1952)
    Sabre and the Arrow, The
Last of the Redmen (1947)
    Last of the Redskins
Latin Love (1930, Brit.)
    Greek Street
Laugh It Off (1939)
    Lady Be Gay
Laughing Policeman, The (1973)
    Investigation of Murder, An
Law and Order (1940)
    Lucky Ralston
Law and Order (1943)
    Double Alibi, The
Law of the Rio Grande (1931)
    Wanted Men
Lawless, The (1950)
    Dividing Line, The
Lawless Border (1935)
    Border Patrol, The
Lawless Empire (1945)
    Power of Possession
Lawless Plainsmen (1942)
    Roll On
Le Petit Soldat (1965, Fr.)
    Little Soldier, The
Leather Gloves (1948)
    Loser Take All
Leathernecking (1930)
    Present Arms
Leathernecks Have Landed, The (1936)
    Marines Have Landed, The
Leave It to Smith (1934)
    Just Smith
Leftover Ladies (1931)
    Broken Links
Let 'Em Have It (1935)
    False Faces
Let's Be Ritzy (1934)
    Millionaire for a Day

Let's Go Collegiate (1941)
  Farewell to Fame
Let's Go Places (1929)
  Mirth and Melody
Let's Make Up (1955, Brit.)
  Lilacs in the Spring
Let's Rock (1958)
  Keep It Cool
Let's Try Again (1934)
  Marriage Symphony
Life Begins (1932)
  Dawn of Life, The
Life Begins (1932)
  Dream of Life
Life Begins at 8:30 (1942)
  Light of the Heart, The
Life Begins in College (1937)
  Joy Parade, The
Life of Jimmy Dolan, The (1933)
  Kid's Last Fight, The
Light Touch, The (1955, Brit.)
  Touch and Go
Lightning Guns (1950)
  Taking Sides
Li'l Abner (1940)
  Trouble Chaser
Limping Man, The (1939)
  Creeping Shadows
Line-Up, The (1934)
  Identity Parade
Lion Hunters (1951)
  Bomba and the Lion Hunters
Lisa (1962, Brit.)
  Inspector, The
Little Big Horn (1951)
  Fighting Seventh, The
Little Egypt (1951)
  Chicago Masquerade
Little Giant (1946)
  On the Carpet
Little Kidnappers, The (1954, Brit.)
  Kidnappers, The
Little Miss Big (1946)
  Baxter Millions, The
Little Miss Marker (1934)
  Girl in Pawn
Little Miss Molly (1940)
  My Irish Molly
Little Red Schoolhouse, The (1936)
  Schoolboy Penitentiary
Littlest Horse Thieves, The (1977)
  Escape from the Dark
Living Dead, The (1936, Brit.)
  Scotland Yard Mystery, The
Living Ghost, The (1942)
  Lend Me Your Ear
Lola (1971, Brit./Ital.)
  Twinky
Lola Montes (1955, Fr./Ger.)
  Fall of Lola Montes, The
London Blackout Murders (1942)
  Secret Motive
Lone Hand Texan, The (1947)
  Cheat, The
Lone Prairie, The (1942)
  Inside Information
Lone Rider in Frontier Fury (1941)
  Frontier Fury
Lone Star Moonlight (1946)
  Amongst the Thieves
Lone Star Pioneers (1939)
  Unwelcome Visitors
Lone Star Vigilantes (1941)
  Devil's Price, The
Lone Wolf Spy Hunt, The (1939)
  Lone Wolf's Daughter, The
Long Ago, Tomorrow (1971, Brit.)
  Raging Moon, The
Long Ride Home, The (1968)
  Time for a Killing, A
Looking Forward (1933)
  Service
Lord Byron of Broadway (1930)
  What Price Melody?
Lord Jeff (1938)
  Boy from Barnardo's, The
Loss of Innocence (1961, Brit.)
  Greengage Summer, The
Lost in Alaska (1952)
  Abbott and Costello Lost in Alaska
Lost Lady, A (1934)
  Courageous
Lost on the Western Front (1940, Brit.)
  Romance in Flanders, A
Loudspeaker, The (1934)
  Radio Star, The
Love Begins at Twenty (1936)
  All One Night
Love From a Stranger (1947)
  Stranger Walked In, A

Love in Morocco (1933, Fr.)
  Baroud
Love Is a Ball (1963)
  All This and Money Too
Love Is a Racket (1932)
  Such Things Happen
Love Is Better Than Ever (1952)
  Light Fantastic, The
Love Is My Profession (1959, Fr.)
  In Case of Adversity
Love Is On the Air (1937)
  Radio Murder Mystery, The
Love Kiss, The (1930)
  Kiss Me
Love Me Forever (1935)
  On Wings of Song
Love Storm, The (1931, Brit.)
  Cape Forlorn
Love Trader, The (1930)
  Island of Desire
Lovebound (1932)
  Souls for Sables
Lovely Way to Die, A (1968)
  Lovely Way to Go, A
Lovers, Happy Lovers! (1955, Brit.)
  Knave of Hearts
Lover's Net (1957, Fr.)
  Lovers of Lisbon
Loves of Madame DuBarry, The (1938, Brit.)
  Give Me Your Heart
Loves of Madame DuBarry, The (1938, Brit.)
  I Give My Heart
Lucky Nick Cain (1951)
  I'll Get You For This
Lured (1947)
  Personal Column

M (1933, Ger.)
  Murderer Among Us
Ma and Pa Kettle Go to Town (1950)
  Going to Town
Ma and Pa Kettle On Vacation (1953)
  Ma and Pa Kettle Go to Paris
MacArthur (1977)
  MacArthur the Rebel General
Mad Doctor, The (1941)
  Date With Destiny, A
Mad Empress, The (1939)
  Carlotta, the
Mad Empress Mad Love (1935)
  Hands of Orlac
Mad Men of Europe (1940, Brit.)
  Englishman's Home, An
Mad Parade, The (1931)
  Forgotten Women
Madame Racketeer (1932)
  Sporting Widow, The
Made on Broadway (1933)
  Girl I Made, The
Magnificent Matador, The (1955)
  Brave and the Beautiful, The
Magnificent Yankee, The (1950)
  Man With Thirty Sons, The
Mail Order Bride (1964)
  West of Montana
Mail Train (1941, Brit.)
  Inspector Hornleigh Goes to It
Mailbag Robbery (1957, Brit.)
  Flying Scot, The
Main Street Lawyer (1939)
  Small Town Lawyer
Maisie Gets Her Man (1942)
  She Got Her Man
Maisie Goes to Reno (1944)
  You Can't Do That to Me
Malay Nights (1932)
  Shadows of Singapore
Malaya (1949)
  East of the Rising Sun
Man Bait (1952, Brit.)
  Last Page, The
Man Betrayed, A (1941)
  Citadel of Crime
Man from Dakota, The (1940)
  Arouse and Beware
Man From Montana
  Montana Justice
Man From Sundown, The (1939)
  Woman's Vengeance, A
Man in a Cocked Hat (1960, Brit.)
  Carlton Browne of the F.O.
Man in the Dinghy, The (1951, Brit.)
  Into the Blue
Man in the Saddle (1951)
  Outcast, The
Man in the Shadow (1957)
  Pay the Devil

Man Made Monster (1941)
  Electric Man, The
Man of Affairs (1937, Brit.)
  His Lordship
Man of Evil (1948, Brit.)
  Fanny by Gaslight
Man on a String (1960)
  Confessions of a Counterspy
Man on the Flying Trapeze (1935)
  Memory Expert, The
Man Who Lived Again, The (1936, Brit.)
  Man Who Changed His Mind, The
Man Who Played God, The (1932)
  Silent Voice, The
Man Who Won, The (1933, Brit.)
  Mr. Bill the Conqueror
Man with a Million (1954, Brit.)
  Million Pound Note, The
Man with Nine Lives, The (1940)
  Behind the Door
Man with 100 Faces, The (1938, Brit.)
  Crackerjack
Man With the Gun, The (1955)
  Trouble Shooter, The
Manfish (1956)
  Calypso
Manhattan Merry-Go-Round (1937)
  Manhattan Music Box
Manhattan Moon (1935)
  Sing Me a Love Song
Mania (1961, Brit.)
  Flesh and the Fiends, The
Maniacs on Wheels (1951, Brit.)
  Once a Jolly Swagman
Man-Trap (1961)
  Man in Hiding
Mark of the Hawk, The (1958)
  Accused
Mark of the Whistler, The (1944)
  Marked Man, The
Marriage on Approval (1934)
  Married in Haste
Mars Attacks the World (1938)
  Rocket Ship
Mary Jane's Pa (1935)
  Wanderlust
Massacre Hill (1949, Brit.)
  Eureka Stockade
Matrimonial Bed, The (1930)
  Matrimonial Problem, A
Matter of Innocence, A (1968, Brit.)
  Pretty Polly
Maxwell Archer, Detective (1942, Brit.)
  Meet Maxwell Archer
McConnell Story, The (1955)
  Tiger in the Sky
McGuire, Go Home! (1966, Brit.)
  High Bright Sun, The
Me and My Gal (1932)
  Pier 13
Medico of Painted Springs, The (1941)
  Doctor's Alibi
Meet Me in Las Vegas (1956)
  Viva Las Vegas!
Men Are Children Twice (1953, Brit.)
  Valley of Song
Men Are Like That (1931)
  Virtuous Wife, The
Men Of America (1933)
  Great Decision, The
Men of Ireland (1938, Ireland)
  Island Man
Men of Ireland (1938, Ireland)
  West of Kirby
Men of Texas (1942)
  Men of Destiny
Men of the Sea (1951, Brit.)
  Midshipman Easy
Men With Steel Faces (1940)
  Couldn't Possibly Happen
Menace in the Night (1958, Brit.)
  Face in the Night
Mercy Plane (1939)
  Wonder Plane
Merrily We Go to Hell (1932)
  Merrily We Go to...
Merry Comes to Stay (1937, Brit.)
  Merry Comes to Town
Merry Frinks, The (1934)
  Happy Family, The
Mesa of Lost Women (1952)
  Lost Women
Mexicali Rose (1929)
  Girl From Mexico, The
Midnight at the Wax Museum (1936, Brit.)
  Midnight at Madame Tussaud's
Midnight Lady (1932)
  Dream Mother
Midnight Story, The (1957)
  Appointment With a Shadow

Midshipmaid Gob (1932, Brit.)
  Midshipmaid, The
Midway (1976)
  Battle of Midway, The
Military Academy With That 10th Avenue Gang (1950)
  Sentence Suspended
Million Dollar Manhunt (1962, Brit.)
  Assignment Redhead
Million Dollar Mermaid (1952)
  One-Piece Bathing Suit, The
Million Eyes of Su-Muru, The (1967, Brit.)
  Sumuru
Millionaire Playboy (1940)
  Glamour Boy
Miracle of Our Lady of Fatima (1952)
  Miracle of Fatima, The
Miracle on 34th Street (1947)
  Big Heart, The
Miss Fane's Baby is Stolen (1934)
  Kidnapped
Miss Grant Takes Richmond (1949)
  Innocence is Bliss
Missing Girls (1936)
  When Girls Leave Home
Missing Ten Days (1941, Brit.)
  Spy in the Pantry
Missing Ten Days (1941, Brit.)
  Ten Days in Paris
Mission Over Korea (1953)
  Eyes of the Skies
Mr. Arkadin (1962, Brit./Fr./Span.)
  Confidential Report
Mister Buddwing (1966)
  Woman Without a Face
Mr. Bug Goes to Town (1941)
  Hoppity Goes to Town
Mr. District Attorney in the Carter Case (1941)
  Carter Case
Mr. Hex (1946)
  Pride of the Bowery, The
Mister Hobo (1936, Brit.)
  Guv'Nor, The
Mr. Imperium (1951)
  You Belong to My Heart
Mr. Lord Says No (1952, Brit.)
  Happy Family, The
Mr. Mom (1983)
  Mr. Mum
Mr. Moto in Danger Island (1939)
  Mr. Moto on Danger Island
Mr. Potts Goes to Moscow (1953, Brit.)
  Top Secret
Mr. Soft Touch (1949)
  House of Settlement
Mr. Winkle Goes to War (1944)
  Arms and the Woman
Mob, The (1950)
  Remember That Face
Mobs, Inc. (1956)
  Mobs Incorporated
Model Murder Case, The (1964, Brit.)
  Girl in the Headlines
Models, Inc. (1952)
  That Kind of Girl
Mom and Dad (1944)
  Family Story, A
Monster Walks, The (1932)
  Monster Walked, The
Moonlight and Pretzels (1933)
  Moonlight and Melody
Morals for Women (1931)
  Farewell Party
Morgan! (1966, Brit.)
  Morgan: A Suitable Case for Treatment
Morgan! (1966, Brit.)
  Suitable Case for Treatment, A
Moscow Does Not Believe in Tears (1980, USSR)
  Moscow Distrusts Tears
Most Dangerous Game, The (1932)
  Hounds of Zaroff, The
Most Wanted Man in the World, The (1962, Fr./Ital.)
  Most Wanted Man, The
Moth, The (1934)
  Seeing It Through
Mother Is a Freshman (1949)
  Mother Knows Best
Mountain Moonlight (1941)
  Moving in Society
Mountain Rhythm (1942)
  Harvest Days
Mozart (1940, Brit.)
  Whom the Gods Love
Murder at Dawn (1932)
  Death Ray, The
Murder at the Baskervilles (1941, Brit.)
  Silver Blaze
Murder Can Be Deadly (1963, Brit.)
  Painted Smile, The

Murder in the Big House (1942)
  Human Sabotage
Murder in the Night (1940, Brit.)
  Murder in Soho
Murder in the Private Car (1934)
  Murder on the Runaway Train
Murder in the Red Barn (1936, Brit.)
  Maria Marten
Murder, Inc. (1960)
  Murder, Incorporated
Murder My Sweet (1931)
  Farewell, My Lovely
Murder on Approval (1956, Brit.)
  Barbados Quest
Murder on Campus (1934)
  On the Stroke of Nine
Murder on Diamond Row (1937, Brit.)
  Squeaker, The
Murder on Monday (1953, Brit.)
  Home at Seven
Murder on the Campus (1963, Brit.)
  Out of the Shadow
Murder on the Set (1936, Brit.)
  Death on the Set
Murder Will Out (1953, Brit.)
  Voice of Merrill, The
Murderers Are Amongst Us, The (1948, Ger.)
  Murderers Among Us
Murieta (1965, Span.)
  Vendetta
Muss 'Em Up (1936)
  House of Fate
My Heart Goes Crazy (1953, Brit.)
  London Town
My Life to Live (1963, Fr.)
  It's My Life
My Son Is Guilty (1939)
  Crime's End
Myrt and Marge (1934)
  Laughter in the Air
Mysterious Mr. Davis, The (1936, Brit.)
  My Partner, Mr. Davis
Mysterious Mr. Reeder, The (1940, Brit.)
  Mind of Mr. Reeder, The
Mystery at the Burlesque (1950, Brit.)
  Murder at the Windmill
Mystery Liner (1934)
  Ghost of John Holling, The
Mystery of Room 13 (1941, Brit.)
  Mr. Reeder in Room 13
Mystery at the Villa Rose (1930, Brit.)
  At the Villa Rose
Mystic Hour, The (1933)
  At Twelve Midnight

Nabonga (1944)
  Jungle Woman, The
Naked Night, The (1956, Swed.)
  Sawdust and Tinsel
Nana (1934)
  Lady of the Boulevards
Nate and Hayes (1983, U.S./New Zealand)
  Savage Islands
Naughty Arlette (1951, Brit.)
  Romantic Age, The
Navy Wife (1956)
  Mother-Sir!
Nelson Affair, The (1973, Brit.)
  Bequest to the Nation
Nevadan, The (1950)
  Man from Nevada, The
Never Give a Sucker an Even Break (1941)
  What a Man
Never Take Candy from a Stranger (1961, Brit.)
  Never Take Sweets From a Stranger
Never Wave at a WAC (1952)
  Private Wore Skirts, The
New Orleans Uncensored (1955)
  Riot on Pier 6
New Wine (1941)
  Great Awakening, The
Newly Rich (1931)
  Forbidden Adventure
Next Time We Love (1936)
  Next Time We Live
Nice Little Bank that Should Be Robbed, A (1958)
  How to Rob a Bank
Night Ambush (1958, Brit.)
  Ill Met by Moonlight
Night and Day (1933, Brit.)
  Jack's the Boy
Night Court (1932)
  Justice for Sale
Night Creatures (1962, Brit.)
  Captain Clegg
Night Editor (1946)
  Trespasser, The

Night Fighters, The (1960)
  Terrible Beauty, A
Night Heaven Fell, The (1958, Fr.)
  Heaven Fell That Night
Night of the Shooting Stars, The (1982, Ital.)
  Night of San Lorenzo, The
Night Parade (1929)
  Sporting Life
Night They Raided Minsky's, The (1968)
  Night They Invented Striptease, The
Night Train (1940, Brit.)
  Night Train to Munich
Night Train (1940, Brit.)
  Gestapo
Nightmare Castle (1966, Ital.)
  Night of the Doomed
99 and 44/100% Dead (1974)
  Call Harry Crown
No Greater Love (1932)
  Divine Love
No Greater Sin (1941)
  Social Enemy No. 1
No Highway in the Sky (1951, Brit.)
  No Highway
No Man Is an Island (1962)
  Island Escape
No Place to Land (1958)
  Man Mad
No Ransom (1934)
  Bonds of Honour
No Time to be Young (1957)
  Teenage Delinquents
No Tree in the Street (1964, Brit.)
  No Trees in the Street
Norah O'Neale (1934, Brit.)
  Irish Hearts
Norman Conquest (1953, Brit.)
  Park Plaza 605
North of the Rockies (1942)
  False Clues
North Sea Patrol (1939, Brit.)
  Luck of the Navy
Northwest Outpost (1947)
  End of the Rainbow
Not Exactly Gentlemen (1931)
  Three Rogues
Notorious Gentleman (1945, Brit.)
  Rake's Progress, The
Now I'll Tell (1934)
  When New York Sleeps
Now I'll Tell (1934)
  While New York Sleeps
Nuisance, The (1933)
  Accidents Wanted
Number One (1969)
  Pro, The

O'Henry's Full House (1952)
  Full House
Obey the Law (1933)
  East of Fifth Avenue
Obsessed (1951, Brit.)
  Late Edwina Black, The
Off Limits (1953)
  Military Policeman
Oh Yeah! (1929)
  No Brakes
Okay America (1932)
  Penalty of Fame
Oklahoma Raiders (1944)
  Midnight Raiders
Old Corral, The (1937)
  Texas Serenade
Old Dracula (1975, Brit.)
  Old Drac
Old Dracula (1975, Brit.)
  Vampira
Old Louisiana (1938)
  Treason
Old Mother Riley (1952, Brit.)
  Old Mother Riley's New Venture
Old Spanish Custom, An (1936, Brit.)
  Invader, The
Old Swimmin' Hole, The (1941)
  When Youth Conspires
Old Texas Trail, The (1944)
  Stagecoach Line
Omoo, Omoo, the Shark God (1949)
  Shark God, The
One Embarrassing Night (1930, Brit.)
  Rookery Nook
One for the Book (1947)
  Voice of the Turtle
One Million B.C. (1940)
  Man and His Mate
One More River (1934)
  Over the River

One Mysterious Night (1944)
  Behind Closed Doors
One New York Night (1935)
  Trunk Mystery, The
One Night in Paris (1940, Brit.)
  Premiere
One Too Many (1950)
  Killer With a Label
One Woman's Story (1949, Brit.)
  Passionate Friends, The
Only When I Laugh (1981)
  It Only Hurts When I Laugh
Operation (1951, Brit.)
  My Daughter Joy
Operation Conspiracy (1957, Brit.)
  Cloak Without Dagger
Operation Dames (1959)
  Girls in Action
Operation Disaster (1951, Brit.)
  Morning Departure
Operation Snafu (1965, Brit.)
  On the Fiddle
Operator 13 (1934)
  Spy 13
Optimists, The (1973, Brit.)
  Optimists of Nine Elms, The
Other Side of the Mountain, The (1975)
  Window to the Sky, A
Our Daily Bread (1934)
  Miracle of Life
Out of the Night (1945)
  Strange Illusion
Out of the Past (1947)
  Build My Gallows High
Outcast, The (1954)
  Fortune Hunter, The
Outcast Lady (1934)
  Woman of the World, A
Outcast of Black Mesa (1950)
  Clue, The
Outlaws of the Panhandle (1941)
  Faro Jack
Outlaws of the Range (1936)
  Call of Justice, The
Outlaws of the Rockies (1945)
  Roving Rogue, A
Outpost in Malaya (1952, Brit.)
  Planter's Wife, The
Outpost of the Mounties (1939)
  On Guard
Outside the 3-Mile Limit (1940)
  Mutiny on the Seas
Outsider, The (1949, Brit.)
  Guinea Pig, The
Overland to Deadwood (1942)
  Falling Stones
Overnight (1933, Brit.)
  That Night in London
Ox-Bow Incident, The (1943)
  Strange Incident

P.J. (1968)
  New Face in Hell
Pacific Adventure (1947, Aus.)
  Smithy
Pack Up Your Troubles (1939)
  We're in the Army Now
Paid (1930)
  Within the Law
Paid to Kill (1954, Brit.)
  Five Days
Palm Springs (1936)
  Palms Springs Affair
Palomino, The (1950)
  Hills of the Brave
Palooka (1934)
  Great Schnozzle, The
Panic in the Parlour (1957, Brit.)
  Sailor Beware!
Paper Gallows (1950, Brit.)
  Torment
Paradise for Three (1938)
  Romance for Three
Paratrooper (1954, Brit.)
  Red Beret, The
Pardon My French (1951, U.S./Fr.)
  Lady From Boston, The
Pardon Us (1931)
  Gaol Birds
Pardon Us (1931)
  Jailbirds
Paris After Dark (1943)
  Night Is Ending, The
Paris Express, The (1953, Brit.)
  Man Who Watched Trains Go By, The
Paris in Spring (1935)
  Paris Love Song

Paris Underground (1945)
  Madame Pimpernel
Park Avenue Logger (1937)
  Millionaire Playboy
Parlor, Bedroom and Bath (1931)
  Romeo in Pyjamas
Paroled From the Big House (1938)
  Main Street Girl
Passage West (1951)
  High Venture
Passionate Sentry, The (1952, Brit.)
  Who Goes There?
Passport to Alcatraz (1940)
  Alien Sabotage
Passport to China (1961, Brit.)
  Visa to Canton
Passport to Hell, A (1932)
  Burnt Offering
Patterns (1956)
  Patterns of Power
Patton (1970)
  Patton—Lust for Glory
Paula (1952)
  Silent Voice, The
Pawnee (1957)
  Pale Arrow
Pay Off, The (1930)
  Losing Game, The
Pecos River (1951)
  Without Risk
Penguin Pool Murder, The (1932)
  Penguin Pool Mystery, The
Penthouse (1933)
  Crooks in Clover
Penthouse Party (1936)
  Without Children
People vs. Dr. Kildare, The (1941)
  My Life Is Yours
Perfect Alibi, The (1931, Brit.)
  Birds of Prey
Perfect Furlough, The (1958)
  Strictly for Pleasure
Perfect Gentleman, The (1935)
  Imperfect Lady, The
Perfect Strangers (1950)
  Too Dangerous to Love
Persecution and Assassination of Jean-Paul Marat
  as Performed by the Inmates of the Asylum of
  Charenton Under the Direction of the Marquis de
  Sade, The (1967, Brit.)
  Marat/Sade
Personal Property (1937)
  Man in Possession, The
Peter Rabbit and Tales of Beatrix Potter (1971,
  Brit.)
  Tales of Beatrix Potter
Petty Girl, The (1950)
  Girl of the Year
Phantom Broadcast, The (1933)
  Phantom of the Air
Phantom Fiend, The (1935, Brit.)
  Lodger, The
Phantom Strikes, The (1939, Brit.)
  Gaunt Stranger, The
Pickup Alley (1957, Brit.)
  Interpol
Pickup Alley (1957, Brit.)
  International Police
Picnic on the Grass (1960, Fr.)
  Lunch on the Grass
Pigskin Parade (1936)
  Harmony Parade
Pillars of the Sky (1956)
  Tomahawk and the Cross, The
Pinto Kid, The (1940)
  All Square
Pioneers of the Frontier (1940)
  Anchor, The
Pirates of Capri, The (1949)
  Masked Pirate, The
Pirates of the Seven Seas (1941, Brit.)
  Queer Cargo
Playboy, The (1942, Brit.)
  Kicking the Moon Around
Pleasure Lovers, The (1964, Brit.)
  Naked Fury
Plot Thickens, The (1936)
  Swinging Pearl Mystery, The
Poacher's Daughter, The (1960, Brit.)
  Sally's Irish Rogue
Police Call (1933)
  Wanted
Police Court (1932)
  Son of Mine
Pony Soldier (1952)
  MacDonald of the Canadian Mounties
Pope Joan (1972, Brit.)
  Devil's Imposter, The
Portia on Trial (1937)
  Trial of Portia Merriman, The

Portrait in Smoke (1957, Brit.)
  Wicked as They Come
Portrait of a Sinner (1961, Brit,)
  Rough and the Smooth, The
Portrait of Jennie (1948)
  Jennie
Postmark for Danger (1956, Brit.)
  Portrait of Alison
Pot O' Gold (1941)
  Golden Hour, The
Power (1934, Brit.)
  Jew Suss
Power and the Glory, The (1933)
  Power and Glory
Powers Girl, The (1942)
  Hello! Beautiful
Prairie Raiders (1947)
  Forger, The
Prairie Schooners (1940)
  Through the Storm
Prairie Stranger (1941)
  Marked Bullet, The
Prehistoric Women (1967, Brit.)
  Slave Girls
President Vanishes, The (1934)
  Strange Conspiracy
President's Mystery, The (1936)
  One for All
Pride of the Blue Grass (1954)
  Prince of the Blue Grass
Pride of the Bowery (1941)
  Here We Go Again
Pride of the Marines (1945)
  Forever in Love
Prisoner of Corbal (1939, Brit.)
  Marriage of Corbal, The
Prisoner of Japan (1942)
  Last Command, The
Private Number (1936)
  Secret Interlude
Prizefighter and the Lady, The (1933)
  Every Woman's Man
Probation (1932)
  Second Chances
Professional Sweetheart (1933)
  Imaginary Sweetheart
Project M7 (1953, Brit.)
  Net, The
Promise, The (1979)
  Face of a Stranger
Promoter, The (1952, Brit.)
  Card, The
Psycho-Circus (1967, Brit.)
  Circus of Fear
Public Enemy, The (1931)
  Enemies of the Public
Public Enemy's Wife (1936)
  G-Man's Wife
Public Eye, The (1972, Brit.)
  Follow Me
Public Stenographer (1935)
  Private Affairs
Puddin' Head (1941)
  Judy Goes to Town
Purple Heart Diary (1951)
  No Time for Tears
Purple Vigilantes, The (1938)
  Purple Riders, The
Pursuit of the Graf Spee (1957, Brit.)
  Battle of the River Plate, The
Pussycat Alley (1965, Brit.)
  World Ten Times Over, The

Quick on the Trigger (1948)
  Condemned in Error
Quincannon, Frontier Scout (1956)
  Frontier Scout

Race for Life, A (1955, Brit.)
  Mask of Dust
Racers, The (1955)
  Such Men Are Dangerous
Radio Follies (1935, Brit.)
  Radio Parade of 1935
Raiders of Tomahawk Creek (1950)
  Circle of Fear
Randolph Family, The (1945, Brit.)
  Dear Octopus
Rasputin and the Empress (1932)
  Rasputin the Mad Monk
Raton Pass (1951)
  Canyon Pass
Reckless Rider (1931)
  Law Demands, The
Record 413 (1936, Fr.)
  Disque 413
Red Hot Tires (1935)
  Racing Luck

Red Menace, The (1949)
  Enemy Within, The
Red Salute (1935)
  Arms and the Girl
Regal Cavalcade (1935, Brit.)
  Royal Cavalcade
Remarkable Mr. Kipps, The (1942, Brit.)
  Kipps
Renegades of the Rio Grande (1945)
  Bank Robbery
Renegades of the Sage (1949)
  Fort, The
Report to the Commissioner (1975)
  Operation Undercover
Requiem for a Heavyweight (1962)
  Blood Money
Reserved for Ladies (1932, Brit.)
  Service for Ladies
Restless Years, The (1958)
  Wonderful Years, The
Return of Casey Jones, The (1933)
  Train 2419
Return of Daniel Boone, The (1941)
  Mayor's Nest, The
Return of Dracula, The (1958)
  Fantastic Disappearing Man, The
Return of Jack Slade, The (1955)
  Texas Rose
Return of Monte Cristo, The (1946)
  Monte Cristo's
Revenge Return of October, The (1948)
  Date With Destiny, A
Return of Wild Bill, The (1940)
  False Evidence
Return of Wildfire, The (1948)
  Black Stallion
Reunion (1936)
  Hearts in Reunion
Reunion in France (1943)
  Mademoiselle France
Revenge at Monte Carlo (1933)
  Mystery at Monte Carlo
Revenge of the Zombies (1943)
  Corpse Vanished, The
Rhodes (1936, Brit.)
  Rhodes of Africa
Rhythm Round-Up (1945)
  Honest John
Ride a Crooked Mile (1938)
  Escape From Yesterday
Ride Him Cowboy (1932)
  Hawk, The
Riders of the Northland (1942)
  Next in Line
Rider of the Plains (1931)
  Greater Love, The
Riders of the Rio (1931)
  Law of the Rio
Riders of the Santa Fe (1944)
  Mile a Minute
Riders of the Whistling Skull, The (1937)
  Golden Trail, The
Riding High (1943)
  Melody Inn
Riding West (1944)
  Fugitive From Time
Right to Live, The (1935)
  Sacred Flame, The
Ring of Spies (1964, Brit.)
  Ring of Treason
Ring-A-Ding Rhythm (1962, Brit.)
  It's Trad, Dad!
Ringside Maisie (1941)
  Cash and Carry
Rip Roaring Riley (1935)
  Mystery of Diamond Island, The
Risk, The (1961, Brit.)
  Suspect
River Gang (1945)
  Fairy Tale Murder
River of Unrest (1937, Brit.)
  Ourselves Alone
Road Gang (1936)
  Injustice
Roaring Rangers (1946)
  False Hero
Rock Around the World (1957, Brit.)
  Tommy Steele Story, The
Rock Island Trail (1950)
  Transcontinent Express
Rockin' in the Rockies (1945)
  Partners in Fortune
Roger Touhy, Gangster (1944)
  Last Gangster, The
Romance on the High Seas (1948)
  It's Magic
Roogie's Bump (1954)
  Kid Colossus, The
Rookie Cop, The (1939)
  Swift Vengeance

Rookies on Parade (1941)
  Jamboree
Room 43 (1959, Brit.)
  Passport to Shame
Roommates (1962, Brit.)
  Raising the Wind
Rootin' Tootin' Rhythm (1937)
  Rhythm on the Ranch
Rose Bowl (1936)
  O'Riley's Luck
Rosie the Riveter (1944)
  In Rosie's Room
Rough Ridin' Justice (1945)
  Decoy Rough
Riding Ranger (1935)
  Secret Stranger, The
Rough, Tough and Ready (1945)
  Men of the Deep
Royal African Rifles (1953)
  Storm Over Africa
Royal Bed, The (1931)
  Queen's Husband, The
Royal Family of Broadway, The (1930)
  Theatre Royal
Royal Mounted Patrol (1941)
  Giants A'Fire
Royal Scandal, A (1945)
  Czarina
Royal Wedding (1951)
  Wedding Bells
Runaround, The (1931)
  Waiting for the Bride
Runaway Queen, The (1935, Brit.)
  Queen's Affair, The
Rustlers of the Badlands (1945)
  By Whose Hand
RX Murder (1958, Brit.)
  Family Doctor

S.O.S. Tidal Wave (1939)
  Tidal Wave
Sabotage (1939)
  Spies at Work
Sabrina (1954)
  Sabrina Fair
Safari Drums (1953)
  Bomba and the Safari Drums
Safe in Hell (1931)
  Lost Lady, The
Sailor of the King
  Single-Handed
St. Benny the Dip (1951)
  Escape If You Can
St. Louis Kid, The (1934)
  Perfect Weekend, A
Saint's Girl Friday, The (1954, Brit.)
  Saint's Return, The
Salt to the Devil (1949, Brit.)
  Give Us the Day
Salvation Nell (1931)
  Men Women Love
Sandra (1966, Ital.)
  Of a Thousand Delights
Santa Fe Trail, The (1930)
  Law Rides West, The
Santiago (1956)
  Gun Runners, The
Sap from Syracuse, The (1930)
  Sap from Abroad, The
Saraband (1949, Brit.)
  Saraband for Dead Lovers
Saskatchewan (1954)
  O'Rourke of the Royal Mounted
Satan Never Sleeps (1962)
  Devil Never Sleeps, The
Saturday's Hero (1951)
  Idols in the Dust
Scandal Sheet (1931)
  Dark Page, The
Scandal Sheet (1952)
  Dark Page, The
Scandals of Paris (1934, Brit.)
  There Goes Susie
Scareheads (1931)
  Speed Reporter, The
School for Brides (1952, Brit.)
  Two on the Tiles
School for Unclaimed Girls (1973, Brit.)
  Smashing Bird I Used to Know, The
Scotch on the Rocks (1954, Brit.)
  Laxdale Hall
Scotland Yard (1930)
  "Detective Clive" Bart
Scotland Yard Commands (1937, Brit.)
  Lonely Road, The
Scotland Yard Dragnet (1957, Brit.)
  Hypnotist, The

Scotland Yard Inspector (1952, Brit.)
  Lady in the Fog
Scream of Fear (1961, Brit.)
  Taste of Fear
Scudda-Hoo! Scudda-Hay! (1948)
  Summer Lightning
Sea Gypsies, The (1978)
  Shipwreck
Sea Wife (1957, Brit.)
  Sea Wyf and Biscuit
Seaside Swingers (1965, Brit)
  Every Day's a Holiday
Second Best Secret Agent in the Whole Wide World,
  The (1965, Brit.)
  Licensed to Kill
Second Face (1954)
  Double Profile
Second Hand Wife (1933)
  Illegal Divorce, The
Second Woman, The (1950)
  Ellen
Secret Agent (1933, Brit.)
  On Secret Service
Secret Bride, The (1935)
  Concealment
Secret Four, The (1940, Brit.)
  Four Just Men, The
Secret of Monte Cristo, The (1961, Brit.)
  Treasure of Monte Cristo, The
Secret Valley (1937)
  Gangster's Bride, The
Secrets of a Co-Ed (1943)
  Silent Witness
Secrets of a Sorority Girl (1946)
  Secret of Linda Hamilton
Secrets of the Lone Wolf (1941)
  Secrets
See No Evil (1971, Brit.)
  Blind Terror
Senator Was Indiscreet, The (1947)
  Mr. Ashton Was Indiscreet
Seven Days Leave (1930)
  Medals
Sez O'Reilly to MacNab (1938, Brit.)
  Said O'Reilly to MacNab
Shadow, The (1937)
  Circus Shadow, The
Shadow Man (1953, Brit.)
  Streets of Shadows
Shadow of Fear (1956, Brit.)
  Before I Wake
Shanghai Lady (1929)
  Girl from China, The
She Beast, The (1966, Brit./Ital./Yugo.)
  Revenge of the Blood Beast, The
She Couldn't Say No (1954)
  Beautiful But Dangerous
She Couldn't Take It (1935)
  Woman Tamer
She Gods of Shark Reef (1958)
  Shark Reef
She Played with Fire (1957, Brit.)
  Fortune Is a Woman
Shepherd of the Ozarks (1942)
  Susanna
Sherlock Holmes and the Spider Woman (1944)
  Spider Woman
Sherlock Holmes' Fatal Hour (1931, Brit.)
  Sleeping Cardinal, The
She-Wolf of London (1946)
  Curse of the Allenbys, The
Shoot First (1953, Brit.)
  Rough Shoot
Shoot the Piano Player (1962, Fr.)
  Shoot the Pianist
Shoot the Works (1934)
  Thank Your Stars
Show Goes On, The (1938, Brit.)
  Three Maxims, The
Show Them No Mercy (1935)
  Tainted Money
Showtime (1948, Brit.)
  Gaiety George
Side Street (1929)
  Three Brothers
Side Streets (1934)
  Woman in Her Thirties
Sidewalks of London (1940, Brit.)
  St. Martin's Lane
Silent Barriers (1937, Brit.)
  Great Barrier, The
Silk Noose, The (1950, Brit.)
  Noose
Silks and Saddles (1936)
  College Racehorse
Silver City (1951)
  High Vermilion
Silver City Raiders (1943)
  Legal Larceny

Sin of Madelon Claudet, The (1931)
  Lullaby, The
Sing a Jingle (1943)
  Lucky Days
Sing and Swing (1964, Brit.)
  Live It Up
Sing, Dance, Plenty Hot (1940)
  Melody Girl
Sing Me a Love Song (1936)
  Come Up Smiling
Sing Me a Song of Texas (1945)
  Fortune Hunter
Sing Sing Nights (1935)
  Reprieved
Singin' in the Corn (1946)
  Give and Take
Singing on the Trail (1946)
  Lookin' for Someone
Singing Through (1935, Brit.)
  Be Careful, Mr. Smith
Sins of the Children (1930)
  Richest Man in the World, The
Sisters (1973)
  Blood Sisters
Sisters Under the Skin (1934)
  Romantic Age, The
Skin Game, The (1965, Brit.)
  Kil 1
Sky Racket (1937)
  Flight into Danger
Slasher, The (1953, Brit.)
  Cosh Boy
Smart Guy (1943)
  You Can't Beat the Law
Smarty (1934)
  Hit Me Again
Smash-Up, the Story of a Woman (1947)
  Woman Destroyed, A
Smiling Along (1938, Brit.)
  Keep Smiling
Smokey and the Bandit II (1980)
  Smokey and the Bandit Ride Again
Smoking Guns (1934)
  Doomed to Die
Smugglers, The (1948, Brit.)
  Man Within, The
Snafu (1945)
  Welcome Home
Snow Job (1972)
  Ski Raiders, The
Snow White and the Three Stooges (1961)
  Snow White and the Three Clowns
Snuffy Smith, Yard Bird (1942)
  Snuffy Smith
So Goes My Love (1946)
  Genius in the Family, A
So This Is Love (1953)
  Grace Moore Story, The
Sob Sister (1931)
  Blonde Reporter, The
Society Doctor (1935)
  After Eight Hours
Soft Skin, The (1964, Fr.)
  Silken Skin
Soldier, The (1982)
  Codename: The Soldier
Soldier and the Lady, The (1937)
  Michael Strogoff
Soldier's Plaything, A (1931)
  Soldier's Pay
Somewhere in France (1943, Brit.)
  Foreman Went to France, The
Son of Davy Crockett, The (1941)
  Blue Clay
Son of the Plains (1931)
  Vultures of the Law
Song of the Gringo (1936)
  Old Corral, The
Sons of New Mexico (1949)
  Brat, The
Sons of the Desert (1933)
  Fraternally Yours
Sons of the Sea (1941, Brit.)
  Atlantic Ferry
Sophie's Place (1970, Brit.)
  Crooks and Coronets
Sorcerer (1977)
  Wages of Fear
Sorority Girl (1957)
  Bad One, The
Sorority House (1939)
  That Girl from College
Soul of the Slums (1931)
  Samaritan, The
Sound of Fury, The (1950)
  Try and Get Me
South of Death Valley (1950)
  River of Poison
South of Tahiti (1941)
  White Savage

South Sea Sinner (1949)
  East of Java
Southern Yankee, A (1948)
  My Hero
Southside 1-1000 (1950)
  Forgery
Southwest Passage (1954)
  Camels West
Spell of Amy Nugent, The (1945, Brit.)
  Spellbound
Spin a Dark Web (1956, Brit.)
  Soho Incident
Spinout (1966)
  California Holiday
Spirit of Culver (1939)
  Man's Heritage
Spirit of Notre Dame (1931)
  Vigour of Youth
Spitfire (1942, Brit.)
  First of the Few
Spooks Run Wild (1941)
  Ghosts on the Loose
Sport of Kings (1947)
  Heart Royal
Springtime (1948, Brit.)
  Spring Song
Spy Hunt (1950)
  Panther's Moon
Spylarks (1965, Brit.)
  Intelligence Men, The
Squaw Man, The (1931)
  White Man, The
Stage to Tucson (1950)
  Lost Stage Valley
Stairway to Heaven (1946, Brit.)
  Matter of Life and Death, A
Stand By for Action (1942)
  Cargo of Innocents
Stars and Stripes Forever (1952)
  Marching Along
State Department-File 649 (1949)
  Assignment in China
State of the Union (1948)
  World and His Wife, The
State Street Sadie (1928)
  Girl from State Street, The
State's Attorney (1932)
  Cardigan's Last Case
Steel Lady, The (1953)
  Treasure of Kalifa
Sterile Cuckoo, The (1969)
  Pookie
Stick 'Em Up (1950, Brit.)
  Let's Have a Murder
Stop Me Before I Kill (1961, Brit.)
  Full Treatment, The
Story of Alexander Graham Bell, The (1939)
  Modern Miracle, The
Story of Seabiscuit, The (1949)
  Pride of Kentucky
Stowaway Girl (1957, Brit.)
  Manuela
Straight, Place and Show (1938)
  They're Off
Strange Affection (1957, Brit.)
  Scamp, The
Strange Case of Dr. Manning, The (1958, Brit.)
  Morning Call
Strange Holiday (1945)
  Day After Tomorrow, The
Strange Interlude (1932)
  Strange Interval
Strange One, The (1957)
  End as a Man
Stranger from Texas, The (1940)
  Stranger, The
Stranger in Between, The (1952, Brit.)
  Hunted
Stranger on the Prowl (1953, Ital.)
  Encounter
Strangler, The (1941, Brit.)
  East of Piccadilly
Strauss' Great Waltz (1934, Brit.)
  Waltzes from Vienna
Strawberry Roan (1933)
  Flying Fury
Strike! (1934, Brit.)
  Red Ensign
Such a Gorgeous Kid Like Me (1973, Fr.)
  Gorgeous Kid Like Me, A
Sucker Money (1933)
  Victims of the Beyond
Suicide Legion (1940, Brit.)
  Sunset in Vienna
Suicide Squadron (1942, Brit.)
  Dangerous Moonlight
Summer Stock (1950)
  If You Feel Like Singing
Summertime (1955)
  Summer Madness

Sundowners, The (1950)
  Thunder in the Dust
Superman and the Mole-Men (1951)
  Superman and the Strange People
Susan and God (1940)
  Gay Mrs. Trexel, The
Susan Lenox—Her Fall and Rise (1931)
  Rise of Helga, The
Susan Lenox, Her Fall and Rise (1931)
  Rising to Fame
Swamp Water (1941)
  Man Who Came Back, The
Swappers, The (1970, Brit.)
  Wife Swappers, The
Swashbuckler (1976)
  Scarlet Buccaneer, The
Sweet Mama (1930)
  Conflict
Sweetheart of Sigma Chi (1933)
  Girl of My Dreams
Sweetheart of the Campus (1941)
  Broadway Ahead
Sweethearts of the U.S.A. (1944)
  Sweethearts on Parade
Swellhead, The (1930)
  Counted Out
Swing in the Saddle (1944)
  Swing and Sway
Swing it Professor (1937)
  Swing it Buddy
Swing it Soldier (1941)
  Radio Revels of 1942
Swing Shift Maisie (1943)
  Girl in Overalls, The
Swinger's Paradise (1965, Brit.)
  Wonderful Life
Swingin' Maiden, The (1963, Brit.)
  Iron Maiden, The
Sword and the Rose, The (1953)
  When Knighthood Was in Flower
Sword of Lancelot (1963, Brit.)
  Lancelot and Guinevere
Sword of Venus (1953)
  Island of Monte Cristo
Symphony of Six Million (1932)
  Melody of Life

T.R. Baskin (1971)
  Date With a Lonely Girl
Take a Letter, Darling (1942)
  Green-Eyed Woman
Take It from Me (1937, Brit.)
  Transatlantic Trouble
Take Me Out to the Ball Game (1949)
  Everybody's Cheering
Take the Stand (1934)
  Great Radio Mystery, The
Tale of Five Women, A (1952, Brit.)
  Tale of Five Cities, A
Talent Scout (1937)
  Studio Romance
Taming of Dorothy, The (1950, Brit.)
  Her Favourite Husband
Taming the Wild (1937)
  Madcap
Tammy and the Bachelor (1957)
  Tammy
Tank Battalion (1958)
  Valley of Death, The
Tank Commandos (1959)
  Tank Commando
Tank Force (1958, Brit.)
  No Time to Die
Tarzan's Peril (1951)
  Tarzan and the Jungle Queen
Tears for Simon (1957, Brit.)
  Lost
Teenage Bad Girl (1959, Brit.)
  My Teenage Daughter
Teenage Caveman (1958)
  Out of Darkness
Teenage Caveman (1958)
  Prehistoric World Out of the Darkness
Teenagers from Outer Space (1959)
  Gargon Terror, The
Temptation (1930)
  So Like a Woman
Ten Cents a Dance (1945)
  Dancing Ladies
$10 Raise (1935)
  Mr. Faintheart
Tennessee Johnson (1942)
  Man on America's Conscience, The
Terror from the Year 5000 (1958)
  Cage of Doom
Terror From Under the House (1971, Brit.)
  Revenge

Terror House (1943)
  Night Has Eyes, The
Terror on a Train (1953, Brit.)
  Time Bomb
Terror Ship (1954, Brit.)
  Dangerous Voyage
Terror Street (1953)
  Thirty-Six Hours
Terror Trail (1946)
  Hands of Menace
Terrorists, The (1975, Brit.)
  Ransom
Tex Takes a Holiday (1932)
  Dolores the Beautiful
Texan, The (1930)
  Big Race, The
Texas Bad Man, The (1932)
  Defiance
Texas, Brooklyn and Heaven (1948)
  Girl from Texas, The
Texas Dynamo (1950)
  Suspected
Texas Pioneers (1932)
  Blood Brothers, The
Texas Stagecoach (1940)
  Two Roads
Texas to Bataan (1942)
  Long, Long Trail, The
Thank You All Very Much (1969, Brit.)
  Touch of Love, A
Thanks for Listening (1937)
  Partly Confidential
That Forsyte Woman (1949)
  Forsyte Saga, The
That Hamilton Woman (1941)
  Lady Hamilton
That's My Man (1947)
  Will Tomorrow Ever Come?
Their Big Moment (1934)
  Afterwards
Thelma Jordan (1949)
  File on Thelma Jordan, The
There's That Woman Again (1938)
  What a Woman
These Are the Damned (1965, Brit.)
  Damned, The
They Call It Sin (1932)
  Way of Life
They Drive by Night (1940)
  Road to Frisco, The
They Live by Night (1948)
  Twisted Road, The
They Shall Have Music (1939)
  Melody of Youth
Thief (1981)
  Violent Streets
Thieves' Holiday (1946)
  Scandal in Paris, A
Thin Ice (1937)
  Lovely to Look At
Thing, The (1951)
  Thing from Another World, The
Thirteenth Guest, The (1932)
  Lady Beware
-30- (1959)
  Deadline Midnight
This Is My Affair (1937)
  His Affair
This, That and the Other (1970, Brit.)
  Promise of a Bed, A
This Thing Called Love (1940)
  Married But Single
Those Daring Young Men in Their Jaunty Jalopies
(1969, Fr./Brit./Ital.)
  Monte Carlo or Bust
Those Fantastic Flying Fools (1967, Brit.)
  Jules Verne's Rocket to the Moon
Those Were the Days (1940)
  Good Old School Days
Three Cockeyed Sailors (1940, Brit.)
  Sailors Three
Three Daring Daughters (1948)
  Birds and the Bees, The
Three Kids and a Queen (1935)
  Baxter Millions, The
Three Legionnaires (1937)
  Three Crazy Legionnaires
Three Russian Girls (1943)
  She Who Dares
Three Stripes in the Sun (1955)
  Gentle Sergeant, The
Three Texas Steers (1939)
  Danger Rides the Range
Thunder in the Valley (1947)
  Bob, Son of Battle
Thunder on the Hill (1951)
  Bonaventure
Thunder Over Tangier (1957, Brit.)
  Man from Tangier

Thunderhoof (1948)
  Fury
Thundering Trail, The (1951)
  Thunder on the Trail
Tight Little Island (1949, Brit.)
  Whiskey Galore
Timber Terrors (1935)
  Morton of the Mounted
Time Lost and Time Remembered (1966, Brit.)
  I Was Happy Here
Times Square Playboy (1936)
  His Best Man
Tip on a Dead Jockey (1957)
  Time for Action
Tip-Off, The (1931)
  Looking for Trouble
To the Victor (1938, Brit.)
  Owd Bob
Tomahawk (1951)
  Battle of Powder River
Tomahawk Trail (1957)
  Mark of the Apache
Tonight at 8:30 (1952, Brit.)
  Meet Me Tonight
Tonight's the Night (1954, Brit.)
  Happy Ever After
Too Many Husbands (1940)
  My Two Husbands
Too Soon to Love (1960)
  Teenage Lovers
Top Man (1943)
  Man of the Family
Top Secret Affair (1957)
  Their Secret Affair
Topa Topa (1938)
  Children of the Wild
Torch, The (1950)
  Bandit General
Torch Singer (1933)
  Broadway Singer
Torchy Blane in Panama (1938)
  Trouble in Panama
Tornado in the Saddle, A (1942)
  Ambushed
Torpedoed (1939, Brit.)
  Our Fighting Navy
Torso Murder Mystery, The (1940, Brit.)
  Traitor Spy
Touch Me Not (1974, Brit.)
  Hunted, The
Touchdown (1931)
  Playing the Game
Touchdown Army (1938)
  Generals of Tomorrow
Tough Kid (1939)
  Fifth Round, The
Toward the Unknown (1956)
  Brink of Hell
Toy Wife, The (1938)
  Frou Frou
Trail of Terror (1935)
  Gangster's Enemy No. 1
Trail of the Rustlers (1950)
  Lost River
Trail Riders (1942)
  Overland Trail
Trail to Vengeance (1945)
  Vengeance
Trailin' West (1936)
  On Secret Service
Trails of the Wild (1935)
  Arrest at Sundown
Transient Lady (1935)
  False Witness
Trap, The (1947)
  Murder at Malibu Beach
Trap, The (1958)
  Baited Trap, The
Trapped by Television (1936)
  Caught by Television
Treachery on the High Seas (1939, Brit.)
  Not Wanted on Voyage
Trial and Error (1962, Brit.)
  Dock Brief, The
Trigger Tom (1935)
  Dangerous Mission
Triple Deception (1957, Brit.)
  House of Deception
Troopship (1938, Brit.)
  Farewell Again
Trouble Ahead (1936, Brit.)
  Falling in Love
Trouble for Two (1936)
  Suicide Club, The
Trouble in the Sky (1961, Brit.)
  Cone of Silence
True Story of Jesse James, The (1957)
  James Brothers, The
Truth About Murder, The (1946)
  Lie Detector, The

Try and Get Me (1950)
  Sound of Fury, The
Tundra (1936)
  Mighty Tundra, The
Tuxedo Junction (1941)
  Gang Made Good, The
24 Hours (1931)
  Hours Between, The
Twenty-One Days Together (1939, Brit.)
  First and the Last, The
Twilight of Honor (1963)
  Charge is Murder, The
Twilight Women (1953, Brit.)
  Women of Twilight
Two Against the World (1936)
  Case of Mrs. Pembrook, The
Two Dollar Bettor (1951)
  Beginner's Luck
Two English Girls (1972, Fr.)
  Anne and Muriel
Two Girls on Broadway (1940)
  Choose Your Partner
Two Grooms for a Bride (1957)
  Reluctant Bride, The
Two Guys from Milwaukee (1946)
  Royal Flush
Two Guys from Texas (1948)
  Two Texas Knights
Two Senoritas from Chicago (1943)
  Two Senoritas
Two Sinners (1935)
  Two Black Sheep
Two Who Dared (1937, Brit.)
  Woman Alone, A
Two-Fisted Rangers (1939)
  Forestalled
Two-Fisted Stranger (1946)
  High Stakes
Two-Gun Troubadour (1939)
  Lone Troubadour, The

U-Boat Prisoner (1944)
  Dangerous Mists
U-Boat 29 (1939, Brit.)
  Spy in Black, The
Under Secret Orders (1943, Brit.)
  Mademoiselle Docteur
Under the Big Top (1938)
  Circus Comes to Town
Undercover Agent (1939)
  Sweepstake Racketeers
Undercover Agent (1953, Brit.)
  Counterspy
Undercover Maisie (1947)
  Undercover Girl
Undercovers Hero (1975, Brit.)
  Soft Beds and Hard Battles
Underground Guerrillas (1944, Brit.)
  Undercover
Underworld Informers (1965, Brit.)
  Informers, The
Underworld Informers (1965, Brit.)
  Snout, The
Undying Monster, The (1942)
  Hammond Mystery, The
Unexpected Father (1939)
  Sandy Takes a Bow
Unholy Four, The (1954, Brit.)
  Stranger Came Home, The
Unholy Love (1932)
  Deceit
Unidentified Flying Oddball, The (1979, Brit.)
  Spaceman and King Arthur, The
Union Depot (1932)
  Gentleman for a Day
Unknown Blonde (1934)
  Man Who Pawned His Soul, The
Unmarried (1939)
  Night Club Hostess
Up Goes Maisie (1946)
  Up She Goes

Vacation from Marriage (1945, Brit.)
  Perfect Strangers
Valley of Vengeance (1944)
  Vengeance
Vanessa, Her Love Story (1935)
  Vanessa
Vengeance of the West (1942)
  Black Shadow, The
Vice Squad (1953)
  Girl in Room 17, The
Vicious Circle (1948)
  Woman in Brown

Victory (1981)
  Escape to Victory
View from Pompey's Head, The (1955)
  Secret Interlude
Vigilantes Return, The (1947)
  Return of the Vigilantes, The
Violent Men, The (1954)
  Rough Company
Violent Stranger (1957, Brit.)
  Man in the Shadow
Virtuous Husband, The (1931)
  What Wives Don't Want
Virtuous Sin, The (1930)
  Cast Iron
Viva Las Vegas (1964)
  Love in Las Vegas
Voice in the Night (1941, Brit.)
  Freedom Radio
Von Richthofen and Brown (1971)
  Red Baron, The

WAC from Walla Walla, The (1952)
  Army Capers
Waco (1952)
  Outlaw and the Lady, The
Walk in the Shadow (1966, Brit.)
  Life for Ruth
Wanted by Scotland Yard (1939, Brit.)
  Dangerous Fingers
Walk East on Beacon! (1952)
  Crime of the Century, The
War Correspondent (1932)
  Soldiers of Fortune
War of the Colossal Beast (1958)
  Terror Strikes, The
Warriors, The (1955)
  Dark Avenger
Washington Masquerade, The (1932)
  Mad Masquerade
Washington Merry-Go-Round (1932)
  Invisible Power
Washington Story (1952)
  Target for Scandal
Waterfront Women (1952, Brit.)
  Waterfront
Way Back Home (1932)
  Old Greatheart
Way of All Men, The (1930)
  Sin Flood
Way of Lost Souls, The (1929, Brit.)
  Woman He Scorned, The
Way Out, The (1956, Brit.)
  Dial 999
We Went to College (1936)
  Old School Tie, The
Wee Geordie (1956, Brit.)
  Geordie
Week-End Marriage (1932)
  Weekend Lives
Week-End Marriage (1932)
  Working Wives
Weekend Millionaire (1937, Brit.)
  Once in a Million
West of Abilene (1940)
  Showdown, The
West Point Story, The (1950)
  Fine and Dandy
Western Gold (1937)
  Mysterious Stranger, The
Western Limited, The (1932)
  Night Express, The
We've Never Been Licked (1943)
  Texas to Tokyo
What a Man (1930)
  Gentleman Chauffeur, The
What a Woman! (1943)
  Beautiful Cheat, The
What Becomes of the Children? (1935)
  Children of Divorce
What Price Innocence? (1933)
  Shall the Children Pay?
What's Cookin' (1942)
  Wake Up and Dream
When a Feller Needs a Friend (1932)
  When a Fellow Needs a Friend
When London Sleeps (1934, Brit.)
  Sabotage
When Thief Meets Thief (1937, Brit.)
  Jump for Glory
When You're in Love (1937)
  For You Alone
Where Sinners Meet (1934)
  Dover Road, The
Where There's a Will (1937, Brit.)
  Good Morning, Boys
Whirlwind Raiders (1948)
  State Police

Whispering Smith Versus Scotland Yard (1952, Brit.)
  Whispering Smith Hits London
Whistle at Eaton Falls, The (1951)
  Richer than the Earth
White Huntress (1954, Brit.)
  Golden Ivory
White Pongo (1945)
  Adventure Unlimited
White Savage (1943)
  White Captive
Who Is Guilty? (1939, Brit.)
  I Killed the Count
Who Is Killing the Great Chefs of Europe? (1978, US/Ger.)
  Too Many Chefs
Who Killed Doc Robbin? (1948)
  Sinister House
Who Slew Auntie Roo? (1971, Brit.)
  Whoever Slew Auntie Roo?
Whole Town's Talking, The (1935)
  Passport to Fame
Who'll Stop the Rain? (1978)
  Dog Soldiers
Why Bother to Knock (1964, Brit.)
  Don't Bother to Knock
Wicked Wife (1953, Brit.)
  Grand National Night
Widow is Willing, The (1961, Fr./Ital.)
  Violent Summer
Wife Takes a Flyer, The (1942)
  Yank in Dutch, A
Wild Blue Yonder, The (1952)
  Thunder Across the Pacific
Wild Boys of the Road (1933)
  Danger Age
Wild Boys of the Road (1933)
  Dangerous Days
Wild Girl (1932)
  Salomy Jane
Wild Heart, The (1950, US/Brit.)
  Gone to Earth
Wild Weed (1949)
  Devil's Weed, The
Wildfire (1945)
  Wildfire: The Story of a Horse
Will Success Spoil Rock Hunter? (1957)
  Oh! For a Man!
Willie and Joe Back at the Front (1952)
  Willie and Joe in Tokyo
Wings and the Woman (1942, Brit.)
  They Flew Alone Wistful
Widow of Wagon Gap, The (1947)
  Wistful Widow, The
Wives Beware (1933, Brit.)
  Two White Arms
Wolves of the Sea (1938)
  Jungle Island
Wolves of the Underworld (1935, Brit.)
  Puppets of Fate
Woman Between, The (1931)
  Madame Julie
Woman Decides, The (1931, Brit.)
  Woman Between, The
Woman Hungry (1931)
  Challenge, The
Woman I Love, The (1937)
  Woman Between, The
Woman in Chains (1932, Brit.)
  Impassive Footman, The
Woman in Command (1934, Brit.)
  Soldiers of the King
Woman in Hiding (1953, Brit.)
  Mantrap
Woman Racket, The (1930)
  Lights and Shadows
Woman Who Wouldn't Die, The (1965, Brit.)
  Catacombs
Woman's Devotion, A (1956)
  War Shock
Wonderful to Be Young (1962, Brit.)
  Young Ones, The
World Gone Mad, The (1933)
  Public Be Hanged, The
Wrath of Jealousy (1936, Brit.)
  Wedding Group
Wrong Is Right (1982)
  Man with the Deadly Lens, The
Wyoming (1940)
  Bad Man of Wyoming

X Y & Zee (1972, Brit.)
  Zee & Co.

Yank in Indo China, A (1952)
  Hidden Secret
Yank in Korea, A (1951)
  Letter from Korea
Yank in London, A (1946, Brit.)
  I Live in Grosvenor Square
Yank on Burma Road, A (1942)
  China Caravan
Yankee Don (1931)
  Daredevil Dick
Yellow Ticket, The (1931)
  Yellow Passport, The
Yodelin' Kid from Pine Ridge (1937)
  Hero of Pine Ridge, The
Yokel Boy (1942)
  Hitting the Headlines
You Belong to Me (1941)
  Good Morning, Doctor
You Can't Beat the Irish (1952, Brit.)
  Talk of a Million
You May Be Next! (1936)
  Panic on the Air
You Never Can Tell (1951)
  You Never Know
Young America (1942)
  We Humans
Young and Willing (1964, Brit.)
  Wild and the Willing, The
Young Blood (1933)
  Lola
Young Donovan's Kid (1931)
  Donovan's Kid
Young Man with a Horn (1950)
  Young Man of Music
Young Philadelphians, The (1959)
  City Jungle, The
Young, Willing and Eager (1962, Brit.)
  Rag Doll
Your Past Is Showing (1958, Brit.)
  Naked Truth, The
You're in the Army Now (1937, Brit.)
  O.H.M.S.

Zamba (1949)
  Zamba the Gorilla
Zamboanga (1937)
  Fury in Paradise
Zenobia (1939)
  Elephants Never Forget
Zigzag (1970)
  False Witness
Zombies of Mora Tau (1957)
  Dead That Walk, The
Zombies on Broadway (1945)
  Loonies on Broadway

GREAT BRITAIN TITLE (GB) TO MPG TITLE

Below is a listing of Great Britain titles followed by title under which the film is listed in the MPG.

Abbott and Costello Lost in Alaska
  Lost in Alaska (1952)
Abbott and Costello Meet the Ghosts
  Abbott and Costello Meet Frankenstein (1948)
ABC Murders, The
  Alphabet Murders, The (1966)
Above All Laws
  Adventures in Silverado (1948)
Above All Things
  Flood Tide (1957)
Accent on Crime
  Delinquent Daughters (1944)
Accidents Wanted
  Nuisance, The (1933)
Accused
  Mark of the Hawk, The (1958)
Ace in the Hole
  Big Carnival, The (1951)
Ace Lucky
  Feudin' Rhythm (1949)
Adventure Unlimited
  White Pongo (1945)
Affairs of Sally, The
  Fuller Brush Gal, The (1950)
Affairs of Sally, The
  Fuller Brush Girl, The (1950)
After Eight Hours
  Society Doctor (1935)
After Midnight
  Captain Carey, U.S.A. (1950)
After Midnight
  After Midnight with Boston Blackie (1943)
Afterwards
  Their Big Moment (1934)
Air Patrol
  Happy Landing (1934)
Air Patrol, The
  Air Police (1931)
Airport '80: The Concorde
  Concorde—Airport '79, The (1979)
All One Night
  Love Begins at Twenty (1936)
All This and Money Too
  Love Is a Ball (1963)
Amateur Detective
  Irish Luck (1939)
Amazon
  Amazon Quest (1949)
Ambushed
  Tornado in the Saddle, A (1942)
Among Those Present
  Headleys At Home, The (1938)
Amongst the Thieves
  Lone Star Moonlight (1946)
Anatolian Smile, The
  America, America (1963)
Angels and the Pirates
  Angels in the Outfield (1951)
Anne and Muriel
  Two English Girls (1972, Fr.)
Anne of Windy Willows
  Anne of Windy Poplars (1940)
Appointment With a Shadow
  Midnight Story, The (1957)
Appointment with Venus
  Island Rescue (1952, Brit.)
Are These Our Children?
  Age of Consent (1932)
Arms and the Girl
  Red Salute (1935)
Arms and the Woman
  Mr. Winkle Goes to War (1944)
Army Capers
  WAC from Walla Walla, The (1952)
Arouse and Beware
  Man from Dakota, The (1940)
Arrest at Sundown
  Trails of the Wild (1935)
Assassin, The
  Gunfighters (1947)
Assignment in China
  State Department-File 649 (1949)
Assignment Redhead
  Million Dollar Manhunt (1962, Brit.)
At the Villa Rose
  Mystery at the Villa Rose (1930, Brit.)
At the Villa Rose
  House of Mystery (1941, Brit.)
At Twelve Midnight
  Mystic Hour, The (1933)

Atlantic City Romance
  Convention Girl (1934)
Atlantic Ferry
  Sons of the Sea (1941, Brit.)
Attorney's Dilemma, The
  False Faces (1943)
Avenging Stranger, The
  God's Country and the Man (1937)

Baby Be Good
  Brother Rat and a Baby (1940)
Baby Vanishes, The
  Broadway Limited (1941)
Bachelor Bait
  Adventure in Baltimore (1949)
Bachelor Girl Apartment
  Any Wednesday (1966)
Bachelor Girls
  Bachelor's Daughters, The (1946)
Bachelor Knight
  Bachelor and the Bobby-Soxer, The (1947)
Bad Man of Wyoming
  Wyoming (1940)
Bad One, The
  Sorority Girl (1957)
Baited Trap, The
  Trap, The (1958)
Bale Out at 43,000
  Bail Out at 43,000 (1957)
Bandit General
  Torch, The (1950)
Bank Detective, The
  Bank Dick, The (1940)
Bank Robbery
  Renegades of the Rio Grande (1945)
Barbados Quest
  Murder on Approval (1956, Brit.)
Barnacle Bill (1957)
  All at Sea (1958, Brit.)
Baroud
  Love in Morocco (1933, Fr.)
Battle for Anzio, The
  Anzio (1968, Ital.)
Battle of Midway, The
  Midway (1976)
Battle of Powder River
  Tomahawk (1951)
Battle of the River Plate, The
  Pursuit of the Graf Spee (1957, Brit.)
Battle on the Beach
  Battle of Bloody Beach (1961)
Baxter Millions, The
  Three Kids and a Queen (1935)
Baxter Millions, The
  Little Miss Big (1946)
Be Careful, Mr. Smith
  Singing Through (1935, Brit.)
Beautiful But Dangerous
  She Couldn't Say No (1954)
Beautiful Cheat, The
  What a Woman! (1943)
Beauty
  Beauty for Sale (1933)
Before I Wake
  Shadow of Fear (1956, Brit.)
Beginner's Luck
  Two Dollar Bettor (1951)
Behind Closed Doors
  One Mysterious Night (1944)
Behind the Counter
  Daring Daughters (1933)
Behind the Door
  Man with Nine Lives, The (1940)
Behold We Live
  If I Were Free (1933)
Beneath the Starry Skies
  Cowboy Blues (1946)
Bengal Rifles
  Bengal Brigade (1954)
Bequest to the Nation
  Nelson Affair, The (1973, Brit.)
Beyond the Border
  Honor of the Mounted (1932)
Beyond the Law
  Californian, The (1937)
Beyond the River
  Bottom of the Bottle, The (1956)

Beyond the Seven Seas
  Beyond the Pecos (1944)
Big Bankroll, The
  King of the Roaring Twenties—The Story of
    Arnold Rothstein (1961)
Big Deal at Dodge City
  Big Hand for the Little Lady, A (1966)
Big Deal, The
  Blondie's Big Deal (1949)
Big Decision, The
  Basketball Fix, The (1951)
Big Heart, The
  Miracle on 34th Street (1947)
Big Race, The
  Texan, The (1930)
Big Search, The
  East of Kilimanjaro (1962, Brit./Ital.)
Big Story, The
  Appointment With a Shadow (1958)
Big Thrill, The
  High Gear (1933)
Birds and the Bees, The
  Three Daring Daughters (1948)
Birds of Prey
  Perfect Alibi, The (1931, Brit.)
Bishop's Misadventures, The
  Bishop Misbehaves, The (1935)
Black Arrow Strikes, The
  Black Arrow, The (1948)
Black Bart, Highwayman
  Black Bart (1948)
Black Jack
  Captain Black Jack (1951)
Black Shadow, The
  Vengeance of the West (1942)
Black Stallion
  Return of Wildfire, The (1948)
Blackie and the Law
  Boston Blackie and the Law (1946)
Blackie Goes Hollywood
  Boston Blackie Goes Hollywood (1942)
Blackie's Rendezvous
  Boston Blackie's Rendezvous (1945)
Blake Murder Mystery, The
  Haunted House (1940)
Blarney
  Ireland's Border Line (1939, Ireland)
Blarney Stone, The
  Blarney Kiss, The (1933, Brit.)
Blaze of Glory
  Boy from Indiana (1950)
Blind Terror
  See No Evil (1971, Brit.)
Blind Wives
  Lady Surrenders, A (1930)
Blonde Bombshell
  Bombshell (1933)
Blonde Reporter, The
  Sob Sister (1931)
Blood Brothers
  Brothers (1930)
Blood Brothers, The
  Texas Pioneers (1932)
Blood Is My Heritage
  Blood of Dracula (1957)
Blood Money
  Requiem for a Heavyweight (1962)
Blood on My Hands
  Kiss the Blood Off My Hands (1948)
Blood Sisters
  Sisters (1973)
Blue and the Gold, The
  Annapolis Story, An (1955)
Blue Clay
  Son of Davy Crockett, The (1941)
Blue Jeans
  Blue Denim (1959)
Blue Streak, The
  Kentucky Blue Streak (1935)
Bob, Son of Battle
  Thunder in the Valley (1947)
Bold Cavalier, The
  Bold Caballero, The (1937)
Bomba and the African Treasure
  African Treasure (1952)
Bomba and the Elephant Stampede
  Elephant Stampede (1951)
Bomba and the Lion Hunters
  Lion Hunters (1951)
Bomba and the Safari Drums
  Safari Drums (1953)

Bonaventure
  Thunder on the Hill (1951)
Bonds of Honour
  No Ransom (1934)
Booked on Suspicion
  Boston Blackie Booked on Suspicion (1945)
Border Patrol, The
  Lawless Border (1935)
Borderlines
  Caretakers, The (1963)
Boss Said 'No', The
  Blondie Goes to College (1942)
Both Ends of the Candle
  Helen Morgan Story, The (1959)
Boy from Barnardo's, The
  Lord Jeff (1938)
Brat, The
  Sons of New Mexico (1949)
Brave and the Beautiful, The
  Magnificent Matador, The (1955)
Breach of Promise
  Adventure in Blackmail (1943, Brit.)
Breath of Scandal
  His Glorious Night (1929)
Bride Wasn't Willing, The
  Frontier Gal (1945)
Brigham Young
  Brigham Young—Frontiersman (1940)
Brink of Hell
  Toward the Unknown (1956)
Britannia Mews
  Affairs of Adelaide (1949, U.S./Brit.)
Broadway Ahead
  Sweetheart of the Campus (1941)
Broadway Singer
  Torch Singer (1933)
Broken Links
  Leftover Ladies (1931)
Brown on Resolution
  Born for Glory (1935, Brit.)
Build My Gallows High
  Out of the Past (1947)
Bulldog Jack
  Alias Bulldog Drummond (1935, Brit.)
Bundle of Trouble, A
  Blondie's Blessed Event (1942)
Burning Arrows
  Captain John Smith and Pocahontas (1953)
Burnt Offering
  Passport to Hell, A (1932)
Busybody, The
  Kibitzer, The (1929)
By Hook or by Crook
  I Dood It (1943)
By Whose Hand
  Rustlers of the Badlands (1945)

Cage of Doom
  Terror from the Year 5000 (1958)
Calendar, The
  Bachelor's Folly (1931, Brit.)
California Dolls, The
  ...All the Marbles (1981)
California Holiday
  Spinout (1966)
Call Harry Crown
  99 and 44/100% Dead (1974)
Call Me a Cab
  Carry on Cabbie (1963, Brit.)
Call of Justice, The
  Outlaws of the Range (1936)
Call of the Ring, The
  Duke Comes Back, The (1937)
Calling All Ma's
  Biter Bit, The (1937, Brit.)
Calypso
  Manfish (1956)
Camels West
  Southwest Passage (1954)
Campsite Massacre
  Final Terror, The (1983)
Canyon Pass
  Raton Pass (1951)
Cap'n Jericho
  Hell and High Water (1933)
Cape Forlorn
  Love Storm, The (1931, Brit.)
Captain Blood, Fugitive
  Captain Pirate (1952)
Captain Clegg
  Night Creatures (1962, Brit.)
Captain Horatio Hornblower, R.N.
  Captain Horatio Hornblower (1951, Brit.)
Card, The
  Promoter, The (1952, Brit.)
Cardigan's Last Case
  State's Attorney (1932)

Caretaker, The
  Guest, The (1963, Brit.)
Cargo of Innocents
  Stand By for Action (1942)
Caribbean Gold
  Caribbean (1952)
Carlotta, the Mad Empress
  Mad Empress, The (1939)
Carlton Browne of the F.O.
  Man in a Cocked Hat (1960, Brit.)
Carnival Nights
  Carnival (1935)
Carnival of Thieves
  Caper of the Golden Bulls, The (1967)
Carquake
  Cannonball (1976, Hong Kong, U.S.)
Carrington V.C.
  Court Martial (1954, Brit.)
Carry on Henry
  Carry on Henry VIII (1970, Brit.)
Carter Case
  Mr. District Attorney in the Carter Case (1941)
Case of Mrs. Pembrook, The
  Two Against the World (1936)
Case of the Missing Brides, The
  Corpse Vanishes, The (1942)
Case of the Missing Blonde, The
  Lady in the Morgue (1938)
Cash and Carry
  Ringside Maisie (1941)
Casino De Paree
  Go into Your Dance (1935)
Cast Iron
  Virtuous Sin, The (1930)
Catacombs
  Woman Who Wouldn't Die, The (1965, Brit.)
Catch Us If You Can
  Having a Wild Weekend (1965, Brit.)
Caught by Television
  Trapped by Television (1936)
Cave In, The
  Draegerman Courage (1936)
Challenge, The
  Across the Badlands (1950)
Challenge, The
  Woman Hungry (1931)
Charge is Murder, The
  Twilight of Honor (1963)
Charley's American Aunt
  Charley's Aunt (1941)
Charm School, The
  Collegiate (1936)
Cheat, The
  Lone Hand Texan, The (1947)
Cheat's Last Throw, The
  Heading West (1946)
Checkmate
  Desert Horseman, The (1946)
Chicago, Chicago
  Gaily, Gaily (1969)
Chicago Masquerade
  Little Egypt (1951)
Children of Divorce
  What Becomes of the Children? (1935)
Children of the Wild
  Topa Topa (1938)
Chin Chin Chinaman
  Boat from Shanghai (1931, Brit.)
China Caravan
  Yank on Burma Road, A (1942)
Chinese Adventure
  Boston Blackie's Chinese Venture (1949)
Chinese Bungalow, The
  Chinese Den, The (1940, Brit.)
Choose Your Partner
  Two Girls on Broadway (1940)
Circle of Fear
  Raiders of Tomahawk Creek (1950)
Circus Comes to Town
  Under the Big Top (1938)
Circus of Fear
  Psycho-Circus (1967, Brit.)
Circus Shadow, The
  Shadow, The (1937)
Cisco Kid in Old New Mexico, The
  In Old New Mexico (1945)
Citadel of Crime
  Man Betrayed, A (1941)
City is Dark, The
  Crime Wave (1954)
City Jungle, The
  Young Philadelphians, The (1959)
City of Song
  Farewell to Love (1931, Brit.)
City of the Dead, The
  Horror Hotel (1960, Brit.)
Clash by Night
  Escape by Night (1965, Brit.)
Claw Strikes, The
  Landrush (1946)

Clean Slate
  Coup de Torchon (1981, Fr.)
Clipped Wings
  Hello Sister (1930)
Cloak Without Dagger
  Operation Conspiracy (1957, Brit.)
Clock Strikes Eight, The
  College Scandal (1935)
Close Call, A
  Close Call for Ellery Queen, A (1942)
Close Harmony
  Cowboy Canteen (1944)
Clue, The
  Outcast of Black Mesa (1950)
Codename: The Soldier
  Soldier, The (1982)
College Racehorse
  Silks and Saddles (1936)
Come Back to Me
  Doll Face (1945)
Come Up Smiling
  Sing Me a Love Song (1936)
Company of Cowards
  Advance to the Rear (1964)
Compromising Daphne
  Compromised (1931, Brit.)
Concealment
  Secret Bride, The (1935)
Concerto
  I've Always Loved You (1946)
Condemned in Error
  Quick on the Trigger (1948)
Cone of Silence
  Trouble in the Sky (1961, Brit.)
Confession
  Deadliest Sin, The (1956, Brit.)
Confessions
  Confessions of Boston Blackie (1942)
Confessions of a Counterspy
  Man on a String (1960)
Confidential Report
  Mr. Arkadin (1962, Brit./Fr./Span.)
Conflict
  Sweet Mama (1930)
Conflict of Wings
  Fuss Over Feathers (1954, Brit.)
Conga Swing
  Blondie Goes Latin (1941)
Contact Man, The
  Alias Nick Beal (1949)
Contraband
  Blackout (1940, Brit.)
Corky
  Corky of Gasoline Alley (1951)
Corpse, The
  Crucible of Horror (1971, Brit.)
Corpse Vanished, The
  Revenge of the Zombies (1943)
Cosh Boy
  Slasher, The (1953, Brit.)
Costello Murder Case, The
  Costello Case, The (1930)
Cottage on Dartmoor, A
  Escaped from Dartmoor (1930, Brit.)
Cottage to Let
  Bombsight Stolen (1941, Brit.)
Cougar
  Cougar, The King Killer (1933)
Couldn't Possibly Happen
  Men With Steel Faces (1940)
Counted Out
  Swellhead, The (1930)
Counterblast
  Devil's Plot, The (1948, Brit.)
Counterspy
  Undercover Agent (1953, Brit.)
Country Bumpkin
  All American Chump (1936)
Country Dance
  Brotherly Love (1970)
Courageous
  Lost Lady, A (1934)
Courtneys of Curzon Street, The
  Courtney Affair, The (1947, Brit.)
Crackerjack
  Man with 100 Faces, The (1938, Brit.)
Crazy to Kill
  Dr. Gillespie's Criminal Case (1943)
Creeping Shadows
  Limping Man, The (1939)
Crime in the Clouds
  Fly-Away Baby (1937)
Crime of the Century, The
  Walk East on Beacon! (1952)
Crime Smasher
  Cosmo Jones—Crime Smasher (1943)
Crime's End
  My Son Is Guilty (1939)
Crime's Highway
  Desert Justice (1936)

Criminal, The
  Concrete Jungle, The (1962, Brit.)
Crooked but Dumb
  Amateur Crook (1937)
Crooked Ring
  Double Jeopardy (1955)
Crooked Way, The
  Gang Bullets (1938)
Crooks and Coronets
  Sophie's Place (1970, Brit.)
Crooks in Clover
  Penthouse (1933)
Crosby Murder Case, The
  Crosby Case, The (1934)
Cruising Casanovas
  Gobs and Gals (1952)
Cupid in the Rough
  Aggie Appleby, Maker of Men (1933)
Curse of the Allenbys, The
  She-Wolf of London (1946)
Cutter's Way
  Cutter and Bone (1981)
Cynthia's Secret
  Dark Delusion (1947)
Czarina
  Royal Scandal, A (1945)

Daisy Goes Hollywood
  Hollywood and Vine (1945)
Damned, The
  These Are the Damned (1965, Brit.)
Dance of the Vampires
  Fearless Vampire Killers, or Pardon Me but Your
  Teeth Are in my Neck, The(1967)
Dancing Feet
  Broadway Hoofer, The (1929)
Dancing Fool, The
  Harold Teen (1934)
Dancing Ladies
  Ten Cents a Dance (1945)
Dancing Partner, The
  Just a Gigolo (1931)
Danger Age
  Wild Boys of the Road (1933)
Danger Rides the Range
  Three Texas Steers (1939)
Danger Within
  Breakout (1960, Brit.)
Dangerous Age, A
  Beloved Brat (1938)
Dangerous Days
  Wild Boys of the Road (1933)
Dangerous Enemy
  Fighting Rookie, The (1934)
Dangerous Fingers
  Wanted by Scotland Yard (1939, Brit.)
Dangerous Ground
  Escapade (1932)
Dangerous Inheritance
  Girls' School (1950)
Dangerous Mission
  Trigger Tom (1935)
Dangerous Mists
  U-Boat Prisoner (1944)
Dangerous Moonlight
  Suicide Squadron (1942, Brit.)
Dangerous Voyage
  Terror Ship (1954, Brit.)
Daredevil Dick
  Yankee Don (1931)
Dark Avenger
  Warriors, The (1955)
Dark Eyes of London
  Human Monster, The (1940, Brit.)
Dark Page, The
  Scandal Sheet (1931)
Dark Page, The
  Scandal Sheet (1952)
Dark, The
  Horror House (1970, Brit.)
Date With a Lonely Girl
  T.R. Baskin (1971)
Date with an Angel, A
  It Comes Up Love (1942)
Date With Destiny, A
  Return of October, The (1948)
Date With Destiny, A
  Mad Doctor, The (1941)
Daughter of Luxury
  Five and Ten (1931)
Daughter of the Orient
  Daughter of Shanghai (1937)
Dawn of Life, The
  Life Begins (1932)
Dawn, The
  Dawn Over Ireland (1938, Irish)

Day After Tomorrow, The
  Strange Holiday (1945)
Day They Gave Babies Away, The
  All Mine to Give (1957)
Day Will Dawn, The
  Avengers, The (1942, Brit.)
Dead Image
  Dead Ringer (1964)
Dead That Walk, The
  Zombies of Mora Tau (1957)
Deadline
  Deadline U.S.A. (1952)
Deadline Midnight
  -30- (1959)
Dear Octopus
  Randolph Family, The (1945, Brit.)
Death on the Set
  Murder on the Set (1936, Brit.)
Death Ray, The
  Murder at Dawn (1932)
Deceit
  Unholy Love (1932)
Decoy
  Rough Ridin' Justice (1945)
Defiance
  Texas Bad Man, The (1932)
Demi-Paradise, The
  Adventure for Two (1945)
Demons of the Swamp
  Attack of the Giant Leeches (1958)
Denny of the Railroad
  Dynamite Denny (1932)
Dentist on the Job
  Get On with It (1963, Brit.)
Derby Day
  Four Against Fate (1952, Brit.)
Desert Patrol
  El Alamein (1953)
Desperate Chance, A
  Desperate Chance for Ellery Queen, A (1942)
Desperate Men
  El Dorado Pass (1948)
Destiny Danger
  Eyes of the Jungle (1953)
Detective Clive
  Scotland Yard (1930)
Determination
  Final Edition, The (1932)
Devil Never Sleeps, The
  Satan Never Sleeps (1962)
Devil on Wheels
  Indianapolis Speedway (1939)
Devil Rides Out, The
  Devil's Bride, The (1968, Brit.)
Devil Takes the Count, The
  Devil is a Sissy, The (1936)
Devil's Imposter, The
  Pope Joan (1972, Brit.)
Devil's Point
  Devil's Harbor (1954, Brit.)
Devil's Price, The
  Lone Star Vigilantes (1941)
Devil's Weed, The
  Wild Weed (1949)
Devils on Wheels
  Burn-'Em-Up Barnes (1934)
Dial 999
  Way Out, The (1956, Brit.)
Diamond Cut Diamond
  Blame the Woman (1932, Brit.)
Diamond, The
  Diamond Wizard, The (1954, Brit.)
Diary of a Bride
  I, Jane Doe (1948)
Dick Tracy's Amazing Adventure
  Dick Tracy Meets Gruesome (1947)
Dick Turpin's Ride
  Lady and the Bandit, The (1951)
Disc Jockey Jamboree
  Jamboree (1957)
Disque 413
  Record 413 (1936, Fr.)
Dividing Line, The
  Lawless, The (1950)
Divine Love
  No Greater Love (1932)
Dock Brief, The
  Trial and Error (1962, Brit.)
Doctor and the Debutante, The
  Dr. Kildare's Victory (1941)
Doctor in Clover
  Carnaby, M.D. (1967, Brit.)
Doctor's Alibi
  Medico of Painted Springs, The (1941)
Doctor's Courage, The
  Crime Doctor's Courage, The (1945)
Doctor's Gamble, The
  Crime Doctor's Gamble, The (1947)
Doctor's Sacrifice, The
  Klondike (1932)

Doctor's Warning, The
  Crime Doctor's Warning, The (1945)
Dog Soldiers
  Who'll Stop the Rain? (1978)
Dolores the Beautiful
  Tex Takes a Holiday (1932)
Domino Killings, The
  Domino Principle, The (1977)
Don't Bother to Knock
  Why Bother to Knock (1964, Brit.)
Don't Pull Your Punches
  Kid Comes Back, The (1937)
Donovan's Kid
  Young Donovan's Kid (1931)
Doomed to Die
  Smoking Guns (1934)
Door with Seven Locks, The
  Chamber of Horrors, The (1941, Brit.)
Doppelganger
  Journey to the Far Side of the Sun (1969, Brit.)
Double Alibi, The
  Law and Order (1943)
Double Daring
  Fixer Dugan (1939)
Double Exposure
  Corruption (1933)
Double Profile
  Second Face (1954)
Double Punch, The
  Down Rio Grande Way (1942)
Dove, The
  Girl of the Rio (1932)
Dover Road, The
  Where Sinners Meet (1934)
Down Cuban Way
  Cuban Pete (1946)
Down Went McGinty
  Great McGinty, The (1940)
Downbeat
  Daddy O (1959)
Dracula
  Horror of Dracula, The (1958, Brit.)
Drake of England
  Drake the Pirate (1935, Brit.)
Dream Mother
  Midnight Lady (1932)
Dream of Life
  Life Begins (1932)
Dreyfus
  Dreyfus Case, The (1931, Brit.)
Drum Crazy
  Gene Krupa Story, The (1959)
Drum, The
  Drums (1938, Brit.)
Drums Along the Amazon
  Angel on the Amazon (1948)
Du Barry
  Du Barry, Woman of Passion (1930)
Dusty Ermine
  Hideout in the Alps (1938, Brit.)
Dynamite Man from Glory Jail
  Fools' Parade (1971)

Eagles of the Fleet
  Flat Top (1952)
East of Fifth Avenue
  Obey the Law (1933)
East of Java
  South Sea Sinner (1949)
East of Piccadilly
  Strangler, The (1941, Brit.)
East of the Rising Sun
  Malaya (1949)
Easy Money
  Big Money (1930)
Eight on the Run
  Eight on the Lam (1967)
Electric Man, The
  Man Made Monster (1941)
Elephants Never Forget
  Zenobia (1939)
Ellen
  Second Woman, The (1950)
Elusive Pimpernel, The
  Fighting Pimpernel, The (1950, Brit.)
Embassy Girl
  Hat Check Girl (1932)
Emergency Call
  Hundred Hour Hunt (1953, Brit.)
Emil and the Detectives
  Emil (1938, Brit.)
Encounter
  Stranger on the Prowl (1953, Ital.)
End as a Man
  Strange One, The (1957)
End of the Rainbow
  Northwest Outpost (1947)

Enemies of Society
    Big Brain, The (1933)
Enemies of the Public
    Public Enemy, The (1931)
Enemy Agent
    British Intelligence (1940)
Enemy Within, The
    Red Menace, The (1949)
English without Tears
    Her Man Gilbey (1949, Brit.)
Englishman's Home, An
    Mad Men of Europe (1940, Brit.)
Escape from the Dark
    Littlest Horse Thieves, The (1977)
Escape From Yesterday
    Ride a Crooked Mile (1938)
Escape If You Can
    St. Benny the Dip (1951)
Escape to Happiness
    Intermezzo (1939)
Escape to Victory
    Victory (1981)
Escapement
    Electronic Monster, The (1960, Brit.)
Eureka Stockade
    Massacre Hill (1949, Brit.)
Eventful Journey
    Hitch Hike Lady (1936)
Every Day's a Holiday
    Seaside Swingers (1965, Brit.)
Every Minute Counts
    Count the Hours (1953)
Every Other Inch a Lady
    Dancing Co-Ed (1939)
Every Woman's Man
    Prizefighter and the Lady, The (1933)
Everybody's Cheering
    Take Me Out to the Ball Game (1949)
Everything Happens to Us
    Hi'Ya, Chum (1943)
Evidence in Camera
    Headline Shooter (1933)
Evil Force, The
    4D Man (1959)
Evils of Chinatown
    Confessions of an Opium Eater (1962)
Eyes of the Skies
    Mission Over Korea (1953)

Face in the Night
    Menace in the Night (1958, Brit.)
Face of a Stranger
    Promise, The (1979)
Face of Eve, The
    Eve (1968, Brit./Span.)
Face the Music
    Black Glove, The (1954, Brit.)
Fairy Tale Murder
    River Gang (1945)
Faithful Heart, The
    Faithful Hearts (1933, Brit.)
Fall of Lola Montes, The
    Lola Montes (1955, Fr./Ger.)
Falling in Love
    Trouble Ahead (1936, Brit.)
Falling Stones
    Overland to Deadwood (1942)
False Clues
    North of the Rockies (1942)
False Evidence
    Return of Wild Bill, The (1940)
False Faces
    Let 'Em Have It (1935)
False Hero
    Roaring Rangers (1946)
False Idol, The
    False Madonna, The (1931)
False News
    Barbed Wire (1952)
False Witness
    Zigzag (1970)
False Witness
    Transient Lady (1935)
False Witness
    Arkansas Judge (1941)
Family Doctor
    RX Murder (1958, Brit.)
Family Story, A
    Mom and Dad (1944)
Fanatic
    Die, Die My Darling (1965, Brit.)
Fanny by Gaslight
    Man of Evil (1948, Brit.)
Fantastic Disappearing Man, The
    Return of Dracula, The (1958)
Farewell Again
    Troopship (1938, Brit.)

Farewell, My Lovely
    Murder My Sweet (1931)
Farewell Party
    Morals for Women (1931)
Farewell to Fame
    Let's Go Collegiate (1941)
Farmyard Follies
    Hoosier Holiday (1943)
Faro Jack
    Outlaws of the Panhandle (1941)
Fast Play
    Campus Confessions (1938)
Father Brown
    Detective, The (1954, Brit.)
Fearless Deputy, The
    Lariats and Six Shooters (1931)
Female Correspondent
    Adventure in Washington (1941)
Feminine Touch
    Dude Wrangler, The (1930)
Feminine Touch, The
    Gentle Touch (1956, Brit.)
Fifth Chair, The
    It's in the Bag (1945)
Fifth Round, The
    Tough Kid (1939)
Fighting Chump, The
    Dynamite Delany (1938)
Fighting Marshal
    Cherokee Strip (1940)
Fighting Seventh, The
    Little Big Horn (1951)
Fighting Test, The
    Cheyenne Kid, The (1931)
File on Thelma Jordan, The
    Thelma Jordan (1949)
Fine and Dandy
    West Point Story, The (1950)
Fire Fighters
    Arson Racket Squad (1938)
First and the Last, The
    Twenty-One Days Together (1939, Brit.)
First Gentleman, The
    Affairs of a Rogue, The (1949, Brit.)
First Great Train Robbery, The
    Great Train Robbery, The (1979, Brit.)
First of the Few
    Spitfire (1942, Brit.)
First Rebel, The
    Allegheny Uprising (1939)
Fitzwilly Strikes Back
    Fitzwilly (1967)
Five Days
    Paid to Kill (1954, Brit.)
Flaming Torch, The
    Bob Mathias Story, The (1954)
Flesh and the Fiends, The
    Mania (1961, Brit.)
Flight from Justice
    Federal Man Hunt (1938)
Flight into Danger
    Sky Racket (1937)
Flying Circus, The
    Flying Devils (1933)
Flying Fury
    Strawberry Roan (1933)
Flying Scot, The
    Mailbag Robbery (1957, Brit.)
Foget Me Not
    Forever Yours (1937, Brit.)
Follow Me
    Public Eye, The (1972, Brit.)
Football Coach
    College Coach (1933)
Footlights and Shadows
    Hitch Hike to Heaven (1935)
For Me and My Girl
    For Me and My Gal (1942
For You Alone
    When You're in Love (1937)
Forbidden Adventure
    Newly Rich (1931)
Foreman Went to France, The
    Somewhere in France (1943, Brit.)
Forestalled
    Two-Fisted Rangers (1939)
Forever England
    Born for Glory (1935, Brit.)
Forever in Love
    Pride of the Marines (1945)
Forged Will, The
    Blazing Trail, The (1949)
Forger, The
    Prairie Raiders (1947)
Forgery
    Southside 1-1000 (1950)
Forgotten Women
    Mad Parade, The (1931)
Forsyte Saga, The
    That Forsyte Woman (1949)

Fort, The
    Renegades of the Sage (1949)
Fortune Hunter
    Sing Me a Song of Texas (1945)
Fortune Hunter, The
    Outcast, The (1954)
Fortune Is a Woman
    She Played with Fire (1957, Brit.)
Forward March
    Dough Boys (1930)
Four Just Men, The
    Secret Four, The (1940, Brit.)
Fra Diavolo
    Devil's Brother, The (1933)
Frank James Rides Again
    Gunfire (1950)
Fraternally Yours
    Sons of the Desert (1933)
Free to Live
    Holiday (1938)
Freedom Radio
    Voice in the Night (1941, Brit.)
Frightened City
    Killer That Stalked New York, The (1950)
Frontier Fury
    Lone Rider in Frontier Fury (1941)
Frontier Scout
    Quincannon, Frontier Scout (1956)
Frou Frou
    Toy Wife, The (1938)
Fugitive From Time
    Riding West (1944)
Fugitive Lady
    Female Fugitive (1938)
Full House
    O'Henry's Full House (1952)
Full Treatment, The
    Stop Me Before I Kill (1961, Brit.)
Funny Face
    Bright Lights (1935)
Fury
    Thunderhoof (1948)
Fury in Paradise
    Zamboanga (1937)
Fury Unleashed
    Hot Rod Gang (1958)

G-Man's Wife
    Public Enemy's Wife (1936)
Gaiety George
    Showtime (1948, Brit.)
Gamblers, The
    Judge, The (1948)
Gang Made Good, The
    Tuxedo Junction (1941)
Gang Show, The
    Gang, The (1938, Brit.)
Gangster's Bride, The
    Secret Valley (1937)
Gangster's Enemy No. 1
    Trail of Terror (1935)
Gaol Birds
    Pardon Us (1931)
Gargon Terror, The
    Teenagers from Outer Space (1959)
Gaunt Stranger, The
    Phantom Strikes, The (1939, Brit.)
Gay City, The
    Las Vegas Nights (1941)
Gay Divorce, The
    Gay Divorcee, The (1934)
Gay Imposters
    Gold Diggers in Paris (1938)
Gay Lady, The
    Lady Tubbs (1935)
Gay Mrs. Trexel, The
    Susan and God (1940)
Gay Nineties, The
    Floradora Girl, The (1930)
Generals of Tomorrow
    Touchdown Army (1938)
Genius in the Family, A
    So Goes My Love (1946)
Gentle Sergeant, The
    Three Stripes in the Sun (1955)
Gentleman Chauffeur, The
    What a Man (1930)
Gentleman for a Day
    Union Depot (1932)
Gentleman of Venture
    It Happened to One Man (1941, Brit.)
Gentlemen of the Navy
    Annapolis Farewell (1935)
Geordie
    Wee Geordie (1956, Brit.)
Georgia's Friends
    Four Friends (1981)

Gestapo
  Night Train (1940, Brit.)
Get that Girl
  Caryl of the Mountains (1936)
Get that Girl
  Caryl of the Mountains (1936)
Ghost of John Holling, The
  Mystery Liner (1934)
Ghosts in the Night
  Ghosts on the Loose (1943)
Ghosts on the Loose
  Spooks Run Wild (1941)
Giants A'Fire
  Royal Mounted Patrol (1941)
Gibraltar Adventure
  Clue of the Missing Ape, The (1953, Brit.)
Gibraltar Adventure
  Clue of the Missing Ape, The (1953, Brit.)
Gideon's Day
  Gideon of Scotland Yard (1959, Brit.)
Gift Horse, The
  Glory at Sea (1952, Brit.)
Gipsy Blood
  Carmen (1931, Brit.)
Gipsy Blood
  Carmen (1931, Brit.)
Girl for Joe, A
  Force of Arms (1951)
Girl from China, The
  Shanghai Lady (1929)
Girl From Ireland, The
  Kathleen Mavourneen (1930)
Girl From Mexico, The
  Mexicali Rose (1929)
Girl from State Street, The
  State Street Sadie (1928)
Girl from Texas, The
  Texas, Brooklyn and Heaven (1948)
Girl I Made, The
  Made on Broadway (1933)
Girl in Overalls, The
  Swing Shift Maisie (1943)
Girl in Pawn
  Little Miss Marker (1934)
Girl in Room 17, The
  Vice Squad (1953)
Girl in the Headlines
  Model Murder Case, The (1964, Brit.)
Girl of My Dreams
  Sweetheart of Sigma Chi (1933)
Girl of the Year
  Petty Girl, The (1950)
Girls He Left Behind, The
  Gang's All Here, The (1943)
Girls in Action
  Operation Dames (1959)
Girls Never Tell
  Her First Romance (1951)
Give and Take
  Singin' in the Corn (1946)
Give Me Your Heart
  Loves of Madame DuBarry, The (1938, Brit.)
Give Us the Day
  Salt to the Devil (1949, Brit.)
Glamour Boy
  Millionaire Playboy (1940)
Glorious Sacrifice, The
  Glory Trail, The (1936)
God Gave Him a Dog
  Biscuit Eater, The (1940)
Godzilla
  Godzilla, King of the Monsters (1956, Jap.)
Going Gay
  Kiss Me Goodbye (1935, Brit.)
Going to Town
  Ma and Pa Kettle Go to Town (1950)
Golden Arrow
  Gay Adventure, The (1953, Brit.)
Golden Disc, The
  Inbetween Age, The (1958, Brit.)
Golden Gloves
  Ex-Champ (1939)
Golden Hour, The
  Pot O' Gold (1941)
Golden Ivory
  White Huntress (1954, Brit.)
Golden Lady
  Fighting Frontiersman, The (1946)
Golden Trail, The
  Riders of the Whistling Skull, The (1937)
Gone to Earth
  Wild Heart, The (1950, US/Brit.)
Good Morning, Boys
  Where There's a Will (1937, Brit.)
Good Morning, Doctor
  You Belong to Me (1941)
Good Old School Days
  Those Were the Days (1940)
Gorgeous Kid Like Me, A
  Such a Gorgeous Kid Like Me (1973, Fr.)

Grace Moore Story, The
  So This Is Love (1953)
Grand National Night
  Wicked Wife (1953, Brit.)
Great Awakening, The
  New Wine (1941)
Great Barrier, The
  Silent Barriers (1937, Brit.)
Great Decision, The
  Men Of America (1933)
Great Manhunt, The
  Doolins of Oklahoma, The (1949)
Great Radio Mystery, The
  Take the Stand (1934)
Great Schnozzle, The
  Palooka (1934)
Greater Love, The
  Rider of the Plains (1931)
Greek Street
  Latin Love (1930, Brit.)
Green-Eyed Woman
  Take a Letter, Darling (1942)
Greengage Summer, The
  Loss of Innocence (1961, Brit.)
Grip of the Strangler
  Haunted Strangler, The (1958, Brit.)
Guest House, The
  In Old Cheyenne (1931)
Guilty as Charged
  Guilty as Hell (1932)
Guinea Pig, The
  Outsider, The (1949, Brit.)
Gun Runners, The
  Santiago (1956)
Gunpoint
  At Gunpoint (1955)
Guns of Wyoming
  Cattle King (1963)
Guns of Wyoming
  Cattle King (1963)
Guv'Nor, The
  Mister Hobo (1936, Brit.)

Hallelujah I'm a Tramp
  Hallelujah, I'm a Bum (1933)
Hammond Mystery, The
  Undying Monster, The (1942)
Handful of Clouds, A
  Doorway to Hell (1930)
Hands of Menace
  Terror Trail (1946)
Hands of Orlac
  Mad Love (1935)
Happy Ever After
  Tonight's the Night (1954, Brit.)
Happy Family, The
  Merry Frinks, The (1934)
Happy Family, The
  Mr. Lord Says No (1952, Brit.)
Happy Landing
  Flying High (1931)
Hardcore Life, The
  Hardcore (1979)
Harem Holiday
  Harem Scarum (1965)
Harmony Parade
  Pigskin Parade (1936)
Harry Black
  Harry Black and the Tiger (1958, Brit.)
Harvest Days
  Mountain Rhythm (1942)
Hats Off to Rhythm
  Earl Carroll Sketchbook (1946)
Haunted and the Hunted, The
  Dementia 13 (1963)
Haunted Honeymoon
  Busman's Honeymoon (1940, Brit.)
Haunted House of Horror, The
  Horror House (1970, Brit.)
Hawaiian Nights
  Down to Their Last Yacht (1934)
Hawk, The
  Ride Him Cowboy (1932)
He Knew Too Much
  Devil's Mate (1933)
Heads We Go
  Charming Deceiver, The (1933, Brit.)
Heart Royal
  Sport of Kings (1947)
Hearts in Reunion
  Reunion (1936)
Hearts in Springtime
  Glamour Boy (1941)
Heaven Bound
  Big Time or Bust (1933)
Heaven Fell That Night
  Night Heaven Fell, The (1958, Fr.)

Heist, The
  $ (Dollars) (1971)
Held for Murder
  Her Mad Night (1932)
Hell Bent for Glory
  Lafayette Escadrille (1957)
Hell's Cargo
  Dangerous Cargo (1939, Brit.)
Hello! Beautiful
  Powers Girl, The (1942)
Henpecked
  Blondie in Society (1941)
Henry Gets Glamour
  Henry Aldrich Gets Glamour (1943)
Henry Haunts a House
  Henry Aldrich Haunts a House (1943)
Henry Plays Cupid
  Henry Aldrich Plays Cupid (1943)
Henry Swings It
  Henry Aldrich Swings It (1943)
Henry's Little Secret
  Henry Aldrich's Little Secret (1944)
Henry—Boy Scout
  Henry Aldrich, Boy Scout (1944)
Her Child
  Her Unborn Child (1929)
Her Dilemna
  Confessions of a Co-Ed (1931)
Her Favourite Husband
  Taming of Dorothy, The (1950, Brit.)
Her Reputation
  Broadway Bad (1933)
Her Sacrifice
  Blind Date (1934)
Here I Come
  Harvard, Here I Come (1941)
Here We Go Again
  Pride of the Bowery (1941)
Hero of Pine Ridge, The
  Yodelin' Kid from Pine Ridge (1937)
Hidden Secret
  Yank in Indo China, A (1952)
High Bright Sun, The
  McGuire, Go Home! (1966, Brit.)
High Road, The
  Lady of Scandal, The (1930)
High Stakes
  Two-Fisted Stranger (1946)
High Venture
  Passage West (1951)
High Vermilion
  Silver City (1951)
High Window, The
  Brasher Doubloon, The (1947)
Highway to Freedom
  Joe Smith, American (1942)
Hill in Korea, A
  Hell in Korea (1956, Brit.)
Hills of the Brave
  Palomino, The (1950)
Hindle Wakes
  Holiday Week (1952, Brit.)
His Affair
  This Is My Affair (1937)
His Best Man
  Times Square Playboy (1936)
His Ferocious Pal
  Ferocious Pal, The (1934)
His Last Adventure
  Battling Buckaroo (1934)
His Lordship
  Man of Affairs (1937, Brit.)
His Majesty Bunker Bean
  Bunker Bean (1936)
His Other Woman
  Desk Set (1957)
Hit Me Again
  Smarty (1934)
Hitting the Headlines
  Yokel Boy (1942)
Hitting the Jackpot
  Blondie Hits the Jackpot (1949)
HMS Defiant
  Damn the Defiant (1962, Brit.)
Hold That Girl
  Hold That Co-ed (1938)
Home at Seven
  Murder on Monday (1953, Brit.)
Honest John
  Rhythm Round-Up (1945)
Honeymoon Adventure, A
  Footsteps in the Night (1932, Brit.)
Honorable Mr. Wong, The
  Hatchet Man, The (1932)
Honorary Consul, The
  Beyond the Limit (1983)
Honourable Mr. Wong, The
  Hatchet Man, The (1932)
Hoppity Goes to Town
  Mr. Bug Goes to Town (1941)

Hot Enough for June
Agent 8-3/4 (1963, Brit.)
Hot One, The
Corvette Summer (1978)
Hot Pearls
Blonde from Singapore, The (1941)
Hot Spot
I Wake Up Screaming (1942)
Hounded
Johnny Allegro (1949)
Hounds of Zaroff, The
Most Dangerous Game, The (1932)
Hours Between, The
24 Hours (1931)
House Across the Lake, The
Heatwave (1954, Brit.)
House in the Square, The
I'll Never Forget You (1951)
House of Chance
Cheating Blondes (1933)
House of Connelly
Carolina (1934)
House of Deception
Triple Deception (1957, Brit.)
House of Doom, The
Black Cat, The (1934)
House of Evil
House on Sorority Row, The (1983)
House of Fate
Muss 'Em Up (1936)
House of Settlement
Mr. Soft Touch (1949)
House of Tao Ling, The
Dangerous Millions (1946)
House of the Arrow
Castle of Crimes (1941, Brit.)
How to Rob a Bank
Nice Little Bank that Should Be Robbed, A (1958)
How to Steal a Diamond in Four Easy Lessons
Hot Rock, The (1972)
Human Sabotage
Murder in the Big House (1942)
Humphrey Takes a Chance
Joe Palooka in Humphrey Takes a Chance (1950)
Hunted
Stranger in Between, The (1952, Brit.)
Hunted, The
Touch Me Not (1974, Brit.)
Husbands or Lovers
Honeymoon in Bali (1939)
Hypnotist, The
Scotland Yard Dragnet (1957, Brit.)

I Am a Fugitive from the Chain Gang
I Am a Fugitive from a Chain Gang (1932)
I Give My Heart
Loves of Madame DuBarry, The (1938, Brit.)
I Killed the Count
Who Is Guilty? (1939, Brit.)
I Live for You
I Live for Love (1945)
I Live in Grosvenor Square
Yank in London, A (1946, Brit.)
I Shall Return
American Guerrilla in the Philippines, An (1950)
I Was Happy Here
Time Lost and Time Remembered (1966, Brit.)
I Was Monty's Double
Hell, Heaven or Hoboken (1958, Brit.)
I'll Get You For This
Lucky Nick Cain (1951)
Ice Cold in Alex
Desert Attack (1958, Brit.)
Identity Parade
Line-Up, The (1934)
Idols in the Dust
Saturday's Hero (1951)
If You Feel Like Singing
Summer Stock (1950)
Ill Met by Moonlight
Night Ambush (1958, Brit.)
Illegal Divorce, The
Second Hand Wife (1933)
Imaginary Sweetheart
Professional Sweetheart (1933)
Impassive Footman, The
Woman in Chains (1932, Brit.)
Imperfect Lady, The
Perfect Gentleman, The (1935)
Impossible Lover
Huddle (1932)
In Case of Adversity
Love Is My Profession (1959, Fr.)
In Rosie's Room
Rosie the Riveter (1944)
In Strange Company
First Aid (1931)

In the Night
Gang's All Here, The (1941)
Indian Scout
Davy Crockett, Indian Scout (1950)
Indian Summer
Judge Steps Out, The (1949)
Indiscretion
Christmas in Connecticut (1945)
Informers, The
Underworld Informers (1965, Brit.)
Injustice
Road Gang (1936)
Innocence is Bliss
Miss Grant Takes Richmond (1949)
Inside Information
Lone Prairie, The (1942)
Inspector Hornleigh Goes to It
Mail Train (1941, Brit.)
Inspector, The
Lisa (1962, Brit.)
Intelligence Men, The
Spylarks (1965, Brit.)
International Police
Pickup Alley (1957, Brit.)
Interpol
Pickup Alley (1957, Brit.)
Interrupted Honeymoon, An
Homicide for Three (1948)
Intimate Stranger, The
Finger of Guilt (1956, Brit.)
Into the Blue
Man in the Dinghy, The (1951, Brit.)
Invader, The
Old Spanish Custom, An (1936, Brit.)
Invasion of the Hell Creatures, The
Invasion of the Saucermen (1957)
Investigation of Murder, An
Laughing Policeman, The (1973)
Invisible Message, The
Gun Play (1936)
Invisible Power
Washington Merry-Go-Round (1932)
Irish Hearts
Norah O'Neale (1934, Brit.)
Iron Fist
Awakening of Jim Burke (1935)
Iron Maiden, The
Swingin' Maiden, The (1963, Brit.)
Iron Road, The
Buckskin Frontier (1943)
Island Escape
No Man Is an Island (1962)
Island Man
Men of Ireland (1938, Ireland)
Island of Desire
Love Trader, The (1930)
Island of Monte Cristo
Sword of Venus (1953)
It Comes Up Love
Get Hep to Love (1942)
It Happened in Hollywood
Another Face (1935)
It Happened in Paris
Desperate Adventure, A (1938)
It Only Hurts When I Laugh
Only When I Laugh (1981)
It's a Dog's Life
Bar Sinister, The (1955)
It's All Happening
Dream Maker, The (1963, Brit.)
It's Magic
Romance on the High Seas (1948)
It's My Life
My Life to Live (1963, Fr.)
It's Trad, Dad!
Ring-A-Ding Rhythm (1962, Brit.)

Jack's the Boy
Night and Day (1933, Brit.)
Jailbirds
Pardon Us (1931)
Jamboree
Rookies on Parade (1941)
James Brothers, The
True Story of Jesse James, The (1957)
Janitor, The
Eyewitness (1981)
Java Seas
East of Java (1935)
Jazzboat
Jazz Boat (1960, Brit.)
Jealousy
Emergency Wedding (1950)
Jeannie
Girl in Distress (1941, Brit.)
Jennie
Portrait of Jennie (1948)

Jenny Lind
Lady's Morals, A (1930)
Jet Men of the Air
Air Cadet (1951)
Jew Suss
Power (1934, Brit.)
Joan Medford is Missing
House of Horrors (1946)
Joe Palooka in Fighting Mad
Fighting Mad (1948)
Johnny Vagabond
Johnny Come Lately (1943)
Jolly Old Higgins
Earl of Puddlestone (1940)
Joy Parade, The
Life Begins in College (1937)
Judy Goes to Town
Puddin' Head (1941)
Jules Verne's Rocket to the Moon
Those Fantastic Flying Fools (1967, Brit.)
Jump for Glory
When Thief Meets Thief (1937, Brit.)
Jungle Island
Wolves of the Sea (1938)
Jungle Street
Jungle Street Girls (1963, Brit.)
Jungle Woman, The
Nabonga (1944)
Jury of the Jungle
Fury of the Jungle (1934)
Just Smith
Leave It to Smith (1934)
Justice for Sale
Night Court (1932)

Katina
Iceland (1942)
Keep It Cool
Let's Rock (1958)
Keep Smiling
Smiling Along (1938, Brit.)
Kicking the Moon Around
Playboy, The (1942, Brit.)
Kid Colossus, The
Roogie's Bump (1954)
Kid's Last Fight, The
Life of Jimmy Dolan, The (1933)
Kidnapped
Miss Fane's Baby is Stolen (1934)
Kidnappers, The
Little Kidnappers, The (1954, Brit.)
Kil 1
Skin Game, The (1965, Brit.)
Killer Dino
Dino (1957)
Killer With a Label
One Too Many (1950)
Killers on the Prairie
King of the Sierras (1938)
Kilroy on Deck
French Leave (1948)
King of the Alcatraz
King of Alcatraz (1938)
King of the Ice Rink
King of Hockey (1936)
King of the Khyber Rifles
Black Watch, The (1929)
King of the Wild
King of the Wild Horses (1933)
Kipps
Remarkable Mr. Kipps, The (1942, Brit.)
Kiss Me
Love Kiss, The (1930)
Kiss of the Vampire
Kiss of Evil (1963, Brit.)
Knave of Hearts
Lovers, Happy Lovers! (1955, Brit.)
Konga
Konga, the Wild Stallion (1939)

Lady and the Doctor, The
Lady and the Monster, The (1944)
Lady Be Gay
Laugh It Off (1939)
Lady Beware
Thirteenth Guest, The (1932)
Lady From Boston, The
Pardon My French (1951, U.S./Fr.)
Lady Godiva of Coventry
Lady Godiva (1955)
Lady Hamilton
That Hamilton Woman (1941)
Lady in the Fog
Scotland Yard Inspector (1952, Brit.)

Lady in the Morgue
  Corpse in the Morgue (1938)
Lady of Deceit
  Born to Kill (1947)
Lady of Mystery
  Close Call for Boston Blackie, A (1946)
Lady of the Boulevards
  Nana (1934)
Lady of the Night
  Lady of the Pavements (1929)
Lady of the Rose
  Bride of the Regiment (1930)
Lady Reporter
  Bulldog Edition (1936)
Lady Windermere's Fan
  Fan, The (1949)
Lancelot and Guinevere
  Sword of Lancelot (1963, Brit.)
Land and the Law
  Black Market Rustlers (1943)
Land Without Music
  Forbidden Music (1936, Brit.)
Larceny Lane
  Blonde Crazy (1931)
Last Command, The
  Prisoner of Japan (1942)
Last Gangster, The
  Roger Touhy, Gangster (1944)
Last of the Cavalry, The
  Army Girl (1938)
Last of the Redskins
  Last of the Redmen (1947)
Last Page, The
  Man Bait (1952, Brit.)
Last Warrior, The
  Flap (1970)
Late Edwina Black, The
  Obsessed (1951, Brit.)
Latin Quarter
  Frenzy (1946, Brit.)
Laughter in the Air
  Myrt and Marge (1934)
Law and Order
  Fast Bullets (1936)
Law and Order
  Fugitive Sheriff, The (1936)
Law Demands, The
  Reckless Rider (1931)
Law of the Rio
  Riders of the Rio (1931)
Law Rides West, The
  Santa Fe Trail, The (1930)
Laxdale Hall
  Scotch on the Rocks (1954, Brit.)
Lazy Bones
  Hallelujah, I'm a Bum (1933)
Lead Law
  Crooked Trail (1936)
Legal Larceny
  Silver City Raiders (1943)
Lend Me Your Ear
  Living Ghost, The (1942)
Let's Have a Murder
  Stick 'Em Up (1950, Brit.)
Let's Love and Laugh
  Bridegroom for Two (1932, Brit.)
Letter from Korea
  Yank in Korea, A (1951)
Licensed to Kill
  Second Best Secret Agent in the Whole Wide
  World, The (1965, Brit.)
Lido Mystery, The
  Enemy Agents Meet Ellery Queen (1942)
Lie Detector, The
  Truth About Murder, The (1946)
Life After Dark
  Girls in the Night (1953)
Life and Death of Colonel Blimp, The
  Colonel Blimp (1945, Brit.)
Life at Stake, A
  Key Man (1955)
Life for Ruth
  Walk in the Shadow (1966, Brit.)
Life with the Lyons
  Family Affair (1954, Brit.)
Light Fantastic, The
  Love Is Better Than Ever (1952)
Light of the Heart, The
  Life Begins at 8:30 (1942)
Lighthouse Keeper's Daughter, The
  Girl in the Bikini, The (1958, Fr.)
Lights and Shadows
  Woman Racket, The (1930)
Lights Out
  Bright Victory (1951)
Lilacs in the Spring
  Let's Make Up (1955, Brit.)
Lily of Killarney
  Bride of the Lake (1934, Brit.)

Little Soldier, The
  Le Petit Soldat (1965, Fr.)
Live It Up
  Sing and Swing (1964, Brit.)
Lock Your Doors
  Ape Man, The (1943)
Lodger, The
  Phantom Fiend, The (1935, Brit.)
Lola
  Young Blood (1933)
London Belongs to Me
  Dulcimer Street (1948, Brit.)
London Melody
  Girl in the Street (1938, Brit.)
London Town
  My Heart Goes Crazy (1953, Brit.)
Lone Troubadour, The
  Two-Gun Troubadour (1939)
Lone Wolf's Daughter, The
  Lone Wolf Spy Hunt, The (1939)
Lonely Road, The
  Scotland Yard Commands (1937, Brit.)
Long Distance
  Hot Money Girl (1962, Brit./Ger.)
Long, Long Trail, The
  Texas to Bataan (1942)
Lookin' for Someone
  Singing on the Trail (1946)
Looking for Trouble
  Tip-Off, The (1931)
Loonies on Broadway
  Zombies on Broadway (1945)
Loser Take All
  Leather Gloves (1948)
Losing Game, The
  Pay Off, The (1930)
Lost
  Tears for Simon (1957, Brit.)
Lost Lady, The
  Safe in Hell (1931)
Lost Men
  Homicide Squad, The (1931)
Lost River
  Trail of the Rustlers (1950)
Lost Stage Valley
  Stage to Tucson (1950)
Lost Treasure of the Amazon
  Jivaro (1954)
Lost Women
  Mesa of Lost Women (1952)
Loudest Whisper, The
  Children's Hour, The (1961)
Love at Second Sight
  Girl Thief, The (1938)
Love Eternal
  Eternal Return, The (1943, Fr.)
Love Finds a Way
  Alias French Gertie (1930)
Love in Las Vegas
  Viva Las Vegas (1964)
Love is Like That
  Jazz Cinderella (1930)
Love Race, The
  Girl O' My Dreams (1934)
Love Redeemed
  Dragnet Patrol (1932)
Love Story
  Lady Surrenders, A (1947)
Love's a Luxury
  Caretaker's Daughter, The (1952, Brit.)
Lovely to Look At
  Thin Ice (1937)
Lovely Way to Go, A
  Lovely Way to Die, A (1968)
Lovers of Lisbon
  Lover's Net (1957, Fr.)
Luck of the Game, The
  Gridiron Flash (1935)
Luck of the Navy
  North Sea Patrol (1939, Brit.)
Lucky
  Boy, a Girl, and a Dog, A (1946)
Lucky Days
  Sing a Jingle (1943)
Lucky Ralston
  Law and Order (1940)
Lullaby, The
  Sin of Madelon Claudet, The (1931)
Lunch on the Grass
  Picnic on the Grass (1960, Fr.)

Ma and Pa Kettle Go to Paris
  Ma and Pa Kettle On Vacation (1953)
MacArthur the Rebel General
  MacArthur (1977)
MacDonald of the Canadian Mounties
  Pony Soldier (1952)

Mad Hatter
  Breakfast in Hollywood (1946)
Mad Masquerade
  Washington Masquerade, The (1932)
Madame Julie
  Woman Between, The (1931)
Madame Pimpernel
  Paris Underground (1945)
Madcap
  Taming the Wild (1937)
Mademoiselle Docteur
  Under Secret Orders (1943, Brit.)
Mademoiselle France
  Reunion in France (1943)
Magnificent Outcast
  Almost a Gentleman (1939)
Magnificent Showman, The
  Circus World (1964)
Main Street Girl
  Paroled From the Big House (1938)
Malaga
  Fire Over Africa (1954, Brit.)
Man and His Mate
  One Million B.C. (1940)
Man at Six, The
  Gables Mystery, The (1931, Brit.)
Man Called Sullivan, A
  Great John L., The (1945)
Man from Nevada, The
  Nevadan, The (1950)
Man from Tangier
  Thunder Over Tangier (1957, Brit.)
Man from the Big City, The
  It Happened Out West (1937)
Man from the Folies Bergere, The
  Folies Bergere (1935)
Man I Killed, The
  Broken Lullaby (1932)
Man in Hiding
  Man-Trap (1961)
Man in Possession, The
  Personal Property (1937)
Man in the Shadow
  Violent Stranger (1957, Brit.)
Man in the Sky, The
  Decision Against Time (1957, Brit.)
Man Is Ten Feet Tall, A
  Edge of the City (1956)
Man Mad
  No Place to Land (1958)
Man of Bronze
  Jim Thorpe—All American (1951)
Man of the Family
  Top Man (1943)
Man of the Hour
  Colonel Effingham's Raid (1945)
Man on America's Conscience, The
  Tennessee Johnson (1942)
Man Who Came Back, The
  Swamp Water (1941)
Man Who Changed His Mind, The
  Man Who Lived Again, The (1936, Brit.)
Man Who Pawned His Soul, The
  Unknown Blonde (1934)
Man Who Watched Trains Go By, The
  Paris Express, The (1953, Brit.)
Man with the Deadly Lens, The
  Wrong Is Right (1982)
Man With Thirty Sons, The
  Magnificent Yankee, The (1950)
Man Within, The
  Smugglers, The (1948, Brit.)
Man's Heritage
  Spirit of Culver (1939)
Mandy
  Crash of Silence (1952, Brit.)
Manhattan Madness
  Adventure in Manhattan (1936)
Manhattan Music Box
  Manhattan Merry-Go-Round (1937)
Manhunt
  From Hell to Texas (1958)
Mantrap
  Woman in Hiding (1953, Brit.)
Manuela
  Stowaway Girl (1957, Brit.)
Marat/Sade
  Persecution and Assassination of Jean-Paul
  Marat as Performed by the Inmates of the
  Asylum of Charenton Under the Direction of the
  Marquis de Sade, The (1967, Brit.)
Marching Along
  Stars and Stripes Forever (1952)
Maria Marten
  Murder in the Red Barn (1936, Brit.)
Marie Walewska
  Conquest (1937)
Marines Have Landed, The
  Leathernecks Have Landed, The (1936)

Mark of the Apache
  Tomahawk Trail (1957)
Mark of the Claw
  Dick Tracy's Dilemma (1947)
Marked Bullet, The
  Prairie Stranger (1941)
Marked Man, The
  Mark of the Whistler, The (1944)
Marriage Forbidden
  Damaged Goods (1937)
Marriage of Convenience
  Hired Wife (1934)
Marriage of Corbal, The
  Prisoner of Corbal (1939, Brit.)
Marriage Symphony
  Let's Try Again (1934)
Married But Single
  This Thing Called Love (1940)
Married in Haste
  Marriage on Approval (1934)
Married in Haste
  Consolation Marriage (1931)
Marshmallow Moon
  Aaron Slick from Punkin Crick (1952)
Marx Brothers Go West, The
  Go West (1940)
Mary Names the Day
  Dr. Kildare's Wedding Day (1941)
Mask of Dust
  Race for Life, A (1955, Brit.)
Mask of Fury
  First Yank into Tokyo (1945)
Masked Pirate, The
  Pirates of Capri, The (1949)
Masked Stranger, The
  Durango Kid, The (1940)
Master of Lassie
  Hills of Home (1948)
Master of the Islands
  Hawaiians, The (1970)
Matrimonial Problem, A
  Matrimonial Bed, The (1930)
Matter of Life and Death, A
  Stairway to Heaven (1946, Brit.)
Mayor's Nest, The
  Return of Daniel Boone, The (1941)
McGlusky the Sea Rover
  Hell's Cargo (1935, Brit.)
Medals
  Seven Days Leave (1930)
Meet Maxwell Archer
  Maxwell Archer, Detective (1942, Brit.)
Meet Me Tonight
  Tonight at 8:30 (1952, Brit.)
Meet Whiplash Willie
  Fortune Cookie, The (1966)
Melody Girl
  Sing, Dance, Plenty Hot (1940)
Melody Inn
  Riding High (1943)
Melody Maker
  Ding Dong Williams (1946)
Melody of Life
  Symphony of Six Million (1932)
Melody of Youth
  They Shall Have Music (1939)
Melting Pot, The
  Betty Co-Ed (1946)
Memory Expert, The
  Man on the Flying Trapeze (1935)
Memory for Two
  I Love a Bandleader (1935)
Men Behind Bars
  Duffy of San Quentin (1954)
Men of Destiny
  Men of Texas (1942)
Men of Steel
  Bill Cracks Down (1937)
Men of the Deep
  Rough, Tough and Ready (1945)
Men of Two Worlds
  Kisenga, Man of Africa (1952, Brit.)
Men on Her Mind
  Girl from Tenth Avenue, The (1935)
Men Women Love
  Salvation Nell (1931)
Mercenaries, The
  Dark of the Sun (1968, Brit.)
Mermaids of Tiburon, The
  Aqua Sex, The (1962)
Merrily We Go to...
  Merrily We Go to Hell (1932)
Merry Comes to Town
  Merry Comes to Stay (1937, Brit.)
Mexican, The
  Hurricane Horseman (1931)
Michael Strogoff
  Soldier and the Lady, The (1937)
Midnight at Madame Tussaud's
  Midnight at the Wax Museum (1936, Brit.)

Midnight Menace
  Bombs Over London (1937, Brit.)
Midnight Raiders
  Oklahoma Raiders (1944)
Midshipmaid, The
  Midshipmaid Gob (1932, Brit.)
Midshipman Easy
  Men of the Sea (1951, Brit.)
Mighty Tundra, The
  Tundra (1936)
Mile a Minute
  Riders of the Santa Fe (1944)
Military Policeman
  Off Limits (1953)
Million Pound Note, The
  Man with a Million (1954, Brit.)
Millionaire for a Day
  Let's Be Ritzy (1934)
Millionaire Playboy
  Park Avenue Logger (1937)
Mind of Mr. Reeder, The
  Mysterious Mr. Reeder, The (1940, Brit.)
Miracle of Fatima, The
  Miracle of Our Lady of Fatima (1952)
Miracle of Life
  Our Daily Bread (1934)
Mirth and Melody
  Let's Go Places (1929)
Miss Fix-It
  Keep Smiling (1938)
Mrs. Loring's Secret
  Imperfect Lady, The (1947)
Mr. Ashton Was Indiscreet
  Senator Was Indiscreet, The (1947)
Mr. Bill the Conqueror
  Man Who Won, The (1933, Brit.)
Mr. Drew
  For Them that Trespass (1949, Brit.)
Mr. Faintheart
  $10 Raise (1935)
Mr. Griggs Returns
  Cockeyed Miracle, The (1946)
Mr. Moto on Danger Island
  Mr. Moto in Danger Island (1939)
Mr. Mum
  Mr. Mom (1983)
Mr. Reeder in Room 13
  Mystery of Room 13 (1941, Brit.)
Mr. Topaze
  I Like Money (1962, Brit.)
Mr. Wong at Headquarters
  Fatal Hour (1940)
Mobs Incorporated
  Mobs, Inc. (1956)
Modern Hero, A
  Knute Rockne—All American (1940)
Modern Madness
  Big Noise, The (1936)
Modern Miracle, The
  Story of Alexander Graham Bell, The (1939)
Money for Jam
  It Ain't Hay (1943)
Money Isn't Everything
  Jeepers Creepers (1939)
Monster
  Humanoids from the Deep (1980)
Monster Meets the Gorilla
  Bela Lugosi Meets a Brooklyn Gorilla (1952)
Monster Walked, The
  Monster Walks, The (1932)
Montana Justice
  Man From Montana
Monte Carlo or Bust
  Those Daring Young Men in their Jaunty Jalo-
  pies (1969, Fr./Brit./Ital.)
Monte Cristo's Revenge
  Return of Monte Cristo, The (1946)
Moonlight and Melody
  Moonlight and Pretzels (1933)
Moonlight Raid
  Challenge of the Range (1949)
Morgan: A Suitable Case for Treatment
  Morgan! (1966, Brit.)
Morning Call
  Strange Case of Dr. Manning, The (1958, Brit.)
Morning Departure
  Operation Disaster (1951, Brit.)
Morton of the Mounted
  Timber Terrors (1935)
Moscow Distrusts Tears
  Moscow Does Not Believe in Tears (1980, USSR)
Moscow Nights
  I Stand Condemned (1936, Brit.)
Most Wanted Man, The
  Most Wanted Man in the World, The (1962,
  Fr./Ital.)
Mother Knows Best
  Mother Is a Freshman (1949)
Mother-Sir!
  Navy Wife (1956)

Mountain Desperadoes
  Laramie Mountains (1952)
Movietone Follies of 1929
  Fox Movietone Follies (1929)
Movietone Follies of 1930
  Fox Movietone Follies of 1930 (1930)
Moving in Society
  Mountain Moonlight (1941)
Moving Target, The
  Harper (1966)
Murder at Malibu Beach
  Trap, The (1947)
Murder at the Windmill
  Mystery at the Burlesque (1950, Brit.)
Murder by Proxy
  Blackout (1954)
Murder in Soho
  Murder in the Night (1940, Brit.)
Murder in the Big House
  Jailbreak (1936)
Murder in Thornton Square, The
  Gaslight (1944)
Murder, Inc.
  Enforcer, The (1951)
Murder, Incorporated
  Murder, Inc. (1960)
Murder on the Runaway Train
  Murder in the Private Car (1934)
Murder Ring, The
  Ellery Queen and the Murder Ring (1941)
Murderer Among Us
  M (1933, Ger.)
Murderers Among Us
  Murderers Are Amongst Us, The (1948, Ger.)
Mutiny on the Seas
  Outside the 3-Mile Limit (1940)
My Daughter Joy
  Operation (1951, Brit.)
My Hero
  Southern Yankee, A (1948)
My Irish Molly
  Little Miss Molly (1940)
My Life Is Yours
  People vs. Dr. Kildare, The (1941)
My Old Man's a Fireman
  Chief, The (1933)
My Partner, Mr. Davis
  Mysterious Mr. Davis, The (1936, Brit.)
My Son Alone
  American Empire (1942)
My Teenage Daughter
  Teenage Bad Girl (1959, Brit.)
My Two Husbands
  Too Many Husbands (1940)
Mysterious Invader
  Astounding She-Monster, The (1958)
Mysterious Stranger, The
  Western Gold (1937)
Mysterious Stranger, The
  Code of the Lawless (1945)
Mystery at Monte Carlo
  Revenge at Monte Carlo (1933)
Mystery of Diamond Island, The
  Rip Roaring Riley (1935)
Mystery of Wentworth Castle, The
  Doomed to Die (1940)

Naked Fury
  Pleasure Lovers, The (1964, Brit.)
Naked Truth, The
  Your Past Is Showing (1958, Brit.)
Natural Born Salesman, A
  Earthworm Tractors (1936)
Navy Steps Out, The
  Girl, A Guy, and A Gob, A (1941)
Nelson Touch, The
  Corvette K-225 (1943)
Net, The
  Project M7 (1953, Brit.)
Never Take Sweets From a Stranger
  Never Take Candy from a Stranger (1961, Brit.)
New Adventures of Don Juan, The
  Adventures of Don Juan (1949)
New Face in Hell
  P.J. (1968)
Next in Line
  Riders of the Northland (1942)
Next Time We Live
  Next Time We Love (1936)
Night Club
  Gigolette (1935)
Night Club Girl
  Glamour Girl (1947)
Night Club Hostess
  Unmarried (1939)
Night Express, The
  Western Limited, The (1932)

Night Has Eyes, The
  Terror House (1943)
Night in Cairo, A
  Barbarian, The (1933)
Night in Havana
  Big Boodle, The (1957)
Night Is Ending, The
  Paris After Dark (1943)
Night of San Lorenzo, The
  Night of the Shooting Stars, The (1982, Ital.)
Night of the Big Heat
  Island of the Burning Damned (1971, Brit.)
Night of the Doomed
  Nightmare Castle (1966, Ital.)
Night of the Eagle
  Burn, Witch, Burn (1962, Brit.)
Night They Invented Striptease, The
  Night They Raided Minsky's, The (1968)
Night Train to Munich
  Night Train (1940, Brit.)
Nipper, The
  Brat, The (1930, Brit.)
No Brakes
  Oh Yeah! (1929)
No Greater Love
  Aloha (1931)
No Highway
  No Highway in the Sky (1951, Brit.)
No Kidding
  Beware of Children (1961, Brit.)
No Sleep Till Dawn
  Bombers B-52 (1957)
No Time for Tears
  Purple Heart Diary (1951)
No Time to Die
  Tank Force (1958, Brit.)
No Trees in the Street
  No Tree in the Street (1964, Brit.)
Nobody Runs Forever
  High Commissioner, The (1968, U.S./Brit.)
None but the Brave
  For the Love of Mike (1960)
Noose
  Silk Noose, The (1950, Brit.)
North Sea Hijack
  Ffolkes (1980, Brit.)
Not Wanted on Voyage
  Treachery on the High Seas (1939, Brit.)

O.H.M.S.
  You're in the Army Now (1937, Brit.)
O'Riley's Luck
  Rose Bowl (1936)
O'Rourke of the Royal Mounted
  Saskatchewan (1954)
Obsession
  Hidden Room, The (1949, Brit.)
Of a Thousand Delights
  Sandra (1966, Ital.)
Off the Beaten Track
  Behind the Eight Ball (1942)
Oh! For a Man!
  Will Success Spoil Rock Hunter? (1957)
Old Corral, The
  Song of the Gringo (1936)
Old Drac
  Old Dracula (1975, Brit.)
Old Greatheart
  Way Back Home (1932)
Old Mother Riley's New Venture
  Old Mother Riley (1952, Brit.)
Old School Tie, The
  We Went to College (1936)
On Guard
  Outpost of the Mounties (1939)
On Secret Service
  Secret Agent (1933, Brit.)
On Secret Service
  Trailin' West (1936)
On Special Duty
  Bullets for Rustlers (1940)
On the Carpet
  Little Giant (1946)
On the Fiddle
  Operation Snafu (1965, Brit.)
On the Night of the Fire
  Fugitive, The (1940, Brit.)
On the Stroke of Nine
  Murder on Campus (1934)
On Top of the World
  Everything Okay (1936, Brit.)
On Wings of Song
  Love Me Forever (1935)
Once a Hero
  It Happened in Hollywood (1937)
Once a Jolly Swagman
  Maniacs on Wheels (1951, Brit.)

Once in a Million
  Weekend Millionaire (1937, Brit.)
Once Upon a Thursday
  Affairs of Martha, The (1942)
One Against Seven
  Counter-Attack (1945)
One Born Every Minute
  Flim-Flam Man, The (1967)
One for All
  President's Mystery, The (1936)
One Hour to Doom's Day
  City Beneath the Sea (1953)
One Hundred Percent Pure
  Girl from Missouri, The (1934)
One Man Mutiny
  Court Martial of Billy Mitchell, The (1955)
One of the Many
  He Couldn't Take It (1933)
One-Piece Bathing Suit, The
  Million Dollar Mermaid (1952)
Operation Undercover
  Report to the Commissioner (1975)
Optimist, The
  Big Shot, The (1931)
Optimists of Nine Elms, The
  Optimists, The (1973, Brit.)
Oracle, The
  Horse's Mouth, The (1953, Brit.)
Orphan of the Ring, The
  Kid From Kokomo, The (1939)
Our Fighting Navy
  Torpedoed (1939, Brit.)
Our Girl Friday
  Adventures of Sadie, The (1955, Brit.)
Ourselves Alone
  River of Unrest (1937, Brit.)
Out of Darkness
  Teenage Caveman (1958)
Out of the Shadow
  Murder on the Campus (1963, Brit.)
Outcast, The
  Man in the Saddle (1951)
Outlaw and the Lady, The
  Waco (1952)
Outlaws of the West
  Call the Mesquiteers (1938)
Outside the Law
  Citadel of Crime (1941)
Over the River
  One More River (1934)
Overland Trail
  Trail Riders (1942)
Owd Bob
  To the Victor (1938, Brit.)

Perfect Strangers
  Vacation from Marriage (1945, Brit.)
Perfect Weekend, A
  St. Louis Kid, The (1934)
Perilous Journey
  Bad Boy (1939)
Personal Column
  Lured (1947)
Personal Honour
  Hello Annapolis (1942)
Phantom Horseman, The
  Border Outlaws (1950)
Phantom of the Air
  Phantom Broadcast, The (1933)
Pier 13
  Me and My Gal (1932)
Planter's Wife, The
  Outpost in Malaya (1952, Brit.)
Playing the Game
  Touchdown (1931)
Plot Thickens, The
  Here Comes Cookie (1935)
Pluck of the Irish
  Great Guy (1936)
Polly Fulton
  B. F.'s Daughter (1948)
Pookie
  Sterile Cuckoo, The (1969)
Porridge
  Doing Time (1979, Brit.)
Port O' Dreams
  Girl Overboard (1929)
Portrait from Life
  Girl in the Painting, The (1948, Brit.)
Portrait of Alison
  Postmark for Danger (1956, Brit.)
Potiphar's Wife
  Her Strange Desire (1931, Brit.)
Power and Glory
  Power and the Glory, The (1933)
Power of Justice
  Beyond the Sacramento (1940)

Power of Possession
  Lawless Empire (1945)
Prehistoric World Out of the Darkness
  Teenage Caveman (1958)
Premiere
  One Night in Paris (1940, Brit.)
Present Arms
  Leathernecking (1930)
Pretty Polly
  Matter of Innocence, A (1968, Brit.)
Pride of Kentucky
  Story of Seabiscuit, The (1949)
Pride of the Bowery, The
  Mr. Hex (1946)
Prince and the Pauper, The
  Crossed Swords (1978)
Prince of the Blue Grass
  Pride of the Blue Grass (1954)
Private Affairs
  Public Stenographer (1935)
Private Wore Skirts, The
  Never Wave at a WAC (1952)
Pro, The
  Number One (1969)
Professional Bride
  Hard Guy (1941)
Promise of a Bed, A
  This, That and the Other (1970, Brit.)
Public Be Hanged, The
  World Gone Mad, The (1933)
Puppets of Fate
  Wolves of the Underworld (1935, Brit.)
Purple Riders, The
  Purple Vigilantes, The (1938)
Pagliacci
  Clown Must Laugh, A (1936, Brit.)
Painted Boats
  Girl on the Canal, The (1947, Brit.)
Painted Smile, The
  Murder Can Be Deadly (1963, Brit.)
Pale Arrow
  Pawnee (1957)
Palms Springs Affair
  Palm Springs (1936)
Panic on the Air
  You May Be Next! (1936)
Panther's Moon
  Spy Hunt (1950)
Paradise for Two
  Gaiety Girls, The (1938, Brit.)
Paris Love Song
  Paris in Spring (1935)
Park Plaza 605
  Norman Conquest (1953, Brit.)
Partly Confidential
  Thanks for Listening (1937)
Partners in Fortune
  Rockin' in the Rockies (1945)
Pass to Romance
  Hi Beautiful (1944)
Passing Show, The
  Hotel Variety (1933)
Passionate Friends, The
  One Woman's Story (1949, Brit.)
Passport to Fame
  Whole Town's Talking, The (1935)
Passport to Shame
  Room 43 (1959, Brit.)
Patterns of Power
  Patterns (1956)
Patton—Lust for Glory
  Patton (1970)
Paula
  Framed (1947)
Pay the Devil
  Man in the Shadow (1957)
Penalty of Fame
  Okay America (1932)
Penguin Pool Mystery, The
  Penguin Pool Murder, The (1932)
Perfect Strangers
  Vacation from Marriage (1945, Brit.)
Perfect Weekend, A
  St. Louis Kid, The (1934)
Perilous Journey
  Bad Boy (1939)
Personal Column
  Lured (1947)
Personal Honour
  Hello Annapolis (1942)
Phantom Horseman, The
  Border Outlaws (1950)
Phantom of the Air
  Phantom Broadcast, The (1933)
Pier 13
  Me and My Gal (1932)
Planter's Wife, The
  Outpost in Malaya (1952, Brit.)
Playing the Game
  Touchdown (1931)

Plot Thickens, The
  Here Comes Cookie (1935)
Pluck of the Irish
  Great Guy (1936)
Polly Fulton
  B. F.'s Daughter (1948)
Pookie
  Sterile Cuckoo, The (1969)
Porridge
  Doing Time (1979, Brit.)
Port O' Dreams
  Girl Overboard (1929)
Portrait from Life
  Girl in the Painting, The (1948, Brit.)
Portrait of Alison
  Postmark for Danger (1956, Brit.)
Potiphar's Wife
  Her Strange Desire (1931, Brit.)
Power and Glory
  Power and the Glory, The (1933)
Power of Justice
  Beyond the Sacramento (1940)
Power of Possession
  Lawless Empire (1945)
Prehistoric World Out of the Darkness
  Teenage Caveman (1958)
Premiere
  One Night in Paris (1940, Brit.)
Present Arms
  Leathernecking (1930)
Pretty Polly
  Matter of Innocence, A (1968, Brit.)
Pride of Kentucky
  Story of Seabiscuit, The (1949)
Pride of the Bowery, The
  Mr. Hex (1946)
Prince and the Pauper, The
  Crossed Swords (1978)
Prince of the Blue Grass
  Pride of the Blue Grass (1954)
Private Affairs
  Public Stenographer (1935)
Private Wore Skirts, The
  Never Wave at a WAC (1952)
Pro, The
  Number One (1969)
Professional Bride
  Hard Guy (1941)
Promise of a Bed, A
  This, That and the Other (1970, Brit.)
Public Be Hanged, The
  World Gone Mad, The (1933)
Puppets of Fate
  Wolves of the Underworld (1935, Brit.)
Purple Riders, The
  Purple Vigilantes, The (1938)
Q Planes
  Clouds Over Europe (1939, Brit.)
Q-Ships
  Blockade (1928, Brit.)
Quatermass and the Pit
  Five Million Miles to Earth (1968, Brit.)
Quatermass II
  Enemy from Space (1957, Brit.)
Queen of Spies
  Joan of Ozark (1942)
Queen of the West
  Cattle Queen (1950)
Queen's Affair, The
  Runaway Queen, The (1935, Brit.)
Queen's Husband, The
  Royal Bed, The (1931)
Queer Cargo
  Pirates of the Seven Seas (1941, Brit.)

Racing Luck
  Red Hot Tires (1935)
Radio Murder Mystery, The
  Love Is On the Air (1937)
Radio Parade of 1935
  Radio Follies (1935, Brit.)
Radio Revels of 1942
  Swing it Soldier (1941)
Radio Star, The
  Loudspeaker, The (1934)
Rag Doll
  Young, Willing and Eager (1962, Brit.)
Raging Moon, The
  Long Ago, Tomorrow (1971, Brit.)
Raging Waters
  Green Promise, The (1949)
Raising the Wind
  Roommates (1962, Brit.)
Raising the Wind
  Big Race, The (1933)
Rake's Progress, The
  Notorious Gentleman (1945, Brit.)

Randy Strikes Oil
  Fighting Texans (1933)
Ransom
  Terrorists, The (1975, Brit.)
Rasputin the Mad Monk
  Rasputin and the Empress (1932)
Re-Union
  In Love With Life (1934)
Rebel, The
  Call Me Genius (1961, Brit.)
Rebel, The
  Bushwhackers, The (1952)
Reckless Age, The
  Dragstrip Riot (1958)
Red Baron, The
  Von Richthofen and Brown (1971)
Red Beret, The
  Paratrooper (1954, Brit.)
Red Ensign
  Strike! (1934, Brit.)
Reluctant Bride, The
  Two Grooms for a Bride (1957)
Remember Me
  Horsemen of the Sierras (1950)
Remember That Face
  Mob, The (1950)
Rendezvous
  Darling, How Could You? (1951)
Reprieved
  Sing Sing Nights (1935)
Reputation
  Lady With a Past (1932)
Return of a Stranger
  Face Behind the Scar, The (1940, Brit.)
Return of the Corsican Brothers
  Bandits of Corsica, The (1953)
Return of the Vigilantes, The
  Vigilantes Return, The (1947)
Revenge
  Terror From Under the House (1971, Brit.)
Revenge
  End of the Trail (1936)
Revenge of the Blood Beast, The
  She Beast, The (1966, Brit./Ital./Yugo.)
Rhodes of Africa
  Rhodes (1936, Brit.)
Rhythm Hits the Ice
  Ice-Capades Revue (1942)
Rhythm on the Ranch
  Rootin' Tootin' Rhythm (1937)
Rhythm on the River
  Freshman Love (1936)
Rich, Full Life, The
  Cynthia (1947)
Richer than the Earth
  Whistle at Eaton Falls, The (1951)
Richest Man in the World, The
  Sins of the Children (1930)
Right to Live, The
  Forever Yours (1945)
Ring of Treason
  Ring of Spies (1964, Brit.)
Ring up the Curtain
  Broadway to Hollywood (1933)
Riot on Pier 6
  New Orleans Uncensored (1955)
Rise of Catherine the Great, The
  Catherine the Great (1934, Brit.)
Rise of Helga, The
  Susan Lenox—Her Fall and Rise (1931)
Rising to Fame
  Susan Lenox, Her Fall and Rise (1931)
River of Poison
  South of Death Valley (1950)
Road to Frisco, The
  They Drive by Night (1940)
Rocket Ship
  Mars Attacks the World (1938)
Rocks of Valpre, The
  High Treason (1937, Brit.)
Rogues' Gallery
  Devil's Trail, The (1942)
Roll On
  Lawless Plainsmen (1942)
Romance and Rhythm
  Cowboy from Brooklyn (1938)
Romance for Three
  Paradise for Three (1938)
Romance in Flanders, A
  Lost on the Western Front (1940, Brit.)
Romance is Sacred
  King and the Chorus Girl, The (1937)
Romantic Age, The
  Sisters Under the Skin (1934)
Romantic Age, The
  Naughty Arlette (1951, Brit.)
Romeo in Pyjamas
  Parlor, Bedroom and Bath (1931)
Rommel—Desert Fox
  Desert Fox, The (1951)

Rookery Nook
  One Embarrassing Night (1930, Brit.)
Rookies
  Buck Privates (1941)
Rookies Come Home
  Buck Privates Come Home (1947)
Rough and the Smooth, The
  Portrait of a Sinner (1961, Brit,)
Rough Company
  Violent Men, The (1954)
Rough Riding Romeo
  Flaming Guns (1932)
Rough Shoot
  Shoot First (1953, Brit.)
Roving Rogue, A
  Outlaws of the Rockies (1945)
Royal Cavalcade
  Regal Cavalcade (1935, Brit.)
Royal Flush
  Two Guys from Milwaukee (1946)

Sabotage
  When London Sleeps (1934, Brit.)
Sabre and the Arrow, The
  Last of the Comanches (1952)
Sabrina Fair
  Sabrina (1954)
Sacred Flame, The
  Right to Live, The (1935)
Said O'Reilly to MacNab
  Sez O'Reilly to MacNab (1938, Brit.)
Sailor Beware!
  Panic in the Parlour (1957, Brit.)
Sailors Three
  Three Cockeyed Sailors (1940, Brit.)
St. Martin's Lane
  Sidewalks of London (1940, Brit.)
Saint's Return, The
  Saint's Girl Friday, The (1954, Brit.)
Sally's Irish Rogue
  Poacher's Daughter, The (1960, Brit.)
Salomy Jane
  Wild Girl (1932)
Salute to Romance
  Annapolis Salute (1937)
Samaritan, The
  Soul of the Slums (1931)
Sandy Takes a Bow
  Unexpected Father (1939)
Sap from Abroad, The
  Sap from Syracuse, The (1930)
Saraband for Dead Lovers
  Saraband (1949, Brit.)
Satan's Skin
  Blood on Satan's Claws, The (1970, Brit.)
Savage Islands
  Nate and Hayes (1983, U.S./New Zealand)
Sawdust and Tinsel
  Naked Night, The (1956, Swed.)
Scamp, The
  Strange Affection (1957, Brit.)
Scandal in Paris, A
  Thieves' Holiday (1946)
Scar, The
  Hollow Triumph (1948)
Scarlet Buccaneer, The
  Swashbuckler (1976)
School for Violence
  High School Hellcats (1958)
Schoolboy Penitentiary
  Little Red Schoolhouse, The (1936)
Schoolmaster, The
  Hoosier Schoolmaster, The (1935)
Scoop, The
  Honor of the Press (1932)
Scotland Yard Mystery, The
  Living Dead, The (1936, Brit.)
Scoundrel in White
  Docteur Popaul (1972, Fr.)
Scouts of the Air
  Danger Flight (1939)
Sea of Sand
  Desert Patrol (1962, Brit.)
Sea Wyf and Biscuit
  Sea Wife (1957, Brit.)
Sealed Lips
  After Tonight (1933)
Second Chances
  Probation (1932)
Second Thoughts
  Crime of Peter Frame, The (1938, Brit.)
Secret Enemy
  Enemy Agent (1940)
Secret Four, The
  Kansas City Confidential (1952)
Secret Interlude
  Private Number (1936)

Secret Interlude
  View from Pompey's Head, The (1955)
Secret Lives
  I Married a Spy (1938)
Secret Motive
  London Blackout Murders (1942)
Secret of Linda Hamilton
  Secrets of a Sorority Girl (1946)
Secret Stranger, The
  Rough Riding Ranger (1935)
Secrets
  Secrets of the Lone Wolf (1941)
Secrets of G32
  Fly By Night (1942)
See You in Hell, Darling
  American Dream, An (1966)
Seeing It Through
  Moth, The (1934)
Seekers, The
  Land of Fury (1955, Brit.)
Sentence Suspended
  Military Academy With That 10th Avenue Gang
  (1950)
Serenade of the West
  Git Along Little Dogies (1937)
Serenade of the West
  Cowboy Serenade (1942)
Serious Charge
  Immoral Charge (1962, Brit.)
Service
  Looking Forward (1933)
Service for Ladies
  Reserved for Ladies (1932, Brit.)
Seven Sinners
  Doomed Cargo (1936, Brit.)
Seven Thunders
  Beasts of Marseilles, The (1959, Brit.)
Seven Waves Away
  Abandon Ship (1957, Brit.)
Shadows of Singapore
  Malay Nights (1932)
Shall the Children Pay?
  What Price Innocence? (1933)
Shark God, The
  Omoo, Omoo, the Shark God (1949)
Shark Reef
  She Gods of Shark Reef (1958)
She Got Her Man
  Maisie Gets Her Man (1942)
She Who Dares
  Three Russian Girls (1943)
She's My Lovely
  Get Hep to Love (1942)
Sherlock Holmes
  Adventures of Sherlock Holmes, The (1939)
Sherlock Holmes and the Secret Code
  Dressed to Kill (1946)
Shipwreck
  Sea Gypsies, The (1978)
Shoot the Pianist
  Shoot the Piano Player (1962, Fr.)
Showdown, The
  West of Abilene (1940)
Siege of Pinchgut, The
  Four Desperate Men (1960, Brit.)
Signed Judgment
  Cowboy from Lonesome River (1944)
Silent Battle, The
  Continental Express (1939, Brit.)
Silent Voice, The
  Paula (1952)
Silent Voice, The
  Man Who Played God, The (1932)
Silent Witness
  Secrets of a Co-Ed (1943)
Silken Skin
  Soft Skin, The (1964, Fr.)
Silver Blaze
  Murder at the Baskervilles (1941, Brit.)
Silver Chains
  Kid From Amarillo, The (1951)
Silver City
  Albuquerque (1948)
Silver Key, The
  Girl in the Case (1944)
Sin Flood
  Way of All Men, The (1930)
Sing Me a Love Song
  Manhattan Moon (1935)
Single-Handed
  Sailor of the King
Sinister House
  Who Killed Doc Robbin? (1948)
Sinner, The
  Desert Desperados (1959)
Six Inches Tall
  Attack of the Puppet People (1958)
Ski Raiders, The
  Snow Job (1972)

Sky West and Crooked
  Gypsy Girl (1966, Brit.)
Slade
  Jack Slade (1953)
Slave Girls
  Prehistoric Women (1967, Brit.)
Sleeping Cardinal, The
  Sherlock Holmes' Fatal Hour (1931, Brit.)
Small Back Room, The
  Hour of Glory (1949, Brit.)
Small Town Lawyer
  Main Street Lawyer (1939)
Small Voice, The
  Hideout (1948, Brit.)
Smash and Grab
  Larceny Street (1941, Brit.)
Smashing Bird I Used to Know, The
  School for Unclaimed Girls (1973, Brit.)
Smashing Through
  Cheyenne Cyclone (1932)
Smithy
  Pacific Adventure (1947, Aus.)
Smokey and the Bandit Ride Again
  Smokey and the Bandit II (1980)
Snout, The
  Underworld Informers (1965, Brit.)
Snow White and the Three Clowns
  Snow White and the Three Stooges (1961)
Snuffy Smith
  Snuffy Smith, Yard Bird (1942)
So Bright the Flame
  Girl in White, The (1952)
So Like a Woman
  Temptation (1930)
Social Enemy No. 1
  No Greater Sin (1941)
Soft Beds and Hard Battles
  Undercovers Hero (1975, Brit.)
Soho Incident
  Spin a Dark Web (1956, Brit.)
Soldier's Pay
  Soldier's Plaything, A (1931)
Soldiers of Fortune
  War Correspondent (1932)
Soldiers of the King
  Woman in Command (1934, Brit.)
Son of Mine
  Police Court (1932)
Song of the Plough
  County Fair (1933, Brit.)
Sons of the Musketeers
  At Sword's Point (1951)
Sons of the Sea
  Atlantic Ferry (1941, Brit.)
Souls for Sables
  Lovebound (1932)
Sound of Fury, The
  Try and Get Me (1950)
South of Algiers
  Golden Mask, The (1954, Brit.)
Southwest to Sonora
  Appaloosa, The (1966)
Spaceman and King Arthur, The
  Unidentified Flying Oddball, The (1979, Brit.)
Spats to Spurs
  Henry Goes to Arizona (1939)
Speed Brent Wins
  Breed of the Border (1933)
Speed Reporter, The
  Scareheads (1931)
Spellbound
  Spell of Amy Nugent, The (1945, Brit.)
Spider Woman
  Sherlock Holmes and the Spider Woman (1944)
Spies at Work
  Sabotage (1939)
Spin of a Coin
  George Raft Story, The (1961)
Spirit of the People
  Abe Lincoln in Illinois, (1940)
Splitface
  Dick Tracy (1945)
Sport of a Nation
  All American, The (1932)
Sporting Life
  Night Parade (1929)
Sporting Widow, The
  Madame Racketeer (1932)
Spring Song
  Springtime (1948, Brit.)
Spy 13
  Operator 13 (1934)
Spy in Black, The
  U-Boat 29 (1939, Brit.)
Spy in the Pantry
  Missing Ten Days (1941, Brit.)
Squared Circle, The
  Joe Palooka in the Squared Circle (1950)
Squeaker, The
  Murder on Diamond Row (1937, Brit.)

Stage Whispers
  Grief Street (1931)
Stagecoach Line
  Old Texas Trail, The (1944)
Stampeded
  Big Land, The (1957)
Stand and Deliver
  Bowery Blitzkreig (1941)
Star of the Circus
  Hidden Menace, The (1940, Brit.)
Star Said No, The
  Callaway Went Thataway (1951)
State Police
  Whirlwind Raiders (1948)
State Secret
  Great Manhunt, The (1951, Brit.)
Stepping into Society
  Doughnuts and Society (1936)
Stolen Time
  Blonde Blackmailer (1955, Brit.)
Stolen Wealth
  Blazing Six Shooters (1940)
Stooges Go West
  Gold Raiders (1952)
Storm Over Africa
  Royal African Rifles (1953)
Story of Dr. Ehrlich's Magic Bullet
  Dr. Ehrlich's Magic Bullet (1940)
Story of Gilbert and Sullivan, The
  Great Gilbert and Sullivan, The (1953, Brit.)
Stranded in Paris
  Artists and Models Abroad (1938)
Strange Awakening, The
  Female Fiends (1958, Brit.)
Strange Conspiracy
  President Vanishes, The (1934)
Strange Illusion
  Out of the Night (1945)
Strange Incident
  Ox-Bow Incident, The (1943)
Strange Interval
  Strange Interlude (1932)
Strange Laws
  Cherokee Strip, The (1937)
Strange Roads
  Exposed (1932)
Stranger Came Home, The
  Unholy Four, The (1954, Brit.)
Stranger in the House
  Cop-Out (1967, Brit.)
Stranger, The
  Stranger from Texas, The (1940)
Stranger, The
  Intruder, The (1962)
Stranger Walked In, A
  Love From a Stranger (1947)
Strangest Case, The
  Crime Doctor's Strangest Case, The (1943)
Street Corner
  Both Sides of the Law (1953, Brit.)
Streets of Shadows
  Shadow Man (1953, Brit.)
Strictly Confidential
  Broadway Bill (1934)
Strictly for Pleasure
  Perfect Furlough, The (1958)
Strip Poker
  Big Swithch, The (1970, Brit.)
Strip-Tease Lady
  Lady of Burlesque (1943)
Stronger than Fear
  Edge of Doom (1950)
Studio Romance
  Talent Scout (1937)
Such Men Are Dangerous
  Racers, The (1955)
Such Things Happen
  Love Is a Racket (1932)
Suicide Club, The
  Trouble for Two (1936)
Suitable Case for Treatment, A
  Morgan! (1966, Brit.)
Summer Interlude
  Illicit Interlude (1954, Swed.)
Summer Lightning
  Scudda-Hoo! Scudda-Hay! (1948)
Summer Madness
  Summertime (1955)
Sumuru
  Million Eyes of Su-Muru, The (1967, Brit.)
Sunset in Vienna
  Suicide Legion (1940, Brit.)
Superman and the Strange People
  Superman and the Mole-Men (1951)
Susanna
  Shepherd of the Ozarks (1942)
Suspect
  Risk, The (1961, Brit.)
Suspected
  Texas Dynamo (1950)

Sweeney Todd, the Demon Barber of Fleet Street
  Demon Barber of Fleet Street, The (1939, Brit.)
Sweepstake Racketeers
  Undercover Agent (1939)
Sweet Aloes
  Give Me Your Heart (1936)
Sweet Revenge
  Dandy, the All American Girl (1976)
Sweethearts on Parade
  Sweethearts of the U.S.A. (1944)
Swift Vengeance
  Rookie Cop, The (1939)
Swing and Sway
  Swing in the Saddle (1944)
Swing High
  Jive Junction (1944)
Swing it Buddy
  Swing it Professor (1937)
Swing, Teacher, Swing
  College Swing (1938)
Swinging Pearl Mystery, The
  Plot Thickens, The (1936)

Tainted Money
  Show Them No Mercy (1935)
Take the Stage
  Curtain Call at Cactus Creek (1950)
Taking Sides
  Lightning Guns (1950)
Tale of Five Cities, A
  Tale of Five Women, A (1952, Brit.)
Tales of Beatrix Potter
  Peter Rabbit and Tales of Beatrix Potter (1971,
  Brit.)
Talk of a Million
  You Can't Beat the Irish (1952, Brit.)
Tall Headlines
  Frightened Bride, The (1952, Brit.)
Tall Trouble, The
  Hell Canyon Outlaws (1957)
Tamlin
  Devil's Widow, The (1972, Brit.)
Tammy
  Tammy and the Bachelor (1957)
Tank Commando
  Tank Commandos (1959)
Target for Scandal
  Washington Story (1952)
Tarzan and the Jungle Queen
  Tarzan's Peril (1951)
Taste of Fear
  Scream of Fear (1961, Brit.)
Tea Leaves in the Wind
  Hate in Paradise (1938, Brit.)
Teenage Delinquents
  No Time to be Young (1957)
Teenage Frankenstein
  I Was a Teenage Frankenstein (1958)
Teenage Lovers
  Too Soon to Love (1960)
Tell It to the Marines
  Here Come the Marines (1952)
Tell-Tale Heart, The
  Bucket of Blood (1934, Brit.)
Ten Days in Paris
  Missing Ten Days (1941, Brit.)
Ten Little Niggers
  And Then There Were None (1945)
Terrible Beauty, A
  Night Fighters, The (1960)
Terror Strikes, The
  War of the Colossal Beast (1958)
Texas Kid, Outlaw
  Kid From Texas, The (1950)
Texas Rose
  Return of Jack Slade, The (1955)
Texas Serenade
  Old Corral, The (1937)
Texas to Tokyo
  We've Never Been Licked (1943)
Thank Your Stars
  Shoot the Works (1934)
That Dangerous Age
  If This Be Sin (1950, Brit.)
That Girl from College
  Sorority House (1939)
That Kind of Girl
  Models, Inc. (1952)
That Mad Mr. Jones
  Fuller Brush Man, The (1948)
That Navy Spirit
  Hold 'Em Navy (1937)
That Night in London
  Overnight (1933, Brit.)
That Woman Opposite
  City After Midnight (1957, Brit.)

Theatre Royal
  Royal Family of Broadway, The (1930)
Their Secret Affair
  Top Secret Affair (1957)
There Goes Susie
  Scandals of Paris (1934, Brit.)
These Dangerous Years
  Dangerous Youth (1958, Brit.)
They Are Guilty
  Are These Our Parents? (1944)
They Flew Alone
  Wings and the Woman (1942, Brit.)
They Passed This Way
  Four Faces West (1948)
They're Off
  Straight, Place and Show (1938)
Thing from Another World, The
  Thing, The (1951)
Third Party Risk
  Deadly Game, The (1955, Brit.)
Thirty-Six Hours
  Terror Street (1953)
This is My Affair
  I Can Get It for You Wholesale (1951)
This Man Reuter
  Dispatch From Reuters, A (1940)
Three Brothers
  Side Street (1929)
Three Crazy Legionnaires
  Three Legionnaires (1937)
Three Maxims, The
  Show Goes On, The (1938, Brit.)
Three Men and a Girl
  Kentucky Moonshine (1938)
Three Rogues
  Not Exactly Gentlemen (1931)
Through Hell to Glory
  Jet Attack (1958)
Through the Storm
  Prairie Schooners (1940)
Thunder Across the Pacific
  Wild Blue Yonder, The (1952)
Thunder in the Dust
  Sundowners, The (1950)
Thunder on the Trail
  Thundering Trail, The (1951)
Tidal Wave
  S.O.S. Tidal Wave (1939)
Tiger in the Sky
  McConnell Story, The (1955)
Tiger of Bengal
  Journey to the Lost City (1960, Ger./Fr./Ital.)
Time Bomb
  Terror on a Train (1953, Brit.)
Time for a Killing, A
  Long Ride Home, The (1968)
Time for Action
  Tip on a Dead Jockey (1957)
Time for Giving, A
  Generation (1969)
Timeslip
  Atomic Man, The (1955, Brit.)
To Dorothy, A Son
  Cash on Delivery (1956, Brit.)
Toast of the Legion
  Kiss Me Again (1931)
Tomahawk and the Cross, The
  Pillars of the Sky (1956)
Tomahawk Trail, The
  Iroquois Trail (1950)
Tommy Steele Story, The
  Rock Around the World (1957, Brit.)
Tomorrow at Midnight
  For Love or Money (1939)
Too Dangerous to Love
  Perfect Strangers (1950)
Too Many Chefs
  Who Is Killing the Great Chefs of Europe? (1978,
  US/Ger.)
Too Many Women
  God's Gift to Women (1931)
Top of the Bill
  Fanny Foley Herself (1931)
Top Secret
  Mr. Potts Goes to Moscow (1953, Brit.)
Torment
  Paper Gallows (1950, Brit.)
Touch and Go
  Light Touch, The (1955, Brit.)
Touch of Love, A
  Thank You All Very Much (1969, Brit.)
Train 2419
  Return of Casey Jones, The (1933)
Traitor Spy
  Torso Murder Mystery, The (1940, Brit.)
Traitors, The
  Accursed, The (1958, Brit.)
Transatlantic Trouble
  Take It from Me (1937, Brit.)

Transcontinent Express
  Rock Island Trail (1950)
Treason
  Old Louisiana (1938)
Treason
  Guilty of Treason (1950)
Treasure of Kalifa
  Steel Lady, The (1953)
Treasure of Monte Cristo, The
  Secret of Monte Cristo, The (1961, Brit.)
Treasure of San Teresa, The
  Hot Money Girl (1962, Brit./Ger.)
Tree of Liberty, The
  Howards of Virginia, The (1940)
Trespasser, The
  Night Editor (1946)
Trial of Portia Merriman, The
  Portia on Trial (1937)
Tricked
  Bandits of El Dorado (1949)
Triple Cross, The
  Joe Palooka in Triple Cross (1951)
Triple Trouble
  Kentucky Kernels (1935)
Trollenberg Terror, The
  Crawling Eye, The (1958, Brit.)
Trooper, The
  Fighting Trooper, The (1935)
Tropicana
  Heat's On, The (1943)
Trottie True
  Gay Lady, The (1949, Brit.)
Trouble Chaser
  Li'l Abner (1940)
Trouble in Panama
  Torchy Blane in Panama (1938)
Trouble Shooter, The
  Man With the Gun, The (1955)
Trouble with Eve
  In Trouble with Eve (1964, Brit.)
Troubles Through Billets
  Blondie for Victory (1942)
Trunk Crime
  Design for Murder (1940, Brit.)
Trunk Mystery, The
  One New York Night (1935)
Trust Your Wife
  Fall Guy, The (1930)
Try and Get Me
  Sound of Fury, The (1950)
Tudor Rose
  Lady Jane Grey (1936, Brit.)
Twinky
  Lola (1971, Brit./Ital.)
Twisted Road, The
  They Live by Night (1948)
Two Black Sheep
  Two Sinners (1935)
Two Faces of Dr. Jekyll
  House of Fright (1961)
Two Fisted Agent
  Bonanza Town (1951)
Two in a Million
  East of Fifth Avenue (1933)
Two Men and a Girl
  Honeymoon (1947)
Two on the Tiles
  School for Brides (1952, Brit.)
Two Roads
  Texas Stagecoach (1940)
Two Senoritas
  Two Senoritas from Chicago (1943)
Two Texas Knights
  Two Guys from Texas (1948)
Two White Arms
  Wives Beware (1933, Brit.)
Two-Gun Cupid
  Bad Man, The (1941)

Uncle Silas
  Inheritance, The (1951, Brit.)
Unconventional Linda
  Holiday (1938)
Under the Clock
  Clock, The (1945)
Undercover
  Underground Guerrillas (1944, Brit.)
Undercover Girl
  Undercover Maisie (1947)
Uniform Lovers
  Hold 'Em Yale (1935)
Unvanquished, The
  Aparajito (1959, India)
Unwelcome Visitors
  Lone Star Pioneers (1939)
Up She Goes
  Up Goes Maisie (1946)

Valley of Death, The
  Tank Battalion (1958)
Valley of Fury
  Chief Crazy Horse (1955)
Valley of Gold, The
  Gold (1932)
Valley of Song
  Men Are Children Twice (1953, Brit.)
Vampira
  Old Dracula (1975, Brit.)
Vanessa
  Vanessa, Her Love Story (1935)
Vendetta
  Murieta (1965, Span.)
Vengeance
  Valley of Vengeance (1944)
Vengeance
  Trail to Vengeance (1945)
Vengeance of Gregory Walters, The
  Feud of the West (1936)
Very Important Person, A
  Coming-Out Party, A (1962, Brit.)
Victims of the Beyond
  Sucker Money (1933)
Victory
  Escape to Victory (1981)
Vigour of Youth
  Spirit of Notre Dame (1931)
Violent City
  Family, The (1974, Fr./Ital.)
Violent Hour, The
  Dial 1119 (1950)
Violent Streets
  Thief (1981)
Violent Summer
  Widow is Willing, The (1961, Fr./Ital.)
Virtuous Tramps, The
  Devil's Brother, The (1933)
Virtuous Wife, The
  Men Are Like That (1931)
Visa to Canton
  Passport to China (1961, Brit.)
Viva Las Vegas!
  Meet Me in Las Vegas (1956)
Voice of Merrill, The
  Murder Will Out (1953, Brit.)
Voice of Scandal
  Here Comes Carter (1936)
Voice of the Turtle
  One for the Book (1947)
Vultures of the Law
  Son of the Plains (1931)

Wages of Fear
  Sorcerer (1977)
Waiting for the Bride
  Runaround, The (1931)
Wake Up and Dream
  What's Cookin' (1942)
Waltzes from Vienna
  Strauss' Great Waltz (1934, Brit.)
Wanderlust
  Mary Jane's Pa (1935)
Wanted
  Police Call (1933)
Wanted
  High Voltage (1929)
Wanted Men
  Law of the Rio Grande (1931)
War Shock
  Woman's Devotion, A (1956)
Waterfront
  Waterfront Women (1952, Brit.)
Way of Life
  They Call It Sin (1932)
Way to the Stars, The
  Johnny in the Clouds (1945, Brit.)
We Humans
  Young America (1942)
We Three
  Compromised! (1931)
We're in the Army Now
  Pack Up Your Troubles (1939)
Wedding Bells
  Royal Wedding (1951)
Wedding Breakfast
  Catered Affair, The (1956)
Wedding Group
  Wrath of Jealousy (1936, Brit.)
Wednesday's Child
  Family Life (1971, Brit.)
Week-End Madness
  August Week-End (1936)
Weekend Lives
  Week-End Marriage (1932)
Welcome Home
  Snafu (1945)

Welcome Stranger
  Across the Sierras (1941)
Went the Day Well?
  48 Hours (1944, Brit.)
West of Kirby
  Men of Ireland (1938, Ireland)
West of Montana
  Mail Order Bride (1964)
West of Suez
  Fighting Wildcats, The (1957, Brit.)
What a Man
  Never Give a Sucker an Even Break (1941)
What a Woman
  There's That Woman Again (1938)
What a Woman!
  Beautiful Cheat, The (1946)
What Lola Wants
  Damn Yankees (1958)
What Price Melody?
  Lord Byron of Broadway (1930)
What Wives Don't Want
  Virtuous Husband, The (1931)
When a Fellow Needs a Friend
  When a Feller Needs a Friend (1932)
When Blonde Meets Blonde
  Anybody's Blonde (1931)
When Girls Leave Home
  Missing Girls (1936)
When Knighthood Was in Flower
  Sword and the Rose, The (1953)
When New York Sleeps
  Now I'll Tell (1934)
When Strangers Marry
  Betrayed (1944)
When We Look Back
  Frisco Waterfront (1935)
Where No Vultures Fly
  Ivory Hunter (1952, Brit.)
Where the River Bends
  Bend of the River (1952)
While New York Sleeps
  Now I'll Tell (1934)
Whiskey Galore
  Tight Little Island (1949, Brit.)
Whispering Smith Hits London
  Whispering Smith Versus Scotland Yard (1952,
  Brit.)
White Captive
  White Savage (1943)
White Cradle Inn
  High Fury (1947, Brit.)
White Man, The
  Squaw Man, The (1931)
White Savage
  South of Tahiti (1941)
Who Dares Wins
  Final Option, The (1983, Brit.)
Who Goes There?
  Passionate Sentry, The (1952, Brit.)
Whoever Slew Auntie Roo?
  Who Slew Auntie Roo? (1971, Brit.)
Whom the Gods Love
  Mozart (1940, Brit.)
Why Change Your Husband?
  Gold Dust Gertie (1931)
Wicked as They Come
  Portrait in Smoke (1957, Brit.)
Wife Swappers, The
  Swappers, The (1970, Brit.)
Wild and the Willing, The
  Young and Willing (1964, Brit.)
Wildfire: The Story of a Horse
  Wildfire (1945)
Will Tomorrow Ever Come?
  That's My Man (1947)
Willie and Joe in Tokyo
  Willie and Joe Back at the Front (1952)
Win, Place and Show
  Crazy Over Horses (1951)
Window in London, A
  Lady in Distress (1942, Brit.)
Winged Devils
  Above the Clouds (1933)
Wings of Song
  Ladies in Love (1930)
Winner Take All
  Joe Palooka in Winner Take All (1948)
Winning Way, The
  All American, The (1953)
Wistful Widow, The
  Wistful Widow of Wagon Gap, The (1947)
Witches, The
  Devil's Own, The (1967, Brit.)
Witchfinder General
  Conqueror Worm, The (1968, Brit.)
Within the Law
  Paid (1930)
Without Children
  Penthouse Party (1936)

Without Risk
  Pecos River (1951)
Woman Alone, A
  Two Who Dared (1937, Brit.)
Woman Between, The
  Woman Decides, The (1931, Brit.)
Woman Between, The
  Woman I Love, The (1937)
Woman Destroyed, A
  Smash-Up, the Story of a Woman (1947)
Woman He Scorned, The
  Way of Lost Souls, The (1929, Brit.)
Woman in Brown
  Vicious Circle (1948)
Woman in Her Thirties
  Side Streets (1934)
Woman in Question, The
  Five Angles on Murder (1950, Brit.)
Woman in the Case, The
  Headline Woman, The (1935)
Woman in the Case
  Allotment Wives (1945)
Woman Tamer
  She Couldn't Take It (1935)
Woman with No Name, The
  Her Panelled Door (1951, Brit.)
Woman Without a Face
  Mister Buddwing (1966)
Woman's Vengeance, A
  Man From Sundown, The (1939)
Women in His House, The
  Animal Kingdom, The (1932)
Women of Twilight
  Twilight Women (1953, Brit.)
Wonder Plane
  Mercy Plane (1939)
Wonderful Life
  Swinger's Paradise (1965, Brit.)
Wonderful Years, The
  Restless Years, The (1958)
Working Wives
  Week-End Marriage (1932)
World and His Wife, The
  State of the Union (1948)
World Ten Times Over, The
  Pussycat Alley (1965, Brit.)
Worthy Deceiver
  Big Bluff, The (1933)
Wrongly Accused
  Bad Men of the Hills (1942)

X-Ray
  Hospital Massacre (1982)

Yank in Dutch, A
  Wife Takes a Flyer, The (1942)
Yankee in King Arthur's Court, The
  Connecticut Yankee, A (1931)
Years without Days
  Castle on the Hudson (1940)
Yellow Passport, The
  Yellow Ticket, The (1931)
Yellow Teddybears, The
  Gutter Girls (1964, Brit.)
Yesterday's Hero
  Hoosier Schoolboy, The (1937)
You Belong to My Heart
  Mr. Imperium (1951)
You Can't Beat the Law
  Smart Guy (1943)
You Can't Do That to Me
  Maisie Goes to Reno (1944)
You Can't Sleep Here
  I Was a Male War Bride (1949)
You Can't Take Money
  Internes Can't Take Money (1937)
You Don't Need Pajamas at Rosie's
  First Time, The (1969)
You Never Know
  You Never Can Tell (1951)
Young and Eager
  Claudelle Inglish (1961)
Young Invaders
  Darby's Rangers (1958)
Young Lovers, The
  Chance Meeting (1954, Brit.)
Young Man of Music
  Young Man with a Horn (1950)
Young Ones, The
  Wonderful to Be Young (1962, Brit.)
Young Paul Baroni
  Kid Monk Baroni (1952)
Youth Takes a Hand
  Behind Prison Walls (1943)

Zamba the Gorilla
  Zamba (1949)
Zee & Co.
  X Y & Zee (1972, Brit.)
Zoltan, Hound of Dracula
  Dracula's Dog (1978)

Series Index

The following list has been compiled to furnish the reader with a concise reference guide to the titles of movies which form series. We have taken a few liberties with the general characteristics that have traditionally been attributed to a series in order to include those movies we feel should be grouped together under a common heading, and which are closely related to a series. There may be some argument about whether ABBOTT AND COSTELLO, ROY ROGERS, GENE AUTRY, LAUREL AND HARDY, and THE RITZ BROTHERS qualify to be included in this list, but the films under these headings have actors who are repeating the same roles throughout, and they have been produced in association with the same studios. To keep all movies in the proper sequential order, films of British series are listed by the year in which they were released in Britain, occasionally disagreeing with individual entries in the MPG having an American release date. In a few instances, entries in the MPG will have a reference to this index, yet are not included. Further research made it evident that these films could not justifiably be considered part of a series. We also apologize for films listed here which do not have references in their individual entries. Though we have attempted to be all-encompassing with this list, undoubtedly some series films will be left out. We regret any such omission, and can only blame this on lack of necessary information at the time of compilation.

ABBOTT AND COSTELLO
ONE NIGHT IN THE TROPICS (1940); BUCK PRIVATES; IN THE NAVY; HOLD THAT GHOST; KEEP EM' FLYING (1941); RIDE EM' COWBOY; RIO RITA; PARDON MY SARONG; WHO DONE IT? (1942); IT AIN'T HAY; HIT THE ICE (1943); IN SOCIETY; LOST IN A HAREM; HERE COME THE CO-EDS; THE NAUGHTY NINETIES; ABBOTT AND COSTELLO IN HOLLYWOOD (1945); LITTLE GIANT; THE TIME OF THEIR LIVES (1946); BUCK PRIVATES COME HOME; THE WISTFUL WIDOW OF WAGON GAP (1947); THE NOOSE HANGS HIGH; ABBOTT AND COSTELLO MEET FRANKENSTEIN; MEXICAN HAYRIDE (1948); AFRICA SCREAMS; ABBOTT AND COSTELLO MEET THE KILLER, BORIS KARLOFF (1949); ABBOTT AND COSTELLO IN THE FOREIGN LEGION (1950); ABBOTT AND COSTELLO MEET THE INVISIBLE MAN; COMIN' ROUND THE MOUNTAIN (1951); JACK AND THE BEANSTALK; LOST IN ALASKA; ABBOTT AND COSTELLO MEET CAPTAIN KIDD (1952); ABBOTT AND COSTELLO GO TO MARS; ABBOTT AND COSTELLO MEET DR. JEKYLL AND MR. HYDE (1953); ABBOTT AND COSTELLO MEET THE KEYSTONE KOPS; ABBOTT AND COSTELLO MEET THE MUMMY (1955); DANCE WITH ME HENRY (1956).

ANDY HARDY
A FAMILY AFFAIR (1937); YOU'RE ONLY YOUNG ONCE; JUDGE HARDY'S CHILDREN; LOVE FINDS ANDY HARDY; OUT WEST WITH THE HARDYS (1938); THE HARDYS RIDE HIGH; ANDY HARDY GETS SPRING FEVER; JUDGE HARDY AND SON (1939); ANDY HARDY MEETS DEBUTANTE (1940); ANDY HARDY'S PRIVATE SECRETARY; LIFE BEGINS FOR ANDY HARDY (1941); THE COURTSHIP OF ANDY HARDY; ANDY HARDY'S DOUBLE LIFE (1942); ANDY HARDY'S BLONDE TROUBLE (1944); LOVE LAUGHS AT ANDY HARDY (1946); ANDY HARDY COMES HOME (1958).

ANTOINE DOINEL
THE 400 BLOWS (1959); LOVE AT TWENTY ["Antoine and Colette" episode] (1962); STOLEN KISSES (1968); BED AND BOARD (1970); LOVE ON THE RUN (1979).

GENE AUTRY
IN OLD SANTE FE (1934); TUMBLING TUMBLEWEEDS; MELODY TRAIL; SAGEBRUSH TROUBADOR; THE SINGING VAGABOND (1935); RED RIVER VALLEY; COMIN' ROUND THE MOUNTAIN; THE SINGING COWBOY; GUNS AND GUITARS (1936); THE BIG SHOW; GIT ALONG, LITTLE DOGIES; ROUNDUP TIME IN TEXAS; ROOTIN' TOOTIN' RHYTHM; YODELIN' KID FROM PINE RIDGE; OH, SUSANNA; PUBLIC COWBOY NO. 1; RIDE, RANGER, RIDE; BOOTS AND SADDLES; MANHATTAN MERRY-GO-ROUND; SPRINGTIME IN THE ROCKIES; THE OLD CORRAL (1937); THE OLD BARN DANCE; GOLD MINE IN THE SKY; MAN FROM MUSIC MOUNTAIN; PRAIRIE MOON; RHYTHM OF THE SADDLE; WESTERN JAMBOREE (1938); HOME ON THE PRAIRIE; MEXICALI ROSE; BLUE MONTANA SKIES; MOUNTAIN RHYTHM; COLORADO SUNSET; IN OLD MONTEREY; ROVIN' TUMBLEWEEDS; SOUTH OF THE BORDER (1939); RANCHO GRANDE; SHOOTING HIGH; GAUCHO SERENADE; CAROLINA MOON; RIDE, TENDERFOOT, RIDE; MELODY RANCH (1940); RIDIN' ON A RAINBOW; BACK IN THE SADDLE; THE SINGING HILL; SUNSET IN WYOMING; UNDER FIESTA STARS; DOWN MEXICO WAY; SIERRA SUE (1941); COWBOY SERENADE; HEART OF THE RIO GRANDE; HOME IN WYOMIN'; STARDUST ON THE SAGE; CALL OF THE CANYON; BELLS OF CAPISTRANO (1942); SIOUX CITY SUE (1946); TRAIL TO SAN ANTONE; TWILIGHT ON THE RIO GRANDE; SADDLE PALS; ROBIN HOOD OF TEXAS; THE LAST ROUND-UP (1947); LOADED PISTOLS; THE STRAWBERRY ROAN (1948); SONS OF NEW MEXICO; THE BIG SOMBRERO; RIDERS OF THE WHISTLING PINES; RIM OF THE CANYON; THE COWBOY AND THE INDIANS; RIDERS IN THE SKY (1949); MULE TRAIN; COW TOWN; BEYOND THE PURPLE HILLS; INDIAN TERRITORY; THE BLAZING SUN (1950); GENE AUTRY AND THE MOUNTIES; TEXANS NEVER CRY; WHIRLWIND; SILVER CANYON; HILLS OF UTAH; VALLEY OF FIRE (1951); THE OLD WEST; NIGHT STAGE TO GALVESTON; APACHE COUNTRY; BARBED WIRE; WAGON TEAM; BLUE CANADIAN ROCKIES (1952); WINNING OF THE WEST; ON TOP OF OLD SMOKY; GOLDTOWN GHOST RIDERS; PACK TRAIN; SAGINAW TRAIL; LAST OF THE PONY RIDERS (1953).

BILL CRANE
THE WESTLAND CASE (1937); LADY IN THE MORGUE; THE LAST WARNING (1938).

BILLY CARSON
See: BILLY THE KID

BILLY JACK
BILLY JACK (1971); THE TRIAL OF BILLY JACK (1974); BILLY JACK GOES TO WASHINGTON (1978).

BILLY THE KID
BILLY THE KID OUTLAWED; BILLY THE KID IN TEXAS; BILLY THE KID'S GUN JUSTICE (1940); BILLY THE KID'S RANGE WAR; BILLY THE KID'S FIGHTING PALS; BILLY THE KID IN SANTE FE; BILLY THE KID WANTED; BILLY THE KID'S ROUNDUP (1941); BILLY THE KID TRAPPED; BILLY THE KID'S SMOKING GUNS; LAW AND ORDER; SHERIFF OF SAGE VALLEY; THE MYSTERIOUS RIDER (1942); THE KID RIDES AGAIN; FUGITIVE OF THE PLAINS; WESTERN CYCLONE; CATTLE STAMPEDE; THE RENEGADE; DEVIL RIDERS (1943); FRONTIER OUTLAWS; THUNDERING GUN SLINGERS; VALLEY OF VENGEANCE; THE DRIFTER; FUZZY SETTLES DOWN; BLAZING FRONTIER; RUSTLER'S HIDEOUT; WILD HORSE PHANTOM; OATH OF VENGEANCE (1944); LIGHTNING RAIDERS; HIS BROTHER'S GHOST; SHADOWS OF DEATH; GANGSTER'S DEN; STAGECOACH OUTLAWS; BORDER BADMEN; FIGHTING BILL CARSON; PRAIRIE RUSTLERS (1945); GENTLEMEN WITH GUNS; TERRORS ON HORSEBACK; GHOST OF HIDDEN VALLEY; PRAIRIE BADMEN; OVERLAND RIDERS; OUTLAW OF THE PLAINS (1946).

BLONDIE
BLONDIE (1938); BLONDIE MEETS THE BOSS; BLONDIE TAKES A VACATION; BLONDIE BRINGS UP BABY (1939); BLONDIE ON A BUDGET; BLONDIE HAS SERVANT TROUBLE; BLONDIE PLAYS CUPID (1940); BLONDIE GOES LATIN; BLONDIE IN SOCIETY (1941); BLONDIE GOES TO COLLEGE; BLONDIE'S BLESSED EVENT; BLONDIE FOR VICTORY (1942); IT'S A GREAT LIFE; FOOTLIGHT GLAMOUR (1943); LEAVE IT TO BLONDIE (1945); LIFE WITH BLONDIE; BLONDIE'S LUCKY DAY; BLONDIE KNOWS BEST (1946); BLONDIE'S BIG MOMENT; BLONDIE'S HOLIDAY; BLONDIE IN THE DOUGH; BLONDIE'S ANNIVERSARY (1947); BLONDIE'S REWARD; BLONDIE'S SECRET (1948); BLONDIE'S BIG DEAL; BLONDIE HITS THE JACKPOT (1949); BLONDIE'S HERO; BEWARE OF BLONDIE (1950).

BOMBA THE JUNGLE BOY
BOMBA THE JUNGLE BOY; BOMBA ON PANTHER ISLAND (1949); THE LOST VOLCANO; BOMBA AND THE HIDDEN CITY (1950); ELEPHANT STAMPEDE; THE LION HUNTERS (1951); AFRICAN TREASURE; BOMBA AND THE JUNGLE GIRL (1952); SAFARI DRUMS (1953); THE GOLDEN IDOL; KILLER LEOPARD (1954); LORD OF THE JUNGLE (1955).

BOSTON BLACKIE
Silents: BOSTON BLACKIE'S LITTLE PAL (1918); BLACKIE'S REDEMPTION (1919); MISSING MILLIONS; THE FACE IN THE FOG (1922); BOSTON BLACKIE; CROOKED ALLEY (1923); THROUGH THE DARK; (1924); THE RETURN OF BOSTON BLACKIE (1927). Sound Films: MEET BOSTON BLACKIE; CONFESSIONS OF BOSTON BLACKIE; ALIAS BOSTON BLACKIE; BOSTON BLACKIE GOES HOLLYWOOD (1942); AFTER MIDNIGHT WITH BOSTON BLACKIE (1943); ONE MYSTERIOUS NIGHT (1944); BOSTON BLACKIE BOOKED ON SUSPICION; BOSTON BLACKIE'S RENDEZVOUS (1945); A CLOSE CALL FOR BOSTON BLACKIE; THE PHANTOM THIEF; BOSTON BLACKIE AND THE LAW (1946); TRAPPED BY BOSTON BLACKIE (1948); BOSTON BLACKIE'S CHINESE VENTURE (1949).

BOWERY BOYS
The following are ordered chronologically with abbreviations following each title to signify the series to which each film belongs: THE DEAD END KIDS—dek; THE DEAD END KIDS AND LITTLE TOUGH GUYS—dek/ltg; LITTLE TOUGH GUYS—ltg; EAST SIDE KIDS—esk)
DEAD END [dek] (1937); CRIME SCHOOL [dek]; LITTLE TOUGH GUY [dek/ltg]; ANGELS WITH DIRTY FACES [dek]; LITTLE TOUGH GUYS IN SOCIETY [ltg] (1938); NEWSBOYS' HOME [ltg]; CODE OF THE STREETS [ltg]; HELL'S KITCHEN [dek]; ANGELS WASH THEIR FACES [dek]; DEAD END KIDS ON DRESS PARADE [dek]; CALL A MESSENGER [ltg] (1939); EAST SIDE KIDS [esk]; BOYS OF THE CITY [esk]; YOU'RE NOT SO TOUGH [dek/ltg]; THAT GANG OF MINE [esk]; GIVE US WINGS [dek/ltg] (1940); PRIDE OF THE BOWERY [esk]; FLYING WILD [esk]; HIT THE ROAD [dek/ltg]; BOWERY BLITZKREIG [esk]; MOB TOWN [dek/ltg]; SPOOKS RUN WILD [esk] (1941); MR. WISE GUY [esk]; LET'S GET TOUGH [esk]; TOUGH AS THEY COME [dek/ltg]; SMART ALECKS [esk]; 'NEATH BROOKLYN BRIDGE [esk] (1942); KID DYNAMITE [esk]; KEEP 'EM SLUGGING [dek/ltg]; CLANCY STREET BOYS [esk]; GHOSTS ON THE LOOSE [esk]; MR. MUGGS STEPS OUT [esk] (1943); MILLION DOLLAR KID [esk]; FOLLOW THE LEADER [esk]; BLOCK BUSTERS [esk]; BOWERY CHAMPS [esk] (1944); DOCKS OF NEW YORK [esk]; MR. MUGGS RIDES AGAIN [esk]; COME OUT FIGHTING [esk] (1945).
The following titles are all part of the BOWERY BOYS series) LIVE WIRES; IN FAST COMPANY; BOWERY BOMBSHELL; SPOOK BUSTERS; MR. HEX (1946); HARD BOILED MAHONEY; NEWS HOUNDS; BOWERY BUCKAROOS (1947); ANGELS ALLEY; JINX MONEY; SMUGGLERS COVE; TROUBLE MAKERS (1948); FIGHTING FOOLS; HOLD THAT BABY!; ANGELS IN DISGUISE; MASTER MINDS (1949); BLONDE DYNAMITE; LUCKY LOSERS; TRIPLE TROUBLE; BLUES BUSTERS (1950); BOWERY BATTALION; GHOST CHASERS; LET'S GO NAVY; CRAZY OVER HORSES (1951); HOLD THAT LINE; HERE COME THE MARINES; FEUDIN'

FOOLS; NO HOLDS BARRED (1952); JALOPY; LOOSE IN LONDON; CLIPPED WINGS; PRIVATE EYES (1953); PARIS PLAYBOYS; THE BOWERY BOYS MEET THE MONSTERS; JUNGLE GENTS (1954); BOWERY TO BAGDAD; HIGH SOCIETY; SPY CHASERS; JAIL BUSTERS (1955); DIG THAT URANIUM; CRASHING LAS VEGAS; FIGHTING TROUBLE; HOT SHOTS (1956); HOLD THAT HYPNOTIST; SPOOK CHASERS; LOOKING FOR DANGER (1957); UP IN SMOKE; IN THE MONEY (1958).

BULLDOG DRUMMOND
Silents: BULLDOG DRUMMOND (1923); BULLDOG DRUMMOND'S THIRD ROUND (1927); TEMPLE TOWER (1930). Sound Films: BULLDOG DRUMMOND (1929); THE RETURN OF BULLDOG DRUMMOND; BULLDOG DRUMMOND STRIKES BACK (1934); ALIAS BULLDOG DRUMMOND (1935); BULLDOG DRUMMOND ESCAPES; BULLDOG DRUMMOND AT BAY; BULLDOG DRUMMOND COMES BACK; BULLDOG DRUMMOND'S REVENGE (1937); BULLDOG DRUMMOND'S PERIL; BULLDOG DRUMMOND IN AFRICA (1938); BULLDOG DRUMMOND'S SECRET POLICE; BULLDOG DRUMMOND'S BRIDE; ARREST BULLDOG DRUMMOND (1939); BULLDOG DRUMMOND AT BAY; BULLDOG DRUMMOND STRIKES BACK (1947); THE CHALLENGE; 13 LEAD SOLDIERS (1948); CALLING BULLDOG DRUMMOND (1951); DEADLIER THAN THE MALE (1967); SOME GIRLS DO (1969).

CARRY ON
CARRY ON SERGEANT; CARRY ON NURSE; CARRY ON TEACHER (1959); CARRY ON CONSTABLE (1960); CARRY ON REGARDLESS (1961); CARRY ON CRUISING (1962); CARRY ON CABBIE; CARRY ON JACK (1963); CARRY ON SPYING; CARRY ON CLEO (1964); CARRY ON COWBOY (1965); CARRY ON SCREAMING; DON'T LOSE YOUR HEAD (1966); FOLLOW THAT CAMEL; CARRY ON DOCTOR (1967); CARRY ON, UP THE KHYBER (1968); CARRY ON CAMPING; CARRY ON AGAIN, DOCTOR (1969); CARRY ON LOVING; CARRY ON UP THE JUNGLE; CARRY ON HENRY VIII (1970); CARRY ON 'ROUND THE BEND (1972); CARRY ON AT YOUR CONVENIENCE (1972?); CARRY ON MATRON (1973); CARRY ON ABROAD; CARRY ON GIRLS (1974); CARRY ON DICK; CARRY ON BEHIND (1975); CARRY ON ENGLAND (1976); CARRY ON EMMANNUELLE (1978).

CHARLIE CHAN
BEHIND THAT CURTAIN (1929); CHARLIE CHAN CARRIES ON; THE BLACK CAMEL (1931); CHARLIE CHAN'S CHANCE (1932); CHARLIE CHAN'S GREATEST CASE (1933); CHARLIE CHAN'S COURAGE; CHARLIE CHAN IN LONDON (1934); CHARLIE CHAN IN PARIS; CHARLIE CHAN IN EGYPT; CHARLIE CHAN IN SHANGHAI (1935); CHARLIE CHAN'S SECRET; CHARLIE CHAN AT THE CIRCUS; CHARLIE CHAN AT THE RACE TRACK; CHARLIE CHAN AT THE OPERA (1936); CHARLIE CHAN AT THE OLYMPICS; CHARLIE CHAN ON BROADWAY; CHARLIE CHAN AT MONTE CARLO (1937); CHARLIE CHAN IN HONOLULU (1938); CHARLIE CHAN IN RENO; CHARLIE CHAN AT TREASURE ISLAND; CHARLIE CHAN IN THE CITY OF DARKNESS (1939); CHARLIE CHAN IN PANAMA; CHARLIE CHAN'S MURDER CRUISE; CHARLIE CHAN AT THE WAX MUSEUM; MURDER OVER NEW YORK (1940); DEAD MEN TELL; CHARLIE CHAN IN RIO (1941); CASTLE IN THE DESERT (1942); CHARLIE CHAN IN THE SECRET SERVICE; THE CHINESE CAT; CHARLIE CHAN IN BLACK MAGIC (1944); THE JADE MASK; THE SCARLET CLUE; THE SHANGHAI COBRA (1945); THE RED DRAGON; DARK ABILI; SHADOWS OVER CHINATOWN; DANGEROUS MONEY (1946); THE TRAP; THE CHINESE RING (1947); DOCKS OF NEW ORLEANS; THE SHANGHAI CHEST; THE MYSTERY OF THE GOLDEN EYE; THE FEATHERED SERPENT; (1948); SKY DRAGON (1949); CHARLIE CHAN AND THE CURSE OF THE DRAGON QUEEN (1981).

CISCO KID
IN OLD ARIZONA (1929); CISCO KID (1931); RETURN OF THE CISCO KID; THE CISCO KID AND THE LADY (1939); VIVA CISCO KID; LUCKY CISCO KID; THE GAY CABALLERO (1940); ROMANCE OF THE RIO GRANDE; RIDE ON VAQUERO (1941); THE CISCO KID RETURNS; IN OLD NEW MEXICO; SOUTH OF THE RIO GRANDE (1945); THE GAY CAVALIER; SOUTH OF MONTEREY; BEAUTY AND THE BANDIT (1946); RIDING THE CALIFORNIA TRAIL; ROBIN HOOD OF MONTEREY; KING OF THE BANDITS (1947); THE VALIANT HOMBRE; THE GAY AMIGO; THE DARING CABALLERO; SATAN'S CRADLE (1949); THE GIRL FROM SAN LORENZO (1950).

THE COHENS AND KELLYS
THE COHENS AND KELLYS IN ATLANTIC CITY (1929); THE COHENS AND KELLYS IN SCOTLAND; THE COHENS AND KELLYS IN AFRICA (1930); THE COHENS AND KELLYS IN HOLLYWOOD (1932); THE COHENS AND KELLYS IN TROUBLE (1933).

CONFESSIONS OF
CONFESSIONS OF A WINDOW CLEANER (1973); CONFESSIONS OF A POP PERFORMER (1975); CONFESSIONS OF A DRIVING INSTRUCTOR (1976); CONFESSIONS FROM A HOLIDAY CAMP (1977)

CRIME DOCTOR
CRIME DOCTOR; CRIME DOCTOR'S STRANGEST CASE (1943); SHADOWS IN THE NIGHT; CRIME DOCTOR'S COURAGE; CRIME DOCTOR'S WARNING (1945); CRIME DOCTOR'S MAN HUNT; JUST BEFORE DAWN (1946); THE MILLERSON CASE; THE CRIME DOCTOR'S GAMBLE (1947); THE CRIME DOCTOR'S DIARY (1949).

DEAD END KIDS
See: BOWERY BOYS

DICK BARTON
DICK BARTON—SPECIAL AGENT (1948); DICK BARTON STRIKES BACK (1949); DICK BARTON AT BAY (1950).

DICK TRACY
DICK TRACY (1945); DICK TRACY VS. CUEBALL (1946); DICK TRACY'S DILEMMA; DICK TRACY MEETS GRUESOME (1947).

DOCTOR
DOCTOR IN THE HOUSE (1954); DOCTOR AT SEA (1955); DOCTOR AT LARGE (1957); DOCTOR IN LOVE (1960); DOCTOR IN DISTRESS (1963); CARNABY, M.D. (1966); DOCTOR IN TROUBLE (1970).

DOCTOR CHRISTIAN
MEET DR. CHRISTIAN (1939); THE COURAGEOUS DR. CHRISTIAN; DR. CHRIS-

TIAN MEETS THE WOMEN (1940); REMEDY FOR RICHES; MELODY FOR THREE; THEY MEET AGAIN (1941).

DOCTOR KILDARE (DOCTOR GILLESPIE)
INTERNES CAN'T TAKE MONEY (1937); YOUNG DR. KILDARE (1938); CALLING DOCTOR KILDARE; SECRET OF DR. KILDARE (1939); DR. KILDARE'S STRANGE CASE; DR. KILDARE GOES HOME; DR. KILDARE'S CRISIS (1940); THE PEOPLE VS. DR. KILDARE; DR. KILDARE'S WEDDING DAY; DR. KILDARE'S VICTORY (1941); CALLING DR. GILLESPIE; DR. GILLESPIE'S NEW ASSISTANT (1942); DR. GILLESPIE'S CRIMINAL CASE (1943); THREE MEN IN WHITE; BETWEEN TWO WOMEN (1944); DARK DELUSION (1947).

DOCTOR MABUSE
THE TESTAMENT OF DR. MABUSE (1933); THE THOUSAND EYES OF DR. MABUSE (1960); THE RETURN OF DR. MABUSE (1961); THE INVISIBLE DR. MABUSE; THE TERROR OF DR. MABUSE (1962); SCOTLAND YARD HUNTS DR. MABUSE (1963); DR. MABUSE'S RAYS OF DEATH (1964).

DRACULA
Universal: DRACULA (1931); DRACULA'S DAUGHTER (1936); SON OF DRACULA (1943); HOUSE OF FRANKENSTEIN (1944); HOUSE OF DRACULA (1945); ABBOTT AND COSTELLO MEET FRANKENSTEIN (1948).Hammer: THE HORROR OF DRACULA (1958); THE BRIDES OF DRACULA (1960); DRACULA—PRINCE OF DARK (1968); TASTE THE BLOOD OF DRACULA; THE SCARS OF DRACULA (1970); DRACULA A.D. 1972; COUNT DRACULA AND HIS VAMPIRE BRIDE; DRACULA AND THE SEVEN GOLDEN VAMPIRES (1973).

DURANGO KID
THE DURANGO KID (1940); RETURN OF THE DURANGO KID; BOTH BARRELS BLAZING; RUSTLERS OF THE BADLANDS; BLAZING THE WESTERN TRAIL; OUTLAWS OF THE ROCKIES; LAWLESS EMPIRE (1945); FRONTIER GUNLAW; ROARING RANGERS; GUNNING FOR VENGEANCE; GALLOPING THUNDER; TWO-FISTED STRANGER; THE DESERT HORSEMAN; HEADING WEST; LANDRUSH; TERROR TRAIL; THE FIGHTING FRONTIERSMAN (1946); SOUTH OF THE CHISHOLM TRAIL; THE LONE HAND TEXAN; WEST OF DODGE CITY; LAW OF THE CANYON; PRAIRIE RAIDERS; THE STRANGER FROM PONCA CITY; RIDERS OF THE LONE STAR; BUCKAROO FROM POWDER RIVER; LAST DAYS OF BOOT HILL (1947); SIX GUN LAW; PHANTOM VALLEY; WEST OF SONORA; WHIRLWIND RAIDERS; BLAZING ACROSS THE PECOS; TRAIL TO LAREDO; EL DORADO PASS; QUICK ON THE TRIGGER (1948); CHALLENGE OF THE RANGE; LARAMIE; THE BLAZING TRAIL; SOUTH OF DEATH VALLEY; BANDITS OF ELDORADO; DESERT VIGILANTE; HORSEMEN OF THE SIERRAS; RENEGADES OF THE SAGE (1949); TRAIL OF THE RUSTLERS; OUTCAST OF BLACK MESA; TEXAS DYNAMO; STREETS OF GHOST TOWN; ACROSS THE BADLANDS; RAIDERS OF TOMAHAWK CREEK; LIGHTNING GUNS; FRONTIER OUTPOST (1950); PRAIRIE ROUNDUP; RIDIN' THE OUTLAW TRAIL; FORT SAVAGE RAIDERS; SNAKE RIVER DESPERADOES; BONANZA TOWN; CYCLONE FURY; THE KID FROM AMARILLO; PECOS RIVER (1951); SMOKY CANYON; THE HAWK OF WILD RIVER; LARAMIE MOUNTAINS; THE ROUGH, TOUGH WEST; JUNCTION CITY; THE KID FROM BROKEN GUN (1952).

EASTSIDE KIDS
See: BOWERY BOYS

ELLERY QUEEN
ELLERY QUEEN, MASTER DETECTIVE (1940); ELLERY QUEEN'S PENTHOUSE MYSTERY; ELLERY QUEEN AND THE PERFECT CRIME; ELLERY QUEEN AND THE MURDER RING (1941); A CLOSE CALL FOR ELLERY QUEEN; A DESPERATE CHANCE FOR ELLERY QUEEN; ENEMY AGENTS MEET ELLERY QUEEN (1942).

THE FALCON
THE GAY FALCON; A DATE WITH THE FALCON (1941); THE FALCON TAKES OVER; THE FALCON'S BROTHER (1942); THE FALCON STRIKES BACK; THE FALCON IN DANGER; THE FALCON AND THE CO-EDS (1943); THE FALCON OUT WEST; THE FALCON IN MEXICO; THE FALCON IN HOLLYWOOD (1944); THE FALCON IN SAN FRANCISCO (1945); THE FALCON'S ALIBI; THE FALCON'S ADVENTURE (1946); DEVIL'S CARGO; APPOINTMENT WITH MURDER (1948); SEARCH FOR DANGER (1949).

FIVE LITTLE PEPPERS
FIVE LITTLE PEPPERS AND HOW THEY GREW (1939); FIVE LITTLE PEPPERS AT HOME; OUT WEST WITH THE PEPPERS; FIVE LITTLE PEPPERS IN TROUBLE (1940).

FRANCIS THE TALKING MULE
FRANCIS (1949); FRANCIS GOES TO THE RACES (1951); FRANCIS GOES TO WEST POINT (1952); FRANCIS COVERS THE BIG TOWN (1953); FRANCIS JOINS THE WACS (1954); FRANCIS IN THE NAVY (1955); FRANCIS IN THE HAUNTED HOUSE (1956).

FRANKENSTEIN
Universal: FRANKENSTEIN (1931); THE BRIDE OF FRANKENSTEIN (1935); SON OF FRANKENSTEIN (1939); THE GHOST OF FRANKENSTEIN (1942); FRANKENSTEIN MEETS THE WOLF MAN (1943); HOUSE OF FRANKENSTEIN (1944); HOUSE OF DRACULA (1945); ABBOTT AND COSTELLO MEET FRANKENSTEIN (1948). Hammer: THE CURSE OF FRANKENSTEIN (1957); THE REVENGE OF FRANKENSTEIN (1958); THE EVIL OF FRANKENSTEIN (1964); FRANKENSTEIN CREATED WOMAN (1966); FRANKENSTEIN MUST BE DESTROYED (1969); THE HORROR OF FRANKENSTEIN (1970); FRANKENSTEIN AND THE MONSTER FROM HELL (1973).

FRIDAY THE 13TH
FRIDAY THE 13TH (1980); FRIDAY THE 13TH PART II (1981); FRIDAY THE 13TH PART III (1982); FRIDAY THE 13TH—THE FINAL CHAPTER (1984); FRIDAY THE 13TH—A NEW BEGINNING (1985); FRIDAY THE 13TH PART VI—JASON LIVES! (1986).

FRONTIER MARSHALS
TEXAS MAN HUNT; RAIDERS OF THE WEST; ROLLING DOWN THE GREAT DIVIDE; TUMBLEWEED TRAIL; PRAIRIE PALS; ALONG THE SOUTHERN TRAIL (1942).

FU MANCHU
THE MYSTERIOUS FU MANCHU (1929); THE RETURN OF DR. FU MANCHU

(1930); DAUGHTER OF THE DRAGON (1931); THE MASK OF FU MANCHU; DRUMS OF FU MANCHU (1932); THE FACE OF FU MANCHU (1965); THE BRIDES OF FU MANCU (1966); THE VENGEANCE OF FU MANCHU; THE BLOOD OF FU MANCHU; THE CASTLE OF FU MANCHU (1968).

GAMERA
GAMERA THE INVINCIBLE; GAMERA VERSUS BARUGON (1966); GAMERA VERSUS GAOS (1967); GAMERA VERSUS VIRAS (1968); GAMERA VERSUS GUIRON (1969); GAMERA VERSUS MONSTER X (1970); GAMERA VERSUS ZIGRA (1971).

GAS HOUSE KIDS
GAS HOUSE KIDS (1946); GAS HOUSE KIDS GO WEST; GAS HOUSE KIDS IN HOLLYWOOD (1947).

GIDGET
GIDGET (1959); GIDGET GOES HAWAIIAN (1961); GIDGET GOES TO ROME (1963).

GODZILLA
GODZILLA, KING OF THE MONSTERS (1954); GIGANTIS, THE FIRE MONSTER (1955); KING KONG VS. GODZILLA (1962); GODZILLA VS. THE THING (1964); GHIDRAH, THE THREE-HEADED MONSTER (1965); MONSTER ZERO (1965); GO SEA MONSTER (1966); SON OF GODZILLA; DESTROY ALL MONSTERS (1968); GODZILLA'S REVENGE (1969); GODZILLA VERSUS THE SMOG MONSTER; WAR OF THE MONSTERS (1971); GODZILLA VS. MEGALON (1973); GODZILLA VERSUS THE COSMIC MONSTER (1974); MONSTERS FROM THE UNKNOWN PLANET (1975); GODZILLA 1985 (1985).

THE GREAT GILDERSLEEVE
LOOK WHO'S LAUGHING (1941); THE GREAT GILDERSLEEVE (1942); GILDERSLEEVE'S BAD DAY; GILDERSLEEVE ON BROADWAY (1943); GILDERSLEEVE'S GHOST (1944).

HENRY ALDRICH
WHAT A LIFE (1939); LIFE WITH HENRY; HENRY ALDRICH FOR PRESIDENT (1941); HENRY AND DIZZY; HENRY ALDRICH, EDITOR; HENRY ALDRICH GETS GLAMOUR (1942); HENRY ALDRICH SWINGS IT; HENRY ALDRICH HAUNTS A HOUSE (1943); HENRY ALDRICH, BOY SCOUT; HENRY ALDRICH PLAYS CUPID; HENRY ALDRICH'S LITTLE SECRET (1944).

HENRY LATHAM
HENRY, THE RAINMAKER; LEAVE IT TO HENRY (1949); FATHER MAKES GOOD; FATHER'S WILD GAME (1950); FATHER TAKES THE AIR (1951).

HIGGINS FAMILY
THE HIGGINS FAMILY (1938); MY WIFE'S RELATIVES; SHOULD HUSBANDS WORK?; THE COVERED TRAILER (1939); MONEY TO BURN; GRANDPA GOES TO TOWN; EARL OF PUDDLESTONE; MEET THE MISSUS (1940); PETTICOAT POLITICS (1941).

HILDEGARDE WITHERS
THE PENGUIN POOL MURDER (1932); MURDER ON THE BLACKBOARD (1934); MURDER ON A HONEYMOON (1935); MURDER ON A BRIDLE PATH; THE PLOT THICKENS (1936); 40 NAUGHTY GIRLS (1937).

HIT PARADE
THE HIT PARADE (1937); HIT PARADE OF 1941 (1940); HIT PARADE OF 1943 (1943); HIT PARADE OF 1947 (1947); HIT PARADE OF 1951 (1950).

HOPALONG CASSSIDY
HOPALONG CASSIDY; THE EAGLE'S BROOD; BAR 20 RIDES AGAIN (1935); CALL OF THE PRAIRIE; THREE ON THE TRAIL; HEART OF THE WEST; HOPALONG CASSIDY RETURNS; TRAIL DUST (1936); BORDERLAND; HILLS OF OLD WYOMING; NORTH OF THE RIO GRANDE; RUSTLER'S VALLEY; HOPALONG RIDES AGAIN; TEXAS TRAIL (1937); HEART OF ARIZONA; BAR 20 JUSTICE; PRIDE OF THE WEST; IN OLD MEXICO; SUNSET TRAIL; THE FRONTIERSMAN; PARTNERS OF THE PLAINS; CASSIDY OF BAR 20 (1938); RANGE WAR; LAW OF THE PAMPAS; SILVER ON THE SAGE; THE RENEGADE TRAIL (1939); SANTE FE MARSHAL; THE SHOWDOWN; HIDDEN GOLD; STAGECOACH WAR; THREE MEN FROM TEXAS (1940); DOOMED CARAVAN; IN OLD COLORADO; BORDER VIGILANTES; PIRATES ON HORSEBACK; WIDE OPEN TOWN; OUTLAWS OF THE DESERT; RIDERS OF THE TIMBERLINE; SECRET OF THE WASTELANDS; STICK TO YOUR GUNS; TWILIGHT ON THE TRAIL (1941); UNDERCOVER MAN; LOST CANYON (1942); COLT COMRADES; BAR 20; HOPPY SERVES A WRIT; BORDER PATROL; THE LEATHER BURNERS; FALSE COLORS; RIDERS OF THE DEADLINE (1943); MYSTERY MAN; FORTY THIEVES; TEXAS MASQUERADE; LUMBERJACK (1944); THE DEVIL'S PLAYGROUND; FOOL'S GOLD (1946); UNEXPECTED GUEST; DANGEROUS VENTURE; HOPPY'S HOLIDAY; THE MARAUDERS (1947); SILENT CONFLICT; THE DEAD DON'T DREAM; SINISTER JOURNEY; BORROWED TROUBLE; FALSE PARADISE; STRANGE GAMBLE (1948).

HUGGETTS FAMILY
HOLIDAY CAMP (1947); HERE COME THE HUGGETTS (1948); VOTE FOR HUGGETT (1948); THE HUGGETTS ABROAD (1949).

INNER SANCTUM
CALLING DR. DEATH (1943); WEIRD WOMAN; DEAD MAN'S EYES (1944); THE FROZEN GHOST; STRANGE CONFESSION; PILLOW OF DEATH (1945).

INSPECTOR HORNLEIGH
INSPECTOR HORNLEIGH (1938); INSPECTOR HORNLEIGH ON HOLIDAY (1939); MAIL TRAIN (1940).

INVISIBLE MAN
INVISIBLE MAN (1933); THE INVISIBLE MAN RETURNS (1940); THE INVISIBLE WOMAN (1941); INVISIBLE AGENT (1942); INVISIBLE MAN'S REVENGE (1944); ABBOTT AND COSTELLO MEET THE INVISIBLE MAN (1951).

JAMES BOND
DR. NO (1962); FROM RUSSIA WITH LOVE (1963); GOLDFINGER (1964); THUNDERBALL (1965); YOU ONLY LIVE TWICE; CASINO ROYALE (1967); ON HER MAJESTY;S SECRET SERVICE (1969); DIAMONDS ARE FOREVER (1971); LIVE AND LET DIE (1973); THE MAN WITH THE GOLDEN GUN (1974); THE SPY WHO LOVED ME (1977); MOONRAKER (1979); FOR YOUR EYES ONLY (1981); NEVER SAY NEVER AGAIN; OCTOPUSSY (1983); A VIEW TO A KILL (1985).

JOE PALOOKA
PALOOKA (1934); JOE PALOOKA, CHAMP (1946); FIGHTING MAD; JOE PALOOKA IN WINNER TAKE ALL (1948); JOE PALOOKA IN THE COUNTERPUNCH; JOE PALOOKA IN THE BIG FIGHT (1949); JOE PALOOKA MEETS HUMPHREY; JOE PALOOKA IN HUMPHREY TAKES A CHANCE; JOE PALOOKA IN THE SQUARED CIRCLE (1950); JOE PALOOKA IN TRIPLE CROSS (1951).

JOHN PAUL REVERE
BEYOND THE LAST FRONTIER; RAIDERS OF SUNSET PASS (1943); PRIDE OF THE PLAINS; BENEATH WESTERN SKIES (1944).

THE JONES FAMILY
EVERY SATURDAY NIGHT; EDUCATING FATHER; BACK TO NATURE (1936); OFF TO THE RACES; BIG BUSINESS; HOT WATER; BORROWING TROUBLE (1937); LOVE ON A BUDGET; A TRIP TO PARIS; SAFETY IN NUMBERS; DOWN ON THE FARM (1938); EVERYBODY'S BABY; THE JONES FAMILY IN HOLLYWOOD; QUICK MILLIONS; TOO BUSY TO WORK (1939); YOUNG AS YOU FEEL; ON THEIR OWN (1940).

JOSSER
P.C. JOSSER; DR. JOSSER KC (1931); JOSSER JOINS THE NAVY; JOSSER ON THE RIVER; JOSSER IN THE ARMY (1932); JOSSER ON THE FARM (1934).

JUNGLE JIM
JUNGLE JIM (1948); THE LOST TRIBE (1949); MARK OF THE GORILLA; CAPTIVE GIRL; PYGMY ISLAND (1950); FURY OF THE CONGO; JUNGLE MANHUNT (1951); JUNGLE JIM IN THE FORBIDDEN LAND; VOODOO TIGER (1952); SAVAGE MUTINY; VALLEY OF THE HEADHUNTERS; KILLER APE (1953); JUNGLE MAN-EATERS; CANNIBAL ATTACK (1954); JUNGLE MOON MEN; DEVIL GODDESS (1955).

LASSIE
LASSIE COME HOME (1943); SON OF LASSIE (1945); COURAGE OF LASSIE (1946); HILLS OF HOME (1948); CHALLENGE TO LASSIE; THE SUN COMES UP (1949); THE PAINTED HILLS (1951); LASSIE'S GREAT ADVENTURE (1963).

LAUREL AND HARDY
PARDON US (1931); PACK UP YOUR TROUBLES (1932); THE DEVIL'S BROTHER; SONS OF THE DESERT (1933); HOLLYWOOD PARTY; BABES IN TOYLAND (1934); BONNIE SCOTLAND (1935); THE BOHEMIAN GIRL; OUR RELATIONS (1936); WAY OUT WEST; PICK A STAR (1937); SWISS MISS; BLOCKHEADS (1938); THE FLYING DEUCES (1939); A CHUMP AT OXFORD; SAPS AT SEA (1940); GREAT GUNS; A-HAUNTING WE WILL GO (1942); AIR-RAID WARDENS; JITTERBUGS; THE DANCING MASTERS; (1943); THE BIG NOISE (1944); NOTHING BUT TROUBLE; THE BULLFIGHTERS (1945); UTOPIA (1952).

LITTLE TOUGH GUYS
See: BOWERY BOYS

LONE RIDER
THE LONE RIDER RIDES ON; THE LONE RIDER CROSSES THE RIO; THE LONE RIDER IN GHOST TOWN; THE LONE RIDER IN FRONTIER FURY; THE LONE RIDER AMBUSHED; THE LONE RIDER FIGHTS BACK (1941); THE LONE RIDER AND THE BANDIT; THE LONE RIDER IN CHEYENNE; THE LONE RIDER IN TEXAS JUSTICE; OVERLAND STAGECOACH (1942); WILD HORSE RUSTLERS; DEATH RIDES THE PLAINS; WOLVES OF THE RANGE; LAW OF THE SADDLE; RAIDERS OF RED GAP (1943).

LONE WOLF
Silents: THE LONE WOLF (1917); FALSE FACES; THE LONE WOLF'S DAUGHTER (1919); THE LONE WOLF (1924); THE LONE WOLF RETURNS (1926); ALIAS THE LONE WOLF (1927). Sound Films: THE LONE WOLF'S DAUGHTER (1929); LAST OF THE LONE WOLF (1930); CHEATERS AT PLAY (1932); THE LONE WOLF RETURNS (1936); THE LONE WOLF IN PARIS (1938); THE LONE WOLF SPY HUNT (1939); THE LONE WOLF KEEPS A DATE; THE LONE WOLF STRIKES; THE LONE WOLF MEETS A LADY (1940); THE LONE WOLF TAKES A CHANCE; SECRETS OF THE LONE WOLF (1941); COUNTER-ESPIONAGE (1942); ONE DANGEROUS NIGHT; PASSPORT TO SUEZ (1943); THE NOTORIOUS LONE WOLF (1946); THE LONE WOLF IN MEXICO; THE LONE WOLF IN LONDON; (1947); THE LONE WOLF AND HIS LADY (1949); THE NOTORIOUS LONE WOLF (1964).

MA AND PA KETTLE
THE EGG AND I (1947); MA AND PA KETTLE (1949); MA AND PA KETTLE GO TO TOWN (1950); MA AND PA KETTLE BACK ON THE FARM (1951); MA AND PA KETTLE AT THE FAIR (1952); MA AND PA KETTLE ON VACATION (1953); MA AND PA KETTLE AT HOME (1954); MA AND PA KETTLE AT WAIKIKI (1955); THE KETTLES IN THE OZARKS (1956); THE KETTLES ON OLD MACDONALD'S FARM (1957).

MAISIE
MAISIE (1939); CONGO MAISIE; GOLD RUSH MAISIE (1940); MAISIE WAS A LADY; RINGSIDE MAISIE (1941); MAISIE GETS HER MAN (1942); SWING SHIFT MAISIE (1943); MAISIE GOES TO RENO (1944); UP GOES MAISIE (1946); UNDERCOVER MAISIE (1947).

MEXICAN SPITFIRE
THE GIRL FROM MEXICO; MEXICAN SPITFIRE (1939); MEXICAN SPITFIRE OUT WEST (1940); MEXICAN SPITFIRE AT SEA; MEXICAN SPITFIRE SEES A GHOST; MEXICAN SPITFIRE'S ELEPHANT (1942); MEXICAN SPITFIRE'S BABY; MEXICAN SPITFIRE'S BLESSED EVENT (1943).

MICHAEL SHAYNE
MICHAEL SHAYNE, PRIVATE DETECTIVE (1940); SLEEPERS WEST; DRESSED TO KILL; BLUE, WHITE AND PERFECT (1941); THE MAN WHO WOULDN'T DIE; JUST OFF BROADWAY; TIME TO KILL (1942); MURDER IS MY BUSINESS; LARCENY IN HER HEART; BLONDE FOR A DAY (1946); THREE ON A TICKET; TOO MANY WINNERS (1947).

MR. DISTRICT ATTORNEY
MR. DISTRICT ATTORNEY; THE CARTER CASE (1941); SECRETS OF THE UNDERGROUND (1943).

MR. MOTO
THINK FAST, MR. MOTO (1937); THANK YOU, MR. MOTO; MR. MOTO'S GAMBLE; MR. MOTO TAKES A CHANCE; THE MYSTERIOUS MR. MOTO (1938);

MR. MOTO'S LAST WARNING; MR. MOTO IN DANGER ISLAND; MR. MOTO TAKES A VACATION (1939); THE RETURN OF MR. MOTO (1965).

MR. WONG
MR. WONG, DETECTIVE (1938); MYSTERY OF MR. WONG; MR. WONG IN CHINATOWN (1939); THE FATAL HOUR; DOOMED TO DIE (1940); PHANTOM OF CHINATOWN (1941).

THE MUMMY
Universal: THE MUMMY (1933); THE MUMMY'S HAND (1940); THE MUMMY'S TOMB (1942); THE MUMMY'S GHOST; THE MUMMY'S CURSE (1944); ABBOTT AND COSTELLO MEET THE MUMMY (1955). Hammer: THE MUMMY (1959); THE CURSE OF THE MUMMY'S TOMB (1964); THE MUMMY'S SHROUD (1967); BLOOD FROM THE MUMMY'S TOMB (1972).

MURDER ON
See: HILDEGARDE WITHERS

NANCY DREW
NANCY DREW—DETECTIVE (1938); NANCY DREW—REPORTER; NANCY DREW, TROUBLE SHOOTER; NANCY DREW AND THE HIDDEN STAIRCASE (1939).

NICK CARTER
NICK CARTER, MASTER DETECTIVE (1939); PHANTOM RAIDERS; SKY MURDER (1940).

OLD MOTHER RILEY
OLD MOTHER RILEY (1937); OLD MOTHER RILEY IN PARIS (1938); OLD MOTHER RILEY MP; OLD MOTHER RILEY JOINS UP (1939); OLD MOTHER RILEY IN SOCIETY; OLD MOTHER RILEY IN BUSINESS (1940); OLD MOTHER RILEY'S GHOSTS; OLD MOTHER RILEY'S CIRCUS (1941); OLD MOTHER RILEY, DETECTIVE; OLD MOTHER RILEY OVERSEAS (1943); OLD MOTHER RILEY AT HOME (1945); OLD MOTHER RILEY (1949); OLD MOTHER RILEY, HEADMISTRESS (1950); OLD MOTHER RILEY'S JUNGLE TREASURE (1951); MY SON, THE VAMPIRE (1952).

PERRY MASON
THE CASE OF THE HOWLING DOG (1934); THE CASE OF THE CURIOUS BRIDE; THE CASE OF THE LUCKY LEGS (1935); THE CASE OF THE VELVET CLAWS; THE CASE OF THE BLACK CAT (1936); THE CASE OF THE STUTTERING BISHOP (1937).

PHILO VANCE
THE CANARY MURDER CASE; THE GREENE MURDER CASE (1929); THE BISHOP MURDER CASE; THE BENSON MURDER CASE (1930); THE KENNEL MURDER CASE (1933); THE DRAGON MURDER CASE (1934); THE CASINO MURDER CASE (1935); THE GARDEN MURDER CASE; THE SCARAB MURDER CASE (1936); NIGHT OF MYSTERY (1937); GRACIE ALLEN MURDER CASE (1939); CALLING PHILO VANCE (1940); PHILO VANCE RETURNS; PHILO VANCE'S GAMBLE; PHILO VANCE'S SECRET MISSION (1947).

PINK PANTHER
THE PINK PANTHER; A SHOT IN THE DARK (1964); INSPECTOR CLOUSEAU (1968); THE RETURN OF THE PINK PANTHER (1975); THE PINK PANTHER STRIKES AGAIN (1976); REVENGE OF THE PINK PANTHER (1978); THE TRAIL OF THE PINK PANTHER (1982); CURSE OF THE PINK PANTHER (1983).

PLANET OF THE APES
PLANET OF THE APES (1968); BENEATH THE PLANET OF THE APES (1970); ESCAPE FROM THE PLANET OF THE APES (1971); CONQUEST OF THE PLANET OF THE APES (1972); BATTLE FOR THE PLANET OF THE APES (1973).

PSYCHO
PSYCHO (1960); PSYCHO II (1983); PSYCHO III (1986).

RANGE BUSTERS
THE RANGE BUSTERS; TRAILING DOUBLE TROUBLE; WEST OF PINTO BASIN (1940); TRAIL OF THE SILVER SPURS; THE KID'S LAST RIDE; TUMBLEDOWN RANCH IN ARIZONA; WRANGLER'S ROOST; FUGITIVE VALLEY; SADDLE MOUNTAIN ROUNDUP; TONTO BASIN OUTLAWS; UNDERGROUND RUSTLERS (1941); THUNDER RIVER FEUD; BOOT HILL BANDITS; TEXAS TROUBLE SHOOTERS; TEXAS TO BATAAN; TRAIL RIDERS (1942); TWO FISTED JUSTICE; THE HAUNTED RANCH; LAND OF HUNTED MEN; COWBOY COMMANDOS; BLACK MARKET RUSTLERS; BULLETS AND SADDLES (1943).

RED RYDER
TUSCON RAIDERS; MARSHAL OF RENO; THE SAN ANTONIO KID; CHEYENNE WILDCAT; VIGILANTES OF DODGE CITY; SHERIFF OF LAS VEGAS (1944); GREAT STAGECOACH ROBBERY; LONE TEXAS RANGER; PHANTOM OF THE PLAINS; MARSHAL OF LAREDO; COLORADO PIONEERS; WAGON WHEELS WESTWARD (1945); CALIFORNIA GOLD RUSH; SUN VALLEY CYCLONE; CONQUEST OF CHEYENNE; SHERIFF OF REDWOOD VALLEY; SANTE FE UPRISING; STAGECOACH TO DENVER (1946); VIGILANTES OF BOOMTOWN; HOMESTEADERS OF PARADISE VALLEY; OREGON TRAIL SCOUTS; RUSTLERS OF DEVIL'S CANYON; THE MARSHAL OF CRIPPLE CREEK (1947); RIDE, RYDER, RIDE!; ROLL, THUNDER, ROLL (1949); COWBOY AND THE PRIZEFIGHTER; THE FIGHTING REDHEAD (1950).

RENFREW OF THE MOUNTIES
RENFREW OF THE ROYAL MOUNTED (1937); ON THE GREAT WHITE TRAIL (1938); FIGHTING MAD; CRASHING THRU (1939); YUKON FLIGHT; MURDER ON THE YUKON; DANGER AHEAD; THE SKY BANDITS (1940).

RITZ BROTHERS
SING, BABY, SING (1936); ONE IN A MILLION; ON THE AVENUE; YOU CAN'T HAVE EVERYTHING; LIFE BEGINS IN COLLEGE (1937); THE GOLDWYN FOLLIES; KENTUCKY MOONSHINE; STRAIGHT PLACE AND SHOW (1938); THE THREE MUSKETEERS; THE GORILLA; PACK UP YOUR TROUBLES (1939); ARGENTINE NIGHTS (1940); BEHIND THE EIGHT BALL (1942); HI'YA, CHUM; NEVER A DULL MOMENT (1943).

ROAD TO
ROAD TO SINGAPORE (1940); ROAD TO ZANZIBAR (1941); ROAD TO MOROCCO (1942); ROAD TO UTOPIA (1945); ROAD TO RIO (1947); ROAD TO BALI (1952); THE ROAD TO HONG KONG (1962).

ROCKY
ROCKY (1976); ROCKY II (1979); ROCKY III (1982); ROCKY IV (1985).

ROY ROGERS
UNDER WESTERN SKIES; COME ON RANGERS; SHINE ON HARVEST MOON (1938); ROUGH RIDERS' ROUNDUP; FRONTIER PONY EXPRESS; SOUTHWARD, HO!; IN OLD CALIENTE; WALL STREET COWBOY; THE ARIZONA KID; JEEPERS CREEPERS; SAGA OF DEATH VALLEY (1939); CARSON CITY KID; THE RANGER AND THE LADY; COLORADO; THE BORDER LEGION (1940); ROBIN HOOD OF THE PECOS; ARKANSAS JUDGE; IN OLD CHEYENNE; SHERIFF OF TOMBSTONE; NEVADA CITY; BAD MAN OF DEADWOOD; JESSE JAMES AT BAY; RED RIVER VALLEY (1941); MAN FROM CHEYENNE; SOUTH OF SANTE FE; SUNSET ON THE DESERT; ROMANCE ON THE RANGE; SONS OF THE PIONEERS; SUNSET SERENADE; HEART OF THE GOLDEN WEST; RIDIN' DOWN THE CANYON (1942); IDAHO; KING OF THE COWBOYS; SONG OF TEXAS; SILVER SPURS; MAN FROM MUSIC MOUNTAIN (1943); HANDS ACROSS THE BORDER; COWBOY AND THE SENORITA; THE YELLOW ROSE OF TEXAS; SONG OF NEVADA; SAN FERNANDO VALLEY; LIGHTS OF OLD SANTE FE (1944); UTAH; BELLS OF ROSARITA; THE MAN FROM OKLAHOMA; SUNSET IN EL DORADO; DON'T FENCE ME IN (1945); ALONG THE NAVAJO TRAIL; SONG OF ARIZONA; RAINBOW OVER TEXAS; MY PAL TRIGGER; UNDER NEVADA SKIES; ROLL ON TEXAS MOON; HOME IN OKLAHOMA; HELLDORADO (1946); APACHE ROSE; HIT PARADE OF 1947; BELLS OF SAN ANGELO; SPRINGTIME IN THE SIERRAS; ON THE OLD SPANISH TRAIL (1947); THE GAY RANCHERO; UNDER CALIFORNIA STARS; EYES OF TEXAS; NIGHTTIME IN NEVADA; GRAND CANYON TRAIL (1948); THE FAR FRONTIER; SUSANNA PASS; DOWN DAKOTA WAY; THE GOLDEN STALLION (1949); BELLS OF CORONADO; TWILIGHT IN THE SIERRAS; TRIGGER, JR.; SUNSET IN THE WEST; NORTH OF THE GREAT DIVIDE; TRAIL OF ROBIN HOOD (1950); SPOILERS OF THE PLAINS; HEART OF THE ROCKIES; IN OLD AMARILLO; SOUTH OF CALIENTE; PALS OF THE GOLDEN WEST (1951).

ROUGH RIDERS
ARIZONA BOUND; THE GUN MAN FROM BODIE; FORBIDDEN TRAILS (1941); BELOW THE BORDER; GHOST TOWN LAW; DOWN TEXAS WAY; RIDERS OF THE WEST; WEST OF THE LAW (1942).

ROUGH-RIDIN' KIDS
BUCKAROO SHERIFF OF TEXAS; THE DAKOTA KID; ARIZONA MANHUNT (1951); WILD HORSE AMBUSH (1952).

THE SAINT
THE SAINT IN NEW YORK (1938); THE SAINT STRIKES BACK; THE SAINT IN LONDON (1939); THE SAINT'S DOUBLE TROUBLE; THE SAINT TAKES OVER (1940); THE SAINT IN PALM SPRINGS; THE SAINT'S VACATION; THE SAINT MEETS THE TIGER (1941); THE SAINT'S GIRL FRIDAY (1953).

SCATTERGOOD BAINES
SCATTERGOOD BAINES; SCATTERGOOD PULLS THE STRINGS; SCATTERGOOD MEETS BROADWAY (1941); SCATTERGOOD RIDES HIGH; SCATTERGOOD SURVIVES A MURDER (1942).

SEXTON BLAKE
Silents: SEXTON BLAKE (1909); SEXTON BLAKE VS. BARON KETTLER (1912); THE FURTHER EXPLOITS OF SEXTON BLAKE (1919); THE CLUE OF THE SECOND GOBLET; BLAKE THE LAWBREAKER; SEXTON BLAKE, GAMBLER; SILKEN THREADS; THE GREAT OFFICE MYSTERY; THE MYSTERY OF THE SILENT DEATH (1928). Sound films: SEXTON BLAKE AND THE BEARDED DOCTOR; SEXTON BLAKE AND THE MADEMOISELLE (1935); SEXTON BLAKE AND THE HOODED TERROR (1938); MEET SEXTON BLAKE (1944); THE ECHO MURDERS (1945); MURDER AT SITE THREE (1959).

SHERLOCK HOLMES
Clive Brook: THE RETURN OF SHERLOCK HOLMES (1929); SHERLOCK HOLMES (1932). Arthur Wontner: SHERLOCK HOLMES' FATAL HOUR (1931); THE MISSING REMBRANDT; THE SIGN OF FOUR (1932); THE TRIUMPH OF SHERLOCK HOLMES (1935); MURDER AT THE BASKERVILLES (1937).
Basil Rathbone/Nigel Bruce: THE HOUND OF THE BASKERVILLES; THE ADVENTURES OF SHERLOCK HOLMES (1939); SHERLOCK HOLMES AND THE VOICE OF TERROR; SHERLOCK HOLMES AND THE SECRET WEAPON (1942); SHERLOCK HOLMES IN WASHINGTON; SHERLOCK HOLMES FACES DEATH (1943); SHERLOCK HOLMES AND THE SPIDER WOMAN; THE SCARLET CLAW; THE PEARL OF DEATH (1944); THE HOUSE OF FEAR; THE WOMAN IN GREEN; PURSUIT TO ALGIERS (1945); TERROR BY NIGHT; DRESSED TO KILL (1946).

SOMEWHERE
SOMEWHERE IN ENGLAND (1940); SOMEWHERE IN CAMP; SOMEWHERE ON LEAVE (1942); SOMEWHERE IN CIVVIES (1943); SOMEWHERE IN POLITICS (1949).

SOPHIE LANG
THE NOTORIOUS SOPHIE LANG (1934); THE RETURN OF SOPHIE LANG (1936); SOPHIE LANG GOES WEST (1937).

STAR TREK
STAR TREK: THE MOTION PICTURE (1979); STAR TREK II: THE WRATH OF KHAN (1982); STAR TREK III: THE SEARCH FOR SPOCK (1984); STAR TREK IV: THE VOYAGE HOME (1985).

STAR WARS
STAR WARS (1977); THE EMPIRE STRIKES BACK (1980); RETURN OF THE JEDI (1983).

SUPERMAN
SUPERMAN (1978); SUPERMAN II (1980); SUPERMAN III (1983); SUPERGIRL (1984).

TAMMY
TAMMY AND THE BACHELOR (1957); TAMMY, TELL ME TRUE (1961); TAMMY AND THE DOCTOR (1963); TAMMY AND THE MILLIONAIRE (1967).

TARZAN
Silents: TARZAN OF THE APES; THE ROMANCE OF TARZAN (1918); THE RETURN OF TARZAN (1920); TARZAN AND THE GOLDEN LION (1927). Sound Films: TARZAN, THE APE MAN (1932); TARZAN THE FEARLESS (1933); TARZAN AND HIS MATE (1934); NEW ADVENTURES OF TARZAN (1935); TARZAN

ESCAPES (1936); TARZAN AND THE GREEN GODDESS; TARZAN'S REVENGE; (1938); TARZAN FINDS A SON! (1939); TARZAN'S SECRET TREASURE (1941); TARZAN'S NEW YORK ADVENTURE (1942); TARZAN TRIUMPHS; TARZAN'S DESERT MYSTERY (1943); TARZAN AND THE AMAZONS (1945); TARZAN AND THE LEOPARD WOMAN (1946); TARZAN AND THE HUNTRESS (1947); TARZAN AND THE MERMAIDS (1948); TARZAN'S MAGIC FOUNTAIN (1949); TARZAN AND THE SLAVE GIRL (1950); TARZAN'S PERIL (1951); TARZAN'S SAVAGE FURY (1952); TARZAN AND THE SHE-DEVIL (1953); TARZAN'S HIDDEN JUNGLE (1955); TARZAN AND THE LOST SAFARI (1957); TARZAN'S FIGHT FOR LIFE (1958); TARZAN'S GREATEST ADVENTURE; TARZAN, THE APE MAN (1959); TARZAN THE MAGNIFICENT (1960); TARZAN GOES TO INDIA (1962); TARZAN'S THREE CHALLENGES (1963); TARZAN AND THE VALLEY OF GOLD (1966); TARZAN AND THE GREAT RIVER (1967); TARZAN AND THE JUNGLE BOY (1968); TARZAN'S JUNGLE REBELLION; TARZAN'S DEADLY SILENCE (1970); TARZAN, THE APE MAN (1981); GREYSTOKE: THE LEGEND OF TARZAN, LORD OF THE APES (1984).

TEXAS RANGERS
RANGERS TAKE OVER; BAD MEN OF THUNDER GAP; WEST OF TEXAS; BORDER BUCKAROOS; FIGHTING VALLEY (1943); TRAIL OF TERROR; THE RETURN OF THE RANGERS; BOSS OF THE RAWHIDE; GUNSMOKE MESA; OUTLAW ROUNDUP; GUNS OF THE LAW; THE PINTO BANDIT; SPOOK TOWN; BRAND OF THE DEVIL; GANGSTERS OF THE FRONTIER; DEAD OR ALIVE; THE WHISPERING SKULL (1944); MARKED FOR MURDER; ENEMY OF THE LAW; THREE IN THE SADDLE; FRONTIER FUGITIVES; FLAMING BULLETS (1945).

THE THIN MAN
THE THIN MAN (1934); AFTER THE THIN MAN (1936); ANOTHER THIN MAN (1939); SHADOW OF THE THIN MAN (1941); THE THIN MAN GOES HOME (1945); SONG OF THE THIN MAN (1947).

THREE MESQUITEERS
POWDERSMOKE RANGE (1935); THE THREE MESQUITEERS; GHOST TOWN GOLD; ROARIN' LEAD (1936); RIDERS OF THE WHISTLING SKULL; HIT THE SADDLE; GUNSMOKE RANCH; COME ON, COWBOYS; RANGE DEFENDERS; HEART OF THE ROCKIES; THE TRIGGER TRIO; WILD HORSE RODEO (1937); THE PURPLE VIGILANTES; CALL THE MESQUITEERS; OUTLAWS OF SONORA; RIDERS OF THE BLACK HILLS; HEROES OF THE HILLS; PALS OF THE SADDLE; OVERLAND STAGE RAIDERS; SANTA FE STAMPEDE; RED RIVER RANGE (1938); THE NIGHT RIDERS; THREE TEXAS STEERS; WYOMING OUTLAWS; NEW FRONTIER; THE KANSAS TERRORS; COWBOYS FROM TEXAS (1939); HEROES OF THE SADDLE; PIONEERS OF THE WEST; COVERED WAGON DAYS; ROCKY MOUNTAIN RANGERS; OKLAHOMA RENEGADES; UNDER TEXAS SKIES; THE TRAIL BLAZERS; LONE STAR RAIDERS (1940); PRAIRIE PIONEERS; SADDLEMATES; GANGS OF SONORA; OUTLAWS OF THE CHEROKEE TRAIL; GAUCHOS OF EL DORADO; WEST OF CIMARRON (1941); CODE OF THE OUTLAW; RAIDERS OF THE RANGE; WESTWARD HO; THE PHANTOM PLAINSMEN; SHADOWS ON THE SAGE; VALLEY OF HUNTED MEN (1942); THUNDERING TRAILS; THE BLOCKED TRAIL; SANTA FE SCOUTS; RIDERS OF THE RIO GRANDE (1943).

TOPPER
TOPPER (1937); TOPPER TAKES A TRIP (1939); TOPPER RETURNS (1941).

TORCHY BLANE
SMART BLONDE (1936); FLY-AWAY BABY; ADVENTUROUS BLONDE (1937); BLONDES AT WORK; TORCHY BLANE IN PANAMA; TORCHY GETS HER MAN (1938); TORCHY BLANE IN CHINATOWN; TORCHY RUNS FOR MAYOR; TORCHY PLAYS WITH DYNAMITE (1939).

TRAIL BLAZERS
BLAZING GUNS; THE LAW RIDES AGAIN; WILD HORSE STAMPEDE (1943); ARIZONA WHIRLWIND; DEATH VALLEY RANGERS; OUTLAW TRAIL; WESTWARD BOUND (1944).

WALLY BENTON
WHISTLING IN THE DARK (1941); WHISTLING IN DIXIE (1942); WHISTLING IN BROOKLYN (1943).

THE WEAVER FAMILY AND ELVIRY
SWING YOUR LADY; DOWN IN ARKANSAW (1938); JEEPER CREEPERS (1939); IN OLD MISSOURI; GRAND OLE OPRY; FRIENDLY NEIGHBORS (1940); ARKANSAS JUDGE; MOUNTAIN MOONLIGHT; TUXEDO JUNCTION (1941); SHEPHERD OF THE OZARKS; THE OLD HOMESTEAD; MOUNTAIN RHYTHM (1942).

THE WHISTLER
THE WHISTLER; MARK OF THE WHISTLER (1944); POWER OF THE WHISTLER; VOICE OF THE WHISTLER (1945); MYSTERIOUS INTRUDER; SECRET OF THE WHISTLER (1946); THE 13TH HOUR; THE RETURN OF THE WHISTLER (1948).

THE WOLF MAN
THE WOLF MAN (1941); FRANKENSTEIN MEETS THE WOLF MAN (1943); HOUSE OF FRANKENSTEIN (1944); HOUSE OF DRACULA (1945); ABBOTT AND COSTELLO MEET FRANKENSTEIN (1948).

Awards Index

Organizations offering special awards and honors to films and filmmakers are legion. We have selected the six most prestigious awards organizations for inclusion in the Motion Picture Guide; each has a different method of selecting its annual prize winners. Two of these are industry associations; one is an affiliation of movie critics; the others are festival connected, conferring their honors in conjunction with selective screenings. The Academy Awards, presented annually since 1928 by the Academy of Motion Picture Arts and Sciences, offer Oscar statuettes in as many as 20 categories with up to five nominees in each, selected by their peers where applicable (coworkers in each of the 13 different filmmaking occupations). The winners are decided by secret ballot of the entire membership. Additional honors for special achievement and overall achievement are sometimes awarded by the organization's board of governors. Foreign-language pictures were first honored by the Academy in 1947. The British Film Academy, founded in 1946, offers similar annual awards for excellence. The New York Film Critics Circle has offered award plaques annually for excellence in the creation and performance of commercial movies since 1935. The top-prize Golden Bear statuettes and lesser Silver and Bronze Bears are awarded by a nine-member jury at the annual Berlin International Film Festival, which began in 1951. The Cannes Film Festival offers grand prizes and Golden Palm awards in a number of filmmaking categories; honorees are selected by a jury of international filmmakers. Since its first offerings in 1946, these categories have changed significantly. With awards ceremonies beginning in 1932, the Venice Film Festival is the oldest of the international film festivals conferring honors on film and filmmakers. Its Golden Lions, Silver Lions, and other honors are awarded through a tightly managed local jury.
NOTE: Where appropriate, winning entries are in italic.

ACADEMY AWARDS-

ACADEMY AWARDS

1927-28
Best Production
THE LAST COMMAND, PAR. Produced by J.G. Bachmann and B.P. Schulberg.
THE RACKET, UA. Produced by Howard Hughes.
SEVENTH HEAVEN, FOX. Produced by William Fox.
THE WAY OF ALL FLESH, PAR. Produced by Adolph Zukor and Jesse L. Lasky.
WINGS, PAR. Produced by Lucien Hubbard.
Most Artistic Quality of Production
CHANG, PAR.
THE CROWD, MGM.
SUNRISE, FOX.
Best Actor
Richard Barthelmess for THE NOOSE and THE PATENT LEATHER KID.
Charles Chaplin for THE CIRCUS.
Emil Jannings for THE LAST COMMAND and THE WAY OF ALL FLESH.
Best Actress
Louise Dresser for A SHIP COMES IN.
Janet Gaynor for SEVENTH HEAVEN, STREET ANGEL, and SUNRISE.
Gloria Swanson for SADIE THOMPSON.
Best Direction
Frank Borzage for SEVENTH HEAVEN.
Herbert Brenon for SORRELL AND SON.
King Vidor for THE CROWD.
Best Comedy Direction
Charles Chaplin for THE CIRCUS.
Lewis Milestone for TWO ARABIAN KNIGHTS.
Ted Wilde for SPEEDY.
Writing Awards
Best Adaptation
GLORIOUS BETSY, by Anthony Coldeway.
THE JAZZ SINGER, by Alfred Cohn.
SEVENTH HEAVEN, by Benjamin Glazer.
Best Original Story
THE LAST COMMAND, by Lajos Biro.
THE PATENT LEATHER KID, by Rupert Hughes.
UNDERWORLD, by Ben Hecht.
Best Title Writing
THE FAIR CO-ED by Joseph Farnham.
LAUGH, CLOWN, LAUGH, by Joseph Farnham.
OH KAY! by George Marion, Jr.
THE PRIVATE LIFE OF HELEN OF TROY, by Gerald Duffy.
TELLING THE WORLD by Joseph Farnham.
Best Cinematography
DEVIL DANCER. George Barnes.
DRUMS OF LOVE. Karl Struss.
MAGIC FLAME. George Barnes.
MY BEST GIRL. Charles Rosher.
SADIE THOMPSON. George Barnes.
SUNRISE. Charles Rosher and Karl Struss.
THE TEMPEST. Charles Rosher.
Best Interior Decoration
THE DOVE. William Cameron Menzies.
SEVENTH HEAVEN. Harry Oliver.
SUNRISE. Rochus Gliese.
THE TEMPEST. William Cameron Menzies.
Best Engineering Effects
THE JAZZ SINGER, Nugent Slaughter.
THE PRIVATE LIFE OF HELEN OF TROY, Ralph Hammeras.
WINGS. Roy Pomeroy.
Special Awards
Warner Bros. for producing THE JAZZ SINGER, the outstanding pioneer talking picture which has revolutionized the industry.
Charles Chaplin for versatility and genius in writing, acting, directing, and producing

THE CIRCUS.

1928-29
Best Production
ALIBI, UA. Produced by Roland West.
BROADWAY MELODY, MGM. Produced by Harry Rapt.
HOLLYWOOD REVUE, MGM. Produced by Harry Rapt.
IN OLD ARIZONA, FOX. Winfield Sheehan, studio head.
THE PATRIOT, PAR. Produced by Ernst Lubitsch.
Best Actor
George Bancroft for THUNDERBOLT.
Warner Baxter for IN OLD ARIZONA.
Chester Morris for ALIBI.
Paul Muni for THE VALIANT.
Lewis Stone for THE PATRIOT.
Best Actress
Ruth Chatterton for MADAM X.
Betty Compson for THE BARKER.
Jeanne Eagels for THE LETTER.
Bessie Love for BROADWAY MELODY.
Mary Pickford for COQUETTE.
Best Direction
Lionel Barrymore for MADAME X.
Harry Beaumont for BROADWAY MELODY.
Irving Cummings for IN OLD ARIZONA.
Frank Lloyd for THE DIVINE LADY, WEARY RIVER, and DRAG.
Ernst Lubitsch for THE PATRIOT.
Best Writing Achievement
IN OLD ARIZONA, by Tom Barry.
THE LEATHERNECK, by Elliott Clawson.
OUR DANCING DAUGHTERS, by Josephine Lovett.
THE PATRIOT, by Hans Kraly.
THE VALIANT, by Tom Barry.
WONDER OF WOMEN, by Bess Meredyth.
Best Cinematography
THE DIVINE LADY. John Seitz.
FOUR DEVILS. Ernest Palmer.
IN OLD ARIZONA. Arthur Edeson.
OUR DANCING DAUGHTERS. George Barnes.
STREET ANGEL. Ernest Palmer.
WHITE SHADOWS IN THE SOUTH SEAS. Clyde DeVinna.
Best Interior Decoration
THE BRIDGE OF SAN LUIS REY. Cedric Gibbons.
DYNAMITE. Mitchell Leisen.
HOLLYWOOD REVUE. Cedric Gibbons.
THE IRON MASK. William Cameron Menzies.
THE PATRIOT. Hans Dreier.
STREET ANGEL. Harry Oliver.

1929-30
Best Production
ALL QUIET ON THE WESTERN FRONT, UNIV. Produced by Carl Laemmle, Jr.
THE BIG HOUSE, MGM. Produced by Irving G. Thalberg.
DISRAELI, WB. Produced by Jack L. Warner and Daryl F. Zanuck.
THE DIVORCEE, MGM. Produced by Robert Z. Leonard.
THE LOVE PARADE, PAR. Produced by Ernst Lubitsch.
Best Actor
George Arliss for DISRAELI.
George Arliss for THE GREEN GODDESS.
Wallace Beery for THE BIG HOUSE.
Maurice Chevalier for THE LOVE PARADE.
Maurice Chevalier for THE BIG POND.
Ronald Colman for BULLDOG DRUMMOND.
Ronald Colman for CONDEMNED.
Lawrence Tibbett for THE ROGUE SONG.

Best Actress
Nancy Carroll for THE DEVIL'S HOLIDAY.
Ruth Chatterton for SARAH AND SON.
Greta Garbo for ANNA CHRISTIE.
Greta Garbo for ROMANCE.
Norma Shearer for THE DIVORCEE.
Norma Shearer for THEIR OWN DESIRE.
Gloria Swanson for THE TRESPASSER.
Best Direction
Clarence Brown for ANNA CHRISTIE.
Clarence Brown for ROMANCE.
Robert Z. Leonard for THE DIVORCEE.
Ernst Lubitsch for THE LOVE PARADE.
Lewis Milestone for ALL QUIET ON THE WESTERN FRONT.
King Vidor for HALLELUJAH.
Best Writing Achievement
ALL QUIET ON THE WESTERN FRONT, by George Abbott, Maxwell Anderson, and Dell Andrews.
THE BIG HOUSE, by Frances Marion.
DISRAELI, by Julian Josephson.
THE DIVORCEE, by John Meehan.
STREET OF CHANCE, by Howard Estabrook.
Best Cinematography
ALL QUIET ON THE WESTERN FRONT. Arthur Edeson.
ANNA CHRISTIE. William Daniels.
HELL'S ANGELS. Gaetano Gaudio and Harry Perry.
THE LOVE PARADE. Victor Milner.
WITH BYRD AT THE SOUTH POLE. Joseph T. Rucker and Willard Van Der Veer.
Best Interior Decoration
BULLDOG DRUMMOND. William Cameron Menzies.
KING OF JAZZ. Herman Rosse.
THE LOVE PARADE. Hans Dreier.
SALLY. Jack Okey.
THE VAGABOND KING. Hans Dreier.
Best Sound Recording
THE BIG HOUSE. Douglas Shearer.
THE CASE OF SERGEANT GRISCHA. John Tribby.
THE LOVE PARADE. Franklin Hansen.
RAFFLES. Oscar Lagerstrom.
SONG OF THE FLAME. George Groves.

1930-31
Best Picture
CIMARRON, RKO. Produced by William LeBaron.
EAST LYNNE, FOX. Winfield Sheehan, studio head.
THE FRONT PAGE, UA. Produced by Howard Hughes.
SKIPPY, PAR. Adolph Zukor, studio head.
TRADER HORN, MGM. Produced by Irving G. Thalberg.
Best Actor
Lionel Barrymore for A FREE SOUL.
Jackie Cooper for SKIPPY.
Richard Dix for CIMARRON.
Fredric March for THE ROYAL FAMILY OF BROADWAY.
Adolphe Menjou for THE FRONT PAGE.
Best Actress
Marlene Dietrich for MOROCCO.
Marie Dressler for MIN AND BILL.
Irene Dunne for CIMARRON.
Ann Harding for HOLIDAY.
Norma Shearer for A FREE SOUL.
Best Direction
Clarence Brown for A FREE SOUL.
Lewis Milestone for THE FRONT PAGE.
Wesley Ruggles for CIMARRON.
Norman Taurog for SKIPPY.
Josef Von Sternberg for MOROCCO.
Writing
Best Screen Adaptation
CIMARRON, by Howard Estabrook.
THE CRIMINAL CODE, by Seton Miller and Fred Niblo, Jr.
HOLIDAY, by Horace Jackson.
LITTLE CAESAR, by Francis Faragoh and Robert N. Lee.
SKIPPY, by Joseph L. Mankiewicz and Sam Mintz.
Best Original Story
THE DAWN PATROL, by John Monk Saunders.
DOORWAY TO HELL, by Rowland Brown.
LAUGHTER, by Harry D'Abbadie D'Arrast, Douglas Doty, and Donald Ogden Stewart.
THE PUBLIC ENEMY, by John Bright and Kubec Glasmon.
SMART MONEY, by Lucien Hubbard and Joseph Jackson.
Best Cinematography
CIMARRON. Edward Cronjager.
MOROCCO. Lee Garmes.
THE RIGHT TO LOVE. Charles Lang.
SVENGALI. Barney "Chick" McGill.
TABU. Floyd Crosby.
Best Interior Decoration
CIMARRON. Max Ree.
JUST IMAGINE. Stephen Goosson and Ralph Hammeras.
MOROCCO. Hans Dreier.
SVENGALI. Anton Grot.
WHOOPEE. Richard Day.
Best Sound Recording
MGM Studio Sound Department.
Paramount Studio Sound Department.
RKO Radio Studio Sound Department.
Samuel Goldwyn Sound Department.
Scientific or Technical
Class I
Electrical Research Products, Inc., RCA-Photophone, Inc., and RKO Radio Pictures,

Inc., for noise reduction recording equipment.
DuPont Film Manufacturing Corp. and Eastman Kodak Co., for supersensitive panchromatic film.
Class II
Fox Film Corp. for effective use of synchro-projection composite photography.
Class III
Electrical Research Products, Inc., for moving coil microphone transmitters.
RKO Radio Pictures, Inc., for reflex type microphone concentrators.
RCA-Photophone, Inc., for ribbon microphone transmitters.

1931-32
Best Picture
ARROWSMITH, UA. Produced by Samuel Goldwyn.
BAD GIRL, FOX. Winfield Sheehan, studio head.
THE CHAMP, MGM. Produced by King Vidor.
FIVE STAR FINAL, FN. Produced by Hal B. Wallis.
GRAND HOTEL, MGM. Produced by Irving Thalberg.
ONE HOUR WITH YOU, PAR. Produced by Ernst Lubitsch.
SHANGHAI EXPRESS, PAR. Adolph Zukor, studio head.
SMILING LIEUTENANT, PAR. Produced by Ernst Lubitsch.
Best Actor
Wallace Beery for THE CHAMP.
Alfred Lunt for THE GUARDSMAN.
Fredric March for DR. JEKYLL AND MR. HYDE.
Best Actress
Marie Dressler for EMMA.
Lynn Fontanne for THE GUARDSMAN.
Helen Hayes for THE SIN OF MADELON CLAUDET.
Best Direction
Frank Borzage for BAD GIRL
King Vidor for THE CHAMP.
Josef Von Sternberg for SHANGHAI EXPRESS.
Writing Awards
Best Screen Adaptation
ARROWSMITH, by Sidney Howard.
BAD GIRL, by Edwin Burke.
DR. JEKYLL AND MR. HYDE, by Percy Heath and Samuel Hoffenstein.
Best Original Story
THE CHAMP, by Frances Marion.
LADY AND GENT, by Grover Jones and William Slavens McNutt.
STAR WITNESS, by Lucien Hubbard.
WHAT PRICE HOLLYWOOD, by Adela Rogers St. John.
Best Cinematography
ARROWSMITH. Ray June.
DR. JEKYLL AND MR. HYDE. Karl Struss.
SHANGHAI EXPRESS. Lee Garmes.
Best Interior Decoration
A NOUS LA LIBERTE. Lazare Meerson.
ARROWSMITH. Richard Day.
TRANSATLANTIC. Gordon Wiles.
Best Sound Recording
Paramount Studio Sound Department.
Short Subjects
Best Cartoon
FLOWERS AND TREES. Walt Disney.
MICKEY'S ORPHANS. Walt Disney.
IT'S GOT ME AGAIN. Leon Schlesinger.
Best Comedy
THE LOUD MOUTH. Mack Sennett.
THE MUSIC BOX. Hal Roach (Laurel and Hardy Series).
STOUT HEARTS AND WILLING HANDS. RKO Radio (Masquers Comedies).
Best Novelty Item
SCREEN SOUVENIRS, PAR.
SWING HIGH, MGM (Sport Champions Series).
WRESTLING SWORDFISH, Mack Sennett (Cannibals of the Deep Series).
Special Award
Walt Disney for the creation of Mickey Mouse.
Scientific or Technical
Class II
Technicolor Motion Picture Corp. for their color cartoon process. Class III
Eastman Kodak Co. for the Type II-B Sensitometer.

1932-33
Best Picture
CAVALCADE, FOX. Winfield Sheehan, studio head.
A FAREWELL TO ARMS, PAR. Adolph Zukor, studio head.
42ND STREET, WB. Produced by Darryl F. Zanuck.
I AM A FUGITIVE FROM A CHAIN GANG, WB. Produced by Hal B. Wallis.
LADY FOR A DAY, COL. Produced by Frank Capra.
LITTLE WOMEN, RKO. Produced by Merian C. Cooper and Kenneth MacGowan.
THE PRIVATE LIFE OF HENRY VIII, London Films/UA. Produced by Alexander Korda.
SHE DONE HIM WRONG, PAR. Produced by William Le Baron.
SMILIN' THRU, MGM. Produced by Irving Thalberg.
STATE FAIR, FOX. Winfield Sheehan, studio head.
Best Actor
Leslie Howard for BERKELEY SQUARE.
Charles Laughton for THE PRIVATE LIFE OF HENRY VIII.
Paul Muni for I AM A FUGITIVE FROM A CHAIN GANG.
Best Actress
Katharine Hepburn for MORNING GLORY.
May Robson for LADY FOR A DAY.
Diana Wynyard for CAVALCADE.
Best Direction
Frank Capra for LADY FOR A DAY.
George Cukor for LITTLE WOMEN.
Frank Lloyd for CAVALCADE.
Writing Awards
Best Screen Adaptation
LADY FOR A DAY, by Robert Riskin.
LITTLE WOMEN, by Victor Heerman and Sarah Y. Mason.

STATE FAIR, by Paul Green and Sonya Levien.
Best Original Story
ONE WAY PASSAGE, by Robert Lord.
THE PRIZEFIGHTER AND THE LADY, by Frances Marion.
RASPUTIN AND THE EMPRESS, by Charles MacArthur.
Best Cinematography
A FAREWELL TO ARMS. Charles Bryant Lang, Jr.
REUNION IN VIENNA. George J. Folsey, Jr.
SIGN OF THE CROSS. Karl Struss.
Best Interior Decoration
CAVALCADE. William S. Darling.
A FAREWELL TO ARMS. Hans Dreier and Roland Anderson.
WHEN LADIES MEET. Cedric Gibbons.
Best Sound Recording
A FAREWELL TO ARMS. Harold C. Lewis.
42ND STREET. Nathan Levinson.
GOLDDIGGERS OF 1933. Nathan Levinson.
I AM A FUGITIVE FROM A CHAIN GANG. Nathan Levinson.
Best Assistant Director
Charles Barton, PAR.
Scott Beal, UNIV.
Charles Dorian, MGM.
Fred Fox, UA.
Gordon Hollingshead, WB.
Dewey Starkey, RKO.
William Tummel, FOX.
Short Subjects
Best Cartoon
BUILDING A BUILDING, Walt Disney.
THE MERRY OLD SOUL, Walter Lantz.
THE THREE LITTLE PIGS, Walt Disney.
Best Comedy
MISTER MUGGS, UNIV.
PREFERRED LIST, RKO (Headliner Series No.5).
SO THIS IS HARRIS, RKO.
Best Novelty Item
KRAKATOA, Educational.
MENU, Pete Smith.
THE SEA, Educational (Battle for Life Series).
Scientific or Technical
Class II
Electrical Research Products, Inc., for their wide range recording and reproducing system.
RCA-Victor Company, Inc., for their high-fidelity recording and reproducing system.
Class III
Fox Film Corporation, Fred Jackman, and Warner Bros. Pictures, Inc, and Sidney Sanders of RKO Studios, Inc. for their development and effective use of the translucent cellulose screen in composite photography.

1934
Best Picture
THE BARRETTS OF WIMPOLE STREET, MGM. Produced by Irving Thalberg.
CLEOPATRA, PAR. Produced by Cecil B. DeMille.
FLIRTATION WALK, FN. Produced by Jack L. Warner and Hal Wallis, with Robert Lord.
THE GAY DIVORCEE, RKO. Produced by Pandro S. Berman.
HERE COMES THE NAVY, WB. Produced by Lou Edelman.
THE HOUSE OF ROTHSCHILD, FOX-UA. Produced by Darryl F. Zanuck, with William Goetz and Raymond Griffith.
IMITATION OF LIFE, UNIV. Produced by John M. Stahl.
IT HAPPENED ONE NIGHT, COL. Produced by Harry Cohn.
ONE NIGHT OF LOVE, COL. Produced by Harry Cohn, with Everett Riskin.
THE THIN MAN, MGM. Produced by Hunt Stromberg.
VIVA VILLA, MGM. Produced by David O. Selznick.
THE WHITE PARADE, FOX. Produced by Jesse L. Lasky.
Best Actor
Clark Gable for IT HAPPENED ONE NIGHT.
Frank Morgan for AFFAIRS OF CELLINI.
William Powell for THE THIN MAN.
Best Actress
Claudette Colbert for IT HAPPENED ONE NIGHT.
Grace Moore for ONE NIGHT OF LOVE.
Norma Shearer for THE BARRETTS OF WIMPOLE STREET.
Best Direction
Frank Capra for IT HAPPENED ONE NIGHT.
Victor Schertzinger for ONE NIGHT OF LOVE.
W.S. Van Dyke for THE THIN MAN.
Writing Awards
Best Screen Adaptation
IT HAPPENED ONE NIGHT, by Robert Riskin.
THE THIN MAN, by Frances Goodrich and Albert Hackett.
VIVA VILLA, by Ben Hecht.
Best Original Story
HIDE-OUT, by Mauri Grashin.
MANHATTAN MELODRAMA, by Arthur Caesar.
THE RICHEST GIRL IN THE WORLD, by Norman Krasna.
Best Cinematography
AFFAIRS OF CELLINI. Charles Rosher.
CLEOPATRA. Victor Milner.
OPERATOR 13. George Folsey.
Best Interior Decoration
AFFAIRS OF CELLINI. Richard Day.
THE GAY DIVORCEE. Van Nest Polglase and Carroll Clark.
THE MERRY WIDOW. Cedric Gibbons and Frederic Hope.
Best Sound Recording
AFFAIRS OF CELLINI. Thomas T. Moulton.
CLEOPATRA. Franklin Hansen.
FLIRTATION WALK. Nathan Levinson.
THE GAY DIVORCEE. Carl Dreher.
IMITATION OF LIFE. Gilbert Kurland.

ONE NIGHT OF LOVE. Paul Neal.
VIVA VILLA. Douglas Shearer.
Best Assistant Director
Scott Beal for IMITATION OF LIFE.
Cullen Tate for CLEOPATRA.
John Waters for VIVA VILLA.
Music Awards
Best Song
"Carioca" from FLYING DOWN TO RIO. Music by Vincent Youmans; lyrics by Edward Eliscu and Gus Kahn.
The Continental" from THE GAY DIVORCEE. Music by Con Conrad; lyrics by Herb Magidson.
"Love in Bloom" from SHE LOVES ME NOT. Music by Ralph Rainger; lyrics by Leo Robin.
Best Score
THE GAY DIVORCEE. RKO Radio Studio Music Department; Max Steiner, head. Score by Kenneth Webb and Samuel Hoffenstein.
THE LOST PATROL. RKO Radio Studio Music Department; Max Steiner, head. Score by Steiner.
ONE NIGHT OF LOVE. Columbia Studio Music Department; Louis Silvers, head. Thematic music by Victor Schertzinger and Gus Kahn.
Best Film Editing
CLEOPATRA. Anne Bauchens.
ESKIMO. Conrad Nervig.
ONE NIGHT OF LOVE. Gene Milford.
Short Subjects
Best Cartoon
HOLIDAY LAND. Mintz.
JOLLY LITTLE ELVES, UNIV
THE TORTOISE AND THE HARE, Walt Disney.
Best Comedy
LA CUCARACHA, RKO.
MEN IN BLACK, COL (Broadway Comedies).
WHAT, NO MEN! WB (Broadway Brevities).
Best Novelty Item
BOSOM FRIENDS, Educational (Treasure Chest Series).
CITY OF WAX, Educational (Battle for Life Series).
STRIKES AND SPARES, MGM.
Special Award
Shirley Temple, in grateful recognition of her outstanding contribution to screen entertainment during the year 1934.
Scientific or Technical
Class II
Electrical Research Products, Inc., for their development of the vertical cut disc method of recording sound for motion pictures
Class III
Columbia Pictures Corporation for their application of the vertical cut disc method to actual studio production, with their recording of the sound on the picture ONE NIGHT OF LOVE.
Bell and Howell Company for their development of the Bell and Howell fully automatic sound and picture printer.

1935
Best Picture
ALICE ADAMS, RKO. Produced by Pandro S. Berman.
BROADWAY MELODY OF 1936, MGM. Produced by John W. Considine, Jr.
CAPTAIN BLOOD, WB. Produced by Hal Wallis, with Harry Joe Brown and Gordon Hollingshead.
DAVID COPPERFIELD, MGM. Produced by David O. Selznick.
THE INFORMER, RKO. Produced by Cliff Reid.
LES MISERABLES, FOX-UA. Produced by Darryl F. Zanuck.
LIVES OF A BENGAL LANCER, PAR. Produced by Louis D. Lighton.
A MIDSUMMER NIGHT'S DREAM, WB. Produced by Henry Blanke.
MUTINY ON THE BOUNTY, MGM. Produced by Irving Thalberg with Albert Lewin.
NAUGHTY MARIETTA, MGM. Produced by Hunt Stromberg.
RUGGLES OF RED GAP, PAR. Produced by Arthur Hornblow, Jr.
TOP HAT, RKO. Produced by Pandro S. Berman.
Best Actor
Clark Gable for MUTINY ON THE BOUNTY.
Charles Laughton for MUTINY ON THE BOUNTY.
Victor McLaglen for THE INFORMER.
Franchot Tone for MUTINY ON THE BOUNTY.
Best Actress
Elisabeth Bergner for ESCAPE ME NEVER.
Claudette Colbert for PRIVATE WORLDS.
Bette Davis for DANGEROUS.
Katharine Hepburn for ALICE ADAMS.
Miriam Hopkins for BECKY SHARP.
Merle Oberon for THE DARK ANGEL.
Best Direction
John Ford for THE INFORMER.
Henry Hathaway for LIVES OF A BENGAL LANCER.
Frank Lloyd for MUTINY ON THE BOUNTY.
Writing Awards
Best Original Story
BROADWAY MELODY OF 1936, by Moss Hart.
THE GAY DECEPTION, by Don Hartman and Stephen Avery.
THE SCOUNDREL, by Ben Hecht and Charles MacArthur.
Screenplay
THE INFORMER, by Dudley Nichols.
LIVES OF A BENGAL LANCER, by Achmed Abdullah, John L. Balderston, Grover Jones, William Slavens McNutt, and Waldemar Young.
MUTINY ON THE BOUNTY, by Jules Furthman, Talbot Jennings, and Carey Wilson.
Best Cinematography
BARBARY COAST. Ray June.
THE CRUSADES. Victor Milner.
LES MISERABLES. Gregg Toland.
A MIDSUMMER NIGHT'S DREAM. Hal Mohr.
Best Interior Decoration

THE DARK ANGEL. Richard Day.
LIVES OF A BENGAL LANCER. Hans Dreier and Roland Anderson.
TOP HAT. Carroll Clark and Van Nest Polglase.
Best Sound Recording
THE BRIDE OF FRANKENSTEIN. Gilbert Kurland.
CAPTAIN BLOOD. Nathan Levinson.
THE DARK ANGEL. Goldwyn Sound Department, Thomas T. Moulton.
I DREAM TOO MUCH. Carl Dreher.
LIVES OF A BENGAL LANCER. Franklin Hansen.
LOVE ME FOREVER. John Livadary.
NAUGHTY MARIETTA. Douglas Shearer.
1,000 DOLLARS A MINUTE. Republic Sound Department.
THANKS A MILLION. E.H. Hansen.
Best Assistant Director
Clem Beauchamp for LIVES OF A BENGAL LANCER.
Joseph Newman for DAVID COPPERFIELD.
Eric Stacey for LES MISERABLES.
Paul Wing for LIVES OF A BENGAL LANCER.
Music Awards
  Best Song
    "Cheek to Cheek" from TOP HAT. Music and lyrics by Irving Berlin.
    "Lovely to Look At" from ROBERTA. Music by Jerome Kern; lyrics by Dorothy
    Fields and Jimmy McHugh.
    "Lullaby of Broadway" from GOLD DIGGERS OF 1935. Music by Harry Warren;
    lyrics by Al Dubin.
  Best Score
    *THE INFORMER. RKO Studio Music Department; Max Steiner, head. Score by Max
    Steiner.*
    MUTINY ON THE BOUNTY. MGM Studio Music Department; Nat W. Finston,
    head. Score by Herbert Stothart.
    PETER IBBETSON. Paramount Studio Music Department; Irvin Talbot, head. Score
    by Ernst Toch.
Best Film Editing
  DAVID COPPERFIELD. Robert J. Kern.
  THE INFORMER. George Hively.
  LES MISERABLES. Barbara McLean.
  LIVES OF A BENGAL LANCER. Ellsworth Hoagland.
  A MIDSUMMER NIGHT'S DREAM. Ralph Dawson.
  MUTINY ON THE BOUNTY. Margaret Booth.
Best Dance Direction
  Busby Berkeley for "Lullaby of Broadway" number and "The Words Are in My
  Heart" number from GOLD DIGGERS OF 1935.
  Bobby Connolly for "Latin from Manhattan" number from GO INTO YOUR DANCE
  and "Playboy from Paree" from BROADWAY HOSTESS.
  David Gould for "I've Got a Feeling You're Fooling" number from BROADWAY
  MELODY OF 1936 and "Straw Hat" from FOLIES BERGERE.
  Sammy Lee for "Lovely Lady" number and "Too Good to Be True" number from
  KING OF BURLESQUE.
  Hermes Pan for "Piccolino" number and "Top Hat" number from TOP HAT.
  Leroy Prinz for "Elephant Number - It's the Animal in Me" from BIG BROADCAST
  OF 1936 and "Viennese Waltz" number from ALL THE KING'S HORSES.
  B. Zemach for "Hall of Kings" number from SHE.
Short Subjects
  Best Cartoon
    THE CALICO DRAGON, Harman-Ising.
    THREE ORPHAN KITTENS, Walt Disney.
    WHO KILLED COCK ROBIN, Walt Disney.
  Best Comedy
    HOW TO SLEEP, MGM.
    OH, MY NERVES, COL. (Broadway Comedies).
    TIT FOR TAT, Hal Roach (Laurel and Hardy).
  Best Novelty Film
    AUDIOSCOPIKS, MGM.
    CAMERA THRILLS, UNIV.
    WINGS OVER MT. EVEREST, Educational.
Special Award
  D.W. Griffith, for his distinguished creative achievements as director and producer
  and his invaluable initiative and lasting contributions to the progress of the motion
  picture arts.
Scientific or Technical
  Class II
    Agfa Ansco Corporation for their development of the Agfa infrared film.
    Eastman Kodak Company for their development of the Eastman Pola-Screen.
  Class III
    Metro-Goldwyn-Mayer Studio for the development of antidirectional negative and
    positive development by means of jet turbulation, and the application of the method
    to all negative and print processing of the entire product of a major producing
    company.
    William A. Mueller of Warner Bros.-First National Studio Sound Department for his
    method of dubbing, in which the level of the dialog automatically controls the level
    of the accompanying music and sound effects.
    Mole-Richardson Company for their development of the "Solarspot" spot lamps.
    Douglas Shearer and MGM Studio Sound Department for their automatic control
    system for cameras and sound recording machines and auxiliary stage equipment.
    Electrical Research Products, Inc., for their study and development of equipment to
    analyze and measure flutter resulting from the travel of the film through the
    mechanisms used in the recording and reproduction of sound.
    Paramount Productions, Inc., for the design and construction of the Paramount
    transparency air turbine developing machine.
    Nathan Levinson, director of Sound Recording for Warner Bros. First National
    Studio for the method of intercutting variable area sound tracks to secure an
    increase in the effective volume range of sound recorded for motion pictures.

1936
Best Picture
  ANTHONY ADVERSE, WB. Produced by Henry Blanke.
  DODSWORTH, UA. Produced by Samuel Goldwyn, with Merritt Hulbert.
  THE GREAT ZIEGFELD, MGM. Produced by Hunt Stromberg.
  LIBELED LADY, MGM. Produced by Lawrence Weingarten.
  MR. DEEDS GOES TO TOWN, COL. Produced by Frank Capra.

ROMEO AND JULIET, MGM. Produced by Irving Thalberg.
SAN FRANCISCO, MGM. Produced by John Emerson and Bernard H. Hyman.
THE STORY OF LOUIS PASTEUR, WB. Produced by Henry Blanke.
A TALE OF TWO CITIES, MGM. Produced by David O. Selznick.
THREE SMART GIRLS, UNIV. Produced by Joseph Pasternak, with Charles Rogers.
Best Actor
  Gary Cooper for MR. DEEDS GOES TO TOWN.
  Walter Huston for DODSWORTH.
  Paul Muni for THE STORY OF LOUIS PASTEUR.
  William Powell for MY MAN GODFREY.
  Spencer Tracy for SAN FRANCISCO.
Best Actress
  Irene Dunne for THEODORA GOES WILD.
  Gladys George for VALIANT IS THE WORD FOR CARRIE.
  Carole Lombard for MY MAN GODFREY.
  Luise Rainer for THE GREAT ZIEGFELD.
  Norma Shearer for ROMEO AND JULIET.
Best Supporting Actor
  Mischa Auer for MY MAN GODFREY.
  Walter Brennan for COME AND GET IT.
  Stuart Erwin for PIGSKIN PARADE.
  Basil Rathbone for ROMEO AND JULIET.
  Akim Tamiroff for THE GENERAL DIED AT DAWN.
Best Supporting Actress
  Beulah Bondi for THE GORGEOUS HUSSY.
  Alice Brady for MY MAN GODFREY.
  Bonita Granville for THESE THREE.
  Maria Ouspenskaya for DODSWORTH.
  Gale Sondergaard for ANTHONY ADVERSE.
Best Direction
  Frank Capra for MR. DEEDS GOES TO TOWN.
  Gregory La Cava for MY MAN GODFREY.
  Robert Z. Leonard for THE GREAT ZIEGFELD.
  W.S. Van Dyke for SAN FRANCISCO.
  William Wyler for DODSWORTH.
Writing Awards
  Best Original Story
    FURY, by Norman Krasna.
    THE GREAT ZIEGFELD, by William Anthony McGuire.
    SAN FRANCISCO, by Robert Hopkins.
    THE STORY OF LOUIS PASTEUR, by Pierre Collings and Sheridan Gibney.
    THREE SMART GIRLS, by Adele Commandini.
  Best Screenplay
    AFTER THE THIN MAN, by Frances Goodrich and Albert Hackett.
    DODSWORTH, by Sidney Howard.
    MR DEEDS GOES TO TOWN, by Robert Riskin.
    MY MAN GODFREY, by Eric Hatch and Morris Ryskind.
    THE STORY OF LOUIS PASTEUR, by Pierre Collings and Sheridan Gibney.
  Best Cinematography
    ANTHONY ADVERSE. Gaetano Guido.
    THE GENERAL DIED AT DAWN. Victor Milner.
    THE GORGEOUS HUSSY. George Folsey.
  Best Interior Decoration
    ANTHONY ADVERSE. Anton Grot.
    DODSWORTH. Richard Day.
    THE GREAT ZIEGFELD. Cedric Gibbons, Eddie Imazu, and Edwin B. Willis.
    LLOYDS OF LONDON. William S. Darling.
    THE MAGNIFICENT BRUTE. Albert S. D'Agostino and Jack Otterson.
    ROMEO AND JULIET. Cedric Gibbons, Frederic Hope, and Edwin B. Willis.
    WINTERSET. Perry Ferguson.
  Best Sound Recording
    BANJO ON MY KNEE. E.H. Hansen.
    THE CHARGE OF THE LIGHT BRIGADE. Nathan Levinson.
    DODSWORTH. Oscar Lagerstrom.
    GENERAL SPANKY. Elmer A. Raguse.
    MR. DEEDS GOES TO TOWN. John Livadary.
    SAN FRANCISCO. Douglas Shearer.
    THE TEXAS RANGERS. Franklin Hansen.
    THAT GIRL FROM PARIS. J.O. Aalberg.
    THREE SMART GIRLS. Homer G. Tasker.
  Best Assistant Director
    Clem Beauchamp for LAST OF THE MOHICANS.
    William Cannon for ANTHONY ADVERSE.
    Joseph Newman for SAN FRANCISCO.
    Eric G. Stacey for GARDEN OF ALLAH.
    Jack Sullivan for THE CHARGE OF THE LIGHT BRIGADE.
Music Awards
  Best Song
    "Did I Remember" from SUZY. Music by Walter Donaldson; lyrics by Harold
    Adamson.
    "I've Got You Under My Skin" from BORN TO DANCE. Music and lyrics by Cole
    Porter.
    "A Melody from the Sky" from TRAIL OF THE LONESOME PINE. Music by Louis
    Alter; lyrics by Sidney Mitchell.
    "Pennies from Heaven" from PENNIES FROM HEAVEN. Music by Arthur
    Johnston; lyrics by Johnny Burke.
    *The Way You Look Tonight" from SWING TIME. Music by Jerome Kern; lyrics by
    Dorothy Fields.*
    "When Did You Leave Heaven" from SING BABY SING. Music by Richard A.
    Whiting; lyrics by Walter Bullock.
  Best Score
    *ANTHONY ADVERSE; Warner Bros. Studio Music Department, Leo Forbstein,
    head. Score by Erich Wolfgang Korngold.*
    THE CHARGE OF THE LIGHT BRIGADE, Warner Bros. Studio Music Depart-
    ment, Leo Forbstein, head. Score by Max Steiner.
    THE GARDEN OF ALLAH, Selznick International Pictures Music Department,
    Max Steiner, head. Score by Max Steiner.
    THE GENERAL DIED AT DAWN, Paramount Studio Music Department, Boris
    Morros, head. Score by Werner Janssen.
    WINTERSET, RKO Radio Music Department, Nathaniel Shilkret, head. Score by

Nathaniel Shilkret.
Best Film Editing
ANTHONY ADVERSE. Ralph Dawson.
COME AND GET IT. Edward Curtiss.
THE GREAT ZIEGFELD. William S. Gray.
LLOYDS OF LONDON. Barbara McLean.
A TALE OF TWO CITIES. Conrad A. Nervig.
THEODORA GOES WILD. Otto Meyer.
Best Dance Direction
Busby Berkeley for "Love and War" number from GOLD DIGGERS OF 1937.
Bobby Connolly for "1000 Love Songs" number from CAIN AND MABEL.
Seymour Felix for "A Pretty Girl Is Like a Melody" number from THE GREAT ZIEGFELD.
Dave Gould for "Swingin' the Jinx" number from BORN TO DANCE.
Jack Haskell for "Skating Ensemble" number from ONE IN A MILLION.
Russell Lewis for "The Finale" number from DANCING PIRATE.
Hermes Pan for "Bojangles" number from SWING TIME.
Short Subjects
Best Cartoon
COUNTRY COUSIN, Walt Disney.
OLD MILL POND, Harman-Ising.
SINBAD THE SAILOR, PAR.
Best One-Reel Film
BORED OF EDUCATION, Hal Roach (Our Gang Series).
MOSCOW MOODS, PAR (Headliners Series).
WANTED, A MASTER, Pete Smith (Pete Smith Specialties).
Best Two-Reel Film
DOUBLE OR NOTHING, WB (Broadway Brevities).
DUMMY ACHE, RKO Radio (Edgar Kennedy Comedies).
THE PUBLIC PAYS, MGM (Crime Doesn't Pay Series).
Best Color Short
GIVE ME LIBERTY, WB (Broadway Brevities).
LA FIESTA DE SANTA BARBARA, MGM (Musical Revues).
POPULAR SCIENCE J-6-2, PAR.
Special Awards
March of Time for its significance to motion pictures and for having revolutionized one of the most important branches of the industry—the newsreel.
W. Howard Greene and Harold Rosson for the color cinematography of the Selznick International Production, THE GARDEN OF ALLAH.
Scientific or Technical
Class I
Douglas Shearer and MGM Studio Sound Department for the development of a practical two-way horn system and a biased Class A push-pull recording system.
Class II
E.C. Wente and the Bell Telephone Laboratories for their multicellular high-frequency horn and receiver.
RCA Manufacturing Company, Inc, for their rotary stabilizer sound head. Class III
RCA Manufacturing Company, Inc., for their development of a method of recording and printing sound records utilizing a restricted spectrum (known as ultra-violet light recording).
Electrical Research Products, Inc, for the ERPI "Type Q" portable recording channel.
RCA Manufacturing Company, Inc., for furnishing a practical design and specifications for a non-slip printer.
United Artists Studio Corporation for the development of a practical, efficient, and quiet wind machine.

1937
Best Picture
THE AWFUL TRUTH, COL. Produced by Leo McCarey, with Everett Riskin.
CAPTAINS COURAGEOUS, MGM. Produced by Louis D. Lighton.
DEAD END, UA. Produced by Samuel Goldwyn, with Merritt Hulbert.
THE GOOD EARTH, MGM. Produced by Irving Thalberg, with Albert Lewin.
IN OLD CHICAGO, FOX. Produced by Darryl F. Zanuck, with Kenneth MacGowan.
THE LIFE OF EMILE ZOLA, WB. Produced by Henry Blanke.
LOST HORIZON, COL. Produced by Frank Capra.
100 MEN AND A GIRL, UNIV. Produced by Charles R. Rogers, with Joe Pasternak.
STAGE DOOR, RKO. Produced by Pandro S. Berman.
A STAR IS BORN, Selznick International. Produced by David O. Selznick.
Best Actor
Charles Boyer for CONQUEST.
Fredric March for A STAR IS BORN.
Robert Montgomery for NIGHT MUST FALL.
Paul Muni for THE LIFE OF EMILE ZOLA.
Spencer Tracy for CAPTAINS COURAGEOUS.
Best Actress
Irene Dunne for THE AWFUL TRUTH.
Greta Garbo for CAMILLE.
Janet Gaynor for A STAR IS BORN.
Luis Rainer for THE GOOD EARTH.
Barbara Stanwyck for STELLA DALLAS.
Best Supporting Actor
Ralph Bellamy for THE AWFUL TRUTH.
Thomas Mitchell for THE HURRICANE.
Joseph Schildkraut for THE LIFE OF EMILE ZOLA.
H.B. Warner for LOST HORIZON.
Roland Young for TOPPER.
Best Supporting Actress
Alice Brady for IN OLD CHICAGO.
Andrea Leeds for STAGE DOOR.
Anne Shirley for STELLA DALLAS.
Claire Trevor for DEAD END.
Dame May Whitty for NIGHT MUST FALL.
Best Direction
William Dieterle for THE LIFE OF EMILE ZOLA.
Sidney Franklin for THE GOOD EARTH.
Gregory La Cava for STAGE DOOR.
Leo McCarey for THE AWFUL TRUTH.
William Wellman for A STAR IS BORN.
Writing Awards

Best Original Story
BLACK LEGION, by Robert Lord.
IN OLD CHICAGO, by Niven Busch.
THE LIFE OF EMILE ZOLA, by Heinz Herald and Geza Herczeg.
100 MEN AND A GIRL, by Hans Kraly.
A STAR IS BORN, by William A. Wellman and Robert Carson.
Best Screenplay
THE AWFUL TRUTH, by Vina Delmar.
CAPTAINS COURAGEOUS, by Marc Connolly, John Lee Mahin, and Dale Van Every.
THE LIFE OF EMILE ZOLA, by Heinz Herald, Geza Herczeg, and Norman Reilly Raine.
STAGE DOOR, by Morris Ryskind and Anthony Veiller.
A STAR IS BORN, by Alan Campbell, Robert Carson, and Dorothy Parker.
Best Cinematography
DEAD END. Gregg Toland.
THE GOOD EARTH. Karl Freund.
WINGS OVER HONOLULU. Joseph Valentine.
Best Interior Decoration
CONQUEST. Cedric Gibbons and William Horning.
A DAMSEL IN DISTRESS. Carroll Clark.
DEAD END. Richard Day.
EVERY DAY'S A HOLIDAY. Wiard Ihnen.
LOST HORIZON. Stephen Goosson.
MANHATTAN MERRY-GO-ROUND. John Victor MacKay.
THE PRISONER OF ZENDA. Lyle Wheeler.
SOULS AT SEA. Hans Dreier and Roland Anderson.
VOGUES OF 1938. Alexander Toluboff.
WEE WILLIE WINKIE. William S. Darling and David Hall.
YOU'RE A SWEETHEART. Jack Otterson.
Best Sound Recording
THE GIRL SAID NO. A.E. Kaye.
HITTING A NEW HIGH. John Aalberg.
THE HURRICANE. Thomas Moulton.
IN OLD CHICAGO. E.H. Hansen.
THE LIFE OF EMILE ZOLA. Nathan Levinson.
LOST HORIZON. John Livadary.
MAYTIME. Douglas Shearer.
100 MEN AND A GIRL. Homer Tasker.
TOPPER. Elmer Raguse.
WELLS FARGO. L.L. Ryder.
Best Assistant Director
C.C. Coleman, Jr. for LOST HORIZON.
Russ Saunders for THE LIFE OF EMILE ZOLA.
Eric Stacey for A STAR IS BORN.
Hal Walker for SOULS AT SEA.
Robert Webb for IN OLD CHICAGO.
Music Awards
Best Song
"Remember Me" from MR. DODD TAKES THE AIR. Music by Harry Warren; lyrics by Al Dubin.
Sweet Leilani" from WAIKIKI WEDDING; Music and lyrics by Harry Owens.
"That Old Feeling" from VOGUES OF 1938. Music by Sammy Fain; lyrics by Lew Brown.
"They Can.t Take That Away from Me" from SHALL WE DANCE. Music by George Gershwin; lyrics by Ira Gershwin.
"Whispers in the Dark" from ARTISTS AND MODELS. Music by Frederick Hollander; lyrics by Leo Robin.
Best Score
THE HURRICANE, Samuel Goldwyn Studio Music Dept., Alfred Newman, head. Score by Alfred Newman.
IN OLD CHICAGO, 20th Century-Fox Studio Music Dept., Louis Silvers, head.
THE LIFE OF EMILE ZOLA, Warner Bros. Studio Music Dept., Leo Forbstein, head. Score by Max Steiner.
LOST HORIZON, Columbia Studio Music Dept. Morris Stollof, head. Score by Dimitri Tiomkin.
MAKE A WISH, Principal Productions: Lesser, RKO Radio, Dr. Hugo Riesenfield, musical director. Score by Riesenfield.
MAYTIME, MGM Studio Music Dept., Nat W. Finston, head. Score by Herbert Stothart.
100 MEN AND A GIRL, Universal Studio Music Dept., Charles Previn, head.
PORTIA ON TRIAL, Republic Studio Music Dept., Alberto Colombo, head. Score by Colombo.
THE PRISONER OF ZENDA, Selznick International Pictures Music Dept., Alfred Newman, musical director. Score by Newman.
QUALITY STREET, RKO Radio Studio Music Dept., Roy Webb, musical director. Score by Roy Webb.
SNOW WHITE AND THE SEVEN DWARFS, Walt Disney Studio Music Dept., Leigh Harline, head. Score by Frank Churchill, Leigh Harline, and Paul J. Smith.
SOMETHING TO SING ABOUT, Grand National Studio Music Dept., C. Bakaleinik-off, musical director. Score by Victor Schertzinger.
SOULS AT SEA, Paramount Studio Music Dept., Boris Morros, head. Score by W. Franke Harling and Milan Roder.
WAY OUT WEST, Hal Roach Studio Music Dept., Marvin Hatley, head. Score by Marvin Hatley.
Best Film Editing
THE AWFUL TRUTH. Al Clark.
CAPTAINS COURAGEOUS. Elmo Vernon.
THE GOOD EARTH. Basil Wrangell.
LOST HORIZON. Gene Havlick and Gene Milford.
100 MEN AND A GIRL. Bernard W. Burton.
Best Dance Direction
Busby Berkeley for "The Finale" number from VARSITY SHOW.
Bobby Connolly for "Too Marvelous for Words" number from READY, WILLING AND ABLE.
Dave Gould for "All God's Children Got Rhythm" number from A DAY AT THE RACES.
Sammy Lee for "Swing Is Here to Stay" number from ALI BABA GOES TO TOWN.
Harry Losee for "Prince Igor Suite" number from THIN ICE.
Hermes Pan for "Fun House" number from DAMSEL IN DISTRESS.

Leroy Prinz for "Luau" number from WAIKIKI WEDDING.

Short Subjects

Best Cartoon

EDUCATED FISH, PAR.
THE LITTLE MATCH GIRL, Charles Mintz.
THE OLD MILL, Walt Disney.

Best One-Reel Film

A NIGHT AT THE MOVIES, MGM. Produced by Robert Benchley.
PRIVATE LIFE OF THE GANNETTS, Educational.
ROMANCE OF RADIUM, Pete Smith.

Best Two-Reel Film

DEEP SOUTH, RKO (Radio Musical Comedies).
SHOULD WIVES WORK, RKO (Leon Errol Comedies).
TORTURE MONEY, MGM (Crime Doesn't Pay Series).

Best Color Short

THE MAN WITHOUT A COUNTRY, WB.
PENNY WISDOM, Pete Smith.
POPULAR SCIENCE J-7-1, PAR.

Irving G. Thalberg Memorial Award

Darryl F. Zanuck.

Special Awards

Mack Sennett for his lasting contribution to the comedy technique of the screen, the basic principles of which are as important today as when they were first put into practice, the Academy presents a Special Award to that master of fun, discoverer of stars, sympathetic, kindly, understanding comedy genius—Mack Sennett.

Edgar Bergen for his outstanding comedy creation, Charlie McCarthy.

The Museum of Modern Art Film Library for its significant work in collecting films dating from 1895 to the present and for the first time making available to the public the means of studying the historical and aesthetic development of the motion picture as one of the major arts.

W. Howard Greene for the color photography of A STAR IS BORN. (This Award was recommended by a committee of leading cinematographers after viewing all the color pictures made during the year.)

Scientific or Technical

Class I

Agfa ANSCO Corp. for Agfa Supreme and Agfa Ultra Speed pan motion picture negatives.

Class II

Walt Disney Productions, Ltd., for the design and application to production of the Multi-Plane Camera.
Eastman Kodak Company for two fine-grain duplicating film stocks.
Farciot Edouart and Paramount Pictures, Inc., for the development of the Paramount dual screen transparency camera setup.
Douglas Shearer and the MGM Studio Sound Dept. for a method of varying the scanning width of variable density sound tracks (squeeze tracks) for the purpose of obtaining an increased amount of noise reduction.

Class III

John Arnold and the MGM Studio Camera Dept. for their improvement of the semi-automatic follow focus device and its application to all of the cameras used by the MGM Studio.
John Livadary, Director of Sound Recording for Columbia Pictures Corp., for the application of the biplanar light valve to motion picture sound recording.
Thomas T. Moulton and the United Artists Studio Sound Dept. for the application to motion picture sound recording of volume indicators which have peak reading response and linear decibel scales.
RCA Manufacturing Company, Inc., for the introduction of the modulated high-frequency method of determining optimum photographic process conditions for variable width sound tracks.
Joseph E. Robbins and Paramount Pictures, Inc., for an exceptional application of acoustic principles to the soundproofing of gasoline generators and water pumps.
Douglas Shearer and the MGM Studio Sound Dept. for the design of the film drive mechanism as incorporated in the ERPI 1010 reproducer.

1938

Best Picture

THE ADVENTURES OF ROBIN HOOD, WB. Produced by Hal B. Wallis, with Henry Blanke.
ALEXANDER'S RAGTIME BAND, FOX. Produced by Darryl F. Zanuck, with Harry Joe Brown.
BOYS TOWN, MGM. Produced by John W. Considine, Jr.
THE CITADEL, MGM. Produced by Victor Saville.
FOUR DAUGHTERS, WB-FN. Produced by Hal B. Wallis, with Henry Blanke.
GRAND ILLUSION, R.A.O., World Pictures. Produced by Frank Rollmer and Albert Pinkovitch.
JEZEBEL, WB. Produced by Hal B. Wallis, with Henry Blanke.
PYGMALION, MGM. Produced by Gabriel Pascal.
TEST PILOT, MGM. Produced by Louis D. Lighton.
YOU CAN'T TAKE IT WITH YOU, COL. Produced by Frank Capra.

Best Actor

Charles Boyer for ALGIERS.
James Cagney for ANGELS WITH DIRTY FACES.
Robert Donat for THE CITADEL.
Leslie Howard for PYGMALION.
Spencer Tracy for BOYS TOWN.

Best Actress

Fay Bainter for WHITE BANNERS.
Bette Davis for JEZEBEL.
Wendy Hiller for PYGMALION.
Norma Shearer for MARIE ANTOINETTE.
Margaret Sullavan for THREE COMRADES.

Best Supporting Actor

Walter Brennan for KENTUCKY.
John Garfield for FOUR DAUGHTERS.
Gene Lockhart for ALGIERS.
Robert Morley for MARIE ANTOINETTE.
Basil Rathbone for IF I WERE KING.

Best Supporting Actress

Fay Bainter for JEZEBEL.
Beulah Bondi for OF HUMAN HEARTS.
Billie Burke for MERRILY WE LIVE.

Spring Byington for YOU CAN'T TAKE IT WITH YOU.
Miliza Korjus for THE GREAT WALTZ.

Best Direction

Frank Capra for YOU CAN'T TAKE IT WITH YOU.
Michael Curtiz for ANGELS WITH DIRTY FACES.
Michael Curtiz for FOUR DAUGHTERS.
Norman Taurog for BOYS TOWN.
King Vidor for THE CITADEL.

Writing Awards

Best Original Story

ALEXANDER'S RAGTIME BAND, by Irving Berlin.
ANGELS WITH DIRTY FACES, by Rowland Brown.
BLOCKADE, by John Howard Lawson.
BOYS TOWN, by Eleanore Griffin and Dore Schary.
MAD ABOUT MUSIC, by Marcella Burke and Frederick Kohner.
TEST PILOT, by Frank Wead.

Best Screenplay

BOYS TOWN, by John Meehan and Dore Schary.
THE CITADEL, by Ian Dalrymple, Elizabeth Hill, and Frank Wead.
FOUR DAUGHTERS, by Lenore Coffee and Julius J. Epstein.
PYGMALION, by George Bernard Shaw; adapted by Ian Dalrymple, Cecil Lewis, and W.P. Lipscomb.
YOU CAN'T TAKE IT WITH YOU, by Robert Riskin.

Best Cinematography

ALGIERS. James Wong Howe.
ARMY GIRL. Ernest Miller and Harry Wild.
THE BUCCANEER. Victor Milner.
THE GREAT WALTZ. Joseph Ruttenberg.
JEZEBEL. Ernest Haller.
MAD ABOUT MUSIC. Joseph Valentine.
MERRILY WE LIVE. Norbert Brodine.
SUEZ. Peverell Marley.
VIVACIOUS LADY. Robert de Grasse.
YOU CAN'T TAKE IT WITH YOU. Joseph Walker.
THE YOUNG IN HEART. Leon Shamroy.

Best Interior Decoration

THE ADVENTURES OF ROBIN HOOD. Carl J. Weyl.
THE ADVENTURES OF TOM SAWYER. Lyle Wheeler.
ALEXANDER'S RAGTIME BAND. Bernard Herzbrun and Boris Leven.
ALGIERS. Alexander Toluboff.
CAREFREE. Van Nest Polglase.
GOLDWYN FOLLIES. Richard Day.
HOLIDAY. Stephen Goosson and Lionel Banks.
IF I WERE KING. Hans Dreier and John Goodman.
MAD ABOUT MUSIC. Jack Otterson.
MARIE ANTOINETTE. Cedric Gibbons.
MERRILY WE LIVE. Charles D. Hall.

Music Awards

Best Song

"Always and Always" from MANNEQUIN. Music by Edward Ward; lyrics by Chet Forrest and Bob Wright.
"Change Partners and Dance with Me" from CAREFREE. Music and lyrics by Irving Berlin.
"The Cowboy and the Lady" from THE COWBOY AND THE LADY. Music by Lionel Newman; lyrics by Arthur Quenzer.
"Dust" from UNDER WESTERN STARS. Music and lyrics by Johnny Marvin.
"Jeepers Creepers" from GOING PLACES. Music by Harry Warren; lyrics by Johnny Mercer.
"Merrily We Live" from MERRILY WE LIVE. Music by Phil Craig; lyrics by Arthur Quenzer.
"A Mist over the Moon" from THE LADY OBJECTS. Music by Ben Oakland; lyrics by Oscar Hammerstein II.
"My Own" from THAT CERTAIN AGE. Music by Jimmy McHugh; lyrics by Harold Adamson.
"Now It Can Be Told" from ALEXANDER'S RAGTIME BAND. Music and lyrics by Irving Berlin.
"Thanks for the Memory" from BIG BROADCAST OF 1938. Music by Ralph Rainger; lyrics by Leo Robin.

Best Score

ALEXANDER'S RAGTIME BAND. Alfred Newman.
CAREFREE. Victor Baravalle.
GIRLS SCHOOL. Morris Stoloff and Gregory Stone.
GOLDWYN FOLLIES. Alfred Newman.
JEZEBEL. Max Steiner.
MAD ABOUT MUSIC. Charles Previn and Frank Skinner.
STORM OVER BENGAL. Cy Feuer.
SWEETHEARTS. Herbert Stothart.
THERE GOES MY HEART. Marvin Hatley.
TROPIC HOLIDAY. Boria Morros.
THE YOUNG IN HEART. Frank Waxman.

Best Original Score

THE ADVENTURES OF ROBIN HOOD. Erich Wolfgang Korngold.
ARMY GIRL. Victor Young.
BLOCKADE. Werner Janssen.
BLOCKHEADS. Marvin Hatley.
BREAKING THE ICE. Victor Young.
THE COWBOY AND THE LADY. Alfred Newman.
IF I WERE KING. Richard Hageman.
MARIE ANTOINETTE. Herbert Stothart.
PACIFIC LINER. Russell Bennett.
SUEZ. Louis Silvers.
THE YOUNG IN HEART. Franz Waxman.

Best Film Editing

THE ADVENTURES OF ROBIN HOOD. Ralph Dawson.
ALEXANDER'S RAGTIME BAND. Barbara McLean.
THE GREAT WALTZ. Tom Held.
TEST PILOT. Tom Held.
YOU CAN'T TAKE IT WITH YOU. Gene Havlick.

Short Subjects

Best Cartoon

BRAVE LITTLE TAILOR, Walt Disney.
FERDINAND THE BULL, Walt Disney.
GOOD SCOUTS, Walt Disney.
HUNKY AND SPUNKY, PAR.
MOTHER GOOSE GOES HOLLYWOOD, Walt Disney.
Best One-Reel Film
THE GREAT HEART, MGM.
THAT MOTHERS MIGHT LIVE, MGM.
TIMBER TOPPERS, FOX (Ed Thorgensen-Sports Series).
Best Two-Reel Film
DECLARATION OF INDEPENDENCE, WB.
SWINGTIME IN THE MOVIES, WB (Broadway Brevities).
THEY'RE ALWAYS CAUGHT, MGM (Crime Doesn't Pay Series).
Irving G. Thalberg Memorial Award
Hal B. Wallis.
Special Awards
Deanna Durbin and Mickey Rooney for their significant contribution in bringing to the screen the spirit and personification of youth, and as juvenile players setting a high standard of ability and achievement.
Harry M. Warner in recognition of patriotic service in the production of historical short subjects presenting significant episodes in the early struggle of the American people for liberty.
Walt Disney for SNOW WHITE AND THE SEVEN DWARFS, recognized as a significant screen innovation which has charmed millions and pioneered a great new entertainment field for the motion picture cartoon.
Oliver Marsh and Allen Davey for the color cinematography of the MGM production SWEETHEARTS.
For outstanding achievement in creating special photographic and sound effects in the Paramount production SPAWN OF THE NORTH: special effects by Gordon Jennings, assisted by Jan Domela, Dev Jennings, Irmin Roberts, and Art Smith; transparencies by Farciot Edouart, assisted by Loyal Griggs; sound effects by Loren Ryder, assisted by Harry Mills, Louis H. Mesenkop, and Walter Oberst.
J. Arthur Ball for his outstanding contributions to the advancement of color in motion picture photography.
Scientific or Technical
Class III
John Aalberg and the RKO Radio Studio Sound Department for the application of compression to variable area recording in motion picture production.
Byron Haskin and the Special Effects Department of Warner Bros. Studio for pioneering the development and for the first practical application to motion picture production of the triple head background projector.

1939
Best Picture
DARK VICTORY, WB. Produced by David Lewis.
GONE WITH THE WIND, MGM. Produced by David O. Selznick.
GOODBYE, MR. CHIPS, MGM. Produced by Victor Saville.
LOVE AFFAIR, RKO. Produced by Leo McCarey.
MR. SMITH GOES TO WASHINGTON, COL. Produced by Frank Capra.
NINOTCHKA, MGM. Produced by Sidney Franklin.
OF MICE AND MEN, UA. Produced by Lewis Milestone.
STAGECOACH, UA. Produced by Walter Wanger.
THE WIZARD OF OZ, MGM. Produced by Mervyn LeRoy.
WUTHERING HEIGHTS, UA. Produced by Samuel Goldwyn.
Best Actor
Robert Donat for GOODBYE, MR. CHIPS.
Clark Gable for GONE WITH THE WIND.
Laurence Olivier for WUTHERING HEIGHTS.
Mickey Rooney for BABES IN ARMS.
James Stewart for MR. SMITH GOES TO WASHINGTON.
Best Actress
Bette Davis for DARK VICTORY.
Irene Dunne for LOVE AFFAIR.
Greta Garbo for NINOTCHKA.
Greer Garson for GOODBYE, MR. CHIPS.
Vivien Leigh for GONE WITH THE WIND.
Best Supporting Actor
Brian Aherne for JUAREZ.
Harry Carey for MR. SMITH GOES TO WASHINGTON.
Brian Donlevy for BEAU GESTE.
Thomas Mitchell for STAGECOACH.
Claude Rains for MR. SMITH GOES TO WASHINGTON.
Best Supporting Actress
Olivia de Havilland for GONE WITH THE WIND.
Geraldine Fitzgerald for WUTHERING HEIGHTS.
Hattie McDaniel for GONE WITH THE WIND.
Edna May Oliver for DRUMS ALONG THE MOHAWK.
Maria Ouspenskaya for LOVE AFFAIR.
Best Direction
Frank Capra for MR. SMITH GOES TO WASHINGTON.
Victor Fleming for GONE WITH THE WIND.
John Ford for STAGECOACH.
Sam Wood for GOODBYE, MR. CHIPS.
William Wyler for WUTHERING HEIGHTS.
Writing Awards
Best Original Story
BACHELOR MOTHER, by Felix Jackson.
LOVE AFFAIR, by Mildred Cram and Leo McCarey.
MR. SMITH GOES TO WASHINGTON, by Lewis R. Foster.
NINOTCHKA, by Melchior Lengyel.
YOUNG MR. LINCOLN, by Lamar Trotti.
Best Screenplay
GONE WITH THE WIND, by Sidney Howard.
GOODBYE, MR. CHIPS, by Eric Maschwitz, R.C. Sherriff, and Claudine West.
MR. SMITH GOES TO WASHINGTON, by Sidney Buchman.
NINOTCHKA, by Charles Brackett, Walter Reisch and Billy Wilder.
WUTHERING HEIGHTS, by Ben Hecht and Charles MacArthur.
Best Cinematography
Black-and-White
FIRST LOVE. Joseph Valentine.

THE GREAT VICTOR HERBERT. Victor Milner.
GUNGA DIN. Joseph H. August.
INTERMEZZO: A LOVE STORY. Gregg Toland.
JUAREZ. Tony Gaudio.
LADY OF THE TROPICS. Norbert Brodine.
ONLY ANGELS HAVE WINGS. Joseph Walker.
THE RAINS CAME. Arthur Miller.
STAGECOACH. Bert Glennon.
WUTHERING HEIGHTS. Gregg Toland.
Color
DRUMS ALONG THE MOHAWK. Ray Rennahan and Bert Glennon.
FOUR FEATHERS. Georges Perinal and Osmond Borradaile.
GONE WITH THE WIND. Ernest Haller and Ray Rennahan.
THE MIKADO. William V. Skall.
THE PRIVATE LIVES OF ELIZABETH AND ESSEX. Sol Polito and W. Howard Greene.
THE WIZARD OF OZ. Hal Rosson.
Best Interior Decoration
BEAU GESTE. Hans Dreier and Robert Odell.
CAPTAIN FURY. Charles D. Hall.
FIRST LOVE. Jack Otterson and Martin Obzina.
GONE WITH THE WIND. Lyle Wheeler.
LOVE AFFAIR. Van Nest Polglase and Al Herman.
MAN OF CONQUEST. John Victor Mackay.
MR. SMITH GOES TO WASHINGTON. Lionel Banks.
THE PRIVATE LIVES OF ELIZABETH AND ESSEX. Anton Grot.
THE RAINS CAME. William Darling and George Dudley.
STAGECOACH. Alexander Toluboff.
THE WIZARD OF OZ. Cedric Gibbons and William A. Horning.
WUTHERING HEIGHTS. James Basevi.
Best Sound Recording
BALALAIKA. Douglas Shearer.
GONE WITH THE WIND. Thomas T. Moulton.
GOODBYE, MR. CHIPS. A.W. Watkins.
THE GREAT VICTOR HERBERT. Loren Ryder.
THE HUNCHBACK OF NOTRE DAME. John Aalberg.
MAN OF CONQUEST. C.L. Lootens.
MR. SMITH GOES TO WASHINGTON. John Livadary.
OF MICE AND MEN. Elmer Raguse.
THE PRIVATE LIVES OF ELIZABETH AND ESSEX. Nathan Levinson.
THE RAINS CAME. E.H. Hansen.
WHEN TOMORROW COMES. Bernard B. Brown.
Music Awards
Best Song
"Faithful Forever" from GULLIVER'S TRAVELS. Music by Ralph Rainger; lyrics by Leo Robin.
"I Poured My Heart into a Song" from SECOND FIDDLE. Music and lyrics by Irving Berlin.
Over the Rainbow" from THE WIZARD OF OZ. Music by Harold Arlen; lyrics by E.Y. Harburg.
"Wishing" from LOVE AFFAIR. Music and lyrics by Buddy De Sylva.
Best Score
BABES IN ARMS. Roger Edens and George E. Stoll.
FIRST LOVE. Charles Previn.
THE GREAT VICTOR HERBERT. Phil Boutelje and Arthur Lange.
THE HUNCHBACK OF NOTRE DAME. Alfred Newman.
INTERMEZZO: A LOVE STORY. Lou Forbes.
MR. SMITH GOES TO WASHINGTON. Dimitri Tiomkin.
OF MICE AND MEN. Aaron Copland.
THE PRIVATE LIVES OF ELIZABETH AND ESSEX. Erich Wolfgang Korngold.
SHE MARRIED A COP. Cy Feuer.
STAGECOACH. Richard Hageman, Frank Harling, John Leipold, and Leo Shuken.
SWANEE RIVER. Louis Silvers.
THEY SHALL HAVE MUSIC. Alfred Newman.
WAY DOWN SOUTH. Victor Young.
Best Original Score
DARK VICTORY. Max Steiner.
ETERNALLY YOURS. Werner Janssen.
GOLDEN BOY. Victor Young.
GONE WITH THE WIND. Max Steiner.
GULLIVER'S TRAVELS. Victor Young.
THE MAN IN THE IRON MASK. Lud Gluskin and Lucien Moraweck.
MAN OF CONQUEST. Victor Young.
NURSE EDITH CAVELL. Anthony Collins.
OF MICE AND MEN. Aaron Copland.
THE RAINS CAME. Alfred Newman.
THE WIZARD OF OZ. Herbert Stothart.
WUTHERING HEIGHTS. Alfred Newman.
Best Film Editing
GONE WITH THE WIND. Hal C. Kern and James E. Newcom.
GOODBYE, MR. CHIPS. Charles Frend.
MR. SMITH GOES TO WASHINGTON. Gene Havlick and Al Clark.
THE RAINS CAME. Barbara McLean.
STAGECOACH. Otho Lovering and Dorothy Spencer.
Best Special Effects
GONE WITH THE WIND. Photographic: John R. Cosgrove; sound: Fred Albin and Arthur Johns.
ONLY ANGELS HAVE WINGS. Photographic: Roy Davidson; sound: Edwin C. Hahn.
THE PRIVATE LIVES OF ELIZABETH AND ESSEX. Photographic: Byron Haskin; sound: Nathan Levinson.
THE RAINS CAME. Photographic: E.H. Hansen; sound: Fred Sersen.
TOPPER TAKES A TRIP. Roy Seawright.
UNION PACIFIC. Photographic: Farciot Edouart and Gordon Jennings; sound: Loren Ryder.
THE WIZARD OF OZ. Photographic: A. Arnold Gillespie; sound: Douglas Shearer.
Short Subjects
Best Cartoon
DETOURING AMERICA, WB.
PEACE ON EARTH, MGM.
THE POINTER, Walt Disney.

THE UGLY DUCKLING, Walt Disney.
Best One-Reel Film
   BUSY LITTLE BEARS, PAR (Paragraphics Series).
   INFORMATION PLEASE, RKO.
   PROPHET WITHOUT HONOR, MGM.
   SWORD FISHING, WB (Vitaphone Varieties).
Best Two-Reel Film
   DRUNK DRIVING, MGM (Crime Doesn't Pay Series).
   FIVE TIMES FIVE, RKO.
   SONS OF LIBERTY, WB.
Irving G. Thalberg Memorial Award
   David O. Selznick.
Special Awards
   Douglas Fairbanks (Commemorative Award)—recognizing the unique and outstanding contribution of Douglas Fairbanks, first president of the Academy, to the international development of the motion picture.
   The Motion Picture Relief Fund—acknowledging the outstanding services to the industry during the past year of the Motion Picture Relief Fund and its progressive leadership. Presented to Jean Hersholt, President; Ralph Morgan, Chairman of the Executive Committee; Ralph Block, First Vice-President; Conrad Nagel.
   Judy Garland for her outstanding performance as a screen juvenile during the past year.
   William Cameron Menzies for outstanding achievement in the use of color for the enhancement of dramatic mood in the production of GONE WITH THE WIND.
   The Technicolor Company for its contributions in successfully bringing three-color feature production to the screen.
Scientific or Technical
   Class III
      George Anderson of Warner Bros. Studio for an improved positive head for sun arcs.
      John Arnold of MGM Studio for the MGM mobile camera crane.
      Thomas T. Moulton, Fred Albin, and the Sound Department of the Samuel Goldwyn Studio for the origination and application of the Delta db test to sound recording in motion pictures.
      Farciot Edouart, Joseph E. Robbins, William Rudolph, and Paramount Pictures, Inc., for the design and construction of a quiet portable treadmill.
      Emery House and Ralph B. Atkinson of Eastman Kodak Co. for their specifications for chemical analysis of photographic developers and fixing baths.
      Harold Nye of Warner Bros. Studio for a miniature incandescent spot lamp.
      A. J. Tondreau of Warner Bros. Studio for the design and manufacture of an improved sound track printer.
      Multiple Award for important contributions in cooperative development of new improved Process Projection Equipment:
         F.R. Abbott, Haller Belt, Alan Cook, and Bausch & Lomb Optical Co. for faster projection lenses.
         Mitchell Camera Co. for a new type process projection head.
         Mole-Richardson Co. for a new type automatically controlled projection arc lamp.
         Charles Handley, David Joy, and National Carbon Co. for improved and more table high-intensity carbons.
         Winton Hoch and Technicolor Motion Picture Corp. for an auxiliary optical system.
         Don Musgrave and Selznick International Pictures, Inc., for pioneering in the use of coordinated equipment in the production GONE WITH THE WIND.

1940
Best Picture
   ALL THIS AND HEAVEN TOO, WB. Produced by Jack L. Warner and Hal B. Wallis, with David Lewis.
   FOREIGN CORRESPONDENT, UA. Produced by Walter Wanger.
   THE GRAPES OF WRATH, FOX. Produced by Darryl F. Zanuck, with Nunnally Johnson.
   THE GREAT DICTATOR, UA. Produced by Charles Chaplin.
   KITTY FOYLE, RKO. Produced by David Hempstead.
   THE LETTER, WB. Produced by Hal B. Wallis.
   THE LONG VOYAGE HOME, UA. Produced by John Ford.
   OUR TOWN, UA. Produced by Sol Lesser.
   THE PHILADELPHIA STORY, MGM. Produced by Joseph L. Mankiewicz.
   REBECCA, UA. Produced by David O. Selznick.
Best Actor
   Charles Chaplin for THE GREAT DICTATOR.
   Henry Fonda for THE GRAPES OF WRATH.
   Raymond Massey for ABE LINCOLN IN ILLINOIS.
   Laurence Olivier for REBECCA.
   James Stewart for THE PHILADELPHIA STORY
Best Actress
   Bette Davis for THE LETTER.
   Joan Fontaine for REBECCA.
   Katharine Hepburn for THE PHILADELPHIA STORY.
   Ginger Rogers for KITTY FOYLE.
   Martha Scott for OUR TOWN.
Best Supporting Actor
   Albert Basserman for FOREIGN CORRESPONDENT.
   Walter Brennan for THE WESTERNER.
   William Gargan for THEY KNEW WHAT THEY WANTED.
   Jack Oakie for THE GREAT DICTATOR.
   James Stephenson for THE LETTER.
Best Supporting Actress
   Judith Anderson for REBECCA.
   Jane Darwell for THE GRAPES OF WRATH.
   Ruth Hussey for THE PHILADELPHIA STORY.
   Barbara O'Neil for ALL THIS, AND HEAVEN TOO.
   Marjorie Rambeau for PRIMROSE PATH.
Best Direction
   George Cukor for THE PHILADELPHIA STORY.
   John Ford for THE GRAPES OF WRATH.
   Alfred Hitchcock for REBECCA.
   Sam Wood for KITTY FOYLE.
   William Wyler for THE LETTER.
Writing Awards
   Best Original Story
      ARISE, MY LOVE, by Benjamin Glazer and John S. Toldy.
      COMRADE X, by Walter Reisch.

EDISON THE MAN, by Hugo Butler and Dore Schary.
   MY FAVORITE WIFE, by Leo McCarey, Bella Spewack, and Samuel Spewack.
   THE WESTERNER, by Stuart N. Lake.
Best Original Screenplay
   ANGELS OVER BROADWAY, by Ben Hecht.
   DR. EHRLICH'S MAGIC BULLET, by Norman Burnside, Heinz Herald, and John Huston.
   FOREIGN CORRESPONDENT, by Charles Bennett and Joan Harrison.
   THE GREAT DICTATOR, by Charles Chaplin.
   THE GREAT MCGINTY, by Preston Sturges.
Best Screenplay
   THE GRAPES OF WRATH, by Nunnally Johnson.
   KITTY FOYLE, by Dalton Trumbo.
   THE LONG VOYAGE HOME, by Dudley Nichols.
   THE PHILADELPHIA STORY, by Donald Ogden Stewart.
   REBECCA, by Robert E. Sherwood and Joan Harrison.
Best Cinematography
   Black-and-White
      ABE LINCOLN IN ILLINOIS. James Wong Howe.
      ALL THIS, AND HEAVEN TOO. Ernest Haller.
      ARISE, MY LOVE. Charles B. Lang, Jr.
      BOOM TOWN. Harold Rosson.
      FOREIGN CORRESPONDENT. Rudolph Mate.
      THE LETTER. Gaetano Gaudio.
      THE LONG VOYAGE HOME. Gregg Toland.
      REBECCA. George Barnes.
      SPRING PARADE. Joseph Valentine.
      WATERLOO BRIDGE. Joseph Ruttenberg.
   Color
      BITTER SWEET. Oliver T. Marsh and Allen Davey.
      THE BLUE BIRD. Arthur Miller and Ray Rennahan.
      DOWN ARGENTINE WAY. Leon Shamroy and Ray Rennahan.
      NORTH WEST MOUNTED POLICE. Victor Milner and W. Howard Greene.
      NORTHWEST PASSAGE. Sidney Wagner and William V. Skall.
      THE THIEF OF BAGDAD. George Perinal.
Best Interior Decoration
   Black-and-White
      ARISE, MY LOVE. Hans Dreier and Robert Usher.
      ARIZONA. Lionel Banks and Robert Peterson.
      THE BOYS FROM SYRACUSE. John Otterson.
      DARK COMMAND. John Victor Mackay.
      FOREIGN CORRESPONDENT. Alexander Golitzen.
      LILLIAN RUSSELL. Richard Day and Joseph C. Wright.
      MY FAVORITE WIFE. Van Nest Polglase and Mark-Lee Kirk.
      MY SON, MY SON. John DuCasse Schulze.
      OUR TOWN. Lewis J. Rachmil.
      PRIDE AND PREJUDICE. Cedric Gibbons and Paul Groesse.
      REBECCA. Lyle Wheeler.
      SEA HAWK. Anton Grot.
      THE WESTERNER. James Basevi.
   Color
      BITTER SWEET. Cedric Gibbons and John S. Detlie.
      DOWN ARGENTINE WAY. Richard Day and Joseph C. Wright.
      NORTH WEST MOUNTED POLICE. Hans Dreier and Roland Anderson.
      THE THIEF OF BAGDAD. Vincent Korda.
Best Sound Recording
   BEHIND THE NEWS. Charles Lootens.
   CAPTAIN CAUTION. Elmer Raguse.
   THE GRAPES OF WRATH. E.H. Hansen.
   THE HOWARDS OF VIRGINIA. Jack Whitney, General Service.
   KITTY FOYLE. John Aalberg.
   NORTH WEST MOUNTED POLICE. Loren Ryder.
   OUR TOWN. Thomas Moulton.
   THE SEA HAWK. Nathan Levinson.
   SPRING PARADE. Bernard B. Brown.
   STRIKE UP THE BAND. Douglas Shearer.
   TOO MANY HUSBANDS. John Livadary.
Music Awards
   Best Song
      "Down Argentine Way" from DOWN ARGENTINE WAY. Music by Harry Warren; lyrics by Mack Gordon.
      "I'd Know You Anywhere" from YOU'LL FIND OUT. Music by Jimmy McHugh; lyrics by Johnny Mercer.
      "It's a Blue World" from MUSIC IN MY HEART. Music and lyrics by Chet Forrest and Bob Wright.
      "Love of My Life" from SECOND CHORUS. Music by Artie Shaw; lyrics by Johnny Mercer.
      "Only Forever" from RHYTHM ON THE RIVER. Music by James Monaco; lyrics by Johnny Burke.
      "Our Love Affair" from STRIKE UP THE BAND. Music and lyrics by Roger Edens and Georgie Stoll.
      "Waltzing in the Clouds" from SPRING PARADE. Music by Robert Stolz; lyrics by Gus Kahn.
      When You Wish Upon a Star" from PINOCCHIO. Music by Leigh Harline; lyrics by Ned Washington.
      "Who Am I?" from HIT PARADE OF 1941. Music by Jule Styne; lyrics by Walter Bullock.
   Best Score
      ARISE, MY LOVE. Victor Young.
      HIT PARADE OF 1941. Cy Feuer.
      IRENE. Anthony Collins.
      OUR TOWN. Aaron Copland.
      THE SEA HAWK. Erich Wolfgang Korngold.
      SECOND CHORUS. Artie Shaw.
      SPRING PARADE. Charles Previn.
      STRIKE UP THE BAND. Georgie Stoll and Roger Edens.
      TIN PAN ALLEY. Alfred Newman.
   Best Original Score
      ARIZONA. Victor Young.
      DARK COMMAND. Victor Young.

THE FIGHT FOR LIFE. Louis Gruenberg.
THE GREAT DICTATOR. Meredith Willson.
THE HOUSE OF SEVEN GABLES. Frank Skinner.
THE HOWARDS OF VIRGINIA. Richard Hageman.
THE LETTER. Max Steiner.
THE LONG VOYAGE HOME. Richard Hageman.
THE MARK OF ZORRO. Alfred Newman.
MY FAVORITE WIFE. Roy Webb.
NORTH WEST MOUNTED POLICE. Victor Young.
ONE MILLION B.C. Werner Heymann.
OUR TOWN. Aaron Copland.
PINOCCHIO. Leigh Harline, Paul J. Smith, and Ned Washington.
REBECCA. Franz Waxman.
THE THIEF OF BAGDAD. Miklos Rozsa.
WATERLOO BRIDGE. Herbert Stothart.

Best Film Editing
THE GRAPES OF WRATH. Robert E. Simpson.
THE LETTER. Warren Low.
THE LONG VOYAGE HOME. Sherman Todd.
NORTH WEST MOUNTED POLICE. Anne Bauchens.
REBECCA. Hal C. Kern.

Best Special Effects
THE BLUE BIRD. Photographic: Fred Sersen; sound: E.H. Hansen.
BOOM TOWN. Photographic: A. Arnold Gillespie; sound: Douglas Shearer.
THE BOYS FROM SYRACUSE. Photographic: John P. Fulton; sound: Bernard B. Brown and Joseph Lapis.
DR. CYCLOPS. Photographic: Farciot Edouart and Gordon Jennings.
FOREIGN CORRESPONDENT. Photographic: Paul Eagler; sound: Thomas T. Moulton.
THE INVISIBLE MAN RETURNS. Photographic: John P. Fulton; sound: Bernard B. Brown and William Hedgecock.
THE LONG VOYAGE HOME. Photographic: R.T. Layton and R.O. Binger; sound: Thomas T. Moulton.
ONE MILLION B.C. Photographic: Roy Seawright; sound: Elmer Raguse.
REBECCA: Photographic: Jack Cosgrove; sound: Arthur Johns.
THE SEA HAWK. Photographic: Byron Haskin; sound: Nathan Levinson.
SWISS FAMILY ROBINSON. Photographic: Vernon L. Walker; sound: John O. Aalberg.
THE THIEF OF BAGDAD. Photographic: Lawrence Butler; sound: Jack Whitney.
TYPHOON. Photographic: Farciot Edouart and Gordon Jennings; sound: Loren Ryder.
WOMEN IN WAR. Photographic: Howard J. Lydecker, William Bradford, and Ellis J. Thackery; sound: Herbert Norsch.

Short Subjects
Best Cartoon
MILKY WAY, MGM (Rudolph Ising Series).
PUSS GETS THE BOOT, MGM (Cat and Mouse Series).
A WILD HARE. WB.

Best One-Reel Film
LONDON CAN TAKE IT, WB (Vitaphone Varieties).
MORE ABOUT NOSTRADAMUS, MGM.
QUICKER 'N A WINK, Pete Smith.
SIEGE, RKO (Reelism Series).

Best Two-Reel Films
EYES OF THE NAVY, MGM (Crime Doesn't Pay Series).
SERVICE WITH THE COLORS, WB (National Defense Series).
TEDDY, THE ROUGH RIDER, WB.

Special Awards
Bob Hope, in recognition of his unselfish services to the motion picture industry.
Colonel Nathan Levinson for his outstanding service to the industry and the Army during the past nine years, which has made possible the present efficient mobilization of the motion picture industry facilities for the production of Army training films.

Scientific or Technical
Class I
20th Century-Fox Film Corporation for the design and construction of the 20th Century Silenced Camera developed by Daniel Clark, Grover Laube, Charles Miller, and Robert W. Stevens.

Class III
Warner Bros. Studio Art Department and Anton Grot for the design and perfection of the Warner Bros. water ripple and wave illusion machine.

1941

Best Picture
BLOSSOMS IN THE DUST, MGM. Produced by Irving Asher.
CITIZEN KANE, RKO. Produced by Orson Welles.
HERE COMES MR. JORDAN, COL. Produced by Everett Riskin.
HOLD BACK THE DAWN, PAR. Produced by Arthur Hornblow, Jr.
HOW GREEN WAS MY VALLEY, FOX. Produced by Darryl F. Zanuck.
THE LITTLE FOXES, RKO. Produced by Samuel Goldwyn.
THE MALTESE FALCON, WB. Produced by Hal B. Wallis.
ONE FOOT IN HEAVEN, WB. Produced by Hal B. Wallis.
SERGEANT YORK, WB. Produced by Jesse L. Lasky and Hal B. Wallis.
SUSPICION, RKO. Produced by RKO.

Best Actor
Gary Cooper for SERGEANT YORK.
Cary Grant for PENNY SERENADE.
Walter Huston for THE DEVIL AND DANIEL WEBSTER.
Robert Montgomery for HERE COMES MR. JORDAN.
Orson Welles for CITIZEN KANE.

Best Actress
Bette Davis for THE LITTLE FOXES.
Joan Fontaine for SUSPICION.
Greer Garson for BLOSSOMS IN THE DUST.
Olivia de Havilland for HOLD BACK THE DAWN.
Barbara Stanwyck for BALL OF FIRE.

Best Supporting Actor
Walter Brennan for SERGEANT YORK.
Charles Coburn for THE DEVIL AND MISS JONES.
Donald Crisp for HOW GREEN WAS MY VALLEY.
James Gleason for HERE COMES MR. JORDAN.

Sydney Greenstreet for THE MALTESE FALCON.

Best Supporting Actress
Sara Allgood for HOW GREEN WAS MY VALLEY.
Mary Astor for THE GREAT LIE.
Patricia Collinge for THE LITTLE FOXES.
Teresa Wright for THE LITTLE FOXES.
Margaret Wycherly for SERGEANT YORK.

Best Direction
John Ford for HOW GREEN WAS MY VALLEY.
Alexander Hall for HERE COMES MR. JORDAN.
Howard Hawks for SERGEANT YORK.
Orson Welles for CITIZEN KANE.
William Wyler for THE LITTLE FOXES.

Writing Awards
Best Original Story
BALL OF FIRE, by Thomas Monroe and Billy Wilder.
HERE COMES MR. JORDAN, by Harry Segall.
THE LADY EVE, by Monckton Hoffe.
MEET JOHN DOE, by Richard Connell and Robert Presnell.
NIGHT TRAIN, by Gordon Wellesley.

Best Original Screenplay
CITIZEN KANE, by Herman J. Mankiewicz and Orson Welles.
THE DEVIL AND MISS JONES, by Norman Krasna.
SERGEANT YORK, by Harry Chandlee, Abem Finkel, John Huston, and Howard Koch.
TALL, DARK, AND HANDSOME, by Karl Tunberg and Darrell Ware.
TOM, DICK AND HARRY, by Paul Jarrico.

Best Screenplay
HERE COMES MR. JORDAN, by Sidney Buchman and Seton I. Miller.
HOLD BACK THE DAWN, by Charles Brackett and Billy Wilder.
HOW GREEN WAS MY VALLEY, by Philip Dunne.
THE LITTLE FOXES, by Lillian Hellman.
THE MALTESE FALCON, by John Huston.

Best Cinematography
Black-and-White
THE CHOCOLATE SOLDIER, Karl Freund.
CITIZEN KANE. Gregg Toland.
DR. JEKYLL AND MR. HYDE. Joseph Ruttenberg.
HERE COMES MR. JORDAN. Joseph Walker.
HOLD BACK THE DAWN. Leo Tover.
HOW GREEN WAS MY VALLEY. Arthur Miller.
SERGEANT YORK. Sol Polito.
SUN VALLEY SERENADE. Edward Cronjager.
SUNDOWN. Charles Lang.
THAT HAMILTON WOMAN. Rudolph Mate.

Color
ALOMA OF THE SOUTH SEAS. Wilfred M. Cline, Karl Struss, and William Snyder.
BILLY THE KID. William V. Skall and Leonard Smith.
BLOOD AND SAND. Ernest Palmer and Ray Rennahan.
BLOSSOMS IN THE DUST. Karl Freund and W. Howard Greene.
DIVE BOMBER. Bert Glennon.
LOUISIANA PURCHASE. Harry Hallenberger and Ray Rennahan.

Best Interior Decoration
Black-and-White
CITIZEN KANE. Perry Ferguson and Van Nest Polglase; Al Fields and Darrell Silvera.
FLAME OF NEW ORLEANS. Martin Obzina and Jack Otterson; Russell A. Gausman.
HOLD BACK THE DAWN. Hans Dreier and Robert Usher; Sam Comer.
HOW GREEN WAS MY VALLEY. Richard Day and Nathan Juran; Thomas Little.
LADIES IN RETIREMENT. Lionel Banks, George Montgomery.
THE LITTLE FOXES. Stephen Goosson; Howard Bristol.
SERGEANT YORK. John Hughes; Fred MacLean.
SON OF MONTE CRISTO. John DuCasse Schulze; Edward G. Boyle.
SUNDOWN. Alexander Golitzen; Richard Irvine.
THAT HAMILTON WOMAN. Vincent Korda, Julia Heron.
WHEN LADIES MEET. Cedric Gibbons and Randall Duell; Edwin B. Willis.

Color
BLOOD AND SAND. Richard Day and Joseph C. Wright; Thomas Little.
BLOSSOMS IN THE DUST. Cedric Gibbons and Urie McCleary; Edwin B. Willis.
LOUISIANA PURCHASE. Raoul Pene du Bois; Stephen A. Seymour.

Best Sound Recording
APPOINTMENT FOR LOVE. Bernard B. Brown.
BALL OF FIRE. Thomas Moulton.
THE CHOCOLATE SOLDIER. Douglas Shearer.
CITIZEN KANE. John Aalberg.
THE DEVIL PAYS OFF. Charles Lootens.
HOW GREEN WAS MY VALLEY. E.H. Hansen.
THE MEN IN HER LIFE. John Livadary.
SERGEANT YORK. Nathan Levinson.
SKYLARK. Loren Ryder.
THAT HAMILTON WOMAN. Jack Whitney, General Service.
TOPPER RETURNS. Elmer Raguse.

Music Awards
Best Song
"Baby Mine" from DUMBO. Music by Frank Churchill; lyrics by Ned Washington.
"Be Honest with Me" from RIDIN' ON A RAINBOW. Music and lyrics by Gene Autry and Fred Rose.
"Blues in the Night" from BLUES IN THE NIGHT. Music by Harold Arlen; lyrics by Johnny Mercer.
"Boogie Woogie Bugle Boy of Company B" from BUCK PRIVATES. Music by Hugh Prince; lyrics by Don Raye.
"Chattanooga Choo Choo" from SUN VALLEY SERENADE. Music by Harry Warren; lyrics by Mack Gordon.
"Dolores" from LAS VEGAS NIGHTS. Music by Lou Alter; lyrics by Frank Loesser.
"The Last Time I Saw Paris" from LADY BE GOOD. Music by Jerome Kern; lyrics by Oscar Hammerstein II.
"Out of the Silence" from ALL AMERICAN CO-ED. Music and lyrics by Lloyd B. Norlind.
"Since I Kissed My Baby Goodbye" from YOU'LL NEVER GET RICH. Music and

lyrics by Cole Porter.

Best Scoring of a Dramatic Picture

BACK STREET. Frank Skinner.
BALL OF FIRE. Alfred Newman.
CHEERS FOR MISS BISHOP. Edward Ward.
CITIZEN KANE. Bernard Herrmann.
THE DEVIL AND DANIEL WEBSTER. Bernard Herrmann.
DR. JEKYLL AND MR. HYDE. Franz Waxman.
HOLD BACK THE DAWN. Victor Young.
HOW GREEN WAS MY VALLEY. Alfred Newman.
KING OF THE ZOMBIES. Edward Kay.
LADIES IN RETIREMENT. Morris Stoloff and Ernst Toch.
THE LITTLE FOXES. Meredith Willson.
LYDIA. Miklos Rozsa.
MERCY ISLAND. Cy Feuer and Walter Scharf.
SERGEANT YORK. Max Steiner.
SO ENDS OUR NIGHT. Louis Gruenberg.
SUNDOWN. Miklos Rozsa.
SUSPICION. Franz Waxman.
TANKS A MILLION. Edward Ward.
THAT UNCERTAIN FEELING. Werner Heymann.
THAT WOMAN IS MINE. Richard Hageman.

Best Scoring of a Musical Picture

ALL AMERICAN CO-ED. Edward Ward.
BIRTH OF THE BLUES. Robert Emmett Dolan.
BUCK PRIVATES. Charles Previn.
THE CHOCOLATE SOLDIER. Herbert Stothart and Bronislau Kaper.
DUMBO. Frank Churchill and Oliver Wallace.
ICE CAPADES. Cy Feuer.
THE STRAWBERRY BLONDE. Heinz Roemheld.
SUN VALLEY SERENADE. Emil Newman.
SUNNY. Anthony Collins.
YOU'LL NEVER GET RICH. Morris Stoloff.

Best Film Editing

CITIZEN KANE. Robert Wise.
DR. JEKYLL AND MR. HYDE. Harold F. Kress.
HOW GREEN WAS MY VALLEY. James B. Clark.
THE LITTLE FOXES. Daniel Mandell.
SERGEANT YORK. William Holmes.

Best Special Effects

ALOMA OF THE SOUTH SEAS. Photographic: Farciot Edouart and Gordon Jennings; sound: Louis Mesenkop.
FLIGHT COMMAND. Photographic: A. Arnold Gillespie; sound: Douglas Shearer.
I WANTED WINGS. Photographic: Farciot Edouart and Gordon Jennings; sound: Louis Mesenkop.
THE INVISIBLE WOMAN. Photographic: John Fulton; sound: John Hall.
THE SEA WOLF. Photographic: Byron Haskin; sound: Nathan Levinson.
THAT HAMILTON WOMAN. Photographic: Lawrence Butler; sound: William H. Wilmarth.
TOPPER RETURNS. Photographic: Roy Seawright; sound: Elmer Raguse.
A YANK IN THE R.A.F. Photographic: Fred Sersen; sound: E.H. Hansen.

Short Subjects

Best Cartoon

BOOGIE WOOGIE BUGLE BOY OF COMPANY B, Lantz.
HIAWATHA'S RABBIT HUNT, Schlesinger.
HOW WAR CAME, COL (Raymond Gram Swing Series).
LEND A PAW, Walt Disney.
THE NIGHT BEFORE CHRISTMAS, MGM (Tom and Jerry Series).
RHAPSODY IN RIVETS, Schlesinger.
THE ROOKIE BEAR, MGM.
RHYTHM IN THE RANKS, PAR (George Pal Puppetoon Series).
SUPERMAN NO.1, PAR.
TRUANT OFFICER DONALD, Disney (Donald Duck).

Best One-Reel Film

ARMY CHAMPIONS, Pete Smith.
BEAUTY AND THE BEACH, PAR (Headliner Series).
DOWN ON THE FARM, PAR (Speaking of Animals Series).
FORTY BOYS AND A SONG, WB (Melody Master Series).
KINGS OF THE TURF, WB (Color Parade Series).
OF PUPS AND PUZZLES, MGM (Passing Parade Series).
SAGEBRUSH AND SILVER, FOX (Magic Carpet Series).

Best Two-Reel Film

ALIVE IN THE DEEP, Woodard Productions.
FORBIDDEN PASSAGE, MGM (Crime Doesn't Pay Series).
THE GAY PARISIAN, WB.
MAIN STREET ON THE MARCH, WB.
THE TANKS ARE COMING, WB (National Defense Series).

Best Documentary

ADVENTURES IN THE BRONX, Film Assocs.
BOMBER, U.S. Office for Emergency Management Film Unit.
CHRISTMAS UNDER FIRE, British Ministry of Information, WB.
CHURCHILL'S ISLAND, Canadian Film Board, UA.
LETTER FROM HOME, British Ministry of Information.
LIFE OF A THOROUGHBRED, FOX.
NORWAY IN REVOLT, March of Time, RKO.
SOLDIERS OF THE SKY, FOX.
WAR CLOUDS IN THE PACIFIC, Canadian Film Board.

Irving G. Thalberg Memorial Award

Walt Disney.

Special Awards

Rey Scott for his extraordinary achievement in producing KUKAN, the film record of China's struggle, including its photography with a 16mm camera under the most difficult and dangerous conditions.
The British Ministry of Information for its vivid and dramatic presentation of the heroism of the RAF in the documentary film TARGET FOR TONIGHT.
Leopold Stokowski and his associates for their unique achievement in the creation of a new form of visualized music in Walt Disney's production FANTASIA, thereby widening the scope of the motion picture as entertainment and as an art form.
Walt Disney, William Garity, John N.A. Hawkins and the RCA manufacturing Company, for their outstanding contribution to the advancement of the use of sound

in motion pictures through the production of FANTASIA.

Scientific or Technical

Class II

Electrical Research Products Division of Western Electric Company, Inc., for the development of the precision integrating sphere densitometer.
RCA Manufacturing Co. for the design and development of the MI-3043 Unidirectional microphone.

Class III

Ray Wilkinson and the Paramount Studio Laboratory for pioneering in the use of and for the first practical application to release printing of fine grain positive stock.
Charles Lootens and the Republic Studio Sound Department for pioneering the use of and for the first practical application to motion picture production of Class B push-pull variable area recording.
Wilber Silvertooth and the Paramount Studio Engineering Department for the design and computation of a relay condenser system applicable to transparency process projection, delivering considerably more usable light.
Paramount Pictures, Inc., and 20th Century-Fox Film Corporation for the development and first practical application to motion picture production of an automatic scene slating device.
Douglas Shearer and the MGM Studio Sound Department and to Loren Ryder and the Paramount Studio Sound Department for pioneering the development of fine grain emulsions for variable density original sound recording in studio production.

1942

Best Picture

THE INVADERS, COL. Produced by Michael Powell.
KINGS ROW, WB. Produced by Hal B. Wallis.
THE MAGNIFICENT AMBERSONS, RKO. Produced by Orson Welles.
MRS. MINIVER, MGM. Produced by Sidney Franklin.
THE PIED PIPER, FOX. Produced by Nunnally Johnson.
THE PRIDE OF THE YANKEES, RKO. Produced by Samuel Goldwyn.
RANDOM HARVEST, MGM. Produced by Sidney Franklin.
THE TALK OF THE TOWN, COL. Produced by George Stevens.
WAKE ISLAND, PAR. Produced by Joseph Sistrom.
YANKEE DOODLE DANDY, WB. Produced by Jack Warner and Hal B. Wallis, with William Cagney.

Best Actor

James Cagney for YANKEE DOODLE DANDY.
Ronald Colman for RANDOM HARVEST.
Gary Cooper for THE PRIDE OF THE YANKEES.
Walter Pidgeon for MRS. MINIVER.
Monty Woolley for THE PIED PIPER.

Best Actress

Bette Davis for NOW, VOYAGER.
Greer Garson for MRS. MINIVER.
Katharine Hepburn for WOMAN OF THE YEAR.
Rosalind Russell for MY SISTER EILEEN.
Teresa Wright for PRIDE OF THE YANKEES.

Best Supporting Actor

William Bendix for WAKE ISLAND.
Van Heflin for JOHNNY EAGER.
Walter Huston for YANKEE DOODLE DANDY.
Frank Morgan for TORTILLA FLAT.
Henry Travers for MRS. MINIVER.

Best Supporting Actress

Gladys Cooper for NOW, VOYAGER.
Agnes Moorehead for THE MAGNIFICENT AMBERSONS.
Susan Peters for RANDOM HARVEST.
Dame May Whitty for MRS. MINIVER.
Teresa Wright for MRS. MINIVER.

Best Direction

Michael Curtiz for YANKEE DOODLE DANDY.
John Farrow for WAKE ISLAND.
Mervyn LeRoy for RANDOM HARVEST.
Sam Wood for KINGS ROW.
William Wyler for MRS. MINIVER.

Writing Awards

Best Original Story

HOLIDAY INN, by Irving Berlin.
THE INVADERS, by Emeric Pressburger.
THE PRIDE OF THE YANKEES, by Paul Gallico.
THE TALK OF THE TOWN, by Sidney Harmon.
YANKEE DOODLE DANDY, by Robert Buckner.

Best Original Screenplay

ONE OF OUR AIRCRAFT IS MISSING, by Michael Powell and Emeric Pressburger.
THE ROAD TO MOROCCO, by Frank Butler and Don Hartman.
WAKE ISLAND, by W.R. Burnett and Frank Butler.
THE WAR AGAINST MRS. HADLEY, by George Oppenheimer.
WOMAN OF THE YEAR, by Michael Kanin and Ring Lardner, Jr.

Best Screenplay

THE INVADERS, by Rodney Ackland and Emeric Pressburger.
MRS. MINIVER, by George Froeschel, James Hilton, Claudine West, and Arthur Wimperis.
THE PRIDE OF THE YANKEES, by Herman J. Mankiewicz and Jo Swerling.
RANDOM HARVEST, by George Froeschel, Claudine West, and Arthur Wimperis.
THE TALK OF THE TOWN, by Sidney Buchman and Irwin Shaw.

Best Cinematography

Black-and-White

KINGS ROW. James Wong Howe.
THE MAGNIFICENT AMBERSONS. Stanley Cortez.
MRS. MINIVER. Joseph Ruttenberg.
MOONTIDE. Charles Clarke.
THE PIED PIPER. Edward Cronjager.
THE PRIDE OF THE YANKEES. Rudolph Mate.
TAKE A LETTER, DARLING. John Mescall.
THE TALK OF THE TOWN. Ted Tetzlaff.
TEN GENTLEMEN FROM WEST POINT. Leon Shamroy.
THIS ABOVE ALL. Arthur Miller.

Color

ARABIAN NIGHTS. Milton Krasner, William V. Skall, and W. Howard Greene.

THE BLACK SWAN. Leon Shamroy.
CAPTAINS OF THE CLOUDS. Sol Polito.
JUNGLE BOOK. W. Howard Greene.
REAP THE WILD WIND. Victor Milner and William V. Skall.
TO THE SHORES OF TRIPOLI. Edward Cronjager and William V. Skall.
Best Interior Decoration
  Black-and-White
    GEORGE WASHINGTON SLEPT HERE. Max Parker and Marke-Lee Kirk; Casey Roberts.
    THE MAGNIFICENT AMBERSONS. Albert S. D'Agostino; Al Fields and Darrell Silvera.
    THE PRIDE OF THE YANKEES. Perry Ferguson; Howard Bristol.
    RANDOM HARVEST. Cedric Gibbons and Randall Duell; Edwin B. Willis and Jack Moore.
    THE SHANGHAI GESTURE. Boris Leven.
    SILVER QUEEN. Ralph Berger; Emile Kuri.
    THE SPOILERS. John B. Goodman and Jack Otterson; Russell A. Gausman and Edward R. Robinson.
    TAKE A LETTER, DARLING. Hans Dreier and Roland Anderson; Sam Comer.
    THE TALK OF THE TOWN. Lionel Banks and Rudolph Sternad; Fay Babcock.
    THIS ABOVE ALL. Richard Day and Joseph Wright; Thomas Little.
  Color
    ARABIAN NIGHTS. Alexander Golitzen and Jack Otterson; Russell A. Gausman and Ira S. Webb.
    CAPTAINS OF THE CLOUDS. Ted Smith; Casey Roberts.
    JUNGLE BOOK. Vincent Korda; Julia Heron.
    MY GAL SAL. Richard Day and Joseph Wright; Thomas Little.
    REAP THE WILD WIND. Hans Dreier and Roland Anderson; George Sawley.
Best Sound Recording
  ARABIAN NIGHTS. Bernard Brown.
  BAMBI. Sam Slyfield.
  FLYING TIGERS. Daniel Bloomberg.
  FRIENDLY ENEMIES. Jack Whitney, Sound Service, Inc.
  THE GOLD RUSH. James Fields, RCA Sound.
  MRS. MINIVER. Douglas Shearer.
  ONCE UPON A HONEYMOON. Steve Dunn.
  THE PRIDE OF THE YANKEES. Thomas Moulton.
  ROAD TO MOROCCO. Loren Ryder.
  THIS ABOVE ALL. E.H. Hansen.
  YANKEE DOODLE DANDY. Nathan Levinson.
  YOU WERE NEVER LOVELIER. John Livadary.
Music Awards
  Best Song
    "Always in My Heart" from ALWAYS IN MY HEART. Music by Ernesto Lecuona; lyrics by Kim Gannon.
    "Dearly Beloved" from YOU WERE NEVER LOVELIER. Music by Jerome Kern; lyrics by Johnny Mercer.
    "How About You?" from BABES ON BROADWAY. Music by Burton Lane; lyrics by Ralph Freed.
    "It Seems I Heard That Song Before" from YOUTH ON PARADE. Music by Jule Styne; lyrics by Sammy Cahn.
    "I've Got a Gal in Kalamazoo" from ORCHESTRA WIVES. Music by Harry Warren; lyrics by Mack Gordon.
    "Love Is a Song" from BAMBI. Music by Frank Churchill; lyrics by Larry Morey.
    "Pennies for Peppino" from FLYING WITH MUSIC. Music by Edward Ward; lyrics by Chet Forrest and Bob Wright.
    "Pig Foot Pete" from HELLZAPOPPIN. Music by Gene de Paul; lyrics by Don Raye.
    "There's a Breeze on Lake Louise" from THE MAYOR OF 44TH STREET. Music by Harry Revel; lyrics by Mort Greene.
    'White Christmas" from HOLIDAY INN. Music and lyrics by Irving Berlin.
  Best Scoring of a Dramatic or Comedy Picture
    ARABIAN NIGHTS. Frank Skinner.
    BAMBI. Frank Churchill and Edward Plumb.
    THE BLACK SWAN. Alfred Newman.
    THE CORSICAN BROTHERS. Dimitri Tiomkin.
    FLYING TIGERS. Victor Young.
    THE GOLD RUSH. Max Terr.
    I MARRIED A WITCH. Roy Webb.
    JOAN OF PARIS. Roy Webb.
    JUNGLE BOOK. Miklos Rozsa.
    KLONDIKE FURY. Edward Kay.
    NOW, VOYAGER. Max Steiner.
    THE PRIDE OF THE YANKEES. Leigh Harline.
    RANDOM HARVEST. Herbert Stothart.
    THE SHANGHAI GESTURE. Richard Hageman.
    SILVER QUEEN. Victor Young.
    TAKE A LETTER, DARLING. Victor Young.
    THE TALK OF THE TOWN. Frederick Hollander and Morris Stoloff.
    TO BE OR NOT TO BE. Werner Heymann.
  Best Scoring of a Musical Picture
    FLYING WITH MUSIC. Edward Ward.
    FOR ME AND MY GAL. Roger Edens and Georgie Stoll.
    HOLIDAY INN. Robert Emmett Dolan.
    IT STARTED WITH EVE. Charles Previn and Hans Salter.
    JOHNNY DOUGHBOY. Walter Scharf.
    MY GAL SAL. Alfred Newman.
    YANKEE DOODLE DANDY. Ray Heindorf and Heinz Roemheld.
    YOU WERE NEVER LOVELIER. Leigh Harline.
Best Film Editing
  MRS. MINIVER. Harold F. Kress.
  THE PRIDE OF THE YANKEES. Daniel Mandell.
  THE TALK OF THE TOWN. Otto Meyer.
  THIS ABOVE ALL. Walter Thompson.
  YANKEE DOODLE DANDY. George Amy.
Best Special Effects
  THE BLACK SWAN. Photographic: Fred Sersen; sound: Roger Heman and George Leverett.
  DESPERATE JOURNEY. Photographic: Byron Haskin; sound: Nathan Levinson.
  FLYING TIGERS. Photographic: Howard Lydecker; sound: Daniel J. Bloomberg.
  INVISIBLE AGENT. Photographic: John Fulton; sound: Bernard B. Brown.

JUNGLE BOOK. Photographic: Lawrence Butler; sound: William H. Wilmarth.
MRS. MINIVER. Photographic: A. Arnold Gillespie and Warren Newcombe; sound: Douglas Shearer.
THE NAVY COMES THROUGH. Photographic: Vernon L. Walker; sound: James G. Stewart.
ONE OF OUR AIRCRAFT IS MISSING. Photographic: Ronald Neame; sound: C.C. Stevens.
PRIDE OF THE YANKEES. Photographic: Jack Cosgrove; sound: Thomas T. Moulton.
REAP THE WILD WIND. Photographic: Farciot Edouart, Gordon Jennings, and William L. Pereira; sound: Louis Meisenkop.
Short Subjects
  Best Cartoon
    ALL OUT FOR V, FOX.
    THE BLITZ WOLF, MGM.
    DER FUEHRER'S FACE, Disney.
    JUKE BOX JAMBOREE, Lanin, UNIV.
    PIGS IN A POLKA, Schlesinger.
    TULIPS SHALL GROW, PAR (George Pal Puppetoon).
  Best One-Reel Film
    DESERT WONDERLAND, FOX (Magic Carpet Series).
    MARINES IN THE MAKING, MGM. (Pete Smith Specialities).
    SPEAKING OF ANIMALS AND THEIR FAMILIES, PAR (Speaking of Animals Series).
    UNITED STATES MARINE BAND, WB (Melody Master Bands).
  Best Two-Reel Film
    BEYOND THE LINE OF DANCE, WB (Broadway Brevities).
    DON'T TALK, MGM.
    PRIVATE SMITH OF THE U.S.A., RKO (This Is America Series).
Best Documentary
  AFRICA, PRELUDE TO VICTORY, March of Time, FOX.
  BATTLE OF MIDWAY, U.S. Navy, FOX.
  COMBAT REPORT, U.S. Army Signal Corps.
  CONQUER BY THE CLOCK, Office of War Information, RKO, Frederic Ulman, Jr.
  THE GRAIN THAT BUILT A HEMISPHERE, Coordinator's Office, Motion Picture Society for the Americas, Walt Disney.
  HENRY BROWNE, FARMER, U.S. Department of Agriculture, Republic.
  HIGH OVER THE BORDER, Canadian National Film Board.
  HIGH STAKES IN THE EAST, Netherlands Information Bureau.
  INSIDE FIGHTING CHINA, Canadian National Film Board.
  IT'S EVERYBODY'S WAR, Office of War Information, FOX.
  KOKODA FRONT LINE, Australian News Information Bureau.
  LISTEN TO BRITAIN, British Ministry of Information.
  LITTLE BELGIUM, Belgian Ministry of Information.
  LITTLE ISLES OF FREEDOM, WB, Victor Stoloff, and Edgar Loew.
  MR. BLABBERMOUTH, Office of War Information, MGM.
  MR. GARDENIA JONES, Office of War Information, MGM.
  MOSCOW STIKES BACK (USSR), Artkino.
  NEW SPIRIT, U.S. Treasury Department, Walt Disney.
  PRELUDE TO WAR, U.S. Army Special Services.
  THE PRICE OF VICTORY, Office of War Information, PAR, Pine-Thomas.
  A SHIP IS BORN, U.S. Merchant Marines, WB.
  TWENTY-ONE MILES, British Ministry of Information.
  WE REFUSE TO DIE, Office of War Information, PAR. William C. Thomas.
  WHITE EAGLE, Cocanen Films.
  WINNING YOUR WINGS, U.S. Army Air Force, WB.
Irving G. Thalberg Memorial Award
  Sidney Franklin.
Special Awards
  Charles Boyer for his progressive cultural achievement in establishing the French Research Foundation in Los Angeles as a source of reference for the Hollywood motion picture industry.
  Noel Coward for his outstanding production achievement in IN WHICH WE SERVE.
  MGM Studio for its achievement in representing the American way of life in the production of the ANDY HARDY series of films.
Scientific or Technical
  Class II
    Carroll Clark, F. Thomas Thompson, and the RKO Radio Studio Art and Miniature Departments for the design and construction of a moving cloud and horizon machine.
    Daniel B. Clark and the 20th Century-Fox Film Corp. for the development of a lens calibration system and the application of this system to exposure control in cinematography.
  Class III
    Robert Henderson and the Paramount Studio Engineering and Transparency Departments for the design and construction of adjustable light bridges and screen frames for transparency process photography.
    Daniel J. Bloomberg and the Republic Studio Sound Department for the design and application to motion picture production of a device for marking action negatives for pre-selection purposes.

1943
Best Picture
  CASABLANCA, WB. Produced by Hal B. Wallis.
  FOR WHOM THE BELL TOLLS, PAR. Produced by Sam Wood.
  HEAVEN CAN WAIT, FOX. Produced by Ernst Lubitsch.
  THE HUMAN COMEDY, MGM. Produced by Clarence Brown.
  IN WHICH WE SERVE, TC-UA. Produced by Noel Coward.
  MADAME CURIE, MGM. Produced by Sidney Franklin.
  THE MORE THE MERRIER, COL. Produced by George Stevens.
  THE OX-BOW INCIDENT, FOX. Produced by Lamar Trotti.
  THE SONG OF BERNADETTE, FOX. Produced by William Perlberg.
  WATCH ON THE RHINE, WB. Produced by Hal B. Wallis.
Best Actor
  Humphrey Bogart for CASABLANCA.
  Gary Cooper for FOR WHOM THE BELL TOLLS.
  Paul Lukas for WATCH ON THE RHINE.
  Walter Pidgeon for MADAME CURIE.
  Mickey Rooney for THE HUMAN COMEDY.
Best Actress

Jean Arthur for THE MORE THE MERRIER.
Ingrid Bergman for FOR WHOM THE BELL TOLLS.
Joan Fontaine for THE CONSTANT NYMPH.
Greer Garson for MADAME CURIE.
Jennifer Jones for THE SONG OF BERNADETTE.

Best Supporting Actor
Charles Bickford for THE SONG OF BERNADETTE.
Charles Coburn for THE MORE THE MERRIER.
J. Carrol Naish for SAHARA.
Claude Rains for CASABLANCA.
Akim Tamiroff for FOR WHOM THE BELL TOLLS.

Best Supporting Actress
Gladys Cooper for THE SONG OF BERNADETTE.
Paulette Goddard for SO PROUDLY WE HAIL.
Katina Paxinou for FOR WHOM THE BELL TOLLS.
Anne Revere for THE SONG OF BERNADETTE.
Lucile Watson for WATCH ON THE RHINE.

Best Direction
Clarence Brown for THE HUMAN COMEDY.
Michael Curtiz for CASABLANCA.
Henry King for THE SONG OF BERNADETTE.
Ernst Lubitsch for HEAVEN CAN WAIT.
George Stevens for THE MORE THE MERRIER.

Writing Awards
  Best Original Story
    ACTION IN THE NORTH ATLANTIC, by Guy Gilpatric.
    DESTINATION TOKYO, by Steve Fisher.
    THE HUMAN COMEDY, by William Saroyan.
    THE MORE THE MERRIER, by Frank Ross and Robert Russell.
    SHADOW OF A DOUBT, by Gordon McDonnell.
  Best Original Screenplay
    AIR FORCE, by Dudley Nichols.
    IN WHICH WE SERVE, by Noel Coward.
    THE NORTH STAR, by Lillian Hellman.
    PRINCESS O'ROURKE, by Norman Krasna.
    SO PROUDLY WE HAIL, by Allan Scott.
  Best Screenplay
    CASABLANCA, by Julius J. Epstein, Philip G. Epstein, and Howard Koch.
    HOLY MATRIMONY, by Nunnally Johnson.
    THE MORE THE MERRIER, by Richard Flournoy, Lewis R. Foster, Frank Ross, and Robert Russell.
    THE SONG OF BERNADETTE, by George Seaton.
    WATCH ON THE RHINE, by Lillian Hellman and Dashiell Hammett.

Best Cinematography
  Black-and-White
    AIR FORCE. James Wong Howe, Elmer Dyer, and Charles Marshall.
    CASABLANCA. Arthur Edeson.
    CORVETTE K-225. Tony Gaudio.
    FIVE GRAVES TO CAIRO. John Seitz.
    THE HUMAN COMEDY. Harry Stradling.
    MADAME CURIE. Joseph Ruttenberg.
    THE NORTH STAR. James Wong Howe.
    SAHARA. Rudolph Mate.
    SO PROUDLY WE HAIL. Charles Lang.
    THE SONG OF BERNADETTE. Arthur Miller.
  Color
    FOR WHOM THE BELL TOLLS. Ray Rennahan.
    HEAVEN CAN WAIT. Edward Cronjager.
    HELLO, FRISCO, HELLO. Charles G. Clarke and Allen Davey.
    LASSIE COME HOME. Leonard Smith.
    THE PHANTOM OF THE OPERA. Hal Mohr and W. Howard Greene.
    THOUSANDS CHEER. George Folsey.

Best Interior Decoration
  Black-and-White
    FIVE GRAVES TO CAIRO. Hans Dreier and Ernst Fegte; Bertram Granger.
    FLIGHT FOR FREEDOM. Albert S. D'Agostino and Carroll Clark; Darrell Silvera and Harley Miller.
    MADAME CURIE. Cedric Gibbons and Paul Groesse; Edwin B. Willis and Hugh Hunt.
    MISSION TO MOSCOW. Carl Weyl; George J. Hopkins.
    THE NORTH STAR. Perry Ferguson; Howard Bristol.
    THE SONG OF BERNADETTE. James Basevi and William Darling; Thomas Little.
  Color
    FOR WHOM THE BELL TOLLS. Hans Dreier and Haldane Douglas; Bertram Granger.
    THE GANG'S ALL HERE. James Basevi and Joseph C. Wright; Thomas Little.
    THE PHANTOM OF THE OPERA. Alexander Golitzen and John B. Goodman; Russell A. Gausman and Ira S. Webb.
    THIS IS THE ARMY. John Hughes and Lt. John Koenig; George J. Hopkins.
    THOUSANDS CHEER. Cedric Gibbons and Daniel Cathcart; Edwin B. Willis and Jacques Mersereau.

Best Sound Recording
    HANGMEN ALSO DIE. Jack Whitney, Sound Service, Inc.
    IN OLD OKLAHOMA. Daniel J. Bloomberg.
    MADAME CURIE. Douglas Shearer.
    THE NORTH STAR. Thomas Moulton.
    THE PHANTOM OF THE OPERA. Bernard B. Brown.
    RIDING HIGH. Loren L. Ryder.
    SAHARA. John Livadary.
    SALUDOS AMIGOS. C.O. Slyfield.
    SO THIS IS WASHINGTON. J.L. Fields, RCA Sound.
    THE SONG OF BERNADETTE. E.H. Hansen.
    THIS IS THE ARMY. Nathan Levinson.
    THIS LAND IS MINE. Stephen Dunn.

Music Awards
  Best Song
    "Change of Heart" from HIT PARADE OF 1943. Music by Jule Styne; lyrics by Harold Adamson.
    "Happiness is a Thing Called Joe" from CABIN IN THE SKY. Music by Harold

Arlen; lyrics by E.Y. Harburg.
    "My Shining Hour" from THE SKY'S THE LIMIT. Music by Harold Arlen; lyrics by Johnny Mercer.
    "Saludos Amigos" from SALUDOS AMIGOS. Music by Charles Wolcott; lyrics by Ned Washington.
    "Say a Prayer for the Boys over There" from HERS TO HOLD. Music by Jimmy McHugh; lyrics by Herb Magidson.
    "That Old Black Magic" from STAR SPANGLED RHYTHM. Music by Harold Arlen; lyrics by Johnny Mercer.
    "They're Either Too Young or Too Old" from THANK YOUR LUCKY STARS. Music by Arthur Schwartz; lyrics by Frank Loesser.
    "We Mustn't Say Good Bye" from STAGE DOOR CANTEEN. Music by James Monaco; lyrics by Al Dubin.
    "You'd Be So Nice To Come Home To" from SOMETHING TO SHOUT ABOUT. Music and lyrics by Cole Porter.
    You'll Never Know" from HELLO, FRISCO, HELLO. Music by Harry Warren; lyrics by Mack Gordon.

Best Scoring of a Dramatic or Comedy Picture
    THE AMAZING MRS. HOLLIDAY. Hans J. Salter and Frank Skinner.
    CASABLANCA. Max Steiner.
    THE COMMANDOS STRIKE AT DAWN. Louis Gruenberg and Morris Stoloff.
    THE FALLEN SPARROW. C. Bakaleinikoff and Roy Webb.
    FOR WHOM THE BELL TOLLS. Victor Young.
    HANGMEN ALSO DIE. Hanns Eisler.
    HI DIDDLE DIDDLE. Phil Boutelje.
    IN OLD OKLAHOMA. Walter Scharf.
    JOHNNY COME LATELY. Leigh Harline.
    THE KANSAN. Gerard Carbonara.
    LADY OF BURLESQUE. Arthur Lange.
    MADAME CURIE. Herbert Stothart.
    THE MOON AND SIXPENCE. Dimitri Tiomkin.
    THE NORTH STAR. Aaron Copland.
    THE SONG OF BERNADETTE. Alfred Newman.
    VICTORY THROUGH AIR POWER. Edward H. Plumb, Paul J. Smith, and Oliver G. Wallace.

Best Scoring of a Musical Picture
    CONEY ISLAND. Alfred Newman.
    HIT PARADE OF 1943. Walter Scharf.
    THE PHANTOM OF THE OPERA. Edward Ward.
    SALUDOS AMIGOS. Edward H. Plumb, Paul J. Smith, and Charles Wolcott.
    THE SKY'S THE LIMIT. Leigh Harline.
    SOMETHING TO SHOUT ABOUT. Morris Stoloff.
    STAGE DOOR CANTEEN. Frederic E. Rich.
    STAR SPANGLED RHYTHM. Robert Emmett Dolan.
    THIS IS THE ARMY. Ray Heindorf.
    THOUSANDS CHEER. Herbert Stothart.

Best Film Editing
    AIR FORCE. George Amy.
    CASABLANCA. Owen Marks.
    FIVE GRAVES TO CAIRO. Doane Harrison.
    FOR WHOM THE BELL TOLLS. Sherman Todd and John Link.
    THE SONG OF BERNADETTE. Barbara McLean.

Best Special Effects
    AIR FORCE. Photograohic: Hans Koenekamp and Rex Wimpy; sound: Nathan Levinson.
    BOMBARDIER. Photographic: Vernon L. Walker; sound: James G. Stewart and Roy Granville.
    CRASH DIVE. Photographic: Fred Sersen; sound: Roger Heman.
    THE NORTH STAR. Photographic: Clarence Slifer and R.O. Binger; sound: Thomas T. Moulton.
    SO PROUDLY WE HAIL. Photographic: Farciot Edouart and Gordon Jennings; sound: George Dutton.
    STAND BY FOR ACTION. Photographic: A. Arnold Gillespie and Donald Jahraus; sound: Michael Steinore.

Short Subjects
  Best Cartoon
    THE DIZZY ACROBAT, UNIV. Produced by Walter Lantz.
    THE FIVE HUNDRED HATS OF BARTHOLOMEW CUBBINS, PAR. Produced by George Pal (Puppetoon).
    GREETINGS, BAIT, WB. Produced by Leon Schlesinger.
    IMAGINATION, COL. Produced by Dave Fleischer.
    REASON AND EMOTION, RKO. Produced by Walt Disney.
    YANKEE DOODLE MOUSE, MGM. Produced by Frederick Quimby.
  Best One-Reel Film
    AMPHIBIOUS FIGHTERS, PAR. Produced by Grantland Rice.
    CAVALCADE OF THE DANCE WITH VELOZ AND YOLANDA, WB. Produced by Gordon Hollingshead (Melody Master Bands).
    CHAMPIONS CARRY ON, FOX. Produced by Edmund Reek (Sports Reviews).
    HOLLYWOOD IN UNIFORM, COL. Produced by Ralph Staub (Screen Snapshots No.1, Series 22).
    SEEING HANDS, MGM. Produced by Pete Smith.
  Best Two-Reel Film
    HEAVENLY MUSIC, MGM. Produced by Jerry Bresler and Sam Coslow.
    LETTER TO A HERO, RKO. Produced by Fred Ullman.
    MARDI GRAS, PAR. Produced by Walter MacEwen.
    WOMEN AT WAR, WB. Produced by Gordon Hollingshead (Technicolor Special).

Documentary
  Best Short Subject Documentary
    CHILDREN OF MARS, This Is America Series, RKO.
    DECEMBER 7TH, U.S. Navy, Field Photographic Branch, Office of Strategic Services.
    PLAN FOR DESTRUCTION, MGM.
    SWEDES IN AMERICA, Office of War Information, Overseas Motion Picture Bureau.
    TO THE PEOPLE OF THE UNITED STATES, U.S. Public Health Service, Walter Wanger, Prods.
    TOMORROW WE FLY, U.S. Navy, Bureau of Aeronautics.
    YOUTH IN CRISIS, March of Time, FOX.
  Best Feature Documentary
    BAPTISM OF FIRE, U.S. Army, Fighting Men Series.

BATTLE OF RUSSIA, Special Service Division of the War Department.
DESERT VICTORY, British Ministry of Information.
REPORT FROM THE ALEUTIANS, U.S. Army Pictorial Service, Combat Film Series.
WAR DEPARTMENT REPORT, Field Photographic Branch, Office of Strategic Services.
Irving G. Thalberg Memorial Award
Hal B. Wallis.
Special Award
George Pal for the development of novel methods and techniques in the production of short subjects known as Puppetoons.
Scientific or Technical
Class II
Farciot Edouart, Earle Morgan, Barton Thompson, and the Paramount Studio Engineering and Transparency Departments for the development and practical application to motion picture production of a method of duplicating and enlarging natural color photographs, transferring the image emulsions to glass plates, and projecting these slides by specially designed stereopticon equipment.
Photo Products Department, E.I. duPont de Nemours and Company, Incorporated for the development of fine-grain motion picture films.
Class III
Daniel J. Bloomberg and the Republic Studio Sound Department for the design and development of an inexpensive method of converting Moviolas to Class B push-pull reproduction.
Charles Galloway Clarke and the 20th Century-Fox Studio Camera Department for the development and practical application of a device for composing artificial clouds into motion picture scenes during production photography.
Farciot Edouart and the Paramount Studio Transparency Department for an automatic electric transparency cueing timer.
Willard H. Turner and the RKO Radio Studio Sound Department for the design and construction of the phono-cue starter.

1944
Best Picture
DOUBLE INDEMNITY, PAR. Produced by Joseph Sistrom.
GASLIGHT, MGM. Produced by Arthur Hornblow, Jr.
GOING MY WAY, PAR. Produced by Leo McCarey.
SINCE YOU WENT AWAY, UA. Produced by David O. Selznick.
WILSON, FOX. Produced by Darryl F. Zanuck.
Best Actor
Charles Boyer for GASLIGHT.
Bing Crosby for GOING MY WAY.
Barry Fitzgerald for GOING MY WAY.
Cary Grant for NONE BUT THE LONELY HEART.
Alexander Knox for WILSON.
Best Actress
Ingrid Bergman for GASLIGHT.
Claudette Colbert for SINCE YOU WENT AWAY.
Bette Davis for MR. SKEFFINGTON.
Greer Garson for MRS. PARKINGTON.
Barbara Stanwyck for DOUBLE INDEMNITY.
Best Supporting Actor
Hume Cronyn for THE SEVENTH CROSS.
Barry Fitzgerald for GOING MY WAY.
Claude Rains for MR. SKEFFINGTON.
Clifton Webb for LAURA.
Monty Woolley for SINCE YOU WENT AWAY.
Best Supporting Actress
Ethel Barrymore for NONE BUT THE LONELY HEART.
Jennifer Jones for SINCE YOU WENT AWAY.
Angela Lansbury for GASLIGHT.
Aline MacMahon for DRAGON SEED.
Agnes Moorehead for MRS. PARKINGTON.
Best Direction
Alfred Hitchcock for LIFEBOAT.
Henry King for WILSON.
Leo McCarey for GOING MY WAY.
Otto Preminger for LAURA.
Billy Wilder for DOUBLE INDEMNITY.
Writing Awards
Best Original Story
GOING MY WAY, by Leo McCarey.
A GUY NAMED JOE, by David Boehm and Chandler Sprague.
LIFEBOAT, by John Steinbeck.
NONE SHALL ESCAPE, by Alfred Neumann and Joseph Than.
THE SULLIVANS, by Edward Doherty and Jules Schermer.
Best Original Screenplay
HAIL THE CONQUERING HERO, by Preston Sturges.
THE MIRACLE OF MORGAN'S CREEK, by Preston Sturges.
TWO GIRLS AND A SAILOR, by Richard Connell and Gladys Lehman.
WILSON, by Lamar Trotti.
WING AND A PRAYER, by Jerome Cady.
Best Screenplay
DOUBLE INDEMNITY, by Raymond Chandler and Billy Wilder.
GASLIGHT, by John L. Balderston, Walter Reisch, and John Van Druten.
GOING MY WAY, by Frank Butler and Frank Cavett.
LAURA, by Jay Dratler, Samuel Hoffenstein, and Betty Reinhardt.
MEET ME IN ST. LOUIS, by Irving Brecher and Fred F. Finkelhoffe.
Best Cinematography
Black-and-White
DOUBLE INDEMNITY. John Seitz.
DRAGON SEED. Sidney Wagner.
GASLIGHT. Joseph Ruttenberg.
GOING MY WAY. Lionel Lindon.
LAURA. Joseph LaShelle.
LIFEBOAT. Glen MacWilliams.
SINCE YOU WENT AWAY. Stanley Cortez and Lee Garmes.
THIRTY SECONDS OVER TOKYO. Robert Surtees and Harold Rosson.
THE UNINVITED. Charles Lang.
THE WHITE CLIFFS OF DOVER. George Folsey.

Color
COVER GIRL. Rudolph Mate and Allen M. Davey.
HOME IN INDIANA. Edward Cronjager.
KISMET. Charles Rosher.
LADY IN THE DARK. Ray Rennahan.
MEET ME IN ST. LOUIS. George Folsey.
WILSON. Leon Shamroy.
Best Interior Decoration
Black-and-White
ADDRESS UNKNOWN. Lionel Banks and Walter Holscher; Joseph Kish.
THE ADVENTURES OF MARK TWAIN. John J. Hughes; Fred MacLean.
CASANOVA BROWN. Perry Ferguson; Julia Heron.
GASLIGHT. Cedric Gibbons and William Ferrari; Edwin B. Willis and Paul Huldschinsky.
LAURA. Lyle Wheeler and Leland Fuller; Thomas Little.
NO TIME FOR LOVE. Hans Dreier and Robert Usher; Sam Comer.
SINCE YOU WENT AWAY. Mark-Lee Kirk; Victor A. Gangelin.
STEP LIVELY. Albert S. D'Agostino and Carroll Clark; Darrell Silvera and Claude Carpenter.
Color
THE CLIMAX. John B. Goodman and Alexander Golitzen; Russell A. Gausman and Ira S. Webb.
COVER GIRL. Lionel Banks and Cary Odell; Fay Babcock.
THE DESERT SONG. Charles Novi; Jack McConaghy.
KISMET. Cedric Gibbons and Daniel B. Cathcart; Edwin B. Willis and Richard Pefferle.
LADY IN THE DARK. Hans Dreier and Raoul Pene du Bois; Ray Moyer.
THE PRINCESS AND THE PIRATE. Ernst Fegte; Howard Bristol.
WILSON. Wiard Ihnen; Thomas Little.
Best Sound Recording
BRAZIL. Daniel J. Bloomberg.
CASANOVA BROWN. Thomas T. Moulton, Goldwyn Sound Department.
COVER GIRL. John Livadary.
DOUBLE INDEMNITY. Loren Ryder.
HIS BUTLER'S SISTER. Bernard B. Brown.
HOLLYWOOD CANTEEN. Nathan Levinson.
IT HAPPENED TOMORROW. Jack Whitney, Sound Service, Inc.
KISMET. Douglas Shearer.
MUSIC IN MANHATTAN. Stephen Dunn.
VOICE IN THE WIND. W.M. Dalgleish, RCA Sound.
WILSON. E.H. Hansen.
Music Awards
Best Song
"I Couldn't Sleep a Wink Last Night" from HIGHER AND HIGHER. Music by Jimmy McHugh; lyrics by Harold Adamson.
"I'll Walk Alone" from FOLLOW THE BOYS. Music by Jule Styne; lyrics by Sammy Cahn.
"I'm Making Believe" from SWEET AND LOWDOWN. Music by James V. Monaco; lyrics by Mack Gordon.
"Long Ago and Far Away" from COVER GIRL. Music by Jerome Kern; lyrics by Ira Gershwin.
"Now I Know" from UP IN ARMS. Music by Harold Arlen; lyrics by Ted Koehler.
"Remember Me to Carolina" from MINSTREL MAN. Music by Harry Revel; lyrics by Paul Webster.
"Rio de Janeiro" from BRAZIL. Music by Ary Barroso; lyrics by Ned Washington.
"Silver Shadows and Golden Dreams" from LADY LET'S DANCE. Music by Lew Pollack; lyrics by Charles Newman.
"Sweet Dreams Sweetheart" from HOLLYWOOD CANTEEN. Music by M.K. Jerome; lyrics by Ted Koehler.
Swinging on a Star" from GOING MY WAY. Music by James Van Heusen; lyrics by Johnny Burke.
"Too Much in Love" from SONG OF THE OPEN ROAD. Music by Walter Kent; lyrics by Kim Gannon.
"The Trolley Song" from MEET ME IN ST. LOUIS. Music and lyrics by Ralph Blane and Hugh Martin.
Best Scoring of a Dramatic or Comedy Picture
ADDRESS UNKNOWN. Morris Stoloff and Ernst Toch.
THE ADVENTURES OF MARK TWAIN. Max Steiner.
THE BRIDGE OF SAN LUIS REY. Dimitri Tiomkin.
CASANOVA BROWN. Arthur Lange.
CHRISTMAS HOLIDAY. H.J. Salter.
DOUBLE INDEMNITY. Miklos Rozsa.
THE FIGHTING SEABEES. Walter Scharf and Roy Webb.
THE HAIRY APE. Michel Michelet and Edward Paul.
IT HAPPENED TOMORROW. Robert Stolz.
JACK LONDON. Frederic E. Rich.
KISMET. Herbert Stothart.
NONE BUT THE LONELY HEART. Constantin Bakaleinikoff and Hanns Eisler.
THE PRINCESS AND THE PIRATE. David Rose.
SINCE YOU WENT AWAY. Max Steiner.
SUMMER STORM. Karl Hajos.
THREE RUSSIAN GIRLS. Franke Harling.
UP IN MABLE'S ROOM. Edward Paul.
VOICE IN THE WIND. Michel Michelet.
WILSON. Alfred Newman.
WOMAN OF THE TOWN. Miklos Rozsa.
Best Scoring of a Musical Picture
BRAZIL. Walter Scharf.
COVER GIRL. Carmen Dragon and Morris Stoloff.
HIGHER AND HIGHER. Constantin Bakaleinikoff.
HOLLYWOOD CANTEEN. Ray Heindorf.
IRISH EYES ARE SMILING. Alfred Newman.
KNICKERBOCKER HOLIDAY. Werner R. Heymann and Kurt Weill.
LADY IN THE DARK. Robert Emmett Dolan.
LADY LET'S DANCE. Edward Kay.
MEET ME IN ST. LOUIS. Georgie Stoll.
THE MERRY MONAHANS. H.J. Salter.
MINSTREL MAN. Leo Erdody and Ferde Grofe.
SENSATIONS OF 1945. Mahlon Merrick.
SONG OF THE OPEN ROAD. Charles Previn.

UP IN ARMS. Louis Forbes and Ray Heindorf.

Best Film Editing
GOING MY WAY. Leroy Stone.
JANIE. Owen Marks.
NONE BUT THE LONELY HEART. Roland Gross.
SINCE YOU WENT AWAY. Hal C. Kern and James E. Newcom.
WILSON. Barbra McLean.

Best Special Effects
THE ADVENTURES OF MARK TWAIN. Photographic: Paul Detlefsen and John Crouse; sound: Nathan Levinson.
DAYS OF GLORY. Photographic: Vernon L. Walker; sound: James G. Stewart and Roy Granville.
SECRET COMMAND. Photographic: David Allen, Ray Cory, and Robert Wright; sound: Russell Malmgren and Harry Kusnick.
SINCE YOU WENT AWAY. Photographic: John R. Cosgrove; sound: Arthur Johns.
THE STORY OF DR. WASSELL. Photographic: Farciot Edouart and Gordon Jennings; sound: George Dutton.
THIRTY SECONDS OVER TOKYO. Photographic: A. Arnold Gillespie, Donald Jahraus, and Warren Newcombe; sound: Douglas Shearer.
WILSON. Photographic: Fred Sersen; sound: Roger Heman.

Short Subjects
Best Cartoon
AND TO THINK I SAW IT ON MULBERRY STREET, PAR. Produced by George Pal (Puppetoon).
THE DOG, CAT AND CANARY, COL (Screen Gems).
FISH FRY, UNIV. Produced by Walter Lantz.
HOW TO PLAY FOOTBALL, RKO. Produced by Walt Disney.
MOUSE TROUBLE, MGM. Produced by Frederick C. Quimby.
MY BOY, JOHNNY, FOX. Produced by Paul Terry.
SWOONER CROONER, WB.

Best One-Reel Film
BLUE GRASS GENTLEMEN, FOX. Produced for Edmund Reek (Sports Review).
50TH ANNIVERSARY OF MOTION PICTURES, COL. Produced by Ralph Staub (Screen Snapshots No. 9, Series 23).
JAMMIN' THE BLUES, WB. Produced by Gordon Hollingshead (Melody Masters).
MOVIE PESTS, MGM. Produced by Pete Smith.
WHO'S WHO IN ANIMAL LAND, PAR. Produced by Jerry Fairbanks (Speaking of Animals Series).

Best Two-Reel Film
BOMBALERA, PAR. Produced by Louis Harris (Musical Parade).
I WON'T PLAY, WB. Produced by Gordon Hollingshead.
MAIN STREET TODAY, MGM. Produced by Jerry Bresler.

Documentary
Best Short Subject Documentary
ARTURO TOSCANINI, Motion Picture Bureau, Overseas Branch, Office of War Information.
NEW AMERICANS, This Is America Series, RKO Radio.
WITH THE MARINES AT TARAWA, U.S. Marine Corps.

Best Feature Documentary
THE FIGHTING LADY, FOX and U.S. Navy.
RESISTING ENEMY INTERROGATION, U.S. Army Air Force.

Irving G. Thalberg Memorial Award
Darryl F. Zanuck.

Special Awards
Margaret O'Brien, outstanding child actress of 1944.
Bob Hope for his many services (a Life Membership in The Academy of Motion Pictures Arts and Sciences)

Scientific or Technical
Class II
Stephen Dunn and the RKO Radio Studio Sound Department and Radio Corporation of America for the design and development of the electronic compressor-limiter.

Class III
Linwood Dunn, Cecil Love and Acme Tool Manufactoring Co. for the design and construction of the Acme-Dunn Optical Printer.
Grover Laube and the 20th Century-Fox Studio Camera Department for the development of a continuous loop projection device.
Western Electric Co. for the design and construction of the 1126A Limiting Amplifier for variable density sound recording.
Russell Brown, Ray Hinsdale and Joseph E. Robbins for the development and production use of the Paramount floating hydraulic boat rocker.
Gordon Jennings for the design and construction of the Paramount nodal point tripod.
Radio Corporation of America and the RKO Radio Studio Sound Department for the design and construction of the RKO reverberation chamber.
Daniel J. Bloomberg and the Republic Studio Sound Department for the design and development of a multi-interlock selector switch.
Bernard B. Brown and John P. Livadary for the design and engineering of a separate soloist and chorus recording room.
Paul Zeff, S.J. Twining and George Seid of the Columbia Studio Laboratory for the formula and application to production of a simplified variable area sound negative developer.
Paul Lerpae for the design and construction of the Paramount traveling matte projection and photographing device.

1945

Best Picture
ANCHORS AWEIGH, MGM. Produced by Joe Pasternak.
THE BELLS OF ST. MARY'S, RKO. Produced by Leo McCarey.
THE LOST WEEKEND, PAR. Produced by Charles Brackett.
MILDRED PIERCE, WB. Produced by Jerry Wald.
SPELLBOUND, UA. Produced by David O. Selznick.

Best Actor
Bing Crosby for THE BELLS OF ST. MARY'S.
Gene Kelly for ANCHORS AWEIGH.
Ray Milland for THE LOST WEEKEND.
Gregory Peck for THE KEYS OF THE KINGDOM.
Cornel Wilde for A SONG TO REMEMBER.

Best Actress
Ingrid Bergman for THE BELLS OF ST. MARY'S.
Joan Crawford for MILDRED PIERCE.

Greer Garson for THE VALLEY OF DECISION.
Jennifer Jones for LOVE LETTERS.
Gene Tierney for LEAVE HER TO HEAVEN.

Best Supporting Actor
Michael Chekhov for SPELLBOUND.
John Dall for THE CORN IS GREEN.
James Dunn for A TREE GROWS IN BROOKLYN.
Robert Mitchum for THE STORY OF G.I. JOE.
J. Carrol Naish for A MEDAL FOR BENNY.

Best Supporting Actress
Eve Arden for MILDRED PIERCE.
Ann Blyth for MILDRED PIERCE.
Angela Lansbury for THE PICTURE OF DORIAN GRAY.
Joan Lorring for THE CORN IS GREEN.
Anne Revere for NATIONAL VELVET.

Best Direction
Clarence Brown for NATIONAL VELVET.
Alfred Hitchcock for SPELLBOUND.
Leo McCarey for THE BELLS OF ST. MARY'S.
Jean Renoir for THE SOUTHERNER.
Billy Wilder for THE LOST WEEKEND.

Writing Awards
Best Original Story
THE AFFAIRS OF SUSAN, by Laszlo Gorog and Thomas Monroe.
THE HOUSE ON 92ND STREET, by Charles G. Booth.
A MEDAL FOR BENNY, by John Steinbeck and Jack Wagner.
OBJECTIVE, BURMA, by Alvah Bessie.
A SONG TO REMEMBER, by Ernst Marischka.

Best Original Screenplay
DILLINGER, by Philip Yordan.
MARIE-LOUISE, by Richard Schweizer.
MUSIC FOR MILLIONS, by Myles Connolly.
SALTY O'ROURKE, by Milton Holmes.
WHAT NEXT, CORPORAL HARGROVE?, by Harry Kurnitz.

Best Screenplay
THE LOST WEEKEND, by Charles Brackett and Billy Wilder.
MILDRED PIERCE, by Ronald MacDougall.
PRIDE OF THE MARINES, by Albert Maltz.
THE STORY OF G.I. JOE, by Leopold Atlas, Guy Endore, and Philip Stevenson.
A TREE GROWS IN BROOKLYN, by Frank Davis and Tess Slesinger.

Best Cinematography
Black-and-White
THE KEYS OF THE KINGDOM. Arthur Miller.
THE LOST WEEKEND. John F. Seitz.
MILDRED PIERCE. Ernest Haller.
THE PICTURE OF DORIAN GRAY. Harry Stradling.
Color
ANCHORS AWEIGH. Robert Planck and Charles Boyle.
LEAVE HER TO HEAVEN. Leon Shamroy.
NATIONAL VELVET. Leonard Smith.
A SONG TO REMEMBER. Tony Gaudio and Allen M. Davey.
THE SPANISH MAIN. George Barnes.

Best Interior Decoration
Black-and-White
BLOOD ON THE SUN. Wiard Ihnen and A. Roland Fields.
EXPERIMENT PERILOUS. Albert S. D'Agostino and Jack Okey; Darrell Silvera and Claude Carpenter.
THE KEYS OF THE KINGDOM. James Basevi and William Darling; Thomas Little and Frank E. Hughes.
LOVE LETTERS. Hans Dreier and Roland Anderson; Sam Comer and Ray Moyer.
THE PICTURE OF DORIAN GRAY. Cedric Gibbons and Hans Peters; Edwin B. Willis, John Bonar, and Hugh Hunt.
Color
FRENCHMAN'S CREEK. Hans Dreier and Ernst Fegte; Sam Comer.
LEAVE HER TO HEAVEN. Lyle Wheeler and Maurice Ransford; Thomas Little.
NATIONAL VELVET. Cedric Gibbons and Urie McCleary; Edwin B. Willis and Mildred Griffiths.
SAN ANTONIO. Ted Smith and Jack McConaghy.
A THOUSAND AND ONE NIGHTS. Stephen Goosson and Rudolph Sternad; Frank Tuttle.

Best Sound Recording
THE BELLS OF ST. MARY'S. Stephen Dunn.
THE FLAME OF THE BARBARY COAST. Daniel J. Bloomberg.
LADY ON A TRAIN. Bernard B. Brown.
LEAVE HER TO HEAVEN. Thomas T. Moulton.
RHAPSODY IN BLUE. Nathan Levinson.
A SONG TO REMEMBER. John Livadary.
THE SOUTHERNER. Jack Whitney, General Service.
THEY WERE EXPENDABLE. Douglas Shearer.
THE THREE CABALLEROS. C.O. Slyfield.
THREE IS A FAMILY. W.V. Wolfe, RCA Sound.
THE UNSEEN. Loren L. Ryder.
WONDER MAN. Gordon Sawyer.

Music Awards
Best Song
"Accentuate the Positive" from HERE COME THE WAVES. Music by Harold Arlen; lyrics by Johnny Mercer.
"Anywhere" from TONIGHT AND EVERY NIGHT. Music by Jule Styne; lyrics by Sammy Cahn.
"Aren't You Glad You're You" from THE BELLS OF ST. MARY'S. Music by James Van Heusen; lyrics by Johnny Burke.
"The Cat and the Canary" from WHY GIRLS LEAVE HOME. Music by Jay Livingston; lyrics by Ray Evans.
"Endlessly" from EARL CARROLL VANITIES. Music by Walter Kent; lyrics by Kim Gannon.
"I Fall in Love Too Easily" from ANCHORS AWEIGH. Music by Jule Styne; lyrics by Sammy Cahn.
"I'll Buy That Dream" from SING YOUR WAY HOME. Music by Allie Wrubel; lyrics by Herb Magidson.
It Might as Well Be Spring" from STATE FAIR. Music by Richard Rodgers; lyrics

by Oscar Hammerstein, II.
"Linda" from THE STORY OF G.I. JOE. Music and lyrics by Ann Ronell.
"Love Letters" from LOVE LETTERS. Music by Victor Young; lyrics by Edward Heyman.
"More and More" from CAN'T HELP SINGING. Music by Jerome Kern; lyrics by E.Y. Harburg.
"Sleighride in July" from BELLE OF THE YUKON. Music by James Van Heusen; lyrics by Johnny Burke.
"So in Love" from WONDER MAN. Music by David Rose; lyrics by Leo Robin.
"Some Sunday Morning" from SAN ANTONIO. Music by Ray Heindorf and M.K. Jerome; lyrics by Ted Koehler.

Best Scoring of a Dramatic or Comedy Picture
THE BELLS OF ST. MARY'S. Robert Emmet Dolan.
BREWSTER'S MILLIONS. Lou Forbes.
CAPTAIN KIDD. Werner Janssen.
ENCHANTED COTTAGE. Roy Webb.
FLAME OF THE BARBARY COAST. Dale Butts and Morton Scott.
G.I. HONEYMOON. Edward J. Kay.
GUEST IN THE HOUSE. Werner Janssen.
GUEST WIFE. Daniele Amfitheatrof.
THE KEYS OF THE KINGDOM. Alfred Newman.
THE LOST WEEKEND. Miklos Rozsa.
LOVE LETTERS. Victor Young.
THE MAN WHO WALKED ALONE. Karl Hajos.
OBJECTIVE, BURMA. Franz Waxman.
PARIS UNDERGROUND. Alexander Tansman.
A SONG TO REMEMBER. Miklos Rozsa and Morris Stoloff.
THE SOUTHERNER. Werner Janssen.
SPELLBOUND. Miklos Rozsa.
THE STORY OF G.I. JOE. Louis Applebaum and Ann Ronell.
THIS LOVE OF OURS. H.J. Salter.
THE VALLEY OF DECISION. Herbert Stothart.
THE WOMAN IN THE WINDOW. Hugo Friedhofer and Arthur Lange.

Best Scoring of a Musical Picture
ANCHORS AWEIGH. Georgie Stoll.
BELLE OF THE YUKON. Arthur Lange.
CAN'T HELP SINGING. Jerome Kern and H.J. Salter.
HITCHHIKE TO HAPPINESS. Morton Scott.
INCENDIARY BLONDE. Robert Emmett Dolan.
RHAPSODY IN BLUE. Ray Heindorf and Max Steiner.
STATE FAIR. Charles Henderson and Alfred Newman.
SUNBONNET SUE. Edward J. Kay.
THE THREE CABALLEROS. Edward Plumb, Paul J. Smith, and Charles Wolcott.
TONIGHT AND EVERY NIGHT. Marlin Skiles and Morris Stoloff.
WHY GIRLS LEAVE HOME. Walter Greene.
WONDER MAN. Lou Forbes and Ray Heindorf.

Best Film Editing
THE BELLS OF ST. MARY'S. Harry Marker.
THE LOST WEEKEND. Doane Harrison.
NATIONAL VELVET. Robert J. Kern.
OBJECTIVE, BURMA. George Amy.
A SONG TO REMEMBER. Charles Nelson.

Best Special Effects
CAPTAIN EDDIE. Photographic: Fred Sersen and Sol Halprin; sound: Roger Heman and Harry Leonard.
SPELLBOUND. Photographic: Jack Cosgrove.
THEY WERE EXPENDABLE. Photographic: A. Arnold Gillespie, Donald Jahraus, and R.A. MacDonald; sound: Michael Steinore.
A THOUSAND AND ONE NIGHTS. Photographic: L.W. Butler; sound: Ray Momba.
WONDER MAN. Photographic: John Fulton; sound: A.W. Johns.

Short Subjects
Best Cartoon
DONALD'S CRIME, RKO. Produced by Walt Disney.
JASPER AND THE BEANSTALK, PAR. Produced by George Pal (Jasper Puppetoon).
LIFE WITH FEATHERS, WB. Produced by Eddie Selzer (Merrie Melodies).
MIGHTY MOUSE IN GYPSY LIFE, FOX. Produced by Paul Terry (Terrytoon).
POET AND PEASANT, UNIV. Produced by Walter Lantz.
QUIET PLEASE, MGM. Produced by Frederick Quimby (Tom and Jerry Series).
RIPPLING ROMANCE, COL (Color Rhapsodies).

Best One-Reel Film
ALONG THE RAINBOW TRAIL, FOX. Produced by Edmund Reek.
SCREEN SNAPSHOTS 25TH ANNIVERSARY, COL. Produced by Ralph Straub (Screen Snapshots).
STAIRWAY TO LIGHT, MGM. Produced by Herbert Moulton (John Nesbitt Passing Parade).
STORY OF A DOG, WB. Produced by Gordon Hollingshead (Vitaphone Varieties).
WHITE RHAPSODY, PAR. Produced by Grantland Rice (Sportlights).
YOUR NATIONAL GALLERY, UNIV. Produced by Joseph O'Brien and Thomas Mead (Variety Views).

Best Two-Reel Film
A GUN IN HIS HAND, MGM. Produced by Chester Franklin (Crime Does Not Pay Series).
THE JURY GOES ROUND 'N' ROUND, COL. Produced by Jules White (All Star Comedies).
THE LITTLE WITCH, PAR. Produced by George Templeton (Musical Parade).
STAR IN THE NIGHT, WB. Produced by Gordon Hollingshead (Broadway Brevities).

Documentary
Best Short Subject Documentary
HITLER LIVES?, WB.
LIBRARY OF CONGRESS, Overseas Motion Picture Bureau, Office of War Information.
TO THE SHORES OF IWO JIMA, U.S. Marine Corps. Best Feature Documentary
THE LAST BOMB, U.S. Army Air Force
THE TRUE GLORY, Governments of Great Britain and USA.

Irving G. Thalberg Memorial Award
None awarded.

Special Award
Walter Wanger for his six years service as President of the Academy of Motion Picture Arts and Sciences.
Peggy Ann Garner, outstanding child actress of 1945.
THE HOUSE I LIVE IN, tolerance short subject; produced by Frank Ross and Mervyn LeRoy; directed by Mervyn LeRoy; screenplay by Albert Maltz; song "The House I Live In," music by Earl Robinson, lyrics by Lewis Allen; starring Frank Sinatra; released by RKO.
Republic Studio, Daniel J. Bloomberg and the Republic Sound Department for the building of an outstanding musical scoring auditorium which provides optimum recording conditions and combines all elements of acoustic and engineering design.

Scientific or Technical
Class III
Loren L. Ryder, Charles R. Daily and the Paramount Studio Sound Department for the design, construction and use of the first dial-controlled step-by-step sound channel line-up and test circuit.
Michael S. Leshing, Benjamin C. Robinson, Arthur B. Chatelain and Robert C. Stevens of 20th Century-Fox Studio and John G. Capstaff of Eastman Kodak & Co. for the 20th Century-Fox film processing machine.

1946

Best Picture
THE BEST YEARS OF OUR LIVES, RKO. Produced by Samuel Goldwyn.
HENRY V, Rank-UA. Produced by Laurence Olivier.
IT'S A WONDERFUL LIFE, RKO. Produced by Frank Capra.
THE RAZOR'S EDGE, FOX. Produced by Darryl F. Zanuck.
THE YEARLING, MGM. Produced by Sidney Franklin.

Best Actor
Fredric March for THE BEST YEARS OF OUR LIVES.
Laurence Olivier for HENRY V.
Larry Parks for THE JOLSON STORY.
Gregory Peck for THE YEARLING.
James Stewart for IT'S A WONDERFUL LIFE.

Best Actress
Olivia de Havilland for TO EACH HIS OWN.
Celia Johnson for BRIEF ENCOUNTER.
Jennifer Jones for DUEL IN THE SUN.
Rosalind Russell for SISTER KENNY.
Jane Wyman for THE YEARLING.

Best Supporting Actor
Charles Coburn for THE GREEN YEARS.
William Demarest for THE JOLSON STORY.
Claude Rains for NOTORIOUS.
Harold Russell for THE BEST YEARS OF OUR LIVES.
Clifton Webb for THE RAZOR'S EDGE.

Best Supporting Actress
Ethel Barrymore for THE SPIRAL STAIRCASE.
Anne Baxter for THE RAZOR'S EDGE.
Lillian Gish for DUEL IN THE SUN.
Flora Robson for SARATOGA TRUNK.
Gale Sondergaard for ANNA AND THE KING OF SIAM.

Best Direction
Clarence Brown for THE YEARLING.
Frank Capra for IT'S A WONDERFUL LIFE.
David Lean for BRIEF ENCOUNTER.
Robert Siodmak for THE KILLERS.
William Wyler for THE BEST YEARS OF OUR LIVES.

Writing Awards
Best Original Story
THE DARK MIRROR, by Vladimir Pozner.
THE STRANGE LOVE OF MARTHA IVERS, by Jack Patrick.
THE STRANGER, by Victor Trivas.
TO EACH HIS OWN, by Charles Brackett.
VACATION FROM MARRIAGE, by Clemence Dane.

Best Original Screenplay
THE BLUE DAHLIA, by Raymond Chandler.
CHILDREN OF PARADISE, by Jacques Prevert.
NOTORIOUS, by Ben Hecht.
THE ROAD TO UTOPIA, by Norman Panama and Melvin Frank.
THE SEVENTH VEIL, by Muriel Box and Sydney Box. Best Screenplay
ANNA AND THE KING OF SIAM, by Sally Benson and Talbot Jennings.
THE BEST YEARS OF OUR LIVES, by Robert E. Sherwood.
BRIEF ENCOUNTER, by Anthony Havelock-Allan, David Lean and Ronald Neame.
THE KILLERS, by Anthony Veiller.
OPEN CITY, by Sergio Amidei and Federico Fellini.

Best Cinematography
Black-and-White
ANNA AND THE KING OF SIAM. Arthur Miller.
THE GREEN YEARS. George Folsey.
Color
THE JOLSON STORY. Joseph Walker.
THE YEARLING. Charles Rosher, Leonard Smith, and Arthur Arling.

Best Interior Decoration
Black-and-White
ANNA AND THE KING OF SIAM. Lyle Wheeler and William Darling; Thomas Little and Frank E. Hughes.
KITTY. Hans Dreier and Walter Tyler; Sam Comer and Ray Moyer.
THE RAZOR'S EDGE. Richard Day and Nathan Juran; Thomas Little and Paul S. Fox.
Color
CAESAR AND CLEOPATRA. John Bryan.
HENRY V. Paul Sheriff and Carmen Dillon.
THE YEARLING. Cedric Gibbons and Paul Groesse; Edwin B. Willis.

Best Sound Recording
THE BEST YEARS OF OUR LIVES. Gordon Sawyer.
IT'S A WONDERFUL LIFE. John Aalberg.
THE JOLSON STORY. John Livadary.

Music Awards
Best Song
"All Through the Day" from CENTENNIAL SUMMER. Music by Jerome Kern; lyrics by Oscar Hammerstein II.
"I Can't Begin to Tell You" from THE DOLLY SISTERS. Music by James Monaco;

lyrics by Mack Gordon.

"Ole Buttermilk Sky" from CANYON PASSAGE. Music by Hoagy Carmichael; lyrics by Jack Brooks.

On the Atchison, Topeka and Sante Fe" from THE HARVEY GIRLS. Music by Harry Warren; lyrics by Johnny Mercer.

"You Keep Coming Back Like a Song" from BLUE SKIES. Music and lyrics by Irving Berlin.

Best Scoring of a Dramatic or Comedy Picture
ANNA AND THE KING OF SIAM. Bernard Herrmann.
THE BEST YEARS OF OUR LIVES. Hugo Friedhofer.
HENRY V. William Walton.
HUMORESQUE. Franz Waxman.
THE KILLERS. Miklos Rozsa.

Best Scoring of a Musical Picture
BLUE SKIES. Robert Emmett Dolan.
CENTENNIAL SUMMER. Alfred Newman.
THE HARVEY GIRLS. Lennie Hayton.
THE JOLSON STORY. Morris Stoloff.
NIGHT AND DAY. Ray Heindorf and Max Steiner.

Best Film Editing
THE BEST YEARS OF OUR LIVES. Daniel Mandell.
IT'S A WONDERFUL LIFE. William Hornbeck.
THE JOLSON STORY. William Lyon.
THE KILLERS. Arthur Hilton.
THE YEARLING. Harold Kress.

Best Special Effects
BLITHE SPIRIT. Visual: Thomas Howard.
A STOLEN LIFE. Visual: William McGann; audio: Nathan Levinson.

Short Subjects

Best Cartoon
THE CAT CONCERTO, MGM. Produced by Frederick Quimby (Tom and Jerry Series).
CHOPIN'S MUSICAL MOMENTS, UNIV. Produced by Walter Lantz.
JOHN HENRY AND THE INKY POO, PAR. Produced by George Pal (Puppetoon).
SQUATTER'S RIGHTS, RKO. Produced by Walt Disney (Mickey Mouse).
WALKY TALKY HAWKY, WB. Produced by Edward Selzer (Merrie Melodies).

Best One-Reel Film
DIVE-HI CHAMPS, PAR. Produced by Jack Eaton (Sportlights).
FACING YOUR DANGER, WB. Produced by Gordon Hollingshead (Sports Parade).
GOLDEN HORSES, FOX. Produced by Edmund Reek (Movietone Sports Review).
SMART AS A FOX, WB. Produced by Gordon Hollingshead.
SURE CURES, MGM. Produced by Pete Smith.

Best Two-Reel Film
A BOY AND HIS DOG, WB. Produced by Gordon Hollingshead.
COLLEGE QUEEN, PAR. Produced by George Templeton (Musical Parade).
HISS AND YELL, COL. Produced by Jules White (All Star Comedies).
THE LUCKIEST GUY IN THE WORLD, MGM. Produced by Jerry Bresler.

Documentary

Best Short Subject Documentary
ATOMIC POWER, FOX.
LIFE AT THE ZOO, Artkino.
PARAMOUNT NEWS ISSUE NO. 37, PAR.
SEEDS OF DESTINY, U.S. War Department.
TRAFFIC WITH THE DEVIL, MGM.

Irving G. Thalberg Memorial Award
Samuel Goldwyn.

Special Awards
Laurence Olivier for his outstanding achievement as actor, producer and director in bringing HENRY V to the screen.
Harold Russell for bringing hope and courage to his fellow veterans through his appearance in THE BEST YEARS OF OUR LIVES.
Ernst Lubitsch for his distinguished contribution to the art of the motion picture.
Claude Jarman, Jr., outstanding child actor of 1946.

Scientific or Technical

Class III
Harlan L. Baumbach and the Paramount West Coast Laboratory for an improved method for the quantitative determination of hydroquinone and metol in photographing developing baths.
Herbert E. Britt for the development and application of formulas and equipment for producing cloud and smoke effects.
Burton F. Miller and the Warner Bros. Studio Sound and Electrical Departments for the design and construction of a motion picture arc lighting generator filter.
Carl Faulkner of the 20th Century-Fox Studio Sound Department for the reversed bias method, including a double bias method for light valve galvanometer density recording.
Mole Richardson Co. for the type 450 super high intensity carbon arc lamp.
Arthur F. Blinn, Robert O. Cook, C.O. Slyfield and the Walt Disney Studio Sound Department for the design and development of an audio finder and track viewer for checking and locating noise in sound tracks.
Burton F. Miller and the Warner Bros. Studio Sound Department for the design and application of an equalizer to eliminate relative spectral energy distortion in electronic compressors.
Marty Martin and Hal Adkins of the RKO Radio Studio Miniature Department for the design and construction of equipment providing visual bullet effects.
Harold Nye and the Warner Bros. Studio Electrical Department for the development of the electronically controlled fire and gaslight effect.

1947

Best Picture
THE BISHOP'S WIFE, RKO. Produced by Samuel Goldwyn.
CROSSFIRE, RKO. Produced by Adrian Scott.
GENTLEMAN'S AGREEMENT, FOX. Produced by Darryl F. Zanuck.
GREAT EXPECTATIONS, RANK. Produced by Ronald Neame.
MIRACLE ON 34TH STREET, FOX. Produced by William Perlberg.

Best Actor
Ronald Colman for A DOUBLE LIFE.
John Garfield for BODY AND SOUL.
Gregory Peck for GENTLEMAN'S AGREEMENT.
William Powell for LIFE WITH FATHER.
Michael Redgrave for MOURNING BECOMES ELECTRA.

Best Actress
Joan Crawford for POSSESSED.
Susan Hayward for SMASH UP—THE STORY OF A WOMAN.
Dorothy McGuire for GENTLEMAN'S AGREEMENT.
Rosalind Russell for MOURNING BECOMES ELECTRA.
Loretta Young for THE FARMER'S DAUGHTER.

Best Supporting Actor
Charles Bickford for THE FARMER'S DAUGHTER.
Thomas Gomez for RIDE THE PINK HORSE.
Edmund Gwenn for MIRACLE ON 34TH STREET.
Robert Ryan for CROSSFIRE.
Richard Widmark for KISS OF DEATH.

Best Supporting Actress
Ethel Barrymore for THE PARADINE CASE.
Gloria Grahame for CROSSFIRE.
Celeste Holm for GENTLEMAN'S AGREEMENT.
Marjorie Main for THE EGG AND I.
Ann Revere for GENTLEMAN'S AGREEMENT.

Best Direction
George Cukor for A DOUBLE LIFE.
Edward Dmytryk for CROSSFIRE.
Elia Kazan for GENTLEMAN'S AGREEMENT.
Henry Koster for THE BISHOP'S WIFE.
David Lean for GREAT EXPECTATIONS.

Writing Awards

Best Original Story
A CAGE OF NIGHTINGALES, by Georges Chaperot and Rene Wheeler.
IT HAPPENED ON FIFTH AVENUE, by Herbert Clyde Lewis and Frederick Stephani.
KISS OF DEATH, by Eleazar Lipsky.
MIRACLE ON 34TH STREET, by Valentine Davies.
SMASH UP—THE STORY OF A WOMAN, by Dorothy Parker and Frank Cavett.

Best Original Screenplay
THE BACHELOR AND THE BOBBY-SOXER, by Sidney Sheldon.
BODY AND SOUL, by Abraham Polonsky.
A DOUBLE LIFE, by Ruth Gordon and Garson Kanin.
MONSIEUR VERDOUX, by Charles Chaplin.
SHOESHINE, by Sergio Amidei, Adolofo Franci, C.G. Viola, and Cesare Zavattini.

Best Screenplay
BOOMERANG!, by Richard Murphy.
CROSSFIRE, by John Paxton.
GENTLEMAN'S AGREEMENT, by Moss Hart.
GREAT EXPECTATIONS, by David Lean, Ronald Neame, and Anthony Havelock-Allan.
MIRACLE ON 34TH STREET, by George Seaton.

Best Cinematography

Black-and-White
THE GHOST AND MRS. MUIR. Charles Lang, Jr.
GREAT EXPECTATIONS. Guy Green.
GREEN DOLPHIN STREET. George Folsey.

Color
BLACK NARCISSUS. Jack Cardiff.
LIFE WITH FATHER. Peverell Marley and William V. Skall.
MOTHER WORE TIGHTS. Harry Jackson.

Best Art Direction—Set Decoration

Black-and-White
THE FOXES OF HARROW. Lyle Wheeler and Maurice Ransford; Thomas Little and Paul S. Fox.
GREAT EXPECTATIONS. John Bryan; Wilfred Shingleton.

Color
BLACK NARCISSUS. Alfred Junge.
LIFE WITH FATHER. Robert M. Haas; George James Hopkins.

Best Sound Recording
THE BISHOP'S WIFE. Goldwyn Sound Department.
GREEN DOLPHIN STREET. MGM Sound Department.
T-MEN. Eagle-Lion, Sound Services, Inc.

Music Awards

Best Song
"A Gal in Calico" from THE TIME, THE PLACE AND THE GIRL. Music by Arthur Schwartz; lyrics by Leo Robin.
"I Wish I Didn't Love You So" from THE PERILS OF PAULINE. Music and lyrics by Frank Loesser.
"Pass That Peace Pipe" from GOOD NEWS. Music and lyrics by Ralph Blane, Hugh Martin and Roger Edens.
"You Do" from MOTHER WORE TIGHTS. Music by Josef Myrow; lyrics by Mack Gordon.
Zip-A-Dee-Doo-Dah" from SONG OF THE SOUTH. Music by Allie Wrubel; lyrics by Ray Gilbert.

Best Scoring of a Dramatic or Comedy Picture
THE BISHOP'S WIFE. Hugo Friedhofer.
CAPTAIN FROM CASTILE. Alfred Newman.
A DOUBLE LIFE. Miklos Rozsa.
FOREVER AMBER. David Raksin.
LIFE WITH FATHER. Max Steiner.

Best Scoring of a Musical Picture
FIESTA. Johnny Green.
MOTHER WORE TIGHTS. Alfred Newman.
MY WILD IRISH ROSE. Ray Heindorf and Max Steiner.
ROAD TO RIO. Robert Emmett Dolan.
SONG OF THE SOUTH. Daniele Amfitheatrof, Paul J. Smith and Charles Wolcott.

Best Film Editing
THE BISHOP'S WIFE. Monica Collingwood.
BODY AND SOUL. Francis Lyon and Robert Parrish.
GENTLEMAN'S AGREEMENT. Harmon Jones.
GREEN DOLPHIN STREET. George White.
ODD MAN OUT. Fergus McDonnell.

Best Special Effects
GREEN DOLPHIN STREET. Visual: A. Arnold Gillespie and Warren Newcombe; audible: Douglas Shearer and Michael Steinore.
UNCONQUERED. Visual: Farciot Edouart, Devereux Jennings, Gordon Jennings,

Wallace Kelly, and Paul Lerpae; audible: George Dutton.
Short Subjects
Best Cartoon
CHIP AN' DALE, RKO. Produced by Walt Disney (Donald Duck).
DR. JEKYLL AND MR. MOUSE, MGM. Produced by Frederick Quimby (Tom and Jerry Series).
PLUTO'S BLUE NOTE, RKO. Produced by Walt Disney.
TUBBY THE TUBA, PAR. Produced by George Pal (Puppetoon).
TWEETIE PIE, WB. Produced by Edward Selzer (Merrie Melodies).
Best One-Reel Film
BROOKLYN, U.S.A., U-I. Produced by Thomas Mead (Variety Series).
GOODBYE MISS TURLOCK, MGM. Produced by Herbert Moulton (John Nesbitt Passing Parade).
MOON ROCKETS, PAR. Produced by Jerry Fairbanks (Popular Science).
NOW YOU SEE IT, MGM. Produced by Pete Smith.
SO YOU WANT TO BE IN PICTURES, WB. Produced by Gordon Hollingshead (Joe McDoakes Series).
Best Two-Reel Film
CHAMPAGNE FOR TWO, PAR. Produced by Harry Grey (Musical Parade).
CLIMBING THE MATTERHORN, MON. Produced by Irving Allen.
FIGHT OF THE WILD STALLIONS, U-I. Produced by Thomas Mead.
GIVE US THE EARTH, MGM. Produced by Herbert Morgan.
A VOICE IS BORN, COL. Produced by Ben Blake.
Documentary
Best Short Subject Documentary
FIRST STEPS, United Nations Division of Films and Visual Education.
PASSPORT TO NOWHERE, RKO. Produced by Frederic Ullman, Jr. (This Is America Series).
SCHOOL IN THE MAILBOX, Australian News and Information Bureau.
Best Feature Documentary
DESIGN FOR DEATH, RKO. Sid Rogell, executive producer; produced by Theron Warth and Richard O. Fleischer.
JOURNEY INTO MEDICINE, U.S. Department of State, Office of Information and Educational Exchange.
THE WORLD IS RICH, British Information Services. Produced by Paul Rotha.
Irving G. Thalberg Award
None awarded.
Special Awards
James Baskette for his able and heart-warming characterization of Uncle Remus, friend and storyteller to the children of the world.
BILL AND COO, in which artistry and patience blended in a novel and entertaining use of the medium of motion pictures.
SHOESHINE—the high quality of this motion picture, brought to eloquent life in a country scarred by war, is proof to the world that the creative spirit can triumph over adversity.
Colonel William N. Selig, Albert E. Smith, Thomas Armat and George K. Spoor, the small group of pioneers whose belief in a new medium, and whose contributions to its development, blazed the trail along which the motion picture has progressed, in their lifetime, from obscurity to world-wide acclaim.
Scientific or Technical
Class II
C.C. Davis and Electrical Research Products, Division of Western Electric Co., for the development and application of an improved film drive filter mechanism.
C.R. Daily and the Paramount Studio Film Laboratory, Still and Engineering Departments for the development and first practical application to motion picture and still photography of a method of increasing film speed as first suggested to the industry by E.I. duPont de Nemours & Co.
Class III
Nathan Levinson and the Warner Bros. Studio Sound Department for the design and construction of a constant-speed sound editing machine.
Farciot Edouart, C.R. Daily, Hal Corl, H.G. Cartwright and the Paramount Studio Transparency and Engineering Departments for the first application of a special antisolarizing glass to high intensity background and spot arc projectors.
Fred Ponedel of Warner Bros. Studio for pioneering the fabrication and practical application to motion picture color photography of large translucent photographic backgrounds.
Kurt Singer and the RCA-Victor Division of the Radio Corporation of America for the design and development of a continuously variable band elimination filter.
James Gibbons of Warner Bros. Studio for the development and production of large dyed plastic filters for motion picture photography.

1948
Best Picture
HAMLET, RANK-TC. Produced by Laurence Olivier.
JOHNNY BELINDA, WB. Produced by Jerry Wald.
THE RED SHOES, EL. Produced by Michael Powell and Emeric Pressburger.
THE SNAKE PIT, FOX. Produced by Anatole Litvak and Robert Bassler.
TREASURE OF SIERRA MADRE, WB. Produced by Henry Blanke.
Best Actor
Lew Ayres for JOHNNY BELINDA.
Montgomery Clift for THE SEARCH.
Dan Dailey for WHEN MY BABY SMILES AT ME.
Laurence Olivier for HAMLET.
Clifton Webb for SITTING PRETTY.
Best Actress
Ingrid Bergman for JOAN OF ARC.
Olivia de Havilland for THE SNAKE PIT.
Irene Dunne for I REMEMBER MAMA.
Barbara Stanwyck for SORRY, WRONG NUMBER.
Jane Wyman for JOHNNY BELINDA.
Best Supporting Actor
Charles Bickford for JOHNNY BELINDA.
Jose Ferrer for JOAN OF ARC.
Oscar Homolka for I REMEMBER MAMA.
Walter Huston for TREASURE OF SIERRA MADRE.
Cecil Kellaway for THE LUCK OF THE IRISH.
Best Supporting Actress
Barbara Bel Geddes for I REMEMBER MAMA.
Ellen Corby for I REMEMBER MAMA.
Agnes Moorehead for JOHNNY BELINDA.

Jean Simmons for HAMLET.
Claire Trevor for KEY LARGO.
Best Direction
John Huston for TREASURE OF SIERRA MADRE.
Anatole Litvak for THE SNAKE PIT.
Jean Negulesco for JOHNNY BELINDA.
Laurence Olivier for HAMLET.
Fred Zinnemann for THE SEARCH.
Writing Awards
Best Motion Picture Story
THE LOUISIANA STORY, by Frances Flaherty and Robert Flaherty.
THE NAKED CITY, by Malvin Ward.
RED RIVER, by Borden Chase.
THE RED SHOES, by Emeric Pressburger.
THE SEARCH, by Richard Schwiezer and David Wechsler.
Best Screenplay
A FOREIGN AFFAIR, by Charles Brackett, Billy Wilder, and Richard L. Breen.
JOHNNY BELINDA, by Irmgard Von Cube and Allen Vincent.
THE SEARCH, by Richard Schweizer and David Wechsler.
THE SNAKE PIT, by Frank Partos and Millen Brand.
TREASURE OF SIERRA MADRE, by John Huston.
Best Cinematography
Black-and-White
A FOREIGN AFFAIR. Charles B. Lang, Jr.
I REMEMBER MAMA. Nicholas Musuraca.
JOHNNY BELINDA. Ted McCord.
THE NAKED CITY. William Daniels.
PORTRAIT OF JENNIE. Joseph August.
Color
GREEN GRASS OF WYOMING. Charles G. Clarke.
JOAN OF ARC. Joseph Valentine, William V. Skall, and Winton Hoch.
THE LOVES OF CARMEN. William Snyder.
THE THREE MUSKETEERS. Robert Planck.
Best Art Direction—Set Direction
Black-and-White
HAMLET. Roger K. Furse; Carmen Dillon.
JOHNNY BELINDA. Robert Haas; William Wallace.
Color
JOAN OF ARC. Richard Day; Edwin Casey Roberts and Joseph Kish.
THE RED SHOES. Hein Heckroth; Arthur Lawson.
Best Sound Recording
JOHNNY BELINDA. Warner Bros. Sound Department.
MOONRISE. Republic Sound Department.
THE SNAKE PIT. 20th Century-Fox Sound Department.
Music Awards
Best Song
Buttons and Bows" from THE PALEFACE. Music and lyrics by Jay Livingston and Ray Evans.
"For Every Man There's a Woman" from CASBAH. Music by Harold Arlen; lyrics by Leo Robin.
"It's Magic" from ROMANCE ON THE HIGH SEAS. Music by Jule Styne; lyrics by Sammy Cahn.
"This is the Moment" from THAT LADY IN ERMINE. Music by Frederick Hollander; lyrics by Leo Robin.
"The Woody Woodpecker Song" from WET BLANKET POLICY. Music and lyrics by Ramey Idriss and George Tibbles.
Best Scoring of a Dramatic or Comedy Picture
HAMLET. William Walton.
JOAN OF ARC. Hugo Friedhofer.
JOHNNY BELINDA. Max Steiner.
THE RED SHOES. Brian Easdale.
THE SNAKE PIT. Alfred Newman.
Best Scoring of a Musical Picture
EASTER PARADE. Johnny Green and Roger Edens.
THE EMPEROR WALTZ. Victor Young.
THE PIRATE. Lennie Hayton.
ROMANCE ON THE HIGH SEAS. Ray Heindorf.
WHEN MY BABY SMILES AT ME. Alfred Newman.
Best Film Editing
JOAN OF ARC. Frank Sullivan.
JOHNNY BELINDA. David Weisbart.
THE NAKED CITY. Paul Weatherwax.
RED RIVER. Christian Nyby.
THE RED SHOES. Reginald Mills.
Best Costume Design
Black-and-White
B.F.'S DAUGHTER. Irene.
HAMLET. Roger K. Furse.
Color
THE EMPEROR WALTZ. Edith Head and Gile Steele.
JOAN OF ARC. Dorothy Jeakins and Karinska.
Best Special Effects
DEEP WATERS. Visual: Ralph Hammeras, Fred Sersen, and Edward Snyder; audible: Roger Heman.
PORTRAIT OF JENNIE. Visual: Paul Eagler, J. McMillan Johnson, Russell Shearman and Clarence Slifer; audible: Charles Freeman and James G. Stewart.
Short Subjects
Best Cartoon
THE LITTLE ORPHAN, MGM. Produced by Fred Quimby (Tom and Jerry Series).
MICKEY AND THE SEAL, RKO. Produced by Walt Disney.
MOUSE WRECKERS, WB. Produced by Edward Selzer (Looney Tunes).
ROBIN HOODLUM, COL. Produced by United Productions of America (Fox and Crow Series).
TEA FOR TWO HUNDRED, RKO. Produced by Walt Disney (Donald Duck).
Best One-Reel Film
ANNIE WAS A WONDER, MGM. Produced by Herbert Moulton (John Nesbitt Passing Parade).
CINDERELLA HORSE, WB. Produced by Gordon Hollingshead (Sports Parade).
SO YOU WANT TO BE ON THE RADIO, WB. Produced by Gordon Hollingshead (Joe McDoakes Series).

SYMPHONY OF A CITY, FOX. Produced by Edmund H. Reek.
YOU CAN'T WIN, MGM. Produced by Pete Smith.
Best Two-Reel Film
    CALGARY STAMPEDE, WB. Produced by Gordon Hollingshead.
    GOING TO BLAZES, MGM. Produced by Herbert Morgan.
    SAMBA-MANIA, PAR. Produced by Harry Grey (Musical Parade).
    SEAL ISLAND, RKO. Produced by Walt Disney (True Life Adventure Series).
    SNOW CAPERS, UNIV. Produced by Thomas Mead.
Documentary
  Best Short Subject Documentary
    HEART TO HEART, Fact Film Organization. Produced by Herbert Morgan.
    OPERATION VITTLES, U.S. Army Air Force.
    TOWARD INDEPENDENCE, U.S. Army.
  Best Feature Documentary
    THE QUIET ONE, Mayer-Burstyn. Produced by Janice Loeb.
    THE SECRET LAND, U.S. Navy, MGM. Produced by O.O. Dull.
Irving G. Thalberg Memorial Award
    Jerry Wald.
Special Awards
    MONSIEUR VINCENT (Fr.)—voted by the Academy Board of Governors as the most
    outstanding foreign language film released in the United States during 1948.
    Ivan Jandl for the outstanding juvenile performance of 1948 in THE SEARCH.
    Sid Grauman, master showman, who raised the standard of exhibition of motion
    pictures.
    Adolph Zukor, a man who has been called the father of feature film in America, for
    his services to the industry over a period of forty years.
    Walter Wanger for distinguished service to the industry in adding to its moral stature
    in the world community by his production of the picture JOAN OF ARC.
Scientific or Technical
  Class II
    Victor Caccialanza, Maurice Ayers and the Paramount Studio Set Construction
    Department for the development and application of "Paralite," a new lightweight
    plaster process for set construction.
    Nick Kalten, Louis J. Witti and the 20th Century-Fox Studio Mechanical Effects
    Department for a process of preserving and flame-proofing foliage.
  Class III
    Marty Martin, Jack Lannon, Russell Shearman and the RKO Radio Studio Special
    Effects Department for the development of a new method of simulating falling snow
    on motion picture sets.
    A.J. Moran and the Warner Bros. Studio Electrical Department for a method of
    remote control for shutters on motion picture arc lighting equipment.

1949
Best Picture
    ALL THE KING'S MEN, COL. Produced by Robert Rossen.
    BATTLEGROUND, MGM. Produced by Dore Schary.
    THE HEIRESS, PAR. Produced by William Wyler.
    A LETTER TO THREE WIVES, FOX. Produced by Sol C. Siegel.
    12 O'CLOCK HIGH, FOX. Produced by Darryl F. Zanuck.
Best Actor
    Broderick Crawford for ALL THE KING'S MEN.
    Kirk Douglas for CHAMPION.
    Gregory Peck for 12 O'CLOCK HIGH.
    Richard Todd for THE HASTY HEART.
    John Wayne for SANDS OF IWO JIMA.
Best Actress
    Jeanne Crain for PINKY.
    Olivia de Havilland for THE HEIRESS.
    Susan Hayward for MY FOOLISH HEART.
    Deborah Kerr for EDWARD MY SON.
    Loretta Young for COME TO THE STABLE.
Best Supporting Actor
    John Ireland for ALL THE KING'S MEN.
    Dean Jagger for 12 O'CLOCK HIGH.
    Arthur Kennedy for CHAMPION.
    Ralph Richardson for THE HEIRESS.
    James Whitmore for BATTLEGROUND.
Best Supporting Actress
    Ethel Barrymore for PINKY.
    Celeste Holm for COME TO THE STABLE.
    Elsa Lanchester for COME TO THE STABLE.
    Mercedes McCambridge for ALL THE KING'S MEN.
    Ethel Waters for PINKY.
Best Direction
    Joseph L. Mankiewicz for A LETTER TO THREE WIVES.
    Carol Reed for THE FALLEN IDOL.
    Robert Rossen for ALL THE KING'S MEN.
    William A. Wellman for BATTLEGROUND.
    William Wyler for THE HEIRESS.
Writing Awards
  Best Motion Picture Story
    COME TO THE STABLE, by CLare Booth Luce.
    IT HAPPENS EVERY SPRING, by Shirley W. Smith and Valentine Davies.
    SANDS OF IWO JIMA, by Harry Brown.
    THE STRATTON STORY, by Douglas Marrow.
    WHITE HEAT, by Virginia Kellogg.
  Best Screenplay
    ALL THE KING'S MEN, by Robert Rossen.
    THE BICYCLE THIEF, by Cesare Zavattini.
    CHAMPION, by Carl Foreman.
    THE FALLEN IDOL, by Graham Greene.
    A LETTER TO THREE WIVES, by Joseph L. Mankiewicz.
  Best Story and Screenplay
    BATTLEGROUND, by Robert Pirosh.
    JOLSON SINGS AGAIN, by Sidney Buchman.
    PAISAN, by Alfred Hayes, Federico Fellini, Sergio Amidei, Marcello Pagliero and
    Roberto Rossellini.
    PASSPORT TO PIMLICO, by T.E.B. Clarke.
    THE QUIET ONE, by Janice Loeb, Helen Levitt, and Sidney Meyers.
Best Cinematography

Black-and-White
    BATTLEGROUND. Paul Vogel.
    CHAMPION. Frank Planer.
    COME TO THE STABLE. Joseph LaShelle.
    THE HEIRESS. Leo Tover.
    PRINCE OF FOXES. Leon Shamroy.
Color
    THE BARKLEYS OF BROADWAY. Harry Stradling.
    JOLSON SINGS AGAIN. William Snyder.
    LITTLE WOMEN. Robert Planck and Charles Schoenbaum.
    SAND. Charles G. Clarke.
    SHE WORE A YELLOW RIBBON. Winton Hoch.
Best Art Direction-Set Decoration
  Black-and-White
    COME TO THE STABLE. Lyle Wheeler and Joseph C. Wright; Thomas Little and
    Paul S. Fox.
    THE HEIRESS. John Meehan and Harry Horner; Emile Kuri.
    MADAME BOVARY. Cedric Gibbons and Jack Martin Smith; Edwin B. Willis and
    Richard A. Pefferle.
  Color
    ADVENTURES OF DON JUAN. Edward Carrere; Lyle Reifsnider.
    LITTLE WOMEN. Cedric Gibbons and Paul Groesse; Edwin B. Willis and Jack D.
    Moore.
    SARABAND. Jim Morahan, William Kellner, and Michael Relph.
Best Sound Recording
    ONCE MORE, MY DARLING. Universal-International Sound Department.
    SANDS OF IWO JIMA. Republic Sound Department.
    12 O'CLOCK HIGH. 20th Century-Fox Sound Department.
Music Awards
  Best Song
    Baby, It's Cold Outside" from NEPTUNE'S DAUGHTER. Music and lyrics by Frank
    Loesser.
    "It's a Great Feeling" from IT'S A GREAT FEELING. Music by Jule Styne; lyrics
    by Sammy Cahn.
    "Lavender Blue" from SO DEAR TO MY HEART. Music by Eliot Daniel; lyrics by
    Larry Morey.
    "My Foolish Heart" from MY FOOLISH HEART. Music by Victor Young; lyrics by
    Ned Washington.
    "Through a Long and Sleepless Night" from COME TO THE STABLE. Music by
    Alfred Newman; lyrics by Mack Gordon.
  Best Scoring of a Dramatic or Comedy Picture
    BEYOND THE FOREST. Max Steiner.
    CHAMPION. Dimitri Tiomkin.
    THE HEIRESS. Aaron Copland.
  Best Scoring of a Musical Picture
    JOLSON SINGS AGAIN, Morris Stoloff and George Duning.
    LOOK FOR THE SILVER LINING. Ray Heindorf.
    ON THE TOWN. Roger Edens and Lennie Hayton.
Best Film Editing
    ALL THE KING'S MEN. Robert Parrish and Al Clark.
    BATTLEGROUND. John Dunning.
    CHAMPION. Harry Gerstad.
    SANDS OF IWO JIMA. Richard L. Van Enger.
    THE WINDOW. Frederic Knudtson.
Best Costume Design
  Black-and-White
    THE HEIRESS. Edith Head and Gile Steele.
    PRINCE OF FOXES. Vittorio Nino Novarese.
  Color
    ADVENTURES OF DON JUAN. Leah Rhodes, Travilla and Marjorie Best.
    MOTHER IS A FRESHMAN. Kay Nelson.
Best Special Effects
    MIGHTY JOE YOUNG, RKO.
    TULSA, EL.
Short Subjects
  Best Cartoon
    FOR SCENT-IMENTAL REASONS, WB. Produced by Edward Selzer (Looney
    Tunes).
    HATCH UP YOUR TROUBLES, MGM. Produced by Fred Quimby (Tom and Jerry
    Series).
    MAGIC FLUKE, COL. Produced by Stephen Bosustow (Fox and Crow Series).
    TOY TINKERS, RK0. Produced by Walt Disney.
  Best One-Reel Film
    AQUATIC HOUSE-PARTY, PAR. Produced by Jack Eaton (Grantland Rice
    Sportlights).
    ROLLER DERBY GIRL, PAR. Produced by Justin Herman (Pacemaker Series).
    SO YOU THINK YOU'RE NOT GUILTY, WB. Produced by Gordon Hollingshead
    (Joe McDoakes Series).
    SPILLS AND CHILLS, WB. Produced by Walton C. Ament.
    WATER TRIX, MGM. Produced by Pete Smith.
  Best Two-Reel Film
    BOY AND THE EAGLE, RKO. Produced by William Lasky.
    CHASE OF DEATH. Produced by Irving Allen.
    THE GRASS IS ALWAYS GREENER, WB. Produced by Gordon Hollingshead.
    SNOW CARNIVAL, WB. Produced by Gordon Hollingshead.
    VAN GOGH. Produced by Gaston Diehl and Robert Haessens.
Documentary
  Best Short Subject Documentary
    A CHANCE TO LIVE, March of Time, FOX. Produced by Richard de Rochemont.
    1848, A.F. Films, Inc. Produced by French Cinema General Cooperative.
    THE RISING TIDE, National Film Board of Canada, Produced by St. Francis-Xavier
    University.
    SO MUCH FOR SO LITTLE, WB. Produced by Edward Selzer.
  Best Feature Documentary
    DAYBREAK IN UDI, British Information Services. Produced by Crown Film Unit.
    KENJI COMES HOME, A Protestant Film Commission Prod. Produced by Paul F.
    Heard.
Irving G. Thalberg Award
    None awarded.
Special Awards

THE BICYCLE THIEF (Ital.)—voted by the Academy Board of Governors as the most outstanding foreign language film released in the United States during 1949.

Bobby Driscoll, as the outstanding juvenile actor of 1949.

Fred Astaire for his unique artistry and his contributions to the technique of musical pictures.

Cecil B. DeMille, distinguished motion picture pioneer, for thirty-seven years of brilliant showmanship.

Jean Hersholt for distinguished service to the motion-picture industry.

Scientific or Technical
Class I
Eastman Kodak Co. for the development and introduction of an improved safety base motion picture film.
Class III
Loren L. Ryder, Bruce H. Denney, Robert Carr and the Paramount Studio Sound Department for the development and application of the supersonic playback and public address system.

M.B. Paul for the first successful large-area seamless translucent backgrounds.

Herbert Britt for the development and application of formulas and equipment producing artificial snow and ice for dressing motion-picture sets.

Andre Coutant and Jacques Mathot for the design of the Eclair Camerette.

Charles R. Daily, Steve Csillag and the Paramount Studio Engineering, Editorial and Music Departments for a new precision method of computing variable tempo-click tracks.

International Projector Corp. for a simplified and self-adjusting take-up device for projection machines.

Alexander Velcoff for the application to production of the infrared photographic evaluator.

1950

Best Picture
ALL ABOUT EVE, FOX. Produced by Darryl F. Zanuck.
BORN YESTERDAY, COL. Produced by S. Sylvan Simon.
FATHER OF THE BRIDE, MGM. Produced by Pandro S. Berman.
KING SOLOMON'S MINES, MGM. Produced by Sam Zimbalist.
SUNSET BOULEVARD, PAR. Produced by Charles Brackett.

Best Actor
Louis Calhern for THE MAGNIFICENT YANKEE.
Jose Ferrer for CYRANO DE BERGERAC.
William Holden for SUNSET BOULEVARD.
James Stewart for HARVEY.
Spencer Tracy for FATHER OF THE BRIDE.

Best Actress
Anne Baxter for ALL ABOUT EVE.
Bette Davis for ALL ABOUT EVE.
Judy Holliday for BORN YESTERDAY.
Eleanor Parker for CAGED.
Gloria Swanson for SUNSET BOULEVARD.

Best Supporting Actor
Jeff Chandler for BROKEN ARROW.
Edmund Gwenn for MISTER 880.
Sam Jaffe for THE ASPHALT JUNGLE.
George Sanders for ALL ABOUT EVE.
Erich von Stroheim for SUNSET BOULEVARD.

Best Supporting Actress
Hope Emerson for CAGED.
Celeste Holm for ALL ABOUT EVE.
Josephine Hull for HARVEY.
Nancy Olson for SUNSET BOULEVARD.
Thelma Ritter for ALL ABOUT EVE.

Best Direction
George Cukor for BORN YESTERDAY.
John Huston for THE ASPHALT JUNGLE.
Joseph L. Mankiewicz for ALL ABOUT EVE.
Carol Reed for THE THIRD MAN.
Billy Wilder for SUNSET BOULEVARD.

Writing Awards
Best Motion Picture Story
BITTER RICE, by Giuseppe De Santis and Carlo Lizzani.
THE GUNFIGHTER, by William Bowers and Andre de Toth.
MYSTERY STREET, by Leonard Spigelgass.
PANIC IN THE STREETS, by Edna Anhalt and Edward Anhalt.
WHEN WILLIE COMES MARCHING HOME, by Sy Gomberg.

Best Screenplay
ALL ABOUT EVE, by Joseph L. Mankiewicz.
THE ASPHALT JUNGLE, by Ben Maddow and John Huston.
BORN YESTERDAY, by Albert Mannheimer.
BROKEN ARROW, by Michael Blankfort.
FATHER OF THE BRIDE, by Frances Goodrich and Albert Hackett.

Best Story and Screenplay
ADAM'S RIB, by Ruth Gordon and Garson Kanin.
CAGED, by Virginia Kellogg and Bernard C. Schoenfeld.
THE MEN, by Carl Foreman.
NO WAY OUT, by Joseph L. Mankiewicz and Lesser Samuels.
SUNSET BOULEVARD, by Charles Brackett, Billy Wilder and D.M. Marshman, Jr.

Best Cinematography
Black-and-White
ALL ABOUT EVE. Milton Krasner.
THE ASPHALT JUNGLE. Harold Rosson.
THE FURIES. Victor Milner.
SUNSET BOULEVARD. John F. Seitz.
THE THIRD MAN. Robert Krasker.
Color
ANNIE GET YOUR GUN. Charles Rosher.
BROKEN ARROW. Ernest Palmer.
THE FLAME AND THE ARROW. Ernest Haller.
KING SOLOMON'S MINES. Robert Surtees.
SAMSON AND DELILAH. George Barnes.

Best Art Direction—Set Decoration
Black-and-White
ALL ABOUT EVE. Lyle Wheeler and George Davis; Thomas Little and Walter M.

Scott.
THE RED DANUBE. Cedric Gibbons and Hans Peters; Edwin B. Willis and Hugh Hunt.
SUNSET BOULEVARD. Hans Dreier and John Meehan; Sam Comer and Ray Moyer.
Color
ANNIE GET YOUR GUN. Cedric Gibbons and Paul Groesse; Edwin B. Willis and Richard A. Pefferle.
DESTINATION MOON. Ernst Fegte; George Sawley.
SAMSON AND DELILAH. Hans Dreier and Walter Tyler; Sam Comer and Ray Moyer.

Best Sound Recording
ALL ABOUT EVE. 20th Century-Fox Sound Department.
CINDERELLA. Disney Sound Department.
LOUISA. Universal-International Sound Deartment.
OUR VERY OWN. Goldwyn Sound Department.
TRIO. Paramount.

Music Awards
Best Song
"Be My Love" from THE TOAST OF NEW ORLEANS. Music by Nicholas Brodszky; lyrics by Sammy Cahn.
"Bibbidy-Bobbidi-Boo" from CINDERELLA. Music and lyrics by Mack David, Al Hoffman, and Jerry Livingston.
Mona Lisa from CAPTAIN CAREY. Music and lyrics by Ray Evans and Jay Livingston.
"Mule Train" from SWINGING GUNS. Music and lyrics by Fred Glickman, Hy Heath, and Johnny Lange.
"Wilhelmina" from WABASH AVENUE. Music by Josef Myrow; lyrics by Mack Gordon.

Best Scoring of a Dramatic or Comedy Picture
ALL ABOUT EVE. Alfred Newman.
THE FLAME AND THE ARROW. Max Steiner.
NO SAD SONGS FOR ME. George Duning.
SAMSON AND DELILAH. Victor Young.
SUNSET BOULEVARD. Franz Waxman.

Best Scoring of a Musical Picture
ANNIE GET YOUR GUN. Adolph Deutsch and Roger Edens.
CINDERELLA. Oliver Wallace and Paul J. Smith.
I'LL GET BY. Lionel Newman.
THREE LITTLE WORDS. Andre Previn.
THE WEST POINT STORY. Ray Heindorf.

Best Film Editing
ALL ABOUT EVE. Barbara McLean.
ANNIE GET YOUR GUN. James E. Newcom.
KING SOLOMON'S MINES. Ralph E. Winters and Conrad A. Nervig.
SUNSET BOULEVARD. Arthur Schmidt and Doane Harrison.
THE THIRD MAN. Oswald Hafenrichter.

Best Costume Design
Black-and-White
ALL ABOUT EVE. Edith Head and Charles LeMaire.
BORN YESTERDAY. Jean Louis.
THE MAGNIFICENT YANKEE. Walter Plunkett.
Color
THE BLACK ROSE. Michael Whittaker.
SAMSON AND DELILAH. Edith Head, Dorothy Jeakins, Elois Jenssen, Gile Steele and Gwen Wakeling.
THAT FORSYTE WOMAN. Walter Plunkett and Valles.

Best Special Effects
DESTINATION MOON, Eagle-Lion.
SAMSON AND DELILAH, DeMille. PAR.

Short Subjects
Best Cartoon
GERALD MCBOING-BOING, COL. Produced by Stephen Bosustow (Jolly Frolics Series).
JERRY'S COUSIN, MGM. Produced by Fred Quimby (Tom and Jerry Series).
TROUBLE INDEMNITY, COL. Produced by Stephen Bosustow (Mr. Magoo Series).

Best One-Reel Film
BLAZE BUSTERS, WB. Produced by Robert Youngson (Vitaphone Novelties).
GRANDAD OF RACES, WB. Produced by Gordon Hollingshead (Sports Parade).
WRONG WAY BUTCH, MGM. Produced by Pete Smith.

Best Two-Reel Film
GRANDMA MOSES. Produced by Falcon Films, Inc.
IN BEAVER VALLEY, RKO. Produced by Walt Disney (True-Life Adventures Series).
MY COUNTRY 'TIS OF THEE, WB. Produced by Gordon Hollingshead.

Documentary
Best Short Subject Documentary
THE FIGHT: SCIENCE AGAINST CANCER, National Film Board of Canada in cooperation with the Medical Film Institute of the Association of American Medical Colleges.
THE STAIRS, Film Documents, Inc.
WHY KOREA?, FOX-Movietone. Produced by Edmund Reek.

Best Feature Documentary
THE TITAN: STORY OF MICHELANGELO. Produced by Robert Snyder.
WITH THESE HANDS. Produced by Jack Arnold and Lee Goodman.

Irving G. Thalberg Memorial Award
Darryl F. Zanuck

Honorary Awards
George Murphy for his services in interpreting the film industry to the country at large.
Louis B. Mayer for distinguished service to the motion picture industry.
THE WALLS OF MALAPAGA—voted by the Board of Governors as the most outstanding foreign language film released in the United States in 1950.

Scientific or Technical
Class II
James B. Gordon and the 20th Century-Fox Studio Camera Department for the design and development of a multiple image film viewer.
John Paul Livadary, Floyd Campbell, L.W. Russell and the Columbia Studio Sound Department for the development of a multitrack magnetic re-recording system.
Loren L. Ryder and the Paramount Studio Sound Department for the first

studio-wide application of magnetic sound recording to motion picture production.

1951

Best Picture
AN AMERICAN IN PARIS, MGM. *Produced by Arthur Freed.*
DECISION BEFORE DAWN, FOX. Produced by Anatole Litvak and Frank McCarthy.
A PLACE IN THE SUN, PAR. Produced by George Stevens.
QUO VADIS, MGM. Produced by Sam Zimbalist.
A STREETCAR NAMED DESIRE, WB. Produced by Charles K. Feldman.

Best Actor
Humphrey Bogart for THE AFRICAN QUEEN.
Marlon Brando for A STREETCAR NAMED DESIRE.
Montgomery Clift for A PLACE IN THE SUN.
Arthur Kennedy for BRIGHT VICTORY.
Frederic March for DEATH OF A SALESMAN.

Best Actress
Katharine Hepburn for THE AFRICAN QUEEN.
Vivien Leigh for A STREETCAR NAMED DESIRE.
Eleanor Parker for DETECTIVE STORY.
Shelley Winters for A PLACE IN THE SUN.
Jane Wyman for THE BLUE VEIL.

Best Supporting Actor
Leo Genn for QUO VADIS.
Karl Malden for A STREETCAR NAMED DESIRE.
Kevin McCarthy for DEATH OF A SALESMAN.
Peter Ustinov for QUO VADIS.
Gig Young for COME FILL THE CUP.

Best Supporting Actress
Joan Blondell for THE BLUE VEIL.
Mildred Dunnock for DEATH OF A SALESMAN.
Lee Grant for DETECTIVE STORY.
Kim Hunter for A STREETCAR NAMED DESIRE.
Thelma Ritter for THE MATING SEASON.

Best Direction
John Huston for THE AFRICAN QUEEN.
Elia Kazan for A STREETCAR NAMED DESIRE.
Vincente Minnelli for AN AMERICAN IN PARIS.
George Stevens for A PLACE IN THE SUN.
William Wyler for DETECTIVE STORY.

Writing Awards
Best Motion Picture Story
THE BULLFIGHTER AND THE LADY, by Budd Boetticher and Ray Nazarro.
THE FROGMEN, by Oscar Millard.
HERE COMES THE GROOM, by Robert Riskin and Liam O'Brian.
SEVEN DAYS TO NOON, by Paul Dehn and James Bernard.
TERESA, by Alfred Hayes and Stewart Stern.

Best Screenplay
THE AFRICAN QUEEN, by James Agee and John Huston.
DETECTIVE STORY, by Philip Yordan and Robert Wyler.
LA RONDE, by Jacques Natanson and Max Ophuls.
A PLACE IN THE SUN, by Michael Wilson and Harry Brown.
A STREETCAR NAMED DESIRE, by Tennessee Williams.

Best Story and Screenplay
AN AMERICAN IN PARIS, by Alan Jay Lerner.
THE BIG CARNIVAL, by Billy Wilder, Lesser Samuels and Walter Newman.
DAVID AND BATHSHEBA, by Philip Dunne.
GO FOR BROKE!, by Robert Pirosh.
THE WELL, by Clarence Greene and Russell Rouse.

Best Cinematography
Black-and-White
DEATH OF A SALESMAN. Frank Planer.
THE FROGMEN. Norbert Brodine.
A PLACE IN THE SUN. William C. Mellor.
STRANGERS ON A TRAIN. Robert Burks.
A STREETCAR NAMED DESIRE. Harry Stradling.

Color
AN AMERICAN IN PARIS. Alfred Gilks and John Alton.
DAVID AND BATHSHEBA. Leon Shamroy.
QUO VADIS. Robert Surtees and William V. Skall.
SHOW BOAT. Charles Rosher.
WHEN WORLDS COLLIDE. John F. Seitz and W. Howard Greene.

Best Art Direction—Set Decoration
Black-and-White
FOURTEEN HOURS. Lyle Wheeler and Leland Fuller; Thomas Little and Fred J. Rode.
HOUSE ON TELEGRAPH HILL. Lyle Wheeler and John DeCuir; Thomas Little and Paul S. Fox.
LA RONDE. D'Eaubonne.
A STREETCAR NAMED DESIRE. Richard Day; George James Hopkins.
TOO YOUNG TO KISS. Cedric Gibbons and Paul Groesse; Edwin B. Willis and Jack D. Moore.

Color
AN AMERICAN IN PARIS. Cedric Gibbons and Preston Ames; Edwin B. Willis and Keogh Gleason.
DAVID AND BATHSHEBA. Lyle Wheeler and George Davis; Thomas Little and Paul S. Fox.
ON THE RIVIERA. Lyle Wheeler and Leland Fuller; Joseph C. Wright, Thomas Little and Walter M. Scott.
QUO VADIS. William A. Horning, Cedric Gibbons and Edward Carfagno; Hugh Hunt.
TALES OF HOFFMAN. Hein Heckroth.

Best Sound Recording
BRIGHT VICTORY. Leslie I. Carey, sound director.
THE GREAT CARUSO. Douglas Shearer, sound director.
I WANT YOU. Gordon Sawyer, sound director.
A STREETCAR NAMED DESIRE. Col. Nathan Levinson, sound director.
TWO TICKETS TO BROADWAY. John O. Aalberg, sound director.

Music Awards
Best Song
In the Cool, Cool, Cool of the Evening" from HERE COMES THE GROOM. Music by Hoagy Carmichael; lyrics by Johnny Mercer.
"A Kiss to Build a Dream On" from THE STRIP. Music and lyrics by Bert Kalmar, Harry Ruby and Oscar Hammerstein II.
"Never" from GOLDEN GIRL. Music by Lionel Newman; lyrics by Eliot Daniel.
"Too Late Now" from ROYAL WEDDING. Music by Burtin Lane; lyrics by Alan Jay Lerner.
"Wonder Why" from RICH, YOUNG AND PRETTY. Music by Nicholas Brodszky; lyrics by Sammy Cahn.

Best Scoring of a Dramatic or Comedy Picture
DAVID AND BATHSHEBA. Alfred Newman.
DEATH OF A SALESMAN. Alex North.
A PLACE IN THE SUN. Franz Waxman.
QUO VADIS. Miklos Rozsa.
A STREETCAR NAMED DESIRE. Alex North.

Best Scoring of a Musical Picture
ALICE IN WONDERLAND. Oliver Wallace.
AN AMERICAN IN PARIS. Johnny Green and Saul Chaplin.
THE GREAT CARUSO. Peter Herman Adler and Johnny Green.
ON THE RIVIERA. Alfred Newman.
SHOW BOAT. Adolph Deutsch and Conrad Salinger.

Best Film Editing
AN AMERICAN IN PARIS. Adrienne Fazan.
DECISION BEFORE DAWN. Dorothy Spencer.
A PLACE IN THE SUN. William Hornbeck.
QUO VADIS. Ralph E. Winters.
THE WELL. Chester Schaeffer.

Best Costume Design
Black-and-White
KIND LADY. Walter Plunkett and Gile Steele.
THE MODEL AND THE MARRIAGE BROKER. Charles LeMaire and Renie.
THE MUDLARK. Edward Stevenson and Margaret Furse.
A PLACE IN THE SUN. Edith Head.
A STREETCAR NAMED DESIRE. Lucinda Ballard.

Color
AN AMERICAN IN PARIS. Walter Plunkett and Irene Sharaff.
DAVID AND BATHSHEBA. Charles LeMaire and Edward Stevenson.
THE GREAT CARUSO. Helen Rose and Gile Steele.
QUO VADIS. Herschel McCoy.
TALES OF HOFFMAN. Hein Heckroth.

Best Special Effects.
WHEN WORLDS COLLIDE, Pal, PAR.

Short Subjects
Best Cartoon
LAMBERT, THE SHEEPISH LION, RKO. Produced by Walt Disney.
ROOTY TOOT TOOT, COL. Produced by Stephen Bosustow. (Jolly Frolics).
TWO MOUSEKETEERS, MGM. Produced by Fred Quimby (Tom and Jerry Series).

Best One Reel Film
RIDIN' THE RAILS, PAR. Produced by Jack Eaton (Sportlights).
THE STORY OF TIME. A Signal Films Production by Robert G. Leffingwell.
WORLD OF KIDS, WB. Produced by Robert Youngson (Vitaphone Novelties).

Best Two-Reel Film
BALZAC (Fr.). Produced by Les Films Du Compass.
DANGER UNDER THE SEA, UI. Produced by Tom Mead.
NATURE'S HALF ACRE, RKO. Produced by Walt Disney (True-Life Adventure Series).

Documentary
Best Short Subject Documentary
BENJY. Made by Fred Zinnemann with the cooperation of Paramount Pictures Corp. for the Los Angeles Orthopaedic Hospital.
ONE WHO CAME BACK, Owen Crump, producer. (Film sponsored by the Disabled American Veterans, in cooperation with the United States Department of Defense and the Association of Motion Picture Producers.)
THE SEEING EYE, WB. Produced by Gordon Hollingshead.

Best Feature Documentary
I WAS A COMMUNIST FOR THE F.B.I., WB. Produced by Bryan Foy.
KON-TIKI (Nor.), RKO. Produced by Olle Nordemar.

Irving G. Thalberg Memorial Award
Arthur Freed

Honorary Awards
Gene Kelly in appreciation of his versatilty as an actor, singer, director, and dancer, and specifically for his brilliant achievements in the art of choreography on film.
RASHOMON (Jap.)—voted by the Board of Governors as the most outstanding foreign language film released in the United States in 1951.

Scientific or Technical
Class II
Gordon Jennings, S.L. Stancliffe and the Paramount Studio Special Photographic and Engineering Departments for the design, construction and application of a servo-operated recording and repeating device.
Olin L. Dupy of MGM Studio for the design, construction and application of a motion picture reproducing system.
Radio Corporation of America, Victor Division, for pioneering direct positive recording with anticipatory noise reduction.

Class III
Richard M. Haff, Frank P. Herrnfeld, Garland C. Misener and the Ansco Film Division of General Aniline and Film Corp. for the development of the Ansco color scene tester.
Fred Ponedel, Ralph Ayres and George Brown of Warner Bros. Studio for an air-driven water motor to provide flow, wake and white water for marine sequences in motion pictures.
Glen Robinson and the MGM Studio Construction Department for the development of a new music wire and cable cutter.
Jack Gaylord and the MGM Studio Construction Department for the development of balsa falling snow.
Carlos Riva of MGM Studios for the development of an automatic magnetic film splicer.

1952
Best Picture
THE GREATEST SHOW ON EARTH, PAR. Produced by Cecil B. DeMille.

HIGH NOON, UA. Produced by Stanley Kramer.
IVANHOE, MGM. Produced by Pandro S. Berman.
MOULIN ROUGE, UA. Produced by John Huston.
THE QUIET MAN, REP. Produced by John Ford, and Merian C. Cooper.

Best Actor
Marlon Brando for VIVA ZAPATA!
Gary Cooper for HIGH NOON.
Kirk Douglas for THE BAD AND THE BEAUTIFUL.
Jose Ferrer for MOULIN ROUGE.
Alec Guinness for THE LAVENDER HILL MOB.

Best Actor
Shirley Booth for COME BACK, LITTLE SHEBA.
Joan Crawford for SUDDEN FEAR.
Bette Davis for THE STAR.
Julie Harris for THE MEMBER OF THE WEDDING.
Susan Hayward for WITH A SONG IN MY HEART.

Best Supporting Actor
Richard Burton for MY COUSIN RACHEL.
Arthur Hunnicutt for THE BIG SKY.
Victor McLaglen for THE QUIET MAN.
Jack Palance for SUDDEN FEAR.
Anthony Quinn for VIVA ZAPATA!

Best Supporting Actress
Gloria Grahame for THE BAD AND THE BEAUTIFUL.
Jean Hagen for SINGIN' IN THE RAIN.
Colette Marchand for MOULIN ROUGE.
Terry Moore for COME BACK, LITTLE SHEBA.
Thelma Ritter for WITH A SONG IN MY HEART.

Best Direction
Cecil B. DeMille for THE GREATEST SHOW ON EARTH.
John Ford for THE QUIET MAN.
John Huston for MOULIN ROUGE.
Joseph L. Mankiewicz for FIVE FINGERS.
Fred Zinnemann for HIGH NOON.

Writing Awards
Best Motion Picture Story
THE GREATEST SHOW ON EARTH, by Frederic M. Frank, Theodore St. John and Frank Cavett.
MY SON JOHN, by Leo McCarey.
THE NARROW MARGIN, by Martin Goldsmith and Jack Leonard.
THE PRIDE OF ST. LOUIS, by Guy Trosper.
THE SNIPER, by Edna Anhalt and Edward Anhalt.

Best Screenplay
THE BAD AND THE BEAUTIFUL, by Charles Schnee.
FIVE FINGERS, by Michael Wilson.
HIGH NOON, by Carl Foreman.
THE MAN IN THE WHITE SUIT, by Roger MacDougall, John Dighton, and Alexander Mackendrick.
THE QUIET MAN, by Frank S. Nugent.

Best Story and Screenplay
THE ATOMIC CITY, by Sydney Boehm.
BREAKING THE SOUND BARRIER, by Terence Rattigan.
THE LAVENDER HILL MOB, by T.E.B. Clarke.
PAT AND MIKE, by Ruth Gordon and Garson Kanin.
VIVA ZAPATA!, by John Steinbeck.

Best Cinematography
Black-and-White
THE BAD AND THE BEAUTIFUL. Robert Surtees.
THE BIG SKY. Russell Harlan.
MY COUSIN RACHEL. Joseph LaShelle.
NAVAJO. Virgil E. Miller.
SUDDEN FEAR. Charles B. Lang, Jr.
Color
HANS CHRISTIAN ANDERSEN. Harry Stradling.
IVANHOE. F.A. Young.
MILLION DOLLAR MERMAID. George J. Folsey.
THE QUIET MAN. Winton C. Hoch and Archie Stout.
THE SNOWS OF KILIMANJARO. Leon Shamroy.

Best Art Direction—Set Decoration
Black-and-White
THE BAD AND THE BEAUTIFUL. Cedric Gibbons and Edward Carfagno; Edwin B. Willis and Keogh Gleason.
CARRIE. Hal Pereira and Roland Anderson; Emile Kuri.
MY COUSIN RACHEL. Lyle Wheeler and John DeCuir; Walter M. Scott.
RASHOMON. Matsuyama H. Motsumoto.
VIVA ZAPATA! Lyle Wheeler and Leland Fuller; Thomas Little and Claude Carpenter.
Color
HANS CHRISTIAN ANDERSON. Richard Day and Clave; Howard Bristol.
THE MERRY WIDOW. Cedric Gibbons and Paul Groesse; Edwin B. Willis and Arthur Krams.
MOULIN ROUGE. Paul Sheriff; Marcel Vertes.
THE QUIET MAN. Frank Hotaling; John McCarthy, Jr., and Charles Thompson.
THE SNOWS OF KILIMANJARO. Lyle Wheeler and John Deucir; Thomas Little and Paul S. Fox.

Best Sound Recording
BREAKING THE SOUND BARRIER. London Film Sound Department.
HANS CHRISTIAN ANDERSEN. Goldwyn Sound Department; Gordon Sawyer, sound director.
THE PROMOTER. Pinewood Studios Sound Department.
THE QUIET MAN. Republic Sound Department; Daniel J. Bloomberg, sound director.
WITH A SONG IN MY HEART. 20th Century-Fox Sound Department; Thomas T. Moulton, sound director.

Music Awards
Best Song
"Am I in Love" from SON OF PALEFACE. Music and lyrics by Jack Brooks.
"Because You're Mine" from BECAUSE YOU'RE MINE. Music by Nicholas Brodszky; lyrics by Sammy Cahn.
High Noon (Do Not Forsake Me, Oh My Darlin')" from HIGH NOON. Music by Dimitri Tiomkin; lyrics by Ned Washington.

"Thumbelina" from HANS CHRISTIAN ANDERSEN. Music and lyrics by Frank Loesser.
"Zing a Little Zong" from JUST FOR YOU. Music by Harry Warren; lyrics by Leo Robin.

Best Scoring of a Dramatic or Comedy Picture
HIGH NOON. Dimitri Tiomkin.
IVANHOE. Miklos Rozsa.
THE MIRACLE OF OUR LADY OF FATIMA. Max Steiner.
THE THIEF. Herschel Burke Gilbert.
VIVA ZAPATA! Alex North.

Best Scoring of a Musical Picture
HANS CHRISTIAN ANDERSEN. Walter Scharf.
THE JAZZ SINGER. Ray Heindorf and Max Steiner.
THE MEDIUM. Gian-Carlo Menotti.
SINGIN' IN THE RAIN. Lennie Hayton.
WITH A SONG IN MY HEART. Alfred Newman.

Best Film Editing
COME BACK, LITTLE SHEBA. Warren Low.
FLAT TOP. William Austin.
THE GREATEST SHOW ON EARTH. Anne Bauchens.
HIGH NOON. Elmo Williams and Harry Gerstad.
MOULIN ROUGE. Ralph Kemplen.

Best Costume Design
Black-and-White
AFFAIR IN TRINIDAD. Jean Louis.
THE BAD AND THE BEAUTIFUL. Helen Rose.
CARRIE. Edith Head.
MY COUSIN RACHEL. Charles LeMaire and Dorothy Jeakins.
SUDDEN FEAR. Sheila O'Brien.
Color
THE GREATEST SHOW ON EARTH. Edith Head, Dorothy Jeakins, and Miles White.
HANS CHRISTIAN ANDERSEN. Clave, Mary Wills and Madame Karinska.
THE MERRY WIDOW. Helen Rose and Gile Steele.
MOULIN ROUGE. Marcel Vertes.
WITH A SONG IN MY HEART. Charles LeMaire.

Best Special Effects
PLYMOUTH ADVENTURE, MGM.

Short Subjects
Best Cartoon
JOHANN MOUSE, MGM. Produced by Fred Quimby (Tom and Jerry Series).
LITTLE JOHNNY JET, MGM. Produced by Fred Quimby.
MADELINE, COL. Produced by Stephen Bosustow (Jolly Frolics).
PINK AND BLUE BLUES, COL. Produced by Stephen Bosustow (Mister Magoo Series).
ROMANCE OF TRANSPORTATION (Can.), National Film Board of Canada. Produced by Tom Daly.

Best One-Reel Film
ATHLETES OF THE SADDLE, PAR. Produced by Jack Eaton (Sportlights).
DESERT KILLER, WB. Produced by Gordon Hollingshead (Sports Parade).
LIGHT IN THE WINDOW, FOX. Produced by Boris Vermont (Art Series).
NEIGHBOURS (Can.), National Film Board of Canada. Produced by Norman McLaren.
ROYAL SCOTLAND (Brit.), Crown Film Unit, British Information Services.

Best Two-Reel Film
BRIDGE OF TIME, London Film Prod., British Information Services.
DEVIL TAKE US, Theatre of Life Prod. Produced by Herbert Morgan.
THAR SHE BLOWS!, WB. Produced by Gordon Hollingshead.
WATER BIRDS, RKO. Produced by Walt Disney (True-Life Adventure Series).

Documentary
Best Short Subject Documentary
DEVIL TAKE US, Theatre of Life Prod. Produced by Herbert Morgan.
THE GARDEN SPIDER (EPEIRA DIADEMA) (Ital.), Cristallo Films, I.F.E. Releasing Corp. Produced by Alberto Ancilotto.
MAN ALIVE! UPA for the American Cancer Society. Produced by Stephen Bosustow.
NEIGHBOURS (Can.), National Film Board of Canada. Produced by Norman McLaren.

Best Feature Documentary
THE HOAXTERS, MGM. Produced by Dore Schary.
NAVAJO, Lippert Pictures, Inc. Produced by Hall Bartlett.
THE SEA AROUND US, RKO. Produced by Irwin Allen.

Irving G. Thalberg Memorial Award
Cecil B. DeMille.

Honorary Awards
George Alfred Mitchell for the design and development of the camera which bears his name and for his continued and dominant presence in the field of cinematography.
Joseph M. Schenck for long and distinguished service to the motion picture industry.
Merian C. Cooper for his many innovations and contributions to the art of motion pictures.
Harold Lloyd, master comedian and good citizen.
Bob Hope for his contribution to the laughter of the world, his service to the motion picture industry, and his devotion to the American premise.
FORBIDDEN GAMES (Fr.)—Best Foreign Language Film released in the United States in 1952.

Scientific or Technical
Class I
Eastman Kodak Co. for the introduction of Eastman color negative and Eastman color print film.
Ansco Division, General Aniline and Film Corp., for the introduction of Ansco color negative and Ansco color print film.
Class II
Technicolor Motion Picture Corp. for an improved method of color motion picture photography under incandescent light.
Class III
Projection, Still Photographic and Development Engineering Departments of MGM Studio for an improved method of projecting photographic backgrounds.
John G. Frayne and R.R. Scoville and Westrex Corp. for a method of measuring distortion in sound reproduction.
Photo Research Corp. for creating the Spectra color temperature meter.

Gustav Jirouch for the design of the Robot automatic film splicer.
Carlos Rivas of MGM Studio for the development of a sound reproducer for magnetic film.

1953
Best Picture
FROM HERE TO ETERNITY, COL. Produced by Buddy Adler.
JULIUS CAESAR, MGM. Produced by John Houseman.
THE ROBE, FOX. Produced by Frank Ross.
ROMAN HOLIDAY, PAR. Produced by William Wyler.
SHANE, PAR. Produced by George Stevens.
Best Actor
Marlon Brando for JULIUS CAESAR.
Richard Burton for THE ROBE.
Montgomery Clift for FROM HERE TO ETERNITY.
William Holden for STALAG 17.
Burt Lancaster for FROM HERE TO ETERNITY.
Best Actress
Leslie Caron for LILI.
Ava Gardner for MOGAMBO.
Audrey Hepburn for ROMAN HOLIDAY.
Deborah Kerr for FROM HERE TO ETERNITY.
Maggie McNamara for THE MOON IS BLUE.
Best Supporting Actor
Eddie Albert for ROMAN HOLIDAY.
Brandon de Wilde for SHANE.
Jack Palance for SHANE.
Frank Sinatra for FROM HERE TO ETERNITY.
Robert Strauss for STALAG 17.
Best Supporting Actress
Grace Kelly for MOGAMBO.
Geraldine Page for HONDO.
Marjorie Rambeau for TORCH SONG.
Donna Reed for FROM HERE TO ETERNITY.
Thelma Ritter for PICKUP ON SOUTH STREET.
Best Direction
George Stevens for SHANE.
Charles Walters for LILI.
Billy Wilder for STALAG 17.
William Wyler for ROMAN HOLIDAY.
Fred Zinnemann for FROM HERE TO ETERNITY.
Writing Awards
Best Motion Picture Story
ABOVE AND BEYOND, by Beirne Lay, Jr.
THE CAPTAIN'S PARADISE, by Alec Coppel.
LITTLE FUGITIVE, by Ray Ashley, Morris Engel and Ruth Orkin.
ROMAN HOLIDAY, by Ian McLellan Hunter. Best Screenplay
THE CRUEL SEA, by Eric Ambler.
FROM HERE TO ETERNITY, by Daniel Taradash.
LILI, by Helen Deutsch.
ROMAN HOLIDAY, by Ian McLellan Hunter and John Dighton.
SHANE, by A.B. Guthrie, Jr.
Best Story and Screenplay
THE BAND WAGON, by Betty Comden and Adolph Green.
THE DESERT RATS, by Richard Murphy.
THE NAKED SPUR, by Sam Rolfe and Harold Jack Bloom.
TAKE THE HIGH GROUND, by Millard Kaufman.
TITANIC, by Charles Brackett, Walter Reisch and Richard Breen.
Best Cinematography
Black-and-White
THE FOUR POSTER. Hal Mohr.
FROM HERE TO ETERNITY. Burnett Guffey.
JULIUS CAESAR. Joseph Ruttenberg.
MARTIN LUTHER. Joseph C. Brun.
ROMAN HOLIDAY. Frank Planer and Henry Alekan.
Color
ALL THE BROTHERS WERE VALIANT. George Folsey.
BENEATH THE 12 MILE REEF. Edward Cronjager.
LILI. Robert Planck.
THE ROBE. Leon Shamroy.
SHANE. Loyal Griggs.
Best Art Direction—Set Direction
Black-and-White
JULIUS CAESAR. Cedric Gibbons and Edward Carfagno; Edwin B. Willis and Hugh Hunt.
MARTIN LUTHER. Fritz Maurischat and Paul Markwitz.
THE PRESIDENT'S LADY. Lyle Wheeler and Leland Fuller; Paul S. Fox.
ROMAN HOLIDAY. Hal Pereira and Walter Tyler.
TITANIC. Lyle Wheeler and Maurice Ransford; Stuart Reiss.
Color
KNIGHTS OF THE ROUND TABLE. Alfred Junge and Hans Peters; John Jarvis.
LILI. Cedric Gibbons and Paul Groesse; Edwin B. Willis and Arthur Krams.
THE ROBE. Lyle Wheeler and George W. Davis; Walter M. Scott and Paul S. Fox.
THE STORY OF THREE LOVES. Cedric Gibbons, Preston Ames, Edward Carfagno and Gabriel Scognamillo; Edwin B. Willis, Keogh Gleason, Arthur Krams, and Jack D. Moore.
YOUNG BESS. Cedric Gibbons and Urie McCleary; Edwin B. Willis and Jack D. Moore.
Best Sound Recording
CALAMITY JANE. Warner Bros. Sound Department; William A. Mueller, sound director.
FROM HERE TO ETERNITY. Columbia Sound Department; John P. Livadary, sound director.
KNIGHTS OF THE ROUND TABLE. MGM Sound Department; A.W. Watkins, sound director.
MISSISSIPPI GAMBLER. Universal International Sound Department; Leslie I. Carey, sound director.
WAR OF THE WORLDS. Paramount Sound Department; Loren L. Ryder, sound director.
Music Awards

Best Song
"The Moon Is Blue" from FROM THE MOON IS BLUE. Music by Herschel Burke Gilbert; lyrics by Sylvia Fine.
"My Flaming Heart" from SMALL TOWN GIRL. Music by Nicholas Brodszky; lyrics by Leo Robin.
"Sadie Thompson's Song (Blue Pacific Blues)" from MISS SADIE THOMPSON. Music by Lester Lee; lyrics by Ned Washington.
Secret Love" from CALAMITY JANE. Music by Sammy Fain; lyrics by Paul Francis Webster.
"That's Amore" from THE CADDY. Music by Harry Warren; lyrics by Jack Brooks.
Best Scoring of a Dramatic or Comedy Picture
ABOVE AND BEYOND. Hugo Friedhofer.
FROM HERE TO ETERNITY. Morris Stoloff and George Duning.
JULIUS CAESAR. Miklos Rozsa.
LILI. Bronislau Kaper.
THIS IS CINERAMA. Louis Forbes.
Best Scoring of a Musical Picture
THE BAND WAGON. Adolph Deutsch.
CALAMITY JANE. Ray Heindorf.
CALL ME MADAM. Alfred Newman.
5,000 FINGERS OF DR. T. Frederick Hollander and Morris Stoloff.
KISS ME KATE. Andre Previn and Saul Chapin.
Best Film Editing
CRAZYLEGS. Irvine "Cotton" Warburton.
FROM HERE TO ETERNITY. William Lyon.
THE MOON IS BLUE. Otto Ludwig.
ROMAN HOLIDAY. Robert Swink.
WAR OF THE WORLDS. Everett Douglas.
Best Costume Design
Black-and-White
THE ACTRESS. Walter Plunkett.
DREAM WIFE. Helen Rose and Herschel McCoy.
FROM HERE TO ETERNITY. Jean Louis.
THE PRESIDENT'S LADY. Charles LeMaire and Renie.
ROMAN HOLIDAY. Edith Head.
Color
THE BAND WAGON. Mary Ann Nyberg.
CALL ME MADAM. Irene Sharaff.
HOW TO MARRY A MILLIONAIRE. Charles LeMaire and Travilla.
THE ROBE. Charles LeMaire and Emile Santiago.
YOUNG BESS. Walter Plunkett.
Best Special Effects
WAR OF THE WORLDS, Pal.
Short Subjects
Best Cartoon
CHRISTOPHER CRUMPET, COL. Produced by Stephen Bosustow (Jolly Frolics).
FROM A TO Z-Z-Z-Z, WB. Produced by Edward Selzer (Looney Tunes).
RUGGED BEAR, RKO. Produced by Walt Disney (Donald Duck).
THE TELL-TALE HEART, COL. Produced by Stephen Bosustow.
TOOT, WHISTLE, PLUNK AND BOOM, Buena Vista. Produced by Walt Disney.
Best One-Reel Film
CHRIST AMONG THE PRIMITIVES (Ital.), IFE Releasing Corp. Produced by Vincenzo Lucci-Chiarissi.
HERRING HUNT, National Film Board of Canada (Canada Carries On Series).
JOY OF LIVING, FOX. Produced by Boris Vermont (Art Film Series).
THE MERRY WIVES OF WINDSOR OVERTURE, MGM. Produced by Johnny Green (Overture Series).
WEE WATER WONDERS, PAR. Produced by Jack Eaton (Grantland Rice Sportlights Series).
Best Two-Reel Film
BEAR COUNTRY, RKO. Produced by Walt Disney (True-Life Adventure Series).
BEN AND ME, Buena Vista. Produced by Walt Disney.
RETURN TO GLENNASCAUL, Dublin Gate Theatre Prod.
VESUVIUS EXPRESS, FOX. Produced by Otto Lang.
WINTER PARADISE, WB. Produced by Cedric Francis.
Documentary
Best Short Subject Documentary
THE ALASKAN ESKIMO, RKO. Produced by Walt Disney.
THE LIVING CITY, Encyclopaedia Britannica Films, Inc. Produced by John Barnes.
OPERATION BLUE JAY, U.S. Army Signal Corps.
THEY PLANTED A STONE, British Information Services. Produced by James Carr.
THE WORD, FOX. Produced by John Healy and John Adams.
Best Feature Documentary
THE CONQUEST OF EVEREST (Brit.), Countryman Films and Group 3 Ltd. Produced by John Taylor, Leon Clore, and Grahame Tharp.
THE LIVING DESERT, Buena Vista. Produced by Walt Disney.
A QUEEN IS CROWNED (Brit.), RANK. Produced by Castleton Knight.
Irving G. Thalberg Memorial Award
George Stevens.
Honorary Awards
Pete Smith for his witty and pungent observations on the American scene in his series of "Pete Smith Specialties."
20th Century-Fox Film Corporation in recognition of their imagination, showmanship and foresight in introducing the revolutionary process known as CinemaScope.
Joseph I. Breen for his conscientious, open-minded and dignified management of the Motion Picture Production Code.
Bell and Howell Company for their pioneering and basic achievements in the advancement of the motion picture industry.
Scientific or Technical
Class I
Professor Henri Chretien and Earl Sponable, Sol Halprin, Lorin Grignon, Herbert Bragg and Carl Faulkner of 20th Century-Fox Studios for creating, developing and engineering the equipment, processes and techniques known as CinemaScope.
Fred Waller for designing and developing the multiple photographic and projection systems which culminated in Cinerama.
Class II
Reeves Soundcraft Corp. for their development of a process of applying stripes of magnetic oxide to motion picture film for sound recording and reproduction.
Class III
Westrex Corp. for the design and construction of a new film editing machine.

1954 Best Picture

THE CAINE MUTINY, COL. Produced by Stanley Kramer.
THE COUNTRY GIRL, PAR. Produced by William Perlberg.
ON THE WATERFRONT, COL. Produced by Sam Spiegel.
SEVEN BRIDES FOR SEVEN BROTHERS, MGM. Produced by Jack Cummings.
THREE COINS IN THE FOUNTAIN, FOX. Produced by Sol C. Siegel.

Best Actor

Humphrey Bogart for THE CAINE MUTINY.
Marlon Brando for ON THE WATERFRONT.
Bing Crosby for THE COUNTRY GIRL.
James Mason for A STAR IS BORN.
Dan O'Herlihy for ADVENTURES OF ROBINSON CRUSOE.

Best Actress

Dorothy Dandridge for CARMEN JONES.
Judy Garland for A STAR IS BORN.
Grace Kelly for THE COUNTRY GIRL.
Jane Wyman for MAGNIFICENT OBSESSION.

Best Supporting Actor

Lee J. Cobb for ON THE WATERFRONT.
Karl Malden for ON THE WATERFRONT.
Edmond O'Brien for THE BAREFOOT CONTESSA.
Rod Steiger for ON THE WATERFRONT.
Tom Tully for THE CAINE MUTINY.

Best Supporting Actress

Nina Foch for EXECUTIVE SUITE.
Katy Jurado for BROKEN LANCE.
Eva Marie Saint for ON THE WATERFRONT.
Jan Sterling for THE HIGH AND THE MIGHTY.
Claire Trevor for THE HIGH AND THE MIGHTY.

Best Direction

Alfred Hitchcock for REAR WINDOW.
Elia Kazan for ON THE WATERFRONT.
George Seaton for THE COUNTRY GIRL.
William Wellman for THE HIGH AND THE MIGHTY.
Billy Wilder for SABRINA.

Writing Awards

Best Motion Picture Story
BREAD, LOVE AND DREAMS (Ital.), by Ettore Margadonna.
BROKEN LANCE, by Philip Yordan.
FORBIDDEN GAMES, by Francois Boyer.
NIGHT PEOPLE, by Jed Harris and Tom Reed.
THERE'S NO BUSINESS LIKE SHOW BUSINESS, by Lamar Trotti.

Best Screenplay
THE CAINE MUTINY, by Stanley Roberts.
THE COUNTRY GIRL, by George Seaton.
REAR WINDOW, by John Michael Hayes.
SABRINA, by Billy Wilder, Samuel Taylor, and Ernest Lehman.
SEVEN BRIDES FOR SEVEN BROTHERS, by Albert Hackett, Frances Goodrich and Dorothy Kingsley.

Best Story and Screenplay
THE BAREFOOT CONTESSA, by Joseph Mankiewicz.
GENEVIEVE, by William Rose.
THE GLENN MILLER STORY, by Valentine Davies and Oscar Brodney.
KNOCK ON WOOD, by Norman Panama and Melvin Frank.
ON THE WATERFRONT, by Budd Schulberg.

Best Cinematography

Black-and-White
THE COUNTRY GIRL. John F. Warren
EXECUTIVE SUITE. George Folsey.
ON THE WATERFRONT. Boris Kaufman.
ROGUE COP. John Seitz.
SABRINA. Charles Lang, Jr.

Color
THE EGYPTIAN. Leon Shamroy.
REAR WINDOW. Robert Burks.
SEVEN BRIDES FOR SEVEN BROTHERS. George Folsey.
THE SILVER CHALICE. William V. Skall.
THREE COINS IN THE FOUNTAIN. Milton Krasner.

Best Art Direction—Set Decoration

Black-and-White
THE COUNTRY GIRL. Hal Pereira and Roland Anderson; Sam Comer and Grace Gregory.
EXECUTIVE SUITE. Cedric Gibbons and Edward Carfagno; Edwin B. Willis and Emile Kuri.
LE PLAISIR. Max Ophuls.
ON THE WATERFRONT. Richard Day.
SABRINA. Hal Pereira and Walter Tyler; Sam Comer and Ray Moyer.

Color
BRIGADOON. Cedric Gibbons and Preston Ames; Edwin B. Willis and Keogh Gleason.
DESIREE. Lyle Wheeler and Leland Fuller; Walter M. Scott and Paul S. Fox.
RED GARTERS. Hal Pereira and Roland Anderson; Sam Comer and Ray Moyer.
A STAR IS BORN. Malcolm Bert, Gene Allen and Irene Sharaff; George James Hopkins.
20,000 LEAGUES UNDER THE SEA. John Meehan; Emile Kuri.

Best Sound Recording

BRIGADOON. Wesley C. Miller, sound director.
THE CAINE MUTINY. John P. Livadary, sound director.
THE GLENN MILLER STORY. Leslie I. Carey, sound director.
REAR WINDOW. Loren L Ryder, sound director.
SUSAN SLEPT HERE. John O Aalberg, sound director.

Music Awards

Best Song
"Count Your Blessings Instead of Sheep" from WHITE CHRISTMAS. Music and lyrics by Irving Berlin.
"The High and the Mighty" from THE HIGH AND THE MIGHTY. Music by Dimitri Tiomkin; lyrics by Ned Washington.
"Hold My Hand" from SUSAN SLEPT HERE. Music and lyrics by Jack Lawrence and Richard Myers.
"The Man That Got Away" from A STAR IS BORN. Music by Harold Arlen; lyrics

by Ira Gershwin.
Three Coins in the Fountain" from THREE COINS IN THE FOUNTAIN. Music by Jule Styne; lyrics by Sammy Cahn.

Best Scoring of a Dramatic or Comedy Picture
THE CAINE MUTUINY. Max Steiner.
GENEVIEVE. Muir Mathieson.
THE HIGH AND THE MIGHTY. Dimitri Tiomkin.
ON THE WATERFRONT. Leonard Bernstein.
THE SILVER CHALICE. Franz Waxman.

Best Scoring of a Musical Picture
CARMEN JONES. Herschel Burke Gilbert.
THE GLENN MILLER STORY. Joseph Gershenson and Henry Mancini.
SEVEN BRIDES FOR SEVEN BROTHERS. Adolph Deutsch and Saul Chaplin.
A STAR IS BORN. Ray Heindorf.
THERE'S NO BUSINESS LIKE SHOW BUSINESS. Alfred Newman and Lionel Newman.

Best Film Editing

THE CAINE MUTINY. William A. Lyon and Henry Batista.
THE HIGH AND THE MIGHTY. Ralph Dawson.
ON THE WATERFRONT. Gene Milford.
SEVEN BRIDES FOR SEVEN BROTHERS. Ralph E. Winters.
20,000 LEAGUES UNDER THE SEA. Elmo Williams.

Best Costume Design

Black-and-White
THE EARRINGS OF MADAME DE.... Georges Annenkov and Rosine Delamare.
EXECUTIVE SUITE. Helen Rose.
INDISCRETION OF AN AMERICAN WIFE. Christian Dior.
IT SHOULD HAPPEN TO YOU. Jean Louis.
SABRINA. Edith Head.

Color
BRIGADOON. Irene Sharaff.
DESIREE. Charles LeMaire and Rene Hubert.
GATE OF HELL. Sanzo Wada.
A STAR IS BORN. Jean Louis, Mary Ann Nyberg and Irene Sharaff.
THERE'S NO BUSINESS LIKE SHOW BUSINESS. Charles LeMaire, Travilla and Miles White.

Best Special Effects

HELL AND HIGH WATER. Fox.
THEM! WB.
20,000 LEAGUES UNDER THE SEA. Disney.

Short Subjects

Best Cartoon
CRAZY MIXED UP PUP, U-I. Produced by Walter Lantz.
PIGS IS PIGS, RKO. Produced by Walt Disney.
SANDY CLAWS, WB. Produced by Edward Selzer.
TOUCHE, PUSSY CAT, MGM. Produced by Fred Quimby.
WHEN MAGOO FLEW, UPA. Produced by Stephen Bosustow.

Best One-Reel Film
THE FIRST PIANO QUARTETTE, FOX. Produced by Otto Lang.
THE STRAUSS FANTASY, MGM. Produced by Johnny Green.
THIS MECHANICAL AGE, WB. Produced by Robert Youngson.

Best Two-Reel Film
BEAUTY AND THE BULL, WB. Produced by Cedric Francis.
JET CARRIER, FOX. Produced by Otto Lang.
SIAM, Buena Vista. Produced by Walt Disney.
A TIME OUT OF WAR. Produced by Denis and Terry Sanders.

Documentary

Best Short Subject Documentary
JET CARRIER, FOX. Produced by Otto Lang.
REMBRANDT: A SELF PORTRAIT, Distributors Corp. of America. Produced by Morrie Roizman.
THURSDAY'S CHILDREN. Produced by World Wide Pictures and Morse Films.

Best Feature Documentary
THE STRATFORD ADVENTURE, National Film Board of Canada. Produced by Guy Glover.
THE VANISHING PRAIRIE, Buena Vista. Produced by Walt Disney.

Irving G. Thalberg Memorial Award

None awarded.

Honorary Awards

Bausch & Lomb Optical Company for their contributions to the advancement of the motion picture industry.
Kemp R. Niver for the development of the Renovare Process which has made possible the restoration of the Library of Congress Paper Film Collection.
Greta Garbo for her unforgettable screen performances.
Danny Kaye for his unique talents, his service to the Academy, the motion picture industry, and the American people.
Jon Whiteley for his outstanding juvenile performance in THE LITTLE KIDNAPPERS.
Vincent Winter for his outstanding performance in THE LITTLE KIDNAPPERS.
GATE OF HELL - Best Foreign Language Film released in the United States in 1954.

Scientific or Technical

Class I
Paramount Pictures, Inc., Loren L. Ryder, John R. Bishop and all the members of the technical and engineering staff for developing a method of producing and exhibiting motion pictures known as VistaVision.

Class III
David S. Horsley and the Universal-International Studio Special Photographic Department for a portable remote control device for process projectors.
Karl Freund and Frank Crandell of Photo Research Corp. for the design and development of a direct reading brightness meter.
Wesley C. Miller, J.W. Stafford, K.M. Frierson and the MGM Studio Sound Department for an electronic sound printing comparison device.
John P. Livadary, Lloyd Russell and the Columbia Studio Sound Department for an improved limiting amplifier as applied to sound level comparison devices.
Roland Miller and Max Goeppinger of the Magnascope Corp. for the design and development of a cathode ray magnetic sound track viewer.
Carlos Rivas, G.M. Sprague and the MGM Studio Sound Department for the design of a magnetic sound editing machine.
Fred Wilson of the Samuel Goldwyn Studio Sound Department for the design of a variable multi-band equalizer.

P.C. Young of the MGM Studio Projection Department for the practical application of a variable focal length attachment to motion picture projector lenses.

Fred Knoth and Orien Ernest of the Universal-International Studio Technical Department for the development of a hand portable, electric, dry oil-fog machine.

1955
Best Picture
LOVE IS A MANY-SPLENDORED THING, FOX. Produced by Buddy Adler.
MARTY, UA. Produced by Harold Hecht.
MISTER ROBERTS, WB. Produced by Leland Hayward.
PICNIC, COL. Produced by Fred Kohlmar.
THE ROSE TATTOO, PAR. Produced by Hal Wallis.

Best Actor
Ernest Borgnine for MARTY.
James Cagney for LOVE ME OR LEAVE ME.
James Dean for EAST OF EDEN.
Frank Sinatra for THE MAN WITH THE GOLDEN ARM.
Spencer Tracy for BAD DAY AT BLACK ROCK.

Best Actress
Susan Hayward for I'LL CRY TOMORROW.
Katharine Hepburn for SUMMERTIME.
Jennifer Jones for LOVE IS A MANY-SPLENDORED THING.
Anna Magnani for THE ROSE TATTOO.
Eleanor Parker for INTERRUPTED MELODY.

Best Supporting Actor
Arthur Kennedy for TRIAL.
Jack Lemmon for MISTER ROBERTS.
Joe Mantell for MARTY.
Sal Mineo for REBEL WITHOUT A CAUSE.
Arthur O'Connell for PICNIC.

Best Supporting Actress
Betsy Blair for MARTY.
Peggy Lee for PETE KELLY'S BLUES.
Marisa Pavan for THE ROSE TATTOO.
Jo Van Fleet for EAST OF EDEN.
Natalie Wood for REBEL WITHOUT A CAUSE.

Best Direction
Elia Kazan for EAST OF EDEN.
David Lean for SUMMERTIME.
Joshua Logan for PICNIC.
Delbert Mann for MARTY.
John Sturges for BAD DAY AT BLACK ROCK.

Writing Awards
Best Motion Picture Story
LOVE ME OR LEAVE ME, by Daniel Fuchs.
THE PRIVATE WAR OF MAJOR BENSON, by Joe Connelly and Bob Mosher.
REBEL WITHOUT A CAUSE, by Nicholas Ray.
THE SHEEP HAS FIVE LEGS, by Jean Marsan, Henry Troyat, Jacques Perret, Henri Verneuil, and Raoul Ploquin.
STRATEGIC AIR COMMAND, by Beirne Lay, Jr.

Best Screenplay
BAD DAY AT BLACK ROCK, by Millard Kaufman.
BLACKBOARD JUNGLE, by Richard Brooks.
EAST OF EDEN, by Paul Osborn.
LOVE ME OR LEAVE ME, by Daniel Fuchs and Isobel Lennart.
MARTY, by Paddy Chayefsky.

Best Story and Screenplay
THE COURT-MARTIAL OF BILLY MITCHELL, by Milton Sperling and Emmet Lavery.
INTERRUPTED MELODY, by William Ludwig and Sonya Levien.
IT'S ALWAYS FAIR WEATHER, by Betty Comden and Adolph Green.
MR. HULOT'S HOLIDAY, by Jacques Tati and Henri Marquet.
THE SEVEN LITTLE FOYS, by Melville Shavelson and Jack Rose.

Best Cinematography
Black-and-White
BLACKBOARD JUNGLE. Russell Harlan.
I'LL CRY TOMORROW. Arthur E. Arling.
MARTY. Joseph LaShelle.
QUEEN BEE. Charles Lang.
THE ROSE TATTOO. James Wong Howe.
Color
GUYS AND DOLLS. Harry Stradling.
LOVE IS A MANY-SPLENDORED THING. Leon Shamroy.
A MAN CALLED PETER. Harold Lipstein.
OKLAHOMA! Robert Surtees.
TO CATCH A THIEF. Robert Burks.

Best Art Direction—Set Decoration
Black-and-White
BLACKBOARD JUNGLE. Cedric Gibbons and Randall Duell; Edwin B. Willis and Henry Grace.
I'LL CRY TOMORROW. Cedric Gibbons and Malcolm Brown; Edwin B. Willis and Hugh B. Hunt.
THE MAN WITH THE GOLDEN ARM. Joseph C. Wright; Darrell Silvera.
MARTY. Edward S. Haworth and Walter Simonds; Robert Priestly.
THE ROSE TATTOO. Hal Pereira and Tambi Larsen; Sam Comer and Arthur Krams.
Color
DADDY LONG LEGS. Lyle Wheeler and John DeCuir; Walter M. Scott and Paul S. Fox.
GUYS AND DOLLS. Oliver Smith and Joseph C. Wright; Howard Bristol.
LOVE IS A MANY-SPLENDORED THING. Lyle Wheeler and George W. Davis; Walter M. Scott and Jack Stubbs.
PICNIC. William Flannery and Jo Mielziner; Robert Priestley.
TO CATCH A THIEF. Hal Pereira and Joseph McMillan Johnson; Sam Comer and Arthur Krams.

Best Sound Recording
LOVE IS A MANY SPLENDORED THING. Carl W. Faulkner, sound director.
LOVE ME OR LEAVE ME. Wesley C. Miller, sound director.
MISTER ROBERTS. William A. Mueller, sound director.
NOT AS A STRANGER. Watson Jones, sound director.
OKLAHOMA! Fred Hynes, sound director.

Music Awards
Best Song
"I'll Never Stop Loving You" from LOVE ME OR LEAVE ME. Music by Nicholas Brodszky; lyrics by Sammy Cahn.
Love Is a Many-Splendored Thing" from LOVE IS A MANY-SPLENDORED THING. Music by Sammy Fain; lyrics by Paul Francis Webster.
"Something's Gotta Give" from DADDY LONG LEGS. Music and lyrics by Johnny Mercer.
"(Love Is) The Tender Trap" from THE TENDER TRAP. Music by James Van Heusen; lyrics by Sammy Cahn.
"Unchained Melody" from UNCHAINED. Music by Alex North; lyrics by Hy Zaret.

Best Scoring of a Dramatic or Comedy Picture
BATTLE CRY. Max Steiner.
LOVE IS A MANY-SPLENDORED THING. Alfred Newman.
THE MAN WITH THE GOLDEN ARM. Elmer Bernstein.
PICNIC. George Duning.
THE ROSE TATTOO. Alex North.

Best Scoring of a Musical Picture
DADDY LONG LEGS. Alfred Newman.
GUYS AND DOLLS. Jay Blackton and Cyril J. Mockridge.
IT'S ALWAYS FAIR WEATHER. Andre Previn.
LOVE ME OR LEAVE ME. Percy Faith and George Stoll.
OKLAHOMA! Robert Russell Bennett, Jay Blackton, and Adolph Deutsch.

Best Film Editing
BLACKBOARD JUNGLE. Ferris Webster.
THE BRIDGES AT TOKO-RI. Alma Macrorie.
OKLAHOMA! Gene Ruggiero and George Boemler.
PICNIC. Charles Nelson and William A. Lyon.
THE ROSE TATTOO. Warren Low.

Best Costume Design
Black-and-White
I'LL CRY TOMORROW. Helen Rose.
THE PICKWICK PAPERS. Beatrice Dawson.
QUEEN BEE. Jean Louis.
THE ROSE TATTOO. Edith Head.
UGETSU (Jap.). Tadao-to Kainoscho.
Color
GUYS AND DOLLS. Irene Sharaff.
INTERRUPTED MELODY. Helen Rose.
LOVE IS A MANY-SPLENDORED THING. Charles LeMaire.
TO CATCH A THIEF. Edith Head.
THE VIRGIN QUEEN. Charles LeMaire and Mary Wills.

Best Special Effects
THE BRIDGES AT TOKO-RI, PAR.
THE DAM BUSTERS, AB-WB.
THE RAINS OF RANCHIPUR, FOX.

Short Subjects
Best Cartoon
GOOD WILL TO MEN, MGM. Produced by Fred Quimby, William Hanna, and Joseph Barbera.
THE LEGEND OF ROCK-A-BYE POINT. Produced by Walter Lantz.
NO HUNTING, RKO. Produced by Walt Disney.
SPEEDY GONZALES, WB. Produced By Edward Selzer.

Best One-Reel Film
GADGETS GALORE, WB. Produced by Robert Youngson.
SURVIVAL CITY, FOX. Produced by Edmund Reek.
3RD AVE, Ardee Films. Produced by Carson Davidson.
THREE KISSES, PAR. Produced by Justin Herman.

Best Two-Reel Film
THE BATTLE OF GETTYSBURG, MGM. Produced by Dore Schary.
THE FACE OF LINCOLN, University of Southern California, Cavalcade Pictures. Produced by Wilbur T. Blume.
ON THE TWELFTH DAY..., Go Pictures, George Brest & Assoc. Produced by George K. Arthur.

Documentary
Best Short Subject Documentary
THE BATTLE OF GETTYSBURG, MGM. Produced by Dore Schary.
THE FACE OF LINCOLN, University of Southern California, Cavalcade Pictures. Produced by Wilbur T. Blume.
MEN AGAINST THE ARCTIC, Buena Vista. Produced by Walt Disney.

Best Feature Documentary
HEARTBREAK RIDGE, Tudor Pictures. Produced by Rene Risacher.
HELEN KELLER IN HER STORY. Produced by Nancy Hamilton.

Irving G. Thalberg Memorial Award
None awarded.

Honorary Award
SAMURAI, THE LEGEND OF MUSASHI—Best Foreign Language Film first released in the United States during 1955.

Scientific or Technical
Class I
National Carbon Co. for the development and production of a high-efficiency yellow flame carbon for motion picture color photography.

Class II
Eastman Kodak Co. for Eastman Tri-X panchromatic negative film.
Farciot Edouart, Hal Corl and the Paramount Studio Transparency Dept. for the engineering and development of a double-frame, triple-head background projector.

Class III
20th Century-Fox Studio and Bausch & Lomb Co. for the new combination lenses for CinemaScope photography.
Walter Jolley, Maurice Larson and R.H. Spies of 20th Century-Fox Studio for a spraying process which creates simulated metallic surfaces.
Steve Krilanovich for an improved camera dolly incorporating multi-directional steering.
Dave Anderson of 20th Century-Fox Studio for an improved spotlight capable of maintaining a fixed circle of light at constant intensity over varied distances.
Loren L. Ryder, Charles West, Henry Fracker and Paramount Studio for a projection film index to establish proper framing for various aspect ratios.
Farciot Edouart, Hal Corl and the Paramount Studio Transparency Department for an improved dual stereopticon background projector.

1956

Best Picture
AROUND THE WORLD IN 80 DAYS, UA. Produced by Michael Todd.
FRIENDLY PERSUASION, AA. Produced by William Wyler.
GIANT, WB. Produced by George Stevens and Henry Ginsberg.
THE KING AND I, FOX. Produced by Charles Brackett.
THE TEN COMMANDMENTS, PAR. Produced by Cecil B. DeMille.

Best Actor
Yul Brynner for THE KING AND I.
James Dean for GIANT.
Kirk Douglas for LUST FOR LIFE.
Rock Hudson for GIANT.
Sir Laurence Olivier for RICHARD III.

Best Actress
Carroll Baker for BABY DOLL.
Ingrid Bergman for ANASTASIA.
Katharine Hepburn for THE RAINMAKER.
Nancy Kelly for THE BAD SEED.
Deborah Kerr for THE KING AND I.

Best Supporting Actor
Don Murray for BUS STOP.
Anthony Perkins for FRIENDLY PERSUASION.
Anthony Quinn for LUST FOR LIFE.
Mickey Rooney for THE BOLD AND THE BRAVE.
Robert Stack for WRITTEN ON THE WIND.

Best Supporting Actress
Mildred Dunnock for BABY DOLL.
Eileen Heckart for THE BAD SEED.
Mercedes McCambridge for GIANT.
Patty McCormack for THE BAD SEED.
Dorothy Malone for WRITTEN ON THE WIND.

Best Direction
Michael Anderson for AROUND THE WORLD IN 80 DAYS.
Walter Lang for THE KING AND I.
George Stevens for GIANT.
King Vidor for WAR AND PEACE.
William Wyler for FRIENDLY PERSUASION.

Writing Awards
Best Motion Picture Story
THE BRAVE ONE, by Robert Rich [Dalton Trumbo].
THE EDDY DUCHIN STORY, by Leo Katcher.
HIGH SOCIETY, by Edward Bernds and Elwood Ullman.
THE PROUD AND THE BEAUTIFUL, by Jean-Paul Sartre.
UMBERTO D (Ital.), by Cesare Zavattini.

Adapted Screenplay
AROUND THE WORLD IN 80 DAYS, by James Poe, John Farrow and S.J. Perelman.
BABY DOLL, by Tennessee Williams.
GIANT, by Fred Guiol and Ivan Moffat.
LUST FOR LIFE, by Norman Corwin.
FRIENDLY PERSUASION, by Michael Wilson (though ineligible for nomination).

Best Original Screenplay
THE BOLD AND THE BRAVE, by Robert Lewin.
JULIE, by Andrew L. Stone.
LA STRADA (Ital.), by Federico Fellini and Tullio Pinelli.
THE LADY KILLERS, by William Rose.
THE RED BALLOON, by Albert Lamorisse.

Best Cinematography
Black-and-White
BABY DOLL. Boris Kaufman.
THE BAD SEED. Hal Rosson.
THE HARDER THEY FALL. Burnett Guffey.
SOMEBODY UP THERE LIKES ME. Joseph Ruttenberg.
STAGECOACH TO FURY. Walter Strenge.

Color
AROUND THE WORLD IN 80 DAYS. Lionel Lindon.
THE EDDY DUCHIN STORY. Harry Stradling.
THE KING AND I. Leon Shamroy.
THE TEN COMMANDMENTS. Loyal Griggs.
WAR AND PEACE. Jack Cardiff.

Best Art Direction—Set Decoration
Black-and-White
THE SEVEN SAMURAI. Takashi Matsuyama.
THE PROUD AND THE PROFANE. Hal Pereira and A. Earl Hedrick; Samuel M. Comer and Frank R. McKelvy.
THE SOLID GOLD CADILLAC. Ross Bellah; William R. Kiernan and Louis Diage.
SOMEBODY UP THERE LIKES ME. Cedric Gibbons and Malcolm F. Brown; Edwin B. Willis and F. Keogh Gleason.
TEENAGE REBEL. Lyle R. Wheeler and Jack Martin Smith; Walter M. Scott and Stuart A. Reiss.

Color
AROUND THE WORLD IN 80 DAYS. James W. Sullivan and Ken Adam; Ross J. Dowd.
GIANT. Boris Leven; Ralph S. Hurst.
THE KING AND I. Lyle R. Wheeler and John DeCuir; Walter M. Scott and Paul S. Fox.
LUST FOR LIFE. Cedric Gibbons, Hans Peters and Preston Ames; Edwin B. Willis and F. Keogh Gleason.
THE TEN COMMANDMENTS. Hal Pereira, Walter H. Tyler and Albert Nozaki; Sam M. Comer and Ray Moyer.

Best Sound Recording
THE BRAVE ONE. John Myers, sound director.
THE EDDY DUCHIN STORY. John Livadary, sound director.
FRIENDLY PERSUASION. Westrex Sound Services Inc., Gordon R. Glenman, sound director; and Samuel Goldwyn Studio Sound Department, Gordon Sawyer, sound director.
THE KING AND I. Carl Faulkner, sound director.
THE TEN COMMANDMENTS. Loren L. Ryder, sound director.

Music Awards
Best Song

"Friendly Persuasion (Thee I Love)" from FRIENDLY PERSUASION. Music by Dimitri Tiomkin; lyrics by Paul Francis Webster.
"Julie" from JULIE. Music by Leith Stevens; lyrics by Tom Adair.
"True Love" from HIGH SOCIETY. Music and lyrics by Cole Porter.
"Whatever Will Be, Will Be (Que Sera, Sera)" from THE MAN WHO KNEW TOO MUCH. Music and lyrics by Jay Livingston and Ray Evans.
"Written on the Wind" from WRITTEN ON THE WIND. Music by Victor Young; lyrics by Sammy Cahn.

Best Scoring of a Dramatic or Comedy Picture
ANASTASIA. Alfred Newman.
AROUND THE WORLD IN 80 DAYS. Victor Young.
BETWEEN HEAVEN AND HELL. Hugo Friedhofer.
GIANT. Dimitri Tiomkin.
THE RAINMAKER. Alex North.

Best Scoring of a Musical Picture
THE BEST THINGS IN LIFE ARE FREE. Lionel Newman.
THE EDDY DUCHIN STORY. Morris Stoloff and George Duning.
HIGH SOCIETY. Johnny Green and Saul Chaplin.
THE KING AND I. Alfred Newman and Ken Darby.
MEET ME IN LAS VEGAS. George Stoll and Johnny Green.

Best Film Editing
AROUND THE WORLD IN 80 DAYS. Gene Ruggiero and Paul Weatherwax.
THE BRAVE ONE. Merrill G. White.
GIANT. William Hornbeck, Philip W. Anderson and Fred Bohanan.
SOMEBODY UP THERE LIKES ME. Albert Akst.
THE TEN COMMANDMENTS. Anne Bauchens.

Best Costume Design
Black-and-White
THE SEVEN SAMURAI. Kohei Ezaki.
THE POWER AND THE PRIZE. Helen Rose.
THE PROUD AND THE PROFANE. Edith Head.
THE SOLID GOLD CADILLAC. Jean Louis.
TEENAGE REBEL. Charles LeMaire and Mary Wills.

Color
AROUND THE WORLD IN 80 DAYS. Miles White.
GIANT. Moss Mabry and Marjorie Best.
THE KING AND I. Irene Sharaff.
THE TEN COMMANDMENTS. Edith Head, Ralph Jester, John Jensen, Dorothy Jeakins and Arnold Friberg.
WAR AND PEACE. Marie De Matteis.

Best Special Effects
FORBIDDEN PLANET. A. Arnold Gillespie, Irving Ries and Wesley C. Miller.
THE TEN COMMANDMENTS. John Fulton.

Short Subjects
Best Cartoon
GERALD MCBOING-BOING ON PLANET MOO, COL. Produced by Stephen Bosustow.
THE JAYWALKER, Col. Produced by Stephen Bosustow.
MISTER MAGOO'S PUDDLE JUMPER, COL. Produced by Stephen Bosustow.

Best One-Reel Film
CRASHING THE WATER BARRIER, WB. Produced by Konstantin Kalser.
I NEVER FORGET A FACE. WB. Produced by Robert Youngson.
TIME STOOD STILL. WB. Produced by Cedric Francis.

Best Two-Reel Film
THE BESPOKE OVERCOAT, Romulus Films. Produced by George K. Arthur.
COW DOG, Buena Vista. Produced by Larry Lansburgh.
THE DARK WAVE, FOX. Produced by John Healy.
SAMOA, Buena Vista. Produced by Walt Disney.

Documentary
Best Short Subject Documentary
A CITY DECIDES, Charles Guggenheim & Assocs.
THE DARK WAVE, FOX. Produced by John Healy.
THE HOUSE WITHOUT A NAME, U-I. Produced by Valentine Davies.
MAN IN SPACE, Buena Vista. Produced by Ward Kimball.
THE TRUE STORY OF THE CIVIL WAR, Camera Eye Pictures. Produced by Louis Clyde Stoumen.

Best Feature Documentary
THE NAKED EYE, Camera Eye Pictures. Produced by Louis Clyde Stoumen.
THE SILENT WORLD (Fr.), COL. Produced by Jacques-Yves Cousteau.
WHERE MOUNTAINS FLOAT (Den.), Brandon Films. Produced by The Government Film Committee of Denmark.

Best Foreign Language Film
THE CAPTAIN OF KOPENICK (Ger.)—Helmut Kaeutner.
GERVAISE (Fr.)—Rene Clement.
HARP OF BURMA (Jap.)—Kon Ichikawa.
LA STRADA (Ital.)—Federico Fellini.
QIVITOQ (Den.)—Eric Balling.

Irving G. Thalberg Memorial Award
Buddy Adler.

Jean Hersholt Humanitarian Award
Y. Frank Freeman.

Honorary Award
Eddie Cantor for distinguished service to the film industry.

Scientific or Technical
Class III
Richard H. Ranger of Rangertone, Inc., for the development of a synchronous recording and reproducing system for quarter-inch magnetic tape.
Ted Hirsch, Carl Hauge, and Edward Reichard of Consolidated Film Industries for an automatic scene counter for laboratory projection rooms.
The Technical Departments of Paramount Pictures Corp. for the engineering and development of the Paramount lightweight horizontal-movement VistaVision camera.
Roy C. Stewart and Sons of Stewart-Trans Lux Corp., Dr. C.R. Daily and the Transparency Department of Paramount Pictures Corp. for the engineering and development of the HiTrans and Para-HiTrans rear projection screens.
The Construction Department of MGM Studio for a new hand-portable fog machine.
Daniel J. Bloomberg, John Pond, William Wade and the Engineering and Camera Departments of Republic Studio for the Naturama adaptation to the Mitchell camera.

1957
Best Picture
THE BRIDGE ON THE RIVER KWAI, COL. Produced by Sam Spiegel.
PEYTON PLACE, FOX. Produced by Jerry Wald.
SAYONARA, WB. Produced by William Goetz.
12 ANGRY MEN, UA. Produced by Henry Fonda and Reginald Rose.
WITNESS FOR THE PROSECUTION, UA. Produced by Arthur Hornblow, Jr.
Best Actor
Marlon Brando for SAYONARA.
Anthony Franciosa for A HATFUL OF RAIN.
Alec Guinness for THE BRIDGE ON THE RIVER KWAI.
Charles Laughton for WITNESS FOR THE PROSECUTION.
Anthony Quinn for WILD IS THE WIND.
Best Actress
Deborah Kerr for HEAVEN KNOWS, MR. ALLISON.
Anna Magnani for WILD IS THE WIND.
Elizabeth Taylor for RAINTREE COUNTY.
Lana Turner for PEYTON PLACE.
Joanne Woodward for THE THREE FACES OF EVE.
Best Supporting Actor
Red Buttons for SAYONARA.
Vittorio de Sica for A FAREWELL TO ARMS.
Sessue Hayakawa for THE BRIDGE ON THE RIVER KWAI.
Arthur Kennedy for PEYTON PLACE.
Russ Tamblyn for PEYTON PLACE.
Best Supporting Actress
Carolyn Jones for THE BACHELOR PARTY.
Elsa Lanchester for WITNESS FOR THE PROSECUTION.
Hope Lange for PEYTON PLACE.
Miyoshi Umeki for SAYONARA.
Diane Varsi for PEYTON PLACE.
Best Direction
David Lean for THE BRIDGE ON THE RIVER KWAI.
Joshua Logan for SAYONARA.
Sidney Lumet for 12 ANGRY MEN.
Mark Robson for PEYTON PLACE.
Billy Wilder for WITNESS FOR THE PROSECUTION.
Writing Awards
Best Screenplay, Based on Material from Another Medium
THE BRIDGE ON THE RIVER KWAI, by Pierre Boulle.
HEAVEN KNOWS, MR. ALLISON, by John Lee Mahin and John Huston.
PEYTON PLACE, by John Michael Hayes.
SAYONARA, by Paul Osborn.
12 ANGRY MEN, by Reginald Rose.
Best Story and Screenplay, Written Directly for the Screen
DESIGNING WOMAN, by George Wells.
FUNNY FACE, by Leonard Gershe.
MAN OF A THOUSAND FACES, by Ralph Wheelright, R. Wright Campbell, Ivan Goff,and Ben Roberts.
THE TIN STAR, by Barney Slater and Joel Kane; Dudley Nichols.
VITELLONI (Ital.), by Federico Fellini, Ennio Flaiano and Tullio Pinelli.
Best Cinematography
AN AFFAIR TO REMEMBER. Milton Krasner.
THE BRIDGE ON THE RIVER KWAI. Jack Hildyard.
FUNNY FACE. Ray June.
PEYTON PLACE. William Mellor.
SAYONARA. Ellsworth Fredericks.
Best Art Direction—Set Decoration
FUNNY FACE. Hal Pereira and George W. Davis; Sam Comer and Ray Moyer.
LES GIRLS. William A. Horning and Gene Allen; Edwin B. Willis and Richard Pefferle.
PAL JOEY. Walter Holscher; William Kiernan and Louis Diage.
RAINTREE COUNTY. William A. Horning and Urie McCleary; Edwin B. Willis and Hugh Hunt.
SAYONARA. Ted Haworth; Robert Priestley.
Best Sound
GUNFIGHT AT THE O.K. CORRAL. Paramount Studio Sound Department; George Dutton, sound director.
LES GIRLS. MGM Studio Sound Department; Dr. Wesley C. Miller, sound director.
PAL JOEY. Columbia Studio Sound Department; John P. Livadary, sound director.
SAYONARA. Warner Bros. Studio Sound Department; George Groves, sound director.
WITNESS FOR THE PROSECUTION. Samuel Goldwyn Studio Sound Department; Gordon Sawyer, sound director.
Music Awards
Best Song
"An Affair to Remember" from AN AFFAIR TO REMEMBER. Music by Harry Warren; lyrics by Harold Adamson and Leo McCarey.
▌All the Way" from THE JOKER IS WILD. Music by James Van Heusen; lyrics by Sammmy Cahn.
"April Love" from APRIL LOVE. Music by Sammy Fain; lyrics by Paul Francis Webster.
"Tammy" from TAMMY AND THE BACHELOR. Music and lyrics by Ray Evans and Jay Livingston.
"Wild is the Wind" from WILD IS THE WIND. Music by Dimitri Tiomkin; lyrics by Ned Washington.
Best Score
AN AFFAIR TO REMEMBER. Hugo Friedhofer.
BOY ON A DOLPHIN. Hugo Friedhofer.
THE BRIDGE ON THE RIVER KWAI. Malcolm Arnold.
PERRI. Paul Smith.
RAINTREE COUNTY. Johnny Green.
Best Film Editing
THE BRIDGE ON THE RIVER KWAI. Peter Taylor.
GUNFIGHT AT THE O.K. CORRAL. Warren Low.
PAL JOEY. Viola Lawrence and Jerome Thoms.
SAYONARA. Arthur P. Schmidt and Philip W. Anderson.
WITNESS FOR THE PROSECUTION. Daniel Mandell.
Best Costume Design
AN AFFAIR TO REMEMBER. Charles LeMaire.
FUNNY FACE. Edith Head and Hubert de Givenchy.

LES GIRLS. Orry-Kelly.
PAL JOEY. Jean Louis.
RAINTREE COUNTY. Walter Plunkett.
Best Special Effects
THE ENEMY BELOW, Walter Rossi.
THE SPIRIT OF ST. LOUIS, Louis Lichtenfield.
Short Subjects
Best Cartoon
BIRDS ANONYMOUS, WB. Produced by Edward Selzer.
ONE DROOPY KNIGHT, MGM. Produced by William Hanna and Joseph Barbera.
TABASCO ROAD, WB. Produced by Edward Selzer.
TREES AND JAMAICA DADDY, COL. Produced by Stephen Bosustow.
THE TRUTH ABOUT MOTHER GOOSE, Buena Vista. Produced by Walt Disney.
Best Live Action Subject
A CHARITY TALE, National Film Board of Canada. Produced by Norman McLaren.
CITY OF GOLD, National Film Board of Canada. Produced by Tom Daly.
FOOTHOLD ON ANTARCTICA, World Wide Pictures. Produced by James Carr.
PORTUGAL, Buena Vista. Produced by Ben Sharpsteen.
THE WETBACK HOUND, Buena Vista. Produced by Larry Lansburgh.
Documentary
Best Feature Documentary
ALBERT SCHWEITZER, Louis de Rochemont Assocs.. Produced by Jerome Hill.
ON THE BOWERY. Produced by Lionel Rogosin.
TORERO! (Mex.), Producciones Barbachano Ponce, COL. Produced by Manuel Barbachano Ponce, producer.
Best Foreign Language Film
THE DEVIL CAME AT NIGHT (Ger.).
GATES OF PARIS (Fr.)—Rene Clair.
MOTHER INDIA (India)—Mehboob.
NIGHTS OF CABIRIA (Ital.)—Federico Fellini.
NINE LIVES (Nor.)—Arne Skouen.
Irving G. Thalberg Memorial Award
None Awarded.
Jean Hersholt Humanitarian Award
Samuel Goldwyn.
Honorary Awards
Charles Brackett for outstanding service to the Academy.
B.B. Kahane for distinguished service to the motion picture industry.
Gilbert M. (Broncho Billy.) Anderson, motion picture pioneer, for his contributions to the development of motion pictures as entertainment.
The Society of Motion Picture and Television Engineers for their contributions to the advancement of the motion picture industry.
Scientific or Technical
Class I
Todd-AO Corp. and Westrex Corp. for developing a method of producing and exhibiting wide-film motion pictures known as the Todd-AO System.
Motion Picture Research Council for the design and development of a high efficiency projection screen for drive-in theaters.
Class II
Societe D'Optique et de Mecanique de Haute Precision for the development of a high speed vari-focal photographic lens.
Harlan L. Baumbach, Lorand Wargo, Howard M. Little, and the Unicorn Engineering Corp. for the development of an automatic printer light selector.
Class III
Charles E. Sutter, William B. Smith, Paramount Pictures Corp., and General Cable Corp. for the engineering and application to studio use of aluminum lightweight electrical cable and connectors.

1958
Best Picture
AUNTIE MAME, WB. Jack L. Warner, studio head,
CAT ON A HOT TIN ROOF, MGM. Produced by Lawrence Weingarten.
THE DEFIANT ONES, UA. Produced by Stanley Kramer.
GIGI, MGM. Produced by Arthur Freed.
SEPARATE TABLES, UA. Produced by Harold Hecht.
Best Actor
Tony Curtis for THE DEFIANT ONES.
Paul Newman for CAT ON A HOT TIN ROOF.
David Niven for SEPARATE TABLES.
Sidney Poitier for THE DEFIANT ONES.
Spencer Tracy for THE OLD MAN AND THE SEA.
Best Actress
Susan Hayward for I WANT TO LIVE!
Deborah Kerr for SEPARATE TABLES.
Shirley MacLaine for SOME CAME RUNNING.
Rosalind Russell for AUNTIE MAME.
Elizabeth Taylor for CAT ON A HOT TIN ROOF.
Best Supporting Actor
Theodore Bikel for THE DEFIANT ONES.
Lee J. Cobb for THE BROTHERS KARAMAZOV.
Burl Ives for THE BIG COUNTRY.
Arthur Kennedy for SOME CAME RUNNING.
Gig Young for TEACHER'S PET.
Best Supporting Actress
Peggy Cass for AUNTIE MAME.
Wendy Hiller for SEPARATE TABLES.
Martha Hyer for SOME CAME RUNNING.
Maureen Stapleton for LONELY HEARTS.
Cara Williams for THE DEFIANT ONES.
Best Direction
Richard Brooks for CAT ON A HOT TIN ROOF.
Stanley Kramer for THE DEFIANT ONES.
Vincente Minnelli for GIGI.
Mark Robson for THE INN OF THE SIXTH HAPPINESS.
Robert Wise for I WANT TO LIVE!
Writing Awards
Best Screenplay, Based on Material from Another Medium
CAT ON A HOT TIN ROOF, by Richard Brooks and James Poe.
GIGI, by Alan Jay Lerner.
THE HORSE'S MOUTH, by Alec Guinness.

I WANT TO LIVE!, by Nelson Gidding and Don Mankiewicz.
SEPARATE TABLES, by Terence Rattigan and John Gay.
Best Story and Screenplay, Written Directly for the Screen
THE DEFIANT ONES, by Nathan E. Douglas and Harold Jacob Smith.
THE GODDESS, by Paddy Chayefsky.
HOUSEBOAT, by Melville Shavelson and Jack Rose.
THE SHEEPMAN, by James Edward Grant and William Bowers.
TEACHER'S PET, by Fay and Michael Kanin.
Best Cinematography
Black-and-White
THE DEFIANT ONES. Sam Leavitt.
DESIRE UNDER THE ELMS. Daniel L. Fapp.
I WANT TO LIVE!. Lionel Lindon.
SEPARATE TABLES. Charles Lang, Jr.
THE YOUNG LIONS. Joe MacDonald.
Color
AUNTIE MAME. Harry Stradling, Sr.
CAT ON A HOT TIN ROOF. William Daniels.
GIGI. Joseph Ruttenberg.
THE OLD MAN AND THE SEA. James Wong Howe.
SOUTH PACIFIC. Leon Shamroy.
Best Art Direction—Set Decoration
Black-and-White or Color
AUNTIE MAME. Malcolm Bert; George James Hopkins.
BELL, BOOK AND CANDLE. Cary Odell; Louis Diage.
A CERTAIN SMILE. Lyle R. Wheeler and John DeCuir; Walter M. Scott and Paul S. Fox.
GIGI. William Horning and Preston Ames; Henry Grace and Keogh Gleason.
VERTIGO. Hal Pereira and Henry Bumstead; Sam Comer and Frank McKelvy.
Best Sound
I WANT TO LIVE!. Samuel Goldwyn Studio Sound Department; Gordon E. Sawyer, sound director.
SOUTH PACIFIC. Todd-AO Sound Department; Fred Hynes, sound director.
A TIME TO LIVE AND A TIME TO DIE. Universal-International Studio Sound Department; Leslie I. Carey, sound director.
VERTIGO. Paramount Studio Sound Department; George Dutton, sound director.
THE YOUNG LIONS. 20th Century-Fox Studio Sound Department; Carl Faulkner, sound director.
Music Awards
Best Song
"Almost in Your Arms" from HOUSEBOAT. Music and lyrics by Jay Livingston and Ray Evans.
"A Certain Smile" from A CERTAIN SMILE. Music by Sammy Fain; lyrics by Paul Francis Webster.
"Gigi" from GIGI. Music by Frederick Loewe; lyrics by Alan Jay Lerner.
"To Love and Be Loved" from SOME CAME RUNNING. Music by James Van Heusen; lyrics by Sammy Cahn.
"A Very Precious Love" from MARJORIE MORNINGSTAR. Music by Sammy Fain; lyrics by Paul Francis Webster.
Best Scoring of a Dramatic or Comedy Picture
THE BIG COUNTRY. Jerome Moross.
THE OLD MAN AND THE SEA. Dimitri Tiomkin.
SEPARATE TABLES. David Raksin.
WHITE WILDERNESS. Oliver Wallace.
THE YOUNG LIONS. Hugo Friedhofer.
Best Scoring of a Musical Picture
THE BOLSHOI BALLET. Yuri Faier and G. Rozhdestvensky.
DAMN YANKEES. Ray Reindorf.
GIGI. Andre Previn.
MARDI GRAS. Lionel Newman.
SOUTH PACIFIC. Alfred Newman and Ken Darby.
Best Film Editing
AUNTIE MAME. William Ziegler.
COWBOY. William A. Lyon and Al Clark.
THE DEFIANT ONES. Frederick Knudtson.
GIGI. Adrienne Fazan.
I WANT TO LIVE!. William Hornbeck.
Best Costume Design
Black-and-White or Color
BELL, BOOK AND CANDLE. Jean Louis.
THE BUCCANEER. Ralph Jester, Edith Head, and John Jensen.
A CERTAIN SMILE. Charles LeMaire and Mary Willis.
GIGI. Cecil Beaton.
SOME CAME RUNNING. Walter Plunkett.
Best Special Effects
TOM THUMB, MGM. Tom Howard.
TORPEDO RUN, MGM. A. Arnold Gillespie; Harold Humbrock.
Short Subjects
Best Cartoon
KNIGHTY KNIGHT BUGS, WB. Produced by John W. Burton.
PAUL BUNYAN, Buena Vista. Produced by Walt Disney.
SIDNEY'S FAMILY TREE, FOX. Produced by William M. Weiss.
Best Live Action Subject
GRAND CANYON, Buena Vista. Produced by Walt Disney.
JOURNEY INTO SPRING, British Transport Films. Produced by Ian Ferguson.
THE KISS, Continental Distribution, Inc. Produced by John Patrick Hayes.
SNOWS OF AORANGI, New Zealand Screen Board. George Brest Assocs.
T IS FOR TUMBLEWEED, Continental Distribution, Inc. Produced by James A. Lebenthal.
Documentary
Best Short Subject Documentary
AMA GIRLS, Buena Vista. Produced by Ben Sharpsteen.
EMPLOYEES ONLY, Hughes Aircraft Co. Produced by Kenneth G. Brown.
JOURNEY INTO SPRING, British Transport Films. Produced by Ian Ferguson.
THE LIVING STONE, National Film Board of Canada. Produced by Tom Daly.
OVERTURE, United Nations Film Service. Produced by Thorold Dickinson.
Best Feature Documentary
ANTARCTIC CROSSING, World Wide Pictures. Produced by James Carr.
THE HIDDEN WORLD, Small World Co. Produced by Robert Snyder.
PSYCHIATRIC NURSING, Dynamic Films, Inc. Produced by Nathan Zucker.

WHITE WILDERNESS, Buena Vista. Produced by Ben Sharpsteen.
Best Foreign Language Film
ARMS AND THE MAN (Ger.).
BIG DEAL ON MADONNA STREET (Ital.), Mario Monicelli.
MY UNCLE (Fr.), Jacques Tati.
THE ROAD A YEAR LONG (Yugo.), Giuseppe de Santis.
THE VENGEANCE (Span.), Juan Bardem.
Irving G. Thalberg Memorial Award
Jack L. Warner.
Jean Hersholt Humanitarian Award
None awarded.
Honorary Award
Maurice Chevalier for his contributions to the world of entertainment for more than half a century.
Scientific or Technical
Class II
Don W. Prideaux, Leory G. Leighton, and the Lamp Division of General Electric Co. for the development of an improved 10-kilowatt lamp for motion picture set lighting.
Panavision, Inc., for the design and development of the Auto Panatar anamorphic photographic lens for 35mm CinemaScope photography.
Class III
Willy Borberg of the General Precision Laboratory, Inc., for the development of a high speed intermittent movement for 35mm motion picture theater projection equipment.
Fred Ponedel, George Brown, and Conrad Boye of the Warner Bros. Special Effects Department for the design and fabrication of a new rapid-fire marble gun.

1959
Best Picture
ANATOMY OF A MURDER, COL. Produced by Otto Preminger.
BEN-HUR, MGM. Produced by Sam Zimbalist.
THE DIARY OF ANNE FRANK, FOX. Produced by George Stevens.
THE NUN'S STORY, WB. Produced by Henry Blanke.
ROOM AT THE TOP, Continental. Produced by John and James Woolf.
Best Actor
Laurence Harvey for ROOM AT THE TOP.
Charlton Heston for BEN-HUR.
Jack Lemmon for SOME LIKE IT HOT.
Paul Muni for THE LAST ANGRY MAN.
James Stewart for ANATOMY OF A MURDER.
Best Actress
Doris Day for PILLOW TALK.
Audrey Hepburn for THE NUN'S STORY.
Katharine Hepburn for SUDDENLY, LAST SUMMER.
Simone Signoret for ROOM AT THE TOP.
Elizabeth Taylor for SUDDENLY, LAST SUMMER.
Best Supporting Actor
Hugh Griffith for BEN-HUR.
Arthur O'Connell for ANATOMY OF A MURDER.
George C. Scott for ANATOMY OF A MURDER.
Robert Vaughn for THE YOUNG PHILADELPHIANS.
Ed Wynn for THE DIARY OF ANNE FRANK.
Best Supporting Actress
Hermione Baddeley for ROOM AT THE TOP.
Susan Kohner for IMITATION OF LIFE.
Juanita Moore for IMITATION OF LIFE.
Thelma Ritter for PILLOW TALK.
Shelley Winters for THE DIARY OF ANNE FRANK.
Best Direction
Jack Clayton for ROOM AT THE TOP.
George Stevens for THE DIARY OF ANNE FRANK.
Billy Wilder for SOME LIKE IT HOT.
William Wyler for BEN-HUR.
Fred Zinnemann for THE NUN'S STORY.
Writing Awards
Best Screenplay, Based on Material from another Medium
ANATOMY OF A MURDER, by Wendell Mayes.
BEN-HUR, by Karl Tunberg.
THE NUN'S STORY, by Robert Anderson.
ROOM AT THE TOP, by Neil Paterson.
SOME LIKE IT HOT, by Billy Wilder and I.A.L. Diamond.
Best Story and Screenplay, Written Directly for the Screen
THE 400 BLOWS (Fr.), by Francois Truffaut and Marcel Moussy.
NORTH BY NORTHWEST, by Ernest Lehman.
OPERATION PETTICOAT, by Paul King and Joseph Stone; Stanley Shapiro and Maurice Richlin.
PILLOW TALK, by Russell Rouse and Clarence Greene; Stanley Shapiro and Maurice Richlin.
WILD STRAWBERRIES, by Ingmar Bergman.
Best Cinematography
Black-and-White
ANATOMY OF A MURDER. Sam Leavitt.
CAREER. Joseph LaShelle.
THE DIARY OF ANNE FRANK. William C. Mellor.
SOME LIKE IT HOT. Charles Lang, Jr.
THE YOUNG PHILADELPHIANS. Harry Stradling, Sr.
Color
BEN-HUR. Robert L. Surtees.
THE BIG FISHERMAN. Lee Garmes.
THE FIVE PENNIES. Daniel L. Fapp.
THE NUN'S STORY. Franz Planer.
PORGY AND BESS. Leon Shamroy.
Best Art Direction—Set Decoration
Black-and-White
CAREER. Hal Pereira and Walter Tyler; Sam Comer and Arthur Krams.
THE DIARY OF ANNE FRANK. Lyle R. Wheeler and George W. Davis; Walter M. Scott and Stuart A. Reiss.
THE LAST ANGRY MAN. Carl Anderson; William Kiernan.
SOME LIKE IT HOT. Ted Haworth; Edward G. Boyle.
SUDDENLY, LAST SUMMER. Oliver Messel and William Kellner; Scot Slimon.

Color
   BEN-HUR. William A. Horning and Edward Carfagno; Hugh Hunt.
   THE BIG FISHERMAN. John DeCuir; Julia Heron.
   JOURNEY TO THE CENTER OF THE EARTH. Lyle R. Wheeler, Franz Bachelin
   and Herman A. Blumenthal; Walter M. Scott and Joseph Kish.
   NORTH BY NORTHWEST. William A. Horning, Robert Boyle, and Merrill Pye;
   Henry Grace and Frank McKelvy.
   PILLOW TALK. Richard H. Riedel; Russell A. Gausman and Rudy R. Levitt.
Best Sound
   BEN-HUR. MGM Studio Sound Department; Franklin E. Milton, sound director.
   JOURNEY TO THE CENTER OF THE EARTH. 20th Century-Fox Sound Depart-
   ment; Carl Faulkner, sound director.
   LIBEL! MGM London Sound Department; A.W. Watkins, sound director.
   THE NUN'S STORY. Warner Bros. Studio Sound department; George R. Groves,
   sound director.
   PORGY AND BESS. Samuel Goldwyn Studio Sound Department; Gordon E. Sawyer,
   sound director; and Todd-AO Sound Department; Fred Hynes, sound director.
Music Awards
   Best Song
      "The Best of Everything" from THE BEST OF EVERYTHING. Music by Alfred
      Newman; lyrics by Sammy Cahn.
      "The Five Pennies" from THE FIVE PENNIES. Music and lyrics by Sylvia Fine.
      "The Hanging Tree" from THE HANGING TREE. Music by Jerry Livingston; lyrics
      by Mack David.
      *High Hopes" from A HOLE IN THE HEAD. Music by James Van Heusen; lyrics by
      Sammy Cahn.*
      "Strange Are the Ways of Love" from THE YOUNG LAND. Music by Dimitri
      Tiomkin; lyrics by Ned Washington.
   Best Scoring of a Dramatic or Comedy Picture
      BEN-HUR. Miklos Rozsa.
      THE DIARY OF ANNE FRANK. Alfred Newman.
      THE NUN'S STORY. Franz Waxman.
      ON THE BEACH. Ernest Gold.
      PILLOW TALK. Frank DeVol.
   Best Scoring of a Musical Picture
      THE FIVE PENNIES. Leith Stevens.
      LI'L ABNER. Nelson Riddle and Joseph J. Lilley.
      PORGY AND BESS. Andre Previn and Ken Darby.
      SAY ONE FOR ME. Lionel Newman.
      SLEEPING BEAUTY. George Bruns.
Best Film Editing
   ANATOMY OF A MURDER. Louis R. Loeffler.
   BEN-HUR. Ralph E. Winters and John D. Dunning.
   NORTH BY NORTHWEST. George Tomasini.
   THE NUN'S STORY. Walter Thompson.
   ON THE BEACH. Frederic Knudtson.
Best Costume Design
   Black-and-White
      CAREER. Edith Head.
      THE DIARY OF ANNE FRANK. Charles LeMaire and Mary Willis.
      THE GAZEBO. Helene Rose.
      SOME LIKE IT HOT. Orry-Kelly.
      THE YOUNG PHILADELPHIANS. Howard Shoup.
   Color
      BEN-HUR. Elizabeth Haffenden.
      THE BEST OF EVERYTHING. Adele Palmer.
      THE BIG FISHERMAN. Renie.
      THE FIVE PENNIES. Edith Head.
      PORGY AND BESS. Irene Sharaff.
Best Special Effects
   BEN-HUR. Visual: A. Arnold Gillespie and Robert MacDonald; Audible: Milo Lory.
   JOURNEY TO THE CENTER OF THE EARTH. Visual: L.B. Abbott and James B.
   Gordon; Audible: Carl Faulkner.
Short Subjects
   Best Cartoon
      MEXICALI SHMOES, WB. Produced by John W. Burton.
      MOONBIRD. Produced by John Hubley.
      NOAH'S ARK, Buena Vista. Produced by Walt Disney.
      THE VIOLINIST, Kingsley International. Produced by Ernest Pintoff.
   Best Live Action Subject
      BETWEEN THE TIDES, British Transport Films, Schoenfeld Films. Produced by
      Ian Ferguson.
      *THE GOLDEN FISH (Fr.), Les Requins Assoc., COL. Produced by Jacques-Yves
      Cousteau.*
      MYSTERIES OF THE DEEP, Buena Vista. Produced by Walt Disney.
      THE RUNNING, JUMPING AND STANDING-STILL FILM, Lion International,
      Kingsley-Union Films (British). Produced by Peter Sellers.
      SKYSCRAPER, Burstyn Film Enterprises. Produced by Shirley Clarke, Willard Van
      Dyke and Irving Jacoby.
Documentary
   Best Short Subject Documentary
      DONALD IN MATHMAGIC LAND, Buena Vista. Produced by Walt Disney.
      FROM GENERATION TO GENERATION, Maternity Center Assoc. produced by
      Edward F. Cullen.
      *GLASS, Netherlands Government, George K. Arthur-Go Pictures. Produced by Burt
      Haanstra.*
   Best Feature Documentary
      THE RACE FOR SPACE. Produced by David L. Wolper.
      SERENGETI SHALL NOT DIE, Transocean Film. Produced by Bernhard Grzimek.
Best Foreign Language Film
   BLACK ORPHEUS (Fr.), Marcel Camus.
   THE BRIDGE (Ger.), Bernhard Wicki.
   THE GREAT WAR (Ital.), Mario Monicelli.
   PAW (Den.), Astrid Henning-Jensen.
   THE VILLAGE ON THE RIVER (Neth.), Fons Rademaker.
Irving G. Thalberg Memorial Award
   None awarded.
Jean Hersholt Humanitarian Award
   Bob Hope.
Honorary Awards

Lee de Forest for his pioneering inventions which brought sound to the motion
picture.
Buster Keaton for his unique talents which brought immortal comedies to the screen.
Scientific or Technical
   Class II
      Douglas G. Shearer of MGM, Inc., and Robert E. Gottschalk and John R. Moore of
      Panavision, Inc., for the development of a system of producing and exhibiting wide
      film motion pictures known as Camera 65.
      Wadsworth E. Pohl, William Evams, Werner Hopf, S.E. Howse, Thomas P. Dixon,
      Stanford Research Institute, and Technicolor Corp. for the design and development
      of the Technicolor electronic printing timer.
      Wadsworth E. Pohl, Jack Alford, Henry Imus, Joseph Schmit, Paul Fassnacht, Al
      Lofquist and Technicolor Corp. for the development and practical application of
      equipment for wet printing.
      Dr. Howard S. Coleman, Dr. A. Francis Turner, Harold H. Schroeder, James R.
      Benford, and Harold E. Rosenberger of the Bausch & Lomb Optical Co. for the design
      and development of the Balcold projection mirror.
      Robert P. Guterman of general Kinetics, Inc., and the Lipsner Smith Corp. for the
      design and development of the CF-2 Ultra-sonic Film Cleaner.
   Class III
      Ub Iwerks of Walt Disney Prods. for the design of an improved optical printer for
      special effects and matte shots.
      E.L. Stones, Glen Robinson, Winfield Hubbard, and Luther Newman of the MGM
      Studio Construction Department for the design of a multiple-cable remote-controlled
      winch.

1960
Best Picture
   THE ALAMO, UA. Produced by John Wayne.
   THE APARTMENT, UA. Produced by Billy Wilder.
   ELMER GANTRY, UA. Produced by Bernard Smith.
   SONS AND LOVERS, FOX. Produced by Jerry Wald.
   THE SUNDOWNERS, WB. Produced by Fred Zinnemann.
Best Actor
   Trevor Howard for SONS AND LOVERS.
   Burt Lancaster for ELMER GANTRY.
   Jack Lemmon for THE APARTMENT.
   Laurence Olivier for THE ENTERTAINER.
   Spencer Tracy for INHERIT THE WIND.
Best Actress
   Greer Garson for SUNRISE AT CAMPOBELLO.
   Deborah Kerr for THE SUNDOWNERS.
   Shirley MacLaine for THE APARTMENT.
   Melina Mercouri for NEVER ON SUNDAY.
   Elizabeth Taylor for BUTTERFIELD 8.
Best Supporting Actor
   Peter Falk for MURDER, INC.
   Jack Kruschen for THE APARTMENT.
   Sal Mineo for EXODUS.
   Peter Ustinov for SPARTACUS.
   Chill Wills for THE ALAMO.
Best Supporting Actress
   Glynis Johns for THE SUNDOWNERS.
   Shirley Jones for ELMER GANTRY.
   Shirley Knight for THE DARK AT THE TOP OF THE STAIRS.
   Janet Leigh for PSYCHO.
   Mary Ure for SONS AND LOVERS.
Best Direction
   Jack Cardiff for SONS AND LOVERS.
   Jules Dassin for NEVER ON SUNDAY.
   Alfred Hitchcock for PSYCHO.
   Billy Wilder for THE APARTMENT.
   Fred Zinnemann for THE SUNDOWNERS.
Writing Awards
   Best Screenplay, Based on Material from Another Medium
      ELMER GANTRY, by Richard Brooks.
      INHERIT THE WIND, by Nathan E. Douglas and Harold Jacob Smith.
      SONS AND LOVERS, by Gavin Lambert and T.E.B. Clarke.
      THE SUNDOWNERS, by Isobel Lannart.
      TUNES OF GLORY, by James Kennaway.
   Story and Screenplay, Written Directly for the Screen
      THE ANGRY SILENCE, by Richard Gregson and Michael Craig; Bryan Forbes.
      THE APARTMENT, by Billy Wilder and I.A.L. Diamond.
      THE FACTS OF LIFE, by Norman Panama and Melvin Frank.
      HIROSHIMA, MON AMOUR (Fr./Jap.), by Marguerite Duras.
      NEVER ON SUNDAY, by Jules Dassin.
Best Cinematography
   Black-and-White
      THE APARTMENT. Joseph LaShelle.
      THE FACTS OF LIFE. Charles B. Lang, Jr.
      INHERIT THE WIND. Ernest Laszlo.
      PSYCHO. John L. Russell.
      SONS AND LOVERS. Freddie Francis.
   Color
      THE ALAMO. William H. Clothier.
      BUTTERFIELD 8. Joseph Ruttenberg and Charles Harten.
      EXODUS. Sam Leavitt.
      PEPE. Joe MacDonald.
      SPARTACUS. Russell Metty.
Best Art Direction—Set Decoration
   Black-and-White
      THE APARTMENT. Alexander Trauner; Edward G. Boyle.
      THE FACTS OF LIFE. Joseph McMillan Johnson and Kenneth A. Reid; Ross Dowd.
      PSYCHO. Joseph Hurley and Robert Clatworthy; George Milo.
      SONS AND LOVERS. Tom Morahan; Lionel Couch.
      VISIT TO A SMALL PLANET. Hal Pereira and Walter Tyler; Sam Comer and
      Arthur Krams.
   Color
      CIMARRON. George W. Davis and Addison Hehr; Henry Grace, Hugh Hunt, and
      Otto Siegel.

IT STARTED IN NAPLES. Hal Pereira and Roland Anderson; Sam Comer and Arrigo Breschi.
PEPE. Ted Haworth; William Kiernan.
SPARTACUS. Alexander Golitzen and Eric Orbom; Russell A. Gausman and Julia Heron.
SUNRISE AT CAMPOBELLO. Edward Carrere; George James Hopkins.
Best Sound
THE ALAMO. Samuel Goldwyn Studio Sound Department; Gordon E. Sawyer, sound director; and Todd-AO Sound Department; Fred Hynes, sound director.
THE APARTMENT. Samuel Goldwyn Studio Sound Department; Gordon E. Sawyer, sound director.
CIMARRON. MGM Studio Sound Department; Franklin E. Milton, sound director.
PEPE. Columbia Studio Sound Department; Charles Rice, sound director.
SUNRISE AT CAMPOBELLO. Warner Bros Studio Sound Department; George R. Groves, sound director.
Music Awards
Best Song
"The Facts of Life" from THE FACTS OF LIFE. Music and lyrics by Johnny Mercer.
"Faraway Part of Town" from PEPE. Music by Andre Previn; lyrics by Dory Langdon.
"The Green Leaves of Summer" from THE ALAMO. Music by Dimitri Tiomkin; lyrics by Paul Francis Webster.
"Never on Sunday" from NEVER ON SUNDAY. Music and lyrics by Manos Hadjidakis.
"The Second Time Around" from HIGH TIME. Music by James Van Heusen; lyrics by Sammy Cahn.
Best Scoring of a Dramatic or Comedy Picture
THE ALAMO. Dimitri Tiomkin.
ELMER GANTRY. Andre Previn.
EXODUS. Ernest Gold.
THE MAGNIFICENT SEVEN. Elmer Bernstein.
SPARTACUS. Alex North.
Best Scoring of a Musical Picture
BELLS ARE RINGING. Andre Previn.
CAN-CAN. Nelson Riddle.
LET'S MAKE LOVE. Lionel Newman and Earle H. Hagen.
PEPE. Johnny Green.
SONG WITHOUT END. Morris Stoloff and Harry Sukman.
Best Film Editing
THE ALAMO. Stuart Gilmore.
THE APARTMENT. Daniel Mandell.
INHERIT THE WIND. Frederic Knudtson.
PEPE. Viola Lawrence and Al Clark.
SPARTACUS. Robert Lawrence.
Best Costume Design
Black-and-White
THE FACTS OF LIFE. Edith Head and Edward Stevenson.
NEVER ON SUNDAY. Denny Vachlioti.
THE RISE AND FALL OF LEGS DIAMOND. Howard Shoup.
SEVEN THIEVES. Bill Thomas.
THE VIRGIN SPRING. Marik Vos.
Color
CAN-CAN. Irene Sharaff.
MIDNIGHT LACE. Irene.
PEPE. Edith Head.
SPARTACUS. Valles and Bill Thomas.
SUNRISE AT CAMPOBELLO. Marjorie Best.
Best Special Effects
THE LAST VOYAGE. A.J. Lohman.
THE TIME MACHINE. Gene Warren and Tim Bear.
Short Subjects
Best Cartoon
GOLIATH II, Buena Vista. Produced by Walt Disney.
HIGH NOTE, WB.
MOUSE AND GARDEN, WB.
MUNRO, Rembrandt Films. Produced by William L. Snyder.
A PLACE IN THE SUN (Czech.), George K. Arthur-Go Pictures. Produced by Frantisek Vystrecil.
Best Live Action Subject
THE CREATION OF WOMAN (India), Trident Films, Sterling World Distributors. Produced by Charles F. Schwep and Ismail Merchant.
DAY OF THE PAINTER, Kingsley-Union Films. Produced by Ezra R. Baker.
ISLAND OF THE SEA, Buena Vista. Produced by Walt Disney.
A SPORT IS BORN, PAR. Produced by Leslie Winik.
Documentary
Best Short Subject Documentary
BEYOND SILENCE, U.S. Information Agency.
A CITY CALLED COPENHAGEN (Den.), Statens Filmcentral, Danish Film Office.
GEORGE GROSZ' INTERREGNUM, Educational Communications Corp. Produced by Charles and Altina Carey.
GIUSEPPINA (Brit.), Schoenfeld Films. Produced by James Hill.
UNIVERSE, National Film Board of Canada, Schoenfeld Films. Produced by Colin Low.
Best Feature Documentary
THE HORSE WITH THE FLYING TAIL, Buena Vista. Produced by Larry Lansburgh.
REBEL IN PARADISE, Tiare Co. Produced by Robert D. Fraser.
Best Foreign Language Film
KAPO (Ital.), Gillo Pontecorvo.
LA VERITE (Fr.), Henri-Georges Clouzot.
MACARIO (Mex.), Roberto Gavalson.
THE NINTH CIRCLE (Yugo.), Frances Stiglic.
THE VIRGIN SPRING (Swed.), Ingmar Bergman.
Irving G. Thalberg Memorial Award
None awarded.
Jean Hersholt Humanitarian Award
Sol Lesser.
Honorary Awards
Gary Cooper for his many memorable screen performances and the international recognition he, as an individual, has gained for the motion picture industry.

Stan Laurel for his creative pioneering in the field of cinema comedy.
Hayley Mills for POLLYANA, the most outstanding juvenile performance during 1960.
Scientific and Technical
Class II
Ampex Professional Products Co. for the production of a well-engineered multi-purpose sound system combining high standards of quality with convenience of control, dependable operation, and simplified emergency provisions.
Arthur Holcomb, Petro Vlahos and Columbia Studio Camera Department for a camera flicker indicating device.
Anthony Paglia and the 20th Century-Fox Studio Mechanical Effects Department for the design and construction of a miniature flak gun and ammunition.
Carl Hauge, Robert Grubel, and Edward Reichard of Consolidated Film Industries for the development of an automatic developer replenisher system.

1961
Best Picture
FANNY, WB. Produced by Joshua Logan.
THE GUNS OF NAVARONE, COL. Produced by Carl Foreman.
THE HUSTLER, FOX. Produced by Robert Rossen.
JUDGMENT AT NUREMBERG, UA. Produced by Stanley Kramer.
WEST SIDE STORY, UA. Produced by Robert Wise.
Best Actor
Charles Boyer for FANNY.
Paul Newman for THE HUSTLER.
Maximilian Schell for JUDGMENT AT NUREMBERG.
Spencer Tracy for JUDGMENT AT NUREMBERG.
Stuart Whitman for THE MARK.
Best Actress
Audrey Hepburn for BREAKFAST AT TIFFANY'S.
Piper Laurie for THE HUSTLER.
Sophia Loren for TWO WOMEN.
Geraldine Page for SUMMER AND SMOKE.
Natalie Wood for SPLENDOR IN THE GRASS.
Best Supporting Actor
George Chakiris for WEST SIDE STORY.
Montgomery Clift for JUDGMENT AT NUREMBERG.
Peter Falk for POCKETFUL OF MIRACLES.
Jackie Gleason for THE HUSTLER.
George C. Scott for THE HUSTLER.
Best Supporting Actress
Fay Bainter for THE CHILDREN'S HOUR.
Judy Garland for JUDGMENT AT NUREMBERG.
Lotte Lenya for THE ROMAN SPRING OF MRS. STONE.
Una Merkel for SUMMER AND SMOKE.
Rita Moreno for WEST SIDE STORY.
Best Direction
Federico Fellini for LA DOLCE VITA.
Stanley Kramer for JUDGMENT AT NUREMBERG.
Robert Rossen for THE HUSTLER.
J. Lee Thompson for THE GUNS OF NAVARONE.
Robert Wise and Jerome Robbins for WEST SIDE STORY.
Writing Awards
Best Screenplay, Based on Material from Another Medium
BREAKFAST AT TIFFANY'S, by George Axelrod.
THE GUNS OF NAVARONE, by Carl Foreman.
THE HUSTLER, by Sidney Carroll and Robert Rossen.
JUDGMENT AT NUREMBERG, by Abby Mann.
WEST SIDE STORY, by Ernest Lehman.
Best Story and Screenplay, Written Directly for the Screen
BALLAD OF A SOLDIER, by Valentin Yoshov and Grigori Chukhrai.
GENERAL DELLA ROVERE, by Sergio Amidei, Diego Fabbri, and Indro Montanelli.
LA DOLCE VITA, by Federico Fellini, Tullio Pinelli, Ennio Flaiano, and Brunello Rondi.
LOVER COME BACK, by Stanley Shapiro and Paul Henning.
SPLENDOR IN THE GRASS, by William Inge.
Best Cinematography
Black-and-White
THE ABSENT-MINDED PROFESSOR. Edward Colman.
THE CHILDREN'S HOUR. Franz F. Planer.
THE HUSTLER. Eugen Shuftan.
JUDGMENT AT NUREMBERG. Ernest Laszlo.
ONE, TWO, THREE. Daniel L. Fapp.
Color
FANNY. Jack Cardiff.
FLOWER DRUM SONG. Russell Metty.
A MAJORITY OF ONE. Harry Stradling, Sr.
ONE-EYED JACKS. Charles Lang, Jr.
WEST SIDE STORY. Daniel L. Fapp.
Best Art Direction—Set Decoration
Black-and-White
THE ABSENT-MINDED PROFESSOR. Carroll Clark; Emile Kuri and Hal Gausman.
THE CHILDREN'S HOUR. Fernando Carrere; Edward G. Boyle.
THE HUSTLER. Harry Horner; Gene Callahan.
JUDGMENT AT NUREMBERG. Rudolph Sternad; George Milo.
LA DOLCE VITA. Piero Gherardi.
Color
BREAKFAST AT TIFFANY'S. Hal Pereira and Roland Anderson; Sam Comer and Ray Moyer.
EL CID. Veniero Colasanti and John Moore.
FLOWER DRUM SONG. Alexander Golitzen and Joseph Wright; Howard Bristol.
SUMMER AND SMOKE. Hal Pereira and Walter Tyler; Sam Comer and Arthur Krams.
WEST SIDE STORY. Boris Leven; Victor A. Gangelin.
Best Sound
THE CHILDREN'S HOUR. Samuel Goldwyn Studio Sound Department; Gordon E. Sawyer, sound director.
FLOWER DRUM SONG. Revue Studio Sound Department; Waldon O. Watson, sound

director.

THE GUNS OF NAVARONE. Shepperton Studio Sound Department; John Cox, sound director.

THE PARENT TRAP. Walt Disney Studio Sound Department; Robert O. Cook, sound director.

WEST SIDE STORY. Todd-AO Sound Department; Fred Hynes, sound director; and Samuel Goldwyn Studio Sound Department; Gordon E. Sawyer, sound director.

Music Awards

Best Song

"Bachelor in Paradise" from BACHELOR IN PARADISE. Music by Henry Mancini; lyrics by Mack David.

"Love Theme from EL CID (The Falcon and the Dove)" from EL CID. Music by Miklos Rozsa; lyrics by Paul Francis Webster.

Moon River" from BREAKFAST AT TIFFANY'S. Music by Henry Mancini; lyrics by Johnny Mercer.

"Pocketful of Miracles" from POCKETFUL OF MIRACLES. Music by James Van Heusen; lyrics by Sammy Cahn.

"Town Without Pity" from TOWN WITHOUT PITY. Music by Dimitri Tiomkin; lyrics by Ned Washington.

Best Scoring of a Dramatic or Comedy Picture

BREAKFAST AT TIFFANY'S. Henry Mancini.

EL CID. Miklos Rozsa.

FANNY. Morris Stoloff and Harry Sukman.

THE GUNS OF NAVARONE. Dimitri Tiomkin.

SUMMER AND SMOKE. Elmer Bernstein.

Best Scoring of a Musical Picture

BABES IN TOYLAND. George Bruns.

FLOWER DRUM SONG. Alfred Newman and Ken Darby.

KHOVANSHCHINA (USSR). Dimitri Shostakovich.

PARIS BLUES. Duke Ellington.

WEST SIDE STORY. Saul Chaplin, Johnny Green, Sid Ramin, and Irwin Kostal.

Best Film Editing

FANNY. William H. Reynolds.

THE GUNS OF NAVARONE. Alan Osbiston.

JUDGMENT AT NUREMBERG. Frederic Knudtson.

THE PARENT TRAP. Phillip W. Anderson.

WEST SIDE STORY. Saul Chaplin, Johnny Green, Sid Ramin, and Irwin Kostal.

Best Costume Design

Black-and-White

THE CHILDREN'S HOUR. Dorothy Jeakins.

CLAUDELLE INGLISH. Howard Shoup.

JUDGMENT AT NUREMBERG. Jean Louis.

LA DOLCE VITA. Piero Gherardi.

YOJIMBO (Jap.). Yoshiro Muraki.

Color

BABES IN TOYLAND. Bill Thomas.

BACK STREET. Jean Louis.

FLOWER DRUM SONG. Irene Sharaff.

POCKETFUL OF MIRACLES. Edith Head and Walter Plunkett.

WEST SIDE STORY. Irene Sharaff.

Best Special Effects

THE ABSENT-MINDED PROFESSOR. Robert A. Mattey and Eustace Lycett.

THE GUNS OF NAVARONE. Visual: Bill Warrington; Audible: Vivian C. Greenham.

Short Subjects

Best Cartoon

AQUAMANIA, Buena Vista. Produced by Walt Disney.

BEEP PREPARED, WB. Produced by Chuck Jones.

ERSATZ (THE SUBSTITUTE), Zagreb Film, Herts-Lion International Corp.

NELLY'S FOLLY, WB. Produced by Chuck Jones.

PIED PIPER OF GUADALUPE, WB. Produced by Friz Freleng.

Best Live Action Subject

BALLON VOLE (PLAY BALL), Cine-Documents, Kingsley International.

THE FACE OF JESUS. Produced by Dr. John D. Jennings.

ROOFTOPS OF NEW YORK, McCarty-Rush-Gaffney, COL.

SEAWARDS THE GREAT SHIPS, Templar Film Studios, Schoenfeld Films.

VERY NICE, VERY NICE, National Film Board of Canada, Kingsley International.

Documentary

Best Short Subject Documentary

BREAKING THE LANGUAGE BARRIER, U.S. Air Force.

CRADLE OF GENIUS (Irish), Lesser Films. Produced by Jim O'Connor and Tom Hayes.

KAHL (Ger.), Dido-Film-GmbH., AEG-Filmdienst.

L'UOMO IN GRIGIO (THE MAN IN GRAY) (Ital.). Produced by Benedetto Benedetti.

PROJECT HOPE, Klaeger Films. Produced by Frank P. Bibas.

Best Feature Documentary

OLYMPIC GAMES 1960 (Ital.), Cineriz.

SKY ABOVE AND MUD BENEATH, Rank Films (Fr.). Produced by Arthur Cohn and Rene Lafuite.

Best Foreign Language Film

HARRY AND THE BUTLER (Den.).

IMMORTAL LOVE (Jap.), Keisuke Kinoshita.

THE IMPORTANT MAN (Mex.), Ismael Rodriguez.

PLACIDO (Span.), Luis Barlanga.

THROUGH A GLASS DARKLY (Swed.), Ingmar Bergman.

Irving G. Thalberg Memorial Award

Stanley Kramer.

Jean Hersholt Humanitarian Award

George Seaton.

Honorary Awards

William Hendricks for his outstanding patriotic service in the conception, writing, and production of the Marine Corps film, A FORCE IN READINESS, which has brought honor to the Academy and the motion picture industry.

Fred L. Metzler for his dedication and outstanding service to the Academy of Motion Picture Arts and Sciences.

Jerome Robbins for his brilliant achievements in the art of choreography on film.

Scientific or Technical

Class II

Sylvania Electric Products, Inc., for the development of a hand held high-power

photographic lighting unit known as the Sun Gun Professional.

James Dale, S. Wilson, H.E. Rice, John Rude, Laurie Atkin, Wadsworth E. Pohl, H. Peasgood, and Technicolor Corp. for a process of automatic selective printing.

20th Century-Fox Research Department, under the direction of E.I. Sponable and Herbert E. Bragg, and Deluxe Laboratories, Inc. with the assistance of F.D. Leslie, R.D. Whitmore, A.A. Alden, Endel Pool, and James B. Gordon for a system of decompressing and recompressing CinemaScope pictures for conventional aspect ratios.

Class III

Hurletron, Inc., Electric Eye Equipment Division, for an automatic light changing system for motion picture printers.

Wadsworth E. Pohl and Technicolor Corp. for an integrated sound and picture transfer process.

1962

Best Picture

LAWRENCE OF ARABIA, COL. Produced by Sam Spiegel.

THE LONGEST DAY, FOX. Produced by Darryl F. Zanuck.

THE MUSIC MAN, WB. Produced by Morton Da Costa.

MUTINY ON THE BOUNTY, MGM. Produced by Aaron Rosenberg.

TO KILL A MOCKINGBIRD, U-I. Produced by Alan J. Pakula.

Best Actor

Burt Lancaster for BIRD MAN OF ALCATRAZ.

Jack Lemmon for DAYS OF WINE AND ROSES.

Marcello Mastroianni for DIVORCE—ITALIAN STYLE.

Peter O'Toole for LAWRENCE OF ARABIA.

Gregory Peck for TO KILL A MOCKINGBIRD.

Best Actress

Ann Bancroft for THE MIRACLE WORKER.

Bette Davis for WHAT EVER HAPPENED TO BABY JANE?

Katharine Hepburn for LONG DAYS JOURNEY INTO NIGHT.

Geraldine Page for SWEET BIRD OF YOUTH.

Lee Remick for DAYS OF WINE AND ROSES.

Best Supporting Actor

Ed Begley for SWEET BIRD OF YOUTH.

Victor Buono for WHAT EVER HAPPENED TO BABY JANE?

Telly Savalas for BIRD MAN OF ALCATRAZ.

Omar Sharif for LAWRENCE OF ARABIA.

Terence Stamp for BILLY BUDD.

Best Supporting Actress

Mary Badham for TO KILL A MOCKINGBIRD.

Patty Duke for THE MIRACLE WORKER.

Shirley Knight for SWEET BIRD OF YOUTH.

Angela Lansbury for THE MANCHURIAN CANDIDATE.

Thelma Ritter for BIRD MAN OF ALCATRAZ.

Best Direction

Pietro Germi for DIVORCE—ITALIAN STYLE.

David Lean for LAWRENCE OF ARABIA.

Robert Mulligan for TO KILL A MOCKINGBIRD.

Arthur Penn for THE MIRACLE WORKER.

Frank Perry for DAVID AND LISA.

Writing Awards

Best Screenplay, Based on Material from Another Medium

DAVID AND LISA, by Eleanor Perry.

LAWRENCE OF ARABIA, by Robert Bolt.

LOLITA, by Vladimir Nabokov.

THE MIRACLE WORKER, by William Gibson.

TO KILL A MOCKINGBIRD, by Horton Foote.

Best Story and Screenplay, Written Directly for the Screen

DIVORCE—ITALIAN STYLE (Ital.), by Ennio de Concini, Alfredo Gianetti, and Pietro Germi.

FREUD, by Charles Kaufman and Wolfgang Reinhardt.

LAST YEAR AT MARIENBAD (Fr.), by Alain Robbe-Grillet.

THAT TOUCH OF MINK, by Stanley Shapiro and Nate Monaster.

THROUGH A GLASS DARKLY (Swed.), by Ingmar Bergman.

Best Cinematography

Black-and-White

BIRD MAN OF ALCATRAZ. Burnett Guffey.

THE LONGEST DAY. Jean Bourgoin and Walter Wottitz.

TO KILL A MOCKINGBIRD. Russell Harlan.

TWO FOR THE SEESAW. Ted McCord.

WHAT EVER HAPPENED TO BABY JANE? Ernest Haller.

Color

GYPSY. Harry Stradling, Sr.

HATARI! Russell Harlan.

LAWRENCE OF ARABIA. Fred A. Young.

MUTINY ON THE BOUNTY. Robert L. Surtees.

THE WONDERFUL WORLD OF THE BROTHERS GRIMM. Paul C. Vogel.

Best Art Direction—Set Decoration

Black-and-White

DAYS OF WINE AND ROSES. joseph Wright; George James Hopkins.

THE LONGEST DAY. Ted Haworth, Leon Barasa and Vincent Korda; Gabriel Bechir.

PERIOD OF ADJUSTMENT. George W. Davis and Edward Carfagno; Henry Grace and Dick Pefferle.

THE PIGEON THAT TOOK ROME. Hal Pereira and Roland Anderson; Sam Comer and Frank R. McKelvy.

TO KILL A MOCKINGBIRD. Alexander Golitzen and Henry Bumstead; Oliver Emert.

Color

LAWRENCE OF ARABIA. John Box and John Stoll; Dario Simoni.

THE MUSIC MAN. Paul Groesse; George James Hopkins.

MUTINY ON THE BOUNTY. George W. Davis and J. McMillan Johnson; Henry Grace and Hugh Hunt.

THAT TOUCH OF MINK. Alexander Golitzen and Robert Clatworthy; George Milo.

THE WONDERFUL WORLD OF THE BROTHERS GRIMM. Georg W. Davis and Edward Carfagno; Henry Grace and Dick Pefferle.

Best Sound

BON VOYAGE. Walt Disney Studio Sound Department; Robert O. Cook, sound director.

LAWRENCE OF ARABIA. *Shepperton Studio Sound Department; John Cox, sound director.*

THE MUSIC MAN. Warner Bros. Studio Sound Department; George R. Groves, sound director.

THAT TOUCH OF MINK. Universal City Studio Sound Department; Waldon O. Watson, sound director.

WHAT EVER HAPPENED TO BABY JANE? Warner Bros. Glenn Glenn Sound Department; Joseph Kelly, sound director.

Music Awards
Best Song
Days of Wine and Roses" from DAYS OF WINE AND ROSES. Music by Henry Mancini; lyrics by Jonny Mercer.
"Love Song from MUTINY ON THE BOUNTY (Follow Me). Music by Bronislau Kaper; lyrics by Paul Francis Webster.
"Song from TWO FOR THE SEESAW (Second Chance). Music by Andre Previn; lyrics by Dory Langdon.
"Tender Is the Night" from TENDER IS THE NIGHT. Music by Sammy Fain; lyrics by Paul Francis Webster.
"Walk on the Wild Side" from WALK ON THE WILD SIDE. Music by Elmer Bernstein; lyrics by Mack David.

Best Music Score, Substantially Original
FREUD. Jerry Goldsmith.
LAWRENCE OF ARABIA. Maurice Jarre.
MUTINY ON THE BOUNTY. Bronislau Kaper.
TARAS BULBA. Franz Waxman.
TO KILL A MOCKINGBIRD. Elmer Bernstein.

Best Scoring of Music, Adaptation or Treatment
BILLY ROSE'S JUMBO. George Stoll.
GIGOT. Michel Magne.
GYPSY. Frank Perkins.
THE MUSIC MAN. Ray Heindorf.
THE WONDERFUL WORLD OF THE BROTHERS GRIMM. Leigh Harline.

Best Film Editing
LAWRENCE OF ARABIA. Anne Coates.
THE LONGEST DAY. Samuel E. Beetley.
THE MANCHURIAN CANDIDATE. Ferris Webster.
THE MUSIC MAN. William Ziegler.
MUTINY ON THE BOUNTY. John McSweeney, Jr.

Best Costume Design
Black-and-White
DAYS OF WINE AND ROSES. Don Feld.
THE MAN WHO SHOT LIBERTY VALANCE. Edith Head.
THE MIRACLE WORKER. Ruth Morley.
PHAEDRA. Denny Vachlioti.
WHAT EVER HAPPENED TO BABY JANE? Norma Koch.
Color
BON VOYAGE. Bill Thomas.
GYPSY. Orry-Kelly.
THE MUSIC MAN. Dorothy Jeakins.
MY GEISHA. Edith Head.
THE WONDERFUL WORLD OF THE BROTHERS GRIMM. Mary Wills.

Best Special Effects
THE LONGEST DAY. Visual: Robert MacDonald; Audible: Jacques Maumont.
MUTINY ON THE BOUNTY. Visual: A.Arnold Gillespie; Audible: Milo Lory.

Short Subjects
Best Cartoon
THE HOLE, *Storyboard Inc.,* Brandon Films. Produced by John and Faith Hubley.
ICARUS MONTGOLFIER WRIGHT, Format Films, UA. Produced by Jules Engel.
NOW HEAR THIS, WB.
SELF-DEFENSE FOR COWARDS, Rembrandt Films, Film Representations. Produced by William L. Snyder.
SYMPOSIUM ON POPULAR SONGS, Buena Vista. Produced by Walt Disney.

Best Live Action Subject
BIG CITY BLUES, Mayfair Pictures. Produced by Martina and Charles Huguenot van der Linden.
THE CADILLAC, United Producers Releasing. Produced by Robert Clouse.
THE CLIFF DWELLERS, Group II Film Productions. Produced by Hayward Anderson.
HAPPY ANNIVERSARY (Fr.). Atlantic Pictures. Produced by Pierre Etaix and J.C. Carriere.
PAN, Mayfair Pictures. Produced by Herman van der Horst.

Documentary
Best Short Subject Documentary
DYLAN THOMAS, Janus Films (Welsh). Produced by Jack Howells.
THE JOHN GLENN STORY, Department of the Navy, WB. Produced by William L. Hendricks.
THE ROAD TO THE WALL, CBS Films, Department of Defense. Produced by Robert Saudek.

Best Feature Documentary
ALVORADA (Brazil's Changing Face), MW Filmproduktion. Produced by Hugo Niebeling.
BLACK FOX, Image Productions, Heritage Films. Produced by Louis Clyde Stoumen.

Best Foreign Language Film
ELECTRA (Gr.), Michael Cacoyannis.
THE FOUR DAYS OF NAPLES (Ital.), Nanni Loy.
THE GIVEN WORD (Bra.), Anselmo Duarte.
SUNDAYS AND CYBELE (Fr.), Serge Bourguignon.
TLAYUCAN (Mex.), Luis Alcoriza.

Irving G. Thalberg Memorial Award
None awarded.

Jean Hersholt Humanitarian Award
Steve Broidy.

Scientific or Technical
Class II
Ralph Chapman for the design and development of an advanced motion picture camera crane.
Albert S. Pratt, James L. Wassell, and Hans C. Wohlrab of the Professional Division, Bell & Howell Co., for the design and development of a new and improved automatic motion picture additive color printer.

North American Phillips Co., Inc., for the design and engineering of the Norelco Universal 70/35mm motion picture projector.
Charles E. Sutter, William Bryson Smith, and Louis C. Kennell of Paramount Pictures Corp. for the engineering and application to motion picture production of a new system of electric power distribution.
Class III
Electro-Voice, Inc., for a highly directional dynamic line microphone.
Louis G. MacKenzie for a selective sound effects repeater.

1963
Best Picture
AMERICA, AMERICA, WB. Produced by Elia Kazan.
CLEOPATRA, FOX. Produced by Walker Wanger.
HOW THE WEST WAS WON, MGM and Cinerama. Produced by Bernard Smith.
LILIES OF THE FIELD, UA. Produced by Ralph Nelson.
TOM JONES (Brit.), UA-Lopert. Produced by Tony Richardson.

Best Actor
Albert Finney for TOM JONES (Brit.).
Richard Harris for THIS SPORTING LIFE (Brit.).
Rex Harrison for CLEOPATRA.
Paul Newman for HUD.
Sidney Poitier for LILIES OF THE FIELD.

Best Actress
Leslie Caron for THE L-SHAPED ROOM (Brit.)
Shirley MacLaine for IRMA LA DOUCE.
Patricia Neal for HUD.
Rachel Roberts for THIS SPORTING LIFE.
Natalie Wood for LOVE WITH THE PROPER STRANGER.

Best Supporting Actor
Nick Adams for TWILIGHT OF HONOR.
Bobby Darin for CAPTAIN NEWMAN, M.D.
Melvyn Douglas for HUD.
Hugh Griffith for TOM JONES (Brit.).
John Huston for THE CARDINAL.

Best Supporting Actress
Diane Cilento for TOM JONES (Brit.).
Dame Edith Evans for TOM JONES (Brit.).
Joyce Redman for TOM JONES (Brit.).
Margaret Rutherford for THE V.I.P.S.
Lilia Skala for LILIES OF THE FIELD.

Best Direction
Federico Fellini for 8 1/2 (Ital.).
Elia Kazan for AMERICA, AMERICA.
Otto Preminger for THE CARDINAL.
Tony Richardson for TOM JONES.
Martin Ritt for HUD.

Writing Awards
Best Screenplay, Based on Material from Another Medium
CAPTAIN NEWMAN, M.D., by Richard L. Breen, Phoebe and Henry Ephron.
HUD, by Irving Ravetch and Harriet Frank, Jr.
LILIES OF THE FIELDS, by James Poe.
SUNDAYS AND CYBELE (Fr.), by Serge Bourguigon and Antoine Tudal.
TOM JONES (Brit.), by John Osborne.

Best Story and Screenplay, Written Directly for the Screen
AMERICA, AMERICA, by Elia Kazan.
8 1/2 (Ital.), by Federico Fellini, Ennio Flaiano, Tullio Pinelli, and Brunello Rondi.
FOUR DAYS OF NAPLES (Ital.), by Pasquale Festa Campanile, Massimo Franciosa, Nanni Loy, Vasco Pratolini and Carlo Bernari.
HOW THE WEST WAS WON, by James R. Webb.
LOVE WITH THE PROPER STRANGER, by Arnold Schulman.

Best Cinematography
Black-and-White
THE BALCONY. George Folsey.
THE CARETAKERS. Lucien Ballard.
HUD. James Wong Howe.
LILIES OF THE FIELD. Ernest Haller.
LOVE WITH THE PROPER STRANGER. Milton Krasner.
Color
THE CARDINAL. Leon Shamroy.
CLEOPATRA. Leon Shamroy.
HOW THE WEST WAS WON. William H. Daniels, Milton Krasner, Charles Lang, Jr., and Joseph LaShelle.
IRMA LA DOUCE. Joseph LaShelle.
IT'S A MAD, MAD, MAD, MAD WORLD. Ernest Laszlo.

Best Art Direction—Set Decoration
Black-and-White
AMERICA, AMERICA. Gene Callahan.
8 1/2 (Ital.). Piero Gherardi.
HUD. Hal Pereira and Tambi Larsen; Sam Comer and Robert Benton.
LOVE WITH THE PROPER STRANGER. Hal Pereira and Roland Anderson; Sam Comer and Grace Gregory.
TWILIGHT OF HONOR. George W. Davis and Paul Groesse; Henry Grace and Hugh Hunt.
Color
THE CARDINAL. Lyle Wheeler; Gene Callahan.
CLEOPATRA. John DeCuir, Jack Martin Smith, Hilyard Brown, Herman Blumenthal, Elven Webb, Maurice Pelling, and Boris Juraga; Walter M. Scott, Paul S. Fox and Ray Moyer.
COME BLOW YOUR HORN. Hal Pereira and Roland Anderson; Sam Comer and James Payne.
HOW THE WEST WAS WON. George W. Davis, William Ferrari, and Addison Hehr; Henry Grace, Don Greenwood, Jr., and Jack Mills.
TOM JONES. Ralph Brinton, Ted Marshall, and Jocelyn Herbert; Josie MacAvin.

Best Sound
BYE BYE BIRDIE. Columbia Studio Sound Department; Charles Rice, sound director.
CAPTAIN NEWMAN, M.D. Universal City Studio Sound Department; Waldon O. Watson, sound director.
CLEOPATRA. 20th Century-Fox Studio Sound Department; James P. Corcoran, sound director; and Todd-AO Sound Department; Fred Hynes, sound director.

HOW THE WEST WAS WON. MGM Studio Sound Department; Franklin E. Milton, sound director.
IT'S A MAD, MAD, MAD, MAD WORLD. Samuel Golgwyn Studio Sound Department; Gordon E. Sawyer, sound director.
Music Awards
  Best Song
    'Call Me Irresponsible" from PAPA'S DELICATE CONDITION. Music by James Van Heusen; lyrics by Sammy Cahn.
    "Charade" from CHARADE. Music by Henry Mancini; lyrics by Johnny Mercer.
    "It's a Mad, Mad, Mad, Mad World" from IT'S A MAD, MAD, MAD, MAD WORLD. Music by Ernest Gold; lyrics by Mack David.
    "More" from MONDO CANE (Ital.). Music by Riz Ortolani and Nino Oliviero; lyrics by Norman Newell.
    "So Little Time" from 55 DAYS AT PEKING. Music by Dimitri Tiomkin; lyrics by Paul Francis Webster.
  Best Music Score, Substantially Original
    CLEOPATRA. Alex North.
    55 DAYS AT PEKING. Dimitri Tiomkin.
    HOW THE WEST WAS WON. Alfred Newman and Ken Darby.
    IT'S A MAD, MAD, MAD, MAD WORLD. Ernest Gold.
    TOM JONES (Brit.). John Addison.
  Best Scoring of Music, Adaptation or Treatment
    BYE BYE BIRDIE. John Green.
    IRMA LA DOUCE. Andre Previn.
    A NEW KIND OF LOVE. Leith Stevens.
    SUNDAYS AND CYBELE (Fr.). Maurice Jarre.
    THE SWORD IN THE STONE. George Bruns.
  Best Film Editing
    THE CARDINAL. Louis R. Loeffler.
    CLEOPATRA. Dorothy Spencer.
    THE GREAT ESCAPE. Ferris Webster.
    HOW THE WEST WAS WON. Harold F. Kress.
    IT'S A MAD, MAD, MAD, MAD WORLD. Frederic Knudtson, Robert C. Jones, and Gene Fowler, Jr.
  Best Costume Design
    Black-and-White
      8 1/2 (Ital.). Piero Gherardi.
      LOVE WITH THE PROPER STRANGER. Edith Head.
      THE STRIPPER. Travilla.
      TOYS IN THE ATTIC. Bill Thomas.
      WIVES AND LOVERS. Edith Head.
    Color
      THE CARDINAL. Donald Brooks.
      CLEOPATRA. Irene Sharaff, Vittorio Nino Novarese, and Renie.
      HOW THE WEST WAS WON. Walter Plunkett.
      THE LEOPARD (Ital.). Piero Tosi.
      A NEW KIND OF LOVE. Edith Head.
  Best Special Visual Effects
    THE BIRDS. Ub Iwerks.
    CLEOPATRA. Emil Kosa, Jr.
  Best Sound Effects
    A GATHERING OF EAGLES. Robert L. Bratton.
    IT'S A MAD, MAD, MAD, MAD WORLD. Walter G. Elliott.
Short Subjects
  Best Cartoon
    AUTOMANIA 2000, Pathe Contemporary Films. Produced by John Halas.
    THE CRITIC, COL. Produced by Ernest Pintoff.
    THE GAME, Rembrandt Films-Film Representations. Produced by Dusan Vukotic.
    MY FINANCIAL CAREER, National Film Board of Canada. Walter Reade-Sterling-Continental Distributing. Produced by Colin Low and Tom Daly.
    PIANOSSIMO, Cinema 16. Produced by Carmen D'Avino.
  Best Live Action Subject
    THE CONCERT, King Corp., George K. Arthur-Go Pictures. Produced by Ezra Baker.
    HOME-MADE CAR, Schoenfeld Films. Produced by James Hill.
    AN OCCURRENCE AT OWL CREEK BRIDGE, Janus Films. Produced by Paul de Roubaix and Marcel Ichac.
    SIX-SIDED TRIANGLE, Lion International. Produced by Christopher Miles.
    THAT'S ME, Pathe Contemporary Films. Produced by Walker Stuart.
Documentary
  Best Short Subject Documentary
    CHAGALL, Auerbach-Flag Films. Produced by Simon Schiffrin.
    THE FIVE CITIES OF JUNE, U.S. Information Agency. Produced by George Stevens, Jr.
    THE SPIRIT OF AMERICA, Spotlite News. Produced by Algernon G. Walker.
    THIRTY MILLION LETTERS, British Transport Films. Produced by Edgar Anstey.
    TO LIVE AGAIN, Wilding Inc. Produced by Mel London.
  Best Feature Documentary
    THE LINK AND THE CHAIN (Fr.), Films du Centaure-Filmartic. Produced by Paul de Roubaix.
    ROBERT FROST: A LOVER'S QUARREL WITH THE WORLD, WGBH Educational Foundation. Produced by Robert Hughes.
    THE YANKS ARE COMING, David L. Wolper Productions. Produced by Marshall Flaum.
  Best Foreign Language Film
    8 1/2 (Ital.), Federico Fellini.
    KNIFE IN THE WATER (Pol.), Roman Polanski.
    LOS TARANTOS (Span.), Rovira-Beleta.
    THE RED LANTERNS (Gr.), Vassilis Georgiades.
    TWIN SISTERS OF KYOTO (Jap.), Noboru Nakamura.
Irving G. Thalberg Memorial Award
  Sam Spiegel.
Jean Hersholt Humanitarian Award
  None given.
Scientific and Technical Awards
  Class III
    Douglas G. Shearer and A. Arnold Gillespie of MGM Studio for the engineering of an improved Background Process Projection System.

1964
Best Picture
  BECKET, PAR. Produced by Hal B. Wallis.
  DR. STRANGELOVE OR: HOW I LEARNED TO STOP WORRYING AND LOVE THE BOMB, COL. Produced by Stanley Kubrick.
  MARY POPPINS, Buena Vista. Produced by Walt Disney.
  MY FAIR LADY, WB. Produced by Jack L. Warner.
  ZORBA THE GREEK, FOX. Produced by Michael Cacoyannis.
Best Actor
  Richard Burton for BECKET.
  Rex Harrison for MY FAIR LADY.
  Peter O'Toole for BECKET.
  Anthony Quinn for ZORBA THE GREEK.
  Peter Sellers for DR. STRANGELOVE.
Best Actress
  Julie Andrews for MARY POPPINS.
  Anne Bancroft for THE PUMPKIN EATER.
  Sophia Loren for MARRIAGE ITALIAN STYLE.
  Debbie Reynolds for THE UNSINKABLE MOLLY BROWN.
  Kim Stanley for SEANCE ON A WET AFTERNOON.
Best Supporting Actor
  John Gielgud for BECKET.
  Stanley Holloway for MY FAIR LADY.
  Edmond O'Brien for SEVEN DAYS IN MAY.
  Lee Tracy for THE BEST MAN.
  Peter Ustinov for TOPKAPI.
Best Supporting Actress
  Gladys Cooper for MY FAIR LADY.
  Dame Edith Evans for THE CHALK GARDEN.
  Grayson Hall for THE NIGHT OF THE IGUANA.
  Lila Kedrova for ZORBA THE GREEK.
  Agnes Moorehead for HUSH...HUSH, SWEET CHARLOTTE.
Best Direction
  Michael Cacoyannis for ZORBA THE GREEK.
  George Cukor for MY FAIR LADY.
  Peter Glenville for BECKET.
  Stanley Kubrick for DR. STRANGELOVE.
  Robert Stevenson for MARY POPPINS.
Writing Awards
  Best Screenplay, Based on Material from Another Medium
    BECKET, by Edward Anhalt.
    DR. STRANGELOVE, by Stanley Kubrick, Peter George, and Terry Southern.
    MARY POPPINS, by Bill Walsh and Don DaGradi.
    MY FAIR LADY, by Alan Jay Lerner.
    ZORBA THE GREEK, by Michael Cacoyannis.
  Best Story and Screenplay, Written Directly for the Screen
    FATHER GOOSE, by S.H. Barnett; Peter Stone and Frank Tarloff.
    A HARD DAY'S NIGHT, by Alan Owen.
    ONE POTATO, TWO POTATO, by Orville H. Hampton and Raphael Hayes.
    THE ORGANIZER (Ital.), by Age, Scarpelli, and Mario Monicelli.
    THAT MAN FROM RIO (Fr.), by Jean-Paul Rappeneau, Ariane Mnouchkine, Daniel Boulanger, and Philippe De Broca.
Best Cinematography
  Black-and-White
    THE AMERICANIZATION OF EMILY. Philip H. Lathrop.
    FATE IS THE HUNTER. Milton Krasner.
    HUSH...HUSH, SWEET CHARLOTTE. Joseph Biroc.
    THE NIGHT OF THE IGUANA. Gabriel Figueroa.
    ZORBA THE GREEK. Walter Lassally.
  Color
    BECKET. Geoffrey Unsworth.
    CHEYENNE AUTUMN. William H. Clothier.
    MARY POPPINS. Edward Colman.
    MY FAIR LADY. Harry Stradling.
    THE UNSINKABLE MOLLY BROWN. Daniel L. Fapp.
Best Art Direction—Set Decoration
  Black-and-White
    THE AMERICANIZATION OF EMILY. George W. Davis, Hans Peters, and Elliot Scott; Henry Grace and Robert R. Benton.
    HUSH...HUSH, SWEET CHARLOTTE. William Glasgow; Raphael Bretton.
    THE NIGHT OF THE IGUANA. Stephen Grimes.
    SEVEN DAYS IN MAY. Cary Odell; Edward G. Boyle.
    ZORBA THE GREEK. Vassilis Fotopoulos.
  Color
    BECKET. John Bryan and Maurice Carter; Patrick McLoughlin and Robert Cartwright.
    MARY POPPINS. Carroll Clark and William H. Tuntke; Emile Kuri and Hal Gausman.
    MY FAIR LADY. Gene Allen and Cecil Beaton; George James Hopkins.
    THE UNSINKABLE MOLLY BROWN. George W. Davis and Preston Ames; Henry Grace and Hugh Hunt.
    WHAT A WAY TO GO. Jack Martin Smith and Ted Haworth; Walter M. Scott and Stuart A. Reiss.
Best Sound
  BECKET. Shepperton Studio Sound Department; John Cox, sound director.
  FATHER GOOSE. Universal City Studio Sound Department; Waldon O. Watson, sound director.
  MARY POPPINS. Walt Disney Studio Sound Department; Robert O. Cook, sound director.
  MY FAIR LADY. Warner Bros. Studio Sound Department; George R. Groves, sound director.
  THE UNSINKABLE MOLLY BROWN. MGM Studio Sound Department; Franklin E. Milton, sound director.
Music Awards
  Best Song
    Chim Chim Cher-ee" from MARY POPPINS. Music and lyrics by Richard M. Sherman and Robert B. Sherman.
    "Dear Heart" from DEAR HEART. Music by Henry Mancini; lyrics by Jay Livingston and Ray Evans.
    "Hush...Hush, Sweet Charlotte" from HUSH...HUSH, SWEET CHARLOTTE. Music by Frank DeVol; lyrics by Mack David.

"My Kind of Town" from ROBIN AND THE 7 HOODS. Music by James Van Heusen; lyrics by Sammy Cahn.

"Where Love Has Gone" from WHERE LOVE HAS GONE. Music by James Van Heusen; lyrics by Sammy Cahn.

Best Music Score, Substantially Original

BECKET. Laurence Rosenthal.

THE FALL OF THE ROMAN EMPIRE. Dimitri Tiomkin.

HUSH...HUSH, SWEET CHARLOTTE. Frank DeVol.

MARY POPPINS. Richard M. Sherman and Robert B. Sherman.

THE PINK PANTHER. Henry Mancini.

Best Scoring of Music, Adaptation or Treatment

A HARD DAY'S NIGHT (Brit.). George Martin.

MARY POPPINS. Irwin Kostal.

MY FAIR LADY. Andre Previn.

ROBIN AND THE 7 HOODS. Nelson Riddle.

THE UNSINKABLE MOLLY BROWN. Robert Armbruster, Leo Arnaud, Jack Elliott, Jack Hayes, Calvin Jackson, and Leo Shuken.

Best Film Editing

BECKET. Anne Coates.

FATHER GOOSE. Ted J. Kent.

HUSH...HUSH, SWEET CHARLOTTE. Michael Luciano.

MARY POPPINS. Cotton Warburton.

MY FAIR LADY. William Ziegler.

Best Costume Design

Black-and-White

A HOUSE IS NOT A HOME. Edith Head.

HUSH...HUSH, SWEET CHARLOTTE. Norma Koch.

KISSES FOR MY PRESIDENT. Howard Shoup.

THE NIGHT OF THE IGUANA. Dorothy Jeakins.

THE VISIT. Rene Hubert.

Color

BECKET. Margaret Furse.

MARY POPPINS. Tony Walton.

MY FAIR LADY. Cecil Beaton.

THE UNSINKABLE MOLLY BROWN. Morton Haack.

WHAT A WAY TO GO. Edith Head and Moss Mabry.

Best Special Visual Effects

MARY POPPINS. Peter Ellenshaw, Hamilton Luske, and Eustace Lycett.

7 FACES OF DR. LAO. Jim Danforth.

Best Sound Effects

GOLDFINGER (Brit.). Norman Wanstall.

THE LIVELY SET. Robert L. Bratton.

Short Subjects

Best Cartoon

CHRISTMAS CRACKER, National Film Board of Canada, Favorite Films of California.

HOW TO AVOID FRIENDHSIP, Rembrandt Films, Film Representations. Produced by William L. Snyder.

NUDNIK NO. 2, Rembrandt Films, Film Representations. Produced by William L. Snyder.

THE PINK PHINK, Mirisch-Geoffrey, UA. Produced by David H. DePatie and Friz Freleng.

Best Live Action Subject

CASALS CONDUCTS: 1964, Thalia Film Corp., Beckman Film Corp. Produced by Edward Schreiber.

HELP! MY SNOWMAN'S BURNING DOWN, Pathe Contemporary Films. Produced by Carson Davidson.

THE LEGEND OF JIMMY BLUE EYES, Topaz Film Corp. Produced by Robert Clouse.

Documentary

Best Short Subject Documentary

BREAKING THE HABIT. American Cancer Society, Modern Talking Picture Service. Produced by Henry Jacobs and John Korty.

CHILDREN WITHOUT. National Education Association, Guggenheim Productions.

KENOJUAK, National Film Board of Canada.

NINE FROM LITTLE ROCK, U.S. Information Agency, Guggenheim Productions.

140 DAYS UNDER THE WORLD, New Zealand National Film Unit, Rank Film Distributors of New Zealand. Produced by Geoffrey Scott and Oxley Hughan.

Best Feature Documentary

THE FINEST HOURS, COL. Produced by Jack Le Vien.

FOUR DAYS IN NOVEMBER, David L. Wolper Productions, UA. Produced by Mel Stuart.

THE HUMAN DUTCH. Produced by Bert Haanstra.

JACQUES-YVES COUSTEAU'S WORLD WITHOUT SUN, COL. Produced by Jacues-Yves Cousteau.

OVER THERE, 1914-18. Zodiac Productions, Pathe Contemporary Films. Produced by Jean Aurel.

Best Foreign Language Films

RAVEN'S END (Swed.). Bo Widerberg.

SALLAH (Israel). Ephraim Kishon.

THE UMBRELLAS OF CHERBOURG (Fr.). Jacques Demy.

WOMAN IN THE DUNES (Jap.). Hiroshi Teshigahara.

YESTERDAY, TODAY, AND TOMORROW (Ital.). Vittorio De Sica.

Irving G. Thalberg Memorial Award

None awarded.

Jean Hersholt Humanitarian Award

None awarded.

Honorary Award

William Tuttle for his outstanding makeup achievement for 7 FACES OF DR. LAO.

Scientific or Technical

Class I

Petro Vlahos, Wadsworthj E. Pohl, and Ub Iwerks for the conception and perfection of techniques for Color Traveling Matte Composite Cinematography.

Class II

Sidney P. Solow, Edward H. Reichard, Carl W. Hauge and Job Sanderson of Consolidated Film Industries for the design and development of the versatile Automatic 35mm Composite Color Printer.

Pierre Angenieux for the development of a ten-to-one Zoom Lens for cinematography.

Class III

Milton Forman, Richard B. Glickman and Daniel J. Pearlman of ColorTran Industries for the advancements in the design and application to motion picture photography of lighting units using quartz iodine lamps.

Stewart Filmscreen for a seamless translucent Blue Screen for Traveling Matte Color Cinematography.

Anthony Paglia and the 20th Century-Fox Studio Mechanical Effects Department for an improved method of producing Explosion Flash Effects for motion pictures.

Edward H. Reichard and Carl W. Hauge of Consolidated Film Industries for the design of a Proximity Cue Detector and its application to motion picture printers.

Edward H. Reichard, Leonard L. Sokolow and Carl W. Hauge od Consolidated Film Industries for the design and application to motion picture laboratory practice of a Stroboscopic Scene Tester for color and black-and-white.

Nelson Tyler for the design and construction of an improved Helicopter Camera System.

1965

Best Picture

DARLING (Brit.), Embassy. Produced by Joseph Janni.

DOCTOR ZHIVAGO, MGM. Produced by Carlo Ponti.

SHIP OF FOOLS, COL. Produced by Stanley Kramer.

THE SOUND OF MUSIC, FOX. Produced by Robert Wise.

A THOUSAND CLOWNS, UA. Produced by Fred Coe.

Best Actor

Richard Burton for THE SPY WHO CAME IN FROM THE COLD.

Lee Marvin for CAT BALLOU.

Laurence Olivier for OTHELLO.

Rod Steiger for THE PAWNBROKER.

Oskar Werner for SHIP OF FOOLS.

Best Actress

Julie Andrews for THE SOUND OF MUSIC.

Julie Christie for DARLING (Brit.).

Samantha Eggar for THE COLLECTOR.

Elizabeth Hartman for A PATCH OF BLUE.

Simone Signoret for SHIP OF FOOLS.

Best Supporting Actor

Martin Balsam for A THOUSAND CLOWNS.

Ian Bannen for THE FLIGHT OF THE PHOENIX.

Tom Courtenay for DOCTOR ZHIVAGO.

Michael Dunn for SHIP OF FOOLS.

Frank Finlay for OTHELLO (Brit.).

Best Supporting Actress

Ruth Gordon for INSIDE DAISY CLOVER.

Joyce Redman for OTHELLO (Brit.).

Maggie Smith for OTHELLO (Brit.).

Shelley Winters for A PATCH OF BLUE.

Peggy Wood for THE SOUND OF MUSIC.

Best Direction

David Lean for DOCTOR ZHIVAGO.

John Schlesinger for DARLING (Brit.).

Hiroshi Teshigahara for WOMAN IN THE DUNES (Jap.).

Robert Wise for THE SOUND OF MUSIC.

William Wyler for THE COLLECTOR.

Writing Awards

Best Screenplay, Based on Material from Another Medium

CAT BALLOU, by Walter Newman and Frank R. Pierson.

THE COLLECTOR, by Stanley Mann and John Kohn.

DOCTOR ZHIVAGO by Robert Bolt.

SHIP OF FOOLS, by Abby Mann.

A THOUSAND CLOWNS, by Herb Gardner.

Best Story and Screenplay, Written Directly for the Screen.

CASANOVA '70 (Ital.), by Age, Scarpelli, Mario Monicelli, Tonino Guerra, Giorgio Salvioni and Suso Cecchi D'Amico.

DARLING (Brit.), by Frederic Raphael.

THOSE MAGNIFICENT MEN IN THEIR FLYING MACHINES, by Jack Davies and Ken Annakin.

THE TRAIN, by Franklin Coen and Frank Davis.

THE UMBRELLAS OF CHERBOURG (Fr.), by Jacques Demy.

Best Cinematography

Black-and-White

IN HARM'S WAY. Loyal Griggs.

KING RAT. Burnett Guffey.

MORITURI. Conrad Hall.

A PATCH OF BLUE. Robert Burks.

SHIP OF FOOLS. Ernest Laszlo.

Color

THE AGONY AND THE ECSTASY. Leon Shamroy.

DOCTOR ZHIVAGO. Freddie Young.

THE GREAT RACE. Russell Harlan.

THE GREATEST STORY EVER TOLD. William C. Mellor and Loyal Griggs.

THE SOUND OF MUSIC. Ted McCord.

Best Art Direction—Set Decoration

Black-and-White

KING RAT. Robert Emmet Smith; Frank Tuttle.

A PATCH OF BLUE. George W. Davis and Urie McCleary; Henry Grace and Charles S. Thompson.

SHIP OF FOOLS. Robert Clatworthy; Joseph Kish.

THE SLENDER THREAD. Hal Pereira and Jack Poplin; Robert Benton and Joseph Kish.

THE SPY WHO CAME IN FROM THE COLD. Hal Pereira, Tambi Larsen and Edward Marshall; Josie MacAvin.

Color

THE AGONY AND THE ECSTASY. John DeCuir and Jack Martin Smith; Dario Simoni.

DOCTOR ZHIVAGO. John Box and Terry Marsh; Dario Simoni.

THE GREATEST STORY EVER TOLD. Richard Day, William Creber, and David Hall; Ray Moyer, Fred MacLean and Norman Rockett.

INSIDE DAISY CLOVER. Robert Clatworthy; George James Hopkins.

THE SOUND OF MUSIC. Boris Leven; Walter M. Scott and Ruby Levitt.

Best Sound

THE AGONY AND THE ECSTASY. 20th Century-Fox Studio Sound Department;

James P. Corcoran, sound director.
DOCTOR ZHIVAGO. MGM British Studio Sound Department; A.W. Watkins, sound director; and MGM Studio Sound Department; Franklin E. Milton, sound director.
THE GREAT RACE. Warner Bros. Studio Sound Department; George R. Groves, sound director.
SHENANDOAH. Universal City Sound Department; Waldon O. Watson, sound director.
THE SOUND OF MUSIC. 20th Century-Fox Studio Sound Department; James P. Corcoran, sound director; and Todd-AO Sound Department; Fred Hynes, sound director.
Music Awards
  Best Song
    "The Ballad of Cat Ballou" from CAT BALLOU. Music by Jerry Livingston; lyrics by Mack David.
    "I Will Wait for You" from THE UMBRELLAS OF CHERBOURG. Music by Michel Legrand; lyrics by Jacques Demy.
    The Shadow of Your Smile" from THE SANDPIPER. Music by Johnny Mandel; lyrics by Paul Francis Webster.
    "The Sweetheart Tree" from THE GREAT RACE. Music by Henry Mancini; lyrics by Johnny Mercer.
    "What's New Pussycat?" from WHAT'S NEW PUSSYCAT? Music by Burt Bacharach; lyrics by Hal David.
  Best Music Score, Substantially Original
    THE AGONY AND THE ECSTASY. Alex North.
    DOCTOR ZHIVAGO. Maurice Jarre.
    THE GREATEST STORY EVER TOLD. Alfred Newman.
    A PATCH OF BLUE. Jerry Goldsmith.
    THE UMBRELLAS OF CHERBOURG (Fr.). Michel Legrand and Jacques Demy.
  Best Scoring of Music, Adaptation or Treatment
    CAT BALLOU. DeVol.
    THE PLEASURE SEEKERS. Lionel Newman and Alexander Courage.
    THE SOUND OF MUSIC. Irwin Kostal.
    A THOUSAND CLOWNS. Don Walker.
    THE UMBRELLAS OF CHERBOURG (Fr.). Michel Legrand.
Best Film Editing
  CAT BALLOU. Charles Nelson.
  DOCTOR ZHIVAGO. Norman Savage.
  THE FLIGHT OF THE PHOENIX. Michael Luciano.
  THE GREAT RACE. Ralph E. Winters.
  THE SOUND OF MUSIC. William Reynolds.
Best Costume Design
  Black-and-White
    DARLING (Brit.). Julie Harris.
    MORITURI. Moss Mabry.
    A RAGE TO LIVE. Howard Shoup.
    SHIP OF FOOLS. Bill Thomas and Jean Louis.
    THE SLENDER THREAD. Edith Head.
  Color
    THE AGONY AND THE ECSTASY. Vittorio Nino Novarese.
    DOCTOR ZHIVAGO. Phyllis Dalton.
    THE GREATEST STORY EVER TOLD. Vittorio Nino Novarese and Marjorie Best.
    INSIDE DAISY CLOVER. Edith Head and Bill Thomas.
    THE SOUND OF MUSIC. Dorothy Jeakins.
Best Special Visual Effects
  THE GREATEST STORY EVER TOLD. J. McMillan Johnson.
  THUNDERBALL. John Stears.
Best Sound Effects
  THE GREAT RACE. Tregoweth Brown.
  VON RYAN'S EXPRESS. Walter A. Rossi.
Short Subjects
  Best Cartoon
    CLAY OR THE ORIGIN OF SPECIES, Harvard University, Pathe Contemporary Films. Produced by Eliot Noyes, Jr.
    THE DOT AND THE LINE, MGM. Produced by Chuck Jones and Les Goldman.
    THE THIEVING MAGPIE, AA. Produced by Emanuele Luzzati.
  Live Action Subjects
    THE CHICKEN (Fr.), Pathe Contemporary Films. Produced by Claude Berri.
    FORTRESS OF PEACE, Farner-Looser Films, Cinerama. Produced by Lothar Wolff.
    SKATERDATER, Byway Productions, UA. Produced by Marshall Backlar and Noel Black.
    SNOW, Manson Distributing. Produced by Edgar Anstey.
    TIME PIECE, Muppets, Inc., Pathe Contemporary Films. Produced by Jim Henson.
Documentary
  Best Short Subject Documentary
    MURAL ON OUR STREET, Henry Street Settlement, Pathe Contemporary Films. Produced by Kirk Smallman.
    OUVERTURE, Mafilm Prods., Hungarofilm-Pathe Contemporary Films.
    POINT OF VIEW, Vision Associates Prod., National Tuberculosis Assoc.
    TO BE ALIVE!, Johnson Wax. Produced by Francis Thompson, Inc..
    YEATS COUNTRY, Aengus Films for the Department of External Affairs of Ireland. Produced by Patrick Carey and Joe Mendoza.
  Best Feature Documentary
    THE BATTLE OF THE BULGE...THE BRAVE RIFLES, Mascott Productions. Produced by Laurence E. Mascott.
    THE ELEANOR ROOSEVELT STORY, American International. Produced by Sidney Glazier.
    THE FORTH ROAD BRIDGE, Randon Films Productions, Shell-Max and B.P. Film Library. Produced by Peter Mills.
    LET MY PEOPLE GO, David L. Wolper Productions. Produced by Marshall Flaum.
    TO DIE IN MADRID, Altura Films International. Produced by Frederic Rossif.
Best Foreign Language Films
  BLOOD ON THE LAND (Gr.).
  DEAR JOHN (Swed.). Lars Magnus Lindgren.
  KWAIDAN (Jap.). Masaki Kobayashi.
  MARRIAGE ITALIAN STYLE (Ital.). Vittorio De Sica.
  THE SHOP ON MAIN STREET (Czech.). Jan Kadar and Elmar Klos.
Irving G. Thalberg Memorial Award
  William Wyler.
Jean Hersholt Humanitarian Award
  Edmond L. DePatie.

Honorary Award
  Bob Hope for unique and distinguished service to our industry and the Academy.
Scientific or Technical
  Class II
    Arthur J. Hatch of Strong Electric, subsidiary of General Precision Equipment, for the design and development of an Air Blown Carbon Arc Projection Lamp.
    Stefan Kudelski for the design and development of the Nagra portable 1/4" tape recording system for motion picture sound recording.

1966
Best Picture
  ALFIE (Brit.), PAR. Produced by Lewis Gilbert.
  A MAN FOR ALL SEASONS, COL. Produced by Fred Zinnemann.
  THE RUSSIANS ARE COMING, THE RUSSIANS ARE COMING, UA. Produced by Norman Jewison.
  THE SAND PEBBLES, FOX. Produced by Robert Wise.
  WHO'S AFRAID OF VIRGINIA WOOLF? WB. Porduced by Ernest Lehman.
Best Actor
  Alan Arkin for THE RUSSIANS ARE COMING, THE RUSSIANS ARE COMING.
  Richard Burton for WHO'S AFRAID OF VIRGINIA WOOLF?
  Michael Caine for ALFIE (Brit.).
  Steve McQueen for THE SAND PEBBLES.
  Paul Scofield for A MAN FOR ALL SEASONS.
Best Actress
  Anouk Aimee for A MAN AND A WOMAN (Fr.).
  Ida Kaminska for THE SHOP ON MAIN STREET (Czech.).
  Lynn Redgrave for GEORGY GIRL (Brit.).
  Vanessa Redgrave for MORGAN! (Brit.).
  Elizabeth Taylor for WHO'S AFRAID OF VIRGINIA WOOLF?
Best Supporting Actor
  Mako for THE SAND PEBBLES.
  James Mason for GEORGY GIRL (Brit.).
  Walter Matthau for THE FORTUNE COOKIE.
  George Segal for WHO'S AFRAID OF VIRGINIA WOOLF?
  Robert Shaw for A MAN FOR ALL SEASONS.
Best Supporting Actress
  Sandy Dennis for WHO'S AFRAID OF VIRGINIA WOOLF?
  Wendy Hiller for A MAN FOR ALL SEASONS.
  Jocelyn Lagarde for HAWAII.
  Vivien Merchant for ALFIE (Brit.).
  Geraldine Page for YOU'RE A BIG BOY NOW.
Best Direction
  Michelangelo Antonioni for BLOW-UP. (Brit./Ital.).
  Richard Brooks for THE PROFESSIONALS.
  Claude Lelouch for A MAN AND A WOMAN (Fr.).
  Mike Nichols for WHO'S AFRAID OF VIRGINIA WOOLF?
  Fred Zinneman for A MAN FOR ALL SEASONS.
Writing Awards
  Best Screenplay, Based on Material from Another Medium
    ALFIE (Brit.), by Bill Naughton.
    A MAN FOR ALL SEASONS, by Robert Bolt.
    THE PROFESSIONALS, by Richard Brooks.
    THE RUSSIANS ARE COMING, THE RUSSIANS ARE COMING, by William Rose.
    WHO'S AFRAID OF VIRGINIA WOOLF?, by Ernest Lehman.
  Best Story and Screenplay, Written Directly for the Screen
    BLOW-UP (Brit./Ital.), by Michelangelo Antonioni, Tonino Guerra, and Edward Bond.
    THE FORTUNE COOKIE, by Billy Wilder and I.A.L. Diamond.
    KHARTOUM, by Robert Ardrey.
    A MAN AND A WOMAN (Fr.), by Claude Lelouch and Pierre Uytterhoeven.
    THE NAKED PREY, by Clint Johnson and Don Peters.
Best Cinematography
  Black-and-White
    THE FORTUNE COOKIE. Joseph LaShelle.
    GEORGY GIRL (Brit.). Ken Higgins.
    IS PARIS BURNING? Marcel Grignon.
    SECONDS. James Wong Howe.
    WHO'S AFRAID OF VIRGINIA WOOLF? Haskell Wexler.
  Color
    FANTASTIC VOYAGE. Ernest Laszlo.
    HAWAII. Russell Harlan.
    A MAN FOR ALL SEASONS. Ted Moore.
    THE PROFESSIONALS. Conrad Hall.
    THE SAND PEBBLES. Joseph MacDonald.
Best Art Direction—Set Decoration
  Black-and-White
    THE FORTUNE COOKIE. Robert Luthardt and Edward G. Boyle.
    THE GOSPEL ACCORDING TO ST. MATTHEW (Ital.). Luigi Scaccianoce.
    IS PARIS BURNING? Willy Holt; Marc Frederix and Pierre Guffroy.
    MR. BUDDWING. George W. Davis and Paul Groesse; Henry Grace and Hugh Hunt.
    WHO'S AFRAID OF VIRGINIA WOOLF? Richard Sylbert; George James Hopkins.
  Color
    FANTASTIC VOYAGE. Jack Martin Smith and Dale Hennesy; Walter M. Scott and Stuart A. Reiss.
    GAMBIT. Alexander Golitzen and George C. Webb; John McCarthy and John Austin.
    JULIET OF THE SPIRITS (Ital.). Piero Gherardi.
    THE OSCAR. Hal Pereira and Arthur Lonergan; Robert Benton and James Payne.
    THE SAND PEBBLES. Boris Leven; Walter M. Scott, John Sturtevant and William Kiernan.
Best Sound
  GAMBIT. Universal Sound Department; Waldon O. Watson, sound director.
  GRAND PRIX. MGM Studio Sound Department; Franklin E. Milton, sound director.
  HAWAII. Samuel Goldwyn Studio Sound Department; Gordon E. Sawyer, sound director.
  THE SAND PEBBLES. 20th Sentury-Fox Studio Sound Department; James P. Corcoran, sound director.
  WHO'S AFRAID OF VIRGINIA WOOLF? Warner Bros. Studio Sound Department; George R. Groves, sound director.

Music Awards
Best Song
"Alfie" from ALFIE (Brit.). Music by Burt Bacharach; lyrics by Hal David.
Born Free" from BORN FREE (Brit.). Music by John Barry; lyrics by Don Black.
"Georgy Girl" from GEORGY GIRL (Brit.). Music by Tom Springfield; lyrics by Jim Dale.
"My Wishing Doll" from HAWAII. Music by Elmer Bernstein; lyrics by Mack David.
"A Time for Love" from AN AMERICAN DREAM. Music by Johnny Mandel; lyrics by Paul Francis Webster.
Best Original Music Score
THE BIBLE. Toshiro Mayuzumi.
BORN FREE. John Barry.
HAWAII. Elmer Bernstein.
THE SAND PEBBLES. Jerry Goldsmith.
WHO'S AFRAID OF VIRGINIA WOOLF? Alex North.
Best Scoring of Music, Adaptation or Treatment
A FUNNY THING HAPPENED ON THE WAY TO THE FORUM. Ken Thorne.
THE GOSPEL ACCORDING TO ST. MATTHEW (Ital.). Luis Enrique Bacalov.
RETURN OF THE SEVEN. Elmer Bernstein.
THE SINGING NUN. Harry Sukman.
STOP THE WORLD—I WANT TO GET OFF. Al Ham.
Best Film Editing
FANTASTIC VOYAGE. William B. Murphy.
GRAND PRIX. Fredric Steinkamp, Henry Berman, Stewart Linder and Frank Santillo.
THE RUSSIANS ARE COMING, THE RUSSIANS ARE COMING. Hal Ashby and J. Terry Williams.
THE SAND PEBBLES. William Reynolds.
WHO'S AFRAID OF VIRGINIA WOOLF? Sam O'Steen.
Best Costume Design
Black-and-White
THE GOSPEL ACCORDING TO ST. MATTHEW (Ital.). Danilo Donati.
MANDRAGOLA (Ital.). Danilo Donati.
MISTER BUDDWING. Helen Rose.
MORGAN! Jocelyn Rickards.
WHO'S AFRAID OF VIRGINIA WOOLF? Irene Sharaff.
Color
GAMBIT. Jean Louis.
HAWAII. Dorothy Jeakins.
JULIET OF THE SPIRITS (Ital.). Piero Gherardi.
A MAN FOR ALL SEASONS. Elizabeth Haffenden and Joan Bridge.
THE OSCAR. Edith Head.
Best Special Visual Effects
FANTASTIC VOYAGE. Art Cruikshank.
HAWAII. Linwood G. Dunn.
Best Sound Effects
FANTASTIC VOYAGE. Walter Rossi.
GRAND PRIX. Gordon Daniel.
Short Subjects
Best Cartoon
THE DRAG, National Film Board of Canada, Favorite Films. Produced by Wolf Koenig and Robert Verall.
HERB ALBERT AND THE TIJUANA BRASS DOUBLE FEATURE, PAR. Produced by John and Faith Hubley.
THE PINK BLUEPRINT, Mirisch-Geoffrey-DePatie-Freleng, UA. Produced by David H. DePatie and Friz Freleng.
Best Live Action Subject
TURKEY THE BRIDGE, Samaritan Productions, Schoenfeld Films. Produced by Derek Williams.
WILD WINGS, British Transport Films, Manson Distributing. Produced by Edgar Anstey.
THE WINNING STRAIN, Winik Films, PAR. Produced by Leslie Winik.
Documentary
Best Short Subject Documentary
ADOLESCENCE, M.K. Productions. Produced by Marin Karmitz and Vladimir Forgency.
COWBOY, U.S. Information Agency. Produced by Michael Ahnemann and Gary Schlosser.
THE ODDS AGAINST, Vision Associates Production for the American Foundation Institute of Corrections. Produced by Lee R. Bobker and Helen Kristt Radin.
SAINT MATTHEW PASSION. Mafilm Studio, Hungarofilm.
A YEAR TOWARD TOMORROW, Sun Dial Films for Office of Economic Opportunity. Produced by Edmund A. Levy.
Best Feature Documentary
THE FACE OF GENIUS, WBZ-TV, Group W, Boston. Produced by Alfred R. Kelman.
HELICOPTER CANADA, Centennial Commission, National Film Board of Canada. Produced by Peter Jones and Tom Daly.
LE VOLCAN INTERDIT (THE FORBIDDEN VOLCANO), Cine Documents Tazieff, Athos Films. Produced by Haroun Tazieff.
THE REALLY BIG FAMILY, David L. Wolper Productions. Produced by Alex Grasshoff.
THE WAR GAME, BBC Productions of the British Film Institute, Pathe Contemporary Films. Produced by Peter Watkins.
Best Foreign Language Film
THE BATTLE OF ALGIERS (Ital.). Gillo Pontecorvo.
LOVES OF A BLONDE (Czech.). Milos Forman.
A MAN AND A WOMAN (Fr.). Claude Lelouch.
PHARAOH (Pol.). Jerzy Kawalerowicz.
THREE (Yugo.). Alejsandar Petrovic.
Irving G. Thalberg Memorial Award
Robert Wise.
Jean Hersholt Humanitarian Award
George Bagnall.
Honorary Awards
Y. Frank Freeman for unusual and outstanding service to the Academy during his 30 years in Hollywood.
Yakima Canutt for achievements as a stunt man and for developing safety devices to protect stunt men everywhere.
Scientific or Technical

Class II
Mitchell Camera for the design and development of the Mitchell Mark II 35mm Portable Motion Picture Reflex Camera.
Arnold & Richter KG for the design and development of the Arriflex 35mm Portable Motion Picture Reflex Camera.
Class III
Panavision for the design of the Panatron Power Inverter and its application to motion picture camera operation.
Carroll Knudson for the production of a Composers Manual for Motion Picture Music Synchronization.
Ruby Raksin for the production of a Composers Manual for Motion Picture Music Synchronization.

1967
Best Picture
BONNIE AND CLYDE, WB. Produced by Warren Beatty.
DOCTOR DOLITTLE, FOX. Produced by Arthur P. Jacobs.
THE GRADUATE, Embassy. Produced by Lawrence Turman.
GUESS WHO'S COMING TO DINNER?, COL. Produced by Stanley Kramer.
IN THE HEAT OF THE NIGHT, UA. Produced by Walter Mirisch.
Best Actor
Warren Beatty for BONNIE AND CLYDE.
Dustin Hoffman for THE GRADUATE.
Paul Newman for COOL HAND LUKE.
Rod Steiger for IN THE HEAT OF THE NIGHT.
Spencer Tracy for GUESS WHO'S COMING TO DINNER?
Best Actress
Anne Bancroft for THE GRADUATE.
Faye Dunaway for BONNIE AND CLYDE.
Dame Edith Evans for THE WHISPERERS (Brit.).
Audrey Hepburn for WAIT UNTIL DARK.
Katharine Hepburn for GUESS WHO'S COMING TO DINNER?
Best Supporting Actor
John Cassavetes for THE DIRTY DOZEN.
Gene Hackman for BONNIE AND CLYDE.
Cecil Kellaway for GUESS WHO'S COMING TO DINNER?
George Kennedy for COOL HAND LUKE.
Michael J. Pollard for BONNIE AND CLYDE.
Best Supporting Actress
Carol Channing for THOROUGHLY MODERN MILLIE.
Mildred Natwick for BAREFOOT IN THE PARK.
Estelle Parsons for BONNIE AND CLYDE.
Beah Richards for GUESS WHO'S COMING TO DINNER?
Katharine Ross for THE GRADUATE.
Best Direction
Richard Brooks for IN COLD BLOOD.
Norman Jewison for IN THE HEAT OF THE NIGHT.
Stanley Kramer for GUESS WHO'S COMING TO DINNER?
Mike Nichols for THE GRADUATE.
Arthur Penn for BONNIE AND CLYDE.
Writing Awards
Best Screenplay, Based on Material from Another Medium
COOL HAND LUKE, by Donn Pearce and Frank R. Pierson.
THE GRADUATE, by Calder Willingham and Buck Henry.
IN COLD BLOOD, by Richard Brooks.
IN THE HEAT OF THE NIGHT, by Stirling Silliphant.
ULYSSES, by Joseph Strick and Fred Haines.
Best Story and Screenplay, Written Directly for the Screen
BONNIE AND CLYDE, by David Newman and Robert Benton.
DIVORCE AMERICAN STYLE, by Robert Kaufman; Norman Lear.
GUESS WHO'S COMING TO DINNER?, by William Rose.
LA GUERRE EST FINIE (Fr.). by Jorge Semprun.
TWO FOR THE ROAD, by Frederic Raphael.
Best Cinematography
BONNIE AND CLYDE. Burnett Guffey.
CAMELOT. Richard H. Kline.
DOCTOR DOLITTLE. Robert Surtees.
THE GRADUATE. Robert Surtees.
IN COLD BLOOD. Conrad Hall.
Best Art Direction—Set Decoration
CAMELOT. John Truscott and Edward Carrere; John W. Brown.
DOCTOR DOLITTLE. Mario Chiari, Jack Martin Smith, and Ed Graves; Walter M. Scott and Stuart A. Reiss.
GUESS WHO'S COMING TO DINNER? Robert Clatworthy; Frank Tuttle.
THE TAMING OF THE SHREW. Renzo Mongiardino, John DeCuir, Elven Webb, and Giuseppe Mariani; Dario Simoni and Luigi Gervasi.
THOROUGHLY MODERN MILLIE. Alexander Golitzen and George C. Webb; Howard Bristol.
Best Sound
CAMELOT. Warner Bros.-Seven Arts Studio Sound Department.
THE DIRTY DOZEN. MGM Studio Sound Department.
DOCTOR DOLITTLE. 20th Century-Fox Studio Sound Department.
IN THE HEAT OF THE NIGHT. Samuel Goldwyn Studio Sound Department.
THOROUGHLY MODERN MILLIE. Universal City Studio Sound Department.
Music Awards
Best Song
"The Bare Necessities" from THE JUNGLE BOOK. Music and lyrics by Terry Gilkyson.
"The Eyes of Love" from BANNING. Music by Quincy Jones; lyrics by Bob Russell.
"The Look of Love" from CASINO ROYALE. Music by Burt Bacharach; lyrics by Hal David.
Talk to the Animals" from DOCTOR DOLITTLE. Music and lyrics by Leslie Bricusse.
"Thoroughly Modern Millie" from THOROUGHLY MODERN MILLIE. Music and lyrics by James Van Heusen and Sammy Cahn.
Best Original Music Score
COOL HAND LUKE. Lalo Schifrin.
DOCTOR DOLITTLE. Leslie Bricusse.
FAR FROM THE MADDING CROWD. Richard Rodney Bennett.
IN COLD BLOOD. Quincy Jones.

THOROUGHLY MODERN MILLIE. Elmer Bernstein.
Best Scoring of Music, Adaptation or Treatment
    CAMELOT. Alfred Newman and Ken Darby.
    DOCTOR DOLITTLE. Lionel Newman and Alexander Courage.
    GUESS WHO'S COMING TO DINNER? DeVol.
    THOROUGHLY MODERN MILLIE. Andre Previn and Joseph Gershenson.
    VALLEY OF THE DOLLS. John Williams.
Best Film Editing
    BEACH RED. Frank P. Keller.
    THE DIRTY DOZEN. Michael Luciano.
    DOCTOR DOLITTLE. Samuel E. Beetley and Marjorie Fowler.
    GUESS WHO'S COMING TO DINNER? Robert C. Jones.
    IN THE HEAT OF THE NIGHT. Hal Ashby.
Best Costume Design
    BONNIE AND CLYDE. Theadora Van Runkle.
    CAMELOT. John Truscott.
    THE HAPPIEST MILLIONAIRE. Bill Thomas.
    THE TAMING OF THE SHREW. Irene Sharaff and Danilo Donati.
    THOROUGHLY MODERN MILLIE. Jean Louis.
Best Special Visual Effects
    DOCTOR DOLITTLE. L.B. Abbott.
    TOBRUK. Howard A. Anderson, Jr. and Albert Whitlock.
Best Sound Effects
    THE DIRTY DOZEN. John Poyner.
    IN THE HEAT OF THE NIGHT. James A. Richard.
Short Subjects
Best Cartoon
    THE BOX, Brandon Films. Produced by Fred Wolf.
    HYPOTHESE BETA, Films Orzeaux, Pathe Contemporary Films. Produced by Jean-Charles Meunier.
    WHAT ON EARTH!, National Film Board of Canada, COL. Produced by Robert Verrall and Wolf Koenig.
Best Live Action Subject
    PADDLE TO THE SEA, National Film Board of Canada, Favorite Films. Produced by Julian Biggs.
    A PLACE TO STAND, T.D.F. Productions for Ontario Department of Economics and Development, COL. Produced by Christopher Chapman.
    SKY OVER HOLLAND, Ferno Productions for The Netherlands, Seneca International. Produced by John Ferno.
    STOP, LOOK AND LISTEN, MGM. Produced by Len Janson and Chuck Menville.
Documentary
Best Short Subject Documentary
    MONUMENT TO THE DREAM. Produced by Charles E. Guggenheim.
    A PLACE TO STAND, T.D.F. Productions for the Ontario Department of Economics and Development. Produced by Christopher Chapman.
    THE REDWOODS, King Screen Productions. Produced by Mark Harris and Trevor Greenwood.
    SEE YOU AT THE PILLAR, Associated British-Pathe Productions. Produced by Robert Fitchett.
    WHILE I RUN THIS RACE, Sun Dial Films for VISTA. Produced by Carl V. Ragsdale.
Best Feature Documentary
    THE ANDERSON PLATOON, French Broadcasting System. Produced by Pierre Schoendoerffer.
    FESTIVAL, Patchke Productions. Produced by Murray Lerner.
    HARVEST, U.S. Information Agency. Produced by Carroll Ballard.
    A KING'S STORY. Produced by Jack Le Vien.
    A TIME FOR BURNING, Quest Productions for Lutheran Film Associates. Produced by William C. Jersey.
Best Foreign Language Film
    CLOSELY WATCHED TRAINS (Czech.). Jiri Menzel.
    EL AMOR BRUJO (Span.). Rovira Beleta.
    I EVEN MET HAPPY GYPSIES (Yugo.). Aleksandar Petrovic.
    LIVE FOR LIFE (Fr.). Claude Lelouch.
    PORTRAIT OF CHIEKO (Jap.). Noboru Nakamura.
Irving G. Thalberg Memorial Award
    Alfred Hitchcock.
Jean Hersholt Humanitarian Award
    Gregory Peck.
Honorary Award
    Arthur Freed for distinguished service to the Academy and the production of six top-rated Awards telecasts.
Scientific or Technical
Class III
    Electro-Optical Division of the Kollmorgen Corporation for the design and development of a series of Motion Picture Projection Lenses.
    Panavision Incorporated for a Variable Speed Motor for Motion Picture Cameras.
    Fred R. Wilson of the Samuel Goldwyn Studio Sound Department for an Audio Level Clamper.
    Waldon O. Watson and the Universal City Studio Sound Department for new concepts in the design of a Music Scoring Stage.

1968

Best Picture
    FUNNY GIRL, COL. Produced by Ray Stark.
    THE LION IN WINTER, Avco-Embassy. Produced by Martin Poll.
    OLIVER!, COL. Produced by John Woolf.
    RACHEL, RACHEL, WB. Produced by Paul Newman.
    ROMEO AND JULIET, PAR. Produced by Anthony Havelock-Allan and John Brabourne.
Best Actor
    Alan Arkin for THE HEART IS A LONELY HUNTER.
    Alan Bates for THE FIXER.
    Ron Moody for OLIVER!
    Peter O'Toole for THE LION IN WINTER.
    Cliff Robertson for CHARLY.
Best Actress
    Katharine Hepburn for THE LION IN WINTER.
    Patricia Neal for THE SUBJECT WAS ROSES.
    Vanessa Redgrave for ISADORA.

Barbra Streisand for FUNNY GIRL.
Joanne Woodward for RACHEL, RACHEL.
Best Supporting Actor
    Jack Albertson for THE SUBJECT WAS ROSES.
    Seymour Cassel for FACES.
    Daniel Massey for STAR!
    Jack Wild for OLIVER!
    Gene Wilder for THE PRODUCERS.
Best Supporting Actress
    Lynn Carlin for FACES.
    Ruth Gordon for ROSEMARY'S BABY.
    Sondra Locke for THE HEART IS A LONELY HUNTER.
    Kay Medford for FUNNY GIRL.
    Estelle Parsons for RACHEL, RACHEL.
Best Direction
    Anthony Harvey for THE LION IN WINTER.
    Stanley Kubrick for 2001: A SPACE ODYSSEY.
    Gillo Pontecorvo for THE BATTLE OF ALGIERS (Ital.).
    Carol Reed for OLIVER!
    Franco Zeffirelli for ROMEO AND JULIET.
Writing Awards
Best Screenplay, Based on Material from Another Medium
    THE LION IN WINTER, by James Goldman.
    THE ODD COUPLE, by Neil Simon.
    OLIVER!, by Vernon Harris.
    RACHEL, RACHEL, by Stewart Stern.
    ROSEMARY'S BABY, by Roman Polanski.
Best Story and Screenplay, Written Directly for the Screen
    THE BATTLE OF ALGIERS (Ital.), by Franco Solinas and Gillo Pontecorvo.
    FACES, by John Cassavetes.
    HOT MILLIONS, by Ira Wallach and Peter Ustinov.
    THE PRODUCERS, by Mel Brooks.
    2001: A SPACE ODYSSEY, by Arthur C. Clarke and Stanley Kubrick.
Best Cinematography
    FUNNY GIRL. Harry Stradling.
    ICE STATION ZEBRA. Daniel L. Fapp.
    OLIVER! Oswald Morris.
    ROMEO AND JULIET. Pasqualino De Santis.
    STAR! Ernest Laszlo.
Best Art Direction—Set Decoration
    OLIVER! John Box and Terence Marsh; Vernon Dixon and Ken Muggleston.
    THE SHOES OF THE FISHERMAN. George W. Davis and Edward Carfagno.
    STAR! Boris Leven; Walter M. Scott and Howard Bristol.
    2001: A SPACE ODYSSEY. Tony Masters, Harry Lange, and Ernie Archer.
    WAR AND PEACE (USSR). Mikhail Bogdanov and Gennady Myasnikov; G. Koshelev and V. Uvarov.
Best Sound
    BULLITT. Warner Bros.-Seven Arts Studio Sound Department.
    FINIAN'S RAINBOW. Warner Bros.-Seven Arts Studio Sound Department.
    FUNNY GIRL. Columbia Studio Sound Department.
    OLIVER! Shepperton Studio Sound Department.
    STAR! 20th Century-Fox Studio Sound Department.
Music Award
Best Song
    "Chitty Chitty Bang Bang" from CHITTY CHITTY BANG BANG. Music and lyrics by Richard M. Sherman and Robert B. Sherman.
    "For Love of Ivy" from FOR LOVE OF IVY. Music by Quincy Jones; lyrics by Bob Russell.
    "Funny Girl" from FUNNY GIRL. Music by Jule Styne; lyrics by Bob Merrill.
    "Star!" from STAR! Music by Jimmy Van Heusen; lyrics by Sammy Cahn.
    The Windmills of Your Mind" from THE THOMAS CROWN AFFAIR. Music by Michel Legrand; lyrics by Alan and Marilyn Bergman.
Best Original Score, for a Nonmusical Motion Picture
    THE FOX. Lalo Schifrin.
    THE LION IN WINTER. John Barry.
    PLANET OF THE APES. Jerry Goldsmith.
    THE SHOES OF THE FISHERMAN. Alex North.
    THE THOMAS CROWN AFFAIR. Michel Legrand.
Best Score of a Musical Picture, Original or Treatment
    FINIAN'S RAINBOW. Ray Heindorf.
    FUNNY GIRL. Walter Scharf.
    OLIVER! John Green.
    STAR! Lennie Hayton.
    THE YOUNG GIRLS OF ROCHEFORT (Fr.). Michel Legrand and Jacques Demy.
Best Film Editing
    BULLITT. Frank P. Keller.
    FUNNY GIRL. Robert Swink, Maury Winetrobe, and William Sands.
    THE ODD COUPLE. Frank Bracht.
    OLIVER! Ralph Kemplen.
    WILD IN THE STREETS. Fred Feitshans and Eve Newman.
Best Costume Design
    THE LION IN WINTER. Margaret Furse.
    OLIVER! Phyllis Dalton.
    PLANET OF THE APES. Morton Haack.
    ROMEO AND JULIET. Danilo Donati.
    STAR! Donald Brooks.
Best Special Visual Effects
    ICE STATION ZEBRA. Hal Millar and J. McMillan Johnson.
    2001: A SPACE ODYSSEY. Stanley Kubrick.
Short Subjects
Best Cartoon
    THE HOUSE THAT JACK BUILT, National Film Board of Canada, COL. Produced by Wolf Koenig and Jim Mackay.
    THE MAGIC PEAR TREE, Bing Crosby Productions. Produced by Jimmy Murakami.
    WINDY DAY, PAR. Produced by John and Faith Hubley.
    WINNIE THE POO AND THE BLUSTERY DAY, Buena Vista. Produced by Walt Disney.
Best Live Action Subject
    THE DOVE, Schoenfeld Films. Produced by George Coe, Sidney Davis, and Anthony

Lover.
DUO, National Film Board of Canada, COL.
PRELUDE, Prelude Company, Excelsior. Produced by John Astin.
ROBERT KENNEDY REMEMBERED, National General. Produced by Charles Guggenheim.

Documentary
Best Short Subject Documentary
THE HOUSE THAT AMANDA BUILT, Films Division, Government of India. Produced by Fali Bilimoria.
THE REVOLVING DOOR, Vision Associates for the American Foundation Institute of Corrections. Produced by Lee R. Bobker.
A SPACE TO GROW, Office of Economic Opportunity for Project Upward Bound. Produced by Thomas P. Kelly, Jr.
A WAY OUT OF THE WILDERNESS, John Sutherland Productions. Produced by Dan E. Weisburd.
WHY MAN CREATES. Produced by Saul Bass.

Best Feature Documentary
A FEW NOTES ON THE FOOD PROBLEM, U.S. Information Agency. Produced by James Blue.
JOURNEY INTO SELF, Western Behavioral Sciences Institute. Produced by Bill McGaw.
THE LEGENDARY CHAMPIONS, Turn of the Century Fights. Produced by William Cayton.
OTHER VOICES, DHS Films. Produced by David H. Sawyer.
YOUNG AMERICANS. Produced by Robert Cohn and Alex Grasshoff.

Best Foreign Language Film
THE BOYS OF PAUL STREET (Hung.). Zoltan Fabri.
THE FIREMAN'S BALL (Czech.). Milos Forman.
THE GIRL WITH A PISTOL (Ital.). Mario Monicelli.
STOLEN KISSES (Fr.). Francois Truffaut.
WAR AND PEACE (USSR). Serge Bondarchuk.

Irving G. Thalberg Memorial Award
None awarded.

Jean Hersholt Humanitarian Award
Martha Raye.

Honorary Awards
John Chambers for his oustanding makeup achievements for PLANET OF THE APES.
Onna White for her outstanding choreography for OLIVER!

Scientific or Technical
Class I
Philip V. Palmquist of Minnesota Mining and Manufacturing Company, to Herbert Meyer of the Motion Picture and Television Research Center, and to Charles D. Staffell of the Rank Organization for the development of a successful embodiment of the reflex background projection system for composite cinematography.

Class II
Donald W. Norwood for the design and development of the Norwood Photographic Exposure Meters.
Eastman Kodak Company and Producers Service Company for the development of a new high-speed step-optical reduction printer.
Edmund M. DiGiulio, Niels G. Petersen, and Norman S. Hughes of the Cinema Product Development Company for the design and application of a conversion which makes available the reflex viewing system for motion picture cameras.
Optical Coating Laboratories, Inc., for the development of an improved anti-reflection coating for photographic and projection lens system
Eastman Kodak Company for the introduction of a new high speed motion picture color negative film.
Panavision Incorporated for the conception, design, and introduction of a 65mm hand-held motion picture camera.
Todd-AO Company and the Mitchell Camera Company for the design and engineering of the Todd-AO hand-held motion picture camera.

Class III
Carl W. Hauge and Edward H. Reichard of Consolidated Film Industries and E. Michael Meahl and Roy J. Ridenour of Ramtronics for engineering an automatic exposure control for printing-machine lamps.
Eastman Kodak Company for a new direct positive film, and to Consolidated Film Industries for the application of this film to the making of post-production work prints.

1969

Best Picture
ANNE OF THE THOUSAND DAYS, UNIV. Produced by Hal B. Wallis.
BUTCH CASSIDY AND THE SUNDANCE KID, FOX. Produced by John Foreman.
HELLO, DOLLY!, FOX. Produced by Ernest Lehman.
MIDNIGHT COWBOY, UA. Produced by Jerome Hellman.
Z (Fr./Algerian). Produced by Jacques Perrin and Hamed Rachedi.

Best Actor
Richard Burton for ANNE OF THE THOUSAND DAYS.
Dustin Hoffman for MIDNIGHT COWBOY.
Peter O'Toole for GOODBYE, MR. CHIPS.
Jon Voight for MIDNIGHT COWBOY.
John Wayne for TRUE GRIT.

Best Actress
Genevieve Bujold for ANNE OF THE THOUSAND DAYS.
Jane Fonda for THEY SHOOT HORSES, DON'T THEY?
Liza Minnelli for THE STERILE CUCKOO.
Jean Simmons for THE HAPPY ENDING.
Maggie Smith for THE PRIME OF MISS JEAN BRODIE.

Best Supporting Actor
Rupert Crosse for THE REIVERS.
Elliott Gould for BOB & CAROL & TED & ALICE.
Jack Nicholson for EASY RIDER.
Anthony Quayle for ANNE OF THE THOUSAND DAYS.
Gig Young for THEY SHOOT HORSES, DON'T THEY?

Best Supporting Actress
Catherine Burns for LAST SUMMER.
Dyan Cannon for BOB & CAROL & TED & ALICE.
Goldie Hawn for CACTUS FLOWER.
Sylvia Miles for MIDNIGHT COWBOY.
Susannah York for THEY SHOOT HORSES, DON'T THEY?

Best Direction
Costa-Gavras for Z (Fr./Algeria).
George Roy Hill for BUTCH CASSIDY AND THE SUNDANCE KID.
Arthur Penn for ALICE'S RESTAURANT.
Sydney Pollack for THEY SHOOT HORSES, DON'T THEY?
John Schlesinger for MIDNIGHT COWBOY.

Writing Awards
Best Screenplay, Based on Material from Another Medium
ANNE OF THE THOUSAND DAYS, by John Hale, Bridget Boland, and Richard Sokolove.
GOODBYE, COLUMBUS, by Arnold Schulman.
MIDNIGHT COWBOY, by Waldo Salt.
THEY SHOOT HORSES, DON'T THEY?, by James Poe and Robert E. Thompson.
Z (Fr./Algeria), by Jorge Semprun and Costa-Gavras.

Best Story and Screenplay, Based on Material not Previously Published or Produced
BOB & CAROL & TED & ALICE, by Paul Mazursky and Larry Tucker.
BUTCH CASSIDY AND THE SUNDANCE KID, by William Goldman.
THE DAMNED (Ital.), by Nicola Badalucco, Enrico Medioli, and Luchino Visconti.
EASY RIDER, by Peter Fonda, Dennis Hopper, and Terry Southern.
THE WILD BUNCH, by Walon Green, Roy N. Sickner, and Sam Peckinpah.

Best Cinematography
ANNE OF THE THOUSAND DAYS. Arthur Ibbetson.
BOB & CAROL & TED & ALICE. Charles B. Lang.
BUTCH CASSIDY AND THE SUNDANCE KID. Conrad Hall.
HELLO, DOLLY! Harry Stradling.
MAROONED. Daniel Fapp.

Best Art Direction—Set Decoration
ANNE OF THE THOUSAND DAYS. Maurice Carter and Lionel Couch; Patrick McLoughlin.
GAILY, GAILY. Robert Boyle and George B. Chan; Edward Boyle and Carl Biddiscombe.
HELLO, DOLLY! John DeCuir, Jack Martin Smith, and Herman Blumenthal; Walter M. Scott, George Hopkins, and Raphael Bretton.
SWEET CHARITY. Alexander Golitzen and George C. Webb; Jack D. Moore.
THEY SHOOT HORSES, DON'T THEY? Harry Horner; Frank McKelvy.

Best Sound
ANNE OF THE THOUSAND DAYS. John Aldred.
BUTCH CASSIDY AND THE SUNDANCE KID. William Edmundson and David Dockendorf.
GAILY, GAILY. Robert Martin and Clem Portman.
HELLO, DOLLY! Jack Solomon and Murray Spivack.
MAROONED. Les Fresholtz and Arthur Piantadosi.

Music Awards
Best Song
"Come Saturday Morning" from THE STERILE CUCKOO. Music by Fred Karlin; lyrics by Dory Previn.
"Jean" from THE PRIME OF MISS JEAN BRODIE. Music and lyrics by Rod McKuen.
"Raindrops Keep Fallin' on My Head" from BUTCH CASSIDY AND THE SUNDANCE KID. Music by Burt Bacharach; lyrics by Hal David.
"True Grit" from TRUE GRIT. Music by Elmer Bernstein; lyrics by Don Black.
"What Are You Doing the Rest of Your Life?" from THE HAPPY ENDING. Music by Michel Legrand; lyrics by Alan and Marilyn Bergman.

Best Original Score, for a Nonmusical Motion Picture
ANNE OF THE THOUSAND DAYS. Georges Delerue.
BUTCH CASSIDY AND THE SUNDANCE KID. Burt Bacharach.
THE REIVERS. John Williams.
THE SECRET OF SANTA VITTORIA. Ernest Gold.
THE WILD BUNCH. Jerry Fielding.

Best Score of a Musical Picture, Original or Adaptation
GOODBYE, MR. CHIPS. Leslie Bricusse and John Williams.
HELLO, DOLLY! Lennie Hayton and Lionel Newman.
PAINT YOUR WAGON. Nelson Riddle.
SWEET CHARITY. Cy Coleman.
THEY SHOOT HORSES, DON'T THEY? John Green and Albert Woodbury.

Best Film Editing
HELLO, DOLLY! William Reynolds.
MIDNIGHT COWBOY. Hugh A. Robertson.
THE SECRET OF SANTA VITTORIA. William Lyon and Earle Herdan.
THEY SHOOT HORSES, DON'T THEY? Fredric Steinkamp.
Z (Fr./Algeria). Francoise Bonnot.

Best Costume Design
ANNE OF THE THOUSAND DAYS. Margaret Furse.
GAILY, GAILY. Ray Aghayan.
HELLO, DOLLY! Irene Sharaff.
SWEET CHARITY. Edith Head.
THEY SHOOT HORSES, DON'T THEY? Donfeld.

Best Special Visual Effects
KRAKATOA, EAST OF JAVA. Eugene Lourie and Alex Weldon.
MAROONED. Robbie Robertson.

Short Subjects
Best Cartoon
IT'S TOUGH TO BE A BIRD, Buena Vista. Produced by Ward Kimball.
OF MEN AND DEMONS, PAR. Produced by John and Faith Hubley.
WALKING, National Film Board of Canada, COL. Produced by Ryan Larkin.

Best Live Action Subject
BLAKE, National Film Board of Canada, Vaudeo, Inc.. Produced by Doug Jackson.
THE MAGIC MACHINES, Fly-By-Night Productions, Manson Distributing. Produced by Joan Keller Stern.
PEOPLE SOUP, Pangloss Productions, COL. Produced by Marc Merson.

Documentary
Best Short Subject Documentary
CZECHOSLOVAKIA 1968, Sanders-Fresco Film Makers for U.S. Information Agency. Produced by Denis Sanders and Robert M. Fresco.
AN IMPRESSION OF JOHN STEINBECK: WRITER, Donald Wrye Productions for U.S. Information Agency. Produced by Donald Wrye.
JENNY IS A GOOD THING, A.C.I. Productions for Project Head Start. Produced by Joan Horvath.
LEO BEUERMAN, Centron Productions. Produced by Arthur H. Wolf and Russell A. Mosser.

THE MAGIC MACHINES, Fly-By-Night Productions, Manson Distributing. Produced by Joan Keller Stern.
Best Feature Documentary
ARTHUR RUBINSTEIN—THE LOVE OF LIFE, Midem Productions. Produced by Bernard Chevry.
BEFORE THE MOUNTAIN WAS MOVED, Robert K. Sharpe Productions for the Office of Economic Opportunity. Produced by Robert K. Sharpe.
IN THE YEAR OF THE PIG. Produced by Emile de Antonio.
THE OLYMPICS IN MEXICO, Film Section of the Organizing Committee for the XIX Olympic Games.
THE WOLF MEN, MGM. Produced by Irwin Rosten.
Best Foreign Language Film
ADALEN 31 (Swed.). Bo Widerberg.
THE BATTLE OF THE NERETVA (Yugo.). Veljko Bulajic.
THE BROTHERS KARAMAZOV (USSR). Ivan Piriev.
MY NIGHT AT MAUDS (Fr.). Eric Rohmer.
Z (Fr./Algeria). Constantin Costa-Gavras.
Irving G. Thalberg Memorial Award
None Awarded.
Jean Hersholt Humanitarian Award
George Jessel.
Honorary Award
Cary Grant for his unique mastery of the art of screen acting with the respect and affection of his colleagues.
Scientific or Technical
Class II
Hazeltine Corporation for the design and development of the Hazeltine Color Film Analyzer.
Fouad Said for the design and introduction of the Cinemobile series of equipment trucks for location motion picture production.
Juan de la Cierva and Dynasciences Corporation for the design and development of the Dynalens optical image motion compensator.
Class III
Otto Popelka of Magna-Tech Electronics Co., Inc., for the development of an Electronically Controlled Looping System.
Fenton Hamilton of MGM Studio for the concept and engineering of a mobile battery power unit for location lighting.
Panavision Incorporated for the design and development of the Panaspeed Motion Picture Camera Motor.
Robert M. Flynn and Russell Hessy of Universal City Studios, Inc., for a machine-gun modification for motion picture photography.

1970
Best Picture
AIRPORT, UNIV. Produced by Ross Hunter.
FIVE EASY PIECES, COL. Produced by Bob Rafelson and Richard Wechsler.
LOVE STORY, PAR. Produced by Howard G. Minsky.
M*A*S*H, FOX. Produced by Ingo Preminger.
PATTON, FOX. Produced by Frank McCarthy.
Best Actor
Melvyn Douglas for I NEVER SANG FOR MY FATHER.
James Earl Jones for THE GREAT WHITE HOPE.
Jack Nicholson for FIVE EASY PIECES.
Ryan O'Neal for LOVE STORY.
George C. Scott for PATTON.
Best Actress
Jane Alexander for THE GREAT WHITE HOPE.
Glenda Jackson for WOMEN IN LOVE.
Ali MacGraw for LOVE STORY.
Sarah Miles for RYAN'S DAUGHTER.
Carrie Snodgress for DIARY OF A MAD HOUSEWIFE.
Best Supporting Actor
Richard Castellano for LOVERS AND OTHER STRANGERS.
Chief Dan George for LITTLE BIG MAN.
Gene Hackman for I NEVER SANG FOR MY FATHER.
John Marley for LOVE STORY.
John Mills for RYAN'S DAUGHTER.
Best Supporting Actress
Karen Black for FIVE EASY PIECES.
Lee Grant for THE LANDLORD.
Helen Hayes for AIRPORT.
Sally Kellerman for M*A*S*H.
Maureen Stapleton for AIRPORT.
Best Direction
Robert Altman for M*A*S*H.
Federico Fellini for FELLINI SATYRICON (Ital.).
Arthur Hiller for LOVE STORY.
Ken Russell for WOMEN IN LOVE.
Franklin J. Schaffner for PATTON.
Writing Awards
Best Screenplay, Based on Material from Another Source
AIRPORT, by George Seaton.
I NEVER SANG FOR MY FATHER, by Robert Anderson.
LOVERS AND OTHER STRANGERS, by Renee Taylor, Joseph Bologna, and David Zelag Goodman.
*M*A*S*H, by Ring Lardner, Jr.*
WOMEN IN LOVE, by Larry Kramer. Best Story and screenplay, Based on Factual Material or Material not Previously Published or Produced
FIVE EASY PIECES, by Bob Rafelson and Adrien Joyce.
JOE, by Norman Wexler.
LOVE STORY, by Erich Segal.
MY NIGHT AT MAUD'S (Fr.), by Erich Rohmer.
PATTON, by Francis Ford Coppola and Edmund H. North.
Best Cinematography
AIRPORT. Ernest Laszlo.
PATTON. Fred Koenekamp.
RYAN'S DAUGHTER. Freddie Young.
TORA! TORA! TORA! Jack Martin Smith, Yoshiro Muraki, Richard Day, and Taizoh Kawashima; Walter M. Scott, Norman Rockett and Carl Biddiscombe.
WOMEN IN LOVE. Billy Williams

Best Art Direction—Set Decoration
AIRPORT. Alexander Golitzen and E. Preston Ames; Jack D. Moore and Mickey S. Michaels.
THE MOLLY MAGUIRES. Tambi Larsen; Darrell Silvera.
PATTON. Urie McCleary and Gil Parrondo; Antonio Mateos and Pierre Louis Thevent.
SCROOGE. Terry Marsh and Bob Cartwright; Pamela Cornell.
TORA! TORA! TORA! Jack Martin Smith, Yoshiro Muraki, Richard Day, and Taizoh Kawashima; Walter M. Scott, Norman Rockett and Carl Biddiscombe.
Best Sound
AIRPORT. Ronald Pierce and David Moriarty.
PATTON. Douglas Williams and Don Bassman.
RYAN'S DAUGHTER. Gordon K. McCallum and John Bramall.
TORA! TORA! TORA! Murray Spivack and Herman Lewis.
WOODSTOCK. Dan Wallin and Larry Johnson.
Music Awards
Best Song
For All We Know" from LOVERS AND OTHER STRANGERS. Music by Fred Karlin; lyrics by Robb Royer [Robb Wilson] and James Griffin [Arthur James].
"Pieces of Dreams" from PIECES OF DREAMS. Music by Michel Legrand. Lyrics by Alan and Marilyn Bergman.
"Thank You Very Much" from SCROOGE. Music and lyrics by Leslie Bricusse.
"Till Love Touches Your Life" from MADRON. Music by Riz Ortolani; lyrics by Arthur Hamilton.
"Whistling Away the Dark" from DARLING LILI. Music by Henry Mancini; lyrics by Johnny Mercer.
Best Original Score
AIRPORT. Alfred Newman.
CROMWELL. Frank Cordell.
LOVE STORY. Francis Lai.
PATTON. Jerry Goldsmith.
SUNFLOWER. Henry Mancini.
Best Original Song Score
THE BABY MAKER. Fred Karlin and Tylwyth Kymry.
A BOY NAMED CHARLIE BROWN. Rod McKuen, John Scott Trotter, Bill Melendez, Al Shean, Vince Guaraldi.
DARLING LILI. Henry Mancini and Johnny Mercer.
LET IT BE. The Beatles.
SCROOGE. Leslie Bricusse, Ian Fraser and Herbert W. Spencer.
Best Film Editing
AIRPORT. Stuart Gilmore.
M*A*S*H. Danford B. Greene.
PATTON. Hugh S. Fowler.
TORA! TORA! TORA! James E. Newcom, Pembroke J. Herring, and Inoue Chikaya.
WOODSTOCK. Thelma Schoonmaker.
Best Costume Design
AIRPORT. Edith Head.
CROMWELL. Nino Novarese.
DARLING LILI. Donald Brooks and Jack Bear.
THE HAWAIIANS. Bill Thomas.
SCROOGE. Margaret Furse.
Best Special Visual Effects
PATTON. Alex Weldon.
TORA! TORA! TORA! A.D. Flowers and L.B. Abbott.
Short Subjects
Best Cartoon
THE FURTHER ADVENTURES OF UNCLE SAM: PART TWO, Haboush Company, Goldstone Films. Produced by Robert Mitchell and Dale Case.
IS IT ALWAYS RIGHT TO BE RIGHT?, Stephen Bosustow Productions, Schoenfeld Films. Produced by Nick Bosustow.
THE SHEPHERD, Brandon Films. Produced by Cameron Guess.
Best Live Action Subject
THE RESURRECTION OF BRONCHO BILLY, University of Southern California, Department of Cinema, UNIV, Produced by John Longenecker.
SHUT UP...I'M CRYING, Schoenfeld Films. Produced by Robert Siegler.
STICKY MY FINGERS..FLEET MY FEET, American Film Institute, Schoenfeld Films. Produced by John Hancock.
Documentary
Best Short Subject Documentary
THE GIFTS, Richter-McBride Productions for the Water Quality Office of the Environmental Protection Agency. Produced by Robert McBride.
INTERVIEWS WITH MY LAI VETERANS, Laser Film Corporation. Produced by Joseph Strick.
A LONG WAY FROM NOWHERE. Produced by Bob Aller.
OISIN, Aengus Film. Produced by Vivien and Patrick Carey.
TIME IS RUNNING OUT, Gesellschaft fur bildende Filme. Produced by Horst Dallmayr and Robert Mengoz. Best Feature Documentary
CHARIOTS OF THE GODS, Terra-Filmkunst GmbH. Produced by Dr. Harald Reini.
JACK JOHNSON, THE BIG FIGHTS. Produced by Jim Jacobs.
KING: A FILMED RECORD...MONTGOMERY TO MEMPHIS, Commonwealth United Productions. Produced by Ely Landau.
SAY GOODBYE, Wolper Productions. Produced by David H. Vowell.
WOODSTOCK, Wadleigh-Maurice, WB. Produced by Bob Maurice.
Best Foreign Language Film
FIRST LOVE (Switz.). Maximilian Schell.
HOA-BINH (Fr.). Raoul Coutard.
INVESTIGATION OF A CITIZEN ABOVE SUSPICION (Ital.). Elio Petri.
PAIX SUR LES CHAMPS (Bel.).
TRISTANA (Span.). Luis Bunuel.
Irving G. Thalberg Memorial Award
Ingmar Bergman.
Jean Hersholt Humanitarian Award
Frank Sinatra.
Honorary Awards
Lillian Gish for superlative artistry and for distinguished contribution to the progress of motion pictures.
Orson Welles for superlative artistry and versatility in the creation of motion pictures.
Scientific or Technical

Class II
Leonard Sokolow and Edward H. Reichard of Consolidated Film Industries for the concept and engineering of the Color Proofing Printer for motion pictures.

Class III
Sylvania Electric Products, Inc., for the development and introduction of a series of compact tungsten halogen lamps for motion picture production.

B.J. Losmandy for the concept, design and application of micro-miniature solid state amplifier modules used in motion picture recording equipment.

Eastman Kodak Company and Photo Electronics Corporation for the design and engineering of an improved video color analyzer for motion picture laboratories.

Electro Sound Incorporated for the design and introduction of the Series 8000 Sound System for motion picture theaters.

1971

Best Picture
A CLOCKWORK ORANGE, WB. Produced by Stanley Kubrick.
FIDDLER ON THE ROOF, UA. Produced by Norman Jewison.
THE FRENCH CONNECTION, FOX. Produced by Philip D'Antoni.
THE LAST PICTURE SHOW, COL. Produced by Stephen J. Friedman.
NICHOLAS AND ALEXANDRA, COL. Produced by Sam Spiegel.

Best Actor
Peter Finch for SUNDAY, BLOODY SUNDAY.
Gene Hackman for THE FRENCH CONNECTION.
Walter Matthau for KOTCH.
George C. Scott for THE HOSPITAL.
Topol for FIDDLER ON THE ROOF.

Best Actress
Julie Christie for MCCABE & MRS. MILLER.
Jane Fonda for KLUTE.
Glenda Jackson for SUNDAY, BLOODY SUNDAY.
Vanessa Redgrave for MARY, QUEEN OF SCOTS.
Janet Suzman for NICHOLAS AND ALEXANDRA.

Best Supporting Actor
Jeff Bridges for THE LAST PICTURE SHOW.
Leonard Frey for FIDDLER ON THE ROOF.
Richard Jaeckel for SOMETIMES A GREAT NOTION.
Ben Johnson for THE LAST PICTURE SHOW.
Roy Scheider for THE FRENCH CONNECTION.

Best Supporting Actress
Ellen Burstyn for THE LAST PICTURE SHOW.
Barbara Harris for WHO IS HARRY KELLERMAN, AND WHY IS HE SAYING THOSE TERRIBLE THINGS ABOUT ME?
Cloris Leachman for THE LAST PICTURE SHOW.
Margaret Leighton for THE GO-BETWEEN.
Ann-Margret for CARNAL KNOWLEDGE.

Best Direction
Peter Bogdanovich for THE LAST PICTURE SHOW.
William Friedkin for THE FRENCH CONNECTION.
Norman Jewison for FIDDLER ON THE ROOF.
Stanley Kubrick for A CLOCKWORK ORANGE.
John Schlesinger for SUNDAY, BLOODY SUNDAY.

Writing Awards
Best Screenplay, Based on Material from Another Medium
A CLOCKWORK ORANGE, by Stanley Kubrick.
THE CONFORMIST (Ital.), by Bernardo Bertolucci.
THE FRENCH CONNECTION, by Ernest Tidyman.
THE GARDEN OF THE FINZI-CONTINIS (Ital.), by Ugo Pirro and Vittorio Bonicelli.
THE LAST PICTURE SHOW, by Larry McMurtry and Peter Bogdanovich.

Best Story and Screenplay, Based on Factual Material or Material not Previously Published or Produced
THE HOSPITAL, by Paddy Chayefsky.
INVESTIGATION OF A CITIZEN ABOVE SUSPICION (Ital.), by Elio Petri and Ugo Pirro.
KLUTE, by Andy and Dave Lewis.
SUMMER OF '42, by Herman Raucher.
SUNDAY, BLOODY SUNDAY, by Penelope Gilliatt.

Best Cinematography
FIDDLER ON THE ROOF. Oswald Morris.
THE FRENCH CONNECTION. Owen Roizman.
THE LAST PICTURE SHOW. Robert Surtees.
NICHOLAS AND ALEXANDRA. Freddie Young.
SUMMER OF '42. Robert Surtees.

Best Art Direction—Set Decoration
THE ANDROMEDA STRAIN. Boris Leven and William Tuntke; Ruby Levitt.
BEDKNOBS AND BROOMSTICKS. John B. Mansbridge and Peter Ellenshaw; Emile Kuri and Hal Gausman.
FIDDLER ON THE ROOF. Robert Boyle and Michael Stringer; Peter Lamont.
MARY, QUEEN OF SCOTS. Terence Marsh and Robert Cartwright; Peter Howitt.
NICHOLAS AND ALEXANDRA. John Box, Ernest Archer, Jack Maxsted and Gil Parrondo; Vernon Dixon.

Best Sound
DIAMONDS ARE FOREVER. Gordon K. McCallum, John Mitchell, and Alfred J. Overton.
FIDDLER ON THE ROOF. Gordon K. McCallum and David Hildyard.
THE FRENCH CONNECTION. Theodore Soderberg and Christopher Newman.
KOTCH. Richard Portman and Jack Solomon.
MARY, QUEEN OF SCOTS. Bob Jones and John Aldred.

Music Awards
Best Song
"The Age of Not Believing" from BEDKNOBS AND BROOMSTICKS. Music and lyrics by Richard M. Sherman and Robert B. Sherman.
"All His Children" from SOMETIMES A GREAT NOTION. Music by Henry Mancini; lyrics by Alan and Marilyn Bergman.
"Bless the Beasts and Children" from BLESS THE BEAST AND CHILDREN. Music and lyrics by Barry DeVorzon and Perry Botkin, Jr.
"Life Is What You Make It" from KOTCH. Music by Marvin Hamlisch; lyrics by Johnny Mercer.
■*Theme from SHAFT." Music and lyrics by Issac Hayes.*

Best Original Dramatic Score

MARY, QUEEN OF SCOTS. John Barry.
NICHOLAS AND ALEXANDRA. Richard Rodney Bennett.
SHAFT. Issac Hayes.
STRAW DOGS. Jerry Fielding.
SUMMER OF '42. Michel Legrand.

Best Scoring: Adaptation and Original Song Score
BEDKNOBS AND BROOMSTICKS. Richard M. Sherman, Robert B. Sherman, and Irwin Kostal.
THE BOY FRIEND. Peter Maxwell Davies and Peter Greenwell.
FIDDLER ON THE ROOF. John Williams.
TCHAIKOVSKY (USSR). Dimitri Tiomkin.
WILLIE WONKA AND THE CHOCOLATE FACTORY. Leslie Bricusse, Anthony Newley, and Walter Scharf.

Best Film Editing
THE ANDROMEDA STRAIN. Stuart Gilmore and John W. Holmes.
A CLOCKWORK ORANGE. Bill Butler.
THE FRENCH CONNECTION. Jerry Greenberg.
KOTCH. Ralph E. Winters.
SUMMER OF '42. Folmar Blangsted.

Best Costume Design
BEDKNOBS AND BROOMSTICKS. Bill Thomas.
DEATH IN VENICE (Ital.). Piero Tosi.
MARY, QUEEN OF SCOTS. Margaret Furse.
NICHOLAS AND ALEXANDRA. Yvonne Blake and Antonio Castillo.
WHAT'S THE MATTER WITH HELEN? Morton Haack.

Best Special Visual Effects
BEDKNOBS AND BROOMSTICKS. Alan Maley, Eustace Lycett, and Danny Lee.
WHEN DINOSAURS RULED THE EARTH. Jim Danforth and Roger Dicken.

Short Subjects
Best Animated Film
THE CRUNCH BIRD, Maxwell-Petok-Petrovich Productions, Regency Films. Produced by Ted Petok.
EVOLUTION, National Film Board of Canada, COL. Produced by Michael Mills.
THE SELFISH GIANT, Potterton Productions, Pyramid Films. Produced by Peter Sander and Murray Shostak.

Best Live Action Film
GOOD MORNING, E/G Films, Seymour Borde & Associates. Produced by Denny Evans and Ken Greenwald.
THE REHEARSAL, Cinema Verona Production, Schoenfeld Films. Produced by Stephen F. Verona.
THE NUMBERS START WITH THE RIVER, a WH Picture for U.S. Information Agency. Produced by Donald Wrye.
SENTINELS OF SILENCE, Producciones Concord, PAR. Produced by Manuel Arango and Robert Amram.

Documentary
Best Short Subject Documentary
ADVENTURES IN PERCEPTION, Han van Gelder Filmproduktie for Netherlands Information Service. Produced by Han van Gelder.
ART IS..., Henry Strauss Associates for Sears, Roebuck Foundation. Produced by Julian Krainin and DeWitt L. Sage, Jr.
SENTINELS OF SILENCE, Producciones Concord, PAR. Produced by Manuel Arango and Robert Amram.
SOMEBODY WAITING. Snider Productions for the University of California Medical Film Library. Produced by Hal Riney, Dick Snider and Sherwood Omens.

Best Feature Documentary
ALASKA WILDERNESS LAKE. Produced by Alan Landsburg.
THE HELLSTROM CHRONICLE, David L. Wolper, Cinema V. Produced by Walon Green.
ON ANY SUNDAY, Brown-Solar, Cinema V. Produced by Bruce Brown.
THE RA EXPEDITIONS, Swedish Broadcasting Company, Interwest Film Corp. Produced by Lennart Ehrenborg and Thor Heyerdahl.
THE SORROW AND THE PITY (Fr.), Cinema V. Produced by Marcel Ophuls.

Best Foreign Language Film
DODES'KA-DEN (Jap.). Akira Kurosawa.
THE EMIGRANTS (Swed.). Jan Troell.
THE GARDEN OF THR FINZI-CONTINIS (Ital.). Vittorio De Sica.
THE POLICEMAN (Israel). Ephraim Kishon.
TCHAIKOVSKY (USSR). Igor Talankan.

Irving G. Thalberg Memorial Award
None awarded.

Jean Hersholt Humanitarian Award
None awarded.

Honorary Award
Charles Chaplin for the incalculable effect he has had in making motion pictures the art form of this century.

Scientific or Technical
Class II
John N. Wilkinson of Optical Radiation Corporation for the development and engineering of a system of xenon arc lamphouses for motion picture projection.

Class III
Thomas Jefferson Hutchinson, James R. Rochester, and Fenton Hamilton for the development and introduction of the Sunbrute system of xenon arc lamps for location lighting in motion picture production.

Photo Research, a Division of Kollmorgen Corporation, for the development and introduction of the film-lens balanced Three Color Meter.

Robert D. Auguste and Cinema Products Co. for the development and introduction of a new crystal controlled lightweight motor for the 35mm motion picture Arriflex camera.

Producers Service Corporation and Consolidated Film Industries, and to Cinema Research Corporation and Research Products, Inc., for the engineering and implementation of fully automated blow-up motion picture printing systems.

Cinema Products Co. for a control to actuate zoom lenses on motion picture cameras.

1972

Best Picture
CABARET, AA. Produced by Cy Feuer.
DELIVERANCE, WB. Produced by John Boorman.
THE EMIGRANTS (Swed.), WB. Produced by Bengt Forslund.
THE GODFATHER, PAR. Produced by Albert S. Ruddy.
SOUNDER, FOX. Produced by Robert B. Radnitz.

Best Actor

Marlon Brando for THE GODFATHER.
Michael Caine for SLEUTH.
Laurence Olivier for SLEUTH.
Peter O'Toole for THE RULING CLASS.
Paul Winfield for SOUNDER.
Best Actress
Liza Minelli for CABARET.
Diana Ross for LADY SINGS THE BLUES.
Maggie Smith for TRAVELS WITH MY AUNT.
Cicely Tyson for SOUNDER.
Liv Ullmann for THE EMIGRANTS (Swed.).
Best Supporting Actor
Eddie Albert for THE HEARTBREAK KID.
James Caan for THE GODFATHER.
Robert Duvall for THE GODFATHER.
Joel Grey for CABARET.
Al Pacino for THE GODFATHER.
Best Supporting Actress
Jeannie Berlin for THE HEARTBREAK KID.
Eileen Heckart for BUTTERFLIES ARE FREE.
Geraldine Page for PETE 'N' TILLIE.
Susan Tyrrell for FAT CITY.
Shelley Winters for THE POSEIDON ADVENTURE.
Best Direction
John Boorman for DELIVERANCE.
Francis Ford Coppola for THE GODFATHER.
Bob Fosse for Cabaret.
Joseph L. Mankiewicz for SLEUTH.
Jan Troell for THE EMIGRANTS (Swed.).
Writing Awards
Best Screenplay, Based on Material from Another Medium
CABARET, by Jay Allen.
THE EMIGRANTS (Swed.), by Jan Troell and Bengt Forslund.
THE GODFATHER, by Mario Puzo and Francis Ford Coppola.
Pete 'N' TILLIE, by Julius J. Epstein.
SOUNDER, by Lonne Elder, III.
Best Story and Screenplay, Based on Factual Material or Material not Previously
Published or Released
THE CANDIDATE, by Jeremy Larner.
THE DISCREET CHARM OF THE BOURGEOISIE (Fr.), by Luis Bunuel and
Jean-Claude Carriere.
LADY SINGS THE BLUES, by Terence McCoy, Chris Clark, and Suzanne de
Passe.
MURMUR OF THE HEART (Fr.), by Louis Malle.
YOUNG WINSTON, by Carl Foreman.
Best Cinematography
BUTTERFLIES ARE FREE. Charles B. Lang.
CABARET. Geoffrey Unsworth.
THE POSEIDON ADVENTURE. Harold E. Stine.
"1776." Harry Stradling, Jr.
TRAVELS WITH MY AUNT. Douglas Slocombe.
Best Art Direction—Set Decoration
CABARET. Rolf Zehetbauer and Jurgen Kiebach; Herbert Strabel.
LADY SINGS THE BLUES. Carl Anderson; Reg Allen.
THE POSEIDON ADVENTURE. William Creber; Raphael Bretton.
TRAVELS WITH MY AUNT. John Box, Gil Parrondo, and Robert W. Laing.
YOUNG WINSTON. Don Ashton, Geoffrey Drake, John Graysmark, and William
Hutchinson; Peter James.
Best Sound
BUTTERFLIES ARE FREE. Arthur Piantadosi and Charles Knight.
CABARET. Robert Knudson and David Hildyard.
THE CANDIDATE. Richard Portman and Gene Cantamessa.
THE GODFATHER. Bud Grenzbach, Richard Portman, and Christopher Newman.
THE POSEIDON ADVENTURE. Theodore Soderberg and Herman Lewis.
Music Awards
Best Song
"Ben" from BEN. Music by Walter Scharf; lyrics by Don Black.
"Come Follow, Follow Me" from THE LITTLE ARK. Music by Fred Karlin; lyrics
by Marsha Karlin.
"Marmalade, Molasses & Honey" from THE LIFE AND TIME OF JUDGE ROY
BEAN. Music by Maurice Jarre; lyrics by Marily and Alan Bergman.
·The Morning After" from THE POSEIDON ADVENTURE. Music and lyrics by Al
Kasha and Joel Hirschborn.
"Strange Are the Ways of Love" from THE STEPMOTHER. Music by Sammy
Fain; lyrics by Paul Francis Webster.
Best Original Dramatic Score
IMAGES. John Williams.
LIMELIGHT. Charles Chaplin, Raymond Rasch and Larry Russell.
NAPOLEON AND SAMANTHA. Buddy Baker.
THE POSEIDON ADVENTURE. John Williams.
SLEUTH. John Addison
Best Scoring: Adaptation and Original Song Score
CABARET. Ralph Burns.
LADY SINGS THE BLUES. Gil Askey.
MAN OF LA MANCHA. Laurence Rosenthal.
Best Film Editing
CABARET. David Bretherton.
DELIVERANCE. Tom Priestley.
THE GODFATHER. William Reynolds and Peter Zinner.
THE HOT ROCK. Frank P. Keller and Fred W. Berger.
THE POSEIDON ADVENTURE. Harold F. Kress.
Best Costume Design
THE GODFATHER. Anna Hill Johnstone.
LADY SINGS THE BLUES. Bob Mackie, Ray Aghayan, and Norma Koch.
THE POSEIDON ADVENTURE. Paul Zastupnevich.
TRAVELS WITH MY AUNT. Anthony Powell.
YOUNG WINSTON. Anthony Mendleson.
Short Subjects
Best Animated Film
A CHRISTMAS CAROL, American Broadcasting Company Film Services. Produced

by Richard Williams.
KAMA SUTRA RIDES AGAIN, Lion International Films. Produced by Bob Godfrey.
TUP TUP. Zagreb Film-Corona Cinematografica, Manson Distributing. Produced by
Nedeljko Dragic.
Best Live Action Film
FROG STORY, Gidron Productions, Schoenfeld Films. Produced by Ron Satlof and
Ray Gideon.
*NORMAN ROCKWELL'S WORLD...AN AMERICAN DREAM, Concepts Unlimit-
ed, COL. Produced by Richard Barclay.*
SOLO, Pyramid Films, UA. Produced by David Adams.
Documentary
Best Short Subject Documentary
HUNDERTWASSER'S RAINY DAY, Argos films-Schamoni Film Productions.
Produced by Peter Schamoni.
K-Z, Nexus Films. Produced by Giorgio Treves.
SELLING OUT, Unit Productions Film. Produced by Tadfeusz Jaworski.
THIS TINY WORLD. Produced by Charles and Martina Huguenot van der Linden.
THE TIDE OF TRAFFIC. BP-Greenpark. Produced by Humphrey Swingler.
Best Feature Documentary
APE AND SUPER-APE, Netherlands Ministry of Culture, Recreation and Social
Welfare. Produced by Bert Haanstra.
MALCOLM X, WB. Produced by Marvin Worth and Arnold Perl.
MANSON, Merrick International. Produced by Robert Hendrickson and Laurence
Merrick.
*MARJOE, Cinema X, Cinema V. Produced by Howard Smith and Sarah
Kernochan.*
THE SILENT REVOLUTION, Leonaris Films. Produced by Eckehard Munck.
Best Foreign Language Film
THE DAWNS HERE ARE QUIET (USSR).
THE DISCREET CHARM OF THE BOURGEOISIE (Fr.). Luis Bunuel.
I LOVE YOU ROSA (Israel). Moshe Mizrahi.
MY DEAREST SENORITA (Span.). Jaime de Arminan.
THE NEW LAND (Swed.). Jan Troell.
Irving G. Thalberg Memorial Award
None Awarded.
Jean Hersholt Humanitarian Award
Rosalind Russell.
Honorary Awards
Charles S. Boren, leader for 38 years of the industry's enlightened labor relations
and architect of its policy of nondiscrimination. With the respect and affection of all
who work in films.
Edward G. Robinson, who achieved greatness as a player, a patron of the arts and
a dedicated citizen...in sum, a Renaissance man. From the friends in the industry he
loves.
Special Achievement Award
For Visual Effects: L.B. Abbott and A.D. Flowers for THE POSEIDON ADVEN-
TURE.
Scientific or Technical
Class II
Joseph E. Bluth for research and development in the field of electronic photogra-
phy and transfer of video tape to motion picture film.
Edward H. Reichard and Howard T. La Zare of Consolidated Film Industries and
Edward Efron of IBM for the engineering of a computerized light valve monitoring
system for motion picture printing.
Panavision Incorporated for the development and engineering of the Panaflex
motion picture camera.
Class III
Photo Research, a Division of Kollmorgen Corporation, and PSC Technology, Inc.,
Acme Products Division, for the Spectra Film gate Photometer for motion picture
printing.
Carter Equipment Company, Inc., and Ramtronics for the Ramtronics light-valve
photometer for motion picture printers.
David Degenkolb, Harry Larson Manfred Michelson, and Fred Scobey of DeLuxe
General Incorporated for the development of a computerized motion picture
printer and process control system.
Jiro Mukai and Ryusho Hirose of Canon, Inc., and Wilton R. Holm of the AMPTP
Motion Picture and Television Research Center for development of the Canon
Macro Zoom lens for motion picture photography.
Philip V. Palmquist and Leonard L. Olson of the 3M Company, and Frank P. Clark
of the AMPTP Motion Picture and Television Research Center for the development
of the Nextel simulated blood for motion picture color photography.
E.H. Geissler and G.M. Berggren of Wil-Kin, Inc., for engineering of the
Ultra-Vision Motion Picture Theater Projection System.

1973
Best Picture
AMERICAN GRAFFITI, UNIV. Produced by Francis Ford Coppola.
CRIES AND WHISPERS (Swed.). Produced by Ingmar Bergman.
THE EXORCIST, WB. Produced by William Peter Blatty.
THE STING, UNIV. Produced by Tony Bill, Michael and Julia Phillips.
A TOUCH OF CLASS, Avco Embassy. Produced by Melvin Frank.
Best Actor
Marlon Brando for LAST TANGO IN PARIS (Fr./Ital.).
Jack Lemmon for SAVE THE TIGER.
Jack Nicholson for THE LAST DETAIL.
Al Pacino for SERPICO.
Robert Redford for THE STING.
Best Actress
Ellen Burstyn for THE EXORCIST.
Glenda Jackson for A TOUCH OF CLASS.
Marsha Mason for CINDERELLA LIBERTY.
Barbra Streisand for THE WAY WE WERE.
Joanne Woodward for SUMMER WISHES, WINTER DREAMS.
Best Supporting Actor
Vincent Gardenia for BANG THE DRUM SLOWLY.
Jack Gilford for SAVE THE TIGER.
John Houseman for THE PAPER CHASE.
Jason Miller for THE EXORCIST.
Randy Quaid for THE LAST DETAIL.
Best Supporting Actress

Linda Blair for THE EXORCIST.
Candy Clark for AMERICAN GRAFFITI.
Madeline Kahn for PAPER MOON.
Tatum O'Neal for PAPER MOON.
Sylvia Sidney for SUMMER WISHES, WINTER DREAMS.
Best Direction
Ingmar Bergman for CRIES AND WHISPERS (Swed.).
Bernardo Bertolucci for LAST TANGO IN PARIS (Fr./Ital.).
William Friedkin for THE EXORCIST.
George Roy Hill for THE STING.
George Lucas for AMERICAN GRAFFITI.
Writing Awards
Best Screenplay, Based on Material from Another Medium
THE EXORCIST, by William Peter Blatty.
THE LAST DETAIL, by Robert Towne.
THE PAPER CHASE, by James Bridges.
PAPER MOON, by Alvin Sargent.
SERPICO, by Waldo Salt and Norman Wexler.
Best Story and Screenplay, Based on Factual Material or Material not Previously Published or Produced.
AMERICAN GRAFFITI, by George Lucas, Gloria Katz, and Willard Huyck.
CRIES AND WHISPERS (Swed.), by Ingmar Bergman.
SAVE THE TIGER, by Steve Shagan.
THE STING, by David S. Ward.
A TOUCH OF CLASS, by Melvin Frank and Jack Rose.
Best Cinematography
CRIES AND WHISPERS (Swed.). Sven Nykvist.
THE EXORCIST. Owen Roizman.
JONATHAN LIVINGSTON SEAGULL. Jack Couffer.
THE STING. Robert Surtees.
THE WAY WE WERE. Harry Stradling, Jr.
Best Art Direction—Set Decoration
BROTHER SUN, SISTER MOON (Ital.). Lorenzo Mongiardino and Gianni Quaranta; Carmelo Patrono.
THE EXORCIST. Bill Malley; Jerry Wunderlich.
THE STING. Henry Bumstead; James Payne.
TOM SAWYER. Philip Jefferies; Robert de Vestel.
THE WAY WE WERE. Stephen Grimes; William Kiernan.
Best Sound
THE DAY OF THE DOLPHIN. Richard Portman and Lawrence O. Jost.
THE EXORCIST. Robert Knudson and Chris Newman.
THE PAPER CHASE. Donald O. Mitchell and Lawrence O. Jost.
PAPER MOON. Richard Portman and Les Fresholtz.
THE STING. Ronald K. Pierce and Robert Bertrand.
Music Awards
Best Song
"All That Love Went to Waste" from A TOUCH OF CLASS. Music by George Barrie; lyrics by Sammy Cahn.
"Live and Let Die" from LIVE AND LET DIE. Music and lyrics by Paul and Linda McCartney.
"Love" from ROBIN HOOD. Music by George Bruns; lyrics by Floyd Huddleston.
The Way We Were" from THE WAY WE WERE. Music by Marvin Hamlisch; lyrics by Alan and Marilyn Bergman.
"You're So Nice to Be Around" from CINDERELLA LIBERTY. Music by John Williams; lyrics by Paul Williams.
Best Original Dramatic Score
CINDERELLA LIBERTY. John Williams.
THE DAY OF THE DOLPHIN. Georges Delerue.
PAPILLON. Jerry Goldsmith.
A TOUCH OF CLASS. John Cameron.
THE WAY WE WERE. Marvin Hamlisch.
Best Scoring: Original Song Score and/or Adaptation
JESUS CHRIST SUPERSTAR. Andre Previn, Herbert Spencer and Andrew Lloyd Webber.
THE STING. Marvin Hamlisch.
TOM SAWYER. Richard M. Sherman, Robert B. Sherman, and John Williams.
Best Film Editing
AMERICAN GRAFFITI. Verna Fields and Marcia Lucas.
THE DAY OF THE JACKAL. Ralph Kemplen.
THE EXORCIST. Jordan Leondopoulos, Bud Smith, Evan Lottman, and Norman Gay.
JOHNATHAN LIVINGSTON SEAGULL. Frank P. Keller and James Galloway.
THE STING. William Reynolds.
Best Costume Design
CRIES AND WHISPERS (Swed.). Marik Vos.
LUDWIG. Piero Tosi.
THE STING. Edith Head.
TOM SAWYER. Donfeld.
THE WAY WE WERE. Dorothy Jeakins and Moss Mabry.
Short Subjects
Best Animated Film
FRANK FILM. Produced by Frank Mouris.
THE LEGEND OF JOHN HENRY, Bosustow-Pyramid Films. Produced by Nick Bosustow and David Adams.
PULCINELLA. Produced by Emanuele Luzzati and Guilo Gianini.
Best Live Action Film
THE BOLERO. Produced by Allan Miller and William Fertik.
CLOCKMAKER, James Street Productions. Produced by Richard Gayer.
LIFE TIMES NINE, Insight Productions. Produced by Pen Densham and John Watson.
Documentary
Best Short Subject Documentary
BACKGROUND, D'Avino and Fucci-Stone Productions. Produced by Carmen D'Avino.
CHILDREN AT WORK. Gael-Linn Films. Produced by Louis Marcus.
CHRISTO'S VALLEY CURTAIN. Produced by Albert and David Maysles.
FOUR STONES FOR KANEMITSU, Tamarind Productions.
PRINCETON: A SEARCH FOR ANSWERS. Produced by Julian Krainin and DeWitt L. Sage, Jr.
Best Feature Documentary
ALWAYS A NEW BEGINNING. Produced by John D. Goodell.

BATTLE OF BERLIN, Chronos Film. Produced by Bengt von zur Muehlen.
THE GREAT AMERICAN COWBOY, Merrill-Rodeo Film Productions. Produced by Keith Merrill.
JOURNEY TO THE OUTER LIMITS, National Geographic Society and Wolper Productions. Produced by Alex Grasshoff.
WALLS OF FIRE, Mentor Productions. Produced by Gertrude Ross Marks and Edmund F. Penney.
Best Foreign Language Film
DAY FOR NIGHT (Fr.). Francois Trufffaut.
THE HOUSE ON CHELOUCHE STREET (Israel). Moshe Mizrahi.
L'INVITATION (Switz.). Claude Goretta.
THE PEDESTRIAN (Ger.). Maximilian Schell.
TURKISH DELIGHT (Neth.). Paul Vehoeven.
Irving G. Thalberg Memorial Award
Lawrence Weingarten.
Jean Hersholt Humanitarian Award
Lew Wasserman.
Honorary Awards
Henri Langlois for his devotion to the art of film, his massive contributions in preserving its past and his unswerving faith in its future.
Groucho Marx in recognition of his brilliant creativity and for the unequalled achievements of the Marx Brothers in the art of motion picture comedy.
Scientific or Technical
Class II
Joachim Gerb and Erich Kastner of the Arnold and Richter Company for the development and engineering of the Arriflex 35BL motion picture camera.
Magna-Tech Electronic Company, Inc. for the engineering and development of a high-speed re-recording system for motion-picture production.
William W. Valliant of PSC Technology, Incorporated, Howard F. Ott of Eastman Kodak Company, and Gerry Diebold of the Richmark Camera Service for the development of a liquid-gate system for motion picture printers.
Harold A. Scheiv, Clifford H. Ellis, and Roger W. Banks of Research Products Incorporated for the concept and engineering of the Model 2101 optical printer for motion-picture optical effects.
Class III
Rosco Laboratories, Inc., for the technical advances and the development of a complete system of light-control materials for motion-picture photography.
Richard H. Vetter of the Todd-AO Corporation for the design of an improved anamorphic focusing system for motion-picture photography.

1974
Best Picture
CHINATOWN, PAR. Produced by Robert Evans.
THE CONVERSATION, PAR. Produced by Francis Ford Coppola.
THE GODFATHER PART II, PAR. Produced by Francis Ford Coppola; Gray Frederickson and Fred Roos.
LENNY, UA. Produced by Marvin Worth.
THE TOWERING INFERNO, FOX-WB. Produced by Irwin Allen.
Best Actor
Art Carney for HARRY AND TONTO.
Albert Finney for MURDER ON THE ORIENT EXPRESS.
Dustin Hoffman for LENNY.
Jack Nicholson for CHINATOWN.
Al Pacino for THE GODFATHER PART II.
Best Actress
Ellen Burstyn for ALICE DOESN'T LIVE HERE ANYMORE.
Diahann Carroll for CLAUDINE.
Faye Dunaway for CHINATOWN.
Valerie Perrine for LENNY.
Gena Rowlands for A WOMAN UNDER THE INFLUENCE.
Best Supporting Actor
Fred Astaire for THE TOWERING INFERNO.
Jeff Bridges for THUNDERBOLT AND LIGHTFOOT.
Robert De Niro for THE GODFATHER PART II.
Michael V. Gazzo for THE GODFATHER PART II.
Lee Strasberg for THE GODFATHER PART II.
Best Supporting Actress
Ingrid Bergman for MURDER ON THE ORIENT EXPRESS.
Valentina Cortese for DAY FOR NIGHT.
Madeline Kahn for BLAZING SADDLES.
Diane Ladd for ALICE DOESN'T LIVE HERE ANYMORE.
Talia Shire for THE GODFATHER PART II.
Best Direction
John Cassavetes for A WOMAN UNDER THE INFLUENCE.
Francis Ford Coppola for THE GODFATHER PART II.
Bob Fosse for LENNY.
Roman Polanski for CHINATOWN.
Francois Truffaut for DAY FOR NIGHT (Fr.).
Writing Awards
Best Original Screenplay
ALICE DOESN'T LIVE HERE ANYMORE, by Robert Getchell.
CHINATOWN, by Robert Towne.
THE CONVERSATION, by Francis Ford Coppola.
DAY FOR NIGHT (Fr.), by Francois Truffaut, Jean-Louis Richard, and Suzanne Schiffman.
HARRY AND TONTO, by Paul Mazursky and Josh Greenfeld.
Best Screenplay Adapted from Other Material
THE APPRENTICESHIP OF DUDDY KRAVITZ, by Mordecai Richler and Lionel Chetwynd.
THE GODFATHER PART II, by Francis Ford Coppola and Mario Puzo.
LENNY, by Julian Barry.
MURDER ON THE ORIENT EXPRESS, by Paul Dehn.
YOUNG FRANKENSTEIN, by Gene Wilder and Mel Brooks.
Best Cinematography
CHINATOWN. John A. Alonzo.
EARTHQUAKE. Philip Lathrop.
LENNY. Bruce Surtees.
MURDER ON THE ORIENT EXPRESS. Geoffrey Unsworth.
THE TOWERING INFERNO. Fred Koenekamp and Joseph Biroc.
Best Art Direction—Set Decoration

CHINATOWN. Richard Sylbert and W. Stewart Campbell; Ruby Levitt.
EARTHQUAKE. Alexander Golitzen and E. Preston Ames; Frank McKelvy.
THE GODFATHER PART II. Dean Tavoularis and Angelo Graham; George R. Nelson.
THE ISLAND AT THE TOP OF THE WORLD. Peter Ellenshaw, John B. Mansbridge, Walter Tyler, and Al Roelofs; Hal Gausman.
THE TOWERING INFERNO. William Creber and Ward Preston; Raphael Bretton.
Best Sound
CHINATOWN. Bud Grenzbach and Larry Jost.
THE CONVERSATION. Walter Murch and Arthur Rochester.
EARTHQUAKE. Ronald Pierce and Melvin Metcalfe, Sr.
THE TOWERING INFERNO. Theodore Soderberg and Herman Lewis.
YOUNG FRANKENSTEIN. Richard Portman and Gene Cantamessa.
Music Awards
Best Song
"Benji's Theme (I Feel Love)" from BENJI. Music by Euel Box; lyrics by Betty Box.
"Blazing Saddles" from BLAZING SADDLES. Music by John Morris; lyrics by Mel Brooks.
"Little Prince" from THE LITTLE PRINCE. Music by Frederick Loewe; lyrics by Alan Jay Lerner.
.We May Never Love Like This Again" from THE TOWERING INFERNO. Music and lyrics by Al Kasha and Joel Hirschhorn.
"Wherever Love Takes Me" from GOLD. Music by Elmer Bernstein; lyrics by Don Black.
Best Original Dramatic Score
CHINATOWN. Jerry Goldsmith.
THE GODFATHER PART II. Nino Rota and Carmine Coppola.
MURDER ON THE ORIENT EXPRESS. Richard Rodney Bennett.
SHANKS. Alex North.
THE TOWERING INFERNO. John Williams.
Best Scoring: Original Song Score and/or Adaptation
THE GREAT GATSBY. Nelson Riddle.
THE LITTLE PRINCE. Alan Jay Lerner, Frederick Loewe, Angela Morly, and Douglas Gamley.
PHANTOM OF THE PARADISE. Paul Williams and George Aliceson Tipton.
Best Film Editing
BLAZING SADDLES. John C. Howard and Danford Greene.
CHINATOWN. Sam O'Steen.
EARTHQUAKE. Dorothy Spencer.
THE LONGEST YARD. Michael Luciano.
THE TOWERING INFERNO. Harold F. Kress and Carl Kress.
Best Costume Design
CHINATOWN. Anthea Sylbert.
DAISY MILLER. John Furness.
THE GODFATHER PART II. Theadora Van Runkle.
THE GREAT GATSBY. Theoni V. Aldredge.
MURDER ON THE ORIENT EXPRESS. Tony Walton.
Short Films
Best Animated Film
CLOSED MONDAYS, Lighthouse Productions. Produced by Will Vinton and Bob Gardiner.
THE FAMILY THAT DWELT APART, National Film Board of Canada. Produced by Yvon Mallette and Robert Verrall.
HUNGER, National Film Board of Canada. Produced by Peter Foldes and Rene Jodoin.
VOYAGE TO NEXT. Produced by Faith and John Hubley.
WINNIE THE POOH AND TIGGER TOO, Buena Vista. Produced by Wolfgang Reitherman.
Best Live Action Film
CLIMB. Produced by Dewitt Jones.
THE CONCERT, The Black and White Colour Film Company, Ltd. Produced by Julian and Claude Chagrin.
ONE-EYED MEN ARE KINGS (Fr.), C.A.P.A.C. Productions. Produced by Paul Claudon and Edmond Sechan.
PLANET OCEAN, Graphic Films. Produced by George V. Casey.
THE VIOLIN, Sincinkin, Ltd. Produced by Andrew Welsh and George Pastic.
Documentary
Best Short Subject Documentary
CITY OUT OF WILDERNESS. Produced by Francis Thompson.
DON'T, R.A. Films. Produced by Robin Lehman.
EXPLORATORIUM. Produced by Jon Boorstin.
JOHN MUIR'S HIGH SIERRA. Produced by DeWitt Jones and Lesley Foster.
NAKED YOGA, Filmshop Productions. Produced by Ronald S. Kass and Mervyn Lloyd.
Best Feature Documentary
ANTONIA: A PORTRAIT OF THE WOMAN, Rocky Mountain Productions. Produced by Judy Collins and Jill Godmilow.
THE CHALLENGE...A TRIBUTE TO MODERN ART, World View. Produced by Herbert Kline.
THE 81ST BLOW, Ghetto Fighters House. Produced by Jacquot Ehrlich, David Bergman,and Haim Gouri.
HEARTS AND MINDS, Touchstone-Audjeff-BBS Productions, Zuker/Jaglom-Rainbow Pictures, WB. Produced by Peter Davis and Bert Schneider.
THE WILD AND THE BRAVE, E.S.J.-Tomorrow Entertainment-Jones/Howard Ltd. Produced by Natalie R. Jones and Eugene S. Jones.
Best Foreign Language Film
AMARCORD (Ital.). Federico Fellini.
CATSPLAY (Hung.). Karely Makk.
THE DELUGE (Pol.). Jerzy Hoffman.
LACOMBE, LUCIEN (Fr.). Louis Malle.
THE TRUCE (Arg.). Sergio Renen.
Irving G. Thalberg Memorial Award
None awarded.
Jean Hersholt Humanitarian Award
Arthur B. Krim.
Honorary Awards
Howard Hawks—A master American filmmaker whose creative efforts hold a distinguished place in world cinema.
Jean Renoir—a genius who, with grace, responsibility and enviable devotion through silent film, sound film, feature, documentary and television, has won the world's

admiration.
Special Achievement Awards
For Visual Effects: Frank Brendel, Glen Robinson and Albert Whitlock for EARTH-QUAKE.
Scientific or Technical
Class II
Joseph D. Kelly of Glen Glenn Sound for the design of new audio control consoles which have advanced the state of the art of sound recording and recording for motion picture production.
The Burbank Studios Sound Department for the design of new audio control consoles engineered and constructed by the Quad-Eight Sound Corporation.
Samuel Goldwyn Studios Sound Department for the design of a new audio control console engineered and constructed by the Quad-Eight Sound Corporation.
Quad-Eight Sound Corporation for the engineering and construction of new audio control consoles designed by the Burbank Studios Sound Department and the Samuel Goldwyn Studios Sound Department.
Waldon O. Watson, Richard J. Stumpf, Robert J. Leonard and the Universal City Studios Sound Department for the development and engineering of the Sensurround System for motion picture presentation.
Class III
Elemack Company of Rome, Italy, for the design and development of their Spyder camera dolly.
Louis Ami of the Universal City Studios for the design and construction of a reciprocating camera platform used when photographing special visual effects for motion pictures.

1975
Best Picture
BARRY LYNDON, WB. Produced by Stanley Kubrick.
DOG DAY AFTERNOON, WB. Produced by Martin Bregman and Martin Elfand.
JAWS, UNIV. Produced by Richard D. Zanuck and David Brown.
NASHVILLE, PAR. Produced by Robert Altman.
ONE FLEW OVER THE CUCKOO'S NEST, UA. Produced by Saul Zaentz and Michael Douglas.
Best Actor
Walter Matthau for THE SUNSHINE BOYS.
Jack Nicholson for ONE FLEW OVER THE CUCKOO'S NEST.
Al Pacino for DOG DAY AFTERNOON.
Maximilian Schell for THE MAN IN THE GLASS BOOTH.
James Whitmore for GIVE 'EM HELL, HARRY!
Best Actress
Isabelle Adjani for THE STORY OF ADELE H (Fr.).
Ann-Margret for TOMMY.
Louise Fletcher for ONE FLEW OVER THE CUCKOO'S NEST.
Glenda Jackson for HEDDA.
Carol Kane for HESTER STREET.
Best Supporting Actor
George Burns for THE SUNSHINE BOYS.
Brad Dourif for ONE FLEW OVER THE CUCKOO'S NEST.
Burgess Meredith for THE DAY OF THE LOCUST.
Chris Sarandon for DOG DAY AFTERNOON.
Jack Warden for SHAMPOO.
Best Supporting Actress
Ronee Blakley for NASHVILLE.
Lee Grant for SHAMPOO.
Sylvia Miles for FAREWELL, MY LOVELY.
Lily Tomlin for NASHVILLE.
Brenda Vaccaro for JACQUELINE SUSANN'S ONCE IS NOT ENOUGH.
Best Direction
Robert Altman for NASHVILLE.
Federico Fellini for AMARCORD (Ital.).
Milos Forman for ONE FLEW OVER THE CUCKOO'S NEST.
Stanley Kubrick for BARRY LYNDON.
Sidney Lumet for DOG DAY AFTERNOON.
Writing Awards
Best Original Screenplay
AMARCORD (Ital.), by Federico Fellini and Tonino Guerra.
AND NOW MY LOVE (Fr.), by Claude Lelouch and Pierre Uytterhoeven.
DOG DAY AFTERNOON, by Frank Pierson.
LIES MY FATHER TOLD ME, by Ted Allan.
SHAMPOO, by Robert Towne and Warren Beatty.
Best Screenplay Adapted from Other Material
BARRY LYNDON, by Stanley Kubrick.
THE MAN WHO WOULD BE KING, by John Huston and Gladys Hill.
ONE FLEW OVER THE CUCKOO'S NEST, by Lawrence Hauben and Bo Goldman.
SCENT OF A WOMAN (Ital.), by Ruggero Maccari and Dino Risi.
THE SUNSHINE BOYS, by Neil Simon.
Best Cinematography
BARRY LYNDON. John Alcott.
THE DAY OF THE LOCUST. Conrad Hall.
FUNNY LADY. James Wong Howe.
THE HINDENBURG. Robert Surtees.
ONE FLEW OVER THE CUCKOO'S NEST. Haskell Wexler and Bill Butler.
Best Art Direction—Set Decoration
BARRY LYNDON. Ken Adam and Roy Walker; Vernon Dixon.
THE HINDENBURG. Edward Carfagno; Frank McKelvy.
THE MAN WHO WOULD BE KING. Alexander Trauner and Tony Inglis; Peter James.
SHAMPOO. Richard Sylbert and W. Stewart Campbell; George Gaines.
THE SUNSHINE BOYS. Albert Brenner; Marvin March.
Best Sound
BITE THE BULLET. Arthur Piantodosi, Les Fresholtz, Richard Tyler, and Al Overton, Jr.
FUNNY LADY. Richard Portman, Don MacDougall, Curly Thirlwell, and Jack Solomon.
THE HINDENBURG. Leonard Peterson, John A. Bolger, Jr., John Mack, and Don K. Sharpless.
JAWS. Robert L. Hoyt, Roger Heman, Earl Madery, and John Carter.
THE WIND AND THE LION. Harry W. Tetrick, Aaron Rochin, William McCaughey, and Roy Charman.

Music Awards
  Best Original Song
    "How Lucky Can You Get" from FUNNY LADY. Music and lyrics by Fred Ebb and John Kander.
    ■I'm Easy" from NASHVILLE. Music and lyrics by Keith Carradine.
    "Now That We're in Love" from WHIFFS. Music by George Barrie; lyrics by Sammy Cahn.
    "Richard's Window" from THE OTHER SIDE OF THE MOUNTAIN. Music by Charles Fox; lyrics by Norman Gimbel.
    "Do You Know Where You're Going To" from MAHOGANY. Music by Michael Masser; lyrics by Gerry Goffin.
  Best Original Score
    BIRDS DO IT, BEES DO IT. Gerald Fried.
    BITE THE BULLET. Alex North.
    JAWS. John Williams.
    ONE FLEW OVER THE CUCKOO'S NEST. Jack Nitzsche.
    THE WIND AND THE LION. Jerry Goldsmith.
  Best Scoring: Original Song Score and/or Adaptation
    BARRY LYNDON. Leonard Rosenman.
    FUNNY LADY. Peter Matz.
    TOMMY. Peter Townshend.
Best Film Editing
    DOG DAY AFTERNOON. Dede Allen.
    JAWS. Verna Fields.
    THE MAN WHO WOULD BE KING. Russell Lloyd.
    ONE FLEW OVER THE CUCKOO'S NEST. Richard Chew, Lynzee Klingman, and Sheldon Kahn.
    THREE DAYS OF THE CONDOR. Frederic Steinkamp and Don Guidice.
Best Costume Design
    BARRY LYNDON. Ulla-Britt Soderlund and Milena Canonero.
    THE FOUR MUSKETEERS. Yvonne Blake and Ron Talsky.
    FUNNY LADY. Ray Aghayan and Bob Mackie.
    THE MAGIC FLUTE (Swed.). Henny Noremark and Karin Erskine.
    THE MAN WHO WOULD BE KING. Edith Head.
Short Films
  Best Animated Film
    GREAT, Grantstern, British Lion Films Ltd. Produced by Bob Godfrey.
    KICK ME. Produced by Robert Swarthe.
    MONSIEUR POINTU, National Film Board of Canada. Produced by Rene Jodoin, Bernard Longpre and Andre Leduc.
    SISYPHUS, Hungarofilms. Produced by Marcell Jankovics.
  Best Live Action Film
    ANGEL AND BIG JOE. Produced by Bert Salzman.
    CONQUEST OF LIGHT. Produced by Louis Marcus.
    DAWN FLIGHT. Produced by Lawrence M. Lansburgh and Brian Lansburgh.
    A DAY IN THE LIFE OF BONNIE CONSOLO, Barr Films. Produced by Barry Spinello.
    DOUBLETALK. Produced by Alan Beattie.
Documentary
  Best Short Subject Documentary
    ARTHUR AND LILLIE, Department of Communication, Stanford University. Produced by Jon Else, Steven Kovacs, and Kristine Samuelson.
    THE END OF THE GAME, Opus Films Ltd. Produced by Claire Wilbur and Robin Lehman.
    MILLIONS OF YEARS AHEAD OF MAN, BASF. Produced by Manfred Baier.
    PROBES IN SPACE, Graphic Films. Produced by George V. Casey.
    WHISTLING SMITH, National Film Board of Canada. Produced by Barrie Howells and Michael Scott.
  Best Feature Documentary
    THE CALIFORNIA REICH, Yasny Talking Pictures. Produced by Walter F. Parkes and Keith F. Critchlow.
    FIGHTING FOR OUR LIVES, Farm Worker Films. Produced by Glen Pearcy.
    THE INCREDIBLE MACHINE, The National Geographic Society, Wolper Productions. Produced by Irwin Rosten.
    THE MAN WHO SKIED DOWN EVEREST, Crawley Films. Produced by F.R. Crawley, James Hager, and Dale Hartleben.
    THE OTHER HALF OF THE SKY: A CHINA MEMOIR. Produced by Shirley MacLaine.
Best Foreign Language Film
    DERSU UZALA (USSR). Akira Kurosawa.
    LAND OF PROMISE (Pol.). Andrzej Wajda.
    LETTERS OF MARUSIA (Mex.). Miguel Littin.
    SANDAKAN NO.8 (Jap.). Kei Kumai.
    SCENT OF A WOMAN (Ital.). Dino Risi.
Irving G. Thalberg Memorial Award
    Mervyn LeRoy.
Jean Hersholt Humanitarian Award
    Jules C. Stein.
Honorary Award
    Mary Pickford, in recognition of her unique contributions to the film industry and the development of film as an artistic medium.
Special Achievement Awards
    For Sound Effects: Peter Berkos for THE HINDENBURG.
    For Visual Effects: Albert Whitlock and Glen Robinson for THE HINDENBURG.
Scientific or Technical
  Class II
    Chadwell O'Connor of the O'Connor Engineering Laboratories for the concept and engineering of a fluid-damped camera-head for motion-picture photography.
    William F. Miner of Universal City Studios, Inc. and the Westinghouse Electric Corporation for the development and engineering of a solid-state, 500 kilowatt, direct-current static rectifier for motion-picture lighting.
  Class III
    Lawrence W. Butler and Roger Banks for the concept of applying low inertia and stepping electric motors to film transport systems and optical printers for motion-picture production.
    David J. Degenkolb and Fred Scobey of Deluxe General, Inc., and John C. Dolan and Richard Dubois of the Akwaklame Company for the development of a technique for silver recovery from photographic wash-waters by ion exchange.
    Joseph Westheimer for the development of a device to obtain shadowed titles on motion-picture films.

Carter Equipment Company, Inc., and Ramtronics for the engineering and manufacture of a computerized tape punching system for programming laboratory printing machines.
The Hollywood Film Company for the engineering and manufacture of a computerized tape punching system for programming laboratory printing machines.
Bell & Howell for the engineering and manufacture of a computerized tape punching system for programming laboratory printing machines.
Fredrik Schlyter for the engineering and manufacture of a computerized tape punching system for programming laboratory printing machines.

1976
Best Picture
    ALL THE PRESIDENT'S MEN, WB. Produced by Walter Coblenz.
    BOUND FOR GLORY, UA. Produced by Robert F. Blumofe and Harold Leventhal.
    NETWORK, MGM/UA. Produced by Howard Gottfried.
    ROCKY, UA. Produced by Irwin Winkler and Robert Chartoff.
    TAXI DRIVER, COL. Produced by Michael Phillips and Julia Phillips.
Best Actor
    Robert De Niro for TAXI DRIVER.
    Peter Finch for NETWORK.
    Giancarlo Giannini for SEVEN BEAUTIES (Ital.).
    William Holden for NETWORK.
    Sylvester Stallone for ROCKY.
Best Actress
    Marie-Christine Barrault for COUSIN, COUSINE (Fr.).
    Faye Dunaway for NETWORK.
    Talia Shire for ROCKY.
    Sissy Spacek for CARRIE.
    Liv Ullman for FACE TO FACE (Swed.).
Best Supporting Actor
    Ned Beatty for NETWORK
    Burgess Meredith for ROCKY.
    Laurence Olivier for MARATHON MAN.
    Jason Robards for ALL THE PRESIDENT'S MEN.
    Burt Young for ROCKY.
Best Supporting Actress
    Jane Alexander for ALL THE PRESIDENT'S MEN.
    Jodie Foster for TAXI DRIVER.
    Lee Grant for VOYAGE OF THE DAMNED.
    Piper Laurie for CARRIE.
    Beatrice Straight for NETWORK.
Best Direction
    John G. Avildsen for ROCKY.
    Ingmar Bergman for FACE TO FACE (Swed.).
    Sidney Lumet for NETWORK.
    Alan J. Pakula for ALL THE PRESIDENT'S MEN.
    Lina Wertmuller for SEVEN BEAUTIES.
Writing Award
  Best Screenplay Written Directly for the Screen
    COUSIN, COUSINE, by Jean-Charles Tachella and Daniele Thompson.
    THE FRONT, by Walter Bernstein.
    NETWORK, by Paddy Chayefsky.
    ROCKY, by Sylvester Stallone.
    SEVEN BEAUTIES (Ital.), by Lina Wertmuller.
  Best Screenplay Based on Material from Another Medium
    ALL THE PRESIDENT'S MEN, by William Goldman.
    BOUND FOR GLORY, by Robert Getchell.
    FELLINI'S CASANOVA (Ital.), by Federico Fellini and Bernadino Zapponi.
    THE SEVEN-PER-CENT SOLUTION, by Nicholas Meyer.
    VOYAGE OF THE DAMNED, by Steve Shagan and David Butler.
Best Cinematography
    BOUND FOR GLORY. Haskell Wexler.
    KING KONG. Richard H. Kline.
    LOGAN'S RUN. Ernest Laszlo.
    NETWORK. Owen Roizman.
    A STAR IS BORN. Robert Surtees.
Best Art Direction—Set Decoration
    ALL THE PRESIDENT'S MEN. George Jenkins; George Gaines.
    THE INCREDIBLE SARAH. Elliot Scott and Norman Reynolds.
    THE LAST TYCOON. Gene Callahan and Jack Collis; Jerry Wunderlich.
    LOGAN'S RUN. Dale Hennesy; Robert de Vestel.
    THE SHOOTIST. Robert F. Boyle; Arthur Jeph Parker.
Best Sound
    ALL THE PRESIDENT'S MEN. Arthur Piantadosi, Les Fresholtz, Dick Alexander, and Jim Webb.
    KING KONG. Harry Warren Tetrick, William McCaughey, Aaron Rochin, and Jack Solomon.
    ROCKY. Harry Warren Tetrick, William McCaughey, Lyle Burbridge, and Bud Alper.
    SILVER STREAK. Donald Mitchell, Douglas Williams, Richard Tyler, and Hal Etherington.
    A STAR IS BORN. Robert Knudson, Dan Wallin, Robert Glass, and Tom Overton.
Music Award
  Best Original Song
    "Ave Satani" from THE OMEN. Music and lyrics by Jerry Goldsmith.
    "Come to Me" from THE PINK PANTHER STRIKES AGAIN. Music by Henry Mancini; lyrics by Don Black.
    Evergreen (Love Theme from A STAR IS BORN.)" Music by Barbra Streisand; lyrics by Paul Williams.
    "Gonna Fly Now" from ROCKY. Music by Bill Conti; lyrics by Carol Connors and Ayn Robbins.
    "A World That Never Was" from HALF A HOUSE. Music by Sammy Fain; lyrics by Paul Francis Webster.
  Best Original Score
    OBSESSION. Bernard Herrmann.
    THE OMEN. Jerry Goldsmith.
    THE OUTLAW JOSEY WALES. Jerry Fielding.
    TAXI DRIVER. Bernard Herrmann.
    VOYAGE OF THE DAMNED. Lalo Schifrin.
  Best Original Song Score and Its Adaptation or Adaptation Score
    BOUND FOR GLORY. Leonard Rosenman.

BUGSY MALONE. Paul Williams.
A STAR IS BORN. Roger Kellaway.
Best Film Editing
ALL THE PRESIDENT'S MEN. Robert L. Wolfe.
BOUND FOR GLORY. Robert Jones and Pembroke J. Herring.
NETWORK. Alan Heim.
ROCKY. Richard Halsey and Scott Conrad.
TWO-MINUTE WARNING. Eve Newman and Walter Hannemann.
Best Costume Design
BOUND FOR GLORY. William Theiss.
FELLINI'S CASANOVA (Ital.). Danilo Donati.
THE INCREDIBLE SARAH. Anthony Mendleson.
THE PASSOVER PLOT. Mary Wills.
THE SEVEN-PER-CENT SOLUTION. Alan Barrett.
Short Films
Best Animated Film
DEDALO, Cineteam Realizzzazioni. Produced by Manfredo Manfredi.
LEISURE, Film Australia. Produced by Suzanne Baker.
THE STREET, National Film Board of Canada. Produced by Caroline Leaf and Guy Glover.
Best Live Action Film
IN THE REGION OF ICE, American Film Institute. Produced by Andre Guttgreund and Peter Werner.
KUDZU. Produced by Marjori Anne Short.
THE MORNING SPIDER, The Black and White Color Film Company. Produced by Julian Chagrin and Claude Chagrin.
NIGHTLIFE, Opus Films, Ltd. Produced by Claire Wilbur and Robin Lehman.
NUMBER ONE, Number One Productions. Produced by Dyan Cannon and Vince Cannon.
Documentary
Best Short Subject Documentary
AMERICAN SHOESHINE, Titan Films. Produced by Sparky Greene.
BLACKWOOD, National Film Board of Canada. Produced by Tony Ianzelo and Andy Thompson.
THE END OF THE ROAD, Pelican Films. Produced by John Armstrong.
NUMBER OUR DAYS, Community Television of Southern California. Produced by Lynne Littman.
UNIVERSE, Graphic Films Corp for NASA. Produced by Lester Novros.
Best Feature Documentary
HARLAN COUNTY, U.S.A., Cabin Creek Films. Barbara Kopple, producer.
HOLLYWOOD ON TRIAL, October Films/Cinema Associates. Produced by James Gutman and David Helpern, Jr..
OFF THE EDGE, Pentacle Films. Produced by Michael Firth.
PEOPLE OF THE WIND, Elizabeth E. Rogers Productions. Produced by Anthony Howart and Davud Koff.
VOLCANO; AN INQUIRY INTO THE LIFE AND DEATH OF MALCOLM LOWRY, National Film Board of Canada. Produced by Donald Brittain and Robert Duncan.
Best Foreign Language Film
BLACK AND WHITE IN COLOR (Ivory Coast). Jean-Jacques Annaud.
COUSIN, COUSINE (Fr.). Jean-Charles Tacchella.
JACOB THE LIAR (Ger.). Frank Beyer.
NIGHTS AND DAYS (Pol.). Jerzy Antezak.
SEVEN BEAUTIES (Ital.). Lina Wertmuller.
Irving G. Thalberg Memorial Award
Pandro S. Berman.
Jean Hersholt Humanitarian Award
None awarded.
Special Achievement Award
For Visual Effects: Carlo Rambaldi, Glen Robinson and Frank Van Der Veer for KING KONG.
For Visual Effects: L.B. Abbott, Glen Robinson and Matthew Yuricich for LOGAN'S RUN.
Scientific or Technical
Class II
Consolidated Film Industries and the Barnebey-Cheney Company for the development of a system for the recovery of film cleaning solvent vapors in a motion picture laboratory.
William L. Graham, Manfred G. Michelson, Geoffrey F. Norman and Siegfried Seibert of Technicolor for the development and engineering of a continuous, high-speed, Color Motion Picture Printing System.
Class III
Fred Bartscher of the Kollmorgen Corporation and to Glenn Berggren of the Schneider Corporation for the design and development of a single-lens magnifier for motion picture projection lenses.
Panavision Incorporated for the design and development of super-speed lenses for motion picture photography.
Hiroshi Suzukawa of Canon and Wilton R. Holm of AMPTP Motion Picture and Television Research Center for the design and development of super-speed lenses for motion picture photography.
Carl Zeiss Company for the design and development of super-speed lenses for motion picture photography.
Photo Research Division of the Kollmorgen Corporation for the engineering and manufacture of the spectra TriColor Meter.

1977
Best Picture
ANNIE HALL, UA. Produced by Charles H. Joffe.
THE GOODBYE GIRL, MGM/WB. Produced by Ray Stark.
JULIA, FOX. Produced by Richard Roth.
STAR WARS, FOX. Produced by Gary Kurtz.
THE TURNING POINT, FOX. Produced by Herbert Ross and Arthur Laurents.
Best Actor
Woody Allen for ANNIE HALL.
Richard Burton for EQUUS.
Richard Dreyfuss for THE GOODBYE GIRL.
Marcello Mastroianni for A SPECIAL DAY (Ital.).
John Travolta for SATURDAY NIGHT FEVER.
Best Actress
Anne Bancroft for THE TURNING POINT.
Jane Fonda for JULIA.

Diane Keaton for ANNIE HALL.
Shirley MacLaine for THE TURNING POINT.
Marsha Mason for THE GOODBYE GIRL.
Best Supporting Actor
Mikhail Baryshnikov for THE TURNING POINT.
Peter Firth for EQUUS.
Alec Guinness for STAR WARS.
Jason Robards for JULIA.
Maximilian Schell for JULIA.
Best Supporting Actress
Leslie Browne for THE TURNING POINT.
Quinn Cummings for THE GOODBYE GIRL.
Melinda Dillon for CLOSE ENCOUNTERS OF THE THIRD KIND.
Vanessa Redgrave for JULIA.
Tuesday Weld for LOOKING FOR MR. GOODBAR.
Best Direction
Woody Allen for ANNIE HALL.
George Lucas for STAR WARS.
Herbert Ross for THE TURNING POINT.
Steven Spielberg for CLOSE ENCOUNTERS OF THE THIRD KIND.
Fred Zinnemann for JULIA.
Writing Awards
Best Screenplay Written Directly for the Screen
ANNIE HALL, by Woody Allen and Marshall Brickman.
THE GOODBYE GIRL, by Neil Simon.
THE LATE SHOW, by Robert Benton.
STAR WARS, by George Lucas.
THE TURNING POINT, by Arthur Laurents.
Best Screenplay Based on Material from Another Source
EQUUS, by Peter Shaffer.
I NEVER PROMISED YOU A ROSE GARDEN, by Gavin Lambert and Lewis John Carlino.
JULIA, by Alvin Sargent.
OH, GOD! by Larry Gelbart.
THAT OBSCURE OBJECT OF DESIRE (Span.), by Luis Bunuel and Jean-Claude Carriere.
Best Cinematography
ISLANDS IN THE STREAM. Fred J. Koenekamp.
JULIA. Douglas Slocombe.
LOOKING FOR MR. GOODBAR. William A. Fraker.
CLOSE ENCOUNTERS OF THE THIRD KIND. Vilmos Zsigmund.
THE TURNING POINT. Robert Surtees.
Best Art Direction—Set Decoration
AIRPORT '77. George C. Webb; Mickey S. Michaels
CLOSE ENCOUNTERS OF THE THIRD KIND. Joe Alves and Dan Lomino; Phil Abramson.
THE SPY WHO LOVED ME. Ken Adam and Peter Lamont; Hugh Scaife.
STAR WARS. John Barry, Norman Reynolds and Leslie Dilley; Roger Christian.
THE TURNING POINT. Albert Brenner; Marvin March.
Best Sound
CLOSE ENCOUNTERS OF THE THIRD KIND. Robert Knudson, Robert J. Glass, Don MacDougall, and Gene S. Cantamessa.
THE DEEP. Walter Goss, Dick Alexander, Tom Beckert, and Robin Gregory.
SORCERER. Robert Knudson, Robert J. Glass, Richard Tyler, and Jean-Louis Ducarme.
STAR WARS. Don MacDougall, Ray West, Bob Minkler, and Derek Ball.
THE TURNING POINT. Theodore Soderberg, Paul Wells, Douglas O. Williams, and Jerry Jost.
Music Awards
Best Original Song
"Candle on the Water" from PETE'S DRAGON. Music and lyrics by Al Kasha and Joel Hirschhorn.
"Nobody Does It Better" from THE SPY WHO LOVED ME. Music by Marvin Hamlisch; lyrics by Carole Bayer Sager.
"The Slipper and the Rose Waltz (He Danced with Me/She Danced with Me)" from THE SLIPPER AND THE ROSE—THE STORY OF CINDERELLA. Music and lyrics by Richard M. Sherman and Robert B. Sherman.
"Someone's Waiting for You" from THE RESCUERS. Music by Sammy Fain; lyrics by Carol Connors and Ayn Robbins.
"You Light Up My Life" from YOU LIGHT UP MY LIFE. Music and lyrics by Joseph Brooks.
Best Original Score
CLOSE ENCOUNTERS OF THE THIRD KIND. John Williams.
JULIA. Georges Delerue.
MOHAMMAD—MESSENGER OF GOD. Maurice Jarre.
THE SPY WHO LOVED ME. Marvin Hamlisch.
STAR WARS. John Williams.
Best Original Song Score and Its Adaptation or Adaptation Score
A LITTLE NIGHT MUSIC. Jonathan Tunick.
PETE'S DRAGON. Al Kasha, Joel Hirschborn, and Irwin Kostal.
THE SLIPPER AND THE ROSE—THE STORY OF CINDERELLA. Richard M. Sherman, Robert B. Sherman, and Angela Morley.
Best Film Editing
CLOSE ENCOUNTERS OF THE THIRD KIND. Michael Kahn.
JULIA. Walter Murch and Marcel Durham.
SMOKEY AND THE BANDIT. Walter Hannemann and Angelo Ross.
STAR WARS. Paul Hirsch, Marcia Lucas and Richard Chew.
THE TURNING POINT. William Reynolds.
Best Costume Design
AIRPORT '77. Edith Head and Burton Miller.
JULIA. Anthea Sylbert.
A LITTLE NIGHT MUSIC. Florence Katz.
THE OTHER SIDE OF MIDNIGHT. Irene Sharaff.
STAR WARS. John Mollo. Best Visual Effects
CLOSE ENCOUNTERS OF THE THIRD KIND. Roy Arbogast, Douglas Trumbull, Matthew Yuricich, Gregory Jein, and Richard Yuricich.
STAR WARS. John Stears, John Dykstra, Richard Edlund, Grant McCune, and Robert Blalack.
Short Films
Best Animated Film

THE BEAD GAME, National Film Board of Canada. Produced by Ishu Patel.
THE DOONESBURY SPECIAL, Hubley Studio. Produced by John and Faith Hubley, and Garry Trudeau.
JIMMY THE C, Motionpicker Production. Produced by James Picker, Robert Grossman, and Craig Whitaker.
SAND CASTLE, National Film Board of Canada. Produced by Co Hoedeman.
Best Live Action Film
THE ABSENT-MINDED WAITER, Aspen Film Society. Produced by William E. McEuen.
FLOATING FREE, Trans World International. Produced by Jerry Butts.
'LL FIND A WAY, National Film BVoard of Canada. Produced by Beverly Shaffer and Yuki Yoshida.
NOTES ON THE POPULAR ARTS. Produced by Saul Bass.
SPACEBORNE, Lawrence Hall of Science Production for the Regents of the University of California with the cooperation of NASA. Produced by Philip Dauber.
Documentary
Best Short Subject Documentary
AGUEDA MARTINEZ: OUR PEOPLE. OUR COUNTRY. Produced by Moctesuma Esparza.
FIRST EDITION, Sage Productions. Produced by Helen Whitney and DeWitt L. Sage, Jr.
GRAVITY IS MY ENEMY, Joseph Production. Produced by John Joseph and Jan Stussy.
OF TIME, TOMBS AND TREASURE, Charlie/Papa Productions. Produced by James R. Messenger and Paul N. Raimondi.
THE SHETLAND EXPERIENCE, Balfour Films. Produced by Douglas Gordon.
Best Feature Documentary
THE CHILDREN OF THEATER STREET, Mack-Vaganova Company. Produced by Robert Dornhelm and Earle Mack.
HIGH GRASS CIRCUS, National Film Board of Canada. Produced by Bill Brind, Torben Schioler and Tony Ianzelo.
HOMAGE TO CHAGALL—THE COLOURS OF LOVE, a CBC Production. Produced by Harry Rasky.
UNION MAIDS. Produced by James Klein, Julia Reichert and Miles Mogulescu.
WHO ARE THE DEABOLTS? AND WHERE DID THEY GET 19 KIDS? Korty Films/Charles M. Schultz, Sanrio Films. Produced by John Korty, Dan McCann and Warren L. Lockhart.
Best Foreign Language Film
IPHIGENIA (Gr.). Michael Cacoyannis.
MADAME ROSA (Fr.). Moishe Mizrahi.
OPERATION THUNDERBOLT (Israel). Menahem Golan.
A SPECIAL DAY (Ital.). Ettore Scola.
THAT OBSCURE OBJECT OF DESIRE (Span.). Luis Bunuel.
Irving G. Thalberg Memorial Award
Walter Mirisch.
Jean Hersholt Humanitarian Award
Charlton Heston.
Honorary Awards
Margaret Booth for her exceptional contribution to the art of film editing in the motion picture industry.
Gordon E. Sawyer and Sidney P. Solow in appreciation for outstanding service and dedication in upholding the high standards of the Academy of Motion Picture Arts and Sciences.
Special Achievement Awards
For Sound Effects Editing: Frank Warner for CLOSE ENCOUNTERS OF THE THIRD KIND.
For Sound Effects: Benjamin Burtt, Jr. for the creation of the alien, creature and robot voices in STAR WARS.
Scientific or Technical
Class I
Garrett Brown and the Cinema Products Corp. engineering staff under the supervision of John Jurgens for the invention and development of Steadicam.
Class II
Joseph D. Kelly, Emory M. Cohen, Barry K. Hneley, Hammond H. Holt and John Agalsoff of Glen Glenn Sound for the concept and develpment of a post-production audio processing system for motion picture film
Panavision, Incorporated for the concept and engineering of the improvements in the Panaflex Motion Picture Camera.
N. Paul Kenworthy, Jr. and William R. Latady for the invention and development of the Kenworthy Snorkel Camera System for motion picture photography.
The Eastman Kodak Company for the development and introduction of a new duplicating film for motion pictures.
Stefan Kudelski of Nagra Magnetic Recorders, Incorporated, for the engineering of the improvements incorporated in the Nagra 4.2L sound recorder for motion picture production.
Class III
Ernest Nettmann of the Astrovision Division of Continental Camera Systems, Inc., for the engineering of its Snorkel Aerial Camera System.
EECO (Electronic Engineering Company of California) for developing a method for interlocking non-sprocketed film and tape media used in motion picture production.
Dr. Bernhard Kuhl and Werner Block of Osram, GmbH for the development of the HMI high-efficiency discharge lamp for motion picture lighting.
Panavision, Incorporated, for the design of Panalite, a camera-mounted controllable light for motion picture photography and for the engineering of the Panahead gearhead for motion picture cameras.
Piclear, Inc., for originating and developing an attachment to motion picture projectors to improve screen image quality.

1978
Best Picture
COMING HOME, UA. Produced by Jerome Hellman.
THE DEER HUNTER, UNIV. Produced by Barry Spikings, Michael Deeley, Michael Cimino, and John Peverall.
HEAVEN CAN WAIT, PAR. Produced by Warren Beatty.
MIDNIGHT EXPRESS, COL. Produced by Alan Marshall and David Puttnam.
AN UNMARRIED WOMAN, FOX. Produced by Paul Mazursky and Tony Ray.
Best Actor
Warren Beatty for HEAVEN CAN WAIT.
Gary Busey for THE BUDDY HOLLY STORY.
Robert De Niro for THE DEER HUNTER.

Laurence Olivier for THE BOYS FROM BRAZIL.
Jon Voight for COMING HOME.
Best Actress
Ingrid Bergman for AUTUMN SONATA (Swed.).
Ellen Burstyn for SAME TIME, NEXT YEAR.
Jill Clayburgh for AN UNMARRIED WOMAN.
Jane Fonda for COMING HOME.
Geraldine Page for INTERIORS.
Best Supporting Actor
Bruce Dern for COMING HOME.
Richard Farnsworth for COMES A HORSEMAN.
John Hurt for MIDNIGHT EXPRESS.
Christopher Walken for THE DEER HUNTER.
Jack Warden for HEAVEN CAN WAIT.
Best Supporting Actress
Dyan Cannon for HEAVEN CAN WAIT.
Penelope Milford for COMING HOME.
Maggie Smith for CALIFORNIA SUITE.
Maureen Stapleton for INTERIORS.
Meryl Streep for THE DEER HUNTER.
Best Direction
Woody Allen for INTERIORS.
Hal Ashby for COMING HOME.
Warren Beatty and Buck Henry for HEAVEN CAN WAIT.
Michael Cimino for THE DEER HUNTER
Alan Parker for MIDNIGHT EXPRESS.
Writing Awards
Best Screenplay Written Directly for the Screen
AUTUMN SONATA, by Ingmar Bergman.
COMING HOME, by Waldo Salt and Robert C. Jones from a story by Nancy Dowd.
THE DEER HUNTER, by Michael Cimino, Deric Washburn, Louis Garfinkle and Quinn K. Redeker.
INTERIORS, by Woody Allen.
AN UNMARRIED WOMAN, by Paul Mazursky.
Best Screenplay Based on Material from Another Source
BLOODBROTHERS, by Walter Newman.
CALIFORNIA SUITE, by Neil Simon.
HEAVEN CAN WAIT, by Elaine May and Warren Beatty.
MIDNIGHT EXPRESS, by Oliver Stone.
SAME TIME, NEXT YEAR, by Bernard Slade.
Best Cinematography
DAYS OF HEAVEN. Nestor Almendros.
THE DEER HUNTER. Vilmos Zsigmond.
HEAVEN CAN WAIT. William A. Fraker.
SAME TIME, NEXT YEAR. Robert Surtees.
THE WIZ. Oswald Morris.
Best Art Direction
THE BRINK'S JOB. Dean Tavoularis and Angelo Graham; George R. Nelson.
CALIFORNIA SUITE. Albert Brenner; Marvin March.
HEAVEN CAN WAIT. Paul Sylbert and Edwin O'Donovan, George Gaines.
INTERIORS. Mel Bourne; Daniel Robert.
THE WIZ. Tony Walton and Philip Rosenberg; Edward Stewart and Robert Drumheller.
Best Sound
THE BUDDY HOLLY STORY. Tex Rudloff, Joel Fein, Curly Thirlwell, and Willie Barry Thomas.
THE DEER HUNTER. Richard Portman, William McCaughey, Aaron Rochin and Darrin Knight.
HOOPER. Robert Knudson, Robert J. Glass, Don MacDougall and Jack Solomon.
SUPERMAN. Gordon K. McCallum, Graham Hartstone, Nicholas LeMessurier, and Roy Charman.
Music Awards
Best Original Song
"Hopelessly Devoted to You" from GREASE. Music and lyrics by John Farrar.
Last Dance" from THANK GOD IT'S FRIDAY. Music and lyrics by Paul Jabara.
"The Last Time I Felt Like This" from SAME TIME, NEXT YEAR. Music by Marvin Hamlisch; lyrics by Alan and Marilyn Bergman.
"Ready to Take a Chance Again" from FOUL PLAY. Music by Charles Fox; lyrics by Norman Gimbel.
"When You're Loved" from THE MAGIC OF LASSIE. Music and lyrics by Richard M. Sherman and Robert B. Sherman.
Best Original Score
THE BOYS FROM BRAZIL. Jerry Goldsmith.
THE DAYS OF HEAVEN. Ennio Morricone.
HEAVEN CAN WAIT. Dave Grusin.
MIDNIGHT EXPRESS. Giorgio Moroder.
SUPERMAN. John Williams.
Best Original Song Score and Its Adaptation or Adaptation Score
THE BUDDY HOLLY STORY; Joe Renzetti.
PRETTY BABY. Jerry Wexler.
THE WIZ. Quincy Jones.
Best Film Editing
THE BOYS FROM BRAZIL. Robert E. Swink.
COMING HOME. Don Zimmerman.
THE DEER HUNTER. Peter Zinner.
MIDNIGHT EXPRESS. Gerry Hambling.
SUPERMAN. Stuart Baird.
Best Costume Design
CARAVANS. Renie Conley.
DAYS OF HEAVEN. Patricia Norris.
DEATH ON THE NILE. Anthony Powell.
THE SWARM. Paul Zastupnevich.
THE WIZ. Tony Walton.
Short Films
Best Animated Film
OH MY DARLING. Produced by Nico Crama.
RIP VAN WINKEL. Wil vinton/Billy Budd. Produced by Will Vinton.
SPECIAL DELIVERY. National Film Board of Canada. Produced by Eunice Macaulay and John Weldon.
Best Live Action Film

A DIFFERENT APPROACH, Jim Belcher/Brookfield. Produced by Jim Belcher, Fern Feld.
MANDY's GRANDMOTHER, Illuminaton Films. Produced by Andrew Sugerman.
STRANGE FRUIT, The American Film Institute. Produced by Seth Pinsker.
TEENAGE FATHER, New Visions Inc. for the Children's Home Society of California. Produced by Taylor Hackford.

Documentary

Best Short Subject Documentary
THE DIVIDED TRAIL. Produced by Jerry Aronson.
AN ENCOUNTER WITH FACES, Films Division, Government of India. Produced by K. Kapil.
THE FLIGHT OF THE GOSSAMER CONDOR. Produced by Jacqueline Phillips Shedd.
GOODNIGHT MISS ANN. Produced by August Cinquegrana.
SQUIRES OF SAN QUENTIN. Produced by J. Gary Mitchell.

Best Feature Documentary
THE LOVERS' WIND, Ministry of Culture & Arts of Iran. Produced by Albert Lamorisse.
MYSTERIOUS CASTLES OF CLAY, Survival Anglia Ltd. Produced by Alan Root.
RAONI, a Franco-Brazilian Production. Produced by Michel Gast, Barry Williams and Jean-Pierre Dutilleuz.
SCARED STRAIGHT! Golden West Television. Produced by Arnold Shapiro.
WITH BABIES AND BANNERS: STORY OF THE WOMEN'S EMERGENCY BRIGADE, a woman's Labor History Film Project Production. Produced by Anne Bohlen, Lyn Goldfarb and Lorraine Gray.

Best Foreign Language Film
GET OUT YOUR HANDKERCHIEFS (Fr.). Bertrand Blier.
THE GLASS CELL (Ger.). Hans C. Geissendoerfer.
HUNGARIANS (Hung.). Zoltan Fabri.
VIVA ITALIA! (Ital.). Mario Monicelli.
WHITE BIM BLACK EAR (USSR). Stanislas Rosototzki.

Irving G. Thalberg Memorial Award
None awarded.

Jean Hersholt Humanitarian Award
Leo Jaffe.

Honorary Awards
Walter Lantz for bringing joy and laughter to every part of the world through his unique animated motion pictures.
Laurence Olivier for the full body of his work, for the unique achievements of his entire career and his lifetime of contribution to the art of film.
King Vidor for incomparable achievements as a cinematic creator and innovator.
The Museum of Modern Art Department of Film for the contribution it has made to the public's perception of movies as an art form.
Linwood G. Dunn, Loren L. Ryder, and Waldon O. Watson in appreciation for outstanding service and dedication in upholding the high standards of the Academy of Motion Picture Arts and Sciences.

Special Achievement Awards
For Visual Effects: Les Bowie, Colin Chilvers, Denys Coop, Roy Field, Derek Meddings, and Zoran Perisic for SUPERMAN. Scientific or Technical

Academy Award of Merit
Eastman Kodak Company for the research and development of a Duplicating Color Film for Motion Pictures.
Stefan Kudelski of Nagra Magnetic Recorders, Inc., for the continuing research, design and development of the Nagra Production Sound Recorder for Motion Pictures.
Panavision, Inc., and its engineering staff under the direction of Robert E. Gottschalk, for the concept, design and continuous development of the Panaflex Motion Picture Camera System.

Scientific and Engineering
Ray M. Dolby, Ioan R. Allen, David P. Robinson, Stephen M. Katz and Philip S.J. Boole of Dolby Laboratories, Inc., for the development and implementation of an improved Sound Recording and Reproducing System for Motion Picture Production and Exhibition.

Technical Achievement Award
Karl Macher and Glenn M. Berggren of Isco Optische Werke for the development and introduction of the Cinelux-ULTRA lens for 35mm Motion Picture Projection.
David J. Degenkolb, Arthur L. Ford and Fred J. Scobey of Deluxe General, Inc., for the development of a Method to Recycle Motion Picture Laboratory Photographic Wash Water by Ion Exchange.
Kiichi Sekiguchi of Cine-Fi International for the development of the Cine-Fi Auto Radio Sound System for Drive-in Theaters.
Leonard Chapman of Leonard Equipment for the design and manufacture of a small mobile motion picture camera platform known as the Chapman Hustler Dolly.
James L. Fisher of J.L. Fisher, Inc., for the design and manufacture of a small mobile motion picture camera platform known as the Fisher Model Ten Dolly.
Robert Stindt of Production Grip Equipment Company for the design and manufacture of a small mobile motion picture camera platform known as the Stindt Dolly.

1979

Best Picture
ALL THAT JAZZ, FOX. Produced by Robert Alan Aurthur.
APOCALYPSE NOW, Zoetrope/UA. Produced by Francis Coppola; coproduced by Fred Roos, Gray Frederickson, and Tom Sternberg.
BREAKING AWAY, FOX. Produced by Peter Yates.
KRAMER VS. KRAMER, COL. Produced by Stanley R. Jaffe.
NORMA RAE, FOX. Produced by Tamara Asseyev and Alex Rose.

Best Actor
Dustin Hoffman for KRAMER VS. KRAMER.
Jack Lemmon for THE CHINA SYNDROME.
Al Pacino for...AND JUSITCE FOR ALL.
Roy Scheider for ALL THAT JAZZ.
Peter Sellers for BEING THERE.

Best Actress
Jill Clayburgh for STARTING OVER.
Sally Field for NORMA RAE.
Jane Fonda for THE CHINA SYNDROME.
Marsha Mason for CHAPTER TWO.
Bette Midler for THE ROSE.

Best Supporting Actor
Melvyn Douglas for BEING THERE.
Robert Duvall for APOCALYPSE NOW.
Frederic Forrest for THE ROSE.
Justin Henry for KRAMER VS. KRAMER.
Mickey Rooney for THE BLACK STALLION.

Best Supporting Actress
Jane Alexander for KRAMER VS. KRAMER.
Barbara Barrie for BREAKING AWAY.
Candice Bergen for STARTING OVER.
Mariel Hemingway for MANHATTAN.
Meryl Streep for KRAMER VS. KRAMER.

Best Direction
Robert Benton for KRAMER VS. KRAMER.
Francis Coppola for APOCALYPSE NOW.
Bob Fosse for ALL THAT JAZZ.
Edouard Molinaro for LA CAGE AUX FOLLES (Fr.).
Peter Yates for BREAKING AWAY.

Writing Awards

Best Screenplay Written Directly for the Screen
ALL THAT JAZZ, by Robert Alan Aurthur and Bob Fosse.
...AND JUSTICE FOR ALL, by Valerie Curtin and Barry Levinson.
BREAKING AWAY, by Steve Tesich.
THE CHINA SYNDROME, by Mike Gray, T.S. Cook and James Bridges.
MANHATTAN, by Woody Allen and Marshall Brickman.

Best Screenplay Based on Material from Another Medium
APOCALYPSE NOW, by John Milius and Francis Coppola.
KRAMER VS. KRAMER, by Robert Benton.
LA CAGE AUX FOLLES (Fr.), by Francis Veber, Edouard Molinaro, Marcello Danon and Jean Poiret.
A LITTLE ROMANCE, by Allan Burns.
NORMA RAE, by Irving Ravetch and Harriet Frank, Jr.

Best Cinematography
ALL THAT JAZZ. Giuseppe Rotunno.
APOCALYPSE NOW. Vittorio Storaro.
THE BLACK HOLE. Frank Phillips.
KRAMER VS. KRAMER. Nestor Almendros.
1941. William A. Fraker.

Best Art Direction—Set Decoration
ALIEN. Michael Seymour, Les Dilley and Roger Christian; Ian Whittaker.
ALL THAT JAZZ. Philip Rosenberg and Tony Walton; Edward Stewart and Gary Brink.
APOCALYPSE NOW. Dean Tavoularis and Angelo Graham; George R. Nelson.
THE CHINA SYNDROME. George Jenkins; Arthur Jeph Parker.
STAR TREK—THE MOTION PICTURE. Harold Michelson, Joe Jennings, Leon Harris, and John Vallone; Linda Descenna.

Best Sound
APOCALYPSE NOW. Walter Murch, Mark Berger, Richard Beggs and Nat Boxer.
THE ELECTRIC HORSEMAN. Arthur Piantadosi, Les Fresholtz, Michael Minkler and Al Overton.
METEOR. William McCaughey, Aaron rochin, Michael J. Kohut and Jack Solomon.
1941. Robert Knudson, Robert J. Glass, Don MacDougall, and Gene S. Cantamessa.
THE ROSE. Theodore Soderberg, Douglas Williams, Paul Wells, and Jim Webb.

Music Award

Best Original Song
It Goes Like It Goes" from NORMA RAE. Music by David Shire; lyrics by Norman Gimbel.
"The Rainbow Connection" from THE MUPPET MOVIE. Music and lyrics by Paul Williams and Kenny Ascher.
"Song from 10 (It's Easy to Say)." Music by Henry Mancini; lyrics by Robert Wells.
"Theme from ICE CASTLES (Through the Eyes of Love)." Music by Marvin Hamlisch; lyrics by Carole Bayer Sager.
"Theme from THE PROMISE (I'll Never Say 'Goodbye')." Music by David Shire; lyrics by Alan and Marilyn Bergman.

Best Original Score
THE AMITYVILLE HORROR. Lalo Schifrin.
THE CHAMP. Dave Grusin.
A LITTLE ROMANCE. George Delerue.
STAR TREK—THE MOTION PICTURE. Jerry Goldsmith.

Best Original Song Score and Its Adaptation or Adaptation Score
ALL THAT JAZZ. Ralph Burns.
BREAKING AWAY. Patrick Williams.
THE MUPPET MOVIE. Paul Williams and Kenny Ascher.

Best Film Editing
ALL THAT JAZZ. Alan Heim.
APOCALYPSE NOW. Richard Marks, Walter Murch, Gerald B. Greenberg, and Lisa Fruchtman.
THE BLACK STALLION. Robert Dalva.
KRAMER VS. KRAMER. Jerry Greenberg.
THE ROSE. Robert L. Wolfe and C. Timothy O'Meara.

Best Costume Design
AGATHA. Shirley Russell.
ALL THAT JAZZ. Albert Wolsky.
BUTCH AND SUNDANCE: THE EARLY DAYS. William Theiss.
THE EUROPEANS. Judy Moorcroft.
LA CAGE AUX FOLLES. Piero Tosi and Ambra.

Best Visual Effects
ALIEN. Carlo Rimbaldi, Brian Johnson, Nick Allder, and Denys Ayling.
THE BLACK HOLE. Peter Ellenshaw, Art Cruickshank, Eustace Lycett, Danny Lee, Harrison Ellenshaw, and Joe Hale.
MOONRAKER. Derek Meddings, Paul Wilson, and John Evans.
1941. William A. Fraker, A.D. Flowers, and Gregory Jein.
STAR TREK—THE MOTION PICTURE. Douglas Trumbull, John Dykstra, Richard Yuricich, Robert Swarthe, Dave Stewart and Grant McCune.

Short Films

Best Animated Film
DREAM DOLL, Godfrey Films/Zagreb Films/Halas and Batchelor, Film Wright. Produced by Bob Godfrey and Zlatko Grgic.
EVERY CHILD, National Film Board of Canada. Produced by Derek Lamb.
IT'S SO NICE TO HAVE A WOLF AROUND THE HOUSE, AR&T Productions for

Learning Corporation of America. Produced by Paul Fierlinger.
Best Live Action Film
BOARD AND CARE, Ron Ellis Films. Produced by Sarah Pillsbury and Ron Ellis.
BRAVERY IN THE FIELD, National Film Board of Canada. Produced by Roman Kroitor and Stefan Wodoslawsky.
OH BROTHER, MY BROTHER, Ross Lowell Productions, Pyramid Films, Inc. Produced by Carol and Ross Lowell.
THE SOLAR FILM, Woldwood Enterprises Inc. Produced by Saul Bass and Michael Britton.
SOLLY'S DINER. Produced by Harry Mathias, Jay Zukerman, and Larry Hankin.
Documentary
Best Short Subject Documentary
DAE, Vardar Film/Skopje.
KORYO CELADON, Charlie/Papa Productions, Inc.
NAILS, National Film Board of Canada.
PAUL ROBESON: TRIBUTE TO AN ARTIST, Janus Films, Inc.
REMEMBER ME. Produced by Dick Young.
Best Feature Documentary
BEST BOY, Only Child Motion Pictures, Inc. Produced by Ira Wohl.
GENERATION ON THE WIND, More Than One Medium. Produced by David A. Vassar.
GOING THE DISTANCE, National Film Board of Canada.
THE KILLING GROUND, ABC News Closeup Unit. Produced by Steve Singer and Tom Priestly.
THE WAR AT HOME, Catalyst Films/Madison Film Production Co. Produced by Glenn Silber and Barry Alexander Brown.
Best Foreign Language Film
THE MAIDS OF WILKO (Pol.).
MAMA TURNS A HUNDRED (Span.). Carlos Saura.
A SIMPLE STORY (Fr.). Claude Sautet.
THE TIN DRUM (Ger.). Volker Schlondorf.
TO FORGET VENICE (Ital.). Franco Brusati.
Irving G. Thalberg Memorial Award
Ray Stark.
Jean Hersholt Humanitarian Award
Robert Benjamin.
Honorary Awards
Hal Elias for his dedication and distinguised service to the Academy of Motion Picture Arts and sciences.
Alec Guinness for advancing the art of screen acting through a host of memorable and distinguised performances.
John O. Aalberg, Charles G. Clarke and John G. Frayne in appreciation for outstanding service and dedication in upholding the high standard of the Academy of Motion Picture Arts and Sciences.
Special Achievement Award
Sound Editing: Alan Splet for THE BLACK STALLION.
Scientific or Technical
Academy Award of Merit
Mark Serrurier for the progressive development of the Moviola from the 1924 invention of his father, Iwan Serrurier, to the present Series 20 sophisticated film editing equipment.
Scientific and Engineering Award
Neiman-Tillar Associated for the creative development, and to Mini-Micro Systems, Inc., for the design and engineering of an Automated Computer Controlled Editing Sound System (ACCESS) for motion picture post-production.
Technical Achievement Award
Michael V. Chewey, Walter G. Eggers and Allen Hecht of MGM Laboratories for the development of a Computer-controlled Paper Tape Programmer System and its applications in the motion picture laboratory.
Irwin Young, Paul Kaufman and Fredrik Schlyter of Du Art Film Laboratoires, Inc., for the development of a computer-controlled Papter Tape Programmer System and its applications in the motion picture laboratory.
James S. Stanfield and Paul W. Trester for the development and manufacture of a device for the repair or protection of sprocket holes in motion picture film.
Zoran Perisic of Courier Films, Litmited, for the Zoptic Special Optical Effects Device for motion picture photography.
A.D. Flowers and Logan R. Frazee for the development of a device to control flight patterns of miniature airplanes during motion-picture photography.
Photo Research Division of Killmorgen Corporation for the development of the Spectra Series II Cine Special Exposure Meter for motion picture photography.
Bruce Lyon and John Lamb for the development of a Video Animation System for testing motion picture animation sequences.
Ross Lowell of Lowell-Light Manufacturing, Inc., for the development of compact lighting equipment for motion picture photography.

1980
Best Picture
COAL MINER'S DAUGHTER. UNIV. Produced by Bernard Schwartz.
THE ELEPHANT MAN, PAR. Produced by Jonathan Sanser.
ORDINARY PEOPLE, PAR. Produced by Ronald L. Schwary.
RAGING BULL, UA. Produced by Irwin Winkler and Robert Chartoff.
TESS, COL. Produced by Claude Berri; Timothy Burrill, co-producer.
Best Actor
Robert De Niro for RAGING BULL.
Robert Duvall for THE GREAT SANTINI.
John Hurt for THE ELEPHANT MAN.
Jack Lemmon for TRIBUTE.
Peter O'Toole for THE STUNT MAN.
Best Actress
Ellen Burstyn for RESURRECTION.
Goldie Hawn for PRIVATE BENJAMIN.
Mary Tyler Moore for ORDINARY PEOPLE.
Gena Rowlands for GLORIA.
Sissy Spacek for COAL MINER'S DAUGHTER.
Best Supporting Actor
Judd Hirsch for ORDINARY PEOPLE.
Timothy Hutton for ORDINARY PEOPLE.
Michael O'Keefe for THE GREAT SANTINI.
Joe Pesci for RAGING BULL.
Jason Robards for MELVIN AND HOWARD.

Best Supporting Actress
Eileen Brennan for PRIVATE BENJAMIN.
Eva Le Gallienne for RESURRECTION.
Cathy Moriarty for RAGING BULL.
Diana Scarwid for INSIDE MOVES.
Mary Steenburgen for MELVIN AND HOWARD.
Best Direction
David Lynch for THE ELEPHANT MAN.
Roman Polanski for TESS.
Robert Redford for ORDINARY PEOPLE.
Richard Rush for THE STUNT MAN.
Martin Scorsese for RAGING BULL.
Writing Awards
Best Screenplay, Written Directly for the Screen
BRUBAKER, by W.D. Richter and Arthur Ross.
FAME, by Christopher Gore.
MELVIN AND HOWARD, by Bo Goldman.
MON ONCLE D'AMERIQUE (Fr.), by Jean Gruault.
PRIVATE BENJAMIN, by Nancy Meyers, Charles Shyer, and Harvey Miller.
Best Screenplay, Based on Material from Another Medium
BREAKER MORANT (Aus.), by Jonathan Hardy, David Stevens, and Bruce Beresford.
COAL MINER'S DAUGHTER, Tom Rickman.
THE ELEPHANT MAN, by Christopher Devore, Eric Bergren, and David Lynch.
ORDINARY PEOPLE, by Alvin Sargent.
THE STUNT MAN, by Lawrence B. Marcus and Richard Rush.
Best Cinematography
THE BLUE LAGOON. Nestor Almendros.
COAL MINER'S DAUGHTER. Ralf D. Bode.
THE FORMULA. James Crabe.
RAGING BULL. Michael Chapman.
TESS. Geoffrey Unsworth and Ghislain Cloquet.
Best Art Direction—Set Decoration
COAL MINER'S DAUGHTER. John W. Corso; John M. Dwyer.
THE ELEPHANT MAN. Stuart Craig and Bob Cartwright; Hugh Scaife.
THE EMPIRE STRIKES BACK. Norman Reynolds, Leslie Dilley, Harry Lange and Alan Tomkins; Michael Ford.
KAGEMUSHA (Jap.). Yoshiro Muraki.
TESS. Pierre Guffroy and Jack Stevens.
Best Sound
ALTERED STATES. Arthur Piantadosi, Les Fresholtz, Michael Minkler and Willie D. Burton.
COAL MINER'S DAUGHTER. Richard Portman, Roger Heman, Willie D. Burton.
THE EMPIRE STRIKES BACK. Bill Varney, Steve Maslow, Gregg Landaker and Peter Sutton.
FAME. Michael J. Kohut, Aaron Rochin, Jay M. Harding, and Chris Newman.
RAGING BULL. Donald O. Mitchell, Bill Nicholson, David J. Kimball, and Les Lazarowitz.
Music Awards
Best Song
FAME" from FAME. Music by Michael Gore; lyrics by Dean Pitchford.
"Nine to Five" from NINE TO FIVE. Music and lyrics by Dolly Parton.
"On the Road Again" from HONEYSUCKLE ROSE. Music and lyrics by Willie Nelson.
"Out Here on My Own" from FAME. Music by Michael Gore; lyrics by Lesliey Gore.
"People Alone" from THE COMPETITION. Music by Lalo Schifrin; lyrics by Wilbur Jennings.
Best Original Score
ALTERED STATES. John Corigliano.
THE ELEPHANT MAN. John Morris.
THE EMPIRE STRIKES BACK. John Williams.
FAME. Michael Gore.
TESS. Philippe Sarde.
Best Film Editing
COAL MINER'S DAUGHTER. Arthur Schmidt.
THE COMPETITION. David Blewitt.
THE ELEPHANT MAN. Anne V. Coates.
FAME. Gerry Hambling.
RAGING BULL. Thelma Schoonmaker.
Best Costume Design
THE ELEPHANT MAN. Patricia Norris.
MY BRILLIANT CAREER (Aus.). Anna Senior.
SOMEWHERE IN TIME. Jean-Pierre Dorleac.
TESS. Anthony Powell.
WHEN TIME RAN OUT. Paul Zastupnevich.
Short Films
Best Animated Film
ALL NOTHING, Radio Canada. Produced by Frederic Back.
THE FLY, Pannonia Film, Budapest. Produced by Ferenc Rofusz.
HISTORY OF THE WORLD IN THREE MINUTES FLAT. Michael Mills, producer.
Best Live Action Film
THE DOLLAR BOTTOM, Rocking Horse Films, Ltd., PAR. Produced by Llyod Phillips.
FALL LINE, Sports Imagery, Inc. Produced by Bob Carmichael and Greg Lowe.
A JURY OF HER PEERS. Produced by Sally Heckel.
Documentary
Best Short Subject Documentary
DON'T MISS WITH BILL. Produced by John Watson and Pen Densham.
THE ERUPTION OF MOUNT ST. HELENS, Graphic Films Corp. Produced by George Casey.
IT'S THE SAME WORLD. Produced by Dick Young.
KARL HESS: TOWARD LIBERTY. Produced by Peter W. Ladue and Roland Halle.
LUTHER METKE AT 94, Ethnographic Program. Produced by Richard Hawkins and Jorge Prelpran.
Best Feature Documentary
AGEE, James Agee Film Project. Produced by Ross Spears.
THE DAY AFTER TRINITY. Produced by Jon Else.
FROM MAO TO MOZART: ISSAC STERN IN CHINA. The Hopewell Foundation. Produced by Murray Lerner.
FRONT LINE. Produced by David Bradbury.

YELLOW STAR— THE PERSECUTION OF EUROPEAN JEWS 1933-45, Chronos Films. Produced by Bengt von zur Muehlen.

Best Foreign Language Film
CONFIDENCE (Hung.), Istvan Szabo.
KAGEMUSHA (Jap.), Akari Kurosawa.
THE LAST METRO (Fr.), Francois Truffaut.
MOSCOW DOES NOT BELIEVE IN TEARS (USSR), Vladimir Menshov.
THE NEST (Span.), Jaime De Arminan.

Irving G. Thalberg Memorial Award
None awarded.

Jean Hersholt Humanitarian Award
None awarded.

Special Achievement Award
For Visual Effects: Brian Johnson, Richard Edlund, Dennis Muren, and Bruce Nicholson for THE EMPIRE STRIKES BACK.

Honorary Award
Henry Fonda, the consummate actor, in recognition of his brilliant accomplishments and enduring contributions to the art of motion pictures.
Fred Hynes in appreciation for outstanding service and dedication in upholding the high standards of the Academy of Motion Picture Arts and Sciences.

Scientific or Technical
Academy Award of Merit
Linwood G. Dunn, Cecil D. Love and Acme Tool and Manufacturing Company for the concept, engineering and development of the Acme-Dunn Optical Printer for motion picture special effects.

Scientific and Engineering Award
Jean-Marie Lavalou, Alan Masseron and David Samuelson of Samuelson Alga Cinema S.A. and Samuelson Film Service, Ltd., for the engineering and development of the Louma Crane and remote control system for motion picture projection.
Edward B. Krause of Filmline Corp. for the engineering and manufacture of the micro-demand drive for continuous motion film processors.
Ross Taylor for the concept and development of a system of air guns for propelling objects in special-effects motion picture production.
Dr. Bernard Kuhl and Dr. Warner Block of Osram GmbH for the progressive engineering and manufacture of the Osram HMI light source for motion picture color photography.
David A. Grafton for the optical design and engineering of a telecentric anamorphic lens for motion picture optical effects.

Technical Achievement Award
Carter Equipment Company for the development of a continuous contact, total immersion, additive-color motion picture printer.
Hollywood Film company for the development of a continuous contact, total immersion, additive-color motion picture printer.
Andre DeBrie S.A. for the development of a continuous contact, total immersion, additive-color motion picture printer.
Charles Vaughn and Eugene Nottingham of Cinetron Computer Systems, Inc., for the development of a versatile general purpose computer system for animation and optical effects motion picture photography.
John W. Lang, Walter Hrastnik and Charles J. Watson of Bell and Howell Company for the development and manufacture of a modular continuous contact motion picture film printer.
Worth Baird of LaVezzi Machine Works, Inc. for the advanced design and manufacture of a film sprocket for motion picture projectors.
Peter A. Regla and Dan Slater of Elicon for the development of a follow focus system for motion picture optical effects printers and animation stands.

1981
Best Picture
ATLANTIC CITY, PAR. Produced by Denis Heroux.
CHARIOTS OF FIRE, The Ladd Company/WB. Produced by David Puttnam.
ON GOLDEN POND, UNIV. produced by Bruce Gilbert.
RAIDERS OF THE LOST ARK, PAR. Produced by Frank Marshall.
REDS, PAR. Produced by Warren Beatty.

Best Actor
Warren Beatty for REDS.
Henry Fonda for ON GOLDEN POND.
Burt Lancaster for ATLANTIC CITY.
Dudley Moore for ARTHUR.
Paul Newman for ABSENCE OF MALICE.

Best Actress
Katharine Hepburn for ON GOLDEN POND.
Diane Keaton for REDS.
Marsha Mason for ONLY WHEN I LAUGH.
Susan Sarandon for ATLANTIC CITY.
Meryl Streep for THE FRENCH LIEUTENANT'S WOMAN.

Best Supporting Actor
James Coco for ONLY WHEN I LAUGH.
John Gielgud for ARTHUR.
Ian Holm for CHARIOTS OF FIRE.
Jack Nicholson for REDS.
Howard E. Rollins, Jr. for RAGTIME.

Best Supporting Actress
Melinda Dillon for ABSENCE OF MALICE.
Jane Fonda for ON GOLDEN POND.
Joan Hackett for ONLY WHEN I LAUGH.
Elizabeth McGovern for RAGTIME.
Maureen Stapleton for REDS.

Best Direction
Warren Beatty for REDS.
Hugh Hudson for CHARIOTS OF FIRE.
Louis Malle for ATLANTIC CITY.
Mark Rydell for ON GOLDEN POND.
Steven Spielberg for RAIDERS OF THE LOST ARK.

Writing Awards
Best Screenplay, Written Directly for the Screen
ABSENCE OF MALICE, by Kurt Luedtke.
ARTHUR, by Steven Gordon.
ATLANTIC CITY, by John Guare.
CHARIOTS OF FIRE, by Colin Welland.
REDS, by Warren Beatty and Trevor Griffiths.

Best Screenplay, Based on Material from Another Medium
THE FRENCH LIEUTENANT'S WOMAN, by Harold Pinter.
ON GOLDEN POND, by Ernest Thompson.
PENNIES FROM HEAVEN, by Dennis Potter.
PRINCE OF THE CITY, by Jay Presson Allen and Sidney Lumet.
RAGTIME, by Michael Weller.

Best Cinematography
EXCALIBUR. Alex Thomson.
ON GOLDEN POND. Billy Williams.
RAGTIME. Miroslav Ondricek.
RAIDERS OF THE LOST ARK. Douglas Slocombe.
REDS. Vittorio Storaro.

Best Art Direction
THE FRENCH LIEUTENANT'S WOMAN. Asheton Gorton; Ann Mollo.
HEAVEN'S GATE. Tambi Larsen; Jim Berkey.
RAGTIME. John Graysmark, Patrizia Von Brandenstein and Anthony Reading; George De Titta, Sr., George De Titta, Jr. and Peter Howitt.
RAIDERS OF THE LOST ARK. Norman Reynolds and Leslie Dilley; Michael Ford.
REDS. Richard Sylbert; Michael Seirton.

Best Sound
ON GOLDEN POND. Richard Portman and David Ronne.
OUTLAND. John K. Wilkinson, Robert W. Glass, Jr., Robert M. Thirlwell and Robin Gregory.
PENNIES FROM HEAVEN. Michael J. Kohut, Jay M. Harding, Richard tyler and Al Overton.
RAIDERS OF THE LOST ARK. Bill Varney, Steve Maslow, Greg Landaker, and Roy Charman.
REDS. Dick Vorisek, Tom Fleischman and Simon Kaye.

Music Awards
Best Original Song
Arthur's Theme (Best That You Can Do)" from ARTHUR. Music and lyrics by Burt Bacharach, Carole Bayer Sager, Christopher Cross and Peter Allen.
"Endless Love" from ENDLESS LOVE. Music and lyrics by Lionel Ritchie.
"The First Time It Happens" from THE GREAT MUPPET CAPER. Music and lyrics by Joe Raposo.
"For Your Eyes Only" from FOR YOUR EYES ONLY. Music by Bill Conti; lyrics by Mick Leeson.
"One More Hour" from RAGTIME. Music and lyrics by Randy Newman.

Best Original Score
CHARIOTS OF FIRE. Vangelis.
DRAGONSLAYER. Alex North.
ON GOLDEN POND. Dave Grusin.
RAGTIME. Randy Newman.
RAIDERS OF THE LOST ARK. John Williams.

Best Film Editing
CHARIOTS OF FIRE. Terry Rawlings.
THE FRENCH LIEUTENANT'S WOMAN. John Bloom.
ON GOLDEN POND. Robert Wolfe.
RAIDERS OF THE LOST ARK. Michael Kahn.
REDS. Dede Allen and Craig McKay.

Best Costume Design
CHARIOTS OF FIRE. Milena Canonero.
THE FRENCH LIEUTENANT'S WOMAN. Tom Rand.
PENNIES FROM HEAVEN. Bob Mackie.
RAGTIME. Anna Hill Johnstone.
REDS. Shirley Russell.

Best Make-Up
AN AMERICAN WEREWOLF IN LONDON. Rick Baker.
HEARTBEEPS. Stan Winston.

Best Visual Effects
DRAGONSLAYER. Dennis Muren, Phil Tippett, Ken Ralston and Brian Johnson.
RAIDERS OF THE LOST ARK. Richard Edlund, Kit West, Bruce Nicholson and Joe Johnston.

Short Films
Best Animation Film
CRAC, Societe Radio-Canada. Produced by Frederic Back.
THE CREATION. Produced by Will Vinton.
THE TENDER TALE OF CINDERELLA PENGUIN, National Film Board of Canada. Produced by Janet Perlman.

Best Live Action Film
COUPLES AND ROBBERS, Flamingo Pictures, Ltd. Produced by Christine Oestreicher.
FIRST WINTER, National Film Board of Canada. Produced by John H. Smith.
VIOLET, American Film Institute. Produced by Paul Kamp and shelley Levinson.

Documentary
Best Short Subject Documentary
AMERICAS IN TRANSITION, Americas in Transition, Inc. Produced by Obie Benz.
CLOSE HARMONY, Nobel Enterprise. Produced by Nigel Noble.
JOURNEY FOR SURVIVAL. Produced by Dick Young.
SEE WHAT I SAY, Michigan Women Filmmakers Productions. Produced by Linda Chapman, Pam LeBlanc and Freddi Stevens.
URGE TO BUILD, Roland Halle Productions, Inc. Produced by Roland Halle and John Hoover.

Best Feature Documentary
AGAINST WIND AND TIDE: A CUBAN ODYSSEY, Seven League Productions, Inc. Produced by Susanne Bauman and Paul Neshamkin.
BROOKLYN BRIDGE, Florentine Films. Produced by Ken Burns.
EIGHT MINUTES TO MIDNIGHT: A PORTRAIT OF DR. HELEN CALDICOTT, The Caldicott Project. Produced by Mary Benjamin, Susanne Simpson, and Boyd Estus.
EL SALVADOR: ANOTHER VIETNAM, Catalyst Media Productions. Produced by Glenn Silver and Tete Vasconcellos.
GENOCIDE, Arnold Schwartzman Productions, Inc. Produced by Arnold Schwartzman and Rabbi Marvin Hier.

Best Foreign Language Film
THE BOAT IS FULL (Switz.), Markus Imhoof.
MAN OF IRON (Pol.), Andrjez Wajda.
MEPHISTO (Hung.), Istvan Szabo.
MUDDY RIVER (Jap.), Kohei Oguri.
THREE BROTHERS (Ital.), Francesco Rosi.

Irving G. Thalberg Memorial Award
  Albert R. "Cubby" Broccoli.
Jean Hersholt Humanitarian Award
  Danny Kaye.
Gordon E. Sawyer Award
  Joseph B. Walker.
Honorary Award
  Barbara Stanwyck, for superlative creativity and unique contribution to the art of
  screen acting.
Special Achievement Award
  For Sound Effects Editing: Benjamin P. Burtt, Jr., and Richard L. Anderson for
  RAIDERS OF THE LOST ARK.
Scientific or Technical
  Academy Award of Merit
    Fuji Photo Film Company, Ltd. for the research, development and introduction of
    a new ultra-high speed color negative film for motion pictures.
  Scientific and Engineering Award
    Leonard Sokolow for the concept and design and Howard Lazare for the develop-
    ment of the Consolidated Film Industries' Stroboscan motion picture film viewer.
    Richard Edlund and Industrial Light and Magic, Inc., for the concept and
    engineering of a beam-splitter optical composite motion picture printer.
    Richard Edlund Industrial Light and Magic, Inc., for the engineering of the Empire
    motion picture camera system.
    Edward J. Blasko and Dr. Roderick T. Ryan of the Eastman Kodak Company for the
    application of the Prostar Microfilm Processor for motion picture title and special
    optical effects production.
    Nelson Tyler for the progressive development and improvement of the Tyler
    Helicopter motion picture camera platform.
  Technical Achievement Award
    Hal Landaker for the concept and Alan D. Landaker for the engineering of the
    Burbank Studio's Production Sound Department 24-frame color video system.
    Bill Hogan of Ruxton, Ltd. and Richard J. Stumpf and Daniel R. Brewer of Universal
    City Studio's production Sound department for the engineering of a 24-frame color
    video system.
    Ernst F. Nettman of Continental Camera Systems, Inc., for the development of a
    pitching lens for motion picture photography.
    Bill Taylor of Universal Studios for the concept and specifications for a Two Format,
    Rotating Head, Aerial Image Optical Printer.
    Peter D. Parks of Oxford Scientific Films for the development of the OSF microscopic
    photography.
    Dr. Louis Stankiewicz and H.L. Blanchford for the development of Baryfol sound
    barrier materials.
    Dennis Muren and Stuart Ziff of Industrial Light and Magic Inc., for the
    development of a Motion Picture Figure Mover for animation photography.

1982

Best Picture
  E.T.—EXTRA-TERRESTRIAL, UNIV. Produced by Steven Spielberg and Kathleen
  Kennedy.
  GANDHI, COL. Produced by Richard Attenborough.
  MISSING, UNIV. Produced by Edward and Mildred Lewis.
  TOOTSIE, COL. Produced by Sydney Pollack and Dick Richards.
  THE VERDICT, FOX. Produced by Richard D. Zanuck and David Brown.
Best Actor
  Dustin Hoffman for TOOTSIE.
  Ben Kingsley for GHANDI.
  Jack Lemmon for MISSING.
  Paul Newman for THE VERDICT.
  Peter O'Toole for MY FAVORITE YEAR.
Best Actress
  Julie Andrew for VICTOR/VICTORIA.
  Jessica Lange for FRANCES.
  Sissy Spacek for MISSING.
  Meryl Streep for SOPHIE'S CHOICE.
  Debra Winger for AN OFFICER AND A GENTLEMAN.
Best Supporting Actor
  Charles Durning for THE BEST LITTLE WHOREHOUSE IN TEXAS.
  Louis Gossett, Jr. for AN OFFICER AND A GENTLEMAN.
  John Lithgow for THE WORLD ACCORDING TO GARP.
  James Mason for THE VERDICT.
  Robert Preston for VICTOR/VICTORIA.
Best Supporting Actress
  Glenn Close for THE WORLD ACCORDING TO GARP.
  Teri Garr for TOOTSIE.
  Jessica Lange for TOOTSIE.
  Kim Stanley for FRANCES.
  Lesly Ann Warren for VICTOR/VICTORIA.
Best Direction
  Richard Attenborough for GANDHI.
  Sidney Lumet for THE VERDICT.
  Wolfgang Petersen for DAS BOOT (Ger.).
  Sydney Pollack for TOOTSIE.
  Steven Spielberg for E.T.—THE EXTRA-TERRESTRIAL.
Writing Awards
  Best Screenplay, Written Directly for the Screen
    DINER, by Barry Levinson.
    E.T.—THE EXTRA-TERRESTRIAL, by Melissa Matheson.
    GANDHI, by John Briley.
    AN OFFICER AND A GENTLEMAN, by Douglas Day Stewart.
    TOOTSIE, by Don McGuire, Larry Gelbart and Murray Schisgal.
  Best Screenplay, Based on Material from Another Medium
    DAS BOOT (Ger.), by Wolfgang Petersen.
    MISSING, by Constantin Costa-Gravas and Donald Stewart.
    SOPHIE'S CHOICE, by Alan J. Pakula.
    THE VERDICT, by David Mamet.
    VICTOR/VICTORIA, by Blake Edwards.
Best Cinematography
  DAS BOOT (Ger.). Jost Vacano.
  E.T.—THE EXTRA-TERRESTRIAL. Allen Daviau.
  GANDHI. Billy Williams and Ronnie Taylor.

SOPHIE'S CHOICE. Nestor Almendros.
TOOTSIE. Owen Roizman.
Best Art Direction - Set Decoration
  ANNIE. Dale Hennesy; Marvin March.
  BLADE RUNNER. Lawrence G. Paull and David Snyder; Linda De Scenna.
  GANDHI. Stuart Craig and Bob Laing; Michael Seirton.
  LA TRAVIATA (Ital.). Franco Zeffirelli; Gianni Quaranta.
  VICTOR/VICTORIA. Rodger Maus, Tim Hutchinson and William Crai Smith; Harry
  Cordwell.
Best Sound
  DAS BOOT (GER.). Milan Bor, Trevor Pyke and Mike LeMare.
  E.T.—THE EXTRA-TERRESTRIAL. Buzz Knudson, Robert Glass, Don Digirolamo
  and Gene Cantamessa.
  GANDHI. Gerry Humphreys, Robin O'Donoghue, Jonathan Bates, and Simon Kaye.
  TOOTSIE. Arthur Piantadosi, Les Fresholt, Dick Alexander and Les Lazarowitz.
  TRON. Michael Minkler, Bob Minkler, Lee Minkler, and Jim La Rue.
Music Awards Best Song
  "Eye of the Tiger" from ROCKY III. Music and lyrics by Jim Peterik and Frankie
  Sullivan III.
  "How Do You Keep the Music Playing?" from BEST FRIENDS. Music by Michel
  Legrand; lyrics by Alan and Marilyn Bergman.
  "If We Were in Love" from YES GIORGIO. Music by John Williams; lyrics by Alan
  and Marilyn Bergman.
  "It Might Be You" from TOOTSIE. Music by Dave Grusin; lyrics by Alan and Marilyn
  Bergman.
  "Up Where You Belong" from AN OFFICER AND A GENTLEMAN. Music by Jack
  Nitzsche and Buffy Sainte-Marie. Lyrics by Will Jennings.
Best Original Score
  E.T.—THE EXTRA-TERRESTRIAL. John Williams.
  GANDHI. Ravi Shankar and George Fenton.
  AN OFFICER AND A GENTLEMAN. Jack Nitzsche.
  POLTERGEIST. Jerry Goldsmith.
  SOPHIE'S CHOICE. Marvin Hamlisch. Best Original Score and Its Adaptation or
  Adaptation Score
  ANNIE. Ralph Burns.
  ONE FROM THE HEART. Tom Waits
  VICTOR/VICTORIA. Leslie Bricusse and Henry Mancini.
Best Film Editing
  DAS BOOT (Ger.). Hannes Nikel.
  GANDHI. John Bloom.
  AN OFFICER AND A GENTLEMAN. Peter Zinner.
  TOOTSIE. Frederic Steinkamp and William Steinkamp.
Best Costume Design
  GANDHI. John Bloom.
  LA TRAVIATA (Ital.). Piero Tosi.
  SOPHIE'S CHOICE. Albert Wolsky.
  TRON. Elois Jenssen and Rosanna Norton.
  VICTOR/VICTORIA. Patricia Norris.
Best Make-Up
  GANDHI. Tom Smith.
  QUEST FOR FIRE. (controversial credits).
Best Visual Effects
  BLADE RUNNER. Douglas Trumbull, Richard Yuricich and David Dryer.
  E.T.—THE EXTRA-TERRESTRIAL. Carlo Rambaldi, Dennis Murren, and Kenneth
  F. Smith.
  POLTERGIEST. Richard Edlund, Michael Wood, and Bruce Nicholson.
Best Sound Effects Editing
  DAS BOOT (Ger.). Mike Le-Mare
  E.T.—THE EXTRA-TERRESTRIAL. Charles A. Campbell and Ben Burtt.
  POLTERGEIST. Stephen Hunter Flick and Richard L. Anderson.
Short Films
  THE GREAT COGNITO. Produced by Will Vinton.
  THE SNOWMAN. Snowman Enterprises Ltd. Produced by John Coates.
  TANGO. Film Polski. Produced by Zbignew Rybczynski.
Best Live Action Film
  BALLET ROBOTIQUE. Produced by Bob Rogers.
  A SHOCKING ACCIDENT. Flamingo Pictures, Ltd. Produced by Christine Oes-
  treichner.
  THE SILENCE. American Film Institute. Produced by Michael Toshiyuki Uno and
  Joseph Benson.
  SPLIT CHERRY TREE. Learning Corp. of America. Produced by Jan Saunders.
  SREDNI VASHTAR. Lauretic Film Productions, Ltd. Produced by Andrew Birkin.
Documentary
  Best Short Subject Documentary
    GODS OF METAL. Produced by Robert Richter.
    IF YOU LOVE THIS PLANET. National Film Board of Canada. Produced by
    Edward Le Lorrain.
    THE KLAN: A LEGACY OF HATE IN AMERICA. Guggenheim Prods., Inc.
    Produced by Charles Guggenheim and Werner Schumann.
    TO LOVE OR LET DIE. American Film Foundation. Produced by Freida Lee Mock.
    TRAVELING HOPEFULLY, Arnuthfonyus Films, Inc. Produced by John G.
    Avildsen.
  Best Feature Documentary
    AFTER THE AXE. National Film Board of Canada. Produced by Sturla Gunnar-
    sson.
    BEN'S MILL. Public Broadcasting Associates, Odyssey. Produced by John Karol
    and Michael Chalufour.
    IN OUR WATER. Foresight Films. Produced by Meg Switzgable.
    JUST ANOTHER MISSING KID. Canadian Broadcasting Corp. Produced by John
    Zaritsky.
    A PORTRAIT OF GISELLE. Wishup Prods. Produced by Joseph Wishy.
Best Foreign Language Film
  ALSINO AND THE CONDOR (Nicaragua)—Miguel Littin.
  COUP DE TORCHON (Fr.)—Bernard Travernier.
  THE FLIGHT OF THE EAGLE (Swed.)—Jan Troell.
  PRIVATE LIFE (USSR)—Julij Rajzman.
  VOLVER A EMPEZAR (TO BEGIN AGAIN) (Span.)—Jose Luis Garci.
Irving G. Thalberg Memorial Award
  None awarded.
Jean Hersholt Humanitarian Award

Walter Mirsch.
Gordon E. Sawyer Award
John O. Aalberg for his technological contributions to the motion picture industry.
Honorary Award
Mickey Rooney for 50 years of versatility in a variety of memorable films performances.
Scientific or Technical
Academy Award of Merit
August Arnold and Erich Kaestner for the concept and engineering of the first operational 35mm, hand-held, spinning mirror reflex, motion picture camera.
Scientific and Engineering
Colin F. Mossman and the Research & Development group of Rank Film Laboratories, London, for the engineering and implementation of a 4000-meter printing system for motion picture laboratories.
Santee Zelli and Salvatore Zelli of Elemack Italia, S.R.L., Rome, Italy for the continuing engineering design, development, and manufacture of the PeeWee Camera Dolly for motion picture production.
Dr. Mohammad S. Nozari of Minnesota Mining & Manufacturing Co. for research and devlopment of the 3M Photogard protective coating for motion picture film.
Brianne Murphy and Donald Schisler of Mitchell Insert Systems, Inc., for the concept design and manufacture of the MSI Camera Insert Car and Process Trailer.
Jacobus L. Dimmers for the engineering and manufacutre of the Teccon Enterprises' magnetic transducer for motion picture sound recording and playback.
Technical Achievement Award
Richard W. Deats for the design and manufacture of the "Little Big Crane" for motion picture production.
Constant Tresfon and Adriaan De Rooy of Egripment, and Ed Phillips and Carlos de Mattos of Matthews Studio Equipment, Inc., for the design and manufacture of the "Tulip Crane" for motion picture production.
Bran Ferren of Associates and Ferren for the design and devlopment of a computerized lighting-effect system for motion picture photography.
Christie Electric Corp. and LaVezzi Machine Works, Inc. for the design and manufacture of the Ultramittent film transport for Christie motion picture projectors.

1983
Best Picture
THE BIG CHILL, COL. Produced by Michael Shamberg.
THE DRESSER, COL. Produced by Peter Yates.
THE RIGHT STUFF, WB. Produced by Irwin Winkler and Robert Chartoff.
TENDER MERCIES, UNIV/AFD. Produced by Philip S. Hobel.
TERMS OF ENDEARMENT, PAR. Produced by James L. Brooks.
Best Actor
Michael Caine for EDUCATING RITA.
Tom Conti for REUBEN, REUBEN.
Tom Courtenay for THE DRESSER
Robert Duvall for TENDER MERCIES.
Albert Finney for THE DRESSER
Best Actress
Jane Alexander for TESTAMENT.
Shirley MacLaine for TERMS OF ENDEARMENT.
Meryl Streep for SILKWOOD
Julie Waters for EDUCATING RITA.
Debra Winger for TERMS OF ENDEARMENT.
Best Supporting Actor
Charles Durning for TO BE OR NOT TO BE.
John Lithgow for TERMS OF ENDEARMENT.
Jack Nicholson for TERMS OF ENDEARMENT.
Sam Shepard for THE RIGHT STUFF.
Rip Torn for CROSS CREEK.
Best Supporting Actress
Cher for SILKWOOD.
Glenn Close for THE BIG CHILL.
Linda Hunt for THE YEAR OF LIVING DANGEROUSLY.
Amy Irving for YENTL.
Alfre Woodard for CROSS CREEK.
Best Direction
Bruce Beresford for TENDER MERCIES.
Ingmar Bergman for FANNY AND ALEXANDER.
James L. Brooks for TERMS OF ENDEARMENT.
Mike Nichols for SILKWOOD.
Peter Yates for THE DRESSER.
Writing Awards
Best Screenplay, Written Directly for the Screen
THE BIG CHILL, by Lawrence Kasdan and Barbara Benedek.
FANNY AND ALEXANDER (Swed.), by Ingmar Bergman.
SILKWOOD by Nora Ephron and Alice Arlen.
TENDER MERCIES, by Horton Foote.
WARGAMES by Lawrence Lasker and Walter F. Parkes.
Best Screenplay, Based on Material from Another Medium
BETRAYAL, by Harold Pinter.
THE DRESSER, by Ronald Harwood.
EDUCATING RITA, by Willy Russell.
REUBEN, REUBEN, by Julius Epstein.
TERMS OF ENDEARMENT, by James L. Brooks.
Best Cinematography
FANNY AND ALEXANDER (Swed.). Sven Nykvist.
FLASHDANCE. Don Peterman.
THE RIGHT STUFF. Caleb Deschanel.
WARGAMES. Willam A. Fraker.
ZELIG. Gordon Willis.
Best Art Direction - Set Decoration
FANNY AND ALEXANDER (Swed.) Anna Asp; Susan Lindheim.
RETURN OF THE JEDI. Norman Reynolds, Fred Hole and James Schoppe; Michael Ford.
THE RIGHT STUFF. Geoffrey Kirkland, Richard J. Lawrence, W. Stewart Campbell, and Peter Romero; Pat Pending and George R. Nelson.
TERMS OF ENDEARMENT. Polly Platt; Tom Pedigo.
YENTL. Roy Walker and Leslie Tomkins; Tessa Davies.
Best Sound

NEVER CRY WOLF. Alan R. Splet, Todd Boekelheide, Randy Thom, and David Parker.
RETURN OF THE JEDI. Ben Burtt, Gary Summers, Randy Thom and Tony Dawe.
THE RIGHT STUFF. Mark Berger, Tom Scott, Randy Thom, and David MacMillan.
TERMS OF ENDEARMENT. Donald O. Mitchell, Rick Kline, Kevin O'Connell, and James Alexander.
WARGAMES. Michael J. Kohut, Carlos de Larios, Aaron Rochin, and Willie D. Burton.
Music Awards Best Song
Flashdance" from FLASHDANCE. Music by Giorgio Moroder; lyrics by Keith Forsey and Irene Cara.
"Maniac" from FLASHDANCE. Music and lyrics by Michael Sembello and Dennis Matkosky.
"Over You" from TENDER MERCIES. Music and lyrics by Austin Roberts and Bobby Hart.
"Papa Can You Hear Me" from YENTL. Music by Michel Legrand; lyrics by Alan and Marilyn Bergman.
"The Way He Makes Me Feel" from YENTL. Music by Michel Legrand; lyrics by Alan and Marilyn Bergman.
Best Original Score
CROSS CREEK. Leonard Rosenman.
RETURN OF THE JEDI. John Williams.
THE RIGHT STUFF. Bill Conti.
TERMS OF ENDEARMENT. Michael Gore.
UNDER FIRE. Jerry Goldsmith. Best Original Score and Adaptation Score
THE STING II. Lalo Schifrin.
TRADING PLACES. Elmer Bernstein.
YENTL. Michel Legrand, Alan and Marilyn Bergman.
Best Film Editing
BLUE THUNDER. Frank Morris and Edward Abroms.
FLASHDANCE. Bud Smith and Walt Mulconery.
THE RIGHT STUFF. Glenn Farr, Lisa Fruchtman, Stephen A. Rotter, Douglas Steward, and Sam Rolfe.
SILKWOOD. Sam O'Steen.
TERMS OF ENDEARMENT. Richard Marks.
Best Costume Design
CROSS CREEK. Joe I. Tompkins.
FANNY AND ALEXANDER (Swed.). Marik Vos.
HEART LIKE A WHEEL. William Ware Theiss.
THE RETURN OF MARTIN GUERRE (Fr.). Anne-Marie Marchand.
ZELIG. Santo Loquasto.
Best Sound Effects Editing
RETURN OF THE JEDI. Ben Burtt.
THE RIGHT STUFF. Jay Boekelheide.
Short Films
Best Animated Film
MICKEY'S CHRISTMAS CAROL, Walt Disney. Produced by Burny Mattinson.
SOUND OF SUNSHINE-SOUND OF RAIN, Hallinan Plus. Produced by Eda Hallinan.
SUNDAE IN NEW YORK, Motionpickture Productions. Produced by Jimmy Picker.
Best Live Action Film
BOYS AND GIRLS, Atlantis Films Ltd. Produced by Janice L. Platt.
GOODIE-TWO-SHOES, Timeless Films, PAR. Produced by Ian Emes.
OVERNIGHT SENSATION. Produced by Jon N. Bloom.
Documentary
Best Short Subject Documentary
FLAMENCO AT 5:15, National Board of Canada. Produced by Cynthia Scott and Adam Symansky.
IN THE NUCLEAR SHADOW: WHAT CAN THE CHILDREN TELL US?, Impact Productions. Produced by Vivienne Verdon-Roe and Eric Thiermann.
SEWING WOMAN, DeepFocus Productions. Produced by Arthur Dong.
SPACES: THE ARCHITECTURE OF PAUL RUDOLPH. Eisenhardt Productions Inc. Produced by Robert Eisenhardt.
YOU ARE FREE. Produced by Dea Brokman and Ilene Landis.
Best Feature Documentary
CHILDREN OF DARKNESS, Children of Darkness Productions. Produced by Richard Kotuk and Ara Chekmayan.
FIRST CONTACT, Arundel Productions. Produced by Bob Connolly and Robin Anderson.
HE MAKES ME FEEL LIKE DANCIN', Edgar J. Scherick Associates. Produced by Emile Ardolino.
THE PROFESSION OF ARMS. (War Series Films No. 3), National Film Board of Canada. Produced by Michael Bryans and Tina Viljoen.
SEEING RED. Heartland Productions. Produced by James Klein and Julie Reichert.
Best Foreign Language Film
CARMEN (Span.)—Carlos Saura.
ENTRE NOUS (Fr.)—Diane Kurys.
FANNY AND ALEXANDER (Swed.)—Ingmar Bergman.
JOB'S REVOLT (Hung.)-
LE BAL (Alg.)—Ettore Scola.
Irving G. Thalberg Memorial Award
None awarded.
Jean Hersholt Humanitarian Award
M.J. "Mike" Frankovich.
Gordon E. Sawyer Award
Dr. John G. Frayne.
Honorary Award
Hal Roach, in recognition of his unparalleled record of distinguished contribution to the motion picture art form.
Special Achievement Awards
Visual Effects: Richard Edlund, Dennis Muren, Ken Ralston, and Phil Tippett for RETURN OF THE JEDI.
Scientific or Technical
Academy Award of Merit
Dr. Kurt Larch of OSMAN GmBH, for the research and development of xenon short-arc discharge lamps for motion picture projection.
Scientific and Engineering
Jonathan Erland and Roger Dorney of Apogee, Inc. for the engineering and development of a reverse bluescreen traveling matte process for motion picture

photography.

Gunnar P: Michelson for the engineering and development of an improved, electronic, high-speed, precision light valve for use in motion picture printing machines.

Gerald L. Turpin of Lightflex International Ltd. for the design, engineering and development of an on-camera device providing contrast control, sourceless fill light and special effects for motion picture photography.

Technical Achievement Award

William G. Krokaugger of Mole-Richardson Co. for the design and engineering of a portable, 12,000 watt, lighting control dimmer for use in motion picture production.

Charles L. Watson, Larry L. Langrehr and John H. Steiner for the development of the BHP electro-mechanical fader for use on continuous motion picture contact printers.

Elizabeth D. De La Mare of De La Mare Engineering, Inc., for the progressive development and continuous research of special effects pyrotechnics originally designed by Glenn W. De La Mare for motion picture production.

Douglas Fries, John Lacey and Michael Sicrist for the design and engineering of a 35mm reflex conversion camera system for special effects photography.

Jack Cashin of Ultra-Stereo Labs, Inc. for the engineering and development of a 4-channel, stereophonic decoding system for optical motion picture sound track reproduction.

David J. Degenkolb for the design and development of an automated device used in the silver recovery process in motion picture laboratories.

1984

Best Picture

AMADEUS, Orion. Produced by Saul Zaentz.
THE KILLING FIELDS, WB. Produced by David Puttnam.
A PASSAGE TO INDIA, COL. Produced by John Brabourne and Richard Goodwin.
PLACES IN THE HEART, Tri-Star. Produced by Arlene Donovan.
A SOLDIER'S STORY, COL. Produced by Norman Jewison, Ronald L. Scwary and Patrick Palmer.

Best Actor

F. Murray Abraham for AMADEUS.
Jeff Bridges for STARMAN.
Albert Finney for UNDER THE VOLCANO.
Tom Hulce for AMADEUS.
Sam Waterston for THE KILLING FIELDS.

Best Actress

Judy Davis for PASSAGE TO INDIA.
Sally Field for PLACES IN THE HEART.
Jessica Lange for COUNTRY.
Vanessa Redgrave for THE BOSTONIANS.
Sissy Spacek for THE RIVER.

Best Supporting Actor

Adolph Caesar for A SOLDIER'S STORY.
John Malkovich for PLACES IN THE HEART.
Noriyuki "Pat" Morita for THE KARATE KID.
Haing S. Ngor for THE KILLING FIELD.
Ralph Richardson for GREYSTOKE: THE LEGEND OF TARZAN, LORD OF THE APES.

Best Supporting Actress

Peggy Ashcroft for A PASSAGE TO INDIA.
Glenn Close for THE NATURAL.
Lindsay Crouse for PLACES IN THE HEART.
Christine Lahti for SWING SHIFT.
Geraldine Page for THE POPE OF GREENWICH VILLAGE.

Best Direction

Woody Allen for BROADWAY DANNY ROSE.
Robert Benton for PLACES IN THE HEART.
Milos Forman for AMADEUS.
Roland Joffe for THE KILLING FIELDS.
David Lean for A PASSAGE TO INDIA.

Writing Awards

Best Screenplay, Written Directly for the Screen

BEVERLY HILLS COP, by Daniel Petrie, Jr.,; story by Danilo Bach and Daniel Petrie, Jr.
BROADWAY DANNY ROSE, by Woody Allen.
EL NORTE, by Gregory Nava and Anna Thomas.
PLACES IN THE HEART, by Robert Benton.
SPLASH, by Lowell Ganz, Babaloo Mandel, and Bruce Jay Friedman; screen story by Friedman, story by Brian Grazer.

Best Screenplay, Based on Material from Another Medium

AMADEUS, by Peter Shaffer.
GREYSTOKE: THE LEGEND OF TARZAN, LORD OF THE APES, by P.H. Vazak and Michael Austin.
THE KILLING FIELDS, by Bruce Robinson.
A PASSAGE TO INDIA, by David Lean.
A SOLDIER'S STORY, by Charles Fuller.

Best Cinematography

AMADEUS. Miroslav Ondricek.
THE KILLING FIELDS. Chris Menges.
THE NATURAL. Angelo Graham and Mel Bourne.
A PASSAGE TO INDIA. Ernest Day.
THE RIVER. Vilmos Zsigmond.

Best Art Direction—Set Decoration

AMADEUS. Patrizia Von Bradenstein; Karel Cerny.
THE COTTON CLUB. Richard Sylbert; George Gaines.
THE NATURAL. Anegelo Graham and Mel Bourne; Bruch Weintraub.
A PASSAGE TO INDIA. John Box; Hugh Scaife.
2010. Albert Brenner; Rick Simpson.

Best Sound

AMADEUS. Mark Berger, Tom Scott, Todd Boekelheide, and Chris Newman.
DUNE. Bill Varney, Steve Maslow, Kevin O'Connell, and Nelson Stoll.
A PASSAGE TO INDIA. Graham Hairstone, Nicholas Le Messurier, Michael A. Carter and John Mitchell.
THE RIVER. Nick Alphin, Robert Thirwell, Richard Portman, and David Ronne.
2010. Michael J. Kohut, Carlos de Larios, Aaron Rochin, and Gene S. Cantamessa.

Music Awards

Best Song

Against All Odds (Take a Look at Me Now)" from AGAINST ALL ODDS. Music and lyrics by Phil Collins.
"Footloose" from FOOTLOOSE. Music and lyrics by Kenny Loggins and Dean Pitchford.
"Ghostbusters" from GHOSTBUSTERS. Music and lyrics by Ray Parker, Jr.
"I Just Called to Say I Love You" from THE WOMAN IN RED. Music and lyrics by Stevie Wonder.
"Let's Hear It for the Boy" from FOOTLOOSE. Music and lyrics by Dean Pitchford and Tom Snow. Marilyn Bergman.

Best Original Score

INDIANA JONES AND THE TEMPLE OF DOOM. John Williams.
THE NATURAL. Randy Newman.
A PASSAGE TO INDIA. Maurice Jarre.
THE RIVER. John Williams.

Best Original Song Score

THE MUPPETS TAKE MANAHATTAN. Jeffrey Moss.
PURPLE RAIN. Prince.
SONGWRITER. Kris Kristofferson.

Best Film Editing

AMADEUS. Nena Danevic and Michael Chandler.
THE COTTON CLUB. Barry Malkin and Robert O. Lovett.
THE KILLING FIELDS. Jim Clark.
A PASSAGE TO INDIA. David Lean.
ROMANCING THE STONE. Donn Cambern and Frank Morriss.

Best Costume Design

AMADEUS. Theodor Pistek.
THE BOSTONIANS. Jerry Beavan and John Bright.
A PASSAGE TO INDIA. Judy Moorcroft.
PLACES IN THE HEART. Ann Roth.
2010. Patricia Norris.

Best Makeup

AMADEUS. Paul LeBlanc and Dick Smith.
GREYSTOKE: THE LEGEND OF TARZAN, LORD OF THE APES. Rick Baker and Paul Engelen.
2010. Michael Westmore.

Best Visual Effects

GHOSTBUSTERS. Richard Edlund, John Bruno, Mark Vargo, and Chuck Gasper.
INDIANA JONES AND THE TEMPLE OF DOOM. Dennis Muren, Michael McAlister, Lorne Peterson, and George Gibbs.
2010. Richard Edlund, Neil Krepela, George Jensen and Mark Stetson.

Short Films

Best Animated Film

CHARADE, Sheridan College. Produced by Jon Minnis.
DOCTOR DESOTO, Sporn Animation. Produced by Morton Schindel and Michael Sporn.
PARADISE, National Film Board of Canada. Produced by Ishu Patel.
THE PAINTED DOOR, Atlantis Films Ltd., National Film Board of Canada. Produced by Michael MacMillan and Janice L. Platt.
TALES OF MEETING AND PARTING, American Film Institute—Directing Workshop for Women. Produced by Sharon Orcek and Lesli Linka Glatter.
UP, Pyramid Films. Produced by Mike Hoover.

Documentary

Best Short Subject Documentary

THE CHILDREN OF SOONG CHING LING, UNICEF and the Soong Ching Ling Foundation.
CODE GRAY: ETHICAL DILEMMAS IN NURSING, The Nursing Ethics Project/Fanlight Prods. Produced by Ben Achtenberg and Joan Sawyer.
THE GARDEN OF EDEN, Florentine Films. Produced by Lawrence R. Hott and Roger M. Sherman.
RECOLLECTIONS OF PAVLOVSK, Leningrad Documentary Film Studio. Produced by Irina Kalinina.
THE STONE CARVERS. Wagner Productions. Produced by Marjorie Hunt and Paul Wagner.

Best Feature Documentary

HIGH SCHOOLS, Guggenheim Productions. Produced by Charles Guggenheim and Nancy Sloss.
IN THE NAME OF THE PEOPLE, Pan American Films. Produced by Alex W. Drehsler and Frank Christopher.
MARLENE, Braun Pictures/OKO Film Production. Produced by Karel Dirka and Zev Braun.
STREETWISE, Bear Creek Productions. Produced by Cheryl McCall.
THE TIMES OF HARVEY MILK. Black Sand Educations Productions, Inc. Produced by Robert Epstein and Richard Schmiechen.

Best Foreign Language Film

BEYOND THE WALLS (Israel).
CAMILA (Arg.).
DANGEROUS MOVES (Switz.).
DOUBLE FEATURE (Span.).
WAR-TIME ROMANCE (USSR).

Irving G. Thalberg Memorial Award

None awarded.

Jean Hersholt Humanitarian Award

David L. Wolper

Gordon E. Sawyer Award

Linwood G. Dunn.

Honorary Award

National Endowment for the arts.
James Stewart for 50 years of meaningful performances, for his high ideals, both on and off the screen, with the respect and admiration of his colleagues.

Special Achievement Award

Sound Effects Editing: Kay Rose for THE RIVER.

Scientific or Technical

Academy Award of Merit

None Awarded

Scientific and Engineering Award

Donald A. Anderson and Diana Reiners of 3M Co. for the development of "Cinetrak" Magnetic Film 351 for motion picture sound recording.
Barry M. Stultz, Ruebn Avial, and Wes Kennedy of Film Processing Corp. for the formulation and application of an improved soundtrack stripe to 70mm motion

picture film, and John Mosely for the engineering research involved therein.

Kenneth Richter of Richter Cine Equipment for the design and engineering of the R-2 Auto-Collimator for examining image quality at the focal plane of motion picture camera lenses.

Gunther Schaidt and Rosco Laboratories, Inc., for the devlopment of an improved, nontoxic fluid for creating fog and smoke for motion picture production.

John Whitney, Jr. and Gary Demos of Digital Prods., Inc., for the practical simulation of motion picture photography by means of computer-generated images.

Technical Achievement Awards

Nat Tiffen of Tiffen Manufacturing Corp. for the production of high-quality, durable, laminated color filters for motion picture photography.

Donald Trumbull, Jonathan Erland, Stephen Fog and Paul Burk of Apogee, Inc., for the design and development of the "Blue Max" high-power blue-flux projector for traveling matte composite photography.

Jonathan Erland and Robert Bealmear of Apogee, Inc., for an innovative design for front projection screens and an improved method for their construction.

Howard J. Preston of Preston Cinema Systems for the design and devlopment of a variable speed control device with automatic exposure compensation for motion picture cameras.

BRITISH ACADEMY AWARDS

1947
Best Film, Any Source
THE BEST YEARS OF OUR LIVES (U.S.)—William Wyler.
Best British Film
ODD MAN OUT—Carol Reed.
Best Documentary
THE WORLD IS RICH.

1948
Best Film, Any Source
HAMLET (Brit.)—Laurence Olivier.
Nominees
CROSSFIRE (U.S.)—Edward Dmytryk.
THE LOST ILLUSION (Brit.)—Carol Reed.
FOUR STEPS IN THE CLOUDS (Ital.)—Alessandro Blasetti.
MONSIEUR VINCENT (Fr.)—Leon Carre.
THE NAKED CITY (U.S.)—Jules Dassin.
PAISAN (Ital.)—Roberto Rossellini.
Best British Film
THE LOST ILLUSION—Carol Reed.
Nominees
MANIACS ON WHEELS—Jack Lee.
THE RED SHOES—Michael Powell and Emeric Pressburger.
SCOTT OF THE ANTARCTIC—Charles Frend.
HIDEOUT—Fergus McDonnell.
OLIVER TWIST—David Lean.
Best Documentary
THE LOUISIANA STORY (U.S.)—Robert Flaherty.
Best Specialized Film
ATOMIC PHYSICS.

1949
Best Film, Any Source
BICYCLE THIEVES (Ital.)—Vittorio de Sica.
Nominees
THE LAST STAGE (Pol.)—Wanda Jakubowska.
THE SET UP (U.S.)—Robert Wise.
THE THIRD MAN (Brit.)—Carol Reed.
THE TREASURE OF THE SIERRA MADRE (U.S.)—John Huston.
THE WINDOW (U.S.)—Ted Tetzlaff.
Best British Film
THE THIRD MAN—Carol Reed.
Nominees
KIND HEARTS AND CORONETS—Robert Hamer.
PASSPORT TO PIMLICO—Henry Cornelius.
THE QUEEN OF SPADES—Thorold Dickinson.
HOUR OF GLORY—Michael Powell and Emeric Pressburger.
TIGHT LITTLE ISLAND—Alexander Mackendrick.
Best Documentary
DAYBREAK IN UDI.
Best Specialized Film
LA FAMILIE MARTIN.
United Nations Award
THE SEARCH (U.S./Switz.)—Fred Zinnemann.

1950
Best Film, Any Source
ALL ABOUT EVE (U.S.)—Joseph L. Mankiewicz.
Nominees
THE ASPHALT JUNGLE (U.S.)—John Huston.
BEAUTY AND THE DEVIL (Fr.)—Rene Clair.
INTRUDER IN THE DUST (U.S.)—Clarence Brown.
BATTLE STRIPE (U.S.)—Stanley Kramer.
ON THE TOWN (U.S.)—Gene Kelly and Stanley Donen.
ORPHEUS (Fr.)—Jean Cocteau.
Best British Film
THE BLUE LAMP—Basil Dearden.
Nominees
CHANCE OF A LIFETIME—Bernard Miles.
SEVEN DAYS TO NOON—The Boulting Brothers.
THE GREAT MANHUNT—Sidney Gilliat.
THE WOODEN HORSE—Jack Lee.
Best Documentary
THE UNDEFEATED.
Best Specialized Film
THE TRUE FACE OF JAPAN.
United Nations Award
INTRUDER IN THE DUST (U.S.)—Clarence Brown.

1951
Best Film, Any Source
LA RONDE (Fr.)—Max Ophuls.
Best British Film
THE LAVENDER HILL MOB—Charles Crichton.
Nominees
AN AMERICAN IN PARIS (U.S.)—Vincente Minnelli.
THE BROWNING VERSION (Brit.)—Anthony Asquith.
DETECTIVE STORY (U.S.)—William Wyler.
SUNDAY IN AUGUST (Ital.)—Luciano Emmer.
EDOUARD ET CAROLINE (Fr.)—Jacques Becker.
FOURTEEN HOURS (U.S.)—Henry Hathaway.
THE MAGIC BOX (Brit.)—John Boulting.
THE MAN IN THE WHITE SUIT (Brit.)—Alexander Mackendrick.
MISS JULIE (Swed.)—Alf Sjoberg.
NEVER TAKE NO FOR AN ANSWER (Brit.)—Maurice Cloche and Ralph Smart.
NO RESTING PLACE (Brit.)—Paul Rotha.
THE RED BADGE OF COURAGE (U.S.)—John Huston.
THE SOUND OF FURY (U.S.)—Cyril Endfield.

A WALK IN THE SUN (U.S.)—Lewis Milestone.
WHITE CORRIDORS (Brit.)—Pat Jackson.
Best Documentary
BEAVER VALLEY.
Best Specialized Film
GERALD MCBOING BOING.
United Nations Award
FOUR IN A JEEP (Switz.)—Leopold Lindtberg.

1952
Best Film
BREAKING THE SOUND BARRIER (Brit.)—David Lean (Both Any Source and British Categories).
Nominees
THE AFRICAN QUEEN (U.S.)—John Huston.
ANGELS ONE FIVE (Brit.)—George More O'Ferrall.
CARRIE (U.S.)—William Wyler.
AFRICAN FURY (Brit.)—Zoltan Korda.
DEATH OF A SALESMAN (U.S.)—Laslo Benedek.
LIMELIGHT (U.S.)—Charles Chaplin.
THE CRASH OF SILENCE (Brit.)—Alexander Mackendrick.
AN OUTCAST OF THE ISLANDS (Brit.)—Carol Reed.
THE RIVER (India)—Jean Renoir.
SINGIN' IN THE RAIN (U.S.)—Gene Kelly and Stanley Donen.
A STREETCAR NAMED DESIRE (U.S.)—Elia Kazan.
VIVA ZAPATA (U.S.)—Elia Kazan.
Best British Actor
Ralph Richardson for BREAKING THE SOUND BARRIER (Brit.).
Best British Actress
Vivien Leigh for A STREETCAR NAMED DESIRE (U.S.).
Best Foreign Actor
Marlon Brando for VIVA ZAPATA! (U.S.).
Best Foreign Actress
Simone Signoret for CASQUE D'OR (Fr.).
Best Documentary
ROYAL JOURNEY.
Best Specialized Film
ANIMATED GENESIS.
United Nations Award
AFRICAN FURY (Brit.)—Zoltan Korda.

1953
Best Film, Any Source
FORBIDDEN GAMES (Fr.)—Rene Clement.
Best British Film
GENEVIEVE—Henry Cornelius.
Nominees
COME BACK, LITTLE SHEBA (U.S.)—Daniel Mann.
THE BAD AND THE BEAUTIFUL (U.S.)—Vincente Minnelli.
THE CRUEL SEA (Brit.)—Charles Frend.
THE HEART OF THE MATTER (Brit.)—George More O'Ferrall.
JULIUS CAESAR (U.S.)—Joseph L. Mankiewicz.
THE LITTLE WORLD OF DON CAMILLO (Fr./Ital.)—Julien Duvivier.
THE MEDIUM (Ital.)—Gian-Carlo Menotti.
MOGAMBO (U.S.)—John Ford.
MOULIN ROUGE (Brit.)—John Huston.
ARE WE ALL MURDERERS? (Fr.)—Andre Cayatte.
ROMAN HOLIDAY (U.S.)—William Wyler.
SHANE (U.S.)—George Stevens.
TWO PENNYWORTH OF HOPE (Ital.)—Renato Castellani.
Best British Actor
John Gielgud for JULIUS CAESAR (U.S.).
Best British Actress
Audrey Hepburn for ROMAN HOLIDAY (U.S.).
Best Foreign Actor
Marlon Brando for JULIUS CAESAR (U.S.).
Best Foreign Actress
Leslie Caron for LILI (U.S.).
Most Promising Newcomer
David Kossoff as revealed in CHANCE MEETING (Brit.).
Best Documentary
CONQUEST OF EVEREST (Brit.)—Thomas Stobart.
Best Specialized Film
ROMANCE OF TRANSPORTATION.
United Nations Award
WORLD WITHOUT END (U.S.)—Edward Bernds.

1954
Best Film, Any Source
THE WAGES OF FEAR (Fr./Ital.)—Henri-Georges Clouzot.
Best British Film
HOBSON'S CHOICE—David Lean.
Nominees
THE ADVENTURES OF ROBINSON CRUSOE (Mex.)—Luis Bunuel.
BREAD, LOVE AND DREAMS (Ital.)—Luigi Comencini.
THE CAINE MUTINY (U.S.)—Edward Dmytryk.
COURT MARTIAL (Brit.)—Anthony Asquith.
THE DIVIDED HEART (Brit.)—Charles Crichton.
DOCTOR IN THE HOUSE (Brit.)—Ralph Thomas.
EXECUTIVE SUITE (U.S.)—Robert Wise.
COCKTAILS IN THE KITCHEN (Brit.)—J. Lee-Thompson.
GATE OF HELL (Jap.)—Teinosuke Kinugasa.
HOW TO MARRY A MILLIONAIRE (U.S.)—Jean Negulesco.
HIGH AND DRY (Brit.)—Alexander Mackendrick.
THE MOON IS BLUE (U.S.)—Otto Preminger.
ON THE WATERFRONT (U.S.)—Elia Kazan.
THE PURPLE PLAIN (Brit.)—Robert Parrish.

REAR WINDOW (U.S.)—Alfred Hitchcock.
RIOT IN CELL BLOCK ELEVEN (U.S.)—Don Siegel.
ROMEO AND JULIET (Brit./Ital.)—Renato Castellani.
SEVEN BRIDES FOR SEVEN BROTHERS (U.S.)—Stanley Donen.
CHANCE MEETING (Brit.)—Anthony Asquith.
Best British Actor
Kenneth More for DOCTOR IN THE HOUSE (Brit.).
Best British Actress
Yvonne Mitchell for THE DIVIDED HEART (Brit.).
Best Foreign Actor
Marlon Brando for ON THE WATERFRONT (U.S.).
Best Foreign Actress
Cornell Borchers for THE DIVIDED HEART (Brit.).
Most Promising Newcomer
Norman Wisdom as revealed in TROUBLE IN STORE (Brit.).
Best Screenplay
CHANCE MEETING by Robin Estridge, from a story by George Tabori.
Best Documentary
THE GREAT ADVENTURE (Swed.)—Arne Sucksdorff.
Best Animated Film
SONG ON THE PRAIRIE.
United Nations Award
THE DIVIDED HEART (Brit.)—Charles Crichton.

1955
Best Film
RICHARD III (Brit.)—Laurence Olivier (Both Any Source and British Categories).
Nominees
BAD DAY AT BLACK ROCK (U.S.)—John Sturges.
CARMEN JONES (U.S.)—Otto Preminger.
THE COLDITZ STORY (Brit.)—Guy Hamilton.
EAST OF EDEN (U.S.)—Elia Kazan.
THE LADYKILLERS (Brit.)—Alexander Mackendrick.
MARTY (U.S.)—Delbert Mann.
THE NIGHT MY NUMBER CAME UP (Brit.)—Leslie Norman.
THE PRISONER (Brit.)—Peter Glenville.
SEVEN SAMURAI (Jap.)—Akira Kurosawa.
SIMBA (Brit.)—Brian Desmond Hurst.
LA STRADA (Ital.)—Federico Fellini.
SUMMERTIME (U.S.)—David Lean.
Best British Actor
Laurence Olivier for RICHARD III (Brit.).
Best British Actress
Katie Johnson for THE LADYKILLERS (Brit.).
Best Foreign Actor
Ernest Borgnine for MARTY (U.S.).
Best Foreign Actress
Betsy Blair for MARTY (U.S.).
Most Promising Newcomer
Paul Scofield as revealed in THAT LADY (Brit.).
Best Screenplay
THE LADYKILLERS (Brit.) by William Rose.
Best Documentary
THE VANISHING PRAIRIE.
Best Specialized Film
THE BESPOKEN OVERCOAT.
Best Animated Film
BLINKITY BLANK.
United Nations Award
CHILDREN OF HIROSHIMA (Jap.)—Kaneto Shindo.

1956
Best Film, Any Source
GERVAIS (Fr.)—Rene Clement.
Best British Film
REACH FOR THE SKY—Lewis Gilbert.
Nominees
BABY DOLL (U.S.)—Elia Kazan.
PURSUIT OF THE GRAF SPREE (Brit.)—Michael Powell and Emeric Pressburger.
LE DEFROQUE (Fr.)—Leo Joannon.
GUYS AND DOLLS (U.S.)—Joseph L. Mankiewicz.
THE KILLING (U.S.)—Stanley Kubrick.
THE MAN WITH THE GOLDEN ARM (U.S.)—Otto Preminger.
PICNIC (U.S.)—Joshua Logan.
REBEL WITHOUT A CAUSE (U.S.)—Nicholas Ray.
SMILES OF A SUMMER NIGHT (Swed.)—Ingmar Bergman.
THE RAPE OF MALAYA (Brit.)—Jack Lee.
BLONDE SINNER (Brit.)—J. Lee-Thompson.
Best British Actor
Peter Finch for THE RAPE OF MALAYA (Brit.).
Best British Actress
Virginia McKenna for THE RAPE OF MALAYA (Brit.).
Best Foreign Actor
Francois Perier for GERVAISE (Fr.).
Best Foreign Actress
Anna Magnani for THE ROSE TATTOO (U.S.).
Most Promising Newcomer
Eli Wallach as revealed in BABY DOLL (U.S.).
Best Screenplay
THE MAN WHO NEVER WAS (Brit.) by Nigel Balchin.
Best Documentary
ON THE BOWERY.
Best Specialized Film
THE RED BALLOON (Fr.)—Albert Lamorisse.
Best Animated Film
GERALD MCBOING BOING ON PLANET MOO.
United Nations Award
REACH FOR THE SKY (Brit.)—Lewis Gilbert.

1957
Best Film, Both Any Source and British Categories
THE BRIDGE ON THE RIVER KWAI (Brit.)—David Lean

Nominees
THE BACHELOR PARTY (U.S.)—Delbert Mann.
A MAN ESCAPED (Fr.)—Robert Bresson.
HE WHO MUST DIE (Fr./Ital.)—Jules Dassin.
HEAVEN KNOWS MR. ALLISON (U.S.)—John Huston.
EDGE OF THE CITY (U.S.)—Martin Ritt.
PATHS OF GLORY (U.S.)—Stanley Kubrick.
PATHER PANCHALI (India)—Satyajit Ray.
GATE OF LILACS (Fr./Ital.)—Rene Clair.
THE PRINCE AND THE SHOWGIRL (Brit.)—Laurence Olivier.
THE SHIRALEE (Brit.)—Leslie Norman.
THE TIN STAR (U.S.)—Anthony Mann.
3:10 TO YUMA (U.S.)—Delmer Daves.
TWELVE ANGRY MEN (U.S.)—Sidney Lumet.
WINDOM'S WAY (Brit.)—Ronald Neame.
Best British Actor
Alec Guinness for THE BRIDGE ON THE RIVER KWAI (Brit.).
Best British Actress
Heather Sears for THE STORY OF ESTHER COSTELLO (Brit.).
Best Foreign Actor
Henry Fonda for TWELVE ANGRY MEN (U.S.).
Best Foreign Actress
Simone Signoret for THE WITCHES OF SALEM (Fr.).
Most Promising Newcomer
Eric Baker as revealed in BROTHERS IN LAW (Brit.).
Best Screenplay
THE BRIDGE ON THE RIVER KWAI (Brit.) by Pierre Boulle.
Best Documentary
JOURNEY INTO SPRING.
Best Specialized Film
A CHAIRY TALE.
Best Animated Film
PAN-TELE-TRON.

1958
Best Film Both Any Source and British Categories
ROOM AT THE TOP (Brit.)—Jack Clayton
Nominees
CAT ON A HOT TIN ROOF (U.S.)—Richard Brooks.
THE CRANES ARE FLYING (U.S.S.R.)—Mikhail Kalatozov.
THE DEFIANT ONES (U.S.)—Stanley Kramer.
DESERT ATTACK (Brit.)—J. Lee-Thompson.
NIGHTS OF CABIRIA (Ital./Fr.)—Federico Fellini.
DESERT PATROL (Brit.)—Guy Green.
THE SHEEPMAN (U.S.)—George Marshall.
APARAJITO (India)—Satyajit Ray.
WILD STRAWBERRIES (Swed.)—Ingmar Bergman.
THE YOUNG LIONS (U.S.)—Edward Dmytryk.
Best British Actor
Trevor Howard for THE KEY (Brit.).
Best British Actress
Irene Worth for ORDERS TO KILL (Brit.).
Best Foreign Actor
Sidney Poitier for THE DEFIANT ONES (U.S.).
Best Foreign Actress
Simone Signoret for ROOM AT THE TOP (Brit.).
Most Promising Newcomer
Paul Massie for ORDERS TO KILL (Brit.).
Best Screenplay
ORDERS TO KILL (Brit.) by Paul Dehn.
Best Documentary
GLASS.
Best Specialized Film
THE CHILDREN'S FILM FOUNDATION.
Best Animated Film
THE LITTLE ISLAND.
United Nations Award
THE DEFIANT ONES (U.S.)—Stanley Kramer.

1959
Best Film, Any Source
BEN-HUR (U.S.)—William Wyler and Andrew Marton.
Best British Film
SAPPHIRE—Basil Dearden.
Nominees
ANATOMY OF A MURDER (U.S.)—Otto Preminger.
ASHES AND DIAMONDS (Pol.)—Andrzej Wajda.
THE BIG COUNTRY (U.S.)—William Wyler.
COMPULSION (U.S.)—Richard Fleischer.
THE MAGICIAN (Swed.)—Ingmar Bergman.
GIGI (U.S.)—Vincente Minnelli.
LOOK BACK IN ANGER (Brit.)—Tony Richardson.
MAIGRET SETS A TRAP (Fr.)—Jean Delannoy.
FLAME OVER INDIA (Brit.)—J. Lee-Thompson.
THE NUN'S STORY (U.S.)—Fred Zinnemann.
SOME LIKE IT HOT (U.S.)—Billy Wilder.
TIGER BAY (Brit.)—J. Lee-Thompson.
YESTERDAY'S ENEMY (Brit.)—Val Guest.
Best British Actor
Peter Sellers for I'M ALL RIGHT JACK (Brit.).
Best British Actress
Audrey Hepburn for THE NUN'S STORY (U.S.).
Best Foreign Actor
Jack Lemmon for SOME LIKE IT HOT (U.S.).
Best Foreign Actress
Shirley MacLaine for ASK ANY GIRL (U.S.).
Most Promising Newcomer
Hayley Mills as revealed in TIGER BAY.

Best Screenplay
I'M ALL RIGHT JACK (Brit.) by Frank Harvey, John Boulting, and Alan Hockney.
Robert Flaterly Award for Best Feature Length Documentary
THE SAVAGE EYE (U.S.)—Ben Maddow, Joseph Strick, and Sidney Meyers.
Best Short Film
SEVEN CITIES OF ANTARCTICA.
Best Specialized Film
THIS IS THE BBC.
Best Animated Film
THE VIOLINIST.
United Nations Award
ON THE BEACH (U.S.)—Stanley Kramer.

1960
Best Film, Any Source
THE APARTMENT (U.S.)—Billy Wilder.
Best British Film
SATURDAY NIGHT AND SUNDAY MORNING—Karel Reisz.
Nominees
THE ANGRY SILENCE (Brit.)—Guy Green.
L'AVVENTURA (Ital./Fr.)—Michelangelo Antonioni.
LA DOLCE VITA (Ital./Fr.)—Federico Fellini.
HIROSHIMA MON AMOUR (Fr./Jap.)—Alain Resnais.
ELMER GANTRY (U.S.)—Richard Brooks.
INHERIT THE WIND (U.S.)—Stanley Kramer.
LET'S MAKE LOVE (U.S.)—George Cukor.
NEVER ON SUNDAY (Gr.)—Jules Dassin.
BLACK ORPHEUS (Fr./Ital.)—Marcel Camus.
THE 400 BLOWS (Fr.)—Francois Truffaut.
SHADOWS (U.S.)—John Cassavetes.
TESTAMENT OF ORPHEUS (Fr.)—Jean Cocteau.
THE MAN WITH THE GREEN CARNATION (Brit.)—Ken Hughes.
TUNES OF GLORY (Brit.)—Ronald Neame.
Best British Actor
Peter Finch for THE MAN WITH THE GREEN CARNATION (Brit.).
Best British Actress
Rachel Roberts for SATURDAY NIGHT AND SUNDAY MORNING (Brit.).
Best Foreign Actor
Jack Lemmon for THE APARTMENT (U.S.).
Best Foreign Actress
Shirley MacLaine for THE APARTMENT (U.S.).
Most Promising Newcomer
Albert Finney as revealed in SATURDAY NIGHT AND SUNDAY MORNING (Brit.).
Best Screenplay
THE ANGRY SILENCE (Brit.) by Bryan Forbes.
Robert Flaterly Award for Best Feature Length Documentary
None awarded.
Best Short Film
NIGHT JOURNEY.
Best Animated Film
UNIVERSE.
Best Specialized Film
DISPUTE.
United Nations Award
HIROSHIMA, MON AMOUR (Fr.)—Alain Resnais.

1961
Best Film, Any Source
BALLAD OF A SOLDIER (U.S.S.R.)—Grigori Chukarai.
THE HUSTLER (U.S.)—Robert Rossen.
Best British Film
A TASTE OF HONEY—Tony Richardson.
Nominees
THE INNOCENTS (Brit.)—Jack Clayton.
JUDGMENT AT NUREMBURG (U.S.)—Stanley Kramer.
JUNGLE FIGHTERS (Brit.)—Leslie Norman.
ROCCO AND HIS BROTHERS (Ital.)—Luchino Visconti.
THE SUNDOWNERS (Brit./Aus.)—Fred Zinnemann.
LE TROU (Fr.)—Jacques Becker.
WHISTLE DOWN THE WIND (Brit.)—Bryan Forbes.
THE WORLD OF APU (India)—Satyajit Ray.
Best British Actor
Peter Finch for NO LOVE FOR JOHNNIE (Brit.).
Best British Actress
Dora Bryan for A TASTE OF HONEY (Brit.).
Best Foreign Actor
Paul Newman for THE HUSTLER (U.S.).
Best Foreign Actress
Sophia Loren for TWO WOMEN (Fr./Ital.).
Most Promising Newcomer
Rita Tushingham as revealed in A TASTE OF HONEY (Brit.).
Best Screenplay
THE DAY THE EARTH CAUGHT FIRE (Brit.) by Val Guest and Wolf Mankowitz.
A TASTE OF HONEY (Brit.) by Shelagh Delaney and Tony Richardson.
Robert Flaterly Award for Feature Documentary
VOLCANO.
Best Short Film
TERMINUS.
Best Animated Film
101 DALMATIONS (U.S.)—Walt Disney.
United Nations Award
LET MY PEOPLE GO.

1962
Best Film, Both Any Source and British Categories
LAWRENCE OF ARABIA (Brit.)—David Lean
Nominees
BILLY BUDD (Brit.)—Peter Ustinov.
THE ISLAND (Jap.)—Kaneto Shindo.
JULES AND JIM (Fr.)—Francois Truffaut.
A KIND OF LOVING (Brit.)—John Schlesinger.
THE L-SHAPED ROOM (Brit.)—Bryan Forbes.

THE LADY WITH THE LITTLE DOG (U.S.S.R.)—Josef Heifits.
LAST YEAR AT MARIENBAD (Fr./Ital.)—Alain Resnais.
THE LONG ABSENCE (Fr./Ital.)—Henri Colpi.
THE MANCHURIAN CANDIDATE (U.S.)—John Frankenheimer.
THE MIRACLE WORKER (U.S.)—Arthur Penn.
ONLY TWO CAN PLAY (Brit.)—Sidney Gilliat.
PHAEDRA (Gr.)—Jules Dassin.
THOU SHALT NOT KILL (Ital./Yugo./Lichenstein)—Claude Autant-Lara.
THROUGH A GLASS DARKLY (Swed.)—Ingmar Bergman.
THE VANISHING CORPORAL (Fr.)—Jean Renoir.
WEST SIDE STORY (U.S.)—Robert Wise and Jerome Robbins.
Best British Actor
Peter O'Toole for LAWRENCE OF ARABIA (Brit.).
Best British Actress
Leslie Caron for THE L-SHAPED ROOM (Brit.).
Best Foreign Actor
Burt Lancaster for BIRDMAN OF ALCATRAZ (U.S.).
Best Foreign Actress
Anne Bancroft for THE MIRACLE WORKER (U.S.).
Most Promising Newcomer
Tom Courtenay as revealed in THE LONELINESS OF THE LONG DISTANCE
RUNNER (Brit.).
Best Screenplay
LAWRENCE OF ARABIA (Brit.) by Robert Bolt.
Robert Flaterly Award for Best Feature Length Documentary
None awarded.
Best Short Film
INCIDENT AT OWL CREEK.
Best Animated Film
THE APPLE.
Best Specialized Film
FOUR LINE CONICS.
United Nations Award
REACH FOR GLORY (Brit.)—Philip Leacock.

1963
Best Film, Both Any Source and British Categories
TOM JONES (Brit.)—Tony Richardson.
Nominees
BILLY LIAR (Brit.)—John Schlesinger.
DAVID AND LISA (U.S.)—Frank Perry.
DAYS OF WINE AND ROSES (U.S.)—Blake Edwards.
DIVORCE ITALIAN STYLE (Ital.)—Pietro Germi.
8 1/2 (Ital.)—Federico Fellini.
FOUR DAYS OF NAPLES (Ital.)—Nanni Loy.
HUD (U.S.)—Martin Ritt.
KNIFE IN THE WATER (Pol.)—Roman Polanski.
THE SERVANT (Brit.)—Joseph Losey.
THIS SPORTING LIFE (Brit.)—Lindsay Anderson.
TO KILL A MOCKINGBIRD (U.S.)—Robert Mulligan.
Best British Actor
Dirk Bogarde for THE SERVANT (Brit.).
Best British Actress
Rachel Roberts for THIS SPORTING LIFE (Brit.).
Best Foreign Actor
Marcello Mastroianni for DIVORCE ITALIAN STYLE (Ital.).
Best Foreign Actress
Patricia Neal for HUD (U.S.).
Most Promising Newcomer
John Fox as revealed in THE SERVANT (Brit.).
Best Screenplay
TOM JONES (Brit.) by John Osborne.
Best Cinematography
(Black-and-White)
Douglas Slocombe for THE SERVANT (Brit.).
(Color)
Ted Moore for FROM RUSSIA WITH LOVE (Brit.).
Robert Flaterly Award for Best Documentary
None Awarded.
Best Specialized Film
None Awarded.
Best Animated Film
THE CRITIC.
AUTOMANIA 2000.
Best Short Film
HAPPY ANNIVERSARY.
United Nations Award
INHERITANCE.

1964
Best Film, Any Source
DR. STRANGELOVE OR: HOW I LEARNED TO STOP WORRYING AND LOVE
THE BOMB (Brit.)—Stanley Kubrick.
Nominees
BECKET (Brit.)—Peter Glenville.
THE PUMPKIN EATER (Brit.)—Jack Clayton.
THE TRAIN (U.S.)—John Frankenheimer.
Best British Film
DR. STRANGELOVE OR: HOW I LEARNED TO STOP WORRYING AND LOVE
THE BOMB—Stanley Kubrick.
Nominees
BECKET—Peter Glenville.
THE PUMPKIN EATER—Jack Clayton.
KING AND COUNTRY—Joseph Losey.
Best British Actor
Richard Attenborough for GUNS AT BATASI (Brit.), and SEANCE ON A WET
AFTERNOON (Brit.).
Best British Actress
Audrey Hepburn for CHARADE (U.S.).
Best Foreign Actor
Marcello Mastroianni for YESTERDAY TODAY AND TOMORROW (Ital./Fr.).

Best Foreign Actress
    Anne Bancroft for THE PUMPKIN EATER (Brit.).
Most Promising Newcomer
    Julie Andrews as revealed in MARY POPPINS (U.S.).
Best Screenplay
    THE PUMPKIN EATER (Brit.) by Harold Pinter.
Best Cinematography
    (Black-and-White)
    Oswald Morris for THE PUMPKIN EATER (Brit.).
    (Color)
    Geoffrey Unsworth for BECKET (Brit.).
Best Art Direction
    (Black-and-White)
    Ken Adam for DR STRANGELOVE OR: HOW I LEARNED TO STOP WORRYING
        AND LOVE THE BOMB (Brit.).
    (Color)
    John Bryan for BECKET (Brit.).
Best Costume Design
    (Black-and-White)
    Motley for THE PUMPKIN EATER (Brit.).
    (Color)
    Margaret Furse for BECKET (Brit.).
Robert Flaterly Award for Best Feature Length Documentary
    NOBODY WAVED GOODBYE.
Best Short
    KENOJUAK.
Best Animated Film
    THE INSECTS.
Best Specialized Film
    DRIVING TECHNIQUE—PASSENGER TRAINS.

1965
Best Film, Any Source
    MY FAIR LADY (U.S.)—George Cukor.
    Nominees
    HAMLET (U.S.S.R.)—Grigori Kozintsev.
    THE HILL (Brit.)—Sidney Lumet.
    ZORBA THE GREEK (Gr./U.S.)—Michael Cacoyannis.
Best British Film
    THE IPCRESS FILE—Sidney J. Furie.
    Nominees
    DARLING—John Schlesinger.
    THE HILL—Sidney Lumet.
    THE KNACK—Richard Lester.
Best British Actor
    Dirk Bogarde for DARLING (Brit.).
Best British Actress
    Julie Christie for DARLING (Brit.).
Best Foreign Actor
    Lee Marvin for THE KILLERS (U.S.), and CAT BALLOU (U.S.).
Best Foreign Actress
    Patricia Neal for IN HARM'S WAY. (U.S.).
Most Promising Newcomer
    Judi Dench as revealed in FOUR IN THE MORNING (Brit.).
Best Screenplay for a British Film
    DARLING by Frederic Raphael.
Best Photography for A British Film
    (Black-and-White)
    Oswald Morris for THE HILL.
    (Color)
    Otto Heller for THE IPCRESS FILE.
Best Art Direction of a British Film
    (Black-and-White)
    Ray Simm for DARLING.
    (Color)
    Ken Adam for THE IPCRESS FILE.
Best Costume Design in a British Film
    (Black-and-White)
    None awarded.
    (Color)
    Osbert Lancaster and Dinah Greet for THOSE MAGNIFICENT MEN IN THEIR
    FLYING MACHINES.
Robert Flaterly Award for Best Feature Length Documentary
    TOYKO OLYMPIAD (Jap.)—Kon Ichikawa.
Best Short Film
    BE CAREFUL BOYS.
Best Specialized Film
    I DO—AND I UNDERSTAND.
United Nations Award
    TOKYO OLYMPIAD (Jap.)—Kon Ichikawa.

1966
Best Film, Any Source
    WHO'S AFRAID OF VIRGINIA WOOLF? (U.S.)—Mike Nichols.
    Nominees
    DR. ZHIVAGO (U.S.)—David Lean.
    MORGAN! (Brit.)—Karel Reisz.
    THE SPY WHO CAME IN FROM THE COLD (Brit.)—Martin Ritt.
Best British Film
    THE SPY WHO CAME IN FROM THE COLD—Martin Ritt.
    Nominees
    ALFIE—Lewis Gilbert.
    GEORGY GIRL—Silvio Narizzano.
    MORGAN!—Karel Reisz.
Best British Actor
    Richard Burton for WHO'S AFRAID OF VIRGINIA WOOLF? (U.S.).
Best British Actress
    Elizabeth Taylor for WHO'S AFRAID OF VIRGINIA WOOLF? (U.S.).
Best Foreign Actor
    Rod Steiger for THE PAWNBROKER (U.S.).

Best Foreign Actress
    Jeanne Moreau for VIVA MARIA (Fr./Ital.).
Most Promising Newcomer
    Vivien Merchant as revealed in ALFIE (Brit.).
Best Screenplay for a British Film
    MORGAN! by David Mercer.
Best Cinematography of a British Film
    (Black-and-White)
    Oswald Morris for THE SPY WHO CAME IN FROM THE COLD.
    (Color)
    Christopher Challis for ARABESQUE.
Best Art Direction for a British Film
    (Black-and-White)
    Tambi Larsen for THE SPY WHO CAME IN FROM THE COLD.
    (Color)
    Wilfred Shingleton for THE BLUE MAX.
Best Costume Design for a British Film
    (Black-and-White)
    None awarded.
    (Color)
    Julie Harris for THE WRONG BOX.
Best Editing of a British Film
    Tom Priestly for MORGAN!
Robert Flaterly Award for Best Feature Length Documentary
    GOALL THE WORLD CUP.
Best Short Film
    THE WAR GAME.
Best Specialized Film
    EXPLORING CHEMISTRY.
United Nations Award
    THE WAR GAME.

1967
Best Film, Any Source
    A MAN FOR ALL SEASONS (Brit.)—Fred Zinnemann.
    Nominees
    BONNIE AND CLYDE (U.S.)—Arthur Penn.
    A MAN AND A WOMAN (Fr.)—Claude Lelouch.
    IN THE HEAT OF THE NIGHT (U.S.)—Norman Jewison.
Best British Film
    A MAN FOR ALL SEASONS—Fred Zinnemann.
    Nominees
    ACCIDENT—Joseph Losey.
    BLOW-UP—Michelangelo Antonioni.
    THE DEADLY AFFAIR—Sidney Lumet.
Best British Actor
    Paul Scofield for A MAN FOR ALL SEASONS.
Best British Actress
    Edith Evans for THE WHISPERERS.
Best Foreign Actor
    Rod Steiger for IN THE HEAT OF THE NIGHT (U.S.).
Best Foreign Actress
    Anouk Aimee for A MAN AND A WOMAN (Fr.).
Most Promising Newcomer
    Faye Dunaway as revealed in BONNIE AND CLYDE (U.S.).
Best Screenplay for a British Film
    A MAN FOR ALL SEASONS by Robert Bolt.
Best Cinematography for a British Film
    (Black-and-White)
    Gerry Turpin for THE WHISPERERS.
    (Color)
    Ted Moore for A MAN FOR ALL SEASONS.
Best Art Direction for a British Film
    (Black-and-White)
    None awarded.
    (Color)
    John Box for A MAN FOR ALL SEASONS.
Best Costume Design in a British Film
    (Black-and-White)
    Jocelyn Rickards for MADEMOISELLE.
    (Color)
    None.

Robert Flaterly Award for Best Feature Length Documentary
    TO DIE IN MADRID.
Best Short Film
    INDUS WATERS.
Best Specialized Film
    ENERGY AND WATER.
Best Animated Film
    NOTES ON A TRIANGLE.
United Nations Award
    IN THE HEAT OF THE NIGHT (U.S.)—Norman Jewison.

1968
Best Film
    THE GRADUATE (U.S.)—Mike Nichols.
    Nominees
    CLOSELY WATCHED TRAINS (Czech.)—Jiri Menzel.
    OLIVER (Brit.)—Carol Reed.
    2001: A SPACE ODYSSEY (Brit.)—Stanley Kubrick.
Best Actor
    Spencer Tracy for GUESS WHO'S COMING TO DINNER? (U.S.).
Best Actress
    Katharine Hepburn for GUESS WHO'S COMING TO DINNER? (U.S.), and THE
    LION IN WINTER (Brit.).
Best Supporting Actor
    Ian Holm for THE BOFORS GUN (Brit.).
Best Supporting Actress
    Billie Whitelaw for TWISTED NERVE (Brit.), and CHARLIE BUBBLES (Brit.).

Most Promising Newcomer
Dustin Hoffman as revealed in THE GRADUATE (U.S.).
Best Direction
Mike Nichols for THE GRADUATE (U.S.).
Best Screenplay
THE GRADUATE (U.S.) by Calder Willingham and Buck Henry.
Best Cinematography
Geoffrey Unsworth for 2001: A SPACE ODYSSEY (Brit.).
Best Art Direction
Tony Masters, Harry Lange, and Ernie Archer for 2001: A SPACE ODYSSEY (Brit.).
Best Costume Design
Danilo Donati for ROMEO AND JULIET (Brit.).
Best Soundtrack
Winston Ryder for 2001: A SPACE ODYSSEY (Brit.).
Best Film Editing
Sam O'Steen for THE GRADUATE (U.S.).
Anthony Asquith Award for Original Film Music
John Barry for THE LION IN WINTER (Brit.).
Robert Flaterly Award for Feature Length Documentary
IN NEED OF SPECIAL CARE.
Best Specialized Film
THE THREAT IN WATER.
Best Animated Film
PAS DE DEUX (Can.)—Norman Mclaren.
United Nations Award
GUESS WHO'S COMING TO DINNER? (U.S.)—Stanley Kramer.

1969
Best Film
MIDNIGHT COWBOY (U.S.)—John Schlesinger.
Nominees
OH, WHAT A LOVELY WAR (Brit.)—Richard Attenborough.
WOMEN IN LOVE (Brit.)—Ken Russell.
Z (Fr./Algeria)—Constantin Costa-Gavras.
Best Actor
Dustin Hoffman for MIDNIGHT COWBOY (U.S.), and JOHN AND MARY (U.S.).
Best Actress
Maggie Smith for THE PRIME OF MISS JEAN BRODIE (Brit.).
Best Supporting Actor
Laurence Olivier for OH, WHAT A LOVELY WAR (Brit.).
Best Supporting Actress
Celia Johnson for THE PRIME OF MISS JEAN BRODIE (Brit.).
Most Promising Newcomer
Jon Voight as revealed in MIDNIGHT COWBOY (U.S.).
Best Direction
John Schlesinger for MIDNIGHT COWBOY (U.S.).
Best Screenplay
MIDNIGHT COWBOY (U.S.) by Waldo Salt.
Best Cinematography
Gerry Turping for OH, WHAT A LOVELY WAR (Brit.).
Best Art Direction
Don Ashton for OH, WHAT A LOVELY WAR (Brit.).
Best Costume Design
Anthony Mendelson for OH, WHAT A LOVELY WAR (Brit.).
Best Film Editing
Hugh A. Robertson for MIDNIGHT COWBOY (U.S.).
Anthony Asquith Award for Original Film Music
Mikis Theodorakis for Z (Fr./Alg.).
Robert Flaterly Award for Best Feature Length Documentary
PROLOGUE.
Best Specialized Film
LET THERE BE LIGHT.
Best Short Film
PICTURE TO POST.
United Nations Award
OH, WHAT A LOVELY WAR (Brit.)—Richard Attenborough.

1970
Best Film
BUTCH CASSIDY AND THE SUNDANCE KID (U.S.)—George Roy Hill.
Nominees
KES (Brit.)—Ken Loach.
M.A.S.H. (U.S.)—Robert Altman.
RYAN'S DAUGHTER (Brit.)—David Lean.
Best Actor
Robert Redford for BUTCH CASSIDY AND THE SUNDANCE KID (U.S.), TELL THEM WILLIE BOY IS HERE (U.S.) and DOWNHILL RACER (U.S.).
Best Actress
Katharine Ross for BUTCH CASSIDY AND THE SUNDANCE KID (U.S.) and TELL THEM WILLIE BOY IS HERE (U.S.).
Best Supporting Actor
Colin Welland for KES (Brit.)
Best Supporting Actress
Susannah York for THEY SHOOT HORSES, DON'T THEY? (U.S.).
Most Promising Newcomer
David Bradley as revealed in KES (Brit.).
Best Direction
George Roy Hill for BUTCH CASSIDY AND THE SUNDANCE KID (U.S.).
Best Screenplay
BUTCH CASSIDY AND THE SUNDANCE KID (U.S.) by William Goldman.
Best Cinematography
Conrad Hall for BUTCH CASSIDY AND THE SUNDANCE KID (U.S.).
Best Art Direction
Mario Garbuglia for WATERLOO (Ital./U.S.S.R.).
Best Costume Design
Maria de Metteis for WATERLOO. (Ital./U.S.S.R.).
Best Film Editing
John C. Howard and Richard C. Meyer for BUTCH CASSIDY AND THE SUNDANCE KID (U.S.).

Best Soundtrack
Don Hall, David Dockendorf, and William Edmundson for BUTCH CASSIDY AND THE SUNDANCE KID (U.S.).
Anthony Asquith Award for Original Film Music
Burt Bacharach for BUTCH CASSIDY AND THE SUNDANCE KID (U.S.).
Robert Flaterly Award for Best Feature Length Documentary
SAD SONG OF YELLOW SKIN.
Best Specialized Film
THE RISE AND FALL OF THE GREAT LAKES.
Best Short Film
SHADOW OF PROGRESS.
United Nations Award
M.A.S.H. (U.S.)—Robert Altman.

1971
Best Film
SUNDAY, BLOODY SUNDAY (Brit.)—John Schlesinger.
Nominees
A DEATH IN VENICE (Ital.)—Luchino Visconti.
THE GO-BETWEEN (Brit.)—Joseph Losey.
TAKING OFF (U.S.)—Milos Forman.
Best Actor
Peter Finch for SUNDAY, BLOODY SUNDAY.
Best Actress
Glenda Jackson for SUNDAY, BLOODY SUNDAY.
Best Supporting Actor
Edward Fox for THE GO-BETWEEN.
Best Supporting Actress
Margaret Leighton for THE GO-BETWEEN.
Most Promising Newcomer
Dominic Guard as revealed in THE GO-BETWEEN.
Best Direction
John Schlesinger for SUNDAY, BLOODY SUNDAY.
Best Screenplay
THE GO-BETWEEN by Harold Pinter.
Best Cinematography
Pasquale de Santis for DEATH IN VENICE.
Best Art Direction
Ferdinando Scarfiotti for DEATH IN VENICE.
Best Costume Design
Piero Tosi for DEATH IN VENICE.
Best Film Editing
Richard Marden for SUNDAY, BLOODY SUNDAY.
Best Soundtrack
Giuseppe Muratori for DEATH IN VENICE.
Anthony Asquith Award for Original Film Music
Michael Legrand for SUMMER OF '42.
Robert Flaterly Award for Best Feature Length Documentary
THE HELLSTROM CHRONICLE—Walon Green.
Best Specialized Film
THE SAVAGE VOYAGE.
Best Short Film
ALASKA—THE GREAT LAND.
United Nations Award
THE BATTLE OF ALGIERS (Alg./Ital.)—Gillo Pontecorvo.

1972
Best Film
CABARET (U.S.)—Bob Fosse.
Nominees
A CLOCKWORK ORANGE (Brit.)—Stanley Kubrick.
THE FRENCH CONNECTION (U.S.)—William Friedkin.
THE LAST PICTURE SHOW (U.S.)—Peter Bogdanovich.
Best Actor
Gene Hackman for THE FRENCH CONNECTION and THE POSEIDON ADVENTURE (U.S.).
Best Actress
Liza Minnelli for CABARET.
Best Supporting Actor
Ben Johnson for THE LAST PICTURE SHOW.
Best Supporting Actress
Cloris Leachman for THE LAST PICTURE SHOW.
Most Promising Newcomer
Joel Grey as revealed in CABARET.
Best Direction
Bob Fosse for CABARET.
Best Screenplay
THE HOSPITAL (U.S.) by Paddy Chayefsky; and THE LAST PICTURE SHOW by Larry McMurtry and Peter Bogdanovich.
Best Cinematography
Geoffrey Unsworth for CABARET and ALICE'S ADVENTURES IN WONDERLAND.
Best Art Direction
Rolf Zehetbauer for CABARET.
Best Costume Design
Anthony Mendelson for YOUNG WINSTON (Brit.), MACBETH, and ALICE'S ADVENTURES IN WONDERLAND.
Best Film Editing
Jerry Greenberg for THE FRENCH CONNECTION.
Best Soundtrack
David Hildyard, Robert Knudson, and Arthur Piantadosi for CABARET.
Anthony Asquith Award for Original Film Music
Nino Rota for THE GODFATHER (U.S.).
John Grierson Award for Best Short Film
MEMORIAL.
Best Specialized Film
CUTTING OILS AND FLUIDS.
United Nations Award
THE GARDEN OF THE FINZI-CONTINIS (Ital./Ger.)—Vittorio de Sica.

1973
Best Film
    DAY FOR NIGHT (Fr./Ital.)—Francois Truffaut.
    Nominees
    THE DAY OF THE JACKAL (Brit./Fr.)—Fred Zinnemann.
    THE DISCREET CHARM OF THE BOURGEOISIE (Fr.)—Luis Bunuel.
    DON'T LOOK NOW (Brit.)—Nicholas Roeg.
Best Actor
    Walter Matthau for PETE N' TILLIE (U.S.) and CHARLEY VARRICK (U.S.)
Best Actress
    Stephane Audran for THE DISCREET CHARM OF THE BOURGEOISIE and JUST
    BEFORE NIGHTFALL (Fr./Ital.).
Best Supporting Actor
    Arthur Lowe for O LUCKY MAN (Brit.).
Best Supporting Actress
    Valentina Cortese for DAY FOR NIGHT.
Most Promising Newcomer
    Peter Egan for THE HIRELING (Brit.).
Best Direction
    Francois Truffaut for DAY FOR NIGHT.
Best Screenplay
    THE DISCREET CHARM OF THE BOURGEOISIE by Luis Bunuel and Jean-Claude
    Carriere.
Best Cinematography
    Anthony Richmond for DON'T LOOK NOW.
Best Art Direction
    Natasha Kroll for THE HIRELING (Brit.).
Best Costume Design
    Phyllis Dalton for THE HIRELING.
Best Film Editing
    Ralph Kemplen for THE DAY OF THE JACKAL.
Best Soundtrack
    Les Wiggins, Keith Grant, and Gordon K. McCallum for JESUS CHRIST SUPER-
    STAR (U.S.).
Anthony Asquith Award for Original Film Music
    Alan Price for O LUCKY MAN.
Robert Flaterly Award for Best Feature Length Documentary
    GRIERSON.
John Grierson Award for Best Short Film
    CARING FOR HISTORY.
Best Specialized Film
    A MAN'S WORLD.
Best Animated Film
    TCHOU-TCHOU.
United Nations Award
    STATE OF SIEGE (Fr.)—Constantin Costa-Gavras.

1974
Best Film
    LACOMBE LUCIEN (Fr./Ital./Ger.)—Louis Malle.
    Nominees
    CHINATOWN (U.S.)—Roman Polanski.
    THE LAST DETAIL (U.S.)—Hal Ashby.
    MURDER ON THE ORIENT EXPRESS (Brit.)—Sidney Lumet.
Best Actor
    Jack Nicholson for CHINATOWN, and THE LAST DETAIL.
Best Actress
    Joanne Woodward for SUMMER WISHES, WINTER DREAMS.
Best Supporting Actor
    John Gielgud for MURDER ON THE ORIENT EXPRESS.
Best Supporting Actress
    Ingrid Bergman for MURDER ON THE ORIENT EXPRESS.
Best Direction
    Roman Polanski for CHINATOWN.
Best Screenplay
    Robert Towne for CHINATOWN and THE LAST DETAIL.
Best Cinematography
    Douglas Slocombe for THE GREAT GATSBY (US).
Best Art Direction
    John Box for THE GREAT GATSBY.
Best Costume Design
    Theoni V. Aldredge for THE GREAT GATSBY.
Best Film Editing
    Walter Murch and Richard Crew for THE CONVERSATION.
Best Soundtrack
    Art Rochester, Nat Boxer, Mike Evoe, and Walter Murch for THE CONVERSATION.
Anthony Asquith Award for Original Film Music

    Richard Rodney Bennett for MURDER ON THE ORIENT EXPRESS.
United Nations Award
    LACOMBE, LUCIEN—Louis Malle.

1975
Best Film
    ALICE DOESN'T LIVE HERE ANYMORE (U.S.)—Martin Scorsese.
    Nominees
    BARRY LYNDON (Brit.)—Stanley Kubrick.
    DOG DAY AFTERNOON (U.S.)—Sidney Lumet.
    JAWS (U.S.)—Steven Spielberg.
Best Actor
    Al Pacino for THE GODFATHER PART II (U.S.) and DOG DAY AF
Best Actress
    Ellen Burstyn for ALICE DOESN'T LIVE HERE ANYMORE.
Best Supporting Actor
    Fred Astaire for THE TOWERING INFERNO (U.S.).
Best Supporting Actress
    Diane Ladd for ALICE DOESN'T LIVE HERE ANYMORE.
Most Promising Newcomer
    Valerie Perrine as revealed in LENNY (U.S.).
Best Direction
    Stanley Kubrick for BARRY LYNDON.

Best Screenplay
    Robert Getchell for ALICE DOESN'T LIVE HERE ANYMORE.
Best Cinematography
    John Alcott for BARRY LYNDON.
Best Art Direction
    John Box for ROLLERBALL (U.S.).
Best Costume Design
    Ann Roth for DAY OF THE LOCUST.
Best Film Editing
    Dede Allen for DOG DAY AFTERNOON.
Best Soundtrack
    William Sawyer, Jon Webb, Chris McLaughlin, and Richard Portman for NASH-
    VILLE (U.S.).
Anthony Asquith Award for Original Film Music
    John Williams for JAWS and THE TOWERING INFERNO.
Robert Flaterly Award for Best Feature Length Documentary
    THE EARLY AMERICANS.
John Grierson Award for Best Short Film
    SEA AREA FORTIES.
Best Animated Film
    GREAT.
Best Specialized Film
    THE CURIOSITY THAT KILLS THE CAT.

1976
Best Film
    ONE FLEW OVER THE CUCKOO'S NEST (U.S.)—Milos Forman.
    Nominees
    ALL THE PRESIDENT'S MEN (U.S.)—Alan J. Pakula.
    BUGSY MALONE (Brit.)—Alan Parker.
    TAXI DRIVER (U.S.)—Martin Scorsese.
Best Actor
    Jack Nicholson for ONE FLEW OVER THE CUCKOO'S NEST (U.S.).
Best Actress
    Louise Fletcher for ONE FLEW OVER THE CUCKOO'S NEST (U.S.).
Best Supporting Actor
    Brad Dourif for ONE FLEW OVER THE CUCKOO'S NEST (U.S.).
Best Supporting Actress
    Jodie Foster for BUGSY MALONE and TAXI DRIVER.
Most Promising Newcomer
    Jodie Foster as revealed in BUGSY MALONE (Brit.) and TAXI DRIVER (U.S.).
Best Direction
    Milos Forman for ONE FLEW OVER THE CUCKOO'S NEST (U.S.).
Best Screenplay
    Alan Parker for BUGSY MALONE (Brit.).
Best Cinematography
    Russell Boyd for PICNIC AT HANGING ROCK (Aus.).
Best Art Direction
    Geoffrey Kirkland for BUGSY MALONE.
Best Costume Design
    Moidele Bickel for THE MARQUISE OF O (Fr./Ger.).
Best Film Editing
    Richard Chew, Lynzee Klingman, and Sheldon Kahn for ONE FLEW OVER THE
    CUCKOO'S NEST (U.S.).
Best Soundtrack
    Les Wiggins, Clive Winter, and Ken Barker for BUGSY MALONE (Brit.).
Best Specialized Film
    HYDRAULICS.
Best Short Factual Film
    THE END OF THE ROAD.
Anthony Asquith Award for Original Film Music
    Bernard Herrmann for TAXI DRIVER.
Robert Flaherty Award for Best Feature Length Documentary
    LOS CANADIENSES—Albert Kish.

1977
Best Film
    ANNIE HALL (U.S.)—Woody Allen.
    Nominees
    A BRIDGE TOO FAR (Brit.)—Richard Attenborough.
    NETWORK (Brit.)—Sidney Lumet.
    ROCKY (U.S.)—John G. Avildsen.
Best Actor
    Peter Finch for NETWORK (U.S.).
Best Actress
    Diane Keaton for ANNIE HALL (U.S.).
Best Supporting Actor
    Edward Fox for A BRIDGE TOO FAR (Brit.).
Best Supporting Actress
    Jenny Agutter for EQUUS (Brit.).
Most Promising Newcomer
    Isabelle Huppert as revealed in THE LACEMAKER (Fr./Switz./Ger.).
Best Direction
    Woody Allen for ANNIE HALL (U.S.).
Best Screenplay
    Woody Allen and Marshall Brickman for ANNIE HALL (U.S.).
Best Cinematography
    Geoffrey Unsworth for A BRIDGE TOO FAR (Brit.).
Best Art Direction
    Danilo Donati for FELLINI'S CASANOVA (Ital.).
Best Costume Design
    Danilo Donati for FELLINI'S CASANOVA (Ital.).
Best Editing
    Ralph Rosenblum and Wendy Greene Bricmount for ANNIE HALL (U.S.).
Best Soundtrack
    Peter Horrocks, Gerry Humphrey, Simon Kaye, Robin O'Donaoghue, and Les
    Wiggins for A BRIDGE TOO FAR (Brit.).
Best Specialized Film
    PATH OF THE POODLE.
Best Short Factual Film
    THE LIVING CITY.

Anthony Asquith Award for Original Film Music
John Addison for A BRIDGE TOO FAR.
Fellowship Award
Fred Zinnemann.

1978
Best Film
JULIA (U.S.)—Fred Zinnemann.
Nominees
CLOSE ENCOUNTERS OF THE THIRD KIND (U.S.)—Steven Spielberg.
MIDNIGHT EXPRESS (Brit.)—Alan Parker.
STAR WARS (U.S.)—George Lucas.
Best Actor
Richard Dreyfuss for THE GOODBYE GIRL (U.S.).
Best Actress
Jane Fonda for JULIA (U.S.).
Best Supporting Actor
John Hurt for MIDNIGHT EXPRESS (Brit.).
Best Supporting Actress
Geraldine Page for INTERIORS (U.S.).
Most Promising Newcomer
Christopher Reeve as revealed in SUPERMAN (U.S.).
Best Direction
Alan Parker for MIDNIGHT EXPRESS (Brit.).
Best Screenplay
Alvin Sargent for JULIA (U.S.).
Best Cinematography
Douglas Slocombe for JULIA (U.S.).
Best Art Direction
Joe Alves for CLOSE ENCOUNTERS OF THE THIRD KIND (U.S.).
Best Costume Design
Anthony Powell for DEATH ON THE NILE (Brit.).
Best Film Editing
Gerry Hambling for MIDNIGHT EXPRESS (Brit.).
Best Soundtrack
Don MacDougall, Ray West, Bob Minkler, and Derek Ball for STAR WARS (U.S.).
Anthony Asquith Award for Original Film Music
John Williams for STAR WARS (U.S.).
Michael Balcon Award for Outstanding British Contribution to Cinema
Les Bowie, Colin Chilvers, Deny Coops, Roy Field, Derek Meddings and Zoran Perisic
for the special Effects of SUPERMAN (U.S./Brit.).

1979
Best Film
MANHATTAN (U.S.)—Woody Allen.
Nominees
APOCALYPSE NOW (U.S.)—Francis Ford Coppola.
THE CHINA SYNDROME (U.S.)—James Bridges.
THE DEER HUNTER (U.S.)—Michael Cimino.
Best Actor
Jack Lemmon for THE CHINA SYNDROME (U.S.).
Best Actress
Jane Fonda for THE CHINA SYNDROME (U.S.).
Best Supporting Actor
Robert Duvall for APOCALYPSE NOW (U.S.).
Best Supporting Actress
Rachel Roberts for YANKS (Brit.).
Most Promising Newcomer
Dennis Christopher for BREAKING AWAY (U.S.).
Best Screenplay
Woody Allen and Marshall Brickman for MANHATTAN (U.S.).
Best Cinematography
Vilmos Zsigmond for THE DEER HUNTER (U.S.).
Best Art Direction
Michael Seymour for ALIEN (U.S.).
Best Costume Design
Shirley Russell for YANKS (Brit.).
Best Film Editing
Peter Zinner for THE DEER HUNTER (U.S.).
Best Sound
Derrick Leather, Jim Shields, and Bill Rowe for ALIEN (U.S.).
Anthony Asquith Award for Original Film Music
Ennio Morricone for DAYS OF HEAVEN (U.S.).
Robert Flaherty Award for Best Feature Length Documentary
TREE OF WOODEN CLOGS (Ital.)—Ermanno Olmi.

1980
Best Film
THE ELEPHANT MAN (U.S.)—David Lynch.
Best Actor
John Hurt for THE ELEPHANT MAN (U.S.).
Best Actress
Judy Davis for MY BRILLIANT CAREER (Aus.).
Best Supporting Actor
None awarded.
Best Supporting Actress
None awarded.
Most Promising Newcomer
Judy Davis as revealed in MY BRILLIANT CAREER (Aus.).
Best Direction
Akira Kurosawa for KAGEMUSHA (Jap.).
Best Screenplay
Jerzy Kosinski for BEING THERE (U.S.).
Best Cinematography
Giuseppe Rotunno for ALL THAT JAZZ (U.S.).
Best Art Direction
Stuart Craig for THE ELEPHANT MAN (U.S.).
Best Costume Design
Seiichiro Momosawa for KAGEMUSHA (Jap.).
Best Film Editing
Alan Heim for ALL THAT JAZZ (U.S.).

Best Sound
Michael J. Kohut, Aaron Rochin, Jay M. Harding, and Chris Newman for FAME (U.S.).
Anthony Asquith Award for Original Film Music
John Williams for THE EMPIRE STRIKES BACK (U.S.).
Michael Balcon Award for Outstanding British Contribution to Cinema
Kevin Brownlow for reassembling Abel Gance's NAPOLEON.
Special Film Award
Jimmy Wright.
Fellowship Award
Michael Powell and Emeric Pressburger.

1981
Best Film
CHARIOTS OF FIRE—Hugh Hudson.
Best Actor
Burt Lancaster for ATLANTIC CITY (Can.).
Best Actress
Meryl Streep for THE FRENCH LIEUTENANT'S WOMAN (U.S.).
Best Supporting Artist
Ian Holm for CHARIOTS OF FIRE (Brit.).
Most Promising Newcomer
Joe Pesci as revealed in RAGING BULL (U.S.).
Best Direction
Louis Malle for ATLANTIC CITY (Can.).
Best Screenplay
Bill Forsyth for GREGORY'S GIRL (Scot.).
Best Cinematography
Geoffrey Unsworth, Ghislain Cloquet for TESS (Brit.).
Best Production Design/Art Direction
Norman Reynolds for RAIDERS OF THE LOST ARK (U.S.).
Best Costume Design
Milena Canonero for CHARIOTS OF FIRE (Brit.).
Best Film Editing
Thelma Shoonmaker for RAGING BULL (U.S.).
Best Sound
Don Sharpe, Ivon Sharrock, and Bill Rowe for THE FRENCH LIEUTENANT'S WOMAN (U.S.).
Anthony Asquith Award for Original Film Music
Carl Davis for THE FRENCH LIEUTENANT'S WOMAN (U.S.).
Best Short Film
RECLUSE by Bob Bentley.
Best Animated Film
THE SWEATER by Sheldon Cohen.
Michael Balcon Award for Outstanding British Contribution to the Cinema
David Puttnam.
Robert Flaherty Award for Best Feature Length Documentary
SOLDIER GIRLS by Nick Broomfield and Joan Churchill.
Fellowship Award
Andrzej Wajda.

1982
Best Film
GANDHI (Brit.)—Richard Attenborough.
Best Actor
Ben Kingsley for GANDHI (Brit.).
Best Actress
Katharine Hepburn for ON GOLDEN POND (U.S.).
Best Supporting Actor
Jack Nicholson for REDS (U.S.).
Best Supporting Actress
Maureen Stapleton for REDS (U.S.).
Rohini Hattangandy for GANDHI (Brit.).
Best Direction
Richard Attenborough for GANDHI (Brit.).
Best Screenplay
Constantin Costa-Gavras and Donald Stewart for MISSING (U.S.).
Best Cinematography
Jordan Cronenweth for BLADE RUNNER (U.S.).
Best Production Design/Art Direction
Lawrence G. Paull for BLADE RUNNER (U.S.).
Best Costume Design
Michael Kaplan and Charles Knode for BLADE RUNNER (U.S.).
Best Film Editing
Francoise Bonnot for MISSING (U.S.).
Best Sound
James Guthrie, Eddy Joseph, Clive Winter, Graham Hartsone, and Nicholas Le Mussurier for PINK FLOYD THE WALL (Brit.).
Anthony Asquith Award for Original Film Music
John Williams for E.T. THE EXTRA-TERRESTRIAL (U.S.).
Best Short Film
Ian Knox for THE PRIVILEGE.
Best Animated Film
David Anderson for DREAMLAND EXPRESS.
Michael Balcon Award for Outstanding British Contribution to Cinema
Arthur Wooster.
Fellowship Award
Richard Attenborough.

1983
Best Film
EDUCATING RITA (Brit.)—Lewis Gilbert.
Best Actor
Michael Caine for EDUCATING RITA (Brit.).
Dustin Hoffman for TOOTSIE (U.S.).
Best Actress
Julie Walters for EDUCATING RITA (Brit.).
Best Supporting Actor
Denholm Elliott for TRADING PLACES (U.S.).
Best Supporting Actress
Jamie Lee Curtis for TRADING PLACES (U.S.).

Most Promising Newcomer
    Phyllis Logan as revealed in ANOTHER TIME, ANOTHER PLACE (Brit.).
Best Direction
    Bill Forsyth for LOCAL HERO (Brit.).
Best Original Screenplay
    Paul D. Zimmermann for THE KING OF COMEDY (U.S.).
Best Adapted Screenplay
    Ruth Prawer Jhabvala for HEAT AND DUST (Brit.).
Best Cinematography
    Sven Nykvist for FANNY AND ALEXANDER (Swed./Ger.).
Best Art Direction
    Franco Zeffirelli and Gianni Quaranta for LA TRAVIATA (Ital.).
Best Costume Design
    Piero Tosi for LA TRAVIATA (Ital.).
Best Film Editing
    Bud Smith and Walt Mulconery for FLASHDANCE (U.S.)
Best Score
    Ryuichi Sakamoto for MERRY CHRISTMAS, MISTER LAWRENCE (Jap./Brit.).
Best Original Song Written for a Film
    Jack Nitzche, Buffe Sainte-Marie, and Will Jennings for "Up Where We Belong" from AN OFFICER AND A GENTLEMAN (U.S.).
Best Sound
    Willie D. Burton for WARGAMES (U.S.).
Best Foreign Language Film
    DANTON (Fr.)—Andrzej Wajda.
Best Short Film
    Ian Emes for GOODIE TWO SHOES.
Best Animated Film
    Bob Godfrey for HENRY'S CAT.
The Michael Balcon Award for Outstanding British Contribution to Cinema
    Colin Young.
Fellowship Awards
    Sir Hugh Greene, and Sam Spiegel.

1984
Best Film
    THE KILLING FIELDS (Brit.)—Roland Joffe.
Best Actor
    Dr. Haing S. Ngor for THE KILLING FIELDS (Brit.).
Best Actress
    Maggie Smith for A PRIVATE FUNCTION (Brit.).
Best Supporting Actor
    Denholm Elliott for A PRIVATE FUNCTION (Brit.).
Best Supporting Actress
    Liz Smith for A PRIVATE FUNCTION (Brit.).
Most Promising Newcomer
    Dr. Haing S. Ngor as revealed in THE KILLING FIELDS (Brit.).
Best Direction
    Wim Wenders for PARIS, TEXAS.
Best Original Screenplay
    Woody Allen for BROADWAY DANNY ROSE (U.S.).
Best Adapted Screenplay
    Bruce Robinson for THE KILLING FIELDS (U.S.).
Best Cinematography
    Chris Menges for THE KILLING FIELDS (Brit.).
Best Production Design
    Roy Walker for THE KILLING FIELDS (Brit.).
Best Film Editing
    Jim Clark for THE KILLING FIELDS (Brit.).
Best Sound
    Ian Fuller, Clive Winter, and Bill Rowe for THE KILLING FIELDS (Brit.).
Best Foreign Language Film
    CARMEN (Span.)—Carlos Saura.

NEW YORK FILM CRITICS CIRCLE AWARDS

1935
Best Film
 INFORMER, John Ford; the unanimous choice on the 1st ballot.
Best Actor
 Laughton for MUTINY ON THE BOUNTY and RUGGLES OF RED GAP.
Best Actress
 Garbo for ANNA KARENINA.
Best Direction
 John Ford for THE INFORMER.

1936
Best Film
 MR. DEEDS GOES TO TOWN, Frank Capra; 11 votes on 2nd ballot.
 FURY, Fritz Lang; 4 Votes.
 WINTERSET, Alfred Santell; 1 vote.
 DODSWORTH, William Wyler; 1 vote.
 THESE THREE, William Wyler.
Best Actor
 Walter Huston for DODSWORTH; 12 votes on 5th ballot.
 Spencer Tracy; 6 votes.
 Gary Cooper, Burgess Meredith, and Charles Laughton were also considered.
Best Actress
 Luise Rainer for THE GREAT ZIEGFELD; 13 votes on 4th ballot.
 Ruth Chatterton; 4 votes.
 Norma Shearer, Katharine Hepburn and Carole Lombard were also considered.
Best Direction
 Rouben Mamoulian for THE GAY DESPERADO; 12 votes on 10th ballot.
 William Wyler for THESE THREE and DODSWORTH.
 Fritz Lang for FURY; 6 votes.
 George Cukor for ROMEO AND JULIET.
 Frank Capra for MR. DEEDS GOES TO TOWN.
Best Foreign Language Film
 CARNIVAL IN FLANDERS (Fr.), Jacques Feyder; 15 votes on 1st ballot.
 TONI (Fr.), Jean Renoir; 1 vote.
 REVOLUTIONISTS (USSR), Vera Stroyeva; 1 vote.

1937
Best Film
 THE LIFE OF EMILE ZOLA, William Dieterle; on 2nd ballot.
 CAPTAINS COURAGEOUS, Victor Fleming.
 THE GOOD EARTH, Sidney Franklin.
 STAGE DOOR, Gregory La Cava.
 NIGHT MUST FALL, Richard Thorpe.
Best Actor
 Paul Muni for THE LIFE OF EMILE ZOLA; on 12th ballot.
 Spencer Tracy, Fredric March, Charles Boyer, and Robert Montgomery were also considered.
Best Actress
 Greta Garbo for CAMILLE; on 5th ballot.
 Katharine Hepburn, Carole Lombard, Deanna Durbin, and Erin O'Brien-Moore were also considered.
Best Direction
 Gregory La Cava for STAGE DOOR; on 1st ballot.
 Victor Fleming for CAPTAINS COURAGEOUS.
 Henry Koster for 100 MEN AND A GIRL.
 William Dieterle for THE LIFE OF EMILE ZOLA.
 Leo McCarey for MAKE WAY FOR TOMORROW and THE AWFUL TRUTH.
Best Foreign Language Film
 MAYERLING (Fr.), Anatole Litvak.
 BALTIC DEPUTY (USSR), Alexander Zharbi and Josef Heifits.
 THE ETERNAL MASK (Switz.), Walter Hochbaum.
 THE WAVE (Mex.), Fred Zinnemann and Gomez Muriel.
 RAZUMOV (Fr.), Marc Allegret.

1938
Best Film
 THE CITADEL (Brit.), King Vidor; on 4th ballot.
 THE LADY VANISHES (Brit.), Alfred Hitchcock.
 TO THE VICTOR (Brit.), George Archainbaud.
 SING YOU SINNERS, Wesley Ruggles.
 IN OLD CHICAGO, Henry King.
 BLOCKADE, William Dieterle.
 THREE ON A WEEKEND (Brit.), Carol Reed.
Best Actor
 James Cagney for ANGELS WITH DIRTY FACES; on 9th ballot.
 Spencer Tracy, John Garfield, Will Fyffe, John Barrymore, Franchot Tone, Robert Morley, Edward Ellis, Charles Laughton, Gene Lockhart, Robert Montgomery, and Ralph Richardson were also considered.
Best Actress
 Margaret Sullavan for THREE COMRADES.
 Wendy Hiller, Katharine Hepburn, and Norma Shearer were also considered.
Best Direction
 Alfred Hitchcock for THE LADY VANISHES (Brit.); on 1st ballot.
 Garson Kanin for A MAN TO REMEMBER.
 Frank Capra for YOU CAN'T TAKE IT WITH YOU.
 John Cromwell for ALGIERS.
 Michael Curtiz for FOUR DAUGHTERS.
Best Foreign Language Film
 GRAND ILLUSION (Fr.), Jean Renoir; on 7th ballot.
 PROFESSOR MAMLOCK (USSR), Adolph Minkin and Herbert Rappaport.
 BALLERINA (Fr.), M. Benoit-Levy.
 CARNET DE BAL (Fr.), Julien Duvivier.
Special Award
 Walt Disney, for the production of SNOW WHITE AND THE SEVEN DWARFS.
 The documentary THE RIVER by Pare Lorentz was also considered.

1939
Best Film

WUTHERING HEIGHTS, William Wyler; on 14th ballot.
 GONE WITH THE WIND, David O. Selznick, producer; Victor Fleming, director.
 MR. SMITH GOES TO WASHINGTON, Frank Capra.
Best Actor
 James Stewart for MR. SMITH GOES TO WASHINGTON; on 3rd ballot.
 Robert Donat for GOOD-BYE MR. CHIPS.
 Henry Fonda for YOUNG MR. LINCOLN.
Best Actress
 Vivien Leigh for GONE WITH THE WIND; on 2nd ballot.
 Greta Garbo for NINOTCHKA.
Best Direction
 John Ford for STAGECOACH; 12 votes on 3rd ballot.
 Ernst Lubitsch for NINOTCHKA; 3 votes.
 Victor Fleming for GONE WITH THE WIND; 2 votes.
Best Foreign Language Film
 HARVEST (Fr.), Marcel Pagnol; on 12th ballot.
 THE END OF THE DAY (Fr.), Julien Duvivier.

1940
Best Film
 THE GRAPES OF WRATH, John Ford.
Best Actor
 Charles Chaplin for THE GREAT DICTATOR (Refused).
Best Actress
 Katharine Hepburn for THE PHILADELPHIA STORY.
Best Direction
 John Ford for THE GRAPES OF WRATH and THE LONG VOYAGE HOME.
Best Foreign Language Film
 THE BAKER'S WIFE (Fr.), Marcel Pagnol.
Special Award
 Walt Disney and Leopold Stokowski for the production of FANTASIA.

1941
Best Film
 CITIZEN KANE, Orson Welles; 10 votes on 6th ballot.
 HOW GREEN WAS MY VALLEY, John Ford; 7 votes.
 SERGEANT YORK, Howard Hawks.
 HERE COMES MR. JORDAN, Alexander Hall.
 THE STARS LOOK DOWN (Brit.), Carol Reed.
 THE LITTLE FOXES, William Wyler.
 MAJOR BARBARA (Brit.), Gabriel Pascal, Harold French, and David Lean.
 THE LADY EVE, Preston Sturges.
 BLOSSOMS IN THE DUST, Mervyn LeRoy.
Best Actor
 Gary Cooper for SERGEANT YORK; 14 votes on 1st ballot.
 Orson Welles for CITIZEN KANE; 2 votes.
 Cary Grant and Robert Montgomery were also considered.
Best Actress
 Joan Fontaine for SUSPICION; 12 votes on 6th ballot.
 Olivia de Havilland for HOLD BACK THE DAWN; 3 votes.
 Greta Garbo for TWO FACED WOMAN; 2 votes.
 Dorothy Comingore for CITIZEN KANE; 1 vote.
Best Direction
 John Ford for HOW GREEN WAS MY VALLEY; 10 votes on 6th ballot.
 Orson Welles for CITIZEN KANE; 7 votes.
 Carol Reed for THE STARS LOOK DOWN (Brit.).
 Alexander Hall for HERE COMES MR. JORDAN.
 Alfred Hitchcock for SUSPICION.
 Preston Sturges for THE LADY EVE.
The war necessitated the discontinuation of the award for Best Foreign Language Film.

1942
Best Film
 IN WHICH WE SERVE (Brit.), Noel Coward; 11 votes on 5th ballot.
 WAKE ISLAND, John Farrow; 7 votes.
 THE MOON AND SIXPENCE, Albert Levin.
Best Actor
 James Cagney for YANKEE DOODLE DANDY; 13 votes on 1st ballot.
 Humphrey Bogart for CASABLANCA and ACROSS THE PACIFIC; 2 votes.
 Monty Woolley for THE MAN WHO CAME TO DINNER; 1 vote.
 Ronald Colman for RANDOM HARVEST; 1 vote.
 Brian Donlevy for WAKE ISLAND; 1 vote.
Best Actress
 Agnes Moorhead for THE MAGNIFICENT AMBERSONS; 11 votes on 6th ballot.
 Greer Garson for MRS. MINIVER; 7 votes.
 Katharine Hepburn for WOMAN OF THE YEAR.
 Ingrid Bergman for CASABLANCA.
 Teresa Wright for THE PRIDE OF THE YANKEES and MRS. MINIVER.
 Anna Neagle for WINGS AND THE WOMAN (Brit.).
 Rosalind Russell for MY SISTER EILEEN.
 Joan Fontaine for THIS ABOVE ALL.
Best Direction
 John Farrow for WAKE ISLAND; 12 votes on 4th ballot.
 David Lean and Noel Coward for IN WHICH WE SERVE (Brit.); 6 votes.
 William Wyler for MRS. MINIVER.
 Orson Welles for THE MAGNIFICENT AMBERSONS.
 Michael Curtiz for YANKEE DOODLE DANDY and CASABLANCA.
 Preston Sturges for SULLIVAN'S TRAVELS.
 Michael Powell for THE INVADERS (Brit.).
Best War Film
 MOSCOW STRIKES BACK; 13 votes on 1st ballot.
 THE WORLD AT WAR, Office of War information; 2 votes.
 LETTER FROM HOME (Brit.), 2 votes.
 THE BATTLE OF MIDWAY, John Ford; 1 vote.

1943

Best Film
WATCH ON THE RHINE, Herman Shulin; 11 votes on 5th ballot.
THE HUMAN COMEDY, Clarence Brown; 5 votes.
HANGMEN ALSO DIE, Fritz Lang.
MISSION TO MOSCOW, Michael Curtiz.
CLAUDIA, Edmund Goulding.
CORVETTE K-225, Richard Rossen.
ACTION IN THE NORTH ATLANTIC, Lloyd Bacon.
HOLY MATRIMONY, John Stahl.
AIR FORCE, Howard Hawks.

Best Actor
Paul Lukas for WATCH ON THE RHINE; 15 votes on 1st ballot.
Monty Woolley for HOLY MATRIMONY; 1 vote.
Sonny Tufts for SO PROUDLY WE HAIL; 1 vote.

Best Actress
Ida Lupino for THE HARD WAY; 11 votes on 6th ballot.
Katina Paxinou for FOR WHOM THE BELLS TOLL; 6 votes.
Joan Fontaine for THE CONSTANT NYMPH.
Gracie Fields for HOLY MATRIMONY.
Teresa Wright, Ingrid Bergman, Margo, Lucille Watson, and Claudette Colbert were
also considered.

Best Direction
George Stevens for THE MORE THE MERRIER.

Special Award
Army Signal Corps for the WHY WE FIGHT Series.

1944

Best Film
GOING MY WAY, Leo McCarey; 11 votes on 3rd ballot.
HAIL THE CONQUERING HERO, Preston Sturges; 3 votes.
WILSON, Henry King; 2 votes.
DOUBLE INDEMNITY, Billy Wilder.
THUNDER ROCK, Roy Boulting.

Best Actor
Barry Fitzgerald for GOING MY WAY; 11 votes on 1st ballot.
Bing Crosby for GOING MY WAY; 2 votes.
Alexander Knox for WILSON; 2 votes.
Fred MacMurray for DOUBLE INDEMNITY; 1 vote.

Best Actress
Tallulah Bankhead for LIFEBOAT; 10 votes on 6th ballot.
Ingrid Bergman for GASLIGHT; 5 votes.
Barbara Stanwyck for DOUBLE INDEMNITY.
Jennifer Jones for THE SONG OF BERNADETTE.

Best Direction
Leo McCarey for GOING MY WAY; 7 votes on 5th ballot.
Preston Sturges for THE MIRACLE OF MORGAN'S CREEK and HAIL THE
CONQUERING HERO.
Henry King for THE SONG OF BERNADETTE and WILSON.
Otto Preminger for LAURA.
Billy Wilder for DOUBLE INDEMNITY.
Henry Koster for MUSIC FOR MILLIONS.
John Boulting for THUNDER ROCK (Brit.).
Vincente Minnelli for MEET ME IN ST. LOUIS.

1945

Best Film
THE LOST WEEKEND, Billy Wilder; 9 votes on 6th ballot.
THE STORY OF G.I. JOE, William A. Wellman; 8 votes.
COLONEL BLIMP (Brit.), Michael Powell and Emeric Pressburger.
STATE FAIR, Walter Lang.

Best Actor
Ray Milland for THE LOST WEEKEND; 13 votes on 4th ballot.
Robert Mitchum for THE STORY OF G.I. JOE; 4 votes.
Zachary Scott for THE SOUTHERNER and MILDRED PIERCE.
James Dunn for A TREE GROWS IN BROOKLYN.
Roger Livesy for COLONEL BLIMP (Brit.).
Gary Cooper for ALONG CAME JONES.
James Mason for THE SEVENTH VEIL (Brit.).

Best Actress
Ingrid Bergman for SPELLBOUND and THE BELLS OF ST. MARY; 9 votes on 6th
ballot.
Joan Crawford for MILDRED PIERCE; 6 votes.
Deborah Kerr for COLONEL BLIMP (Brit.) and LOVE ON THE DOLE (Brit.).
Peggy Ann Garner for A TREE GROWS IN BROOKLYN.
Bette Davis for THE CORN IS GREEN and THE SUSPECT.
Margaret Rutherford for BLITHE SPIRIT (Brit.).

Best Direction
Billy Wilder for THE LOST WEEKEND; 9 votes on 5th ballot.
William A. Wellman for THE STORY OF G.I. JOE.
Jean Renoir for THE SOUTHERNER.
Michael Powell and Emeric Pressburger for COLONEL BLIMP (Brit.).
Henry Hathaway for THE HOUSE ON NINETY-SECOND STREET.
Raoul Walsh for SALTY O'ROURKE.
Leopold Lindtberg for THE LAST CHANCE (Switz.).

Special Awards
Dwight D. Eisenhower and the British and United States Armies for the production
of the documentary THE TRUE GLORY.
The United States Navy and 20th Century Fox for the production of the documentary
THE FIGHTING LADY.

1946

Best Film
THE BEST YEARS OF OUR LIVES, William Wyler; 12 votes on 2nd ballot.
HENRY V (Brit.), Laurence Olivier; 6 votes.
STAIRWAY TO HEAVEN (Brit.), Michael Powell and Emeric Pressburger.

Best Actor
Laurence Olivier for HENRY V (Brit.); 12 votes on 2nd ballot.
Fredric March for THE BEST YEARS OF OUR LIVES; 6 votes.
Rex Harrison for ANNA AND THE KING OF SIAM .

Best Actress
Celia Johnson for BRIEF ENCOUNTER (Brit.); 11 votes on 6th ballot.
Olivia de Havilland for TO EACH HIS OWN; 7 votes.
Teresa Wright for THE BEST YEARS OF OUR LIVES.
Ann Baxter for THE RAZOR'S EDGE.
Rosalind Russell for SISTER KENNY.
Ingrid Bergman for NOTORIOUS.
Renee Asherson for HENRY V (Brit.).
Francoise Rosay for PORTRAIT OF A WOMAN (Fr.) and JOHNNY FRENCHMAN.

Best Direction
William Wyler for THE BEST YEARS OF OUR LIVES; 12 votes on 1st ballot.
Laurence Olivier for HENRY V (Brit.); 4 votes.
Michael Powell and Emeric Pressburger for STAIRWAY TO HEAVEN (Brit.).
Frank Capra for IT'S A WONDERFUL LIFE.

Best Foreign Language Film
OPEN CITY (Ital.), Roberto Rossellini; 10 votes on 6th ballot.
THE WELL-DIGGER'S DAUGHTER (Fr.), Marcel Pagnol; 7 votes.

1947

Best Film
GENTLEMAN'S AGREEMENT, Elia Kazan; 9 votes on 6th ballot.
GREAT EXPECTATIONS (Brit.), David Lean; 7 votes.
ODD MAN OUT (Brit.), Carol Reed.
CROSSFIRE, Edward Dmytryk.
MIRACLE ON 34TH STREET, George Seaton.
THE FUGITIVE, John Ford.
BOOMERANG, Elia Kazan.

Best Actor
William Powell for LIFE WITH FATHER and THE SENATOR WAS INDISCREET;
10 votes on 6th ballot.
John Garfield for BODY AND SOUL; 6 votes.
Gregory Peck for GENTLEMAN'S AGREEMENT and THE YEARLING.
Robert Ryan for CROSSFIRE.
Bernard Miles for TAWNY PIPIT (Brit.), GREAT EXPECTATIONS (Brit.), and
NICHOLAS NICKLEBY (Brit.).

Best Actress
Deborah Kerr for BLACK NARCISSUS (Brit.) and THE ADVENTURESS (Brit.); on
2nd ballot.
Anne Revere for GENTLEMAN'S AGREEMENT.
Martita Hunt for GREAT EXPECTATIONS (Brit.).
Celeste Holm for GENTLEMAN'S AGREEMENT.
Loretta Young for THE FARMER'S DAUGHTER.
Kathleen Byron for BLACK NARCISSUS (Brit.).
Dorothy Maguire for GENTLEMAN'S AGREEMENT.

Best Direction
Elia Kazan for GENTLEMAN'S AGREEMENT and BOOMERANG; 11 votes on 6th
ballot.
Edward Dmytryk for CROSSFIRE; 3 votes.
John Ford for THE FUGITIVE; 2 votes.
Carol Reed for ODD MAN OUT (Brit.).

Best Foreign Language Film
TO LIVE IN PEACE (Ital.), Luigi Zampa; 12 votes on 4th ballot.
SHOE-SHINE (Ital.), Vittorio de Sica.
PANIQUE (Fr.), Julien Duvivier.
CHILDREN OF PARADISE (Fr.), Marcel Carne.

1948

Best Film
THE TREASURE OF THE SIERRA MADRE, John Huston; 9 votes on 6th ballot.
HAMLET (Brit.), Laurence Olivier; 8 votes.
THE SNAKE PIT, Anatole Litvak.
THE SEARCH (U.S./Switz.), Fred Zinnemann.

Best Actor
Laurence Olivier for HAMLET (Brit.).
Walter Huston for TREASURE OF THE SIERRA MADRE.
Ivan Jandl for THE SEARCH (U.S./Switz.).

Best Actress
Olivia de Havilland for THE SNAKE PIT, a unanimous choice on the 1st ballot.

Best Direction
John Huston for TREASURE OF THE SIERRA MADRE.
Laurence Olivier for HAMLET (Brit.).
Anatole Litvak for THE SNAKE PIT.
Fred Zinnemann for THE SEARCH (U.S./Switz.).

Best Foreign Language Film
PAISAN (Ital.), Roberto Rossellini; 12 votes on 3rd ballot.
MONSIEUR VINCENT (Fr.), Leon Carre.
SYMPHONIE PASTORALE (Fr.), Jean Delannoy.
FOUR STEPS IN THE CLOUDS (Ital.), Alessandro Blasetti.
FARREBIQUE (Fr.), Georges Rouquier.
FANNY (Fr.), Marc Allegret.
DAY OF WRATH (Den.), Carl Dreyer.

1949

Best Film
ALL THE KING'S MEN,Robert Rossen; 9 votes on 6th ballot.
INTRUDER IN THE DUST, Clarence Brown; 5 votes.
THE FALLEN IDOL (Brit.), Carol Reed; 3 votes.
LOST BOUNDARIES, Alfred Werker.
BATTLEGROUND, William Wellman.
HOME OF THE BRAVE, Mark Robson.
FAME IS THE SPUR (Brit.), Roy Boulting.
QUARTET (Brit.), James Ivory.

Best Actor
Broderick Crawford for ALL THE KING'S MEN; 9 votes on 6th ballot.
Ralph Richardson for THE FALLEN IDOL (Brit.) and THE HEIRESS (Brit.); 5 votes.
Juano Hernandez for INTRUDER IN THE DUST.
Mel Ferrer for LOST BOUNDARIES.
Michael Redgrave for FAME IS THE SPUR (Brit).
James Whitmore for BATTLEGROUND.

Best Actress
  Olivia de Havilland for THE HEIRESS; 12 votes on 5th ballot.
  Edith Evans for DOLWYN (Brit.) and QUEEN OF SPADES (Brit.); 5 votes.
  Mercedes McCambridge for ALL THE KING'S MEN.
  Lea Padovani for SALT TO THE DEVIL (Brit.).
  Nora Swinburne for QUARTET (Brit.).
  Judy Holliday for ADAM'S RIB.
  Deborah Kerr for EDWARD MY SON (Brit.).
Best Direction
  Carol Reed for THE FALLEN IDOL (Brit.).
  Clarence Brown for INTRUDER IN THE DUST.
  Robert Rossen for ALL THE KING'S MEN.
  Alfred Werker for LOST BOUNDARIES.
  Roy Boulting for FAME IS THE SPUR (Brit.).
  Mark Robson for HOME OF THE BRAVE and CHAMPION.
  Elia Kazan for PINKY.
Best Foreign Language Film
  BICYCLE THIEF (Ital.), Vittorio de Sica; 13 votes on 1st ballot.
  DEVIL IN THE FLESH (Fr.), Claude Autant-Lara.
  THE LAST STAGE (Pol.), Wanda Jakubowska.
  AFFAIRE BLUM (Ger.), Erich Engel.

1950
Best Film
  ALL ABOUT EVE, Joseph L. Mankiewicz; 11 votes on 1st ballot.
  SUNSET BOULEVARD, Billy Wilder; 3 votes.
  THE ASPHALT JUNGLE, John Huston; 2 votes.
  DEVIL'S DOORWAY, Anthony Mann; 1 vote.
Best Actor
  Gregory Peck for TWELVE O'CLOCK HIGH; 9 votes on 6th ballot.
  Broderick Crawford for BORN YESTERDAY; 6 votes.
  Jose Ferrer for CYRANO DE BERGERC.
  Alec Guinness for KIND HEARTS AND CORONETS (Brit.); 1 vote.
  William Holden for SUNSET BOULEVARD.
  Louis Calhern for THE ASPHALT JUNGLE.
  Sam Jaffe for THE ASPHALT JUNGLE.
  James Stewart for HARVEY.
Best Actress
  Bette Davis for ALL ABOUT EVE; 10 votes on 6th ballot.
  Judy Holliday for BORN YESTERDAY; 6 votes.
  Gloria Swanson for SUNSET BOULEVARD.
Best Direction
  Joseph L. Mankiewicz for ALL ABOUT EVE; 11 votes on 4th ballot.
  John Huston for THE ASPHALT JUNGLE; 3 votes.
  Billy Wilder for SUNSET BOULEVARD; 1 vote.
Best Foreign Language Film
  WAYS OF LOVE (Fr./Ital.) - "The Miracle" by Roberto Rossellini; "Jofroi" by Marcel Pagnol; and "A Day in The Country" by Jean Renoir.

1951
Best Film
  A STREETCAR NAMED DESIRE - Elia Kazan; 8 votes on 6th ballot.
  THE RIVER (India) - Jean Renoir; 7 votes.
  AN AMERICAN IN PARIS - Vincente Minnelli.
  A PLACE IN THE SUN - George Stevens.
  DEATH OF A SALESMAN - Laslo Benedek.
Best Actor
  Arthur Kennedy for LIGHTS OUT; 10 votes on 3rd ballot.
  Marlon Brando for A STREETCAR NAMED DESIRE; 5 votes.
  Fredric March for DEATH OF A SALESMAN.
  Kirk Douglas for DETECTIVE STORY.
  Richard Basehart for FOURTEEN HOURS.
  Charles Laughton for THE BLUE VEIL.
Best Actress
  Vivien Leigh for A STREETCAR NAMED DESIRE; 10 votes on 5th ballot.
  Shelley Winters for A PLACE IN THE SUN; 5 votes.
  Mildred Dunnock for DEATH OF A SALESMAN.
  Katherine Locke for TRY AND GET ME.
Best Direction
  Elia Kazan for A STREETCAR NAMED DESIRE; 9 votes on 6th ballot.
  George Stevens for A PLACE IN THE SUN; 6 votes.
  Jean Renoir for THE RIVER (India).
  William Wyler for DETECTIVE STORY.
Best Foreign Language Film
  MIRACLE IN MILAN (Ital.), Vittorio de Sica; 10 votes on 4th ballot.
  RASHOMON (Jap.), Akira Kurosawa; 5 votes.
  LA MARIE DU PORT (Fr.), Marcel Carne.
  THE SECRET OF MAYERLING (Fr.), M. Delannoy.
  PASSION FOR LIFE (Fr.), Jean-Paul le Chanois.

1952
Best Film
  HIGH NOON, Fred Zinnemann; 10 votes on 6th ballot.
  THE AFRICAN QUEEN (U.S./Brit.), John Huston; 5 votes.
  THE QUIET MAN, John Ford.
  THE GREATEST SHOW ON EARTH, Cecil B. DeMille.
  THE MAN IN THE WHITE SUIT (Brit.), Alexander Mackendrick.
  COME BACK, LITTLE SHEBA, Daniel Mann.
  BREAKING THE SOUND BARRIER (Brit.), David Lean.
  HANS CHRISTIAN ANDERSEN, Charles Vidor.
  SINGIN' IN THE RAIN, Gene Kelly.
Best Actor
  Ralph Richardson for BREAKING THE SOUND BARRIER; 10 votes on 5th ballot.
  Charlie Chaplin for LIMELIGHT (Brit.); 5 votes.
  Laurence Olivier for CARRIE.
  Gary Cooper for HIGH NOON.
  Alec Guinness for THE MAN IN THE WHITE SUIT (Brit.) and THE PROMOTER (Brit.).
  Barry Fitzgerald for THE QUIET MAN.
  Millard Mitchell for MY SIX CONVICTS.
  Marlon Brando for VIVA ZAPATA.

Best Actress
  Shirley Booth for COME BACK, LITTLE SHEBA; 12 votes on 1st ballot.
  Katharine Hepburn for THE AFRICAN QUEEN (U.S./Brit.); 3 votes.
Best Direction
  Fred Zinnemann for HIGH NOON; 10 votes on 2nd ballot.
  John Huston for THE AFRICAN QUEEN (Brit.); 2 votes.
  William Wyler for CARRIE; 1 vote.
  Charlie Chaplin for LIMELIGHT (Brit.); 1 vote.
  Cecil B. DeMille for THE GREATEST SHOW ON EARTH; 1 vote.
  Alexander Mackendrick for THE MAN IN THE WHITE SUIT.
  David Lean for BREAKING THE SOUND BARRIER (Brit.).
Best Foreign Language Film
  FORBIDDEN GAMES (Fr.), Rene Clement; 8 votes on 6th ballot.
  THE WHITE LINE (Ital.), Luigi Zampa.
  TWO CENTS WORTH OF HOPE (Ital.), Renato Castellani.

1953
Best Film
  FROM HERE TO ETERNITY, Fred Zinnemann; 11 votes on 2nd ballot.
  CONQUEST OF EVEREST (Brit.), Thomas Stobart; 2 votes.
  ROMAN HOLIDAY, William Wyler; 1 vote.
  MOULIN ROUGE (Brit.), John Huston.
  THE ROBE, Henry Koster.
Best Actor
  Burt Lancaster for FROM HERE TO ETERNITY.
  James Mason for JULIUS CAESAR.
  John Gielgud for JULIUS CAESAR.
  Spencer Tracy for THE ACTRESS.
  William Holden for STALAG 17.
Best Actress
  Audrey Hepburn for ROMAN HOLIDAY.
  Ava Gardner for MOGAMBO.
  Jean Simmons for THE ACTRESS and YOUNG BESS.
  Anna Magnani for BELLISSIMA (Ital.).
  Leslie Caron for LILI.
  Colette Marchand for MOULIN ROUGE (Brit.).
Best Direction
  Fred Zinnemann for FROM HERE TO ETERNITY.
  George Stevens for SHANE.
  William Wyler for ROMAN HOLIDAY.
  Joseph L. Mankiewicz for JULIUS CAESAR.
  John Huston for MOULIN ROUGE (Brit.).
Best Foreign Language Film
  JUSTICE IS DONE (Fr.), Andre Cayatte.
  THE LITTLE WORLD OF DON CAMILLO (Fr.), Julien Duvivier.
  THE SEVEN DEADLY SINS (Ital.), Various artists.
Special Citations for their Contributions to the Documentary
  A QUEEN IS CROWNED (Brit.).
  THE CONQUEST OF EVEREST (Brit.).

1954
Best Film
  ON THE WATERFRONT, Elia Kazan; 12 votes on 1st ballot.
  THE COUNTRY GIRL, George Seaton; 2 votes.
  ROMEO AND JULIET (Brit./Ital.), Renato Castellani; 1 vote.
  CARMEN JONES, Otto Preminger; 1 vote.
Best Actor
  Marlon Brando for ON THE WATERFRONT; 1st ballot.
  James Mason for A STAR IS BORN; 3 votes.
  Edmond O'Brien for THE BAREFOOT CONTESSA; 1 vote.
  Humphrey Bogart for THE CAINE MUTINY; 1 vote.
Best Actress
  Grace Kelly for THE COUNTRY GIRL, REAR WINDOW, and DIAL M FOR MURDER; 12 votes on 2nd ballot.
  Eva Marie Saint for ON THE WATERFRONT; 1 vote.
  Audrey Hepburn for SABRINA; 1 vote.
  Ava Gardner for THE BAREFOOT CONTESSA.
  Dorothy McGuire for THREE COINS IN THE FOUNTAIN.
  June Allyson for THE GLENN MILLER STORY.
  Dorothy Dandridge for CARMEN JONES.
  Judy Garland for A STAR IS BORN.
Best Direction
  Elia Kazan for ON THE WATERFRONT; 11 votes on 1st ballot.
  George Seaton for THE COUNTRY GIRL.
  Renato Castellani for ROMEO AND JULIET (Brit./Ital.).
  Otto Preminger for CARMEN JONES.
  Alfred Hitchcock for REAR WINDOW.
  Edward Dmytryk for THE CAINE MUTINY.
Best Foreign Language Film
  GATE OF HELL (Jap.), Yeinosuke Kinugasa; 11 votes on 2nd ballot.
  MONSIEUR HULOT'S HOLIDAY (Fr.), Jacques Tati; 5 votes.
  BREAD, LOVE AND DREAMS (Ital.), Luigi Comencini.

1955
Best Film
  MARTY, Delbert Mann; 12 votes on 3rd ballot.
  MISTER ROBERTS, John Ford and Mervyn Le Roy; 4 votes.
  SUMMERTIME, David Lean.
  THE ROSE TATTOO, Daniel Mann.
  OKLAHOMA, Fred Zinnemann.
Best Actor
  Ernest Borgnine for MARTY; 9 votes on 6th ballot.
  Frank Sinatra for THE MAN WITH THE GOLDEN ARM; 4 votes.
  Alec Guinness for THE PRISONER; 3 votes.
  Jose Ferrer for THE SHRIKE.
  Spencer Tracy for BAD DAY AT BLACK ROCK.
  Jack Hawkins for THE PRISONER (Brit.).
  Fredric March for THE DESPERATE HOURS.
  Richard Todd for A MAN CALLED PETER.
  James Cagney for LOVE ME OR LEAVE ME.

Best Actress
Anna Magnani for THE ROSE TATOO; 13 votes on 1st ballot.
Katharine Hepburn for SUMMERTIME; 2 votes.
Jennifer Jones for LOVE IS A MANY SPLENDORED THING; 1 vote.
Best Direction
David Lean for SUMMERTIME; 9 votes on 6th ballot.
William Wyler for THE DESPERATE HOURS; 1 vote.
Delbert Mann for MARTY.
John Sturges for BAD DAY AT BLACK ROCK.
John Ford and Mervyn Le Roy for MISTER ROBERTS.
Otto Preminger for THE COURT MARTIAL OF BILLY MITCHELL and THE MAN WITH THE GOLDEN ARM.
Daniel Mann for THE ROSE TATTOO.
Peter Glenville for THE PRISONER (Brit.).
Nicholas Ray for REBEL WITHOUT A CAUSE.
Best Foreign Language Film
UMBERTO D (Ital.), Vittorio de Sica; 5 votes.
LES DIABOLIQUES (Fr.), Henri-Georges Clouzot; 5 votes.
LETTERS FROM MY WINDMILL (Fr.), Marcel Pagnol; 3 votes.
THE GREAT ADVENTURE (Swed.), Arne Sucksdorf; 2 votes.
THE SHEEP HAS FIVE LEGS (Fr.), Henri Verneuil; 1 vote.

1956
Best Film
AROUND THE WORLD IN 80 DAYS, Michael Anderson and Kevin McClory; 2nd ballot.
GIANT, George Stevens.
THE KING AND I, Walter Lang.
LUST FOR LIFE, Vincente Minnelli.
MOBY DICK (Brit.), John Huston.
Best Actor
Kirk Douglas for LUST FOR LIFE; 11 votes on 6th ballot.
Yul Brynner for THE KING AND I; 3 votes.
Laurence Olivier for RICHARD III (Brit.); 2 votes.
James Dean for GIANT.
Gregory Peck for MOBY DICK (Brit.).
Eli Wallach for BABY DOLL.
Best Actress
Ingrid Bergman for ANASTASIA; 13 votes on 3rd ballot.
Deborah Kerr for THE KING AND I; 2 votes.
Audrey Hepburn for WAR AND PEACE (U.S./Ital.).
Carroll Baker for BABY DOLL.
Best Direction
John Huston for MOBY DICK (Brit.).
Elia Kazan for BABY DOLL.
Walter Lang for THE KING AND I.
Anatole Litvak for ANASTASIA.
Alfred Hitchcock for THE WRONG MAN.
Michael Anderson for AROUND THE WORLD IN 80 DAYS.
Best Screenwriting
AROUND THE WORLD IN 80 DAYS by S.J. Perelman, James Poe, and John Farrow, based on a novel by Jules Verne.
Best Foreign Language Film
LA STRADA (Ital.), Federico Fellini; 12 votes on 1st ballot.

1957
Best Film
THE BRIDGE ON THE RIVER KWAI (Brit.), David Lean; 13 votes on 2nd ballot.
TWELVE ANGRY MEN, Sidney Lumet; 2 votes.
SAYONARA, Joshua Logan; 1 vote.
A HATFUL OF RAIN, Fred Zinnemann.
HEAVEN KNOWS MR. ALLISON, John Huston.
Best Actor
Alec Guinness for THE BRIDGE ON THE RIVER KWAI; 10 votes on 6th ballot.
Marlon Brando for SAYONARA; 6 votes.
James Cagney for THE MAN OF 1,000 FACES.
Henry Fonda for TWELVE ANGRY MEN.
Robert Mitchum for HEAVEN KNOWS MR. ALLISON.
Anthony Franciosa for A HATFUL OF RAIN.
James Stewart for THE SPIRIT OF ST. LOUIS.
Sidney Poitier for SOMETHING OF VALUE.
Best Actress
Deborah Kerr for HEAVEN KNOWS MR. ALLISON; 12 votes on 5th ballot.
Eva Marie Saint for A HATFUL OF RAIN; 3 votes.
Anna Magnani for WILD IS THE WIND.
Kay Kendall for LES GIRLS; 1 vote.
Audrey Hepburn for LOVE IN THE AFTERNOON.
Best Direction
David Lean for THE BRIDGE ON THE RIVER KWAI; 13 votes on 6th ballot.
Sidney Lumet for TWELVE ANGRY MEN; 3 votes.
Joshua Logan for SAYONARA.
John Sturges for GUNFIGHT AT THE O.K. CORRAL.
Best Foreign Language Film
GERVAISE (Fr.), Rene Clement; 8 votes on 6th ballot.
THE RED BALLOON (Fr.), Albert Lamorisse; 5 votes.
ORDET (Den.), Carl Dreyer; 3 votes.
THE GOLD OF NAPLES (Ital.), Vittorio de Sica.
ARE WE ALL MURDERERS (Fr.), Andre Cayatte.
THE NIGHTS OF CABIRIA (Ital.), Federico Fellini.
THE LAST BRIDGE (Aust./Yugo.), Helmut Kautner.
TORERO (Mex.), Carlos Velo.

1958
Best Film
THE DEFIANT ONES, Stanley Kramer; 10 votes on 3rd ballot.
THE HORSE'S MOUTH (Brit.), Ronald Neame.
SEPARATE TABLES, Delbert Mann; 5 votes.
THE LAST HURRAH, John Ford.
GIGI, Vincente Minnelli.
HOT SPELL, William Wyler.

Best Actor
David Niven for SEPARATE TABLES; 8 votes on 6th ballot.
Alec Guinness for THE HORSE'S MOUTH; 7 votes.
Spencer Tracy for THE LAST HURRAH and THE OLD MAN AND THE SEA.
Sidney Poitier for THE DEFIANT ONES.
Anthony Quinn for HOT SPELL.
Best Actress
Susan Hayward for I WANT TO LIVE; 4th ballot.
Shirley Booth for HOT SPELL and THE MATCHMAKER.
Joanne Woodward for THE LONG HOT SUMMER.
Elizabeth Taylor for CAT ON A HOT TIN ROOF.
Kim Stanley for THE GODDESS.
Deborah Kerr for SEPARATE TABLES.
Rosalind Russell for AUNTIE MAME.
Jean Simmons for HOME BEFORE DARK.
Best Direction
Stanley Kramer for THE DEFIANT ONES; 4th ballot.
Richard Brooks for THE BROTHERS KARAMAZOV.
Delbert Mann for SEPARATE TABLES.
John Ford for THE LAST HURRAH.
Robert Wise for I WANT TO LIVE.
Daniel Mann for HOT SPELL.
Vincente Minnelli for GIGI.
Best Screenwriting
THE DEFIANT ONES by Nathan E. Douglas and Jacob Smith; 6th ballot.
SEPARATE TABLES by Terence Rattigan and John Gay based on a play by Rattigan.
THE GODDESS by Paddy Chayevsky.
Best Foreign Language Film
MY UNCLE (Fr.), Jacques Tati; on 6th ballot.
HE WHO MUST DIE (Fr.), Jules Dassin.
PATHER PANCHALI (India), Satyajit Ray.

1959
Best Film
BEN-HUR, William Wyler and Andrew Marton; 10 votes on 5th ballot.
ROOM AT THE TOP (Brit.), Jack Clayton; 5 votes.
ON THE BEACH, Stanley Kramer.
ANATOMY OF A MURDER, Otto Preminger.
THE NUN'S STORY, Fred Zinnemann.
SUDDENLY, LAST SUMMER (Brit.), Joseph L. Mankiewicz.
CAREER, Joseph Anthony.
THE DIARY OF ANNE FRANK, George Stevens.
Best Actor
James Stewart for ANATOMY OF A MURDER; 10 votes on 5th ballot.
Paul Muni for THE LAST ANGRY MAN; 5 votes.
Charlton Heston for BEN-HUR.
Laurence Harvey for ROOM AT THE TOP (Brit.).
Joseph N. Welch for ANATOMY OF A MURDER.
Jack Lemmon for SOME LIKE IT HOT.
Orson Welles for COMPULSION.
Richard Burton for LOOK BACK IN ANGER (Brit.).
Best Actress
Audrey Hepburn for THE NUN'S STORY; 8 votes on 6th ballot.
Simone Signoret for ROOM AT THE TOP (Brit.); 7 votes.
Millie Perkins for DIARY OF ANNE FRANK.
Lee Remick for ANATOMY OF A MURDER.
Elizabeth Taylor for SUDDENLY, LAST SUMMER (Brit.).
Best Direction
Fred Zinnemann for THE NUN'S STORY; 8 votes on 6th ballot.
Jack Clayton for ROOM AT THE TOP (Brit.); 5 votes.
William Wyler for BEN-HUR; 1 vote.
Basil Dearden for SAPPHIRE (Brit.); 1 vote.
Alfred Hitchcock for NORTH BY NORTHWEST.
Otto Preminger for ANATOMY OF A MURDER.
George Stevens for THE DIARY OF ANNE FRANK.
Joseph L. Mankiewicz for SUDDENLY, LAST SUMMER (Brit.).
Joseph Anthony for CAREER.
Best Screenwriting
ANATOMY OF A MURDER by Wendell Mayes, based on a book by Robert Traver; 10 votes on 3rd ballot.
BEN-HUR by Karl Tunberg; 3 votes.
THE DIARY OF ANNE FRANK by Francis Goodrich and Albert Hackett, from the actual diaries.
SAPPHIRE (Brit.) by Janet Green.
ROOM AT THE TOP (Brit.) by Neil Paterson, based on a novel by John Braine.
CAREER by James Lee.
LOOK BACK IN ANGER (Brit.) by Nigel Kneale, based on a play by John Osborne.
SUDDENLY, LAST SUMMER (Brit.) by Gore Vidal, based on a play by Tennessee Williams.
Best Foreign Language Film
THE 400 BLOWS (Fr.), Francois Truffaut; 12 votes on 3rd ballot.
BLACK ORPHEUS (Fr./Ital.), Marcel Camus; 3 votes.
WILD STRAWBERRIES (Swed.), Ingmar Bergman.
APARJITO (India), Satyajit Ray.
THE MAGICIAN (Swed.), Ingmar Bergman.
IVAN THE TERRIBLE PART II (USSR), Sergei Eisenstein.

1960
Best Film
THE APARTMENT, Billy Wilder.
SONS AND LOVERS (Brit.), Jack Cardiff.
ELMER GANTRY, Richard Brooks.
SUNRISE AT CAMPOBELLO, Vincent J. Donehue.
EXODUS, Otto Preminger.
INHERIT THE WIND, Stanley Kramer.
PSYCHO, Alfred Hitchcock.
TUNES OF GLORY (Brit.), Ronald Neame.
Best Actor
Burt Lancaster for ELMER GANTRY.
Trevor Howard for SONS AND LOVERS (Brit.).

Fredric March for INHERIT THE WIND.
Alec Guinness for TUNES OF GLORY (Brit.).
John Mills for TUNES OF GLORY (Brit.).
Jack Lemmon for THE APARTMENT.
Laurence Olivier for THE ENTERTAINER (Brit.).
James Cagney for THE GALLANT HOURS.
Best Actress
Deborah Kerr for THE SUNDOWNERS (Brit./Aus.).
Melina Mercouri for NEVER ON SUNDAY (Gr.).
Greer Garson for SUNRISE AT CAMPOBELLO.
Shirley MacLaine for THE APARTMENT.
Wendy Hiller for SONS AND LOVERS (Brit.).
Hayley Mills for POLLYANNA.
Luana Patton for HOME FROM THE HILL.
Jean Simmons for ELMER GANTRY.
Best Direction
Billy Wilder for THE APARTMENT.
Jack Cardiff for SONS AND LOVERS (Brit.).
Fred Zinnemann for THE SUNDOWNERS (Brit./Aus.)
Ronald Neame for TUNES OF GLORY (Brit.).
Richard Brooks for ELMER GANTRY.
Stanley Kramer for INHERIT THE WIND.
Best Screenwriting
THE APARTMENT by Billy Wilder and I.A.L. Diamond.
SONS AND LOVERS (Brit.) by Gavin Lambert and T.E.B. Clark, based on a novel by
D.H. Lawrence.
ELMER GANTRY by Richard Brooks.
TUNES OF GLORY (Brit.) by James Kennaway, from his novel.
THE ANGRY SILENCE (Brit.) by Bryan Forbes, based on a story by Michael Craig
and Richard Gregson.
INHERIT THE WIND by Nathan E. Douglas and Harold Jacob Smith, based on the
play by Jerome Lawrence.
Best Foreign Language Film
HIROSHIMA MON AMOUR (Fr./Ital.), Alain Resnais; 11 votes on 3rd ballot.
GENERAL DELLA ROVERE (Ital./Fr.), Roberto Rossellini.
THE VIRGIN SPRING (Swed.), Ingmar Bergman.
NEVER ON SUNDAY (Gr.), Jules Dassin.
BIG DEAL ON MADONNA STREET (Ital.), Mario Monicelli.
IKURU (Jap.), Akira Kurosawa.
BALLAD OF A SOLDIER (USSR), Grigori Chukrai.
THE WORLD OF APU (India), Satyajit Ray.

1961
Best Film
WEST SIDE STORY, Robert Wise; 11 votes on 3rd ballot.
JUDGMENT AT NUREMBERG, Stanley Kramer.
LOSS OF INNOCENCE (Brit.), Lewis Gilbert.
THE GUNS OF NAVARONE (Brit.), J. Lee Thompson.
A RAISIN IN THE SUN, Daniel Petrie.
SATURDAY NIGHT AND SUNDAY MORNING (Brit.), Karel Reisz.
THE MARK (Brit.), Guy Green.
Best Actor
Maximilian Schell for JUDGMENT AT NUREMBERG.
James Cagney for ONE, TWO, THREE; 4 votes.
Paul Newman for THE HUSTLER.
Best Actress
Sophia Loren for TWO WOMEN (Fr./Ital.); 11 votes.
Geraldine Page for SUMMER AND SMOKE; 7 votes.
Piper Laurie for THE HUSTLER; 1 vote.
Best Direction
Robert Rossen for THE HUSTLER.
Robert Wise and Jerome Robbins for WEST SIDE STORY.
Stanley Kramer for JUDGMENT AT NUREMBERG.
Guy Green for THE MARK.
John Ford for TWO RODE TOGETHER.
Billy Wilder for ONE, TWO, THREE.
Karel Reisz for SATURDAY NIGHT AND SUNDAY MORNING.
Best Screenwriting
JUDGMENT AT NUREMBERG by Abby Mann, based on a television play.
ONE, TWO, THREE by Billy Wilder and I.A.C. Diamond, based on a play by Ferenc
Molnar.
THE MARK by Sidney Buchman and Stanley Mann.
THE MISFITS by Arthur Miller.
THE HUSTLER by Robert Rossen and Sidney Carrol, based on a novel by Walter
Tevis.
SATURDAY NIGHT AND SUNDAY MORNING by Alan Sillitoe based on his novel.
THE INNOCENTS by William Archibald and Truman Capote.
A RAISIN IN THE SUN by Lorraine Hansbury, based on her play.
WEST SIDE STORY by Ernest Lehman, based on a play by Arthur Laurents.
Best Foreign Language Film
LA DOLCE VITA (Fr./Ital.), Federico Fellini; on 3rd ballot.
TWO WOMEN (Fr./Ital.), Vittorio de Sica.
L'AVVENTURA (Ital.), Michelangelo Antonioni.

1962
Awards presentation cancelled because of the the New York newspaper strike.

1963
Best Film
TOM JONES (Brit.), Tony Richardson.
HUD, Martin Ritt.
TO KILL A MOCKINGBIRD, Robert Mulligan.
IT'S A MAD, MAD, MAD, MAD WORLD, Stanley Kramer.
THE BIRDS, Alfred Hitchcock.
Best Actor
Albert Finney for TOM JONES (Brit.).
Sidney Poitier for LILIES OF THE FIELD.
Melvyn Douglas for HUD.
Paul Newman for HUD.
Richard Harris for THIS SPORTING LIFE (Brit.).
Gregory Peck for TO KILL A MOCKINGBIRD.
Jason Robards, Jr. for ACT ONE.

Best Actress
Patricia Neal for HUD.
Leslie Caron for THE L-SHAPED ROOM (Brit.).
Best Direction
Tony Richardson for TOM JONES.
Martin Ritt for HUD.
Alfred Hitchcock for THE BIRDS.
Stanley Kramer for IT'S A MAD, MAD, MAD, MAD WORLD.
Ralph Nelson for LILIES OF THE FIELD.
John Schlesinger for BILLY LIAR (Brit.).
Best Screenwriting
HUD by Irving Ravetch and Harriet Frank, Jr., based on a novel by Larry McMurtry.
TO KILL A MOCKINGBIRD by Horton Foote, based on a novel by Harper Lee.
IT'S A MAD, MAD, MAD, MAD WORLD by William and Tania Rose
THIS SPORTING LIFE (Brit.) by David Storey.
THE L-SHAPED ROOM (Brit.) by Bryan Forbes, based on a novel by Lynn Reid
Banks.
IRMA LA DOUCE by Billy Wilder and I.A.L. Diamond.
Best Foreign Language Film
8 1/2 (Ital.), Federico Fellini.
THE SOUND OF TRUMPETS (Ital.), Ermanno Olmi.
THE ELUSIVE CORPORAL (Fr.), Jean Renoir.
THE EASY LIFE (Ital.), Dino Risi.
THE DEVIL (Ital.), Gian Luigi Polidoro.
THE IMPORTANT MAN (Mex.), Ismael Rodriguez.

1964
Best Film
MY FAIR LADY, George Cukor; 8 votes on 4th ballot.
DR. STRANGELOVE: OR HOW I LEARNED TO STOP WORRYING AND LOVE
THE BOMB (Brit.), Stanley Kubrick; 5 votes.
THE SERVANT (Brit.), Joseph Losey.
ZORBA THE GREEK (U.S./Gr.), Michael Cacoyannis.
BECKET (Brit.), Peter Glenville.
Best Actor
Rex Harrison for MY FAIR LADY; 7 votes on 6th ballot.
Dirk Bogarde for THE SERVANT (Brit.); 6 votes.
Richard Attenborough for SEANCE ON A WET AFTERNOON (Brit.).
Marcello Mastroianni for THE ORGANIZER (Ital.).
Sterling Hayden for DR. STRANGELOVE (Brit.).
George C. Scott for DR. STRANGELOVE (Brit.).
Peter O'Toole for BECKET (Brit.).
Richard Burton for BECKET (Brit.).
Anthony Quinn for ZORBA THE GREEK.
Harry H. Corbett for RATTLE OF A SIMPLE MAN (Brit.).
Best Actress
Kim Stanley for SEANCE ON A WET AFTERNOON (Brit.).
Julie Andrews for MARY POPPINS.
Sophia Loren for MARRIAGE, ITALIAN STYLE (Ital.).
Audrey Hepburn for MY FAIR LADY.
Barbara Barrie for ONE POTATO, TWO POTATO.
Best Direction
*Stanley Kubrick for DR. STRANGELOVE: OR HOW I LEARNED TO STOP
WORRYING AND LOVE THE BOMB (Brit.).*
George Cukor for MY FAIR LADY.
Joseph Losey for THE SERVANT (Brit.).
Michael Cacoyannis for ZORBA THE GREEK.
Sidney Lumet for FAIL SAFE.
Peter Glenville for BECKET (Brit.).
Best Screenwriting
THE SERVANT (Brit.) by Harold Pinter.
THE AMERICANIZATION OF EMILY by Paddy Chayevsky, based on a novel by
William Bradford.
GOLDFINGER (Brit.) by Richard Maibaum and Paul Dehn, based on a novel by Ian
Fleming.
ZORBA THE GREEK by Michael Cacoyannis, based on a novel by Nikos Kazantzakis.
MY FAIR LADY by Alan Jay Lerner, based on the play "Pygmalion" by George
Bernard Shaw.
Best Foreign Language Film
THAT MAN FROM RIO (Fr./Ital.), Philippe de Broca.
SEDUCED AND ABANDONED (Fr./Ital.), Pietro Germi.
THE ORGANIZER (Fr./Ital./Yugo.), Mario Monicelli.
THE UMBRELLAS OF CHERBOURG (Fr./Ger.), Jacques Demy.
MARRIAGE - ITALIAN STYLE (Ital.), Vittorio de Sica.
YESTERDAY, TODAY AND TOMORROW (Ital.), Vittorio de Sica.
Special Citation

Johnson's Wax for the production of TO BE ALIVE, produced by Francis Thompson
and Alexander Hammid.

1965
Best Film
DARLING (Brit.), John Schlesinger; 8 votes on 6th ballot.
THE PAWNBROKER, Sidney Lumet; 5 votes.
THOSE MAGNIFICENT MEN IN THEIR FLYING MACHINES (Brit.), Ken Anna-
kin.
A THOUSAND CLOWNS, Fred Coe.
THE KNACK (Brit.), Richard Lester.
DOCTOR ZHIVAGO, David Lean.
SHIP OF FOOLS, Stanley Kramer.
THE COLLECTOR, William Wyler.
Best Actor
Oskar Werner for SHIP OF FOOLS; 11 votes on 3rd ballot.
Laurence Harvey for DARLING (Brit.).
Rod Steiger for THE PAWNBROKER; 3 votes.
Lee Marvin for CAT BALLOU; 3 votes.
Richard Widmark for THE BEDFORD INCIDENT.
Sean Connery for THE HILL (Brit.).
Terence Stamp for THE COLLECTOR.
Rex Harrison for THE AGONY AND THE ECSTASY.

Best Actress
Julie Christie for DARLING (Brit.); 11 votes on 3rd ballot.
Julie Andrews for THE SOUND OF MUSIC; 4 votes.
Catherine Deneuve for REPULSION (Brit.); 1 vote.
Vivien Leigh for SHIP OF FOOLS.
Rita Tushingham for THE KNACK (Brit.) and THE LEATHER BOYS (Brit.).
Simone Signoret for SHIP OF FOOLS.
Elizabeth Hartman for A PATCH OF BLUE.
Geraldine Chaplin for DOCTOR ZHIVAGO.
Best Direction
John Schlesinger for DARLING (Brit.); 10 votes on 6th ballot.
Roman Polanski for REPULSION (Brit.).
David Lean for DOCTOR ZHIVAGO.
Sidney Lumet for THE PAWNBROKER and THE HILL (Brit.).
Stanley Kramer for SHIP OF FOOLS.
Sidney Furie for THE IPCRESS FILE (Brit.) and THE LEATHER BOYS (Brit.).
William Wyler for THE COLLECTOR.
Best Screenwriting
(After 6 ballots DARLING and SHIP OF FOOLS were tied and the Critics Circle decided against having the award shared between two films, so no award was given.)
DARLING (Brit.) by Frederic Raphael.
SHIP OF FOOLS by Abby Mann, based on a novel by Katherine Anne Porter.
REPULSION (Brit.) by Roman Polanski and Gerard Brach.
THE LEATHER BOYS (Brit.) by Gillian Freeman, based on a novel by Elliott George.
KING RAT by Bryan Forbes, based on a novel by James Clavell.
DOCTOR ZHIVAGO by Robert Bolt, based on a novel by Boris Pasternak.
HELP (Brit.) by Charles Wood and Marc Bohm.
THE SPY WHO CAME IN FROM THE COLD (Brit.) by Paul Dehn and Guy Trosper based on a novel by John Le Carre.
A THOUSAND CLOWNS by Herb Gardner, based on his play.
Best Foreign Language Film
JULIET OF THE SPIRITS (Fr./Ital./Ger.), Federico Fellini; 11 votes on 2nd ballot.
THE RED DESERT (Ital./Fr.), Michelangelo Antonioni; 2 votes.
SALLAH (Israel), Ephraim Kishon.
LIFE UPSIDE DOWN (Fr.), Alain Jessua.
KWAIDAN (Jap.), Masaki Kobayashi.
VIVA MARIA (Fr.), Louis Malle.
A MARRIED WOMAN (Fr.), Jean-Luc Godard.

1966
Best Film
A MAN FOR ALL SEASONS (Brit.), Fred Zinnemann; 10 votes on 1st ballot.
WHO'S AFRAID OF VIRGINIA WOOLF?, Mike Nichols.
BLOW-UP (Brit./Ital.), Michelangelo Antonioni.
Best Actor
Paul Scofield for A MAN FOR ALL SEASONS (Brit.).
Richard Burton for WHO'S AFRAID OF VIRGINIA WOOLF?
Alan Arkin for THE RUSSIANS ARE COMING, THE RUSSIANS ARE COMING.
Best Actress
Lynn Redgrave for GEORGY GIRL (Brit.).
Elizabeth Taylor for WHO'S AFRAID OF VIRGINIA WOOLF?
Ida Kaminska for THE SHOP ON MAIN STREET (Czech.).
Vanessa Redgrave for MORGAN! (Brit.).
Wendy Hiller for A MAN FOR ALL SEASONS (Brit.).
Best Direction
Fred Zinnemann for A MAN FOR ALL SEASONS (Brit.).
Edward Albee for WHO'S AFRAID OF VIRGINIA WOOLF?
Michelangelo Antonioni for BLOW-UP (Brit.).
Karel Reisz for MORGAN! (Brit.).
Jan Kadar and Elmar Klos for THE SHOP ON MAIN STREET (Czech.).
Best Screenwriting
A MAN FOR ALL SEASONS (Brit.) by Robert Bolt.
MORGAN! (Brit.) by David Mercer.
Best Foreign Language Film
THE SHOP ON MAIN STREET (Czech.), Jan Kadar and Elmar Klos; 11 votes on 1st ballot.
THE GOSPEL ACCORDING TO ST. MATTHEW (Fr./Ital.), Pier Paolo Pasolini; 2 votes.
A MAN AND A WOMAN (Fr.), Claude Lelouch; 1 vote.

1967
Best Film
IN THE HEAT OF THE NIGHT, Norman Jewison; on 6th ballot.
BONNIE AND CLYDE, Arthur Penn.
ULYSSES (Brit./U.S.), Joseph Strick.
IN COLD BLOOD, Richard Brooks.
GUESS WHO'S COMING TO DINNER?, Stanley Kramer.
THE GRADUATE, Mike Nichols.
Best Actor
Rod Steiger for IN THE HEAT OF THE NIGHT.
Spencer Tracy for GUESS WHO'S COMING TO DINNER?
Yves Montand for THE WAR IS OVER (Fr./Swed.).
Paul Newman for COOL HAND LUKE.
Dustin Hoffman for THE GRADUATE.
Best Actress
Edith Evans for THE WHISPERERS (Brit.).
Sandy Dennis for UP THE DOWN STAIRCASE.
Annie Girardot for LIVE FOR LIFE (Fr./Ital.).
Audrey Hepburn for WAIT UNTIL DARK.
Anne Jackson for THE TIGER MAKES OUT.
Barbara Jefford for ULYSSES (Brit.).
Jo Van Fleet for COOL HAND LUKE.
Best Direction
Mike Nichols for THE GRADUATE.
Arthur Penn for BONNIE AND CLYDE.
Norman Jewison for IN THE HEAT OF THE NIGHT.
Richard Brooks for IN COLD BLOOD.
Alain Resnais for THE WAR IS OVER (Fr./Swed.).
Best Screenwriting
BONNIE AND CLYDE by David Newman and Robert Benton.

THE GRADUATE by Calder Willingham and Buck Henry from the novel by Charles Webb.
TWO FOR THE ROAD by Frederic Raphael.
ULYSSES (Brit.) by Joseph Strick, based on a novel by James Joyce.
HOW I WON THE WAR (Brit.) by Charles Wood, based on a novel by Patrick Ryan.
CLOSELY WATCHED TRAINS (Czech.) by Jiri Menzel, based on a novel by Bohumil Hrabal.
IN THE HEAT OF THE NIGHT by Stirling Silliphant.
THE WAR IS OVER (Fr./Swed.) by Jorge Semprun.
Best Foreign Language Film
THE WAR IS OVER (Fr./Swed.), Alain Resnais.
ELVIRA MADIGAN (Swed.), Bo Weiderberg.
THE BATTLE OF ALGIERS (Alg./Ital.), Gillo Pontecorvo.
THE HUNT (Span.), Carlos Saura.
CLOSELY WATCHED TRAINS (Czech.), Jiri Menzel.
LA VIE DE CHATEAU (Fr.), Jean-Paul Rappeneau.
Special Award
New York Times film reviewer Bosley Crowther.

1968
Best Film
THE LION IN WINTER (Brit.), Anthony Harvey; 13 votes on 6th ballot.
FACES, John Cassavetes; 11 votes.
OLIVER! (Brit.), Carol Reed.
2001: A SPACE ODYSSEY (Brit.), Stanley Kubrick.
RACHEL, RACHEL, Paul Newman.
THE SEAGULL (U.S./Brit.), Sidney Lumet.
THE FIXER, John Frankenheimer.
SECRET CEREMONY (Brit.), Joseph Losey.
Best Actor
Alan Arkin for THE HEART IS A LONELY HUNTER; 13 votes.
George C. Scott for PETULIA; 8 votes.
Peter O'Toole for THE LION IN WINTER (Brit.); 2 votes.
Per Oscarsson for HUNGER (Den.).
Best Actress
Joanne Woodward for RACHEL, RACHEL; 18 votes on 3rd ballot.
Tuesday Weld for PRETTY POISON; 5 votes.
Barbara Streisand for FUNNY GIRL.
Billie Whitelaw for CHARLIE BUBBLES.
Beryl Reid for THE KILLING OF SISTER GEORGE.
Liv Ullman for SHAME (Swed.).
Patricia Neal for THE SUBJECT WAS ROSES.
Maggie Smith for HOT MILLIONS.
Lynn Carlin for FACES.
Katharine Hepburn for THE LION IN WINTER (Brit.).
Best Direction
Paul Newman for RACHEL, RACHEL; 11 votes on 6th ballot.
John Cassavetes for FACES; 9 votes.
Carol Reed for OLIVER! (Brit.); 3 votes.
Stanley Kubrick for 2001: A SPACE ODYSSEY (Brit.).
Anthony Harvey for A LION IN WINTER (Brit.).
Allen King for WARRENDALE.
Mel Brooks for THE PRODUCERS.
Joseph McGrath for THE BLISS OF MRS. BLOSSOM (Brit.).
Michael Sarne for JOANNA.
John Frankenheimer for THE FIXER.
Peter Yates for BULLITT.
Robert Ellis Miller for THE HEART IS A LONELY HUNTER.
Best Screenwriting
PRETTY POISON by Lorenzo Semple, based on his novel; 10 votes on 6th ballot.
THE LION IN WINTER (Brit.) by John Goldman, based on his play; 8 votes.
FACES by John Cassavetes.
THE PRODUCERS by Mel Brooks.
THE BIRTHDAY PARTY (Brit.) by Harold Pinter, based on his play.
THE CHARGE OF THE LIGHT BRIGADE (Brit.) by Charles Wood.
THE HEART IS A LONELY HUNTER by Thomas C. Ryan, based on a novel by Carson McCullers.
RACHEL, RACHEL by Stewart Stern, based on a novel by Margaret Laurence.
2001: A SPACE ODYSSEY (Brit.) by Stanley Kubrick and Arthur C. Clarke, based on a story by Clarke.
CHARLIE BUBBLES (Brit.) by Shelagh Delaney.
Best Foreign Language Film
WAR AND PEACE (USSR), Sergei Bondarchuk; 12 votes on 7th ballot.
SHAME (Swed.), Ingmar Bergman; 11 votes.
BELLE DE JOUR (Fr./Ital.), Luis Bunuel.
WEEKEND (Fr./Ital.), Jean-Luc Godard.
HOUR OF THE WOLF (Swed.), Ingmar Bergman.
LES CARABINIERS (Fr./Ital.), Jean-Luc Godard.
THE TWO OF US (Fr.), Claude Berri.

1969
In 1969 a new balloting system was initiated. Critics cast one vote in each category on the first ballot, but if there is no majority, on the second ballot, they assign points (from one to three) for several choices.
Best Film
Z (Fr./Alg.), Constantin Costa-Gavras; 39 pts. on 2nd ballot.
OH! WHAT A LOVELY WAR (Brit.), Richard Attenborough; 18 pts.
THE DAMNED (Ital./Ger.), Luchino Visconti; 17 pts.
MIDNIGHT COWBOY, John Schlesinger; 15 pts.
EASY RIDER, Dennis Hopper; 9 pts.
STOLEN KISSES (Fr.), Francois Truffaut; 4 pts.
ADALEN 31 (Swed.), Bo Widerberg; 2 pts.
THE WILD BUNCH, Sam Peckinpah; 2 pts.
THEY SHOOT HORSES, DON'T THEY?, Sydney Pollack; 2 pts.
LA FEMME INFIDELE (Fr.), Claude Chabrol; 2 pts.
THE SECRET OF SANTA VITTORIA, Stanley Kramer; 2 pts.
MEDIUM COOL, Haskell Wexler; 2 pts.
IF (Brit.), Lindsay Anderson; 2 pts.
Best Actor
Jon Voight for MIDNIGHT COWBOY; 34 pts.

Dustin Hoffman for MIDNIGHT COWBOY; 28 pts.
Robert Redford for DOWNHILL RACER; 18 pts.
Nicol Williamson for HAMLET (Brit.); 10 pts.
Helmut Berger for THE DAMNED (Ital./Ger.); 9 pts.
Jean-Louis Trintignant for Z (Fr./Alg.); 7 pts.
Peter O'Toole for GOODBYE MR. CHIPS (Brit.); 6 pts.
John Wayne for TRUE GRIT; 4 pts.
Richard Benjamin, Anthony Quinn, Henry Fonda, and Elliott Gould each received one point.

Best Actress
Jane Fonda for THEY SHOOT HORSES, DON'T THEY?; 38 pts.
Vanessa Redgrave for ISADORA (Brit.); 24 pts.
Maggie Smith for OH! WHAT A LOVELY WAR (Brit.); 23 pts.
Liza Minnelli for THE STERILE CUCKOO; 17 pts.
Barbra Streisand for HELLO, DOLLY!; 4 pts.
Geraldine Page for TRILOGY; 2 pts.
Jean Simmons for THE HAPPY ENDING; 2 pts.
Pat Quinn for ALICE'S RESTAURANT; 2 pts.
Verna Bloom for MEDIUM COOL; 2 pts.
Dyan Cannon for BOB & CAROL & TED & ALICE; 1 pt.
Ingrid Thulin for ADALEN 31 (Swed.); 1 pt.

Best Supporting Actor
Jack Nicholson for EASY RIDER; 17 votes on 1st ballot.
Elliott Gould for BOB & CAROL & TED & ALICE; 2 votes.
Robert Blake for TELL THEM WILLIE BOY IS HERE; 1 vote.
Dustin Hoffman for MIDNIGHT COWBOY; 1 vote.
Gene Hackman for DOWNHILL RACERS; 1 vote.
Gig Young for THEY SHOOT HORSES, DON'T THEY?; 1 vote.
Helmut Berger for THE DAMNED (Ital./Ger.); 1 vote.
Brian Keith for GAILY, GAILY; 1 vote.

Best Supporting Actress
Dyan Cannon for BOB & CAROL & TED & ALICE; 23 pts. on 2nd ballot.
Cathy Burns for LAST SUMMER; 19 pts.
Delphine Seyrig for STOLEN KISSES (Fr.); 16 pts.
Goldie Hawn for CACTUS FLOWER; 15 pts.
Maggie Smith for OH! WHAT A LOVELY WAR (Brit.); 12 pts.
Irene Papas for Z (Fr./Alg.); 6 pts.
Verna Bloom for MEDIUM COOL; 6 pts.
Pat Quinn for ALICE'S RESTAURANT; 6 pts.
Bonnie Bedelia, Rita Moreno, Shelley Winters, Ingrid Thulin, and Sylvia Miles each received a point.

Best Direction
Constantin Costa-Gavras for Z (Fr./Alg.); 34 pts. on 2nd ballot.
Richard Attenborough for OH! WHAT A LOVELY WAR (Brit.); 24 pts.
Luchino Visconti for THE DAMNED (Ital./Ger.); 13 pts.
Francois Truffaut for STOLEN KISSES (Fr.); 10 pts.
Lindsay Anderson for IF (Brit.); 9 pts.
Claude Chabrol for LA FEMME INFIDELE (Fr.); 8 pts.
Sam Peckinpah for THE WILD BUNCH; 3 pts.
Bo Widerberg for ADALEN 31 (Swed.); 3 pts.
Haskell Wexler for MEDIUM COOL; 3 pts.
John Schlesinger for MIDNIGHT COWBOY; 3 pts.
Tony Richardson for HAMLET (Brit.); 2 pts.
Jean-Luc Godard for PIERROT LE FOU (Fr.); 2 pts.
Gene Kelly for HELLO, DOLLY!; 1 pt.

Best Screenwriting
BOB & CAROL & TED & ALICE by Larry Tucker and Paul Mazursky; 14 pts.
STOLEN KISSES (Fr.) by Francois Truffaut, Claude de Givray, and Bernard Revon; 12 pts.
THE DAMNED (Ital./Ger.) by Nicola Badalucco, Enrico Medioli, and Luchino Visconti; 12 pts.
Z (Fr./Alg.) by Constantin Costa-Gavras and Jorge Semprun, based on a novel by Vassili Vassilakis; 11 pts.
TELL THEM WILLIE BOY IS HERE by Abraham Polonsky, based on a novel by Harry Lawton; 9 pts.
MIDNIGHT COWBOY by Waldo Salt, based on a novel by James Leo Herlihy; 7 pts.
IF (Brit.) by David Sherwin; 7 pts.
BUTCH CASSIDY AND THE SUNDANCE KID by Allan Burns; 7 pts.
ALICE'S RESTAURANT by Venable Herndon and Arthur Penn; 5 pts.
EASY RIDER by Peter Fonda, Dennis Hopper, and Terry Southern; 3 pts.
THE STERILE CUCKOO by Alvin Sargent and John Nicholson; 2 pts.
LA FEMME INFIDELE (Fr.) by Claude Chabrol; 1 pt.

1970
Best Film
FIVE EASY PIECES, Bob Rafelson; 27 pts. on 2nd ballot.
PASSION OF ANNA (Swed.), Ingmar Bergman; 12 pts.
M.A.S.H., Robert Altman; 11 pts.
PATTON, Franklin Schaffner; 9 pts.
THE CONFESSION (Fr./Ital.), Constantin Costa-Gavras; 8 pts.
TRISTANA (Fr./Ital./Span.), Luis Bunuel.
MY NIGHT AT MAUD'S (Fr.), Eric Rohmer; 6 pts.
AU HAZARD BALTHAZAR (Fr.), Robert Bresson; 6 pts.
RYAN'S DAUGHTER, David Lean; 5 pts.
CATCH-22, Mike Nichols; 4 pts.
FELLINI'S SATYRICON (Ital.), Federico Fellini; 4 pts.

Best Actor
George C. Scott for PATTON; 31 pts. on 2nd ballot.
Melvin Douglas for I NEVER SANG FOR MY FATHER; 20 pts.
Jack Nicholson for FIVE EASY PIECES; 17 pts.
Marcello Mastroianni for THE PIZZA TRIANGLE (Span./Ital.); 10 pts
George Segal for THE OWL AND THE PUSSYCAT, LOVING, and POPPA?; 9 pts.
Yves Montand for THE CONFESSION (Fr./Ital.); 7 pts.
Gian Maria Volante for THE INVESTIGATION OF A CITIZEN ABOVE (Ital.); 7 pts.
Jean-Louis Trintignant for MY NIGHT AT MAUD'S (Fr.); 6 pts.
Robert Redford for LITTLE FAUSS AND BIG HALSY; 6 pts.
Peter Boyle for JOE; 6 pts.
Alan Arkin for CATCH-22; 4 pts.

John Cassavetes for HUSBANDS; 2 pts.
James Earl Jones for THE GREAT WHITE HOPE; 1 pt.

Best Actress
Glenda Jackson for WOMEN IN LOVE (Brit.); 22 pts.
Karen Black for FIVE EASY PIECES; 16 pts.
Liv Ullman for THE PASSION OF ANNA (Swed.); 14 pts.
Francoise Fabian for MY NIGHT AT MAUD'S (Fr.); 12 pts.

Best Supporting Actor
Chief Dan George for LITTLE BIG MAN; 32 pts.
Paul Mazursky for ALEX IN WONDERLAND; 17 pts.

Best Supporting Actress
Karen Black for FIVE EASY PIECES; 38 pts on 2nd ballot.
Francoise Fabian for MY NIGHT AT MAUD'S (Fr.); 18 pts.

Best Direction
Bob Rafelson for FIVE EASY PIECES; 23 pts. on 2nd ballot.
Federico Fellini for FELLINI SATYRICON (Ital./Fr.); 21 pts.
Robert Altman for M.A.S.H. and BREWSTER McCLOUD; 15 pts.
Luis Bunuel for TRISTANA (Fr./Ital./Span.); 13 pts.
Ingmar Bergman for THE PASSION OF ANNA (Swed.); 9 pts.
Francois Truffaut for THE WILD CHILD (Fr.); 8 pts.
Franklin Schaffner for PATTON; 7 pts.
Constantin Costa-Gavras for THE CONFESSION (Fr./Ital.); 6 pts.

Best Screenwriting
MY NIGHT AT MAUD'S (Fr.) by Eric Rohmer; 34 pts. on 2nd ballot.
INVESTIGATION OF A CITIZEN ABOVE SUSPICION (Ital.) by Ugo Pirro and Elio Petri; 19 pts.

1971
Best Film
A CLOCKWORK ORANGE (Brit.), Stanley Kubrick; 31 pts.
THE LAST PICTURE SHOW, Peter Bogdanovich; 24 pts.
THE FRENCH CONNECTION, William Friedkin; 11 pts.
SUNDAY, BLOODY SUNDAY (Brit.), John Schlesinger; 8 pts.
McCABE AND MRS. MILLER, Robert Altman; 5 pts.
CLAIRE'S KNEE (Fr.), Eric Rohmer; 5 pts.
THE CONFORMIST (Ital./Fr./Ger.), Bernardo Bertolucci; 4 pts.
DEEP END (U.S./Ger.), Jerzy Skolimowski; 4 pts.
TAKING OFF, Milos Forman; 4 pts.
PANIC IN NEEDLE PARK, Jerry Schatzberg; 3 pts.
FIDDLER ON THE ROOF, Norman Jewison; 2 pts.
DESPERATE CHARACTERS, Frank D. Gilroy; 2 pts.
BANANAS, Woody Allen; 2 pts.
THE CROOK (Fr.), Claude Lelouch; 2 pts.
MINNIE AND MOSKOWITZ, John Cassavetes; 2 pts.
MACBETH (Brit.), Roman Polanski; 1 pt.
"$, Richard Brooks; 1 pt.
THE BOY FRIEND (Brit.), Ken Russell; 1 pt.
KING LEAR (Brit./Den.), Peter Brook; 1 pt.
LE BOUCHER (Fr.), Claude Chabrol; 1 pt.

Best Actor
Gene Hackman for THE FRENCH CONNECTION; 31 pts.
Peter Finch for SUNDAY, BLOODY SUNDAY (Brit.); 25 pts.
Malcolm McDowell for A CLOCKWORK ORANGE (Brit.); 18 pts.
Paul Scofield for KING LEAR (Brit./Den.); 13 pts.
Jean-Louis Trintignant for THE CONFORMIST (Ital./Fr./Ger.); 13 pts.
George C. Scott for THE HOSPITAL; 6 pts.
Topol for FIDDLER ON THE ROOF; 6 pts.
Seymour Cassell for MINNIE AND MOSKOWITZ; 5 pts.
Jean-Claude Brialy for CLAIRE'S KNEE (Fr.); 3 pts.

Best Actress
Jane Fonda for KLUTE; 38 pts.
Gena Rowlands for MINNIE AND MOSKOWITZ; 21 pts.
Shirley MacLaine for DESPERATE CHARACTERS; 22 pts.

Best Supporting Actor
Ben Johnson for THE LAST PICTURE SHOW; 31 pts.
Warren Oates for THE HIRED HAND and TWO-LANE BLACKTOP; 27 pts.
Alan Webb for KING LEAR (Brit./Den.); 22 pts.

Best Supporting Actress
Ellen Burstyn for THE LAST PICTURE SHOW; 37 pts.
Cloris Leachman for THE LAST PICTURE SHOW; 30 pts.
Ann-Margret for CARNAL KNOWLEDGE; 11 pts.
Margaret Leighton for THE GO-BETWEEN (Brit.); 8 pts.
Beatrice Romand for CLAIRE'S KNEE (Fr.); 7 pts.
Lee Grant for PLAZA SUITE; 7 pts.

Best Direction
Stanley Kubrick for A CLOCKWORK ORANGE (Brit.); 38 pts.
Peter Bogdanovich for THE LAST PICTURE SHOW; 21 pts.
Bernardo Bertolucci for THE CONFORMIST (Ital./Fr./Ger.); 12 pts.
William Friedkin for THR FRENCH CONNECTION; 11 pts.
Jerzy Skolimowski for DEEP END (U.S./Ger.); 5 pts.
John Schlesinger for SUNDAY, BLOODY SUNDAY (Brit.); 5 pts.
Eric Rohmer for CLAIRE'S KNEE (Fr.); 5 pts.
Milos Forman for TAKING OFF; 4 pts.
Roman Polanski for MACBETH; 3 pts.
Louis Malle for MURMUR OF THE HEART (Fr./Ger./Ital.); 3 pts.
Claude Lelouch for THE CROOK; 2 pts.
Robert Altman for McCABE AND MRS. MILLER; 2 pts.
Richard Brooks for "$; 1 pt.
Norman Jewison for FIDDLER ON THE ROOF; 1 pt.
Vittorio de Sica for GARDEN OF THE FINZI CONTINIS (Ital./Ger.); 1 pt.
Ken Russell for THE BOY FRIEND (Brit.); 1 pt.

Best Screenwriting
THE LAST PICTURE SHOW by Peter Bogdanovich and Larry McMurtry; 22 pts.
SUNDAY, BLOODY SUNDAY (Brit.) by Penelope Gilliatt; 22 pts.
CLAIRE'S KNEE (Fr.) by Eric Rohmer; 20 pts.
BANANAS by Woody Allen and Mickey Rose.
A CLOCKWORK ORANGE (Fr.) by Stanley Kubrick, based on a novel by Anthony Burgess.
BED AND BOARD (Fr.) by Francois Truffaut, Claude de Givray, and Bernard Roven.
CARNAL KNOWLEDGE by Jules Feiffer.

MURMUR OF THE HEART by Louis Malle.
THE CROOK by Claude Lelouch, Pierre Vy Herhovenm, and Claude Pinoteau.

1972
Best Film
CRIES AND WHISPERS (Swed.), Ingmar Bergman; 40 pts.
THE GODFATHER, Francis Ford Coppola; 24 pts.
THE EMIGRANTS (Swed.), Jan Troell; 15 pts.
THE DISCREET CHARM OF THE BOURGEOISIE (Fr.), Luis Bunuel; 13 pts.
CABARET, Bob Fosse; 8 pts.
THE HEARTBREAK KID, Elaine May; 4 pts.
THE EFFECT OF GAMMA RAYS ON MAN IN THE MOON MARIGOLDS, Paul
Newman; 3 pts.
ROMA (Ital.), Federico Fellini; 3 pts.
THE SORROW AND THE PITY (Switz.), Marcel Ophuls; 2 pts.
DELIVERANCE, John Boorman; 1 pt.
FRENZY (Brit.), Alfred Hitchcock; 1 pt.
FOUR NIGHTS OF A DREAMER (Fr.), Robert Bresson; 1 pt.
SLEUTH (Brit.), Joseph L. Mankiewicz; 1 pt.
Best Actor
Laurence Olivier for SLEUTH (Brit.); 30 pts on 5th ballot.
Marlon Brando for THE GODFATHER; 27 pts.
James Mason for CHILD'S PLAY; 20 pts.
Peter O'Toole for THE RULING CLASS (Brit.); 15 pts.
Paul Winfield for SOUNDER.
Al Pacino for THE GODFATHER.
Burt Lancaster for ULZANA'S RAID.
Jacques Tati for TRAFFIC (Fr.).
Best Actress
Liv Ullman for CRIES AND WHISPERS (Swed.) and THE EMIGRANTS (Swed.); 38
pts. on 2nd ballot.
Cicely Tyson for SOUNDER; 14 pts.
Harriet Anderson for CRIES AND WHISPERS (Swed.); 11 pts.
Janet Suzman for A DAY IN THE LIFE OF JOE EGG; 11 pts.
Joanne Woodward for THE EFFECT OF GAMMA RAYS ON MAN IN THE MOON
MARIGOLDS; 10 pts.
Diana Ross for LADY SINGS THE BLUES; 10 pts.
Liza Minnelli for CABARET; 9 pts.
Bulle Ogier for LE SALAMANDRE (Switz.) and L'AMOUR FOU (Fr.); 6 pts.
Susannah York for IMAGES (Ireland); 5 pts.
Best Supporting Actor
Robert Duvall for THE GODFATHER; 22 pts. on 3rd ballot.
Eddie Albert for THE HEARTBREAK KID; 18 pts.
Robert Shaw for YOUNG WINSTON (Brit.); 13 pts.
Alec McCowan for FRENZY.
Fernando Rey for THE DISCREET CHARM OF THE BOURGEOISIE (Fr./Span./
Ital.).
Robert Preston for JUNIOR BONNER.
Joel Grey for CABARET.
Best Supporting Actress
Jeannie Berlin for THE HEARTBREAK KID; 12 votes on 1st ballot.
Susan Tyrrell for FAT CITY; 4 1/2 votes.
Ida Lupino for JUNIOR BONNER; 1 1/2 votes.
Vivian Merchant for FRENZY (Brit.); 1 vote.
Valentina Cortese for THE ASSASSINATION OF TROTSKY (Ital./Brit./Fr.); 1 vote.
Best Direction
Ingmar Bergman for CRIES AND WHISPERS (Swed.); 36 pts.
Francis Ford Coppola for THE GODFATHER; 26 pts.
Luis Bunuel for THE DISCREET CHARM OF THE BOURGEOISIE (Fr./Span./Ital.);
16 pts.
Bob Fosse for CABARET; 10 pts.
Jan Troell for THE EMIGRANTS (Swed.); 10 pts.
Alfred Hitchcock for FRENZY (Brit.); 5 pts.
Martin Ritt for SOUNDER; 3 pts.
Elaine May for THE HEARTBREAK KID; 3 pts.
Federico Fellini for ROMA (Ital.); 2 pts.
John Boorman for DELIVERANCE; 1 pt.
Robert Bresson for FOUR NIGHTS OF A DREAMER (Fr.); 1 pt.
Best Screenwriting
CRIES AND WHISPERS (Swed.) by Ingmar Bergman; 37 pts.
THE DISCREET CHARM OF THE BOURGEOISIE (Fr./Span./Ital.) by Luis Bunuel
and Jean-Claude Carriere; 23 pts.
THE EMIGRANTS (Swed.) by Jan Troell; 13 pts.
THE GODFATHER by Francis Ford Coppola and Mario Puzo, based on Puzo's novel;
9 pts.
THE HEARTBREAK KID by Neil Simon, based on a story by Bruce Jay Friedman;
9 pts.
SOUNDER by Lonne Elder III, based on a novel by William H. Armstrong; 4 pts.
CABARET by Jay Presson Allen, based on a book by Christopher Isherwood.
MY UNCLE ANTOINE (Can.) by Clement Perron.
BAD COMPANY by David Newman and Robert Benton.
LE SALAMANDRE (Switz.) by Alain Tanner.
EVERYTHING YOU ALWAYS WANTED TO KNOW ABOUT SEX BUT WERE
AFRAID TO ASK by Woody Allen, based on a book by Dr. David Reuben.
Special Citation
Marcel Ophuls for the Documentary THE SORROW AND THE PITY.

1973
Best Film
DAY FOR NIGHT (Fr./Ital.), Francois Truffaut; 40 pts.
LAST TANGO IN PARIS (Fr./Ital./U.S.), Bernardo Bertolucci; 30 pts.
MEAN STREETS, Martin Scorsese.
AMERICAN GRAFFITI, George Lucas.
Best Actor
Marlon Brando for LAST TANGO IN PARIS (Fr./Ital./U.S.); 38 pts.
Al Pacino for SERPICO; 33 pts.
Best Actress
Joanne Woodward for SUMMER WISHES, WINTER DREAMS; 28 pts.
Glenda Jackson for A TOUCH OF CLASS; 26 pts.
Best Supporting Actor
Robert De Niro for BANG THE DRUM SLOWLY.

John Houseman for THE PAPER CHASE.
Best Supporting Actress
Valentina Cortese for DAY FOR NIGHT (Fr./Ital.).
Best Direction
Francois Truffaut for DAY FOR NIGHT (Fr./Ital.); 41 pts.
Constantin Costa-Gavras for STATE OF SIEGE (Fr.); 27 pts.
Best Screenwriting
AMERICAN GRAFFITI by George Lucas, Gloria Katz, and Willard Huyck.

1974
Best Film
AMARCORD (Fr./Ital.), Federico Fellini; 43 pts.
SCENES FROM A MARRIAGE (Swed.), Ingmar Bergman; 38 pts.
THE GODFATHER PART II, Francis Ford Coppola; 17 pts.
THE CONVERSATION, Francis Ford Coppola; 12 pts.
CHINATOWN, Roman Polanski; 10 pts.
Best Actor
Jack Nicholson for CHINATOWN and THE LAST DETAIL; 32 pts for each.
Gene Hackman for THE CONVERSATION; 19 pts.
Richard Dreyfuss for THE APPRENTICESHIP OF DUDDY KRAVITZ (Can.); 19 pts.
Best Actress
Liv Ullman for SCENES FROM A MARRIAGE (Swed.); 52 pts.
Gena Rowlands for A WOMAN UNDER THE INFLUENCE; 42 pts.
Best Supporting Actor
Charles Boyer for STAVISKY (Fr./Ital.); 43 pts.
Robert De Niro for THE GODFATHER PART II; 35 pts.
Lee Strasberg for THE GODFATHER PART II; 16 pts.
Holger Lowenaeller for LACOMBE, LUCIEN (Fr.); 12 pts.
Randy Quaid for THE LAST DETAIL; 12 pts.
Best Supporting Actress
Valerie Perrine for LENNY; 45 pts.
Bibi Andersson for SCENES FROM A MARRIAGE (Swed.); 20 pts.
Madeline Kahn for YOUNG FRANKENSTEIN; 18 pts.
Ellen Burstyn for HARRY AND TONTO; 10 pts.
Best Direction
Federico Fellini for AMARCORD; 48 pts.
Ingmar Bergman for SCENES FROM A MARRIAGE (Swed.); 25 pts.
Best Screenwriting
SCENES FROM A MARRIAGE (Swed.) by Ingmar Bergman; 45 pts.
CHINATOWN by Robert Towne; 32 pts.
THE CONVERSATION by Francis Ford Coppola; 30 pts.
THE APPRENTICESHIP OF DUDDY KRAVITZ (Can.) by Mordecai Richler from his
novel; 10 pts.
BADLANDS by Terrence Malick; 10 pts.
Special Award
Fabiano Canosa, for his innovative programs at the First Ave. Screening Room.

1975
Best Film
NASHVILLE, Robert Altman; 45 pts.
BARRY LYNDON (Brit.), Stanley Kubrick; 30 pts.
Best Actor
Jack Nicholson for ONE FLEW OVER THE CUCKOO'S NEST; 41 pts.
Al Pacino for DOG DAY AFTERNOON; 26 pts.
Best Actress
Isabelle Adjani for THE STORY OF ADELE H. (Fr.); 44 pts.
Florinda Bolkan for A BRIEF VACATION (Ital.); 29 pts.
Best Supporting Actor
Alan Arkin for HEARTS OF THE WEST; 30 pts. on 3rd ballot.
Henry Gibson for NASHVILLE; 21 pts.
Best Supporting Actress
Lily Tomlin for NASHVILLE; 49 pts.
Louise Fletcher for ONE FLEW OVER THE CUCKOO'S NEST; 28 pts.
Best Direction
Robert Altman for NASHVILLE; 44 pts.
Stanley Kubrick for BARRY LYNDON (Brit.); 28 pts.
Best Screenwriting
*THE STORY OF ADELE H. (Fr.) by Francois Truffaut, Jean Grualt, and Suzanne
Schiffman;* 28 pts on 4th ballot.
SWEPT AWAY (Ital.) by Lina Wertmuller; 26 pts.

1976
Best Film
ALL THE PRESIDENT'S MEN, Alan Pakula; 40 pts on 2nd ballot.
NETWORK, Sidney Lumet; 26 pts.
SEVEN BEAUTIES (Ital.), Lina Wertmuller; 18 pts.
TAXI DRIVER, Martin Scorsese; 14 pts.
THE MEMORY OF JUSTICE (Ger./U.S.), Marcel Ophuls; 10 pts.
THE MARQUISE OF O (Fr./Ger.), Eric Rohmer; 7 pts.
ROCKY, John Avildsen; 6 pts.
Best Actor
Robert De Niro for TAXI DRIVER; 33 pts on 2nd ballot.
David Carradine for BOUND FOR GLORY; 19 pts.
William Holden for NETWORK; 12 pts.
Philippe Noiret for THE CLOCKMAKER (Switz.); 12 pts.
Giancarlo Giannini for SEVEN BEAUTIES (Ital.); 12 pts.
Best Actress
Liv Ullmann for FACE TO FACE (Swed.).
Faye Dunaway for NETWORK; 28 pts.
Sissy Spacek for CARRIE; 24 pts.
Talia Shire for ROCKY; 14 pts.
Best Supporting Actor
Jason Robards for ALL THE PRESIDENT'S MEN; 37 pts. on 2nd ballot.
Harvey Keitel for TAXI DRIVER; 12 pts.
Richard Pryor for SILVER STREAK; 11 pts.
Laurence Olivier for MARATHON MAN; 9 pts.
Robert Duvall for NETWORK; 9 pts.
Laurence Olivier for THE SEVEN PER CENT SOLUTION; 8 pts.
Robert Duvall for THE SEVEN PER CENT SOLUTION; 8 pts.
Best Supporting Actress
Talia Shire for ROCKY; 41 pts. on 3rd ballot.
Jodie Foster for TAXI DRIVER; 32 pts.
Marie-France Pisier for COUSIN COUSINE (Fr.); 21 pts.

Beatrice Straight for NETWORK; 9 pts.
Shelley Winters for NEXT STOP, GREENWICH VILLAGE; 7 pts.
Best Direction
Alan Pakula for ALL THE PRESIDENT'S MEN; 37 pts. on 2nd ballot.
Martin Scorsese for TAXI DRIVER; 22 pts.
Lina Wertmuller for SEVEN BEAUTIES (Ital.); 21 pts.
Sidney Lumet for NETWORK; 20 pts.
Marcel Ophuls for THE MEMORY OF JUSTICE (Ger./U.S.).
Nicholas Roeg for THE MAN WHO FELL TO EARTH (Brit.).
Eric Rohmer for THE MARQUISE OF O (Fr./Ger.).
Alfred Hitchcock for FAMILY PLOT.
Brian De Palma for CARRIE and OBSESSION.
Best Screenwriting
NETWORK by Paddy Chayefsky; 38 pts.
THE LAST TYCOON by Harold Pinter, based on a book by F. Scott Fitzgerald; 20 pts.
SEVEN BEAUTIES (Ital.) by Lina Wertmuller; 16 pts.
ALL THE PRESIDENT'S MEN by William Goldman; 13 pts.
JONAH WHO WILL BE 25 IN THE YEAR 2000 (Switz.) by Alain Tanner and John Berger; 10 pts.
ROCKY by Sylvester Stallone; 9 pts.

1977
Best Film
ANNIE HALL, Woody Allen; 46 pts.
THAT OBSCURE OBJECT OF DESIRE (Span./Fr.), Luis Bunuel.
CLOSE ENCOUNTERS OF THE THIRD KIND, Steven Spielberg.
Best Actor
John Gielgud for PROVIDENCE (Fr./Switz.); 37 pts.
Fernando Rey for THAT OBSCURE OBJECT OF DESIRE (Span./Fr.); 31 pts.
John Travolta for SATURDAY NIGHT FEVER; 25 pts.
Best Actress
Diane Keaton for ANNIE HALL; 34 pts.
Shelley Duvall for THREE WOMEN; 27 pts.
Diane Keaton for LOOKING FOR MR. GOODBAR; 25 pts.
Best Supporting Actor
Maximilian Schell for JULIA; 30 pts.
Billy Macy for THE LATE SHOW; 17 pts.
David Hemmings for ISLANDS IN THE STREAM; 14 pts.
Best Supporting Actress
Sissy Spacek for THREE WOMEN; 31 pts.
Vanessa Redgrave for JULIA; 25 pts.
Donna Pescoe for SATURDAY NIGHT FEVER; 22 pts.
Best Direction
Woody Allen for ANNIE HALL; 35 pts.
Luis Bunuel for THAT OBSCURE OBJECT OF DESIRE (Span./Fr.); 33 pts.
Steven Spielberg for CLOSE ENCOUNTERS OF THE THIRD KIND; 16 pts.
Best Screenwriting
ANNIE HALL by Woody Allen and Marshall Brickman.

1978
Best Film
THE DEER HUNTER, Michael Cimino; 29 pts. on 3rd ballot.
DAYS OF HEAVEN, Terrence Malick; 24 pts.
AN UNMARRIED WOMAN, Paul Mazursky; 20 pts.
COMING HOME, Hal Ashby; 15 pts.
INTERIORS, Woody Allen; 9 pts.
WHO'LL STOP THE RAIN, Karel Reisz; 8 pts.
Best Actor
Jon Voight for COMING HOME; 40 pts. on 2nd ballot.
Gary Busey for THE BUDDY HOLLY STORY; 32 pts.
Robert De Niro for THE DEER HUNTER; 19 pts.
Nino Manfredi for BREAD AND CHOCOLATE (Ital.); 16 pts.
Nick Nolte for WHO'LL STOP THE RAIN; 13 pts.
Best Actress
Ingrid Bergman for AUTUMN SONATA (Swed.); 14 votes on 1st ballot.
Jill Clayburgh for AN UNMARRIED WOMAN; 4 votes.
Jane Fonda for COMING HOME; 3 votes.
Jane Fonda for COMES A HORSEMAN; 2 votes.
Best Supporting Actor
Christopher Walken for THE DEER HUNTER; 35 pts.
Richard Farnsworth for COMES A HORSEMAN; 24 pts.
Barry Bostwick for MOVIE, MOVIE; 23 pts.
Gene Hackman, John Belushi, Charles Grodin, Laurence Olivier, and Rex Reed were also considered.
Best Supporting Actress
Maureen Stapleton for INTERIORS; 34 pts.
Maggie Smith for CALIFORNIA SUITE; 26 pts.
Meryl Streep for THE DEER HUNTER; 25 pts.

Lis Lucas for AN UNMARRIED WOMAN; 18 pts.
Best Direction
Terrence Malick for DAYS OF HEAVEN; 29 pts. on 4th ballot.
Paul Mazursky for AN UNMARRIED WOMAN; 20 pts.
Ingmar Bergman for AUTUMN SONATA (Swed.); 18 pts.
Michael Cimino for THE DEER HUNTER; 17 pts.
Bertrand Blier for GET OUT YOUR HANDKERCHIEFS (Fr.); 16 pts.
Best Screenwriting
AN UNMARRIED WOMAN by Paul Mazursky; 30 pts.
MOVIE, MOVIE by Larry Gelbart and Sheldon Keller.
BREAD AND CHOCOLATE (Ital.) by Franco Brusati, Iaia Fiastri, and Nino Manfredi.
GET OUT YOUR HANDKERCHIEFS (Fr.) by Bertrand Blier.
WHO'LL STOP THE RAIN by Judith Roscoe, based on a book by Robert Stone.
INTERIORS by Woody Allen.
Best Foreign Language Film
BREAD AND CHOCOLATE (Ital.), Franco Brusati; 35 pts. on 2nd ballot.
AUTUMN SONATA (Swed.), Ingmar Bergman.
A SLAVE OF LOVE (USSR), Nikita Mikhalkov.
GET OUR YOUR HANDKERCHIEFS (Fr.), Bertrand Blier.

1979
Best Film
KRAMER VS. KRAMER, Robert Benton; 30 pts, on 2nd ballot.
BREAKING AWAY, Peter Yates; 29 pts.
MANHATTAN, Woody Allen; 26 pts.
ALL THAT JAZZ, Bob Fosse; 17 pts.
"10", Blake Edwards; 13 pts.
BEING THERE, Hal Ashby; 11 pts.
Best Actor
Dustin Hoffman for KRAMER VS. KRAMER; 13 votes on 1st ballot.
Peter Sellers for BEING THERE; 3 votes.
Nick Nolte for NORTH DALLAS FORTY; 2 votes.
Robert Duvall for APOCALYPSE NOW; 1 vote.
Peter Falk for THE IN-LAWS; 1 vote.
Burt Reynolds for STARTING OVER; 1 vote.
Ben Gazzara for SAINT JACK; 1 vote.
Best Actress
Sally Field for NORMA RAE; 42 pts. on 2nd ballot.
Bette Midler for THE ROSE; 34 pts.
Hanna Schygulla for THE MARRIAGE OF MARIA BRAUN (Ger.); 31 pts.
Nathalie Nell for RAPE OF LOVE (Fr.); 13 pts.
Diane Keaton for MANHATTAN; 8 pts.
Mary Beth Hurt for HEAD OVER HEELS; 5 pts.
Best Supporting Actor
Melvyn Douglas for BEING THERE; 46 pts.
Frederic Forrest for THE ROSE; 17 pts.
Melvyn Douglas for THE SEDUCTION OF JOE TYNAN; 16 pts.
James Woods for THE ONION FIELD; 16 pts.
Paul Dooley for BREAKING AWAY; 15 pts.
Robert Duvall for APOCALYPSE NOW; 15 pts.
Best Supporting Actress
Meryl Streep for KRAMER VS. KRAMER and THE SEDUCTION OF JOE TYNAN; 33 pts. and 32 pts. respectively.
Jane Alexander for KRAMER VS. KRAMER; 27 pts.
Barbara Barrie for BREAKING AWAY; 15 pts.
Mariel Hemingway for MANHATTAN; 9 pts.
Best Direction
Woody Allen for MANHATTAN; 28 pts.
Robert Benton for KRAMER VS. KRAMER; 23 pts.
Bob Fosse for ALL THAT JAZZ; 13 pts.
Ermanno Olmi for THE TREE OF WOODEN CLOGS (Ital.); 12 pts.
Hal Ashby for BEING THERE; 11 pts.
Francis Ford Coppola for APOCALYPSE NOW; 10 pts.
Blake Edwards for "10; 8 pts.
Best Screenplay
BREAKING AWAY by Steve Tesich; 41 pts.
MANHATTAN by Woody Allen and Marshall Brickman; 38 pts.
BEING THERE by Jerzy Kosinski, from his novel; 27 pts.
KRAMER VS. KRAMER by Robert Benton; 12 pts.
Best Foreign Language Film
THE TREE OF WOODEN CLOGS (Ital.), Ermanno Olmi; 22 pts.
LA CAGE AUX FOLLES (Fr.), Edouard Molinaro; 19 pts.
PEPPERMINT SODA (Fr.), Diane Kurys; 19 pts.
SOLDIER OF ORANGE (Neth.), Paul Verhoeven; 18 pts.

1980
Best Picture
ORDINARY PEOPLE, Robert Redford; 31 pts on 3rd ballot.
MELVIN AND HOWARD, Jonathan Demme; 22 pts.
RAGING BULL, Martin Scorsese; 12 pts.
WISE BLOOD, John Huston; 11 pts.
MON ONCLE D'AMERIQUE (Fr.), Alain Resnais; 10 pts.
DRESSED TO KILL, Brian De Palma; 10 pts.
Best Actor
Robert De Niro for RAGING BULL; 33 pts.
Robert Duvall for THE GREAT SANTINI; 29 pts.
Peter O'Toole for THE STUNT MAN; 24 pts.
Best Actress
Sissy Spacek for COAL MINER'S DAUGHTER; 37 pts. on 2nd ballot.
Goldie Hawn for PRIVATE BENJAMIN; 20 pts.
Mary Tyler Moore for ORDINARY PEOPLE; 20 pts.
Shelley Duvall for POPEYE; 14 pts.
Best Supporting Actor
Joe Pesci for RAGING BULL; 33 pts.
Jason Robards for MELVIN AND HOWARD; 27 pts.
Timothy Hutton for ORDINARY PEOPLE; 25 pts.
Tommy Lee Jones for COAL MINER'S DAUGHTER; 11 pts.
Levon Helm for COAL MINER'S DAUGHTER; 8 pts.
Best Supporting Actress
Mary Steenburgen for MELVIN AND HOWARD; 31 pts.
Debra Winger for URBAN COWBOY; 24 pts.
Mary Nell Santacroce for WISE BLOOD; 17 pts.
Eva Le Gallienne for RESURRECTION; 12 pts.
Cathy Moriarty for RAGING BULL; 8 pts.
Best Direction
Jonathan Demme for MELVIN AND HOWARD; 27 pts.
Martin Scorsese for RAGING BULL; 25 pts.
Robert Redford for ORDINARY PEOPLE; 19 pts.
Brian De Palma for DRESSED TO KILL; 11 pts.
Roman Polanski for TESS; 9 pts.
Best Screenplay
MELVIN AND HOWARD by Bo Goldman; 34 pts.
MON ONCLE D'AMERIQUE (Fr.) by Jean Grualt, based on the works of Henri Laborit; 19 pts.
RETURN OF THE SECAUCUS SEVEN by John Sayles; 17 pts.
Best Foreign Language Film
MON ONCLE D'AMERIQUE (Fr.), Alain Resnais; 28 pts. on 4th ballot.
BREAKER MORANT (Aus.), Bruce Beresford; 27 pts.

TESS (Fr./Brit.), Roman Polanski; 16 pts.
KAGEMUSHA (Jap.), Akira Kurosawa; 10 pts.
CHANT OF JIMMIE BLACKSMITH (Aus.), Fred Schepisi; 10 pts.
Best Cinematography
Geoffrey Unsworth and Ghislain Cloquet for TESS (Fr./Brit.); on 1st ballot.
Best Documentary
BEST BOY, Ira Wohl.

1981
Best Film
REDS, Warren Beatty: 37 pts. on 2nd ballot.
PRINCE OF THE CITY, Sidney Lumet; 25 pts.
ATLANTIC CITY, Louis Malle; 24 pts.
CHARIOTS OF FIRE (Brit.), Hugh Hudson; 23 pts.
Best Actor
Burt Lancaster for ATLANTIC CITY; 58 pts on 2nd ballot.
Henry Fonda for ON GOLDEN POND; 27 pts.
Robert Duvall for TRUE CONFESSIONS; 12 pts.
Best Actress
Glenda Jackson for STEVIE (Brit.); 36 pts. on 2nd ballot.
Faye Dunaway for MOMMIE DEAREST; 34 pts.
Diane Keaton for REDS; 15 pts.
Best Supporting Actor
John Gielgud for ARTHUR; 36 pts. on 2nd ballot.
Jack Nicholson for REDS; 29 pts.
Jerry Orbach for PRINCE OF THE CITY; 28 pts.
Howard E. Rollins, Jr. for RAGTIME; 21 pts.
Best Supporting Actress
Mona Washbourne for STEVIE (Brit.); 52 pts. on 2nd ballot.
Marilia Pera for PIXOTE (Braz.); 19 pts.
Maureen Stapleton for REDS; 19 pts.
Elizabeth McGovern for RAGTIME; 15 pts.
Best Direction
Sidney Lumet for PRINCE OF THE CITY; 33 pts. on 2nd ballot.
Louis Malle for ATLANTIC CITY; 26 pts.
Hugh Hudson for CHARIOTS OF FIRE (Brit.); 25 pts.
Warren Beatty for REDS; 20 pts.
Best Screenplay
ATLANTIC CITY by John Guare; 48 pts. on 2nd ballot.
PRINCE OF THE CITY by Jay Presson Allen and Sidney Lumet; 25 pts.
ARTHUR by Steve Gordon; 10 pts.
PENNIES FROM HEAVEN by Dennis Potter; 10 pts.
Best Foreign Film
PIXOTE (Braz.), Hector Babenco; 34 pts. on 2nd ballot.
MAN OF IRON (Pol.), Andrej Wajda; 20 pts.
MAN OF MARBLE (Pol.), Andrej Wajda; 20 pts.
THE LAST METRO (Fr.), Francois Truffaut; 16 pts.
CONTRACT (Pol.), Krysztof Zanussi; 15 pts.
Best Cinematography
David Watkin for CHARIOTS OF FIRE (Brit.).
Special Awards
In recognition of the artistry and independent spirit of the Polish Film makers Krystof Zanussi and Andrzej Wajda, as recognized in Zanussi's films CONTRACT and CAMOUFLAGE, and Wajda's MAN OF MARBLE and MAN OF IRON.
Abel Gance's NAPOLEON (1927).

1982
Best Film
GANDHI, Richard Attenborough; 36 pts. on 2nd ballot.
TOOTSIE, Sydney Pollack; 32 pts.
E.T., Steven Spielberg; 28 pts.
MISSING, Constantin Costa-Gavras; 11 pts.
VICTOR/VICTORIA, Blake Edwards; 7 pts.
MOONLIGHTING (Brit.), Jerzy Skolimowski; 6 pts.
DINER, Barry Levinson; 6 pts.
Best Actor
Ben Kingsley for GANDHI; 14 votes on 1st ballot.
Dustin Hoffman for TOOTSIE; 5 votes.
Peter O'Toole for MY FAVORITE YEAR; 2 votes.
Paul Newman for THE VERDICT; 1 vote.
Eddie Murphy for 48 HOURS; 1 vote.
Best Actress
Meryl Streep for SOPHIE'S CHOICE; 14 votes on 1st ballot.
Diane Keaton for SHOOT THE MOON; 3 votes.
Jessica Lange for TOOTSIE; 3 votes.
Debra Winger for AN OFFICER AND A GENTLEMAN; 2 votes.
Best Supporting Actor
John Lithgow for THE WORLD ACCORDING TO GARP; 33 pts..
George Gaynes for TOOTSIE; 21 pts.
Robert Preston for VICTOR/VICTORIA; 20 pts.
Louis Gossett, Jr. for AN OFFICER AND A GENTLEMAN; 17 pts.
Best Supporting Actress
Jessica Lange for TOOTSIE; 39 pts. on 2nd ballot.

Glenn Close for THE WORLD ACCORDING TO GARP; 34 pts.
Best Direction
Sydney Pollack for TOOTSIE; with 14 votes on a 4th ballot tie breaking vote.
Steven Spielberg for E.T.; 11 votes.
Best Screenplay
TOOTSIE by Larry Gelbart and Murray Schisgal; 42 pts.
DINER by Barry Levinson; 31 pts.
Best Foreign Language Film
TIME STANDS STILL (Hung.), Peter Gothar; 31 pts.
LE BEAU MARIAGE (Fr.), Eric Rohmer; 24 pts.
THREE BROTHERS (Ital./Fr.), Francesco Rosi; 22 pts.
Best Cinematography
Nestor Almendros for SOPHIE'S CHOICE; 30 pts.
Philippe Rousselot for DIVA (Fr.); 20 pts.
Jordan Cronenweth for BLADE RUNNER; 17 pts.
Lajos Koltai for TIME STANDS STILL (Hung.); 16 pts.

1983
Best Film
TERMS OF ENDEARMENT, James L. Brooks.
Best Actor
Robert Duvall for TENDER MERCIES.
Best Actress
Shirley MacLaine for TERMS OF ENDEARMENT.
Best Supporting Actor
Jack Nicholson for TERMS OF ENDEARMENT.
Best Supporting Actress
Linda Hunt for THE YEAR OF LIVING DANGEROUSLY (Aus.).
Best Direction
Ingmar Bergman for FANNY AND ALEXANDER (Swed./Fr./Ger.).
Best Screenplay
Bill Forsyth for LOCAL HERO (Brit.).
Best Foreign Language Film
FANNY AND ALEXANDER (Swed./Fr./Ger.), Ingmar Bergman.
Best Cinematography
Gordon Willis for ZELIG.

1984
Best Film
A PASSAGE TO INDIA (Brit.), David Lean.
THE KILLING FIELDS (Brit.), Roland Joffe.
Best Actor
Steve Martin for ALL OF ME.
Best Actress
Peggy Ashcroft for A PASSAGE TO INDIA.
Vanessa Redgrave for THE BOSTONIANS.
Best Supporting Actor
Sir Ralph Richardson for GREYSTOKE (Brit.).
John Malkovich for PLACES IN THE HEART.
Best Supporting Actress
Christine Lahti for SWING SHIFT.
Melanie Griffith for BODY DOUBLE.
Best Direction
David Lean for A PASSAGE TO INDIA (Brit.).
Bertrand Tavernier for A SUNDAY IN THE COUNTRY (Fr.).
Best Screenplay
PLACES IN THE HEART by Robert Benton.
Best Cinematography
Chris Menges for THE KILLING FIELDS.
Best Foreign Language Film
SUNDAY IN THE COUNTRY (Fr.), Bertrand Tavernier.
Best Documentary
THE TIMES OF HARVEY MILK, Robert Epstein.

BERLIN INTERNATIONAL FILM FESTIVAL

1951
Best of Festival According to Appropriate Categories
Dramatic Film
Golden Bear: FOUR IN A JEEP (Switz.)—Leopold Lindtberg.
Silver Bear: THE WAY OF HOPE (Ital.)—Pietro Germi.
Bronze Bear: THE BROWNING VERSION (Brit.)—Anthony Asquith.
Comedy
Golden Bear: SANS LAISSER D'ADRESSE (Fr.)—Jean-Paul Le Chanois.
Silver Bear: L'ESPOIRE FAIT VIVRE (Swed.)—
Bronze Bear: THE MATING SEASON (U.S.)—Mitchell Leisen.
Crime and Adventure
Golden Bear: JUSTICE IS DONE (Fr.)—Andre Cayatte.
Silver Bear: None awarded.
Bronze Bear: DESTINATION MOON (U.S.)—Irving Pichel.
Musical
Golden Bear: CINDERELLA (U.S.)—Wilfred Jackson, Hamilton Luske, and Clyde
Geronimi for Walt Disney.
Silver Bear: TALES OF HOFFMAN (Brit.)—Michael Powell and Emeric Pressburger.
Bronze Bear: None Awarded.
Feature Documentary
Golden Bear: BEAVER VALLEY (U.S.).
Silver Bear: None awarded.
Bronze Bear: THE UNDEFEATED (Brit.).
Best of Festival According to Public Poll
Golden Bear: CINDERELLA (U.S.)—Walt Disney.
Silver Bear: THE BROWNING VERSION (Brit.)—Anthony Asquith.
Bronze Bear: JUSTICE IS DONE (Fr.)—Andre Cayatte.
4) FOUR IN A JEEP (Switz.)—Leopold Lindtberg.
5) LIGHTS OUT (U.S.).
6) SANS LAISSER D'ADRESSE (Fr.)—Jean-Paul Le Chanois.
7) GOD NEEDS MEN (Fr.)—Jean Delannoy.
8) DR. HOLL (Ger.)—Rolf Hansen.
9) STRANGE DECEPTION (Ital.)—Curzio Malaparte.
10) THE MATING SEASON (U.S.)—Mitchell Leisen.
Competing Films
BRIGHT VICTORY (U.S.)—Mark Robson.
THE BROWNING VERSION (Brit.)—Anthony Asquith.
CINDERELLA (U.S.)—Walt Disney.
CRIMEN Y CASTIGO (Mex.)—Fernando de Fuentes.
CUDOTVORNO MAC (Yugo.)—Vojislav Nanovic.
DAS GESTOHLENE JAHR (Ger./Aust.)—Wilfried Frass.
DAS JAHR DAS HERRN (Aust.)—Alfred Stoger.
DAS SELTSAME LEBEN DES HERRN BRUGGS (Ger.)—Erich Engel.
DESTINATION MOON (U.S.)—Irving Pichel.
DIE EROBERUNG VON BYZANZ (Turkey)—Aydin Gyarakon.
DR. HOLL (Ger.)—Rolf Hansen.
FATHER'S LITTLE DIVIDEND (U.S.)—Vincente Minnelli.
FOUR IN A JEEP (Switz.)—Leopold Lindtberg.
GOD NEEDS MEN (Fr.)—Jean Delannoy.
JUSTICE IS DONE (Fr.)—Andre Cayatte.
LADY PANAME (Fr.)—Henri Jeanson.
LEVA PA "HOPPET" (Swed.)—Goran Gentele.
MALAIRE (Span./Fr.)—Alejandro Perla and Gilbert Dupe.
MARIA MONTECRISTO (Mex.)—Luis Cesart Amadori.
THE MATING SEASON (U.S.)—Mitchell Leisen.
MIN KONE ER USKYLDIG (Den.)—Johan Jacobsen.
MISS JULIE (Swed.)—Alf Sjoberg.
MUCHACHAS DE UNIFORME (Mex.)—Alfredo B. Crevenna.
PASSPORT TO PIMLICO (Brit.)—Henry Cornelius.
POR LA PUERTA FALSA (Mex.)—Fernando de Fuentes.
SANS LAISSER D'ADRESSE (Fr.)—Jean-Paul Le Chanois.
STRANGE DECEPTION (Ital.)—Curzio Malaparte.
TALES OF HOFFMAN (Brit.)—Michael Powell and Emeric Pressburger.
TRIO (Brit.)—Ken Annakin and Harold French.
VITA DA CANI (Ital.)—Mario Monicelli and Steno.
THE WAY OF HOPE (Ital.)—Pietro Germi.
WIEN TANZT (Aust.)—Emile Edwin Reinert.

1952
Best of Festival According to Public Poll
Golden Bear: ONE SUMMER OF HAPPINESS (Swed.)—Arne Mattsson.
Silver Bear: FANFAN THE TULIP (Fr.)—Christian-Jaque.
Bronze Bear: AFRICAN FURY (Brit.)—Zoltan Korda.
4) THE VOICE OF THE OTHER (Ger.)—Erich Engel.
5) MIRACLE IN MILAN (Ital.)—Vittorio de Sica.
6) THE WELL (U.S.)—Leo Popkin.
7) DEATH OF A SALESMAN (U.S.)—Laslo Benedek.
8) THREE FORBIDDEN STORIES (Ital.)—Augusto Genina.
9) THE DESERTED COURT (Mex.)—Alfredo B. Crevenna.
10) ROSHOMON (Jap.)—Akira Kurosawa.
Competing Films
AFRICAN FURY (Brit.)—Zoltan Korda.
AGENCE MATRIMONIALE (Fr.)—Jean-Paul Chanois.
BALARASA (Span.)—Jose Antonio Nieves Conde.
BELLISSIMA (Ital.)—Luchino Visconti.
DEATH OF A SALESMAN (U.S.)—Laslo Benedek.
THE DESERTED COURT (Mex.)—Alfredo B. Crevenna.
FANFAN, LA TULIPE (Fr.)—Christian-Jaque.
KANGAROO (U.S.)—Lewis Milestone.
L'AMOUR, MADAME (Fr.)—Gilles Grangier.
LA VERITE SUR BEBE DONGE (Fr.)—Henri Decoin.
LE BANQUET DES FRAUDEURS (Ger./Bel.)—Henri Storck.
LOLA, LA PICONERA (Span.)—Luis Lucia.
THE MAGIC BOX (Brit.)—John Boulting.

MIRACLE IN MILAN (Ital.)—Vittorio de Sica.
MY FAVORITE WIFE (U.S.)—Garson Kanin.
ONE SUMMER OF HAPPINESS (Swed.)—Arne Mattsson.
THE OVERCOAT (Ital.)—Alberto Lattuada.
THE PERFECTIONIST (Fr.)—Yves Ciampi.
POSTLAGERND: TURTELTAUBE (Ger.)—Gerhard T. Buckholz.
RASHOMON (Jap.)—Akira Kurosawa.
THE RIVER (U.S./India)—Jean Renoir.
SENSUALITA (Ital.)—Clemente Fracassi.
THREE FORBIDDEN STORIES (Ital.)—Augusto Genina.
THREE GIRLS FROM ROME (Ital.)—Luciano Emmer.
TREASURE ISLAND (U.S.)—Byron Haskin.
TROIS FEMMES (Fr.)—Andre Michel.
UNMARRIED (Swed.)—Gustaf Molander.
THE VOICE OF THE OTHER (Ger.)—Erich Engel.
THE WELL (U.S.)—Leo Popkin.
WHITE CORRIDORS (Brit.)—Pat Jackson.
WIFE FOR A NIGHT (Ital.)—Franco Brusati.
YHDEN YON HINTA (Fin.)—Edvin Laine.
ZEINAB (Egypt)—Mohamed Korayem.

1953
Best of Festival According to Public Poll
Golden Bear: THE WAGES OF FEAR (Fr./Ital.)—Henri-Georges Clouzot.
Silver Bear: GREEN MAGIC (Ital.)—Gian Gaspare Napolitano.
Bronze Bear: THEY FOUND A HOME (Switz.)—Leopold Lindtberg.
4) FORBIDDEN FRUIT (Fr.)—Henri Verneuil.
5) TIMES GONE BY (Ital.)—Alessandro Blassetti.
6) A HEART PLAYS FALSE (Ger.)—Rudolf Jugert.
7) THE CAPTAIN'S PARADISE (Brit.)—Anthony Kimmins.
8) THE SUN SHINES BRIGHT (U.S.)—John Ford.
9) MR. HULOT'S HOLIDAY (Fr.)—Jacques Tati.
10) MAN ON A TIGHTROPE (U.S.)—Elia Kazan.
International Delegation
MAN ON A TIGHTROPE (U.S.)—Elia Kazan.
CITY ON TRIAL (Ital.)—Luigi Zampa.
FOUR CHIMNEYS (Jap.)—Heinosuke Gosho.
Competing Films
THE BAD AND THE BEAUTIFUL (U.S.)—Vincente Minnelli.
BONGOLO (Bel.)—Andre Cauvin.
THE BOY KUMASENU—Sean Graham.
THE CAPTAIN'S PARADISE (Brit.)—Anthony Kimmins.
CARNAVAL (Fr.)—Henri Verneuil.
CITY ON TRIAL (Ital.)—Luigi Zampa.
CRIMES OF LOVE (Fr.)—Maurice Clavel and Maurice Barry.
DER KAMPF DER TERTIA (Ger.)—Erik Ode.
FORBIDDEN FRUIT (Fr.)—Henri Verneuil.
FOUR CHIMNEYS (Jap.)—Heinosuke Gosho.
A HEART PLAYS FALSE (Ger.)—Rudolf Jugert.
HELL RAIDERS OF THE DEEP (Ital.)—Duilio Coletti.
HO SCELTO L'AMORE (Ital.)—Mario Zampi.
LES AMANTS DE MINUIT (Fr.)—Roger Richebe.
LOS OJOS DEJAN HUELLAS (Span.)—Jose Luis Saenz de Heredia.
MAN ON A TIGHTROPE (U.S.)—Elia Kazan.
MANON DES SOURCES ET UGOLIN (Fr.)—Marcel Pagnol.
THE MEMBER OF THE WEDDING (U.S.)—Fred Zinnemann.
MEN GEHR WEDSDA (Egypt)—Ahmed Dia El Dine.
MR. HULOT'S HOLIDAY (Fr.)—Jacques Tati.
THE MOON IS BLUE (U.S.)—Otto Preminger.
THE NET (Mex.)—Emilio Fernandez.
THE NIGHT IS MY KINGDOM (Fr.)—Georges Lacombe.
O CANGACEIRO (Bra.)—Limo Barreto.
PEPPINO AND VIOLETTA (Ital./Fr./Brit.)—Maurice Cloche.
THE PICKWICK PAPERS (Brit.)—Noel Langley.
RAYA AND SEKINA (Egypt)—Salah Abu Seif.
THE RETURN OF DON CAMILLO (Fr./Ital.)—Julien Duvivier.
SENGOKU BURAI (Jap.)—Hiroshi Inagaki.
SHANE (U.S.)—George Stevens.
THE SUN SHINES BRIGHT (U.S.)—John Ford.
TIMES GONE BY (Alessandro Blasetti.
TRINE (Nor.)—Toralf Sando.
THE VILLAGE (Switz./Brit.)—Leopold Lindtberg.
WAGES OF FEAR (Fr.)—Henri-Georges Clouzot.
YOUR DAY WILL COME (Egypt)—Salah Abu Seif.
ZWERG NASE (Ger.)—Francesco Stefani.

1954
Best of Festival According to Public Poll
Golden Bear: HOBSON'S CHOICE (Brit.)—David Lean.
Silver Bear: BREAD, LOVE AND DREAMS (Ital.)—Luigi Comencini.
Bronze Bear: THE RENEGADE (Fr.)—Leo Joannon.
4) THE LIGHT OF LOVE (Aust.)—R.A. Stemmle.
5) THE GREAT HOPE (Ital.)—Duilio Coletti.
6) JULIETTA (Fr.)—Marc Allegret.
7) WILD FRUIT (Fr.)—Herve Bromberger.
8) NO WAY BACK (Ger.)—Victor Vicas.
9) NEAPOLITAN CAROUSEL (Ital.)—Ettore Giannini.
10) KONIG DROSSELBART (Ger.)—Herbert B. Fredersdorf.

Documentary
    Golden Plaque: THE LIVING DESERT (U.S.)—James Algar for Walt Disney.
    Silver Plaque: THE GREAT ADVENTURE (Swed.)—Arne Sucksdorff.
    Bronze Plaque: UN SIECLE D'OR (Belg.) -
International Delegation Jury
    THE GREAT HOPE (Ital.)—Duilio Coletti.
    SINHA MOCA (Brazil)—Tom Payne.
    IKURU (Jap.)—Akira Kurosawa.
    Walt Disney.
Honorable Mentions
    THE GREAT ADVENTURE (Swed.)—Arne Sucksdorff.
    LE DEFROQUE (Fr.)—Leo Joannon.
Catholic Film Office Prize
    THE GREAT HOPE (Ital.)—Duilio Coletti.
Competing Films
    BETTY SLOW DRAG (Brit.)—Ernest Borneman.
    BHAGWAN SHREE KRISHNA CHAITANYA (India)—Raja Yagnik.
    BREAD, LOVE AND DREAMS (Ital.)—Luigi Comencini.
    DECAMERON NIGHTS (U.S.)—Hugo Fragonese.
    ELEPHANT WALK (U.S.)—William Dieterle.
    GARDEN OF EVIL (U.S.)—Henry Hathaway.
    GATE OF HELL (Jap.)—Teinosuke Kinugasa.
    THE GREAT HOPE (Ital.)—Duilio Coletti.
    HOBSON'S CHOICE (Brit.)—David Lean.
    IKURU (Jap.)—Akira Kurosawa.
    JULIETTA (Fr.)—Marc Allegret.
    KNIGHTS OF THE ROUND TABLE (U.S.)—Richard Thorpe.
    KONIG DROSSELBART (Ger.)—Herbert B. Fredersdorf.
    KUSA WO KARU MUSUME (Jap.)—Nebuo Nakagawa.
    LE DEFROQUE (Fr.)—Leo Joannon.
    LES FEMMES S'EN BALANCENT (Fr.)—Bernard Borderie.
    THE LIGHT OF LOVE (Aust.)—R.A. Stemmle.
    MADDALENA (Ital.)—Augusto Genina.
    MAGNIFICENT OBSESSION (U.S.)—Douglas Sirk.
    NEOPOLITAN CAROUSEL (Ital.)—Ettore Giannini.
    NISKAVUOREN HETA (Fin.)—Edvin Laine.
    NO WAY BACK (Ger.)—Victor Vicas.
    ON TRIAL (Fr.)—Julien Duvivier.
    PAMPOSH—LOTOS OF KASHMIR (India)—Ezra Mir.
    SINHA MOCA (Bra.)—Tom Payne.
    VALPARAISO EXPRESS (Arg.)—Daniel Tianyre.
    WHAT EVERY WOMAN WANTS (Brit.)—Maurice Elvey.
    WILD FRUIT (Fr.)—Herve Bromberger.

1955
Best of Festival According to Audience Poll
    Golden Bear: THE RATS (Ger.)—Robert Siodmak.
    Silver Bear: MARCELINO (Span.)—Ladislao Vajda.
    Bronze Bear: CARMEN JONES (US)—Otto Preminger.
    4) BREAD, LOVE AND JEALOUSY (Ital.)—Luigi Comencini.
    5) THREE MEN IN THE SNOW (Aust.)—Kurt Hoffmann.
    6) HIROSHIMA (Jap.)—Hideo Sekigawa.
    7) THE DIVIDED HEART (Brit.)—Charles Crichton.
    8) CHANCE MEETING (Brit.)—Anthony Asquith.
    9) PAPA, MAMA, THE MAID AND I (Fr.)—Jean-Paul Le Chanois.
    10) ANIMAL FARM (Brit.)—John Halas and Joy Batchclor.
Feature Documentary
    Golden Plaque: THE VANISHING PRAIRIE (US)—James Algar
    Silver Plaque: THE LOST CONTINENT (Ital.)—Leonardo Bonzi.
    Bronze Plaque: IM SCHATTEN DES KARAKORUM (Ger.)—Eugen Schumacher.
Short Film
    Golden Plaque: ZIMMERLEUTE DES WALDES (Ger.)
    Silver Plaque: SIAM (US)
    Bronze Plaque: PANTOMIMES (Fr.)—featuring Marcel Marceau.
Competing Films
    ANIMAL FARM (Brit.)—John Halas and Joy Batchelor.
    BEAU BRUMMEL (U.S.)—Curtis Bernhardt.
    THE CONSTANT HUSBAND (Brit.)—Sidney Gilliat.
    THE DIVIDED HEART (Brit.)—Charles Crichton.
    DJEVOJKA I HRAST (Yugo.)—Kreso Golik.
    FROU-FROU (Fr./Ital.)—Augusto Genina.
    FRUITS OF SUMMER (Fr.)—Raymond Bernard.
    HIROSHIMA (Jap.)—Hideo Sekigawa.
    LE RAGAZZE DI SAN FREDIANO (Ital.)—Valerio Zurlini.
    LOVE, BREAD AND JEALOUSY (Ital.)—Luigi Comencini.
    MAMA, PAPA, THE MAID AND I (Fr.)—Jean-Paul Le Chanois.
    MARCELINO (Span.)—Ladislav Vajda.
    MERAPI (Indonesia)—Soedarso W.K.
    NO EXIT (Fr.)—Jacqueline Audry.
    NUKKEKAUPPIAS JA KAUNIS LILITH (Fin.)—Jack Witikka.
    THE RATS (Ger.)—Robert Siodmak.
    RAZZIA IN PARIS (Fr.)—Henri Decoin.
    THE SEVEN YEAR ITCH (U.S.)—Billy Wilder.
    STRATEGIC AIR COMMAND (U.S.)—Anthony Mann.
    THREE MEN IN THE SNOW (Aust.)—Kurt Hoffmann.
    TOO BAD SHE'S A WOMAN (Ital.)—Alessandro Blasetti.
    TUNNEL NO. 6 (Mex.)—Chano Urueta.
    THE 20TH OF JULY (Ger.)—Falk Harnack.
    THE YOUNG LOVERS (Brit.)—Anthony Asquith.

1956
Prizes of the International Jury
    Golden Bear for Best Film: INVITATION TO THE DANCE (U.S.)—Gene Kelly.
    International Prize, Silver Bear: RICHARD III (Brit.)—Laurence Olivier.
    Silver Bear for Male Performance: Burt Lancaster for TRAPEZE (U.S.).
    Silver Bear for Female Performance: Elsa Martinella for DONATELLA (Ital.).
    Silver Bear for Best Direction and Screenwriting: Robert Aldrich for AUTUMN LEAVES (U.S.)
Honorary Award, Silver Bear
    1) THE THIRD KEY (Brit.)—Charles Frend.
    2) THE SORCERESS (Fr.)—Andre Michel.
Honorable Mention
    Best Direction: Alfonso Corona Blake for THE ROAD TO LIFE (Mex.).
    Best Comedy: SCANDAL IN SORRENTO (Ital.)—Marcello Girosi.
Feature Documentary
    Golden Bear: NO SPACE FOR WILD ANIMALS (Ger.)—Bernhard and Michael Grzimek.
    Silver Bear) THE AFRICAN LION (US)—James Algar for Walt Disney.
Short Films
    Golden Bear: PARIS AT NIGHT (Fr.)—Jacques Baratier and Jean Valerie.
    Silver Bears
        RHYTHMETIC (Can.)—Norman McLaren.
        SPRING COMES TO KASHMIR (India)
        HITIT GUNESEI (Turkey)
    Honorable Mentions
        ...ERWACHSEN SEIN DAGEGEN SEHR (Ger.)—Wolf Hart.
        LE SABOTIER DU VAL DE LOIRE (Fr.)—Jacques Demy.
        THE LONG JOURNEY

Catholic Film Office Prize
    THE UNKNOWN SOLDIER (Fin.)—Edvin Laine.
    THE ROAD TO LIFE (Mex.)—Alfonso Corona Blake (Honorable Mention).
Best of Festival According to Audience Poll
    Golden Bear: BEFORE SUNSET (Ger.)—Gottfried Reinhardt.
    Runners up
        MY UNCLE, JACINTO (Span.)—Ladislao Vajda.
        TRAPEZE (U.S.)—Carol Reed.
        INVITATION TO THE DANCE (U.S.)—Gene Kelly.
        THE SORCERESS (Fr.)—Andre Michel.
        THE UNKNOWN SOLDIER (Fin.)—Edvin Laine.
        KISPUS (Den.)—Erik Balling.
        THE ROAD TO LIFE (Mex.)—Alfonso Corona Blake.
        THE THIRD KEY (Brit.)—Charles Frend.
        RICHARD III (Brit.)—Laurence Olivier.
    Feature Documentary
        Golden Bear: NO SPACE FOR WILD ANIMALS (Ger.—Bernhard and Michael Grzimek.
        Runners Up
        THE AFRICAN LION (U.S.)—James Algar.
        ZAUBER DER NATUR (Ger.)—Richard Mostler.
    Short Films
        Golden Plaque: MAN AGAINST THE ARCTIC (U.S.).
        Runners Up
        ERNST REUTER (Ger.)—Wolfgang Kiepenheuer.
        LES TRES RICHES HEURES DE L'AFRIQUE ROMAINE (Fr.)—Jean Leherissey.

Competing Films
    ADAM AND EVA (Mex.)—Alberto Gout.
    AINA OMRI (Egypt)—Ahmed Dia Eddin.
    AUTUMN LEAVES (U.S.)—Robert Aldrich.
    AYER FUE PRIMAVERA (Arg.)—Fernando Ayala.
    BANDISH (India)—Satyen Bose.
    BEFORE SUNSET (Swed.)—Gottfried Reinhardt.
    BYAKUFUJIN NO YOREN (Jap.)—Schiro Tanaka.
    CELA S'APPELLE L'AURORE (Fr./Ital.)—Luis Bunuel.
    DONATELLA (Ital.)—Mario Monicelli.
    DONNE SOLE (Ital.)—Vittorio Sala.
    GIFTAS (Swed.)—Anders Henrikson.
    INVITATION TO THE DANCE (U.S.)—Gene Kelly.
    THE IRON PETTICOAT (Brit.)—Ralph Thomas.
    KARAKORUM (Jap.)—Shigeo Hayashida.
    KISPUS (Den.)—Erik Balling.
    LE SALAIRE DU PECHE (Fr.)—Denys de la Patelliere.
    LE TOUBIB (Bel.)—Yvan Govar.
    LO SCAPOLO (Ital.)—Antonio Pietrangeli.
    LOSER TAKES ALL (Brit.)—Ken Annakin.
    MY UNCLE, JACINTO (Span./Ital.)—Ladislao Vajda.
    PESMA SA KUMBARE (Yugo.)—Rados Novakovic.
    RAI KAMAL (India)—Subodh Mittra.
    RICHARD III (Brit.)—Laurence Olivier.
    THE ROAD TO LIFE (Mex.)—Alfonso Corona Blake.
    SCANDAL IN SORRENTO (Ital.)—Marcello Girosi.
    THE SECRET OF SISTER ANGELE (Fr./Ital.)—Leo Joannon.
    SERENADE IN MEXICO (Mex.)—Chano Urveta.
    THE SORCERESS (Fr.)—Andre Michel.
    THE THIRD KEY (Brit.)—Charles Frend.
    TRAPEZE (U.S.)—Carol Reed.
    25 PACES TO BAKER STREET (U.S.)—Henry Hathaway.

THE UNKNOWN SOLDIER (Fin.)—Edvin Laine.
WILHELM TELL (Aust.)—Alfred Stogert

1957
Prizes of the International Jury
Golden Bear for Best Film: TWELVE ANGRY MEN (U.S.)—Sidney Lumet.
Silver Bear for Best Male Performance: Pedro Infante for TIZOC (Mex.).
Silver Bear for Best Female Performance: Yvonne Mitchell for WOMAN IN A DRESSING GOWN (Brit.).
Silver Bear for Best Direction: Mario Monicelli for FATHER AND SONS (Ital.).
Silver Bear for Best Music: Ravi Shankar for KABULIWALA (India).
Silver Bear for WHOM GOD FORGIVES (Span.)—Jose Urana Forque.
Feature Documentary
Golden Bear: SECRETS OF LIFE (U.S.)—James Algar for Walt Disney.
Silver Bear: THE LAST PARADISE (Ital.)—Folco Quilici.
Short Films
Golden Bear: FAR-OFF PEOPLE (Ital.).
Silver Bears
BIG BILL BLUES (Belg.).
ONE THOUSAND SMALL CHARACTERS (Ger.)—Herbert Seggelke.
PLITVICE LAKES (Yugo.)—Dragoslav Holub. Catholic Film Office Award
TWELVE ANGRY MEN (U.S.)—Sidney Lumet.
WOMAN IN A DRESSING GOWN (Brit.)—J. Lee Thompson. (Mention) FIPRESCI Prizes
WOMAN IN A DRESSING GOWN (Brit.)—J. Lee Thompson.
INGEN TID TIL KA ERTEGN (Den.)—Annelise Hovmand.
Competing Films
ABAREMBO KAIDO (Jap.)—Tomu Uchida.
THE ADVENTURES OF ARSENE LUPIN (Fr./Ital.)—Jacques Becker.
DAT LANH (Vietnam)
DIE LETZTEN WERDEN DIE ERSTEN SEIN (Ger.)—Rolf Hansen.
EL FETTOWA (Bel.)—Salah Abu Seif.
EL HOMBRE SENALADO (Arg.)—Francis Lauric.
FATHER AND SONS (Ital.)—Mario Monicelli.
FELICIDAD (Mex.)—Alfonso Corona Blake.
FREEDOM (Nigeria)
THE GIRL OF KORFU (Gr.)—Jannis Petropoulakis.
HANG TUAH (Malaya)—M.C. Sheppard.
INGEN TID TIL KA ERTEGN (Den.)—Annelise Hovmand.
KABULIWALA (India)—Tapan Sinha.
LA FINESTRA SUL LUNAPARK (Ital.)—Luigi Comencini.
THE MAN IN THE RAINCOAT (Fr./Ital.)—Julien Duvivier.
NIJE BILO UZALUD (Yugo.)—Nikola Tanhofer.
NO SUN IN VENICE (Fr./Ital.)—Roger Vadim.
SISTA PARET UT (Swed.)—Alf Sjoberg.
THE SPANISH GARDENER (Brit.)—Philip Leacock.
STEVNEMOTE MET GLEMTE AR (Nor.)—Jon Lennart Mjoen.
THE STORM (Jap.)—Hiroshi Inagaki.
STOWAWAY GIRL (Brit.)—Guy Hamilton.
THE TEAHOUSE OF THE AUGUST MOON (U.S.)—Daniel Mann.
TIZOC (Mex.)—Ismael Rodriguez.
TWELVE ANGRY MEN (U.S.)—Sidney Lumet.
THE VALLEY OF LOST SOULS (Hong Kong)—Yien Chuen.
THE WAYWARD BUS (U.S.)—Victor Vicas.
THE WEDDING DAY (Kor.)—Lee Byung Il.
WHOM GOD FORGIVES (Span.)—Jose Urana Forque.
WOMAN IN A DRESSING GOWN (Brit.)—J. Lee Thompson.

1958
Prizes of the International Jury
Golden Bear for Best Film: WILD STRAWBERRIES (Swed.)—Ingmar Bergman.
Silver Bear for Best Male Performance: Sidney Poitier for THE DEFIANT ONES (U.S.).
Silver Bear for Best Female Performance: Anna Magnani for WILD IS THE WIND (U.S.)
Silver Bear for Best Direction: Tadashi Imai for STORY OF TRUE LOVE (Jap.).
Silver Bear: TWO EYES, TWELVE HANDS (India)—V. Shantaram.
Feature Documentary
Golden Bear: PERRI (U.S.)—N. Paul Kenworthy and Rakph Wright for Walt Disney.
Silver Bear: TRAUMSTRASSE DER WELT (Ger.)—Hans Domnick.
Short Films
Golden Bear: OLIVE HARVEST IN CALABRIA (Ital.)—Lionetto Fabbri.
Silver Bears
KONIGEN IM FRAUENREICH (Switz.)—H. Zickendraht.
GLAS (Neth.)—Bert Haanstra.
Catholic Film Office Award
TWO EYES, TWELVE HANDS (India)—V. Shantaram.
FIPRESCI Award
ICE COLD IN ALEX (Brit.)—J. Lee Thompson.
JAGUAR (Ghana)—Sean Graham (Special Mention)
Special Award: Victor Sjostrom for his life work and performance in WILD STRAWBERRIES (Swed.).
Prize of the Senators for Volsbildung, for the Best Youthfilm
LA PASSE DU DIABLE (Fr.)—Jacques Dupont and Pierre Schoendoerffer.
Competing Films
ANNA OF BROOKLYN (Ital.)—Carlo Lastricati and Vittorio de Sica.
BAB EL-HADID (Egypt)—Youssef Chahine.
BYAKUA NO YO-JO (Jap.)—Eisuke Takizawa.
THE DEFIANT ONES (U.S.)—Stanley Kramer.
DJAJAPRANA (Indonesia)—Kotot Soekardi.
FEAR OF POWER (Switz.)—Franz Schnyder.
GOLDEN MOUNTAINS (Den.)—Gabriel Axel.
THE HUNTED (Gr.)—Nikos Koundouros.
ICE COLD IN ALEX (Brit.)—J. Lee Thompson.
IT HAPPENED IN BROAD DAYLIGHT (Switz.)—Ladislao Vajda.
THE LAW IS THE LAW (Fr.)—Christian-Jaque.
LOS DIOS ES AJENOS (Arg.)—Roman Vinoly Barreto.
MADCHEN IN UNIFORM (Ger.)—Geza Radvanyi.
MIERCOLES DE CENIZA (Mex.)—Roberto Galvaldon.
MIRIAM (Fin.)—William Markus.
PASSION OF THE WILDERNESS (Brazil)— Zygmunt Sulistrowski.

SCHAB NESCHINI DAR DJAHANNAM (Iran)—Samuel Khotschikian.
STORY OF TRUE LOVE (Jap.)—Tadashi Imai.
TWO EYES, TWELVE HANDS (India)—V. Shantaram.
UNA CITA DE AMOR (Mex.)—Emilio Fernandez.
UT AV MORKET (Nor.)—Alex and Arild Brinchmann.
VIVA LO IMPOSIBLE! (Span.)—Rafael Gil.
WILD IS THE WIND (U.S.)—George Cukor.
WILD STRAWBERRIES (Swed.)—Ingmar Bergman.

1959
Prizes of the International Jury
Golden Bear for Best Film: COUSINS (Fr.)—Claude Chabrol.
Silver Bear for Best Male Performance: Jean Gabin for THE MAGNIFICENT TRAMP (Fr.).
Silver Bear for Best Female Performance: Shirley MacLaine for ASK ANY GIRL (U.S.).
Silver Bear for Best Direction: Akira Kurosawa for THE HIDDEN FORTRESS.
Special Silver Bear: Hayley Mills for TIGER BAY.
Documentary and Short Films
Golden Bear for Best Feature Documentary: WHITE WILDERNESS (U.S.)—James Algar for Walt Disney.
Golden Bear for Best Short Film: PRAISE THE SEA (Neth.)—Herman van der Horst.
Silver Bear for Short Film: HEST PAA FERIE (Neth.)—Astrid Henning-Jensen.
Prizes for Short Films
DAS KNALLEIDOSKOP (Ger.)—Herbert Hunger.
RADHA AND KRISHNA (India)—J.S. Bhownagary.
I DITTERI (Ital.)—Alberto Ancilotto.
Catholic Film Office Award
PARADIES UND FEUEROFEN (Ger.)—Herbert Viktor.
FIPRESCI Award
THE HIDDEN FORTRESS (Jap.)—Akira Kurosawa.
Competing Films
ALLE LIEBEN PETER (Ger.)—Wolfgang Becker.
ASK ANY GIRL (U.S.)—Charles Walters.
ASTERO (Gr.)—Dinos Dimopoulos.
BEYOND ALL LIMITS (Mex.)—Roberto Gavaldon.
CHONGKACK (Korea)—Chunam Yang.
COUSINS (Fr.)—Claude Chabrol.
DIEZ FUSILES ESPERAN (Span./Ital.)—Jose Luis Saenz de Heredia.
DOORP AAN DE RIVIER (Neth.)—Fons Rademaker.
HASSAN AND NAYIMA (Egypt)—Henry Barakat.
HERREN OG HANS SEINE TJENERE (Nor.)—Arne Skouen.
THE HIDDEN FORTRESS (Jap.)—Akira Kurosawa.
HOME IS THE HERO (Brit.)—J. Fielder Cook.
KORKARLEN (Swed.)—Arne Mattsson.
LOVE IN RIO (Brazil)—Carlos Hugo Cristiensen.
THE MAGNIFICENT TRAMP (Fr./Ital.)—Gilles Grangier.
MUNCHHAUSEN (Ger.)—Josef von Baky.
THE NAKED SUN (Jap.)—Miyoji Ieki.
PANOPTIKUM 59 (Aust.)—Walter Kolm-Veltee.
POETEN OG LILLEMOR (Den.)—Erik Balling.
POWER AMONG MEN (Ital.)—Alexander Hammid and G. L. Polidoro.
THE REST IS SILENCE (Ger.)—Helmut Kautner.
SAGAR SANGAME (India)—Debaki Kumar Bose.
THE SIEGE OF PINCHGUT (Brit.)—Harry Watt.
STRANGE GUESTS (Arg.)—Leopoldo Torre-Nilsson.
SVEN TUUVA (Fin.)—Edvin Laine.
TELESME SCHEKASTE (Iran)—Syamak Yassami.
THAT KIND OF WOMAN (U.S.)—Sidney Lumet.
TIGER BAY (Brit.)—J. Lee Thompson.
UND DAS AM MONTAGMORGEN (Ger.)—Luigi Comencini.
UN UOMO FACILE (Ital.)—Paojo Heusch.
WOLVES IN THE DEPTHS (Ital./Fr.)—Silvio Amadio.

1960
Prizes of the International Jury
Golden Bear for Best Film: LAZARILLO (Span.)—Cesar Ardavin.
Silver Bear for Best Male Performance: Fredric March for INHERIT THE WIND (U.S.).
Silver Bear for Best Female Performance: Juliette Mayniel for COUNTY FAIR (Ger.).
Silver Bear for Best Direction: Jean-Luc Godard for BREATHLESS (Fr.).
Silver Bear for Best Film Comedy: THE LOVE GAME (Fr.)—Philippe de Broca.
Documentary and Short Films
Golden Bear for Best Feature Documentary: ARDENT LOVE (Neth.)—Herman van der Horst.
Honorable Mention for Feature Documentary: MANDARA (Switz.)—Rene Gardi.
Honorable Mention for Best Short Film: LE SONGE DES CHEVAUX SAUVAGES (Fr.)—Denys Colomb Daunant.
Silver Bears for Short Films
DER SPIELVERDERBER (Ger.)—Boris von Borrisholm.
I VECCHI (Ital.)—Raffaele Andreassi.
DIARO (Arg.)—Juan Berend.
Honorable Mentions
HAFENRHYTHMUS (Ger.)—Wolf Hart.
AUSTRIA GLORIOSA (Aust.)
Catholic Film Office Award
THE ANGRY SILENCE (Brit.)—Guy Green.
FIPRESCI Prize
THE ANGRY SILENCE (Brit.)—Guy Green.
Competing Films
THE ANGRY SILENCE (Brit.)—Guy Green.
BIYAYA NG LUPA (Phil.)—Manuel Silos.
THE BLOOD FEAST (Arg.)—Leopoldo Torre –Nilsson.
BREATHLESS (Fr.)—Jean-Luc Godard.
DOA EL KARAWAN (Egypt)—H. Barakat.
GURUM EUN HEULLEO DO (Korea)—Yu Hyun-Mok.
INHERIT THE WIND (US)—Stanley Kramer.
KAKS' TAVALLISTA LAHTISTA (Fin.)—Ville Salminen.
KIRMES (Ger.)—Wolfgang Staudte.

LAZARILLO (Span.)—Cesar Ardavin.
LOVE AND LARCENY (Ital.)—Dino Risi.
THE LOVE GAME (Fr.)—Philippe de Broca.
MEN OF RIO (Brazil)—Nelson Marcellino de Carvalho.
MOULIN ROUGE (Brit.)—John Huston.
MY SECOND BROTHER (Jap.)—Shohei Imamura.
MY SLAVE (Thai.)—Ubol Yugala.
NAI KIRAN (Pakistan)—S.M. Agha.
OUR LAST SPRING (Gr.)—Michael Cacoyannis.
PENSION SCHOLLER (Ger.)—Georg Jacoby.
PICKPOCKET (Fr.)—Robert Bresson.
PUBERUN (India)—P. Mukherjee.
SANGKAMMARTJUVEN (Swed.)—Goran Gentele.
TRO, HAB OG TROLLDOM (Den.)—Erik Balling.
UNDER TEN FLAGS (Ital.)—Duilio Coletti.
VENNER (Nor.)—Tancred Ibsen.
VILLAGE SUNDAY (U.S.)—Stewart Wilensky.
WILD RIVER (U.S.)—Elia Kazan.
A WOMAN'S TESTAMENT (Jap.)—Kozaburo Yoshimura, Kon Ichikawa, and Yasuzo Masumura.

1961
Prizes of the International Jury
  Golden Bear for Best Film: LA NOTTE (Ital.)—Michelangelo Antonioni.
  Silver Bear for Best Male Performance: Peter Finch for NO LOVE FOR JOHNNIE (Brit.).
  Silver Bear for Best Female Performance: Anna Karina for A WOMAN IS A WOMAN (Fr.).
  Silver Bear for Best Direction: Bernhard Wicki for THE MIRACLE OF FATHER MALACHIAS (Ger.).
  Silver Bears for Special Jury Prize
    A WOMAN IS A WOMAN (Fr.)—Jean-Luc Godard.
    MABU (Korea)—Dae Jin-Kang.
    MAKKERS, STAAKT UW WILD GERASS (Neth.)—Fons Rademakers.
Feature Documentary and Culture Films
  Golden Bear for Best Feature Documentary: DESCRIPTION OF A STRUGGLE (Israel)—Chris Marker.
  Silver Bear for Feature Documentary: TRAUMLAND DER SEHNSUCHT (Ger.)—Wolfgang Mueller-Sehn.
Short Films
  Golden Bear for Best Short Film: GESICHT VON DER STANGE? (Ger.)—Raimond Ruehl.
  Silver Bears
    CHIMICHIMITO (Ven.)—Jose Martin.
    DE LAGE LANDEN (Neth.)—George Sluizer.
    LO SPECCHIO, LA TIGRE, ET LA PIANURA (Ital.).
    SIRENES (Belg.)—Emile Degelin.
    MORNING ON THE LIEVRE (Can.)—David Bairstow.
Catholic Film Office Award
  QUESTION 7 (U.S.)—Stuart Rosenberg. FIPRESCI Prize
Michelangelo Antonioni for his body of work.
Competing Films
AMELIE OR THE TIME TO LOVE (Fr.)—Michel Drach.
ANTIGONE (Gr.)—George Tzavellas.
ANURADHA (India)—Hrishikesh Mukerjee.
THE BAD SLEEP WELL (Jap.)—Akira Kurosawa.
BLACK SILK (Thai.)—Ratana Pestonji, Ratanavadi Ratanabhand, and Thom Viswachart.
DIE EHE DES HERRN MISSISSIPPI (Switz./Ger.)—Kurt Hoffmann.
THE END OF THE CANGACEIROS (Brazil)—Walter Guimaraes Motta.
THE FIVE DAY LOVERS (Fr.)—Philippe de Broca.
IKURU (Jap.)—Akira Kurosawa.
KRIK CANAKLAR (Turkey)—Memduh Un.
LA NOTTE (Ital.)—Michelangelo Antonioni.
LA POTOTA (Arg.)—Daniel Tinayre.
THE LADY KILLERS OF ROME (Ital./Fr.)—Elio Petri.
LOS JOVENES (Mex.)—Luis Alcoriza.
MABU (Korea)—Dae Jin-Kang.
MACBETH (Brit.)—George Schaeffer.
MAKKERS, STAAKT UW WILD GERAAS (Neth.)—Fons Rademakers.
THE MIRACLE OF FATHER MALACHIAS (Ger.)—Bernhard Wicki.
NO LOVE FOR JOHNNIE (Brit.)—Ralph Thomas.
THE PLEASURE OF HIS COMPANY (US)—George Seaton.
QUESTION 7 (U.S./Ger.)—Stuart Rosenberg.
THE RED DOVE (Fin.)—Matti Kassila.
ROMANOFF AND JULIET (U.S.)—Peter Ustinov.
TEENAGER (Egypt)—Ahmed Dhia El Din.
TWO LOVES (U.S.)—Charles Walters.
ZONE OF DANGER (Nor.)—Bjorn Breigutu.

1962
Prizes of the International Jury
  Golden Bear for Best Film: A KIND OF LOVING (Brit.)—John Schlesinger.
  Silver Bear for Best Male Performance: James Stewart for MR. HOBBS TAKES A VACATION (US).
  Silver Bear for Best Female Performance: Viveca Landfors and Rita Gam for NO EXIT (Arg.).
  Silver Bear for Best Direction: Francesco Rosi for SALVATORE GIULIANO (Ital.).
  Silver Bear for Most Promising Newcomer: Jon Young Sun as revealed in TO THE LAST DAY (Korea).
Documentary and Short Films
  Silver Bear for Feature Length Documentary: GALAPAGOS (Ger.)—Heinz Sielmann.
  Golden Bear for Best Short Film: THE WORK OF KAREL APPEL (Neth.)—Jan Vrijman.
  Silver Bears for Short Films
    LE GRANDE MAGAL DE TOUBE (Senegal)—Blaise Senghor.
    NAHANNI (Can.)—Nicholas Balla.
    THE ANCESTORS (Nigeria)—Andre Libik.
    VENEDIG (Aust.)—Kurt Steinwender.
    TEST FOR THE WEST: BERLIN (Ger.)—Franz Baake.

Catholic Film Office Award
  THROUGH A GLASS DARKLY (Swed.)—Ingmar Bergman.
FIPRESCI Prize
  ZOO (Neth.)—Bert Haanstra.
Competing Films
AL ZOUGA TALATTASHAR—Fatin Abdel Wahab.
BADAI-SELATAN (Indonesia)—Sofia Waldi.
DONNEZ-MOI DIX HOMMES DESESPERES (Fr./Israel)—Pierre Zimmer.
DUELLEN (Den.)—Knud Leif Thomsen.
EARLY AUTUMN (Jap.)—Yasujiro Ozu.
EL TEJEDOR DE MILAGROS (Mex.)—Francisco del Villar.
HUM DONO (India)—Amar Jeet.
IL Y A UN TRAIN TOUTES LES HEURES (Belg.)—Andre Cavens.
LA BELLEZA DI IPPOLITA (Ital.)—Giancarlo Zagni.
LA POUPEE (Fr.)—Jacques Baratier.
LAS HERMANAS (Arg.)—Daniel Tinayre.
LOS ATRACADORES (Span.)—Rovira Beleta.
LOVE AT TWENTY (Fr.)—Francois Truffaut, Andrzej Wajda, Renzo Rossellini, Shintaro Ishihara, Marcel Ophuls.
MR. HOBBS TAKES A VACATION (U.S.)—Henry Koster.
NO EXIT (Arg.)—Tad Danielewski.
OS CAFAJESTES (Brazil)—Ruy Guerra.
OUT OF THE TIGER'S MOUTH (U.S.)—Tim Whelan, Jr.
PIKKU PIETARIN PIEHA (Fin.)—Jack Wirikka.
THE REDHEAD (Ger./Ital.)—Helmut Kautner.
SALVATORE GIULIANO (Ital.)—Francesco Rosi.
THE STEPPE (Ital.)—Alberto Lattuada.
TA CHERIA (Gr.)—John G. Contes.
THROUGH A GLASS DARKLY (Swed.)—Ingmar Bergman.
TO THE LAST DAY (Korea)—Shin Sang Okk.
TONNY (Nor.)—Nils R. Muller.
THE VANISHING CORPORAL (Fr.)—Jean Renoir.

1963
Prizes of the International Jury
  Golden Bear for Best Film
    BUSHIDO (Jap.)—Tadashi Imai.
    THE DEVIL (Ital.)—Gian Luigi Polidoro.
  Silver Bear for Best Male Performance: Sidney Poitier for LILIES OF THE FIELD (U.S.).
  Silver Bear for Best Female Performance: Bibi Andersson for THE SWEDISH MISTRESS.
  Silver Bear for Best Direction: Nikos Koundouras for YOUNG APHRODITES (Gr.).
  Special Jury Prize: THE GUEST (Brit.)—Clive Donner.
Documentary and Short Films
  Golden Bear for Feature Documentary: THE GREAT ATLANTIC (Ger.)—Peter Baylis.
  Golden for Best Short Film: BOUWSPELEMENT (Neth.)—Charles Huguenot van de Linden.
  Silver Bears
    THE HOME-MADE CAR (Brit.)—James Hill.
    FLAMING POPPIES (Iran)—Houshang Shafti.
    TOVI (Fin.)—Errko Kivikoski.
Catholic Film Office Award
  LILIES OF THE FIELD (US)—Ralph Nelson.
FIPRESCI Prize
  YOUNG APHRODITES (Gr.)—Nikos Koundouras.
  THE REUNION (Ital.)—Damiano Damiani (Honorable Mention).
Competing Films
BUSHIDO (Jap.)—Tadashi Imai.
THE COUNTRY DOCTOR (Por.)—Jorge Brum do Canto.
DELAY IN MARIENBORN (Ger.)—Rolf Haedrich.
THE DEVIL (Ital.)—Gian Luigi Polidoro.
EL LESS WAL KILAB (Egypt)—Kamal El Sheikh.
FREUD (US)—John Huston.
GARRINCHA—ALEGRIA DO POVO (Brazil)—Joaquim Pedro.
HA'MARTEFF (Israel)—Natan Gross.
THE INNOCENTS (Span.)—Juan Antonio Bardem.
KING, QUEEN, AND SLAVE (India)—Abrar Alvi.
LEVEN IN DOOD OP HET LAND (Bel.)—Emile Degelin.
L'IMMORTELLE (Fr.)—Alain Robbe-Grillet.
THE LILIES OF THE FIELD (U.S.)—Ralph Nelson.
MENSCH UND BESTIE (Ger.)—Edwin Zbonek.
THE REUNION (Ital.)—Damiano Damiani.
THE ROOF GARDEN (Arg.)—Leopoldo Torre Nilsson.
THE SUITOR (Fr.)—Pierre Etaix.
THE SWEDISH MISTRESS (Swed.)—Vilgot Sjoman.
THANK HEAVEN FOR SMALL FAVORS (Fr.)—Jean-Pierre Mocky.
YKSIT YISALUE (Fin.)—Maunu Kurkvaara.
YOLLYOMOON (Korea)—Shin Sang Ok.
YOUNG APHRODITES (Gr.)—Nicos Koundouros.

1964
Prizes of the International Jury
  Golden Bear for Best Film: DRY SUMMER (Turkey)—Ismail Metin.
  Silver Bear for Best Male Performance: Rod Steiger for THE PAWNBROKER (U.S.).
  Silver Bear for Best Female Performance: Sachiko Hidari for SHE AND HE (Jap.) and THE INSECT WOMAN (Jap.).
  Silver Bear for Best Direction: Satyajit Ray for MAHANAGAR (India).
  Silver Bear for Special Jury Prize: THE GUNS (Bra.)—Ruy Guerra.
Documentary and Short Films
  Golden Bear for Feature Documentary: ALLEMAN (Neth.)—Bert Haanstra.
  Golden Bear for Best Short Film: KIRDI (Aust.)—Max Lersch.
  Silver Bears
    SUNDAY LARK (U.S.)—Sanford Semel.
    KONTRASTE (Ger.)—Wolfgang Urchs.
    AANMELDING (Neth.)—Bob Houwer.
Catholic Film Office Award
  SHE AND HE (Jap.)—Susumu Hani.
FIPRESCI Prize

THE VISIT (Ital.)—Antonio Pietrangeli.
HERRENPARTIE (Ger/Yugo.)—Wolfgang Staudte.
Competing Films
BEBO'S GIRL (Ital.)—Luigi Comencini.
CIRCE (Arg.)—Manuel Antin.
DRY SUMMER (Turkey)—Ismail Metin.
THE ESCAPED (Arg.)—Enrique Carreras.
FAUST (U.S.)—Michael Suman.
THE GUNS (Brazil)—Riy Guerra.
HERRENPARTIE (Ger./Yugo.)—Wolfgang Stadte.
THE INSECT WOMAN (Jap.)—Shohei Imamura.
LA DIFFICULTE D'ETRE INFIDELE (Fr./Ital.)—Bernard T. Michel.
LAMENT FOR A BANDIT (Span./Fr./Ital.)—Carlos Saura.
L'AMOUR AVEC DES SI... (Fr.)—Claude Lelouch.
MAHANGAR (India)—Satyajit Ray.
NIGHT MUST FALL (Brit.)—Karel Reisz.
OF HUMAN BONDAGE (Brit.)—Ken Hughes and Henry Hathaway.
OLLE OLSON HAGELUND (Swed.)—Rune Ericsson.
THE PAWNBROKER (U.S.)—Sidney Lumet.
SELVMORDSSKOLEN (Den.)—Knud Leif Thomsen.
SHE AND HE (Jap.)—Susumu Hani.
SOFT HANDS (Egypt)—Mahmoud Zoulfikar.
THIS SUMMER AT FIVE (Fin.)—Erkko Kivikoski.
TONIO KROGER (Ger./Fr.)—Rolf Thiele.
THE VISIT (Ital.)—Antonio Pietrangeli.
ZEIT DER SCHULDLOSEN (Ger.)—Thomas Fantl.

1965
Prizes of the International Jury
Golden Bear for Best Film: ALPHAVILLE (Fr.)—Jean-Luc Godard.
Special Jury Award, Silver Bear
    LE BONHEUR (Fr.)—Agnes Varda.
    REPULSION (Brit.)—Roman Polanski.
Silver Bear for Best Male Performance: Lee Marvin for CAT BALLOU (U.S.).
Silver Bear for Best Female Performance: Madhur Jaffrey for SHAKESPEARE WALLAH. (India).
Silver Bear for Best Direction: Satyajit Ray for CHARULATA (India).
Honorable Mentions: Walter Newman, Frank Pierson for the screenplay of CAT BALLOU (U.S.).
Golden Bear for Best Short Film: YEATS COUNTRY (Ireland)—Patrick Carey.
Silver Bear for Best Short Film: EEN ZONDAG OP HET EILAND VAN DE GRANDE JATTE (Neth.)—Frans Weisz.
Short Film Honorable Mention: THE RAILROADER (Can.)—Gerald Potterton.
Catholic Film Office Award
CHARULATA (India)—Satyajit Ray.
FIPRESCI Prize
REPULSION (Brit.)—Roman Polanski.
LOVE 65 (Swed.)—Bo Widerberg (Honorable Mention).
Competing Films
ALPHAVILLE (Fr./Ital.)—Jean-Luc Godard.
CAT BALLOU (U.S.)—Elliot Silverstein.
CHARULATA (India)—Satyajit Ray.
THE DRESS (Swed.)—Vilgot Sjoman.
EL ARTE DE VIVIR (Span.)—Julio Diamante.
KABE NO NAKANO HIMEGOTO (Jap.)—Koji Wakamatsu.
THE KNACK...AND HOW TO GET IT (Brit.)—Richard Lester.
KUNGSLEDEN (Swed.)—Gunnar Hoglund.
LE BONHEUR (Fr.)—Agnes Varda.
THE LIFE OF PAJARITO GOMEZ (Arg.)—Rodolfo Kuhn.
LOVE 65 (Swed.)—Bo Widerberg.
THE RECKLESS (Ital.)—Giuliano Montaldo.
REPULSION (Brit.)—Roman Polanski.
SHAKESPEARE WALLAH (India)—James Ivory.
THOMAS THE IMPOSTER (Fr.)—Georges Franju.
TWO (Den.)—Palle Kjaerulff-Schmidt.
VEREDA DA SALVACAO (Brazil)—Anselmo Duarte.
WALSUNGENBLUT (Ger.)—Rolf Thiele.

1966
Prizes of the International Jury
Golden Bear for Best Film: CUL-DE-SAC (Brit.)—Roman Polanski.
Silver Bear for Best Male Performance: Jean-Pierre Leaud for MASCULIN-FEMI-NIN (Fr.).
Silver Bear for Best Female Performance: Lola Albright for LORD LOVE A DUCK (U.S.).
Silver Bear for Best Direction: Carlos Saura for THE HUNT (Span.).
Special Jury Prize, Silver Bear
    OFFSEASON FOR FOXES (Ger.)—Peter Schamoni.
    Lars Passgard for MANHUNT (Swed.).
Honorable Mention: Satyajit Ray for THE HERO (India), and his entire body of work.
Golden Bear for Best Short: KNUD (Den.)—Jorgen Roos.
Silver Bear for Best Short: ROSALIE (Fr.)—Walerian Borowczyk.
Catholic Film Office Award
GEORGY GIRL (Brit.)—Silvio Narizzano.
FIPRESCI Prize
SEASONS OF OUR LOVE (Ital.)—Florestano Vancini.
Honorary Award: Max Ophuls for his body of work.
Competing Films
CUL-DE-SAC (Brit.)—Roman Polanski.
GEORGY GIRL (Brit.)—Silvio Narrizzano.
THE GROUP (U.S.)—Sidney Lumet.
THE HERO (India)—Satyajit Ray.
THE HUNT (Span.)—Carlos Saura.
LES COEURS VERTS (Fr.)—Edouard Luntz.
LORD LOVE A DUCK (U.S.)—George Axelrod.
MANHUNT (Swed.)—Yngue Gamlin.
MASCULIN-FEMININ (Fr./Swed.)—Jean-Luc Godard.
O FOVOS (Gr.)—Costas Manoussakis.
OFFSEASON FOR FOXES (Ger.)—Peter Schamoni.
THE PRIEST AND THE GIRL (Bra.)—Joaquin Pedro de Andrade.
SEASONS OF OUR LOVE (Ital.)—Florestano Vancini.

1967
Prizes of the International Jury
Golden Bear for Best Film: LE DEPART (Belg.)—Jerzy Skolimowski.
Silver Bear for Best Male Performance: Michel Simon for THE OLD MAN AND THE BOY (Fr.).
Silver Bear for Best Female Performance: Edith Evans for THE WHISPERERS (Brit.).
Silver Bear for Best Direction: Zivojin Pavlovic for THE RATS AWAKEN.
Special Jury Prize: LA COLLECTIONEUSE (Fr.)—Eric Rohmer.
    Michael Lentz for the idea and Screenplay for EVERY YEAR AGAIN (Ger.).
Golden Bear for Best Short Film: THROUGH THE EYES OF A PAINTER (India)—M.F. Hussain.
Silver Bear for Short Film: FLEA CEOIL (Ireland)—Louis Marcus.
Catholic Film Office Award
THE WHISPERERS (Brit.)—Bryan Forbes. FIPRESCI Prize
EVERY YEAR AGAIN (Ger.)—Ulrich Schamoni.
Competing Films
EVERY YEAR AGAIN (Ger.)—Ulrich Schamoni.
FACE OF MEDUSA (Gr.)—Nikos Koundouros.
HERE IS YOUR LIFE (Swed.)—Jan Troell.
HET GANGSTERMEISJE (Neth.)—Frans Weisz.
HISTORY OF BARBARA (Den.)—Palle Kjaerulff-Schmidt.
IL FISCHIO AL NASO (Ital.)—Ugo Tognazzi.
LA COLLECTIONNEUSE (Fr.)—Eric Rohmer.
LA NOTTE PAZZA DEL CONGLIACCIO (Ital.)—Alfredo Angeli.
LE DEPART (Bel.)—Jerzy Skolimowski.
LE MUR (Fr.)—Serge Roullet.
LIV (Nor.)—Pal Lakkeberg.
LIVET AR STENKUL (Swed.)—Jan Halldoff.
NOCHE TERRIBLE (Arg.)—Rodolfo Kuhn.
THE OLD MAN AND THE BOY (Fr.)—Claude Berri.
PARANOIA (Neth.)—Adriaan Ditvoorst.
THE RATS AWAKEN (Yugo.)—Zivojin Pavlovic.
SAN (Yugo.)—Purisa Djordjevic.
SEKISHUN (Jap.)—Noboru Nakamura.
TATOWIERUNG (Ger.)—Johannes Schaaf.
THE WHISPERERS (Brit.)—Bryan Forbes.

1968
Prizes of the International Jury
Golden Bear for Best Film: EENY MEANY MINY MOE (Swed.)—Jan Troell.
Silver Bear for Best Male Performance: Jean-Louis Trintignant for THE MAN WHO LIES (Fr./Czech.).
Silver Bear for Best Female Performance: Stephane Audran for LES BICHES (Fr.).
Silver Bear for Best Direction: Carlos Saura for PEPPERMINT FRAPPE (Span.).
Special Jury Prize, Silver Bear:
    INNOCENCE UNPROTECTED (Yugo.)—Dusan Makavejev.
    COME L'AMORE (Ital.)—Enzo Muzii.
    SIGNS OF LIFE (Ger.)—Werner Herzog (For First Feature).
Short Films:
    Golden Bear for Best Short Film: PORTRAIT OF ORSON WELLES (Fr.)—Francois Reichenbach and Fr. Rossif.
    Silver Bears
        TOETS (Neth.)—Tom Tholen.
        KREK (Yugo.)—Borivoj Dovnikovic-Bordo.
        Honorable Mention: ASTA NIELSEN (Den.)—Asta Nielsen.
Catholic Film Office Award
EENY MEANY MINY MOE (Swed.)—Jan Troell. FIPRESCI Prize
INNOCENCE UNPROTECTED (Yugo.)—Dusan Makavejev.
    Honorary Mention: Asta Nielsen for her short film ASTA NIELSEN (Den.).
Competing Films
CHARLY (U.S.)—Ralph Nelson.
CHRONICLE OF ANNA MAGDALENA BACH (Ger./Ital.)—Jean-Marie Straub.
COME L'AMORE (Ital.)—Enzo Muzii.
EENY MEANY MINY MOE (Swed.)—Jan Troell.
THE ERNIE GAME (Can.)—Don Owen.
GATES TO PARADISE (Brit.)—Andrzej Wajda.
HUNGER FOR LOVE (Bra.)—Nelson Pereira dos Santos.
IL GIORNO DELLA CIVETTA (Ital./Fr.)—Damiano Damiani.
THE IMMORTAL STORY (Fr.)—Orson Welles.
INNOCENCE UNPROTECTED (Yugo.)—Dusan Makavejev.
LES BICHES (Fr./Ital.)—Claude Chabrol.
THE MAN WHO LIES (Fr.)—Alain Robbe-Grillet.
PEPPERMINT FRAPPE (Span.)—Carlos Saura.
SIGNS OF LIFE (Ger.)—Werner Herzog.
TO GRAB THE RING (Neth.)—Nikolai van der Heyde.
THE VIOLENT FOUR (Ital.)—Carlo Lizzani.
WEEKEND (Fr.)—Jean-Luc Godard.

1969
Prizes of the International Jury
Golden Bear for Best Film: EARLY WORKS (Yugo.)—Zelimir Zilnik.
Silver Bears
    BRAZIL YEAR 2000 (Brazil)—Walter Jima, Jr.
    MADE IN SWEDEN (Swed.)—Johan Bergenstrahle.
    I AM AN ELEPHANT, MADAME (Ger.)—Peter Zadek.
    A QUIET PLACE IN THE COUNTRY (Ital.)—Elio Petri.
    GREETINGS (U.S.)—Brian De Palma.
(No Awards named for Best Actor, Actress, or Direction
Golden Bear for Best Short Subject: TO SEE OR NOT TO SEE (Can.)—
Silver Bear for Best Short Subject: PRESADJIVANJE OSECANJA (Yugo.)—Dejan Djurkovic.
Catholic Film Office Award
MIDNIGHT COWBOY (U.S.)—John Schlesinger.
FIPRESCI Prize
The Series on Yugoslavian Youth Films:
    RONDO—Zvonimir Berkovic.
    JUTRO—Purisa Djordjevic.
    HOROSKOP—Boro Drascovic.
    GRAVITATION—Branko Ivanda.
    BAJKA—Gordan Mihic and Ljubisa Kozomara.

KAD BUDEN MRTAV I BEO—Zivojin Pavlovic.
SEDMINA—Matjaz Klopcic.
Luis Bunuel received an Honorable Mention for his contribution to film.
Competing Films
THE ADVENTURES OF GOOPY AND BAGHA (India)—Satyajit Ray.
AIDO, SLAVE OF LOVE (Jap.)—Susumu Hani.
THE BALLAD OF CARL-HENNING (Den.)—Lene and Sven Gronlykke.
THE BED SITTING ROOM (Brit.)—Richard Lester.
BRAZIL YEAR 2000 (Brazil)—Walter Lima, Jr.
COUP DE GRACE (Arg.)—Ricardo Becher.
EROTISSMO (Fr./Ital.)—Gerard Pires.
GREETINGS (U.S.)—Brian De Palma.
HONEYCOMB (Span.)—Carlos Saura.
I AM AN ELEPHANT, MADAME (Ger.)—Peter Zadek.
LA SUA GIORNATA DI GLORIA (Ital.)—Edoardo Bruno.
LE GAI SAVIOR (Fr.)—Jean-Luc Godard.
LOVE AND ANGER (Ital./Fr.)—Carlo Lizzani, Pier Paolo Pasolini, Bernardo Bertolucci, Jean-Luc Godard, Marco Bellocchio.
LOVE IS COLDER THAN DEATH (Ger.)—Rainer Werner Fassbinder.
MADE IN SWEDEN (Swed.)—Johann Bergenstrahle.
MIDNIGHT COWBOY (U.S.)—John Schlesinger.
RANI RADOVI (Yugo.)—Zelemir Zilnik.
THANK YOU ALL VERY MUCH (Brit./U.S.)—Waris Hussein.
THREE INTO TWO WON'T GO (Brit.)—Peter Hall.
WE ARE ALL DEMONS (Den.)—Henning Carlsen.

1970
The International Jury was unable to name any Official Prizes as a result of political unrest that forced the festival to shut down.
Catholic Film Office Awards
WHY DOES HERR R RUN AMOK? (Ger.)—Rainer Werner Fassbinder.
THE TRAVELLER (Israel/Fr.)—Moshe Mizrahi.
EL CHACAL DE NAHUELTORO (Chile)—Miguel Littin Cucumides.
OUT OF IT (U.S.)—Paul Williams.
Competing Films
BALTUTLAMNINGEN (Swed.)—Johan Bergenstrahle.
BLACK OUT (Switz.)—Jean-Louis Roy.
CHI NO MURE (Jap.)—Kei Kumai.
THE CONFORMIST (Ital./Fr.)—Bernardo Bertolucci.
DAYS AND NIGHTS IN THE FOREST (India)—Satyajit Ray.
DIONYSUS IN 69 (U.S.)—Brian De Palma.
EL CHACAL DE NAHUELTORO (Chile)—Miguel Littin Cucumides.
EN KARLEKSHUSTORIA (Swed.)—Roy Andersson.
L'EDEN ET APRES (Fr.)—Alain Robbe-Grillet.
LE TEMPS DE MOURIR (Fr.)—Andre Farwagi.
LOS HEREDEROS (Arg.)—David Stivel.
L'URLO (Ital.)—Tinto Brass.
O.K. (Ger.)—Michael Verhoeven.
O PROFETA DA FOME (Brasil)—Maurice Capovilla.
OS DEUSES E OS MORTOS (Brasil)—Ruy Guerra.
OUT OF IT (US)—Paul Williams.
THE TRAVELLER (Israel/Fr.)—Moshe Mirahi.
WHY DOES HERR R RUN AMOK? (Ger.)—Rainer Werner Fassbinder.

1971
Prizes of the International Jury
Golden Bear for Best Film: THE GARDEN OF THE FINZI-CONTINIS (Ital.)—Vittorio de Sica.
Special Jury Prize, Silver Bear: DECAMERON (Ital.)—Pier Paolo Pasolini.
Silver Bear for Best Male Performance: Jean Gabin for LE CHAT (Fr.).
Silver Bear for Best Female Performance: Simone Signoret for LE CHAT (Fr.), and Shirley MacLaine for DESPERATE CHARACTERS (U.S.).
Silver Bear for Best Screenplay: Frank Gilroy for DESPERATE CHARACTERS (U.S.).
Silver Bear for Best Camerawork: Ragner Lasse for LOVE IS WAR (Nor.).
Golden Bear for Best Short Film: 1501 1/2 (U.S.)—Paul B. Brice.
Silver Bear for Short Film: IN CONTINUO (Yugo.)—Vlatko Gilic.
Silver Bear for Animated Film: DIE ORDNUNG (Ger.)—Boris von Borresholm and Bohumil Stepan.
Honorable Mention: ANG.: LONE (Den.)—Franz Ernst.
Catholic Film Office Award
BLESS THE BEASTS AND THE CHILDREN (U.S.)—Stanley Kramer.
FOUR NIGHTS OF A DREAMER (Fr.)—Robert Bresson.
Empfehlungen Forum
BANANERA LIBERTAD (Switz.)
REMPARTS D'ARGILE (Fr.)
TROPICI (Ital.)
LA SALAMANDRE (Switz.)—Alain Tanner.
FIPRESCI Prize
International Forum on Youth Films:
ANAPARASTASSI (Gr.)—
W.R.—MYSTERIES OF THE ORGANISM (Yugo.)—Dusan Makavejev.
ARGENTINA, MAYO (Arg.)
Competing Films
ANG.: LONE (Den.)—Franz Ernst.
BLESS THE BEASTS AND THE CHILDREN (U.S.)—Stanley Kramer.
BLUSHING CHARLIE (Swed.)—Vilgot Sjoman.
COMO ERA GOSTOSO O MEU FRANCIS (Brazil)—Nelson Pereira dos Santos.
DECAMERON (Ital./Fr./Ger.)—Pier Paolo Pasolini.
DESPERATE CHARACTERS (U.S.)—Frank Gilroy.
DULCIMA (Brit.)—Frank Nesbitt.
THE FIRST DAY (Aust.)—Herbert Holba.
FOUR NIGHTS OF A DREAMER (Fr.)—Robert Bresson.
THE GARDEN OF THE FINZI-CONTINIS (Ital.)—Vittorio de Sica.
THE HERO (Israel/Brit.)—Richard Harris.
JAIDER—DER EINSAME JAGER (Ger.)—Volker Vogeler.
LE CHAT (Fr./Ital.)—Pierre Granier-Deferre.
LOVE IS WAR (Nor.)—Ragnar Lasse.
NINI TIRABUSCIO (Ital.)—Marcello Fondato.
RDECE KLASJE (Yugo.)—Zivojin Pavlovic.
RENDEZVOUS IN BRAY (Belg./Fr.)—Andre Delvaux.

TO LOVE AGAIN (Jap.)—Kon Ichikawa.
WER IM GLASHAUS LIEBT...DER GRABEN (Ger.)—Michael Verhoeven.
WHITY (Ger.)—Rainer Werner Fassbinder.

1972
Prizes of the International Film Jury
Golden Bear for Best Film: THE CANTERBURY TALES (Ital./Fr.)—Pier Paolo Pasolini.
Special Jury Prize, Silver Bear: HOSPITAL (U.S.)—Arthur Hiller.
Silver Bear for Best Male Performance: Alberto Sordi for WHY (Ital.)
Silver Bear for Best Female Performance: Elizabeth Taylor for HAMMERSMITH IS OUT (U.S.)
Silver Bear for Best Direction: Jean-Pierre Blanc for THE SPINSTER (Fr.).
Documentary
WEEKEND OF A CHAMPION (Brit.)—Roman Polanski and Frank Simon (Honorable Mention).
OLYMPIA (Ger.)—Jochen Bauer (Honorable Mention).
Short Subjects
Golden Bear: FLYAWAY (Brit.)—R.O. Lehman.
Silver Bears
THE SELFISH GIANT (Can.)—Peter Sander.
TRI ETIDE ZA MILOSA I CATHY (Yugo.)—Joze Pognacnik.
A Special Silver Bear was awarded to Peter Ustinov for his creative work and for the direction of HAMMERSMITH IS OUT.
Catholic Film Office Awards
Competing Films: DEN FORSVUNDNE FULDMAEGTIG (Den.)—Gert Fredholm.
THE SPINSTER (Fr.)—Jean-Pierre Blanc.
HOSPITAL (US)—Arthur Hiller.
Forum Films: EL CORAJE DEL PUEBLO (Bolivia).
LES CAMISARDES (Fr.).
LOS DIAS DEL AGUA (Cuba).
EMITAI (Senegal).
FAMILY LIFE (Brit.).
GAV (Iran).
YOUNG LORDS (U.S.).
Competing Films
THE AUDIENCE (Ital.)—Marco Ferreri.
THE BITTERS TEARS OF PETRA VAN KANT (Ger.)—Rainer Werner Fassbinder.
THE CANTERBURY TALES (Ital.)—Pier Paolo Pasolini.
DEN FORSVUNDNE FULDMAEGTIG (Den.)—Marco Ferreri.
HAMMERSMITH IS OUT (Brit.)—Peter Ustinov.
HOSPITAL (U.S.)—Arthur Hiller.
JOAO EN HET MES (Brasil/Neth.)—George Sluizer.
LA CASA SIN FRONTERAS (Span.)—Pedro Olea.
LE BAR DE LA ROURCHE (Fr.)—Alain Levent.
LUNKET AVDELING (Nor.)—Arnljot Berg.
MAN SKU' VAERE NOGET VED MUSIKKEN (Den.)—Henning Carlsen.
NEITHER BY DAY NOR BY NIGHT (US/Israel)—Steven Hillard Stern.
THE POSSESSION OF JOEL DELANEY (U.S.)—Waris Hussein.
THE RENDEZVOUS (Jap.)—Koichi Saito.
RESHMA AND SHERA (India)—Sunil Dutt.
SEOK HWA TOCHON (Korea)—Zin-Uh Zeong.
SMEKMANAD (Swed.)—Claes Lundberg.
THE SPINSTER (Fr./Ital.)—Jean-Pierre Blanc.
TOP OF THE HEAP (U.S.)—Christopher St. John.
TRAGOVI CRNE DEVOJKE (Yugo.)—Zdravko Randic.
WHY (Ital.)—Nanni Loy.

1973
Prizes of the International Jury
Golden Bear for Best Film: DISTANT THUNDER (India)—Satyajit Ray.
Special Jury Prize, Silver Bear: WHERE THERE'S SMOKE (Fr.)—Andre Cayatte.
Silver Bears
THE REVOLUTION OF THE SEVEN MADMEN (Arg.)—Leopoldo Torre-Nilsson.
THE TALL BLONDE MAN WITH THE ONE BLACK SHOE (Fr.)—Yves Robert.
THE EXPERTS (Ger.)—Norbert Kackelmann.
ALL NUDITY SHALL BE PUNISHED (Brazil)—Arnaldo Jabor.
THE 14 (Brit.)—David Hemmings.
Short Subjects
Golden Bear: COLTER'S HELL (Brit.)—Robin Lehman.
Silver Bears
SOVA (Yugo.)—Aleksandar Ilic.
JOSEPH SULC (Yugo.)—Pedrag Golubovic.
Catholic Film Office Awards
Competing Films
WHERE THERE'S SMOKE (Fr.)—Andre Cayatte.
DIE SACHVERSTANDIGEN (Ger.)—Norbert Kuckelmann.
THE 14 (Brit.)—David Hemmings.
Forum Films
LE TOUR D'AFRIQUE (Switz.).
LE CHARBONNIER (Algeria).
LO STAGIONALE (Switz.)—Alvo Bizzarai.
SAMBIZANGA (Fr./Congo).
FIPRESCI Prizes
Competing Films
WEDDING IN BLOOD (Fr.)—Claude Chabrol.
Forum Films:
LO STAGIONALE (Switz.)—Alvo Bizzarai.
MERES TOU '36 (Gr.).
Competing Films
ALL NUDITY SHALL BE PUNISHED (Brazil)—Arnaldo Jabor.
ANGELA (LOVE COMES QUIETLY: Neth./Bel.)—Nikolai van der Heyde.
BELLADONNA (Jap.)—Eiichi Yamamoto.
THE BLOCKHOUSE (Brit.)—Clive Rees.
DIE SACHVERSTANDIGEN (Ger.)—Norbert Kuckelmann.
DISTANT THUNDER (India)—Satyajit Ray.
THE 14 (Brit.)—David Hemmings.
GEORGIA, GEORGIA (U.S./Swed.)—Stig Bjorkman.
HABLA MUDITA (Span.)—Manuel Gutierrez Aragon.
LONG LIVE THE ISLAND FROGS (Korea)—Chinwoo Chung.
MALIZIA (Ital.)—Salvatore Samperi.

PEEPING TOMS (Israel)—Uri Zohar.
THE REVOLUTION OF THE SEVEN MADMEN (Arg.)—Leopoldo Torre-Nilsson.
THE TALL BLONDE MAN WITH THE ONE BLACK SHOE (Fr.)—Yves Robert.
TENDERNESS OF WOLVES (Ger.)—Ulli Lommel.
U-TURN (Can.)—George Kaczender.
WEDDING IN BLOOD (Fr.)—Claude Chabrol.
WHERE THERE'S SMOKE (Fr.)—Andre Cayatte.
THE WORKING CLASS GOES TO HEAVEN (Ital.)—Elio Petri.

1974
Prizes of the International Jury
Golden Bear for Best Film: THE APPRENTICESHIP OF DUDDY KRAVITZ (Can.)—Ted Kotcheff.
Special Jury Prize, Silver Bear: THE CLOCKMAKER (Fr.)—Bertrand Tavernier.
Silver Bears
    IN THE NAME OF THE PEOPLE (Ger.)—Ottokar Runze.
    LITTLE MALCOLM (Brit.)—Stuart Cooper.
    BREAD AND CHOCOLATE (Ital.)—Franco Brusati.
    STILL LIFE (Iran)—Sohrab Shahid-Saless.
    REBELLION IN PATAGONIA (Arg.)—Hector Olivera.
Short Subjects
Golden Bear: THE CONCERT (Brit.)—Claude Chagrin.
Silver Bears
    SEA CREATURES (Brit.)—Robin Lehman.
    STRAF (Neth.)—Olga Madsen.
Special Mention: Richard Dreyfuss for his performance in THE APPRENTICESHIP OF DUDDY KRAVITZ (Can.).
Catholic Film Office Awards
Competing Films
    THE CLOCKMAKER (Fr.)—Bertrand Tavernier.
    STILL LIFE (Iran)—Sohrab Shahid-Saless.
    BREAD AND CHOCOLATE (Ital.)—Franco Brusati.
FIPRESCI Prize
    STILL LIFE (Iran)—Sohrab Shahid-Saless.
    Special Award: TO PROXENIO TIS ANNAS (Gr.).
Competing Films
    THE AMLASH ENCHANTED FOREST (Israel)—Shlomo Soriano.
    ANKUR (India)—Shyan Benegal.
    THE APPRENTICESHIP OF DUDDY KRAVITZ (Can.)—Ted Kotcheff.
    ASAYAKE NO UTA (Jap.)—Kei Kumai.
    BOBBYS WAR (Nor.)—Arnljot Berg.
    BREAD AND CHOCOLATE (Ital.)—Franco Brusati.
    CHARLEY-ONE-EYE (Brit.)—Don Chaffey.
    THE CLOCKMAKER (Fr.)—Bertrand Tavernier.
    DE LOTELING (Bel.)—Roland Verhaevert.
    EFFI BRIEST (Ger.)—Rainer Werner Fassbinder.
    IN THE NAME OF THE PEOPLE (Ger.)—Ottokar Runze.
    LES GUICHETS DU LOUVRE (Fr.)—Michel Mitrani.
    LITTLE MALCOLM (Brit.)—Stuart Cooper.
    THE LOVE OF CAPTAIN BRANDO (Span.)—Jaime de Arminan.
    MAA ON SYNTINEN LAULU (Fin.)—Rauni Mollberg.
    THE PELICAN (Fr.)—Gerard Blain.
    PREDSTAVA HAMLETA U MRDUSI DONJOJ (Yugo.)—Krsto Papic.
    SAGARANA, THE DUEL (Brazil)—Paolo Thiago Paes de Oliveira.
    STILL LIFE (Iran)—Sohrab Shahid-Saless.
    THERE IS NO 13 (U.S.)—William Sachs.
    TWO (U.S.)—Charles Trieschmann.
    ZEAMI (Jap.)—Susumu Harada.

1975
Prizes of the International Jury
Golden Bear for Best Film: ADOPTION (Hung.)—Marta Meszaros.
Special Jury Prizes, Silver Bear
    OVERLORD (Brit.)—Stuart Cooper.
    RAPE OF INNOCENCE (Fr.)—Yves Boisset.
Silver Bear for Best Male Performance: Vlastimil Brodsky for JACOB, THE LIAR (E. Ger.)
Silver Bear for Best Female Performance: Kinuyo Tanaka for SANDAKAN 8 (Jap.).
Silver Bear for Best Direction: Sergei Solovyov for A HUNDRED DAYS AFTER CHILDHOOD (U.S.S.R.).
Special Award, Silver Bear: Woody Allen for his body of work.
Short Subjects
Golden Bear: SEE (US)—Robin Lehman.
Silver Bears
    SSS (Czech)—Vaclav Bedrich.
    STRAST (Yugo.)—Aleksandar Illic.
Catholic Film Office Awards
Competing Films
    QUARTERLY BALANCE (Pol.)—Krysztof Zanussi.
    ALIEN (Iran/Ger.)—Sohrab Shahid-Saless.
    SANDAKAN 8 (Jap.)—Kei Kumai.
    THE ADOPTION (Hung.)—Marta Meszaros.
Forum Films
    NESSUNO O TUTTI (Ital.).
    LINA BRAAKE (Ger.).
    FAMILIENGLUCK (Ger.)
    KALINA KRASNAJA (U.S.S.R.).
FIPRESCI Prizes
Competing Film
    ALIEN (Iran/Ger.)—Sohrab Shahid-Saless.
Forum Films
    KALINA KRASNAJA (U.S.S.R.).
    TAGEBUCH (Ger.).
    ISTENMEZEJEN 1972-73-BAN (Hung.).
    NESSUNO O TUTTI (Ital.).
Competing Films
ADOPTION (Hung.)—Marta Meszaros.
ALIEN (Iran/Ger.)—Sohrab Shahid-Saless.
CHILDREN OF THE GRASSLAND (China)—Ru Djia.
FANTASTIC COMEDY (Rum.)—Ion Popescu Gopo.
THE FIRST TIME ON THE GREEN GRASS (Ital.)—Gian Luigi Calderone.

GANGSTERFILMEN (Swed.)—Lars G. Thelestam.
THE GREAT HOUSE (Span.)—Francisco Rodrigues.
ICE-AGE (Nor.)—Peter Zadek.
IL PIATTO PIANGE (Ital.)—Paolo Nuzzi.
JACOB, THE LIAR (E. Ger.)—Frank Beyer.
JOHN GLUECKSTADT (Ger.)—Ulf Miehe.
LA' OS VAERE (Den.)—Lasse Nielsen and Ernst Johansen.
LILY AIME-MOI (Fr.)—Maurice Dugowson.
LOVE AND DEATH (U.S.)—Woody Allen.
OUT OF SEASON (Brit.)—Alan Bridges.
OVERLORD (Brit.)—Stuart Cooper.
POSSE (U.S.)—Kirk Douglas.
QUARTERLY BALANCE (Pol.)—Krysztof Zanussi.
RAPE OF INNOCENCE (Fr.)—Yves Boisset.
SAMNA (India)—Jabber Patel.
SANDAKAN 8 (Jap.)—Kei Kumai.
TO SEARCH FOR A GOLDEN EARTH (Czech.)—Jiri Menzel.

1976
Prizes of the International Jury
Golden Bear for Best Film: BUFFALO BILL AND THE INDIANS OR SITTING BULL'S HISTORY LESSON (U.S.)—Robert Altman.
Special Jury Prize, Silver Bear: CANOA (Mex.)—Felipe Cazals.
Silver Bear: GARDEN OF STONES (Iran)—Parviz Kimiavi.
Silver Bear for Best Male Performance: Gerhard Olschewski for LOST LIFE (Ger.).
Silver Bear for Best Female Performance: Jadwiga Baranska for NIGHTS AND DAYS (Pol.).
Silver Bear for Best Direction: Mario Monicelli for DEAR MICHAEL (Ital.).
Silver Bear for a Director's First Film: MAN WITHOUT A NAME (Hung.)—Laszlo Lugossy.
Short Subjects
Golden Bear: MUNAKATA, THE WOODCARVER (Jap.)—Takeo Yanagawa.
Silver Bears
    TRAINS (U.S.)—Caleb Deschanel.
    OMINIDE (Ital.)—Master Programmi Audiovisivi S.R.L.
Catholic Film Office Award
Competing Films
    THE LONELINESS OF KONRAD STEINER (Switz.)—Kurt Gloor.
    F COMME FAIRBANKS (Fr.)—Maurice Dugowson.
    MAN WITHOUT A NAME (Hung.)—Lazlo Lugossy.
    SMALL CHANGE (Fr.)—Francois Truffaut.
Forum Films: KADDU BEYKAT (Senegal).
FIPRESCI Prize
Competing Film: LAS LARGAS VACACIONES DEL 36 (Span.)—Jaime Camino.
Forum Films
    CHHATRABHANG (India).
    KADDU BEYKAT (Senegal).
Competing Films
THE BEACH GUARD IN WINTER (Yugo.)—Goran Paskaljevic.
BUFFALO BILL AND THE INDIANS OR SITTING BULL'S HISTORY LESSON (U.S.)—Robert Altman.
CANOA (Mex.)—Felipe Cazals.
DEAR MICHAEL (Ital.)—Mario Monicelli.
DEATH AT THE OLD MANSION (Jap.)—Yoichi Takabayashi.
DIVINE CREATURE (Ital.)—Giuseppe Patroni Griffi.
DVOJI SVET HOTELU PACIFIK (Czech./Pol.)—Janusz Majewski.
EXPROPIACION (Ven./Peru)—Mario Robles.
F COMME FAIRBANKS (Fr.)—Maurice Dugowson.
GARDEN OF STONES (Iran)—Parviz Kimiavi.
LAS LARGAS VACACIONES DEL 36 (Span.)—Jaime Camino.
THE LAST PLANTATION (Brazil)—Marcos Farias.
THE LONELINESS OF KONRAD STEINER (Switz.)—Kurt Gloor.
THE MAN WHO FELL TO EARTH (Brit.)—Nicolas Roeg.
MAN WITHOUT A NAME (Hung.)—Lazlo Lugossy.
MOZART—A CHILDHOOD CHRONICLE (Ger.)—Klaus Kirschner.
NIGHT AND DAY (Pol.)—Jerzy Antczak.
SLEDOVATELYAT Y GORATA (Bulg.)—Ranguel Valtchanov.
SMALL CHANGE (Fr.)—Francois Truffaut.
VERLORENES LEBEN (Ger.)—Ottokar Runze.
WHEN THE POPPIES BLOOM AGAIN (Neth.)—Bert Haanstra.
THE WHITE SHIP (U.S.S.R.)—Bolotbek Schamschiev.

1977
Prizes of the International Jury
Golden Bear for Best Film: THE ASCENT (U.S.S.R.)—Larissa Schepitko.
Special Jury Prize, Silver: THE DEVIL PROBABLY (Fr.)—Robert Bresson.
Silver Bears
    THE BRICKLAYERS (Mex.)—Jorge Fons.
    A STRANGE ROLE (Hung.)—Pal Sandor.
Silver Bear for Best Actor: Fernando Fernan Gomez for THE ANCHORITE (Span.).
Silver Bear for Best Actress: Lily Tomlin for THE LATE SHOW (U.S.).
Silver Bear for Best Direction: Manuel Aragon for BLACK LITTER (Span.).
Short Subjects
Golden Bear: NOT KNOWN AT THIS ADDRESS (Ger.)—Hans Sachs and Hedda Rinneberg.
Silver Bears
    ETUDA O ZKOUSCE (Czech.)—Evald Schorm.
    PHOENIX (Yugo.)—Peter Gligorovski.
Catholic Film Office Award
Competing Films
    THE ASCENT (U.S.S.R.)—Larissa Schepitko.
    DEN PRO MOU LASKU (Czech.)—Juraj Herz.
    THE DEVIL PROBABLY (Fr.)—Robert Bresson.
    A STRANGE ROLE (Hung.)—Pal Sandor.
    NOT KNOWN AT THIS ADDRESS (Ger.)—Hans Sachs and Hedda Rinneberg.
Forum Films
    NOUS AURONS TOUTE LA MORT POUR DORMIR (Fr.).
    KILENC HONAP (Hung.).
    MABABANGONG BANGUNGOT (Phil.).
FIPRESCI Prize
Competing Film: THE ASCENT (U.S.S.R.)—Larissa Schepitko.

Forum Films: MABABANGONG BANGUNGOT (Phil.).
Honorary Award: Yilmaz Guney of Turkey for his body of work.
Competing Films
THE ASCENT (U.S.S.R.)—Larissa Schepitko.
BETWEEN THE LINES (U.S.)—Joan Micklin Silver.
THE BRICKLAYER (Mex.)—Jorge Fons.
CAMADA NEGRA (Span.)—Manuel Guitierrez Aragon.
THE CONQUEST OF CITADEL (Ger.)—Bernard Wicki.
CYKLOPAT (Bulg.)—Christo Christov.
DEN PRO MOU LASKU (Czech.)—Juraj Herz.
THE DEVIL PROBABLY (Fr.)—Robert Bresson.
DIE VERTREIBUNG AUS DEM PARADIES (Ger.)—Niklaus Schilling.
DON'S PARTY (Aus.)—Bruce Beresford.
EL ANACORETA (Span./Fr.)—Juan Estelrich.
THE FIFTH SEAL (Hung.)—Zoltan Fabri.
GRETE MINDE—DER WALD IST VOLLER WOLFE.
THE LATE SHOW (U.S.)—Robert Benton.
MAMA, ICH LEBE (E. Ger.)—Konrad Wolfe.
THE MAN WHO LOVED WOMEN (Fr.)—Francois Truffaut.
NICKELODEON (U.S./Brit.)—Peter Bogdanovich.
PORCI CON LE ALI (Ital.)—Paolo Pietrangeli.
SENTIMENTALJNYI ROMAN (U.S.S.R.)—Igor Maslennikow.
TENDA DOS MILAGRES (Brazil)—Nelson Pereira dos Santos.
VDOVSTVO KAROLINE ZASLER (Yugo.)—Matjaz Klopcic.

1978
Prizes of the International Jury
Golden Bear for Best Film, Awarded to all Spanish entries in the festival:
THE TROUT—Jose Luis Garcia Sanchez.
WHAT MAX SAID -Emilio Martinez Lazaro.
THE LIFT (Short)—Tomas Munoz.
Special Jury Prize, Silver Bear: THE FALL (Brazil)—Ray Guerra and Nelson Xavier.
Silver Bear for Best Actor: Graig Russell for OUTRAGEOUS (Can.).
Silver Bear for Best Actress: Gena Rowlands for OPENING NIGHT (U.S.).
Silver Bear for Best Direction: Georgi Djulgerov for ADVANTAGE (Bulg.).
Silver Bear for First Feature: Octavio Cortazar for THE TEACHER (Cuba).
Special Silver Bear: Jerzy Kawalerowicz for THE DEATH OF THE PRESIDENT (Pol.) and his entire film oeuvre.
Honorable Mention: GERMANY IN AUTUMN (Ger.)—Various Prominent German Directors.
Short Subjects
Golden Bear: WHAT HAVE YOU DONE TO THE HENS (Czech.)—Josef Hekrdla and Vladimir Jiranek.
Silver Bears
THE CONTRAPTION (Brit.)—James Dearden.
UNE VIELLE SOUPIERE (Fr.)—Michel Longuet.
Catholic Film Office Awards
Competing Films
WHAT MAX SAID (Span.)—Emilio Martinez Lazaro.
APAM NEHANY BOLDOG EVE (Hung.)—Sandor Simo.
BRODERNA LEJONHJARTA (Swed.)—Olle Hellbom.
Forum Films: DAYEREH MINA (Iran)
FIPRESCI Prize
Competing Films: APAM NEHANY BOLDOG EVE (Hung.)—Sandor Simo.
Forum Films: DAYEREH MINA.
Competing Films
ADVANTAGE (Bulg.)—Georgi Djulgerov.
APAM NEHANY BOLDOG EVE (Hung.)—Sandor Simo.
BIRJUK (U.S.S.R.)—Roman Balaian.
BRODERNA LEJONHJARTA (Swed.)—Olle Hellbom.
THE CHESS PLAYERS (India)—Satyajit Ray.
CIRCUITO CHIUOSO (Ital.)—Giulano Montaldo.
THE DEATH OF THE PRESIDENT (Pol.)—Jerzy Kawalerowicz.
THE END OF THE WORLD IN OUR USUAL BED IN A NIGHT FULL OF RAIN (U.S./Ital.)—Lina Wertmuller.
THE FALL (Brazil)—Ruy Guerra and Nelson Xavier.
FLAMMENDE HERZEN (Ger.)—Walter Bockmeyer and Rolf Buhrmann.
GERMANY IN AUTUMN (Ger.)—Various Artists.
JORG RATGEB, MALER (E. Ger.)—Bernhard Stephan.
LEMON POPSICLE (Israel)—Boaz Davidson.
MORITZ, DEAR MORITZ (Ger.)—Hark Bohm.
OPENING NIGHT (U.S.)—John Cassavetes.
OUTRAGEOUS (Can.)—Richard Benner.
PAPER FLOWERS (Mex.)—Gabriel Retes.
PAS KOJI JE VELEO VOZOVE (Yugo.)—Goran Paskaljevic.
RHEINGOLD (Ger.)—Niklaus Schilling.
THE TEACHER (Cuba)—Octavio Cortazar.
TOI IPPON NO MICHI (Jap.)—Sachiko Hidari.
THE TROUT (Span.)—Jose Luis Sanchez.
UNE PAGE D'AMOUR (Belg./Fr.)—Maurice Rabinowicz.
WHAT MAX SAID (Span.)—Emilio Martinez Lazaro.

1979
Prizes of the International Jury
Golden Bear for Best Film: DAVID (Ger.)—Peter Lilienthal.
Special Jury Award, Silver Bear: ALEXANDRIA—WHY? (Egypt)—Youssef Chahine.
Silver Bear for Best Actor: Michele Placido for ERNESTO (Ital.).
Silver Bear for Best Actress: Hanna Schygulla for THE MARRIAGE OF MARIA BRAUN (Ger.).
Silver Bear for Best Direction: Astrid Henning-Jensen.
Silver Bear for Best Photography: Sten Holmberg for THE EMPEROR (Swed.).
Silver Bear for Best Art Direction: Henning Von Gierke for NOSFERATU—THE VAMPYRE (Ger./Fr.).
Silver Bear for Best Whole Technical Team: THE MARRIAGE OF MARIA BRAUN (Ger.)—Rainer Werner Fassbinder, director.
Short Subjects
Golden Bear: UBU (Brit.)—Geoff Dunbar.
Silver Bear: PHANTOM (Ger.)—Rene Perraudin and Uwe Schrader.
Catholic Film Office Awards

Competing Films
WINTER CHILDREN (Den.)—Astrid Henning-Jensen.
DAVID (Ger.)—Peter Lilienthal (Honorable Mention).
Forum Films: SURU (Turkey)
FIPRESCI Prize
Competing Films: ALBERT—WHY? (Ger.)—Joseph Rodel.
Forum Films
MY WAY HOME (Brit.)—Bill Douglas.
LA MACCHINA CINEMA (Ital.).
Competing Films
ALEXANDRIA—WHY? (Egypt)—Youssef Chahine.
DAVID (Ger)—Peter Lilienthal.
EL CORAZON DEL BOSQUE (Span.)—Manuel Gutierrez Aragon.
ERNESTO (Ital.)—Salvatore Samperi.
THE FIRST POLKA (Ger.)—Klaus Emmerich.
HARDCORE (U.S.)—Paul Schrader.
KASSBACH (Aust.)—Peter Patzak.
KEJSAREN (Swed.)—Josta Hagelback.
L'ADOLESCENTE (Fr./Ger.)—Jeanne Moreau.
LOVE ON THE RUN (Fr.)—Francois Truffaut.
THE MARRIAGE OF MARIA BRAUN (Ger.)—Rainer Werner Fassbinder.
MEETINGS WITH REMARKABLE MEN (Brit.)—Peter Brook.
MESSIDOR (Switz./Fr.)—Alain Tanner.
MOVIE, MOVIE (U.S.)—Stanley Donen.
NOSFERATU—THE VAMPYRE (Ger./Fr.)—Werner Herzog.
WINTER CHILDREN (Den.)—Astrid Henning-Jensen.

1980
Prizes of the International Jury
Golden Bear for Best Film
HEARTLAND (U.S.)—Richard Pearce.
PALERMO OR WOLFSBURG (Ger.)—Werner Schroeter.
Special Jury Prize, Silver Bear: CHIEDO ASILO (Ital./Fr.)—Marco Ferreri.
Silver Bear for Best Actor: Andrzej Seweryn for THE CONDUCTOR (Pol.).
Silver Bear for Best Actress: Renate Krossner for SOLO SUNNY (E. Ger.).
Silver Bear for Best Direction: Istvan Szabo for CONFIDENCE (Hung.).
Special Jury Mentions
THE ENEMY (Turkey)—Zeki Okten.
THE RAVEN'S DANCE (Fin./Swed.)—Markko Lehmuskallio.
RUDE BOY (Brit.)—Jack Hazan and David Mingay.
Special Prize: Athol Fugard in recognition of his artistic work and achievement, and for the film MARIGOLDS IN AUGUST (S. Africa).
Short Subjects
Golden Bear: THE HEADS (Czech.)—Peter Sis.
Silver Bear for the Best Direction of a Short Film: Jorg Moser-Metius for ROD GROTH (Ger.).
Catholic Film Office Award
Competing Films
THE ENEMY (Turkey)—Zeki Okten.
THE RAVEN'S DANCE (Fin./Swed.)—Markko Lehmuskallio (Honorable Mention).
Forum Films: THE CHILDREN OF NO. 67 (Ger.)
FIPRESCI Prize
Competing Films: SOLO SUNNY (E. Ger.)—Konrad Wolf.
Forum Films
HUNGER YEARS (Ger.)—Jutta Bruckner.
ON COMPANY BUSINESS (U.S.)—John Frankovich.
Competing Films
CHIEDO ASILO (Ital./Fr.)—Marco Ferreri.
THE CONDUCTOR (Pol.)—Andrzej Wajda.
CONFIDENCE (Hung.)—Istvan Szabo.
DEATH WATCH (Ger./Fr.)—Bertrand Tavernier.
EL CRIMEN DE CUENCA (Span.)—Pilar Miro.
THE ENEMY (Turkey)—Zeki Okten.
GERMANY, PALE MOTHER (Ger.)—Helma Sanders-Brahms.
HEARTLAND (U.S.)—Richard Pearce.
LE VOYAGE EN DOUCE (Fr.)—Michel Deville.
LES BONS DEBARRAS (Can.)—Francis Mankiewicz.
MARIGOLDS IN AUGUST (S. Africa)—Ross Devenish.
THE MARMALADE REVOLUTION (Swed.)—Erland Josephson and Sven Nykvist.
MOSCOW DOES NOT BELIEVE IN TEARS (U.S.S.R.)—Vladimir Menshov.
POLERMO OR WOLFSBURG (Ger.)—Werner Schroeter.
THE PRICE OF SURVIVAL (Ger./Fr.)—Hans Noever.
THE RAVEN'S DANCE (Swed./Fin.)—Markko Lehmuskallio.
RUDE BOY (Brit.)—Jack Hazan and David Mingay.
SOLO SUNNY (E. Ger.)—Konrad Wolf.
TRANSIT (Israel)—Daniel Wachsmann and Daniel Horowitz.
THE WIDOW MONTIEL (Mex./Cuba/Ven./Col.)—Miguel Littin.

1981
Prizes of the International
Golden Bear for Best Film: DEPRESA, DEPRISA! (Span.)—Carlos Saura.
Special Jury Prize, Silver Bear: IN SEARCH OF FAMINE (India)—Mrinal Sen.
Silver Bear for Best Actor
Jack Lemmon for TRIBUTE (Can.).
Anitoli Solonizyn for 26 DAYS IN THE LIFE OF DOSTOEVSKY (USSR).
Silver Bear for Best Actress: Barbara Grabowski for FEVER (Pol.).
Silver Bear for Best Screenplay: Markus Imhoof for THE BOAT IS FULL (Switz.).
Honorable Mention
ZIGEUNERWEISEN (Jap.)—Seijun Suzuki.
LE GRAND PAYSAGE D'ALEXIS DROEVEN (Belg.)—Jean-Jacques Andrien.
Short Subjects
Golden Bear: HISTORY OF THE WORLD IN THREE MINUTES FLAT (Can.)—Michael Mills.
Silver Bear for Best Direction of a Short Film: Paul Driessen for ON LAND, AT SEA, AND IN THE AIR (Neth.).
Catholic Film Office Award
THE BOAT IS FULL (Switz)—Markus Imhoof.
IN SEARCH OF FAMINE (India)—Mrinal Sen (Honorable Mention).
FIPRESCI Prize
Special Mentions

Competing Films

THE BOAT IS FULL (Switz.)—Markus Imhoof.

I'M ALL RIGHT (Hung.)—Laszlo Lugossy.

Forum Films

DIALOGUE WITH A WOMAN DEPARTED (U.S.).

KILLER OF SHEEP (U.S.).

Yilmaz Guney received an Honorable Mention for his work.

Competing Films

BARNENS O (Swed.)—Kay Pollack.

THE BOAT IS FULL (Switz.)—Markus Imhoof.

DEPRISA, DEPRISA (Span.)—Carlos Saura.

DER ERFINDER (Switz.)—Kurt Gloor.

DER NEGER ERWIN (Ger.)—Herbert Achternbusch.

FEVER (Pol.)—Agnieszka Holland.

FRIDAY (Bel.)—Hugo Claus.

HEAD ON (Can.)—Michael Grant.

IL MINISTRONE (Ital.)—Sergio Citti.

I'M ALL RIGHT (Hung.)—Laszlo Lugossy.

IN SEARCH OF FAMINE (India)—Mrinal Sen.

KAMIONAT (Bulg.)—Christo Christov.

LA PROVINCIALE (Fr./Switz.)—Claude Goretta.

LE GRAND PAYSAGE D'ALEXIS DROEVEN (Bel.)—Jean-Jacques Andrien.

LUANG TA (Thai.)—Pempol Cheyaroon.

MARAVILLAS (Span.)—Manuel Gutierrez Aragon.

MIKA—ELOKUVA TABUISTA (Fin.)—Rauni Mollberg.

TRIBUTE (Can.)—Bob Clark.

YEN GUI LAI (China)—Fu Jinggong.

ZIGEUNERWEISEN (Jap.)—Seijun Suzuki.

1982

Prizes of the International Jury

Golden Bear for Best Film: VERONIKA VOSS (Ger.)—Rainer Werner Fassbinder.

Special Jury Prize for the Most Originality, Silver Bear: DRESZCZE (Pol.)—Wojciech Marcewski.

Silver Bear for Best Actor

Michel Piccoli for A STRANGE AFFAIR (Fr.).

Stellan Skarsgaard for DEN ENFALDIGE MORDAREN (Swed.).

Silver Bear for Best Actress: Katrin Sass for BURGSCHAFT FUR AIN JAHR (E. Ger.)

Silver Bear for Best Direction: Mario Monicelli for IL MARCHESE DEL GRILLO (Ital.).

Silver Bear for Best Screenplay: Zoltan Fabri for REQUIEM (Hung.).

Honorable Mentions

ABSENCE OF MALICE (U.S.)—Sidney Pollack.

THE KILLING OF ANGEL STREET (Aus.)—Donald Crombie.

MUZHYKI (U.S.S.R.)—Iskra Babitsch.

Short Subjects

Golden Bear: LOUTKA, PRITEL CLOVEKA (Czech.)—Ivan Renc.

Silver Bear for Best Screenplay of a Short Film: Bao Lei for SAN GE HESHANG (China).

Catholic Film Office Award

Competing Films

BURGSCHAFT FUR EIN JAHR (E. Ger.)—Herrmann Zschoche.

DEN ENFALDIGE MORDAREN (Swed.)—Hans Alfredson (Honorable Mention).

Forum Films: NUESTRA VOZ DE TIERRA, MEMORIA Y FUTURO (Col.)

PASTORALE (U.S.S.R.)—Otar Ioseliani (Honorable Mention).

FIPRESCI Prize

Competing Films: DRESZCZE (Pol.)—Wojciech Marcewski.

Forum Film: PASTORALE (U.S.S.R.)—Otar Ioseliani.

Competing Films

ABSENCE OF MALICE (U.S.)—Sidney Pollack.

BEYROUTOU EL LIKA (Lebanon/Tunisia/Bel.)—Borhane Alaouie.

BOSATSU:SHIMOYAMA JIKEN (Jap.)—Kei Kumai.

BURGSCHAFT FUR EIN JAHR (E. Ger.)—Herrmann Zschoche.

DEN ENFALDIGE MORDAREN (Swed.)—Hans Alfredson.

DRESZCZE (Pol.)—Wojciech Marcewski.

THE GIRL WITH THE RED HAIR (Neth.)—Ben Verbong.

IL MARCHESE DEL GRILLO (Ital.)—Mario Monicelli.

THE KILLING OF ANGEL STREET (Aus.)—Donald Crombie.

KRAFTPROBE (Ger.)—Heidi Genee.

L'AMOUR DES FEMMES (Switz.)—Michael Soutter.

MUZHYKI (U.S.S.R.)—Iskra Babitsch.

REQUIEM (Hung.)—Zoltan Fabri.

ROMANZE MIT AMELIE (E. Ger.)—Ulrich Thein.

SARABA ITOSHIKI DAICHI (Jap.)—Mitsuo Yanagimachi.

A STRANGE AFFAIR (Fr.)—Pierre Granier-Deferre.

AN UNSUITABLE JOB FOR A WOMAN (Brit.)—Christopher Petit.

VERONIKA VOSS (Ger.) Rainer Werner Fassbinder.

XIANG QING (China)—Hu Bingliu and Wang Jin.

ZLILA CHOSERET (Israel)—Shimon Dotan.

1983

Prizes of the International Jury

Golden Bear for Best Film

ASCENDANCY (Brit.)—Edward Bennett.

LA COLMENA (Span.)—Mario Camus.

Special Jury Prize, Silver Bear: HAKKARI'DE BIR MEVSIM (Turkey)—Erden Kiral.

Silver Bear for Best Actor: Bruce Dern for THAT CHAMPIONSHIP SEASON (U.S.).

Silver Bear for Best Female Performance: Jewgenija Gluschenko for VLUBLEN PO SOBSTVENNOMU ZELANIJ (U.S.S.R.).

Silver Bear for Best Direction: Eric Rohmer for PAULINE AT THE BEACH (Fr.).

Silver Bear for Outstanding Single Achievement: Xaver Schwarzenberger for DER STILLE OZEAN (Aust.).

Honorable Mentions

MO SHENG DE PENG YOU (China)—Xu Lei.

DER ER ET YNDIGT LAND (Den.)—Morten Arnfred.

DIES RIGOROSE LEBEN (Ger.)—Vadim Glowna.

Short Subjects

Golden Bear: MOZNOSTI DIALOGU (Czech.)—Jan Svankmajer.

Silver Bear for Best Direction of a Short Film: WAS DAS LEBEN SO VERSPRICHT

(Ger.)—Egon Haase.

Catholic Film Office Award

Competing Films: DER STILLE OZEAN (Aust.)—Xaver Schwarzenberger.

Honorable Mentions

PRA FRENTE BRASIL (Brazil)—Roberto Farias.

IN THE KING OF PRUSSIA (US)—Emile de Antonio.

Forum Films

CHOKH (India)

LA ZERDA OU LES CHANTES DE L'OUBLI (Algeria) (Honorable Mention).

Honorary Award for Direction

Eric Rohmer

Margarethe von Trotta

Chris Marker.

FIPRESCI Prize

Competing Films

HAKKARI'DE BIR MEVSIM (Turkey)—Erden Kiral.

PAULINE AT THE BEACH (Fr.)—Eric Rohmer.

Forum Films:

ASHES AND EMBERS (U.S.).

BUSCH SINGT (E. Ger.).

Competing Films

ASCENDANCY (Brit.)—Edward Bennett.

CAP CANAILLE (Fr./Bel.)—Jean-Henri Roger and Juliet Berto.

DAS GESPENST (Ger.)—Herbert Achternbusch.

DER ER ET YNDIGT LAND (Den.)—Morten Arnfred.

DER STILLE OZEAN (Aust.)—Xaver Schwarzenberger.

DIES RIGOROSE LEBEN (Ger.)—Vadim Glowna.

DOGKELSELYU (Hung.)—Ferenc Andras.

FERESTADEH (Ger./U.S.)—Parviz Sayyad.

HAKKARI'DE BIR MEVSIM (Turkey)—Erden Kiral.

HECATE (Switz./Fr.)—Daniel Schmid.

HIMALA (Phil.)—Ishmael Bernal.

IN THE WHITE CITY (Switz./Por.)—Alain Tanner.

KOYAANISQATSI (U.S.)—Godfrey Reggio.

LA BELLE CAPTIVE (Fr.)—Alain Robbe-Grillet.

LA COLMENA (Span.)—Mario Camus.

MO SHENG DE PENG YOU (China)—Xu Lei.

NEUPLNE ZATMENI (Czech.)—Jaromil Jires.

PAULINE AT THE BEACH (Fr.)—Eric Rohmer.

PRA FRENTE BRASIL (Brazil)—Roberto Farias.

SHEER MADNESS (Ger./Fr.)—Michael Ballhaus.

THAT CHAMPIONSHIP SEASON (U.S.)—Jason Miller.

UTOPIA (Ger.)—Sohrab Shahid Saless.

VIA DEGLI SPECCHI (Ital.)—Giovanni Gagliardo.

VLUBEN PO SOBSTVENNOMU ZELANIJ (U.S.S.R.)—Sergei Mikaeljan.

YAJU-DEKA (Jap.)—Eiichi Kudo.

1984

Prizes of the International Jury

Golden Bear for Best Film: LOVE STREAMS (U.S.)—John Cassavetes.

Special Jury Prize, Silver Bear: FUNNY DIRTY LITTLE WAR (Arg.)—Hector Olivera.

Silver Bears

Ettore Scola for LE BAL (Fr./Ital./Alg.).

Monica Vitti for FLIRT (Ital.).

MORNING IN ALABAMA (Ger.)—Norbert Kuckelmann.

REMBETIKO (Gr.)—Costas Ferris.

Silver Bear for Best Actor: Albert Finney for THE DRESSER (Brit.).

Silver Bear for Best Actress: Inna Tschurikova for FRONT ROMANCE (USSR).

Special Award: Jean-Marie Straub and Daniele Huillet for CLASS RELATIONS (Ger.).

Short Subjects

Golden Bear: BICYCLE SYMPHONY (Den.)—Ake Sandgren.

Silver Bear: YU BANG XIANG ZHENG (China)—Hu Jinqing.

Catholic Film Office Award

Competing Films

MANN OHNE GEDACHTNIS (Switz.)—Kurt Gloor.

AH YING (Hong Kong)—Allen Fong and Fong Yuk-Ping.

Forum Films

TIZNAO (Ven.).

BLESS THEIR LITTLE HEARTS (U.S.).

FIPRESCI Prize

Competing Films

LOVE STREAMS (U.S.)—John Cassavetes.

FUNNY DIRTY LITTLE WAR (Arg.)—Hector Olivera.

Forum Films: NIPPON-KOKU FURUYASHIKI-MURA (Jap.).

Competing Films

A NOS AMOURS (Fr.)—Maurice Pialat.

AH YING (Hong Kong)—Allen Fong and Fong Yuk-Ping.

AKELARRE (Span.)—Pedro Olea.

ARZTINNEN (E. Ger.)—Horst Seemann.

CHAMPIONS (Brit.)—John Irvin.

CLASS RELATIONS (Ger.)—Jean-Marie Straub and Daniele Huillet.

CRACKERS (U.S.)—Louis Malle.

DAS ARCHE NOAH PRINZIP (Ger.)—Roland Emmerich.

DAS AUTOGRAMM (Ger./Por.)—Peter Lilienthal.

DE STILLE OCEAAN (Neth./Belg.)—Digna Sinke.

THE DRESSER (Brit.)—Peter Yates.

FLIRT (Ital.)—Roberto Russo.

FRONT ROMANCE (U.S.S.R.)—Pjotr Todorovskij.

FUNNY DIRTY LITTLE WAR (Arg.)—Hector Olivera.

KONNYU TESTI SERTEA (Hung.)—Gyorgy Szomjas.

LE BAL (Fr./Ital./Alg.)—Ettore Scola.

LOVE STREAMS (U.S.)—John Cassavetes.

MANN OHNE GEDACHTNIS (Switz.)—Kurt Gloor.

MORNING IN ALABAMA (Ger.)—Norbert Kuckelmann.

NANKYOKU MONOGATARI (Jap.)—Koreyoshi Kurahara.

REMBETIKO (Gr.)—Costas Ferris.

SKONHEDEN OG UDYRET (Den.)—Nils Malmros.

STAR 80 (U.S.)—Bob Fosse.

XUE, ZONG SHI RE DE (China)—Wen Yan.

CANNES INTERNATIONAL FILM FESTIVAL

1946
Grand Prix
THE RED EARTH (Den.)—Lau Lauritzen.
THE LOST WEEK-END (U.S.)—Billy Wilder.
SYMPHONIE PASTORALE (Fr.)—Jean Delannoy.
BRIEF ENCOUNTER (Brit.)—David Lean.
NEECHA NAGAR (India)—Chetan Anand.
OPEN CITY (Ital.)—Roberto Rossellini.
MARIA CANDELARIA (Mex.)—Emilio Fernandez.
THE PRIZE (Swed.)—Alf Sjoberg.
THE LAST CHANCE (Switz.)—Leopold Lindtberg.
MEN WITHOUT WINGS (Czech.)—M. Cap.
THE GREAT TURNING POINT (U.S.S.R.)—Friedrich Ermler.
Grand Prix of the International Jury
Direction: Rene Clement for BATTLE OF THE RAILS (Fr.).
Male Performance: Ray Milland for THE LOST WEEK-END (U.S.).
Female Performance: Michele Morgan for SYMPHONIE PASTORALE (Fr.).
Screenplay: Tchirskov for THE GREAT TURNING POINT (U.S.S.R.).
Music: Georges Auric.
Cinematography: Gabriel Figueroa for MARIA CANDELARIA and THE THREE MUSKETEERS (Mex.).
Color: THE STONE FLOWER (U.S.S.R.), directed by Alexander Ptouchko.
Documentary: BERLIN (U.S.S.R.)—J. Raisman.
Animation: MAKE MINE MUSIC (U.S.)—Walt Disney.
Special Jury Prize: BATTLE OF THE RAILS (Fr.)—Rene Clement.
Grand Prix for Peace: THE LAST CHANCE (Switz.)—Leopold Lindtberg.
CIDALC Prize: EPAVES (Fr.)—J.Y. Cousteau, Frederic Dumas, Philippe Tailliez, and Roger Gary.
Competing Films
AMANTI IN FUGA (Ital.)—Giacomo Gentilomo.
ANNA AND THE KING OF SIAM (Brit.)—John Cromwell.
BATTLE OF THE RAILS (Fr.)—Rene Clement.
BEAUTY AND THE BEAST (Fr.)—Jean Cocteau.
BLOOD AND FIRE (Swed.)—Anders Henrikson.
BRIEF ENCOUNTER (Brit.)—David Lean.
CAMOENS (Por.)—Leitao de Barros.
THE CAPTIVE HEART (Brit.)—Basil Dearden.
CAESAR AND CLEOPATRA (Brit.)—Gabriel Pascal.
DONIA (Egypt)—Mohammed Kalim.
GASLIGHT (U.S.)—George Cukor.
GILDA (U.S.)—Charles Vidor.
GIRL NO. 217 (U.S.S.R.)—Mikhail Romm.
GLINKA (U.S.S.R.)—Lev Arnchtam.
THE GREAT TURNING POINT (U.S.S.R.)—Friedrich Ermler.
IL BANDITO (Ital.)—Dino de Laurentis.
LA LETTRE (Den.)—Johan Jacobsen.
THE LAST CHANCE (Switz.)—Leopold Lindtberg.
LE BACHELIER MALICIEUX (Czech.)—Otakar Vavra.
LES ENNUIS DE MONSIEUR TRAVET (Ital.)—Dino de Laurentis.
LOST WEEKEND (U.S.)—Billy Wilder.
A LOVER'S RETURN (Fr.)—Christian-Jaque.
THE MAGIC BOW (Brit.)—Bernard Knowles.
MAKE MINE MUSIC (U.S.)—Walt Disney.
MARIA CANDELARIA (Mex.)—Emilio Fernandez.
MEN WITHOUT WINGS (Czech.)—M. Cap.
NEECHA NAGAR (India)—Chetan Anand.
NOTORIOUS (U.S.)—Alfred Hitchcock.
OPEN CITY (Ital.)—Roberto Rosselini.
PATRIE (Fr.)—Louis Daquin.
THE RED EARTH (Den.)—Lau Lauritzen.
RHAPSODY IN BLUE (U.S.)—Irving Rapper.
SALUT, MOSCOU (U.S.S.R.)—Serge Youtkevitch.
THE SEVENTH VEIL (Brit.)—Compton Bennet.
THE STONE FLOWER (U.S.S.R.)—Alexander Ptouchko.
SYMPHONIE PASTORALE (Fr.)—Jean Delannoy.
THE THREE MUSKETEERS (Mex.)—Miguel Delgado.
TROIS JOURS SANS DIEU (Por.)—Barbara Virginia.
UN GIORNO NELLA VITA (Ital.)—Alexandre Blasetti.
WONDER MAN (U.S.)—Bruce Hunderstone.
ZOYA (U.S.S.R.)—Lev Arnstam.

1947
Grand Prix of the International Jury
Psychological and Love Film: ANTOINE ET ANTOINETTE (Fr.)—Jacques Becker.
Adventure and Detective Film: THE DAMNED (Fr.)—Rene Clement.
Social Film: CROSSFIRE (U.S.)—Edward Dmytryk.
Musical: ZIEGFELD FOLLIES (U.S.)—Vincente Minnelli.
Animated Film: DUMBO (U.S.)—Ben Sharpsteen for Walt Disney.
Honorable Mentions:
MINE OWN EXECUTIONER (Brit.)—Anthony Kimmins.
THE LAND OF DESIRE/A TRIP TO INDIA (Swed.)—Ingmar Bergman.
Competing Films
THE AL JOLSON STORY (U.S.)—Alfred E. Green.
ANTOINE ET ANTOINETTE (Fr.)—Jacques Becker.
BOOMERANG (U.S.)—Elia Kazan.
THE CAPTAIN'S DAUGHTER (Ital.)—Mario Camerini.
THE CHASE (U.S.)—Seymour Nebenzahl.
THE CHIPS ARE DOWN (Fr.)—Jean Delannoy.
CROSSFIRE (U.S.)—Edward Dmytryk.
THE DAMNED (Fr.)—Rene Clement.
DUMBO (U.S.)—Walt Disney.
FLESH WILL SURRENDER (Ital.)—Alberto Lattuada.
IVY (U.S.)—Sam Wood.
LA COLPA DE LA DOLORES (Arg.)—Benito Petojo.
LA GATA (Arg.)—Mario Soffici.
THE LAND OF DESIRE (Swed.)—Ingmar Bergman.

LES AMANTS DU PONT SAINT-JEAN (Fr.)—Henri Decoin.
MAROUF SAVETIER DU CAIRE (Mor.)—Jean Mauran.
MINE OWN EXECUTIONER (Brit.)—Anthony Kimmins.
PARIS 1900 (Fr.)—Nicole Vedres.
POSSESSED (U.S.)—Curtis Bernhardt.
SPERDUTI NEL BUIO (Ital.)—Camilio Mastrocinque.
THE STRANGE LOVE OF MARTHA IVERS (U.S.)—Lewis Milestone.
TANITONO (Hung.)—Marton Keleti.
TWO WOMEN (Swed.)—Arnold Sjostrand.
ZIEGFELD FOLLIES (U.S.)—Vincente Minnelli.

1948
Festival not held due to lack of funding.

1949
Prizes of the International Jury
Grand Prix: THE THIRD MAN (Brit.)—Carol Reed.
Male Performance: Edward G. Robinson for HOUSE OF STRANGERS (U.S.).
Female Performance: Isa Miranda for THE WALLS OF MALAPAGA (Fr./Ital.).
Direction: Rene Clement for THE WALLS OF MALAPAGA (Fr./Ital.).
Screenplay: Virginia Shaler and Eugene Ling for LOST BOUNDARIES (U.S.).
Music: PUEBLERINA (Mex.), directed by Emilio Fernandez.
Decor: OH, AMELIA (Fr.), directed by Claude Autant-Lara.
Competing Films
AN ACT OF MURDER (U.S.)—Michael Gordon.
ACT OF VIOLENCE (U.S.)—Fred Zinnemann.
THE ADVENTURES OF ANTAR AND ABLA (Egypt)—Salah Abou Seif.
ALMA FUERTE (Arg.)—Luis Cesar Amadori.
AU GRAND BALCON (Fr.)—Henri Decoin and Marcel Rivet.
BITTER RICE (Ital.)—Giuseppe De Santis.
DIE BUNTKARIERTEN (Ger.)—Kurt Maetzig.
EL BEIT EL KEBIR (Egypt).
EROICA (Aust.)—Walter Kolm-Veltee and Karl Hartl.
A GREAT LOVE (Ger.)—Hans Bertram.
HOUSE OF STRANGERS (U.S.)—Joseph L. Mankiewicz.
IMAGES OF ETHIOPIA (Bel.)—Paul Pichonnier.
L'AMOROSA MENZOGNA (Ital.)—Michelangelo Antonioni.
THE LAST ILLUSION (Ger.)—Josef von Baky.
LOST BOUNDARIES (U.S.)—Alfred Wecker.
OBSESSION (Brit.)—Edward Dmytryk.
OH, AMELIA (Fr.)—Claude Autant-Lara.
THE ORIGINAL SIN (Ger.)—Helmut Kautner.
THE PASSIONATE FRIENDS (Brit.)—David Lean.
PUEBLERINA (Mex.)—Emilio Fernandez.
THE QUEEN OF SPADES (Brit.)—Thorold Dickinson.
RENDEZ-VOUS DE JUILLET (Fr.)—Jacques Becker.
RETOUR A LA VIE (Fr.)—Andre Cayatte, Henri-Georges Clouzot, Jean Dreville, and Georges Lampin.
SERTAO (Bra.)—Joao C. Martin.
THE SET UP (U.S.)—Robert Wise.
SUR LE SOL NATAL (Yugo.)—France Stiglic.
TILL FRAMMANDE HAMM (Swed.)—Hampe Faustman.
THE THIRD MAN (Brit.)—Carol Reed.
TWILIGHT (U.S.)—Irving Pichel.
THE WALLS OF MALAPAGA (Ital.)—Rene Clement.

1950
Festival not held due to lack of funds, and other problems in the film industry of France.

1951
Prizes of the International Jury
Grand Prix:
MIRACLE IN MILAN (Ital.)—Vittorio De Sica.
MISS JULIE (Swed.)—Alf Sjoberg.
Special Jury Prize: ALL ABOUT EVE (U.S.)—Joseph L. Mankiewicz.
Male Performance: Michael Redgrave for THE BROWNING VERSION (Brit.).
Female Performance: Bette Davis for ALL ABOUT EVE (U.S.).
Direction: Luis Bunuel for LOS OLVIDADOS (Mex.).
Screenplay: Terence Rattigan for THE BROWNING VERSION (Brit.).
Music: Joseph Kosma for JULIETTE OU LA CLEF DES SONGES (Fr.).
Cinematography: Luis-Maria Beltran for LA CARAVELLE ISABEL PARTIRA CE SOIR (Ven.).
Decor: Souvorov A. Veksler for MOUSSORGSKY (U.S.S.R.).
Special Prize for Originality of Lyrical Adaptation to Film: TALES OF HOFFMAN (Brit.)—Michael Powell and Emeric Pressburger.
Special Award: The entire selection of films presented at the festival by Italy.

Competing Films
ALL ABOUT EVE (U.S.)—Joseph L. Mankiewicz.
BALLARASA (Span.)—Jose Antonio Nieves Conde.
THE BROWNING VERSION (Brit.)—Anthony Asquith.
CAICARA (Bra.)—Adolfo Celi.
DANZA DEL FUEGO (Arg.)—Daniel Tinayre.
DEBLA LA VIRGEN GITANA (Span.)—Ramon Torrado.
DIE TODLICHEN TRAUME (Ger.)—Paul Martin.

DREAM OF A COSSACK (U.S.S.R.)—Yuli Raizman.
EDOUARD AND CAROLINE (Fr.)—Jacques Becker.
THE FALLING STAR (Ger.)—Jacob Geis.
FOUR IN A JEEP (Switz.)—Leopold Lindtberg.
IDENTITE JUDICIAIRE (Fr.)—Herve Bromberger.
JULIETTE OU LA CLEF DES SONGES (Fr.)—Marcel Carne.
LA BALANDRA ISABEL LLEGO ESTA TARDE (Ven.)—Carlos H. Christensen and Luis G. Villegas Blanco.
LA CHINE LIBEREE (U.S.S.R.)—Serge Guerassimov.
LA HONRADEZ DELLA CERRADURA (Span.)—Luis Escobar.
LA VILLE INDOMPTEE (Pol.)—Jerzy Zarzychi.
LIGHTS OUT (U.S.)—Mark Robson.
LOS ISLEROS (Arg.)—Lucas Demare.
MAD WEDNESDAY (U.S.)—Preston Sturges.
MARIHUANA (Arg.)—Leon Klimovsky.
MIRACLE IN MILAN (Ital.)—Vittorio De Sica.
MISS JULIE (Swed.)—Alf Sjoberg.
MOUSSORSKY (U.S.S.R.)—Grigori Rochal.
THE PATH OF HOPE (Ital.)—Pietro Germi.
A PLACE IN THE SUN (U.S.)—George Stevens.
RUMBO (Span.)—Ramon Torrado.
SIDE STREET STORY (Ital.)—Eduardo De Filippo.
STRANGE DECEPTION (Ital.)—Curzio Malaparte.
THE TALES OF HOFFMAN (Brit.)—Michael Powell and Emeric Pressburger.
TELEFTEA APOSTOLI (Gr.)—Nicolas Tsiforos.
UN DROLE DE MARIAGE (Hung.)—Marton Keleti.

1952
Prizes of the International Jury
Grand Prix:
TWO PENNYWORTH OF HOPE (Ital.)—Renato Castellani.
OTHELLO (Morocco)—Orson Welles.
Special Jury Prize: WE ARE ALL MURDERERS (Fr.)—Andre Cayatte.
Film Lyricism: THE MEDIUM (U.S.)—Gian Carlo Menotti.
Male Performance: Marlon Brando for VIVA ZAPATA (U.S.).
Female Performance: Lee Grant for DETECTIVE STORY (U.S.).
Direction: Christian-Jaque for FANFAN LA TULIPE (Fr.).
Scenario: Piero Fellini for COPS AND ROBBERS (Ital.).
Music: Sven Skold for ONE SUMMER OF HAPPINESS (Swed.).
Photography and Composition: Kohei Sugiyama for A TALE OF GENJI (Jap.).
Competing Films
AMAR BHOOPALI (India)—V. Shantaram.
AM AMERICAN IN PARIS (U.S.)—Vincente Minnelli.
CRY, THE BELOVED COUNTRY (Brit.)—Zoltan Korda.
COPS AND ROBBERS (Ital.)—Mario Monicelli.
DAS LETZTE REZEPT (Ger.)—Rolf Hansen.
DER WEIBSTEUFEL (Aust.)—Wolfgang Liebeneiner.
DETECTIVE STORY (U.S.)—William Wyler.
ENCORE (Brit.)—Pat Jackson, Anthony Pelissier, and Harold French.
FANFAN LA TULIPE (Fr.)—Christian-Jaque.
HERZ DER WELT (Ger.)—Harald Braun.
IBN EL NIL (Egypt)—Youssef Chahine.
LA AUSENTE (Mex.)—Julio Bracho.
LE BANQUET DES FRAUDEURS (Bel.)—Henri Storck.
LEILET GHARAM (Egypt)—Badrakhan.
MARIA MORENA (Span.)—Lazaga and Forque.
THE MEDIUM (U.S.)—Gian Carlo Menotti.
MEXICAN BUS RIDE (Mex.)—Luis Bunuel.
MOTHERS IN A STORM (Jap.)—Kiyoshi Saheki.
NAMI (Jap.)—Noburo Nakamura.
NEKRI POLITEIA (Gr.)—Frixos Heliades.
NODLANDING (Nor.)—Arne Skouen.
ONE SUMMER OF HAPPINESS (Swed.)—Arne Mattson.
OTHELLO (Mor.)—Orson Welles.
THE OVERCOAT (Ital.)—Alberto Lattuada.
PARSIFAL (Span.)—Daniel Mangrane and Carlos Serrano de Osma.
PASO EN MI BARRIO (Arg.)—Mario Soffici.
SURCOS (Span.)—Jose Antonio Nieves-Conde.
A TALE OF GENJI (Jap.)—Kosaburo Yoshimura.
TICO TICO NO FUBA (Bra.)—Adolfo Celi.
TROIS FEMMES (Fr.)—Andre Michel.
TWO CENTS WORTH OF HOPE (Ital.)—Renato Castellani.
UMBERTO D. (Ital.)—Vittorio De Sica.
VIVA ZAPATA (U.S.)—Elia Kazan.
VOICE OF ANOTHER (Ger.)—Erich Engel.
WE ARE ALL MURDERERS (Fr.)—Andre Cayatte

1953
Prizes of the International Jury
Grand Prix: THE WAGES OF FEAR (Fr./Ital.)—Henri-Georges Clouzot.
Adventure Film: O CANGACEIRO (Brazil)—Lima Barreto.
Entertainment Film: LILI (U.S.)—Charles Walters.
Dramatic Film: COME BACK LITTLE SHEBA (U.S.)—Daniel Mann.
Mythical Film: THE WHITE REINDEER (U.S.)—Erik Blomberg.
Exploration Film: MAGIA VERDE (Ital.)—Gian Gaspare Napolitano.
Prize for Good Humor: BIENVENUDO, MISTER MARSHALL (Span.)—Luis Berlanga.
Le Mieux Raconte Par L'Image: THE NET (Mex.)—Emilio Fernandez.

Male Performance: Charles Vanel for THE WAGES OF FEAR (Fr./Ital.).
Female Performance: Shirley Booth for COME BACK LITTLE SHEBA (U.S.).
Scenario: Luis Berlanga for BIENVENUDO, MISTER MARSHALL (Span.).
Music: O CANGACEIRO (Span.), directed by L. Barreto.
Color Film: MAGIA VERDE (Ital.)—Gian Gaspare Napolitano.
Special Homage:
Walt Disney, for the entire ensemble of his work.
DUENDE Y MISTERIO DEL FLAMENCO (Span.)—Edgar Neville.
Competing Films
BARABBAS (Swed.)—Alf Sjoberg.
BIENVENUDO MISTER MARSHALL (Span.)—Luis Berlanga.
BONGOLO (Bel.)—Andre Cauvin.
CALL ME MADAM (U.S.)—Walter Lang.
THE CHILDREN OF HIROSHIMA (Jap.) Kaneto Shindo.
COME BACK LITTLE SHEBA (U.S.)—Daniel Mann.
DONA FRANCISQUITA (Span.)—Ladislao Vajda.
EL (Mex.)—Luis Bunuel.
EQUINOX (Yugo.)—Vladimir Pogacic.
FOR MIN HETA UNGSDOMS SKULL (Swed.)—Arne Mattson.
THE HEART OF THE MATTER (Brit.)—George More O'Ferrall.
HORIZON'S SANS FIN—HELENE BOUCHER (Fr.)—Jean Dreville.
I CONFESS (U.S.)—Alfred Hitchcock.
INDISCRETION OF AN AMERICAN WIFE (U.S.)—Vittorio De Sica.
INTIMATE RELATIONS (Brit.)—Charles Frank.
LA VIE PASSIONNEE DE CLEMENCEAU (Fr.)—Gilbert Prouteau.
LAS TRES PERFECTAS CASADAS (Mex.)—Roberto Gavaldon.
LILI (U.S.)—Charles Walters.
LUZ EN EL PARAMO (Ven.)—Victor Urruchua.
MAGIA VERDE (Ital.)—Gian Gaspare Napolitano.
MR. HULOT'S HOLIDAY (Fr.)—Jacques Tati.
THE MODERNS (Jap.)—Minoru Shibuya.
THE NET (Mex.)—Emilio Fernandez.
O CANGACEIRO (Bra.)—Lima Barreto.
IER AVRIL AN 2.000 (Aust.)—Wolfgang Liebeneiner.
PETER PAN (U.S.)—Walt Disney.
SAGA OF THE GREAT BUDDHA (Jap.)—Teinosuke Kinugasa.
SALA DE GUARDIA (Arg.)—Tulio Demicheli.
THE SUN SHINES BRIGHT (U.S.)—John Ford.
THE VAGABOND (India)—Raj Kapoor.
THE VILLAGE (Switz.)—Leopold Lindtberg.
THE WAYWARD WIFE (Ital.)—Mario Soldati.
THE WHITE REINDEER (Fin.)—Erik Blomberg.

1954
Prizes of the International Jury
Grand Prix: GATE OF HELL (Jap.)—Teinosuke Kinugasa.
Special Jury Prizes:
Rene Clement for the Direction of KNAVE OF HEARTS (Brit.).
International Prize: THE LAST BRIDGE (Aust.)—Helmut Kautner.
Maria Schell for her performance in THE LAST BRIDGE (Aust.).
National Recognition Awards:
THE LIVING DESERT (U.S.)—James Algar for Walt Disney.
AVANT LE DELUGE (Fr.)—Andre Cayatte.
TWO ACRES OF LAND (India)—Bimal Roy.
NEAPOLITAN CAROUSEL (Ital.)—Ettore Giannini.
CHRONICLE OF POOR LOVERS (Ital.)—Carlo Lizzani.
FIVE BOYS FROM BARSKA STREET (Pol.)—Aleksander Ford.
THE GREAT ADVENTURE (Swed.)—Arne Sucksdorff.
THE GREAT WARRIOR, SKANDERBERG (U.S.S.R.)—Serge Youtkevitch.
Special Recognition Prize:
FROM HERE TO ETERNITY (U.S.)—Fred Zinnemann.
Competing Films
AL WAHCHE (Egypt)—Salah Abou Seif.
AS LONG AS YOU ARE THERE (Ger.)—Dr. Harald Braun.
AVANT LE DELUGE (Fr.)—Andre Cayatte.
BENEATH THE TWELVE MILE REEF (U.S.)—Robert D. Webb.
THE BREAD OF LOVE (Swed.)—Arne Mattson.
CHRONICLE OF POOR LOVERS (Ital.)—Carlo Lizzani.
COMICOS (Span.)—Juan Bardem.
EL NINO Y LA NIEBLA (Mex.)—Roberto Gavaldon.
ET LE COEUR DANSE (Ger.).
FIVE BOYS FROM BARSKA STREET (Pol.)—Aleksander Ford.
FLESH AND THE WOMAN (Fr.)—Robert Siodmak.
FROM HERE TO ETERNITY (U.S.)—Fred Zinnemann.
GATE OF HELL (Jap.)—Teinosuke Kinugasa.
THE GREAT ADVENTURE (Swed.)—Arne Sucksdorff.
THE GREAT WARRIOR, SKANDERBERG (U.S.S.R.)—Serge Youtkevitch.
THE KIDNAPPERS (Brit.)—Philip Leacock.
KIRIAKATIKO XIPNIMA (Gr.)—Michael Cacoyannis.
KISKRAJCAAR (Hung.)—Marton Keleti.
KNAVE OF HEARTS (Brit.)—Rene Clement.
KNIGHTS OF THE ROUND TABLE (U.S.)—Richard Thorpe.
KOMEDIANTI (Czech.)—V. Vlek.
LAS AVENTURAS DEL BARBERO DE SEVILLA (Span.)—Ladislao Vajda.
THE LAST BRIDGE (Aust.)—Helmut Kautner.
LOVE LETTER (Jap.)—Kinuyo Tanaka.
LITTLE BOY LOST (U.S.)—George Seaton.
THE LIVING DESERT (U.S.)—James Algar for Walt Disney.
MADDALENA (Ital.)—Augusto Genina.
MAN OF AFRICA (Brit.)—D. Cyrio Frankio.
MARTIR DEL CALVARIO (Mex.)—Miguel Morayta.
MAYUR PANKI (India)—Kishore Sahu.
MEMORIES OF MEXICO (Mex.)—Carmen Toscano.
MUDDY WATERS (Jap.)—Tadashi Imai.
NAKED AMAZON (Bra.)—Zygmont Sulistrowski.

NEAPOLITAN CAROUSEL (Ital.)—Ettore Giannini.
PAMPOSH: LOTUS OF FLOWERS (India)—Ezra Mir.
SANG ET LUMIERE (Fr.)—Georges Rouquier and R. Munoz-Suay.
SERA'A FIL WADIE (Egypt)—Youssef Chahine.
SI MIS CAMPOS HABLARAN (Chili)—Jose Bohr.
SOUDBA MARINY (U.S.S.R.)—I. Schmarouk and V. Ivtchenko.
STARS OF THE RUSSIAN BALLET (U.S.S.R.)—Gerbert Rappoport.
TODO ES POSIBLE EN GRANADA (Span.)—Carlos Blanco.
TWO ACRES OF LAND (India)—Bismal Roy.

1955
Prizes of the International Jury
Golden Palm: MARTY (U.S.)
    particular praise for the following contributions:
        Screenplay by Paddy Chayevski.
        Mise-en-Scene by Delbert Mann.
        Performances of Ernest Borgnine and Betsy Blair.
Special Jury Prize: THE LOST CONTINENT (Ital.)—Leonardo Bonzi, Mario Craveri, Enrico Gras, F. Lavagnino, and G. Moser.
Mise-en-Scene: Sergei Vassiliev for THE HEROES OF SHIPKA (Bulg.).
Direction: Jules Dassin for RIFIFI (Fr.).
Performances:
    Spencer Tracy for BAD DAY AT BLACK ROCK (U.S.)
    The ensemble of actors for THE BIG FAMILY (U.S.S.R.), directed by Joseph Heifitz.
Dramatic Film: EAST OF EDEN (U.S.)—Elia Kazan.
Film Lyricism: ROMEO AND JULIET (U.S.S.R.), directed by L. Arnchtam and L. Lavrovsky; choreographed by Gabila Oulanova.
Special Jury Mentions:
    Baby Naaz for BOOT POLISH (India).
    Haya Havarit for HILL 24 DOESN'T ANSWER (Israel).
    MARCELINO (Span.)—Ladislao Vajda.
Competing Films
    ROMEO AND JULIET (U.S.S.R.)—L. Arnchtam and L. Lavrovsky.
    BAD DAY AT BLACK ROCK (U.S.)—John Sturges.
    BIRAJ BAHU (India)—Bimal Roy.
    BOOT POLISH (India)—Prakah Arora.
    COUNTRY LIFE (U.S.)—George Seaton.
    DET BRENNER I NATT (Nor.)—Arne Skouen.
    DIE MUECKE (Ger.)—Walter Reisch.
    DOG HEADS (Czech.)—Martin Fric.
    EAST OF EDEN (U.S.)—Elia Kazan.
    THE END OF THE AFFAIR (Brit.)—Edward Dmytryk.
    THE GOLD OF NAPLES (Ital.)—Vittorio De Sica.
    HAYAAII AW MOUT (Egypt)—Kamal El Cheikh.
    THE HEROES OF SHIPKA (Bulg.)—Sergei Vassiliev.
    HILL 24 DOESN'T ANSWER (Israel)—Thorold Dickinson.
    JEDDA (Aus.)—Charles Chauvel.
    LE DOSSIER NOIR (Fr.)—Andre Cayatte.
    LILIOMFI (Hung.)—Karoly Makk.
    THE LOST CONTINENT (Ital.)—Leonardo Bonzi, Mario Craveri, Enrico Gras, F. Lavagnino, and G. Moser.
    LUDWIG II (Ger.)—Helmut Kautner.
    MARCELINO (Span.)—Ladislao Vajda.
    MARTY (U.S.)—Delbert Mann.
    ONNA NO KOYOMI (Jap.)—Seiji Hisamatsu.
    PRINCESS SEN (Jap.)—Keigo Kimura.
    RIFIFI (Fr.)—Jules Dassin.
    THE ROOTS (Mex.)—Benito Alazraki.
    SAMBA FANTASTICO (Brazil)—Rene Persin and Jean Manzon.
    THE SIGN OF VENUS (Ital.)—Dino Risi.
    STELLA (Gr.)—Michael Cacoyannis.
    UN EXTRANO EN LA ESCALERA (Mex.)—Gregorio Walerteins.

1956
Prizes of the International Jury
Golden Palm: THE SILENT WORLD (Fr.)—Jacques Yves Cousteau and Louis Malle.
Special Jury Prize: THE MYSTERY OF PICASSO (Fr.)—Henri-Georges Clouzot.
Direction: Serge Youtkevitch for OTHELLO (U.S.S.R.).
Female Performance: Susan Hayward for I'LL CRY TOMORROW (U.S.).
Poetic Humor Film: SMILES OF A SUMMER NIGHT (Swed.)—Ingmar Bergman.
Human Document: PATHER PANCHALI (India)—Satyajit Ray.
Competing Films
    AFACEREA PROTAR (Rum.)—Haralambie Boros.
    BLONDE SINNER [YIELD TO THE NIGHT] (Brit.)—J. Lee Thompson.
    CHABAB EMRAA (Egypt)—Salah Abou Seif.
    CHRIST IN BRONZE (Jap.)—Minoru Shibuya.
    DALIBOR (Czech.)—Vaclav Krska.
    EL ULTIMO PERRO (Arg.)—Lucas Demare.
    THE GIRL IN BLACK (Gr.)—Michael Cacoyannis.
    THE HARDER THEY FALL (U.S.)—Mark Robson.
    I LIVE IN FEAR (Jap.)—Akira Kurosawa.
    I'LL CRY TOMORROW (U.S.)—Daniel Mann.
    LA ESCONDIDA (Mex.)—Roberto Gavaldon.
    MABOROSHI (Jap.)—Koji Shima.
    THE MAN IN THE GREY FLANNEL SUIT (U.S.)—Nunnally Johnson.
    THE MAN WHO KNEW TOO MUCH (U.S.)—Alfred Hitchcock.
    THE MAN WHO NEVER WAS (Brit.)—Ronald Neame.
    MARIE ANTOINETTE (Fr.)—Jean Delannoy.
    MEEUWEN STERVEN IN DE HAVEN (Belg.)—Rik Kuypers, Ivo Michiels, Roland Verhavert.
    MERRY-GO-ROUND (India)—Zoltan Fabri.
    MOTHER (U.S.S.R.)—Mark Donskoi.
    MOZART (Aust.)—Karl Hartl.
    THE MYSTERY OF PICASSO (Fr.)—Henri-Georges Clouzot.
    OTHELLO (U.S.S.R.)—Serge Youtkevitch.
    PATHER PANCHALI (India)—Satyajit Ray.
    PEDAGOGUITCHESKAIA POEMA (U.S.S.R.)—A. Masiioukov and M. Maievskaia.
    THE RAILROAD MAN (Ital.)—Pietro Germi.
    THE ROOF (Ital.)—Vittorio De Sica.
    SEVEN YEARS IN TIBET (Brit.)—Hans Nieter.
    THE SHADOW (Pol.)—Jerzy Kawalerowicz.

SHEVGYACHYA SHENGA (India)—Shantaram Athavale.
THE SILENT WORLD (Fr.)—Jacques Yves Cousteau and Louis Malle.
SMILES OF A SUMMER NIGHT (Swed.)—Ingmar Bergman.
SOB O CEU DA BAHIA (Brazil)—Ernesto Remani.
TALPA (Mex.)—Alfredo B. Crevenna.
TARDE DE TOROS (Span.)—Ladislao Vajda.
TOTCHA PARVA OT DNEVNIA (Bulg.)—Boian Danowski.
TOUBIB EL AFFIA (Mor.)—Henri Jacques.
WALK INTO PARADISE (Aus.)—Lee Robinson.
WILD LOVE (Ital.)—Mauro Bolognini.

1957
Prizes of the International Jury
Golden Palm: FRIENDLY PERSUASION (U.S.)—William Wyler.
Special Jury Prize:
    KANAL (Pol.)—Andrzej Wajda.
    THE SEVENTH SEAL (Swed.)—Ingmar Bergman.
Special Prize: THE FORTY-FIRST (U.S.S.R.)—Grigori Chukhrai.
Direction: Robert Bresson for A MAN ESCAPED (Fr.).
Female Performance: Giuletta Masina for NIGHTS OF CABIRIA (Ital./Fr.).
Male Performance: John Kitzmiller for VALLEY OF FACES (Yugo.).
Documentary: THE ROOF OF JAPAN (Jap.)—Sadao Imamura.
    QIVITOQ (Den.)—Erik Balling.
Special Mention: GOTOMA THE BUDDHA (India)—Rajbans Khanna.
Country Selection: France.
    HE WHO MUST DIE - Jules Dassin.
    A MAN ESCAPED - Robert Bresson.
    TOUTE LA MEMOIRE DU MONDE - Alain Resnais.
    NIOK - Edmond Sechan.
Competing Films
    BACHELOR PARTY (U.S.)—Delbert Mann.
    BATTLE HELL (Brit.)—Michael Anderson.
    DOLINA MIRU (Yugo.)—France Stiglic.
    DON QUIXOTE (U.S.S.R.)—Grigori Kozintsev.
    ELOKUU (Fin.)—Matti Kassila.
    FAUSTINA (Span.)—Jose Luis Saenz de Heredia.
    THE FORTY-FIRST (U.S.S.R.)—Grigori Chukhrai.
    FRIENDLY PERSUASION (U.S.)—William Wyler.
    FUNNY FACE (U.S.)—Stanley Donen.
    GOTOMA THE BUDDHA (India)—Rajbans Khanna.
    GUENDALINA (Ital.)—Alberto Lattuada.
    HE WHO MUST DIE (Fr.)—Jules Dassin.
    HIGH TIDE AT NOON (Brit.)—Philip Leacock.
    THE HOUSE OF THE ANGEL (Arg.)—Leopoldo Torre Nilsson.
    KANAL (Pol.)—Andrzej Wajda.
    KET VALLOMAS (Hung.)—Marton Keleti.
    LES ENFANTS PERDUS (Czech.)—Milos Makovec.
    MOARA CU NOROC (Rum.)—Victor Iliu.
    NIGHTS OF CABIRIA (Ital./Fr.)—Federico Fellini.
    QIVITOQ (Den.)—Erik Balling.
    REKAVA (Ceylon)—Lester James Peries.
    RICE (Jap.)—Tadashi Imai.
    THE ROOF OF JAPAN (Jap.)—Sadao Imamura.
    SAME JAKKI (Nor.)—Per Host.
    SEMIA (Bulg.)—Zahari Jandov.
    THE SEVENTH SEAL (Swed.)—Ingmar Bergman.
    THE SINS OF ROSE BERND (Ger.)—Wolfgang Staudte.
    SISSI DIE JUNGE KAISERIN (Aust.)—Ernst Marischka.

1958
Prizes of the International Jury
Golden Palm: THE CRANES ARE FLYING (U.S.S.R.)—Mikhail Kalatozov, with an Honorary Award to Tatiana Samoilova for her superb performance.
Special Jury Prize: MY UNCLE (Fr.)—Jacques Tati.
Direction: Ingmar Bergman for BRINK OF LIFE (Swed.).
Original Scenario: Pier Paolo Pasolini, Massimo Franciosa, and P. Festa Campanile for YOUNG HUSBANDS (Ital.).
Female Performance: Bibi Andersson, Eva Dahlbeck, Ingrid Thulin and Barbro Hiort-Af-Ornas for their combined performances in BRINK OF LIFE (Swed.).
Male Performance: Paul Newman for THE LONG HOT SUMMER (U.S.).
Special Prizes:
    GOHA (Tunisia)—Jacques Baratier.
    BRONZE FACES (Switz.)—Bernard Taisant.
FIPRESCI Award
    VENGEANCE (Span.)—Juan Bardem.
Competing Films
    BRINK OF LIFE (Swed.)—Ingmar Bergman.
    BRONZE FACES (Switz.)—Bernard Taisant.
    THE BROTHERS KARAMAZOV (U.S.)—Richard Brooks.
    CIULINII BARAGANULUI (Rum.)—Louis Daquin.
    THE CRANES ARE FLYING (U.S.S.R.)—Mikhail Kalatozov.
    DESIRE UNDER THE ELMS (U.S.)—Delbert Mann.
    THE FLUTE AND THE ARROW (Swed.)—Arne Sucksdorff.
    GIGI (U.S.)—Vincente Minnelli.
    HORYU-JI (Jap.)—Susumu Hani.
    THE IRON FLOWER (Hung.)—Janos Hersko.
    L'HUOMO DI PAGLIA (Ital.)—Pietro Germi.
    LA CALETA OLVIDADA (Chili)—Bruno Gebel.
    THE LONG HOT SUMMER (U.S.)—Martin Ritt.
    MY UNCLE (Fr.)—Jacques Tati.
    NI LIV (Nor.)—Arne Skouen.
    ORDERS TO KILL (Brit.)—Anthony Asquith.
    PARAS PATHAR (India)—Satyajit Ray.
    PARDESI (India)—Abbas and Pronin.
    ROSAURA A LAS DIEZ (Arg.)—Mario Soffici.
    SNOW COUNTRY (Jap.)—Shido Toyoda.
    VENGEANCE (Span.)—Juan Bardem.
    YOUNG HUSBANDS (Ital.)—Mauro Bolognini.
    ZIZKOVSKA ROMANCE (Czech.)—Zbynek Brynych.

1959

Prizes of the International Jury
Golden Palm: BLACK ORPHEUS (Fr.)—Marcel Camus.
Special Jury Prize: STARS (Bulg.)—Konrad Wolf.
International Prize: NAZARIN (Mex.)—Luis Bunuel.
Mise-en-Scene: Francois Truffaut for THE 400 BLOWS (Fr.).
Female Performance: Simone Signoret for ROOM AT THE TOP (Brit.).
Male Performance: Dean Stockwell, Bradford Dillman, and Orson Welles for their combined performances in COMPULSION (U.S.).
Comedy: POLICARPO (Ital.)—Mario Soldati.
Special Mention: THE WHITE HERON (Jap.)—Teinosuke Kinugasa.
FIPRESCI Award
HIROSHIMA MON AMOUR (Fr./Jap.)—Alain Resnais.
ARAYA (Ven.)—Margot Benaceraf.
Catholic Film Office Award
THE 400 BLOWS (Fr.)—Francois Truffaut.
Film Writers Award
Margerite Duras and Alain Resnais for HIROSHIMA MON AMOUR.
Competing Films
AND THE WILD, WILD WOMEN (Ital.)—Renato Castellani.
ANNA (Hung.)—Zoltan Fabri.
ARAYA (Ven.)—Margot Benaceraf.
BLACK ORPHEUS (Fr.)—Marcel Camus.
COMPULSION (U.S.)—Richard Fleisher.
DESIRE (Czech.)—Vojtech Jasny.
DIE HALBZARTE (Aust.)—Rolf Thiele.
FANFARE (Neth.)—Bert Haanstra.
THE 400 BLOWS (Fr.)—Francois Truffaut.
HELDEN (Ger.)—Frantz Peter Wirth.
HONEYMOON (Span.)—Michael Powell.
KRIEGSGERICHT (Ger.)—Kurt Meisel.
LA CUCARACHA (Mex.)—Ismael Rodriguez.
LAJWANTI (India)—Narendra Suri.
LAW AND DISORDER (Brit.)—Charles Crichton.
MATOMENO HELIOVASILEMA (Gr.)—Andreas Lambrinos.
MIDDLE OF THE NIGHT (U.S.)—Delbert Mann.
MISS APRIL (Swed.)—Goran Gentele.
NAZARIN (Mex.)—Luis Bunuel.
OTCHII DOM (U.S.S.R.)—L. Koulidjanov.
POLYCARPO (Ital.)—Mario Soldati.
RAPSODIA PORTUGUESA (Por.)—Joao Menses.
ROOM AT THE TOP (Brit.)—Jack Clayton.
STARS (Bulg.)—Konrad Wolf.
TANG FU YU SHENG NU (China)—Tien Shen.
TRAIN WITHOUT A TIMETABLE (Yugo.)—Veljko Bulajic.
THE WHITE HERON (Jap.)—Teinosuke Kinugasa.
ZAFRA (Arg.)—Lucas Demare.

1960

Prizes of the International Jury
Golden Palm: LA DOLCE VITA (Ital.)—Federico Fellini.
Special Jury Prizes:
BALLAD OF A SOLDIER (U.S.S.R.)—Grigori Chukrai.
LADY WITH A PET DOG (U.S.S.R.)—Josef Heifitz.
KAGI (Jap.)—Kon Ichikawa.
L'AVVENTURA (Ital.)—Michelangelo Antonioni, for its contribution to film language.
Female Performance:
Melina Mercouri for NEVER ON SUNDAY (Gr.).
Jeanne Moreau for MODERATO CANTABILE (Fr.).
Special Homage Awards:
Ingmar Bergman for THE VIRGIN SPRING (Swed.).
Luis Bunuel for THE YOUNG ONE (Mex.).
Competing Films
BALLAD OF A SOLDIER (U.S.S.R.)—Grigori Chukrai.
CIDADE AMEACADA (Brazil)—Roberto Faria.
DEVETI KRUG (Yugo.)—France Stiglic.
HOME FROM THE HILL (U.S.)—Vincente Minnelli.
JAKTEN (Nor.)—Erik Lochen.
KAGI (Jap.)—Kon Ichikawa.
KAM CERT NEMUZE (Czech.)—Zdenek Podskalsky.
L'AMERIQUE INSOLITE (Fr.)—Francois Reichenbach.
L'AVVENTURA (Ital.)—Michelangelo Antonioni.
LA DOLCE VITA (Ital.)—Federico Fellini.
LADY WITH A PET DOG (U.S.S.R.)—Josef Heifitz.
LE TROU (Fr.)—Jacques Becker.
LOS GOLFOS (Span.)—Carlos Saura.
MACARIO (Mex.)—Roberto Gavaldon.
MODERATO CANTABILE (Fr.)—Peter Brook.
NEVER ON SUNDAY (Gr.)—Jules Dassin.
PARVI UROK (Bulg.)—Ranguel Valtchanov.
PAW, BOY OF TWO WORLDS (Den.)—Astrid Henning-Jensen.
THE PROCESSION (Arg.)—Francis Lauric.
THE SAVAGE INNOCENTS (It./Fr./Brit.)—Nicholas Ray and Baccio Bandini.
SI LE VENT TE FAIT PEUR (Bel.)—Emile Degelin.
SONS AND LOVERS (Brit.)—Jack Cardiff.
SUJATA (India)—Bimal Roy.
TCHIEN GNU YOU HOUN (China)—Li Han-Hsiang.
TELEGRAMELE (Rum.)—Gheorghe Naghi and Aurel Miheles.
THE VIRGIN SPRING (Swed.)—Ingmar Bergman.
THE YOUNG ONE (Mex.)—Luis Bunuel.
ZEZOWATE SZCZESCIE (Pol.)—Andrzej Munk.

1961

Prizes of the International Jury
Golden Palm:
VIRIDIANA (Span.)—Luis Bunuel.
A LONG ABSENCE (Fr./Ital.)—Henri Colpi.
Special Jury Prize: MOTHER JOAN OF THE ANGELS (Pol.)—Jerzy Kawalerowicz.
Mise-en-Scene: Julia Solntzeva for HISTORY OF THE BURNING YEARS (U.S.S.R.).
Female Performance: Sophia Loren for TWO WOMEN (Fr./Ital.).
Male Performance: Anthony Perkins for GOODBYE AGAIN (Fr./U.S.).

National Selection: Italy.
NEBBIA - Raffaele Andreassi.
GIOVEDI: PASSEGIATA - Vincenzo Gamma.
GIRL WITH A SUITCASE - Valerio Zurlini.
CHE GIOIA VIVERE - Rene Clement.
THE LOVE MAKERS - Mauro Bolognini.
Gary Cooper Award for Human Values: A RAISIN IN THE SUN (U.S.)—Daniel Petrie.
FIPRESCI Awards
HANDS IN THE TRAP (Arg.)—Leopoldo Torre Nilsson.
CHRONICLE OF A SUMMER (Fr.)—Jean Rouch.
Catholic Film Office Award
THE HOODLUM PRIEST (U.S.)—Irvin Kershner.
Competing Films
CHE GIOIA VIVERE (Ital.)—Rene Clement.
DAN CETRNAESTI (Yugo.)—Zdravko Velimirovic.
DARCLEE (Rum.)—Mihai Iacob.
DUVAD (Hung.)—Zoltan Fabri.
EL CENTROFORWARD MURIO AL AMANECER (Arg.)—Rene Mujica.
THE FIRST MASS (Bra.)—Lima Barreto.
GIRL WITH A SUITCASE (Ital.)—Valerio Zurlini.
GOODBYE AGAIN (U.S.)—Anatole Litvak.
HANDS IN THE TRAP (Arg.)—Leopoldo Torre Nilsson.
HER BROTHER (Jap.)—Kon Ichikawa.
HET MES (Neth.)—Fons Rademakers.
HISTORY OF THE BURNING YEARS (U.S.S.R.)—Julia Solntzeva.
THE HOODLUM PRIEST (U.S.)—Irvin Kershner.
I LIKE MIKE (Israel)—Peter Frye.
THE JUDGE (Swed.)—Alf Sjoberg.
THE LAST WITNESS (Ger.)—Wolfgang Staudte.
LE CIEL ET LA BOUE (Fr.)—Pierre-Dominique Gaisseau.
LES COSAQUES (U.S.S.R.)—Vassili Pronine.
THE LOVEMAKERS (Ital.)—Mauro Bolognini.
MADALENA (Gr.)—Dinos Dimopoulos.
THE MARK (Brit.)—Guy Green.
MOTHER JOAN OF THE ANGELS (Pol.)—Jerzy Kawalerowicz.
THE PASSIONATE DEMONS (Nor.)—Nils Reinhardt Christensen.
PLEIN SUD (Bel.)—Commandant de Gerlache.
SONG OF THE GRAY PIGEON (Czech.)—Stanislas Barabas.
VIRIDIANA (Span.)—Luis Bunuel.
THE WASTREL (Cyprus)—Michael Cacoyannis.

1962

Prizes of the International Jury
Golden Palm: THE GIVEN WORD (Brazil)—Anselmo Duarte.
Special Jury Prize:
THE TRIAL OF JOAN OF ARC (Fr.)—Robert Bresson.
L'ECLIPSE (Ital./Fr.)—Michelangelo Antonioni.
Performances:
The combined performances of Katharine Hepburn, Ralph Richardson, Jason Robards, Jr., and Dean Stockwell in LONG DAY'S JOURNEY INTO NIGHT (U.S.).
The combined performances of Rita Tushingham and Murray Melvin for A TASTE OF HONEY (Brit.).
Adaptation: ELECTRA (Gr.)—Michael Cacoyannis.
Comedy: DIVORCE - ITALIAN STYLE (Ital.)—Pietro Germi.
FIPRESCI Award
THE EXTERMINATING ANGEL (Mex.)—Luis Bunuel.
Catholic Film Office Award
L'ECLIPSE (Ital./Fr.)—Michelangelo Antonioni.
Competing Films
ADORABLE JULIA (Aust.)—Alfred Weidenmann.
ADVISE AND CONSENT (U.S.)—Otto Preminger.
ALL FALL DOWN (U.S.)—John Frankenheimer.
BAAL HA KHALOMOT (Israel)—Alina and Yoram Gross.
BREAD OF THE EARLY YEARS (Ger.)—Herbert Vesely.
CLEO FROM 5 TO 7 (Fr.)—Agnes Varda.
CUPOLA (Jap.)—Urayama Kiriro.
DIVORCE—ITALIAN STYLE (Ital.)—Pietro Germi.
DOM BEZ OKIEN (Pol.).
DVOJE (Yugo.)—Aleksandar Petrovic.
ELECTRA (Gr.)—Michael Cacoyannis.
THE EXTERMINATING ANGEL (Mex.)—Luis Bunuel.
THE FEMALE: SEVENTY TIMES SEVEN (Arg.)—Leopoldo Torre Nilsson.
THE GODDESS (India)—Satyajit Ray.
HARRY OG KAMMERTJENEREN (Den.)—Bent Christensen.
THE INNOCENTS (Brit.)—Jack Clayton.
KONGA YO (Congo)—Yves Allegret.
L'ECLIPSE (Ital.)—Michelangelo Antonioni.
LE PETIT ETRANGER (Libya)—George Michel Nasser.
LES ENFANTS DU SOLEIL (Mor.)—Jacques Severac.
LIBERTE I (Senegal)—Yves Ciampi.
LONG DAY'S JOURNEY INTO NIGHT (U.S.)—Sidney Lumet.
THE LOVERS OF TERUEL (Fr.)—Raymond Rouleau.
THE MAN FROM THE FIRST CENTURY (Czech.)—Oldrich Lipsky.
MONDO CANE (Ital.)—Gualtiero Jacopetti, Paolo Cavara, and Franco Prosperi.
O PAGALOR DE PROMESSAS (Bra.)—Anselmo Duarte.
PLACIDO (Span.)—Luis G. Berlanga.
PLENENO YATO (Bul.)—Doutcho Mundrov.
QUAND LES ARBRES ETAIENT GRANDS (U.S.S.R.)—Lev Koulidjanov.
THE TRIAL OF JOAN OF ARC (Fr.)—Robert Bresson.
YANK KWEI FEI (China)—Li Han-Hsiang.

1963

Prizes of the International Jury
Golden Palm: THE LEOPARD (Fr./Ital.)—Luchino Visconti.
Special Jury Award:
HARAKIRI (Jap.)—Masaki Kobayashi.
A CAT (Czech.)—Vojtech Jasny.
Female Performance: Marina Vlady for THE CONJUGAL BED (Ital.).
Male Performance: Richard Harris for THIS SPORTING LIFE (Brit.).
Scenario: CODINE (Rum.)—Yves Jamiaque. Dumuitru Carabat, and Henri Colpi.
Evocation D'unwe Epopee Revolutionnaire: THE OPTIMISTIC TRAGEDY (U.S.S.R.).

Gary Cooper Award for Human Values: TO KILL A MOCKINGBIRD (U.S.)—Robert Mulligan.
FIPRESCI Awards
THIS SPORTING LIFE (Brit.)—Lindsay Anderson.
LE JOLI MAI (Fr.)—Chris Marker.
Catholic Film Office Award
THE FIANCES (Ital.)—Ermanno Olmi.
Competing Films
ALVORADA - AUFBRUCK IN BRASILIEN (Ger.)—Hugo Niebeiling.
CARAMBOLAGES (Fr.)—Marcel Bluwald.
CODINE (Rum.)—Henri Colpi.
THE CONJUGAL BED (Ital.)—Marco Ferreri.
EL BUEN AMOR (Span.)—Francisco Regueiro.
EL OTRO CRISTOBAL (Cuba)—Armand Gatti.
THE FIANCES (Ital.)—Ermanno Olmi.
HARAKIRI (Jap.)—Masaki Kobayashi.
HOW TO BE LOVED (Pol.)—Wojciech J. Has.
KERTES HAZAK UTCAJA (Hung.)—Tamas Fejer.
LA CAGE (Gabon)—Robert Darene.
LA REINE DIABOLIQUE (China)—Li Han-Hsiang.
LE RAT D'AMERIQUE (Fr.)—Jean-Gabriel Albicoco.
THE LEOPARD (Ital.)—Luchino Visconti.
LES ABYSSES (Fr.)—Nico Papatakis.
LIKE TWO DROPS OF WATER (Neth.)—Fons Rademakers.
LORD OF THE FLIES (Brit.)—Peter Brook.
LOS VENERBLES TODOS (Arg.)—Manuel Antin.
THE OPTIMISTIC TRAGEDY (U.S.S.R.)—Samson Samsonov.
OURANOS (Gr.)—Takis Kanellopoulos.
THIS SPORTING LIFE (Brit.)—Lindsay Anderson.
TO KILL A MOCKINGBIRD (U.S.)—Robert Mulligan.
TUTUNE (Bul.)—Nicolas Korabov.
WHAT EVER HAPPENED TO BABY JANE? (U.S.)—Robert Aldrich.

1964
Prizes of the International Jury
Golden Palm: THE UMBRELLAS OF CHERBOURG (Fr./Ger.)—Jacques Demy.
Special Jury Award: WOMAN OF THE DUNES (Jap.)—Hiroshi Teshigahara.
Female Performance:
Anne Bancroft for THE PUMPKIN EATER (U.S.).
Barbara Barrie for ONE POTATO-TWO POTATO (U.S.).
Male Performance:
Antal Pager for PACSIRTA (Hung.).
Saro Urzi for SEDUCED AND ABANDONED (Ital.).
Special Homage: Andrzej Munk for THE PASSENGER (Pol.).
Special Jury Mention:
Jaromil Jires for KRIK (Czech.).
Georgui Danelia for ROMANCE A MOSCOU (U.S.S.R.).
Manuel Summers for LA NINA DE LUTO (Span.).
FIPRESCI Award
THE PASSENGER (Pol.)—Andrzej Munk.
Catholic Film Office Award
THE UMBRELLAS OF CHERBOURG (Fr.)—Jacques Demy.
STERILE LIVES (Brazil)—Nelson Pereira dos Santos.
Competing Films
ALONE ON THE PACIFIC (Jap.)—Kon Ichikawa.
ANY NUMBER CAN PLAY (Fr.)—Henri Verneuil.
THE APE WOMAN (Ital.)—Marco Ferreri.
BLACK GOD - WHITE GOD (Bra.)—Glauber Rocha.
THE DEAD OF BEVERLY HILLS (Ger.)—Michael Pfleghar.
EL LEILA EL AKHIRA (Egypt)—Kamal El Sheikh.
KOKKINA FANARIA (Gr.)—Vassili Georgiades.
KRIK (Czech.)—Jaromil Jires.
KVARTERET KORPEN (Swed.)—Bo Widerberg.
LA CARAVANE BLANCHE (U.S.S.R.)—Eldar Chenguelaia and Tomaz Meliava.
LA NINA DE LUTO (Span.)—Manuel Summers.
MUJHE JEENE DO (India)—Moni Battacharjee.
ONE POTATO - TWO POTATO (U.S.)—Larry Pierce.
PACSIRTA (Hung.)—Laszlo Ranody.
THE PASSENGER (Pol.)—Andrzej Munk.
PRIMERO YO (Arg.)—Fernando Ayala.
THE PUMPKIN EATER (Brit.)—Jack Clayton.
SEDUCED AND ABANDONED (Ital.)—Pietro Germi.
THE SOFT SKIN (Fr.)—Francois Truffaut.
STERILE LIVES (Bra.)—Nelson Pereira dos Santos.
THE UMBRELLAS OF CHERBOURG (Fr.)—Jacques Demy.
THE VISIT (Ger.)—Bernhard Wicki.
WOMAN OF THE DUNES (Jap.)—Hiroshi Teshigahara.
THE WORLD OF HENRY ORIENT (U.S.)—George Roy Hill.

1965
Prizes of the International Jury
Golden Palm: THE KNACK (Brit.)—Richard Lester.
Special Jury Prize: KWAIDAN (Jap.)—Masaki Kobayashi.
Male and Female Performances: Samantha Eggar and Terence Stamp for THE COLLECTOR (U.S.).
Mise-en-Scene: Liviu Ciulei for THE LOST FOREST (Rum.).
Scenario:
THE HILL (Brit.), written by Ray Rigby.
317TH SECTION (Fr.), written by Pierre Schoendoerffer.
Special Jury Mentions:
Josef Kroner of Czechoslovakia.
Ida Kaminska of Czechoslovakia.
Vera Kouznetsova of The U.S.S.R.
FIPRESCI Prize
TARAHUMARA (Mex.)—Luis Alcoriza.
Catholic Film Office Awards
YOYO (Fr.)—Pierre Etaix.
TOKYO OLYMPICS (Jap.)—Kon Ichikawa.
Competing Films
CLAY (Aus.)—Giorgio Mangiamele.
THE COLLECTOR (U.S.)—William Wyler.

EL HARAM (Egypt)—Henri Barakat.
EL JUEGO DE LA OCA (Span.)—Manuel Summers.
EL RENIDERO (Arg.)—Rene Mujica.
ELETBETANCOLTATOTT LANY (Hung.)—Tamas Banovich.
FIFI LA PLUME (Fr.)—Albert Lamorisse.
THE FIRST DAY OF FREEDOM (Pol.)—Aleksander Ford.
GILI-BILI STARIK SO STAROUKHOI (U.S.S.R.)—Grigori Chukrai.
GORECHTO PLANE (Bul.)—Zako Heskia.
THE HILL (Brit.)—Sydney Lumet.
THE IPCRESS FILE (Brit.)—Sydney J. Furie.
JAVORONOK (U.S.S.R.)—Nikita Kourikhine and Leonide Menaker.
THE KNACK (Brit.)—Richard Lester.
KWAIDAN (Jap.)—Masaki Kobayashi.
THE LOST FOREST (Rum.)—Liviu Ciulei.
LOVING COUPLES (Swed.)—Mai Zetterling.
THE MOMENT OF TRUTH (Ital.)—Francisco Rosi and Antonio Cervi.
MY HOME IN COPACABANA (Swed.)—Arne Sucksdorff.
NOITE VAZIA (Bra.)—Walter Hugo Khouri.
PRODOSSIA (Gr.)—Costas Manoussakis.
THE SHOP ON MAIN STREET (Czech.)—Jan Kadar and Elmar Klos.
TARAHUMARA (Mex.)—Luis Alcoriza.
THE UNINHIBITED (Span.)—Juan Bardem.
YOYO (Fr.)—Pierre Etaix.

1966
Prizes of the International Jury
Golden Palm:
A MAN AND A WOMAN (Fr.)—Claude Lelouch.
THE BIRDS, THE BEES, AND THE ITALIANS (Fr./Ital.)—Pietro Germi.
Special Jury Prize: ALFIE (Brit.)—Lewis Gilbert.
Female Performance: Vanessa Redgrave for MORGAN! (Brit.).
Male Performance: Per Oscarsson for HUNGER (Den.).
Mise-en-Scene: Serge Youtkevitch for PORTRAIT OF LENIN (U.S.S.R.).
Directorial Debut: RASCOALA (Rum.)—Mircea Muresan.
Special Acting Mention: Toto of Italy.
20th Anniversary Tribute: Orson Welles, in recognition of his outstanding contribution to Cinema.
FIPRESCI Prize
YOUNG TORLESS (Ger.)—Volker Schloendorff.
THE WAR IS OVER (Fr.)—Alain Resnais.
Catholic Film Office Award
A MAN AND A WOMAN (Fr.)—Claude Lelouch.
Competing Films
ALFIE (Brit.)—Lewis Gilbert.
ASHES (Pol.)—Andrzej Wajda.
THE BIRDS, THE BEES, AND THE ITALIANS (Ital.)—Pietro Germi.
BONJOUR, C'EST MOI (U.S.S.R.)—Dovlatiane Frounze.
CON EL VIENTO SOLANO (Span.)—Mario Camus.
ES (Ger.)—Ulrich Schamoni.
FALSTAFF (Span.)—Orson Welles.
THE HAWKS AND THE SPARROWS (Ital.)—Pier Paolo Pasolini.
HUNGER (Den.)—Henning Carlsen.
THE ISLAND (Swed.)—Alf Sjoberg.
L'ARMATA BRANCALEONE (Ital.)—Mario Monicelli.
MADEMOISELLE (Fr./Brit.)—Tony Richardson.
MODESTY BLAISE (Brit.)—Joseph Losey.
MORGAN! (Brit.)—Harold Karel Reisz.
THE NUN (Fr.)—Jacques Rivette.
PHARAOH (Pol.)—Jerzy Kawalerowicz.
PORTRAIT OF LENIN (U.S.S.R.)—Serge Youtkevitch.
RASCOALA (Rum.)—Mircea Muresan.
THE ROUND-UP (Hung.)—Miklos Jancso.
SECONDS (U.S.)—John Frankenheimer.
YOUNG TORLESS (Ger.)— Volker Schloendorff.

1967
Prizes of the International Jury
Golden Palm: BLOW-UP (Brit./Ital.)—Michelangelo Antonioni.
Special Jury Prize:
ACCIDENT (Brit.)—Joseph Losey.
I EVEN MET HAPPY GYPSIES (Yugo.)—Aleksandar Petrovic.
Female Performance: Pia Degermark for ELVIRA MADIGAN (Den.).
Male Performance: Odded Kotler for THREE DAYS AND A CHILD (Israel).
Mise-en-Scene: Ferenc Kosa for TEN THOUSAND SUNS (Hung.).
Scenario:
Alain Jessua for THE KILLING GAME (Fr.).
Elio Petri and Ugo Pirro for WE STILL KILL THE OLD WAY (Ital.).
Film Debut: LE VENT DES AURES (Algeria)—Mohammed Lakhdar Hamina.
Special Homage Award: Robert Bresson.
Competing Films
ACCIDENT (Brit.)—Joseph Losey.
BLOW-UP (Ital./Brit.)—Michelangelo Antonioni.
DEN RODE KAPPE (Den.)—Gabriel Axel.
EARTH ENTRANCED (Brazil)—Glauber Rocha.
ELVIRA MADIGAN (Swed.)—Bo Widerberg.
HOTEL PRO CIZINCE (Czech.)—Antonin Masa.
I EVEN MET SOME HAPPY GYPSIES (Yugo.)—Aleksandar Petrovic.
THE IMMORAL MAN (Ital.)—Pietro Germi.
KATERINA IZMAILOVA (U.S.S.R.)—Mikhail Shapiro.
THE KILLING GAME (Fr.)—Alain Jessua.
LE VENT DES AURES (Algeria)—Mohammed Lakhdar Hamina.
L'INCOMPRESO (Ital.)—Luigi Comencini.
L'INCONNU DE SHANDIGOR (Switz.)—Jean-Louis Roy.
MON AMOUR, MON AMOUR (Fr.)—Nadine Trintignant.
MONDAY'S CHILD (Arg.)—Leopoldo Torre Nilsson.
MOUCHETTE (Fr.)—Robert Bresson.
PEDRO PARAMO (Mex.)—Carlos Velo.
TEN THOUSAND SUNS (Hung.)—Ferenc Kosa.
THREE DAYS AND A CHILD (Israel)—Uri Zohar.
ULYSSES (Brit.)—Joseph Strick.
WE STILL KILL THE OLD WAY (Ital.)—Elio Petri.

YOU'RE A BIG BOY NOW (U.S.)—Francis Ford Coppola.

1968
Festival cancelled because of the unstable political climate in Paris.
Films Presented in Competition
ANNA KARENINA (U.S.S.R.)—Alexandre Zarkhi.
BLACK CAT (Jap.)—Kaneto Shindo.
BLACK JESUS (Ital.)—Valerio Zurlini.
CAPRICIOUS SUMMER (Czech.)—Jiri Menzel.
THE CASTLE (Ger.)—R. Nolte.
CHARLIE BUBBLES (Brit.)—Albert Finney.
DOCTEUR GLAS (Den.)—Mai Zetterling.
THE FIREMEN'S BALL (Czech.)—Milos Forman.
THE GIRL ON THE MOTORCYCLE (Brit.)—Jack Cardiff.
GRAZIE ZIA (Ital.)—Salvatore Samperi.
HERE WE GO AROUND THE MULBERRY BUSH (Brit.)—C. Donner.
HISTOIRES EXTRAORDINAIRES (Fr.)—Federico Fellini, Louis Malle, and Roger Vadim.
JE T'AIME, JE T'AIME (Fr.)—Alain Resnais.
JOANNA (Brit.)—Michael Sarn.
LES GAULOISES BLEUES (Fr.)—M. Cournot.
THE LONG DAY'S DYING (Brit.)—Peter Collinson.
MALI VOJNICI (Yugo.)—Bata Cengic.
O SLAVNOSTI A HOSTECH (Czech.)—Jean Nemec.
PEPPERMINT FRAPPE (Span.)—Carlos Saura.
PETULIA (U.S.)—Richard Lester.
THE RED AND THE WHITE (Hung.)—Miklos Jancso.
TRILOGY (U.S.)—Frank Perry.
TUVYA AND HIS 7 DAUGHTERS (Israel)—Menahem Golan.
THE VIOLENT FOUR (Ital.)—Carlo Lizzani.
ZYWOT MATEUSZA (Pol.)—Witold Leszczynski.

1969
Prizes of the International Jury
Golden Palm: IF (Brit.)—Lindsay Anderson.
Special Jury Prize: ADALEN 31 (Swed.)—Bo Widerberg.
Female Performance: Vanessa Redgrave for ISADORA (Brit.).
Male Performance: Jean-Louis Trintignant for Z (Fr.).
Jury Prize: Z (Fr.)—Constantin Costa-Gavras.
Mise-en-Scene:
    ANTONIO DAS MORTES (Brazil)—Glauber Rocha.
    ALL GOOD CITIZENS (Czech.)—Vojtech Jasny.
Film Debut: EASY RIDER (U.S.)—Dennis Hopper.
FIPRESCI Prize
    ANDREI ROUBLEV (U.S.S.R.)—Andrei Tarkovsky.
Competing Films
ADALEN 31 (Swed.)—Bo Widerberg.
ALL GOOD CITIZENS (Czech.)—Vojtech Jasny.
ANTONIO DAS MORTES (Brazil)—Glauber Rocha.
THE APPOINTMENT (U.S.)—Sydney Lumet.
THE CONFRONTATION (Hung.)—Miklos Jancso.
DILLINGER IS DEAD (Ital.)—Marco Ferreri.
DON'T LET THE ANGELS FALL (Can.)—George Kaczender.
EASY RIDER (U.S.)—Dennis Hopper.
END OF A PRIEST (Czech.)—Evald Schorm.
FELDOBOTT KO (Hung.)—Sandor Sara.
FLASHBACK (Ital.)—Raffaele Andreassi.
FOR A PRICE (Ital.)—Guilano Montaldo.
HUNTING FLIES (Pol.)—Andrzej Wajda.
HYMN OF A TIRED MAN (Jap.)—Masaki Kobayashi.
IF (Brit.)—Lindsay Anderson.
ISADORA (Brit.)—Karel Reisz.
IT RAINS IN MY VILLAGE (Yugo.)—Aleksandar Petrovic.
LE GRAND AMOUR (Fr.)—Pierre Etaix.
THE MAN WHO THOUGHT THINGS (Den.)—Jens Raun.
MATZOR (Israel)—Gilberto Tofano.
METTI, UNA SERA A CENA (Ital.)—Guiseppe Patroni Griffi.
MICHAEL KOHLHAAS, THE REBEL (Ger.)—Volker Schlondorff.
MY NIGHT AT MAUD'S (Fr.)—Eric Rohmer.
THE PRIME OF MISS JEAN BRODIE (Brit.)—Ronald Neame.
SLAVES (U.S.)—Herbert Biberman.
SPAIN AGAIN (Span.)—Jaime Camino.
Z (Fr.)—Constantin Costa-Gavras.

1970
Prizes of the International Jury
Golden Palm: M.A.S.H. (U.S.)—Robert Altman.
Special Jury Prize: INVESTIGATION OF A CITIZEN ABOVE SUSPICION (Ital.)—Elio Petri.
Female Performance: Ottavia Piccolo for METELLO (Ital.).
Male Performance: Marcello Mastroianni for DRAMA OF JEALOUSY (Ital.).
Mise-en-Scene: John Boorman for LEO THE LAST (Brit.).
Jury Prizes:
    THE FALCONS (Hung.)—Istvan Gal.
    THE STRAWBERRY STATEMENT (U.S.)—Stuart Hagmann.
Film Debut: HOA-BINH (Fr.)—Raoul Coutard.
Competing Films
THE ALIENIST (Brazil)—Nelson Pereira dos Santos.
BUTTERCUP CHAIN (Brit.)—Robert Ellis Miller.
DON SEGUNDO SOMBRA (Arg.)—Manuel Antin.
DRAMA OF JEALOUSY (Ital.)—Ettore Scola.
THE DREAMER (Israel)—Dan Wolman.
THE EARTH (Egypt)—Youssef Chahine.
ELISE, OR REAL LIFE (Fr.)—Michel Drach.
THE FALCONS (Hung.)—Istvan Cal.
HARRY MUNTER (Swed.)—Kjell Grede.
HOA-BINH (Fr.)—Raoul Coutard.
INVESTIGATION OF A CITIZEN ABOVE SUSPICION (Ital.)—Elio Petri.
LANDSCAPE AFTER THE BATTLE (Pol.)—Andrzej Wajda.
THE LAST LEAP (Fr.)—Edouard Luntz.
LEO THE LAST (Brit.)—John Boorman.

LONG LIVE THE BRIDE AND GROOM (Span.)—Luis Garcia Berlanga.
M.A.S.H. (U.S.)—Robert Altman.
MALATESTA (Ger.)—Peter Lilienthal.
METELLO (Ital.)—Mauro Bolognini.
THE PALACE OF ANGELS (Brazil)—Walter Hugo Khouri.
THE STRAWBERRY STATEMENT (U.S.)—Stuart Hagmann.
TELL ME THAT YOU LOVE ME, JUNIE MOON (U.S.)—Otto Preminger.
THE THINGS OF LIFE (Fr.)—Claude Sautet.
THE TULIPS OF HAARLEM (Ital.)—Franco Brusati.
UNE SI SIMPLE HISTOIRE (Tunisia)—Abdel Tif Ben Ammar.
WE'LL EAT THE FRUIT OF PARADISE (Bel./Czech.)—Vera Chytilova.

1971
Prizes of the International Jury
25th Anniversary Prize: Luchino Visconti for DEATH IN VENICE (Ital.), as well as his complete Oeuvre.
Golden Palm: THE GO-BETWEEN (Brit.)—Joseph Losey.
Special Jury Prize:
    TAKING OFF (U.S.)—Milos Forman.
    JOHNNY GOT HIS GUN (U.S.)—Dalton Trumbo.
Female Performance: Kitty Winn for PANIC IN NEEDLE PARK (U.S.).
Male Performance: Riccardo Cucciolla for SACCO AND VANZETTI (Ital.).
Jury Prize:
    LOVE (Hung.)—Karoly Makk, with a special mention for the performances of Lily Darvas and Mari Torocsik.
    JOE HILL (Swed.)—Bo Widerberg.
Film Debut: BY GRACE RECEIVED (Ital.)—Nino Manfredi.
Competing Films
ANIMALE BOLNAVE (Rum.)—Nicolae Breban.
APOKAL (Ger.)—Paul Anczykowski.
BY GRACE RECEIVED (Ital.)—Nino Manfredi.
DEATH IN VENICE (Ital.)—Luchino Visconti.
DRIVE, HE SAID (U.S.)—Jack Nicholson.
FAMILY LIFE (Pol.)—Krzysztof Zanussi.
THE FLIGHT (U.S.S.R.)—Alexandre Alov and Vladimir Naoumov.
THE GO-BETWEEN (Brit.)—Joseph Losey.
GOYA—HISTORIA DE UNA SOLEDAD (Span.)—Nino Quevedo.
JOE HILL (Swed.)—Bo Widerberg.
JOHNNY GOT HIS GUN (U.S.)—Dalton Trumbo.
LA CALIFFA (Ital.)—Alberto Bevilacqua.
LE BATEAU SUR L'HERBE (Fr.)—Gerard Brach.
LES MARIES DE L'AN II (Fr.)—Jean-Paul Rappeneau.
LOOT (Brit.)—Silvio Narizzano.
LOVE (Hung.)—Karoly Makk.
MIRA (Bel.)—Fons Rademakers.
MURMUR OF THE HEART (Fr.)—Louis Malle.
OUT BACK (Aus.)—Ted Kotcheff.
PANIC IN NEEDLE PARK (U.S.)—Jerry Shatzberg.
PINDORAMA (Bra.)—Arnaldo Jabor.
RAPHAEL OU LE DEBAUCHE (Fr.)—Michel Deville.
SACCO AND VANZETTI (Ital.)—Giuliano Montaldo.
TAKING OFF (U.S.)—Milos Forman.
WALKABOUT (Brit.)—Nicolas Roeg.

1972
Prizes of the International Jury
Golden Palm:
    THE MATTEI AFFAIR (Ital.)—Francesco Rosi; with a Special Jury Mention for the performance of Gian Maria Volonte.
    THE WORKING CLASS GO TO HEAVEN (Ital.)—Elio Petri.
Special Jury Prize: SOLARIS (U.S.S.R.)—Andrei Tarkovsky.
Female Performance: Susannah York for IMAGES (Ireland).
Male Performance: Jean Yanne for WE WILL NOT GROW OLD TOGETHER (Fr.).
Mise-en-Scene: RED PSALM (Hung.)—Miklos Jancso.
Jury Prize: SLAUGHTERHOUSE-FIVE (U.S.)—George Roy Hill.
Competing Films
CHERE LOUISE (Fr.)—Philippe de Broca.
IMAGES (Ireland)—Robert Altman.
I LOVE YOU ROSA (Israel)—Moshe Mizrahi.
JEREMIAH JOHNSON (U.S.)—Sydney Pollack.
KING, QUEEN, KNAVE (Ger.)—Jerzy Skolimowski.
LES FEUX DE LA CHANDELEUR (Fr.)—Serge Korber.
MALPERTUIS (Bel.)—Harry Kumel.
THE MATTEI AFFAIR (Ital.)—Francesco Rosi.
PEARL IN THE CROWN (Pol.)—Kazimierz Kutz.
PETROLEJOVE LAMPY (Czech.)—Juraj Herz.
RED PSALM (Hung.)—Miklos Jancso.
THE RULING CLASS (Brit.)—Peter Medak.
THE SEDUCTION OF MIMI (Ital.)—Lina Wertmuller.
SLAUGHTERHOUSE-FIVE (U.S.)—George Roy Hill.
SOLARIS (U.S.S.R.)—Andrei Tarkovsky.
THE SURVEYORS (Switz.)—Michel Soulter.
TO FIND A MAN (U.S.)—Buzz Kulik.
TROTTA (Ger.)—Johannes Schaaf.
THE TRUE NATURE OF BERNADETTE (Can.)—Gilles Carle.
THE VISITORS (U.S.)—Elia Kazan.
WE WILL NOT GROW OLD TOGETHER (Fr.)—Maurice Pialat.
THE WORKING CLASS GO TO HEAVEN (Ital.)—Elio Petri.

1973
Prizes of the International Jury
Golden Palm:
    SCARECROW (U.S.)—Jerry Schatzberg.
    THE HIRELING (Brit.)—Alan Bridges.
Special Jury Prize: THE MOTHER AND THE WHORE (Fr.)—Jean Eustache.
Female Performance: Joanne Woodward for THE EFFECT OF GAMMA RAYS ON MAN-IN-THE-MOON MARIGOLDS (U.S.).
Male Performance: Giancarlo Giannini for LOVE AND ANARCHY (Ital.).
Special Prize: LA PLANETE SAUVAGE (Fr.)—Rene Laloux.
Jury Prize:
    HOUR GLASS SANATORIUM (Pol.)—Wojciech Has.

THE INVITATION (Switz.)—Claude Goretta.
Film Debut: JEREMY (U.S.)—Arthur Barron.
FIPRESCI Prize
THE MOTHER AND THE WHORE (Fr.)—Jean Eustache.
LA GRANDE BOUFFE (Fr.)—Marco Ferreri.
Competing Films
AMLETO (Ital.)—Carmelo Bene.
ANNA AND THE WOLVES (Span.)—Carlos Saura.
BELLE (Bel.)—Andre Delvaux.
BISTURI, LA MAFIA BIANCA (Ital.)—Luigi Zampa.
THE EFFECT OF GAMMA RAYS ON MAN-IN-THE-MOON MARIGOLDS (U.S.)—Paul Newman.
ELECTRA GLIDE IN BLUE (U.S.)—James Guercio.
THE HIRELING (Brit.)—Alan Bridges.
HOUR GLASS SANATORIUM (Pol.)—Wojciech Has.
THE INVITATION (Switz.)—Claude Goretta.
JEREMY (U.S.)—Arthur Barron.
LA GRANDE BOUFFE (Fr.)—Marco Ferreri.
LA MORT D'UN BUCHERON (Can.)—Gilles Carle.
LA OTRA IMAGEN (Span.)—Antonio Ribas.
LA PLANETE SAUVAGE (Fr.)—Rene Laloux.
LE FAR WEST (Bel.)—Jacques Brel.
LOVE AND ANARCHY (Ital.)—Lina Wertmuller.
THE MOTHER AND THE WHORE (Fr.)—Jean Eustache.
O LUCKY MAN! (Brit.)—Lindsay Anderson.
PETOFI 73 (Hung.)—Ferenc Kardos.
SCARECROW (U.S.)—Jerry Schatzberg.
UN MONOLOGUE (U.S.S.R.)—Ylia Averbakh.
VOGLIAMO I COLONNELLI (Ital.)—Mario Monicelli.
THE VOWS (Por.)—Antonio de Macedo.

1974
Prizes of the International Jury
Golden Palm: THE CONVERSATION (U.S.)—Francis Ford Coppola.
Special Jury Prize: ONE THOUSAND AND ONE NIGHTS (Ital.)—Pier Paolo Pasolini.
Female Performance: Marie-Jose Nat for LES VIOLONS DU BAL (Fr.).
Male Performance: Jack Nicholson for THE LAST DETAIL (U.S.).
Jury Prize: Carlos Saura for COUSIN ANGELICA (Span.).
Scenario: THE SUGARLAND EXPRESS (U.S.), written by Hal Barwood and Matthew Robbins.
Grand Prix de la Commission Superieure Technique du Cinema Francais: MAHLER (Brit.)—Ken Russell.
Special Tribute: Charles Boyer, in recognition of his portrayal in STAVISKY (Fr.).
FIPRESCI Prize
LANCELOT OF THE LAKE (Fr.)—Robert Bresson.
FEAR EATS THE SOUL (Ger.)—Rainer Werner Fassbinder.
Competing Films
ABOU EL BANAT (Israel)—Moshe Mizrahi.
CAT'S PLAY (Hung.)—Karoly Makk.
THE CONVERSATION (U.S.)—Francis Ford Coppola.
COUSIN ANGELICA (Span.)—Carlos Saura.
DELITTO D'AMORE (Ital.)—Luigi Comencini.
FEAR EATS THE SOUL (Ger.)—Rainer Werner Fassbinder.
GARM HAVA (India)—M.S. Satyyu.
HIMIKO (Jap.)—Masahiro Shinoda.
THE HOLY OFFICE (Mex.)—Arturo Ripstein.
LA CAGE AUX OURS (Bel.)—Marian Handwerker.
THE LAST DETAIL (U.S.)—Hal Ashby.
THE LAST WORD (Bulg.)—Binka Jeliaskova.
LES VIOLONS DU BAL (Fr.)—Michel Drach.
THE LOST BOY (U.S.S.R.)—Gueorguy Danelia.
MAHLER (Brit.)—Ken Russel.
MILAREPA (Ital.)—Liliana Cavani.
THE NICKEL RIDE (U.S.)—Robert Mulligan.
THE NINE LIVES OF FRITZ THE CAT (U.S.)—Robert Taylor.
THE OTHERS (Fr.)—Hugo Santiago.
ONCE UPON A TIME IN THE EAST (Can.)—Andre Brassard.
ONE THOUSAND AND ONE NIGHTS (Ital.)—Pier Paolo Pasolini.
STAVISKY (Fr.)—Alain Resnais.
THE SUGARLAND EXPRESS (U.S.)—Steven Spielberg.
SYMPTOMS (Brit.)—Jose Larraz.
THIEVES LIKE US (U.S.)—Robert Altman.

1975
Prizes of the International Jury
Golden Palm: CHRONICLE OF THE BURNING YEARS (Algeria)—Mohammed Lakhdar-Hamina.
Special Jury Prize: EVERY MAN FOR HIMSELF AND GOD AGAINST ALL (Ger.)—Werner Herzog.
Female Performance: Valerie Perrine for LENNY (U.S.).
Male Performance: Vittorio Gassman for SCENT OF A WOMAN (Ital.).
Mise-en-Scene:
Constantin Costa-Gavras for SPECIAL SECTION (Fr.).
Michel Brault for THE ORDER (Can.).
Honorable Mention: Delphine Seyrig.
FIPRESCI Prize
EVERY MAN FOR HIMSELF AND GOD AGAINST ALL (Ger.)—Werner Herzog.
Ecumenical Prize (Mixed Catholic and Protestant Jury):
EVERY MAN FOR HIMSELF AND GOD AGAINST ALL (Ger.)—Werner Herzog.
Competing Films
ALICE DOESN'T LIVE HERE ANYMORE (U.S.)—Martin Scorsese.
ALOISE (Fr.)—Liliane de Kermadec.
THE AMULET OF OGUM (Brazil)—Nelson Pereira dos Santos.
CHRONICLE OF THE BURNING YEARS (Algeria)—Mohammed Lakhdar-Hamina.
DO YOU HEAR THE DOGS BARKING? (Mex.)—Francois Reichenbach.
ELECTRA (Hung.)–Miklos Jancso.
EVERY MAN FOR HIMSELF AND GOD AGAINST ALL (Ger.)—Werner Herzog.
LENNY (U.S.)—Bob Fosse.
LOTTE IM WEIMAR (E. Ger.)—Egon Gunther.
MAN FRIDAY (Brit.)—Jack Gold.
MARIKEN VAN NIEUMEGHEN (Neth.)—Jos Stelling.

THE ORDER (Can.)—Michel Brault.
PASTORAL HIDE AND SEEK (Jap.)—Shuji Terayama.
THE SCENT OF A WOMAN (Ital.)—Dino Risi.
SPECIAL SECTION (Fr.)—Constantin Costa-Gavras.
STORY OF A SIN (Pol.)—Walerian Borowczyk.
THAT DEAR VICTOR (Fr.)—Robin Davis.
THEY FOUGHT FOR THEIR COUNTRY (U.S.S.R.)—Serge Bondartchouk.
UN DIVORCE HEUREUX (Den.)—Henning Carlsen.
YUPPI DU (Ital.)—Adriano Celentano.

1976
Prizes of the International Jury
Golden Palm: TAXI DRIVER (U.S.)—Martin Scorsese.
Special Jury Prize:
CRIA CUERVOS (Span.)—Carlos Saura.
THE MARQUISE OF O (Ger./Fr.)—Eric Rohmer.
Female Performance:
Dominique Sanda for THE INHERITANCE (Ital.).
Mari Torocsik for MRS. DERY, WHERE ARE YOU? (Hung.).
Male Performance: Jose Luis Gomez for PASCUAL DUARTE (Span.).
Mise-en-Scene: Ettore Scola for UGLY, DIRTY, AND MEAN (Ital.).
FIPRESCI Prize
FERDINAND THE STRONGMAN (Ger.)—Alexander Kluge.
KINGS OF THE ROAD (Ger.)—Wim Wenders.
Competing Films
BABATOU (Nigeria)—Jean Rouch.
BUGSY MALONE (Brit.)—Alan Parker.
CRIA CUERVOS (Span.)—Carlos Saura.
DANDY, THE ALL-AMERICAN GIRL (U.S.)—Jerry Schatzberg.
END OF NIGHT (India)—Shyam Benegal.
KINGS OF THE ROAD (Ger.)—Wim Wenders.
LA GRIFFE ET LA DENT—Francois Bel and Gerard Vienne.
L'EREDITA FERRAMONTI (Ital.)—Mauro Bolognini.
LETTERS FROM MARUSIA (Mex.)—Miguel Littin.
THE MARQUISE OF O (Fr./Ger.)—Eric Rohmer.
MR. KLEIN (Fr.)—Joseph Losey.
MRS. DERY, WHERE ARE YOU? (Hung.)—Gyula Maar.
NEXT STOP, GREENWICH VILLAGE (U.S.)—Paul Mazursky.
PASCUAL DUARTE (Span.)—Ricardo Franco.
PRIVATE VICES, PUBLIC VIRTUES (Ital./Yugo.)—Miklos Jancso.
SHADOW OF ANGELS (Ger./Switz.)—Daniel Schmid.
TAXI DRIVER (U.S.)—Martin Scorsese.
THE TENANT (Fr./U.S.)—Roman Polanski.
UGLY, DIRTY, AND MEAN (Ital.)—Ettore Scola.

1977
Prizes of the International Jury
Golden Palm: PADRE PADRONE (Ital.)—Paolo and Vittorio Taviani.
Female Performance:
Shelley Duvall for THREE WOMEN (U.S.).
Monique Mercure for J.A. MARTIN, PHOTOGRAPHER (Can.).
Male Performance: Fernando Rey for ELISA, MY LOVE (Span.).
Film Debut: THE DUELLISTS (Brit.)—Ridley Scott.
Musical Score: Norman Whitfield for CAR WASH (U.S.).
FIPRESCI Prize
PADRE PADRONE (Ital.)—Paolo and Vittorio Taviani.
Ecumenical Award (Mixed Catholic and Protestant Jury):
THE LACEMAKER (Switz.)—Claude Goretta.
Competing Films
THE AMERICAN FRIEND (Ger.)—Wim Wenders.
BANG! (Swed.)—Jan Troell.
BLACK JOY (Brit.)—Anthony Simmons.
BOUND FOR GLORY (U.S.)—Hal Ashby.
CAR WASH (U.S.)—Michael Schultz.
THE DUELLISTS (Brit.)—Ridley Scott.
ELISA, MY LOVE (Span.)—Carlos Saura.
GRUPPENBILD MIT DAME (Ger.)—Aleksandar Petrovic.
THE HUNTERS (Gr.)—Theodor Angelopoulos.
IPHIGENIE (Gr.)—Michael Cacoyannis.
KICMA (Yugo.)—Vlatko Gilic.
LA COMMUNION SOLENNELLE (Fr.)—Rene Feret.
THE LACEMAKER (Switz.)—Claude Goretta.
THE OLD COUNTRY WHERE RIMBAUD DIED (Can.)—Jean-Pierre Lefebvre.
ORPHANS (U.S.S.R.)—Nicolai Goubenko.
PADRE PADRONE (Ital.) Paolo and Vittorio Taviani.
THE PURPLE TAXI (Fr.)—Yves Boisset.
TALES OF BUDAPEST (Hung.)—Istvan Szabo.
THREE WOMEN (U.S.)—Robert Altman.
THE TRUCK (Fr.)—Marguerite Duras.
UN BORGHESE PICCOLO PICCOLO (Ital.)—Mario Monicelli.

1978
Prizes of the International Jury
Golden Palm: THE TREE OF WOODEN CLOGS (Ital.)—Ermanno Olmi.
Special Jury Prize:
BYE BYE MONKEY (Ital.)—Marco Ferreri.
THE SHOUT (Brit.)—Jerzy Skolimowski.
Female Performance:
Jill Clayburgh for AN UNMARRIED WOMAN (U.S.).
Isabelle Huppert for VIOLETTE (Fr.).
Male Performance: Jon Voight for COMING HOME (U.S.).
Mise-en-Scene: Nagisa Oshima for EMPIRE OF PASSION (Jap.).
FIPRESCI Prize
MAN OF MARBLE (Pol.)—Andrzej Wajda.
SMELL OF WILD FLOWERS (Ital.)—Srdan Karanovic.
Ecumenical Award
THE TREE OF WOODEN CLOGS (Ital.)—Ermanno Olmi.
Competing Films
AN UNMARRIED WOMAN (U.S.)—Paul Mazursky.
BLINDFOLDED (Span.)—Carlos Saura.
BRAVO MAESTRO (Yugo.)—Rajko Grlic.

BYE BYE MONKEY (Ital.)—Marco Ferreri.
THE CHANT OF JIMMIE BLACKSMITH (Aus.)—Fred Schepisi.
COMING HOME (U.S.)—Hal Ashby.
DESPAIR (Ger.)—Rainer Werner Fassbinder.
EMPIRE OF PASSION (Jap.)—Nagisa Oshima.
THE LEFT-HANDED WOMAN (Ger.)—Peter Handke.
LOS RESTOS DEL NAUFRAGIO (Span.)—Ricardo Franco.
MIDNIGHT EXPRESS (Brit.)—Alan Parker.
MOLIERE (Fr.)—Ariane Mnouchkine.
PRETTY BABY (U.S.)—Louis Malle.
THE RECOURSE TO THE METHOD (Mex.)—Miguel Littin.
THE SHOUT (Brit.)—Jerzy Skolimowski.
SPIRAL (Pol.)—Krzysztof Zanussi.
THE TREE OF WOODEN CLOGS (Ital.)—Ermanno Olmi.
UN ACCIDENT DE CHASSE (U.S.S.R.)—Emil Lotianou.
VIOLETTE NOZIERE (Fr.)—Claude Chabrol.
WHO'LL STOP THE RAIN (U.S.)—Karel Reisz.

1979
Prizes of the International Jury
Golden Palm:
THE TIN DRUM (Ger.)—Volker Schloendorff.
APOCALYPSE NOW (U.S.)—Francis Ford Coppola.
Special Jury Prize: SIBERAID (U.S.S.R.)—Andrei Mikhalkov Kontchalovsky.
Female Performance: Sally Field for NORMA RAE (U.S.).
Male Performance: Jack Lemmon for THE CHINA SYNDROME (U.S.).
Supporting Female Performance: Eva Mattes for WOYZECK (Ger.).
Supporting Male Performance: Stefano Madia for DEAR PAPA (Ital.).
Mise-en-Scene: Terrence Malick for DAYS OF HEAVEN (U.S.).
Camera D'Or for Film Debut: NORTHERN LIGHTS (U.S.)—John Hanson and Rob Nilsson.
Grand Prix de La Commission Superieure Technique du Cinema Francais:
NORMA RAE (U.S.)—Martin Ritt.
Special Homage: Miklos Jancso in recognition of his ensemble of work.
FIPRESCI Prize
Competing Film: APOCALYPSE NOW (U.S.)—Francis Ford Coppola.
Out of Competition:
ANGI VERA (Hung.)—Pal Gabor.
BLACK JACK (Brit.)—Ken Loach.
Ecunemical Award
ROUGH TREATMENT (Pol.)—Andrzej Wajda.
Competing Films
APOCALYPSE NOW (U.S.)—Francis Ford Coppola.
THE BRONTE SISTERS (Fr.)—Andre Techine.
THE CHINA SYNDROME (U.S.)—James Bridges.
DAYS OF HEAVEN (U.S.)—Terrence Malick.
DEAR PAPA (Ital.)—Dino Risi.
THE EUROPEANS (Brit.)—James Ivory.
THE HERITAGE (Nor.)—Anja Breien.
HUNGARIAN RHAPSODY (Hung.)—Miklos Jancso.
L'INGORGO (Ital.)—Luigi Comencini.
LA DROLESSE (Fr.)—Jacques Doillon.
LOS SOBREVIVIENTES (Cuba)—Tomas Gutierres Alea.
MY BRILLIANT CAREER (Aus.)—Gill Armstrong.
NORMA RAE (U.S.)—Martin Ritt.
THE OCCUPATION IN 26 IMAGES (Yugo.)—Lordan Zafranovic.
ROUGH TREATMENT (Pol.)—Andrzej Wajda.
SERIE NOIRE (Fr.)—Alain Corneau.
SIBERAID (U.S.S.R.)—Andrei Mikhalkov Kontchalovsky.
THE TIN DRUM (Ger.)—Volker Schloendorff.
VICTORIA (Swed.)—Bo Widerberg.
WOYZECK (Ger.)—Werner Herzog.

1980
Prizes of the International Jury
Golden Palm:
KAGEMUSHA (Jap.)—Akira Kurosawa.
ALL THAT JAZZ (U.S.)—Bob Fosse.
Special Jury Prize: MON ONCLE D'AMERIQUE (Fr.)—Alain Resnais.
Female Performance: Anouk Aimee for LEAP INTO THE VOID (Ital.).
Male Performance: Michel Piccoli for LEAP INTO THE VOID (Ital.).
Scenario: Ettore Scola, Agenore Incrocci, and Furio Scarpelli for THE TERRACE (Ital.).
Mise-en-Scene: Krzysztof Zanussi for THE CONSTANT FACTOR (Pol.).
Second Female Role:
Carla Gravina for THE TERRACE (Ital.).
Milena Dravic for SPECIAL THERAPY (Yugo.).
Second Male Role: Jack Thompson for BREAKER MORANT (Aus.).
Camera D'Or for Debut Film: HISTOIRE D'ADRIEN (Fr.)—Jean-Pierre Denis.
Grand Prix de la Commission Superieure Technique du Cinema Francais: LE RISQUE DE VIVRE (Fr.)—Gerald Calderon.
FIPRESCI Prize
MON ONCLE D'AMERIQUE (Fr.)—Alain Resnais.
PROVINCIAL ACTORS (Pol.)—Agniezka Holland.
Competing Films
ALL THAT JAZZ (U.S.)—Bob Fosse.
BEING THERE (U.S.)—Hal Ashby.
THE BIG RED ONE (U.S.)—Samuel Fuller.
BREAKER MORANT (Aus.)—Bruce Beresford.
BYE BYE BRASIL (Bra.)—Carlos Diegues.
THE CONSTANT FACTOR (Pol.)—Krzysztof Zanussi.
EK DIN PRATIDIN (India)—Mrinal Sen.
EVERY MAN FOR HIMSELF (Switz.)—Jean-Luc Godard.
THE HERITAGE (Hung.)—Marta Meszaros.
JAGUAR (Phil.)—Lino Brocka.
KAGEMUSHA (Jap.)—Akira Kurosawa.
LA DEDICATORIA (Span.)—Jaime Chavari.
LEAP INTO THE VOID (Ital.)—Marco Bellocchio.
THE LONG RIDERS (U.S.)—Walter Hill.
LOULOU (Fr.)—Maurice Pialat.
THE MISSING LINK (Fr./Bel.)—Picha.
MON ONCLE D'AMERIQUE (Fr.)—Alain Resnais.

OUT OF THE BLUE (Can.)—Dennis Hopper.
PUT ON ICE (Ger.)—Bernhard Sinkel.
SPECIAL THERAPY (Yugo.)—Goran Paskaljevic.
THE TERRACE (Ital.)—Ettore Scola.

1981
Prizes of the International Jury
Golden Palm: MAN OF IRON (Pol.)—Andrzej Wajda
Special Jury Prize: LIGHT YEARS AWAY (Fr./Switz.)—Alain Tanner.
Female Performance: Isabelle Adjani for QUARTET (Brit./Fr.) and POSSESSION (Fr./Ger.).
Male Performance: Ugo Tognazzi for THE TRAGEDY OF A RIDICULOUS MAN (Ital.).
Scenario: Istvan Szabo and Peter Dobai for MEPHISTO (Hung.).
Artistic Contribution to the Poetics of Cinema: John Boorman for EXCALIBUR (Ireland).
Contemporary Cinema:
LOOKS AND SMILES (Brit.)—Ken Loach.
NEIGE (Fr.)—Juliet Berto and Jean-Henri Roger.
Second Female Role: Elena Solovei for BLOOD GROUP ZERO (U.S.S.R.).
Second Male Role: Ian Holm for CHARIOTS OF FIRE (Brit.).
Camera D'Or for Debut Film: DESPERADO CITY (Ger.)—Vadim Glowna.
Grand Prix de la Commission Superieure Technique du Cinema Francais: LES UNS ET LES AUTRES (Fr.)—Claude Lelouch.
FIPRESCI Prize
MEPHISTO (Hung.)—Istvan Szabo.
Competing Films
BEAU-PERE (Fr.)—Bertrand Blier.
BLOOD GROUP ZERO (U.S.S.R.)—Almantas Grikiavicius.
CHARIOTS OF FIRE (Brit.)—Hugh Hudson.
ENGEL AUS EISEN (Ger.)—Thomas Brasch.
EXCALIBUR (Ireland)—John Boorman.
HEAVEN'S GATE (U.S.)—Michael Cimino.
LA PELLE (Ital.)—Liliana Cavani.
LES UNS ET LES AUTRES (Fr.)—Claude Lelouch.
LIGHT YEARS AWAY (Switz./Fr.)—Alain Tanner.
LOOKS AND SMILES (Brit.)—Ken Loach.
MAN OF IRON (Pol.)—Andrzej Wajda.
MEPHISTO (Hung.)—Istvan Szabo.
MONTENEGRO (Swed.)—Dusan Makavejev.
NEIGE (Fr.)—Juliet Berto and Jean-Henri Roger.
PASSIONE D'AMORE (Ital.)—Ettore Scola.
PATRIMONIO NACIONAL (Span.)—Luis G. Berlanga.
POSSESSION (Ger./Fr.)—Andrzej Zulawski.
QUARANTINE (Hung.)—Istvan Gaal.
QUARTET (Brit.)—James Ivory.
THE TRAGEDY OF A RIDICULOUS MAN (Ital.)—Bernardo Bertolucci.
TULIPAA (Fin.)—Pirjo Honkasalo and Pekka Lehto.
VIOLENT STREETS (U.S.)—Michael Mann.

1982 Prizes of the International Jury
Golden Palm:
MISSING (U.S.)—Constantin Costa-Gavras.
YOL (Turkey)—Yilmaz Guney.
Special Jury Prize: NIGHT OF THE SHOOTING STARS (Ital.)—Paolo and Vittorio Taviani.
Mise-en-Scene: Werner Herzog for FITZCARRALDO (Ger.).
Female Performance: Jadwiga Jankowska-Cieslak for ANOTHER WAY (Hung.).
Male Performance: Jack Lemmon for MISSING (U.S.).
Artistic Contribution: For the Photography of Bruno Nuytten in INVITATION AU VOYAGE (Fr.).
Scenario: Jerzy Skolimowski for MOONLIGHTING (Brit.).
Camera D'Or for Film Debut: MOURIR A TRENTE ANS—Romain Goupil.
Grand Prix de la Commission Superieure Technique du Cinema Francais:
Raoul Coutard for the Photography of PASSION (Fr.).
Special 35th Anniversary Award:
Michelangelo Antonioni for IDENTIFICATION OF A WOMAN (Ital.).
FIPRESCI Prize
YOL (Turkey)—Yilmaz Guney.
Special Awards:
ANOTHER WAY (Hung.)—Karoly Makk.
LES FLEURS SAUVAGES (Can.).
Competing Films
AH Q ZHEN ZHUAN (China)—Cen Fan.
ANOTHER WAY (Hung.)—Karoly Makk.
BRITANNIA HOSPITAL (Brit.)—Lindsay Anderson.
CECILIA (Cuba)—Humberto Solas.
DOUCE ENQUETE SUR LA VIOLENCE (Fr.)—Gerard Guerin.
FITZCARRALDO (Ger.)—Werner Herzog.
HAMMETT (U.S.)—Wim Wenders.
IDENTIFICATION OF A WOMAN (Ital.)—Michelangelo Antonioni.
INVITATION AU VOYAGE (Fr.)—Peter Del Monte.
LA NUIT DE VARENNES (Ital.)—Ettore Scola.
MISSING (U.S.)—Constantin Costa-Gavras.
MOONLIGHTING (Brit.)—Jerzy Skolimowski.
THE NIGHT OF THE SHOOTING STARS (Ital.)—Paolo and Vittorio Taviani.
PASSION (Switz./Fr.)—Jean-Luc Godard.
THE RETURN OF THE SOLDIER (Brit.)—Alan Bridges.
SHOOT THE MOON (U.S.)—Alan Parker.
SMITHEREENS (U.S.)—Susan Seidelman.
TAG DER IDIOTEN (Ger.)—Werner Schroeter.
VENT DE SABLE (Algeria)—Mohammed Lakhdar Hamina.
YOL (Turkey)—Yilmaz Guney and Serif Goren.

1983
Prizes of the International Jury
Golden Palm: THE BALLAD OF NARAYAMA (Jap.)—Shohei Imamura.
Grand Prix du Cinema de Creation:
Robert Bresson for L'ARGENT (Fr.).
Andrei Tarkovsky for NOSTALGHIA (Ital.).
Special Jury Prize: MONTY PYTHON—THE MEANING OF LIFE (Brit.)—Terry Jones.

Female Performance: Hanna Schygulla for THE STORY OF PIERA (Ital.)—Marco Ferreri.

Male Performance: Gian Maria Volonte for THE DEATH OF MARIO RICCI (Switz./Fr.).

Jury Prize: KHARIJ (India)—Mrinal Sen.

Artistic Contribution: CARMEN (Span.)—Carlos Saura.

Camera D'Or for Film Debut: LA PRINCESSE—Pal Erdoss.

Grand Prix de la Commission Superieure Technique du Cinema Francais:
  CARMEN (Span.)—Carlos Saura.

FIPRESCI Prize
  NOSTALGHIA (Ital.)—Andrei Tarkovsky.
  SZERENCSES DANIEL (Hung.)—Pal Sandor.

Competing Films
  BALLAD OF NARAYAMA (Jap.)—Shohei Imamura.
  CARMEN (Span.)—Carlos Saura.
  CROSS CREEK (U.S.)—Martin Ritt.
  THE DEATH OF MARIO RICCI (Switz./Fr.)—Claude Goretta.
  EL SUR (Span.)—Victor Erice.
  ERENDIRA (Mex./Fr./Ger.)—Ruy Guerra.
  HEAT AND DUST (Brit.)—James Ivory.
  HISTORY OF PIERA (Ital.)—Marco Ferreri.
  KHARIJ (India)—Mrinal Sen.
  KING OF COMEDY (U.S.)—Martin Scorsese.
  L'ARGENT (Fr.)—Robert Bresson.
  L'ETE MEUTRIER (Fr.)—Jean Becker.
  L'HOMME BLESSE (Fr.)—Patrice Chereau.
  LE MUR—Yilmaz Guney.
  MERRY CHRISTMAS, MR. LAWRENCE (Brit./Jap./New Zealand)—Nagisa Oshima.
  MONTY PYTHON—THE MEANING OF LIFE (Brit.)—Terry Jones.
  MOON IN THE GUTTER (Fr.)—Jean-Jacques Beineix.
  NOSTALGHIA (Ital.)—Andrei Tarkovsky.
  TENDER MERCIES (U.S./Aus./Brit.)—Bruce Beresford
  UNE GARE POUR DEUX (U.S.S.R.)—Eldar Riazanov.
  VISSZAESOK (Hung.)—Zsolt Kezdi-Kovacs.
  THE YEAR OF LIVING DANGEROUSLY (Aus./U.S.)—Peter Weir.

1984

Prizes of the International Jury
  Golden Palm: PARIS, TEXAS (Ger./Fr.)—Wim Wenders.
  Special Jury Prize: NAPLO (Hung.)—Marta Meszaros.
  Female Performance: Helen Mirren for CAL (Ireland).
  Male Performance: Alfredo Landa and Francisco Rabal for THE HOLY INNOCENTS (Span.).
  Mise-en-Scene: Bertrand Tavernier for A SUNDAY IN THE COUNTRY (Fr.).
  Artistic Contribution: Peter Biziou for the cinematography of ANOTHER COUNTRY (Brit.).
  Original Scenario: Theo Angelopoulos, Theo Valtinos, and Tonino Guerra for VOYAGE TO CYTHERA (Gr.).
  Technique: Lars von Trier for THE ELEMENT OF CRIME (Den.).
  Camera D'Or for film debut: STRANGER THAN PARADISE (U.S.)—Jim Jarmush.

FIPRESCI Prize
  Competing Films:
    PARIS, TEXAS (Ger./Fr.)—Wim Wenders.
    VOYAGE TO CYTHERA (Gr.)—Theo Angelopoulos.
  Non-competing: MEMORIAS DO CACERE.

Competing Films
  ANOTHER COUNTRY (Brit.)—Marek Kanievska.
  BAYAN KO (Phil./Fr.)—Lino Brocka.
  THE BOUNTY (U.S.)—Roger Donaldson.
  CAL (Brit.)—Pat O'Connor.
  THE DAY LONGER THAN THE NIGHT (U.S.S.R.)—Lana Gogoberidze.
  THE ELEMENT OF CRIME (Den.)—Lars von Trier.
  GHARE BAIRE (India)—Satyajit Ray.
  HENRY IV (Ital.)—Marco Bellocchio.
  THE HOLY INNOCENTS (Span.)—Mario Camus.
  LA PIRATE (Fr.)—Jacques Doillon.
  NAPLO (Hung.)—Marta Meszaros.
  PARIS, TEXAS (Ger./Fr.)—Wim Wenders.
  QUILOMBO (Bra.)—Carlos Diegues.
  SUCCESS IS THE BEST REVENGE (Brit./Fr.)—Jerzy Skolimowski.
  UNDER THE VOLCANO (U.S.)—John Huston.
  VIGIL (New Zealand)—Vincent Ward.
  VOYAGE TO CYTHERA (Gr.)—Theo Angelopoulos.
  WHERE THE GREEN ANTS DREAM (Ger.)—Werner Herzog.

VENICE FILM FESTIVAL

1932
Best of Festival According to Public Poll
  Favorite Actress: Helen Hayes.
  Favorite Actor: Fredric March.
  Most Effective Direction: Nikolai Ekk.
  Most Amusing Film: A NOUS LA LIBERTE (Fr.)—Rene Clair.
  Most Touching Film: THE SIN OF MADELON CLAUDET (U.S.)—Edgar Selwyn.
  Most Original Film: DR. JEKYLL AND MR. HYDE (U.S.)—Rouben Mamoulian.
Films Presented
  A NOUS LA LIBERTE (Fr.)—Rene Clair.
  AU NOM DE LA LOI (Fr.)—Maurice Tourneur.
  AZAIS (Fr.)—Rene Hervil.
  BE MINE TONIGHT (Ger.)—Anatole Litvak.
  BIALY SLAD (Pol.)—Adam Krzeptowski.
  THE BLUE LIGHT (Ger.)—Leni Riefenstahl.
  BRING 'EM BACK ALIVE (U.S.)—Clayde E. Elliot.
  BROKEN LULLABY (U.S.)—Ernst Lubitsch.
  THE CHAMP (U.S.)—King Vidor.
  THE CONGRESS DANCES (Ger.)—Eric Charell.
  THE CROWD ROARS (U.S.)—Howard Hawks.
  DAVID GOLDER (Fr.)—Julien Duvivier.
  THE DEVIL TO PAY (U.S.)—George Fitzmaurice.
  DR. JEKYLL AND MR. HYDE (U.S.)—Rouben Mamoulian.
  DUE CUORI FELICI (Ital.)—Baldassare Negroni.
  EARTH (U.S.S.R.)—Aleksandr Dovzenko.
  THE FAITHFUL HEART (Brit.)—Victor Saville.
  FORBIDDEN (U.S.)—Frank Capra.
  FRANKENSTEIN (U.S.)—James Whale.
  GLI UOMINI, CHE MASCALZONI! (Ital.)—Mario Camerini.
  GRAND HOTEL (U.S.)—Edmund Goulding.
  HOTEL DES ETUDIANTS (Fr.)—Victor Tourjansky.
  MADCHEN IN UNIFORM (Ger.)—Leontine Sagan.
  THE QUIET DON (U.S.S.R.)—Olga Preobrazensckaja and Ivan Provov.
  ROAD TO LIFE (U.S.S.R.)—Nikolai Ekk.
  THE SIN OF MADELON CLAUDET (U.S.)—Edgar Selwyn.
  STRANGE INTERLUDE (U.S.)—Robert Z. Leonard.
  YELLOW TICKET (U.S.)—Raoul Walsh.
  ZWEI MENSCHEN (Ger.)—Erich Waschneck.

1934
Prizes of the International Jury
  Mussolini Cup: MAN OF ARAN (Brit.)—Robert J. Flaherty.
  Best Italian Film: TERESA CONFALONIERI (Ital.)—Guido Brignone.
  Biennial Cup for Best State Entry: U.S.S.R.
    Films of special mention
      CELJUSKIN (Short)—Jacov Posel'skij
      PETERBURGSKAJA NOC - Grigorij Roscial.
      IVAN, BOULE DE SUIF.
      GULIVER.
  Biennial Cup for Largest Industrial Entry:
    Motion Picture Producers and Distributors of America.
  Cup of City of Venice for Best Direction: Czechoslovakia
    Films Include
      Josef Rovensky for YOUNG LOVE.
      Gustav Machaty for EXTASE.
      Tomas Tinka for HURRICANE IN THE TATRAS.
      Karel Plicka for ZEM SPIEVA.
  Cup of the Istituto Nazionale LUCE for Best Photography:
    Andor Van Barsy and Alfons Lusteck for DOOD WATER (Neth.).
  Gold Medals
    Best Actor: Wallace Beery for VIVA VILLA! (U.S.).
    Best Actress: Katharine Hepburn for LITTLE WOMEN (U.S.).
    Best Animated Cartoon: THREE LITTLE PIGS (U.S.)—Walt Disney.
    Best Documentary: MANOVRE NAVALI (Ital.)—Istuto Nazionale LUCE.
    Best Story: MASKERADE (Aust.)—Willi Forst.
    Best Short: The Films of Marcel de Hubsch.
  Medal of the Festival for Best Absolute First Screening: THE PRIVATE LIFE OF DON JUAN (Brit.)—Alexander Korda.
Films Presented
  AMOK (Fr.)—Fedor Ozep.
  BLOSSOM TIME (Brit.)—Paul L. Stein.
  BROKEN DREAMS (U.S.)—Robert G. Vignola.
  BY CANDLELIGHT (U.S.)—James Whale.
  DEATH TAKES A HOLIDAY (U.S.)—Mitchell Leisen.
  DIE WEISSE MAJESTAT (Switz.)—Anton Kutter.
  DOOD WATER (Neth.)—Gerard Rutten.
  EN STILLA FLIRT (Swed.)—Gustaf Molandaro.
  EXTASE (Czech.)—Gustav Machaty.
  FLUCHTLINGE (Ger.)—Gustav Ucicky.
  GOING HOLLYWOOD (U.S.)—Raoul Walsh.
  IL CANALE DEGLI ANGELI (Ital.)—Francesco Pasinetti.
  THE INVISIBLE MAN (U.S.)—James Whale.
  IT HAPPENED ONE NIGHT (U.S.)—Frank Capra.
  JEUNESSE (Fr.)—Georges Lacombe.
  JOLLY FELLOWS (U.S.S.R.)—Grigorij Aleksandrov.
  LE PAQUEBOT TENACITY (Fr.)—Julien Duvivier.
  LA SIGNORA DI TUTTI (Ital.)—Max Ophuls.
  LE GRAND JEU (Fr.)—Jacques Feyder.
  LEBLEBLICI HORHOR AGA (Turkey)—Ertugrul Muhsin.
  LITTLE WOMEN (U.S.)—George Cukor.
  MAN OF ARAN (Brit.)—Robert J. Flaherty.
  MASKERADE (Aust.)—Willi Forst.
  PETERBURGSKAJA NOC (U.S.S.R.)—Grigorij Roscial and Vera Strojeva.
  THE PRIVATE LIFE OF DON JUAN (Brit.)—Alexander Korda.
  PUBERHEIT (Neth.)—Hans Sluizer.
  QUEEN CHRISTINA (U.S.)—Rouben Mamoulian.
  REIFENDE JUGEND (Ger.)—Carl Froelich.

TAVASZI PARADE (Hung.)—Geza von Bolvary.
TERESA CONFALONIERI (Ital.)—Guido Brignone.
THUNDERSTORM (U.S.S.R.)—Vladimir Petrov.
TWENTIETH CENTURY (U.S.)—Howard Hawks.
VIVA VILLA! (U.S.)—Jack Conway.
WHITE HEAT (U.S.)—Lois Weber.
WONDER BAR (U.S.)—Lloyd Bacon.
THE WORLD MOVES ON (U.S.)—John Ford.
YOUNG LOVE (Czech.)—Josef Rovensky.

1935
Prizes of the International Jury
  Mussolini Cup: ANNA KARENINA (U.S.)—Clarence Brown.
  Best Italian Film: CASTA DIVA - Carmine Gallone.
  Volpi Cup for Best Actress: Paula Wessely for EPISODE (Aust.).
  Volpi Cup for Best Actor: Pierre Blanchar for CRIME AND PUNISHMENT (Fr.).
  Best Direction: King Vidor for WEDDING NIGHT (U.S.).
  Best Screenplay: Dudley Nichols for THE INFORMER (U.S.).
  Best Music: SANDERS OF THE RIVER (Brit.)—produced by Alexander Korda.
  Cups of the Third International Exhibition of Cinematographic Art
    Color: BECKY SHARP (U.S.), Rouben Mamoulian, photographed by Ray Rennahan.
    Photography: Josef von Sternberg, Lucien Ballard, and Hans Dreier for THE DEVIL IS A WOMAN (U.S.).
  Gold Medals of the International Institute for Educational Cinematography
    Short: MONT SAINT-MICHEL (Fr.)—Maurice Cloche.
    Animated Cartoon: BAND CONCERT (U.S.)—Walt Disney.
  Cup of the Biennial for Best Documentary: RISCATTO (Ital.)
  Other Cups Awarded
    DER VERLORENE SOHN (Ger.)—Luis Trenker.
    TRIUMPH OF THE WILL (Ger.)—Leni Riefenstahl.
    LE SCARPE AL SOLE (Ital.)—Marco Elter.
    PASSAPORTO ROSSO (Ital.)—Guido Brignone.
    DARO UN MILIONE (Ital.)—Mario Camerini.
    NO GREATER GLORY (U.S.)—Frank Borzage.
    THE DAY OF THE GREAT ADVENTURE (Pol.)—Josef Lejtes.
    THE ETERNAL MASK (Switz.)—Werner Hochbaum.
    ITTO (Fr.)—Jean Benoit-Levy.
    ESCAPE ME NEVER (Brit.)—Paul Czinner.
  Special Mention for Exceptional Qualities
    MARIE CHAPDELAINE (Fr.)—Julien Duvivier.
    UN VOYAGE IMPREVU (Fr.)—Simon Barstoff.
    HERMINE UND DIE SIEBEN AUFRECHTEN (Ger.)—Frank Wysbar.
    DER AMEINSENSTAAT (Ger.,Short).
    THE PRIVATE LIFE OF THE GANNETS (Brit.)—Julian Huxley (Short).
    THE GOOD HOPE (Neth.)—A. Benno.
    SWEDENHIELMS (Swed.)—Gustav Molander.
    HALLALI (Hung.)—Magyar Film Iroda (Short).
    THE PROMISED LAND (Palestine)—Juda Lehmann (Short).
Competing Films
  AMORE (Ital.)—Carlo Ludovico Bragaglia.
  ANNA KARENINA (U.S.)—Clarence Brown.
  BECKY SHARP (U.S.)—Rouben Mamoulian.
  BLACK FURY (U.S.)—Michael Curtiz.
  CASTA DIVA (Ital.)—Carmine Gallone.
  CHINA SEAS (U.S.)—Tay Garnett.
  CRIME AND PUNISHMENT (Fr.)—Pierre Chenal.
  THE CRUSADES (U.S.)—Cecil B. DeMille.
  CURLY TOP (U.S.)—Irving Cummings.
  DANTE'S INFERNO (U.S.)—Harry Lachman.
  DARO UN MILIONE (Ital.)—Mario Camerini.
  DAVID COPPERFIELD (U.S.)—George Cukor.
  THE DAY OF THE GREAT ADVENTURE (Pol.)—Jozef Lejtes.
  DER VERLORENE SOHN (Ger.)—Luis Trenker.
  DER ZERBROCHENE KRUG (Aust.)—Gustav Ucicky.
  THE DEVIL IS A WOMAN (U.S.)—Josef von Sternberg.
  EPISODE (Aust.)—Walter Reisch.
  ESCAPE ME NEVER (Brit.)—Paul Czinner.
  THE ETERNAL MASK (Switz.)—Werner Hochbaum.
  FOLIES BERGERE (U.S.)—Roy Del Ruth.
  FRECCIA D'ORO (Ital.)—Corrado D'Errico and Piero Ballerini.
  THE GOOD HOPE (Neth.)—A. Benno.
  HEJ RUP! (Czech.)—Martin Fric.
  HERMINE UND DIE SIEBEN AUFRECHTEN (Ger.)—Frank Wysbar.
  THE INFORMER (U.S.)—John Ford.
  ITTO (Fr.)—Jean Benoit-Levy and Marie Epstein.
  LA DAME AUX CAMELIAS (Fr.)—Fernand Rivers.
  LA MASCOTTE (Fr.)—Leon Mathot.
  LE BONHEUR (Fr.)—Marcel L'Herbier.
  LE SCARPE AL SOLE (Ital.)—Marco Elter.
  LE VOYAGE IMPREVU (Fr.)—Jean de Limur.
  LITTLE MOTHER (Hung.)—Herman Kosterlitz [Henry Koster].
  MARIE CHAPDELAINE (Fr.)—Julien Duvivier.
  MARIE DES ANGOISSES (Fr.)—Michel Bernheim.
  ME FOR YOU - YOU FOR ME (Ger.)—Carl Froelich.
  NO GREATER GLORY (U.S.)—Frank Borzage.
  OBERWACHTMEISTER SCHWENKE (Ger.)—Carl Froelich.
  THE OLD AND THE YOUNG KING (Ger.)—Hans Steinhoff.
  PASSAPORTO ROSSO (Ital.)—Guido Brignone.
  PEER GYNT (Ger.)—Fritz Wendhausen.
  REGINE (Ger.)—Erich Waschneck.
  SANDERS OF THE RIVER (Brit.)—Zoltan Korda.
  STRICTLY CONFIDENTIAL (U.S.)—Frank Capra.
  THE STUDENT'S ROMANCE (Brit.)—Otto Kanturek.
  SWEDENHIELMS (Swed.)—Gustaf Molander.
  SZERELMI ALMON (Hung.)—Heinz Hille.
  TATRA ROMANCE (Czech.)—Josef Rovensky.

THE WEDDING NIGHT (U.S.)—King Vidor.

1936

Prizes of the International Jury

   Mussolini Cups

      Foreign Film: DER KAISER VON KALIFORNIEN (Ger.)—Luis Trenker.

      Italian Film: SQUADRONE BIANCO - Augusto Genina.

   Other Cups Awarded

      Volpi Cup for Best Actress: Annabella for VEILLE D'ARMES (Fr.).

      Volpi Cup for Best Actor: Paul Muni for THE STORY OF LOUIS PASTEUR (U.S.).

      Direction: Jacques Feyder for CARNIVAL IN FLANDERS (Fr.).

      Photography: M. Greenbaum for NINE DAYS A QUEEN (Brit.).

      Musical: NINTH SYMPHONY (Ger.)—Detlef Sierck [Douglas Sirk].

      Political/Social Film: IL CAMINO DEGLI EROI (Ital.)—Corrado D'Errico.

      Documentary: JUGEND DER WELT (Ger.)—Hans Weidemann.

      Scientific Film: UNO SGUARDO AL FONDO MARINO (Ital.)—Roberto Omegna.

      Ministry Cup: CAVALLERIA (Ital.)—Goffredo Alessandrini.

   Special Mention Medals

      THANK YOU, MADAME (Aust.)—Carmine Gallone.

      AVE MARIE (Ger.)—Johannes Riemann.

      VERRATER (Ger.)—Karl Ritter.

      SCROOGE (Brit.)—Henry Edwards.

      THE ROBBER SYMPHONY (Brit.)—Friedrich Feher.

      THE TRAIL OF THE LONESOME PINE (U.S.)—Henry Hathaway.

      MR. DEEDS GOES TO TOWN (U.S.)—Frank Capra.

      MARY OF SCOTLAND (U.S.)—John Ford.

      PACSIRTA (Hung.)—Karl Lamac.

Films Presented

   ANNE-MARIE (Fr.)—Raymond Bernard.

   AVE MARIA (Ger.)—Johannes Riemann.

   AZ UJ FOLDESUR (Hung.)—Bela Gaal.

   BALLERINE (Ital.)—Gustav Machaty.

   THE BELOVED VAGABOND (Brit.)—Curtis Kurt Bernhardt.

   THE CALL (Fr.)—Leon Poirier.

   THE CARDINAL (Brit.)—Sinclair Hill.

   CARNIVAL IN FLANDERS (Fr.)—Jacques Feyder.

   CAVALLERIA (Ital.)—Goffredo Alessandrini.

   DER BETTELSTUDENT (Ger.)—Georg Jacoby.

   DER KAISER VON KALIFORNIEN (Ger.)—Luis Trenker.

   EN VOLTAM! (Hung.)—Arthur Bardos.

   THE GHOST GOES WEST (Brit.)—Rene Clair.

   THE GREAT ZIEGFELD (U.S.)—Robert Z. Leonard.

   JANOSIK (Czech.)—Martin Fric.

   JONGE HARTEN (Neth.)—A. Charles Huguenot van der Linden.

   THE KING STEPS OUT (U.S.)—Josef von Sternberg.

   LA DAMIGELLA DI BARD (Ital.)—Mario Mattoli.

   THE MAN WHO COULD WORK MIRACLES (Brit.)—Lothar Mendes.

   MANJA WALEWSKA (Aust.)—Josef Rovensky.

   MARY OF SCOTLAND (U.S.)—John Ford.

   MARYSA (Czech.)—Josef Rovensky.

   MAYERLING (Fr.)—Anatole Litvak.

   MORENA CLARA (Span.)—Florian Rey.

   MR. DEEDS GOES TO TOWN (U.S.)—Frank Capra.

   NINE DAYS A QUEEN (Brit.)—Robert Stevenson.

   NINTH SYMPHONY (Ger.)—Dietlef Sierck [Douglas Sirk].

   PACSIRTA (Hung.)—Karel Lamac.

   THE ROBBER SYMPHONY (Brit.)—Friedrich Feher.

   RUBBER (Neth.)—Gerard Rutten and Johan de Meester.

   SAN FRANCISCO (U.S.)—W. S. Van Dyke.

   SCHATTEN DER VERGANGENHEIT (Aust.)—Werner Hochbaum.

   SCROOGE (Brit.)—Henry Edwards.

   SHOW BOAT (U.S.)—James Whale.

   SILHOUETTEN (Aust.)—Walter Reisch.

   SINGING YOUTH (Aust.)—Max Neufeld.

   SQUADRONE BIANCO (Ital.)—Augusto Genina.

   THE STORY OF A CHEAT (Fr.)—Sacha Guitry.

   THE STORY OF LOUIS PASTEUR (U.S.)—William Dieterle.

   THE TENDER ENEMY (Fr.)—Max Ophuls.

   THANK YOU, MADAME (Aust.)—Carmine Gallone.

   THE TRAIL OF THE LONESOME PINE (U.S.)—Henry Hathaway.

   TRAUMULUS (Ger.)—Carl Froelich.

   TREDICI UOMINI E UN CANNONE (Ital.)—Giovacchino Forzano.

   VEILLE D'ARMES (Fr.)—Marcel L'Herbier.

   VERRATER (Ger.)—Karl Ritter.

   THE WHITE ANGEL (U.S.)—William Dieterle.

   WHOM THE GODS LOVE (Brit.)—Basil Dean.

   A WOMAN ALONE (Brit.)—Eugene Franke.

1937

Prizes of the International Jury

   Mussolini Cups

      Foreign Film: UN CARNET DE BAL (Fr.)—Julien Duvivier.

      Italian Film: DEFEAT OF HANNIBAL - Carmine Gallone.

   Cup of Nations for Best Film screened for the very first time:

      VICTORIA THE GREAT (Brit.)—Herbert Wilcox.

   Best Documentary: MANNESMANN (Ger.)—Walter Ruttmann.

   Best Direction: Robert J. Flaherty and Zoltan Korda for ELEPHANT BOY (Brit.).

   Best Italian Direction: Mario Camerini for IL SIGNOR MAX.

   Prize of the Ministry for Italian East Africa for the Best Film with a Colonial Subject: SENTINELLE DI BRONZO (Ital.)—Romolo Marcellini.

   Best Artistic Ensemble: GRAND ILLUSION (Fr.)—Jean Renoir.

   Best Screenplay: Sacha Guitry for THE PEARLS OF THE CROWN (Fr.).

   Best Film Interpreting Natural and Artistic Beauties: CONDOTTIERI (Ital.)—Luis Trenker.

   Best Educational Film: The group of films entered by the Instituto Nazionale LUCE.

   Volpi Cup for Best Actor: Emil Jannings for DER HERRSCHER (Ger.).

   Volpi Cup for Best Actress: Bette Davis for MARKED WOMAN (U.S.), and KID GALAHAD (U.S.).

   Best Photography: Peverell Marley for WINTERSET (U.S.).

   Cup of the General Management of the Theater for Best Animated Film:

      Walt Disney's Productions, which include: HAWAIIAN HOLIDAY; MUSIC LAND;

OLD MILL; ALPINE CLIMBERS; COUNTRY COUSIN; and MICKEY'S POLO TEAM.

Special Mention)—(mainly a form of recognition for the smaller film producing countries

   SISTER MARY (Hung.)—Viktor Gertler.

   BATALION (Czech.)—Miroslav Cikan.

   SENT TUKARAM (India)—Shante Apte.

   BARBARA DE RADZIWELL (Pol.)—Jozef Lejtes.

   MOON ON THE RUINS (Jap.)—Keisuke Sasaki.

   THE FLYING DOCTOR (Aus.)—Miles Mander.

   THREE CHOPIN STUDIES (Pol.)—Laboratorium Filmowo Sektor (Short).

Films Presented

   ARANYEMBER (Hung.)—Bela Gaal.

   BARBARA DE RADZIWELL (Pol.)—Jozef Lejtes.

   BATALION (Czech.)—Miroslav Cikan.

   CONDOTTIERI (Ital.)—Luis Trenker.

   DEFEAT OF HANNIBAL (Ital.)—Carmine Gallone.

   DER HERRSCHER (Ger.)—Veit Harlan.

   DIE WARSCHAUER ZITADELLE (Ger.)—Fritz Peter Bruch.

   THE EDGE OF THE WORLD (Brit.)—Michael Powell.

   ELEPHANT BOY (Brit.)—Robert J. Flaherty and Zoltan Korda.

   FAREWELL AGAIN (Brit.)—Tim Whelan.

   THE FLYING DOCTOR (Aus.)—Miles Mander.

   GRAND ILLUSION (Fr.)—Jean Renoir.

   HELENE (Fr.)—Jean Benoit-Levy and Marie Epstein.

   IF WE ALL WERE ANGELS (Ger.)—Carl Froelich.

   IL SIGNOR MAX (Ital.)—Mario Camerini.

   KID GALAHAD (U.S.)—Michael Curtiz.

   KING SOLOMON'S MINES (Brit.)—Robert Stevenson.

   LE MESSAGER (Fr.)—Raymond Rouleau.

   LIDE NA KRE (Czech.)—Martin Fric.

   LLOYDS OF LONDON (U.S.)—Henry King.

   MARKED WOMAN (U.S.)—Lloyd Bacon.

   MOON ON THE RUINS (Jap.)—Keisuke Sasaki.

   PATRIOTEN (Ger.)—Karl Ritter.

   THE PEARLS OF THE CROWN (Fr.)—Sacha Guitry and Christian Jaque.

   SANT TUKARAM (India)—V. Damle and S. Fathelal.

   SENTINELLE DI BRONZO (Ital.)—Romolo Marcellini.

   SEVENTH HEAVEN (U.S.)—Henry King.

   SHALL WE DANCE (U.S.)—Mark Sandrich.

   SHERLOCK HOLMES (Ger.)—Karl Hartl.

   SISTER MARY (Hung.)—Viktor Gertler.

   A STAR IS BORN (U.S.)—William A. Wellman.

   THEODORA GOES WILD (U.S.)—Richard Boleslawski.

   THIS IS MY AFFAIR (U.S.)—William A. Seiter.

   THREE SMART GIRLS (U.S.)—Henry Koster.

   TO NEW SHORES (Ger.)—Detlef Sierck [Douglas Sirk].

   UN CARNET DE BAL (Fr.)—Julien Duvivier.

   VERSPRICH MIR NICHTS (Ger.)—Wolfgang Liebeneiner.

   VICTORIA THE GREAT (Brit.)—Herbert Wilcox.

   WINGS OF THE MORNING (U.S.)—Harold Schuster.

   WINTERSET (U.S.)—Alfred Santell.

1938

Prizes of the International Jury

   Mussolini Cup: OLYMPIA (Ger.)—Leni Riefenstahl.

   Mussolini Cup for Best Italian Film: LUCIANO SERRA PILOTA - Goffredo Alessandrini.

   Great Art Trophy of the Biennial: SNOW WHITE AND THE SEVEN DWARFS (U.S.)—Walt Disney.

   Volpi Cup for Best Actor: Leslie Howard for PYGMALION (Brit.).

   Volpi Cup for Best Actress: Norma Shearer for MARIE ANTOINETTE (U.S.).

   Minister of Popular Culture Awards

      FIVE SCOUTS (Jap.)—Tazaka Tomotaka.

      THE ADVENTURES OF TOM SAWYER (U.S.)—Norman Taurog.

      THE DRUM (Brit.)—Zoltan Korda.

      PRISON WITHOUT BARS (Fr.)—Leonide Moguy.

      GIUSEPPE VERDI (Ital.)—Carmine Gallone.

      THE MERRY WIVES (Czech.)—Otakar Vavra.

      HEIMAT (Ger.)—Carl Froelich.

   Special Mention Medals

      Direction

         Karl Ritter for URLAUB AUF EHRENWORT (Ger.).

         Marcel Carne for PORT OF SHADOWS (Fr.).

      Artistic Ensemble

         A WOMAN'S FACE (Swed.)—Gustaf Molander.

         ALLA EN EL RANCHO GRANDE (Mex.)—Fernando de Fuentes.

         FAHRENDES VOLK (Ger.)—Jacques Feyder.

         VIVACIOUS LADY (U.S.)—George Stevens.

         JEZEBEL (U.S.)—William Wyler.

      Acting

         THE RAGE OF PARIS (U.S.)—Henry Koster.

         HANNO RAPITO UN UOMO (Ital.)—Gennaro Righelli.

         DER MUSTERGATTE (Ger.)—Wolfgang Liebeneiner.

      Technique

         THE GOLDWYN FOLLIES (U.S.)—George Marshall.

         SOTTO LA CROCE DEL SUD (Ital.)—Guido Brignone.

      Story

         BREAK THE NEWS (Brit.)—Rene Clair.

         STAGE GENIUS (Pol.)—Romuald Gantkowski.

Competing Films

   ABUSED CONFIDENCE (Fr.)—Henri Decoin.

   THE ADVENTURES OF TOM SAWYER (U.S.)—Norman Taurog.

   ALEXANDER'S RAGTIME BAND (U.S.)—Henry King.

   ALLA EN EL RANCHO GRANDE (Mex.)—Fernando de Fuentes.

   BALLERINA (Fr.)—Jean Benoit-Levy and Marie Epstein.

   BREAK THE NEWS (Brit.)—Rene Clair.

   CHILDREN IN THE WIND (Jap.)—Hiroschi Shimizu.

   THE CURTAIN RISES (Fr.)—Marc Allegret.

   DER MUSTERGATTE (Ger.)—Wolfgang Liebeneiner.

THE DEVIL IS AN EMPRESS (Fr.)—Jean Dreville.
THE DRUM (Brit.)—Zoltan Korda.
FAHRENDES VOLK (Ger.)—Jacques Feyder.
FIVE SCOUTS (Jap.)—Tazaka Tomotaka.
FRIDAY ROSE (Hung.)—Laszlo Vajda.
GIUSEPPE VERDI (Ital.)—Carmine Gallone.
THE GOLDWYN FOLLIES (U.S.)—George Marshall.
HALKA (Pol.)—Juliusz Gardan.
HANNO RAPITO UN UOMO (Ital.)—Gennaro Righelli.
HEIMAT (Ger.)—Carl Froelich.
HORDUBALOVE (Czech.)—Martin Fric.
JEZEBEL (U.S.)—William Wyler.
KUNKU (India)—V. Shantaram.
LA CHIMOSA (Arg.)—Enrique T. Susini.
L'INNOCENT (Fr.)—Maurice Cammage.
LUCIANO SERRA PILOT (Ital.)—Goffredo Alessandrini.
MARIE ANTOINETTE (U.S.)—W. S. Van Dyke II.
THE MERRY WIVES (Czech.)—Otakar Vavra.
MOTHER CAREY'S CHICKENS (U.S.)—Rowland V. Lee.
OLYMPIA (Ger.)—Leni Riefenstahl.
ORA PONCIANO! (Mex.)—Gabriel Soria.
PORT OF SHADOWS (Fr.)—Marcel Carne.
PRISON WITHOUT BARS (Fr.)—Leonide Moguy.
THE PRISONER OF ZENDA (U.S.)—John Cromwell.
PYGMALION (Brit.)—Anthony Asquith.
THE RAGE OF PARIS (U.S.)—Henry Koster.
RAMUNTCHO (Fr.)—Rene Barberis.
SNOW WHITE AND THE SEVEN DWARFS (U.S.)—David Hand for Walt Disney.
SOTTO LA CROCE DEL SUD (Ital.)—Guido Brignone.
STAGE GENIUS (Pol.)—Romuald Gantkowski.
SVET KDE SE ZEBRA (Czech.)—Miroslav Cikan.
TEST PILOT (U.S.)—Victor Fleming.
URLAUB AUF EHRENWORT (Ger.)—Karl Ritter.
VERWEHTE SPUREN (Ger.)—Veit Harlan.
VIRGINITY (Czech.)—Otakar Vavra.
VIVACIOUS LADY (U.S.)—George Stevens.
WHITE BANNERS (U.S.)—Edmund Goulding.
YVETTE (Ger.)—Wolfgang Liebeneiner.

1939

Prizes of the International Jury
Mussolini Cup for Best Italian Film: ABUNA MESSIAS - Goffredo Alessandrini.
Best Cameraman: Ubaldo Arata for DERNIERE JEUNESSE.
Cups of the Biennial
    THE END OF THE DAY (Fr.)—Julien Duvivier.
    ROBERT KOCH (Ger.)—Hans Steinhoff.
    THE FOUR FEATHERS (Brit.)—Zoltan Korda.
    YOUTH, ENJOY YOUR YOUTH (Swed.)—Per Lindberg.
    A HANDFUL OF RICE (Swed.)—Paul Fejos and Gunnar Skoglund.
Special Mention Medals
    MARGARITA, ARMANDO Y SU PADRE (Arg.)—Francisco Mugica.
    MACOUN THE TRAMP (Bohemia)—Ladislav Brom.
    JEUNES FILLES EN DETRESSE (Fr.)—G.W. Pabst.
    FORTY YEARS (Neth.)—Edmond T. Greville.
    THE GOLDEN HARVEST OF THE WITWATERSRAND (S. Africa)—Le Cserep[i and L. Nago.
    THE MIKADO (Brit.)—Victor Schertzinger.
Competing Films
    ABUNA MESSIAS (Ital.)—Goffredo Alessandrini.
    AMBICION (Arg.)—Adelqui Millar.
    THE BANDITS (Arg.)—Orestes Caviglia.
    BEL AMI (Ger.)—Willi Forst.
    BORIS ISTVAN (Hung.)—Viktor Banky.
    CASTELLI IN ARIA (Ital.)—Augusto Genina.
    DE LA SIERRA AL VALLE (Arg.)—Anton Ber Ciani.
    DERNIERE JEUNESSE (Ital.)—Jeff Musso.
    DERRIERE LA FACADE (Fr.)—Georges Lacombe and Yves Mirande.
    DIVORCIO EN MONTEVIDEO (Arg.)—Manuel Romero.
    THE DREAM OF BUTTERFLY (Ital.)—Carmine Gallone.
    THE EARTH (Jap.)—Tomu Uchida.
    THE END OF THE DAY (Fr.)—Julien Duvivier.
    ES WAR EINE RAUSCHENDE BALLNACHT (Ger.)—Carl Froelich.
    FASCHING (Ger.)—Hans Schweikart.
    FORTY YEARS (Neth.)—Edmond T. Greville.
    THE FOUR FEATHERS (Brit.)—Zoltan Korda.
    THE GOVERNOR (Ger.)—Viktor Turjansky.
    GRANDI MAGAZZINI (Ital.)—Mario Camerini.
    THE GREAT LIGHT (Ital.)—Carlo Campogalliani.
    HUMORESQUE (Bohemia)—Otakar Vavra.
    JEUNES FILLES EN DETRESSE (Fr.)—G.W. Pabst.
    L'OR DANS LA MONTAGNE (Switz.)—Max Haufler.
    LA BETE HUMAINE (Fr.)—Jean Renoir.
    LAUTER LUGEN (Ger.)—Heinz Ruhmann.
    LE JOUR SE LEVE (Fr.)—Marcel Carne.
    MACOUN THE TRAMP (Bohemia)—Ladislav Brom.
    MARGARITA, ARMANDO Y SU PADRE (Arg.)—Francisco Mugica.
    THE MIKADO (Brit.)—Victor Schertzinger.
    OT ORA 40 (Hung.)—Endre Toth [Andre De Toth].
    PICCOLO HOTEL (Ital.)—Piero Ballerini.
    POUR LE MERITE (Ger.)—Karl Ritter.
    ROBERT KOCH (Ger.)—Hans Steinhoff.
    SHANGHAI RIKUSENTAI (Jap.)—Hisatoka Kumagai.
    TAJYO NO KORU (Jap.)—Yutaka Abe.
    VALFANGARE (Swed.)—Tancred Ibsen.
    VISION LOINE (Switz.)—Leo Lapaire.
    YOUNG MAN'S FANCY (Brit.)—Robert Stevenson.
    YOUTH, ENJOY YOUR YOUTH (Swed.)—Per Lindberg.

1940-42

World War II saw the end of the festival as an international event, but it remained open serving mainly the films of Italy and its Allies. The name was temporarily changed to the Italian-German Festival.

1940

Best Italian Film: THE SEIGE OF THE ALCAZAR - Augusto Genina. Best Foreign Film: THE POSTMASTER (Ger.)—Gustav Ucicky.
Competing Films
    ABBANDONO (Ital.)—Mario Mattoli.
    ACHTUNG! FEINDHORT MIT! (Ger.)—Arthur Maria Rabenalt.
    BEFREITE HANDE (Ger.)—Hans Schweikart.
    DANKO PISTA (Hung.)—Laszlo Kalmar.
    DON PASQUALE (Ital.)—Camillo Mastrocinque.
    GUL BABA (Hung.)—Kalman Nadasdy.
    IL CAVALIERE DI KRUJA (Ital.)—Carlo Campogalliani.
    JUD SUSS (Ger.)—Veit Harlan.
    KADETTKAMRATER (Swed.)—Weyler Hildebrand.
    LA PECCATRICE (Ital.)—Amleto Palermi.
    LUPII DIN MUNTELE SURUL (Rum.)—Joup Rubner and Angela Popescu.
    MOTHER LOVE (Ger.)—Gustav Ucicky.
    MUZ Z NEZNAMA (Bohemia)—Martin Fric.
    OLTRE L'AMORE (Ital.)—Carmine Gallone.
    OPERNBALL (Ger.)—Geza von Bolvary.
    THE POSTMASTER (Ger.)—Gustav Ucicky.
    THE SEIGE OF THE ALCAZAR (Ital.)—Augusto Genina.
    STEEL (Swed.)—Per Lindberg.
    TRENCK, DER PANDUR (Ger.)—Herbert Selpin.
    UNA ROMANTICA AVVENTURA (Ital.)—Mario Camerini.
    VERENA-STADLER (Switz.)—Hermann Haller.

1941

Mussolini Cup for Best Italian Film: HELMUT OF IRON, Alessandro Blasetti.
Mussolini Cup for Best Foreign Film: OHM KRUGER (Ger.)—Hans Steinhoff.
Volpi Cup for Best Actor: Ermete Zacconi for DON BUONAPARTE (Ital.).
Volpi Cup for Best Actress: Luise Ullrich for ANNELIE (Ger.). Cups of the Biennial
    DIE MISSBRAUCHTEN LIEBESBRIEFE (Switz.)—Leopold Lindtberg.
    ALTER EGO (Hung.)—Frigyes Ban.
    MARIANELA (Span.)—Benito Perojo.
    ICH KLAGE AN (Ger.)—Wolfgang Liebeneiner.
    I MARITI-TEMPESTA D'AMORE (Ital.)—Camillo Mastrocinque. Trophy of the Biennial: Istituto LUCE for its selection of films. Gold Medal for Best Direction: G.W. Pabst for KOMODIANTEN (Ger.). Special Mention Plaques
    SWING IT, MAGISTERN! (Swed.)—Schamyl Bauman.
    THE MOTH (Bohemia)—Frantisek Cap.
    BASTARD (Nor.)—Helge Lunde.
Other Films to receive Cups for their excellence
    LA NAVE BIANCA (Ital.)—Roberto Rossellini.
    HEIMKEHR (Ger.)—Gustav Ucicky.
Competing Films
    ADVOKAT CHUDYCH (Bohemia)—Vladimir Slavinsky.
    ALLE GAARRUNDT OG FORELSKER SIG (Den.)—Emanuel Gregers.
    ALTER EGO (Hung.)—Frigyes Ban.
    ANNELIE (Ger.)—Josef von Baky.
    BASTARD (Nor.)—Helge Lunde.
    CLOSED DOOR (Arg.)—Luis Saslavsky.
    DAS MENSCHLEIN MATTHIAS (Switz.)—Edmond Heuberger.
    DIE MISSBRAUCHTEN LIEBESBRIEFE (Switz.)—Leopold Lindtberg.
    DON BUONAPARTE (Ital.)—Flavio Calzavra.
    ETT BROTT (Swed.)—Anders Henrikson.
    HEIMKEHR (Ger.)—Gustav Ucicky.
    HELMUT OF IRON (Ital.)—Alessandro Blasetti.
    I MARITI-TEMPESTA D'AMORE (Ital.)—Camillo Mastrocinque.
    ICH KLAGE AN (Ger.)—Wolfgang Liebeneiner.
    IMMER NUR DU (Ger.)—Karl Karel Anton.
    KAIVOPUISTON KAUNIS REGINA (Fin.)—Toivo Sarkka.
    KARL FOR SIN HATT (Swed.)—Schamyl Bauman.
    KOMODIANTEN (Ger.)—G.W. Pabst.
    LA NAVE BIANCA (Ital.)—Roberto Rossellini.
    LANGOK (Hung.)—Laszlo Kalmar.
    MADRESELVA (Arg.)—Luis Cesar Amadori.
    MARIANELA (Span.)—Benito Perojo.
    THE MOTH (Bohemia)—Frantisek Cap.
    NOZZE DI SANGUE (Ital.)—Goffredo Alessandrini.
    OHM KRUGER (Ger.)—Hans Steinhoff.
    OPERETTE (Ger.)—Willi Forst.
    ORE 9 LEZIONE DI CHIMICA (Ital.)—Mario Mattoli.
    RAGAZZA CHE DORME (Ital.)—Andrea Forzano.
    SOMEWHERE IN EUROPE (Hung.)—Geza Radvanyi.
    SWING IT, MAGISTERN! (Swed.)—Schamyl Bauman.
    WUNSCHKONZERT (Ger.)—Eduard von Borsody.

1942

Mussolini Cup for Best Italian Film: BENGASI, Augusto Genina. Mussolini Cup for Best Foreign Film: THE GREAT KING (Ger.)—Veit Harlan.
Volpi Cup for Best Actor: Fosco Glachetti for UN COLPI DI PISTOLA (Ital.), BENGASI (Ital.), and NOI VIVI (Ital.).
Volpi Cup for Best Actress: Kristina Soderbaum for THE GREAT KING (Ger.), and DIE GOLDENE STADT (Ger.).
International Film Chamber Prizes
    Best Color: DIE GOLDENE STADT (Ger.)—Veit Harlan, photographed by Bruno Mondi.
    Best Technique: ALFA TAU! (Ital.)—Francesco de Robertis.
Biennial Prizes
    EMBEREK A HAVASON (Hung.)—Istvan Szots.
    NOI VIVI (Ital.)—Goffredo Alessandrini.
    WIENER BLUT (Ger.)—Willy Forst.
    GOYESCAS (Span.)—Benito Perojo.
    DIE GROSSE SCHATTEN (Ger.)—Paul Verhoven.
    ALA-ARRIBA (Por.)—Leitao de Barros.
    ODESSA IN FLAMES (Rum.)—Carmine Gallone.
Medals of the Biennial
    SNIPERS (Switz.)—Ake Ohberg.
    YLI RAJAN (Fin.)—Vilho Ilmari.

NEGYEDIZIGLEN (Hung.)—Zoltan Farkas.
Medals of the Biennial for Documentaries
MUSICA NEL TEMPO (Ital.)—Edmondo Cancellieri.
COMACCHIO (Ital.)—Ferdinando Cerchio.
DER SEEADLER (Ger.)—W. Hege and V. Lowenstein.
BUNTER REIGEN (Ger.).
LE DRAPEAU DE L'HUMANITE (Switz.)—Arthur Porchet.
ROMAN COUNTRYSIDE (Rum.).
ROCCIATORI ED AQUILE (Ital.)—Arturo Gemmiti.
ERDE AUF GEWALTMARSCHEN (Ger.)—Victor Borel.
WATCH ON THE DRINA (Croatia)—Marjan Mikac.
FUNERAL OF ISTVAN HORTY (Hung.)—Magyar Films.
Medals of the Biennial for Animation
ANACLETO E LA FAINA (Ital.)—Roberto Sgrilli.
NEL PAESE DEI RANOCCHI (Ital.)—Antonio Rubino.
Competing Films
AFSPORET (Den.)—Bodil Ipsen and Lau Lauritzen.
ALA-ARRIBA (Por.)—Leitao de Barros.
ALFA TAU! (Ital.)—Francesco De Robertis.
ANDREAS SCHLUTER (Ger.)—Herbert Maisch.
BENGASI (Ital.)—Augusto Genina.
BODA EN EL INFIERNO (Span.)—Antonio Roman.
THE COURIER OF THE INDIES (Span.)—Edgar Neville.
DER GROSSE SCHATTEN (Ger.)—Paul Verhoeven.
DIE GOLDENE STADT (Ger.)—Veit Harlan.
EMBEREK A HAVASON (Hung.)—Istvan Szots.
GOYESCAS (Span.)—Benito Perojo.
THE GREAT KING (Ger.)—Veit Harlan.
THE GREAT LOVE (Ger.)—Rolf Hansen.
GULA KLINIKEN (Swed.)—Ivar Johansson.
JACOB'S LADDER (Swed.)—Gustaf Molander.
KVINNA OM BORD (Swed.)—Gunnar Skoglund.
LA ALDEA MALDITA (Span.)—Florian Rey.
LANDAMANN STAUFFACHER (Switz.)—Leopold Lindtberg.
LE VIE DEL CUORE (Ital.)—Camillo Mastrocinque.
NEGYEDIZIGLEN (Hung.)—Zoltan Farkas.
NOI VIVI (Ital.)—Goffredo Alessandrini.
ODESSA IN FLAMES (Rum.)—Carmine Gallone.
PASSERS-BY (Switz.)—Max Haufler.
RAZA (Span.)—Jose Luis Saenz de Heredia.
SLEEPING BEAUTY (Ital.)—Luigi Chiarini.
SNIPERS (Swed.)—Ake Ohberg.
SZIRIUSZ (Hung.)—D. Akos Hamza.
UN COLPO DI PISTOLA (Ital.)—Renato Castellani.
UNA STORIA D'AMORE (Ital.)—Mario Camerini.
WIENER BLUT (Ger.)—Willi Forst.
YLI RAJAN (Fin.)—Vilho Ilmari.

1943-45
Festival cancelled.

1946
International Prize: THE SOUTHERNER (U.S.)—Jean Renoir. Special Mention by the
International Delegation
CHILDREN OF PARADISE (Fr.)—Marcel Carne.
THE OATH (U.S.S.R.)—Mikhail Caureli.
HANGMEN ALSO DIE (U.S.)—Fritz Lang.
HENRY V (Brit.)—Laurence Olivier.
THE UNDAUNTED (U.S.S.R.)—Mark Donskoi.
PAISAN (Ital.)—Roberto Rossellini.
PANIQUE (Fr.)—Julien Duvivier.
OUTCRY (Ital.)—Aldo Vergano.
Best Documentary
IN THE SANDS OF CENTRAL ASIA (U.S.S.R.)—Alexandr Zguridi.
Special Mention Documentaries
BAMBINI IN CITTA (Ital.)—Luigi Comencini.
BARBONI (Ital.)—Dino Risi.
GIORDNALI DI ATTUALITA (Ital.)—Instituto Nazionale LUCE.
SPORTS REVIEW (U.S.S.R.)—V. Beljaev, I. Venzer, and I. Posselsky.
LE RHONE (Switz.)—C.G. Duvanel.
Films Presented
BALTIC DEPUTY (1936, U.S.S.R.)—Alexander Zarkhi and Jossif Chejfiz.
BAMBI (U.S.)—David Hand for Walt Disney.
THE BELLS OF ST. MARY'S (U.S.)—Leo McCarey.
BLOOD AND SAND (U.S.)—Rouben Mamoulian.
CAPAJEV (1934, U.S.S.R.)—Sergei; and Gheroghij Vasiliev.
CHILDREN OF PARADISE (Fr.)—Marcel Carne.
EUGENIA GRANDET (Ital.)—Mario Soldati.
GUILTY WITHOUT GUILT (U.S.S.R.)—Vladimir Petrov.
HANGMEN ALSO DIE (U.S.)—Fritz Lang.
HENRY V (Brit.)—Laurence Olivier.
LASSIE COME HOME (U.S.)—Fred McLeod Wilcox.
THE LIFE OF EMILE ZOLA (U.S.)—William Dieterle.
LOVE LETTERS (U.S.)—William Dieterle.
MEN OF TWO WORLDS (Brit.)—Thorold Dickinson.
MONTECASSINO (Ital.)—Arturo Gemmiti.
NATHALIE (Fr.)—Pierre Billon.
THE OATH (U.S.S.R.)—Mikhail Caureli.
OLD ACQUAINTANCE (U.S.)—Vincent Sherman.
OUTCRY (Ital.)—Aldo Vergano.
PAISAN (Ital.)—Roberto Rossellini.
PANIQUE (Fr.)—Julien Duvivier.
PIAN DELLE STELLE (Ital.)—Giorgio Ferroni.
THE PICTURE OF DORIAN GRAY (U.S.)—Albert Lewin.
SCARLET STREET (U.S.)—Fritz Lang.
SISTER KENNY (U.S.)—Dudley Nichols.
A SONG TO REMEMBER (U.S.)—Charles Vidor.
THE SOUTHERNER (U.S.)—Jean Renoir.
STAIRWAY TO HEAVEN (Brit.)—Anthony Asquith.
SYLVIE AND THE PHANTOM (Fr.)—Claude Autant-Lara.
THERE WAS ONCE A CHILD (U.S.S.R.)—Viktor Ejzimont.

THE THIEF OF BAGDAD (Brit.)—Ludwig Berger, Tim Whelan, and Michael Powell.
THIS LOVE OF OURS (U.S.)—William Dieterle.
THE UNDAUNTED (U.S.S.R.)—Mark Donskoy.
WONDER MAN (U.S.)—H. Bruce Humberstone.

1947
Prizes of the International Jury
International Grand Prix: SIRENA (Czech.)—Karel Stekly.
International Prizes
Best Original Contribution to the Progress of Cinematography:
LA PERLA (Mex.)—Emilio Fernandez.
DREAMS THAT MONEY CAN BUY (U.S.)—Hans Richter.
Direction: Henri-Georges Clouzot for JENNY LAMOUR.
Most Original Story: Gregorij Alexandrov, A. Raskin, and M. Slobodskoj for SPRING
(U.S.S.R.), directed by Alexandrov.
Actress: Anna Magnani for HONORABLE ANGELINA (Ital.).
Actor: Pierre Fresnay for MONSIEUR VINCENT (Fr.).
Photography: Gabriel Figueroa in connection with LA PERLA (Mex.).
Music: E.F. Burian for SIRENA (Czech.).
Prize of the Presidency of the Council of Ministers for
Best Italian Film:
TRAGIC HUNT, Giuseppe de Santis.
Prizes of the Biennial
ADMIRAL NAKHIMOV (U.S.S.R.)—Vsevolod Pudovkin.
PENGAR (Swed.)—Nils Poppe.
THE OVERLANDERS (Brit.)—Harry Watt.
FARREBIQUE (Fr.)—Georges Rouquier.
Prizes of Special Artistic Merit:
Acting
Mai Zetterling
Maria Elena Marques
Ingrid Bergman
Aldo Fabrizi
Alexei Dikii
Pedro Armendariz
Direction
Martin Fric
Bjarne Henning-Jensen
Astrid Henning-Jensen
Carol Reed
Special Homage Award: Carl Dreyer for DAY OF WRATH (Den.). Prizes of the Special
Jury for Shorts and Documentaries
International Grand Prix of Venice for Best Feature Documentary:
ON THE TRAIL OF THE ANIMALS (U.S.S.R.)—Boris Dolin.
Short Documentary: PIAZZA SAN MARCO (Ital.)—Francesco Pasinetti.
Shorts
LA ROSE ET LE RESEDA (Fr.)—Andre Michel.
PRISONERS OF THE MSITS (Bul.)—Zaharii Giandov.
SPORTS NEWS REEL (USSR)
LE MONDE DE PAUL DELVAUX (Bel.)—Henri Storck.
Animated Cartoon Short: THE ATOM AT THE CROSSROADS (Czech.)—Cenek
Duba.
Puppet Short: POSVICENI (Czech.)—Jiri Trnka.
Competing Films
ADMIRAL NAKHIMOV (U.S.S.R.)—Vsevolod Pudovkin.
BETHSABEE (Fr.)—Leonide Moguy.
CREPUSCOLO (Mex.)—Julio Bracho.
DEVIL IN THE FLESH (Fr.)—Claude Autant-Lara.
DITTE: CHILD OF MAN (Den.)—Bjarne and Astrid Henning-Jensen.
DREAMS THAT MONEY CAN BUY (U.S.)—Hans Richter.
ENAMORADA (Mex.)—Emilio Fernandez.
FLESH WILL SURRENDER (Ital.)—Alberto Lattuada.
FRIEDA (Brit.)—Basil Dearden.
GALLANT JOURNEY (U.S.)—William A. Wellman.
GLINKA (U.S.S.R.)—Leo Arnstam.
HONORABLE ANGELINA (Ital.)—Luigi Zampa.
IRIS AND THE LIEUTENANT (Swed.)—Alf Sjoberg.
IT HAPPENED ON FIFTH AVENUE (U.S.)—Roy Del Ruth.
JENNY LAMOUR (Fr.)—Henri-Georges Clouzot.
THE JOURNEY OF DR. KOTNIS (India)—V. Shantaram.
LA MUJER DE TODOS (Mex.)—Julio Bracho.
LA SELVA DE FUEGO (Mex.)—Fernando de Fuentes.
LEAVE HER TO HEAVEN (U.S.)—John M. Stahl.
LES FRERES BOUQUINQUANT (Fr.)—Louis Daquin.
THE LITTLE BALLERINA (Brit.)—Lewis Gilbert.
MAJOR BARBARA (Brit.)—Gabriel Pascal.
MATTO REGIERT (Switz.)—Leopold Lindtberg.
MONSIEUR VINCENT (Fr.)—Maurice Cloche.
ODD MAN OUT (Brit.)—Carol Reed.
THE OVERLANDERS (Brit.)—Harry Watt.
THE PEARL (Mex.)—Emilio Fernandez.
PENGAR (Swed.)—Nils Poppe.
SHAKUNTALA (India)—V. Shantaram.
SIRENA (Czech.)—Karel Stekly.
SPELLBOUND (U.S.)—Alfred Hitchcock.
SPRING (U.S.S.R.)—Grigorij Alexandrov.
THE STORY OF G.I. JOE (U.S.)—William A. Wellman.
THE STRANGER (U.S.)—Orson Welles.
TALES FROM CAPEK (Czech.)—Martin Fric.
TEMPTATION HARBOUR (Brit.)—Lance Comfort.
THEY MADE ME A FUGITIVE (Brit.)—Alberto Cavalcanti.
THOSE BLASTED KIDS (Den.)—Bjarne and Astrid Henning-Jensen.
TOMORROW IS FOREVER (U.S.)—Irving Pichel.
TORMENT (Swed.)—Alf Sjoberg.
TRAGIC HUNT (Ital.)—Giuseppe De Sanctis.
UOMINI SENZA DOMANI (Ital.)—Gianni Vernuccio.

1948
Prizes of the International Jury
International Grand Prix: HAMLET (Brit.)—Laurence Olivier.
Prize of the Presidency for Best Italian Film: UNDER THE SUN OF ROME, Renato

Castellani.
International Prizes
THE FUGITIVE (U.S.)—John Ford, for figurative and dramatic qualities.
LOUISIANA STORY (U.S.)—Robert J. Flaherty, for its lyrical beauty.
LA TERRA TREMA (Ital.)—Luchino Visconti, for its choral qualities and style.
Direction: G.W. Pabst for THE TRIAL (Aust.).
Actress: Jean Simmons for HAMLET (Brit.).
Actor: Ernst Deutsch for THE TRIAL (Aust.).
Story and Screenplay: Graham Greene for THE FALLEN IDOL (Brit.).
Musical Comment: Max Steiner for THE TREASURE OF THE SIERRA MADRE (U.S.).
Scenography: John Bryan for OLIVER TWIST (Brit.).
Photography: Desmond Dickinson for HAMLET (Brit.).
Documentary: GOEMENS (Fr.)—Yamick Bellon.
Animated Cartoon
MELODY TIME (U.S.)—Walt Disney.
LE PETIT SOLDAT (Fr.)—Paul Grimault.
Shorts
LANDSBYKIRCHEN (Den.)—Carl Dreyer.
TARGET (Swed.)—Gosta Werner.
VENTE AUX ENCHERES (Fr.)—Jean Mousselle.
Medals of the Presidency of the Council of Ministers
ULICA GRANICZNA (Pol.)—Alexander Ford.
MACLOVIA (Mex.)—Emilio Fernandez.
NOCES DE SABLE (Mor.)—Andre Zwobada.
Medals of the Biennial
THE SEARCH (Switz.)—Fred Zinnemann.
MUSIC IN THE SHADOWS (Swed.)—Gustaf Molander.
Competing Films
AMORE (Ital.)—Roberto Rossellini.
THE BIG CLOCK (U.S.)—John Farrow.
DAS ANDERE LEBEN (Aust.)—Rudolf Steinbock.
DEDEE D'ANVERS (Fr.)—Yves Allegret.
DER ENGEL MIT DER POSAUNE (Aust.)—Karl Hartl.
DIFFICULT YEARS (Ital.)—Luigi Zampa.
DOUBLE LIFE (U.S.)—George Cukor.
DUEL IN THE SUN (U.S.)—King Vidor.
EAGLE WITH TWO HEADS (Fr.)—Jean Cocteau.
EHE IM SCHATTEN (E. Ger.)—Kurt Maetzig.
THE FACELESS WOMAN (Swed.)—Gustaf Molander.
THE FALLEN IDOL (Brit.)—Carol Reed.
FINALE (Ger.)—Ulrich Erfurth.
FLIGHT INTO FRANCE (Ital.)—Mario Soldati.
FORTUNE LANE (Brit.)—John Baxter.
THE FUGITIVE (U.S.)—John Ford.
GENTLEMAN'S AGREEMENT (U.S.)—Elia Kazan.
HAMLET (Brit.)—Laurence Olivier.
LA TERRA TREMA (Ital.)—Luchino Visconti.
LOUISIANA STORY (U.S.)—Robert J. Flaherty.
MACBETH (U.S.)—Orson Welles.
MACLOVIA (Mex.)—Emilio Fernandez.
MORITURI (Ger.)—Eugen York.
MUSIC IN THE SHADOWS (Swed.)—Ingmar Bergman.
NATIONAL VELVET (U.S.)—Clarence Brown.
NOCES DE SABLE (Mor.)—Andre Zwobada.
NOCTURNO DE AMOR (Mex.)—Emilio Gomez Muriel.
OLIVER TWIST (Brit.)—David Lean.
OSTATNI ETAP (Pol.)—Wanda Jakubowska.
PASSEURS D'OR (Bel.)—E.G. de Meyst.
THE RED SHOES (Brit.)—Michael Powell and Emeric Pressburger.
THE SEARCH (Switz.)—Fred Zinnemann.
SPRING IN PARK LANE (Brit.)—Herbert Wilcox.
TO THE ENDS OF THE EARTH (U.S.)—Robert Stevenson.
THE TREASURE OF THE SIERRA MADRE (U.S.)—John Huston.
THE TRIAL (Aust.)—G.W. Pabst.
ULICA GRANICZNA (Pol.)—Aleksander Ford.
UNDER THE SUN OF ROME (Ital.)—Renato Castellani.
THE WINSLOW BOY (Brit.)—Anthony Asquith.

1949
Prizes of the International Jury:
Golden Lion: MANON (Fr.)—Henri-Georges Clouzot, for the masterly way in which the director has narrated in cinematographic form his version of Prevost's novel.
Prize of the Presidency of the Council of Ministers for
Best Italian Film:
HEAVEN OVER THE MARSHES—Augusto Genina, for the delicate rendering of the very human story of Maria Goretti and the delicate environment in which it took place.
International Prizes
THE QUIET ONE (U.S.)—Sidney Meyers, for the poetical intentions so successfully achieved at the essential points of the film.
THE SNAKE PIT (U.S.)—Anatole Litvak, for a daring enquiry into a clinical case dramatically performed.
BERLINER BALLADE (Ger.)—Robert A. Stemmle, for the original interpretation of some aspects of the post war years in Germany.
Direction: Augusto Genina for HEAVEN OVER THE MARSHES (Ital.).
Actor: Joseph Cotten for PORTRAIT OF JENNIE (U.S.).
Actress: Olivia De Havilland for THE SNAKE PIT (U.S.).
Scenario: Jacques Tati for JOUR DE FETE (Fr.).
Photography: Gabriel Figueroa for LA MALQUERIDA (Mex.).
Scenography: William Kellner for KIND HEARTS AND CORONETS (Brit.).
Music: John Greenwood for THE LAST DAYS OF DOLWYN (Brit.).
Documentary: L'EQUATEUR AUX CENTS VISAGES (Bel.)—Andre Cauvin.
Short Subjects
HOULES CELESTES (Switz.)—Martin Rikli.
1848 (Fr.)—Spiri Mercanton.
ZINGARESCA (Swed.)—Arne Sucksdorff.
TIBET PROIBITO (Ital.)—Pietro Mele.
Competing Films
BERLINER BALLADE (Ger.)—Robert A. Stemmle.

THE BLUE LAGOON (Brit.)—Frank Launder.
CHAMPION (U.S.)—Mark Robson.
THE ELUSIVE PIMPERNEL (Brit.)—Michael Powell and Emeric Pressburger.
EVA (Swed.)—Gustaf Molander.
EYN BREIRA (Israel)—Jozef Leytes.
THE FOOL AND THE PRINCESS (Brit.)—William C. Hammond.
GEHEIMNISVOLLE TIEFE (Aust.)—G.W. Pabst.
HARDLY A CRIMINAL (Arg.)—Hugo Fegonese.
HEAVEN OVER THE MARSHES (Ital.)—Augusto Genina.
HOUSE ON THE WASTELANDS (Pol.)—Jan Rybkowski.
JOHNNY BELINDA (U.S.)—Jean Negulesco.
JOUR DE FETE (Fr.)—Jacques Tati.
KIND HEARTS AND CORONETS (Brit.)—Robert Hamer.
LA FIAMMA CHE NON SI SPEGNE (Ital.)—Vittorio Cottafavi.
LA MALQUERIDA (Mex.)—Emilio Fernandez.
THE LAST DAYS OF DOLWYN (Brit.)—Elmyn Williams.
LE SORCIER DU CIEL (Fr.)—Marcel Blistene.
LOOK FOR THE SILVER LINING (U.S.)—David Butler.
MANON (Fr.)—Henri-Georges Clouzot.
MEERA (India)—Ellis R. Dungan.
THE MILL ON THE PO (Ital.)—Alberto Lattuada.
PATTO COL DIAVOLO (Ital.)—Luigi Chiarini.
PORTRAIT OF JENNIE (U.S.)—William Dieterle.
THE QUIET ONE (U.S.)—Sidney Meyers.
SCOTT OF THE ANTARCTIC (Brit.)—Charles Frend.
THE SINNERS (Fr.)—Julien Duvivier.
THE SNAKE PIT (U.S.)—Anatole Litvak.
SOFIA (Yugo.)—Rados Novakovic.
SOUVENIR (Fr.)—Jean Delannoy.
UN HOMME ET SON PECHE (Can.)—Paul L'Anglais.

1950
Prizes of the International Jury
Golden Lion: JUSTICE IS DONE (Fr.)—Andre Cayatte.
Prize of the Presidency of the Council of Ministers for
Best Italian Film:
TOMORROW IS TOO LATE—Leonide Moguy.
International Prizes
PANIC IN THE STREETS (U.S.)—Elia Kazan.
GOD NEEDS MEN (Fr.)—Jean Delannoy.
FATHER'S DILEMMA (Ital.)—Alessandro Blasetti.
Actress: Eleanor Parker for CAGED (U.S.).
Actor: Sam Jaffe for THE ASPHALT JUNGLE (U.S.).
Story and Screenplay: Jacques Natanson and Max Ophuls for LA RONDE (Fr.).
Photography: Martin Bodin for ONLY A MOTHER (Swed.).
Music: Brian Easdale for GONE TO EARTH (Brit.).
Scenography: Jean d'Eaubonne for LA RONDE (Fr.).
Documentary: VISIT WITH PICASSO (Bel.)—Paul Haesaerts.
Short Subjects:
LES CHARMES DE L'EXISTENCE (Fr.)—Jean Gremillon.
MILLESIMO DI MILLIMETRO (Ital.)—Leonardo Sinisgalli.
Special Jury Prize: Walt Disney for CINDERELLA and BEAVER VALLEY (U.S.).
FIPRESCI Prize
ORPHEUS (Fr.)—Jean Cocteau.
Competing Films
ALL THE KING'S MEN (U.S.)—Robert Rossen.
THE ASPHALT JUNGLE (U.S.)—John Huston.
THE BLUE LAMP (Brit.)—Basil Dearden.
CAGED (U.S.)—John Cromwell.
CE SIECLE A CINQUANTE ANS (Fr.)—Denise and Roland Tual.
CINDERELLA (U.S.)—Ben Sharpsteen for Walt Disney.
THE DANCING YEARS (Brit.)—Harold French.
DAS VIERTE GEBOT (Aust.)—Eduard von Borsody.
DON JUAN (Span.)—Jose Luis Saenz de Heredia.
EL HOMBRE SIN ROSTRO (Mex.)—Juan Bustillo Oro.
EPILOG (Ger.)—Helmut Kautner.
FATHER'S DILEMMA (Ital.)—Alessandro Blasetti.
FLOWERS OF ST. FRANCIS (Ital.)—Roberto Rossellini.
FRAUENARZT DR. PRATORIUS (Ger.)—Curt Goetz and Karl Peter Gillmann.
GIVE US THIS DAY (Brit.)—Edward Dmytryk.
GONE TO EARTH (Brit.)—Michael Powell and Emeric Pressburger.
HIS LAST TWELVE HOURS (Ital.)—Luigi Zampa.
JUSTICE IS DONE (Fr.)—Andre Cayatte.
LA NOCHE DEL SABADO (Span.)—Rafael Gil.
LA RONDE (Fr.)—Max Ophuls.
LIFE BEGINS TOMORROW (Fr.)—Nicole Vedres.
MORNING DEPARTURE (Brit.)—Roy Baker.
MY FATHER'S HOUSE (Israel)—Herbert Kline.
ONCE A THIEF (U.S.)—William Lee Wilder.
ONLY A MOTHER (Swed.)—Alf Sjoberg.
ORPHEUS (Fr.)—Jean Cocteau.
OUT OF EVIL (Israel)—Joseph Krumgold.
PANIC IN THE STREETS (U.S.)—Elia Kazan.
PASSPORT TO PIMLICO (Brit.)—Henry Cornelius.
ROSARIO CASTRO (Mex.)—Roberto Gavaldon.
SEPTEMBER AFFAIR (U.S.)—William Dieterle.
SEVEN DAYS TO NOON (Brit.)—Roy Boulting.
SOBRE LAS OLAS (Mex.)—Ismael Rodriguez.
STATE SECRET (Brit.)—Sidney Gilliat.
STROMBOLI (Ital.)—Roberto Rossellini.
TOMORROW IS TOO LATE (Ital.)—Leonide Moguy.

1951
Prizes of the International Jury
Golden Lion: RASHOMON (Jap.)—Akira Kurosawa.
Special Jury Prize: A STREETCAR NAMED DESIRE (U.S.)—Elia Kazan, for having reproduced a stageplay on the screen, poetically interpreting the lost humanity of the characters thanks to the masterly direction.
Prize of the Presidency of the Council of Ministers for
Best Italian Film
FOUR WAYS OUT—Pietro Germi.

International Prizes
- THE BIG CARNIVAL (U.S.)—Billy Wilder.
- THE DIARY OF A COUNTRY PRIEST (Fr.)—Robert Bresson.
- THE RIVER (India)—Jean Renoir.

Jury Prizes
- Volpi Prize for Best Actor: Jean Gabin for THE NIGHT IS MY KINGDOM (Fr.).
- Volpi Prize for Best Actress: Vivien Leigh for A STREETCAR NAMED DESIRE (U.S.).
- Story and Screenplay: T.E.B. Clarke for THE LAVENDER HILL MOB (Brit.).
- Photography: Leonce-Henry Burel for THE DIARY OF A COUNTRY PRIEST (Fr.).
- Music: Hugo Friedholfer for THE BIG CARNIVAL (U.S.).
- Scenography: Peter Pendry for MURDER IN THE CATHEDRAL (Brit.).

Prizes of the Jury of Scientific Film and Art Documentary
- Golden Lion for Feature Documentary: NATURE'S HALF ACRE (U.S.)—James Algar for Walt Disney.
- International Prize for Feature Documentary: ABENTEUER IM ROTEN MEER (Aust.)—Hans Hass.
- Prize for Best National Selection: Great Britain.

Catholic Film Office Award
- THE DIARY OF A COUNTRY PRIEST (Fr.)—Robert Bresson.
- Special Mention: THE NIGHT IS MY KINGDOM (Fr.)—Georges Lacombe.

Competing Films
- ALICE IN WONDERLAND (U.S.)—Clyde Geronimi, Hamilton Luske, and Wilfred Jackson for Walt Disney.
- THE BIG CARNIVAL (U.S.)—Billy Wilder.
- BLUEBEARD (Fr.)—Christian-Jaque.
- BORN YESTERDAY (U.S.)—George Cukor.
- CAFE PARADISE (Den.)—Bodil Ipsen and Lau Lauritzen.
- DAS DOPPELTE LOTTCHEN (Ger.)—Josef von Baky.
- DECAK MITA (Yugo.)—Rados Novakovic.
- THE DIARY OF A COUNTRY PRIEST (Fr.)—Robert Bresson.
- FOUR WAYS OUT (Ital.)—Pietro Germi.
- FOURTEEN HOURS (U.S.)—Henry Hathaway.
- LA CORONA NEGRA (Span.)—Luis Saslavsky.
- THE LAVENDER HILL MOB (Brit.)—Charles Crichton.
- LOCKENDE GEFAHR (Ger.)—Eugen York.
- THE LOST ONE (Ger.)—Peter Lorre.
- MURDER IN THE CATHEDRAL (Brit.)—George Hoellering.
- NATIVE SON (Arg.)—Pierre Chenal.
- NIEBLA Y SOL (Span.)—Jose Maria Forque.
- THE NIGHT IS MY KINGDOM (Fr.)—Georges Lacombe.
- NO RESTING PLACE (Brit.)—Paul Rotha.
- OMBRE SUL CANAL GRANDE (Ital.)—Glauco Pellegrini.
- OTHELLO (Mor.)—Orson Welles.
- PARIGI E SEMPRE PARIGI (Ital.)—Luciano Emmer.
- RASHOMON (Jap.)—Akira Kurosawa.
- THE RIVER (India)—Jean Renoir.
- SAVAGE TRIANGLE (Fr.)—Jean Delannoy.
- A STREETCAR NAMED DESIRE (U.S.)—Elia Kazan.
- TERESA (U.S.)—Fred Zinnemann.
- WHITE CORRIDORS (Brit.)—Pat Jackson.

1952

Prizes of the International Jury
- Golden Lion: FORBIDDEN GAMES (Fr.)—Rene Clement.

International Prizes
- THE QUIET MAN (U.S.)—John Ford.
- EUROPA '51 (Ital.)—Roberto Rossellini.
- THE LIFE OF OHARU (Jap.)—Kenji Mizoguchi.
- Volpi Cup for Best Actor: Fredric March for DEATH OF A SALESMAN (U.S.).

Jury Prizes
- Scenario: Nunnally Johnson for PHONE CALL FROM A STRANGER (U.S.).
- Music: Georges Auric for THE RESPECTFUL PROSTITUTE (Fr.).
- Decor: Carmen Dillon for THE IMPORTANCE OF BEING EARNEST (Brit.).

FIPRESCI Prize
- BEAUTIES OF THE NIGHT (Fr.)—Rene Clair.
- Special Prize: LA BERGERE ET LE RAMONEUR (Fr.)—Paul Grimault.
- Special Mention: LAS AGUAS BAJAN TURBIAS (Arg.)—Hugo del Carril.

Competing Films
- AANDHIYAN (India)—Anand Chetan.
- ANATOMY OF LOVE (Ital.)—Alessandro Blasetti.
- AREIAO (Bra.)—Camillo Mastrocinque.
- BEAUTIES OF THE NIGHT (Fr.)—Rene Clair.
- THE BRAVE DON'T CRY (Brit.)—Philip Leacock.
- CARRIE (U.S.)—William Wyler.
- CRASH OF SILENCE (Brit.)—Alexander Mackendrick.
- DEATH OF A SALESMAN (U.S.)—Laslo Benedek.
- DESHONRA (Arg.)—Daniel Tinayre.
- EL JUDAS (Span.)—Ignacio F. Iquino.
- EL REBOZO DE SOLEDAD (Ital.)—Roberto Gavaldon.
- EUROPA '51 (Ital.)—Roberto Rossellini.
- FORBIDDEN GAMES (Fr.)—Rene Clement.
- GENGIS KAHN (Phil.)—Lou Salvador [Manuel Conde].
- IL BRIGANTE DI TACCA DEL LUPO (Ital.)—Pietro Germi.
- THE IMPORTANCE OF BEING EARNEST (Brit.)—Anthony Asquith.
- IVANHOE (U.S.)—Richard Thorpe.
- KIR'YA NE'EMANA (Israel)—Josef Leytes.
- LA BERGERE ET LE RAMONEUR (Fr.)—Paul Grimault.
- LAS AGUAS BAJAN TURBIAS (Arg.)—Hugo del Carril.
- LES CONQUERANTS SOLITAIRES (Fr.)—Claude Vermoral.
- THE LIFE OF OHARU (Jap.)—Kenji Mizoguchi.
- LOS OJOS DEJAN HUELLAS (Span.)—Jose Luis Saenz de Heredia.
- THE MIRACLE OF OUR LADY OF FATIMA (U.S.)—John Brahm.
- NDRINE OG KJELL (Nor.)—Kaare Bergstrom.
- PHONE CALL FROM A STRANGER (U.S.)—Jean Negulesco.
- THE QUIET MAN (U.S.)—John Ford.
- THE RESPECTFUL PROSTITUTE (Fr.)—Marcello Pagliero.
- SUMMER INTERLUDE (Swed.)—Ingmar Bergman.
- SUNDIGE GRENZE (Ger.)—Robert A. Stemmle.

THE WHITE SHEIK (Ital.)—Federico Fellini.

1953

Prizes of the International Jury
Silver Lions
- UGETSU MONOGATARI (Jap.)—Kenji Mizoguchi.
- THE VITELLONI (Ital.)—Federico Fellini.
- THE LITTLE FUGITIVE (U.S.)—Ray Ashley, Morris Engel, and Ruth Orkin.
- MOULIN ROUGE (Brit.)—John Huston.
- THERESE RAQUIN (Fr.)—Marcel Carne.
- SADKO (U.S.S.R.)—Aleksandr Ptusko.
- Volpi Cup for Best Actor: Henri Vilbert for ABSOLUTION WITHOUT CONFESSION (Fr.).
- Volpi Cup for Best Actress: Lilli Palmer for THE FOURPOSTER (U.S.).

Bronze Medals
- WAR OF GOD (Span.)—Rafael Gil.
- THE PROUD AND THE BEAUTIFUL (Fr.)—Yves Allegret.
- LANDOWNER'S DAUGHTER (Brazil)—Tom Payne.
- PICKUP ON SOUTH STREET (U.S.)—Samuel Fuller.

Catholic Film Office Award
- WAR OF GOD (Span.)—Rafael Gil.

Competing Films
- ABSOLUTION WITHOUT CONFESSION (Fr.)—Claude Autant-Lara.
- THE BAD AND THE BEAUTIFUL (U.S.)—Vincente Minnelli.
- DIE GROSSE VERSUCHUNG (Ger.)—Rolf Hansen.
- EASY YEARS (Ital.)—Luigi Zampa.
- FOLTAMADOTT A TENGER (Hung.)—Kalman Nadasdy, Laszlo Ranody, and Mihaly Szemes.
- THE FOUR POSTER (U.S.)—Irving Reis.
- HEIGHTS OF DANGER (Brit.)—Peter Bradford.
- JARA GOSPODA (Yugo.)—Bojan Stupica.
- JHANSI KI RANI (India)—Sohrab M. Modi and Rusi K. Banker.
- JOHNNY ON THE RUN (Brit.)—Lewis Gilbert, Vernon Harris, and Patricia Latham.
- LA PASION DESNUDA (Arg.)—Luis Cesar Amadori.
- LANDOWNER'S DAUGHTER (Bra.)—Tom Payne.
- THE LITTLE FUGITIVE (U.S.)—Ray Ashley, Morris Engel, and Ruth Orkin.
- MOULIN ROUGE (Brit.)—John Huston.
- THE MYSTERY OF THE BLOOD (Czech.)—Martin Fric.
- NAPOLETANI A MILANO (Ital.)—Eduardo De Filippo.
- OLD CZECH LEGENDS (Czech.)—Jiri Trnka.
- PICKUP ON SOUTH STREET (U.S.)—Samuel Fuller.
- THE PROUD AND THE BEAUTIFUL (Fr.)—Yves Allegret.
- THE RETURN OF VASILI BORTNIKOV (U.S.S.R.)—Vsevolod J. Pudovkin.
- RIMSKIJ-KORSAKOV (U.S.S.R.)—Grigorij Rosal.
- SADKO (U.S.S.R.)—Aleksandr Ptusko.
- THE SAGA OF ANATAHAN (Jap.)—Josef von Sternberg.
- SECRETS OF WOMEN (Swed.)—Ingmar Bergman.
- THERESE RAQUIN (Fr.)—Marcel Carne.
- UGETSU MONOGATARI (Jap.)—Kenji Mizoguchi.
- THE VANQUISHED (Ital.)—Michelangelo Antonioni.
- VERGISS DER LIEBE NICHT (Ger.)—Paul Antonioni Verhoeven.
- THE VITELLONI (Ital.)—Federico Fellini.
- WAR OF GOD (Span.)—Rafael Gil.
- YOUNG CHOPIN (Pol.)—Aleksander Ford.

1954

Prizes of the International Jury
- Golden Lion: ROMEO AND JULIET (Ital./Brit.)—Renato Castellani.

Silver Lion
- SEVEN SAMURAI (Jap.)—Akira Kurosawa.
- SANSHO THE BAILIFF (Jap.)—Kenji Mizoguchi.
- LA STRADA (Ital.)—Federico Fellini.
- ON THE WATERFRONT (U.S.)—Elia Kazan.
- Volpi Cup for Best Actor: Jean Gabin for GRISBI (Fr.) and L'AIR DE PARIS (Fr.).
- Special Jury Prize for Ensemble Acting: EXECUTIVE SUITE (U.S.)—with William Holden, June Allyson, Barbara Stanwyck, Fredric March, Walter Pidgeon, and Shelley Winters.

Competing Films
- THE CAINE MUTINY (U.S.)—Edward Dmytryk.
- CAMELIA (Mex.)—Roberto Gavaldon.
- EL BESO DE JUDAS (Span.)—Rafael Gil.
- EL GAUCHO (Arg.)—Lucas Demare.
- EXECUTIVE SUITE (U.S.)—Robert Wise.
- FATHER BROWN (Brit.)—Robert Hamer.
- GRISBI (Fr.)—Jacques Becker.
- AN INN AT OSAKA (Jap.)—Heinosuke Gosho.
- KONIGLICHE HOHEIT (Ger.)—Harald Braun.
- L'AIR DE PARIS (Fr.)—Marcel Carne.
- LA QUINTRALA (Arg.)—Hugo del Carril.
- LA REBELION DE LOS COLGADOS (Mex.)—Alfredo B. Crevenna and Emilio Fernandez.
- MAFTEAM MAZAMAV (Israel)—Eascha Alexander.
- MAGIC CITY (Gr.)—Nikos Koundouros.
- ON THE WATERFRONT (U.S.)—Elia Kazan.
- PESSEN ZA COVEKA (Bul.)—Borislav Sciaraliev.
- PUNKTCHEN UND ANTON (Aust.)—Thomas Engel.
- REAR WINDOW (U.S.)—Alfred Hitchcock.
- THE RIVER AND DEATH (Mex.)—Luis Bunuel.
- ROMEO AND JULIET (Brit./Ital.)—Renato Castellani.
- SANSHO THE BAILIFF (Jap.)—Kenji Mizoguchi.
- SENSO (Ital.)—Luchino Visconti.
- SEVEN SAMURAI (Jap.)—Akira Kurosawa.
- SIMON MENYHERT SZULETESE (Hung.)—Zoltan Varkonyi.
- SOM I DROMMAR (Swed.)—Carl Gyllenberg.
- SURANG (India)—V. Shantaram.
- THREE COINS IN THE FOUNTAIN (U.S.)—Jean Negulesco.
- UNSTERBLICHEN MOZART (Aust.)—Alfred Stogen.
- WOMAN OF ROME (Ital.)—Luigi Zampa.

1955

Prizes of the International Jury

Golden Lion: ORDET (Den.)—Carl Dreyer.
Silver Lions
  THE BIG KNIFE (U.S.)—Robert Aldrich.
  LE AMICHE (Ital.)—Michelangelo Antonioni.
  THE GRASSHOPPER (U.S.S.R.)—Samson Samsonov.
  CISKE DE RAT (Neth.)—Wolfgang Staudte.
Volpi Cup for Best Actor
  Curt Jurgens for THE DEVIL'S GENERAL (Ger.) and THE HEROES ARE TIRED (Fr.).
  Kenneth More for THE DEEP BLUE SEA (Brit.).
Most Promising New Directors
  Vaclav Krska of Czechoslovakia.
  Alexandre Astruc of France.
  William Fairchild of Britain.
  Francesco Maselli of Italy.
  Andrzej Munk of Poland.
Competing Films
  THE BIG KNIFE (U.S.)—Robert Aldrich.
  BLEKITNY KRZYZ (Pol.)—Andrzej Munk.
  BORIS GODUNOV (U.S.S.R.)—Vera Stroeva.
  CHIENS PERDUS SANS COLLIER (Fr.)—Jean Delannoy.
  CISKE DE RAT (Neth.)—Wolfgang Staudte.
  DANCE OF SHIVA (India)—V. Shantaram.
  THE DEEP BLUE SEA (Brit.)—Anatole Litvak.
  DESPUES DE LA TORMENTA (Mex.)—Roberto Gavaldon.
  THE DEVIL'S GENERAL (Ger.)—Helmut Kautner.
  DJEVOJKA I HRAST (Yugo.)—Kreso Golik.
  DOCTOR AT SEA (Brit.)—Ralph Thomas.
  DVA DRUGA (U.S.S.R.)—E. Eijsymont.
  GLI SBANDATI (Ital.)—Francesco Maselli.
  THE GRASSHOPPER (U.S.S.R.)—Samson Samsonov.
  GROWING UP (Jap.)—Heinosuke Gosho.
  THE HEROES ARE TIRED (Fr.)—Yves Ciampi.
  IL BIDONE/THE SWINDLER (Ital.)—Federico Fellini.
  INTERRUPTED MELODY (U.S.)—Curtis Bernhardt.
  JOHN AND JULIE (Brit.)—William Fairchild.
  THE KENTUCKIAN (U.S.)—Burt Lancaster.
  LA TIERRA DEL FUEGO SE APAGA (Arg.)—Emilio Fernandez.
  LE AMICHE (Ital.)—Michelangelo Antonioni.
  LES MAUVAISES RENCONTRES (Fr.)—Alexandre Astruc.
  MAOS SANGRENTAS (Bra.)—Carlos Hugo Christensen.
  ORDET (Den.)—Carl Dreyer.
  PRINCESS YANG KWEI FEI (Jap./Hong Kong)—Kenji Mizoguchi.
  SHUZENJI MONOGATARI (Jap.)—Noboru Nakamura.
  TO CATCH A THIEF (U.S.)—Alfred Hitchcock.
  TOWARD NEW SHORES (U.S.S.R.)—Leonild Lukov.
  THE WOMAN IN THE PAINTING (Ital.)—Franco Rossi.
  ZAKONAT POSVOLIAVA (Bul.)—Dako Dakovski.

1956
Prizes of the International Jury
  Volpi Cup for Best Actor: Bourvil for FOUR BAGS FULL (Fr.).
  Volpi Cup for Best Actress: Maria Schell for GERVAISE (Fr.).
  Documentary: ON THE BOWERY (U.S.)—Lionel Rogosin.
  Special Mentions
    HARP OF BURMA (Jap.)—Kon Ichikawa.
    STREET OF SHAME (Jap.)—Kenji Mizoguchi.
    O DRAKOS (Gr.)—Nikos Koundouros.
    TORERO (Mex.)—Carlos Velo.
    CALABUCH (Span.)—Luis Berlanga.
    MAIN STREET (Span.)—Juan Bardem, with a special mention for the performance of Betsy Blair.
FIPRESCI Prize
  GERVAISE (Fr.)—Rene Clement.
  MAIN STREET (Span.)—Juan Bardem.
Catholic Film Office Award
  CALABUCH (Span.)—Luis Berlanga.
Italian Film Critics Award
  ATTACK! (U.S.)—Robert Aldrich.
San Giorgio Prize
  HARP OF BURMA (Jap.)—Kon Ichikawa.
Competing Films
  ATTACK! (U.S.)—Robert Aldrich.
  THE AWAKENING (Ital.)—Mario Camerini.
  BESSMERTNJI GARNIZON (U.S.S.R.)—Zachar Agranenko.
  BIGGER THAN LIFE (U.S.)—Nicholas Ray.
  CALABUCH (Span.)—Luis Berlanga.
  THE CAPTAIN FROM KOPENICK (Ger.)—Helmut Kautner.
  FOUR BAGS FULL (Fr.)—Claude Autant-Lara.
  GERVAISE (Fr.)—Rene Clement.
  HARP OF BURMA (Jap.)—Kon Ichikawa.
  L'IMPERO DEL SOLE (Ital.)—Mario Cravei and Enrico Gras.
  MAIN STREET (Span.)—Juan Bardem.
  O DRAKOS (Gr.)—Nikos Koundouros.
  STREET OF SHAME (Jap.)—Kenji Mizoguchi.
  TORERO (Mex.)—Carlos Velo.

1957
Prizes of the International Jury
  Golden Lion: APARAJITO (India)—Satyajit Ray.
  Silver Lion: WHITE NIGHTS (Ital.)—Luchino Visconti.
  Volpi Cup for Best Actor: Anthony Franciosa for A HATFUL OF RAIN (U.S.).
  Volpi Cup for Best Actress: Zidra Ritenberg for MALVA (U.S.S.R.).
FIPRESCI Award
  APARAJITO (India)—Satyajit Ray.
Catholic Film Office Award
  A HATFUL OF RAIN (U.S.)—Fred Zinneman.
Italian Film Critics Award
  A HATFUL OF RAIN (U.S.)—Fred Zinneman.
San Giorgio Prize
  SOMETHING OF VALUE (U.S.)—Richard Brooks.

Competing Films
  AN ANGEL PASSES OVER BROOKLYN (Span.)—Ladislao Vajda.
  AN EYE FOR AN EYE (Fr.)—Andre Cayatte.
  APARAJITO (India)—Satyajit Ray.
  THE BABY CARRIAGE (Jap.)—Tomotoka Tasaka.
  BITTER VICTORY (Fr.)—Nicholas Ray.
  A HATFUL OF RAIN (U.S.)—Fred Zinneman.
  I SOGNI NEL CASSETTO (Ital.)—Renato Castellani.
  LOS SALVAJES (Mex.)—Rafael Baledon.
  MALVA (U.S.S.R.)—Vladimir Braun.
  SAMO LJUDI (Yugo.)—Branko Bauer.
  SOMETHING OF VALUE (U.S.)—Richard Brooks.
  THE STORY OF ESTHER COSTELLO (Brit.)—David Miller.
  THRONE OF BLOOD (Jap.)—Akira Kurosawa.
  WHITE NIGHTS (Ital.)—Luchino Visconti.

1958
Prizes of the International Jury
  Golden Lion: THE RICKSHAW MAN (Jap.)—Iroshi Inagaki.
  Silver Lions
    Special Jury Prize: LES AMANTS (Fr.)—Louis Malle.
    Special Prize: THE CHALLENGE (Ital.)—Francesco Rosi.
  Volpi Cup for Best Actor: Alec Guinness for THE HORSE'S MOUTH (Brit.).
  Volpi Cup for Best Actress: Sophia Loren for BLACK ORCHID (U.S.).
  Documentary: THE LAST DAYS OF SUMMER (Pol.)—Tadeusz Konwicki and Jan Laskowski.
FIPRESCI Prize
  THE WOLF TRAP (Czech.)—Jiri Weiss.
Competing Films
  THE BALLAD OF NARAYAMA (Jap.)—Keisuke Kinoshita.
  BLACK ORCHID (U.S.)—Martin Ritt.
  THE CHALLENGE (Ital.)—Francesco Rosi.
  THE EIGHTH DAY OF THE WEEK (Pol.)—Aleksander Ford.
  END OF DESIRE (Fr.)—Aklexandr Astruc.
  GOD'S LITTLE ACRE (U.S.)—Anthony Mann.
  THE HORSE'S MOUTH (Brit.)—Ronald Neame.
  LES AMANTS (Fr.)—Louis Malle.
  LOVE IS MY PROFESSION (Fr.)—Claude Autant-Lara.
  NATTENS LJUS (Swed.)—Lars-Eric Kjellegren.
  OTAROVA VDOVA (U.S.S.R.)—Mikhail Caureli.
  THE RICKSHAW MAN (Jap.)—Iroshi Inagaki.
  ROSEMARY (Ger.)—Rolf Thiele.
  THE WOLF TRAP (Czech.)—Jiri Weiss.

1959
Prizes of the International Jury
  Golden Lion
    GENERAL DELLA ROVERE (Ital./Fr.)—Roberto Rossellini.
    THE GREAT WAR (Ital.)—Mario Monicelli.
  Special Jury Prize: THE MAGICIAN (Swed.)—Ingmar Bergman.
  Volpi Cup for Best Actor: James Stewart for ANATOMY OF A MURDER (U.S.).
  Volpi Cup for Best Actress: Madeleine Robinson for LEDA (Fr.).
  Short: PAVUCINA (Czech.)—Zbynek Brynych.
FIPRESCI Prize
  ASHES AND DIAMONDS (Pol.)—Andrjez Wajda.
  THE SAVAGE EYE (U.S.)—Ben Maddow, Sidney Meyers, and Joseph Strick.
Catholic Film Office Award
  GENERAL DELLA ROVERE (Ital.)—Roberto Rossellini.
Prizes of the Italian Film Critics
  In competition: THE MAGICIAN (Swed.)—Ingmar Bergman.
  Out of competition: COME BACK AFRICA (U.S.)—Lionel Rogosin.
Competing Films
  ANATOMY OF A MURDER (U.S.)—Otto Preminger.
  THE BOY AND THE BRIDGE (Brit.)—Kevin McClory.
  CAMPO ARADO (Arg.)—Leo Fleider.
  ESTERINA (Ital.)—Carlo Lizzani.
  GENERAL DELLA ROVERE (Ital.)—Roberto Rossellini.
  THE GREAT WAR (Ital.)—Mario Monicelli.
  LEDA (Fr.)—Claude Chabrol.
  THE MAGICIAN (Swed.)—Ingmar Bergman.
  NIGHT ENCOUNTER (Fr.)—Robert Hossein.
  NIGHT TRAIN (Pol.)—Jerzy Kawalerowicz.
  THE SLEEPLESS YEARS (Hung.)—Felix Mariassy.

1960
Prizes of the International Jury
  Golden Lion: TOMORROW IS MY TURN (Fr.)—Andre Cayatte.
  Special Prize: ROCCO AND HIS BROTHERS (Ital.)—Luchino Visconti.
  Volpi Cup for Best Actor: John Mills for TUNES OF GLORY (Brit.).
  Volpi Cup for Best Actress: Shirley MacLaine for THE APARTMENT (U.S.).
  Film Debut: THAT LONG NIGHT IN '43 (Ital.)—Florestano Vancini.
  Culture and Information Film: LES ANNEES FOLLES (Fr.)—Mirca Alexandresco and Henri Torrent.FIPRESCI Prize
  ROCCO AND HIS BROTHERS (Ital.)—Luchino Visconti.Catholic Film Office Award
  STOWAWAY IN THE SKY (Fr.)—Albert Lamorisse.
San Giorgio Prize:
  THE HUMAN CONDITION PART I, NO GREATER LOVE (Jap.)—Masaki Kobayashi.
Competing Films
  THE APARTMENT (U.S.)—Billy Wilder
  BILA HOLUBICE (Czech.)—Frantisek Vlacil.
  BRAINWASHED (Ger.)—Gerd Oswald.
  THE HUMAN CONDITION PART I, NO GREATER LOVE (Jap.)—Masaki Kobayashi
  I DELFINI (Ital.)—Francesco Maselli.
  KNIGHTS OF THE TEUTONIC ORDER (Pol.)—Aleksander Ford.
  LENINGRAD'S SKY (U.S.S.R.)—Vladimir Vengerov.
  LOVE A LA CARTE (Ital.)—Antonio Pietrangeli.
  RAT (Yugo.)—Veljko Bulajic.
  STOWAWAY IN THE SKY (Fr.)—Albert Lamorisse.
  THAT LONG NIGHT IN '43 (Ital.)—Florestano Vancini.

TOMORROW IS MY TURN (Fr.)—Andre Cayatte.

1961
Prizes of the International Jury
Golden Lion: LAST YEAR AT MARIENBAD (Fr.)—Alain Resnais.
Special Jury Prize: PEACE TO ALL WHO ENTER (U.S.S.R.)—Aleksander Alov and Vladimir Naumov.
Film Debut: BANDITS OF ORGOSOLO (Ital.)—Vittorio De Seta.
Volpi Cup for Best Actress: Suzanne Flon for THOU SHALT NOT KILL (Yugo./Lichtenstein).
Cinema Nuovo Special Mentions
Toshiro Mifune for his performance in YOJIMBO (Jap.).
Geraldine Page for her performance in SUMMER AND SMOKE (U.S.).
FIPRESCI Prize
IL BRIGANTE (Ital.)—Renato Castellani .
Catholic Film Office Award
THE SOUND OF THE TRUMPETS (Ital.)—Ermanno Olmi.
San Giorgio Prize
BANDITS OF ORGOSOLO (Ital.)—Vittorio De Seta.
Federation of Italian Film Critics Prize
BANDITS OF ORGOSOLO (Ital.)—Vittorio De Seta.
National Syndication of Italian Film Journalists
PEACE TO ALL WHO ENTER (U.S.S.R.)—Aleksander Alov and Vladimir Naumov.
Competing Films
BANDITS OF ORGOSOLO (Ital.)—Vittorio De Seta.
BRIDGE TO THE SUN (U.S./Fr.)—Etienne Perier.
IL BRIGANTE (Ital.)—Renato Castellani.
IL GIUDIZIO UNIVERSALE (Ital.)—Vittorio De Sica.
KDE REKY MAJI SLUNCE (Czech.)—Vaclav Krska.
LAST YEAR AT MARIENBAD (Fr.)—Alain Resnais.
PEACE TO ALL WHO ENTER (U.S.S.R.)—Aleksander Alov and Vladimir Naumov.
SAMSON (Pol.)—Andrzej Wajda.
SUMMER AND SMOKE (U.S.)—Peter Glenville.
THE GIRL WITH THE GOLDEN EYES (Fr.)—Jean-Gabriel Albicocco.
THOU SHALT NOT KILL (Yugo./Lichtenstein)—Claude Autant-Lara.
VANINA VANINI (Ital.)—Roberto Rossellini.
VICTIM (Brit.)—Basil Dearden.
YOJIMBO (Jap.)—Akira Kurosawa.

1962
Prizes of the International Jury
Golden Lion
CHILDHOOD OF IVAN (U.S.S.R.)—Andrei Tarkovsky.
FAMILY DIARY (Ital.)—Valerio Zurlini.
Special Jury Prize: MY LIFE TO LIVE (Fr.)—Jean-Luc Godard.
Volpi Cup for Best Actor: Burt Lancaster for THE BIRDMAN OF ALCATRAZ (U.S.).
Volpi Cup for Best Actress: Emmanuelle Riva for THERESE DESQUEYROUX (Fr.).
Film Debut:
DAVID AND LISA (U.S.)—Frank Perry.
LOS INNUNDADOS (Arg.)—Fernando Birri.
FIPRESCI Prize
KNIFE IN THE WATER (Pol.)—Roman Polanski.
Catholic Film Office Award
TERM OF TRIAL (Brit.)—Peter Glenville.
San Giorgio Prize
BIRDMAN OF ALCATRAZ (U.S.)—John Frankenheimer.
Competing Films
BIRDMAN OF ALCATRAZ (U.S.)—John Frankenheimer.
CHILDHOOD OF IVAN (U.S.S.R.)—Andrei Tarkovsky.
DAVID AND LISA (U.S.)—Frank Perry.
FAMILY DIARY (Ital.)—Valerio Zurlini.
HOMAGE AT SIESTA TIME (Arg.)—Leopoldo Torre-Nilsson.
KOIYA KOI NASUMA KOI (Jap.)—Tomu Uchida.
LOLITA (U.S.)—Stanley Kubrick.
LOS INUNDADOS (Arg.)—Fernando Birri.
MAMMA ROMA (Ital.)—Pier Paolo Pasolini.
MEN AND BEASTS (U.S.S.R.)—Sergej Gerasimov.
MY LIFE TO LIVE (Fr.)—Jean-Luc Godard.
SMOG (Ital./US)—Franco Rossi.
TERM OF TRIAL (Brit.)—Peter Glenville.
THERESE DESQUEYROUX (Fr.)—Georges Franju.
THIRD OF A MAN (U.S.)—Robert Lewin.
UNA STORIA MILANESE (Ital.)—Eriprando Visconti.

1963
Prizes of the International Jury
Golden Lion: THE BATTLE OF ALGIERS (Fr./Ital.)—Francesco Rosi.
Special Jury Prizes
INTRODUCTION TO LIFE (U.S.S.R.)—Igor Talankin.
THE FIRE WITHIN (Fr.)—Louis Malle.
Volpi Cup for Best Actor: Albert Finney for TOM JONES (Brit.).
Volpi Cup for Best Actress: Delphine Seyrig for MURIEL (Fr.).
Film Debut
A SUNDAY IN SEPTEMBER (Swed.)—Jorn Donner.
LE JOLI MAI (Fr.)—Chris Marker.
FIPRESCI Prize
THE HANGMAN (Span.)—Luis Berlanga.
Catholic Film Office Award
HUD (U.S.)—Martin Ritt.
National Syndication of Italian Film Journalists Prize
IL TERRORISTA (Ital.)—Gianfranco De Bosio.
Competing Films
THE BATTLE OF ALGIERS (Fr./Ital.)—Francesco Rosi.
BILLY LIAR (Brit.)—John Schlesinger.
BOLSAJA DOROGA (U.S.S.R.)—Jurij Ozerov.
THE COOL WORLD (U.S.)—Shirley Clarke.
THE FIRE WITHIN (Fr.)—Louis Malle.
THE GOLDEN FERN (Czech.)—Jiri Weiss.
THE HANGMAN (Span.)—Luis Berlanga.
HIGH AND LOW (Jap.)—Akira Kurosawa.
HUD (U.S.)—Martin Ritt.

IL TERRORISTA (Ital.)—Gianfranco De Bosio.
INTRODUCTION TO LIFE (U.S.S.R.)—Igor Talankin.
LE JOLI MAI (Fr.)—Chris Marker.
THE MAN (Jap.)—Kaneto Shindo.
MARE MOTTO (Ital.)—Renato Castellani.
MURIEL (Fr.)—Alain Resnais.
NUNCA PASA NADA (Span.)—Juan Bardem.
OMICRON (Ital.)—Ugo Gregoretti.
POUR LA SUITE DU MONDE (Can.)—Pierre Perrault, Michel Brault, and Marcel Carriere.
THE SERVANT (Brit.)—Joseph Losey.
SILENCE (Pol.)—Kazimierz Kutz.
SWEET AND SOUR (Fr.)—Jacques Baratier.
TOM JONES (Brit.)—Tony Richardson.
UN TENTATIVO SENTIMENTALE (Ital./Fr.)—Pasquale Festa Campanile and Massimo Franciosa.

1964
Prizes of the International Jury
Golden Lion: RED DESERT (Ital./Fr.)—Michelangelo Antonioni.
Special Jury Prizes
THE GOSPEL ACCORDING TO SAINT MATTHEW (Fr./Ital.)—Pier Paolo Pasolini.
HAMLET (U.S.S.R.)—Grigorij Kozintsev.
Volpi Cup for Best Actor: Tom Courtenay for KING AND COUNTRY (Brit.).
Volpi Cup for Best Actress: Harriet Andersson for TO LOVE (Swed.).
Film Debut: LIFE UPSIDE DOWN (Fr.)—Alain Jessua.
FIPRESCI Prize
RED DESERT (Ital.)—Michelangelo Antonioni.
Catholic Film Office Award
THE GOSPEL ACCORDING TO SAINT MATTHEW (Fr./Ital.)—Pier Paolo Pasolini.
San Giorgio Prize
NOTHING BUT A MAN (U.S.)—Michael Roemer.
Federation of Italian Film Critics Prize
CERNY PETR (Czech.)—Milos Forman.
Competing Films
ALL THESE WOMEN (Swed.)—Ingmar Bergman.
GIRL WITH GREEN EYES (Brit.)—Desmond Davis.
THE GOSPEL ACCORDING TO SAINT MATTHEW (Ital.)—Pier Paolo Pasolini.
HAMLET (U.S.S.R.)—Grigorij Kozinstev.
KING AND COUNTRY (Brit.)—Joseph Losey.
KRADEZAT NA PRASKOVI (Bul.)—Veulo Radev.
LIFE UPSIDE DOWN (Fr.)—Alain Jessua.
NOTHING BUT A MAN (U.S.)—Michael Roemer.
RED DESERT (Ital.)—Michelangelo Antonioni.
THIS SPECIAL FRIENDSHIP (Fr.)—Jean Delannoy.
TO LOVE (Swed.)—Jorn Donner.

1965
Prizes of the International Film Jury
Golden Lion: SANDRA (Ital.)—Luchino Visconti.
Special Jury Prizes
SIMON OF THE DESERT (Mex.)—Luis Bunuel.
I'M TWENTY (U.S.S.R.)—Marlen Khitziev.
Volpi Cup for Best Actor: Toshiro Mifune for RED BEARD (Jap.).
Volpi Cup for Best Actress: Annie Girardot for THREE ROOMS IN MANHATTAN (Fr.).
Film Debut: FAITHFULNESS (U.S.S.R.)—Pavel Todorovskij.
Cinema Nuovo Prize: SANDRA (Ital.)—Luchino Visconti.
FIPRESCI Prize
SIMON OF THE DESERT (Mex.)—Luis Bunuel.
Film Critics Prizes
GERTRUD (Den.)—Carl Dreyer.
PIERROT LE FOU (Fr.)—Jean-Luc Godard.
Catholic Film Office Award
RED BEARD (Jap.)—Akira Kurosawa.
Competing Films
FAITHFULNESS (U.S.S.R.)—Pavel Todorovskij.
KAPURUSH (India)—Satyajit Ray.
LOVES OF A BLONDE (Czech.)—Milos Forman.
MICKEY ONE (U.S.)—Arthur Penn.
PIERROT LE FOU (Fr.)—Jean-Luc Godard.
RED BEARD (Jap.)—Akira Kurosawa.
SANDRA (Ital.)—Luchino Visconti.
THE SHAMELESS OLD LADY (Fr.)—Rene Allio.
THREE ROOMS IN MANHATTAN (Fr.)—Marcel Carne.

1966
Prizes of the International Jury
Golden Lion: BATTLE OF ALGIERS (Ital./Alg.)—Gillo Pontecorvo.
Special Jury Prize
CHAPPAQUA (U.S.)—Conrad Rooks.
YESTERDAY GIRL (Ger.)—Alexander Kluge.
Volpi Cup for Best Actor: Jacques Perrin for THE SEARCH (Span.) and HALF A MAN (Ital.).
Volpi Cup for Best Actress: Natalia Arinbasarova for THE FIRST TEACHER (U.S.S.R.).
Special Homage Award: Robert Bresson for his complete work on film.
FIPRESCI Prize
BATTLE OF ALGIERS (Ital./Alg.)—Gillo Pontecorvo.
Catholic Film Office Award
AU HASARD BALTHAZAR (Fr./Swed.)—Robert Bresson.
YESTERDAY GIRL (Ger.)—Alexander Kluge.
San Giorgio Prize
AU HASARD, BALTHAZAR (Fr./Swed.)—Robert Bresson.
National Syndication of Italian Film Journalist Prize
AU HASARD, BALTHAZAR (Fr.)—Robert Bresson.
For Films not in competition: CUL-DE-SAC (Brit.)—Roman Polanski.
Federation of Italian Film Critics Prize
YESTERDAY GIRL (Ger.)—Alexander Kluge.
Cinema Nuovo Special Mentions

Oskar Werner for his performance in FAHRENHEIT 451 (Brit.).
Alexander Kluge for the direction of YESTERDAY GIRL (Ger.).
Competing Films
ALMOST A MAN (Ital.)—Vittorio de Seta.
AU HASARD, BALTHAZAR (Fr./Swed.)—Robert Bresson.
BATTLE OF ALGIERS (Ital./Alg.)—Gillo Pontecorvo.
CHAPPAQUA (U.S.)—Conrad Rooks.
FAHRENHEIT 451 (Brit.)—Francois Truffaut.
LES CREATURES (Fr.)—Agnes Varda.
NIGHT GAMES (Swed.)—Mai Zetterling.
THE GAME IS OVER (Fr.)—Roger Vadim.
THE SEARCH (Span.)—Angelino Fons.
THE WILD ANGELS (U.S.)—Roger Corman.
YESTERDAY GIRL (Ger.)—Alexander Kluge.

1967
Prizes of the International Jury
Golden Lion: BELLE DE JOUR (Fr.)—Luis Bunuel.
Special Jury Prize
CHINA IS NEAR (Ital.)—Marco Bellocchio.
LA CHINOISE (Fr.)—Jean-Luc Godard.
Volpi Cup for Best Actor: Ljubisa Samardzic for DAWN (Yugo.).
Volpi Cup for Best Actress: Shirley Knight for DUTCHMAN (Brit.).
Film Debut: MAHLZEITEN (Ger.)—Edgar Reitz.
FIPRESCI Prize
CHINA IS NEAR (Fr.)—Marco Bellocchio.
Catholic Film Office Award
SILENT VOYAGER (Fr.)—Christian De Chalonge.
Cinema Nuovo Prize
DAWN (Yugo.)—Purisa Djordjevic.
Competing Films
BELLE DE JOUR (Fr.)—Luis Bunuel.
CHINA IS NEAR (Ital.)—Marco Bellocchio.
DAWN (Yugo.)—Purisa Djordjevic.
DEADLY SWEET (Ital.)—Tinto Brass.
DUTCHMAN (Brit.)—Anthony Harvey.
THE HEAD OF THE FAMILY (Ital.)—Nanni Loy.
I SOVVERSIVI (Ital.)—Paolo and Vittorio Taviani.
LA CHINOISE (Fr.)—Jean-Luc Godard.
LATE SEASON (Hung.)—Zoltan Fabri.
MAHLZEITEN (Ger.)—Edgar Reitz.
THE NIGHT OF THE BRIDE (Czech.)—Karel Kachyna.
OUR MOTHER'S HOUSE (Brit.)—Jack Clayton.
OTKLONENIE (Bul.)—Griscia Ostrovski and Todor Stoianov.
SILENT VOYAGER (Fr.)—Christian De Chalonge.
THE STRANGER (Ital.)—Luchino Visconti.
THANOS AND DESPINA (Fr.)—Niko Papatakis.
THREE NIGHTS IN LOVE (Hung.)—Gyorgy Revesz.

1968
Prizes of the International Jury
Golden Lion: ARTISTS AT THE TOP OF THE WORLD: DISORIENTED (Ger.).—
Alexander Kluge.
Special Jury Prize
OUR LADY OF THE TURKS (Ital.)—Carmelo Bene.
LE SOCRATE (Fr.)—Robert Lapoujade.
Volpi Cup for Best Actor: John Marley for FACES (U.S.).
Volpi Cup for Best Actress: Laura Betti for TEOREMA (Ital.).
Honorable Mention: KIERION (Gr.)—Dimosthenis Theos.
Competing Films
ARTISTS AT THE TOP OF THE WORLD: DISORIENTED (Ger.)—Alexander Kluge.
BALLADE POUR UN CHIEN (Fr.)—Gerard Vergez.
THE CASTLE (Ger.)—Rudolf Noelte.
THE DESERTER (Czech.)—Juraj Jakubisko.
DESPUES DEL DILUVIO (Span.)—Jacinto Esteva Grewe.
DIARY OF A SCHIZOPHRENIC (Ital.)—Nelo Risi.
FACES (U.S.)—John Cassavetes.
FALAK (Hung.)—Andras Kovacs.
KIERION (Gr.)—Dimosthenis Theos.
L'ECUME DES JOURS (Fr.)—Charles Belmont.
LE MANDAT MANDABI (Senegal)—Ousmane Sembene.
LE SOCRATE (Fr.)—Robert Lapoujade.
ME AND MY BROTHER (U.S.)—Robert Frank.
NAKED CHILDHOOD (Fr.)—Maurice Pialat.
O SLAVNOSTI A HOSTECH (Czech.)—Jan Nemec.
OUR LADY OF THE TURKS (Ital.)—Carmelo Bene.
PARTNER (Ital.)—Bernardo Bertolucci.
PODNE (Yugo.)—Purisa Djordjevic.
SILENCE AND CRY (Hung.)—Miklos Jancso.
SUMMIT (Ital.)—Giorgio Bontempi.
TELL ME LIES (Brit.)—Peter Brook.
TEOREMA (Ital.)—Pier Paolo Pasolini.
UN AMICO (Ital.)—Ernesto Guida.
WHEEL OF ASHES (U.S.)—Peter Emanuel Goldman.
WILD IN THE STREETS (U.S.)—Barry Shear.

1969-78
Festival held but no official prizes were named; with the festival completely closing its
doors in 1973, 1977, and 1978.

1969
CIDALC Prize
ZASEDA (Yugo.)—Zivojin Pavlovic.
Films Presented
BENITO CERENO (Fr.)—Serge Roullet.
BOY (Jap.)—Nagisa Oshima.
CARDILLAC (Ger.)—Edgar Reitz.
CEST A SLAVA (Czech.)—Hynek Bocan.
CHILDREN'S GAMES (U.S.)—Walter Welebit.
DAY STARS (U.S.S.R.)—Igor Talankin.
DEL AMOR Y OTRAS SOLEDADES (Span.)—Basilio Martin Patino.
DOGADJAJ (Yugo.)—Vatroslav Mimica.

THE FATHER (Swed.)—Alf Sjoberg.
GENIUS (Czech.)—Stefan Uher.
LA PRIMERA CARGA AL MACHETE (Cuba)—Manuel Octavio Gomez.
OS HERDEIROS (Bra.)—Carlos Diegues.
PAULINA S'EN VA (Fr.)—Andre Techine.
PIG PEN (Ital.)—Pier Paolo Pasolini.
PROLOGUE (Can.)—Robin Spry.
SIERRA MAESTRA (Ital.)—Ansano Giannarelli.
SIROKKO (Hung.)—Miklos Jancso.
SJUGET DLJA NEBOLSOVO RASSKAZA (U.S.S.R.)—Sergei Jutkevic.
SWEET HUNTERS (Pan.)—Ruy Guerra.
TILTOTT TERULET (Hung.)—Pal Gabor.
TWO GENTLEMEN SHARING (Brit.)—Ted Kotcheff.
UMANO, NON UMANO (Ital.)—Mario Schifano.
UNDER THE SIGN OF SCORPIO (Ital.)—Paolo and Vittorio Taviani.
YAWAR MALLKU (Bol.)—Jorge Sanjines.
ZASEDA (Yugo.)—Zivojin Pavlovic.

1970
Films Presented
BEBE U GLAVI (Yugo.)—Milos Radivojevic.
CRIME AND PUNISHMENT (U.S.S.R.)—Lev Kulidzanov.
DEEP END (Ger.)—Jerzy Skolimowski.
EL HOMBRE OCULTO (Span.)—Alfonso Ungria.
EL SENOR PRESIDENTE (Arg.)—Marcos Madanes.
I CLOWNS (Ital.)—Federico Fellini.
KESAKAPINA (Fin.)—Jaakko Pakkasvirta.
L'ALLIANCE (Fr.)—Christian De Chalonge.
LE COEUR FOU (Fr.)—Jean-Gabriel Albicocco.
THE LION HAS SEVEN HEADS (Ital./Fr.)—Glauber Rocha.
LOKIS (Pol.)—Janusz Majewski.
PECADO MORTAL (Bra.)—Miguel Faria.
PETIT A PETIT (Fr.)—Jean Rouch.
THE SPIDER'S STRATAGEM (Ital.)—Bernardo Bertolucci.
THREE SISTERS (Brit.)—Laurence Olivier.
UOMINI CONTRO (Ital.)—Francesco Rosi.
WANDA (U.S.)—Barbara Loden.

1971
Films Presented
THE ADVERSARY (India)—Satyajit Ray.
ANNA (Fin.)—Jorn Donner.
ARDE (Mex.)—Jose Bolanos.
THE ARP STATUES (Brit.)—Alan Sekers.
BEWARE THE HOLY WHORE (Ger.)—Rainer Werner Fassbinder.
THE BIG MESS (Ger.)—Alexander Kluge.
CARA IRENE (Den.)—Christian Brad Thomsen.
THE DEVILS (Brit.)—Ken Russell.
DODES'KA-DEN (Jap.)—Akira Kurosawa.
DURING THE SUMMER (Ital.)—Ermanno Olmi.
FORTUNE AND MEN'S EYES (Can.)—Harvey Hart.
GAV (Iran)—Daryush Mehrjui.
HORIZONT (Hung.)—Pal Gabor.
IL POTERE (Ital.)—Augusto Tretti.
L'HUMEUR VAGABONDE (Fr.)—Edouard Luntz.
L'OSPITE (Ital.)—Liliana Cavani.
LA PIAZZA VUOTA (Ital.)—Giuseppe Recchia.
THE LAST MOVIE (U.S.)—Dennis Hopper.
LE PRINTEMPS (Fr.)—Marcel Hanoun.
LENZ (Ger.)—George Moorse.
LES ASSASSINS DE L'ORDRE (Fr.)—Marcel Carne.
LIBERXINA 90 (Span.)—Carlos Duran.
LIEBE SO SCHON DIE LIEBE (Ger.)—Klaus Lemke.
THE LITTLE MOTHER (Fr.)—Jean-Gabriel Albicocco.
NACALO (U.S.S.R.)—Gleb Panfilov.
THE NIGHTCOMERS (Brit.)—Michael Winner.
ON N'ARRETE PAS LE PRINTEMPS (Fr.)—Rene Gilson.
SMIC, SMAC, SMOC (Fr.)—Claude Lelouch.
SUNDAY, BLOODY SUNDAY (Brit.)—John Schlesinger.
THE TOUCH (Swed.)—Ingmar Bergman.
TRZECIA CZESC NOCY (Pol.)—Andrzej Zulawski.
ULOGA MOJE PORODIGE U SVETSKOJ REVOLUCIJI (Yugo.)—Bata Cengic.
UNDER MILK WOOD (Brit.)—Andrew Sinclair.
USKI ROTI (India)—Mani Kaul.
THE VACATION (Ital.)—Tinto Brass.
WHO IS HARRY KELLERMAN AND WHY IS HE SAYING THOSE TERRIBLE
THINGS ABOUT ME? (U.S.)—Ulu Grosbard.
Y QUE PATATIN Y QUE PATATAN (Arg.)—Mario Sabato.

1972
CIDALC Prize
THE MASTER AND MARGERITA (Yugo./Ital.)—Aleksander Petrovic.
Films Presented
ACADIA, ACADIA (Can.)—Pierre Perrault and Michel Brault.
AGIT (Turkey)—Yilmaz Guney.
AMICHE, ANDIAMO ALLA FESTA (Ital.)—Giorgio Trentin.
THE CANDIDATE (U.S.)—Michael Ritchie.
CABARET (U.S.)—Bob Fosse.
CALCUTTA 71 (India)—Murial Sen.
DEAD LANDSCAPE (Hung.)—Istvan Gaal.
DIE VERWEIGERUNG (Aust.)—Alex Corti.
FELICE AND OTILIA (Rum.)—Julian Mihu.
FLOCH (Israel)—Dan Wolman.
KLARA LUST (Swed.)—Kjell Grede.
KOCKSGATAN 48 (Swed.)—Johan Bergenstrahle.
LA NOCE EST PAS FINIE (Can.)—Leonard Forest.
LA VALLEE (Fr.)—Barbet Schroeder.
LALIE POLNE (Czech.)—Elo Havetta.
LE GRANDE SABORDAGE (Can.)—Alain Perisson.
MADE (Brit.)—John Mackenzie.
THE MASTER AND MARGERITA (Yugo./Ital.)—Aleksander Petrovic.

MEIN LIEBER ROBINSON (E. Ger.)—Roland Graf.
THE MERCHANT OF FOUR SEASONS (Ger.)—Rainer Werner Fassbinder.
NATHALIE GRAGGIER (Fr.)—Marguerite Duras.
OS INCONFIDENTES (Braz.)—Joaquin Pedro de Andrade.
PLAY IT AS IT LAYS (U.S.)—Frank Perry.
SALOME (Ital.)—Carmelo Bene.
SAVAGE MESSIAH (Brit.)—Ken Russell.
SIDDHARTHA (U.S.)—Conrad Rooks.
SLIKE IZ ZIVOTA UDARNIKA (Yugo.)—Bata Cengic.
STUNDENTEN AUF SCHAFOTT (Ger.)—Gustav Ehmck.
SUMMER LIGHTNING (Ger.)—Volker Schlondorff.
SUMMER SISTER (Jap.)—Nagisa Oshima.
SZINDBAD (Hung.)—Zoltan Huszarik.
TCHESHMEH (Iran)—Arbi Avanessian.
TOUT VA BIEN (Fr.)—Jean-Pierre Gorin and Jean-Luc Godard.
TUTTE LE DOMENICHE MATTINA (Ital.)—Carlo Tuzi.
UN DOPPIO A META (Ital.)—Gianfranco Piccioli.

1974
Films Presented
ALOISE (Fr.)—Liliane de Kermadec.
CHAMULA (Mex.)—Archibaldo Burns.
DI SHAUL E DEI SICARI DOVE FINISCONO LE VIE DA DAMASCO (Ital.)—Gianni Toti.
E COMINCIO IL VIAGGIO NELLA VERTIGINE (Ital.)—Toni De Gregorio.
GENERAL IDI AMIN DADA (Fr.)—Barbet Schroeder.
IL TEMPO DELL'INIZIO (Ital.)—Luigi Di Gianni.
THE INVITATION (Switz.)—Claude Goretta.
L'ETA DELLA PACE (Ital.)—Fabio Carpi.
LA COURSE EN TETE (Fr.)—Joel Santoni.
MARIE (Ger.)—Hans W. Geissendorfer.
MERIDIANO 100 (Mex.)—Alfredo Joskowicz.
PART-TIME WORLD OF A DOMESTIC SLAVE (Ger.)—Alexander Kluge.
VERMISAT (Ital.)—Mario Brenta.

1975
Films Presented
BADLANDS (U.S.)—Terrence Malick.
BORN TO KILL (U.S.)—Monte Hellman.
CHILD'S PLAY (U.S.)—Sidney Lumet.
DEATH RACE 2000 (U.S.)—Paul Bartel.
DI ASSIMANTON AFORMIN (Gr.)—Tassos Psarras.
I GIORNI DELLA CHIMERA (Ital.)—Franco Corona.
IL CASO RAOUL (Ital.)—Maurizio Ponzi.
IL FRATELLO (Ital.)—Massimo Mida.
THE KING OF MARVIN GARDENS (U.S.)—Bob Rafelson.
L'ALTRO DIO (Ital.)—Elio Bartolini.
LES DOIGTS DANS LA TETE (Fr.)—Jacques Doillon.
LILY, AIME-MOI (Fr.)—Maurice Dugowson.
MEGARA (Gr.)—Saki Maniatis and Yorgos Tseberopoulos.
MUNA-MOTO (Cameroon)—J.P. Dikongue-Pipa.
NESSUNO O TUTTI—MATTI DA SLEGARE (Ital.)—Silvano Agosti, Marco Bellocchio, Stefano Rulli, and Sandro Petraglia.
NON SI SCRIVE SUI MURI A MILANO (Ital.)—Raffaele Maiello.
PREMJIA (U.S.S.R.)—Sergej Mikaelian.
SISTERS (U.S.)—Brian De Palma.
TABI'AT-E BI JAN (Iran)—Sohrab Shahid-Salesa.
TERMINAL (Ital.)—Paolo Breccia.
THOMAS (Fr.)—Jean-Francois Dion.
TO PROXENIO TIS ANNAS (Gr.)—Pantelis Vulgaris.
VARAKOZOK (Hung.)—Imre Gyongyossy.

1976
Films Presented
ALLE ORIGINI DELLA MAFIA (Ital.)—Enzo Muzii.
BAKS (Senegal)—Momar Thiam.
CAMBIAR LA VIDA (Cuba)—Jesus Diaz.
CANTATA DE CHILE (Cuba)—Humberto Solas.
COMMENT YUKONG DEPLACA LES MONTAGNES (Fr.)—Joris Ivens and Marceline Loridan; a film in twelve episodes.
CRIA CUERVOS (Span.)—Carlos Saura.
DAKOI NINGEN BUSHI (Jap.)—Yuji Okumura, Marco Yumoto, Takaoki Watanabe, and Tadashi Hara.
DER PROTOTIP (Ger.)—Sven Severin.
DINCOLO DE PAD (Rum.)—Mircea Veroiu.
EDINSTVENNAJA (U.S.S.R.)—Josif Cheific.
EIN TODSICHERES SYSTEM (Ger.)—Carlo Di Carlo.
GLI ALTRI (Ital.)—Marina Malfatti and Riccardo Tortora.
JARVANYI (Hung.)—Pal Gabor.
JE SUIS PIERRE RIVIERE (Fr.)—Christine Lipinska.
THE JUDGE AND THE ASSASSIN (Fr.)—Bertrand Tavernier.
JULIO ANTONIO NIELLA (Cuba)—Enrique Pineda Barnet.
LA VIE TRES BREVE DE JOSEPH BIZOUARD (Fr.)—Jean-Louis Daniel.
LAS LARGAS VACACIONES DEL '36 (Span.)—Jaime Camino.
THE LAST WOMAN (Ital.)—Marco Ferreri.
LE CINQUE STAGIONI (Ital.)—Gianni Amico.
LOVIN' MOLLY (U.S.)—Sidney Lumet.
MALADIE MORTELLE (Fr.)—Francois Weyergans.
MURDER BY DEATH (U.S.)—Robert Moore.
NEL CERCHIO (Ital.)—Gianni Minello.
NEL PIU ALTO DEI CIELI (Ital.)—Silvano Agosti.
ODE TO BILLY JOE (U.S.)—Max Baer.
PARTITA NA INSTRUMENT DREWNIANY (Pol.)—Janusz Zaorski.
PASCUAL DUARTE (Span.)—Ricardo Franco.
SMILE (U.S.)—Michael Ritchie.
THE SPIRIT OF THE BEEHIVE (Span.)—Victor Erice.
STAY HUNGRY (U.S.)—Bob Rafelson.
UN SAC DE BILLES (Fr.)—Jacques Doillon.
UNA VITA VENDUTA (Ital.)—Aldo Florio.
WALANDA (Mali)—Alkaly Kaba.
WAMBA (Mali)—Alkaly Kaba.

WAN PIPEL (Neth.)—Pim De La Parra, Jr.

1979
FIPRESCI Prize
LA NOUBA (Algeria)—Assia Djebar.
PASSE MONTAGNE (Fr.)—Jean-Francois Stevenin.
Italian Film Critic's Prizes
Best Film: SAINT JACK (U.S.)—Peter Bogdanovich.
Best Actor: Evgenij Leonov for AUTUMN MARATHON (U.S.S.R.)
Best Actress: Nobuko Otowa for THE STRANGLER (Jap.).
Competing Films
ARCHIETA JOSE DO BRASIL (Bra.)—Paulo Cesar Saraceni.
AUTUMN MARATHON (U.S.S.R.)—Georgij Danelija.
CINEMA (U.S.S.R.)—Liana Eliava.
EL SUPER (U.S.)—Leon Ichaso and Orlando Jimenez.
ESCAPE FROM ALCATRAZ (U.S.)—Don Siegel.
ESSAKKAMAT (Egypt)—Salah Abu Sayf.
IL FIUME (Iraq)—Feisal Yasini.
LA LUNA (Ital.)—Bernardo Bertolucci.
MAGICIAN OF LUBLIN (U.S.)—Menahem Golan.
THE MEADOW (Ital.)—Paolo and Vittorio Taviani.
MORE AMERICAN GRAFFITI (U.S.)—B.W.L. Norton.
OGRO (Ital.)—Gillo Pontecorvo.
PASSE MONTAGNE (Fr.)—Jean-Francois Stevenin.
SAINT JACK (U.S.)—Peter Bogdanovich.
SAMBA LE GRAND (Niger)—Mustapha Alassane.
SOLDADOS (Span.)—Alfonso Ungria.
THE STRANGLER (Jap.)—Kaneto Shindo.
UN DRAMMA BORGHESE (Ital.)—Florestano Vancini.
VEREDA TROPICAL (Bra.)—Joaquim Pedro de Andrade.
THE WANDERERS (U.S.)—Philip Kaufman.
ZEMALJSKI DANI TEKU (Yugo.)—Goran Paskaljevic.

1980
Prizes of the International Jury
Golden Lion: GLORIA (U.S.)—John Cassavetes.
Cinema 80 Series Golden Lion: ALEXANDER THE GREAT (Gr.)—Theodoros Anghelopoulos.
Golden Lion for First Film: AJANDEK EZ A NAP (Hung.)—Peter Gothar.
AGIS Prize
MON ONCLE D'AMERIQUE (Fr.)—Alain Resnais.
Competing Films
A IDADE DA TERRA (Bra.)—Glauber Rocha.
ATLANTIC CITY (Can.)—Louis Malle.
DEUX LIONS AU SOLEIL (Fr.)—Claude Faraldo.
GLORIA (U.S.)—John Cassavetes.
GOING IN STYLE (U.S.)—Martin Brest.
LA PETITE SIRENE (Fr.)—Roger Andrieux.
LASKI MEZI KAPKAMI DESTE (Czech.)—Karel Kachyna.
MELVIN AND HOWARD (U.S.)—Jonathan Demme.
OXALA (Por.)—Antonio-Pedro de Vasconcelos.
RASSKAZ O NEISVESTNOM CELOVEKE (U.S.S.R.)—Vitautas Zalakjavicjus.
UN'ALTRA ITALIA NELLE BANDIERE DEI LAVORATORI (Ital.)—Archivio Nazionale Cinematografico.
VOLTATI EUGENIO (Ital.)—Luigi Comencini.
Cinema 80 Series
AL AYYAM AL TEWIL (Iraq)—Tawfiq Salah.
ALEXANDER THE GREAT (Gr.)—Theodoros Anghelopoulos.
RICHARD'S THINGS (Brit.)—Anthony Harvey.

1981
Prizes of the International Jury
Golden Lion: DIE BLEIERNE ZEIT (Ger.)—Margarethe von Trotta.
Special Jury Prize
SOGNI D'ORO (Ital.)—Nanni Moretti.
ELES NAO USAM BLACK-TIE (Bra.)—Leon Hirszman.
Golden Lion for First Film: SJECAS LI SE DOLLY BELL? (Yugo.)—Emir Kusturica.
I.S.D.A.P. Prize: VISOKI NAPON (Yugo.)—Veljko Bulajic (for its documentary story).
Competing Films
BEYRUTH EL-LIKAA (Libya)—Borhane Alauiye.
BOSCO D'AMORE (Ital.)—Alberto Bevilacqua.
DIE BLEIERNE ZEIT (Ger.)—Margarethe von Trotta.
DU ZAIRE AU CONGO (Bel.)—Christian Mesnil.
ELES NAO USAM BLACK-TIE (Bra.)—Leon Hirszman.
FORFOLGELSEN (Nor.)—Anja Brein.
KARGUS (Span.)—Juan Minon and Miguel A. Trujillo.
LA CADUTA DEGLI ANGELI RIBELLI (Ital.)—Marco Tullio Giordana.
LE OCCASIONI DI ROSA (Ital.)—Salvatore Piscicelli.
LES JEUX DE LA COMTESSE DOLINGEN DE GRATZ (Fr.)—Catherine Binet.
PISO PISELLO (Ital.)—Peter Del Monte.
POSTRIZINY (Czech.)—Jiri Menzel.
PRINCE OF THE CITY (U.S.)—Sidney Lumet.
SILVESTRE (Por.)—Joao Cesar Monteiro.
SJECAS LI SE DOLLY BELL? (Yugo.)—Emir Kusturica.
SOGNI D'ORO (Ital.)—Nanni Moretti.
TRUE CONFESSIONS (U.S.)—Ulu Grosbard.
ZVEZDOPAD (U.S.S.R.)—Igor Talankin.

1982
Prizes of the International Jury
Golden Lion: THE STATE OF THINGS (Ger.)—Wim Wenders.
Special Jury Prize: IMPERATIVE (Ger.)—Krzystof Zanussi.
Golden Lion for First Film
DE SMAAK VAN WATER (Neth.)—Orlow Seunke.
SCIOPEN (Ital.)—Luciano Odorisio.
Special Prize for a Professional Contribution: Michail Ul'janov for his performance in CESTNAJA ZIZN (U.S.S.R.).
FIPRESCI Prize
AGONIJA (U.S.S.R.)—Elem Klimov.
THE STATE OF THINGS (Ger.)—Wim Wenders.
Competing Films
AGONIJA (U.S.S.R.)—Elem Klimov.

BLADE RUNNER (U.S.)—Ridley Scott.
CESTNAJA ZIZN (U.S.S.R.)—Julij Rajzman.
COLPIRE AL CUORE (Ital.)—Gianni Amelio.
DIE BEUNRUHIGUNG (E. Ger.)—Lothar Warneke.
DE SMAAK VAN WATER (Neth.)—Orlow Seunke.
THE DRAUGHTSMAN'S CONTRACT (Brit.)—Peter Greenaway.
ESTOY EN CRISIS! (Span.)—Fernando Colomo.
FIVE LAST DAYS (Ger.)—Percy Adlon.
GOLOS (U.S.S.R.)—Il'ja Averbach.
GRIHAYUDDA (India)—Buddhadeb Dasgupta.
GUERNICA (Hung.)—Ferenc Kosa.
HADDUTA MISRIYA (Egypt)—Yussef Sahine.
HERO (Brit.)—Barney Platt-Mills.
IL BUON SOLDATO (Ital.)—Franco Brusati.
IMPERATIVE (Ger.)—Krzysztof Zanussi.
INGENJOR ANDREES LUFTFARD (Swed.)—Jan Troell.
LA TRUITE (Fr.)—Joseph Losey.
LE BEAU MARIAGE (Fr.)—Eric Rohmer.
LE GRAN FRERE (Fr.)—Francis Girod.
QU'EST-CE QU'ON ATTEND POUR ETRE HEREUX? (Fr.)—Coline Serreau.
QUERELLE (Ger.)—Rainer Werner Fassbinder.
THE STATE OF THINGS (Ger.)—Wim Wenders.
TEMPEST (U.S.)—Paul Mazursky.
TO PHRAGMA (Gr.)—Dimitri Makris.

1983
Prizes of the International Jury
    Golden Lion: FIRST NAME, CARMEN (Fr./Switz.)—Jean-Luc Godard.
    Special Jury Prize: BIQUEFARRE (Fr.)—Georges Rouquier.
    Best Actor: The Cast of STREAMERS (U.S.), directed by Robert Altman.
    Best Actress: Darling Legitimus for RUE CASES NEGRES (Fr./Martinique).
    Silver Lion for First and Second Works: RUE CASES NEGRES (Fr./Martinique)—
    Euzhan Palcy.
Career Award: Michelangelo Antonioni.
FIPRESCI Prize
    FANNY AND ALEXANDER (Swed.)—Ingmar Bergman.
    DIE MACHT DER GEFUHLE (Ger.)—Alexander Kluge.
Competing Films
    BIQUEFARRE (Fr.)—Georges Rouquier.
    CAREFUL, HE MIGHT HEAR YOU (Aus.)—Carl Schultz.
    DER AUFENTHALT (E. Ger.)—Frank Beyer.
    DIE MACHT DER GEFUHLE (Ger.)—Alexander Kluge.
    EDITH'S DIARY (Ger.)—Hans W. Geissendorfer.
    FAVORITI E VINCENTI (Ital.)—Salvatore Maira.
    FIRST NAME, CARMEN (Fr.)—Jean-Luc Godard.
    GLUT (Switz.)—Thomas Koerfer.

HANNA K (Fr.)—Constantin Costa-Gavras.
IL DISERTORE (Ital.)—Giuliana Berlinguer.
JOGO DE MAO (Por.)—Monique Rutler.
LA VILLE DES PIRATES (Por.)—Raul Ruiz.
LIFE IS A BED OF ROSES (Fr.)—Alain Resnais.
MARIA CHAPDELAINE (Can.)—Gilles Carle.
MOTHER MARIA (U.S.S.R.)—Sergej Kolosov.
SASAME YUKI (Jap.)—Kon Ichikawa.
STREAMERS (U.S.)—Robert Altman.
TISICROCNA VCELA (Czech.)—Juraj Jakubisko.
ZELIG (U.S.)—Woody Allen.

1984
Prizes of the International Jury
    Golden Lion: YEAR OF THE QUIET SUN (Pol./Ger./U.S.)—Krzysztof Zanussi.
    Special Jury Prize: FAVORITES OF THE MOON (Fr.)—Otar Ioseliani.
    Best Female Performance: Pascale Ogier for FULL MOON IN PARIS (Fr.).
    Best Male Performance: Naseeruddin Shah for THE CROSSING (India).
    Film Debut: SONATINE (Can.)—Micheline Lanctot.
    Special Award for Technical Merit: WE THREE (Ital.)—Pupi Avati.
Competing Films
    ANGELAS KRIG (Fin.)—Eija-Elina Bergholm.
    ANGYALI UDVOZLET (Hung.)—Andras Jeles.
    BEREG (U.S.S.R.)—Aleksandr Alov and Vladimir Naumov.
    CARMEN (Fr.)—Francesco Rosi.
    CLARETTA (Ital.)—Pasquale Squitieri.
    THE CROSSING (India)—Goutam Ghosh.
    CUORE (Ital.)—Luigi Comencini.
    DER SPIEGEL (Ger.)—Erden Kiral.
    DIONYSOS (Fr.)—Jean Rouch.
    GREYSTOKE—THE LEGEND OF TARZAN (Brit.)—Hugh Hudson.
    HEIMAT (Ger.)—Edgar Reitz.
    IL FUTURO E DONNA (Ital.)—Marco Ferreri.
    KAOS (Ital.)—Paolo and Vittorio Taviani.
    L'AMOUR A MORT/LOVE UNTO DEATH (Fr.)—Alain Resnais.
    L'AMOUR PAR TERRE (Fr.)—Jacques Rivette.
    LA NEVE NEL BICCHIERE (Ital.)—Florestano Vancini.
    LOS ZANCOS (Span.)—Carlos Saura.
    MARIA'S LOVERS (U.S.)—Andrej Koncalovskij.
    NINGUEM DUAS VEZES (Por.)—Jorge Silva Melo.
    PIRATA! (CULT MOVIE) (Ital.)—Paolo Ricagno.
    SANGANDAAN (Phil.)—Mike de Leon.
    SONATINE (Can.)—Micheline Lanctot.
    TUKUMA (Den.)—Palle Kjaerulff-Schmidt.
    UNO SCANDALO PER BENE (Ital.)—Pasquale Festa Campanile.
    WE THREE (Ital.)—Pupi Avati.
    YBRIS (Ital.)—Gavino Ledda.
    YEAR OF THE QUIET SUN (Pol.)—Krzysztof Zanussi.

MPG Name Index

The MPG Name Index, offering complete filmographies for nearly 180,000 individuals involved in filmmaking from 1910 to 1984, has film credits relating to each of the five sections of the Motion Picture Guide.

Unless otherwise noted, the film credits refer to the major sound films listed alphabetically in Volumes I through IX. Credits for Silents, Miscellaneous Silents, Miscellaneous Talkies, and 1984 releases are listed separately within a name entry. Those sections are contained in the following volumes:

Miscellaneous Talkies: Page 4123, Volume IX
1984: Page 4006, Volume XI
Silents: Volume X
Miscellaneous Silents: Page 317, Volume X

Pseudonyms and Variant Spellings

Many individuals used more than one name or changed their names during their film careers. In such cases, bracketed names have been used to indicate cross references (ie, Casey Adams [Max Showalter]).

Slight variations in name forms (ie, Ernest Adams, Ernest S. Adams, Ernie Adams) have been preserved to reflect different billing choices over the course of a career.

In some cases, particularly with respect to foreign productions, name variations have occurred due to conflicting spellings in the wide variety of source materials used to compile cast and credits. Since it was often not feasible to determine a standard spelling, these variations were used in the entries and so appear in this index.

Credits

If no abbreviation appears after a film title, the credit is for acting in the film listed. Acting credits are only noted when an individual acted in *and* performed other functions on the film. In those cases, the film title is followed by an "a" and then abbreviations for the other functions performed on the film.

The following is an alphabetical listing of the production credits included in this index:

anim: animation
anim d: animation director
animal d: animal director
animal t: animal trainer
art d: art director
ch: choreographer
cons: consultant
cos: costumes
d: director
ed: editor
m: musical score composer
makeup
md: musical director
p: producer
ph: cinematographer
prod d: production design
set d: set decorator
spec eff: special effects
staging: staging of special sequences
stunts
sup: supervisor (Silent films)
t: titles (Silent films)
titles: English subtitles
tech adv: technical adviser
titles: English subtitles
w: writer (both screenplay and source material)

A

Robert A'Dair
MYSTERY OF MR. X, THE(1934); RIP TIDE(1934); SONS O' GUNS(1936); SUZY(1936)

Robert "Bob" A'Dair
LIMEHOUSE BLUES(1934)

Paddy A'Hearne
CAT GIRL(1957), ph

Lejaren a'Hiller
Misc. Silents
DEVIL'S ANGEL, THE(1920), d

Lejaren A'Hiller, Jr.
TIME OF THE HEATHEN(1962), m

Hank Aabel
WHALERS, THE(1942, Swed.)

Dennis Aaberg
BIG WEDNESDAY(1978), w

Beverly Aadland
SOUTH PACIFIC(1958); CUBAN REBEL GIRLS(1960)

Erik Aaes
WHILE THE ATTORNEY IS ASLEEP(1945, Den.), art d; HIDDEN FEAR(1957), art d; ORDET(1957, Den.), art d; WEEKEND(1964, Den.), art d; HUNGER(1968, Den./Norway/Swed.), art d

Dee Aaker
MR. SCOUTMASTER(1953); BIGGER THAN LIFE(1956)

Lee Aaker
ATOMIC CITY, THE(1952); DESPERATE SEARCH(1952); GREATEST SHOW ON EARTH, THE(1952); NO ROOM FOR THE GROOM(1952); O. HENRY'S FULL HOUSE(1952); SOMETHING TO LIVE FOR(1952); ARENA(1953); HONDO(1953); JEOPARDY(1953); TAKE ME TO TOWN(1953); DESTRY(1954); RICOCHET RO-MANCE(1954)

Aileen Aalbu
YOUNG MAN OF MANHATTAN(1930)

Fern Aalbu
YOUNG MAN OF MANHATTAN(1930)

Harriet Aalbu
YOUNG MAN OF MANHATTAN(1930)

Lorraine Aalbu
YOUNG MAN OF MANHATTAN(1930)

Mariann Aalda
WIZ, THE(1978)

Angela Aamers
H.O.T.S.(1979)

Marlene Aames
TIME OF YOUR LIFE, THE(1948); BEST YEARS OF OUR LIVES, THE(1946)

Willie Aames
SCAVENGER HUNT(1979); PARADISE(1982); ZAPPED!(1982)

Mathaleen Aamold
Silents
LITTLE GRAY LADY, THE(1914)

Frank Aanucci
KING OF THE STALLIONS(1942), m, md

Abraxas Aaran
PATTON(1970)

Ed Aardal
MELODY TIME(1948), animators; LADY AND THE TRAMP(1955), anim

Edwin Aardal
FANTASIA(1940), anim, anim; THREE CABALLEROS, THE(1944), anim; HEY THERE, IT'S YOGI BEAR(1964), anim; MAN CALLED FLINTSTONE, THE(1966), anim; PHANTOM TOLLBOOTH, THE(1970), anim

Annu Aarnela
MAKE LIKE A THIEF(1966, Fin.)

Caroline Aaron
COME BACK TO THE 5 & DIME, JIMMY DEAN, JIMMY DEAN(1982); BABY, IT'S YOU(1983); WITHOUT A TRACE(1983)
1984
BROTHER FROM ANOTHER PLANET, THE(1984)

Charles Aaron
DO YOU LOVE ME?(1946)

Jack Aaron
LADY LIBERTY(1972, Ital./Fr.); SPOOK WHO SAT BY THE DOOR, THE(1973); FAT ANGELS(1980, U.S./Span.)
Misc. Talkies
FAT CHANCE(1982)

James Aaron
TENDER MERCIES(1982)

Levy Aaron
GUIDE, THE(1965, U.S./India)

Lindy Aaron
COP-OUT(1967, Brit.)

Paul Aaron
DIFFERENT STORY, A(1978), d; FORCE OF ONE, A(1979), d; OCTAGON, THE(1980), w; DEADLY FORCE(1983), d

Sidney Aaron [Paddy Chayefsky]
ALTERED STATES(1980), w

Steve Aaron
1984
SLAPSTICK OF ANOTHER KIND(1984)

Aaron Gonzalez and his Tango-Rumba Band
FIFTH AVENUE GIRL(1939)

Michael Aarons
LEAP OF FAITH(1931, Brit.), ed

Alan Aaronson
UNDERWORLD U.S.A.(1961)

John Aasen
Silents
WHY WORRY(1923); TWO FLAMING YOUTHS(1927)

G.S. Aasie
KENNER(1969)

Mohamed Aazzi
PIRATES OF PENZANCE, THE(1983)

Teruaki Aba
MYSTERIANS, THE(1959, Jap.), art d

Samba Ababaka
CHECKERBOARD(1969, Fr.)

Appollonio Abadesa
1984
HUNTERS OF THE GOLDEN COBRA, THE(1984, Ital.), spec eff

Julio Abadia
GILDA(1946)

Tim Abadie
TAKE A GIRL LIKE YOU(1970, Brit,), set d

Temple Abady
DEAR MR. PROHACK(1949, Brit.), m; MIRANDA(1949, Brit.), m; WOMAN IN THE HALL, THE(1949, Brit.), m; NEVER LOOK BACK(1952, Brit.), m; FOLLY TO BE WISE(1953), m; LOVE IN PAWN(1953, Brit.), m; KILL ME TOMORROW(1958, Brit.), m

Sonny Abagnale
1984
FALLING IN LOVE(1984)

Assi Abaiov
1984
AMBASSADOR, THE(1984)

Mayya Abar-Baranovskaya
RED AND THE WHITE, THE(1969, Hung./USSR), cos

Judith Abarbanel
CANTOR'S SON, THE(1937)
Misc. Talkies
AMERICAN MATCHMAKER(1940); UNCLE MOSES(1932)

Lorraine Abarbanel
CANTOR'S SON, THE(1937)

Sam X. Abarbanel
ARGYLE SECRETS, THE(1948), p; PREHISTORIC WOMEN(1950), p, w; SOUND OF HORROR(1966, Span.), w; LAST DAY OF THE WAR, THE(1969, U.S./Ital./Span.), p, w; NARCO MEN, THE(1969, Span./Ital.), p

Boleslaw Abart
TEST OF PILOT PIRX, THE(1978, Pol./USSR)

Natividad Abascal
BANANAS(1971)

D. Abashidze
DRAGONFLY, THE(1955 USSR)

Lina Abashidze
DRAGONFLY, THE(1955 USSR)

T. Abashidze
DRAGONFLY, THE(1955 USSR)

Loraine Abate
LOVE WITH THE PROPER STRANGER(1963)

Dario Abatello
OPERATION KID BROTHER(1967, Ital.), p

Tony Abatemarco
1984
UNFAITHFULLY YOURS(1984)

Marta Abba
LOYALTY OF LOVE(1937, Ital.)

Claudio Abbado
BARBER OF SEVILLE, THE(1973, Ger./Fr.), md

Marcello Abbado
VIOLATED PARADISE(1963, Ital./Jap.), m

Abdullah Abbas
LADY EVE, THE(1941); WE WERE STRANGERS(1949); MY FAVORITE SPY(1951); MACAO(1952); KING RICHARD AND THE CRUSADERS(1954); AUTUMN LEA-VES(1956)

Hector Abbas
SCHOOL FOR SCANDAL, THE(1930, Brit.); GENTLEMAN OF PARIS, A(1931); MADAME GUILLOTINE(1931, Brit.); ROOF, THE(1933, Brit.); WANDERING JEW, THE(1935, Brit.); REMBRANDT(1936, Brit.); MAN WHO MADE DIAMONDS, THE(1937, Brit.); OLD MOTHER RILEY'S CIRCUS(1941, Brit.); ONE OF OUR AIR-CRAFT IS MISSING(1942, Brit.); PIMPERNEL SMITH(1942, Brit.)
Silents
FATE'S PLAYTHING(1920, Brit.); BOLIBAR(1928, Brit.)
Misc. Silents
FIRST MEN IN THE MOON, THE(1919, Brit.)

Hector Abbass
GYPSY MELODY(1936, Brit.)

Pam Abbass
BRONCO BILLY(1980)

Charles Abbe
Silents
NIOBE(1915); BAB'S CANDIDATE(1920); CAPPY RICKS(1921); BACK HOME AND BROKE(1922)
Misc. Silents
HOMEWARD BOUND(1923)

Jack Abbe
Silents
TALE OF TWO WORLDS, A(1921)
Misc. Silents
MYSTIC FACES(1918); WHO IS TO BLAME?(1918); PAGAN GOD, THE(1919); LOTUS BLOSSOM(1921)

James Abbe
Silents
WHITE SISTER, THE(1923)

Abbey
TONY DRAWS A HORSE(1951, Brit.), cos

Edward Abbey
LONELY ARE THE BRAVE(1962), w

Eleanor Abbey
HUNGRY HILL(1947, Brit.), cos; MARK OF CAIN, THE(1948, Brit.), cos; WOMAN HATER(1949, Brit.), cos; NAUGHTY ARLETTE(1951, Brit.), cos; DANGEROUS EXILE(1958, Brit.), cos; OPERATION AMSTERDAM(1960, Brit.), cos; THREE WORLDS OF GULLIVER, THE(1960, Brit.), cos

John Abbey
MISTER FREEDOM(1970, Fr.)

Leo Abbey
GENERAL DIED AT DAWN, THE(1936); SAIGON(1948); I WAS AN AMERICAN SPY(1951)

William Abbey
HAWAII CALLS(1938)

Monks of Abbey at Casamari
CARDINAL, THE(1963)

Members of the Abbey Theatre Company
YOUNG CASSIDY(1965, U.S./Brit.)

The Abbey Theatre Company
RISING OF THE MOON, THE(1957, Ireland)

Ernest Abbeyquaye
HAMILE(1965, Ghana)

Franco Abbinia
PRESIDENT'S MYSTERY, THE(1936), w; THAT SPLENDID NOVEMBER(1971, Ital./Fr.)

Jerry Abbot
TENDER MERCIES(1982)

Spud Abbot
LAST GUNFIGHTER, THE(1961, Can.)

Virginia Abbot
Misc. Silents
DRIFTWOOD(1924); HARBOR PATROL(1924)

Aimee Abbott
Silents
DOING THEIR BIT(1918)

Anthony Abbott [Fulton Oursler]
NIGHT CLUB LADY(1932), w; CIRCUS QUEEN MURDER, THE(1933), w; PRESIDENT'S MYSTERY, THE(1936), w; PANTHER'S CLAW, THE(1942), w; BOOMERANG!(1947), w

Brian Abbott
ORPHAN OF THE WILDERNESS(1937, Aus.); WILD INNOCENCE(1937, Aus.)

Bruce Abbott
T.A.G.: THE ASSASSINATION GAME(1982)
1984
LAST STARFIGHTER, THE(1984)

Bud Abbott
ONE NIGHT IN THE TROPICS(1940); BUCK PRIVATES(1941); HOLD THAT GHOST(1941); IN THE NAVY(1941); KEEP 'EM FLYING(1941); PARDON MY SARONG(1942); RIDE 'EM COWBOY(1942); RIO RITA(1942); WHO DONE IT?(1942); HIT THE ICE(1943); IT AIN'T HAY(1943); IN SOCIETY(1944); LOST IN A HAREM(1944); ABBOTT AND COSTELLO IN HOLLYWOOD(1945); HERE COME THE CO-EDS(1945); NAUGHTY NINETIES, THE(1945); LITTLE GIANT(1946); TIME OF THEIR LIVES, THE(1946); BUCK PRIVATES COME HOME(1947); WISTFUL WIDOW OF WAGON GAP, THE(1947); ABBOTT AND COSTELLO MEET FRANKENSTEIN(1948); MEXICAN HAYRIDE(1948); NOOSE HANGS HIGH, THE(1948); ABBOTT AND COSTELLO MEET THE KILLER, BORIS KARLOFF(1949); AFRICA SCREAMS(1949); ABBOTT AND COSTELLO IN THE FOREIGN LEGION(1950); ABBOTT AND COSTELLO MEET THE INVISIBLE MAN(1951); COMIN' ROUND THE MOUNTAIN(1951); ABBOTT AND COSTELLO MEET CAPTAIN KIDD(1952); JACK AND THE BEANSTALK(1952); LOST IN ALASKA(1952); ABBOTT AND COSTELLO GO TO MARS(1953); ABBOTT AND COSTELLO MEET DR. JEKYLL AND MR. HYDE(1954); ABBOTT AND COSTELLO MEET THE KEYSTONE KOPS(1955); ABBOTT AND COSTELLO MEET THE MUMMY(1955); DANCE WITH ME, HENRY(1956)

Charles Abbott
FIGHTING TEXAN(1937), d; HIGH HAT(1937), ed
Misc. Talkies
ADVENTURES OF THE MASKED PHANTOM, THE(1939), d

David Abbott
1984
KARATE KID, THE(1984)

Diahann Abbott
WELCOME TO L.A.(1976)

Diahnne Abbott
TAXI DRIVER(1976); NEW YORK, NEW YORK(1977); KING OF COMEDY, THE(1983)

Dianne Abbott
1984
LOVE STREAMS(1984)

Dorothy Abbott
RAZOR'S EDGE, THE(1946); NIGHT HAS A THOUSAND EYES(1948); NEPTUNE'S DAUGHTER(1949); RED, HOT AND BLUE(1949); TAKE ME OUT TO THE BALL GAME(1949); LIFE OF HER OWN, A(1950); PETTY GIRL, THE(1950); WHERE DANGER LIVES(1950); MY FAVORITE SPY(1951); LAS VEGAS STORY, THE(1952); LOVE ME OR LEAVE ME(1955); REBEL WITHOUT A CAUSE(1955); EVERYTHING BUT THE TRUTH(1956); GUNFIGHT AT THE O.K. CORRAL(1957); JAILHOUSE ROCK(1957); JET PILOT(1957); PILLOW TALK(1959); APARTMENT, THE(1960); PEPE(1960); SERGEANTS 3(1962); THAT TOUCH OF MINK(1962); GATHERING OF EAGLES, A(1963)

Elizabeth Abbott
CHAD HANNA(1940)

Fred Abbott
FOUR DESPERATE MEN(1960, Brit.)

Frederick Abbott
1,000 CONVICTS AND A WOMAN zero(1971, Brit.)

Fredric Abbott
BEYOND THE FOG(1981, Brit.)

George Abbott
BROADWAY(1929), w; COQUETTE(1929), w; HALF WAY TO HEAVEN(1929), d&w; NIGHT PARADE(1929), w; SATURDAY NIGHT KID, THE(1929), w; WHY BRING THAT UP?(1929), d, w; ALL QUIET ON THE WESTERN FRONT(1930), w; FALL GUY, THE(1930), w; MANSLAUGHTER(1930), p,d&w; SEA GOD, THE(1930), d&w; CHEAT, THE(1931), d; MY SIN(1931), d, w; SECRETS OF A SECRETARY(1931), d, w; STOLEN HEAVEN(1931), d, w; THOSE WE LOVE(1932), w; LILLY TURNER(1933), w; HEAT LIGHTNING(1934), w; STRAIGHT IS THE WAY(1934), w; THREE MEN ON A HORSE(1936), w; ON YOUR TOES(1939), w; BOYS FROM SYRACUSE(1940), w; TOO MANY GIRLS(1940), p, d; HIGHWAY WEST(1941), w; BROADWAY(1942), w; BEAT THE BAND(1947), w; WHERE'S CHARLEY?(1952, Brit.), w; PAJAMA GAME, THE(1957), w; DAMN YANKEES(1958), p&d, w
Silents
FOUR WALLS(1928), w

Gypsie Abbott
Silents
MAN WHO COULD NOT LOSE, THE(1914)

H. Abbott
Silents
RAIDERS, THE(1921)

Imogene Abbott
FOR LOVE OR MONEY(1963), makeup

J. F. Abbott
Silents
JUST JIM(1915)

Jamie Abbott
TESTAMENT(1983)
1984
MICKI AND MAUDE(1984)

Jane Abbott
ROLLING THUNDER(1977); HARD COUNTRY(1981)

Jess Abbott
OKEFENOKEE(1960), w

John Abbott
SAINT IN LONDON, THE(1939, Brit.); CONQUEST OF THE AIR(1940); MISSING TEN DAYS(1941, Brit.); SHANGHAI GESTURE, THE(1941); GET MY LOVE(1942); GORILLA MAN(1942); JOAN OF PARIS(1942); LONDON BLACKOUT MURDERS(1942); MRS. MINIVER(1942); NIGHTMARE(1942); RUBBER RACKETEERS(1942); THIS ABOVE ALL(1942); DANGEROUS BLONDES(1943); MISSION TO MOSCOW(1943); THEY GOT ME COVERED(1943); UNDER SECRET ORDERS(1943, Brit.); ABROAD WITH TWO YANKS(1944); CRY OF THE WEREWOLF(1944); END OF THE ROAD(1944); FALCON IN HOLLYWOOD, THE(1944); JANE EYRE(1944); MASK OF DIMITRIOS, THE(1944); ONCE UPON A TIME(1944); SECRETS OF SCOTLAND YARD(1944); SUMMER STORM(1944); U-BOAT PRISONER(1944); CRIME DOCTOR'S WARNING(1945); HONEYMOON AHEAD(1945); POWER OF THE WHISTLER, THE(1945); PURSUIT TO ALGIERS(1945); SARATOGA TRUNK(1945); THOUSAND AND ONE NIGHTS, A(1945); VAMPIRE'S GHOST, THE(1945); ANNA AND THE KING OF SIAM(1946); BANDIT OF SHERWOOD FOREST, THE(1946); DECEPTION(1946); HUMORESQUE(1946); NOTORIOUS LONE WOLF, THE(1946); ONE MORE TOMORROW(1946); ADVENTURE ISLAND(1947); IF WINTER COMES(1947); TIME OUT OF MIND(1947); WEB, THE(1947); WOMAN IN WHITE, THE(1948); MADAME BOVARY(1949); SIDESHOW(1950); CROSSWINDS(1951); NAVY BOUND(1951); THUNDER ON THE HILL(1951); MERRY WIDOW, THE(1952); ROGUE'S MARCH(1952); SOMBRERO(1953); STEEL LADY, THE(1953); THUNDER IN THE EAST(1953); OMAR KHAYYAM(1957); PUBLIC PIGEON NO. 1(1957); GIGI(1958); WHO'S MINDING THE STORE?(1963); GREATEST STORY EVER TOLD, THE(1965); GAMBIT(1966); JUNGLE BOOK, THE(1967); THREE GUNS FOR TEXAS(1968); 2000 YEARS LATER(1969); BLACK BIRD, THE(1975)
1984
SLAPSTICK OF ANOTHER KIND(1984)
Misc. Talkies
TWO THOUSAND YEARS LATER(1969)

L. B. Abbott
ENEMY BELOW, THE(1957), spec eff; FORTY GUNS(1957), spec eff; KISS THEM FOR ME(1957), spec eff; NO DOWN PAYMENT(1957), spec eff; PEYTON PLACE(1957), spec eff; WAYWARD BUS, THE(1957), spec eff; WILL SUCCESS SPOIL ROCK HUNTER?(1957), spec eff; FIEND WHO WALKED THE WEST, THE(1958), spec eff; FRAULEIN(1958), spec eff; LONG, HOT SUMMER, THE(1958), spec eff; RALLY 'ROUND THE FLAG, BOYS!(1958), spec eff; ROOTS OF HEAVEN, THE(1958), spec eff; SOUTH PACIFIC(1958), spec eff; YOUNG LIONS, THE(1958), spec eff; 10 NORTH FREDERICK(1958), spec eff; DIARY OF ANNE FRANK, THE(1959), spec eff; HOLIDAY FOR LOVERS(1959), spec eff; JOURNEY TO THE CENTER OF THE EARTH(1959), spec eff; MAN WHO UNDERSTOOD WOMEN, THE(1959), spec eff; WARLOCK(1959), spec eff; WOMAN OBSESSED(1959), spec eff; FROM THE TERRACE(1960), spec eff; LOST WORLD, THE(1960), spec eff; NORTH TO ALASKA(1960), spec eff; WIZARD OF BAGHDAD, THE(1960), spec eff; SNOW WHITE AND THE THREE STOOGES(1961), spec eff; TENDER IS THE NIGHT(1961), spec eff; VOYAGE TO THE BOTTOM OF THE SEA(1961), spec eff; MR. HOBBS TAKES A VACATION(1962), spec eff; STATE FAIR(1962), spec eff; CLEOPATRA(1963), spec eff; MOVE OVER, DARLING(1963), spec eff; TAKE HER, SHE'S MINE(1963), spec eff; FATE IS THE HUNTER(1964), spec eff; GOODBYE CHARLIE(1964), spec eff; JOHN GOLDFARB, PLEASE COME HOME(1964), spec eff; SHOCK TREATMENT(1964), spec eff; WHAT A WAY TO GO(1964), spec eff; AGONY AND THE ECSTASY, THE(1965), spec eff; DEAR BRIGETTE(1965), spec eff; DO NOT DISTURB(1965), spec eff; FLIGHT OF THE PHOENIX, THE(1965), sp eff; MORITURI(1965), spec eff; REWARD, THE(1965), spec eff; SOUND OF MUSIC, THE(1965), spec eff; VON RYAN'S EXPRESS(1965), spec eff; FANTASTIC VOYAGE(1966), spec eff; OUR MAN FLINT(1966), spec eff; STAGECOACH(1966), spec eff; WAY...WAY OUT(1966), spec eff; DOCTOR DOLITTLE(1967), spec eff; FLIM-FLAM MAN, THE(1967), spec eff; GUIDE FOR THE MARRIED MAN, A(1967), spec eff; IN LIKE FLINT(1967), spec eff; ST. VALENTINE'S DAY MASSACRE, THE(1967), spec eff; VALLEY OF THE DOLLS(1967), spec eff; DETECTIVE, THE(1968), spec eff; LADY IN CEMENT(1968), spec eff; PLANET OF THE APES(1968), spec eff; SECRET LIFE OF AN AMERICAN WIFE, THE(1968), spec eff; STAR!(1968), spec eff; THE BOSTON STRANGLER, THE(1968), spec eff; BUTCH CASSIDY AND THE SUNDANCE KID(1969), spec eff; HARD CONTRACT(1969), spec eff; HELLO, DOLLY!(1969), spec eff; JOHN AND MARY(1969), spec eff; UNDEFEATED, THE(1969), spec eff; 100 RIFLES(1969), spec eff; M(1970), spec eff; MOVE(1970), spec eff; ONLY GAME IN TOWN, THE(1970), spec eff; PATTON(1970), spec eff; TORA! TORA! TORA!(1970, U.S./Jap.), spec eff; POSEIDON ADVENTURE, THE(1972), spec eff; TOWERING INFERNO, THE(1974), spec eff;

LOGAN'S RUN(1976), spec eff; VIVA KNIEVEL!(1977), spec eff; SWARM, THE(1978), spec eff; WHEN TIME RAN OUT(1980), spec eff

Lenwood Abbott
Silents
ROMANCE ROAD(1925), ph

Lyle B. Abbott
FLY, THE(1958), spec eff

Margaret Abbott
1984
LOVE STREAMS(1984)

Marion Abbott
Silents
TOL'ABLE DAVID(1921)

Mia Abbott
UNHOLY ROLLERS(1972)

Norman Abbott
KEEP 'EM SLUGGING(1943); WALKING MY BABY BACK HOME(1953); LAST OF THE SECRET AGENTS?, THE(1966), p&d, w

Pamela Abbott
MAROC 7(1967, Brit.); OH! WHAT A LOVELY WAR(1969, Brit.)

Philip Abbott
BACHELOR PARTY, THE(1957); INVISIBLE BOY, THE(1957); SPIRAL ROAD, THE(1962); SWEET BIRD OF YOUTH(1962); MIRACLE OF THE WHITE STALLIONS(1963); THOSE CALLOWAYS(1964); SAVANNAH SMILES(1983)

Phillip Abbott
HANGAR 18(1980)

Polly Abbott
1984
PLOUGHMAN'S LUNCH, THE(1984, Brit.)

Richard Abbott
FOUNTAIN, THE(1934); HAPPY LAND(1943); SCARLET STREET(1945); VALLEY OF DECISION, THE(1945); EXILE, THE(1947); HUCKSTERS, THE(1947); I'LL BE YOURS(1947); LAST ESCAPE, THE(1970, Brit.)

Ruth Abbott
ONE IS GUILTY(1934)

Sandra Abbott
ONE HUNDRED AND ONE DALMATIANS(1961)

Stephen Abbott
ESCAPADE(1955, Brit.)

Sylvia Abbott
COMIN' THRU' THE RYE(1947, Brit.)

Tom Abbott
FIDDLER ON THE ROOF(1971), ch

Tommy Abbott
WEST SIDE STORY(1961)

Vic Abbott
MACBETH(1971, Brit.)

W. J. Abbott
SCARED TO DEATH(1947), w

Walter Abbott
STOP THAT CAB(1951), w

William Abbott
SEA WOLF, THE(1930), ph

The Abbottiers
ROMAN SCANDALS(1933)

Mona Abboud
WEDDING, A(1978)

Giuseppe Abbrescia
SEVEN SEAS TO CALAIS(1963, Ital.)

Mario Abdah
WAY OF A GAUCHO(1952)

Abdallah
EAGLE WITH TWO HEADS(1948, Fr.)

Pepe Abded
FEMMINA(1968 Fr./Ital./Ger.)

Ahmed Abdelhalim
MOHAMMAD, MESSENGER OF GOD(1976, Lebanon/Brit.)

Tony Abdenour
PASSPORT TO SUEZ(1943)

Eddie Abdo
FOUR MEN AND A PRAYER(1938); RAINS CAME, THE(1939); KISMET(1944); LOST IN A HAREM(1944); TEMPTATION(1946); SINBAD THE SAILOR(1947); SLAVE GIRL(1947)

Ol Abdou
FREUD(1962)

Paula Abdul
PRIVATE SCHOOL(1983), ch

Abdul the Turk
Silents
ONE-ROUND HOGAN(1927)

Kareem Abdul-Jabbar
FISH THAT SAVED PITTSBURGH, THE(1979); GAME OF DEATH, THE(1979); AIRPLANE!(1980)
1984
FLETCH(1984)

Abdulla
I COVER THE WAR(1937)

Achmed Abdulla
Silents
CHANG(1927), t

Achmed Abdullah
HATCHET MAN, THE(1932), w; LIVES OF A BENGAL LANCER(1935), w

Eve Abdullah
KANGAROO(1952)

Joe Abdullah
MOMMIE DEAREST(1981)

Joseph Abdullah
MOLE PEOPLE, THE(1956); LEGION OF THE DOOMED(1958)

Mohammed Abdullah
AFRICA–TEXAS STYLE!(1967 U.S./Brit.)

Mohsen Ben Abdullah
PLAY DIRTY(1969, Brit.)

Sarah Abdullah
MATTER OF INNOCENCE, A(1968, Brit.)

Omar Abdulov
MILITARY SECRET(1945, USSR)

Vsevolod Abdulov
ARMED AND DANGEROUS(1977, USSR)

S. Abduzhalilov
MORNING STAR(1962, USSR)

Harry Abdy
ORPHAN OF THE WILDERNESS(1937, Aus.); WILD INNOCENCE(1937, Aus.); FORTY THOUSAND HORSEMEN(1941, Aus.)

Iya Abdy
NORAH O'NEALE(1934, Brit.)

Kazao Abe
IKIRU(1960, Jap.)

Kimei Abe
MOTHRA(1962, Jap.), art d

Kobo Abe
WOMAN IN THE DUNES(1964, Jap.), w; FACE OF ANOTHER, THE(1967, Jap.), w

Kusuo Abe
SAMURAI(1955, Jap.)

Naoyuki Abe
GAMERA VERSUS GAOS(1967, Jap.)

Toru Abe
HUMAN CONDITION, THE(1959, Jap.); MAN FROM THE EAST, THE(1961, Jap.); DUEL AT EZO(1970, Jap.); FRIENDLY KILLER, THE(1970, Jap.); HARBOR LIGHT YOKOHAMA(1970, Jap.); TOKYO STORY(1972, Jap.); BANISHED(1978, Jap.)

Yutaka Abe
Misc. Silents
WOMAN WHO TOUCHED THE LEGS, THE(1926, Jap.), d

Abe Lyman and Band
MADAME SATAN(1930)

Abe Lyman and His Band
GOOD NEWS(1930); PARDON MY GUN(1930); TEN CENTS A DANCE(1931), a, m

Abe Lyman Orchestra
JUNIOR PROM(1946)

Henri Abehsera
ROUND TRIP(1967)

Alan Abel
PUTNEY SWOPE(1969)
Misc. Talkies
IS THERE SEX AFTER DEATH(1971), a, d; FAKING OF THE PRESIDENT, THE(1976), d

Alfred Abel
DOLLY GETS AHEAD(1931, Ger.); BEAUTIFUL ADVENTURE(1932, Ger.); JOHNNY STEALS EUROPE(1932, Ger.); TRUNKS OF MR. O.F., THE(1932, Ger.); WHITE DEMON, THE(1932, Ger.); 1914(1932, Ger.); COURT CONCERT, THE(1936, Ger.)
Silents
METROPOLIS(1927, Ger.)
Misc. Silents
DR. MABUSE, THE GAMBLER(1922, Ger.); PHANTOM, THE(1922, Ger.); CAGLIOSTRO(1928, Fr.); MODERN DU BARRY, A(1928, Ger.), d; L'ARGENT(1929, Fr.); STRAUSS, THE WALTZ KING(1929, Ger.)

Allen Abel
NO MORE EXCUSES(1968)

Bob Abel
MAN FROM TORONTO, THE(1933, Brit.)

Dave Abel
SQUARE SHOULDERS(1929), ph; HER PRIVATE AFFAIR(1930), ph; SWING HIGH(1930), ph

David Abel
SHOW FOLKS(1928), ph; AWFUL TRUTH, THE(1929), ph; GERALDINE(1929), ph; RACKETEER, THE(1929), ph; GRAND PARADE, THE(1930), ph; GRUMPY(1930), ph; SANTA FE TRAIL, THE(1930), ph; VIRTUOUS SIN, THE(1930), ph; HUCKLEBERRY FINN(1931), ph; RICH MAN'S FOLLY(1931), ph; SCANDAL SHEET(1931), ph; SECRET CALL, THE(1931), ph; LADIES OF THE BIG HOUSE(1932), ph; MADAME BUTTERFLY(1932), ph; MERRILY WE GO TO HELL(1932), ph; MIRACLE MAN, THE(1932), ph; PHANTOM PRESIDENT, THE(1932), ph; SKY BRIDE(1932), ph; ANN VICKERS(1933), ph; CRIME OF THE CENTURY, THE(1933), ph; PICK-UP(1933), ph; BACHELOR BAIT(1934), ph; GAY DIVORCEE, THE(1934), ph; HIPS, HIPS, HOORAY(1934), ph; RAFTER ROMANCE(1934), ph; THIS MAN IS MINE(1934), ph; CASE OF THE CURIOUS BRIDE, THE(1935), ph; I DREAM TOO MUCH(1935), ph; NOTORIOUS GENTLEMAN, A(1935), ph; TOP HAT(1935), ph; BUNKER BEAN(1936), ph; FOLLOW THE FLEET(1936), ph; MAKE WAY FOR A LADY(1936), ph; SWING TIME(1936), ph; CRIMINAL LAWYER(1937), ph; SHALL WE DANCE(1937), w; HOLIDAY INN(1942), ph; FOLLOW THE BOYS(1944), ph; AFFAIRS OF SUSAN(1945), ph
Silents
HUN WITHIN, THE(1918), ph; ISLE OF CONQUEST(1919), ph; NEW MOON, THE(1919), ph; WAY OF A WOMAN(1919), ph; SHE LOVES AND LIES(1920), ph; COURAGE(1921), ph; RIP VAN WINKLE(1921), ph; GREAT NIGHT, THE(1922), ph; LITTLE MISS SMILES(1922), ph; MIXED FACES(1922), ph; BABBITT(1924), ph; BEAU BRUMMEL(1924), ph; LOST LADY, A(1924), ph; COMPROMISE(1925), ph; RECOMPENSE(1925), ph; ROSE OF THE WORLD(1925), ph; CAVEMAN, THE(1926), ph; HIS JAZZ BRIDE(1926), ph; WHAT EVERY GIRL SHOULD KNOW(1927), ph; CRAIG'S WIFE(1928), ph; MIDNIGHT MADNESS(1928), ph; STAND AND DELIVER(1928), ph; NED MCCOBB'S DAUGHTER(1929), ph

Frank Abel
THRILL OF A LIFETIME(1937)

Fritz Abel
Misc. Silents
GUARDSMAN, THE(1927, Aust.)

Jeanne Abel
Misc. Talkies
IS THERE SEX AFTER DEATH(1971), d; FAKING OF THE PRESIDENT, THE(1976), d

Jose Abel
  GULLIVER'S TRAVELS(1977, Brit., Bel.), anim
Michael Abel
  BLUEPRINT FOR MURDER, A(1953), p; SILVER WHIP, THE(1953), p
Randolph E. Abel
  LAST CROOKED MILE, THE(1946), p
Robert Abel
  GREENWOOD TREE, THE(1930, Brit.); UNDER THE GREENWOOD TREE(1930, Brit.); BREAKDOWN(1953), w; ROAR OF THE CROWD(1953), w; PRIME TIME, THE(1960), w
Rudolph E. Abel
  GIRL WHO DARED, THE(1944), p; STRANGERS IN THE NIGHT(1944), p; FATAL WITNESS, THE(1945), p; GIRLS OF THE BIG HOUSE(1945), p; SPORTING CHANCE, A(1945), p; VAMPIRE'S GHOST, THE(1945), p; UNDERCOVER WOMAN, THE(1946), p
Walter Abel
  LILIOM(1930); THREE MUSKETEERS, THE(1935); FURY(1936); LADY CONSENTS, THE(1936); SECOND WIFE(1936); TWO IN THE DARK(1936); WE WENT TO COLLEGE(1936); WITNESS CHAIR, THE(1936); GREEN LIGHT(1937); PORTIA ON TRIAL(1937); WISE GIRL(1937); LAW OF THE UNDERWORLD(1938); MEN WITH WINGS(1938); RACKET BUSTERS(1938); FIRST OFFENDERS(1939); KING OF THE TURF(1939); ARISE, MY LOVE(1940); DANCE, GIRL, DANCE(1940); MICHAEL SHAYNE, PRIVATE DETECTIVE(1940); MIRACLE ON MAIN STREET, A(1940); WHO KILLED AUNT MAGGIE?(1940); GLAMOUR BOY(1941); HOLD BACK THE DAWN(1941); SKYLARK(1941); BEYOND THE BLUE HORIZON(1942); HOLIDAY INN(1942); STAR SPANGLED RHYTHM(1942); WAKE ISLAND(1942); FIRED WIFE(1943); SO PROUDLY WE HAIL(1943); AMERICAN ROMANCE, AN(1944); AFFAIRS OF SUSAN(1945); DUFFY'S TAVERN(1945); KISS AND TELL(1945); KID FROM BOOKLYN, THE(1946); 13 RUE MADELEINE(1946); DREAM GIRL(1947); THAT LADY IN ERMINE(1948); ISLAND IN THE SKY(1953); SO THIS IS LOVE(1953); NIGHT PEOPLE(1954); INDIAN FIGHTER, THE(1955); STEEL JUNGLE, THE(1956); BERNARDINE(1957); RAINTREE COUNTY(1957); HANDLE WITH CARE(1958); MIRAGE(1965); QUICK, LET'S GET MARRIED(1965); SILENT NIGHT, BLOODY NIGHT(1974)
1984
  ULTIMATE SOLUTION OF GRACE QUIGLEY, THE(1984)
Misc. Talkies
  FABULOUS JOE, THE(1946)
Silents
  OUT OF A CLEAR SKY(1918)
Dave Abela
  NOISY NEIGHBORS(1929), ph
Emanuel Abela
  TRENCHCOAT(1983)
Joe Abela
  TRENCHCOAT(1983)
Richard Abelardo
  SURRENDER–HELL!(1959), art d
Edward Abeles
Silents
  BREWSTER'S MILLIONS(1914); READY MONEY(1914); AFTER FIVE(1915)
Misc. Silents
  MAKING OF BOBBY BURNIT, THE(1914); MILLION, THE(1915); LONE WOLF, THE(1917); OPPORTUNITY(1918)
Alan Abelew
  FIRST NUDIE MUSICAL, THE(1976)
S. Abelian
Misc. Silents
  NAMUS(1926, USSR)
Walter Abell
Silents
  NORTH WIND'S MALICE, THE(1920)
Amado Abello
  AMBUSH BAY(1966)
Peter Abenheim
  THIS IS NOT A TEST(1962), w
Angela Aber
  FRATERNITY ROW(1977)
Bestor Aber
  STRAIGHT FROM THE HEART(1935)
Chuck Aber
  CREEPSHOW(1982)
Nestor Aber
  HALF WAY TO HEAVEN(1929); PENROD AND SAM(1931); CHANDU THE MAGICIAN(1932)
J. Abercomie
  BREAK THE NEWS(1938, Brit.)
Jabee Abercrombe
Misc. Talkies
  FUGITIVE GIRLS(1975)
Ian Abercrombie
  YOUNG FRANKENSTEIN(1974); PRISONER OF ZENDA, THE(1979)
1984
  ICE PIRATES, THE(1984)
J. Abercrombie
  MUSEUM MYSTERY(1937, Brit.)
Sir Patrick Abercrombie
  WAY WE LIVE, THE(1946, Brit.)
Robert Aberdeen
  SATURDAY NIGHT AT THE BATHS(1975)
Keith Aberdein
  MIDDLE AGE SPREAD(1979, New Zealand), w; SMASH PALACE(1982, New Zealand)
1984
  UTU(1984, New Zealand), w; WILD HORSES(1984, New Zealand)
John Einar Aberg
  LOVE MATES(1967, Swed.), w

Lars Aberg
  VIBRATION(1969, Swed.), a, w
Lasse Aberg
  MONTENEGRO(1981, Brit./Swed.)
Myra Aberg
Silents
  AUTOCRAT, THE(1919, Brit.)
Siv Marta Aberg
  I'LL TAKE SWEDEN(1965)
Sivi Aberg
  DOCTOR DEATH: SEEKER OF SOULS(1973); TEACHER, THE(1974); SILENT MOVIE(1976)
Tom Abernathy
  SIX PACK(1982)
Luis Aberni
  WONDER MAN(1945)
Arline Abers
  PICK A STAR(1937)
Frank Aberschal
  TORN CURTAIN(1966)
Richard Abert
  DYNAMITE DELANEY(1938)
Lawrence J. Aberwood
  LIVING VENUS(1961); SOMETHING WEIRD(1967)
Antonio Abeyta
  SECOND-HAND HEARTS(1981)
Marie-Annick Abgrall
  PASSION(1983, Fr./Switz.)
Abou Saud Abiari
  LITTLE MISS DEVIL(1951, Egypt), w
Shirley Abicair
  ONE GOOD TURN(1955, Brit.)
Hans Abich
  SINS OF ROSE BERND, THE(1959, Ger.), p; DAY WILL COME, A(1960, Ger.), p
Paolo Abicocco
  ALLEGRO NON TROPPO(1977, Ital.), anim
Princess Aicha Abidir
  PIERROT LE FOU(1968, Fr./Ital.)
Abigail
  ALVIN RIDES AGAIN(1974, Aus.); TRUE STORY OF ESKIMO NELL, THE(1975, Aus.); ELIZA FRASER(1976, Aus.)
1984
  MELVIN, SON OF ALVIN(1984, Aus.)
Jytte Abildstrom
  ERIC SOYA'S "17"(1967, Den.)
Daniel Abineri
  INTERNATIONAL VELVET(1978, Brit.)
John Abineri
  DEAD MAN'S CHEST(1965, Brit.); MC KENZIE BREAK, THE(1970); DIAMONDS ARE FOREVER(1971, Brit.); OPERATION DAYBREAK(1976, U.S./Brit./Czech.)
W. L. Abingdon
Silents
  MANON LESCAUT(1914)
William L. Abingdon
Misc. Silents
  KISS OF HATE, THE(1916)
Nana Abiri
1984
  WHITE ELEPHANT(1984, Brit.)
Rafael Ablanque
  LAST DAY OF THE WAR, THE(1969, U.S./Ital./Span.), art d
Albert Able
  SHAGGY D.A., THE(1976)
Will B. Able
  NIGHT THEY RAIDED MINSKY'S, THE(1968)
N. Ablov
  LOSS OF FEELING(1935, USSR)
A. Ablova
  NIGHT BEFORE CHRISTMAS, A(1963, USSR)
Jean Abney
  ONLY WAY HOME, THE(1972)
William Abney
  NEVER TAKE CANDY FROM A STRANGER(1961, Brit.); TROUBLE IN THE SKY(1961, Brit.); TWO-WAY STRETCH(1961, Brit.); FLIGHT FROM SINGAPORE(1962, Brit.); WE SHALL SEE(1964, Brit.); ON THE RUN(1967, Brit.); HITLER: THE LAST TEN DAYS(1973, Brit./Ital.); LEGACY, THE(1979, Brit.); FFOLKES(1980, Brit.); CURSE OF THE PINK PANTHER(1983)
Klevor Abo
1984
  WHITE ELEPHANT(1984, Brit.)
Noerena Abookire
1984
  TEACHERS(1984)
Aborigines of the Pitjantara Tribe
  JEDDA, THE UNCIVILIZED(1956, Aus.)
Emile Abossolo
1984
  GREYSTOKE: THE LEGEND OF TARZAN, LORD OF THE APES(1984)
Charles Abou
  SAVAGE WILD, THE(1970)
Colin Abraham
  WILD GEESE, THE(1978, Brit.)
David Abraham
  JUNGLE, THE(1952); NINE HOURS TO RAMA(1963, U.S./Brit.)
Dawn Abraham
1984
  MIKE'S MURDER(1984)

Edward Abraham
TRUNK, THE(1961, Brit.), d&w; SERENA(1962, Brit.), w; DOMINIQUE(1978, Brit.), w; MONSTER CLUB, THE(1981, Brit.), w

F. Murray Abraham
THEY MIGHT BE GIANTS(1971); SERPICO(1973); SUNSHINE BOYS, THE(1975); ALL THE PRESIDENT'S MEN(1976); RITZ, THE(1976); BIG FIX, THE(1978); SCARFACE(1983)
1984
AMADEUS(1984)

J. Johnson Abraham
NORAH O'NEALE(1934, Brit.), w

Jack Abraham
Misc. Silents
GENTLEMAN'S AGREEMENT, A(1918)

Jake Abraham
Silents
BY THE WORLD FORGOT(1918)
Misc. Silents
GIRL IN HIS HOUSE, THE(1918)

John Abraham
Silents
PUPPET CROWN, THE(1915)

Josef Abraham
OPERATION DAYBREAK(1976, U.S./Brit./Czech.)

Nik Abraham
FLASH GORDON(1980)

Paul Abraham
OFFICE GIRL, THE(1932, Brit.), m; BALL AT SAVOY(1936, Brit.), m; AFFAIRS OF MAUPASSANT(1938, Aust.), m

Valerie Abraham
TRUNK, THE(1961, Brit.), d&w; SERENA(1962, Brit.), w; DOMINIQUE(1978, Brit.), w; MONSTER CLUB, THE(1981, Brit.), w

Zaky Abraham
LITTLE MISS DEVIL(1951, Egypt)

Derwin Abrahams
BORDER VIGILANTES(1941), d; SECRETS OF THE WASTELANDS(1941), d; NORTHWEST TRAIL(1945), d; COWBOY CAVALIER(1948), d; DOCKS OF NEW ORLEANS(1948), d; RANGERS RIDE, THE(1948), d; MISSISSIPPI RHYTHM(1949), d; GIRL FROM SAN LORENZO, THE(1950), d; WHISTLING HILLS(1951), d
Misc. Talkies
BOTH BARRELS BLAZING(1945), d; RETURN OF THE DURANGO KID(1945), d; ROUGH RIDIN' JUSTICE(1945), d; RUSTLERS OF THE BADLANDS(1945), d; FIGHTING FRONTIERSMAN, THE(1946), d; FRONTIER GUNLAW(1946), d; HAUNTED MINE, THE(1946), d; PRAIRIE RAIDERS(1947), d; RIDERS OF THE LONE STAR(1947), d; SMOKY RIVER SERENADE(1947), d; SOUTH OF THE CHISHOLM TRAIL(1947), d; STRANGER FROM PONCA CITY, THE(1947), d; SWING THE WESTERN WAY(1947), d

Derwin M. Abrahams
DRIFTING ALONG(1946), d

Jim Abrahams
KENTUCKY FRIED MOVIE, THE(1977), a, w; AIRPLANE!(1980), d&w
1984
TOP SECRET!(1984), d, w

Mort Abrahams
CHAIRMAN, THE(1969), p

Nancy Abrahams
1984
TOP SECRET!(1984)

Arne Abrahamsen
GERTRUD(1966, Den.), ph; OPERATION LOVEBIRDS(1968, Den.), ph; VENOM(1968, Den.), ph

Eric Abrahamson
COUNT OF THE MONK'S BRIDGE, THE(1934, Swed.)

S. Abramouitch-Bleck
HEROES OF THE SEA(1941), w

N. Abramov
LAST GAME, THE(1964, USSR)

Natasha Abramova
STALKER(1982, USSR)

Bina Abramowitz
Silents
BROKEN HEARTS(1926)

Barry Abrams
HERE COME THE TIGERS(1978), ph; CHILDREN, THE(1980), ph; FRIDAY THE 13TH(1980), ph; STRANGER IS WATCHING, A(1982), ph

Ed Abrams
DOUBLE NICKELS(1977)

Edward R. Abrams
Misc. Silents
GUNSAULUS MYSTERY, THE(1921); SPORT OF THE GODS, THE(1921)

Jacob Abrams
Silents
OUTSIDE WOMAN, THE(1921); PAWN TICKET 210(1922)

Jeffrey Abrams
NIGHTBEAST(1982), m

Jessie Abrams
CHILDREN, THE(1980)

Leon Abrams
HIGHWAY WEST(1941), w; MISSING JUROR, THE(1944), w; MUMMY'S CURSE, THE(1944), w; SUNSET IN EL DORADO(1945), w
Silents
ADVENTURER, THE(1928), w

Margaret Abrams
UNCLE, THE(1966, Brit.), w

Martin Abrams
LADY LIBERTY(1972, Ital./Fr.)

Michael Abrams
SUMMER CAMP(1979)

Richard Abrams
I WALKED WITH A ZOMBIE(1943); MEDIUM COOL(1969)

Rita Abrams
AT LONG LAST LOVE(1975), ch; NICKELODEON(1976)

Robert Abrams
CRIME AND PASSION(1976, U.S., Ger.)

Robert L. Abrams
CRIME AND PASSION(1976, U.S., Ger.), p

Steve Abrams
SLAP SHOT(1977), makeup

Bernie Abramson
BAKER'S HAWK(1976), ph; PONY EXPRESS RIDER(1976), ph

Ivan Abramson
ENLIGHTEN THY DAUGHTER(1934), w
Silents
SHOULD A WOMAN DIVORCE?(1914), d; ONE LAW FOR BOTH(1917), d&w; CHILD FOR SALE, A(1920), d&w
Misc. Silents
CONCEALED TRUTH, THE(1915), d; UNWELCOME WIFE, THE(1915), d; CITY OF ILLUSION, THE(1916), d; FADED FLOWER, THE(1916), d; FORBIDDEN FRUIT(1916), d; HERE SURRENDER(1916), d; IMMORTAL FLAME, THE(1916), d; SEX LURE, THE(1916), d; ENLIGHTEN THY DAUGHTER(1917), d; MORAL SUICIDE(1918), d; ECHO OF YOUTH, THE(1919), d; SOMEONE MUST PAY(1919), d; WRONG WOMAN, THE(1920), d; BRIDE'S CONFESSION, THE(1921), d; MOTHER ETERNAL(1921), d; WILDNESS OF YOUTH(1922), d; I AM THE MAN(1924), d; MEDDLING WOMEN(1924), d; LYING WIVES(1925), d

Max Abramson
Silents
MY BOY(1922), t; TROUBLE(1922), t; IS YOUR DAUGHTER SAFE?(1927), w

Phil Abramson
LE MANS(1971), prod d; DROWNING POOL, THE(1975), set d; EMBRYO(1976), set d; CLOSE ENCOUNTERS OF THE THIRD KIND(1977), set d; RAGING BULL(1980), set d; SHARKY'S MACHINE(1982), set d

Philip Abramson
FINIAN'S RAINBOW(1968), set d; REIVERS, THE(1969), set d; MONTE WALSH(1970), set d; SPORTING CLUB, THE(1971), set d; FUZZ(1972), set d; SEPARATE PEACE, A(1972), set d; THEY ONLY KILL THEIR MASTERS(1972), set d; ASH WEDNESDAY(1973), art d; OTHER SIDE OF THE MOUNTAIN, THE(1975), set d; JAWS II(1978), set d; JAWS 3-D(1983), cons
1984
HARD TO HOLD(1984), set d

Phillip Abramson
REFLECTION OF FEAR, A(1973), set d; LEGEND OF THE LONE RANGER, THE(1981), set d

Richard C. Abramson
LAST WORD, THE(1979), p

Raymond Abrashkin
SON OF FLUBBER(1963), w

Sarah Abrell
1984
LONELY GUY, THE(1984)

Ronaldo Abrev
LUMIERE(1976, Fr.), makeup

Josef Abrham
TRANSPORT FROM PARADISE(1967, Czech.); HAPPY END(1968, Czech.); NIGHTS OF PRAGUE, THE(1968, Czech.)

Andrei Abrikosov
IVAN THE TERRIBLE(Part I, 1947, USSR); SWORD AND THE DRAGON, THE(1960, USSR)

M. Abrikosov
COSSACKS OF THE DON(1932, USSR)

A.L. Abrikossov
ALEXANDER NEVSKY(1939)

A. Garcia Abril
HORROR OF THE ZOMBIES(1974, Span.), m

Anton Garcia Abril
SAVAGE GUNS, THE(1962, U.S./Span.), m; ISLAND OF THE DOOMED(1968, Span./Ger.), m; MISSION STARDUST(1968, Ital./Span./Ger.), m; WEREWOLF VS. THE VAMPIRE WOMAN, THE(1970, Span./Ger.), m
1984
HOLY INNOCENTS, THE(1984, Span.), m

Dorothea Abril
Misc. Silents
HOSTAGE, THE(1917)

Dorothy Abril
Silents
ALIEN SOULS(1916); THOSE WITHOUT SIN(1917)
Misc. Silents
ROGUE AND RICHES(1920)

Jose Antonio Abril
COBRA, THE(1968), m

Victoria Abril
COMIN' AT YA!(1981); MOON IN THE GUTTER, THE(1983, Fr./Ital.)
1984
ON THE LINE(1984, Span.)

Holger Abro
WALK, DON'T RUN(1966)

Werner Abrolat
FOR A FEW DOLLARS MORE(1967, Ital./Ger./Span.); FOUNTAIN OF LOVE, THE(1968, Aust.)

Edward Abroms
BLUE THUNDER(1983), ed; OSTERMAN WEEKEND, THE(1983), ed

Edward M. Abroms
TARZAN'S DEADLY SILENCE(1970), ed; GROUNDSTAR CONSPIRACY, THE(1972, Can.), ed; YOU'LL LIKE MY MOTHER(1972), ed; SUGARLAND EXPRESS, THE(1974), ed

Dr. William Abruzzi
BELIEVE IN ME(1971)

A. Absolon
SEVEN BRAVE MEN(1936, USSR)
Ab Abspoel
LIFT, THE(1983, Neth.)
Albert Abspoel
SPETTERS(1983, Holland)
Tengiz Abuladze
STEPCHILDREN(1962, USSR), d, w
Elsa Abutal
IGOROTA, THE LEGEND OF THE TREE OF LIFE(1970, Phil.), ed
Mario Abutelli
MAN FROM CAIRO, THE(1953), ph
Earl Aby
HEARTS IN BONDAGE(1936)
Bella Abzug
MANHATTAN(1979)
Robert Acacio
VIOLENT AND THE DAMNED, THE(1962, Braz.), p
Franco Acampora
DEAD OF SUMMER(1970 Ital./Fr.); AVANTI!(1972)
Acappella Singers
ONE-TRICK PONY(1980)
Felix Acaso
REDEEMER, THE(1965, Span.)
Paul Acciari
NEXT ONE, THE(1982, U.S./Gr.), prod d
Miguel Accion
SURRENDER-HELL!(1959), ph
Mike Accion
CRY FREEDOM(1961, Phil.), ph; FLIGHT TO FURY(1966, U.S./Phil.), ph; CURSE OF
THE VAMPIRES(1970, Phil., U.S.), ph
Vitto Acconci
JOURNEYS FROM BERLIN-1971(1980)
Art Accord
Misc. Silents
RIDIN' RASCAL, THE(1926); WESTERN PLUCK(1926); SET FREE(1927)
Claude Accursi
GUTS IN THE SUN(1959, Fr.), w; WHERE THE TRUTH LIES(1962, Fr.), w; POST-
MAN GOES TO WAR, THE(1968, Fr.), w; CHECKERBOARD(1969, Fr.), w
Ace
ORPHANS OF THE STREET(1939); GIRL FROM GOD'S COUNTRY(1940); MON-
STER MAKER, THE(1944); ADVENTURES OF RUSTY(1945)
Goodman Ace
I MARRIED A WOMAN(1958), w
Rosemary Ace
GIRL IN THE RED VELVET SWING, THE(1955)
Ace the Dog
PRIDE OF THE ARMY(1942); DANNY BOY(1946); GOD'S COUNTRY(1946)
Ace the Wonder Dog
BLIND ALIBI(1938); ALMOST A GENTLEMAN(1939); ROOKIE COP, THE(1939)
The Ace Trucking Company
PETULIA(1968, U.S./Brit.); HARRAD EXPERIMENT, THE(1973)
Del Acerdo
OREGON TRAIL, THE(1959), makeup
Ricardo Acero
MAD QUEEN, THE(1950, Span.)
Carlos Acevedo
ALEXANDER THE GREAT(1956)
Del Acevedo
LOVE HAS MANY FACES(1965), makeup; NEVADA SMITH(1966), makeup; SAND
PEBBLES, THE(1966), makeup; PATTON(1970), makeup; LAST RUN, THE(1971),
makeup; SEVEN MINUTES, THE(1971), makeup; VANISHING POINT(1971), make-
up; NEW CENTURIONS, THE(1972), makeup; POSEIDON ADVENTURE, THE(1972),
makeup; RAGE(1972), makeup; SLEEPER(1973), makeup; ISLANDS IN THE
STREAM(1977), makeup; DEER HUNTER, THE(1978), makeup
John Acevedo
WHERE THE BUFFALO ROAM(1980)
Manuel Acevedo
DOLORES(1949, Span.), w
Miriam Acevedo
MAN OF LA MANCHA(1972)
Harold Aceves
MORE AMERICAN GRAFFITI(1979)
Robert Acey
1984
ANGEL(1984)
Said Achaibou
OLIVE TREES OF JUSTICE, THE(1967, Fr.)
Marcel Achard
ALIBI, THE(1939, Fr.), w; HEART OF PARIS(1939, Fr.), w; ALIBI, THE(1943,
Brit.), w; HEART OF A NATION, THE(1943, Fr.), w; THREE HOURS(1944, Fr.), w;
MEET ME AT DAWN(1947, Brit.), w; FEMALE, THE(1960, Fr.), w; SHOT IN THE
DARK, A(1964), w; FRIEND OF THE FAMILY(1965, Fr./Ital.), w
Oliver Achard
1984
CHEECH AND CHONG'S THE CORSICAN BROTHERS(1984)
Army Acherd
TEACHER'S PET(1958)
Jim Acheson
SIR HENRY AT RAWLINSON END(1980, Brit.), art d; MONTY PYTHON'S THE
MEANING OF LIFE(1983, Brit.), cos
John Acheson
YOU CAN'T WIN 'EM ALL(1970, Brit.)
Kamaunani Achi
WHITE HEAT(1934)
Freddy Achiang
WILBY CONSPIRACY, THE(1975, Brit.)

Peter Achilles
ALL NIGHT LONG(1961, Brit.), w
James Achley
1984
BLACK ROOM, THE(1984), m
Werner Achmann
TOWN WITHOUT PITY(1961, Ger./Switz./U.S.), set d; FAUST(1963, Ger.), art d;
BLOOD DEMON(1967, Ger.), art d; SERPENT'S EGG, THE(1977, Ger./U.S.), art d;
TWILIGHT'S LAST GLEAMING(1977, U.S./Ger.), art d; WHO IS KILLING THE
GREAT CHEFS OF EUROPE?(1978, US/Ger.), art d; AMERICAN SUCCESS COMPA-
NY, THE(1980), art d; PARSIFAL(1983, Fr.), set d
M. Torres Acho
MANHUNT IN THE JUNGLE(1958)
Members of the Acholi Tribes
SANDERS OF THE RIVER(1935, Brit.)
John Achorn
1984
BEVERLY HILLS COP(1984); NIGHT OF THE COMET(1984)
Monica Achterberg
LITTLE ARK, THE(1972)
Herbert Achternbusch
YOUNG MONK, THE(1978, Ger.), a, p,d&w
Arnie Achtman
HEARTACHES(1981, Can.)
1984
COVERGIRL(1984, Can.)
Eugene Acker
Silents
MY FOUR YEARS IN GERMANY(1918); MAN WORTH WHILE, THE(1921)
Misc. Silents
SYLVIA ON A SPREE(1918); TRAIL OF THE CIGARETTE, THE(1920); CHARMING
DECEIVER, THE(1921); BLOW YOUR OWN HORN(1923)
Jean Acker
NO MORE LADIES(1935); HIS BROTHER'S WIFE(1936); SAN FRANCISCO(1936);
VOGUES OF 1938(1937); GOOD GIRLS GO TO PARIS(1939); MY FAVORITE WI-
FE(1940); OBLIGING YOUNG LADY(1941); THIN MAN GOES HOME, THE(1944);
MASQUERADE IN MEXICO(1945); SPELLBOUND(1945); MATING SEASON,
THE(1951)
Silents
$5,000,000 COUNTERFEITING PLOT, THE(1914); ARE YOU A MASON?(1915);
NEVER SAY QUIT(1919); ABABIAN KNIGHT, AN(1920); HELP WANTED-MA-
LE!(1920); ROUND UP, THE(1920); BREWSTER'S MILLIONS(1921); WEALTH(1921);
NEST, THE(1927)
Misc. Silents
BLUE BANDANNA, THE(1919); CHECKERS(1919); LOMBARDI, LTD.(1919); LAD-
DER OF LIES, THE(1920); SEE MY LAWYER(1921)
Joan Acker
REMEMBER THE NIGHT(1940)
Kathy Acker
1984
VARIETY(1984), w
Martha Acker
SERENADE(1956)
Norman Acker
Misc. Silents
HATE(1917)
Sharon Acker
LUCKY JIM(1957, Brit.); ONE PLUS ONE(1961, Can.); POINT BLANK(1967); DON'T
LET THE ANGELS FALL(1969, Can.); FIRST TIME, THE(1969); WAITING FOR
CAROLINE(1969, Can.); ACT OF THE HEART(1970, Can.); HAPPY BIRTHDAY TO
ME(1981); THRESHOLD(1983, Can.)
Bill Ackeridge
NORTHERN LIGHTS(1978)
Bettye Ackerman
FACE OF FIRE(1959, U.S./Brit.); RASCAL(1969)
Boyd Ackerman
UP IN CENTRAL PARK(1948); SHOW BOAT(1951)
Dave Ackerman
RAVAGER, THE(1970), p; THREE-WAY SPLIT(1970), p
Forrest J. Ackerman
TIME TRAVELERS, THE(1964); QUEEN OF BLOOD(1966); MAD MONSTER
PARTY(1967), w; SCHLOCK(1973); SCALPS(1983)
Hal Ackerman
SECOND WIND(1976, Can.), w
Hildegard Ackerman
KILLER AT LARGE(1947)
Homer Ackerman
GAMBLING SEX(1932), ed
J. Forrest Ackerman
BLOOD OF FRANKENSTEIN(1970)
Jack Ackerman
SHADOWS(1960); FACES(1968), m, md; HUSBANDS(1970), md; MACHINE GUN
McCAIN(1970, Ital.); LEPKE(1975, U.S./Israel); KILLING OF A CHINESE BOOKIE,
THE(1976)
James Ackerman
WARGAMES(1983)
Jean Ackerman
GIRL HABIT(1931)
Leonard J. Ackerman
AL CAPONE(1959), p; EVERY LITTLE CROOK AND NANNY(1972), p
Leslie Ackerman
LAW AND DISORDER(1974); FIRST NUDIE MUSICAL, THE(1976); CRACKING
UP(1977); HARDCORE(1979)
1984
BLAME IT ON THE NIGHT(1984)
Misc. Talkies
JOY RIDE TO NOWHERE(1978); BABY DOLLS(1982)

THEY WON'T FORGET(1937); WHAT PRICE VENGEANCE?(1937); CHASER, THE(1938); FOUR DAUGHTERS(1938); HIS EXCITING NIGHT(1938); INVISIBLE MENACE, THE(1938); KING OF ALCATRAZ(1938); LADIES IN DISTRESS(1938); LAW OF THE UNDERWORLD(1938); RHYTHM OF THE SADDLE(1938); YOUNG FUGITIVES(1938); COWBOY QUARTERBACK(1939); DAYS OF JESSE JAMES(1939); ESPIONAGE AGENT(1939); HERO FOR A DAY(1939); MEET DR. CHRISTIAN(1939); MIRACLES FOR SALE(1939); MYSTERIOUS MISS X, THE(1939); ROUGH RIDERS' ROUNDUP(1939); SOCIETY SMUGGLERS(1939); TOO BUSY TO WORK(1939); TWO BRIGHT BOYS(1939); WHEN TOMORROW COMES(1939); BANK DICK, THE(1940); CAFE HOSTESS(1940); CHARLIE CHAN IN PANAMA(1940); DR. KILDARE'S CRISIS(1940); FIGHTING 69TH, THE(1940); IT'S A DATE(1940); MA, HE'S MAKING EYES AT ME(1940); ONE NIGHT IN THE TROPICS(1940); SAILOR'S LADY(1940); SHOOTING HIGH(1940); TEXAS RANGERS RIDE AGAIN(1940); THEY DRIVE BY NIGHT(1940); BLONDIE GOES LATIN(1941); DR. KILDARE'S VICTORY(1941); DR. KILDARE'S WEDDING DAY(1941); GREAT AMERICAN BROADCAST, THE(1941); HELLZAPOPPIN(1941); HERE COMES HAPPINESS(1941); HIGH SIERRA(1941); PEOPLE VS. DR. KILDARE, THE(1941); RAGS TO RICHES(1941); ROBIN HOOD OF THE PECOS(1941); SIX LESSONS FROM MADAME LA ZONGA(1941); WAGONS ROLL AT NIGHT, THE(1941); BELLS OF CAPISTRANO(1942); CALLING DR. GILLESPIE(1942); DR. GILLESPIE'S NEW ASSISTANT(1942); GIRL TROUBLE(1942); IN THIS OUR LIFE(1942); LADY IS WILLING, THE(1942); PARDON MY SARONG(1942); SLEEPYTIME GAL(1942); TAKE A LETTER, DARLING(1942); THEY DIED WITH THEIR BOOTS ON(1942); TRAITOR WITHIN, THE(1942); TRUE TO THE ARMY(1942); YANKEE DOODLE DANDY(1942); FLESH AND FANTASY(1943); GOOD MORNING, JUDGE(1943); GUADALCANAL DIARY(1943); HE HIRED THE BOSS(1943); HEADIN' FOR GOD'S COUNTRY(1943); HERS TO HOLD(1943); PILOT NO. 5(1943); SLIGHTLY DANGEROUS(1943); YOUTH ON PARADE(1943); CAROLINA BLUES(1944); FOUR JILLS IN A JEEP(1944); HAT CHECK HONEY(1944); IN THE MEANTIME, DARLING(1944); IRISH EYES ARE SMILING(1944); IT HAPPENED TOMORROW(1944); ONCE UPON A TIME(1944); RAINBOW ISLAND(1944); SEE HERE, PRIVATE HARGROVE(1944); SOMETHING FOR THE BOYS(1944); SOUTH OF DIXIE(1944); WEEKEND PASS(1944); WING AND A PRAYER(1944); DIAMOND HORSESHOE(1945); DON JUAN QUILLIGAN(1945); HER LUCKY NIGHT(1945); HIDDEN EYE, THE(1945); HONEYMOON AHEAD(1945); JUNGLE CAPTIVE(1945); LADY ON A TRAIN(1945); LEAVE IT TO BLONDIE(1945); ON STAGE EVERYBODY(1945); SAN ANTONIO(1945); SERGEANT MIKE(1945); SHADOW OF TERROR(1945); SHE GETS HER MAN(1945); WITHOUT LOVE(1945); WONDER MAN(1945); BAD BASCOMB(1946); DANGER WOMAN(1946); FLYING SERPENT, THE(1946); HELLDORADO(1946); LIFE WITH BLONDIE(1946); NOTORIOUS LONE WOLF, THE(1946); THREE LITTLE GIRLS IN BLUE(1946); WAKE UP AND DREAM(1946); BANDITS OF DARK CANYON(1947); BELLS OF SAN ANGELO(1947); BLONDIE IN THE DOUGH(1947); BLONDIE'S ANNIVERSARY(1947); BLONDIE'S BIG MOMENT(1947); BLONDIE'S HOLIDAY(1947); CARTER CASE, THE(1947); DOWN TO EARTH(1947); LADY IN THE LAKE(1947); SEA OF GRASS, THE(1947); SECRET LIFE OF WALTER MITTY, THE(1947); SUDDENLY IT'S SPRING(1947); WYOMING(1947); BLONDIE'S REWARD(1948); BLONDIE'S SECRET(1948); BUNGALOW 13(1948); LEATHER GLOVES(1948); SLIPPY MCGEE(1948); SONG OF IDAHO(1948); TIMBER TRAIL, THE(1948); BLONDIE'S BIG DEAL(1949); JOHNNY ALLEGRO(1949); MISS GRANT TAKES RICHMOND(1949); SMOKY MOUNTAIN MELODY(1949); MILKMAN, THE(1950); PAINTING THE CLOUDS WITH SUNSHINE(1951)

Edward Acuff
LAUGHING AT TROUBLE(1937)
Misc. Talkies
BEHIND PRISON BARS(1937)
Edward "Eddie" Acuff
OUTER GATE, THE(1937); SMASHING THE RACKETS(1938)
Roy Acuff
HI, NEIGHBOR(1942); O, MY DARLING CLEMENTINE(1943); NIGHT TRAIN TO MEMPHIS(1946); SMOKY MOUNTAIN MELODY(1949)
Misc. Talkies
HOME IN SAN ANTONE(1949)
O. Acursio
MAN COULD GET KILLED, A(1966)
Ann Aczel
SET, THE(1970, Aus.)
Ada-May [Weeks]
MONSIEUR VERDOUX(1947)
Masao Adachi
DIARY OF A SHINJUKU BURGLAR(1969, Jap.), w
Alan Adair
LOOK BEFORE YOU LOVE(1948, Brit.); WEEKEND AT DUNKIRK(1966, Fr./Ital.); JE T'AIME, JE T'AIME(1972, Fr./Swed.)
Alice Adair
WILD PARTY, THE(1929); SATURDAY NIGHT KID, THE(1929); FAREWELL TO ARMS, A(1932); NIGHT WORLD(1932); PICK-UP(1933)
Silents
NONE BUT THE BRAVE(1928)
Belle Adair
Silents
MOTHER(1914)
Dick Adair
Misc. Talkies
BLIND RAGE(1978)
Frank Adair
Silents
ARTISTIC TEMPERAMENT, THE(1919, Brit.); FLAG LIEUTENANT, THE(1919, Brit.)
Hazel Adair
MY BROTHER JONATHAN(1949, Brit.); LIFE IN EMERGENCY WARD 10(1959, Brit.), w; GET ON WITH IT(1963, Brit.), w; GAME FOR VULTURES, A(1980, Brit.), p
Jack Adair
LADY IN SCARLET, THE(1935); MANHATTAN MERRY-GO-ROUND(1937); WE'RE ON THE JURY(1937); 52ND STREET(1937); STRANGE CARGO(1940)
Misc. Talkies
DRAGNET, THE(1936)
Jan Adair
CLOCKWORK ORANGE, A(1971, Brit.)

Jane Adair
Silents
GIRL'S FOLLY, A(1917)
Janice Adair
ALF'S CARPET(1929, Brit.); INFORMER, THE(1929, Brit.); TO WHAT RED HELL(1929, Brit.); SUCH IS THE LAW(1930, Brit.); CONTRABAND LOVE(1931, Brit.); DEADLOCK(1931, Brit.); LUCKY LADIES(1932, Brit.); THIS ACTING BUSINESS(1933, Brit.); NINE FORTY-FIVE(1934, Brit.); FLOOD TIDE(1935, Brit.)
Misc. Silents
RED ACES(1929, Brit.)
Jean Adair
ADVICE TO THE LOVELORN(1933); ARSENIC AND OLD LACE(1944); LIVING IN A BIG WAY(1947); SOMETHING IN THE WIND(1947); NAKED CITY, THE(1948)
Joe Adair
SOMEONE(1968); DRIFTER(1975)
John Adair
RAMPARTS WE WATCH, THE(1940)
Josephine Adair
Silents
ONLY A SHOP GIRL(1922); THIRD ALARM, THE(1922); MAILMAN, THE(1923)
Misc. Silents
IN THE NAME OF THE LAW(1922)
Maryon Adair
UP IN ARMS(1944)
Molly Adair
Silents
PUPPET MAN, THE(1921, Brit.); MARRIED TO A MORMAN(1922, Brit.)
Misc. Silents
STELLA(1921); SINISTER STREET(1922, Brit.)
Phyllis Adair
WILD HORSE VALLEY(1940); BILLY THE KID'S FIGHTING PALS(1941); LAND OF HUNTED MEN(1943); GOD IS MY CO-PILOT(1945); RIDERS OF THE DAWN(1945); GLASS ALIBI, THE(1946)
"Red" Adair
HELLFIGHTERS(1968), tech adv
Robert Adair
JOURNEY'S END(1930); KING OF THE JUNGLE(1933); KISS BEFORE THE MIRROR, THE(1933); STUDENT TOUR(1934); TREASURE ISLAND(1934); WHERE SINNERS MEET(1934); CRUSADES, THE(1935); FARMER TAKES A WIFE, THE(1935); FATHER BROWN, DETECTIVE(1935); GIRL WHO CAME BACK, THE(1935); LAST OUTPOST, THE(1935); BRILLIANT MARRIAGE(1936); CALL IT A DAY(1937); EMPTY SADDLES(1937); PRINCE AND THE PAUPER, THE(1937); TICKET OF LEAVE MAN, THE(1937, Brit.); WHAT A MAN!(1937, Brit.); FACE AT THE WINDOW, THE(1939, Brit.); JAMAICA INN(1939, Brit.); ME AND MY PAL(1939, Brit.); WHO IS GUILTY?(1940, Brit.); MAN ON THE RUN(1949, Brit.); SILK NOOSE, THE(1950, Brit.); MADAME LOUISE(1951, Brit.); PORTRAIT OF CLARE(1951, Brit.); GAMBLER AND THE LADY, THE(1952, Brit.); SCOTLAND YARD INSPECTOR(1952, Brit.); CAPTAIN'S PARADISE, THE(1953, Brit.); NORMAN CONQUEST(1953, Brit.); THERE WAS A YOUNG LADY(1953, Brit.); EIGHT O'CLOCK WALK(1954, Brit.); MEET MR. CALLAGHAN(1954, Brit.); INTRUDER, THE(1955, Brit.)
Robert "Bob" Adair
SYLVIA SCARLETT(1936)
Robin Adair
LIBELED LADY(1936); WHIPSAW(1936)
Robyn Adair
Silents
GIRL FROM HIS TOWN, THE(1915)
Misc. Silents
BOOTS AND SADDLES(1916); YELLOW BULLET, THE(1917)
Ronald Adair
Silents
GIRL WHO TOOK THE WRONG TURNING, THE(1915, Brit.)
Sugar Adair
WORDS AND MUSIC(1929)
Tim Adair
CANARY MURDER CASE, THE(1929)
Tom Adair
JULIE(1956), m
Virginia Adair
Silents
WESTERN FIREBRANDS(1921); SECOND HAND ROSE(1922); TILLIE(1922)
Y. Adaki
MY FATHER'S HOUSE(1947, Palestine)
Max Adalbert
CAPTAIN FROM KOEPENICK(1933, Ger.)
Ricardo Adalid
TOAST TO LOVE(1951, Mex.); SIERRA BARON(1958); SLAUGHTER(1972)
Jack Adalist
LIQUID SKY(1982)
Adam
NIGHT AND DAY(1946); CHILD IS A WILD THING, A(1976)
Alfred Adam
CARNIVAL IN FLANDERS(1936, Fr.); LA FERME DU PENDU(1946, Fr.); ANGEL AND SINNER(1947, Fr.); ROYAL AFFAIR, A(1950); SYLVIA AND THE PHANTOM(1950, Fr.), w; CADET-ROUSSELLE(1954, Fr.); LA BELLE AMERICAINE(1961, Fr.), a, w; LOVE AND THE FRENCHWOMAN(1961, Fr.); MOST WANTED MAN, THE(1962, Fr./Ital.); STRANGER, THE(1967, Algeria/Fr./Ital.); LET JOY REIGN SUPREME(1977, Fr.)
Camile Adam
TAKE IT ALL(1966, Can.), ed
Carl Adam
TWO GENTLEMEN SHARING(1969, Brit.)
Dorothee Adam
LOVE AT FIRST SIGHT(1930)
Gabriele Adam
SHADOWS GROW LONGER, THE(1962, Switz./Ger.)
Gordon Adam
ROCKETS IN THE DUNES(1960, Brit.)

Graham Adam
IT HAPPENED HERE(1966, Brit.)

Jan Adam
MIDSUMMERS NIGHT'S DREAM, A(1961, Czech), anim

Jason Adam
1984
NIGHTMARE ON ELM STREET, A(1984)

Jean-Francois Adam
CLEO FROM 5 TO 7(1961, Fr.), prod d; LOVE AT TWENTY(1963, Fr./Ital./Jap./Pol./Ger.); STOLEN KISSES(1969, Fr.)

Ken Adam
SPIN A DARK WEB(1956, Brit.), art d; CURSE OF THE DEMON(1958), set d; GIDEON OF SCOTLAND YARD(1959, Brit.), art d; TEN SECONDS TO HELL(1959), art d; MAN WITH THE GREEN CARNATION, THE(1960, Brit.), art d; PORTRAIT OF A SINNER(1961, Brit.), art d; DR. NO(1962, Brit.), prod d; SODOM AND GOMOR-RAH(1962, U.S./Fr./Ital.), art d; IN THE COOL OF THE DAY(1963), prod d; GOLDFIN-GER(1964, Brit.), prod d; WOMAN OF STRAW(1964, Brit.), prod d; IPCRESS FILE, THE(1965, Brit.), prod d; THUNDERBALL(1965, Brit.), prod d; FUNERAL IN BER-LIN(1966, Brit.), prod d; YOU ONLY LIVE TWICE(1967, Brit.), prod d; SLEUTH(1972, Brit.), prod d; LAST OF SHEILA, THE(1973), prod d; BARRY LYNDON(1975, Brit.), prod d; SEVEN-PER-CENT SOLUTION, THE(1977, Brit.), prod d; SPY WHO LOVED ME, THE(1977, Brit.), prod d; MOONRAKER(1979, Brit.), prod d

Ladislav Adam
FIREMAN'S BALL, THE(1968, Czech.); MOST BEAUTIFUL AGE, THE(1970, Czech.)

Michal Bat Adam
MADAME ROSA(1977, Fr.)

Noelle Adam
WONDERS OF ALADDIN, THE(1961, Fr./Ital.); LA PRISONNIERE(1969, Fr./Ital.)

Peter Adam
BULLWHIP(1958)

Ronald Adam
DRUMS(1938, Brit.); KATE PLUS TEN(1938, Brit.); SONG OF FREEDOM(1938, Brit.); STRANGE BOARDERS(1938, Brit.); CLOUDS OVER EUROPE(1939, Brit.); DANGER-OUS CARGO(1939, Brit.); INSPECTOR HORNLEIGH(1939, Brit.); TOO DANGEROUS TO LIVE(1939, Brit.); LION HAS WINGS, THE(1940, Brit.); MISSING PEOPLE, THE(1940, Brit.); HOUSE OF MYSTERY(1941, Brit.); MAXWELL ARCHER, DETEC-TIVE(1942, Brit.); ESCAPE TO DANGER(1943, Brit.); GREEN FOR DANGER(1946, Brit.); BONNIE PRINCE CHARLIE(1948, Brit.); COUNTER BLAST(1948, Brit.); DE-VIL'S PLOT, THE(1948, Brit.); TAKE MY LIFE(1948, Brit.); ALL OVER THE TOWN(1949, Brit.); BLACK MAGIC(1949); CASE OF CHARLES PEACE, THE(1949, Brit.); CHRISTOPHER COLUMBUS(1949, Brit.); DIAMOND CITY(1949, Brit.); HID-DEN ROOM, THE(1949, Brit.); UNDER CAPRICORN(1949); IF THIS BE SIN(1950, Brit.); PINK STRING AND SEALING WAX(1950, Brit.); SEVEN DAYS TO NOON(1950, Brit.); SHADOW OF THE PAST(1950, Brit.); ADVENTURERS, THE(1951, Brit.); CAPTAIN HORATIO HORNBLOWER(1951, Brit.); HELL IS SOLD OUT(1951, Brit.); I'LL NEVER FORGET YOU(1951); LAUGHTER IN PARADISE(1951, Brit.); LAVEND-ER HILL MOB, THE(1951, Brit.); OBSESSED(1951, Brit.); OPERATION X(1951, Brit.); HOLIDAY WEEK(1952, Brit.); FLANNELFOOT(1953, Brit.); MR. DENNING DRIVES NORTH(1953, Brit.); MR. POTTS GOES TO MOSCOW(1953, Brit.); ANGELS ONE FIVE(1954, Brit.); BLACK KNIGHT, THE(1954); CIRCUMSTANIAL EVIDENCE(1954, Brit.); ESCAPE BY NIGHT(1954, Brit.); FRONT PAGE STORY(1954, Brit.); JOHNNY ON THE SPOT(1954, Brit.); MALTA STORY(1954, Brit.); MAN WITH A MILLION(1954, Brit.); CASH ON DELIVERY(1956, Brit.); LUST FOR LIFE(1956); MAN WHO NEVER WAS, THE(1956, Brit.); PRIVATE'S PROGRESS(1956, Brit.); TONS OF TROUBLE(1956, Brit.); CARRY ON ADMIRAL(1957, Brit.); REACH FOR THE SKY(1957, Brit.); SEA WIFE(1957, Brit.); SURGEON'S KNIFE, THE(1957, Brit.); INBETWEEN AGE, THE(1958, Brit.); KILL ME TOMORROW(1958, Brit.); MAN WHO COULD CHEAT DEATH, THE(1959, Brit.); AND THE SAME TO YOU(1960, Brit.); MAN IN A COCKED HAT(1960, Bri.); PLEASE TURN OVER(1960, Brit.); SNOWBALL(1960, Brit.); OFF-BEAT(1961, Brit.); SHOOT TO KILL(1961, Brit.); THREE ON A SPREE(1961, Brit.); GOLDEN RABBIT, THE(1962, Brit.); MILLION DOLLAR MANHUNT(1962, Brit.); POSTMAN'S KNOCK(1962, Brit.); SATAN NEVER SLEEPS(1962); TWO LETTER ALIBI(1962, Brit.); HAUNTING, THE(1963); TOMB OF LIGEIA, THE(1965, Brit.); WHO KILLED THE CAT?(1966, Brit.); SONG OF NORWAY(1970); ZEPPELIN(1971, Brit.); RULING CLASS, THE(1972, Brit.)
Misc. Talkies
MAN FROM NOWHERE, THE(1976, Brit.)

Wing Commander Ronald Adam
JOURNEY TOGETHER(1946, Brit.)

Ruth Adam
QUIET WOMAN, THE(1951, Brit.), d&w

Tempe Adam
MILLIONAIRESS, THE(1960, Brit.)

Theo Adam
FIDELIO(1970, Ger.)

Adam and the Ants
JUBILEE(1978, Brit.), m

Ava Adamaz
MANOLETE(1950, Span.)

Samuel Adamcik
DESERTER AND THE NOMADS, THE(1969, Czech./Ital.)

Olga Adamcikova
DESERTER AND THE NOMADS, THE(1969, Czech./Ital.)

Juan Adames
GLORIA(1980)

Addi Adametz
SNOW WHITE(1965, Ger.)

Alfredo Adami
WAR ITALIAN STYLE(1967, Ital.); ROMA(1972, Ital./Fr.)

Sbarra Adami
ROMA(1972, Ital./Fr.)

Bojan Adamic
CROOKED ROAD, THE(, m; GREH(1962, Ger./Yugo.), m

Robert Adamina
NEVER TAKE NO FOR AN ANSWER(1952, Brit./Ital.)

Jiri Adamira
FIFTH HORSEMAN IS FEAR, THE(1968, Czech.); SIGN OF THE VIRGIN(1969, Czech.); DIVINE EMMA, THE(1983, Czech,)

Frank Adamo
SIX WEEKS(1982)

Joe Adamo
NUNZIO(1978)

Helenka Adamowska
Silents .
SECOND FIDDLE(1923); GRIT(1924)

Adams
TUTTLES OF TAHITI(1942)

Abigail Adams [Tommye Adams&rb
OUR VINES HAVE TENDER GRAPES(1945); OVER 21(1945); COLORADO SERE-NADE(1946); MARY LOU(1948); TRAPPED BY BOSTON BLACKIE(1948)

Ada Adams
SCARLET ANGEL(1952); THREE HOURS TO KILL(1954)

Alan Adams
THREE SISTERS(1974, Brit.)

Alicia Adams
HEADLEYS AT HOME, THE(1939)

Arthur Adams
GREATEST, THE(1977, U.S./Brit.); METEOR(1979); LAST FLIGHT OF NOAH'S ARK, THE(1980); FIRST MONDAY IN OCTOBER(1981); GETTING OVER(1981)
1984
STRANGERS KISS(1984)

Ashby Adams
WITHOUT A TRACE(1983)

Bee Adams
NO ROOM AT THE INN(1950, Brit.)

Ben Adams
SCAVENGERS, THE(1969); MACHISMO–40 GRAVES FOR 40 GUNS(1970), art d, set d

Berle Adams
LOOK OUT SISTER(1948), p

Bernard Adams
MURDER AHOY(1964, Brit.); WILD AFFAIR, THE(1966, Brit.)

Bertram Adams
FLASH GORDON(1980)

Betty [Julie] Adams
DALTON GANG, THE(1949); COLORADO RANGER(1950); CROOKED RIVER(1950); FAST ON THE DRAW(1950); FOR HEAVEN'S SAKE(1950); HOSTILE COUN-TRY(1950); MARSHAL OF HELDORADO(1950); WEST OF THE BRAZOS(1950)

Beverly Adams
SILENCERS, THE(; ROUSTABOUT(1964); HOW TO STUFF A WILD BIKINI(1965); WINTER A GO-GO(1965); BIRDS DO IT(1966); MURDERERS' ROW(1966); AMBUSH-ERS, THE(1967); DEVIL'S ANGELS(1967); KISS THE GIRLS AND MAKE THEM DIE(1967, U.S./Ital.); HAMMERHEAD(1968); TORTURE GARDEN(1968, Brit.)

Bob Adams
CAPETOWN AFFAIR(1967, U.S./South Afr.), m

Brass Adams
IN-LAWS, THE(1979); ROMANTIC COMEDY(1983)
1984
HARD TO HOLD(1984)

Brian Adams
1984
PHAR LAP(1984, Aus.); RAZORBACK(1984, Aus.)

Brooke Adams
SHOCK WAVES(1977); DAYS OF HEAVEN(1978); INVASION OF THE BODY SNATCHERS(1978); CUBA(1979); MAN, A WOMAN, AND A BANK, A(1979, Can.); TELL ME A RIDDLE(1980); DEAD ZONE, THE(1983); UTILITIES(1983, Can.)
1984
ALMOST YOU(1984)

Carol Adams
DANCING ON A DIME(1940); BAD MAN OF DEADWOOD(1941); GAY VAGABOND, THE(1941); ICE-CAPADES(1941); RIDIN' ON A RAINBOW(1941); SIS HOPKINS(1941); EVER SINCE VENUS(1944); ULTIMATE THRILL, THE(1974)

Caroll Adams
HALLELUJAH TRAIL, THE(1965)

Carolyn Adams
CLAUDINE(1974)

Casey Adams [Max Showalter]
MY WIFE'S BEST FRIEND(1952); WHAT PRICE GLORY?(1952); DANGEROUS CROSSING(1953); DESTINATION GOBI(1953); NIAGARA(1953); VICKI(1953); DOWN THREE DARK STREETS(1954); NAKED ALIBI(1954); NIGHT PEOPLE(1954); RE-TURN OF JACK SLADE, THE(1955); BUS STOP(1956); INDESTRUCTIBLE MAN, THE(1956); NEVER SAY GOODBYE(1956); DRAGON WELLS MASSACRE(1957); MONSTER THAT CHALLENGED THE WORLD, THE(1957); FEMALE ANIMAL, THE(1958); NAKED AND THE DEAD, THE(1958); VOICE IN THE MIRROR(1958); IT HAPPENED TO JANE(1959); RETURN TO PEYTON PLACE(1961); SUMMER AND SMOKE(1961); BON VOYAGE(1962); MUSIC MAN, THE(1962)

Caswell Adams
SOMEBODY UP THERE LIKES ME(1956)

Catherine Adams
Misc. Silents
SILVER GIRL, THE(1919)

Catlin Adams
JERK, THE(1979); JAZZ SINGER, THE(1980)

Chalmers Adams
PARTNERS(1976, Can.), p

Christopher Adams
SINCE YOU WENT AWAY(1944)

Claire Adams
Silents
PENALTY, THE(1920); RIDERS OF THE DAWN(1920); KILLER, THE(1921); DO AND DARE(1922); JUST TONY(1922); CLEAN UP, THE(1923); LEGALLY DEAD(1923); SCARLET CAR, THE(1923); STEPPING FAST(1923); HELEN'S BABIES(1924); OH, YOU TONY!(1924); PAINTED FLAPPER, THE(1924); BIG PARADE, THE(1925); DEVIL'S CARGO, THE(1925); KISS BARRIER, THE(1925); YELLOW FINGERS(1926); MARRIED ALIVE(1927)
Misc. Silents
KEY TO POWER, THE(1918); SPEEDY MEADE(1919); DWELLING PLACE OF LIGHT, THE(1920); GREAT LOVER, THE(1920); INVISIBLE BOND, THE(1920);

MONEY CHANGERS, THE(1920); WHITE DOVE, THE(1920); CERTAIN RICH MAN, A(1921); LURE OF EGYPT, THE(1921); MAN OF THE FOREST, THE(1921); MYSTERIOUS RIDER(1921); SPENDERS, THE(1921); GOLDEN DREAMS(1922); GRAY DAWN, THE(1922); HEART'S HAVEN(1922); WHEN ROMANCE RIDES(1922); BRASS COMMANDMENTS(1923); WHERE THE NORTH BEGINS(1923); BRASS BOWL, THE(1924); GIRL IN THE LIMOUSINE, THE(1924); HONOR AMONG MEN(1924); MISSING DAUGHTERS(1924); NIGHT HAWK, THE(1924); MEN AND WOMEN(1925); SOULS FOR SABLES(1925); WHEEL, THE(1925); SEA WOLF, THE(1926); COMBAT(1927)

Clay Adams
HONEYMOON'S OVER, THE(1939), w; GIRL IN 313(1940), w

Cleve F. Adams
FATAL WITNESS, THE(1945), w

Clifton Adams
DESPERADO, THE(1954), w; OUTLAW'S SON(1957), w; COLE YOUNGER, GUNFIGHTER(1958), w

Col. William Adams
HONEYMOON KILLERS, THE(1969)

Colin Adams
ORGANIZATION, THE(1971)

Constance Adams
Silents
WHERE THE TRAIL DIVIDES(1914)

Coolidge Adams
BERMUDA AFFAIR(1956, Brit.), p

Cora Mills Adams
Misc. Silents
RECOIL, THE(1917)

Dallas Adams
ABOMINABLE DR. PHIBES, THE(1971, Brit.)

Dave Adams
I WANNA HOLD YOUR HAND(1978); PENNIES FROM HEAVEN(1981)
1984
SAM'S SON(1984)

David Adams
FINAL CHAPTER–WALKING TALL zero(1977); THOSE LIPS, THOSE EYES(1980); LOOKER(1981); PURSUIT OF D.B. COOPER, THE(1981); SOME KIND OF HERO(1982)
1984
TOP SECRET!(1984)

Dell Adams
INVASION OF THE STAR CREATURES(1962), cos

Dennis Adams
AMAZING TRANSPARENT MAN, THE(1960); FREE, WHITE AND 21(1963), art d

Diana Adams
KNOCK ON WOOD(1954); INVITATION TO THE DANCE(1956)

Dixon Adams
MYSTERY SUBMARINE(1963, Brit.)

Don Adams
NUDE BOMB, THE(1980); JIMMY THE KID(1982)

Donald Adams
MIKADO, THE(1967, Brit.); CURTAINS(1983, Can.)

Dora Adams
Misc. Silents
QUEEN X(1917); DETERMINATION(1920)

Dora M. Adams
Silents
MOTH AND THE FLAME, THE(1915)

Dora Mills Adams
Silents
MY LADY INCOG(1916)

Dorothy Adams
BROADWAY MUSKETEERS(1938); DISPUTED PASSAGE(1939); NINOTCHKA(1939); WOMEN, THE(1939); CHILD IS BORN, A(1940); LUCKY PARTNERS(1940); NOBODY'S CHILDREN(1940); UNTAMED(1940); WE WHO ARE YOUNG(1940); DEVIL COMMANDS, THE(1941); FLAME OF NEW ORLEANS, THE(1941); MY LIFE WITH CAROLINE(1941); PENNY SERENADE(1941); SHEPHERD OF THE HILLS, THE(1941); TOBACCO ROAD(1941); WHISTLING IN THE DARK(1941); BEDTIME STORY(1942); LADY GANGSTER(1942); SO PROUDLY WE HAIL(1943); LAURA(1944); SINCE YOU WENT AWAY(1944); CIRCUMSTANTIAL EVIDENCE(1945); FALLEN ANGEL(1945); MISS SUSIE SLAGLE'S(1945); BEST YEARS OF OUR LIVES, THE(1946); INNER CIRCLE, THE(1946); NOCTURNE(1946); O.S.S.(1946); SENTIMENTAL JOURNEY(1946); FOXES OF HARROW, THE(1947); THAT'S MY MAN(1947); TROUBLE WITH WOMEN, THE(1947); UNCONQUERED(1947); HE WALKED BY NIGHT(1948); SAINTED SISTERS, THE(1948); SITTING PRETTY(1948); DOWN TO THE SEA IN SHIPS(1949); NOT WANTED(1949); SAMSON AND DELILAH(1949); CARIBOO TRAIL, THE(1950); MONTANA(1950); PAID IN FULL(1950); FIRST LEGION, THE(1951); CARRIE(1952); FORT OSAGE(1952); GREATEST SHOW ON EARTH, THE(1952); JET JOB(1952); WINNING TEAM, THE(1952); PRODIGAL, THE(1955); BROKEN STAR, THE(1956); JOHNNY CONCHO(1956); MAN IN THE GREY FLANNEL SUIT, THE(1956); TEN COMMANDMENTS, THE(1956); THESE WILDER YEARS(1956); THREE FOR JAMIE DAWN(1956); BUCKSKIN LADY, THE(1957); BIG COUNTRY, THE(1958); GUNMAN'S WALK(1958); UNWED MOTHER(1958); FROM THE TERRACE(1960); PEEPER(1975)

Dwight Adams
STRATTON STORY, THE(1949)

Eadie Adams
SINNER TAKE ALL(1936); THIRTEENTH MAN, THE(1937)

Ed Adams
1984
FLESHBURN(1984)

Eddie Adams
Silents
RACKET, THE(1928), t

Eddy Adams
ROAD AGENT(1941)

Edgar Adams
ALL QUIET ON THE WESTERN FRONT(1930), ed

Edie Adams
UP IN SMOKE(1978); APARTMENT, THE(1960); LOVER COME BACK(1961); CALL ME BWANA(1963, Brit.); IT'S A MAD, MAD, MAD, MAD WORLD(1963); LOVE WITH THE PROPER STRANGER(1963); UNDER THE YUM-YUM TREE(1963); BEST MAN, THE(1964); MADE IN PARIS(1966); OSCAR, THE(1966); HONEY POT, THE(1967, Brit.); RACQUET(1979); HAPPY HOOKER GOES TO HOLLYWOOD, THE(1980); BOXOFFICE(1982)

Edward L. Adams
SHIPMATES FOREVER(1935), tech adv

Edwin M. Adams
FIRST MONDAY IN OCTOBER(1981)

Elayne Adams
MISSING CORPSE, THE(1945)

Elsie Adams
MINNIE AND MOSKOWITZ(1971)

Ernest Adams
FOR THE DEFENSE(1930); FAIR WARNING(1931); LAW OF THE RANGER(1937); ROLLIN' PLAINS(1938); YANKEE FAKIR(1947)
Misc. Silents
HUTCH OF THE U.S.A.(1924)

Ernest S. Adams
GOOD DAME(1934); HERE COMES THE GROOM(1934); RUGGLES OF RED GAP(1935)

Ernie Adams
FIGHTING LEGION, THE(1930); SHADOW RANCH(1930); FIRST AID(1931); GANG BUSTER, THE(1931); LITTLE CAESAR(1931); TIP-OFF, THE(1931); BEYOND THE ROCKIES(1932); FREAKS(1932); HOLD'EM JAIL(1932); MILLION DOLLAR LEGS(1932); NIGHT BEAT(1932); ONE-MAN LAW(1932); PANAMA FLO(1932); UNWRITTEN LAW, THE(1932); BREED OF THE BORDER(1933); GALLOPING ROMEO(1933); RANGER'S CODE, THE(1933); SHE DONE HIM WRONG(1933); WEST OF SINGAPORE(1933); FOUND ALIVE(1934); HELL BENT FOR LOVE(1934); IT HAPPENED ONE NIGHT(1934); LITTLE MISS MARKER(1934); MEN OF THE NIGHT(1934); OPERATOR 13(1934); WE'RE NOT DRESSING(1934); CASINO MURDER CASE, THE(1935); LAST OF THE CLINTONS, THE(1935); MEN OF THE HOUR(1935); PERFECT CLUE, THE(1935); SHE MARRIED HER BOSS(1935); HOPALONG CASSIDY RETURNS(1936); MY MAN GODFREY(1936); PRESCOTT KID, THE(1936); RIO GRANDE ROMANCE(1936); THREE ON THE TRAIL(1936); ARIZONA GUNFIGHTER(1937); BAR Z BAD MEN(1937); COME ON, COWBOYS(1937); DODGE CITY TRAIL(1937); GUN LORDS OF STIRRUP BASIN(1937); GUN RANGER, THE(1937); HOPALONG RIDES AGAIN(1937); LIGHTNIN' CRANDALL(1937); MAN WHO CRIED WOLF, THE(1937); OLD WYOMING TRAIL, THE(1937); RANGE DEFENDERS(1937); RIDIN' THE LONE TRAIL(1937); SAN QUENTIN(1937); SHADOW, THE(1937); STARS OVER ARIZONA(1937), w; TWO-FISTED SHERIFF(1937); COLORADO KID(1938); DANGER VALLEY(1938); DURANGO VALLEY RAIDERS(1938); GUN PACKER(1938); LAND OF FIGHTING MEN(1938); MAN'S COUNTRY(1938); MEXICALI KID, THE(1938); PAINTED TRAIL, THE(1938); PURPLE VIGILANTES, THE(1938); TEXANS, THE(1938); THUNDER IN THE DESERT(1938); WEST OF CHEYENNE(1938); WHERE THE BUFFALO ROAM(1938); YOU AND ME(1938); DOWN THE WYOMING TRAIL(1939); FRONTIER PONY EXPRESS(1939); I STOLE A MILLION(1939); MAN FROM SUNDOWN, THE(1939); PHANTOM STAGE, THE(1939); SONG OF THE BUCKAROO(1939); ST. LOUIS BLUES(1939); SUNDOWN ON THE PRAIRIE(1939); TEXAS STAMPEDE(1939); TOWER OF LONDON(1939); TRIGGER PALS(1939); UNION PACIFIC(1939); YOU CAN'T CHEAT AN HONEST MAN(1939); 6000 ENEMIES(1939); ENEMY AGENT(1940); HE STAYED FOR BREAKFAST(1940); INVISIBLE MAN RETURNS, THE(1940); MAN FROM TUMBLEWEEDS, THE(1940); MAN WITH NINE LIVES, THE(1940); OUT WEST WITH THE PEPPERS(1940); RIDERS FROM NOWHERE(1940); SON OF MONTE CRISTO(1940); WEST OF CARSON CITY(1940); BURY ME NOT ON THE LONE PRAIRIE(1941); FACE BEHIND THE MASK, THE(1941); FARGO KID, THE(1941); HONOLULU(1941); INVISIBLE GHOST, THE(1941); PINTO KID, THE(1941); RICHEST MAN IN TOWN(1941); RIDE, KELLY, RIDE(1941); ROAD AGENT(1941); ROBBERS OF THE RANGE(1941); SEA WOLF, THE(1941); TWO LATINS FROM MANHATTAN(1941); ALIAS BOSTON BLACKIE(1942); BANDIT RANGER(1942); ISLE OF MISSING MEN(1942); LADY IS WILLING, THE(1942); LONE PRAIRIE, THE(1942); MAN WHO CAME TO DINNER, THE(1942); MAN WITH TWO LIVES, THE(1942); MY GAL SAL(1942); ONE THRILLING NIGHT(1942); PRIDE OF THE YANKEES, THE(1942); RIDING THE WIND(1942); SABOTAGE SQUAD(1942); STAGECOACH BUCKAROO(1942); THEY ALL KISSED THE BRIDE(1942); WEST OF TOMBSTONE(1942); BEYOND THE LAST FRONTIER(1943); HAIL TO THE RANGERS(1943); HEADIN' FOR GOD'S COUNTRY(1943); JACK LONDON(1943); KEEP 'EM SLUGGING(1943); MISSION TO MOSCOW(1943); MUG TOWN(1943); SAGEBRUSH LAW(1943); SHE HAS WHAT IT TAKES(1943); WINGS OVER THE PACIFIC(1943); BLACK PARACHUTE, THE(1944); GHOST GUNS(1944); GIRL RUSH(1944); GOIN' TO TOWN(1944); LAKE PLACID SERENADE(1944); LOUISIANA HAYRIDE(1944); MAN IN HALF-MOON STREET, THE(1944); MARSHAL OF GUNSMOKE(1944); OUTLAWS OF SANTA FE(1944); PRINCESS AND THE PIRATE, THE(1944); RAIDERS OF THE BORDER(1944); RETURN OF THE APE MAN(1944); ALONG CAME JONES(1945); ESCAPE IN THE FOG(1945); FRISCO SAL(1945); JOHNNY ANGEL(1945); JUNGLE CAPTIVE(1945); MURDER, MY SWEET(1945); PATRICK THE GREAT(1945); BLUE DAHLIA, THE(1946); DEADLINE AT DAWN(1946); DO YOU LOVE ME?(1946); FEAR(1946); GIRL ON THE SPOT(1946); KILLERS, THE(1946); LAWLESS BREED, THE(1946); MYSTERIOUS MR. VALENTINE, THE(1946); SUSPENSE(1946); DESPERATE(1947); PRETENDER, THE(1947); SECRET LIFE OF WALTER MITTY, THE(1947); SMASH-UP, THE STORY OF A WOMAN(1947); TRAIL STREET(1947); 13TH HOUR, THE(1947); RETURN OF THE BADMEN(1948)
Misc. Talkies
TRAIL'S END(1935)
Silents
PONY EXPRESS, THE(1925); HAIR TRIGGER BAXTER(1926); JAZZ GIRL, THE(1926); VALLEY OF BRAVERY, THE(1926); JEWELS OF DESIRE(1927); SO THIS IS LOVE(1928); WHAT A NIGHT!(1928)

Ernie S. Adams
SATURDAY NIGHT KID, THE(1929); VIRGINIAN, THE(1929); STORM, THE(1930); MERRILY WE GO TO HELL(1932); LOST JUNGLE, THE(1934); ANNIE OAKLEY(1935); NIGHT WAITRESS(1936); DARK COMMAND, THE(1940); HERS TO HOLD(1943); GREAT JOHN L. THE(1945)
Silents
BLACK BIRD, THE(1926); NEVADA(1927); SPEEDY(1928); ONE SPLENDID HOUR(1929)

Eustace Adams
DOWN TO THE SEA(1936), w

Eustace L. Adams
UNDER SECRET ORDERS(1933), w; SIXTEEN FATHOMS DEEP(1934), w; DESPERATE CARGO(1941), w; SIXTEEN FATHOMS DEEP(1948), w

Fay Adams
Misc. Silents
DAUGHTER OF THE SIOUX, A(1925)

Francis Adams
WOMAN TO WOMAN(1946, Brit.)

Frank Adams
SHE GETS HER MAN(1935); VIRGINIA JUDGE, THE(1935), w

Frank R. Adams
TIME, THE PLACE AND THE GIRL, THE(1929), w; PEG O' MY HEART(1933), w; SHE MADE HER BED(1934), w; LOVE IN BLOOM(1935), w; CIRCUS GIRL(1937), w; OUTCAST(1937), w; COWBOY AND THE LADY, THE(1938), w; TRADE WINDS(1938), w
Silents
NEAR LADY, THE(1923), w; ALMOST A LADY(1926), w

Frank Ramsay Adams
Silents
ENCHANTMENT(1921), w

Frankie Adams
FORGOTTEN COMMANDMENTS(1932)

Gary Adams
GROUND ZERO(1973)

Geoffrey Adams
LIFE IN EMERGENCY WARD 10(1959, Brit.); THIRD SECRET, THE(1964, Brit.)

Gerald Adams
DEAD RECKONING(1947), w; GALLANT LEGION, THE(1948), w; OLD LOS ANGELES(1948), w; PLUNDERERS, THE(1948), w; GOLDENGIRL(1979), set d

Gerald D. Adams
DUKE OF THE NAVY(1942), w

Gerald Drayson Adams
MIRACLE KID(1942), w; GUY, A GAL AND A PAL, A(1945), w; TELL IT TO A STAR(1945), w; INVISIBLE INFORMER(1946), w; MAGNIFICENT ROGUE, THE(1946), w; BIG STEAL, THE(1949), w; ARMORED CAR ROBBERY(1950), w; BETWEEN MIDNIGHT AND DAWN(1950), w; DESERT HAWK, THE(1950), w; FLAME OF ARABY(1951), p; FLAMING FEATHER(1951), w; GOLDEN HORDE, THE(1951), w; HIS KIND OF WOMAN(1951), w; LADY FROM TEXAS, THE(1951), w; PRINCE WHO WAS A THIEF, THE(1951), w; SEA HORNET, THE(1951), w; BATTLE AT APACHE PASS, THE(1952), w; DUEL AT SILVER CREEK, THE(1952), w; SON OF ALI BABA(1952), w; STEEL TOWN(1952), w; UNTAMED FRONTIER(1952), w; WINGS OF THE HAWK(1953), w; GAMBLER FROM NATCHEZ, THE(1954), w; PRINCESS OF THE NILE(1954), w; TAZA, SON OF COCHISE(1954), w; THREE YOUNG TEXANS(1954), w; CHIEF CRAZY HORSE(1955), w; DUEL ON THE MISSISSIPPI(1955), w; GUN BROTHERS(1956), w; THREE BAD SISTERS(1956), w; AFFAIR IN RENO(1957), w; WAR DRUMS(1957), w; GUN FIGHT(1961), w; WILD WESTERNERS, THE(1962), w; KISSIN' COUSINS(1964), w; HARUM SCARUM(1965), w

Gil Adams
OLGA'S GIRLS(1964)

Gloria Adams
NATCHEZ TRACE(1960)

Glyn Adams
MIKADO, THE(1967, Brit.)

Greg Adams
QUIET DAY IN BELFAST, A(1974, Can.), m

Hank Adams
MACHISMO–40 GRAVES FOR 40 GUNS(1970), a, set d

Harold Adams
HOLD 'EM NAVY!(1937)

Harry Adams
REUNION IN FRANCE(1942); THANK YOUR LUCKY STARS(1943); GASLIGHT(1944); MRS. PARKINGTON(1944); TWO GIRLS AND A SAILOR(1944)

Harvey Adams
IT ISN'T DONE(1937, Aus.); TALL TIMBERS(1937, Aus.); FORTY THOUSAND HORSEMEN(1941, Aus.); HIS MAJESTY O'KEEFE(1953); LONG JOHN SILVER(1954, Aus.); ON THE BEACH(1959)

Hazel Adams
Misc. Silents
DEBT OF HONOR, THE(1918)

Helen Adams
TORTURE DUNGEON(1970)

Henry Adams
DANGEROUS PASSAGE(1944), ed; DARK MOUNTAIN(1944), ed; DOUBLE EXPOSURE(1944), ed; FOLLOW THAT WOMAN(1945), ed; HIGH POWERED(1945), ed; ONE EXCITING NIGHT(1945), ed; PEOPLE ARE FUNNY(1945), ed; SCARED STIFF(1945), ed; TOKYO ROSE(1945), ed; HOT CARGO(1946), ed; THEY MADE ME A KILLER(1946), ed; SEA OF GRASS, THE(1947); TOP GUN(1955), ed

Hugh Allen Adams
PAINTED DESERT, THE(1931)

Jack Adams
FAST COMPANY(1929); AMAZING DOBERMANS, THE(1976), ph
Silents
GOLD RUSH, THE(1925)

James Adams
Silents
KISMET(1920)

James W. Adams
Silents
TIGER WOMAN, THE(1917), w

Jane Adams [Poni Adams]
HOUSE OF DRACULA(1945); SALOME, WHERE SHE DANCED(1945); THIS LOVE OF OURS(1945); BRUTE MAN, THE(1946); GUNMAN'S CODE(1946); LAWLESS BREED, THE(1946); NIGHT IN PARADISE, A(1946); RUNAROUND, THE(1946); RUSTLER'S ROUNDUP(1946); SMOOTH AS SILK(1946); HE WALKED BY NIGHT(1948); ANGELS IN DISGUISE(1949); GUN LAW JUSTICE(1949); MASTER MINDS(1949); WESTERN RENEGADES(1949); GIRL FROM SAN LORENZO, THE(1950); LAW OF THE PANHANDLE(1950); OUTLAW GOLD(1950); STREET BANDITS(1951)

Misc. Talkies
SECRET OF OUTLAW FLATS(1953)

Jeb Adams
RUN, ANGEL, RUN(1969)

Jennifer Adams
SIX WEEKS(1982)

Jerry Adams
PARADISE ALLEY(1978), set d

Jessie Adams
JUNE BRIDE(1948); MONTANA(1950); MOTHER DIDN'T TELL ME(1950)

Jill Adams
CHANCE MEETING(1954, Brit.); CONSTANT HUSBAND, THE(1955, Brit.); COUNT OF TWELVE(1955, Brit.); DOCTOR AT SEA(1955, Brit.); LOVE MATCH, THE(1955, Brit.); ONE JUMP AHEAD(1955, Brit.); ONE WAY OUT(1955, Brit.); PRIVATE'S PROGRESS(1956, Brit.); BROTHERS IN LAW(1957, Brit.); GREEN MAN, THE(1957, Brit.); VALUE FOR MONEY(1957, Brit.); DEATH OVER MY SHOULDER(1958, Brit.); STRANGE AFFECTION(1959, Brit.); CARRY ON CONSTABLE(1960, Brit.); CROSSTRAP(1962, Brit.); DOCTOR IN DISTRESS(1963, Brit.); COMEDY MAN, THE(1964); GUTTER GIRLS(1964, Brit.); PROMISE HER ANYTHING(1966, Brit.)

Jim Adams
DESTRUCTORS, THE(1968); MONEY JUNGLE, THE(1968); PANIC IN THE CITY(1968)

Jimmie Adams
OFFICE SCANDAL, THE(1929)
Misc. Silents
HOLD YOUR BREATH(1924); HER MAN O'WAR(1926)

Jimmy Adams
GRAND PARADE, THE(1930)

Joe Adams
RINGSIDE(1949); DISC JOCKEY(1951); CARMEN JONES(1954); MANCHURIAN CANDIDATE, THE(1962); BLUES FOR LOVERS(1966, Brit.)

Joey Adams
SINGING IN THE DARK(1956), a, p; DON'T WORRY, WE'LL THINK OF A TITLE(1966); EXORCIST II: THE HERETIC(1977)

John Adams
1984
DEATHSTALKER, THE(1984), ed

John Destry Adams
GROUNDSTAR CONSPIRACY, THE(1972, Can.)

Jonathan Adams
ROCKY HORROR PICTURE SHOW, THE(1975, Brit.)

Joseph Adams [Josef Adamovic]
VOYAGE TO THE END OF THE UNIVERSE(1963, Czech.)

Joyce Adams
ENEMY FROM SPACE(1957, Brit.)

Judith Adams
CARRIE(1952)

Julia [Julie] Adams
RED, HOT AND BLUE(1949); BRIGHT VICTORY(1951); FINDERS KEEPERS(1951); HOLLYWOOD STORY(1951); BEND OF THE RIVER(1952); HORIZONS WEST(1952); LAWLESS BREED, THE(1952); TREASURE OF LOST CANYON, THE(1952); MAN FROM THE ALAMO, THE(1953); MISSISSIPPI GAMBLER, THE(1953); STAND AT APACHE RIVER, THE(1953); WINGS OF THE HAWK(1953); CREATURE FROM THE BLACK LAGOON(1954); FRANCIS JOINS THE WACS(1954); LOOTERS, THE(1955); ONE DESIRE(1955); PRIVATE WAR OF MAJOR BENSON, THE(1955); SIX BRIDGES TO CROSS(1955); AWAY ALL BOATS(1956); FOUR GIRLS IN TOWN(1956); SLAUGHTER ON TENTH AVENUE(1957); SLIM CARTER(1957); TARAWA BEACHHEAD(1958); GUNFIGHT AT DODGE CITY, THE(1959); RAYMIE(1960); UNDERWATER CITY, THE(1962); TICKLE ME(1965); VALLEY OF MYSTERY(1967); LAST MOVIE, THE(1971); MC Q(1974); PSYCHIC KILLER(1975); WILD McCULLOCHS, THE(1975); KILLER INSIDE ME, THE(1976); GOODBYE FRANKLIN HIGH(1978); FIFTH FLOOR, THE(1980)
1984
CHAMPIONS(1984)

Katherine Adams
Misc. Silents
VALENTINE GIRL, THE(1917); TRUE BLUE(1918); GENTLEMAN OF QUALITY, A(1919); RESTLESS SOULS(1919); ROGUE'S ROMANCE, A(1919)

Katheryn Adams
Silents
SHOOTING OF DAN McGREW, THE(1915)

Kathlyn Adams
Misc. Silents
HINTON'S DOUBLE(1917)

Kathryn Adams
FIFTH AVENUE GIRL(1939); THAT'S RIGHT–YOU'RE WRONG(1939); ARGENTINE NIGHTS(1940); BLACK DIAMONDS(1940); IF I HAD MY WAY(1940); LOVE, HONOR AND OH, BABY(1940); SKI PATROL(1940); ARIZONA CYCLONE(1941); BACHELOR DADDY(1941); BURY ME NOT ON THE LONE PRAIRIE(1941); INVISIBLE WOMAN, THE(1941); MEET THE CHUMP(1941); MODEL WIFE(1941); RAWHIDE RANGERS(1941); UNFINISHED BUSINESS(1941); SABOTEUR(1942); YOU'RE TELLING ME(1942); BLONDE FOR A DAY(1946)
Silents
BABY MINE(1917); FORBIDDEN WOMAN, THE(1920); SILVER CAR, THE(1921)
Misc. Silents
BIRD OF PREY, A(1916); DIVORCE AND THE DAUGHTER(1916); POTS AND PANS PEGGIE(1917); VICAR OF WAKEFIELD, THE(1917); WOMAN AND THE BEAST, THE(1917); BRUTE BREAKER, THE(1919); COWARDICE COURT(1919); LITTLE BROTHER OF THE RICH, A(1919); WHOM THE GODS WOULD DESTROY(1919); "813"(1920); BEST OF LUCK, THE(1920); BIG HAPPINESS(1920); UNCHARTED CHANNELS(1920)

Ken Adams
FLASHING GUNS(1947); PRAIRIE EXPRESS(1947); AROUND THE WORLD IN 80 DAYS(1956), art d; DR. STRANGELOVE: OR HOW I LEARNED TO STOP WORRYING AND LOVE THE BOMB(1964), prod d; GOODBYE MR. CHIPS(1969, U.S./Brit.), prod d; DIAMONDS ARE FOREVER(1971, Brit.), prod d

Kitty Adams
LAWLESS WOMAN, THE(1931)

Lawrence Adams
WHIP'S WOMEN(1968)
Leon Adams
HEAT LIGHTNING(1934), w
Leslie Adams
CRIME WITHOUT PASSION(1934)
Lillian Adams
WILD AND THE INNOCENT, THE(1959); TORMENTED(1960); MAJORITY OF ONE, A(1961); ENTER LAUGHING(1967); LEPKE(1975, U.S./Israel); HUNTER, THE(1980); PRIVATE BENJAMIN(1980); HEY, GOOD LOOKIN'(1982)
Lionel Adams
Silents
ONE OF OUR GIRLS(1914); IMPOSTER, THE(1918); SUCCESS(1923); JANICE MEREDITH(1924)
Misc. Silents
COMING POWER, THE(1914); SPITFIRE, THE(1914); CLOSED ROAD, THE(1916); GREAT PROBLEM, THE(1916); THAIS(1917); UNFORSEEN, THE(1917)
Lola Adams
MY BODY HUNGERS(1967)
Lowden Adams
SILENT WITNESS, THE(1932); BARRETTS OF WIMPOLE STREET, THE(1934); GREAT IMPERSONATION, THE(1935); RENDEZVOUS(1935); GENTLEMAN FROM LOUISIANA(1936); WE ARE NOT ALONE(1939); EARL OF CHICAGO, THE(1940); I TAKE THIS WOMAN(1940); PRIDE AND PREJUDICE(1940); STRIKE UP THE BAND(1940); RANDOM HARVEST(1942)
Lynn G. Adams
Misc. Silents
TROOPER 44(1917)
Mack Adams
PASTOR HALL(1940, Brit.), m
Margaret Adams
MY SIN(1931); THAT SINKING FEELING(1979, Brit.)
Marla Adams
SPLENDOR IN THE GRASS(1961); SPECIAL DELIVERY(1976)
Mary Adams
FOR THE LOVE OF MARY(1948); HAZARD(1948); NIGHT HAS A THOUSAND EYES(1948); STARLIFT(1951); BUGLES IN THE AFTERNOON(1952); EXECUTIVE SUITE(1954); MOUNTAIN, THE(1956); REBEL IN TOWN(1956); BLOOD OF DRACULA(1957); CLOWN AND THE KID, THE(1961); DIARY OF A MADMAN(1963)
Mason Adams
DREAM NO MORE(1950, Palestine); GOD TOLD ME TO(1976); RAGGEDY ANN AND ANDY(1977); FINAL CONFLICT, THE(1981)
Maud Adams
CHRISTIAN LICORICE STORE, THE(1971); U-TURN(1973, Can.); MAN WITH THE GOLDEN GUN, THE(1974, Brit.); KILLER FORCE(1975, Switz./Ireland); ROLLERBALL(1975); TATTOO(1981); OCTOPUSSY(1983, Brit.)
Misc. Talkies
GIRL IN BLUE, THE(1974); TARGET EAGLE(1982)
Max Adams
CRAZY OVER HORSES(1951), w; LET'S GO NAVY(1951), w
Michael Adams
NORMAN LOVES ROSE(1982, Aus.)
Michael Gene Adams
1984
RHINESTONE(1984)
Mike Adams
LEGEND OF THE LONE RANGER, THE(1981); WARGAMES(1983)
Mrs. Adams
Silents
DEVIL'S PLAYGROUND, THE(1918)
Myrtle Adams
EARLY BIRD, THE(1936, Brit.)
Nan Adams
FORBIDDEN ISLAND(1959)
Nate Adams
SUPERFLY(1972), a, cos
Neile Adams
THIS COULD BE THE NIGHT(1957); FUZZ(1972)
Nick Adams
JUST FOR A SONG(1930, Brit.); SOMEBODY LOVES ME(1952); I DIED A THOUSAND TIMES(1955); MISTER ROBERTS(1955); PICNIC(1955); REBEL WITHOUT A CAUSE(1955); STRANGE LADY IN TOWN(1955); LAST WAGON, THE(1956); OUR MISS BROOKS(1956); STRANGE ADVENTURE, A(1956); FURY AT SHOWDOWN(1957); NO TIME FOR SERGEANTS(1958); SING, BOY, SING(1958); TEACHER'S PET(1958); FBI STORY, THE(1959); PILLOW TALK(1959); HELL IS FOR HEROES(1962); HOOK, THE(1962); INTERNS, THE(1962); TWILIGHT OF HONOR(1963); FRANKENSTEIN CONQUERS THE WORLD(1964, Jap./US); YOUNG LOVERS, THE(1964); DIE, MONSTER, DIE(1965, Brit.); YOUNG DILLINGER(1965); DON'T WORRY, WE'LL THINK OF A TITLE(1966); FEVER HEAT(1968); MISSION MARS(1968); MONSTER ZERO(1970, Jap.)
Pamela Adams
BLOOD(1974, Brit.)
Peggy Adams
Silents
CHRIS AND THE WONDERFUL LAMP(1917)
Misc. Silents
SALT OF THE EARTH(1917); YOUR OBEDIENT SERVANT(1917)
Peter Adams
DONOVAN'S BRAIN(1953); PROJECT MOONBASE(1953); WAR OF THE WORLDS, THE(1953); COURT-MARTIAL OF BILLY MITCHELL, THE(1955); FLAME OF THE ISLANDS(1955); SCARLET COAT, THE(1955); HELL ON DEVIL'S ISLAND(1957); JAILHOUSE ROCK(1957); OMAR KHAYYAM(1957); BIG FISHERMAN, THE(1959)
Misc. Talkies
ALTERNATIVE(1976)
Phil Adams
HOT ROD RUMBLE(1957); TOBRUK(1966); IN THE HEAT OF THE NIGHT(1967); KELLY'S HEROES(1970, U.S./Yugo.); BUCK AND THE PREACHER(1972); SHANKS(1974); STUNTS(1977); THANK GOD IT'S FRIDAY(1978), stunts; TO BE OR NOT TO BE(1983)

Philip Adams
DON'S PARTY(1976, Aus.), p
1984
RACING WITH THE MOON(1984)
Phillip Adams
ADVENTURES OF BARRY McKENZIE(1972, Austral.), p; GETTING OF WISDOM, THE(1977, Aus.), p; GRENDEL GRENDEL GRENDEL(1981, Aus.), p
Polly Adams
NEVER PUT IT IN WRITING(1964)
Poni Adams [Jane Adams]
CODE OF THE LAWLESS(1945); LADY ON A TRAIN(1945); TRAIL TO VENGEANCE(1945)
R.C. Adams
GUN RUNNER(1969)
Reetsy Adams
KID RANGER, THE(1936)
Richard Adams
SONG OF THE GRINGO(1936); PAROLED FROM THE BIG HOUSE(1938); PORT OF HATE(1939); EAST SIDE KIDS(1940); FALLGUY(1962), w; ADVANCE TO THE REAR(1964); RED TENT, THE(1971, Ital./USSR), w; COMMITMENT, THE(1976); WATERSHIP DOWN(1978, Brit.), w; LOST AND FOUND(1979); MERRY CHRISTMAS MR. LAWRENCE(1983, Jap./Brit.)
1984
CHAMPIONS(1984); PLAGUE DOGS, THE(1984, U.S./Brit.), w
Richard C. Adams
LEPKE(1975, U.S./Israel); PANDEMONIUM(1982); STING II, THE(1983); TWO OF A KIND(1983)
Richard L. Adams
I ESCAPED FROM DEVIL'S ISLAND(1973), w; SLAMS, THE(1973), w
Ritchie Adams
HUNTING PARTY, THE(1977, Brit.)
Robert Adams
KING SOLOMON'S MINES(1937, Brit.); OLD BONES OF THE RIVER(1938, Brit.); SONG OF FREEDOM(1938, Brit.); DREAMING(1944, Brit.); IT HAPPENED ONE SUNDAY(1944, Brit.); CAESAR AND CLEOPATRA(1946, Brit.); OLD MOTHER RILEY'S JUNGLE TREASURE(1951, Brit.); KISENGA, MAN OF AFRICA(1952, Brit.); SAPPHIRE(1959, Brit.); TOY, THE(1982)
Misc. Silents
SUPREME PASSION, THE(1921)
Ron Adams
1984
KILLPOINT(1984), spec eff
Ronald Adams
SOMEWHERE IN FRANCE(1943, Brit.)
Rush Adams
METALSTORM: THE DESTRUCTION OF JARED-SYN(1983)
Sam Adams
GOLDEN WEST, THE(1932); MILLION DOLLAR LEGS(1932); LOVE IS LIKE THAT(1933); MAN OF SENTIMENT, A(1933); MIGHTY BARNUM, THE(1934); IT'S A SMALL WORLD(1935); PICK A STAR(1937); $1,000,000 RACKET(1937); THANK YOUR LUCKY STARS(1943)
Samuel Adams
FOREIGN CORRESPONDENT(1940)
Samuel Hopkins Adams
YOU CAN'T RUN AWAY FROM IT(1956), w; IT HAPPENED ONE NIGHT(1934), w; IN PERSON(1935), w; GORGEOUS HUSSY, THE(1936), w; PRESIDENT'S MYSTERY, THE(1936), w; PERFECT SPECIMEN, THE(1937), w; HARVEY GIRLS, THE(1946), w
Silents
CLARION, THE(1916), w
Shawn Adams
SMITHEREENS(1982)
Sheila K. Adams
PSYCHO II(1983)
Simon Adams
1984
BOUNTY, THE(1984)
Stanley Adams
ATOMIC KID, THE(1954); HELL'S HORIZON(1955); BOLD AND THE BRAVE, THE(1956); HELL ON FRISCO BAY(1956); BLACK PATCH(1957); HELL BOUND(1957); HELL SHIP MUTINY(1957); TROOPER HOOK(1957); VALERIE(1957); I MARRIED A WOMAN(1958); SADDLE THE WIND(1958); HIGH SCHOOL BIG SHOT(1959); NORTH BY NORTHWEST(1959); NORTH TO ALASKA(1960); STUDS LONIGAN(1960); WIZARD OF BAGHDAD, THE(1960); BREAKFAST AT TIFFANY'S(1961); PIRATES OF TORTUGA(1961); YOUNG SAVAGES, THE(1961); OUTSIDER, THE(1962); REQUIEM FOR A HEAVYWEIGHT(1962); THIRTEEN WEST STREET(1962); CRITIC'S CHOICE(1963); LILIES OF THE FIELD(1963); FATE IS THE HUNTER(1964); HOUSE IS NOT A HOME, A(1964); WILD AND WONDERFUL(1964); SHIP OF FOOLS(1965); WHEN THE BOYS MEET THE GIRLS(1965); NEVADA SMITH(1966); DOUBLE TROUBLE(1967); THUNDER ALLEY(1967); GRASSHOPPER, THE(1970); MACHISMO-40 GRAVES FOR 40 GUNS(1970); MOVE(1970); SEVEN MINUTES, THE(1971); EVERYTHING YOU ALWAYS WANTED TO KNOW ABOUT SEX, BUT WE'RE AFRAID TO ASK(1972); CLONES, THE(1973); ACT OF VENGEANCE(1974); DIXIE DYNAMITE(1976); GREAT GUNDOWN, THE(1977)
Misc. Talkies
WOMAN IN THE RAIN(1976)
Stella Adams
BACHELOR MOTHER(1933); SING SINNER, SING(1933); VAMPIRE BAT, THE(1933); THEODORA GOES WILD(1936)
Misc. Silents
ME, GANGSTER(1928)
Steve Adams
1984
KILLPOINT(1984)
Suzi Adams
Misc. Talkies
TANYA(1976)
T C. Adams
CARNIVAL OF SOULS(1962)

Ted Adams

CYCLONE KID(1931); GOD'S COUNTRY AND THE MAN(1931); RIDER OF THE PLAINS(1931); SHIPS OF HATE(1931); BATTLING BUCKAROO(1932); BEYOND THE ROCKIES(1932); GHOST VALLEY(1932); WAR OF THE RANGE(1933); HIS FIGHTING BLOOD(1935); HOPALONG CASSIDY(1935); LAWLESS BORDER(1935); BORDER CABALLERO(1936); CROOKED TRAIL, THE(1936); THREE ON THE TRAIL(1936); TOLL OF THE DESERT(1936); TRAIL DUST(1936); UNDERCOVER MAN(1936); ARIZONA GUNFIGHTER(1937); BOSS OF LONELY VALLEY(1937); DESERT PHANTOM(1937); GAMBLING TERROR, THE(1937); GUNS IN THE DARK(1937); HEART OF THE WEST(1937); LAWLESS LAND(1937); RUSTLER'S VALLEY(1937); SMOKE TREE RANGE(1937); COLORADO KID(1938); DESERT PATROL(1938); DURANGO VALLEY RAIDERS(1938); GUNSMOKE TRAIL(1938); PALS OF THE SADDLE(1938); SUDDEN BILL DORN(1938); CODE OF THE CACTUS(1939); CRASHING THRU(1939); EL DIABLO RIDES(1939); FIGHTING MAD(1939); FIGHTING RENEGADE(1939); MESQUITE BUCKAROO(1939); OUTLAW'S PARADISE(1939); PAL FROM TEXAS, THE(1939); SIX-GUN RHYTHM(1939); SMOKY TRAILS(1939); TEXAS WILDCATS(1939); THREE TEXAS STEERS(1939); TRIGGER FINGERS ½(1939); TRIGGER PALS(1939); FRONTIER CRUSADER(1940); GAUCHO SERENADE(1940); GUN CODE(1940); LAW AND ORDER(1940); PHANTOM RANCHER(1940); PINTO CANYON(1940); PIONEER DAYS(1940); RIDERS FROM NOWHERE(1940); RIDERS OF PASCO BASIN(1940); SKY BANDITS, THE(1940); STRAIGHT SHOOTER(1940); WILD HORSE VALLEY(1940); WYOMING(1940); BILLY THE KID(1941); BILLY THE KID'S RANGE WAR(1941); LONE RIDER AMBUSHED, THE(1941); RIDERS OF BLACK MOUNTAIN(1941); ROYAL MOUNTED PATROL, THE(1941); THUNDER OVER THE PRAIRIE(1941); BILLY THE KID TRAPPED(1942); FIGHTING BILL FARGO(1942); KING OF THE STALLIONS(1942); LAW AND ORDER(1942); MYSTERIOUS RIDER, THE(1942); OVERLAND STAGECOACH(1942); ROLLING DOWN THE GREAT DIVIDE(1942); SUNDOWN KID, THE(1942); CATTLE STAMPEDE(1943); HAIL TO THE RANGERS(1943); KID RIDES AGAIN, THE(1943); GENTLEMAN FROM TEXAS(1946); RED RIVER RENEGADES(1946); STAGECOACH TO DENVER(1946); TUMBLEWEED TRAIL(1946); UNDER ARIZONA SKIES(1946); BUFFALO BILL RIDES AGAIN(1947); CODE OF THE SADDLE(1947); FLASHING GUNS(1947); LAST ROUND-UP, THE(1947); PRAIRIE EXPRESS(1947); RAIDERS OF THE SOUTH(1947); RANGE BEYOND THE BLUE(1947); SONG OF THE WASTELAND(1947); UNDER COLORADO SKIES(1947); VIGILANTES OF BOOMTOWN(1947); BACK TRAIL(1948); BUCKAROO FROM POWDER RIVER(1948); CHECK YOUR GUNS(1948); CROSSED TRAILS(1948); FRONTIER AGENT(1948); GUN TALK(1948); GUNNING FOR JUSTICE(1948); ACROSS THE RIO GRANDE(1949); DEPUTY MARSHAL(1949); GUN RUNNER(1949); MUTINEERS, THE(1949); NAVAJO TRAIL RAIDERS(1949); OUTLAW COUNTRY(1949); QUICK ON THE TRIGGER(1949); SHADOWS OF THE WEST(1949); STALLION CANYON(1949); HILLS OF OKLAHOMA(1950); I KILLED GERONIMO(1950); LAW OF THE PANHANDLE(1950); ABILENE TRAIL(1951); NIGHT RIDERS OF MONTANA(1951); VANISHING OUTPOST, THE(1951); KANSAS TERRITORY(1952)
Misc. Talkies
LAW OF THE 45'S(1935); LION MAN, THE(1936); LIGHTNING CARSON RIDES AGAIN(1938); LONE RIDER IN FRONTIER FURY, THE(1941); BILLY THE KID'S SMOKING GUNS(1942)

Terry Adams

HERE COME THE WAVES(1944); I LOVE A SOLDIER(1944); LAURA(1944)

Tessa Adams
Misc. Talkies
BLACK BIRD DESCENDING: TENSE ALIGNMENT(1977)

Theodore [Ted] Adams

CAVALIER OF THE WEST(1931); SAVAGE GIRL, THE(1932); EASY MILLIONS(1933)

Thomas Adams
1984
NO SMALL AFFAIR(1984)

Tom Adams

PRIZE OF ARMS, A(1962, Brit.); GREAT ESCAPE, THE(1963); THIS IS MY STREET(1964, Brit.); SECOND BEST SECRET AGENT IN THE WHOLE WIDE WORLD, THE(1965, Brit.); FIGHTING PRINCE OF DONEGAL, THE(1966, Brit.); WHERE THE BULLETS FLY(1966, Brit.); FATHOM(1967); JOURNEY INTO MIDNIGHT(1968, Brit.); SUBTERFUGE(1969, US/Brit.); VON RICHTHOFEN AND BROWN(1970); HOUSE THAT DRIPPED BLOOD, THE(1971, Brit.)
Misc. Talkies
FAST KILL(1973)

Tommey Adams

TAHITI HONEY(1943)

Tommye Adams [Abigail Adams]

MOONLIGHT MASQUERADE(1942); LET'S FACE IT(1943); OLD ACQUAINTANCE(1943)

Tony Adams

REVENGE OF THE PINK PANTHER(1978), p; 10(1979), p; HARDLY WORKING(1981); S.O.B.(1981), p; TRAIL OF THE PINK PANTHER, THE(1982), p; VICTOR/VICTORIA(1982), p; CURSE OF THE PINK PANTHER(1983), p; MAN WHO LOVED WOMEN, THE(1983), p
1984
MICKI AND MAUDE(1984), p

Trevor Adams

JULIUS CAESAR(1970, Brit.)

Victor Adams

COUNSELLOR-AT-LAW(1933); DUKE COMES BACK, THE(1937); FIREFLY, THE(1937); HERE'S FLASH CASEY(1937); HOLY TERROR, THE(1937); LAST GANGSTER, THE(1937); LITTLE TOUGH GUY(1938); YOUNG FUGITIVES(1938); SARABAND(1949, Brit.)

Victoria Adams

ANGEL BABY(1961)

W. Robert Adams

MEN OF THE SEA(1951, Brit.)

Warren Adams

JOE PALOOKA IN THE COUNTERPUNCH(1949), ed; BRIDE OF THE MONSTER(1955), ed; HELL ON DEVIL'S ISLAND(1957), ed; PARSON AND THE OUTLAW, THE(1957), ed; PLUNDER ROAD(1957), ed; GREAT ST. LOUIS BANK ROBBERY, THE(1959), ed; FLIPPER(1963), ed; FLIPPER'S NEW ADVENTURE(1964), ed; RHINO(1964), ed; CLARENCE, THE CROSS-EYED LION(1965), ed; THREE WEEKS OF LOVE(1965), ed; ZEBRA IN THE KITCHEN(1965), ed; AROUND THE WORLD UNDER THE SEA(1966), ed; NAMU, THE KILLER WHALE(1966), ed; GENTLE GIANT(1967), ed; COLOR ME DEAD(1969, Aus.), ed

Warren Frederick Adams

PICNIC(1955)

William Adams [William S. Adams]

SWEET SURRENDER(1935); HOUSE ON 92ND STREET, THE(1945); ODDS AGAINST TOMORROW(1959)
Silents
BRIDE OF THE STORM(1926), ph; GRIT WINS(1929), ph; SKY SKIDDER, THE(1929), ph

William S. Adams [William Adams]
Silents
MAN AND HIS WOMAN(1920), ph; DESTINY'S ISLE(1922), ph; SKY-HIGH SAUNDERS(1927), ph; AIR PATROL, THE(1928), ph

Willie Adams

NATCHEZ TRACE(1960); FRIDAY THE 13TH(1980)

Yvonne Adams
1984
CAL(1984, Ireland)

Zachary Adams

CAMILLE 2000(1969)

Al Adamson

PSYCHO A GO-GO!(1965), P&d, w; BLOOD OF DRACULA'S CASTLE(1967), p, d; FEMALE BUNCH, THE(1969), d; GUN RIDERS, THE(1969), p&d; SATAN'S SADISTS(1969), p&d; BLOOD OF FRANKENSTEIN(1970), p, d; HELL'S BLOODY DEVILS(1970), p&d; HORROR OF THE BLOOD MONSTERS(1970, U.S./Phil.), p, d; BRAIN OF BLOOD(1971, Phil.), p, d; DOOMSDAY VOYAGE(1972), p; HAMMER(1972), p; JESSIE'S GIRLS(1976), p, d; NURSE SHERRI(1978), d; SUNSET COVE(1978), d
Misc. Talkies
BLOOD SEEKERS, THE(1971), d; ANGELS' WILD WOMEN(1972), d; NAUGHTY STEWARDESSES, THE(1973), d; DYNAMITE BROTHERS, THE(1974), d; GIRLS FOR RENT(1974), d; BLAZING STEWARDESSES(1975), d; JESSE'S GIRLS(1975), d; BLACK HEAT(1976), d; BLACK SAMURAI(1977), d; FREEZE BOMB(1980), d

Betty Adamson

VOYAGE OF THE DAMNED(1976, Brit.), cos

Chuck Adamson

THIEF(1981)
1984
BEVERLY HILLS COP(1984)

Ewart Adamson

PERFECT CRIME, THE(1928), w; BARNUM WAS RIGHT(1929), w; INSIDE THE LINES(1930), w; ANNIE OAKLEY(1935), w; CIRCUMSTANTIAL EVIDENCE(1935), w; FALSE PRETENSES(1935), w; GIRL WHO CAME BACK, THE(1935), w; BELOW THE DEADLINE(1936), w; DARK HOUR, THE(1936), w; EASY MONEY(1936), w; WALKING DEAD, THE(1936), w; LONG SHOT, THE(1939), w; EARL OF PUDDLESTONE(1940), w; MEET THE MISSUS(1940), w; GAY VAGABOND, THE(1941), w; PETTICOAT POLITICS(1941), w; HOUSE OF ERRORS(1942), w; CAMPUS RYTHM(1943), w
Silents
SINGED WINGS(1922), w; SOUTH OF SUVA(1922), w; NIGHT CRY, THE(1926), w; AFLAME IN THE SKY(1927), w; HOME STRUCK(1927), w; OUTLAW DOG, THE(1927), w; RANGER OF THE NORTH(1927), w; DEAD MAN'S CURVE(1928), w, ed

Frank Adamson

CHRISTINA(1974, Can.); SILENCE OF THE NORTH(1981, Can.)
1984
MRS. SOFFEL(1984)

George Adamson

BORN FREE(1966), tech adv; ELEPHANT CALLED SLOWLY, AN(1970, Brit.); CHRISTIAN THE LION(1976, Brit.)

Hans Christian Adamson

HELLCATS OF THE NAVY(1957), w

Harold Adamson

UNDER-PUP, THE(1939), m; HIT PARADE OF 1943(1943), md; SCENT OF MYSTERY(1960), m

James Adamson

FUGITIVE LADY(1934); LONE COWBOY(1934); HANDS ACROSS THE TABLE(1935); DARK MANHATTAN(1937); IN NAME ONLY(1939); WHISTLING IN THE DARK(1941); JUNGLE SIREN(1942); RINGS ON HER FINGERS(1942); DOUBLE INDEMNITY(1944); COLONEL EFFINGHAM'S RAID(1945); LETTER TO THREE WIVES, A(1949); I WANT YOU(1951); I WAS A COMMUNIST FOR THE F.B.I.(1951); AFRICAN TREASURE(1952); SAFARI DRUMS(1953); GOLDEN IDOL, THE(1954); LORD OF THE JUNGLE(1955)

John Adamson

HER FIRST ROMANCE(1940)

Joy Adamson

BORN FREE(1966), w; LIVING FREE(1972, Brit.), w

Peter F. Adamson

TAKE HER BY SURPRISE(1967, Can.)

Raymond Adamson

ECHO OF DIANA(1963, Brit.); IT!(1967, Brit.)

Robert Adamson

FARMER'S OTHER DAUGHTER, THE(1965)

Rod Adamson

BLUE FIN(1978, Aus.), ed; WEEKEND OF SHADOWS(1978, Aus.), ed

Roger Adamson

REMEMBRANCE(1982, Brit.)

Terence Adamson

CHRISTIAN THE LION(1976, Brit.)

Victor Adamson [Denver Dixon]

SAGEBRUSH POLITICS(1930), p&d; FIGHTING COWBOY(1933), p; CIRCLE CANYON(1934), p&d; LIGHTNING RANGE(1934), p&d; RIDING SPEED(1934), p; ARIZONA TRAILS(1935), p; DESERT MESA(1935), p; ROLL, WAGONS, ROLL(1939), w
Misc. Talkies
BOSS COWBOY(1934), d; PECOS DANDY, THE(1934), d; RAWHIDE ROMANCE(1934), d

Misc. Silents
COMPASSION(1927), d
Laura Adani
BORSALINO(1970, Fr.)
Ted Adanis
HUMAN TARGETS(1932)
Ralph Adano
SPEEDWAY(1968)
Larry Adare
PRIZE, THE(1963)
Robin Adare
PRIZE, THE(1963)
K. Adashevskiy
KATERINA IZMAILOVA(1969, USSR)
Abi Adatsi
1984
WHITE ELEPHANT(1984, Brit.)
James Aday
HOW TO BEAT THE HIGH COST OF LIVING(1980)
Harry Adby
ANTS IN HIS PANTS(1940, Aus.)
Chris Adcock
TREASURE ISLAND(1950, Brit.)
Danny Adcock
ON THE RUN(1983, Aus.); WE OF THE NEVER NEVER(1983, Aus.)
David Adcock
KITTY AND THE BAGMAN(1983, Aus.)
Jean Adcock
SUMMER STOCK(1950)
W. Adcook
Misc. Silents
FIGHTING JIM GRANT(1923), d
Duke Addabayo
1984
ELEMENT OF CRIME, THE(1984, Den.)
Dawn Addams
NIGHT INTO MORNING(1951); UNKNOWN MAN, THE(1951); HOUR OF THIRTEEN, THE(1952); PLYMOUTH ADVENTURE(1952); SINGIN' IN THE RAIN(1952); MOON IS BLUE, THE(1953); ROBE, THE(1953); YOUNG BESS(1953); KHYBER PATROL(1954); RETURN TO TREASURE ISLAND(1954); RIDERS TO THE STARS(1954); SECRETS D'ALCOVE(1954, Fr./Ital.); KING IN NEW YORK, A(1957, Brit.); HOUSE OF INTRIGUE, THE(1959, Ital.); SILENT ENEMY, THE(1959, Brit.); COME DANCE WITH ME(1960, Fr.); PRISONER OF THE VOLGA(1960, Fr./Ital.); THOUSAND EYES OF DR. MABUSE, THE(1960, Fr./Ital./Ger.); FOLLOW THAT MAN(1961, Brit.); HOUSE OF FRIGHT(1961); HOT MONEY GIRL(1962, Brit./Ger.); ROMMEL'S TREASURE(1962, Ital.); TEMPTATION(1962, Fr.); COME FLY WITH ME(1963); LIARS, THE(1964, Fr.); 20,000 POUNDS KISS, THE(1964, Brit.); BLUES FOR LOVERS(1966, Brit.); WHERE THE BULLETS FLY(1966, Brit.); VAMPIRE LOVERS, THE(1970, Brit.); VAULT OF HORROR, THE(1973, Brit.)
James Addams
L'AVVENTURA(1960, Ital.)
Lee Addams
DIARY OF A MAD HOUSEWIFE(1970)
John Adderley
SPANISH GARDENER, THE(1957, Span.)
Giovanni Addessi
LE AMICHE(1962, Ital.), p
Malcolm Addey
IF EVER I SEE YOU AGAIN(1978)
Elizabeth Addeyman
SECRET TENT, THE(1956, Brit.), w
Johnny Addie
GANG THAT COULDN'T SHOOT STRAIGHT, THE(1971)
Robert Addie
EXCALIBUR(1981)
1984
ANOTHER COUNTRY(1984, Brit.)
Everett Addington
WOMEN AND BLOODY TERROR(1970)
Misc. Talkies
KEEP OFF! KEEP OFF!(1975)
Ken Addington
WOMEN AND BLOODY TERROR(1970)
Sarah Addington
DANCE TEAM(1932), w; AND SO THEY WERE MARRIED(1936), w
Richard Addinsel
FIRE OVER ENGLAND(1937, Brit.), m
A. Trevor Addinsell
Misc. Silents
TOUCH OF A CHILD, THE(1918, Brit.)
Richard Addinsell
DARK JOURNEY(1937, Brit.), m; SOUTH RIDING(1938, Brit.), m; THE BEACHCOMBER(1938, Brit.), m; TROOPSHIP(1938, Brit.), m; GOODBYE MR. CHIPS(1939, Brit.), m; GASLIGHT(1940), m; LION HAS WINGS, THE(1940, Brit.), m; SUICIDE SQUADRON(1942, Brit.), m; BLITHE SPIRIT(1945, Brit.), m; LOVE ON THE DOLE(1945, Brit.), m; ONE WOMAN'S STORY(1949, Brit.), m; UNDER CAPRICORN(1949), m; BLACK ROSE, THE(1950), m; CHRISTMAS CAROL, A(1951, Brit.), m; ENCORE(1951, Brit.), m; TOM BROWN'S SCHOOLDAYS(1951, Brit.), m; SEA DEVILS(1953), m; BEAU BRUMMELL(1954), m; OUT OF THE CLOUDS(1957, Brit.), m; PRINCE AND THE SHOWGIRL, THE(1957, Brit.), m; TALE OF TWO CITIES, A(1958, Brit.), m; LOSS OF INNOCENCE(1961, Brit.), m; ROMAN SPRING OF MRS. STONE, THE(1961, U.S./Brit.), m; WALTZ OF THE TOREADORS(1962, Brit.), m; WAR LOVER, THE(1962, U.S./Brit.), m; MACBETH(1963), m; LIFE AT THE TOP(1965, Brit.), m
Cecil Addis
HELL SQUAD(1958)
David Addis
TANK COMMANDOS(1959)

H. B. Addis [Hugo Butler]
YOUNG ONE, THE(1961, Mex.), w
Joan Addis
TERROR IN THE JUNGLE(1968)
Michael Scott Addis
EUREKA(1983, Brit.)
Darline Addison
WORDS AND MUSIC(1929)
Edward Addison
ESCAPE(1930, Brit.)
Jeff Addison
Misc. Talkies
TAKE ONE(1977)
John Addison
HELL, HEAVEN OR HOBOKEN(1958, Brit.), m, md; SEVEN DAYS TO NOON(1950, Brit.), m; HIGH TREASON(1951, Brit.), m; POOL OF LONDON(1951, Brit.), m; BRANDY FOR THE PARSON(1952, Brit.), m; HOUR OF THIRTEEN, THE(1952), m, md; MAN BETWEEN, THE(1953, Brit.), m; TERROR ON A TRAIN(1953), m; TIME GENTLEMEN PLEASE!(1953, Brit.), m; BLACK KNIGHT, THE(1954), m; END OF THE ROAD, THE(1954, Brit.), m; HIGH AND DRY(1954, Brit.), m; MAKE ME AN OFFER(1954, Brit.), m; PARATROOPER(1954, Brit.), m; COCKLESHELL HEROES, THE(1955), m; JOSEPHINE AND MEN(1955, Brit.), m; LIGHT TOUCH, THE(1955, Brit.), m; ONE GOOD TURN(1955, Brit.), m; THAT LADY(1955, Brit.), m, md; PRIVATE'S PROGRESS(1956, Brit.), m; LUCKY JIM(1957, Brit.), m; REACH FOR THE SKY(1957, Brit.), m; SHIRALEE, THE(1957, Brit.), m; ALL AT SEA(1958, Brit.), m; THREE MEN IN A BOAT(1958, Brit.), m; LOOK BACK IN ANGER(1959), md; ENTERTAINER, THE(1960, Brit.), m; FRENCH MISTRESS(1960, Brit.), m; MAN IN A COCKED HAT(1960, Bri.), m; SCHOOL FOR SCOUNDRELS(1960, Brit.), m; HIS AND HERS(1961, Brit.), m; GO TO BLAZES(1962, Brit.), m; LONELINESS OF THE LONG DISTANCE RUNNER, THE(1962, Brit.), m; TASTE OF HONEY, A(1962, Brit.), m, md; TOM JONES(1963, Brit.), m, md; GIRL WITH GREEN EYES(1964, Brit.), m&md; GUNS AT BATASI(1964, Brit.), m&md; MODEL MURDER CASE, THE(1964, Brit.), m, md; AMOROUS ADVENTURES OF MOLL FLANDERS, THE(1965), m; LOVED ONE, THE(1965), m; FINE MADNESS, A(1966), m; TIME LOST AND TIME REMEMBERED(1966, Brit.), m; TORN CURTAIN(1966), m; HONEY POT, THE(1967, Brit.), m; SMASHING TIME(1967 Brit.), m; CHARGE OF THE LIGHT BRIGADE, THE(1968, Brit.), m; BROTHERLY LOVE(1970, Brit.), m; START THE REVOLUTION WITHOUT ME(1970), m, md; CRY OF THE PENGUINS(1972, Brit.), m; SLEUTH(1972, Brit.), m; LUTHER(1974), m; RIDE A WILD PONY(1976, U.S./Aus.), m; SWASHBUCKLER(1976), m; BRIDGE TOO FAR, A(1977, Brit.), m; JOSEPH ANDREWS(1977, Brit.), m; SEVEN-PER-CENT SOLUTION, THE(1977, Brit.), m; PILOT, THE(1979), m; STRANGE INVADERS(1983), m
1984
HIGHPOINT(1984, Can.), m; ULTIMATE SOLUTION OF GRACE QUIGLEY, THE(1984), m
Patrick Addison
GREED OF WILLIAM HART, THE(1948, Brit.)
Jus Addiss
CRY BABY KILLER, THE(1958), d
Mario Addobati
WAR AND PEACE(1956, Ital./U.S.)
Aldo Addobbati
FANTASTIC THREE, THE(1967, Ital./Ger./Fr./Yugo.), p
Giuseppe Addobbati
KILL BABY KILL(1966, Ital.); MISSION STARDUST(1968, Ital./Span./Ger.); TO COMMIT A MURDER(1970, Fr./Ital./Ger.); CONFORMIST, THE(1971, Ital., Fr); NIGHT PORTER, THE(1974, Ital./U.S.)
Wesley Addy
FIRST LEGION, THE(1951); BIG KNIFE, THE(1955); KISS ME DEADLY(1955); TIMETABLE(1956); GARMENT JUNGLE, THE(1957); TEN SECONDS TO HELL(1959); WHATEVER HAPPENED TO BABY JANE?(1962); FOUR FOR TEXAS(1963); HUSH... HUSH, SWEET CHARLOTTE(1964); MISTER BUDDWING(1966); SECONDS(1966); TORA! TORA! TORA!(1970, U.S./Jap.); GRISSOM GANG, THE(1971); NETWORK(1976); EUROPEANS, THE(1979, Brit.); VERDICT, THE(1982)
1984
BOSTONIANS, THE(1984)
George Ade
YOUNG AS YOU FEEL(1931), w; COUNTY CHAIRMAN, THE(1935), w; FRESHMAN LOVE(1936), w
Silents
COUNTY CHAIRMAN, THE(1914), w; SLIM PRINCESS, THE(1915), w; ARTIE, THE MILLIONAIRE KID(1916), w; JUST OUT OF COLLEGE(1921), w; BACK HOME AND BROKE(1922), w; OUR LEADING CITIZEN(1922), w; OLD HOME WEEK(1925), w; FAIR CO-ED, THE(1927), w
Obaka Adedunyo
NIGHTHAWKS(1981)
Richard Adee
PEOPLE NEXT DOOR, THE(1970), set d
Remi Adefarasin
1984
FOUR DAYS IN JULY(1984), ph
Adele
MYSTERY BROADCAST(1943), cos
Blanche Adele
THOSE WHO LOVE(1929, Brit.); EAST LYNNE ON THE WESTERN FRONT(1931, Brit.); BROTHER ALFRED(1932, Brit.); NEW HOTEL, THE(1932, Brit.); I'M AN EXPLOSIVE(1933, Brit.)
Silents
BROKEN ROMANCE, A(1929, Brit.)
Jan Adele
CADDIE(1976, Aus.)
Tamara Adelheim
Misc. Silents
JEWISH LUCK(1925, USSR); SEEDS OF FREEDOM(1929, USSR)
Sherri Adeline
PHANTOM OF THE PARADISE(1974)
Hirsch Adell
ON THE NICKEL(1980)

Joe Adelman
COOL AND THE CRAZY, THE(1958)
Joseph Adelman
Misc. Silents
CONTINENTAL GIRL, A(1915), d; WHERE IS MY FATHER?(1916), d
Julius Adelman
KILLER'S KISS(1955)
Gary Adelson
1984
LAST STARFIGHTER, THE(1984), p
Maude Adelson
OBSESSION(1968, Swed.)
Merv Adelson
CHOIRBOYS, THE(1977), p; TWILIGHT'S LAST GLEAMING(1977, U.S./Ger.), p
Dapo Adelugba
KONGI'S HARVEST(1971, U.S./Nigeria)
A. Adelung
CAPTAIN GRANT'S CHILDREN(1939, USSR)
Yashar Adem
KEEP, THE(1983)
Yasher Adem
SPY WHO LOVED ME, THE(1977, Brit.)
Robin Aden
TOUCH OF HER FLESH, THE(1967), m
Eric Adeney
CASTLE SINISTER(1932, Brit.)
Funso Adeolu
COUNTDOWN AT KUSINI(1976, Nigerian)
Jack Ader
PAWNBROKER, THE(1965)
Frank Aderias
Silents
GOLD RUSH, THE(1925)
Leona Aderias
Silents
GOLD RUSH, THE(1925)
Dan Ades
MISSOURI BREAKS, THE(1976); PASSOVER PLOT, THE(1976, Israel)
Daniel Ades
ST. VALENTINE'S DAY MASSACRE, THE(1967); TARGETS(1968); LAST MOVIE, THE(1971); 10 TO MIDNIGHT(1983)
Danny Ades
AGUIRRE, THE WRATH OF GOD(1977, W. Ger.); ON THE NICKEL(1980); SURVIVAL RUN(1980)
Vivienne Ades
DUAL ALIBI(1947, Brit.), w
Lilias Adeson
GRANDAD RUDD(1935, Aus.)
Giovanni Adessi
WEB OF THE SPIDER(1972, Ital./Fr./Ger.), p, w
Georges Adet
UP FROM THE BEACH(1965); TASTE FOR WOMEN, A(1966, Fr./Ital.); LOVE AND DEATH(1975); ZIG-ZAG(1975, Fr/Ital.)
Frank Adey
NEW HOTEL, THE(1932, Brit.)
Ilma Adey
KING OF THE CORAL SEA(1956, Aus.)
Del Adey-Jones
10 TO MIDNIGHT(1983), cos
Sally Adez
CHATO'S LAND(1972)
John Adiar
MUSS 'EM UP(1936)
Patrick Adiarte
KING AND I, THE(1956); HIGH TIME(1960); FLOWER DRUM SONG(1961); JOHN GOLDFARB, PLEASE COME HOME(1964)
Egbert Adieso
HAMILE(1965, Ghana), ed
Ugo Adinolfi
GIRL WHO COULDN'T SAY NO, THE(1969, Ital.); PLUCKED(1969, Fr./Ital.); INVESTIGATION OF A CITIZEN ABOVE SUSPICION(1970, Ital.); KILL THEM ALL AND COME BACK ALONE(1970, Ital./Span.); MERCENARY, THE(1970, Ital./Span.)
Patricia Adiutori
TORSO(1974, Ital.)
Vern Adix
BEYOND AND BACK(1978)
Eric Adjani
DON GIOVANNI(1979, Fr./Ital./Ger.)
Isabelle Adjani
STORY OF ADELE H., THE(1975, Fr.); BAROCCO(1976, Fr.); TENANT, THE(1976, Fr.); DRIVER, THE(1978); BRONTE SISTERS, THE(1979, Fr.); NOSFERATU, THE VAMPIRE(1979, Fr./Ger.); POSSESSION(1981, Fr./Ger.); QUARTET(1981, Brit./Fr.)
1984
ONE DEADLY SUMMER(1984, Fr.)
Don Adkins
TOWN THAT DREADED SUNDOWN, THE(1977)
Ella Adkins
TIME IS MY ENEMY(1957, Brit.), w
Lt. Joseph D. Adkins, USN
ETERNAL SEA, THE(1955), tech adv
Suzanne Adkinson
1984
RACING WITH THE MOON(1984)
Paul Adkonas
Misc. Silents
HANDS OF ORLAC, THE(1925, Aust.)
Basil Adlam
SHIP AHOY(1942), m

Darrel Adleman
CROSS AND THE SWITCHBLADE, THE(1970)
Joe Adleman
DELINQUENTS, THE(1957)
Robert H. Adleman
DEVIL'S BRIGADE, THE(1968), w
Alan Adler
PARASITE(1982), w
Alan J. Adler
CONCRETE JUNGLE, THE(1982), w; METALSTORM: THE DESTRUCTION OF JARED-SYN(1983), p, w
Allen Adler
FORBIDDEN PLANET(1956), w
Ben Adler
WANDERING JEW, THE(1933)
Misc. Talkies
JOSEPH IN THE LAND OF EGYPT(1932); ABRAHAM OUR PATRIARCH(1933); PEOPLE THAT SHALL NOT DIE, A(1939)
Bill Adler
POM POM GIRLS, THE(1976); VAN, THE(1977); LOVE AND THE MIDNIGHT AUTO SUPPLY(1978); MALIBU BEACH(1978); VAN NUYS BLVD.(1979)
Bob Adler
SHOCK(1946); BRASHER DOUBLOON, THE(1947); FOREVER AMBER(1947); DANCING IN THE DARK(1949); FATHER WAS A FULLBACK(1949); OUTCASTS OF POKER FLAT, THE(1952); PEYTON PLACE(1957); WILL SUCCESS SPOIL ROCK HUNTER?(1957); 10 NORTH FREDERICK(1958); BANDOLERO!(1968)
Bud Adler
SAM WHISKEY(1969)
Buddy Adler
DARK PAST, THE(1948), p; TELL IT TO THE JUDGE(1949), p; NO SAD SONGS FOR ME(1950), p; WOMAN OF DISTINCTION, A(1950), p; HARLEM GLOBETROTTERS, THE(1951), p; SATURDAY'S HERO(1951), p; LAST OF THE COMANCHES(1952), p; PAULA(1952), p; FROM HERE TO ETERNITY(1953), p; SALOME(1953), p; HOUSE OF BAMBOO(1955), p; LEFT HAND OF GOD, THE(1955), p; LOVE IS A MANY-SPLENDORED THING(1955), p; SOLDIER OF FORTUNE(1955), p; VIOLENT SATURDAY(1955), p; ANASTASIA(1956), p; BOTTOM OF THE BOTTLE, THE(1956), p; BUS STOP(1956), p; LIEUTENANT WORE SKIRTS, THE(1956), p; REVOLT OF MAMIE STOVER, THE(1956), p; HATFUL OF RAIN, A(1957), p; HEAVEN KNOWS, MR. ALLISON(1957), p; INN OF THE SIXTH HAPPINESS, THE(1958), p; SOUTH PACIFIC(1958), p
Celia Adler
WHERE IS MY CHILD?(1937); NAKED CITY, THE(1948)
Charles Adler
VICTIMS OF PERSECUTION(1933); THANKS A MILLION(1935)
Misc. Silents
LOOPED FOR LIFE(1924)
Clyde Adler
PATSY, THE(1964)
Cynthia Adler
KNIGHTRIDERS(1981)
Dick Adler
WILD 90(1968)
Ernest Adler
CATCH-22(1970), cos
Fay Adler
BANK DICK, THE(1940); MY LITTLE CHICKADEE(1940); TEN DAYS TO TULA-RA(1958), m
Felicity Adler
I, THE JURY(1982)
Felix Adler
WELCOME DANGER(1929), w; FEET FIRST(1930), w; MOVIE CRAZY(1932), w; OUR RELATIONS(1936), w; WAY OUT WEST(1937), w; BLOCKHEADS(1938), w; SWISS MISS(1938), w; CHUMP AT OXFORD, A(1940), w; SAPS AT SEA(1940), w; COWBOY CANTEEN(1944), w; GREATEST SHOW ON EARTH, THE(1952); JACK AND THE BEANSTALK(1952), w
Gil Adler
HOME MOVIES(1979), p
Hans Adler
FOLIES DERGERE(1935), w; THAT NIGHT IN RIO(1941), w; ON THE RIVE-RA(1951), w
Harry Adler
BY WHOSE HAND?(1932), w
Ida Adler
TWO SISTERS(1938)
Jay Adler
NO TIME TO MARRY(1938); PENROD AND HIS TWIN BROTHER(1938); CRY DANGER(1951); MOB, THE(1951); ASSIGNMENT–PARIS(1952); DREAMBOAT(1952); MY PAL GUS(1952); MY SIX CONVICTS(1952); PRISONER OF ZENDA, THE(1952); SCANDAL SHEET(1952); TURNING POINT, THE(1952); JUGGLER, THE(1953); VICE SQUAD(1953); 99 RIVER STREET(1953); DOWN THREE DARK STREETS(1954); LONG WAIT, THE(1954); BIG COMBO, THE(1955); ILLEGAL(1955); LOVE ME OR LEAVE ME(1955); LUCY GALLANT(1955); MAN WITH THE GUN(1955); MURDER IS MY BEAT(1955); CATERED AFFAIR, THE(1956); KILLING, THE(1956); LUST FOR LIFE(1956); CRIME OF PASSION(1957); HELL ON DEVIL'S ISLAND(1957); RUNAWAY DAUGHTERS(1957); SWEET SMELL OF SUCCESS(1957); BROTHERS KARAMAZOV, THE(1958); SADDLE THE WIND(1958); SEVEN GUNS TO MESA(1958); CURSE OF THE UNDEAD(1959); STORY ON PAGE ONE, THE(1959); DIME WITH A HALO(1963); FAMILY JEWELS, THE(1965); GRAVE OF THE VAMPIRE(1972)
Misc. Talkies
BELLE SOMMERS(1962)
Jerry Adler
TOKYO AFTER DARK(1959); FLAP(1970), p
Jimmy Adler
1984
HOME FREE ALL(1984)
Joseph Adler
SCREAM, BABY, SCREAM(1969), p&d, ed

Misc. Talkies
REVENGE IS MY DESTINY(1971), d; SAMMY SOMEBODY(1976), d; CONVENTION GIRLS(1978), d

Judy Adler
UNDER AGE(1964); SATAN'S BED(1965)

Julius Adler
TEVYA(1939); CATSKILL HONEYMOON(1950)
Silents
BROKEN HEARTS(1926)

Kurt Adler
YES, GIORGIO(1982)

Larry Adler
MANY HAPPY RETURNS(1934); BIG BROADCAST OF 1937, THE(1936); SINGING MARINE, THE(1937); SIDEWALKS OF LONDON(1940, Brit.); MUSIC FOR MILLIONS(1944); THREE DARING DAUGHTERS(1948); GENEVIEVE(1953, Brit.), m; JUMPING FOR JOY(1956, Brit.), m; CRY FROM THE STREET, A(1959, Brit.), m; HELLIONS, THE(1962, Brit.), m; HOOK, THE(1962), m; KING AND COUNTRY(1964, Brit.), m; HIGH WIND IN JAMAICA, A(1965), m

Lou Adler
UP IN SMOKE(1978), p, d; BREWSTER McCLOUD(1970), p; LADIES AND GENTLEMEN, THE FABULOUS STAINS(1982), d

Lulla Adler
PARIS BLUES(1961), w

Luther Adler
LANCER SPY(1937); CORNERED(1945); LOVES OF CARMEN, THE(1948); SAIGON(1948); HOUSE OF STRANGERS(1949); WAKE OF THE RED WITCH(1949); D.O.A.(1950); KISS TOMORROW GOODBYE(1950); SOUTH SEA SINNER(1950); UNDER MY SKIN(1950); DESERT FOX, THE(1951); M(1951); MAGIC FACE, THE(1951, Aust.); HOODLUM EMPIRE(1952); TALL TEXAN, THE(1953); MIAMI STORY, THE(1954); CRASHOUT(1955); GIRL IN THE RED VELVET SWING, THE(1955); HOT BLOOD(1956); LAST ANGRY MAN, THE(1959); CAST A GIANT SHADOW(1966); BROTHERHOOD, THE(1968); CRAZY JOE(1974); MURPH THE SURF(1974); MAN IN THE GLASS BOOTH, THE(1975); MEAN JOHNNY BARROWS(1976); VOYAGE OF THE DAMNED(1976, Brit.); THREE SISTERS, THE(1977); ABSENCE OF MALICE(1981)

Nathan Adler
ON THE NICKEL(1980)

Polly Adler
HOUSE IS NOT A HOME, A(1964), w

Robert Adler
MY DARLING CLEMENTINE(1946); CAPTAIN FROM CASTILE(1947); KISS OF DEATH(1947); CRY OF THE CITY(1948); FURY AT FURNACE CREEK(1948); GREEN GRASS OF WYOMING(1948); IRON CURTAIN, THE(1948); LUCK OF THE IRISH(1948); SCUDDA-HOO! SCUDDA-HAY!(1948); YELLOW SKY(1948); BROKEN ARROW(1950); NO WAY OUT(1950); TICKET TO TOMAHAWK(1950); TWO FLAGS WEST(1950); FROGMEN, THE(1951); RAWHIDE(1951); LES MISERABLES(1952); LURE OF THE WILDERNESS(1952); RED SKIES OF MONTANA(1952); RETURN OF THE TEXAN(1952); CITY OF BAD MEN(1953); HOW TO MARRY A MILLIONAIRE(1953); INFERNO(1953); POWDER RIVER(1953); SILVER WHIP, THE(1953); VICKI(1953); BROKEN LANCE(1954); HELL AND HIGH WATER(1954); PRINCE VALIANT(1954); TALL MEN, THE(1955); UNTAMED(1955); VIOLENT SATURDAY(1955); VIRGIN QUEEN, THE(1955); FURY AT SHOWDOWN(1957); TRUE STORY OF JESSE JAMES, THE(1957); VALERIE(1957); BRAVADOS, THE(1958); JOURNEY TO THE CENTER OF THE EARTH(1959); WARLOCK(1959); STORY OF RUTH, THE(1960); FATE IS THE HUNTER(1964)

Robin Adler
TWO OF A KIND(1983)

Robin D. Adler
1984
RHINESTONE(1984)

Ruth Adler
I MARRIED AN ANGEL(1942)

Sandy Hendrick Adler
VAN NUYS BLVD.(1979), ch

Sarah Adler
Misc. Silents
SINS OF THE PARENTS(1914)

Stanislaw Adler
KANAL(1961, Pol.), p; EROICA(1966, Pol.), p; LOTNA(1966, Pol.), p

Stella Adler
LOVE ON TOAST(1937); SHADOW OF THE THIN MAN(1941); MY GIRL TISA(1948)

Toby Adler
GOOD MORNING... AND GOODBYE(1967)

William F. Adler
Silents
SECOND IN COMMAND, THE(1915), ph

Ahmed Adley
LITTLE MISS DEVIL(1951, Egypt), ph

Georges Adlin
MR. HULOT'S HOLIDAY(1954, Fr.)

Duke Adlon
ICELAND(1942)

Duke Louis Adlon
FIRST COMES COURAGE(1943)

Eleanore Adlon
CELESTE(1982, Ger.), p

Louis Adlon
DRAMATIC SCHOOL(1938); ESPIONAGE AGENT(1939); MYSTERY SEA RAIDER(1940); MY FAVORITE SPY(1942); HOSTAGES(1943); BIG SHOW-OFF, THE(1945); COUNTER-ATTACK(1945)

Percy Adlon
CELESTE(1982, Ger.), d&w

Adlum
SHRIEK OF THE MUTILATED(1974), w

Ed Adlum
INVASION OF THE BLOOD FARMERS(1972), p&d, w; SHRIEK OF THE MUTILATED(1974), p

Ernie Admas
COWBOY AND THE LADY, THE(1938)

Henry Adnes
GOOD COMPANIONS(1933, Brit.); LITTLE DOLLY DAYDREAM(1938, Brit.); ROSE OF TRALEE(1938, Ireland)

John Adolfi
COLLEGE LOVERS(1930), d; COMPROMISED(1931), d; CENTRAL PARK(1932), d; KING'S VACATION, THE(1933), d
Silents
MAN AND HIS MATE, A(1915), d
Misc. Silents
CHILD OF GOD, A(1915), d; LITTLE MISS HAPPINESS(1916), d; MERELY MARY ANN(1916), d; SPHINX, THE(1916), d; QUEEN OF THE SEA(1918), d; BEFORE MIDNIGHT(1925), d; PHANTOM EXPRESS, THE(1925), d

John G. Adolfi
MIDNIGHT TAXI, THE(1928), d; EVIDENCE(1929), d; FANCY BAGGAGE(1929), d; IN THE HEADLINES(1929), d; DUMBBELLS IN ERMINE(1930), d; RECAPTURED LOVE(1930), d; SINNER'S HOLIDAY(1930), d; ALEXANDER HAMILTON(1931), d; MILLIONAIRE, THE(1931), d; MAN WHO PLAYED GOD, THE(1932), d; SUCCESSFUL CALAMITY, A(1932), d; VOLTAIRE(1933), d; WORKING MAN, THE(1933), d
Silents
CAPRICE OF THE MOUNTAINS(1916), d; MISCHIEF MAKER, THE(1916), d&w; MODERN CINDERELLA, A(1917), d; LITTLE 'FRAID LADY, THE(1920), d; DARLING OF THE RICH, THE(1923), d; BIG PAL(1925), d; HUSBAND HUNTERS(1927), d; WHAT HAPPENED TO FATHER(1927), d; SINNER'S PARADE(1928), d
Misc. Silents
MAN INSIDE, THE(1916), d; MODERN THELMA, A(1916), d; RAGGED PRINCESS, THE(1916), d; CHILD OF THE WILD, A(1917), d; PATSY(1917), d; SMALL TOWN GIRL, A(1917), d; HEART OF A GIRL(1918), d; WOMAN THE GERMANS SHOT(1918), d; WHO'S YOUR BROTHER?(1919), d; WONDER MAN, THE(1920), d; LITTLE RED SCHOOLHOUSE, THE(1923), d; CHALK MARKS(1924), d; WHAT SHALL I DO?(1924), d; SCARLET WEST, THE(1925), d; CHECKERED FLAG, THE(1926), d; DEVIL'S SKIPPER, THE(1928), d; LITTLE SNOB, THE(1928), d; PROWLERS OF THE SEA(1928), d

Heidi Adolph
RADIO ON(1980, Brit./Ger.), w

Hylette Adolphe
FELLINI SATYRICON(1969, Fr./Ital.); UNDERCOVERS HERO(1975, Brit.)

Edvin Adolphson
COUNT OF THE MONK'S BRIDGE, THE(1934, Swed.), a, d; ON THE SUNNYSIDE(1936, Swed.); DOLLAR(1938, Swed.); ONLY ONE NIGHT(1942, Swed.); GYPSY FURY(1950, Fr.); MAKE WAY FOR LILA(1962, Swed./Ger.); SWEDISH WEDDING NIGHT(1965, Swed.); LOVE MATES(1967, Swed.); LURE OF THE JUNGLE, THE(1970, Den.)
Misc. Talkies
BOY OF TWO WORLDS(1970)

Kristina Adolphson
FACE TO FACE(1976, Swed.)

Kristina Adolphsson
DEVIL'S EYE, THE(1960, Swed.)

Lan Adomian
DREAM NO MORE(1950, Palestine), m; YOUNG AND EVIL(1962, Mex.), m

Frank Adonis
EYES OF LAURA MARS(1978); RAGING BULL(1980); WOLFEN(1981)

Rene Adore
Silents
MAN AND MAID(1925)

Andre Adoree
ESCAPE FROM RED ROCK(1958)

Rene Adoree
Silents
ON ZE BOULEVARD(1927)

Renee Adoree
PAGAN, THE(1929); SPIELER, THE(1929); CALL OF THE FLESH(1930); REDEMPTION(1930)
Silents
MADE IN HEAVEN(1921); MIXED FACES(1922); WEST OF CHICAGO(1922); ETERNAL STRUGGLE, THE(1923); BIG PARADE, THE(1925); BLACK BIRD, THE(1926); EXQUISITE SINNER, THE(1926); TIN GODS(1926); MR. WU(1927); MICHIGAN KID, THE(1928); SHOW PEOPLE(1928)
Misc. Silents
STRONGEST, THE(1920); HONOR FIRST(1922); SELF-MADE MAN, A(1922); SIX-FIFTY, THE(1923); DEFYING THE LAW(1924); MAN'S MATE, A(1924); WOMEN WHO GIVE(1924); EXCHANGE OF WIVES(1925); EXCUSE ME(1925); BLARNEY(1926); FLAMING FOREST, THE(1926); LA BOHEME(1926); BACK TO GOD'S COUNTRY(1927); HEAVEN ON EARTH(1927); SHOW, THE(1927); CERTAIN YOUNG MAN, A(1928); COSSACKS, THE(1928); FORBIDDEN HOURS(1928); PAGAN, THE(1929); TIDE OF EMPIRE(1929)

Renne Adoree
Misc. Silents
MATING CALL, THE(1928)

Mario Adorf
DEVIL STRIKES AT NIGHT, THE(1959, Ger.); ROSEMARY(1960, Ger.); THREE MOVES TO FREEDOM(1960, Ger.); BRAINWASHED(1961, Ger.); LULU(1962, Aus.); STATION SIX-SAHARA(1964, Brit./Ger.); APACHE GOLD(1965, Ger.); MAJOR DUNDEE(1965); TEN LITTLE INDIANS(1965, Brit.); GIRL AND THE LEGEND, THE(1966, Ger.); LA VISITA(1966, Ital./Fr.); SUNSCORCHED(1966, Span./Ger.); THAT MAN IN ISTANBUL(1966, Fr./Ital./Span.); THE DIRTY GAME(1966, Fr./Ital./Ger.); ROSE FOR EVERYONE, A(1967, Ital.); ANYONE CAN PLAY(1968, Ital.); TREASURE OF SAN GENNARO(1968, Fr./Ital./Ger.); DROP THEM OR I'LL SHOOT(1969, Fr./Ger./Span.); GHOSTS, ITALIAN STYLE(1969, Ital./Fr.); BIRD WITH THE CRYSTAL PLUMAGE, THE(1970, Ital./Ger.); RED TENT, THE(1971, Ital./USSR); KING, QUEEN, KNAVE(1972, Ger./U.S.); ITALIAN CONNECTION, THE(1973, U.S./Ital.); LOST HONOR OF KATHARINA BLUM, THE(1975, Ger.); FEDORA(1978, Ger./Fr.); GERMANY IN AUTUMN(1978, Ger.); TIN DRUM, THE(1979, Ger./Fr./Yugo./Pol.); LOLA(1982, Ger.)

Andrew Adorian
MAIN ATTRACTION, THE(1962, Brit.), m

Dina Adorni
AMARCORD(1974, Ital.)

Guido Adorni
GET CHARLIE TULLY(1976, Brit.); NEVER SAY NEVER AGAIN(1983)

Anatoli Adoskine
THREE TALES OF CHEKHOV(1961, USSR)

Adrainne
DRACULA(THE DIRTY OLD MAN) (1969)

Franklin Adreon
SONS OF ADVENTURE(1948), p, w; DAUGHTER OF THE JUNGLE(1949), p; ARIZONA COWBOY, THE(1950), p; HILLS OF OKLAHOMA(1950), p; REDWOOD FOREST TRAIL(1950), p; NO MAN'S WOMAN(1955), d; MAN IS ARMED, THE(1956), d; TERROR AT MIDNIGHT(1956), d; HELL'S CROSSROADS(1957), d; SATAN'S SATELLITES(1958), p; NUN AND THE SERGEANT, THE(1962), d; DIMENSION 5(1966), d
Misc. Talkies
COMMANDO CODY(1953), d; CLAW MONSTERS, THE(1966), d

Franklyn Adreon
HI-YO SILVER(1940), w; DRUMS OF FU MANCHU(1943), w

Danie Adrewmah
CRY, THE BELOVED COUNTRY(1952, Brit.)

Adrian
LADY OF CHANCE, A(1928), cos; DEVIL MAY CARE(1929), cos; LAST OF MRS. CHEYNEY, THE(1929), cos; MARIANNE(1929), cos; OUR MODERN MAIDENS(1929), cos; THEIR OWN DESIRE(1929), cos; TRIAL OF MARY DUGAN, THE(1929), cos; UNHOLY NIGHT, THE(1929), cos; UNTAMED(1929), cos; ANNA CHRISTIE(1930), cos; DIVORCEE, THE(1930), cos; LADY OF SCANDAL, THE(1930), cos; LADY'S MORALS, A(1930), cos; LET US BE GAY(1930), cos; MADAME SATAN(1930), cos; MONTANA MOON(1930), cos; NOT SO DUMB(1930), cos; OUR BLUSHING BRIDES(1930), cos; PAID(1930), cos; PASSION FLOWER(1930), cos; REDEMPTION(1930), cos; ROGUE SONG, THE(1930), cos; THIS MAD WORLD(1930), cos; FREE SOUL, A(1931), cos; PRIVATE LIVES(1931), cos; STRANGERS MAY KISS(1931), cos; THIS MODERN AGE(1931), cos; BLONDIE OF THE FOLLIES(1932), cos; GRAND HOTEL(1932), cos; LETTY LYNTON(1932), cos; MASK OF FU MANCHU, THE(1932), cos; RASPUTIN AND THE EMPRESS(1932), cos; RED DUST(1932), cos; SMILIN' THROUGH(1932), cos; STRANGE INTERLUDE(1932), cos; DANCING LADY(1933), cos; DINNER AT EIGHT(1933), cos; HOLD YOUR MAN(1933), cos; MIDNIGHT MARY(1933), cos; QUEEN CHRISTINA(1933), cos; SECRETS(1933), cos; STAGE MOTHER(1933), cos; TODAY WE LIVE(1933), cos; WHEN LADIES MEET(1933), cos; BARRETTS OF WIMPOLE STREET, THE(1934), cos; CAT AND THE FIDDLE(1934), cos; CHAINED(1934), cos; HOLLYWOOD PARTY(1934), cos; MERRY WIDOW, THE(1934), cos; NANA(1934), cos; OPERATOR 13(1934), cos; OUTCAST LADY(1934), cos; PAINTED VEIL, THE(1934), cos; PARIS INTERLUDE(1934), cos; RIP TIDE(1934), cos; SADIE MCKEE(1934), cos; WOMEN IN HIS LIFE, THE(1934), cos; CHINA SEAS(1935), cos; FORSAKING ALL OTHERS(1935), cos; I LIVE MY LIFE(1935), art d & cos; NAUGHTY MARIETTA(1935), cos; NO MORE LADIES(1935), cos; RECKLESS(1935), cos; GORGEOUS HUSSY, THE(1936), cos; GREAT ZIEGFELD, THE(1936), cos; LOVE ON THE RUN(1936), cos; ROMEO AND JULIET(1936), cos; ROSE MARIE(1936), cos; SAN FRANCISCO(1936), cos; WIFE VERSUS SECRETARY(1936), cos; BRIDE WORE RED, THE(1937), cos; FIREFLY, THE(1937), cos; LAST OF MRS. CHEYNEY, THE(1937), cos; MANNEQUIN(1937), cos; MAYTIME(1937), cos; PARNELL(1937), cos; DRAMATIC SCHOOL(1938), cos; GIRL OF THE GOLDEN WEST, THE(1938), cos; MARIE ANTOINETTE(1938), cos; SHINING HOUR, THE(1938), cos; SHOPWORN ANGEL(1938), cos; SWEETHEARTS(1938), cos; THREE LOVES HAS NANCY(1938), cos; ICE FOLLIES OF 1939(1939), cos; IDIOT'S DELIGHT(1939), cos; IT'S A WONDERFUL WORLD(1939), cos; LADY OF THE TROPICS(1939), cos; NINOTCHKA(1939), cos; WIZARD OF OZ, THE(1939), cos; WOMEN, THE(1939), cos; BOOM TOWN(1940), cos; ESCAPE(1940), cos; I TAKE THIS WOMAN(1940), cos; MORTAL STORM, THE(1940), cos; NEW MOON(1940), cos; PHILADELPHIA STORY, THE(1940), cos; PRIDE AND PREJUDICE(1940), cos; SUSAN AND GOD(1940), cos; WATERLOO BRIDGE(1940), cos; BLOSSOMS IN THE DUST(1941), cos; CHOCOLATE SOLDIER, THE(1941), cos; COME LIVE WITH ME(1941), cos; DR. JEKYLL AND MR. HYDE(1941), cos; LADY BE GOOD(1941), cos; RAGE IN HEAVEN(1941), cos; SMILIN' THROUGH(1941), cos; TWO-FACED WOMAN(1941), cos; WHEN LADIES MEET(1941), cos; WOMAN'S FACE(1941), cos; ZIEGFELD GIRL(1941), cos; KEEPER OF THE FLAME(1942), cos; WE WERE DANCING(1942), cos; WOMAN OF THE YEAR(1942), cos; THEY GOT ME COVERED(1943), cos; POSSESSED(1947), cos; ROPE(1948), cos; SMART WOMAN(1948), cos; LOVELY TO LOOK AT(1952), cos
Silents
EAGLE, THE(1925), cos; VOLGA BOATMAN, THE(1926), cos; VANITY(1927), cos; CHICAGO(1928), cos; STAND AND DELIVER(1928), cos; WALKING BACK(1928), cos; KISS, THE(1929), cos; SINGLE MAN, A(1929), cos; WILD ORCHIDS(1929), cos

Allan Adrian
CODE OF SILENCE(1960), w

Arnold Adrian
DEVIL'S HARBOR(1954, Brit.); BLONDE BLACKMAILER(1955, Brit.)

Christine Adrian
WOMANHOOD(1934, Brit.); AULD LANG SYNE(1937, Brit.); TERROR STREET(1953); HEATWAVE(1954, Brit.)

George Adrian
MY SISTER EILEEN(1942); FIGHTER SQUADRON(1948); MISTER 880(1950); TO CATCH A THIEF(1955)

Iris Adrian
RUMBA(1935); GOLD DIGGERS OF 1937(1936); LADY LUCK(1936); MESSAGE TO GARCIA, A(1936); MISTER CINDERELLA(1936); MURDER AT GLEN ATHOL(1936); ONE RAINY AFTERNOON(1936); OUR RELATIONS(1936); STAGE STRUCK(1936); BACK DOOR TO HEAVEN(1939); ONE THIRD OF A NATION(1939); MEET THE WILDCAT(1940); HARD GUY(1941); HORROR ISLAND(1941); LADY FROM CHEYENNE(1941); MEET THE CHUMP(1941); ROAD TO ZANZIBAR(1941); SING ANOTHER CHORUS(1941); SWING IT SOLDIER(1941); TOO MANY BLONDES(1941); WILD GEESE CALLING(1941); BROADWAY(1942); I KILLED THAT MAN(1942); JUKE BOX JENNY(1942); RINGS ON HER FINGERS(1942); ROXIE HART(1942); THUNDER BIRDS(1942); TO THE SHORES OF TRIPOLI(1942); ACTION IN THE NORTH ATLANTIC(1943); CRYSTAL BALL, THE(1943); HERS TO HOLD(1943); HIS BUTLER'S SISTER(1943); LADIES' DAY(1943); LADY OF BURLESQUE(1943); SPOTLIGHT SCANDALS(1943); SUBMARINE BASE(1943); ALASKA(1944); BLUEBEARD(1944); CAREER GIRL(1944); I'M FROM ARKANSAS(1944); MILLION DOLLAR KID(1944); ONCE UPON A TIME(1944); SHAKE HANDS WITH MURDER(1944); SINGING SHERIFF, THE(1944); SWING HOSTESS(1944); BOSTON

BLACKIE'S RENDEZVOUS(1945); IT'S A PLEASURE(1945); ROAD TO ALCATRAZ(1945); STEPPIN' IN SOCIETY(1945); STORK CLUB, THE(1945); WOMAN IN THE WINDOW, THE(1945); BAMBOO BLONDE, THE(1946); CROSS MY HEART(1946); VACATION IN RENO(1946); FALL GUY(1947); PHILO VANCE RETURNS(1947); TROUBLE WITH WOMEN, THE(1947); WISTFUL WIDOW OF WAGON GAP, THE(1947); OUT OF THE STORM(1948); PALEFACE, THE(1948); SMART WOMAN(1948); ALWAYS LEAVE THEM LAUGHING(1949); FLAMINGO ROAD(1949); LOVABLE CHEAT, THE(1949); MIGHTY JOE YOUNG(1949); MISS MINK OF 1949(1949); MY DREAM IS YOURS(1949); SKY DRAGON(1949); THERE'S A GIRL IN MY HEART(1949); TOUGH ASSIGNMENT(1949); TRAIL OF THE YUKON(1949); BLONDIE'S HERO(1950); HI-JACKED(1950); HUMPHREY TAKES A CHANCE(1950); ONCE A THIEF(1950); SIDESHOW(1950); WOMAN ON PIER 13, THE(1950); G.I. JANE(1951); MY FAVORITE SPY(1951); RACKET, THE(1951); STOP THAT CAB(1951); CRIME WAVE(1954); FAST AND THE FURIOUS, THE(1954); HIGHWAY DRAGNET(1954); CARNIVAL ROCK(1957); BUCCANEER, THE(1958); BLUE HAWAII(1961); ERRAND BOY, THE(1961); FATE IS THE HUNTER(1964); THAT DARN CAT(1965); LOVE BUG, THE(1968); ODD COUPLE, THE(1968); BAREFOOT EXECUTIVE, THE(1971); SCANDALOUS JOHN(1971); APPLE DUMPLING GANG, THE(1975); FREAKY FRIDAY(1976); SHAGGY D.A., THE(1976); HERBIE GOES BANANAS(1980)

Jane Adrian
TYCOON(1947); GUNFIRE(1950); SNOW DOG(1950)

Kay Adrian
SCREAM AND SCREAM AGAIN(1970, Brit.); TALES FROM THE CRYPT(1972, Brit.)

Lillian Adrian
Silents
GOLD RUSH, THE(1925)

Max Adrian
PRIMROSE PATH, THE(1934, Brit.); HAPPY FAMILY, THE(1936, Brit.); NOTHING LIKE PUBLICITY(1936, Brit.); TO CATCH A THIEF(1936, Brit.); TOUCH OF THE MOON, A(1936, Brit.); MACUSHLA(1937, Brit.); WHEN THE DEVIL WAS WELL(1937, Brit.); WHY PICK ON ME?(1937, Brit.); MERELY MR. HAWKINS(1938, Brit.); COURAGEOUS MR. PENN, THE(1941, Brit.); REMARKABLE MR. KIPPS(1942, Brit.); TALK ABOUT JACQUELINE(1942, Brit.); YOUNG MR. PITT, THE(1942, Brit.); HENRY V(1946, Brit.); TAMING OF DOROTHY, THE(1950, Brit.); POOL OF LONDON(1951, Brit.); PICKWICK PAPERS, THE(1952, Brit.); DR. TERROR'S HOUSE OF HORRORS(1965, Brit.); DEADLY AFFAIR, THE(1967, Brit.); TERRORNAUTS, THE(1967, Brit.); BOY FRIEND, THE(1971, Brit.); MUSIC LOVERS, THE(1971, Brit.); UNCLE VANYA(1977, Brit.)
Misc. Talkies
DEVILS, THE(1971)

Michael Adrian
Misc. Talkies
HEROWORK(1977), d

Adrian Teen Models
CATALINA CAPER, THE(1967)

Adriana
REBELLION OF THE HANGED, THE(1954, Mex.)

Ermanno Adriani
MYTH, THE(1965, Ital.)

Patricia Adriani
NEST, THE(1982, Span.)

Christine Adrien
UNHOLY QUEST, THE(1934, Brit.)

Philippe Adrien
COCKTAIL MOLOTOV(1980, Fr.), w

Jean Adrienne
AFTER THE BALL(1932, Brit.); BROKEN ROSARY, THE(1934, Brit.); BARNACLE BILL(1935, Brit.); SHIPMATES O' MINE(1936, Brit.); FATHER O'FLYNN(1938, Irish)
Misc. Talkies
HOUSE OF DREAMS(1933)

Henry Adries
WHERE THERE'S A WILL(1936, Brit)

Lucien Adriot
HALLELUJAH, I'M A BUM(1933), ph

Gui Adrisano
NEXT STOP, GREENWICH VILLAGE(1976)

Kay Adshead
ACCEPTABLE LEVELS(1983, Brit.)

Frank Adu
LOVE AND DEATH(1975); TAXI DRIVER(1976); NIGHT OF THE JUGGLER(1980); FORT APACHE, THE BRONX(1981)
1984
C.H.U.D.(1984)

Jab Adu
COUNTDOWN AT KUSINI(1976, Nigerian)

Samuel Adumuah
HAMILE(1965, Ghana)

Kwame Adunuo
HAMILE(1965, Ghana)

Vicenta Advincula
NO PLACE TO HIDE(1956)

Marina Adzhubey
VIOLIN AND ROLLER(1962, USSR)

Alar Aedma
1984
MRS. SOFFEL(1984)

Werner Aellen
WOLFPEN PRINCIPLE, THE(1974, Can.), p; SALLY FIELDGOOD & CO.(1975, Can.), p; BY DESIGN(1982), p

Ben Aerden
SPETTERS(1983, Holland)

Elizabeth Aeriens
Silents
JANE EYRE(1921)

Aerosmith
SGT. PEPPER'S LONELY HEARTS CLUB BAND(1978)

Aeschylus
ILLIAC PASSION, THE(1968), w
Barbro Hiort af Ornas
LOVING COUPLES(1966, Swed.); SHAME(1968, Swed.); PASSION OF ANNA, THE(1970, Swed.); TOUCH, THE(1971, U.S./Swed.)
Barbro Hjort af Ornas
ALL THESE WOMEN(1964, Swed.)
Leonid Afansyev
WHEN THE TREES WERE TALL(1965, USSR), m
S. Afansyev
GARNET BRACELET, THE(1966, USSR)
Neil Affleck
OH, HEAVENLY DOG!(1980); MY BLOODY VALENTINE(1981, Can.); VISITING HOURS(1982, Can.)
Declan Affley
1984
STRIKEBOUND(1984, Aus.), a, m
Therese Affolter
FRIENDS AND HUSBANDS(1983, Ger.)
Max Afford
SMITHY(1946, Aus.), w; PACIFIC ADVENTURE(1947, Aus.), w
Mindy Affrime
TELL ME A RIDDLE(1980), p
Tybee Afra
SILK STOCKINGS(1957)
Spike Africa
CINDERELLA LIBERTY(1973)
The African Brothers
1984
WHITE ELEPHANT(1984, Brit.), m
Afrika Bambaataa/Soul Sonic Force/Shango
1984
BEAT STREET(1984)
N. Afrikyants
WAR AND PEACE(1968, USSR)
Afrique
GRAND FINALE(1936, Brit.); LET'S MAKE A NIGHT OF IT(1937, Brit.); DISCOVERIES(1939, Brit.)
Effie Afton
HERE COMES CARTER(1936); MIDDLE OF THE NIGHT(1959); PRETTY BOY FLOYD(1960)
Richard Afton
UPTURNED GLASS, THE(1947, Brit.)
Florence L. Afuma
LIKE A TURTLE ON ITS BACK(1981, Fr.)
Safira Afzal
OCTOPUSSY(1983, Brit.)
Izhak Agadati
TEL AVIV TAXI(1957, Israel), p; PILLAR OF FIRE, THE(1963, Israel), p
Nina Agadzhanova
DESERTER(1934, USSR), w
Nina Agadzhanova-Shutko
Silents
BATTLESHIP POTEMKIN, THE(1925, USSR), w
D. Agafonova
SPRINGTIME ON THE VOLGA(1961, USSR)
M. Agafonova
SOUND OF LIFE, THE(1962, USSR), makeup
Koula Agagiotou
SERENITY(1962)
Christopher J.C. Agajanian
GONE IN 60 SECONDS(1974)
J.C. Agajanian, Jr.
GONE IN 60 SECONDS(1974)
J.C. Agajanian, Sr.
GONE IN 60 SECONDS(1974)
Wladimir Agajeff
Misc. Silents
ASIAN SUN, THE(1921, Ger.)
Giorgio Agamben
GOSPEL ACCORDING TO ST. MATTHEW, THE(1966, Fr., Ital.)
Isac Agami
I SPIT ON YOUR GRAVE(1983)
T. Agamirova
DON QUIXOTE(1961, USSR)
N. Agapova
RESURRECTION(1963, USSR)
John Agar
FORT APACHE(1948); ADVENTURE IN BALTIMORE(1949); SANDS OF IWO JIMA(1949); SHE WORE A YELLOW RIBBON(1949); BREAKTHROUGH(1950); WOMAN ON PIER 13, THE(1950); ALONG THE GREAT DIVIDE(1951); MAGIC CARPET, THE(1951); WOMAN OF THE NORTH COUNTRY(1952); MAN OF CONFLICT(1953); BAIT(1954); GOLDEN MISTRESS, THE(1954); ROCKET MAN, THE(1954); SHIELD FOR MURDER(1954); HOLD BACK TOMORROW(1955); LONESOME TRAIL, THE(1955); REVENGE OF THE CREATURE(1955); TARANTULA(1955); MOLE PEOPLE, THE(1956); STAR IN THE DUST(1956); DAUGHTER OF DR. JEKYLL(1957); FLESH AND THE SPUR(1957); JOE BUTTERFLY(1957); RIDE A VIOLENT MILE(1957); ATTACK OF THE PUPPET PEOPLE(1958); BRAIN FROM THE PLANET AROUS, THE(1958); FRONTIER GUN(1958); JET ATTACK(1958); INVISIBLE INVADERS(1959); RAYMIE(1960); LISETTE(1961); HAND OF DEATH(1962); JOURNEY TO THE SEVENTH PLANET(1962, U.S./Swed.); CAVALRY COMMAND(1963, U.S./Phil.); OF LOVE AND DESIRE(1963); YOUNG AND THE BRAVE, THE(1963); LAW OF THE LAWLESS(1964); STAGE TO THUNDER ROCK(1964); YOUNG FURY(1965); CURSE OF THE SWAMP CREATURE(1966); JOHNNY RENO(1966); WACO(1966); WOMEN OF THE PREHISTORIC PLANET(1966); ZONTAR, THE THING FROM VENUS(1966); ST. VALENTINE'S DAY MASSACRE, THE(1967); HELL RAIDERS(1968); UNDEFEATED, THE(1969); CHISUM(1970); BIG JAKE(1971); KING KONG(1976)

Mona Agar
FUNHOUSE, THE(1981)
Gabor Agardy
ROUND UP, THE(1969, Hung.)
Cesar Agarte
JET OVER THE ATLANTIC(1960)
Shri Agarwal
GURU, THE(1969, U.S./India)
Mohan Agashe
SEA WOLVES, THE(1981, Brit.)
May Agate
SCHOOL FOR SCANDAL, THE(1930, Brit.); FRENCH LEAVE(1931, Brit.); ARE YOU A MASON?(1934, Brit.); I WAS A SPY(1934, Brit.)
Irene Agay
FABULOUS SUZANNE, THE(1946)
Age
IT HAPPENED IN ROME(1959, Ital.), w; LAW IS THE LAW, THE(1959, Fr.), w; GREAT WAR, THE(1961, Fr., Ital.), w; ORGANIZER, THE(1964, Fr./Ital./Yugo.), w; PIZZA TRIANGLE, THE(1970, Ital./Span.), w; VIVA ITALIA(1978, Ital.), w
1984
JOKE OF DESTINY LYING IN WAIT AROUND THE CORNER LIKE A STREETBANDIT, A(1984, Ital.), w
Age & Scarpelli
MAFIOSO(1962, Ital.), w; FIASCO IN MILAN(1963, Fr./Ital.), w; SEDUCED AND ABANDONED(1964, Fr./Ital.), w; GOOD, THE BAD, AND THE UGLY, THE(1967, Ital./Span.), w; OPIATE '67(1967, Fr./Ital.), w; MOTIVE WAS JEALOUSY, THE(1970 Ital./Span.), w; GOODNIGHT, LADIES AND GENTLEMEN(1977, Ital.), d&w; SUNDAY LOVERS(1980, Ital./Fr.), w
N. Agedzanov
SEEDS OF FREEDOM(1943, USSR), w
James Agee
AFRICAN QUEEN, THE(1951, U.S./Brit.), w; FACE TO FACE(1952), a, w; NIGHT OF THE HUNTER, THE(1955), w; ALL THE WAY HOME(1963), w
Henri Agel
MAN WHO LOVED WOMEN, THE(1977, Fr.)
Habib Ageli
MOHAMMAD, MESSENGER OF GOD(1976, Lebanon/Brit.)
Agena
JAWS OF THE JUNGLE(1936)
Hy R. Agens
WITHOUT A TRACE(1983)
Pat Agers
Misc. Talkies
BACCHANALE(1970)
Sol-Britt Agerup
NIGHT IN JUNE, A(1940, Swed.)
Hanne Agesen
ORDET(1957, Den.)
S. Ageyeva
DIMKA(1964, USSR)
Exel Aggebrecht
OPERETTA(1949, Ger.), w
Ray Aghayan
FATHER GOOSE(1964), cos; DO NOT DISTURB(1965), cos; GLASS BOTTOM BOAT, THE(1966), cos; OUR MAN FLINT(1966), cos; CAPRICE(1967), cos; DOCTOR DOLITTLE(1967), cos; IN LIKE FLINT(1967), cos; GAILY, GAILY(1969), cos; HANNIE CALDER(1971, Brit.), cos; LADY SINGS THE BLUES(1972), cos; FUNNY LADY(1975), cos
Jabler Agirresarobe
1984
ESCAPE FROM SEGOVIA(1984, Span.), ph
G.G. Agliani
OUTCRY(1949, Ital.), p
Giorgio Agliani
MINOTAUR, THE(1961, Ital.), p; WHITE SLAVE SHIP(1962, Fr./Ital.), p; GLADIATOR OF ROME(1963, Ital.), p
Agnanenko
IMMORTAL GARRISON, THE(1957, USSR), d
Louis Agnel
THEY MET ON SKIS(1940, Fr.)
Irene Agnelli
FIST IN HIS POCKET(1968, Ital.)
Marie-Ange Agnes
CHAMPAGNE MURDERS, THE(1968, Fr.)
Agnes the Horse
MILKY WAY, THE(1936)
Bobbie Agnew
MIDNIGHT TAXI, THE(1928)
Bobby Agnew
WOMAN RACKET, THE(1930)
Misc. Silents
TESSIE(1925); HEART OF BROADWAY, THE(1928)
Brendan Agnew
BLUES FOR LOVERS(1966, Brit.)
Frances Agnew
RAINBOW MAN(1929), w; SYNCOPATION(1929), w
Silents
ARE PARENTS PEOPLE?(1925), w; PARADISE(1926), t; JOY GIRL, THE(1927), w; SILK LEGS(1927), w; NONE BUT THE BRAVE(1928), w
Robert Agnew
EXTRAVAGANCE(1930); NAUGHTY FLIRT, THE(1931); GOLD DIGGERS OF 1933(1933)
Silents
SIN THAT WAS HIS, THE(1920); KICK IN(1922); PAWN TICKET 210(1922); WITHOUT FEAR(1922); ONLY 38(1923); GREAT LOVE, THE(1925); TAXI MYSTERY, THE(1926); WILD OATS LANE(1926); DOWN THE STRETCH(1927); SLIGHTLY USED(1927); WANDERING GIRLS(1927)
Misc. Silents
HIGHEST LAW, THE(1921); DANGEROUS ADVENTURE, A(1922); MARRIAGE MAKER, THE(1923); TRIMMED IN SCARLET(1923); GOLD HEELS(1924); LOVE'S

WHIRLPOOL(1924); THOSE WHO DANCE(1924); TROUBLES OF A BRIDE(1924); LOST - A WIFE(1925); PRIVATE AFFAIRS(1925); STEPPIN' OUT(1925); RACING BLOOD(1926); UNKNOWN TREASURES(1926); HEART OF SALOME, THE(1927); QUARANTINED RIVALS(1927); SHE'S MY BABY(1927); SNOWBOUND(1927)

Valerie Agnew
GIRL IS MINE, THE(1950, Brit.)

Armando Agnini
LOST WEEKEND, THE(1945), set d

Braccio Agnoletti
RETURN OF THE BLACK EAGLE(1949, Ital.), w

Joel Agona
YEAR OF LIVING DANGEROUSLY, THE(1982, Aus.)

Carlos Agosti
INVASION OF THE VAMPIRES, THE(1961, Mex.); SANTO CONTRA LA HIJA DE FRANKENSTEIN(1971, Mex.)

Silvano Agosti
N. P.(1971, Ital.), d&w

Bruno Agostini
8 ½(1963, Ital.)

Claude Agostini
BLACK AND WHITE IN COLOR(1976, Fr.), ph; SUNDAY LOVERS(1980, Ital./Fr.), ph; QUEST FOR FIRE(1982, Fr./Can.), ph
1984
BAY BOY(1984, Can.), ph; LES COMPERES(1984, Fr.), ph

Didier Agostini
INQUISITOR, THE(1982, Fr.)

Lucio Agostini
AGE OF INNOCENCE(1977, Can.), m

Philip Agostini
MONSEIGNEUR(1950, Fr.), ph

Philippe Agostini
UN CARNET DE BAL(1938, Fr.), ph; LES DERNIERES VACANCES(1947, Fr.), ph; LOVE STORY(1949, Fr.), ph; ANGELS OF THE STREETS(1950, Fr.); GATES OF THE NIGHT(1950, Fr.), ph; SYLVIA AND THE PHANTOM(1950, Fr.), ph; LE PLAISIR(1954, Fr.), ph; IF PARIS WERE TOLD TO US(1956, Fr.), ph; RIFIFI(1956, Fr.), ph; LADIES OF THE PARK(1964, Fr.), ph

Louis Agotay
DIRTY HEROES(1971, Ital./Fr./Ger.), w

Sid Ahmed Agoumi
Z(1969, Fr./Algeria)

S. Agoyan
VIOLIN AND ROLLER(1962, USSR), art d

Frank Agrama
SKI FEVER(1969, U.S./Aust./Czech.), w

V. Agranov
SONG OF THE FOREST(1963, USSR), art d

Mohammed Agrebi
THIEF OF BAGHDAD, THE(1961, Ital./Fr.)

Janet Agren
AVANTI!(1972); MOST WONDERFUL EVENING OF MY LIFE, THE(1972, Ital./Fr.); PULP(1972, Brit.)

Ed Agresti
ARTISTS AND MODELS ABROAD(1938); FLIGHT FOR FREEDOM(1943); MADAME BOVARY(1949); SUN COMES UP, THE(1949); STORY OF THREE LOVES, THE(1953)

Edward Agresti
MY FAVORITE SPY(1951)

Jackie Agrique
LONG AGO, TOMORROW(1971, Brit.)

Martin Agronsky
FIRST MONDAY IN OCTOBER(1981)

Toon Agterberg
SPETTERS(1983, Holland)

Jose Aguayo
GIRL FROM VALLADOLIO(1958, Span.), ph

Jose F. Aguayo
MAD QUEEN, THE(1950, Span.), ph; GUNFIGHTERS OF CASA GRANDE(1965, U.S./Span.), ph; TRISTANA(1970, Span./Ital./Fr.), ph; DON'T TURN THE OTHER CHEEK(1974, Ital./Ger./Span.), ph

Jose Fernandez Aguayo
FACE OF TERROR(1964, Span.), ph; MINNESOTA CLAY(1966, Ital./Fr./Span.), ph

Jose F. Aguayo, Jr.
MAN FROM O.R.G.Y., THE(1970), ph

Laurie Agudo
SECRET OF THE SACRED FOREST, THE(1970)

Theodore Aguelopoulos
RECONSTRUCTION OF A CRIME(1970, Ger.), d, w

Lucien Aguettand
LE DENIER MILLIARDAIRE(1934, Fr.), art d; LOVE AND THE FRENCH-WOMAN(1961, Fr.), art d, art d

Mimi Aguglia
OUTLAW, THE(1943); CAPTAIN FROM CASTILE(1947); CARNIVAL IN COSTA RICA(1947); UNCONQUERED(1947); CRY OF THE CITY(1948); THAT MIDNIGHT KISS(1949); WE WERE STRANGERS(1949); BLACK HAND, THE(1950); DEPORTED(1950); RIGHT CROSS(1950); CUBAN FIREBALL(1951); MAN WHO CHEATED HIMSELF, THE(1951); WHEN IN ROME(1952); ROSE TATTOO, THE(1955); BROTHERS RICO, THE(1957)

Alfredo Aguilar
BRAVE BULLS, THE(1951)

Amalia Aguilar
LOS PLATILLOS VOLADORES(1955, Mex.)

Antonio Aguilar
IMPORTANT MAN, THE(1961, Mex.); LA CUCARACHA(1961, Mex.)

Cesar Aguilar
PASSIONATE STRANGERS, THE(1968, Phil.)

Eduardo Aguilar
DANCERS IN THE DARK(1932)

George Aguilar
ULZANA'S RAID(1972); TRIAL OF BILLY JACK, THE(1974)

Jorge "Ranchero" Aguilar
MAGNIFICENT MATADOR, THE(1955)

Luz Maria Aguilar
SURVIVE!(1977, Mex.)

Pedro Aguilar
SCALPHUNTERS, THE(1968)

Perfideo Aguilar
GIANT(1956)

Rich Aguilar
LAST MOVIE, THE(1971)

Richmond Aguilar
MACHISMO–40 GRAVES FOR 40 GUNS(1970), ph

Silvia Aguilar
THAT HOUSE IN THE OUTSKIRTS(1980, Span.)

Tony Aguilar
UNDEFEATED, THE(1969)

Beatriz Aguirre
MADCAP OF THE HOUSE(1950, Mex.); LITTLE RED RIDING HOOD(1963, Mex.); LITTLE RED RIDING HOOD AND HER FRIENDS(1964, Mex.); SPIRITISM(1965, Mex.)

Delores Aguirre
HARD COUNTRY(1981)

Dolores Aguirre
HERBIE GOES BANANAS(1980); SEEMS LIKE OLD TIMES(1980)

Fred Aguirre
FUN IN ACAPULCO(1963)

Isidora Aguirre
ALSINO AND THE CONDOR(1983, Nicaragua), w

Javier Aguirre
DRACULA'S GREAT LOVE(1972, Span.), d, w; HUNCHBACK OF THE MORGUE, THE(1972, Span.), d, w

Alfonso Agullo
MONSTER ISLAND(1981, Span./U.S.), m

Christopher Agunda
LION, THE(1962, Brit.)

Gianni Agus
FASCIST, THE(1965, Ital.)

Agust Agustsson
MAYA(1982), d

Jenny Agutter
EAST OF SUDAN(1964, Brit.); MAN COULD GET KILLED, A(1966); GATES TO PARADISE(1968, Brit./Ger.); STAR!(1968); I START COUNTING(1970, Brit.); RAILWAY CHILDREN, THE(1971, Brit.); WALKABOUT(1971, Aus./U.S.); EAGLE HAS LANDED, THE(1976, Brit.); LOGAN'S RUN(1976); "EQUUS"(1977); CHINA 9, LIBERTY 37(1978, Ital.); DOMINIQUE(1978, Brit.); SURVIVOR(1980, Aus.); SWEET WILLIAM(1980, Brit.); AMERICAN WEREWOLF IN LONDON, AN(1981); AMY(1981)
1984
RIDDLE OF THE SANDS, THE(1984, Brit.); SECRET PLACES(1984, Brit.)

Aguvaluk
Misc. Silents
KIVALINA OF THE ICE LANDS(1925)

Kong Ah
Silents
TABU(1931)

Ah-Yue-Lou
CORRUPT ONES, THE(1967, Ger.)

Jim Ahart
HONKYTONK MAN(1982)

David Ahdar
DOWN AMONG THE SHELTERING PALMS(1953); SALOME(1953); SABRINA(1954)

Daniel Ahearn
WILD BOYS OF THE ROAD(1933), w

Danny Ahearn
PICTURE SNATCHER(1933), w; BULLDOG EDITION(1936), w; ESCAPE FROM CRIME(1942), w

George Ahearn
Misc. Silents
STRENGTH OF DONALD MCKENZIE, THE(1916); SEA MASTER, THE(1917)

Gladys Ahearn
GIT ALONG, LITTLE DOGIES(1937)

John Ahearn
TRAP DOOR, THE(1980)

Thomas Ahearn
BEHIND THE HEADLINES(1937), w; BIG SHOT, THE(1937), w; FRESHMAN YEAR(1938), w; SWING THAT CHEER(1938), w; DISASTER(1948), w

Tom Ahearn
PROJECT X(1949)

Will Ahearn
GIT ALONG, LITTLE DOGIES(1937)

Thomas Ahearne
LET'S MAKE A MILLION(1937), w

Tom Ahearne
CRY MURDER(1936); BUTTERFIELD 8(1960); HUSTLER, THE(1961); NO WAY TO TREAT A LADY(1968); THREE IN THE ATTIC(1968); WHAT'S SO BAD ABOUT FEELING GOOD?(1968); APRIL FOOLS, THE(1969); TREE, THE(1969)

Allegra Ahern
SAND CASTLE, THE(1961)

Alston Ahern
PRIVATE BENJAMIN(1980); WHOSE LIFE IS IT ANYWAY?(1981)

Gladys Ahern
ONE YEAR LATER(1933); PICTURE BRIDES(1934)

Jack Ahern
IN COLD BLOOD(1967), set d; TIME FOR KILLING, A(1967), set d

Lassie Lou Ahern
Misc. Silents
ROBES OF SIN(1924); LITTLE MICKEY GROGAN(1927)

Lloyd Ahern
BRASHER DOUBLOON, THE(1947), ph; MIRACLE ON 34TH STREET, THE(1947), ph; FATHER WAS A FULLBACK(1949), ph; MR. BELVEDERE GOES TO COLLEGE(1949), ph; FOR HEAVEN'S SAKE(1950), ph; LOVE THAT BRUTE(1950), ph; LOVE NEST(1951), ph; O. HENRY'S FULL HOUSE(1952), ph; SILVER WHIP, THE(1953), ph; GAMBLER FROM NATCHEZ, THE(1954), ph; GORILLA AT LARGE(1954), ph; PRINCESS OF THE NILE(1954), ph; LOOTERS, THE(1955), ph; SAND CASTLE, THE(1961), ph; HOT RODS TO HELL(1967), ph; KLANSMAN, THE(1974), ph

Patrick Ahern
ROCKETSHIP X-M(1950)

Will Ahern
ONE YEAR LATER(1933), a, w; PICTURE BRIDES(1934), a, w

Brian Aherne
"W" PLAN, THE(1931, Brit.); MADAME GUILLOTINE(1931, Brit.); CONSTANT NYMPH, THE(1933, Brit.); SONG OF SONGS(1933); FOUNTAIN, THE(1934); WHAT EVERY WOMAN KNOWS(1934); I LIVE MY LIFE(1935); BELOVED ENEMY(1936); SYLVIA SCARLETT(1936); GREAT GARRICK, THE(1937); MERRILY WE LIVE(1938); CAPTAIN FURY(1939); JUAREZ(1939); HIRED WIFE(1940); LADY IN QUESTION, THE(1940); MY SON, MY SON!(1940); VIGIL IN THE NIGHT(1940); MAN WHO LOST HIMSELF, THE(1941); SKYLARK(1941); SMILIN' THROUGH(1941); MY SISTER EILEEN(1942); NIGHT TO REMEMBER, A(1942); FIRST COMES COURAGE(1943); FOREVER AND A DAY(1943); WHAT A WOMAN!(1943); LOCKET, THE(1946); ANGEL ON THE AMAZON(1948); SMART WOMAN(1948); I CONFESS(1953); TITANIC(1953); BULLET IS WAITING, A(1954); PRINCE VALIANT(1954); SWAN, THE(1956); BEST OF EVERYTHING, THE(1959); SUSAN SLADE(1961); SWORD OF LANCELOT(1963, Brit.); CAVERN, THE(1965, Ital./Ger.); ROSIE!(1967); SLIPSTREAM(1974, Can.), m

Silents
ELEVENTH COMMANDMENT, THE(1924, Brit.); KING OF THE CASTLE(1925, Brit.); SAFETY FIRST(1926, Brit.)

Misc. Silents
SQUIRE OF LONG HADLEY, THE(1925, Brit.); WOMAN REDEEMED, A(1927, Brit.); SHOOTING STARS(1928); UNDERGROUND(1928, Brit.)

Lloyd Aherne, Jr.
PRINCE VALIANT(1954)

Pat Aherne
AULD LANG SYNE(1929, Brit.); CITY OF PLAY(1929, Brit.); MY OLD DUCHESS(1933, Brit.); PRIDE OF THE FORCE, THE(1933, Brit.); OUTCAST, THE(1934, Brit.); RETURN OF BULLDOG DRUMMOND, THE(1934, Brit.); STOKER, THE(1935, Brit.); TROUBLE AHEAD(1936, Brit.); ASK A POLICEMAN(1939, Brit.); CLOUDS OVER EUROPE(1939, Brit.); THURSDAY'S CHILD(1943, Brit.); WARN THAT MAN(1943, Brit.); GREEN DOLPHIN STREET(1947); IF WINTER COMES(1947); PARADINE CASE, THE(1947); SINGAPORE(1947); CHALLENGE, THE(1948); ROGUES OF SHERWOOD FOREST(1950); LORNA DOONE(1951); SOLDIERS THREE(1951); SON OF DR. JEKYLL, THE(1951); BWANA DEVIL(1953); ROYAL AFRICAN RIFLES, THE(1953); TITANIC(1953)

Silents
THOU FOOL(1926, Brit.); DAUGHTER IN REVOLT, A(1927, Brit.); HUNTINGTOWER(1927, Brit.); VIRGINIA'S HUSBAND(1928, Brit.); INSEPARABLES, THE(1929, Brit.)

Misc. Silents
BLINKEYES(192?); SILVER LINING, THE(1927, Brit.); LOVE'S OPTION(1928, Brit.)

Patrick Aherne
ROGUE'S MARCH(1952); COURT JESTER, THE(1956); MAN WHO KNEW TOO MUCH, THE(1956)

Richard Aherne
MY HANDS ARE CLAY(1948, Irish); CHRISTOPHER COLUMBUS(1949, Brit.); D-DAY, THE SIXTH OF JUNE(1956); PARDNERS(1956); BUSTER KEATON STORY, THE(1957)

Bernice Ahi
MURDER, MY SWEET(1945)

Jo Ahl
SIX PACK(1982)

Mac Ahlberg
TIME IN THE SUN, A(1970, Swed.), ph; NOCTURNA(1979), ph; HELL NIGHT(1981), ph; PARASITE(1982), ph; SEDUCTION, THE(1982), ph; CHAINED HEAT(1983 U.S./Ger.), ph; METALSTORM: THE DESTRUCTION OF JARED-SYN(1983), ph; MY TUTOR(1983), ph; YOUNG WARRIORS(1983), ph

1984
SWORDKILL(1984), ph

Karl Gustav Ahlefeldt
GERTRUD(1966, Den.)

David Ozzie Ahlers
NORTHERN LIGHTS(1978), m

Mme. Alice Ahlers
WUTHERING HEIGHTS(1939)

Ozzie Ahlers
OVER-UNDER, SIDEWAYS-DOWN(1977), m

Harry Ahlin
RAILROAD WORKERS(1948, Swed.); PORT OF CALL(1963, Swed.)

Jean Ahlin
JOAN OF ARC(1948)

Philip Ahlin
FOREVER AND A DAY(1943)

Philip Ahlm
THIS LAND IS MINE(1943); O.S.S.(1946); JOAN OF ARC(1948); GAL WHO TOOK THE WEST, THE(1949); WHERE DANGER LIVES(1950); LAS VEGAS STORY, THE(1952)

Phillip Ahlm
POSTMAN ALWAYS RINGS TWICE, THE(1946)

Boerje Ahlstedt
FANNY AND ALEXANDER(1983, Swed./Fr./Ger.)

Linne Ahlstrand
LIVING VENUS(1961)

Ahmang
SHARK WOMAN, THE(1941)

Philip Ahn
YESTERDAY'S ENEMY(1959, Brit.); THOROUGHLY MODERN MILLIE(1967); GENERAL DIED AT DAWN, THE(1936); KLONDIKE ANNIE(1936); CHINA PASSAGE(1937); GOOD EARTH, THE(1937); ROARING TIMBER(1937); SOMETHING TO SING ABOUT(1937); TEX RIDES WITH THE BOY SCOUTS(1937); THANK YOU, MR. MOTO(1937); HAWAII CALLS(1938); BARRICADE(1939); DISPUTED PASSAGE(1939); ISLAND OF LOST MEN(1939); PANAMA PATROL(1939); THEY MET IN BOMBAY(1941); ACROSS THE PACIFIC(1942); CHINA GIRL(1942); LET'S GET TOUGH(1942); SHIP AHOY(1942); SUBMARINE RAIDER(1942); WE WERE DANCING(1942); YANK ON THE BURMA ROAD, A(1942); AROUND THE WORLD(1943); BEHIND THE RISING SUN(1943); CHINA(1943); FIVE GRAVES TO CAIRO(1943); SCREAM IN THE NIGHT(1943); THEY GOT ME COVERED(1943); DRAGON SEED(1944); KEYS OF THE KINGDOM, THE(1944); PURPLE HEART, THE(1944); STORY OF DR. WASSELL, THE(1944); BACK TO BATAAN(1945); BETRAYAL FROM THE EAST(1945); BLOOD ON THE SUN(1945); CHINA SKY(1945); GOD IS MY CO-PILOT(1945); CHINESE RING, THE(1947); INTRIGUE(1947); SINGAPORE(1947); CREEPER, THE(1948); MIRACLE OF THE BELLS, THE(1948); ROGUES' REGIMENT(1948); SAIGON(1948); WOMEN IN THE NIGHT(1948); BOSTON BLACKIE'S CHINESE VENTURE(1949); IMPACT(1949); STATE DEPARTMENT-FILE 649(1949); CHINA CORSAIR(1951); HALLS OF MONTEZUMA(1951); I WAS AN AMERICAN SPY(1951); SECRETS OF MONTE CARLO(1951); BATTLE ZONE(1952); JAPANESE WAR BRIDE(1952); MACAO(1952); RED SNOW(1952); TARGET HONG KONG(1952); BATTLE CIRCUS(1953); CHINA VENTURE(1953); FAIR WIND TO JAVA(1953); HIS MAJESTY O'KEEFE(1953); HELL'S HALF ACRE(1954); SHANGHAI STORY, THE(1954); LEFT HAND OF GOD, THE(1955); LOVE IS A MANY-SPLENDORED THING(1955); BATTLE HYMN(1957); WAY TO THE GOLD, THE(1957); HONG KONG CONFIDENTIAL(1958); NEVER SO FEW(1959); GREAT IMPOSTOR, THE(1960); ONE-EYED JACKS(1961); CONFESSIONS OF AN OPIUM EATER(1962); DIAMOND HEAD(1962); GIRL NAMED TAMIRO, A(1962); SHOCK CORRIDOR(1963); PARADISE, HAWAIIAN STYLE(1966); KARATE KILLERS, THE(1967); VOODOO HEARTBEAT(1972); JONATHAN LIVINGSTON SEAGULL(1973); WORLD'S GREATEST ATHLETE, THE(1973)

Phillip Ahn
STOWAWAY(1936); DAUGHTER OF SHANGHAI(1937); CHARLIE CHAN IN HONOLULU(1938); KING OF CHINATOWN(1939); THEY WERE EXPENDABLE(1945); COBRA STRIKES, THE(1948); BIG HANGOVER, THE(1950)

Philson Ahn
DISPUTED PASSAGE(1939); PANAMA PATROL(1939); INTRIGUE(1947)

Ralph Ahn
PRISONER OF WAR(1954); CONFESSIONS OF AN OPIUM EATER(1962)

Robert Ahola
1984
NOT FOR PUBLICATION(1984)

Mary Ahor
FIESTA(1947)

Ron Ahran
SWEET BEAT(1962, Brit.), w

George Ahren
Silents
OVERALLS(1916)

Jimmy Ahrens
RACE FOR YOUR LIFE, CHARLIE BROWN(1977)

Monique Ahrens
DOG OF FLANDERS, A(1959)

Thekla Ahrens
ETERNAL MASK, THE(1937, Swiss)

Inga-Lill Ahstrom
GUILT(1967, Swed.)

Wong Ahtarre
DRAGON'S GOLD(1954)

Julio Ahuet
PORTRAIT OF MARIA(1946, Mex.)

Ahui
Misc. Talkies
ROBINSON CRUSOE AND THE TIGER(1972)

Kyoko Ai
DESTROY ALL MONSTERS(1969, Jap.)

Tomoko Ai
MONSTERS FROM THE UNKNOWN PLANET(1975, Jap.)

Federico Aicardi
LOVES AND TIMES OF SCARAMOUCHE, THE(1976, Ital.), p

Julius Aicardi
JOAN OF ARC(1948)

Gopa Aich
1984
HOME AND THE WORLD, THE(1984, India)

Ken Aichele
I'M DANCING AS FAST AS I CAN(1982), set d

Marius Aicher
AMERICAN SOLDIER, THE(1970 Ger.); SOMETHING FOR EVERYONE(1970)

Elma Aicklen
GREAT WALDO PEPPER, THE(1975)

Aida
HANNIBAL BROOKS(1969, Brit.)

The Aida Broadbent Girls
STORM OVER LISBON(1944)

Aida Foster Girls
COME DANCE WITH ME(1950, Brit.)

Betsy Aidem
LITTLE SEX, A(1982)

Charles Aidman
WRONG MAN, THE(1956); PORK CHOP HILL(1959); WAR HUNT(1962); HOUR OF THE GUN(1967); COUNTDOWN(1968); SERGEANT RYKER(1968); ANGEL, ANGEL, DOWN WE GO(1969); TELL THEM WILLIE BOY IS HERE(1969); ADAM AT 6 A.M.(1970); KOTCH(1971); DIRTY LITTLE BILLY(1972); TWILIGHT'S LAST GLEAMING(1977, U.S./Ger.); ZOOT SUIT(1981); UNCOMMON VALOR(1983)

Misc. Talkies
ALIEN ZONE(1978); HOUSE OF THE DEAD(1980)

Michele Delle Aie
TAKE ALL OF ME(1978, Ital.), w
Danny Aiello
BANG THE DRUM SLOWLY(1973); GODFATHER, THE, PART II(1974); FRONT, THE(1976); BLOODBROTHERS(1978); FINGERS(1978); DEFIANCE(1980); HIDE IN PLAIN SIGHT(1980); CHU CHU AND THE PHILLY FLASH(1981); FORT APACHE, THE BRONX(1981)
1984
OLD ENOUGH(1984); ONCE UPON A TIME IN AMERICA(1984)
Misc. Talkies
HOOCH(1977)
Laurie Aiello
1984
DELIVERY BOYS(1984), makeup
Pierfrancesco Aiello
IDENTIFICATION OF A WOMAN(1983, Ital.)
Thomas Aiello
WHO'S THAT KNOCKING AT MY DOOR?(1968)
Danny Aiello III
1984
NATURAL, THE(1984)
Franz Aigner
GREAT WALTZ, THE(1972)
Janeth Aigren
PUSSYCAT, PUSSYCAT, I LOVE YOU(1970)
Alma Aiken
Silents
MASTER MIND, THE(1920)
Elaine Aiken
LONELY MAN, THE(1957); CADDY SHACK(1980)
Hugh Aiken
HIGH LONESOME(1950)
Robert Aiken
GAMES(1967)
Van Aikens
REVOLT OF THE SLAVES, THE(1961, Ital./Span./Ger.); GOLIATH AND THE VAMPIRES(1964, Ital.)
Vanore Aikens
I EAT YOUR SKIN(1971)
Alvin Ailey
TURNING POINT, THE(1977), ch
Monique Aime
HOUSE OF 1,000 DOLLS(1967, Ger./Span./Brit.)
Anouk Aimee
LOVERS OF VERONA, THE(1951, Fr.); PARIS EXPRESS, THE(1953, Brit.); FOREVER MY HEART(1954, Brit.); CONTRABAND SPAIN(1955, Brit.); JOURNEY, THE(1959, U.S./Aust.); JOKER, THE(1961, Fr.); LA DOLCE VITA(1961, Ital./Fr.); LOLA(1961, Fr./Ital.); MODIGLIANI OF MONTPARNASSE(1961, Fr./Ital.); SODOM AND GOMORRAH(1962, U.S./Fr./Ital.); 8 ½(1963, Ital.); OF FLESH AND BLOOD(1964, Fr./Ital.); WHITE VOICES(1965, Fr./Ital.); LA FUGA(1966, Ital.); MAN AND A WOMAN, A(1966, Fr.); VERY HANDY MAN, A(1966, Fr./Ital.); ONE NIGHT... A TRAIN(1968, Fr./Bel.); APPOINTMENT, THE(1969); JUSTINE(1969); MODEL SHOP, THE(1969); MY FIRST LOVE(1978, Fr.); LEAP INTO THE VOID(1982, Ital.); TRAGEDY OF A RIDICULOUS MAN, THE(1982, Ital.)
1984
SUCCESS IS THE BEST REVENGE(1984, Brit.)
Blanche Aimee
Misc. Silents
GREEN CLOAK, THE(1915)
Elizabeth Aimers
MY FAIR LADY(1964)
Hardy Aimes
AMOROUS MR. PRAWN, THE(1965, Brit.), cos
Jean-Claude Aimimi
ADIEU PHILLIPINE(1962, Fr./Ital.)
Aimos
LE DENIER MILLIARDAIRE(1934, Fr.); GOLEM, THE(1937, Czech./Fr.); ESCAPE FROM YESTERDAY(1939, Fr.); MAN OF THE HOUR, THE(1940, Fr.); ULTIMATUM(1940, Fr.); FIRE IN THE STRAW(1943); YOUNG MAN'S FANCY(1943, Brit.); THREE HOURS(1944, Fr.); FRENCH WAY, THE(1952, Fr.)
Raymond Aimos
UNDER THE ROOFS OF PARIS(1930, Fr.); COURRIER SUD(1937, Fr.); PORT OF SHADOWS(1938, Fr.); THEY WERE FIVE(1938, Fr.)
Anthony Ainley
EXORCISM AT MIDNIGHT(1966, Brit. revised 1973, U.S.); INSPECTOR CLOUSEAU(1968, Brit.); JOANNA(1968, Brit.); OH! WHAT A LOVELY WAR(1969, Brit.); BLOOD ON SATAN'S CLAW, THE(1970, Brit.); ASSAULT(1971, Brit.); LAND THAT TIME FORGOT, THE(1975, Brit.)
Clarissa Ainley
HOT TIMES(1974)
Henry Ainley
FIRST MRS. FRASER, THE(1932, Brit.); GOOD COMPANIONS(1933, Brit.); AS YOU LIKE IT(1936, Brit.)
Silents
GREAT ADVENTURE, THE(1915, Brit.); IRIS(1915, Brit.); PRISONER OF ZENDA, THE(1915, Brit.); RUPERT OF HENTZAU(1915, Brit.); PRINCE AND THE BEGGARMAID, THE(1921, Brit.); ROYAL OAK, THE(1923, Brit.)
Misc. Silents
CALLED BACK(1914, Brit.); SHE STOOPS TO CONQUER(1914, Brit.); MAN OF HIS WORD, A(1915, Brit.); SWEET LAVENDER(1915, Brit.); MANXMAN, THE(1916, Brit.); MARRIAGE OF WILLIAM ASHE, THE(1916, Brit.); SOWING THE WIND(1916, Brit.); BUILD THY HOUSE(1920, Brit.); MONEY(1921, Brit.); SALLY BISHOP(1923, Brit.)
Joe Ainley
DANIEL BOONE, TRAIL BLAZER(1957)
Lynn Ainley
UNDERCOVER GIRL(1950); MAN WITH MY FACE, THE(1951)
Owen Ainley
SQUATTER'S DAUGHTER(1933, Aus.)

Pekoe Ainley
BRIDAL PATH, THE(1959, Brit.)
Richard Ainley
AS YOU LIKE IT(1936, Brit.); FROG, THE(1937, Brit.); GANG, THE(1938, Brit.); LILY OF LAGUNA(1938, Brit.); OLD IRON(1938, Brit.); STOLEN LIFE(1939, Brit.); THERE AIN'T NO JUSTICE(1939, Brit.); TORPEDOED!(1939, Brit.); LADY WITH RED HAIR(1940); MAD MEN OF EUROPE(1940, Brit.); BULLETS FOR O'HARA(1941); HERE COMES HAPPINESS(1941); KNOCKOUT(1941); PASSAGE FROM HONG KONG(1941); SHINING VICTORY(1941); SINGAPORE WOMAN(1941); SMILING GHOST, THE(1941); WHITE CARGO(1942); ABOVE SUSPICION(1943); I DOOD IT(1943); THREE HEARTS FOR JULIA(1943)
Tony Ainley
SOMEWHERE IN FRANCE(1943, Brit.)
Marguerite Ainslee
FIREBRAND JORDAN(1930)
Marian Ainslee
BRIDGE OF SAN LUIS REY, THE(1929), w; OUR MODERN MAIDENS(1929), titles
Silents
FOOLISH WIVES(1920), t; MERRY WIDOW, THE(1925), t; TOWER OF LIES, THE(1925), t; FLESH AND THE DEVIL(1926), t; TEMPTRESS, THE(1926), t; ANNIE LAURIE(1927), t; CALIFORNIA(1927), t; FOREIGN DEVILS(1927), w; LOVE(1927), t; QUALITY STREET(1927), t; MYSTERIOUS LADY, THE(1928), t; OUR DANCING DAUGHTERS(1928), t; WOMAN OF AFFAIRS, A(1928), t; KISS, THE(1929), t; OUR MODERN MAIDENS(1929), t; QUEEN KELLY(1929), t; WILD ORCHIDS(1929), t
Marion Ainslee
Silents
FOREIGN DEVILS(1927), t; SINGLE STANDARD, THE(1929), t
Mary Ainslee
EARL OF PUDDLESTONE(1940); MAD YOUTH(1940); WHEN THE DALTONS RODE(1940); SAILORS ON LEAVE(1941); SIS HOPKINS(1941); HARVARD, HERE I COME(1942)
Norman Ainslee
INTERNATIONAL HOUSE(1933)
Ian Ainsley
UGLY DUCKLING, THE(1959, Brit.); INVASION QUARTET(1961, Brit.)
Marian Ainsley
Silents
IN OLD KENTUCKY(1927), t
Mary Ainsley
PRIDE OF THE BOWERY(1941)
Norman Ainsley
GAY BRIDE, THE(1934); GIRL FROM MISSOURI, THE(1934); NOTORIOUS SOPHIE LANG, THE(1934); MAN WHO RECLAIMED HIS HEAD, THE(1935); LOVE ON THE RUN(1936); SWORN ENEMY(1936); WIDOW FROM MONTE CARLO, THE(1936); CAPTAINS COURAGEOUS(1937); SHADOW STRIKES, THE(1937); SHALL WE DANCE(1937); ADVENTURE IN DIAMONDS(1940); DISPATCH FROM REUTERS, A(1940); LADY EVE, THE(1941); GOOD FELLOWS, THE(1943); MAN IN HALF-MOON STREET, THE(1944); UNINVITED, THE(1944); CLUNY BROWN(1946); MOSS ROSE(1947); SINGAPORE(1947)
Paul Ainsley
Misc. Talkies
AMERICAN RASPBERRY(1980)
Norman Ainslie
MYSTERY OF MR. X, THE(1934)
Carole Ainsworth
PETER RABBIT AND TALES OF BEATRIX POTTER(1971, Brit.)
Cupid Ainsworth
BIG NEWS(1929); TIP-OFF, THE(1931); GOLD MINE IN THE SKY(1938); CAFE SOCIETY(1939)
Fred Ainsworth
ME AND MY BROTHER(1969)
Harrison Ainsworth
Silents
KING CHARLES(1913, Brit.), w
Helen Ainsworth
DOCTOR TAKES A WIFE(1940); LADY IS WILLING, THE(1942); HARD MAN, THE(1957), p; 27TH DAY, THE(1957), p; BULLWHIP(1958), p
John Ainsworth
FORCES' SWEETHEART(1953, Brit.); MURDER AT 3 A.M.(1953, Brit.), p, w; BAY OF SAINT MICHEL, THE(1963, Brit.), p&d; HELL IS EMPTY(1967, Brit./Ital), d, w
Phil Ainsworth
Silents
CHORUS GIRL'S ROMANCE, A(1920)
Sidney Ainsworth
Silents
ACCORDING TO THE CODE(1916); ON TRIAL(1917); BRANDING IRON, THE(1920); OUT OF THE STORM(1920)
Misc. Silents
MISLEADING LADY, THE(1916); TWO-BITS SEATS(1917); LITTLE ROWDY, THE(1919); MAN AND HIS MONEY, A(1919); ONE WEEK OF LIFE(1919); HALF A CHANCE(1920)
Sydney Ainsworth
Silents
DOUBLING FOR ROMEO(1921); INVISIBLE POWER, THE(1921)
Misc. Silents
CHAPERON, THE(1916); PRINCE OF GRAUSTARK, THE(1916); TRUFFLERS, THE(1917); BOYS WILL BE BOYS(1921); POOR RELATION, A(1921)
Virginia Ainsworth
RENO(1930)
Misc. Silents
SELF-MADE WIFE, THE(1923)
W. Harrison Ainsworth
DICK TURPIN(1933, Brit.), w
Silents
DICK TURPIN(1925), w
Roberto Airaldi
AVENGERS, THE(1950)

Jane Aird
STRANGER IN BETWEEN, THE(1952, Brit.); DEATM GOES TO SCHOOL(1953, Brit.); DANCE LITTLE LADY(1954, Brit.); ENEMY FROM SPACE(1957, Brit.); X THE UNKNOWN(1957, Brit.); DAY THE EARTH CAUGHT FIRE, THE(1961, Brit.)
Bon Aires
ROCK BABY, ROCK IT(1957)
Mireille Airgoz
MADLY(1970, Fr.), w
Ted Airhart
SOUNDER, PART 2(1976)
Teddy Airhart
SOUNDER(1972)
Jacques Airic
ENTRE NOUS(1983, Fr.)
Mark Airlie
1984
EVERY PICTURE TELLS A STORY(1984, Brit.)
The Airliners
JUNIOR PROM(1946)
Jean-Pierre Airola
MOON IN THE GUTTER, THE(1983, Fr./Ital.)
Christina Airoldi
NEXT!(1971, Ital./Span.)
Conchita Airoldi
HUMAN FACTOR, THE(1975)
Cristina Airoldi
DEAF SMITH AND JOHNNY EARS(1973, Ital.); TORSO(1974, Ital.)
Sohi-Ichi Aisaka
BUDDHA(1965, Jap.), spec eff
Sylvianne Aisenstein
FRANTIC(1961, Fr.)
Robert Aisner
CASABLANCA(1942), tech adv; CROSS OF LORRAINE, THE(1943), w
Mlle. Aisse
Misc. Silents
ROSE FRANCE(1919, Fr.)
Vincenzo Aita
MARRIAGE–ITALIAN STYLE(1964, Fr./Ital.)
Peggy Aitchison
LOLA(1971, Brit./Ital.); GREAT MUPPET CAPER, THE(1981)
Garrick Aitken
Silents
JACK, SAM AND PETE(1919, Brit.)
H. E. Aitken
Silents
HOME SWEET HOME(1914), w
Harvey Aitken
NEON PALACE, THE(1970, Can.)
John Aitken
SUMMER OF SECRETS(1976, Aus.), w
Kelly Aitken
BLUE FIN(1978, Aus.)
Maria Aitken
MARY, QUEEN OF SCOTS(1971, Brit.)
Marie Aitken
DOCTOR FAUSTUS(1967, Brit.)
Robert Aitken
LET THE PEOPLE SING(1942, Brit.)
Spotiswoode Aitken
Silents
ACQUITTED(1916)
Spottiswoode Aitken
Silents
AVENGING CONSCIENCE, THE(1914); HOME SWEET HOME(1914); BIRTH OF A NATION, THE(1915); FLYING TORPEDO, THE(1916); INNOCENT MAGDALENE, AN(1916); INTOLERANCE(1916); OLD FOLKS AT HOME, THE(1916); AMERICANO, THE(1917); JANE GOES A' WOOING(1919); NOMADS OF THE NORTH(1920); BEYOND(1921); REPUTATION(1921); TRAP, THE(1922); MERRY-GO-ROUND(1923); SIX DAYS(1923); LURE OF THE YUKON(1924); EAGLE, THE(1925); POWER OF THE WEAK, THE(1926)
Misc. Silents
CAPTAIN MACKLIN(1915); HER SHATTERED IDOL(1915); OUTCAST, THE(1915); SOULS TRIUMPHANT(1915); PRICE OF POWER, THE(1916); WHARF RAT, THE(1916); CHEERFUL GIVERS(1917); GAME OF WITS, A(1917); MELISSA OF THE HILLS(1917); WOMAN'S AWAKENING, A(1917); HOW COULD YOU, JEAN?(1918); BONNIE, BONNIE LASSIE(1919); CALEB PIPER'S GIRL(1919); CAPTAIN KIDD, JR.(1919); EVANGELINE(1919); HAY FOOT, STRAW FOOT(1919); HER KINGDOM OF DREAMS(1919); ROUGH RIDING ROMANCE(1919); SECRET GARDEN, THE(1919); THUNDERBOLT, THE(1919); WHO CARES?(1919); WICKED DARLING, THE(1919); WOMAN OF PLEASURE, A(1919); WHITE CIRCLE, THE(1920); UNKNOWN WIFE, THE(1921); DANGEROUS GAME, A(1922); MAN OF COURAGE(1922); PRICE OF YOUTH, THE(1922); FIRE PATROL, THE(1924); COAST PATROL, THE(1925); TWO-GUN MAN(1926)
Valerie Aitken
NIJINSKY(1980, Brit.); RETURN OF THE SOLDIER, THE(1983, Brit.)
Michael Aitkens
DEATHCHEATERS(1976, Aus.)
Michael Aitkin
DEMONSTRATOR(1971, Aus.)
Michael Aitkins
LONG WEEKEND(1978, Aus.)
Adam Aivazian
TEARS OF HAPPINESS(1974)
Arshalouis Aivazian
MOTOR PSYCHO(1965)
Emiko Aizawa
INSECT WOMAN, THE(1964, Jap.)

Jo [Yuzuru] Aizawa
SCHOOL FOR SEX(1966, Jap.), ph; TWO IN THE SHADOW(1968, Jap.), ph; WAR OF THE PLANETS(1977, Jap.), ph
Yuzuri Aizawa
YOUNG GUY GRADUATES(1969, Jap.), ph
Yuzuru Aizawa
WESTWARD DESPERADO(1961, Jap.), ph; OPERATION X(1963, Jap.), ph; LET'S GO, YOUNG GUY!(1967, Jap.), ph; GODZILLA VERSUS THE COSMIC MONSTER(1974, Jap.), ph; GODZILLA VS. MEGALON(1976, Jap.), ph
Mashood Ajala
WHITE WITCH DOCTOR(1953)
Emile Ajar [Romain Gary]
MADAME ROSA(1977, Fr.), w
Irene Ajay
STRONGHOLD(1952, Mex.)
Franklyn Ajaye
CARWASH(1976); DANDY, THE ALL AMERICAN GIRL(1976); CONVOY(1978); JAZZ SINGER, THE(1980); STIR CRAZY(1980); GET CRAZY(1983); HYSTERICAL(1983)
Afolabi Ajayi
FRIDAY THE 13TH... THE ORPHAN(1979)
Yadigar Ajder
YOR, THE HUNTER FROM THE FUTURE(1983, Ital.)
Yemi Ajibade
CALL HIM MR. SHATTER(1976, Hong Kong)
Daniele Ajoret
BERNADETTE OF LOURDES(1962, Fr.)
Aka
SOME KIND OF HERO(1982)
Riba Akabusi
CLASS OF MISS MAC MICHAEL, THE(1978, Brit./U.S.)
Tarik Akan
YOL(1982, Turkey)
John Akana
NASTY RABBIT, THE(1964)
John Akar
HEART OF THE MATTER, THE(1954, Brit.)
Sergei Akasakov
ADVENTURE IN ODESSA(1954, USSR), w
Mitsuyo Akashi
IDIOT, THE(1963, Jap.)
Ushio Akashi
EMPEROR AND A GENERAL, THE(1968, Jap.); SNOW COUNTRY(1969, Jap.); SONG FROM MY HEART, THE(1970, Jap.)
Yasushi Akatagawa
ANGRY ISLAND(1960, Jap.), m; ALONE ON THE PACIFIC(1964, Jap.), m
Mostafa Akavan
INVINCIBLE SIX, THE(1970, U.S./Iran), p
Miyoko Akaza
FIGHT FOR THE GLORY(1970, Jap.)
Tuncay Akca
YOL(1982, Turkey)
Adnan Akdemir
YOR, THE HUNTER FROM THE FUTURE(1983, Ital.)
Herent Akdemir
YOR, THE HUNTER FROM THE FUTURE(1983, Ital.)
Muriel Aked
BED AND BREAKFAST(1930, Brit.); MIDDLE WATCH, THE(1930, Brit.); HER FIRST AFFAIRE(1932, Brit.); INDISCRETIONS OF EVE(1932, Brit.); MAGIC NIGHT(1932, Brit.); MAYOR'S NEST, THE(1932, Brit.); GOOD COMPANIONS(1933, Brit.); ROME EXPRESS(1933, Brit.); TROUBLE(1933, Brit.); EVENSONG(1934, Brit.); FRIDAY THE 13TH(1934, Brit.); JOSSER ON THE FARM(1934, Brit.); NIGHT OF THE PARTY, THE(1934, Brit.); NO FUNNY BUSINESS(1934, Brit.); CAN YOU HEAR ME MOTHER?(1935, Brit.); RUNAWAY QUEEN, THE(1935, Brit.); DON'T RUSH ME(1936, Brit.); FAME(1936, Brit.); PUBLIC NUISANCE NO. 1(1936, Brit.); ROYAL EAGLE(1936, Brit.); MR. STRINGFELLOW SAYS NO(1937, Brit.); CONTINENTAL EXPRESS(1939, Brit.); GIRL WHO FORGOT, THE(1939, Brit.); BOMBSIGHT STOLEN(1941, Brit.); GIRL MUST LIVE, A(1941, Brit.); REMARKABLE MR. KIPPS(1942, Brit.); 2,000 WOMEN(1944, Brit.); ADVENTURE FOR TWO(1945, Brit.); COLONEL BLIMP(1945, Brit.); THEY KNEW MR. KNIGHT(1945, Brit.); JUST WILLIAM'S LUCK(1948, Brit.); SISTER TO ASSIST'ER, A(1948, Brit.); SO EVIL MY LOVE(1948, Brit.); WILLIAM COMES TO TOWN(1948, Brit.); HAPPIEST DAYS OF YOUR LIFE(1950, Brit.); IT'S HARD TO BE GOOD(1950, Brit.); FLESH AND BLOOD(1951, Brit.); WONDER BOY(1951, Brit./Aust.); GREAT GILBERT AND SULLIVAN, THE(1953, Brit.)
Silents
SISTER TO ASSIST 'ER, A(1922, Brit.)
Agnes Aker
Silents
GENTLE JULIA(1923)
Mya Akerling
MAN WITH TWO BRAINS, THE(1983)
Arne Akermark
TORMENT(1947, Swed.), art d; SCOTT OF THE ANTARCTIC(1949, Brit.), art d
Andra Akers
MURDER A LA MOD(1968); WEDDING PARTY, THE(1969); MOMENT BY MOMENT(1978)
George Akers
ASCENDANCY(1983, Brit.), ed
I.W. Akers
KENTUCKY BLUE STREAK(1935), ph
Irving Akers
LOVE PAST THIRTY(1934), ph
Donna Akersten
SLEEPING DOGS(1977, New Zealand); MIDDLE AGE SPREAD(1979, New Zealand)
Pamela Akert
BLUE HAWAII(1961)

Ital./Span.), ed; NEXT!(1971, Ital./Span.), ed; ALMOST HUMAN(1974,Ital.), ed; MAN FROM THE EAST, A(1974, Ital./Fr.), ed; SONNY AND JED(1974, Ital.), ed; SCREAMERS(1978, Ital.), ed; SILHOUETTES(1982), ed
1984
    AFTER THE FALL OF NEW YORK(1984, Ital./Fr.), ed

Salvatore Alabiso
    TWO SUPER COPS(1978, Ital.), p

Wojciech Alaborski
    MAN OF IRON(1981, Pol.)

Rinaldo Alacorn
    ROSE MARIE(1936)

Laszlo Aladar
    TROUBLE IN PARADISE(1932), w

Johnny Aladdin
    NEW ORLEANS AFTER DARK(1958)

G. Aladov
    TRAIN GOES TO KIEV, THE(1961, USSR)

Geoffrey Alah
    RED DANUBE, THE(1949)

Iris Alahanti
    WARRIORS, THE(1979)

Marc Alaimo
    WHICH WAY IS UP?(1977); MEAN DOG BLUES(1978); HARDCORE(1979); SEEMS LIKE OLD TIMES(1980)
1984
    LAST STARFIGHTER, THE(1984)

Michael Alaimo
    CHINA SYNDROME, THE(1979); MR. MOM(1983)

Steve Alaimo
    WILD REBELS, THE(1967); HOOKED GENERATION, THE(1969); NAKED ZOO, THE(1970); STANLEY(1973)

Claude Alain
    PORTRAIT OF A WOMAN(1946, Fr.)

Michael Alain
    PARIS EXPRESS, THE(1953, Brit.)

V. Alakhverdova
    WAR AND PEACE(1968, USSR)

B. Q. Alakija
    CAESAR AND CLEOPATRA(1946, Brit.)

Robin Alalouf
    PARIS EXPRESS, THE(1953, Brit.); 23 PACES TO BAKER STREET(1956)

John Shamsul Alam
    NIGHTHAWKS(1981)

Humberto Alamazan
    PANCHO VILLA RETURNS(1950, Mex.)

Richard Alameda
    OLD MAN AND THE SEA, THE(1958)

James Alamo
Silents
    TIPPED OFF(1923)

Buddy Alan
    FROM NASHVILLE WITH MUSIC(1969)

Cameron Alan
    NIGHT OF THE PROWLER, THE zero(1979, Aus.), m

Clark Alan
    DIARY OF A HIGH SCHOOL BRIDE(1959)

Drew Alan
    TILL THE END OF TIME(1946)

Rick Alan
    SATAN'S MISTRESS(1982)

Wolf Alan
    SMITHEREENS(1982)

Alan K. Foster Girls
    COCOANUTS, THE(1929)

Douglas Alan-Mann
    ENDLESS LOVE(1981)

Lissi Alandh
    SILENCE, THE(1964, Swed.); LOVING COUPLES(1966, Swed.)

Annick Alane
1984
    AMERICAN DREAMER(1984)

Rico Alaniz
    MISTER 880(1950); CALIFORNIA CONQUEST(1952); FIGHTER, THE(1952); MACAO(1952); APPOINTMENT IN HONDURAS(1953); COLUMN SOUTH(1953); CONQUEST OF COCHISE(1953); JEOPARDY(1953); TROPIC ZONE(1953); WINGS OF THE HAWK(1953); JUBILEE TRAIL(1954); SIEGE AT RED RIVER, THE(1954); GREEN FIRE(1955); SANTIAGO(1956); STAGECOACH TO FURY(1956); WOMEN OF PITCAIRN ISLAND, THE(1957); HONG KONG CONFIDENTIAL(1958); TOUGHEST GUN IN TOMBSTONE(1958); WAR OF THE COLOSSAL BEAST(1958); WOLF LARSEN(1958); MAGNIFICENT SEVEN, THE(1960); SUMMER AND SMOKE(1961)

Enrique [Henry] Alarcon
    GIRL FROM VALLADOLIO(1958, Span.), art d; COMMANDO(1962, Ital., Span., Bel., Ger.), art d; DEVIL MADE A WOMAN, THE(1962, Span.), set d; SON OF CAPTAIN BLOOD, THE(1964, U.S./Ital./Span.), art d; MURIETA(1965, Span.), set d; REDEEMER, THE(1965, Span.), art d; EVERY DAY IS A HOLIDAY(1966, Span.), art d; PLACE CALLED GLORY, A(1966, Span./Ger.), art d; 10:30 P.M. SUMMER(1966, U.S./Span.), art d; UNINHIBITED, THE(1968, Fr./Ital./Span.), art d; YOUNG REBEL, THE(1969, Fr./Ital./Span.), art d; TRISTANA(1970, Span./Ital./Fr.), art d; LIGHT AT THE EDGE OF THE WORLD, THE(1971, U.S./Span./Lichtenstein), art d; RED SUN(1972, Fr./Ital./Span.), art d; LOVE AND PAIN AND THE WHOLE DAMN THING(1973), art d; HUNTING PARTY, THE(1977, Brit.), art d

Frankie Alarcon
    CHAN IS MISSING(1982)

Jose Maria Alarcon
    DOC(1971), art d; VALDEZ IS COMING(1971), art d; TREASURE ISLAND(1972, Brit./Span./Fr./Ger.), set d; THAT HOUSE IN THE OUTSKIRTS(1980, Span.), set d
1984
    CONAN THE DESTROYER(1984), art d

Luis Alarcon
    LOVE HUNGER(1965, Arg.)

Nadine Alari
    MR. ORCHID(1948, Fr.); PERFECTIONIST, THE(1952, Fr.); GAMBLER, THE(1958, Fr.); BERNADETTE OF LOURDES(1962, Fr.); SLEEPING CAR MURDER THE(1966, Fr.)

John Alarimo
    VALACHI PAPERS, THE(1972, Ital./Fr.)

Faruk Alatan
    SUPERSONIC MAN(1979, Span.), p

Gustavo Alatriste
    EXTERMINATING ANGEL, THE(1967, Mex.), p

Max Alautdinov
    RED TENT, THE(1971, Ital./USSR), makeup

Mori Alavi
    CHILD, THE(1977), ph

Benito Alazraki
    FRANKENSTEIN, THE VAMPIRE AND CO.(1961, Mex.), d; SPIRITISM(1965, Mex.), d; CURSE OF THE DOLL PEOPLE, THE(1968, Mex.), d

Robert Alazraki
1984
    LA PETIT SIRENE(1984, Fr.), ph

Alba
    BEDAZZLED(1967, Brit.); PRIVILEGE(1967, Brit.); LEO THE LAST(1970, Brit.)
Misc. Talkies
    SWEET SOUND OF DEATH(1965, U.S./Span.)

Alfredo Alba
Misc. Talkies
    TO LOVE, PERHAPS TO DIE(1975)

Alney Alba
    SPELL OF THE HYPNOTIST(1956)

Armando Orive Alba
    MACARIO(1961, Mex.), p; TOM THUMB(1967, Mex.), p

Armando Ozive Alba
    ILLUSION TRAVELS BY STREETCAR, THE(1977, Mex.), p

Jamie Alba
    NUNZIO(1978)

Julia Caba Alba
    THUNDERSTORM(1956); TEACHER AND THE MIRACLE, THE(1961, Ital./Span.); NOT ON YOUR LIFE(1965, Ital./Span.)

Julius Alba
    FAR FROM THE MADDING CROWD(1967, Brit.)

Luz Alba
    SOFIA(1948); DAUGHTER OF THE WEST(1949); SOMBRERO(1953)

Maria Alba
    HELL'S HEROES(1930); GOLDIE(1931); JUST A GIGOLO(1931); ALMOST MARRIED(1932); MR. ROBINSON CRUSOE(1932); HYPNOTIZED(1933); FLIRTING WITH DANGER(1935); GREAT GOD GOLD(1935); WEST OF THE PECOS(1935)
Silents
    ROAD HOUSE(1928); JOY STREET(1929)
Misc. Silents
    BLINDFOLD(1928)

Orpha Alba
Silents
    WELCOME CHILDREN(1921)
Misc. Silents
    LOOK YOUR BEST(1923)

Rafael Morena Alba
    EXORCISM'S DAUGHTER(1974, Span.), d&w

Ricardo Alba
    SECOND CHANCE(1953); WINGS OF THE HAWK(1953)

Rose Alba
    SHADOW OF A MAN(1955, Brit.); MARY HAD A LITTLE(1961, Brit.); THUNDERBALL(1965, Brit.); SCHOOL FOR SEX(1969, Brit.); PASSAGE, THE(1979, Brit.); FUNNY MONEY(1983, Brit.)

Sylvia Alba
    RETURN OF SABATA(1972, Ital./Fr./Ger.)

Tito Alba
    GODFATHER, THE, PART II(1974)

Rosa Albach-Retty
    MONEY ON THE STREET(1930, Aust.); MOZART STORY, THE(1948, Aust.)

Wolf Albach-Retty
    BEAUTIFUL ADVENTURE(1932, Ger.)

Maria Albaicin
    UNINHIBITED, THE(1968, Fr./Ital./Span.)

Rafael Albaicin
    SAVAGE GUNS, THE(1962, U.S./Span.); CEREMONY, THE(1963, U.S./Span.); NAVAJO JOE(1967, Ital./Span.); PLAY DIRTY(1969, Brit.); EL CONDOR(1970); CHARLEY-ONE-EYE(1973, Brit.)

Dick Albain
    ZAPPED!(1982), spec eff

Dick Albain, Jr.
    FOG, THE(1980), spec eff

Richard Albain
    VALLEY OF THE DRAGONS(1961), spec eff; MAN FROM THE DINERS' CLUB, THE(1963), spec eff; THREE STOOGES GO AROUND THE WORLD IN A DAZE, THE(1963), spec eff; STRAIT-JACKET(1964), spec eff; OUTLAWS IS COMING, THE(1965), spec eff; WHO'S MINDING THE MINT?(1967), spec eff; GIANT SPIDER INVASION, THE(1975), spec eff; NEW YORK, NEW YORK(1977), spec eff; KIDNAPPING OF THE PRESIDENT, THE(1980, Can.), spec eff

Richard F. Albain
    MECHANIC, THE(1972), spec eff; UP THE SANDBOX(1972), spec eff

John Alban
    POSTMAN ALWAYS RINGS TWICE, THE(1946); TILL THE CLOUDS ROLL BY(1946); SENATOR WAS INDISCREET, THE(1947)

Dion Albanese
    WANDERERS, THE(1979)

Licia Albanese
SERENADE(1956)
Meggie Albanesi
Silents
MR. WU(1919, Brit.)
Misc. Silents
DARBY AND JOAN(1919, Brit.)
Elsa Albani
GIRL WITH A SUITCASE(1961, Fr./Ital.); ANZIO(1968, Ital.); WITCHES, THE(1969, Fr./Ital.)
Guardo Albani
COUNTERPLOT(1959)
Marcella Albani
Misc. Silents
RUSSIA(1929, Ger.); SECRETS OF THE ORIENT(1932, Ger.)
Romano Albani
INFERNO(1980, Ital.), ph
Mary Albano
CURIOUS DR. HUMPP(1967, Arg.)
Pietro Albano
PRISONER OF THE IRON MASK(1962, Fr./Ital.)
K. Albanov
HUNTING IN SIBERIA(1962, USSR)
Albarado
HORSE IN THE GRAY FLANNEL SUIT, THE(1968)
Celeste Albaret
CELESTE(1982, Ger.), w
John Albasiny
1984
KIPPERBANG(1984, Brit.)
Freddy Albech
WHILE THE ATTORNEY IS ASLEEP(1945, Den.)
J. Frederik Albeck
TRUE STORY OF JESSE JAMES, THE(1957)
Edward Albee
WHO'S AFRAID OF VIRGINIA WOOLF?(1966), w; DELICATE BALANCE, A(1973), w
Josh Albee
JEREMIAH JOHNSON(1972)
The Albee Sisters
TURN OFF THE MOON(1937)
Joe Alben, Jr.
BIG TOWN AFTER DARK(1947)
Hans Alberg
F.P. 1 DOESN'T ANSWER(1933, Ger.)
Mildred Freed Alberg
HOT MILLIONS(1968, Brit.), p
Somer Alberg
SHRIKE, THE(1955)
Anna Maria Alberghetti
HERE COMES THE GROOM(1951); MEDIUM, THE(1951); STARS ARE SINGING, THE(1953); LAST COMMAND, THE(1955); DUEL AT APACHE WELLS(1957); TEN THOUSAND BEDROOMS(1957); CINDERFELLA(1960)
Luis Alberni
SANTA FE TRAIL, THE(1930); LAST FLIGHT, THE(1931); MAD GENIUS, THE(1931); MANHATTAN PARADE(1931); MEN IN HER LIFE(1931); ONE HEAVENLY NIGHT(1931); SIDE SHOW(1931); SVENGALI(1931); TIP-OFF, THE(1931); BIG STAMPEDE, THE(1932); COCK OF THE AIR(1932); COHENS, AND KELLYS IN HOLLYWOOD, THE(1932); HIGH PRESSURE(1932); PARISIAN ROMANCE, A(1932); TROUBLE IN PARADISE(1932); WEEK-END MARRIAGE(1932); WOMAN IN ROOM 13, THE(1932); CALIFORNIA TRAIL, THE(1933); CHILD OF MANHATTAN(1933); FLYING DOWN TO RIO(1933); HYPNOTIZED(1933); I LOVE THAT MAN(1933); LADY KILLER(1933); MAN FROM MONTEREY, THE(1933); MEN MUST FIGHT(1933); SPHINX, THE(1933); TOPAZE(1933); TRICK FOR TRICK(1933); WHEN LADIES MEET(1933); ABOVE THE CLOUDS(1934); BLACK CAT, THE(1934); CAPTAIN HATES THE SEA, THE(1934); COUNT OF MONTE CRISTO, THE(1934); GLAMOUR(1934); GOODBYE LOVE(1934); I BELIEVED IN YOU(1934); LAST TRAIL, THE(1934); ONE NIGHT OF LOVE(1934); WHEN STRANGERS MEET(1934); BAD BOY(1935); GAY DECEPTION, THE(1935); GILDED LILY, THE(1935); GOIN' TO TOWN(1935); IN CALIENTE(1935); LET'S LIVE TONIGHT(1935); LOVE ME FOREVER(1935); LOVE ME FOREVER(1935); MANHATTAN MOON(1935); MUSIC IS MAGIC(1935); PUBLIC OPINION(1935); ROBERTA(1935); WINNING TICKET, THE(1935); ANTHONY ADVERSE(1936); COLLEEN(1936); DANCING PIRATE(1936); FOLLOW YOUR HEART(1936); TICKET TO PARADISE(1936); EASY LIVING(1937); GREAT GARRICK, THE(1937); HATS OFF(1937); HITTING A NEW HIGH(1937); KING AND THE CHORUS GIRL, THE(1937); LOVE ON TOAST(1937); MADAME X(1937); MANHATTAN MERRY-GO-ROUND(1937); MR. DODD TAKES THE AIR(1937); SING AND BE HAPPY(1937); TWO WISE MAIDS(1937); UNDER SUSPICION(1937); WHEN YOU'RE IN LOVE(1937); I'LL GIVE A MILLION(1938); GREAT MAN VOTES, THE(1939); HOUSEKEEPER'S DAUGHTER(1939); LET FREEDOM RING(1939); NAUGHTY BUT NICE(1939); ENEMY AGENT(1940); LONE WOLF MEETS A LADY, THE(1940); PUBLIC DEB NO. 1(1940); SCATTERBRAIN(1940); BABES ON BROADWAY(1941); LADY EVE, THE(1941); LAW OF THE TROPICS(1941); OBLIGING YOUNG LADY(1941); ROAD TO ZANZIBAR(1941); SAN ANTONIO ROSE(1941); SHE KNEW ALL THE ANSWERS(1941); THAT HAMILTON WOMAN(1941); THEY MET IN ARGENTINA(1941); THEY MET IN BOMBAY(1941); WORLD PREMIERE(1941); I MARRIED AN ANGEL(1942); MEXICAN SPITFIRE'S ELEPHANT(1942); HARVEST MELODY(1943); HERE COMES ELMER(1943); HERE COMES KELLY(1943); MY SON, THE HERO(1943); NEARLY EIGHTEEN(1943); SUBMARINE BASE(1943); TWO WEEKS TO LIVE(1943); YOU'RE A LUCKY FELLOW, MR. SMITH(1943); HENRY ALDRICH PLAYS CUPID(1944); IN SOCIETY(1944); MACHINE GUN MAMA(1944); MEN ON HER MIND(1944); RAINBOW ISLAND(1944); VOICE IN THE WIND(1944); WHEN THE LIGHTS GO ON AGAIN(1944); BELL FOR ADANO, A(1945); HIT THE HAY(1945); IN FAST COMPANY(1946); NIGHT SONG(1947); CAPTAIN CAREY, U.S.A(1950); WHEN WILLIE COMES MARCHING HOME(1950); WHAT PRICE GLORY?(1952); TEN COMMANDMENTS, THE(1956)
Misc. Talkies
GUILTY OR NOT GUILTY(1932); PASSPORT TO HEAVEN(1943)

Silents
MAN FROM BEYOND, THE(1922)
Sherri Alberoni
THREE WORLDS OF GULLIVER, THE(1960, Brit.)
Sherry Alberoni
DANCE WITH ME, HENRY(1956); PAY OR DIE(1960); MR. HOBBS TAKES A VACATION(1962); CYBORG 2087(1966); BARN OF THE NAKED DEAD Zero(1976)
Ellie Albers
WEDDING, A(1978)
Hans Albers
BLUE ANGEL, THE(1930, Ger.); COPPER, THE(1930, Brit.); BOMBARDMENT OF MONTE CARLO, THE(1931, Ger.); WHITE DEMON, THE(1932, Ger.); GOLD(1934, Ger.); MAN WHO WAS SHERLOCK HOLMES, THE(1937, Ger.); SERGEANT BERRY(1938, Ger.), a, p; WATER FOR CANITOGA(1939, Ger.); CITY OF TORMENT(1950, Ger.); VOR SONNENUNTERGANG(1961, Ger)
Harry Albers
WORDS AND MUSIC(1929)
Albert
OH, YOU BEAUTIFUL DOLL(1949), w
Annie Albert
TOMB OF TORTURE(1966, Ital.)
Arnold Albert
MAN I LOVE, THE(1946), p
Arthur Albert
PLEASE STAND BY(1972), ph
1984
NIGHT OF THE COMET(1984), ph
Carlos Albert
WHERE DANGER LIVES(1950); FRENCH LINE, THE(1954); SO THIS IS PARIS(1954)
Eddie Albert
CONCORDE, THE–AIRPORT '79(; BROTHER RAT(1938); FOUR WIVES(1939); ANGEL FROM TEXAS, AN(1940); BROTHER RAT AND A BABY(1940); DISPATCH FROM REUTERS, A(1940); MY LOVE CAME BACK(1940); FOUR MOTHERS(1941); GREAT MR. NOBODY, THE(1941); OUT OF THE FOG(1941); THIEVES FALL OUT(1941); WAGONS ROLL AT NIGHT, THE(1941); EAGLE SQUADRON(1942); LADY BODYGUARD(1942); TREAT EM' ROUGH(1942); BOMBARDIER(1943); LADIES' DAY(1943); STRANGE VOYAGE(1945); PERFECT MARRIAGE, THE(1946); RENDEZVOUS WITH ANNIE(1946); HIT PARADE OF 1947(1947); SMASH-UP, THE STORY OF A WOMAN(1947); TIME OUT OF MIND(1947); DUDE GOES WEST, THE(1948); YOU GOTTA STAY HAPPY(1948); FULLER BRUSH GIRL, THE(1950); MEET ME AFTER THE SHOW(1951); YOU'RE IN THE NAVY NOW(1951); CARRIE(1952); ROMAN HOLIDAY(1953); GIRL RUSH, THE(1955); I'LL CRY TOMORROW(1955); OKLAHOMA(1955); ATTACK!(1956); TEAHOUSE OF THE AUGUST MOON, THE(1956); JOKER IS WILD, THE(1957); GUN RUNNERS, THE(1958); ORDERS TO KILL(1958, Brit.); ROOTS OF HEAVEN, THE(1958); BELOVED INFIDEL(1959); TWO LITTLE BEARS, THE(1961); YOUNG DOCTORS, THE(1961); LONGEST DAY, THE(1962); MADISON AVENUE(1962); WHO'S GOT THE ACTION?(1962); CAPTAIN NEWMAN, M.D.(1963); MIRACLE OF THE WHITE STALLIONS(1963); PARTY'S OVER, THE(1966, Brit.); SEVEN WOMEN(1966); HEARTBREAK KID, THE(1972); LONGEST YARD, THE(1974); MC Q(1974); TAKE, THE(1974); DEVIL'S RAIN, THE(1975, U.S./Mex.); ESCAPE TO WITCH MOUNTAIN(1975); HUSTLE(1975); WHIFFS(1975); BIRCH INTERVAL(1976); MOVING VIOLATION(1976); FOOLIN' AROUND(1980); HOW TO BEAT THE HIGH COST OF LIVING(1980); YESTERDAY(1980, Can.); TAKE THIS JOB AND SHOVE IT(1981); YES, GIORGIO(1982)
1984
ACT, THE(1984); DREAMSCAPE(1984)
Misc. Talkies
THIS TIME FOREVER(1981)
Edward Albert
FOOL KILLER, THE(1965); BUTTERFLIES ARE FREE(1972); FORTY CARATS(1973); MIDWAY(1976); DOMINO PRINCIPLE, THE(1977); GREEK TYCOON, THE(1978); SQUEEZE, THE(1980, Ital.); WHEN TIME RAN OUT(1980); GALAXY OF TERROR(1981); BUTTERFLY(1982); HOUSE WHERE EVIL DWELLS, THE(1982)
1984
ELLIE(1984)
Elsie Albert
Silents
WELCOME CHILDREN(1921)
Emeric Albert
CHALLENGE, THE(1939, Brit.)
Emmerich Albert
REBEL, THE(1933, Ger.)
Frankie Albert
SPIRIT OF STANFORD, THE(1942)
Germaine Albert
DR. KNOCK(1936, Fr.)
Gina Albert
MARIZINIA(1962, U.S./Braz.); MAEDCHEN IN UNIFORM(1965, Ger./Fr.)
Jerry Albert
MAKO: THE JAWS OF DEATH(1976)
Misc. Talkies
BLOODSTALKERS(1976)
John A. Albert
DOUBLE CROSS(1941), w
John Albert
SHAME OF THE SABINE WOMEN, THE(1962, Mex.), art d
Julius Albert
DAISIES(1967, Czech.)
Katherine Albert
ON THE LOOSE(1951), w; HOW TO MARRY A MILLIONAIRE(1953), w; SABRE JET(1953), w; STAR, THE(1953), w
Silents
SAPHEAD, THE(1921)
Marvin Albert
FISH THAT SAVED PITTSBURGH, THE(1979)

Marvin H. Albert
LAW AND JAKE WADE, THE(1958), w; BULLET FOR A BADMAN(1964), w; DUEL AT DIABLO(1966), w; ROUGH NIGHT IN JERICHO(1967), w; TONY ROME(1967), w; LADY IN CEMENT(1968), w; TWIST OF SAND, A(1968, Brit.), w; UGLY ONES, THE(1968, Ital./Span.), w; DON IS DEAD, THE(1973), w

Michelle Albert
TAKE HER BY SURPRISE(1967, Can.)

Paule Albert
HOUSE OF CARDS(1969)

Ronnie Albert
SWEET BEAT(1962, Brit.), d

Ross Albert
1984
SUBURBIA(1984), ed

Susan Albert
LOVE IS A FUNNY THING(1970, Fr./Ital.)

Vic Albert
VALDEZ IS COMING(1971)

Wil Albert
FOR PETE'S SAKE(1977); I WANNA HOLD YOUR HAND(1978); WACKO(1983)
Misc. Talkies
AMERICAN RASPBERRY(1980)

Albert Sandler & The Palm Court Orchestra
I'LL TURN TO YOU(1946, Brit.)

Albert Sandler and His Orchestra
SMALL MAN, THE(1935, Brit.)

Linda Albertano
BEACH RED(1967)

Giorgia Albertazzi
BLOOD, SWEAT AND FEAR(1975, Ital.)

Giorgio Albertazzi
EVA(1962, Fr./Ital.); LAST YEAR AT MARIENBAD(1962, Fr./Ital.); RED LIPS(1964, Fr./Ital.)

Albertelli
13 MEN AND A GUN(1938, Brit.), ph

Mario Albertelli
ROSSINI(1948, Ital.), ph; BURIED ALIVE(1951, Ital.), ph

Anna Alberti
GUNS OF THE BLACK WITCH(1961, Fr./Ital.); LOST SOULS(1961, Ital.)

Barbara Alberti
NIGHT PORTER, THE(1974, Ital./U.S.), w; ERNESTO(1979, Ital.), w

Fritz Alberti
BECAUSE I LOVED YOU(1930, Ger.); KARAMAZOV(1931, Ger.); 1914(1932, Ger.)
Silents
KRIEMHILD'S REVENGE(1924, Ger.); METROPOLIS(1927, Ger.)
Misc. Silents
CAFE ELECTRIC(1927, Aust.)

Guido Alberti
8 ½(1963, Ital.); CASANOVA '70(1965, Ital.); NOT ON YOUR LIFE(1965, Ital./Span.); LA FUGA(1966, Ital.); MARCO THE MAGNIFICENT(1966, Ital./Fr./Yugo./Egypt/ Afghanistan); SHOOT LOUD, LOUDER... I DON'T UNDERSTAND(1966, Ital.); TASTE FOR WOMEN, A(1966, Fr./Ital.); NO ROSES FOR OSS 117(1968, Fr.); FINE PAIR, A(1969, Ital.); TEN DAYS' WONDER(1972, Fr.); CHE?(1973, Ital./Fr./Ger.); ALMOST HUMAN(1974,Ital.); NO WAY OUT(1975, Ital./Fr.); BOBBY DEERFIELD(1977)
Misc. Talkies
SPASMO(1976)

Rudo Alberti
MOON IN THE GUTTER, THE(1983, Fr./Ital.)

Albertina Rasch Ballet
SALLY(1929)

Albertina Rasch Dancers
BROADWAY TO HOLLYWOOD(1933); MADAME DU BARRY(1934), ch

The Albertina Rasch Dancers
ROSALIE(1937)

Adalberto Albertini
BRIEF RAPTURE(1952, Ital.), ph; DAVID AND GOLIATH(1961, Ital.), ph; RED CLOAK, THE(1961, Ital./Fr.), ph; NIGHT THEY KILLED RASPUTIN, THE(1962, Fr./Ital.), ph; LADY DOCTOR, THE(1963, Fr./Ital./Span.), ph; GLADIATORS 7(1964, Span./Ital.), ph; 00-2 MOST SECRET AGENTS(1965, Ital.), ph; SEVEN REVENGES, THE(1967, Ital.), ph; GLASS SPHINX, THE(1968, Egypt/Ital./Span.), w

Edda Albertini
BEFORE HIM ALL ROME TREMBLED(1947, Ital.)

Giamopiero Albertini
ORGANIZER, THE(1964, Fr./Ital./Yugo.)

Giampiero Albertini
MADE IN ITALY(1967, Fr./Ital.); ITALIAN SECRET SERVICE(1968, Ital.); SEVEN GOLDEN MEN(1969, Fr./Ital./Span.)

Gian Pier Albertini
MINUTE TO PRAY, A SECOND TO DIE, A(1968, Ital.)

Gianpiero Albertini
BURN(1970); RETURN OF SABATA(1972, Ital./Fr./Ger.)

Michel Albertini
VERDICT(1975, Fr./Ital.)

Jean Alberto [Juan Alberto Soler]
THAT MAN IN ISTANBUL(1966, Fr./Ital./Span.), art d

Anita Alberts
STERILE CUCKOO, THE(1969); STEAGLE, THE(1971); HOUSE CALLS(1978)

Karl-Erik Alberts
PIMPERNEL SVENSSON(1953, Swed.), ph

Mal Alberts
MIDNIGHT MAN, THE(1974)

Arthur Albertson
Silents
ARGYLE CASE, THE(1917)
Misc. Silents
LOTUS WOMAN, THE(1916)

Coit Albertson
Silents
SILVER LINING, THE(1921); AVERAGE WOMAN, THE(1924); LEND ME YOUR HUSBAND(1924); MAD DANCER(1925); JAZZ GIRL, THE(1926)

Misc. Silents
FOR FREEDOM(1919); FACE TO FACE(1920); SUNSHINE HARBOR(1922); ERMINE AND RHINESTONES(1925); SCANDAL STREET(1925); SUBSTITUTE WIFE, THE(1925); RETURN OF BOSTON BLACKIE, THE(1927)

Crank Albertson
CONNECTICUT YANKEE, A(1931)

E. Coit Albertson
Misc. Silents
WHO'S YOUR BROTHER?(1919); WITS VS. WITS(1920)

Eric Albertson
SIN OF MONA KENT, THE(1961), ed; HOSPITAL, THE(1971), ed; EVERYTHING YOU ALWAYS WANTED TO KNOW ABOUT SEX, BUT WE'RE AFRAID TO ASK(1972), ed; FROM THE MIXED-UP FILES OF MRS. BASIL E. FRANK-WEILER(1973), ed; GORDON'S WAR(1973), ed; SUNNYSIDE(1979), ed; FIRST DEADLY SIN, THE(1980), ed; UNION CITY(1980), ed

Frank Albertson
SALUTE(1929); WORDS AND MUSIC(1929); BIG PARTY, THE(1930); BORN RECK-LESS(1930); HAPPY DAYS(1930); JUST IMAGINE(1930); MEN WITHOUT WO-MEN(1930); SO THIS IS LONDON(1930); SON OF THE GODS(1930); SPRING IS HERE(1930); WILD COMPANY(1930); BIG BUSINESS GIRL(1931); BRAT, THE(1931); TRAVELING HUSBANDS(1931); AIR MAIL(1932); BILLION DOLLAR SCAN-DAL(1932); HUDDLE(1932); RACING YOUTH(1932); WAY BACK HOME(1932); ANN CARVER'S PROFESSION(1933); COHENS AND KELLYS IN TROUBLE, THE(1933); EVER IN MY HEART(1933); KING FOR A NIGHT(1933); MIDSHIPMAN JACK(1933); RAINBOW OVER BROADWAY(1933); HOLLYWOOD MYSTERY(1934); LAST GEN-TLEMAN, THE(1934); LIFE OF VERGIE WINTERS, THE(1934); AH, WILDER-NESS!(1935); ALICE ADAMS(1935); DOUBTING THOMAS(1935); EAST OF JAVA(1935); ENTER MADAME(1935); KIND LADY(1935); PERSONAL MAID'S SE-CRET(1935); WATERFRONT LADY(1935); FARMER IN THE DELL, THE(1936); FURY(1936); NAVY BLUE AND GOLD(1937); PLAINSMAN, THE(1937); FUGITIVES FOR A NIGHT(1938); HOLD THAT KISS(1938); MOTHER CAREY'S CHICKENS(1938); ROOM SERVICE(1938); SHINING HOUR, THE(1938); SPRING MADNESS(1938); BACHELOR MOTHER(1939); DR. CHRISTIAN MEETS THE WOMEN(1940); FRAMED(1940); GHOST COMES HOME, THE(1940); WHEN THE DALTONS RO-DE(1940); BEHIND THE NEWS(1941); BURMA CONVOY(1941); CITADEL OF CRI-ME(1941); ELLERY QUEEN'S PENTHOUSE MYSTERY(1941); FLYING CADETS(1941); LOUISIANA PURCHASE(1941); MAN MADE MONSTER(1941); CITY OF SILENT MEN(1942); MAN FROM HEADQUARTERS(1942); SHEPHERD OF THE OZARKS(1942); UNDERGROUND AGENT(1942); WAKE ISLAND(1942); HERE COMES ELMER(1943); KEEP 'EM SLUGGING(1943); MYSTERY BROADCAST(1943); O, MY DARLING CLEMENTINE(1943); AND THE ANGELS SING(1944); I LOVE A SOLDIER(1944); ROSIE THE RIVETER(1944); ARSON SQUAD(1945); GAY BLA-DES(1946); HOW DO YOU DO?(1946); IT'S A WONDERFUL LIFE(1946); THEY MADE ME A KILLER(1946); GINGER(1947); HUCKSTERS, THE(1947); KILLER DILL(1947); SHED NO TEARS(1948); NIGHTFALL(1956); ENEMY BELOW, THE(1957); LAST HURRAH, THE(1958); PSYCHO(1960); GIRL ON THE RUN(1961); DON'T KNOCK THE TWIST(1962); BYE BYE BIRDIE(1963); JOHNNY COOL(1963)
Misc. Talkies
CITY LIMITS(1941); FATHER STEPS OUT(1941)
Silents
PREP AND PEP(1928)
Misc. Silents
FARMER'S DAUGHTER, THE(1928); BLUE SKIES(1929)

George Albertson
HOT CAR GIRL(1958)

Grace Albertson
DUFFY'S TAVERN(1945); ANGEL IN MY POCKET(1969)

Grace Gillern Albertson
FANCY PANTS(1950)

Jack Albertson
YOU CAN'T RUN AWAY FROM IT(1956); NEXT TIME I MARRY(1938); STRIKE UP THE BAND(1940); MIRACLE ON 34TH STREET, THE(1947); TOP BANANA(1954); BRING YOUR SMILE ALONG(1955); EDDY DUCHIN STORY, THE(1956); HARDER THEY FALL, THE(1956); OVER-EXPOSED(1956); UNGUARDED MOMENT, THE(1956); MAN OF A THOUSAND FACES(1957); MONKEY ON MY BACK(1957); TEACHER'S PET(1958); NEVER STEAL ANYTHING SMALL(1959); SHAGGY DOG, THE(1959); GEORGE RAFT STORY, THE(1961); LOVER COME BACK(1961); MAN-TRAP(1961); CONVICTS FOUR(1962); DAYS OF WINE AND ROSES(1962); PERIOD OF ADJUSTMENT(1962); WHO'S GOT THE ACTION?(1962); SON OF FLUB-BER(1963); KISSIN' COUSINS(1964); PATSY, THE(1964); ROUSTABOUT(1964); TIG-ER WALKS, A(1964); HOW TO MURDER YOUR WIFE(1965); FLIM-FLAM MAN, THE(1967); HOW TO SAVE A MARRIAGE–AND RUIN YOUR LIFE(1968); SUBJECT WAS ROSES, THE(1968); CHANGES(1969); JUSTINE(1969); RABBIT, RUN(1970); SQUEEZE A FLOWER(1970, Aus.); LATE LIZ, THE(1971); WILLY WONKA AND THE CHOCOLATE FACTORY(1971); PICKUP ON 101(1972); POSEIDON ADVENTURE, THE(1972); DON'T GO NEAR THE WATER(1975); DEAD AND BURIED(1981); FOX AND THE HOUND, THE(1981)

Lillian Albertson
STORM WARNING(1950); GREATEST SHOW ON EARTH, THE(1952); TEN COM-MANDMENTS, THE(1956)

Mabel Albertson
GANG WAR(1928); MUTINY ON THE BLACKHAWK(1939); MY PAL GUS(1952); SHE'S BACK ON BROADWAY(1953); SO THIS IS LOVE(1953); ABOUT MRS. LESLIE(1954); BLACK WIDOW(1954); COBWEB, THE(1955); MA AND PA KETTLE AT WAIKIKI(1955); FOREVER DARLING(1956); FOUR GIRLS IN TOWN(1956); RANSOM(1956); MAN AFRAID(1957); FEMALE ANIMAL, THE(1958); HOME BEFORE DARK(1958); LONG, HOT SUMMER, THE(1958); DON'T GIVE UP THE SHIP(1959); GAZEBO, THE(1959); HANGMAN, THE(1959); ALL THE FINE YOUNG CANNIBALS(1960); ALL IN A NIGHT'S WORK(1961); PERIOD OF ADJUST-MENT(1962); FINE MADNESS, A(1966); BAREFOOT IN THE PARK(1967); ON A CLEAR DAY YOU CAN SEE FOREVER(1970); WHAT'S UP, DOC?(1972)

Mitzi Albertson
TEENAGE ZOMBIES(1960)

Karl Otto Alberty
GREAT ESCAPE, THE(1963); PHONY AMERICAN, THE(1964, Ger.); BATTLE OF THE BULGE(1965); IS PARIS BURNING?(1966, U.S./Fr.); ASSIGNMENT K(1968, Brit.); BATTLE OF BRITAIN, THE(1969, Brit.); MIDAS RUN(1969); SECRET OF SANTA VITTORIA, THE(1969); DAY OF ANGER(1970, Ital./Ger.); GREAT WHITE HOPE, THE(1970); KELLY'S HEROES(1970, U.S./Yugo.); RAID ON ROMMEL(1971); SALZBURG CONNECTION, THE(1972); SLAUGHTERHOUSE-FIVE(1972)

Jean-Gabriel Albicocco
GIRL WITH THE GOLDEN EYES, THE(1962, Fr.), d, w; WANDERER, THE(1969, Fr.), d, w

Quinto Albicocco
GIRL WITH THE GOLDEN EYES, THE(1962, Fr.), ph; PROSTITUTION(1965, Fr.), ph; WANDERER, THE(1969, Fr.), ph

Peter Albiez
BLUE THUNDER(1983), spec eff

Elsie Albiin
HIDDEN FEAR(1957)

Elsy Albin
RAPTURE(1950, Ital.); TERROR STREET(1953); WHAT EVERY WOMAN WANTS(1954, Brit.)

Emmy Albiin
OCEAN BREAKERS(1949, Swed.)

Andy Albin
NORTH BY NORTHWEST(1959); GUN FIGHT(1961); CONVICTS FOUR(1962); CINCINNATI KID, THE(1965); MC HALE'S NAVY JOINS THE AIR FORCE(1965); DON'T WORRY, WE'LL THINK OF A TITLE(1966); TAMMY AND THE MILLIONAIRE(1967); 1776(1972); GABLE AND LOMBARD(1976)

Charles Albin
TOY WIFE, THE(1938)

Dolores Albin
1984
ICE PIRATES, THE(1984)

Elsy Albin
DISOBEDIENT(1953, Brit.)

Hans Albin
NO SURVIVORS, PLEASE(1963, Ger.), p, d

Peter Albin
MORE AMERICAN GRAFFITI(1979)

Ricardo Albinana
UNSATISFIED, THE(1964, Span.), ph

John Albineri
ATTACK ON THE IRON COAST(1968, U.S./Brit.)

Tomaso Giovanni Albinoni
ROLLERBALL(1975), md

Tommaso Albinoni
TRIAL, THE(1963, Fr./Ital./Ger.), m

Mark Albiston
LIBIDO(1973, Aus.)

Elsie Alblin
CRIME AND PUNISHMENT(1948, Swed.)

Julio Albo
YOUNG AND EVIL(1962, Mex.), w

Isabella Albonica
WATERLOO(1970, Ital./USSR)

Giulio Albonico
CANNIBALS, THE(1970, Ital.), ph; DEAD OF SUMMER(1970 Ital./Fr.), ph; GUN, THE(1978, Ital.), ph

Isabella Albonico
THAT TOUCH OF MINK(1962)

Rene Albouze
RAPTURE(1965), spec eff; SHOCK TROOPS(1968, Ital./Fr.), spec eff; FORCE 10 FROM NAVARONE(1978, Brit.), spec eff

Martha Albrand
CAPTAIN CAREY, U.S.A(1950), w; DESPERATE MOMENT(1953, Brit.), w

Maurice Albray
LANDRU(1963, Fr./Ital), cos; LA BONNE SOUPE(1964, Fr./Ital.), cos; CHAMPAGNE MURDERS, THE(1968, Fr.), cos; LES BICHES(1968, Fr.), cos

Edward Albrecht
END, THE(1978)

Ernst Albrecht
LA HABANERA(1937, Ger.), set d

Heidi Albrecht
THOSE LIPS, THOSE EYES(1980)

Helen Albrecht
MY FAIR LADY(1964)

Marcy Albrecht
HOLLYWOOD HIGH(1977)
Misc. Talkies
HOLLYWOOD HIGH(1976)

Oscar Albrecht
TOMORROW IS MY TURN(1962, Fr./Ital./Ger.)

Patricia Alice Albrecht
FORCE: FIVE(1981)

Peter Albrecht
SARABAND(1949, Brit.)

Michael Albrechtsen
ISLAND OF TERROR(1967, Brit.), spec eff; CORRUPTION(1968, Brit.), spec eff; UNCANNY, THE(1977, Brit./Can.), spec eff

Mike Albrechtsen
DEATH SHIP(1980, Can.), spec eff

Carlton J. Albright
CHILDREN, THE(1980), p, w

Daniel Albright
1984
TANK(1984)

Hardie Albright
HEARTBREAK(1931); HUSH MONEY(1931); SKYLINE(1931); YOUNG SINNERS(1931); CABIN IN THE COTTON(1932); JEWEL ROBBERY(1932); MATCH KING, THE(1932); PURCHASE PRICE, THE(1932); SO BIG(1932); SUCCESSFUL CALAMITY, A(1932); THE CRASH(1932); THIS SPORTING AGE(1932); THREE ON A MATCH(1932); HOUSE ON 56TH STREET, THE(1933); SONG OF SONGS(1933); THREE-CORNERED MOON(1933); WORKING MAN, THE(1933); CRIMSON ROMANCE(1934); NANA(1934); NINTH GUEST, THE(1934); SCARLET LETTER, THE(1934); TWO HEADS ON A PILLOW(1934); WHITE HEAT(1934); CALM YOURSELF(1935); CHAMPAGNE FOR BREAKFAST(1935); LADIES LOVE DANGER(1935); RED SALUTE(1935); SILVER STREAK, THE(1935); SING SING NIGHTS(1935); WOMEN MUST DRESS(1935); CAROLINA MOON(1940); GRANNY GET YOUR

GUN(1940); SKI PATROL(1940); BACHELOR DADDY(1941); FLIGHT FROM DESTINY(1941); MARRY THE BOSS' DAUGHTER(1941); MEN OF THE TIMBERLAND(1941); NAVY BLUES(1941); CAPTAINS OF THE CLOUDS(1942); LADY IN A JAM(1942); LOVES OF EDGAR ALLAN POE, THE(1942); MAD DOCTOR OF MARKET STREET, THE(1942); PRIDE OF THE YANKEES, THE(1942); ARMY WIVES(1944); CAPTAIN TUGBOAT ANNIE(1945); JADE MASK, THE(1945); SUNSET IN EL DORADO(1945); ANGEL ON MY SHOULDER(1946); MOM AND DAD(1948)
Misc. Talkies
BEGGAR'S HOLIDAY(1934)

John Albright
COLLEEN(1936); DON JUAN QUILLIGAN(1945); TILL THE CLOUDS ROLL BY(1946); FLAME, THE(1948); I, JANE DOE(1948); KING OF THE GAMBLERS(1948); PERFECT STRANGERS(1950); PEOPLE AGAINST O'HARA, THE(1951)

Johnny Albright
HOMECOMING(1948)

Larry Albright
ONE FROM THE HEART(1982)

Lois Albright
WHAT PRICE VENGEANCE?(1937)

Lola Albright
EASTER PARADE(1948); JULIA MISBEHAVES(1948); CHAMPION(1949); GIRL FROM JONES BEACH, THE(1949); TULSA(1949); BEAUTY ON PARADE(1950); BODYHOLD(1950); GOOD HUMOR MAN, THE(1950); KILLER THAT STALKED NEW YORK, THE(1950); WHEN YOU'RE SMILING(1950); SIERRA PASSAGE(1951); ARCTIC FLIGHT(1952); SILVER WHIP, THE(1953); MAGNIFICENT MATADOR, THE(1955); TENDER TRAP, THE(1955); TREASURE OF RUBY HILLS(1955); MONOLITH MONSTERS, THE(1957); PAWNEE(1957); OREGON PASSAGE(1958); SEVEN GUNS TO MESA(1958); COLD WIND IN AUGUST(1961); KID GALAHAD(1962); JOY HOUSE(1964, Fr.); LORD LOVE A DUCK(1966); WAY WEST, THE(1967); HELICOPTER SPIES, THE(1968); IMPOSSIBLE YEARS, THE(1968); MONEY JUNGLE, THE(1968); WHERE WERE YOU WHEN THE LIGHTS WENT OUT?(1968)

Nathanael Albright
CHILDREN, THE(1980)

Sarah Albright
CHILDREN, THE(1980)

Vicky Albright
TROUBLE WITH ANGELS, THE(1966); WILD, WILD WINTER(1966)

Victoria Albright
SNAKE PIT, THE(1948)

Wallie Albright
SOB SISTER(1931); WRECKER, THE(1933)

Wally Albright
TRESPASSER, THE(1929); EAST LYNNE(1931); SALVATION NELL(1931); CONQUERORS, THE(1932); END OF THE TRAIL(1932); LAW OF THE SEA(1932); REBECCA OF SUNNYBROOK FARM(1932); SILVER LINING(1932); THIRTEEN WOMEN(1932); ZOO IN BUDAPEST(1933); KID MILLIONS(1934); WATERFRONT LADY(1935); COWBOY STAR, THE(1936); CAPTAINS COURAGEOUS(1937); MAID OF SALEM(1937); WHAT PRICE VENGEANCE?(1937); WOMAN I LOVE, THE(1937); OLD LOUISIANA(1938); SONS OF THE LEGION(1938); MEXICALI ROSE(1939); GRAPES OF WRATH(1940); JOHNNY APOLLO(1940); PUBLIC ENEMIES(1941); WILD ONE, THE(1953)

Wally Albright, Jr.
WONDER OF WOMEN(1929); PRODIGAL, THE(1931); O'SHAUGHNESSY'S BOY(1935); ROLL ALONG, COWBOY(1938)
Silents
THUNDER(1929)

Arthur Albro
Silents
DAMSEL IN DISTRESS, A(1919)

Sidney D. Albrook
THIRTEENTH MAN, THE(1937)

Ruth Albu
HOTEL BERLIN(1945)

Albuquerque Polo Club
COVENANT WITH DEATH, A(1966)

Tory Alburn
WEEKEND OF FEAR(1966)

Chris Alcaide
KID FROM BROKEN GUN, THE(1952); MASSACRE CANYON(1954); MIAMI STORY, THE(1954); OUTLAW STALLION, THE(1954); OVERLAND PACIFIC(1954); CHICAGO SYNDICATE(1955); DUEL ON THE MISSISSIPPI(1955); I DIED A THOUSAND TIMES(1955); ILLEGAL(1955); GUNSLINGER(1956); HOUSTON STORY, THE(1956); MIAMI EXPOSE(1956); CARNIVAL ROCK(1957); ROCK ALL NIGHT(1957); DAY OF THE BAD MAN(1958); VICE RAID(1959); OSCAR, THE(1966)

Cris Alcaide
GLASS MENAGERIE, THE(1950); CRIPPLE CREEK(1952); JUNCTION CITY(1952); SMOKY CANYON(1952); BIG HEAT, THE(1953); FORTY-NINTH MAN, THE(1953); BAD FOR EACH OTHER(1954); JUPITER'S DARLING(1955)

Don Alcaide
GUILTY MELODY(1936, Brit.)

Mary Alcaide
LUXURY GIRLS(1953, Ital.)

Jose Luis Alcaine
ISLAND OF THE DAMNED(1976, Span.), ph; FROM HELL TO VICTORY(1979, Fr./Ital./Span.), ph
1984
DEMONS IN THE GARDEN(1984, Span.), ph

Chris Alcalde
BLACK DAKOTAS, THE(1954)

Mario Alcalde
CROWDED PARADISE(1956); DEAD RINGER(1964); HAIL, HERO!(1969); CLAY PIGEON(1971)

Marlo Alcalde
ALL THE YOUNG MEN(1960)

Luana Alcaniz
DEVIL WITH WOMEN, A(1930); NADA MAS QUE UNA MUJER(1934); DOCTOR ZHIVAGO(1965)

Eduardo Alcaraz
  LITTLE RED RIDING HOOD AND HER FRIENDS(1964, Mex.); ZORRO, THE GAY BLADE(1981)
Rosita Alcaraz
  LA HABANERA(1937, Ger.)
Rafael Alcarde
  JET OVER THE ATLANTIC(1960)
Jose Antonio Alcarz
  EL TOPO(1971, Mex.)
Rafael Alcayde
  PANCHO VILLA RETURNS(1950, Mex.); LAST OF THE FAST GUNS, THE(1958); TEN DAYS TO TULARA(1958); VILLA!(1958)
Diego Alchimede
  LEGEND OF THE WOLF WOMAN, THE(1977, Span.), p
Murie Alcid
1984
  MISSION, THE(1984)
Bob Alcivar
  BUTTERFLIES ARE FREE(1972), m; CRAZY WORLD OF JULIUS VROODER, THE(1974), m; OLLY, OLLY, OXEN FREE(1978), m
Robert Alcivar
  HYSTERICAL(1983), m
Santos Alcocer [Edward Mann]
  CAULDRON OF BLOOD(1971. Span.), d
Teresa Alcocer
  SOFT SKIN ON BLACK SILK(1964, Fr./Span.), ed; SUPERARGO VERSUS DIABOLICUS(1966, Ital./Span.), ed; TEXICAN, THE(1966, U.S./Span.), ed; DAY THE HOTLINE GOT HOT, THE(1968, Fr./Span.), ed; JETLAG(1981, U.S./Span.), ed
Terese Alcocer
  PLACE CALLED GLORY, A(1966, Span./Ger.), ed
Victor Alcocer
  UNDER FIRE(1983)

Alfredo Alcon
  SUMMERSKIN(1962, Arg.); MAFIA, THE(1972, Arg.)
Manuel Alcon
  DESERT WARRIOR(1961 Ital./Span.)
Maria Alcorcha
1984
  CRACKERS(1984)
Luis Alcoriza
  LOS OLVIDADOS(1950, Mex.), w; BRUTE, THE(1952, Mex.), w; EL(1955, Mex.), w; UNTOUCHED(1956), w; GINA(1961, Fr./Mex.), w; PEARL OF TLAYUCAN, THE(1964, Mex.), d&w; EXTERMINATING ANGEL, THE(1967, Mex.), w; DAUGHTER OF DECEIT(1977, Mex.), w; DEATH IN THE GARDEN(1977, Fr./Mex.), w
Bill Alcorn
  I'LL REMEMBER APRIL(1945)
Cherokee Alcorn
  WHISTLING BULLETS(1937)
Olive Ann Alcorn
  PHANTOM OF THE OPERA, THE(1929)
Silents
  PHANTOM OF THE OPERA, THE(1925)
Misc. Silents
  LONG ARM OF MANNISTER, THE(1919)
R. W. Alcorn
  JOHNNY HOLIDAY(1949), p, w
Ron W. Alcorn
  ARMORED COMMAND(1961), p&w
William Alcorn
  MILDRED PIERCE(1945)
Arthur Alcott
  DEVIL'S BAIT(1959, Brit.), p; BIG DAY, THE(1960, Brit.), p; LINDA(1960, Brit.), p; OCTOBER MOTH(1960, Brit.), p; ECHO OF BARBARA(1961, Brit.), p
John Alcott
  2001: A SPACE ODYSSEY(1968, U.S./Brit.), ph; CLOCKWORK ORANGE, A(1971, Brit.), ph; LITTLE MALCOLM(1974, Brit.), ph; BARRY LYNDON(1975, Brit.), ph; OVERLORD(1975, Brit.), ph; MARCH OR DIE(1977, Brit.), ph; WHO IS KILLING THE GREAT CHEFS OF EUROPE?(1978, US/Ger.), ph; SHINING, THE(1980), ph; TERROR TRAIN(1980, Can.), ph; DISAPPEARANCE, THE(1981, Brit./Can.), ph; FORT APACHE, THE BRONX(1981), ph; BEASTMASTER, THE(1982), ph; VICE SQUAD(1982), ph; TRIUMPHS OF A MAN CALLED HORSE(1983, US/Mex.), ph; UNDER FIRE(1983), ph
1984
  GREYSTOKE: THE LEGEND OF TARZAN, LORD OF THE APES(1984), ph
Louisa May Alcott
  LITTLE WOMEN(1933), w; LITTLE MEN(1935), w; LITTLE MEN(1940), w; LITTLE WOMEN(1949), w
Robert Alcott
  UNDER AGE(1964); IT'S ALIVE(1968), ph
Robert B. Alcott
  ZONTAR, THE THING FROM VENUS(1966), ph
Alcover
  LILIOM(1935, Fr.); COURIER OF LYONS(1938, Fr.); BIZARRE BIZARRE(1939, Fr.)
Catherine Alcover
  BEAU PERE(1981, Fr.); CHANEL SOLITAIRE(1981)
Pierre Alcover
  SECOND BUREAU(1936, Fr.)
Misc. Silents
  L'ARGENT(1929, Fr.)
Alan Alda
  GONE ARE THE DAYS(1963); PAPER LION(1968); EXTRAORDINARY SEAMAN, THE(1969); JENNY(1969); MOONSHINE WAR, THE(1970); MEPHISTO WALTZ, THE(1971); TO KILL A CLOWN(1972); CALIFORNIA SUITE(1978); SAME TIME, NEXT YEAR(1978); SEDUCTION OF JOE TYNAN, THE(1979), a, w; FOUR SEASONS, THE(1981)

Antony Alda
  MELVIN AND HOWARD(1980)
Beatrice Alda
  FOUR SEASONS, THE(1981)
Elizabeth Alda
  FOUR SEASONS, THE(1981)
Robert Alda
  RHAPSODY IN BLUE(1945); BEAST WITH FIVE FINGERS, THE(1946); CINDERELLA JONES(1946); CLOAK AND DAGGER(1946); MAN I LOVE, THE(1946); NORA PRENTISS(1947); APRIL SHOWERS(1948); HOMICIDE(1949); TARZAN AND THE SLAVE GIRL(1950); MR. UNIVERSE(1951); TWO GALS AND A GUY(1951); IMITATION OF LIFE(1959); DEVIL'S HAND, THE(1961); FORCE OF IMPULSE(1961); CLEOPATRA'S DAUGHTER(1963, Fr., Ital.); ALL WOMAN(1967); GIRL WHO KNEW TOO MUCH, THE(1969); SERPENT, THE(1973, Fr./Ital./Ger.); CAGLIOSTRO(1975, Ital.); BITTERSWEET LOVE(1976); HOUSE OF EXORCISM, THE(1976, Ital.); I WILL ...I WILL ...FOR NOW(1976); WON TON TON, THE DOG WHO SAVED HOLLYWOOD(1976); SQUEEZE, THE(1980, Ital.)
Misc. Talkies
  ASSIGNMENT ABROAD(1955)
Rutanya Alda
  LONG GOODBYE, THE(1973); PAT GARRETT AND BILLY THE KID(1973); SCARECROW(1973); NEXT STOP, GREENWICH VILLAGE(1976); DEER HUNTER, THE(1978); FURY, THE(1978); WHEN A STRANGER CALLS(1979); MOMMIE DEAREST(1981); AMITYVILLE II: THE POSSESSION(1982); VIGILANTE(1983)
1984
  GIRLS NIGHT OUT(1984); RACING WITH THE MOON(1984)
Ruth Alda
  HI, MOM!(1970); PANIC IN NEEDLE PARK(1971)
Misc. Talkies
  LOVE AND KISSES(?)
Gillian Aldam
  FAHRENHEIT 451(1966, Brit.)
Julio Aldama
  PEARL OF TLAYUCAN, THE(1964, Mex.); GUNS FOR SAN SEBASTIAN(1968, U.S./Fr./Mex./Ital.)
Carl Aldana
  VALLEY GIRL(1983), set d
Vida Aldana
  BEAUTY AND THE BANDIT(1946)
Nat Aldeen
  MAN IN THE WATER, THE(1963), m
Betty Alden
  LIGHTNIN'(1930); FOUNTAIN, THE(1934); FUGITIVE LADY(1934); NUT FARM, THE(1935); CAPTAINS COURAGEOUS(1937)
Bob Alden
  TWO O'CLOCK COURAGE(1945); FALCON'S ALIBI, THE(1946); WIFE WANTED(1946); UNFAITHFUL, THE(1947); UNSUSPECTED, THE(1947); VARIETY GIRL(1947); FOUNTAINHEAD, THE(1949); CARBINE WILLIAMS(1952); COUNTRY GIRL, THE(1954); THESE WILDER YEARS(1956)

Bobby Alden
  TOGETHER AGAIN(1944)
Charles Alden
  THIS IS A HIJACK(1973), m
Chuck Alden
  FAT SPY(1966)
Clare Alden
  DOUBLE LIFE, A(1947)
Debra Alden
  CODE OF THE WEST(1947)
Diana Alden
Silents
  RIP-TIDE, THE(1923); DYNAMITE DAN(1924)
Edward Keane Alden
  WHEN TOMORROW COMES(1939)
Eric Alden
  WITHOUT RESERVATIONS(1946); SCARLET EMPRESS, THE(1934); GARDEN OF ALLAH, THE(1936); LITTLE LORD FAUNTLEROY(1936); WOMEN OF GLAMOUR(1937); LET US LIVE(1939); NORTHWEST MOUNTED POLICE(1940); BROADWAY LIMITED(1941); PARIS CALLING(1941); JOAN OF OZARK(1942); CRYSTAL BALL, THE(1943); LAKE PLACID SERENADE(1944); STORY OF DR. WASSELL, THE(1944); MONSIEUR BEAUCAIRE(1946); PERILS OF PAULINE, THE(1947); UNCONQUERED(1947); VARIETY GIRL(1947); WHERE THERE'S LIFE(1947); BIG CLOCK, THE(1948); JOAN OF ARC(1948); PALEFACE, THE(1948); SEALED VERDICT(1948); CHICAGO DEADLINE(1949); SAMSON AND DELILAH(1949); FILE ON THELMA JORDAN, THE(1950); LET'S DANCE(1950); UNION STATION(1950); FAT MAN, THE(1951); RACKET, THE(1951); CARRIE(1952); HAS ANYBODY SEEN MY GAL?(1952); HURRICANE SMITH(1952); PRISONER OF ZENDA, THE(1952); FLIGHT TO TANGIER(1953); PONY EXPRESS(1953); WAR OF THE WORLDS, THE(1953); COURT JESTER, THE(1956); TEN COMMANDMENTS, THE(1956); THAT CERTAIN FEELING(1956); FEAR STRIKES OUT(1957); JOKER IS WILD, THE(1957); LAST TRAIN FROM GUN HILL(1959)
Ginger Alden
  LADY GREY(1980); LIVING LEGEND(1980)
Glen Alden
  HAPPY DAYS(1930)
Hazel Alden
Silents
  ALL WOMAN(1918)
Honey Alden
  THREE IN THE ATTIC(1968)
Jerome Alden
  O.S.S.(1946); 300 YEAR WEEKEND(1971), w
Joan Alden
Misc. Silents
  CALL OF THE HEART(1928)

John Alden
  MAKING THE GRADE(1929); YOUNG WARRIORS(1983)
June Alden
  TAKE CARE OF MY LITTLE GIRL(1951)
Junior Alden
  Silents
  PENROD(1922)
Lester Alden
  UNDERGROUND(1941)
Louis Alden
  UNDERGROUND(1941)
Mari Alden
  THIS WOMAN IS DANGEROUS(1952)
Marian Alden
  GIRLS ON PROBATION(1938); DARK VICTORY(1939); WOMEN IN THE WIND(1939)
Mary Alden
  POLITICS(1931); HELL'S HOUSE(1932); STRANGE INTERLUDE(1932)
  Silents
  BATTLE OF THE SEXES, THE(1914); HOME SWEET HOME(1914); BIRTH OF A NATION, THE(1915); LILY AND THE ROSE, THE(1915); MAN'S PREROGATIVE, A(1915); ACQUITTED(1916); GOOD BAD MAN, THE(1916); HELL-TO-PAY AUSTIN(1916); INNOCENT MAGDALENE, AN(1916); INTOLERANCE(1916); ARGYLE CASE, THE(1917); NARROW PATH, THE(1918); NAULAHKA, THE(1918); ERSTWHILE SUSAN(1919); INFERIOR SEX, THE(1920); SNOWBLIND(1921); WITCHING HOUR, THE(1921); NOTORIETY(1922); EAGLE'S FEATHER, THE(1923); HAS THE WORLD GONE MAD!(1923); PLEASURE MAD(1923); STEADFAST HEART, THE(1923); BABBITT(1924); PAINTED PEOPLE(1924); PLASTIC AGE, THE(1925); APRIL FOOL(1926); BROWN OF HARVARD(1926); JOY GIRL, THE(1927); POTTERS, THE(1927); LADIES OF THE MOB(1928)
  Misc. Silents
  GHOSTS(1915); OUTCAST, THE(1915); LESS THAN THE DUST(1916); PILLARS OF SOCIETY(1916); BROKEN BUTTERFLY, THE(1919); HONEST HUTCH(1920); NOBODY'S GIRL(1920); SILK HUSBANDS AND CALICO WIVES(1920); OLD NEST, THE(1921); PARTED CURTAINS(1921); TRUST YOUR WIFE(1921); MAN WITH TWO MOTHERS, THE(1922); WOMAN'S WOMAN, A(1922); EMPTY CRADLE, THE(1923); TENTS OF ALLAH, THE(1923); FOOL'S AWAKENING, A(1924); FAINT PERFUME(1925); HAPPY WARRIOR, THE(1925); SIEGE(1925); UNWRITTEN LAW, THE(1925); EARTH WOMAN, THE(1926); LOVEY MARY(1926)
Norm Alden
  SEMI-TOUGH(1977)
Norman Alden
  MAN'S FAVORITE SPORT(?)**1/2 (1964); WALKING TARGET, THE(1960); OPERATION BOTTLENECK(1961); PORTRAIT OF A MOBSTER(1961); SECRET OF DEEP HARBOR(1961); NUTTY PROFESSOR, THE(1963); SWORD IN THE STONE, THE(1963); BEDTIME STORY(1964); PATSY, THE(1964); ANDY(1965); RED LINE 7000(1965); WILD ANGELS, THE(1966); FIRST TO FIGHT(1967); GOOD TIMES(1967); CHUBASCO(1968); DEVIL'S BRIGADE, THE(1968); FEVER HEAT(1968); KILLERS THREE(1968); GREAT BANK ROBBERY, THE(1969); TORA! TORA! TORA!(1970, U.S./Jap.); BEN(1972); KANSAS CITY BOMBER(1972); WHERE DOES IT HURT?(1972); I NEVER PROMISED YOU A ROSE GARDEN(1977); BORDERLINE(1980); CLOUD DANCER(1980)
Priscilla Alden
  1984
  BIRDY(1984)
Richard Alden
  CANADIANS, THE(1961, Brit.); TWO LITTLE BEARS, THE(1961); SADIST, THE(1963); MC MASTERS, THE(1970)
Robert Alden
  MAKER OF MEN(1931); SHOPWORN(1932)
  Misc. Silents
  UNCHARTED SEAS(1921)
Terry Alden
  Misc. Talkies
  LAST GAME, THE(1983)
Lisa Aldenhoven
  MAD MAX(1979, Aus.)
Byron Aldenn
  Silents
  PAIR OF SIXES, A(1918)
Alan Alder
  DON QUIXOTE(1973, Aus.)
Allen Alder
  MAKING LOVE(1982), p
Bob Alder
  SMOKY(1946)
Clyde Alder
  BEACH GIRLS AND THE MONSTER, THE(1965)
Cynthia Alder
  FANTASTIC PLANET(1973, Fr./Czech.)
Robert Alder
  THESE THOUSAND HILLS(1959)
Ruth Alder
  BRINGING UP BABY(1938); DRAMATIC SCHOOL(1938); WOMEN, THE(1939); DESIGN FOR SCANDAL(1941)
Steve Alder
  1984
  SCRUBBERS(1984, Brit.)
Bob Alderette
  VIOLENT ROAD(1958)
Clorinda Alderette
  SALT OF THE EARTH(1954)
Don Alderette
  FALLGUY(1962)
Larry Alderette
  MY SIX LOVES(1963)
Robert Alderette
  OLD MAN AND THE SEA, THE(1958)

Joseph Alderham
  FINNEGANS WAKE(1965)
Jane Alderman
  T.R. BASKIN(1971)
John Alderman
  PORK CHOP HILL(1959); THRILL OF IT ALL, THE(1963); HOT SPUR(1968); DIAMOND STUD(1970); HARD ROAD, THE(1970); TRADER HORNEE(1970); ESCAPE FROM THE PLANET OF THE APES(1971); LAST MOVIE, THE(1971); CLEOPATRA JONES(1973); STACEY!(1973); THIS IS A HIJACK(1973); BLACK SAMSON(1974); CANNONBALL(1976, U.S./Hong Kong); SWINGING BARMAIDS, THE(1976); NEW YEAR'S EVIL(1980); STUNT MAN, THE(1980)
  Misc. Talkies
  DIAMOND STUD(1970); PINK ANGELS, THE(1971); DANDY(1973); LITTLE MISS INNOCENCE(1973); ALPHA INCIDENT, THE(1976); C.B. HUSTLERS(1978)
Rex Alderman
  OLD MOTHER RILEY IN PARIS(1938, Brit.); OLD MOTHER RILEY MP(1939, Brit.)
Thomas Alderman
  Misc. Talkies
  SEVERED ARM(1973), d
Tom Alderman
  SPOOK WHO SAT BY THE DOOR, THE(1973)
Brooke Alderson
  URBAN COWBOY(1980); INDEPENDENCE DAY(1983)
  1984
  MIKE'S MURDER(1984)
Carole Alderson
  1984
  POLICE ACADEMY(1984)
Erville Alderson
  SERGEANT YORK(; SPEAKEASY(1929); GUILTY?(1930); LASH, THE(1930); DAWN TRAIL, THE(1931); SHANGHAIED LOVE(1931); HAUNTED GOLD(1932); I AM A FUGITIVE FROM A CHAIN GANG(1932); THEY CALL IT SIN(1932); THIRTEENTH GUEST, THE(1932); STATE FAIR(1933); TO THE LAST MAN(1933); FIGHTING CODE, THE(1934); LAZY RIVER(1934); SCARLET EMPRESS, THE(1934); PUBLIC OPINION(1935); PURSUIT(1935); SEVEN KEYS TO BALDPATE(1935); SOCIETY FEVER(1935); WOMAN WANTED(1935); CAREER WOMAN(1936); EDUCATING FATHER(1936); FURY(1936); HEARTS IN BONDAGE(1936); JUNGLE PRINCESS, THE(1936); EMPEROR'S CANDLESTICKS, THE(1937); MIGHTY TREVE, THE(1937); SMALL TOWN BOY(1937); GOLD IS WHERE YOU FIND IT(1938); LOVE FINDS ANDY HARDY(1938); MARIE ANTOINETTE(1938); JESSE JAMES(1939); NANCY DREW, TROUBLE SHOOTER(1939); ROMANCE OF THE REDWOODS(1939); DOCTOR TAKES A WIFE(1940); GRAPES OF WRATH(1940); MARYLAND(1940); RANGERS OF FORTUNE(1940); SANTA FE TRAIL(1940); WHEN THE DALTONS RODE(1940); BAD MEN OF MISSOURI(1941); HIGH SIERRA(1941); HONKY TONK(1941); LADY FROM CHEYENNE(1941); LAST OF THE DUANES(1941); PARACHUTE BATTALION(1941); RICHEST MAN IN TOWN(1941); COMMANDOS STRIKE AT DAWN, THE(1942); GAY SISTERS, THE(1942); LOVES OF EDGAR ALLAN POE, THE(1942); MY FAVORITE BLONDE(1942); YOU CAN'T ESCAPE FOREVER(1942); ARIZONA TRAIL(1943); FIRST COMES COURAGE(1943); HANGMEN ALSO DIE(1943); WHAT'S BUZZIN COUSIN?(1943); AND THE ANGELS SING(1944); DESTINY(1944); HEAVENLY DAYS(1944); MAN FROM FRISCO(1944); RATIONING(1944); TALL IN THE SADDLE(1944); ALONG CAME JONES(1945); BACK TO BATAAN(1945); INCENDIARY BLONDE(1945); OBJECTIVE, BURMA!(1945); CANYON PASSAGE(1946); MAGNIFICENT DOLL(1946); SPIRAL STAIRCASE, THE(1946); TWO SISTERS FROM BOSTON(1946); DESPERATE(1947); HIGH WALL(1947); SEA OF GRASS, THE(1947); SMASH-UP, THE STORY OF A WOMAN(1947); UNCONQUERED(1947); WELCOME STRANGER(1947); FEATHERED SERPENT, THE(1948); KIDNAPPED(1948); SHANGHAI CHEST, THE(1948); DANCING IN THE DARK(1949); SUMMER STOCK(1950); SOMETHING TO LIVE FOR(1952); SPIRIT OF ST. LOUIS, THE(1957)
  Misc. Talkies
  SQUARE SHOOTER(1935)
  Silents
  EXCITERS, THE(1923); WHITE ROSE, THE(1923); AMERICA(1924); ISN'T LIFE WONDERFUL(1924); SALLY OF THE SAWDUST(1925); WHITE BLACK SHEEP, THE(1926); FORTUNE HUNTER, THE(1927); GIRL FROM CHICAGO, THE(1927); SALVATION JANE(1927)
Erville Alderson, Sr.
  POSTMAN DIDN'T RING, THE(1942)
George Alderson
  DIAL M FOR MURDER(1954)
John Alderson
  AGAINST ALL FLAGS(1952); DESERT RATS, THE(1953); SOUTH SEA WOMAN(1953); KING RICHARD AND THE CRUSADERS(1954); LIVING IT UP(1954); MOONFLEET(1955); SCARLET COAT, THE(1955); TARGET ZERO(1955); TO CATCH A THIEF(1955); VIOLENT SATURDAY(1955); LAST STAGECOACH WEST, THE(1957); SHOOT-OUT AT MEDICINE BEND(1957); SPOILERS OF THE FOREST(1957); WOLF LARSEN(1958); YOUNG LIONS, THE(1958); NO NAME ON THE BULLET(1959); ROMANOFF AND JULIET(1961); MY FAIR LADY(1964); WAR LORD, THE(1965); I DEAL IN DANGER(1966); DOUBLE TROUBLE(1967); HELLFIGHTERS(1968); MOLLY MAGUIRES, THE(1970); YOU CAN'T WIN 'EM ALL(1970, Brit.); DESERTER, THE(1971 Ital./Yugo.); TOP OF THE HEAP(1972); KLANSMAN, THE(1974); DON'T GO NEAR THE WATER(1975); DUCHESS AND THE DIRTWATER FOX, THE(1976); VALENTINO(1977, Brit.); CANDLESHOE(1978); CAT FROM OUTER SPACE, THE(1978); ALL THINGS BRIGHT AND BEAUTIFUL(1979, Brit.); EVIL UNDER THE SUN(1982, Brit.)
Judith Alderson
  FRENCH LIEUTENANT'S WOMAN, THE(1981); OUTLAND(1981)
Elizabeth Alderton
  HIGH COUNTRY, THE(1981, Can.)
John Alderton
  ZARDOZ(; CLEOPATRA(1963); GIRL GETTERS, THE(1966, Brit.); ASSIGNMENT K(1968, Brit.); DUFFY(1968, Brit.); HANNIBAL BROOKS(1969, Brit.); PLEASE SIR(1971, Brit.)
Louis Aldez
  GARDEN OF ALLAH, THE(1936)
Gillian Aldham
  CONQUEROR WORM, THE(1968, Brit.)

James Aldine
LEATHERNECK, THE(1929)
Jimmy Aldine
GODLESS GIRL, THE(1929); OFFICE SCANDAL, THE(1929)
Richard Aldington
ALL MEN ARE ENEMIES(1934), w
Barry Aldis
MAN IN THE DARK(1963, Brit.)
G. R. Aldo
LA TERRA TREMA(1947, Ital.), ph   INDISCRETION OF AN
AMERICAN WIFE(1954, U.S./Ital.), ph

Aldo Graziati [G.R. Aldo]
OTHELLO(1955, U.S./Fr./Ital.), ph
Duke Aldon
VALLEY OF HUNTED MEN(1942)
Louis Aldon
ICE FOLLIES OF 1939(1939); LADY IN QUESTION, THE(1940)
Lynda Aldon
DOCTOR DETROIT(1983)
Mari Aldon
LOCKET, THE(1946); DISTANT DRUMS(1951); TANKS ARE COMING, THE(1951);
TANGIER INCIDENT(1953); BAREFOOT CONTESSA, THE(1954); RACE FOR LIFE,
A(1955, Brit.); SUMMERTIME(1955)
Frank Aldous
HOMER(1970)
Harry Aldous
DON'T PANIC CHAPS!(1959, Brit.), ed; NOWHERE TO GO(1959, Brit.), ed
Lucette Aldous
DON QUIXOTE(1973, Aus.); TURNING POINT, THE(1977)
Joel Aldred
SECRET DOOR, THE(1964)
John Aldredge
GOD IS MY WITNESS(1931)
Kay Aldredge
FALCON'S BROTHER, THE(1942)
Michael Aldredge
SHOOT THE MOON(1982)
Theoni V. Aldredge
GIRL OF THE NIGHT(1960), cos; YOU'RE A BIG BOY NOW(1966), cos; NO WAY TO
TREAT A LADY(1968), cos; UPTIGHT(1968), cos; LAST SUMMER(1969), cos; I NEV-
ER SANG FOR MY FATHER(1970), cos; PROMISE AT DAWN(1970, U.S./Fr.), cos;
HARRY AND WALTER GO TO NEW YORK(1976), cos; NETWORK(1976), cos; SEMI-
TOUGH(1977), cos; CHEAP DETECTIVE, THE(1978), cos; EYES OF LAURA
MARS(1978), cos; FURY, THE(1978), cos; CHAMP, THE(1979), cos; ROSE, THE(1979),
cos; CAN'T STOP THE MUSIC(1980), cos; RICH AND FAMOUS(1981), cos; AN-
NIE(1982), cos; MONSIGNOR(1982), cos
1984
GHOSTBUSTERS(1984), cos
Tom Aldredge
MOUSE ON THE MOON, THE(1963, Brit.); TROUBLEMAKER, THE(1964); WHO
KILLED TEDDY BEAR?(1965); RAIN PEOPLE, THE(1969); HAPPINESS CAGE,
THE(1972); COUNTDOWN AT KUSINI(1976, Nigerian)
Alden Aldrich
PERILOUS JOURNEY, A(1953)
Alida Aldrich
HUSH... HUSH, SWEET CHARLOTTE(1964)
Bess Streeter Aldrich
CHEERS FOR MISS BISHOP(1941), w
Charles T. Aldrich
LADY FROM CHEYENNE(1941)
Charlie Aldrich
BALLAD OF A GUNFIGHTER(1964)
David Aldrich
MAN IN THE WATER, THE(1963)
Davie Aldrich
STAR PACKER, THE(1934)
Frank Aldrich
AARON LOVES ANGELA(1975)
Fred Aldrich
ONCE UPON A HONEYMOON(1942); DEADLINE AT DAWN(1946); IN FAST
COMPANY(1946); TYCOON(1947); MRS. MIKE(1949); DARK CITY(1950); TRAVEL-
ING SALESWOMAN(1950); 711 OCEAN DRIVE(1950); JOURNEY INTO LIGHT(1951);
UNKNOWN MAN, THE(1951); LOST IN ALASKA(1952); FARMER TAKES A WIFE,
THE(1953); SON OF SINBAD(1955)
Georganne Aldrich
COME SPY WITH ME(1967), cos
Hank Aldrich
WHO KILLED TEDDY BEAR?(1965), art d; GAMERA THE INVINCIBLE(1966,
Jap.), art d; PAPER LION(1968), set d; I NEVER SANG FOR MY FATHER(1970), art
d; LORD SHANGO(1975), art d; NATURAL ENEMIES(1979), art d
Misc. Talkies
ROBIN(1979), d
Kate Aldrich
COME SPY WITH ME(1967)
Katharine Aldrich
HERE I AM A STRANGER(1939)
Kelly Aldrich
HUSH... HUSH, SWEET CHARLOTTE(1964)
Mariska Aldrich
EVELYN PRENTICE(1934); LADY BY CHOICE(1934); UNDER YOUR SPELL(1936);
EMPEROR'S CANDLESTICKS, THE(1937); EXCLUSIVE(1937); I'LL TAKE RO-
MANCE(1937); LIVE, LOVE AND LEARN(1937); MAYTIME(1937); PARADISE FOR
THREE(1938); FORGOTTEN WOMAN, THE(1939); STRONGER THAN DESIRE(1939);
WOMEN, THE(1939); WHISTLING IN THE DARK(1941); YOU'RE THE ONE(1941);
SHIP AHOY(1942); MADAME CURIE(1943); SONG OF THE SARONG(1945)
Meeka Aldrich
I'LL TAKE ROMANCE(1937); FOREIGN CORRESPONDENT(1940); WE WERE
DANCING(1942)

Mika Aldrich
Silents
LOVES OF RICARDO, THE(1926)
Rhonda Aldrich
BOOGEYMAN II(1983)
Robert Aldrich
BIG LEAGUER(1953), d; APACHE(1954), d; VERA CRUZ(1954), d; WORLD FOR
RANSOM(1954), p, d; BIG KNIFE, THE(1955), p&d; KISS ME DEADLY(1955), p&d;
ATTACK!(1956), p&d; AUTUMN LEAVES(1956), d; GARMENT JUNGLE, THE(1957),
d; ANGRY HILLS, THE(1959, Brit.), d; TEN SECONDS TO HELL(1959), d, w; LAST
SUNSET, THE(1961), d; SODOM AND GOMORRAH(1962, U.S./Fr./Ital.), d; WHA-
TEVER HAPPENED TO BABY JANE?(1962), p&d; FOUR FOR TEXAS(1963), p&d, w;
HUSH... HUSH, SWEET CHARLOTTE(1964), p&d; FLIGHT OF THE PHOENIX,
THE(1965), p&d; DIRTY DOZEN, THE(1967, Brit.), d; LEGEND OF LYLAH CLARE,
THE(1968), p&d; WHAT EVER HAPPENED TO AUNT ALICE?(1969), p; TOO LATE
THE HERO(1970), p&d, w; GRISSOM GANG, THE(1971), p&d; ULZANA'S
RAID(1972), d; EMPEROR OF THE NORTH POLE(1973), d; LONGEST YARD,
THE(1974), d; HUSTLE(1975), p&d; CHOIRBOYS, THE(1977), d; TWILIGHT'S LAST
GLEAMING(1977, U.S./Ger.), d; FRISCO KID, THE(1979), d; ...ALL THE MAR-
BLES(1981), d
Roma Aldrich
PARACHUTE NURSE(1942); DOUBLE EXPOSURE(1944)
Thomas Bailey Aldrich
Silents
JUDITH OF BETHULIA(1914), w
Waldon Bailey Aldrich
Silents
HEART OF THE BLUE RIDGE, THE(1915), w
William Aldrich
WHATEVER HAPPENED TO BABY JANE?(1962); HUSH... HUSH, SWEET CHAR-
LOTTE(1964); FLIGHT OF THE PHOENIX, THE(1965); WHO IS KILLING THE
GREAT CHEFS OF EUROPE?(1978, US/Ger.), p; ...ALL THE MARBLES(1981), p
William E. Aldrich
Misc. Silents
PURPLE DAWN(1923)
Alfred Aldridge
Silents
IT CAN BE DONE(1921)
Charles W. Aldridge
GUNS OF A STRANGER(1973), w
Charley Aldridge
GUNS OF A STRANGER(1973)
Ernest Aldridge
TROUBLE BREWING(1939, Brit.), ed
James Aldridge
RIDE A WILD PONY(1976, U.S./Aus.), w
Jane Aldridge
OCTOPUSSY(1983, Brit.)
Jess Aldridge
Silents
BIG TOWN IDEAS(1921)
Katharine Aldridge
ROSALIE(1937); HOTEL FOR WOMEN(1939); DOWN ARGENTINE WAY(1940);
FREE, BLONDE AND 21(1940); GIRL FROM AVENUE A(1940); GIRL IN 313(1940);
SAILOR'S LADY(1940); SHOOTING HIGH(1940); YESTERDAY'S HEROES(1940);
DEAD MEN TELL(1941); GOLDEN HOOFS(1941); NAVY BLUES(1941)
Kay Aldridge
VOGUES OF 1938(1937); LOUISIANA PURCHASE(1941); YOU'RE IN THE ARMY
NOW(1941); DU BARRY WAS A LADY(1943); MAN WHO WALKED ALONE,
THE(1945); PHANTOM OF 42ND STREET, THE(1945)
Michael Aldridge
NOTHING VENTURE(1948, Brit.); MURDER IN THE CATHEDRAL(1952, Brit.);
SUICIDE MISSION(1956, Brit.); WALK IN THE SHADOW(1966, Brit.); CHIMES AT
MIDNIGHT(1967, Span.,Switz.); PUBLIC EYE, THE(1972, Brit.); BULLSHOT(1983)
Richard Aldridge
WOLFMAN(1979), ed; LIVING LEGEND(1980), ed
Virginia Aldridge
HIGH SCHOOL BIG SHOT(1959); RIOT IN JUVENILE PRISON(1959); GNOME-
MOBILE, THE(1967)
Leo C. Aldridge-Milas
WHITE WITCH DOCTOR(1953)
George Aldwin
REUNION IN FRANCE(1942)
Irene Aldwyn
Silents
NARROW PATH, THE(1918)
Tomas Guttierez Alea
DEATH OF A BUREAUCRAT(1979, Cuba), d, w
Emil Alegata
MARLOWE(1969)
Augusto Alegero
ANTONY AND CLEOPATRA(1973, Brit.), m
Anna Maria Alegiani
LADY OF MONZA, THE(1970, Ital.)
Christian Alegny
CONFORMIST, THE(1971, Ital., Fr)
Alona Alegre
BLACK MAMA, WHITE MAMA(1973)
Alegrina
ZAZIE(1961, Fr.)
W. Schultz Porto Alegro
STRANGE WORLD(1952), m
Sholem Aleichem
TEVYA(1939), d&w; FIDDLER ON THE ROOF(1971), w
Aleinikov
SKI BATTALION(1938, USSR)
P. Aleinikov
CITY OF YOUTH(1938, USSR)

Peter Aleinikov
NO GREATER LOVE(1944, USSR)
Rodolfo Alejandre
1984
EL NORTE(1984)
Julio Alejandro
INVISIBLE MAN, THE(1958, Mex.), w; VIRIDIANA(1962, Mex./Span.), w; NAZARIN(1968, Mex.), w; TRISTANA(1970, Span./Ital./Fr.), w
Miguel Alejandro
POPI(1969); LAST VALLEY, THE(1971, Brit.)
Henri Alekan
ROMA RIVUOLE CESARE(, ph; BEAUTY AND THE BEAST(1947, Fr.), ph; DAMNED, THE(1948, Fr.), ph; BATTLE OF THE RAILS(1949, Fr.), ph; JUST ME(1950, Fr.), ph; LA MARIE DU PORT(1951, Fr.), ph; LOVERS OF VERONA, THE(1951, Fr.), ph; VOYAGE TO AMERICA(1952, Fr.), ph; STRANGER ON THE PROWL(1953, Ital.), a, ph; FROU-FROU(1955, Fr.), ph; JULIETTA(1957, Fr.), ph; CASE OF DR. LAURENT(1958, Fr.), ph; AUSTERLITZ(1960, Fr./Ital./Yugo.), ph; WOULD-BE GENTLEMAN, THE(1960, Fr.), ph; TALES OF PARIS(1962, Fr./Ital.), ph; FIVE MILES TO MIDNIGHT(1963, U.S./Fr./Ital.), ph; MARRIAGE OF FIGARO, THE(1963, Fr.), ph; TOPKAPI(1964), ph; LADY L(1965, Fr./Ital.), ph; POPPY IS ALSO A FLOWER, THE(1966), ph; TRIPLE CROSS(1967, Fr./Brit.), ph; CHRISTMAS TREE, THE(1969, Fr.), ph; FIGURES IN A LANDSCAPE(1970, Brit.), ph; RED SUN(1972, Fr./Ital./Span.), ph; TROUT, THE(1982, Fr.), ph; BEAUTIFUL PRISONER, THE(1983, Fr.), ph; STATE OF THINGS, THE(1983), ph
Henri Alekana
ANNA KARENINA(1948, Brit.), ph
Henri Alekhan
MAYERLING(1968, Brit./Fr.), ph
M. Alekian
COLOR OF POMEGRANATES, THE(1980, Armenian)
Boris Alekin
LA HABANERA(1937, Ger.)
R. Aleksandrov
WAR AND PEACE(1968, USSR)
K. Aleksandrova
LITTLE HUMPBACKED HORSE, THE(1962, USSR), anim
N. Aleksandrova
STEPCHILDREN(1962, USSR), w
Ye. Aleksandrova
DAY THE WAR ENDED, THE(1961, USSR), cos; HOME FOR TANYA, A(1961, USSR), cos
A. Aleksandrovich
SONG OVER MOSCOW(1964, USSR)
A. Alekseyev
LAD FROM OUR TOWN(1941, USSR)
G. Alekseyev
JACK FROST(1966, USSR), animal t
K. Alekseyev
DESTINY OF A MAN(1961, USSR)
P. Alekseyev
WAR AND PEACE(1968, USSR)
V. Alekseyeva
MUMU(1961, USSR), spec eff
Dragoljub Aleksic
INNOCENCE UNPROTECTED(1971, Yugo.)
Mija Aleksic
I EVEN MET HAPPY GYPSIES(1968, Yugo.)
Zivojin Aleksic
LOVE AFFAIR; OR THE CASE OF THE MISSING SWITCHBOARD OPERATOR(1968, Yugo.)
Paul Alelyanes
PUNISHMENT PARK(1971)
Julio Aleman
LOS AUTOMATAS DE LA MUERTE(1960, Mex.); NEUTRON CONTRA EL DR. CARONTE(1962, Mex.); NEUTRON EL ENMASCARADO NEGRO(1962, Mex.)
Rick Alemany
KILLER ELITE, THE(1975); DR. JEKYLL'S DUNGEON OF DEATH(1982), ch
Nestor Alemendros
MORE(1969, Luxembourg), art d
Sango Alemez
INCREDIBLE INVASION, THE(1971, Mex./U.S.)
Arlene Alen
SATURDAY THE 14TH(1981), art d
Inga Alenius
FANNY AND ALEXANDER(1983, Swed./Fr./Ger.)
Vera Alentova
MOSCOW DOES NOT BELIEVE IN TEARS(1980, USSR)
Aki Aleong
MOTORCYCLE GANG(1957); NO DOWN PAYMENT(1957); NEVER SO FEW(1959); OPERATION BIKINI(1963); BUCKSKIN(1968)
1984
OVER THE BROOKLYN BRIDGE(1984)
Georges Alepee
TIME BOMB(1961, Fr./Ital.), ed; MATTER OF DAYS, A(1969, Fr./Czech.), ed
Alerme
COUNSEL FOR ROMANCE(1938, Fr.); MAN OF THE HOUR, THE(1940, Fr.); CONFESSIONS OF A NEWLYWED(1941, Fr.); BLUE VEIL, THE(1947, Fr.)
Andre Alerme
CARNIVAL IN FLANDERS(1936, Fr.)
Christian Alers
OTHER ONE, THE(1967,Fr.); GOING PLACES(1974, Fr.)
Prince Alert
DAY THE BOOKIES WEPT, THE(1939)
John Alese
JENNY(1969), makeup; STILETTO(1969), makeup; SIDELONG GLANCES OF A PIGEON KICKER, THE(1970), makeup; LITTLE MURDERS(1971), makeup; NETWORK(1976), makeup

Harold Aleshire
NORTHERN LIGHTS(1978)
Liliya Aleshnikova
SUN SHINES FOR ALL, THE(1961, USSR); GROWN-UP CHILDREN(1963, USSR)
Frank Alesia
PAJAMA PARTY(1964); GHOST IN THE INVISIBLE BIKINI(1966); C'MON, LET'S LIVE A LITTLE(1967); RIOT ON SUNSET STRIP(1967); MARYJANE(1968); R.P.M.(1970); TUNNELVISION(1976)
George Alesko
JOHNNY O'CLOCK(1947)
R. Alessandri
MAN COULD GET KILLED, A(1966)
Roberto Alessandri
GOD FORGIVES–I DON'T!(1969, Ital./Span.)
Geofredo Alessandrini
FURIA(1947, Ital.), d&w
Goffredo Alessandrini
WANDERING JEW, THE(1948, Ital.), d, w; RAPTURE(1950, Ital.), a, d; ANITA GARIBALDI(1954, Ital.), d; DESERT WARRIOR(1961 Ital./Span.), d; THREE FACES OF A WOMAN(1965, Ital.)
Franco Alessandro
MAGIC WORLD OF TOPO GIGIO, THE(1961, Ital.), ed
Alessandro Alessandroni
LADY FRANKENSTEIN(1971, Ital.), m
Ottavio Alessi
MAN WHO WAGGED HIS TAIL, THE(1961, Ital./Span.), w; NUDE ODYSSEY(1962, Fr./Ital.), w; FRIENDS FOR LIFE(1964, Ital.), w; MONGOLS, THE(1966, Fr./Ital.), w; TIKO AND THE SHARK(1966, U.S./Ital./Fr.), w
Paul Alessi
CHILD'S PLAY(1972)
Rino Alessi
LOYALTY OF LOVE(1937, Ital.), w
Frank Aletter
MISTER ROBERTS(1955); TIGER WALKS, A(1964); TORA! TORA! TORA!(1970, U.S./Jap.); NOW YOU SEE HIM, NOW YOU DON'T(1972); PRIVATE SCHOOL(1983)
Ken Aleuto
FORTY DEUCE(1982), ed
Nicos Alewras
RECONSTRUCTION OF A CRIME(1970, Ger.)
Emile Alex
PARDON MY FRENCH(1951, U.S./Fr.), art d
Miriam Alex
WOMAN ON FIRE, A(1970, Ital.)
Alex Hyde and his Original New York Jazz Orchestra
Silents
VARIETY(1925, Ger.)
Alex Nahera Dancers
SONG OF TEXAS(1943)
Karin Alexana
WIZARD OF GORE, THE(1970)
Alexander
TARZAN AND THE VALLEY OF GOLD(1966 U.S./Switz.), md
Silents
LAW FORBIDS, THE(1924)
A. Alexander
Misc. Silents
WHY AMERICA WILL WIN(1918)
A.L. Alexander
WAR IS A RACKET(1934)
Alex Alexander
RED SNOW(1952), m; ALASKA PASSAGE(1959), m; OPERATION EICHMANN(1961), md
Alicia Alexander
Misc. Talkies
LONE STAR COUNTRY(1983)
Alphonso Alexander
BUSTIN' LOOSE(1981)
Andrew Alexander
ISLAND WOMEN(1958), w
Angela Alexander
BLACK SLEEP, THE(1956), cos; HOT CARS(1956), cos; LONELYHEARTS(1958), cos; SERGEANTS 3(1962), cos; WINTER A GO-GO(1965), cos; ORGANIZATION, THE(1971), cos
Annette Alexander
NATCHEZ TRACE(1960)
Arthur Alexander
COWBOY HOLIDAY(1934), p; THUNDER OVER TEXAS(1934), p; DANGER TRAILS(1935), p; GUN PLAY(1936), p; MEN OF THE PLAINS(1936), p; STORMY TRAILS(1936), p; TOO MUCH BEEF(1936), p; WEST OF NEVADA(1936), p; HERE'S FLASH CASEY(1937), p; IDAHO KID, THE(1937), p; LAW AND LEAD(1937), p; SHADOW STRIKES, THE(1937), p; INTERNATIONAL CRIME(1938), p; SIX SHOOTIN' SHERIFF(1938), p; WHIRLWIND HORSEMAN(1938), p; FLAMING LEAD(1939), p; DEATH RIDES THE RANGE(1940), p; LIGHTNING STRIKES WEST(1940), p; PHANTOM RANCHER(1940), p; HARD GUY(1941), p; BOMBS OVER BURMA(1942), p; RANGERS TAKE OVER, THE(1942), p; SECRETS OF A CO-ED(1942), p; BAD MEN OF THUNDER GAP(1943), p; BORDER BUCKAROOS(1943), p; FIGHTING VALLEY(1943), p; GHOST AND THE GUEST(1943), p; LADY FROM CHUNGKING(1943), p; RETURN OF THE RANGERS(1943), p; WEST OF TEXAS(1943), p; BRAND OF THE DEVIL(1944), p; DEAD OR ALIVE(1944), p; GANGSTERS OF THE FRONTIER(1944), p; GUNS OF THE LAW(1944), p; GUNSMOKE MESA(1944), p; SPOOK TOWN(1944), p; TRAIL OF TERROR(1944), p; WATERFRONT(1944), p; WHISPERING SKULL, THE(1944), p; ARSON SQUAD(1945), p; ENEMY OF THE LAW(1945), p; FLAMING BULLETS(1945), p; FRONTIER FUGITIVES(1945), p; MARKED FOR MURDER(1945), p; THREE IN THE SADDLE(1945), p; AMBUSH TRAIL(1946), p; NAVAJO KID, THE(1946), p; QUEEN OF BURLESQUE(1946), p; SIX GUN MAN(1946), p; THUNDER TOWN(1946), p
Ben Alexander
ALL QUIET ON THE WESTERN FRONT(1930); ARE THESE OUR CHILDREN?(1931); IT'S A WISE CHILD(1931); MANY A SLIP(1931); SUICIDE FLEET(1931); HIGH PRESSURE(1932); STRANGE LOVE OF MOLLY LOUVAIN,

THE(1932); TOM BROWN OF CULVER(1932); VANISHING FRONTIER, THE(1932); WET PARADE, THE(1932); STAGE MOTHER(1933); THIS DAY AND AGE(1933); WHAT PRICE INNOCENCE?(1933); LIFE OF VERGIE WINTERS, THE(1934); MOST PRECIOUS THING IN LIFE(1934); ONCE TO EVERY WOMAN(1934); ANNAPOLIS FAREWELL(1935); BORN TO GAMBLE(1935); FIRETRAP, THE(1935); GRAND OLD GIRL(1935); RECKLESS ROADS(1935); HEARTS IN BONDAGE(1936); LEGION OF MISSING MEN(1937); OUTER GATE, THE(1937); RED LIGHTS AHEAD(1937); SHALL WE DANCE(1937); WESTERN GOLD(1937); MR. DOODLE KICKS OFF(1938); SPY RING, THE(1938); CONVICT'S CODE(1939); DARK COMMAND, THE(1940); LEATHER-PUSHERS, THE(1940); CRIMINALS WITHIN(1941); DRAGNET(1954); MAN IN THE SHADOW(1957)

Misc. Talkies
BEHIND PRISON BARS(1937)

Silents
EACH PEARL A TEAR(1916); HEARTS OF THE WORLD(1918); NOTORIOUS MRS. SANDS, THE(1920); BOY OF MINE(1923); JEALOUS HUSBANDS(1923); PENROD AND SAM(1923)

Misc. Silents
LADY OF THE DUGOUT(1918); MAYOR OF FILBERT, THE(1919); TURN IN THE ROAD, THE(1919); WHITE HEATHER, THE(1919); FAMILY HONOR, THE(1920); THRU THE EYES OF MEN(1920); TRIFLERS, THE(1920); IN THE NAME OF THE LAW(1922); SELF-MADE FAILURE, A(1924); FRIVOLOUS SAL(1925); PAMPERED YOUTH(1925); SHINING ADVENTURE, THE(1925); HIGHBINDERS, THE(1926)

Betty Alexander
PRINCESS AND THE PIRATE, THE(1944); UP IN ARMS(1944); CHRISTMAS IN CONNECTICUT(1944); MILDRED PIERCE(1945); KID FROM BOOKLYN, THE(1946); DANGEROUS VENTURE(1947); TRESPASSER, THE(1947)

Bill Alexander
NAKED RUNNER, THE(1967, Brit.), art d; BLISS OF MRS. BLOSSOM, THE(1968, Brit.), art d; MC MASTERS, THE(1970); SWEENEY(1977, Brit.), art d; SWEENEY 2(1978, Brit.), art d; LADY VANISHES, THE(1980, Brit.), art d

Bob Alexander
TEA AND SYMPATHY(1956); WILD IS MY LOVE(1963)

Bruce Alexander
GIRO CITY(1982, Brit.); LONG GOOD FRIDAY, THE(1982, Brit.)

Cathy Alexander
ROVER, THE(1967, Ital.)

Charles Alexander
JUST IMAGINE(1930)

Chick Alexander
CAESAR AND CLEOPATRA(1946, Brit.)

Claire Alexander
Silents
CHILD OF M'SIEU(1919)

Claude Alexander
NAKED WITCH, THE(1964), p

Clifford Alexander
Silents
ALIEN ENEMY, AN(1918)

Curt Alexander
JAZZBAND FIVE, THE(1932, Ger,), w

Dalton Alexander
1984
MISSION, THE(1984)

David Alexander
VICIOUS CIRCLE, THE(1948)

Dean Alexander
GIRL, THE BODY, AND THE PILL, THE(1967), art d

Denise Alexander
CRIME IN THE STREETS(1956)

Denyse Alexander
MEDUSA TOUCH, THE(1978, Brit.)

Dick Alexander
GODLESS GIRL, THE(1929); CITY GIRL(1930); SEE AMERICA THIRST(1930); FRONT PAGE, THE(1931); HURRICANE HORSEMAN(1931); SHANGHAIED LOVE(1931); SUNRISE TRAIL(1931); ONE-MAN LAW(1932); SUNSET TRAIL(1932); QUEEN CHRISTINA(1933); ROMAN SCANDALS(1933); CLEOPATRA(1934); COWBOY HOLIDAY(1934); FIGHTING CODE, THE(1934); GEORGE WHITE'S SCANDALS(1934); WE LIVE AGAIN(1934); COWBOY AND THE BANDIT, THE(1935); COYOTE TRAILS(1935); RUMBA(1935); EVERYMAN'S LAW(1936); MODERN TIMES(1936); ROARIN' GUNS(1936); MYSTERY RANGE(1937); OUTCAST(1937); THINK FAST, MR. MOTO(1937); TWO-FISTED SHERIFF(1937); ADVENTURES OF MARCO POLO, THE(1938); CHARLIE CHAN IN HONOLULU(1938); FEUD OF THE TRAIL(1938); MARIE ANTOINETTE(1938); MYSTERIOUS RIDER, THE(1938); OUTLAWS OF THE PRAIRIE(1938); SANTA FE STAMPEDE(1938); SIX SHOOTIN' SHERIFF(1938); DESTRY RIDES AGAIN(1939); FRONTIER MARSHAL(1939); UNION PACIFIC(1939); DARK COMMAND, THE(1940); DEATH RIDES THE RANGE(1940); SON OF ROARING DAN(1940); WYOMING(1940); BOSS OF BULLION CITY(1941); DOUBLE TROUBLE(1941); FORBIDDEN TRAILS(1941); IN THE NAVY(1941); LADY FROM CHEYENNE(1941); MAN FROM MONTANA(1941); PARIS CALLING(1941); CODE OF THE OUTLAW(1942); GHOST OF FRANKENSTEIN, THE(1942); IN OLD CALIFORNIA(1942); LADY IN A JAM(1942); RAIDERS OF THE RANGE(1942); REAP THE WILD WIND(1942); ROMANCE ON THE RANGE(1942); WE WERE DANCING(1942); DU BARRY WAS A LADY(1943); RETURN OF THE RANGERS, THE(1943); CALL OF THE SOUTH SEAS(1944); GUNSMOKE MESA(1944); LOST IN A HAREM(1944); MAN FROM FRISCO(1944); OKLAHOMA RAIDERS(1944); RAIDERS OF THE BORDER(1944); RIDERS OF THE SANTA FE(1944); STORM OVER LISBON(1944); TRIGGER TRAIL(1944); ABBOTT AND COSTELLO IN HOLLYWOOD(1945); BOSTON BLACKIE'S RENDEZVOUS(1945); FLAMING BULLETS(1945); HIS BROTHER'S GHOST(1945); HOUSE OF FEAR, THE(1945); RENEGADES OF THE RIO GRANDE(1945); SALOME, WHERE SHE DANCED(1945); SENORITA FROM THE WEST(1945); CANYON PASSAGE(1946); NIGHT IN PARADISE, A(1946); MARAUDERS, THE(1947); NORTHWEST OUTPOST(1947); SONG OF SCHEHERAZADE(1947); UNCONQUERED(1947); FALSE PARADISE(1948); JOAN OF ARC(1948); LOADED PISTOLS(1948); SOUTHERN YANKEE, A(1948); HELLFIRE(1949); MADAME BOVARY(1949); RIMFIRE(1949); FATHER OF THE BRIDE(1950); NIGHT STAGE TO GALVESTON(1952); BAND WAGON, THE(1953); PACK TRAIN(1953); PERILOUS JOURNEY, A(1953); SO BIG(1953); LONG, LONG TRAILER, THE(1954); LES GIRLS(1957); GREAT RACE, THE(1965); REQUIEM FOR A GUNFIGHTER(1965); MOONCHILD(1972), p

Misc. Talkies
RIDING WILD(1935)

Silents
LEOPARD LADY, THE(1928)

Don Alexander
WIZARD OF GORE, THE(1970)

Ed Alexander
Silents
BY THE WORLD FORGOT(1918)

Edward Alexander
Silents
ISLAND OF INTRIGUE, THE(1919); PUTTING IT OVER(1919); SAPHEAD, THE(1921)

Misc. Silents
NORTH OF FIFTY-THREE(1917); IN JUDGEMENT OF(1918); WILD STRAIN, THE(1918)

Elizabeth Alexander
SECOND CHOICE(1930); YOU BELONG TO ME(1934), w; SUMMERFIELD(1977, Aus.); CHANT OF JIMMIE BLACKSMITH, THE(1980, Aus.)

Misc. Talkies
SCALP MERCHANT, THE(1977)

Ernest Alexander
AFTER THE THIN MAN(1936); KILL, THE(1968), m, md

Ernie Alexander
TEN CENTS A DANCE(1931); SONS OF THE DESERT(1933); CAT'S PAW, THE(1934); GAMBLING LADY(1934); HOLLYWOOD PARTY(1934); OPERATOR 13(1934); SHE LEARNED ABOUT SAILORS(1934); MUSIC IS MAGIC(1935); O'SHAUGHNESSY'S BOY(1935); PAGE MISS GLORY(1935); SHIPMATES FOREVER(1935); AND SO THEY WERE MARRIED(1936); HERE COMES TROUBLE(1936); OUR RELATIONS(1936); ROSE MARIE(1936); I AM THE LAW(1938); TEST PILOT(1938); ONE HOUR TO LIVE(1939); TELL NO TALES(1939); DR. KILDARE'S CRISIS(1940); SAPS AT SEA(1940); THIRD FINGER, LEFT HAND(1940); DOWN IN SAN DIEGO(1941); MR. AND MRS. SMITH(1941); SUN VALLEY SERENADE(1941); TRIAL OF MARY DUGAN, THE(1941); NAZI AGENT(1942); BATAAN(1943); DU BARRY WAS A LADY(1943); FLIGHT FOR FREEDOM(1943); THREE HEARTS FOR JULIA(1943)

Fatty Alexander
Silents
PLAY SAFE(1927)

Fay Alexander
VARIETY GIRL(1947); TRAPEZE(1956)

Frank Alexander
Silents
WIZARD OF OZ, THE(1925); OH, WHAT A NIGHT!(1926)

Misc. Silents
MELTING MILLIONS(1917)

Fred Alexander
YOUNG FURY(1965)

Frederick Alexander
1984
ANOTHER COUNTRY(1984, Brit.)

Gary Alexander
GO, JOHNNY, GO!(1959), w; CHEAP DETECTIVE, THE(1978)

Georg Alexander
LOVE WALTZ, THE(1930, Ger.); MONEY ON THE STREET(1930, Aust.)

Misc. Silents
ART OF LOVE, THE(1928, Ger.)

George Alexander
WHISPERING CITY(1947, Can.); THIRTEENTH LETTER, THE(1951); WAR OF THE COLOSSAL BEAST(1958)

Georges Alexander
MY UNCLE ANTOINE(1971, Can.)

Gerard Alexander
Silents
SAVING THE FAMILY NAME(1916)

Gerhard Alexander
BUT NOT IN VAIN(1948, Brit.)

Gerry Alexander
VIKING QUEEN, THE(1967, Brit.); GUNS IN THE HEATHER(1968, Brit.); UNDERGROUND(1970, Brit.)

Gilbert Alexander
HUNTING PARTY, THE(1977, Brit.), w

Gina Alexander
URBAN COWBOY(1980)

Gus Alexander
Silents
LES MISERABLES(1918)

Misc. Silents
LIFE'S GREATEST PROBLEM(1919)

Helen Alexander
GANGSTER, THE(1947)

Hilton Alexander
Misc. Talkies
STREETS OF HONG KONG(1979), d

Howard Alexander
EXCUSE MY GLOVE(1936, Brit.), w

Hugh Alexander
HAMLET(1964)

J. G. Alexander
IT'S A DEAL(1930), w; HATCHET MAN, THE(1932), w

J. Grubb Alexander
EVIDENCE(1929), w; GAMBLERS, THE(1929), w; GENERAL CRACK(1929), w; ISLE OF ESCAPE(1930), w; MOBY DICK(1930), w; MURDER WILL OUT(1930), w; NOTORIOUS AFFAIR, A(1930), w; OUTWARD BOUND(1930), w; SWEET KITTY BELLAIRS(1930), w; MAD GENIUS, THE(1931), w; ROAD TO SINGAPORE(1931), w; SVENGALI(1931), w; SO BIG(1932), w

Silents
MOON MADNESS(1920), w; PURPLE CIPHER, THE(1920), w; NOT GUILTY(1921), w; SWAMP, THE(1921), w; CHAIN LIGHTNING(1922), w; IMPULSE(1922), w; RIPTIDE, THE(1923), w; PASSIONATE YOUTH(1925), w; KING OF THE TURF, THE(1926), w; LADY FROM HELL, THE(1926), w; MAN WHO LAUGHS, THE(1927),

w; FREEDOM OF THE PRESS(1928), w; MICHIGAN KID, THE(1928), w

Jack Alexander
OPERATION MANHUNT(1954), d

James Alexander
JACK AND THE BEANSTALK(1952); LAS VEGAS SHAKEDOWN(1955); TREASURE OF RUBY HILLS(1955)

Jamie Alexander
CHILD'S PLAY(1972)

Jane Alexander
GREAT WHITE HOPE, THE(1970); GUNFIGHT, A(1971); MOONCHILD(1972), cos, makeup; NEW CENTURIONS, THE(1972); ALL THE PRESIDENT'S MEN(1976); BETSY, THE(1978); KRAMER VS. KRAMER(1979); BRUBAKER(1980); NIGHT CROSSING(1982); TESTAMENT(1983)
1984
CITY HEAT(1984)

Janet Alexander
HIGH SEAS(1929, Brit.); COMPULSORY HUSBAND, THE(1930, Brit.); NO EXIT(1930, Brit.)
Silents
QUEEN OF THE WICKED(1916, Brit.); QUEEN'S EVIDENCE(1919, Brit.); NOT QUITE A LADY(1928, Brit.)
Misc. Silents
FALLEN STAR, A(1916, Brit.); TREASURE OF HEAVEN, THE(1916, Brit.); WHAT'S BRED...COMES OUT IN THE FLESH(1916, Brit.); FOR ALL ETERNITY(1917, Brit.); STRONG MAN'S WEAKNESS, A(1917, Brit.); SECRET WOMAN, THE(1918, Brit.); GOD'S CLAY(1919, Brit.); I HEAR YOU CALLING ME(1919, Brit.); HOUR OF THE TRIAL, THE(1920, Brit.)

Janie Alexander
GREAT MAN, THE(1957)

Janie Leslie Alexander
NAKED CITY, THE(1948)

Jason Alexander
BURNING, THE(1981)

Jean Alexander
FAMILY SECRET, THE(1951); MOB, THE(1951); TALES OF HOFFMANN, THE(1951, Brit.)

Jeff Alexander
WESTWARD THE WOMEN(1951), m; AFFAIRS OF DOBIE GILLIS, THE(1953), md; ESCAPE FROM FORT BRAVO(1953), m; REMAINS TO BE SEEN(1953), md; PRISONER OF WAR(1954), m; ROGUE COP(1954), m; KISMET(1955), md; TENDER TRAP, THE(1955), m; GREAT AMERICAN PASTIME, THE(1956), m; RANSOM(1956), m; SLANDER(1956), m; THESE WILDER YEARS(1956), m; GUN GLORY(1957), m; JAILHOUSE ROCK(1957), md; WINGS OF EAGLES, THE(1957), m; HIGH COST OF LOVING, THE(1958), m; PARTY GIRL(1958), m; SADDLE THE WIND(1958), m; SHEEPMAN, THE(1958), m; ASK ANY GIRL(1959), m; GAZEBO, THE(1959), m; IT STARTED WITH A KISS(1959), m, md; MATING GAME, THE(1959), m; ALL THE FINE YOUNG CANNIBALS(1960), m; GEORGE RAFT STORY, THE(1961), m; KID GALAHAD(1962), m; ROUNDERS, THE(1965), m; CURSE OF THE SWAMP CREATURE(1966), m; CLAMBAKE(1967), m; DOUBLE TROUBLE(1967), m; DAY OF THE EVIL GUN(1968), m; SPEEDWAY(1968), m; SUPPORT YOUR LOCAL SHERIFF(1969), m; BULLET FOR PRETTY BOY, A(1970); DIRTY DINGUS MAGEE(1970), m

Jeffrey Alexander
FLAMING FRONTIER(1958, Can.)

Jim Alexander
NIGHT FREIGHT(1955); PORT OF HELL(1955); DIARY OF A BACHELOR(1964); SKULLDUGGERY(1970)

Jimmy Alexander
ROOKIES ON PARADE(1941); EARL CARROLL'S VANITIES(1945)

Jock Alexander
RAILWAY CHILDREN, THE(1971, Brit.), makeup

John Alexander
BABY, TAKE A BOW(1934); GHOST RIDER, THE(1935); SPECIAL AGENT(1935); PETRIFIED FOREST, THE(1936); POLO JOE(1936); SATAN MET A LADY(1936); STAGE STRUCK(1936); MEN IN EXILE(1937); ON SUCH A NIGHT(1937); CALLING ALL HUSBANDS(1940); FLOWING GOLD(1940); ARSENIC AND OLD LACE(1944); DOUGHGIRLS, THE(1944); MR. SKEFFINGTON(1944); HORN BLOWS AT MIDNIGHT, THE(1945); JUNIOR MISS(1945); TREE GROWS IN BROOKLYN, A(1945); IT SHOULDN'T HAPPEN TO A DOG(1946); JOLSON STORY, THE(1946); CASS TIMBERLANE(1947); LIVING IN A BIG WAY(1947); NEW ORLEANS(1947); WHERE THERE'S LIFE(1947); NIGHT HAS A THOUSAND EYES(1948); SUMMER HOLIDAY(1948); FANCY PANTS(1950); SLEEPING CITY, THE(1950); WINCHESTER '73(1950); MODEL AND THE MARRIAGE BROKER, THE(1951); MARRYING KIND, THE(1952); UNTAMED FRONTIER(1952); MUGGER, THE(1958); MAN IN THE NET, THE(1959); ONE FOOT IN HELL(1960); PLAYERS(1979)
1984
GREYSTOKE: THE LEGEND OF TARZAN, LORD OF THE APES(1984)
Silents
FOX FARM(1922, Brit.)

Julie Alexander
PURE HELL OF ST. TRINIAN'S, THE(1961, Brit.); MATTER OF WHO, A(1962, Brit.); OPERATION BULLSHINE(1963, Brit.)

K.C. Alexander
MAKE-UP(1937, Brit.), p; SONS OF THE SEA(1939, Brit.), p; LAW AND DISORDER(1940, Brit.), p

Kart Alexander
TIME AFTER TIME(1979, Brit.), w

Katharine Alexander
SHOULD LADIES BEHAVE?(1933); BARRETTS OF WIMPOLE STREET, THE(1934); DEATH TAKES A HOLIDAY(1934); OPERATOR 13(1934); PAINTED VEIL, THE(1934); AFTER OFFICE HOURS(1935); ALIAS MARY DOW(1935); CARDINAL RICHELIEU(1935); ENCHANTED APRIL(1935); GINGER(1935); GIRL FROM TENTH AVENUE, THE(1935); SHE MARRIED HER BOSS(1935); SPLENDOR(1935); DEVIL IS A SISSY, THE(1936); MOONLIGHT MURDER(1936); REUNION(1936); SUTTER'S GOLD(1936); AS GOOD AS MARRIED(1937); DOUBLE WEDDING(1937); GIRL FROM SCOTLAND YARD(1937); STAGE DOOR(1937); THAT CERTAIN WOMAN(1937); RASCALS(1938); BROADWAY SERENADE(1939); GREAT MAN VOTES, THE(1939); HUNCHBACK OF NOTRE DAME, THE(1939); IN NAME ONLY(1939); THREE SONS(1939); ANNE OF WINDY POPLARS(1940); DANCE, GIRL, DANCE(1940); PLAY GIRL(1940); ANGELS WITH BROKEN WINGS(1941); SIS HOPKINS(1941); SMALL

TOWN DEB(1941); VANISHING VIRGINIAN, THE(1941); NOW, VOYAGER(1942); ON THE SUNNY SIDE(1942); HUMAN COMEDY, THE(1943); KISS AND TELL(1945); FOR THE LOVE OF MARY(1948); JOHN LOVES MARY(1949)

Keith Alexander
THUNDERBIRD 6(1968, Brit.); SUMARINE X-1(1969, Brit.); SUPERMAN(1978); HANOVER STREET(1979, Brit.)

Kenneth Alexander
SUN VALLEY SERENADE(1941)

Larry Alexander
GAMBLING SHIP(1933); STOOLIE, THE(1972), w

Liz Alexander
KILLING OF ANGEL STREET, THE(1983, Aus.)

Lois Alexander
Silents
FORGIVEN, OR THE JACK O'DIAMONDS(1914); 20,000 LEAGUES UNDER THE SEA(1916); ALL WOMAN(1918)

Louis Alexander
JOHNNY ON THE RUN(1953, Brit.); PRINCE OF PLAYERS(1955)

Mac Alexander
Silents
CASSIDY(1917)

Mara Alexander
RAINS CAME, THE(1939); PRIMROSE PATH(1940)

Marc Alexander
PAWNBROKER, THE(1965)

Marie Alexander
Misc. Silents
LIBERTINE, THE(1916)

Mary Alexander
MY FAIR LADY(1964)

Max Alexander
COWBOY HOLIDAY(1934), p; THUNDER OVER TEXAS(1934), p; TICKET TO CRIME(1934), p; DANGER TRAILS(1935), p; WHAT PRICE CRIME?(1935), p; MEN OF THE PLAINS(1936), p; STORMY TRAILS(1936), p; TOO MUCH BEEF(1936), p; HERE'S FLASH CASEY(1937), p; LAW AND LEAD(1937), p; SHADOW STRIKES, THE(1937), p; INTERNATIONAL CRIME(1938), p; SIX SHOOTIN' SHERIFF(1938), p; WHIRLWIND HORSEMAN(1938), p; FLAMING LEAD(1939), p; DEATH RIDES THE RANGE(1940), p; LIGHTNING STRIKES WEST(1940), p; PHANTOM RANCHER(1940), p; CITY OF MISSING GIRLS(1941), p; SWAMP WOMAN(1941), p; DAWN EXPRESS, THE(1942), p; UNDERDOG, THE(1943), p; I ACCUSE MY PARENTS(1945), p; MASK OF DIIJON, THE(1946), p; AMAZON QUEST(1949), p

Maxwell Alexander
1984
GARBO TALKS(1984)

May Alexander
Silents
YELLOW STAIN, THE(1922)

Melanie Alexander
COOL ONES THE(1967)

Mello Alexander
THX 1138(1971)

Michael Alexander
GILDED CAGE, THE(1954, Brit.); WEDDINGS AND BABIES(1960), ed; THREE MUSKETEERS, THE(1974, Panama), p

Muriel Alexander
Misc. Silents
SCALLYWAG, THE(1921, Brit.)

Newell Alexander
HOMEWORK(1982)

Nick Alexander
LOVE WITH THE PROPER STRANGER(1963)

Norman Alexander
CRIME OVER LONDON(1936, Brit.), w

Paris Alexander
IT HAPPENED IN ATHENS(1962); DAY THE FISH CAME OUT, THE(1967. Brit./Gr.)
Misc. Talkies
ALIKI-MY LOVE(1963, U.S./Gr.)

Patrick Alexander
ROOM 43(1959, Brit.), w

Paul Alexander
SCHIZO(1977, Brit.)

Pero Alexander
THEY WERE SO YOUNG(1955); 5 SINNERS(1961, Ger.)

Peter Alexander
DIE FLEDERMAUS(1964, Aust.); HOW TO SEDUCE A PLAYBOY(1968, Aust./Fr./Ital.); DIVINE MR. J., THE(1974), p&d

Philip Alexander
MAN WHO LOVED WOMEN, THE(1983); TRENCHCOAT(1983)

Phoebe Alexander
CONVERSATION, THE(1974)

R. Alexander
BOUNTY KILLER, THE(1965), w; REQUIEM FOR A GUNFIGHTER(1965), w

R. Howard Alexander
EXCUSE MY GLOVE(1936, Brit.), p; TELEVISION TALENT(1937, Brit.), p, d&w; DANCE LITTLE LADY(1954, Brit.), w

R. P. Alexander
MYSTERY LAKE(1953)

Rhys Alexander
Misc. Silents
GALLOPER, THE(1915); SECRET CODE, THE(1918)

Richard Alexander
ALL QUIET ON THE WESTERN FRONT(1930); ARE YOU THERE?(1930); LONE STAR RANGER, THE(1930); ROUGH WATERS(1930); LAW OF THE TONG(1931); YOUNG DONOVAN'S KID(1931); DARING DANGER(1932); LAW AND ORDER(1932); SCARLET DAWN(1932); SIGN OF THE CROSS(1932); TEXAS BAD MAN(1932); TWO-FISTED LAW(1932); DESTINATION UNKNOWN(1933); SCARLET EMPRESS, THE(1934); SIXTEEN FATHOMS DEEP(1934); FRECKLES(1935); KENTUCKY KERNELS(1935); SHE GETS HER MAN(1935); TALE OF TWO CITIES, A(1935); DANGEROUS WATERS(1936); DRIFT FENCE(1936); FLASH GORDON(1936); SILLY

BILLIES(1936); STORY OF LOUIS PASTEUR, THE(1936); WILD BRIAN KENT(1936); ON THE GREAT WHITE TRAIL(1938); WHERE THE BUFFALO ROAM(1938); WHERE THE WEST BEGINS(1938); KANSAS TERRORS, THE(1939); STRANGE CARGO(1940); SPOOK TOWN(1944); SPOOK BUSTERS(1946); DEAD DON'T DREAM, THE(1948); SILENT CONFLICT(1948); LUST FOR GOLD(1949); SILVER CANYON(1951); DANGEROUS WHEN WET(1953); FLESH AND THE SPUR(1957)
Silents
KING OF KINGS, THE(1927); MYSTERIOUS LADY, THE(1928); SIN SISTER, THE(1929)

Richard "Dick" Alexander
PRINCESS AND THE PIRATE, THE(1944)

Robert Alexander
CRIME IN THE STREETS(1956); BLOOMFIELD(1971, Brit./Israel)

Robert D. E. Alexander
FOES(1977), p

Rod Alexander
BEST THINGS IN LIFE ARE FREE, THE(1956), ch; CAROUSEL(1956), ch

Rolf Alexander
HAPPY GO LOVELY(1951, Brit.)

Ronald Alexander
LADY IN QUESTION, THE(1940); HOLIDAY FOR LOVERS(1959), w; RETURN TO PEYTON PLACE(1961), w; BILLIE(1965), w

Ross Alexander
WISER SEX, THE(1932); FLIRTATION WALK(1934); GENTLEMEN ARE BORN(1934); SOCIAL REGISTER(1934); CAPTAIN BLOOD(1935); GOING HIGH-BROW(1935); MAYBE IT'S LOVE(1935); MIDSUMMER'S NIGHT'S DREAM, A(1935); SHIPMATES FOREVER(1935); WE'RE IN THE MONEY(1935); BOULDER DAM(1936); BRIDES ARE LIKE THAT(1936); HERE COMES CARTER(1936); CHINA CLIPPER(1936); HOT MONEY(1936); I MARRIED A DOCTOR(1936); READY, WILLING AND ABLE(1937)

Ruth Alexander
UNDERWATER CITY, THE(1962), w

Sandy Alexander
PEOPLE NEXT DOOR, THE(1970)

Sara Alexander
Silents
CAPRICE OF THE MOUNTAINS(1916); JUNGLE TRAIL, THE(1919)
Misc. Silents
LITTLE MISS HAPPINESS(1916)

Sean Alexander
1984
CANNONBALL RUN II(1984)

Shana Alexander
SLENDER THREAD, THE(1965), w

Sidney Alexander
PIRATES OF CAPRI, THE(1949), w

Sir George Alexander
Misc. Silents
SECOND MRS. TANQUERAY, THE(1916, Brit.)

Sooren Alexander
LAST AFFAIR, THE(1976), m

Stan Alexander
BAMBI(1942)

Stephen Alexander
SLENDER THREAD, THE(1965), p

Suzanne Alexander
CAT WOMEN OF THE MOON(1953); LATIN LOVERS(1953); DOWN THREE DARK STREETS(1954); FRENCH LINE, THE(1954); PRINCESS OF THE NILE(1954); GIRL IN THE RED VELVET SWING, THE(1955); SON OF SINBAD(1955); SOLID GOLD CADILLAC, THE(1956); GARMENT JUNGLE, THE(1957)

Tad Alexander
AMBASSADOR BILL(1931); RASPUTIN AND THE EMPRESS(1932); STRANGE INTERLUDE(1932); TOMORROW AND TOMORROW(1932); BROADWAY TO HOLLY-WOOD(1933); BUREAU OF MISSING PERSONS(1933); STRANGER'S RETURN(1933); I GIVE MY LOVE(1934); YOU CAN'T BUY EVERYTHING(1934); LITTLE MEN(1935)

Terence Alexander
FIGHTING PIMPERNEL, THE(1950, Brit.); DEATH IS A NUMBER(1951, Brit.); HER PANELLED DOOR(1951, Brit.); TALE OF FIVE WOMEN, A(1951, Brit.); GENTLE GUNMAN, THE(1952, Brit.); GLAD TIDINGS(1953, Brit.); MR. POTTS GOES TO MOSCOW(1953, Brit.); NORMAN CONQUEST(1953, Brit.); DANGEROUS CAR-GO(1954, Brit.); GREEN SCARF, THE(1954, Brit.); HANDS OF DESTINY(1954, Brit.); RUNAWAY BUS, THE(1954, Brit.); POSTMARK FOR DANGER(1956, Brit.); GREEN MAN, THE(1957, Brit.); DOCTOR'S DILEMMA, THE(1958, Brit.); ONE THAT GOT AWAY, THE(1958, Brit.); SQUARE PEG, THE(1958, Brit.); DON'T PANIC CHAPS!(1959, Brit.); BULLDOG BREED, THE(1960, Brit.); PRICE OF SILENCE, THE(1960, Brit.); CARRY ON REGARDLESS(1961, Brit.); LEAGUE OF GENTLEMEN, THE(1961, Brit.); MAN AT THE CARLTON TOWER(1961, Brit.); GENTLE TERROR, THE(1962, Brit.); ON THE BEAT(1962, Brit.); SHE ALWAYS GETS THEIR MAN(1962, Brit.); BITTER HARVEST(1963, Brit.); FAST LADY, THE(1963, Brit.); MIND BEND-ERS, THE(1963, Brit.); V.I.P.s, THE(1963, Brit.); JUDITH(1965); SPYLARKS(1965, Brit.); LONG DUEL, THE(1967, Brit.); ONLY WHEN I LARF(1968, Brit.); WHAT'S GOOD FOR THE GOOSE(1969, Brit.); ALL THE WAY UP(1970, Brit.); MAGIC CHRISTIAN, THE(1970, Brit.); WATERLOO(1970, Ital./USSR); DAY OF THE JACKAL, THE(1973, Brit./Fr.); VAULT OF HORROR, THE(1973, Brit.); INTERNECINE PRO-JECT, THE(1974, Brit.)
Misc. Talkies
BREAKOUT(1959); CORVINI INHERITANCE(1984, Brit.)

Terrence Alexander
COMIN' THRU' THE RYE(1947, Brit.)

Terry Alexander
CLAUDINE(1974)
1984
FLASHPOINT(1984)

Van Alexander
ATOMIC KID, THE(1954), m; TWINKLE IN GOD'S EYE, THE(1955), m; JA-GUAR(1956), m, md; WHEN GANGLAND STRIKES(1956), md; BABY FACE NEL-SON(1957), m; BIG OPERATOR, THE(1959), m; GIRLS' TOWN(1959), m&md; LAST MILE, THE(1959), m; PLATINUM HIGH SCHOOL(1960), m; PRIVATE LIVES OF ADAM AND EVE, THE(1961), m; SAFE AT HOME(1962), m; THIRTEEN FRIGHT-ENED GIRLS(1963), m; STRAIT-JACKET(1964), m; I SAW WHAT YOU DID(1965), m;

TARZAN AND THE VALLEY OF GOLD(1966 U.S./Switz.), m; TIME FOR KILLING, A(1967), m; STRANGE HOLIDAY(1969, Aus.)

William Alexander
INGAGI(1931), p; KLANSMAN, THE(1974), p
Misc. Talkies
THAT MAN OF MINE(1947), d

Zoe Alexander
NIGHT DIGGER, THE(1971, Brit.)

Hope Alexander-Willis
PACK, THE(1977)

Charles Alexandra
Silents
OUT WITH THE TIDE(1928)

Sandra Alexandra
Misc. Talkies
BLACK HOOKER(1974)

Jacqueline Alexandre
RETURN OF SABATA(1972, Ital./Fr./Ger.)

Manuel Alexandre
MAIN STREET(1956, Span.)

Patrice Alexandre
TENANT, THE(1976, Fr.)

Raymond Alexandre
LUCKY TO BE A WOMAN(1955, Ital.), p

Roland Alexandre
PERFECTIONIST, THE(1952, Fr.)

Alexandresco
Silents
ARAB, THE(1924)

Mello Alexandria
UPTIGHT(1968); COVER ME BABE(1970); PSYCHIC KILLER(1975); SLITHIS(1978)

Queen Alexandria
Silents
GREAT LOVE, THE(1918)

Victor Alexandroff
DAMNED, THE(1948, Fr.), w

Antoll Alexandrov
THIRTEEN, THE(1937, USSR), m

G. Alexandrov
SEEDS OF FREEDOM(1943, USSR)

Gregori Alexandrov
Misc. Silents
STRIKE(1925, USSR)

Gregory Alexandrov
SPRING(1948, USSR), d, w; MAN OF MUSIC(1953, USSR), d, w

Grigori Alexandrov
Silents
TEN DAYS THAT SHOOK THE WORLD(1927, USSR), w
Misc. Silents
OLD AND NEW(1930, USSR), d

Grigory Alexandrov
Silents
BATTLESHIP POTEMKIN, THE(1925, USSR)

Inga Alexandrova
MASOCH(1980, Ital.)

Yekaterina Alexandrovskaya
FATHERS AND SONS(1960, USSR)

Doris Alexaner
BUDDY HOLLY STORY, THE(1978), makeup

Nathalie Alexeeff
LOWER DEPTHS, THE(1937, Fr.)

Irina Alexeieva
JULIET OF THE SPIRITS(1965, Fr./Ital./W.Ger.)

Inna Alexeiff
GARDEN OF THE FINZI-CONTINIS, THE(1976, Ital./Ger.)

Ina Alexeiva
WAR AND PEACE(1956, Ital./U.S.)

Andrei Alexeyev
DAYS AND NIGHTS(1946, USSR)

E. Alexeyeva
CHILDHOOD OF MAXIM GORKY(1938, Russ.)

Alexia
1984
HERE COMES SANTA CLAUS(1984)

Anna Alexiadis
FANTASIES(1981)

Nikos Alexiou
DAY THE FISH CAME OUT, THE(1967. Brit./Gr.)

Alvin Alexis
WIZ, THE(1978); WILLIE AND PHIL(1980)
1984
BROTHER FROM ANOTHER PLANET, THE(1984)

Brian Alexis
HIDE AND SEEK(1964, Brit.)

Demetrius Alexis
LOVE CAPTIVE, THE(1934); WONDER BAR(1934); PADDY O'DAY(1935); HONKY TONK(1941); GOVERNMENT GIRL(1943); LAKE PLACID SERENADE(1944); SPAN-ISH MAIN, THE(1945); RAZOR'S EDGE, THE(1946)
Misc. Silents
RED SWORD, THE(1929)

Dimitrios Alexis
BEDSIDE MANNER(1945)

Dimitris Alexis
MISSION TO MOSCOW(1943)

Dmitri Alexis
TORTURE SHIP(1939)

Laura Alexis
1984
LA PETIT SIRENE(1984, Fr.)

Martine Alexis
LYONS IN PARIS, THE(1955, Brit.); FRENCH CANCAN(1956, Fr.); ROYAL AF-
FAIRS IN VERSAILLES(1957, Fr.); CRACK IN THE MIRROR(1960)
Yuri Alexis
Misc. Talkies
FOX AFFAIR, THE(1978)
Patrice Alexsandre
LUMIERE(1976, Fr.)
Albert Aley
UGLY DACHSHUND, THE(1966), w
Maxwell Aley
YOU'RE NOT SO TOUGH(1940), w
K. Aleyeva
RESURRECTION(1963, USSR), ed; LAST GAME, THE(1964, USSR), ed
Pytor Aleynikov
HOME FOR TANYA, A(1961, USSR)
A. Aleynikova
WELCOME KOSTYA!(1965, USSR); MEET ME IN MOSCOW(1966, USSR); GIRL AND
THE BUGLER, THE(1967, USSR)
Benito Alezraki
TIME AND THE TOUCH, THE(1962), d, w
Gina R. Alfano
1984
BROTHER FROM ANOTHER PLANET, THE(1984), set d
Henry Alfaro
TELEFON(1977)
Rhonda Alfaro
SAFE PLACE, A(1971)
Rosa Alfaro
STUCK ON YOU(1983), cos
J. Alfasa
POCKET MONEY(1972)
Joe Alfasa
WHAT'S UP, DOC?(1972); HOW TO SEDUCE A WOMAN(1974)
Norman Alfe
SLAUGHTER(1972)
Richard Alfieri
CHILDREN OF RAGE(1975, Brit.-Israeli); IN SEARCH OF HISTORIC JESUS(1980);
ECHOES(1983)
L. Alfimova
KIEV COMEDY, A(1963, USSR)
Yves Alfonse
ZIG-ZAG(1975, Fr./Ital.)
Enzo Alfonsi
PIRATE OF THE BLACK HAWK, THE(1961, Fr./Ital.), w, ed; HUNS, THE(1962,
Fr./Ital.), ed; MISSION BLOODY MARY(1967, Fr./Ital./Span.), ed
Lidia Alfonsi
HERCULES(1959, Ital.); WHERE THE HOT WIND BLOWS(1960, Fr., Ital.); MORGAN
THE PIRATE(1961, Fr./Ital.); TROJAN HORSE, THE(1962, Fr./Ital.); BLACK SAB-
BATH(1963, Ital.); MYTH, THE(1965, Ital.)
Antonio Alfonso
WHITE SISTER(1973, Ital./Span./Fr.)
Omar Alfonso
DEATH OF A BUREAUCRAT(1979, Cuba)
Yves Alfonso
MADE IN U.S.A.(1966, Fr.); WEEKEND(1968, Fr./Ital.)
1984
ONE DEADLY SUMMER(1984, Fr.)
Enzo Alfonzi
LOVES OF SALAMMBO, THE(1962, Fr./Ital.), ed
Harold Alford
TITFIELD THUNDERBOLT, THE(1953, Brit.)
Les Alford
JAWS 3-D(1983)
Lucie Alford
ELEPHANT MAN, THE(1980, Brit.)
Max Alford
FLASH GORDON(1980)
Philip Alford
SHENANDOAH(1965)
Phillip Alford
TO KILL A MOCKINGBIRD(1962)
Tommy Alford
CROSS CREEK(1983)
Vi Alford
LIBERATION OF L.B. JONES, THE(1970), cos
Jack Alfred
FOREIGN CORRESPONDENT(1940)
Neil Russell Alfred
NOW YOU SEE HIM, NOW YOU DON'T(1972)
Alfred Rode and his Tzigane Band
CARNIVAL(1931, Brit.); BLUE DANUBE(1932, Brit.)
Alfred Rode and His Tzigane Orchestra
TEMPTATION(1935, Brit.)
Alfred Wright & Co
BOB'S YOUR UNCLE(1941, Brit.)
Alfreda
SHRIEK IN THE NIGHT, A(1933), cos
Sam Alfredo
SIN OF MONA KENT, THE(1961)
Alfredo and His Gypsy Orchestra
MAID OF THE MOUNTAINS, THE(1932, Brit.)
Alfredo Campoli and his Tzigane Orchestra
HIS MAJESTY AND CO(1935, Brit.)
Hans Alfredson
SHAME(1968, Swed.); EMIGRANTS, THE(1972, Swed.); NEW LAND, THE(1973,
Swed.); ADVENTURES OF PICASSO, THE(1980, Swed.), a, w

Aina Alfredsson
EMIGRANTS, THE(1972, Swed.)
Arnold Alfredsson
EMIGRANTS, THE(1972, Swed.)
Gisli Alfredsson
HAGBARD AND SIGNE(1968, Den./Iceland/Swed.)
Hugo Alfven
GYPSY FURY(1950, Fr.), m
Gabor Algacs
FATHER(1967, Hung.)
James Algar
SNOW WHITE AND THE SEVEN DWARFS(1937), anim; FANTASIA(1940), d;
BAMBI(1942), d; ADVENTURES OF ICHABOD AND MR. TOAD(1949), d; LEGEND
OF LOBO, THE(1962), d, w; INCREDIBLE JOURNEY, THE(1963), p, w; GNOME-
MOBILE, THE(1967), p; RASCAL(1969), p
Robert Algar
WINDMILL, THE(1937, Brit.)
John H. Algate
SNIPER, THE(1952)
Sepp Algier
REBEL, THE(1933, Ger.), ph
Sidney Algier
WILD HORSE(1931), d
Nelson Algren
MAN WITH THE GOLDEN ARM, THE(1955), w; WALK ON THE WILD SIDE(1962),
w; GOLDSTEIN(1964); FEARLESS FRANK(1967)
Augusto Alguero
EVERY DAY IS A HOLIDAY(1966, Span.), m
Jose Alguero
THIN RED LINE, THE(1964), art d; RETURN OF THE SEVEN(1966, Span.), art d;
VILLA RIDES(1968), art d; DESPERADOS, THE(1969), art d; LAND RAIDERS(1969),
art d; HANNIE CALDER(1971, Brit.), art d; ANTONY AND CLEOPATRA(1973,
Brit.), art d
Iris Alhanti
KRAMER VS. KRAMER(1979); PARTNERS(1982)
Ali
RANGO(1931)
Bobker Ben Ali
SALOME(1953); ISTANBUL(1957)
Fatima Bint Ali
ISLAND OF ALLAH(1956)
George Ali
Silents
PETER PAN(1924)
Hadji Ali
SCARLET DAWN(1932)
Hakmeh Abou Ali
CIRCLE OF DECEIT(1982, Fr./Ger.)
Jamal Ali
BLACK JOY(1977, Brit.), w
Khalilah Ali
CHINA SYNDROME, THE(1979)
Muhammad Ali
BLACK RODEO(1972); GREATEST, THE(1977, U.S./Brit.); BODY AND SOUL(1981)
Rahaman Ali
GREATEST, THE(1977, U.S./Brit.)
Robert Ben Ali
THUNDER IN THE EAST(1953)
Useff Ali
FALCON IN HOLLYWOOD, THE(1944)
Yussef Ali
SLAVE GIRL(1947)
Yussuf Ali
SONG OF SCHEHERAZADE(1947)
Hrant Alianak
SPACEHUNTER: ADVENTURES IN THE FORBIDDEN ZONE(1983)
Carl Alianello
SENSO(1968, Ital.), w
Angelina Alias
CATHERINE & CO.(1976, Fr.)
Alibe
TREASURE ISLAND(1972, Brit./Span./Fr./Ger.)
Alibert
Misc. Silents
PARIS(1924, Fr.)
Bozidar Alic
1984
MEMED MY HAWK(1984, Brit.)
Mario Alicata
OSSESSIONE(1959, Ital.), w
Mary Alice
EDUCATION OF SONNY CARSON, THE(1974); SPARKLE(1976)
1984
BEAT STREET(1984); TEACHERS(1984)
Alice the Horse
MAD WEDNESDAY(1950)
Ana Alicia
HALLOWEEN II(1981)
Kamee Aliessa
HARRY'S WAR(1981)
Carlo Alighiero
FIVE MAN ARMY, THE(1970, Ital.); CAT O'NINE TAILS(1971, Ital./Ger./Fr.);
NEXT!(1971, Ital./Span.)
Slobodan Aligrudic
LOVE AFFAIR; OR THE CASE OF THE MISSING SWITCHBOARD OPERA-
TOR(1968, Yugo.); EARLY WORKS(1970, Yugo.)
O. Alikin
RESURRECTION(1963, USSR), set d; GARNET BRACELET, THE(1966, USSR), art
d

The Alilena twins
GODZILLA VERSUS THE SEA MONSTER(1966, Jap.)

Jeff Alin
Misc. Talkies
MATTER OF LOVE, A(1979)

Anne Alinatt
MURDER IN THE CATHEDRAL(1952, Brit.), ed

Dallas Alinder
BLACK MARBLE, THE(1980); FIRST MONDAY IN OCTOBER(1981)

Kemal Alinoren
TARGET: HARRY(1980)

Claude Aliotti
CAST A GIANT SHADOW(1966); THREE BITES OF THE APPLE(1967)

Marcello Aliprandi
TIN GIRL, THE(1970, Ital.), p&d, w

Ted Alires
MC MASTERS, THE(1970), spec eff

Jill Alis
LUM AND ABNER ABROAD(1956)

Dorothy Alisen
GENTLE TOUCH, THE(1956, Brit.)

Sadri Alisik
THERE IS STILL ROOM IN HELL(1963, Ger.)

Bart Alison
O LUCKY MAN!(1973, Brit.)

Dave Alison
DISPUTED PASSAGE(1939)

David Alison
NEW MOON(1940); DESTROYER(1943); MARGIN FOR ERROR(1943); GAL WHO TOOK THE WEST, THE(1949); PEGGY(1950)

Dayle Alison
WE OF THE NEVER NEVER(1983, Aus.)

Dorothy Alison
CRASH OF SILENCE(1952, Brit.); CHILD'S PLAY(1954, Brit.); COMPANIONS IN CRIME(1954, Brit.); HIGH AND DRY(1954, Brit.); PURPLE PLAIN, THE(1954, Brit.); TURN THE KEY SOFTLY(1954, Brit.); PICKUP ALLEY(1957, Brit.); REACH FOR THE SKY(1957, Brit.); THIRD KEY, THE(1957, Brit.); LIFE IN EMERGENCY WARD 10(1959, Brit.); MAN UPSTAIRS, THE(1959, Brit.); NUN'S STORY, THE(1959); STRANGE AFFECTION(1959, Brit.); TWO LIVING, ONE DEAD(1964, Brit./Swed.); GEORGY GIRL(1966, Brit.); MATTER OF INNOCENCE, A(1968, Brit.); DR. JEKYLL AND SISTER HYDE(1971, Brit.); SEE NO EVIL(1971, Brit.); AMAZING MR. BLUNDEN, THE(1973, Brit.); RETURN OF THE SOLDIER, THE(1983, Brit.)

Eric Alison
CREMATORS, THE(1972)

Joan Alison
CASABLANCA(1942), w

Patricia Alison
ALL WOMAN(1967)

Natalia Alisova
RAINBOW, THE(1944, USSR); MILITARY SECRET(1945, USSR)

Nina Alisova
LADY WITH THE DOG, THE(1962, USSR); SHADOWS OF FORGOTTEN ANCESTORS(1967, USSR)

Florence Aliston
Misc. Silents
TRUTH AND JUSTICE(1916, Brit.)

Victor Alix
Silents
PASSION OF JOAN OF ARC, THE(1928, Fr.), m

Ben Aliza
GREAT BANK ROBBERY, THE(1969)

Howard Alk
RENALDO AND CLARA(1978), ph, ed; KING OF THE MOUNTAIN(1981)

Mosko Alkalai
JESUS(1979)

Mosko Alkalay
MADRON(1970, U.S./Israel)

John Alkin
GAMES, THE(1970); SWEENEY(1977, Brit.); NO LONGER ALONE(1978); SWEENEY 2(1978, Brit.)

Candy All
HIT MAN(1972)

Paul Alladice
PUTNEY SWOPE(1969)

Johnny Alladin
YOUNG WARRIORS, THE(1967)

Ben Allah
Silents
PASSIONATE YOUTH(1925), t

Bruno Allain
1984
LES COMPERES(1984, Fr.)

Marcel Allain
FANTOMAS(1966, Fr./Ital.), w

Keith Allams
HEROSTRATUS(1968, Brit.), ph

Alex Allan
FLASH THE SHEEPDOG(1967, Brit.)

Andrea Allan
HOUSE THAT VANISHED, THE(1974, Brit.); OLD DRACULA(1975, Brit.)

Anita Allan
LOVE ON THE RIVIERA(1964, Fr./Ital.)

Anne Allan
SILVER DARLINGS, THE(1947, Brit.)

Anthony [John Hubbard] Allan
DRAMATIC SCHOOL(1938); OUT WEST WITH THE HARDYS(1938); FAST AND LOOSE(1939); KID FROM TEXAS, THE(1939); MAISIE(1939)

Arthur Allan
NAKED WOMAN, THE(1950, Fr.)

Bebe Allan
STATE FAIR(1962)

Bill Allan
FLOODTIDE(1949, Brit.), ph; POET'S PUB(1949, Brit.), ph; STOP PRESS GIRL(1949, Brit.), ph

Cameron Allan
STIR(1980, Aus.), m; HEATWAVE(1983, Aus.), m

Claire Allan
IT HAPPENED HERE(1966, Brit.)

Dick Allan
LOVE CRAZY(1941)

Elizabeth Allan
ALIBI(1931, Brit.); BLACK COFFEE(1931, Brit.); BOAT FROM SHANGHAI(1931, Brit.); MANY WATERS(1931, Brit.); ROSARY, THE(1931, Brit.); CHINESE PUZZLE, THE(1932, Brit.); DOWN OUR STREET(1932, Brit.); INSULT(1932, Brit.); MICHAEL AND MARY(1932, Brit.); NINE TILL SIX(1932, Brit.); RESERVED FOR LADIES(1932, Brit.); ACE OF ACES(1933); LOOKING FORWARD(1933); NO MARRIAGE TIES(1933); SOLITAIRE MAN, THE(1933); MEN IN WHITE(1934); MYSTERY OF MR. X, THE(1934); OUTCAST LADY(1934); DAVID COPPERFIELD(1935); JAVA HEAD(1935, Brit.); MARK OF THE VAMPIRE(1935); PHANTOM FIEND, THE(1935, Brit.); TALE OF TWO CITIES, A(1935); SHADOW, THE(1936, Brit.); WOMAN REBELS, A(1936); CAMILLE(1937); LOST CHORD, THE(1937, Brit.); SLAVE SHIP(1937); SOLDIER AND THE LADY, THE(1937); DANGEROUS MEDICINE(1938, Brit.); GIRL WHO FORGOT, THE(1939, Brit.); INQUEST(1939, Brit.); SALOON BAR(1940, Brit.); GREAT MR. HANDEL, THE(1942, Brit.); HE SNOOPS TO CONQUER(1944, Brit.); 48 HOURS(1944, Brit.); NO HIGHWAY IN THE SKY(1951, Brit.); FOLLY TO BE WISE(1953); TWICE UPON A TIME(1953, Brit.); FRONT PAGE STORY(1954, Brit.); HEART OF THE MATTER, THE(1954, Brit.); BRAIN MACHINE, THE(1955, Brit.); HAUNTED STRANGLER, THE(1958, Brit.)

Eric Allan
TELL ME LIES(1968, Brit.); MC KENZIE BREAK, THE(1970); BLEAK MOMENTS(1972, Brit.)

Fleming Allan
STUNT PILOT(1939), m

George Allan
MY SIDE OF THE MOUNTAIN(1969)

Hayes Allan
Misc. Silents
WILD BEAUTY(1927)

Hugh Allan
Silents
WHAT FOOLS MEN(1925); DRESS PARADE(1927); WHAT HAPPENED TO FATHER(1927); ANNAPOLIS(1928); HOLD 'EM YALE!(1928); OBJECT–ALIMONY(1929)
Misc. Silents
BLOCK SIGNAL, THE(1926); BIRDS OF PREY(1927); WILD BEAUTY(1927); SIN TOWN(1929); VOICE OF THE STORM, THE(1929)

Jack Allan
INN OF THE DAMNED(1974, Aus.)

James Allan
LADIES OF THE PARK(1964, Fr.), art d

Jane Allan
GOOD SAM(1948)

Janet Allan
LITTLE BIG SHOT(1952, Brit.), w

Jed Allan
ICE STATION ZEBRA(1968)
Misc. Talkies
NEEKA(1968)

Jerry Allan
OUTLAWS IS COMING, THE(1965)

Jill Allan
WALKING ON AIR(1946, Brit.); MANIACS ON WHEELS(1951, Brit.)

John Allan
HONEYMOON HOTEL(1946, Brit.)

Julie Allan
1984
LOVE STREAMS(1984)

Lane Allan
I WANTED WINGS(1941); MAC ARTHUR(1977)

Marguerite Allan
PLAYTHING, THE(1929, Brit.); ROMANCE OF SEVILLE, A(1929, Brit.); GREENWOOD TREE, THE(1930, Brit.); SLEEPING PARTNERS(1930, Brit.); UNDER THE GREENWOOD TREE(1930, Brit.); DAUGHTERS OF TODAY(1933, Brit.); MATINEE IDOL(1933, Brit.); DOCTOR'S ORDERS(1934, Brit.); THOSE WERE THE DAYS(1934, Brit.); BIG SPLASH, THE(1935, Brit.); GAY OLD DOG(1936, Brit.); PRISON BREAKER(1936, Brit.); APRIL BLOSSOMS(1937, Brit.); FORBIDDEN TERRITORY(1938, Brit.); ADVENTURE IN BLACKMAIL(1943, Brit.)
Misc. Silents
WIDECOMBE FAIR(1928, Brit.)

Michael Allan
DEAD OF NIGHT(1946, Brit.); BROKEN JOURNEY(1948, Brit.); WHILE THE SUN SHINES(1950, Brit.); CALLING BULLDOG DRUMMOND(1951, Brit.); SECRET PEOPLE(1952, Brit.)

Nancy Allan
HAPPY BIRTHDAY TO ME(1981)

Pamela Allan
DEATM GOES TO SCHOOL(1953, Brit.); NOOSE FOR A LADY(1953, Brit.)

Patrick Allan
FLIGHT FROM SINGAPORE(1962, Brit.)

Paul Allan
Silents
ARIZONA DAYS(1928), ph

Phillip L. Allan
WHERE THE BUFFALO ROAM(1980)

Ray Allan
FINNEGANS WAKE(1965)

Richard Allan
FROGMEN, THE(1951); HALLS OF MONTEZUMA(1951); BLOODHOUNDS OF BROADWAY(1952); DREAMBOAT(1952); SNOWS OF KILIMANJARO, THE(1952); WITH A SONG IN MY HEART(1952); NIAGARA(1953); RACERS, THE(1955); REST IS SILENCE, THE(1960, Ger.)

Ross Allan
NO BLADE OF GRASS(1970, Brit.)

Sean Allan
LEGACY(1976)

Seth Allan
ALICE'S RESTAURANT(1969)

Shirley Allan
QUARTET(1981, Brit./Fr.)

Ted Allan
BANDIT OF SHERWOOD FOREST, THE(1946); BRIDE OF THE MONSTER(1955), ph; 1001 ARABIAN NIGHTS(1959), w; LIES MY FATHER TOLD ME(1960, Brit.), w; LIES MY FATHER TOLD ME(1975, Can.), a, w; FALLING IN LOVE AGAIN(1980), w
1984
LOVE STREAMS(1984), w

Wayne Allan
1984
UTU(1984, New Zealand)

Guy Alland
LETTERS FROM MY WINDMILL(1955, Fr.)

William Alland
CITIZEN KANE(1941); DEVIL AND DANIEL WEBSTER, THE(1941); TOM, DICK AND HARRY(1941); LADY FROM SHANGHAI, THE(1948); MACBETH(1948), a, d; BLACK CASTLE, THE(1952), p; FLESH AND FURY(1952), w; LAWLESS BREED, THE(1952), p, w; RAIDERS, THE(1952), p; IT CAME FROM OUTER SPACE(1953), p; STAND AT APACHE RIVER, THE(1953), p; CREATURE FROM THE BLACK LAGOON(1954), p; DAWN AT SOCORRO(1954), p; FOUR GUNS TO THE BORDER(1954), p; JOHNNY DARK(1954), p; CHIEF CRAZY HORSE(1955), p; REVENGE OF THE CREATURE(1955), p, w; TARANTULA(1955), p; THIS ISLAND EARTH(1955), p; CREATURE WALKS AMONG US, THE(1956), p; MOLE PEOPLE, THE(1956), p; DEADLY MANTIS, THE(1957), p, w; GUN FOR A COWARD(1957), p; LAND UNKNOWN, THE(1957), p; AS YOUNG AS WE ARE(1958), p, w; COLOSSUS OF NEW YORK, THE(1958), p; LADY TAKES A FLYER, THE(1958), p; PARTY CRASHERS, THE(1958), p; RAW WIND IN EDEN(1958), p; SPACE CHILDREN, THE(1958), p; LOOK IN ANY WINDOW(1961), p, d; LIVELY SET, THE(1964), p, w; RARE BREED, THE(1966), p

Merja Allanen
CASTLE KEEP(1969)

Susan Allanson
JESUS CHRIST, SUPERSTAR(1973)

John Allansu
PIRATE MOVIE, THE(1982, Aus.)

Eric Allard
STRANGE BREW(1983), spec eff

Georges Allard
FORTUNE AND MEN'S EYES(1971, U.S./Can.)

Jeanne Allard
ZAZIE(1961, Fr.); VERY PRIVATE AFFAIR, A(1962, Fr./Ital.); LES CREATURES(1969, Fr./Swed.)

Michael Allard
Silents
APACHE, THE(1925, Brit.), w

Shirlee Allard
I CAN GET IT FOR YOU WHOLESALE(1951); SCANDAL SHEET(1952); PHFFFT!(1954)

James Allardice
SAILOR BEWARE(1951), w; JUMPING JACKS(1952), w; MONEY FROM HOME(1953), w

James B. Allardice
AT WAR WITH THE ARMY(1950), w

Albert Allardt
Silents
ALIEN ENEMY, AN(1918)

Arthur Allardt
Silents
INSIDE THE LINES(1918); LOUISIANA(1919)

Grace Allardyce
MILLIONS LIKE US(1943, Brit.); YELLOW CANARY, THE(1944, Brit.); SEVENTH VEIL, THE(1946, Brit.); DULCIMER STREET(1948, Brit.)

Marisa Allasio
WAR AND PEACE(1956, Ital./U.S.); SEVEN HILLS OF ROME, THE(1958)

Louise Allbritton
DANGER IN THE PACIFIC(1942); PARACHUTE NURSE(1942); PITTSBURGH(1942); WHO DONE IT?(1942); FIRED WIFE(1943); GOOD MORNING, JUDGE(1943); IT COMES UP LOVE(1943); SON OF DRACULA(1943); BOWERY TO BROADWAY(1944); FOLLOW THE BOYS(1944); HER PRIMITIVE MAN(1944); SAN DIEGO, I LOVE YOU(1944); THIS IS THE LIFE(1944); MEN IN HER DIARY(1945); THAT NIGHT WITH YOU(1945); TANGIER(1946); EGG AND I, THE(1947); DON'T TRUST YOUR HUSBAND(1948); SITTING PRETTY(1948); WALK A CROOKED MILE(1948); DOOLINS OF OKLAHOMA, THE(1949)

Nick Allder
TWIST OF SAND, A(1968, Brit.), spec eff; MOON ZERO TWO(1970, Brit.), spec eff; SENDER, THE(1982, Brit.), spec eff; KEEP, THE(1983), makeup
1984
TOP SECRET!(1984), spec eff

Michael Alldredge
RUBY(1977); INCREDIBLE MELTING MAN, THE(1978); ENTITY, THE(1982); SCARFACE(1983)

Michael D. Alldredge
STING II, THE(1983)

Florence Nightingale Allebeury
LADY WITH A LAMP, THE(1951, Brit.)

Elizabeth Allee
TERROR EYES(1981)

Lisa Allee
TERROR EYES(1981)

Tony Allef
FUNNY MONEY(1983, Brit.)

Tony Alleff
NEVER SAY NEVER AGAIN(1983)

Henri Alleg
QUESTION, THE(1977, Fr.), w

Sepp Allegeler
DOOMED BATTALION, THE(1932), ph

A. Allegier
LOVE IN MOROCCO(1933, Fr.), ph

Jean-Marc Allegre
HAIL MAFIA(1965, Fr./Ital.); LIFE LOVE DEATH(1969, Fr./Ital.)

Allegret
LOVES OF THREE QUEENS, THE(1954, Ital./Fr.), w

Catherine Allegret
LADY L(1965, Fr./Ital.); SLEEPING CAR MURDER THE(1966, Fr.); IT ONLY HAPPENS TO OTHERS(1971, Fr./Ital.); PAUL AND MICHELLE(1974, Fr./Brit.); CHANEL SOLITAIRE(1981)

Marc Allegret
CURTAIN RISES, THE(1939, Fr.), d; HEART OF PARIS(1939, Fr.), d; BLANCHE FURY(1948, Brit.), d; FANNY(1948, Fr.), d; BLACKMAILED(1951, Brit.), d; LOVES OF THREE QUEENS, THE(1954, Ital./Fr.), d, w; NAKED HEART, THE(1955, Brit.), d, w; JULIETTA(1957, Fr.), d; PLEASE! MR. BALZAC(1957, Fr.), d, w; LADY CHATTERLEY'S LOVER(1959, Fr.), d&w; BLOOD AND ROSES(1961, Fr./Ital.); MIDNIGHT FOLLY(1962, Fr.), d; TALES OF PARIS(1962, Fr./Ital.), d, w

Yves Allegret
CONFESSIONS OF A NEWLYWED(1941, Fr.), w; DEDEE(1949, Fr.), d, w; CHEAT, THE(1950, Fr.), d; SEVEN DEADLY SINS, THE(1953, Fr./Ital.), d; DESPERATE DECISION(1954, Fr.), d; PORT OF DESIRE(1960, Fr.), d; GERMINAL(1963, Fr.), d; JOHNNY BANCO(1969, Fr./Ital./Ger.), d, w

Cosmo Allegretti
PRINCE OF THE CITY(1981)

Cosmo F. Allegretti
AUTHOR! AUTHOR!(1982)

Gus Allegretti
SORCERER(1977)

Alfred Allegro
OVER 21(1945); SONG TO REMEMBER, A(1945)

Joseph Allegro
GREAT ADVENTURE, THE(1976, Span./Ital.), p

W.A. Alleman
Misc. Silents
FIGHTING STRANGER, THE(1921)

Adrianne Allen
LOOSE ENDS(1930, Brit.); BLACK COFFEE(1931, Brit.); STRONGER SEX, THE(1931, Brit.); NIGHT OF JUNE 13(1932); WOMAN DECIDES, THE(1932, Brit.); MORALS OF MARCUS, THE(1936, Brit.); BOND STREET(1948, Brit.); OCTOBER MAN, THE(1948, Brit.); VOTE FOR HUGGETT(1948, Brit.); FINAL TEST, THE(1953, Brit.); MEET MR. MALCOLM(1954, Brit.)

Adrienne Allen
MERRILY WE GO TO HELL(1932)

Alex Allen
DEPTH CHARGE(1960, Brit.)

Alfred Allen
Silents
FLASHLIGHT, THE(1917); GIRL IN THE DARK, THE(1918); RIDERS OF VENGEANCE(1919); OLD FASHIONED BOY, AN(1920); NEW DISCIPLE, THE(1921); O'MALLEY OF THE MOUNTED(1921); PRIDE OF PALOMAR, THE(1922); SHATTERED IDOLS(1922); GENTLEMAN OF LEISURE, A(1923); NOISE IN NEWBORO, A(1923); SHOOTIN' FOR LOVE(1923); ABRAHAM LINCOLN(1924); ROLLING HOME(1926); OUT ALL NIGHT(1927); OUTLAW DOG, THE(1927); SINGED(1927); FIFTY-FIFTY GIRL, THE(1928); HOT NEWS(1928); FLYING FEET, THE(1929); SUNSET PASS(1929)
Misc. Silents
BARRIERS OF SOCIETY(1916); YOKE OF GOLD, A(1916); REED CASE, THE(1917); BRACE UP(1918); GUILT OF SILENCE, THE(1918); KISS OR KILL(1918); PAINTED LIPS(1918); SEA FLOWER, THE(1918); WINNER TAKES ALL(1918); HIS DIVORCED WIFE(1919); LOOT(1919); MAN IN THE MOONLIGHT, THE(1919); TONGUES OF FLAME(1919); BLACKMAIL(1920); BURNING DAYLIGHT(1920); COLLEEN OF THE PINES(1922); GRUB STAKE, THE(1923); BUSTIN' THRU(1925); DANGEROUS INNOCENCE(1925); GOLDEN YUKON, THE(1927); UNDER THE TONTO RIM(1928)

Ali Allen
SALVAGE GANG, THE(1958, Brit.)

Alicia Allen
1984
CALIFORNIA GIRLS(1984)

Allen D. Allen
SPECTRE OF EDGAR ALLAN POE, THE(1974), m

Alta Allen
Silents
SHOCKING NIGHT, A(1921); DARING CHANCES(1924)
Misc. Silents
BE MY WIFE(1921); SEVEN YEARS BAD LUCK(1921); MARRIAGE CHANCE, THE(1922); SET-UP, THE(1926)

Andrea Allen
WRONG BOX, THE(1966, Brit.); ASSIGNMENT K(1968, Brit.)

Ann E. Allen
HARLEM GLOBETROTTERS, THE(1951)

Anna Lou Allen
Misc. Silents
HEARTS OF THE WOODS(1921)

Anne Allen
ESCAPADE(1955, Brit.)

Anthony Allen
ROSSITER CASE, THE(1950, Brit.); MAFIA GIRLS, THE(1969); FLAME(1975, Brit.)

April Allen
SKATETOWN, U.S.A.(1979)
Argy Allen
NO WAY BACK(1976)
Ariane Allen
GALLOPING DYNAMITE(1937)
Arthur Allen
EBB TIDE(1937); OUR TOWN(1940); RANGERS OF FORTUNE(1940)
Audrey Allen
SON OF SINBAD(1955)
Austen Allen
PLEASURE CRUISE(1933), w
Bambi Allen
SOMEONE(1968); SATAN'S SADISTS(1969); ANGELS DIE HARD(1970); HELL'S
BLOODY DEVILS(1970); TOM(1973); DRIFTER(1975)
Misc. Talkies
OUTLAW RIDERS(1971)
Barbara Allen
BUY ME THAT TOWN(1941); OKLAHOMA JUSTICE(1951); DEAD MAN'S
TRAIL(1952); FORT OSAGE(1952); IT STARTED IN PARADISE(1952, Brit.); HOME-
STEADERS, THE(1953)
Misc. Talkies
STAGECOACH DRIVER(1951)
Misc. Silents
HER HUSBAND'S HONOR(1918)
Barbara Jo Allen
ICE-CAPADES(1941); SWORD IN THE STONE, THE(1963)
Barry Allen
SUNNY(1930)
Bea Allen
BLUE DAHLIA, THE(1946); WELCOME STRANGER(1947); SOMEBODY LOVES
ME(1952); WHITE CHRISTMAS(1954)
Beatrice Allen
Silents
ANNE OF GREEN GABLES(1919)
Misc. Silents
WEAVERS OF LIFE(1917); FANGS OF FATE(1925)
Bebe Allen
OPERATION MAD BALL(1957)
Becky Allen
HARD TIMES(1975)
Bee Allen
ROYAL WEDDING(1951)
Bernie Allen
PRODUCERS, THE(1967); RAGING BULL(1980)
Betty Allen
SCARLET ANGEL(1952); REDHEAD FROM WYOMING, THE(1953)
Beverly Allen
SCREAMS OF A WINTER NIGHT(1979)
Bill Allen
STREAMERS(1983)
Billie Allen
WIZ, THE(1978); WINTER KILLS(1979)
Misc. Talkies
SOULS OF SIN(1949); LOSING GROUND(1982)
Billy Allen
PRINCESS AND THE MAGIC FROG, THE(1965), m; SHE FREAK(1967), m; DE-
VIL'S MISTRESS, THE(1968), m; TRADER HORNEE(1970), md
Bob Allen
UNKNOWN RANGER, THE(1936); LAW OF THE RANGER(1937); RANGER COUR-
AGE(1937); RANGERS STEP IN, THE(1937); RECKLESS RANGER(1937); RIO
GRANDE RANGER(1937); SHE GETS HER MAN(1945); WEB, THE(1947); DIR-
TYMOUTH(1970)
C. J. Allen
1984
LAUGHTER HOUSE(1984, Brit.)
Silents
FOOLISH WIVES(1920)
Cameron Allen
SUMMER OF SECRETS(1976, Aus.), m
Carlo Allen
HEARTBREAKER(1983)
Celena Allen
NEW YEAR'S EVIL(1980)
Chesney Allen
WILD BOY(1934, Brit.); FIRE HAS BEEN ARRANGED, A(1935, Brit.); OKAY FOR
SOUND(1937, Brit.), a, w; UNDERNEATH THE ARCHES(1937, Brit.); ALF'S BUTTON
AFLOAT(1938, Brit.); GASBAGS(1940, Brit.); WE'LL SMILE AGAIN(1942, Brit.);
THEATRE ROYAL(1943, Brit.); HERE COMES THE SUN(1945, Brit.); DUNKIRK(1958,
Brit.); LIFE IS A CIRCUS(1962, Brit.)
Chet Allen
MEET ME AT THE FAIR(1952); DELINQUENTS, THE(1957), art d
Chris Allen
MAN FROM MUSIC MOUNTAIN(1938); GENE AUTRY AND THE MOUN-
TIES(1951); TERMINAL ISLAND(1973); LAST REMAKE OF BEAU GESTE,
THE(1977), w; IN GOD WE TRUST(1980), w
Misc. Silents
DEADSHOT CASEY(1928)
Christi Michelle Allen
1984
INITIATION, THE(1984)
Christine Allen
ONE, TWO, THREE(1961)
Christopher Allen
SEVENTH DAWN, THE(1964)
Cliff Allen
ANGEL COMES TO BROOKLYN, AN(1945)

Corey Allen
NIGHT OF THE HUNTER, THE(1955); REBEL WITHOUT A CAUSE(1955); BIG
CAPER, THE(1957); SHADOW ON THE WINDOW, THE(1957); DARBY'S RAN-
GERS(1958); JUVENILE JUNGLE(1958); PARTY GIRL(1958); KEY WITNESS(1960);
PRIVATE PROPERTY(1960); CHAPMAN REPORT, THE(1962); SWEET BIRD OF
YOUTH(1962); THUNDER AND LIGHTNING(1977), d; AVALANCHE(1978), d, w
Dave Allen
LITTLE JOE, THE WRANGLER(1942); SQUEEZE A FLOWER(1970, Aus.); LASER-
BLAST(1978), spec eff & makeup
David Allen
FEAR AND DESIRE(1953); FORTY POUNDS OF TROUBLE(1962); EQUINOX(1970),
spec eff; THREE DAYS OF THE CONDOR(1975); CRATER LAKE MONSTER,
THE(1977), anim; CAVEMAN(1981), spec eff; Q(1982), spec eff
Dayton Allen
1984
COTTON CLUB, THE(1984)
Debbie Allen
FAME(1980); RAGTIME(1981)
Debra Allen
FISH THAT SAVED PITTSBURGH, THE(1979), a, ch
Dede Allen
WIZ, THE(1978), ed; BECAUSE OF EVE(1948), ed; TERROR FROM THE YEAR
5,000(1958), ed; ODDS AGAINST TOMORROW(1959), ed; HUSTLER, THE(1961), ed;
AMERICA, AMERICA(1963), ed; BONNIE AND CLYDE(1967), ed; RACHEL, RACH-
EL(1968), ed; ALICE'S RESTAURANT(1969), ed; LITTLE BIG MAN(1970), ed;
SLAUGHTERHOUSE-FIVE(1972), ed; SERPICO(1973), ed; DOG DAY AFTER-
NOON(1975), ed; NIGHT MOVES(1975), ed; MISSOURI BREAKS, THE(1976), ed;
SLAP SHOT(1977), ed; REDS(1981), ed
1984
HARRY AND SON(1984), ed; MIKE'S MURDER(1984), ed
Dennis Allen
ME, NATALIE(1969)
Diana Allen
Silents
AMAZING LOVERS(1921); KENTUCKIANS, THE(1921); WAY OF A MAID,
THE(1921); EXCITERS, THE(1923); ROULETTE(1924)
Misc. Silents
(; HELIOTROPE(1920); MAN AND WOMAN(1920); VOICES(1920); GET-RICH-QUICK
WALLINGFORD(1921); MAN AND WOMAN(1921); BEYOND THE RAINBOW(1922);
DIVORCE COUPONS(1922); MALE WANTED(1923); SALOME(1923)
Dick Allen
FOLIES DERGERE(1935); SPLENDOR(1935); KLONDIKE ANNIE(1936); ETERNAL-
LY YOURS(1939); STRIKE UP THE BAND(1940)
Dominic Allen
GIRL WITH A PISTOL, THE(1968, Ital.); RAILWAY CHILDREN, THE(1971, Brit.)
Don Allen
MAN'S FAVORITE SPORT(?)**1/2 (1964)
Donald V. Allen
1984
SUBURBIA(1984)
Donnie Allen
MELODY FOR THREE(1941)
Dorothy Allen
Silents
OVER THE HILL TO THE POORHOUSE(1920); BEYOND PRICE(1921); SECOND
YOUTH(1924); YOUTH FOR SALE(1924)
Misc. Silents
DYNAMITE ALLEN(1921); POWER WITHIN, THE(1921)
Drew Allen
RENDEZVOUS 24(1946); SONG OF MY HEART(1947)
Duane Allen
MANDINGO(1975)
Ed Allen
COVER GIRL(1944); KANSAS CITY KITTY(1944); MADEMOISELLE FIFI(1944);
COLONEL EFFINGHAM'S RAID(1945)
Eddie Allen
SOMETHING TO SING ABOUT(1937); LEAVE IT TO THE IRISH(1944); PERFECT
STRANGERS(1950), makeup; EMMA MAE(1976)
Edgar Allen
MANDARIN MYSTERY, THE(1937)
Silents
SPITFIRE OF SEVILLE, THE(1919)
Edith Allen
RICH ARE ALWAYS WITH US, THE(1932); TENDERFOOT, THE(1932)
Silents
SCARAMOUCHE(1923)
Misc. Silents
VIRTUOUS LIARS(1924)
Edwin Allen
SUDDEN FEAR(1952), makeup
Elizabeth Allen
THREE WEIRD SISTERS, THE(1948, Brit.); IF THIS BE SIN(1950, Brit.); FROM THE
TERRACE(1960); DIAMOND HEAD(1962); DONOVAN'S REEF(1963); CHEYENNE
AUTUMN(1964); STAR SPANGLED GIRL(1971); CAREY TREATMENT, THE(1972)
Misc. Talkies
BORN FOR TROUBLE(1955)
Eric Allen
SMOKE IN THE WIND(1975), w; OUT OF THE BLUE(1982)
Estelle Allen
Silents
OVERALLS(1916)
Misc. Silents
LAST ACT, THE(1916); ROAD TO LOVE, THE(1916)
Ethan Allen
BORDER LEGION, THE(1930); ALIAS THE BAD MAN(1931); FLOOD, THE(1931);
LIGHTNING FLYER(1931); TWO GUN MAN, THE(1931); FLAMING LEAD(1939);
RIDERS OF BLACK RIVER(1939); SINGING COWGIRL, THE(1939); TAMING OF
THE WEST, THE(1939); TRIGGER PALS(1939); WATER RUSTLERS(1939); BULLET
FOR PRETTY BOY, A(1970)

Eugene Allen
RODEO RHYTHM(1941), w; BREATH OF SCANDAL, A(1960), art d; HELLER IN PINK TIGHTS(1960), art d

Fletcher Allen
QUICK, BEFORE IT MELTS(1964)
Florence Allen
LONE WOLF'S DAUGHTER, THE(1929); THAT HAGEN GIRL(1947)
Silents
AVENGING RIDER, THE(1928); JOY STREET(1929)
Frank Allen
SOUTH OF SONORA(1930)
Fred Allen
SENOR AMERICANO(1929), ed; WAGON MASTER, THE(1929), ed; FIGHTING LEGION, THE(1930), ed; HEADIN' NORTH(1930), ed; MOUNTAIN JUSTICE(1930), ed; PARADE OF THE WEST(1930), ed; PARDON MY GUN(1930), ed; SONG OF THE CABELLERO(1930), ed; SONS OF THE SADDLE(1930), ed; SUNDOWN TRAIL(1931), p; WOMAN OF EXPERIENCE, A(1931), ed; BEYOND THE ROCKIES(1932), d; FREIGHTERS OF DESTINY(1932), d; GHOST VALLEY(1932), d; PARTNERS(1932), d; RIDE HIM, COWBOY(1932), d; SADDLE BUSTER, THE(1932), d; MYSTERIOUS RIDER, THE(1933), d; THANKS A MILLION(1935); THIS IS THE LIFE(1935), ed; COUNTRY BEYOND, THE(1936), ed; EVERY SATURDAY NIGHT(1936), ed; GENTLE JULIA(1936), ed; PEPPER(1936), ed; UNDER YOUR SPELL(1936), ed; CHARLIE CHAN AT THE OLYMPICS(1937), ed; CRACK-UP, THE(1937), ed; ONE MILE FROM HEAVEN(1937), ed; STEP LIVELY, JEEVES(1937), ed; ADVENTURES OF MARCO POLO, THE(1938), ed; ARIZONA WILDCAT(1938), ed; FIVE OF A KIND(1938), ed; MEET THE GIRLS(1938), ed; SALLY, IRENE AND MARY(1938); SPEED TO BURN(1938), ed; CHARLIE CHAN IN RENO(1939), ed; CHICKEN WAGON FAMILY(1939), ed; ESCAPE, THE(1939), ed; TOO BUSY TO WORK(1939), ed; 20,000 MEN A YEAR(1939), ed; CHARLIE CHAN IN PANAMA(1940), ed; CHARTER PILOT(1940), ed; LOVE THY NEIGHBOR(1940), ed; LUCKY CISCO KID(1940), ed; PIER 13(1940), ed; SAILOR'S LADY(1940), ed; CADET GIRL(1941), ed; DRESSED TO KILL(1941), ed; ROMANCE OF THE RIO GRANDE(1941), ed; SLEEPERS WEST(1941), ed; WE GO FAST(1941), ed; BERLIN CORRESPONDENT(1942), ed; DR. RENAULT'S SECRET(1942), ed; LIFE BEGINS AT 8:30(1942), ed; LOVES OF EDGAR ALLAN POE, THE(1942), ed; MAN WHO WOULDN'T DIE, THE(1942), ed; ON THE SUNNY SIDE(1942), ed; GUADALCANAL DIARY(1943), ed; BRAZIL(1944), ed; CHINESE CAT, THE(1944), ed; SECRETS OF SCOTLAND YARD(1944), ed; THREE LITTLE SISTERS(1944), ed; DAKOTA(1945), ed; GANGS OF THE WATERFRONT(1945), ed; HITCHHIKE TO HAPPINESS(1945), ed; IT'S IN THE BAG(1945), a, w; SCOTLAND YARD INVESTIGATOR(1945, Brit.), ed; SWINGIN' ON A RAINBOW(1945), ed; TIGER WOMAN, THE(1945), ed; IN OLD SACRAMENTO(1946), ed; MADONNA'S SECRET, THE(1946), ed; PLAINSMAN AND THE LADY(1946), ed; SIOUX CITY SUE(1946), ed; UNDERCOVER WOMAN, THE(1946), ed; CALENDAR GIRL(1947), ed; GHOST GOES WILD, THE(1947), ed; LOVE FROM A STRANGER(1947), ed; RED STALLION, THE(1947), ed; T-MEN(1947), ed; HOLLOW TRIUMPH(1948), ed; BLACK BOOK, THE(1949), ed; VICIOUS YEARS, THE(1950), ed; ENFORCER, THE(1951), ed; SLAUGHTER TRAIL(1951), ed; GOLD RAIDERS, THE(1952), ed; I DREAM OF JEANIE(1952), ed; O. HENRY'S FULL HOUSE(1952); RIDE THE MAN DOWN(1952), ed; WE'RE NOT MARRIED(1952); CHAMP FOR A DAY(1953), ed; CITY THAT NEVER SLEEPS(1953), ed; FLIGHT NURSE(1953), ed; LADY WANTS MINK, THE(1953), ed; SWEETHEARTS ON PARADE(1953), ed; WOMAN THEY ALMOST LYNCHED, THE(1953), ed; HELL'S HALF ACRE(1954), ed; MAKE HASTE TO LIVE(1954), ed; ETERNAL SEA, THE(1955), ed; WAGON WHEELS WESTWARD(1956), ed
Silents
SHADOWS OF CONSCIENCE(1921), ed; BULLDOG COURAGE(1922), ed; CORPORAL KATE(1926); LAWLESS LEGION, THE(1929), w, ed; ROYAL RIDER, THE(1929), ed
Frederick Allen
HANGMAN'S WHARF(1950, Brit.); SEVEN DAYS TO NOON(1950, Brit.); FORT APACHE, THE BRONX(1981)
Frederick Lewis Allen
ONLY YESTERDAY(1933), w
Gary Allen
WICKED DIE SLOW, THE(1968), a, w; NIGHT THEY ROBBED BIG BERTHA'S, THE(1975); ANNIE HALL(1977); SENTINEL, THE(1977); ALICE, SWEET ALICE(1978); DON'T ANSWER THE PHONE(1980); BUDDY BUDDY(1981); MOMMIE DEAREST(1981); PANDEMONIUM(1982)
Gene Allen
STAR IS BORN, A(1954), prod d; LES GIRLS(1957), art d; MERRY ANDREW(1958), art d; LET'S MAKE LOVE(1960), art d; CHAPMAN REPORT, THE(1962), art d; MY FAIR LADY(1964), art d; CHEYENNE SOCIAL CLUB, THE(1970), art d
George Allen
TWO YANKS IN TRINIDAD(1942); SOUL OF NIGGER CHARLEY, THE(1973)
Georgia Allen
TOGETHER FOR DAYS(1972); GREASED LIGHTNING(1977); MARVIN AND TIGE(1983)
Georgina Allen
STOP THE WORLD-I WANT TO GET OFF(1966, Brit.)
Gertrude Allen
Silents
HER BOY(1915, Brit.), w
Glen Allen
BURNING CROSS, THE(1947)
Glenn Allen
LOOK OUT SISTER(1948)
Gracie Allen
BIG BROADCAST, THE(1932); COLLEGE HUMOR(1933); INTERNATIONAL HOUSE(1933); MANY HAPPY RETURNS(1934); SIX OF A KIND(1934); WE'RE NOT DRESSING(1934); BIG BROADCAST OF 1936, THE(1935); HERE COMES COOKIE(1935); LOVE IN BLOOM(1935); BIG BROADCAST OF 1937, THE(1936); COLLEGE HOLIDAY(1936); DAMSEL IN DISTRESS, A(1937); COLLEGE SWING(1938); GRACIE ALLEN MURDER CASE(1939); HONOLULU(1939); MR. AND MRS. NORTH(1941); TWO GIRLS AND A SAILOR(1944)
Harry Allen
IN OLD CALIFORNIA(1929); STRANGE CARGO(1929); DAWN PATROL, THE(1930); HEADIN' NORTH(1930); HELL HARBOR(1930); HELL'S ISLAND(1930); RICH MAN'S FOLLY(1931); SECOND HONEYMOON(1931); TEXAS PIONEERS(1932); FOURTH HORSEMAN, THE(1933); KENNEL MURDER CASE, THE(1933); MONKEY'S PAW,

THE(1933); RIP TIDE(1934); ANNA KARENINA(1935); FEATHER IN HER HAT, A(1935); GREAT IMPERSONATION, THE(1935); NIGHT AT THE OPERA, A(1935); SILVER STREAK, THE(1935); GIRL FROM MANDALAY(1936); LOVE ON THE RUN(1936); RETURN OF SOPHIE LANG, THE(1936); WHITE ANGEL, THE(1936); WHITE LEGION, THE(1936); CALIFORNIA STRAIGHT AHEAD(1937); GIRL WITH IDEAS, A(1937); OUTSIDE OF PARADISE(1938); RECKLESS LIVING(1938); LITTLE PRINCESS, THE(1939); RAFFLES(1939); STAND UP AND FIGHT(1939); EARL OF CHICAGO, THE(1940); MOON OVER BURMA(1940); ONE NIGHT IN LISBON(1941); RAGE IN HEAVEN(1941); MRS. MINIVER(1942); BUCKSKIN FRONTIER(1943); FOREVER AND A DAY(1943); HOUR BEFORE THE DAWN, THE(1944); JANE EYRE(1944); LODGER, THE(1944); NATIONAL VELVET(1944); SCARLET CLAW, THE(1944); WHITE CLIFFS OF DOVER, THE(1944); LOVE LETTERS(1945); MINISTRY OF FEAR(1945); MOSS ROSE(1947); SWORDSMAN, THE(1947); EMPEROR WALTZ, THE(1948); JULIA MISBEHAVES(1948); KISS THE BLOOD OFF MY HANDS(1948); NIGHT HAS A THOUSAND EYES(1948); TAKE ME OUT TO THE BALL GAME(1949)
Silents
AFTER MIDNIGHT(1921); ENCHANTED COTTAGE, THE(1924); ELLA CINDERS(1926); ADORABLE CHEAT, THE(1928); SWEET SIXTEEN(1928); TWO LOVERS(1928)
Misc. Silents
SCORCHER, THE(1927)
Henry Allen
HOLIDAY(1938)
Hervey Allen
ANTHONY ADVERSE(1936), w
Hilary Allen
MOULIN ROUGE(1952)
Howard Allen
CEILNG ZERO(1935)
Howie Allen
WARGAMES(1983)
Hugh Allen
THIS MAN'S NAVY(1945), w; MISS TATLOCK'S MILLIONS(1948); WAR OF THE WORLDS, THE(1953)
Hylton Allen
CAESAR AND CLEOPATRA(1946, Brit.); SEND FOR PAUL TEMPLE(1946, Brit.); HANGMAN WAITS, THE(1947, Brit.); SCARLET THREAD(1951, Brit.)
Ira Allen
Silents
IN THE DAYS OF SAINT PATRICK(1920, Brit.)
Irene Allen
TOY WIFE, THE(1938)
Irvin Allen
LOLITA(1962); ON HER MAJESTY'S SECRET SERVICE(1969, Brit.); SPY WHO LOVED ME, THE(1977, Brit.); REVENGE OF THE PINK PANTHER(1978)
Irving Allen
SILENCERS, THE(, p; GENGHIS KHAN(U.S./Brit./Ger./Yugo), p; STRANGE VOYAGE(1945), d; AVALANCHE(1946), d; HIGH CONQUEST(1947), p, d; SIXTEEN FATHOMS DEEP(1948), p, d; MAN ON THE EIFFEL TOWER, THE(1949), p; NEW MEXICO(1951), p; SLAUGHTER TRAIL(1951), p&d; BLACK KNIGHT, THE(1954), p; HELL BELOW ZERO(1954, Brit.), p; PARATROOPER(1954, Brit.), p; COCKLESHELL HEROES, THE(1955), p; PRIZE OF GOLD, A(1955), p; ZARAK(1956, Brit.), p; FIRE DOWN BELOW(1957, U.S./Brit.), p; HIGH FLIGHT(1957, Brit.), p; PICKUP ALLEY(1957, Brit.), p; MAN INSIDE, THE(1958, Brit.), p; TANK FORCE(1958, Brit.), p; BANDIT OF ZHOBE, THE(1959), p; ROAD TO HONG KONG, THE(1962, U.S./Brit.), p; LONG SHIPS, THE(1964, Brit./Yugo.), p; MURDERERS' ROW(1966), p; HAMMERHEAD(1968), p; WRECKING CREW, THE(1968), p; DESPERADOS, THE(1969), p; CROMWELL(1970, Brit.), p
Irwin Allen
GIRL IN EVERY PORT, A(1952), p; DANGEROUS MISSION(1954), p; STORY OF MANKIND, THE(1957), p&d, w; BIG CIRCUS, THE(1959), p, w; LOST WORLD, THE(1960), p&d, w; VOYAGE TO THE BOTTOM OF THE SEA(1961), p&d, w; FIVE WEEKS IN A BALLOON(1962), p&d, w; AMBUSHERS, THE(1967), p; POSEIDON ADVENTURE, THE(1972), p; TOWERING INFERNO, THE(1974), p, d; SWARM, THE(1978), p&d; BEYOND THE POSEIDON ADVENTURE(1979), p&d; WHEN TIME RAN OUT(1980), p
J.H. Allen
VIRGINIA JUDGE, THE(1935); SATAN MET A LADY(1936)
Jack Allen
WHO KILLED FEN MARKHAM?(1937, Brit.); FOUR FEATHERS, THE(1939, Brit.); SPY FOR A DAY(1939, Brit.); CONSPIRATOR(1949, Brit.); ELIZABETH OF LADYMEAD(1949, Brit.); SHE SHALL HAVE MURDER(1950, Brit.); BREAKING THE SOUND BARRIER(1952, Brit.); DEAD ON COURSE(1952, Brit.); IT STARTED IN PARADISE(1952, Brit.); HEART OF THE MATTER, THE(1954, Brit.); RADIO CAB MURDER(1954, Brit.); IMPULSE(1955, Brit.); THUNDER OVER TANGIER(1957, Brit.); JACK THE RIPPER(1959, Brit.); WHITE TRAP, THE(1959, Brit.); BOMB IN THE HIGH STREET(1961, Brit.); BREAKING POINT, THE(1961, Brit.); QUEEN'S GUARDS, THE(1963, Brit.); GREAT ARMORED CAR SWINDLE, THE(1964); LIFE IN DANGER(1964, Brit.); THEY'RE A WEIRD MOB(1966, Aus.); BIG SWITCH, THE(1970, Brit.); NED KELLY(1970, Brit.); SUNSTRUCK(1973, Aus.); CONFESSIONAL, THE(1977, Brit.)
James Allen
CLUE OF THE MISSING APE, THE(1953, Brit.), ph; PERIL FOR THE GUY(1956, Brit.), ph; SALVAGE GANG, THE(1958, Brit.), ph; BELSTONE FOX, THE(1976, 1976), ph
1984
STREETS OF FIRE(1984), art d
Jane Allen
WITHOUT RESERVATIONS(1946), w; SHE KNEW ALL THE ANSWERS(1941), w; JOAN OF OZARK(1942); WONDER MAN(1945); THEY LIVE BY NIGHT(1949)
Janis Allen
MEATBALLS(1979, Can.), w; DOUBLE NEGATIVE(1980, Can.), w
Jared Allen
MAN IN THE MIDDLE(1964, U.S./Brit.); BOY TEN FEET TALL, A(1965, Brit.)
Jay Presson Allen
WIVES AND LOVERS(1963), w; MARNIE(1964), w; PRIME OF MISS JEAN BRODIE, THE(1969, Brit.), w; CABARET(1972), w; TRAVELS WITH MY AUNT(1972, Brit.), w; FORTY CARATS(1973), w; FUNNY LADY(1975), w; JUST TELL ME WHAT YOU WANT(1980), p, w; PRINCE OF THE CITY(1981), w; DEATHTRAP(1982), w

Jean Allen
KID FROM SPAIN, THE(1932); MY WEAKNESS(1933)
Jeffrey Allen
MOONSHINE MOUNTAIN(1964); TWO THOUSAND MANIACS!(1964); THIS STUFF'LL KILL YA!(1971); YEAR OF THE YAHOO(1971)
Jill Allen
MARRY ME!(1949, Brit.); SALUTE THE TOFF(1952, Brit.)
Jimmie Allen
SKY PARADE(1936)
Joe Allen, Jr.
DANGEROUS MONEY(1946); ROAD TO THE BIG HOUSE(1947)
Joel Allen
FOLLOW THE BOYS(1944); STORY OF DR. WASSELL, THE(1944); GOD IS MY CO-PILOT(1945); OBJECTIVE, BURMA!(1945); PATRICK THE GREAT(1945); FIGHTER SQUADRON(1948); MALAYA(1950); SUNSET BOULEVARD(1950); STRANGERS ON A TRAIN(1951); STRIP, THE(1951); CONFIDENCE GIRL(1952); MAN FROM BLACK HILLS, THE(1952); MAVERICK, THE(1952); WILD BLUE YONDER, THE(1952); ONE DESIRE(1955)
Johannes Allen
GOLDEN MOUNTAINS(1958, Den.), w
John Allen
I'LL TURN TO YOU(1946, Brit.); SECRET PEOPLE(1952, Brit.); ONE, TWO, THREE(1961); ODD ANGRY SHOT, THE(1979, Aus.)
Misc. Talkies
ROSES BLOOM TWICE(1977)
John E. Allen
EYES OF LAURA MARS(1978)
John Edward Allen
BLADE RUNNER(1982)
John H. Allen
CHARLIE CHAN AT THE RACE TRACK(1936); MR. MUGGS RIDES AGAIN(1945)
John Henry Allen
WEDDING PRESENT(1936)
Jonelle Allen
CROSS AND THE SWITCHBLADE, THE(1970); COME BACK CIHARLESTON BLUE(1972); RIVER NIGER, THE(1976)
1984
HOTEL NEW HAMPSHIRE, THE(1984)
Joseph Allen
SEVEN KEYS TO BALDPATE(1930); GAMBLING(1934); ALL WOMEN HAVE SECRETS(1939)
Silents
GOOD-BYE, BILL(1919)
Joseph Allen, Jr.
DESPERATE WOMEN, THE(?); DEATH OF A CHAMPION(1939); LUCKY NIGHT(1939); OUR LEADING CITIZEN(1939); IT HAPPENED IN FLATBUSH(1942); MOUNTAIN RHYTHM(1942); NIGHT BEFORE THE DIVORCE, THE(1942); RIGHT TO THE HEART(1942); WHO IS HOPE SCHUYLER?(1942); MANTRAP, THE(1943); MY SON, THE HERO(1943); VALLEY OF THE HEADHUNTERS(1953)
Joseph A. Allen, Jr.
CANNIBAL ATTACK(1954)
Josephine Allen
WIFE TAKES A FLYER, THE(1942)
Joy Allen
MAN IN THE DARK(1963, Brit.)
Misc. Talkies
NIGHT OF THE DEMON(1980)
Joyce Allen
NAKED CITY, THE(1948)
Judith Allen
HELL AND HIGH WATER(1933); THIS DAY AND AGE(1933); TOO MUCH HARMONY(1933); BRIGHT EYES(1934); DANCING MAN(1934); MARRYING WIDOWS(1934); MEN OF THE NIGHT(1934); OLD-FASHIONED WAY, THE(1934); SHE LOVES ME NOT(1934); THUNDERING HERD, THE(1934); WITCHING HOUR, THE(1934); YOUNG AND BEAUTIFUL(1934); BEHIND GREEN LIGHTS(1935); HEALER, THE(1935); NIGHT ALARM(1935); RECKLESS ROADS(1935); BURNING GOLD(1936); BEWARE OF LADIES(1937); BILL CRACKS DOWN(1937); BOOTS AND SADDLES(1937); GIT ALONG, LITTLE DOGIES(1937); IT HAPPENED OUT WEST(1937); NAVY SPY(1937); TEXAS TRAIL(1937); PORT OF MISSING GIRLS(1938); TELEPHONE OPERATOR(1938); TOUGH KID(1939); WOMEN, THE(1939); FRAMED(1940); SKY MURDER(1940); TRAIN TO TOMBSTONE(1950); SOMETHING TO LIVE FOR(1952)
Misc. Talkies
PORT OF MISSING GIRLS(1938)
June Allen
AFFAIRS OF ADELAIDE(1949, U. S./Brit); TAKING TIGER MOUNTAIN(1983, U.S./Welsh)
Karen Allen
NATIONAL LAMPOON'S ANIMAL HOUSE(1978); MANHATTAN(1979); WANDERERS, THE(1979); CRUISING(1980); SMALL CIRCLE OF FRIENDS, A(1980); RAIDERS OF THE LOST ARK(1981); SHOOT THE MOON(1982); SPLIT IMAGE(1982)
1984
STARMAN(1984); UNTIL SEPTEMBER(1984)
Katherine Allen
NONE BUT THE LONELY HEART(1944)
Keith Allen
1984
LOOSE CONNECTIONS(1984, Brit.)
Ken Allen
PARRISH(1961)
Kim Allen
ONE IS A LONELY NUMBER(1972)
Kip Allen
THOMASINE AND BUSHROD(1974)
Lane Allen
NAVY BLUES(1941); NEW WINE(1941)
Larry Allen
BECAUSE OF EVE(1948), w

Lee Allen
BATTLE FLAME(1955); FUNNY GIRL(1968)
1984
STREETS OF FIRE(1984)
Leigh Allen
REBOUND(1931); SOOKY(1931); DOUBLE HARNESS(1933)
Les Allen
ROSARY, THE(1931, Brit.); HEAT WAVE(1935, Brit.)
Leslie Allen
GIRL ON THE CANAL, THE(1947, Brit.), ed; CANDIDATE, THE(1972)
Lester Allen
HEAT'S ON, THE(1943); KLONDIKE KATE(1944); DOLLY SISTERS, THE(1945); GREAT FLAMARION, THE(1945); DARK MIRROR, THE(1946); PIRATE, THE(1948); THAT LADY IN ERMINE(1948); MA AND PA KETTLE(1949); LOVE THAT BRUTE(1950); FUN ON A WEEKEND(1979)
Lewis Allen
OUR HEARTS WERE YOUNG AND GAY(1944), d; UNINVITED, THE(1944), d; THOSE ENDEARING YOUNG CHARMS(1945), d; UNSEEN, THE(1945), d; PERFECT MARRIAGE, THE(1946), d; DESERT FURY(1947), d; IMPERFECT LADY, THE(1947), d; SEALED VERDICT(1948), d; SO EVIL MY LOVE(1948, Brit.), d; CHICAGO DEADLINE(1949), d; APPOINTMENT WITH DANGER(1951), d; AT SWORD'S POINT(1951), d; VALENTINO(1951), d; SUDDENLY(1954), d; BULLET FOR JOEY, A(1955), d; ILLEGAL(1955), d; ANOTHER TIME, ANOTHER PLACE(1958), p, d; WHIRLPOOL(1959, Brit.), d; CONNECTION, THE(1962), p; LORD OF THE FLIES(1963, Brit.), p; FAHRENHEIT 451(1966, Brit.), p; NEVER CRY WOLF(1983), p
Lewis M. Allen
FORTUNE AND MEN'S EYES(1971, U.S./Can.), p
Lillian Allen
Misc. Silents
SHADOW OF DOUBT, THE(1916)
Lucille Allen
COVER GIRL(1944)
M. Alfred Allen
Silents
KAISER, BEAST OF BERLIN, THE(1918)
Mabel Allen
Silents
SOUL OF BROADWAY, THE(1915)
MacKenzie Allen
WITHOUT A TRACE(1983)
Madeline Allen
YANKEE DON(1931), w
Marguerite Allen
NORTH SEA PATROL(1939, Brit.)
Mark Allen
WHO WAS THAT LADY?(1960); GAMBLER WORE A GUN, THE(1961); HOW THE WEST WAS WON(1962); CLARENCE, THE CROSS-EYED LION(1965); MARLOWE(1969); FAREWELL, MY LOVELY(1975)
Marsh Allen
Misc. Silents
THELMA(1918, Brit.); TOWARDS THE LIGHT(1918, Brit.)
Martin Allen
MAME(1974), ch
Marty Allen
LAST OF THE SECRET AGENTS?, THE(1966); GREAT WALTZ, THE(1972); HARRAD SUMMER, THE(1974); WHALE OF A TALE, A(1977); DR. JEKYLL'S DUNGEON OF DEATH(1982), m
1984
CANNONBALL RUN II(1984)
Misc. Talkies
BALLAD OF BILLIE BLUE(1972)
Mary Allen
TOWN LIKE ALICE, A(1958, Brit.); PERSECUTION AND ASSASSINATION OF JEAN-PAUL MARAT AS PERFORMED BY THE INMATES OF THE ASYLUM OF CHARENTON UNDER THE DIRECTION OF THE MARQUIS DE SADE, THE(1967, Brit.); TELL ME LIES(1968, Brit.)
Mary Marsh Allen
Misc. Silents
WAGES OF SIN, THE(1918, Brit.); WHOSOEVER SHALL OFFEND(1919, Brit.)
Maude Allen
SMILING LIEUTENANT, THE(1931); COWBOY MILLIONAIRE(1935); IT'S IN THE AIR(1935); WHISPERING SMITH SPEAKS(1935); SAN FRANCISCO(1936); SHOW BOAT(1936); CAPTAIN'S KID, THE(1937); SECRET VALLEY(1937); PAINTED DESERT, THE(1938); LET FREEDOM RING(1939); WOMEN, THE(1939); BLACK DIAMONDS(1940); DANGER AHEAD(1940); INVISIBLE STRIPES(1940); I MARRIED AN ANGEL(1942)
Maureen Allen
SING ALONG WITH ME(1952, Brit.)
McKenzie Allen
EASY MONEY(1983)
Mel Allen
BABE RUTH STORY, THE(1948); RETURN OF DRACULA, THE(1958)
1984
FLAMINGO KID, THE(1984)
Melvin Allen
CLAMBAKE(1967)
Melvin F. Allen
ON THE NICKEL(1980)
Michael Allen
THURSDAY'S CHILD(1943, Brit.); SAN DEMETRIO, LONDON(1947, Brit.)
Mike Allen
Misc. Talkies
DEATH DRIVER(1977); HOOCH(1977)
Nancy Allen
LAST DETAIL, THE(1973); FORCED ENTRY(1975); CARRIE(1976); I WANNA HOLD YOUR HAND(1978); HOME MOVIES(1979); 1941(1979); DRESSED TO KILL(1980); BLOW OUT(1981); STRANGE INVADERS(1983)
1984
BUDDY SYSTEM, THE(1984); NOT FOR PUBLICATION(1984); PHILADELPHIA EXPERIMENT, THE(1984)

Misc. Talkies
  MONEY IN MY POCKET(1962)
Nellie Allen
Misc. Silents
  STATION CONTENT(1918)
Oliver C. Allen
Misc. Silents
  BAIT, THE(1916)
Patrick Allen
  HELL, HEAVEN OR HOBOKEN(1958, Brit.); DIAL M FOR MURDER(1954); CROSS CHANNEL(1955, Brit.); DEADLIEST SIN, THE(1956, Brit.); 1984(1956, Brit.); HIGH TIDE AT NOON(1957, Brit.); LONG HAUL, THE(1957, Brit.); PORTRAIT IN SMOKE(1957, Brit.); DUNKIRK(1958, Brit.); HIGH HELL(1958); MAN WHO WOULDN'T TALK, THE(1958, Brit.); MARK OF THE HAWK, THE(1958); TREAD SOFTLY STRANGER(1959, Brit.); JET STORM(1961, Brit.); NEVER TAKE CANDY FROM A STRANGER(1961, Brit.); NIGHT CREATURES(1962, Brit.); TRAITORS, THE(1963, Brit.); SINISTER MAN, THE(1965, Brit.); NIGHT OF THE GENERALS, THE(1967, Brit./Fr.); BODY STEALERS, THE(1969); ISLAND OF THE BURNING DAMNED(1971, Brit.); PUPPET ON A CHAIN(1971, Brit.); WHEN DINOSAURS RULED THE EARTH(1971, Brit.); PERSECUTION(1974, Brit.); WILBY CONSPIRACY, THE(1975, Brit.); WILD GEESE, THE(1978, Brit.); SEA WOLVES, THE(1981, Brit.); FINAL OPTION, THE(1983, Brit.)
Misc. Talkies
  OUT OF THIN AIR(1969)
Patrie Allen
1984
  NIGHT PATROL(1984)
Paul Allen
Silents
  ORPHANS OF THE STORM(1922), ph; DOWN TO THE SEA IN SHIPS(1923), ph; OUTLAWS OF THE SEA(1923), ph; LAST CHANCE, THE(1926), ph; LAW OF THE MOUNTED(1928), ph; ON THE DIVIDE(1928), ph; WEST OF SANTA FE(1928), ph; HEADIN' WESTWARD(1929), ph
Paul H. Allen
  LONESOME TRAIL, THE(1930), ph
Paula Allen
  NATIONAL VELVET(1944); STORY OF THREE LOVES, THE(1953)
Penelope Allen
  DOC(1971); IT AIN'T EASY(1972); ON THE NICKEL(1980); RESURRECTION(1980)
Penny Allen
  OH! WHAT A LOVELY WAR(1969, Brit.); SCARECROW(1973); DOG DAY AFTERNOON(1975); PROPERTY(1979), p,d&w
Peter Allen
  HANDS ACROSS THE TABLE(1935); SGT. PEPPER'S LONELY HEARTS CLUB BAND(1978)
Phil Allen
Misc. Talkies
  INTERPLAY(1970)
Phillip R. Allen
  MIDWAY(1976); SPECIAL DELIVERY(1976); ONION FIELD, THE(1979); MOMMIE DEAREST(1981)
Phillip Richard Allen
1984
  STAR TREK III: THE SEARCH FOR SPOCK(1984)
Phyllis Allen
Silents
  TILLIE'S PUNCTURED ROMANCE(1914); SUBMARINE PIRATE, A(1915); WHITE YOUTH(1920); PILGRIM, THE(1923)
R. S. Allen
  GIRL HAPPY(1965), w; WITH SIX YOU GET EGGROLL(1968), w; DON'T DRINK THE WATER(1969), w; HILL, THE(1965, Brit.), w; MAN CALLED FLINTSTONE, THE(1966), w; WHO'S MINDING THE MINT?(1967), w

Radford Allen
  EARL OF CHICAGO, THE(1940)
Rae Allen
  DAMN YANKEES(1958); TIGER MAKES OUT, THE(1967); WHERE'S POPPA?(1970); TAKING OFF(1971)
Silents
  INNOCENT(1918); RIGHT TO LIE, THE(1919)
Randa Allen
  YOUNGEST PROFESSION, THE(1943)
Randi Allen
  CATHY'S CURSE(1977, Can.)
Randy Allen
  SON OF SINBAD(1955)
Ray Allen
Silents
  SPITFIRE, THE(1924)
Misc. Silents
  REMORSELESS LOVE(1921)
Rebecca Allen
  FRENCH QUARTER(1978)
Reg Allen
  WHAT DID YOU DO IN THE WAR, DADDY?(1966), set d; GUNN(1967), set d; WATERHOLE NO. 3(1967), set d; DARLING LILI(1970), set d; PLAZA SUITE(1971), set d; STAR SPANGLED GIRL(1971), set d; WILD ROVERS(1971), set d; LADY SINGS THE BLUES(1972), set d; PARALLAX VIEW, THE(1974), set d; SHEILA LEVINE IS DEAD AND LIVING IN NEW YORK(1975), set d; SEXTETTE(1978), set d; 10(1979), set d
Reginald Allen
  PINK PANTHER, THE(1964), set d
Rex Allen
  ARIZONA COWBOY, THE(1950); HILLS OF OKLAHOMA(1950); REDWOOD FOREST TRAIL(1950); TRAIL OF ROBIN HOOD(1950); UNDER MEXICALI STARS(1950); RODEO KING AND THE SENORITA(1951); SILVER CITY BONANZA(1951); THUNDER IN GOD'S COUNTRY(1951); UTAH WAGON TRAIN(1951); BORDER SADDLEMATES(1952); COLORADO SUNDOWN(1952); I DREAM OF JEANIE(1952); LAST MUSKETEER, THE(1952); OLD OKLAHOMA PLAINS(1952); SOUTH PACIFIC

TRAIL(1952); DOWN LAREDO WAY(1953); IRON MOUNTAIN TRAIL(1953); OLD OVERLAND TRAIL(1953); RED RIVER SHORE(1953); SHADOWS OF TOMBSTONE(1953); PHANTOM STALLION, THE(1954); FOR THE LOVE OF MIKE(1960); TOMBOY AND THE CHAMP(1961); LEGEND OF LOBO, THE(1962); INCREDIBLE JOURNEY, THE(1963); SWAMP COUNTRY(1966); CHARLIE, THE LONESOME COUGAR(1967); CHARLOTTE'S WEB(1973); LEGEND OF COUGAR CANYON(1974)
Misc. Talkies
  LAST MUSKETEER, THE(1952); SECRET OF NAVAJO CAVE(1976)
Rica Allen
Silents
  MAD DANCER(1925)
Ricca Allen
  CLOSE HARMONY(1929); PURSUIT OF HAPPINESS, THE(1934); MEN WITHOUT NAMES(1935); TRAIL OF THE LONESOME PINE, THE(1936); EXCLUSIVE(1937); ROSALIE(1937); THREE COMRADES(1938); ONE MILLION B.C.(1940); THEY KNEW WHAT THEY WANTED(1940)
Silents
  FORGIVEN, OR THE JACK O'DIAMONDS(1914); ALADDIN'S OTHER LAMP(1917); LIFE'S WHIRLPOOL(1917); OUTWITTED(1917); OUR MRS. McCHESNEY(1918)
Misc. Silents
  POWER AND THE GLORY, THE(1918); HEADIN' HOME(1920); SONG OF THE SOUL, THE(1920)
Ricca K. Allen
  MAID OF SALEM(1937)
Richard Allen
  EXCLUSIVE(1937); NORTHERN PURSUIT(1943); O. HENRY'S FULL HOUSE(1952); EYES OF A STRANGER(1980)
Misc. Talkies
  METAL MESSIAH(1978)
Richard D. Allen
  SPRING FEVER(1983, Can.), set d
Richard E. Allen
  TIP-OFF GIRLS(1938)
Rick Allen
  TALL STORY(1960); SMOKEY AND THE BANDIT II(1980)
Ricky Allen
  PLUNDERERS OF PAINTED FLATS(1959)
Rita Allen
Silents
  SALAMANDER, THE(1915)
Robert Allen
  RECKLESS HOUR, THE(1931); MENACE(1934); AIR HAWKS(1935); BLACK ROOM, THE(1935); CRIME AND PUNISHMENT(1935); FIGHTING SHADOWS(1935); GUARD THAT GIRL(1935); I'LL LOVE YOU ALWAYS(1935); LAW BEYOND THE RANGE(1935); LOVE ME FOREVER(1935); PARTY WIRE(1935); REVENGE RIDER, THE(1935); WHITE LIES(1935); CRAIG'S WIFE(1936); LADY OF SECRETS(1936); PRIDE OF THE MARINES(1936); AWFUL TRUTH, THE(1937); HOLD'EM NAVY!(1937); LET'S GET MARRIED(1937); KEEP SMILING(1938); MEET THE GIRLS(1938); PENITENTIARY(1938); UP THE RIVER(1938); EVERYBODY'S BABY(1939); FIGHTING THOROUGHBREDS(1939); WINNER TAKE ALL(1939); WINTER CARNIVAL(1939); CITY OF CHANCE(1940); DEATH VALLEY RANGERS(1944); HAPPY ANNIVERSARY(1959), m, md; PIE IN THE SKY(1964)
1984
  FOOTLOOSE(1984)
Robert J. Allen
  PEACE FOR A GUNFIGHTER(1967), p, ph
Robert Lee Allen
Misc. Silents
  CHAMBER OF MYSTERY, THE(1920)
Roger Allen
  STUDENT PRINCE, THE(1954); LORD OF THE FLIES(1963, Brit.)
Ron Allen
  ANGEL, ANGEL, DOWN WE GO(1969)
Ronald Allen
  NIGHT TO REMEMBER, A(1958, Brit.); CIRCLE OF DECEPTION(1961, Brit.); PROJECTED MAN, THE(1967, Brit.); HELL BOATS(1970, Brit.)
Rose Allen
  DARK HOUR, THE(1936); MY FAVORITE BLONDE(1942); MIRACLE IN THE RAIN(1956)
Russ Allen
  DEAD ON COURSE(1952, Brit.); FORCES' SWEETHEART(1953, Brit.); WILL ANY GENTLEMAN?(1955, Brit.)
Russell Allen
Misc. Silents
  ROBES OF SIN(1924), d; VALLEY OF HATE, THE(1924), d
Rusty Allen
  BLACK SPURS(1965); GIRL HAPPY(1965)
Ruth Allen
  SWEETHEART OF SIGMA CHI(1946); GANGSTER, THE(1947)
Silents
  DOWN TO EARTH(1917)
Sally Allen
1984
  BREAKIN' 2: ELECTRIC BOOGALOO(1984), ed
Sam Allen
  SEA WOLF, THE(1930); LAST ROUND-UP, THE(1934)
Silents
  CONFLICT, THE(1921); SON OF THE WOLF, THE(1922); VIRGINIAN, THE(1923); BASHFUL BUCCANEER(1925); GOLD RUSH, THE(1925); SEA BEAST, THE(1926)
Misc. Silents
  TIMBER WOLF(1925); CALL OF THE KLONDIKE, THE(1926); MAN RUSTLIN'(1926); MIDNIGHT LIMITED(1926); DEATH VALLEY(1927)
Samm Allen
  COWBOY COUNSELOR(1933)
Samuel Allen
Silents
  ARE YOU A FAILURE?(1923)

Scott Arthur Allen
S.O.B.(1981)
Seth Allen
MADIGAN(1968); ME AND MY BROTHER(1969); CATCH-22(1970); HOT ROCK, THE(1972); HONEYBABY, HONEYBABY(1974)
1984
ALMOST YOU(1984); FLAMINGO KID, THE(1984)
Sheila Allen
DEADLIEST SIN, THE(1956, Brit.); CHILDREN OF THE DAMNED(1963, Brit.); ALPHABET MURDERS, THE(1966); MALPAS MYSTERY, THE(1967, Brit.); THREE INTO TWO WON'T GO(1969, Brit.); OTHER SIDE OF THE UNDERNEATH, THE(1972, Brit.); VIVA KNIEVEL!(1977); WHEN TIME RAN OUT(1980)
Sheldon Allen
END OF THE LINE, THE(1959, Brit.)
Sian Barbara Allen
YOU'LL LIKE MY MOTHER(1972); BILLY TWO HATS(1973, Brit.)
Sonny Allen
SEA GYPSIES, THE(1978), animal t
Stan Allen
HOLLYWOOD KNIGHTS, THE(1980), ed
Stanford Allen
FIFTH FLOOR, THE(1980), ed
Stanford C. Allen
TAKE A HARD RIDE(1975, U.S./Ital.), ed; BLUE BIRD, THE(1976), ed; SILENT MOVIE(1976), ed; MARCH OR DIE(1977, Brit.), ed; RABBIT TEST(1978), ed; ROCKY II(1979), ed; MORTUARY(1983), ed
Steve Allen
DOWN MEMORY LANE(1949); I'LL GET BY(1950); BENNY GOODMAN STORY, THE(1956); BIG CIRCUS, THE(1959); COLLEGE CONFIDENTIAL(1960); DON'T WORRY, WE'LL THINK OF A TITLE(1966); MAN CALLED DAGGER, A(1967), m; WARNING SHOT(1967); WHERE WERE YOU WHEN THE LIGHTS WENT OUT?(1968); COMIC, THE(1969); SUNSHINE BOYS, THE(1975); HEART BEAT(1979)
Stewart Allen
RICHARD III(1956, Brit.)
Sue Allen
DRACULA(THE DIRTY OLD MAN) (1969); YOUNG GIRLS OF ROCHEFORT, THE(1968, Fr.)
1984
RACING WITH THE MOON(1984)
Ta-Ronce Allen
HICKEY AND BOGGS(1972)
Ted Allen
GREAT RUPERT, THE(1950), w; WEBSTER BOY, THE(1962, Brit.), w
Theresa Allen
HAPPY DAYS(1930); VAGABOND KING, THE(1930)
Todd Allen
48 HOURS(1982); UNCOMMON VALOR(1983)
1984
ICE PIRATES, THE(1984); SWING SHIFT(1984)
Tom Allen
FLAMING STAR(1960); SHADOWS(1960)
1984
SPLITZ(1984), art d
Tommy Allen
STATE FAIR(1962)
Tony Allen
YOUNGBLOOD(1978)
Tyrees Allen
UP THE ACADEMY(1980)
Valeria Allen
OMAR KHAYYAM(1957)
Valerie Allen
PARDNERS(1956); THAT CERTAIN FEELING(1956); JOKER IS WILD, THE(1957); HOT SPELL(1958); I MARRIED A MONSTER FROM OUTER SPACE(1958); FIVE PENNIES, THE(1959); PILLOW TALK(1960); BELLS ARE RINGING(1960); SHOTGUN WEDDING, THE(1963); DEVIL'S BEDROOM, THE(1964); BIRDS AND THE BEES, THE(1965); COME SPY WITH ME(1967); WHAT EVER HAPPENED TO AUNT ALICE?(1969)
Vera Allen
DR. BULL(1933)
Vernett Allen
UPTIGHT(1968)
Vic Allen
Silents
OUTLAW DOG, THE(1927); SONORA KID, THE(1927)
Misc. Silents
VIC DYSON PAYS(1925)
Victor Allen
COME ON, COWBOYS(1937)
Silents
RAINBOW RANGERS(1924); DON X(1925)
Viola Allen
Silents
SCALES OF JUSTICE, THE(1914); OPEN YOUR EYES(1919)
Misc. Silents
WHITE SISTER, THE(1915)
Vivian Allen
DOC(1971)

Winifred Allen
Silents
MAN HATER, THE(1917); MAN WHO MADE GOOD, THE(1917); SECOND YOUTH(1924)
Misc. Silents
SEVENTEEN(1916); AMERICA - THAT'S ALL(1917); FOR VALOUR(1917); HAUNTED HOUSE, THE(1917); JINX JUMPER, THE(1917); LONG TRAIL, THE(1917); SUCCESSFUL FAILURE, A(1917); FROM TWO TO SIX(1918)

Woody Allen
WHAT'S NEW, PUSSYCAT?(1965, U.S./Fr.), a, w; WHAT'S UP, TIGER LILY?(1966), a, p, w; CASINO ROYALE(1967, Brit.); DON'T DRINK THE WATER(1969), w; TAKE THE MONEY AND RUN(1969), a, d, w; PUSSYCAT, PUSSYCAT, I LOVE YOU(1970), w; BANANAS(1971), a, d, w; EVERYTHING YOU ALWAYS WANTED TO KNOW ABOUT SEX, BUT WE'RE AFRAID TO ASK(1972), a, d&w; PLAY IT AGAIN, SAM(1972), a, w; SLEEPER(1973), a, d, w, m; LOVE AND DEATH(1975), a, d&w; FRONT, THE(1976); ANNIE HALL(1977), a, d, w; INTERIORS(1978), d&w; MANHATTAN(1979), a, d, w; STARDUST MEMORIES(1980), a, d&w; MIDSUMMER NIGHT'S SEX COMEDY, A(1982), a, d&w; ZELIG(1983), a, d&w
1984
BROADWAY DANNY ROSE(1984), a, d&w
Robert Allen [Craig Reynolds]
SATURDAY'S MILLIONS(1933)
Allen & Allen
Misc. Talkies
BEALE STREET MAMA(1946)
Frank Allenby
FIVE POUND MAN, THE(1937, Brit.); CRIME OF PETER FRAME, THE(1938, Brit.); RETURN OF THE SCARLET PIMPERNEL(1938, Brit.); BLACK SHEEP OF WHITEHALL, THE(1941 Brit.); NEXT OF KIN(1942, Brit.); MADAME BOVARY(1949); FLAME AND THE ARROW, THE(1950); SOLDIERS THREE(1951)
Peter Allenby
ZOO BABY(1957, Brit.); GUNS OF DARKNESS(1962, Brit.); INFORMATION RECEIVED(1962, Brit.); GREAT VAN ROBBERY, THE(1963, Brit.); SECRET DOOR, THE(1964)
Fernando Allende
MUSHROOM EATER, THE(1976, Mex.); HEARTBREAKER(1983)
Ali Alleney
PERIL FOR THE GUY(1956, Brit.)
Tamba Alleney
BEGGAR'S OPERA, THE(1953); MOBY DICK(1956, Brit.)
Bert Allens
FRAMED(1975), set d
Hazel Allensworth
NAKED KISS, THE(1964), cos
Katherine Allentuck
SUMMER OF '42(1971)
Chris Aller
WIND AND THE LION, THE(1975)
Luis Aller
TRISTANA(1970, Span./Ital./Fr.); CHARLEY-ONE-EYE(1973, Brit.); SONNY AND JED(1974, Ital.)
Michelle Aller
LADY SINGS THE BLUES(1972)
Paulette Aller
MADMAN(1982), cos
Byron Allerd
DON'T ANSWER THE PHONE(1980), m
Alexander Allerson
I DEAL IN DANGER(1966); BATTLE OF BRITAIN, THE(1969, Brit.); MC KENZIE BREAK, THE(1970); LUDWIG(1973, Ital./Ger./Fr.); WHO?(1975, Brit./Ger.); CHINESE ROULETTE(1977, Ger.); DESPAIR(1978, Ger.); LILI MARLEEN(1981, Ger.)
Jacqueline Allerton
NAUGHTY ARLETTE(1951, Brit.)
Art Allessi
CANDIDATE, THE(1964)
Johnny Allett
MY SIDE OF THE MOUNTAIN(1969), set d
Danilo Alleva
ACCATTONE!(1961, Ital.)
Alley
OFFENDERS, THE(1980), m
Kirstie Alley
STAR TREK II: THE WRATH OF KHAN(1982)
1984
BLIND DATE(1984); CHAMPIONS(1984); RUNAWAY(1984)
Ralph Alley
LAS VEGAS STORY, THE(1952)
S. Alley
THE BEACHCOMBER(1938, Brit.)
Sepp Allgeir
SILENT BARRIERS(1937, Brit.), ph
Sara Allgood
UNCLE HARRY(1945); BLACKMAIL(1929, Brit.); TO WHAT RED HELL(1929, Brit.); JUNO AND THE PAYCOCK(1930, Brit.); WORLD, THE FLESH, AND THE DEVIL, THE(1932, Brit.); FORTUNATE FOOL, THE(1933, Brit.); BRIDE OF THE LAKE(1934, Brit.); LAZYBONES(1935, Brit.); IT'S LOVE AGAIN(1936, Brit.); PASSING OF THE THIRD FLOOR BACK, THE(1936, Brit.); PEG OF OLD DRURY(1936, Brit.); SOUTHERN ROSES(1936, Brit.); SABOTAGE(1937, Brit.); SKY'S THE LIMIT, THE(1937, Brit.); STORM IN A TEACUP(1937, Brit.); KATHLEEN(1938, Ireland); FUGITIVE, THE(1940, Brit.); DR. JEKYLL AND MR. HYDE(1941); HOW GREEN WAS MY VALLEY(1941); LYDIA(1941); THAT HAMILTON WOMAN(1941); IT HAPPENED IN FLATBUSH(1942); LIFE BEGINS AT 8:30(1942); ROXIE HART(1942); THIS ABOVE ALL(1942); WAR AGAINST MRS. HADLEY, THE(1942); CITY WITHOUT MEN(1943); FOREVER AND A DAY(1943); BETWEEN TWO WORLDS(1944); JANE EYRE(1944); KEYS OF THE KINGDOM, THE(1944); LODGER, THE(1945); KITTY(1945); CLUNY BROWN(1946); SPIRAL STAIRCASE, THE(1946); FABULOUS DORSEYS, THE(1947); IVY(1947); MOTHER WORE TIGHTS(1947); MOURNING BECOMES ELECTRA(1947); MY WILD IRISH ROSE(1947); GIRL FROM MANHATTAN(1948); MAN FROM TEXAS, THE(1948); ONE TOUCH OF VENUS(1948); ACCUSED, THE(1949); CHALLENGE TO LASSIE(1949); CHEAPER BY THE DOZEN(1950); SIERRA(1950)
Sarah Allgood
NORAH O'NEALE(1934, Brit.); POT LUCK(1936, Brit.)
Fred Allhoff
I AM THE LAW(1938), w
Francesco Alliata
GOLDEN COACH, THE(1953, Fr./Ital.), p

Jean-Louis Allibert
LA MARSEILLAISE(1938, Fr.); PASSION FOR LIFE(1951, Fr.); ROYAL AFFAIRS IN VERSAILLES(1957, Fr.)
Louis Allibert
MILLION, THE(1931, Fr.)
Anick Allieres
1984
MISUNDERSTOOD(1984)
Annick Allieres
LOVE IS MY PROFESSION(1959, Fr.)
Alex Allin
Misc. Silents
MAUPRAT(1926, Fr.); LA CIQUILLE ET LE CLERGYMAN(1928, Fr.)
Michael Allin
ENTER THE DRAGON(1973), w; TRUCK TURNER(1974), w; CHECKERED FLAG OR CRASH(1978), w; FLASH GORDON(1980), w
Norman Allin
REINCARNATE, THE(1971, Can.), ph
Richard Allin
WHITE LIGHTNING(1973)
Gabriela Allina
CONTRACT, THE(1982, Pol.), art d
Margery Allingham
ROOM TO LET(1949, Brit.), w; TIGER IN THE SMOKE(1956, Brit.), w
Mark Allington
MAN OF VIOLENCE(1970, Brit.)
Michael Allinson
THREE CROOKED MEN(1958, Brit.)
Vera Allinson
CRIME ON THE HILL(1933, Brit.), w; MONEY FOR SPEED(1933, Brit.), w; BELLA DONNA(1934, Brit.), w; BLIND JUSTICE(1934, Brit.), w; BROKEN MELODY, THE(1934, Brit.), w; LASH, THE(1934, Brit.), w; TEN MINUTE ALIBI(1935, Brit.), w; GRAND FINALE(1936, Brit.), w; HOUSE BROKEN(1936, Brit.), w; ROMANCE A LA CARTE(1938, Brit.), w; BOB'S YOUR UNCLE(1941, Brit.), w; DANNY BOY(1941, Brit.), w; SHEEPDOG OF THE HILLS(1941, Brit.), w
Rene Allio
SHAMELESS OLD LADY, THE(1966, Fr.), d&w; OTHER ONE, THE(1967,Fr.), d&w
Arlene Allison
KILLING OF A CHINESE BOOKIE, THE(1976)
Bart Allison
VENGEANCE IS MINE(1948, Brit.); SKIMPY IN THE NAVY(1949, Brit.); KID FOR TWO FARTHINGS, A(1956, Brit.); TWO-HEADED SPY, THE(1959, Brit.); IT HAPPENED HERE(1966, Brit.); SMASHING TIME(1967 Brit.); RITZ, THE(1976)
Bill Allison
BONNIE PRINCE CHARLIE(1948, Brit.)
Bonny Allison
WOMEN OF DESIRE(1968)
Charles Gary Allison
FRATERNITY ROW(1977), p, w
Cindy Allison
Misc. Talkies
69 MINUTES(1977)
Cynthia Allison
LOVE AND MONEY(1982)
Dorothy Allison
MASSACRE HILL(1949, Brit.); SILKEN AFFAIR, THE(1957, Brit.)
Edmund Allison
THREE IN ONE(1956, Aus.)
Eric Allison
SCHLOCK(1973)
Hart Allison
GIDEON OF SCOTLAND YARD(1959, Brit.)
Jean Allison
DEVIL'S PARTNER, THE(1958); EDGE OF FURY(1958); STEAGLE, THE(1971); BAD COMPANY(1972); HARDCORE(1979)
Jerry Allison
GIRLS ON THE BEACH(1965)
Joe Allison
DISC JOCKEY(1951)
John Allison
SUDDEN TERROR(1970, Brit.)
Keith Allison
WHERE DOES IT HURT?(1972), a, m; PHANTOM OF THE PARADISE(1974); SEXTETTE(1978); NIGHT THE LIGHTS WENT OUT IN GEORGIA, THE(1981)
Marie Allison
WHERE DANGER LIVES(1950); TWO TICKETS TO BROADWAY(1951)
Mary Allison
Silents
WOMAN WHO FOOLED HERSELF, THE(1922); YOUTH FOR SALE(1924)
Misc. Silents
EXTRAVAGANCE(1921)
May Allison
Silents
DAVID HARUM(1915); FOOL THERE WAS, A(1915); BIG TREMAINE(1916); ALMOST MARRIED(1919); IN FOR THIRTY DAYS(1919); ISLAND OF INTRIGUE, THE(1919); ARE ALL MEN ALIKE?(1920); MARRIAGE OF WILLIAM ASHE, THE(1921); TELEPHONE GIRL, THE(1927)
Misc. Silents
BUZZARD'S SHADOW, THE(1915); END OF THE ROAD, THE(1915); SECRETARY OF FRIVOLOUS AFFAIRS, THE(1915); LIFE'S BLIND ALLEY(1916); MASKED RIDER, THE(1916); MISTER 44(1916); OTHER SIDE OF THE DOOR, THE(1916); PIDGIN ISLAND(1916); RIVER OF ROMANCE, THE(1916); HIDDEN CHILDREN, THE(1917); PROMISE, THE(1917); RETURN OF MARY, THE(1918); SOCIAL HYPOCRITES(1918); SUCCESSFUL ADVENTURE, THE(1918); TESTING OF MILDRED VANE, THE(1918); WINNING OF BEATRICE, THE(1918); CASTLES IN THE AIR(1919); FAIR AND WARMER(1919); PEGGY DOES HER DARNDEST(1919); UPLIFTERS, THE(1919); CHEATER, THE(1920); HELD IN TRUST(1920); WALK-OFFS, THE(1920); LAST CARD, THE(1921); BROAD ROAD, THE(1923); FLAPPER WIVES(1924); I WANT MY MAN(1925); WRECKAGE(1925); GREATER GLORY, THE(1926); MEN OF STEEL(1926); MISMATES(1926); HER INDISCRETIONS(1927);

ONE INCREASING PURPOSE(1927)
Patricia Allison
RUBY(1977)
1984
RACING WITH THE MOON(1984)
Steve Allison
BURGLAR, THE(1956)
Tony Allison
STORM BOY(1976, Aus.)
Vera Allison
TICKET OF LEAVE(1936, Brit.), w
Bunny Allister
CURIOUS FEMALE, THE(1969)
Claud Allister
BULLDOG DRUMMOND(1929); THREE LIVE GHOSTS(1929); CZAR OF BRODWAY, THE(1930); FLORODORA GIRL, THE(1930); SLIGHTLY SCARLET(1930); I LIKE YOUR NERVE(1931); SEA GHOST, THE(1931); MIDSHIPMAID GOB(1932, Brit.); EXCESS BAGGAGE(1933, Brit.); MEDICINE MAN, THE(1933, Brit.); SLEEPING CAR(1933, Brit.); THAT'S MY WIFE(1933, Brit.); WIVES BEWARE(1933, Brit.); LADY IS WILLING, THE(1934, Brit.); RETURN OF BULLDOG DRUMMOND, THE(1934, Brit.); THOSE WERE THE DAYS(1934, Brit.); DARK ANGEL, THE(1935); AWFUL TRUTH, THE(1937); BULLDOG DRUMMOND AT BAY(1937, Brit.); LET'S MAKE A NIGHT OF IT(1937, Brit.); LILLIAN RUSSELL(1940); NEVER GIVE A SUCKER AN EVEN BREAK(1941); YANK IN THE R.A.F., A(1941); FOREVER AND A DAY(1943); HUNDRED POUND WINDOW, THE(1943, Brit.); KISS THE BRIDE GOODBYE(1944, Brit.); DON CHICAGO(1945, Brit.); SHOWTIME(1948, Brit.); DOWN AMONG THE SHELTERING PALMS(1953); KISS ME KATE(1953); BLACK SHIELD OF FALWORTH, THE(1954)
Claude Allister
CHARMING SINNERS(1929); TRIAL OF MARY DUGAN, THE(1929); IN THE NEXT ROOM(1930); LADIES LOVE BRUTES(1930); MONTE CARLO(1930); MURDER WILL OUT(1930); SUCH MEN ARE DANGEROUS(1930); CAPTAIN APPLEJACK(1931); MEET THE WIFE(1931); PLATINUM BLONDE(1931); REACHING FOR THE MOON(1931); BLAME THE WOMAN(1932, Brit.); RETURN OF RAFFLES, THE(1932, Brit.); UNEXPECTED FATHER(1932); PRIVATE LIFE OF HENRY VIII, THE(1933); PRIVATE LIFE OF DON JUAN, THE(1934, Brit.); EVERY NIGHT AT EIGHT(1935); THREE LIVE GHOSTS(1935); DRACULA'S DAUGHTER(1936); LADY LUCK(1936); YELLOWSTONE(1936); DANGER–LOVE AT WORK(1937); KENTUCKY MOON-SHINE(1938); MEN ARE SUCH FOOLS(1938); STORM OVER BENGAL(1938); ARREST BULLDOG DRUMMOND(1939, Brit.); CAPTAIN FURY(1939); PRIDE AND PREJUDICE(1940); CHARLEY'S AUNT(1941); CONFIRM OR DENY(1941); RELUCTANT DRAGON, THE(1941); ADVENTURES OF ICHABOD AND MR. TOAD(1949); QUARTET(1949, Brit.); HONG KONG(1951)
David Allister
STATUE, THE(1971, Brit.)
1984
JIGSAW MAN, THE(1984, Brit.)
Ray Allister
MAGIC BOX, THE(1952, Brit.), w
Elvia Allman
YOU CAN'T RUN AWAY FROM IT(1956); NIGHT AT EARL CARROLL'S, A(1940); ROAD TO SINGAPORE(1940); MELODY FOR THREE(1941); SIS HOPKINS(1941); SWING IT SOLDIER(1941); SWEETHEART OF THE FLEET(1942); THREE HEARTS FOR JULIA(1943); IN SOCIETY(1944); NOOSE HANGS HIGH, THE(1948); WEEKEND WITH FATHER(1951); KETTLES IN THE OZARKS, THE(1956); BREAKFAST AT TIFFANY'S(1961); PLEASURE OF HIS COMPANY, THE(1961); NUTTY PROFESSOR, THE(1963); HONEYMOON HOTEL(1964)
Robert Allman
HONG KONG NIGHTS(1935), w; SLIGHTLY HONORABLE(1940), w
Roger Allman
FEUD OF THE WEST(1936), w; LUCKY TERROR(1936), w; SWIFTY(1936), w
Sheldon Allman
INSIDE THE MAFIA(1959); HUD(1963); SONS OF KATIE ELDER, THE(1965); NEVADA SMITH(1966); IN COLD BLOOD(1967); JONIKO AND THE KUSH TA KA(1969)
John Allmond
ATLANTIC CITY(1981, U.S./Can.)
Wendy Allnut
WHEN EIGHT BELLS TOLL(1971, Brit.)
Wendy Allnutt
OH! WHAT A LOVELY WAR(1969, Brit.); WUTHERING HEIGHTS(1970, Brit.); FROM BEYOND THE GRAVE(1974, Brit.)
The Allon Trio
THIS IS THE ARMY(1943)
Richard Allord
NORTHERN PURSUIT(1943)
William Allot
1984
SHEENA(1984)
Christopher Allport
MAN ON A SWING(1974); LINCOLN CONSPIRACY, THE(1977); DEAD AND BURIED(1981); SAVAGE WEEKEND(1983)
Misc. Talkies
BRAINWASH(1982, Brit.); CIRCLE OF POWER(1984)
Bruce Allpress
BEYOND REASONABLE DOUBT(1980, New Zeal.); SCARECROW, THE(1982, New Zealand); NATE AND HAYES(1983, U.S./New Zealand)
Julie Allred
WHATEVER HAPPENED TO BABY JANE?(1962)
Sam Allred
HONEYSUCKLE ROSE(1980)
Sammy Allred
1984
SONGWRITER(1984)
Eric Allright
TO THE DEVIL A DAUGHTER(1976, Brit./Ger.), makeup
Tyre Alls
REACHING OUT(1983)

David Allshoru
NEXT OF KIN(1983, Aus.)

May Allsion
Misc. Silents
COME-BACK, THE(1916)

Allan Allter
I'M GOING TO GET YOU ... ELLIOT BOY(1971, Can.), m

Eric Allum
EDVARD MUNCH(1976, Norway/Swed.)

Kerstii Allum
EDVARD MUNCH(1976, Norway/Swed.)

Victoria Allum
SCHIZO(1977, Brit.)

Sherry Allurd
HONKYTONK MAN(1982)

Glendon Allvine
SILVER STREAK, THE(1935), p

Pernilla Allwin
FANNY AND ALEXANDER(1983, Swed./Fr./Ger.)

Frederick Allwood
NO HAUNT FOR A GENTLEMAN(1952, Brit.), w

Peter Allwork
VON RICHTHOFEN AND BROWN(1970), ph; JUGGERNAUT(1974, Brit.), ph; EAGLE HAS LANDED, THE(1976, Brit.), ph; ACES HIGH(1977, Brit.), ph; HIGH ROAD TO CHINA(1983), aerial ph

Frank Allworth
Silents
"THAT ROYLE GIRL"(1925)

Margaret Allworthy
UNEASY TERMS(1948, Brit.); HOUR OF DECISION(1957, Brit.)

Christophe Allwright
1984
LE BAL(1984, Fr./Ital./Algeria)

Eric Allwright
GRASS IS GREENER, THE(1960), makeup; ROAD TO HONG KONG, THE(1962, U.S./Brit.), makeup; V.I.P.s, THE(1963, Brit.), makeup; NIGHT OF THE IGUANA, THE(1964), makeup; MAN FOR ALL SEASONS, A(1966, Brit.), makeup; THERE'S A GIRL IN MY SOUP(1970, Brit.), makeup; TALES THAT WITNESS MADNESS(1973, Brit.), makeup; OCTOPUSSY(1983, Brit.), makeup
1984
PASSAGE TO INDIA, A(1984, Brit.), makeup

Astrid Allwyn
GIRL FROM CALGARY(1932); HAT CHECK GIRL(1932); LADY WITH A PAST(1932); LOVE AFFAIR(1932); NIGHT MAYOR, THE(1932); BACHELOR MOTHER(1933); HELLO SISTER!(1933); IRON MASTER, THE(1933); BEGGARS IN ERMINE(1934); HE COULDN'T TAKE IT(1934); MONTE CARLO NIGHTS(1934); MYSTERY LINER(1934); SERVANTS' ENTRANCE(1934); WHITE PARADE, THE(1934); ACCENT ON YOUTH(1935); DANTE'S INFERNO(1935); HANDS ACROSS THE TABLE(1935); IT'S A SMALL WORLD(1935); ONE MORE SPRING(1935); WAY DOWN EAST(1935); CHARLIE CHAN'S SECRET(1936); DIMPLES(1936); FLYING HOSTESS(1936); FOLLOW THE FLEET(1936); STAR FOR A NIGHT(1936); STOWAWAY(1936); IT COULD HAPPEN TO YOU(1937); LOVE TAKES FLIGHT(1937); MURDER GOES TO COLLEGE(1937); VENUS MAKES TROUBLE(1937); WESTLAND CASE, THE(1937); WOMAN-WISE(1937); INTERNATIONAL CRIME(1938); HONEYMOON IN BALI(1939); LOVE AFFAIR(1939); MIRACLES FOR SALE(1939); MR. SMITH GOES TO WASHINGTON(1939); RENO(1939); GANGS OF CHICAGO(1940); LEATHER-PUSHERS, THE(1940); LONE WOLF STRIKES, THE(1940); MEET THE MISSUS(1940); CITY OF MISSING GIRLS(1941); CRACKED NUTS(1941); MELODY FOR THREE(1941); NO HANDS ON THE CLOCK(1941); PUDDIN' HEAD(1941); THERE'S MAGIC IN MUSIC(1941); UNEXPECTED UNCLE(1941); HIT PARADE OF 1943(1943)

William Allwyn
WAY AHEAD, THE(1945, Brit.), m; ISLAND OF DESIRE(1952, Brit.), m

Alice Allyn
OPERATION DAMES(1959)

Robin Allyn
1984
UNFAITHFULLY YOURS(1984)

Sandra Smith Allyn
RICH AND FAMOUS(1981)

Tony Allyn
STRANGE HOLIDAY(1969, Aus.); STONE(1974, Aus.); STUD, THE(1979, Brit.)

William Allyn
UNDER FIRE(1957); RICH AND FAMOUS(1981), p

June Allyson
YOU CAN'T RUN AWAY FROM IT(1956); BEST FOOT FORWARD(1943); GIRL CRAZY(1943); THOUSANDS CHEER(1943); MEET THE PEOPLE(1944); MUSIC FOR MILLIONS(1944); TWO GIRLS AND A SAILOR(1944); HER HIGHNESS AND THE BELLBOY(1945); SAILOR TAKES A WIFE, THE(1946); SECRET HEART, THE(1946); TILL THE CLOUDS ROLL BY(1946); TWO SISTERS FROM BOSTON(1946); GOOD NEWS(1947); HIGH BARBAREE(1947); BRIDE GOES WILD, THE(1948); THREE MUSKETEERS, THE(1948); LITTLE WOMEN(1949); STRATTON STORY, THE(1949); REFORMER AND THE REDHEAD, THE(1950); RIGHT CROSS(1950); TOO YOUNG TO KISS(1951); GIRL IN WHITE, THE(1952); BATTLE CIRCUS(1953); GLENN MILLER STORY, THE(1953); REMAINS TO BE SEEN(1953); EXECUTIVE SUITE(1954); WOMAN'S WORLD(1954); MC CONNELL STORY, THE(1955); SHRIKE, THE(1955); STRATEGIC AIR COMMAND(1955); OPPOSITE SEX, THE(1956); INTERLUDE(1957); MY MAN GODFREY(1957); STRANGER IN MY ARMS(1959); THEY ONLY KILL THEIR MASTERS(1972); BLACKOUT(1978, Fr./Can.)

Alma and Bobby
UP WITH THE LARK(1943, Brit.)

Gila Almagor
SALLAH(1965, Israel); TRUNK TO CAIRO(1966, Israel/Ger.); ESCAPE TO THE SUN(1972, Fr./Ger./Israel); OPERATION THUNDERBOLT(1978, ISRAEL)
Misc. Talkies
DEATH OF A STRANGER(1976)

Loren Almaguer
SCARFACE(1983)

Almaini
1984
COVERGIRL(1984, Can.)

Ann Alman
INCUBUS(1966)

Robert Almanza
YOUNG GRADUATES, THE(1971)

James Almanzar
INVASION OF THE STAR CREATURES(1962); QUICK AND THE DEAD, THE(1963); CHARRO(1969); WEEKEND WITH THE BABYSITTER(1970); ISLAND AT THE TOP OF THE WORLD, THE(1974); PONY EXPRESS RIDER(1976); APPLE DUMPLING GANG RIDES AGAIN, THE(1979)

Henry Almar
BUT NOT IN VAIN(1948, Brit.)

Marvin Almars
GHOST OF DRAGSTRIP HOLLOW(1959)

Almas
M(1933, Ger.)

Josef Almas
HOTEL RESERVE(1946, Brit.); MAN FROM MOROCCO, THE(1946, Brit.)

Joseph Almas
SCHOOL FOR SECRETS(1946, Brit.)

Noam Almaz
1984
LITTLE DRUMMER GIRL, THE(1984)

Humberto Almazan
RAIN FOR A DUSTY SUMMER(1971, U.S./Span.)
Misc. Talkies
DAMIEN'S ISLAND(1976)

Laurindo Almeida
STAR IS BORN, A(1954); GOODBYE, MY LADY(1956), m; MARACAIBO(1958), m; CRY TOUGH(1959), m; FLIGHT(1960), m

Antonio Almeijeiras
1984
MEMOIRS OF PRISON(1984, Braz.)

Laurindo Almenda
ESCAPE FROM SAN QUENTIN(1957), m

Nestor Almendros
SIX IN PARIS(1968, Fr.), ph; WILD RACERS, THE(1968), ph; MY NIGHT AT MAUD'S(1970, Fr.), ph; WILD CHILD, THE(1970, Fr.), ph; BED AND BOARD(1971, Fr.), ph; CLAIRE'S KNEE(1971, Fr.), ph; LA COLLECTIONNEUSE(1971, Fr.), ph; CHLOE IN THE AFTERNOON(1972, Fr.), ph; TWO ENGLISH GIRLS(1972, Fr.), ph; BORN TO KILL(1975), ph; STORY OF ADELE H., THE(1975, Fr.), ph; MADAME ROSA(1977, Fr.), ph; MAN WHO LOVED WOMEN, THE(1977, Fr.), ph; DAYS OF HEAVEN(1978), ph; GOIN' SOUTH(1978), ph; GREEN ROOM, THE(1979, Fr.), ph; KRAMER VS. KRAMER(1979), ph; BLUE LAGOON, THE(1980), ph; LOVE ON THE RUN(1980, Fr.), ph; LAST METRO, THE(1981, Fr.), ph; SOPHIE'S CHOICE(1982), ph; STILL OF THE NIGHT(1982), ph; CONFIDENTIALLY YOURS(1983, Fr.), ph; PAULINE AT THE BEACH(1983, Fr.), ph
1984
PLACES IN THE HEART(1984), ph

Ermanno Almi
CAMMINA CAMMINA(1983, Ital.), d,w,ph,ed,set d,&cos

Almine
NIGHTS OF SHAME(1961, Fr.), cos

Almirante
THREE CABALLEROS, THE(1944)

Ernesto Almirante
TO LIVE IN PEACE(1947, Ital.); ANGELINA(1948, Ital.); CHILDREN OF CHANCE(1950, Ital.); DIFFICULT YEARS(1950, Ital.); FATHER'S DILEMMA(1952, Ital.); WHITE LINE, THE(1952, Ital.); CENTO ANNI D'AMORE(1954, Ital.); WHITE SHEIK, THE(1956, Ital.)

Luigi Almirante
DREAM OF BUTTERFLY, THE(1941, Ital.); MY WIDOW AND I(1950, Ital.)

Danny Almond
HELP!(1965, Brit.)

Erin Almond
SLENDER THREAD, THE(1965)

Paul Almond
BACKFIRE!(1961, Brit.), d; ISABEL(1968, Can.), p,d&w; ACT OF THE HEART(1970, Can.), p,d&w; JOURNEY(1977, Can.), p,d&w, ed; FINAL ASSIGNMENT(1980, Can.), d
Misc. Talkies
UPS AND DOWNS(1981), d

Michael Almont
TALES THAT WITNESS MADNESS(1973, Brit.), set d

Rosario Almontes
SORCERER(1977)

Tchaka Almoravids
FIVE ON THE BLACK HAND SIDE(1973)

Antonio Almoros
CONTRABAND SPAIN(1955, Brit.)

Edith Almoslino-Assmann
WILD DUCK, THE(1977, Ger./Aust.), cos

Dean L. Almquist
SPELL OF THE HYPNOTIST(1956)

Greta Almroth
Misc. Silents
PARSON'S WIDOW, THE(1920, Den.)

Murray Alner
BIG TOWN GIRL(1937)

Wendy Alnutt
PRIEST OF LOVE(1981, Brit.)

Jean Aloise
I'LL TELL THE WORLD(1945)

John Aloisi
TOTO AND THE POACHERS(1958, Brit.)

Ray Alon
1984
COMFORT AND JOY(1984, Brit.)

Ygal Alon
CLOUDS OVER ISRAEL(1966, Israel)

Aminadav Aloni
ONCE(1974), m

Alicia Alonso
MAD DOCTOR OF BLOOD ISLAND, THE(1969, Phil./U.S.)

Arsenio Alonso
LOST BATTALION(1961, U.S./Phil.); WALLS OF HELL, THE(1964, U.S./Phil.)

Chelo Alonso
SIGN OF THE GLADIATOR(1959, Fr./Ger./Ital.); GOLIATH AND THE BARBARI-ANS(1960, Ital.); MORGAN THE PIRATE(1961, Fr./Ital.); PIRATE AND THE SLAVE GIRL(1961, Fr./Ital.); HUNS, THE(1962, Fr./Ital.); SON OF SAMSON(1962, Fr./Ital./Yugo.); ATLAS AGAINST THE CYCLOPS(1963, Ital.); GOOD, THE BAD, AND THE UGLY, THE(1967, Ital./Span.)

Ernesto Alonso
CRIMINAL LIFE OF ARCHIBALDO DE LA CRUZ, THE(1962, Mex.)

Francisco Alonso
FLAMING SIGNAL(1933)

Maria Conchita Alonso
1984
MOSCOW ON THE HUDSON(1984)

Mercedes Alonso
GUNFIGHTERS OF CASA GRANDE(1965, U.S./Span.); NARCO MEN, THE(1969, Span./Ital.), ed; NEST, THE(1982, Span.)

Pablito Alonso
COMMANDO(1962, Ital., Span., Bel., Ger.)

Trini Alonso
WEEKEND, ITALIAN STYLE(1967, Fr./Ital./Span.)

Virginia Alonso
CROSS AND THE SWITCHBLADE, THE(1970)

Cecil Alonzo
BLACK CAESAR(1973)

Gilbert Alonzo
FANCY PANTS(1950)

Jesus Alonzo, Jr.
CHANGES(1969)

John Alonzo
LONG ROPE, THE(1961); HAND OF DEATH(1962); TERROR AT BLACK FALLS(1962); INVITATION TO A GUNFIGHTER(1964); HAROLD AND MAU-DE(1971), ph; GET TO KNOW YOUR RABBIT(1972), ph; SOUNDER(1972), ph; NAKED APE, THE(1973), ph; CONRACK(1974), ph; TOM HORN(1980), ph; BLUE THUNDER(1983), ph

John A. Alonzo
BLOODY MAMA(1970), ph; VANISHING POINT(1971), ph; LADY SINGS THE BLUES(1972), ph; PETE 'N' TILLIE(1972), ph; HIT(1973), ph; CHINATOWN(1974), ph; FAREWELL, MY LOVELY(1975), ph; FORTUNE, THE(1975), ph; ONCE IS NOT ENOUGH(1975), ph; BAD NEWS BEARS, THE(1976), ph; I WILL ...I WILL ...FOR NOW(1976), ph; BLACK SUNDAY(1977), ph; CLOSE ENCOUNTERS OF THE THIRD KIND(1977), ph; WHICH WAY IS UP?(1977), ph; CASEY'S SHADOW(1978), ph; CHEAP DETECTIVE, THE(1978), ph; FM(1978), d; NORMA RAE(1979), ph; BACK ROADS(1981), ph; ZORRO, THE GAY BLADE(1981), ph; CROSS CREEK(1983), ph; SCARFACE(1983), ph
1984
RUNAWAY(1984), ph

Nora Alonzo
DEVIL'S SISTERS, THE(1966); WILD REBELS, THE(1967)

Giorgio Alorio
GOLDEN ARROW, THE(1964, Ital.), w

Matty Alou
ODD COUPLE, THE(1968)

Aleksandr Alov
PEACE TO HIM WHO ENTERS(1963, USSR), d, w

Gitta Alpar
EVERYTHING IN LIFE(1936, Brit.); GUILTY MELODY(1936, Brit.); RECORD 413(1936, Fr.); LOVES OF MADAME DUBARRY, THE(1938, Brit.); FLAME OF NEW ORLEANS, THE(1941)

Mumtaz Alpaslan
YOU CAN'T WIN 'EM ALL(1970, Brit.)

Colleen Alpaugh
DARK CORNER, THE(1946); EGG AND I, THE(1947)

Alan Alper
WILD RIDERS(1971), m

Allan Alper
SUPERCHICK(1973), m, md

Linda Alper
CHILLY SCENES OF WINTER(1982)

Mac Alper
GIRL CRAZY(1943), set d; YOUNG IDEAS(1943), set d; SEVENTH CROSS, THE(1944), set d; CLOCK, THE(1945), set d; ZIEGFELD FOLLIES(1945), set d; SO DEAR TO MY HEART(1949), set d

Murray Alper
SERGEANT YORK(; ROYAL FAMILY OF BROADWAY, THE(1930); GIRL HA-BIT(1931); HANDS ACROSS THE TABLE(1935); LITTLE BIG SHOT(1935); PUBLIC MENACE(1935); SEVEN KEYS TO BALDPATE(1935); AFTER THE THIN MAN(1936); HIGH TENSION(1936); MILKY WAY, THE(1936); NAVY WIFE(1936); TWO IN REVOLT(1936); WINTERSET(1936); ESCAPE BY NIGHT(1937); SEA DEVILS(1937); SINGING MARINE, THE(1937); THAT'S MY STORY(1937); YOU CAN'T BUY LUCK(1937); 23 ½ HOURS LEAVE(1937); COCOANUT GROVE(1938); NEXT TIME I MARRY(1938); ROAD DEMON(1938); SUBMARINE PATROL(1938); YOUNG DR. KILDARE(1938); ANOTHER THIN MAN(1939); BACHELOR MOTHER(1939); KING OF THE UNDERWORLD(1939); NIGHT OF NIGHTS, THE(1939); ROARING TWEN-TIES, THE(1939); ROSE OF WASHINGTON SQUARE(1939); TWELVE CROWDED HOURS(1939); BLACK FRIDAY(1940); BLONDIE HAS SERVANT TROUBLE(1940); GAMBLING ON THE HIGH SEAS(1940); I CAN'T GIVE YOU ANYTHING BUT LOVE, BABY(1940); LONE WOLF STRIKES, THE(1940); LUCKY PARTNERS(1940); MAN-HATTAN HEARTBEAT(1940); MY FAVORITE WIFE(1940); SAILOR'S LADY(1940); TURNABOUT(1940); AFFECTIONATELY YOURS(1941); CAUGHT IN THE DRAFT(1941); CITY, FOR CONQUEST(1941); DOWN MEXICO WAY(1941); MALTESE FALCON, THE(1941); MANPOWER(1941); MARRIED BACHELOR(1941); MR. AND MRS. SMITH(1941); MY LIFE WITH CAROLINE(1941); NAVY BLUES(1941); OBLIG-ING YOUNG LADY(1941); OUT OF THE FOG(1941); YOU'RE IN THE ARMY NOW(1941); BIG SHOT, THE(1942); DANGEROUSLY THEY LIVE(1942); GAY SIS-TERS, THE(1942); LADY BODYGUARD(1942); LADY IS WILLING, THE(1942); MY FAVORITE SPY(1942); SABOTEUR(1942); YANKEE DOODLE DANDY(1942); AIR FORCE(1943); CORVETTE K-225(1943); GOOD MORNING, JUDGE(1943); HERS TO HOLD(1943); LARCENY WITH MUSIC(1943); MUG TOWN(1943); NO TIME FOR LOVE(1943); SLIGHTLY DANGEROUS(1943); SWING FEVER(1943); THIS IS THE ARMY(1943); ARMY WIVES(1944); EVE OF ST. MARK, THE(1944); LADY IN THE DARK(1944); MOONLIGHT AND CACTUS(1944); ONCE UPON A TIME(1944); ROGER TOUHY, GANGSTER!(1944); SOMETHING FOR THE BOYS(1944); WING AND A PRAYER(1944); GOD IS MY CO-PILOT(1945); HONEYMOON AHEAD(1945); HORN BLOWS AT MIDNIGHT, THE(1945); POWER OF THE WHISTLER, THE(1945); THEY WERE EXPENDABLE(1945); ANGEL ON MY SHOULDER(1946); GALLANT BESS(1946); PHANTOM THIEF, THE(1946); GANGSTER, THE(1947); LONG NIGHT, THE(1947); BLONDIE'S SECRET(1948); FORCE OF EVIL(1948); RETURN OF OCTO-BER, THE(1948); SLEEP, MY LOVE(1948); SLIPPY MCGEE(1948); ABBOTT AND COSTELLO MEET THE KILLER, BORIS KARLOFF(1949); FREE FOR ALL(1949); ON THE TOWN(1949); TAKE ME OUT TO THE BALL GAME(1949); BLONDE DYNA-MITE(1950); LET'S GO NAVY(1951); LOST CONTINENT(1951); LULLABY OF BROADWAY, THE(1951); NAVY BOUND(1951); STRANGERS ON A TRAIN(1951); HERE COME THE MARINES(1952); NO HOLDS BARRED(1952); STEEL FIST, THE(1952); DEVIL'S CANYON(1953); JALOPY(1953); MURDER WITHOUT TEARS(1953); THREE SAILORS AND A GIRL(1953); TROUBLE ALONG THE WAY(1953); HIGHWAY DRAGNET(1954); JUNGLE GENTS(1954); SECURITY RISK(1954); TANGANYIKA(1954); BIG TIP OFF, THE(1955); JAIL BUSTERS(1955); LAS VEGAS SHAKEDOWN(1955); WOMEN'S PRISON(1955); BABY FACE NEL-SON(1957); CALYPSO JOE(1957); HOLD THAT HYPNOTIST(1957); SAY ONE FOR ME(1959); LEECH WOMAN, THE(1960); OCEAN'S ELEVEN(1960); ERRAND BOY, THE(1961); WALK ON THE WILD SIDE(1962); NUTTY PROFESSOR, THE(1963); THREE STOOGES GO AROUND THE WORLD IN A DAZE, THE(1963); DISORDERLY ORDERLY, THE(1964); PATSY, THE(1964); OUTLAWS IS COMING, THE(1965)
Misc. Talkies
BEHIND SOUTHERN LINES(1952); BORDER CITY RUSTLERS(1953)

Murry Alper
UP GOES MAISIE(1946)

Allan Alperin
SHERIFF OF REDWOOD VALLEY(1946), set d

Alperov
Misc. Silents
DAREDEVIL(1919, USSR)

Edward L. Alperson
FRONTIER DAYS(1934), p; DEVIL ON HORSEBACK, THE(1936), p; BLACK BEAU-TY(1946), p; BELLE STARR'S DAUGHTER(1947), p; TENDER YEARS, THE(1947), p; DAKOTA LIL(1950), p; SWORD OF MONTE CRISTO, THE(1951), p; ROSE OF CIMARRON(1952), p; INVADERS FROM MARS(1953), p; NEW FACES(1954), p; MO-HAWK(1956), p; COURAGE OF BLACK BEAUTY(1957), p; RESTLESS BREED, THE(1957), p; I, MOBSTER(1959), p; SEPTEMBER STORM(1960), p

Edward Alperson, Jr.
MAGNIFICENT MATADOR, THE(1955), m

Edward L. Alperson, Jr.
THREE FOR BEDROOM C(1952), p; MAGNIFICENT MATADOR, THE(1955), p; MOHAWK(1956), m; COURAGE OF BLACK BEAUTY(1957), m; RESTLESS BREED, THE(1957), m; I, MOBSTER(1959), m; SEPTEMBER STORM(1960), m

Chava Alperstein
DREAM NO MORE(1950, Palestine)

Charlotte Alpert
TWO TICKETS TO BROADWAY(1951); SON OF SINBAD(1955)

David Alpert
MAGNIFICENT YANKEE, THE(1950); IT'S A BIG COUNTRY(1951); DEATH OF A SALESMAN(1952); CHARGE AT FEATHER RIVER, THE(1953); MOONLIGHTER, THE(1953); REDHEAD FROM WYOMING, THE(1953); STAR, THE(1953); CAINE MUTINY, THE(1954); GOG(1954); BLACKBOARD JUNGLE, THE(1955); OUR MISS BROOKS(1956)

Dennis Alpert
ICE STATION ZEBRA(1968)

Gerald Alpert
LAST MOVIE, THE(1971), cos

Harvey Alpert
GONG SHOW MOVIE, THE(1980)

Henry J. Alpert
SCARECROW IN A GARDEN OF CUCUMBERS(1972), p

Herb Alpert
TEN COMMANDMENTS, THE(1956)

Herbert Alpert
CLEGG(1969, Brit.), p

Herbert S. Alpert
LAST GUNFIGHTER, THE(1961, Can.), ph; MASK, THE(1961, Can.), ph

Herman Alpert
GONG SHOW MOVIE, THE(1980)

Jerry Alpert
SOLDIER IN THE RAIN(1963), cos; GREEN BERETS, THE(1968), cos; 2000 YEARS LATER(1969), cos

Lynne Alpert
WARM IN THE BUD(1970)

Mike Alpert
1984
HOME FREE ALL(1984)

Trigger Alpert
SUN VALLEY SERENADE(1941)

Aliki Alpha
ANNA OF RHODES(1950, Gr.)

Corinne Alphen
BRAINWAVES(1983); SPRING BREAK(1983)
1984
NEW YORK NIGHTS(1984)

Jean-Paul Alphen
Misc. Talkies
HOT T-SHIRTS(1980); C.O.D.(1983)

Jean-Paul Alphen
LA MARSEILLAISE(1938, Fr.), ph; BOUDU SAVED FROM DROWNING(1967, Fr.), ph

Pat Alphin
LOVER COME BACK(1946)

Patricia Alphin
IDEA GIRL(1946); WHITE TIE AND TAILS(1946); I'LL BE YOURS(1947); SOMETHING IN THE WIND(1947); WEB, THE(1947); LARCENY(1948); UP IN CENTRAL PARK(1948); JOHNNY STOOL PIGEON(1949); MA AND PA KETTLE(1949); YES SIR, THAT'S MY BABY(1949)

Donatien Alphonse
VICE AND VIRTUE(1965, Fr./Ital.), w

Arnold Alpiger
DOWNHILL RACER(1969)

Bert Alpino
Silents
TORRENT, THE(1921)

Tony Alpino
WHERE THE BULLETS FLY(1966, Brit.)

Catherine Alric
DEAR DETECTIVE(1978, Fr.); WE'LL GROW THIN TOGETHER(1979, Fr.); ASSOCIATE, THE(1982 Fr./Ger.)

Jacques Alric
DAY OF THE JACKAL, THE(1973, Brit./Fr.)

Alsab
WINNER'S CIRCLE, THE(1948)

Arthur Alsberg
GUS(1976), w; NO DEPOSIT, NO RETURN(1976), w; HERBIE GOES TO MONTE CARLO(1977), w; HOT LEAD AND COLD FEET(1978), w

Donald Alsdurf
HAIR(1979)

Elsa Alsen
ROGUE SONG, THE(1930)

Gerhard Alsen
TAKE HER BY SURPRISE(1967, Can.), ph

Martin Alsop
Misc. Silents
HER GREAT HOUR(1916)

Martin J. Alsop
Misc. Silents
GREAT DIAMOND ROBBERY, THE(1914)

Peter Alsop
ON THE NICKEL(1980)

William Alspaugh
KILLERS THREE(1968)
1984
FIRESTARTER(1984)

Andy Alston
DR. BLOOD'S COFFIN(1961)

Barbara Alston
HERO AIN'T NOTHIN' BUT A SANDWICH, A(1977)

Bill Alston
BANK DICK, THE(1940)

Emmett Alston
MOONCHILD(1972), ph; NEW YEAR'S EVIL(1980), d, w
Misc. Talkies
THREE WAY WEEKEND(1979), d

Jim Alston
SOLOMON KING(1974), w

William Alston
ONE NIGHT IN THE TROPICS(1940)

Tommy Alsup
HONKYTONK MAN(1982)

Al Alt
HIS PRIVATE SECRETARY(1933), p
Misc. Silents
MOVING GUEST, THE(1927); RILEY OF THE RAINBOW DIVISION(1928)

Alexander Alt
Silents
DEVIL DOGS(1928)

Greg Alt
ZORRO, THE GAY BLADE(1981), w

Sarah Alt
MICROWAVE MASSACRE(1983)

Alicia Altabella
NUN AT THE CROSSROADS, A(1970, Ital./Span.)

Joe Altadonna
FINAL CHAPTER–WALKING TALL zero(1977), art d; BIG BRAWL, THE(1980), art d

Joseph M. Altadonna
MOTEL HELL(1980), art d

Vera Altaiskaya
ONCE THERE WAS A GIRL(1945, USSR)

Roberto Altamura
SWORD OF THE CONQUEROR(1962, Ital.)

Tullio Altamura
GUNS OF THE BLACK WITCH(1961, Fr./Ital.); REBEL GLADIATORS, THE(1963, Ital.); RED LIPS(1964, Fr./Ital.); BLACK VEIL FOR LISA, A(1969 Ital./Ger.)

Francesco Tullio Altan
TROPICS(1969, Ital.), w

Laura Altan
HERCULES AND THE CAPTIVE WOMEN(1963, Fr./Ital.)

Beatrice Altariba
HORROR CHAMBER OF DR. FAUSTUS, THE(1962, Fr./Ital.); YOUNG RACERS, THE(1963); CRAZY DESIRE(1964, Ital.)

Vera Altayskaya
NIGHT BEFORE CHRISTMAS, A(1963, USSR); HOUSE WITH AN ATTIC, THE(1964, USSR); MAGIC WEAVER, THE(1965, USSR); JACK FROST(1966, USSR)

Ron Altbach
ALMOST SUMMER(1978), m

Edneh Altemus
Silents
AS MAN DESIRES(1925)

Frank Alten
DESPERATE JOURNEY(1942); ONCE UPON A HONEYMOON(1942); WIFE TAKES A FLYER, THE(1942); THIS LAND IS MINE(1943); RED, HOT AND BLUE(1949)

Ronnaug Alten
PASSIONATE DEMONS, THE(1962, Norway)

Enver Altenbay
GREEN SLIME, THE(1969)

Phyllis Altenhaus
SUMMER RUN(1974)

F. Altenkirch
HIS MAJESTY, KING BALLYHOO(1931, Ger.), w

Deborah Alter
DEMENTED(1980)

Dr. Dinsmore Alter
ROPE(1948), tech adv

Eric Alter
1984
HARDBODIES(1984), w

Lou Alter
TAKE A CHANCE(1933), m

Robert Edmond Alter
RAVAGERS, THE(1979), w

Tom Alter
CHESS PLAYERS, THE(1978, India)

Hector Alterio
MAFIA, THE(1972, Arg.); NEST, THE(1982, Span.)
1984
BASILEUS QUARTET(1984, Ital.)

Gerald Alters
YOU'VE GOT TO BE SMART(1967), m&md

James Altgens
BEYOND THE TIME BARRIER(1960); FREE, WHITE AND 21(1963)

Rudy Althoff
MAN IN THE WILDERNESS(1971, U.S./Span.)

Tedi Altice
THOMASINE AND BUSHROD(1974)

Anne Altieri
BOY NAMED CHARLIE BROWN, A(1969)

Elena Altieri
BICYCLE THIEF, THE(1949, Ital.); GOLDEN COACH, THE(1953, Fr./Ital.); HIS LAST TWELVE HOURS(1953, Ital.)

Ezio Altieri
YESTERDAY, TODAY, AND TOMORROW(1964, Ital./Fr.), set d; TIGER AND THE PUSSYCAT, THE(1967, U.S., Ital.), set d&cos; PIZZA TRIANGLE, THE(1970, Ital./Span.), cos; MALICIOUS(1974, Ital.), art d; GIRL FROM TRIESTE, THE(1983, Ital.), prod d
1984
LE BAL(1984, Fr./Ital./Algeria), cos

Maj. James Altieri
DARBY'S RANGERS(1958), w

Rzio Altieri
ERNESTO(1979, Ital.), prod d

Henry Altimus
MAN WHO LIVED TWICE(1936), w; CRIME TAKES A HOLIDAY(1938), w; THEY ALL KISSED THE BRIDE(1942), w; MAN IN THE DARK(1953), w

Alaettin Altiok
DRY SUMMER(1967, Turkey)

Phyllis Altivo
INTERRUPTED MELODY(1955)

Christine Altman
DELINQUENTS, THE(1957)

Frieda Altman
HOUSE ON 92ND STREET, THE(1945); GO, MAN, GO!(1954); FAIL SAFE(1964)

Herbert S. Altman
MURDER IN MISSISSIPPI(1965), p, w; DIRTYMOUTH(1970), p,d&w

Ian Altman
PLAYERS(1979)

Jeff Altman
AMERICAN HOT WAX(1978); WACKO(1983)

Jeffrey Altman
EASY MONEY(1983)

John Altman
GREAT TRAIN ROBBERY, THE(1979, Brit.); MEMOIRS OF A SURVIVOR(1981, Brit.); REMEMBRANCE(1982, Brit.)

Karin Altman
NED KELLY(1970, Brit.)

Kate Altman
1984
PARIS, TEXAS(1984, Ger./Fr.), art d

Phil Altman
MITCHELL(1975); NIGHT MOVES(1975)

Richard Altman
ROLLERCOASTER(1977); DIFFERENT STORY, A(1978); MAIN EVENT, THE(1979); HAND, THE(1981)

Robert Altman
CHRISTMAS EVE(1947), w; DELINQUENTS, THE(1957), p,d&w; COUNTDOWN(1968), d; THAT COLD DAY IN THE PARK(1969, U.S./Can.), d; BREWSTER McCLOUD(1970), d; EVENTS(1970); M(1970), d; MC CABE AND MRS. MILLER(1971), d, w; IMAGES(1972, Ireland), d&w; LONG GOODBYE, THE(1973), d; CALIFORNIA SPLIT(1974), p, d; THIEVES LIKE US(1974), d, w; NASHVILLE(1975), p&d; BUFFALO BILL AND THE INDIANS, OR SITTING BULL'S HISTORY LESSON(1976), p&d; WELCOME TO L.A.(1976), p; LATE SHOW, THE(1977), p; THREE WO-

MEN(1977), p,d&w; REMEMBER MY NAME(1978), p; WEDDING, A(1978), p&d, w; PERFECT COUPLE, A(1979), p&d, w; QUINTET(1979), p&d, w; HEALTH(1980), d, w; POPEYE(1980), d; ENDLESS LOVE(1981); COME BACK TO THE 5 & DIME, JIMMY DEAN, JIMMY DEAN(1982), d; STREAMERS(1983), p, d
1984
  SECRET HONOR(1984), p&d
Robert B. Altman
  BODYGUARD(1948), w
Robin Altman
  GONG SHOW MOVIE, THE(1980)
Sharon Jan Altman
  STARS AND STRIPES FOREVER(1952)
Stephen Altman
  M(1970)
1984
  SECRET HONOR(1984), art d
Steve Altman
  STREAMERS(1983), art d
William Altman
  THAT CERTAIN FEELING(1956), w
Dora Altmann
  WILLY WONKA AND THE CHOCOLATE FACTORY(1971)
Bobby Alto
  MADE FOR EACH OTHER(1971); DEATH COLLECTOR(1976); PRINCE OF THE CITY(1981)
Jeannine Altobelli
  MISTER BROWN(1972)
Peter Altobelli
1984
  STARMAN(1984), makeup
Carmel Altomare
  MADE FOR EACH OTHER(1971)
Monsignor Altomonto
  ROMAN HOLIDAY(1953)
Alton
  I LOVE MELVIN(1953), ch
Bob Alton
  TWO-FACED WOMAN(1941), ch
Jack Alton
  LOVE, HONOR AND GOODBYE(1945), ph
Jeralyn Alton
  IT'S A BIG COUNTRY(1951)
John Alton
  COURAGEOUS DR. CHRISTIAN, THE(1940), ph; DR. CHRISTIAN MEETS THE WOMEN(1940), ph; THREE FACES WEST(1940), ph; DEVIL PAYS OFF, THE(1941), ph; FORCED LANDING(1941), ph; MELODY FOR THREE(1941), ph; POWER DIVE(1941), ph; REMEDY FOR RICHES(1941), ph; ICE-CAPADES REVUE(1942), ph; MOONLIGHT MASQUERADE(1942), ph; PARDON MY STRIPES(1942), ph; JOHNNY DOUGHBOY(1943), ph; SULTAN'S DAUGHTER, THE(1943), ph; ATLANTIC CITY(1944), ph; ENEMY OF WOMEN(1944), ph; LADY AND THE MONSTER, THE(1944), ph; LAKE PLACID SERENADE(1944), ph; STORM OVER LISBON(1944), ph; GIRLS OF THE BIG HOUSE(1945), ph; SONG OF MEXICO(1945), ph; AFFAIRS OF GERALDINE(1946), ph; GUY COULD CHANGE, A(1946), ph; MADONNA'S SECRET, THE(1946), ph; MAGNIFICENT ROGUE, THE(1946), ph; MURDER IN THE MUSIC HALL(1946), ph; ONE EXCITING WEEK(1946), ph; BURY ME DEAD(1947), ph; CARTER CASE, THE(1947), ph; DRIFTWOOD(1947), ph; GHOST GOES WILD, THE(1947), ph; HIT PARADE OF 1947(1947), ph; PRETENDER, THE(1947), ph; T-MEN(1947), ph; TRESPASSER, THE(1947), ph; WINTER WONDERLAND(1947), ph; WYOMING(1947), ph; CANON CITY(1948), ph; HE WALKED BY NIGHT(1948), ph; HOLLOW TRIUMPH(1948), ph; RAW DEAL(1948), ph; SPIRITUALIST, THE(1948), ph; BLACK BOOK, THE(1949), ph; BORDER INCIDENT(1949), ph; CAPTAIN CHINA(1949), ph; CROOKED WAY, THE(1949), ph; RED STALLION IN THE ROCKIES(1949), ph; DEVIL'S DOORWAY(1950), ph; FATHER OF THE BRIDE(1950), ph; GROUNDS FOR MARRIAGE(1950), ph; MYSTERY STREET(1950), ph; AMERICAN IN PARIS, AN(1951), ph; FATHER'S LITTLE DIVIDEND(1951), ph; IT'S A BIG COUNTRY(1951), ph; PEOPLE AGAINST O'HARA, THE(1951), ph; APACHE WAR SMOKE(1952), ph; TALK ABOUT A STRANGER(1952), ph; WASHINGTON STORY(1952), ph; BATTLE CIRCUS(1953), ph; COUNT THE HOURS(1953), ph; I, THE JURY(1953), ph; TAKE THE HIGH GROUND(1953), ph; CATTLE QUEEN OF MONTANA(1954), ph; DUFFY OF SAN QUENTIN(1954), ph; PASSION(1954), ph; SILVER LODE(1954), ph; STEEL CAGE, THE(1954), ph; WITNESS TO MURDER(1954), ph; BIG COMBO, THE(1955), ph; ESCAPE TO BURMA(1955), ph; PEARL OF THE SOUTH PACIFIC(1955), ph; TENNESSEE'S PARTNER(1955), ph; CATERED AFFAIR, THE(1956), ph; SLIGHTLY SCARLET(1956), ph; TEA AND SYMPATHY(1956), ph; TEAHOUSE OF THE AUGUST MOON, THE(1956), ph; DESIGNING WOMAN(1957), ph; BROTHERS KARAMAZOV, THE(1958), ph; LONELYHEARTS(1958), ph; ELMER GANTRY(1960), ph; TWELVE TO THE MOON(1960), ph
Ken Alton
  ABBOTT AND COSTELLO MEET THE MUMMY(1955); NEVER SAY GOODBYE(1956)
Kenneth Alton
  KRONOS(1957); TIME LIMIT(1957)
Leon Alton
  MAN IN THE GREY FLANNEL SUIT, THE(1956); PAL JOEY(1957); MADISON AVENUE(1962); SWEET CHARITY(1969)
Maxine Alton
  HOLD YOUR MAN(1929), w; CALL OF THE CIRCUS(1930), w
Silents
  DEVIL DOGS(1928), w; MASKED ANGEL(1928), w; LINDA(1929), w
Robert Alton
  STRIKE ME PINK(1936), ch; TWO-FACED WOMAN(1941); YOU'LL NEVER GET RICH(1941), ch; ZIEGFELD FOLLIES(1945), w, ch; HARVEY GIRLS, THE(1946), ch; TILL THE CLOUDS ROLL BY(1946), ch; MERTON OF THE MOVIES(1947), ch; EASTER PARADE(1948), ch; PIRATE, THE(1948), ch; IN THE GOOD OLD SUMMERTIME(1949), ch; ANNIE GET YOUR GUN(1950), ch; PAGAN LOVE SONG(1950), ch; SHOW BOAT(1951), ch; BELLE OF NEW YORK, THE(1952), ch; CALL ME MADAM(1953), ch; TITANIC(1953), ch; COUNTRY GIRL, THE(1954), ch; THERE'S NO BUSINESS LIKE SHOW BUSINESS(1954), ch; WHITE CHRISTMAS(1954), ch; GIRL RUSH, THE(1955), ch

Walter George Alton
  10(1979)
Misc. Talkies
  PUMA MAN, THE(1980)
Sam Altonian
  QUICK AND THE DEAD, THE(1963), p; SHELL SHOCK(1964), spec eff
Kenneth Altose
  RIDER ON A DEAD HORSE(1962), p
Antonio Altoviti
  WOMAN OF THE RIVER(1954, Fr./Ital.), w; MAN WITH THE BALLOONS, THE(1968, Ital./Fr.); THAT SPLENDID NOVEMBER(1971, Ital./Fr.), w
Lutz Altschul
  QUESTION 7(1961, U.S./Ger.)
Alice Altschuler
  MICKEY, THE KID(1939), w; SABOTAGE(1939), w; WOMAN DOCTOR(1939), w
Jane Brodsky Altschuler
  GETTING TOGETHER(1976), ed
Modest Altschuler
  FOOLS OF DESIRE(1941), md
Robert Altuna
  RING, THE(1952)
E. Altus
  GREAT CITIZEN, THE(1939, USSR)
James Altweid
  GHOST AND THE GUEST(1943), art d
James Altwell
  DAWN EXPRESS, THE(1942), set d
James Altwies
  WITHOUT RESERVATIONS(1946), set d; LADY LUCK(1946), set d; NOCTURNE(1946), set d; BACHELOR AND THE BOBBY-SOXER, THE(1947), set d; RETURN OF THE BADMEN(1948), set d; STATION WEST(1948), set d; FOLLOW ME QUIETLY(1949), set d; SET-UP, THE(1949), set d; WOMAN ON PIER 13, THE(1950), set d
Griffiths Alun
  SEVENTH DAWN, THE(1964)
Frank Alustiza
  BIG GAME, THE(1936)
Baudelio Alva
  RAINBOW ISLAND(1944)
Joseph Alva
1984
  HARRY AND SON(1984)
Luigi Alva
  BARBER OF SEVILLE, THE(1973, Ger./Fr.)
Tony Alva
  SKATEBOARD(1978)
Jon Alvar
  THIRTEEN FRIGHTENED GIRLS(1963); ISLAND OF THE BLUE DOLPHINS(1964); SHIP OF FOOLS(1965)
Carlos Alvarado
  SAILOR BE GOOD(1933)
Charles Alvarado
  ARABIAN NIGHTS(1942)
Crox Alvarado
  TOAST TO LOVE(1951, Mex.); AZTEC MUMMY, THE(1957, Mex.); CURSE OF THE AZTEC MUMMY, THE(1965, Mex.); ROBOT VS. THE AZTEC MUMMY, THE(1965, Mex.)
David Alvarado
  FANCY PANTS(1950)
Don Alvarado
  BRIDGE OF SAN LUIS REY, THE(1929); RIO RITA(1929); BAD ONE, THE(1930); BEAU IDEAL(1931); CAPTAIN THUNDER(1931); BACHELOR'S AFFAIRS(1932); KING MURDER, THE(1932); LADY WITH A PAST(1932); WESTWARD PASSAGE(1932); BLACK BEAUTY(1933); MORNING GLORY(1933); SECRET AGENT(1933, Brit.); UNDER SECRET ORDERS(1933); DEMON FOR TROUBLE, A(1934); ONCE TO EVERY BACHELOR(1934); DEVIL IS A WOMAN, THE(1935); I LIVE FOR LOVE(1935); SWEET ADELINE(1935); FEDERAL AGENT(1936); PUT ON THE SPOT(1936); RED WAGON(1936); RIO GRANDE ROMANCE(1936); ROSE OF THE RANCHO(1936); LADY ESCAPES, THE(1937); LOVE UNDER FIRE(1937); NOBODY'S BABY(1937); ROSE OF THE RIO GRANDE(1938); CAFE SOCIETY(1939); ONE NIGHT IN THE TROPICS(1940); BIG STEAL, THE(1949)
Silents
  HIS JAZZ BRIDE(1926); NIGHT CRY, THE(1926); MONKEY TALKS, THE(1927); APACHE, THE(1928); BATTLE OF THE SEXES, THE(1928); NO OTHER WOMAN(1928); SCARLET LADY, THE(1928)
Misc. Silents
  HERO OF THE BIG SNOWS, A(1926); LOVES OF CARMEN(1927); DRIFTWOOD(1928); DRUMS OF LOVE(1928)
Fernando Alvarado
  WITHOUT RESERVATIONS(1946); BARRIER, THE(1937); FALCON IN MEXICO, THE(1944); MEDAL FOR BENNY, A(1945); THRILL OF A ROMANCE(1945); GALLANT JOURNEY(1946); JEWELS OF BRANDENBURG(1947); STALLION ROAD(1947); TYCOON(1947); WAKE OF THE RED WITCH(1949); GIANT(1956)
Gina Alvarado
  SECOND THOUGHTS(1983)
Jose Alvarado
  WITHOUT RESERVATIONS(1946); LAST ROUND-UP, THE(1947); RIDE THE PINK HORSE(1947); WAKE OF THE RED WITCH(1949)
Manuel Alvarado
  POR MIS PISTOLAS(1969, Mex.); SHARK(1970, U.S./Mex.)
Trini Alvarado
  RICH KIDS(1979); TIMES SQUARE(1980)
1984
  MRS. SOFFEL(1984)
Tony Alvarenga
  WHICH WAY IS UP?(1977); WALK PROUD(1979)
Luis Alvares
  SECOND CHANCE(1953)

Abraham Alvarez
BABY BLUE MARINE(1976)

Angel Alvarez
NOT ON YOUR LIFE(1965, Ital./Span.); DJANGO(1966 Ital./Span.); OPERATION DELILAH(1966, U.S./Span.); NAVAJO JOE(1967, Ital./Span.); MERCENARY, THE(1970, Ital./Span.); CAULDRON OF DEATH, THE(1979, Ital.)

Art Alvarez
1984
FLASH OF GREEN, A(1984), set d

Carmen Alvarez
STARLIGHT OVER TEXAS(1938); LI'L ABNER(1959)

Dale Alvarez
ESCAPE FROM ALCATRAZ(1979)

Edmundo Rivera Alvarez
COUNTERPLOT(1959); CREATURE FROM THE HAUNTED SEA(1961); FIEND OF DOPE ISLAND(1961); POSSESSION OF JOEL DELANEY, THE(1972)

Elroy Alvarez
DARK RIVER(1956, Arg.)

Enrico Garcia Alvarez
EXTERMINATING ANGEL, THE(1967, Mex.)

Enrique Garcia Alvarez
INVASION OF THE VAMPIRES, THE(1961, Mex.); MACARIO(1961, Mex.)

Felix Jose Alvarez
ALAMBRISTA!(1977)

Irma Alvarez
EARTH ENTRANCED(1970, Braz.)

James Alvarez
EVIL, THE(1978), cos

Juanita Alvarez
FALCON AND THE CO-EDS, THE(1943); CURSE OF THE CAT PEOPLE, THE(1944); FALCON IN MEXICO, THE(1944); YOUTH RUNS WILD(1944)

Lily Alvarez
ALAMBRISTA!(1977)

Louis Alvarez
MIDSTREAM(1929)

Luis Alvarez
MANHUNT IN THE JUNGLE(1958); REDEEMER, THE(1965, Span.)

Miami Alvarez
LAST DANCE, THE(1930); WHARF ANGEL(1934); WEDDING NIGHT, THE(1935)

Michael Alvarez
TOO MANY GIRLS(1940)

Miguel Angel Alvarez
COUNTERPLOT(1959); FIEND OF DOPE ISLAND(1961); MADAME DEATH(1968, Mex.)

Mimi Alvarez
Misc. Talkies
DEVIL'S CANYON(1935)

Mirko Alvarez
HAND IN THE TRAP, THE(1963, Arg./Span.)

Nilda Alvarez
TOWN CALLED HELL, A(1971, Span./Brit.)

Oscar Alvarez
ROYAL HUNT OF THE SUN, THE(1969, Brit.)

Paul Alvarez
1984
WHERE THE BOYS ARE '84(1984)

Robert Alvarez
ILLIAC PASSION, THE(1968)

Ruth Alvarez
FALCON AND THE CO-EDS, THE(1943); FALCON IN MEXICO, THE(1944)

Tere Alvarez
CAVEMAN(1981)

Anne Alvaro
DANTON(1983)

Arnold Alvaro
BIONIC BOY, THE(1977, Hong Kong/Phil.), ph

Corrado Alvaro
CARMELA(1949, Ital.), w

Miami Alverez
GOOD DAME(1934)

Charles Alverson
JABBERWOCKY(1977, Brit.), w

Joe Alves
WINNING(1969), art d; PUFNSTUF(1970), art d; EMBRYO(1976), art d; CLOSE ENCOUNTERS OF THE THIRD KIND(1977), prod d; JAWS II(1978), prod d; ESCAPE FROM NEW YORK(1981), prod d; JAWS 3-D(1983), d

Joseph Alves
COMPANY OF KILLERS(1970), art d

Joseph Alves, Jr.
SUGARLAND EXPRESS, THE(1974), art d; JAWS(1975), prod d

Lidia Alves
NATIVE SON(1951, U.S., Arg.)

Vern Alves
BIG NIGHT, THE(1960), p

Piper Alvez
SLAUGHTER'S BIG RIP-OFF(1973)

Ruy Alvez
VIOLENT AND THE DAMNED, THE(1962, Braz.), m

Alvici
SCHLOCK(1973)

Tommaso Alvieri
UPPER HAND, THE(1967, Fr./Ital./Ger.); WAR ITALIAN STYLE(1967, Ital.)

Dave Alvin
1984
STREETS OF FIRE(1984)

John Alvin
NORTHERN PURSUIT(1943); DESTINATION TOKYO(1944); JANIE(1944); SULLIVANS, THE(1944); VERY THOUGHT OF YOU, THE(1944); OBJECTIVE, BURMA!(1945); ROUGHLY SPEAKING(1945); SAN ANTONIO(1945); BEAST WITH FIVE FINGERS, THE(1946); NIGHT AND DAY(1946); ONE MORE TOMORROW(1946);

SHADOW OF A WOMAN(1946); THREE STRANGERS(1946); CHEYENNE(1947); DEEP VALLEY(1947); LOVE AND LEARN(1947); UNDER COLORADO SKIES(1947); BOLD FRONTIERSMAN, THE(1948); OPEN SECRET(1948); ROCKY(1948); ROMANCE ON THE HIGH SEAS(1948); SHANGHAI CHEST, THE(1948); TRAIN TO ALCATRAZ(1948); TWO GUYS FROM TEXAS(1948); FOUNTAINHEAD, THE(1949); THIS SIDE OF THE LAW(1950); CLOSE TO MY HEART(1951); COME FILL THE CUP(1951); GOODBYE, MY FANCY(1951); MISSING WOMEN(1951); UNKNOWN MAN, THE(1951); CARRIE(1952); APRIL IN PARIS(1953); DREAM WIFE(1953); TORPEDO ALLEY(1953); DEEP IN MY HEART(1954); SHANGHAI STORY, THE(1954); BULLET FOR JOEY, A(1955); KENTUCKY RIFLE(1956); COUCH, THE(1962); IRMA LA DOUCE(1963); SOMEWHERE IN TIME(1980)

Phil Alvin
1984
STREETS OF FIRE(1984)

Alvin Saxon's Murray Club Band
STRANGE CARGO(1936, Brit.)

Anicee Alvina
FRIENDS(1971, Brit.); PAUL AND MICHELLE(1974, Fr./Brit.); SECOND WIND, A(1978, Fr.)

Kathe Alving
JUDGE AND THE SINNER, THE(1964, Ger.)

Alvino Rey and his Orchestra
LARCENY WITH MUSIC(1943)

Alvino Rey Orchestra
JAM SESSION(1944)

Alvino Rey Orchestra with the King Sisters
SING YOUR WORRIES AWAY(1942)

Rafael Alvir
FLYING DOWN TO RIO(1933)

Alfonso Alvirez
BRAVE BULLS, THE(1951)

Alvis and Capla
MURDER AT THE CABARET(1936, Brit.)

David Alvizu
SANTO Y BLUE DEMON CONTRA LOS MONSTRUOS(1968, Mex.)

Eva Alw
LOVING COUPLES(1966, Swed.)

Gabriel Alw
NIGHT IN JUNE, A(1940, Swed.); WALPURGIS NIGHT(1941, Swed.)

Sven-Goran Alw
NIGHT IN JUNE, A(1940, Swed.)

Dick Alweis
LAND OF NO RETURN, THE(1981), ed

William Bengal Alwis
ELEPHANT WALK(1954)

Jean Alwyn
Silents
GREATEST WISH IN THE WORLD, THE(1918, Brit.)

Wiliam Alwyn
MAGIC BOX, THE(1952, Brit.), m

William Alwyn
SQUADRON LEADER X(1943, Brit.), m; ON APPROVAL(1944, Brit.), m; GREAT DAY(1945, Brit.), m; NOTORIOUS GENTLEMAN(1945, Brit.), m; ADVENTURESS, THE(1946, Brit.), m; GREEN FOR DANGER(1946, Brit.), m; CAPTAIN BOYCOTT(1947, Brit.), m; ODD MAN OUT(1947, Brit.), m; ESCAPE(1948, Brit.), m; SO EVIL MY LOVE(1948, Brit.), m; TAKE MY LIFE(1948, Brit.), m; FALLEN IDOL, THE(1949, Brit.), m; HISTORY OF MR. POLLY, THE(1949, Brit.), m; CURE FOR LOVE, THE(1950, Brit.), m; GOLDEN SALAMANDER(1950, Brit.), m; MADELEINE(1950, Brit.), m; MAGNET, THE(1950, Brit.), m; MUDLARK, THE(1950, Brit.), m; ROCKING HORSE WINNER, THE(1950, Brit.), m; WINSLOW BOY, THE(1950), m; GREAT MANHUNT, THE(1951, Brit.), m; I'LL NEVER FORGET YOU(1951), m; CRASH OF SILENCE(1952, Brit.), m; CRIMSON PIRATE, THE(1952), m; NO RESTING PLACE(1952, Brit.), m; PROMOTER, THE(1952, Brit.), m; LONG MEMORY, THE(1953, Brit.), m; MASTER OF BALLANTRAE, THE(1953, U.S./Brit.), m; NIGHT WITHOUT STARS(1953, Brit.), m; MALTA STORY(1954, Brit.), m; MAN WITH A MILLION(1954, Brit.), m; PERSONAL AFFAIR(1954, Brit.), m; RAINBOW JACKET, THE(1954, Brit.), m; BEDEVILLED(1955), m; LADY GODIVA RIDES AGAIN(1955, Brit.), m; LAND OF FURY(1955 Brit.), m; SVENGALI(1955, Brit.), m, md; BLACK TENT, THE(1956, Brit.), m; SAFARI(1956), m; SHIP THAT DIED OF SHAME, THE(1956, Brit.), m; WEE GEORDIE(1956, Brit.), m; SHE PLAYED WITH FIRE(1957, Brit.), m; SMALLEST SHOW ON EARTH, THE(1957, Brit.), m; SMILEY(1957, Brit.), m; STOWAWAY GIRL(1957, Brit.), m; CARVE HER NAME WITH PRIDE(1958, Brit.), m; I ACCUSE(1958, Brit.), m; NIGHT TO REMEMBER, A(1958, Brit.), m; MAN WITH A MILLION(1954, Brit.), m; SHAKE HANDS WITH THE DEVIL(1959, Ireland), m; SILENT ENEMY, THE(1959, Brit.), m; THIRD MAN ON THE MOUNTAIN(1959), m; KILLERS OF KILIMANJARO(1960, Brit.), m; SWISS FAMILY ROBINSON(1960), m; NAKED EDGE, THE(1961), m; IN SEARCH OF THE CASTAWAYS(1962, Brit.), m; RUNNING MAN, THE(1963, Brit.), m; WALK IN THE SHADOW(1966, Brit.), m

Marthe Alycia
24 HOURS IN A WOMAN'S LIFE(1968, Fr./Ger.)

Glen Alyn
HEAD OF THE FAMILY(1933, Brit.); MAYFAIR GIRL(1933, Brit.); GRAND FINALE(1936, Brit.); IT'S IN THE BAG(1936, Brit.); DON'T GET ME WRONG(1937, Brit.); GYPSY(1937, Brit.); MAYFAIR MELODY(1937, Brit.); PERFECT CRIME, THE(1937, Brit.); SWEET DEVIL(1937, Brit.); WINDMILL, THE(1937, Brit.); YOU LIVE AND LEARN(1937, Brit.); DARK STAIRWAY, THE(1938, Brit.); IT'S IN THE BLOOD(1938, Brit.); SIMPLY TERRIFIC(1938, Brit.); SINGING COP, THE(1938, Brit.); THANK EVANS(1938, Brit.); OLD MOTHER RILEY JOINS UP(1939, Brit.); WARE CASE, THE(1939, Brit.); LAW AND DISORDER(1940, Brit.); LADY IN DISTRESS(1942, Brit.); MAYTIME IN MAYFAIR(1952, Brit.); THERE'S ALWAYS A THURSDAY(1957, Brit.)

Kirk Alyn
LUCKY JORDAN(1942); MY SISTER EILEEN(1942); YOU WERE NEVER LOVELIER(1942); GUY NAMED JOE, A(1943); IRON MAJOR, THE(1943); IS EVERYBODY HAPPY?(1943); MAN FROM THE RIO GRANDE(1943); OVERLAND MAIL ROBBERY(1943); PISTOL PACKIN' MAMA(1943); FORTY THIEVES(1944); FOUR JILLS IN A JEEP(1944); GIRL WHO DARED, THE(1944); ONCE UPON A TIME(1944); STORM OVER LISBON(1944); TIME OF THEIR LIVES, THE(1946); LITTLE MISS BROADWAY(1947); TRAP, THE(1947); THREE MUSKETEERS, THE(1948); GAMBLING HOUSE(1950); WHEN WORLDS COLLIDE(1951); EDDY DUCHIN STORY, THE(1956); SUPERMAN(1978); SCALPS(1983)

Misc. Talkies
CALL OF THE ROCKIES(1944); GOLDEN HANDS OF KURIGAL, THE(1949)
Alexei [Alyosha]
ON HIS OWN(1939, USSR)
A. Alyoshin
MAGIC WEAVER, THE(1965, USSR)
Lyle Alzado
THE DOUBLE McGUFFIN(1979)
Armand Alzamora
PUBLIC AFFAIR, A(1962); SERGEANTS 3(1962); DUEL AT DIABLO(1966); BAR-QUERO(1970); SOMETHING BIG(1971)
Claudius Alzner
FOUNTAIN OF LOVE, THE(1968, Aust.), m
Mickey Alzola
ELECTRA GLIDE IN BLUE(1973)
Howard Amacker
NO NAME ON THE BULLET(1959), w
Raymond Amade
BARBER OF SEVILLE(1949, Fr.)
Giovanni Amadei
SEVEN TASKS OF ALI BABA, THE(1963, Ital.), art d
Silvio Amadio
MINOTAUR, THE(1961, Ital.), d; PRISONER OF THE IRON MASK(1962, Fr./Ital.), w; WHITE SLAVE SHIP(1962, Fr./Ital.), d; ALL THE OTHER GIRLS DO!(1967, Ital.), d, w; MANIAC MANSION(1978, Ital.)
Jorge Amado
WILD PACK, THE(1972), w; DONA FLOR AND HER TWO HUSHANDS(1977, Braz.), d&w; KISS ME GOODBYE(1982), w
1984
GABRIELA(1984, Braz.), w
Lupe Amador
SOMETHING BIG(1971)
Ron Amador
COMING HOME(1978)
Zenaida Amador
SECRET OF THE SACRED FOREST, THE(1970)
Luis Amadori
GIRL FROM VALLADOLIO(1958, Span.), d, w
Ugo Amadoro
ATOM AGE VAMPIRE(1961, Ital.), spec eff; HERCULES AGAINST THE MOON MEN(1965, Fr./Ital.), spec eff; WAR OF THE ZOMBIES, THE(1965 Ital.), spec eff
Nydia Amagas
PHANTOM OF THE PARADISE(1974)
Nanjiwarra Amagula
LAST WAVE, THE(1978, Aus.)
Walter Amagula
LAST WAVE, THE(1978, Aus.)
Vance Amaker
PUTNEY SWOPE(1969)
O. Amalina
YOLANTA(1964, USSR); THERE WAS AN OLD COUPLE(1967, USSR)
Eugenie Amami
LADY FROM THE SEA, THE(1929, Brit.)
Eisei Amamoto
EMPEROR AND A GENERAL, THE(1968, Jap.); KING KONG ESCAPES(1968, Jap.)
Hideo Amamoto
KILL(1968, Jap.)
Hideyo Amamoto
MESSAGE FROM SPACE(1978, Jap.)
Sara Aman
PUSHER, THE(1960)
Fajni Amand
WOMAN TO WOMAN(1946, Brit.)
Lia Amanda
ALERT IN THE SOUTH(1954, Fr.); COUNT OF MONTE-CRISTO(1955, Fr., Ital.)
Amanda Productions
TURN ON TO LOVE(1969), m
Antigone Amanitis
1984
BLIND DATE(1984)
Bee Amann
Silents
KICK-OFF, THE(1926)
Misc. Silents
TRAIL OF THE HORSE THIEVES, THE(1929)
Betty Amann
PERFECT LADY, THE(1931, Brit.); RICH AND STRANGE(1932, Brit.); IN OLD MEXICO(1938); NANCY DREW–REPORTER(1939); ISLE OF FORGOTTEN SINS(1943)
Lucas Amann
DEVIL STRIKES AT NIGHT, THE(1959, Ger.)
Pelham Leigh Amann
CROSS CURRENTS(1935, Brit.), w
Marcella Saint Amant
1984
PROTOCOL(1984)
Rudolph [Anders] Amant
I MET HIM IN PARIS(1937)
Leonora Amar
CAPTAIN SCARLETT(1953)
Tarak Ben Amar
1984
MISUNDERSTOOD(1984), p
Nestor Amarale
THREE CABALLEROS, THE(1944)
Amarande
TIGHT SKIRTS, LOOSE PLEASURES(1966, Fr.); PARIS IN THE MONTH OF AUGUST(1968, Fr.)

Henry Amargo
NAKED AND THE DEAD, THE(1958)
Mario Amari
GUNMEN OF THE RIO GRANDE(1965, Fr./Ital./Span.), set d
Florencio Amarilla
EL CONDOR(1970); CHINO(1976, Ital., Span., Fr.)
Joao Amaro
KILL OR BE KILLED(1950)
John Amaro
Misc. Talkies
BACCHANALE(1970), d
Lem Amaro
Misc. Talkies
BACCHANALE(1970), d
Amaru
STILETTO(1969)
Michele Amas
ELEPHANT MAN, THE(1980, Brit.)
Rod Amateau
BUSHWHACKERS, THE(1952), d, w; HOOK, LINE AND SINKER(1969), w; PUSSYCAT, PUSSYCAT, I LOVE YOU(1970), d&w; STATUE, THE(1971, Brit.), d; WHERE DOES IT HURT?(1972), p, d, w; WILBY CONSPIRACY, THE(1975, Brit.), w; DRIVE-IN(1976), d; SENIORS, THE(1978), d
1984
LOVELINES(1984), d
Misc. Talkies
SENIORS, THE(1978), d
Rodney Amateau
IN A LONELY PLACE(1950), tech adv; MONSOON(1953), d
Edmondo Amati
HE WHO SHOOTS FIRST(1966, Ital.), p; KILL THEM ALL AND COME BACK ALONE(1970, Ital./Span.), p; EAGLE OVER LONDON(1973, Ital.), p; DON'T OPEN THE WINDOW(1974, Ital.), p; STRANGE SHADOWS IN AN EMPTY ROOM(1977, Can./Ital.), p; TEMPTER, THE(1978, Ital.), p
Edmundo Amati
DIRTY HEROES(1971, Ital./Fr./Ger.), p; CHOSEN, THE(1978, Brit./Ital.), p
Maurizio Amati
CANNIBALS IN THE STREETS(1982, Ital./Span.), p; GREAT WHITE, THE(1982, Ital.), p
Sandro Amati
CANNIBALS IN THE STREETS(1982, Ital./Span.), p
Amato
DEVIL'S DAUGHTER(1949, Fr.); INNOCENTS IN PARIS(1955, Brit.)
G. Amato
ETERNAL MELODIES(1948, Ital.), p
Gerardo Amato
PASSION OF LOVE(1982, Ital./Fr.)
Giueseppi Amato
SEVEN HILLS OF ROME, THE(1958), w
Giuseppe Amato
ANGELS OF DARKNESS(1956, Ital.), p&d, w; LA DOLCE VITA(1961, Ital./Fr.), p; FACTS OF MURDER, THE(1965, Ital.), p
Guiseppe Amato
AND THE WILD, WILD WOMEN(1961, Ital.), p
Julie Amato
Misc. Talkies
GHOST DANCE(1982)
Maria Rosa Amato
THAT SPLENDID NOVEMBER(1971, Ital./Fr.)
Mary Margaret Amato
HEART BEAT(1979); SMALL CIRCLE OF FRIENDS, A(1980); CANNERY ROW(1982); I, THE JURY(1982)
Nicolas Amato
RULES OF THE GAME, THE(1939, Fr.)
Stefano Amato
MALICIOUS(1974, Ital.)
Tony Amato, Jr.
SHAMUS(1973)
Tony Amato, Sr.
SHAMUS(1973)
Pearl Amatore
DAMSEL IN DISTRESS, A(1937)
Shichisaburo Amatsu
HAHAKIRI(1963, Jap.)
Antonio S. Amaya
SPANISH AFFAIR(1958, Span.)
Carmen Amaya
SEE MY LAWYER(1945)
Remy Amazan
LOST BATTALION(1961, U.S./Phil.), makeup; MORO WITCH DOCTOR(1964, U.S./Phil.), makeup; RAVAGERS, THE(1965, U.S./Phil.), makeup
Genevieve Ambas
LITTLE ARK, THE(1972)
Aubrey Amber
Misc. Talkies
TERROR IN THE CRYPT(1963, Span./Ital.)
Eve Amber
SUSPECT, THE(1944); WOMAN IN GREEN, THE(1945)
Gale Amber
UP IN ARMS(1944)
Jo Amber
WIDE BOY(1952, Brit.), ph
Joseph Amber
CASE OF CHARLES PEACE, THE(1949, Brit.), ph
Julie Amber
SWEET BEAT(1962, Brit.)
Lee Amber
TOUCH OF SATAN, THE(1971)

Misc. Talkies
TOUCH OF SATAN, THE(1974)

Toni Amber
MAHOGANY(1975), w

Van Amberg
CANDIDATE, THE(1972)

Aubrey Ambert
MALENKA, THE VAMPIRE(1972, Span./Ital.), p

Adriana Ambesi
BIBLE...IN THE BEGINNING, THE(1966); SECRET AGENT SUPER DRAGON(1966, Fr./Ital./Ger./Monaco); 10,000 DOLLARS BLOOD MONEY(1966, Ital.); TALL WOMEN, THE(1967, Aust./Ital./Span.); MALENKA, THE VAMPIRE(1972, Span./Ital.)

Mark Ambient
Silents
ARCADIANS, THE(1927, Brit.), w

Lars Amble
SHAME(1968, Swed.)

Dail Ambler
TAKE ME OVER(1963, Brit.), w; NIGHT AFTER NIGHT AFTER NIGHT(1970, Brit.), w

Eric Ambler
JOURNEY INTO FEAR(1942), w; BACKGROUND TO DANGER(1943), w; MASK OF DIMITRIOS, THE(1944), w; WAY AHEAD, THE(1945, Brit.), w; HOTEL RESERVE(1946, Brit.), w; OCTOBER MAN, THE(1948, Brit.), p, w; ONE WOMAN'S STORY(1949, Brit.), w; CLOUDED YELLOW, THE(1950, Brit.), w; HIGHLY DANGEROUS(1950, Brit.), w; ENCORE(1951, Brit.), w; MAGIC BOX, THE(1952, Brit.), w; PROMOTER, THE(1952, Brit.), w; CRUEL SEA, THE(1953, Brit.), w; SHOOT FIRST(1953, Brit.), w; LEASE OF LIFE(1954, Brit.), w; PURPLE PLAIN, THE(1954, Brit.), w; BATTLE HELL(1956, Brit.), w; NIGHT TO REMEMBER, A(1958, Brit.), w; WRECK OF THE MARY DEAR, THE(1959), w; MUTINY ON THE BOUNTY(1962), w; TOPKAPI(1964), w; JOURNEY INTO FEAR(1976, Can), w

Jerry Ambler
BOY FROM INDIANA(1950); FORT DEFIANCE(1951); BRONCO BUSTER(1952); GIRL IN GOLD BOOTS(1968)

Joseph Ambler
AMONG HUMAN WOLVES(1940 Brit.)

Joss Ambler
CAPTAIN'S ORDERS(1937, Brit.); LAST CURTAIN, THE(1937, Brit.); BREAK THE NEWS(1938, Brit.); CITADEL, THE(1938); CLAYDON TREASURE MYSTERY, THE(1938, Brit.); MEET MR. PENNY(1938, Brit.); COME ON GEORGE(1939, Brit.); TROUBLE BREWING(1939, Brit.); FINGERS(1940, Brit.); MURDER IN THE NIGHT(1940, Brit.); ONE NIGHT IN PARIS(1940, Brit.); BLACK SHEEP OF WHITEHALL, THE(1941 Brit.); COURAGEOUS MR. PENN, THE(1941, Brit.); GIRL IN DISTRESS(1941, Brit.); ONCE A CROOK(1941, Brit.); PRIME MINISTER, THE(1941, Brit.); BIG BLOCKADE, THE(1942, Brit.); FLYING FORTRESS(1942, Brit.); GERT AND DAISY CLEAN UP(1942, Brit.); MUCH TOO SHY(1942, Brit.); NEXT OF KIN(1942, Brit.); PETERVILLE DIAMOND, THE(1942, Brit.); BATTLE FOR MUSIC(1943, Brit.); HAPPIDROME(1943, Brit.); HEADLINE(1943, Brit.); RHYTHM SERENADE(1943, Brit.); SOMEWHERE IN CIVVIES(1943, Brit.); CANDLES AT NINE(1944, Brit.); GIVE ME THE STARS(1944, Brit.); WORLD OWES ME A LIVING, THE(1944, Brit.); HALF-WAY HOUSE, THE(1945, Brit.); HERE COMES THE SUN(1945, Brit.); I'LL BE YOUR SWEETHEART(1945, Brit.); SILVER FLEET, THE(1945, Brit.); THEY WERE SISTERS(1945, Brit.); HONEYMOON HOTEL(1946, Brit.); YEARS BETWEEN, THE(1947, Brit.); MINE OWN EXECUTIONER(1948, Brit.); AGITATOR, THE(1949); MAGNET, THE(1950, Brit.); TAMING OF DOROTHY, THE(1950, Brit.); PASSIONATE SENTRY, THE(1952, Brit.); SOMETHING MONEY CAN'T BUY(1952, Brit.); CAPTAIN'S PARADISE, THE(1953, Brit.); GHOST SHIP(1953, Brit.); HARASSED HERO, THE(1954, Brit.); JOHN WESLEY(1954, Brit.); MISS TULIP STAYS THE NIGHT(1955, Brit.); GENTLE TOUCH, THE(1956, Brit.); SPIN A DARK WEB(1956, Brit.); THIRD KEY, THE(1957, Brit.); DUNKIRK(1958, Brit.)

Kim Ambler
HOME MOVIES(1979), w

William Ambler
NONE BUT THE LONELY HEART(1944)

Caiyu Ambol
REAL GLORY, THE(1939)

Jo "Joe" Ambor
TERROR SHIP(1954, Brit.), ph

Joe Ambor
FLOATING DUTCHMAN, THE(1953, Brit.), ph; COSMIC MONSTERS(1958, Brit.), w; JOHN OF THE FAIR(1962, Brit.), ph

Josef Ambor
BRAIN MACHINE, THE(1955, Brit.), ph; CASE OF THE RED MONKEY(1955, Brit.), ph; WRONG NUMBER(1959, Brit.), ph

Domingo Ambriz
ALAMBRISTA!(1977); JERK, THE(1979); METEOR(1979); WALK PROUD(1979); GREEN ICE(1981, Brit.); BEYOND THE LIMIT(1983); STAR CHAMBER, THE(1983); TWILIGHT ZONE–THE MOVIE(1983)

Hal Ambro
MAKE MINE MUSIC(1946), anim; SONG OF THE SOUTH(1946), anim; MELODY TIME(1948), animators; CINDERELLA(1950), anim; ALICE IN WONDERLAND(1951), anim; PETER PAN(1953), anim; LADY AND THE TRAMP(1955), anim; SLEEPING BEAUTY(1959), anim; ONE HUNDRED AND ONE DALMATIANS(1961), anim; GAY PURR-EE(1962), anim; MARY POPPINS(1964), anim; PHANTOM TOLLBOOTH, THE(1970), anim; RAGGEDY ANN AND ANDY(1977), anim; HEIDI'S SONG(1982), anim

Will Ambro
HER PANELLED DOOR(1951, Brit.); FRANCHISE AFFAIR, THE(1952, Brit.); TRAIN OF EVENTS(1952, Brit.)

Adriano Ambrogi
PRINCE OF FOXES(1949); DEPORTED(1950); THREE STEPS NORTH(1951); WHEN IN ROME(1952)

Armando Ambrogi
ROMAN HOLIDAY(1953)

Rinaldo Ambrogi
VOLCANO(1953, Ital.)

Otto Ambros
HOW TO SEDUCE A PLAYBOY(1968, Aust./Fr./Ital.)

Ambrose
PLAYBOY, THE(1942, Brit.); MEN AGAINST THE SUN(1953, Brit.)

Anna Ambrose
Misc. Talkies
PHOELIX(1979), d

David Ambrose
BEHIND THE IRON MASK(1977), w; FINAL COUNTDOWN, THE(1980), w; SURVIVOR(1980, Aus.), w

Elwyn Ambrose
CARETAKERS DAUGHTER, THE(1952, Brit.), w

Paul Ambrose
LADY LIBERTY(1972, Ital./Fr.)
1984
SECRET PLACES(1984, Brit.)

Tish Ambrose
Misc. Talkies
IN LOVE(1983)

Valerie Ambrose
SALLY FIELDGOOD & CO.(1975, Can.)

Ambrose's Orchestra
PLAYBOY, THE(1942, Brit.)

Ezio Ambrosetti
PASSION(1983, Fr./Switz.)

Guglielmo Ambrosi
WATERLOO(1970, Ital./USSR)

Maria Ambrosino
DORIAN GRAY(1970, Ital./Brit./Ger./Liechtenstein), art d

Mario Ambrosino
WHITE SISTER(1973, Ital./Span./Fr.), cos

Arturo Ambrosio
Misc. Silents
QUO VADIS?(1925, Ital.), d

Irene Ambrus
VIENNA, CITY OF SONGS(1931, Ger.)

Don Ameche
CLIVE OF INDIA(1935); LADIES IN LOVE(1936); ONE IN A MILLION(1936); RAMONA(1936); SINS OF MAN(1936); FIFTY ROADS TO TOWN(1937); LOVE IS NEWS(1937); LOVE UNDER FIRE(1937); YOU CAN'T HAVE EVERYTHING(1937); ALEXANDER'S RAGTIME BAND(1938); GATEWAY(1938); HAPPY LANDING(1938); IN OLD CHICAGO(1938); JOSETTE(1938); HOLLYWOOD CAVALCADE(1939); MIDNIGHT(1939); STORY OF ALEXANDER GRAHAM BELL, THE(1939); SWANEE RIVER(1939); THREE MUSKETEERS, THE(1939); DOWN ARGENTINE WAY(1940); FOUR SONS(1940); LILLIAN RUSSELL(1940); CONFIRM OR DENY(1941); FEMININE TOUCH, THE(1941); KISS THE BOYS GOODBYE(1941); MOON OVER MIAMI(1941); THAT NIGHT IN RIO(1941); GIRL TROUBLE(1942); MAGNIFICENT DOPE, THE(1942); HAPPY LAND(1943); HEAVEN CAN WAIT(1943); SOMETHING TO SHOUT ABOUT(1943); GREENWICH VILLAGE(1944); WING AND A PRAYER(1944); GUEST WIFE(1945); IT'S IN THE BAG(1945); SO GOES MY LOVE(1946); THAT'S MY MAN(1947); SLEEP, MY LOVE(1948); SLIGHTLY FRENCH(1949); FEVER IN THE BLOOD, A(1961); PICTURE MOMMY DEAD(1966); BOATNIKS, THE(1970); SUPPOSE THEY GAVE A WAR AND NOBODY CAME?(1970); TRADING PLACES(1983)

Jim Ameche
STORY OF MANKIND, THE(1957)

Amedde
GREEN MARE, THE(1961, Fr./Ital.)

Amedee
FORBIDDEN GAMES(1953, Fr.); GERVAISE(1956, Fr.); GATES OF PARIS(1958, Fr./Ital.); LONG ABSENCE, THE(1962, Fr./Ital.); NUDE IN HIS POCKET(1962, Fr.)

Sergio Amedei
DIFFICULT YEARS(1950, Ital.), w; STROMBOLI(1950, Ital.), w; SECRETS D'ALCOVE(1954, Fr./Ital.), w

Salamon Amedeo
DAISY MILLER(1974)

Pehelwan Ameer
TARZAN GOES TO INDIA(1962, U.S./Brit./Switz.)

Rafi Ameer
GURU, THE(1969, U.S./India)

Gianni Amelio
BLOW TO THE HEART(1983, Ital.), d, w

Lucio Amelio
END OF THE WORLD(in Our Usual Bed In a Night Full of Rain), THE*1/2 (1978, Ital.); SEVEN BEAUTIES(1976, Ital.)

Sonia Amelio
WILD BUNCH, THE(1969)

Carol Amen
TESTAMENT(1983), w

The Amen Corner
SCREAM AND SCREAM AGAIN(1970, Brit.)

Nick Amend
BUGSY MALONE(1976, Brit.)

Anna Amendola
FRENCH CANCAN(1956, Fr.)

Ferruccio Amendola
GREAT WAR, THE(1961, Fr., Ital.)

Mario Amendola
TEACHER AND THE MIRACLE, THE(1961, Ital./Span.), w; KILL OR BE KILLED(1967, Ital.), w; BATTLE OF THE AMAZONS(1973, Ital./Span.), w; SONNY AND JED(1974, Ital.), w; CRIME AT PORTA ROMANA(1980, Ital.), w

Don Amendolia
WITHOUT A TRACE(1983)

Rudolf Amendt
STAMBOUL QUEST(1934)

Rudolf Amendt [Anders]
WHEN STRANGERS MARRY(1933); FOUNTAIN, THE(1934); GOLDEN ARROW, THE(1936); WE'RE IN THE LEGION NOW(1937); MAD EMPRESS, THE(1940)

Don Ament
DRAGSTRIP GIRL(1957), art d; INVASION OF THE SAUCER MEN(1957), art d; MOTORCYCLE GANG(1957), art d; REFORM SCHOOL GIRL(1957), art d; HIGH SCHOOL HELLCATS(1958), art d; HOT ROD GANG(1958), art d; JET ATTACK(1958), art d; SUICIDE BATTALION(1958), art d; ATOMIC SUBMARINE, THE(1960), art d;

VALLEY OF THE DRAGONS(1961), art d; DON'T KNOCK THE TWIST(1962), art d; INTERNS, THE(1962), art d; THREE STOOGES IN ORBIT, THE(1962), art d; THREE STOOGES MEET HERCULES, THE(1962), art d; UNDERWATER CITY, THE(1962), art d; MAN FROM THE DINERS' CLUB, THE(1963), art d; THIRTEEN FRIGHTENED GIRLS(1963), art d; THREE STOOGES GO AROUND THE WORLD IN A DAZE, THE(1963), art d; NEW INTERNS, THE(1964), art d; REQUIEM FOR A GUNFIGHTER(1965), art d; YOUNG DILLINGER(1965), art d

Duane Ament
THREE STOOGES IN ORBIT, THE(1962); BEACH PARTY(1963); OPERATION BIKINI(1963); MUSCLE BEACH PARTY(1964)

Ahmed Amer
RED SHEIK, THE(1963, Ital.)

Nicholas Amer
HENRY VIII AND HIS SIX WIVES(1972, Brit.); MOHAMMAD, MESSENGER OF GOD(1976, Lebanon/Brit.); DRAUGHTSMAN'S CONTRACT, THE(1983, Brit.)

Alex Ameri
THIS STUFF'LL KILL YA!(1971), ph; YEAR OF THE YAHOO(1971), ph

Paul America
CIAO MANHATTAN(1973)

The American Ballet of the Metropolitan Opera
GOLDWYN FOLLIES, THE(1938)

The American Clippers Band
FLYING DOWN TO RIO(1933)

Members of the American Conservatory Theatre
PETULIA(1968, U.S./Brit.)

The American GI Chorus
NORTHWEST OUTPOST(1947)

The American Legion Zouaves
COURT JESTER, THE(1956)

American military personnel stationed in Germany
BIG LIFT, THE(1950)

American Music Band
TRIP, THE(1967), m

The American Revolution
BORN WILD(1968)

Alex Ameripoor
WIZARD OF GORE, THE(1970), a, ph

Eskandar Ameripoor
WIZARD OF GORE, THE(1970), ed; THIS STUFF'LL KILL YA!(1971), ed; YEAR OF THE YAHOO(1971), ed

Frank Amerise
UNDER THE PAMPAS MOON(1935)

Cecilia Amerling
1984
BROADWAY DANNY ROSE(1984)

Kathy Amerman
JOHNNY VIK(1973)

Lockhart Amerman
GUNS IN THE HEATHER(1968, Brit.), w

John Amero
CHECKMATE(1973), p

Lem Amero
SATAN'S BED(1965), makeup; CHECKMATE(1973), d, ed
Misc. Talkies
R.S.V.P.(1984), d

Albert Amerson
KNIGHTRIDERS(1981)

Adrianne Ames
FUGITIVES FOR A NIGHT(1938)

Adrienne Ames
GIRLS ABOUT TOWN(1931); HUSBAND'S HOLIDAY(1931); 24 HOURS(1931); GUILTY AS HELL(1932); SINNERS IN THE SUN(1932); TWO KINDS OF WOMEN(1932); AVENGER, THE(1933); BEDTIME STORY, A(1933); BROADWAY BAD(1933); DEATH KISS, THE(1933); DISGRACED(1933); FROM HELL TO HEAVEN(1933); GEORGE WHITE'S SCANDALS(1934); OLD-FASHIONED WAY, THE(1934); YOU'RE TELLING ME(1934); ABDUL THE DAMNED(1935, Brit.); BLACK SHEEP(1935); GIGOLETTE(1935); HARMONY LANE(1935); LADIES LOVE DANGER(1935); WOMAN WANTED(1935); CITY GIRL(1938); SLANDER HOUSE(1938); PANAMA PATROL(1939); ZERO HOUR, THE(1939)

Alice Ames
Misc. Talkies
TEASERS, THE(1977)

Allyson Ames
PHANTOM PLANET, THE(1961); TOO LATE BLUES(1962); HOUSE IS NOT A HOME, A(1964); INCUBUS(1966); SIMON, KING OF THE WITCHES(1971)

Amanda Ames
GERONIMO(1962)

Barbara Ames
BACHELOR PARTY, THE(1957)

Carolyn Ames
Misc. Talkies
MY FRIENDS NEED KILLING(1984)

Christine Ames [Margaret Morrison Smith]
HUMAN SIDE, THE(1934), w

Cindy Ames
BELOVED INFIDEL(1959); CAREER GIRL(1960)

Delano Ames
SHE SHALL HAVE MURDER(1950, Brit.), w

Don Ames
HARRY AND WALTER GO TO NEW YORK(1976)

E. Preston Ames
EARTHQUAKE(1974), art d

Ed Ames
Misc. Talkies
CRICKET OF THE HEARTH, THE(1968)

Elsie Ames
HOUDINI(1953); WOMAN UNDER THE INFLUENCE, A(1974)

Florenz Ames
VIVA ZAPATA!(1952); HUMAN JUNGLE, THE(1954); MAN WITH THE GUN(1955); TEXAS LADY(1955); FASTEST GUN ALIVE(1956); GIRL HE LEFT BEHIND, THE(1956); HE LAUGHED LAST(1956); THAT CERTAIN FEELING(1956); BIG CAPER, THE(1957); DEADLY MANTIS, THE(1957); TEACHER'S PET(1958)

Floyd Ames
Misc. Silents
LOVE OF PAQUITA, THE(1927)

Francine Ames
OVER 21(1945)

Gerald Ames
Silents
LOVE IN A WOOD(1915, Brit.); PRISONER OF ZENDA, THE(1915, Brit.); RUPERT OF HENTZAU(1915, Brit.); ARSENE LUPIN(1916, Brit.); GREATER NEED, THE(1916, Brit.); KING'S DAUGHTER, THE(1916, Brit.); PRINCESS OF HAPPY CHANCE, THE(1916, Brit.); RAGGED MESSENGER, THE(1917, Brit.); ADAM BEDE(1918, Brit.); MISSING THE TIDE(1918, Brit.); PEEP BEHIND THE SCENES, A(1918, Brit.); RED POTTAGE(1918, Brit.); NATURE OF THE BEAST, THE(1919, Brit.); POSSESSION(1919, Brit.); ALF'S BUTTON(1920, Brit.); ANNA THE ADVENTURESS(1920, Brit.); AYLWIN(1920, Brit.); ONCE ABOARD THE LUGGER(1920, Brit.), d; MR. JUSTICE RAFFLES(1921, Brit.), a, d
Misc. Silents
CHRISTIAN, THE(1915, Brit.); DERBY WINNER, THE(1915, Brit.); HIS VINDICATION(1915, Brit.); MAN OF HIS WORD, A(1915, Brit.); MIDDLEMAN, THE(1915, Brit.); SHULMATE, THE(1915); SONS OF SATAN, THE(1915, Brit.); WHOSO DIGGETH A PIT(1915, Brit.); 1914(1915, Brit.); FOLLY OF DESIRE, THE OR THE SHULAMITE(1916); ME AND M'PAL(1916, Brit.); UNDER SUSPICION(1916, Brit.); WHEN KNIGHTS WERE BOLD(1916, Brit.); GAMBLE FOR LOVE, A(1917, Brit.); BOUNDARY HOUSE(1918, Brit.); FORTUNE AT STAKE, A(1918, Brit.); TURF CONSPIRACY, A(1918, Brit.); COMRADESHIP(1919, Brit.); FOREST ON THE HILL, THE(1919, Brit); IRRESISTIBLE FLAPPER, THE(1919, Brit.); SHEBA(1919, Brit.); SUNKEN ROCKS(1919, Brit.); HELEN OF FOUR GATES(1920, Brit.); JOHN FORREST FINDS HIMSELF(1920, Brit.); TANSY(1921, Brit.); WILD HEATHER(1921, Brit.); GOD'S PRODIGAL(1923, Brit.); LOVES OF MARY, QUEEN OF SCOTS, THE(1923); ROYAL DIVORCE, A(1923, Brit.); LITTLE PEOPLE, THE(1926, Brit.); KING'S HIGHWAY, THE(1927, Brit.); DOLORES(1928, Brit.)

Heather Ames
BLOOD OF DRACULA(1957); HIGH SCHOOL HELLCATS(1958); HOT ANGEL, THE(1958); HOW TO MAKE A MONSTER(1958)

James Ames
CANON CITY(1948)

Jean Ames
INTERNATIONAL SQUADRON(1941); MANPOWER(1941); MILLION DOLLAR BABY(1941); NAVY BLUES(1941); ALL THROUGH THE NIGHT(1942); LARCENY, INC.(1942); MALE ANIMAL, THE(1942); POWERS GIRL, THE(1942); FOLLOW THE BAND(1943); TRUCK BUSTERS(1943)

Jim Ames
SILVER RIVER(1948)

Jimmy Ames
LOVE CRAZY(1941); SLEEPYTIME GAL(1942); KISMET(1944); TIMBER QUEEN(1944); CHASE, THE(1946); WHISTLE STOP(1946); DAISY KENYON(1947); FOREVER AMBER(1947); RIDE THE PINK HORSE(1947); RIVER LADY(1948); SMART WOMAN(1948); LUCKY STIFF, THE(1949); TOO LATE FOR TEARS(1949); HE RAN ALL THE WAY(1951); TOO YOUNG TO KISS(1951); SHE'S WORKING HER WAY THROUGH COLLEGE(1952); ROGUE COP(1954); WOMAN OBSESSED(1959); SWINGIN' ALONG(1962)

Joyce Ames
HELLO, DOLLY!(1969); TODD KILLINGS, THE(1971)

Judith Ames
WHEN WORLDS COLLIDE(1951); TURNING POINT, THE(1952); RICOCHET ROMANCE(1954); OREGON PASSAGE(1958); GUNFIGHTERS OF ABILENE(1960)

Julia Ames
JUST FOR THE HELL OF IT(1968)

Leon Ames
QUICK MILLIONS(1931); CANNONBALL EXPRESS(1932); THIRTEEN WOMEN(1932); NOW I'LL TELL(1934); GET THAT MAN(1935); MUTINY AHEAD(1935); STRANGERS ALL(1935); CHARLIE CHAN ON BROADWAY(1937); DANGEROUSLY YOURS(1937); DEATH IN THE SKY(1937); MURDER IN GREENWICH VILLAGE(1937); 45 FATHERS(1937); CIPHER BUREAU(1938); COME ON, LEATHERNECKS(1938); INTERNATIONAL SETTLEMENT(1938); ISLAND IN THE SKY(1938); MYSTERIOUS MR. MOTO(1938); SECRETS OF A NURSE(1938); SPY RING, THE(1938); STRANGE FACES(1938); SUEZ(1938); WALKING DOWN BROADWAY(1938); CALLING ALL MARINES(1939); CODE OF THE STREETS(1939); FUGITIVE AT LARGE(1939); I WAS A CONVICT(1939); LEGION OF LOST FLYERS(1939); MAN OF CONQUEST(1939); MARSHAL OF MESA CITY, THE(1939); MR. MOTO IN DANGER ISLAND(1939); PACK UP YOUR TROUBLES(1939); PANAMA PATROL(1939); RISKY BUSINESS(1939); THUNDER AFLOAT(1939); EAST SIDE KIDS(1940); ELLERY QUEEN AND THE MURDER RING(1941); NO GREATER SIN(1941); CRIME DOCTOR(1943); IRON MAJOR, THE(1943); MEET ME IN ST. LOUIS(1944); THIN MAN GOES HOME, THE(1944); THIRTY SECONDS OVER TOKYO(1944); ANCHORS AWEIGH(1945); SON OF LASSIE(1945); THEY WERE EXPENDABLE(1945); WEEKEND AT THE WALDORF(1945); YOLANDA AND THE THIEF(1945); COCKEYED MIRACLE, THE(1946); NO LEAVE, NO LOVE(1946); POSTMAN ALWAYS RINGS TWICE, THE(1946); SHOW-OFF, THE(1946); LADY IN THE LAKE(1946); MERTON OF THE MOVIES(1947); SONG OF THE THIN MAN(1947); UNDERCOVER MAISIE(1947); ALIAS A GENTLEMAN(1948); DATE WITH JUDY, A(1948); ON AN ISLAND WITH YOU(1948); VELVET TOUCH, THE(1948); ANY NUMBER CAN PLAY(1949); BATTLEGROUND(1949); LITTLE WOMEN(1949); SCENE OF THE CRIME(1949); AMBUSH(1950); BIG HANGOVER, THE(1950); CRISIS(1950); DIAL 1119(1950); HAPPY YEARS, THE(1950); SKIPPER SURPRISED HIS WIFE, THE(1950); WATCH THE BIRDIE(1950); CATTLE DRIVE(1951); IT'S A BIG COUNTRY(1951); ON MOONLIGHT BAY(1951); ANGEL FACE(1953); BY THE LIGHT OF THE SILVERY MOON(1953); LET'S DO IT AGAIN(1953); SABRE JET(1953); PEYTON PLACE(1957); FROM THE TERRACE(1960); ABSENT-MINDED PROFESSOR, THE(1961); SON OF FLUBBER(1963); MISADVENTURES OF MERLIN JONES, THE(1964); MONKEY'S UNCLE, THE(1965); ON A CLEAR DAY YOU CAN SEE FOREVER(1970); TORA! TORA! TORA!(1970, U.S./Jap.); HAMMERSMITH IS OUT(1972); MEAL, THE(1975); JUST YOU AND ME, KID(1979); TESTAMENT(1983)

Misc. Talkies
DEATH IN THE AIR(1937); TIMBER TRAMPS(1975); CLAWS(1977); DEADLY ENCOUNTER(1979)
Lew Ames
Misc. Silents
FAR WESTERN TRAILS(1929)
Lionel Ames
THUNDERING JETS(1958); THIS EARTH IS MINE(1959); WHY MUST I DIE?(1960)
Michael Ames [Tod Andrews]
BODY DISAPPEARS, THE(1941); BULLET SCARS(1942); CAPTAINS OF THE CLOUDS(1942); I WAS FRAMED(1942); MURDER IN THE BIG HOUSE(1942); NOW, VOYAGER(1942); SPY SHIP(1942); TRUCK BUSTERS(1943); LAST RIDE, THE(1944); RETURN OF THE APE MAN(1944); VOODOO MAN(1944)
Percy Ames
GAMBLING(1934)
Silents
ADAM AND EVA(1923)
Misc. Silents
SOUL-FIRE(1925)
Preston Ames
HIDDEN EYE, THE(1945), art d; SHE WENT TO THE RACES(1945), art d; SHOW-OFF, THE(1946), art d; LADY IN THE LAKE(1947), art d; THREE DARING DAUGHTERS(1948), art d; DOCTOR AND THE GIRL, THE(1949), art d; THAT MIDNIGHT KISS(1949), art d; CRISIS(1950), art d; TWO WEEKS WITH LOVE(1950), art d; AMERICAN IN PARIS, AN(1951), art d; WILD NORTH, THE(1952), art d; STORY OF THREE LOVES, THE(1953), art d; TORCH SONG(1953), art d; BRIGADOON(1954), art d; KISMET(1955), art d; LUST FOR LIFE(1956), art d; THESE WILDER YEARS(1956), art d; GIGI(1958), art d; GREEN MANSIONS(1959), art d; BELLS ARE RINGING(1960), art d; HOME FROM THE HILL(1960), art d; WHERE THE BOYS ARE(1960), art d; HONEYMOON MACHINE, THE(1961), art d; WILD IN THE COUNTRY(1961), art d; ALL FALL DOWN(1962), art d; JUMBO(1962), art d; IT HAPPENED AT THE WORLD'S FAIR(1963), art d; GLOBAL AFFAIR, A(1964), art d; QUICK, BEFORE IT MELTS(1964), art d; UNSINKABLE MOLLY BROWN, THE(1964), art d; MADE IN PARIS(1966), art d; PENELOPE(1966), art d; IMPOSSIBLE YEARS, THE(1968), art d; LIVE A LITTLE, LOVE A LITTLE(1968), art d; AIRPORT(1970), art d; BREWSTER McCLOUD(1970), art d; STRAWBERRY STATEMENT, THE(1970), art d; PRETTY MAIDS ALL IN A ROW(1971), art d; DON IS DEAD, THE(1973), art d; LOST HORIZON(1973), art d; PRISONER OF SECOND AVENUE, THE(1975), art d; ROOSTER COGBURN(1975), art d; DAMNATION ALLEY(1977), prod d; CAT FROM OUTER SPACE, THE(1978), art d; OH GOD! BOOK II(1980), prod d; PURSUIT OF D.B. COOPER, THE(1981), prod d
Rachel Ames
DADDY'S GONE A-HUNTING(1969)
Ramsay Ames
CALLING DR. DEATH(1943); FOLLOW THE BOYS(1944); HAT CHECK HONEY(1944); MUMMY'S GHOST, THE(1944); WAVE, A WAC AND A MARINE, A(1944); MILDRED PIERCE(1945); BEAUTY AND THE BANDIT(1946); VICKI(1953); RUNNING MAN, THE(1963, Brit.)
Ramsey Ames
TWO SENORITAS FROM CHICAGO(1943); ALI BABA AND THE FORTY THIEVES(1944); TOO YOUNG TO KNOW(1945); BELOW THE DEADLINE(1946); GREEN DOLPHIN STREET(1947); PHILO VANCE RETURNS(1947); ALEXANDER THE GREAT(1956)
Misc. Talkies
GAY CAVALIER, THE(1946)
Robert Ames
BLACK WATERS(1929); NIX ON DAMES(1929); RICH PEOPLE(1929); TRESPASSER, THE(1929); VOICE OF THE CITY(1929); DOUBLE CROSS ROADS(1930); HOLIDAY(1930); LADY TO LOVE, A(1930); MADONNA OF THE STREETS(1930); NOT DAMAGED(1930); WAR NURSE(1930); BEHIND OFFICE DOORS(1931); MILLIE(1931); REBOUND(1931); RICH MAN'S FOLLY(1931); SMART WOMAN(1931); THREE WHO LOVED(1931); TOMORROW AND TOMORROW(1932); ZIEGFELD FOLLIES(1945)
Silents
WEDDING SONG, THE(1925)
Misc. Silents
WITHOUT MERCY(1925); CROWN OF LIES, THE(1926); THREE FACES EAST(1926)
Rosemary Ames
LOVE ON THE SPOT(1932, Brit.); MR. QUINCEY OF MONTE CARLO(1933, Brit.); I BELIEVED IN YOU(1934); PURSUED(1934); SUCH WOMEN ARE DANGEROUS(1934); GREAT HOTEL MURDER(1935); ONE MORE SPRING(1935); OUR LITTLE GIRL(1935)
Seneca Ames
WHY RUSSIANS ARE REVOLTING(1970)
Stephen Ames
SPANISH MAIN, THE(1945), p; SINBAD THE SAILOR(1947), p; TYCOON(1947), p; BOY WITH THE GREEN HAIR, THE(1949), p; MAN WITH A CLOAK(1951), p; MY MAN AND I(1952), p; WILD NORTH, THE(1952), p; CONFIDENTIAL CONNIE(1953), p; RIDE, VAQUERO!(1953), p
Suzanne Ames
TWO TICKETS TO BROADWAY(1951); LAS VEGAS STORY, THE(1952); FRENCH LINE, THE(1954)
Totty Ames
IN LIKE FLINT(1967); SKULLDUGGERY(1970)
Trudi Ames
GYPSY(1962); GIDGET GOES TO ROME(1963); IMPOSSIBLE YEARS, THE(1968)
Trudy Ames
BYE BYE BIRDIE(1963)
Ames and Arno
DOUBLE OR NOTHING(1937)
Ebba Amfeldt
LURE OF THE JUNGLE, THE(1970, Den.)
Daniele Amfitheatrof
GET-AWAY, THE(1941), m; ANDY HARDY'S DOUBLE LIFE(1942), m; CALLING DR. GILLESPIE(1942), m; DR. GILLESPIE'S NEW ASSISTANT(1942), m; CRY HAVOC(1943), m; DR. GILLESPIE'S CRIMINAL CASE(1943), m, md; HARRIGAN'S KID(1943), m; HIGH EXPLOSIVE(1943), m; LASSIE, COME HOME(1943), m; STRANGER IN TOWN, A(1943), m; I'LL BE SEEING YOU(1944), m; LOST ANGEL(1944), m; GUEST WIFE(1945), m; MISS SUSIE SLAGLE'S(1945), m; O.S.S.(1946), m; SONG OF THE SOUTH(1946), m; SUSPENSE(1946), m; TEMPTATION(1946), m; VIRGINIAN,

THE(1946), m; BEGINNING OR THE END, THE(1947), m; IVY(1947), m; LOST MOMENT, THE(1947), m; SENATOR WAS INDISCREET, THE(1947), m; SINGAPORE(1947), m; SMASH-UP, THE STORY OF A WOMAN(1947), m; ACT OF MURDER, AN(1948), m; ANOTHER PART OF THE FOREST(1948), m; LETTER FROM AN UNKNOWN WOMAN(1948), m; ROGUES' REGIMENT(1948), m; YOU GOTTA STAY HAPPY(1948), m; FAN, THE(1949), m; HOUSE OF STRANGERS(1949), md; SAND(1949), m, md; CAPTURE, THE(1950), m; DAMNED DON'T CRY, THE(1950), m; DEVIL'S DOORWAY(1950), m; STORM WARNING(1950), m; UNDER MY SKIN(1950), m; ANGELS IN THE OUTFIELD(1951), m; BIRD OF PARADISE(1951), m; DESERT FOX, THE(1951), m; PAINTED HILLS, THE(1951), m; TOMORROW IS ANOTHER DAY(1951), m; BIG HEAT, THE(1953), m; DEVIL'S CANYON(1953), m; NAKED JUNGLE, THE(1953), m; SALOME(1953), m; SCANDAL AT SCOURIE(1953), m; DAY OF TRIUMPH(1954), m; HUMAN DESIRE(1954), m; TRIAL(1955), m, md; LAST HUNT, THE(1956), m, md; MOUNTAIN, THE(1956), m; UNHOLY WIFE, THE(1957), m, md; FRAULEIN(1958), m; FROM HELL TO TEXAS(1958), m; SPANISH AFFAIR(1958, Span.), m; EDGE OF ETERNITY(1959), m; THAT KIND OF WOMAN(1959), m; HELLER IN PINK TIGHTS(1960), m; MAJOR DUNDEE(1965), m
Bat Ami
TEL AVIV TAXI(1957, Israel)
Vanio Amici
CHINO(1976, Ital., Span., Fr.), ed
Gianni Amico
TROPICS(1969, Ital.), d, w
Gian-franco Amicucci
LOVES AND TIMES OF SCARAMOUCHE, THE(1976, Ital.), ed
Gianfranco Amicucci
COUNTERFEIT COMMANDOS(1981, Ital.), ed; NEW BARBARIANS, THE(1983, Ital.), ed; 1990: THE BRONX WARRIORS(1983, Ital.), ed
1984
WARRIORS OF THE WASTELAND(1984, Ital.), ed
Anna Amidei
ROMEO AND JULIET(1968, Ital./Span.), ed
Sergio Amidei
OPEN CITY(1946, Ital.), w; SHOE SHINE(1947, Ital.), w; PAISAN(1948, Ital.), w; UNDER THE SUN OF ROME(1949, Ital.), w; DAUGHTERS OF DESTINY(1954, Fr./Ital.), w; FEAR(1956, Ger.), w; GENERALE DELLA ROVERE(1960, Ital./Fr.), w; LOVE ON THE RIVIERA(1964, Fr./Ital.), w; LA FUGA(1966, Ital.), w; VERY HANDY MAN, A(1966, Fr./Ital.), w; GIRL GAME(1968, Braz./Fr./Ital.), w; SINGAPORE, SINGAPORE(1969, Fr./Ital.), w; MOST WONDERFUL EVENING OF MY LIFE, THE(1972, Ital./Fr.), w; LA NUIT DE VARENNES(1983, Fr./Ital.), w; TALES OF ORDINARY MADNESS(1983, Ital.), w
Byron Amidon
THESE WILDER YEARS(1956)
Amidou
CROOK, THE(1971, Fr.); ROSEBUD(1975); SORCERER(1977); VICTORY(1981)
Souad Amidou
MAN AND A WOMAN, A(1966, Fr.); LIFE LOVE DEATH(1969, Fr./Ital.)
Alan Amiel
ENTER THE NINJA(1982); REVENGE OF THE NINJA(1983)
1984
NINJA III-THE DOMINATION(1984)
J.J. Amiel
DAUGHTERS OF DARKNESS(1971, Bel./ Fr./ Ger./ Ital.), w
Jean Pierre Amiel
DARK CRYSTAL, THE(1982, Brit.), a, ch
Sibyl Amiel
BLESS 'EM ALL(1949, Brit.)
Caroline Amies
1984
1919(1984, Brit.), art d
Hardy Amies
GRASS IS GREENER, THE(1960), cos; TWO FOR THE ROAD(1967, Brit.), cos; 2001: A SPACE ODYSSEY(1968, U.S./Brit.), cos
Angel Amigo
1984
ESCAPE FROM SEGOVIA(1984, Span.), p, w
Cesar Amigo
LOST BATTALION(1961, U.S./Phil.), w; RAVAGERS, THE(1965, U.S./Phil.), w; BLOOD DRINKERS, THE(1966, U.S./Phil.), w; PASSIONATE STRANGERS, THE(1968, Phil.), d&w
Cesar J. Amigo
WALLS OF HELL, THE(1964, U.S./Phil.), w
Amilcar
JUBILEE(1978, Brit.), m
Henri Amilien
LAFAYETTE(1963, Fr.)
Abbas Amin
SPECTRE OF EDGAR ALLAN POE, THE(1974), ed
Usha Amin
HOUSEHOLDER, THE(1963, US/India)
Georges Aminel
LEATHER AND NYLON(1969, Fr./Ital.); POPSY POP(1971, Fr.)
Richard Amington
1984
PURPLE RAIN(1984), makeup
Marianne Aminoff
NIGHT IN JUNE, A(1940, Swed.); FANNY AND ALEXANDER(1983, Swed./Fr./Ger.)
Paul Amiot
CROSSROADS(1938, Fr.); J'ACCUSE(1939, Fr.)
Gideon Amir
HANNAH K.(1983, Fr.)
Khalil Amir
KENNER(1969)
Kingsley Amis
LUCKY JIM(1957, Brit.), w; ONLY TWO CAN PLAY(1962, Brit.), w; TELL ME LIES(1968, Brit.); TAKE A GIRL LIKE YOU(1970, Brit.), w

Martin Amis
HIGH WIND IN JAMAICA, A(1965); SATURN 3(1980), w
Alicia Amman
JOURNEY INTO FEAR(1976, Can)
Betty Amman
DAUGHTERS OF TODAY(1933, Brit.)
Gary Ammann
MA BARKER'S KILLER BROOD(1960)
Lukas Ammann
DAY OF ANGER(1970, Ital./Ger.); MARK OF THE DEVIL II(1975, Ger./Brit.)
Roger Ammann
1984
FLETCH(1984)
Tarak Ben Ammar
LA TRAVIATA(1982), p
1984
PAR OU T'ES RENTRE? ON T'A PAS VUE SORTIR(1984, Fr./Tunisia), p
Harry Ammerlaan
LIFT, THE(1983, Neth.), art d
1984
FOURTH MAN, THE(1984, Neth.), set d; QUESTION OF SILENCE(1984, Neth.), prod d
Dan Ammerman
LOCAL HERO(1983, Brit.)
Tony Ammirati
LA TRAVIATA(1982)
Alica Ammon
WOLFPEN PRINCIPLE, THE(1974, Can.)
Alicia Ammon
THAT COLD DAY IN THE PARK(1969, U.S./Can.)
Princess Vanessa Ammon
TIN PAN ALLEY(1940)
Ruth Ammon
1984
HARD CHOICES(1984), prod d
Mario Ammonini
WONDERS OF ALADDIN, THE(1961, Fr./Ital.), md; TROJAN HORSE, THE(1962, Fr./Ital.), m
Walter Amner
MUSIC HALL(1934, Brit.); JUBILEE WINDOW(1935, Brit.); SMALL MAN, THE(1935, Brit.); TALKING FEET(1937, Brit.)
Krisana Amnueyporn
S.T.A.B.(1976, Hong Kong/Thailand)
Samuel Amoah
1984
WHITE ELEPHANT(1984, Brit.)
Amedeo Amodio
NIGHT PORTER, THE(1974, Ital./U.S.)
1984
BEYOND GOOD AND EVIL(1984, Ital./Fr./Ger.)
Paul Amoit
RUY BLAS(1948, Fr.)
Chris Amon
GRAND PRIX(1966)
Robert Amon
DEVIL AND THE TEN COMMANDMENTS, THE(1962, Fr.), p; MALE HUNT(1965, Fr./Ital.), p
Marlene Among
TIKO AND THE SHARK(1966, U.S./Ital./Fr.)
Viraj Amonsin
PORK CHOP HILL(1959); ECHOES OF SILENCE(1966)
Duane Amont
BOUNTY KILLER, THE(1965)
Marcel Amont
BRIDE IS MUCH TOO BEAUTIFUL, THE(1958, Fr.)
Carlos Amor
Silents
RAMONA(1928)
Christine Amor
TOUCH AND GO(1955); PETERSEN(1974, Aus.); DAY AFTER HALLOWEEN, THE(1981, Aus.); NOW AND FOREVER(1983, Aus.)
Jay Amor
SPRING BREAK(1983), stunts
Jim Amormino
NEW YEAR'S EVIL(1980)
Roberto Amoroso
MELODY OF LOVE(1954, Ital.), p, w; DONATELLA(1956, Ital.), p, w; SECRET AGENT SUPER DRAGON(1966, Fr./Ital./Ger./Monaco), p, w
Richard Amory
SONG OF THE LOON(1970), p, w
Albert Amos
CLARENCE, THE CROSS-EYED LION(1965)
Beth Amos
NOW THAT APRIL'S HERE(1958, Can.); INCREDIBLE JOURNEY, THE(1963); PROM NIGHT(1980)
1984
POLICE ACADEMY(1984)
Janet Amos
HIGH(1968, Can.); WINTER KEPT US WARM(1968, Can.); SILENCE OF THE NORTH(1981, Can.)
Jean Amos
JUDGE AND THE ASSASSIN, THE(1979, Fr.)
John Amos
WORLD'S GREATEST ATHLETE, THE(1973); LET'S DO IT AGAIN(1975); TOUCHED BY LOVE(1980); BEASTMASTER, THE(1982); DANCE OF THE DWARFS(1983, U.S., Phil.)
Tom Amos
Misc. Silents
SHOT IN THE NIGHT, A(1923)

Amos & Arno
RHYTHM INN(1951)
Amos 'n Andy
BIG BROADCAST OF 1936, THE(1935)
Dahn Ben Amotz
EXODUS(1960)
Louis L. Amour
STRANGER ON HORSEBACK(1955), w
Fahimeh Amouzandeh
CARAVANS(1978, U.S./Iranian)
Amparo
SHE-DEVIL ISLAND(1936, Mex.)
Pierre Ampeles
ELECTRA(1962, Gr.)
Christina Amphlett
MONKEY GRIP(1983, Aus.)
John Amplas
MARTIN(1979); BLOODEATERS(1980); KNIGHTRIDERS(1981); CREEPSHOW(1982)
John Amplos
MIDNIGHT(1983)
David Amram
SPLENDOR IN THE GRASS(1961), m, md; YOUNG SAVAGES, THE(1961), m; MANCHURIAN CANDIDATE, THE(1962), m, md; ARRANGEMENT, THE(1969), m
Robert G. Amram
MINI-AFFAIR, THE(1968, Brit.), d&w
Gabi Amrani
SINAI COMMANDOS: THE STORY OF THE SIX DAY WAR(1968, Israel/Ger.); MADRON(1970, U.S./Israel)
1984
BEST DEFENSE(1984); SAHARA(1984)
Vijay Amritraj
PLAYERS(1979); OCTOPUSSY(1983, Brit.)
Joe Amsler
WHAT'S UP, DOC?(1972); NICKELODEON(1976); MAIN EVENT, THE(1979)
Jane Amsten
SLOW RUN(1968)
Lewis Amster
TOUGH AS THEY COME(1942), w; MUG TOWN(1943), w
Greg Amsterdam
AMBUSH BAY(1966)
Gregg Amsterdam
DON'T WORRY, WE'LL THINK OF A TITLE(1966)
Morey Amsterdam
GHOST AND THE GUEST(1943), w; KID DYNAMITE(1943), w; IT CAME FROM OUTER SPACE(1953); MACHINE GUN KELLY(1958); MURDER, INC.(1960); GAY PURR-EE(1962); BEACH PARTY(1963); MUSCLE BEACH PARTY(1964); DON'T WORRY, WE'LL THINK OF A TITLE(1966), a, p, w; HORSE IN THE GRAY FLANNEL SUIT, THE(1968); MR. MAGOO'S HOLIDAY FESTIVAL(1970); WON TON TON, THE DOG WHO SAVED HOLLYWOOD(1976)
Roland Amstut
1984
HEAT OF DESIRE(1984, Fr.)
Roland Amstutz
EVERY MAN FOR HIMSELF(1980, Fr.)
1984
PERILS OF GWENDOLINE, THE(1984, Fr.)
Mitchell Amundsen
ONE FROM THE HEART(1982)
Barbara Amusen
LAST HOUSE ON DEAD END STREET(1977)
Christopher Amy
1984
ANGEL(1984), set d; CRIMES OF PASSION(1984), set d
George Amy
THOSE WHO DANCE(1930), ed; GORILLA, THE(1931), ed; RULING VOICE, THE(1931), ed; CABIN IN THE COTTON(1932), ed; DOCTOR X(1932), ed; MOUTHPIECE, THE(1932), ed; FOOTLIGHT PARADE(1933), ed; GOLD DIGGERS OF 1933(1933), ed; LADY KILLER(1933), ed; MYSTERY OF THE WAX MUSEUM, THE(1933), ed; SHE HAD TO SAY YES(1933), d; 20,000 YEARS IN SING SING(1933), ed; HE WAS HER MAN(1934), ed; HERE COMES THE NAVY(1934), ed; SIX-DAY BIKE RIDER(1934), ed; WONDER BAR(1934), ed; BROADWAY GONDOLIER(1935), ed; CAPTAIN BLOOD(1935), ed; GOLD DIGGERS OF 1935(1935), ed; CHARGE OF THE LIGHT BRIGADE, THE(1936), ed; HOLLYWOOD HOTEL(1937), ed; KID GALAHAD(1937), ed; MOUNTAIN JUSTICE(1937), ed; VARSITY SHOW(1937), ed; GARDEN OF THE MOON(1938), ed; GOLD DIGGERS IN PARIS(1938), ed; DODGE CITY(1939), ed; KID NIGHTINGALE(1939), ed; OLD MAID, THE(1939), ed; GAMBLING ON THE HIGH SEAS(1940), d; GRANNY GET YOUR GUN(1940), d; LETTER, THE(1940), ed; SANTA FE TRAIL(1940), ed; SEA HAWK, THE(1940), ed; VIRGINIA CITY(1940), ed; DIVE BOMBER(1941), ed; SEA WOLF, THE(1941), ed; CAPTAINS OF THE CLOUDS(1942), ed; YANKEE DOODLE DANDY(1942), ed; ACTION IN THE NORTH ATLANTIC(1943), ed; AIR FORCE(1943), ed; THIS IS THE ARMY(1943), ed; UNCERTAIN GLORY(1944), ed; CONFIDENTIAL AGENT(1945), ed; OBJECTIVE, BURMA!(1945), ed; CINDERELLA JONES(1946), ed; THREE STRANGERS(1946), ed; LIFE WITH FATHER(1947), ed; CAPTURE, THE(1950), ed; SOUND OF FURY, THE(1950), ed; LADY SAYS NO, THE(1951), ed; QUEEN FOR A DAY(1951), ed; AFFAIR WITH A STRANGER(1953), ed; LION IS IN THE STREETS, A(1953), ed; SHE COULDN'T SAY NO(1954), ed
George J. Amy
BLUE VEIL, THE(1951), ed; CLASH BY NIGHT(1952), ed
Gilbert Amy
LA PRISONNIERE(1969, Fr./Ital.), md
Nita Amy
1984
1919(1984, Brit.), p
Julian Amyes
HELL IN KOREA(1956, Brit.), d; MIRACLE IN SOHO(1957, Brit.), d
Max Amyl
SHAMELESS OLD LADY, THE(1966, Fr.); PARIS IN THE MONTH OF AUGUST(1968, Fr.); THINGS OF LIFE, THE(1970, Fr./Ital./Switz.)

R. Vild An
FATHER OF A SOLDIER(1966, USSR)

Ana
TAHITIAN, THE(1956)

Bill Anagnos
SOMEBODY KILLED HER HUSBAND(1978); TIMES SQUARE(1980); ROL-
LOVER(1981)
1984
ALPHABET CITY(1984); BEAT STREET(1984); FIRSTBORN(1984); POPE OF
GREENWICH VILLAGE, THE(1984), stunts

Billy Anagnos
WARRIORS, THE(1979)

William Anagos
SOLDIER, THE(1982)

Gordon Analla
AMERICAN GRAFFITI(1973)

Eugenie Anami
ROMANCE OF SEVILLE, A(1929, Brit.)

Cpl. Munto Anampio
KING SOLOMON'S MINES(1950)

Junko Anan
TOKYO STORY(1972, Jap.)

Dev Anand
GUIDE, THE(1965, U.S./India)

Jafeth Ananda
IVORY HUNTER(1952, Brit.)

V. Ananina
HOUSE WITH AN ATTIC, THE(1964, USSR); MEET ME IN MOSCOW(1966, USSR)

Spero Anast
THIEF(1981)

Andrea Anastassatos
LOVE CYCLES(1969, Gr.), ph

Georg Anaya
NEW LAND, THE(1973, Swed.)

Yano Anaya
CHRISTMAS STORY, A(1983)

Y. Anazhevskaya
DIARY OF A NAZI(1943, USSR)

Andre Ancel
LES GAULOISES BLEUES(1969, Fr.)

Philippe Ancellin
MYSTERIOUS ISLAND OF CAPTAIN NEMO, THE(1973, Fr./Ital. 87m Span./
Cameroon), prod d
1984
TO CATCH A COP(1984, Fr.), art d

Pergiovanni Anchisi
GIORDANO BRUNO(1973, Ital.), w

Piero Anchisi
BLINDMAN(1972, Ital.), w

Leo Anchoriz
COMMANDO(1962, Ital., Span., Bel., Ger.); INVINCIBLE GLADIATOR, THE(1963,
c.u. Ital./Span.); SANDOKAN THE GREAT(1964, Fr./Ital./Span.); FINGER ON THE
TRIGGER(1965, US/Span.); UP THE MACGREGORS(1967, Ital./Span.); SEVEN GUNS
FOR THE MACGREGORS(1968, Ital./Span.); VENGEANCE IS MINE(1969, Ital./
Span.); BULLET FOR SANDOVAL, A(1970, Ital./Span.); KILL THEM ALL AND COME
BACK ALONE(1970, Ital./Span.)

Carlos Ancira
VAMPIRE'S COFFIN, THE(1958, Mex.); ORLAK, THE HELL OF FRANKEN-
STEIN(1960, Mex.); LIVING COFFIN, THE(1965, Mex.); SANTO Y BLUE DEMON
CONTRA LOS MONSTRUOS(1968, Mex.)

Ricardo Ancona
YANCO(1964, Mex.)

Richard Anconina
CHOICE OF ARMS(1983, Fr.)

Joseph Ancore, Jr.
REVENGE OF THE CHEERLEADERS(1976), ed

F.D. Andam
MAEDCHEN IN UNIFORM(1932, Ger.), w; ONE NIGHT IN PARIS(1940, Brit.), w;
MAEDCHEN IN UNIFORM(1965, Ger./Fr.), w

David Andar
HOUSE OF USHER(1960)

Michael Ande
TRAPP FAMILY, THE(1961, Ger.)

Franco Andei
PLANET OF THE VAMPIRES(1965, U.S./Ital./Span.)

James Andelin
CITY THAT NEVER SLEEPS(1953); ON THE RIGHT TRACK(1981)

Juli Andelman
SILENT SCREAM(1980); WHERE THE BUFFALO ROAM(1980); WHOSE LIFE IS IT
ANYWAY?(1981)

Julie Andelman
MEAN STREETS(1973)

Mathew Anden
NICKELODEON(1976)

Matthew Anden
DAVID AND LISA(1962)

Calvin Ander
TROUBLEMAKER, THE(1964); TIMES SQUARE(1980); I OUGHT TO BE IN PIC-
TURES(1982)

Charlotte Ander
ELISABETH OF AUSTRIA(1931, Ger.); VIENNA, CITY OF SONGS(1931, Ger.);
RASPUTIN(1932, Ger.); MAID HAPPY(1933, Brit.); MY SONG GOES ROUND THE
WORLD(1934, Brit.); DANCING HEART, THE(1959, Ger.)

Bertil Anderberg
SEVENTH SEAL, THE(1958, Swed.); JUST ONCE MORE(1963, Swed.); HOUR OF
THE WOLF, THE(1968, Swed.)

Jacqueline Andere
EXTERMINATING ANGEL, THE(1967, Mex.)

Maria Andergast
PRODIGAL SON, THE(1935); LITTLE MELODY FROM VIENNA(1948, Aust.)

Maureen Anderman
SEDUCTION OF JOE TYNAN, THE(1979); MAN, WOMAN AND CHILD(1983)

Bill Anders
EVERYTHING BUT THE TRUTH(1956); I'VE LIVED BEFORE(1956); SCARLET
HOUR, THE(1956)

Cal Anders
GIRL IN LOVER'S LANE, THE(1960)

Chris Anders
36 HOURS(1965); AGENT FOR H.A.R.M.(1966); SECRET OF SANTA VITTORIA,
THE(1969); RAID ON ROMMEL(1971); HEARTBREAKER(1983), p

Christian Anders
WHY DOES HERR R. RUN AMOK?(1977, Ger.), m

Derek Anders
THIRTY NINE STEPS, THE(1978, Brit.)

Dick Anders
DEVIL'S ANGELS(1967)

Donna Anders
COUNT YORGA, VAMPIRE(1970)

Glen Anders
BY YOUR LEAVE(1935)

Glenn Anders
LAUGHTER(1930); NOTHING BUT THE TRUTH(1941); LADY FROM SHANGHAI,
THE(1948); NANCY GOES TO RIO(1950); BEHAVE YOURSELF(1951); M(1951);
TARZAN'S PERIL(1951)
Silents
SALLY OF THE SAWDUST(1925)

Guenther Anders
WHITE HORSE INN, THE(1959, Ger.), ph

Gunther Anders
WONDER BOY(1951, Brit./Aust.), ph; LAST TEN DAYS, THE(1956, Ger.), ph;
HIPPODROME(1961, Aust./Ger.), ph; VIENNA WALTZES(1961, Aust.), ph; GLASS
OF WATER, A(1962, Cgr.), ph; END OF MRS. CHENEY(1963, Ger.), ph; FAUST(1963,
Ger.), ph; MIRACLE OF THE WHITE STALLIONS(1963), ph; GIRL AND THE
LEGEND, THE(1966, Ger.), ph; SWAN LAKE, THE(1967), ph

Harris Anders
SHE MAN, THE(1967), w

Helga Anders
HOW TO SEDUCE A PLAYBOY(1968, Aust./Fr./Ital.)
Misc. Talkies
BEYOND CONTROL(1971)

Ina Anders
RACERS, THE(1955); BLUE ANGEL, THE(1959); 48 HOURS TO LIVE(1960, Brit./
Swed.)

Irene Anders
MAN CRAZY(1953)

Jan Anders
THREES, MENAGE A TROIS(1968), d

Karen Anders
SHEILA LEVINE IS DEAD AND LIVING IN NEW YORK(1975); AUDREY RO-
SE(1977); PROMISES IN THE DARK(1979)

Kristoffer Anders
VICE SQUAD(1982)

Laurie Anders
MARSHAL'S DAUGHTER, THE(1953)

Luana Anders
REFORM SCHOOL GIRL(1957); LIFE BEGINS AT 17(1958); MAN WHO DIED
TWICE, THE(1958); NOTORIOUS MR. MONKS, THE(1958); PIT AND THE PEN-
DULUM, THE(1961); DEMENTIA 13(1963); NIGHT TIDE(1963); YOUNG RACERS,
THE(1963); GAMES(1967); TRIP, THE(1967); HOW SWEET IT IS(1968); EASY RI-
DER(1969); THAT COLD DAY IN THE PARK(1969, U.S./Can.); GREASER'S PALA-
CE(1972); WHEN THE LEGENDS DIE(1972); KILLING KIND, THE(1973); LAST
DETAIL, THE(1973); SHAMPOO(1975); MISSOURI BREAKS, THE(1976); GOIN'
SOUTH(1978); PERSONAL BEST(1982)
1984
IRRECONCILABLE DIFFERENCES(1984)
Misc. Talkies
B.J. LANG PRESENTS(1971)

Lynn Anders
GIRL FROM SCOTLAND YARD, THE(1937); SHADOW STRIKES, THE(1937)

Merry Anders
LES MISERABLES(1952); WAIT 'TIL THE SUN SHINES, NELLIE(1952); FARMER
TAKES A WIFE, THE(1953); HOW TO MARRY A MILLIONAIRE(1953); TITA-
NIC(1953); PHFFFT!(1954); PRINCESS OF THE NILE(1954); THREE COINS IN THE
FOUNTAIN(1954); CALYPSO HEAT WAVE(1957); DALTON GIRLS, THE(1957);
DEATH IN SMALL DOSES(1957); DESK SET(1957); ESCAPE FROM SAN QUEN-
TIN(1957); HEAR ME GOOD(1957); NIGHT RUNNER, THE(1957); NO TIME TO BE
YOUNG(1957); VIOLENT ROAD(1958); FIVE BOLD WOMEN(1960); SPRING AF-
FAIR(1960); THE HYPNOTIC EYE(1960); WALKING TARGET, THE(1960); YOUNG
JESSE JAMES(1960); GAMBLER WORE A GUN, THE(1961); POLICE DOG STORY,
THE(1961); SECRET OF DEEP HARBOR(1961); WHEN THE CLOCK STRIKES(1961);
20,000 EYES(1961); AIR PATROL(1962); CASE OF PATTY SMITH(1962); BEAU-
TY AND THE BEAST(1963); HOUSE OF THE DAMNED(1963); POLICE NURSE(1963);
FBI CODE 98(1964); QUICK GUN, THE(1964); RAIDERS FROM BENEATH THE
SEA(1964); TIGER WALKS, A(1964); TIME TRAVELERS, THE(1964); TICKLE
ME(1965); YOUNG FURY(1965); WOMEN OF THE PREHISTORIC PLANET(1966);
LEGACY OF BLOOD(1973)

Richard Anders
HELL'S ANGELS ON WHEELS(1967); SAVAGE SEVEN, THE(1968); GETTING
STRAIGHT(1970)

Rudolph Anders [RobertO. Davis]
RENDEZVOUS(1935); CHAMPAGNE WALTZ(1937); THIN ICE(1937); MAN I MAR-
RIED, THE(1940); STRANGE DEATH OF ADOLF HITLER, THE(1943); COUNTER-
ATTACK(1945); ESCAPE IN THE DESERT(1945); DANGEROUS MILLIONS(1946);
HER SISTER'S SECRET(1946); UNDER NEVADA SKIES(1946); KILL OR BE
KILLED(1950); ACTORS AND SIN(1952); PHANTOM FROM SPACE(1953); JUNGLE
GENTS(1954); KING RICHARD AND THE CRUSADERS(1954); MAGNIFICENT
OBSESSION(1954); SNOW CREATURE, THE,(1954); STAR IS BORN, A(1954); FRAN-
KENSTEIN 1970(1958); SHE DEMONS(1958); PRIVATE'S AFFAIR, A(1959); ON THE

DOUBLE(1961); PIGEON THAT TOOK ROME, THE(1962); PRIZE, THE(1963); 36 HOURS(1965)

Tom Anders
DIRT GANG, THE(1972)

Vern Anders
O.S.S.(1946)

Asbjorn Andersen
REPTILICUS(1962, U.S./Den.); LURE OF THE JUNGLE, THE(1970, Den.)

Bjarne Andersen
HUNGER(1968, Den./Norway/Swed.)

Bridgette Andersen
NIGHTMARES(1983); SAVANNAH SMILES(1983)

Dana Andersen
1984
KARATE KID, THE(1984)

Elga Andersen
FRANTIC(1961, Fr.); EMPIRE OF NIGHT, THE(1963, Fr.); YOUR TURN, DARLING(1963, Fr.); GLOBAL AFFAIR, A(1964); COAST OF SKELETONS(1965, Brit.); LE MANS(1971); SERPENT, THE(1973, Fr./Ital./Ger.)

Gerald Andersen
PORT OF ESCAPE(1955, Brit.); YOU CAN'T ESCAPE(1955, Brit.); IN THE DOGHOUSE(1964, Brit.); SINISTER MAN, THE(1965, Brit.)

Hans Christian Andersen
SNOW QUEEN, THE(1959, USSR), w; DAYDREAMER, THE(1966), w; TINDER BOX, THE(1968, E. Ger.), w; SCANDAL IN DENMARK(1970, Den.), p,d&w; THUMBELINA(1970), w; STORIES FROM A FLYING TRUNK(1979, Brit.), d&w

Inga Andersen
TAKE OFF THAT HAT(1938, Brit.)

Jurgen Andersen
SEA WOLVES, THE(1981, Brit.); VICTORY(1981)
1984
LASSITER(1984); RIDDLE OF THE SANDS, THE(1984, Brit.)

Lale Andersen
LILI MARLEEN(1981, Ger.), w

Lawrence Andersen
LIVING DANGEROUSLY(1936, Brit.)

M. A. Andersen
LAST DANCE, THE(1930), ph; FIFTEEN WIVES(1934), ph; GIRL WHO CAME BACK, THE(1935), ph; HAPPINESS C.O.D.(1935), ph; SHOT IN THE DARK, A(1935), ph; DEATH FROM A DISTANCE(1936), ph; EASY MONEY(1936), ph; HITCH HIKE TO HEAVEN(1936), ph; IT COULDN'T HAVE HAPPENED–BUT IT DID(1936), ph; LADY LUCK(1936), ph; TANGO(1936), ph; THREE OF A KIND(1936), ph; SLANDER HOUSE(1938), ph

Michael Andersen
WINGS OF CHANCE(1961, Can.), m; TOWER OF LONDON(1962), m; TERRIFIED!(1963), m; TELL ME IN THE SUNLIGHT(1967), m

Susy Andersen
MAGNIFICENT CUCKOLD, THE(1965, Fr./Ital.); WAR OF THE ZOMBIES, THE(1965 Ital.)

A. Anderson
CROSS-EXAMINATION(1932), ph

Agnes Anderson
I LIVE MY LIFE(1935); VANESSA, HER LOVE STORY(1935); WEDDING NIGHT, THE(1935); DRACULA'S DAUGHTER(1936); PLOT THICKENS, THE(1936)

Alan Anderson
THIS IS THE ARMY(1943)

Allan Anderson
CHRISTINA(1974, Can.)

Allegretti Anderson
Misc. Talkies
GEORGIA ROSE(1930)

Andy Anderson
MAN FROM PLANET X, THE(1951), spec eff
Silents
PATCHWORK GIRL OF OZ, THE(1914)

Anita Anderson
SHUTTERED ROOM, THE(1968, Brit.)

Anna Anderson
EYES OF LAURA MARS(1978)

Anne Anderson
NORTH BY NORTHWEST(1959); TATTOO(1981)

Arline Anderson
EDDY DUCHIN STORY, THE(1956); NIGHTFALL(1956); BILLIE(1965)

Arthur Anderson
GROUP, THE(1966); MIDNIGHT COWBOY(1969); SIDELONG GLANCES OF A PIGEON KICKER, THE(1970)

Audley Anderson
ON STAGE EVERYBODY(1945); IDEA GIRL(1946); KILLERS, THE(1946); OUTLAW'S SON(1957)

Augusta Anderson
BELLE OF THE NINETIES(1934); RUGGLES OF RED GAP(1935)
Silents
RAINBOW PRINCESS, THE(1916); AMATEUR WIFE, THE(1920); GUILTY OF LOVE(1920)
Misc. Silents
SEVEN SWANS, THE(1918); ROMANTIC ADVENTURESS, A(1920); SINNERS(1920)

Axel Anderson
THUNDER ISLAND(1963); FINGER ON THE TRIGGER(1965, US/Span.); BANANAS(1971)

Barbara Anderson
CREEPSHOW(1982), cos

Beau Anderson
TATTERED DRESS, THE(1957)

Beaudine Anderson
BAND PLAYS ON, THE(1934); NO GREATER GLORY(1934); TRUE CONFESSION(1937)

Bernadine Anderson
JULIA(1977), makeup

Betty Anderson
IN THE WAKE OF A STRANGER(1960, Brit.)

Bill Anderson
FORBIDDEN ISLAND(1959); SWISS FAMILY ROBINSON(1960), p; MOON PILOT(1962), p; SAVAGE SAM(1963), p; MOON-SPINNERS, THE(1964), p; TIGER WALKS, A(1964), p; FORTY ACRE FEUD(1965); FIGHTING PRINCE OF DONEGAL, THE(1966, Brit.), p; GOLD GUITAR, THE(1966); LAS VEGAS HILLBILLYS(1966); ADVENTURES OF BULLWHIP GRIFFIN, THE(1967), p; HAPPIEST MILLIONAIRE, THE(1967), p; ONE AND ONLY GENUINE ORIGINAL FAMILY BAND, THE(1968), p; FROM NASHVILLE WITH MUSIC(1969); SMITH(1969), p; COMPUTER WORE TENNIS SHOES, THE(1970), p; BAREFOOT EXECUTIVE, THE(1971), p; YOUNG GRADUATES, THE(1971), ed; $1,000,000 DUCK(1971), p; BISCUIT EATER, THE(1972), p; CHARLEY AND THE ANGEL(1973), p; SUPERDAD(1974), p; APPLE DUMPLING GANG, THE(1975), p; DR. SYN, ALIAS THE SCARECROW(1975), p; STRONGEST MAN IN THE WORLD, THE(1975), p; DON'S PARTY(1976, Aus.), ed; SHAGGY D.A., THE(1976), p; TREASURE OF MATECUMBE(1976), p; YEAR OF LIVING DANGEROUSLY, THE(1982, Aus.), ed
Misc. Talkies
MONEY IN MY POCKET(1962)

Bill Anderson, Jr.
COAL MINER'S DAUGHTER(1980)

Billey Anderson
RECOMMENDATION FOR MERCY(1975, Can.)

Billy Anderson
WONDER BAR(1934)

Birgitta Anderson
ADVENTURES OF PICASSO, THE(1980, Swed.)

Blair Anderson
1984
ICEMAN(1984)

Blondie Anderson
THEY SHOOT HORSES, DON'T THEY?(1969), spec eff

Bob Anderson
TREASURE ISLAND(1934); RUTHLESS(1948); DESERT HAWK, THE(1950); WINCHESTER '73(1950); PLACE IN THE SUN, A(1951); LAWLESS BREED, THE(1952); BORN TO THE SADDLE(1953); SOMETHING OF VALUE(1957); LEFT-HANDED GUN, THE(1958); MAN WHO DIED TWICE, THE(1958); GAMBLER WORE A GUN, THE(1961); STAGECOACH TO DANCER'S PARK(1962); ADVANCE TO THE REAR(1964); YOUNG BILLY YOUNG(1969); KIDNAPPED(1971, Brit.), stunts
Silents
NON-STOP FLIGHT, THE(1926)

Bobby Anderson
MARYLAND(1940); YOUNG PEOPLE(1940); COLORADO PIONEERS(1945); IT'S A WONDERFUL LIFE(1946); KIDNAPPED(1948)

Booker T. Anderson
Misc. Talkies
ENFORCER FROM DEATH ROW, THE(1978)

Brian Anderson
SIDECAR RACERS(1975, Aus.); LET THE BALLOON GO(1977, Aus.); ODD ANGRY SHOT, THE(1979, Aus.); CHANT OF JIMMIE BLACKSMITH, THE(1980, Aus.); PUBERTY BLUES(1983, Aus.)
1984
PHAR LAP(1984, Aus.)

Bronco Billy Anderson
Misc. Silents
HUMANITY(1917); SON OF A GUN, THE(1919); ESCAPED CONVICT, THE(1927)

Bruce Anderson
CRY, THE BELOVED COUNTRY(1952, Brit.); 2,000 WEEKS(1970, Aus.)

Bull Anderson
MYSTERY OF THE WAX MUSEUM, THE(1933); MILKY WAY, THE(1936); HOTEL IMPERIAL(1939)

C. Anderson
Silents
OVERLAND RED(1920)

C. E. Anderson
LET FREEDOM RING(1939)
Silents
CONFLICT, THE(1921); WALLOP, THE(1921)

C.B. Anderson
COUNTRY BOY(1966)

C.E. Anderson
FOURTH HORSEMAN, THE(1933)
Misc. Silents
COMBAT, THE(1926); SCRAPPIN' KID, THE(1926); TERROR, THE(1926); RAMBLING RANGER, THE(1927)

Cap Anderson
SPURS(1930); RED RIVER VALLEY(1936); REAP THE WILD WIND(1942); OX-BOW INCIDENT, THE(1943)
Silents
NIGHT HORSEMAN, THE(1921); LOVE GAMBLER, THE(1922); CLEARING THE TRAIL(1928); LARIAT KID, THE(1929)

Capt. Anderson
WILD GEESE CALLING(1941)
Silents
KAISER, BEAST OF BERLIN, THE(1918)

Capt. C.E. Anderson
TEXAS BAD MAN(1932); WESTERNER, THE(1940)
Misc. Silents
BORDER CAVALIER, THE(1927)

Capt. Donald Anderson
FOUR FEATHERS, THE(1939, Brit.), tech adv

Captain Anderson
STEAMBOAT ROUND THE BEND(1935)

Carl Anderson
BLACK PARACHUTE, THE(1944), art d; MEET MISS BOBBY SOCKS(1944), art d; THEY LIVE IN FEAR(1944), art d; EADIE WAS A LADY(1945), art d; EVE KNEW HER APPLES(1945), art d; I LOVE A BANDLEADER(1945), art d; CLOSE CALL FOR BOSTON BLACKIE, A(1946), art d; GALLANT JOURNEY(1946), art d; RETURN OF MONTE CRISTO, THE(1946), art d; SO DARK THE NIGHT(1946), art d; TARS AND SPARS(1946), art d; HER HUSBAND'S AFFAIRS(1947), art d; DAY OF WRATH(1948,

Ester Anderson
GENGHIS KHAN(U.S./Brit./Ger./Yugo.)
Esther Anderson
TWO GENTLEMEN SHARING(1969, Brit.); ONE MORE TIME(1970, Brit.); WARM DECEMBER, A(1973, Brit.)
Misc. Talkies
TOUCHABLES, THE(1968, Brit.)
Eugene Anderson
I AM THE LAW(1938); YOU CAN'T TAKE IT WITH YOU(1938); COVER GIRL(1944); OUTLAW'S DAUGHTER, THE(1954)
Eunice Anderson
JEREMY(1973)
Evert Anderson
JOE HILL(1971, Swed./U.S.)
Ezeret Anderson
CARIBBEAN(1952)
Ferris Anderson, Jr.
WALK IN THE SPRING RAIN, A(1970), ed
Floyd Anderson
RAGING BULL(1980)
Silents
KINGFISHER'S ROOST, THE(1922)
Frank Anderson
NORSEMAN, THE(1978)
Fred Anderson
HOLD'EM YALE(1935)
Frederick Irving Anderson
NOTORIOUS SOPHIE LANG, THE(1934), w; RETURN OF SOPHIE LANG, THE(1936), w; SOPHIE LANG GOES WEST(1937), w
G.M. [Bronco Billy] Anderson
Silents
GOOD-FOR-NOTHING, THE(1914)
Misc. Silents
VERA, THE MEDIUM(1916), d; ASHES(1922), d
Gene Anderson
FLANNELFOOT(1953, Brit.); LAUGHING IN THE SUNSHINE(1953, Brit./Swed.); TALE OF THREE WOMEN, A(1954, Brit.); INTRUDER, THE(1955, Brit.); DOUBLE CROSS(1956, Brit.); LONG HAUL, THE(1957, Brit.); SHAKEDOWN, THE(1960, Brit.); DAY THE EARTH CAUGHT FIRE, THE(1961, Brit.); BREAK, THE(1962, Brit.)
George Anderson
HOTEL HAYWIRE(1937); NIGHT OF MYSTERY(1937); UNDER SUSPICION(1937); BORN TO BE WILD(1938); KING OF ALCATRAZ(1938); KING OF CHINATOWN(1939); LADY'S FROM KENTUCKY, THE(1939); MILLION DOLLAR LEGS(1939); OUR NEIGHBORS-THE CARTERS(1939); EARL OF CHICAGO, THE(1940); HIDDEN GOLD(1940); SANTA FE MARSHAL(1940); SECRET SEVEN, THE(1940); WOMEN WITHOUT NAMES(1940); MAJOR AND THE MINOR, THE(1942); DIXIE(1943); HENRY ALDRICH HAUNTS A HOUSE(1943); UNDERDOG, THE(1943); DESTINATION TOKYO(1944); HAIL THE CONQUERING HERO(1944); HENRY ALDRICH PLAYS CUPID(1944); ONCE UPON A TIME(1944); WILSON(1944); MASQUERADE IN MEXICO(1945); MILDRED PIERCE(1945); MURDER, MY SWEET(1945); NOB HILL(1945); ROAD TO UTOPIA(1945); THOSE ENDEARING YOUNG CHARMS(1945); KILLERS, THE(1946); DESPERATE(1947); SONG OF THE THIN MAN(1947); ARGYLE SECRETS, THE(1948); KING OF THE GAMBLERS(1948)
Silents
LITTLE PAL(1915); QUESTION, THE(1916)
Misc. Silents
ALMIGHTY DOLLAR, THE(1916); SHADOW OF DOUBT, THE(1916); CO-RESPONDENT, THE(1917); HER MAN(1918)
Georgine Anderson
1984
SECRETS(1984, Brit.)
Gerald Anderson
DARK MAN, THE(1951, Brit.); FOUR AGAINST FATE(1952, Brit.); STRANGER IN BETWEEN, THE(1952, Brit.); PASSAGE HOME(1955, Brit.); HORRORS OF THE BLACK MUSEUM(1959, U.S./Brit.); MOUSE ON THE MOON, THE(1963, Brit.); VIOLENT MOMENT(1966, Brit.)
Gerry Anderson
CROSSROADS TO CRIME(1960, Brit.), p, d; THUNDERBIRD 6(1968, Brit.), p&w; THUNDERBIRDS ARE GO(1968, Brit.), w; JOURNEY TO THE FAR SIDE OF THE SUN(1969, Brit.), p, w
Gilda Anderson
LAS RATAS NO DUERMEN DE NOCHE(1974, Span./Fr.)
Gloria Anderson
SHOW BUSINESS(1944); UP IN ARMS(1944); TWO SMART PEOPLE(1946)
Gordon Anderson
REFLECTION OF FEAR, A(1973)
Gus Anderson
RIDERS OF THE CACTUS(1931)
Guy Anderson
BATTLEGROUND(1949); LAWLESS, THE(1950); MAGNIFICENT YANKEE, THE(1950); YELLOW CAB MAN, THE(1950); EXCUSE MY DUST(1951); GIRL IN WHITE, THE(1952); ISLAND IN THE SKY(1953); CAINE MUTINY, THE(1954)
H. C. Anderson
WHITE DEATH(1936, Aus.), ph
Hans Christian Anderson
EMPEROR AND THE NIGHTINGALE, THE(1949, Czech.), w
Harry Anderson
TOUGH TO HANDLE(1937); PRISON TRAIN(1938); HONOLULU LU(1941); MEET BOSTON BLACKIE(1941); DOUGHBOYS IN IRELAND(1943); REVEILLE WITH BEVERLY(1943); FIRST YANK INTO TOKYO(1945); GOLDEN EARRINGS(1947); BIG CLOCK, THE(1948); STATE OF THE UNION(1948); ESCAPE ARTIST, THE(1982)
Haskell Anderson
1984
SCARRED(1984)
Haylely Anderson
MY BRILLIANT CAREER(1980, Aus.)
Hedli Anderson
COLONEL BOGEY(1948, Brit.)

Herb Anderson
I BURY THE LIVING(1958); SUNRISE AT CAMPOBELLO(1960)
Herbert Anderson
DR. EHRLICH'S MAGIC BULLET(1940); FIGHTING 69TH, THE(1940); NO TIME FOR COMEDY(1940); SEA HAWK, THE(1940); BODY DISAPPEARS, THE(1941); BRIDE CAME C.O.D., THE(1941); DIVE BOMBER(1941); HONEYMOON FOR THREE(1941); KNOCKOUT(1941); NAVY BLUES(1941); STRAWBERRY BLONDE, THE(1941); MALE ANIMAL, THE(1942); THIS IS THE ARMY(1943); LOVE AND LEARN(1947); THAT WAY WITH WOMEN(1947); GIVE MY REGARDS TO BROADWAY(1948); YOU WERE MEANT FOR ME(1948); SET-UP, THE(1949); FINDERS KEEPERS(1951); BENNY GOODMAN STORY, THE(1956); FOUR GIRLS IN TOWN(1956); JOE BUTTERFLY(1957); KELLY AND ME(1957); MY MAN GODFREY(1957); NIGHT PASSAGE(1957); SPRING REUNION(1957); HOLD ON(1966); RASCAL(1969)
Hesper Anderson
TOUCHED BY LOVE(1980), w
Hillyard Anderson
COMPUTER WORE TENNIS SHOES, THE(1970)
Howard A. Anderson
KIT CARSON(1940), spec eff; UNKNOWN ISLAND(1948), spec eff; LOVE HAPPY(1949), spec eff; INVASION OF THE SAUCER MEN(1957), spec eff; TWELVE TO THE MOON(1960), spec eff; JACK THE GIANT KILLER(1962), spec eff; WOMEN OF THE PREHISTORIC PLANET(1966), spec eff; VENUS IN FURS(1970, Ital./Brit./Ger.), spec eff; MEPHISTO WALTZ, THE(1971), spec eff; DOC SAVAGE... THE MAN OF BRONZE(1975), spec eff
Howard Anderson
WHITE ZOMBIE(1932), spec eff; NEW ADVENTURES OF TARZAN(1935), spec eff; PRISON TRAIN(1938), spec eff; FLYING DEUCES, THE(1939), spec eff; MAN IN THE IRON MASK, THE(1939), spec eff; BEYOND TOMORROW(1940), spec eff; MY SON, MY SON!(1940), spec eff; CORSICAN BROTHERS, THE(1941), spec eff; GENTLEMAN AFTER DARK, A(1942), spec eff; STRANGE HOLIDAY(1945), spec eff; PHANTOM FROM SPACE(1953), spec eff; X-15(1961), ph; VARAN THE UNBELIEVABLE(1962, U.S./Jap.), spec eff; WILD HARVEST(1962), spec eff
Hyde Anderson
ZAPPED!(1982)
Ian Anderson
ROAD TO SALINA(1971, Fr./Ital.), m
Ida Anderson
Misc. Silents
SON OF SATAN, A(1924)
Inez Anderson
HANSEL AND GRETEL(1954), anim
Inga Anderson
DON CHICAGO(1945, Brit.)
Ingrid Anderson
HERCULES(1983)
Ira Anderson
FRANKENSTEIN'S DAUGHTER(1958), spec eff; MISSILE TO THE MOON(1959), spec eff; TARZAN AND THE VALLEY OF GOLD(1966 U.S./Switz.), spec eff; TARZAN AND THE GREAT RIVER(1967, U.S./Switz.), spec eff; GETTING STRAIGHT(1970), spec eff; GOING HOME(1971), spec eff; JENNIFER ON MY MIND(1971), spec eff; MURPHY'S WAR(1971, Brit.), spec eff
Ira Anderson, Jr.
TARZAN AND THE VALLEY OF GOLD(1966 U.S./Switz.), spec eff; SILENT MOVIE(1976), spec eff; MODERN PROBLEMS(1981), spec eff
Irv Anderson
MOUSE AND HIS CHILD, THE(1977), anim
Isabelle Anderson
1984
CAREFUL, HE MIGHT HEAR YOU(1984, Aus.)
Ivie Anderson
DAY AT THE RACES, A(1937)
J.L. Anderson
MISS JESSICA IS PREGNANT(1970), p, d, w, ed
Jack Anderson
PROMISES IN THE DARK(1979)
James Anderson
SERGEANT YORK(; DIVE BOMBER(1941); GREAT SINNER, THE(1949); TIGHT LITTLE ISLAND(1949, Brit.); HUNT THE MAN DOWN(1950); ALONG THE GREAT DIVIDE(1951); FIVE(1951); DUEL AT SILVER CREEK, THE(1952); LAST MUSKETEER, THE(1952); RUBY GENTRY(1952); CHINA VENTURE(1953); FLIGHT TO TANGIER(1953); GREAT JESSE JAMES RAID, THE(1953); DRAGNET(1954); DRUMS ACROSS THE RIVER(1954); PUSHOVER(1954); RIOT IN CELL BLOCK 11(1954); SCOTCH ON THE ROCKS(1954, Brit.); AT GUNPOINT(1955); MARAUDERS, THE(1955); SEVEN ANGRY MEN(1955); VIOLENT MEN, THE(1955); FRIENDLY PERSUASION(1956); FURY AT GUNSIGHT PASS(1956); RAWHIDE YEARS, THE(1956); RUNNING TARGET(1956); BIG LAND, THE(1957); I MARRIED A MONSTER FROM OUTER SPACE(1958); THING THAT COULDN'T DIE, THE(1958); CONNECTION, THE(1962); PRESSURE POINT(1962); TO KILL A MOCKINGBIRD(1962); TAKE THE MONEY AND RUN(1969); BALLAD OF CABLE HOGUE, THE(1970); LITTLE BIG MAN(1970)
Misc. Talkies
LAST MUSKETEER, THE(1952)
Silents
FRESHMAN, THE(1925)
Jamie Anderson
WHITE LINE FEVER(1975, Can.); GREAT TEXAS DYNAMITE CHASE, THE(1976), ph; HOLLYWOOD BOULEVARD(1976), ph; MALIBU BEACH(1978), ph; PIRANHA(1978), ph
Jane E. Anderson
1984
RUNNING HOT(1984), cos
Jean Anderson
MARK OF CAIN, THE(1948, Brit.); LIFE IN HER HANDS(1951, Brit.); NAUGHTY ARLETTE(1951, Brit.); BRAVE DON'T CRY, THE(1952, Brit.); FRANCHISE AFFAIR, THE(1952, Brit.); WHITE CORRIDORS(1952, Brit.); JOHNNY ON THE RUN(1953, Brit.); LEASE OF LIFE(1954, Brit.); LITTLE KIDNAPPERS, THE(1954, Brit.); SECRET TENT, THE(1956, Brit.); BARRETTS OF WIMPOLE STREET, THE(1957); LUCKY JIM(1957, Brit.); HEART OF A CHILD(1958, Brit.); ROBBERY UNDER ARMS(1958, Brit.); TOWN LIKE ALICE, A(1958, Brit.); S.O.S. PACIFIC(1960, Brit.); SPARE THE

ROD(1961, Brit.); LISA(1962, Brit.); WALTZ OF THE TOREADORS(1962, Brit.); THREE LIVES OF THOMASINA, THE(1963, U.S./Brit.); SILENT PLAYGROUND, THE(1964, Brit.); HALF A SIXPENCE(1967, Brit.); BROTHERLY LOVE(1970, Brit.); NIGHT DIGGER, THE(1971, Brit.); LADY VANISHES, THE(1980, Brit.)
Misc. Talkies
SCREAMTIME(1983, Brit.)

Jeannie Anderson
FANDANGO(1970)
Misc. Talkies
DOUBLE INITIATION(1970)

Jennie Anderson
NEW YEAR'S EVIL(1980)

Jerry Anderson
ROSEANNA McCOY(1949); ATTACK OF THE KILLER TOMATOES(1978); CHU CHU AND THE PHILLY FLASH(1981)

Jim Anderson
VILLAIN, THE(1979)
Misc. Talkies
BRIG, THE(1965)

Jim Cassett Anderson
1984
CANNONBALL RUN II(1984)

Jimmy Anderson
YOU CAN'T TAKE IT WITH YOU(1938)
Misc. Silents
COLLEGE BOOB, THE(1926)

Joan Anderson
LONNIE(1963)

Jock Anderson
VISIT TO A CHIEF'S SON(1974)

Jodi Anderson
PERSONAL BEST(1982)

John A. Anderson
JOHNNY RENO(1966), cos; WILL PENNY(1968), cos; STERILE CUCKOO, THE(1969), cos; MAN IN THE GLASS BOOTH, THE(1975); CHEAP DETECTIVE, THE(1978), cos

John Anderson
TREASURE ISLAND(1934); TRUE STORY OF LYNN STUART, THE(1958); PSYCHO(1960); GERONIMO(1962); RIDE THE HIGH COUNTRY(1962); WALK ON THE WILD SIDE(1962); HALLELUJAH TRAIL, THE(1965); SATAN BUG, THE(1965); COVENANT WITH DEATH, A(1966); NAMU, THE KILLER WHALE(1966); WELCOME TO HARD TIMES(1967); DAY OF THE EVIL GUN(1968); FIVE CARD STUD(1968); GREAT BANK ROBBERY, THE(1969); HEAVEN WITH A GUN(1969); MAN CALLED GANNON, A(1969); YOUNG BILLY YOUNG(1969); COTTON COMES TO HARLEM(1970); SOLDIER BLUE(1970); ANIMALS, THE(1971); KOTCH(1971), cos; MAN AND BOY(1972); MOLLY AND LAWLESS JOHN(1972); EXECUTIVE ACTION(1973); DOVE, THE(1974, Brit.); SPECIALIST, THE(1975); AIRPORT '77(1977), cos; LINCOLN CONSPIRACY, THE(1977); IN SEARCH OF HISTORIC JESUS(1980); SMOKEY AND THE BANDIT II(1980); PATERNITY(1981), set d; ZOOT SUIT(1981); OUT OF THE BLUE(1982); SOME KIND OF HERO(1982), set d; LONE WOLF McQUADE(1983)
1984
KARATE KID, THE(1984), set d
Misc. Talkies
STEPMOTHER, THE(1973); SPECIALIST, THE(1975); ASHES AND EMBERS(1982)

John H. Anderson
UNCOMMON VALOR(1983), set d

John Murray Anderson
ZIEGFELD FOLLIES(1945), w

John R. Anderson
LAST TRAIN FROM GUN HILL(1959)

Judith Anderson
BLOOD MONEY(1933); FORTY LITTLE MOTHERS(1940); REBECCA(1940); FREE AND EASY(1941); LADY SCARFACE(1941); ALL THROUGH THE NIGHT(1942); KING'S ROW(1942); EDGE OF DARKNESS(1943); STAGE DOOR CANTEEN(1943); LAURA(1944); AND THEN THERE WERE NONE(1945); DIARY OF A CHAMBERMAID(1946); SPECTER OF THE ROSE(1946); STRANGE LOVE OF MARTHA IVERS, THE(1946); PURSUED(1947); RED HOUSE, THE(1947); TYCOON(1947); FURIES, THE(1950); SALOME(1953); TEN COMMANDMENTS, THE(1956); CAT ON A HOT TIN ROOF(1958); CINDERFELLA(1960); MACBETH(1963); WHY BOTHER TO KNOCK(1964, Brit.); MAN CALLED HORSE, A(1970); INN OF THE DAMNED(1974, Aus.)

Jurgen Anderson
BOYS FROM BRAZIL, THE(1978)

Kate Anderson
Silents
MAN'S LAW AND GOD'S(1922)

Katherine Anderson
QUEEN BEE(1955); TIGHT SPOT(1955)

Keigh Anderson
MYSTERY SUBMARINE(1963, Brit.)

Ken Anderson
RELUCTANT DRAGON, THE(1941), anim d; MELODY TIME(1948), w; STORY OF THREE LOVES, THE(1953); SLEEPING BEAUTY(1959), prod d; ONE HUNDRED AND ONE DALMATIANS(1961), prod d&art d; SWORD IN THE STONE, THE(1963), art d; JUNGLE BOOK, THE(1967), w; ARISTOCATS, THE(1970), w, prod d; ROBIN HOOD(1973), w; PETE'S DRAGON(1977), anim; RESCUERS, THE(1977), w; PHOBIA(1980, Can.)

Kenneth Anderson
SNOW WHITE AND THE SEVEN DWARFS(1937), art d; FANTASIA(1940), art d; PINOCCHIO(1940), art d; CINDERELLA(1950), w
1984
STONE BOY, THE(1984)

Kevin C. Anderson
RISKY BUSINESS(1983)

Kimelle Anderson
FIRE SALE(1977)

Ladd Anderson
REVENGE OF THE NINJA(1983)

Lance Anderson
PARASITE(1982), spec eff; MAN WITH TWO BRAINS, THE(1983), makeup

Larry Anderson
1984
HOT MOVES(1984), w

Laurence Anderson
FIRE RAISERS, THE(1933, Brit.); NIGHT OF THE PARTY, THE(1934, Brit.); GANGWAY(1937, Brit.)

Lawrence Anderson
THREADS(1932, Brit.); MAYFAIR GIRL(1933, Brit.); RIGHT TO LIVE, THE(1933, Brit.); CASE FOR THE CROWN, THE(1934, Brit.); MONEY MAD(1934, Brit.); EXPERT'S OPINION(1935, Brit.); MARRY THE GIRL(1935, Brit.); NELL GWYN(1935, Brit.); ROYAL EAGLE(1936, Brit.); LET'S MAKE A NIGHT OF IT(1937, Brit.); MAKE-UP(1937, Brit.); MAN OF AFFAIRS(1937, Brit.); YOU'RE IN THE ARMY NOW(1937, Brit.)
Silents
INNOCENT(1921, Brit.)
Misc. Silents
BLUFF(1921, Brit.); RECOIL, THE(1922, Brit.)

Leif Anderson
OF UNKNOWN ORIGIN(1983, Can.)

Leona Anderson
HOUSE ON HAUNTED HILL(1958)
Misc. Silents
ASHES(1922)

Leonard Anderson
CITIZEN SAINT(1947), ed; SINGING IN THE DARK(1956), ed; BRAIN THAT WOULDN'T DIE, THE(1959), ed

Les "Carrot Top" Anderson
KENTUCKY JUBILEE(1951)

Leslie Anderson
FAR FROM THE MADDING CROWD(1967, Brit.); WOMEN IN LOVE(1969, Brit.)

Lindsay Anderson
TOGETHER(1956, Brit.), ed; PRIVATE POOLEY(1962, Brit./E. Ger.); THIS SPORTING LIFE(1963, Brit.), d; SHOP ON MAIN STREET, THE(1966, Czech.), titles; IF ...(1968, Brit.), p, d; INADMISSIBLE EVIDENCE(1968, Brit.); MARTYRS OF LOVE(1968, Czech.); O LUCKY MAN!(1973, Brit.), a, p, d; IN CELEBRATION(1975, Brit.), d; CHARRIOTS OF FIRE(1981, Brit.); BRITTANIA HOSPITAL(1982, Brit.), d

Lita Anderson
Misc. Talkies
BELOW THE HILL(1974)

Loni Anderson
STROKER ACE(1983)

Louis Anderson
1984
CLOAK AND DAGGER(1984)

Louise Anderson
1984
RIVER RAT, THE(1984)

Lynn Anderson
Misc. Silents
TEXAS TOMMY(1928)

M.A. Anderson
JAZZ CINDERELLA(1930), ph; LADIES IN LOVE(1930), ph; LOTUS LADY(1930), ph; GRIEF STREET(1931), ph; LADY FROM NOWHERE(1931), ph; MIDNIGHT SPECIAL(1931), ph; BEAUTY PARLOR(1932), ph; ESCAPADE(1932), ph; FORBIDDEN COMPANY(1932), ph; KING MURDER, THE(1932), ph; LAST RIDE, THE(1932), ph; MIDNIGHT LADY(1932), ph; PROBATION(1932), ph; SECRETS OF WU SIN(1932), ph; THRILL OF YOUTH(1932), ph; BY APPOINTMENT ONLY(1933), ph; DANCE, GIRL, DANCE(1933), ph; FORGOTTEN(1933), ph; I HAVE LIVED(1933), ph; LOVE IS LIKE THAT(1933), ph; MAN OF SENTIMENT, A(1933), ph; RAINBOW OVER BROADWAY(1933), ph; SLIGHTLY MARRIED(1933), ph; STRANGE PEOPLE(1933), ph; WOMEN WON'T TELL(1933), ph; CROSS STREETS(1934), ph; FUGITIVE ROAD(1934), ph; GREEN EYES(1934), ph; IN LOVE WITH LIFE(1934), ph; IN THE MONEY(1934), ph; MURDER ON THE CAMPUS(1934), ph; NOTORIOUS BUT NICE(1934), ph; QUITTERS, THE(1934), ph; STOLEN SWEETS(1934), ph; CIRCUMSTANTIAL EVIDENCE(1935), ph; CONDEMNED TO LIVE(1935), ph; CURTAIN FALLS, THE(1935), ph; FALSE PRETENSES(1935), ph; GHOST WALKS, THE(1935), ph; LADY IN SCARLET, THE(1935), ph; ONE IN A MILLION(1935), ph; PORT OF LOST DREAMS(1935), ph; PUBLIC OPINION(1935), ph; SOCIETY FEVER(1935), ph; SONS OF STEEL(1935), ph; SYMPHONY OF LIVING(1935), ph; WORLD ACCUSES, THE(1935), ph; AUGUST WEEK-END(1936, Brit.), ph; BELOW THE DEADLINE(1936), ph; BRIDGE OF SIGHS(1936), ph; BRILLIANT MARRIAGE(1936), ph; DARK HOUR, THE(1936), ph; LITTLE RED SCHOOLHOUSE(1936), ph; MISSING GIRLS(1936), ph; MURDER AT GLEN ATHOL(1936), ph; RING AROUND THE MOON(1936), ph; HOUSE OF SECRETS, THE(1937), ph; RED LIGHTS AHEAD(1937), ph; DELINQUENT PARENTS(1938), ph; BETTY CO-ED(1946), ph; WHIRLWIND RAIDERS(1948), ph
Silents
ADORABLE CHEAT, THE(1928), ph; SKY RIDER, THE(1928), ph; CAMPUS KNIGHTS(1929), ph; JUST OFF BROADWAY(1929), ph; PEACOCK FAN(1929), ph

M.A. "Andy" Anderson
TWIN HUSBANDS(1934), ph

M.S. Anderson
LAWLESS WOMAN, THE(1931), ph

Maceo Anderson
RHYTHM OF THE ISLANDS(1943)

Maceo Edward Anderson
HERE COME THE GIRLS(1953)

Marc Anderson
BRAIN THAT WOULDN'T DIE, THE(1959), ed
Misc. Talkies
MATTER OF LOVE, A(1979)

Margaret Anderson
HAPPIEST DAYS OF YOUR LIFE(1950, Brit.); NAUGHTY ARLETTE(1951, Brit.); LARGE ROPE, THE(1953, Brit.); BAREFOOT CONTESSA, THE(1954); RIVER BEAT(1954); ROOM IN THE HOUSE(1955, Brit.); REVENGE OF THE PINK PANTHER(1978)

Marilyn Anderson
FOREST, THE(1983)
Marion Clayton Anderson
CROWNING EXPERIENCE, THE(1960), d
Mark Anderson
SECOND THOUGHTS(1983)
Mary Anderson
GONE WITH THE WIND(1939); ALL THIS AND HEAVEN TOO(1940); DISPATCH FROM REUTERS, A(1940); FLIGHT ANGELS(1940); SEA HAWK, THE(1940); 'TIL WE MEET AGAIN(1940); BAHAMA PASSAGE(1941); CHEERS FOR MISS BISHOP(1941); HENRY ALDRICH FOR PRESIDENT(1941); UNDER AGE(1941); HENRY AND DIZZY(1942); SONG OF BERNADETTE, THE(1943); LIFEBOAT(1944); WILSON(1944); WITHIN THESE WALLS(1945); BEHIND GREEN LIGHTS(1946); TO EACH HIS OWN(1946); WHISPERING CITY(1947, Can.); HUNT THE MAN DOWN(1950); LAST OF THE BUCCANEERS(1950); WHIPPED, THE(1950); CHICAGO CALLING(1951); PASSAGE WEST(1951); ONE BIG AFFAIR(1952); DANGEROUS CROSSING(1953); I, THE JURY(1953); JET OVER THE ATLANTIC(1960)
Silents
BY RIGHT OF POSSESSION(1917); FALSE FACES(1919); JOHNNY GET YOUR GUN(1919); TWO MINUTES TO GO(1921); ENEMIES OF CHILDREN(1923)
Misc. Silents
BLUEBEARD, JR.(; LAST MAN, THE(1916); DIVORCEE, THE(1917); FLAMING OMEN, THE(1917); MAGNIFICENT MEDDLER, THE(1917); SUNLIGHT'S LAST RAID(1917); HIS BIRTHRIGHT(1918); WHEN MEN ARE TEMPTED(1918); SPENDER, THE(1919); BUBBLES(1920); TOO MUCH MARRIED(1921); HALF BREED, THE(1922); WILDNESS OF YOUTH(1922); SHELL SHOCKED SAMMY(1923)
Maurice Anderson
HONEYSUCKLE ROSE(1980)
Max Anderson
TREASURE AT THE MILL(1957, Brit.), d; CAUGHT IN THE NET(1960, Brit.), w; HIGH YELLOW(1965); IN THE YEAR 2889(1966); STUDENT TEACHERS, THE(1973)
1984
PHILADELPHIA EXPERIMENT, THE(1984), spec eff
Max W. Anderson
1984
CHILDREN OF THE CORN(1984), spec eff; ICE PIRATES, THE(1984), spec eff
Maxine Anderson
POLO JOE(1936)
Maxwell Anderson
COCK-EYED WORLD, THE(1929), w; SATURDAY'S CHILDREN(1929), w; ALL QUIET ON THE WESTERN FRONT(1930), w; RAIN(1932), w; WASHINGTON MERRY-GO-ROUND(1932), w; HOT PEPPER(1933), w; DEATH TAKES A HOLIDAY(1934), w; WE LIVE AGAIN(1934), w; MAYBE IT'S LOVE(1935), w; SO RED THE ROSE(1935), w; MARY OF SCOTLAND(1936), w; WINTERSET(1936), w; PRIVATE LIVES OF ELIZABETH AND ESSEX, THE(1939), w; SATURDAY'S CHILDREN(1940), w; EVE OF ST. MARK, THE(1944), w; KNICKERBOCKER HOLIDAY(1944), w; JOAN OF ARC(1948), w; KEY LARGO(1948), w; WHAT PRICE GLORY?(1952), w; WRONG MAN, THE(1956), w; NEVER STEAL ANYTHING SMALL(1959), w; ANNE OF THE THOUSAND DAYS(1969, Brit.), w; LOST IN THE STARS(1974), w
Silents
WHAT PRICE GLORY(1926), w
Mel Anderson
DARK, THE(1979)
Melissa Sue Anderson
HAPPY BIRTHDAY TO ME(1981)
1984
CHATTANOOGA CHOO CHOO(1984)
Melody Anderson
FLASH GORDON(1980); DEAD AND BURIED(1981)
Mia Anderson
CURSE OF THE FLY(1965, Brit.)
Michael Anderson
PRIVATE ANGELO(1949, Brit.), d, w; HELL IS SOLD OUT(1951, Brit.), d; NIGHT WAS OUR FRIEND(1951, Brit.), d; WATERFRONT WOMEN(1952, Brit.), d; HOUSE OF THE ARROW, THE(1953, Brit.), d; WILL ANY GENTLEMAN?(1955, Brit.), d; AROUND THE WORLD IN 80 DAYS(1956), d; BATTLE HELL(1956, Brit.), d; 1984(1956, Brit.), d; CHASE A CROOKED SHADOW(1958, Brit.), d; SHAKE HANDS WITH THE DEVIL(1959, Ireland), p&d; WRECK OF THE MARY DEAR, THE(1959), d; ALL THE FINE YOUNG CANNIBALS(1960), d; TWELVE TO THE MOON(1960), m; NAKED EDGE, THE(1961), d; FLIGHT FROM ASHIYA(1964, U.S./Jap.), d; WILD AND WONDERFUL(1964), d; OPERATION CROSSBOW(1965, U.S./Ital.), d; QUILLER MEMORANDUM, THE(1966, Brit.), d; SHOES OF THE FISHERMAN, THE(1968), d; POPE JOAN(1972, Brit.), d; HUCKLEBERRY FINN(1974), ed; CONDUCT UNBECOMING(1975, Brit.), d; DOC SAVAGE... THE MAN OF BRONZE(1975), d; REINCARNATION OF PETER PROUD, THE(1975), d; LOGAN'S RUN(1976), d; ORCA(1977), d; LULU(1978); LOVE AND BULLETS(1979, Brit.), ed; BELLS(1981, Can.), d
1984
SECOND TIME LUCKY(1984, Aus./New Zealand), d
Michael Anderson, Jr.
MOONRAKER, THE(1958, Brit.); SUNDOWNERS, THE(1960); IN SEARCH OF THE CASTAWAYS(1962, Brit.); PLAY IT COOL(1963, Brit.); REACH FOR GLORY(1963, Brit.); DEAR HEART(1964); GLORY GUYS, THE(1965); GREATEST STORY EVER TOLD, THE(1965); MAJOR DUNDEE(1965); SONS OF KATIE ELDER, THE(1965); WUSA(1970); LAST MOVIE, THE(1971); LOGAN'S RUN(1976)
Michael Anderson, Sr.
DAM BUSTERS, THE(1955, Brit.), d
Michael F. Anderson
ECHOES OF A SUMMER(1976), ed; ST. IVES(1976), ed; WHITE BUFFALO, THE(1977), ed; CABOBLANCO(1981), ed; SPHINX(1981), ed; YES, GIORGIO(1982), ed
Micheal Anderson
DOMINIQUE(1978, Brit.), d
Mignon Anderson
Silents
EVEN AS YOU AND I(1917); KING SPRUCE(1920); KISSES(1922)
Misc. Silents
NAIDRA, THE DREAM WOMAN(1914, Ger.); MILESTONES OF LIFE(1915); MILL ON THE FLOSS, THE(1915); PRICE OF HER SILENCE, THE(1915); CITY OF ILLUSION, THE(1916); PAMELA'S PAST(1916); WOMAN IN POLITICS, THE(1916); CIRCUS OF LIFE, THE(1917); PHANTOM'S SECRET, THE(1917); WIFE ON TRAIL,

A(1917); CLAIM, THE(1918); MIDNIGHT STAGE, THE(1919); HEART OF A WOMAN, THE(1920); MOUNTAIN MADNESS(1920); CUPID'S BRAND(1921)
Miles Anderson
THIRTY NINE STEPS, THE(1978, Brit.)
Milford Anderson
BORDER FEUD(1947), ph; WEST TO GLORY(1947), ph
Milo Anderson
KID FROM SPAIN, THE(1932), cos; CAPTAIN BLOOD(1935), cos; ANTHONY ADVERSE(1936), cos; CHARGE OF THE LIGHT BRIGADE, THE(1936), cos; STORY OF LOUIS PASTEUR, THE(1936), cos; BLACK LEGION, THE(1937), cos; GREAT GARRICK, THE(1937), cos; GREAT O'MALLEY, THE(1937), cos; LIFE OF EMILE ZOLA, THE(1937), cos; MELODY FOR TWO(1937), cos; MOUNTAIN JUSTICE(1937), cos; MR. DODD TAKES THE AIR(1937), cos; ONCE A DOCTOR(1937), cos; PRINCE AND THE PAUPER, THE(1937), cos; ADVENTURES OF ROBIN HOOD, THE(1938), cos; AMAZING DR. CLITTERHOUSE, THE(1938), cos; BOY MEETS GIRL(1938), cos; FOOLS FOR SCANDAL(1938), cos; NANCY DREW–DETECTIVE(1938), cos; DODGE CITY(1939), cos; HELL'S KITCHEN(1939), cos; RETURN OF DR. X, THE(1939), cos; ROARING TWENTIES, THE(1939), cos; THEY MADE ME A CRIMINAL(1939), cos; WATERFRONT(1939), cos; YOU CAN'T GET AWAY WITH MURDER(1939), cos; INVISIBLE STRIPES(1940), cos; LADY WITH RED HAIR(1940), cos; SANTA FE TRAIL(1940), cos; SATURDAY'S CHILDREN(1940), cos; THEY DRIVE BY NIGHT(1940), cos; THREE CHEERS FOR THE IRISH(1940), cos; HIGH SIERRA(1941), cos; MANPOWER(1941), cos; ACROSS THE PACIFIC(1942), cos; BIG SHOT, THE(1942), cos; DESPERATE JOURNEY(1942), cos; GENTLEMAN JIM(1942), cos; SPY SHIP(1942), cos; THEY DIED WITH THEIR BOOTS ON(1942), cos; YANKEE DOODLE DANDY(1942), cos; YOU CAN'T ESCAPE FOREVER(1942), cos; ACTION IN THE NORTH ATLANTIC(1943), cos; MYSTERIOUS DOCTOR, THE(1943), cos; THANK YOUR LUCKY STARS(1943), cos; TRUCK BUSTERS(1943), cos; HOLLYWOOD CANTEEN(1944), cos; TO HAVE AND HAVE NOT(1944), cos; VERY THOUGHT OF YOU, THE(1944), cos; CONFLICT(1945), cos; DANGER SIGNAL(1945), cos; MILDRED PIERCE(1945), cos; PILLOW TO POST(1945), cos; SAN ANTONIO(1945), cos; NIGHT AND DAY(1946), cos; NOBODY LIVES FOREVER(1946), cos; LIFE WITH FATHER(1947), cos; TWO MRS. CARROLLS, THE(1947), cos; UNSUSPECTED, THE(1947), cos; JOHNNY BELINDA(1948), cos; ROMANCE ON THE HIGH SEAS(1948), cos; TO THE VICTOR(1948), cos; WHIPLASH(1948), cos; FOUNTAINHEAD, THE(1949), cos; IT'S A GREAT FEELING(1949), cos; JOHN LOVES MARY(1949), cos; LADY TAKES A SAILOR, THE(1949), cos; MY DREAM IS YOURS(1949), cos; ONE LAST FLING(1949), cos; SOUTH OF ST. LOUIS(1949), cos; MONTANA(1950), cos; PERFECT STRANGERS(1950), cos; STAGE FRIGHT(1950, Brit.), cos; STORM WARNING(1950), cos; WEST POINT STORY, THE(1950), cos; YOUNG MAN WITH A HORN(1950), cos; JIM THORPE–ALL AMERICAN(1951), cos; LULLABY OF BROADWAY(1951), cos; ON MOONLIGHT BAY(1951), cos; PAINTING THE CLOUDS WITH SUNSHINE(1951), cos; MARA MARU(1952), cos; STORY OF WILL ROGERS, THE(1952), cos; SO BIG(1953), cos; MIRACLE IN THE RAIN(1956), cos
Morgan Anderson
DEAR JOHN(1966, Swed.)
Mrs. R. S. Anderson
Silents
DOLL'S HOUSE, A(1918)
Myrtle Anderson
GREEN PASTURES(1936); TOY WIFE, THE(1938); LADY IS WILLING, THE(1942); PERILS OF PAULINE, THE(1947); SEA OF GRASS, THE(1947); OH, YOU BEAUTIFUL DOLL(1949); WHIRLPOOL(1949); FOLLOW THE SUN(1951); WHITE WITCH DOCTOR(1953); JEANNE EAGELS(1957)
Myrtle D. Anderson
BRIDE WORE BOOTS, THE(1946)
Nancy Anderson
GHOST OF DRAGSTRIP HOLLOW(1959); COME SEPTEMBER(1961)
Neal Anderson
1984
MISUNDERSTOOD(1984)
Nellie Anderson
Silents
TWO-EDGED SWORD, THE(1916); HOODLUM THE(1919); WITHOUT LIMIT(1921); ANGEL OF CROOKED STREET, THE(1922)
Nina Anderson
DAY THE EARTH FROZE, THE(1959, Fin./USSR)
P. Kip Anderson
DOUBLES(1978), ph
Pat Anderson
DIRTY O'NEIL(1974); NEWMAN'S LAW(1974); TNT JACKSON(1975); SUMMER SCHOOL TEACHERS(1977)
Misc. Talkies
COVER GIRL MODELS(1975)
Paul Anderson
ONCE UPON A HORSE(1958); HARRY'S WAR(1981)
1984
PURPLE HEARTS(1984)
Pershing P. Anderson
DOCTOR DETROIT(1983)
Peter Anderson
GOLDEN SEAL, THE(1983)
1984
BIG MEAT EATER(1984, Can.)
Phil Anderson
GIANT(1956), ed
Philip Anderson
HAPPENING, THE(1967), ed; HOW TO SAVE A MARRIAGE–AND RUIN YOUR LIFE(1968), ed
Philip W Anderson
CASH McCALL(1960), ed
Philip W. Anderson
OCEAN BREAKERS(1949, Swed.), ed; SAYONARA(1957), ed; FBI STORY, THE(1959), ed; WESTBOUND(1959), ed; OCEAN'S ELEVEN(1960), ed; TALL STORY(1960), ed; MAJORITY OF ONE, A(1961), ed; PARENT TRAP, THE(1961), ed; ONE MAN'S WAY(1964), ed; MISTER MOSES(1965), ed; MOMENT TO MOMENT(1966), ed; NIGHT OF THE GRIZZLY, THE(1966), ed; SWEET RIDE, THE(1968), ed; MAN CALLED HORSE, A(1970), ed; MRS. POLLIFAX-SPY(1971), ed

Phillip W. Anderson
HOME BEFORE DARK(1958), ed; GYPSY(1962), ed
Ralph Anderson
SECOND THOUGHTS(1983)
Randy Anderson
1984
HOT AND DEADLY(1984)
Reginald Price Anderson
GHOST, THE(1965, Ital.)
Reid Anderson
SECRETS OF SEX(1970, Brit.)
Relyea Anderson
Silents
SHOULD A WOMAN TELL?(1920)
Rhoda Anderson
GLASS HOUSES(1972)
Richard Anderson
TWELVE O'CLOCK HIGH(1949); LIFE OF HER OWN, A(1950); MAGNIFICENT YANKEE, THE(1950); VANISHING WESTERNER, THE(1950); ACROSS THE WIDE MISSOURI(1951); CAUSE FOR ALARM(1951); NO QUESTIONS ASKED(1951); PAYMENT ON DEMAND(1951); PEOPLE AGAINST O'HARA, THE(1951); RICH, YOUNG AND PRETTY(1951); UNKNOWN MAN, THE(1951); FEARLESS FAGAN(1952); HOLIDAY FOR SINNERS(1952); JUST THIS ONCE(1952); SCARAMOUCHE(1952); DREAM WIFE(1953); ESCAPE FROM FORT BRAVO(1953); GIVE A GIRL A BREAK(1953); I LOVE MELVIN(1953); STORY OF THREE LOVES, THE(1953); STUDENT PRINCE, THE(1954); BAR SINISTER, THE(1955); HIT THE DECK(1955); CRY IN THE NIGHT, A(1956); FORBIDDEN PLANET(1956); SEARCH FOR BRIDEY MURPHY, THE(1956); BUSTER KEATON STORY, THE(1957); PATHS OF GLORY(1957); THREE BRAVE MEN(1957); CURSE OF THE FACELESS MAN(1958); LONG, HOT SUMMER, THE(1958); COMPULSION(1959); GUNFIGHT AT DODGE CITY, THE(1959); WACKIEST SHIP IN THE ARMY, THE(1961); GATHERING OF EAGLES, A(1963); JOHNNY COOL(1963); KITTEN WITH A WHIP(1964); SEVEN DAYS IN MAY(1964); SECONDS(1966); RIDE TO HANGMAN'S TREE, THE(1967); MACHO CALLAHAN(1970); TORA! TORA! TORA!(1970, U.S./Jap.); DOCTORS' WIVES(1971); HONKERS, THE(1972); PLAY IT AS IT LAYS(1972); BLACK EYE(1974)
Rick Anderson
KING OF DODGE CITY(1941); RIDERS OF THE BADLANDS(1941); COWBOY SERENADE(1942); LONE STAR VIGILANTES, THE(1942); THUNDER RIVER FEUD(1942)
Robert Anderson
UNCLE HARRY(1945); UNTIL THEY SAIL(1957), w; WHITE SHADOWS IN THE SOUTH SEAS(1928); CLEAR THE DECKS(1929); WINGS OVER HONOLULU(1937); ADVENTURES OF A ROOKIE(1943); HIGHER AND HIGHER(1943); IRON MAJOR, THE(1943); LEOPARD MAN, THE(1943); MEXICAN SPITFIRE'S BLESSED EVENT(1943); TENDER COMRADE(1943); ACTION IN ARABIA(1944); BRIDE BY MISTAKE(1944); FALCON OUT WEST, THE(1944); MARINE RAIDERS(1944); SINCE YOU WENT AWAY(1944); JOHNNY ANGEL(1945); TREE GROWS IN BROOKLYN, A(1945); WEST OF THE PECOS(1945); COCKEYED MIRACLE, THE(1946); NOCTURNE(1946); WOMAN ON THE BEACH, THE(1947); JOAN OF ARC(1948); FRANCIS(1949); UNDERTOW(1949); BRIGHT VICTORY(1951); MOB, THE(1951); TWO OF A KIND(1951); LAWLESS BREED, THE(1952); UNTAMED FRONTIER(1952); TAKE ME TO TOWN(1953); LONG, LONG TRAILER, THE(1954); OUTLAW STALLION, THE(1954); FURY AT GUNSIGHT PASS(1956); TEA AND SYMPATHY(1956), w; TOY TIGER(1956); NIGHT RUNNER, THE(1957); PAL JOEY(1957); PHANTOM STAGECOACH, THE(1957); TALL T, THE(1957); BUCHANAN RIDES ALONE(1958); HIGH SCHOOL HELLCATS(1958); JOY RIDE(1958); NUN'S STORY, THE(1959), w; CROWNING EXPERIENCE, THE(1960); YOUNG GRADUATES, THE(1971), p, d, w; HOAX, THE(1972), p&d
Misc. Talkies
CINDY AND DONNA(1971), d
Silents
HEARTS OF THE WORLD(1918); HUN WITHIN, THE(1918); PETAL ON THE CURRENT, THE(1919); DR. JIM(1921); TILLIE(1922); ETERNAL STRUGGLE, THE(1923); SLANDER THE WOMAN(1923); LULLABY, THE(1924); BEAUTIFUL CHEAT, THE(1926); TEMPTRESS, THE(1926); LOVE ME AND THE WORLD IS MINE(1928)
Misc. Silents
COMMON PROPERTY(1919); HEART OF HUMANITY, THE(1919); RIGHT TO HAPPINESS, THE(1919); BELOW THE DEAD LINE(1921); GIRL IN HIS ROOM, THE(1922); UP IN THE AIR ABOUT MARY(1922)
Robert "Bob" Anderson
WITHOUT RESERVATIONS(1946)
Robert G. Anderson
PEGGY(1950); SILVER CITY(1951); CRIPPLE CREEK(1952); MISS SADIE THOMPSON(1953); SHOWDOWN AT ABILENE(1956)
Robert J. Anderson
AARON LOVES ANGELA(1975), p
Robert S. Anderson
MONEY TRAP, THE(1966)
Robert W. Anderson
SAND PEBBLES, THE(1966), w; I NEVER SANG FOR MY FATHER(1970), w
Roger Anderson
NOT WANTED(1949); TWELVE O'CLOCK HIGH(1949); GUNFIRE(1950); CATTLE QUEEN(1951); LES MISERABLES(1952); RANCHO NOTORIOUS(1952)
Roland Anderson
FAREWELL TO ARMS, A(1932), art d; LIVES OF A BENGAL LANCER(1935), art d; GIVE US THIS NIGHT(1936), art d; LADY BE CAREFUL(1936), art d; YOURS FOR THE ASKING(1936), art d; INTERNES CAN'T TAKE MONEY(1937), art d; PLAINSMAN, THE(1937), art d; SOULS AT SEA(1937), art d; OUR LEADING CITIZEN(1939), art d; UNION PACIFIC(1939), art d; NORTHWEST MOUNTED POLICE(1940), art d; REMEMBER THE NIGHT(1940), art d; SHEPHERD OF THE HILLS, THE(1941), art d; SKYLARK(1941), art d; HOLIDAY INN(1942), art d; MAJOR AND THE MINOR, THE(1942), art d; REAP THE WILD WIND(1942), art d; TAKE A LETTER, DARLING(1942), art d; CRYSTAL BALL, THE(1943), art d; HERE COME THE WAVES(1944), art d; STORY OF DR. WASSELL, THE(1944), art d; LOVE LETTERS(1945), art d; MASQUERADE IN MEXICO(1945), art d; ROAD TO UTOPIA(1945), art d; CALIFORNIA(1946), art d; TO EACH HIS OWN(1946), art d; PERILS OF PAULINE, THE(1947), art d; BIG CLOCK, THE(1948), art d; BRIDE OF VENGEANCE(1949), art d; CONNECTICUT YANKEE IN KING ARTHUR'S COURT, A(1949), art d; GREAT GATSBY, THE(1949), art d; LET'S DANCE(1950), art d;

DARLING, HOW COULD YOU!(1951), art d; MATING SEASON, THE(1951), art d; MY FAVORITE SPY(1951), art d; CARRIE(1952), art d; JUST FOR YOU(1952), art d; SON OF PALEFACE(1952), art d; GIRLS OF PLEASURE ISLAND, THE(1953), art d; HERE COME THE GIRLS(1953), art d; COUNTRY GIRL, THE(1954), art d Hal Pereira; RED GARTERS(1954), art d; WHITE CHRISTMAS(1954), art d; WE'RE NO ANGELS(1955), art d; PARDNERS(1956), art d; JOKER IS WILD, THE(1957), art d; LONELY MAN, THE(1957), art d; SHORT CUT TO HELL(1957), art d; MATCHMAKER, THE(1958), art d; SPACE CHILDREN, THE(1958), art d; ST. LOUIS BLUES(1958), art d; ALIAS JESSE JAMES(1959), art d; BLACK ORCHID(1959), art d; JAYHAWKERS, THE(1959), art d; THAT KIND OF WOMAN(1959), art d; IT STARTED IN NAPLES(1960), art d; LOVE IN A GOLDFISH BOWL(1961), art d; POCKETFUL OF MIRACLES(1961), art d; PIGEON THAT TOOK ROME, THE(1962), art d; COME BLOW YOUR HORN(1963), art d; LOVE WITH THE PROPER STRANGER(1963), art d; MY SIX LOVES(1963), art d; WHO'S MINDING THE STORE?(1963), art d; BABY, THE RAIN MUST FALL(1965), art d; HARLOW(1965), art d; SYLVIA(1965), art d; LAST OF THE SECRET AGENTS?, THE(1966), art d; WARNING SHOT(1967), art d; WILL PENNY(1968), art d; STALKING MOON, THE(1969), art d; STERILE CUCKOO, THE(1969), art d; GREAT GATSBY, THE(1974), art d
Rona Anderson
FLOODTIDE(1949, Brit.); POET'S PUB(1949, Brit.); SLEEPING CAR TO TRIESTE(1949, Brit.); PAPER GALLOWS(1950, Brit.); TAMING OF DOROTHY, THE(1950, Brit.); TWENTY QUESTIONS MURDER MYSTERY, THE(1950, Brit.); CHRISTMAS CAROL, A(1951, Brit.); HOME TO DANGER(1951, Brit.); WHISPERING SMITH VERSUS SCOTLAND YARD(1952, Brit.); NOOSE FOR A LADY(1953, Brit.); BLACK RIDER, THE(1954, Brit.); BLACK 13(1954, Brit.); CIRCUMSTANIAL EVIDENCE(1954, Brit.); DOUBLE EXPOSURE(1954, Brit.); CASE OF THE RED MONKEY(1955, Brit.); FLAW, THE(1955, Brit.); SHADOW OF A MAN(1955, Brit.); STOCK CAR(1955, Brit.); TIME TO KILL, A(1955, Brit.); HIDEOUT, THE(1956, Brit.); SPIN A DARK WEB(1956, Brit.); MAN WITH A GUN(1958, Brit.); SOLITARY CHILD, THE(1958, Brit.); BAY OF SAINT MICHEL, THE(1963, Brit.); DEVILS OF DARKNESS, THE(1965, Brit.); PRIME OF MISS JEAN BRODIE, THE(1969, Brit.)
Ronald Anderson
DISPUTED PASSAGE(1939), art d; WALK LIKE A DRAGON(1960), art d
Rosemary Anderson
CONSCIENCE BAY(1960, Brit.)
S. Newton Anderson
WICKER MAN, THE(1974, Brit.)
Sam Anderson
SAM'S SONG(1971)
Sara Anderson
BATTLE AT BLOODY BEACH(1961); NAME OF THE GAME IS KILL, THE(1968), cos
Seicland Anderson
HARDER THEY COME, THE(1973, Jamaica), ed
Sharon Anderson
ABSENCE OF MALICE(1981); SMOKEY AND THE BANDIT-PART 3(1983)
Sheila Anderson
STAR 80(1983)
Shelby Anderson
TREASURE OF MATECUMBE(1976), cos
Shirley Anderson
MAN WHO BROKE THE BANK AT MONTE CARLO, THE(1935)
Slim Anderson
ROLLIN' HOME TO TEXAS(1941)
Steve "Nasty" Anderson
1984
KILLPOINT(1984)
Steven Anderson
WHEN A STRANGER CALLS(1979)
Steven W. Anderson
Misc. Talkies
TWO CATCH TWO(1979)
Stuart Anderson
TEXAS ACROSS THE RIVER(1966)
Sugarfoot Anderson
STORY OF SEABISCUIT, THE(1949); I WAS A COMMUNIST FOR THE F.B.I.(1951); AFRICAN TREASURE(1952)
Susy Anderson
BLACK SABBATH(1963, Ital.)
Misc. Talkies
THOR AND THE AMAZON WOMEN(1960); TWO VIOLENT MEN(1964)
Sylvia Anderson
THUNDERBIRD 6(1968, Brit.), a, p&w; THUNDERBIRDS ARE GO(1968, Brit.), a, p, w; JOURNEY TO THE FAR SIDE OF THE SUN(1969, Brit.), p, w; ANGELS BRIGADE(1980)
Misc. Talkies
THUNDERBIRDS 6(1968); EBONY, IVORY AND JADE(1977)
Tekla Anderson
MID-DAY MISTRESS(1968)
Terry Anderson
YOUNG GRADUATES, THE(1971), p, w
Thomas Anderson
LEARNING TREE, THE(1969); LEGEND OF NIGGER CHARLEY, THE(1972); SHAFT'S BIG SCORE(1972)
Tobias Anderson
HARPER VALLEY, P.T.A.(1978)
Toby Anderson
OUTFIT, THE(1973)
Tom Anderson
TRICK BABY(1973)
Toyce Anderson
1984
EXTERMINATOR 2(1984), cos
U. S. Anderson
HIGHWAY DRAGNET(1954), w
Vass Anderson
SUPERMAN(1978)

Verily Anderson
BEWARE OF CHILDREN(1961, Brit.), w
Veronica Anderson
SOME CALL IT LOVING(1973)
Warner Anderson
THIS IS THE ARMY(1943); DESTINATION TOKYO(1944); ABBOTT AND COSTELLO IN HOLLYWOOD(1945); DANGEROUS PARTNERS(1945); HER HIGHNESS AND THE BELLBOY(1945); OBJECTIVE, BURMA!(1945); WEEKEND AT THE WALDORF(1945); BAD BASCOMB(1946); FAITHFUL IN MY FASHION(1946); MY REPUTATION(1946); THREE WISE FOOLS(1946); ARNELO AFFAIR, THE(1947); BEGINNING OR THE END, THE(1947); DARK DELUSION(1947); HIGH WALL, THE(1947); SONG OF THE THIN MAN(1947); ALIAS A GENTLEMAN(1948); COMMAND DECISION(1948); TENTH AVENUE ANGEL(1948); DOCTOR AND THE GIRL, THE(1949); LUCKY STIFF, THE(1949); DESTINATION MOON(1950); BANNERLINE(1951); BLUE VEIL, THE(1951); DETECTIVE STORY(1951); GO FOR BROKE(1951); ONLY THE VALIANT(1951); SANTA FE(1951); LAST POSSE, THE(1953); LION IS IN THE STREETS, A(1953); STAR, THE(1953); CAINE MUTINY, THE(1954); CITY STORY(1954); DRUM BEAT(1954); YELLOW TOMAHAWK(1954); BLACKBOARD JUNGLE, THE(1955); LAWLESS STREET, A(1955); VIOLENT MEN, THE(1955); LINEUP, THE(1958); ARMORED COMMAND(1961); RIO CONCHOS(1964)
Wesley Anderson
PILLOW TO POST(1945), ph; BEAST WITH FIVE FINGERS, THE(1946), ph; LOVE AND LEARN(1947), ph; THAT HAGEN GIRL(1947), spec eff; WALLFLOWER(1948), spec eff
Will R. Anderson
Silents
TAKE IT FROM ME(1926), w
William Anderson
MEET NERO WOLFE(1936); BARRY MC KENZIE HOLDS HIS OWN(1975, Aus.), ed; GRIZZLY(1976), ph; GETTING OF WISDOM, THE(1977, Aus.), ed; MONEY MOVERS(1978, Aus.), ed; BREAKER MORANT(1980, Aus.), ed; CLUB, THE(1980, Aus.), ed; GALLIPOLI(1981, Aus.), ed; TENDER MERCIES(1982), ed; PUBERTY BLUES(1983, Aus.), ed
1984
RAZORBACK(1984, Aus.), ed
Silents
BAR SINISTER, THE(1917); MAN IN HOBBLES, THE(1928)
Misc. Silents
FORBIDDEN GRASS(1928)
William E. Anderson
AARON LOVES ANGELA(1975), ed
William H. Anderson
THIRD MAN ON THE MOUNTAIN(1959), p; SIGN OF ZORRO, THE(1960), p
Nick Anderson [Nazareno Zamperla]
UP THE MACGREGORS(1967, Ital./Span.); SEVEN GUNS FOR THE MACGREGORS(1968, Ital./Span.)
Jeffrey Anderson-Gunter
JUST TELL ME WHAT YOU WANT(1980)
Annie Andersson
OSS 117–MISSION FOR A KILLER(1966, Fr./Ital.)
Bibi Andersson
SMILES OF A SUMMER NIGHT(1957, Swed.); SEVENTH SEAL, THE(1958, Swed.); MAGICIAN, THE(1959, Swed.); WILD STRAWBERRIES(1959, Swed.); BRINK OF LIFE(1960, Swed.); DEVIL'S EYE, THE(1960, Swed.); SQUARE OF VIOLENCE(1963, U.S./Yugo.); ALL THESE WOMEN(1964, Swed.); SWEDISH MISTRESS, THE(1964, Swed.); DUEL AT DIABLO(1966); PERSONA(1967, Swed.); LE VIOL(1968, Fr./Swed.); SHORT IS THE SUMMER(1968, Swed.); KREMLIN LETTER, THE(1970); PASSION OF ANNA, THE(1970, Swed.); STORY OF A WOMAN(1970, U.S./Ital.); TOUCH, THE(1971, U.S./Swed.); GIRLS, THE(1972, Swed.); SCENES FROM A MARRIAGE(1974, Swed.); I NEVER PROMISED YOU A ROSE GARDEN(1977); ENEMY OF THE PEOPLE, AN(1978); QUINTET(1979); EXPOSED(1983)
Birgitta Andersson
COTTONPICKIN' CHICKENPICKERS(1967)
Brigitta Andersson
NO TIME TO KILL(1963, Brit./Swed./Ger.)
Evald Andersson
SEVENTH SEAL, THE(1958, Swed.), spec eff; GUILT(1967, Swed.), spec eff; PERSONA(1967, Swed.), spec eff; HOUR OF THE WOLF, THE(1968, Swed.), spec eff; SHAME(1968, Swed.), spec eff
Gerd Andersson
SECRETS OF WOMEN(1961, Swed.)
Harriet Andersson
NAKED NIGHT, THE(1956, Swed.); SMILES OF A SUMMER NIGHT(1957, Swed.); DREAMS(1960, Swed.); LESSON IN LOVE, A(1960, Swed.); THROUGH A GLASS DARKLY(1962, Swed.); ALL THESE WOMEN(1964, Swed.); TO LOVE(1964, Swed.); LOVING COUPLES(1966, Swed.); DEADLY AFFAIR, THE(1967, Brit.); FIGHT FOR ROME(1969, Ger./Rum.); PEOPLE MEET AND SWEET MUSIC FILLS THE HEART(1969, Den./Swed.); CRIES AND WHISPERS(1972, Swed.); GIRLS, THE(1972, Swed.); SABINA, THE(1979, Span./Swed.); FANNY AND ALEXANDER(1983, Swed./Fr./Ger.)
Laila Andersson
SUDDENLY, A WOMAN!(1967, Den.)
Lars-Olof Andersson
WINTER LIGHT, THE(1963, Swed.)
Max Andersson
LIFE STUDY(1973)
Mona Andersson
FANNY AND ALEXANDER(1983, Swed./Fr./Ger.)
Olga Andersson
ON THE SUNNYSIDE(1936, Swed.)
Torbjoern Andersson
ELVIS! ELVIS!(1977, Swed.), ph
Ulla Andersson
DEVIL, THE(1963)
Viktor Andersson
ON THE SUNNYSIDE(1936, Swed.); OCEAN BREAKERS(1949, Swed.)
Viktor "Kulorten" Andersson
COUNT OF THE MONK'S BRIDGE, THE(1934, Swed.); ONLY ONE NIGHT(1942, Swed.)

Keith Andes
FARMER'S DAUGHTER, THE(1947); PROJECT X(1949); BLACKBEARD THE PIRATE(1952); CLASH BY NIGHT(1952); SPLIT SECOND(1953); SECOND GREATEST SEX, THE(1955); AWAY ALL BOATS(1956); BACK FROM ETERNITY(1956); PILLARS OF THE SKY(1956); GIRL MOST LIKELY, THE(1957); INTERLUDE(1957); DAMN CITIZEN(1958); SURRENDER–HELL!(1959); MODEL FOR MURDER(1960, Brit.); HELL'S BLOODY DEVILS(1970); TORA! TORA! TORA!(1970, U.S./Jap.); ...AND JUSTICE FOR ALL(1979)
Misc. Talkies
HOMEWARD BORNE(1957)
Philemon Blake Andhoua
1984
GREYSTOKE: THE LEGEND OF TARZAN, LORD OF THE APES(1984)
Hellmut Andics
$100 A NIGHT(1968, Ger.), w
Marie Andjaparidze
THREE TALES OF CHEKHOV(1961, USSR), d, w
Veriko Andjaparidze
Misc. Silents
SABA(1929, USSR)
Zurab Andjaparidze
YOLANTA(1964, USSR)
Ando
PAPER TIGER(1975, Brit.)
Eiko Ando
BARBARIAN AND THE GEISHA, THE(1958)
Shohei Ando
GIRL I ABANDONED, THE(1970, Jap.), ph; MUDDY RIVER(1982, Jap.), ph
Teruaki Ando
BATTLE IN OUTER SPACE(1960), art d
R. Andom
Silents
FOUR MEN IN A VAN(1921, Brit.), w
Kurt Andon
HERO AT LARGE(1980)
Ian Andonov
WINDOWS OF TIME, THE(1969, Hung.)
Ivan Andonov
DETOUR, THE(1968, Bulgarian)
Lotte Palfi Andor
LOVESICK(1983)
Paul Andor
CONCORDE, THE–AIRPORT '79(; ENEMY OF WOMEN(1944); COUNTER-ATTACK(1945); HOTEL BERLIN(1945); WALK EAST ON BEACON(1952); SINGING IN THE DARK(1956); MISTER BUDDWING(1966); UNION CITY(1980); LOVESICK(1983)
Lotta Andor-Palfi
MARATHON MAN(1976)
Peter Andorai
CONFIDENCE(1980, Hung.); MEPHISTO(1981, Ger.)
Fern Andra
EYES OF THE WORLD, THE(1930); LOTUS LADY(1930)
Silents
UNCLE TOM'S CABIN(1914)
Misc. Silents
GENUINE(1920, Ger.); BURGOMASTER OF STILEMONDE, THE(1928, Brit.); SPANGLES(1928, Brit.); WARNING, THE(1928, Brit.)
Alyce Andrace
HELL'S BLOODY DEVILS(1970)
Rhae Andrace
HELL'S BLOODY DEVILS(1970)
David Andrada
Silents
WITHOUT HOPE(1914)
Cisco Andrade
WORLD IN MY CORNER(1956)
Flavia Andrade
MEN AGAINST THE SUN(1953, Brit.)
Richard Andrade
EL DORADO(1967)
Manfred Andrae
I DEAL IN DANGER(1966)
Paule Andral
DAVID GOLDER(1932, Fr.); WITH A SMILE(1939, Fr.)
Marta Andras
ONCE IN PARIS(1978)
Anette Andre
Misc. Talkies
MISSION: MONTE CARLO(1981, Brit.)
Annette Andre
THIS IS MY STREET(1964, Brit.); HEROES OF TELEMARK, THE(1965, Brit.); UP JUMPED A SWAGMAN(1965, Brit.); FUNNY THING HAPPENED ON THE WAY TO THE FORUM, A(1966); HE WHO RIDES A TIGER(1966, Brit.); MISTER TEN PERCENT(1967, Brit.)
Beverly Andre
POT O' GOLD(1941); I MARRIED A WITCH(1942)
Carl Andre
TWO IN A CROWD(1936); O.S.S.(1946); PALEFACE, THE(1948); STREETS OF LAREDO(1949); COLT .45(1950); DALLAS(1950); SON OF PALEFACE(1952); WORLD IN HIS ARMS, THE(1952); CHARGE AT FEATHER RIVER, THE(1953); THUNDER OVER THE PLAINS(1953); TALL MAN RIDING(1955); VIOLENT MEN, THE(1955)
Carol Andre
DEATH IN VENICE(1971, Ital./Fr.)
Misc. Talkies
ONE RUSSIAN SUMMER(1973); ENCOUNTERS OF THE DEEP(1984)
Carole Andre
FACE TO FACE(1967, Ital.); YOR, THE HUNTER FROM THE FUTURE(1983, Ital.)
Charles Andre
SEVEN DAYS LEAVE(1942); MASK OF DIMITRIOS, THE(1944); PARIS UNDERGROUND(1945); SECRET OF ST. IVES, THE(1949); ON THE RIVERA(1951); SOMETHING TO LIVE FOR(1952); I CONFESS(1953)

Claire Andre
RIVER OF NO RETURN(1954)
Colette Andre
FIRST TASTE OF LOVE(1962, Fr.)
Dominique Andre
DEVIL BY THE TAIL, THE(1969, Fr./Ital.), art d; LA VIE CONTINUE(1982, Fr.), art d; L'ETOILE DU NORD(1983, Fr.), art d
Dorothy Andre
WILDCAT OF TUCSON(1941); CALLAWAY WENT THATAWAY(1951); CATTLE QUEEN OF MONTANA(1954)
E.J. Andre
BATTLE AT BLOODY BEACH(1961); SHOWDOWN(1963); SHAKIEST GUN IN THE WEST, THE(1968); ARRANGEMENT, THE(1969); LAWYER, THE(1969); PAPILLON(1973); DUCHESS AND THE DIRTWATER FOX, THE(1976); NICKELODEON(1976); HAUNTS(1977); LINCOLN CONSPIRACY, THE(1977); MOONSHINE COUNTY EXPRESS(1977); MAGIC(1978)
Francois Andre
FATE IS THE HUNTER(1964)
Gaby Andre
HIGHWAY 301(1950); PLEASE BELIEVE ME(1950); GREEN GLOVE, THE(1952); COSMIC MONSTERS(1958, Brit.); GOLIATH AND THE DRAGON(1961, Ital./Fr.); EAST OF KILIMANJARO(1962, Brit./Ital.); GUILT IS NOT MINE(1968, Ital.); PUSSYCAT, PUSSYCAT, I LOVE YOU(1970)
Misc. Talkies
CRAWLING TERROR, THE(1958, Brit.)
George Andre
ONCE IN A BLUE MOON(1936); FALLGUY(1962); WILD WORLD OF BATWOMAN, THE(1966)
Gwili Andre
ROAR OF THE DRAGON(1932); SECRETS OF THE FRENCH POLICE(1932); NO OTHER WOMAN(1933); MEET THE BOY FRIEND(1937); WOMAN'S FACE(1941); FALCON'S BROTHER, THE(1942)
Gwill Andre
GIRL SAID NO, THE(1937)
Jackie Andre
GNOME-MOBILE, THE(1967)
Jan Andre
LITTLE ARK, THE(1972), set d
Jean Andre
AND GOD CREATED WOMAN(1957, Fr.), art d; PARIS DOES STRANGE THINGS(1957, Fr./Ital.), set d; LA PARISIENNE(1958, Fr./Ital.), art d; NIGHT HEAVEN FELL, THE(1958, Fr.), art d; BLOOD AND ROSES(1961, Fr./Ital.), prod d; TRUTH, THE(1961, Fr./Ital.), art d; TALES OF PARIS(1962, Fr./Ital.), art d; LOVE ON A PILLOW(1963, Fr./Ital.), art d; JOY HOUSE(1964, Fr.), art d; MODERATO CANTABILE(1964, Fr./Ital.), art d; NUTTY, NAUGHTY CHATEAU(1964, Fr./Ital.), art d; OF FLESH AND BLOOD(1964, Fr./Ital.), art d; HAIL MAFIA(1965, Fr./Ital.), art d; RAPTURE(1965), art d; VICE AND VIRTUE(1965, Fr./Ital.), set d; RAVISHING IDIOT, A(1966, Ital./Fr.), art d; GAME IS OVER, THE(1967, Fr.), art d; BRAIN, THE(1969, Fr./US), art d; DON'T LOOK NOW(1969, Brit./Fr.), art d; SPIRITS OF THE DEAD(1969, Fr./Ital.), set d; DEADLY TRAP, THE(1972, Fr./Ital.), art d; JACQUES BREL IS ALIVE AND WELL AND LIVING IN PARIS(1975), art d
Jill Andre
TWO OF A KIND(1983)
Joyce Andre
EIGHTEEN AND ANXIOUS(1957)
Julia Andre
PIRATES OF MONTEREY(1947)
Lona Andre
COLLEGE HUMOR(1933); INTERNATIONAL HOUSE(1933); MYSTERIOUS RIDER, THE(1933); PICK-UP(1933); TAKE A CHANCE(1933); WOMAN ACCUSED(1933); COME ON, MARINES(1934); MERRY WIDOW, THE(1934); MURDER AT THE VANITIES(1934); TWO HEADS ON A PILLOW(1934); WOMAN UNAFRAID(1934); BORDER BRIGANDS(1935); BY YOUR LEAVE(1935); HAPPINESS C.O.D.(1935); LOST IN THE STRATOSPHERE(1935); SCHOOL FOR GIRLS(1935); UNDER THE PAMPAS MOON(1935); LUCKY TERROR(1936); OUR RELATIONS(1936); CRUSADE AGAINST RACKETS(1937); DEATH IN THE SKY(1937); HIGH HAT(1937); PLAINSMAN, THE(1937); TRAILING TROUBLE(1937); GHOST VALLEY RAIDERS(1940); SUNSET MURDER CASE(1941)
Misc. Talkies
SKYBOUND(1935); DEATH IN THE AIR(1937)
Marcel Andre
HEART OF PARIS(1939, Fr.); ULTIMATUM(1940, Fr.); BEAUTY AND THE BEAST(1947, Fr.); FRIEND WILL COME TONIGHT, A(1948, Fr.); ROOM UPSTAIRS, THE(1948, Fr.); LES PARENTS TERRIBLES(1950, Fr.); PERFECTIONIST, THE(1952, Fr.); LES MAINS SALES(1954, Fr.)
Marvel Andre
MANIAC(1934); OUR RELATIONS(1936); KENTUCKY JUBILEE(1951)
Marvelle Andre
GAMBLING DAUGHTERS(1941); HOLD THAT LINE(1952)
Mary Andre
UNSINKABLE MOLLY BROWN, THE(1964)
Michael Andre
FIRST OFFENCE(1936, Brit.)
Michel Andre
IDIOT, THE(1948, Fr.)
Monya Andre
ESCAPADE(1935); PRINCESS COMES ACROSS, THE(1936); FIREFLY, THE(1937); NINOTCHKA(1939); NOCTURNE(1946); DAISY KENYON(1947); STRANGERS ON A TRAIN(1951); UNKNOWN MAN, THE(1951); ONE MINUTE TO ZERO(1952)
Moyna Andre
UNDERCURRENT(1946)
Nicki [Nicole] Andre
PHANTOM OF THE OPERA(1943)
Nicolle Andre
HILLBILLY BLITZKRIEG(1942)
Olga Andre
WHAT PRICE GLORY?(1952)

Pierre Andre
TANGIER(1946); MY WILD IRISH ROSE(1947)
Raoul Andre
NIGHTS OF SHAME(1961, Fr.), p&d; VICE DOLLS(1961, Fr.), d
Robert Andre
CHRISTMAS TREE, THE(1969, Fr.), art d; DEADLY TRAP, THE(1972, Fr./Ital.), set d; FEDORA(1978, Ger./Fr.), art d
Vittorio Andre
PLUCKED(1969, Fr./Ital.); SABATA(1969, Ital.)
Yvonee Andre
RED SHOES, THE(1948, Brit.)
Yvonne Andre
PACK UP YOUR TROUBLES(1940, Brit.); NEUTRAL PORT(1941, Brit.); SECRET MISSION(1944, Brit.); PORTRAIT OF CLARE(1951, Brit.); FEMALE FIENDS(1958, Brit.); MIDDLE COURSE, THE(1961, Brit.); RETURN FROM THE ASHES(1965, U.S./Brit.)
Andre and Curtis
MOUNTAINS O'MOURNE(1938, Brit.)
Andre Kostelanetz and His Orchestra
MUSIC IN MY HEART(1940)
Andre Kostelanetz and Orchestra
ARTISTS AND MODELS(1937)
Andre-ani
WIND, THE(1928), cos; MONEY TALKS(1933, Brit.), cos
Silents
RED MILL, THE(1927), cos
Manfred Andrea
FREUD(1962)
Elsie Andrean
Silents
DUCKS AND DRAKES(1921)
Rudolph Andrean
KID FROM BOOKLYN, THE(1946)
Henri Andreani
Misc. Silents
MIMI TROTTIN(1922, Fr.), d; L'AUTRE AILE(1924, Fr.), d; FLAMENCA LA GITANE(1928, Fr.), d; LA PENTE(1928, Fr.), d
Jean-Pierre Andreani
SIX IN PARIS(1968, Fr.)
Demitri Andreas
NIGHT AMBUSH(1958, Brit.)
Dimitri Andreas
EVIL UNDER THE SUN(1982, Brit.)
1984
TOP SECRET!(1984)
Dimitris Andreas
PRIVATE RIGHT, THE(1967, Brit.)
Elena Andreas
GHOST IN THE INVISIBLE BIKINI(1966)
Herb Andreas
GHOST IN THE INVISIBLE BIKINI(1966)
Hern Andreas
WHAT DID YOU DO IN THE WAR, DADDY?(1966)
Luke Andreas
STILETTO(1969); I WANNA HOLD YOUR HAND(1978); ROSE, THE(1979); UP THE ACADEMY(1980); BUSTIN' LOOSE(1981); GOING APE!(1981); MODERN PROBLEMS(1981); PENNIES FROM HEAVEN(1981)
Michael Andreas
DAY OF THE ANIMALS(1977)
Felice Andreasi
CLARETTA AND BEN(1983, Ital., Fr.)
Mylee Andreason
PHFFFT!(1954)
Raffaele Andreassi
DOWN THE ANCIENT STAIRCASE(1975, Ital.), w
Rune Andreasson
NIGHT IS MY FUTURE(1962, Swed.)
Ulla Andreasson
NIGHT IS MY FUTURE(1962, Swed.)
Ingrid Andree
CONFESSIONS OF FELIX KRULL, THE(1957, Ger.); REST IS SILENCE, THE(1960, Ger.); ROSES FOR THE PROSECUTOR(1961, Ger.)
Monya Andree
Silents
POLICE PATROL, THE(1925)
Yvonne Andree
COLONEL BLIMP(1945, Brit.)
Serge Andreguy
DEVIL'S DAUGHTER(1949, Fr.)
Aamir Andrei
HAPPY BIRTHDAY TO ME(1981)
Damir Andrei
VISITING HOURS(1982, Can.)
France Andrei
REQUIEM FOR A SECRET AGENT(1966, Ital.)
Franco Andrei
BIG SHOW, THE(1961)
Frederic Andrei
DIVA(1982, Fr.)
Marcello Andrei
EYE OF THE NEEDLE, THE(1965, Ital./Fr.), d, w
Yannik Andrei
BEYOND FEAR(1977, Fr.), d&w
Andre Andrieu
MURDERER LIVES AT NUMBER 21, THE(1947, Fr.), art d
Andre Andreiev
MOZART(1940, Brit.), set d

Andrei Andreiev
THREEPENNY OPERA, THE(1931, Ger./U.S.), prod d
Silents
PANDORA'S BOX(1929, Ger.), art d
Aleksander Andreievsky
LOSS OF FEELING(1935, USSR), d
Gabriella Andreini
INVASION 1700(1965, Fr./Ital./Yugo.)
Andre Andrejeff
MAMBO(1955, Ital.), art d
Andrejev
GOLEM, THE(1937, Czech./Fr.), set d
Andre Andrejew
DARK JOURNEY(1937, Brit.), prod d; STORM IN A TEACUP(1937, Brit.), prod d; MAN ABOUT THE HOUSE, A(1947, Brit.), art d; ANNA KARENINA(1948, Brit.), prod d; IF THIS BE SIN(1950, Brit.), art d; WINSLOW BOY, THE(1950), prod d; OPERATION X(1951, Brit.), set d; MAN BETWEEN, THE(1953), art d; MELBA(1953, Brit.), art d; ALEXANDER THE GREAT(1956), set d
Andrei Andrejew
ANASTASIA(1956), art d
Jean Andren
THEY WON'T BELIEVE ME(1947); DARK MIRROR, THE(1946); TILL THE CLOUDS ROLL BY(1946); TWO SMART PEOPLE(1946); UNDERCURRENT(1946); HIGH WALL, THE(1947); LIFE WITH FATHER(1947); TOO MANY WINNERS(1947); UNSUSPECTED, THE(1947); EVERY GIRL SHOULD BE MARRIED(1948); STREET CORNER(1948); BARKLEYS OF BROADWAY, THE(1949); IT'S A GREAT FEELING(1949); I KILLED GERONIMO(1950); NO MAN OF HER OWN(1950); I WANT YOU(1951); UNKNOWN MAN, THE(1951); RAINBOW 'ROUND MY SHOULDER(1952); SCARLET ANGEL(1952); DREAM WIFE(1953); GOOD MORNING, MISS DOVE(1955); INVASION OF THE BODY SNATCHERS(1956); OPPOSITE SEX, THE(1956)
Joan Andren
IT HAPPENED ON 5TH AVENUE(1947)
Annabella Andreoli
ANZIO(1968, Ital.); FIVE MAN ARMY, THE(1970, Ital.); MACHINE GUN McCAIN(1970, Ital.)
Franklin Andreon
CYBORG 2087(1966), d
Marc Andreoni
1984
CHEECH AND CHONG'S THE CORSICAN BROTHERS(1984)
Paul Andreota
JULIE THE REDHEAD(1963, Fr.), w; DON'T TEMPT THE DEVIL(1964, Fr./Ital.), w; VERDICT(1975, Fr./Ital.), w
Errikos Andreou
SISTERS, THE(1969, Gr.), d
Andres
DOULOS–THE FINGER MAN(1964, Fr./Ital.)
Alfredo Andres
HEAT(1970, Arg.), m
Elvira Andres
BLOOD WEDDING(1981, Sp.)
Eva Marie Andres
DECISION BEFORE DAWN(1951)
Gumer Andres
MONSTER ISLAND(1981, Span./U.S.), art d
Gumersindo Andres
MAN IN THE WILDERNESS(1971, U.S./Span.), art d
Luis San Andres
NIGHT FLOWERS(1979), d&ed
Mason Andres
TOWN THAT DREADED SUNDOWN, THE(1977)
Michael Andres
TERMINAL ISLAND(1973), m
Richard Andres
Silents
TWO MINUTES TO GO(1921), w; ALIAS JULIUS CAESAR(1922), w
Rivera Andres
LA VIE CONTINUE(1982, Fr.)
Rudolph Andres
SOUTH SEA WOMAN(1953)
Stanley Andres
ACROSS THE BADLANDS(1950)
Tod Andres
BENEATH THE PLANET OF THE APES(1970)
Bjorn Andresen
DEATH IN VENICE(1971, Ital./Fr.)
Barbara Andress
LOOKING UP(1977)
Herb Andress
LAST REBEL, THE(1971); WHO?(1975, Brit./Ger.); LILI MARLEEN(1981, Ger.)
Ursula Andress
DR. NO(1962, Brit.); FOUR FOR TEXAS(1963); FUN IN ACAPULCO(1963); NIGHTMARE IN THE SUN(1964); SHE(1965, Brit.); TENTH VICTIM, THE(1965, Fr./Ital.); WHAT'S NEW, PUSSYCAT?(1965, U.S./Fr.); BLUE MAX, THE(1966); UP TO HIS EARS(1966, Fr./Ital.); CASINO ROYALE(1967, Brit.); ONCE BEFORE I DIE(1967, U.S./Phil.); ANYONE CAN PLAY(1968, Ital.); SOUTHERN STAR, THE(1969, Fr./Brit.); PERFECT FRIDAY(1970, Brit.); RED SUN(1972, Fr./Ital./Span.); LOVES AND TIMES OF SCARAMOUCHE, THE(1976, Ital.); STATELINE MOTEL(1976, Ital.); BEHIND THE IRON MASK(1977); SLAVE OF THE CANNIBAL GOD(1979, Ital.); CLASH OF THE TITANS(1981); MEXICO IN FLAMES(1982, USSR/Mex./Ital.)
Misc. Talkies
LOADED GUNS(1975); PRISONER OF THE CANNIBAL GOD(1978, Ital.)
Clara Andressa
CARNIVAL ROCK(1957)
Gaby Andreu
END OF A DAY, THE(1939, Fr.)
Simon Andreu
WEB OF FEAR(1966, Fr./Span.); BAD MAN'S RIVER(1972, Span.); OPEN SEASON(1974, U.S./Span.); CHILDREN OF RAGE(1975, Brit.-Israeli); JAGUAR LIVES(1979); TRIUMPHS OF A MAN CALLED HORSE(1983, US/Mex.)

April Andrew
1984
VARIETY(1984)
Jorge Hernandez Andrew
HIGH RISK(1981)
Josy Andrew
CHARLES AND LUCIE(1982, Fr.)
Lona Andrew
GREAT HOSPITAL MYSTERY, THE(1937)
Margo Andrew
VIRGIN AND THE GYPSY, THE(1970, Brit.)
Michael Andrew
1984
HOLLYWOOD HOT TUBS(1984)
Simon Andrew
BLOOD SPATTERED BRIDE, THE(1974, Span.); THOSE DIRTY DOGS(1974, U.S./Ital./Span.)
Sylvia Andrew
UNDERCURRENT(1946); SNAKE PIT, THE(1948); THREE CAME HOME(1950)
Tom Andrew
SILVER BEARS(1978)
A.G. Andrews
Misc. Silents
MISS NOBODY(1917)
Adora Andrews
MIDDLETON FAMILY AT THE N.Y. WORLD'S FAIR(1939)
Andy Andrews
23 ½ HOURS LEAVE(1937); GANGSTER, THE(1947); GOG(1954); BATTLE TAXI(1955); CRAWLING HAND, THE(1963)
Ann Andrews
CHEAT, THE(1931)
Misc. Silents
GIRL BY THE ROADSIDE, THE(1918)
Anthony Andrews
TAKE ME HIGH(1973, Brit.); OPERATION DAYBREAK(1976, U.S./Brit./Czech.)
1984
UNDER THE VOLCANO(1984)
Arkansas "Slim" Andrews
PIONEERS, THE(1941)
Barbara Andrews
EVIL, THE(1978), cos
1984
FEAR CITY(1984); WOMAN IN RED, THE(1984)
Barry Andrews
DRACULA HAS RISEN FROM HIS GRAVE(1968, Brit.); BLOOD ON SATAN'S CLAW, THE(1970, Brit.); TERROR FROM UNDER THE HOUSE(1971, Brit.); SPY WHO LOVED ME, THE(1977, Brit.)
Betti Andrews
MADISON AVENUE(1962)
Betty Andrews
REACHING OUT(1983)
Beverly Andrews
FLASH GORDON(1980)
Bill Andrews
ANASTASIA(1956), art d; HORSE'S MOUTH, THE(1958, Brit.), set d; SILENT ENEMY, THE(1959, Brit.), art d; DENTIST IN THE CHAIR(1960, Brit.), art d; MYSTERIOUS ISLAND(1961, U.S./Brit.), art d; LOLITA(1962), art d; WAR LOVER, THE(1962, U.S./Brit.), art d; FOLLOW THE BOYS(1963), art d; MURDER AHOY(1964, Brit.), art d; ATTACK ON THE IRON COAST(1968, U.S./Brit.), art d; HOT MILLIONS(1968, Brit.), art d; CAPTAIN NEMO AND THE UNDERWATER CITY(1969, Brit.), art d; SUMARINE X-1(1969, Brit.), art d; MOSQUITO SQUADRON(1970, Brit.), art d; MY LOVER, MY SON(1970, Brit.), art d; I WANT WHAT I WANT(1972, Brit.), art d
Bob Andrews
SCHOOL FOR SEX(1969, Brit.); SOLDIER, THE(1982)
Bobbie Andrews
Silents
FIRES OF INNOCENCE(1922, Brit.)
Misc. Silents
SWORD OF DAMOCLES, THE(1920, Brit.)
Brian Andrews
HALLOWEEN(1978); GREAT SANTINI, THE(1979); HALLOWEEN II(1981)
Carol Andrews
BULLFIGHTERS, THE(1945); COLONEL EFFINGHAM'S RAID(1945); LADY CONFESSES, THE(1945); NOB HILL(1945); MURDER IS MY BUSINESS(1946)
Caroline Andrews
GUILTY, THE(1947)
Cathy Andrews
DO NOT THROW CUSHIONS INTO THE RING(1970)
Charles Andrews
GREEN PASTURES(1936); TOY WIFE, THE(1938); REFORM SCHOOL(1939)
Silents
PIRATES OF THE SKY(1927), d
Charles C. Andrews
SLENDER THREAD, THE(1965)
Charles E. Andrews
INNOCENTS OF PARIS(1929), w
Charlton Andrews
BLUEBEARD'S EIGHTH WIFE(1938), w
Christopher Andrews
MS. 45(1981), ed
Clark Andrews
MANHATTAN HEARTBEAT(1940), w; PIER 13(1940), w
Daisy H. Andrews
SHANGHAI LADY(1929), w
Dana Andrews
KIT CARSON(1940); LUCKY CISCO KID(1940); SAILOR'S LADY(1940); WESTERNER, THE(1940); BALL OF FIRE(1941); BELLE STARR(1941); SWAMP WATER(1941); TOBACCO ROAD(1941); BERLIN CORRESPONDENT(1942); CRASH DIVE(1943); NORTH STAR, THE(1943); OX-BOW INCIDENT, THE(1943); LAURA(1944); PURPLE

HEART, THE(1944); UP IN ARMS(1944); WING AND A PRAYER(1944); FALLEN ANGEL(1945); STATE FAIR(1945); WALK IN THE SUN, A(1945); BEST YEARS OF OUR LIVES, THE(1946); CANYON PASSAGE(1946); BOOMERANG(1947); DAISY KENYON(1947); NIGHT SONG(1947); DEEP WATERS(1948); IRON CURTAIN, THE(1948); NO MINOR VICES(1948); AFFAIRS OF ADELAIDE(1949, U. S./Brit); MY FOOLISH HEART(1949); SWORD IN THE DESERT(1949); EDGE OF DOOM(1950); WHERE THE SIDEWALK ENDS(1950); FROGMEN, THE(1951); I WANT YOU(1951); SEALED CARGO(1951); ASSIGNMENT-PARIS(1952); DUEL IN THE JUNGLE(1954, Brit.); ELEPHANT WALK(1954); THREE HOURS TO KILL(1954); SMOKE SIGNAL(1955); STRANGE LADY IN TOWN(1955); BEYOND A REASONABLE DOUBT(1956); COMANCHE(1956); WHILE THE CITY SLEEPS(1956); SPRING REUNION(1957); ZERO HOUR!(1957); CURSE OF THE DEMON(1958); ENCHANTED ISLAND(1958); FEARMAKERS, THE(1958); CROWDED SKY, THE(1960); MADISON AVENUE(1962); BATTLE OF THE BULGE(1965); BRAINSTORM(1965); CRACK IN THE WORLD(1965); IN HARM'S WAY(1965); LOVED ONE, THE(1965); SATAN BUG, THE(1965); TOWN TAMER(1965); JOHNNY RENO(1966); SPY IN YOUR EYE(1966, Ital.); FROZEN DEAD, THE(1967, Brit.); HOT RODS TO HELL(1967); COBRA, THE(1968); DEVIL'S BRIGADE, THE(1968); INNOCENT BYSTANDERS(1973, Brit.); AIRPORT 1975(1974); TAKE A HARD RIDE(1975, U.S./Ital.); LAST TYCOON, THE(1976); BORN AGAIN(1978); GOOD GUYS WEAR BLACK(1978); PILOT, THE(1979)
Misc. Talkies
TEN MILLION DOLLAR GRAB(1966, Ital.); NO DIAMONDS FOR URSULA(1967)
David Andrews
WHILE THE CITY SLEEPS(1956); PLACE TO GO, A(1964, Brit.); SOME PEOPLE(1964, Brit.); DRACULA A.D. 1972(1972, Brit.)
1984
BODY ROCK(1984); NIGHTMARE ON ELM STREET, A(1984)
Del Andrews
ALL QUIET ON THE WESTERN FRONT(1930), w
Silents
BRONZE BELL, THE(1921), w; JUDGMENT OF THE STORM(1924), d; RIDIN' THE WIND(1925), d; IS THAT NICE?(1926), d; YELLOW BACK, THE(1926), d&w; AIN'T LOVE FUNNY?(1927), d; RACKET, THE(1928), w; RAWHIDE KID, THE(1928), d
Misc. Silents
GALLOPING FISH(1924), w; NO MAN'S LAW(1925), d; RIDIN' STREAK, THE(1925), d; THAT DEVIL QUEMADO(1925), d; WILD BULL'S LAIR, THE(1925), d; COLLEGIATE(1926), d; MAN RUSTLIN'(1926), d; TIMID TERROR, THE(1926), d; HERO ON HORSEBACK, A(1927), d; WILD WEST SHOW, THE(1928), d
Dell Andrews
OUTLAW DEPUTY, THE(1935), w
Eamonn Andrews
LEFT, RIGHT AND CENTRE(1959)
Edward Andrews
TROUBLE WITH GIRLS(AND HOW TO GET INTO IT), THE*1/2 (1969); PHENIX CITY STORY, THE(1955); HARDER THEY FALL, THE(1956); TEA AND SYMPATHY(1956); TENSION AT TABLE ROCK(1956); THESE WILDER YEARS(1956); UNGUARDED MOMENT, THE(1956); HOT SUMMER NIGHT(1957); TATTERED DRESS, THE(1957); THREE BRAVE MEN(1957); TROOPER HOOK(1957); FIEND WHO WALKED THE WEST, THE(1958); NIGHT OF THE QUARTER MOON(1959); ELMER GANTRY(1960); ABSENT-MINDED PROFESSOR, THE(1961); LOVE IN A GOLDFISH BOWL(1961); YOUNG DOCTORS, THE(1961); YOUNG SAVAGES, THE(1961); ADVISE AND CONSENT(1962); FORTY POUNDS OF TROUBLE(1962); SON OF FLUBBER(1963); THRILL OF IT ALL, THE(1963); BRASS BOTTLE, THE(1964); GOOD NEIGHBOR SAM(1964); KISSES FOR MY PRESIDENT(1964); MAN FROM GALVESTON, THE(1964); SEND ME NO FLOWERS(1964); TIGER WALKS, A(1964); YOUNGBLOOD HAWKE(1964); FLUFFY(1965); BIRDS DO IT(1966); GLASS BOTTOM BOAT, THE(1966); TORA! TORA! TORA!(1970, U.S./Jap.); HOW TO FRAME A FIGG(1971); $1,000,000 DUCK(1971); AVANTI!(1972); NOW YOU SEE HIM, NOW YOU DON'T(1972); CHARLEY AND THE ANGEL(1973); SENIORS, THE(1978)
1984
GREMLINS(1984); SIXTEEN CANDLES(1984)
Felicia Andrews
FIVE WILD GIRLS(1966, Fr.)
Frank Andrews
Silents
NIGHTINGALE, THE(1914); POOR LITTLE RICH GIRL, A(1917); OLDEST LAW, THE(1918); WARRENS OF VIRGINIA, THE(1924)
Misc. Silents
ROAD BETWEEN, THE(1917); EYES OF MYSTERY, THE(1918); WHEN MY SHIP COMES IN(1919)
Frank B. Andrews
Silents
CAPTAIN SWIFT(1914)
Geno Andrews
AMERICATHON(1979)
Hanley Andrews
WINGS IN THE DARK(1935)
Harry Andrews
BLACK KNIGHT, THE(1954); PARATROOPER(1954, Brit.); MAN WHO LOVED REDHEADS, THE(1955, Brit.); ALEXANDER THE GREAT(1956); HELEN OF TROY(1956, Ital); HELL IN KOREA(1956, Brit.); MOBY DICK(1956, Brit.); SAINT JOAN(1957); DESERT ATTACK(1958, Brit.); I ACCUSE(1958, Brit.); DEVIL'S DISCIPLE, THE(1959); IN THE NICK(1960, Brit.); TOUCH OF LARCENY, A(1960, Brit.); CIRCLE OF DECEPTION(1961, Brit.); BARABBAS(1962, Ital.); BEST OF ENEMIES, THE(1962); LISA(1962, Brit.); NINE HOURS TO RAMA(1963, U.S./Brit.); REACH FOR GLORY(1963, Brit.); 55 DAYS AT PEKING(1963); NOTHING BUT THE BEST(1964, Brit.); SQUADRON 633(1964, U.S./Brit.); 633 SQUADRON(1964); AGONY AND THE ECSTASY, THE(1965); HILL, THE(1965, Brit.); SANDS OF THE KALAHARI(1965, Brit.); TRUTH ABOUT SPRING, THE(1965, Brit.); UNDERWORLD INFORMERS(1965, Brit.); GIRL GETTERS, THE(1966, Brit.); MODESTY BLAISE(1966, Brit.); DEADLY AFFAIR, THE(1967, Brit.); I'LL NEVER FORGET WHAT'S 'IS NAME(1967, Brit.); JOKERS, THE(1967, Brit.); LONG DUEL, THE(1967, Brit.); NIGHT OF THE GENERALS, THE(1967, Brit./Fr.); CHARGE OF THE LIGHT BRIGADE, THE(1968, Brit.); DANDY IN ASPIC, A(1968, Brit.); DANGER ROUTE(1968, Brit.); NIGHT THEY RAIDED MINSKY'S, THE(1968); SEA GULL, THE(1968); BATTLE OF BRITAIN, THE(1969, Brit.); NICE GIRL LIKE ME, A(1969, Brit.); PLAY DIRTY(1969, Brit.); SOUTHERN STAR, THE(1969, Fr./Brit.); BROTHERLY LOVE(1970, Brit.); ENTERTAINING MR. SLOANE(1970, Brit.); TOO LATE THE HERO(1970); WUTHERING HEIGHTS(1970, Brit.); NICHOLAS AND ALEXANDRA(1971, Brit.); NIGHT COMERS,

THE(1971, Brit.); NIGHT HAIR CHILD(1971, Brit.); BURKE AND HARE(1972, Brit.); I WANT WHAT I WANT(1972, Brit.); MAN OF LA MANCHA(1972); RULING CLASS, THE(1972, Brit.); MACKINTOSH MAN, THE(1973, Brit.); MAN AT THE TOP(1973, Brit.); THEATRE OF BLOOD(1973, Brit.); INTERNECINE PROJECT, THE(1974, Brit.); LAST DAYS OF MAN ON EARTH, THE(1975, Brit.); BLUE BIRD, THE(1976); PASSOVER PLOT, THE(1976, Israel); SKY RIDERS(1976, U.S./Gr.); "EQUUS"(1977); BIG SLEEP, THE½(1978, Brit.); CROSSED SWORDS(1978); DEATH ON THE NILE(1978, Brit.); MEDUSA TOUCH, THE(1978, Brit.); SUPERMAN(1978); WATERSHIP DOWN(1978, Brit.); HAWK THE SLAYER(1980, Brit.)
Misc. Talkies
PLAY IT COOLER(1961)
Helen Andrews
FOUR GIRLS IN TOWN(1956)
Herbert Andrews
LOST BOUNDARIES(1949), art d; WHISTLE AT EATON FALLS(1951), art d; WALK EAST ON BEACON(1952), art d
Jack Andrews
BORN RECKLESS(1937), w; MARYLAND(1940), w; CADET GIRL(1941), w; MARRY THE BOSS' DAUGHTER(1941), w; BERLIN CORRESPONDENT(1942), w; CHETNIKS(1943), w; JOHNNY COMES FLYING HOME(1946), w; STRANGE TRIANGLE(1946), w; DARK DELUSION(1947), w; JOHNNY HOLIDAY(1949), w; SUBWAY IN THE SKY(1959, Brit.), w; HOT MONEY GIRL(1962, Brit./Ger.), w
Silents
DEMOCRACY(1918, Brit.)
James Andrews
O.S.S.(1946)
Janine Andrews
OCTOPUSSY(1983, Brit.)
Joanie Andrews
RUBY(1971)
Joel Andrews
HILDUR AND THE MAGICIAN(1969), a, m
John Andrews
ORGY OF THE DEAD(1965)
Julie Andrews
THOROUGHLY MODERN MILLIE(1967); AMERICANIZATION OF EMILY, THE(1964); MARY POPPINS(1964); SOUND OF MUSIC, THE(1965); HAWAII(1966); TORN CURTAIN(1966); SINGING PRINCESS, THE(1967, Ital.); STAR!(1968); DARLING LILI(1970); TAMARIND SEED, THE(1974, Brit.); 10(1979); LITTLE MISS MARKER(1980); S.O.B.(1981); VICTOR/VICTORIA(1982); MAN WHO LOVED WOMEN, THE(1983)
LaVerne Andrews
HER LUCKY NIGHT(1945)
Lawrence Andrews
GRAND PRIX(1934, Brit.)
Lewis Andrews
RAT FINK(1965), p
Lloyd "Arkansas Slim" Andrews
RHYTHM OF THE RIO GRANDE(1940)
Lloyd "Slim" Andrews
CYCLONE KID, THE(1942); SOMBRERO KID, THE(1942)
Lois Andrews
DIXIE DUGAN(1943); ROGER TOUHY, GANGSTER!(1944); WESTERN HERITAGE(1948); RUSTLERS(1949); DESERT HAWK, THE(1950); MEET ME AFTER THE SHOW(1951)
Loretta Andrews
PALMY DAYS(1931); KID FROM SPAIN, THE(1932); GOLD DIGGERS OF 1933(1933); LITTLE GIANT, THE(1933); 42ND STREET(1933)
Maidie Andrews
SYMPHONY IN TWO FLATS(1930, Brit.)
Margaret Andrews
Misc. Talkies
CURSE OF KILIMANJARO(1978)
Marie Andrews
Misc. Talkies
TANYA(1976)
Mark Andrews
HOT ROD GIRL(1956); 9/30/55(1977); ATTIC, THE(1979)
1984
UP THE CREEK(1984)
Mary Andrews
ONE FROM THE HEART(1982)
Matthew Andrews
FAT SPY(1966), w
Maxine Andrews
HER LUCKY NIGHT(1945)
Michael Andrews
TOGETHER(1956, Brit.)
Mike Andrews
HUMAN FACTOR, THE(1979, Brit.)
Nancy Andrews
SIDELONG GLANCES OF A PIGEON KICKER, THE(1970); MADE FOR EACH OTHER(1971); SUMMER WISHES, WINTER DREAMS(1973); WEREWOLF OF WASHINGTON(1973); W. W. AND THE DIXIE DANCEKINGS(1975); NIGHT OF THE JUGGLER(1980)
Nancy Lee Andrews
SATURDAY THE 14TH(1981)
Patty Andrews
HER LUCKY NIGHT(1945); PHYNX, THE(1970); GONG SHOW MOVIE, THE(1980)
Peter Andrews
BLOOD ON SATAN'S CLAW, THE(1970, Brit.), p
Peter L. Andrews
BLACK BEAUTY(1971, Brit./Ger./Span.), p
Ray Andrews
SUNSET COVE(1978)
Real Andrews
1984
ICEMAN(1984); LISTEN TO THE CITY(1984, Can.)

Robert Andrews

I LIVE FOR LOVE(1935), w; LITTLE BIG SHOT(1935), w; RECKLESS(1935); ISLE OF FURY(1936), w; LONGEST NIGHT, THE(1936), w; WALKING DEAD, THE(1936), w; GEEK MAGGOT BINGO(1983)

Silents

WARRENS OF VIRGINIA, THE(1924)

Misc. Silents

RUBBER HEELS(1927); BURGOMASTER OF STILEMONDE, THE(1928, Brit.)

Robert D. Andrews

THREE GIRLS LOST(1931), w; IF I HAD A MILLION(1932), w; JAILBREAK(1936), w; FLIGHT FROM GLORY(1937), w; GANGSTER'S BOY(1938), w; I WAS A CONVICT(1939), w; MUTINY IN THE BIG HOUSE(1939), w; STREETS OF NEW YORK(1939), w; BABIES FOR SALE(1940), w; BEFORE I HANG(1940), w; DREAMING OUT LOUD(1940), w; GIRLS OF THE ROAD(1940), w; ISLAND OF DOOMED MEN(1940), w; MEN WITHOUT SOULS(1940), w; DEVIL COMMANDS, THE(1941), w; SWEETHEART OF THE CAMPUS(1941), w; UNDER AGE(1941), w; MAYOR OF 44TH STREET, THE(1942), w; ROAD TO HAPPINESS(1942), w; SHERLOCK HOLMES AND THE VOICE OF TERROR(1942), w; BATAAN(1943), w; CROSS OF LORRAINE, THE(1943), w; POWER OF THE PRESS(1943), w; SALUTE TO THE MARINES(1943), w; HAIRY APE, THE(1944), w; TALK ABOUT A LADY(1946), w; MAN FROM COLORADO, THE(1948), w

Robert H. Andrews

BAGDAD(1949), w; TROUBLE ALONG THE WAY(1953), w

Robert Hardy Andrews

BAD BOY(1949), w; KID FROM TEXAS, THE(1950), w; UNDERCOVER GIRL(1950), w; WOMAN ON PIER 13, THE(1950), w; WYOMING MAIL(1950), w; BEST OF THE BADMEN(1951), w; MARK OF THE RENEGADE(1951), w; TANKS ARE COMING, THE(1951), w; HALF-BREED, THE(1952), w; KING'S THIEF, THE(1955), w; GREAT DAY IN THE MORNING(1956), w; GIRLS' TOWN(1959), w; TARZAN GOES TO INDIA(1962, U.S./Brit./Switz.), w

Roger Andrews

ONE BRIEF SUMMER(1971, Brit.), art d

Rose Andrews

PEER GYNT(1965)

Roy Andrews

OVER-UNDER, SIDEWAYS-DOWN(1977)

Slim Andrews

ARIZONA FRONTIER(1940); COWBOY FROM SUNDOWN(1940); GOLDEN TRAIL, THE(1940); PALS OF THE SILVER SAGE(1940); RAINBOW OVER THE RANGE(1940); DRIFTIN' KID, THE(1941); DYNAMITE CANYON(1941); RIDING THE CHEROKEE TRAIL(1941); RIDING THE SUNSET TRAIL(1941); WANDERERS OF THE WEST(1941); COWBOY SERENADE(1942); LONE RIDER AND THE BANDIT, THE(1942); KENTUCKY JUBILEE(1951); BUFFALO BILL IN TOMAHAWK TERRITORY(1952)

Misc. Talkies

TAKE ME BACK TO OKLAHOMA(1940)

Stanley Andrews

TRUE TO LIFE(1943); ROMAN SCANDALS(1933); EVELYN PRENTICE(1934); ALL THE KING'S HORSES(1935); COLLEGE SCANDAL(1935); CRUSADES, THE(1935); ESCAPE FROM DEVIL'S ISLAND(1935); GOIN' TO TOWN(1935); HOLD'EM YALE(1935); IN OLD KENTUCKY(1935); MEN WITHOUT NAMES(1935); MISSISSIPPI(1935); MURDER MAN(1935); PEOPLE WILL TALK(1935); PETER IBBETSON(1935); PRIVATE WORLDS(1935); SHE COULDN'T TAKE IT(1935); SHE GETS HER MAN(1935); STOLEN HARMONY(1935); WANDERER OF THE WASTELAND(1935); WINGS IN THE DARK(1935); DANGEROUS INTRIGUE(1936); DESIRE(1936); DRIFT FENCE(1936); FLORIDA SPECIAL(1936); IN HIS STEPS(1936); MR. DEEDS GOES TO TOWN(1936); NEVADA(1936); PAROLE(1936); TEXAS RANGERS, THE(1936); WILD BRIAN KENT(1936); DEVIL'S PLAYGROUND(1937); DOUBLE OR NOTHING(1937); EASY LIVING(1937); HAPPY-GO-LUCKY(1937); HIGH, WIDE AND HANDSOME(1937); JOHN MEADE'S WOMAN(1937); MAN WHO CRIED WOLF, THE(1937); MAN WHO FOUND HIMSELF, THE(1937); NANCY STEELE IS MISSING(1937); SHE'S DANGEROUS(1937); ADVENTURE IN SAHARA(1938); ALEXANDER'S RAGTIME BAND(1938); BLONDIE(1938); BUCCANEER, THE(1938); COCOANUT GROVE(1938); FORBIDDEN VALLEY(1938); HOLD THAT CO-ED(1938); I'LL GIVE A MILLION(1938); JUVENILE COURT(1938); KENTUCKY(1938); LADY OBJECTS, THE(1938); MYSTERIOUS RIDER, THE(1938); PENITENTIARY(1938); PRAIRIE MOON(1938); SHINE ON, HARVEST MOON(1938); SPAWN OF THE NORTH(1938); STABLEMATES(1938); TIP-OFF GIRLS(1938); WHEN G-MEN STEP IN(1938); YOU CAN'T TAKE IT WITH YOU(1938); ANDY HARDY GETS SPRING FEVER(1939); BEAU GESTE(1939); COAST GUARD(1939); GERONIMO(1939); GOLDEN BOY(1939); HOMICIDE BUREAU(1939); HOTEL IMPERIAL(1939); LADY'S FROM KENTUCKY, THE(1939); MR. SMITH GOES TO WASHINGTON(1939); PIRATES OF THE SKIES(1939); RACKETEERS OF THE RANGE(1939); UNION PACIFIC(1939); BRIGHAM YOUNG–FRONTIERSMAN(1940); HI-YO SILVER(1940); JOHNNY APOLLO(1940); KIT CARSON(1940); LITTLE OLD NEW YORK(1940); MARK OF ZORRO, THE(1940); MARYLAND(1940); PLAY GIRL(1940); SON OF MONTE CRISTO(1940); STRANGE CARGO(1940); WESTERNER, THE(1940); BORROWED HERO(1941); IN OLD COLORADO(1941); MEET JOHN DOE(1941); STRANGE ALIBI(1941); TIME OUT FOR RHYTHM(1941); WILD GEESE CALLING(1941); CANAL ZONE(1942); FLEET'S IN, THE(1942); MAJOR AND THE MINOR, THE(1942); MY GAL SAL(1942); NORTH TO THE KLONDIKE(1942); PANAMA HATTIE(1942); POSTMAN DIDN'T RING, THE(1942); REAP THE WILD WIND(1942); TEN GENTLEMEN FROM WEST POINT(1942); TO THE SHORES OF TRIPOLI(1942); VALLEY OF THE SUN(1942); CANYON CITY(1943); CRASH DIVE(1943); DIXIE(1943); FLIGHT FOR FREEDOM(1943); IN OLD OKLAHOMA(1943); OX-BOW INCIDENT, THE(1943); RIDING HIGH(1943); ATLANTIC CITY(1944); FOLLOW THE BOYS(1944); LAKE PLACID SERENADE(1944); MAN FROM FRISCO(1944); PRACTICALLY YOURS(1944); PRINCESS AND THE PIRATE, THE(1944); SENSATIONS OF 1945(1944); TUCSON RAIDERS(1944); VIGILANTES OF DODGE CITY(1944); WING AND A PRAYER(1944); ADVENTURE(1945); CODE OF THE LAWLESS(1945); DALTONS RIDE AGAIN, THE(1945); ROAD TO UTOPIA(1945); TRAIL TO VENGEANCE(1945); BAD BASCOMB(1946); GOD'S COUNTRY(1946); HOODLUM SAINT, THE(1946); IT'S A WONDERFUL LIFE(1946); SMOKY(1946); TILL THE CLOUDS ROLL BY(1946); TWO YEARS BEFORE THE MAST(1946); WAKE UP AND DREAM(1946); DESIRE ME(1947); EASY COME, EASY GO(1947); FABULOUS TEXAN, THE(1947); FRAMED(1947); HIGH BARBAREE(1947); KILLER DILL(1947); MICHIGAN KID, THE(1947); ROAD TO RIO(1947); ROBIN OF TEXAS(1947); SCARED TO DEATH(1947); SEA OF GRASS, THE(1947); TRAIL STREET(1947); BEST MAN WINS(1948); DEAD DON'T DREAM, THE(1948); DOCKS OF NEW ORLEANS(1948); FULLER BRUSH MAN(1948); I REMEMBER MAMA(1948); JINX MONEY(1948); LAST OF THE WILD HORSES(1948); LEATHER GLOVES(1948); MAN FROM COLORADO, THE(1948); MR. BLANDINGS BUILDS HIS DREAM HOUSE(1948); MY DEAR SECRETARY(1948); NORTHWEST STAMPEDE(1948); PALEFACE, THE(1948); PANHANDLE(1948); PERILOUS WATERS(1948); RETURN OF WILDFIRE, THE(1948); SINISTER JOURNEY(1948); SOUTHERN YANKEE, A(1948); STATE OF THE UNION(1948); VALIANT HOMBRE, THE(1948); BLONDIE'S BIG DEAL(1949); BRIMSTONE(1949); BROTHERS IN THE SADDLE(1949); FIGHTING FOOLS(1949); LAST BANDIT, THE(1949); TOUGH ASSIGNMENT(1949); TRAIL OF THE YUKON(1949); ARIZONA COWBOY, THE(1950); BLONDE DYNAMITE(1950); COPPER CANYON(1950); MULE TRAIN(1950); NEVADAN, THE(1950); OUTCAST OF BLACK MESA(1950); SALT LAKE RAIDERS(1950); SHORT GRASS(1950); STREETS OF GHOST TOWN(1950); TRAVELING SALESWOMAN(1950); TRIGGER, JR.(1950); TWO FLAGS WEST(1950); UNDER MEXICALI STARS(1950); WEST OF WYOMING(1950); WHERE DANGER LIVES(1950); AL JENNINGS OF OKLAHOMA(1951); HOT LEAD(1951); SADDLE LEGION(1951); SILVER CANYON(1951); SUPERMAN AND THE MOLE MEN(1951); TEXAS RANGERS, THE(1951); UTAH WAGON TRAIN(1951); VENGEANCE VALLEY(1951); BAD AND THE BEAUTIFUL, THE(1952); FARGO(1952); GREATEST SHOW ON EARTH, THE(1952); KANSAS TERRITORY(1952); LONE STAR(1952); MAN FROM BLACK HILLS, THE(1952); MONTANA BELLE(1952); TALK ABOUT A STRANGER(1952); THUNDERING CARAVANS(1952); WACO(1952); APPOINTMENT IN HONDURAS(1953); DANGEROUS CROSSING(1953); EL PASO STAMPEDE(1953); RIDE, VAQUERO!(1953); DAWN AT SOCORRO(1954); SOUTHWEST PASSAGE(1954); STEEL CAGE, THE(1954); TREASURE OF RUBY HILLS(1955); FRONTIER GAMBLER(1956); STAR IN THE DUST(1956); THREE OUTLAWS, THE(1956)

Misc. Talkies

AND NOW TOMORROW(1952)

Stella Andrews

THEY WERE NOT DIVIDED(1951, Brit.); DEVIL'S HARBOR(1954, Brit.)

Sylvia Andrews

COURAGEOUS DR. CHRISTIAN, THE(1940)

Ted Andrews

WINGS AND THE WOMAN(1942, Brit.)

Tige Andrews

UNTIL THEY SAIL(1957); MISTER ROBERTS(1955); WINGS OF EAGLES, THE(1957); CHINA DOLL(1958); IMITATION GENERAL(1958); ONIONHEAD(1958); PRIVATE'S AFFAIR, A(1959); IN ENEMY COUNTRY(1968); LAST TYCOON, THE(1976)

Tina Andrews

HIT(1973); CONRACK(1974); CARNY(1980)

Tod Andrews

DIVE BOMBER(1941); INTERNATIONAL SQUADRON(1941); DANGEROUSLY THEY LIVE(1942); THEY DIED WITH THEIR BOOTS ON(1942); HEAVEN CAN WAIT(1943); OUTRAGE(1950); BETWEEN HEAVEN AND HELL(1956); FROM HELL IT CAME(1957); IN HARM'S WAY(1965)

Todd Andrews

MALE ANIMAL, THE(1942); HANG'EM HIGH(1968)

W. Andrews

BLACK ROSE, THE(1950), art d

W.C. Andrews

SQUADRON LEADER X(1943, Brit.), art d; YELLOW CANARY, THE(1944, Brit.), art d; HOTEL RESERVE(1946, Brit.), art d; SPRING IN PARK LANE(1949, Brit.), art d

William Andrews

SEALED CARGO(1951); GEISHA GIRL(1952); LAST OF THE COMANCHES(1952); GAMBLER, THE(1974); SATURDAY NIGHT FEVER(1977); WANDERERS, THE(1979)

William C. Andrews

GREAT DAY(1945, Brit.), art d; MINE OWN EXECUTIONER(1948, Brit.), art d; PICCADILLY INCIDENT(1948, Brit.), art d; SHOWTIME(1948, Brit.), art d; ODETTE(1951, Brit.), art d; TRENT'S LAST CASE(1953, Brit.), art d; KING'S RHAPSODY(1955, Brit.), art d; ISLAND IN THE SUN(1957), art d

The Andrews Sisters

ARGENTINE NIGHTS(1940); BUCK PRIVATES(1941); HOLD THAT GHOST(1941); IN THE NAVY(1941); PRIVATE BUCKAROO(1942); WHAT'S COOKIN'?(1942); ALWAYS A BRIDESMAID(1943); HOW'S ABOUT IT?(1943); FOLLOW THE BOYS(1944); MOONLIGHT AND CACTUS(1944); SWINGTIME JOHNNY(1944); MAKE MINE MUSIC(1946); ROAD TO RIO(1947); MELODY TIME(1948)

Andrex

LA MARSEILLAISE(1938, Fr.); FRIC FRAC(1939, FR.); MANON(1950, Fr.); MY WIFE'S HUSBAND(1965, Fr./Ital.); TONI(1968, Fr.); LE PETIT THEATRE DE JEAN RENOIR(1974, Fr.)

Boris Andreyev

LAST HILL, THE(1945, USSR); DARK IS THE NIGHT(1946, USSR); SYMPHONY OF LIFE(1949, USSR); SWORD AND THE DRAGON, THE(1960, USSR); GORDEYEV FAMILY, THE(1961, U.S.S.R.); OPTIMISTIC TRAGEDY, THE(1964, USSR)

Leonid Andreyev

Silents

HE WHO GETS SLAPPED(1924), w

S. Andreyev

SANDU FOLLOWS THE SUN(1965, USSR)

Galina Andreyeva

SUNFLOWER(1970, Fr./Ital.)

Helena Andreyko

ZOOT SUIT(1981)

Yvette Andreyor

FRIEND WILL COME TONIGHT, A(1948, Fr.)

Misc. Silents

AME D'ARTISTE(1925, Fr.)

Andrez

ANGELE(1934 Fr.)

Marayat Andriane [Emmanuelle Arsan]

SAND PEBBLES, THE(1966)

Oscar Andriani

ANGELO IN THE CROWD(1952, Ital.); TIMES GONE BY(1953, Ital.); ULYSSES(1955, Ital.); LADY WITHOUT CAMELLIAS, THE(1981, Ital.)

Miodrag Andric

LOVE AFFAIR; OR THE CASE OF THE MISSING SWITCHBOARD OPERATOR(1968, Yugo.)

Zoran Andric

GIRL FROM PETROVKA, THE(1974)

A. A. Andrienkov
MYSTERIOUS ISLAND(1941, USSR)
Andrei Andrieu
SYMPHONIE FANTASTIQUE(1947, Fr.), art d
Andrieux
THEY ARE NOT ANGELS(1948, Fr.)
Roger Andrieux
MISTER BROWN(1972), p,d,w&ph, ed
1984
LA PETIT SIRENE(1984, Fr.), p,d&w
E. Andrikanis
CONCENTRATION CAMP(1939, USSR), ph; OTHELLO(1960, U.S.S.R.), ph
Eugene Andrikanis
LUCKY BRIDE, THE(1948, USSR), ph
Yevgeni Andrikanis
DAYS AND NIGHTS(1946, USSR), ph
Frank Andrina
SHINBONE ALLEY(1971), anim
Lucien Andriot
CHRISTINA(1929), ph; LOVE, LIVE AND LAUGH(1929), ph; VALIANT, THE(1929), ph; BIG TRAIL, THE(1930), ph; GOLDEN CALF, THE(1930), ph; HAPPY DAYS(1930), ph; DADDY LONG LEGS(1931), ph; DON'T BET ON WOMEN(1931), ph; BIRD OF PARADISE(1932), ph; COCK OF THE AIR(1932), ph; PRESTIGE(1932), ph; WESTWARD PASSAGE(1932), ph; BEFORE DAWN(1933), ph; BONDAGE(1933), ph; PENTHOUSE(1933), ph; RIGHT TO ROMANCE(1933), ph; TOPAZE(1933), ph; ANNE OF GREEN GABLES(1934), ph; LIFE OF VERGIE WINTERS, THE(1934), ph; STRAIGHT IS THE WAY(1934), ph; TWO ALONE(1934), ph; CHASING YESTERDAY(1935), ph; GRAND OLD GIRL(1935), ph; HOORAY FOR LOVE(1935), ph; RETURN OF PETER GRIMM, THE(1935), ph; CASE AGAINST MRS. AMES, THE(1936), ph; CHARLIE CHAN AT THE OPERA(1936), ph; GAY DESPERADO, THE(1936), ph; HIS FAMILY TREE(1936), ph; BIG TOWN GIRL(1937), ph; CAFE METROPOLE(1937), ph; I'LL TAKE ROMANCE(1937), ph; LADY ESCAPES, THE(1937), ph; ON THE AVENUE(1937), ph; YOU CAN'T HAVE EVERYTHING(1937), ph; ALWAYS IN TROUBLE(1938), ph; ARIZONA WILDCAT(1938), ph; I'LL GIVE A MILLION(1938), ph; INTERNATIONAL SETTLEMENT(1938), ph; MR. MOTO'S GAMBLE(1938), ph; THANKS FOR EVERYTHING(1938), ph; WHILE NEW YORK SLEEPS(1938), ph; BOY FRIEND(1939), ph; MR. MOTO IN DANGER ISLAND(1939), ph; PACK UP YOUR TROUBLES(1939), ph; QUICK MILLIONS(1939), ph; STOP, LOOK, AND LOVE(1939), ph; CHARTER PILOT(1940), ph; CITY OF CHANCE(1940), ph; EARTHBOUND(1940), ph; GIRL FROM AVENUE A(1940), ph; HIGH SCHOOL(1940), ph; LADY IN QUESTION, THE(1940), ph; LUCKY CISCO KID(1940), ph; DANCE HALL(1941), ph; GOLDEN HOOFS(1941), ph; MOON OVER HER SHOULDER(1941), ph; RIDE ON VAQUERO(1941), ph; RIDERS OF THE PURPLE SAGE(1941), ph; LONE STAR RANGER(1942), ph; LOVES OF EDGAR ALLAN POE, THE(1942), ph; MAD MARTINDALES, THE(1942), ph; MANILA CALLING(1942), ph; ON THE SUNNY SIDE(1942), ph; OVER MY DEAD BODY(1942), ph; SECRET AGENT OF JAPAN(1942), ph; JITTERBUGS(1943), ph; PARIS AFTER DARK(1943), ph; THEY CAME TO BLOW UP AMERICA(1943), ph; HAIRY APE, THE(1944), ph; SULLIVANS, THE(1944), ph; AND THEN THERE WERE NONE(1945), ph; SOUTHERNER, THE(1945), ph; DIARY OF A CHAMBERMAID(1946), ph; LADY LUCK(1946), ph; STRANGE WOMAN, THE(1946), ph; DISHONORED LADY(1947), ph; INTRIGUE(1947), ph; NEW ORLEANS(1947), ph; OUTPOST IN MOROCCO(1949), ph; BORDERLINE(1950), ph; JOHNNY ONE-EYE(1950), ph
Silents
FOOL THERE WAS, A(1915), ph; POOR LITTLE RICH GIRL, A(1917), ph; OH, BOY!(1919), ph; RIGHT TO LIE, THE(1919), ph; HELP WANTED--MALE!(1920), ph; CONNECTICUT YANKEE AT KING ARTHUR'S COURT, A(1921), ph; LAST TRAIL(1921), ph; SHAME(1921), ph; RAGGED HEIRESS, THE(1922), ph; EAST OF BROADWAY(1924), ph; NELLIE, THE BEAUTIFUL CLOAK MODEL(1924), ph; ROUGH SHOD(1925), ph; WHITE GOLD(1927), ph; LET 'ER GO GALLEGHER(1928), ph
Lueien Andriot
CORPSE CAME C.O.D., THE(, ph; WOMEN OF ALL NATIONS(1931), ph; CRIME DOCTOR, THE(1934), ph; CAPTAIN HURRICANE(1935), ph; JUST OFF BROADWAY(1942), ph; HOME TOWN STORY(1951), ph
Silents
PRIDE OF THE CLAN, THE(1917), ph; WEST OF CHICAGO(1922), ph; RED DICE(1926), ph; VOLCANO(1926), ph
Poupee Andriot
ALL QUIET ON THE WESTERN FRONT(1930)
Thomas Andrisano
TEENAGE GANG DEBS(1966)
Poupee Androit
Silents
BAIT, THE(1921)
James Andronica
NUNZIO(1978), a, w
1984
ACT, THE(1984)
Randall Andronica
NUNZIO(1978)
Enzo Andronico
00-2 MOST SECRET AGENTS(1965, Ital.); ITALIAN SECRET SERVICE(1968, Ital.)
Livio Andronico
ONCE UPON A TIME IN THE WEST(1969, U.S./Ital.)
Kira Andronikashvili
Misc. Silents
IN THE PILLORY(1924, USSR); ELISO(1928, USSR)
Spiros Andros
MATTER OF TIME, A(1976, Ital./U.S.)
Hans Androschin
ECSTASY(1940, Czech.), ph
Carol Androsky
FUNNYMAN(1967); ALL-AMERICAN BOY, THE(1973); I NEVER PROMISED YOU A ROSE GARDEN(1977); SATURDAY THE 14TH(1981)
Carole Androsky
LITTLE BIG MAN(1970)

Simon Andrue
Misc. Talkies
NIGHT OF THE SORCERORS(1970)
Kelly Andrus
1984
WOMAN IN RED, THE(1984)
Malon Andrus
Misc. Silents
ACE OF CACTUS RANGE(1924), d
Richie Andrusco
LITTLE FUGITIVE, THE(1953)
Nina Andrycz
CONTRACT, THE(1982, Pol.)
Jerzy Andrzejewski
ASHES AND DIAMONDS(1961, Pol.), w; GATES TO PARADISE(1968, Brit./Ger.), w
Carlos Anduze
ILLIAC PASSION, THE(1968)
Andy
KLUTE(1971), w
Bob Andy
CHILDREN OF BABYLON(1980, Jamaica)
Peter Gwynne Andy
NICKEL QUEEN, THE(1971, Aus.)
Andy Cavell and the Saints
SING AND SWING(1964, Brit.)
Andy Parker and the Plainsmen
CHECK YOUR GUNS(1948); HAWK OF POWDER RIVER, THE(1948); TIOGA KID, THE(1948); TORNADO RANGE(1948); WESTWARD TRAIL, THE(1948)
Zurab Andzhaparidze
QUEEN OF SPADES(1961, USSR)
Anel
SANTO CONTRA LA HIJA DE FRANKENSTEIN(1971, Mex.); INTERVAL(1973, Mex./U.S.)
Antonio Anelli
WATERLOO(1970, Ital./USSR); VOYAGE, THE(1974, Ital.)
Anemone
FRENCH POSTCARDS(1979)
Claude Anet
ARIANE(1931, Ger.), w; ARIANE, RUSSIAN MAID(1932, Fr.), w; MAYERLING(1937, Fr.), w; LOVE IN THE AFTERNOON(1957), w; MAYERLING(1968, Brit./Fr.), w
Genica Anet
DON QUIXOTE(1935, Fr.)
L. Anfilova
TRAIN GOES TO KIEV, THE(1961, USSR)
Tom Anfinsen
BAREFOOT EXECUTIVE, THE(1971)
Gerard Anfosso
COUSIN, COUSINE(1976, Fr.), m; BLUE COUNTRY, THE(1977, Fr.), m
Elizabeth Ang
SAINT JACK(1979)
Darien Angadi
BUTLEY(1974, Brit.)
Adele Angard
KING LEAR(1971, Brit./Den.), cos
Richard Angarola
GAMBIT(1966); MOMENT TO MOMENT(1966); VALLEY OF THE DOLLS(1967); DON'T JUST STAND THERE!(1968); HANG'EM HIGH(1968); STAR!(1968); CHE!(1969); SWEET CHARITY(1969); UNDEFEATED, THE(1969); WHAT EVER HAPPENED TO AUNT ALICE?(1969); SEVEN MINUTES, THE(1971); JEREMIAH JOHNSON(1972); PAPILLON(1973); THREE THE HARD WAY(1974); MASTER GUNFIGHTER, THE(1975)
Julie Ange
GIRL ON A CHAIN GANG(1966); TEENAGE MOTHER(1967)
Angel
ATTIC, THE(1979)
Daniel M. Angel
BODY SAID NO!, THE(1950, Brit.), p; MISS PILGRIM'S PROGRESS(1950, Brit.), p; MR. DRAKE'S DUCK(1951, Brit.), p; ANOTHER MAN'S POISON(1952, Brit.), p; SLASHER, THE(1953, Brit.), p; TWILIGHT WOMEN(1953, Brit.), p; ESCAPADE(1955, Brit.), p; SEA SHALL NOT HAVE THEM, THE(1955, Brit.), p; REACH FOR THE SKY(1957, Brit.), p; CARVE HER NAME WITH PRIDE(1958, Brit.), p; CAST A DARK SHADOW(1958, Brit.), p; SHERIFF OF FRACTURED JAW, THE(1958, Brit.), p; BEASTS OF MARSEILLES, THE(1959, Brit.), p; WE JOINED THE NAVY(1962, Brit.), p; WEST 11(1963, Brit.), p; ROMANTIC ENGLISHWOMAN, THE(1975, Brit./Fr.), p
Daniel N. Angel
MYSTERY AT THE BURLESQUE(1950, Brit.), p
Engineer Angel
FOR FREEDOM(1940, Brit.)
Ernest Angel
LOVE ON WHEELS(1932, Brit.), w
Ernst Angel
MARRY ME(1932, Brit.), w
Heather Angel
FAREWELL TO LOVE(1931, Brit.); NIGHT IN MONTMARTE, A(1931, Brit.); AFTER OFFICE HOURS(1932, Brit.); HOUND OF THE BASKERVILLES(1932, Brit.); MEN OF STEEL(1932, Brit.); SELF-MADE LADY(1932, Brit.); BERKELEY SQUARE(1933); CHARLIE CHAN'S GREATEST CASE(1933); EARLY TO BED(1933, Brit./Ger.); MAN WHO WON, THE(1933, Brit.); PILGRIMAGE(1933); MURDER IN TRINIDAD(1934); ORIENT EXPRESS(1934); ROMANCE IN THE RAIN(1934); SPRINGTIME FOR HENRY(1934); HEADLINE WOMAN, THE(1935); INFORMER, THE(1935); IT HAPPENED IN NEW YORK(1935); MYSTERY OF EDWIN DROOD, THE(1935); PERFECT GENTLEMAN, THE(1935); THREE MUSKETEERS, THE(1935); BOLD CABALLERO(1936); DANIEL BOONE(1936); LAST OF THE MOHICANS, THE(1936); BULLDOG DRUMMOND ESCAPES(1937); DUKE COMES BACK, THE(1937); PORTIA ON TRIAL(1937); WESTERN GOLD(1937); ARMY GIRL(1938); BULLDOG DRUMMOND IN AFRICA(1938); ARREST BULLDOG DRUMMOND(1939); BULLDOG DRUMMOND'S BRIDE(1939); BULLDOG DRUMMOND'S SECRET POLICE(1939); UNDERCOVER DOCTOR(1939); HALF A SINNER(1940); KITTY FOYLE(1940); PRIDE AND

PREJUDICE(1940); SHADOWS ON THE STAIRS(1941); SINGAPORE WOMAN(1941); SUSPICION(1941); THAT HAMILTON WOMAN(1941); TIME TO KILL(1942); UNDYING MONSTER, THE(1942); CRY HAVOC(1943); IN THE MEANTIME, DARLING(1944); LIFEBOAT(1944); SAXON CHARM, THE(1948); ALICE IN WONDERLAND(1951); PETER PAN(1953); PREMATURE BURIAL, THE(1962)

Jack Angel
YOUNG SAVAGES, THE(1961), cos; ONE MAN'S WAY(1964), cos; THANK GOD IT'S FRIDAY(1978), cos; NUTCRACKER FANTASY(1979)
Misc. Talkies
TEENAGE TEASERS(1982), d

Marguerite Angel
AFFAIR LAFONT, THE(1939, Fr.)

Michel Angel
CURIOUS DR. HUMPP(1967, Arg.)

Mike Angel
GUNN(1967); PSYCHIC KILLER(1975), w

Mikel Angel
AIRBORNE(1962); VALLEY OF THE DOLLS(1967); TELL THEM WILLIE BOY IS HERE(1969); ANGELS DIE HARD(1970); HARD RIDE, THE(1971); LOVE BUTCHER, THE(1982), d

Morris Angel
TORPEDOED!(1939), cos; CHANCE MEETING(1960, Brit.), cos; PAYROLL(1962, Brit.), cos

Super Swedish Angel
ALIAS THE CHAMP(1949)

Simone Angele
DEMONIAQUE(1958, Fr.)

Lia Angeleri
DISORDER(1964, Fr./Ital.); LIPSTICK(1965, Fr./Ital.)

Luz Angeles
CURSE OF THE VAMPIRES(1970, Phil., U.S.)

Carlo Angeletti
VERY HANDY MAN, A(1966, Fr./Ital.)

Marietto Angeletti
BEHOLD A PALE HORSE(1964)

Pio Angeletti
MOTIVE WAS JEALOUSY, THE(1970 Ital./Span.), p; PIZZA TRIANGLE, THE(1970, Ital./Span.), p; ROCCO PAPALEO(1974, Ital./Fr.), p; SCENT OF A WOMAN(1976, Ital.), p; VIVA ITALIA(1978, Ital.), p; TILL MARRIAGE DO US PART(1979, Ital.), p

Fabrizio Angeli
SPIRITS OF THE DEAD(1969, Fr./Ital.)

Pier Angeli
LIGHT TOUCH, THE(1951); TERESA(1951); DEVIL MAKES THREE, THE(1952); SOMBRERO(1953); STORY OF THREE LOVES, THE(1953); FLAME AND THE FLESH(1954); SILVER CHALICE, THE(1954); PORT AFRIQUE(1956, Brit.); SOMEBODY UP THERE LIKES ME(1956); VINTAGE, THE(1957); MERRY ANDREW(1958); ANGRY SILENCE, THE(1960, Brit.); S.O.S. PACIFIC(1960, Brit.); SODOM AND GOMORRAH(1962, U.S./Fr./Ital.); WHITE SLAVE SHIP(1962, Fr./Ital.); BATTLE OF THE BULGE(1965); SPY IN YOUR EYE(1966, Ital.); SHADOW OF EVIL(1967, Fr./Ital.); EVERY BASTARD A KING(1968, Israel); ONE STEP TO HELL(1969, U.S./Ital./Span.); OCTAMAN(1971)

Siro Angeli
GUILT IS NOT MINE(1968, Ital.), w

Norma Angelica
PEARL OF TLAYUCAN, THE(1964, Mex.)

Edy Angelillo
RATATAPLAN(1979, Ital.)

Luciana Angelillo
GIRL WITH A SUITCASE(1961, Fr./Ital.); TROJAN HORSE, THE(1962, Fr./Ital.); LOVE AND MARRIAGE(1966, Ital.); WILD EYE, THE(1968, Ital.)

Rick Angeline
LOVE HUNGER(1965, Arg.)

Luciano Angelini
WAR AND PEACE(1956, Ital./U.S.)

Nando Angelini
GUNS OF THE BLACK WITCH(1961, Fr./Ital.); PHAROAH'S WOMAN, THE(1961, Ital.); LA VIACCIA(1962, Fr./Ital.); DUEL OF THE TITANS(1963, Ital.); EASY LIFE, THE(1963, Ital.); DUEL OF CHAMPIONS(1964 Ital./Span.); HERCULES, SAMSON & ULYSSES(1964, Ital.); INVASION 1700(1965, Fr./Ital./Yugo.); 00-2 MOST SECRET AGENTS(1965, Ital.); SIX DAYS A WEEK(1966, Fr./Ital./Span.); OPERATION KID BROTHER(1967, Ital.)

Camillo Angelini-Rota
GARDEN OF THE FINZI-CONTINIS, THE(1976, Ital./Ger.)

Angelique
TOUCH OF HER FLESH, THE(1967)

Mike Angelis
Misc. Talkies
ALF GARNETT SAGA, THE(1972)

Paul Angelis
OTLEY(1969, Brit.); SWEENEY(1977, Brit.); FOR YOUR EYES ONLY(1981); RUNNERS(1983, Brit.)

Buckley Angell
HIRED GUN, THE(1957), w

Jeffery B. Angell
RUBY(1977), makeup

Bob Angelle
SWEET JESUS, PREACHER MAN(1973)

Lou Angelli
SLASHER, THE(1975), w

Angelo
LIQUID SKY(1982)
1984
STREETS OF FIRE(1984)

Dom Angelo
1984
OH GOD! YOU DEVIL(1984)

Edmond Angelo
BREAKDOWN(1953), p&d

Jean Angelo
Misc. Silents
DIVINE SACRIFICE, THE(1918); L'ATLANTIDE(1921, Fr.); LE CHANT DE L'AMOUR TRIOMPHANT(1923, Fr.); NANA(1926, Fr.); MARQUITTA(1927, Fr.); LA VIERGE FOLLE(1929, Fr.); MONTE-CRISTO(1929, Fr.); STRANGE CASE OF DISTRICT ATTORNEY M.(1930)

Liberty Angelo
MACHISMO–40 GRAVES FOR 40 GUNS(1970)

Little Angelo
ANGELO(1951, Ital.)

Michelle Angelo
FOR LOVE AND MONEY(1967)

Miguel Angelo
TRAIN ROBBERY CONFIDENTIAL(1965, Braz.)

Robert Angelo
YOUNG SINNER, THE(1965)

Tony Angelo
RABID(1976, Can.); ATLANTIC CITY(1981, U.S./Can.); GAS(1981, Can.)

Angelo-Galassi
WHITE NIGHTS(1961, Ital./Fr.)

Theodor Angelopoulos
DAYS OF 36(1972, Gr.), d&w

Mario Angelotti
COUNTERFEITERS, THE(1953, Ital.)

Maya Angelou
CALYPSO HEAT WAVE(1957); GEORGIA, GEORGIA(1972), w

Muriel Angelus
NO EXIT(1930, Brit.); HINDLE WAKES(1931, Brit.); NIGHT BIRDS(1931, Brit.); BLIND SPOT(1932, Brit.); BRIDEGROOM FOR TWO(1932, Brit.); DON'T BE A DUMMY(1932, Brit.); MY WIFE'S FAMILY(1932, Brit.); SO YOU WON'T TALK?(1935, Brit.); LIGHT THAT FAILED, THE(1939); GREAT McGINTY, THE(1940); SAFARI(1940); WAY OF ALL FLESH, THE(1940)
Silents
RINGER, THE(1928, Brit.)
Misc. Silents
INFAMOUS LADY, THE(1928, Brit.); RED ACES(1929, Brit.)

Paul Angelus
YELLOW SUBMARINE(1958, Brit.)

Barbara Angely
BLUE DEMON VERSUS THE INFERNAL BRAINS(1967, Mex.)

Mark Anger
LITTLE MISS MARKER(1980)

Oliver A. Anger
MOZAMBIQUE(1966, Brit.), p

Heinz Angermeyer
DREAM TOWN(1973, Ger.), p

Avril Angers
SKIMPY IN THE NAVY(1949, Brit.); MISS PILGRIM'S PROGRESS(1950, Brit.); LUCKY MASCOT, THE(1951, Brit.); SIX MEN, THE(1951, Brit.); DON'T BLAME THE STORK(1954, Brit.); BLONDE BAIT(1956, U.S./Brit.); BOND OF FEAR(1956, Brit.); GREEN MAN, THE(1957, Brit.); LIGHT FINGERS(1957, Brit.); BE MY GUEST(1965, Brit.); DEVILS OF DARKNESS, THE(1965, Brit.); FAMILY WAY, THE(1966, Brit.); THREE BITES OF THE APPLE(1967); TWO A PENNY(1968, Brit.); BEST HOUSE IN LONDON, THE(1969, Brit.); STAIRCASE(1969 U.S./Brit./Fr.); THERE'S A GIRL IN MY SOUP(1970, Brit.); CRY OF THE PENGUINS(1972, Brit.)

Harry Angers
MY AIN FOLK(1944, Brit.)

Bobby Angew
Misc. Silents
COLLEGE HERO, THE(1927)

Angie
BANDIT QUEEN(1950)

G.B. Angioletti
WANDERING JEW, THE(1948, Ital.), w

Luciana Angiolillo
EASY LIFE, THE(1963, Ital.); HERCULES AND THE CAPTIVE WOMEN(1963, Fr./Ital.); DISORDER(1964, Fr./Ital.); SPY IN YOUR EYE(1966, Ital.); GRAND SLAM(1968, Ital., Span., Ger.)

Renato Angiolini
TO KILL OR TO DIE(1973, Ital.), p

France Anglade
SUNDAYS AND CYBELE(1962, Fr.); 24 HOURS TO KILL(1966, Brit.); CAROLINE CHERIE(1968, Fr.); OLDEST PROFESSION, THE(1968, Fr./Ital./Ger.)

Frances Anglade
DOUBLE BED, THE(1965, Fr./Ital.)

Chuck Angle
TERROR IN THE JUNGLE(1968)

Jimmy Angle
TERROR IN THE JUNGLE(1968)

Philip Anglim
TESTAMENT(1983)

Sally Anglim
THUNDERING TRAIL, THE(1951); YES SIR, MR. BONES(1951)

Dan Anglin
EDDIE MACON'S RUN(1983)

Florence Anglin
TRADING PLACES(1983)
1984
FALLING IN LOVE(1984)

Edith Angold
TWO WEEKS IN ANOTHER TOWN(1962); SO ENDS OUR NIGHT(1941); UNDERGROUND(1941); ABOVE SUSPICION(1943); TOMORROW THE WORLD(1944); SUSPENSE(1946); RINGSIDE(1949); TOUGH ASSIGNMENT(1949); GOLDBERGS, THE(1950); SECRET FURY, THE(1950); WHITE TOWER, THE(1950); GREAT CARUSO, THE(1951); WOMAN IN THE DARK(1952); MURDER WITHOUT TEARS(1953); BERNARDINE(1957); BLUE ANGEL, THE(1959)

Conrad E. Angone
BEASTMASTER, THE(1982), prod d

Michele Angot
AMELIE OR THE TIME TO LOVE(1961, Fr.), w
Nick Angotti
FIRST MONDAY IN OCTOBER(1981)
Francesco Angrisano
MONSIGNOR(1982)
Franco Angrisano
AVANTI!(1972)
Richard Angst
S.O.S. ICEBERG(1933), ph; REMBRANDT(1936, Brit.), ph; NEW EARTH, THE(1937, Jap./Ger.), ph; HIGH CONQUEST(1947), ph; STORM OVER TIBET(1952), ph; SCHLAGER-PARADE(1953), ph; ARENT WE WONDERFUL?(1959, Ger.), ph; MISTRESS OF THE WORLD(1959, Ital./Fr./Ger.), ph; JOURNEY TO THE LOST CITY(1960, Ger./Fr./Ital.), ph; SPESSART INN, THE(1961, Ger.), ph; GOOD SOLDIER SCHWEIK, THE(1963, Ger.), ph; MAD EXECUTIONERS, THE(1965, Ger.), ph; THE DIRTY GAME(1966, Fr./Ital./Ger.), ph; PHANTOM OF SOHO, THE(1967, Ger.), ph; HEIDI(1968, Aust.), ph; FIGHT FOR ROME(1969, Ger./Rum.), ph
Axel Angstfeld
WAR AND PEACE(1983, Ger.), d&w
Albert Angus
SILENCE OF THE NORTH(1981, Can.); RUNNING BRAVE(1983, Can.)
Bernadine Angus
FOG ISLAND(1945), w
Robert Angus
ARMORED CAR ROBBERY(1950), w; TIMETABLE(1956), w; CANDIDATE, THE(1964), d; SKATEBOARD(1978), ed
Angwin
LAST WAVE, THE(1978, Aus.), spec eff
Neil Angwin
LAST WAVE, THE(1978, Aus.), art d; MANGANINNIE(1982, Aus.), art d; SCARECROW, THE(1982, New Zealand), prod d; LONELY HEARTS(1983, Aus.), art d
1984
RAZORBACK(1984, Aus.), art d
Laszlo Angyal
SPRING SHOWER(1932, Hung.), m
Kieu Anh
HOA-BINH(1971, Fr.)
Edna Anhalt
EMBRACEABLE YOU(1948), w; YOUNGER BROTHERS, THE(1949), w; PANIC IN THE STREETS(1950), w; RETURN OF THE FRONTIERSMAN(1950), w; SIERRA(1950), w; MEMBER OF THE WEDDING, THE(1952), w; SNIPER, THE(1952), w; NOT AS A STRANGER(1955), w; PRIDE AND THE PASSION, THE(1957), w
Edward Anhalt
GENTLEMAN FROM NOWHERE, THE(1948), w; CRIME DOCTOR'S DIARY, THE(1949), w; PANIC IN THE STREETS(1950), w; MEMBER OF THE WEDDING, THE(1952), w; SNIPER, THE(1952), w; NOT AS A STRANGER(1955), w; PRIDE AND THE PASSION, THE(1957), w; IN LOVE AND WAR(1958), w; RESTLESS YEARS, THE(1958), w; YOUNG LIONS, THE(1958), w; SINS OF RACHEL CADE, THE(1960), w; YOUNG SAVAGES, THE(1961), w; GIRL NAMED TAMIRO, A(1962), w; GIRLS! GIRLS! GIRLS!(1962), w; WIVES AND LOVERS(1963), w; BECKET(1964, Brit.), w; BOEING BOEING(1965), w; SATAN BUG, THE(1965), w; HOUR OF THE GUN(1967), a, w; IN ENEMY COUNTRY(1968), w; THE BOSTON STRANGLER, THE(1968), w; MADWOMAN OF CHAILLOT, THE(1969), w; JEREMIAH JOHNSON(1972), w; LUTHER(1974), w; MAN IN THE GLASS BOOTH, THE(1975), w; ESCAPE TO ATHENA(1979, Brit.), w; GREEN ICE(1981, Brit.), w; RIGHT STUFF, THE(1983)
Sukumar Anhana
TUSK(1980, Fr.)
Tony Anholt
FEAR IS THE KEY(1973)
Stella Anicette
MADAME ROSA(1977, Fr.)
Anick
ODYSSEY OF THE PACIFIC(1983, Can./Fr.)
Marie-Ange Anies
LEGEND OF FRENCHIE KING, THE(1971, Fr./Ital./Span./Brit.), w
N. Anikeyeva
PEACE TO HIM WHO ENTERS(1963, USSR), ed; FORTY-NINE DAYS(1964, USSR), ed
N. Anikina
LETTER THAT WAS NEVER SENT, THE(1962, USSR), ed
Paul Anil
1984
PASSAGE TO INDIA, A(1984, Brit.)
The Animals
GET YOURSELF A COLLEGE GIRL(1964); IT'S A BIKINI WORLD(1967)
Mario Aniouv
STUDENT NURSES, THE(1970)
Mario Aniov
RED SKY AT MORNING(1971)
Anisha
WELCOME TO THE CLUB(1971)
N. Anisimova
DON QUIXOTE(1961, USSR)
Irina Anisimova-Wolf
UNCLE VANYA(1972, USSR)
A. Aleksandrushkin V Anisko
CLEAR SKIES(1963, USSR)
Paul Anka
LET'S ROCK(1958); GIRLS' TOWN(1959); PRIVATE LIVES OF ADAM AND EVE, THE(1961); LONGEST DAY, THE(1962)

Anker
SUDDENLY, A WOMAN!(1967, Den.), d, w; LURE OF THE JUNGLE, THE(1970, Den.), ed
Marshall Anker
SHAMUS(1973)
Misc. Talkies
FORBIDDEN UNDER THE CENSORSHIP OF THE KING(1973)

William Anker
Misc. Silents
WILD OATS(1916)
Evelyn Ankers
REMBRANDT(1936, Brit.); FIRE OVER ENGLAND(1937, Brit.); WINGS OF THE MORNING(1937, Brit.); CLAYDON TREASURE MYSTERY, THE(1938, Brit.); COMING OF AGE(1938, Brit.); CRIME OF PETER FRAME, THE(1938, Brit.); MURDER IN THE FAMILY(1938, Brit.); VILLIERS DIAMOND, THE(1938, Brit.); OVER THE MOON(1940, Brit.); BACHELOR DADDY(1941); BURMA CONVOY(1941); HIT THE ROAD(1941); HOLD THAT GHOST(1941); WOLF MAN, THE(1941); EAGLE SQUADRON(1942); GHOST OF FRANKENSTEIN, THE(1942); GREAT IMPERSONATION, THE(1942); NORTH TO THE KLONDIKE(1942); PIERRE OF THE PLAINS(1942); SHERLOCK HOLMES AND THE VOICE OF TERROR(1942); ALL BY MYSELF(1943); CAPTIVE WILD WOMAN(1943); HERS TO HOLD(1943); HIS BUTLER'S SISTER(1943); KEEP 'EM SLUGGING(1943); MAD GHOUL, THE(1943); SON OF DRACULA(1943); YOU'RE A LUCKY FELLOW, MR. SMITH(1943); BOWERY TO BROADWAY(1944); FOLLOW THE BOYS(1944); INVISIBLE MAN'S REVENGE(1944); JUNGLE WOMAN(1944); LADIES COURAGEOUS(1944); PARDON MY RHYTHM(1944); PEARL OF DEATH, THE(1944); WEIRD WOMAN(1944); FATAL WITNESS, THE(1945); FROZEN GHOST, THE(1945); BLACK BEAUTY(1946); FLIGHT TO NOWHERE(1946); FRENCH KEY, THE(1946); QUEEN OF BURLESQUE(1946); LAST OF THE REDMEN(1947); LONE WOLF IN LONDON(1947); SPOILERS OF THE NORTH(1947); PAROLE, INC.(1949); TARZAN'S MAGIC FOUNTAIN(1949); TEXAN MEETS CALAMITY JANE, THE(1950)
Camille Ankewich
Silents
STELLA MARIS(1918)
Camille Ankewitch
Silents
ONE MORE AMERICAN(1918)
James Anklam
1984
REVENGE OF THE NERDS(1984)
Bob Ankrom
CAYMAN TRIANGLE, THE(1977)
David Ankrum
ROOMMATES, THE(1973); STUDENT BODY, THE(1976); STING II, THE(1983)
Morris Ankrum
STAND UP AND CHEER(1934 80m FOX bw); HILLS OF OLD WYOMING(1937); RUSTLER'S VALLEY(1937); BUCK BENNY RIDES AGAIN(1940); CHEROKEE STRIP(1940); KNIGHTS OF THE RANGE(1940); LIGHT OF WESTERN STARS, THE(1940); SHOWDOWN, THE(1940); THREE MEN FROM TEXAS(1940); BANDIT TRAIL, THE(1941); BORDER VIGILANTES(1941); DOOMED CARAVAN(1941); IN OLD COLORADO(1941); PIRATES ON HORSEBACK(1941); ROAD AGENT(1941); ROUNDUP, THE(1941); THIS WOMAN IS MINE(1941); WIDE OPEN TOWN(1941); I WAKE UP SCREAMING(1942); LOVES OF EDGAR ALLAN POE, THE(1942); OMAHA TRAIL, THE(1942); REUNION IN FRANCE(1942); RIDE 'EM COWBOY(1942); ROXIE HART(1942); TALES OF MANHATTAN(1942); TEN GENTLEMEN FROM WEST POINT(1942); TENNESSEE JOHNSON(1942); TIME TO KILL(1942); BEST FOOT FORWARD(1943); DIXIE DUGAN(1943); HEAVENLY BODY, THE(1943); HUMAN COMEDY, THE(1943); SWING FEVER(1943); BARBARY COAST GENT(1944); GENTLE ANNIE(1944); MARRIAGE IS A PRIVATE AFFAIR(1944); MEET THE PEOPLE(1944); RATIONING(1944); SEE HERE, PRIVATE HARGROVE(1944); THIN MAN GOES HOME, THE(1944); THIRTY SECONDS OVER TOKYO(1944); ADVENTURE(1945); HIDDEN EYE, THE(1945); BLUE SIERRA(1946); COCKEYED MIRACLE, THE(1946); COURAGE OF LASSIE(1946); HARVEY GIRLS, THE(1946); LITTLE MISTER JIM(1946); MIGHTY MCGURK, THE(1946); POSTMAN ALWAYS RINGS TWICE, THE(1946); DESIRE ME(1947); GOOD NEWS(1947); HIGH WALL, THE(1947); LADY IN THE LAKE(1947); SEA OF GRASS, THE(1947); SONG OF THE THIN MAN(1947); UNDERCOVER MAISIE(1947); FIGHTING BACK(1948); FOR THE LOVE OF MARY(1948); JOAN OF ARC(1948); COLORADO TERRITORY(1949); FOUNTAINHEAD, THE(1949); SLATTERY'S HURRICANE(1949); WE WERE STRANGERS(1949); BORDERLINE(1950); CHAIN LIGHTNING(1950); DAMNED DON'T CRY, THE(1950); IN A LONELY PLACE(1950); REDHEAD AND THE COWBOY, THE(1950); ROCKETSHIP X-M(1950); SHORT GRASS(1950); SOUTHSIDE 1-1000(1950); ALONG THE GREAT DIVIDE(1951); FIGHTING COAST GUARD(1951); FLIGHT TO MARS(1951); LION HUNTERS, THE(1951); MY FAVORITE SPY(1951); TOMORROW IS ANOTHER DAY(1951); FORT OSAGE(1952); HIAWATHA(1952); MAN BEHIND THE GUN, THE(1952); MUTINY(1952); RAIDERS, THE(1952); RED PLANET MARS(1952); SON OF ALI BABA(1952); DEVIL'S CANYON(1953); FORT VENGEANCE(1953); INVADERS FROM MARS(1953); MEXICAN MANHUNT(1953); MOONLIGHTER, THE(1953); SKY COMMANDO(1953); APACHE(1954); DRUMS ACROSS THE RIVER(1954); OUTLAW STALLION, THE(1954); SILVER LODE(1954); SOUTHWEST PASSAGE(1954); STEEL CAGE, THE(1954); TAZA, SON OF COCHISE(1954); THREE YOUNG TEXANS(1954); TWO GUNS AND A BADGE(1954); VERA CRUZ(1954); CHIEF CRAZY HORSE(1955); CRASHOUT(1955); ETERNAL SEA, THE(1955); HALF HUMAN(1955, Jap.); NO MAN'S WOMAN(1955); SILVER STAR, THE(1955); TENNESSEE'S PARTNER(1955); DEATH OF A SCOUNDREL(1956); DESPERADOES ARE IN TOWN, THE(1956); EARTH VS. THE FLYING SAUCERS(1956); FURY AT GUNSIGHT PASS(1956); NAKED GUN, THE(1956); QUINCANNON, FRONTIER SCOUT(1956); WALK THE PROUD LAND(1956); WHEN GANGLAND STRIKES(1956); BEGINNING OF THE END(1957); DRANGO(1957); GIANT CLAW, THE(1957); HELL'S CROSSROADS(1957); KRONOS(1957); OMAR KHAYYAM(1957); ZOMBIES OF MORA TAU(1957); BADMAN'S COUNTRY(1958); FROM THE EARTH TO THE MOON(1958); FRONTIER GUN(1958); GIANT FROM THE UNKNOWN(1958); HOW TO MAKE A MONSTER(1958); SAGA OF HEMP BROWN, THE(1958); TWILIGHT FOR THE GODS(1958); YOUNG AND WILD(1958); LITTLE SHEPHERD OF KINGDOM COME(1961); MOST DANGEROUS MAN ALIVE, THE(1961); "X"-THE MAN WITH THE X-RAY EYES(1963)
Misc. Talkies
AND NOW TOMORROW(1952)
Anni Ann
TREMENDOUSLY RICH MAN, A(1932, Ger.)
Pock Rock Ann
UGLY AMERICAN, THE(1963)
Priscilla Ann
SPLIT, THE(1968)

Ann Cornell and the International Jittebugs
  BOY! WHAT A GIRL(1947)
Tracy Ann-King
  HIT MAN(1972)
Ann-Margret
  POCKETFUL OF MIRACLES(1961); STATE FAIR(1962); BYE BYE BIRDIE(1963); KITTEN WITH A WHIP(1964); PLEASURE SEEKERS, THE(1964); VIVA LAS VEGAS(1964); BUS RILEY'S BACK IN TOWN(1965); CINCINNATI KID, THE(1965); ONCE A THIEF(1965); MADE IN PARIS(1966); MURDERERS' ROW(1966); STAGECOACH(1966); SWINGER, THE(1966); TIGER AND THE PUSSYCAT, THE(1967, U.S., Ital.); R.P.M.(1970); C. C. AND COMPANY(1971); CARNAL KNOWLEDGE(1971); OUTSIDE MAN, THE(1973, U.S./FR.); TRAIN ROBBERS, THE(1973); TOMMY(1975, Brit.); TWIST, THE(1976, Fr.); JOSEPH ANDREWS(1977, Brit.); LAST REMAKE OF BEAU GESTE, THE(1977); CHEAP DETECTIVE, THE(1978); MAGIC(1978); VILLAIN, THE(1979); MIDDLE AGE CRAZY(1980, Can.); I OUGHT TO BE IN PICTURES(1982); LOOKIN' TO GET OUT(1982); RETURN OF THE SOLDIER, THE(1983, Brit.)
Misc. Talkies
  REBUS(1969, Ger./Ital./Span./Arg.); PROPHET, THE(1976)
Christie Anna
Misc. Talkies
  MIDNIGHT PLOWBOY(1973)
Julie Anna
  RABID(1976, Can.); ONE MAN(1979, Can.)
Anna-Lisa
  HAVE ROCRET, WILL TRAVEL(1959); TWELVE TO THE MOON(1960)
Annabella
  DRAGNET NIGHT(1931, Fr.); MILLION, THE(1931, Fr.); SPRING SHOWER(1932, Hung.); ANNE-MARIE(1936, Fr.); DINNER AT THE RITZ(1937, Brit.); UNDER THE RED ROBE(1937, Brit.); WINGS OF THE MORNING(1937, Brit.); BARONESS AND THE BUTLER, THE(1938); SACRIFICE OF HONOR(1938); SUEZ(1938); BRIDAL SUITE(1939); ESCAPE FROM YESTERDAY(1939, Fr.); BOMBER'S MOON(1943); TONIGHT WE RAID CALAIS(1943); 13 RUE MADELEINE(1946)
Misc. Silents
  MALDONE(1928, Fr.)
Annaconda
  SHADOW MAN(1953, Brit.)
Ken Annakin
  HOLIDAY CAMP(1947, Brit.), d; BROKEN JOURNEY(1948, Brit.), d; HERE COME THE HUGGETTS(1948, Brit.), d; VOTE FOR HUGGETT(1948, Brit.), d; HUGGETTS ABROAD, THE(1949, Brit.), d; MIRANDA(1949, Brit.), d; QUARTET(1949, Brit.), d; TRIO(1950, Brit.), d; HOTEL SAHARA(1951, Brit.), d; OUTPOST IN MALAYA(1952, Brit.), d; STORY OF ROBIN HOOD, THE(1952, Brit.), d; DOUBLE CONFESSION(1953, Brit.), d; LANDFALL(1953, Brit.), d; SWORD AND THE ROSE, THE(1953), d; YOU KNOW WHAT SAILORS ARE(1954, Brit.), d; LAND OF FURY(1955 Brit.), d; LOSER TAKES ALL(1956, Brit.), d; ACROSS THE BRIDGE(1957, Brit.), d; VALUE FOR MONEY(1957, Brit.), d; THREE MEN IN A BOAT(1958, Brit.), d; ELEPHANT GUN(1959, Brit.), d; THIRD MAN ON THE MOUNTAIN(1959), d; SWISS FAMILY ROBINSON(1960), d; HELLIONS, THE(1962, Brit.), d; LONGEST DAY, THE(1962), d; CROOKS ANONYMOUS(1963, Brit.), d; FAST LADY, THE(1963, Brit.), d; BATTLE OF THE BULGE(1965), d; THOSE MAGNIFICENT MEN IN THEIR FLYING MACHINES; OR HOW I FLEWFROM LONDON TO PARIS IN 25 HOURS AND 11 MINUTES(1965, Brit.), d, w; UNDERWORLD INFORMERS(1965, Brit.), d; LONG DUEL, THE(1967, Brit.), p&d; BIGGEST BUNDLE OF THEM ALL, THE(1968), d; THOSE DARING YOUNG MEN IN THEIR JAUNTY JALOPIES(1969, Fr./Brit./ Ital.), p, d, w; CALL OF THE WILD(1972, Ger./ Span./Ital./Fr.), d; PAPER TIGER(1975, Brit.), d; BEHIND THE IRON MASK(1977), d; CHEAPER TO KEEP HER(1980), d; PIRATE MOVIE, THE(1982, Aus.), d
Kenn Annakin
  COMING-OUT PARTY, A(, d
Michael Annals
  JOSEPH ANDREWS(1977, Brit.), prod d, cos
Annamode
  MARRIAGE–ITALIAN STYLE(1964, Fr./Ital.), cos; YESTERDAY, TODAY, AND TOMORROW(1964, Ital./Fr.), cos
Charles Annan
1984
  WHITE ELEPHANT(1984, Brit.)
James Annand
Silents
  ANNA THE ADVENTURESS(1920, Brit.); PIPES OF PAN, THE(1923, Brit.)
Jean-Jacques Annaud
  BLACK AND WHITE IN COLOR(1976, Fr.), d, w; QUEST FOR FIRE(1982, Fr./Can.), d
Annazette
  DON'T WORRY, WE'LL THINK OF A TITLE(1966)
Dennis Anndel
  HISTORY OF MR. POLLY, THE(1949, Brit.)
Anne
  DONKEY SKIN(1975, Fr.), ed
Beth Anne
Misc. Talkies
  CHORUS CALL(1979)
Beverly Anne
Misc. Talkies
  DISCO 9000(1977)
Carol Anne
  CRIMSON CULT, THE(1970, Brit.)
Cheryl Anne
  SATAN'S SADISTS(1969); OCTOPUSSY(1983, Brit.)
Lilli Anne
  WATER GYPSIES, THE(1932, Brit.)
Peggy Anne
  YOU CAN'T DO WITHOUT LOVE(1946, Brit.)
Anne-Wiazemsky
  WIND FROM THE EAST(1970, Fr./Ital./Ger.)
Paul Annell
  NEVER NEVER LAND(1982), d

Bill Anneman
  CORPSE GRINDERS, THE(1972), ph
Glory Annen
  SPACED OUT(1981, Brit.); LONELY LADY, THE(1983)
1984
  SUPERGIRL(1984)
Georges Annenkov
  LE PLAISIR(1954, Fr.), cos; LOLA MONTES(1955, Fr./Ger.), cos; MODIGLIANI OF MONTPARNASSE(1961, Fr./Ital.), cos
I. Annensky
  ANNA CROSS, THE(1954, USSR), d&w
Mark Annerl
  JIM, THE WORLD'S GREATEST(1976)
Fred Annerly
Silents
  PURSUING VENGEANCE, THE(1916)
Misc. Silents
  MAN FROM MEXICO, THE(1914)
Jeremy Annett
  WOMAN HATER(1949, Brit.)
Paul Annett
  BEAST MUST DIE, THE(1974, Brit.), d
Misc. Talkies
  AND THE WALL CAME TUMBLING DOWN(1984), d
Annette [Funicello]
  MONKEY'S UNCLE, THE(1965)
Corrado Annicelli
  GUNS OF THE BLACK WITCH(1961, Fr./Ital.); LAST OF THE VIKINGS, THE(1962, Fr./Ital.)
Vito Annichiarico
  OPEN CITY(1946, Ital.)
Yvonne Annie
Misc. Silents
  RAMUNTCHO(1919, Fr.)
Annie-Savarin
  MADEMOISELLE(1966, Fr./Brit.)
Joanna Annin
  NO BLADE OF GRASS(1970, Brit.)
Francesca Annis
  CAT GANG, THE(1959, Brit.); HIS AND HERS(1961, Brit.); CLEOPATRA(1963); EYES OF ANNIE JONES, THE(1963, Brit.); WEST 11(1963, Brit.); CROOKS IN CLOISTERS(1964, Brit.); FLIPPER'S NEW ADVENTURE(1964); MURDER MOST FOUL(1964, Brit.); SATURDAY NIGHT OUT(1964, Brit.); PLEASURE GIRLS, THE(1966, Brit.); RUN WITH THE WIND(1966, Brit.); SKY PIRATE, THE(1970); WALKING STICK, THE(1970, Brit.); MACBETH(1971, Brit.); STRONGER THAN THE SUN(1980, Brit.); KRULL(1983)
1984
  DUNE(1984)
Misc. Talkies
  YOUNG JACOBITES(1959)
Mimosa Annis
  PUMPKIN EATER, THE(1964, Brit.)
Paul Annixter
  THOSE CALLOWAYS(1964), w
Hidiaki Anno
1984
  WARRIORS OF THE WIND(1984, Jap.), anim
Armando Annuale
  ROMAN HOLIDAY(1953); LOVE AND LARCENY(1963, Fr./Ital.)
Giuseppe Annunziata
  ROMANOFF AND JULIET(1961), makeup; TWO WOMEN(1961, Ital./Fr.), makeup; MARRIAGE–ITALIAN STYLE(1964, Fr./Ital.), makeup; LADY L(1965, Fr./Ital.), makeup; MORE THAN A MIRACLE(1967, Ital./Fr.), makeup; LADY LIBERTY(1972, Ital./Fr.), makeup
Guiseppe Annunziata
  PRIEST'S WIFE, THE(1971, Ital./Fr.), makeup
Guisse Giuseppe Annunziata
  MAN OF LA MANCHA(1972), makeup
John Annus
  LOOKING UP(1977), art d
Jack Ano
  JEANNE EAGELS(1957); VERTIGO(1958)
Marisol Anon
  HOUSE OF 1,000 DOLLS(1967, Ger./Span./Brit.)
Catherine Anouilh
  GRAND MANEUVER, THE(1956, Fr.)
Jean Anouilh
  ANNA KARENINA(1948, Brit.), w; MONSIEUR VINCENT(1949, Fr.), w; CAROLINE CHERIE(1951, Fr.), w; MONSOON(1953), w; PASSION OF SLOW FIRE, THE(1962, Fr.), w; WALTZ OF THE TOREADORS(1962, Brit.), w; BECKET(1964, Brit.), w; CIRCLE OF LOVE(1965, Fr.), w; TIME FOR LOVING, A(1971, Brit.), w
Anouk
  GOLDEN SALAMANDER(1950, Brit.)
Eleni Anousaki
  ZORBA THE GREEK(1964, U.S./Gr.); RED LANTERNS(1965, Gr.)
Malena Anousaki
  LYDIA(1964, Can.)
Paddy Madden Victoria Anoux
  TRUE STORY OF ESKIMO NELL, THE(1975, Aus.)
Victoria Anoux
  STONE(1974, Aus.)
Michel Anphoux
  LA BALANCE(1983, Fr.)
Tommy Ansah
  ONE PLUS ONE(1969, Brit.); TWO GENTLEMEN SHARING(1969, Brit.); BUSHBABY, THE(1970); 10 RILLINGTON PLACE(1971, Brit.)
Alan Ansara
  MOVING FINGER, THE(1963)

Edward Ansara
RABBIT TEST(1978)
Michael Ansara
INTRIGUE(1947); DESERT HAWK, THE(1950); KIM(1950); BANNERLINE(1951); MY FAVORITE SPY(1951); ONLY THE VALIANT(1951); SOLDIERS THREE(1951); BRAVE WARRIOR(1952); DIPLOMATIC COURIER(1952); GOLDEN HAWK, THE(1952); LAWLESS BREED, THE(1952); ROAD TO BALI(1952); YANKEE BUCCANEER(1952); BANDITS OF CORSICA, THE(1953); DIAMOND QUEEN(1953); JULIUS CAESAR(1953); ROBE, THE(1953); SERPENT OF THE NILE(1953); SLAVES OF BABYLON(1953); WHITE WITCH DOCTOR(1953); BENGAL BRIGADE(1954); EGYPTIAN, THE(1954); PRINCESS OF THE NILE(1954); SARACEN BLADE, THE(1954); SIGN OF THE PAGAN(1954); THREE YOUNG TEXANS(1954); ABBOTT AND COSTELLO MEET THE MUMMY(1955); DIANE(1955); JUPITER'S DARLING(1955); LONE RANGER, THE(1955); NEW ORLEANS UNCENSORED(1955); GUN BROTHERS(1956); PILLARS OF THE SKY(1956); TEN COMMANDMENTS, THE(1956); LAST OF THE BADMEN(1957); QUANTEZ(1957); TALL STRANGER, THE(1957); COMANCHEROS, THE(1961); VOYAGE TO THE BOTTOM OF THE SEA(1961); GREATEST STORY EVER TOLD, THE(1965); HARUM SCARUM(1965); QUICK, LET'S GET MARRIED(1965); AND NOW MIGUEL(1966); TEXAS ACROSS THE RIVER(1966); DARING GAME(1968); DESTRUCTORS, THE(1968); PINK JUNGLE, THE(1968); SOL MADRID(1968); GUNS OF THE MAGNIFICENT SEVEN(1969); PHYNX, THE(1970); DEAR, DEAD DELILAH(1972); STAND UP AND BE COUNTED(1972); DOLL SQUAD, THE(1973); BEARS AND I, THE(1974); IT'S ALIVE(1974); MOHAMMAD, MESSENGER OF GOD(1976, Lebanon/Brit.); DAY OF THE ANIMALS(1977); MANITOU, THE(1978); TARGET: HARRY(1980); GUNS AND THE FURY, THE(1983)
Misc. Talkies
CONFESSION, THE(1964); ACCESS CODE(1984)
Michael G. Ansara
SAD SACK, THE(1957)
Mike Ansara
ACTION IN ARABIA(1944)
Huspin Ansari
ROAD TO SINGAPORE(1931)
Ronald Anscombe
SUSPECTED PERSON(1943, Brit.), ph
Hy Ansel
ANNIE HALL(1977)
Bernard Ansell
M'BLIMEY(1931, Brit.); MONEY TALKS(1933, Brit.); IT HAPPENED IN PARIS(1935, Brit.); LAST ADVENTURERS, THE(1937, Brit); LOST CHORD, THE(1937, Brit.); SONG OF FREEDOM(1938, Brit.)
Eric Ansell
TIGER BAY(1933, Brit.), w; BIG FELLA(1937, Brit.), m; I MET A MURDERER(1939, Brit.), m
Gail Ansell
MY LOVER, MY SON(1970, Brit.), cos
Louis K. Ansell
WOMEN IN THE NIGHT(1948), p
Joe Ansen
GOLDEN GLOVES STORY, THE(1950), w
S. Ansky
DYBBUK THE(1938, Pol.), w
Daniel Ansley
MOONSHINE COUNTY EXPRESS(1977), w
Sara Ansley
UNHINGED(1982)
Commissioner Harry J. Anslinger
TO THE ENDS OF THE EARTH(1948)
Julie Anslow
LOVERS, HAPPY LOVERS!(1955, Brit.)
A.C. Anson
ARROWSMITH(1931)
A.E. Anson
ROAD TO SINGAPORE(1931)
Barbara Anson
OWL AND THE PUSSYCAT, THE(1970)
Bill Anson
DISC JOCKEY(1951)
Bruce Anson
RAIDERS FROM BENEATH THE SEA(1964)
Ina Anson
Silents
JIMMIE'S MILLIONS(1925)
Jay Anson
AMITYVILLE HORROR, THE(1979), w
Joe Anson
BABES IN BAGDAD(1952), w
Laura Anson
Silents
CRAZY TO MARRY(1921); EASY ROAD, THE(1921); LITTLE CLOWN, THE(1921); IF YOU BELIEVE IT, IT'S SO(1922); SILENT PARTNER, THE(1923); SKID PROOF(1923)
Misc. Silents
BLUEBEARD, JR.; GREAT ALONE, THE(1922)
Robert Anson
HAPPY MOTHER'S DAY... LOVE, GEORGE(1973), cos
Misc. Talkies
MONEY IN MY POCKET(1962)
Anson Weeks and His Orchestra
MELODY PARADE(1943)
Anson Weeks and Orchestra
RHYTHM INN(1951)
Susan Anspach
FIVE EASY PIECES(1970); LANDLORD, THE(1970); PLAY IT AGAIN, SAM(1972); BLUME IN LOVE(1973); BIG FIX, THE(1978); RUNNING(1979, Can.); DEVIL AND MAX DEVLIN, THE(1981); GAS(1981, Can.); MONTENEGRO(1981, Brit./Swed.)
1984
MISUNDERSTOOD(1984)

Louis K. Anspacher
Silents
EMBARRASSMENT OF RICHES, THE(1918), w
Louis Kaufman Anspacher
Silents
UNCHASTENED WOMAN(1925), w
Gary Anstaett
JAWS 3-D(1983)
Melva Anstead
MAN FROM OKLAHOMA, THE(1945)
F. Anstey
MAN FROM BLANKLEY'S, THE(1930), w; GUEST OF HONOR(1934, Brit.), w; ONE TOUCH OF VENUS(1948), w; VICE VERSA(1948, Brit.), d&w; BRASS BOTTLE, THE(1964), w
Jill Anstey
MYSTERY AT THE BURLESQUE(1950, Brit.)
Gerald Anstruther
THIRD VISITOR, THE(1951, Brit.), w; DANGEROUS AFTERNOON(1961, Brit.), w; MASTER SPY(1964, Brit.), w
Harold Anstruther
INQUEST(1939, Brit.); THUNDER ROCK(1944, Brit.)
Adam Ant
JUBILEE(1978, Brit.)
Giulio Antamoro
Misc. Silents
PASSION OF ST. FRANCIS(1932, Ital.), d
Gulio Antamoro
Misc. Silents
CHRISTUS(1917, Ital.), d
Matia Antar
SONG OF SCHEHERAZADE(1947)
Frank Antel
Misc. Talkies
NAUGHTY NYMPHS(1974), d
Franz Antel
SOME LIKE IT COOL(1979, Ger./Aust./Ital./Fr.), p
Amparo Antenercruz
SO PROUDLY WE HAIL(1943)
Joan Antequera
LA DOLCE VITA(1961, Ital./Fr.)
Jerry Antes
REAR WINDOW(1954); LAWLESS STREET, A(1955), ch; OPPOSITE SEX, THE(1956); UNDER THE YUM-YUM TREE(1963)
George Antheil
ONCE IN A BLUE MOON(1936), m; MAKE WAY FOR TOMORROW(1937), m; PLAINSMAN, THE(1937), m; THUNDER TRAIL(1937), m; BUCCANEER, THE(1938), m; UNION PACIFIC(1939), m; ANGELS OVER BROADWAY(1940), m; PLAINSMAN AND THE LADY(1946), m; SPECTER OF THE ROSE(1946), m; THAT BRENNAN GIRL(1946), m; REPEAT PERFORMANCE(1947), m; FIGHTING KENTUCKIAN, THE(1949), m; KNOCK ON ANY DOOR(1949), m; TOKYO JOE(1949), m; WE WERE STRANGERS(1949), m; HOUSE BY THE RIVER(1950), m; IN A LONELY PLACE(1950), m; SIROCCO(1951), m; ACTORS AND SIN(1952), m; SNIPER, THE(1952), m; JUGGLER, THE(1953), m; DEMENTIA(1955), m; NOT AS A STRANGER(1955), m, md; PRIDE AND THE PASSION, THE(1957), m; YOUNG DON'T CRY, THE(1957), m
Paul Anthelme
I CONFESS(1953), w
Ingrid Anthofer
IT'S ALL OVER TOWN(1963, Brit.); RATTLE OF A SIMPLE MAN(1964, Brit.); LIFE AT THE TOP(1965, Brit.)
Anthony
CITY ACROSS THE RIVER(1949)
B. Leon Anthony
NOAH'S ARK(1928), w
Bill Anthony
MANHATTAN(1979)
Bob G. Anthony
MIXED COMPANY(1974)
Brian Anthony
DARWIN ADVENTURE, THE(1972, Brit.); ALFIE DARLING(1975, Brit.)
C.L. Anthony [Dodie Smith]
LOOKING FORWARD(1933), w; AUTUMN CROCUS(1934, Brit.), d
Carl Anthony
SINISTER URGE, THE(1961)
Christopher Anthony
Misc. Silents
DOWN CHANNEL(1929, Brit.)
Clariette Anthony
Silents
MARRIAGE PRICE(1919)
David Anthony
BANK HOLIDAY(1938, Brit.); FRONT LINE KIDS(1942, Brit.); MIDNIGHT MAN, THE(1974), w
1984
ANGEL(1984)
David F. Anthony
1984
SOLE SURVIVOR(1984), m
De Leon Anthony
SACRED FLAME, THE(1929), titles
Silents
AIR PATROL, THE(1928), ed; MANHATTAN KNIGHTS(1928), ed
Dee Anthony
COUNTRYMAN(1982, Jamaica)
DeLeon Anthony
AVIATOR, THE(1929), w
Silents
ADORABLE CHEAT, THE(1928), t, ed

Dianne Anthony
HARD COUNTRY(1981), cos
Dick Anthony
LADY AND THE TRAMP(1955), art d; SLEEPING BEAUTY(1959), art d
Edward Anthony
BIG CAGE, THE(1933), w
Edwin Anthony
CRIME AFLOAT(1937), w; MILE A MINUTE LOVE(1937), w
Elizabeth Anthony
GLASS MOUNTAIN, THE(1950, Brit), m
Emmett Anthony
MAKE A MILLION(1935), w
Evelyn Anthony
TAMARIND SEED, THE(1974, Brit.), d&w
Hilda Anthony
Silents
PUPPET MAN, THE(1921, Brit.)
Misc. Silents
MARRIED LIFE(1921, Brit.)
Jack Anthony
Misc. Silents
GUN-HAND GARRISON(1927); RIDIN' LUCK(1927); WILD BORN(1927); TEXAS TORNADO, THE(1928)
James Anthony
YOUNG NURSES, THE(1973); NUNZIO(1978)
Jeremy Anthony
TELL ME LIES(1968, Brit.)
Joe Anthony
SCAVENGERS, THE(1969), set d
John Anthony
GREAT POWER, THE(1929); JACKTOWN(1962); FORTY DEUCE(1982)
John J. Anthony
DIVORCE AMERICAN STYLE(1967)
Joseph Anthony
HAT, COAT AND GLOVE(1934); CRIME AND PUNISHMENT(1935), w; ONE-WAY TICKET(1935), w; AND SO THEY WERE MARRIED(1936), w; LADY OF SECRETS(1936), w; MEET NERO WOLFE(1936), w; WEDDING PRESENT(1936), w; DOCTOR'S DIARY, A(1937), w; WOMAN CHASES MAN(1937), w; SPELLBINDER, THE(1939), w; SHADOW OF THE THIN MAN(1941); JOE SMITH, AMERICAN(1942); RAINMAKER, THE(1956), d; MATCHMAKER, THE(1958), d; CAREER(1959), d; ALL IN A NIGHT'S WORK(1961), d; CAPTIVE CITY, THE(1963, Ital.), d; CONQUERED CITY(1966, Ital.), d; TOMORROW(1972), d
Silents
WHEEL OF DESTINY, THE(1927), w
June-Ellen Anthony
BAND OF ANGELS(1957)
Lee Anthony
Silents
MAKING THE VARSITY(1928), t, ed
Leigh Anthony
GAMES THAT LOVERS PLAY(1971, Brit.)
Leslie Anthony
KISMET(1944)
Lon Anthony
MEET NERO WOLFE(1936), cos; TWO-FISTED GENTLEMAN(1936), cos; SHED NO TEARS(1948), cos
Lysette Anthony
KRULL(1983)
Marcus Anthony
NOCTURNA(1979)
Mark Anthony
IT'S A DATE(1940); MY LITTLE CHICKADEE(1940)
Michael Anthony
FLAMINGO AFFAIR, THE(1948, Brit.); IDEAL HUSBAND, AN(1948, Brit.); TO PARIS WITH LOVE(1955, Brit.); LET'S BE HAPPY(1957, Brit.); I ACCUSE(1958, Brit.); INDISCREET(1958); QUESTION OF ADULTERY, A(1959, Brit.); KHARTOUM(1966, Brit.); NIGHT OF BLOODY HORROR zero(1969); MOSQUITO SQUADRON(1970, Brit.); WOMEN AND BLOODY TERROR(1970); S(1974); NIGHT OF THE STRANGLER(1975)
Olga Anthony
MACBETH(1971, Brit.); MUTATIONS, THE(1974, Brit.)
Pat Anthony
JUMBO(1962)
Paul Anthony
MADNESS OF THE HEART(1949, Brit.)
Philip Anthony
FILE OF THE GOLDEN GOOSE, THE(1969, Brit.); INTERNECINE PROJECT, THE(1974, Brit.)
Misc. Silents
SAVED FROM THE SEA(1920, Brit.); RIVER OF STARS, THE(1921, Brit.); WAY OF A MAN, THE(1921, Brit.)
Phillip Anthony
PRIVATE LIFE OF SHERLOCK HOLMES, THE(1970, Brit.)
Ray Anthony
SUN VALLEY SERENADE(1941); GIRL CAN'T HELP IT, THE(1956); HIGH SCHOOL CONFIDENTIAL(1958); BEAT GENERATION, THE(1959); BIG OPERATOR, THE(1959); FIVE PENNIES, THE(1959); GIRLS' TOWN(1959); NIGHT OF THE QUARTER MOON(1959)
Richard J. Anthony
ECHOES(1983), w
Rick Anthony
NIGHT OF THE JUGGLER(1980)
Robert Anthony
HATE IN PARADISE(1938, Brit.); HOSPITAL, THE(1971); FRIENDS OF EDDIE COYLE, THE(1973)
Rory Anthony
VOICES(1979)
Sal Anthony
TIME AFTER TIME(1979, Brit.), cos

Salvatore Anthony
RUMBLE ON THE DOCKS(1956)
Shirley Anthony
NINE TO FIVE(1980)
Stuart Anthony
BORDER LAW(1931), w; DESERT VENGEANCE(1931), w; FIGHTING SHERIFF, THE(1931), w; END OF THE TRAIL(1932), w; FAME STREET(1932), w; LENA RIVERS(1932), w; MC KENNA OF THE MOUNTED(1932), w; STRANGERS OF THE EVENING(1932), w; VANISHING FRONTIER, THE(1932), w; WHISTLIN' DAN(1932), w; LIFE IN THE RAW(1933), w; LOVE IS LIKE THAT(1933), w; SMOKY(1933), w; STATE TROOPER(1933), w; EVER SINCE EVE(1934), w; FRONTIER MARSHAL(1934), w; HAPPY LANDING(1934), w; LAST TRAIL, THE(1934), w; PURSUED(1934), w; BORDER BRIGANDS(1935), w; CHARLIE CHAN IN PARIS(1935), w; MOTIVE FOR REVENGE(1935), w; MUTINY AHEAD(1935), w; WANDERER OF THE WASTELAND(1935), w; ARIZONA MAHONEY(1936), w; BORDER FLIGHT(1936), w; BURNING GOLD(1936), w; DESERT GOLD(1936), w; DRIFT FENCE(1936), w; GIRL OF THE OZARKS(1936), w; NEVADA(1936), w; BORN TO THE WEST(1937), w; FORLORN RIVER(1937), w; THUNDER TRAIL(1937), w; HIGHWAY PATROL(1938), w; ILLEGAL TRAFFIC(1938), w; PRISON FARM(1938), w; TIP-OFF GIRLS(1938), w; SAGA OF DEATH VALLEY(1939), w; TOM SAWYER, DETECTIVE(1939), w; BISCUIT EATER, THE(1940), w; RANGER AND THE LADY, THE(1940), w; WHEN THE DALTONS RODE(1940), w; ALONG THE RIO GRANDE(1941), w; MONSTER AND THE GIRL, THE(1941), w; SHEPHERD OF THE HILLS, THE(1941), w
Silents
FLOATING COLLEGE, THE(1928), w
Tom Anthony
STRANGERS WHEN WE MEET(1960); GOOD NEIGHBOR SAM(1964)
Tony Anthony
FORCE OF IMPULSE(1961), a, p, w; WITHOUT EACH OTHER(1962), a, w; ENGAGEMENT ITALIANO(1966, Fr./Ital.); SHOOT FIRST, LAUGH LAST(1967, Ital./Ger./U.S.); STRANGER IN TOWN, A(1968, U.S./Ital.); STRANGER RETURNS, THE(1968, U.S./Ital./Ger./Span.), a, w; COMETOGETHER(1971), a, p&w; BLINDMAN(1972, Ital.), a, p, w; GET MEAN(1976, Ital.), a, p; COMIN' AT YA!(1981), a, p; TREASURE OF THE FOUR CROWNS(1983, Span./U.S.), a, p
Misc. Talkies
PITY ME NOT(1960); SILENT STRANGER, THE(1975)
Walter Anthony
GENERAL CRACK(1929), w; LAST PERFORMANCE, THE(1929), w; SCANDAL(1929), w; COURAGE(1930), w; GOLDEN DAWN(1930), w; OLD ENGLISH(1930), w; SCARLET PAGES(1930), w; PAROLED FROM THE BIG HOUSE(1938); STRANGER FROM ARIZONA, THE(1938)
Silents
OLIVER TWIST(1922), t; AFTER BUSINESS HOURS(1925), t; BELOVED ROGUE, THE(1927), t; CAT AND THE CANARY, THE(1927), t; CHEATING CHEATERS(1927), t; MAN WHO LAUGHS, THE(1927), t; ALIAS THE DEACON(1928), t; FREEDOM OF THE PRESS(1928), t; JAZZ MAD(1928), t; LOVE ME AND THE WORLD IS MINE(1928), t; MICHIGAN KID, THE(1928), t; 13 WASHINGTON SQUARE(1928), t
Walther Anthony
Silents
DON JUAN(1926), t
William Anthony
PILGRIMAGE(1972), p
LeRoi Antienne
MISSISSIPPI GAMBLER, THE(1953)
Lisa Antille
VALLEY GIRL(1983)
Steve Antin
LAST AMERICAN VIRGIN, THE(1982); SWEET SIXTEEN(1983)
Maria Antinea
GAMES MEN PLAY, THE(1968, Arg.)
Lamberto Antinori
SWORD OF THE CONQUEROR(1962, Ital.); CONQUERED CITY(1966, Ital.)
Maria Antippas
IRON PETTICOAT, THE(1956, Brit.)
Mary Antoianette
SONG AND THE SILENCE, THE(1969)
Antoine
BONNE CHANCE(1935, Fr.)
Andre Antoine
Misc. Silents
LE COUPABLE(1917, Fr.), d; LES FRERES CORSES(1917, Fr.), d; LES TRAVAILLEURS DE LA MER(1918, Fr.), d; LA TERRE(1921, Fr.), d; MADEMOISELLE DE LA SEIGLIERE(1921, Fr.), d; QUATRE-VINGT TREIZE(1921, Fr.), d; L'ARLESIENNE(1922, Fr.), d
Andre-Paul Antoine
GOLEM, THE(1937, Czech./Fr.), w; LA FERME DU PENDU(1946, Fr.), w; FRENCH CANCAN(1956, Fr.), w
Jacques Antoine
COW AND I, THE(1961, Fr., Ital., Ger.), w
LeRol Antoine
CITY BENEATH THE SEA(1953)
Michel Antoine
ALL THE WAY, BOYS(1973, Ital.)
Vladimir Antolek-Oresek
LANCELOT OF THE LAKE(1975, Fr.)
Davor Antolic
RAMPAGE AT APACHE WELLS(1966, Ger./Yugo.); SCALAWAG(1973, Yugo.); TWILIGHT TIME(1983, U.S./Yugo.)
A. Antomov
ADVENTURE IN ODESSA(1954, USSR)
Amerigo Anton
CAESAR THE CONQUEROR(1963, Ital.), d; ATLAS AGAINST THE CZAR(1964, Ital.), d; KILL OR BE KILLED(1967, Ital.), d
Bob Anton
END OF AUGUST, THE(1982), cos
Dorothy Anton
1984
AMERICAN TABOO(1984)

Edoardo Anton
COUNTERFEITERS, THE(1953, Ital.), w; ANGELA(1955, Ital.), w; LOVE ON THE RIVIERA(1964, Fr./Ital.), w

Francisco Anton
RETURN OF THE SEVEN(1966, Span.)

Matthew Anton
BELIEVE IN ME(1971); PRETTY BABY(1978)

Matthew Douglas Anton
BAD NEWS BEARS GO TO JAPAN, THE(1978)

Ronald Anton
DIANE(1955); HURRY UP OR I'LL BE 30(1973)

Susan Anton
GOLDENGIRL(1979); SPRING FEVER(1983, Can.)
1984
CANNONBALL RUN II(1984)

Greg Antonacci
SUMMER SOLDIERS(1972, Jap.)

L. Antonakis
ELECTRA(1962, Gr.), ed

A. Antonelli
SLAVE, THE(1963, Ital.), cos

Alessandro Antonelli
INDISCRETION OF AN AMERICAN WIFE(1954, U.S./Ital.), cos

Ennio Antonelli
MATCHLESS(1967, Ital.); WAR ITALIAN STYLE(1967, Ital.)

Filippo Antonelli
STRANGER RETURNS, THE(1968, U.S./Ital./Ger./Span.)

Franco Antonelli
LONG RIDE FROM HELL, A(1970, Ital.), cos; HIGH ROAD TO CHINA(1983), cos

Laura Antonelli
DR. GOLDFOOT AND THE GIRL BOMBS(1966, Ital.); MAN CALLED SLEDGE, A(1971, Ital.); DOCTEUR POPAUL(1972, Fr.); WITHOUT APPARENT MOTIVE(1972, Fr.); MALICIOUS(1974, Ital.); DIVINE NYMPH, THE(1979, Ital.); INNOCENT, THE(1979, Ital.); TILL MARRIAGE DO US PART(1979, Ital.); WIFEMISTRESS(1979, Ital.); PASSION OF LOVE(1982, Ital./Fr.)

Roberto Antonelli
TAMING OF THE SHREW, THE(1967, U.S./Ital.); ROMEO AND JULIET(1968, Brit./Ital.); TIN GIRL, THE(1970, Ital.)

Lt. John W. Antonelli, USMC
PROUD AND THE PROFANE, THE(1956), tech adv

Dusan Antonijevic
FLAMING FRONTIER(1968, Ger./Yugo.)

Alfredo Antonini
WHERE THE SPIES ARE(1965, Brit.), md

Carlo Antonini
CONDEMNED OF ALTONA, THE(1963)

Gabriele Antonini
HERCULES(1959, Ital.); HEAD OF A TYRANT(1960, Fr./Ital.); HERCULES UN-CHAINED(1960, Ital./Fr.); SAMSON AND THE SEVEN MIRACLES OF THE WORLD(1963, Fr./Ital.); EIGHTEEN IN THE SUN(1964, Ital.); MONGOLS, THE(1966, Fr./Ital.); SEVEN REVENGES, THE(1967, Ital.)

Antonio
NEOPOLITAN CAROUSEL(1961, Ital.)

James Antonio
GREASER'S PALACE(1972)

Jim Antonio
TERMINAL MAN, THE(1974); FORTUNE, THE(1975); FUTUREWORLD(1976)
1984
DADDY'S DEADLY DARLING(1984); RIVER, THE(1984)

Jose Antonio
KING OF KINGS(1961)

Lew Antonio
MISSION BATANGAS(1968), w

Lou Antonio
AMERICA, AMERICA(1963); HAWAII(1966); COOL HAND LUKE(1967); PHYNX, THE(1970)

Marco Antonio
DEADLY DUO(1962); CHUKA(1967); WAR WAGON, THE(1967)

Modica Antonio
DRUMS OF TABU, THE(1967, Ital./Span.), ph

Phaedros Antonio
SECRET PEOPLE(1952, Brit.)

Pistillo Antonio
STATUE, THE(1971, Brit.)

Antonio and Rosario
ZIEGFELD GIRL(1941)

Antonio Gades Dance Company
1984
BIZET'S CARMEN(1984, Fr./Ital.)

Antonio Triana and Montes
ALLERGIC TO LOVE(1943)

Michaelangelo Antonioni
PASSENGER, THE(1975, Ital.), d, w, ed

Michelangelo Antonioni
L'AVVENTURA(1960, Ital.), d, w; LA NOTTE(1961, Fr./Ital.), d, w; ECLIPSE(1962, Fr./Ital.), d, w; IL GRIDO(1962, U.S./Ital.), d, w; LE AMICHE(1962, Ital.), d, w; RED DESERT(1965, Fr./Ital.), d, w; THREE FACES OF A WOMAN(1965, Ital.), d&w; BLOW-UP(1966, Brit.), d, w; ZABRISKIE POINT(1970), d, w; LADY WITHOUT CA-MELLIAS, THE(1981, Ital.), d, w; IDENTIFICATION OF A WOMAN(1983, Ital.), d, w, ed

Ruth Antonofsky
BELL JAR, THE(1979)

A. Antonov
GENERAL SUVOROV(1941, USSR); SEEDS OF FREEDOM(1943, USSR); TWELFTH NIGHT(1956, USSR)

Alexander Antonov
Silents
BATTLESHIP POTEMKIN, THE(1925, USSR)

N. Antonova
KIEV COMEDY, A(1963, USSR); MOTHER AND DAUGHTER(1965, USSR)

Alessandro Antonucci
LEAP INTO THE VOID(1982, Ital.)

Piero Antonucci
WHITE SHEIK, THE(1956, Ital.)

Vittorio Antonucci
BICYCLE THIEF, THE(1949, Ital.)

Omero Antonutti
PADRE PADRONE(1977, Ital.); NIGHT OF THE SHOOTING STARS, THE(1982, Ital.)
1984
BASILEUS QUARTET(1984, Ital.)

Charles Antony
LA TRAVIATA(1982)

Scott Antony
SAVAGE MESSIAH(1972, Brit.); MUTATIONS, THE(1974, Brit.)
Misc. Talkies
DEAD CERT(1974, Brit.)

Harry Antrim
MIRACLE ON 34TH STREET, THE(1947); LARCENY(1948); LET'S LIVE A LITT-LE(1948); LUCK OF THE IRISH(1948); ACT OF VIOLENCE(1949); CHICAGO DEAD-LINE(1949); FREE FOR ALL(1949); HEIRESS, THE(1949); INTRUDER IN THE DUST(1949); JOHNNY ALLEGRO(1949); MA AND PA KETTLE(1949); PRISON WARDEN(1949); DEVIL'S DOORWAY(1950); FILE ON THELMA JORDAN, THE(1950); NO MAN OF HER OWN(1950); SIDE STREET(1950); APPOINTMENT WITH DANGER(1951); FOLLOW THE SUN(1951); I'LL SEE YOU IN MY DREAMS(1951); MEET ME AFTER THE SHOW(1951); MR. BELVEDERE RINGS THE BELL(1951); NIGHT INTO MORNING(1951); TOMORROW IS ANOTHER DAY(1951); LION AND THE HORSE, THE(1952); MUTINY(1952); WE'RE NOT MARRIED(1952); BOUNTY HUNTER, THE(1954); LAWLESS STREET, A(1955); SOLID GOLD CADIL-LAC, THE(1956); TEACHER'S PET(1958); GUNMEN FROM LAREDO(1959); FOR THOSE WHO THINK YOUNG(1964); MONKEY'S UNCLE, THE(1965)

Henry Antrim
DESIRE(1936); ANGELS OVER BROADWAY(1940)

Henry "Harry" Antrim
TRAPPED(1949)

Paul Antrim
MAN WHO WOULD BE KING, THE(1975, Brit.); MARCH OR DIE(1977, Brit.); EVIL UNDER THE SUN(1982, Brit.)
1984
LASSITER(1984)

John Antrobus
IDOL ON PARADE(1959, Brit.), w; JAZZ BOAT(1960, Brit.), w; ROOMMATES(1962, Brit.); WRONG ARM OF THE LAW, THE(1963, Brit.), w; BED SITTING ROOM, THE(1969, Brit.), w

Yvonne Antrobus
DR. WHO AND THE DALEKS(1965, Brit.); HAPPY DEATHDAY(1969, Brit.); MR. QUILP(1975, Brit.)

M. Antropova
ROAD TO LIFE(1932, USSR)

Michael "Tunes" Antunes
EDDIE AND THE CRUISERS(1983)

Nemesio Antunes
STATE OF SIEGE(1973, Fr./U.S./Ital./Ger.)

Melvin Antwerp
99 WOUNDS(1931), ph

Van Antwerp
WING AND A PRAYER(1944)

Anthony Antypas
SKY RIDERS(1976, U.S./Gr.)

Louis Antzes
JOE(1970), spec eff

Jim Anuao
AMBUSH BAY(1966)

Ye. Anufriyev
FAREWELL, DOVES(1962, USSR)

Anulka
VAMPYRES, DAUGHTERS OF DRACULA(1977, Brit.)

Hatam Anvar
1984
MISSION, THE(1984)

Hedyeh Anvar
1984
MISSION, THE(1984)

Rafik Anwar
LORD JIM(1965, Brit.)

Rafiq Anwar
LONG DUEL, THE(1967, Brit.); CONDUCT UNBECOMING(1975, Brit.); SPY WHO LOVED ME, THE(1977, Brit.)

Anyaogu
WHITE WITCH DOCTOR(1953)

Georgette Anys
FANFAN THE TULIP(1952, Fr.); DAY TO REMEMBER, A(1953, Brit.); LITTLE BOY LOST(1953); INNOCENTS IN PARIS(1955, Brit.); TO CATCH A THIEF(1955); FOUR BAGS FULL(1957, Fr./Ital.); MIRROR HAS TWO FACES, THE(1959, Fr.); FAN-NY(1961); BON VOYAGE(1962); JESSICA(1962, U.S./Ital./Fr.); LOVE IS A BALL(1963); MOMENT TO MOMENT(1966); ZIG-ZAG(1975, Fr./Ital.)

Andy Anza
MURIETA(1965, Span.); SON OF A GUNFIGHTER(1966, U.S./Span.); CRY BLOOD, APACHE(1970)

Kyoko Anzai
WOMEN IN PRISON(1957, Jap.); BATTLE IN OUTER SPACE(1960)

Larry Anzalone
STREET WITH NO NAME, THE(1948); WHIPLASH(1948); FIGHTING FOOLS(1949)

Ray Anzalone
STUCKEY'S LAST STAND(1980); SAVANNAH SMILES(1983)

Governor Anzani
TANGA-TIKA(1953)

Hy Anzel
PARTY GIRL(1958); DEATH PLAY(1976)
Hy Anzell
WHAT'S SO BAD ABOUT FEELING GOOD?(1968)
Yvette Anziani
LOLA(1961, Fr./Ital.)
Miguel Anzures
AMERICAN GUERRILLA IN THE PHILIPPINES, AN(1950)
Mike Anzures
NO MAN IS AN ISLAND(1962)
Kumi Aoichi
ALL RIGHT, MY FRIEND(1983, Japan)
Dan Aoki
BEACHHEAD(1954)
Hidemi Aoki
SEVEN NIGHTS IN JAPAN(1976, Brit./Fr.)
Junko Aoki
MY GEISHA(1962)
Nozumi Aoki
GALAXY EXPRESS(1982, Jap.), m
Tsura Aoki
Misc. Silents
BLACK ROSES(1921)
Tsuru Aoki
Silents
TYPHOON, THE(1914); WRATH OF THE GODS, THE or THE DESTRUCTION OF
SAKURA JIMA(1914); ALIEN SOULS(1916); EACH TO HIS KIND(1917); BRAVEST
WAY, THE(1918); NIGHT LIFE IN HOLLYWOOD(1922)
Misc. Silents
BECKONING FLAME, THE(1916); HONORABLE FRIEND, THE(1916); SOUL OF
KURA SAN, THE(1916); CALL OF THE EAST, THE(1917); CURSE OF IKU, THE(1918);
ASHES OF DESIRE(1919); BONDS OF HONOR(1919); COURAGEOUS COWARD,
THE(1919); DRAGON PAINTER, THE(1919); GRAY HORIZON, THE(1919); HEART IN
PAWN, A(1919); BREATH OF THE GODS, THE(1920); LOCKED LIPS(1920); TOKIO
SIREN, A(1920); FIVE DAYS TO LIVE(1922); DANGER LINE, THE(1924); GREAT
PRINCE SHAN, THE(1924, Brit.); SEN YAN'S DEVOTION(1924, Brit.)
Yoshio Aoki
HAHAKIRI(1963, Jap.)
Hirayoshi Aono
EAST CHINA SEA(1969, Jap.)
Kazuya Aoyama
GODZILLA VERSUS THE COSMIC MONSTER(1974, Jap.)
Kyoko Aoyama
NAKED GENERAL, THE(1964, Jap.); I LIVE IN FEAR(1967, Jap.)
Sugisaku Aoyama
UGETSU(1954, Jap.)
Yoshihiko Aoyama
MAJIN(1968, Jap.)
Yoshio Aoyama
MADAME BUTTERFLY(1955 Ital./Jap.), ch
Yukio Aoyama
Silents
BRAVEST WAY, THE(1918)
Misc. Silents
JAPANESE NIGHTINGALE, A(1918); WHO'S YOUR SERVANT?(1920)
Apache
WESTERN TRAILS(1938)
Apache the Horse
OUTLAW EXPRESS(1938)
Reed Apaghian
GENTLE PEOPLE AND THE QUIET LAND, THE(1972)
Katherine Apanowicz
BUGSY MALONE(1976, Brit.)
Manuel Aparico
JIGSAW(1949)
N. Aparin
DESTINY OF A MAN(1961, USSR); WAR AND PEACE(1968, USSR)
Kogar the Swinging Ape
RAT PFINK AND BOO BOO(1966)
Pierre Apesteguy
NATHALIE(1958, Fr.), w; NATHALIE, AGENT SECRET(1960, Fr.), w
Oscar Apfel
HALF WAY TO HEAVEN(1929); MARIANNE(1929); NOT QUITE DECENT(1929);
SMILING IRISH EYES(1929); ABRAHAM LINCOLN(1930); MAN TROUBLE(1930);
PUTTIN' ON THE RITZ(1930); SPOILERS, THE(1930); TEXAN, THE(1930); VIRTU-
OUS SIN, THE(1930); BIG BUSINESS GIRL(1931); FINGER POINTS, THE(1931); FIVE
STAR FINAL(1931); HUCKLEBERRY FINN(1931); INSPIRATION(1931); MALTESE
FALCON, THE(1931); MEN IN HER LIFE(1931); MISBEHAVING LADIES(1931);
RIGHT TO LOVE, THE(1931); SIDEWALKS OF NEW YORK(1931); SOOKY(1931);
WICKED(1931); ALIAS THE DOCTOR(1932); BUSINESS AND PLEASURE(1932);
FALSE FACES(1932); FELLER NEEDS A FRIEND(1932); HEART OF NEW
YORK(1932); HIGH PRESSURE(1932); HOT SATURDAY(1932); IT'S TOUGH TO BE
FAMOUS(1932); MAKE ME A STAR(1932); MAN WHO PLAYED GOD, THE(1932);
SHOPWORN(1932); SUCCESSFUL CALAMITY, A(1932); SYMPHONY OF SIX MIL-
LION(1932); TWO AGAINST THE WORLD(1932); WAY BACK HOME(1932); WOMAN
FROM MONTE CARLO, THE(1932); WORLD AND THE FLESH, THE(1932); YOU
SAID A MOUTHFUL(1932); BEFORE DAWN(1933); BOWERY, THE(1933); EMER-
GENCY CALL(1933); HOLD THE PRESS(1933); LADIES MUST LOVE(1933); ONE
MAN'S JOURNEY(1933); ONLY YESTERDAY(1933); PICK-UP(1933); STORY OF
TEMPLE DRAKE, THE(1933); TOMORROW AT SEVEN(1933); TUGBOAT AN-
NIE(1933); WORLD CHANGES, THE(1933); BELOVED(1934); BIG SHAKEDOWN,
THE(1934); CRIMSON ROMANCE(1934); FIFTEEN WIVES(1934); HOUSE OF ROTH-
SCHILD, THE(1934); MADAME SPY(1934); MANHATTAN MELODRAMA(1934); OLD-
FASHIONED WAY, THE(1934); TAKE THE STAND(1934); TWENTY MILLION
SWEETHEARTS(1934); WHIRLPOOL(1934); ANOTHER FACE(1935); BORDER-
TOWN(1935); CAPPY RICKS RETURNS(1935); DANTE'S INFERNO(1935); DEATH
FLIES EAST(1935); FIRETRAP, THE(1935); HIS NIGHT OUT(1935); I AM A
THIEF(1935); I DREAM TOO MUCH(1935); MAN ON THE FLYING TRAPEZE,
THE(1935); MARY JANE'S PA(1935); NUT FARM, THE(1935); O'SHAUGHNESSY'S
BOY(1935); ROMANCE IN MANHATTAN(1935); WHITE LIES(1935); AND SUDDEN

DEATH(1936); BULLDOG EDITION(1936); EVERY SATURDAY NIGHT(1936); GOR-
GEOUS HUSSY, THE(1936); HEARTS IN BONDAGE(1936); HOLLYWOOD BOULE-
VARD(1936); MURDER AT GLEN ATHOL(1936); PLOT THICKENS, THE(1936); SAN
FRANCISCO(1936); SUTTER'S GOLD(1936); CONQUEST(1937); CRACK-UP,
THE(1937); FIFTY ROADS TO TOWN(1937); JIM HANVEY, DETECTIVE(1937);
RUSTLER'S VALLEY(1937); SHADOWS OF THE ORIENT(1937); TOAST OF NEW
YORK, THE(1937); TROUBLE IN MOROCCO(1937)
Silents
BREWSTER'S MILLIONS(1914), d; CIRCUS MAN, THE(1914), d; LAST VOLUN-
TEER, THE(1914), d; MAN FROM HOME, THE(1914), d; MASTER MIND, THE(1914),
d; READY MONEY(1914), d; ROSE OF THE RANCHO(1914), d; SQUAW MAN,
THE(1914), p,d&w; AFTER FIVE(1915), d; KILMENY(1915), d; SNOBS(1915), d; END
OF THE TRAIL, THE(1916), d&w; FIRES OF CONSCIENCE(1916), d; AMATEUR
WIDOW, AN(1919), d; OAKDALE AFFAIR, THE(1919), d; LION'S MOUSE, THE(1922,
Brit.), d; BULLDOG DRUMMOND(1923, Brit.), d; IN SEARCH OF A THRILL(1923), d;
SOCIAL CODE, THE(1923), d; BORROWED FINERY(1925), d; LAST ALARM,
THE(1926), d; PERILS OF THE COAST GUARD(1926), d; CHEATERS(1927), d;
WHEN SECONDS COUNT(1927), d
Misc. Silents
LOST PARADISE, THE(1914), d; MAKING OF BOBBY BURNIT, THE(1914), d; MAN
ON THE BOX, THE(1914), d; BROKEN LAW, THE(1915), d; LITTLE GYPSY,
THE(1915), d; BATTLE OF HEARTS(1916), d; MAN FROM BITTER ROOTS,
THE(1916), d; MAN OF SORROW, A(1916), d; HIDDEN CHILDREN, THE(1917), d;
MAN'S MAN, A(1917), d; PRICE OF HER SOUL, THE(1917), d; INTERLOPER,
THE(1918), d; MERELY PLAYERS(1918), d; TINSEL(1918), d; TO HIM THAT
HATH(1918), d; TURN OF THE CARD, THE(1918), d; BRINGING UP BETTY(1919), d;
CROOK OF DREAMS(1919), d; LITTLE INTRUDER, THE(1919), d; MANDARIN'S
GOLD(1919), d; ME AND CAPTAIN KID(1919), d; PHIL-FOR-SHORT(1919), d;
ROUGHNECK, THE(1919), d; STEEL KING, THE(1919), d; TEN NIGHTS IN A BAR
ROOM(1921), d; AUCTION OF SOULS(1922), d; MAN WHO PAID, THE(1922), d;
WOLF'S FANGS, THE(1922), d; HEART BANDIT, THE(1924), d; TRAIL OF THE
LAW(1924), d; SPORTING CHANCE, THE(1925), d; THOROUGHBRED, THE(1925),
d; CALL OF THE KLONDIKE, THE(1926), d; MIDNIGHT LIMITED(1926), d; RACE
WILD(1926), d; SOMEBODY'S MOTHER(1926), d; CODE OF THE COW COUN-
TRY(1927), d; HEART OF BROADWAY, THE(1928); VALLEY OF HUNTED MEN,
THE(1928); TRUE HEAVEN(1929)
Oscar C. Apfel
Misc. Silents
SOLDIER'S OATH, A(1915), d
Oscar Apfel, Sr.
RAINBOW'S END(1935)
Yodying Apibal
GREEN BERETS, THE(1968)
Tina Apicella
BELLISSIMA(1952, Ital.)
Lak Apichat
1 2 3 MONSTER EXPRESS(1977, Thai.)
Mary Apick
RIGHT STUFF, THE(1983)
1984
MISSION, THE(1984)
Bruno Apitz
NAKED AMONG THE WOLVES(1967, Ger.), a, w
Fritz Apking
DANGEROUS MISSION(1954); LONG GRAY LINE, THE(1955)
Bert Apling
Silents
WESTERN FIREBRANDS(1921); NEW CHAMPION(1925); STORMY WATERS(1928)
Misc. Silents
VENGEANCE TRAIL, THE(1921)
Boris Aplon
CITIZEN SAINT(1947); MUGGER, THE(1958); TWO-MINUTE WARNING(1976)
Muang Apollo
1 2 3 MONSTER EXPRESS(1977, Thai.)
Apollo Boy's Choir
HANSEL AND GRETEL(1954)
Uni Apollon
Silents
MARE NOSTRUM(1926)
A. Apone
METALSTORM: THE DESTRUCTION OF JARED-SYN(1983), makeup
Alan Apone
1984
HOSPITAL MASSACRE(1984), makeup
Allan Apone
DEADLY EYES(1982), spec eff; HOSPITAL MASSACRE(1982), makeup; WACK-
O(1983), makeup
John Apone
YOU HAVE TO RUN FAST(1961)
Margo Apostocos
RETURN OF THE JEDI(1983)
Poch Apostol
SECRET OF THE SACRED FOREST, THE(1970)
Stephen C. Apostolof
JOURNEY TO FREEDOM(1957), p, w
Misc. Talkies
FUGITIVE GIRLS(1975), d
Zetta Apostolou
RAPE, THE(1965, Gr.)
Michael Apostoulou
ISLAND OF LOVE(1963)
Paul Apoteker
VERY PRIVATE AFFAIR, A(1962, Fr./Ital.)
Angelika Appel
GOOD SOLDIER SCHWEIK, THE(1963, Ger.), ed
Anna Appel
FAITHLESS(1932); HEART OF NEW YORK(1932); SYMPHONY OF SIX MIL-
LION(1932); GREEN FIELDS(1937); SINGING BLACKSMITH(1938)

Silents
  BROKEN HEARTS(1926)
Arthur Appel
  DRAGONWYCH(1946), ch
Benjamin Appel
  CRY OF BATTLE(1963), w
Chris Appel
  HERE COMES THE GROOM(1951)
Christofer Appel
  STORY OF THREE LOVES, THE(1953)
David Appel
  TONKA(1958), w
Sam Appel
  LOVE COMES ALONG(1930); UNDER A TEXAS MOON(1930); YANKEE DON(1931); IN CALIENTE(1935); UNDER THE PAMPAS MOON(1935); HI GAUCHO!(1936); MESSAGE TO GARCIA, A(1936); FIREFLY, THE(1937); LAST TRAIN FROM MADRID, THE(1937); TWENTY MULE TEAM(1940); DOWN MEXICO WAY(1941); HONOLULU LU(1941); REAP THE WILD WIND(1942); GILDA(1946)
Silents
  GIRL OF THE GOLDEN WEST, THE(1923); LONG LIVE THE KING(1923); WHITE BLACK SHEEP, THE(1926)
Wendy Appel
  PUTNEY SWOPE(1969); PLEASE STAND BY(1972)
L.A. Appelbaum
  SONG YOU GAVE ME, THE(1934, Brit.), ed
George Appelby
  FAR SHORE, THE(1976, Can.), ed; WILD HORSE HANK(1979, Can.), ed
Roy Appelgate
Misc. Silents
  HIS GREAT TRIUMPH(1916)
Arthur Appell
  BIG STORE, THE(1941), ch
Don Appell
  WHERE THE SIDEWALK ENDS(1950)
Sam Appell
Silents
  CODE OF THE SEA(1924)
Len Appelson
  SHADOWS(1960), ed
Marlene Appelt
  DOCTEUR POPAUL(1972, Fr.)
Clyde Apperson
  DOBERMAN GANG, THE(1972)
John Apperson
  JULIA(1977), cos
Leah Appet
  SEPARATE WAYS(1981), w
Jeffrey D. Apple
  ZAPPED!(1982), p
Max Apple
  SMOKEY BITES THE DUST(1981), w
Sam Apple Pie
  TOOMORROW(1970, Brit.)
Harvey Applebaum
  LITTLE DRAGONS, THE(1980), w
Irving A. Applebaum
  STRANGE VOYAGE(1945), ed
Larry Applebaum
  BADGE 373(1973)
Louis Applebaum
  DREAMS THAT MONEY CAN BUY(1948), m; LOST BOUNDARIES(1949), m; TERESA(1951), m; WHISTLE AT EATON FALLS(1951), m; MASK, THE(1961, Can.), m
Louise Applebaum
  STORY OF G.I. JOE, THE(1945), m
Basil Appleby
  INVADERS, THE,(1941); PIMPERNEL SMITH(1942, Brit.); END OF THE RIVER, THE(1947, Brit.); HIGH JINKS IN SOCIETY(1949, Brit.); WEAKER SEX, THE(1949, Brit.); NO HIGHWAY IN THE SKY(1951, Brit.); BLACK KNIGHT, THE(1954); REACH FOR THE SKY(1957, Brit.); HEIGHTS OF DANGER(1962, Brit.); NORMAN LOVES ROSE(1982, Aus.), p; WILD DUCK, THE(1983, Aus.), p
1984
  FANTASY MAN(1984, Aus.), p
Diane Appleby
  NOTHING BUT THE BEST(1964, Brit.)
Dorothy Appleby
  UNDER EIGHTEEN(1932); TRICK FOR TRICK(1933); AS THE EARTH TURNS(1934); I GIVE MY LOVE(1934); KING OF THE WILD HORSES, THE(1934); TWO HEADS ON A PILLOW(1934); CHARLIE CHAN IN PARIS(1935); LET 'EM HAVE IT(1935); SCHOOL FOR GIRLS(1935); RIFF-RAFF(1936); LIVE, LOVE AND LEARN(1937); MAKE A WISH(1937); NORTH OF NOME(1937); PARADISE EXPRESS(1937); SMALL TOWN BOY(1937); MAKING THE HEADLINES(1938); FLYING IRISHMAN, THE(1939); STAGECOACH(1939); WHEN TOMORROW COMES(1939); CONVICTED WOMAN(1940); DOCTOR TAKES A WIFE(1940); HIGH SIERRA(1941); MANPOWER(1941)
Misc. Talkies
  HOUSE OF MYSTERY, THE(1938)
Misc. Silents
  SQUARE CROOKS(1928)
Fred Appleby
Silents
  ANNAPOLIS(1928)
George Appleby
  RECOMMENDATION FOR MERCY(1975, Can.), ed; PARTNERS(1976, Can.), ed; OUTRAGEOUS!(1977, Can.), ed; DOUBLE NEGATIVE(1980, Can.), ed; NOTHING PERSONAL(1980, Can.), ed; INCUBUS, THE(1982, Can.), ed
George R. Appleby
  ISABEL(1968, Can.), ed; WINTER KEPT US WARM(1968, Can.)

James Appleby
  WORLD ACCORDING TO GARP, The(1982)
James S. Appleby
  GREAT WALDO PEPPER, THE(1975), a, stunts
John Appleby
  CAPTIVE CITY, THE(1963, Ital.), w; CONQUERED CITY(1966, Ital.), w
Lucy Appleby
  BLUES FOR LOVERS(1966, Brit.); STITCH IN TIME, A(1967, Brit.)
Michael Appleby
  DOWN OUR ALLEY(1939, Brit.)
Paul Appleby
  MAKING IT(1971); CAT ATE THE PARAKEET, THE(1972)
Stephen Appleby
  MASK, THE(1961, Can.)
Suky Appleby
  EYE OF THE DEVIL(1967, Brit.)
Jonas Applegarth
  BATTLE FLAME(1955)
Annabelle Applegate
  LAS VEGAS STORY, THE(1952)
Charles Applegate
  RED RUNS THE RIVER(1963), a, w, makeup
Christina Applegate
  JAWS OF SATAN(1980)
Eddie Applegate
  TICKLISH AFFAIR, A(1963)
Roy Applegate
  FUZZ(1972); THEY ONLY KILL THEIR MASTERS(1972); HAPPY MOTHER'S DAY... LOVE, GEORGE(1973)
Silents
  UNCLE TOM'S CABIN(1914); ALL FOR A GIRL(1915), a, d; DAUGHTER OF THE SEA, A(1915); BAB'S CANDIDATE(1920); SALLY OF THE SAWDUST(1925)
Misc. Silents
  CHILD OF DESTINY, THE(1916); MAN'S LAW, A(1917); DAREDEVIL, THE(1918); CAMBRIC MASK, THE(1919); UPSIDE DOWN(1919)
Royce Applegate
  BACK ROADS(1981)
Royce D. Applegate
  HARPER VALLEY, P.T.A.(1978); LOOSE SHOES(1980), w
1984
  SPLASH(1984)
Misc. Talkies
  AMERICAN RASPBERRY(1980)
Stanley Appleman
  UP THE SANDBOX(1972)
Peter Applequist
  SPY HUNT(1950)
Mary Ann Appleseth
  SLUMBER PARTY '57(1977)
Mary Appleseth
  PLANET OF DINOSAURS(1978)
Anne Appleton
  DESPERATE WOMEN, THE(?)
Cyril Appleton
  RULING CLASS, THE(1972, Brit.); ROUGH CUT(1980, Brit.)
Elinor Appleton
  YANKEE FAKIR(1947)
Louis B. Appleton, Jr.
  DESPERATE WOMEN, THE(?), p, d; NEVER TRUST A GAMBLER(1951), p
Louise B. Appleton, Jr.
  STRANGE VOYAGE(1945), p
Peter Appleton
  BUFFALO BILL AND THE INDIANS, OR SITTING BULL'S HISTORY LESSON(1976), ed; LATE SHOW, THE(1977), ed
George Applewhite
  FLIPPER(1963)
Ric Applewhite
  X-15(1961); NOBODY'S PERFEKT(1981)
Chris Appley
  FEARMAKERS, THE(1958), w
Arthur Applin
Silents
  LURE OF LONDON, THE(1914, Brit.), w; ALL THE WINNERS(1920, Brit.), w
Bert Appling
Silents
  END OF THE GAME, THE(1919)
Misc. Silents
  LIGHT OF WESTERN STARS, THE(1918)
Edwin Apps
  I THANK A FOOL(1962, Brit.); BARGEE, THE(1964, Brit.); RING OF SPIES(1964, Brit.)
Pier Luigi Apra
  SARDINIA: RANSOM(1968, Ital.)
Pierluigi Apra
  CHINA IS NEAR(1968, Ital.); MACHINE GUN McCAIN(1970, Ital.)
John Aprea
  BULLITT(1968); DARK SIDE OF TOMORROW, THE(1970); AROUSERS, THE(1973); GODFATHER, THE, PART II(1974); RENEGADE GIRLS(1974); CRAZY MAMA(1975); STEPFORD WIVES, THE(1975); IDOLMAKER, THE(1980)
1984
  ACT, THE(1984)
Misc. Talkies
  JUST THE TWO OF US(1975)
Werner Aprelat
  CASTLE OF FU MANCHU, THE(1968, Ger./Span./Ital./Brit.)
Frank Aprigo
  DOWN LAREDO WAY(1953), art d

Renee April
1984
BAY BOY(1984, Can.), cos
Salvatore Aprile
KILLING OF A CHINESE BOOKIE, THE(1976)
Sonny Aprile
WOMAN UNDER THE INFLUENCE, A(1974)
Ted Apstein
WITHOUT EACH OTHER(1962), w
Theodore Apstein
WHAT EVER HAPPENED TO AUNT ALICE?(1969), w
Michael Apted
TRIPLE ECHO, THE(1973, Brit.), d; STARDUST(1974, Brit.), d; SQUEEZE, THE(1977, Brit.), d; AGATHA(1979, Brit.), d; COAL MINER'S DAUGHTER(1980), d; STRONGER THAN THE SUN(1980, Brit.), d; CONTINENTAL DIVIDE(1981), d; GORKY PARK(1983), d
1984
FIRSTBORN(1984), d; KIPPERBANG(1984, Brit.), d
Alain Aptekman
SEASON FOR LOVE, THE(1963, Fr.), w
1984
L'ARGENT(1984, Fr./Switz.)
Jeanne Aptekman
1984
L'ARGENT(1984, Fr./Switz.)
Oscar Aptel
MADAME RACKETEER(1932)
Adam Apul
MADE FOR EACH OTHER(1971)
Apus and Estellita
SEPIA CINDERELLA(1947)
Burnu Aquanetta
CALLAWAY WENT THATAWAY(1951)
Giuseppe Aquari
FRANKENSTEIN-ITALIAN STYLE(1977, Ital.), ph
Louis Aquilina
GYPSY AND THE GENTLEMAN, THE(1958, Brit.)
Umberto Aquilino
IT HAPPENED IN ROME(1959, Ital.)
Aquilliere
END OF A DAY, THE(1939, Fr.)
Raymond Aquilon
DIVA(1982, Fr.)
Butch Aquino
PASSIONATE STRANGERS, THE(1968, Phil.)
Butz Aquino
Misc. Talkies
TOO HOT TO HANDLE(1976)
John Aquino
TRICK BABY(1973); BLOW OUT(1981); FORT APACHE, THE BRONX(1981); DINER(1982)
Robert Aquino
TOWN THAT DREADED SUNDOWN, THE(1977)
Aquistapace
PASSION FOR LIFE(1951, Fr.)
Jean Aquistapace
LA MARSEILLAISE(1938, Fr.)
Arab
Silents
PHANTOM OF THE NORTH(1929)
Fernando Arabal
DIE HAMBURGER KRANKHEIT(1979, Ger./Fr.)
Arabella
ALADDIN AND HIS LAMP(1952)
Sergei Arabeloff
GIRL OF THE GOLDEN WEST, THE(1938)
Michael Aracheguesne
ADOLESCENTS, THE(1967, Can.)
L. Arachtam
ROMEO AND JULIET(1955, USSR), d&w
Izviad Arad
HANNAH K.(1983, Fr.)
Cyril Aradoff
YOU CAN'T FOOL AN IRISHMAN(1950, Ireland), ph
Riccardo Aragno
MILLIONAIRESS, THE(1960, Brit.), w; BIGGEST BUNDLE OF THEM ALL, THE(1968), w
Chico Arago
KILLER FISH(1979, Ital./Braz.)
Angel Aragon
HIGH RISK(1981)
Angelica Aragon
1984
EVIL THAT MEN DO, THE(1984)
Art Aragon
RING, THE(1952); OFF LIMITS(1953); TO HELL AND BACK(1955); WORLD IN MY CORNER(1956); FAT CITY(1972)
Gutierrez Aragon
1984
DEMONS IN THE GARDEN(1984, Span.), w
Jesse Aragon
BOULEVARD NIGHTS(1979); HEART LIKE A WHEEL(1983); LOSIN' IT(1983)
1984
EXTERMINATOR 2(1984)
Joe Aragon
UNHOLY ROLLERS(1972)
Luis Aragon
IMPORTANT MAN, THE(1961, Mex.); CURSE OF THE DOLL PEOPLE, THE(1968, Mex.)

Manuel Gutierrez Aragon
1984
DEMONS IN THE GARDEN(1984, Span.), d
Michael Aragon
THINGS ARE TOUGH ALL OVER(1982)
Ray Aragon
GAY PURR-EE(1962), prod d; CHARLOTTE'S WEB(1973), art d; METAMORPHOSES(1978), prod d; GREAT AMERICAN BUGS BUNNY-ROAD RUNNER CHASE(1979), prod d
Rose Aragon
SGT. PEPPER'S LONELY HEARTS CLUB BAND(1978)
Tita Aragon
CHINA DOLL(1958)
Sergio Aragones
NORMAN...IS THAT YOU?(1976)
Chu Arai
HOTSPRINGS HOLIDAY(1970, Jap.)
Tadashi Arakami
FINAL WAR, THE(1960, Jap.), ph; RIFIFI IN TOKYO(1963, Fr./Ital.), ph
Hagop Arakelian
BEAUTY AND THE BEAST(1947, Fr.), makeup
Shinobu Araki
SANSHO THE BAILIFF(1969, Jap.)
Miguel Arana
MUSHROOM EATER, THE(1976, Mex.), ph
Silvia Arana
SMOKEY AND THE BANDIT–PART 3(1983)
Aranda
JEDDA, THE UNCIVILIZED(1956, Aus.)
Angel Aranda
LAST DAYS OF POMPEII, THE(1960, Ital.); COLOSSUS OF RHODES, THE(1961, Ital., Fr.); GOLIATH AGAINST THE GIANTS(1963, Ital./Span.); PLANET OF THE VAMPIRES(1965, U.S./Ital./Span.); EL GRECO(1966, Ital., Fr.); HELLBENDERS, THE(1967, U.S./Ital./Span.); FROM HELL TO VICTORY(1979, Fr./Ital./Span.)
Rene Aranda
FIENDISH PLOT OF DR. FU MANCHU, THE(1980)
Vincent Aranda
BLOOD SPATTERED BRIDE, THE(1974, Span.), d&w
Stole Arandjelovic
FRONTIER HELLCAT(1966, Fr./Ital./Ger./Yugo.); SCALAWAG(1973, Yugo.); TWILIGHT TIME(1983, U.S./Yugo.)
Roque Aranjo
TROPICS(1969, Ital.)
Ricardo Aranovich
WOMANLIGHT(1979, Fr./Ger./Ital.), ph; CLAIR DE FEMME(1980,Fr.), ph
Jack Aranson
MURDER IN EDEN(1962, Brit.)
Shirley Aranson
DANCING LADY(1933)
Romulo Arantes
1984
BLAME IT ON RIO(1984)
Arantza
NEST, THE(1982, Span.)
Kanjuro Arashi
EAST CHINA SEA(1969, Jap.); KURAGEJIMA–LEGENDS FROM A SOUTHERN ISLAND(1970, Jap.); ZATOICHI MEETS YOJIMBO(1970, Jap.)
Sanemon Arashi
BUDDHA(1965, Jap.)
Clifford Arashiro
HOUSE OF BAMBOO(1955)
Jenny Arasse
PAUL AND MICHELLE(1974, Fr./Brit.)
Ernest Arata
GROUND ZERO(1973)
Frank Arata
COMMITMENT, THE(1976)
Ubaldo Arata
DEFEAT OF HANNIBAL, THE(1937, Ital.), ph; UNA SIGNORA DELL'OVEST(1942, Ital), ph; CARMEN(1946, Ital.), ph; OPEN CITY(1946, Ital.), ph; KING'S JESTER, THE(1947, Ital.), ph; BLACK MAGIC(1949), ph
Michiyo Aratama
ENJO(1959, Jap.); HUMAN CONDITION, THE(1959, Jap.); DANGEROUS KISS, THE(1961, Jap.); EARLY AUTUMN(1962, Jap.); ROAD TO ETERNITY(1962, Jap.); TWILIGHT STORY, THE(1962, Jap.); CHUSHINGURA(1963, Jap.); MADAME AKI(1963,Jap.); PRODIGAL SON, THE(1964, Jap.); KWAIDAN(1965, Jap.); SAMURAI ASSASSIN(1965, Jap.); GAMBLING SAMURAI, THE(1966, Jap.); SWORD OF DOOM, THE(1967, Jap.); THIN LINE, THE(1967, Jap.); EMPEROR AND A GENERAL, THE(1968, Jap.); ONCE A RAINY DAY(1968, Jap.); DEVIL'S TEMPLE(1969, Jap.); SOLDIER'S PRAYER, A(1970, Jap.)
Paul Aratow
1984
SHEENA(1984), p
Misc. Talkies
LUCIFER'S WOMEN(1978), d
Alfonso Arau
WILD BUNCH, THE(1969); SCANDALOUS JOHN(1971); POSSE(1975); USED CARS(1980)
1984
ROMANCING THE STONE(1984)
Marilena Aravantinou
IT HAPPENED IN ATHENS(1962), art d; SAILOR FROM GIBRALTAR, THE(1967, Brit.), set d; WHO'S GOT THE BLACK BOX?(1970, Fr./Gr./Ital.), art d
Ben Arbeid
CLOUDED CRYSTAL, THE(1948, Brit.), p; VENGEANCE IS MINE(1948, Brit.), p; BARBER OF STAMFORD HILL, THE(1963, Brit.), p; CHILDREN OF THE DAMNED(1963, Brit.), p; PRIVATE POTTER(1963, Brit.), p; MURDER MOST FOUL(1964, Brit.), p; JOKERS, THE(1967, Brit.), p; ASSIGNMENT K(1968, Brit.), p; HOFFMAN(1970, Brit.), p; HIRELING, THE(1973, Brit.), p; EAGLE'S WING(1979, Brit.), p; ENIGMA(1983), p

Gerry Arbeid
DISAPPEARANCE, THE(1981, Brit./Can.), p

Stella Arbenia
Misc. Silents
BEYOND THE VEIL(1925, Brit.)

Arbenina
OUTSIDER, THE(1940, Brit.)

Stella Arbenina
BRACELETS(1931, Brit.); STAMBOUL(1931, Brit.); COLONEL BLOOD(1934, Brit.); WHAT HAPPENED THEN?(1934, Brit.); CRIME UNLIMITED(1935, Brit.); FINE FEATHERS(1937, Brit.); MERRY COMES TO STAY(1937, Brit.); MURDER IN THE FAMILY(1938, Brit.); STOLEN LIFE(1939, Brit.)
Silents
LAST WITNESS, THE(1925, Brit.)
Misc. Silents
WOMAN REDEEMED, A(1927, Brit.)

Arbessier
DEMONIAQUE(1958, Fr.)

Louis Arbessier
ROYAL AFFAIRS IN VERSAILLES(1957, Fr.); WE ARE ALL MURDERERS(1957, Fr.); TRUTH, THE(1961, Fr./Ital.); END OF DESIRE(1962 Fr./Ital.); THE DIRTY GAME(1966, Fr./Ital./Ger.)

Azis Arbia
1984
LE BAL(1984, Fr./Ital./Algeria)

Johnny Arbid
1984
LITTLE DRUMMER GIRL, THE(1984)

Marta Arbin
TORMENT(1947, Swed.); SECRETS OF WOMEN(1961, Swed.)

Petronius Arbiter
FELLINI SATYRICON(1969, Fr./Ital.), w

Linda Arbizu
Misc. Talkies
LEGEND OF THE WILD(1981)

Ronald Arblaster
HAVING A WILD WEEKEND(1965, Brit.)

Manuel Arbo
MAD QUEEN, THE(1950, Span.); GOLIATH AGAINST THE GIANTS(1963, Ital./Span.)

Miguel Asins Arbo
NOT ON YOUR LIFE(1965, Ital./Span.), m

Annie Arbogast
RETURN OF THE JEDI(1983)

Hortense Arbogast
DISPUTED PASSAGE(1939)

Lewis Arbogast
WIRE SERVICE(1942), stunts

Roy Arbogast
CLOSE ENCOUNTERS OF THE THIRD KIND(1977), spec eff; JAWS II(1978), spec eff; DRACULA(1979), spec eff; CAVEMAN(1981), spec eff; THING, THE(1982), spec eff; CHRISTINE(1983), spec eff; JAWS 3-D(1983), cons; RETURN OF THE JEDI(1983), spec eff
1984
STARMAN(1984), spec eff

Andrew Arbuckle
Silents
BIG TREMAINE(1916); FAMILY SKELETON, THE(1918); NAUGHTY, NAUGHTY!(1918); HOODLUM THE(1919); ROMANCE OF HAPPY VALLEY, A(1919); SPIDER AND THE ROSE, THE(1923); FIGHTING BOOB, THE(1926); HAZARDOUS VALLEY(1927); JAZZ MAD(1928)
Misc. Silents
LITTLE MARY SUNSHINE(1916); MATRIMONIAL MARTYR, A(1916); HAPPINESS(1917); PEGGY LEADS THE WAY(1917); DENNY FROM IRELAND(1918); CLEAN HEART, THE(1924); DANGEROUS COWARD, THE(1924)

Andy Arbuckle
DARK ANGEL, THE(1935)

James Arbuckle, Jr.
Silents
IDOL OF THE STAGE, THE(1916)

Macklyn Arbuckle
Silents
COUNTY CHAIRMAN, THE(1914); IT'S NO LAUGHING MATTER(1915)
Misc. Silents
REFORM CANDIDATE, THE(1915)

Maclyn Arbuckle
Silents
JANICE MEREDITH(1924); GILDED HIGHWAY, THE(1926)
Misc. Silents
SQUIRE PHIN(1921); MR. BINGLE(1922); MR. POTTER OF TEXAS(1922); PRODIGAL JUDGE, THE(1922); WELCOME TO OUR CITY(1922); YOUNG DIANA, THE(1922); YOLANDA(1924); LURE OF THE TRACK(1925); THAT OLD GANG OF MINE(1925); THOROUGHBRED, THE(1925)

Minta Durfee Arbuckle
MY DOG RUSTY(1948); KING CREOLE(1958); STEAGLE, THE(1971); WHAT'S THE MATTER WITH HELEN?(1971); WILLARD(1971)

Mrs. Maclyn Arbuckle
Silents
JANICE MEREDITH(1924)

Roscoe Arbuckle
Silents
BREWSTER'S MILLIONS(1921); GASOLINE GUS(1921)

Roscoe "Fatty" Arbuckle
Silents
ROUND UP, THE(1920); CRAZY TO MARRY(1921)
Misc. Silents
LIFE OF THE PARTY, THE(1920); DOLLAR-A-YEAR MAN, THE(1921); LEAP YEAR(1921); TRAVELING SALESMAN, THE(1921)

Alan Arbus
HEY, LET'S TWIST!(1961); CHRISTIAN LICORICE STORE, THE(1971); LAW AND DISORDER(1974); DAMIEN–OMEN II(1978); LAST MARRIED COUPLE IN AMERICA, THE(1980)

Allan Arbus
PUTNEY SWOPE(1969); CISCO PIKE(1971); GREASER'S PALACE(1972); CINDERELLA LIBERTY(1973); COFFY(1973); YOUNG NURSES, THE(1973); W.C. FIELDS AND ME(1976); AMERICATHON(1979); ELECTRIC HORSEMAN, THE(1979)

Mollie Arbuthnot
THESE ARE THE DAMNED(1965, Brit.), cos

Molly Arbuthnot
HORROR OF DRACULA, THE(1958, Brit.), cos; SNORKEL, THE(1958, Brit.), cos; CASH ON DEMAND(1962, Brit.), cos; KISS OF EVIL(1963, Brit.), cos; JIG SAW(1965, Brit.), cos

Aleksei Arbuzov
PROMISE, THE(1969, Brit.), d&w

Franco Arcali
PASSENGER, THE(1975, Ital.), ed

Franco Arcalli
DJANGO KILL(1967, Ital./Span.), w; SEATED AT HIS RIGHT(1968, Ital.), ed; GIRL WHO COULDN'T SAY NO, THE(1969, Ital.), ed; PLUCKED(1969, Fr./Ital.), w, ed; SPIRITS OF THE DEAD(1969, Fr./Ital.), ed; ZABRISKIE POINT(1970), ed; NIGHT PORTER, THE(1974, Ital./U.S.), ed; 1900(1976, Ital.), w, ed; LUNA(1979, Ital.), w
1984
BEYOND GOOD AND EVIL(1984, Ital./Fr./Ger.), w, ed; ONCE UPON A TIME IN AMERICA(1984), w

Kim Arcalli
'TIS A PITY SHE'S A WHORE(1973, Ital.), ed; VOYAGE, THE(1974, Ital.), ed

Bernard Arcand
ADOLESCENTS, THE(1967, Can.)

Gabriel Arcand
SUZANNE(1980, Can.)

Luis Arcaraz
CHA-CHA-CHA BOOM(1956)

Flavia Arcaro
Silents
PLUNDERER, THE(1915)

Berett Arcaya
JOY HOUSE(1964, Fr.)

Gil Arceo
DANCE OF THE DWARFS(1983, U.S., Phil.)
1984
MISSING IN ACTION(1984)

Nonong Arceo
AMBUSH BAY(1966)

Albert H. Arch
PICCADILLY NIGHTS(1930, Brit.), p&d, w

Robert Arch
MELODY OF LOVE, THE(1928), w

Edward J. Montgue Archainbaud
Silents
ONE WEEK OF LOVE(1922), w

George Archainbaud
BROADWAY HOOFER, THE(1929), d; BROADWAY SCANDALS(1929), d; TWO MEN AND A MAID(1929), d; ALIAS FRENCH GERTIE(1930), d; FRAMED(1930), d; SHOOTING STRAIGHT(1930), d; SILVER HORDE, THE(1930), d; LADY REFUSES, THE(1931), d; THREE WHO LOVED(1931), d; LOST SQUADRON, THE(1932), d; MEN OF CHANCE(1932), d; PENGUIN POOL MURDER, THE(1932), d; STATE'S ATTORNEY(1932), d; THIRTEEN WOMEN(1932), d; AFTER TONIGHT(1933), d; BIG BRAIN, THE(1933), d; KEEP 'EM ROLLING(1934), d; MURDER ON THE BLACKBOARD(1934), d; THUNDER IN THE NIGHT(1935), d; MY MARRIAGE(1936), d; RETURN OF SOPHIE LANG, THE(1936), d; BLONDE TROUBLE(1937), d; CLARENCE(1937), d; HIDEAWAY GIRL(1937), d; HOTEL HAYWIRE(1937), d; THRILL OF A LIFETIME(1937), d; CAMPUS CONFESSIONS(1938), d; HER JUNGLE LOVE(1938), d; THANKS FOR THE MEMORY(1938), d; BOY TROUBLE(1939), d; NIGHT WORK(1939), d; SOME LIKE IT HOT(1939), d; COMIN' ROUND THE MOUNTAIN(1940), d; OPENED BY MISTAKE(1940), d; UNTAMED(1940), d; FLYING WITH MUSIC(1942), d; FALSE COLORS(1943), d; HOPPY SERVES A WRIT(1943), d; KANSAN, THE(1943), d; WOMAN OF THE TOWN, THE(1943), d; ALASKA(1944), d; BIG BONANZA, THE(1944), d; MYSTERY MAN(1944), d; TEXAS MASQUERADE(1944), d; GIRLS OF THE BIG HOUSE(1945), d; DEVIL'S PLAYGROUND, THE(1946), d; FOOL'S GOLD(1946), d; UNEXPECTED GUEST(1946), d; DANGEROUS VENTURE(1947), d; HOPPY'S HOLIDAY(1947), d; KING OF THE WILD HORSES(1947), d; MARAUDERS, THE(1947), d; MILLERSON CASE, THE(1947), d; BORROWED TROUBLE(1948), d; DEAD DON'T DREAM, THE(1948), d; FALSE PARADISE(1948), d; SILENT CONFLICT(1948), d; SINISTER JOURNEY(1948), d; STRANGE GAMBLE(1948), d; BORDER TREASURE(1950), d; HUNT THE MAN DOWN(1950), d; APACHE COUNTRY(1952), d; BARBED WIRE(1952), d; BLUE CANADIAN ROCKIES(1952), d; NIGHT STAGE TO GALVESTON(1952), d; OLD WEST, THE(1952), d; WAGON TEAM(1952), d; GOLDTOWN GHOST RIDERS(1953), d; LAST OF THE PONY RIDERS(1953), d; ON TOP OF OLD SMOKY(1953), d; PACK TRAIN(1953), d; SAGINAW TRAIL(1953), d; WINNING OF THE WEST(1953), d
Misc. Talkies
VOICE WITHIN, THE(1929), d
Silents
AWAKENING, THE(1917), d; IRON RING, THE(1917), d; DAMSEL IN DISTRESS, A(1919), d; IN WALKED MARY(1920), d; CLAY DOLLARS(1921), d; ONE WEEK OF LOVE(1922), d; COMMON LAW, THE(1923), d; STORM DAUGHTER, THE(1924), d; NECESSARY EVIL, THE(1925), d; WHAT FOOLS MEN(1925), d; PUPPETS(1926), d; SILENT LOVER, THE(1926), d; EASY PICKINGS(1927), d; NIGHT LIFE(1927), d; BACHELOR'S PARADISE(1928), d; GRAIN OF DUST, THE(1928), d; MAN IN HOBBLES, THE(1928), d; TRAGEDY OF YOUTH, THE(1928), d
Misc. Silents
AS MAN MADE HER(1917), d; BRAND OF SATAN, THE(1917), d; MAID OF BELGIUM, THE(1917), d; YANKEE PLUCK(1917), d; CROSS BEARER, THE(1918), d; DIAMONDS AND PEARLS(1918), d; DIVINE SACRIFICE, THE(1918), d; TRAP, THE(1918), d; LOVE CHEAT, THE(1919), d; MAROONED HEARTS(1920), d; PLEASURE SEEKERS(1920), d; SHADOW OF ROSALIE BYRNES, THE(1920), d; WHAT WOMEN WANT(1920), d; WONDERFUL CHANCE, THE(1920), d; GIRL FROM NOWHERE, THE(1921), d; MAN OF STONE, THE(1921), d; MIRACLE OF MANHAT-

TAN, THE(1921), d; EVIDENCE(1922), d; POWER OF A LIE, THE(1922), d; UNDER OATH(1922), d; CORDELIA THE MAGNIFICENT(1923), d; MIDNIGHT GUEST, THE(1923), d; CHRISTINE OF THE HUNGRY HEART(1924), d; FOR SALE(1924), d; MIRAGE, THE(1924), d; PLUNDERER, THE(1924), d; SHADOW OF THE EAST, THE(1924), d; SINGLE WIVES(1924), d; ENTICEMENT(1925), d; SCARLET SAINT(1925), d; MEN OF STEEL(1926), d; GEORGE WASHINGTON COHEN(1928), d; LADIES OF THE NIGHT CLUB(1928), d; WOMAN AGAINST THE WORLD, A(1928), d

Alex Archambault
FRENCH CONNECTION 11(1975), makeup

Arch Archambault
ANGELS DIE HARD(1970), ph; COUNT YORGA, VAMPIRE(1970), ph; DO NOT THROW CUSHIONS INTO THE RING(1970), ph; MARIGOLD MAN(1970), ph

Clifton Archambault
DO NOT THROW CUSHIONS INTO THE RING(1970)

Harold Archambault
GUN RUNNER(1969), ph

Joseph Archambault
DO NOT THROW CUSHIONS INTO THE RING(1970)

Monique Archambault
ZORBA THE GREEK(1964, U.S./Gr.), makeup; 25TH HOUR, THE(1967, Fr./Ital./ Yugo.), makeup; MADWOMAN OF CHAILLOT, THE(1969), makeup; VIVA MAX!(1969), makeup; TWO PEOPLE(1973), makeup; FRENCH CONNECTION 11(1975), makeup

George Archambeault
MACHINE GUN KELLY(1958)

Bernard Archard
SECRET MAN, THE(1958, Brit.); VILLAGE OF THE DAMNED(1960, Brit.); CLUE OF THE NEW PIN, THE(1961, Brit.); MAN DETAINED(1961, Brit.); FLAT TWO(1962, Brit.); PASSWORD IS COURAGE, THE(1962, Brit.); TWO LETTER ALIBI(1962); LIST OF ADRIAN MESSENGER, THE(1963); FACE OF A STRANGER(1964, Brit.); SILENT PLAYGROUND, THE(1964, Brit.); SPY WITH A COLD NOSE, THE(1966, Brit.); MINI-AFFAIR, THE(1968, Brit.); FILE OF THE GOLDEN GOOSE, THE(1969, Brit.); HORROR OF FRANKENSTEIN, THE(1970, Brit.); SONG OF NORWAY(1970); FRAGMENT OF FEAR(1971, Brit.); MACBETH(1971, Brit.); SEA WOLVES, THE(1981, Brit.); KRULL(1983)

Marcel Archard
LADY IN QUESTION, THE(1940), w; UNDER SECRET ORDERS(1943, Brit.), w; EARRINGS OF MADAME DE..., THE(1954, Fr.), w

Don Archbold
PARALLELS(1980, Can.), m

Alexander Archdale
LUCKY DAYS(1935, Brit.); HOUSE OF DARKNESS(1948, Brit.); FLOODTIDE(1949, Brit.); HIS MAJESTY O'KEEFE(1953); HEADLESS GHOST, THE(1959, Brit.); SCAPEGOAT, THE(1959, Brit.); WRECK OF THE MARY DEAR, THE(1959, Brit.); VILLAGE OF THE DAMNED(1960, Brit.); INVASION QUARTET(1961, Brit.); MARRIAGE OF CONVENIENCE(1970, Brit.); KILLING OF ANGEL STREET, THE(1983, Aus.)

Mabel Archdale
Silents
GOD IN THE GARDEN, THE(1921, Brit.)

Bernard Archeard
PLAY DIRTY(1969, Brit.)

Anne Archer
CANCEL MY RESERVATION(1972); HONKERS, THE(1972); ALL-AMERICAN BOY, THE(1973); LIFEGUARD(1976); TRACKDOWN(1976); GOOD GUYS WEAR BLACK(1978); PARADISE ALLEY(1978); HERO AT LARGE(1980); RAISE THE TITANIC(1980, Brit.); GREEN ICE(1981, Brit.); WALTZ ACROSS TEXAS(1982), a, w
1984
NAKED FACE, THE(1984)

Barbara Archer
GENTLE TOUCH, THE(1956, Brit.); JUMPING FOR JOY(1956, Brit.); KID FOR TWO FARTHINGS, A(1956, Brit.); GOOD COMPANIONS, THE(1957, Brit.); MIRACLE IN SOHO(1957, Brit.); NOVEL AFFAIR, A(1957, Brit.); SHIRALEE, THE(1957, Brit.); STRANGER'S MEETING(1957, Brit.); HORROR OF DRACULA, THE(1958, Brit.); THREE MEN IN A BOAT(1958, Brit.); DEVIL'S BAIT(1959, Brit.); LIBEL(1959, Brit.); IN THE WAKE OF A STRANGER(1960, Brit.); MODEL FOR MURDER(1960, Brit.); RATTLE OF A SIMPLE MAN(1964, Brit.); SQUADRON 633(1964, U.S./Brit.); 633 SQUADRON(1964); UP THE JUNCTION(1968, Brit.)

Bruce Archer
SMILEY(1957, Brit.); SMILEY GETS A GUN(1959, Brit.)

Carolyn Archer
HALF A SIXPENCE(1967, Brit.)

Edward Archer
1984
ALLEY CAT(1984)

Elizabeth Archer [Scherbachova]
MISSION TO MOSCOW(1943)

Ernest Archer
HELL DRIVERS(1958, Brit.), art d; ZULU(1964, Brit.), art d; LORD JIM(1965, Brit.), art d; 2001: A SPACE ODYSSEY(1968, U.S./Brit.), prod d; ALFRED THE GREAT(1969, Brit.), art d; TOOMORROW(1970, Brit.), art d; NICHOLAS AND ALEXANDRA(1971, Brit.), art d; DAY OF THE JACKAL, THE(1973, Brit./Fr.), art d; PIRATES OF PENZANCE, THE(1983), art d

Ernie Archer
SHOUT AT THE DEVIL(1976, Brit.), art d

Eugene Archer
TEN DAYS' WONDER(1972, Fr.), w

Graham Archer
Misc. Talkies
MONEY IN MY POCKET(1962)

H.E. Archer
Misc. Silents
WANTED - A BROTHER(1918)

Harry Archer
Silents
JOYOUS TROUBLEMAKERS, THE(1920); ONCE A PLUMBER(1920)

Jeri Archer
TWO TICKETS TO PARIS(1962); SQUARE ROOT OF ZERO, THE(1964); SWEET LOVE, BITTER(1967)

Misc. Talkies
MORALS SQUAD(1960)

Jillian Archer
DEVIL'S PLAYGROUND, THE(1976, Aus.)

Jimmy Archer
BADGE 373(1973); FAREWELL, MY LOVELY(1975)

John Archer
LETTER OF INTRODUCTION(1938); CAREER(1939); CURTAIN CALL(1940); CITY OF MISSING GIRLS(1941); KING OF THE ZOMBIES(1941); MOUNTAIN MOONLIGHT(1941); PAPER BULLETS(1941); SCATTERGOOD BAINES(1941); BOWERY AT MIDNIGHT(1942); HI, NEIGHBOR(1942); MRS. WIGGS OF THE CABBAGE PATCH(1942); POLICE BULLETS(1942); SCATTERGOOD SURVIVES A MURDER(1942); CRASH DIVE(1943); GUADALCANAL DIARY(1943); HELLO, FRISCO, HELLO(1943); PURPLE V, THE(1943); SHANTYTOWN(1943); SHERLOCK HOLMES IN WASHINGTON(1943); EVE OF ST. MARK, THE(1944); ROGER TOUHY, GANGSTER!(1944); I'LL REMEMBER APRIL(1945); LOST MOMENT, THE(1947); COLORADO TERRITORY(1949); WHITE HEAT(1949); DESTINATION MOON(1950); GREAT JEWEL ROBBER, THE(1950); HIGH LONESOME(1950); BEST OF THE BADMEN(1951); MY FAVORITE SPY(1951); SANTA FE(1951); BIG TREES, THE(1952); RODEO(1952); SEA TIGER(1952); SOUND OFF(1952); YANK IN INDO-CHINA, A(1952); STARS ARE SINGING, THE(1953); DRAGON'S GOLD(1954); NO MAN'S WOMAN(1955); EMERGENCY HOSPITAL(1956); ROCK AROUND THE CLOCK(1956); AFFAIR IN RENO(1957); DECISION AT SUNDOWN(1957); SHE DEVIL(1957); TEN THOUSAND BEDROOMS(1957); CITY OF FEAR(1959); BLUE HAWAII(1961); I SAW WHAT YOU DID(1965); HOW TO FRAME A FIGG(1971)

Juanita Archer
Misc. Silents
GHOSTS(1915); PILLARS OF SOCIETY(1916)

June Archer
INNOCENT SINNERS(1958, Brit.)

Karen Archer
MOUSE AND THE WOMAN, THE(1981, Brit.); GIRO CITY(1982, Brit.)
1984
FOREVER YOUNG(1984, Brit.)

Kate Archer
TWO-MINUTE WARNING(1976)
Misc. Talkies
SATAN'S CHILDREN(1975)

Laurence Archer
LAUGHING LADY, THE(1950, Brit.)

Lou Archer
Silents
LIGHTNING REPORTER(1926); BABE COMES HOME(1927)
Misc. Silents
DUTY'S REWARD(1927)

Mel Archer
UNDERCOVER GIRL(1950); WINCHESTER '73(1950); DISTANT DRUMS(1951); STREETCAR NAMED DESIRE, A(1951); BLADES OF THE MUSKETEERS(1953)

Nick Archer
DOWNHILL RACER(1969), ed; MAGIC GARDEN OF STANLEY SWEETHART, THE(1970), ed

Peter Archer
ENTER THE DRAGON(1973)

Polly Archer
Silents
JAVA HEAD(1923)

Robin Archer
JULIUS CAESAR(1970, Brit.), cos

Sandra Archer
FUNNYMAN(1967)

Steve Archer
1984
NEVERENDING STORY, THE(1984, Ger.), anim

Venna Archer
I'LL REMEMBER APRIL(1945)

Vernon Archer
SILENT RUNNING(1972), spec eff

William Archer
GREEN GODDESS, THE(1930), w; ADVENTURES IN IRAQ(1943), w

Army Archerd
NEW KIND OF LOVE, A(1963); UNDER THE YUM-YUM TREE(1963); WHAT A WAY TO GO(1964); WILD IN THE STREETS(1968); YOUNG RUNAWAYS(1968); ESCAPE FROM THE PLANET OF THE APES(1971); OUTFIT, THE(1973); WON TON TON, THE DOG WHO SAVED HOLLYWOOD(1976); CALIFORNIA SUITE(1978)

Bernard Archerd
DAD'S ARMY(1971, Brit.)

Selma Archerd
CONCORDE, THE–AIRPORT '79(; HARRY AND WALTER GO TO NEW YORK(1976); FIRE SALE(1977); FUN WITH DICK AND JANE(1977); NEW YORK, NEW YORK(1977); METEOR(1979); MOMMIE DEAREST(1981)
1984
HARD TO HOLD(1984)

The Archers
NASTY RABBIT, THE(1964)

Alberto Archetti
RED SHEIK, THE(1963, Ital.); INVASION 1700(1965, Fr./Ital./Yugo.)

Cheryl Archibald
COVER GIRL(1944)

Dawn Archibald
MISSIONARY, THE(1982); REMEMBRANCE(1982, Brit.); UNSUITABLE JOB FOR A WOMAN, AN(1982, Brit.)
1984
SCRUBBERS(1984, Brit.)

Freddie Archibald
HEARTS DIVIDED(1936)

Gilda Varesi Archibald
ENTER MADAME(1935), w

James Archibald
SOME PEOPLE(1964, Brit.), p
Myra Archibald
RAMPARTS WE WATCH, THE(1940)
Stephen Archibald
MY CHILDHOOD(1972, Brit.); MY AIN FOLK(1974, Brit.)
William Archibald
I CONFESS(1953), w; INNOCENTS, THE(1961, U.S./Brit.), w
Silents
REPUTATION(1921)
Ben Archibek
LITTLE FAUSS AND BIG HALSY(1970); DIRT GANG, THE(1972); NIGHT MO-VES(1975)
John Archie
ABSENCE OF MALICE(1981); NOBODY'S PERFEKT(1981); LOVE CHILD(1982); NIGHT IN HEAVEN, A(1983); SPRING BREAK(1983)
Will Archie
Misc. Silents
FAIRY AND THE WAIF, THE(1915)
Archie Savage Dancers
GLENN MILLER STORY, THE(1953)
Archie's Juvenile Band
DODGING THE DOLE(1936, Brit.)
George Archinbaund
COLLEGE COQUETTE, THE(1929), d
Piero Archisi
SACCO AND VANZETTI(1971, Ital./Fr.)
Arline Archuletta
LAST ROUND-UP, THE(1947)
Beulah Archuletta
FOXFIRE(1955); SEARCHERS, THE(1956); JEANNE EAGELS(1957); HOW THE WEST WAS WON(1962)
James Archuletta
WYOMING(1947)
Louis Arco
DR. EHRLICH'S MAGIC BULLET(1940); UNDERGROUND(1941); DESPERATE JOURNEY(1942); PACIFIC RENDEZVOUS(1942); MISSION TO MOSCOW(1943); MOON IS DOWN, THE(1943); SONG OF BERNADETTE, THE(1943); BIG NOISE, THE(1944)
Louis V. Arco
NICK CARTER, MASTER DETECTIVE(1939); SECRETS OF SCOTLAND YARD(1944)
Rafael Arcos
Silents
WOMAN WHO FOOLED HERSELF, THE(1922)
Hugh Ardale
TOMORROW WE LIVE(1936, Brit.)
Michel Ardan
PANIQUE(1947, Fr.); ROOM UPSTAIRS, THE(1948, Fr.); NIGHTS OF SHAME(1961, Fr.); RAVISHING IDIOT, A(1966, Ital./Fr.), p; WISE GUYS(1969, Fr./Ital.), p
Fanny Ardant
WOMAN NEXT DOOR, THE(1981, Fr.); BENVENUTA(1983, Fr.); CONFIDENTIAL-LY YOURS(1983, Fr.)
1984
LIFE IS A BED OF ROSES(1984, Fr.); SWANN IN LOVE(1984, Fr.Ger.)
Cesar Ardavin
LAZARILLO(1963, Span.), d&w
Henri Ardel
Silents
LIFTING SHADOWS(1920), w
Hugh Ardele
YOUNG MR. PITT, THE(1942, Brit.)
Alice Ardell
FLYING DOWN TO RIO(1933); IMITATION OF LIFE(1934); MAGNIFICENT OBSES-SION(1935); NOTORIOUS GENTLEMAN, A(1935); PARIS IN SPRING(1935); REMEM-BER LAST NIGHT(1935); RUGGLES OF RED GAP(1935); GO WEST, YOUNG MAN(1936); LOVE ON THE RUN(1936); WE HAVE OUR MOMENTS(1937); SONGS AND BULLETS(1938)
Alyce Ardell
FIND THE WITNESS(1937)
Deirdre Ardell
CANNONBALL(1976, U.S./Hong Kong)
Franklin Ardell
MARK OF THE VAMPIRE(1935)
Franklyn Ardell
LOOKING FOR TROUBLE(1934); LOVE CAPTIVE, THE(1934); MIGHTY BARNUM, THE(1934); PALOOKA(1934); READY FOR LOVE(1934); SHE LOVES ME NOT(1934); METROPOLITAN(1935); GREAT ZIEGFELD, THE(1936); IT HAD TO HAPPEN(1936); SARATOGA(1937); WINGS OVER HONOLULU(1937)
Gretchen Ardell
CANNONBALL(1976, U.S./Hong Kong)
John Ardell
WILSON(1944); CRACK-UP(1946); T-MEN(1947)
Maxine Ardell
TRUE TO LIFE(1943); MELODY RANCH(1940); JOAN OF OZARK(1942); STAR SPANGLED RHYTHM(1942); CRYSTAL BALL, THE(1943); FOR WHOM THE BELL TOLLS(1943); SALUTE FOR THREE(1943); LADY IN THE DARK(1944); HOUSE OF STRANGERS(1949)
Arianne Arden
BEYOND THE TIME BARRIER(1960)
Bob Arden
2,000 WOMEN(1944, Brit.)
Clive Arden
Silents
SINNERS IN HEAVEN(1924), w
Curtis Arden
VALLEY OF GWANGI, THE(1969)

Donn Arden
FRESH FROM PARIS(1955), ch; PARIS FOLLIES OF 1956(1955), ch
Doris Arden
CARMEN, BABY(1967, Yugo./Ger.)
Eddie Arden
KID MILLIONS(1934); REPENT AT LEISURE(1941); RACE STREET(1948)
Edwin Arden
Silents
SIMON THE JESTER(1915)
Misc. Silents
BELOVED VAGABOND, THE(1912); EAGLE'S NEST(1915); IRON HEART, THE(1917); VIRTUOUS WIVES(1919)
Elaine Arden
HEADIN' EAST(1937)
Eve Arden
THAT UNCERTAIN FEELING(1941); DANCING LADY(1933); OH DOCTOR(1937); STAGE DOOR(1937); COCOANUT GROVE(1938); HAVING WONDERFUL TI-ME(1938); LETTER OF INTRODUCTION(1938); AT THE CIRCUS(1939); BIG TOWN CZAR(1939); ETERNALLY YOURS(1939); FORGOTTEN WOMAN, THE(1939); WOM-EN IN THE WIND(1939); CHILD IS BORN, A(1940); COMRADE X(1940); NO, NO NANETTE(1940); SLIGHTLY HONORABLE(1940); LAST OF THE DUANES(1941); MANPOWER(1941); OBLIGING YOUNG LADY(1941); SAN ANTONIO ROSE(1941); SHE COULDN'T SAY NO(1941); SHE KNEW ALL THE ANSWERS(1941); SING FOR YOUR SUPPER(1941); WHISTLING IN THE DARK(1941); ZIEGFELD GIRL(1941); BEDTIME STORY(1942); HIT PARADE OF 1943(1943); LET'S FACE IT(1943); COVER GIRL(1944); DOUGHGIRLS, THE(1944); EARL CARROLL'S VANITIES(1945); MIL-DRED PIERCE(1945); PAN-AMERICANA(1945); PATRICK THE GREAT(1945); KID FROM BOOKLYN, THE(1946); MY REPUTATION(1946); NIGHT AND DAY(1946); ARNELO AFFAIR, THE(1947); SONG OF SCHEHERAZADE(1947); UNFAITHFUL, THE(1947); VOICE OF THE TURTLE, THE(1947); ONE TOUCH OF VENUS(1948); WHIPLASH(1948); LADY TAKES A SAILOR, THE(1949); OUR MISS BROOKS(1956); YOURS(1949); CURTAIN CALL AT CACTUS CREEK(1950); PAID IN FULL(1950); TEA FOR TWO(1950); THREE HUSBANDS(1950); GOODBYE, MY FANCY(1951); WE'RE NOT MARRIED(1952); LADY WANTS MINK, THE(1953); OUR MISS BROOKS(1956); ANATOMY OF A MURDER(1959); DARK AT THE TOP OF THE STAIRS, THE(1960); SERGEANT DEADHEAD(1965); BEAUTY JUNGLE, THE(1966, Brit.); STRONGEST MAN IN THE WORLD, THE(1975); GREASE(1978); UNDER THE RAINBOW(1981); GREASE 2(1982); PANDEMONIUM(1982)
Gisella Arden
TERROR OF THE BLACK MASK(1967, Fr./Ital.)
Gloria Joy Arden
TILL THE CLOUDS ROLL BY(1946)
Hunter Arden
Silents
INNOCENT LIE, THE(1916)
Jane Arden
JAZZ SINGER, THE(1927); BLACK MEMORY(1947, Brit.); GUNMAN HAS ES-CAPED, A(1948, Brit.); SEPARATION(1968, Brit.), a, w; OTHER SIDE OF THE UNDERNEATH, THE(1972, Brit.), d&w; ANTI-CLOCK(1980), d, w&m
Jean Arden
STATE DEPARTMENT–FILE 649(1949)
Lyn Arden
$1,000,000 RACKET(1937)
Lynne Arden
BROTHER JOHN(1971)
Mary Arden
FATHER TAKES A WIFE(1941); JEALOUSY(1945); MISSING CORPSE, THE(1945); YOUTH AFLAME(1945); BLOOD AND BLACK LACE(1965, Ital.)
Maurice Arden
MARCH OR DIE(1977, Brit.)
Mildred Arden
Silents
SISTERS(1922); JANICE MEREDITH(1924)
Misc. Silents
UNRESTRAINED YOUTH(1925)
Neal Arden
SECRET FOUR, THE(1940, Brit.); YOUNG MR. PITT, THE(1942, Brit.); TRAIN OF EVENTS(1952, Brit.); SOULS IN CONFLICT(1955, Brit.); MAN WHO WOULDN'T TALK, THE(1958, Brit.); SHAKEDOWN, THE(1960, Brit.); FRIGHTENED CITY, THE(1961, Brit.); NIGHT TRAIN TO PARIS(1964, Brit.); THIRD SECRET, THE(1964, Brit.); BEST HOUSE IN LONDON, THE(1969, Brit.)
Neil Arden
JOHN WESLEY(1954, Brit.)
Patty Lou Arden
DEAR WIFE(1949); DEAR BRAT(1951)
Pauline Arden
TOP FLOOR GIRL(1959, Brit.)
Ricky Arden
HELLIONS, THE(1962, Brit.); AFTER YOU, COMRADE(1967, S. Afr.)
Robert Arden
MAN FROM MOROCCO, THE(1946, Brit.); JOE MACBETH(1955); BERMUDA AF-FAIR(1956, Brit.); SPIN A DARK WEB(1956, Brit.); COUNTERFEIT PLAN, THE(1957, Brit.); DEPRAVED, THE(1957, Brit.); KING IN NEW YORK, A(1957, Brit.); CHILD AND THE KILLER, THE(1959, Brit.); NEVER TAKE CANDY FROM A STRAN-GER(1961, Brit.); MR. ARKADIN(1962, Brit./Fr./Span.); CALL ME BWANA(1963, Brit.); SANDERS(1963, Brit.); CONDORMAN(1981); FINAL CONFLICT, THE(1981); RAGTIME(1981)
Toni Arden
SUNNY SIDE OF THE STREET(1951); SENIOR PROM(1958)
Jacques Ardennes
GIRL CAN'T STOP, THE(1966, Fr./Gr.)
Allessandro Ardenti
HERCULES(1983)
Pinuccio Ardia
10,000 DOLLARS BLOOD MONEY(1966, Ital.); OPERATION ST. PETER'S(1968, Ital.); TREASURE OF SAN GENNARO(1968, Fr./Ital./Ger.)
Tom Ardies
RUSSIAN ROULETTE(1975), w

Osvaldo Ardiles
VICTORY(1981)
Mildred Ardin
Silents
STEADFAST HEART, THE(1923)
Robert Ardis
BLOODY PIT OF HORROR, THE(1965, Ital.), ed; TERROR-CREATURES FROM THE GRAVE(1967, U.S./Ital.), ed
Valerie Ardis
NIGHT AND DAY(1946); WIFE WANTED(1946)
Victoria Ardiss
WILD IS MY LOVE(1963)
Ardisson
LA MARSEILLAISE(1938, Fr.); PASSION FOR LIFE(1951, Fr.); MY WIFE'S HUS-BAND(1965, Fr./Ital.)
Edmond Ardisson
LADY IN THE CAR WITH GLASSES AND A GUN, THE(1970, U.S./Fr.); LE PETIT THEATRE DE JEAN RENOIR(1974, Fr.); LOVE AND DEATH(1975)
Giorgio Ardisson
MORGAN THE PIRATE(1961, Fr./Ital.); LAST OF THE VIKINGS, THE(1962, Fr./Ital.); ERIK THE CONQUEROR(1963, Fr./Ital.); HERCULES IN THE HAUNTED WORLD(1964, Ital.); JULIET OF THE SPIRITS(1965, Fr./Ital./W.Ger.)
Mario Arditi
PLAYGIRLS AND THE VAMPIRE(1964, Ital.), ed
Pierre Arditi
MON ONCLE D'AMERIQUE(1980, Fr.)
1984
LIFE IS A BED OF ROSES(1984, Fr.)
Gino Ardito
ER LOVE A STRANGER(1958); ALEX AND THE GYPSY(1976); TAXI DRIVER(1976); CALIFORNIA SUITE(1978); WHY WOULD I LIE(1980)
1984
HARD TO HOLD(1984)
Gino Arditto
DOUBLE STOP(1968)
John Ardizoni
ONE NIGHT OF LOVE(1934); MADAME BOVARY(1949)
Silents
AMERICAN WAY, THE(1919)
Misc. Silents
WITCH WOMAN, THE(1918)
Louis Ardizoni
WONDER BAR(1934)
John Ardizonia
Silents
MAN HUNT, THE(1918)
Misc. Silents
GLORY OF YOLANDA, THE(1917)
Mika Ardova
RED AND THE WHITE, THE(1969, Hung./USSR)
Dean Ardow
WHAT!(1965, Fr./Brit./Ital.); ROAD TO FORT ALAMO, THE(1966, Fr./Ital.)
Peter Ardran
YOUNG GIRLS OF ROCHEFORT, THE(1968, Fr.)
Robert Ardrey
THEY KNEW WHAT THEY WANTED(1940), w; LADY TAKES A CHANCE, A(1943), w; THUNDER ROCK(1944, Brit.), w; GREEN YEARS, THE(1946), w; THREE MUS-KETEERS, THE(1948), w; MADAME BOVARY(1949), w; SECRET GARDEN, THE(1949), w; QUENTIN DURWARD(1955), w; POWER AND THE PRIZE, THE(1956), w; WONDERFUL COUNTRY, THE(1959), w; FOUR HORSEMEN OF THE APOCALYPSE, THE(1962), w; KHARTOUM(1966, Brit.), w
Suzanne Arduini
LAFAYETTE(1963, Fr.), w; THAT MAN GEORGE!(1967, Fr./Ital./Span.), w
Trini Ardura
NEST, THE(1982, Span.), cos
Antonio Areero
BLOOD WEDDING(1981, Sp.), w
Dita Arel
1984
DRIFTING(1984, Israel)
Fabienne Arel
WILD RACERS, THE(1968); CATHERINE & CO.(1976, Fr.)
Jack Arel
EROTIQUE(1969, Fr.), m
Rosita Aremas
NEUTRON CONTRA EL DR. CARONTE(1962, Mex.)
R. Aren
HAMLET(1966, USSR)
Anna Arena
WHERE THE HOT WIND BLOWS(1960, Fr., Ital.); PIRATE AND THE SLAVE GIRL, THE(1961, Fr./Ital.)
Carl Arena
CHU CHU AND THE PHILLY FLASH(1981)
1984
HOT DOG...THE MOVIE(1984), set d
Fortunato Arena
HERCULES, SAMSON & ULYSSES(1964, Ital.); STRANGER IN TOWN, A(1968, U.S./Ital.); STATUE, THE(1971, Brit.)
James Arena
HOT SPUR(1968)
Maurizio Arena
ROMAN HOLIDAY(1953); MAN WHO WAGGED HIS TAIL, THE(1961, Ital./Span.); COMMANDO(1962, Ital., Span., Bel., Ger.); BAMBOLE!(1965, Ital.); LA FUGA(1966, Ital.); CORRUPT ONES, THE(1967, Ger.); THEY CAME TO ROB LAS VEGAS(1969, Fr./Ital./Span./Ger.)
Rodolfo Arena
LOLLIPOP(1966, Braz.); BYE-BYE BRASIL(1980, Braz.); XICA(1982, Braz.)

Rosita Arena
BRUTE, THE(1952, Mex.)
Sammy Arena
STRANGE FETISHES, THE(1967)
Julie Arenal
KING OF THE GYPSIES(1978), ch; FOUR FRIENDS(1981), ch
Miguel Arenas
LEGEND OF A BANDIT, THE(1945, Mex.); TOAST TO LOVE(1951, Mex.)
Paco Arenas
TEN DAYS TO TULARA(1958)
Robert Arenas
LONE WOLF McQUADE(1983)
Rosita Arenas
AZTEC MUMMY, THE(1957, Mex.); WITCH'S MIRROR, THE(1960, Mex.); NEUTRON EL ENMASCARADO NEGRO(1962, Mex.); CURSE OF THE AZTEC MUMMY, THE(1965, Mex.); ROBOT VS. THE AZTEC MUMMY, THE(1965, Mex.); CURSE OF THE CRYING WOMAN, THE(1969, Mex.)
Ekkehard Arend
ELISABETH OF AUSTRIA(1931, Ger.)
Elke Arendt
FURY OF HERCULES, THE(1961, Ital.); SNOW WHITE(1965, Ger.)
E. Arene
ROYAL AFFAIR, A(1950), w
Lois Areno
ELECTRIC HORSEMAN, THE(1979); CANNONBALL RUN, THE(1981); STRI-PES(1981)
John Datu Arensma
RED RIVER(1948), art d; SPIRAL ROAD, THE(1962), tech adv
Brad Arensman
PARASITE(1982), ed; METALSTORM: THE DESTRUCTION OF JARED-SYN(1983), ed
1984
SWORDKILL(1984), ed
Marek Arenstein
DYBBUK THE(1938, Pol.), w
Arthur Arent
ONE THIRD OF A NATION(1939), w
Eddi Arent
DARK EYES OF LONDON(1961, Ger.); TREASURE OF SILVER LAKE(1965, Fr./Ger./Yugo.); LAST OF THE RENEGADES(1966, Fr./Ital./Ger./Yugo.); TRAITOR'S GATE(1966, Brit./Ger.); PSYCHO-CIRCUS(1967, Brit.); FOUNTAIN OF LOVE, THE(1968, Aust.); TRYGON FACTOR, THE(1969, Brit.)
Misc. Talkies
SPY TODAY, DIE TOMORROW(1967)
Laurie Arent
FOG, THE(1980)
Lindsey Arent
FOG, THE(1980)
John W. Arents
TWO GALS AND A GUY(1951), p
Sonja Arentzson
SWEET SUBSTITUTE(1964, Can.), anim
Francisco Arenzana
REDEEMER, THE(1965, Span.)
Helene Areon
LAST TEN DAYS, THE(1956, Ger.)
Joey Aresco
1984
SWING SHIFT(1984)
Niels Arestrup
LUMIERE(1976, Fr.)
Bert Aretsky
HOW SWEET IT IS(1968)
Bubby Arett
TO BE FREE(1972)
Tito Arevaldo
BLOOD DRINKERS, THE(1966, U.S./Phil.), md
Mario Arevalo
1984
UNDER THE VOLCANO(1984)
Robert Arevalo
RAVAGERS, THE(1965, U.S./Phil.)
Tito Arevalo
CAVALRY COMMAND(1963, U.S./Phil.), m; RAIDERS OF LEYTE GULF(1963 U.S./Phil.), m; WALLS OF HELL, THE(1964, U.S./Phil.), m; RAVAGERS, THE(1965, U.S./Phil.), m; MAD DOCTOR OF BLOOD ISLAND, THE(1969, Phil./U.S.), m; BEAST OF BLOOD(1970, U.S./Phil.), m; CURSE OF THE VAMPIRES(1970, Phil., U.S.), m; IGOROTA, THE LEGEND OF THE TREE OF LIFE(1970, Phil.), m
Mark Arevan
SORCERESS(1983)
Wayne Arey
Silents
KING LEAR(1916)
Misc. Silents
FLIGHT OF THE DUCHESS, THE(1916); SAINT, DEVIL AND WOMAN(1916); SHINE GIRL, THE(1916); WORLD AND THE WOMAN, THE(1916); HER BELOVED ENEMY(1917); HINTON'S DOUBLE(1917); POTS AND PANS PEGGIE(1917); WAR AND THE WOMAN(1917)
Mario Arezney
STRANGER IN HOLLYWOOD(1968)
Dominique Arfi
1984
SUGAR CANE ALLEY(1984, Fr.)
Else Argal
KATHLEEN(1941)
Danielle Argence
SHERLOCK HOLMES AND THE DEADLY NECKLACE(1962, Ger.)

Maurice Argent
PAL JOEY(1957); ONE IS A LONELY NUMBER(1972); DIE LAUGHING(1980)

Maurice S. Argent
DIRTY HARRY(1971)

Argentin
CROSSROADS(1938, Fr.); LA CHIENNE(1975, Fr.)

Imperio Argentina
CARMEN(1949, Span.); DOLORES(1949, Span.)

Alberto Argentino
ARABIAN NIGHTS(1980, Ital./Fr.)

Claudio Argento
SUSPIRIA(1977, Ital.), p; INFERNO(1980, Ital.), p

Dario Argento
TODAY IT'S ME...TOMORROW YOU!(1968, Ital.), w; ONCE UPON A TIME IN THE WEST(1969, U.S./Ital.), w; BIRD WITH THE CRYSTAL PLUMAGE, THE(1970, Ital./Ger.), d&w; FIVE MAN ARMY, THE(1970, Ital.), w; CAT O'NINE TAILS(1971, Ital./Ger./Fr.), d&w; FOUR FLIES ON GREY VELVET(1972, Ital.), d&w; DEEP RED(1976, Ital.), d, w; SUSPIRIA(1977, Ital.), d, w, m; DAWN OF THE DEAD(1979), m; INFERNO(1980, Ital.), d&w

Salvatore Argento
BIRD WITH THE CRYSTAL PLUMAGE, THE(1970, Ital./Ger.), p; CAT O'NINE TAILS(1971, Ital./Ger./Fr.), p; FOUR FLIES ON GREY VELVET(1972, Ital.), p; DEEP RED(1976, Ital.), p

Carmen Argenziano
COVER ME BABE(1970); JESUS TRIP, THE(1971); PUNISHMENT PARK(1971); HOT BOX, THE(1972, U.S./Phil.); GODFATHER, THE, PART II(1974); RENEGADE GIRLS(1974); CRAZY MAMA(1975); SHARK'S TREASURE(1975); VIGILANTE FORCE(1976); WHEN A STRANGER CALLS(1979); SUDDEN IMPACT(1983)
1984
HEARTBREAKERS(1984)
Misc. Talkies
DEATH FORCE(1978)

Carmine Argenziano
OUTSIDE MAN, THE(1973, U.S./FR.)

Yannis Arghyris
THANOS AND DESPINA(1970, Fr./Gr.)

Alberto Argibay
ALIAS BIG SHOT(1962, Argen.)

Vinny Argiro
1984
FEAR CITY(1984)

George Arglen
MA AND PA KETTLE(1949); MA AND PA KETTLE AT THE FAIR(1952); MEET ME AT THE FAIR(1952); MA AND PA KETTLE ON VACATION(1953); MA AND PA KETTLE AT WAIKIKI(1955); KETTLES IN THE OZARKS, THE(1956); KETTLES ON OLD MACDONALD'S FARM, THE(1957)

Leif Argo
PAN-AMERICANA(1945)

Vic Argo
UNHOLY ROLLERS(1972); TAXI DRIVER(1976)

Victor Argo
BOXCAR BERTHA(1972); DON IS DEAD, THE(1973); MEAN STREETS(1973); TERMINAL MAN, THE(1974); WHICH WAY IS UP?(1977); HOT TOMORROWS(1978); FIREPOWER(1979, Brit.); HANKY-PANKY(1982)
1984
FALLING IN LOVE(1984)

Sebastian Argol
YOL(1982, Turkey), m

Sacha Argov
IMPOSSIBLE ON SATURDAY(1966, Fr./Israel), m

David Argue
GALLIPOLI(1981, Aus.); BMX BANDITS(1983)
1984
MELVIN, SON OF ALVIN(1984, Aus.); RAZORBACK(1984, Aus.)

Luis Arguello
GUNMEN OF THE RIO GRANDE(1965, Fr./Ital./Span.), art d; FICKLE FINGER OF FATE, THE(1967, Span./U.S.), set d; TALL WOMEN, THE(1967, Aust./Ital./Span.), art d; GLASS SPHINX, THE(1968, Egypt/Ital./Span.), art d; YOUNG REBEL, THE(1969, Fr./Ital./Span.), cos; TRISTANA(1970, Span./Ital./Fr.), set d

Argus
TAKE ME TO PARIS(1951, Brit.)

Edwin Argus
SMART MONEY(1931); MOTIVE FOR REVENGE(1935); SPECIAL AGENT(1935); WHAT PRICE CRIME?(1935)
Silents
SCARAMOUCHE(1923); JANICE MEREDITH(1924)

Fred Argus
DOORWAY TO HELL(1930)

Jean Argyle
NEW KIND OF LOVE, A(1963); SUPPOSE THEY GAVE A WAR AND NOBODY CAME?(1970)

John Argyle
LOVE'S OLD SWEET SONG(1933, Brit.), p; SONG AT EVENTIDE(1934, Brit.), p; VARIETY(1935, Brit.), p; HAPPY DAYS ARE HERE AGAIN(1936, Brit.), p; OLD MOTHER RILEY(1937, Brit.), w; KATHLEEN(1938, Ireland), p; LITTLE DOLLY DAYDREAM(1938, Brit.), p; MUTINY OF THE ELSINORE, THE(1939, Brit.), p; WANTED BY SCOTLAND YARD(1939, Brit.), p; HUMAN MONSTER, THE(1940, Brit.), p, w; LITTLE MISS MOLLY(1940), p, w; TORSO MURDER MYSTERY, THE(1940, Brit.), p, w; CHAMBER OF HORRORS(1941, Brit.), p, w; TERROR HOUSE(1942, Brit.), p, w; TOWER OF TERROR, THE(1942, Brit.), p, w; THURSDAY'S CHILD(1943, Brit.), p; SEND FOR PAUL TEMPLE(1946, Brit.), p&d, w; HILLS OF DONEGAL, THE(1947, Brit.), p&d; PATIENT VANISHES, THE(1947, Brit.), p, w; CASE OF CHARLES PEACE, THE(1949, Brit.), p; GIRL WHO COULDN'T QUITE, THE(1949, Brit.), p; ONCE A SINNER(1952, Brit.), p
Silents
FLAMES OF FEAR(1930, Brit.); PARADISE ALLEY(1931, Brit.), a, p, d, w
Misc. Silents
LAST TIDE, THE(1931, Brit.), d

John F. Argyle
FINAL RECKONING, THE(1932, Brit.), p,d&w; GAME OF CHANCE, A(1932, Brit.), a, w; THOROUGHBRED(1932, Brit.), a, p, w
Silents
FLAMES OF FEAR(1930, Brit.), p&w

Pearl Argyle
OVERNIGHT(1933, Brit.); ADVENTURE LIMITED(1934, Brit.); CHU CHIN CHOW(1934, Brit.); REGAL CAVALCADE(1935, Brit.); THINGS TO COME(1936, Brit.)

Minos Argyrakis
OEDIPUS THE KING(1968, Brit.)

James R. Argyras
SAFE AT HOME!(1962)

Christian Arhoff
WHILE THE ATTORNEY IS ASLEEP(1945, Den.)

Ari
CHELSEA GIRLS, THE(1967)

Ben Ari
AL CAPONE(1959)

Raiken Ben Ari
GANGSTER STORY(1959)

Reza Aria
1984
MISSION, THE(1984), p, ph

Marc Arian
BURGLARS, THE(1972, Fr./Ital.)
1984
SWANN IN LOVE(1984, Fr.Ger.)

Imanol Arias
1984
DEMONS IN THE GARDEN(1984, Span.)

Maria Luisa Arias
ISLAND OF THE DAMNED(1976, Span.)

Vincent Arias
PETULIA(1968, U.S./Brit.)

Alan Aric
SUBMARINE SEAHAWK(1959)

Piera Arico
LOVE AND LARCENY(1963, Fr./Ital.)

Bruno Arie
GOD FORGIVES–I DON'T!(1969, Ital./Span.)

Brigitte Ariel
ROSEBUD(1975); PIAF–THE EARLY YEARS(1982, U.S./Fr.)

Claude Ariel
LOVE IN THE AFTERNOON(1957)

Harriett Ariel
MADWOMAN OF CHAILLOT, THE(1969)

Clea Ariell
WILD PARTY, THE(1975)

Francis K. Arien
ROAD TO ALCATRAZ(1945), w

Anna Aries
OMEGA MAN, THE(1971); RAGE(1972); INVASION OF THE BEE GIRLS(1973)

Nicola Arigliano
GREAT WAR, THE(1961, Fr., Ital.)

Sadamasa Arikawa
GODZILLA VS. THE THING(1964, Jap.), spec eff; SON OF GODZILLA(1967, Jap.), spec eff; DESTROY ALL MONSTERS(1969, Jap.), spec eff; SPACE AMOEBA, THE(1970, Jap.), spec eff; YOG-MONSTER FROM SPACE(1970, Jap.), spec eff; WAR OF THE WIZARDS(1983, Taiwan), d, spec eff

Ineko Arima
HUMAN CONDITION, THE(1959, Jap.); LOVE UNDER THE CRUCIFIX(1965, Jap.); TWILIGHT PATH(1965, Jap.)

Midorri Arimoto
KRAKATOA, EAST OF JAVA(1969)

John Arineri
POPE JOAN(1972, Brit.)

Ken Ariola
DEVIL'S BEDROOM, THE(1964)

Ben Aris
TOM BROWN'S SCHOOLDAYS(1951, Brit.); PLAGUE OF THE ZOMBIES, THE(1966, Brit.); CHARGE OF THE LIGHT BRIGADE, THE(1968, Brit.); IF ...(1968, Brit.); LIONHEART(1968, Brit.); HAMLET(1969, Brit.); GET CARTER(1971, Brit.); MUSIC LOVERS, THE(1971, Brit.); SAY HELLO TO YESTERDAY(1971, Brit.); SAVAGE MESSIAH(1972, Brit.); O LUCKY MAN!(1973, Brit.); DIGBY, THE BIGGEST DOG IN THE WORLD(1974, Brit.); THREE MUSKETEERS, THE(1974, Panama); ALFIE DARLING(1975, Brit.); TOMMY(1975, Brit.); RITZ, THE(1976); SIR HENRY AT RAWLINSON END(1980, Brit.)

Doreen Aris
NIGHT MY NUMBER CAME UP, THE(1955, Brit.)

Ichiro Arishima
DANGEROUS KISS, THE(1961, Jap.); DIPLOMAT'S MANSION, THE(1961, Jap.); TATSU(1962, Jap.); CHUSHINGURA(1963, Jap.); KING KONG VERSUS GODZILLA(1963, Jap.); LOST WORLD OF SINBAD, THE(1965, Jap.); RABBLE, THE(1965, Jap.); IT STARTED IN THE ALPS(1966, Jap.); YOUNG GUY GRADUATES(1969, Jap.); YOUNG GUY ON MT. COOK(1969, Jap.)

Christopher Ariss
UNCLE, THE(1966, Brit.)

Guido Aristarco
OUTCRY(1949, Ital.), w

R. Aristarkhova
THERE WAS AN OLD COUPLE(1967, USSR)

John Aristedes
MOONLIGHTING WIVES(1966); MY BODY HUNGERS(1967)

Alisa Aristi
GUILTY PARENTS(1934)

Trio Ariston
OPPOSITE SEX, THE(1956)

Aristophanes
SECOND GREATEST SEX, THE(1955), w
Arius
PASSION FOR LIFE(1951, Fr.); CARNIVAL(1953, Fr.); LETTERS FROM MY WIND-MILL(1955, Fr.)
Henri Arius
LAW IS THE LAW, THE(1959, Fr.); MY WIFE'S HUSBAND(1965, Fr./Ital.)
Roman Ariz-Navarreta
1984
YELLOW HAIR AND THE FORTRESS OF GOLD(1984)
Roman Ariznavaretta
RUN LIKE A THIEF(1968, Span.)
P. Arjanov
SECRET MISSION(1949, USSR)
Arjay
PSYCHO FROM TEXAS(1982), ed
Tony Arjuna
OCTOPUSSY(1983, Brit.)
A.A. Arkadev
HEROES OF THE SEA(1941)
Natalya Arkangelskaya
AND QUIET FLOWS THE DON(1960 USSR)
Alexander Arkatov
Misc. Silents
BLOODY EAST, THE(1915, USSR), d; TALE OF PRIEST PANKRATI(1918, USSR), d
Elizabeth Arkell
LOVE ON THE SPOT(1932, Brit.); LAST WALTZ, THE(1936, Brit.); MURDER ON THE SET(1936, Brit.)
Marie-Monique Arkell
DIARY OF A COUNTRY PRIEST(1954, Fr.)
Reginald Arkell
LAST WALTZ, THE(1936, Brit.), w; STREET SINGER, THE(1937, Brit.), w; CHARLEY MOON(1956, Brit.), w
Alan Arken
WOMAN TIMES SEVEN(1967, U.S./Fr./Ital.)
Nina Arkhangelskaya
VIOLIN AND ROLLER(1962, USSR)
Yu Arkhintsev
HOME FOR TANYA, A(1961, USSR)
L. Arkhipova
RESURRECTION(1963, USSR)
N. Arkhipova
BOUNTIFUL SUMMER(1951, USSR)
Sandy Arkhurst
HAMILE(1965, Ghana)
Adam Arkin
MONITORS, THE(1969); MADE FOR EACH OTHER(1971); BABY BLUE MARINE(1976); CHU CHU AND THE PHILLY FLASH(1981); UNDER THE RAINBOW(1981); FULL MOON HIGH(1982)
Alan Arkin
RUSSIANS ARE COMING, THE RUSSIANS ARE COMING, THE(1966); WAIT UNTIL DARK(1967); HEART IS A LONELY HUNTER, THE(1968); INSPECTOR CLOUSEAU(1968, Brit.); MONITORS, THE(1969); POPI(1969); CATCH-22(1970); LITTLE MURDERS(1971), a, d; LAST OF THE RED HOT LOVERS(1972); FREEBIE AND THE BEAN(1974); HEARTS OF THE WEST(1975); RAFFERTY AND THE GOLD DUST TWINS(1975); FIRE SALE(1977), a, d; SEVEN-PER-CENT SOLUTION, THE(1977, Brit.); IN-LAWS, THE(1979); MAGICIAN OF LUBLIN, THE(1979, Israel/Ger.); SIMON(1980); CHU CHU AND THE PHILLY FLASH(1981); IMPROPER CHANNELS(1981, Can.); DEADHEAD MILES(1982); FULL MOON HIGH(1982); LAST UNICORN, THE(1982); RETURN OF CAPTAIN INVINCIBLE, THE(1983, Aus./U.S.)
David Arkin
I LOVE YOU, ALICE B. TOKLAS!(1968); M(1970); UP IN THE CELLAR(1970); LONG GOODBYE, THE(1973); NASHVILLE(1975); ALL THE PRESIDENT'S MEN(1976); CANNONBALL(1976, U.S./Hong Kong)
Jack Arkin
LADY LUCK(1946); LIKELY STORY, A(1947)
Matthew Arkin
UNMARRIED WOMAN, AN(1978); CHU CHU AND THE PHILLY FLASH(1981)
Tony Arkin
CHU CHU AND THE PHILLY FLASH(1981)
Pervis Arkins
LONGEST YARD, THE(1974)
Robert Arkless
MAN WHO WOULD NOT DIE, THE(1975), p, d, w
Israel Arko
Misc. Silents
HIS WIFE'S HUSBAND(1913, Pol.)
Arko the Dog
Silents
ANYTHING ONCE(1925)
Louis S. Arkoff
GORP(1980), p
Samuel Z. Arkoff
SHE-CREATURE, THE(1956), p; REFORM SCHOOL GIRL(1957), p; HIGH SCHOOL HELLCATS(1958), p; HOW TO MAKE A MONSTER(1958), p; PARATROOP COMMAND(1959), p; BIKINI BEACH(1964), p; PAJAMA PARTY(1964), p; BEACH BLANKET BINGO(1965), p; DR. GOLDFOOT AND THE BIKINI MACHINE(1965), p; HOW TO STUFF A WILD BIKINI(1965), p; SERGEANT DEADHEAD(1965), p; FIREBALL 590(1966), p; GHOST IN THE INVISIBLE BIKINI(1966), p; WILD IN THE STREETS(1968), p; DE SADE(1969), p; DUNWICH HORROR, THE(1970), p; UP IN THE CELLAR(1970), p; WUTHERING HEIGHTS(1970, Brit.), p; WHO SLEW AUNTIE ROO?(1971, U.S./Brit.), p; RETURN TO MACON COUNTY(1975), p
Alan Arkush
HEARTBEEPS(1981), d
Allan Arkush
CANNONBALL(1976, U.S./Hong Kong); HOLLYWOOD BOULEVARD(1976), d, ed; DEATHSPORT(1978), d; ROCK 'N' ROLL HIGH SCHOOL(1979), d, w; GET CRAZY(1983), d

Nigel Arkwright
ROOMMATES(1962, Brit.)
Iris Arlan
BARBERINA(1932, Ger.)
Johnny Arlan
TERROR OF THE TONGS, THE(1961, Brit.)
R. M. Arlaud
MAIGRET LAYS A TRAP(1958, Fr.), w IMPERIAL VENUS(1963, Ital./Fr.), w
R.M. Arlaud

Rodolphe M. Arlaud
PARIS IN THE MONTH OF AUGUST(1968, Fr.), w; MATTER OF DAYS, A(1969, Fr./Czech.), w
Johh Arledge
WE'RE ONLY HUMAN(1936)
John Arledge
DADDY LONG LEGS(1931); HEARTBREAK(1931); SPIDER, THE(1931); YOUNG SINNERS(1931); CARELESS LADY(1932); HUDDLE(1932); WEEK-ENDS ONLY(1932); JIMMY AND SALLY(1933); FLIRTATION WALK(1934); OLSEN'S BIG MOMENT(1934); BACHELOR OF ARTS(1935); DEVIL DOGS OF THE AIR(1935); OLD MAN RHYTHM(1935); SHIPMATES FOREVER(1935); BIG GAME, THE(1936); DON'T TURN'EM LOOSE(1936); MURDER ON A BRIDLE PATH(1936); TWO IN REVOLT(1936); YOU MAY BE NEXT(1936); BIG CITY(1937); COUNTY FAIR(1937); SATURDAY'S HEROES(1937); CAMPUS CONFESSIONS(1938); PRISON NURSE(1938); ALL WOMEN HAVE SECRETS(1939); GONE WITH THE WIND(1939); TWELVE CROWDED HOURS(1939); YOU CAN'T CHEAT AN HONEST MAN(1939); 6000 ENEMIES(1939); FIGHTING 69TH, THE(1940); FLIGHT ANGELS(1940); GRAPES OF WRATH(1940); IT'S A DATE(1940); SKI PATROL(1940); STRANGE CARGO(1940); CHEERS FOR MISS BISHOP(1941); CITY, FOR CONQUEST(1941); DARK PASSAGE(1947); I WONDER WHO'S KISSING HER NOW(1947)
Johnny Arledge
MARY JANE'S PA(1935)
Alice Arlen
SILKWOOD(1983), w
Bette Arlen
NEPTUNE'S DAUGHTER(1949); SCENE OF THE CRIME(1949); MRS. O'MALLEY AND MR. MALONE(1950); SUMMER STOCK(1950); SHOW BOAT(1951); STRIP, THE(1951); SON OF SINBAD(1955); LIEUTENANT WORE SKIRTS, THE(1956)
Betty Arlen
SHE'S WORKING HER WAY THROUGH COLLEGE(1952); CAT WOMEN OF THE MOON(1953)
Dee Arlen
LADIES MAN, THE(1961)
Elizabeth Arlen
1984
JOHNNY DANGEROUSLY(1984)
Harold Arlen
STRIKE ME PINK(1936), m; STAR IS BORN, A(1954), m
Joan Arlen
STUDENT TOUR(1934)
Judith Arlen
KISS AND MAKE UP(1934); YOUNG AND BEAUTIFUL(1934)
Lynn Arlen
MAISIE GOES TO RENO(1944); MARRIAGE IS A PRIVATE AFFAIR(1944); TWO GIRLS AND A SAILOR(1944)
Lynne Arlen
KISMET(1944)
Michael Arlen
THESE CHARMING PEOPLE(1931, Brit.), w; LILY CHRISTINE(1932, Brit.), w; OUTCAST LADY(1934), w; GOLDEN ARROW, THE(1936), w; CAVALIER OF THE STREETS, THE(1937, Brit.), w; DATE WITH THE FALCON, A(1941), w; GAY FALCON, THE(1941), w; FALCON TAKES OVER, THE(1942), w; FALCON'S BROTHER, THE(1942), w; FALCON AND THE CO-EDS, THE(1943), w; FALCON IN DANGER, THE(1943), w; FALCON STRIKES BACK, THE(1943), w; HEAVENLY BODY, THE(1943), w; FALCON IN HOLLYWOOD, THE(1944), w; FALCON IN MEXICO, THE(1944), w; FALCON IN SAN FRANCISCO, THE(1945), w; FATAL NIGHT, THE(1948, Brit.), w; SEARCH FOR DANGER(1949), w
Silents
ACE OF CADS, THE(1926), w; WOMAN OF AFFAIRS, A(1928), w
Richard Arlen
BEGGARS OF LIFE(1928); MANHATTAN COCKTAIL(1928); DANGEROUS CURVES(1929); MAN I LOVE, THE(1929); THUNDERBOLT(1929); VIRGINIAN, THE(1929); BORDER LEGION, THE(1930); BURNING UP(1930); DANGEROUS PARADISE(1930); LIGHT OF WESTERN STARS, THE(1930); ONLY SAPS WORK(1930); SANTA FE TRAIL, THE(1930); SEA GOD, THE(1930); CAUGHT(1931); CONQUERING HORDE, THE(1931); GUN SMOKE(1931); LAWYER'S SECRET, THE(1931); SECRET CALL, THE(1931); TOUCHDOWN!(1931); ALL-AMERICAN, THE(1932); GUILTY AS HELL(1932); SKY BRIDE(1932); TIGER SHARK(1932); WAYWARD(1932); ALICE IN WONDERLAND(1933); COLLEGE HUMOR(1933); GOLDEN HARVEST(1933); HELL AND HIGH WATER(1933); ISLAND OF LOST SOULS(1933); SONG OF THE EAGLE(1933); THREE-CORNERED MOON(1933); COME ON, MARINES(1934); READY FOR LOVE(1934); SHE MADE HER BED(1934); HELLDORADO(1935); LET 'EM HAVE IT(1935); THREE LIVE GHOSTS(1935); DAN MATTHEWS(1936); MINE WITH THE IRON DOOR, THE(1936); ARTISTS AND MODELS(1937); MURDER IN GREENWICH VILLAGE(1937); SECRET VALLEY(1937); SILENT BARRIERS(1937, Brit.); CALL OF THE YUKON(1938); NO TIME TO MARRY(1938); STRAIGHT, PLACE AND SHOW(1938); LEGION OF LOST FLYERS(1939); MISSING DAUGHTERS(1939); MUTINY ON THE BLACKHAWK(1939); TROPIC FURY(1939); BLACK DIAMONDS(1940); DANGER ON WHEELS(1940); DEVIL'S PIPELINE, THE(1940); HOT STEEL(1940); LEATHER-PUSHERS, THE(1940); MAN FROM MONTREAL, THE(1940); DANGEROUS GAME, A(1941); FLYING BLIND(1941); FORCED LANDING(1941); LUCKY DEVILS(1941); MEN OF THE TIMBERLAND(1941); MUTINY IN THE ARCTIC(1941); POWER DIVE(1941); RAIDERS OF THE DESERT(1941); TORPEDO BOAT(1942); WILDCAT(1942); WRECKING CREW(1942); AERIAL GUNNER(1943); ALASKA HIGHWAY(1943); MINESWEEPER(1943); SUBMARINE ALERT(1943); BIG BONANZA, THE(1944); LADY AND THE MONSTER, THE(1944); STORM OVER LISBON(1944); THAT'S MY BABY(1944); TIMBER QUEEN(1944); IDENTITY UNKNOWN(1945); PHANTOM SPEAKS, THE(1945); ACCOMPLICE(1946); BUFFALO BILL RIDES AGAIN(1947); RETURN OF WILDFIRE, THE(1948); SPEED TO SPARE(1948); WHEN MY BABY SMILES AT ME(1948); GRAND CANYON(1949);

KANSAS RAIDERS(1950); FLAMING FEATHER(1951); SILVER CITY(1951); BLAZING FOREST, THE(1952); HURRICANE SMITH(1952); SABRE JET(1953); DEVIL'S HARBOR(1954, Brit.); BLONDE BLACKMAILER(1955, Brit.); HIDDEN GUNS(1956); MOUNTAIN, THE(1956); WARLOCK(1959); RAYMIE(1960); LAST TIME I SAW ARCHIE, THE(1961); CAVALRY COMMAND(1963, U.S.); CRAWLING HAND, THE(1963); YOUNG AND THE BRAVE, THE(1963); BEST MAN, THE(1964); LAW OF THE LAWLESS(1964); SHEPHERD OF THE HILLS, THE(1964); BLACK SPURS(1965); BOUNTY KILLER, THE(1965); HUMAN DUPLICATORS, THE(1965); TOWN TAMER(1965); YOUNG FURY(1965); APACHE UPRISING(1966); JOHNNY RENO(1966); TO THE SHORES OF HELL(1966); WACO(1966); FORT UTAH(1967); HOSTILE GUNS(1967); RED TOMAHAWK(1967); BUCKSKIN(1968); WON TON TON, THE DOG WHO SAVED HOLLYWOOD(1976); WHALE OF A TALE, A(1977)
Misc. Talkies
CALLING OF DAN MATTHEWS, THE(1936); ROAD TO NASHVILLE(1967)
Silents
IN THE NAME OF LOVE(1925); BEHIND THE FRONT(1926); ENCHANTED HILL, THE(1926); ROLLED STOCKINGS(1927); SALLY IN OUR ALLEY(1927); SHE'S A SHEIK(1927); WINGS(1927); LADIES OF THE MOB(1928); FOUR FEATHERS(1929)
Misc. Silents
BLOOD SHIP, THE(1927); FIGURES DON'T LIE(1927); MANHATTAN COCKTAIL(1928); UNDER THE TONTO RIM(1928)
Robert [Bob] Arlen
HILLS OF DONEGAL, THE(1947, Brit.)
Roxanne Arlen
ILLEGAL(1955); SON OF SINBAD(1955); BEST THINGS IN LIFE ARE FREE, THE(1956); EVERYTHING BUT THE TRUTH(1956); HOT ROD GIRL(1956); BIG CAPER, THE(1957); SLIM CARTER(1957); BACHELOR FLAT(1962); GYPSY(1962); HOUSE IS NOT A HOME, A(1964); LOVED ONE, THE(1965)
Layne Arlene
ONE SUNDAY AFTERNOON(1948)
Dimitra Arless
SKI BUM, THE(1971)
Jean Arless
HOMICIDAL(1961)
Arletty
PEARLS OF THE CROWN(1938, Fr.); FRIC FRAC(1939, FR.); DAYBREAK(1940, Fr.); CHILDREN OF PARADISE(1945, Fr.); DEVIL'S ENVOYS, THE(1947, Fr.); FLESH AND THE WOMAN(1954, Fr./Ital.); LONGEST DAY, THE(1962); MAXIME(1962, Fr.)
Anita Arley
KID FOR TWO FARTHINGS, A(1956, Brit.)
Catherine Arley
WOMAN OF STRAW(1964, Brit.), w
Arley Welfare Band
BLOW YOUR OWN TRUMPET(1958, Brit.)
Georg Arlin
SWEDISH WEDDING NIGHT(1965, Swed.)
George Arlin
CRIES AND WHISPERS(1972, Swed.)
Alfred E. Arling
KETTLES ON OLD MACDONALD'S FARM, THE(1957), ph
Arthur Arling
MERELY MARY ANN(1931), ph; YEARLING, THE(1946), ph; HOMESTRETCH, THE(1947), ph; RED GARTERS(1954), ph; THREE FOR THE SHOW(1955), ph; TAKE A GIANT STEP(1959), ph; WHEN THE GIRLS TAKE OVER(1962), ph; STRAITJACKET(1964), ph; ONCE BEFORE I DIE(1967, U.S./Phil.), ph
Arthur E. Arling
CAPTAIN FROM CASTILE(1947), ph; MOTHER IS A FRESHMAN(1949), ph; YOU'RE MY EVERYTHING(1949), ph; MY BLUE HEAVEN(1950), ph; WABASH AVENUE(1950), ph; CALL ME MISTER(1951), ph; MEET ME AFTER THE SHOW(1951), ph; BELLES ON THEIR TOES(1952), ph; I DON'T CARE GIRL, THE(1952), ph; FARMER TAKES A WIFE, THE(1953), ph; GLASS SLIPPER, THE(1955), ph; I'LL CRY TOMORROW(1955), ph; LOVE ME OR LEAVE ME(1955), ph; GREAT AMERICAN PASTIME, THE(1956), ph; RANSOM(1956), ph; MAN IN THE SHADOW(1957), ph; TAMMY AND THE BACHELOR(1957), ph; FLOOD TIDE(1958), ph; KATHY O'(1958), ph; ONCE UPON A HORSE(1958), ph; THIS HAPPY FEELING(1958), ph; PILLOW TALK(1959), ph; STORY OF RUTH, THE(1960), ph; LOVER COME BACK(1961), ph; BOYS' NIGHT OUT(1962), ph; NOTORIOUS LANDLADY, THE(1962), ph; SWINGIN' ALONG(1962), ph; MY SIX LOVES(1963), ph; SECRET INVASION, THE(1964), ph; SKI PARTY(1965), ph
Charles Arling
Silents
AND A STILL, SMALL VOICE(1918); IN OLD KENTUCKY(1920); JACK KNIFE MAN, THE(1920); PENROD(1922); WONDERFUL WIFE, A(1922)
Misc. Silents
QUEST OF THE SACRED GEM, THE(1914); LONE STAR RUSH, THE(1915); SELFISH WOMAN, THE(1916); BORDER WIRELESS, THE(1918); MILE-A-MINUTE KENDALL(1918); NO MAN'S LAND(1918); SNARES OF PARIS(1919); BEGGAR IN PURPLE, A(1920); BLUE STREAK MCCOY(1920); NO.99(1920); WOMAN IN ROOM 13, THE(1920); VENGEANCE TRAIL, THE(1921)
Joyce Arling
GIRL OF THE LIMBERLOST, THE(1945); ROMANCE OF ROSY RIDGE, THE(1947); RUTHLESS(1948); VELVET TOUCH, THE(1948)
Adrian Arlington
THOSE KIDS FROM TOWN(1942, Brit.), w; MY BROTHER JONATHAN(1949, Brit.), w; PORTRAIT OF CLARE(1951, Brit.), w
Arthur Arlington
OUR LEADING CITIZEN(1939)
Julie Arlington
DOUGHGIRLS, THE(1944)
Paul Arlington
PROSTITUTE(1980, Brit.)
Dimitra Arliss
STING, THE(1973); OTHER SIDE OF MIDNIGHT, THE(1977); PERFECT COUPLE, A(1979); FALL OF THE HOUSE OF USHER, THE(1980); XANADU(1980); FIREFOX(1982)
Florence Arliss
DISRAELI(1929); MILLIONAIRE, THE(1931); KING'S VACATION, THE(1933); HOUSE OF ROTHSCHILD, THE(1934)

Misc. Silents
DISRAELI(1921)
George Arliss
DISRAELI(1929); GREEN GODDESS, THE(1930); OLD ENGLISH(1930); ALEXANDER HAMILTON(1931), a, w; MILLIONAIRE, THE(1931); MAN WHO PLAYED GOD, THE(1932); SUCCESSFUL CALAMITY, A(1932); KING'S VACATION, THE(1933); VOLTAIRE(1933); WORKING MAN, THE(1933); HOUSE OF ROTHSCHILD, THE(1934); LAST GENTLEMAN, THE(1934); CARDINAL RICHELIEU(1935); IRON DUKE, THE(1935, Brit.); TRANSATLANTIC TUNNEL(1935, Brit.); EAST MEETS WEST(1936, Brit.); MISTER HOBO(1936, Brit.); DOCTOR SYN(1937, Brit.); MAN OF AFFAIRS(1937, Brit.)
Silents
MAN WHO PLAYED GOD, THE(1922); RULING PASSION, THE(1922)
Misc. Silents
DEVIL, THE(1921); DISRAELI(1921); GREEN GODDESS, THE(1923); $20 A WEEK(1924)
Joan Arliss
Silents
MAN WORTH WHILE, THE(1921)
Leslie Arliss
JOSSER ON THE RIVER(1932, Brit.), w; TONIGHT'S THE NIGHT(1932, Brit.), w; WHY SAPS LEAVE HOME(1932, Brit.), w; MY OLD DUTCH(1934, Brit.), w; ORDERS IS ORDERS(1934, Brit.), w; ROAD HOUSE(1934, Brit.), w; HEAT WAVE(1935, Brit.), w; JACK AHOY!(1935, Brit.), w; ALL IN(1936, Brit.), w; EVERYBODY DANCE(1936, Brit.), w; RHODES(1936, Brit.), w; WHERE THERE'S A WILL(1936, Brit), w; WHERE THERE'S A WILL(1937, Brit.), w; WINDBAG THE SAILOR(1937, Brit.), w; SEZ O'REILLY TO MACNAB(1938, Brit.), w; COME ON GEORGE(1939, Brit.), w; TOO DANGEROUS TO LIVE(1939, Brit.), w; FOR FREEDOM(1940, Brit.), w; PASTOR HALL(1940, Brit.), w; SECOND MR. BUSH, THE(1940, Brit.), w; FARMER'S WIFE, THE(1941, Brit.), d, w; SOUTH AMERICAN GEORGE(1941, Brit.), w; TERROR HOUSE(1942, Brit.), d, w; MAN IN GREY, THE(1943, Brit.), d, w; SAINT MEETS THE TIGER, THE(1943, Brit.), w; SOMEWHERE IN FRANCE(1943, Brit.), w; WICKED LADY, THE(1946, Brit.), d, w; LADY SURRENDERS, A(1947, Brit.), d, w; MAN ABOUT THE HOUSE, A(1947, Brit.), d, w; IDOL OF PARIS(1948, Brit.), d; SAINTS AND SINNERS(1949, Brit.), p&d, w; TOP OF THE FORM(1953, Brit.), w; DESTINATION MILAN(1954, Brit.), d; FOREVER MY HEART(1954, Brit.), d; WOMAN'S ANGLE, THE(1954, Brit.), d, w; MISS TULIP STAYS THE NIGHT(1955, Brit.), d, w; SEE HOW THEY RUN(1955, Brit.), d, w; WICKED LADY, THE(1983, Brit.), w
Pamela Arliss
SAINTS AND SINNERS(1949, Brit.); MUDLARK, THE(1950, Brit.)
Ralph Arliss
LAST VALLEY, THE(1971, Brit.); ASPHYX, THE(1972, Brit.)
Georgio Arlorio
HEAD OF THE FAMILY(1967, Ital./Fr.), w
Giorgio Arlorio
SUBVERSIVES, THE(1967, Ital.); BURN(1970), w; MERCENARY, THE(1970, Ital./Span.), w
John Arlott
1984
KIPPERBANG(1984, Brit.)
Rodolphe M. Arloud
RIFIFI IN TOKYO(1963, Fr./Ital.), w
Lewis Arlt
HE KNOWS YOU'RE ALONE(1980)
Frank Arlton
LAST HOUR, THE(1930, Brit.)
Silents
DON QUIXOTE(1923, Brit.); NELSON(1926, Brit.)
Misc. Silents
HARD CASH(1921, Brit.)
Elliott Arluck
YANK IN LONDON, A(1946, Brit.)
The Armadillo
WOMEN AND BLOODY TERROR(1970)
Judy Arman
NIGHT IN HEAVEN, A(1983)
Mary Bea Arman
PURPLE HAZE(1982)
Alice Armand
WIFE, HUSBAND AND FRIEND(1939); LILLIAN RUSSELL(1940)
Alon Armand
TERROR OF DR. MABUSE, THE(1965, Ger.)
Corinne Armand
ANATOMY OF A MARRIAGE(MY DAYS WITH JEAN-MARC AND MY NIGHTS WITH FRANCOISE)**1/2 (1964 Fr.); ZITA(1968, Fr.)
Eddie Armand
PORK CHOP HILL(1959), cos
Edward Armand
GUNFIGHT AT COMANCHE CREEK(1964), cos; JOURNEY TO SHILOH(1968), cos
Jacques Armand
TALES OF PARIS(1962, Fr./Ital.), w
Jean-Marie Armand
YOUNG GIRLS OF ROCHEFORT, THE(1968, Fr.), cos
Margot Armand
Misc. Silents
SIR OR MADAM(1928, Brit.)
Philip Armand
Silents
IS LOVE EVERYTHING?(1924), ph
Armando & Lita
YOU'RE IN THE ARMY NOW(1941)
Armando and Lita
IT CAN'T LAST FOREVER(1937); CASA MANANA(1951)
L. Armando, Jr.
QUEENS, THE(1968, Ital./Fr.), ph; POCKET MONEY(1972)
Andre Armandy
RENEGADES(1930), w

Giorgio Armani
LONELY LADY, THE(1983), cos
Lucine Armara
GREAT CARUSO, THE(1951)
Sammy Armaro
WRONG MAN, THE(1956)
Mabel Armatage
Silents
MEG(1926, Brit.)
Cyril Armbrister
Misc. Talkies
CHANDU ON THE MAGIC ISLAND(1934)
Robert Armbruster
NORTHWEST OUTPOST(1947), md; I DREAM OF JEANIE(1952), md; SWEET-
HEARTS ON PARADE(1953), md; MUTINY ON THE BOUNTY(1962), md; SUNDAY
IN NEW YORK(1963), md; UNSINKABLE MOLLY BROWN, THE(1964), md
Robert Armbuster
SWEET BIRD OF YOUTH(1962), md
Yvette Armel
Misc. Silents
ANTOINETTE SABRIER(1927, Fr.)
Raymond Armelino
SOUNDER, PART 2(1976)
Kay Armen
HIT THE DECK(1955); HEY, LET'S TWIST!(1961); PATERNITY(1981)
Pedro Armendariz
SHE-DEVIL ISLAND(1936, Mex.); GUADALAJARA(1943, Mex.); PASSION IS-
LAND(1943, Mex.); PORTRAIT OF MARIA(1946, Mex.); FUGITIVE, THE(1947); FORT
APACHE(1948); PEARL, THE(1948, U.S./Mex.); THREE GODFATHERS, THE(1948);
TULSA(1949); WE WERE STRANGERS(1949); MADCAP OF THE HOUSE(1950, Mex.);
TORCH, THE(1950); BRUTE, THE(1952, Mex.); LUCRECE BORGIA(1953, Ital./Fr.);
BORDER RIVER(1954); LOVERS OF TOLEDO, THE(1954, Fr./Span./Ital.); REBEL-
LION OF THE HANGED, THE(1954, Mex.); DIANE(1955); LITTLEST OUTLAW,
THE(1955); CONQUEROR, THE(1956); BIG BOODLE, THE(1957); STOWAWAY
GIRL(1957, Brit.); LITTLE SAVAGE, THE(1959); WONDERFUL COUNTRY,
THE(1959); FRANCIS OF ASSISI(1961); LA CUCARACHA(1961, Mex.); CAPTAIN
SINBAD(1963); FROM RUSSIA WITH LOVE(1963, Brit.); MY SON, THE HERO(1963,
Ital./Fr.); DOGS OF WAR, THE(1980, Brit.)
Pedro Armendariz, Jr.
GUNS FOR SAN SEBASTIAN(1968, U.S./Fr./Mex./Ital.); UNDEFEATED,
THE(1969); VAMPIRES, THE(1969, Mex.); CHISUM(1970); MACHO CAL-
LAHAN(1970); MAGNIFICENT SEVEN RIDE, THE(1972); DEADLY TRACK-
ERS(1973); SOUL OF NIGGER CHARLEY, THE(1973); CHOSEN SURVIVORS(1974
U.S.-Mex.); EARTHQUAKE(1974); SURVIVAL RUN(1980)
Rudolph Armendt
HELL IN THE HEAVENS(1934)
Victor Armenise
CRIME OVER LONDON(1936, Brit.), ph; WHEN THIEF MEETS THIEF(1937, Brit.),
ph
Don Arment
LEGEND OF TOM DOOLEY, THE(1959), art d
Gwen Arment
MARDI GRAS MASSACRE(1978)
F. A. Armenta

F.A. Armenta
LAUGHING BOY(1934) |LIVES OF A BENGAL LANCER(1935)
Mario Armenta
THIRD VOICE, THE(1960)
Phillip Armenta
GIRL OF THE GOLDEN WEST, THE(1938)
Russell Armes
COVER-UP(1949)
Xavier Armet
CORRUPTION OF CHRIS MILLER, THE(1979, Span.), p
Henry Armetta
STREET ANGEL(1928); IN OLD ARIZONA(1929); JAZZ HEAVEN(1929); LADY OF
THE PAVEMENTS(1929); LOVE, LIVE AND LAUGH(1929); TRESPASSER,
THE(1929); CLIMAX, THE(1930); LADIES LOVE BRUTES(1930); LADY TO LOVE,
A(1930); LITTLE ACCIDENT(1930); LOVIN' THE LADIES(1930); ROMANCE(1930);
SINS OF THE CHILDREN(1930); FIVE AND TEN(1931); HUSH MONEY(1931); JUST
A GIGOLO(1931); LAUGHING SINNERS(1931); STRANGERS MAY KISS(1931); TAIL-
OR MADE MAN, A(1931); UNHOLY GARDEN, THE(1931); ARSENE LUPIN(1932);
CENTRAL PARK(1932); DOOMED BATTALION, THE(1932); FAREWELL TO ARMS,
A(1932); HAT CHECK GIRL(1932); HUDDLE(1932); OKAY AMERICA(1932); PAS-
SIONATE PLUMBER(1932); PROSPERITY(1932); SCARFACE(1932); SPEAK EASI-
LY(1932); STEADY COMPANY(1932); UPTOWN NEW YORK(1932); WEEK-ENDS
ONLY(1932); COHENS AND KELLYS IN TROUBLE, THE(1933); DECEPTION(1933);
DEVIL'S BROTHER, THE(1933); DON'T BET ON LOVE(1933); HER FIRST MA-
TE(1933); LAUGHING AT LIFE(1933); MEN OF AMERICA(1933); SO THIS IS
AFRICA(1933); THEY JUST HAD TO GET MARRIED(1933); TOO MUCH HAR-
MONY(1933); WHAT! NO BEER?(1933); BLACK CAT, THE(1934); CAT AND THE
FIDDLE(1934); CHEATING CHEATERS(1934); CROSS COUNTRY CRUISE(1934);
EMBARRASSING MOMENTS(1934); GIFT OF GAB(1934); HIDE-OUT(1934); IMITA-
TION OF LIFE(1934); KISS AND MAKE UP(1934); LET'S TALK IT OVER(1934);
MERRY WIDOW, THE(1934); ONE NIGHT OF LOVE(1934); POOR RICH, THE(1934);
ROMANCE IN THE RAIN(1934); TWO HEADS ON A PILLOW(1934); VIVA VIL-
LA!(1934); WAKE UP AND DREAM(1934); AFTER OFFICE HOURS(1935); DIN-
KY(1935); I'VE BEEN AROUND(1935); MAGNIFICENT OBSESSION(1935); MAN
WHO RECLAIMED HIS HEAD, THE(1935); MANHATTAN MOON(1935); NIGHT
LIFE OF THE GODS(1935); PRINCESS O'HARA(1935); STRAIGHT FROM THE
HEART(1935); THREE KIDS AND A QUEEN(1935); UNKNOWN WOMAN(1935);
CRIME OF DR. FORBES(1936); LET'S SING AGAIN(1936); MAGNIFICENT BRUTE,
THE(1936); POOR LITTLE RICH GIRL(1936); TWO IN A CROWD(1936); MAKE A
WISH(1937); MANHATTAN MERRY-GO-ROUND(1937); TOP OF THE TOWN(1937);
EVERYBODY SING(1938); ROAD DEMON(1938); SPEED TO BURN(1938); SUBMA-
RINE PATROL(1938); DUST BE MY DESTINY(1939); ESCAPE, THE(1939); FISHER-
MAN'S WHARF(1939); I STOLE A MILLION(1939); LADY AND THE MOB, THE(1939);
RIO(1939); WINNER TAKE ALL(1939); MAN WHO TALKED TOO MUCH, THE(1940);
THREE CHEERS FOR THE IRISH(1940); WE WHO ARE YOUNG(1940); YOU'RE NOT

SO TOUGH(1940); CAUGHT IN THE ACT(1941); ALLERGIC TO LOVE(1943); GOOD
LUCK, MR. YATES(1943); STAGE DOOR CANTEEN(1943); THANK YOUR LUCKY
STARS(1943); GHOST CATCHERS(1944); ONCE UPON A TIME(1944); ANCHORS
AWEIGH(1945); BELL FOR ADANO, A(1945); COLONEL EFFINGHAM'S RAID(1945);
PENTHOUSE RHYTHM(1945)
Silents
ETERNAL SIN, THE(1917); JUNGLE TRAIL, THE(1919); SILENT COMMAND,
THE(1923); DESERT'S PRICE, THE(1926); SEVENTH HEAVEN(1927); HOME-
SICK(1928)
Misc. Silents
STREET ANGEL(1928)
Sal Armetta
PAY OR DIE(1960)
Armida
GENERAL CRACK(1929); BORDER ROMANCE(1930); UNDER A TEXAS
MOON(1930); WINGS OF ADVENTURE(1930); MARINES ARE COMING, THE(1935);
UNDER THE PAMPAS MOON(1935); BORDER CAFE(1937); ROOTIN' TOOTIN'
RHYTHM(1937); LA CONGA NIGHTS(1940); SOUTH OF TAHITI(1941); ALWAYS IN
MY HEART(1942); GIRL FROM MONTEREY, THE(1943); HERE COMES KEL-
LY(1943); MELODY PARADE(1943); MACHINE GUN MAMA(1944); BAD MEN OF
THE BORDER(1945); SOUTH OF THE RIO GRANDE(1945); JUNGLE GOD-
DESS(1948); GAY AMIGO, THE(1949); RHYTHM INN(1951)
Martin Armiger
PURE S(1976, Aus.), m
Armillita
BLOOD AND SAND(1941)
Victor Arminese
ACCUSED(1936, Brit.), ph
Buford Armitage
STOLEN HEAVEN(1931)
Frank Armitage
SLEEPING BEAUTY(1959), art d
George Armitage
GAS-S-S-S!(1970), a, w; VON RICHTHOFEN AND BROWN(1970); HIT MAN(1972),
d&w; PRIVATE DUTY NURSES(1972), p,d&w; NIGHT CALL NURSES(1974), w;
RENEGADE GIRLS(1974); DARKTOWN STRUTTERS(1975), w; VIGILANTE FOR-
CE(1976), d&w
Gordon Armitage
GOLDEN BOY(1939)
Graham Armitage
PRIVATE LIFE OF SHERLOCK HOLMES, THE(1970, Brit.); BOY FRIEND,
THE(1971, Brit.); GAMES THAT LOVERS PLAY(1971, Brit.); MUSIC LOVERS,
THE(1971, Brit.); SPANISH FLY(1975, Brit.); ZULU DAWN(1980, Brit.)
Jennifer Armitage
BROTHERS AND SISTERS(1980, Brit.)
Walter Armitage
HER STRANGE DESIRE(1931, Brit.); LOVE HABIT, THE(1931, Brit.); FOOTSTEPS
IN THE NIGHT(1932, Brit.); BOMBAY MAIL(1934); GREAT EXPECTATIONS(1934);
WHERE SINNERS MEET(1934)
Mary Armiyn
Silents
LAST OF THE INGRAHAMS, THE(1917)
John Armond
PSYCHO A GO-GO!(1965); TWO-MINUTE WARNING(1976)
Lyn Armondo
MANTIS IN LACE(1968)
P. Armont
FRENCH TOUCH, THE(1954, Fr.), w
Paul Armont
LOVE ME TONIGHT(1932), w; PURPLE MASK, THE(1955), w
Silents
FRENCH DOLL, THE(1923), w
Armontel
LOVERS OF VERONA, THE(1951, Fr.); BEAST, THE(1975, Fr.)
Roland Armontel
MAN ABOUT TOWN(1947, Fr.); CHEATERS, THE(1961, Fr.); DEVIL AND THE TEN
COMMANDMENTS, THE(1962, Fr.); SHERLOCK HOLMES AND THE DEADLY
NECKLACE(1962, Ger.)
Annabel Armour
DOCTOR DETROIT(1983)
David Armour
NICE GIRL LIKE ME, A(1969, Brit.)
Jean Armour
Silents
BRANDED WOMAN, THE(1920)
Misc. Silents
AMATEUR ORPHAN, AN(1917); WINCHESTER WOMAN, THE(1919); OTHER
MEN'S SHOES(1920)
Kay Armour
NEW KIND OF LOVE, A(1963)
Keith Armour
Silents
ATTA BOY'S LAST RACE(1916)
Misc. Silents
CHILDREN PAY, THE(1916)
Maxine Armour
UP IN ARMS(1944)
Frances Arms
NEVER SAY DIE(1939)
Russell Arms
ALWAYS IN MY HEART(1942); CAPTAINS OF THE CLOUDS(1942); MAN WHO
CAME TO DINNER, THE(1942); WINGS FOR THE EAGLE(1942); DECEPTION(1946);
FIGHTING VIGILANTES, THE(1947); HIGH WALL, THE(1947); LIFE WITH FA-
THER(1947); STAGE TO MESA CITY(1947); DAREDEVILS OF THE CLOUDS(1948);
LOADED PISTOLS(1948); TORNADO RANGE(1948); JOHN LOVES MARY(1949);
QUICK ON THE TRIGGER(1949); SMOKY MOUNTAIN MELODY(1949); SONS OF
NEW MEXICO(1949); BY THE LIGHT OF THE SILVERY MOON(1953)

Stan Armsted
PUNISHMENT PARK(1971)
Armstrong
SINGER AND THE DANCER, THE(1977, Aus.), w
Alun Armstrong
GET CARTER(1971, Brit.); FOURTEEN, THE(1973, Brit.); DUELLISTS, THE(1977, Brit.); FRENCH LIEUTENANT'S WOMAN, THE(1981); KRULL(1983)
1984
NUMBER ONE(1984, Brit.)
Anthony Armstrong
ORDERS IS ORDERS(1934, Brit.), w; TEN MINUTE ALIBI(1935, Brit.), w; DON'T EVER LEAVE ME(1949, Brit.), w; MAN IN THE ROAD, THE(1957, Brit.), w; ORDERS ARE ORDERS(1959, Brit.), w; MAN WHO HAUNTED HIMSELF, THE(1970, Brit.), w
Antony Armstrong
YOUNG AND INNOCENT(1938, Brit.), w
Arnold B. Armstrong
RAW DEAL(1948), w
Audrey Armstrong
TO HAVE AND HAVE NOT(1944)
Bess Armstrong
FOUR SEASONS, THE(1981); JEKYLL AND HYDE...TOGETHER AGAIN(1982); HIGH ROAD TO CHINA(1983); JAWS 3-D(1983)
1984
HOUSE OF GOD, THE(1984)
Misc. Talkies
HOUSE OF GOD, THE(1979)
Bill Armstrong
NAKED IN THE SUN(1957); HISTORY OF THE WORLD, PART 1(1981)
Bridget Armstrong
LIVE NOW–PAY LATER(1962, Brit.); HARD DAY'S NIGHT, A(1964, Brit.); WE SHALL SEE(1964, Brit.); AMOROUS MR. PRAWN, THE(1965, Brit.); HALF A SIXPENCE(1967, Brit.); INCREDIBLE SARAH, THE(1976, Brit.); FOR THE LOVE OF BENJI(1977); MIDDLE AGE SPREAD(1979, New Zealand)
Bunny Armstrong
LOVED ONE, THE(1965), makeup
Carl Armstrong
WOMAN ON THE BEACH, THE(1947)
Charlotte Armstrong
UNSUSPECTED, THE(1947), w; THREE WEIRD SISTERS, THE(1948, Brit.), w; DON'T BOTHER TO KNOCK(1952), w; TALK ABOUT A STRANGER(1952), w
Cheryl Armstrong
THOSE LIPS, THOSE EYES(1980)
Curtis Armstrong
RISKY BUSINESS(1983)
1984
REVENGE OF THE NERDS(1984)
Dale Armstrong
HERO FOR A DAY(1939); SLIGHTLY HONORABLE(1940)
Darrell Armstrong
$(DOLLARS)**1/2 (1971)
Dave Armstrong
CAREER GIRL(1960)
David Armstrong
ON THE THRESHOLD OF SPACE(1956); HELLER IN PINK TIGHTS(1960); WOMAN UNDER THE INFLUENCE, A(1974), ed; NEW YORK, NEW YORK(1977)
Del Armstrong
NORTHWEST STAMPEDE(1948), makeup; TULSA(1949), makeup; WOMAN IN HIDING(1949), makeup; SHAKEDOWN(1950), makeup; STAR, THE(1953), makeup; BY LOVE POSSESSED(1961), makeup; WHO'S GOT THE ACTION?(1962), makeup; LOVE HAS MANY FACES(1965), makeup; RUSSIANS ARE COMING, THE RUSSIANS ARE COMING, THE(1966), makeup; IN THE HEAT OF THE NIGHT(1967), makeup; GAILY, GAILY(1969), makeup; STALKING MOON, THE(1969), makeup; SOLDIER BLUE(1970), makeup; ORGANIZATION, THE(1971), makeup; WRATH OF GOD, THE(1972), makeup; DOMINO PRINCIPLE, THE(1977), makeup; LAST REMAKE OF BEAU GESTE, THE(1977), makeup
Derek Armstrong
PARDON MY FRENCH(1951, U.S./Fr.), ed
Dick Armstrong
POSSE(1975); VILLAIN, THE(1979)
Edwina Armstrong
ONCE IN A BLUE MOON(1936)
Gary Armstrong
COLORADO PIONEERS(1945); MOONRISE(1948)
Gillian Armstrong
SINGER AND THE DANCER, THE(1977, Aus.), p&d; MY BRILLIANT CAREER(1980, Aus.), d; STARSTRUCK(1982, Aus.), d
1984
MRS. SOFFEL(1984), d
H.C. Armstrong
DEAD MEN ARE DANGEROUS(1939, Brit.), w
Harry Armstrong
Silents
SWEET ADELINE(1926), w
Henry Armstrong
NEW ADVENTURES OF GET-RICH-QUICK WALLINGFORD, THE(1931); PITTSBURGH KID, THE(1941); JOE PALOOKA, CHAMP(1946)
Misc. Talkies
KEEP PUNCHING(1939)
Herb Armstrong
ROOKIE, THE(1959); YOUNG CAPTIVES, THE(1959); CAPE FEAR(1962); GUN STREET(1962); FOR PETE'S SAKE(1977); SEEMS LIKE OLD TIMES(1980)
Herbert Armstrong
PARTY GIRL(1958)
Hugh Armstrong
PRUDENCE AND THE PILL(1968, Brit.); TELL ME LIES(1968, Brit.); MUMSY, NANNY, SONNY, AND GIRLY(1970, Brit.); EAGLE IN A CAGE(1971, U.S./Yugo.); DEATHLINE(1973, Brit.)

Jack "Wildman" Armstrong
1984
MICKI AND MAUDE(1984)
Jo Armstrong
NO RETURN ADDRESS(1961)
Joan Armstrong
TAKE HER BY SURPRISE(1967, Can.)
Joanna Armstrong
OPERATION HAYLIFT(1950)
John Armstrong
PRIVATE LIFE OF HENRY VIII, THE(1933), cos; CATHERINE THE GREAT(1934, Brit.), cos; SCARLET PIMPERNEL, THE(1935, Brit.), cos; AS YOU LIKE IT(1936, Brit.), cos; GHOST GOES WEST, THE(1936), cos; I STAND CONDEMNED(1936, Brit.), cos; REMBRANDT(1936, Brit.), cos; THINGS TO COME(1936, Brit.), cos; THIEF OF BAGHDAD, THE(1940, Brit.), cos; HOBSON'S CHOICE(1954, Brit.), cos; BUTTERFIELD 8(1960); HUSBANDS(1970); OUTBACK(1971, Aus.); SUNSTRUCK(1973, Aus.)
John M. Armstrong
STUDENT BODIES(1981)
Kathleen Armstrong
Misc. Silents
CRUISKEEN LAWN(1922, Brit.)
Kerry Armstrong
GETTING OF WISDOM, THE(1977, Aus.)
Leslie Armstrong
FATAL NIGHT, THE(1948, Brit.)
Louis Armstrong
PENNIES FROM HEAVEN(1936); DR. RHYTHM(1938); EVERY DAY'S A HOLIDAY(1938); GOING PLACES(1939); CABIN IN THE SKY(1943); COWBOY CAVALIER(1948); OUTLAW BRAND(1948); HERE COMES THE GROOM(1951); GLORY ALLEY(1952); GLENN MILLER STORY, THE(1953); HIGH SOCIETY(1956); BEAT GENERATION, THE(1959); FIVE PENNIES, THE(1959); PARIS BLUES(1961); WHEN THE BOYS MEET THE GIRLS(1965); MAN CALLED ADAM, A(1966); HELLO, DOLLY!(1969)
Louis W. Armstrong
RANGERS RIDE, THE(1948)
Margaret Armstrong
TOMORROW AND TOMORROW(1932); THREE-CORNERED MOON(1933); SHE LOVES ME NOT(1934); ANNIE OAKLEY(1935); LIGHTNING STRIKES TWICE(1935); OUR LITTLE GIRL(1935); AND SO THEY WERE MARRIED(1936); GRAND JURY(1936); M'LISS(1936); TRAIL OF THE LONESOME PINE, THE(1936); GO CHASE YOURSELF(1938); LITTLE ORPHAN ANNIE(1938); WESTERN JAMBOREE(1938); WOMEN IN PRISON(1938); SORORITY HOUSE(1939); NO, NO NANETTE(1940); LADY FOR A NIGHT(1941); MAN WHO LOST HIMSELF, THE(1941); UNFINISHED BUSINESS(1941); DUKE OF THE NAVY(1942)
Mary Armstrong
CHATTERBOX(1943)
Michael Armstrong
HORROR HOUSE(1970, Brit.), d, w; MARK OF THE DEVIL(1970, Ger./Brit.), d; BLACK PANTHER, THE(1977, Brit.), w; HOUSE OF LONG SHADOWS, THE(1983, Brit.), m
Mike Armstrong
HARD TRAIL(1969); EMPIRE OF THE ANTS(1977)
Paul Armstrong
WILD GIRL(1932), w; EVER SINCE EVE(1934), w; HOLD THAT BLONDE(1945), w; CAPTAIN'S PARADISE, THE(1953, Brit.); MAN OUTSIDE, THE(1968, Brit.)
Silents
ESCAPE, THE(1914), w; GREYHOUND, THE(1914), w; SALOMY JANE(1914), w; ALIAS JIMMY VALENTINE(1920), w; PATHS TO PARADISE(1925), w; ESCAPE, THE(1928), w
Perry Armstrong
SOLO(1978, New Zealand/Aus.)
Peter Armstrong
BLOOD AND LACE(1971); CARS THAT ATE PARIS, THE(1974, Aus,); STONE(1974, Aus.), stunts; NATURAL ENEMIES(1979)
R. Dale Armstrong
Misc. Silents
CRUCIFIX OF DESTINY, THE(1920), d; FALSE WOMEN(1921), d
R.G. Armstrong
GARDEN OF EDEN(1954); ER LOVE A STRANGER(1958); FROM HELL TO TEXAS(1958); NO NAME ON THE BULLET(1959); FUGITIVE KIND, THE(1960); TEN WHO DARED(1960); RIDE THE HIGH COUNTRY(1962); HE RIDES TALL(1964); MAJOR DUNDEE(1965); EL DORADO(1967); 80 STEPS TO JONAH(1969); ANGELS DIE HARD(1970); BALLAD OF CABLE HOGUE, THE(1970); GREAT WHITE HOPE, THE(1970); MC MASTERS, THE(1970); TIGER BY THE TAIL(1970); J.W. COOP(1971); FINAL COMEDOWN, THE(1972); GREAT NORTHFIELD, MINNESOTA RAID, THE(1972); WHO FEARS THE DEVIL(1972); PAT GARRETT AND BILLY THE KID(1973); WHITE LIGHTNING(1973); BOSS NIGGER(1974); MY NAME IS NOBODY(1974, Ital./Fr./Ger.); RACE WITH THE DEVIL(1975); WHITE LINE FEVER(1975, Can.); DIXIE DYNAMITE(1976); MEAN JOHNNY BARROWS(1976); STAY HUNGRY(1976); CAR, THE(1977); MR. BILLION(1977); PACK, THE(1977); HEAVEN CAN WAIT(1978); FAST CHARLIE... THE MOONBEAM RIDER(1979); STEEL(1980); WHERE THE BUFFALO ROAM(1980); PURSUIT OF D.B. COOPER, THE(1981); RAGGEDY MAN(1981); REDS(1981); BEAST WITHIN, THE(1982); EVILSPEAK(1982); HAMMETT(1982); LONE WOLF McQUADE(1983)
1984
CHILDREN OF THE CORN(1984)
Misc. Talkies
DELIVER US FROM EVIL(1975); TEXAS DETOUR(1978)
R.L. Armstrong
SWAMP COUNTRY(1966); HARD RIDE, THE(1971); J.W. COOP(1971); ULZANA'S RAID(1972); MISSOURI BREAKS, THE(1976); SLUMBER PARTY '57(1977); GOIN' SOUTH(1978)
Ray Armstrong
RETURN OF THE JEDI(1983)
Raymond Armstrong
WHERE HAS POOR MICKEY GONE?(1964, Brit.)
Richard Armstrong
PASSAGE HOME(1955, Brit.), w; TENTH VICTIM, THE(1965, Fr./Ital.); CHASTITY(1969)

Robert Armstrong
SHOW FOLKS(1928); BIG NEWS(1929); LEATHERNECK, THE(1929); OH, YEAH!(1929); RACKETEER, THE(1929); SHADY LADY, THE(1929); SO THIS IS COLLEGE(1929); BE YOURSELF(1930); BIG MONEY(1930); DANGER LIGHTS(1930); DUMBBELLS IN ERMINE(1930); PAID(1930); EX-BAD BOY(1931); IRON MAN, THE(1931); SUICIDE FLEET(1931); TIP-OFF, THE(1931); BILLION DOLLAR SCANDAL(1932); HOLD'EM JAIL(1932); IS MY FACE RED?(1932); LOST SQUADRON, THE(1932); MOST DANGEROUS GAME, THE(1932); PANAMA FLO(1932); PENGUIN POOL MURDER, THE(1932); RADIO PATROL(1932); BLIND ADVENTURE(1933); FAST WORKERS(1933); I LOVE THAT MAN(1933); KING KONG(1933); SON OF KONG(1933); ABOVE THE CLOUDS(1934); HELL CAT, THE(1934); KANSAS CITY PRINCESS(1934); MANHATTAN LOVE SONG(1934); PALOOKA(1934); SEARCH FOR BEAUTY(1934); SHE MADE HER BED(1934); FLIRTING WITH DANGER(1935); G-MEN(1935); GIGOLETTE(1935); LITTLE BIG SHOT(1935); MYSTERY MAN, THE(1935); REMEMBER LAST NIGHT(1935); SWEET MUSIC(1935); ALL-AMERICAN CHUMP(1936); DANGEROUS WATERS(1936); EX-MRS. BRADFORD, THE(1936); PUBLIC ENEMY'S WIFE(1936); WITHOUT ORDERS(1936); GIRL SAID NO, THE(1937); IT CAN'T LAST FOREVER(1937); NOBODY'S BABY(1937); SHE LOVED A FIREMAN(1937); THREE LEGIONNAIRES, THE(1937); NIGHT HAWK, THE(1938); THERE GOES MY HEART(1938); CALL A MESSENGER(1939); FLIGHT AT MID-NIGHT(1939); FLYING IRISHMAN, THE(1939); MAN OF CONQUEST(1939); UNMAR-RIED(1939); WINTER CARNIVAL(1939); BRIDE WORE CRUTCHES, THE(1940); ENEMY AGENT(1940); FORGOTTEN GIRLS(1940); FRAMED(1940); BEHIND THE NEWS(1941); CITADEL OF CRIME(1941); DIVE BOMBER(1941); MR. DYNAMI-TE(1941); SAN FRANCISCO DOCKS(1941); BABY FACE MORGAN(1942); IT HAP-PENED IN FLATBUSH(1942); LET'S GET TOUGH(1942); MY FAVORITE SPY(1942); AROUND THE WORLD(1943); KANSAN, THE(1943); MAD GHOUL, THE(1943); WINGS OVER THE PACIFIC(1943); ACTION IN ARABIA(1944); BELLE OF THE YUKON(1944); MR. WINKLE GOES TO WAR(1944); NAVY WAY, THE(1944); ARSON SQUAD(1945); BLOOD ON THE SUN(1945); FALCON IN SAN FRANCISCO, THE(1945); GANGS OF THE WATERFRONT(1945); BLONDE ALIBI(1946); CRIMI-NAL COURT(1946); DECOY(1946); GAY BLADES(1946); G.I. WAR BRIDES(1946); EXPOSED(1947); FALL GUY(1947); FUGITIVE, THE(1947); SEA OF GRASS, THE(1947); PALEFACE, THE(1948); RETURN OF THE BADMEN(1948); CAPTAIN CHINA(1949); CRIME DOCTOR'S DIARY, THE(1949); LUCKY STIFF, THE(1949); MIGHTY JOE YOUNG(1949); SONS OF NEW MEXICO(1949); STREETS OF SAN FRANCISCO(1949); DESTINATION BIG HOUSE(1950); PACE THAT THRILLS, THE(1952); LAS VEGAS SHAKEDOWN(1955); PEACEMAKER, THE(1956); CROOKED CIRCLE, THE(1958); JOHNNY COOL(1963); FOR THOSE WHO THINK YOUNG(1964)
Silents
GIRL IN EVERY PORT, A(1928); LEOPARD LADY, THE(1928); NED MCCOBB'S DAUGHTER(1929)
Misc. Silents
BABY CYCLONE, THE(1928); CELEBRITY(1928); COP, THE(1928); SQUARE CROOKS(1928); WOMAN FROM HELL, THE(1929)
Ron Armstrong
NIGHT OF THE ZOMBIES(1981)
Sam Armstrong
SEQUOIA(1934), w; DUMBO(1941), d; BAMBI(1942), d
Silents
FRESHIE, THE(1922)
Samuel Armstrong
SNOW WHITE AND THE SEVEN DWARFS(1937), anim; FANTASIA(1940), d
Sean Armstrong
GOSPEL ROAD, THE(1973)
Sir Orville Armstrong
PATRICK THE GREAT(1945)
Sue Armstrong
SINGER AND THE DANCER, THE(1977, Aus.), art d
Tex Armstrong
TO KILL A MOCKINGBIRD(1962); BLACK KLANSMAN, THE(1966); DIMENSION 5(1966); FIREBALL 590(1966); RARE BREED, THE(1966); DESTRUCTORS, THE(1968); MONEY JUNGLE, THE(1968); PANIC IN THE CITY(1968)
Thomas Armstrong
MASTER OF BANKDAM, THE(1947, Brit.), w
Todd Armstrong
SILENCERS, THE(; FIVE FINGER EXERCISE(1962); WALK ON THE WILD SI-DE(1962); JASON AND THE ARGONAUTS(1963, Brit.); KING RAT(1965); DEAD HEAT ON A MERRY-GO-ROUND(1966); THUNDER AT THE BORDER(1966, Ger./ Yugo.); TIME FOR KILLING, A(1967)
Tony Armstrong
YOU MUST BE JOKING!(1965, Brit.), cos; JOKERS, THE(1967, Brit.), cos
Vaughn Armstrong
TRIUMPHS OF A MAN CALLED HORSE(1983, US/Mex.)
1984
PHILADELPHIA EXPERIMENT, THE(1984)
Vic Armstrong
RAIDERS OF THE LOST ARK(1981)
1984
CONAN THE DESTROYER(1984), stunts
Will Armstrong
RED FORK RANGE(1931)
Silents
CLANCY'S KOSHER WEDDING(1927)
William H. Armstrong
SOUNDER(1972), w; SOUNDER, PART 2(1976), w
William S. Armstrong
BREAKING AWAY(1979)
Paul Armstrong, Jr.
RETURN OF JIMMY VALENTINE, THE(1936), w
Sidney Armus
THOMAS CROWN AFFAIR, THE(1968); WHO IS HARRY KELLERMAN AND WHY IS HE SAYING THOSE TERRIBLE THINGS ABOUT ME?(1971); NICK-ELODEON(1976)
Army Personnel of 16th Field Artillery
KEEP 'EM ROLLING(1934)

Army Polo Team
FLIRTATION WALK(1934)
Lissi Arna
BEYOND VICTORY(1931); LIFE BEGINS ANEW(1938, Ger.)
Silents
PHYSICIAN, THE(1928, Brit.)
Beatrice Arnac
LOLA MONTES(1955, Fr./Ger.)
Marcel Arnac
STEPPIN' IN SOCIETY(1945), w
Helene Arnai
EGLANTINE(1972, Fr.), ed
Helene Arnal
VOYAGE OF SILENCE(1968, Fr.), ed
Issa Arnal
DR. GOLDFOOT AND THE BIKINI MACHINE(1965); HARD ROAD, THE(1970)
Julia Arnall
I AM A CAMERA(1955, Brit.); MAN OF THE MOMENT(1955, Brit.); SIMON AND LAURA(1956, Brit.); MAN WITHOUT A BODY(1957, Brit.); TEARS FOR SIMON(1957, Brit.); TRIPLE DECEPTION(1957, Brit.); VALUE FOR MONEY(1957, Brit.); MARK OF THE PHOENIX(1958, Brit.); MODEL FOR MURDER(1960, Brit.); CARRY ON REGARDLESS(1961, Brit.); TRUNK, THE(1961, Brit.); DOUBLE MAN, THE(1967)
Russell Arnas
CHECKERED COAT, THE(1948)
John Arnatt
DICK BARTON AT BAY(1950, Brit.); CRY, THE BELOVED COUNTRY(1952, Brit.); HOUSE OF BLACKMAIL(1953, Brit.); CIRCUMSTANIAL EVIDENCE(1954, Brit.); NOVEL AFFAIR, A(1957, Brit.); THIRD ALIBI, THE(1961, Brit.); WHISTLE DOWN THE WIND(1961, Brit.); IMPERSONATOR, THE(1962, Brit.); ONLY TWO CAN PLAY(1962, Brit.); OUT OF THE FOG(1962, Brit.); DR. CRIPPEN(1963, Brit.); SET-UP, THE(1963, Brit.); SHADOW OF FEAR(1963, Brit.); ESCAPE BY NIGHT(1965, Brit.); HYSTERIA(1965, Brit.); JOEY BOY(1965, Brit.); SECOND BEST SECRET AGENT IN THE WHOLE WIDE WORLD, THE(1965, Brit.); WHERE THE BULLETS FLY(1966, Brit.); OUR MOTHER'S HOUSE(1967, Brit.); CHALLENGE FOR ROBIN HOOD, A(1968, Brit.)
B. J. Arnau
LIVE AND LET DIE(1973, Brit.)
Brenda Arnau
FINIAN'S RAINBOW(1968)
Christiane Arnaud
NIGHT OF LUST(1965, Fr.)
Fede Arnaud
SON OF THE RED CORSAIR(1963, Ital.), w
Florence Arnaud
SELLERS OF GIRLS(1967, Fr.)
Francis Arnaud
RETURN OF MARTIN GUERRE, THE(1983, Fr.)
G. J. Arnaud
SIN ON THE BEACH(1964, Fr.), w
Georges Arnaud
WAGES OF FEAR, THE(1955, Fr./Ital.), w; SORCERER(1977), w
Irene Arnaud
OBSESSED(1951, Brit.)
Leo Arnaud
SHIP AHOY(1942), m; THRILL OF BRAZIL, THE(1946), md; CALENDAR GIRL(1947), md; ONE TOUCH OF VENUS(1948), md; SOMBRERO(1953), md
Marie-Helene Arnaud
FANTOMAS(1966, Fr./Ital.)
Yvonne Arnaud
CANARIES SOMETIMES SING(1930, Brit.); ON APPROVAL(1930, Brit.); TONS OF MONEY(1931, Brit.); CUCKOO IN THE NEST, THE(1933, Brit.); LADY IN DAN-GER(1934, Brit.); WIDOW'S MIGHT(1934, Brit.); PRINCESS CHARMING(1935, Brit.); STORMY WEATHER(1935, Brit.); GAY ADVENTURE, THE(1936, Brit.); IMPROPER DUCHESS, THE(1936, Brit.); NEUTRAL PORT(1941, Brit.); AT DAWN WE DIE(1943, Brit.); WOMAN TO WOMAN(1946, Brit.); GHOSTS OF BERKELEY SQUARE(1947, Brit.); MY UNCLE(1958, Fr.)
Misc. Silents
TEMPTRESS, THE(1920, Brit.)
The Arnaut Brothers
MUSIC HALL PARADE(1939, Brit.)
Claude Arnay
FRENCH CANCAN(1956, Fr.)
Desi Arnaz
TOO MANY GIRLS(1940); FATHER TAKES A WIFE(1941); FOUR JACKS AND A JILL(1941); NAVY COMES THROUGH, THE(1942); BATAAN(1943); CUBAN PE-TE(1946); HOLIDAY IN HAVANA(1949); LONG, LONG TRAILER(1954); FOREV-ER DARLING(1956), a, p
Desi Arnaz, Jr.
RED SKY AT MORNING(1971); BILLY TWO HATS(1973, Brit.); MARCO(1973); JOYRIDE(1977); WEDDING, A(1978); HOUSE OF LONG SHAD-OWS, THE(1983, Brit.)
Desiderio Arnaz
ESCAPE ARTIST, THE(1982)
Lucie Arnaz
BILLY JACK GOES TO WASHINGTON(1977); JAZZ SINGER, THE(1980); SECOND THOUGHTS(1983)
Charles Arndt
SOMEWHERE IN THE NIGHT(1946); SUN SETS AT DAWN, THE(1950)
Ernst Arndt
Misc. Silents
SAMSON AND DELILAH(1922, Aust.)
Helga Arndt
EIGHT GIRLS IN A BOAT(1932, Ger.)
John Arndt
APPLE DUMPLING GANG RIDES AGAIN, THE(1979)
Jurgen Arndt
CELESTE(1982, Ger.)

Peter Arne

FOR THOSE IN PERIL(1944, Brit.); MYSTERY ON BIRD ISLAND(1954, Brit.); PURPLE PLAIN, THE(1954, Brit.); YOU KNOW WHAT SAILORS ARE(1954, Brit.); ATOMIC MAN, THE(1955, Brit.); COCKLESHELL HEROES, THE(1955); HIGH TIDE AT NOON(1957, Brit.); MEN OF SHERWOOD FOREST(1957, Brit.); STRANGER'S MEETING(1957, Brit.); TARZAN AND THE LOST SAFARI(1957, Brit.); DESERT ATTACK(1958, Brit.); INTENT TO KILL(1958, Brit.); MOONRAKER, THE(1958, Brit.); BREAKOUT(1960, Brit.); CONSPIRACY OF HEARTS(1960, Brit.); SANDS OF THE DESERT(1960, Brit.); SCENT OF MYSTERY(1960); STORY OF DAVID, A(1960, Brit.); SECRET OF MONTE CRISTO, THE(1961, Brit.); PIRATES OF BLOOD RIVER, THE(1962, Brit.); HELLFIRE CLUB, THE(1963, Brit.); VICTORS, THE(1963); MODEL MURDER CASE, THE(1964, Brit.); BLACK TORMENT, THE(1965, Brit.); KHARTOUM(1966, Brit.); SANDWICH MAN, THE(1966, Brit.); BATTLE BENEATH THE EARTH(1968, Brit.); CHITTY CHITTY BANG BANG(1968, Brit.); OBLONG BOX, THE(1969, Brit.); MURDERS IN THE RUE MORGUE(1971); STRAW DOGS(1971, Brit.); WHEN EIGHT BELLS TOLL(1971, Brit.); POPE JOAN(1972, Brit.); RETURN OF THE PINK PANTHER, THE(1975, Brit.); PROVIDENCE(1977, Fr.); PASSAGE, THE(1979, Brit.); TRAIL OF THE PINK PANTHER, THE(1982); VICTOR/VICTORIA(1982); CURSE OF THE PINK PANTHER(1983)

Leon Arnel

LILIOM(1935, Fr.)

France Arnell

SUITOR, THE(1963, Fr.)

Richard Arnell

THIRD SECRET, THE(1964, Brit.), m, md; VISIT, THE(1964, Ger./Fr./Ital./U.S.), m, md; MAN OUTSIDE, THE(1968, Brit.), m; BLACK PANTHER, THE(1977, Brit.), m

Robert Arnell

MUSTANG(1959), p

Gwen Arner

TRIAL OF THE CATONSVILLE NINE, THE(1972); MAKING LOVE(1982)

Neda Arneric

SHAFT IN AFRICA(1973); LEGEND OF SPIDER FOREST, THE(1976, Brit.)

James Arness

ROSES ARE RED(1947); WAGONMASTER(1950); WYOMING MAIL(1950); CAVALRY SCOUT(1951); PEOPLE AGAINST O'HARA, THE(1951); THING, THE(1951); BIG JIM McLAIN(1952); CARBINE WILLIAMS(1952); GIRL IN WHITE, THE(1952); HORIZONS WEST(1952); HONDO(1953); ISLAND IN THE SKY(1953); VEILS OF BAGDAD, THE(1953); HER TWELVE MEN(1954); THEM!(1954); FLAME OF THE ISLANDS(1955); MANY RIVERS TO CROSS(1955); SEA CHASE, THE(1955); FIRST TRAVELING SALESLADY, THE(1956); GUN THE MAN DOWN(1957); ALIAS JESSE JAMES(1959)

Jim [James] Arness

TWO LOST WORLDS(1950); HELLGATE(1952)

Jim Arness

SIERRA(1950); IRON MAN, THE(1951); LONE HAND, THE(1953)

James Arnett

LIFE AND TIMES OF JUDGE ROY BEAN, THE(1972), stunts; JACKSON COUNTY JAIL(1976), a, stunts; NIGHTWING(1979); STEEL(1980), stunts

1984

ADVENTURES OF BUCKAROO BANZAI: ACROSS THE 8TH DIMENSION, THE(1984), stunts

Jim Arnett

SOMETIMES A GREAT NOTION(1971), stunts; TAPS(1981)

Leslie Arnett

1984

FIRSTBORN(1984)

M. James Arnett

FOUL PLAY(1978); WHEN TIME RAN OUT(1980)

1984

WHERE THE BOYS ARE '84(1984); 2010(1984), stunts

Paul Arnett

SIERRA BARON(1958)

Jeanetta Arnette

Misc. Talkies

TEENAGE GRAFFITI(1977)

Jeannetta Arnette

REDEEMER, THE(1978); SMALL CIRCLE OF FRIENDS, A(1980); YOUNG GIANTS(1983)

Karen Arney

ON HER BED OF ROSES(1966)

Stefan Arngrim

WAY WEST, THE(1967); FEAR NO EVIL(1981); CLASS OF 1984(1982, Can.)

Gus Arnheim

SCARFACE(1932), m

Carlos Arniches

DAUGHTER OF DECEIT(1977, Mex.), w

Harry Arnie

OPERATION SECRET(1952)

Walter Arnim

BIG TOWN(1932)

Vic Arnley

CUP-TIE HONEYMOON(1948, Brit.)

Arnley & Gloria

HOME SWEET HOME(1945, Brit.)

Frank Arno

KARATE KILLERS, THE(1967); HUNTER, THE(1980); POSTMAN ALWAYS RINGS TWICE, THE(1981)

Louis Arno

THIS LAND IS MINE(1943)

Nellie Arno

GIRL IN THE PAINTING, THE(1948, Brit.); LOVE LOTTERY, THE(1954, Brit.)

Nelly Arno

LOST PEOPLE, THE(1950, Brit.); THIRD MAN, THE(1950, Brit.); GREAT MANHUNT, THE(1951, Brit.); SO LONG AT THE FAIR(1951, Brit.); TREAD SOFTLY(1952, Brit.); PRIZE OF GOLD, A(1955)

Nick Arno

HOUDINI(1953)

Peter Arno

ARTISTS AND MODELS(1937); ANTONY AND CLEOPATRA(1973, Brit.)

Siegfried [Sig] Arno

VIENNA, CITY OF SONGS(1931, Ger.); STAR MAKER, THE(1939); DIAMOND FRONTIER(1940); MUMMY'S HAND, THE(1940); AND THE ANGELS SING(1944)

Silents

PANDORA'S BOX(1929, Ger.)

Sig Arno

DARK STREETS OF CAIRO(1940); LITTLE BIT OF HEAVEN, A(1940); THIS THING CALLED LOVE(1940); CHOCOLATE SOLDIER, THE(1941); GAMBLING DAUGHTERS(1941); HELLZAPOPPIN'(1941); IT STARTED WITH EVE(1941); NEW WINE(1941); RAIDERS OF THE DESERT(1941); SING FOR YOUR SUPPER(1941); TWO LATINS FROM MANHATTAN(1941); DEVIL WITH HITLER(1942); I MARRIED AN ANGEL(1942); JUKE BOX JENNY(1942); PALM BEACH STORY, THE(1942); PARDON MY SARONG(1942); TALES OF MANHATTAN(1942); TWO YANKS IN TRINIDAD(1942); CRYSTAL BALL, THE(1943); DU BARRY WAS A LADY(1943); HIS BUTLER'S SISTER(1943); LARCENY WITH MUSIC(1943); PASSPORT TO SUEZ(1943); THOUSANDS CHEER(1943); SONG OF THE OPEN ROAD(1944); STANDING ROOM ONLY(1944); UP IN ARMS(1944); BRING ON THE GIRLS(1945); ROUGHLY SPEAKING(1945); SONG TO REMEMBER, A(1945); ONE MORE TOMORROW(1946); GREAT LOVER, THE(1949); HOLIDAY IN HAVANA(1949); DUCHESS OF IDAHO, THE(1950); NANCY GOES TO RIO(1950); TOAST OF NEW ORLEANS, THE(1950); ON MOONLIGHT BAY(1951); DIPLOMATIC COURIER(1952); FAST COMPANY(1953); GREAT DIAMOND ROBBERY(1953)

William Joseph Arno

STUNT MAN, THE(1980)

Grace Arnois

CRASH DRIVE(1959, Brit.)

Alfonso Arnold

CURSE OF THE DOLL PEOPLE, THE(1968, Mex.)

Anton Arnold

WHAT A WAY TO GO(1964)

Bert Arnold

RED SNOW(1952); ROUGH, TOUGH WEST, THE(1952)

Billy Arnold

YELLOW JACK(1938); HIDE-OUT(1934); MANHATTAN MELODRAMA(1934); PERSONALITY KID(1934); SHE MARRIED HER BOSS(1935); GOLDEN ARROW, THE(1936); SING ME A LOVE SONG(1936); CAPTAINS COURAGEOUS(1937); EXCLUSIVE(1937); HOTEL HAYWIRE(1937); KID GALAHAD(1937); LAST GANGSTER, THE(1937); TOAST OF NEW YORK, THE(1937); I AM THE LAW(1938); PENITENTIARY(1938); ST. LOUIS BLUES(1939)

C. W. Arnold

NUMBER SEVENTEEN(1932, Brit.), art d

Silents

CHAMPAGNE(1928, Brit.), art d

C. Wilfred Arnold

RICH AND STRANGE(1932, Brit.), set d

Silents

LODGER, THE(1926, Brit.), art d

Carl Arnold

DAYS OF WINE AND ROSES(1962)

Celia Arnold

WHERE IS MY CHILD?(1937)

Chris Arnold

SEDUCTION OF JOE TYNAN, THE(1979)

Claire Arnold

LUCKY JADE(1937, Brit.); LILY OF LAGUNA(1938, Brit.); MURDER IN THE FAMILY(1938, Brit.)

Claude Arnold

FIRST TASTE OF LOVE(1962, Fr.)

Clint Arnold

NEW YORK, NEW YORK(1977)

Danny Arnold

BREAKTHROUGH(1950); SAILOR BEWARE(1951); JUMPING JACKS(1952); CADDY, THE(1953), w; DESERT SANDS(1955), w; FORT YUMA(1955), w; OUTSIDE THE LAW(1956), w; REBEL IN TOWN(1956), w; LADY TAKES A FLYER, THE(1958), w; WAR BETWEEN MEN AND WOMEN, THE(1972), a, p, w

David Arnold

FIVE POUND MAN, THE(1937, Brit.); LANDSLIDE(1937, Brit.); MURDER IN THE FAMILY(1938, Brit.)

Denny Arnold

CHINATOWN(1974); LOGAN'S RUN(1976); BLUE COLLAR(1978)

Doris Arnold

SUNSHINE AHEAD(1936, Brit.)

Dorothy Arnold

EXPOSED(1938); SECRETS OF A NURSE(1938); STORM, THE(1938); CODE OF THE STREETS(1939); FAMILY NEXT DOOR, THE(1939); HOUSE OF FEAR, THE(1939); PIRATES OF THE SKIES(1939); UNEXPECTED FATHER(1939); YOU CAN'T CHEAT AN HONEST MAN(1939); LIZZIE(1957)

Eddie Arnold

LAST PICTURE SHOW, THE(1971), m

Eddy Arnold

HOEDOWN(1950)

Misc. Talkies

FEUDIN' RHYTHM(1949)

Edith Arnold

COLLEGE SCANDAL(1935)

Edward Arnold

AFRAID TO TALK(1932); OKAY AMERICA(1932); RASPUTIN AND THE EMPRESS(1932); THREE ON A MATCH(1932); BARBARIAN, THE(1933); HER BODYGUARD(1933); I'M NO ANGEL(1933); JENNIE GERHARDT(1933); ROMAN SCANDALS(1933); SECRET OF THE BLUE ROOM(1933); WHISTLING IN THE DARK(1933); WHITE SISTER, THE(1933); HIDE-OUT(1934); MADAME SPY(1934); MILLION DOLLAR RANSOM(1934); PRESIDENT VANISHES, THE(1934); SADIE McKEE(1934); THIRTY-DAY PRINCESS(1934); UNKNOWN BLONDE(1934); WEDNESDAY'S CHILD(1934); BIOGRAPHY OF A BACHELOR GIRL(1935); CARDINAL RICHELIEU(1935); CRIME AND PUNISHMENT(1935); DIAMOND JIM(1935); GLASS KEY, THE(1935); REMEMBER LAST NIGHT(1935); COME AND GET IT(1936); MEET NERO WOLFE(1936); SUTTER'S GOLD(1936); BLOSSOMS ON BROADWAY(1937); EASY LIVING(1937); JOHN MEADE'S WOMAN(1937); TOAST OF NEW

YORK, THE(1937); CROWD ROARS, THE(1938); YOU CAN'T TAKE IT WITH YOU(1938); IDIOT'S DELIGHT(1939); LET FREEDOM RING(1939); MAN ABOUT TOWN(1939); MR. SMITH GOES TO WASHINGTON(1939); EARL OF CHICAGO, THE(1940); JOHNNY APOLLO(1940); LILLIAN RUSSELL(1940); SLIGHTLY HONORABLE(1940); DESIGN FOR SCANDAL(1941); DEVIL AND DANIEL WEBSTER, THE(1941); LADY FROM CHEYENNE(1941); MEET JOHN DOE(1941); NOTHING BUT THE TRUTH(1941); PENALTY, THE(1941); UNHOLY PARTNERS(1941); EYES IN THE NIGHT(1942); JOHNNY EAGER(1942); WAR AGAINST MRS. HADLEY, THE(1942); YOUNGEST PROFESSION, THE(1943); JANIE(1944); KISMET(1944); MAIN STREET AFTER DARK(1944); MRS. PARKINGTON(1944); STANDING ROOM ONLY(1944); HIDDEN EYE, THE(1945); WEEKEND AT THE WALDORF(1945); ZIEGFELD FOLLIES(1945); JANIE GETS MARRIED(1946); MIGHTY MCGURK, THE(1946); MY BROTHER TALKS TO HORSES(1946); NO LEAVE, NO LOVE(1946); THREE WISE FOOLS(1946); DEAR RUTH(1947); HUCKSTERS, THE(1947); BIG CITY(1948); COMMAND DECISION(1948); THREE DARING DAUGHTERS(1948); WALLFLOWER(1948); BIG JACK(1949); DEAR WIFE(1949); JOHN LOVES MARY(1949); TAKE ME OUT TO THE BALL GAME(1949); ANNIE GET YOUR GUN(1950); SKIPPER SURPRISED HIS WIFE, THE(1950); YELLOW CAB MAN(1950); DEAR BRAT(1951); BELLES ON THEIR TOES(1952); CITY THAT NEVER SLEEPS(1953); MAN OF CONFLICT(1953); LIVING IT UP(1954); AMBASSADOR'S DAUGHTER, THE(1956); HOUSTON STORY, THE(1956); MIAMI EXPOSE(1956)
Silents
COST, THE(1920)
Misc. Silents
MISLEADING LADY, THE(1916); RETURN OF EVE, THE(1916)

Edward Arnold, Jr.
BLAZING BARRIERS(1937); LIFE BEGINS IN COLLEGE(1937); DRAMATIC SCHOOL(1938); LITTLE TOUGH GUY(1938); MR. DOODLE KICKS OFF(1938); DANCING CO-ED(1939); MILLION DOLLAR LEGS(1939); RISE AND SHINE(1941)

Elliott Arnold
FIRST COMES COURAGE(1943), w; BROKEN ARROW(1950), w; DEEP IN MY HEART(1954), w; KINGS OF THE SUN(1963), w; FLIGHT FROM ASHIYA(1964, U.S./Jap.), w; ALVAREZ KELLY(1966), w

Eric Arnold
CRIMSON ROMANCE(1934)

Erick Arnold
Silents
MASKED ANGEL(1928)

Ernst Arnold
MONEY ON THE STREET(1930, Aust.)

Frank Arnold
ABOVE SUSPICION(1943); FLESH AND FANTASY(1943); PARIS AFTER DARK(1943); PASSPORT TO SUEZ(1943); THIS LOVE OF OURS(1945); RAZOR'S EDGE, THE(1946); SEARCHING WIND, THE(1946); SO DARK THE NIGHT(1946); MACOMBER AFFAIR, THE(1947), w; HOMECOMING(1948); EMERGENCY WEDDING(1950); UNDER MY SKIN(1950); ON DANGEROUS GROUND(1951); TEN TALL MEN(1951); PHFFFT!(1954); AUTUMN LEAVES(1956); BLOODY PIT OF HORROR, THE(1965, Ital.), art d; HUMANOIDS FROM THE DEEP(1980), a, w

Franz Arnold
WARM CORNER, A(1930, Brit.), w; IT'S A BOY(1934, Brit.), w; INTERRUPTED HONEYMOON, THE(1936, Brit.), w; PUBLIC NUISANCE NO. 1(1936, Brit.), w

Freddy Arnold
JUDGE AND THE SINNER, THE(1964, Ger.), makeup; JAIL BAIT(1977, Ger.), makeup

Gail Arnold
RENDEZVOUS AT MIDNIGHT(1935)

Gertrud Arnold
Silents
SIEGFRIED(1924, Ger.)

Gordon Arnold
MASQUERADE IN MEXICO(1945); DREAM GIRL(1947); GOLDEN EARRINGS(1947); SONG OF SCHEHERAZADE(1947); DARLING, HOW COULD YOU!(1951); MATING SEASON, THE(1951)

Grace Arnold
MEN WITHOUT HONOUR(1939, Brit.); SPARE A COPPER(1940, Brit.); GENTLE SEX, THE(1943, Brit.); LAMP STILL BURNS, THE(1943, Brit.); GIVE ME THE STARS(1944, Brit.); THEY KNEW MR. KNIGHT(1945, Brit.); WAY AHEAD, THE(1945, Brit.); I'LL TURN TO YOU(1946, Brit.); JOHNNY FRENCHMAN(1946, Brit.); TROJAN BROTHERS, THE(1946); GIRL ON THE CANAL, THE(1947, Brit.); LOVES OF JOANNA GODDEN, THE(1947, Brit.); HOUSE OF DARKNESS(1948, Brit.); JASSY(1948, Brit.); LOVE IN WAITING(1948, Brit.); DARK SECRET(1949, Brit.); IT ALWAYS RAINS ON SUNDAY(1949, Brit.); MAN FROM YESTERDAY, THE(1949, Brit.); MY BROTHER JONATHAN(1949, Brit.); PASSPORT TO PIMLICO(1949, Brit.); HUE AND CRY(1950, Brit.); MAGNET, THE(1950, Brit.); LIFE IN HER HANDS(1951, Brit.); PORTRAIT OF CLARE(1951, Brit.); CARETAKERS DAUGHTER, THE(1952, Brit.); STRANGER IN BETWEEN, THE(1952, Brit.); THOSE PEOPLE NEXT DOOR(1952, Brit.); MURDER ON APPROVAL(1956, Brit.); HIGH FLIGHT(1957, Brit.); TOWN ON TRIAL(1957, Brit.); KONGA(1961, Brit.); I THANK A FOOL(1962, Brit.); HEROES OF TELEMARK, THE(1965, Brit.)

Harry Arnold
TIME OF DESIRE, THE(1957, Swed.), m; INVASION OF THE ANIMAL PEOPLE(1962, U.S./Swed.), m; NO TIME TO KILL(1963, Brit./Swed./Ger.), m; TIME IN THE SUN, A(1970, Swed.), m

Helen Arnold
Silents
ONE LAW FOR BOTH(1917)

Henry O. Arnold
PAYDAY(1972); FRAMED(1975)

Irene Arnold
VIOLENT PLAYGROUND(1958, Brit.); NIGHT TRAIN FOR INVERNESS(1960, Brit.)

Ivan Arnold
ONE, TWO, THREE(1961)

Jack Arnold [Vinton Arnold]
ENLIGHTEN THY DAUGHTER(1934); DANGER PATROL(1937); HITTING A NEW HIGH(1937); BLIND ALIBI(1938); CRIME RING(1938); LAW OF THE UNDERWORLD(1938); MR. DOODLE KICKS OFF(1938); TARNISHED ANGEL(1938); THIS MARRIAGE BUSINESS(1938); VIVACIOUS LADY(1938); DAY THE BOOKIES WEPT, THE(1939); FIXER DUGAN(1939); DANGER ON WHEELS(1940); ENEMY AGENT(1940); FRAMED(1940); LOVE, HONOR AND OH, BABY(1940); MARGIE(1940); MILLIONAIRES IN PRISON(1940); OH JOHNNY, HOW YOU CAN

LOVE!(1940); SUED FOR LIBEL(1940); TILLIE THE TOILER(1941); BEHIND THE EIGHT BALL(1942); JUKE BOX JENNY(1942); MEXICAN SPITFIRE'S ELEPHANT(1942); PRIDE OF THE YANKEES, THE(1942); SABOTEUR(1942); THERE'S ONE BORN EVERY MINUTE(1942); TO THE SHORES OF TRIPOLI(1942); YOU'RE TELLING ME(1942); GIRLS IN THE NIGHT(1953), d; GLASS WEB, THE(1953), d; IT CAME FROM OUTER SPACE(1953), d; CREATURE FROM THE BLACK LAGOON(1954), d; MAN FROM BITTER RIDGE, THE(1955), d; REVENGE OF THE CREATURE(1955), d; TARANTULA(1955), d, w; THIS ISLAND EARTH(1955), d; OUTSIDE THE LAW(1956), d; RED SUNDOWN(1956), d; INCREDIBLE SHRINKING MAN, THE(1957), d; MAN IN THE SHADOW(1957), d; MONOLITH MONSTERS, THE(1957), w; TATTERED DRESS, THE(1957), d; HIGH SCHOOL CONFIDENTIAL(1958), d; LADY TAKES A FLYER, THE(1958), d; MONSTER ON THE CAMPUS(1958), d; SPACE CHILDREN, THE(1958), d; MOUSE THAT ROARED, THE(1959, Brit.), d; NO NAME ON THE BULLET(1959), p, d; BACHELOR IN PARADISE(1961), d; GLOBAL AFFAIR, A(1964), d; LIVELY SET, THE(1964), d; HELLO DOWN THERE(1969), d; BLACK EYE(1974), d; BOSS NIGGER(1974), p, d; SWISS CONSPIRACY, THE(1976, U.S./Ger.), d

James Arnold
STRANGERS ON A HONEYMOON(1937, Brit.)

Jeanne Arnold
MUNSTER, GO HOME!(1966); WHAT'S SO BAD ABOUT FEELING GOOD?(1968)

Jeremy Arnold
RETURN OF THE SOLDIER, THE(1983, Brit.)

Jess Arnold
EAGLE AND THE HAWK, THE(1950), w; BRASS LEGEND, THE(1956), w

Jesse Arnold
HARD HOMBRE(1931); FORCE OF EVIL(1948)

Jessie Arnold
BROTHERS(1930); HOT SATURDAY(1932); MADAME RACKETEER(1932); STRANGER IN TOWN(1932); WHISTLIN' DAN(1932); BITTER TEA OF GENERAL YEN, THE(1933); WE LIVE AGAIN(1934); STRANDED(1935); WHITE LIES(1935); STELLA DALLAS(1937); THREE COMRADES(1938); LUCKY NIGHT(1939); THEY SHALL HAVE MUSIC(1939); APE, THE(1940); HAUNTED HOUSE, THE(1940); LITTLE OLD NEW YORK(1940); TWO GIRLS ON BROADWAY(1940); CONFESSIONS OF BOSTON BLACKIE(1941); DESIGN FOR SCANDAL(1941); RICHEST MAN IN TOWN(1941); THREE GIRLS ABOUT TOWN(1941); TRIAL OF MARY DUGAN, THE(1941); WOLF MAN, THE(1941); BOSTON BLACKIE GOES HOLLYWOOD(1942); NAZI AGENT(1942); TISH(1942); WHAT'S BUZZIN' COUSIN?(1943); LOUISIANA HAYRIDE(1944); MRS. PARKINGTON(1944); SUNDOWN VALLEY(1944); TOGETHER AGAIN(1944); BOSTON BLACKIE BOOKED ON SUSPICION(1945); EVE KNEW HER APPLES(1945); KISS AND TELL(1945); HOODLUM SAINT, THE(1946); JOLSON STORY, THE(1946); LAWLESS EMPIRE(1946); LIKELY STORY, A(1947); TRAIL STREET(1947); LADY FROM SHANGHAI, THE(1948); AIR HOSTESS(1949); RECKLESS MOMENTS, THE(1949); STRATTON STORY, THE(1949); SUN COMES UP, THE(1949); TRAVELING SALESWOMAN(1950); GOLDEN GIRL(1951); SHE'S WORKING HER WAY THROUGH COLLEGE(1952); SNIPER, THE(1952)
Silents
TEMPTATION(1915); ROUGH AND READY(1918); DARK MIRROR, THE(1920); IDOL OF THE NORTH, THE(1921)
Misc. Silents
SHOES(1916); BLACKBIRDS(1920)

Jessie Mae Arnold
Silents
TENNESSEE'S PARDNER(1916)

Joan Arnold
HOLIDAY INN(1942); ROCK BABY, ROCK IT(1957)

JoAnn Arnold
TEN TALL MEN(1951); TWO TICKETS TO BROADWAY(1951); STOP, YOU'RE KILLING ME(1952); YOU FOR ME(1952); GREAT JESSE JAMES RAID, THE(1953); SCANDAL AT SCOURIE(1953); SON OF SINBAD(1955)

Joanne Arnold
SON OF PALEFACE(1952); MARRY ME AGAIN(1953)

John Arnold
WIND, THE(1928), ph; BROADWAY MELODY, THE(1929), ph; SILVER FLEET, THE(1945, Brit.); GREAT SINNER, THE(1949); PASSING STRANGER, THE(1954, Brit.), d, w; TIME WITHOUT PITY(1957, Brit.), p; HOT ROD HULLABALOO(1966); HARD KNOCKS(1980, Aus.)
Silents
ALADDIN'S OTHER LAMP(1917), ph; HIS FATHER'S SON(1917), ph; FALSE EVIDENCE(1919), ph; CHORUS GIRL'S ROMANCE, A(1920), ph; DANGEROUS TO MEN(1920), ph; HOME STUFF(1921), ph; LIFE'S DARN FUNNY(1921), ph; OFFSHORE PIRATE, THE(1921), ph; JUNE MADNESS(1922), ph; SEEING'S BELIEVING(1922), ph; CRINOLINE AND ROMANCE(1923), ph; FOG, THE(1923), ph; HER FATAL MILLIONS(1923), ph; IN SEARCH OF A THRILL(1923), ph; NOISE IN NEWBORO, A(1923), ph; SOCIAL CODE, THE(1923), ph; ALONG CAME RUTH(1924), ph; REVELATION(1924), ph; BIG PARADE, THE(1925), ph; BRIGHT LIGHTS(1925), ph; PROUD FLESH(1925), ph; AUCTION BLOCK, THE(1926), ph; LOVE'S BLINDNESS(1926), ph; MR. WU(1927), ph; SHOW PEOPLE(1928), ph

Larry Arnold
SEPTEMBER AFFAIR(1950); THREE COINS IN THE FOUNTAIN(1954)

Leo Arnold
TWO-FACED WOMAN(1941), md

Lester Arnold
THIS DAY AND AGE(1933)

Liselotte Arnold
SISTERS, OR THE BALANCE OF HAPPINESS(1982, Ger.)

Lucy Arnold
PAUL AND MICHELLE(1974, Fr./Brit.)

Madison Arnold
SATAN'S BED(1965); HAIL(1973); ESCAPE FROM ALCATRAZ(1979); DEADHEAD MILES(1982); HANKY-PANKY(1982)
1984
LONELY GUY, THE(1984)

Makolm Arnold
CONSTANT HUSBAND, THE(1955, Brit.), m

Mal Arnold
BLOOD FEAST(1963); SCUM OF THE EARTH(1963)

Malcolm Arnold
AFFAIRS OF ADELAIDE(1949, U. S./Brit), m; EYE WITNESS(1950, Brit.), m; BREAKING THE SOUND BARRIER(1952), m; CURTAIN UP(1952, Brit.), m; IT STARTED IN PARADISE(1952, Brit.), m; STOLEN FACE(1952, Brit.), m; ALBERT, R.N.(1953, Brit.), m; CAPTAIN'S PARADISE, THE(1953, Brit.), m; MURDER ON MONDAY(1953, Brit.), m; RINGER, THE(1953, Brit.), m; BEAUTIFUL STRANGER(1954, Brit.), m; BELLES OF ST. TRINIAN'S, THE(1954, Brit.), m; DEVIL ON HORSEBACK(1954, Brit.), m; HOBSON'S CHOICE(1954, Brit.), m; HOLLY AND THE IVY, THE(1954, Brit.), m; SLEEPING TIGER, THE(1954, Brit.), m; YOU KNOW WHAT SAILORS ARE(1954, Brit.), m; DEEP BLUE SEA, THE(1955, Brit.), m; I AM A CAMERA(1955, Brit.), m; NIGHT MY NUMBER CAME UP, THE(1955, Brit.), m; PRIZE OF GOLD, A(1955), m; SEA SHALL NOT HAVE THEM, THE(1955, Brit.), m; WOMAN FOR JOE, THE(1955, Brit.), m; HELL IN KOREA(1956, Brit.), m; MAN OF AFRICA(1956, Brit.), m; PORT AFRIQUE(1956, Brit.), m; TIGER IN THE SMOKE(1956, Brit.), m; TRAPEZE(1956), m; BRIDGE ON THE RIVER KWAI, THE(1957), m; ISLAND IN THE SUN(1957), m; PORTRAIT IN SMOKE(1957, Brit.), m; VALUE FOR MONEY(1957, Brit.), m; BLUE MURDER AT ST. TRINIAN'S(1958, Brit.), m; DUNKIRK(1958, Brit.), m; INN OF THE SIXTH HAPPINESS, THE(1958), m, md; KEY, THE(1958, Brit.), m, md; ROOTS OF HEAVEN, THE(1958), m; BOY AND THE BRIDGE, THE(1959, Brit.), m; SUDDENLY, LAST SUMMER(1959, Brit.), m; ANGRY SILENCE, THE(1960, Brit.), m; CHANCE MEETING(1960, Brit.), md; TUNES OF GLORY(1960, Brit.), m; NO LOVE FOR JOHNNIE(1961), m, md; WHISTLE DOWN THE WIND(1961, Brit.), m&md; LION, THE(1962, Brit.), m, md; LISA(1962, Brit.), m, md; NINE HOURS TO RAMA(1963, U.S./Brit.), m, md; CHALK GARDEN, THE(1964, Brit.), m; TAMAHINE(1964, Brit.), m; THIN RED LINE, THE(1964), m, md; HEROES OF TELEMARK, THE(1965, Brit.), m; OPERATION SNAFU(1965, Brit.), m, md; GREAT ST. TRINIAN'S TRAIN ROBBERY, THE(1966, Brit.), m; GYPSY GIRL(1966, Brit.), m, md; AFRICA–TEXAS STYLE!(1967 U.S./Brit.), m; BATTLE OF BRITAIN, THE(1969, Brit.), m; DAVID COPPERFIELD(1970, Brit.), m; RECKONING, THE(1971, Brit.), m, md

Malcom Arnold
FOUR SIDED TRIANGLE(1953, Brit.), m; PURE HELL OF ST. TRINIAN'S, THE(1961, Brit.), m, md

Marcella Arnold
Misc. Silents
UNGUARDED GIRLS(1929)

Marcelle Arnold
MR. PEEK-A-BOO(1951, Fr.); BRIDE IS MUCH TOO BEAUTIFUL, THE(1958, Fr.); MONKEY IN WINTER, A(1962, Fr.); SEVEN CAPITAL SINS(1962, Fr./Ital.); THINGS OF LIFE, THE(1970, Fr./Ital./Switz.)

Maria Arnold
FANTASM(1976, Aus.)

Marie Arnold
Misc. Talkies
TOY BOX, THE(1971)

Marilee Arnold
BABES IN TOYLAND(1961)

Mario Arnold
Misc. Talkies
AMAZING LOVE SECRET(1975)

Marion Arnold
LURE OF THE WASTELAND(1939)

Mark Hopson Arnold
ENDLESS LOVE(1981)

Melanie Arnold
BABES IN TOYLAND(1961)

Melbourne Arnold
PSYCHO II(1983), spec eff

Melvyn Arnold
CRAZYLEGS, ALL AMERICAN(1953)

Michael Arnold
MAYERLING(1968, Brit./Fr.), w

Mike Arnold
LADY'S FROM KENTUCKY, THE(1939)

Monroe Arnold
MOVING FINGER, THE(1963); PIE IN THE SKY(1964); FITZWILLY(1967); HOW TO SAVE A MARRIAGE–AND RUIN YOUR LIFE(1968); ALICE'S RESTAURANT(1969); GOODBYE COLUMBUS(1969)

N. Arnold
PLAYTHING, THE(1929, Brit.), prod d

Nancy Arnold
LOVE HUNGER(1965, Arg.)
1984
SAVAGE STREETS(1984), set d; SUBURBIA(1984), set d

Newt Arnold
Misc. Talkies
BLOOD THIRST(1965 Phil./U.S.), d

Newton Arnold
HANDS OF A STRANGER(1962), p, d&w; I WANNA HOLD YOUR HAND(1978)

Newton D. Arnold
SKULLDUGGERY(1970); D.C. CAB(1983)

Norman Arnold
BLACKMAIL(1929, Brit.), set d; JUNO AND THE PAYCOCK(1930, Brit.), art d; WHITE FACE(1933, Brit.), art d; CANDLELIGHT IN ALGERIA(1944, Brit.), art d; MR. EMMANUEL(1945, Brit.), art d; NOTORIOUS GENTLEMAN(1945, Brit.), art d; THEY MET IN THE DARK(1945, Brit.), art d; MEET ME AT DAWN(1947, Brit.), art d; WEE GEORDIE(1956, Brit.), art d; SON OF ROBIN HOOD(1959, Brit.), art d; TIME LOCK(1959, Brit.), art d; TELL-TALE HEART, THE(1962, Brit.), art d; RING OF SPIES(1964, Brit.), art d; STORK TALK(1964, Brit.), art d

Norman J. Arnold
HUE AND CRY(1950, Brit.), art d

Phil Arnold
DR. BROADWAY(1942); GANGSTER, THE(1947); HOLLYWOOD BARN DANCE(1947); KILLER AT LARGE(1947); MAIN STREET KID, THE(1947); DEADLINE(1948); SMART WOMAN(1948); I CHEATED THE LAW(1949); ONCE A THIEF(1950); G.I. JANE(1951); KENTUCKY JUBILEE(1951); YES SIR, MR. BONES(1951); STOP, YOU'RE KILLING ME(1952); BIG HEAT, THE(1953); MONEY FROM HOME(1953); BIG CHASE, THE(1954); STAR IS BORN, A(1954); COURT-MARTIAL OF BILLY MITCHELL, THE(1955); NAVY WIFE(1956); JET PILOT(1957); MY GUN IS QUICK(1957); STUDS LONIGAN(1960); ERRAND BOY, THE(1961);

THREE STOOGES GO AROUND THE WORLD IN A DAZE, THE(1963); UNDER THE YUM-YUM TREE(1963); CANDIDATE, THE(1964); PATSY, THE(1964); ROBIN AND THE SEVEN HOODS(1964); THREE NUTS IN SEARCH OF A BOLT(1964); WHAT A WAY TO GO(1964); ZEBRA IN THE KITCHEN(1965); HOLD ON(1966); COOL ONES THE(1967); GOOD TIMES(1967); SKIDOO(1968)

Phillip Arnold
BUFFALO BILL RIDES AGAIN(1947)

Rick Arnold
BLACK WHIP, THE(1956)

Robert Arnold
LAST PICTURE SHOW, THE(1971)

Sean Arnold
FFOLKES(1980, Brit.); REMEMBRANCE(1982, Brit.)

Seth Arnold
LOST BOUNDARIES(1949); WHISTLE AT EATON FALLS(1951)

Sidney Arnold
LOVE'S OLD SWEET SONG(1933, Brit.); GIVE ME THE STARS(1944, Brit.)

Steve Arnold
1984
TAIL OF THE TIGER(1984, Aus.), m

Susan Arnold
SATAN'S SADISTS(1969), makeup; BLACK EYE(1974); WILD PARTY, THE(1975)

Sydney Arnold
ONE MORE TIME(1970, Brit.)
1984
TOP SECRET!(1984)

Tandy Arnold
PAPER MOON(1973)

Thomas Charles Arnold
HERE'S GEORGE(1932, Brit.), p

Tom Arnold
STRAUSS' GREAT WALTZ(1934, Brit.), p; IT'S A GRAND OLD WORLD(1937, Brit.), p, w; LEAVE IT TO ME(1937, Brit.), p; HAPPIDROME(1943, Brit.), p, w

Victor Arnold
INCIDENT, THE(1967); SHAFT(1971); SEVEN UPS, THE(1973); ...AND JUSTICE FOR ALL(1979); WOLFEN(1981); RETURNING, THE(1983)

Walter Arnold
LILITH(1964); GAMERA THE INVINCIBLE(1966, Jap.)

Ward Arnold
PHANTOM SUBMARINE, THE(1941)

Wilfred Arnold
TALK OF THE DEVIL(1937, Brit.), art d; GHOSTS OF BERKELEY SQUARE(1947, Brit.), art d; GREEN FINGERS(1947), art d; HER PANELLED DOOR(1951, Brit.), set d; SCOTLAND YARD INSPECTOR(1952, Brit.), art d; FINGER OF GUILT(1956, Brit.), art d; MURDER ON APPROVAL(1956, Brit.), art d; WAY OUT, THE(1956, Brit.), art d; SCOTLAND YARD DRAGNET(1957, Brit.), art d; HIDDEN HOMICIDE(1959, Brit.), art d; HORRORS OF THE BLACK MUSEUM(1959, U.S./Brit.), art d; ELECTRONIC MONSTER. THE(1960, Brit.), art d; PASSWORD IS COURAGE, THE(1962, Brit.), art d; SHADOW OF FEAR(1963, Brit.), art d; MARRIAGE OF CONVENIENCE(1970, Brit.), art d

Wilfred C. Arnold
BLACKMAIL(1929, Brit.), set d

William Arnold
GUN SMOKE(1931); RICH MAN'S FOLLY(1931); VICE SQUAD, THE(1931); CROWD ROARS, THE(1932); IN LOVE WITH LIFE(1934); KID MILLIONS(1934); MURDER AT THE VANITIES(1934); THIRTY-DAY PRINCESS(1934); MAGNIFICENT OBSESSION(1935); RENDEZVOUS AT MIDNIGHT(1935); SWEET ADELINE(1935); LOVE BEFORE BREAKFAST(1936); YOURS FOR THE ASKING(1936); SWING HIGH, SWING LOW(1937); OVERLAND EXPRESS, THE(1938); YOU CAN'T TAKE IT WITH YOU(1938); MR. SMITH GOES TO WASHINGTON(1939); SORCERESS(1983)

William R. [Billy] Arnold
SPLENDOR(1935)

Wolf Arnold
CLUE OF THE TWISTED CANDLE(1968, Brit.), art d

Arnold the Horse
ONE GOOD TURN(1936, Brit.)

John Arnoldy
SUPER VAN(1977), w; YOUNG CYCLE GIRLS, THE(1979), w

Mordecai Arnon
SALLAH(1965, Israel); FLYING MATCHMAKER, THE(1970, Israel)

Ricardo Arnonovitch
SWEET HUNTERS(1969, Panama), ph

Rex Arnot
Misc. Silents
KINGDOM OF TWILIGHT, THE(1929, Brit.)

Mark Arnott
RETURN OF THE SECAUCUS SEVEN(1980); TEX(1982)
1984
BEST DEFENSE(1984)

Noel Arnott
Silents
GAY CORINTHIAN, THE(1924)

Francoise Arnoul
NOUS IRONS A PARIS(1949, Fr.); DANGER IS A WOMAN(1952, Fr.); LOVERS OF TOLEDO, THE(1954, Fr./Span./Ital.); SECRETS D'ALCOVE(1954, Fr./Ital.); FRENCH CANCAN(1956, Fr.); IF PARIS WERE TOLD TO US(1956, Fr.); LOVER'S NET(1957, Fr.); CAT, THE(1959, Fr.); FORBIDDEN FRUIT(1959, Fr.); DEVIL AND THE TEN COMMANDMENTS, THE(1962, Fr.); TALES OF PARIS(1962, Fr./Ital.); TESTAMENT OF ORPHEUS, THE(1962, Fr.); SEASON FOR LOVE, THE(1963, Fr.); SLEEPING CAR MURDER THE(1966, Fr.); LE PETIT THEATRE DE JEAN RENOIR(1974, Fr.)

A. Arnoux
SHANGHAI DRAMA, THE(1945, Fr.), w

Alexandre Arnoux
DON QUIXOTE(1935, Fr.), w; ULTIMATUM(1940, Fr.), w

Jean-Marie Arnoux
OPHELIA(1964, Fr.); LA FEMME INFIDELE(1969, Fr./Ital.)

Robert Arnoux
LILIOM(1935, Fr.); DEADLIER THAN THE MALE(1957, Fr.); FOUR BAGS FULL(1957, Fr./Ital.); GIRL IN THE BIKINI, THE(1958, Fr.); BERNADETTE OF LOURDES(1962, Fr.)

Alba Arnova
FUGITIVE LADY(1951); MIRACLE IN MILAN(1951, Ital.); TIMES GONE BY(1953, Ital.); CENTO ANNI D'AMORE(1954, Ital.); LOVES OF THREE QUEENS, THE(1954, Ital./Fr.)

Ricardo Arnovich
MURMUR OF THE HEART(1971, Fr./Ital./Ger.), ph

David Arnsen
CHINA SYNDROME, THE(1979)

Bobbe Arnst
WINE, WOMEN, AND SONG(1934)

Bobby Arnst
TORCH SINGER(1933)

Georges Arnstam
STOP TRAIN 349(1964, Fr./Ital./Ger.), ed

Hansi Arnstead
INTERMEZZO(1937, Ger.)

Stefan Arnstein
TOO SOON TO LOVE(1960), ed; ANY WEDNESDAY(1966), ed; ARRANGEMENT, THE(1969), ed

Jim Arnsten
PAPERBACK HERO(1973, Can.)

Stefan Arnsten
AFFAIR IN HAVANA(1957), ed; HIT AND RUN(1957), ed; TERROR IN A TEXAS TOWN(1958), ed; BORN TO BE LOVED(1959), ed; THIRD DAY, THE(1965), ed; HARPER(1966), ed; WHERE IT'S AT(1969), ed; MRS. POLLIFAX-SPY(1971), ed; VANISHING POINT(1971), ed; KID BLUE(1973), ed

Charles Arnt
WITHOUT RESERVATIONS(1946); ROMAN SCANDALS(1933); HERE IS MY HEART(1934); LADIES SHOULD LISTEN(1934); AND SO THEY WERE MARRIED(1936); AND SUDDEN DEATH(1936); BUNKER BEAN(1936); WITNESS CHAIR, THE(1936); DR. KILDARE'S CRISIS(1940); I LOVE YOU AGAIN(1940); PLAY GIRL(1940); SHOP AROUND THE CORNER, THE(1940); BALL OF FIRE(1941); BLOSSOMS IN THE DUST(1941); DRESSED TO KILL(1941); FOUR JACKS AND A JILL(1941); GREAT GUNS(1941); MARRY THE BOSS' DAUGHTER(1941); MR. DISTRICT ATTORNEY(1941); PARIS CALLING(1941); POT O' GOLD(1941); WE GO FAST(1941); FALCON'S BROTHER, THE(1942); GREAT GILDERSLEEVE, THE(1942); LADY HAS PLANS, THE(1942); MY GAL SAL(1942); PITTSBURGH(1942); REUNION IN FRANCE(1942); TAKE A LETTER, DARLING(1942); THAT OTHER WOMAN(1942); THIS GUN FOR HIRE(1942); TWIN BEDS(1942); YOUNG AMERICA(1942); GANGWAY FOR TOMORROW(1943); GILDERSLEEVE'S BAD DAY(1943); HENRY ALDRICH SWINGS IT(1943); IN OLD OKLAHOMA(1943); DANGEROUS PASSAGE(1944); DOUBLE EXPOSURE(1944); GAMBLER'S CHOICE(1944); IMPATIENT YEARS, THE(1944); MY PAL, WOLF(1944); ONCE UPON A TIME(1944); THREE LITTLE SISTERS(1944); TOGETHER AGAIN(1944); UP IN ARMS(1944); CHRISTMAS IN CONNECTICUT(1945); CRIME DOCTOR'S COURAGE, THE(1945); DANGEROUS INTRUDER(1945); GIRL OF THE LIMBERLOST, THE(1945); PARDON MY PAST(1945); SHE WOULDN'T SAY YES(1945); STRANGE ILLUSION(1945); SUDAN(1945); WITHOUT LOVE(1945); BEHIND GREEN LIGHTS(1946); BLONDIE'S LUCKY DAY(1946); CINDERELLA JONES(1946); HOODLUM SAINT, THE(1946); JUST BEFORE DAWN(1946); THAT BRENNAN GIRL(1946); BIG TOWN(1947); BIG TOWN AFTER DARK(1947); CALENDAR GIRL(1947); FALL GUY(1947); HIGH WALL, THE(1947); MY FAVORITE BRUNETTE(1947); SADDLE PALS(1947); THAT WAY WITH WOMEN(1947); HOLLOW TRIUMPH(1948); MICHAEL O'HALLORAN(1948); SITTING PRETTY(1948); THAT WONDERFUL URGE(1948); BOSTON BLACKIE'S CHINESE VENTURE(1949); BOY WITH THE GREEN HAIR, THE(1949); BRIDE FOR SALE(1949); MASKED RAIDERS(1949); HE'S A COCKEYED WONDER(1950); WABASH AVENUE(1950); MAN WHO CHEATED HIMSELF, THE(1951); GREAT SIOUX UPRISING, THE(1953); VEILS OF BAGDAD, THE(1953); MIRACLE OF THE HILLS, THE(1959); WILD IN THE COUNTRY(1961); SWEET BIRD OF YOUTH(1962)

Charles E. Arnt
READY FOR LOVE(1934); SHE MARRIED HER BOSS(1935); STOLEN HARMONY(1935); TWO FOR TONIGHT(1935); RHYTHM ON THE RANGE(1936); MISS SUSIE SLAGLE'S(1945); FLOOD TIDE(1958)

Charlie Arnt
COLLEGE HOLIDAY(1936); ANGEL'S HOLIDAY(1937); IT HAPPENED IN HOLLYWOOD(1937); MOUNTAIN MUSIC(1937); SWING HIGH, SWING LOW(1937); REMEMBER THE NIGHT(1940)

David Arntzen
PHANTASM(1979)

Aroldino the Comedian
WHITE SHEIK, THE(1956, Ital.)

Adrian Aron
MOMMIE DEAREST(1981)
1984
HOTEL NEW HAMPSHIRE, THE(1984)

Bill Aron
POPDOWN(1968, Brit.)

Jean Aron
DOLL, THE(1962, Fr.); BORSALINO(1970, Fr.)

Arona
NUDE ODYSSEY(1962, Fr./Ital.)

Scott Aronesty
SANTA CLAUS CONQUERS THE MARTIANS(1964)

Michael Aronin
CRUISING(1980); TWO OF A KIND(1983)

Dimitri Aronis
ASSAULT ON AGATHON(1976, Brit./Gr.); IPHIGENIA(1977, Gr.)

Maria Aronoff
Misc. Talkies
AMOROUS ADVENTURES OF DON QUIXOTE AND SANCHO PANZA, THE(1976)

Ricardo Aronovich
WILD PACK, THE(1972), ph; FRENCH CONSPIRACY, THE(1973, Fr.), ph; LUMIERE(1976, Fr.), ph; PROVIDENCE(1977, Fr.), ph; OUTSIDER, THE(1980), ph; YOU BETTER WATCH OUT(1980), ph; CHANEL SOLITAIRE(1981), ph; MISSING(1982), ph; HANNAH K.(1983, Fr.), ph
1984
LE BAL(1984, Fr./Ital./Algeria), ph

Ricardo Aronovitch
MAIN THING IS TO LOVE, THE(1975, Ital./Fr.), ph

Aronson
Silents
STORM OVER ASIA(1929, USSR), set d

Judie Aronson
1984
FRIDAY THE 13TH–THE FINAL CHAPTER(1984)

Anita Aros
THREE DARING DAUGHTERS(1948)

Maria Sanchez Arosa
HUNT, THE(1967, Span.)

Emita Arosemena "Miss Panama"
YANKEE PASHA(1954)

Per-Axel Arosenius
TOPAZ(1969, Brit.)

Olga Aroseva
UNCOMMON THIEF, AN(1967, USSR)

Mario Arosio
DOWN THE ANCIENT STAIRCASE(1975, Ital.), w

Gabriel Arout
GINA(1961, Fr./Mex.), w; RIFF RAFF GIRLS(1962, Fr./Ital.), w; UNKNOWN MAN OF SHANDIGOR, THE(1967, Switz.), p, w

E. Arozamena
BRAVE BULLS, THE(1951)

Alfred Arp
FANNY HILL: MEMOIRS OF A WOMAN OF PLEASURE zero(1965), ed

Clarence Arper
Misc. Silents
HEART OF JUANITA(1919)

Giovanni Arpino
SCENT OF A WOMAN(1976, Ital.), w

Tony Arpino
MEET SEXTON BLAKE(1944, Brit.); ECHO MURDERS, THE(1945, Brit.); SCHOOL FOR SECRETS(1946, Brit.); LONG JOHN SILVER(1954, Aus.); GIRL HUNTERS, THE(1963, Brit.); EVIL OF FRANKENSTEIN, THE(1964, Brit.); SECRET DOOR, THE(1964); LOLA(1971, Brit./Ital.)

Cliff Arquette
COMIN' ROUND THE MOUNTAIN(1940); DRAGNET(1954); SATURDAY NIGHT IN APPLE VALLEY(1965); DON'T WORRY, WE'LL THINK OF A TITLE(1966)

Lewis Arquette
CHINA SYNDROME, THE(1979); LOOSE SHOES(1980); OFF THE WALL(1983)

Rosanna Arquette
MORE AMERICAN GRAFFITI(1979); GORP(1980); S.O.B.(1981); BABY, IT'S YOU(1983); OFF THE WALL(1983)

Alexandre Arquillere
Misc. Silents
LE BLED(1929, Fr.)

Fernando Arrabal
ODYSSEY OF THE PACIFIC(1983, Can./Fr.), d, w

Irene Arranga
I WANNA HOLD YOUR HAND(1978)

Rod Arrants
FOOLS(1970)
1984
VAMPING(1984)
Misc. Talkies
A(1976, U.S./Korea)

Harry Arras
OUR RELATIONS(1936)
Silents
GOLD RUSH, THE(1925)
Misc. Silents
BLIND CIRCUMSTANCES(1922)

Antonio Arriaga
TREASURE OF THE SIERRA MADRE, THE(1948), tech adv

Dolly Arriaga
CAPTAIN FROM CASTILE(1947); IT'S A BIG COUNTRY(1951)

Rosita Arriaga
SANTA(1932, Mex.)

Simon Arriaga
GUNFIGHTERS OF CASA GRANDE(1965, U.S./Span.); HELLBENDERS, THE(1967, U.S./Ital./Span.); NAVAJO JOE(1967, Ital./Span.); MERCENARY, THE(1970, Ital./Span.)

Jorge Arriagada
1984
AVE MARIA(1984, Fr.), m; THREE CROWNS OF THE SAILOR(1984, Fr.), m

Fernando Arribas
OPEN SEASON(1974, U.S./Span.), ph; TEN LITTLE INDIANS(1975, Ital./Fr./Span./Ger.), ph; COMIN' AT YA!(1981), ph; CANNIBALS IN THE STREETS(1982, Ital./Span.), ph; SCARAB(1982, U.S./Span.), ph

Julien Arrichi
MOON IN THE GUTTER, THE(1983, Fr./Ital.)

Rose Arrick
NEW LEAF, A(1971); MIKEY AND NICKY(1976); THOSE LIPS, THOSE EYES(1980)
1984
OVER THE BROOKLYN BRIDGE(1984)

Charles Arrico
DONDI(1961), cos; FORTUNE COOKIE, THE(1966), cos

Chuck Arrico
LONELYHEARTS(1958), cos

Luciana Arrighi
WOMEN IN LOVE(1969, Brit.), set d; SUNDAY BLOODY SUNDAY(1971, Brit.), prod d; MY BRILLIANT CAREER(1980, Aus.), prod d, cos; PRIVATES ON PARADE(1982), prod d, cos; STARSTRUCK(1982, Aus.), cos; RETURN OF THE SOLDIER, THE(1983, Brit.), prod d
1984
MRS. SOFFEL(1984), prod d, cos; PLOUGHMAN'S LUNCH, THE(1984, Brit.), prod d, cos; PRIVATES ON PARADE(1984, Brit.), prod d, cos

Nike Arrighi
DEVIL'S BRIDE, THE(1968, Brit.); DON'T RAISE THE BRIDGE, LOWER THE RIVER(1968, Brit.); ONE PLUS ONE(1969, Brit.); COUNTESS DRACULA(1972, Brit.); DAY FOR NIGHT(1973, Fr.)

Fran Arrigo
BLACKMAIL(1947), art d; DRIFTWOOD(1947), art d; MARSHAL OF CRIPPLE CREEK, THE(1947), art d; RUSTLERS OF DEVIL'S CANYON(1947), art d; SPRINGTIME IN THE SIERRAS(1947), art d; THAT'S MY GAL(1947), art d; THAT'S MY MAN(1947), art d; DENVER KID, THE(1948), art d; INSIDE STORY, THE(1948), art d; LIGHTNIN' IN THE FOREST(1948), art d; MADONNA OF THE DESERT(1948), art d; MARSHAL OF AMARILLO(1948), art d; OKLAHOMA BADLANDS(1948), art d; PLUNDERERS, THE(1948), art d; RENEGADES OF SONORA(1948), art d; SECRET SERVICE INVESTIGATOR(1948), art d; SON OF GOD'S COUNTRY(1948), art d; DUKE OF CHICAGO(1949), art d; LAST BANDIT, THE(1949), art d; OUTCASTS OF THE TRAIL(1949), art d; POST OFFICE INVESTIGATOR(1949), art d; RED MENACE, THE(1949), art d; SHERIFF OF WICHITA(1949), art d; WYOMING BANDIT, THE(1949), art d; FRISCO TORNADO(1950), art d; GUNMEN OF ABILENE(1950), art d; HARBOR OF MISSING MEN(1950), art d; MISSOURIANS, THE(1950), art d; PRISONERS IN PETTICOATS(1950), art d; REDWOOD FOREST TRAIL(1950), art d; ROCK ISLAND TRAIL(1950), art d; RUSTLERS ON HORSEBACK(1950), art d; SAVAGE HORDE, THE(1950), art d; SHOWDOWN, THE(1950), art d; TARNISHED(1950), art d; TRAIL OF ROBIN HOOD(1950), art d; TRIGGER, JR.(1950), art d; UNDER MEXICALI STARS(1950), art d; DESERT OF LOST MEN(1951), art d; OH! SUSANNA(1951), art d; SEA HORNET, THE(1951), art d; STREET BANDITS(1951), art d; HOODLUM EMPIRE(1952), art d; LADY POSSESSED(1952), art d; LAST MUSKETEER, THE(1952), art d; MONTANA BELLE(1952), art d; OKLAHOMA ANNIE(1952), art d; RIDE THE MAN DOWN(1952), art d; WILD HORSE AMBUSH(1952), art d; WOMAN OF THE NORTH COUNTRY(1952), art d; EL PASO STAMPEDE(1953), art d; FAIR WIND TO JAVA(1953), art d; IRON MOUNTAIN TRAIL(1953), art d; OLD OVERLAND TRAIL(1953), art d; PERILOUS JOURNEY, A(1953), art d; SAN ANTONE(1953), art d; SAVAGE FRONTIER(1953), art d; SEA OF LOST SHIPS(1953), art d; JUBILEE TRAIL(1954), art d; UNTAMED HEIRESS(1954), art d; FIGHTING CHANCE, THE(1955), art d; HELL'S OUTPOST(1955), art d; LAST COMMAND, THE(1955), art d; SANTA FE PASSAGE(1955), art d; TIMBERJACK(1955), art d; ACCUSED OF MURDER(1956), art d; LISBON(1956), art d; STRANGE ADVENTURE, A(1956), art d; STRANGER AT MY DOOR(1956), art d; DUEL AT APACHE WELLS(1957), art d; HELL'S CROSSROADS(1957), art d; SPOILERS OF THE FOREST(1957), art d; KILLERS, THE(1964), art d; NIGHT WALKER, THE(1964), art d; LOVE AND KISSES(1965), art d; MIRAGE(1965), art d; TORN CURTAIN(1966), art d; ROUGH NIGHT IN JERICHO(1967), art d; HELLFIGHTERS(1968), art d; SCALPHUNTERS, THE(1968), art d; HOUSE OF CARDS(1969), art d; SOLDIER BLUE(1970), art d; FLIGHT OF THE DOVES(1971), art d

Frank J. Arrigo
TOPEKA TERROR, THE(1945), art d

Helene Arrindell
NOTHING BUT A MAN(1964)

The Arriolas
TRAPEZE(1956)

NIke Arriphi
WOMEN IN LOVE(1969, Brit.)

Carlos Arriya
MAGNIFICENT MATADOR, THE(1955), tech adv

Marcelo Arroita
DIABOLICAL DR. Z, THE(1966 Span./Fr.)

Ann Arrow
BLOODTHIRSTY BUTCHERS(1970)

Jack Arrow
TREASURE ISLAND(1950, Brit.)

Joe Arrowsmith
WILD PARTY, THE(1975); JESSIE'S GIRLS(1976)

Alejandro Arroyo
1984
TOY SOLDIERS(1984)

Luis Arroyo
YOUNG SAVAGES, THE(1961); TOYS ARE NOT FOR CHILDREN(1972)

J.H. Arrufat
SIX PACK ANNIE(1975), ed

Carlos Arruza
ALAMO, THE(1960)

Carmen Arselle
Silents
PRIDE OF PALOMAR, THE(1922)
Misc. Silents
FOUR HEARTS(1922)

Arsenal Football Club, The
LUCKY NUMBER, THE(1933, Brit.); SMALL TOWN STORY(1953, Brit.)

Darren Arsenault
1984
BAY BOY(1984, Can.)

Kitty Arseni
ELECTRA(1962, Gr.)

Vladimir Arseniev
DERSU UZALA(1976, Jap./USSR), w

N.N. Arski
ALEXANDER NEVSKY(1939)

Sylvia Arslan
MOON OVER HER SHOULDER(1941); GREAT IMPERSONATION, THE(1942); IN OUR TIME(1944); MR. SKEFFINGTON(1944); GREAT STAGECOACH ROBBERY(1945); SHERIFF OF CIMARRON(1945); HUMORESQUE(1946)

Petre Arsovski
1984
MEMED MY HAWK(1984, Brit.)

Stefan Arsten
FEDORA(1978, Ger./Fr.), ed

Dennis Art
ANGELS HARD AS THEY COME(1971)

Art Baxter and His Rockin' Sinners
ROCK YOU SINNERS(1957, Brit.)

Art Davis and His Rhythm Riders
TEXAS MARSHAL, THE(1941)

Art Ensemble of Chicago
SOPHIE'S WAYS(1970, Fr.), m

Art Wilcox and his Arizona Rangers
ARIZONA FRONTIER(1940)

Art Wilcox and the Arizona Rangers
RAINBOW OVER THE RANGE(1940)

Duke Art, Jr.
BELLBOY, THE(1960)

Carmelo Artale
LEOPARD, THE(1963, Ital.)

Wong Artarne
CALCUTTA(1947); I WAS AN AMERICAN SPY(1951); KOREA PATROL(1951); MR. WALKIE TALKIE(1952); CHINA VENTURE(1953); HELL AND HIGH WATER(1954)

Antonin Artaud
THREEPENNY OPERA, THE(1931, Ger./U.S.); LILIOM(1935, Fr.)
Silents
NAPOLEON(1927, Fr.)
Misc. Silents
LE JUIF ERRANT(1926, Fr.)

Antonion Artaud
Misc. Silents
VERDUN, VISIONS D'HISTOIRE(1929, Fr.)

E. Artaud
Misc. Silents
DANCER AND THE KING, THE(1914), d

Artault
LUCREZIA BORGIA(1937, Fr.)

Angel Arteaga
PLACE CALLED GLORY, A(1966, Span./Ger.), m; FRANKENSTEIN'S BLOODY TERROR(1968, Span.), m; YOUNG REBEL, THE(1969, Fr./Ital./Span.), m

Angela Arteaga
WHAT CHANGED CHARLEY FARTHING?(1976, Brit.), m

Mario Arteaga
YOUNG LAND, THE(1959); MAN WHO SHOT LIBERTY VALANCE, THE(1962); BITE THE BULLET(1975)

Sophia Artega
Silents
SADIE THOMPSON(1928)

Art Artego
Silents
VALLEY OF BRAVERY, THE(1926)

S. Artemowsky
COSSACKS IN EXILE(1939, Ukrainian), w

Jackie Artemus
GRAND ESCAPADE, THE(1946, Brit.); NOTHING VENTURE(1948, Brit.)

Peter Artemus
GRAND ESCAPADE, THE(1946, Brit.); NOTHING VENTURE(1948, Brit.)

Philip Artemus
GRAND ESCAPADE, THE(1946, Brit.); NOTHING VENTURE(1948, Brit.)

Eduard Artemyer
SOLARIS(1972, USSR), m

Carole Arterbery
CLASS(1983)

Janet Arters
GREAT GATSBY, THE(1974)

Louise Arters
GREAT GATSBY, THE(1974)

Vittorio Artesi
SODOM AND GOMORRAH(1962, U.S./Fr./Ital.)

Alfred Arthur
MY LUCKY STAR(1933, Brit.)

Art Arthur
CHARLIE CHAN ON BROADWAY(1937), w; LOVE AND HISSES(1937), w; KENTUCKY MOONSHINE(1938), w; THANKS FOR EVERYTHING(1938), w; DAY-TIME WIFE(1939), w; EVERYTHING HAPPENS AT NIGHT(1939), w; SAILORS ON LEAVE(1941), w; SUN VALLEY SERENADE(1941), w; TIGHT SHOES(1941), w; DR. BROADWAY(1942), w; LADY BODYGUARD(1942), w; PRIORITIES ON PARADE(1942), w; SLEEPYTIME GAL(1942), w; TRUE TO THE ARMY(1942), w; RIDING HIGH(1943), w; SALUTE FOR THREE(1943), w; LOVE, HONOR AND GOODBYE(1945), w; FABULOUS DORSEYS, THE(1947), w; HEAVEN ONLY KNOWS(1947), w; NORTHWEST STAMPEDE(1948), w; SONG OF INDIA(1949), w; BATTLE TAXI(1955), p, w; FLIPPER'S NEW ADVENTURE(1964), w; RHINO(1964), w; CLARENCE, THE CROSS-EYED LION(1965), w; ZEBRA IN THE KITCHEN(1965), w; AROUND THE WORLD UNDER THE SEA(1966), w; BIRDS DO IT(1966), w; DARING GAME(1968), w; HELLO DOWN THERE(1969), w

Bea Arthur
LOVERS AND OTHER STRANGERS(1970); HISTORY OF THE WORLD, PART 1(1981)

Beatrice Arthur
MAME(1974)

Bill Arthur
GUY NAMED JOE, A(1943)

Bob Arthur
BIG CARNIVAL, THE(1951); SYSTEM, THE(1953); TRUE CONFESSIONS(1981)

Carol Arthur
MAKING IT(1971); OUR TIME(1974); SUNSHINE BOYS, THE(1975); SILENT MOVIE(1976); WORLD'S GREATEST LOVER, THE(1977)

Charles Arthur
SHEILA LEVINE IS DEAD AND LIVING IN NEW YORK(1975)
Misc. Silents
WORMWOOD(1915)

Charlotte Arthur
RESCUE SQUAD(1935), w

Colin Arthur
WHO?(1975, Brit./Ger.), makeup; SINBAD AND THE EYE OF THE TIGER(1977, U.S./Brit.), makeup

Daniel V. Arthur
Misc. Silents
GREAT DIAMOND ROBBERY, THE(1914), d
Daphne Arthur
LOOK BEFORE YOU LOVE(1948, Brit.); IF THIS BE SIN(1950, Brit.)
Donald Arthur
MONTENEGRO(1981, Brit./Swed.), w
Dorothy Arthur
Silents
MANON LESCAUT(1914)
Misc. Silents
GREAT DIAMOND ROBBERY, THE(1914)
Doug Arthur
DISC JOCKEY(1951)
Edward Arthur
MOONLIGHTING(1982, Brit.)
George Arthur
INNOCENTS OF PARIS(1929), ed; COCOANUT GROVE(1938), p; GRACIE ALLEN MURDER CASE(1939), p; OUR LEADING CITIZEN(1939), p; I WANT A DIVORCE(1940), p; MAD DOCTOR, THE(1941), p; POWERS GIRL, THE(1942), ed; JOHNNY COME LATELY(1943), ed; FABULOUS DORSEYS, THE(1947), ed; INTRIGUE(1947), ed; MAN-EATER OF KUMAON(1948), ed; OUTPOST IN MOROCCO(1949), ed
George K. Arthur
LAST OF MRS. CHEYNEY, THE(1929); CHASING RAINBOWS(1930); BLIND ADVENTURE(1933); LOOKING FORWARD(1933); OLIVER TWIST(1933); RIP TIDE(1934); STAND UP AND CHEER(1934 80m FOX bw); VANESSA, HER LOVE STORY(1935)
Misc. Talkies
BROTHERLY LOVE(1928)
Silents
KIPPS(1921, Brit.); FLAMES OF PASSION(1922, Brit.); MADNESS OF YOUTH(1923); PADDY, THE NEXT BEST THING(1923, Brit.); LADY OF THE NIGHT(1925); PRETTY LADIES(1925); SALVATION HUNTERS, THE(1925); ALMOST A LADY(1926); EXQUISITE SINNER, THE(1926); IRENE(1926); KIKI(1926); WANING SEX, THE(1926); WHEN THE WIFE'S AWAY(1926); TILLIE THE TOILER(1927); BABY MINE(1928); SHOW PEOPLE(1928)
Misc. Silents
DEAR FOOL, A(1921, Brit.); LAMP IN THE DESERT(1922, Brit.); LOVE'S INFLUENCE(1922, Brit.); WHEELS OF CHANCE, THE(1922, Brit.); HER SISTER FROM PARIS(1925); LIGHTS OF OLD BROADWAY(1925); BOOB, THE(1926); BOY FRIEND, THE(1926); SUNNYSIDE UP(1926); GINGHAM GIRL, THE(1927); ROOKIES(1927); SPRING FEVER(1927); CIRCUS ROOKIES(1928); DETECTIVES(1928); ALL AT SEA(1929); CHINA BOUND(1929)
George M. Arthur
LAST TRAIN FROM MADRID, THE(1937), p; ARKANSAS TRAVELER, THE(1938), p; HER JUNGLE LOVE(1938), p; NIGHT OF NIGHTS, THE(1939), p
Silents
REPORTED MISSING(1922), ed; CHICAGO AFTER MIDNIGHT(1928), t, ed
Misc. Silents
CROOKS CAN'T WIN(1928), d
Glen Arthur
MAN FROM TEXAS, THE(1948)
Hartney Arthur
DEVOTION(1946)
Helene Arthur
INSIDE AMY(1975), w
Henry Arthur
THIRTEEN HOURS BY AIR(1936); ROAD DEMON(1938); MY WIFE'S RELATIVES(1939)
Indus Arthur
SLENDER THREAD, THE(1965); ALVAREZ KELLY(1966); M(1970)
Jean Arthur
SINS OF THE FATHERS(1928); CANARY MURDER CASE, THE(1929); GREENE MURDER CASE, THE(1929); HALF WAY TO HEAVEN(1929); MYSTERIOUS DR. FU MANCHU, THE(1929); SATURDAY NIGHT KID, THE(1929); DANGER LIGHTS(1930); RETURN OF DR. FU MANCHU, THE(1930); SILVER HORDE, THE(1930); STREET OF CHANCE(1930); YOUNG EAGLES(1930); EX-BAD BOY(1931); GANG BUSTER, THE(1931); LAWYER'S SECRET, THE(1931); VIRTUOUS HUSBAND(1931); PAST OF MARY HOLMES, THE(1933); DEFENSE HESTS, THE(1934); MOST PRECIOUS THING IN LIFE(1934); WHIRLPOOL(1934); DIAMOND JIM(1935); PARTY WIRE(1935); PUBLIC HERO NO. 1(1935); PUBLIC MENACE(1935); WHOLE TOWN'S TALKING, THE(1935); ADVENTURE IN MANHATTAN(1936); EX-MRS. BRADFORD, THE(1936); IF YOU COULD ONLY COOK(1936); MORE THAN A SECRETARY(1936); MR. DEEDS GOES TO TOWN(1936); EASY LIVING(1937); HISTORY IS MADE AT NIGHT(1937); PLAINSMAN, THE(1937); YOU CAN'T TAKE IT WITH YOU(1938); MR. SMITH GOES TO WASHINGTON(1939); ONLY ANGELS HAVE WINGS(1939); ARIZONA(1940); TOO MANY HUSBANDS(1940); DEVIL AND MISS JONES, THE(1941); TALK OF THE TOWN(1942); LADY TAKES A CHANCE, A(1943); MORE THE MERRIER, THE(1943); IMPATIENT YEARS, THE(1944); FOREIGN AFFAIR, A(1948); SHANE(1953)
Misc. Talkies
BROTHERLY LOVE(1928)
Silents
FIGHTING SMILE, THE(1925); MAN OF NERVE, A(1925); SEVEN CHANCES(1925); FIGHTING CHEAT, THE(1926); UNDER FIRE(1926); HUSBAND HUNTERS(1927); WARMING UP(1928); STAIRS OF SAND(1929)
Misc. Silents
BIFF BANG BUDDY(1924); BRINGIN' HOME THE BACON(1924); FAST AND FEARLESS(1924); THUNDERING ROMANCE(1924); TRAVELIN' FAST(1924); DRUG STORE COWBOY(1925); HURRICANE HORSEMAN(1925); TEARIN' LOOSE(1925); THUNDERING THROUGH(1925); BLOCK SIGNAL, THE(1926); BORN TO BATTLE(1926); COLLEGE BOOB, THE(1926); COWBOY COP, THE(1926); DOUBLE DARING(1926); LIGHTING BILL(1926); TWISTED TRIGGERS(1926); BROKEN GATE, THE(1927); FLYING LUCK(1927); POOR NUT, THE(1927); SINS OF THE FATHER(1928); WALLFLOWERS(1928)
John Arthur
MANY HAPPY RETURNS(1934); RENDEZVOUS(1935); KING STEPS OUT, THE(1936); BLOSSOMS ON BROADWAY(1937); SOMETHING TO SING ABOUT(1937); JEEPERS CREEPERS(1939); IT HAPPENED ON 5TH AVENUE(1947); SHARKY'S MACHINE(1982)

Johnny Arthur
ON TRIAL(1928); AVIATOR, THE(1929); DESERT SONG, THE(1929); GAMBLERS, THE(1929); CHEER UP AND SMILE(1930); PERSONALITY(1930); SHE COULDN'T SAY NO(1930); GOING WILD(1931); IT'S A WISE CHILD(1931); PENROD AND SAM(1931); CONVENTION CITY(1933); EASY MILLIONS(1933); DAMES(1934); HELL IN THE HEAVENS(1934); TWENTY MILLION SWEETHEARTS(1934); CRIME AND PUNISHMENT(1935); DOUBTING THOMAS(1935); GHOST WALKS, THE(1935); IT'S IN THE AIR(1935); TOO TOUGH TO KILL(1935); TRAVELING SALESLADY, THE(1935); BRIDE COMES HOME(1936); EX-MRS. BRADFORD, THE(1936); FRESHMAN LOVE(1936); MURDER OF DR. HARRIGAN, THE(1936); OUR RELATIONS(1936); STAGE STRUCK(1936); EXILED TO SHANGHAI(1937); HIT PARADE, THE(1937); IT HAPPENED OUT WEST(1937); MAKE A WISH(1937); PICK A STAR(1937); DANGER ON THE AIR(1938); EVERY DAY'S A HOLIDAY(1938); LI'L ABNER(1940); ROAD TO SINGAPORE(1940); MOUNTAIN MOONLIGHT(1941); HENRY ALDRICH GETS GLAMOUR(1942); SHEPHERD OF THE OZARKS(1942); THAT NAZTY NUISANCE(1943)
Misc. Talkies
DIVORCE MADE EASY(1929); LAST THREE(1942)
Silents
MONSTER, THE(1925)
Jose Arthur
MR. ORCHID(1948, Fr.)
Julia Arthur
Misc. Silents
WOMAN THE GERMANS SHOT(1918)
Karen Arthur
GUIDE FOR THE MARRIED MAN, A(1967); WINNING(1969); LEGACY(1976), d; MAFU CAGE, THE(1978), d
Misc. Talkies
NOT MY DAUGHTER(1975)
Lee Arthur
Silents
JUNE FRIDAY(1915), w; AUCTIONEER, THE(1927), w
Louise Arthur
ROAR OF THE CROWD(1953); LUCY GALLANT(1955); BIG CAPER, THE(1957); JUVENILE JUNGLE(1958); DIARY OF A HIGH SCHOOL BRIDE(1959); SNOW QUEEN, THE(1959, USSR); THAT TOUCH OF MINK(1962)
Misc. Talkies
AND NOW TOMORROW(1952)
Marie Arthur
SUN VALLEY CYCLONE(1946), set d
Mary Arthur
Silents
GENTLE JULIA(1923)
Maureen Arthur
HOT ROD GANG(1958); MAN CALLED DAGGER, A(1967); THUNDER ALLEY(1967); KILLERS THREE(1968); WICKED DREAMS OF PAULA SCHULTZ, THE(1968); HOW TO COMMIT MARRIAGE(1969); LOVE GOD?, THE(1969); LOVE MACHINE, THE,(1971); HARRY AND WALTER GO TO NEW YORK(1976); HOW TO SUCCEED IN BUSINESS WITHOUT REALLY TRYING(1976)
Maurice Arthur
OH! WHAT A LOVELY WAR(1969, Brit.)
Robert Alan Arthur
ALL THAT JAZZ(1979), p, w
Robert Arthur
NEW MOON(1940), w; CHIP OFF THE OLD BLOCK(1944), w; DANGER SIGNAL(1945); MILDRED PIERCE(1945); ROUGHLY SPEAKING(1945); TOO YOUNG TO KNOW(1945); NIGHT AND DAY(1946); NOBODY LIVES FOREVER(1946); SWEETHEART OF SIGMA CHI(1946); BUCK PRIVATES COME HOME(1947), p; DEVIL ON WHEELS, THE(1947); MOTHER WORE TIGHTS(1947); NORA PRENTISS(1947); WISTFUL WIDOW OF WAGON GAP, THE(1947), p; ABBOTT AND COSTELLO MEET FRANKENSTEIN(1948), p; ARE YOU WITH IT?(1948), p; FOR THE LOVE OF MARY(1948), p; GREEN GRASS OF WYOMING(1948); MEXICAN HAYRIDE(1948), p; YELLOW SKY(1948); ABBOTT AND COSTELLO MEET THE KILLER, BORIS KARLOFF(1949), p; BAGDAD(1949), p; FRANCIS(1949), p; GAL WHO TOOK THE WEST, THE(1949), p; MOTHER IS A FRESHMAN(1949); TWELVE O'CLOCK HIGH(1949); YOU'RE MY EVERYTHING(1949); ABBOTT AND COSTELLO IN THE FOREIGN LEGION(1950), p; BUCCANEER'S GIRL(1950), p; CURTAIN CALL AT CACTUS CREEK(1950), p; LOUISA(1950), p; SEPTEMBER AFFAIR(1950); AIR CADET(1951); FRANCIS GOES TO THE RACES(1951), w; GOLDEN HORDE, THE(1951), p; ON THE LOOSE(1951); STARLIFT(1951), p; BELLES ON THEIR TOES(1952); JUST FOR YOU(1952); RING, THE(1952); STORY OF WILL ROGERS, THE(1952), p; BIG HEAT, THE(1953); TAKE THE HIGH GROUND(1953); YOUNG BESS(1953); BLACK SHIELD OF FALWORTH, THE(1954), p; RETURN FROM THE SEA(1954); RICOCHET ROMANCE(1954), p; LADY GODIVA(1955), p; LONG GRAY LINE, THE(1955), p; TOP OF THE WORLD(1955); DAY OF FURY, A(1956), p; DESPERADOES ARE IN TOWN, THE(1956), p; FRANCIS IN THE HAUNTED HOUSE(1956), p; PILLARS OF THE SKY(1956), p; THREE VIOLENT PEOPLE(1956), p; HELLCATS OF THE NAVY(1957); KELLY AND ME(1957), p; MAN OF A THOUSAND FACES(1957), p; MIDNIGHT STORY, THE(1957), p; MISTER CORY(1957), p; FLOOD TIDE(1958), p; PERFECT FURLOUGH, THE(1958), p; TIME TO LOVE AND A TIME TO DIE, A(1958), p; YOUNG AND WILD(1958); OPERATION PETTICOAT(1959), p; GREAT IMPOSTOR, THE(1960), p; COME SEPTEMBER(1961), p; WILD YOUTH(1961); SPIRAL ROAD, THE(1962), p; CAPTAIN NEWMAN, M.D.(1963), p; FOR LOVE OR MONEY(1963), p; BRASS BOTTLE, THE(1964), p; FATHER GOOSE(1964), p; SHENANDOAH(1965), p; MAN COULD GET KILLED, A(1966), p; KING'S PIRATE(1967), p; HELLFIGHTERS(1968), p; SWEET CHARITY(1969), p; ONE MORE TRAIN TO ROB(1971), p
Roy Arthur
GREAT EXPECTATIONS(1946, Brit.)
Victor Arthur
HILLS OF OKLAHOMA(1950), w; LIGHTNING GUNS(1950), w; RIDIN' THE OUTLAW TRAIL(1951), w
Walter Arthur
Silents
IS LOVE EVERYTHING?(1924), ph; SPITFIRE, THE(1924), ph
William Arthur
DEMONS OF LUDLOW, THE(1983), w

Arthur "Fiddlin" Smith Trio
WEST OF THE ALAMO(1946)
Arthur L. Ward and His Band
OFF THE DOLE(1935, Brit.)
Richard Arthure
KING AND COUNTRY(1964, Brit.)
George Arthurs
YELLOW MASK, THE(1930, Brit.), w; THEIR NIGHT OUT(1933, Brit.), W; MARRY THE GIRL(1935, Brit.), w
Philippe Arthuys
PARIS BELONGS TO US(1962, Fr.), m; NIGHT WATCH, THE(1964, Fr./Ital.), spec eff; LES CARABINIERS(1968, Fr./Ital.), m
Judith Arthy
THEY'RE A WEIRD MOB(1966, Aus.); SHUTTERED ROOM, THE(1968, Brit.)
Artie Shaw and His Band
SECOND CHORUS(1940)
Jose Artigas
L'AGE D'OR(1979, Fr.)
Raul Artigot
HORROR OF THE ZOMBIES(1974, Span.), ph
Anoush Artin
INVINCIBLE SIX, THE(1970, U.S./Iran)
Barbara J. Artis
THX 1138(1971)
Studio Artist
RELUCTANT DRAGON, THE(1941)
Giorgio Artorio
AND SUDDENLY IT'S MURDER!(1964, Ital.), w
Antonin Artraud
Silents
PASSION OF JOAN OF ARC, THE(1928, Fr.)
Jose Artur
Z(1969, Fr./Algeria)
Monique Artur
LES MAINS SALES(1954, Fr.)
Germaine Artus
ETERNAL HUSBAND, THE(1946, Fr.), ed; DEADLY DECOYS, THE(1962, Fr.), ed; TRIAL OF JOAN OF ARC(1965, Fr.), ed
Raymond Artus
BLUE VEIL, THE(1947, Fr.), p
Linda Artuso
WANDERERS, THE(1979)
Mary Gail Artz
Misc. Talkies
DON'T GO INTO THE WOODS(1980)
Ami Artzi
DREAMER, THE(1970, Israel), p; SILENT NIGHT, BLOODY NIGHT(1974), p, w
Mudite Arums
SOMETHING WEIRD(1967)
Sybil Arundale
LOOSE ENDS(1930, Brit.); GIRLS PLEASE!(1934, Brit.)
Silents
GOD AND THE MAN(1918, Brit.)
Misc. Silents
TOM JONES(1917, Brit.); CHINESE PUZZLE, THE(1919, Brit.)
Ronald Arunde
FLY NOW, PAY LATER(1969)
Dennis Arundel
MELBA(1953, Brit.), md
E.J. Arundel
Misc. Silents
MAN WHO BOUGHT LONDON, THE(1916, Brit.)
Edith Arundel
GREEN FINGERS(1947), w
Harris Arundel
PIMPERNEL SMITH(1942, Brit.)
Rex Howard Arundel
OVER THE ODDS(1961, Brit.), w
Sidney Arundel
Silents
SENSATION SEEKERS(1927)
Anthony Arundell
PIRATES OF PENZANCE, THE(1983)
Dennis Arundell
SHOW GOES ON, THE(1937, Brit.); GLAMOUR GIRL(1938, Brit.); BLACKOUT(1940, Brit.); COURAGEOUS MR. PENN, THE(1941, Brit.); PIMPERNEL SMITH(1942, Brit.); ADVENTURE IN BLACKMAIL(1943, Brit.); SAINT MEETS THE TIGER, THE(1943, Brit.); MEET SEXTON BLAKE(1944, Brit.); COLONEL BLIMP(1945, Brit.); ECHO MURDERS, THE(1945, Brit.); CARNIVAL(1946, Brit.); MAN FROM MOROCCO, THE(1946, Brit.); END OF THE RIVER, THE(1947, Brit.); SOMETHING MONEY CAN'T BUY(1952, Brit.)
E. C. Arundell
Silents
NEW CLOWN, THE(1916, Brit.)
Edward Arundell
Silents
GREATEST WISH IN THE WORLD, THE(1918, Brit.); LONDON PRIDE(1920, Brit.)
Teddy Arundell
Silents
NELSON(1918, Brit.); ELUSIVE PIMPERNEL, THE(1919, Brit.); MR. WU(1919, Brit.); AMATEUR GENTLEMAN, THE(1920, Brit.); AT THE VILLA ROSE(1920, Brit.); GENERAL POST(1920, Brit.); QUESTION OF TRUST, A(1920, Brit.); AMAZING PARTNERSHIP, THE(1921, Brit.); GENERAL JOHN REGAN(1921, Brit.); KIPPS(1921, Brit.); MYSTERY OF MR. BERNARD BROWN(1921, Brit.); FALSE EVIDENCE(1922, Brit.); PASSIONATE FRIENDS, THE(1922, Brit.); POINTING FINGER, THE(1922, Brit.)
Misc. Silents
SWINDLER, THE(1919, Brit.); TAVERN KNIGHT, THE(1920, Brit.); FOUR JUST MEN, THE(1921, Brit.); RIVER OF STARS, THE(1921, Brit.)

Janos Arva
DIALOGUE(1967, Hung.)
Jan Arvan
DESERT HAWK, THE(1950); HOW TO MARRY A MILLIONAIRE(1953); OTHER WOMAN, THE(1954); ABBOTT AND COSTELLO MEET THE MUMMY(1955); COBWEB, THE(1955); ISTANBUL(1957); 20 MILLION MILES TO EARTH(1957); CURSE OF THE FACELESS MAN(1958); SOME CAME RUNNING(1959); GUNFIGHTERS OF ABILENE(1960); NOOSE FOR A GUNMAN(1960); SIGN OF ZORRO, THE(1960); THREE CAME TO KILL(1960); FRONTIER UPRISING(1961); ISLAND OF LOVE(1963); BRASS BOTTLE, THE(1964); SANDPIPER, THE(1965); SPY WITH MY FACE, THE(1966); POSEIDON ADVENTURE, THE(1972); STONE KILLER, THE(1973); OTHER SIDE OF MIDNIGHT, THE(1977)
Betty Arvaniti
HOT MONTH OF AUGUST, THE(1969, Gr.)
George Arvanitis
RECONSTRUCTION OF A CRIME(1970, Ger.), ph; ASSAULT ON AGATHON(1976, Brit./Gr.), ph; DREAM OF PASSION, A(1978, Gr.), ph
Georges Arvanitis
DAYS OF 36(1972, Gr.), ph
Georges Arvantis
IPHIGENIA(1977, Gr.), ph
Ragnar Arvedson
TRUE AND THE FALSE, THE(1955, Swed.); DEVIL'S EYE, THE(1960, Swed.)
Arvel
CONFLICT(1939, Fr.)
Manuel Arvide
HONEYMOON(1947); SOMBRERO(1953); BEAST OF HOLLOW MOUNTAIN, THE(1956); LAST REBEL, THE(1961, Mex.); NAZARIN(1968, Mex.)
Frank Arvidson
MONSTER OF PIEDRAS BLANCAS, THE(1959); 7TH COMMANDMENT, THE(1961)
Linda Lee Arvidson
1984
FIRSTBORN(1984)
Margareta Arvidssen
1984
SLAYGROUND(1984, Brit.)
John Arville
STARK FEAR(1963)
Steve Arvin
TRUE CONFESSIONS(1981)
Paulita Arvizu
DAUGHTER OF SHANGHAI(1937); TRADE WINDS(1938); COBRA WOMAN(1944)
Jacques Ary
LOVE IN THE AFTERNOON(1957); DYNAMITE JACK(1961, Fr.), w; GIGOT(1962); TALES OF PARIS(1962, Fr./Ital.); SUCKER, THE(1966, Fr./Ital.)
Dr. Usharbudh Arya
1984
VARIETY(1984)
M. Aryss-Nissotti
THEY WERE FIVE(1938, Fr.), p
Randle Aryton
Silents
DECAMERON NIGHTS(1924, Brit.)
Mark L. Arywitz
JUST BEFORE DAWN(1980), w
Marco Antonio Arzate
SCALPHUNTERS, THE(1968); SOLDIER BLUE(1970)
Dorothy Arzner
WILD PARTY, THE(1929), d; MANHATTAN COCKTAIL(1928), d; ANYBODY'S WOMAN(1930), d; SARAH AND SON(1930), d; HONOR AMONG LOVERS(1931), d; WORKING GIRLS(1931), d; MERRILY WE GO TO HELL(1932), d; CHRISTOPHER STRONG(1933), d; NANA(1934), d; CRAIG'S WIFE(1936), d; BRIDE WORE RED, THE(1937), d; DANCE, GIRL, DANCE(1940), d; FIRST COMES COURAGE(1943), d
Silents
BLOOD AND SAND(1922), ed; COVERED WAGON, THE(1923), ed; INEZ FROM HOLLYWOOD(1924), ed; NO-GUN MAN, THE(1924), w; RED KIMONO(1925), w
Misc. Silents
FASHIONS FOR WOMEN(1927), d; GET YOUR MAN(1927), d; TEN MODERN COMMANDMENTS(1927), d; MANHATTAN COCKTAIL(1928), d
Dorthy Arzner
Silents
OLD IRONSIDES(1926), w
Kostas Arzoglou
DREAM OF PASSION, A(1978, Gr.)
Angel Arzuaga
THOSE DIRTY DOGS(1974, U.S./Ital./Span.), set d
Nobutaka Asahara
MUDDY RIVER(1982, Jap.)
Shozaburo Asai
SECRETS OF A WOMAN'S TEMPLE(1969, Jap.), w
Werner Asam
QUERELLE(1983, Ger./Fr.)
Birger Asander
RAILROAD WORKERS(1948, Swed.); CHILDREN, THE(1949, Swed.); LOVING COUPLES(1966, Swed.)
Yuke Asano
WAR OF THE PLANETS(1977, Jap.)
Christopher Asante
DOGS OF WAR, THE(1980, Brit.); LOCAL HERO(1983, Brit.)
Ruriko Asaoka
LONGING FOR LOVE(1966, Jap.); GOYOKIN(1969, Jap.); SUN ABOVE, DEATH BELOW(1969, Jap.); GIRL I ABANDONED, THE(1970, Jap.); VIXEN(1970, Jap.)
Yukiji Asaoka
ZATOICHI CHALLENGED(1970, Jap.)
Nurdan Asar
YOR, THE HUNTER FROM THE FUTURE(1983, Ital.)
Joey Asaro
GETTING TOGETHER(1976), p

Mark Asarow
SONG OF LIFE, THE(1931, Ger.), ed; TRUNKS OF MR. O.F., THE(1932, Ger.), p
L. Asatian
DRAGONFLY, THE(1955 USSR)
Stuart Asbjorsen
FOREST, THE(1983), ph
Adaline Asbury
WESTERN LIMITED(1932)
Adalyn Asbury
BRINGING UP BABY(1938)
Claudia Asbury
1984
COTTON CLUB, THE(1984), ch
Herbert Asbury
AMONG THE MISSING(1934), w; FUGITIVE LADY(1934), w; NAME THE WO-MAN(1934), w; GANGS OF NEW YORK(1938), w
Jody Asbury
REVENGE OF THE NINJA(1983)
Ofelia Ascencio
TROPIC HOLIDAY(1938)
Sara Ascencio
TROPIC HOLIDAY(1938)
Ascencio Del Rio Trio
THREE CABALLEROS, THE(1944)
Jerome Asch
RIVER GANG(1945), ph
Kris Aschan
EAST OF KILIMANJARO(1962, Brit./Ital.)
Rolf Aschan
EAST OF KILIMANJARO(1962, Brit./Ital.)
Oscar Asche
MY LUCKY STAR(1933, Brit.); CHU CHIN CHOW(1934, Brit.), w; TWO HEARTS IN WALTZ TIME(1934, Brit.); DON QUIXOTE(1935, Fr.); PRIVATE SECRETARY, THE(1935, Brit.); SCROOGE(1935, Brit.); ELIZA COMES TO STAY(1936, Brit.); ROBBER SYMPHONY, THE(1937, Brit.)
Emil Ascher
FOUR FOR THE MORGUE(1962), m
Max Ascher
TRIGGER TRICKS(1930); RIDER OF DEATH VALLEY(1932)
Silents
AT DEVIL'S GORGE(1923); DYNAMITE DAN(1924); PAINTING THE TOWN(1927); PLAY SAFE(1927)
Shoshana Ascher
NIGHT OF THE ZOMBIES(1981)
Diane Ascher [Dorothy Costello]
DO YOU LOVE ME?(1946)
Renee Ascherson [Asherson]
WAY AHEAD, THE(1945, Brit.)
Jeb Aschery
HERE COMES KELLY(1943), w
Anthony Ascot
Misc. Talkies
THEY CALL ME HALLELUJAH(1973), d
Charles Ascot
Silents
AMATEUR WIDOW, AN(1919)
Duggie Ascot
TALKING FEET(1937, Brit.); STEPPING TOES(1938, Brit.); DEATH OF AN ANGEL(1952, Brit.)
Hazel Ascot
TALKING FEET(1937, Brit.); STEPPING TOES(1938, Brit.)
Freddie Ascott
OH! WHAT A LOVELY WAR(1969, Brit.)
Edna Aselin
Misc. Talkies
GUNNERS AND GUNS(1935)
Francisco R. Asensio
DESERT WARRIOR(1961 Ital./Span.), art d; REVOLT OF THE SLAVES, THE(1961, Ital./Span./Ger.), art d
Lenora Asereth
Silents
MOONSHINE VALLEY(1922), w
Nikolai Aseyev
Silents
BATTLESHIP POTEMKIN, THE(1925, USSR), t
S. M. Asgaralli
FLAME OVER INDIA(1960, Brit.)
Arte Ash
LOVE LIES(1931, Brit.)
Artie Ash
LOVE RACE, THE(1931, Brit.); RANDOLPH FAMILY, THE(1945, Brit.)
Arty Ash
JOSSER ON THE RIVER(1932, Brit.); WOMAN IN COMMAND, THE(1934 Brit.); HONEYMOON FOR THREE(1935, Brit.); GUILTY MELODY(1936, Brit.); DR. SIN FANG(1937, Brit.); GIVE US THE MOON(1944, Brit.); DULCIMER STREET(1948, Brit.)
Bill Ash
VISITOR, THE(1980, Ital./U.S.); SIX PACK(1982)
Dan Ash
MADIGAN'S MILLIONS(1970, Span./Ital), d
David Ash
JUNKET 89(1970, Brit.), w
E. Hopewell Ash
MAGIC BOX, THE(1952, Brit.), art d
Frances Ash
CALL ME MISTER(1951), m/l Rome
George Ash
DELTA FACTOR, THE(1970)

Jerome Ash
BARNUM WAS RIGHT(1929), ph; DRAKE CASE, THE(1929), ph; SHAKEDOWN, THE(1929), ph; TONIGHT AT TWELVE(1929), ph; UNDERTOW(1930), ph; EX-BAD BOY(1931), ph; GRAFT(1931), ph; MANY A SLIP(1931), ph; VIRTUOUS HUSBAND(1931), ph; COHENS, AND KELLYS IN HOLLYWOOD, THE(1932), ph; UNEXPECTED FATHER(1932), ph; I CAN'T ESCAPE(1934), ph; I'LL TELL THE WORLD(1934), ph; MIGHTY TREVE, THE(1937), ph; TROUBLE AT MIDNIGHT(1937), ph; WHEN LOVE IS YOUNG(1937), ph; LEGION OF LOST FLYERS(1939), ph; OKLAHOMA FRONTIER(1939), ph; ENEMY AGENT(1940), ph; FRAMED(1940), ph; LAW AND ORDER(1940), ph; RAGTIME COWBOY JOE(1940), ph; DON'T GET PERSONAL(1941), ph; HIT THE ROAD(1941), ph; MELODY LANE(1941), ph; ROAD AGENT(1941), ph; SING ANOTHER CHORUS(1941), ph; ALMOST MARRIED(1942), ph; STAGECOACH BUCKAROO(1942), ph; WHAT'S COOKIN'?(1942), ph; YOU'RE TELLING ME(1942), ph; GALS, INCORPORATED(1943), ph; HI'YA, SAILOR(1943), ph; MOONLIGHT IN VERMONT(1943), ph; SING A JINGLE(1943), ph; STRANGE DEATH OF ADOLF HITLER, THE(1943), ph; BABES ON SWING STREET(1944), ph; HI, GOOD-LOOKIN'(1944), ph; IN SOCIETY(1944), ph; MOON OVER LAS VEGAS(1944), ph; MOONLIGHT AND CACTUS(1944), ph; RECKLESS AGE(1944), ph; SOUTH OF DIXIE(1944), ph; SWINGTIME JOHNNY(1944), ph; TWILIGHT ON THE PRAIRIE(1944), ph; CRIMSON CANARY(1945), ph; EASY TO LOOK AT(1945), ph; I'LL REMEMBER APRIL(1945), ph; PILLOW OF DEATH(1945), ph; SHE GETS HER MAN(1945), ph; TIME OF THEIR LIVES, THE(1946), spec eff
Jerry Ash
MODERN LOVE(1929), ph; SHANNONS OF BROADWAY, THE(1929), ph; CLIMAX, THE(1930), ph; EAST IS WEST(1930), ph; FLAMING GUNS(1933), ph; LUCKY DOG(1933), ph; OUT ALL NIGHT(1933), ph; SUCCESSFUL FAILURE, A(1934), ph; FLASH GORDON(1936), ph; DESPERATE TRAILS(1939), ph; PIRATES OF THE SKIES(1939), ph; TROPIC FURY(1939), ph; SOUTH TO KARANGA(1940), ph; WEST OF CARSON CITY(1940), ph; MAD DOCTOR OF MARKET STREET, THE(1942), ph
John Ash
Misc. Talkies
MR. HORATIO KNIBBLES(1971)
Laura Ash
FOOLS(1970)
Leslie Ash
QUADROPHENIA(1979, Brit.); NUTCRACKER(1982, Brit.); CURSE OF THE PINK PANTHER(1983)
Misc. Talkies
BOY WITH TWO HEADS, THE(1974, Brit.)
Monty Ash
NIGHTFALL(1956); 27TH DAY, THE(1957); BELL, BOOK AND CANDLE(1958)
Nathan Ash
I CAN'T ESCAPE(1934), w
Russell Ash
MARJORIE MORNINGSTAR(1958)
Sam Ash
UNMASKED(1929); GIRL WITHOUT A ROOM(1933); LADY KILLER(1933); KISS AND MAKE UP(1934); OPERATOR 13(1934); BROADWAY GONDOLIER(1935); FOUR HOURS TO KILL(1935); HANDS ACROSS THE TABLE(1935); MAD LOVE(1935); MAN WHO BROKE THE BANK AT MONTE CARLO, THE(1935); MILLIONS IN THE AIR(1935); ONE HOUR LATE(1935); PARIS IN SPRING(1935); RECKLESS(1935); RENDEZVOUS(1935); SHE MARRIED HER BOSS(1935); STARS OVER BROADWAY(1935); IT HAD TO HAPPEN(1936); SAN FRANCISCO(1936); CONFESSION(1937); KING AND THE CHORUS GIRL, THE(1937); LOVE IS NEWS(1937); MAN BETRAYED, A(1937); YOU CAN'T HAVE EVERYTHING(1937); ALEXANDER'S RAGTIME BAND(1938); JUVENILE COURT(1938); KING OF CHINATOWN(1939); STAND UP AND FIGHT(1939); FIVE LITTLE PEPPERS AT HOME(1940); HOUSE ACROSS THE BAY, THE(1940); ISLAND OF DOOMED MEN(1940); FACE BEHIND THE MASK, THE(1941); WEST POINT WIDOW(1941); LADY BODYGUARD(1942); TISH(1942); DANCING MASTERS, THE(1943); HEAT'S ON, THE(1943); TWO SENORITAS FROM CHICAGO(1943); COVER GIRL(1944); PRACTICALLY YOURS(1944); DICK TRACY(1945); STORK CLUB, THE(1945); GILDA(1946); DESIRE ME(1947); SADDLE PALS(1947); SECRET LIFE OF WALTER MITTY, THE(1947); FORCE OF EVIL(1948); HAZARD(1948); STREET CORNER(1948); MY FOOLISH HEART(1949); OH, YOU BEAUTIFUL DOLL(1949); MATING SEASON, THE(1951); BIG SKY, THE(1952)
Misc. Silents
UNMASKED(1929)
T. Hopewell Ash
PROMOTER, THE(1952, Brit.), art d
William Ash
LONELINESS OF THE LONG DISTANCE RUNNER, THE(1962, Brit.)
Shief Ashanti
WOMAN EATER, THE(1959, Brit.)
Daphne Ashbrook
1984
GIMME AN 'F'(1984)
Florence Ashbrook
Misc. Silents
RAGGED PRINCESS, THE(1916); UNKNOWN 274(1917)
H. Ashbrook
GREEN EYES(1934), w
Stephen Ashbrook
LULU(1978)
Florence Ashbrooke
Silents
AMATEUR WIDOW, AN(1919)
Carroll Ashburn
SLEEPING CITY, THE(1950)
Michelle Ashburn
POCO...LITTLE DOG LOST(1977)
Carol Ashby
CHARRIOTS OF FIRE(1981, Brit.)
Carole Ashby
OCTOPUSSY(1983, Brit.)
Hal Ashby
CINCINNATI KID, THE(1965), ed; RUSSIANS ARE COMING, THE RUSSIANS ARE COMING, THE(1966), ed; IN THE HEAT OF THE NIGHT(1967), ed; THOMAS CROWN AFFAIR, THE(1968), ed; LANDLORD, THE(1970), d; HAROLD AND

MAUDE(1971), d; LAST DETAIL, THE(1973), d; SHAMPOO(1975), d; BOUND FOR GLORY(1976), d; COMING HOME(1978), d; BEING THERE(1979), d; SECOND-HAND HEARTS(1981), d; LOOKIN' TO GET OUT(1982), d

Jeff Ashby
SQUEEZE A FLOWER(1970, Aus.); ALVIN RIDES AGAIN(1974, Aus.)

Jess Ashby
SUNSTRUCK(1973, Aus.)

John Ashby
J.W. COOP(1971); MITCHELL(1975); UNDER FIRE(1983)

John Russell Ashby
SUN SHINES BRIGHT, THE(1953)

Johnny Ashby
SUCH IS THE LAW(1930, Brit.)
Silents
PHYSICIAN, THE(1928, Brit.)

Sally Ashby
PETER RABBIT AND TALES OF BEATRIX POTTER(1971, Brit.); BIDDY(1983, Brit.)

Mary Ashcraft
LOCKED DOOR, THE(1929); WHOOPEE(1930); DANTE'S INFERNO(1935)

Peggy Ashcroft
WANDERING JEW, THE(1935, Brit.); 39 STEPS, THE(1935, Brit.); RHODES(1936, Brit.); QUIET WEDDING(1941, Brit.); NUN'S STORY, THE(1959); SECRET CEREMONY(1968, Brit.); TELL ME LIES(1968, Brit.); THREE INTO TWO WON'T GO(1969, Brit.); SUNDAY BLOODY SUNDAY(1971, Brit.); PEDESTRIAN, THE(1974, Ger.); JOSEPH ANDREWS(1977, Brit.); HULLABALOO OVER GEORGIE AND BONNIE'S PICTURES(1979, Brit.)
1984
PASSAGE TO INDIA, A(1984, Brit.)

Ronnie Ashcroft
WETBACKS(1956), ed; ASTOUNDING SHE-MONSTER, THE(1958), p&d

Anthony Ashdown
SING AND SWING(1964, Brit.); TOBRUK(1966)

Nadene Ashdown
I WAS AN AMERICAN SPY(1951); SHADOW IN THE SKY(1951); TOUGHEST MAN IN ARIZONA(1952); YOUNG MAN WITH IDEAS(1952); BRIDGES AT TOKO-RI, THE(1954); STAR IS BORN, A(1954); FRONTIER GAMBLER(1956)

Dick Ashe
TRACK OF THE MOONBEAST(1976), d

Eve Brent Ashe
FADE TO BLACK(1980); BRAINWAVES(1983); GOING BERSERK(1983)
1984
RACING WITH THE MOON(1984)

Hopewell Ashe
ONE WOMAN'S STORY(1949, Brit.), art d

Jerry Ashe
CITY LIMITS(1934), ph

Martin Ashe
PANTHER'S CLAW, THE(1942); FLIGHT FOR FREEDOM(1943); GUY NAMED JOE, A(1943); HONEYMOON LODGE(1943); SING A JINGLE(1943); FOLLOW THE BOYS(1944); TIGER BY THE TAIL(1970)

Michael Ashe
JACKSON COUNTY JAIL(1976)

Nancy Ashe
LIMIT, THE(1972)

Sharon Ashe
SOMETHING WICKED THIS WAY COMES(1983)

Warren Ashe
MILITARY ACADEMY(1940); WILDCAT BUS(1940); FACE BEHIND THE MASK, THE(1941); GIRL, A GUY AND A GOB, A(1941); HARMON OF MICHIGAN(1941); HERE COMES MR. JORDAN(1941); I WANTED WINGS(1941); NAVAL ACADEMY(1941); PENALTY, THE(1941); BOMBAY CLIPPER(1942); LADY BODYGUARD(1942); LADY HAS PLANS, THE(1942); PRIORITIES ON PARADE(1942); SUBMARINE RAIDER(1942); UNDERGROUND AGENT(1942); DEERSLAYER(1943); DESTROYER(1943); GUADALCANAL DIARY(1943); ONE DANGEROUS NIGHT(1943); WHAT'S BUZZIN COUSIN?(1943); YOUTH ON PARADE(1943); COVER GIRL(1944); DESTINATION TOKYO(1944); GHOST THAT WALKS ALONE, THE(1944); IMPOSTER, THE(1944); MR. WINKLE GOES TO WAR(1944); PRACTICALLY YOURS(1944); RACKET MAN, THE(1944); BOSTON BLACKIE AND THE LAW(1946); LITTLE MISS BIG(1946)

Ashelbe
DEDEE(1949, Fr.), w

Detective Ashelbe
CASBAH(1948), w

Ron Ashen
DOWN OUR ALLEY(1939, Brit.)

Aerin Asher
STARTING OVER(1979)

Billy Asher
Misc. Silents
WHERE AMBITION LEADS(1919, Brit.), d

David Asher
OUT OF SIGHT(1966), w

E.M. Asher
EAST IS WEST(1930), p; DON'T BET ON LOVE(1933), p; MR. DYNAMITE(1935), p; DRACULA'S DAUGHTER(1936), p; LOVE LETTERS OF A STAR(1936), p; ARMORED CAR(1937), p; LOVE IN A BUNGALOW(1937), p; MAN WHO CRIED WOLF, THE(1937), p; REPORTED MISSING(1937), p; SHE'S DANGEROUS(1937), p; SOME BLONDES ARE DANGEROUS(1937), p
Silents
COHENS AND KELLYS, THE(1926), p; FLYING ROMEOS(1928), p

Guy Asher
MAKE A MILLION(1935)

Irvin Asher
NAZI AGENT(1942), p

Irving Asher
BLIND SPOT(1932, Brit.), p; DON'T BE A DUMMY(1932, Brit.), p; HELP YOURSELF(1932, Brit.), p; HER NIGHT OUT(1932, Brit.), p; HIGH SOCIETY(1932, Brit.), p; ILLEGAL(1932, Brit.), p, w; LUCKY LADIES(1932, Brit.), p; MURDER ON THE SECOND FLOOR(1932, Brit.), p; RIVER HOUSE GHOST, THE(1932, Brit.), p; BERMONDSEY KID, THE(1933, Brit.), p; CALL ME MAME(1933, Brit.), p; ENEMY OF

THE POLICE(1933, Brit.), p; GOING STRAIGHT(1933, Brit.), p; HEAD OF THE FAMILY(1933, Brit.), p; HER IMAGINARY LOVER(1933, Brit.), p; HIGH FINANCE(1933, Brit.), p; I ADORE YOU(1933, Brit.), p; LITTLE MISS NOBODY(1933, Brit.), p; MAYFAIR GIRL(1933, Brit.), p; MELODY MAKER, THE(1933, Brit.), p; MR. QUINCEY OF MONTE CARLO(1933, Brit.), p; NAUGHTY CINDERELLA(1933, Brit.), p; OUT OF THE PAST(1933, Brit.), p; SMITHY(1933, Brit.), p; THIRTEENTH CANDLE, THE(1933, Brit.), p; THIS ACTING BUSINESS(1933, Brit.), p; TOO MANY WIVES(1933, Brit.), p; BIG BUSINESS(1934, Brit.), p; BLUE SQUADRON, THE(1934, Brit.), p; CHURCH MOUSE, THE(1934, Brit.), p; FATHER AND SON(1934, Brit.), p; GIRL IN POSSESSION(1934, Brit.), p; GIRL IN THE CROWD, THE(1934, Brit.), p; GLIMPSE OF PARADISE, A(1934, Brit.), p; GUEST OF HONOR(1934, Brit.), p; LEAVE IT TO BLANCHE(1934, Brit.), p; LIFE OF THE PARTY(1934, Brit.), p; MURDER AT THE INN(1934, Brit.), p; NINE FORTY-FIVE(1934, Brit.), p; NO ESCAPE(1934, Brit.), p; SILVER SPOON, THE(1934, Brit.), p; SOMETHING ALWAYS HAPPENS(1934, Brit.), p; TOO MANY MILLIONS(1934, Brit.), p; WHAT HAPPENED TO HARKNESS(1934, Brit.), p; WIDOW'S MIGHT(1934, Brit.), p; BLACK MASK(1935, Brit.), p; CRIME UNLIMITED(1935, Brit.), p; FULL CIRCLE(1935, Brit.), p; GET OFF MY FOOT(1935, Brit.), p; HELLO SWEETHEART(1935, Brit.), p; MAN OF THE MOMENT(1935, Brit.), p; MR. WHAT'S-HIS-NAME(1935, Brit.), p; MURDER AT MONTE CARLO(1935, Brit.), p; SO YOU WON'T TALK?(1935, Brit.), p; SOME DAY(1935, Brit.), p; BROWN WALLET, THE(1936, Brit.), p; CROWN VS STEVENS(1936, Brit.), p; EDUCATED EVANS(1936, Brit.), p; FAIR EXCHANGE(1936, Brit.), p; FAITHFUL(1936, Brit.), p; GAOL BREAK(1936, Brit.), p; HEAD OFFICE(1936, Brit.), p; IRISH FOR LUCK(1936, Brit.), p; IT'S IN THE BAG(1936, Brit.), p; MR. COHEN TAKES A WALK(1936, Brit.), p; TWELVE GOOD MEN(1936, Brit.), p; WHERE'S SALLY?(1936, Brit.), p; CHANGE FOR A SOVEREIGN(1937, Brit.), p; COMPULSORY WIFE, THE(1937, Brit.), p; DON'T GET ME WRONG(1937, Brit.), p; GYPSY(1937, Brit.), p; IT'S NOT CRICKET(1937, Brit.), p; MAN WHO MADE DIAMONDS, THE(1937, Brit.), p; MAYFAIR MELODY(1937, Brit.), p; PATRICIA GETS HER MAN(1937, Brit.), p; PERFECT CRIME, THE(1937, Brit.), p; SIDE STREET ANGEL(1937, Brit.), p; TAKE IT FROM ME(1937, Brit.), p; VULTURE, THE(1937, Brit.), p; WHO KILLED JOHN SAVAGE?(1937, Brit.), p; WINDMILL, THE(1937, Brit.), p; YOU LIVE AND LEARN(1937, Brit.), p; DARK STAIRWAY, THE(1938, Brit.), p; DOUBLE OR QUITS(1938, Brit.), p; IT'S IN THE BLOOD(1938, Brit.), p; QUIET PLEASE(1938, Brit.), p; SIMPLY TERRIFIC(1938, Brit.), p; SINGING COP, THE(1938, Brit.), p; THANK EVANS(1938, Brit.), p; THISTLEDOWN(1938, Brit.), p; VIPER, THE(1938, Brit.), p; CLOUDS OVER EUROPE(1939, Brit.), p; U-BOAT 29(1939, Brit.), p; BILLY THE KID(1941), p; BLOSSOMS IN THE DUST(1941), p; MISSING TEN DAYS(1941, Brit.), p; MR. AND MRS. NORTH(1941), p; WAR AGAINST MRS. HADLEY, THE(1942), p; ADVENTURES OF TARTU(1943, Brit.), p; REDHEAD AND THE COWBOY, THE(1950), p; TURNING POINT, THE(1952), p; STARS ARE SINGING, THE(1953), p; ELEPHANT WALK(1954), p

Jack Asher
MAGIC BOW, THE(1947, Brit.), ph; GIRL IN THE PAINTING, THE(1948, Brit.), ph; HELTER SKELTER(1949, Brit.), ph; ASTONISHED HEART, THE(1950, Brit.), ph; LOST PEOPLE, THE(1950, Brit.), ph; HELL IS SOLD OUT(1951, Brit.), ph; LILLI MARLENE(1951, Brit.), ph; GIRDLE OF GOLD(1952, Brit.), ph; KILLER WALKS, A(1952, Brit.), ph; ALBERT, R.N.(1953, Brit.), ph; SLASHER, THE(1953, Brit.), ph; TWILIGHT WOMEN(1953, Brit.), ph; CHANCE MEETING(1954, Brit.), ph; FAST AND LOOSE(1954, Brit.), ph; GOOD DIE YOUNG, THE(1954, Brit.), ph; SECRET, THE(1955, Brit.), ph; WICKED WIFE(1955, Brit.), ph; SHADOW OF FEAR(1956, Brit.), ph; AFTER THE BALL(1957, Brit.), ph; CURSE OF FRANKENSTEIN, THE(1957, Brit.), ph; REACH FOR THE SKY(1957, Brit.), ph; CAMP ON BLOOD ISLAND, THE(1958, Brit.), ph; CAST A DARK SHADOW(1958, Brit.), ph; HORROR OF DRACULA, THE(1958, Brit.), ph; REVENGE OF FRANKENSTEIN, THE(1958, Brit.), ph; SNORKEL, THE(1958, Brit.), ph; FOLLOW A STAR(1959, Brit.), ph; HOUND OF THE BASKERVILLES, THE(1959, Brit.), ph; MAN WHO COULD CHEAT DEATH, THE(1959, Brit.), ph; MUMMY, THE(1959, Brit.), ph; ROOM 43(1959, Brit.), ph; BRIDES OF DRACULA, THE(1960, Brit.), ph; BULLDOG BREED, THE(1960, Brit.), ph; HOUSE OF FRIGHT(1961), ph; MAID FOR MURDER(1963, Brit.), p, ph; CRIMSON BLADE, THE(1964, Brit.), ph; EARLY BIRD, THE(1965, Brit.), ph; SECRET OF BLOOD ISLAND, THE(1965, Brit.), ph; SPYLARKS(1965, Brit.), ph; STITCH IN TIME, A(1967, Brit.), ph

Jane Asher
CRASH OF SILENCE(1952, Brit.); ADVENTURE IN THE HOPFIELDS(1954, Brit.); LOSS OF INNOCENCE(1961, Brit.); MASQUE OF THE RED DEATH, THE(1964, U.S./Brit.); MODEL MURDER CASE, THE(1964, Brit.); ALFIE(1966, Brit.); WINTER'S TALE, THE(1968, Brit.); DEEP END(1970 Ger./U.S.); BUTTERCUP CHAIN, THE(1971, Brit.); HENRY VIII AND HIS SIX WIVES(1972, Brit.); RUNNERS(1983, Brit.)
1984
SUCCESS IS THE BEST REVENGE(1984, Brit.)

John Asher
EASY MONEY(1948, Brit.), ph; STEEL BAYONET, THE(1958, Brit.), ph

Marcin Asher
Silents
PLEASURES OF THE RICH(1926); HUSBAND HUNTERS(1927)
Misc. Silents
UNKNOWN DANGERS(1926)

Max Asher
SHOW BOAT(1929); SWEETHEARTS ON PARADE(1930); SOUL OF THE SLUMS(1931); CRASHING BROADWAY(1933); JEALOUSY(1934); LITTLE MAN, WHAT NOW?(1934)
Silents
RIP VAN WINKLE(1921); SILVER CAR, THE(1921); CARNIVAL GIRL, THE(1926); AVENGING FANGS(1927); KID'S CLEVER, THE(1929)

Michael Asher
Misc. Talkies
TENDER LOVING CARE(1974)

Peter Asher
OUTPOST IN MALAYA(1952, Brit.); ISN'T LIFE WONDERFUL!(1953, Brit.); ESCAPADE(1955, Brit.)

Robert Asher
FOLLOW A STAR(1959, Brit.), d; BULLDOG BREED, THE(1960, Brit.), d; MAKE MINE MINK(1960, Brit.), d; ON THE BEAT(1962, Brit.), d; MAID FOR MURDER(1963, Brit.), p, d; EARLY BIRD, THE(1965, Brit.), d; SPYLARKS(1965, Brit.), d; PRESS FOR TIME(1966, Brit.), d; STITCH IN TIME, A(1967, Brit.), d

Roland Asher
LUCKY DOG(1933), w

Ron Asher
ECHOES(1983)
Will Asher
Silents
GRIT OF A JEW, THE(1917, Brit.)
William Asher
BUTCHER BAKER(NIGHTMARE MAKER)* (1982), d; LEATHER GLOVES(1948), p&d; MOBS INC(1956), d; SHADOW ON THE WINDOW, THE(1957), d; 27TH DAY, THE(1957), d; BEACH PARTY(1963), d; JOHNNY COOL(1963), p&d; BIKINI BEACH(1964), d, w; MUSCLE BEACH PARTY(1964), d, w; BEACH BLANKET BINGO(1965), d; HOW TO STUFF A WILD BIKINI(1965), d, w; FIREBALL 590(1966), d, w
Alan Asherman
PRINCE OF FOXES(1949)
David Asherman
MEMENTO MEI(1963)
Misha Asherov
IMPOSSIBLE ON SATURDAY(1966, Fr./Israel); NOT MINE TO LOVE(1969, Israel); KAZABLAN(1974, Israel)
Renee Asherson
JOHNNY IN THE CLOUDS(1945, Brit.); CAESAR AND CLEOPATRA(1946, Brit.); HENRY V(1946, Brit.); HOUR OF GLORY(1949, Brit.); CURE FOR LOVE, THE(1950, Brit.); MANIACS ON WHEELS(1951, Brit.); POOL OF LONDON(1951, Brit.); MAGIC BOX, THE(1952, Brit.); MALTA STORY(1954, Brit.); RED DRESS, THE(1954, Brit.); TIME IS MY ENEMY(1957, Brit.); DAY THE EARTH CAUGHT FIRE, THE(1961, Brit.); RASPUTIN-THE MAD MONK(1966, Brit.); SCHOOL FOR UNCLAIMED GIRLS(1973, Brit.); THEATRE OF BLOOD(1973, Brit.)
Misc. Talkies
HELL HOUSE GIRLS(1975, Brit.)
Donald Ashford
RETURN TO PARADISE(1953)
Murray Ashford
SHE KNEW WHAT SHE WANTED(1936, Brit.)
Ted Ashford
HICKEY AND BOGGS(1972), m
1984
HOT AND DEADLY(1984), m
Isamu Ashida
RODAN(1958, Jap.), ph
Shinsuke Ashida
LAKE, THE(1970, Jap.)
Izumi Ashikawa
NO GREATER LOVE THAN THIS(1969, Jap.)
N. Ashikhmyan
SONS AND MOTHERS(1967, USSR)
Ashininka-Campa Indians
FITZCARRALDO(1982)
Mohammed Ashiq
1984
PASSAGE TO INDIA, A(1984, Brit.)
Gannosuke Ashiya
MUDDY RIVER(1982, Jap.)
Nidal Ashkar
1984
MISUNDERSTOOD(1984)
Irvin Ashkenazy
DAVY CROCKETT AND THE RIVER PIRATES(1956)
Irvin Ashkenszy
27TH DAY, THE(1957)
David Ashkinazi
GARNET BRACELET, THE(1966, USSR)
Camila Ashland
10(1979); ANY WHICH WAY YOU CAN(1980)
Blair Ashleigh
FAST TIMES AT RIDGEMONT HIGH(1982)
April Ashley
ROAD TO HONG KONG, THE(1962, U.S./Brit.)
Arthur Ashley
Silents
LITTLE MADEMOISELLE, THE(1915); SEALED LIPS(1915); GILDED CAGE, THE(1916); MEN SHE MARRIED, THE(1916); TANGLED FATES(1916); DIVORCE GAME, THE(1917); IRON RING, THE(1917); AMERICAN WAY, THE(1919); PRAISE AGENT, THE(1919)
Misc. Silents
REVOLT, THE(1916); STRUGGLE, THE(1916); SUMMER GIRL, THE(1916); WHAT HAPPENED AT 22(1916); BONDAGE OF FEAR, THE(1917); GUARDIAN, THE(1917), a, d; MARRIAGE MARKET, THE(1917), a, d; MORAL COURAGE(1917); PAGE MYSTERY, THE(1917); RASPUTIN, THE BLACK MONK(1917), a, d; SHALL WE FORGIVE HER?(1917), a, d; SOCIAL LEPER, THE(1917); BEAUTIFUL MRS. REYNOLDS, THE(1918), a, d; BROKEN TIES(1918), a, d; FOREST RIVALS(1919); OH MARY BE CAREFUL(1921), d; BREAKING HOME TIES(1922)
Audrey Ashley
RAW DEAL(1948), w
Bob Ashley
FOLLOW THE BOYS(1944)
Carol Ashley
JIVE JUNCTION(1944)
Charles E. Ashley
Silents
PAIR OF SIXES, A(1918)
Cindy Ashley
FIRST NUDIE MUSICAL, THE(1976)
Cynthia Ashley
GREAT MUPPET CAPER, THE(1981)
David Ashley
1984
SOLDIER'S STORY, A(1984)

Diana Ashley
OUR MOTHER'S HOUSE(1967, Brit.); CORRUPTION(1968, Brit.); TARGETS(1968)
Edward Ashley
WHITE LILAC(1935, Brit.); UNDER PROOF(1936, Brit.); SATURDAY NIGHT REVUE(1937, Brit.); SING AS YOU SWING(1937, Brit.); UNDERNEATH THE ARCHES(1937, Brit.); VILLIERS DIAMOND, THE(1938, Brit.); BITTER SWEET(1940); GALLANT SONS(1940); PRIDE AND PREJUDICE(1940); SKY MURDER(1940); SPIES OF THE AIR(1940, Brit.); COME LIVE WITH ME(1941); MAISIE WAS A LADY(1941); BLACK SWAN, THE(1942); PIED PIPER, THE(1942); YOU'RE TELLING ME(1942); LOVE, HONOR AND GOODBYE(1945); GAY BLADES(1946); MADONNA'S SECRET, THE(1946); NOCTURNE(1946); DICK TRACY MEETS GRUESOME(1947); OTHER LOVE, THE(1947); TARZAN AND THE MERMAIDS(1948); TARZAN'S PERIL(1951); MACAO(1952); EL ALAMEIN(1954); ELEPHANT WALK(1954); COURT JESTER, THE(1956); DARBY'S RANGERS(1958); KING RAT(1965); WON TON TON, THE DOG WHO SAVED HOLLYWOOD(1976)
Elizabeth Ashley
CARPETBAGGERS, THE(1964); SHIP OF FOOLS(1965); THIRD DAY, THE(1965); MARRIAGE OF A YOUNG STOCKBROKER, THE(1971); PAPERBACK HERO(1973, Can.); GOLDEN NEEDLES(1974); RANCHO DELUXE(1975); 92 IN THE SHADE(1975, U.S./Brit.); GREAT SCOUT AND CATHOUSE THURSDAY, THE(1976); COMA(1978); WINDOWS(1980); PATERNITY(1981); SPLIT IMAGE(1982)
Eve Ashley
I BECAME A CRIMINAL(1947); SHADOW OF THE PAST(1950, Brit.)
Francine Ashley
LOVE MERCHANT, THE(1966)
Fred Ashley
WANDA NEVADA(1979)
Gene Ashley
LOST WEEKEND, THE(1945); STRANGE LOVE OF MARTHA IVERS, THE(1946)
Gloria Ashley
LOSER TAKES ALL(1956, Brit.)
Grace Ashley
Misc. Silents
SKYLIGHT ROOM, THE(1917)
Graeme Ashley
TRACK THE MAN DOWN(1956, Brit.)
Graham Ashley
MAN ACCUSED(1959); TELL-TALE HEART, THE(1962, Brit.); ALFIE DARLING(1975, Brit.); DEADLY FEMALES, THE(1976, Brit.); STAR WARS(1977)
Helmut Ashley
STOLEN IDENTITY(1953), ph; DAS LETZTE GEHEIMNIS(1959, Ger.), ph
Helmuth Ashley
AS LONG AS YOU'RE NEAR ME(1956, Ger.), ph
Herb Ashley
EVERY NIGHT AT EIGHT(1935); MIDNIGHT LIMITED(1940); RINGS ON HER FINGERS(1942); FALLEN ANGEL(1945)
Herbert Ashley
BRILLIANT MARRIAGE(1936); FURY(1936); KING OF BURLESQUE(1936); RHYTHM ON THE RANGE(1936); ROSE BOWL(1936); STAGE STRUCK(1936); DOUBLE OR NOTHING(1937); IT'S LOVE I'M AFTER(1937); LEAGUE OF FRIGHTENED MEN(1937); LOVE IS NEWS(1937); NIGHT CLUB SCANDAL(1937); SARATOGA(1937); TRUE CONFESSION(1937); WHEN YOU'RE IN LOVE(1937); HARD TO GET(1938); HOTEL FOR WOMEN(1939); CHAD HANNA(1940); HOUSE ACROSS THE BAY, THE(1940); LITTLE OLD NEW YORK(1940); MISSION TO MOSCOW(1943); ROGER TOUHY, GANGSTER!(1944); DOLLY SISTERS, THE(1945)
Iris Ashley
HOURS OF LONELINESS(1930, Brit.); NEVER TROUBLE TROUBLE(1931, Brit.); POOR OLD BILL(1931, Brit.); CHARMING DECEIVER, THE(1933, Brit.); SONG YOU GAVE ME, THE(1934, Brit.); WARREN CASE, THE(1934, Brit.); ME AND MARLBOROUGH(1935, Brit.); PHANTOM FIEND, THE(1935, Brit.); REGAL CAVALCADE(1935, Brit.); BLIND MAN'S BLUFF(1936, Brit.); STUDENT'S ROMANCE, THE(1936, Brit.); ROMANCE AND RICHES(1937, Brit.); LOVES OF MADAME DUBARRY, THE(1938, Brit.)
Jane Ashley
ONE JUMP AHEAD(1955, Brit.); HELL'S PLAYGROUND(1967)
Jean Ashley
PURPLE HAZE(1982)
Jennifer Ashley
YOUR THREE MINUTES ARE UP(1973); BARN OF THE NAKED DEAD(1976); POM POM GIRLS, THE(1976); TINTORERA...BLOODY WATERS(1977, Brit./Mex.); TOWING(1978); GUYANA, CULT OF THE DAMNED(1980, Mex./Span./Panama); HORROR PLANET(1982, Brit.); PARTNERS(1982); MAN WHO LOVED WOMEN, THE(1983)
Misc. Talkies
INSEMINOID(1980)
Joel Ashley
BROKEN STAR, THE(1956); CRIME AGAINST JOE(1956); GHOST TOWN(1956); REBEL IN TOWN(1956); RUMBLE ON THE DOCKS(1956); TEN COMMANDMENTS, THE(1956); VAGABOND KING, THE(1956); ZOMBIES OF MORA TAU(1957); WARLOCK(1959)
John Ashley
DRAGSTRIP GIRL(1957); MOTORCYCLE GANG(1957); ZERO HOUR!(1957); FRANKENSTEIN'S DAUGHTER(1958); HOT ROD GANG(1958); HOW TO MAKE A MONSTER(1958); SUICIDE BATTALION(1958); HIGH SCHOOL CAESAR(1960); BEACH PARTY(1963); HUD(1963); BIKINI BEACH(1964); MUSCLE BEACH PARTY(1964); BEACH BLANKET BINGO(1965); EYE CREATURES, THE(1965); HOW TO STUFF A WILD BIKINI(1965); SERGEANT DEADHEAD(1965); YOUNG DILLINGER(1965); HELL ON WHEELS(1967); BRIDES OF BLOOD(1968, US/Phil.); 2001: A SPACE ODYSSEY(1968, U.S./Brit.); MAD DOCTOR OF BLOOD ISLAND, THE(1969, Phil./U.S.); BEAST OF BLOOD(1970, U.S./Phil.); TWILIGHT PEOPLE(1972, Phil.), a, p; BEYOND ATLANTIS(1973, Phil.), a, p; BLACK MAMA, WHITE MAMA(1973), p; SAVAGE SISTERS(1974), a, p; SMOKE IN THE WIND(1975); WOMAN HUNT, THE(1975, U.S./Phil.), a, p
Misc. Talkies
BEAST OF THE YELLOW NIGHT(1971, U.S./Phil.); SUDDEN DEATH(1977)
June Ashley
DEAD ON COURSE(1952, Brit.); BLUE PARROT, THE(1953, Brit.); I'LL GET YOU(1953, Brit.); CIRCUMSTANIAL EVIDENCE(1954, Brit.); CROSS CHANNEL(1955, Brit.); TIME TO KILL, A(1955, Brit.); NARROWING CIRCLE, THE(1956, Brit.)

Kurek Ashley
TWO OF A KIND(1983)
Liz Ashley
NELSON AFFAIR, THE(1973, Brit.)
Lyn Ashley
I'LL NEVER FORGET WHAT'S 'IS NAME(1967, Brit.); QUEST FOR LOVE(1971, Brit.)
Mary Ashley
MAKING THE GRADE(1929); CRY DR. CHICAGO(1971)
Merri Ashley
LIVE A LITTLE, LOVE A LITTLE(1968)
Mike Ashley
TALL WOMEN, THE(1967, Aust./Ital./Span.), w
Nelroy Ashley
ONCE UPON A TIME(1944)
Peter Ashley
FLIGHT ANGELS(1940); KNUTE ROCKNE–ALL AMERICAN(1940); MONEY AND THE WOMAN(1940); STRAWBERRY BLONDE, THE(1941)
Philip Ashley
ESTHER WATERS(1948, Brit.); TRAIN OF EVENTS(1952, Brit.); CARRY ON ADMIRAL(1957, Brit.)
Ray Ashley
LITTLE FUGITIVE, THE(1953), p, d&w
Robert Ashley
SUCH IS LIFE(1936, Brit.); NORTHERN PURSUIT(1943)
Rosalie Ashley
TOO MANY CROOKS(1959, Brit.); CAPTAIN'S TABLE, THE(1960, Brit.)
Susan Ashley
TOO YOUNG, TOO IMMORAL!(1962)
Wilson Ashley
SEDUCERS, THE(1962), p, w
Michael Ashlin
GLORY AT SEA(1952, Brit.)
Jesse Ashlock
SONG OF THE SIERRAS(1946); RIDIN' DOWN THE TRAIL(1947); SONG OF THE WASTELAND(1947)
Gene Ashman
HEAD(1968), cos; GETTING STRAIGHT(1970), cos; LIBERATION OF L.B. JONES, THE(1970), cos
Frank Ashmore
CLONUS HORROR, THE(1979); AIRPLANE II: THE SEQUEL(1982)
1984
INVISIBLE STRANGLER(1984)
Jonathan Ashmore
KID FOR TWO FARTHINGS, A(1956, Brit.)
Peter Ashmore
IPCRESS FILE, THE(1965, Brit.); JIG SAW(1965, Brit.); BEAUTY JUNGLE, THE(1966, Brit.)
Bob Ashmun
1984
PRODIGAL, THE(1984)
Namonai Ashoona
WHITE DAWN, THE(1974)
L. Ashrafova
OTHELLO(1960, U.S.S.R.)
Al Ashton
REMEMBRANCE(1982, Brit.)
Barry Ashton
DANCING YEARS, THE(1950, Brit.)
Brad Ashton
GIRLS OF LATIN QUARTER(1960, Brit.), w
Charles Ashton
AMERICAN PRISONER, THE(1929 Brit.); KITTY(1929, Brit.)
Silents
MONTY WORKS THE WIRES(1921, Brit.); HEAD OF THE FAMILY, THE(1922, Brit.); MONKEY'S PAW, THE(1923, Brit.); SMASHING THROUGH(1928, Brit.)
Misc. Silents
SAM'S BOY(1922, Brit.); WE WOMEN(1925, Brit.); MARIA MARTEN(1928, Brit.); SWEENEY TODD(1928, Brit.)
David Ashton
EYE OF THE NEEDLE(1981)
Don Ashton
MURDER WITHOUT CRIME(1951, Brit.), art d; PORTRAIT OF CLARE(1951, Brit.), art d; THEY WHO DARE(1954, Brit.), art d; END OF THE AFFAIR, THE(1955, Brit.), art d; PORTRAIT IN SMOKE(1957, Brit.), art d; INDISCREET(1958), art d; COUNT YOUR BLESSINGS(1959), art d; SAVAGE INNOCENTS, THE(1960, Brit.), art d; MAN IN THE MOON(1961, Brit.), prod d; I LIKE MONEY(1962, Brit.), prod d; BUNNY LAKE IS MISSING(1965), prod d; MASQUERADE(1965, Brit.), prod d; COUNTESS FROM HONG KONG, A(1967, Brit.), prod d; MAGUS, THE(1968, Brit.), prod d; OH! WHAT A LOVELY WAR(1969, Brit.), prod d; DEVIL'S WIDOW, THE(1972, Brit.), prod d; YOUNG WINSTON(1972, Brit.), prod d
Frederick Ashton
DANCE PRETTY LADY(1932, Brit.), ch tech adv; TALES OF HOFFMANN, THE(1951, Brit.); STORY OF THREE LOVES, THE(1953), ch; PETER RABBIT AND TALES OF BEATRIX POTTER(1971, Brit.), a, ch; TURNING POINT, THE(1977), ch
Helen Ashton
WHITE CORRIDORS(1952, Brit.), w
Herbert Ashton, Jr.
BROTHERS(1930), w
Horace D. Ashton
SILENT ENEMY, THE(1930), ph
Iris Ashton
WORDS AND MUSIC(1929)
Silents
LAMPLIGHTER, THE(1921)
James Ashton
CAPTAIN MILKSHAKE(1970); DEVIL'S RAIN, THE(1975, U.S./Mex.), w

John Ashton
BREAKING AWAY(1979); BORDERLINE(1980); HONKY TONK FREEWAY(1981)
1984
ADVENTURES OF BUCKAROO BANZAI: ACROSS THE 8TH DIMENSION, THE(1984); BEVERLY HILLS COP(1984)
John D. Ashton
PSYCHOPATH, THE(1973)
Judy Ashton
DEAD AND BURIED(1981)
Marcia Ashton
GREEN BUDDHA, THE(1954, Brit.)
Marie Ashton
DON'T CRY, IT'S ONLY THUNDER(1982)
Natasha Ashton
STOP THE WORLD–I WANT TO GET OFF(1966, Brit.)
Nigel Ashton
MACBETH(1971, Brit.)
Pat Ashton
HALF A SIXPENCE(1967, Brit.); OPTIMISTS, THE(1973, Brit.); PARTY PARTY(1983, Brit.)
1984
BLOODBATH AT THE HOUSE OF DEATH(1984, Brit.)
Peter Ashton
ON THE BEACH(1959)
Queenie Ashton
ALWAYS ANOTHER DAWN(1948, Aus.)
Ray Ashton
NEVER TAKE CANDY FROM A STRANGER(1961, Brit.), makeup
Roy Ashton
MAN WHO LIVED AGAIN, THE(1936, Brit.), makeup; FIRE MAIDENS FROM OUTER SPACE(1956, Brit.), makeup; PICKUP ALLEY(1957, Brit.), makeup; WHOLE TRUTH, THE(1958, Brit.), makeup; MAN WHO COULD CHEAT DEATH, THE(1959, Brit.), makeup; CURSE OF THE WEREWOLF, THE(1961), makeup; PASSPORT TO CHINA(1961, Brit.), makeup; SHADOW OF THE CAT, THE(1961, Brit.), makeup; TERROR OF THE TONGS, THE(1961, Brit.), makeup; DESERT PATROL(1962, Brit.), makeup; PHANTOM OF THE OPERA, THE(1962, Brit.), makeup; PIRATES OF BLOOD RIVER, THE(1962, Brit.), makeup; KISS OF EVIL(1963, Brit.), makeup; NIGHTMARE(1963, Brit.), makeup; PARANOIAC(1963, Brit.), makeup; EVIL OF FRANKENSTEIN, THE(1964, Brit.), makeup; GORGON, THE(1964, Brit.), makeup; SECRET OF BLOOD ISLAND, THE(1965, Brit.), makeup; SHE(1965, Brit.), cos; DRACULA–PRINCE OF DARKNESS(1966, Brit.), makeup; PLAGUE OF THE ZOMBIES, THE(1966, Brit.), makeup; RASPUTIN–THE MAD MONK(1966, Brit.), makeup; REPTILE, THE(1966, Brit.), makeup; KIDNAPPED(1971, Brit.), makeup; TALES FROM THE CRYPT(1972, Brit.), makeup; VAULT OF HORROR, THE(1973, Brit.), makeup; PERSECUTION(1974, Brit.), makeup; LITTLEST HORSE THIEVES, THE(1977), makeup
Sylvia Ashton
BARKER, THE(1928)
Silents
OVERALLS(1916); OLD WIVES FOR NEW(1918); PAIR OF SILK STOCKINGS, A(1918); JOHNNY GET YOUR GUN(1919); JACK STRAW(1920); JENNY BE GOOD(1920); SOUL OF YOUTH, THE(1920); THOU ART THE MAN(1920); BLUSHING BRIDE, THE(1921); LOVE CHARM, THE(1921); PRINCE THERE WAS, A(1921); SHAM(1921); OUR LEADING CITIZEN(1922); SATURDAY NIGHT(1922); WHILE SATAN SLEEPS(1922); YOUTH TO YOUTH(1922); SOULS FOR SALE(1923); WHITE FLOWER, THE(1923); GREED(1925); CHEATING CHEATERS(1927); BACHELOR'S PARADISE(1928); HEAD MAN, THE(1928); LEOPARD LADY, THE(1928); QUEEN KELLY(1929)
Misc. Silents
DON'T CHANGE YOUR HUSBAND(1919); FOR BETTER, FOR WORSE(1919); UNDER THE TOP(1919); HER STURDY OAK(1921); HOLD YOUR HORSES(1921); SNOB, THE(1921); LADIES' NIGHT IN A TURKISH BATH(1928)
Tara Ashton
MARRIAGE ON THE ROCKS(1965); GUN RIDERS, THE(1969)
Tony Ashton
LAST REBEL, THE(1971), m
Warwick Ashton
CRUEL SEA, THE(1953); LIGHT TOUCH, THE(1955, Brit.); TECKMAN MYSTERY, THE(1955, Brit); WHO DONE IT?(1956, Brit.); THIRD KEY, THE(1957, Brit.); DUNKIRK(1958, Brit.)
Sylvia Ashton-Warner
TWO LOVES(1961), w
H. Ashton-Wolfe
SECRETS OF THE FRENCH POLICE(1932), w
Thomas Ashwell
THERE'S ALWAYS VANILLA(1972)
Terry Ashwood
FLOOD, THE(1963, Brit.), p; STOPOVER FOREVER(1964, Brit.), p
Christine Ashworth
WHISTLE DOWN THE WIND(1961, Brit.)
Dicken Ashworth
REMEMBRANCE(1982, Brit.); KRULL(1983)
Ernest Ashworth
FARMER'S OTHER DAUGHTER, THE(1965)
Ernie Ashworth
Misc. Talkies
VALLEY OF BLOOD(1973)
John Ashworth
QUEEN FOR A DAY(1951), w
Ivan Asic
DIAMONDS OF THE NIGHT(1968, Czech.)
Elliott Asinof
BREAKOUT(1975), w
Connie Asins
RIDE THE PINK HORSE(1947)
Miguel Asins-Arbo
FACE OF TERROR(1964, Span.), m

Earl Askam

LET'S GO NATIVE(1930); MADAME SATAN(1930); STOLEN HARMONY(1935); FLASH GORDON(1936); SILVER SPURS(1936); TRAIL DUST(1936); DEAD END(1937); EMPTY SADDLES(1937); THUNDER TRAIL(1937); PRIDE OF THE WEST(1938); RED RIVER RANGE(1938); GOLDEN BOY(1939); RULERS OF THE SEA(1939); UNION PACIFIC(1939); LIGHT OF WESTERN STARS, THE(1940); PIONEERS OF THE WEST(1940)

Perry Askam

SWEET KITTY BELLAIRS(1930); CRUSADES, THE(1935)

Alice Askew

Silents

PLEYDELL MYSTERY, THE(1916, Brit.), w; JOHN HERIOT'S WIFE(1920, Brit.), w

Claude Askew

Silents

PLEYDELL MYSTERY, THE(1916, Brit.), w; JOHN HERIOT'S WIFE(1920, Brit.), w

Desmond Askew

1984

GIVE MY REGARDS TO BROAD STREET(1984, Brit.)

Luke Askew

COOL HAND LUKE(1967); HAPPENING, THE(1967); HURRY SUNDOWN(1967); DEVIL'S BRIGADE, THE(1968); GREEN BERETS, THE(1968); WILL PENNY(1968); EASY RIDER(1969); FLAREUP(1969); ANGEL UNCHAINED(1970); CULPEPPER CATTLE COMPANY, THE(1972); GREAT NORTHFIELD, MINNESOTA RAID, THE(1972); MAGNIFICENT SEVEN RIDE, THE(1972); PAT GARRETT AND BILLY THE KID(1973); SLIPSTREAM(1974, Can.); MACKINTOSH & T.J.(1975); POSSE(1975); WALKING TALL, PART II(1975); ROLLING THUNDER(1977); WANDA NEVADA(1979); BEAST WITHIN, THE(1982)

Nicholas Askew

1984

GIVE MY REGARDS TO BROAD STREET(1984, Brit.)

Anthea Askey

LOVE MATCH, THE(1955, Brit.); RAMSBOTTOM RIDES AGAIN(1956, Brit.); MAKE MINE A MILLION(1965, Brit.)

Arthur Askey

CHARLEY'S(BIG-HEARTED) AUNT*1/2 (1940); BAND WAGGON(1940, Brit.); GHOST TRAIN, THE(1941, Brit.); I THANK YOU(1941, Brit.); BACK ROOM BOY(1942, Brit.); KING ARTHUR WAS A GENTLEMAN(1942, Brit.); MISS LONDON LTD.(1943, Brit.); BEES IN PARADISE(1944, Brit.); LOVE MATCH, THE(1955, Brit.); RAMSBOTTOM RIDES AGAIN(1956, Brit.), a, w; FRIENDS AND NEIGHBORS(1963, Brit.); MAKE MINE A MILLION(1965, Brit.), a, w

David Askey

TAKE ME HIGH(1973, Brit.), d

Phil Askham

GAMEKEEPER, THE(1980, Brit.); LOOKS AND SMILES(1982, Brit.)

Leon Askin

ASSIGNMENT–PARIS(1952); ROAD TO BALI(1952); CHINA VENTURE(1953); DESERT LEGION(1953); ROBE, THE(1953); SOUTH SEA WOMAN(1953); VEILS OF BAGDAD, THE(1953); KNOCK ON WOOD(1954); SECRET OF THE INCAS(1954); VALLEY OF THE KINGS(1954); CAROLINA CANNONBALL(1955); SON OF SINBAD(1955); SPY CHASERS(1956); MY GUN IS QUICK(1957); LAST BLITZKRIEG, THE(1958); ONE, TWO, THREE(1961); LULU(1962, Aus.); SHERLOCK HOLMES AND THE DEADLY NECKLACE(1962, Ger.); JOHN GOLDFARB, PLEASE COME HOME(1964); DO NOT DISTURB(1965); TERROR OF DR. MABUSE, THE(1965, Ger.); WHAT DID YOU DO IN THE WAR, DADDY?(1966); CAPER OF THE GOLDEN BULLS, THE(1967); DOUBLE TROUBLE(1967); PERILS OF PAULINE, THE(1967); GUNS FOR SAN SEBASTIAN(1968, U.S./Fr./Mex./Ital.); WICKED DREAMS OF PAULA SCHULTZ, THE(1968); FINE PAIR, A(1969, Ital.); MALTESE BIPPY, THE(1969); HAMMERSMITH IS OUT(1972); DOCTOR DEATH: SEEKER OF SOULS(1973); WORLD'S GREATEST ATHLETE, THE(1973); YOUNG FRANKENSTEIN(1974); GOING APE!(1981); AIRPLANE II: THE SEQUEL(1982); FRIGHTMARE(1983)

Peter Askin

SMITHEREENS(1982), w

Monroe Askins

BLOOD OF DRACULA(1957), ph; THIS REBEL BREED(1960), ph; HUMAN DUPLICATORS, THE(1965), ph; CAT, THE(1966), ph; THUNDER ALLEY(1967), ph; HOUSE ON SKULL MOUNTAIN, THE(1974), ph

Monroe P. Askins

SAGA OF THE VIKING WOMEN AND THEIR VOYAGE TO THE WATERS OF THE GREAT SEA SERPENT, THE(1957), ph; SORORITY GIRL(1957), ph; NAPOLEON AND SAMANTHA(1972), ph

Robin Askwith

IF ...(1968, Brit.); OTLEY(1969, Brit.); COOL IT, CAROL!(1970, Brit.); SCRAMBLE(1970, Brit.); HORROR HOSPITAL(1973, Brit.); CONFESSIONS OF A WINDOW CLEANER(1974, Brit.); FLESH AND BLOOD SHOW, THE(1974, Brit.); CONFESSIONS OF A POP PERFORMER(1975, Brit.); CONFESSIONS FROM A HOLIDAY CAMP(1977, Brit.); STAND UP VIRGIN SOLDIERS(1977, Brit.); BEYOND THE FOG(1981, Brit.); BRITTANIA HOSPITAL(1982, Brit.)

Misc. Talkies

HANS BRINKER AND THE SILVER SKATES(1969); DIRTIEST GIRL I EVER MET, THE(1973)

Aslan

SLEEPING CAR TO TRIESTE(1949, Brit.)

Coco [Gregoire] Aslan

WHIRLWIND OF PARIS(1946, Fr.); CAIRO ROAD(1950, Brit.); LAST HOLIDAY(1950, Brit.)

Gregoire Aslan

CAGE OF GOLD(1950, Brit.); ADVENTURERS, THE(1951, Brit.); ACT OF LOVE(1953); RED, INN, THE(1954, Fr.); INNOCENTS IN PARIS(1955, Brit.); JOE MACBETH(1955); CASINO DE PARIS(1957, Fr./Ger.); ROOTS OF HEAVEN, THE(1958); SNORKEL, THE(1958, Brit.); WINDOM'S WAY(1958, Brit.); SEA FURY(1959, Brit.); KILLERS OF KILIMANJARO(1960, Brit.); OUR MAN IN HAVANA(1960, Brit.); THREE WORLDS OF GULLIVER, THE(1960, Brit.); UNDER TEN FLAGS(1960, U.S./Ital.); CALL ME GENIUS(1961, Brit.); DEVIL AT FOUR O'CLOCK, THE(1961); INVASION QUARTET(1961, Brit.); KING OF KINGS(1961); CONCRETE JUNGLE, THE(1962, Brit.); HAPPY THIEVES, THE(1962); MR. ARKADIN(1962, Brit./Fr./Span.); VILLAGE OF DAUGHTERS(1962, Brit.); CLEOPATRA(1963); CROOKS IN CLOISTERS(1964, Brit.); PARIS WHEN IT SIZZLES(1964); YELLOW ROLLS-ROYCE, THE(1965, Brit.); BANG, BANG, YOU'RE DEAD(1966); LOST COMMAND, THE(1966); MAIN CHANCE, THE(1966, Brit.); MAN COULD GET KILLED, A(1966); MARCO THE MAGNIFICENT(1966, Ital./Fr./Yugo./Egypt/Afghanistan); MC GUIRE, GO HOME!(1966, Brit.); MOMENT TO MOMENT(1966); RAVISHING IDIOT, A(1966, Ital./Fr.); TASTE FOR WOMEN, A(1966, Fr./Ital.); 25TH HOUR, THE(1967, Fr./Ital./Yugo.); FLEA IN HER EAR, A(1968, Fr.); CHECKERBOARD(1969, Fr.); MARRY ME! MARRY ME!(1969, Fr.); YOU CAN'T WIN 'EM ALL(1970, Brit.); GIRL FROM PETROVKA, THE(1974, Fr.); GOLDEN VOYAGE OF SINBAD, THE(1974, Brit.); RETURN OF THE PINK PANTHER, THE(1975, Brit.); MEETINGS WITH REMARKABLE MEN(1979, Brit.)

Greyoire Aslan

GUTS IN THE SUN(1959, Fr.)

Raoul Aslan

WHITE DEMON, THE(1932, Ger.); INVISIBLE OPPONENT(1933, Ger.)

Misc. Silents

OTHER SELF, THE(1918, Aust.)

Hermin Aslanian

NIGHT GAMES(1980)

Jacques Aslanian

SHOOT THE PIANO PLAYER(1962, Fr.)

Michelle Aslanoff

INTENT TO KILL(1958, Brit.)

Arthur Asley

Misc. Silents

MISS PETTICOATS(1916)

Rita Aslim

UNCIVILISED(1937, Aus.)

Edna Aslin

ARIZONA TRAILS(1935)

Misc. Talkies

RACKETEER ROUND-UP(1934); PHANTOM COWBOY, THE(1935); TRAILS OF ADVENTURE(1935); WESTERN RACKETEERS(1935)

Silents

INVADERS, THE(1929); RIDERS OF THE RIO GRANDE(1929)

Misc. Silents

COWBOY AND THE OUTLAW, THE(1929); BREEZY BILL(1930)

Bub Asman

DAY OF THE ANIMALS(1977), ed; MANITOU, THE(1978), ed

Henry Asman

ABBY(1974), ed; SHEBA BABY(1975), ed

William Asman

ABBY(1974), ph; SHEBA BABY(1975), ph

Herbert Asmodi

YOUNG TORLESS(1968, Fr./Ger.); CROSS OF IRON(1977, Brit., Ger.), w

Ed Asner

DO NOT THROW CUSHIONS INTO THE RING(1970); GUS(1976)

Edward Asner

SATAN BUG, THE(1965); SLENDER THREAD, THE(1965); EL DORADO(1967); GUNN(1967); VENETIAN AFFAIR, THE(1967); CHANGE OF HABIT(1969); HALLS OF ANGER(1970); THEY CALL ME MISTER TIBBS(1970); SKIN GAME(1971); TODD KILLINGS, THE(1971); WRESTLER, THE(1974); FORT APACHE, THE BRONX(1981); DANIEL(1983); O'HARA'S WIFE(1983)

Connie Asnis

SILVER TRAILS(1948)

Asoka

DESERT LEGION(1953), ch; FLAME OF CALCUTTA(1953); SALOME(1953)

Ruriko Asoka

ALONE ON THE PACIFIC(1964, Jap.)

Reiko Asoo

WHISPERING JOE(1969, Jap.)

Anna Asp

AUTUMN SONATA(1978, Swed.), prod d; FANNY AND ALEXANDER(1983, Swed./Fr./Ger.), art d

1984

AFTER THE REHEARSAL(1984, Swed.), art d

Jim Asp

TEEN-AGE STRANGLER(1967)

Fred Asparagus

1984

BREAKIN' 2: ELECTRIC BOOGALOO(1984); THIS IS SPINAL TAP(1984)

Chuck Aspegren

DEER HUNTER, THE(1978)

Michael Aspel

MAGIC CHRISTIAN, THE(1970, Brit.)

Wally Aspell

1984

HOTEL NEW HAMPSHIRE, THE(1984)

Patricia Aspillaga

JORY(1972)

Dale Aspin

DEATHCHEATERS(1976, Aus.)

Max Aspin

DEATHCHEATERS(1976, Aus.); CHAIN REACTION(1980, Aus.), stunts; ROAD WARRIOR, THE(1982, Aus.), stunts

J. Aspinal

VORTEX(1982), makeup

Aspinosa

CARNIVAL(1946, Brit.)

Marger Aspit

TOUCHDOWN!(1931)

Maria Asquerino

THAT OBSCURE OBJECT OF DESIRE(1977, Fr./Span.)

Anthony Asquith

BATTLE OF GALLIPOLI(1931, Brit.), d, w; DANCE PRETTY LADY(1932, Brit.), d&w; MARRY ME(1932, Brit.), w; LETTING IN THE SUNSHINE(1933, Brit.), w; LUCKY NUMBER, THE(1933, Brit.), d; I STAND CONDEMNED(1936, Brit.), d, w; PYGMALION(1938, Brit.), d, w; FRENCH WITHOUT TEARS(1939, Brit.), d; BOMBSIGHT STOLEN(1941, Brit.), d; QUIET WEDDING(1941, Brit.), d; VOICE IN THE NIGHT, A(1941, Brit.), d; WE DIVE AT DAWN(1943, Brit.), d; UNCENSORED(1944, Brit.), d; ADVENTURE FOR TWO(1945, Brit.), d; JOHNNY IN THE CLOUDS(1945, Brit.), d; MAN OF EVIL(1948, Brit.), d; FIVE ANGLES ON MURDER(1950, Brit.), d; WHILE THE SUN SHINES(1950, Brit.), d; WINSLOW BOY, THE(1950), d, w;

BROWNING VERSION, THE(1951, Brit.), d; IMPORTANCE OF BEING EARNEST, THE(1952, Brit.), d&w; FINAL TEST, THE(1953, Brit.), d; PROJECT M7(1953, Brit.), d; UNFINISHED SYMPHONY, THE(1953, Aust./Brit.), d; CHANCE MEETING(1954, Brit.), d; COURT MARTIAL(1954, Brit.), d; DOCTOR'S DILEMMA, THE(1958, Brit.), d; ORDERS TO KILL(1958, Brit.), d; LIBEL(1959, Brit.), d; MILLIONAIRESS, THE(1960, Brit.), d; GUNS OF DARKNESS(1962, Brit.), d; V.I.P.s, THE(1963, Brit.), d; TWO LIVING, ONE DEAD(1964, Brit./Swed.), d; YELLOW ROLLS-ROYCE, THE(1965, Brit.), d
Misc. Silents
SHOOTING STARS(1928), d; UNDERGROUND(1928, Brit.), d; RUNAWAY PRINCESS, THE(1929, Brit.), d

Elizabeth Asquith
Silents
GREAT LOVE, THE(1918)

John Asquith
PIRATES OF PENZANCE, THE(1983)

Lady Cynthia Asquith
DREAMING LIPS(1937, Brit.), w

Mary Asquith
Silents
POWER OF DECISION, THE(1917)

Robert Asquith
JOKER IS WILD, THE(1957)

Robin Asquith
BARTLEBY(1970, Brit.)

Andre Asriel
PRIVATE POOLEY(1962, Brit./E. Ger.), m

Alexander Asro
ROOM SERVICE(1938)

Rafik Assad
LIAR'S DICE(1980)

Juan Assaei
BRAVE BULLS, THE(1951)

Danny Assael
SCHIZOID(1980)

Kobi Assaf
JESUS(1979)

Roger Assaf
CIRCLE OF DECEIT(1982, Fr./Ger.)

Adeeb Assaly
THUNDER OVER TANGIER(1957, Brit.); NIGHT AMBUSH(1958, Brit.)

Edouard Assaly
INTENT TO KILL(1958, Brit.); MARK OF THE PHOENIX(1958, Brit.)

Ratna Assan
PAPILLON(1973)

Armand Assante
LORDS OF FLATBUSH, THE(1974); PARADISE ALLEY(1978); PROPHECY(1979); LITTLE DARLINGS(1980); PRIVATE BENJAMIN(1980); I, THE JURY(1982); LOVE AND MONEY(1982)
1984
UNFAITHFULLY YOURS(1984)

Assault
WINNER'S CIRCLE, THE(1948)

Carlos Asse
1984
FLASH OF GREEN, A(1984), art d

Carly Asse
1984
FLASH OF GREEN, A(1984)

Diane Asselin
HONEYMOON KILLERS, THE(1969)

Georges Asselin
LA MATERNELLE(1933, Fr.), ph

Philippe Asselin
AU HASARD, BALTHAZAR(1970, Fr.)

Robert Asselin
SECOND BUREAU(1936, Fr.), ph

Etienne Assena
MAGNIFICENT ONE, THE(1974, Fr./Ital.)

Tamara Asseyev
PADDY(1970, Irish), p; AROUSERS, THE(1973), p; DRIVE-IN(1976), p; I WANNA HOLD YOUR HAND(1978), p; NORMA RAE(1979), p

Assia
THEY MET ON SKIS(1940, Fr.)

Lya Assia
SCHLAGER-PARADE(1953)

G. Assimakopoulos
ANNA OF RHODES(1950, Gr.), w

Arno Assmann
DECISION BEFORE DAWN(1951)

R. Greenberg Associates
ZELIG(1983), spec eff

Ovidio Assonitis
BEYOND THE DOOR(1975, Ital./U.S.), p; VISITOR, THE(1980, Ital./U.S.), p

Ovidio G. Assonitis
Misc. Talkies
MADHOUSE(1982), d

Jacques Assuerus
1984
HERE COMES SANTA CLAUS(1984), ph

Robert Assumpaco
GENTLE RAIN, THE(1966, Braz.)

Pierre Assy
STORY OF A CHEAT, THE(1938, Fr.)

Margrette Ast
YOUNG LORD, THE(1970, Ger.)

Pat Ast
SIDELONG GLANCES OF A PIGEON KICKER, THE(1970); DUCHESS AND THE DIRTWATER FOX, THE(1976); WHICH WAY IS UP?(1977); WORLD'S GREATEST LOVER, THE(1977); FOUL PLAY(1978); PURSUIT OF D.B. COOPER, THE(1981);

PANDEMONIUM(1982)
Misc. Talkies
HEAT(1972)

Asta
BRINGING UP BABY(1938); ANOTHER THIN MAN(1939)

Asta, Jr.
SONG OF THE THIN MAN(1947)

Adele Astaire
Silents
FANCHON THE CRICKET(1915)

Fred Astaire
DANCING LADY(1933); FLYING DOWN TO RIO(1933); GAY DIVORCEE, THE(1934), a, ch; ROBERTA(1935), a, ch; TOP HAT(1935), a, ch; FOLLOW THE FLEET(1936), a, ch; SWING TIME(1936); DAMSEL IN DISTRESS, A(1937), a, ch; SHALL WE DANCE(1937); CAREFREE(1938), a, ch; STORY OF VERNON AND IRENE CASTLE, THE(1939); BROADWAY MELODY OF 1940(1940); SECOND CHORUS(1940); YOU'LL NEVER GET RICH(1941); HOLIDAY INN(1942); YOU WERE NEVER LOVELIER(1942); SKY'S THE LIMIT, THE(1943), a, ch; YOLANDA AND THE THIEF(1945); ZIEGFELD FOLLIES(1945); BLUE SKIES(1946); EASTER PARADE(1948); BARKLEYS OF BROADWAY, THE(1949); LET'S DANCE(1950); THREE LITTLE WORDS(1950); ROYAL WEDDING(1951); BELLE OF NEW YORK, THE(1952); BAND WAGON, THE(1953); DADDY LONG LEGS(1955), a, ch; FUNNY FACE(1957), a, ch; SILK STOCKINGS(1957); ON THE BEACH(1959); PLEASURE OF HIS COMPANY, THE(1961), a, ch; NOTORIOUS LANDLADY, THE(1962); PARIS WHEN IT SIZZLES(1964); FINIAN'S RAINBOW(1968); MIDAS RUN(1969); TOWERING INFERNO, THE(1974); AMAZING DOBERMANS, THE(1976); PURPLE TAXI, THE(1977, Fr./Ital./Ireland); GHOST STORY(1981)
Silents
FANCHON THE CRICKET(1915)

Fred Astaire, Jr.
MIDAS RUN(1969)

Jarvis Astaire
AGATHA(1979, Brit.), p

Marie Astaire
NIGHT PARADE(1929, Brit.); GRAND PARADE, THE(1930); MILLIE(1931); SOLDIER'S PLAYTHING, A(1931); UPPER WORLD(1934); DR. SOCRATES(1935); G-MEN(1935); MISS PACIFIC FLEET(1935); WOMEN IN THE WIND(1939)
Misc. Silents
LIGHTS OUT(1923)

Thomas Astan
JONATHAN(1973, Ger.)

M. Astangov
GENERAL SUVOROV(1941, USSR); MAGIC VOYAGE OF SINBAD, THE(1962, USSR)

Mikhail Astangov
HYPERBOLOID OF ENGINEER GARIN, THE(1965, USSR)

A. Ben Astar
FIVE FINGERS(1952)

Albert Astar
CARRIE(1952)

Albert Ben Astar
LIGHT TOUCH, THE(1951)

Ben Astar
ASSIGNMENT–PARIS(1952); BAD AND THE BEAUTIFUL, THE(1952); TARGET HONG KONG(1952); CHARGE OF THE LANCERS(1953); FORT TI(1953); MONEY FROM HOME(1953); ROBE, THE(1953); MAN WHO UNDERSTOOD WOMEN, THE(1959); THIS EARTH IS MINE(1959); MARRIAGE-GO-ROUND, THE(1960); STORY OF RUTH, THE(1960); HONEYMOON MACHINE, THE(1961); ON THE DOUBLE(1961); FIVE WEEKS IN A BALLOON(1962); BYE BYE BIRDIE(1963); HOUSE IS NOT A HOME, A(1964); DEAD HEAT ON A MERRY-GO-ROUND(1966); WALK, DON'T RUN(1966)

Betty Astell
CLEANING UP(1933, Brit.); GREAT STUFF(1933, Brit.); I'LL STICK TO YOU(1933, Brit.); MEDICINE MAN, THE(1933, Brit.); STRIKE IT RICH(1933, Brit.); THAT'S MY WIFE(1933, Brit.); THIS IS THE LIFE(1933, Brit.); JOSSER ON THE FARM(1934, Brit.); LIFE OF THE PARTY(1934, Brit.); MAN I WANT, THE(1934, Brit.); ON THE AIR(1934, Brit.); STRICTLY ILLEGAL(1935, Brit.); THAT'S MY UNCLE(1935, Brit.); WIFE OR TWO, A(1935, Brit.); SUNSHINE AHEAD(1936, Brit.); LOST CHORD, THE(1937, Brit.); TWO OF US, THE(1938, Brit.); MYSTERIOUS MR. REEDER, THE(1940, Brit.)

Elizabeth [Betty] Astell
VANDERGILT DIAMOND MYSTERY, THE(1936); BEHIND YOUR BACK(1937, Brit.)

Nils Asther
SEA BAT, THE(1930); BUT THE FLESH IS WEAK(1932); LETTY LYNTON(1932); WASHINGTON MASQUERADE(1932); BITTER TEA OF GENERAL YEN, THE(1933); IF I WERE FREE(1933); RIGHT TO ROMANCE(1933); STORM AT DAYBREAK(1933); BY CANDLELIGHT(1934); CRIME DOCTOR, THE(1934); LOVE CAPTIVE, THE(1934); LOVE TIME(1934); MADAME SPY(1934); ABDUL THE DAMNED(1935, Brit.); GUILTY MELODY(1936, Brit.); MAKE-UP(1937, Brit.); HATE IN PARADISE(1938, Brit.); PRISONER OF CORBAL(1939, Brit.); DR. KILDARE'S WEDDING DAY(1941); FLYING BLIND(1941); FORCED LANDING(1941); MAN WHO LOST HIMSELF, THE(1941); NIGHT OF JANUARY 16TH(1941); NIGHT BEFORE THE DIVORCE, THE(1942); NIGHT MONSTER(1942); SWEATER GIRL(1942); MYSTERY BROADCAST(1943); SUBMARINE ALERT(1943); ALASKA(1944); BLUEBEARD(1944); HOUR BEFORE THE DAWN, THE(1944); MAN IN HALF-MOON STREET, THE(1944); JEALOUSY(1945); LOVE, HONOR AND GOODBYE(1945); SON OF LASSIE(1945); FEATHERED SERPENT, THE(1948); SAMSON AND DELILAH(1949); THAT MAN FROM TANGIER(1953); SUDDENLY, A WOMAN!(1967, Den.)
Silents
LAUGH, CLOWN, LAUGH(1928); OUR DANCING DAUGHTERS(1928); SINGLE STANDARD, THE(1929); WILD ORCHIDS(1929)
Misc. Silents
BLUE DANUBE, THE(1928); CARDBOARD LOVER, THE(1928); COSSACKS, THE(1928); DREAM OF LOVE(1928); LOVES OF AN ACTRESS(1928)

Adriana Asti
ACCATTONE!(1961, Ital.); ROCCO AND HIS BROTHERS(1961, Fr./Ital.); BEFORE THE REVOLUTION(1964, Ital.); DISORDER(1964, Fr./Ital.); DUET FOR CANNIBALS(1969, Swed.); LUDWIG(1973, Ital./Ger./Fr.); PHANTOM OF LIBERTY, THE(1974, Fr.); DOWN THE ANCIENT STAIRCASE(1975, Ital.); INHERITANCE, THE(1978, Ital.)

Emmanuelle Astier
GOODBYE EMMANUELLE(1980, Fr.), w

John Astin
WEST SIDE STORY(1961); THAT TOUCH OF MINK(1962); MOVE OVER, DARLING(1963); WHEELER DEALERS, THE(1963); SPIRIT IS WILLING, THE(1967); CANDY(1968, Ital./Fr.); VIVA MAX!(1969); BUNNY O'HARE(1971); EVERY LITTLE CROOK AND NANNY(1972); GET TO KNOW YOUR RABBIT(1972); BROTHERS O'TOOLE, THE(1973); FREAKY FRIDAY(1976)
Misc. Talkies
PEPPER AND HIS WACKY TAXI(1972)

Patty Duke Astin
SWARM, THE(1978); BY DESIGN(1982)

Nancy Astinger
RED RUNS THE RIVER(1963)

Ed Astley
LIFE AND TIMES OF CHESTER-ANGUS RAMSGOOD, THE(1971, Can.)

Edward Astley
WHAT EVERY WOMAN WANTS(1954, Brit.), m

Edwin Astley
DEVIL GIRL FROM MARS(1954, Brit.), m; TO PARIS WITH LOVE(1955, Brit.), m, md; FUN AT ST. FANNY'S(1956, Brit.), m; KILL HER GENTLY(1958, Brit.), m, md; END OF THE LINE, THE(1959, Brit.), m; MOUSE THAT ROARED, THE(1959, Brit.), m, md; WOMAN EATER, THE(1959, Brit.), m&md; DAY THEY ROBBED THE BANK OF ENGLAND, THE(1960, Brit.), m; FACES IN THE DARK(1960, Brit.), m; IN THE WAKE OF A STRANGER(1960, Brit.), m; LET'S GET MARRIED(1960, Brit.), m; PASSPORT TO CHINA(1961, Brit.), m; MATTER OF WHO, A(1962, Brit.), m; PHANTOM OF THE OPERA, THE(1962, Brit.), m; GREAT VAN ROBBERY, THE(1963, Brit.), m; PLEASURE LOVERS, THE(1964, Brit.), md; PUSSYCAT ALLEY(1965, Brit.), m, m&md; SYNDICATE, THE(1968, Brit.), m

Edwin T. Astley
DIGBY, THE BIGGEST DOG IN THE WORLD(1974, Brit.), m

George Astley
DOUBLE EXPOSURES(1937, Brit.)

John Astley
Silents
JIMMY(1916, Brit.)

Pat Astley
1984
DON'T OPEN TILL CHRISTMAS(1984, Brit.)

Ted Astley
HAPPINESS OF THREE WOMEN, THE(1954, Brit.), m; BEHEMOTH, THE SEA MONSTER(1959, Brit.), m

Gianni Astolfi
FALL OF ROME, THE(1963, Ital.), w

Beatrice Aston
BARRY MC KENZIE HOLDS HIS OWN(1975, Aus.)

Brian Smedly Aston
GIRL STROKE BOY(1971, Brit.), ed

Doug Aston
GOODBYE PORK PIE(1981, New Zealand)

E. Smedley Aston
STRANGER'S MEETING(1957, Brit.), p; STRICTLY FOR THE BIRDS(1963, Brit.), p

E.M. Smedley Aston
OFFBEAT(1961, Brit.), p; TWO LETTER ALIBI(1962), p; GET CHARLIE TULLY(1976, Brit.), p

Joy Aston
STOP TRAIN 349(1964, Fr./Ital./Ger.)

Lucy Aston
DANGEROUS DAVIES–THE LAST DETECTIVE(1981, Brit.)

Paul Aston
UNMAN, WITTERING AND ZIGO(1971, Brit.)

Susan Aston
TENDER MERCIES(1982)

Camile Astor
Misc. Silents
FOR THOSE WE LOVE(1921)

Camille Astor
Silents
CHIMMIE FADDEN(1915); CHIMMIE FADDEN OUT WEST(1915)
Misc. Silents
FOR THE DEFENCE(1916)

Gertrude Astor
FALL OF EVE, THE(1929); FROZEN JUSTICE(1929); TWIN BEDS(1929); TWO WEEKS OFF(1929); UNTAMED(1929); BE YOURSELF(1930); DAMES AHOY(1930); HELL BOUND(1931); THEY NEVER COME BACK(1932); WESTERN LIMITED(1932); CARNIVAL LADY(1933); I HAVE LIVED(1933); SHIP OF WANTED MEN(1933); GUILTY PARENTS(1934); MIGHTY BARNUM, THE(1934); NOW I'LL TELL(1934); WINE, WOMEN, AND SONG(1934); DANTE'S INFERNO(1935); FOUR HOURS TO KILL(1935); I LIVE FOR LOVE(1935); NO MORE LADIES(1935); NORTHERN FRONTIER(1935); GREAT GUY(1936); HIS BROTHER'S WIFE(1936); MILKY WAY, THE(1936); OUR RELATIONS(1936); POSTAL INSPECTOR(1936); SAN FRANCISCO(1936); ALL OVER TOWN(1937); EASY LIVING(1937); EMPTY SADDLES(1937); MAN WHO CRIED WOLF, THE(1937); WOMEN, THE(1939); $1,000 A TOUCHDOWN(1939); HOLD BACK THE DAWN(1941); LADY FOR A NIGHT(1941); MISBEHAVING HUSBANDS(1941); MOONTIDE(1942); SLEEPYTIME GAL(1942); SCARLET CLAW, THE(1944); DRAGONWYCH(1946); SISTER KENNY(1946); JOE PALOOKA IN WINNER TAKE ALL(1948); MUSIC MAN(1948); MY DEAR SECRETARY(1948); SITTING PRETTY(1948); JOLSON SINGS AGAIN(1949); STORY OF SEABISCUIT, THE(1949); FATHER MAKES GOOD(1950); FILE ON THELMA JORDAN, THE(1950); MONTANA(1950); SUNSET BOULEVARD(1950); CRAZY OVER HORSES(1951); PLACE IN THE SUN, A(1951); WHEN WORLDS COLLIDE(1951); PAULA(1952); ANGEL FACE(1953); LOOSE IN LONDON(1953); AT GUNPOINT(1955); EVERYTHING BUT THE TRUTH(1956); OKLAHOMAN, THE(1957); ALL IN A NIGHT'S WORK(1961); MAN WHO SHOT LIBERTY VALANCE, THE(1962)
Misc. Talkies
HIT OF THE SNOW(1928)
Silents
RESCUE, THE(1917); BRAZEN BEAUTY(1918); GIRL WHO WOULDN'T QUIT, THE(1918); BRANDING IRON, THE(1920); OCCASIONALLY YOURS(1920); HER MAD BARGAIN(1921); BEYOND THE ROCKS(1922); IMPOSSIBLE MRS. BELLEW,

THE(1922); KENTUCKY DERBY, THE(1922); NINETY AND NINE, THE(1922); SEEING'S BELIEVING(1922); WALL FLOWER, THE(1922); ALICE ADAMS(1923); RUPERT OF HENTZAU(1923); WANTERS, THE(1923); BORROWED FINERY(1925); CHARMER, THE(1925); EASY MONEY(1925); RECKLESS SEX, THE(1925); BEHIND THE FRONT(1926); DAME CHANCE(1926); KIKI(1926); OLD SOAK, THE(1926); STRONG MAN, THE(1926); CAT AND THE CANARY, THE(1927); GINSBERG THE GREAT(1927); IRRESISTIBLE LOVER, THE(1927); PRETTY CLOTHES(1927); TAXI DANCER, THE(1927); COHENS AND THE KELLYS IN PARIS, THE(1928); STOCKS AND BLONDES(1928)
Misc. Silents
BONDAGE(1917); DEVIL'S PAY DAY, THE(1917); LITTLE ORPHAN, THE(1917); POLLY REDHEAD(1917); PRETTY SMOOTH(1919); LUCKY CARSON(1921); THROUGH THE BACK DOOR(1921); WHO AM I?(1921); NE'ER-DO-WELL, THE(1923); SIX-FIFTY, THE(1923); BROADWAY OR BUST(1924); DARING LOVE(1924); RIDIN' KID FROM POWDER RIVER, THE(1924); SILENT WATCHER, THE(1924); KENTUCKY PRIDE(1925); SATAN IN SABLES(1925); SHIP OF SOULS(1925); STAGE STRUCK(1925); VERDICT, THE(1925); COUNTRY BEYOND, THE(1926); SHANGHAIED(1927); FIVE AND TEN CENT ANNIE(1928)

Gertude Astor
DICK TRACY(1945)

Junie Astor
LOWER DEPTHS, THE(1937, Fr.)

Juny Astor
ENTENTE CORDIALE(1939, Fr.)

Lady Astor
REGAL CAVALCADE(1935, Brit.)

Mary Astor
HOLIDAY(1930); LADIES LOVE BRUTES(1930); LASH, THE(1930); RUNAWAY BRIDE(1930); BEHIND OFFICE DOORS(1931); OTHER MEN'S WOMEN(1931); ROYAL BED, THE(1931); SIN SHIP(1931); SMART WOMAN(1931); WHITE SHOULDERS(1931); LOST SQUADRON, THE(1932); MEN OF CHANCE(1932); RED DUST(1932); SUCCESSFUL CALAMITY, A(1932); THOSE WE LOVE(1932); CONVENTION CITY(1933); JENNIE GERHARDT(1933); KENNEL MURDER CASE, THE(1933); LITTLE GIANT, THE(1933); WORLD CHANGES, THE(1933); CASE OF THE HOWLING DOG, THE(1934); EASY TO LOVE(1934); MAN WITH TWO FACES, THE(1934); RETURN OF THE TERROR(1934); UPPER WORLD(1934); DINKY(1935); I AM A THIEF(1935); MAN OF IRON(1935); PAGE MISS GLORY(1935); RED HOT TIRES(1935); STRAIGHT FROM THE HEART(1935); AND SO THEY WERE MARRIED(1936); DODSWORTH(1936); LADY FROM NOWHERE(1936); MURDER OF DR. HARRIGAN, THE(1936); TRAPPED BY TELEVISION(1936); HURRICANE, THE(1937); PRISONER OF ZENDA, THE(1937); LISTEN, DARLING(1938); NO TIME TO MARRY(1938); PARADISE FOR THREE(1938); THERE'S ALWAYS A WOMAN(1938); WOMAN AGAINST WOMAN(1938); MIDNIGHT(1939); BRIGHAM YOUNG–FRONTIERSMAN(1940); TURNABOUT(1940); GREAT LIE, THE(1941); MALTESE FALCON, THE(1941); ACROSS THE PACIFIC(1942); IN THIS OUR LIFE(1942); PALM BEACH STORY, THE(1942); THOUSANDS CHEER(1943); YOUNG IDEAS(1943); BLONDE FEVER(1944); MEET ME IN ST. LOUIS(1944); CLAUDIA AND DAVID(1946); CASS TIMBERLANE(1947); CYNTHIA(1947); DESERT FURY(1947); ACT OF VIOLENCE(1949); ANY NUMBER CAN PLAY(1949); LITTLE WOMEN(1949); KISS BEFORE DYING, A(1956); POWER AND THE PRIZE, THE(1956); DEVIL'S HAIRPIN, THE(1957); THIS HAPPY FEELING(1958); STRANGER IN MY ARMS(1959); RETURN TO PEYTON PLACE(1961); HUSH... HUSH, SWEET CHARLOTTE(1964); YOUNGBLOOD HAWKE(1964)
Silents
JOHN SMITH(1922); MAN WHO PLAYED GOD, THE(1922); SECOND FIDDLE(1923); SUCCESS(1923); BEAU BRUMMEL(1924); FIGHTING AMERICAN, THE(1924); FIGHTING COWARD, THE(1924); INEZ FROM HOLLYWOOD(1924); OH, DOCTOR(1924); PRICE OF A PARTY, THE(1924); DON Q, SON OF ZORRO(1925); PACE THAT THRILLS, THE(1925); DON JUAN(1926); FOREVER AFTER(1926); ROUGH RIDERS, THE(1927); SEA TIGER, THE(1927); SUNSET DERBY, THE(1927); NEW YEAR'S EVE(1929)
Misc. Silents
BRIGHT SHAWL, THE(1923); HOLLYWOOD(1923); PURITAN PASSIONS(1923); UNGUARDED WOMEN(1924); ENTICEMENT(1925); PLAYING WITH SOULS(1925); SCARLET SAINT(1925); HIGH STEPPERS(1926); WISE GUY, THE(1926); NO PLACE TO GO(1927); ROSE OF THE GOLDEN WEST(1927); TWO ARABIAN KNIGHTS(1927); DRESSED TO KILL(1928); DRY MARTINI(1928); HEART TO HEART(1928); ROMANCE OF THE UNDERWORLD(1928); SAILORS' WIVES(1928); THREE-RING MARRIAGE(1928); WOMAN FROM HELL, THE(1929)

Patti Astor
FOREIGNER, THE(1978); UNDERGROUND U.S.A.(1980)

Raoul Astor
WAY OF A GAUCHO(1952)

Suzanne Astor
ISLAND, THE(1980)

Gabrio Astori
CHASTITY BELT, THE(1968, Ital.), ed

Astradantsev
ENEMIES OF PROGRESS(1934, USSR), m

Edward Astran
WOMAN'S WORLD(1954)

Humbert Astredo
HOUSE OF DARK SHADOWS(1970)

Norman Astridge
LAST HOLIDAY(1950, Brit.); DOUBLE CONFESSION(1953, Brit.)

Pacifico Astrologo
SHOE SHINE(1947, Ital.)

Marianne Astrom-De Fina
NORTHERN LIGHTS(1978)

The Astronauts
SURF PARTY(1964); WILD ON THE BEACH(1965); OUT OF SIGHT(1966); WILD, WILD WINTER(1966)

Alexandre Astruc
END OF DESIRE(1962 Fr./Ital.), d, w

Edith Astruc
EVERY BASTARD A KING(1968, Israel)

Jenny Astruc
SWEET ECSTASY(1962, Fr.); GIRL CAN'T STOP, THE(1966, Fr./Gr.); HIT(1973)

Carpi Asturias
WALLS OF HELL, THE(1964, U.S./Phil.)
Norman Astwood
Misc. Talkies
SUNDAY SINNERS(1941)
Annick Asty
BED AND BOARD(1971, Fr.)
Bobby Astyr
Misc. Talkies
PELVIS(1977)
Asugebe and Jasantua
1984
WHITE ELEPHANT(1984, Brit.)
Maasaki Asukai
GRAND PRIX(1966)
Mukhtar Aswad
LION OF THE DESERT(1981, Libya/Brit.)
Miss Percy Aswell
Silents
DADDY LONG LEGS(1919)
Arno Aszmann
HELP I'M INVISIBLE(1952, Ger.)
Bela Asztalos
AGE OF ILLUSIONS(1967, Hung.); FATHER(1967, Hung.)
Hoang Thanh At
1984
SUGAR CANE ALLEY(1984, Fr.), art d
Lev Atamanov
ADVENTURE IN ODESSA(1954, USSR), d
Robert Atamu
BEYOND THE REEF(1981)
Mayumi Atano
BUSHIDO BLADE, THE(1982 Brit./U.S.)
Dely Atay-Atayan
IMPASSE(1969)
Nadia Atbib
MAN WHO WOULD BE KING, THE(1975, Brit.)
Atcheelak
WHITE DAWN, THE(1974)
Jack Atcheler
HORROR HOUSE(1970, Brit.), ph; SHARK'S TREASURE(1975), ph
Leota Atcher
HAIL TO THE RANGERS(1943)
Robert Owen Atcher
HAIL TO THE RANGERS(1943)
Jeff Atcheson
SUPERMAN(1978)
Evelyn Atchinson
I MARRIED AN ANGEL(1942)
Tex Atchinson
GUN LAW JUSTICE(1949); GUN RUNNER(1949)
Hooper Atchley
SANTA FE TRAIL, THE(1930); ARIZONA TERROR(1931); CLEARING THE RAN-
GE(1931); LADIES' MAN(1931); MEN IN HER LIFE(1931); NEAR THE TRAIL'S
END(1931); SECRET WITNESS, THE(1931); SUNDOWN TRAIL(1931); GOLD(1932);
HAT CHECK GIRL(1932); HELL'S HOUSE(1932); IF I HAD A MILLION(1932); LOCAL
BAD MAN(1932); MIDNIGHT WARNING, THE(1932); PHANTOM PRESIDENT,
THE(1932); RASPUTIN AND THE EMPRESS(1932); SPIRIT OF THE WEST(1932);
TROUBLE IN PARADISE(1932); DRUM TAPS(1933); DUDE BANDIT, THE(1933);
GAMBLING SHIP(1933); LAWYER MAN(1933); SCARLET RIVER(1933); SPHINX,
THE(1933); AGAINST THE LAW(1934); BIG TIME OR BUST(1934); CHAINED(1934);
GUN JUSTICE(1934); I CAN'T ESCAPE(1934); SPEED WINGS(1934); STAMBOUL
QUEST(1934); BEHIND GREEN LIGHTS(1935); MAD LOVE(1935); NEW FRONTIER,
THE(1935); O'SHAUGHNESSY'S BOY(1935); RECKLESS(1935); RUMBA(1935); SAGE-
BRUSH TROUBADOR(1935); STAR OF MIDNIGHT(1935); TWO FOR TONIGHT(1935);
AND SO THEY WERE MARRIED(1936); CRIME PATROL, THE(1936); GORGEOUS
HUSSY, THE(1936); HEARTS IN BONDAGE(1936); NAVY BORN(1936); PRESCOTT
KID, THE(1936); RETURN OF JIMMY VALENTINE, THE(1936); ROSE BOWL(1936);
WESTERNER, THE(1936); WIFE VERSUS SECRETARY(1936); DAY AT THE RACES,
A(1937); FIREFLY, THE(1937); LAST TRAIN FROM MADRID, THE(1937); LOVE AND
HISSES(1937); PORTIA ON TRIAL(1937); ROARIN' LEAD(1937); SARATOGA(1937);
100 MEN AND A GIRL(1937); CIPHER BUREAU(1938); GANGSTER'S BOY(1938);
HAVING WONDERFUL TIME(1938); HUNTED MEN(1938); LITTLE TOUGH
GUY(1938); MR. WONG, DETECTIVE(1938); OLD BARN DANCE, THE(1938); SAY IT
IN FRENCH(1938); TEST PILOT(1938); TRADE WINDS(1938); HONEYMOON IN
BALI(1939); LADY'S FROM KENTUCKY, THE(1939); MOUNTAIN RHYTHM(1939);
MYSTERY OF MR. WONG, THE(1939); PIRATES OF THE SKIES(1939); SAGA OF
DEATH VALLEY(1939); TOO BUSY TO WORK(1939); GAY CABALLERO, THE(1940);
I LOVE YOU AGAIN(1940); HONKY TONK(1941); IN THE NAVY(1941); LITTLE
FOXES, THE(1941); REPENT AT LEISURE(1941); GENTLEMAN JIM(1942); IN OLD
CALIFORNIA(1942); JOHNNY EAGER(1942); QUIET PLEASE, MURDER(1942);
RINGS ON HER FINGERS(1942); BLACK HILLS EXPRESS(1943); GANGWAY FOR
TOMORROW(1943); HONEYMOON LODGE(1943); MISSION TO MOSCOW(1943);
SONG OF BERNADETTE, THE(1943); SWEET ROSIE O'GRADY(1943); THREE
HEARTS FOR JULIA(1943)
Misc. Talkies
FIGHTING FOR JUSTICE(1932)
Hooper L. Atchley
LOVE AT FIRST SIGHT(1930); TRUMPET BLOWS, THE(1934)
Memel Atchori
BLACK AND WHITE IN COLOR(1976, Fr.)
Richard Atckison
GROUNDS FOR MARRIAGE(1950)
Nushet Atear
FROM RUSSIA WITH LOVE(1963, Brit.)
Larry Aten
BEAST OF YUCCA FLATS, THE(1961)

Dorothy Ates
WATERFRONT LADY(1935); HONKY TONK(1941)
Nejla Ates
KING RICHARD AND THE CRUSADERS(1954); SON OF SINBAD(1955)
Rosco [Roscoe] Ates
POLITICS(1931); COME ON DANGER!(1932); FREAKS(1932); RENEGADES OF THE
WEST(1932)
Roscoe Ates
SOUTH SEA ROSE(1929); BIG HOUSE, THE(1930); BILLY THE KID(1930); CITY
GIRL(1930); LOVE IN THE ROUGH(1930); BIG SHOT, THE(1931); CHAMP, THE(1931);
CIMARRON(1931); FREE SOUL, A(1931); GREAT LOVER, THE(1931); TOO MANY
COOKS(1931); HOLD'EM JAIL(1932); LADIES OF THE JURY(1932); RAINBOW
TRAIL(1932); ROADHOUSE MURDER, THE(1932); YOUNG BRIDE(1932); ALICE IN
WONDERLAND(1933); CHEYENNE KID, THE(1933); GOLDEN HARVEST(1933);
LUCKY DEVILS(1933); PAST OF MARY HOLMES, THE(1933); SCARLET RI-
VER(1933); WHAT! NO BEER?(1933); MERRY WIVES OF RENO, THE(1934); SHE
MADE HER BED(1934); WOMAN IN THE DARK(1934); PEOPLE'S ENEMY,
THE(1935); FAIR EXCHANGE(1936, Brit.); GOD'S COUNTRY AND THE WO-
MAN(1937); RIDERS OF THE BLACK HILLS(1938); GONE WITH THE WIND(1939);
THREE TEXAS STEERS(1939); CAPTAIN CAUTION(1940); CHAD HANNA(1940); I
WANT A DIVORCE(1940); RANCHO GRANDE(1940); UNTAMED(1940); BAD MEN
OF MISSOURI(1941); I'LL SELL MY LIFE(1941); MOUNTAIN MOONLIGHT(1941);
ONE FOOT IN HEAVEN(1941); REG'LAR FELLERS(1941); ROBIN HOOD OF THE
PECOS(1941); SHE KNEW ALL THE ANSWERS(1941); SULLIVAN'S TRAVELS(1941);
ZIEGFELD GIRL(1941); PALM BEACH STORY, THE(1942); COLORADO SERENA-
DE(1946); DOWN MISSOURI WAY(1946); DRIFTIN' RIVER(1946); STARS OVER
TEXAS(1946); TUMBLEWEED TRAIL(1946); WILD WEST(1946); RANGE BEYOND
THE BLUE(1947); SHADOW VALLEY(1947); WEST TO GLORY(1947); WILD COUN-
TRY(1947); BLACK HILLS(1948); CHECK YOUR GUNS(1948); HAWK OF POWDER
RIVER, THE(1948); INNER SANCTUM(1948); PRAIRIE OUTLAWS(1948); TIOGA
KID, THE(1948); TORNADO RANGE(1948); WESTWARD TRAIL, THE(1948); THUN-
DER IN THE PINES(1949); FATHER'S WILD GAME(1950); HILLS OF OK-
LAHOMA(1950); HONEYCHILE(1951); BLAZING FOREST, THE(1952); STRANGER
WORE A GUN, THE(1953); THOSE REDHEADS FROM SEATTLE(1953); ABBOTT
AND COSTELLO MEET THE KEYSTONE KOPS(1955); LUCY GALLANT(1955);
COME NEXT SPRING(1956); KETTLES IN THE OZARKS, THE(1956); BIG CAPER,
THE(1957); SHORT CUT TO HELL(1957); SHEEPMAN, THE(1958); LADIES MAN,
THE(1961); SILENT CALL, THE(1961)
Rose Ates
COWBOY FROM SUNDOWN(1940)
Kitty Atfield
Misc. Silents
LITTLE BREADWINNER, THE(1916, Brit.)
Bernard Atha
KES(1970, Brit.)
Bhanu Athaiya
GANDHI(1982), cos
Verne Athanas
PROUD ONES, THE(1956), w
Genica Athanasiou
Misc. Silents
LA CIQUILLE ET LE CLERGYMAN(1928, Fr.); GARDIENS DE PHARE(1929, Fr.)
Gencia Athansaiou
Misc. Silents
MALDONE(1928, Fr.)
Athena
711 OCEAN DRIVE(1950), cos; VOICE OF THE HURRICANE(1964), cos
Vi Athens
CRIME DOCTOR(1943); IS EVERYBODY HAPPY?(1943); COWBOY FROM LONE-
SOME RIVER(1944); ONCE UPON A TIME(1944); SAILOR'S HOLIDAY(1944)
Misc. Talkies
SADDLE LEATHER LAW(1944)
Members of Athens Hellenic Theater
DRY SUMMER(1967, Turkey)
Frank Atherley
BETRAYAL(1932, Brit.); TROUBLE(1933, Brit.)
Basil Atherton
SONG AT EVENTIDE(1934, Brit.)
Effie Atherton
SCHOOL FOR STARS(1935, Brit.); TEMPTATION(1935, Brit.)
Ella Atherton
Misc. Silents
FIRST BORN, THE(1928, Brit.); HUMAN CARGO(1929, Brit.)
Gertrude Atherton
WOMAN ACCUSED(1933), w
Silents
AVALANCHE, THE(1919), w; OUT OF THE STORM(1920), w
Gertrude Franklin Atherton
Silents
CRYSTAL CUP, THE(1927), w
Howard Atherton
RUNNERS(1983, Brit.), ph
Jonathan Atherton
MANGO TREE, THE(1981, Aus.)
Vernie Atherton
Silents
JANE EYRE(1921)
William Atherton
NEW CENTURIONS, THE(1972); CLASS OF '44(1973); SUGARLAND EXPRESS,
THE(1974); DAY OF THE LOCUST, THE(1975); HINDENBURG, THE(1975); LOOKING
FOR MR. GOODBAR(1977)
1984
GHOSTBUSTERS(1984)
Darryl Athons
WORLD'S GREATEST LOVER, THE(1977), cos
1984
UNFAITHFULLY YOURS(1984), cos

Edward Atienza
PURSUIT OF THE GRAF SPEE(1957, Brit.); ROMANOFF AND JULIET(1961); SINISTER MAN, THE(1965, Brit.); LOCK UP YOUR DAUGHTERS(1969, Brit.); SAY HELLO TO YESTERDAY(1971, Brit.)

Frank Atienza
BLUE HAWAII(1961)

Edouard Atiyah
JUST BEFORE NIGHTFALL(1975, Fr./Ital.), d&w

Harvey Atkin
SILVER STREAK(1976); POWER PLAY(1978, Brit./Can.); MEATBALLS(1979, Can.); ATLANTIC CITY(1981, U.S./Can.); IMPROPER CHANNELS(1981, Can.); TICKET TO HEAVEN(1981); FUNERAL HOME(1982, Can.); IF YOU COULD SEE WHAT I HEAR(1982); VISITING HOURS(1982, Can.)
1984
FINDERS KEEPERS(1984)

Feodor Atkine
LOVE AND DEATH(1975); CHARLES AND LUCIE(1982, Fr.); LE BEAU MARIAGE(1982, Fr.); PAULINE AT THE BEACH(1983, Fr.)
1984
AVE MARIA(1984, Fr.)

Albert Atkins
ROSE TATTOO, THE(1955)

Alfred Atkins
LAST BARRICADE, THE(1938, Brit.); NO PARKING(1938, Brit.)

Barbara Atkins
MASK OF THE DRAGON(1951)

Bruce Atkins
FIREBALL JUNGLE(1968); MOMENTS(1974, Brit.), set d; SCALPEL(1976); GREASED LIGHTNING(1977); LINCOLN CONSPIRACY, THE(1977)

Christopher Atkins
BLUE LAGOON, THE(1980); PIRATE MOVIE, THE(1982, Aus.); NIGHT IN HEAVEN, A(1983)

Dave Atkins
BRITTANIA HOSPITAL(1982, Brit.)
1984
KIPPERBANG(1984, Brit.)

David Atkins
BURY ME AN ANGEL(1972); PIRATE MOVIE, THE(1982, Aus.), ch; STARSTRUCK(1982, Aus.), ch
1984
SQUIZZY TAYLOR(1984, Aus.)

Doug Atkins
BREAKHEART PASS(1976)

Eileen Atkins
INADMISSIBLE EVIDENCE(1968, Brit.); DEVIL WITHIN HER, THE(1976, Brit.); "EQUUS"(1977); DRESSER, THE(1983); NELLY'S VERSION(1983, Brit.)
Misc. Talkies
RAKU FIRE(

Felicia Atkins
ERRAND BOY, THE(1961)

Garland Atkins
PREACHERMAN(1971)

Geoffrey Atkins
DANGEROUS CARGO(1939, Brit.); DEAD MAN'S SHOES(1939, Brit.); YOUNG MR. PITT, THE(1942, Brit.)

Gerald A. Atkins
1984
TANK(1984)

Gregory Atkins
YOURS, MINE AND OURS(1968)

Harvey Atkins
INCUBUS, THE(1982, Can.)

Jane Atkins
ONLY WHEN I LAUGH(1981)

LeRoy Atkins
SWING, SISTER, SWING(1938)

Lynnell Atkins
YOURS, MINE AND OURS(1968)

Pervis Atkins
MELINDA(1972), p

Robert Atkins
CARDINAL, THE(1936, Brit.); EVERYTHING IS THUNDER(1936, Brit.); PEG OF OLD DRURY(1936, Brit.); HE FOUND A STAR(1941, Brit.); GREAT MR. HANDEL, THE(1942, Brit.); STAIRWAY TO HEAVEN(1946, Brit.); BLACK MAGIC(1949); IF THIS BE SIN(1950, Brit.); I'LL NEVER FORGET YOU(1951)
Silents
HAMLET(1913, Brit.)

Rubin Atkins
WHIP'S WOMEN(1968)

Ted Atkins
CREEPSHOW(1982)

Thomas Atkins
HI GAUCHO!(1936), d, w

Tom Atkins
DETECTIVE, THE(1968); OWL AND THE PUSSYCAT, THE(1970); WHERE'S POPPA?(1970); SPECIAL DELIVERY(1976); NINTH CONFIGURATION, THE(1980); ESCAPE FROM NEW YORK(1981); HALLOWEEN III: SEASON OF THE WITCH(1982)

Tommy Atkins
MUTINY AHEAD(1935), d; SILVER STREAK, THE(1935), d; FOG, THE(1980)

Zoe Atkins
Silents
EVE'S SECRET(1925), w

Adrienne Atkinson
THAT SINKING FEELING(1979, Brit.), prod d & cos; GREGORY'S GIRL(1982, Brit.), art d; LOCAL HERO(1983, Brit.), art d
1984
COMFORT AND JOY(1984, Brit.), prod d; WINTER FLIGHT(1984, Brit.), art d

Alex Atkinson
WHEEL OF FATE(1953, Brit.), w

Betty Atkinson
MAD YOUTH(1940); YOUTH ON PARADE(1943)

Beverly Hope Atkinson
NEW CENTURIONS, THE(1972)
Misc. Talkies
HEAVY TRAFFIC(1974)

Chris Atkinson
MONDO TRASHO(1970)

David Atkinson
GRENDEL GRENDEL GRENDEL(1981, Aus.), anim

Dawn Atkinson
TWICE UPON A TIME(1983), m

Doris Atkinson
DESIRABLE(1934)

Eleanor Atkinson
CHALLENGE TO LASSIE(1949), w; GREYFRIARS BOBBY(1961, Brit.), w

Frank Atkinson
LONESOME(1928), ed; LADIES' MAN(1931); HELL'S HEADQUARTERS(1932), ed; CAVALCADE(1933); PLEASURE CRUISE(1933); RIGHT TO LIVE, THE(1933, Brit.), a, w; SAILOR'S LUCK(1933); FREEDOM OF THE SEAS(1934, Brit.); GREAT DEFENDER, THE(1934, Brit.); PATH OF GLORY, THE(1934, Brit.); ROAD HOUSE(1934, Brit.); ROLLING IN MONEY(1934, Brit.), a, w; THIRD CLUE, THE(1934, Brit.), a, w; DEATH DRIVES THROUGH(1935, Brit.); NIGHT MAIL(1935, Brit.); PLAY UP THE BAND(1935, Brit.), a, w; SINGING THROUGH(1935, Brit.), a, w; KING OF THE CASTLE(1936, Brit.), w; LIMPING MAN, THE(1936, Brit.); MORALS OF MARCUS, THE(1936, Brit.); NOT SO DUSTY(1936, Brit.), w; SHIPMATES O' MINE(1936, Brit.); INTIMATE RELATIONS(1937, Brit.), w; KNIGHTS FOR A DAY(1937, Brit.), a, w; SCHOONER GANG, THE(1937, Brit.), a, w; TWO WHO DARED(1937, Brit.); I'VE GOT A HORSE(1938, Brit.); PYGMALION(1938, Brit.); YOUNG AND INNOCENT(1938, Brit.); DISCOVERIES(1939, Brit.); LOST ON THE WESTERN FRONT(1940, Brit.); HARD STEEL(1941, Brit.); MISSING TEN DAYS(1941, Brit.); GREAT MR. HANDEL, THE(1942, Brit.); MRS. MINIVER(1942); PLAYBOY, THE(1942, Brit.); GENTLE SEX, THE(1943, Brit.); GIVE US THE MOON(1944, Brit.); HE SNOOPS TO CONQUER(1944, Brit.); KISS THE BRIDE GOODBYE(1944, Brit.); GREAT EXPECTATIONS(1946, Brit.); GREEN COCKATOO, THE(1947, Brit.); LAST LOAD, THE(1948, Brit.); WATERLOO ROAD(1949, Brit.); MAN IN THE WHITE SUIT, THE(1952); FAKE, THE(1953, Brit.); TERROR ON A TRAIN(1953); TITFIELD THUNDERBOLT, THE(1953, Brit.); GREEN BUDDHA, THE(1954, Brit.); LEASE OF LIFE(1954, Brit.); MAN WHO KNEW TOO MUCH, THE(1956); SHADOW OF FEAR(1956, Brit.); TRACK THE MAN DOWN(1956, Brit.); AT THE STROKE OF NINE(1957, Brit.); CAT GIRL(1957); HIGH FLIGHT(1957, Brit.); JUST MY LUCK(1957, Brit.); PORTRAIT IN SMOKE(1957, Brit.); THREE MEN IN A BOAT(1958, Brit.); LEFT, RIGHT AND CENTRE(1959); KITCHEN, THE(1961, Brit.); IN TROUBLE WITH EVE(1964, Brit.)
Misc. Talkies
BE CAREFUL, MR. SMITH(1935)
Silents
COHENS AND THE KELLYS IN PARIS, THE(1928), ed; POWER OF THE PRESS, THE(1928), ed; RUNAWAY GIRLS(1928), ed; SCARLET LADY, THE(1928), ed

G. A. Atkinson
Silents
PASSION ISLAND(1927, Brit.), p

George Atkinson
DISRAELI(1929); RAFFLES(1939); GUY NAMED JOE, A(1943); NONE BUT THE LONELY HEART(1944); I REMEMBER MAMA(1948); CHILDISH THINGS(1969)
Silents
CONQUERING POWER, THE(1921); RACING FOR LIFE(1924)

Hugh Atkinson
GAMES, THE(1970), w; WEEKEND OF SHADOWS(1978, Aus.), w

J. A. Atkinson
Silents
OLD CURIOSITY SHOP, THE(1921, Brit.), w

Jack Atkinson
STAMPEDE(1936)

John Atkinson
TRUNK, THE(1961, Brit.); FRAULEIN DOKTOR(1969, Ital./Yugo.)

Johnny Atkinson
1984
ICE PIRATES, THE(1984)

Keith Atkinson
TILL DEATH(1978)

Martin Atkinson
ZARDOZ(, set d; SOME GIRLS DO(1969, Brit.), set d; FINAL CONFLICT, THE(1981), art d

Michael Atkinson
BLACK MEMORY(1947, Brit.); HAUNTED STRANGLER, THE(1958, Brit.); ROOM AT THE TOP(1959, Brit.)

Mike Atkinson
STATUE, THE(1971, Brit.)

Olive Atkinson
Silents
NOT GUILTY(1919, Brit.)

Owen Atkinson
TWENTY MULE TEAM(1940), w

Ray Atkinson
PAJAMA PARTY(1964); HOW TO STUFF A WILD BIKINI(1965)

Rosalind Atkinson
TOMORROW WE LIVE(1936, Brit.); GOOD TIME GIRL(1950, Brit.); TOM JONES(1963, Brit.); PUMPKIN EATER, THE(1964, Brit.)

Rowan Atkinson
NEVER SAY NEVER AGAIN(1983)

Sara Atkinson
HUNTING PARTY, THE(1977, Brit.)

Sarah Atkinson
DECLINE AND FALL... OF A BIRD WATCHER(1969, Brit.); WHAT'S GOOD FOR THE GOOSE(1969, Brit.); SWEENEY 2(1978, Brit.)

Shelby Atkinson
COWBOY FROM LONESOME RIVER(1944)
Norman Atkyns
IDOL ON PARADE(1959, Brit.); NO BLADE OF GRASS(1970, Brit.); S(1974)
Robert Atlan
LA BALANCE(1983, Fr.)
Rip Atlanta
Misc. Talkies
BED OF VIOLENCE(1967)
The Atlanta Stone Mountain Choir
STARS AND STRIPES FOREVER(1952)
Dorothy Atlas
DESPERATE(1947), w
Larry Atlas
CRUISING(1980)
1984
FIRSTBORN(1984)
Leopold Atlas
MYSTERY OF EDWIN DROOD, THE(1935), w; NOTORIOUS GENTLEMAN, A(1935), w; TOMORROW THE WORLD(1944), w; STORY OF G.I. JOE, THE(1945), w; BOY, A GIRL, AND A DOG, A(1946), w; HER KIND OF MAN(1946), w; RAW DEAL(1948), w; MY FORBIDDEN PAST(1951), w
Leopold L. Atlas
WEDNESDAY'S CHILD(1934), w; CHILD OF DIVORCE(1946), w
Ann Atmar
STREET FIGHTER(1959); COLD WIND IN AUGUST(1961)
Charlie Atom
GREAT MCGONAGALL, THE(1975, Brit.)
Charlie Young Atom
PRIVATE LIFE OF SHERLOCK HOLMES, THE(1970, Brit.)
Teddy Kiss Atom
PRIVATE LIFE OF SHERLOCK HOLMES, THE(1970, Brit.)
Kiyoshi Atsumi
TORA-SAN PART 2(1970, Jap.)
Mari Atsumi
GAMERA VERSUS VIRAS(1968, Jap); PLAY IT COOL(1970, Jap.)
Ushun Atsuta
LATE AUTUMN(1973, Jap.), ph
Yuhara Atsuta
TOKYO STORY(1972, Jap.), ph
Yushun Atsuta
OHAYO(1962, Jap.), ph; TEA AND RICE(1964, Jap.), ph
Spazz Attack
1984
MIKE'S MURDER(1984)
Henri Attal
LANDRU(1963, Fr./Ital); MY LIFE TO LIVE(1963, Fr.); OPHELIA(1964, Fr.); VICE AND VIRTUE(1965, Fr./Ital.); FANTOMAS(1966, Fr./Ital.); LES BICHES(1968, Fr.); PARIS IN THE MONTH OF AUGUST(1968, Fr.); LA FEMME INFIDELE(1969, Fr./Ital.); JUST BEFORE NIGHTFALL(1975, Fr./Ital.); ONCE IN PARIS(1978)
Ugo Attanasio
WHITE SHEIK, THE(1956, Ital.); MAFIOSO(1962, Ital.); MANDRAGOLA(1966 Fr./Ital.); OPIATE '67(1967, Fr./Ital.)
Francis Attard
HOVERBUG(1970, Brit.)
Peter Attard
TO SIR, WITH LOVE(1967, Brit.); UP THE JUNCTION(1968, Brit.); TERROR(1979, Brit.)
Tony Attard
THAT SUMMER(1979, Brit.), w
Ruth Attaway
TAKING OF PELHAM ONE, TWO, THREE, THE(1974); PRESIDENT'S LADY, THE(1953); RAINTREE COUNTY(1957); YOUNG DON'T CRY, THE(1957); PORGY AND BESS(1959); PIE IN THE SKY(1964); CONRACK(1974); BEING THERE(1979)
Duke Atteberry
MOUNTAIN MUSIC(1937), w; TROPIC HOLIDAY(1938), w
Larry Attebery
HERO AT LARGE(1980)
Duke Attebury
COMIN' ROUND THE MOUNTAIN(1940), w
Abu Attef
THEY WERE TEN(1961, Israel)
Toni Attell
THINGS ARE TOUGH ALL OVER(1982)
Charlotte Attenborough
OH! WHAT A LOVELY WAR(1969, Brit.)
Julian Attenborough
WEREWOLF IN A GIRL'S DORMITORY(1961, Ital./Aust.), ed
Richard Attenborough
IN WHICH WE SERVE(1942, Brit.); HUNDRED POUND WINDOW, THE(1943, Brit.); SCHWEIK'S NEW ADVENTURES(1943, Brit.); SCHOOL FOR SECRETS(1946, Brit.); STAIRWAY TO HEAVEN(1946, Brit.); BRIGHTON ROCK(1947, Brit.); DANCING WITH CRIME(1947, Brit.); DULCIMER STREET(1948, Brit.); SMUGGLERS, THE(1948, Brit.); BOYS IN BROWN(1949, Brit.); OUTSIDER, THE(1949, Brit.); LOST PEOPLE, THE(1950, Brit.); HELL IS SOLD OUT(1951, Brit.); OPERATION DISASTER(1951, Brit.); FATHER'S DOING FINE(1952, Brit.); GLORY AT SEA(1952, Brit.); MAGIC BOX, THE(1952, Brit.); EIGHT O'CLOCK WALK(1954, Brit.); PRIVATE'S PROGRESS(1956, Brit.); SHIP THAT DIED OF SHAME, THE(1956, Brit.); BABY AND THE BATTLE-SHIP, THE(1957, Brit.); BROTHERS IN LAW(1957, Brit.); DUNKIRK(1958, Brit.); I'M ALL RIGHT, JACK(1959, Brit.); MAN UPSTAIRS, THE(1959, Brit.); STRANGE AFFECTION(1959, Brit.); ANGRY SILENCE, THE(1960, Brit.), a, p; BREAKOUT(1960, Brit.); S.O.S. PACIFIC(1960, Brit.); ALL NIGHT LONG(1961, Brit.); JET STORM(1961, Brit.); LEAGUE OF GENTLEMEN, THE(1961, Brit.); WHISTLE DOWN THE WIND(1961, Brit.), p; DESERT PATROL(1962, Brit.); L-SHAPED ROOM, THE(1962, Brit.), p; ONLY TWO CAN PLAY(1962, Brit.); TRIAL AND ERROR(1962, Brit.); GREAT ESCAPE, THE(1963, Brit.); GUNS AT BATASI(1964, Brit.); SEANCE ON A WET AFTER-NOON(1964 Brit.), a, p; THIRD SECRET, THE(1964, Brit.); FLIGHT OF THE PHO-ENIX, THE(1965); SAND PEBBLES, THE(1966); DOCTOR DOLITTLE(1967); BLISS OF MRS. BLOSSOM, THE(1968, Brit.); ONLY WHEN I LARF(1968, Brit.); OH! WHAT A LOVELY WAR(1969, Brit.), p, d; DAVID COPPERFIELD(1970, Brit.); LAST GRE-

NADE, THE(1970, Brit.); MAGIC CHRISTIAN, THE(1970, Brit.); LOOT(1971, Brit.); SEVERED HEAD, A(1971, Brit.); 10 RILLINGTON PLACE(1971, Brit.); YOUNG WINSTON(1972, Brit.), d; BRANNIGAN(1975, Brit.); CONDUCT UNBECOMING(1975, Brit.); ROSEBUD(1975); TEN LITTLE INDIANS(1975, Ital./Fr./Span./Ger.); BRIDGE TOO FAR, A(1977, Brit.), d; CHESS PLAYERS, THE(1978, India); MAGIC(1978), d; HUMAN FACTOR, THE(1979, Brit.); GANDHI(1982), p&d
Sgt. Richard Attenborough
JOURNEY TOGETHER(1946, Brit.)
Elsie Attenhofer
HEIDI(1954, Switz.)
Giuliana Attenni
GREAT HOPE, THE(1954, Ital.), ed; PSYCOSISSIMO(1962, Ital.), ed; RUN WITH THE DEVIL(1963, Fr./Ital.), ed; SAUL AND DAVID(1968, Ital./Span.), ed
Duke Atterberry
DOUBLE OR NOTHING(1937), w; I'M FROM MISSOURI(1939), w
Ellen Atterbury
JOY IN THE MORNING(1965)
Malcolm Atterbury
DRAGNET(1954); MAN WITHOUT A STAR(1955); CRIME IN THE STREETS(1956); DAKOTA INCIDENT(1956); RAWHIDE YEARS, THE(1956); REPRISAL(1956); STEEL JUNGLE, THE(1956); STORM CENTER(1956); STRANGER AT MY DOOR(1956); TOWARD THE UNKNOWN(1956); BLOOD OF DRACULA(1957); CRIME OF PAS-SION(1957); DALTON GIRLS, THE(1957); FURY AT SHOWDOWN(1957); I WAS A TEENAGE WEREWOLF(1957); BADMAN'S COUNTRY(1958); FROM HELL TO TEX-AS(1958); HOW TO MAKE A MONSTER(1958); NO TIME FOR SERGEANTS(1958); HIGH SCHOOL BIG SHOT(1959); NORTH BY NORTHWEST(1959); RIO BRAVO(1959); FROM THE TERRACE(1960); HELL BENT FOR LEATHER(1960); WILD RIVER(1960); SUMMER AND SMOKE(1961); ADVISE AND CONSENT(1962); CATTLE KING(1963); SEVEN DAYS IN MAY(1964); CHASE, THE(1966); HAWAII(1966); LEARNING TREE, THE(1969); EMPEROR OF THE NORTH POLE(1973); TOWERING INFERNO, THE(1974)
Miss Atterbury
Silents
KIPPS(1921, Brit.)
Lillian Atterer
IF IT'S TUESDAY, THIS MUST BE BELGIUM(1969)
Harold Atteridge
BIG BOY(1930), w; GOLDEN CALF, THE(1930), w
Carlos Attias
SUPERSONIC MAN(1979, Span.), m
Ken Attiwill
NON-STOP NEW YORK(1937, Brit.), w; HEADLINE(1943, Brit.), w; NOT WANTED ON VOYAGE(1957, Brit.), w
Louis G. Attlee
LITTLE DRAGONS, THE(1980), w
Joe Attles
GOING HOME(1971); ACROSS 110TH STREET(1972)
Joseph Attles
FOR LOVE OF IVY(1968); LIBERATION OF L.B. JONES, THE(1970); PURSUIT OF HAPPINESS, THE(1971); GAMBLER, THE(1974)
Billy Attmore
TREASURE OF MATECUMBE(1976)
Pop Attmore
MAX DUGAN RETURNS(1983)
Harold Attridge
NOT DAMAGED(1930), w
Winifred Attwell
IT'S A GRAND LIFE(1953, Brit.)
Alban Attwood
Misc. Silents
LACKEY AND THE LADY, THE(1919, Brit.)
Kitty Attwood
GET CARTER(1971, Brit.)
Leslie Attwood
Silents
PIPES OF PAN, THE(1923, Brit.)
Hugh Attwooll
THREE LIVES OF THOMASINA, THE(1963, U.S./Brit.), p; MOON-SPINNERS, THE(1964), p
Asushi Atumoto
SAMURAI(PART II)** (1967, Jap.), ph
Andy Aturba
DANCE OF THE DWARFS(1983, U.S., Phil.), spec eff
Edith Atwabter
OUR TIME(1974)
Barry Atwater
EVERYTHING BUT THE TRUTH(1956); MAN FROM DEL RIO(1956); NIGHT-MARE(1956); RACK, THE(1956); SCARLET HOUR, THE(1956); WRONG MAN, THE(1956); HARD MAN, THE(1957); TRUE STORY OF JESSE JAMES, THE(1957); AS YOUNG AS WE ARE(1958); TRUE STORY OF LYNN STUART, THE(1958); PORK CHOP HILL(1959); VICE RAID(1959); BATTLE AT BLOODY BEACH(1961); SWEET BIRD OF YOUTH(1962); CAPTAIN NEWMAN, M.D.(1963); 1,000 PLANE RAID, THE(1969); TEACHER, THE(1974)
Cladys Atwater
NAKED ALIBI(1954), w
Edith Atwater
GORGEOUS HUSSY, THE(1936); HIS BROTHER'S WIFE(1936); WE WENT TO COLLEGE(1936); BODY SNATCHER, THE(1945); C-MAN(1949); TERESA(1951); SWEET SMELL OF SUCCESS(1957); IT HAPPENED AT THE WORLD'S FAIR(1963); STRAIT-JACKET(1964); STRANGE BEDFELLOWS(1965); RIDE A NORTHBOUND HORSE(1969); TRUE GRIT(1969); NORWOOD(1970); PIECES OF DREAMS(1970); LOVE MACHINE, THE(1971); STAND UP AND BE COUNTED(1972); MACKINTOSH & T.J.(1975); FAMILY PLOT(1976); MEAN DOG BLUES(1978)
Misc. Talkies
COMPANION, THE(1976); DIE SISTER, DIE(1978)
G. B. Atwater
ALVAREZ KELLY(1966)

G. V. Atwater
CRIMINAL LAWYER(1937), w; MAN WHO FOUND HIMSELF, THE(1937), w

Gladys Atwater
CRASHING HOLLYWOOD(1937), w; CRIME RING(1938), w; THIS MARRIAGE BUSINESS(1938), w; PARENTS ON TRIAL(1939), w; ARGENTINE NIGHTS(1940), w; AMERICAN EMPIRE(1942), w; IN OLD CALIFORNIA(1942), w; UNDERGROUND AGENT(1942), w; FIRST YANK INTO TOKYO(1945), w; EL PASO(1949), w; GREAT SIOUX UPRISING, THE(1953), w; OVERLAND PACIFIC(1954), w; SIEGE AT RED RIVER, THE(1954), w; TREASURE OF PANCHO VILLA, THE(1955), w

John Atwater
HARD TO GET(1938)

Frederick Atwell
JEALOUSY(1931, Brit.)

Grace Atwell
Silents
ROYAL FAMILY, A(1915)

Roy Atwell
HARVESTER, THE(1936); BEHIND THE MIKE(1937); SNOW WHITE AND THE SEVEN DWARFS(1937); VARSITY SHOW(1937); FLEET'S IN, THE(1942); PEOPLE ARE FUNNY(1945); WHERE THERE'S LIFE(1947)
Silents
DON'T GET PERSONAL(1922); RED HOT ROMANCE(1922); SOUTH OF SUVA(1922); SOULS FOR SALE(1923); OUTSIDER, THE(1926)
Misc. Silents
HEART SPECIALIST, THE(1922)

Ken Atwill
ONCE A CROOK(1941, Brit.), w

LioneI Atwill
CAPTAIN BLOOD(1935)

Lionel Atwill
DOCTOR X(1932); SILENT WITNESS, THE(1932); MURDERS IN THE ZOO(1933); MYSTERY OF THE WAX MUSEUM, THE(1933); SECRET OF MADAME BLANCHE, THE(1933); SECRET OF THE BLUE ROOM(1933); SOLITAIRE MAN, THE(1933); SONG OF SONGS(1933); SPHINX, THE(1933); VAMPIRE BAT, THE(1933); AGE OF INNOCENCE(1934); BEGGARS IN ERMINE(1934); FIREBIRD, THE(1934); NANA(1934); ONE MORE RIVER(1934); STAMBOUL QUEST(1934); DEVIL IS A WOMAN, THE(1935); MAN WHO RECLAIMED HIS HEAD, THE(1935); MARK OF THE VAMPIRE(1935); MURDER MAN(1935); RENDEZVOUS(1935); ABSOLUTE QUIET(1936); LADY OF SECRETS(1936); TILL WE MEET AGAIN(1936); GREAT GARRICK, THE(1937); LANCER SPY(1937); LAST TRAIN FROM MADRID, THE(1937); ROAD BACK, THE(1937); WRONG ROAD, THE(1937); GREAT WALTZ, THE(1938); HIGH COMMAND(1938, Brit.); MR. MOTO TAKES A VACATION(1938); THREE COMRADES(1938); BALALAIKA(1939); GORILLA, THE(1939); HOUND OF THE BASKERVILLES, THE(1939); SECRET OF DR. KILDARE, THE(1939); SON OF FRANKENSTEIN(1939); SUN NEVER SETS, THE(1939); THREE MUSKETEERS, THE(1939); BOOM TOWN(1940); CHARLIE CHAN IN PANAMA(1940); CHARLIE CHAN'S MURDER CRUISE(1940); GIRL IN 313(1940); GREAT PROFILE, THE(1940); JOHNNY APOLLO(1940); MAD EMPRESS, THE(1940); MAN MADE MONSTER(1940); CAIRO(1942); GHOST OF FRANKENSTEIN, THE(1942); MAD DOCTOR OF MARKET STREET, THE(1942); NIGHT MONSTER(1942); PARDON MY SARONG(1942); SHERLOCK HOLMES AND THE SECRET WEAPON(1942); STRANGE CASE OF DR. RX, THE(1942); TO BE OR NOT TO BE(1942); FRANKENSTEIN MEETS THE WOLF MAN(1943); HOUSE OF FRANKENSTEIN(1944); LADY IN THE DEATH HOUSE(1944); SECRETS OF SCOTLAND YARD(1944); CRIME, INC.(1945); FOG ISLAND(1945); HOUSE OF DRACULA(1945); GENIUS AT WORK(1946)
Silents
EVE'S DAUGHTER(1918); MARRIAGE PRICE(1919)
Misc. Silents
FOR SALE(1918); HIGHEST BIDDER, THE(1921); INDISCRETION(1921)

Alban Atwood
Silents
FLAMES OF PASSION(1922, Brit.)
Misc. Silents
BEYOND THE DREAMS OF AVARICE(1920, Brit.)

Bill Atwood
HOODLUM PRIEST, THE(1961)

Colleen C. Atwood
1984
FIRSTBORN(1984), cos

Donna Atwood
ICE-CAPADES REVUE(1942)

Kim Atwood
M(1970)

May Atwood
Silents
NOOSE, THE(1928)

Robert Atwood
Misc. Talkies
BOSS LADY(1982)

Robert Atzorn
FROM THE LIFE OF THE MARIONETTES(1980, Ger.)

Wel P'ing Au
RETURN OF THE DRAGON(1974, Chin.)

Bobby A. Auarez
Misc. Talkies
ONE ARMED EXECUTIONER(1980), d

Tony Aubain
RAVEN, THE(1948, Fr.), m

Joe Aubel
DEAD AND BURIED(1981), art d

Brigitte Auber
TO CATCH A THIEF(1955); TONIGHT THE SKIRTS FLY(1956, Fr.)

Daniel F. Auber
DEVIL'S BROTHER, THE(1933), w, m

Maurice Auberga
DOCTORS, THE(1956, Fr.), w

Maurice Auberge
ANATOMY OF A MARRIAGE(MY DAYS WITH JEAN-MARC AND MY NIGHTS WITH FRANCOISE)**1/2 (1964 Fr.), w; SECRETS D'ALCOVE(1954, Fr./Ital.), w; PORT OF DESIRE(1960, Fr.), w; TOMORROW IS MY TURN(1962, Fr./Ital./Ger.), w

Rene Auberjonois
LILITH(1964); PETULIA(1968, U.S./Brit.); BREWSTER McCLOUD(1970); M(1970); MC CABE AND MRS. MILLER(1971); IMAGES(1972, Ireland); PETE 'N' TILLIE(1972); HINDENBURG, THE(1975); BIG BUS, THE(1976); KING KONG(1976); EYES OF LAURA MARS(1978); WHERE THE BUFFALO ROAM(1980); LAST UNICORN, THE(1982)
Misc. Talkies
TEENAGE TEASE(1983)

Claude-Bernard Aubert
GUTS IN THE SUN(1959, Fr.), d, w

Georges Aubert
MADEMOISELLE(1966, Fr./Brit.); CONFESSION, THE(1970, Fr.)

Jeanne Aubert
YOUNG WORLD, A(1966, Fr./Ital.)

Lenore Aubert
THEY GOT ME COVERED(1943); ACTION IN ARABIA(1944); PASSPORT TO DESTINY(1944); HAVING WONDERFUL CRIME(1945); THE CATMAN OF PARIS(1946); WIFE OF MONTE CRISTO, THE(1946); I WONDER WHO'S KISSING HER NOW(1947); OTHER LOVE, THE(1947); ABBOTT AND COSTELLO MEET FRANKENSTEIN(1948); PRAIRIE, THE(1948); RETURN OF THE WHISTLER, THE(1948); ABBOTT AND COSTELLO MEET THE KILLER, BORIS KARLOFF(1949); BARBARY PIRATE(1949)

Pierre Aubert
MR. HULOT'S HOLIDAY(1954, Fr.), w

Shirley Aubert
Misc. Silents
DODGING A MILLION(1918)

Luce Aubertin
SELLERS OF GIRLS(1967, Fr.)

Pascal Aubier
CHAPPAQUA(1967); PIERROT LE FOU(1968, Fr./Ital.); WINTER WIND(1970, Fr./Hung.)

Henry Aubin
DARK SANDS(1938, Brit.)

Jacques Aubochon
SHAGGY DOG, THE(1959)

Michel Aubossu
CONFIDENTIALLY YOURS(1983, Fr.)

Robert Auboyneau
FRENCH CANCAN(1956, Fr.)

Jacques Aubran
RIDERS OF THE WHISTLING SKULL(1937), m

Patrick Aubree
ONCE IN PARIS(1978)

Paulina Aubret
CONFIDENTIALLY YOURS(1983, Fr.)

Angharad Aubrey
NANNY, THE(1965, Brit.)

Anne Aubrey
HIGH FLIGHT(1957, Brit.); MAN INSIDE, THE(1958, Brit.); SECRET MAN, THE(1958, Brit.); TANK FORCE(1958, Brit.); BANDIT OF ZHOBE, THE(1959); IDOL ON PARADE(1959, Brit.); IN THE NICK(1960, Brit.); JAZZ BOAT(1960, Brit.); KILLERS OF KILIMANJARO(1960, Brit.); LET'S GET MARRIED(1960, Brit.); HELLIONS, THE(1962, Brit.)
Misc. Talkies
PLAY IT COOLER(1961)

Danielle Aubrey
BIKINI BEACH(1964)

Diane Aubrey
HAUNTED STRANGLER, THE(1958, Brit.); CARRY ON CONSTABLE(1960, Brit.); PETTICOAT PIRATES(1961, Brit.); PIRATES OF BLOOD RIVER, THE(1962, Brit.); TAKE ME OVER(1963, Brit.); LITTLE ONES, THE(1965, Brit.); WILD AFFAIR, THE(1966, Brit.)

Eric Aubrey
FLAW, THE(1955, Brit.)

Eve Aubrey
TOMCAT, THE(1968, Brit.)

Gus Aubrey
SOMEWHERE IN CAMP(1942, Brit.); SOMEWHERE IN CIVVIES(1943, Brit.); WHEN YOU COME HOME(1947, Brit.)

Helen Aubrey
Silents
COUNTY CHAIRMAN, THE(1914); RING AND THE MAN, THE(1914)

James A. Aubrey
UNDER MONTANA SKIES(1930), w

James Aubrey
WOMEN MEN MARRY(1931); BACHELOR MOTHER(1933); MYSTIC HOUR, THE(1934); FAST BULLETS(1936); RETURN OF SOPHIE LANG, THE(1936); LEGION OF MISSING MEN(1937); LIGHT THAT FAILED, THE(1939); PORT OF HATE(1939); PIONEER DAYS(1940); DANGEROUS LADY(1941); PICTURE OF DORIAN GRAY, THE(1945); THAT FORSYTE WOMAN(1949); MILLION DOLLAR MERMAID(1952); LORD OF THE FLIES(1963, Brit.); TERROR(1979, Brit.); HUNGER, THE(1983)
1984
FOREVER YOUNG(1984, Brit.)
Misc. Talkies
BORDER MENACE, THE(1934); POTLUCK PARDS(1934)
Silents
WHEN SECONDS COUNT(1927); OUT WITH THE TIDE(1928)

James T. Aubrey
RECORD CITY(1978), p

James T. Aubrey, Jr.
FUTUREWORLD(1976), p

Jean Aubrey
THREE CORNERED FATE(1954, Brit.); AS LONG AS THEY'RE HAPPY(1957, Brit.); DESPERATE MAN, THE(1959, Brit.); LIFE IN EMERGENCY WARD 10(1959, Brit.); DATE AT MIDNIGHT(1960, Brit.); MODEL FOR MURDER(1960, Brit.); MAN DETAINED(1961, Brit.); ON THE BEAT(1962, Brit.); OPERATION SNAFU(1965, Brit.)

Jim Aubrey
SMOKY TRAILS(1939)
Jimmie Aubrey
THANK YOU, JEEVES(1936); LURED(1947)
Jimmy Aubrey
CODE OF HONOR(1930); GRAND PARADE, THE(1930); LONESOME TRAIL, THE(1930); MIDNIGHT SPECIAL(1931); OUT OF SINGAPORE(1932); SONS OF THE DESERT(1933); DEMON FOR TROUBLE, A(1934); FIGHTING HERO(1934); INSIDE INFORMATION(1934); PICTURE BRIDES(1934); WAY OF THE WEST, THE(1934); GILDED LILY, THE(1935); MAKE A MILLION(1935); RESCUE SQUAD(1935); TALE OF TWO CITIES, A(1935); ACES AND EIGHTS(1936); CHARGE OF THE LIGHT BRIGADE, THE(1936); LIGHTNING BILL CARSON(1936); LOVE ON THE RUN(1936); NIGHT CARGO(1936); STORMY TRAILS(1936); TOO MUCH BEEF(1936); AMATEUR CROOK(1937); IDAHO KID, THE(1937); LAW OF THE RANGER(1937); MOONLIGHT ON THE RANGE(1937); PERSONAL PROPERTY(1937); $1,000,000 RACKET(1937); DANGER VALLEY(1938); RANGER'S ROUNDUP, THE(1938); WEST OF RAINBOW'S END(1938); KNIGHT OF THE PLAINS(1939); LET FREEDOM RING(1939); MESQUITE BUCKAROO(1939); CHARLIE CHAN IN PANAMA(1940); EARL OF CHICAGO, THE(1940); INVISIBLE MAN RETURNS, THE(1940); KID FROM SANTA FE, THE(1940); PINTO CANYON(1940); WATERLOO BRIDGE(1940); WILD HORSE VALLEY(1940); RIDING THE SUNSET TRAIL(1941); SCOTLAND YARD(1941); SWAMP WOMAN(1941); BILLY THE KID TRAPPED(1942); BROADWAY BIG SHOT(1942); JOURNEY FOR MARGARET(1942); BAD MEN OF THUNDER GAP(1943); FIGHTING VALLEY(1943); HAUNTED RANCH, THE(1943); MY FRIEND FLICKA(1943); WILD HORSE RUSTLERS(1943); DEATH RIDES THE PLAINS(1944); DRIFTER, THE(1944); LAW OF THE SADDLE(1944); LODGER, THE(1944); PINTO BANDIT, THE(1944); RAIDERS OF RED GAP(1944); TRAIL OF TERROR(1944); HANGOVER SQUARE(1945); VAMPIRE'S GHOST, THE(1945); GHOST OF HIDDEN VALLEY(1946); MR. HEX(1946); RENDEZVOUS 24(1946); THUNDER TOWN(1946); CALCUTTA(1947); I WOULDN'T BE IN YOUR SHOES(1948); JIGGS AND MAGGIE IN SOCIETY(1948); JULIA MISBEHAVES(1948); KISS THE BLOOD OFF MY HANDS(1948); LULLABY OF BROADWAY, THE(1951); DANGEROUS WHEN WET(1953)
Misc. Talkies
SHERIFF'S SECRET, THE(1931); COURAGE OF THE NORTH(1935); DEFYING THE LAW(1935); PHANTOM COWBOY, THE(1935); GO-GET-'EM HAINES(1936)
Silents
BASHFUL BUCCANEER(1925); GALLANT FOOL, THE(1926); LAST ALARM, THE(1926); DOWN GRADE, THE(1927); PIRATES OF THE SKY(1927); LITTLE WILD GIRL, THE(1928)
Misc. Silents
WHO'S YOUR FRIEND(1925); GENTLEMAN PREFFERED, A(1928)
Larry Aubrey
1984
AMERICAN NIGHTMARE(1984)
Oliver Aubrey
Misc. Talkies
BLUE MONEY(1975)
Richard Aubrey
TOWN CALLED HELL, A(1971, Span./Brit.), w
Skye Aubrey
CAREY TREATMENT, THE(1972)
Cecile Aubry
BLACK ROSE, THE(1950); MANON(1950, Fr.)
Danielle Aubry
NEW KIND OF LOVE, A(1963); OPERATION CIA(1965); ANGEL, ANGEL, DOWN WE GO(1969)
Renee Aubry
TWIST AROUND THE CLOCK(1961); GYPSY(1962)
Simone Aubry
POIL DE CAROTTE(1932, Fr.)
Jacques Aubuchon
BENEATH THE 12-MILE REEF(1953); SO BIG(1953); OPERATION MANHUNT(1954); SILVER CHALICE, THE(1954); SCARLET HOUR, THE(1956); BIG BOODLE, THE(1957); GUN GLORY(1957); SHORT CUT TO HELL(1957); WAY TO THE GOLD, THE(1957); THUNDER ROAD(1958); TWENTY PLUS TWO(1961); WILD AND WONDERFUL(1964); MC HALE'S NAVY JOINS THE AIR FORCE(1965); LOVE GOD?, THE(1969); HOAX, THE(1972)
Joy Auburn
MOTHER KNOWS BEST(1928)
Lee Auburn
HAPPY DAYS(1930)
Emile Aucamp
GUEST AT STEENKAMPSKRAAL, THE(1977, South Africa)
1984
GUEST, THE(1984, Brit.)
Jacques Aucante
SWEET ECSTASY(1962, Fr.), w
Gillaume Martin Aucion
OH! CALCUTTA!(1972), d
Michael Auclair
RICE GIRL(1963, Fr./Ital.); IMPOSSIBLE OBJECT(1973, Fr.)
Michel Auclair
BEAUTY AND THE BEAST(1947, Fr.); DAMNED, THE(1948, Fr.); GYPSY FURY(1950, Fr.); MANON(1950, Fr.); HENRIETTE'S HOLIDAY(1953, Fr.); ANITA GARIBALDI(1954, Ital.); HOLIDAY FOR HENRIETTA(1955, Fr.); FUNNY FACE(1957); ROYAL AFFAIRS IN VERSAILLES(1957, Fr.); MIDNIGHT MEETING(1962, Fr.); MISTRESS FOR THE SUMMER, A(1964, Fr./Ital.); MURDER AT 45 R.P.M.(1965, Fr.); SYMPHONY FOR A MASSACRE(1965, Fr./Ital.); DAY OF THE JACKAL, THE(1973, Brit./Fr.); THREE MEN TO DESTROY(1980, Fr.)
1984
LE BON PLAISIR(1984, Fr.)
Adeline Aucoc
LES ENFANTS TERRIBLES(1952, Fr.)
Alexandra Auder
STATE OF THINGS, THE(1983)
Viva Auder
STATE OF THINGS, THE(1983)
1984
PARIS, TEXAS(1984, Ger./Fr.)

Michel Audiard
MR. PEEK-A-BOO(1951, Fr.), w; LOVE IN A HOT CLIMATE(1958, Fr./Span.), w. Maurice Gerry; MAIGRET LAYS A TRAP(1958, Fr.), w; LOVE AND THE FRENCHWOMAN(1961, Fr.), w; NIGHT AFFAIR(1961, Fr.), w; COUNTERFEITERS OF PARIS, THE(1962, Fr., Ital.), w, w; DEVIL AND THE TEN COMMANDMENTS, THE(1962, Fr.), w; MAGNIFICENT TRAMP, THE(1962, Fr./Ital.), w; MONKEY IN WINTER, A(1962, Fr.), w; MOST WANTED MAN, THE(1962, Fr./Ital.), w; ANY NUMBER CAN WIN(1963 Fr.), w; GREED IN THE SUN(1965, Fr./ Ital.), w; MALE HUNT(1965, Fr./Ital.), w; TAXI FOR TOBRUK(1965, Fr./Span./Ger.), w; CLOPORTES(1966, Fr., Ital.), w; GREAT SPY CHASE, THE(1966, Fr.), w; TENDER SCOUNDREL(1967, Fr./Ital.), w; FEMMINA(1968 Fr./Ital./Ger.), w; JOHNNY BANCO(1969, Fr./Ital./Ger.), w; DEAR DETECTIVE(1978, Fr.), w; INCORRIGIBLE(1980, Fr.), w; INQUISITOR, THE(1982, Fr.), w
1984
DOG DAY(1984, Fr.), w
Jacques Audiberti
DOLL, THE(1962, Fr.), w
Gaitano Audiero
SUMMERTIME(1955)
Eleanor Audley
CINDERELLA(1950); GAMBLING HOUSE(1950); NO WAY. OUT(1950); PRETTY BABY(1950); STARLIFT(1951); CELL 2455, DEATH ROW(1955); PRINCE OF PLAYERS(1955); UNTAMED(1955); FULL OF LIFE(1956); UNGUARDED MOMENT, THE(1956); JEANNE EAGELS(1957); SPOILERS OF THE FOREST(1957); HOME BEFORE DARK(1958); SLEEPING BEAUTY(1959); SUMMER PLACE, A(1959); SECOND TIME AROUND, THE(1961); FOR THOSE WHO THINK YOUNG(1964); UNSINKABLE MOLLY BROWN, THE(1964); NEVER A DULL MOMENT(1968); HOOK, LINE AND SINKER(1969)
Hawk Audley
Misc. Talkies
BOARDING HOUSE(1984)
Maxine Audley
SLEEPING TIGER, THE(1954, Brit.); BARRETTS OF WIMPOLE STREET, THE(1957); KING IN NEW YORK, A(1957, Brit.); PRINCE AND THE SHOWGIRL, THE(1957, Brit.); DUNKIRK(1958, Brit.); VIKINGS, THE(1958); BLUEBEARD'S TEN HONEYMOONS(1960, Brit.); HELL IS A CITY(1960, Brit.); MAN WITH THE GREEN CARNATION, THE(1960, Brit.); OUR MAN IN HAVANA(1960, Brit.); PEEPING TOM(1960, Brit.); MAN AT THE CARLTON TOWER(1961, Brit.); PETTICOAT PIRATES(1961, Brit.); JOLLY BAD FELLOW, A(1964, Brit.); NEVER MENTION MURDER(1964, Brit.); AGONY AND THE ECSTASY, THE(1965); BATTLE OF THE VILLA FIORITA, THE(1965, Brit.); BRAIN, THE(1965, Ger./Brit.); RICOCHET(1966, Brit.); HERE WE GO ROUND THE MULBERRY BUSH(1968, Brit.); FRANKENSTEIN MUST BE DESTROYED!(1969, Brit.); HOUSE OF CARDS(1969); SINFUL DAVEY(1969, Brit.); LOOKING GLASS WAR, THE(1970, Brit.); RUNNING SCARED(1972, Brit.)
Michael Audley
MARK OF THE HAWK, THE(1958), d; KISS THE GIRLS AND MAKE THEM DIE(1967, U.S./Ital.)
Edmond Audran
FIGHTING PIMPERNEL, THE(1950, Brit.)
Silents
LA POUPEE(1920, Brit.), w
Edmund Audran
TALES OF HOFFMANN, THE(1951, Brit.)
Stephane Audran
LANDRU(1963, Fr./Ital); THIRD LOVER, THE(1963, Fr./Ital.); CHAMPAGNE MURDERS, THE(1968, Fr.); LES BICHES(1968, Fr.); SIX IN PARIS(1968, Fr.); LA FEMME INFIDELE(1969, Fr./Ital.); LADY IN THE CAR WITH GLASSES AND A GUN, THE(1970, U.S./Fr.); LE BOUCHER(1971, Fr./Ital.); DISCREET CHARM OF THE BOURGEOISIE, THE(1972, Fr.); WITHOUT APPARENT MOTIVE(1972, Fr.); BLACK BIRD, THE(1975); JUST BEFORE NIGHTFALL(1975, Fr./Ital.); TEN LITTLE INDIANS(1975, Ital./Fr./Span./Ger.); TWIST, THE(1976, Fr.); BLOOD RELATIVES(1978, Fr./Can.); SILVER BEARS(1978); VIOLETTE(1978, Fr.); EAGLE'S WING(1979, Brit.); BIG RED ONE, THE(1980); COUP DE TORCHON(1981, Fr.); PARADISE POUR TOUS(1982, Fr.)
1984
BAY BOY(1984, Can.)
Lila Audres
LUM AND ABNER ABROAD(1956)
Michael Audreson
YOUNG WINSTON(1972, Brit.)
Pascale Audret
LAFAYETTE(1963, Fr.); TWO ARE GUILTY(1964, Fr.); LES CARABINIERS(1968, Fr./Ital.)
Colette Audry
BATTLE OF THE RAILS(1949, Fr.), w
Genevieve Audry
PIRATE AND THE SLAVE GIRL, THE(1961, Fr./Ital.)
Mick Audsley
UNSUITABLE JOB FOR A WOMAN, AN(1982, Brit.), ed
Mickey Audsley
BROTHERS AND SISTERS(1980, Brit.), ed
Ariston Auelino
TERROR IS A MAN(1959, U.S./Phil.), m
Bismark Auelua
MALAYA(1950); ROAD TO BALI(1952)
Carl Auen
FINAL CHORD, THE(1936, Ger.)
Signe Auen
Misc. Silents
FOX WOMAN, THE(1915); YANKEE FROM THE WEST, A(1915)
Florence Auer
I MARRIED AN ANGEL(1942); LADY OF BURLESQUE(1943); NORTH STAR, THE(1943); ADVENTURE(1945); YOUTH ON TRIAL(1945); IT HAPPENED ON 5TH AVENUE(1947); NIGHTMARE ALLEY(1947); GOOD SAM(1948); LOVES OF CARMEN, THE(1948); MICHAEL O'HALLORAN(1948); STATE OF THE UNION(1948); BAD BOY(1949); HOLD THAT BABY!(1949); KNOCK ON ANY DOOR(1949); MADAME BOVARY(1949); THAT FORSYTE WOMAN(1949); BLONDE DYNAMITE(1950); LOVE NEST(1951); SILVER LODE(1954)

Silents
MODERN CINDERELLA, A(1917), w; HER MAD BARGAIN(1921), w; "THAT ROYLE GIRL"(1925)
Greg Auer
PHANTOM OF THE PARADISE(1974), spec eff; TRACKDOWN(1976), spec eff; KINGDOM OF THE SPIDERS(1977), spec eff; PROMISE, THE(1979), spec eff
Gregory M. Auer
CARRIE(1976), spec eff
Hannelore Auer
I, TOO, AM ONLY A WOMAN(1963, Ger.); ONLY A WOMAN(1966, Ger.)
Inger Auer
DEVIL, THE(1963)
John Auer
CIRCUS GIRL(1937), d; UNDER STRANGE FLAGS(1937), w; MAN BETRAYED, A(1941), d; GIRL RUSH(1944), p
John H. Auer
CRIME OF DR. CRESPI, THE(1936), p&d; FRANKIE AND JOHNNY(1936), d; MAN BETRAYED, A(1937), d; RHYTHM IN THE CLOUDS(1937), d; DESPERATE ADVENTURE, A(1938), p&d; I STAND ACCUSED(1938), p&d; INVISIBLE ENEMY(1938), d; OUTSIDE OF PARADISE(1938), d; CALLING ALL MARINES(1939), d; FORGED PASSPORT(1939), p&d; ORPHANS OF THE STREET(1939), d; SMUGGLED CARGO(1939), p&d; S.O.S. TIDAL WAVE(1939), d; THOU SHALT NOT KILL(1939), d; HIT PARADE OF 1941(1940), d; WOMEN IN WAR(1940), d; DEVIL PAYS OFF, THE(1941), d; MOONLIGHT MASQUERADE(1942), p&d, w; PARDON MY STRIPES(1942), d; GANGWAY FOR TOMORROW(1943), p&d; JOHNNY DOUGHBOY(1943), p&d; TAHITI HONEY(1943), p&d; MUSIC IN MANHATTAN(1944), p&d; SEVEN DAYS ASHORE(1944), p&d; PAN-AMERICANA(1945), p&d, w; BEAT THE BAND(1947), d; ANGEL ON THE AMAZON(1948), p&d; FLAME, THE(1948), d; I, JANE DOE(1948), p&d; AVENGERS, THE(1950), p, d; HIT PARADE OF 1951(1950), p&d; THUNDERBIRDS(1952), p&d; HELL'S HALF ACRE(1954), p&d; ETERNAL SEA, THE(1955), d; JOHNNY TROUBLE(1957), p&d
John J. Auer
CITY THAT NEVER SLEEPS(1953), p&d
Mischa Auer
BENSON MURDER CASE, THE(1930); INSIDE THE LINES(1930); JUST IMAGINE(1930); COMMAND PERFORMANCE(1931); DELICIOUS(1931); DRUMS OF JEOPARDY(1931); LADY FROM NOWHERE(1931); MATA HARI(1931); NO LIMIT(1931); UNHOLY GARDEN, THE(1931); WOMEN LOVE ONCE(1931); YELLOW TICKET, THE(1931); BEAUTY PARLOR(1932); INTRUDER, THE(1932); MIDNIGHT PATROL, THE(1932); MONSTER WALKS(1932); MURDER AT DAWN(1932); NO GREATER LOVE(1932); RASPUTIN AND THE EMPRESS(1932); SCARLET DAWN(1932); SINISTER HANDS(1932); UNWRITTEN LAW, THE(1932); AFTER TONIGHT(1933); CORRUPTION(1933); DANGEROUSLY YOURS(1933); FLAMING SIGNAL(1933); GIRL WITHOUT A ROOM(1933); INFERNAL MACHINE(1933); STORM AT DAYBREAK(1933); SUCKER MONEY(1933); TARZAN THE FEARLESS(1933); BULLDOG DRUMMOND STRIKES BACK(1934); CHANGE OF HEART(1934); CROSBY CASE, THE(1934); STAMBOUL QUEST(1934); STUDENT TOUR(1934); TRUMPET BLOWS, THE(1934); VIVA VILLA!(1934); WHARF ANGEL(1934); CLIVE OF INDIA(1935); CONDEMNED TO LIVE(1935); CRUSADES, THE(1935); I DREAM TOO MUCH(1935); LIVES OF A BENGAL LANCER(1935); MURDER IN THE FLEET(1935); MYSTERY WOMAN(1935); GAY DESPERADO, THE(1936); HOUSE OF A THOUSAND CANDLES, THE(1936); MY MAN GODFREY(1936); ONE RAINY AFTERNOON(1936); PRINCESS COMES ACROSS, THE(1936); SONS O' GUNS(1936); TOUGH GUY(1936); WE'RE ONLY HUMAN(1936); WINTERSET(1936); IT'S ALL YOURS(1937); MARRY THE GIRL(1937); MERRY-GO-ROUND OF 1938(1937); PICK A STAR(1937); PRESCRIPTION FOR ROMANCE(1937); THAT GIRL FROM PARIS(1937); THREE SMART GIRLS(1937); TOP OF THE TOWN(1937); VOGUES OF 1938(1937); WE HAVE OUR MOMENTS(1937); 100 MEN AND A GIRL(1937); LITTLE TOUGH GUYS IN SOCIETY(1938); RAGE OF PARIS, THE(1938); SERVICE DE LUXE(1938); SWEETHEARTS(1938); YOU CAN'T TAKE IT WITH YOU(1938); DESTRY RIDES AGAIN(1939); EAST SIDE OF HEAVEN(1939); UNEXPECTED FATHER(1939); ALIAS THE DEACON(1940); MARGIE(1940); PUBLIC DEB NO. 1(1940); SANDY IS A LADY(1940); SEVEN SINNERS(1940); SPRING PARADE(1940); TRAIL OF THE VIGILANTES(1940); CRACKED NUTS(1941); DON'T GET PERSONAL(1941); FLAME OF NEW ORLEANS, THE(1941); HELLZAPOPPIN'(1941); HOLD THAT GHOST(1941); MOONLIGHT IN HAWAII(1941); SING ANOTHER CHORUS(1941); TWIN BEDS(1942); AROUND THE WORLD(1943); LADY IN THE DARK(1944); UP IN MABEL'S ROOM(1944); AND THEN THERE WERE NONE(1945); BREWSTER'S MILLIONS(1945); ROYAL SCANDAL, A(1945); SENTIMENTAL JOURNEY(1946); SHE WROTE THE BOOK(1946); FOR YOU I DIE(1947); SOFIA(1948); BACHELOR IN PARIS(1953, Brit.); FROU-FROU(1955, Fr.); MONTE CARLO STORY, THE(1957, Ital.); NATHALIE(1958, Fr.); SPUTNIK(1960, Fr.); MR. ARKADIN(1962, Brit./Fr./Span.); WE JOINED THE NAVY(1962, Brit.); ARRIVEDERCI, BABY!(1966, Brit.); CHRISMAS THAT ALMOST WASN'T, THE(1966, Ital.)
Misc. Talkies
WESTERN CODE(1932)
Stephan Auer
FEDERAL AGENT AT LARGE(1950), p
Stephen Auer
SAN ANTONIO KID, THE(1944), p; SHERIFF OF LAS VEGAS(1944), p; SHERIFF OF SUNDOWN(1944), p; SILVER CITY KID(1944), p; STAGECOACH TO MONTEREY(1944), p; TOPEKA TERROR, THE(1945), p; TRAIL OF KIT CARSON(1945), p; MADONNA'S SECRET, THE(1946), p; DAREDEVILS OF THE CLOUDS(1948), p; HOMICIDE FOR THREE(1948), p; KING OF THE GAMBLERS(1948), p; MADONNA OF THE DESERT(1948), p; ALIAS THE CHAMP(1949), p; DUKE OF CHICAGO(1949), p; ROSE OF THE YUKON(1949), p; LONELY HEARTS BANDITS(1950), p; TRIAL WITHOUT JURY(1950), p; UNMASKED(1950), p; WOMAN FROM HEADQUARTERS(1950), p; MISSING WOMEN(1951), p; WOMAN IN THE DARK(1952), p
Mischa Auer, Jr.
SKY IS RED, THE(1952, Ital.)
Arnold Auerbach
LADY BE GOOD(1941), w
Arnold M. Auerbach
CALL ME MISTER(1951), w
Artie Auerbach
HERE COMES ELMER(1943)
George Auerbach
BISHOP MISBEHAVES, THE(1933), w; HIS BROTHER'S WIFE(1936), w; ST. BENNY THE DIP(1951), w

Lee Auerbach
Misc. Talkies
JUPITER MENACE, THE(1982), d
Leon Auerbach
GIDGET GOES TO ROME(1963)
Stefanie Auerbach
Misc. Talkies
ALIEN ZONE(1978)
Maurice Aufair
JONAH–WHO WILL BE 25 IN THE YEAR 2000(1976, Switz.)
Claude Aufaure
1984
CHEECH AND CHONG'S THE CORSICAN BROTHERS(1984)
Nicole Aufay
FAR FROM DALLAS(1972, Fr.), w
Patrick Auffay
FOUR HUNDRED BLOWS, THE(1959); LOVE AT TWENTY(1963, Fr./Ital./Jap./Pol./Ger.)
Hans Auffenberg
U-47 LT. COMMANDER PRIEN(1967, Ger.), art d
Edna Aug
Misc. Silents
WHERE D'YE GET THAT STUFF?(1916)
Carl Augenstein
EFFECTS(1980), ph
Michael Augenstein
BREAKER! BREAKER!(1977)
Claudine Auger
TESTAMENT OF ORPHEUS, THE(1962, Fr.); IN THE FRENCH STYLE(1963, U.S./Fr.); THUNDERBALL(1965, Brit.); HEAD OF THE FAMILY(1967, Ital./Fr.); THAT MAN GEORGE!(1967, Fr./Ital./Span.); TRIPLE CROSS(1967, Fr./Brit.); YO YO(1967, Fr.); ANYONE CAN PLAY(1968, Ital.); DEVIL IN LOVE, THE(1968, Ital.); KILLING GAME, THE(1968, Fr.); TREASURE OF SAN GENNARO(1968, Fr./Ger.); LISTEN, LET'S MAKE LOVE(1969, Fr./Ital.); SONS OF SATAN(1969, Ital./Fr./Ger.); BLACK BELLY OF THE TARANTULA, THE(1972, Ital.); SUMMERTIME KILLER(1973); TWITCH OF THE DEATH NERVE(1973, Ital.); BUTTERFLY ON THE SHOULDER, A(1978, Fr.); FANTASTICA(1980, Can./Fr.); LOVERS AND LIARS(1981, Ital.); ASSOCIATE, THE(1982 Fr./Ger.)
1984
SECRET PLACES(1984, Brit.)
Germaine Auger
ROTHSCHILD(1938, Fr.)
Jacques Auger
THIRTEENTH LETTER, THE(1951)
Albert Augier
LOVE AND DEATH(1975); CHANEL SOLITAIRE(1981)
1984
AMERICAN DREAMER(1984); UNTIL SEPTEMBER(1984)
Charles Augins
REVENGE OF THE PINK PANTHER(1978)
Mme. Augris
Silents
NAPOLEON(1927, Fr.), cos
Adele August
APACHE AMBUSH(1955); HOLLYWOOD OR BUST(1956)
Adelle August
WOMEN'S PRISON(1955)
Bille August
GRASS IS SINGING, THE(1982, Brit./Swed.), ph
Billie August
1984
KILLING HEAT(1984), ph; ZAPPA(1984, Den.), d, w
E. August
YOLANTA(1964, USSR), spec eff
Edwin August
SIDE STREET(1929); MAGNIFICENT AMBERSONS, THE(1942); OVER MY DEAD BODY(1942); EXILE, THE(1947)
Silents
EVIDENCE(1915), a, d&w; BROADWAY SCANDAL(1918); IDOL OF THE NORTH, THE(1921)
Misc. Silents
WHEN IT STRIKES HOME(1915); PERILS OF DIVORCE(1916), d; SOCIAL HIGHWAYMAN, THE(1916), a, d; SUMMER GIRL, THE(1916), d; YELLOW PASSPORT, THE(1916), d; TALE OF TWO NATIONS, A(1917); CITY OF TEARS, THE(1918); POISON PEN, THE(1919), d; SCANDAL STREET(1925)
Harry August
PLEASURE PLANTATION(1970), ph
Helen August
MISADVENTURES OF MERLIN JONES, THE(1964), w; MONKEY'S UNCLE, THE(1965), w
Joe August
NO MORE ORCHIDS(1933), ph
Silents
TRUTHFUL TULLIVER(1917), ph; BRANDING BROADWAY(1918), ph; TOLL GATE, THE(1920), ph; O'MALLEY OF THE MOUNTED(1921), ph; WHITE OAK(1921), ph; ARABIAN LOVE(1922), ph; LOVE GAMBLER, THE(1922), ph; TRAVELIN' ON(1922), ph; ST. ELMO(1923), ph; BELOVED ROGUE, THE(1927), ph
John H. August
GUNGA DIN(1939), ph
Joseph August
BLACK WATCH, THE(1929), ph; SEVEN FACES(1929), ph; DOUBLE CROSS ROADS(1930), ph; MAN TROUBLE(1930), ph; MEN WITHOUT WOMEN(1930), ph; ON YOUR BACK(1930), ph; BRAT, THE(1931), ph; HEARTBREAK(1931), ph; MR. LEMON OF ORANGE(1931), ph; QUICK MILLIONS(1931), ph; CHARLIE CHAN'S CHANCE(1932), p, ph; MYSTERY RANCH(1932), ph; SILENT WITNESS, THE(1932), ph; THAT'S MY BOY(1932), ph; VANITY STREET(1932), ph; COCKTAIL HOUR(1933), ph; MAN'S CASTLE, A(1933), ph; MASTER OF MEN(1933), ph; AMONG THE MISSING(1934), ph; BLACK MOON(1934), ph; CAPTAIN HATES THE SEA, THE(1934), ph; DEFENSE HESTS, THE(1934), ph; NO GREATER GLORY(1934), ph; TWENTIETH CENTURY(1934), ph; AFTER THE DANCE(1935), ph; EIGHT

BELLS(1935), ph; I'LL LOVE YOU ALWAYS(1935), ph; WHOLE TOWN'S TALKING, THE(1935), ph; EVERY SATURDAY NIGHT(1936), ph; MUSS 'EM UP(1936), ph; SYLVIA SCARLETT(1936), ph; SEA DEVILS(1937), ph; SAINT IN NEW YORK, THE(1938), ph; HUNCHBACK OF NOTRE DAME, THE(1939), ph; MELODY RANCH(1940), ph; DEVIL AND DANIEL WEBSTER, THE(1941), ph; PORTRAIT OF JENNIE(1949), ph

Silents
APOSTLE OF VENGEANCE, THE(1916), ph; ARYAN, THE(1916), ph; CIVILIZATION(1916), ph; HELL'S HINGES(1916), ph; PATRIOT, THE(1916), ph; PRIMAL LURE, THE(1916), ph; BREED OF MEN(1919), ph; MONEY CORRAL, THE(1919), ph; POPPY GIRL'S HUSBAND, THE(1919), ph; SAND(1920), ph; TESTING BLOCK, THE(1920), ph; CALIFORNIA ROMANCE, A(1922), ph; MADNESS OF YOUTH(1923), ph; DANTE'S INFERNO(1924), ph; ANCIENT MARINER, THE(1925), ph; TUMBLEWEEDS(1925), ph; DON'T MARRY(1928), ph; STRONG BOY(1929), ph

Joseph H. August
SALUTE(1929), ph; UP THE RIVER(1930), ph; SEAS BENEATH, THE(1931), ph; INFORMER, THE(1935), ph; MARY OF SCOTLAND(1936), ph; PLOUGH AND THE STARS, THE(1936), ph; DAMSEL IN DISTRESS, A(1937), ph; FIFTY ROADS TO TOWN(1937), ph; MUSIC FOR MADAME(1937), ph; SOLDIER AND THE LADY, THE(1937), ph; SUPER SLEUTH(1937), ph; THERE GOES MY GIRL(1937), ph; BORDER G-MAN(1938), ph; GUN LAW(1938), ph; THIS MARRIAGE BUSINESS(1938), ph; MAN OF CONQUEST(1939), ph; NURSE EDITH CAVELL(1939), ph; PRIMROSE PATH(1940), ph; THEY WERE EXPENDABLE(1945), ph

Kim August
TIGER MAKES OUT, THE(1967); NO WAY TO TREAT A LADY(1968)

Tom August
MISADVENTURES OF MERLIN JONES, THE(1964), w; MONKEY'S UNCLE, THE(1965), w

Karel Augusta
DIVINE EMMA, THE(1983, Czech,)

Ira Augustain
80 STEPS TO JONAH(1969)

Dieter Augustin
1984
LITTLE DRUMMER GIRL, THE(1984)

William Augustin
MANHATTAN MELODRAMA(1934); SIX OF A KIND(1934); THIRTY-DAY PRINCESS(1934)

Carole Augustine
CONFESSIONS OF A WINDOW CLEANER(1974, Brit.)

Christopher Augustine
Misc. Talkies
HOLLYWOOD 90028(1973)

Ken Augustine
COMING HOME(1978)

Kenneth Augustine
HEROES(1977)

Peter Augustine
TECKMAN MYSTERY, THE(1955, Brit); WEAPON, THE(1957, Brit.); NIGHT AMBUSH(1958, Brit.)

Gary Augustynek
1984
LISTEN TO THE CITY(1984, Can.)

David Auker
UNMAN, WITTERING AND ZIGO(1971, Brit.); CONFESSIONS OF A POP PERFORMER(1975, Brit.); EMILY(1976, Brit.); SPY WHO LOVED ME, THE(1977, Brit.); STAND UP VIRGIN SOLDIERS(1977, Brit.)

Liane Aukin
PHANTOM OF THE OPERA, THE(1962, Brit.); SUNDAY BLOODY SUNDAY(1971, Brit.)

Frank Aukor
WANDERING JEW, THE(1933), ph

Olav Aukrust
Misc. Silents
PARSON'S WIDOW, THE(1920, Den.)

Elizabeth Aulajut
1984
ICEMAN(1984)

Lynn Aulbaugh
BUGSY MALONE(1976, Brit.)

Aggie Auld
HAWAII CALLS(1938), a, ch; RAINBOW ISLAND(1944)

Don Auld
PRECIOUS JEWELS(1969); SATIN MUSHROOM, THE(1969)

Donald Auld
UNSTOPPABLE MAN, THE(1961, Brit.)

Georgie Auld
NEW YORK, NEW YORK(1977)

Ewa Aulin
CANDY(1968, Ital./Fr.); PLUCKED(1969, Fr./Ital.); START THE REVOLUTION WITHOUT ME(1970); FEMALE BUTCHER, THE(1972, Ital./Span.)
Misc. Talkies
DEATH SMILES ON A MURDER(1974)

Elise Aulinger
GOLDEN PLAGUE, THE(1963, Ger.)

Elsie Aulinger
FEAR(1956, Ger.)

Joe Aulisi
SHAFT(1971), cos; SHAFT'S BIG SCORE(1972), cos; EASY MONEY(1983), cos

Joseph Aulisi
JENNIFER ON MY MIND(1971), cos; LITTLE DARLINGS(1980), cos

Joseph C. Aulisi
THREE DAYS OF THE CONDOR(1975), cos

Joseph G. Aulisi
SEVEN UPS, THE(1973), cos; DEATH WISH(1974), cos; SOMEBODY KILLED HER HUSBAND(1978), cos; NIGHT THE LIGHTS WENT OUT IN GEORGIA, THE(1981), cos; MAN, WOMAN AND CHILD(1983), cos
1984
BUDDY SYSTEM, THE(1984), cos; POPE OF GREENWICH VILLAGE, THE(1984), cos; SLAYGROUND(1984, Brit.), cos

Joseph Garibaldi Aulisi
GANG THAT COULDN'T SHOOT STRAIGHT, THE(1971), cos; LEGEND OF NIGGER CHARLEY, THE(1972), cos

Joe Aulist
FOREVER YOUNG, FOREVER FREE(1976, South Afr.), cos

Jane Aull
DIRTY HARRY(1971); HIGH PLAINS DRIFTER(1973)

Ann Ault
GREEN SLIME, THE(1969); ONLY WAY HOME, THE(1972)

Marie Ault
KITTY(1929, Brit.); RETURN OF THE RAT, THE(1929, Brit.); YELLOW STOCKINGS(1930, Brit.); CONTRABAND LOVE(1931, Brit.); SPECKLED BAND, THE(1931, Brit.); THIRD TIME LUCKY(1931, Brit.); DAUGHTERS OF TODAY(1933, Brit.); MAID HAPPY(1933, Brit.); MONEY FOR SPEED(1933, Brit.); THEIR NIGHT OUT(1933, Brit.); SONG AT EVENTIDE(1934, Brit.); SWINGING THE LEAD(1934, Brit.); LEND ME YOUR WIFE(1935, Brit.); WINDFALL(1935, Brit.); DAREDEVILS OF EARTH(1936, Brit.); TROPICAL TROUBLE(1936, Brit.); JAMAICA INN(1939, Brit.); MAJOR BARBARA(1941, Brit.); YOU WILL REMEMBER(1941, Brit.); MISSING MILLION, THE(1942, Brit.); WE DIVE AT DAWN(1943, Brit.); IT HAPPENED ONE SUNDAY(1944, Brit.); TWILIGHT HOUR(1944, Brit.); LOVE ON THE DOLE(1945, Brit.); THEY KNEW MR. KNIGHT(1945, Brit.); ADVENTURESS, THE(1946, Brit.); CAESAR AND CLEOPATRA(1946, Brit.); CARNIVAL(1946, Brit.); MAN FROM MOROCCO, THE(1946, Brit.); WALTZ TIME(1946, Brit.); THREE WEIRD SISTERS, THE(1948, Brit.); NO ROOM AT THE INN(1950, Brit.); CHEER THE BRAVE(1951, Brit.)
Silents
IF FOUR WALLS TOLD(1922, Brit.); MONKEY'S PAW, THE(1923, Brit.); PADDY, THE NEXT BEST THING(1923, Brit.); PRUDES FALL, THE(1924, Brit.); RAT, THE(1925, Brit.); LODGER, THE(1926, Brit.); DAUGHTER IN REVOLT(1927, Brit.); MADAME POMPADOUR(1927, Brit.); ROSES OF PICARDY(1927, Brit.); DAWN(1928, Brit.); LIFE(1928, Brit.); VIRGINIA'S HUSBAND(1928, Brit.); ALLEY CAT, THE(1929, Brit.)
Misc. Silents
CLASS AND NO CLASS(1921, Brit.); WOMAN TO WOMAN(1923, Brit.); FANNY HAWTHORNE(1927, Brit.); SILVER LINING, THE(1927, Brit.); VICTORY(1928, Brit.); DOWNSTREAM(1929, Brit.); KITTY(1929, Brit.)

Debbie AuLuce
Misc. Talkies
UP RIVER(1979)

Robert S. Aumen
LOOKIN' TO GET OUT(1982)

Alexandra Aumond
LAST METRO, THE(1981, Fr.)

Stacy Aumonier
DARK RED ROSES(1930, Brit.), w; BROWN WALLET, THE(1936, Brit.), w; SPY FOR A DAY(1939, Brit.), w

Genevieve Aumont
CAPTAIN PIRATE(1952); STRANGE FASCINATION(1952); FORTY-NINTH MAN, THE(1953); LOVE ME OR LEAVE ME(1955); PROUD AND THE PROFANE, THE(1956); AFFAIR TO REMEMBER, AN(1957); FUNNY FACE(1957); JOURNEY TO FREEDOM(1957); PERFECT FURLOUGH, THE(1958)

Jean Pierre Aumont
BIZARRE BIZARRE(1939, Fr.); CROSS OF LORRAINE, THE(1943); HEARTBEAT(1946); SONG OF SCHEHERAZADE(1947); AFFAIRS OF A ROGUE, THE(1949, Brit.); LILI(1953); NAPOLEON(1955, Fr.); HILDA CRANE(1956); SEVENTH SIN, THE(1957); JOHN PAUL JONES(1959); DEVIL AT FOUR O'CLOCK, THE(1961); HAPPY HOOKER, THE(1975)

"Jean" Pierre Aumont
ASSIGNMENT IN BRITTANY(1943)

Jean-Pierre Aumont
DARK EYES(1938, Fr.); THREE HOURS(1944, Fr.); SIREN OF ATLANTIS(1948); LIFE BEGINS TOMORROW(1952, Fr.); CHARGE OF THE LANCERS(1953); GAY ADVENTURE, THE(1953, Brit.); ROYAL AFFAIRS IN VERSAILLES(1957, Fr.); ENEMY GENERAL, THE(1960); SEVEN CAPITAL SINS(1962, Fr./Ital.); FIVE MILES TO MIDNIGHT(1963, U.S./Fr./Ital.); CASTLE KEEP(1969); CAULDRON OF BLOOD(1971, Span.); MAN WITH THE TRANSPLANTED BRAIN, THE(1972, Fr./Ital./Ger.); DAY FOR NIGHT(1973, Fr.); MAHOGANY(1975); CATHERINE & CO.(1976, Fr.); BLACKOUT(1978, Fr./Can.); CAT AND MOUSE(1978, Fr.); TWO SOLITUDES(1978, Can.); SOMETHING SHORT OF PARADISE(1979); NANA(1983, Ital.)

Michel Aumont
NADA GANG, THE(1974, Fr./Ital.); 1★2?(1975, Fr.); POURQUOI PAS!(1979, Fr.); LA VIE CONTINUE(1982, Fr.)
1984
LES COMPERES(1984, Fr.); SUNDAY IN THE COUNTRY, A(1984, Fr.)

Tina Aumont
WHITE SISTER(1973, Ital./Span./Fr.); MALICIOUS(1974, Ital.); TORSO(1974, Ital.); DRAMA OF THE RICH(1975, Ital./Fr.); LIFESPAN(1975, U.S./Brit./Neth.); CASANOVA(1976, Ital.); MATTER OF TIME, A(1976, Ital./U.S.); LA GRANDE BOURGEOISE(1977, Ital.)

Sven Aune
TERRORISTS, THE(1975, Brit.)

Nora Aunor
1984
BONA(1984, Phil.)

Richard Aurandt
GANG BUSTERS(1955), m

Richard D. Aurandt
WALK TALL(1960), m; SILENT CALL, THE(1961), m, md

Claude Aurant-Lara
FOUR BAGS FULL(1957, Fr./Ital.), d

Carlos Aured
HOUSE OF PSYCHOTIC WOMEN, THE(1973, Span.), d; TRIUMPHS OF A MAN CALLED HORSE(1983, US/Mex.), w

Edward J. Auregul
BEN HUR(1959)

Jean Aurel
MATA HARI'S DAUGHTER(1954, Fr./Ital), w; GATES OF PARIS(1958, Fr./Ital.), w; LA PARISIENNE(1958, Fr./Ital.), w; NIGHT WATCH, THE(1964, Fr./Ital.), w; DE L'AMOUR(1968, Fr./Ital.), d, w; MANON 70(1968, Fr.), d, w; LOVE ON THE RUN(1980, Fr.), w; WOMAN NEXT DOOR, THE(1981, Fr.), w; CONFIDENTIALLY YOURS(1983, Fr.), w

Jean-Claude Aurel
LIGHT ACROSSS THE STREET, THE(1957, Fr.), w
Andrea Aureli
HANNIBAL(1960, Ital.); LEGIONS OF THE NILE(1960, Ital.); MIGHTY CRUSADERS, THE(1961, Ital.); PIRATE OF THE BLACK HAWK, THE(1961, Fr./Ital.); QUEEN OF THE PIRATES(1961, Ital./Ger.); LAST OF THE VIKINGS, THE(1962, Fr./Ital.); FALL OF ROME, THE(1963, Ital.); GLADIATOR OF ROME(1963, Ital.); REBEL GLADIATORS, THE(1963, Ital.); SAMSON AND THE SLAVE QUEEN(1963, Ital.); DUEL OF CHAMPIONS(1964 Ital./Span.); TIGER OF THE SEVEN SEAS(1964, Fr./Ital.); RINGO AND HIS GOLDEN PISTOL(1966, Ital.); BIGGEST BUNDLE OF THEM ALL, THE(1968)
Neville Aurelius
POPE JOAN(1972, Brit.); NATIONAL HEALTH, OR NURSE NORTON'S AFFAIR, THE(1973, Brit.)
Jean Aurenche
CONFESSIONS OF A NEWLYWED(1941, Fr.), w; SYMPHONIE PASTORALE(1948, Fr.), w; DEVIL IN THE FLESH, THE(1949, Fr.), w; LOVE STORY(1949, Fr.), w; SYLVIA AND THE PHANTOM(1950, Fr.), w; WALLS OF MALAPAGA, THE(1950, Fr./Ital.), w; FORBIDDEN GAMES(1953, Fr.), w; SEVEN DEADLY SINS, THE(1953, Fr./Ital.), w; DAUGHTERS OF DESTINY(1954, Fr./Ital.), w; GAME OF LOVE, THE(1954, Fr.), w; RED AND THE BLACK, THE(1954, Fr./Ital.), w; RED, INN, THE(1954, Fr.), w; FOUR BAGS FULL(1957, Fr./Ital.), w; GERVAISE(1956, Fr.), w; HUNCHBACK OF NOTRE DAME, THE(1957, Fr.), w; GAMBLER, THE(1958, Fr.), w; LOVE IS MY PROFESSION(1959, Fr.), w; FEMALE, THE(1960, Fr.), w; GREEN MARE, THE(1961, Fr./Ital.), w; CRIME DOES NOT PAY(1962, Fr.), w; IMPERIAL VENUS(1963, Ital./Fr.), w; ENOUGH ROPE(1966, Fr./Ital./Ger.), w; IS PARIS BURNING?(1966, U.S./Fr.), w; THIS SPECIAL FRIENDSHIP(1967, Fr.), w; CLOCKMAKER, THE(1976, Fr.), w; LET JOY REIGN SUPREME(1977, Fr.), w; JUDGE AND THE ASSASSIN, THE(1979, Fr.), w; COUP DE TORCHON(1981, Fr.), w; L'ETOILE DU NORD(1983, Fr.), w
1984
SWANN IN LOVE(1984, Fr.Ger.)
Marc Aurian
LOVE IN THE AFTERNOON(1957); TALES OF PARIS(1962, Fr./Ital.), w
George Auric
ALIBI, THE(1939, Fr.), m; HOLIDAY FOR HENRIETTA(1955, Fr.), m; NIGHT HEAVEN FELL, THE(1958, Fr.), m
Georges Auric
ROMA RIVUOLE CESARE(, m; BLOOD OF A POET, THE(1930, Fr.), m; A NOUS LA LIBERTE(1931, Fr.), m; ETERNAL RETURN, THE(1943, Fr.), m; DEAD OF NIGHT(1946, Brit.), m; BEAUTY AND THE BEAST(1947, Fr.), m; LES JEUX SONT FAITS(1947, Fr.), m; ANOTHER SHORE(1948, Brit.), m; BLIND DESIRE(1948, Fr.), m; CORRIDOR OF MIRRORS(1948, Brit.), m; EAGLE WITH TWO HEADS(1948, Fr.), m; QUEEN OF SPADES(1948, Brit.), m; RUY BLAS(1948, Fr.), m; SYMPHONIE PASTORALE(1948, Fr.), m; IT ALWAYS RAINS ON SUNDAY(1949, Brit.), m; PASSPORT TO PIMLICO(1949, Brit.), m; SILENT DUST(1949, Brit.), m; HUE AND CRY(1950, Brit.), m; LES PARENTS TERRIBLES(1950, Fr.), m; ORPHEUS(1950, Fr.), m; CAROLINE CHERIE(1951, Fr.), m; GALLOPING MAJOR, THE(1951, Brit.), m; LAVENDER HILL MOB, THE(1951, Brit.), m; DAUGHTER OF THE SANDS(1952, Fr.), m; MOULIN ROUGE(1952), m; SPIDER AND THE FLY, THE(1952, Brit.), m; HENRIETTE'S HOLIDAY(1953, Fr.), m; TITFIELD THUNDERBOLT, THE(1953, Brit.), m; DETECTIVE, THE(1954, Qit.), m; GOOD DIE YOUNG, THE(1954, Brit.), md; DIVIDED HEART, THE(1955, Brit.), m; LOLA MONTES(1955, Fr./Ger.), m; WAGES OF FEAR, THE(1955, Fr./Ital.), m, md; ABDULLAH'S HAREM(1956, Brit./Egypt.), m; GERVAISE(1956, Fr.), m; RIFIFI(1956, Fr.), m; HEAVEN KNOWS, MR. ALLISON(1957), m; HUNCHBACK OF NOTRE DAME, THE(1957, Fr.), m; STORY OF ESTHER COSTELLO, THE(1957, Brit.), m; WALK INTO HELL(1957, Aus.), m; BONJOUR TRISTESSE(1958), m; DANGEROUS EXILE(1958, Brit.), m; JOURNEY, THE(1959, U.S./Aust.), m; NEXT TO NO TIME(1960, Brit.), m; S.O.S. PACIFIC(1960, Brit.), m; BRIDGE TO THE SUN(1961), m; GOODBYE AGAIN(1961), m; INNOCENTS, THE(1961, U.S./Brit.), m; TESTAMENT OF ORPHEUS, THE(1962, Fr.), m; MIND BENDERS, THE(1963, Brit.), m; POPPY IS ALSO A FLOWER, THE(1966), m; THERESE AND ISABELLE(1968, U.S./Ger.), m; CHRISTMAS TREE, THE(1969, Fr.), m; DON'T LOOK NOW(1969, Brit./Fr.), m
Jimmy Aurichio
MANIAC(1980)
Lois Aurino
LAST OF THE RED HOT LOVERS(1972)
Jean-Georges Auriol
CHILDREN OF CHAOS(1950, Fr.), w
Mario Auritano
PIRATES OF CAPRI, THE(1949)
James [Arness] Aurness
FARMER'S DAUGHTER, THE(1947)
Soni Aurora
GURU, THE(1969, U.S./India)
Robert Alan Aurther
EDGE OF THE CITY(1957), w
Robert Alan Aurthur
SPRING REUNION(1957), w; WARLOCK(1959), w; GRAND PRIX(1966), w; FOR LOVE OF IVY(1968), w; LOST MAN, THE(1969), d&w
Germaine Aussey
A NOUS LA LIBERTE(1931, Fr.); BELOVED IMPOSTER(1936, Brit.); GOLEM, THE(1937, Czech./Fr.); PEARLS OF THE CROWN(1938, Fr.); CONFESSIONS OF A NEWLYWED(1941, Fr.)
Peter Aust
FRIENDS AND HUSBANDS(1983, Ger.)
Stefan Aust
WAR AND PEACE(1983, Ger.), d&w
Austa
LIVING ON VELVET(1935)
Paul Austad
SNOW TREASURE(1968)
Herve Austen
1984
A NOS AMOURS(1984, Fr.)
Jane Austen
PRIDE AND PREJUDICE(1940), w; JANE AUSTEN IN MANHATTAN(1980), w

Leslie Austen
Silents
MAN AND THE WOMAN, A(1917); SILVER LINING, THE(1921)
Misc. Silents
AUCTION OF VIRTUE, THE(1917); TWO LITTLE IMPS(1917); CAUGHT IN THE ACT(1918); MRS. DANE'S DEFENSE(1918); MARIE, LTD.(1919); MY LITTLE SISTER(1919); RECKLESS WIVES(1921); LET NO MAN PUT ASUNDER(1924)
Peter Austen-Hunt
BIG SWITCH, THE(1970, Brit.), ed; MAN OF VIOLENCE(1970, Brit.), ed
Islen Auster
CHEATING BLONDES(1933), w
Islin Auster
MAYOR OF HELL, THE(1933), w; NAVY COMES THROUGH, THE(1942), p; SUSPECT, THE(1944), p; BRIDE FOR SALE(1949), w; ODONGO(1956, Brit.), p, w
Arthur Austie
FOUR AGAINST FATE(1952, Brit.), w
Al Austin
HOLIDAY FOR LOVERS(1959)
Alan Austin
PAY OR DIE(1960)
1984
DOOR TO DOOR(1984)
Albert Austin
Silents
KID, THE(1921); MY BOY(1922), d; TROUBLE(1922), d; GOLD RUSH, THE(1925); KEEP SMILING(1925), d; CITY LIGHTS(1931)
Misc. Silents
PRINCE OF A KING, A(1923), d
Amber Denyse Austin
MY TUTOR(1983)
Anne Austin
WICKED WOMAN, A(1934), w
Carmen Austin
STEEL CLAW, THE(1961); SAMAR(1962)
Charles Austin
WILD WEST WHOOPEE(1931); IT'S A COP(1934, Brit.), w; ANOTHER DAWN(1937); WE'LL SMILE AGAIN(1942, Brit.); BLOODEATERS(1980)
Charlotte Austin
LES MISERABLES(1952); RAINBOW 'ROUND MY SHOULDER(1952); FARMER TAKES A WIFE, THE(1953); HOW TO MARRY A MILLIONAIRE(1953); DESIREE(1954); GORILLA AT LARGE(1954); THERE'S NO BUSINESS LIKE SHOW BUSINESS(1954); DADDY LONG LEGS(1955); HOW TO BE VERY, VERY, POPULAR(1955); MAN WHO TURNED TO STONE, THE(1957); PAWNEE(1957); BRIDE AND THE BEAST, THE(1958); FRANKENSTEIN 1970(1958)
Chuck Austin
PRETTY BOY FLOYD(1960), ph
Clare Austin
ABANDON SHIP(1957, Brit.); GYPSY AND THE GENTLEMAN, THE(1958, Brit.)
Cornelius H. Austin, Jr.
COMING HOME(1978)
Damian Austin, Jr.
FISH THAT SAVED PITTSBURGH, THE(1979)
David Austin
UNCOMMON VALOR(1983)
Edward R. Austin
DEATH GOES NORTH(1939), w
Ernie Austin
DOUBLE-BARRELLED DETECTIVE STORY, THE(1965)
F. Britten Austin
LAST OUTPOST, THE(1935), w
Silents
LAST WITNESS, THE(1925, Brit.), w
Frank Austin
TERROR, THE(1928); PARDON US(1931); RANGE FEUD, THE(1931); BABES IN TOYLAND(1934); HOLLYWOOD PARTY(1934); DANTE'S INFERNO(1935); IT'S A SMALL WORLD(1935); SHE COULDN'T TAKE IT(1935); YOUNG DYNAMITE(1937); TIP-OFF GIRLS(1938); YOU CAN'T TAKE IT WITH YOU(1938); I WANT A DIVORCE(1940); DEVIL AND DANIEL WEBSTER, THE(1941); MEET JOHN DOE(1941); NEVER GIVE A SUCKER AN EVEN BREAK(1941); SWAMP WATER(1941); TWILIGHT ON THE TRAIL(1941); HILLBILLY BLITZKRIEG(1942); SNUFFY SMITH, YARD BIRD(1942); SLEEPY LAGOON(1943); EXILE, THE(1947); SEA OF GRASS, THE(1947); TRAIL STREET(1947); ARIZONA TERRITORY(1950)
Silents
SEA HORSES(1926)
Misc. Silents
MOCCASINS(1925); CODE OF THE NORTHWEST(1926)
Frederic Austin
MEN OF THE SEA(1951, Brit.), m
Frederick Austin
UNDERGROUND GUERRILLAS(1944, Brit.), m
Gary Austin
THX 1138(1971); CANNONBALL(1976, U.S./Hong Kong)
Gay Austin
HOSPITAL MASSACRE(1982)
1984
HOSPITAL MASSACRE(1984)
Gene Austin
BELLE OF THE NINETIES(1934); GIFT OF GAB(1934); SADIE MCKEE(1934); KLONDIKE ANNIE(1936); MY LITTLE CHICKADEE(1940); FOLLOW THE LEADER(1944); MOON OVER LAS VEGAS(1944)
Misc. Talkies
SONGS AND SADDLES(1938)
George Austin
Silents
MONSTER, THE(1925)
Misc. Silents
SECRET OF BLACK MOUNTAIN, THE(1917)

Gillie Austin
HERE WE GO ROUND THE MULBERRY BUSH(1968, Brit.)
Gordon Austin
Misc. Talkies
THURSDAY MORNING MURDERS, THE(1976)
Guy K. Austin
ROOKIE COP, THE(1939), w
Harold Austin
Silents
BAFFLED(1924); ANYTHING ONCE(1925); NIGHT OWL, THE(1926)
Misc. Silents
RICH GIRL, POOR GIRL(1921); BLACK LIGHTING(1924); LOVE MASTER, THE(1924); NORTH STAR(1925)
Ingrid Austin
BLACK MARKET RUSTLERS(1943)
Irving Austin
BATTLETRUCK(1982), w
J. Welsh Austin
PEARL OF DEATH, THE(1944)
J.W. Austin
HANGOVER SQUARE(1945)
Jack Austin
THEY MADE ME A CRIMINAL(1939)
Misc. Silents
GREEN-EYED MONSTER, THE(1921)
James Austin
ONE FROM THE HEART(1982)
Jane Austin
BUTCH AND SUNDANCE: THE EARLY DAYS(1979)
Jean Austin
BLACK MARKET RUSTLERS(1943); KOTCH(1971), hairstyles
Jeanne Austin
FUNHOUSE, THE(1981)
Jeanne L. Austin
STUCKEY'S LAST STAND(1980)
Jeff Austin
JONI(1980)
Jere Austin
Silents
ALL WOMAN(1918); PERFECT LADY, A(1918); ERSTWHILE SUSAN(1919); CARDIGAN(1922); SPLENDID LIE, THE(1922); PURE GRIT(1923); KING OF KINGS, THE(1927)
Misc. Silents
FEDORA(1918); RESURRECTION(1918); DAY DREAMS(1919); TRAP, THE(1919); WOMAN ON THE INDEX, THE(1919); WOMAN GAME, THE(1920); HIS MYSTERY'S GIRL(1923); DEMON, THE(1926); DESPERATE GAME, THE(1926)
Jerry Austin
SARATOGA TRUNK(1945); ADVENTURES OF DON JUAN(1949); LOVABLE CHEAT, THE(1949)
Silents
REGULAR FELLOW, A(1925)
Jim Austin
BLACK MARKET RUSTLERS(1943)
Joan Austin
LOVE ON SKIS(1933, Brit.)
John Austin
MADE FOR EACH OTHER(1939); DOUBLE LIFE, A(1947), set d; MEXICAN HAYRIDE(1948), set d; SECRET BEYOND THE DOOR, THE(1948), set d; CITY ACROSS THE RIVER(1949), set d; ILLEGAL ENTRY(1949), set d; JOHNNY STOOL PIGEON(1949), set d; SPY HUNT(1950), set d; THUNDER ON THE HILL(1951), set d; HAS ANYBODY SEEN MY GAL?(1952), set d; RAIDERS, THE(1952), set d; SON OF ALI BABA(1952), set d; SEND ME NO FLOWERS(1964), set d; MIRAGE(1965), set d; STRANGE BEDFELLOWS(1965), set d; VERY SPECIAL FAVOR, A(1965), set d; GAMBIT(1966), set d; MOMENT TO MOMENT(1966), set d; SECONDS(1966), set d; GUNFIGHT IN ABILENE(1967), set d; KING'S PIRATE(1967), set d; RELUCTANT ASTRONAUT, THE(1967), set d; COOGAN'S BLUFF(1968), set d; MADIGAN(1968), set d; SECRET WAR OF HARRY FRIGG, THE(1968), set d; EYE OF THE CAT(1969), set d; LOST MAN, THE(1969), set d; TOPAZ(1969, Brit.), set d; DIAMONDS ARE FOREVER(1971, Brit.), set d; RED SKY AT MORNING(1971), set d; PETE 'N' TILLIE(1972), set d; WHAT'S UP, DOC?(1972), set d; PAPER MOON(1973), set d; WESTWORLD(1973), set d; SHANKS(1974), set d; MANDINGO(1975), set d; EXORCIST II: THE HERETIC(1977), set d; 1941(1979), set d
John P Austin
COME SEPTEMBER(1961), set d
John P. Austin
MAN IN THE SHADOW(1957), set d; TATTERED DRESS, THE(1957), set d; TOUCH OF EVIL(1958), set d; YOUNG PHILADELPHIANS, THE(1959), set d; HOUSE OF WOMEN(1962), set d; ROME ADVENTURE(1962), set d; PT 109(1963), set d; WALL OF NOISE(1963), set d; KISSES FOR MY PRESIDENT(1964), set d; KITTEN WITH A WHIP(1964), set d; YOUNGBLOOD HAWKE(1964), set d; MIKEY AND NICKY(1976), set d
Leo Austin
TWO HUNDRED MOTELS(1971, Brit.), art d
1984
BOSTONIANS, THE(1984), prod d
Leslie Austin
YOUNG MAN OF MANHATTAN(1930)
Silents
AMERICAN BUDS(1918); DARLING OF THE RICH, THE(1923); JAMESTOWN(1923)
Misc. Silents
TABLES TURNED(1915); COURAGE OF THE COMMONPLACE(1917); DEMOCRACY(1920); MASKED DANCER, THE(1924)
Lois Austin
WITHOUT RESERVATIONS(1946); FATHER TAKES A WIFE(1941); SWAMP WOMAN(1941); DOWN TEXAS WAY(1942); G.I. HONEYMOON(1945); CENTENNIAL SUMMER(1946); G.I. WAR BRIDES(1946); MAGNIFICENT DOLL(1946); SPIDER WOMAN STRIKES BACK, THE(1946); TOMORROW IS FOREVER(1946); WHITE TIE AND TAILS(1946); HIGH BARBAREE(1947); IVY(1947); THAT HAGEN GIRL(1947); TRAP, THE(1947); UNFAITHFUL, THE(1947); VOICE OF THE TURTLE, THE(1947); FAMILY HONEYMOON(1948); LETTER FROM AN UNKNOWN WOMAN(1948); MYSTERY OF

THE GOLDEN EYE, THE(1948); NOOSE HANGS HIGH, THE(1948); SHANGHAI CHEST, THE(1948); SILVER RIVER(1948); SMART WOMAN(1948); WINTER MEETING(1948); FOUNTAINHEAD, THE(1949); HENRY, THE RAINMAKER(1949); IT'S A GREAT FEELING(1949); NIGHT UNTO NIGHT(1949); FATHER MAKES GOOD(1950); FULLER BRUSH GIRL, THE(1950); ON MOONLIGHT BAY(1951); NIGHT STAGE TO GALVESTON(1952); JET PILOT(1957)
Louis Austin
DECEPTION(1946)
Marie Austin
TRAIL TO GUNSIGHT(1944)
Michael Austin
SHOUT, THE(1978, Brit.), w; FIVE DAYS ONE SUMMER(1982), w
1984
GREYSTOKE: THE LEGEND OF TARZAN, LORD OF THE APES(1984), w
Mike Austin
STAR CHAMBER, THE(1983)
Nana Austin
SONG AND THE SILENCE, THE(1969)
Nancy Austin
CANNONBALL RUN, THE(1981)
Pam Austin
HOOTENANNY HOOT(1963); KISSIN' COUSINS(1964)
Pamela Austin
CHAPMAN REPORT, THE(1962); ROME ADVENTURE(1962); PERILS OF PAULINE, THE(1967)
Paul Austin
MAIDSTONE(1970); REUBEN, REUBEN(1983); TRADING PLACES(1983)
1984
POPE OF GREENWICH VILLAGE, THE(1984)
Peter Austin
HAUNTING OF M, THE(1979)
Philip Austin
ZACHARIAH(1971), w
Phyllis Konstan Austin
CROWNING EXPERIENCE, THE(1960)
Ray Austin
LONELINESS OF THE LONG DISTANCE RUNNER, THE(1962, Brit.); V.I.P.s, THE(1963, Brit.); ESCAPE BY NIGHT(1965, Brit.); 1,000 CONVICTS AND A WOMAN zero(1971, Brit.), d; HOUSE OF THE LIVING DEAD(1973, S. Afr.), d; VIRGIN WITCH, THE(1973, Brit.), d
Rene Austin
TALES OF MANHATTAN(1942); NATIONAL VELVET(1944)
Richard Austin
MUTINY IN THE BIG HOUSE(1939)
Robert Austin
FIRST TO FIGHT(1967); GIRO CITY(1982, Brit.)
1984
JIGSAW MAN, THE(1984, Brit.)
Ron Austin
HARRY IN YOUR POCKET(1973), w
Ronald Austin
HAPPENING, THE(1967), w; MIDAS RUN(1969), w
Sam Austin
Silents
LONG ODDS(1922, Brit.); PRODIGAL SON, THE(1923, Brit.)
Misc. Silents
PEACEMAKER, THE(1922, Brit.)
Steve Austin
NATURAL ENEMIES(1979)
Terence Austin
MURDER WILL OUT(1953, Brit.), w
Terry Austin
BORN TO SPEED(1947); PHILO VANCE RETURNS(1947); PHILO VANCE'S GAMBLE(1947); STEPCHILD(1947)
Vivian Austin
MOONLIGHT IN VERMONT(1943); SING A JINGLE(1943); COBRA WOMAN(1944); DESTINY(1944); HI, GOOD-LOOKIN'(1944); MOON OVER LAS VEGAS(1944); NIGHT CLUB GIRL(1944); TRIGGER TRAIL(1944); TWILIGHT ON THE PRAIRIE(1944); HONEYMOON AHEAD(1945); MEN IN HER DIARY(1945); SHE GETS HER MAN(1945); T-MEN(1947)
Misc. Talkies
BOSS OF BOOMTOWN(1944)
Will Austin
SMART POLITICS(1948), ed
William Austin
ILLUSION(1929); MARRIAGE PLAYGROUND, THE(1929); MYSTERIOUS DR. FU MANCHU, THE(1929); SWEETIE(1929); EMBARRASSING MOMENTS(1930); FLIRTING WIDOW, THE(1930); LET'S GO NATIVE(1930); MAN FROM BLANKLEY'S, THE(1930); RETURN OF DR. FU MANCHU, THE(1930); ALONG CAME YOUTH(1931); CORSAIR(1931); TAILOR MADE MAN, A(1931); DON'T BE A DUMMY(1932, Brit.); HIGH SOCIETY(1932, Brit.); ALICE IN WONDERLAND(1933); DECEPTION(1933), ed; PRIVATE LIFE OF HENRY VIII, THE(1933); THREE MEN IN A BOAT(1933, Brit.); DEMON FOR TROUBLE, A(1934), ed; GAY DIVORCEE, THE(1934); IMITATION OF LIFE(1934), ed; MANIAC(1934), ed; ONCE TO EVERY BACHELOR(1934); GOOSE AND THE GANDER, THE(1935); REDHEADS ON PARADE(1935); SECRETS OF CHINATOWN(1935), ed; $1,000 A MINUTE(1935); GARDEN MURDER CASE, THE(1936); SECRET PATROL(1936), ed; STAMPEDE(1936), ed; FURY AND THE WOMAN(1937), ed; LIVE, LOVE AND LEARN(1937); RENFREW OF THE ROYAL MOUNTED(1937); WHAT PRICE VENGEANCE?(1937), ed; CONVICTED(1938), ed; DR. RHYTHM(1938); EVERY DAY'S A HOLIDAY(1938); WOMAN AGAINST THE WORLD(1938), ed; ADVENTURES OF SHERLOCK HOLMES, THE(1939); DEATH GOES NORTH(1939), ed; MANHATTAN SHAKEDOWN(1939), ed; MURDER IS NEWS(1939), ed; SPECIAL INSPECTOR(1939), ed; DOCTOR TAKES A WIFE(1940); CHARLEY'S AUNT(1941); HI' YA, SAILOR(1943), ed; HOLY MATRIMONY(1943); ARMY WIVES(1944), ed; NATIONAL VELVET(1944); ONCE UPON A TIME(1944); SHADOW OF SUSPICION(1944), ed; WAVE, A WAC AND A MARINE, A(1944), ed; ALLOTMENT WIVES, INC.(1945), ed; COME OUT FIGHTING(1945), ed; DOCKS OF NEW YORK(1945), ed; FASHION MODEL(1945), ed; G.I. HONEYMOON(1945), ed; MR. MUGGS RIDES AGAIN(1945), ed; RIDERS OF THE DAWN(1945), ed; SOUTH OF THE RIO GRANDE(1945), ed; BLACK MARKET BABIES(1946), ed; BOWERY BOMBSHELL(1946,

ed; DANGEROUS MONEY(1946), ed; DON'T GAMBLE WITH STRANGERS(1946), ed; FACE OF MARBLE, THE(1946), ed; IN FAST COMPANY(1946), ed; JUNIOR PROM(1946), ed; MURDER IN THE MUSIC HALL(1946); SPOOK BUSTERS(1946), ed; SWEETHEART OF SIGMA CHI(1946), ed; WEST OF THE ALAMO(1946), ed; FALL GUY(1947), ed; GHOST GOES WILD, THE(1947), ed; HARD BOILED MAHONEY(1947), ed; NEWS HOUNDS(1947), ed; ANGELS ALLEY(1948), ed; CAMPUS SLEUTH(1948), ed; JINX MONEY(1948), ed; MUSIC MAN(1948), ed; SMUGGLERS' COVE(1948), ed; STAGE STRUCK(1948), ed; TROUBLE MAKERS(1948), ed; ANGELS IN DISGUISE(1949), ed; BAD BOY(1949), ed; FIGHTING FOOLS(1949), ed; HOLD THAT BABY!(1949), ed; MASTER MINDS(1949), ed; BLONDE DYNAMITE(1950), ed; BLUES BUSTERS(1950), ed; LAW OF THE PANHANDLE(1950), ed; LUCKY LOSERS(1950), ed; TRIPLE TROUBLE(1950), ed; BOWERY BATTALION(1951), ed; CRAZY OVER HORSES(1951), ed; ELEPHANT STAMPEDE(1951), ed; GHOST CHASERS(1951), ed; G.I. JANE(1951), ed; LET'S GO NAVY(1951), ed; FEUDIN' FOOLS(1952), ed; FLAT TOP(1952), ed; HERE COME THE MARINES(1952), ed; HOLD THAT LINE(1952), ed; NO HOLDS BARRED(1952), ed; RODEO(1952), ed; WILD STALLION(1952), ed; JALOPY(1953), ed; KANSAS PACIFIC(1953), ed; ROAR OF THE CROWD(1953), ed; ADVENTURES OF HAJJI BABA(1954), ed; ARROW IN THE DUST(1954), ed; BOWERY BOYS MEET THE MONSTERS, THE(1954), ed; ANNAPOLIS STORY, AN(1955), ed; DIAL RED O(1955), ed; JAIL BUSTERS(1955), ed; SUDDEN DANGER(1955), ed; WICHITA(1955), ed; CALLING HOMICIDE(1956), ed; DIG THAT URANIUM(1956), ed; FIGHTING TROUBLE(1956), ed; DEATH IN SMALL DOSES(1957), ed; DINO(1957), ed; DISEMBODIED, THE(1957), ed; LAST OF THE BADMEN(1957), ed; SABU AND THE MAGIC RING(1957), ed; TALL STRANGER, THE(1957), ed; UP IN SMOKE(1957), ed; WOMEN OF PITCAIRN ISLAND, THE(1957), ed; COLE YOUNGER, GUNFIGHTER(1958), ed; JOY RIDE(1958), ed; QUANTRILL'S RAIDERS(1958), ed; QUEEN OF OUTER SPACE(1958), ed; REVOLT IN THE BIG HOUSE(1958), ed; BAT, THE(1959), ed; BATTLE CRY(1959), ed; REBEL SET, THE(1959), ed; ATOMIC SUBMARINE, THE(1960), ed; THE HYPNOTIC EYE(1960), ed; PANIC IN YEAR ZERO!(1962), ed; BLOOD ON THE ARROW(1964), ed; GUNFIGHT AT COMANCHE CREEK(1964), ed; TROUBLEMAKER, THE(1964), ed; GREAT SIOUX MASSACRE, THE(1965), ed; EYE FOR AN EYE, AN(1966), ed
Silents
SUDS(1920); HANDLE WITH CARE(1922); RICH MEN'S WIVES(1922); RECKLESS AGE, THE(1924); FAR CRY, THE(1926); WHAT HAPPENED TO JONES(1926); IT(1927); ONE HOUR OF LOVE(1927); FIFTY-FIFTY GIRL, THE(1928); JUST MARRIED(1928); RED HAIR(1928); WHAT A NIGHT!(1928)
Misc. Silents
COWBOY KING, THE(1922); IN LOVE WITH LOVE(1924); FLAMING FOREST, THE(1926); HONEYMOON HATE(1927); RITZY(1927); SILK STOCKINGS(1927); SMALL BACHELOR, THE(1927); SOMEONE TO LOVE(1928)

William C.P. Austin
RETURN OF THE VAMPIRE, THE(1944)
Austin Brothers Circus
HAUNTING OF M, THE(1979)
Nicola Austine
SUBURBAN WIVES(1973, Brit.); OLD DRACULA(1975, Brit.)
The Australian Motor Air Aces
MUSIC HALL PARADE(1939, Brit.)
Amy Austria
JAGUAR(1980, Phil.)
Autant-Lara
RED, INN, THE(1954, Fr.), w
Claude Autant-Lara
MYSTERIOUS MR. DAVIS, THE(1936, Brit.), p&d; FRIC FRAC(1939, FR.), d; DEVIL IN THE FLESH, THE(1949, Fr.), d; LOVE STORY(1949, Fr.), p&d, w; SYLVIA AND THE PHANTOM(1950, Fr.), d; SEVEN DEADLY SINS, THE(1953, Fr./Ital.), w; GAME OF LOVE, THE(1954, Fr.), d, w; RED AND THE BLACK, THE(1954, Fr./Ital.), d; RED, INN, THE(1954, Fr.), d; GAMBLER, THE(1958, Fr.), d; LOVE IS MY PROFESSION(1959, Fr.), d; GREEN MARE, THE(1961, Fr./Ital.), p&d; STORY OF THE COUNT OF MONTE CRISTO, THE(1962, Fr./Ital.), d; ENOUGH ROPE(1966, Fr./Ital./Ger.), d
M. Autant-Lara
SEVEN DEADLY SINS, THE(1953, Fr./Ital.), d
Jean Auteche
COURIER OF LYONS(1938, Fr.), w
Harold Auten
SAVAGE GOLD(1933), w
Leslie Auten
Misc. Silents
CITY OF FAILING LIGHT, THE(1916)
Daniel Auteuil
MEN PREFER FAT GIRLS(1981, Fr.)
Lee Authmar
Silents
CAMPUS KNIGHTS(1929), t; PEACOCK FAN(1929), t
Marie Autl
MADNESS OF THE HEART(1949, Brit.)
Margherita Autori
IT HAPPENED IN ROME(1959, Ital.)
Adolphe Autran
LA MARSEILLAISE(1938, Fr.)
Liliane Autran
PEEK-A-BOO(1961, Fr.)
Paulo Autran
EARTH ENTRANCED(1970, Braz.)
Tanine Autre
LOVE ON A PILLOW(1963, Fr./Ital.), cos; LOST COMMAND, THE(1966), cos; RAVISHING IDIOT, A(1966, Ital./Fr.), cos; TWO WEEKS IN SEPTEMBER(1967, Fr./Brit.), cos; FAREWELL, FRIEND(1968, Fr./Ital.), set d; BRAIN, THE(1969, Fr./US), cos; CHRISTMAS TREE, THE(1969, Fr.), cos; ALMOST PERFECT AFFAIR, AN(1979), cos; GIFT, THE(1983, Fr./Ital.), cos
M. Autret
LIGHT YEARS AWAY(1982, Fr./Switz.), makeup
Jean-Yves Autrey
WHAT'S NEW, PUSSYCAT?(1965, U.S./Fr.)
Waldo Autrey
FREEWHEELIN'(1976)

Alan Autry
1984
ROADHOUSE 66(1984)
Gene Autry
IN OLD SANTA FE(1935); MELODY TRAIL(1935); SAGEBRUSH TROUBADOR(1935); SINGING VAGABOND, THE(1935); TUMBLING TUMBLEWEEDS(1935); COMIN' ROUND THE MOUNTAIN(1936); GUNS AND GUITARS(1936); RED RIVER VALLEY(1936); RIDE, RANGER, RIDE(1936); SINGING COWBOY, THE(1936); BIG SHOW, THE(1937); BOOTS AND SADDLES(1937); GIT ALONG, LITTLE DOGIES(1937); MANHATTAN MERRY-GO-ROUND(1937); OH, SUSANNA(1937); OLD CORRAL, THE(1937); PUBLIC COWBOY NO. 1(1937); ROOTIN' TOOTIN' RHYTHM(1937); ROUNDUP TIME IN TEXAS(1937); SPRINGTIME IN THE ROCKIES(1937); YODELIN' KID FROM PINE RIDGE(1937), a, m/1; GOLD MINE IN THE SKY(1938); MAN FROM MUSIC MOUNTAIN(1938); OLD BARN DANCE, THE(1938); PRAIRIE MOON(1938); RHYTHM OF THE SADDLE(1938); WESTERN JAMBOREE(1938); BLUE MONTANA SKIES(1939); COLORADO SUNSET(1939); HOME ON THE PRAIRIE(1939); IN OLD MONTEREY(1939); MEXICALI ROSE(1939); MOUNTAIN RHYTHM(1939); ROVIN' TUMBLEWEEDS(1939); SOUTH OF THE BORDER(1939); CAROLINA MOON(1940); GAUCHO SERENADE(1940); MELODY RANCH(1940); RANCHO GRANDE(1940); RIDE, TENDERFOOT, RIDE(1940); SHOOTING HIGH(1940); BACK IN THE SADDLE(1941); DOWN MEXICO WAY(1941); RIDIN' ON A RAINBOW(1941); SIERRA SUE(1941); SINGING HILL, THE(1941); SUNSET IN WYOMING(1941); UNDER FIESTA STARS(1941); BELLS OF CAPISTRANO(1942); CALL OF THE CANYON(1942); COWBOY SERENADE(1942); HEART OF THE RIO GRANDE(1942); HOME IN WYOMIN'(1942); STARDUST ON THE SAGE(1942); SIOUX CITY SUE(1946); LAST ROUND-UP, THE(1947); ROBIN OF TEXAS(1947); SADDLE PALS(1947); TRAIL TO SAN ANTONE(1947); TWILIGHT ON THE RIO GRANDE(1947); LOADED PISTOLS(1948); STRAWBERRY ROAN, THE(1948); BIG SOMBRERO, THE(1949); COWBOY AND THE INDIANS, THE(1949); RIDERS IN THE SKY(1949); RIDERS OF THE WHISTLING PINES(1949); RIM OF THE CANYON(1949); SONS OF NEW MEXICO(1949); BEYOND THE PURPLE HILLS(1950); BLAZING SUN, THE(1950); COW TOWN(1950); INDIAN TERRITORY(1950); MULE TRAIN(1950); GENE AUTRY AND THE MOUNTIES(1951); HILLS OF UTAH(1951); SILVER CANYON(1951); TEXANS NEVER CRY(1951); VALLEY OF FIRE(1951); WHIRLWIND(1951); APACHE COUNTRY(1952); BARBED WIRE(1952); BLUE CANADIAN ROCKIES(1952); NIGHT STAGE TO GALVESTON(1952); OLD WEST, THE(1952); WAGON TEAM(1952); GOLDTOWN GHOST RIDERS(1953); LAST OF THE PONY RIDERS(1953); ON TOP OF OLD SMOKY(1953); PACK TRAIN(1953); SAGINAW TRAIL(1953); WINNING OF THE WEST(1953); ALIAS JESSE JAMES(1959)
Misc. Talkies
WHIRLWIND(1951)
Steve Autry
HONKYTONK MAN(1982)
Victor Auz
NUN AT THE CROSSROADS, A(1970, Ital./Span.), w
Maurice Auzel
THIEF OF PARIS, THE(1967, Fr./Ital.)
Michel Auzepi
SUNSCORCHED(1966, Span./Ger.), m
Dana Auzins
MONKEY GRIP(1983, Aus.)
Igor Auzins
HIGH ROLLING(1977, Aus.), d; WE OF THE NEVER NEVER(1983, Aus.), d
Misc. Talkies
NIGHT NURSE, THE(1977), d
Aram A. Avakian
GIRL OF THE NIGHT(1960), ed
Aram Avakian
LAD: A DOG(1962), d; MIRACLE WORKER, THE(1962), ed; LILITH(1964), ed; ANDY(1965), ed; MICKEY ONE(1965), ed; YOU'RE A BIG BOY NOW(1966), ed; COPS AND ROBBERS(1973), d; 11 HARROWHOUSE(1974, Brit.), d; NEXT MAN, THE(1976), ed; HONEYSUCKLE ROSE(1980), ed
Don Avalier
MASQUERADE IN MEXICO(1945); SPANISH MAIN, THE(1945); PERILOUS HOLIDAY(1946); THREE DARING DAUGHTERS(1948); PLAYGIRL(1954)
Al Avalon
BRUSHFIRE(1962); EXPERIMENT IN TERROR(1962)
Frank Burt Avalon
1984
KARATE KID, THE(1984)
Frankie Avalon
JAMBOREE(1957); ALAMO, THE(1960); GUNS OF THE TIMBERLAND(1960); ALAKAZAM THE GREAT!(1961, Jap.); SAIL A CROOKED SHIP(1961); VOYAGE TO THE BOTTOM OF THE SEA(1961); PANIC IN YEAR ZERO!(1962); BEACH PARTY(1963); CASTILIAN, THE(1963, Span./U.S.); DRUMS OF AFRICA(1963); OPERATION BIKINI(1963); BIKINI BEACH(1964); MUSCLE BEACH PARTY(1964); PAJAMA PARTY(1964); BEACH BLANKET BINGO(1965); DR. GOLDFOOT AND THE BIKINI MACHINE(1965); HOW TO STUFF A WILD BIKINI(1965); I'LL TAKE SWEDEN(1965); SERGEANT DEADHEAD(1965); SKI PARTY(1965); FIREBALL 590(1966); MILLION EYES OF SU-MURU, THE(1967, Brit.); SKIDOO(1968); HORROR HOUSE(1970, Brit.); TAKE, THE(1974); GREASE(1978)
Misc. Talkies
BLOOD SONG(1982)
Phil Avalon
INN OF THE DAMNED(1974, Aus.)
The Avalon Boys
NOBODY'S BABY(1937)
Avalon Boys Quartet
WAY OUT WEST(1937)
Luis Avalos
BADGE 373(1973); HOT STUFF(1979); HUNTER, THE(1980); STIR CRAZY(1980); LOVE CHILD(1982)
Avant
NIGHT OF A THOUSAND CATS(1974, Mex.), p
Renzo Avanzo
PAISAN(1948, Ital.); GOLDEN COACH, THE(1953, Fr./Ital.), w; VOLCANO(1953, Ital.), w

Andras Avar
BOYS OF PAUL STREET, THE(1969, Hung./US)

Istvan Avar
DIALOGUE(1967, Hung.); ROUND UP, THE(1969, Hung.)

L. Avdeyeva
BORIS GODUNOV(1959, USSR)

Larisa Avdeyeva
QUEEN OF SPADES(1961, USSR); TSAR'S BRIDE, THE(1966, USSR)

Victor Avdiushko
FATHERS AND SONS(1960, USSR)

Viktor Avdiushko
NAKED AMONG THE WOLVES(1967, Ger.)

Viktor Avdyushko
PEACE TO HIM WHO ENTERS(1963, USSR); RED AND THE WHITE, THE(1969, Hung./USSR)

Hikmet Avedis
TEACHER, THE(1974), p,d&w; DR. MINX(1975), p,d&w; SPECIALIST, THE(1975), p&d, w; SCORCHY(1976), p,d&w
Misc. Talkies
STEPMOTHER, THE(1973), d; TEXAS DETOUR(1978), d

Howard [Hikmet] Avedis
FIFTH FLOOR, THE(1980), p&d; SEPARATE WAYS(1981), a, p&d, w; MORTUARY(1983), p, d, w
1984
THEY'RE PLAYING WITH FIRE(1984), p, d, w
Misc. Talkies
SPECIALIST, THE(1975), d

Doe Avedon
DEEP IN MY HEART(1954); HIGH AND THE MIGHTY, THE(1954); BOSS, THE(1956)
1984
LOVE STREAMS(1984)

Ariston Avelino
CAVALRY COMMAND(1963, U.S./Phil.), m; KIDNAPPERS, THE(1964, U.S./Phil.), m; MORO WITCH DOCTOR(1964, U.S./Phil.), m

Bert [Lamberto V.] Avellana
NO MAN IS AN ISLAND(1962)

Jose Mari Avellana
BOYS IN COMPANY C, THE(1978, U.S./Hong Kong)

Lamberto V Avellana
CRY FREEDOM(1961, Phil.), d

Fausta Avelli
CASSANDRA CROSSING, THE(1977)

P. Avenetti
POCKET MONEY(1972)

Phil Avenetti
SOUL OF NIGGER CHARLEY, THE(1973)

Phillip Avenetti
NIGHT OF THE LEPUS(1972)

Lucie Aveney
INVITATION, THE(1975, Fr./Switz.)

Salvatore Aventario
RETURN OF SABATA(1972, Ital./Fr./Ger.), ed

Stephen Aver
VIGILANTES OF DODGE CITY(1944), p

Hy Averbach
CRY DANGER(1951)

Hy Averback
BENNY GOODMAN STORY, THE(1956); FOUR GIRLS IN TOWN(1956); CHAMBER OF HORRORS(1966), p&d; I LOVE YOU, ALICE B. TOKLAS!(1968), d; WHERE WERE YOU WHEN THE LIGHTS WENT OUT?(1968), d; GREAT BANK ROBBERY, THE(1969), d; SUPPOSE THEY GAVE A WAR AND NOBODY CAME?(1970), d; HOW TO SUCCEED IN BUSINESS WITHOUT REALLY TRYING(1976)
1984
WHERE THE BOYS ARE '84(1984), d

Ruth Avergon
NIGHT SCHOOL(1981), p, w; TERROR EYES(1981), p, w

Anthony Averill
BROADWAY MUSKETEERS(1938); GIRLS ON PROBATION(1938); HEART OF THE NORTH(1938); MYSTERY HOUSE(1938); RACKET BUSTERS(1938); TORCHY BLANE IN PANAMA(1938); WHEN WERE YOU BORN?(1938); BLACKWELL'S ISLAND(1939); SECRET SERVICE OF THE AIR(1939); TORTURE SHIP(1939)

Jackie Averill
HAPPY LAND(1943); HELLO, FRISCO, HELLO(1943)

Lynn Averill
GEORG(1964)

Yuriy Averin
DESTINY OF A MAN(1961, USSR); GARNET BRACELET, THE(1966, USSR)

Andre Aversa
PARDON MY FRENCH(1951, U.S./Fr.)

Roy Aversa
MUSIC MAN(1948)

Ben Avery
SILENT WITNESS, THE(1962)

Bettye Avery
THAT NIGHT IN RIO(1941); THEY GOT ME COVERED(1943)

Brain Avery
GRADUATE, THE(1967)

Brian Avery
FOUR HORSEMEN OF THE APOCALYPSE, THE(1962); JOURNEY TO SHILOH(1968); SLEEPER(1973); FORTUNE, THE(1975)

Charles Avery
Silents
SUBMARINE PIRATE, A(1915), d; WESTERN ROVER, THE(1927)

Dwayne Avery
Misc. Talkies
WEEKEND LOVER(1969), d; YOUNG AND WILD(1975), d

Emile Avery
IT GROWS ON TREES(1952); RUN OF THE ARROW(1957); GREAT BANK ROBBERY, THE(1969)

Garth Avery
TAXI DRIVER(1976)

Harrison Avery
CLAUDINE(1974)

J. Ray Avery
Silents
OUT OF THE STORM(1920)

James Avery
STUNT MAN, THE(1980)
1984
FLETCH(1984)

Linda Avery
HITCHHIKERS, THE(1972)
Misc. Talkies
ATTACK AT NOON SUNDAY(1971); NOON SUNDAY(1971)

Margaret Avery
CURTAIN UP(1952, Brit.); COOL BREEZE(1972); TERROR HOUSE(1972); HELL UP IN HARLEM(1973); MAGNUM FORCE(1973); PSYCHOPATH, THE(1973); SCOTT JOPLIN(1977); WHICH WAY IS UP?(1977); FISH THAT SAVED PITTSBURGH, THE(1979)

Margot Avery
EASY MONEY(1983)

Nettie Avery
COOL WORLD, THE(1963)

Patricia Avery
Silents
ANNIE LAURIE(1927); LIGHT IN THE WINDOW, THE(1927); NIGHT LIFE(1927); ALEX THE GREAT(1928)

Paul Avery
STANLEY(1973); SUPERMAN(1978)

Phyllis Avery
SENSATION HUNTERS(1945), ch; QUEEN FOR A DAY(1951); RUBY GENTRY(1952); BEST THINGS IN LIFE ARE FREE, THE(1956)

Rick Avery
1984
KILLPOINT(1984), stunts

Stephen Avery
GAY DECEPTION, THE(1935), w; OUR LITTLE GIRL(1935), w

Stephen M. Avery
ANNAPOLIS FAREWELL(1935), w

Stephen Morehouse Avery
PURSUIT OF HAPPINESS, THE(1934), w; GORGEOUS HUSSY, THE(1936), w; ONE RAINY AFTERNOON(1936), w; I'LL TAKE ROMANCE(1937), w; HARD TO GET(1938), w; RIO(1939), w; FOUR MOTHERS(1941), w; MALE ANIMAL, THE(1942), w; DEEP VALLEY(1947), w; EVERY GIRL SHOULD BE MARRIED(1948), w; WOMAN IN WHITE, THE(1948), w

Suzanne Avery
Silents
SPEED CRAZED(1926), w; WHEN SECONDS COUNT(1927), w

Ted Avery
LITTLE BIG HORN(1951); NIGHT PEOPLE(1954)

Tex Avery
BUGS BUNNY, SUPERSTAR(1975)

Tol Avery
WHERE DANGER LIVES(1950); HIS KIND OF WOMAN(1951); SCARLET ANGEL(1952); NAKED ALIBI(1954); SHE COULDN'T SAY NO(1954); I'LL CRY TOMORROW(1955); IT CAME FROM BENEATH THE SEA(1955); PAL JOEY(1957); UNHOLY WIFE, THE(1957); BUCHANAN RIDES ALONE(1958); CASE AGAINST BROOKLYN, THE(1958); NORTH BY NORTHWEST(1959); GEORGE RAFT STORY, THE(1961); MAN-TRAP(1961); TWIST AROUND THE CLOCK(1961); FOLLOW ME, BOYS!(1966); HOTEL(1967); DREAM OF KINGS, A(1969); MAURIE(1973)

Val Avery
UP IN SMOKE(1978); FULLER BRUSH GIRL, THE(1950); HARDER THEY FALL, THE(1956); EDGE OF THE CITY(1957); LONG, HOT SUMMER, THE(1958); LAST TRAIN FROM GUN HILL(1959); MAGNIFICENT SEVEN, THE(1960); REQUIEM FOR A HEAVYWEIGHT(1962); TOO LATE BLUES(1962); HUD(1963); LOVE WITH THE PROPER STRANGER(1963); HALLELUJAH TRAIL, THE(1965); SATAN'S BED(1965); SYLVIA(1965); ASSAULT ON A QUEEN(1966); NEVADA SMITH(1966); WILD, WILD WINTER(1966); HOMBRE(1967); BROTHERHOOD, THE(1968); FACES(1968); PINK JUNGLE, THE(1968); DREAM OF KINGS, A(1969); MACHINE GUN McCAIN(1970, Ital.); TRAVELING EXECUTIONER, THE(1970); WUSA(1970); ANDERSON TAPES, THE(1971); MINNIE AND MOSKOWITZ(1971); WHO SAYS I CAN'T RIDE A RAINBOW!(1971); WHO FEARS THE DEVIL(1972); BLACK CAESAR(1973); LAUGHING POLICEMAN, THE(1973); PAPILLON(1973); LET'S DO IT AGAIN(1975); LUCKY LADY(1975); RUSSIAN ROULETTE(1975); HARRY AND WALTER GO TO NEW YORK(1976); KILLING OF A CHINESE BOOKIE, THE(1976); HEROES(1977); AMITYVILLE HORROR, THE(1979); LOVE AND BULLETS(1979, Brit.); WANDERERS, THE(1979); BRUBAKER(1980); CONTINENTAL DIVIDE(1981); CHOSEN, THE(1982); JINXED!(1982); SHARKY'S MACHINE(1982); EASY MONEY(1983); STING II, THE(1983)
1984
POPE OF GREENWICH VILLAGE, THE(1984)
Misc. Talkies
CHOICES(1981)

Nikolai Averyuskin
1984
JAZZMAN(1984, USSR)

Bruno Avesani
ROOTS OF HEAVEN, THE(1958), set d; REFLECTIONS IN A GOLDEN EYE(1967), art d; STATUE, THE(1971, Brit.), art d

A. Avetisian
Misc. Silents
NAMUS(1926, USSR)

N. Avetisova
WAR AND PEACE(1968, USSR)

Frank Avianca
FOURTEEN, THE(1973, Brit.), p; HUMAN FACTOR, THE(1975), a, p; MATILDA(1978)
Max Avieson
OFFICER'S MESS, THE(1931, Brit.); P.C. JOSSER(1931, Brit.); LOVE UP THE POLE(1936, Brit.)
Seymour Avigdor
FEMALE TROUBLE(1975)
Gordan Avil
ZOTZ!(1962), ph
Gordon Avil
HALLELUJAH(1929), ph; BILLY THE KID(1930), ph; CHAMP, THE(1931), ph; CHRISTMAS EVE(1947), ph; ON OUR MERRY WAY(1948), ph; WAR PAINT(1953), ph; BEACHHEAD(1954), ph; OUTLAW'S DAUGHTER, THE(1954), ph; SHIELD FOR MURDER(1954), ph; YELLOW TOMAHAWK, THE(1954), ph; BIG BLUFF, THE(1955), ph; BIG HOUSE, U.S.A.(1955), ph; DESERT SANDS(1955), ph; FORT YUMA(1955), ph; KING DINOSAUR(1955), ph; BLACK SLEEP, THE(1956), ph; REBEL IN TOWN(1956), ph; SIGN OF ZORRO, THE(1960), ph; TEN WHO DARED(1960), ph; TEENAGE MILLIONAIRE(1961), ph; TWIST AROUND THE CLOCK(1961), ph; DEADLY DUO(1962), ph; DON'T KNOCK THE TWIST(1962), ph; UNDERWATER CITY, THE(1962), ph; WILD HARVEST(1962), ph; WILD WESTERNERS, THE(1962), ph; THIRTEEN FRIGHTENED GIRLS(1963), ph; CONVICT STAGE(1965), ph; FORT COURAGEOUS(1965), ph; GIT!(1965), ph; WAR PARTY(1965), ph
Ben Avila
WORLD'S GREATEST SINNER, THE(1962)
Chuco Avila
BOULEVARD NIGHTS(1979)
Enrique Avila
LAZARILLO(1963, Span.); GLADIATORS 7(1964, Span./Ital.); SAVAGE PAMPAS(1967, Span./Arg.); FEW BULLETS MORE, A(1968, Ital./Span.); PLAY DIRTY(1969, Brit.); THEY CAME TO ROB LAS VEGAS(1969, Fr./Ital./Span./Ger.)
Frank Avila
STUNT MAN, THE(1980)
Vicente P. Avila
FLAME OVER VIETNAM(1967, Span./Ger.)
Anthony Avildsen
NIGHT IN HEAVEN, A(1983)
Christopher Avildsen
ROCKY(1976)
John Avildsen
OKAY BILL(1971), d,w&ph, ed
John G. Avildsen
GREENWICH VILLAGE STORY(1963); OUT OF IT(1969), ph; TURN ON TO LOVE(1969), d, ph; GUESS WHAT WE LEARNED IN SCHOOL TODAY?(1970), d, w; JOE(1970), d, ph; STOOLIE, THE(1972), d, ph; SAVE THE TIGER(1973), d; FOREPLAY(1975), d; W. W. AND THE DIXIE DANCEKINGS(1975), d; ROCKY(1976), d; SLOW DANCING IN THE BIG CITY(1978), p, d, ed; FORMULA, THE(1980), d, ed; NEIGHBORS(1981), d; NIGHT IN HEAVEN, A(1983), d&ed
1984
KARATE KID, THE(1984), d, ed
Misc. Talkies
CRY UNCLE(1973), d
Thomas K. Avildsen
THINGS ARE TOUGH ALL OVER(1982), d
Tom Avildsen
1984
CHEECH AND CHONG'S THE CORSICAN BROTHERS(1984), ed
Gordon Avile
CANYON CROSSROADS(1955), ph
Rick Aviles
CANNONBALL RUN, THE(1981)
Lorraine Avins
SMALL HOURS, THE(1962)
Mimi Avins
RUN FOR THE ROSES(1978), w
Anne Marie Avis
WEREWOLF IN A GIRL'S DORMITORY(1961, Ital./Aust.)
John Avison
NO BLADE OF GRASS(1970, Brit.)
Nurith Aviv
ONE SINGS, THE OTHER DOESN'T(1977, Fr.), ph; MAIS OU ET DONC ORNICAR(1979, Fr.), ph
Yael Aviv
IMPOSSIBLE ON SATURDAY(1966, Fr./Israel)
Basil Avlonitis
FORTUNE TELLER, THE(1961, Gr.); WE HAVE ONLY ONE LIFE(1963, Gr.)
John Avnet
COAST TO COAST(1980), p
Jon Avnet
RISKY BUSINESS(1983), p
Stella Avni
NOT MINE TO LOVE(1969, Israel)
Tony Avola
1984
RENO AND THE DOC(1984, Can.)
Roger Avon
FUN AT ST. FANNY'S(1956, Brit.); STARS IN YOUR EYES(1956, Brit.); KILL HER GENTLY(1958, Brit.); STRANGE AFFECTION(1959, Brit.); UGLY DUCKLING, THE(1959, Brit.); WOMAN EATER, THE(1959, Brit.); HARD DAY'S NIGHT, A(1964, Brit.); DALEKS–INVASION EARTH 2155 A.D.(1966, Brit.); FIVE MILLION YEARS TO EARTH(1968, Brit.); CRIMSON CULT, THE(1970, Brit.); DRESSER, THE(1983)
Suzanne Avon
SINS OF THE FATHERS(1948, Can.)
Ricard Avonde
CYRANO DE BERGERAC(1950)
Richard Avonde
TUNA CLIPPER(1949); CAPTAIN CAREY, U.S.A(1950); PETTY GIRL, THE(1950); SNOW DOG(1950); OKLAHOMA JUSTICE(1951); DEAD MAN'S TRAIL(1952); OUTLAW WOMEN(1952); WACO(1952); WILD BLUE YONDER, THE(1952); WILD HORSE AMBUSH(1952); FANGS OF THE ARCTIC(1953); FORTY-NINTH MAN, THE(1953);

SAVAGE FRONTIER(1953); SHADOWS OF TOMBSTONE(1953); VIGILANTE TERROR(1953); PURPLE MASK, THE(1955); LOOKING FOR DANGER(1957); FEMALE ANIMAL, THE(1958)
Misc. Talkies
SECRET OF OUTLAW FLATS(1953)
Don Avory
LATE AT NIGHT(1946, Brit.)
Sally Avory
HERE WE GO ROUND THE MULBERRY BUSH(1968, Brit.)
Anshel Avraham
DREAM NO MORE(1950, Palestine)
Zion Avrahamian
SAVAGE WEEKEND(1983), ed
Chris Avram
SLASHER, THE(1975); TORMENTED, THE(1978, Ital.)
V Avramenko
COSSACKS IN EXILE(1939, Ukrainian), p
Vasile Avramenko
GIRL FROM POLTAVA(1937), w
Peter Avramo
SIX BRIDGES TO CROSS(1955)
Mila Avramovic
ONE-EYED SOLDIERS(1967, U.S./Brit./Yugo.)
Chris Avran
Misc. Talkies
STAR ODYSSEY(1978)
Mira Avrech
MISTER TEN PERCENT(1967, Brit.), w
Robert J. Avrech
1984
BODY DOUBLE(1984), w
Charles Avred
CURSE OF THE DEVIL(1973, Span./Mex.), d
Gine Avril
Misc. Silents
LA FEMME DE NULLE PART(1922, Fr.)
Jane Avril
WOMEN IN CELL BLOCK 7(1977, Ital./U.S.)
Mag Avril
CASE OF DR. LAURENT(1958, Fr.)
Philippe Avron
DE L'AMOUR(1968, Fr./Ital.); BYE BYE BARBARA(1969, Fr.)
Keiko Awaji
BRIDGES AT TOKO-RI, THE(1954); WOMEN IN PRISON(1957, Jap.); TWILIGHT STORY, THE(1962, Jap.); WISER AGE(1962, Jap.); STRAY DOG(1963, Jap.); WHEN A WOMAN ASCENDS THE STAIRS(1963, Jap.); ILLUSION OF BLOOD(1966, Jap.)
Chikage Awashima
HUMAN CONDITION, THE(1959, Jap.); DIPLOMAT'S MANSION, THE(1961, Jap.); TATSU(1962, Jap.); PRESSURE OF GUILT(1964, Jap.); TEA AND RICE(1964, Jap.)
Kiyoshi Awazu
DOUBLE SUICIDE(1970, Jap.), art d; BANISHED(1978, Jap.), art d
Alena Awes
SOUTH SEA WOMAN(1953)
Kanan Awni
STRANGE BEDFELLOWS(1965)
Georgette Awys
1984
CHEECH AND CHONG'S THE CORSICAN BROTHERS(1984)
Eddie Axberg
WINTER LIGHT, THE(1963, Swed.); HERE'S YOUR LIFE(1968, Swed.); EMIGRANTS, THE(1972, Swed.); NEW LAND, THE(1973, Swed.)
Rick Axberg
DOLL, THE(1964, Swed.); HERE'S YOUR LIFE(1968, Swed.)
Carl Axcelle
WHITE ZOMBIE(1932), makeup
Gabriel Axel
GOLDEN MOUNTAINS(1958, Den.), d; CRAZY PARADISE(1965, Den.), d, w; HAGBARD AND SIGNE(1968, Den./Iceland/Swed.), d&w
Violet Axelle
SPLENDOR(1935)
Torbjorn Axelman
VIBRATION(1969, Swed.), p&d, w
Dave Axelrod
WHITE RAT(1972), ph
David A. Axelrod
CANNONBALL(1976, U.S./Hong Kong), m
David Axelrod
CHARLIE CHAN AND THE CURSE OF THE DRAGON QUEEN(1981), w
George Axelrod
PHFFFT!(1954), w; SEVEN YEAR ITCH, THE(1955), w; BUS STOP(1956), w; WILL SUCCESS SPOIL ROCK HUNTER?(1957), w; BREAKFAST AT TIFFANY'S(1961), w; MANCHURIAN CANDIDATE, THE(1962), p, w; GOODBYE CHARLIE(1964), w; PARIS WHEN IT SIZZLES(1964), p, w; HOW TO MURDER YOUR WIFE(1965), p&w; LORD LOVE A DUCK(1966), p&d, w; SECRET LIFE OF AN AMERICAN WIFE, THE(1968), p,d&w; LADY VANISHES, THE(1980, Brit.), w
Jack Axelrod
BANANAS(1971)
Jonathan Axelrod
EVERY LITTLE CROOK AND NANNY(1972), w
Nina Axelrod
ROLLER BOOGIE(1979); MOTEL HELL(1980); TIME WALKER(1982); CROSS COUNTRY(1983, Can.)
Alex Axelson
PHANTOM EXPRESS, THE(1932)
Einar Axelson
ON THE SUNNYSIDE(1936, Swed.)
Mary M. Axelson
LIFE BEGINS(1932), w

Mary McDougal Axelson
CHILD IS BORN, A(1940), w
Eva Axen
SUSPIRIA(1977, Ital.)
Ulf Axen
JOE HILL(1971, Swed./U.S.), art d; FLIGHT OF THE EAGLE(1983, Swed.), art d
George Axiotis
BAREFOOT BATTALION, THE(1954, Gr.)
Savvas Axiotis
DREAM OF PASSION, A(1978, Gr.)
George Axler
DANIEL(1983)
1984
BROADWAY DANNY ROSE(1984)
Hanne Axman
RED MENACE, THE(1949); ASSIGNMENT–PARIS(1952)
Hannelore Axman
FIVE FINGERS(1952); CALL ME MADAM(1953); THEY WERE SO YOUNG(1955)
Hannelore Axmann
GREAT SINNER, THE(1949)
Hanne Axmann-Rezzori
YOUNG TORLESS(1968, Fr./Ger.)
Dr. William Axt
OUR MODERN MAIDENS(1929), m; BLONDIE OF THE FOLLIES(1932), m; WET PARADE, THE(1932), m; BROADWAY TO HOLLYWOOD(1933), md; GABRIEL OVER THE WHITE HOUSE(1933), m; PENTHOUSE(1933), m; SECRET OF MADAME BLANCHE, THE(1933), m; STORM AT DAYBREAK(1933), m; GIRL FROM MISSOURI, THE(1934), m; LAZY RIVER(1934), m; OPERATOR 13(1934), m; RENDEZVOUS(1935), m; ALL-AMERICAN CHUMP(1936), m; LIBELED LADY(1936), m; OLD HUTCH(1936), md; PICCADILLY JIM(1936), m; SUZY(1936), m; THREE GODFATHERS(1936), m; THREE WISE GUYS, THE(1936), m; UNGUARDED HOUR, THE(1936), m; WE WENT TO COLLEGE(1936), m; BETWEEN TWO WOMEN(1937), m; LAST OF MRS. CHEYNEY, THE(1937), m; LONDON BY NIGHT(1937), m; SONG OF THE CITY(1937), m; EVERYBODY SING(1938), md; FAST COMPANY(1938), m; FIRST 100 YEARS, THE(1938), m; RICH MAN, POOR GIRL(1938), m; SPRING MADNESS(1938), m; WOMAN AGAINST WOMAN(1938), m; KID FROM TEXAS, THE(1939), m; SERGEANT MADDEN(1939), m; STAND UP AND FIGHT(1939), m
William Axt
YELLOW JACK(1938), m; FREE SOUL, A(1931), m; MEN IN WHITE(1934), m; FORSAKING ALL OTHERS(1935), m; MURDER MAN(1935), m; O'SHAUGHNESSY'S BOY(1935), m; PURSUIT(1935), m; WHIPSAW(1936), m; BEG, BORROW OR STEAL(1937), md; BIG CITY(1937), m; PARNELL(1937), m; THOROUGHBREDS DON'T CRY(1937), md; TELL NO TALES(1939), m; WITHIN THE LAW(1939), m
Silents
PASSION(1920, Ger.), m; BEN-HUR(1925), m; BIG PARADE, THE(1925), m; MERRY WIDOW, THE(1925), m; DON JUAN(1926), m; OUR MODERN MAIDENS(1929), m; SINGLE STANDARD, THE(1929), m; TRAIL OF '98, THE(1929), m
Kirk Axtel
TAKE, THE(1974), art d
Kurt Axtel
FOXY DROWN(1974), art d
Kirk Axtell
EXECUTIVE ACTION(1973), art d; GATOR(1976), art d; RAGING BULL(1980), art d
Hoyt Axton
SMOKY(1966); BLACK STALLION, THE(1979); ENDANGERED SPECIES(1982); JUNKMAN, THE(1982); LIAR'S MOON(1982); HEART LIKE A WHEEL(1983)
1984
GREMLINS(1984)
Carl Axzell
Silents
ADVENTURES OF CAROL, THE(1917)
Evelyn Axzell
Silents
SAINTED DEVIL, A(1924)
Carl Axzelle
Silents
CHICAGO AFTER MIDNIGHT(1928); DRIFTIN' SANDS(1928)
Violet Axzelle
DAWN TRAIL, THE(1931); WEDDING NIGHT, THE(1935)
Silents
JAVA HEAD(1923)
Misc. Silents
GIRL FROM BOHEMIA, THE(1918); GULF BETWEEN, THE(1918); SACRED FLAME, THE(1919); OLD OAKEN BUCKET, THE(1921)
Tamiko Aya
THREE WEEKS OF LOVE(1965)
Fernando Ayala
NO EXIT(1962, U.S./Arg.), p
Ann Ayars
DR. KILDARE'S VICTORY(1941); APACHE TRAIL(1942); NAZI AGENT(1942); REUNION IN FRANCE(1942); HUMAN COMEDY, THE(1943); YOUNGEST PROFESSION, THE(1943); TALES OF HOFFMANN, THE(1951, Brit.)
Henry Ayau
SEVEN(1979)
William Aydelott
RETURN OF THE SECAUCUS SEVEN(1980), p
Jimmy Aye
CEILNG ZERO(1935); LOVE BEFORE BREAKFAST(1936)
Maryon Aye
Silents
ETERNAL THREE, THE(1923); ROUGHNECK, THE(1924); IRENE(1926)
Misc. Silents
MONTANA BILL(1921); VENGEANCE TRAIL, THE(1921); MEANEST MAN IN THE WORLD, THE(1923)
Aly Ben Ayed
PLAY DIRTY(1969, Brit.)
George Ayer
1984
NEW YORK NIGHTS(1984)

Harold Ayer
GLORY AT SEA(1952, Brit.); ISLAND OF DESIRE(1952, Brit.); DESPERATE MOMENT(1953, Brit.); RIVER BEAT(1954); ORDERS ARE ORDERS(1959, Brit.); MARY-JANE(1968); TIME TO SING, A(1968); GENTLE PEOPLE AND THE QUIET LAND, THE(1972); TARZAN, THE APE MAN(1981)
Hay Ayer
THREE SUNDAYS TO LIVE(1957, Brit.)
Nat D. Ayer
VARIETY JUBILEE(1945, Brit.)
Agnes Ayers
Misc. Silents
HELD BY THE ENEMY(1920)
Curt Ayers
KING OF THE MOUNTAIN(1981); ZAPPED!(1982)
1984
THEY'RE PLAYING WITH FIRE(1984)
Lemuel Ayers
MEET ME IN ST. LOUIS(1944), art d; ZIEGFELD FOLLIES(1945), w, art d
Maurice Ayers
PRIDE AND THE PASSION, THE(1957), spec eff; PAINT YOUR WAGON(1969), spec eff
Ralph Ayers
DIRTY LITTLE BILLY(1972), spec eff
Roy Ayers
COFFY(1973), m
Robert Ayerton
Misc. Silents
REGULAR GIRL, A(1919)
Theo Aygar
SEPARATION(1968, Brit.)
Dan Aykroyd
LOVE AT FIRST SIGHT(1977, Can.); 1941(1979); BLUES BROTHERS, THE(1980), a, w; NEIGHBORS(1981); DOCTOR DETROIT(1983); TRADING PLACES(1983); TWILIGHT ZONE–THE MOVIE(1983)
1984
GHOSTBUSTERS(1984), a, w; NOTHING LASTS FOREVER(1984)
Peter Aykroyd
GAS(1981, Can.); FUNNY FARM, THE(1982, Can.); DOCTOR DETROIT(1983)
Ethel Ayler
TIME OF THE HEATHEN(1962); LORD SHANGO(1975)
Arthur Aylesworth
SERGEANT YORK(; BABBITT(1934); BRITISH AGENT(1934); CASE OF THE HOWLING DOG, THE(1934); DAMES(1934); DESIRABLE(1934); GENTLEMEN ARE BORN(1934); KEY, THE(1934); MAN WITH TWO FACES, THE(1934); MIDNIGHT ALIBI(1934); SIX-DAY BIKE RIDER(1934); ST. LOUIS KID, THE(1934); ESCAPE FROM DEVIL'S ISLAND(1935); FORCED LANDING(1935); I AM A THIEF(1935); MAN ON THE FLYING TRAPEZE, THE(1935); MEN WITHOUT NAMES(1935); NITWITS, THE(1935); RED HOT TIRES(1935); SECRET BRIDE, THE(1935); WOMAN IN RED, THE(1935); ARIZONA RAIDERS, THE(1936); DIMPLES(1936); GIRL OF THE OZARKS(1936); KING OF THE PECOS(1936); LOVE BEGINS AT TWENTY(1936); MAN I MARRY, THE(1936); MISTER CINDERELLA(1936); NEXT TIME WE LOVE(1936); PETRIFIED FOREST, THE(1936); PLOT THICKENS, THE(1936); PRESIDENT'S MYSTERY, THE(1936); ROSE OF THE RANCHO(1936); TO MARY–WITH LOVE(1936); WOMAN TRAP(1936); ESCAPE BY NIGHT(1937); FIFTY ROADS TO TOWN(1937); I COVER THE WAR(1937); LIFE OF EMILE ZOLA, THE(1937); MARKED WOMAN(1937); MARRY THE GIRL(1937); MOUNTAIN JUSTICE(1937); PLAINSMAN, THE(1937); SLAVE SHIP(1937); THAT MAN'S HERE AGAIN(1937); GOLD IS WHERE YOU FIND IT(1938); OF HUMAN HEARTS(1938); PROFESSOR BEWARE(1938); SPAWN OF THE NORTH(1938); TEST PILOT(1938); BEAU GESTE(1939); DRUMS ALONG THE MOHAWK(1939); DUST BE MY DESTINY(1939); FRONTIER MARSHAL(1939); JESSE JAMES(1939); KING OF THE UNDERWORLD(1939); OKLAHOMA KID, THE(1939); RETURN OF DR. X, THE(1939); RETURN OF THE CISCO KID(1939); STRANGE CASE OF DR. MEADE(1939); THEY SHALL HAVE MUSIC(1939); WHAT A LIFE(1939); YOUNG MR. LINCOLN(1939); 6000 ENEMIES(1939); BRIGHAM YOUNG–FRONTIERSMAN(1940); DANCING ON A DIME(1940); GRANNY GET YOUR GUN(1940); LITTLE OLD NEW YORK(1940); NORTHWEST PASSAGE(1940); SKY MURDER(1940); WESTERNER, THE(1940); WOMEN WITHOUT NAMES(1940); YOUNG PEOPLE(1940); HIGH SIERRA(1941); LAST OF THE DUANES(1941); SHADOW OF THE THIN MAN(1941); SMILING GHOST, THE(1941); THREE GIRLS ABOUT TOWN(1941); UNEXPECTED UNCLE(1941); MOONTIDE(1942); ROXIE HART(1942); SCATTERGOOD RIDES HIGH(1942); SIN TOWN(1942); HOME IN INDIANA(1944); ROGER TOUHY, GANGSTER!(1944); CHRISTMAS IN CONNECTICUT(1945); SCARED STIFF(1945)
Bill Aylesworth
MAX DUGAN RETURNS(1983)
Charles Aylesworth
VIRGINIA JUDGE, THE(1935)
Doug Aylesworth
RIDIN' DOWN THE TRAIL(1947)
Douglas Aylesworth
I WANTED WINGS(1941); SMART WOMAN(1948)
Arthur Ayleswroth
SANTA FE TRAIL(1940)
Carole-Ann Aylett
PATRICK(1979, Aus.)
Arthur Ayleworth
DRAGONWYCH(1946)
James Ayling
Silents
$5,000,000 COUNTERFEITING PLOT, THE(1914)
John Ayling
FLAMING TEEN-AGE, THE(1956), ph
David Aylmer
GIRLS AT SEA(1958, Brit.); MAN WHO WOULDN'T TALK, THE(1958, Brit.); GIDEON OF SCOTLAND YARD(1959, Brit.); SWINGIN' MAIDEN, THE(1963, Brit.)
Felix Aylmer
VICTORIA THE GREAT(1937, Brit.); CHARLEY'S(BIG-HEARTED) AUNT*1/2 (1940) ESCAPE(1930, Brit.); TEMPORARY WIDOW, THE(1930, Ger./Brit.); WORLD, THE FLESH, AND THE DEVIL, THE(1932, Brit.); GHOST CAMERA, THE(1933, Brit.); HOME, SWEET HOME(1933, Brit.); DOCTOR'S ORDERS(1934, Brit.); MY OLD

DUTCH(1934, Brit.); NIGHT CLUB QUEEN(1934, Brit.); PATH OF GLORY, THE(1934, Brit.); WHISPERING TONGUES(1934, Brit.); ACE OF SPADES, THE(1935, Brit.); CHECKMATE(1935, Brit.); CLAIRVOYANT, THE(1935, Brit.); DIVINE SPARK, THE(1935, Brit./Ital.); HELLO SWEETHEART(1935, Brit.); HER LAST AFFAIRE(1935, Brit.); IRON DUKE, THE(1935, Brit.); OLD ROSES(1935, Brit.); PRICE OF A SONG, THE(1935, Brit.); SHE SHALL HAVE MUSIC(1935, Brit.); WANDERING JEW, THE(1935, Brit.); AS YOU LIKE IT(1936, Brit.); DOMMED CARGO(1936, Brit.); IMPROPER DUCHESS, THE(1936, Brit.); IN THE SOUP(1936, Brit.); LADY JANE GREY(1936, Brit.); MAN IN THE MIRROR, THE(1936, Brit.); ROYAL EAGLE(1936, Brit.); SENSATION(1936, Brit.); SHADOW, THE(1936, Brit.); ACTION FOR SLANDER(1937, Brit.); DREAMING LIPS(1937, Brit.); FROG, THE(1937, Brit.); GLAMOROUS NIGHT(1937, Brit.); LIVE WIRE, THE(1937, Brit.); VICAR OF BRAY, THE(1937, Brit.); BANK HOLIDAY(1938, Brit.); BREAK THE NEWS(1938, Brit.); CITADEL, THE(1938, Brit.); HIDEOUT IN THE ALPS(1938, Brit.); I'VE GOT A HORSE(1938, Brit.); KATE PLUS TEN(1938, Brit.); RAT, THE(1938, Brit.); SIXTY GLORIOUS YEARS(1938, Brit.); SOUTH RIDING(1938, Brit.); TWO OF US, THE(1938, Brit.); JUST LIKE A WOMAN(1939, Brit.); MILL ON THE FLOSS(1939, Brit.); BRIGGS FAMILY, THE(1940, Brit.); CASE OF THE FRIGHTENED LADY, THE(1940. Brit.); DR. O'DOWD(1940, Brit.); NIGHT TRAIN(1940, Brit.); SALOON BAR(1940, Brit.); SPIES OF THE AIR(1940, Brit.); ATLANTIC FERRY(1941, Brit.); BLACK SHEEP OF WHITEHALL, THE(1941 Brit.); GHOST OF ST. MICHAEL'S. THE(1941, Brit.); GIRL IN THE NEWS, THE(1941, Brit.); HI, GANG!(1941, Brit.); I THANK YOU(1941, Brit.); MAJOR BARBARA(1941, Brit.); ONCE A CROOK(1941, Brit.); SAINT'S VACATION, THE(1941, Brit.); SEVENTH SURVIVOR, THE(1941, Brit.); SOUTH AMERICAN GEORGE(1941, Brit.); PETERVILLE DIAMOND, THE(1942, Brit.); REMARKABLE MR. KIPPS(1942, Brit.); SABOTAGE AT SEA(1942, Brit.); YOUNG MR. PITT, THE(1942, Brit.); ESCAPE TO DANGER(1943, Brit.); THURSDAY'S CHILD(1943, Brit.); TIME FLIES(1944, Brit.); UNCENSORED(1944, Brit.); ADVENTURE FOR TWO(1945, Brit.); COLONEL BLIMP(1945, Brit.); JOHNNY IN THE CLOUDS(1945, Brit.); MR. EMMANUEL(1945, Brit.); SPELL OF AMY NUGENT, THE(1945, Brit.); CAESAR AND CLEOPATRA(1946, Brit.); HENRY V(1946, Brit.); WICKED LADY, THE(1946, Brit.); GHOSTS OF BERKELEY SQUARE(1947, Brit.); GREEN FINGERS(1947, Brit.); MAGIC BOW, THE(1947, Brit.); MAN ABOUT THE HOUSE, A(1947, Brit.); YEARS BETWEEN, THE(1947, Brit.); CALENDAR, THE(1948, Brit.); HAMLET(1948, Brit.); OCTOBER MAN, THE(1948, Brit.); SMUGGLERS, THE(1948, Brit.); CHRISTOPHER COLUMBUS(1949, Brit.); EDWARD, MY SON(1949, U.S./Brit.); HER MAN GILBEY(1949, Brit.); PRINCE OF FOXES(1949); QUARTET(1949, Brit.); EYE WITNESS(1950, Brit.); LAUGHING LADY, THE(1950, Brit.); SHE SHALL HAVE MURDER(1950, Brit.); TRIO(1950, Brit.); ALICE IN WONDERLAND(1951, Fr.); I'LL NEVER FORGET YOU(1951); LADY WITH A LAMP, THE(1951, Brit.); NO HIGHWAY IN THE SKY(1951, Brit.); QUO VADIS(1951); SO LONG AT THE FAIR(1951, Brit.); IVANHOE(1952, Brit.); KNIGHTS OF THE ROUND TABLE(1953); MASTER OF BALLANTRAE, THE(1953, U.S./Brit.); PARIS EXPRESS, THE(1953, Brit.); LOVE LOTTERY, THE(1954, Brit.); ANASTASIA(1956); ANGEL WHO PAWNED HER HARP, THE(1956, Brit.); LOSER TAKES ALL(1956, Brit.); SAINT JOAN(1957); DOCTOR'S DILEMMA, THE(1958, Brit.); I ACCUSE(1958, Brit.); SEPARATE TABLES(1958); MUMMY, THE(1959, Brit.); TWO-HEADED SPY, THE(1959, Brit.); EXODUS(1960); FROM THE TERRACE(1960); BOYS, THE(1962, Brit.); ROAD TO HONG KONG, THE(1962, U.S./Brit.); MACBETH(1963); RUNNING MAN, THE(1963, Brit.); BECKET(1964, Brit.); CHALK GARDEN, THE(1964, Brit.); HANDS OF ORLAC, THE(1964, Brit./Fr.); MASQUERADE(1965, Brit.); HOSTILE WITNESS(1968, Brit.); DECLINE AND FALL... OF A BIRD WATCHER(1969, Brit.)

Felix Aylmer, Sr.
NEVER TAKE CANDY FROM A STRANGER(1961, Brit.)

Dave Aylot
MUDLARK, THE(1950, Brit.), makeup

Dave Aylott
MILLIONAIRESS, THE(1960, Brit.), makeup; ROAD TO HONG KONG, THE(1962, U.S./Brit.), makeup; V.I.P.s, THE(1963, Brit.), makeup
Silents
SOLDIER AND A MAN, A(1916, Brit.), d
Misc. Silents
(; JADE HEART, THE(1915, Brit.), d; SHATTERED IDYLL, A(1916, Brit.), d; TWO LANCASHIRE LASSES IN LONDON(1916, Brit.), a, d; IT'S NEVER TOO LATE TO MEND(1917, Brit.), d; MAN WHO MADE GOOD, THE(1917, Brit.), d; GAMBLERS ALL(1919, Brit.), d

David Aylott
SUDDENLY, LAST SUMMER(1959, Brit.), makeup

Eric Aylott
FOLLOW THAT HORSE!(1960, Brit.), makeup; VILLAGE OF THE DAMNED(1960, Brit.), makeup; OPERATION BULLSHINE(1963, Brit.), makeup

Arthur Aylsworth
SANDFLOW(1937); IN NAME ONLY(1939); EDISON, THE MAN(1940); DANGEROUSLY THEY LIVE(1942)

Derek Aylward
JOHN WESLEY(1954, Brit.); HANDCUFFS, LONDON(1955, Brit.); HOUSE IN MARSH ROAD, THE(1960, Brit.); MAN WITH THE GREEN CARNATION, THE(1960, Brit.); SCHOOL FOR SEX(1969, Brit.); BIG SWITCH, THE(1970, Brit.); COOL IT, CAROL!(1970, Brit.); MAN OF VIOLENCE(1970, Brit.)

Edward Aylward
CAPTAIN LIGHTFOOT(1955)

Sally Aylward
BAY OF SAINT MICHEL, THE(1963, Brit.)

Tony Aylward
SO FINE(1981)

Derek Aylwood
DEVIL'S JEST, THE(1954, Brit.)

Jean Ayme
LE DENIER MILLIARDAIRE(1934, Fr.); LA MARSEILLAISE(1938, Fr.); END OF A DAY, THE(1939, Fr.)

Marcel Ayme
CRIME AND PUNISHMENT(1935, Fr.), w; MR. PEEK-A-BOO(1951, Fr.), w; FOUR BAGS FULL(1957, Fr./Ital.), w; GREEN MARE, THE(1961, Fr./Ital.), w; LOVE AND THE FRENCHWOMAN(1961, Fr.), w; MAN WHO WALKED THROUGH THE WALL, THE(1964, Ger.), w

Juan Aymerich
NUN'S STORY, THE(1959)

Julian Aymes
CRASH OF SILENCE(1952, Brit.)

Felix Aymler
YOUNG MAN'S FANCY(1943, Brit.)

Alan Aynesworth
LAST DAYS OF DOLWYN, THE(1949, Brit.)

Allan Aynesworth
BROWN SUGAR(1931, Brit.); LEAVE IT TO SMITH(1934); LITTLE FRIEND(1934, Brit.); LOVE, LIFE AND LAUGHTER(1934, Brit.); BREWSTER'S MILLIONS(1935, Brit.); IRON DUKE, THE(1935, Brit.); YOUNG MAN'S FANCY(1943, Brit.)
Silents
FLAMES OF PASSION(1922, Brit.); GAME OF LIFE, THE(1922, Brit.)

Michael Ayr
BOARDWALK(1979)

Robert Ayre
MR. SYCAMORE(1975), w

Agnes Ayres
DONOVAN AFFAIR, THE(1929); SMALL TOWN GIRL(1936); MAID OF SALEM(1937); SOULS AT SEA(1937)
Misc. Talkies
BROKEN HEARTED(1929); BYE-BYE BUDDY(1929)
Silents
MISS DULCIE FROM DIXIE(1919); SACRED SILENCE(1919); MODERN SALOME, A(1920); AFFAIRS OF ANATOL, THE(1921); CAPPY RICKS(1921); SHEIK, THE(1921); TOO MUCH SPEED(1921); ORDEAL, THE(1922); HEART RAIDER, THE(1923); RACING HEARTS(1923); TEN COMMANDMENTS, THE(1923); BLUFF(1924); AWFUL TRUTH, THE(1925); SON OF THE SHEIK(1926); INTO THE NIGHT(1928)
Misc. Silents
BOTTOM OF THE WELL(1917); RENAISSANCE AT CHARLEROI, THE(1917); ONE THOUSAND DOLLARS(1918); GAMBLERS, THE(1919); GIRL PROBLEM, THE(1919); IN HONOR'S WEB(1919); STITCH IN TIME, A(1919); FURNANCE, THE(1920); GO AND GET IT(1920); INNER VOICE, THE(1920); FORBIDDEN FRUIT(1921); LOVE SPECIAL, THE(1921); BORDERLAND(1922); BOUGHT AND PAID FOR(1922); CLARENCE(1922); DAUGHTER OF LUXURY, A(1922); LANE THAT HAD NO TURNING, THE(1922); MARRIAGE MAKER, THE(1923); DON'T CALL IT LOVE(1924); GUILTY ONE, THE(1924); STORY WITHOUT A NAME, THE(1924); WHEN A GIRL LOVES(1924); WORLDLY GOODS(1924); HER MARKET VALUE(1925); MORALS FOR MEN(1925); TOMORROW'S LOVE(1925)

Clio Ayres
Silents
PRICE MARK, THE(1917)
Misc. Silents
DEVIL'S PRIZE, THE(1916); MARY JANE'S PA(1917)

Curt Ayres
MORTUARY(1983)

David Ayres
MISS JESSICA IS PREGNANT(1970)

Gerald Ayres
CISCO PIKE(1971), p; LAST DETAIL, THE(1973), p; FOXES(1980), p. David Puttnam, w; RICH AND FAMOUS(1981), w

Gregg Ayres
Misc. Talkies
SKATEBOARD MADNESS(1980)

Herbert Ayres
REUNION(1932, Brit.), w; COMMISSIONAIRE(1933, Brit.), w; DOSS HOUSE(1933, Brit.), w; LEST WE FORGET(1934, Brit.), w; REAL BLOKE, A(1935, Brit.), w; HEARTS OF HUMANITY(1936, Brit.), w; COMMON TOUCH, THE(1941, Brit.), w; JUDGMENT DEFERRED(1952, Brit.), w

Jerry Ayres
ACE ELI AND RODGER OF THE SKIES(1973); HANGUP(1974)

John Ayres
SOMETHING FOR THE BIRDS(1952); HALLIDAY BRAND, THE(1957); EDGE OF ETERNITY(1959)

John H. Ayres
BUREAU OF MISSING PERSONS(1933), w

Leah Ayres
BURNING, THE(1981); EDDIE MACON'S RUN(1983)

Lemuel Ayres
ZIEGFELD FOLLIES(1945), d

Lew Ayres
BIG NEWS(1929); ALL QUIET ON THE WESTERN FRONT(1930); COMMON CLAY(1930); EAST IS WEST(1930); HEAVEN ON EARTH(1931); IRON MAN, THE(1931); MANY A SLIP(1931); SPIRIT OF NOTRE DAME, THE(1931); UP FOR MURDER(1931); IMPATIENT MAIDEN(1932); NIGHT WORLD(1932); OKAY AMERICA(1932); DON'T BET ON LOVE(1933); MY WEAKNESS(1933); STATE FAIR(1933); CROSS COUNTRY CRUISE(1934); LET'S BE RITZY(1934); SERVANTS' ENTRANCE(1934); SHE LEARNED ABOUT SAILORS(1934); LOTTERY LOVER(1935); SILK HAT KID(1935); SPRING TONIC(1935); HEARTS IN BONDAGE(1936); LADY BE CAREFUL(1936); LEATHERNECKS HAVE LANDED, THE(1936); MURDER WITH PICTURES(1936); SHAKEDOWN(1936); CRIME NOBOBY SAW, THE(1937); HOLD-'EM NAVY!(1937); LAST TRAIN FROM MADRID, THE(1937); HOLIDAY(1938); KING OF THE NEWSBOYS(1938); RICH MAN, POOR GIRL(1938); SCANDAL STREET(1938); SPRING MADNESS(1938); YOUNG DR. KILDARE(1938); BROADWAY SERENADE(1939); CALLING DR. KILDARE(1939); ICE FOLLIES OF 1939(1939); REMEMBER?(1939); SECRET OF DR. KILDARE, THE(1939); THESE GLAMOUR GIRLS(1939); DR. KILDARE GOES HOME(1940); DR. KILDARE'S CRISIS(1940); DR. KILDARE'S STRANGE CASE(1940); GOLDEN FLEECING, THE(1940); DR. KILDARE'S VICTORY(1941); DR. KILDARE'S WEDDING DAY(1941); MAISIE WAS A LADY(1941); PEOPLE VS. DR. KILDARE, THE(1941); FINGERS AT THE WINDOW(1942); DARK MIRROR, THE(1946); UNFAITHFUL, THE(1947); JOHNNY BELINDA(1948); CAPTURE, THE(1950); NEW MEXICO(1951); DONOVAN'S BRAIN(1953); NO ESCAPE(1953); ADVISE AND CONSENT(1962); CARPETBAGGERS, THE(1964); BISCUIT EATER, THE(1972); MAN, THE(1972); BATTLE FOR THE PLANET OF THE APES(1973); END OF THE WORLD(1977); DAMIEN–OMEN II(1978); BATTLESTAR GALACTICA(1979)
Misc. Talkies
LAST GENERATION, THE(1971)
Silents
KISS, THE(1929)

Lewis [Lew] Ayres
DOORWAY TO HELL(1930)

Maray Ayres
GIRLS FROM THUNDER STRIP, THE(1966); CYCLE SAVAGES(1969); DIRTY DINGUS MAGEE(1970)

Maurice Ayres
BLUE MAX, THE(1966), spec eff

Mitch Ayres
LADY, LET'S DANCE(1944)

Phyllis Ayres
FEAR(1946); GANGSTER, THE(1947)

Ralph Ayres
THEM!(1954), spec eff; MERRILL'S MARAUDERS(1962), spec eff; THOSE MAGNIFICENT MEN IN THEIR FLYING MACHINES; OR HOW I FLEW FROM LONDON TO PARIS IN 25 HOURS AND 11 MINUTES(1965, Brit.), anim

Richard Ayres
HOUSE BY THE LAKE, THE(1977, Can.)

Robert Ayres
BLACK WIDOW(1951, Brit.); GREAT MANHUNT, THE(1951, Brit.); THEY WERE NOT DIVIDED(1951, Brit.); TO HAVE AND TO HOLD(1951, Brit.); 13 EAST STREET(1952, Brit.); AFFAIR IN MONTE CARLO(1953, Brit.); NIGHT WITHOUT STARS(1953, Brit.); SLASHER, THE(1953, Brit.); WEDDING OF LILLI MARLENE, THE(1953, Brit.); DELAYED ACTION(1954, Brit.); RIVER BEAT(1954); CONTRABAND SPAIN(1955, Brit.); PRIZE OF GOLD, A(1955); CAT GIRL(1957); DEPRAVED, THE(1957, Brit.); OPERATION MURDER(1957, Brit.); STORY OF ESTHER COSTELLO, THE(1957, Brit.); IT'S NEVER TOO LATE(1958, Brit.); NIGHT TO REMEMBER, A(1958, Brit.); FIRST MAN INTO SPACE(1959, Brit.); JOHN PAUL JONES(1959); TIME LOCK(1959, Brit.); WOMAN'S TEMPTATION, A(1959, Brit.); DATE AT MIDNIGHT(1960, Brit.); TRANSATLANTIC(1961, Brit.); ROAD TO HONG KONG, THE(1962, U.S./Brit.); TWO AND TWO MAKE SIX(1962, Brit.); SICILIANS, THE(1964, Brit.); HEROES OF TELEMARK, THE(1965, Brit.); BATTLE BENEATH THE EARTH(1968, Brit.)

Rosalind Ayres
FROM BEYOND THE GRAVE(1974, Brit.); LITTLE MALCOLM(1974, Brit.); STARDUST(1974, Brit.); THAT'LL BE THE DAY(1974, Brit.); SLIPPER AND THE ROSE, THE(1976, Brit.); WEATHER IN THE STREETS, THE(1983, Brit.)

Ruby M. Ayres
SECOND HONEYMOON(1931), w

Susan Ayres
Misc. Talkies
BLACK LOLITA(1975)

Randle Ayrton
FEATHER, THE(1929, Brit.); HIGH SEAS(1929, Brit.); ROMANCE OF SEVILLE, A(1929, Brit.); GREAT GAME, THE(1930); HATE SHIP, THE(1930, Brit.); TWO WORLD(1930, Brit.); DREYFUS CASE, THE(1931, Brit.); POWER(1934, Brit.); ME AND MARLBOROUGH(1935, Brit.); DEBT OF HONOR(1936, Brit.); TALK OF THE DEVIL(1937, Brit.)
Silents
PROFIT AND THE LOSS(1917, Brit.); HANGING JUDGE, THE(1918, Brit.); NO. 5 JOHN STREET(1921, Brit.); WOMAN'S SECRET, A(1924, Brit.); NELL GWYNNE(1926, Brit.); ONE OF THE BEST(1927, Brit.); PASSION ISLAND(1927, Brit.); HIS HOUSE IN ORDER(1928, Brit.), d; MANXMAN, THE(1929, Brit.)
Misc. Silents
MY SWEETHEART(1918, Brit.); GATES OF DUTY(1919, Brit.), d; SANDS OF TIME, THE(1919, Brit.), d; WONDERFUL YEAR, THE(1921, Brit.); CHU CHIN CHOW(1923, Brit.); GLORIOUS YOUTH(1928, Brit.)

Alfred Aysanoa
PAYMENT IN BLOOD(1968, Ital.)

Arthur Aysleworth
GRAPES OF WRATH(1940)

Anyarat Suthat Na Ayudhaya
1 2 3 MONSTER EXPRESS(1977, Thai.)

Manuel Ayulo
ROAR OF THE CROWD(1953)

Surresh Ayyar
1984
TAIL OF THE TIGER(1984, Aus.), ed

G. Ayzenberg
RESURRECTION(1963, USSR), spec eff; FORTY-NINE DAYS(1964, USSR), spec eff

Graham Aza
WINGS OF MYSTERY(1963, Brit.)

Sheila Aza
SCARLET THREAD(1951, Brit.); TIME GENTLEMEN PLEASE!(1953, Brit.)

Georgi Azagarov
Misc. Silents
ANDREI KOZHUKHOV(1917, USSR)

Paul Azais
ANNE-MARIE(1936, Fr.); CASQUE D'OR(1956, Fr.); ROYAL AFFAIRS IN VERSAILLES(1957, Fr.)

Azalea Blossom String Band
GAL YOUNG UN(1979), m

Charles Azanvour
TWIST, THE(1976, Fr.)

Leonid Azar
LOVE IN THE AFTERNOON(1957), ed

Leonide Azar
IDIOT, THE(1948, Fr.), ed; LA MARIE DU PORT(1951, Fr.), ed; LA RONDE(1954, Fr.), ed; LE PLAISIR(1954, Fr.), ed; FROU-FROU(1955, Fr.), ed; LOVERS, THE(1959, Fr.), ed; AUSTERLITZ(1960, Fr./Ital./Yugo.), ed; FRANTIC(1961, Fr.), ed; DOLL, THE(1962, Fr.), ed; RIFF RAFF GIRLS(1962, Fr./Ital.), ed; SUNDAYS AND CYBELE(1962, Fr.), ed; TALES OF PARIS(1962, Fr./Ital.), ed; NAKED AUTUMN(1963, Fr.), ed; TIME OUT FOR LOVE(1963, Ital./Fr.), ed

Villen Azarov
GROWN-UP CHILDREN(1963, USSR), p&d

Martin Azarow
SOME KIND OF HERO(1982); THEY CALL ME BRUCE(1982)

Rafael Azcona
MAFIOSO(1962, Ital.), w; CONJUGAL BED, THE(1963, Ital.), w; APE WOMAN, THE(1964, Ital.), w; NOT ON YOUR LIFE(1965, Ital./Span.), w; RUN FOR YOUR WIFE(1966, Fr./Ital.), w; MAN WITH THE BALLOONS, THE(1968, Ital./Fr.), w; BIG

AND THE BAD, THE(1971, Ital./Fr./Span.), w; LA GRANDE BOUFFE(1973, Fr.), w; DON'T TOUCH WHITE WOMEN!(1974, Fr.), w; BYE BYE MONKEY(1978, Ital/Fr.), w; CLARETTA AND BEN(1983, Ital., Fr.), w

Sandy "Chikaye" Azeka
HOUSE OF BAMBOO(1955)

Sabine Azema
1984
LIFE IS A BED OF ROSES(1984, Fr.); SUNDAY IN THE COUNTRY, A(1984, Fr.)

W. Azenberg
Silents
KING OF KINGS, THE(1927)

Alinor Azevedo
TRAIN ROBBERY CONFIDENTIAL(1965, Braz.), w

Dionisio Azevedo
GIVEN WORD, THE(1964, Braz.)

Odilon Azevedo
LOLLIPOP(1966, Braz.)

Aliza Azikri
KAZABLAN(1974, Israel)

Nissim Azikri
THEY WERE TEN(1961, Israel)

Tony Azito
NIGHT OF THE JUGGLER(1980); UNION CITY(1980); PIRATES OF PENZANCE, THE(1983)
1984
CHATTANOOGA CHOO CHOO(1984)

Shabana Azmi
CHESS PLAYERS, THE(1978, India)

Charles Aznavour
DANIELLA BY NIGHT(1962, Fr/Ger.), m; DEVIL AND THE TEN COMMANDMENTS, THE(1962, Fr.), a, m; SHOOT THE PIANO PLAYER(1962, Fr.); SWEET ECSTASY(1962, Fr.), m; TEMPTATION(1962, Fr.), m; TESTAMENT OF ORPHEUS, THE(1962, Fr.); TOMORROW IS MY TURN(1962, Fr./Ital./Ger.); THREE FABLES OF LOVE(1963, Fr./Ital./Span.), a, m; HIGH INFIDELITY(1965, Fr./Ital.); TAXI FOR TOBRUK(1965, Fr./Span./Ger.); CLOPORTES(1966, Fr., Ital.); CANDY(1968, Ital./Fr.); CAROLINE CHERIE(1968, Fr.); PARIS IN THE MONTH OF AUGUST(1968, Fr.); POSTMAN GOES TO WAR, THE(1968, Fr.); ADVENTURERS, THE(1970); GAMES, THE(1970); TIME OF THE WOLVES(1970, Fr.); BLOCKHOUSE, THE(1974, Brit.); TEN LITTLE INDIANS(1975, Ital./Fr./Span./Ger.); SKY RIDERS(1976, U.S./Gr.); HEIST, THE(1979, Ital.); TIN DRUM, THE(1979, Ger./Fr./Yugo./Pol.); HATTER'S GHOST, THE(1982, Fr.)
1984
EDITH AND MARCEL(1984, Fr.)

Patricia Aznavour
PARIS IN THE MONTH OF AUGUST(1968, Fr.)

Irving Azoff
URBAN COWBOY(1980), p; FAST TIMES AT RIDGEMONT HIGH(1982), p

Joe Azomar
RETURN OF A MAN CALLED HORSE, THE(1976), spec eff

Rafael Azoona
AMERICAN WIFE, AN(1965, Ital.), w

Harry Azorin
1984
SPLITZ(1984), w

Catherine Azoulai
DAY AND THE HOUR, THE(1963, Fr./ Ital.)

Gessie Azoulai
DAY AND THE HOUR, THE(1963, Fr./ Ital.)

Natividad Azro
GUNMEN OF THE RIO GRANDE(1965, Fr./Ital./Span.), w

Hadara Azulai
CLOUDS OVER ISRAEL(1966, Israel)

Ryonosuke Azuma
SANSHO THE BAILIFF(1969, Jap.)

Jo Azumi
HAHAKIRI(1963, Jap.)

Eiko Azusa
THOUSAND CRANES(1969, Jap.); GATEWAY TO GLORY(1970, Jap.); MAGOICHI SAGA, THE(1970, Jap.); VIXEN(1970, Jap.)

Candice Azzara
WORLD'S GREATEST LOVER, THE(1977); HOUSE CALLS(1978); FATSO(1980)

Candy Azzara
MADE FOR EACH OTHER(1971); THEY MIGHT BE GIANTS(1971); WHO IS HARRY KELLERMAN AND WHY IS HE SAYING THOSE TERRIBLE THINGS ABOUT ME?(1971); HEARTS OF THE WEST(1975); PANDEMONIUM(1982); EASY MONEY(1983)

Tho. E. Azzari
1984
CANNONBALL RUN II(1984), art d

Nedo Azzini
CRAZY DESIRE(1964, Ital.), art d; HOURS OF LOVE, THE(1965, Ital.), art d; LA FUGA(1966, Ital.), set d; MISSION BLOODY MARY(1967, Fr./Ital./Span.), art d; LISTEN, LET'S MAKE LOVE(1969, Fr./Ital.), set d; CONFORMIST, THE(1971, Ital., Fr), art d; DEATH IN VENICE(1971, Ital./Fr.), set d; DIRTY HEROES(1971, Ital./Fr./Ger.), art d; NIGHT PORTER, THE(1974, Ital./U.S.), art d

Marcel Azzola
JUDGE AND THE ASSASSIN, THE(1979, Fr.)

Remy Azzolini
JOY(1983, Fr./Can.)

Mario Azzopardi
Misc. Talkies
DEADLINE(1984), d

Nadine Azzopardi
TRENCHCOAT(1983)

The B 52's
ONE-TRICK PONY(1980)

Beth B.
OFFENDERS, THE(1980), d,w&ph m; TRAP DOOR, THE(1980), p,d,w&ph, m; VORTEX(1982), d&w, m, ed

Ida B.
ONLY WAY HOME, THE(1972)

K. C. B.
Silents
SOULS FOR SALE(1923)

Scott B.
OFFENDERS, THE(1980), d,w&ph m; TRAP DOOR, THE(1980), p,d,w&ph, m; VORTEX(1982), a, d&w, m, ed

B.B.B
WIDE OPEN(1930)

Christoph Baal
LOVE FEAST, THE(1966, Ger.), w

Karin Baal
DAS LETZTE GEHEIMNIS(1959, Ger.); ROSEMARY(1960, Ger.); DARK EYES OF LONDON(1961, Ger.); JUDGE AND THE SINNER, THE(1964, Ger.); HANNIBAL BROOKS(1969, Brit.); LILI MARLEEN(1981, Ger.); LOLA(1982, Ger.)

Ace Baandage
REVENGE OF THE CHEERLEADERS(1976), w

Nico A.V. Baarle
DOG OF FLANDERS, A(1959), art d

Lida Baarova
BARCAROLE(1935, Ger.)

Lida Baarowa
VITELLONI(1956, Ital./Fr.)

Balduin Baas
FOUNTAIN OF LOVE, THE(1968, Aust.)

Chris Baay
LAST BLITZKRIEG, THE(1958)

Baba
GIVE HER THE MOON(1970, Fr./Ital.), cos

Masaru Baba
VENGEANCE IS MINE(1980, Jap.), w

N. Babanini
VAMPYR(1932, Fr./Ger.)

Maria Babanova
Misc. Silents
ELDER VASILI GRYAZNOV(1924, USSR)

Joe Babas
SHORT EYES(1977), prod d

Harry Babasin
SONG IS BORN, A(1948)

Dorothy Babb
YOU CAN'T TAKE IT WITH YOU(1938); PLAYMATES(1941); GET HEP TO LOVE(1942); MOONLIGHT IN HAVANA(1942); TALK OF THE TOWN(1942); HOW'S ABOUT IT?(1943); EARL CARROLL SKETCHBOOK(1946); WHEN MY BABY SMILES AT ME(1948)

Ken Babb
SILENCE OF THE NORTH(1981, Can.)

Kroger Babb
MOM AND DAD(1948), p; LAWTON STORY, THE(1949), p; ONE TOO MANY(1950), p, w; PRINCE OF PEACE, THE(1951), p; UNCLE TOM'S CABIN(1969, Fr./Ital./Ger./Yugo.), p

Larry Babb
NIGHT SCHOOL(1981), p; TERROR EYES(1981), p

Maurice Babb
GIRL OF THE OZARKS(1936), w

Robert Babb
SLAYER, THE(1982), spec eff

Sheila Babbage
MAN OF VIOLENCE(1970, Brit.)

Wilfred Babbage
OLD MOTHER RILEY(1952, Brit.); SCHOOL FOR SEX(1969, Brit.); PETER RABBIT AND TALES OF BEATRIX POTTER(1971, Brit.)

Wilfrid Babbage
BRIEF ENCOUNTER(1945, Brit.)

Rosemarie Babbick
SUDAN(1945)

Art Babbitt
FOUR POSTER, THE(1952), anim; RAGGEDY ANN AND ANDY(1977), anim

Arthur Babbitt
SNOW WHITE AND THE SEVEN DWARFS(1937), anim; FANTASIA(1940), anim; PINOCCHIO(1940), anim d; DUMBO(1941), anim d; FUN AND FANCY FREE(1947), anim

George Arthur Babbitt
FANTASIA(1940), anim

Harry Babbitt
THAT'S RIGHT–YOU'RE WRONG(1939); YOU'LL FIND OUT(1940); PLAYMATES(1941); MY FAVORITE SPY(1942); AROUND THE WORLD(1943); SWING FEVER(1943); CAROLINA BLUES(1944)

Natalie Babbitt
EYES OF THE AMARYLLIS, THE(1982), w

Barbara Babcock
DAY OF THE EVIL GUN(1968); HEAVEN WITH A GUN(1969); BANG THE DRUM SLOWLY(1973); CHOSEN SURVIVORS(1974 U.S.-Mex.); BLACK MARBLE, THE(1980); BACK ROADS(1981); LORDS OF DISCIPLINE, THE(1983)

Bill Babcock
TRADER HORNEE(1970)

Dwight Babcock
CORPSE CAME C.O.D., THE(, w; TROUBLE WITH GIRLS(AND HOW TO GET INTO IT), THE*1/2 (1969), w; DEAD MAN'S EYES(1944), w; SO DARK THE NIGHT(1946), w; UNKNOWN, THE(1946), w; FBI GIRL(1951), w; SAVAGE FRONTIER(1953), w

Dwight V. Babcock
MUMMY'S CURSE, THE(1944), w; JUNGLE CAPTIVE(1945), w; PILLOW OF DEATH(1945), w; RIVER GANG(1945), w; ROAD TO ALCATRAZ(1945), w; BRUTE MAN, THE(1946), w; DEVIL'S MASK, THE(1946), w; HOUSE OF HORRORS(1946), w; SHE-WOLF OF LONDON(1946), w; BURY ME DEAD(1947), w; LOOPHOLE(1954), w; JUNGLE MOON MEN(1955), w

Fay Babcock
FIRST COMES COURAGE(1943), set d; COVER GIRL(1944), set d; RETURN OF MONTE CRISTO, THE(1946), set d; FRAMED(1947), set d; NIGHT WIND(1948), set d; SHED NO TEARS(1948), set d; ESCAPE TO BURMA(1955), set d; MAVERICK QUEEN, THE(1956), set d; 23 PACES TO BAKER STREET(1956), set d; IN LOVE AND WAR(1958), set d

Fay C. Babcock
SECOND CHANCE(1947), set d; GOLD OF THE SEVEN SAINTS(1961), set d

Nathan Babcock
WORLD ACCORDING TO GARP, The(1982)

Peggy Babcock
HOW SWEET IT IS(1968)

Ray Babcock
MY SISTER EILEEN(1942), set d; MORE THE MERRIER, THE(1943), set d; TOGETHER AGAIN(1944), set d

Theodore Babcock
Silents
SILVER LINING, THE(1921); SILENT COMMAND, THE(1923)
Misc. Silents
SOUL OF A WOMAN, THE(1915); SHOCK PUNCH, THE(1925)

Angelus Babe
ON WITH THE SHOW(1929)

Little Babe
ESCAPE TO BURMA(1955)

Hector Babenco
PIXOTE(1981, Braz.), d, w

V. Babenko
MEET ME IN MOSCOW(1966, USSR)

Douglas Baber
MY DEATH IS A MOCKERY(1952, Brit.), w

Sidney Baber
Silents
FROM THE MANGER TO THE CROSS(1913)

Vivianne Baber
BLACK KING(1932)

Robert Baberakd
OUR DAILY BREAD(1950, Ger.), ph

Robert Baberske
BEAUTIFUL ADVENTURE(1932, Ger.), ph; SECRET AGENT(1933, Brit.), w; FINAL CHORD, THE(1936, Ger.), ph

Doudou Babet
GREED IN THE SUN(1965, Fr./ Ital.); POSTMAN GOES TO WAR, THE(1968, Fr.); CHECKERBOARD(1969, Fr.)

Howard Loeb Babeuf
EDGE, THE(1968)

Frank Babich
BARQUERO(1970); TIGER BY THE TAIL(1970)

Chris Babida
POWERFORCE(1983), m

E.J. Babiel
NO MORE LADIES(1935)

Jean Babilee
AMELIE OR THE TIME TO LOVE(1961, Fr.); SWEET AND SOUR(1964, Fr./Ital.), a, ch

E. J. Babille
Silents
NO CONTROL(1927), d

Philippe Babin
RETURN OF MARTIN GUERRE, THE(1983, Fr.)

Colette Bablon
COME BACK BABY(1968); HAVE A NICE WEEKEND(1975)

Lill Babs
TURKISH CUCUMBER, THE(1963, Ger.)

Tom Babson
Misc. Talkies
BEASTS(1983)

N. Baburina
WHEN THE TREES WERE TALL(1965, USSR), cos

Hulya Babus
COUNTESS DRACULA(1972, Brit.)

Mark L. Babus
HARD COUNTRY(1981), set d

Nicolas Baby
1984
SWANN IN LOVE(1984, Fr.Ger.)

Baby Rose Marie
INTERNATIONAL HOUSE(1933)

Baby Sandy
BACHELOR DADDY(1941)

S. Babyevsky
DREAM OF A COSSACK(1982, USSR), w

Andre Bac
CROSS OF THE LIVING(, ph; DAUGHTER OF THE SANDS(1952, Fr.), ph; SEVEN DEADLY SINS, THE(1953, Fr./Ital.), ph; RED, INN, THE(1954, Fr.), ph; SPUTNIK(1960, Fr.), ph; PARIS PICK-UP(1963, Fr./Ital.), ph; WAR OF THE BUTTONS(1963 Fr.), ph

Charles Baca
SHOWDOWN(1973)

David Baca
1984
BREAKIN' 2: ELECTRIC BOOGALOO(1984), cos
Dorothy Baca
1984
BREAKIN' 2: ELECTRIC BOOGALOO(1984), cos
E. Baca
POCKET MONEY(1972)
Kathy Baca
PIECES OF DREAMS(1970)
Pasqualita Baca
MOLLY AND LAWLESS JOHN(1972)
Raimundo Baca
PIECES OF DREAMS(1970)
Luis Enriquez Bacalav
KISS THE OTHER SHEIK(1968, Fr./Ital.), m
Lauren Bacall
TO HAVE AND HAVE NOT(1944); CONFIDENTIAL AGENT(1945); BIG SLEEP, THE(1946); DARK PASSAGE(1947); KEY LARGO(1948); BRIGHT LEAF(1950); YOUNG MAN WITH A HORN(1950); HOW TO MARRY A MILLIONAIRE(1953); WOMAN'S WORLD(1954); BLOOD ALLEY(1955); COBWEB, THE(1955); WRITTEN ON THE WIND(1956); DESIGNING WOMAN(1957); GIFT OF LOVE, THE(1958); FLAME OVER INDIA(1960, Brit.); SEX AND THE SINGLE GIRL(1964); SHOCK TREATMENT(1964); HARPER(1966); MURDER ON THE ORIENT EXPRESS(1974, Brit.); SHOOTIST, THE(1976); HEALTH(1980); FAN, THE(1981)
Luis Bacalov
BULLET FOR THE GENERAL, A(1967, Ital.), m; CATCH AS CATCH CAN(1968, Ital.), m; MAN CALLED NOON, THE(1973, Brit.), m; CITY OF WOMEN(1980, Ital./Fr.), m; ENTRE NOUS(1983, Fr.), m
Luis Enriquez Bacalov
ONE MILLION DOLLARS(1965, Ital.), m; GOSPEL ACCORDING TO ST. MATTHEW, THE(1966, Fr., Ital.), m, md; MAIDEN FOR A PRINCE, A(1967, Fr./Ital.), m; ROSE FOR EVERYONE, A(1967, Ital.), m; WE STILL KILL THE OLD WAY(1967, Ital.), m; GHOSTS, ITALIAN STYLE(1969, Ital./Fr.), m; WITCH, THE(1969, Ital.), m
Luis Enriquez Bacalova
EMPTY CANVAS, THE(1964, Fr./Ital.), m, md
Mike Bacarella
THINGS ARE TOUGH ALL OVER(1982); ON THE RIGHT TRACK(1981)
1984
JOHNNY DANGEROUSLY(1984)
Donna Baccala
DUNWICH HORROR, THE(1970); LAST MOVIE, THE(1971)
Baccaloni
MERRY ANDREW(1958); FANNY(1961); PIGEON THAT TOOK ROME, THE(1962)
Salvatore Baccaloni
FULL OF LIFE(1956); ROCK-A-BYE BABY(1958)
Delia Baccardo
TENTACLES(1977, Ital.)
Salvatore Baccaro
ARENA, THE(1973)
Valentino Bacchi
TAMING OF THE SHREW, THE(1967, U.S./Ital.)
Silvana Bacci
GOOD, THE BAD, AND THE UGLY, THE(1967, Ital./Span.); LONG RIDE FROM HELL, A(1970, Ital.)
Erasmo Bacciucchi
GOLD FOR THE CAESARS(1964), spec eff; MINUTE TO PRAY, A SECOND TO DIE, A(1968, Ital.), spec eff
Eros Bacciucchi
MORGAN THE PIRATE(1961, Fr./Ital.), spec eff; SEVEN SEAS TO CALAIS(1963, Ital.), spec eff; GOOD, THE BAD, AND THE UGLY, THE(1967, Ital./Span.), spec eff; VIOLENT FOUR, THE(1968, Ital.), spec eff
F. Bacciucchi
PAYMENT IN BLOOD(1968, Ital.), spec eff
Eros Bacciuchi
DEATH RIDES A HORSE(1969, Ital.), spec eff
Stephen Baccus
HARDLY WORKING(1981)
Annette Bach
WHITE DEVIL, THE(1948, Ital.); DUEL WITHOUT HONOR(1953, Ital.)
Barbara Bach
BLACK BELLY OF THE TARANTULA, THE(1972, Ital.); STATELINE MOTEL(1976, Ital.); SPY WHO LOVED ME, THE(1977, Brit.); FORCE 10 FROM NAVARONE(1978, Brit.); SCREAMERS(1978, Ital.); WOLF LARSEN(1978, Ital.); HUMANOID, THE(1979, Ital.); JAGUAR LIVES(1979); GREAT ALLIGATOR(1980, Ital.); UP THE ACADEMY(1980); CAVEMAN(1981); UNSEEN, THE(1981)
1984
GIVE MY REGARDS TO BROAD STREET(1984, Brit.)
Misc. Talkies
ANONYMOUS AVENGER, THE(1976, Ital.); STREET LAW(1981)
Catherine Bach
MIDNIGHT MAN, THE(1974); THUNDERBOLT AND LIGHTFOOT(1974); HUSTLE(1975)
1984
CANNONBALL RUN II(1984)
Claudia Bach
VIXENS, THE(1969)
Danilo Bach
1984
BEVERLY HILLS COP(1984), w
Ernest Curt Bach
TROUBLE WITH HARRY, THE(1955)
Ernst Bach
WARM CORNER, A(1930, Brit.), w; IT'S A BOY(1934, Brit.), w; INTERRUPTED HONEYMOON, THE(1936, Brit.), w
J. S. Bach
ACCATTONE!(1961, Ital.), m; CRIES AND WHISPERS(1972, Swed.), m

J.S. Bach
20,000 LEAGUES UNDER THE SEA(1954), m
Johann Sebastian Bach
LA MARSEILLAISE(1938, Fr.), m; FANTASIA(1940), w; I'VE ALWAYS LOVED YOU(1946), m; LES ENFANTS TERRIBLES(1952, Fr.), m; LOLA(1961, Fr./Ital.), m; MODIGLIANI OF MONTPARNASSE(1961, Fr./Ital.), m; PHAEDRA(1962, U.S./Gr./Fr.), m; TESTAMENT OF ORPHEUS, THE(1962, Fr.), m; THROUGH A GLASS DARKLY(1962, Swed.), m; SILENCE, THE(1964, Swed.), m; GOSPEL ACCORDING TO ST. MATTHEW, THE(1966, Fr., Ital.), m; CHRONICLE OF ANNA MAGDALENA BACH(1968, Ital., Ger.), m; ISADORA(1968, Brit.), m; NOT RECONCILED, OR "ONLY VIOLENCE HELPS WHERE IT RULES"(1969, Ger.), m; FIVE EASY PIECES(1970), m; TELL ME THAT YOU LOVE ME, JUNIE MOON(1970), m; SLAUGHTERHOUSE-FIVE(1972), m; VISITORS, THE(1972), m; TERMINAL MAN, THE(1974), m; ROLLERBALL(1975), m
1984
L'ARGENT(1984, Fr./Switz.), m
Johanna Sebastien Bach
TREE OF WOODEN CLOGS, THE(1979, Ital.), m
John Bach
BEYOND REASONABLE DOUBT(1980, New Zeal.); GOODBYE PORK PIE(1981, New Zealand); BATTLETRUCK(1982)
1984
HEART OF THE STAG(1984, New Zealand); PALLET ON THE FLOOR(1984, New Zealand); UTU(1984, New Zealand); WILD HORSES(1984, New Zealand)
Muriel Bach
ON THE RIGHT TRACK(1981)
Reginald Bach
GIRL IN THE NIGHT, THE(1931, Brit.); HOBSON'S CHOICE(1931, Brit.); HOUND OF THE BASKERVILLES(1932, Brit.); LET ME EXPLAIN, DEAR(1932); SCOOP, THE(1934, Brit.)
Silents
ONCE ABOARD THE LUGGER(1920, Brit.)
Misc. Silents
BUILD THY HOUSE(1920, Brit.); WE WOMEN(1925, Brit.)
Richard Bach
JONATHAN LIVINGSTON SEAGULL(1973), w
Robin Bach
SMORGASBORD(1983)
Steven Bach
MR. BILLION(1977), p; BUTCH AND SUNDANCE: THE EARLY DAYS(1979), p
Vivi Bach
SANDERS(1963, Brit.); MOZAMBIQUE(1966, Brit.); ASSIGNMENT K(1968, Brit.); SKI FEVER(1969, U.S./Aust./Czech.)
Burt Bacharach
WHAT'S NEW, PUSSYCAT?(1965, U.S./Fr.), m; AFTER THE FOX(1966, U.S./Brit./Ital.), m; CASINO ROYALE(1967, Brit.), m; BUTCH CASSIDY AND THE SUNDANCE KID(1969), m; LOST HORIZON(1973), md; ARTHUR(1981), m; NIGHT SHIFT(1982), m
Don Bachardy
RICH AND FAMOUS(1981)
Gordon Bache
BLONDE SAVAGE(1947), w
Bachelet
COMPLIMENTS OF MR. FLOW(1941, Fr.), ph; PORTRAIT OF INNOCENCE(1948, Fr.), ph
Jean Bachelet
CRIME OF MONSIEUR LANGE, THE(1936, Fr.), ph; RULES OF THE GAME, THE(1939, Fr.), ph; LES MAINS SALES(1954, Fr.), ph
Pierre Bachelet
BLACK AND WHITE IN COLOR(1976, Fr.), m
1984
PERILS OF GWENDOLINE, THE(1984, Fr.), m
Frank Bachelin
ISLAND OF LOST MEN(1939), art d; HENRY ALDRICH SWINGS IT(1943), art d
Franz Bachelin
THRILL OF A LIFETIME(1937), art d; HUNTED MEN(1938), art d; STOLEN HEAVEN(1938), art d; THANKS FOR THE MEMORY(1938), art d; GRAND JURY SECRETS(1939), art d; TELEVISION SPY(1939), art d; EMERGENCY SQUAD(1940), art d; SEVENTEEN(1940), art d; HENRY ALDRICH FOR PRESIDENT(1941), art d; MIDNIGHT ANGEL(1941), art d; HENRY ALDRICH, EDITOR(1942), art d; HOSTAGES(1943), art d; HENRY ALDRICH PLAYS CUPID(1944), art d; HENRY ALDRICH'S LITTLE SECRET(1944), art d; HITLER GANG, THE(1944), art d; SEARCHING WIND, THE(1946), art d; TWO YEARS BEFORE THE MAST(1946), art d; CALCUTTA(1947), art d; IMPERFECT LADY, THE(1947), art d; WELCOME STRANGER(1947), art d; EMPEROR WALTZ, THE(1948), art d; I WALK ALONE(1948), art d; MISS TATLOCK'S MILLIONS(1948), art d; NIGHT HAS A THOUSAND EYES(1948), art d; ALIAS NICK BEAL(1949), art d; CHICAGO DEADLINE(1949), art d; RED, HOT AND BLUE(1949), art d; ROPE OF SAND(1949), art d; COPPER CANYON(1950), art d; DARK CITY(1950), art d; SEPTEMBER AFFAIR(1950), art d; LEMON DROP KID, THE(1951), art d; PEKING EXPRESS(1951), art d; RED MOUNTAIN(1951), art d; SILVER CITY(1951), art d; THAT'S MY BOY(1951), art d; DENVER AND RIO GRANDE(1952), art d; STOOGE, THE(1952), art d; SCARED STIFF(1953), art d; SEA CHASE(1955), art d; WAR AND PEACE(1956, Ital./U.S.), art d; BAND OF ANGELS(1957), art d; UNHOLY WIFE, THE(1957), art d; JOHN PAUL JONES(1959), art d; JOURNEY TO THE CENTER OF THE EARTH(1959), art d; STORY OF RUTH, THE(1960), art d; MAGIC SWORD, THE(1962), art d; BEAUTY AND THE BEAST(1963), art d; TWICE TOLD TALES(1963), art d; VILLAGE OF THE GIANTS(1965), art d
Irving Addison Bacheller
Silents
KEEPING UP WITH LIZZIE(1921), w
Stephanie Bachelor
HIS BUTLER'S SISTER(1943); LADY OF BURLESQUE(1943); EXPERIMENT PERILOUS(1944); HER PRIMITIVE MAN(1944); LAKE PLACID SERENADE(1944); MAN FROM FRISCO(1944); PORT OF 40 THIEVES(1944); SECRETS OF SCOTLAND YARD(1944); EARL CARROLL'S VANITIES(1945); GANGS OF THE WATERFRONT(1945); SCOTLAND YARD INVESTIGATOR(1945, Brit.); CRIME OF THE CENTURY(1946); G.I. WAR BRIDES(1946); I'VE ALWAYS LOVED YOU(1946); MAGNIFICENT ROGUE, THE(1946); PASSKEY TO DANGER(1946); UNDERCOVER WOMAN, THE(1946); BLACKMAIL(1947); GHOST GOES WILD, THE(1947); SPRINGTIME

IN THE SIERRAS(1947); CAMPUS HONEYMOON(1948); HOMICIDE FOR THREE(1948); KING OF THE GAMBLERS(1948); SONS OF ADVENTURE(1948)

The Bachelors
IT'S ALL OVER TOWN(1963, Brit.); I'VE GOTTA HORSE(1965, Brit.)

Anne Bachens
DYNAMITE(1930), ed

William A. Bacher
WING AND A PRAYER(1944), p; LEAVE HER TO HEAVEN(1946), p; CARNIVAL IN COSTA RICA(1947), p; FOXES OF HARROW, THE(1947), p; TALL MEN, THE(1955), p, w; UNTAMED(1955), p, w

Mike Baches
HOT STUFF(1979)

Richard Bachler
JINX MONEY(1948), cos; WILD PARTY, THE(1956), cos

Wolfgang Bachler
SISTERS, OR THE BALANCE OF HAPPINESS(1982, Ger.), w

Bob Bachman
RACE FOR YOUR LIFE, CHARLIE BROWN(1977), anim

Charles A. Bachman
PARDON US(1931); OUR RELATIONS(1936); PICK A STAR(1937); SAPS AT SEA(1940)

J. G. Bachman
MAN HUNT(1933), p; EIGHT BELLS(1935), p

Larry Bachman
JALNA(1935), w; SPEED(1936), w

Werner Bachman
ROMANCE AND RICHES(1937, Brit.), m

Almut Bachmann
DECISION BEFORE DAWN(1951)

Ingeborg Bachmann
YOUNG LORD, THE(1970, Ger.), w

J. G. Bachmann
STRANGE JUSTICE(1932), p; GOLDIE GETS ALONG(1933), p
Silents
LAST COMMAND, THE(1928), sup

John G. Bachmann
DOUBLE CROSS(1941), p

Karl Bachmann
NO TIME FOR FLOWERS(1952)

Larry Bachmann
THEY WANTED TO MARRY(1937), w

Lawrence Bachmann
DEVIL MAKES THREE, THE(1952), w

Lawrence P. Bachmann
DR. KILDARE'S WEDDING DAY(1941), w; PEOPLE VS. DR. KILDARE, THE(1941), w; DR. GILLESPIE'S NEW ASSISTANT(1942), w; FINGERS AT THE WINDOW(1942), w; DR. GILLESPIE'S CRIMINAL CASE(1943), w; SHADOW ON THE WALL(1950), w; TEN SECONDS TO HELL(1959), w; WHIRLPOOL(1959, Brit.), w; FOLLOW THE BOYS(1963), p, w; MURDER AHOY(1964, Brit.), p; MURDER MOST FOUL(1964, Brit.), p; ALPHABET MURDERS, THE(1966), p; WHOSE LIFE IS IT ANYWAY?(1981), p

Silva Bachmann
CHARLES, DEAD OR ALIVE(1972, Switz.), ed

Jack Bachom
FUN AND FANCY FREE(1947), ed; ALIAS JESSE JAMES(1959), ed

Jacques Bachrach
HAPPY(1934, Brit.), w; GIVE US THIS NIGHT(1936), w

Margaret Bachus
1984
FLASH OF GREEN, A(1984)

Michael Bachus
RAINMAKER, THE(1956); COUCH, THE(1962)

Vladimir Bacic
ROMANCE OF A HORSE THIEF(1971); ENGLANO MADE ME(1973, Brit.)

Louis Bacigalupi
HOLY TERROR, THE(1937); WITHIN THESE WALLS(1945); T-MEN(1947); DANCING IN THE DARK(1949); DOUBLE CROSSBONES(1950); TALISMAN, THE(1966)

Chela Bacigalupo
ANGEL IN MY POCKET(1969)

Louis Bacigolupi
RAZOR'S EDGE, THE(1946)

Eros Baciucchi
VALACHI PAPERS, THE(1972, Ital./Fr.), spec eff

Andre Back
OPERATION X(1951, Brit.), ph

Annette Back
MERCHANT OF SLAVES(1949, Ital.)

Helene Back
DOZENS, THE(1981)

Irving Back
GOING HIGHBROW(1935)

George Backahle
SHE MAN, THE(1967), m

Brian Backer
BURNING, THE(1981); FAST TIMES AT RIDGEMONT HIGH(1982)

LaWana Backer
MY FAIR LADY(1964)

Zivia Backer
DREAM NO MORE(1950, Palestine)

Alice Backes
UP IN CENTRAL PARK(1948); I WANT TO LIVE!(1958); IT STARTED WITH A KISS(1959); THAT TOUCH OF MINK(1962); GLORY GUYS, THE(1965); SNOWBALL EXPRESS(1972); GABLE AND LOMBARD(1976); CAT FROM OUTER SPACE, THE(1978)

Marshal Backlar
PRETTY POISON(1968), p; TRICK BABY(1973), p; HOMEBODIES(1974), p

Helen Backlin
AMAZING MR. BEECHAM, THE(1949, Brit.)

Susan Backlinie
JAWS(1975); DAY OF THE ANIMALS(1977); 1941(1979); GREAT MUPPET CAPER, THE(1981)

John Backman
HOME BEFORE DARK(1958), art d

Lanny Backman
WHEN TOMORROW DIES(1966, Can.)

Constance Backner
Silents
LONDON PRIDE(1920, Brit.)
Misc. Silents
LONDON FLAT MYSTERY, A(1915, Brit.); MARRIED FOR MONEY(1915, Brit.); SON OF DAVID, A(1920, Brit.); TWO LITTLE WOODEN SHOES(1920, Brit.)

George Backus
FALL GUY(1947); FIGHTER SQUADRON(1948); JOAN OF ARC(1948); MOONRISE(1948); TOO LATE FOR TEARS(1949)
Silents
ONE OF OUR GIRLS(1914); HABIT OF HAPPINESS, THE(1916); EXCITERS, THE(1923); HER OWN FREE WILL(1924); WARRENS OF VIRGINIA, THE(1924)
Misc. Silents
HOUSE OF A THOUSAND CANDLES, THE(1915); SHIRLEY KAYE(1917); RICH MAN, POOR MAN(1918); EYES OF THE SOUL(1919); INDESTRUCTIBLE WIFE, THE(1919); STOLEN KISS, THE(1920)

Georgia Backus
NOBODY'S CHILDREN(1940); FOOTLIGHT FEVER(1941); REPENT AT LEISURE(1941); YOU BELONG TO ME(1941); BLONDIE FOR VICTORY(1942); I MARRIED A WITCH(1942); LADY IS WILLING, THE(1942); LUCKY JORDAN(1942); MAGNIFICENT AMBERSONS, THE(1942); SHUT MY BIG MOUTH(1942); TALK OF THE TOWN(1942); LADY IN THE DARK(1944); STANDING ROOM ONLY(1944); DREAM GIRL(1947); SUDDENLY IT'S SPRING(1947); FORCE OF EVIL(1948); SONG OF SURRENDER(1949); COPPER CANYON(1950); MOTHER DIDN'T TELL ME(1950); NO MAN OF HER OWN(1950); APACHE DRUMS(1951); CAUSE FOR ALARM(1951); MARK OF THE RENEGADE(1951)

Henny Backus
SKIRTS AHOY!(1952); MEET ME IN LAS VEGAS(1956); HOLIDAY FOR LOVERS(1959); DON'T MAKE WAVES(1967); HELLO DOWN THERE(1969)

Henry Backus
BLACKBOARD JUNGLE, THE(1955); GREAT MAN, THE(1957)

James Backus
DANGEROUS PROFESSION, A(1949); EASY LIVING(1949); FATHER WAS A FULLBACK(1949)

Jim Backus
YOU CAN'T RUN AWAY FROM IT(1956); GREAT LOVER, THE(1949); ONE LAST FLING(1949); CUSTOMS AGENT(1950); EMERGENCY WEDDING(1950); KILLER THAT STALKED NEW YORK, THE(1950); MA AND PA KETTLE GO TO TOWN(1950); BRIGHT VICTORY(1951); HALF ANGEL(1951); HIS KIND OF WOMAN(1951); HOLLYWOOD STORY(1951); I WANT YOU(1951); I'LL SEE YOU IN MY DREAMS(1951); IRON MAN, THE(1951); M(1951); MAN WITH A CLOAK, THE(1951); ANDROCLES AND THE LION(1952); DEADLINE–U.S.A.(1952); DON'T BOTHER TO KNOCK(1952); HERE COME THE NELSONS(1952); PAT AND MIKE(1952); ROSE BOWL STORY, THE(1952); ABOVE AND BEYOND(1953); ANGEL FACE(1953); GERALDINE(1953); I LOVE MELVIN(1953); DEEP IN MY HEART(1954); FRANCIS IN THE NAVY(1955); REBEL WITHOUT A CAUSE(1955); SQUARE JUNGLE, THE(1955); GIRL HE LEFT BEHIND, THE(1956); MEET ME IN LAS VEGAS(1956); NAKED HILLS, THE(1956); OPPOSITE SEX, THE(1956); EIGHTEEN AND ANXIOUS(1957); GREAT MAN, THE(1957); MAN OF A THOUSAND FACES(1957); TOP SECRET AFFAIR(1957); HIGH COST OF LOVING, THE(1958); MACABRE(1958); ASK ANY GIRL(1959); BIG OPERATOR, THE(1959); PRIVATE'S AFFAIR, A(1959); WILD AND THE INNOCENT, THE(1959); 1001 ARABIAN NIGHTS(1959); ICE PALACE(1960); BOYS' NIGHT OUT(1962); HORIZONTAL LIEUTENANT, THE(1962); WONDERFUL WORLD OF THE BROTHERS ERIMM, THE(1962); ZOTZ!(1962); CRITIC'S CHOICE(1963); IT'S A MAD, MAD, MAD, MAD WORLD(1963); JOHNNY COOL(1963); MY SIX LOVES(1963); OPERATION BIKINI(1963); SUNDAY IN NEW YORK(1963); WHEELER DEALERS, THE(1963); ADVANCE TO THE REAR(1964); JOHN GOLDFARB, PLEASE COME HOME(1964); BILLIE(1965); FLUFFY(1965); DON'T MAKE WAVES(1967); HURRY SUNDOWN(1967); WHERE WERE YOU WHEN THE LIGHTS WENT OUT?(1968); HELLO DOWN THERE(1969); COCKEYED COWBOYS OF CALICO COUNTY, THE(1970); MR. MAGOO'S HOLIDAY FESTIVAL(1970); NOW YOU SEE HIM, NOW YOU DON'T(1972); CRAZY MAMA(1975); FRIDAY FOSTER(1975); PETE'S DRAGON(1977); GOOD GUYS WEAR BLACK(1978); C.H.O.M.P.S.(1979); ANGELS BRIGADE(1980); THERE GOES THE BRIDE(1980, Brit.)
1984
SLAPSTICK OF ANOTHER KIND(1984)
Misc. Talkies
MAGIC PONY(1979)

Richard Backus
DEATHDREAM(1972, Can.)

Don Backy
VIOLENT FOUR, THE(1968, Ital.); TRAGEDY OF A RIDICULOUS MAN, THE(1982, Ital.)

Baclanova
DANGEROUS WOMAN(1929)
Misc. Silents
DOCKS OF NEW YORK, THE(1928); FORGOTTEN FACES(1928)

Olga Baclanova
MAN I LOVE, THE(1929); WOLF OF WALL STREET, THE(1929); ARE YOU THERE?(1930); CHEER UP AND SMILE(1930); GREAT LOVER, THE(1931); BILLION DOLLAR SCANDAL(1932); DOWNSTAIRS(1932); FREAKS(1932); CLAUDIA(1943)
Silents
MAN WHO LAUGHS, THE(1927); STREET OF SIN, THE(1928); THREE SINNERS(1928)

Nella Bacmeister
MANIAC(1980)

Arch Bacon
COLD TURKEY(1971), art d; MANCHU EAGLE MURDER CAPER MYSTERY, THE(1975), art d

Archie Bacon
SHOOT OUT AT BIG SAG(1962), art d; WHAT AM I BID?(1967), art d; GAY DECEIVERS, THE(1969), art d

Archie J. Bacon
KING KONG(1976), art d
Buni Bacon
SEX KITTENS GO TO COLLEGE(1960); PRIVATE LIVES OF ADAM AND EVE, THE(1961)
David Bacon
TEN GENTLEMEN FROM WEST POINT(1942); BOSS OF BIG TOWN(1943); CRASH DIVE(1943); GALS, INCORPORATED(1943); SOMEONE TO REMEMBER(1943)
Douglas Bacon
STORY OF SEABISCUIT, THE(1949), art d; DALLAS(1950), art d; DAUGHTER OF ROSIE O'GRADY, THE(1950), art d; TEA FOR TWO(1950), art d; DISTANT DRUMS(1951), art d; I'LL SEE YOU IN MY DREAMS(1951), art d; INSIDE THE WALLS OF FOLSOM PRISON(1951), ard d; LIGHTNING STRIKES TWICE(1951), art d; LULLABY OF BROADWAY, THE(1951), art d; ON MOONLIGHT BAY(1951), art d; ROOM FOR ONE MORE(1952), art d; WINNING TEAM, THE(1952), art d
Dwayne Bacon
FEVER HEAT(1968)
Faith Bacon
PRISON TRAIN(1938)
Frank Bacon
LIGHTNIN'(1930), w
Silents
SILENT VOICE, THE(1915)
Gerald F. Bacon
Misc. Silents
SILENT WITNESS, THE(1917), d
Gwen Bacon
UNDERCOVER AGENT(1935, Brit.); CIRCUS BOY(1947, Brit.); CRASH OF SILENCE(1952, Brit.); BRAIN MACHINE, THE(1955, Brit.)
Irving Bacon
SATURDAY NIGHT KID, THE(1929); SIDE STREET(1929); STREET OF CHANCE(1930); ALIAS THE BAD MAN(1931); BRANDED MEN(1931); FIGHTING CARAVANS(1931); BIG BROADCAST, THE(1932); CENTRAL PARK(1932); FILE 113(1932); I AM A FUGITIVE FROM A CHAIN GANG(1932); IF I HAD A MILLION(1932); MADAME RACKETEER(1932); MILLION DOLLAR LEGS(1932); NO ONE MAN(1932); THIS IS THE NIGHT(1932); ANN VICKERS(1933); BOWERY, THE(1933); HE LEARNED ABOUT WOMEN(1933); HELLO, EVERYBODY(1933); I LOVE THAT MAN(1933); KEYHOLE, THE(1933); LAWYER MAN(1933); PRIVATE DETECTIVE 62(1933); SITTING PRETTY(1933); TILLIE AND GUS(1933); GEORGE WHITE'S SCANDALS(1934); HAT, COAT AND GLOVE(1934); HELL CAT, THE(1934); HOUSE OF MYSTERY(1934); IT HAPPENED ONE NIGHT(1934); LONE COWBOY(1934); MISS FANE'S BABY IS STOLEN(1934); NOW I'LL TELL(1934); PURSUIT OF HAPPINESS, THE(1934); READY FOR LOVE(1934); SHADOWS OF SING SING(1934); SIX OF A KIND(1934); YOU BELONG TO ME(1934); DIAMOND JIM(1935); FARMER TAKES A WIFE, THE(1935); GLASS KEY, THE(1935); GOIN' TO TOWN(1935); HERE COMES COOKIE(1935); IT'S A SMALL WORLD(1935); MANHATTAN MOON(1935); MEN WITHOUT NAMES(1935); MILLIONS IN THE AIR(1935); MURDER MAN(1935); MURDER ON A HONEYMOON(1935); NO RANSOM(1935); PAGE MISS GLORY(1935); POWDERSMOKE RANGE(1935); PRIVATE WORLDS(1935); ROMANCE IN MANHATTAN(1935); SHE COULDN'T TAKE IT(1935); SHY CAFE(1935); TWO FISTED(1935); VIRGINIA JUDGE, THE(1935); WEST OF THE PECOS(1935); ARIZONA MAHONEY(1936); CHINA CLIPPER(1936); DRIFT FENCE(1936); EARTHWORM TRACTORS(1936); HOLLYWOOD BOULEVARD(1936); HOPALONG CASSIDY RETURNS(1936); IT'S A GREAT LIFE(1936); LOVE ON A BET(1936); MR. DEEDS GOES TO TOWN(1936); MURDER WITH PICTURES(1936); PETTICOAT FEVER(1936); RHYTHM ON THE RANGE(1936); SAN FRANCISCO(1936); TEXAS RANGERS, THE(1936); THREE CHEERS FOR LOVE(1936); TIMOTHY'S QUEST(1936); TRAIL OF THE LONESOME PINE, THE(1936); VALIANT IS THE WORD FOR CARRIE(1936); ANGEL'S HOLIDAY(1937); BIG CITY(1937); EXCLUSIVE(1937); INTERNES CAN'T TAKE MONEY(1937); IT'S LOVE I'M AFTER(1937); LET'S MAKE A MILLION(1937); MARRY THE GIRL(1937); PLAINSMAN, THE(1937); SEVENTH HEAVEN(1937); SING AND BE HAPPY(1937); STAR IS BORN, A(1937); THERE GOES MY GIRL(1937); VOGUES OF 1938(1937); AMAZING DR. CLITTERHOUSE, THE(1938); BLONDIE(1938); CHASER, THE(1938); CITY GIRL(1938); EVERY DAY'S A HOLIDAY(1938); EXPOSED(1938); FIRST 100 YEARS, THE(1938); HARD TO GET(1938); KENTUCKY MOONSHINE(1938); LETTER OF INTRODUCTION(1938); MAD MISS MANTON, THE(1938); MAN-PROOF(1938); MIDNIGHT INTRUDER(1938); MR. MOTO'S GAMBLE(1938); PROFESSOR BEWARE(1938); RACKET BUSTERS(1938); SING YOU SINNERS(1938); SISTERS, THE(1938); SPAWN OF THE NORTH(1938); STRANGE FACES(1938); SWEETHEARTS(1938); SWING YOUR LADY(1938); TEXANS, THE(1938); THERE GOES MY HEART(1938); TIP-OFF GIRLS(1938); YOU CAN'T TAKE IT WITH YOU(1938); BLONDIE BRINGS UP BABY(1939); BLONDIE MEETS THE BOSS(1939); BLONDIE TAKES A VACATION(1939); GONE WITH THE WIND(1939); GRACIE ALLEN MURDER CASE(1939); HEAVEN WITH A BARBED WIRE FENCE(1939); HOLLYWOOD CAVALCADE(1939); I STOLE A MILLION(1939); INDIANAPOLIS SPEEDWAY(1939); LADY'S FROM KENTUCKY, THE(1939); LONE WOLF SPY HUNT, THE(1939); LUCKY NIGHT(1939); OKLAHOMA KID, THE(1939); RIO(1939); SECOND FIDDLE(1939); TAIL SPIN(1939); THEY MADE ME A CRIMINAL(1939); TOO BUSY TO WORK(1939); TORCHY RUNS FOR MAYOR(1939); YOU CAN'T CHEAT AN HONEST MAN(1939); BLONDIE HAS SERVANT TROUBLE(1940); BLONDIE ON A BUDGET(1940); BLONDIE PLAYS CUPID(1940); BROTHER RAT AND A BABY(1940); DOCTOR TAKES A WIFE(1940); DREAMING OUT LOUD(1940); EDISON, THE MAN(1940); GOLD RUSH MAISIE(1940); GRAPES OF WRATH(1940); HIS GIRL FRIDAY(1940); HOWARDS OF VIRGINIA, THE(1940); INVISIBLE STRIPES(1940); LILLIAN RUSSELL(1940); LOVE, HONOR AND OH, BABY(1940); MAN WHO WOULDN'T TALK, THE(1940); MANHATTAN HEARTBEAT(1940); MICHAEL SHAYNE, PRIVATE DETECTIVE(1940); RETURN OF FRANK JAMES, THE(1940); SAILOR'S LADY(1940); STAR DUST(1940); YOU CAN'T FOOL YOUR WIFE(1940); YOUNG PEOPLE(1940); ACCENT ON LOVE(1941); BARNACLE BILL(1941); BLONDIE GOES LATIN(1941); BLONDIE IN SOCIETY(1941); CAUGHT IN THE DRAFT(1941); GIRL, A GUY AND A GOB, A(1941); GREAT GUNS(1941); IT STARTED WITH EVE(1941); JENNIE(1941); LONE WOLF TAKES A CHANCE, THE(1941); MEET JOHN DOE(1941); MILLION DOLLAR BABY(1941); MOON OVER HER SHOULDER(1941); NEVER GIVE A SUCKER AN EVEN BREAK(1941); REMEMBER THE DAY(1941); RIDE ON VAQUERO(1941); SHE COULDN'T SAY NO(1941); SKYLARK(1941); TOBACCO ROAD(1941); TOO MANY BLONDES(1941); WESTERN UNION(1941); WILD MAN OF BORNEO, THE(1941); BASHFUL BACHELOR, THE(1942); BETWEEN US GIRLS(1942); BLONDIE FOR VICTORY(1942); BLONDIE'S BLESSED EVENT(1942); DARING YOUNG MAN, THE(1942); FOOTLIGHT SERENADE(1942); FRECKLES COMES HOME(1942); GET HEP TO LOVE(1942); GIVE OUT,

SISTERS(1942); GREAT MAN'S LADY, THE(1942); HOLIDAY INN(1942); LADY IN A JAM(1942); PARDON MY SARONG(1942); SPOILERS, THE(1942); STAR SPANGLED RHYTHM(1942); SWEETHEART OF THE FLEET(1942); THEY DIED WITH THEIR BOOTS ON(1942); THRU DIFFERENT EYES(1942); YOUNG AMERICA(1942); ACTION IN THE NORTH ATLANTIC(1943); DESPERADOES, THE(1943); DIXIE DUGAN(1943); FOLLOW THE BAND(1943); FOOTLIGHT GLAMOUR(1943); GIRL CRAZY(1943); GOOD FELLOWS, THE(1943); GUNG HO!(1943); GUY NAMED JOE, A(1943); HAPPY GO LUCKY(1943); HERS TO HOLD(1943); IN OLD OKLAHOMA(1943); IT'S A GREAT LIFE(1943); JOHNNY COME LATELY(1943); KING OF THE COWBOYS(1943); SHADOW OF A DOUBT(1943); SO'S YOUR UNCLE(1943); STRANGER IN TOWN, A(1943); THIS IS THE ARMY(1943); TWO WEEKS TO LIVE(1943); WHAT A WOMAN!(1943); CASANOVA BROWN(1944); CHIP OFF THE OLD BLOCK(1944); HEAVENLY DAYS(1944); HER PRIMITIVE MAN(1944); KNICKERBOCKER HOLIDAY(1944); PIN UP GIRL(1944); SINCE YOU WENT AWAY(1944); STORY OF DR. WASSELL, THE(1944); THIN MAN GOES HOME, THE(1944); WEEKEND PASS(1944); WING AND A PRAYER(1944); GUEST WIFE(1945); HITCHHIKE TO HAPPINESS(1945); OUT OF THIS WORLD(1945); PATRICK THE GREAT(1945); ROUGHLY SPEAKING(1945); SPELLBOUND(1945); UNDER WESTERN SKIES(1945); WEEKEND AT THE WALDORF(1945); MY BROTHER TALKS TO HORSES(1946); NIGHT TRAIN TO MEMPHIS(1946); ONE WAY TO LOVE(1946); WAKE UP AND DREAM(1946); BACHELOR AND THE BOBBY-SOXER, THE(1947); DEAR RUTH(1947); HIGH WALL, THE(1947); MONSIEUR VERDOUX(1947); ADVENTURES IN SILVERADO(1948); ALBUQUERQUE(1948); DYNAMITE(1948); FAMILY HONEYMOON(1948); GOOD SAM(1948); MOONRISE(1948); ROCKY(1948); STATE OF THE UNION(1948); VELVET TOUCH, THE(1948); BIG CAT, THE(1949); DEAR WIFE(1949); DOWN MEMORY LANE(1949); GREEN PROMISE, THE(1949); IT'S A GREAT FEELING(1949); JOHN LOVES MARY(1949); MANHANDLED(1949); NIGHT UNTO NIGHT(1949); SONS OF NEW MEXICO(1949); WOMAN IN HIDING(1949); BORN TO BE BAD(1950); EMERGENCY WEDDING(1950); NEVER A DULL MOMENT(1950); RIDING HIGH(1950); WABASH AVENUE(1950); CAUSE FOR ALARM(1951); DESERT OF LOST MEN(1951); HERE COMES THE GROOM(1951); HONEYCHILE(1951); KATIE DID IT(1951); O. HENRY'S FULL HOUSE(1952); ROOM FOR ONE MORE(1952); ROSE OF CIMARRON(1952); DEVIL'S CANYON(1953); FORT TI(1953); GLENN MILLER STORY, THE(1953); KANSAS PACIFIC(1953); SWEETHEARTS ON PARADE(1953); BLACK HORSE CANYON(1954); DUFFY OF SAN QUENTIN(1954); MA AND PA KETTLE AT HOME(1954); STAR IS BORN, A(1954); AT GUNPOINT(1955); RUN FOR COVER(1955); DAKOTA INCIDENT(1956); HIDDEN GUNS(1956); AMBUSH AT CIMARRON PASS(1958); FORT MASSACRE(1958)
Silents
CALIFORNIA OR BUST(1927); GOOD-BYE KISS, THE(1928); HEAD MAN, THE(1928)

Iving Bacon
SADDLE PALS(1947)
James Bacon
PEPE(1960); 80 STEPS TO JONAH(1969); SKULLDUGGERY(1970); ESCAPE FROM THE PLANET OF THE APES(1971); OUTFIT, THE(1973); HOW TO SEDUCE A WOMAN(1974); TUNNELVISION(1976); ONE MAN JURY(1978); MAN WITH BOGART'S FACE, THE(1980); CHARLIE CHAN AND THE CURSE OF THE DRAGON QUEEN(1981)
James R. Bacon
UNDERWORLD U.S.A.(1961)
Jim Bacon
SEVEN MINUTES, THE(1971)
Kevin Bacon
NATIONAL LAMPOON'S ANIMAL HOUSE(1978); STARTING OVER(1979); FRIDAY THE 13TH(1980); HERO AT LARGE(1980); ONLY WHEN I LAUGH(1981); DINER(1982); FORTY DEUCE(1982)
1984
FOOTLOOSE(1984)
Lloyd Bacon
LION AND THE MOUSE, THE(1928), d; SINGING FOOL, THE(1928), d; WOMEN THEY TALK ABOUT(1928), d; HONKY TONK(1929), d; NO DEFENSE(1929), d; SAY IT WITH SONGS(1929), d; SO LONG LETTY(1929), d; STARK MAD(1929), d; MOBY DICK(1930), d; NOTORIOUS AFFAIR, A(1930), d; OFFICE WIFE, THE(1930), d; OTHER TOMORROW, THE(1930), d; SHE COULDN'T SAY NO(1930), d; FIFTY MILLION FRENCHMEN(1931), d; GOLD DUST GERTIE(1931), d; HONOR OF THE FAMILY(1931), d; KEPT HUSBANDS(1931), d; MANHATTAN PARADE(1931), d; SIT TIGHT(1931), d; ALIAS THE DOCTOR(1932), d; CROONER(1932), d; FAMOUS FERGUSON CASE, THE(1932), d; FIREMAN, SAVE MY CHILD(1932), d, w; MISS PINKERTON(1932), d; YOU SAID A MOUTHFUL(1932), d; FOOTLIGHT PARADE(1933), d; MARY STEVENS, M.D.(1933), d; PICTURE SNATCHER(1933), d; SON OF A SAILOR(1933), d; 42ND STREET(1933), d; HE WAS HER MAN(1934), d; HERE COMES THE NAVY(1934), d; SIX-DAY BIKE RIDER(1934), d; VERY HONORABLE GUY, A(1934), d; WONDER BAR(1934), d; BROADWAY GONDOLIER(1935), d; DEVIL DOGS OF THE AIR(1935), d; FRISCO KID(1935), d; IN CALIENTE(1935), d; IRISH IN US, THE(1935), d; CAIN AND MABEL(1936), d; GOLD DIGGERS OF 1937(1936), d; SONS O' GUNS(1936), d; EVER SINCE EVE(1937), d; MARKED WOMAN(1937), d; SAN QUENTIN(1937), d; SUBMARINE D-1(1937), d; BOY MEETS GIRL(1938), d; COWBOY FROM BROOKLYN(1938), d; RACKET BUSTERS(1938), d; SLIGHT CASE OF MURDER, A(1938), d; ESPIONAGE AGENT(1939), d; INDIANAPOLIS SPEEDWAY(1939), d; OKLAHOMA KID, THE(1939), d; WINGS OF THE NAVY(1939), d; BROTHER ORCHID(1940), d; CHILD IS BORN, A(1940), d; INVISIBLE STRIPES(1940), d; KNUTE ROCKNE–ALL AMERICAN(1940), d; THREE CHEERS FOR THE IRISH(1940), d; AFFECTIONATELY YOURS(1941), d; FOOTSTEPS IN THE DARK(1941), d; HONEYMOON FOR THREE(1941), d; NAVY BLUES(1941), d; LARCENY, INC.(1942), d; SILVER QUEEN(1942), d; WINGS FOR THE EAGLE(1942), d; ACTION IN THE NORTH ATLANTIC(1943), d; SULLIVANS, THE(1944), d; SUNDAY DINNER FOR A SOLDIER(1944), d; CAPTAIN EDDIE(1945), d; HOME SWEET HOMICIDE(1946), d; WAKE UP AND DREAM(1946), d; I WONDER WHO'S KISSING HER NOW(1947), d; DON'T TRUST YOUR HUSBAND(1948), d; GIVE MY REGARDS TO BROADWAY(1948), d; YOU WERE MEANT FOR ME(1948), d; IT HAPPENS EVERY SPRING(1949), d; MISS GRANT TAKES RICHMOND(1949), d; MOTHER IS A FRESHMAN(1949), d; FULLER BRUSH GIRL, THE(1950), d; GOOD HUMOR MAN, THE(1950), d; KILL THE UMPIRE(1950), d; CALL ME MISTER(1951), d; FROGMEN, THE(1951), d; GOLDEN GIRL(1951), d; I DON'T CARE GIRL, THE(1953), d; GREAT SIOUX UPRISING, THE(1953), d; WALKING MY BABY BACK HOME(1953), d; FRENCH LINE, THE(1954), d; SHE COULDN'T SAY NO(1954), d
Silents
BROKEN HEARTS OF HOLLYWOOD(1926), d; PRIVATE IZZY MURPHY(1926), d; SAILOR'S SWEETHEART, A(1927), d; WHITE FLANNELS(1927), d

Misc. Silents
SQUARE DEAL SANDERSON(1919); WAGON TRACKS(1919); GIRL IN THE RAIN, THE(1920); NOBODY'S GIRL(1920); GREATER PROFIT, THE(1921); HANDS OFF(1921); HEARTS AND MASKS(1921); BRASS KNUCKLES(1927), d; FINGER PRINTS(1927), d; HEART OF MARYLAND, THE(1927), d; PAY AS YOU ENTER(1928), d; NO DEFENSE(1929), d

Mai Bacon
GOOD COMPANIONS(1933, Brit.); PUBLIC LIFE OF HENRY THE NINTH, THE(1934, Brit.); CHICK(1936, Brit.); RIDING HIGH(1937, Brit.); SECOND BEST BED(1937, Brit.); DOUBLE OR QUITS(1938, Brit.); FUGITIVE, THE(1940, Brit.); MISSING TEN DAYS(1941, Brit.); THIS MAN IS MINE(1946 Brit.); UP FOR THE CUP(1950, Brit.); POOL OF LONDON(1951, Brit.); DELAVINE AFFAIR, THE(1954, Brit.); LOVERS, HAPPY LOVERS!(1955, Brit.)

Margaret Bacon
DEEP IN MY HEART(1954)

Max Bacon
KING ARTHUR WAS A GENTLEMAN(1942, Brit.); PLAYBOY, THE(1942, Brit.); MISS LONDON LTD.(1943, Brit.); BEES IN PARADISE(1944, Brit.); GIVE US THE MOON(1944, Brit.); GAMBLER AND THE LADY, THE(1952, Brit.); TAKE A POWDER(1953, Brit.); ENTERTAINER, THE(1960, Brit.); EYES OF ANNIE JONES, THE(1963, Brit.); PLAY IT COOL(1963, Brit.); CROOKS IN CLOISTERS(1964, Brit.); SANDWICH MAN, THE(1966, Brit.); PRIVILEGE(1967, Brit.); WHISPERERS, THE(1967, Brit.); CHITTY CHITTY BANG BANG(1968, Brit.)

Norman Bacon
DRACULA HAS RISEN FROM HIS GRAVE(1968, Brit.)
1984
1984(1984, Brit.)

Paul Bacon
THEY CAME FROM BEYOND SPACE(1967, Brit.); I AM A GROUPIE(1970, Brit.); ASPHYX, THE(1972, Brit.)
Misc. Talkies
CORVINI INHERITANCE(1984, Brit.)

Robert Bacon
STOLEN HOURS(1963)

Rod Bacon
THESE GLAMOUR GIRLS(1939); IRENE(1940); GAY VAGABOND, THE(1941); PUBLIC ENEMIES(1941); YOKEL BOY(1942); SEE HERE, PRIVATE HARGROVE(1944)

Roger Bacon
PAD, THE(AND HOW TO USE IT)* (1966, Brit.); IF A MAN ANSWERS(1962); BEACH PARTY(1963); PALM SPRINGS WEEKEND(1963); PAJAMA PARTY(1964)

Ruth Bacon
SPRINGTIME IN THE ROCKIES(1937)

Selby Bacon
DRAGONWYCH(1946)

Shelby Bacon
HOLIDAY INN(1942); SINCE YOU WENT AWAY(1944); CORPUS CHRISTI BANDITS(1945); GEORGE WHITE'S SCANDALS(1945); SARATOGA TRUNK(1945); PINKY(1949); SURRENDER(1950)

Shelly Bacon
SOUTHERN YANKEE, A(1948)

Sybil Bacon
JOURNEY FOR MARGARET(1942); MRS. MINIVER(1942)

Walter Bacon
HOODLUM SAINT, THE(1946); STORM WARNING(1950)

William V. Bacon III
NIKKI, WILD DOG OF THE NORTH(1961, U.S./Can.), ph; CHARLIE, THE LONESOME COUGAR(1967), ph

Baconnet
PRIZE, THE(1952, Fr.)

Georges Baconnet
LE PLAISIR(1954, Fr.); CRAZY FOR LOVE(1960, Fr.); MARRIAGE OF FIGARO, THE(1963, Fr.)

Palau Baconnet
LE PLAISIR(1954, Fr.)

Italia Bacovich
IT HAPPENED IN CANADA(1962, Can.)

Andre Bacque
GOLGOTHA(1937, Fr.); CARNIVAL OF SINNERS(1947, Fr.)
Misc. Silents
MALDONE(1928, Fr.)

Edgar Bacquet
PEEK-A-BOO(1961, Fr.), p

Harold S. Bacquet
KATHLEEN(1941), d

Jean-Pierre Bacri
ENTRE NOUS(1983, Fr.)

Ferenc Bacs
FORTRESS, THE(1979, Hung.)
1984
BRADY'S ESCAPE(1984, U.S./Hung.)

Juliet Bacskai
INSIDE LOOKING OUT(1977, Aus.)
1984
MAN OF FLOWERS(1984, Aus.)

Peter Bacso
WITNESS, THE(1982, Hung.), d&W

Warner Bacter
CRIME DOCTOR'S DIARY, THE(1949)

Walter Baczynsky
PROUD RIDER, THE(1971, Can.), d

Dessie Bad Bear
LITTLE BIG MAN(1970)

Ina Bad Bear
DIRTY DINGUS MAGEE(1970)

Bad Sign
GORKY PARK(1983)

Major M. Badager
TEN DAYS TO TULARA(1958)

Larry Badagliacca
VARIETY GIRL(1947)

Alexander Badal
PHONY AMERICAN, THE(1964, Ger.), w

Jean Badal
MIDNIGHT MEETING(1962, Fr.), ph; NAKED AUTUMN(1963, Fr.), ph; BEHOLD A PALE HORSE(1964), ph; WHAT'S NEW, PUSSYCAT?(1965, U.S./Fr.), ph; OTHER ONE, THE(1967,Fr.), ph; NAKED HEARTS(1970, Fr.), ph; PROMISE AT DAWN(1970, U.S./Fr.), ph; VERY CURIOUS GIRL, A(1970, Fr.), ph; PLAYTIME(1973, Fr.), ph; VERDICT(1975, Fr./Ital.), ph; GOODBYE EMMANUELLE(1980, Fr.), ph

Tom Badal
1984
LOVE STREAMS(1984)

Andy Badale
LAW AND DISORDER(1974), m

Francisco Badalo
COMPANEROS(1970 Ital./Span./Ger.)

Nicolas Badalucca
LA BABY SITTER(1975, Fr./Ital./Ger.), w

Michael Badalucco
1984
BROADWAY DANNY ROSE(1984)

Niccola Badalucco
STREET PEOPLE(1976, U.S./Ital.), w

Nicol Badalucco
BURNING YEARS, THE(1979, Ital.), w

Nicola Badalucco
DEATH IN VENICE(1971, Ital./Fr.), w; THREE TOUGH GUYS(1974, U.S./Ital.), w

Jacob A. Badaracco
Silents
MISS CRUSOE(1919), ph; AFTER MIDNIGHT(1921), ph; SHADOWS OF THE SEA(1922), ph; SOUTH OF NORTHERN LIGHTS(1922), ph; LOSER'S END, THE(1924), ph; ACROSS THE DEADLINE(1925), ph; KING OF KINGS, THE(1927), ph

Jacob Badaracco
Silents
NOTHING BUT THE TRUTH(1920), ph

Jake Badaracco
OFFICE SCANDAL, THE(1929), ph
Silents
LURE OF GOLD(1922), ph

Ali Badarni
1984
LITTLE DRUMMER GIRL, THE(1984)

Mohammed Ali Badarni
1984
LITTLE DRUMMER GIRL, THE(1984)

Wally Badarou
COUNTRYMAN(1982, Jamaica), m

Raffaele Badassarre
ERIK THE CONQUEROR(1963, Fr./Ital.)

Randall Badat
1984
SURF II(1984), d&w

Peggy Baday
HOMECOMING(1948)

V. Badayev
WAR AND PEACE(1968, USSR)

Badazz
J-MEN FOREVER(1980), m

Angela Baddclay
NO TIME FOR TEARS(1957, Brit.)

Angela Baddeley
SPECKLED BAND, THE(1931, Brit.); ARMS AND THE MAN(1932, Brit.); GHOST TRAIN, THE(1933, Brit.); THOSE WERE THE DAYS(1934, Brit.); CITADEL, THE(1938); QUARTET(1949, Brit.); ZOO BABY(1957, Brit.); TOM JONES(1963, Brit.)

Hermione Baddeley
CASTE(1930, Brit.); REGAL CAVALCADE(1935, Brit.); UNDERCOVER AGENT(1935, Brit.); REMARKABLE MR. KIPPS(1942, Brit.); BRIGHTON ROCK(1947, Brit.); DEAR MR. PROHACK(1949, Brit.); IT ALWAYS RAINS ON SUNDAY(1949, Brit.); PASSPORT TO PIMLICO(1949, Brit.); QUARTET(1949, Brit.); FIVE ANGLES ON MURDER(1950, Brit.); NO ROOM AT THE INN(1950, Brit.); CHRISTMAS CAROL, A(1951, Brit.); HELL IS SOLD OUT(1951, Brit.); TOM BROWN'S SCHOOLDAYS(1951, Brit.); PICKWICK PAPERS, THE(1952, Brit.); BACHELOR IN PARIS(1953, Brit.); SLASHER, THE(1953, Brit.); TIME GENTLEMEN PLEASE!(1953, Brit.); BELLES OF ST. TRINIAN'S, THE(1954, Brit.); EXPRESSO BONGO(1959, Brit.); ROOM AT THE TOP(1959, Brit.); LET'S GET MARRIED(1960, Brit.); MIDNIGHT LACE(1960); JET STORM(1961, Brit.); INFORMATION RECEIVED(1962, Brit.); YOUNG, WILLING AND EAGER(1962, Brit.); MARY POPPINS(1964); UNSINKABLE MOLLY BROWN, THE(1964); DO NOT DISTURB(1965); HARLOW(1965); MARRIAGE ON THE ROCKS(1965); ADVENTURES OF BULLWHIP GRIFFIN, THE(1967); HAPPIEST MILLIONAIRE, THE(1967); ARISTOCATS, THE(1970); UP THE FRONT(1972, Brit.); BLACK WINDMILL, THE(1974, Brit.); THERE GOES THE BRIDE(1980, Brit.); SECRET OF NIMH, THE(1982)
Silents
DAUGHTER IN REVOLT, A(1927, Brit.)
Misc. Silents
GUNS OF LOOS, THE(1928, Brit.)

John Baddeley
DARK CRYSTAL, THE(1982, Brit.)

Annette Bade
Silents
WOMAN'S BUSINESS, A(1920)

Tom Bade
SOME OF MY BEST FRIENDS ARE...(1971)

Alan Badel
SALOME(1953); THREE CASES OF MURDER(1955, Brit.); WILL ANY GENTLEMAN?(1955, Brit.); MAGIC FIRE(1956); BITTER HARVEST(1963, Brit.); CHILDREN OF THE DAMNED(1963, Brit.); THIS SPORTING LIFE(1963, Brit.); ARABE-

SQUE(1966); OTLEY(1969, Brit.); WHERE'S JACK?(1969, Brit.); ADVENTURERS, THE(1970); DAY OF THE JACKAL, THE(1973, Brit./Fr.); LUTHER(1974); TELEFON(1977); FORCE 10 FROM NAVARONE(1978, Brit.); MEDUSA TOUCH, THE(1978, Brit.); AGATHA(1979, Brit.); NIJINSKY(1980, Brit.)
1984
RIDDLE OF THE SANDS, THE(1984, Brit.)

Sarah Badel
THINK DIRTY(1970, Brit.)

Tayfun Bademsoy
1984
CLASS ENEMY(1984, Ger.)

Max Baden
Misc. Talkies
HER SECOND MOTHER(1940)

Lord Baden-Powell
Misc. Silents
WOODPIGEON PATROL, THE(1930, Brit.)

Sir Robert Baden-Powell
Misc. Silents
BOYS OF THE OTTER PATROL(1918, Brit.)

Nina Baden-Semper
KONGI'S HARVEST(1971, U.S./Nigeria)
Misc. Talkies
LOVE THY NEIGHBOUR(1973)

Elizabeth Bader
LILITH(1964)

Terry Bader
STONE(1974, Aus.)

George Badera
WHY RUSSIANS ARE REVOLTING(1970)

Rupert Baderman
1984
1984(1984, Brit.)

Francis Badeschi
GLADIATORS 7(1964, Span./Ital.)

Silvia Badesco
CHLOE IN THE AFTERNOON(1972, Fr.)

Clarence Badger
UNCLE HARRY(1945); PARIS(1929), p&d; BAD MAN, THE(1930), d; MURDER WILL OUT(1930), d; NO, NO NANETTE(1930), d; SWEETHEARTS AND WIVES(1930), d; HOT HEIRESS(1931), d; PARTY HUSBAND(1931), d; WOMAN HUNGRY(1931), d; WHEN STRANGERS MARRY(1933), d; THAT CERTAIN SOMETHING(1941, Aus.), d&w; MY GAL SAL(1942)
Silents
ALMOST A HUSBAND(1919), d; DOUBLING FOR ROMEO(1921), d; GUILE OF WOMEN(1921), d; PAINTED PEOPLE(1924), d; EVE'S SECRET(1925), d; NEW LIVES FOR OLD(1925), d; PATHS TO PARADISE(1925), d; CAMPUS FLIRT, THE(1926), d; MISS BREWSTER'S MILLIONS(1926), d; RAINMAKER, THE(1926), d; IT(1927), d; SHE'S A SHEIK(1927), d; FIFTY-FIFTY GIRL, THE(1928), d; HOT NEWS(1928), d; RED HAIR(1928), d
Misc. Silents
FLOOR BELOW, THE(1918), d; VENUS MODEL, THE(1918), d; HONEST HUTCH(1920), d; JES' CALL ME JIM(1920), d; STRANGE BORDER, THE(1920), d; POOR RELATION, A(1921), d; POTASH AND PERLMUTTER(1923), d; SHOOTING OF DAN MCGREW, THE(1924), d; GOLDEN PRINCESS, THE(1925), d; KISS IN A TAXI, A(1927), d; MAN POWER(1927), d; SENORITA(1927), d; SWIM, GIRL, SWIM(1927), d; THREE WEEK-ENDS(1928), d

Clarence D. Badger
Silents
JUBILO(1919), d

Clarence G. Badger
RANGLE RIVER(1939, Aus.), p&d
Silents
PERFECT LADY, A(1918), d; DAUGHTER OF MINE(1919), d; DON'T GET PERSONAL(1922), d; RED LIGHTS(1923), d
Misc. Silents
MODERN ENOCH ARDEN, A(1916), d; FRIEND HUSBAND(1918), d; KINGDOM OF YOUTH, THE(1918), d; DAY DREAMS(1919), d; LEAVE IT TO SUSAN(1919), d; SIS HOPKINS(1919), d; STRICTLY CONFIDENTIAL(1919), d; THROUGH THE WRONG DOOR(1919), d; CUPID, THE COWPUNCHER(1920), d; WATER, WATER, EVERYWHERE(1920), d; BOYS WILL BE BOYS(1921), d; UNWILLING HERO, AN(1921), d; DANGEROUS LITTLE DEMON, THE(1922), d; QUINCY ADAMS SAWYER(1922), d; YOUR FRIEND AND MINE(1923), d; ONE NIGHT IN ROME(1924), d

Mary Ellen Badger
COLD RIVER(1982)

Will Badger
Silents
HER MAD BARGAIN(1921)

Alice Badgerow
PEER GYNT(1965)

Helen Badgley
Silents
MODERN MONTE CRISTO, A(1917)
Misc. Silents
CANDY GIRL, THE(1917); FIRES OF YOUTH(1917)

John Badham
BINGO LONG TRAVELING ALL-STARS AND MOTOR KINGS, THE(1976), d; SATURDAY NIGHT FEVER(1977), d; DRACULA(1979), d; WHOSE LIFE IS IT ANYWAY?(1981), d; BLUE THUNDER(1983), d; WARGAMES(1983), d

Mary Badham
TO KILL A MOCKINGBIRD(1962); LET'S KILL UNCLE(1966); THIS PROPERTY IS CONDEMNED(1966)

Leopold Badia
GANG THAT COULDN'T SHOOT STRAIGHT, THE(1971)

Laurence Badie
FORBIDDEN GAMES(1953, Fr.); LUST FOR LIFE(1956); FOUR BAGS FULL(1957, Fr./Ital.); MURIEL(1963, Fr./Ital.); BEHOLD A PALE HORSE(1964); SOFT SKIN, THE(1964, Fr.); FRIEND OF THE FAMILY(1965, Fr./Ital.); LA GUERRE EST FINIE(1967, Fr./Swed.); FLEA IN HER EAR, A(1968, Fr.); MON ONCLE D'AMERIQUE(1980, Fr.)

John Badila
SEDUCTION OF JOE TYNAN, THE(1979)

Badin
SWEET SKIN(1965, Fr./Ital.)

Jean Badin
1984
THREE CROWNS OF THE SAILOR(1984, Fr.)

Max Badin
ELI ELI(1940)

Henk Badings
FREUD(1962), md

Klara Badiola
1984
ESCAPE FROM SEGOVIA(1984, Span.)

Carlo Badioli
LA BOHEME(1965, Ital.)

Reza S. Badiyi
TRADER HORN(1973), d

Tod Badker
KILL, THE(1968)

Annette Badland
JABBERWOCKY(1977, Brit.)
1984
SACRED HEARTS(1984, Brit.)

Jane Badler
FIRST TIME, THE(1983)

Peggy Badley
LET'S DANCE(1950)

Maria Badmajev
CLEOPATRA(1963)

Philip Badoc
SPY WHO CAME IN FROM THE COLD, THE(1965, Brit.)

Louis Badolati
BROTHERHOOD, THE(1968)

Mario Badolati
LOVE WITH THE PROPER STRANGER(1963)

Claude Badolle
MY UNCLE(1958, Fr.)

Jessica Badovinac
NINE TO FIVE(1980)

Badri
THIRD LOVER, THE(1963, Fr./Ital.)

Joseph Badrous
LITTLE MISS DEVIL(1951, Egypt), m

Kwasi Badu
FIVE ON THE BLACK HAND SIDE(1973)

Pamela Badyk
ZERO IN THE UNIVERSE(1966)

Wolfgang Baechler
GERMANY IN AUTUMN(1978, Ger.)

Otto Baecker
HAPPY EVER AFTER(1932, Ger./Brit.), ph; F.P. 1 DOESN'T ANSWER(1933, Ger.), ph; GOLD(1934, Ger.), ph

Nicholas E. Baehr
INCIDENT, THE(1967), w

Carlos Baena
ALEXANDER THE GREAT(1956); ADAM AND EVE(1958, Mex.)

Carlos Martinez Baena
CRIMINAL LIFE OF ARCHIBALDO DE LA CRUZ, THE(1962, Mex.)

Juan Julio Baena
HAND IN THE TRAP, THE(1963, Arg./Span.), ph; MISSION BLOODY MARY(1967, Fr./Ital./Span.), ph

Martinez Baena
EL(1955, Mex.)

Sam Baenvitz
CHECKERED COAT, THE(1948), p

Abel Baer
LOVE, LIVE AND LAUGH(1929), m/l; THIS DAY AND AGE(1933), m

Arthur "Bugs" Baer
THEY LEARNED ABOUT WOMEN(1930), w

Bohdan Baer
YELLOW SLIPPERS, THE(1965, Pol.)

Brett Baer
RISKY BUSINESS(1983)

Buddy Baer
TAKE IT FROM ME(1937, Brit.); AFRICA SCREAMS(1949); FLAME OF ARABY(1951); QUO VADIS(1951); TWO TICKETS TO BROADWAY(1951); BIG SKY, THE(1952); JACK AND THE BEANSTALK(1952); FAIR WIND TO JAVA(1953); MARSHAL'S DAUGHTER, THE(1953); JUBILEE TRAIL(1954); SLIGHTLY SCARLET(1956); HELL CANYON OUTLAWS(1957); GIANT FROM THE UNKNOWN(1958); ONCE UPON A HORSE(1958); MAGIC FOUNTAIN, THE(1961); SNOW WHITE AND THE THREE STOOGES(1961); BASHFUL ELEPHANT, THE(1962, Aust.); RIDE BEYOND VENGEANCE(1966)

Byron Baer
BRAIN THAT WOULDN'T DIE, THE(1959), spec eff

Dale Baer
BON VOYAGE, CHARLIE BROWN(AND DON'T COME BACK)***(1980), anim; ROBIN HOOD(1973), anim

Ed Baer
ROCKY II(1979), set d; SCAVENGER HUNT(1979), set d

Ellen Baer
GOLDEN EARRINGS(1947)

Hanania Baer
ECHOES(1983), ph
1984
BREAKIN'(1984), ph; BREAKIN' 2: ELECTRIC BOOGALOO(1984), ph; NIGHT PATROL(1984), ph; NINJA III-THE DOMINATION(1984), ph

Harry Baer
FOX AND HIS FRIENDS(1976, Ger.); JAIL BAIT(1977, Ger.); WHY DOES HERR R. RUN AMOK?(1977, Ger.); OUR HITLER, A FILM FROM GERMANY(1980, Ger.); VERONIKA VOSS(1982, Ger.); QUERELLE(1983, Ger./Fr.)
Misc. Talkies
MISTER SCARFACE(1977)

Jean Paul Baer
Misc. Silents
IN THE SPIDER'S WEB(1924)

Johanna Baer
SNOOPY, COME HOME(1972)

John Baer
ARIZONA MANHUNT(1951); INDIAN UPRISING(1951); SUPERMAN AND THE MOLE MEN(1951); ABOUT FACE(1952); BATTLE AT APACHE PASS, THE(1952); DOWN AMONG THE SHELTERING PALMS(1953); MISSISSIPPI GAMBLER, THE(1953); MIAMI STORY, THE(1954); RIDING SHOTGUN(1954); CITY OF SHADOWS(1955); WE'RE NO ANGELS(1955); HUK(1956); GUNS, GIRLS AND GANGSTERS(1958); NIGHT OF THE BLOOD BEAST(1958); TARAWA BEACHHEAD(1958); CAT BURGLAR, THE(1961); FEAR NO MORE(1961); CHAPMAN REPORT, THE(1962); LATE LIZ, THE(1971)
1984
WEEKEND PASS(1984), m
Misc. Talkies
BIKINI PARADISE(1967)

John W. Baer
ABOVE AND BEYOND(1953)

Kary Baer
LOLA(1982, Ger.)

Manny Baer
MARRIAGE BY CONTRACT(1928), m

Max Baer
PRIZEFIGHTER AND THE LADY, THE(1933); OVER SHE GOES(1937, Brit.); NAVY COMES THROUGH, THE(1942); BUCKSKIN FRONTIER(1943); LADIES' DAY(1943); AFRICA SCREAMS(1949); BRIDE FOR SALE(1949); RIDING HIGH(1950); SKIPALONG ROSENBLOOM(1951); HARDER THEY FALL, THE(1956); UTAH BLAINE(1957); ONCE UPON A HORSE(1958)

Max Baer, Jr.
TIME FOR KILLING, A(1967); MACON COUNTY LINE(1974), a, p, w; WILD McCULLOCHS, THE(1975), a, p,d&w; ODE TO BILLY JOE(1976), p, d; HOMETOWN U.S.A.(1979), d

Meredith Baer
SISTER-IN-LAW, THE(1975); CHICKEN CHRONICLES, THE(1977); COACH(1978); PRIVATE LESSONS(1981)
Misc. Talkies
AMERICAN RASPBERRY(1980)

Norman Baer
DESERTER, THE(1971 Ital./Yugo.), p

Parley Baer
COMMANCHE TERRITORY(1950); AIR CADET(1951); ELOPEMENT(1951); FROGMEN, THE(1951); PEOPLE WILL TALK(1951); DEADLINE–U.S.A.(1952); FEARLESS FAGAN(1952); RED SKIES OF MONTANA(1952); PICKUP ON SOUTH STREET(1953); VICKI(1953); D-DAY, THE SIXTH OF JUNE(1956); DRANGO(1957); YOUNG LIONS, THE(1958); FBI STORY, THE(1959); ADVENTURES OF HUCKLEBERRY FINN, THE(1960); CASH McCALL(1960); WAKE ME WHEN IT'S OVER(1960); FEVER IN THE BLOOD, A(1961); GYPSY(1962); SPIRAL ROAD, THE(1962); BEDTIME STORY(1964); BRASS BOTTLE, THE(1964); THOSE CALLOWAYS(1964); BUS RILEY'S BACK IN TOWN(1965); FLUFFY(1965); MARRIAGE ON THE ROCKS(1965); TWO ON A GUILLOTINE(1965); FOLLOW ME, BOYS!(1966); MONEY TRAP, THE(1966); UGLY DACHSHUND, THE(1966); ADVENTURES OF BULLWHIP GRIFFIN, THE(1967); COUNTERPOINT(1967); GNOME-MOBILE, THE(1967); DAY OF THE EVIL GUN(1968); WHERE WERE YOU WHEN THE LIGHTS WENT OUT?(1968); YOUNG BILLY YOUNG(1969); SKIN GAME(1971); LIKE A CROW ON A JUNE BUG(1972); AMAZING DOBERMANS, THE(1976); CARBON COPY(1981); WHITE DOG(1982); DOCTOR DETROIT(1983)
1984
CHATTANOOGA CHOO CHOO(1984)

Parley E. Baer
UNION STATION(1950)

Richard Baer
LIFE BEGINS AT 17(1958), w

Tim Baer
TIME MACHINE, THE(1960; Brit./U.S.), spec eff

Henry Baerlein
Silents
CHARMER, THE(1925), w

Jerry A. Baerwitz
VARAN THE UNBELIEVABLE(1962, U.S./Jap.), p&d; WILD HARVEST(1962), d

Sam Baerwitz
GAS HOUSE KIDS GO WEST(1947), p, w; GAS HOUSE KIDS IN HOLLYWOOD(1947), p; BUNGALOW 13(1948), p; I CHEATED THE LAW(1949), p, w; GREAT PLANE ROBBERY(1950), p, w

Fred Baes
MURDER IS NEWS(1939)

Edmundo Baez
BIG CUBE, THE(1969), w

Ernesto Baez
PUT UP OR SHUT UP(1968, Arg.)

Freddie Baez
HEROINA(1965)

Joan Baez
RENALDO AND CLARA(1978)

Eugenie Bafaloukos
ROCKERS(1980), cos

Theodoros Bafaloukos
ROCKERS(1980), d&w

Reggie Baff
MADE FOR EACH OTHER(1971)

Regina Baff
WHO IS HARRY KELLERMAN AND WHY IS HE SAYING THOSE TERRIBLE THINGS ABOUT ME?(1971); PAPER CHASE, THE(1973); GREAT GATSBY, THE(1974); ROAD MOVIE(1974); MONEY, THE(1975); BELOW THE BELT(1980)

Gino Baffa
CHICKEN CHRONICLES, THE(1977); FOXES(1980)

Al Baffert
WHAT PRICE CRIME?(1935); PARK AVENUE LOGGER(1937); GOLD RAIDERS, THE(1952); STORM RIDER, THE(1957); ESCAPE FROM RED ROCK(1958); SPACE MASTER X-7(1958)

Gamble Baffert
1984
REVENGE OF THE NERDS(1984)

James A. Baffico
ALL THE RIGHT MOVES(1983)

Francesco Bagarrini
EMBALMER, THE(1966, Ital.)

F. Bagaschvili
THEY WANTED PEACE(1940, USSR)

Spartak Bagashvili
SHADOWS OF FORGOTTEN ANCESTORS(1967, USSR)

Pam Bagby
SLENDER THREAD, THE(1965)

William Bagdad
SHE FREAK(1967); GIRL IN GOLD BOOTS(1968); HEAD(1968); ASTRO-ZOMBIES, THE(1969); DOLL SQUAD, THE(1973)

Cecile Bagdadi
FINAL EXAM(1981)

Carol Bagdasarian
STRAWBERRY STATEMENT, THE(1970); CHARGE OF THE MODEL-T'S(1979); OCTAGON, THE(1980)

Philip Bagenal
IF ...(1968, Brit.)

Vincent Bagetta
EMBRYO(1976)

Jim Bagg
CATALINA CAPER, THE(1967)

Harry Bagge
Silents
ADVENTUROUS YOUTH(1928, Brit.)

Neils Bagge
NIGHT FOR CRIME, A(1942)

Niels Bagge
FIRST COMES COURAGE(1943)

Inger Bagger
SCANDAL IN DENMARK(1970, Den.)

Lynn Baggett
MANPOWER(1941); D.O.A.(1950)

Lynne Baggett
AIR FORCE(1943); THANK YOUR LUCKY STARS(1943); ADVENTURES OF MARK TWAIN, THE(1944); MILDRED PIERCE(1945); JANIE GETS MARRIED(1946); NIGHT AND DAY(1946); ONE MORE TOMORROW(1946); TIME OF THEIR LIVES, THE(1946); FLAME AND THE ARROW, THE(1950); MOB, THE(1951)

Wendell Baggett
SKULLDUGGERY(1970)

Vincent Baggetta
TWO-MINUTE WARNING(1976); MAN WHO WASN'T THERE, THE(1983)

King Baggot
CZAR OF BRODWAY, THE(1930); ONCE A GENTLEMAN(1930); CHINATOWN SQUAD(1935); IT HAPPENED IN NEW YORK(1935); NEXT TIME WE LOVE(1936); CHEECH AND CHONG'S NEXT MOVIE(1980), ph; FAST-WALKING(1982), ph; SOME KIND OF HERO(1982), ph; DOCTOR DETROIT(1983), ph; SECOND THOUGHTS(1983), ph
1984
LAST STARFIGHTER, THE(1984), ph; OH GOD! YOU DEVIL(1984), ph; REVENGE OF THE NERDS(1984), ph
Silents
IVANHOE(1913); SUBURBAN, THE(1915); KILDARE OF STORM(1918); NOBODY'S FOOL(1921), d; KENTUCKY DERBY, THE(1922), d; KISSED(1922), d; LAVENDER BATH LADY, THE(1922), d; LOVE LETTER, THE(1923), d; TOWN SCANDAL, THE(1923), d; RAFFLES, THE AMATEUR CRACKSMAN(1925), d; TUMBLEWEEDS(1925), d; DOWN THE STRETCH(1927), d; NOTORIOUS LADY, THE(1927), d
Misc. Silents
IVANHOE(1913, Brit.); ABSINTHE(1914); MARBLE HEART, THE(1915); HALF A ROGUE(1916); MAN FROM NOWHERE, THE(1916); MAN WHO STAYED AT HOME, THE(1919); CHEATER, THE(1920); DWELLING PLACE OF LIGHT, THE(1920); FORBIDDEN THING, THE(1920); LIFE'S TWIST(1920); THIRTIETH PIECE OF SILVER, THE(1920); BUTTERFLY GIRL, THE(1921); CHEATED LOVE(1921), d; GIRL IN THE TAXI, THE(1921); LURING LIPS(1921), d; MOONLIGHT FOLLIES(1921); DANGEROUS GAME, A(1922), d; HUMAN HEARTS(1922); CROSSED WIRES(1923), d; DARLING OF NEW YORK, THE(1923), d; GOSSIP(1923), d; GAIETY GIRL, THE(1924), d; TORNADO, THE(1924), d; WHISPERED NAME, THE(1924), d; HOME MAKER, THE(1925), d; LOVEY MARY(1926), d; PERCH OF THE DEVIL(1927), d; HOUSE OF SCANDAL, THE(1928), d; ROMANCE OF A ROGUE(1928), d

King Baggott
SCAREHEADS(1931); SPORTING CHANCE(1931), w; SWEEPSTAKES(1931); FAME STREET(1932); HELLO TROUBLE(1932); DEATH KISS, THE(1933); ROMANCE IN THE RAIN(1934); FATHER BROWN, DETECTIVE(1935); MISSISSIPPI(1935); SHE GETS HER MAN(1935); SAN FRANCISCO(1936); EMPEROR'S CANDLESTICKS, THE(1937); COME LIVE WITH ME(1941); TISH(1942); HAND, THE(1981), ph

Luigi Baghetti
ALFREDO, ALFREDO(1973, Ital.)

Giovanni Baghino
GUNS OF THE BLACK WITCH(1961, Fr./Ital.); LOVE AND LARCENY(1963, Fr./Ital.)

Doug Bagier
DAUGHTER OF THE WEST(1949), ed

Douglas Bagier-

Douglas Bagier
WIFE OF MONTE CRISTO, THE(1946), ed; WHISPERING CITY(1947, Can.), ed; LOVABLE CHEAT, THE(1949), ed; KILL OR BE KILLED(1950), ed

Douglas W. Bagier
DEVIL BAT'S DAUGHTER, THE(1946), ed; PICKUP(1951), ed

Marino Bagiola
QUIET PLACE IN THE COUNTRY, A(1970, Ital./Fr.)

Douglas W. Bagler
ENEMY OF WOMEN(1944), ed; PRAIRIE, THE(1948), ed

Ben Bagley
CHAFED ELBOWS(1967)

Desmond Bagley
MACKINTOSH MAN, THE(1973, Brit.), w

Don Bagley
VISIT TO A SMALL PLANET(1960); STUDENT BODY, THE(1976), m
1984
SACRED GROUND(1984), m

Edward Bagley
Misc. Silents
TELL IT TO THE MARINES(1918)

Fuddle Bagley
DIRTYMOUTH(1970); TRICK BABY(1973); DARKTOWN STRUTTERS(1975); FREAKY FRIDAY(1976); J.D.'S REVENGE(1976); MONKEY HUSTLE, THE(1976)

Fuddly Bagley
Misc. Talkies
LINDA LOVELACE FOR PRESIDENT(1975)

Irene Bagley
DRUMS O' VOODOO(1934)

James Bagley
Silents
HOW MOLLY MADE GOOD(1915)

Sam Bagley
LIEUTENANT WORE SKIRTS, THE(1956)

Frank Bagnall
WARN THAT MAN(1943, Brit.)

Vernel Bagneris
FRENCH QUARTER(1978); PENNIES FROM HEAVEN(1981)

Gwen Bagni
CAPTAIN CHINA(1949), w; UNTAMED FRONTIER(1952), w; WITH SIX YOU GET EGGROLL(1968), w

John Bagni
HONEYMOON IN BALI(1939); ALOMA OF THE SOUTH SEAS(1941); NEW YORK TOWN(1941); BOMBAY CLIPPER(1942); MUG TOWN(1943); NORTH STAR, THE(1943); COBRA WOMAN(1944); MY BUDDY(1944); HELLDORADO(1946); PRE-TENDER, THE(1947); SENATOR WAS INDISCREET, THE(1947); CASBAH(1948); CAPTAIN CHINA(1949), a, w; FAR FRONTIER, THE(1949); UNTAMED FRON-TIER(1952), w; LAW AND ORDER(1953), w

Margherita Bagni
ETERNAL MELODIES(1948, Ital.); TOO BAD SHE'S BAD(1954, Ital.); UNFAITH-FULS, THE(1960, Ital.)

Owen Bagni
LAW AND ORDER(1953), w

Carlo Bagno
LOVE IN 4 DIMENSIONS(1965 Fr./Ital.); SHOOT LOUD, LOUDER... I DON'T UNDERSTAND(1966, Ital.); CLIMAX, THE(1967, Fr., Ital.)

Enid Bagnold
NATIONAL VELVET(1944), w; CHALK GARDEN, THE(1964, Brit.), w; INTERNA-TIONAL VELVET(1978, Brit.), p,d&w

Silvio Bagolini
ANGELO IN THE CROWD(1952, Ital.); CROSSED SWORDS(1954); VITELLONI(1956, Ital./Fr.); PRISONER OF THE IRON MASK(1962, Fr./Ital.); SULEIMAN THE CON-QUEROR(1963, Ital.); VARIETY LIGHTS(1965, Ital.)

Nellie Bagor
TEL AVIV TAXI(1957, Israel), ed

Aileen Bagot
Silents
MANCHESTER MAN, THE(1920, Brit.)

Jean Pierre Bagot
TENANT, THE(1976, Fr.)

Salvador Bagues
HELL SHIP MUTINY(1957)

Salvador Baguez
FIVE FINGERS(1952); IRON MISTRESS, THE(1952); SNOWS OF KILIMANJARO, THE(1952); JEOPARDY(1953); SECOND CHANCE(1953); TITANIC(1953); AMERICA-NO, THE(1955); RACERS, THE(1955); FIRST TEXAN, THE(1956); WETBACKS(1956); FROM HELL TO TEXAS(1958)

Clinton Bagwell
DOWN AMONG THE SHELTERING PALMS(1953)

Dodo Assad Bahador
DOCTOR ZHIVAGO(1965)

Homayoon Bahadoran
INVINCIBLE SIX, THE(1970, U.S./Iran)

Kip Bahadun
SEVENTH DAWN, THE(1964)

Lal Bahadur
NINE HOURS TO RAMA(1963, U.S./Brit.)

Shaym Bahadur
PAUL TEMPLE'S TRIUMPH(1951, Brit.); OUTPOST IN MALAYA(1952, Brit.)

Shayn Bahadur
YOU PAY YOUR MONEY(1957, Brit.)

Jose Bahamande
EYES OF A STRANGER(1980)

Jose Bahamonde
HOT STUFF(1979)

Houshang Bahariou
CYCLE, THE(1979, Iran), ph

Bahaya Tribe of Tanganyika
MOGAMBO(1953)

Ellen Bahl
TENDER SCOUNDREL(1967, Fr./Ital.); FAREWELL, FRIEND(1968, Fr./Ital.); MILKY WAY, THE(1969, Fr./Ital.); RIDER ON THE RAIN(1970, Fr./Ital.); DISCREET CHARM OF THE BOURGEOISIE, THE(1972, Fr.); THAT OBSCURE OBJECT OF DESIRE(1977, Fr./Span.)

Hansjoerg Bahl
BLACK SPIDER, THE(1983, Swit.)

Jean Reed Bahle
HARDCORE(1979)

Tom Bahler
MARY, MARY, BLOODY MARY(1975, U.S./Mex.), m

Roma Bahm
TALES OF THE UNCANNY(1932, Ger.)

Roma Bahn
CONFESS DR. CORDA(1960, Ger.)

Jonathan Bahnks
TIMERIDER(1983)

Blay Bahnsen
EFFECTS(1980)

Ralph Bahnsen
DUEL AT DIABLO(1966)

Gilbert Bahon
JUDGE AND THE ASSASSIN, THE(1979, Fr.)

Hermann Bahr
ROMANCE IN THE DARK(1938), w

Bruce Bahrenburg
1984
ONCE UPON A TIME IN AMERICA(1984)

Francesca Bahrle
BANK MESSENGER MYSTERY, THE(1936, Brit.); TWIN FACES(1937, Brit.); WHAT A MAN!(1937, Brit.); FLYING FIFTY-FIVE(1939, Brit.)

Ilse Bahrs
POSSESSION(1981, Fr./Ger.); SISTERS, OR THE BALANCE OF HAPPINESS(1982, Ger.)
1984
LOVE IN GERMANY, A(1984, Fr./Ger.)

Marie Bahruth
SWEET CHARITY(1969)

Benning Bahs
OPERATION LOVEBIRDS(1968, Den.), w, art d

Akhtari Bai
MUSIC ROOM, THE(1963, India)

Rama Bai
SUSAN AND GOD(1940); RAINS OF RANCHIPUR, THE(1955); D-DAY, THE SIXTH OF JUNE(1956)

Yolanda Baiano
DOUGHGIRLS, THE(1944)

Francisco Baiao
IN THE WHITE CITY(1983, Switz./Portugal); STATE OF THINGS, THE(1983)

Doon Baide
CREATURES THE WORLD FORGOT(1971, Brit.)

Georgi Baidukov
WINGS OF VICTORY(1941, USSR), w

Richmond Baier
GROOVE TUBE, THE(1974)

Sybille Baier
ALICE IN THE CITIES(1974, W. Ger.)

Ed Baierlein
ULTIMATE THRILL, THE(1974)

Marguerite Baierski
MELVIN AND HOWARD(1980)

Al Baietti
CHINA SYNDROME, THE(1979)

Harold Baigent
GALLIPOLI(1981, Aus.)

Princess Baigum
CHARGE OF THE LIGHT BRIGADE, THE(1936)

Robert Baikoff
GO WEST, YOUNG MAN(1936)

Ben Bail
Silents
ARE ALL MEN ALIKE?(1920), ph; HILLS OF MISSING MEN(1922), ph; KIS-SED(1922), ph; KING'S CREEK LAW(1923), ph; ACROSS THE DEADLINE(1925), ph

Charles Bail
LAST MOVIE, THE(1971), stunts; BLACK SAMSON(1974), d

Chuck Bail
GREEN BERETS, THE(1968); SAVAGE SEVEN, THE(1968); CYCLE SAVA-GES(1969), stunts; DEVIL'S 8, THE(1969), stunts; SCAVENGERS, THE(1969), stunts; GETTING STRAIGHT(1970), stunts; CLEOPATRA JONES AND THE CASINO OF GOLD(1975 U. S. Hong Kong), d; GUMBALL RALLY, THE(1976), p&d, w; STUNT MAN, THE(1980)

Richard Bail
WHEN A STRANGER CALLS(1979)

Bob Bailan
DEATH COLLECTOR(1976), ph

Dorothy Bailer
VOODOO MAN(1944); MAN FROM OKLAHOMA, THE(1945)

David Bailes
SLAUGHTER IN SAN FRANCISCO(1981), ph

Fred Bailes
RUN FOR COVER(1955)

Alvin E. Bailey
BREAKING AWAY(1979)

Angus Bailey
Misc. Talkies
BELOW THE HILL(1974), d

Anne Edward Bailey
BLOODY BROOD, THE(1959, Can.), w

Anthony Bailey
MAIN CHANCE, THE(1966, Brit.); DEADLY BEES,THE(1967, Brit.); CAPTAIN NEMO AND THE UNDERWATER CITY(1969, Brit.); OBLONG BOX, THE(1969, Brit.)

Barbara Bailey
REAR WINDOW(1954)

Bert Bailey
ON OUR SELECTION(1930, Aus.); GRANDAD RUDD(1935, Aus.), a, p; DAD AND DAVE COME TO TOWN(1938, Aus.)

Bill Bailey
CABIN IN THE SKY(1943); SON OF A BADMAN(1949); GUNFIRE(1950); THREE DESPERATE MEN(1951)

Bill Bailey
GROOVE TUBE, THE(1974); SUPERMAN(1978); SUPERMAN II(1980); OUT-LAND(1981)

Bob Bailey
JITTERBUGS(1943)

Buck Bailey
SATAN'S CRADLE(1949); OVER THE BORDER(1950)

Carmen Bailey
RUSTLER'S PARADISE(1935); DAUGHTER OF SHANGHAI(1937); CALIFORNIA FRONTIER(1938); DRIFTING WESTWARD(1939)

Caryl Bailey
MATING GAME, THE(1959)

Charles Bailey
BOILING POINT, THE(1932); GIRL OF THE NIGHT(1960), art d; MURDER, INC.(1960), set d; FOX, THE(1967), art d; REIVERS, THE(1969), art d; CROSS AND THE SWITCHBLADE, THE(1970), art d; OUT OF TOWNERS, THE(1970), art d; PEOPLE NEXT DOOR, THE(1970), prod d; SERPICO(1973), prod d; DOG DAY AFTER-NOON(1975), prod d; FRONT, THE(1976), art d; SATURDAY NIGHT FEVER(1977), prod d

Cheryl Bailey
MATING GAME, THE(1959)

Claude Bailey
UNHOLY QUEST, THE(1934, Brit.); UNPUBLISHED STORY(1942, Brit.); GENTLE SEX, THE(1943, Brit.); HUNDRED POUND WINDOW, THE(1943, Brit.); IT'S THAT MAN AGAIN(1943, Brit.); SAINT MEETS THE TIGER, THE(1943, Brit.); HE SNOOPS TO CONQUER(1944, Brit.); YELLOW CANARY, THE(1944, Brit.); CALENDAR, THE(1948, Brit.); HATTER'S CASTLE(1948, Brit.); ELIZABETH OF LADYMEAD(1949, Brit.)

Claudie Bailey
BEDELIA(1946, Brit.)

Cliff Bailey
BETWEEN MIDNIGHT AND DAWN(1950)

Consuelo Bailey
Silents
GANGSTERS OF NEW YORK, THE(1914)

Dan Bailey
Misc. Silents
SHEPHERD OF THE HILLS, THE(1920)

Dave Bailey
SUBTERRANEANS, THE(1960)

David Bailey
ONE MAN'S WAY(1964); PRINCESS AND THE MAGIC FROG, THE(1965); FOLLOW ME, BOYS!(1966); UP THE MACGREGORS(1967, Ital./Span.); CHANGE OF MIND(1969); WICKED, WICKED(1973)

Dick Bailey
BURNING CROSS, THE(1947); ROAD TO THE BIG HOUSE(1947)

Don Bailey
Silents
SHOULD A WOMAN TELL?(1920)
Misc. Silents
MONEY MADNESS(1917); MARRIED IN HASTE(1919)

Donna Bailey
Misc. Talkies
JOE'S BED-STUY BARBERSHOP: WE CUT HEADS(1983)

Doug Bailey
VAN NUYS BLVD.(1979)

Elizabeth Bailey
ONE FROM THE HEART(1982)

Ellen Bailey
WEEKEND WITH THE BABYSITTER(1970)

Frank Bailey
ULYSSES(1967, U.S./Brit.)

G.W. Bailey
1984
POLICE ACADEMY(1984); RUNAWAY(1984)

Gail Bailey
STALLION CANYON(1949)

George Bailey
WEDNESDAY'S LUCK(1936, Brit.); DON'T TAKE IT TO HEART(1944, Brit.)
Silents
OVERALLS(1916)

Gordon Bailey
SCOOP, THE(1934, Brit.); WELL DONE, HENRY(1936, Brit.)

Greg Bailey
1984
BIGGER SPLASH, A(1984), m

Harry Bailey
JUVENILE COURT(1938); YOU CAN'T TAKE IT WITH YOU(1938); GOOD GIRLS GO TO PARIS(1939); LET US LIVE(1939); ONLY ANGELS HAVE WINGS(1939); CONFES-SIONS OF BOSTON BLACKIE(1941); HONOLULU LU(1941); LADY EVE, THE(1941); RICHEST MAN IN TOWN(1941); HARVARD, HERE I COME(1942); GOVERNMENT GIRL(1943); THANK YOUR LUCKY STARS(1943)
Silents
EARLY TO WED(1926); BERTHA, THE SEWING MACHINE GIRL(1927); PRINCESS FROM HOBOKEN, THE(1927)

Hilda Bailey
GIRL IN DISTRESS(1941, Brit.)

Hillary Bailey
1984
PURPLE HEARTS(1984)

Horace Bailey
CHANGE OF MIND(1969)

J. Bailey
POCKET MONEY(1972)

Jack Bailey
HE WALKED BY NIGHT(1948); MRS. O'MALLEY AND MR. MALONE(1950); HOW TO SEDUCE A WOMAN(1974)

James Bailey
WILD GEESE, THE(1978, Brit.)

Jeff Bailey
BENGAZI(1955), w

Jim Bailey
1984
SURROGATE, THE(1984, Can.)
Misc. Talkies
VULTURES IN PARADISE(1984)

Joe Bailey
CATTLE QUEEN(1951); HOODLUM EMPIRE(1952); REDHEAD FROM WYOMING, THE(1953); PUSHOVER(1954); SOUTH PACIFIC(1958)

Joel Bailey
1984
BEVERLY HILLS COP(1984)

John Bailey
TILL THE END OF TIME(1946); IT HAPPENED IN SOHO(1948, Brit.); CELIA(1949, Brit.); MAN ON THE RUN(1949, Brit.); MEET SIMON CHERRY(1949, Brit.); CAIRO ROAD(1950, Brit.); CIRCLE OF DANGER(1951, Brit.); HIGH TREASON(1951, Brit.); FRANCHISE AFFAIR, THE(1952, Brit.); NIGHT WON'T TALK, THE(1952, Brit.); ASSASSIN, THE(1953, Brit.); SO LITTLE TIME(1953, Brit.); HOSTAGE, THE(1956, Brit.); NEVER LET GO(1960, Brit.); OPERATION AMSTERDAM(1960, Brit.); MALA-GA(1962, Brit.); RASPUTIN–THE MAD MONK(1966, Brit.); FOURTEEN, THE(1973, Brit.); LEGACY(1976), ph; MAFU CAGE, THE(1978), ph; BOULEVARD NIGHTS(1979), ph; AMERICAN GIGOLO(1980), ph; ORDINARY PEOPLE(1980), ph; CONTINENTAL DIVIDE(1981), ph; HONKY TONK FREEWAY(1981), ph; CAT PEO-PLE(1982), ph; THAT CHAMPIONSHIP SEASON(1982), ph; BIG CHILL, THE(1983), ph; WITHOUT A TRACE(1983), ph
1984
POPE OF GREENWICH VILLAGE, THE(1984), ph; RACING WITH THE MOON(1984), ph; RIDDLE OF THE SANDS, THE(1984, Brit.), w

Julie Bailey
URBAN COWBOY(1980)

Leonard Bailey
TARZAN, THE APE MAN(1981)

Leslie Bailey
GREAT GILBERT AND SULLIVAN, THE(1953, Brit.), w

Lynn Bailey
HAVING WONDERFUL TIME(1938)

Mark Bailey
MARRIAGE-GO-ROUND, THE(1960)

Michael Bailey
PURPLE HAZE(1982)

Mickey Bailey
SEA GYPSIES, THE(1978), animal t

"Miss" Baby Bailey
GARBAGE MAN, THE(1963)

Oliver Bailey
Misc. Silents
BLIND LOVE, THE(1920), d

Oliver D. Bailey
Silents
BRANDED WOMAN, THE(1920), w; IN WALKED MARY(1920), w
Misc. Silents
WHIRL OF LIFE, THE(1915), d

Patrick Bailey
1984
DOOR TO DOOR(1984), d

Paul Bailey
EDGE OF ETERNITY(1959); WHEN THE GIRLS TAKE OVER(1962); KARATE KILLERS, THE(1967)

Pearl Bailey
VARIETY GIRL(1947); ISN'T IT ROMANTIC?(1948); CARMEN JONES(1954); THAT CERTAIN FEELING(1956); ST. LOUIS BLUES(1958); PORGY AND BESS(1959); ALL THE FINE YOUNG CANNIBALS(1960); LANDLORD, THE(1970); NORMAN...IS THAT YOU?(1976); FOX AND THE HOUND, THE(1981)
Misc. Talkies
LAST GENERATION, THE(1971)

Polly Bailey
THEY WON'T BELIEVE ME(1947); THIN MAN, THE(1934); ENEMY AGENT(1940); I TAKE THIS WOMAN(1940); GAY FALCON, THE(1941); NAZI AGENT(1942); THEY ALL KISSED THE BRIDE(1942); WE WERE DANCING(1942); YOUNGEST PROFES-SION, THE(1943); NONE BUT THE LONELY HEART(1944); EASY TO LOOK AT(1945); NOB HILL(1945); LOCKET, THE(1946); EASY COME, EASY GO(1947); SEA OF GRASS, THE(1947); DATE WITH JUDY, A(1948); RETURN OF THE BADMEN(1948); LADY GAMBLES, THE(1949); STRATTON STORY, THE(1949); TELL IT TO THE JUDGE(1949); HARVEY(1950); MISTER 880(1950)

Ray Bailey
ISLAND OF DOOMED MEN(1940); MYSTERY OF MARIE ROGET, THE(1942); GIRL FROM JONES BEACH, THE(1949)

Raymond Bailey
ADVENTURES OF JANE ARDEN(1939); FLIGHT AT MIDNIGHT(1939); HELL'S KITCHEN(1939); I STOLE A MILLION(1939); MADE FOR EACH OTHER(1939); ROARING TWENTIES, THE(1939); SECRET SERVICE OF THE AIR(1939); S.O.S. TIDAL WAVE(1939); I LOVE YOU AGAIN(1940); MALE ANIMAL, THE(1942); GIRL IN THE RED VELVET SWING, THE(1955); PICNIC(1955); RETURN OF JACK SLADE, THE(1955); TARANTULA(1955); CONGO CROSSING(1956); GIRL HE LEFT BEHIND, THE(1956); GREAT AMERICAN PASTIME, THE(1956); I'VE LIVED BEFORE(1956); OUTSIDE THE LAW(1956); BAND OF ANGELS(1957); INCREDIBLE SHRINKING MAN, THE(1957); DARBY'S RANGERS(1958); I WANT TO LIVE!(1958); KING

CREOLE(1958); LAFAYETTE ESCADRILLE(1958); LINEUP, THE(1958); NO TIME FOR SERGEANTS(1958); SPACE CHILDREN, THE(1958); UNDERWATER WARRIOR(1958); VERTIGO(1958); AL CAPONE(1959); FROM THE TERRACE(1960); GALLANT HOURS, THE(1960); WAKE ME WHEN IT'S OVER(1960); ABSENT-MINDED PROFESSOR, THE(1961); FIVE WEEKS IN A BALLOON(1962); HERBIE RIDES AGAIN(1974)

Rex Bailey
FANGS OF THE ARCTIC(1953), d; MEXICAN MANHUNT(1953), d; NORTHERN PATROL(1953), d

Richard Bailey
CITY OF SILENT MEN(1942); RIDERS OF THE NORTHWEST MOUNTED(1943); THAT'S MY BABY(1944); WHAT NEXT, CORPORAL HARGROVE?(1945); DESERT HORSEMAN, THE(1946); NIGHT IN PARADISE, A(1946); YOUNG WIDOW(1946); FOREVER AMBER(1947); LIGHTHOUSE(1947); MARAUDERS, THE(1947); AMBUSH(1950); OUTCAST OF BLACK MESA(1950); TRAIN, THE(1965, Fr./Ital./U.S.); WIN, PLACE, OR STEAL(1975), d, w

Robert B. Bailey
UNDERWATER!(1955), w

Robert Bailey
DANCING MASTERS, THE(1943); EVE OF ST. MARK, THE(1944); LADIES OF WASHINGTON(1944); SUNDAY DINNER FOR A SOLDIER(1944); TAMPICO(1944); WING AND A PRAYER(1944); NO ESCAPE(1953); LINEUP, THE(1958); YOR, THE HUNTER FROM THE FUTURE(1983, Ital.), w

Robin Bailey
SCHOOL FOR SECRETS(1946, Brit.); PRIVATE ANGELO(1949, Brit.); PORTRAIT OF CLARE(1951, Brit.); GLORY AT SEA(1952, Brit.); HIS EXCELLENCY(1952, Brit.); FOLLY TO BE WISE(1953); SAILOR OF THE KING(1953, Brit.); FOR BETTER FOR WORSE(1954, Brit.); JUST MY LUCK(1957, Brit.); ANOTHER TIME, ANOTHER PLACE(1958); DIPLOMATIC CORPSE, THE(1958, Brit.); HELL DRIVERS(1958, Brit.); MOUSE ON THE MOON, THE(1963, Brit.); HAVING A WILD WEEKEND(1965, Brit.); SPY WITH A COLD NOSE, THE(1966, Brit.); WHISPERERS, THE(1967, Brit.); DANGER ROUTE(1968, Brit.); SEE NO EVIL(1971, Brit.)
Misc. Talkies
COMMUTER HUSBANDS(1974); SCREAMTIME(1983, Brit.)

Roy Bailey
MISSISSIPPI(1935)

Sandra K. Bailey
1984
HAMBONE AND HILLIE(1984), w

Shane Bailey
1984
RIVER, THE(1984)

Sheila Bailey
NASHVILLE(1975)

Sherwood Bailey
BIG STAMPEDE, THE(1932); MYSTERIOUS RIDER, THE(1933); LOUDSPEAKER, THE(1934); PADDY O'DAY(1935); DEVIL IS A SISSY, THE(1936); TOO MANY PARENTS(1936); GIRL LOVES BOY(1937); QUALITY STREET(1937); SHALL WE DANCE(1937); QUICK MONEY(1938); KING OF THE UNDERWORLD(1939)

Trevor Bailey
WEDDING NIGHT(1970, Ireland)

Wanda Bailey
ARNOLD(1973)

William Bailey
AVIATOR, THE(1929); BACK PAY(1930); TODAY(1930); GEORGE WHITE'S SCANDALS(1934); CHARLIE CHAN'S SECRET(1936); NATIONAL VELVET(1944); DESPERATE(1947); ACROSS THE RIO GRANDE(1949); BRAND OF FEAR(1949); GAL WHO TOOK THE WEST, THE(1949); STRATTON STORY, THE(1949); FATHER OF THE BRIDE(1950); WHERE DANGER LIVES(1950); DOUBLE DYNAMITE(1951); I WAS A COMMUNIST FOR THE F.B.I.(1951); CARRIE(1952); CLASH BY NIGHT(1952); TALL MAN RIDING(1955)
Silents
SUBURBAN, THE(1915); LEAP TO FAME(1918); ISLE OF CONQUEST(1919); IS MONEY EVERYTHING?(1923); BIG PAL(1925)
Misc. Silents
BANKER'S DAUGHTER, THE(1914); CONSCIENCE(1915); WHEN IT STRIKES HOME(1915); MILLION A MINUTE, A(1916); WAR BRIDES(1916); INEVITABLE, THE(1917); ON DANGEROUS GROUND(1917); PRIDE OF NEW YORK, THE(1917); BLIND ADVENTURE, THE(1918); BONNIE ANNIE LAURIE(1918); I'LL SAY SO(1918); CYCLONE RIDER, THE(1924); DESERT HAWK, THE(1924); UNINVITED GUEST, THE(1924); FLYIN' COWBOY, THE(1928); LONE PATROL, THE(1928)

William N. Bailey
MANHATTAN MELODRAMA(1934); DOUBLE LIFE, A(1947); COURTIN' TROUBLE(1948); CATTLE QUEEN(1951); GUNFIGHT AT THE O.K. CORRAL(1957)
Silents
AGAINST ALL ODDS(1924); QUEEN O' DIAMONDS(1926)
Misc. Silents
HIGH SCHOOL HERO(1927); BURNING BRIDGES(1928)

William Norton Bailey
CENTRAL PARK(1932); MIDNIGHT PATROL, THE(1932); LONE AVENGER, THE(1933); CHANGE OF HEART(1934); LIVING ON VELVET(1935); MURDER MAN(1935); ONE HOUR LATE(1935); STRAIGHT FROM THE HEART(1935); THUNDER MOUNTAIN(1935); MURDER WITH PICTURES(1936); ARSENE LUPIN RETURNS(1938); RHYTHM OF THE SADDLE(1938); MIRACLES FOR SALE(1939); NAZI AGENT(1942); CODE OF THE SADDLE(1947); EGG AND I, THE(1947); ROBIN OF TEXAS(1947); CAMPUS SLEUTH(1948); FALSE PARADISE(1948); FAMILY HONEYMOON(1948); MUSIC MAN(1948); SILVER TRAILS(1948); TRAIL'S END(1949); WEST OF EL DORADO(1949); LIGHTNING GUNS(1950); AL JENNINGS OF OKLAHOMA(1951)
Misc. Talkies
HIT OF THE SNOW(1928); FIGHTING FOR JUSTICE(1932)
Silents
DESERT FLOWER, THE(1925); LAZYBONES(1925); RANSON'S FOLLY(1926); MAN IN THE ROUGH(1928); WAY OF THE STRONG, THE(1928)
Misc. Silents
FLAMING FORTIES, THE(1924); GOLD HEELS(1924); BUSTIN' THRU(1925); FIGHTING YOUTH(1925); STOLEN RANCH(1926)

Charles Waldo Bailey II
SEVEN DAYS IN MAY(1964), w

Peter Bailey-Britton
1984
WEEKEND PASS(1984)

Bob Bailin
GROOVE TUBE, THE(1974), ph; SHOOT IT: BLACK, SHOOT IT: BLUE(1974), ph; STUNTS(1977), ph

Jacob Bailin
REDS(1981)

Denise Baillargeon
LOST AND FOUND(1979)

Suzie Baillargeon
KAMOURASKA(1973, Can./Fr.)

Auguste Bailley
KISS OF FIRE, THE(1940, Fr.), w

David Baillie
HENRY VIII AND HIS SIX WIVES(1972, Brit.)

Elaine Baillie
CONFESSIONS OF A WINDOW CLEANER(1974, Brit.)

Maria Baillie
OUTPOST IN MALAYA(1952, Brit.)

Marianne Baillieu
1984
MAN OF FLOWERS(1984, Aus.)

Alfred Baillou
STEPPENWOLF(1974)

Auguste Bailly
FLAME AND THE FLESH(1954), w

Denise Bailly
LE BEAU MARIAGE(1982, Fr.)

Roland Bailly
LES MAINS SALES(1954, Fr.)

Hugh Baily
MUTATIONS, THE(1974, Brit.)

Rory Baily
Misc. Talkies
JOHNSTOWN MONSTER, THE(1971)

Gary L. Baim
ICE CASTLES(1978), w

Harold Baim
NIGHT COMES TOO SOON(1948, Brit.), p; COOL MIKADO, THE(1963, Brit.), p

O.K. Baime
FLY NOW, PAY LATER(1969)

Beverly Bain
DAY OF THE NIGHTMARE(1965)

Bill Bain
WHAT BECAME OF JACK AND JILL?(1972, Brit.), d

Conrad Bain
COOGAN'S BLUFF(1968); LOVELY WAY TO DIE, A(1968); MADIGAN(1968); STAR!(1968); LAST SUMMER(1969); I NEVER SANG FOR MY FATHER(1970); ANDERSON TAPES, THE(1971); BANANAS(1971); JUMP(1971); WHO KILLED MARY WHAT'SER NAME?(1971); FAN'S NOTES, A(1972, Can.); UP THE SANDBOX(1972); C.H.O.M.P.S.(1979)
Misc. Talkies
PLEASURE DOING BUSINESS, A(1979)

Donald Bain
PROMISE, THE(1969, Brit.)

Fred Bain
OVERLAND BOUND(1929), ed; BAR L RANCH(1930), ed; PHANTOM OF THE DESERT(1930), ed; RIDIN' LAW(1930), ed; CYCLONE KID(1931), ed; HEADIN' FOR TROUBLE(1931), ed; LAW OF THE RIO GRANDE(1931), ed; WESTWARD BOUND(1931), ed; FIGHTING GENTLEMAN, THE(1932), ed; FORTY-NINERS, THE(1932), ed; GAMBLING SEX(1932), ph; HUMAN TARGETS(1932), ed; MURDER AT DAWN(1932), ed; SAVAGE GIRL, THE(1932), ed; SCARLET BRAND(1932), ed; DEADWOOD PASS(1933), ed; HER FORGOTTEN PAST(1933), ed; PENAL CODE, THE(1933), ed; SECRET SINNERS(1933), ed; WAR OF THE RANGE(1933), ed; WHEN A MAN RIDES ALONE(1933), ed; BADGE OF HONOR(1934), ed; FIGHTING HERO(1934), ed; FIGHTING ROOKIE, THE(1934), ed; HOUSE OF DANGER(1934), ed; LOVE PAST THIRTY(1934), ed; MARRIAGE ON APPROVAL(1934), ed; ON PROBATION(1935), ed; FAST BULLETS(1936), ed; MILLIONAIRE KID(1936), ed; NIGHT CARGO(1936), ed; SONG OF THE GRINGO(1936), ed; PINTO RUSTLERS(1937), ed; RIDING ON(1937), ed; TROUBLE IN TEXAS(1937), ed; SKULL AND CROWN(1938), ed; STARLIGHT OVER TEXAS(1938), ed; WHERE THE BUFFALO ROAM(1938), ed; MAN FROM TEXAS, THE(1939), ed; MESQUITE BUCKAROO(1939), ed; RIDERS OF THE FRONTIER(1939), ed; ROLL, WAGONS, ROLL(1939), ed; ROLLIN' WESTWARD(1939), ed; SMOKY TRAILS(1939), ed; SONG OF THE BUCKAROO(1939), ed; SUNDOWN ON THE PRAIRIE(1939), ed; PHANTOM RANCHER(1940), ed; RAINBOW OVER THE RANGE(1940), ed; WESTBOUND STAGE(1940), ed; DRIFTIN' KID, THE(1941), ed; DYNAMITE CANYON(1941), ed; GENTLEMAN FROM DIXIE(1941), ed; PIONEERS, THE(1941), ed; RIDING THE SUNSET TRAIL(1941), ed; RIOT SQUAD(1941), ed; ROLLIN' HOME TO TEXAS(1941), ed; SILVER STALLION(1941), ed; WANDERERS OF THE WEST(1941), ed; GALLANT LADY(1942), ed; KING OF THE STALLIONS(1942), ed; LONE STAR LAW MEN(1942), ed; NIGHT FOR CRIME, A(1942), ed; PANTHER'S CLAW, THE(1942), ed; PRISON GIRL(1942), ed; WESTERN MAIL(1942), ed; YANKS ARE COMING, THE(1942), ed; BLAZING GUNS(1943), ed; LAW RIDES AGAIN, THE(1943), ed; MAN OF COURAGE(1943), ed; SCREAM IN THE NIGHT(1943), ed; WILD HORSE STAMPEDE(1943), ed; ROGUES GALLERY(1945), ed; WHITE STALLION(1947), ed
Silents
PHANTOM OF THE NORTH(1929), ed
Misc. Silents
THUNDERING THROUGH(1925), d; RAMBLIN' GALOOT, THE(1926), d

Frederick Bain
MYSTERY OF THE HOODED HORSEMEN, THE(1937), ed; TEX RIDES WITH THE BOY SCOUTS(1937), ed; FRONTIER TOWN(1938), ed

Gertrude Bain
Silents
PEEP BEHIND THE SCENES, A(1918, Brit.)

Imogen Bain
1984
SCRUBBERS(1984, Brit.)
Michael Bain
NEON PALACE, THE(1970, Can.), art d
Miranda Bain
1984
STRIKEBOUND(1984, Aus.), p
Robert Bain
SUMMER LOVE(1958)
Ron Bain
EXPERIENCE PREFERRED... BUT NOT ESSENTIAL(1983, Brit.)
Sherry Bain
HARD RIDE, THE(1971); WILD RIDERS(1971); YOUR THREE MINUTES ARE UP(1973); PIPE DREAMS(1976); OPENING NIGHT(1977); POCO...LITTLE DOG LOST(1977)
Misc. Talkies
CALLIOPE(1971); POSSE FROM HEAVEN(1975)
Phyllis Bainbride
Misc. Silents
COVERED WAGON TRAILS(1930)
Beryl Bainbridge
SWEET WILLIAM(1980, Brit.), w
Hazel Bainbridge
FAMILY WAY, THE(1966, Brit.); TWISTED NERVE(1969, Brit.)
Phyllis Bainbridge
COVERED WAGON TRAILS(1930)
Misc. Silents
O'MALLEY RIDES ALONE(1930)
Rolinda Bainbridge
Silents
ONE OF OUR GIRLS(1914)
Sherman Bainbridge
Misc. Silents
HEART OF TARA, THE(1916)
W. H. Bainbridge
Silents
BROADWAY SCANDAL(1918); IN FOLLY'S TRAIL(1920)
W.H. Bainbridge
Silents
KAISER, BEAST OF BERLIN, THE(1918)
Misc. Silents
DOOR BETWEEN, THE(1917); HANDS DOWN(1918); HUNGRY EYES(1918); SEEING IT THROUGH(1920)
William Bainbridge
MUTINY ON THE BOUNTY(1935)
Silents
FALSE FACES(1919)
Misc. Silents
GOD'S COUNTRY AND THE WOMAN(1916); BONNIE MAY(1920)
William Herbert Bainbridge
Misc. Silents
DESIRE OF THE MOTH, THE(1917)
Babette Baine
LEATHER SAINT, THE(1956)
Enid Baine
SCANDAL INCORPORATED(1956); SCARLET HOUR, THE(1956)
Fred Baine
FOREIGN AGENT(1942), ed
Hollis Baine
BUFFALO BILL RIDES AGAIN(1947)
John Baines
DEAD OF NIGHT(1946, Brit.), w; COLONEL BOGEY(1948, Brit.), w; BLUE LAGOON, THE(1949, Brit.), w; FOUR AGAINST FATE(1952, Brit.), w; HOLIDAY WEEK(1952, Brit.), w; PRIVATE INFORMATION(1952, Brit.), w; WEDDING OF LILLI MARLENE, THE(1953, Brit.), w; SIMBA(1955, Brit.), w; BEASTS OF MARSEILLES, THE(1959, Brit.), w; BIG MONEY, THE(1962, Brit.), w; HANDS OF ORLAC, THE(1964, Brit./Fr.), w
John V. Baines
I'LL GET YOU(1953, Brit.), w
Beulah Bains
Silents
CHARM SCHOOL, THE(1921); KID, THE(1921)
Fay Bainter
THIS SIDE OF HEAVEN(1934); MAKE WAY FOR TOMORROW(1937); QUALITY STREET(1937); SOLDIER AND THE LADY, THE(1937); ARKANSAS TRAVELER, THE(1938); JEZEBEL(1938); MOTHER CAREY'S CHICKENS(1938); SHINING HOUR, THE(1938); WHITE BANNERS(1938); DAUGHTERS COURAGEOUS(1939); LADY AND THE MOB, THE(1939); OUR NEIGHBORS–THE CARTERS(1939); YES, MY DARLING DAUGHTER(1939); BILL OF DIVORCEMENT(1940); MARYLAND(1940); OUR TOWN(1940); YOUNG TOM EDISON(1940); BABES ON BROADWAY(1941); JOURNEY FOR MARGARET(1942); MRS. WIGGS OF THE CABBAGE PATCH(1942); WAR AGAINST MRS. HADLEY, THE(1942); WOMAN OF THE YEAR(1942); CRY HAVOC(1943); HEAVENLY BODY, THE(1943); HUMAN COMEDY, THE(1943); PRESENTING LILY MARS(1943); SALUTE TO THE MARINES(1943); DARK WATERS(1944); 3 IS A FAMILY(1944); STATE FAIR(1945); KID FROM BROOKLYN, THE(1946); VIRGINIAN, THE(1946); DEEP VALLEY(1947); SECRET LIFE OF WALTER MITTY, THE(1947); GIVE MY REGARDS TO BROADWAY(1948); JUNE BRIDE(1948); CLOSE TO MY HEART(1951); PRESIDENT'S LADY, THE(1953); CHILDREN'S HOUR, THE(1961)
Jimmy Baio
BAD NEWS BEARS IN BREAKING TRAINING, THE(1977)
Scott Baio
BUGSY MALONE(1976, Brit.); SKATETOWN, U.S.A.(1979); FOXES(1980); ZAPPED!(1982)
Alan Bair
TWO LIVING, ONE DEAD(1964, Brit./Swed.)

Alston Bair
COME SPY WITH ME(1967)
Dave Bair
GUN CRAZY(1949)
David Bair
RECKLESS MOMENTS, THE(1949); HAPPY YEARS, THE(1950); ACCUSED OF MURDER(1956)
Tom Bair
LOCAL COLOR(1978)
Anthony Baird
HANGMAN WAITS, THE(1947, Brit.); NIGHT COMES TOO SOON(1948, Brit.); RELUCTANT HEROES(1951, Brit.); OFFBEAT(1961, Brit.); SWINGIN' MAIDEN, THE(1963, Brit.); CARRY ON SPYING(1964, Brit.); IPCRESS FILE, THE(1965, Brit.); CHRISTMAS TREE, THE(1966, Brit.)
Antony Baird
DEAD OF NIGHT(1946, Brit.); DEVIL DOLL(1964, Brit.)
Bill Baird
SOUND OF MUSIC, THE(1965), puppeteer
Brad Baird
DEAD MEN DON'T WEAR PLAID(1982)
Cora Baird
SOUND OF MUSIC, THE(1965), puppeteer
Edward Baird
SCHOOL FOR DANGER(1947, Brit.), a, w
Edwin Baird
Silents
CITY OF PURPLE DREAMS, THE(1918), w
Harry Baird
KID FOR TWO FARTHINGS, A(1956, Brit.); SAPPHIRE(1959, Brit.); KILLERS OF KILIMANJARO(1960, Brit.); TARZAN THE MAGNIFICENT(1960, Brit.); FLAME IN THE STREETS(1961, Brit.); MARK, THE(1961, Brit.); OFFBEAT(1961, Brit.); ROAD TO HONG KONG, THE(1962, U.S./Brit.); SMALL WORLD OF SAMMY LEE, THE(1963, Brit.); STATION SIX-SAHARA(1964, Brit./Ger.); HE WHO RIDES A TIGER(1966, Brit.); TRAITOR'S GATE(1966, Brit./Ger.); WHISPERERS, THE(1967, Brit.); STORY OF A THREE DAY PASS, THE(1968, Fr.); CASTLE KEEP(1969); ITALIAN JOB, THE(1969, Brit.); OBLONG BOX, THE(1969, Brit.); 1,000 CONVICTS AND A WOMAN zero(1971, Brit.); THOSE DIRTY DOGS(1974, U.S./Ital./Span.); COUNT OF MONTE CRISTO(1976, Brit.)
Misc. Talkies
TOUCHABLES, THE(1968, Brit.)
Hugh Baird
Silents
AMERICA(1924)
Jeanne Baird
D.I., THE(1957); ANDY HARDY COMES HOME(1958); GET OUTTA TOWN(1960); BLACK SPURS(1965); GAY DECEIVERS, THE(1969)
Jim Baird
KING OF THE ROARING TWENTIES–THE STORY OF ARNOLD ROTHSTEIN(1961); OPERATION EICHMANN(1961)
Jimmie Baird
RETURN OF DRACULA, THE(1958)
Jimmy Baird
THERE'S NO BUSINESS LIKE SHOW BUSINESS(1954); REBEL WITHOUT A CAUSE(1955); SEVEN LITTLE FOYS, THE(1955); BLACK ORCHID(1959); DOG'S BEST FRIEND, A(1960)
John Baird
KING OF THE NEWSBOYS(1938)
Leah Baird
JUNGLE BRIDE(1933), w; BULLETS FOR O'HARA(1941); MANPOWER(1941); BUSSES ROAR(1942); DANGEROUSLY THEY LIVE(1942); KING'S ROW(1942); LADY GANGSTER(1942); SECRET ENEMIES(1942); AIR FORCE(1943); THANK YOUR LUCKY STARS(1943); THIS IS THE ARMY(1943); WATCH ON THE RHINE(1943); LAST RIDE, THE(1944); MAKE YOUR OWN BED(1944); MILDRED PIERCE(1945); PILLOW TO POST(1945); MY REPUTATION(1946); SHADOW OF A WOMAN(1946)
Silents
IVANHOE(1913); NEPTUNE'S DAUGHTER(1914); LIGHTS OF NEW YORK, THE(1916); ONE LAW FOR BOTH(1917); WHEN THE DEVIL DRIVES(1922), a, w; IS DIVORCE A FAILURE?(1923), a, w; MIRACLE MAKERS, THE(1923), a, w; STOLEN PLEASURES(1927), w
Misc. Silents
IVANHOE(1913, Brit.); ABSINTHE(1914); RETURN OF MAURICE DONNELLY, THE(1915); PEOPLE VS. JOHN DOE, THE(1916); DEVIL'S PAY DAY, THE(1917); FRINGE OF SOCIETY, THE(1918); LIFE OR HONOR?(1918); MORAL SUICIDE(1918); AS A MAN THINKS(1919); ECHO OF YOUTH, THE(1919); VOLCANO(1919); CAPITOL, THE(1920); CYNTHIA-OF-THE-MINUTE(1920); BRIDE'S CONFESSION, THE(1921); HEART LINE, THE(1921); DON'T DOUBT YOUR WIFE(1922); WHEN HUSBANDS DECEIVE(1922); DESTROYING ANGEL, THE(1923); LAW DEMANDS, THE(1924); RADIO FLYER, THE(1924); UNNAMED WOMAN, THE(1925)
Lynn Baird
TAKE DOWN(1979)
Margaret Baird
COUNSEL'S OPINION(1933, Brit.)
Marie Terese Baird
CIRCLE OF TWO(1980, Can.), w
Mary Anne Baird
SECRET LIFE OF WALTER MITTY, THE(1947)
Michael Baird
TOP OF THE WORLD(1955), p; DAKOTA INCIDENT(1956), p
Pamela Baird
REMARKABLE MR. PENNYPACKER, THE(1959)
Paula Baird
RESTLESS ONES, THE(1965)
Philip Baird
ENEMY FROM SPACE(1957, Brit.); FIRE DOWN BELOW(1957, U.S./Brit.); VIOLENT STRANGER(1957, Brit.)
Phillip Baird
TWELVE TO THE MOON(1960); LOVE IN A GOLDFISH BOWL(1961); NIGHTMARE IN WAX(1969); GAME FOR VULTURES, A(1980, Brit.), w

Robert Baird
SEVEN(1979), w
Roy Baird
IF ...(1968, Brit.), p; HENRY VIII AND HIS SIX WIVES(1972, Brit.), p; MAH-LER(1974, Brit.), p; LISZTOMANIA(1975, Brit.), p; QUADROPHENIA(1979, Brit.), p; MC VICAR(1982, Brit.), p
Sharon Baird
BLOODHOUNDS OF BROADWAY(1952); PUFNSTUF(1970)
Stewart Baird
Silents
MOTH AND THE FLAME, THE(1915)
Misc. Silents
RUNAWAY WIFE, THE(1915)
Stuart Baird
LISZTOMANIA(1975, Brit.), ed; TOMMY(1975, Brit.), ed; OMEN, THE(1976), ed; VALENTINO(1977, Brit.), ed; SUPERMAN(1978), ed; OUTLAND(1981), ed; FIVE DAYS ONE SUMMER(1982), ed; BEYOND THE LIMIT(1983), ed
Silents
INCORRIGIBLE DUKANE, THE(1915)
Tadeusz Baird
LOTNA(1966, Pol.), m; PASSENGER, THE(1970, Pol.), m
Teddy Baird
FIVE ANGLES ON MURDER(1950, Brit.), p; BROWNING VERSION, THE(1951, Brit.), p; IMPORTANCE OF BEING EARNEST, THE(1952, Brit.), p; FAST AND LOOSE(1954, Brit.), p; SIMON AND LAURA(1956, Brit.), p; DON'T PANIC CHAPS!(1959, Brit.), p; TWO LIVING, ONE DEAD(1964, Brit./Swed.), p
Thomas Baird
MIDDLE AGE CRAZY(1980, Can.)
Wing Comdr. Edward Baird
SCHOOL FOR DANGER(1947, Brit.), d
Tom Baird-Ferguson
SCOTCH ON THE ROCKS(1954, Brit.)
Colm Bairead
POITIN(1979, Irish), w
William A. Bairn
BARON BLOOD(1972, Ital.), w
Bruce Bairnsfather
OLD BILL AND SON(1940, Brit.), w
Silents
OLD BILL THROUGH THE AGES(1924, Brit.), a, w; BETTER 'OLE, THE(1926), w
Bob Baisa
1984
ALLEY CAT(1984)
Michael Baish
COAL MINER'S DAUGHTER(1980)
Chieko Baisho
SAMURAI FROM NOWHERE(1964, Jap.); TOPSY-TURVY JOURNEY(1970, Jap.); TORA-SAN PART 2(1970, Jap.); YOSAKOI JOURNEY(1970, Jap.)
Mitsuko Baisho
DUEL AT EZO(1970, Jap.); TENCHU!(1970, Jap.); VENGEANCE IS MINE(1980, Jap.)
1984
BALLAD OF NARAYAMA, THE(1984, Jap.)
Angelo Baistrocchi
VAMPIRE AND THE BALLERINA, THE(1962, Ital.), ph
George Baizley
TWO GENTLEMEN SHARING(1969, Brit.)
Anna Baj
THIRTEEN FRIGHTENED GIRLS(1963)
Maria Bajcsay
FORBIDDEN RELATIONS(1983, Hung.)
Don Bajema
1984
SIGNAL 7(1984)
Ramona Bajema
1984
BIRDY(1984)
Nancy Bajer
VAGABOND KING, THE(1956)
Rados Bajic
DAY THAT SHOOK THE WORLD, THE(1977, Yugo./Czech.)
A.J. Bajunas
WARRIORS, THE(1979)
Henryk Bak
EROICA(1966, Pol.); GOLEM(1980, Pol.)
Helmut Bakaitis
SHIRLEY THOMPSON VERSUS THE ALIENS(1968, Aus.), a, w; STORK(1971, Aus.)
Boris Bakal
1984
MEMED MY HAWK(1984, Brit.)
Bakaleinikoff
SWING IT, PROFESSOR(1937), md
C. Bakaleinikoff
WITHOUT RESERVATIONS(1946), md; WELCOME DANGER(1929), m; BOTTOMS UP(1934), md; SOMETHING TO SING ABOUT(1937), m, md; GENTLEMAN FROM ARIZONA, THE(1940), m; MELODY FOR THREE(1941), m, md; REMEDY FOR RICHES(1941), md; THEY MEET AGAIN(1941), md; ARMY SURGEON(1942), md; FALCON TAKES OVER, THE(1942), md; FALCON'S BROTHER, THE(1942), md; GREAT GILDERSLEEVE, THE(1942), md; HERE WE GO AGAIN(1942), m; HIGH-WAYS BY NIGHT(1942), md; HITLER'S CHILDREN(1942), md; MAYOR OF 44TH STREET, THE(1942), md; MEXICAN SPITFIRE SEES A GHOST(1942), md; MEXI-CAN SPITFIRE'S ELEPHANT(1942), md; MY FAVORITE SPY(1942), md; NAVY COMES THROUGH, THE(1942), md; SEVEN DAYS LEAVE(1942), md; SING YOUR WORRIES AWAY(1942), md; AROUND THE WORLD(1943), md; BOMBAR-DIER(1943), md; FALCON AND THE CO-EDS, THE(1943), md; FALCON IN DANGER, THE(1943), md; FALCON STRIKES BACK, THE(1943), md; FALLEN SPARROW, THE(1943), md; FLIGHT FOR FREEDOM(1943), md; GILDERSLEEVE ON BROAD-WAY(1943), md; GILDERSLEEVE'S BAD DAY(1943), md; GOVERNMENT GIRL(1943), md; I WALKED WITH A ZOMBIE(1943), md; IRON MAJOR, THE(1943), md; LADY TAKES A CHANCE, A(1943), md; MEXICAN SPITFIRE'S BLESSED EVENT(1943), md; PETTICOAT LARCENY(1943), md; ROOKIES IN BURMA(1943),

md; SEVENTH VICTIM, THE(1943), md; TENDER COMRADE(1943), md; THEY GOT ME COVERED(1943), md; EXPERIMENT PERILOUS(1944), md; FALCON IN HOL-LYWOOD, THE(1944), md; FALCON IN MEXICO, THE(1944), md; FALCON OUT WEST, THE(1944), md; GILDERSLEEVE'S GHOST(1944), md; MUSIC IN MANHAT-TAN(1944), md; NEVADA(1944), md; NIGHT OF ADVENTURE, A(1944), md; NONE BUT THE LONELY HEART(1944), md; SEVEN DAYS ASHORE(1944), md; SHOW BUSINESS(1944), md; YOUTH RUNS WILD(1944), md; BACK TO BATAAN(1945), md; ENCHANTED COTTAGE, THE(1945), md; FALCON IN SAN FRANCISCO, THE(1945), md; FIRST YANK INTO TOKYO(1945), md; GAME OF DEATH, A(1945), md; HAVING WONDERFUL CRIME(1945), md; MAN ALIVE(1945), md; SING YOUR WAY HOME(1945), md; SPANISH MAIN, THE(1945), md; THOSE ENDEARING YOUNG CHARMS(1945), md; WANDERER OF THE WASTELAND(1945), md; WHAT A BLONDE(1945), md; ZOMBIES ON BROADWAY(1945), md; CRIMINAL COURT(1946), md; DEADLINE AT DAWN(1946), md; DING DONG WILLIAMS(1946), md; FALCON'S ALIBI, THE(1946), md; FROM THIS DAY FORWARD(1946), md; HEARTBEAT(1946), md; LADY LUCK(1946), md; RIVERBOAT RHYTHM(1946), md; SISTER KENNY(1946), md; SPIRAL STAIRCASE, THE(1946), md; SUNSET PASS(1946), md; TILL THE END OF TIME(1946), md; TRUTH ABOUT MURDER, THE(1946), md; BACHELOR AND THE BOBBY-SOXER, THE(1947), md; BORN TO KILL(1947), md; HONEYMOON(1947), md; LIKELY STORY, A(1947), md; MAGIC TOWN(1947), md; MOURNING BECOMES ELECTRA(1947), md; NIGHT SONG(1947), md; RIFFRAFF(1947), md; SEVEN KEYS TO BALDPATE(1947), md; SINBAD THE SAILOR(1947), md; SO WELL REMEMBERED(1947, Brit.), md; THUNDER MOUN-TAIN(1947), md; TYCOON(1947), md; BERLIN EXPRESS(1948), md; FIGHTING FA-THER DUNNE(1948), md; I REMEMBER MAMA(1948), md; IF YOU KNEW SUSIE(1948), md; MIRACLE OF THE BELLS, THE(1948), md; MYSTERY IN MEX-ICO(1948), md; RACE STREET(1948), md; RETURN OF THE BADMEN(1948), md; STATION WEST(1948), md; VELVET TOUCH, THE(1948), md; BRIDE FOR SA-LE(1949), md; DANGEROUS PROFESSION, A(1949), md; HOLIDAY AFFAIR(1949), md; JUDGE STEPS OUT, THE(1949), md; MAN ON THE EIFFEL TOWER, THE(1949), md; MIGHTY JOE YOUNG(1949), md; MYSTERIOUS DESPERADO, THE(1949), md; RUSTLERS(1949), md; STAGECOACH KID(1949), md; THREAT, THE(1949), md; WOMAN'S SECRET, A(1949), md; GAMBLING HOUSE(1950), md; HUNT THE MAN DOWN(1950), md; LAW OF THE BADLANDS(1950), m; OUTRAGE(1950), md; RIDER FROM TUCSON(1950), md; STROMBOLI(1950, Ital.), md; VENDETTA(1950), md; WALK SOFTLY, STRANGER(1950), md; WHITE TOWER, THE(1950), md; FLYING LEATHERNECKS(1951), md; HOT LEAD(1951), m; MY FORBIDDEN PAST(1951), md; ON THE LOOSE(1951), md; PAYMENT ON DEMAND(1951), md; PISTOL HAR-VEST(1951), md; SADDLE LEGION(1951), m; SEALED CARGO(1951), md; DESERT PASSAGE(1952), md; LAS VEGAS STORY, THE(1952), md; LUSTY MEN, THE(1952), md; MACAO(1952), md; ONE MINUTE TO ZERO(1952), md; PACE THAT THRILLS, THE(1952), md; TARGET(1952), md; TRAIL GUIDE(1952), md; FRENCH LINE, THE(1954), md; SON OF SINBAD(1955), md; CONQUEROR, THE(1956), md; BACHE-LOR PARTY, THE(1957), md; JET PILOT(1957), md
Constanin Bakaleinikoff
SET-UP, THE(1949), md
Constanti Bakaleinikoff
WESTERN HERITAGE(1948), md
Constantin Bakaleinikoff
THEY WON'T BELIEVE ME(1947), md; TEN CENTS A DANCE(1931), md; LADY FOR A DAY(1933), md; MAN'S CASTLE, A(1933), m; LET'S FALL IN LOVE(1934), md; MEET DR. CHRISTIAN(1939), md; COURAGEOUS DR. CHRISTIAN, THE(1940), md; DR. CHRISTIAN MEETS THE WOMEN(1940), m, md; ISLE OF DESTINY(1940), md; OBLIGING YOUNG LADY(1941), md; SCATTERGOOD BAINES(1941), m; SCAT-TERGOOD PULLS THE STRINGS(1941), m; JOAN OF PARIS(1942), md; JOURNEY INTO FEAR(1942), md; GANGWAY FOR TOMORROW(1943), md; GHOST SHIP, THE(1943), md; HIGHER AND HIGHER(1943), md; LEOPARD MAN, THE(1943), md; MR. LUCKY(1943), md; STAGE DOOR CANTEEN(1943), md; TARZAN'S DESERT MYSTERY(1943), md; THIS LAND IS MINE(1944), m; GIRL RUSH(1944), md; HEAVENLY DAYS(1944), md; MADEMOISELLE FIFI(1944), md; MARINE RAIDERS(1944), md; MASTER RACE, THE(1944), md; MY PAL, WOLF(1944), md; STEP LIVELY(1944), md; TALL IN THE SADDLE(1944), md; BE-TRAYAL FROM THE EAST(1945), md; BODY SNATCHER, THE(1945), md; CHINA SKY(1945), md; CORNERED(1945), md; DICK TRACY(1945), md; GEORGE WHITE'S SCANDALS(1945), md; ISLE OF THE DEAD(1945), md; JOHNNY ANGEL(1945), md; MURDER, MY SWEET(1945), md; RADIO STARS ON PARADE(1945), md; WEST OF THE PECOS(1945), md; CRACK-UP(1946), md; DICK TRACY VS. CUEBALL(1946), m; GENIUS AT WORK(1946), m; LOCKET, THE(1946), md; NOCTURNE(1946), md; NOTORIOUS(1946), md; STEP BY STEP(1946), md; CROSSFIRE(1947), md; DESPER-ATE(1947), md; DEVIL THUMBS A RIDE, THE(1947), md; DICK TRACY MEETS GRUESOME(1947), md; OUT OF THE PAST(1947), md; TRAIL STREET(1947), md; UNDER THE TONTO RIM(1947), md; WILD HORSE MESA(1947), md; MR. BLAND-INGS BUILDS HIS DREAM HOUSE(1948), md; RACHEL AND THE STRAN-GER(1948), md; BOY WITH THE GREEN HAIR, THE(1949), md; EASY LIVING(1949), md; FOLLOW ME QUIETLY(1949), md; ROUGHSHOD(1949), md; SHE WORE A YELLOW RIBBON(1949), md; STRANGE BARGAIN(1949), md; THEY LIVE BY NIGHT(1949), md; WINDOW, THE(1949), md; DOUBLE DEAL(1950), md; NEVER A DULL MOMENT(1950), md; SECRET FURY, THE(1950), md; STORM OVER WYOMING(1950), md; WHERE DANGER LIVES(1950), md; WOMAN ON PIER 13, THE(1950), md; GUNPLAY(1951), md; HARD, FAST, AND BEAUTI-FUL(1951), md; HIS KIND OF WOMAN(1951), md; ON DANGEROUS GROUND(1951), md; RACKET, THE(1951), md; ROADBLOCK(1951), md; WHIP HAND, THE(1951), md; CLASH BY NIGHT(1952), md; HALF-BREED, THE(1952), md; HITCH-HIKER, THE(1953), md; SECOND CHANCE(1953), md; SHE COULDN'T SAY NO(1954), md; UNDERWATER!(1955), md; GREAT DAY IN THE MOR-NING(1956), md
Constantine Bakaleinikoff
FATHER AND SON(1929), m; LOOK WHO'S LAUGHING(1941), md; TARZAN TRIUMPHS(1943), md; CASS TIMBERLANE(1947), md; WOMAN ON THE BEACH, THE(1947), md; EVERY GIRL SHOULD BE MARRIED(1948), md; SMART WO-MAN(1948), md; DOUBLE DYNAMITE(1951), md; SUSAN SLEPT HERE(1954), md
M. Bakaleinikoff
PALOMINO, THE(1950), md
M. R. Bakaleinikoff
LOUISIANA HAYRIDE(1944), md; GIRL OF THE LIMBERLOST, THE(1945), md
Mischa Bakaleinikoff
MISSING JUROR, THE(1944), md; ONE MYSTERIOUS NIGHT(1944), md; SOUL OF A MONSTER, THE(1944), md; UNWRITTEN CODE, THE(1944), md; BOSTON BLACKIE'S RENDEZVOUS(1945), md; I LOVE A BANDLEADER(1945), md; MY NAME IS JULIA ROSS(1945), m; PRISON SHIP(1945), md; SERGEANT MIKE(1945),

md; VOICE OF THE WHISTLER(1945), md; BLONDIE KNOWS BEST(1946), md; BLONDIE'S LUCKY DAY(1946), md; BOSTON BLACKIE AND THE LAW(1946), md; CLOSE CALL FOR BOSTON BLACKIE, A(1946), md; CRIME DOCTOR'S MAN HUNT(1946), md; DANGEROUS BUSINESS(1946), md; DEVIL'S MASK, THE(1946), ed; JUST BEFORE DAWN(1946), md; LIFE WITH BLONDIE(1946), md; MAN WHO DARED, THE(1946), md; MYSTERIOUS INTRUDER(1946), md; NIGHT EDITOR(1946), m; NOTORIOUS LONE WOLF, THE(1946), md; OUT OF THE DEPTHS(1946), md; PERSONALITY KID(1946), md; PHANTOM THIEF, THE(1946), md; SECRET OF THE WHISTLER(1946), md; SHADOWED(1946), md; UNKNOWN, THE(1946), md; BLONDIE IN THE DOUGH(1947), md; BLONDIE'S BIG MOMENT(1947), md; CRIME DOCTOR'S GAMBLE(1947), md; DEVIL SHIP(1947), md; FOR THE LOVE OF RUSTY(1947), md; GLAMOUR GIRL(1947), md; KEY WITNESS(1947), md; KING OF THE WILD HORSES(1947), md; LAST OF THE REDMEN(1947), md; LAST ROUND-UP, THE(1947), md; LITTLE MISS BROADWAY(1947), md; LONE WOLF IN LONDON(1947), md; LONE WOLF IN MEXICO, THE(1947), md; MILLERSON CASE, THE(1947), md; SPORT OF KINGS(1947), md; TWO BLONDES AND A REDHEAD(1947), md; WHEN A GIRL'S BEAUTIFUL(1947), md; BLONDIE'S REWARD(1948), md; BLONDIE'S SECRET(1948), md; JUNGLE JIM(1948), md; LADIES OF THE CHORUS(1948), md; LOADED PISTOLS(1948), md; MANHATTAN ANGEL(1948), md; MARY LOU(1948), md; MY DOG RUSTY(1948), md; PORT SAID(1948), md; PRINCE OF THIEVES, THE(1948), md; RACING LUCK(1948), md; RETURN OF THE WHISTLER, THE(1948), md; RUSTY LEADS THE WAY(1948), md; SONG OF IDAHO(1948), md; STRAWBERRY ROAN, THE(1948), md; THUNDERHOOF(1948), m; TRAPPED BY BOSTON BLACKIE(1948), md; WOMAN FROM TANGIER, THE(1948), md; BLONDIE HITS THE JACKPOT(1949), m; BOSTON BLACKIE'S CHINESE VENTURE(1949), md; CHINATOWN AT MIDNIGHT(1949), m; CRIME DOCTOR'S DIARY, THE(1949), md; DEVIL'S HENCHMEN, THE(1949), m, md; KAZAN(1949), md; LAW OF THE BARBARY COAST(1949), md; LONE WOLF AND HIS LADY, THE(1949), md; LOST TRIBE, THE(1949), md; MARY RYAN, DETECTIVE(1949), m, md; MUTINEERS, THE(1949), m; PRISON WARDEN(1949), m; RIDERS IN THE SKY(1949), md; RIDERS OF THE WHISTLING PINES(1949), md; RIM OF THE CANYON(1949), md; RUSTY SAVES A LIFE(1949), md; RUSTY'S BIRTHDAY(1949), m, md; SECRET OF ST. IVES, THE(1949), m; SONS OF NEW MEXICO(1949), md; BEAUTY ON PARADE(1950), m; BLONDIE'S HERO(1950), md; CAPTIVE GIRL(1950), md; COUNTERSPY MEETS SCOTLAND YARD(1950), md; COW TOWN(1950), md; FLYING MISSILE(1950), md; GIRLS' SCHOOL(1950), md; HE'S A COCKEYED WONDER(1950), m; HOEDOWN(1950), md; INDIAN TERRITORY(1950), m, md; LAST OF THE BUCCANEERS(1950), md; LIGHTNING GUNS(1950), m; MARK OF THE GORILLA(1950), md; MULE TRAIN(1950), md; ON THE ISLE OF SAMOA(1950), m; PYGMY ISLAND(1950), md; RAIDERS OF TOMAHAWK CREEK(1950), md; REVENUE AGENT(1950), m; ROOKIE FIREMAN(1950), m; STATE PENITENTIARY(1950), md; TRAVELING SALESWOMAN(1950), md; TYRANT OF THE SEA(1950), md; CHINA CORSAIR(1951), md; CORKY OF GASOLINE ALLEY(1951), md; FURY OF THE CONGO(1951), md; GASOLINE ALLEY(1951), md; GENE AUTRY AND THE MOUNTIES(1951), md; HILLS OF UTAH(1951), md; HURRICANE ISLAND(1951), md; JUNGLE MANHUNT(1951), md; KID FROM AMARILLO, THE(1951), md; MAGIC CARPET, THE(1951), md; MY TRUE STORY(1951), md; PECOS RIVER(1951), md; PRAIRIE ROUNDUP(1951), md; RIDIN' THE OUTLAW TRAIL(1951), md; SILVER CANYON(1951), md; SMUGGLER'S GOLD(1951), m; TEXANS NEVER CRY(1951), md; TEXAS RANGERS, THE(1951), md; VALLEY OF FIRE(1951), md; WHEN THE REDSKINS RODE(1951), md; WHIRLWIND(1951), md; BARBED WIRE(1952), m; CALIFORNIA CONQUEST(1952), m; CRIPPLE CREEK(1952), m; GOLDEN HAWK, THE(1952), md; HANGMAN'S KNOT(1952), md; HAREM GIRL(1952), md; HAWK OF WILD RIVER, THE(1952), m; JUNCTION CITY(1952), md; JUNGLE JIM IN THE FORBIDDEN LAND(1952), md; KID FROM BROKEN GUN, THE(1952), md; LARAMIE MOUNTAINS(1952), md; LAST TRAIN FROM BOMBAY(1952), md; MONTANA TERRITORY(1952), md; NIGHT STAGE TO GALVESTON(1952), m; OKINAWA(1952), md; OLD WEST, THE(1952), md; PATHFINDER, THE(1952), md; SMOKY CANYON(1952), m; TARGET HONG KONG(1952), md; THIEF OF DAMASCUS(1952), m; VOODOO TIGER(1952), md; WAGON TEAM(1952), md; BIG HEAT, THE(1953), md; CONQUEST OF COCHISE(1953), m; FLAME OF CALCUTTA(1953), m; GOLDTOWN GHOST RIDERS(1953), m; GUN FURY(1953), md; JACK MCCALL, DESPERADO(1953), md; KILLER APE(1953), md; ON TOP OF OLD SMOKY(1953), md; PRINCE OF PIRATES(1953), m; SAVAGE MUTINY(1953), m; SERPENT OF THE NILE(1953), m; SLAVES OF BABYLON(1953), md; VALLEY OF THE HEADHUNTERS(1953), md; BAD FOR EACH OTHER(1954), m; BLACK DAKOTAS, THE(1954), m; CANNIBAL ATTACK(1954), m; IRON GLOVE, THE(1954), m; JESSE JAMES VERSUS THE DALTONS(1954), m; JUNGLE MAN-EATERS(1954), md; MASSACRE CANYON(1954), m; MIAMI STORY, THE(1954), m; APACHE AMBUSH(1955), m; CELL 2455, DEATH ROW(1955), md; CREATURE WITH THE ATOM BRAIN(1955), md; CROOKED WEB, THE(1955), md; DEVIL GODDESS(1955), md; DUEL ON THE MISSISSIPPI(1955), md; INSIDE DETROIT(1955), md; IT CAME FROM BENEATH THE SEA(1955), md; JUNGLE MOON MEN(1955), md; NEW ORLEANS UNCENSORED(1955), md; PIRATES OF TRIPOLI(1955), md; SEMINOLE UPRISING(1955), md; TEEN-AGE CRIME WAVE(1955), m, md; WOMEN'S PRISON(1955), m; WYOMING RENEGADES(1955), m; BATTLE STATIONS(1956), m; FURY AT GUNSIGHT PASS(1956), m; HOUSTON STORY, THE(1956), m; MIAMI EXPOSE(1956), m, md; OVER-EXPOSED(1956), m; REPRISAL(1956), m, md; SECRET OF TREASURE MOUNTAIN(1956), md; SEVENTH CAVALRY(1956), m; URANIUM BOOM(1956), m; WEREWOLF, THE(1956), m; WHITE SQUAW, THE(1956), m&md; DOMINO KID(1957), m, md; GIANT CLAW, THE(1957), md; GUNS OF FORT PETTICOAT, THE(1957), md; HARD MAN, THE(1957), m; HELLCATS OF THE NAVY(1957), m; NO TIME TO BE YOUNG(1957), m; PHANTOM STAGECOACH(1957), md; TALL T, THE(1957), md; TIJUANA STORY, THE(1957), md; 20 MILLION MILES TO EARTH(1957), m; 27TH DAY, THE(1957), md; CASE AGAINST BROOKLYN, THE(1958), m; CRASH LANDING(1958), m; GOING STEADY(1958), md; LINEUP, THE(1958), m; RETURN TO WARBOW(1958), md; SCREAMING MIMI(1958), md; TRUE STORY OF LYNN STUART, THE(1958), m, md; WORLD WAS HIS JURY, THE(1958), md; FLYING FONTAINES, THE(1959), m; HAVE ROCRET, WILL TRAVEL(1959), m, md; COMANCHE STATION(1960), m; ENEMY GENERAL, THE(1960), m

Misha Bakaleinikoff
  13TH HOUR, THE(1947), md

Mischa Bakaleinkoff
  BODYHOLD(1950), m; EARTH VS. THE FLYING SAUCERS(1956), m, md

Dick Bakalyan
  COOL AND THE CRAZY, THE(1958); CHINATOWN(1974); STRONGEST MAN IN THE WORLD, THE(1975); SHAGGY D.A., THE(1976); RETURN FROM WITCH MOUNTAIN(1978); H.O.T.S.(1979); MAN WITH BOGART'S FACE, THE(1980); FOX

AND THE HOUND, THE(1981)
1984
  BLAME IT ON THE NIGHT(1984)

Ricbard Bakalyan
  NEVER A DULL MOMENT(1968)

Richard Bakalyan
  BROTHERS RICO, THE(1957); DELICATE DELINQUENT, THE(1957); DELINQUENTS, THE(1957); DINO(1957); HEAR ME GOOD(1957); BONNIE PARKER STORY, THE(1958); HOT CAR GIRL(1958); JUVENILE JUNGLE(1958); -30-(1959); PARATROOP COMMAND(1959); UP PERISCOPE(1959); ERRAND BOY, THE(1961); PANIC IN YEAR ZERO!(1962); PRESSURE POINT(1962); OPERATION BIKINI(1963); PATSY, THE(1964); ROBIN AND THE SEVEN HOODS(1964); GREATEST STORY EVER TOLD, THE(1965); NONE BUT THE BRAVE(1965, U.S./Jap.); VON RYAN'S EXPRESS(1965); FOLLOW ME, BOYS!(1966); ST. VALENTINE'S DAY MASSACRE, THE(1967); COMPUTER WORE TENNIS SHOES, THE(1970); ANIMALS, THE(1971), p; NOW YOU SEE HIM, NOW YOU DON'T(1972); CHARLEY AND THE ANGEL(1973)

Paul Bakanas
  THEY LIVE BY NIGHT(1949); JET PILOT(1957)

Robert Bakanic
  GOING BERSERK(1983)

Hartinut Bake
  GIRL FROM HONG KONG(1966, Ger.), cos

Gary Bakeman
  TWO THOUSAND MANIACS!(1964)

Abe Baker
  BRAIN THAT WOULDN'T DIE, THE(1959), m

Albert J. Baker
  SUGAR HILL(1974)

Ann Baker
  MEN OF THE FIGHTING LADY(1954)

Anthony Baker
Misc. Talkies
  BEYOND CONTROL(1971), a, d

Art Baker
  TRADE WINDS(1938); SLIGHTLY HONORABLE(1940); NORTH STAR, THE(1943); ONCE UPON A TIME(1944); SPELLBOUND(1945); ABIE'S IRISH ROSE(1946); BEGINNING OR THE END, THE(1947); DAISY KENYON(1947); DARK DELUSION(1947); FARMER'S DAUGHTER, THE(1947); DECISION OF CHRISTOPHER BLAKE, THE(1948); HOMECOMING(1948); SILVER RIVER(1948); SOUTHERN YANKEE, A(1948); STATE OF THE UNION(1948); WALK A CROOKED MILE(1948); WALLS OF JERICHO(1948); ANY NUMBER CAN PLAY(1949); COVER-UP(1949); EASY LIVING(1949); IMPACT(1949); MASSACRE RIVER(1949); NIGHT UNTO NIGHT(1949); TAKE ONE FALSE STEP(1949); TASK FORCE(1949); HOT ROD(1950); WHIPPED, THE(1950); CAUSE FOR ALARM(1951); HERE COMES THE GROOM(1951); ONLY THE VALIANT(1951); ARTISTS AND MODELS(1955); TWELVE HOURS TO KILL(1960); VOYAGE TO THE BOTTOM OF THE SEA(1961); SWINGIN' ALONG(1962); YOUNG DILLINGER(1965); WILD ANGELS, THE(1966)

Arthur Baker
1984
  BEAT STREET(1984), m

Barry Baker
  RUDE BOY(1980, Brit.)

Belle Baker
  SONG OF LOVE, THE(1929); CHARING CROSS ROAD(1935, Brit.); ATLANTIC CITY(1944)

Ben Baker
  PAINT YOUR WAGON(1969); SCANDALOUS JOHN(1971); JORY(1972)

Bennie Baker
  ROSE OF THE RANCHO(1936)

Benny Baker
  BELLE OF THE NINETIES(1934); HELL CAT, THE(1934); ANNAPOLIS FAREWELL(1935); BIG BROADCAST OF 1936, THE(1935); COLLEGE SCANDAL(1935); LOVE IN BLOOM(1935); MILLIONS IN THE AIR(1935); THANKS A MILLION(1935); WANDERER OF THE WASTELAND(1935); DRIFT FENCE(1936); GIVE US THIS NIGHT(1936); LADY BE CAREFUL(1936); MURDER WITH PICTURES(1936); ROSE BOWL(1936); BLONDE TROUBLE(1937); CHAMPAGNE WALTZ(1937); CRIME NOBODY SAW, THE(1937); DOUBLE OR NOTHING(1937); HOLD'EM NAVY(1937); HOTEL HAYWIRE(1937); LOVE ON TOAST(1937); MIND YOUR OWN BUSINESS(1937); WILD MONEY(1937); HIS EXCITING NIGHT(1938); TIP-OFF GIRLS(1938); TOUCHDOWN, ARMY(1938); DANCING CO-ED(1939); SHE MARRIED A COP(1939); FARMER'S DAUGHTER, THE(1940); SING FOR YOUR SUPPER(1941); CAPTAINS OF THE CLOUDS(1942); UP IN ARMS(1944); HOMICIDE FOR THREE(1948); JINX MONEY(1948); MANHATTAN ANGEL(1948); MY GIRL TISA(1948); SMART WOMAN(1948); INSPECTOR GENERAL, THE(1949); JOE PALOOKA IN THE BIG FIGHT(1949); ROSE OF THE YUKON(1949); FEUDIN' FOOLS(1952); LOAN SHARK(1952); MODELS, INC.(1952); THUNDERBIRDS(1952); PUBLIC PIGEON NO. 1(1957); NO TIME FOR SERGEANTS(1958); PAPA'S DELICATE CONDITION(1963); FOR THOSE WHO THINK YOUNG(1964); BOY, DID I GET A WRONG NUMBER!(1966); WICKED DREAMS OF PAULA SCHULTZ, THE(1968); SOME KIND OF A NUT(1969)

Betsy Baker
  EVIL DEAD, THE(1983)

Betty Baker
  BAR L RANCH(1930)
Silents
  GALLOPING GOBS, THE(1927)
Misc. Silents
  FACE VALUE(1927); SKEDADDLE GOLD(1927); PAINTED TRAIL(1928); TRAIL RIDERS(1928); TRAILIN' BACK(1928)

Blanche Baker
  FRENCH POSTCARDS(1979); SEDUCTION OF JOE TYNAN, THE(1979)
1984
  COLD FEET(1984); SIXTEEN CANDLES(1984)

Bob Baker
  COURAGE OF THE WEST(1937); SINGING OUTLAW(1937); BLACK BANDIT(1938); BORDER WOLVES(1938); GHOST TOWN RIDERS(1938); GUILTY TRAILS(1938); LAST STAND, THE(1938); OUTLAW EXPRESS(1938); PRAIRIE JUSTICE(1938); WESTERN TRAILS(1938); DESPERATE TRAILS(1939); HONOR OF THE WEST(1939); OKLAHOMA FRONTIER(1939); PHANTOM STAGE, THE(1939); BAD MAN FROM RED BUTTE(1940); CHIP OF THE FLYING U(1940); RIDERS OF PASCO BASIN(1940);

WEST OF CARSON CITY(1940); WILD HORSE STAMPEDE(1943); MYSTERY MAN(1944); OKLAHOMA RAIDERS(1944)

Bonnie Baker
YOU'RE THE ONE(1941); SPOTLIGHT SCANDALS(1943)

Bruce Baker
HOW TO STUFF A WILD BIKINI(1965)

Bryden Baker
PHANTOM FROM 10,000 LEAGUES, THE(1956), ph

Brydon Baker
FRONTIER DAYS(1934), ph; SCANDAL INCORPORATED(1956), ph; WALK THE DARK STREET(1956), ph; WETBACKS(1956), ph; COPPER SKY(1957), ph; FROM HELL IT CAME(1957), ph; RIDE A VIOLENT MILE(1957), ph; STORM RIDER, THE(1957), ph; CATTLE EMPIRE(1958), ph; ESCAPE FROM RED ROCK(1958), ph; SNOWFIRE(1958), ph; SPACE MASTER X-7(1958), ph; RETURN OF THE FLY(1959), ph; VALLEY OF THE DRAGONS(1961), ph; 20,000 EYES(1961), ph; MERMAIDS OF TIBURON, THE(1962), ph; RING OF TERROR(1962), ph; BALLAD OF A GUNFIGHTER(1964), ph; TAFFY AND THE JUNGLE HUNTER(1965), ph

Buck Baker
THUNDER IN CAROLINA(1960)

Buddy Baker
WICKED WOMAN(1953), m; TOBY TYLER(1960), m; SUMMER MAGIC(1963), m; MISADVENTURES OF MERLIN JONES, THE(1964), m; TIGER WALKS, A(1964), m; MONKEY'S UNCLE, THE(1965), m; GNOME-MOBILE, THE(1967), m; GUNS IN THE HEATHER(1968, Brit.), m; RASCAL(1969), m; KING OF THE GRIZZLIES(1970), m; $1,000,000 DUCK(1971), m; NAPOLEON AND SAMANTHA(1972), m; CHARLEY AND THE ANGEL(1973), m; BEARS AND I, THE(1974), m; SUPERDAD(1974), m; APPLE DUMPLING GANG, THE(1975), m; NO DEPOSIT, NO RETURN(1976), m; SHAGGY D.A., THE(1976), m; TREASURE OF MATECUMBE(1976), m; HOT LEAD AND COLD FEET(1978), m; DEVIL AND MAX DEVLIN, THE(1981), m; FOX AND THE HOUND, THE(1981), m; SIX PACK(1982)

C. Graham Baker
SINGING FOOL, THE(1928), w; CONQUEST(1929), w; FANCY BAGGAGE(1929), w; SONNY BOY(1929), w; PERSONALITY KID, THE(1934), w; SHADOW OF A WOMAN(1946), w
Silents
INNER CHAMBER, THE(1921), w; RAINBOW(1921), w; SCARAB RING, THE(1921), w; SINGLE TRACK, THE(1921), w; ANGEL OF CROOKED STREET, THE(1922), w; NINETY AND NINE, THE(1922), w; PLAYING IT WILD(1923), w; JUST SUPPOSE(1926), w; GAY OLD BIRD, THE(1927), w; HUSBANDS FOR RENT(1927), w; SLIGHTLY USED(1927), w; WHITE FLANNELS(1927), w

Carl Baker
WOMEN OF DESIRE(1968), w

Carle E. Baker
PICNIC(1955)

Carlos Baker
TALES FROM THE CRYPT(1972, Brit.)

Carrie Baker
DRACULA HAS RISEN FROM HIS GRAVE(1968, Brit.)

Carroll Baker
EASY TO LOVE(1953); BABY DOLL(1956); GIANT(1956); BIG COUNTRY, THE(1958); BUT NOT FOR ME(1959); MIRACLE, THE(1959); BRIDGE TO THE SUN(1961); SOMETHING WILD(1961); HOW THE WEST WAS WON(1962); CARPETBAGGERS, THE(1964); CHEYENNE AUTUMN(1964); STATION SIX-SAHARA(1964, Brit./Ger.); GREATEST STORY EVER TOLD, THE(1965); HARLOW(1965); MISTER MOSES(1965); SYLVIA(1965); JACK OF DIAMONDS(1967, U.S./Ger.); SWEET BODY OF DEBORAH, THE(1969, Ital./Fr.); CAPTAIN APACHE(1971, Brit.); WATCHER IN THE WOODS, THE(1980, Brit.); WORLD IS FULL OF MARRIED MEN, THE(1980, Brit.); RED MONARCH(1983, Brit.); STAR 80(1983)
1984
SECRET DIARY OF SIGMUND FREUD, THE(1984)
Misc. Talkies
DEVIL HAS SEVEN FACES, THE(1977)

Charles Baker
THIS ISLAND EARTH(1955), spec eff

Chet Baker
HELL'S HORIZON(1955); STOLEN HOURS(1963); NIGHT OF LUST(1965, Fr.), m

Chiyoko Tota Baker
HUNTERS, THE(1958)

Colette Baker
GIRO CITY(1982, Brit.)

Consuelo Baker
KID FROM SPAIN, THE(1932); LET'S FALL IN LOVE(1934)

Cynthia Baker
RISKY BUSINESS(1983)

Dan Baker
Silents
SALAMANDER, THE(1915)

David Baker
LOVE IS A SPLENDID ILLUSION(1970, Brit.), w; SOME OF MY BEST FRIENDS ARE...(1971); LIBIDO(1973, Aus.), d; GODFATHER, THE, PART II(1974); GREAT MACARTHY, THE(1975, Aus.), p&d; TIME BANDITS(1981, Brit.)

Del Baker
ATCH ME A SPY(1971, Brit./Fr.); TIME BANDITS(1981, Brit.); OCTOPUSSY(1983, Brit.), stunts

Derek Baker
MAN OUTSIDE, THE(1968, Brit.)

Diane Baker
BEST OF EVERYTHING, THE(1959); DIARY OF ANNE FRANK, THE(1959); JOURNEY TO THE CENTER OF THE EARTH(1959); WIZARD OF BAGHDAD, THE(1960); TESS OF THE STORM COUNTRY(1961); ADVENTURES OF A YOUNG MAN(1962); 300 SPARTANS, THE(1962); NINE HOURS TO RAMA(1963, U.S./Brit.); PRIZE, THE(1963); STOLEN HOURS(1963); MARNIE(1964); REBELS AGAINST THE LIGHT(1964); STRAIT-JACKET(1964); MIRAGE(1965); SANDS OF BEERSHEBA(1966, U.S./Israel); HORSE IN THE GRAY FLANNEL SUIT, THE(1968); KRAKATOA, EAST OF JAVA(1969); BAKER'S HAWK(1976); PILOT, THE(1979); NEVER NEVER LAND(1982), p
Misc. Talkies
SAGITTARIUS MINE, THE(1972)

Dick Baker
MICKEY ONE(1965)

Don Baker
STAR TREK: THE MOTION PICTURE(1979), spec eff

Donald Baker
KETTLES ON OLD MACDONALD'S FARM, THE(1957)

Dora Baker
GUY NAMED JOE, A(1943)
Misc. Silents
ROUGH GOING(1925)

Doria Baker
Silents
ELLA CINDERS(1926)

Doris Baker
HAPPY DAYS(1930)
Silents
DANGEROUS TO MEN(1920)
Misc. Silents
SECRET GIFT, THE(1920); YOUTH'S DESIRE(1920)

Dorothy Baker
YOUNG MAN WITH A HORN(1950), w

Dottie Bee Baker
RAINMAKER, THE(1956)

Doyle Baker
CRIME IN THE STREETS(1956)

Eddie Baker
PARDON US(1931); IF I HAD A MILLION(1932); MILLION DOLLAR LEGS(1932); SONS OF THE DESERT(1933); TILLIE AND GUS(1933); ELMER AND ELSIE(1934); FINISHING SCHOOL(1934); IT'S A GIFT(1934); YOU'RE TELLING ME(1934); IDENTITY UNKNOWN(1945); GIANT(1956); STEEL JUNGLE, THE(1956)

Eddy Baker
WEDDING PRESENT(1936)

Edith Baker
KANSAS CITY PRINCESS(1934)

Edward Baker
LAND OF FURY(1955 Brit.)

Edwin Baker
LEMON DROP KID, THE(1934)
Silents
MOTHER(1914)

Eileen Baker
LAUGHING LADY, THE(1950, Brit.), ch; RETURN OF THE JEDI(1983)

Elaine Baker
SECRET CALL, THE(1931)

Elliot Baker
VIVA MAX!(1969), w; BREAKOUT(1975), w

Elliott Baker
FINE MADNESS, A(1966), w; LUV(1967), w; SKIDOO(1968), w; ENTERTAINER, THE(1975), w

Elsie Baker
MYSTERY STREET(1950); SHAKEDOWN(1950); NO ROOM FOR THE GROOM(1952); THREE HOURS TO KILL(1954)
Misc. Talkies
GHOSTS OF HANLEY HOUSE, THE(1974)

Evadne Baker
SEVEN WOMEN FROM HELL(1961); FATE IS THE HUNTER(1964); SHOCK TREATMENT(1964); SOUND OF MUSIC, THE(1965)

Everett Baker
BEAST WITH A MILLION EYES, THE(1956), ph

F. W. Baker
JAILBIRDS(1939, Brit.), p; OLD MOTHER RILEY MP(1939, Brit.), p; PACK UP YOUR TROUBLES(1940, Brit.), p; SAILOR'S DON'T CARE(1940, Brit.), p; THREE SILENT MEN(1940, Brit.), p; BOB'S YOUR UNCLE(1941, Brit.), p; GERT AND DAISY'S WEEKEND(1941, Brit.), p; SHEEPDOG OF THE HILLS(1941, Brit.), p; GERT AND DAISY CLEAN UP(1942, Brit.), p; ROSE OF TRALEE(1942, Brit.), p; I'LL WALK BESIDE YOU(1943, Brit.), p; IT'S IN THE BAG(1943, Brit.), p; MY AIN FOLK(1944, Brit.), p; FOR YOU ALONE(1945, Brit.), p; VARIETY JUBILEE(1945, Brit.), p; I'LL TURN TO YOU(1946, Brit.), p
Silents
FLAMES(1917, Brit.), p; GRIT OF A JEW, THE(1917, Brit.), p

Fay Baker
NOTORIOUS(1946); FAMILY HONEYMOON(1948); GENTLEMAN FROM NOWHERE, THE(1948); MANHATTAN ANGEL(1948); NO MINOR VICES(1948); SAXON CHARM, THE(1948); TRAPPED BY BOSTON BLACKIE(1948); BLACK MIDNIGHT(1949); TELL IT TO THE JUDGE(1949); CHAIN LIGHTNING(1950); COMPANY SHE KEEPS, THE(1950); DOUBLE DEAL(1950); FATHER OF THE BRIDE(1950); HOUSE ON TELEGRAPH HILL(1951); REUNION IN RENO(1951); DEADLINE-U.S.A.(1952); STAR, THE(1953); PHFFFT!(1954); I DIED A THOUSAND TIMES(1955); DON'T KNOCK THE ROCK(1956); SHE DEVIL(1957); SORORITY GIRL(1957)

Florence Baker
WATERLOO BRIDGE(1940)

Frank Baker
MANDALAY(1934); NEW ADVENTURES OF TARZAN(1935); MARY OF SCOTLAND(1936); PRISONER OF SHARK ISLAND, THE(1936); BULLDOG DRUMMOND COMES BACK(1937); BARONESS AND THE BUTLER, THE(1938); FOUR MEN AND A PRAYER(1938); TARZAN AND THE GREEN GODDESS(1938); ARREST BULLDOG DRUMMOND(1939, Brit.); LONE WOLF SPY HUNT, THE(1939); RAFFLES(1939); CHUMP AT OXFORD, A(1940); EARL OF CHICAGO, THE(1940); ESCAPE TO GLORY(1940); SOUTH OF SUEZ(1940); INTERNATIONAL SQUADRON(1941); MRS. MINIVER(1942); MAN IN HALF-MOON STREET, THE(1944); MINISTRY OF FEAR(1945); CALCUTTA(1947); MOSS ROSE(1947); THAT FORSYTE WOMAN(1949); WHEN WILLIE COMES MARCHING HOME(1950); LES MISERABLES(1952); QUIET MAN, THE(1952); LEASE OF LIFE(1954, Brit.), w; VIRGIN QUEEN, THE(1955); RUN OF THE ARROW(1957); TWO RODE TOGETHER(1961); DONOVAN'S REEF(1963); MY FAIR LADY(1964); SEX AND THE SINGLE GIRL(1964); GIRO CITY(1982, Brit.); YENTL(1983)
Silents
LASH OF THE WHIP(1924); GALLANT FOOL, THE(1926); MILLION FOR LOVE, A(1928)

Kristen Baker
1984
  FRIDAY THE 13TH–THE FINAL CHAPTER(1984)
Misc. Talkies
  GAS PUMP GIRLS(1979); GIRLS NEXT DOOR, THE(1979)
LaVern Baker
  ROCK, ROCK, ROCK!(1956); MISTER ROCK AND ROLL(1957)
Lee Baker
  MOURNING BECOMES ELECTRA(1947); SWORD OF THE AVENGER(1948)
Misc. Silents
  KINGDOM OF YOUTH, THE(1918); FIGHTING BLADE, THE(1923)
Lenny Baker
  HOSPITAL, THE(1971); MALATESTA'S CARNIVAL(1973); PAPER CHASE, THE(1973); NEXT STOP, GREENWICH VILLAGE(1976)
Misc. Talkies
  AWOL(1973)
Leonard Baker
  MAN WHO SHOT LIBERTY VALANCE, THE(1962)
Lewis Baker
  TOY, THE(1982)
Loren Baker
  MYSTERIOUS CROSSING(1937)
Lorin Baker
  BY WHOSE HAND?(1932); LOUDSPEAKER, THE(1934); NO HANDS ON THE CLOCK(1941); WEB, THE(1947)
Lorris Baker
  KISMET(1930)
Louise Baker
  HER TWELVE MEN(1954), w
1984
  HIGHWAY TO HELL(1984); RUNNING HOT(1984)
Lynn Baker
  BILLY JACK(1971); TRIAL OF BILLY JACK, THE(1974)
Misc. Talkies
  JUST BE THERE(1977)
Margot Baker
  BORN TO BE LOVED(1959)
Marie Baker
  TAKE HER, SHE'S MINE(1963)
Marilyn Baker
  BOND OF FEAR(1956, Brit.)
Mark Baker
  STEEL KEY, THE(1953, Brit.); LOVE LOTTERY, THE(1954, Brit.); MAKE ME AN OFFER(1954, Brit.); JOE MACBETH(1955); ACROSS THE BRIDGE(1957, Brit.); AFTER THE BALL(1957, Brit.); MAILBAG ROBBERY(1957, Brit.); FLOODS OF FEAR(1958, Brit.); INTENT TO KILL(1958, Brit.); MAN INSIDE, THE(1958, Brit.); ORDERS ARE ORDERS(1959, Brit.); NEVER TAKE CANDY FROM A STRANGER(1961, Brit.); SWASHBUCKLER(1976); RAGGEDY ANN AND ANDY(1977); VALENTINO(1977, Brit.)
Mark G. Baker
  LAST OF THE SECRET AGENTS?, THE(1966)
Mark Linn Baker
  MANHATTAN(1979)
Melville Baker
  CIRCUS KID, THE(1928), w; DARKENED ROOMS(1929), w,Patrick Konesky; ONE ROMANTIC NIGHT(1930), w; HIS WOMAN(1931), w; DOWNSTAIRS(1932), w; ZOO IN BUDAPEST(1933), w; NOW AND FOREVER(1934), w; GILDED LILY, THE(1935), w; LAST DAYS OF POMPEII, THE(1935), w; MILLS OF THE GODS(1935), w; LADIES IN LOVE(1936), w; NEXT TIME WE LOVE(1936), w; SEVENTH HEAVEN(1937), w; FIRST 100 YEARS, THE(1938), w; JOE AND ETHEL TURP CALL ON THE PRESIDENT(1939), w; ABOVE SUSPICION(1943), w
Melvin Baker
  REACH FOR GLORY(1963, Brit.)
Michael Conway Baker
  DESERTERS(1983, Can.), m; GREY FOX, THE(1983, Can.), m
Mickey Baker
  STORY OF A THREE DAY PASS, THE(1968, Fr.), m; CRY OF THE BANSHEE(1970, Brit.)
Moe Baker
Misc. Talkies
  CAN I DO IT 'TIL I NEED GLASSES?(1977)
Monty Baker
  STRANGER IN TOWN(1957, Brit.), p
Muffett Baker
  JAWS 3-D(1983)
Nancy Baker
  SOMETHING WILD(1961)
Nellie Bly Baker
  PAINTED ANGEL, THE(1929); BISHOP MURDER CASE, THE(1930)
Silents
  KID, THE(1921); WOMAN OF PARIS, A(1923); GOLDFISH, THE(1924); SNOB, THE(1924); SALVATION HUNTERS, THE(1925)
Misc. Silents
  LOVE AND THE DEVIL(1929)
Nicholas Baker
  SWEET SUGAR(1972)
Pat Baker
  TWICE UPON A TIME(1953, Brit.)
Patrick Baker
  EXPOSED(1983)
Phil Baker
  GIFT OF GAB(1934); GOLDWYN FOLLIES, THE(1938); GANG'S ALL HERE, THE(1943); TAKE IT OR LEAVE IT(1944)
Philippa Baker
  NO. 96(1974, Aus.)
Phyllis Baker
  GLIMPSE OF PARADISE, A(1934, Brit.)

Pip Baker
  THIRD ALIBI, THE(1961, Brit.), w; BREAK, THE(1962, Brit.), w; MURDER CAN BE DEADLY(1963, Brit.), w; ISLAND OF THE BURNING DAMNED(1971, Brit.), w
R.C. Baker
Misc. Silents
  WHEN DESTINY WILLS(1921), d
Ray Baker
  SILKWOOD(1983)
Raymond Baker
  DIAMONDS ARE FOREVER(1971, Brit.); LINE, THE(1982)
1984
  C.H.U.D.(1984); PLACES IN THE HEART(1984)
Tarkington Baker
Silents
  HUMAN STUFF(1920), w
Reginald Baker
Misc. Silents
  DIXIE HANDICAP, THE(1925), d
Rex "Snowy" Baker
Silents
  FIGHTING BREED, THE(1921); FIGHTER'S PARADISE(1924); SWORD OF VALOR, THE(1924)
Misc. Silents
  HIS LAST RACE(1923)
Richard A. Baker
  KENTUCKY FRIED MOVIE, THE(1977)
Richard A. "Rick" Baker
  INCREDIBLE SHRINKING WOMAN, THE(1981)
Richard Baker
  THE DOUBLE McGUFFIN(1979), p&d
Richard Foster Baker
Misc. Silents
  BUNCH OF KEYS, A(1915), d
Rick Baker
  OCTAMAN(1971), spec eff & makeup; THING WITH TWO HEADS, THE(1972), a, makeup; EXORCIST, THE(1973), makeup; IT'S ALIVE(1974), spec eff, makeup; FOOD OF THE GODS, THE(1976), spec eff; KING KONG(1976), a, cos; SQUIRM(1976), makeup; TRACK OF THE MOONBEAST(1976), makeup; STAR WARS(1977), makeup; FURY, THE(1978), makeup; INCREDIBLE MELTING MAN, THE(1978), spec eff, makeup; AMERICAN WEREWOLF IN LONDON, AN(1981), makeup; TANYA'S ISLAND(1981, Can.), spec eff
1984
  GREYSTOKE: THE LEGEND OF TARZAN, LORD OF THE APES(1984), cos
Robert Baker
  CONSPIRACY(1930), Beulah M. Dix; MELODY CLUB(1949, Brit.), p; NO TRACE(1950, Brit.), p, w; FRIGHTENED MAN, THE(1952, Brit.), p; DEADLY NIGHTSHADE(1953, Brit.), p; LOVE IN PAWN(1953, Brit.), p; RECOIL(1953), p; DELAYED ACTION(1954, Brit.), p; DOUBLE EXPOSURE(1954, Brit.), p; ESCAPE BY NIGHT(1954, Brit.), p; WINDFALL(1955 Brit.), p; BOND OF FEAR(1956, Brit.), p; HOUR OF DECISION(1957, Brit.), p; PROFESSOR TIM(1957, Ireland), p; BLIND SPOT(1958, Brit.), p, w; CRAWLING EYE, THE(1958, Brit.), p; FISTS OF FURY(1973, Chi.)
Silents
  CONSPIRACY, THE(1914), w; ARMS AND THE GIRL(1917), w; COUNTERFEIT(1919), w
Robert M. Baker
Silents
  FLIRTING WITH FATE(1916), w; FLYING TORPEDO, THE(1916), w; REGGIE MIXES IN(1916), w
Robert S. Baker
  DATE WITH A DREAM, A(1948, Brit.), p, w; BLACKOUT(1950, Brit.), d, w; QUIET WOMAN, THE(1951, Brit.), p; 13 EAST STREET(1952, Brit.), p, d, w; BIG FRAME, THE(1953, Brit.), p; MURDER WILL OUT(1953, Brit.), p; STEEL KEY, THE(1953, Brit.), p, d; WHITE FIRE(1953, Brit.), p; EMBEZZLER, THE(1954, Brit.), p; GILDED CAGE, THE(1954, Brit.), p; IMPULSE(1955, Brit.), p; NO SMOKING(1955, Brit.), p; BREAKAWAY(1956, Brit.), p; MURDER ON APPROVAL(1956, Brit.), p; PASSPORT TO TREASON(1956, Brit.), p, d; HIGH TERRACE(1957, Brit.), p; PROFESSOR TIM(1957, Ireland), w; STRANGER IN TOWN(1957, Brit.), p; TWO GROOMS FOR A BRIDE(1957), p; BLOOD OF THE VAMPIRE(1958, Brit.), p; CROSS-UP(1958), p; HOME IS THE HERO(1959, Ireland), p; JACK THE RIPPER(1959, Brit.), p, d; BOYD'S SHOP(1960, Brit.), p; POACHER'S DAUGHTER, THE(1960, Brit.), p; SIEGE OF SIDNEY STREET, THE(1960, Brit.), p&d, ph, ed; MANIA(1961, Brit.), p; SECRET OF MONTE CRISTO, THE(1961, Brit.), p&d, ph; DESERT PATROL(1962, Brit.), p; WHAT A CARVE UP!(1962, Brit.), p; HELLFIRE CLUB, THE(1963, Brit.), p&d; CROSS-PLOT(1969, Brit.), p
Robyn Baker
  BLACK CAT, THE(1966)
Roy Baker
  OCTOBER MAN, THE(1948, Brit.), d; PAPER ORCHID(1949, Brit.), d; WEAKER SEX, THE(1949, Brit.), d; HIGHLY DANGEROUS(1950, Brit.), d; I'LL NEVER FORGET YOU(1951), d; OPERATION DISASTER(1951, Brit.), d; DON'T BOTHER TO KNOCK(1952), d; NIGHT WITHOUT SLEEP(1952), d; INFERNO(1953), d; PASSAGE HOME(1955, Brit.), d; TIGER IN THE SMOKE(1956, Brit.), d; NIGHT TO REMEMBER, A(1958, Brit.), d; ONE THAT GOT AWAY, THE(1958, Brit.), d; MA BARKER'S KILLER BROOD(1960); FLAME IN THE STREETS(1961, Brit.), p, d; TWO LEFT FEET(1965, Brit.), d, w
Roy [Ward] Baker
  SINGER NOT THE SONG, THE(1961, Brit.), p&d; VALIANT, THE(1962, Brit./Ital.), d; ANNIVERSARY, THE(1968, Brit.), d; FIVE MILLION YEARS TO EARTH(1968, Brit.), d; JOURNEY INTO MIDNIGHT(1968, Brit.), d; MOON ZERO TWO(1970, Brit.), d; SCARS OF DRACULA, THE(1970, Brit.), d; VAMPIRE LOVERS, THE(1970, Brit.), d; DR. JEKYLL AND SISTER HYDE(1971, Brit.), d; ASYLUM(1972, Brit.), d; AND NOW THE SCREAMING STARTS(1973, Brit.), d; VAULT OF HORROR, THE(1973, Brit.), d; MONSTER CLUB, THE(1981, Brit.), d
Misc. Talkies
  MISSION: MONTE CARLO(1981, Brit.), d
Roy Wood Baker
  DRACULA AND THE SEVEN GOLDEN VAMPIRES(1978, Brit./Chi.), d

Russell Baker
  MINX, THE(1969)
Ruth Baker
  LILITH(1964); PERSECUTION AND ASSASSINATION OF JEAN-PAUL MARAT AS PERFORMED BY THE INMATES OF THE ASYLUM OF CHARENTON UNDER THE DIRECTION OF THE MARQUIS DE SADE, THE(1967, Brit.); DEAR, DEAD DELILAH(1972)
Said Baker
  MOHAMMAD, MESSENGER OF GOD(1976, Lebanon/Brit.), ph
Sally Baker
  DETROIT 9000(1973)
Sam Baker
  ISLE OF LOST SHIPS(1929); KING OF THE JUNGLE(1933); PUBLIC HERO NO. 1(1935); STEAMBOAT ROUND THE BEND(1935)
Silents
  THIEF OF BAGDAD, THE(1924); SEA BEAST, THE(1926); FAR CALL, THE(1929)
Scott Baker
1984
  DELIVERY BOYS(1984)
Sharon Baker
Misc. Talkies
  STAR OSYSSEY(1978)
Sharisse Baker
  TERMS OF ENDEARMENT(1983)
Silver Tip Baker
  RIDING TORNADO, THE(1932); POWDERSMOKE RANGE(1935); WAGON TRAIL(1935); LEFT-HANDED LAW(1937); DURANGO KID, THE(1940)
Snowy Baker
  BIG CITY(1937)
Misc. Silents
  BETTER MAN, THE(1921); SHADOW OF LIGHTING RIDGE, THE(1921); EMPIRE BUILDERS(1924)
Sophie Baker
  TWO ENGLISH GIRLS(1972, Fr.)
Stanley Baker
  YESTERDAY'S ENEMY(1959, Brit.); UNDERGROUND GUERRILLAS(1944, Brit.); HIDDEN ROOM, THE(1949, Brit.); EYE WITNESS(1950, Brit.); ROSSITER CASE, THE(1950, Brit.); CAPTAIN HORATIO HORNBLOWER(1951, Brit.); HOME TO DANGER(1951, Brit.); LILLI MARLENE(1951, Brit.); CLOUDBURST(1952, Brit.); WHISPERING SMITH VERSUS SCOTLAND YARD(1952, Brit.); CRUEL SEA, THE(1953); KNIGHTS OF THE ROUND TABLE(1953); BEAUTIFUL STRANGER(1954, Brit.); GOOD DIE YOUNG, THE(1954, Brit.); HELL BELOW ZERO(1954, Brit.); PARATROOPER(1954, Brit.); ALEXANDER THE GREAT(1956); CHILD IN THE HOUSE(1956, Brit.); HELEN OF TROY(1956, Ital); HELL IN KOREA(1956, Brit.); RICHARD III(1956, Brit.); CAMPBELL'S KINGDOM(1957, Brit.); CHECKPOINT(1957, Brit.); HELL DRIVERS(1958, Brit.); VIOLENT PLAYGROUND(1958, Brit.); ANGRY HILLS, THE(1959, Brit.); SEA FURY(1959, Brit.); CHANCE MEETING(1960, Brit.); HELL IS A CITY(1960, Brit.); GUNS OF NAVARONE, THE(1961); JET STORM(1961, Brit.); CONCRETE JUNGLE, THE(1962, Brit.); EVA(1962, Fr./Ital.); PRIZE OF ARMS, A(1962, Brit.); SODOM AND GOMORRAH(1962, U.S./Fr./Ital.); IN THE FRENCH STYLE(1963, U.S./Fr.); ZULU(1964, Brit.), a, p; DINGAKA(1965, South Africa); SANDS OF THE KALAHARI(1965, Brit.), a, p; ACCIDENT(1967, Brit.); MAN WHO FINALLY DIED, THE(1967, Brit.); ROBBERY(1967, Brit.), a, p; GIRL WITH A PISTOL, THE(1968, Ital.); WHERE'S JACK?(1969, Brit.), a, p; GAMES, THE(1970); LAST GRENADE, THE(1970, Brit.); PERFECT FRIDAY(1970, Brit.); POPSY POP(1971, Fr.); INNOCENT BYSTANDERS(1973, Brit.)
Susan Baker
  SEASIDE SWINGERS(1965, Brit.); FUNNY THING HAPPENED ON THE WAY TO THE FORUM, A(1966); BUTTERCUP CHAIN, THE(1971, Brit.); TOMMY(1975, Brit.)
Tarkington Baker
Silents
  HER FIVE-FOOT HIGHNESS(1920), w
Ted Baker
  GAY PURR-EE(1962), ed; MAN FROM BUTTON WILLOW, THE(1965), ed
Terry Baker
  TREAD SOFTLY STRANGER(1959, Brit.)
Thomas Baker
  SIGN OF AQUARIUS(1970), md
Tom Baker
  HALLUCINATION GENERATION(1966); SORCERERS, THE(1967, Brit.), w; CONQUEROR WORM, THE(1968, Brit.), w; ANGELS DIE HARD(1970); LAST MOVIE, THE(1971); NICHOLAS AND ALEXANDRA(1971, Brit.); VAULT OF HORROR, THE(1973, Brit.); WEDNESDAY CHILDREN, THE(1973), m; YOUNG NURSES, THE(1973); GOLDEN VOYAGE OF SINBAD, THE(1974, Brit.); MUTATIONS, THE(1974, Brit.); TWO-MINUTE WARNING(1976); ROLLERCOASTER(1977); MORE AMERICAN GRAFFITI(1979); WHOLLY MOSES(1980)
Misc. Talkies
  RUNAWAY(1971); FYRE(1979)
Tommy Baker
  DANGER FLIGHT(1939); SAGA OF DEATH VALLEY(1939); BROTHER ORCHID(1940); MY LOVE CAME BACK(1940)
Tony Baker
  CRY FROM THE STREET, A(1959, Brit.)
V.C. Graham Baker
  HONKY TONK(1929), w
Valerie Baker
  GIRO CITY(1982, Brit.)
Virginia Baker
  TEN SECONDS TO HELL(1959); SOMETHING WILD(1961); THUNDERBOLT AND LIGHTFOOT(1974); DAY OF THE LOCUST, THE(1975)
W. Howard Baker
  MURDER AT SITE THREE(1959, Brit.), w
Warren Baker
  SECRET OF MAGIC ISLAND, THE(1964, Fr./Ital.), m
Baker & Silvers
Silents
  TWO FLAMING YOUTHS(1927)

Stuart Baker-Bergen
  TOY, THE(1982)
1984
  TIGHTROPE(1984)
Malcolm Baker-Smith
  TRAIN OF EVENTS(1952, Brit.), art d
Sheila Bakerman
  ME, NATALIE(1969), ed; TRUMAN CAPOTE'S TRILOGY(1969), ed
Adam BakerMill
  HERO(1982, Brit.), ph
George Bakes
  RAGGEDY ANN AND ANDY(1977), anim
Billy [William] Bakewell
  SPEED WINGS(1934)
Ernest Bakewell
Silents
  FLAMES OF FEAR(1930, Brit.)
William Bakewell
  GOLD DIGGERS OF BROADWAY(1929); HOT STUFF(1929); IRON MASK, THE(1929); LADY OF THE PAVEMENTS(1929); ON WITH THE SHOW(1929); ALL QUIET ON THE WESTERN FRONT(1930); BAT WHISPERS, THE(1930); LUMMOX(1930); ONLY THE BRAVE(1930); PAID(1930); PLAYING AROUND(1930); DANCE, FOOLS, DANCE(1931); DAYBREAK(1931); GUILTY HANDS(1931); POLITICS(1931); REDUCING(1931); SPIRIT OF NOTRE DAME, THE(1931); WOMAN OF EXPERIENCE, A(1931); BACK STREET(1932); CHEATERS AT PLAY(1932); WHILE PARIS SLEEPS(1932); LUCKY DEVILS(1933); MAN OF SENTIMENT, A(1933); THREE-CORNERED MOON(1933); CRIMSON ROMANCE(1934); GREEN EYES(1934); PARTY'S OVER, THE(1934); QUITTERS, THE(1934); STRAIGHT IS THE WAY(1934); STRAIGHTAWAY(1934); YOU CAN'T BUY EVERYTHING(1934); CURTAIN FALLS, THE(1935); HAPPINESS C.O.D.(1935); ON PROBATION(1935); SONS OF STEEL(1935); STRANGERS ALL(1935); TOGETHER WE LIVE(1935); LADY LUCK(1936); SEA SPOILERS, THE(1936); CRIME AFLOAT(1937); DANGEROUS HOLIDAY(1937); EXILED TO SHANGHAI(1937); MILE A MINUTE LOVE(1937); QUALITY STREET(1937); TRAPPED BY G-MEN(1938); DUKE OF WEST POINT, THE(1938); HIGGINS FAMILY, THE(1938); GONE WITH THE WIND(1939); HOTEL IMPERIAL(1939); KING OF THE TURF(1939); BEYOND TOMORROW(1940); SEVEN SINNERS(1940); DR. KILDARE'S VICTORY(1941); DAWN EXPRESS, THE(1942); I LIVE ON DANGER(1942); SUBMARINE ALERT(1943); YANKS AHOY(1943); BACHELOR AND THE BOBBY-SOXER, THE(1947); FABULOUS DORSEYS, THE(1947); FARMER'S DAUGHTER, THE(1947); TRESPASSER, THE(1947); ARTHUR TAKES OVER(1948); KING OF THE BANDITS(1948); ROMANCE ON THE HIGH SEAS(1948); SO THIS IS NEW YORK(1948); YOU GOTTA STAY HAPPY(1948); CAPTURE, THE(1950); MESSENGER OF PEACE(1950); COME FILL THE CUP(1951); WELLS FARGO GUNMASTER(1951); WHEN THE REDSKINS RODE(1951); ROOM FOR ONE MORE(1952); LUCKY ME(1954); DAVY CROCKETT, KING OF THE WILD FRONTIER(1955)
Misc. Talkies
  MANHATTAN BUTTERFLY(1935)
Silents
  LAST EDITION, THE(1925); SHIELD OF HONOR, THE(1927); ANNAPOLIS(1928); HAROLD TEEN(1928); WEST POINT(1928)
Misc. Silents
  MOTHER(1927); DEVIL'S TRADEMARK, THE(1928)
William Bakewell, Jr.
  LOVES OF EDGAR ALLAN POE, THE(1942); POSTMAN DIDN'T RING, THE(1942)
Ed Bakey
  HEAVEN WITH A GUN(1969); BARQUERO(1970); WILD ROVERS(1971); OTHER, THE(1972); STING, THE(1973); DARKTOWN STRUTTERS(1975); FOR PETE'S SAKE(1977); TELEFON(1977); WHITE BUFFALO, THE(1977); HOT LEAD AND COLD FEET(1978); BALTIMORE BULLET, THE(1980); DEAD AND BURIED(1981); ZAPPED!(1982)
1984
  PHILADELPHIA EXPERIMENT, THE(1984)
A. Bakhar
  WAR AND PEACE(1968, USSR)
Emma Bakhle
  SWEET WILLIAM(1980, Brit.)
S. Bakhmetyeva
  VIOLIN AND ROLLER(1962, USSR), w
D. Bakhtin
  JACK FROST(1966, USSR)
Members of The Bakiga and Batwa Tribes
  MAN OF AFRICA(1956, Brit.)
Claude Bakka
  MADE IN U.S.A.(1966, Fr.)
Don Bakke
  PURPLE HAZE(1982)
Vicki Bakken
  GREATEST SHOW ON EARTH, THE(1952); FROM HERE TO ETERNITY(1953)
Trish Bakker
1984
  RENO AND THE DOC(1984, Can.)
Trysh Bakker
1984
  RENO AND THE DOC(1984, Can.), cos
G. Baklanov
  FORTY-NINE DAYS(1964, USSR), w
Olga Baklanova
Misc. Silents
  SYMPHONY OF LOVE AND DEATH(1914, USSR); WHEN THE STRINGS OF THE HEART SOUND(1914, USSR); GREAT MAGARAZ, THE(1915, USSR); WANDERER BEYOND THE GRAVE(1915, USSR); HE WHO GETS SLAPPED(1916, USSR); FLOWERS ARE LATE, THE(1917, USSR); BREAD(1918, USSR)
Mason Bakman
  NOTORIOUS CLEOPATRA, THE(1970)
Laszlo Bakos
  FATHER(1967, Hung.)
Khaula Bakr
  PUTNEY SWOPE(1969)

Said Abu Bakr
CAIRO(1963)
Mohamed Bakri
HANNAH K.(1983, Fr.)
Shakira Baksh
CARRY ON AGAIN, DOCTOR(1969, Brit.)
Constantine Baksheef
RUSSIANS ARE COMING, THE RUSSIANS ARE COMING, THE(1966)
Pytor Baksheyev
Misc. Silents
TSAR NIKOLAI II(1917, USSR); POWER OF DARKNESS, THE(1918, USSR)
Ralph Bakshi
COONSKIN(1975), d&w; WIZARDS(1977), p,d&w; LORD OF THE RINGS, THE(1978), d; AMERICAN POP(1981), d; HEY, GOOD LOOKIN'(1982), p,d&w; FIRE AND ICE(1983), p, d, w
1984
CANNONBALL RUN II(1984), anim
Misc. Talkies
HEAVY TRAFFIC(1974), d
Shango Baku
STUD, THE(1979, Brit.)
A. J. Bakunas
APPLE DUMPLING GANG RIDES AGAIN, THE(1979); STUNT MAN, THE(1980)
Jeanne Bal
COMPANY OF KILLERS(1970)
Bert Balaban
GENTLE RAIN, THE(1966, Braz.), p, d
Bob Balaban
ME, NATALIE(1969); MIDNIGHT COWBOY(1969); STRAWBERRY STATEMENT, THE(1970); MAKING IT(1971); CLOSE ENCOUNTERS OF THE THIRD KIND(1977); GIRLFRIENDS(1978); ALTERED STATES(1980); ABSENCE OF MALICE(1981); PRINCE OF THE CITY(1981); WHOSE LIFE IS IT ANYWAY?(1981)
1984
2010(1984)
Bruce Balaban
PLACE CALLED GLORY, A(1966, Span./Ger.), p; TEXICAN, THE(1966, U.S./Span.), p
Burt Balaban
DIPLOMATIC PASSPORT(1954, Brit.), p; STRANGER FROM VENUS, THE(1954, Brit.), p, d; LADY OF VENGEANCE(1957, Brit), p, d; HIGH HELL(1958), d; MURDER, INC.(1960), p, d; MAD DOG COLL(1961), d
Robert Balaban
CATCH-22(1970); BANK SHOT(1974); REPORT TO THE COMMISSIONER(1975)
Nadia Balabin
NAKED MAJA, THE(1959, Ital./U.S.)
Nadia Balabine
LA DOLCE VITA(1961, Ital./Fr.)
T. Balach
HOUSE OF GREED(1934, USSR)
Fred Balachine
TURN ON TO LOVE(1969), w
Boris Balachoff
Misc. Talkies
SINTHIA THE DEVIL'S DOLL(1970)
Bela Balacz
BLUE LIGHT, THE(1932, Ger.), p
Kostas Balademas
NAKED BRIGADE, THE(1965, U.S./Gr.)
Kostas Baladimas
PHAEDRA(1962, U.S./Gr./Fr.); ASSAULT ON AGATHON(1976, Brit./Gr.)
Costas Baladinas
ISLAND OF LOVE(1963)
Oleg Balaeff
HEAVENLY DAYS(1944)
B. Balakin
MEET ME IN MOSCOW(1966, USSR)
John Balamos
HERCULES IN NEW YORK(1970), m
A. Balanchiavadze
VOW, THE(1947, USSR.), m
George Balanchine
DARK RED ROSES(1930, Brit.); GOLDWYN FOLLIES, THE(1938), ch; I WAS AN ADVENTURESS(1940), ch; STAR SPANGLED RHYTHM(1942), ch; MIDSUMMER NIGHT'S DREAM, A(1966), d, ch; TURNING POINT, THE(1977), ch
A. Balanchivadze
LAST HILL, THE(1945, USSR), m
Antonio Balandin
OPEN SEASON(1974, U.S./Span.), spec eff
Francisco Balangue
1984
PURPLE HEARTS(1984), art d
Simchah Balanoff
VILNA LEGEND, A(1949, U.S./Pol.)
Jean-Claude Balard
WAR AND PEACE(1968, USSR)
J.J. Balargeon
REQUIEM FOR A HEAVYWEIGHT(1962)
Heinrich Balasch
TRUNKS OF MR. O.F., THE(1932, Ger.), ph
V. Balashov
HEROES ARE MADE(1944, USSR); SECRET BRIGADE, THE(1951 USSR)
Vladimir Balashov
IVAN THE TERRIBLE(Part I, 1947, USSR)
Svetlana Balashova
SONS AND MOTHERS(1967, USSR)
Belinda Balaski
BOBBIE JO AND THE OUTLAW(1976); CANNONBALL(1976, U.S./Hong Kong); FOOD OF THE GODS, THE(1976); PIRANHA(1978); TILL DEATH(1978); HOWLING, THE(1981)

1984
GREMLINS(1984)
Josiane Balasko
TENANT, THE(1976, Fr.); MEN PREFER FAT GIRLS(1981, Fr.), a, w
Gabor Balassa
FORBIDDEN RELATIONS(1983, Hung.)
Bela Balasz
THREEPENNY OPERA, THE(1931, Ger./U.S.), w
Charles Balazs
1984
PARIS, TEXAS(1984, Ger./Fr.), makeup
Lajos Balazsovits
CONFIDENCE(1980, Hung.)
Balbina
BELLES OF ST. TRINIAN'S, THE(1954, Brit.); CITY AFTER MIDNIGHT(1957, Brit.); TRIPLE DECEPTION(1957, Brit.); TRUTH ABOUT WOMEN, THE(1958, Brit.); LOSS OF INNOCENCE(1961, Brit.); FUR COLLAR, THE(1962, Brit.); COUNTESS FROM HONG KONG, A(1967, Brit.)
Ennio Balbo
TERROR-CREATURES FROM THE GRAVE(1967, U.S./Ital.); KISS THE OTHER SHEIK(1968, Fr./Ital.); APPOINTMENT, THE(1969); SEVEN GOLDEN MEN(1969, Fr./Ital./Span.); DAY OF ANGER(1970, Ital./Ger.); YEAR ONE(1974, Ital.); STREET PEOPLE(1976, U.S./Ital.)
Rosangela Balbo
INCREDIBLE INVASION, THE(1971, Mex./U.S.)
Silvano Balboni
Silents
ACQUITTAL, THE(1923), ph; LADY ROBINHOOD(1925), ph; FAR CRY, THE(1926), d
Misc. Silents
MASKED WOMAN, THE(1927), d
Peter Balbursch
BATTLEGROUND(1949), spec eff
Adele Balcan
THREE BRAVE MEN(1957), cos
Francisco Balcasar
DAY THE HOTLINE GOT HOT, THE(1968, Fr./Span.), p
Alfonso Balcazar
FIVE GIANTS FROM TEXAS(1966, Ital./Span.), w; PISTOL FOR RINGO, A(1966, Ital./Span.), w; SUNSCORCHED(1966, Span./Ger.), w; LIGHTNING BOLT(1967, Ital./Sp.), w
J.J. Balcazar
SUPERARGO VERSUS DIABOLICUS(1966, Ital./Span.), p, w
Jesus Jaime Balcazar
SUNSCORCHED(1966, Span./Ger.), d
Balch
SECRETS OF SEX(1970, Brit.), w
Anthony Balch
SECRETS OF SEX(1970, Brit.), p, d; HORROR HOSPITAL(1973, Brit.), d, w
Misc. Talkies
BIZARRE(1969), d
Joe Balch
FOURTH HORSEMAN, THE(1933); RACKETEERS OF THE RANGE(1939)
Slim Balch
HOLLYWOOD COWBOY(1937); SUNSET PASS(1946)
Nigel Balchin
FAME IS THE SPUR(1947, Brit.), w; MINE OWN EXECUTIONER(1948, Brit.), w; HOUR OF GLORY(1949, Brit.), w; CRASH OF SILENCE(1952, Brit.), w; MALTA STORY(1954, Brit.), w; JOSEPHINE AND MEN(1955, Brit.), w; MAN WHO NEVER WAS, THE(1956, Brit.), w; 23 PACES TO BAKER STREET(1956), w; BLUE ANGEL, THE(1959), w; CIRCLE OF DECEPTON(1961, Brit.), w; RISK, THE(1961, Brit.), w; SINGER NOT THE SONG, THE(1961, Brit.), w
Max Balchowsky
LOVE BUG, THE(1968); PROMISE, THE(1979)
Carlyle Balckwell
Misc. Silents
SHE(1925, Brit.)
Michael Balcom
SAILING ALONG(1938, Brit.), p
Jean-Marie Balcon
JOHNNY FRENCHMAN(1946, Brit.)
Jill Balcon
NICHOLAS NICKLEBY(1947, Brit.); SARABAND(1949, Brit.); GOOD TIME GIRL(1950, Brit.); HIGHLY DANGEROUS(1950, Brit.); LOST PEOPLE, THE(1950, Brit.)
Michael Balcon
CITY OF PLAY(1929, Brit.), p; RETURN OF THE RAT, THE(1929, Brit.), p; TAXI FOR TWO(1929, Brit.), p; WOMAN TO WOMAN(1929), p; CROOKED BILLET, THE(1930, Brit.), p; JUST FOR A SONG(1930, Brit.), p; SYMPHONY IN TWO FLATS(1930, Brit.), p; WARM CORNER, A(1930, Brit.), p; GENTLEMAN OF PARIS, A(1931), p; HINDLE WAKES(1931, Brit.), p; NIGHT IN MONTMARTE, A(1931, Brit.), p;P.C. JOSSER(1931, Brit.), p; SPORT OF KINGS, THE(1931, Brit.), p;STRONGER SEX, THE(1931, Brit.), p; THIRD TIME LUCKY(1931, Brit.), p; AFTER THE BALL(1932, Brit.), p; CRIMINAL AT LARGE(1932, Brit.), p; HOUND OF THE BASKERVILLES(1932, Brit.), p; LORD BABS(1932, Brit.), p; LOVE ON WHEELS(1932, Brit.), p; MARRY ME(1932, Brit.), p; MICHAEL AND MARY(1932, Brit.), p; MIDSHIPMAID GOB(1932, Brit.), p; OFFICE GIRL, THE(1932, Brit.), p; RINGER, THE(1932, Brit.), p; BRITANNIA OF BILLINGSGATE(1933, Brit.), p; CONSTANT NYMPH, THE(1933, Brit.), p; FAITHFUL HEART(1933, Brit.), p; FALLING FOR YOU(1933, Brit.), p; GHOST TRAIN, THE(1933, Brit.), p; LUCKY NUMBER, THE(1933, Brit.), p; MAN FROM TORONTO, THE(1933, Brit.), p; MAN THEY COULDN'T ARREST, THE(1933, Brit.), p; NIGHT AND DAY(1933, Brit.), p; ROME EXPRESS(1933, Brit.), p; SLEEPING CAR(1933, Brit.), p; THERE GOES THE BRIDE(1933, Brit.), p; TURKEY TIME(1933, Brit.), p; WHITE FACE(1933, Brit.), p; ALONG CAME SALLY(1934, Brit.), p; CAMELS ARE COMING, THE(1934, Brit.), p; CHU CHIN CHOW(1934, Brit.), p; CUP OF KINDNESS, A(1934, Brit.), p; DIRTY WORK(1934, Brit.), p; EVENSONG(1934, Brit.), p; EVERGREEN(1934, Brit.), p; FRIDAY THE 13TH(1934, Brit.), p; GHOUL, THE(1934, Brit.), p; I WAS A SPY(1934, Brit.), p; IT'S A BOY(1934, Brit.), p; LADY IN DANGER(1934, Brit.), p; LEAVE IT TO SMITH(1934), p; ORDERS IS ORDERS(1934, Brit.), p; POWER(1934, Brit.), p; ROAD HOUSE(1934, Brit.), p;

THINGS ARE LOOKING UP(1934, Brit.), p; WILD BOY(1934, Brit.), p; WOMAN IN COMMAND, THE(1934 Brit.), p; ALIAS BULLDOG DRUMMOND(1935, Brit.), p; BORN FOR GLORY(1935, Brit.), p; CLAIRVOYANT, THE(1935, Brit.), p; FIGHTING STOCK(1935, Brit.), p; FIRST A GIRL(1935, Brit.), p; FOREIGN AFFAIRES(1935, Brit.), p; IRON DUKE, THE(1935, Brit.), p; JACK AHOY!(1935, Brit.), p; MAN WHO KNEW TOO MUCH, THE(1935, Brit.), p; ME AND MARLBOROUGH(1935, Brit.), p; OH DADDY!(1935, Brit.), p; PRINCESS CHARMING(1935, Brit.), p; STORMY WEATHER(1935, Brit.), p; TRANSATLANTIC TUNNEL(1935, Brit.), p; 39 STEPS, THE(1935, Brit.), p; ALL IN(1936, Brit.), p; BOYS WILL BE BOYS(1936, Brit.), p; DOMMED CARGO(1936, Brit.), p; EVERYBODY DANCE(1936, Brit.), p; FIRST OFFENCE(1936, Brit.), p; IT'S LOVE AGAIN(1936, Brit.), p; KING OF THE DAMNED(1936, Brit.), p; LADY JANE GREY(1936, Brit.), p; MAN WHO LIVED AGAIN, THE(1936, Brit.), p; MISTER HOBO(1936, Brit.), p; POT LUCK(1936, Brit.), p; SECRET AGENT, THE(1936, Brit.), p; WHERE THERE'S A WILL(1936, Brit), p; DOCTOR SYN(1937, Brit.), p; GANGWAY(1937, Brit.), p; NON-STOP NEW YORK(1937, Brit.), p; SABOTAGE(1937, Brit.), p; TAKE MY TIP(1937, Brit.), p; WINDBAG THE SAILOR(1937, Brit.), p; CLIMBING HIGH(1938, Brit.), p; TWO OF US, THE(1938, Brit.), p; YANK AT OXFORD, A(1938), p; LET'S BE FAMOUS(1939, Brit.), p; PHANTOM STRIKES, THE(1939, Brit.), p; WARE CASE, THE(1939, Brit.), p; CONVOY(1940), p; LET GEORGE DO IT(1940, Brit.), p; SECRET FOUR, THE(1940, Brit.), p; BLACK SHEEP OF WHITEHALL, THE(1941 Brit.), p; PROUD VALLEY, THE(1941, Brit.), p; NEXT OF KIN(1942, Brit.), p; SHIPS WITH WINGS(1942, Brit.), p; BELLS GO DOWN, THE(1943, Brit.), p; CHAMPAGNE CHARLIE(1944, Brit.), p; THEY CAME TO A CITY(1944, Brit.), p; UNDERGROUND GUERRILLAS(1944, Brit.), p; 48 HOURS(1944, Brit.), p; HALF-WAY HOUSE, THE(1945, Brit.), p; DEAD OF NIGHT(1945, Brit.), p; JOHNNY FRENCHMAN(1946, Brit.), p; OVERLANDERS, THE(1946, Brit./Aus.), p; LOVES OF JOANNA GODDEN, THE(1947, Brit.), p; NICHOLAS NICKLEBY(1947, Brit.), p; ANOTHER SHORE(1948, Brit.), p; CAPTIVE HEART, THE(1948, Brit.), p; KIND HEARTS AND CORONETS(1949, Brit.), p; PASSPORT TO PIMLICO(1949, Brit.), p; SCOTT OF THE ANTARCTIC(1949, Brit.), p; TIGHT LITTLE ISLAND(1949, Brit.), p; BITTER SPRINGS(1950, Aus.), p; BLUE LAMP, THE(1950, Brit.), p; CAGE OF GOLD(1950, Brit.), p; DANCE HALL(1950, Brit.), p; HUE AND CRY(1950, Brit.), p; MAGNET, THE(1950, Brit.), p; PINK STRING AND SEALING WAX(1950, Brit.), p; LAVENDER HILL MOB, THE(1951, Brit.), p; CRASH OF SILENCE(1952, Brit.), p; IVORY HUNTER(1952, Brit.), p; MAN IN THE WHITE SUIT, THE(1952), p; TRAIN OF EVENTS(1952, Brit.), p; GENTLE TOUCH, THE(1956, Brit.), p; ALL AT SEA(1958, Brit.), p; DAVY(1958, Brit.), p; DUNKIRK(1958, Brit.), p; NOWHERE TO GO(1959, Brit.), p; SCAPEGOAT, THE(1959, Brit.), p; LONG AND THE SHORT AND THE TALL, THE(1961, Brit.), p

Silents
PASSIONATE ADVENTURE, THE(1924, Brit.), p; PRUDES FALL, THE(1924, Brit.), p; PLEASURE GARDEN, THE(1925, Brit./Ger.), p; RAT, THE(1925, Brit.), p; FEAR O' GOD(1926, Brit./Ger.), p; LODGER, THE(1926, Brit.), p; EASY VIRTUE(1927, Brit.), p; GHOST TRAIN, THE(1927, Brit.), p; ONE OF THE BEST(1927, Brit.), p; VORTEX, THE(1927, Brit.), p; WHEN BOYS LEAVE HOME(1928, Brit.), p

Misc. Silents
DOLORES(1928, Brit.), d

S. C. Balcon
EVERYTHING IS THUNDER(1936, Brit.), p; MAN OF AFFAIRS(1937, Brit.), p; CHEER BOYS CHEER(1939, Brit.), p; YOUNG MAN'S FANCY(1943, Brit.), p

S.C. Balcon
HEAD OVER HEELS IN LOVE(1937, Brit.), p; RETURN TO YESTERDAY(1940, Brit.), p; GOOSE STEPS OUT, THE(1942, Brit.), p; FOR THOSE IN PERIL(1944, Brit.), p

Gertrud Bald
PEDESTRIAN, THE(1974, Ger.)

Wambly Bald
VIOLATED(1953)

Charles Balda
SECRET MENACE(1931)

Sergio Baldacchini
LIPSTICK(1965, Fr./Ital.), art d

Eddie Baldacchino
TRENCHCOAT(1983)

Anna Baldaccini
EVERY MAN FOR HIMSELF(1980, Fr.)

Bernard Baldan
PURPLE HAZE(1982)

Gianfranco Baldanello
THIS MAN CAN'T DIE(1970, Ital.), d

Barrie Baldaro
TIKI TIKI(1971, Can.); WHY ROCK THE BOAT?(1974, Can.)

Barry Baldaro
APPRENTICESHIP OF DUDDY KRAVITZ, THE(1974, Can.)

Raf Baldassare
FISTFUL OF DOLLARS, A(1964, Ital./Ger./Span.)

Raffaele Baldassare
QUEEN OF THE NILE(1964, Ital.); HERCULES(1983)

Raf Baldassarie
BLINDMAN(1972, Ital.)

Raf Baldassarre
NIGHTS OF LUCRETIA BORGIA, THE(1960, Ital.); SWORD OF THE CONQUEROR(1962, Ital.); SECRET MARK OF D'ARTAGNAN, THE(1963, Fr./Ital.); SULEIMAN THE CONQUEROR(1963, Ital.); STRANGER IN TOWN, A(1968, U.S./Ital.); STRANGER RETURNS, THE(1968, U.S./Ital./Ger./Span.); NARCO MEN, THE(1969, Span./Ital.); MERCENARY, THE(1970, Ital./Span.)

Raffaele Baldassarre
QUEEN OF THE PIRATES(1961, Ital./Ger.); SON OF CAPTAIN BLOOD, THE(1964, U.S./Ital./Span.)

Barbara Baldavin
HANGUP(1974)

Alberto Baldecchi
MAEVA(1961), ph

Francisco Balderas
BRAVE BULLS, THE(1951)

John Balderson
LITTLE OLD NEW YORK(1940), w

John L. Balderson
RED PLANET MARS(1952), w

Robert Balderson
1984
SAM'S SON(1984)

Hamilton Deane, John Balderston
DRACULA(1979), w

John Balderston
DRACULA(1931), w; BELOVED ENEMY(1936), w; DRACULA'S DAUGHTER(1936), w; LAST OF THE MOHICANS, THE(1936), w; PRISONER OF ZENDA, THE(1937), w; GONE WITH THE WIND(1939), w; SCOTLAND YARD(1941), w; SMILIN' THROUGH(1941), w

John C. Balderston
ROMANCE AND RICHES(1937, Brit.), w

John L. Balderston
MUMMY, THE(1932), w; BERKELEY SQUARE(1933), w; BRIDE OF FRANKENSTEIN, THE(1935), w; LIVES OF A BENGAL LANCER(1935), w; MAD LOVE(1935), w; MYSTERY OF EDWIN DROOD, THE(1935), w; MAN WHO LIVED AGAIN, THE(1936, Brit.), w; VICTORY(1940), w; STAND BY FOR ACTION(1942), w; TENNESSEE JOHNSON(1942), w; GASLIGHT(1944), w; I'LL NEVER FORGET YOU(1951), w

John Balderstone
PRISONER OF ZENDA, THE(1952), w

Marion Balderstone
BILL OF DIVORCEMENT, A(1932), tech d

Ferdinando Baldi
DAVID AND GOLIATH(1961, Ital.), d; TARTARS, THE(1962, Ital./Yugo.), d; DUEL OF CHAMPIONS(1964 Ital./Span.), d; SWORD OF EL CID, THE(1965, Span./Ital.), w; AVENGER, THE(1966, Ital.), d, w; BLINDMAN(1972, Ital.), d; GET MEAN(1976, Ital.), d; SICILIAN CONNECTION(1977, d; COMIN' AT YA!(1981), d; TREASURE OF THE FOUR CROWNS(1983, Span./U.S.), d

Gian Vittorio Baldi
ADOLESCENTS, THE(1967, Can.), d&w; CHRONICLE OF ANNA MAGDALENA BACH(1968, Ital., Ger.), p; DIARY OF A SCHIZOPHRENIC GIRL(1970, Ital.), p

Luigi Baldi
LUCIANO(1963, Ital.), d, w

Marcello Baldi
SAUL AND DAVID(1968, Ital./Span.), d, w

Ruggero Baldi
GIRL GAME(1968, Braz./Fr./Ital.)

Constantine Baldimas
SERENITY(1962)

B. Baldin
SUN SHINES FOR ALL, THE(1961, USSR), makeup

Rebecca Balding
SILENT SCREAM(1980); BOOGENS, THE(1982)

Gabriele Baldini
HAWKS AND THE SPARROWS, THE(1967, Ital.)

Oreste Baldini
GODFATHER, THE, PART II(1974)

Renato Baldini
ANGELO(1951, Ital.); BEHIND CLOSED SHUTTERS(1952, Ital.); FOUR WAYS OUT(1954, Ital.); GREAT HOPE, THE(1954, Ital.); ESTHER AND THE KING(1960, U.S./Ital.); HEAD OF A TYRANT(1960, Fr./Ital.); GIRL WITH A SUITCASE(1961, Fr./Ital.); WHITE WARRIOR, THE(1961, Ital./Yugo.); NINE MILES TO NOON(1963); SLAVE, THE(1963, Ital.); AMONG VULTURES(1964, Ger./Ital./Fr./Yugo.); GOLDEN ARROW, THE(1964, Ital.); SNOW DEVILS, THE(1965, Ital.); FRONTIER HELLCAT(1966, Fr./Ital./Ger./Yugo.); LAST OF THE RENEGADES(1966, Fr./Ital./Ger./Yugo.); SECRET SEVEN, THE(1966, Ital./Span.); SPY IN YOUR EYE(1966, Ital.); THAT MAN GEORGE!(1967, Fr./Ital./Span.); ROME WANTS ANOTHER CAESAR(1974, Ital.)

Misc. Talkies
REVENGE OF THE GLADIATORS(1962)

Alvin Baldock
SATURDAY'S HERO(1951)

Saltbush Baldock
GALLIPOLI(1981, Aus.)

Maurizio Baldoni
DAMON AND PYTHIAS(1962)

Charles Baldour
SECRET DOOR, THE(1964), p

Z. Baldova
INSPECTOR GENERAL, THE(1937, Czech.)

Zdenka Baldova
DISTANT JOURNEY(1950, Czech.)

Charles Baldra
FIGHTING THRU(1931); LAWLESS RANGE(1935)

Chuck Baldra
WHEELS OF DESTINY(1934); RIDER OF THE LAW, THE(1935); STORMY(1935); LAWLESS NINETIES, THE(1936); PIONEERS OF THE WEST(1940); RANGER AND THE LADY, THE(1940); PHANTOM COWBOY, THE(1941)

Bert Baldridge
SECRET MENACE(1931), ph

Silents
RACING HEARTS(1923), ph; TO THE LAST MAN(1923), ph; ROMANCE RANCH(1924), ph; RECKLESS SEX, THE(1925), ph; WINGS(1927), ph; LINDA(1929), ph

Frank A. Baldridge
TUCSON(1949), ed

Frank Baldridge
CRIMSON KEY, THE(1947), ed; DANGEROUS YEARS(1947), ed; JEWELS OF BRANDENBURG(1947), ed; ROSES ARE RED(1947), ed; SECOND CHANCE(1947), ed; HALF PAST MIDNIGHT(1948), ed; ROLL, THUNDER, ROLL(1949), ed; YOUNG AND DANGEROUS(1957), ed; GANG WAR(1958), ed; SIERRA BARON(1958), ed; THUNDERING JETS(1958), ed

Sawnie Ruth Baldridge
1984
ON THE LINE(1984, Span.), cos

Armenia Balducci
SACCO AND VANZETTI(1971, Ital./Fr.)

Franco Balducci
STRANGER ON THE PROWL(1953, Ital.); HEAD OF A TYRANT(1960, Fr./Ital.); TWO WOMEN(1961, Ital./Fr.); LA VIACCIA(1962, Fr./Ital.); WARRIORS FIVE(1962); DUEL OF THE TITANS(1963, Ital.); HUNCHBACK OF ROME, THE(1963, Ital.); SLAVE, THE(1963, Ital.); TRAMPLERS, THE(1966, Ital.); QUEENS, THE(1968, Ital./Fr.); ROMEO AND JULIET(1968, Ital./Span.); DEATH RIDES A HORSE(1969, Ital.); DAY OF ANGER(1970, Ital./Ger.); LONG RIDE FROM HELL, A(1970, Ital.)

Richard Balducci
BREATHLESS(1959, Fr.); GENDARME OF ST. TROPEZ, THE(1966, Fr./Ital.), w

Dick Balduzzi
KELLY'S HEROES(1970, U.S./Yugo.); NEWMAN'S LAW(1974); POSTMAN ALWAYS RINGS TWICE, THE(1981); ZORRO, THE GAY BLADE(1981); ZAPPED!(1982)

Adam Baldwin
MY BODYGUARD(1980); ORDINARY PEOPLE(1980); D.C. CAB(1983)
1984
HADLEY'S REBELLION(1984); RECKLESS(1984)

Alan Baldwin
GIRL FROM RIO, THE(1939); WINTER CARNIVAL(1939); FUGITIVE FROM A PRISON CAMP(1940); DEVIL BAT, THE(1941); HILLBILLY BLITZKRIEG(1942); UNDERCOVER MAN(1942)

Ann Baldwin
WALL STREET COWBOY(1939); FORGOTTEN GIRLS(1940); RANCHO GRANDE(1940); WOLF OF NEW YORK(1940)

Beau Baldwin
RHYTHM ON THE RANGE(1936)

Bill Baldwin
ONCE A THIEF(1950); TRIAL WITHOUT JURY(1950); IT'S A BIG COUNTRY(1951); LEATHER SAINT, THE(1956); JOKER IS WILD, THE(1957); ROSEMARY'S BABY(1968); SEVEN MINUTES, THE(1971); DAY OF THE LOCUST, THE(1975); ROCKY(1976); NEW YORK, NEW YORK(1977); ONE AND ONLY, THE(1978); CHAMP, THE(1979); ROCKY II(1979); VOICES(1979); ROCKY III(1982)

Bill Baldwin, Sr.
RIOT ON SUNSET STRIP(1967); HORSE IN THE GRAY FLANNEL SUIT, THE(1968)

Bob Baldwin
NEW LIFE STYLE, THE(1970, Ger.), ph; LET'S SCARE JESSICA TO DEATH(1971), ph; WEREWOLF OF WASHINGTON(1973), ph
1984
EXTERMINATOR 2(1984), ph

Curley Baldwin
Misc. Silents
FIGHTING BACK(1917)

Curly Baldwin
LAWLESS BORDER(1935)

Dick Baldwin
LIFE BEGINS IN COLLEGE(1937); LOVE AND HISSES(1937); INTERNATIONAL SETTLEMENT(1938); MR. MOTO'S GAMBLE(1938); ONE WILD NIGHT(1938); SPRING MADNESS(1938); GOIN' TO TOWN(1944); HAIRY APE, THE(1944)

Don Baldwin
GATOR BAIT(1974)

Dona Baldwin
COOL AND THE CRAZY, THE(1958); BADLANDS(1974)

Douglas Baldwin
BOTTOMS UP(1934)

Earl Baldwin
SOPHOMORE, THE(1929), w; COLLEGE LOVERS(1930), w; RED HOT RHYTHM(1930), w; SWEET MAMA(1930), w; WIDOW FROM CHICAGO, THE(1930), w; BIG SHOT, THE(1931), w; NAUGHTY FLIRT, THE(1931), w; TIP-OFF, THE(1931), w; CENTRAL PARK(1932), w; DOCTOR X(1932), w; LIFE BEGINS(1932), w; MOUTH-PIECE, THE(1932), w; TENDERFOOT, THE(1932), w; THE CRASH(1932), w; BLONDIE JOHNSON(1933), w; HAVANA WIDOWS(1933), w; WILD BOYS OF THE ROAD(1933), w; HERE COMES THE NAVY(1934), w; SIX-DAY BIKE RIDER(1934), w; VERY HONORABLE GUY, A(1934), w; WONDER BAR(1934), w; DEVIL DOGS OF THE AIR(1935), w; GO INTO YOUR DANCE(1935), w; IRISH IN US, THE(1935), w; MISS PACIFIC FLEET(1935), p; EVER SINCE EVE(1937), w; COWBOY FROM BROOKLYN(1938), w; GOLD DIGGERS IN PARIS(1938), w; SLIGHT CASE OF MURDER, A(1938), w; OFF THE RECORD(1939), w; BROTHER ORCHID(1940), w; MY LOVE CAME BACK(1940), w; HONEYMOON FOR THREE(1941), w; SHE COULDN'T SAY NO(1941), w; UNHOLY PARTNERS(1941), w; NAVY COMES THROUGH, THE(1942), w; GREENWICH VILLAGE(1944), w; IRISH EYES ARE SMILING(1944), w; PIN UP GIRL(1944), w; HOLD THAT BLONDE(1945), w; AFRICA SCREAMS(1949), w; LULLABY OF BROADWAY, THE(1951), w; SOUTH SEA WOMAN(1953), w; JUKE BOX RHYTHM(1959), w
Silents
ON ZE BOULEVARD(1927), t

Earl W. Baldwin
BREAKFAST IN HOLLYWOOD(1946), w

Emily Baldwin
LIFE BEGINS AT 40(1935)

Evelyn Baldwin
STRUGGLE, THE(1931)

Faith Baldwin
OFFICE WIFE, THE(1930), w; SKYSCRAPER SOULS(1932), w; WEEK-END MARRIAGE(1932), w; BEAUTY FOR SALE(1933), w; AUGUST WEEK-END(1936, Brit.), w; LOVE BEFORE BREAKFAST(1936), w; MOON'S OUR HOME, THE(1936), w; WIFE VERSUS SECRETARY(1936), w; PORTIA ON TRIAL(1937), w; COMET OVER BROADWAY(1938), w; MEN ARE SUCH FOOLS(1938), w; APARTMENT FOR PEGGY(1948), d&w; QUEEN FOR A DAY(1951), w

Fred Baldwin
END OF AUGUST, THE(1982), prod d

Greta Baldwin
PROJECT X(1968)
Misc. Talkies
ROGUE'S GALLERY(1968)

Homer Baldwin
WEDNESDAY CHILDREN, THE(1973), p, ph, ed

James Baldwin
1984
GO TELL IT ON THE MOUNTAIN(1984), w

Janet Baldwin
GATOR BAIT(1974); HUMONGOUS(1982, Can.)

Janit Baldwin
PRIME CUT(1972); RUBY(1977); WHERE THE BUFFALO ROAM(1980)

Joan Baldwin
MANIAC(1980)

Judith Baldwin
STEPFORD WIVES, THE(1975)

Judy Baldwin
EVEL KNIEVEL(1971); SEVEN MINUTES, THE(1971)
1984
NO SMALL AFFAIR(1984)

Kitty Baldwin
Silents
ARE YOU A MASON?(1915)

Michael Baldwin
THEATRE OF BLOOD(1973, Brit.), cos; PHANTASM(1979)

Mike Baldwin
KENNY AND CO.(1976)

Nell Baldwin
MEN OF THE NIGHT(1934)

Paula Baldwin
LADY GREY(1980)

Peter Baldwin
TURNING POINT, THE(1952); GIRLS OF PLEASURE ISLAND, THE(1953); HOUDINI(1953); LITTLE BOY LOST(1953); STALAG 17(1953); SHORT CUT TO HELL(1957); TIN STAR, THE(1957); I MARRIED A MONSTER FROM OUTER SPACE(1958); TEACHER'S PET(1958); TRAP, THE(1959); GHOST, THE(1965, Ital.); PLACE FOR LOVERS, A(1969, Ital./Fr.), w; WEEKEND MURDERS, THE(1972, Ital.)

R.H. Baldwin
FOXFIRE(1955)

Raaf Baldwin
ECHOES(1983)

Ralph Baldwin
Misc. Talkies
OUR MEN IN BAGHDAD(1967, Ital.)

Richard Baldwin
KNICKERBOCKER HOLIDAY(1944)

Robert Baldwin
GIRL FROM SCOTLAND YARD, THE(1937); MIDNIGHT MADONNA(1937); MIND YOUR OWN BUSINESS(1937); MAIN STREET LAWYER(1939); MEET DR. CHRISTIAN(1939); COURAGEOUS DR. CHRISTIAN, THE(1940); VILLAGE BARN DANCE(1940); GAMBLING DAUGHTERS(1941); REMEDY FOR RICHES(1941); THEY MEET AGAIN(1941); FLIPPER'S NEW ADVENTURE(1964)

Robert M. Baldwin
STIGMA(1972), ph; EXTERMINATOR, THE(1980), ph; REFUGE(1981), ph

Robert M. Baldwin, Jr.
SOLDIER, THE(1982), ph, stunts

Robert Walter Baldwin
DRAGONWYCH(1946)

Roger Baldwin
REDS(1981)

Ruth Ann Baldwin
Silents
MARRIAGE OF WILLIAM ASHE, THE(1921), w
Misc. Silents
WIFE ON TRAIL, A(1917), d; '49 - '17(1917), d

Stacey Baldwin
BLUE COLLAR(1978)

Susan Baldwin
THX 1138(1971)

Therese Baldwin
GRASSHOPPER, THE(1970)

Walter Baldwin
YOU CAN'T RUN AWAY FROM IT(1956); ANGELS OVER BROADWAY(1940); I'M NOBODY'S SWEETHEART NOW(1940); DEVIL AND DANIEL WEBSTER, THE(1941); DEVIL COMMANDS, THE(1941); LOOK WHO'S LAUGHING(1941); HARVARD, HERE I COME(1942); IN THIS OUR LIFE(1942); KING'S ROW(1942); THEY DIED WITH THEIR BOOTS ON(1942); AFTER MIDNIGHT WITH BOSTON BLACKIE(1943); HAPPY LAND(1943); LAUGH YOUR BLUES AWAY(1943); STRANGER IN TOWN, A(1943); DARK MOUNTAIN(1944); HOME IN INDIANA(1944); I'LL BE SEEING YOU(1944); I'M FROM ARKANSAS(1944); LOUISIANA HAYRIDE(1944); MR. WINKLE GOES TO WAR(1944); SINCE YOU WENT AWAY(1944); TALL IN THE SADDLE(1944); TOGETHER AGAIN(1944); CHRISTMAS IN CONNECTICUT(1945); COLONEL EFFINGHAM'S RAID(1945); LOST WEEKEND, THE(1945); MURDER, HE SAYS(1945); STATE FAIR(1945); TRAIL TO VENGEANCE(1945); WHY GIRLS LEAVE HOME(1945); BEST YEARS OF OUR LIVES, THE(1946); CLAUDIA AND DAVID(1946); CROSS MY HEART(1946); JOHNNY COMES FLYING HOME(1946); PERFECT MARRIAGE, THE(1946); SING WHILE YOU DANCE(1946); STRANGE LOVE OF MARTHA IVERS, THE(1946); TIME OF THEIR LIVES, THE(1946); YOUNG WIDOW(1946); FRAMED(1947); MOURNING BECOMES ELECTRA(1947); UNSUSPECTED, THE(1947); ALBUQUERQUE(1948); CRY OF THE CITY(1948); HAZARD(1948); MAN FROM COLORADO, THE(1948); ON OUR MERRY WAY(1948); RACHEL AND THE STRANGER(1948); RETURN OF THE BADMEN(1948); WINTER MEETING(1948); CALAMITY JANE AND SAM BASS(1949); COME TO THE STABLE(1949); GAY AMIGO, THE(1949); ON THE TOWN(1949); SPECIAL AGENT(1949); THIEVES' HIGHWAY(1949); CHEAPER BY THE DOZEN(1950); JACKPOT, THE(1950); STELLA(1950); STORM WARNING(1950); I WANT YOU(1951); MILLIONAIRE FOR CHRISTY, A(1951); RACKET, THE(1951); ROUGH RIDERS OF DURANGO(1951); CARRIE(1952); SOMETHING FOR THE BIRDS(1952); WINNING TEAM, THE(1952); RIDE, VAQUERO!(1953); SCANDAL AT SCOURIE(1953); DESTRY(1954); LIVING IT UP(1954); LONG, LONG TRAILER, THE(1954); DESPERATE HOURS, THE(1955); GLORY(1955); INTERRUPTED MELODY(1955); STRANGER ON HORSEBACK(1955); OKLAHOMA TERRITORY(1960); CHEYENNE AUTUMN(1964); ROSEMARY'S BABY(1968); HAIL, HERO!(1969)

Walter S. Baldwin, Jr.
SCATTERGOOD RIDES HIGH(1942)

Wesley Baldwin
HOW TO BEAT THE HIGH COST OF LIVING(1980)
William Baldwin
MY BLUE HEAVEN(1950); ONE TOO MANY(1950); WITH A SONG IN MY HEART(1952); BREWSTER McCLOUD(1970)
Ernest Bale
MAN WITHOUT A BODY, THE(1957, Brit.); MUSIC LOVERS, THE(1971, Brit.); HAUNTING OF M, THE(1979)
Rafael Baledon
ORLAK, THE HELL OF FRANKENSTEIN(1960, Mex.), p&d; MAN AND THE MONSTER, THE(1965, Mex.), d; CURSE OF THE CRYING WOMAN, THE(1969, Mex.), d, w
Misc. Talkies
BULLET FOR BILLY THE KID(1963), d
W.J. Balef
RETURN OF RAFFLES, THE(1932, Brit.), w
Noelle Balenci
MARCO THE MAGNIFICENT(1966, Ital./Fr./Yugo./Egypt/Afghanistan), ed; LA PRISONNIERE(1969, Fr./Ital.), ed
Balenciaga
EMPTY STAR, THE(1962, Mex.), cos
Carla Balenda
HUNT THE MAN DOWN(1950); SEALED CARGO(1951); WHIP HAND, THE(1951); OUTLAW WOMEN(1952); PACE THAT THRILLS, THE(1952); PRINCE OF PIRATES(1953); PHANTOM STALLION, THE(1954)
Cynthia Bales
UNDER FIRE(1983), cos
Liza Balesca
STREET OF SINNERS(1957)
Wolcott Balestier
Silents
NAULAHKA, THE(1918), w
Balestra
SWEET BODY OF DEBORAH, THE(1969, Ital./Fr.), cos
Virginia Balestrieri
FATAL DESIRE(1953)
Dewey Balfa
SOUTHERN COMFORT(1981)
Michael Balfe
BOHEMIAN GIRL, THE(1936), w
Augustus Balfour
Silents
PORT OF MISSING MEN(1914); ANY WIFE(1922)
Bettly Balfour
Silents
PARADISE(1928, Brit.)
Betty Balfour
BRAT, THE(1930, Brit.), a, p; RAISE THE ROOF(1930); VAGABOND QUEEN, THE(1931, Brit.); EVERGREEN(1934, Brit.); MY OLD DUTCH(1934, Brit.); BORN FOR GLORY(1935, Brit.); SQUIBS(1935, Brit.); ELIZA COMES TO STAY(1936, Brit.); FACTS OF LOVE(1949, Brit.)
Silents
SQUIBS(1921, Brit.); SQUIBS WINS THE CALCUTTA SWEEP(1922, Brit.); SQUIBS, MP(1923, Brit.); SATAN'S SISTER(1925, Brit.), a, p; SQUIBS' HONEYMOON(1926, Brit.), a, w; CHAMPAGNE(1928, Brit.)
Misc. Silents
BLINKEYES(192?); NOTHING ELSE MATTERS(1920, Brit.); MARY-FIND-THE-GOLD(1921, Brit.); WEE MACGREGOR'S SWEETHEART, THE(1922, Brit.); REVEILLE(1924, Brit.); PEARL OF LOVE, THE(1925); SOMEBODY'S DARLING(1925, Brit.); CINDERS(1926, Brit.); SEA URCHIN, THE(1926, Brit.); LE DIABLE AU COEUR(1928, Fr.); SKIRTS(1928, Brit.)
Elsie Balfour
Silents
GOVERNOR'S BOSS, THE(1915)
Misc. Silents
BETTER MAN, THE(1915)
Eve Balfour
Silents
JACK TAR(1915, Brit.); LOVE(1916, Brit.); ALL THE WORLD'S A STAGE(1917, Brit.)
Misc. Silents
MYSTERY OF THE DIAMOND BELT(1914, Brit.); FIVE NIGHTS(1915, Brit.); ROYAL LOVE(1915, Brit.); WOMAN WHO DID, THE(1915, Brit.); BURNT WINGS(1916, Brit.); CYNTHIA IN THE WILDERNESS(1916, Brit.); RUSSIA - LAND OF TOMORROW(1919, Brit.); BLACK SHEEP, THE(1920, Brit.); SCARLET WOOING, THE(1920, Brit.); WOMAN OF THE IRON BRACELETS, THE(1920, Brit.)
Katharine Balfour
MUSIC FOR MILLIONS(1944); AMERICA, AMERICA(1963)
1984
TEACHERS(1984)
Katherine Balfour
ADVENTURERS, THE(1970); LOVE STORY(1970)
Lady Evelyn Balfour
ANYTHING MIGHT HAPPEN(1935, Brit.), w
Lorna Balfour
MERELY MARY ANN(1931)
Michael Balfour
HIDEOUT(1948, Brit.); JUST WILLIAM'S LUCK(1948, Brit.); NO ORCHIDS FOR MISS BLANDISH(1948, Brit.); WILLIAM COMES TO TOWN(1948, Brit.); DON'T EVER LEAVE ME(1949, Brit.); MELODY CLUB(1949, Brit.); SLEEPING CAR TO TRIESTE(1949, Brit.); STOP PRESS GIRL(1949, Brit.); PRELUDE TO FAME(1950, Brit.); TAMING OF DOROTHY, THE(1950, Brit.); CASE FOR PC 49, A(1951, Brit.); QUIET WOMAN, THE(1951, Brit.); HOT ICE(1952, Brit.); MOULIN ROUGE(1952); 13 EAST STREET(1952, Brit.); ALBERT, R.N.(1953, Brit.); ASSASSIN, THE(1953, Brit.); CAPTAIN'S PARADISE, THE(1953, Brit.); GENEVIEVE(1953, Brit.); JOHNNY ON THE RUN(1953, Brit.); MR. POTTS GOES TO MOSCOW(1953, Brit.); NORMAN CONQUEST(1953, Brit.); SMALL TOWN STORY(1953, Brit.); WHITE FIRE(1953, Brit.); BLACK 13(1954, Brit.); DELAVINE AFFAIR, THE(1954, Brit.); DELAYED ACTION(1954, Brit.); DEVIL'S HARBOR(1954, Brit.); DIAMOND WIZARD, THE(1954, Brit.); MEET MR. CALLAGHAN(1954, Brit.); PARATROOPER(1954, Brit.); RIVER BEAT(1954, Brit.); SCARLET WEB, THE(1954, Brit.); GENTLEMEN MARRY BRUNET-

TES(1955); ONE GOOD TURN(1955, Brit.); SEA SHALL NOT HAVE THEM, THE(1955, Brit.); SECRET OF THE FOREST, THE(1955, Brit.); SECRET VENTURE(1955, Brit.); BREAKAWAY(1956, Brit.); IT'S A GREAT DAY(1956, Brit.); MURDER ON APPROVAL(1956, Brit.); TRACK THE MAN DOWN(1956, Brit.); ENEMY FROM SPACE(1957, Brit.); HOUR OF DECISION(1957, Brit.); LIGHT FINGERS(1957, Brit.); REACH FOR THE SKY(1957, Brit.); THUNDER OVER TANGIER(1957, Brit.); TWO GROOMS FOR A BRIDE(1957); FIEND WITHOUT A FACE(1958); STEEL BAYONET, THE(1958, Brit.); LOOK BACK IN ANGER(1959); CARRY ON CONSTABLE(1960, Brit.); MAKE MINE MINK(1960, Brit.); MANIA(1961, Brit.); MONSTER OF HIGHGATE PONDS, THE(1961, Brit.); SECRET OF MONTE CRISTO, THE(1961, Brit.); TOO HOT TO HANDLE(1961, Brit.); DESIGN FOR LOVING(1962, Brit.); SHE ALWAYS GETS THEIR MAN(1962, Brit.); FAST LADY, THE(1963, Brit.); HELLFIRE CLUB, THE(1963, Brit.); RESCUE SQUAD, THE(1963, Brit.); FAHRENHEIT 451(1966, Brit.); KALEIDOSCOPE(1966, Brit.); PRESS FOR TIME(1966, Brit.); STRANGLER'S WEB(1966, Brit.); WHERE THE BULLETS FLY(1966, Brit.); FIXER, THE(1968); OBLONG BOX, THE(1969, Brit.); ADVENTURERS, THE(1970); HOVERBUG(1970, Brit.); MAN OF VIOLENCE(1970, Brit.); PRIVATE LIFE OF SHERLOCK HOLMES, THE(1970, Brit.); MACBETH(1971, Brit.); CANDLESHOE(1978); STICK UP, THE(1978, Brit.); PRISONER OF ZENDA, THE(1979)
Mrs. Balfour
Silents
ORDEAL, THE(1914)
Sue Balfour
Silents
LITTLE GRAY LADY, THE(1914); ALL FOR A GIRL(1915); SPRINGTIME(1915); ALIAS MRS. JESSOP(1917)
Misc. Silents
AVALANCHE, THE(1915); CONCEALED TRUTH, THE(1915); MISS ROBINSON CRUSOE(1917); INDESTRUCTIBLE WIFE, THE(1919)
Virginia Balfour
ONE BRIEF SUMMER(1971, Brit.)
Jennifer Balgobin
1984
REPO MAN(1984)
Michael H. Balham
RETURN OF THE JEDI(1983)
Bob Balhatchet
ESCAPE FROM ALCATRAZ(1979); SERIAL(1980)
1984
WOMAN IN RED, THE(1984)
Sophi Balhetchet
GIRO CITY(1982, Brit.), p
Haig Balian
GIRL WITH THE RED HAIR, THE(1983, Neth.), p
Bob Baliban
LOVERS AND OTHER STRANGERS(1970)
Nikita Balieff
ONCE IN A BLUE MOON(1936)
Barbara Balik
TERMS OF ENDEARMENT(1983)
Jaroslav Balik
DEATH OF TARZAN, THE(1968, Czech), d, w
Shelby Balik
INCREDIBLE SHRINKING WOMAN, THE(1981); I OUGHT TO BE IN PICTURES(1982)
Ina Balin
BLACK ORCHID(1959); FROM THE TERRACE(1960); COMANCHEROS, THE(1961); YOUNG DOCTORS, THE(1961); PATSY, THE(1964); GREATEST STORY EVER TOLD, THE(1965); RUN LIKE A THIEF(1968, Span.); CHARRO(1969); PROJECTIONIST, THE(1970); DON IS DEAD, THE(1973); COMEBACK TRAIL, THE(1982)
Misc. Talkies
ACT OF REPRISAL(1965)
Mireille Balin
PEPE LE MOKO(1937, Fr.); KISS OF FIRE, THE(1940, Fr.); MASK OF KOREA(1950, Fr.)
Richard Balin
SCHIZOID(1980); FIRST MONDAY IN OCTOBER(1981)
James Baline
GAY FALCON, THE(1941)
Art Balinger
SWARM, THE(1978)
Andras Balint
AGE OF ILLUSIONS(1967, Hung.); FATHER(1967, Hung.)
Eszter Balint
1984
STRANGER THAN PARADISE(1984, U.S./Ger.)
Gyorgy Balint
WITNESS, THE(1982, Hung.)
Gigi Balista
STAVISKY(1974, Fr.)
Virginia Balistrieri
Misc. Silents
LOST IN THE DARK(1914, Ital.)
Sasha Balitskiy
GORDEYEV FAMILY, THE(1961, U.S.S.R.)
Adele Balkan
MIGHTY JOE YOUNG(1949), cos; SEVEN CITIES OF GOLD(1955), cos; FIEND WHO WALKED THE WEST, THE(1958), cos; YOUNG LIONS, THE(1958), cos; BLUE ANGEL, THE(1959), cos; JOHN GOLDFARB, PLEASE COME HOME(1964), cos
Gladys Balke
SCENE OF THE CRIME(1949)
Adele Balken
BOY WITH THE GREEN HAIR, THE(1949), cos; FLAMING STAR(1960), cos
Adele Balkin
WAY TO THE GOLD, THE(1957), cos
Karen Balkin
CHILDREN'S HOUR, THE(1961); OUR TIME(1974)

Arlette Balkis
TALL BLOND MAN WITH ONE BLACK SHOE, THE(1973, Fr.)

Arlette Balkiss
ZAZIE(1961, Fr.)

Dick Balkney
JANIE(1944)

Robert Balkoff
MISSION TO MOSCOW(1943)

G. Balkrishna
TWO EYES, TWELVE HANDS(1958, India), ph

Alan Ball
YELLOW SUBMARINE(1958, Brit.), animation

Anty Ball
PEER GYNT(1965)

Betty Ball
HOODLUM EMPIRE(1952)

Bob Ball
PRECIOUS JEWELS(1969)

Dean O. Ball
TELL ME THAT YOU LOVE ME, JUNIE MOON(1970), ed

Earl Poole Ball
THEY ALL LAUGHED(1981)

Frank Ball
FORTY-NINERS, THE(1932); MAN FROM NEW MEXICO, THE(1932); MURDER AT DAWN(1932); SCARLET BRAND(1932); FIGHTING CHAMP(1933); GALLOPING ROMEO(1933); RANGER'S CODE, THE(1933); WHEN A MAN RIDES ALONE(1933); COURAGEOUS AVENGER, THE(1935); DESERT TRAIL(1935); NEW FRONTIER, THE(1935); RAINBOW VALLEY(1935); FUGITIVE SHERIFF, THE(1936); KID RANGER, THE(1936); UNDERCOVER MAN(1936); VALLEY OF THE LAWLESS(1936); BAR Z BAD MEN(1937); BOOTHILL BRIGADE(1937); BORDER PHANTOM(1937); DESERT PHANTOM(1937); GAMBLING TERROR, THE(1937); GUN LORDS OF STIRRUP BASIN(1937); GUN RANGER, THE(1937); LAWLESS LAND(1937); RECKLESS RANGER(1937); RED ROPE, THE(1937); RIDIN' THE LONE TRAIL(1937); ROGUE OF THE RANGE(1937); SUNDOWN SAUNDERS(1937); TRAIL OF VENGEANCE(1937); TRUSTED OUTLAW, THE(1937); COLORADO KID(1938); DURANGO VALLEY RAIDERS(1938); FEUD MAKER(1938); IN EARLY ARIZONA(1938); PAROLED–TO DIE(1938); NICK CARTER, MASTER DETECTIVE(1939)

George Ball
MEN OF THE PLAINS(1936); TOO MUCH BEEF(1936); ROGUE OF THE RANGE(1937)

Henry Ball
Misc. Talkies
GHOST DANCE(1982)

Jane Ball
KEYS OF THE KINGDOM, THE(1944); WINGED VICTORY(1944); FOREVER AMBER(1947)

John Ball
IN THE HEAT OF THE NIGHT(1967), w; THEY CALL ME MISTER TIBBS(1970), w; ORGANIZATION, THE(1971), w. James R. Webb; GRAYEAGLE(1977), art d; NORSEMAN, THE(1978), set d

Larry Ball
STONY ISLAND(1978)

Lucille Ball
ROMAN SCANDALS(1933); BULLDOG DRUMMOND STRIKES BACK(1934); FUGITIVE LADY(1934); JEALOUSY(1934); KID MILLIONS(1934); MEN OF THE NIGHT(1934); NANA(1934); CARNIVAL(1935); I DREAM TOO MUCH(1935); OLD MAN RHYTHM(1935); ROBERTA(1935); TOP HAT(1935); WHOLE TOWN'S TALKING, THE(1935); BUNKER BEAN(1936); CHATTERBOX(1936); FARMER IN THE DELL, THE(1936); FOLLOW THE FLEET(1936); WINTERSET(1936); DON'T TELL THE WIFE(1937); STAGE DOOR(1937); THAT GIRL FROM PARIS(1937); AFFAIRS OF ANNABEL(1938); ANNABEL TAKES A TOUR(1938); GO CHASE YOURSELF(1938); HAVING WONDERFUL TIME(1938); JOY OF LIVING(1938); NEXT TIME I MARRY(1938); ROOM SERVICE(1938); BEAUTY FOR THE ASKING(1939); FIVE CAME BACK(1939); PANAMA LADY(1939); THAT'S RIGHT–YOU'RE WRONG(1939); TWELVE CROWDED HOURS(1939); DANCE, GIRL, DANCE(1940); MARINES FLY HIGH, THE(1940); TOO MANY GIRLS(1940); YOU CAN'T FOOL YOUR WIFE(1940); GIRL, A GUY AND A GOB, A(1941); LOOK WHO'S LAUGHING(1941); BIG STREET, THE(1942); SEVEN DAYS LEAVE(1942); VALLEY OF THE SUN(1942); BEST FOOT FORWARD(1943); DU BARRY WAS A LADY(1943); THOUSANDS CHEER(1943); MEET THE PEOPLE(1944); ABBOTT AND COSTELLO IN HOLLYWOOD(1945); WITHOUT LOVE(1945); ZIEGFELD FOLLIES(1945); DARK CORNER, THE(1946); EASY TO WED(1946); LOVER COME BACK(1946); TWO SMART PEOPLE(1946); HER HUSBAND'S AFFAIRS(1947); LURED(1947); EASY LIVING(1949); MISS GRANT TAKES RICHMOND(1949); SORROWFUL JONES(1949); FANCY PANTS(1950); FULLER BRUSH GIRL, THE(1950); WOMAN OF DISTINCTION, A(1950); MAGIC CARPET, THE(1951); LONG, LONG TRAILER, THE(1954); FOREVER DARLING(1956); FACTS OF LIFE, THE(1960); CRITIC'S CHOICE(1963); GUIDE FOR THE MARRIED MAN, A(1967); YOURS, MINE AND OURS(1968); MAME(1974)

Marshall Ball
MEN, THE(1950)

Nicholas Ball
OVERLORD(1975, Brit.); WHO IS KILLING THE GREAT CHEFS OF EUROPE?(1978, US/Ger.); NELLY'S VERSION(1983, Brit.)

Olive Ball
TOY WIFE, THE(1938); MARYLAND(1940); MAGNIFICENT AMBERSONS, THE(1942); TALES OF MANHATTAN(1942)

Pat Ball
STUCKEY'S LAST STAND(1980)

Ralph Ball
INTERNECINE PROJECT, THE(1974, Brit.)

Rex Ball
Misc. Talkies
FROM BROADWAY TO CHEYENNE(1932)

Robert Ball
BRAIN EATERS, THE(1958); INVASION OF THE STAR CREATURES(1962); MOTHER GOOSE A GO-GO(1966); WHO'S MINDING THE MINT?(1967); MADIGAN(1968); EASY RIDER(1969); ZACHARIAH(1971); GET TO KNOW YOUR RABBIT(1972); OUT(1982), ph

Robert E. Ball
DOCTOR DEATH: SEEKER OF SOULS(1973); NICKELODEON(1976); WORLD'S GREATEST LOVER, THE(1977); LITTLE MISS MARKER(1980)

Rod Ball
PORKY'S(1982); PORKY'S II: THE NEXT DAY(1983)
1984
RHINESTONE(1984)

Sherwood Ball
FOLLOW ME, BOYS!(1966)

Susan Ball
YANKEE BUCCANEER(1952)

Suzan Ball
UNTAMED FRONTIER(1952); CITY BENEATH THE SEA(1953); EAST OF SUMATRA(1953); WAR ARROW(1953); CHIEF CRAZY HORSE(1955)

Tom Ball
CONCRETE JUNGLE, THE(1962, Brit.)

Vincent Ball
COMING-OUT PARTY, A(; INTERRUPTED JOURNEY, THE(1949, Brit.); STOP PRESS GIRL(1949, Brit.); WARNING TO WANTONS, A(1949, Brit.); COME DANCE WITH ME(1950, Brit.); YOU CAN'T BEAT THE IRISH(1952, Brit.); BLACK RIDER, THE(1954, Brit.); DEVIL'S HARBOR(1954, Brit.); TERROR SHIP(1954, Brit.); BLONDE BLACKMAILER(1955, Brit.); SECRET OF THE FOREST, THE(1955, Brit.); JOHN AND JULIE(1957, Brit.); BLOOD OF THE VAMPIRE(1958, Brit.); MENACE IN THE NIGHT(1958, Brit.); ROBBERY UNDER ARMS(1958, Brit.); TOWN LIKE ALICE, A(1958, Brit.); NAVY HEROES(1959, Brit.); BREAKOUT(1959, Brit.); DEAD LUCKY(1960, Brit.); DENTIST IN THE CHAIR(1960, Brit.); FEET OF CLAY(1960, Brit.); IDENTITY UNKNOWN(1960, Brit.); HIGHWAY TO BATTLE(1961, Brit.); MIDDLE COURSE, THE(1961, Brit.); SEASON OF PASSION(1961, Brit.); CARRY ON CRUISING(1962, Brit.); DESERT PATROL(1962, Brit.); MATTER OF WHO, A(1962, Brit.); NEARLY A NASTY ACCIDENT(1962, Brit.); ECHO OF DIANA(1963, Brit.); MOUSE ON THE MOON, THE(1963, Brit.); FOLLOW THAT CAMEL(1967, Brit.); WHERE EAGLES DARE(1968, Brit.); OH! WHAT A LOVELY WAR(1969, Brit.); IRISHMAN, THE(1978, Aus.); BREAKER MORANT(1980, Aus.)
1984
PHAR LAP(1984, Aus.)
Misc. Talkies
SPIRAL BUREAU, THE(1974); DEMOLITION(1977)

Warren Ball
HAREM BUNCH; OR WAR AND PIECE, THE(1969); CORPSE GRINDERS, THE(1972)

Yvonne Ball
MARY HAD A LITTLE(1961, Brit.); IMPERSONATOR, THE(1962, Brit.); JOEY BOY(1965, Brit.)

Zachary Ball
JOE PANTHER(1976), w

Melissa Ballan
ARTHUR(1981)

George Ballanchine
DARK RED ROSES(1930, Brit.), ch; ON YOUR TOES(1939), ch

Ron Ballanger
THIN RED LINE, THE(1964), spec eff; HEROES OF TELEMARK, THE(1965, Brit.), spec eff; THOSE MAGNIFICENT MEN IN THEIR FLYING MACHINES; OR HOW I FLEW FROM LONDON TO PARIS IN 25 HOURS AND 11 MINUTES(1965, Brit.), spec eff; OH! WHAT A LOVELY WAR(1969, Brit.), spec eff; HELL BOATS(1970, Brit.), spec eff; PULP(1972, Brit.), spec eff; UNIDENTIFIED FLYING ODDBALL, THE(1979, Brit.), spec eff

Carl Ballantine
MC HALE'S NAVY(1964); PENELOPE(1966); SHAKIEST GUN IN THE WEST, THE(1968); SPEEDWAY(1968); REVENGE OF THE CHEERLEADERS(1976); WORLD'S GREATEST LOVER, THE(1977); JUST YOU AND ME, KID(1979); NORTH AVENUE IRREGULARS, THE(1979)

E. J. Ballantine
MISS SUSIE SLAGLE'S(1945)

E.J. Ballantine
BOOMERANG(1947); MAGIC TOWN(1947)

Sara Ballantine
PHANTOM OF THE PARADISE(1974)

Sarah Ballantine
NEVER PUT IT IN WRITING(1964)

Sheila Ballantine
REMEMBRANCE(1982, Brit.)

Steve Ballantine
THRESHOLD(1983, Can.)

Elspeth Ballantyne
BLUE FIN(1978, Aus.)

Jane Ballantyne
1984
MAN OF FLOWERS(1984, Aus.), p

Lon Ballantyne
I PASSED FOR WHITE(1960)

Maxine Ballantyne
THE LADY DRACULA(1974)

Neil Ballantyne
MR. EMMANUEL(1945, Brit.); SCOTCH ON THE ROCKS(1954, Brit.)

Nell Ballantyne
SHIPBUILDERS, THE(1943, Brit.); FORTUNE LANE(1947, Brit.); BONNIE PRINCE CHARLIE(1948, Brit.); MAD LITTLE ISLAND(1958, Brit.); BRIDAL PATH, THE(1959, Brit.)

Barbara Ballar
WHAT'S UP FRONT(1964)

Alba Ballard
1984
BROADWAY DANNY ROSE(1984)

Alberta Ballard
Misc. Silents
REVENGE(1918)

Beverly Ballard
TRUMAN CAPOTE'S TRILOGY(1969); DIARY OF A MAD HOUSEWIFE(1970); TRICK BABY(1973)

Carroll Ballard
THREE NUTS IN SEARCH OF A BOLT(1964), art d; BLACK STALLION, THE(1979), d; NEVER CRY WOLF(1983), d
David Ballard
DRAGONWYCH(1946)
Elmer Ballard
ALIBI(1929); FALL GUY, THE(1930); HER PRIVATE AFFAIR(1930); SQUEALER, THE(1930); GREEN EYES(1934); THANK YOUR LUCKY STARS(1943)
Fred Ballard
WHEN'S YOUR BIRTHDAY?(1937), w
Irish Ballard
LIFE IN HER HANDS(1951, Brit.)
Jack Ballard
DOWNHILL RACER(1969); MAHOGANY(1975), p
Jimmy Ballard
DON'T KNOCK THE ROCK(1956)
John Ballard
FRIDAY THE 13TH... THE ORPHAN(1979), d&w
Misc. Talkies
ORPHAN, THE(1979), d
John Frederick Ballard
LADIES OF THE JURY(1932), w; YOUNG AMERICA(1932), w; WE'RE ON THE JURY(1937), w
Jovada Ballard
DON'T KNOCK THE ROCK(1956)
Kay Ballard
FALLING IN LOVE AGAIN(1980)
Kaye Ballard
GIRL MOST LIKELY, THE(1957); HOUSE IS NOT A HOME, A(1964); WHICH WAY TO THE FRONT?(1970); FREAKY FRIDAY(1976); RITZ, THE(1976); PANDEMONIUM(1982)
Lee Ballard
ROPE OF FLESH(1965)
Lucian Ballard
CRIME AND PUNISHMENT(1935), ph; AL CAPONE(1959), ph
Lucien Ballard
MOROCCO(1930), ph; DEVIL IS A WOMAN, THE(1935), ph; CRAIG'S WIFE(1936), ph; FINAL HOUR, THE(1936), ph; KING STEPS OUT, THE(1936), ph; DEVIL'S PLAYGROUND(1937), ph; GIRLS CAN PLAY(1937), ph; I PROMISE TO PAY(1937), ph; LIFE BEGINS WITH LOVE(1937), ph; RACKETEERS IN EXILE(1937), ph; SHADOW, THE(1937), ph; VENUS MAKES TROUBLE(1937), ph; FLIGHT TO FAME(1938), ph; HIGHWAY PATROL(1938), ph; LONE WOLF IN PARIS, THE(1938), ph; PENITENTIARY(1938), ph; SQUADRON OF HONOR(1938), ph; BLIND ALLEY(1939), ph; COAST GUARD(1939), ph; LET US LIVE(1939), ph; OUTSIDE THESE WALLS(1939), ph; RIO GRANDE(1939), ph; TEXAS STAMPEDE(1939), ph; THUNDERING WEST, THE(1939), ph; VILLAIN STILL PURSUED HER, THE(1940), ph; MOONTIDE(1942), ph; ORCHESTRA WIVES(1942), ph; UNDYING MONSTER, THE(1942), ph; WHISPERING GHOSTS(1942), ph; BOMBER'S MOON(1943), ph; HOLY MATRIMONY(1943), ph; TONIGHT WE RAID CALAIS(1943), ph; LODGER, THE(1944), ph; SWEET AND LOWDOWN(1944), ph; THIS LOVE OF OURS(1945), ph; TEMPTATION(1946), ph; NIGHT SONG(1947), ph; BERLIN EXPRESS(1948), ph; FIXED BAYONETS(1951), ph; LET'S MAKE IT LEGAL(1951), ph; DIPLOMATIC COURIER(1952), ph; DON'T BOTHER TO KNOCK(1952), ph; NIGHT WITHOUT SLEEP(1952), ph; O. HENRY'S FULL HOUSE(1952), ph; RETURN OF THE TEXAN(1952), ph; DESERT RATS, THE(1953), ph; GLORY BRIGADE, THE(1953), ph; INFERNO(1953), ph; NEW FACES(1954), ph; PRINCE VALIANT(1954), ph; RAID, THE(1954), ph; MAGNIFICENT MATADOR, THE(1955), ph; SEVEN CITIES OF GOLD(1955), ph; WHITE FEATHER(1955), ph; KILLER IS LOOSE, THE(1956), ph; KILLING, THE(1956), ph; KING AND FOUR QUEENS, THE(1956), ph; KISS BEFORE DYING, A(1956), ph; PROUD ONES, THE(1956), ph; BAND OF ANGELS(1957), ph; UNHOLY WIFE, THE(1957), ph; ANNA LUCASTA(1958), ph; BUCHANAN RIDES ALONE(1958), ph; I MARRIED A WOMAN(1958), ph; MURDER BY CONTRACT(1958), ph; CITY OF FEAR(1959), ph; BRAMBLE BUSH, THE(1960), ph; DESIRE IN THE DUST(1960), ph; PAY OR DIE(1960), ph; RISE AND FALL OF LEGS DIAMOND, THE(1960), ph; MARINES, LET'S GO(1961), ph; PARENT TRAP, THE(1961), ph; SUSAN SLADE(1961), ph; RIDE THE HIGH COUNTRY(1962), ph; CARETAKERS, THE(1963), ph; TAKE HER, SHE'S MINE(1963), ph; WALL OF NOISE(1963), ph; WIVES AND LOVERS(1963), ph; NEW INTERNS, THE(1964), ph; ROUSTABOUT(1964), ph; BOEING BOEING(1965), ph; DEAR BRIGETTE(1965), ph; SONS OF KATIE ELDER, THE(1965), ph; EYE FOR AN EYE, AN(1966), ph; NEVADA SMITH(1966), ph; HOUR OF THE GUN(1967), ph; HOW SWEET IT IS(1968), ph; PARTY, THE(1968), ph; WILL PENNY(1968), ph; TRUE GRIT(1969), ph; WILD BUNCH, THE(1969), ph; BALLAD OF CABLE HOGUE, THE(1970), ph; HAWAIIANS, THE(1970), ph; TIME FOR DYING, A(1971), ph; WHAT'S THE MATTER WITH HELEN?(1971), ph; GETAWAY, THE(1972), ph; JUNIOR BONNER(1972), ph; LADY ICE(1973), ph; THOMASINE AND BUSHROD(1974), ph; THREE THE HARD WAY(1974), ph; BREAKOUT(1975), ph; BREAKHEART PASS(1976), ph; DRUM(1976), ph; FROM NOON TO THREE(1976), ph; ST. IVES(1976), ph; RABBIT TEST(1978), ph
Lucinda Ballard
PORTRAIT OF JENNIE(1949), cos; STREETCAR NAMED DESIRE, A(1951), cos
Manoela Ballard
PONTIUS PILATE(1967, Fr./Ital.)
Manuela Ballard
FRANCIS OF ASSISI(1961)
Pamela Ballard
CARNIVAL OF SOULS(1962)
Ray Ballard
LAWYER, THE(1969); WINNING(1969); COCKEYED COWBOYS OF CALICO COUNTY, THE(1970); LITTLE FAUSS AND BIG HALSY(1970); OUT OF TOWNERS, THE(1970); WATERMELON MAN(1970); SSSSSSSS(1973)
Rex Ballard
Misc. Silents
ACROSS THE DIVIDE(1921)
Shirley Ballard
KID FROM BOOKLYN, THE(1946); JULIA MISBEHAVES(1948); SONG IS BORN, A(1948); IT'S A GREAT FEELING(1949); DESERT HAWK, THE(1950); EMERGENCY WEDDING(1950); PETTY GIRL, THE(1950); TARZAN AND THE SLAVE GIRL(1950); SECOND WOMAN, THE(1951); COP HATER(1958); LAUGHING POLICEMAN, THE(1973)

Terry Ballard
FRIDAY THE 13TH PART III(1982)
Thomas E. Ballard
WINDWALKER(1980), p
Todhunter Ballard
OUTCAST, THE(1954), w
Tommy Ballard
LONE WOLF McQUADE(1983)
James D. Ballas
SHAGGY DOG, THE(1959), ed
John Ballato
REDS(1981)
Peter Ballbasch
SCARLET EMPRESS, THE(1934), art d
Peter Ballbusch
SERGEANT MADDEN(1939), spec eff; DR. JEKYLL AND MR. HYDE(1941), spec eff; TAKE ME OUT TO THE BALL GAME(1949), spec eff; SHOW BOAT(1951), spec eff; SCARAMOUCHE(1952), art d; RHAPSODY(1954), spec eff
Ladislav Ballek
ASSISTANT, THE(1982, Czech.), w
Ruth Ballen
CHILD, THE(1977)
Tony Ballen
OPEN THE DOOR AND SEE ALL THE PEOPLE(1964); RATTLERS(1976)
Misc. Talkies
RATTLERS(1976)
E. J. Ballentine
MOON IS DOWN, THE(1943)
E.J. Ballentine
TAMPICO(1944)
Col. Ugo Ballerini
ROMAN HOLIDAY(1953)
Cecil Ballerino
MR. WINKLE GOES TO WAR(1944); SINCE YOU WENT AWAY(1944)
Walter Ballesten
LEGACY OF BLOOD(1978), makeup
Amparo Ballester
THREE DARING DAUGHTERS(1948); THAT MIDNIGHT KISS(1949)
Antonio Ballesteros
LAST DAYS OF POMPEII, THE(1960, Ital.), ph; COLOSSUS OF RHODES, THE(1961, Ital., Fr., Span.), ph
Antonio L. Ballesteros
DESERT WARRIOR(1961 Ital./Span.), ph; DEVIL MADE A WOMAN, THE(1962, Span.), ph; EVERY DAY IS A HOLIDAY(1966, Span.), ph
Belen Ballesteros
1984
HOLY INNOCENTS, THE(1984, Span.)
Carlos Ballesteros
NARCO MEN, THE(1969, Span./Ital.)
Robert Ballesteros
SORCERESS(1983)
Misc. Talkies
SORCERESS(1983)
The Albertina Rasch Ballet
ROGUE SONG, THE(1930)
Ballet de Paris
GLASS SLIPPER, THE(1955)
Ballet of the Folies Pigalle
PARIS OOH-LA-LA!(1963, U.S./Fr.)
The Ballet Theatre of the Stockholm Royal Opera
ILLICIT INTERLUDE(1954, Swed.)
Ballets Colette Brosset
PEEK-A-BOO(1961, Fr.)
Ballets d'Evelyne Gray
PALACE OF NUDES(1961, Fr./Ital.)
Ballets de la Loie Fuller
PEEK-A-BOO(1961, Fr.)
Ballets de Leon Woizikovski
TWO WHO DARED(1937, Brit.)
Ballett Africain de Keita Fodeba
NEOPOLITAN CAROUSEL(1961, Ital.)
Ruth Ballew
WORLD OF HANS CHRISTIAN ANDERSEN, THE(1971, Jap.)
Smith Ballew
PALM SPRINGS(1936); RACING LADY(1937); WESTERN GOLD(1937); HAWAIIAN BUCKAROO(1938); PANAMINT'S BAD MAN(1938); RAWHIDE(1938); ROLL ALONG, COWBOY(1938); GAUCHO SERENADE(1940); MAN WHO WALKED ALONE, THE(1945); DRIFTING ALONG(1946); MUTINEERS, THE(1949); I KILLED GERONIMO(1950); RED BADGE OF COURAGE, THE(1951)
Allen Balley
BLACK CAESAR(1973)
Carl Ballhaus
JOHNNY STEALS EUROPE(1932, Ger.)
Helga Ballhaus
MARRIAGE OF MARIA BRAUN, THE(1979, Ger.), art d; FRIENDS AND HUSBANDS(1983, Ger.)
Michael Ballhaus
BITTER TEARS OF PETRA VON KANT, THE(1972, Ger.), ph; FOX AND HIS FRIENDS(1976, Ger.), ph; MOTHER KUSTERS GOES TO HEAVEN(1976, Ger.), ph; CHINESE ROULETTE(1977, Ger.), ph; DESPAIR(1978, Ger.), ph; GERMANY IN AUTUMN(1978, Ger.), ph; MARRIAGE OF MARIA BRAUN, THE(1979, Ger.), a, ph; BABY, IT'S YOU(1983), ph; DEAR MR. WONDERFUL(1983, Ger.), ph; FRIENDS AND HUSBANDS(1983, Ger.), ph; MALOU(1983), ph
1984
HEARTBREAKERS(1984), ph; OLD ENOUGH(1984), ph; RECKLESS(1984), ph
Hugo Ballin
Silents
BABY MINE(1917), d; DAUGHTER OF MINE(1919), w; JANE EYRE(1921), p,d&w; JOURNEY'S END, THE(1921), p,d&w; SOULS FOR SALE(1923); PRAIRIE WIFE, THE(1925), d&w

Misc. Silents
HELP YOURSELF(1920), d; PAGAN LOVE(1920), d; EAST LYNNE(1921), d; MARRIED PEOPLE(1922), d; OTHER WOMEN'S CLOTHES(1922), d; VANITY FAIR(1923), d; SHINING ADVENTURE, THE(1925), d

Mabel Ballin
Silents
SPREADING DAWN, THE(1917); JANE EYRE(1921); JOURNEY'S END, THE(1921); SOULS FOR SALE(1923); RIDERS OF THE PURPLE SAGE(1925)
Misc. Silents
FOR VALOUR(1917); ILLUSTRIOUS PRINCE, THE(1919); QUICKENING FLAME, THE(1919); WHITE HEATHER, THE(1919); PAGAN LOVE(1920); UNDER CRIMSON SKIES(1920); EAST LYNNE(1921); MARRIED PEOPLE(1922); OTHER WOMEN'S CLOTHES(1922); VANITY FAIR(1923); BARRIERS BURNED AWAY(1925); BEAUTY AND THE BAD MAN(1925); CODE OF THE WEST(1925); SHINING ADVENTURE, THE(1925)

Erik Balling
OPERATION LOVEBIRDS(1968, Den.), d, w
Misc. Talkies
ONE OF THOSE THINGS(1974, Brit.), d

Art Ballinger
LAST TIME I SAW ARCHIE, THE(1961); TOWERING INFERNO, THE(1974)

Bill S. Ballinger
PORTRAIT IN SMOKE(1957, Brit.), w; STRANGLER, THE(1964), w; OPERATION CIA(1965), w

Irene Ballinger
SHOOT IT: BLACK, SHOOT IT: BLUE(1974)

Ron Ballinger
BLUE MAX, THE(1966), spec eff

William S. Ballinger
PUSHOVER(1954), w

Balliol and Merton
QUEEN OF HEARTS(1936, Brit.)
Silents
ARCADIANS, THE(1927, Brit.); CHAMPAGNE(1928, Brit.)

Balliol and Tiller
OLD MOTHER RILEY(1937, Brit.)

Marc Ballis
LA BALANCE(1983, Fr.)

Socrates Ballis
HOOKED GENERATION, THE(1969); IMPULSE(1975), p

Gigi Ballista
BIRDS, THE BEES AND THE ITALIANS, THE(1967); CLIMAX, THE(1967, Fr., Ital.); GALILEO(1968, Ital./Bul.); QUEENS, THE(1968, Ital./Fr.); SECRET OF SANTA VITTORIA, THE(1969); MIDNIGHT EXPRESS(1978, Brit.); CLARETTA AND BEN(1983, Ital., Fr.)

Fred Ballmeyer
SLEEPING CITY, THE(1950), set d; ODDS AGAINST TOMORROW(1959), set d

Nadine Ballot
ADOLESCENTS, THE(1967, Can.); SIX IN PARIS(1968, Fr.)

David S. Ballou
MASK, THE(1961, Can.), art d

Edward S. Ballou
Silents
KING OF DIAMONDS, THE(1918), w

Marion Ballou
BIG POND, THE(1930); NIGHT WORK(1930); CRADLE SONG(1933); LITTLE WOMEN(1933); MELODY LINGERS ON, THE(1935); CAMILLE(1937); PORTIA ON TRIAL(1937); HOLIDAY(1938)

Don Balluck
FOUR RODE OUT(1969, US/Span.), w

Michele Bally
MAFIOSO(1962, Ital.); CLEOPATRA(1963); STEPPE, THE(1963, Fr./Ital.)

Karyn Balm
TWO FOR THE ROAD(1967, Brit.)

Balmain
NIGHT WITHOUT STARS(1953, Brit.), cos; BETRAYED(1954), cos; FIRE DOWN BELOW(1957, U.S./Brit.), cos; DEVIL'S WIDOW, THE(1972, Brit.), cos

Pierre Balmain
TWO WEEKS IN ANOTHER TOWN(1962), cos; FOREIGN INTRIGUE(1956), cos; PARIS HOLIDAY(1958), cos; RELUCTANT DEBUTANTE, THE(1958), cos; MILLIONAIRESS, THE(1960, Brit.), cos; ROMAN SPRING OF MRS. STONE, THE(1961, U.S./Brit.), cos; TENDER IS THE NIGHT(1961), cos; TIME BOMB(1961, Fr./Ital.), cos; HAPPY THIEVES, THE(1962), cos; I LIKE MONEY(1962, Brit.), cos; COME FLY WITH ME(1963), cos; IN THE COOL OF THE DAY(1963), cos; JOY HOUSE(1964, Fr.), cos

Dagmar Balmer
GEORGE(1973, U.S./Switz.)

Edwin Balmer
WHEN WORLDS COLLIDE(1951), w
Silents
"THAT ROYLE GIRL"(1925), w

Jean Francois Balmer
SNOW(1983, Fr.)

Jean-Francois Balmer
AFRICAN, THE(1983, Fr.)

Jean-Francoise Balmer
1984
SWANN IN LOVE(1984, Fr.Ger.)

Claire Balmford
NED KELLY(1970, Brit.)

G. Balodis
TSAR'S BRIDE, THE(1966, USSR), art d

Peter Baloff
1984
DOOR TO DOOR(1984), w

Judit Balog
FORBIDDEN RELATIONS(1983, Hung.)

Bela Balogh
KIND STEPMOTHER(1936, Hung.), d
Misc. Silents
PAUL STREET BOYS(1929), d

Istvan Balogh
FATHER(1967, Hung.)

Laszlo Balogh
FATHER(1967, Hung.)

Zsuzsa Balogh
FATHER(1967, Hung.)

Miha Baloh
WARRIORS FIVE(1962); DESPERADO TRAIL, THE(1965, Ger./Yugo.); FRONTIER HELLCAT(1966, Fr./Ital./Ger./Yugo.)

Hernando Balon
DAUGHTERS OF SATAN(1972), art d; SUPERBEAST(1972), art d

James Balotto
BADLANDERS, THE(1958), ed

Bruno Balp
FRENCH CANCAN(1956, Fr.)

Balpetre
CASE OF DR. LAURENT(1958, Fr.)

Antoine Balpetre
CARNIVAL OF SINNERS(1947, Fr.); DIARY OF A COUNTRY PRIEST(1954, Fr.); LE PLAISIR(1954, Fr.); RED AND THE BLACK, THE(1954, Fr.); DEVIL'S COMMANDMENT, THE(1956, Ital.); WE ARE ALL MURDERERS(1957, Fr.); COUNTERFEITERS OF PARIS, THE(1962, Fr., Ital.); HANDS OF ORLAC, THE(1964, Brit./Fr.); MISTRESS FOR THE SUMMER, A(1964, Fr./Ital.)

Antonine Balpetre
MAGNIFICENT SINNER(1963, Fr.)

Balpo
PANIQUE(1947, Fr.)

Erica Balque
DEVIL'S GENERAL, THE(1957, Ger.)

Alan Balsam
LOOSE SHOES(1980), ed; DEAD AND BURIED(1981), ed; TO BE OR NOT TO BE(1983), ed
1984
REVENGE OF THE NERDS(1984), ed

Frank Balsam
AT THE RIDGE(1931), ed

Martin Balsam
TAKING OF PELHAM ONE, TWO, THREE, THE(1974); TIME LIMIT(1957); 12 ANGRY MEN(1957); MARJORIE MORNINGSTAR(1958); AL CAPONE(1959); MIDDLE OF THE NIGHT(1959); PSYCHO(1960); ADA(1961); BREAKFAST AT TIFFANY'S(1961); CAPE FEAR(1962); EVERYBODY GO HOME!(1962, Fr./Ital.); CAPTIVE CITY, THE(1963, Ital.); WHO'S BEEN SLEEPING IN MY BED?(1963); CARPETBAGGERS, THE(1964); SEVEN DAYS IN MAY(1964); BEDFORD INCIDENT, THE(1965, Brit.); HARLOW(1965); THOUSAND CLOWNS, A(1965); AFTER THE FOX(1966, U.S./Brit./Ital.); CONQUERED CITY(1966, Ital.); HOMBRE(1967); GOOD GUYS AND THE BAD GUYS, THE(1969); ME, NATALIE(1969); TRUMAN CAPOTE'S TRILOGY(1969); CATCH-22(1970); LITTLE BIG MAN(1970); TORA! TORA! TORA!(1970, U.S./Jap.); ANDERSON TAPES, THE(1971); CONFESSIONS OF A POLICE CAPTAIN(1971, Ital.); MAN, THE(1972); STONE KILLER, THE(1973); SUMMER WISHES, WINTER DREAMS(1973); MURDER ON THE ORIENT EXPRESS(1974, Brit.); MITCHELL(1975); ALL THE PRESIDENT'S MEN(1976); SENTINEL, THE(1977); DEATH RACE(1978, Ital.); SILVER BEARS(1978); CUBA(1979); THERE GOES THE BRIDE(1980, Brit.); SALAMANDER, THE(1983, U.S./Ital./Brit.)
1984
GOODBYE PEOPLE, THE(1984)
Misc. Talkies
EYES BEHIND THE STARS(1972)

Marty Balsam
ON THE WATERFRONT(1954)

Talia Balsam
SUNNYSIDE(1979)
1984
MASS APPEAL(1984); NADIA(1984, U.S./Yugo.)

Humbert Balsan
LANCELOT OF THE LAKE(1975, Fr.); LOULOU(1980, Fr.); CHANEL SOLITAIRE(1981); QUARTET(1981, Brit./Fr.)
1984
SWANN IN LOVE(1984, Fr.Ger.)

Ewald Balser
TRIAL, THE(1948, Aust.); DAS LETZTE GEHEIMNIS(1959, Ger.); HOUSE OF THE THREE GIRLS, THE(1961, Aust.)

Robert Balser
YELLOW SUBMARINE(1958, Brit.), animation d

Fred Balshofer
Silents
SILENT VOICE, THE(1915), d

Fred J. Balshofer
Silents
HAUNTED PAJAMAS(1917), d&w; PARADISE GARDEN(1917), d, w; AVENGING TRAIL, THE(1918), w
Misc. Silents
ROSEMARY(1915), d; COME-BACK, THE(1916), d; CORNER IN COTTON, A(1916), d; MASKED RIDER, THE(1916), d; PIDGIN ISLAND(1916), d; SQUARE DECEIVER, THE(1917), d; UNDER HANDICAP(1917), d; BROADWAY BILL(1918), d; LEND ME YOUR NAME(1918), d; MAN OF HONOR, A(1919), d; ISLE OF LOVE, THE(1922), d; THREE BUCKAROOS, THE(1922), d

David Balsiger
LINCOLN CONSPIRACY, THE(1977), w

Phil Balsley
SMOKEY AND THE BANDIT II(1980)

Allison Balson
HEARSE, THE(1980)

Allsion Balson
LOOKER(1981)

Sandy Balson
LAST OF THE RED HOT LOVERS(1972); THIS IS A HIJACK(1973)
Michael Balston
CAST A GIANT SHADOW(1966)
The Balstons
OLD MOTHER RILEY'S CIRCUS(1941, Brit.)
Christian Baltauss
LACEMAKER, THE(1977, Fr.); LAST METRO, THE(1981, Fr.)
Manuelle Baltazar
PASSION(1983, Fr./Switz.)
James Balter
ANNIE HALL(1977)
Sam Balter
HARMON OF MICHIGAN(1941); PITTSBURGH KID, THE(1941); FORGOTTEN WOMEN(1949); JOE PALOOKA MEETS HUMPHREY(1950); ABBOTT AND COSTELLO MEET THE INVISIBLE MAN(1951); CRAZY OVER HORSES(1951)
Balthaus
M(1933, Ger.)
Conrado Balthazar
JAGUAR(1980, Phil.), ph
1984
BONA(1984, Phil.), ph
Alfred Balthoff
MARRIAGE IN THE SHADOWS(1948, Ger.); HELDINNEN(1962, Ger.)
Franco Baltimor
SPY IN YOUR EYE(1966, Ital.)
Vicki Baltimore
WIZ, THE(1978)
Ray Baltz, Jr.
IT HAPPENED ON 5TH AVENUE(1947), set d
Mark Baltzar
WARRIORS, THE(1979)
Deborah Baltzell
DEVIL AND MAX DEVLIN, THE(1981)
L. Balu
JUNGLE, THE(1952), ed
Cardinal Balue
QUENTIN DURWARD(1955)
Jordan Balurov
SHOP ON MAIN STREET, THE(1966, Czech.), p
Jacques Balutin
CARTOUCHE(1962, Fr./Ital.); ARMY GAME, THE(1963, Fr.); WHAT'S NEW, PUSSYCAT?(1965, U.S./Fr.); GREAT SPY CHASE, THE(1966, Fr.); KING OF HEARTS(1967, Fr./Ital.); BRAIN, THE(1969, Fr./US); DEVIL BY THE TAIL, THE(1969, Fr./Ital.); WHO IS KILLING THE GREAT CHEFS OF EUROPE?(1978, US/Ger.)
Ignazio Balzamo
EYE OF THE NEEDLE, THE(1965, Ital./Fr.)
Catherine M. Balzer
CINDERELLA LIBERTY(1973)
George Balzer
ARE YOU WITH IT?(1948), w
Karl Michael Balzer
BRIDGE, THE(1961, Ger.)
Del Balzo
COME SEPTEMBER(1961)
Martha Bamattre
BOLERO(1934); CHAMPAGNE WALTZ(1937); EVERYTHING HAPPENS AT NIGHT(1939); GOLDEN EARRINGS(1947); GREAT SINNER, THE(1949); AMERICAN IN PARIS, AN(1951); TO CATCH A THIEF(1955)
Johnny Bambary
TERROR OF TINY TOWN, THE(1938)
David Bamber
PRIVATES ON PARADE(1982)
1984
PRIVATES ON PARADE(1984, Brit.)
Dickie Bamber
PRAYING MANTIS(1982, Brit.), p
Judy Bamber
DRAGSTRIP GIRL(1957); UP IN SMOKE(1957); IN THE MONEY(1958); BUCKET OF BLOOD, A(1959); ATOMIC BRAIN, THE(1964)
Sharon Bamber
LITTLE SEX, A(1982)
Walter Bamberg
PAYDAY(1972)
Hilary Bamberger
INN OF THE DAMNED(1974, Aus.)
Joseph Jay Bamberger
Silents
SHEFFIELD BLADE, A(1918, Brit.), d, w
Peter Bamberger
ALWAYS VICTORIOUS(1960, Ital.), p; GREH(1962, Ger./Yugo.), p; ENCOUNTERS IN SALZBURG(1964, Ger.), p
Franco Rossi
THREE NIGHTS OF LOVE(1969, Ital.), d
Ralph Bamble
HARDER THEY FALL, THE(1956)
Gertrude Bambrick
Silents
JUDITH OF BETHULIA(1914)
Misc. Silents
DIVORCONS(1915)
Ben Bambridge
TAHITIAN, THE(1956)
George Bamby
SHADOW VALLEY(1947); SOUTH PACIFIC TRAIL(1952)
Freda Bamford
TIME GENTLEMEN PLEASE!(1953, Brit.); DOCTOR AT LARGE(1957, Brit.); MIRACLE IN SOHO(1957, Brit.); TEARS FOR SIMON(1957, Brit.); SAPPHIRE(1959, Brit.); HEIGHTS OF DANGER(1962, Brit.); IN THE DOGHOUSE(1964, Brit.); IPCRESS FILE, THE(1965, Brit.); THREE BITES OF THE APPLE(1967)

Tom Bamford
LOVE BUG, THE(1968)
Dilys Bamlett
BARBER OF STAMFORD HILL, THE(1963, Brit.)
Gerry Bamman
1984
OLD ENOUGH(1984)
Junzaburo Ban
SNOW IN THE SOUTH SEAS(1963, Jap.); TOPSY-TURVY JOURNEY(1970, Jap.); YOSAKOI JOURNEY(1970, Jap.)
Chaim Banai
MADRON(1970, U.S./Israel)
Ehud Banai
CLOUDS OVER ISRAEL(1966, Israel)
Poori Banai
INVINCIBLE SIX, THE(1970, U.S./Iran)
Yaacov Banai
1984
AMBASSADOR, THE(1984)
Yaakov Banai
MADRON(1970, U.S./Israel)
Joe Banana
Misc. Talkies
ROAD OF DEATH(1977)
Arlene Banas
Misc. Talkies
WASHINGTON AFFAIR, THE(1978)
Bab Banas
DADDY-O(1959)
Bob Banas
GIRL MOST LIKELY, THE(1957); SKATETOWN, U.S.A.(1979), ch
Carl Banas
SUNDAY IN THE COUNTRY(1975, Can.)
Robert Banas
KING AND I, THE(1956); WEST SIDE STORY(1961); SKYDIVERS, THE(1963), ch
Lynn Banashek
Misc. Talkies
FATAL GAMES(1983)
Frith Banbury
COLONEL BLIMP(1945, Brit.); HUGGETTS ABROAD, THE(1949, Brit.)
Jack Banbury
SUPERMAN AND THE MOLE MEN(1951)
Giuseppe Banchelli
ROCCO AND HIS BROTHERS(1961, Fr./Ital.), makeup; MARRIAGE–ITALIAN STYLE(1964, Fr./Ital.), makeup; HOUSE OF CARDS(1969), makeup; PLACE FOR LOVERS, A(1969, Ital./Fr.), makeup; PRIEST'S WIFE, THE(1971, Ital./Fr.), makeup
Guiseppe Banchelli
STORY OF A WOMAN(1970, U.S./Ital.), makeup
Mario Banchelli
CASANOVA '70(1965, Ital.); STRANGER, THE(1967, Algeria/Fr./Ital.), makeup
Anne Bancroft
DON'T BOTHER TO KNOCK(1952); KID FROM LEFT FIELD, THE(1953); TONIGHT WE SING(1953); TREASURE OF THE GOLDEN CONDOR(1953); DEMETRIUS AND THE GLADIATORS(1954); GORILLA AT LARGE(1954); RAID, THE(1954); LAST FRONTIER, THE(1955); LIFE IN THE BALANCE, A(1955); NAKED STREET, THE(1955); NEW YORK CONFIDENTIAL(1955); NIGHTFALL(1956); WALK THE PROUD LAND(1956); GIRL IN BLACK STOCKINGS(1957); RESTLESS BREED, THE(1957); MIRACLE WORKER, THE(1962); PUMPKIN EATER, THE(1964, Brit.); SLENDER THREAD, THE(1965); SEVEN WOMEN(1966); GRADUATE, THE(1967); YOUNG WINSTON(1972, Brit.); HINDENBURG, THE(1975); PRISONER OF SECOND AVENUE, THE(1975); LIPSTICK(1976); SILENT MOVIE(1976); TURNING POINT, THE(1977); ELEPHANT MAN, THE(1980, Brit.), a, d&w; FATSO(1980), a, d&w; TO BE OR NOT TO BE(1983)
1984
GARBO TALKS(1984)
Benjie Bancroft
LIVE A LITTLE, LOVE A LITTLE(1968); ST. IVES(1976); WALK PROUD(1979)
Charles Bancroft
ROMEO AND JULIET(1936); I MARRIED AN ANGEL(1942); MADAME BOVARY(1949)
George Bancroft
MIGHTY, THE(1929); THUNDERBOLT(1929); WOLF OF WALL STREET, THE(1929); DERELICT(1930); LADIES LOVE BRUTES(1930); RICH MAN'S FOLLY(1931); SCANDAL SHEET(1931); SKIN GAME, THE(1931, Brit.); LADY AND GENT(1932); WORLD AND THE FLESH, THE(1932); BLOOD MONEY(1933); ELMER AND ELSIE(1934); HELL-SHIP MORGAN(1936); MR. DEEDS GOES TO TOWN(1936); WEDDING PRESENT(1936); DOCTOR'S DIARY, A(1937); JOHN MEADE'S WOMAN(1937); RACKETEERS IN EXILE(1937); ANGELS WITH DIRTY FACES(1938); SUBMARINE PATROL(1938); EACH DAWN I DIE(1939); ESPIONAGE AGENT(1939); RULERS OF THE SEA(1939); STAGECOACH(1939); GREEN HELL(1940); LITTLE MEN(1940); NORTHWEST MOUNTED POLICE(1940); WHEN THE DALTONS RODE(1940); YOUNG TOM EDISON(1940); BUGLE SOUNDS, THE(1941); TEXAS(1941); SYNCOPATION(1942); WHISTLING IN DIXIE(1942)
Silents
JOURNEY'S END, THE(1921); PONY EXPRESS, THE(1925); RAINBOW TRAIL, THE(1925); SPLENDID ROAD, THE(1925); ENCHANTED HILL, THE(1926); OLD IRONSIDES(1926); RUNAWAY, THE(1926); SEA HORSES(1926); ROUGH RIDERS, THE(1927); UNDERWORLD(1927); WHITE GOLD(1927); DRAGNET, THE(1928)
Misc. Silents
DRIVEN(1923); DEADWOOD COACH, THE(1924); TEETH(1924); TELL IT TO SWEENEY(1927); TOO MANY CROOKS(1927); DOCKS OF NEW YORK, THE(1928); SHOWDOWN, THE(1928)
George Pleydell Bancroft
WARE CASE, THE(1939, Brit.), w
Silents
WARE CASE, THE(1917, Brit.), w
Georgette Bancroft
Silents
JOURNEY'S END, THE(1921)

Harold Bancroft
JOE PALOOKA IN TRIPLE CROSS(1951), w
Henry Bancroft
I KILLED THAT MAN(1942), w
Roy Bancroft
RIDERS OF THE BADLANDS(1941)
Albert Band
RED BADGE OF COURAGE, THE(1951), d&w; YOUNG GUNS, THE(1956), d; FOOTSTEPS IN THE NIGHT(1957), w; I BURY THE LIVING(1958), p, d; FACE OF FIRE(1959, U.S./Brit.), p, d; AVENGER, THE(1962, Fr./Ital.), p; GRINGO(1963, Span./Ital.), p, w; TRAMPLERS, THE(1966, Ital.), p, d, w; HELLBENDERS, THE(1967, U.S./Ital./Span.), p, w; MINUTE TO PRAY, A SECOND TO DIE, A(1968 Ital.), p, w; LITTLE CIGARS(1973), p; DRACULA'S DOG(1978), p, d
Misc. Talkies
MASSACRE AT GRAND CANYON(1965), d; SHE CAME TO THE VALLEY(1979) d
Carmen Miranda Band
DOWN ARGENTINE WAY(1940)
Charles Band
MANSION OF THE DOOMED(1976), p; CRASH(1977), p&d; END OF THE WORLD(1977), p; LASERBLAST(1978), p; PARASITE(1982), p&d; METALSTORM: THE DESTRUCTION OF JARED-SYN(1983), p, d
1984
SWORDKILL(1984), p
Misc. Talkies
ALCHEMIST, THE(1981), d
Edwin Band
UTAH WAGON TRAIN(1951)
Leon Miller Band
LAST PICTURE SHOW, THE(1971)
Michael Overly Band
TUNNELVISION(1976)
OSU Band
RETURN TO CAMPUS(1975), m
Richard Band
LASERBLAST(1978), m; DAY TIME ENDED, THE(1980, Span.), m; DR. HECKYL AND MR. HYPE(1980), m; LUNCH WAGON(1981), m; PARASITE(1982), m; TIME WALKER(1982), m; METALSTORM: THE DESTRUCTION OF JARED-SYN(1983), m
1984
NIGHT SHADOWS(1984), m; SWORDKILL(1984), m
Richard H. Band
HOUSE ON SORORITY ROW, THE(1983), m
The Alice Cooper Band
DIARY OF A MAD HOUSEWIFE(1970)
Band of His Majesty's Coldstream Guards
DREAMING(1944, Brit.)
Band of HM Coldstream Guards
VARIETY JUBILEE(1945, Brit.)
Band of HM Grenadier Guards
YOU WILL REMEMBER(1941, Brit.)
Band of HM Scots Guards
REGAL CAVALCADE(1935, Brit.)
Band of the Royal Marines
TALKING FEET(1937, Brit.)
Band without a Name
THUNDER ALLEY(1967)
Nati Banda
CLUE OF THE MISSING APE, THE(1953, Brit.)
Banda Da Lua
DOWN ARGENTINE WAY(1940)
Mineko Bandai
SNOW COUNTRY(1969, Jap.)
Bibhutibhusan Bandapaddhay
APARAJITO(1959, India), w
Ved Bandbu
ANNIE HALL(1977)
Bandeira
FRANTIC(1961, Fr.)
Desh Bandhu
STRANGE BREW(1983)
Armando Bandini
LOVE AND LARCENY(1963, Fr./Ital.); MANDRAGOLA(1966 Fr./Ital.)
Baccio Bandini
SWORDSMAN OF SIENA, THE(1962, Fr./Ital.), d
Lorenzo Bandini
GRAND PRIX(1966)
Paccio Bandini
APPOINTMENT FOR MURDER(1954, Ital.), d, w
Filiberto Bandino
FRANKENSTEIN-ITALIAN STYLE(1977, Ital.), p
Sierra Bandit
CALIFORNIA SPLIT(1974)
Prison Bandleader
STOLEN HARMONY(1935)
Junosuke Bando
Misc. Silents
CROSSWAYS(1928, Jap.)
Kotaro Bando
GATE OF HELL(1954, Jap.)
Tamasaburo Bando
DEMON POND(1980, Jap.)
J. Bandoh
Misc. Silents
SLUMS OF TOKYO(1930, Jap.)
T. Bandoh
ANATAHAN(1953, Jap.)
Bibhutibhusan Bandopadhaya
PATHER PANCHALI(1958, India), p,d&w; WORLD OF APU, THE(1960, India), w

Eliana Banducci
BANDIT, THE(1949, Ital.)
Beverly Bane
Misc. Silents
WALL BETWEEN, THE(1916); CYCLONE HIGGINS, D.D.(1918)
Bruce Bane
MESQUITE BUCKAROO(1939)
Hollis Bane [Mike Ragan]
WAKE ISLAND(1942); HOPPY'S HOLIDAY(1947); HARPOON(1948)
Holly Bane [Mike Ragan]
CHRISTMAS EVE(1947); SONG OF THE WASTELAND(1947); CARSON CITY RAIDERS(1948); NIGHT TIME IN NEVADA(1948); RENEGADES OF SONORA(1948); RETURN OF WILDFIRE, THE(1948); BRAND OF FEAR(1949); FAR FRONTIER, THE(1949); GRAND CANYON(1949); RED DESERT(1949); RIDERS OF THE DUSK(1949); ROARING WESTWARD(1949); COW TOWN(1950); FENCE RIDERS(1950); RADAR SECRET SERVICE(1950); STORM OVER WYOMING(1950); WEST OF WYOMING(1950); MONTANA BELLE(1952); SPRINGFIELD RIFLE(1952); GHOST OF ZORRO(1959)
Misc. Talkies
SIX GUN MESA(1950)
Honey Bane
1984
SCRUBBERS(1984, Brit.)
Jean Bane
CRISS CROSS(1949)
Monty Bane
STATE OF THINGS, THE(1983)
Haradhan Banerjee
BIG CITY, THE(1963, India)
Tarashankar Banerjee
MUSIC ROOM, THE(1963, India), w
Victor Banerjee
1984
PASSAGE TO INDIA, A(1984, Brit.)
Kanu Banerji
PATHER PANCHALI(1958, India); APARAJITO(1959, India)
Karuna Banerji
PATHER PANCHALI(1958, India); APARAJITO(1959, India)
Runki Banerji
PATHER PANCHALI(1958, India)
Subir Banerji
PATHER PANCHALI(1958, India)
Lionel Banes
LOVES OF JOANNA GODDEN, THE(1947, Brit.), spec eff; NICHOLAS NICKLEBY(1947, Brit.), spec eff; AGAINST THE WIND(1948, Brit.), ph; MAGNET, THE(1950, Brit.), ph; TRAIN OF EVENTS(1952, Brit.), ph; GOOD BEGINNING, THE(1953, Brit.), ph; MEN ARE CHILDREN TWICE(1953, Brit.), ph; NIGHT MY NUMBER CAME UP, THE(1955, Brit.), ph; CITY AFTER MIDNIGHT(1957, Brit.), ph; NO ROAD BACK(1957, Brit.), ph; SURGEON'S KNIFE, THE(1957, Brit.), ph; FIEND WITHOUT A FACE(1958), ph; HAUNTED STRANGLER, THE(1958, Brit.), ph; I ONLY ASKED!(1958, Brit.), ph; THEY WERE TEN(1961, Israel), ph
Lisa Banes
1984
HOTEL NEW HAMPSHIRE, THE(1984)
Agi Banfalvi
PASSION(1983, Fr./Switz.)
Agnes Banfalvi
MEPHISTO(1981, Ger.)
Gyorgy Banffy
WINTER WIND(1970, Fr./Hung.); MEPHISTO(1981, Ger.); FORBIDDEN RELATIONS(1983, Hung.)
Bonnie Banfield
FIVE ON THE BLACK HAND SIDE(1973)
George J. Banfield
Silents
POWER OVER MEN(1929, Brit.), p, d, w
Misc. Silents
BURGOMASTER OF STILEMONDE, THE(1928, Brit.), d; SPANGLES(1928, Brit.), d
Axel Bang
GOLDEN MOUNTAINS(1958, Den.)
Elisabeth Bang
PASSIONATE DEMONS, THE(1962, Norway)
Herman Joachim Bang
FOUR DEVILS(1929), w
Joy Bang
SEPARATION(1968, Brit.); MAIDSTONE(1970); SKY PIRATE, THE(1970); CISCO PIKE(1971); DEALING: OR THE BERKELEY-TO-BOSTON FORTY-BRICK LOST-BAG BLUES(1971); PRETTY MAIDS ALL IN A ROW(1971); RED SKY AT MORNING(1971); PLAY IT AGAIN, SAM(1972); DEAD PEOPLE(1974); NIGHT OF THE COBRA WOMAN(1974, U.S./Phil.)
Oluf Bang
DEVIL'S EYE, THE(1960, Swed.), w
Tove Bang
WEEKEND(1964, Den.)
Jon Bang-Carlsen
1984
ELEMENT OF CRIME, THE(1984, Den.)
Arne Bang-Hansen
AUTUMN SONATA(1978, Swed.)
Arturo Soto Bangel
GARDEN OF EVIL(1954)
Johnny Bangert
FOLLOW ME, BOYS!(1966)
Michael Bangerter
O LUCKY MAN!(1973, Brit.)
Kenneth Banghart
WILD IN THE STREETS(1968)

The Bangles
HOOKED GENERATION, THE(1969)
Russ Banham
MEATBALLS(1979, Can.)
Petar Banicevic
WITNESS OUT OF HELL(1967, Ger./Yugo.)
D. Banionis
UNCOMMON THIEF, AN(1967, USSR)
Donatas Banionis
RED TENT, THE(1971, Ital./USSR); ARMED AND DANGEROUS(1977, USSR)
Donatas Banionys
SOLARIS(1972, USSR)
Arthur Banjamin
FIRE DOWN BELOW(1957, U.S./Brit.), m
Kashka Banjoko
WIZ, THE(1978)
Chris Bank
EMBEZZLER, THE(1954, Brit.)
Douglas Bank
PLUNDER ROAD(1957)
Douglas F. Bank
PURPLE HEART DIARY(1951)
Girl in Bank
1984
LONELY GUY, THE(1984)
Jan Bank
MAN FROM O.R.G.Y., THE(1970)
Yudie Bank
SURVIVORS, THE(1983)
Bill Banker
MAYBE IT'S LOVE(1930); MAN TO MAN(1931)
Tallulah Bankhead
TARNISHED LADY(1931); CHEAT, THE(1931); MY SIN(1931); DEVIL AND THE DEEP(1932); FAITHLESS(1932); MAKE ME A STAR(1932); THUNDER BELOW(1932); STAGE DOOR CANTEEN(1943); LIFEBOAT(1944); ROYAL SCANDAL, A(1945); MAIN STREET TO BROADWAY(1953); DIE, DIE, MY DARLING(1965, Brit.); DAYDREAMER, THE(1966)
Silents
HIS HOUSE IN ORDER(1928, Brit.)
Misc. Silents
THIRTY A WEEK(1918)
Zsu Zsu Banki
CITY OF FEAR(1965, Brit.)
Banks
Silents
KEEP SMILING(1925), w
Aaron Banks
GREENWICH VILLAGE STORY(1963); MEAN JOHNNY BARROWS(1976); FIST OF FEAR, TOUCH OF DEATH(1980); ONE DOWN TWO TO GO(1982)
Misc. Talkies
BODYGUARD, THE(1976)
Anthony Banks
SHOUT, THE(1978, Brit.), m
Bessie Banks
Misc. Silents
DULCIE'S ADVENTURE(1916)
Brenda Banks
WIZARDS(1977), anim; HEY, GOOD LOOKIN'(1982), anim
Brenton Banks
FRAMED(1975)
Charles E. Banks
Silents
CALIFORNIA ROMANCE, A(1922), w; SWEET ADELINE(1926), w
Christopher Banks
THEY CAME FROM BEYOND SPACE(1967, Brit.); DECLINE AND FALL... OF A BIRD WATCHER(1969, Brit.); PROMISE, THE(1969, Brit.)
Cindy Banks
PERSONAL BEST(1982)
David Banks
SOME KIND OF HERO(1982)
David Francis Banks
IN GOD WE TRUST(1980)
Don Banks
PETTICOAT PIRATES(1961, Brit.), m; HOT MONEY GIRL(1962, Brit./Ger.), m; NIGHT CREATURES(1962, Brit.), m; NIGHTMARE(1963, Brit.), m; PUNCH AND JUDY MAN, THE(1963, Brit.), m; CROOKS IN CLOISTERS(1964, Brit.), m; EVIL OF FRANKENSTEIN, THE(1964, Brit.), m; BRIGAND OF KANDAHAR, THE(1965, Brit.), m; DIE, MONSTER, DIE(1965, Brit.), m; HYSTERIA(1965, Brit.), m; RASPUTIN–THE MAD MONK(1966, Brit.), m; REPTILE, THE(1966, Brit.), m; FROZEN DEAD, THE(1967, Brit.), m; MUMMY'S SHROUD, THE(1967, Brit.), m; TORTURE GARDEN(1968, Brit.), m
Doreen Banks
Silents
SAFETY FIRST(1926, Brit.)
Doug Banks
BRAIN EATERS, THE(1958)
Elton Banks [Douglas Fairbanks,]
Silents
HIS MAJESTY THE AMERICAN(1919), w
Emily Banks
PLAINSMAN, THE(1966); GUNFIGHT IN ABILENE(1967); LIVE A LITTLE, LOVE A LITTLE(1968); HELL'S BLOODY DEVILS(1970)
Ernie Banks
SECOND THOUGHTS(1983)
Estar Banks
Silents
KNOW YOUR MEN(1921); JOHN SMITH(1922)
Misc. Silents
SAINTS AND SINNERS(1916)

Gene Banks
TWO TICKETS TO BROADWAY(1951)
Geoffrey Banks
KES(1970, Brit.)
George Banks
HOW COME NOBODY'S ON OUR SIDE?(1975)
Gina Banks
DREAM ON(1981)
Harold Banks
GIANT FROM THE UNKNOWN(1958), spec eff; MISSILE TO THE MOON(1959), spec eff
Henry Banks
TO PLEASE A LADY(1950); ROAR OF THE CROWD(1953)
Howard Banks
HARD GUY(1941); EAGLE SQUADRON(1942); LIVING GHOST, THE(1942); MISS V FROM MOSCOW(1942); YANK IN LIBYA, A(1942); TIGER FANGS(1943); BEDTIME FOR BONZO(1951); DREAMBOAT(1952)
Inman Banks
1984
BEAR, THE(1984)
Jary Banks
NOTHING BUT A MAN(1964)
Jeff Banks
SILENCE OF THE NORTH(1981, Can.)
Joan Banks
BRIGHT VICTORY(1951); CRY DANGER(1951); MY PAL GUS(1952); WASHINGTON STORY(1952); MISTER CORY(1957); RETURN TO PEYTON PLACE(1961)
John Banks
GREAT GILBERT AND SULLIVAN, THE(1953, Brit.)
Jonathan Banks
CHEAP DETECTIVE, THE(1978); ROSE, THE(1979); STIR CRAZY(1980); FRANCES(1982); 48 HOURS(1982)
1984
ADVENTURES OF BUCKAROO BANZAI: ACROSS THE 8TH DIMENSION, THE(1984); BEVERLY HILLS COP(1984); GREMLINS(1984); NADIA(1984, U.S./Yugo.)
Junior Banks
THE BLACK HAND GANG(1930, Brit.)
Keith Banks
FIRE DOWN BELOW(1957, U.S./Brit.; MAN WHO WOULDN'T TALK, THE(1958, Brit.); MOONRAKER, THE(1958, Brit.)
Leslie Banks
MOST DANGEROUS GAME, THE(1932); FIRE RAISERS, THE(1933, Brit.); STRANGE EVIDENCE(1933, Brit.); I AM SUZANNE(1934); NIGHT OF THE PARTY, THE(1934, Brit.); STRIKE!(1934, Brit.); MAN WHO KNEW TOO MUCH, THE(1935, Brit.); SANDERS OF THE RIVER(1935, Brit.); TRANSATLANTIC TUNNEL(1935, Brit.); DEBT OF HONOR(1936, Brit.); FIRE OVER ENGLAND(1937, Brit.); WINGS OF THE MORNING(1937, Brit.); SHOW GOES ON, THE(1938, Brit.); TROOPSHIP(1938, Brit.); ARSENAL STADIUM MYSTERY, THE(1939, Brit.); DEAD MAN'S SHOES(1939, Brit.); JAMAICA INN(1939, Brit.); SONS OF THE SEA(1939, Brit.); BUSMAN'S HONEYMOON(1940, Brit.); TWENTY-ONE DAYS TOGETHER(1940, Brit.); BOMBSIGHT STOLEN(1941, Brit.); CHAMBER OF HORRORS(1941, Brit.); NEUTRAL PORT(1941, Brit.); BIG BLOCKADE, THE(1942, Brit.); SHIPS WITH WINGS(1942, Brit.); 48 HOURS(1944, Brit.); HENRY V(1946, Brit.); EYE WITNESS(1950, Brit.); MADELEINE(1950, Brit.); MRS. FITZHERBERT(1950, Brit.)
Linda Banks
CYCLE SAVAGES(1969)
Lionel Banks
AWFUL TRUTH, THE(1937), art d; I'LL TAKE ROMANCE(1937), art d; SHADOW, THE(1937), art d; HOLIDAY(1938), art d; I AM THE LAW(1938), art d; THERE'S ALWAYS A WOMAN(1938), art d; THERE'S THAT WOMAN AGAIN(1938), art d; AMAZING MR. WILLIAMS(1939), art d; BLONDIE BRINGS UP BABY(1939), art d; GOLDEN BOY(1939), art d; GOOD GIRLS GO TO PARIS(1939), art d; LET US LIVE(1939), art d; LONE WOLF SPY HUNT, THE(1939), art d; MAN THEY COULD NOT HANG, THE(1939), art d; MR. SMITH GOES TO WASHINGTON(1939), art d; ONLY ANGELS HAVE WINGS(1939), art d; SPECIAL INSPECTOR(1939), art d; ANGELS OVER BROADWAY(1940), art d; BEFORE I HANG(1940), art d; BLONDIE ON A BUDGET(1940), art d; GLAMOUR FOR SALE(1940), art d; HE STAYED FOR BREAKFAST(1940), art d; HIS GIRL FRIDAY(1940), art d; ISLAND OF DOOMED MEN(1940), art d; LADY IN QUESTION, THE(1940), art d; MAN WITH NINE LIVES, THE(1940), art d; MUSIC IN MY HEART(1940), art d; NOBODY'S CHILDREN(1940), art d; OUT WEST WITH THE PEPPERS(1940), art d; SO YOU WON'T TALK(1940), art d; THIS THING CALLED LOVE(1940), art d; TOO MANY HUSBANDS(1940), art d; BLONDIE IN SOCIETY(1941), art d; FACE BEHIND THE MASK, THE(1941), art d; GO WEST, YOUNG LADY(1941), art d; HARMON OF MICHIGAN(1941), art d; HERE COMES MR. JORDAN(1941), art d; LADIES IN RETIREMENT(1941), art d; OFFICER AND THE LADY, THE(1941), art d; OUR WIFE(1941), art d; PENNY SERENADE(1941), art d; PHANTOM SUBMARINE, THE(1941), art d; RICHEST MAN IN TOWN(1941), art d; SHE KNEW ALL THE ANSWERS(1941), art d; SING FOR YOUR SUPPER(1941), art d; SWEETHEART OF THE CAMPUS(1941), art d; TEXAS(1941), art d; THREE GIRLS ABOUT TOWN(1941), art d; TILLIE THE TOILER(1941), art d; TIME OUT FOR RHYTHM(1941), art d; TWO IN A TAXI(1941), art d; TWO LATINS FROM MANHATTAN(1941), art d; UNDER AGE(1941), art d; YOU BELONG TO ME(1941), art d; YOU'LL NEVER GET RICH(1941), art d; BOOGIE MAN WILL GET YOU, THE(1942), art d; FLIGHT LIEUTENANT(1942), art d; HARVARD, HERE I COME(1942), art d; HELLO ANNAPOLIS(1942), art d; LADY IS WILLING, THE(1942), art d; LAWLESS PLAINSMEN(1942), art d; MAN WHO RETURNED TO LIFE, THE(1942), art d; MEET THE STEWARTS(1942), art d; MY SISTER EILEEN(1942), art d; NIGHT TO REMEMBER, A(1942), art d; PARACHUTE NURSE(1942), art d; PARDON MY GUN(1942), art d; SABOTAGE SQUAD(1942), art d; SPIRIT OF STANFORD, THE(1942), art d; TALK OF THE TOWN(1942), art d; THEY ALL KISSED THE BRIDE(1942), art d; UNDERGROUND AGENT(1942), art d; WEST OF TOMBSTONE(1942), art d; WIFE TAKES A FLYER, THE(1942), art d; YOU WERE NEVER LOVELIER(1942), art d; AFTER MIDNIGHT WITH BOSTON BLACKIE(1943), art d; DANGEROUS BLONDES(1943), art d; DESPERADOES, THE(1943), art d; DESTROYER(1943), art d; DOUGHBOYS IN IRELAND(1943), art d; FIGHTING BUCKAROO, THE(1943), art d; FIRST COMES COURAGE(1943), art d; FOOTLIGHT GLAMOUR(1943), art d; GOOD LUCK, MR. YATES(1943), art d; HAIL TO THE RANGERS(1943), art d; HEAT'S ON, THE(1943), ait d; IS EVERYBODY HAPPY?(1943), art d; IT'S A GREAT LIFE(1943), art d; LAUGH YOUR BLUES AWAY(1943), art d; LAW OF THE NORTHWEST(1943), art d; MORE THE MERRIER, THE(1943), art d;

MURDER IN TIMES SQUARE(1943), art d; MY KINGDOM FOR A COOK(1943), art d; ONE DANGEROUS NIGHT(1943), art d; POWER OF THE PRESS(1943), art d; REVEILLE WITH BEVERLY(1943), art d; RIDERS OF THE NORTHWEST MOUNTED(1943), art d; ROBIN HOOD OF THE RANGE(1943), art d; SAHARA(1943), art d; SHE HAS WHAT IT TAKES(1943), art d; SOMETHING TO SHOUT ABOUT(1943), art d; SWING OUT THE BLUES(1943), art d; THERE'S SOMETHING ABOUT A SOLDIER(1943), art d; TWO SENORITAS FROM CHICAGO(1943), art d; WHAT A WOMAN!(1943), art d; WHAT'S BUZZIN COUSIN?(1943), art d; BEAUTIFUL BUT BROKE(1944), art d; BLACK PARACHUTE, THE(1944), art d; COVER GIRL(1944), art d; COWBOY FROM LONESOME RIVER(1944), art d; CYCLONE PRAIRIE RANGERS(1944), art d; EVER SINCE VENUS(1944), art d; GHOST THAT WALKS ALONE, THE(1944), art d; GIRL IN THE CASE(1944), art d; HEY, ROOKIE(1944), art d; IMPATIENT YEARS, THE(1944), art d; JAM SESSION(1944), art d; KANSAS CITY KITTY(1944), art d; KLONDIKE KATE(1944), art d; LAST HORSEMAN, THE(1944), art d; LOUISIANA HAYRIDE(1944), art d; MEET MISS BOBBY SOCKS(1944), art d; MR. WINKLE GOES TO WAR(1944), art d; NINE GIRLS(1944), art d; NONE SHALL ESCAPE(1944), art d; ONCE UPON A TIME(1944), art d; ONE MYSTERIOUS NIGHT(1944), art d; RACKET MAN, THE(1944), art d; RETURN OF THE VAMPIRE, THE(1944), art d; RIDING WEST(1944), art d; SAILOR'S HOLIDAY(1944), art d; SECRET COMMAND(1944), art d; SHE'S A SOLDIER TOO(1944), art d; SOUL OF A MONSTER, THE(1944), art d; STARS ON PARADE(1944), art d; STRANGE AFFAIR(1944), art d; SUNDOWN VALLEY(1944), art d; SWING IN THE SADDLE(1944), art d; THEY LIVE IN FEAR(1944), art d; TWO-MAN SUBMARINE(1944), art d; U-BOAT PRISONER(1944), art d; GUEST WIFE(1945), art d; IT'S IN THE BAG(1945), art d; SONG TO REMEMBER, A(1945), art d; TONIGHT AND EVERY NIGHT(1945), art d; HEARTBEAT(1946), art d; PERFECT MARRIAGE, THE(1946), art d; SO GOES MY LOVE(1946), art d; MAGIC TOWN(1947), art d; MOONRISE(1948), prod d; SIREN OF ATLANTIS(1948), prod d; REDHEAD FROM MANHATTAN(1954), art d, art d

Louis Banks
SILENCE OF THE NORTH(1981, Can.)

Lynne Reid Banks
L-SHAPED ROOM, THE(1962, Brit.), d&w

Montague Banks
BELL FOR ADANO, A(1945)

Monty Banks
ATLANTIC(1929 Brit.); ALMOST A HONEYMOON(1930, Brit.), d, w; COMPULSORY HUSBAND, THE(1930, Brit.), a, d; KISS ME, SERGEANT(1930, Brit.), d; NOT SO QUIET ON THE WESTERN FRONT(1930, Brit.), d; THE BLACK HAND GANG(1930, Brit.), d; WHY SAILORS LEAVE HOME(1930, Brit.), d; OLD SOLDIERS NEVER DIE(1931, Brit.), p&d; POOR OLD BILL(1931, Brit.), d; HOLD'EM JAIL(1932) MONEY FOR NOTHING(1932, Brit.), d; MY WIFE'S FAMILY(1932, Brit.), d; TENDERFOOT, THE(1932), w; TONIGHT'S THE NIGHT(1932, Brit.), a, p&d; CHARMING DECEIVER, THE(1933, Brit.), d; FOR THE LOVE OF MIKE(1933, Brit.), a; LEAVE IT TO ME(1933, Brit.), d; CHURCH MOUSE, THE(1934, Brit.), a, d; FATHER AND SON(1934, Brit.), d; GIRL IN POSSESSION(1934, Brit.), a, d&w; YOU MADE ME LOVE YOU(1934, Brit.), a, d; HELLO SWEETHEART(1935, Brit.), d; MAN OF THE MOMENT(1935, Brit.), a, d; NO LIMIT(1935, Brit.), d; SO YOU WON'T TALK?(1935, Brit.), a, d; 18 MINUTES(1935, Brit.), d; KEEP YOUR SEATS PLEASE(1936, Brit.), d; QUEEN OF HEARTS(1936, Brit.), a, d; TROUBLE AHEAD(1936, Brit.), a, d; SMILING ALONG(1938, Brit.), d; WE'RE GOING TO BE RICH(1938, Brit.), d; HONEYMOON MERRY-GO-ROUND(1939, Brit.), a, w; SHIPYARD SALLY(1940, Brit.), a, d; BLOOD AND SAND(1941); GREAT GUNS(1941), d
Silents
KEEP SMILING(1925); ATTA BOY!(1926); HONEYMOON AHEAD(1927, Brit.); PLAY SAFE(1927), a, w; WEEKEND WIVES(1928, Brit.)
Misc. Silents
RACING LUCK(1924); FLYING LUCK(1927); HORSE SHOES(1927); COCTAILS(1928, Brit.), d; PERFECT GENTLEMAN, A(1928)

Mrs. Linnaeus Banks
Silents
MANCHESTER MAN, THE(1920, Brit.), w

Perry Banks
Silents
OVERALLS(1916); ANN'S FINISH(1918)
Misc. Silents
OVERCOAT, THE(1916)

Peter Banks
CARRY ON ENGLAND(1976, Brit.)

Polan Banks
STREET OF WOMEN(1932), w; MY FORBIDDEN PAST(1951), p, w
Silents
STAGE MADNESS(1927), w; NO OTHER WOMAN(1928), w

Richard Banks
WILD WORLD OF BATWOMAN, THE(1966)

Seth Banks
GATHERING OF EAGLES, A(1963), cos; HE RIDES TALL(1964), cos; LOVE AND KISSES(1965), cos; MAROONED(1969), cos; STALKING MOON, THE(1969), cos; LIBERATION OF L.B. JONES, THE(1970), cos; OKLAHOMA CRUDE(1973), cos; SUNSHINE BOYS, THE(1975), cos; STAR IS BORN, A(1976), cos; MAIN EVENT, THE(1979)

Sydney Banks
TOMORROW NEVER COMES(1978, Brit./Can.), w

Terry Banks
SMITHY(1946, Aus.), ed; PACIFIC ADVENTURE(1947, Aus.), ed; RUGGED O'RIORDANS, THE(1949, Aus.), ed

Tony Banks
WICKED LADY, THE(1983, Brit.), m

Russell A. Bankson
FEUD OF THE WEST(1936), w

Evalene Bankston
HAVING WONDERFUL CRIME(1945)

Vilma Banky
THIS IS HEAVEN(1929); LADY TO LOVE, A(1930); REBEL, THE(1933, Ger.)
Silents
DARK ANGEL, THE(1925); EAGLE, THE(1925); SON OF THE SHEIK(1926); WINNING OF BARBARA WORTH, THE(1926); NIGHT OF LOVE, THE(1927); AWAKENING, THE(1928); TWO LOVERS(1928)
Misc. Silents
DARK ANGEL, THE(1925); MAGIC FLAME, THE(1927)

Rolf E. Banloo
GOLD(1934, Ger.), w

Robert Bannard
INCIDENT, THE(1967); FOR LOVE OF IVY(1968)

Bannec
Misc. Silents
FINNIS TERRAE(1929, Fr.)

Ian Bannen
BATTLE HELL(1956, Brit.); PRIVATE'S PROGRESS(1956, Brit.); ROTTEN TO THE CORE(1956, Brit.); MIRACLE IN SOHO(1957, Brit.); THIRD KEY, THE(1957, Brit.); BEHIND THE MASK(1958, Brit.); TALE OF TWO CITIES, A(1958, Brit.); FRENCH MISTRESS(1960, Brit.); RISK, THE(1961, Brit.); SHE DIDN'T SAY NO!(1962, Brit.); WORLD IN MY POCKET, THE(1962, Fr./Ital./Ger.); MACBETH(1963); PSYCHE 59(1964, Brit.); STATION SIX-SAHARA(1964, Brit./Ger.); FLIGHT OF THE PHOENIX, THE(1965); HILL, THE(1965, Brit.); MISTER MOSES(1965); PENELOPE(1966); SAILOR FROM GIBRALTAR, THE(1967, Brit.); LOCK UP YOUR DAUGHTERS(1969, Brit.); TOO LATE THE HERO(1970); DESERTER, THE(1971 Ital./Yugo.); FRIGHT(1971, Brit.); JANE EYRE(1971, Brit.); DOOMWATCH(1972, Brit.); MACKINTOSH MAN, THE(1973, Brit.); OFFENSE, THE(1973, Brit.); FROM BEYOND THE GRAVE(1974, Brit.); VOYAGE, THE(1974, Ital.); BITE THE BULLET(1975); DRIVER'S SEAT, THE(1975, Ital.); SWEENEY(1977, Brit.); WATCHER IN THE WOODS, THE(1980, Brit.); COUNTERFEIT COMMANDOS(1981, Ital.); EYE OF THE NEEDLE(1981); GANDHI(1982); NIGHT CROSSING(1982); GORKY PARK(1983)
1984
PRODIGAL, THE(1984)
Misc. Talkies
WON'T WRITE HOME, MOM–I'M DEAD(1975, Brit.)

Bob Banner
WARNING SHOT(1967), p

Jill Banner
WEEKEND OF FEAR(1966); C'MON, LET'S LIVE A LITTLE(1967); DEADLIER THAN THE MALE(1967, Brit.); PRESIDENT'S ANALYST, THE(1967); SHOOT FIRST, LAUGH LAST(1967, Ital./Ger./U.S.); SPIDER BABY(1968); STRANGER RETURNS, THE(1968, U.S./Ital./Ger./Span.)

John Banner
ONCE UPON A HONEYMOON(1942); SEVEN MILES FROM ALCATRAZ(1942); FALLEN SPARROW, THE(1943); IMMORTAL SERGEANT, THE(1943); MOON IS DOWN, THE(1943); THEY CAME TO BLOW UP AMERICA(1943); THIS LAND IS MINE(1943); TONIGHT WE RAID CALAIS(1943); NOCTURNE(1946); RENDEZVOUS 24(1946); TANGIER(1946); ARGYLE SECRETS, THE(1948); MY GIRL TISA(1948); TO THE VICTOR(1948); GUILTY OF TREASON(1950); KING SOLOMON'S MINES(1950); CALLAWAY WENT THATAWAY(1951); JUGGLER, THE(1953); EXECUTIVE SUITE(1954); RAINS OF RANCHIPUR, THE(1955); NEVER SAY GOODBYE(1956); BEAST OF BUDAPEST, THE(1958); YOUNG LIONS, THE(1958); BLUE ANGEL, THE(1959); WONDERFUL COUNTRY, THE(1959); STORY OF RUTH, THE(1960); OPERATION EICHMANN(1961); 20,000 EYES(1961); HITLER(1962); INTERNS, THE(1962); PRIZE, THE(1963); YELLOW CANARY, THE(1963); 36 HOURS(1965); WICKED DREAMS OF PAULA SCHULTZ, THE(1968)
Misc. Talkies
TOGETHERNESS(1970)

Chandana Bannerjee
TWO DAUGHTERS(1963, India)

Karuna Bannerjee
GODDESS, THE(1962, India)

Karuni Bannerjee
KANCHENJUNGHA(1966, India)

Victor Bannerjee
HULLABALOO OVER GEORGIE AND BONNIE'S PICTURES(1979, Brit.)
1984
HOME AND THE WORLD, THE(1984, India)

Alastair Bannerman
TRAPPED BY THE TERROR(1949, Brit.)

Celia Bannerman
TAMARIND SEED, THE(1974, Brit.); BIDDY(1983, Brit.)

John Bannerman
HUNCH, THE(1967, Brit.)

Kay Bannerman
ALL FOR MARY(1956, Brit.), w; PAIR OF BRIEFS, A(1963, Brit.), w; SWINGIN' MAIDEN, THE(1963, Brit.), w; NO, MY DARLING DAUGHTER(1964, Brit.), w; WHO KILLED VAN LOON?(1984, Brit.)

Margaret Bannerman
LILY CHRISTINE(1932, Brit.); WIVES BEWARE(1933, Brit.); GREAT DEFENDER, THE(1934, Brit.); OVER THE GARDEN WALL(1934, Brit.); REGAL CAVALCADE(1935, Brit.); LOVES OF MADAME DUBARRY, THE(1938, Brit.); CLUNY BROWN(1946); HOMESTRETCH, THE(1947)
Silents
FLAMES(1917, Brit.); GAY LORD QUEX, THE(1917, Brit.); HER SECRET(1919, Brit.)
Misc. Silents
GOODBYE(1918, Brit.); LADY AUDLEY'S SECRET(1920, Brit.); GRASS ORPHAN, THE(1922, Brit.)

Ronald Banneth
TRUE STORY OF ESKIMO NELL, THE(1975, Aus.), p

Leslie Banning
RENEGADES OF THE SAGE(1949); GIRLS' SCHOOL(1950); STAGECOACH TO FURY(1956)

Leslye Banning
HIS KIND OF WOMAN(1951); BLACK HILLS AMBUSH(1952)

Margaret Culkin Banning
WOMAN AGAINST WOMAN(1938), w

Charles Bannister
FIVE POUND MAN, THE(1937, Brit.)

Georgiana Bannister
ON STAGE EVERYBODY(1945)

Harry Bannister
GIRL OF THE GOLDEN WEST(1930); HER PRIVATE AFFAIR(1930); HUSBAND'S HOLIDAY(1931); SUICIDE FLEET(1931); DOUBLE LIFE, A(1947); GIRL ON THE RUN(1961)
Misc. Silents
PORCELAIN LAMP, THE(1921)

Manolo Baolognini
AVENGER, THE(1966, Ital.), p
Ivan Baptie
HALF A SIXPENCE(1967, Brit.); FIDDLER ON THE ROOF(1971)
Jules Baptiste
CITY NEWS(1983), m
Mona Baptiste
$100 A NIGHT(1968, Ger.)
Thomas Baptiste
DR. TERROR'S HOUSE OF HORRORS(1965, Brit.); HELP!(1965, Brit.); IPCRESS FILE, THE(1965, Brit.); TWO GENTLEMEN SHARING(1969, Brit.); SUNDAY BLOODY SUNDAY(1971, Brit.); SHAFT IN AFRICA(1973); SWEET SUZY(1973); HONEYBABY, HONEYBABY(1974); COUNTDOWN AT KUSINI(1976, Nigerian); DOGS OF WAR, THE(1980, Brit.); AMIN–THE RISE AND FALL(1982, Kenya)
Misc. Talkies
BLACKSNAKE(1973)
Antonio Baquero
THEY CAME TO ROB LAS VEGAS(1969, Fr./Ital./Span./Ger.), spec eff
Manolo Baquero
FIGURES IN A LANDSCAPE(1970, Brit.), spec eff
Manuel Baquero
MURIETA(1965, Span.), spec eff; LOST COMMAND, THE(1966), spec eff; ROYAL HUNT OF THE SUN, THE(1969, Brit.), spec eff; MERCENARY, THE(1970, Ital./Span.), spec eff; NUN AT THE CROSSROADS, A(1970, Ital./Span.), spec eff; TOWN CALLED HELL, A(1971, Span./Brit.), spec eff; HUNTING PARTY, THE(1977, Brit.), spec eff
Salvadore Baques
HIRED GUN, THE(1957)
Maurice Baquet
CRIME OF MONSIEUR LANGE, THE(1936, Fr.); ALIBI, THE(1939, Fr.); INNOCENTS IN PARIS(1955, Brit.); STOWAWAY IN THE SKY(1962, Fr.); Z(1969, Fr./Algeria)
Salvador Baquez
VIVA ZAPATA!(1952); SOMBRERO(1953)
Jacques Bar
MR. PEEK-A-BOO(1951, Fr.), p; FERNANDEL THE DRESSMAKER(1957, Fr.), p; WHERE THE HOT WIND BLOWS(1960, Fr., Ital.), p; BRIDGE TO THE SUN(1961), p; COUNTERFEITERS OF PARIS, THE(1962, Fr., Ital.), p; MONKEY IN WINTER, A(1962, Fr.), p; MOST WANTED MAN, THE(1962, Fr./Ital.), p; SWORDSMAN OF SIENA, THE(1962, Fr./Ital.), p; ANY NUMBER CAN WIN(1963 Fr.), p; DAY AND THE HOUR, THE(1963, Fr./ Ital.), p; RIFIFI IN TOKYO(1963, Fr./Ital.), p; JOY HOUSE(1964, Fr.), p; MURDER AT 45 R.P.M.(1965, Fr.); ONCE A THIEF(1965), p; GUNS FOR SAN SEBASTIAN(1968, U.S./Fr./Mex./Ital.), p; MYSTERIOUS ISLAND OF CAPTAIN NEMO, THE(1973, Fr./Ital. 87m Span./Cameroon), p; OUTSIDE MAN, THE(1973, U.S./FR.), p
Robert Bar
SWEET ECSTASY(1962, Fr.)
Roger Bar
FIRST TASTE OF LOVE(1962, Fr.), art d
Tim Bar
WONDERFUL WORLD OF THE BROTHERS ERIMM, THE(1962), spec eff
Jeremy Bar-Illan
ENDLESS LOVE(1981)
Schlomo Bar-Shavit
DREAMER, THE(1970, Israel)
Reuven Bar-Yotam
SINAI COMMANDOS: THE STORY OF THE SIX DAY WAR(1968, Israel/Ger.); HELL BOATS(1970, Brit.)
The Bar-6 Cowboys
OLD TEXAS TRAIL, THE(1944)
Frank Bara
LADY LIBERTY(1972, Ital./Fr.)
Little Bara
ZAZIE(1961, Fr.)
Lona Bara
HATE IN PARADISE(1938, Brit.), w
Lori Bara
SHARK WOMAN, THE(1941), w
Loro Bara
Silents
SEVEN CHANCES(1925)
Margit Bara
DIALOGUE(1967, Hung.)
Nina Bara
GAY SENORITA, THE(1945); PAN-AMERICANA(1945); EASY TO WED(1946); GILDA(1946); THRILL OF BRAZIL, THE(1946); BLACK HILLS(1948); THREE DARING DAUGHTERS(1948); MISSILE TO THE MOON(1959)
Roy Bara
LAST WAVE, THE(1978, Aus.)
Theda Bara
Silents
CLEMENCEAU CASE, THE(1915); DESTRUCTION(1915); FOOL THERE WAS, A(1915); SIN(1915); EAST LYNNE(1916); ETERNAL SAPHO, THE(1916); ROMEO AND JULIET(1916); SERPENT, THE(1916); DARLING OF PARIS, THE(1917); TIGER WOMAN, THE(1917); WHEN A WOMAN SINS(1918); KATHLEEN MAVOURNEEN(1919); UNCHASTENED WOMAN(1925)
Misc. Silents
CARMEN(1915); DEVIL'S DAUGHTER, THE(1915); GALLEY SLAVE, THE(1915); KREUTZER SONATA, THE(1915); TWO ORPHANS, THE(1915); GOLD AND THE WOMAN(1916); HER DOUBLE LIFE(1916); UNDER TWO FLAGS(1916); VIXEN, THE(1916); CAMILLE(1917); CLEOPATRA(1917); HEART AND SOUL(1917); HER GREATEST LOVE(1917); ROSE OF BLOOD, THE(1917); FORBIDDEN PATH, THE(1918); MADAME DUBARRY(1918); SHE DEVIL, THE(1918); SOUL OF BUDDHA, THE(1918); UNDER THE YOKE(1918); LA BELLE RUSSE(1919); LIGHT, THE(1919); LURE OF AMBITION(1919); SALOME(1919); SIREN'S SONG, THE(1919); WHEN MEN DESIRE(1919); WOMAN THERE WAS, A(1919)
Nira Barab
UP IN THE CELLAR(1970); FORTUNE, THE(1975)

Sari Barabas
OH ROSALINDA(1956, Brit.)
Victor Barabelle
STREET GIRL(1929), md
Gilda Baracchi
MANGANINNIE(1982, Aus.), p; BUSH CHRISTMAS(1983, Aus.), p
Adriano Baracco
SPY IN YOUR EYE(1966, Ital.), w; DANGER: DIABOLIK(1968, Ital./Fr.), w; OPERATION ST. PETER'S(1968, Ital.), w; TREASURE OF SAN GENNARO(1968, Fr./Ital./Ger.), w; GHOSTS, ITALIAN STYLE(1969, Ital./Fr.), w; MAN WHO CAME FOR COFFEE, THE(1970, Ital.), w
Lola Barache
GREEN GLOVE, THE(1952), ed
A. Baracq
VOLPONE(1947, Fr.), set d
Baragli
TEOREMA(1969, Ital.), md
Gianna Baragli
ANYONE CAN PLAY(1968, Ital.), ed
Giovanni Baragli
SIGN OF THE GLADIATOR(1959, Fr./Ger./Ital.), ed; SHE AND HE(1969, Ital.), ed; CANNIBALS, THE(1970, Ital.), ed
Nino Baragli
FUGITIVE LADY(1951), ed; ACCATTONE!(1961, Ital.), ed; FROM A ROMAN BALCONY(1961, Fr./Ital.), ed; WARRIOR EMPRESS, THE(1961, Ital./Fr.), ed; AGOSTINO(1962, Ital.), ed; BELL' ANTONIO(1962, Ital.), ed; EVERYBODY GO HOME!(1962, Fr./Ital.), m; LA NOTTE BRAVA(1962, Fr./Ital.), ed; LA VIACCIA(1962, Fr./Ital.), ed; MAFIOSO(1962, Ital.), ed; MAMMA ROMA(1962, Ital.), ed; THREE FABLES OF LOVE(1963, Fr./Ital./Span.), ed; THREE FACES OF A WOMAN(1965, Ital.), ed; GOSPEL ACCORDING TO ST. MATTHEW, THE(1966, Fr., Ital.), ed; LA FUGA(1966, Ital.), ed; MANDRAGOLA(1966 Fr./Ital.), ed; GOOD, THE BAD, AND THE UGLY, THE(1967, Ital./Span.), ed; HAWKS AND THE SPARROWS, THE(1967, Ital.), ed; HELLBENDERS, THE(1967, U.S./Ital./Span.), ed; UP THE MAC-GREGORS(1967, Ital./Span.), ed; DAY OF THE OWL, THE(1968, Ital./Fr.), ed; GALILEO(1968, Ital./Bul.), ed; GRAND SLAM(1968, Ital., Span., Ger.), ed; QUEENS, THE(1968, Ital./Fr.), ed; SEVEN GUNS FOR THE MACGREGORS(1968, Ital./Span.), ed; FRAULEIN DOKTOR(1969, Ital./Yugo.), ed; MAFIA(1969, Fr./Ital.), ed; ONCE UPON A TIME IN THE WEST(1969, U.S./Ital.), ed; WITCH, THE(1969, Ital.), ed; WITCHES, THE(1969, Fr./Ital.), ed; MEDEA(1971, Ital./Fr./Ger.), ed; SACCO AND VANZETTI(1971, Ital./Fr.), ed; DUCK, YOU SUCKER!(1972, Ital.), ed; FAMILY, THE(1974, Fr./Ital.), ed; MY NAME IS NOBODY(1974, Ital./Fr./Ger.), ed; DOWN THE ANCIENT STAIRCASE(1975, Ital.), ed; DRAMA OF THE RICH(1975, Ital./Fr.), ed; GENIUS, THE(1976, Ital./Fr./Ger.), ed; INHERITANCE, THE(1978, Ital.), ed; NEST OF VIPERS(1979, Ital.), ed; TILL MARRIAGE DO US PART(1979, Ital.), ed; WIFEMISTRESS(1979, Ital.), ed; ARABIAN NIGHTS(1980, Ital./Fr.), ed
1984
CORRUPT(1984, Ital.), ed; ONCE UPON A TIME IN AMERICA(1984), ed, cos
John Baragrey
CREEPER, THE(1948); LOVES OF CARMEN, THE(1948); SAXON CHARM, THE(1948); SHOCKPROOF(1949); FOUR DAYS LEAVE(1950, Switz.); TALL MAN RIDING(1955); PARDNERS(1956); COLOSSUS OF NEW YORK, THE(1958); FUGITIVE KIND, THE(1960); GAMERA THE INVINCIBLE(1966, Jap.)
Fausto Barajas
CAT PEOPLE(1982); SIX WEEKS(1982)
Michael Barak
ENIGMA(1983), w
Barakat
LITTLE MISS DEVIL(1951, Egypt), w
Gabor Baraker
WHERE THE SPIES ARE(1965, Brit.); ARRIVEDERCI, BABY!(1966, Brit.); SMASHING TIME(1967 Brit.)
Eileen Baral
MIRAGE(1965)
Lorenzo Baraldi
PRIEST'S WIFE, THE(1971, Ital./Fr.), set d; NIGHT EVELYN CAME OUT OF THE GRAVE, THE(1973, Ital.), art d; DUCH IN ORANGE SAUCE(1976, Ital.), art d; GOODNIGHT, LADIES AND GENTLEMEN(1977, Ital.), art d
Orlando Baralla
FEW BULLETS MORE, A(1968, Ital./Span.)
E. Baramona
UNDER FIRE(1983)
Edward Baran
1984
BROTHER FROM ANOTHER PLANET, THE(1984)
Jack Baran
DAVID HOLZMAN'S DIARY(1968); MARCH OF THE SPRING HARE(1969), d&w; ROOMMATES(1971), d&w; HOT TIMES(1974), a, ed
Leo Baran
MARCH OF THE SPRING HARE(1969), p; ROOMMATES(1971), p
Odette Barancay
MAXIME(1962, Fr.)
Sascha Baranley
BORN TO FIGHT(1938), w
A. Baranov
GORDEYEV FAMILY, THE(1961, U.S.S.R.); MAGIC WEAVER, THE(1965, USSR)
Vera Baranovskaya
Misc. Silents
THIEF(1916, USSR); MOTHER(1926, USSR); END OF ST. PETERSBURG, THE(1927, USSR); SUCH IS LIFE(1929, Czech)
Jadwiga Baranska
WIDOWS' NEST(1977, U.S./Span.)
Christine Baranski
SOUP FOR ONE(1982); LOVESICK(1983)
1984
CRACKERS(1984)
A. Barantsev
DAY THE EARTH FROZE, THE(1959, Fin./USSR)

Yura Barantsev
SONG OF THE FOREST(1963, USSR)

Zova Barantsevich
Misc. Silents
SPECTRE HAUNTS EUROPE, A(1923, USSR)

Zoya Barantsevich
Misc. Silents
ANNA KARENINA(1914, USSR); IN THE WHIRLWIND OF REVOLUTION(1922, USSR); LOCKSMITH AND CHANCELLOR(1923, USSR)

J. Baroness Barany
REMBRANDT(1936, Brit.)

Martine Baraque-Curie
LES MISERABLES(1982, Fr.), ed

Norman Barasch
SEND ME NO FLOWERS(1964), w; THAT FUNNY FEELING(1965), w

Olivia Barash
1984
REPO MAN(1984)

Lev Barashkov
SPRINGTIME ON THE VOLGA(1961, USSR)

Stephane Barat
LUNA(1979, Ital.)

Jean-Paul Barathieu
RETURN OF MARTIN GUERRE, THE(1983, Fr.)

Richard Barathy
FIST OF FEAR, TOUCH OF DEATH(1980)

Jacques Baratier
GOHA(1958, Tunisia), d; DOLL, THE(1962, Fr.), p&d; SWEET AND SOUR(1964, Fr./Ital.), d, w

Nena Baratier
SWEET AND SOUR(1964, Fr./Ital.), ed

Ben-Zvi Baratoff
SINGING BLACKSMITH(1938)

Paul Baratoff
MEN IN HER LIFE, THE(1941); THEY RAID BY NIGHT(1942); ROYAL SCANDAL, A(1945); VICIOUS CIRCLE, THE(1948)

M. Baratshvili
DRAGONFLY, THE(1955 USSR), w

Fred Baratta
ALL THAT HEAVEN ALLOWS(1955), ed; SWEET SUZY(1973), ed

Massimiliano Baratta
LION OF THE DESERT(1981, Libya/Brit.)

Baratti
HERCULES' PILLS(1960, Ital.), w

Bruno Baratti
LOVE IN 4 DIMENSIONS(1965 Fr./Ital.), w; LOVE AND MARRIAGE(1966, Ital.), w; MY WIFE'S ENEMY(1967, Ital.), w; LOVE FACTORY(1969, Ital.), w

Gideon Baratz
DREAM NO MORE(1950, Palestine)

Richard Baratz
KING OF COMEDY, THE(1983)

Victor Baravalle
RIO RITA(1929), md; DIXIANA(1930), md; LEATHERNECKING(1930), md; RECKLESS(1935), md; KING OF BURLESQUE(1936), md; SHOW BOAT(1936), md; CAREFREE(1938), m; RADIO CITY REVELS(1938), md; STORY OF VERNON AND IRENE CASTLE, THE(1939), md

Victor Baravelle
DAMSEL IN DISTRESS, A(1937), md

Jack La Barba
JEALOUSY(1934)

Gino Barbacane
MYTH, THE(1965, Ital.)

Maurizio Barbacini
LA TRAVIATA(1982)

Ron Barbanell
YOUNG AND DANGEROUS(1957)

Rocky Barbanica
Misc. Talkies
ASTROLOGER, THE(1975)

Paola Barbara
KING'S JESTER, THE(1947, Ital.); ROSSINI(1948, Ital.); SWORD OF THE CONQUEROR(1962, Ital.), w; SEVEN REVENGES, THE(1967, Ital.); MAN CALLED SLEDGE, A(1971, Ital.)

Barbara Dean's Girls
NEW HOTEL, THE(1932, Brit.)

Luca Barbareschi
HANNAH K.(1983, Fr.)

David Barbarian
D.C. CAB(1983)

Peter Barbarian
D.C. CAB(1983)

The Barbarian Brothers
1984
FLAMINGO KID, THE(1984)

Ginger Barbarino
UNHOLY ROLLERS(1972)

James Barbarino
UNHOLY ROLLERS(1972)

Tony Barbario
SOL MADRID(1968)

Maria Barbarita
Silents
LOVES OF RICARDO, THE(1926)

Joscik Barbarossa
1984
1984(1984, Brit.)

Bob Barbash
PLUNDERERS, THE(1960), w; TARZAN AND THE GREAT RIVER(1967, U.S./Switz.), w; BLACK HOLE, THE(1979), w; TARGET: HARRY(1980), w

Percy Barbat
NO MAN'S LAND(1964)

Adelino Barbati
IT HAPPENED IN CANADA(1962, Can.)

Olga Barbato
1984
BROADWAY DANNY ROSE(1984)

Raffaele Barbato
FOUR DAYS OF NAPLES, THE(1963, US/Ital.)

Pierre Barbaud
HIROSHIMA, MON AMOUR(1959, Fr./Jap.); LAST YEAR AT MARIENBAD(1962, Fr./Ital.); LES ABYSSES(1964, Fr.), m; LA GUERRE EST FINIE(1967, Fr./Swed.); LES CREATURES(1969, Fr./Swed.), m; THANOS AND DESPINA(1970, Fr./Gr.), m; JE T'AIME, JE T'AIME(1972, Fr./Swed.)

Armand Barbault
CONFIDENTIALLY YOURS(1983, Fr.), p

Carlos Barbe
THEY MET IN ARGENTINA(1941); CORNERED(1945)

Nicole Barbe
TARGET: HARRY(1980), makeup

Adrienne Barbeau
FOG, THE(1980); CANNONBALL RUN, THE(1981); ESCAPE FROM NEW YORK(1981); CREEPSHOW(1982); NEXT ONE, THE(1982, U.S./Gr.); SWAMP THING(1982)

Francois Barbeau
KAMOURASKA(1973, Can./Fr.), art d; LIES MY FATHER TOLD ME(1975, Can.), prod d; JACOB TWO-TWO MEETS THE HOODED FANG(1979, Can.), cos; ATLANTIC CITY(1981, U.S./Can.), cos

Carlos Barbee
CRISIS(1950); SOMBRERO(1953)

Richard Barbee
WEDNESDAY'S CHILD(1934); EASY LIVING(1937)
Misc. Silents
HER GREAT PRICE(1916)

Bobby Barber
GREAT GUY(1936); BREAKFAST FOR TWO(1937); PROFESSOR BEWARE(1938); VIVACIOUS LADY(1938); ROAD TO SINGAPORE(1940); STRANGER ON THE THIRD FLOOR(1940); THEY KNEW WHAT THEY WANTED(1940); GAY FALCON, THE(1941); MY FAVORITE SPY(1942); WHO DONE IT?(1942); HIT THE ICE(1943); REVEILLE WITH BEVERLY(1943); HENRY ALDRICH PLAYS CUPID(1944); I LOVE A SOLDIER(1944); MRS. PARKINGTON(1944); RAINBOW ISLAND(1944); ROAD TO UTOPIA(1945); SHE GETS HER MAN(1945); SUSPENSE(1946); CALCUTTA(1947); VIGILANTES OF BOOMTOWN(1947); ABBOTT AND COSTELLO MEET FRANKENSTEIN(1948); I WALK ALONE(1948); ISN'T IT ROMANTIC?(1948); LET'S DANCE(1950); ABBOTT AND COSTELLO MEET THE INVISIBLE MAN(1951); ABBOTT AND COSTELLO MEET CAPTAIN KIDD(1952); LOST IN ALASKA(1952); ABBOTT AND COSTELLO GO TO MARS(1953); MONEY FROM HOME(1953); YOU'RE NEVER TOO YOUNG(1955); PARDNERS(1956); THIRTY FOOT BRIDE OF CANDY ROCK, THE(1959)

Bonnie Belle Barber
MADE FOR EACH OTHER(1939)

Chris Barber
LOOK BACK IN ANGER(1959), m

Dick Barber
TWO HUNDRED MOTELS(1971, Brit.)

Don Barber
GOLD GUITAR, THE(1966)

Donald Barber
1984
TIGHTROPE(1984)

Ellen Barber
DEALING: OR THE BERKELEY-TO-BOSTON FORTY-BRICK LOST-BAG BLUES(1971); PREMONITION, THE(1976); PRIVATE FILES OF J. EDGAR HOOVER, THE(1978); NATURAL ENEMIES(1979); WITHOUT A TRACE(1983)
1984
FIRSTBORN(1984)

Elsie Oaks Barber
ANGEL BABY(1961), w

Frances Barber
MISSIONARY, THE(1982); ACCEPTABLE LEVELS(1983, Brit.)

Frank Barber
SON OF A GUNFIGHTER(1966, U.S./Span.), md; 1,000 CONVICTS AND A WOMAN(1971, Brit.), md

Gil Barber
TRIPLE CROSS(1967, Fr./Brit.)

Glynis Barber
TERROR(1979, Brit.); YESTERDAY'S HERO(1979, Brit.); HOUND OF THE BASKERVILLES, THE(1983, Brit.); WICKED LADY, THE(1983, Brit.)

Heather Barber
THIS, THAT AND THE OTHER(1970, Brit.)

Ian Barber
SMASH PALACE(1982, New Zealand)

J. Edward Barber
Silents
FRAILTY(1921, Brit.)

J. Edwards Barber
Silents
KNAVE OF HEARTS, THE(1919, Brit.); WON BY A HEAD(1920, Brit.)
Misc. Silents
EARLY BIRDS(1923, Brit.)

James Edwards Barber
Silents
FORBIDDEN CARGOES(1925, Brit.)
Misc. Silents
WARRIOR STRAIN, THE(1919, Brit.)

John Barber
NIGHT OF BLOODY HORROR zero(1969); INCREDIBLE TWO-HEADED TRANSPLANT, THE(1971), m, md; MANDINGO(1975)

Michael Barber
THREE MEN IN A BOAT(1958, Brit.)
Neville Barber
BARTLEBY(1970, Brit.)
Oscar Barber
RACING FEVER(1964), ed
Pam Barber
ZELIG(1983)
Patsy Lou Barber
MARYLAND(1940)
Paul Barber
LONG GOOD FRIDAY, THE(1982, Brit.)
Phil Barber
SOLDIER IN THE RAIN(1963), art d; MAN CALLED HORSE, A(1970), art d; SUPPORT YOUR LOCAL GUNFIGHTER(1971), art d; JIM, THE WORLD'S GREATEST(1976), art d
Philip Barber
ROCK, PRETTY BABY(1956), art d; KETTLES ON OLD MACDONALD'S FARM, THE(1957), art d; MAN AFRAID(1957), art d; RESTLESS YEARS, THE(1958), art d; SUMMER LOVE(1958), art d
Robert Barber
SECRET BEYOND THE DOOR, THE(1948)
Ronald Barber
WITHOUT A TRACE(1983)
Rowland Barber
SOMEBODY UP THERE LIKES ME(1956), w; THIRTY FOOT BRIDE OF CANDY ROCK, THE(1959), w; NIGHT THEY RAIDED MINSKY'S, THE(1968), W; TWILIGHT TIME(1983, U.S./Yugo.), w
Samuel Barber
ELEPHANT MAN, THE(1980, Brit.), m
1984
EL NORTE(1984), m
Sandy Barber
WOLFMAN(1979), makeup
Joe Barbera
DANGEROUS WHEN WET(1953), anim; INVITATION TO THE DANCE(1956), anim.; CHARLOTTE'S WEB(1973), p
Joseph Barbera
HEY THERE, IT'S YOGI BEAR(1964), p&d, w; MAN CALLED FLINTSTONE, THE(1966), p&d, w; C.H.O.M.P.S.(1979), p, w; HEIDI'S SONG(1982), p, w
Michael Barbera
WHAT EVER HAPPENED TO AUNT ALICE?(1969)
Neal F. Barbera
PROWLER, THE(1981), w
Alberto Barberis
OTHELLO(1955, U.S./Fr./Ital.), m
Aldo Barbero
CURIOUS DR. HUMPP(1967, Arg.)
Edmundo Barbero
NAZARIN(1968, Mex.)
Luis Barbero
EVERY DAY IS A HOLIDAY(1966, Span.)
Pedro Barbero
MURIETA(1965, Span.)
Joseph Barbers
PROJECT X(1968), p
Stephen Barbers
1984
MISSING IN ACTION(1984)
Barbette
BLOOD OF A POET, THE(1930, Fr.); BIG CIRCUS, THE(1959), ch
The Barbettes
JUMBO(1962)
Carlo Barbetti
ETERNAL MELODIES(1948, Ital.)
Cesare Barbetti
AFFAIRS OF MESSALINA, THE(1954, Ital.); WAR AND PEACE(1956, Ital./U.S.)
Alex Barbey
ON HER MAJESTY'S SECRET SERVICE(1969, Brit.), ph
Claude Inga Barbey
DEATH OF MARIO RICCI, THE(1983, Ital.)
Michael Barbey
CASE OF DR. LAURENT(1958, Fr.)
Michel Barbey
WEEKEND AT DUNKIRK(1966, Fr./Ital.)
Ciccio Barbi
GIRL WITH A SUITCASE(1961, Fr./Ital.); GIRL WHO COULDN'T SAY NO, THE(1969, Ital.)
Vince Barbi
BLOB, THE(1958); CORPSE GRINDERS, THE(1972); WOMAN UNDER THE INFLUENCE, A(1974); KILLING OF A CHINESE BOOKIE, THE(1976)
Misc. Talkies
MORALS SQUAD(1960)
Vincent Barbi
WAR AND PEACE(1956, Ital./U.S.); PAY OR DIE(1960); CONFESSIONS OF AN OPIUM EATER(1962); BLACK GOLD(1963); PANIC BUTTON(1964); SWAMP COUNTRY(1966); WHAT DID YOU DO IN THE WAR, DADDY?(1966); ASTRO-ZOMBIES, THE(1969); MACHISMO-40 GRAVES FOR 40 GUNS(1970); STUDENT TEACHERS, THE(1973); BLACK BELT JONES(1974)
Misc. Talkies
AFTERMATH, THE(1980)
Bobby Barbier
HONEYMOON AHEAD(1945)
Christian Barbier
WEEKEND AT DUNKIRK(1966, Fr./Ital.); LA VIE DE CHATEAU(1967, Fr.); TRANS-EUROP-EXPRESS(1968, Fr.); L'ARMEE DES OMBRES(1969, Fr./Ital.); TARGET: HARRY(1980)

George Barbier
BIG POND, THE(1930); SAP FROM SYRACUSE, THE(1930); GIRLS ABOUT TOWN(1931); SMILING LIEUTENANT, THE(1931); TOUCHDOWN!(1931); 24 HOURS(1931); BIG BROADCAST, THE(1932); BROKEN WING, THE(1932); CASE OF CLARA DEANE, THE(1932); EVENINGS FOR SALE(1932); MADAME RACKETEER(1932); MILLION DOLLAR LEGS(1932); NO ONE MAN(1932); ONE HOUR WITH YOU(1932); PHANTOM PRESIDENT, THE(1932); SKYSCRAPER SOULS(1932); STRANGE CASE OF CLARA DEANE, THE(1932); STRANGERS IN LOVE(1932); HELLO, EVERYBODY(1933); LOVE, HONOR, AND OH BABY!(1933); MAMA LOVES PAPA(1933); NO MAN OF HER OWN(1933); SUNSET PASS(1933); THIS DAY AND AGE(1933); TILLIE AND GUS(1933); TURN BACK THE CLOCK(1933); UNDER THE TONTO RIM(1933); CAT'S PAW, THE(1934); COLLEGE RHYTHM(1934); ELMER AND ELSIE(1934); JOURNAL OF A CRIME(1934); LADIES SHOULD LISTEN(1934); MANY HAPPY RETURNS(1934); MERRY WIDOW, THE(1934); MISS FANE'S BABY IS STOLEN(1934); SHE LOVES ME NOT(1934); BROADWAY GONDOLIER(1935); CRUSADES, THE(1935); HERE COMES COOKIE(1935); HOLD'EM YALE(1935); LIFE BEGINS AT 40(1935); MC FADDEN'S FLATS(1935); MILLIONS IN THE AIR(1935); EARLY TO BED(1936); MILKY WAY, THE(1936); PREVIEW MURDER MYSTERY(1936); PRINCESS COMES ACROSS, THE(1936); SPENDTHRIFT(1936); THREE MARRIED MEN(1936); WIFE VERSUS SECRETARY(1936); GIRL WITH IDEAS, A(1937); HOTEL HAYWIRE(1937); IT'S LOVE I'M AFTER(1937); ON THE AVENUE(1937); WAIKIKI WEDDING(1937); ADVENTURES OF MARCO POLO, THE(1938); HOLD THAT CO-ED(1938); HOLD THAT KISS(1938); LITTLE MISS BROADWAY(1938); MY LUCKY STAR(1938); STRAIGHT, PLACE AND SHOW(1938); SWEETHEARTS(1938); TARZAN'S REVENGE(1938); THANKS FOR EVERYTHING(1938); NEWS IS MADE AT NIGHT(1939); REMEMBER?(1939); SMUGGLED CARGO(1939); S.O.S. TIDAL WAVE(1939); WIFE, HUSBAND AND FRIEND(1939); RETURN OF FRANK JAMES, THE(1940); VILLAGE BARN DANCE(1940); MARRY THE BOSS' DAUGHTER(1941); MILLION DOLLAR BABY(1941); REPENT AT LEISURE(1941); SING ANOTHER CHORUS(1941); WEEKEND IN HAVANA(1941); MAGNIFICENT DOPE, THE(1942); MAN WHO CAME TO DINNER, THE(1942); SONG OF THE ISLANDS(1942); THUNDER BIRDS(1942); YANKEE DOODLE DANDY(1942); HELLO, FRISCO, HELLO(1943); WEEKEND PASS(1944); BLONDE RANSOM(1945); HER LUCKY NIGHT(1945)
George Barbier
OLD MAN RHYTHM(1935)
Georgie Barbier
LADY'S PROFESSION, A(1933)
Ginette Barbier
RISE OF LOUIS XIV, THE(1970, Fr.)
Jean-Luc Barbier
IN THE WHITE CITY(1983, Switz./Portugal), m
Nella Barbier
MAN WHO LOVED WOMEN, THE(1977, Fr.)
Peter Barbier
Silents
ETERNAL TEMPTRESS, THE(1917)
Charlotte Barbier-Krauss
Misc. Silents
POIL DE CAROTTE(1926, Fr.)
Alberto Albani Barbieri
UMBERTO D(1955, Ital.)
Gato Barbieri
FIREPOWER(1979, Brit.), m
1984
STRANGERS KISS(1984), m
Sonia Barbieri
WHERE THE HOT WIND BLOWS(1960, Fr., Ital.)
Babette Barbin
LOLA(1961, Fr./Ital.)
Amato Barbini
KREMLIN LETTER, THE(1970), makeup
Luigi Barbini
GOSPEL ACCORDING TO ST. MATTHEW, THE(1966, Fr., Ital.); TEOREMA(1969, Ital.)
Gina Barbisan
1984
UP THE CREEK(1984)
Luis Barbo
LIGHT AT THE EDGE OF THE WORLD, THE(1971, U.S./Span./Lichtenstein)
Ugo Barbone
ROMEO AND JULIET(1968, Brit./Ital.)
E. B. Clucher Enzo Barboni
TWO SUPER COPS(1978, Ital.), d&w
Enzo Barboni
DUEL OF THE TITANS(1963, Ital.), ph; GIDGET GOES TO ROME(1963), ph; SLAVE, THE(1963, Ital.), ph; AVENGER, THE(1966, Ital.), ph; DJANGO(1966 Ital./Span.), ph; MAN WHO LAUGHS, THE(1966, Ital.), ph; NIGHTMARE CASTLE(1966, Ital.), ph; HELLBENDERS, THE(1967, U.S./Ital./Span.), ph; ASSIGNMENT TO KILL(1968), ph; UGLY ONES, THE(1968, Ital./Span.), ph; FIVE MAN ARMY, THE(1970, Ital.), ph; LONG RIDE FROM HELL, A(1970, Ital.), ph
Leo Barboni
HELLO GOD(1951, U.S./Ital.), ph
Leonida Barboni
GREAT HOPE, THE(1954, Ital.), ph; ANGELA(1955, Ital.), ph; DREAMS IN A DRAWER(1957, Fr./Ital.), ph; DIVORCE, ITALIAN STYLE(1962, Ital.), ph; LA VIACCIA(1962, Fr./Ital.), ph; HUNCHBACK OF ROME, THE(1963, Ital.), ph; PASSIONATE THIEF, THE(1963, Ital.), ph; RUN WITH THE DEVIL(1963, Fr./Ital.), ph; VERONA TRIAL, THE(1963, Ital.), ph; DISORDER(1964, Fr./Ital.), ph; FACTS OF MURDER, THE(1965, Ital.), ph; RAILROAD MAN, THE(1965, Ital.), ph; AFTER THE FOX(1966, U.S./Brit./Ital.), ph; CONQUERED CITY(1966, Ital.), ph; EL GRECO(1966, Ital., Fr.), ph; VERY HANDY MAN, A(1966, Fr./Ital.), ph; ROVER, THE(1967, Ital.), ph; LA TRAVIATA(1968, Ital.), ph; QUEENS, THE(1968, Ital./Fr.), ph; WITCH, THE(1969, Ital.), ph
Luis Barboo
ANTONY AND CLEOPATRA(1973, Brit.); WIND AND THE LION, THE(1975); SUPERSONIC MAN(1979, Span.); CONAN THE BARBARIAN(1982)

Jadeen Barbor
HALLOWEEN III: SEASON OF THE WITCH(1982)
Jarbas Barbosa
XICA(1982, Braz.), p
Nestor Barbosa
INVISIBLE MAN, THE(1958, Mex.)
Leonida Barboui
CAPTIVE CITY, THE(1963, Ital.), ph
Alan G. Barbour
Misc. Talkies
CAPTAIN CELLULOID VS THE FILM PIRATES(1974)
Bruce Barbour
PIRANHA(1978); WHERE THE BUFFALO ROAM(1980); FIRST BLOOD(1982); UNDER FIRE(1983)
Bruce Paul Barbour
UNCOMMON VALOR(1983)
1984
CHILDREN OF THE CORN(1984), stunts
Carla Barbour
DOCTOR DETROIT(1983)
Dave Barbour
SECRET FURY, THE(1950)
Edwin Barbour
Silents
HOUSE NEXT DOOR, THE(1914)
Jack Barbour
FARMER'S OTHER DAUGHTER, THE(1965)
Joyce Barbour
FOR VALOR(1937, Brit.); SABOTAGE(1937, Brit.); HOUSEMASTER(1938, Brit.); SALOON BAR(1940, Brit.); DON'T TAKE IT TO HEART(1944, Brit.); STOP PRESS GIRL(1949, Brit.); IT STARTED IN PARADISE(1952, Brit.); CAPTAIN'S PARADISE, THE(1953, Brit.); MAIN CHANCE, THE(1966, Brit.)
Silents
ENCHANTMENT(1920, Brit.)
Lyndall Barbour
YOU CAN'T SEE 'ROUND CORNERS(1969, Aus.); DAWN(1979, Aus.)
Mr. Barbour
Silents
KIPPS(1921, Brit.)
Richard Barbour
ROLLOVER(1981)
Roy Barbour
DODGING THE DOLE(1936, Brit.)
Thomas Barbour
ARTHUR(1981); MIDSUMMER NIGHT'S SEX COMEDY, A(1982)
Wanda Barbour
SON OF SINBAD(1955)
The Barbours
MR. QUILP(1975, Brit.)
Madeleine Barbulee
SEVEN DEADLY SINS, THE(1953, Fr./Ital.); EARRINGS OF MADAME DE..., THE(1954, Fr.); HUNCHBACK OF NOTRE DAME, THE(1957, Fr.); LOVE IS MY PROFESSION(1959, Fr.); BIG CHIEF, THE(1960, Fr.); PRICE OF FLESH, THE(1962, Fr.); HOW NOT TO ROB A DEPARTMENT STORE(1965, Fr./Ital.); MURDER AT 45 R.P.M.(1965, Fr.)
Julia Barbuto
1984
BROADWAY DANNY ROSE(1984)
Paul Barby
THOMASINE AND BUSHROD(1974)
Ron Barca
CAPTAIN MILKSHAKE(1970)
Lorenzo Barcalata
GUADALAJARA(1943, Mex.)
Bruno Barcarol
FLYING SAUCER, THE(1964, Ital.), ph
Alberto Barcel
LOVE HUNGER(1965, Arg.); PUT UP OR SHUT UP(1968, Arg.)
Lorenzo Barcelata
SHE-DEVIL ISLAND(1936, Mex.), ph; RANCHO GRANDE(1938, Mex.), a, m
Franck Barcellini
MY UNCLE(1958, Fr.), m
Gianni Barcelloni
TROPICS(1969, Ital.), p; WIND FROM THE EAST(1970, Fr./Ital./Ger.), p; DESIRE, THE INTERIOR LIFE(1980, Ital./Ger.), d, w
Ben Barcelon
BEAST OF BLOOD(1970, U.S./Phil.), ed; CURSE OF THE VAMPIRES(1970, Phil., U.S.), ed; HOT BOX, THE(1972, U.S./Phil.), ed
Dawn Barcelona
HURRY SUNDOWN(1967)
Pauline Barcelona
TOY, THE(1982)
Joel Barcelos
TROPICS(1969, Ital.)
Catalina Barcena
IO ... TU ... Y ... ELLA(1933); SENORA CASADA NECEISITA MARIDO(1935)
Michel Barcet
FAREWELL, FRIEND(1968, Fr./Ital.)
Pete Barcia
LEGACY OF BLOOD(1978)
Igo Barcinszki
DANCING YEARS, THE(1950, Brit.)
J. Barckhausen
FIRST SPACESHIP ON VENUS(1960, Ger./Pol.), w
Barclanova
Silents
AVALANCHE(1928)

Arthur Barclay
TRAITORS, THE(1963, Brit.)
Bill Barclay
1984
BREED APART, A(1984), art d
Clement Barclay
1984
PREPPIES(1984), ed
David Barclay
RENFREW OF THE ROYAL MOUNTED(1937); RETURN OF THE JEDI(1983)
Don Barclay
FRISCO KID(1935); LION'S DEN, THE(1936); MAN HUNT(1936); MURDER OF DR. HARRIGAN, THE(1936); TREACHERY RIDES THE RANGE(1936); WHITE LEGION, THE(1936); BORDER PHANTOM(1937); EVER SINCE EVE(1937); FUGITIVE IN THE SKY(1937); HOLLYWOOD HOTEL(1937); I COVER THE WAR(1937); LIVE, LOVE AND LEARN(1937); MY DEAR MISS ALDRICH(1937); NAVY SPY(1937); SWEETHEART OF THE NAVY(1937); ACCIDENTS WILL HAPPEN(1938); OUTLAW EXPRESS(1938); SPY RING, THE(1938); SWEETHEARTS(1938); THUNDER IN THE DESERT(1938); OKLAHOMA KID, THE(1939); HONKY TONK(1941); BLONDIE'S BLESSED EVENT(1942); FALCON'S BROTHER, THE(1942); LARCENY, INC.(1942); MEXICAN SPITFIRE SEES A GHOST(1942); MEXICAN SPITFIRE'S ELEPHANT(1942); SING YOUR WORRIES AWAY(1942); THIS GUN FOR HIRE(1942); AFTER MIDNIGHT WITH BOSTON BLACKIE(1943); FRANKENSTEIN MEETS THE WOLF MAN(1943); GOOD MORNING, JUDGE(1943); MORE THE MERRIER, THE(1943); THANK YOUR LUCKY STARS(1943); IN SOCIETY(1944); MUMMY'S GHOST, THE(1944); ONCE UPON A TIME(1944); PRACTICALLY YOURS(1944); HAVING WONDERFUL CRIME(1945); MY DARLING CLEMENTINE(1946); SAINTED SISTERS, THE(1948); WHISPERING SMITH(1948); FATHER WAS A FULLBACK(1949); CINDERELLA(1950); LONG GRAY LINE, THE(1955)
Donald Barclay
MR. PERRIN AND MR. TRAILL(1948, Brit.); ONE HUNDRED AND ONE DALMATIANS(1961); MARY POPPINS(1964); HALF A SIXPENCE(1967, Brit.)
Dorothy Barclay
Misc. Silents
SONS OF THE SEA(1925, Brit.)
Eddie Barclay
TEMPTATION(1962, Fr.), m
Elizabeth Barclay
MAN, A WOMAN, AND A BANK, A(1979, Can.)
Eric Barclay
Silents
ENCHANTMENT(1920, Brit.); JUDGE NOT(1920, Brit.)
Misc. Silents
CORNER MAN, THE(1921, Brit.)
Florence L. Barclay
Silents
MISTRESS OF SHENSTONE, THE(1921), w
Frances Barclay
CHINESE PUZZLE, THE(1932, Brit.), w
Frank Barclay
WHEN LONDON SLEEPS(1934, Brit.)
George Barclay
MELODY OF MY HEART(1936, Brit.), p; VILLAGE OF THE DAMNED(1960, Brit.), w; POSTMAN'S KNOCK(1962, Brit.), w; DEVIL DOLL(1964, Brit.), w
Gordon Barclay
COLLECTOR, THE(1965)
James F. Barclay
HANSEL AND GRETEL(1954), ed
Jenny Barclay
SCRUFFY(1938, Brit.)
Jered Barclay
CHILDREN'S HOUR, THE(1961)
Jerry Barclay
MAN WITH THE GOLDEN ARM, THE(1955); UNTAMED YOUTH(1957); VALERIE(1957); YOUNG AND DANGEROUS(1957); GUN FEVER(1958); WAR OF THE SATELLITES(1958); GUNMEN FROM LAREDO(1959)
Joan Barclay
GOLD DIGGERS OF 1933(1933); LITTLE GIANT, THE(1933); FINISHING SCHOOL(1934); MADAME DU BARRY(1934); ST. LOUIS KID, THE(1934); COLLEEN(1936); FEUD OF THE WEST(1936); KID RANGER, THE(1936); MEN OF THE PLAINS(1936); PHANTOM PATROL(1936); PRISON SHADOWS(1936); WEST OF NEVADA(1936); GLORY TRAIL, THE(1937); ISLAND CAPTIVES(1937); SINGING OUTLAW(1937); TRUSTED OUTLAW, THE(1937); $1,000,000 RACKET(1937); PIONEER TRAIL(1938); PURPLE VIGILANTES, THE(1938); SWEETHEARTS(1938); TWO-GUN JUSTICE(1938); WHIRLWIND HORSEMAN(1938); CONVICT'S CODE(1939); OUTLAW'S PARADISE(1939); SIX-GUN RHYTHM(1939); TEXAS WILDCATS(1939); BILLY THE KID'S RANGE WAR(1941); FLYING WILD(1941); LOVE CRAZY(1941); TRIAL OF MARY DUGAN, THE(1941); ZIEGFELD GIRL(1941); BANDIT RANGER(1942); BLACK DRAGONS(1942); CORPSE VANISHES, THE(1942); MR. WISE GUY(1942); AROUND THE WORLD(1943); FALCON IN DANGER, THE(1943); FALCON STRIKES BACK, THE(1943); GILDERSLEEVE'S BAD DAY(1943); LADIES' DAY(1943); MEXICAN SPITFIRE'S BLESSED EVENT(1943); ROOKIES IN BURMA(1943); SAGEBRUSH LAW(1943); SEVENTH VICTIM, THE(1943); THIS LAND IS MINE(1943); FALCON OUT WEST, THE(1944); MUSIC IN MANHATTAN(1944); MY PAL, WOLF(1944); YOUTH RUNS WILD(1944); SHANGHAI COBRA, THE(1945)
Misc. Talkies
RIDIN' ON(1936); LIGHTNING CARSON RIDES AGAIN(1938)
John Barclay
DODSWORTH(1936); MIKADO, THE(1939, Brit.); GENTLEMAN FROM ARIZONA, THE(1940); ALOMA OF THE SOUTH SEAS(1941); DR. JEKYLL AND MR. HYDE(1941); KING RAT(1965); MECHANIC, THE(1972); SOYLENT GREEN(1973)
Lila Barclay
Silents
ROYAL FAMILY, A(1915); SENTIMENTAL LADY, THE(1915)
Lola Barclay
Silents
SEVEN SISTERS, THE(1915)

Marie-Christine Barclay
OPERATION ST. PETER'S(1968, Ital.)

Martha Barclay
Misc. Silents
ACROSS THE PLAINS(1928)

Mary Barclay
SINS OF THE FATHERS(1948, Can.); HEADLESS GHOST, THE(1959, Brit.); REVOLUTIONARY, THE(1970, Brit.); TOUCH OF CLASS, A(1973, Brit.)

McClelland Barclay
ARTISTS AND MODELS(1937)

Per Barclay
EL CONDOR(1970); DOC(1971); VALDEZ IS COMING(1971); BAD MAN'S RIVER(1972, Span.)

Richard Barclay
GREEN FINGERS(1947)
Misc. Silents
THOROUGHBRED, THE(1928, Brit.)

Stephan Barclay
FOOL'S GOLD(1946)

Stephen Barclay
GUY NAMED JOE, A(1943); PRIDE OF THE PLAINS(1944); SEE HERE, PRIVATE HARGROVE(1944); VIGILANTES OF DODGE CITY(1944); DON'T FENCE ME IN(1945); GIRLS OF THE BIG HOUSE(1945); GREAT FLAMARION, THE(1945); SPORTING CHANCE, A(1945); THEY WERE EXPENDABLE(1945); LANDRUSH(1946)

Steve Barclay
IRON MAJOR, THE(1943); LUXURY GIRLS(1953, Ital.); DARK PURPOSE(1964), p, w

Arlene Barco
IT'S A DEAL(1930), art d

John Barcroft
TUNES OF GLORY(1960, Brit.)

Roy Barcroft
ROSALIE(1937); FRONTIERSMAN, THE(1938); HEROES OF THE HILLS(1938); STRANGER FROM ARIZONA, THE(1938); CRASHING THRU(1939); MAN FROM TEXAS, THE(1939); MEXICALI ROSE(1939); RENEGADE TRAIL(1939); RIDERS OF THE FRONTIER(1939); SILVER ON THE SAGE(1939); HIDDEN GOLD(1940); RAGTIME COWBOY JOE(1940); RANCHO GRANDE(1940); SANTA FE TRAIL(1940); SHOWDOWN, THE(1940); STAGE TO CHINO(1940); TRAILING DOUBLE TROUBLE(1940); WEST OF CARSON CITY(1940); YUKON FLIGHT(1940); BANDIT TRAIL, THE(1941); JESSE JAMES AT BAY(1941); LAND OF THE OPEN RANGE(1941); MASKED RIDER, THE(1941); OUTLAWS OF THE CHEROKEE TRAIL(1941); PALS OF THE PECOS(1941); SHERIFF OF TOMBSTONE(1941); WEST OF CIMARRON(1941); WIDE OPEN TOWN(1941); DAWN ON THE GREAT DIVIDE(1942); LONE RIDER IN CHEYENNE, THE(1942); NAZI AGENT(1942); PIRATES OF THE PRAIRIE(1942); RIDIN' DOWN THE CANYON(1942); ROMANCE ON THE RANGE(1942); SILVER QUEEN(1942); STARDUST ON THE SAGE(1942); SUNSET ON THE DESERT(1942); SUNSET SERENADE(1942); TENNESSEE JOHNSON(1942); THEY DIED WITH THEIR BOOTS ON(1942); WEST OF THE LAW(1942); BORDERTOWN GUNFIGHTERS(1943); CALLING WILD BILL ELLIOTT(1943); CANYON CITY(1943); CARSON CITY CYCLONE(1943); CHATTERBOX(1943); CHEYENNE ROUNDUP(1943); FALSE COLORS(1943); HOPPY SERVES A WRIT(1943); MAN FROM THE RIO GRANDE, THE(1943); OLD CHISHOLM TRAIL(1943); OVERLAND MAIL ROBBERY(1943); RAIDERS OF SUNSET PASS(1943); RIDERS OF THE RIO GRANDE(1943); SAGEBRUSH LAW(1943); SIX GUN GOSPEL(1943); STRANGER FROM PECOS, THE(1943); WAGON TRACKS WEST(1943); BIG BONANZA, THE(1944); CALL OF THE SOUTH SEAS(1944); CHEYENNE WILDCAT(1944); CODE OF THE PRAIRIE(1944); FIREBRANDS OF ARIZONA(1944); GIRL WHO DARED, THE(1944); HIDDEN VALLEY OUTLAWS(1944); LARAMIE TRAIL, THE(1944); LIGHTS OF OLD SANTA FE(1944); MAN FROM FRISCO(1944); MARSHAL OF RENO(1944); SHERIFF OF SUNDOWN(1944); STAGECOACH TO MONTEREY(1944); STORM OVER LISBON(1944); TUCSON RAIDERS(1944); ALONG THE NAVAJO TRAIL(1945); BELLS OF ROSARITA(1945); CHEROKEE FLASH, THE(1945); COLORADO PIONEERS(1945); CORPUS CHRISTI BANDITS(1945); DAKOTA(1945); LONE TEXAS RANGER(1945); MARSHAL OF LAREDO(1945); SANTA FE SADDLEMATES(1945); SUNSET IN EL DORADO(1945); TOPEKA TERROR, THE(1945); TRAIL OF KIT CARSON(1945); VAMPIRE'S GHOST, THE(1945); ALIAS BILLY THE KID(1946); HOME ON THE RANGE(1946); MY PAL TRIGGER(1946); NIGHT TRAIN TO MEMPHIS(1946); PLAINSMAN AND THE LADY(1946); STAGECOACH TO DENVER(1946); SUN VALLEY CYCLONE(1946); TRAFFIC IN CRIME(1946); ALONG THE OREGON TRAIL(1947); BANDITS OF DARK CANYON(1947); BLACKMAIL(1947); FABULOUS TEXAN, THE(1947); LAST FRONTIER UPRISING(1947); MAIN STREET KID, THE(1947); MARSHAL OF CRIPPLE CREEK, THE(1947); OREGON TRAIL SCOUTS(1947); RUSTLERS OF DEVIL'S CANYON(1947); SPOILERS OF THE NORTH(1947); SPRINGTIME IN THE SIERRAS(1947); VIGILANTES OF BOOMTOWN(1947); WEB OF DANGER, THE(1947); WILD FRONTIER, THE(1947); WYOMING(1947); BOLD FRONTIERSMAN, THE(1948); DESPERADOES OF DODGE CITY(1948); EYES OF TEXAS(1948); GALLANT LEGION, THE(1948); GRAND CANYON TRAIL(1948); LIGHTNIN' IN THE FOREST(1948); MADONNA OF THE DESERT(1948); MARSHAL OF AMARILLO(1948); OKLAHOMA BADLANDS(1948); OLD LOS ANGELES(1948); OUT OF THE STORM(1948); RENEGADES OF SONORA(1948); SECRET SERVICE INVESTIGATOR(1948); SONS OF ADVENTURE(1948); SUNDOWN IN SANTA FE(1948); TIMBER TRAIL, THE(1948); TRAIN TO ALCATRAZ(1948); DOWN DAKOTA WAY(1949); FAR FRONTIER, THE(1949); FRONTIER INVESTIGATOR(1949); HELLFIRE(1949); LAW OF THE GOLDEN WEST(1949); OUTCASTS OF THE TRAIL(1949); POWDER RIVER RUSTLERS(1949); PRINCE OF THE PLAINS(1949); RANGER OF CHEROKEE STRIP(1949); SAN ANTONE AMBUSH(1949); SHERIFF OF WICHITA(1949); SOUTH OF RIO(1949); ARIZONA COWBOY, THE(1950); CODE OF THE SILVER SAGE(1950); FEDERAL AGENT AT LARGE(1950); GUNMEN OF ABILENE(1950); MISSOURIANS, THE(1950); NORTH OF THE GREAT DIVIDE(1950); PIONEER MARSHAL(1950); ROCK ISLAND TRAIL(1950); RUSTLERS ON HORSEBACK(1950); SALT LAKE RAIDERS(1950); SAVAGE HORDE, THE(1950); SURRENDER(1950); UNDER MEXICALI STARS(1950); VANISHING WESTERNER, THE(1950); VIGILANTE HIDEOUT(1950); ARIZONA MANHUNT(1951); DAKOTA KID, THE(1951); DESERT OF LOST MEN(1951); FORT DODGE STAMPEDE(1951); HONEYCHILE(1951); IN OLD AMARILLO(1951); INSURANCE INVESTIGATOR(1951); NIGHT RIDERS OF MONTANA(1951); RODEO KING AND THE SENORITA(1951); STREET BANDITS(1951); UTAH WAGON TRAIN(1951); WELLS FARGO GUNMASTER(1951); BLACK HILLS AMBUSH(1952); BORDER SADDLEMATES(1952); CAPTIVE OF BILLY THE KID(1952); DESPERADOES OUT-

POST(1952); HOODLUM EMPIRE(1952); LEADVILLE GUNSLINGER(1952); MONTANA BELLE(1952); OKLAHOMA ANNIE(1952); OLD OKLAHOMA PLAINS(1952); PALS OF THE GOLDEN WEST(1952); RIDE THE MAN DOWN(1952); SOUTH PACIFIC TRAIL(1952); THUNDERING CARAVANS(1952); WAC FROM WALLA WALLA, THE(1952); WILD HORSE AMBUSH(1952); BANDITS OF THE WEST(1953); DOWN LAREDO WAY(1953); EL PASO STAMPEDE(1953); IRON MOUNTAIN TRAIL(1953); MARSHAL OF CEDAR ROCK(1953); OLD OVERLAND TRAIL(1953); SAVAGE FRONTIER(1953); SHADOWS OF TOMBSTONE(1953); DESPERADO, THE(1954); ROGUE COP(1954); TWO GUNS AND A BADGE(1954); MAN WITHOUT A STAR(1955); OKLAHOMA(1955); SPOILERS, THE(1955); GUN BROTHERS(1956); LAST HUNT, THE(1956); WAGON WHEELS WESTWARD(1956); BAND OF ANGELS(1957); DOMINO KID(1957); KETTLES ON OLD MACDONALD'S FARM, THE(1957); LAST STAGECOACH WEST, THE(1957); ESCORT WEST(1959); GHOST OF ZORRO(1959); FRECKLES(1960); TEN WHO DARED(1960); WHEN THE CLOCK STRIKES(1961); SIX BLACK HORSES(1962); BILLY THE KID VS. DRACULA(1966); DESTINATION INNER SPACE(1966); GUNPOINT(1966); TEXAS ACROSS THE RIVER(1966); WAY WEST, THE(1967); BANDOLERO!(1968); ROSEMARY'S BABY(1968); GAILY, GAILY(1969); REIVERS, THE(1969); MONTE WALSH(1970)

Victor Barcynska
TESHA(1929, Brit.), w

Bardson Bard
Silents
SANDY(1926)

Ben Bard
BAT WHISPERS, THE(1930); BORN RECKLESS(1930); NIGHT WORK(1930); MEET THE BARON(1933); HOLLYWOOD PARTY(1934); WHITE PARADE, THE(1934); GHOST SHIP, THE(1943); LEOPARD MAN, THE(1943); SEVENTH VICTIM, THE(1943); YOUTH RUNS WILD(1944); BLACK ANGEL(1946)
Silents
ARIZONA WILDCAT(1927); LOVE MAKES 'EM WILD(1927); SEVENTH HEAVEN(1927); NO OTHER WOMAN(1928)
Misc. Silents
COME TO MY HOUSE(1927); SECRET STUDIO, THE(1927); 2 GIRLS WANTED(1927); DRESSED TO KILL(1928); FLEETWING(1928); ROMANCE OF THE UNDERWORLD(1928); LOVE AND THE DEVIL(1929)

Benna Bard
I CAN GET IT FOR YOU WHOLESALE(1951)

E. Bard
TROUBLE AHEAD(1936, Brit.), w

Katharine Bard
DECKS RAN RED, THE(1958); INTERNS, THE(1962); INSIDE DAISY CLOVER(1965); HOW TO SAVE A MARRIAGE–AND RUIN YOUR LIFE(1968)

Katherine Bard
JOHNNY COOL(1963)

Mary Bard
MOTHER DIDN'T TELL ME(1950), d&w

Rachel Bard
SILENT SCREAM(1980)

Antonio Barda
Silents
WHITE SISTER, THE(1923)

George Bardawil
TASTE FOR WOMEN, A(1966, Fr./Ital.), w

Adolfo Bardela.
SALT OF THE EARTH(1954), prod d

Beatrice Bardelli
NIGHT OF THE SHOOTING STARS, THE(1982, Ital.)

Juan A. Bardem
AGE OF INFIDELITY(1958, Span.), d&w

Juan Antonia Bardem
CORRUPTION OF CHRIS MILLER, THE(1979, Span.), d

Juan Antonio Bardem
MAIN STREET(1956, Span.), d&w; UNINHIBITED, THE(1968, Fr./Ital./Span.), d, w, ed; LAST DAY OF THE WAR, THE(1969, U.S./Ital./Span.), d, w; MYSTERIOUS ISLAND OF CAPTAIN NEMO, THE(1973, Fr./Ital. 87m Span./Cameroon), d, w
Misc. Talkies
BEHIND THE SHUTTERS(1976, Span.), d

Rafael Bardem
MYSTERIOUS ISLAND OF CAPTAIN NEMO, THE(1973, Fr./Ital. 87m Span./Cameroon)

Raphael Bardem
SEVEN GUNS FOR THE MACGREGORS(1968, Ital./Span.)

Mercia Barden
SUNDOWNERS, THE(1960)

Trevor Bardette
BORDERLAND(1937); GREAT GARRICK, THE(1937); THEY WON'T FORGET(1937); WHITE BONDAGE(1937); IN OLD MEXICO(1938); JEZEBEL(1938); MARIE ANTOINETTE(1938); MYSTERY HOUSE(1938); BLACKMAIL(1939); CHARLIE CHAN AT TREASURE ISLAND(1939); GONE WITH THE WIND(1939); LET FREEDOM RING(1939); OKLAHOMA KID, THE(1939); STAND UP AND FIGHT(1939); ABE LINCOLN IN ILLINOIS(1940); DARK COMMAND, THE(1940); FIGHTING 69TH, THE(1940); GIRL FROM HAVANA(1940); GRAPES OF WRATH(1940); HE STAYED FOR BREAKFAST(1940); ISLAND OF DOOMED MEN(1940); KILLERS OF THE WILD(1940); NEW MOON(1940); SANTA FE TRAIL(1940); THREE FACES WEST(1940); TORRID ZONE(1940); VIRGINIA CITY(1940); WAGONS WESTWARD(1940); WESTERNER, THE(1940); YOUNG BUFFALO BILL(1940); BUY ME THAT TOWN(1941); DOOMED CARAVAN(1941); INTERNATIONAL LADY(1941); MYSTERY SHIP(1941); RED RIVER VALLEY(1941); ROMANCE OF THE RIO GRANDE(1941); TOPPER RETURNS(1941); APACHE TRAIL(1942); FLIGHT LIEUTENANT(1942); HENRY AND DIZZY(1942); WILD BILL HICKOK RIDES(1942); CHANCE OF A LIFETIME, THE(1943); DEERSLAYER(1943); MOON IS DOWN, THE(1943); BLACK PARACHUTE, THE(1944); NONE SHALL ESCAPE(1944); TAMPICO(1944); U-BOAT PRISONER(1944); UNCERTAIN GLORY(1944); WHISTLER, THE(1944); COUNTER-ATTACK(1945); DICK TRACY(1945); THOUSAND AND ONE NIGHTS, A(1945); BIG SLEEP, THE(1946); DICK TRACY VS. CUEBALL(1946); DRAGONWYCH(1946); HOODLUM SAINT, THE(1946); MAN WHO DARED, THE(1946); SING WHILE YOU DANCE(1946); LAST ROUND-UP, THE(1947); MARSHAL OF CRIPPLE CREEK, THE(1947); RAMROD(1947); SEA OF GRASS, THE(1947); SLAVE GIRL(1947); T-MEN(1947); TYCOON(1947); WYOMING(1947); ALIAS A GENTLEMAN(1948); BEHIND LOCKED DOORS(1948); BLACK EAGLE(1948); GALLANT

LEGION, THE(1948); LOVES OF CARMEN, THE(1948); MARSHAL OF AMARIL-
LO(1948); PALEFACE, THE(1948); RETURN OF THE WHISTLER, THE(1948); SE-
CRET SERVICE INVESTIGATOR(1948); SUNDOWN IN SANTA FE(1948); SWORD OF
THE AVENGER(1948); APACHE CHIEF(1949); BLAZING TRAIL, THE(1949); GUN
CRAZY(1949); HELLFIRE(1949); OMOO OMOO, THE SHARK GOD(1949); RENE-
GADES OF THE SAGE(1949); SAN ANTONE AMBUSH(1949); SHERIFF OF WI-
CHITA(1949); SMOKY MOUNTAIN MELODY(1949); SONG OF INDIA(1949);
WYOMING BANDIT, THE(1949); HILLS OF OKLAHOMA(1950); LADY WITHOUT
PASSPORT, A(1950); PALOMINO, THE(1950); UNION STATION(1950); BAREFOOT
MAILMAN, THE(1951); FORT DODGE STAMPEDE(1951); FORT SAVAGE RAI-
DERS(1951); GENE AUTRY AND THE MOUNTIES(1951); LORNA DOONE(1951);
MASK OF THE AVENGER(1951); SWORD OF MONTE CRISTO, THE(1951); TEXAS
RANGERS, THE(1951); LONE STAR(1952); MACAO(1952); MONTANA TER-
RITORY(1952); SAN FRANCISCO STORY, THE(1952); AMBUSH AT TOMAHAWK
GAP(1953); BANDITS OF THE WEST(1953); DESERT SONG, THE(1953); PERILOUS
JOURNEY, A(1953); RED RIVER SHORE(1953); SUN SHINES BRIGHT, THE(1953);
THUNDER OVER THE PLAINS(1953); DANGEROUS MISSION(1954); DESTRY(1954);
JOHNNY GUITAR(1954); OUTLAW STALLION, THE(1954); MAN FROM BITTER
RIDGE, THE(1955); RAGE AT DAWN(1955); RUN FOR COVER(1955); RACK,
THE(1956); RAWHIDE YEARS, THE(1956); RED SUNDOWN(1956); DRAGON WELLS
MASSACRE(1957); HARD MAN, THE(1957); MONOLITH MONSTERS, THE(1957);
SHOOT-OUT AT MEDICINE BEND(1957); SAGA OF HEMP BROWN, THE(1958);
THUNDER ROAD(1958); MATING GAME, THE(1959); PAPA'S DELICATE CONDI-
TION(1963); RAIDERS, THE(1964); MACKENNA'S GOLD(1969)

Gyorgy Bardi
ROUND UP, THE(1969, Hung.)

Mariemma Bardi
BITTER RICE(1950, Ital.); ANNA(1951, Ital.)

Leo Bardichewski
CELESTE(1982, Ger.)

Mabel Bardine
Silents
NIGHT WORKERS, THE(1917); ROUGH AND READY(1918)
Misc. Silents
MOTHER LOVE AND THE LAW(1917)

Michel Bardinet
HEAT OF THE SUMMER(1961, Fr.); HIRED KILLER, THE(1967, Fr./Ital.); SWEET
BODY OF DEBORAH, THE(1969, Ital./Fr.); WOMAN ON FIRE, A(1970, Ital.); WITH-
OUT APPARENT MOTIVE(1972, Fr.); LITTLE ROMANCE, A(1979, U.S./Fr.)
1984
AMERICAN DREAMER(1984)

Alexander Bardini
CATAMOUNT KILLING, THE(1975, Ger.)

Danny Bardisa
HOT STUFF(1979)

Marie Bardishewski
AMERICAN SUCCESS COMPANY, THE(1980)

Brick Bardo
THRILL KILLERS, THE(1965)

Michele Bardollet
SWEET ECSTASY(1962, Fr.)

John Bardon
S(1974)
1984
ORDEAL BY INNOCENCE(1984, Brit.)

Priscilla Bardonille
LIFE STUDY(1973)

Brigitte Bardot
ACT OF LOVE(1953); DOCTOR AT SEA(1955, Brit.); GRAND MANEUVER,
THE(1956, Fr.); HELEN OF TROY(1956, Ital.); AND GOD CREATED WOMAN(1957,
Fr.); LIGHT ACROSSS THE STREET, THE(1957, Fr.); PLEASE! MR. BALZAC(1957,
Fr.); ROYAL AFFAIRS IN VERSAILLES(1957, Fr.); BRIDE IS MUCH TOO BEAUTI-
FUL, THE(1958, Fr.); GIRL IN THE BIKINI, THE(1958, Fr.); LA PARISIENNE(1958,
Fr./Ital.); NIGHT HEAVEN FELL, THE(1958, Fr.); LOVE IS MY PROFESSION(1959,
Fr.); BABETTE GOES TO WAR(1960, Fr.); COME DANCE WITH ME(1960, Fr.); CRAZY
FOR LOVE(1960, Fr.); FEMALE, THE(1960, Fr.); TRUTH, THE(1961, Fr./Ital.); NERO'S
MISTRESS(1962, Ital.); TESTAMENT OF ORPHEUS, THE(1962, Fr.); VERY PRIVATE
AFFAIR, A(1962, Fr./Ital.); CONTEMPT(1963, Fr./Ital.); LOVE ON A PILLOW(1963,
Fr./Ital.); PLEASE, NOT NOW!(1963, Fr./Ital.); DEAR BRIGETTE(1965); VIVA
MARIA(1965, Fr./Ital.); MASCULINE FEMININE(1966, Fr./Swed.); RAVISHING IDI-
OT, A(1966, Ital./Fr.); TWO WEEKS IN SEPTEMBER(1967, Fr./Brit.); SHALAKO(1968,
Brit.); SPIRITS OF THE DEAD(1969, Fr./Ital.); LEGEND OF FRENCHIE KING,
THE(1971, Fr./Ital./Span./Brit.)

Mijanou Bardot
SEX KITTENS GO TO COLLEGE(1960); PIRATE OF THE BLACK HAWK, THE(1961,
Fr./Ital.); LA COLLECTIONNEUSE(1971, Fr.)

Camille Bardou
Misc. Silents
L'AFFICHE(1925, Fr.)

Alan Bardsley
GLENROWAN AFFAIR, THE(1951, Aus.); KANGAROO(1952)

June Bardsley
HER PANELLED DOOR(1951, Brit.); MANIACS ON WHEELS(1951, Brit.); DEATH
OF AN ANGEL(1952, Brit.); WHISPERING SMITH VERSUS SCOTLAND YARD(1952,
Brit.)

Bobby Bare
DISTANT TRUMPET, A(1964)

Frank Bare
REVENGE OF THE NINJA(1983)

Richard Bare
SMART GIRLS DON'T TALK(1948), d; FLAXY MARTIN(1949), d; HOUSE ACROSS
THE STREET, THE(1949), d; RETURN OF THE FRONTIERSMAN(1950), d; PRISON-
ERS OF THE CASBAH(1953), d; I SAILED TO TAHITI WITH AN ALL GIRL
CREW(1969), p&d, w

Richard L. Bare
TWO-GUN TROUBADOR(1939), w; THIS SIDE OF THE LAW(1950), d; SHOOT-OUT
AT MEDICINE BEND(1957), d; THIS REBEL BREED(1960), d; WICKED, WICK-
ED(1973), p,d&fw

Jean Baree
SINISTER URGE, THE(1961)

Eddie Barefield
SINGING KID, THE(1936)

Adam Bareham
RETURN OF THE JEDI(1983)

Gerty Barek
LITTLE NIGHT MUSIC, A(1977, Aust./U.S./Ger.)

Itzhak Bareket
THEY WERE TEN(1961, Israel)

L.H. Barel
DRAGNET NIGHT(1931, Fr.), ph

Adolfo Barela
SALT OF THE EARTH(1954), a, p

Odette Barencey
CASQUE D'OR(1956, Fr.)

Edda Barends
LITTLE ARK, THE(1972)
1984
QUESTION OF SILENCE(1984, Neth.)

E. Barens
LAST GAME, THE(1964, USSR)

Dora Baret
TERRACE, THE(1964, Arg.); VIOLATED LOVE(1966, Arg.)

Daniel Baretta
BLOOD IN THE STREETS(1975, Ital./Fr.)

Gil Baretto
MERMAIDS OF TIBURON, THE(1962); WORLD'S GREATEST SINNER, THE(1962)

Edward Barge
MAN CALLED FLINTSTONE, THE(1966), anim

Gene Barge
STONY ISLAND(1978), a, m

Gillian Barge
NATIONAL HEALTH, OR NURSE NORTON'S AFFAIR, THE(1973, Brit.)
1984
LAUGHTER HOUSE(1984, Brit.)

Paul Barge
CASQUE D'OR(1956, Fr.); MADEMOISELLE(1966, Fr./Brit.)

Douglas Barger
KILLERS THREE(1968)

Lance Barger
JAZZ BABIES(1932), w

Sonny Barger
HELL'S ANGELS ON WHEELS(1967); HELL'S ANGELS '69(1969)

Robert Bargere
OVER THE EDGE(1979), ed

James Bargington
Misc. Silents
STUDY IN SCARLET, A(1914, Brit.)

Le Bargy
Misc. Silents
L'APPEL DU SANG(1920, Fr.)

Freddie Barholomew
LLOYDS OF LONDON(1936)

Frank Barhydt
QUINTET(1979), w; HEALTH(1980), w

Jade Bari
EASY MONEY(1983)
1984
HOTEL NEW HAMPSHIRE, THE(1984); LONELY GUY, THE(1984)

Len Bari
JEREMY(1973)

Lenny Bari
SKATETOWN, U.S.A.(1979)

Lynn Bari
DANCING LADY(1933); STAND UP AND CHEER(1934 80m FOX bw); DOUBTING
THOMAS(1935); GEORGE WHITE'S 1935 SCANDALS(1935); MAN WHO BROKE THE
BANK AT MONTE CARLO, THE(1935); MUSIC IS MAGIC(1935); GIRLS' DORMITO-
RY(1936); LADIES IN LOVE(1936); MY MARRIAGE(1936); PIGSKIN PARADE(1936);
SING, BABY, SING(1936); LANCER SPY(1937); LOVE IS NEWS(1937); ON THE
AVENUE(1937); SING AND BE HAPPY(1937); THIS IS MY AFFAIR(1937); WIFE,
DOCTOR AND NURSE(1937); ALWAYS GOODBYE(1938); BARONESS AND THE
BUTLER, THE(1938); BATTLE OF BROADWAY(1938); CITY GIRL(1938); I'LL GIVE A
MILLION(1938); JOSETTE(1938); MEET THE GIRLS(1938); MR. MOTO'S GAM-
BLE(1938); SHARPSHOOTERS(1938); SPEED TO BURN(1938); WALKING DOWN
BROADWAY(1938); CHARLIE CHAN IN THE CITY OF DARKNESS(1939); CHASING
DANGER(1939); HOLLYWOOD CAVALCADE(1939); HOTEL FOR WOMEN(1939);
NEWS IS MADE AT NIGHT(1939); PACK UP YOUR TROUBLES(1939); PARDON OUR
NERVE(1939); RETURN OF THE CISCO KID(1939); CHARTER PILOT(1940); CITY OF
CHANCE(1940); EARTHBOUND(1940); FREE, BLONDE AND 21(1940); KIT CAR-
SON(1940); LILLIAN RUSSELL(1940); PIER 13(1940); BLOOD AND SAND(1941);
MOON OVER HER SHOULDER(1941); PERFECT SNOB, THE(1941); SLEEPERS
WEST(1941); SUN VALLEY SERENADE(1941); WE GO FAST(1941); CHINA
GIRL(1942); FALCON TAKES OVER, THE(1942); MAGNIFICENT DOPE, THE(1942);
NIGHT BEFORE THE DIVORCE, THE(1942); ORCHESTRA WIVES(1942); SECRET
AGENT OF JAPAN(1942); HELLO, FRISCO, HELLO(1943); BRIDGE OF SAN LUIS
REY, THE(1944); SWEET AND LOWDOWN(1944); TAMPICO(1944); CAPTAIN ED-
DIE(1945); HOME SWEET HOMICIDE(1946); MARGIE(1946); NOCTURNE(1946);
SHOCK(1946); MAN FROM TEXAS, THE(1948); SPIRITUALIST, THE(1948); KID
FROM CLEVELAND, THE(1949); I'D CLIMB THE HIGHEST MOUNTAIN(1951); ON
THE LOOSE(1951); SUNNY SIDE OF THE STREET(1951); HAS ANYBODY SEEN MY
GAL?(1952); I DREAM OF JEANIE(1952); FRANCIS JOINS THE WACS(1954);
ABBOTT AND COSTELLO MEET THE KEYSTONE KOPS(1955); WOMEN OF
PITCAIRN ISLAND, THE(1957); DAMN CITIZEN(1958); TRAUMA(1962); YOUNG
RUNAWAYS, THE(1968)

Phil Baribault
NOCTURNE(1946)

Robert Barich
MAUSOLEUM(1983), p, w, ph
B.J. Barie
AUTHOR! AUTHOR!(1982)
Nimai Barik
RIVER, THE(1951)
Gerard Baril
FAR COUNTRY, THE(1955)
Chiarina Barile
WEDDINGS AND BABIES(1960)
Joe Barilla
BLOOD AND BLACK LACE(1965, Ital.), w
John Barilla
NIGHT OF THE ZOMBIES(1981)
Pierre Barillet
FORTY CARATS(1973), w
Carlotta Barilli
MORE THAN A MIRACLE(1967, Ital./Fr.)
Francesco Barilli
BEFORE THE REVOLUTION(1964, Ital.)
Aubrey Baring
FOOLS RUSH IN(1949, Brit.), p; SNOWBOUND(1949, Brit.), p; CAIRO ROAD(1950, Brit.), p; SPIDER AND THE FLY, THE(1952, Brit.), p; APPOINTMENT IN LONDON(1953, Brit.), p; SO LITTLE TIME(1953, Brit.), p; GOLDEN MASK, THE(1954, Brit.), a, p; THEY WHO DARE(1954, Brit.), p; KEY, THE(1958, Brit.), p; TROUBLE IN THE SKY(1961, Brit.), p; WRONG ARM OF THE LAW, THE(1963, Brit.), p
Mathilde Baring
Silents
ACCORDING TO LAW(1916); AS A WOMAN SOWS(1916)
Misc. Silents
FEATHERTOP(1916); HAUNTED MANOR, THE(1916)
Matilda Baring
Misc. Silents
PANTHER WOMAN, THE(1919)
Nancy Baring
Misc. Silents
SOUL OF A CHILD, THE(1916)
Nora Baring
ESCAPED FROM DARTMOOR(1930, Brit.)
Norah Baring
MURDER(1930, Brit.); MYSTERY AT THE VILLA ROSE(1930, Brit.); TWO WORLD(1930, Brit.); LYONS MAIL, THE(1931, Brit.); SHOULD A DOCTOR TELL?(1931, Brit.); HOUSE OF TRENT, THE(1933, Brit.); STRANGE EVIDENCE(1933, Brit.); LITTLE STRANGER(1934, Brit.)
Misc. Silents
UNDERGROUND(1928, Brit.); CELESTIAL CITY, THE(1929, Brit.); RUNAWAY PRINCESS, THE(1929, Brit.)
Pat Baring
STRANGLEHOLD(1931, Brit.); SEEING IS BELIEVING(1934, Brit.)
Victor Baring
LITTLE BIG SHOT(1952, Brit.); DEVIL'S HARBOR(1954, Brit.); JOE MACBETH(1955, Brit.); CORRUPTION(1968, Brit.); SILVER BEARS(1978); LION OF THE DESERT(1981, Libya/Brit.)
N.W. Baring-Pemberton
SHE WAS ONLY A VILLAGE MAIDEN(1933, Brit.), w; DESIGNING WOMEN(1934, Brit.), w
Barry Baringer
MURDER AT DAWN(1932), w
Alan Barinholtz
Misc. Talkies
FAKING OF THE PRESIDENT, THE(1976)
Harry Baris
SUSIE STEPS OUT(1946)
Tony Baris
SUPERMAN AND THE MOLE MEN(1951)
Marie-Claude Bariset
OLIVE TREES OF JUSTICE, THE(1967, Fr.), ed
Keith Barish
SOPHIE'S CHOICE(1982), p
Rita Barisse
MIDNIGHT EPISODE(1951, Brit.), w
Rene Barjavel
LITTLE WORLD OF DON CAMILLO, THE(1953, Fr./Ital.), w; CASE OF DR. LAURENT(1958, Fr.), w; DEVIL AND THE TEN COMMANDMENTS, THE(1962, Fr.), w; LOVE ON THE RIVIERA(1964, Fr./Ital.), w
Lucien Barjon
POSTMAN GOES TO WAR, THE(1968, Fr.)
David Barkan
JESUS CHRIST, SUPERSTAR(1973)
Yuda Barkan
ESCAPE TO THE SUN(1972, Fr./Ger./Israel)
Geoffrey Barkas
BLOCKADE(1928, Brit.), d; RHODES(1936, Brit.), p; SILENT BARRIERS(1937, Brit.), d; YOU'RE IN THE ARMY NOW(1937, Brit.), p; LITTLE BALLERINA, THE(1951, Brit.), p
Misc. Silents
PALAVER(1926, Brit.), d; INFAMOUS LADY, THE(1928, Brit.), d
Ronnie Barke
FATHER CAME TOO(1964, Brit.)
Ballard Barkeley
JUST MY LUCK(1957, Brit.); BLOOD BEAST FROM OUTER SPACE(1965, Brit.)
Don Barkemeyer
1984
SOLE SURVIVOR(1984), p
Abe Barker
HIGH AND DRY(1954, Brit.); DOCTOR AT SEA(1955, Brit.); DOCTOR AT LARGE(1957, Brit.); BATTLE OF THE SEXES, THE(1960, Brit.); KIDNAPPED(1960)

Adella Barker
Silents
ONE OF MANY(1917)
Misc. Silents
RED, WHITE AND BLUE BLOOD(1918)
Alex Barker [Lex Barker]
DOLL FACE(1945)
Alfred Barker, Jr.
COWBOYS, THE(1972)
Ambrose Barker
RETURN OF DR. FU MANCHU, THE(1930); UNFAITHFUL(1931); GILDED LILY, THE(1935); PETER IBBETSON(1935); UNDER THE PAMPAS MOON(1935); CONVICTS AT LARGE(1938), w; ADVENTURE IN DIAMONDS(1940); REMEMBER THE NIGHT(1940)
Ann Barker
JUST WILLIAM'S LUCK(1948, Brit.), ed
Antonio Barker
AMAZING MR. BLUNDEN, THE(1973, Brit.), d&w
Art Barker
WILD REBELS, THE(1967); MISSION MARS(1968)
Barklay Barker
Silents
ONE DAY(1916)
Betty Barker
CHEAPER BY THE DOZEN(1950)
Bill Barker
REVOLT AT FORT LARAMIE(1957)
Bobb Barker
JACKASS MAIL(1942)
Bobby Barker
CRACKED NUTS(1941); HOLD THAT GHOST(1941); FOLLOW THE BOYS(1944); TANGIER(1946); ABBOTT AND COSTELLO IN THE FOREIGN LEGION(1950)
Bonita Barker
DANCING LADY(1933)
Bradley Barker
MOTHER'S BOY(1929), d
Silents
MOTH AND THE FLAME, THE(1915); ERSTWHILE SUSAN(1919); AWAY GOES PRUDENCE(1920); MASTER MIND, THE(1920); SECRETS OF PARIS, THE(1922); ADAM AND EVA(1923); PLAYTHINGS OF DESIRE(1924); EARLY BIRD, THE(1925); POLICE PATROL, THE(1925); POTTERS, THE(1927); APE, THE(1928)
Misc. Silents
(; CITY OF ILLUSION, THE(1916); HER AMERICAN PRINCE(1916); LITTLE MISS FORTUNE(1917); ROAD BETWEEN, THE(1917); EYES OF MYSTERY, THE(1918); MILLION DOLLAR DOLLIES, THE(1918); STOLEN KISS, THE(1920); COINCIDENCE(1921); INSINUATION(1922); FIGHTING BLADE, THE(1923); LEAVENWORTH CASE, THE(1923); CRACKERJACK, THE(1925); RAINBOW RILEY(1926); COMBAT(1927); HIS RISE TO FAME(1927)
Corinne Barker
Silents
PECK'S BAD GIRL(1918); CLIMBERS, THE(1919); ENCHANTMENT(1921)
Misc. Silents
WHY I WOULD NOT MARRY(1918); ONE WEEK OF LIFE(1919); PEACE OF ROARING RIVER, THE(1919); BROKEN MELODY, THE(1920); SILENT BARRIER, THE(1920); WHY GIRLS LEAVE HOME(1921)
Daphne Barker
SHOWTIME(1948, Brit.); ENCORE(1951, Brit.); LITTLE BIG SHOT(1952, Brit.); LAST SHOT YOU HEAR, THE(1969, Brit.)
Dave Barker
IRON ANGEL(1964)
Dennis Barker
CHINA SYNDROME, THE(1979)
Dick Barker
VAMPIRE, THE(1968, Mex.); CAYMAN TRIANGLE, THE(1977)
Don Barker
GALLIPOLI(1981, Aus.)
Dorothy Barker
VISITING HOURS(1982, Can.)
Eric Barker
ON VELVET(1938, Brit.); BROTHERS IN LAW(1957, Brit.); BACHELOR OF HEARTS(1958, Brit.); HAPPY IS THE BRIDE(1958, Brit.); CARRY ON SERGEANT(1959, Brit.); LEFT, RIGHT AND CENTRE(1959); CARRY ON CONSTABLE(1960, Brit.); DENTIST IN THE CHAIR(1960, Brit.); PURE HELL OF ST. TRINIAN'S, THE(1961, Brit.); WATCH YOUR STERN(1961, Brit.); CARRY ON CRUISING(1962, Brit.), w; NEARLY A NASTY ACCIDENT(1962, Brit.); ON THE BEAT(1962, Brit.); ROOMMATES(1962, Brit.); FAST LADY, THE(1963, Brit.); GET ON WITH IT(1963, Brit.); HEAVENS ABOVE!(1963, Brit.); MOUSE ON THE MOON, THE(1963, Brit.); BARGEE, THE(1964, Brit.); CARRY ON SPYING(1964, Brit.); FATHER CAME TOO(1964, Brit.); FERRY ACROSS THE MERSEY(1964, Brit.); OPERATION SNAFU(1965, Brit.); THOSE MAGNIFICENT MEN IN THEIR FLYING MACHINES; OR HOW I FLEWFROM LONDON TO PARIS IN 25 HOURS AND 11 MINUTES(1965, Brit.); THREE HATS FOR LISA(1965, Brit.); GREAT ST. TRINIAN'S TRAIN ROBBERY, THE(1966, Brit.); CARNABY, M.D.(1967, Brit.); MAROC 7(1967, Brit.); COOL IT, CAROL!(1970, Brit.); THERE'S A GIRL IN MY SOUP(1970, Brit.); LOLA(1971, Brit./Ital.)
Silents
NELSON(1918, Brit.)
George Barker
VIOLENT STRANGER(1957, Brit.)
Granville Barker
Silents
PRUNELLA(1918), w; AFFAIRS OF ANATOL, THE(1921), w
H. Bradley Barker
Silents
MAN AND THE WOMAN, A(1917)
Howard Barker
COME SPY WITH ME(1967), art d; MADE(1972, Brit.), w; ACES HIGH(1977, Brit.), w

Jack Barker
HOT NEWS(1936, Brit.), ph; SUNSHINE AHEAD(1936, Brit.), ph; WORLD OWES ME A LIVING, THE(1944, Brit.)

James Barker
SPENCER'S MOUNTAIN(1963), makeup

Jane Barker
CAPTAIN NEMO AND THE UNDERWATER CITY(1969, Brit.), w

Jean Barker
ONCE UPON A DREAM(1949, Brit.), ed; TRAVELLER'S JOY(1951, Brit.), ed; INDISCRETION OF AN AMERICAN WIFE(1954, U.S./Ital.), ed; THE BEACHCOMBER(1955, Brit.), ed; EYEWITNESS(1956, Brit.), ed; LOSER TAKES ALL(1956, Brit.), ed; SIMON AND LAURA(1956, Brit.), ed; NOVEL AFFAIR, A(1957, Brit.), ed; SUBWAY IN THE SKY(1959, Brit.), ed; TOO YOUNG TO LOVE(1960, Brit.), ed

Jess Barker
GOOD LUCK, MR. YATES(1943); GOVERNMENT GIRL(1943); COVER GIRL(1944); JAM SESSION(1944); SHE'S A SOLDIER TOO(1944); DALTONS RIDE AGAIN, THE(1945); KEEP YOUR POWDER DRY(1945); SCARLET STREET(1945); SENORITA FROM THE WEST(1945); THIS LOVE OF OURS(1945); GIRL ON THE SPOT(1946); IDEA GIRL(1946); TIME OF THEIR LIVES, THE(1946); BLACK BOOK, THE(1949); TAKE ONE FALSE STEP(1949); MILKMAN, THE(1950); DRAGONFLY SQUADRON(1953); MARRY ME AGAIN(1953); SHACK OUT ON 101(1955); KENTUCKY RIFLE(1956); PEACEMAKER, THE(1956); THREE BAD SISTERS(1956); NIGHT WALKER, THE(1964); MURPH THE SURF(1974)

Jim Barker
MAD MISS MANTON, THE(1938), makeup

Joyce Barker
GIRLS ON THE LOOSE(1958)

Kenneth Barker
Silents
TAILOR OF BOND STREET, THE(1916, Brit.)

Les Barker
DUEL ON THE MISSISSIPPI(1955); 125 ROOMS OF COMFORT(1974, Can.)

Lex Barker
DO YOU LOVE ME?(1946); CROSSFIRE(1947); DICK TRACY MEETS GRUESOME(1947); FARMER'S DAUGHTER, THE(1947); UNCONQUERED(1947); UNDER THE TONTO RIM(1947); MR. BLANDINGS BUILDS HIS DREAM HOUSE(1948); RETURN OF THE BADMEN(1948); VELVET TOUCH, THE(1948); TARZAN'S MAGIC FOUNTAIN(1949); TARZAN AND THE SLAVE GIRL(1950); TARZAN'S PERIL(1951); BATTLES OF CHIEF PONTIAC(1952); TARZAN'S SAVAGE FURY(1952); TARZAN AND THE SHE-DEVIL(1953); THUNDER OVER THE PLAINS(1953); YELLOW MOUNTAIN, THE(1954); MAN FROM BITTER RIDGE, THE(1955); MYSTERY OF THE BLACK JUNGLE(1955); AWAY ALL BOATS(1956); PRICE OF FEAR, THE(1956); DEERSLAYER, THE(1957); GIRL IN BLACK STOCKINGS(1957); GIRL IN THE KREMLIN, THE(1957); JUNGLE HEAT(1957); WAR DRUMS(1957); FEMALE FIENDS(1958, Brit.); LA DOLCE VITA(1961, Ital./Fr.); PIRATE AND THE SLAVE GIRL, THE(1961, Fr./Ital.); RETURN OF DR. MABUSE, THE(1961, Ger./Fr./Ital.); SON OF THE RED CORSAIR(1963, Ital.); CODE 7, VICTIM 5(1964, Brit.); APACHE GOLD(1965, Ger.); DESPERADO TRAIL, THE(1965, Ger./Yugo.); INVISIBLE DR. MABUSE, THE(1965, Ger.); TREASURE OF SILVER LAKE(1965, Fr./Ger./Yugo.); LAST OF THE RENEGADES(1966, Fr./Ital./Ger./Yugo.); PLACE CALLED GLORY, A(1966, Span./Ger.); 24 HOURS TO KILL(1966, Brit.); BLOOD DEMON(1967, Ger.); WOMAN TIMES SEVEN(1967, U.S./Fr./Ital.); OLD SHATTERHAND(1968, Ger./Yugo./Fr./Ital.)
Misc. Talkies
MISSION IN MOROCCO(1959); KILLER'S CARNIVAL(1965); SPY TODAY, DIE TOMORROW(1967)

Margaret Barker
LOST BOUNDARIES(1949)

Patricia Barker
PRESENTING LILY MARS(1943); FRENCHMAN'S CREEK(1944); THREE MEN IN WHITE(1944)

Petronella Barker
OTHELLO(1965, Brit.)

Philip Barker
TRAIL OF THE LONESOME PINE, THE(1936)

Pip Barker
CAPTAIN NEMO AND THE UNDERWATER CITY(1969, Brit.), w

Pippin Barker
Misc. Silents
DO UNTO OTHERS(1915, Brit.)

Rand Barker
MUSIC MAN, THE(1962)

Reginald Barker
MISSISSIPPI GAMBLER(1929), d; NEW ORLEANS(1929), d; GREAT DIVIDE, THE(1930), d; HIDE-OUT(1930), d; SEVEN KEYS TO BALDPATE(1930), d; MOONSTONE, THE(1934), d; HEALER, THE(1935), d; WOMEN MUST DRESS(1935), d; FORBIDDEN HEAVEN(1936), d
Silents
TYPHOON, THE(1914), d; WRATH OF THE GODS, THE or THE DESTRUCTION OF SAKURA JIMA(1914), d; ITALIAN, THE(1915), d; REWARD, THE(1915), d; CIVILIZATION(1916), d; JIM GRIMSBY'S BOY(1916), d; MARKET OF VAIN DESIRE, THE(1916), d; ICED BULLET, THE(1917), d; PAWS OF THE BEAR(1917), d; CARMEN OF THE KLONDIKE(1918), d; BRANDING IRON, THE(1920), d; BUNTY PULLS THE STRINGS(1921), d; POVERTY OF RICHES(1921), d; SNOWBLIND(1921), d; STORM, THE(1922), d; ETERNAL STRUGGLE, THE(1923), d; PLEASURE MAD(1923), d; TOILERS, THE(1928), d
Misc. Silents
BARGAIN, THE(1914), d; COWARD, THE(1915), d; GOLDEN CLAW, THE(1915), d; IRON STRAIN, THE(1915), d; ON THE NIGHT STAGE(1915), d; RUMPELSTILSKIN(1915), d; BUGLE CALL, THE(1916), d; CONQUEROR, THE(1916), d; CRIMINAL, THE(1916), d; SHELL FORTY-THREE(1916), d; STEPPING STONE, THE(1916), d; THOROUGHBRED, THE(1916), d; BACK OF THE MAN(1917), d; GOLDEN RULE KATE(1917), d; HAPPINESS(1917), d; MADAM WHO?(1917), d; STRANGE TRANSGRESSOR, A(1917), d; SWEETHEART OF THE DOOMED(1917), d; THREE OF MANY(1917), d; HELL CAT, THE(1918), d; ONE WOMAN, THE(1918), d; SHACKLED(1918), d; TURN OF THE WHEEL, THE(1918), d; BONDS OF LOVE(1919), d; BRAND, THE(1919), d; CRIMSON GARDENIA, THE(1919), d; FLAME OF THE DESERT(1919), d; GIRL FROM THE OUTSIDE, THE(1919), d; SHADOWS(1919), d; STRONGER VOW, THE(1919), d; DANGEROUS DAYS(1920), d; WOMAN AND THE PUPPET, THE(1920), d; GODLESS MEN(1921), d; OLD NEST, THE(1921), d; HEARTS

AFLAME(1923), d; BROKEN BARRIERS(1924), d; WOMEN WHO GIVE(1924), d; GREAT DIVIDE, THE(1925), d; WHEN THE DOOR OPENED(1925), d; WHITE DESERT, THE(1925), d; FLAMING FOREST, THE(1926), d; BODY AND SOUL(1927), d; FRONTIERSMAN, THE(1927), d; RAINBOW, THE(1929), d

Reginald C. Barker
Silents
QUICKER'N LIGHTNIN'(1925), w

Rick Barker
SPACE RAIDERS(1983), stunts

Ron Barker
DAY OF ANGER(1970, Ital./Ger.), w

Ronnie Barker
WONDERFUL THINGS!(1958, Brit.); KILL OR CURE(1962, Brit.); BARGEE, THE(1964, Brit.); RUNAWAY RAILWAY(1965, Brit.); MAN OUTSIDE, THE(1968, Brit.); ROBIN AND MARIAN(1976, Brit.); DOING TIME(1979, Brit.)

Roy Barker
JACQUELINE(1956, Brit.), d

Shirley Barker
THREE DARING DAUGHTERS(1948), cos

Suzanne Barker
1984
POLICE ACADEMY(1984)

Tita Barker
Misc. Talkies
PERFECT KILLER, THE(1977, Span.)

Warren Barker
STRANGE LOVERS(1963), m; ZEBRA IN THE KITCHEN(1965), m

Will Barker
Misc. Silents
SHE(1916, Brit.), d

William J. Barker
SEARCH FOR BRIDEY MURPHY, THE(1956)

Adam Barker-Mill
1984
EVERY PICTURE TELLS A STORY(1984, Brit.), ph

Adam Barker-Mills
PRIVATE ROAD(1971, Brit.), ph

Geoffrey Barkes
Silents
SOMME, THE(1927, Brit.), w

John Barkes
BLONDE ALIBI(1946)

Beege Barkett
FRISCO KID, THE(1979); ONION FIELD, THE(1979)

Christopher Barkett
Misc. Talkies
AFTERMATH, THE(1980)

Steve Barkett
Misc. Talkies
AFTERMATH, THE(1980), a, d

Beege Barkette
SECOND-HAND HEARTS(1981)

Aram Barkev
HAPPY BIRTHDAY TO ME(1981)

Don Barkham
INN OF THE DAMNED(1974, Aus.); DAWN(1979, Aus.)

Borya Barkhatov
SUMMER TO REMEMBER, A(1961, USSR)

P. Barkhoudian
Misc. Silents
POWER OF EVIL(1929, USSR/Armenian), d

Scott Barkhurst
HOW TO BEAT THE HIGH COST OF LIVING(1980)

Ellen Barkin
DINER(1982); TENDER MERCIES(1982); DANIEL(1983); EDDIE AND THE CRUISERS(1983)
1984
ADVENTURES OF BUCKAROO BANZAI: ACROSS THE 8TH DIMENSION, THE(1984); HARRY AND SON(1984)

Marci Barkin
JACKSON COUNTY JAIL(1976)

Marcie Barkin
CHESTY ANDERSON, U.S. NAVY(1976); NEW GIRL IN TOWN(1977); VAN, THE(1977); FADE TO BLACK(1980)
1984
PROTOCOL(1984)
Misc. Talkies
SMOKEY AND THE GOODTIME OUTLAWS(1978); CARHOPS(1980)

Arthur Barking
WHALERS, THE(1942, Swed.)

Barry Barkla
PETERSEN(1974, Aus.); DIMBOOLA(1979, Aus.)

Dorothy Barkley
WILLARD(1971), cos

Lucille Barkley
VARIETY GIRL(1947); WHERE THERE'S LIFE(1947); SCENE OF THE CRIME(1949); DESERT HAWK, THE(1950); FRENCHIE(1950); GREAT PLANE ROBBERY(1950); MA AND PA KETTLE GO TO TOWN(1950); MILKMAN, THE(1950); PEGGY(1950); ARIZONA MANHUNT(1951); BEDTIME FOR BONZO(1951); FAT MAN, THE(1951); FLIGHT TO MARS(1951); GOLDEN HORDE, THE(1951); PRISONERS OF THE CASBAH(1953); OTHER WOMAN, THE(1954)

Lynne Barkley
ALEXANDER'S RAGTIME BAND(1938)

Roxanne Barkley
IRENE(1940)

Tamara Barkley
Misc. Talkies
SWEATER GIRLS(1978)

Villa Mae Barkley
BEING THERE(1979)
Philip Barknel
VIRGIN WITCH, THE(1973, Brit.), ed
Hildegard Barko
DREAMER, THE(1936, Ger.)
Andrew Barkoulis
TAKE ME AWAY, MY LOVE(1962, Gr.); YOU CAME TOO LATE(1962, Gr.)
Peter Barkworth
TOUCH OF LARCENY, A(1960, Brit.); NO LOVE FOR JOHNNIE(1961, Brit.); SEVEN KEYS(1962, Brit.); TIARA TAHITI(1962, Brit.); PLAY IT COOL(1963, Brit.); DOWNFALL(1964, Brit.); NO, MY DARLING DAUGHTER(1964, Brit.); YOU MUST BE JOKING!(1965, Brit.); TWO A PENNY(1968, Brit.); WHERE EAGLES DARE(1968, Brit.); PATTON(1970); LITTLEST HORSE THIEVES, THE(1977); INTERNATIONAL VELVET(1978, Brit.)
1984
CHAMPIONS(1984)
Andre Barlatier
BORROWED WIVES(1930), ph; REDHEAD(1941), ph
Silents
ARGYLE CASE, THE(1917), ph; OUT OF THE STORM(1920), ph; KENTUCKIANS, THE(1921), ph; WITHOUT LIMIT(1921), ph; MIRACLE MAKERS, THE(1923), ph; PAINTED FLAPPER, THE(1924), ph; SNOB, THE(1924), ph; LADY OF THE NIGHT(1925), ph; EXIT SMILING(1926), ph; ADAM AND EVIL(1927), ph; ON ZE BOULEVARD(1927), ph; TEA FOR THREE(1927), ph; YOUR WIFE AND MINE(1927), ph; SINGLE MAN, A(1929), ph
Kate Barlay
THREE CORNERED FATE(1954, Brit.), w
Edward Barle
KING OF THE COWBOYS(1943)
Mona Barlee
HIS ROYAL HIGHNESS(1932, Aus.)
Ursula Barlem
CITY OF TORMENT(1950, Ger.)
Amelie Barleon
LILITH(1964); PRODUCERS, THE(1967)
Anthony Barletta
CHILD'S PLAY(1972)
Beatrice Barley
SPRING HANDICAP(1937, Brit.)
John Barley
Misc. Silents
RED BLOOD AND BLUE(1925)
Kate Barley
ONE JUST MAN(1955, Brit.), w
Olivia Barley
COMIN' THRU' THE RYE(1947, Brit.)
Bruce Barloe
HEART LIKE A WHEEL(1983)
Alice Barlow
BLOOD ON THE SUN(1945), tech ad
Ann Barlow
FIVE LITTLE PEPPERS IN TROUBLE(1940)
Anne Barlow
TURNING POINT, THE(1977)
Charles Barlow
GOODBYE PORK PIE(1981, New Zealand)
Frances Barlow
YELLOW HAT, THE(1966, Brit.)
Harold Barlow
I WAKE UP SCREAMING(1942), m/l
James Barlow
TERM OF TRIAL(1962, Brit.), d&w; VILLAIN(1971, Brit.), w
Jeff Barlow
Silents
RUPERT OF HENTZAU(1915, Brit.); LOVE'S OLD SWEET SONG(1917, Brit.); MAN AND THE MOMENT, THE(1918, Brit.); ONCE UPON A TIME(1918, Brit.); AS HE WAS BORN(1919, Brit.); GLORIOUS ADVENTURE, THE(1922, U.S./Brit.); SKIPPER'S WOOING, THE(1922, Brit.); SATAN'S SISTER(1925, Brit.); THIS MARRIAGE BUSINESS(1927, Brit.)
Misc. Silents
BONNIE MARY(1918, Brit.); FURTHER EXPLOITS OF SEXTON BLAKE, THE - MYSTERY OF THE S.S. OLYMPIC, THE(1919, Brit.)
Jonathan Barlow
1984
SCANDALOUS(1984)
Joy Barlow
GEORGE WHITE'S SCANDALS(1945)
Kitty Barlow
Silents
FANCY DRESS(1919, Brit.); ICE FLOOD, THE(1926); NIGHT LIFE(1927)
Misc. Silents
LITTLE BIT OF FLUFF, A(1919, Brit.)
Reginald Barlow
AFRAID TO TALK(1932); AGE OF CONSENT(1932); ALIAS THE DOCTOR(1932); EVENINGS FOR SALE(1932); HORSE FEATHERS(1932); I AM A FUGITIVE FROM A CHAIN GANG(1932); IF I HAD A MILLION(1932); SINNERS IN THE SUN(1932); THIS RECKLESS AGE(1932); WASHINGTON MASQUERADE(1932); WET PARADE, THE(1932); WOMAN FROM MONTE CARLO, THE(1932); WORLD AND THE FLESH, THE(1932); ANN VICKERS(1933); BIG CAGE, THE(1933); FLYING DOWN TO RIO(1933); GRAND SLAM(1933); HIS PRIVATE SECRETARY(1933); KING KONG(1933); CHEATING CHEATERS(1934); HALF A SINNER(1934); ONE NIGHT OF LOVE(1934); OPERATOR 13(1934); STAMBOUL QUEST(1934); YOU CAN'T BUY EVERYTHING(1934); CAPTAIN BLOOD(1935); GILDED LILY, THE(1935); MUTINY AHEAD(1935); RED BLOOD OF COURAGE(1935); ROMANCE IN MANHATTAN(1935); STRANGERS ALL(1935); WEREWOLF OF LONDON, THE(1935); GIRL FROM MANDALAY(1936); LAST OF THE MOHICANS, THE(1936); LITTLE LORD FAUNTLEROY(1936); LLOYDS OF LONDON(1936); O'MALLEY OF THE MOUNTED(1936); IT HAPPENED OUT WEST(1937); ROAD BACK,THE(1937); SILENT BARRIERS(1937, Brit.); TOAST OF NEW YORK, THE(1937); ADVENTURES OF

MARCO POLO, THE(1938); HERITAGE OF THE DESERT(1939); MAN IN THE IRON MASK, THE(1939); NEW FRONTIER(1939); ROVIN' TUMBLEWEEDS(1939); TOWER OF LONDON(1939); WALL STREET COWBOY(1939); WITNESS VANISHES, THE(1939); COURAGEOUS DR. CHRISTIAN, THE(1940); SCOTLAND YARD(1941); MAD MONSTER, THE(1942); MAYOR OF 44TH STREET, THE(1942); LAW OF THE NORTHWEST(1943)
Silents
CLOTHES MAKE THE PIRATE(1925)
Misc. Silents
CINEMA MURDER, THE(1920)
Roger Barlow
OEDIPUS REX(1957, Can.), ph; PLASTIC DOME OF NORMA JEAN, THE(1966), ph; ROYAL HUNT OF THE SUN, THE(1969, Brit.), ph
Stuart Barlow
LADY IN THE DARK(1944)
Tim Barlow
EAGLE HAS LANDED, THE(1976, Brit.); WHO IS KILLING THE GREAT CHEFS OF EUROPE?(1978, US/Ger.); PRIVATES ON PARADE(1982)
1984
PRIVATES ON PARADE(1984, Brit.)
William Barlow
Silents
CIRCUS DAYS(1923); GREED(1925)
Barbara Barlowe
WRITTEN LAW, THE(1931, Brit.)
Bonnie Barlowe
UP IN ARMS(1944)
Evelyn Barlowe
MEET JOHN DOE(1941)
Joy Barlowe
THANK YOUR LUCKY STARS(1943); DESTINATION TOKYO(1944); BIG SLEEP, THE(1946); TRESPASSER, THE(1947)
Violet Barlowe
FLOOD, THE(1931)
Claude Barma
TALES OF PARIS(1962, Fr./Ital.), d, w
Ira Barmak
INTERNS, THE(1962); JOY IN THE MORNING(1965)
Ira Richard Barmak
1984
SILENT NIGHT, DEADLY NIGHT(1984), p
Charles Barman
GLADIATOR OF ROME(1963, Ital.)
Valmere Barman
LADY OF BURLESQUE(1943); DUFFY'S TAVERN(1945)
I. Barmin
FATHER OF A SOLDIER(1966, USSR)
N. Barmin
THERE WAS AN OLD COUPLE(1967, USSR)
John F. Barmon, Jr.
CADDY SHACK(1980)
Joseph Barnaba
USED CARS(1980)
Bruno Barnabe
DREAMING LIPS(1937, Brit.); LANDSLIDE(1937, Brit.); SECOND BUREAU(1937, Brit.); WAKE UP FAMOUS(1937, Brit.); VIOLENT STRANGER(1957, Brit.); LADY IS A SQUARE, THE(1959, Brit.); FIVE GOLDEN HOURS(1961, Brit.); PIT OF DARKNESS(1961, Brit.); ARRIVEDERCI, BABY!(1966, Brit.); MUMMY'S SHROUD, THE(1967, Brit.); MOHAMMAD, MESSENGER OF GOD(1976, Lebanon/Brit.); SINBAD AND THE EYE OF THE TIGER(1977, U.S./Brit.)
Guglielmo Barnabo
MIRACLE IN MILAN(1951, Ital.); NEOPOLITAN CAROUSEL(1961, Ital.); MOST WANTED MAN, THE(1962, Fr./Ital.)
Broun Barnaby
BALL AT SAVOY(1936, Brit.)
Paul Barnaby
DIE MANNER UM LUCIE(1931), m
H.B. Barnam III
LOST IN THE STARS(1974)
Derek Barnard
FLAW, THE(1955, Brit.)
Edmond Barnard
DAY OF THE JACKAL, THE(1973, Brit./Fr.)
Evelyn Barnard
ANNIE LAURIE(1936, Brit.)
Ivor Barnard
VICTORIA THE GREAT(1937, Brit.); SALLY IN OUR ALLEY(1931, Brit.); BLIND SPOT(1932, Brit.); ILLEGAL(1932, Brit.); CRIME AT BLOSSOMS, THE(1933, Brit.); GOOD COMPANIONS(1933, Brit.); ROOF, THE(1933, Brit.); SLEEPING CAR(1933, Brit.); WALTZ TIME(1933, Brit.); BRIDES TO BE(1934, Brit.); DEATH AT A BROADCAST(1934, Brit.); LOVE, LIFE AND LAUGHTER(1934, Brit.); FOREIGN AFFAIRES(1935, Brit.); PRICE OF WISDOM, THE(1935, Brit.); PRINCESS CHARMING(1935, Brit.); SOME DAY(1935, Brit.); VILLAGE SQUIRE, THE(1935, Brit.); WANDERING JEW, THE(1935, Brit.); DREAMS COME TRUE(1936, Brit.); HOUSE OF THE SPANIARD, THE(1936, Brit.); MAN BEHIND THE MASK, THE(1936, Brit.); DOUBLE EXPOSURES(1937, Brit.); FAREWELL TO CINDERELLA(1937, Brit.); STORM IN A TEACUP(1937, Brit.); WHAT A MAN!(1937, Brit.); EVERYTHING HAPPENS TO ME(1938, Brit.); I MARRIED A SPY(1938); PYGMALION(1938, Brit.); CHEER BOYS CHEER(1939, Brit.); MILL ON THE FLOSS(1939, Brit.); CASTLE OF CRIMES(1940, Brit.); STARS LOOK DOWN, THE(1940, Brit.); QUIET WEDDING(1941, Brit.); SAINT'S VACATION, THE(1941, Brit.); ESCAPE TO DANGER(1943, Brit.); UNDERGROUND GUERRILLAS(1944, Brit.); GREAT DAY(1945, Brit.); SILVER FLEET, THE(1945, Brit.); VACATION FROM MARRIAGE(1945, Brit.); CAESAR AND CLEOPATRA(1946, Brit.); GRAND ESCAPADE, THE(1946, Brit.); GREAT EXPECTATIONS(1946, Brit.); HOTEL RESERVE(1946, Brit.); MURDER IN REVERSE(1946, Brit.); SO WELL REMEMBERED(1947, Brit.); DULCIMER STREET(1948, Brit.); ESTHER WATERS(1948, Brit.); QUEEN OF SPADES(1948, Brit.); SO EVIL MY LOVE(1948, Brit.); HER MAN GILBEY(1949, Brit.); PAPER ORCHID(1949, Brit.); MADELEINE(1950, Brit.); MRS. FITZHERBERT(1950, Brit.); OLIVER TWIST(1951, Brit.); HOT ICE(1952, Brit.); IMPORTANCE OF BEING EARNEST, THE(1952, Brit.);

BEAT THE DEVIL(1953); SEA DEVILS(1953); TIME GENTLEMEN PLEASE!(1953, Brit.); MALTA STORY(1954, Brit.)

John Barnard
SECRETS OF CHINATOWN(1935)

Michael Barnard
1984
EYES OF FIRE(1984), ed; PREY, THE(1984), ed

Morton Barnard
Silents
PARADISE(1926), t

Nick Barnard
JUBILEE(1978, Brit.), ed

Peter Barnard
WHY SAILORS LEAVE HOME(1930, Brit.); HERE COMES THE SUN(1945, Brit.)

Ralph Barnard
WALKING TARGET, THE(1960)

Maurice Barnathan
NUN'S STORY, THE(1959), set d; ROMANOFF AND JULIET(1961), set d; PHAE-DRA(1962, U.S./Gr./Fr.), set d; IRMA LA DOUCE(1963), set d; LADY L(1965, Fr./Ital.), set d; NIGHT OF THE GENERALS, THE(1967, Brit./Fr.), set d; FLEA IN HER EAR, A(1968, Fr.), set d

Barnborough Colliery Orchestra
BLACK DIAMONDS(1932, Brit.)

Harry Barndollar
DANGER SIGNAL(1945), spec eff; CLOAK AND DAGGER(1946), spec eff; ESCAPE ME NEVER(1947), spec eff; MY WILD IRISH ROSE(1947), art d; NORA PREN-TISS(1947), spec eff; UNSUSPECTED, THE(1947), spec eff; VOICE OF THE TURTLE, THE(1947), spec eff; NIGHT UNTO NIGHT(1949), spec eff; CHAIN LIGHTNING(1950), spec eff; WHEN WORLDS COLLIDE(1951), spec eff

Harry Barndoller
MAN I LOVE, THE(1946), spec eff

Shoshana Barnea
SIMCHON FAMILY, THE(1969, Israel)

Jack Barnell
Silents
GALLOPING GOBS, THE(1927)

Robert Barnell
CHRISTINE(1983)

Ruth Barnell
WAR OF THE WORLDS, THE(1953)

Glen Barner
CRY HAVOC(1943), set d; PILOT NO. 5(1943), set d; SALUTE TO THE MARI-NES(1943), set d; RATIONING(1944), set d; THIS MAN'S NAVY(1945), set d

John Barner
RETURN TO CAMPUS(1975)

Klaus Barner
1984
SECRET PLACES(1984, Brit.)

Rene Barnerias
SMALL CHANGE(1976, Fr.)

A. Barnes
NON-STOP NEW YORK(1937, Brit.), ed

Adrian Barnes
1984
ALLEY CAT(1984)

Al Barnes
IT'S LOVE AGAIN(1936, Brit.), ed; GANGWAY(1937, Brit.), ed; HEAD OVER HEELS IN LOVE(1937, Brit.), ed; SAILING ALONG(1938, Brit.), ed; SAINT'S VACATION, THE(1941, Brit.), ed

Alan Barnes
WHISTLE DOWN THE WIND(1961, Brit.); VICTORS, THE(1963)

Arthur Barnes
WHITE CARGO(1930, Brit.), p&d
Misc. Silents
WHITE CARGO(1929, Brit.), d

Barry K. Barnes
DODGING THE DOLE(1936, Brit.); RETURN OF THE SCARLET PIMPERNEL(1938, Brit.); WHO GOES NEXT?(1938, Brit.); YOU'RE THE DOCTOR(1938, Brit.); PRISON WITHOUT BARS(1939, Brit.); THIS MAN IN PARIS(1939, Brit.); THIS MAN IS NEWS(1939, Brit.); WARE CASE, THE(1939, Brit.); LAW AND DISORDER(1940, Brit.); MIDAS TOUCH, THE(1940, Brit.); SPIES OF THE AIR(1940, Brit.); TWO FOR DANGER(1940, Brit.); GIRL IN THE NEWS, THE(1941, Brit.); BEDELIA(1946, Brit.); DANCING WITH CRIME(1947, Brit.)

Bill Barnes
MACK, THE(1973)

Binnie Barnes
DR. JOSSER KC(1931, Brit.); LOVE LIES(1931, Brit.); NIGHT IN MONTMARTE, A(1931, Brit.); OUT OF THE BLUE(1931, Brit.); DOWN OUR STREET(1932, Brit.); LAST COUPON, THE(1932, Brit.); MURDER AT COVENT GARDEN(1932, Brit.); OLD SPANISH CUSTOMERS(1932, Brit.); WHY SAPS LEAVE HOME(1932, Brit.); CHARM-ING DECEIVER, THE(1933, Brit.); COUNSEL'S OPINION(1933, Brit.); PRIVATE LIFE OF HENRY VIII, THE(1933, Brit.); THEIR NIGHT OUT(1933, Brit.); GIFT OF GAB(1934); LADY IS WILLING, THE(1934, Brit.); NINE FORTY-FIVE(1934, Brit.); NO ES-CAPE(1934, Brit.); PRIVATE LIFE OF DON JUAN, THE(1934, Brit.); SILVER SPOON, THE(1934, Brit.); DIAMOND JIM(1935); ONE EXCITING ADVENTURE(1935); RENDEZVOUS(1935); LAST OF THE MOHICANS, THE(1936); MAGNIFICENT BRUTE, THE(1936); SMALL TOWN GIRL(1936); SUTTER'S GOLD(1936); BREEZING HOME(1937); BROADWAY MELODY OF '38(1937); THREE SMART GIRLS(1937); ADVENTURES OF MARCO POLO, THE(1938); ALWAYS GOODBYE(1938); DIVORCE OF LADY X. THE(1938, Brit.); FIRST 100 YEARS, THE(1938); FORBIDDEN TERRITO-RY(1938, Brit.); GATEWAY(1938); HOLIDAY(1938); THANKS FOR EVERY-THING(1938); THREE BLIND MICE(1938); TROPIC HOLIDAY(1938); DAY-TIME WIFE(1939); FRONTIER MARSHAL(1939); MAN ABOUT TOWN(1939); THREE MUS-KETEERS, THE(1939); WIFE, HUSBAND AND FRIEND(1939); THIS THING CALLED LOVE(1940); 'TIL WE MEET AGAIN(1940); ANGELS WITH BROKEN WINGS(1941); NEW WINE(1941); SKYLARK(1941); THREE GIRLS ABOUT TOWN(1941); TIGHT SHOES(1941); CALL OUT THE MARINES(1942); I MARRIED AN ANGEL(1942); IN OLD CALIFORNIA(1942); MAN FROM DOWN UNDER, THE(1943); BARBARY COAST GENT(1944); HOUR BEFORE THE DAWN, THE(1944); UP IN MABEL'S ROOM(1944); GETTING GERTIE'S GARTER(1945); IT'S IN THE BAG(1945); SPANISH

MAIN, THE(1945); TIME OF THEIR LIVES, THE(1946); IF WINTER COMES(1947); DUDE GOES WEST, THE(1948); MY OWN TRUE LOVE(1948); PIRATES OF CAPRI, THE(1949); FUGITIVE LADY(1951); DECAMERON NIGHTS(1953, Brit.); FIRE OVER AFRICA(1954, Brit.); SHADOW OF THE EAGLE(1955, Brit.); THUNDERSTORM(1956), p; TROUBLE WITH ANGELS, THE(1966); WHERE ANGELS GO...TROUBLE FOL-LOWS(1968); FORTY CARATS(1973)

Bobby Barnes
MALE ANIMAL, THE(1942)

Britta Barnes
ROMA(1972, Ital./Fr.)

C.B. Barnes
1984
AMERICAN DREAMER(1984)

Carver Barnes
1984
NINJA III-THE DOMINATION(1984)

Charles Barnes
INTRUDER, THE(1962); CREATURES THE WORLD FORGOT(1971, Brit.), ed

Charles E. Barnes
IVORY-HANDLED GUN(1935), w

Charles Mercer Barnes
SATURDAY'S HERO(1951)

Cheryl Barnes
HAIR(1979)

Chris Barnes
DRACULA-PRINCE OF DARKNESS(1966, Brit.), ed; PLAGUE OF THE ZOMBIES, THE(1966, Brit.), ed; DEVIL'S OWN, THE(1967, Brit.), ed; CHALLENGE FOR ROBIN HOOD, A(1968, Brit.), ed; LOST CONTINENT, THE(1968, Brit.), ed; HORROR OF FRANKENSTEIN, THE(1970, Brit.), ed; TASTE THE BLOOD OF DRACULA(1970, Brit.), ed; CRESCENDO(1972, Brit.), ed; MAN AT THE TOP(1973, Brit.), ed; BAD NEWS BEARS, THE(1976); BAD NEWS BEARS IN BREAKING TRAINING, THE(1977); SEVEN-PER-CENT SOLUTION, THE(1977, Brit.), ed; COUNT DRACULA AND HIS VAMPIRE BRIDE(1978, Brit.), ed; DRACULA AND THE SEVEN GOLDEN VAMPIRES(1978, Brit./Chi.), ed
1984
LAST HORROR FILM, THE(1984), ed

Chuck Barnes
CHOPPERS, THE(1961)

Clarence Barnes
BLACK BELT JONES(1974); GOLDEN NEEDLES(1974); TRUCK TURNER(1974)

D.P. Barnes
PORTNOY'S COMPLAINT(1972)

Derek Barnes
FOUR DESPERATE MEN(1960, Brit.); CARS THAT ATE PARIS, THE(1974, Aus,); FIGHTING BACK(1983, Brit.)

Deryck Barnes
COURT MARTIAL(1954, Brit.); SEASON OF PASSION(1961, Aus./Brit.)

Deryk Barnes
MAN FROM HONG KONG(1975)

Donna Barnes
1984
FIRST TURN-ON!, THE(1984)

Eddie Barnes
HONOR OF THE RANGE(1934)

Eric Barnes
MR. BILLION(1977); MORE AMERICAN GRAFFITI(1979)

Ernie Barnes
NUMBER ONE(1969); DOCTORS' WIVES(1971)

Forrest Barnes
WESTERN GOLD(1937), w

Francis Barnes
SERENADE(1956)

Frank Barnes
Silents
GENERAL, THE(1927)

Gary Barnes
1984
KILLPOINT(1984)

Gene Barnes
WHERE DANGER LIVES(1950)

Geoffrey Barnes
BATTLE OF GALLIPOLI(1931, Brit.), d; PARTY HUSBAND(1931), w

George Barnes
THAT UNCERTAIN FEELING(1941), ph; BULLDOG DRUMMOND(1929), ph; CON-DEMNED(1929), ph; THIS IS HEAVEN(1929), ph; TRESPASSER, THE(1929), ph; DEVIL TO PAY, THE(1930), ph; LADY'S MORALS, A(1930), ph; RAFFLES(1930), ph; WHAT A WIDOW(1930), ph; FIVE AND TEN(1931), ph; GOD IS MY WITNESS(1931), ph; ONE HEAVENLY NIGHT(1931), ph; STREET SCENE(1931), ph; UNHOLY GAR-DEN, THE(1931), ph; BLONDIE OF THE FOLLIES(1932), ph; POLLY OF THE CIRCUS(1932), ph; SHERLOCK HOLMES(1932), ph; SOCIETY GIRL(1932), ph; WET PARADE, THE(1932), ph; BROADWAY BAD(1933), ph; FOOTLIGHT PARADE(1933), ph; GOODBYE AGAIN(1933), ph; HAVANA WIDOWS(1933), ph; PEG O' MY HEART(1933), ph; FLIRTATION WALK(1934), ph; GAMBLING LADY(1934), ph; HE WAS HER MAN(1934), ph; KANSAS CITY PRINCESS(1934), ph; MASSACRE(1934), ph; SMARTY(1934), ph; BROADWAY GONDOLIER(1935), ph; GOLD DIGGERS OF 1935(1935), ph; I LIVE FOR LOVE(1935), ph; IN CALIENTE(1935), ph; IRISH IN US, THE(1935), ph; STARS OVER BROADWAY(1935), ph; TRAVELING SALESLADY, THE(1935), ph; CAIN AND MABEL(1936), ph; COLLEEN(1936), ph; LOVE BEGINS AT TWENTY(1936), ph; SINGING KID, THE(1936), ph; BARRIER, THE(1937), ph; BLACK LEGION, THE(1937), ph; EVER SINCE EVE(1937), ph; HOLLYWOOD HO-TEL(1937), ph; MARKED WOMAN(1937), ph; VARSITY SHOW(1937), ph; BELOVED BRAT(1938), ph; GOLD DIGGERS IN PARIS(1938), ph; LOVE, HONOR AND BEHAVE(1938), ph; JESSE JAMES(1939), ph; OUR NEIGHBORS–THE CAR-TERS(1939), ph; STANLEY AND LIVINGSTONE(1939), ph; DEVIL'S ISLAND(1940), ph; FREE, BLONDE AND 21(1940), ph; GIRL FROM AVENUE A(1940), ph; HUD-SON'S BAY(1940), ph; MARYLAND(1940), ph; REBECCA(1940), ph; RETURN OF FRANK JAMES, THE(1940), ph; LADIES IN RETIREMENT(1941), ph; MEET JOHN DOE(1941), ph; REMEMBER THE DAY(1941), ph; UNHOLY PARTNERS(1941), ph; BROADWAY(1942), ph; NIGHTMARE(1942), ph; ONCE UPON A HONEY-MOON(1942), ph; RINGS ON HER FINGERS(1942), ph; MR. LUCKY(1943), ph;

FRENCHMAN'S CREEK(1944), ph; JANE EYRE(1944), ph; NONE BUT THE LONELY HEART(1944), ph; BELLS OF ST. MARY'S, THE(1945), ph; SPANISH MAIN, THE(1945), ph; SPELLBOUND(1945), ph; FROM THIS DAY FORWARD(1946), ph; SISTER KENNY(1946), ph; MOURNING BECOMES ELECTRA(1947), ph; SINBAD THE SAILOR(1947), ph; EMPEROR WALTZ, THE(1948), ph; FORCE OF EVIL(1948), ph; GOOD SAM(1948), ph; NO MINOR VICES(1948), ph; BOY WITH THE GREEN HAIR, THE(1949), ph; SAMSON AND DELILAH(1949), ph; FILE ON THELMA JORDAN, THE(1950), ph; LET'S DANCE(1950), ph; MR. MUSIC(1950), ph; RIDING HIGH(1950), ph; HERE COMES THE GROOM(1951), ph; GREATEST SHOW ON EARTH, THE(1952), ph; JUST FOR YOU(1952), ph; ROAD TO BALI(1952), ph; SOMEBODY LOVES ME(1952), ph; SOMETHING TO LIVE FOR(1952), ph; LITTLE BOY LOST(1953), ph; WAR OF THE WORLDS, THE(1953), ph
Silents
HAIRPINS(1920), ph; BEAUTIFUL GAMBLER, THE(1921), ph; BRONZE BELL, THE(1921), ph; REAL ADVENTURE, THE(1922), ph; ALICE ADAMS(1923), ph; JANICE MEREDITH(1924), ph; DARK ANGEL, THE(1925), ph; EAGLE, THE(1925), ph; SON OF THE SHEIK(1926), ph; WINNING OF BARBARA WORTH, THE(1926), ph; NIGHT OF LOVE, THE(1927), ph; AWAKENING, THE(1928), ph; OUR DANCING DAUGHTERS(1928), ph; SADIE THOMPSON(1928), ph; TWO LOVERS(1928), ph; RESCUE, THE(1929), ph
Georgene Barnes
TODD KILLINGS, THE(1971)
Georges Barnes
GREEKS HAD A WORD FOR THEM(1932), ph
Glenn Barnes
NIGHTBEAST(1982)
Goerge Barnes
Silents
ZANDER THE GREAT(1925), ph
Gordon Barnes
RED SNOW(1952); HITCH-HIKER, THE(1953); SUICIDE BATTALION(1958)
Harry Barnes
Silents
GENERAL, THE(1927), ed
Helen Barnes
CALLING ALL CROOKS(1938, Brit.)
Howard Barnes
AMSTERDAM AFFAIR, THE(1968 Brit.), p
Howard McKent Barnes
SHE-WOLF, THE(1931), w
J. H. Barnes
Silents
HAMLET(1913, Brit.)
Jack Barnes
ROMANY LOVE(1931, Brit.)
Jackie Barnes
KEEP MY GRAVE OPEN(1980), makeup
Jake Barnes
DRIVE-IN MASSACRE(1976); SUMMER CAMP(1979)
Misc. Talkies
C.B. HUSTLERS(1978)
James Barnes
TOAST OF NEW YORK, THE(1937)
Silents
JOY STREET(1929)
Jane Barnes
SUCH WOMEN ARE DANGEROUS(1934); WHITE PARADE, THE(1934); MELODY TRAIL(1935); NAUGHTY MARIETTA(1935); YOUR UNCLE DUDLEY(1935); FRONTIER JUSTICE(1936); SAN FRANCISCO(1936); MAN OF THE PEOPLE(1937); STAR IS BORN, A(1937); WHEN TOMORROW COMES(1939)
Jerry Barnes
YOU LIGHT UP MY LIFE(1977)
Jimmie Barnes
CEILNG ZERO(1935)
Joanna Barnes
AUNTIE MAME(1958); HOME BEFORE DARK(1958); VIOLENT ROAD(1958); TARZAN, THE APE MAN(1959); SPARTACUS(1960); PARENT TRAP, THE(1961); PURPLE HILLS, THE(1961); GOODBYE CHARLIE(1964); DON'T MAKE WAVES(1967); WAR WAGON, THE(1967); TOO MANY THIEVES(1968); B.S. I LOVE YOU(1971)
Misc. Talkies
I WONDER WHO'S KILLING HER NOW(1975)
John Barnes
BORDER LAW(1931); WARRIORS, THE(1979)
Johnny Barnes
RAGING BULL(1980)
Julian Barnes
HORROR HOUSE(1970, Brit.); DEVIL'S WIDOW, THE(1972, Brit.)
Misc. Talkies
MISTRESS PAMELA(1974)
Katharine Barnes
DANCING LADY(1933)
Kay Barnes
ISLAND WOMEN(1958)
Kay Lou Barnes
MISS FANE'S BABY IS STOLEN(1934)
Keryck Barnes
STONE(1974, Aus.)
Lee Barnes
Silents
COLLEGE(1927)
Lionel Barnes
PASSPORT TO PIMLICO(1949, Brit.), ph
Lisa Anne Barnes
1984
FIRESTARTER(1984)
Louise Reming Barnes
Silents
TOWN SCANDAL, THE(1923)

Lucile Barnes
DESERT HAWK, THE(1950)
Lucille Barnes
FATHER OF THE BRIDE(1950)
Lucinda Barnes
SCRAMBLE(1970, Brit.)
Luis Barnes
Silents
WESTBOUND(1924)
Mac Barnes
Misc. Silents
FOOD GAMBLERS, THE(1917)
Mae Barnes
ODDS AGAINST TOMORROW(1959)
Margaret Ayer Barnes
WESTWARD PASSAGE(1932), w; DISHONORED LADY(1947), w
Margaret Barnes
DANCE HALL(1950, Brit.)
Marjorie Barnes
ARTHUR(1981)
Michael Barnes
PIPER'S TUNE, THE(1962, Brit.), w; GO KART GO(1964, Brit.), w; RUNAWAY RAILWAY(1965, Brit.), w; CHRISTMAS TREE, THE(1966, Brit.), w; OPERATION THIRD FORM(1966, Brit.), w; HOVERBUG(1970, Brit.), w; SCRAMBLE(1970, Brit.), w
Michael M. Barnes
Silents
LOVE'S REDEMPTION(1921)
Milton Barnes
JOHNNY GOT HIS GUN(1971); BLOOD AND GUTS(1978, Can.), m
Nellie Barnes
THOROUGHBRED(1936, Aus.)
Nicholas Barnes
OUTLAND(1981)
Oscar Barnes
1984
COTTON CLUB, THE(1984)
Paul Barnes
JAMBOREE(1957), art d; LET'S ROCK(1958), art d; LAST MILE, THE(1959), prod d
Peter Barnes
WHITE TRAP, THE(1959, Brit.), w; PROFESSIONALS, THE(1960, Brit.), w; OFFBEAT(1961, Brit.), w; RING OF SPIES(1964, Brit.), w; NOT WITH MY WIFE, YOU DON'T!(1966), w; VIOLENT MOMENT(1966, Brit.), w; RULING CLASS, THE(1972, Brit.), w
Phil Barnes
DESERT HAWK, THE(1950)
Philip Barnes
HAZARD(1948)
Phillip Barnes
VELVET TOUCH, THE(1948)
Pinky Barnes
FIGHTING CABALLERO(1935); DESERT GUNS(1936); SINGING BUCKAROO, THE(1937)
Priscilla Barnes
SENIORS, THE(1978); DELTA FOX(1979); LAST MARRIED COUPLE IN AMERICA, THE(1980); SUNDAY LOVERS(1980, Ital./Fr.)
Misc. Talkies
SENIORS, THE(1978); TEXAS DETOUR(1978)
Rayford Barnes
HONDO(1953); RED RIVER SHORE(1953); STRANGER WORE A GUN, THE(1953); DESPERADO, THE(1954); BOWERY TO BAGDAD(1955); WICHITA(1955); BEHIND THE HIGH WALL(1956); BURNING HILLS, THE(1956); STAGECOACH TO FURY(1956); YOUNG GUNS, THE(1956); GUN GLORY(1957); FORT MASSACRE(1958); LONE TEXAN(1959); NORTH TO ALASKA(1960); THIRTEEN FIGHTING MEN(1960); YOUNG JESSE JAMES(1960); THREE STOOGES IN ORBIT, THE(1962); GUNS OF DIABLO(1964); SHENANDOAH(1965); CAHILL, UNITED STATES MARSHAL(1973); MITCHELL(1975); BREAKHEART PASS(1976); HUNTING PARTY, THE(1977, Brit.); DEATH HUNT(1981)
Raymond Barnes
JESSE JAMES MEETS FRANKENSTEIN'S DAUGHTER(1966)
Robert Barnes
Misc. Silents
SOUTH OF THE EQUATOR(1924)
Rosamund Barnes
18 MINUTES(1935, Brit.); HOUSEMASTER(1938, Brit.)
Sally Barnes
HOLIDAYS WITH PAY(1948, Brit.); SOMEWHERE IN POLITICS(1949, Brit.); MAKE MINE A MILLION(1965, Brit.)
Sanford D. Barnes
Silents
MOLLY O'(1921), art d; SUZANNA(1922), art d
Sidney Barnes
MEET ME IN ST. LOUIS(1944)
Sonny Barnes
FORCE: FIVE(1981)
Susan Barnes
1984
REPO MAN(1984); SWING SHIFT(1984)
Suzanne Barnes
CHILDREN, THE(1980)
1984
GIRLS NIGHT OUT(1984)
T Roy Barnes
CAUGHT SHORT(1930)
T. Roy Barnes
DANGEROUS CURVES(1929); SALLY(1929); WIDE OPEN(1930); ALOHA(1931); WOMEN OF ALL NATIONS(1931); IT'S A GIFT(1934); KANSAS CITY PRINCESS(1934); RIP TIDE(1934); DOUBTING THOMAS(1935); LIFE BEGINS AT 40(1935); VILLAGE TALE(1935)

Silents
EXIT THE VAMP(1921); KISS IN TIME, A(1921); DON'T GET PERSONAL(1922); ADAM AND EVA(1923); SOULS FOR SALE(1923); RECKLESS ROMANCE(1924); SEVEN CHANCES(1925); REGULAR SCOUT, A(1926); UNKNOWN CAVALIER, THE(1926); SMILE, BROTHER, SMILE(1927); TENDER HOUR, THE(1927); CHICAGO(1928); GATE CRASHER, THE(1928)

Misc. Silents
SCRATCH MY BACK(1920); SO LONG LETTY(1920); HER FACE VALUE(1921); SEE MY LAWYER(1921); IS MATRIMONY A FAILURE?(1922); OLD HOMESTEAD, THE(1922); TOO MUCH WIFE(1922); GO-GETTER, THE(1923); GREAT WHITE WAY, THE(1924); YOUNG IDEAS(1924); CROWED HOUR, THE(1925); DANGEROUS FRIENDS(1926); BODY AND SOUL(1927); BLONDE FOR A NIGHT, A(1928)

T.Roy Barnes
Misc. Silents
LADIES OF LEISURE(1926)

Ted Barnes
BRAIN, THE(1965, Ger./Brit.), set d

V. L. Barnes
HIDDEN VALLEY(1932)

V.L. Barnes
Silents
FIGHTING CHEAT, THE(1926)
Misc. Silents
CROSSED TRAILS(1924)

Vinnie Barnes
Silents
MILLION DOLLAR ROBBERY, THE(1914)

Wade Barnes
COLD RIVER(1982); EASY MONEY(1983)
1984
MUPPETS TAKE MANHATTAN, THE(1984)

Walter Barnes
OREGON PASSAGE(1958); REVOLT IN THE BIG HOUSE(1958); WESTBOUND(1959); CAPTAIN SINDBAD(1963); AMONG VULTURES(1964, Ger./Ital./Fr./Yugo.); APACHE GOLD(1965, Ger.); FRONTIER HELLCAT(1966, Fr./Ital./Ger./Yugo.); RAMPAGE AT APACHE WELLS(1966, Ger./Yugo.); BIG GUNDOWN, THE(1968, Ital.); TRAVELING EXECUTIONER, THE(1970); CHRISTIAN LICORICE STORE, THE(1971); CAHILL, UNITED STATES MARSHAL(1973); HIGH PLAINS DRIFTER(1973); ESCAPE TO WITCH MOUNTAIN(1975); MACKINTOSH & T.J.(1975); ANOTHER MAN, ANOTHER CHANCE(1977 Fr/US); DAY OF THE ANIMALS(1977); PETE'S DRAGON(1977); BRONCO BILLY(1980); SMOKEY BITES THE DUST(1981)
1984
DADDY'S DEADLY DARLING(1984)
Misc. Talkies
AVENGER OF THE SEVEN SEAS(1960)

William E. Barnes
RECESS(1967), p

Willie C. Barnes
THX 1138(1971)

Windy Barnes
STONY ISLAND(1978)

Winnington Barnes
Misc. Silents
GRIM JUSTICE(1916, Brit.)

Barbara Barnet
MIX ME A PERSON(1962, Brit.)

Boris Barnet
DARK IS THE NIGHT(1946, USSR), a, d; SECRET MISSION(1949, USSR), a, d; BOUNTIFUL SUMMER(1951, USSR), d
Misc. Silents
EXTRAORDINARY ADVENTURES OF MR. WEST IN THE LAND OF THE BOLSHEVIKS(1924, USSR), d; MISS MEND(1926, USSR); GIRL WITH THE HAT-BOX(1927, USSR), d; MOSCOW IN OCTOBER(1927, USSR), d; HOUSE ON TRUBNAYA SQUARE(1928, USSR), d

Charlie Barnet
SYNCOPATION(1942); FREDDIE STEPS OUT(1946); FABULOUS DORSEYS, THE(1947); MAKE BELIEVE BALLROOM(1949)

Griff Barnet
SAIGON(1948)

Lady Barnet
SIMON AND LAURA(1956, Brit.)

Robert Barnete
SECRET OF MY SUCCESS, THE(1965, Brit.)

Alan Barnett
HAPPY BIRTHDAY TO ME(1981)

Antonina Barnett
NORTHWEST OUTPOST(1947)

Celia Barnett
1984
SCRUBBERS(1984, Brit.), art d

Charles Barnett
GAME OF CHANCE, A(1932, Brit.), d; THOROUGHBRED(1932, Brit.), d
Silents
MUNITION GIRL'S ROMANCE, A(1917, Brit.), w; AMAZING PARTNERSHIP, THE(1921, Brit.), a, w; FLAMES OF FEAR(1930, Brit.), d; PAINTED PICTURES(1930, Brit.), d&w

Charlie Barnett
D.C. CAB(1983)

Chester Barnett
Silents
WISHING RING, THE(1914); HEART OF THE BLUE RIDGE, THE(1915); LITTLE MISS BROWN(1915); TRILBY(1915); GIRL'S FOLLY, A(1917); CHALLENGE ACCEPTED, THE(1918); GREAT ADVENTURE, THE(1918)
Misc. Silents
MARRYING MONEY(1915); INEVITABLE, THE(1917); LAW OF COMPENSATION, THE(1917); OVER THE HILL(1917); PUBLIC BE DAMNED(1917); SALT OF THE EARTH(1917); SUBMARINE EYE, THE(1917); TOGETHER(1918); WOMAN(1919); GIRL OF THE SEA(1920); LAW OF COMPENSATION(1927)

Edith M. Barnett
ROBBERY WITH VIOLENCE(1958, Brit.), w

George Ivan Barnett
ROBBERY WITH VIOLENCE(1958, Brit.), p&d, ph

Gilbert Barnett
FATHER WAS A FULLBACK(1949); SHOCKPROOF(1949); DAVID AND BATHSHEBA(1951)

Griff Barnett
WITHOUT RESERVATIONS(1946); FRONTIER VENGEANCE(1939); ARIZONA(1940); GANGS OF SONORA(1941); LADY FROM CHEYENNE(1941); OUTLAWS OF THE CHEROKEE TRAIL(1941); SHADOWS ON THE SAGE(1942); SOMBRERO KID, THE(1942); STARDUST ON THE SAGE(1942); STORY OF DR. WASSELL, THE(1944); STRANGE HOLIDAY(1945); DANGER WOMAN(1946); DUEL IN THE SUN(1946); TO EACH HIS OWN(1946); CASS TIMBERLANE(1947); DAISY KENYON(1947); GANGSTER, THE(1947); GUNFIGHTERS(1947); MAGIC TOWN(1947); MICHIGAN KID, THE(1947); MILLERSON CASE, THE(1947); POSSESSED(1947); STEPCHILD(1947); SUDDENLY IT'S SPRING(1947); TENDER YEARS, THE(1947); UNCONQUERED(1947); WILD HARVEST(1947); APARTMENT FOR PEGGY(1948); FIGHTING FATHER DUNNE(1948); FOR THE LOVE OF MARY(1948); FURY AT FURNACE CREEK(1948); TAP ROOTS(1948); WALLS OF JERICHO(1948); CRISS CROSS(1949); DOOLINS OF OKLAHOMA, THE(1949); FOUNTAINHEAD, THE(1949); HOLIDAY AFFAIR(1949); MOTHER IS A FRESHMAN(1949); PINKY(1949); CONVICTED(1950); CUSTOMS AGENT(1950); NO MAN OF HER OWN(1950); PEGGY(1950); SIERRA(1950); CATTLE DRIVE(1951); HOME TOWN STORY(1951); PASSAGE WEST(1951); SELLOUT, THE(1951); TWO OF A KIND(1951); WHEN I GROW UP(1951); MARRYING KIND, THE(1952); SCANDAL SHEET(1952); TREASURE OF LOST CANYON, THE(1952); ANGEL FACE(1953); COURT-MARTIAL OF BILLY MITCHELL, THE(1955); SPIRIT OF ST. LOUIS, THE(1957)

Herb Barnett
CLAMBAKE(1967)

Hosea Barnett
TRIAL OF BILLY JACK, THE(1974)

Isobel Barnett
SIMON AND LAURA(1956, Brit.)

Ivan Barnett
FALL OF THE HOUSE OF USHER, THE(1952, Brit.), p&d, ph

Jack Barnett
DO YOU LOVE ME?(1946)

Jackie Barnett
EDDIE CANTOR STORY, THE(1953)

James Barnett
ESCAPE FROM TERROR(1960), w; POWERFORCE(1983)

James R. Barnett
PRIVATE BENJAMIN(1980)

Jim Barnett
BLACK GOLD(1963), p; TERMINAL ISLAND(1973), w

John Barnett
MIDDLE AGE SPREAD(1979, New Zealand), p; BEYOND REASONABLE DOUBT(1980, New Zeal.), p; DEAD KIDS(1981 Aus./New Zealand), p
1984
TREASURE OF THE YANKEE ZEPHYR(1984, New Zealand), p; WILD HORSES(1984, New Zealand), p

Jonnie Barnett
NASHVILLE(1975)

Ken Barnett
DIARY OF A BACHELOR(1964), w; DEADLY FORCE(1983), w
1984
HAMBONE AND HILLIE(1984), w

Laurel Barnett
CHILD, THE(1977)

Linda Barnett
SHOCK CORRIDOR(1963)

Madge Barnett
MUTATIONS, THE(1974, Brit.)

Ray Barnett
EARTHLING, THE(1980)

Robbie Barnett
DARK CRYSTAL, THE(1982, Brit.); YENTL(1983)

Robert Barnett
GREAT MUPPET CAPER, THE(1981)

Ruthie Barnett
FLASH GORDON(1980)

S.H. Barnett
FATHER GOOSE(1964), w

Tom Barnett
MY THIRD WIFE GEORGE(1968), ph

Trevor Barnett
HEADLESS GHOST, THE(1959, Brit.)

Vince Barnett
SIDE SHOW(1931); FLESH(1932); NIGHT MAYOR, THE(1932); SCARFACE(1932); TIGER SHARK(1932); BIG CAGE, THE(1933); DEATH KISS, THE(1933); FAST WORKERS(1933); GIRL IN 419(1933); HERITAGE OF THE DESERT(1933); MADE ON BROADWAY(1933); MAN OF THE FOREST(1933); PRIZEFIGHTER AND THE LADY, THE(1933); SUNSET PASS(1933); TUGBOAT ANNIE(1933); AFFAIRS OF CELLINI, THE(1934); CAT'S PAW, THE(1934); HELL IN THE HEAVENS(1934); KANSAS CITY PRINCESS(1934); MADAME SPY(1934); NOW I'LL TELL(1934); REGISTERED NURSE(1934); SHE LOVES ME NOT(1934); TAKE THE STAND(1934); BLACK FURY(1935); CHAMPAGNE FOR BREAKFAST(1935); DON'T BET ON BLONDES(1935); I LIVE MY LIFE(1935); NO RANSOM(1935); PRINCESS O'HARA(1935); SECRET BRIDE(1935); SILK HAT KID(1935); STREAMLINE EXPRESS(1935); AFTER THE THIN MAN(1936); CAPTAIN CALAMITY(1936); DANCING FEET(1936); DOWN TO THE SEA(1936); RIFF-RAFF(1936); SAN FRANCISCO(1936); YELLOW CARGO(1936); BANK ALARM(1937); BOOTS OF DESTINY(1937); STAR IS BORN, A(1937); TRAILING TROUBLE(1937); WE'RE IN THE LEGION NOW(1937); WOMAN I LOVE, THE(1937); I COVER CHINATOWN(1938); EXILE EXPRESS(1939); HEADLEYS AT HOME, THE(1939); OVERLAND MAIL(1939); RIDE 'EM COWGIRL(1939); SINGING COWGIRL, THE(1939); WATER RUSTLERS(1939); BOYS OF THE CITY(1940); EAST SIDE KIDS(1940); HEROES OF THE SADDLE(1940); SEVEN SINNERS(1940); BLONDE COMET(1941); DANGEROUS GAME, A(1941); GIRL, A GUY AND A GOB, A(1941); JUNGLE MAN(1941); PAPER BULLETS(1941); PUDDIN'

HEAD(1941); SIERRA SUE(1941); SUNSET MURDER CASE(1941); BABY FACE MORGAN(1942); CORPSE VANISHES, THE(1942); GALLANT LADY(1942); GIRLS' TOWN(1942); I KILLED THAT MAN(1942); KLONDIKE FURY(1942); MY FAVORITE SPY(1942); PHANTOM PLAINSMEN, THE(1942); PRISON GIRL(1942); QUEEN OF BROADWAY(1942); STARDUST ON THE SAGE(1942); X MARKS THE SPOT(1942); CAPTIVE WILD WOMAN(1943); DANGER! WOMEN AT WORK(1943); HIGH EXPLOSIVE(1943); KID DYNAMITE(1943); PETTICOAT LARCENY(1943); THUNDERING TRAILS(1943); LEAVE IT TO THE IRISH(1944); MASK OF DIMITRIOS, THE(1944); SWEETHEARTS OF THE U.S.A.(1944); HIGH POWERED(1945); RIVER GANG(1945); SENSATION HUNTERS(1945); THRILL OF A ROMANCE(1945); BOWERY BOMBSHELL(1946); FALCON'S ALIBI, THE(1946); KILLERS, THE(1946); NO LEAVE, NO LOVE(1946); SWELL GUY(1946); TWO SISTERS FROM BOSTON(1946); VIRGINIAN, THE(1946); BIG TOWN AFTER DARK(1947); BRUTE FORCE(1947); GAS HOUSE KIDS GO WEST(1947); HIGH WALL, THE(1947); I COVER BIG TOWN(1947); LITTLE MISS BROADWAY(1947); SHOOT TO KILL(1947); TRESPASSER, THE(1947); FLAME, THE(1948); LOADED PISTOLS(1948); DEPUTY MARSHAL(1949); KNOCK ON ANY DOOR(1949); THUNDER IN THE PINES(1949); BORDER TREASURE(1950); MULE TRAIN(1950); I'LL SEE YOU IN MY DREAMS(1951); KENTUCKY JUBILEE(1951); CARSON CITY(1952); RED PLANET MARS(1952); SPRINGFIELD RIFLE(1952); CHARADE(1953); QUIET GUN, THE(1957); ROOKIE, THE(1959); ZEBRA IN THE KITCHEN(1965); SPY IN THE GREEN HAT, THE(1966); CRAZY MAMA(1975); SUMMER SCHOOL TEACHERS(1977)

Vincent [Vince] Barnett
WIDE OPEN(1930)

Vincent Barnett
DANCING SWEETIES(1930); NIGHT WORK(1930); ONE HEAVENLY NIGHT(1931); RACKETY RAX(1932); CRIMSON ROMANCE(1934); NINTH GUEST, THE(1934); THIRTY-DAY PRINCESS(1934); YOUNG AND BEAUTIFUL(1934); BOWERY AT MIDNIGHT(1942)

Vincent I. Barnett
DR. GOLDFOOT AND THE BIKINI MACHINE(1965)

Griff Barnette
DEATH VALLEY OUTLAWS(1941)

Barney
FIRST BABY(1936), ph

Betty Barney
GANJA AND HESS(1973)

Bill Barney
HOW COME NOBODY'S ON OUR SIDE?(1975)

Brian Barney
FAR SHORE, THE(1976, Can.), w

Jay Barney
CONVICTED(1950); FULLER BRUSH GIRL, THE(1950); JACKPOT, THE(1950); SPY HUNT(1950); BATTLE TAXI(1955); SHRIKE, THE(1955); MISTER ROCK AND ROLL(1957); BIG FISHERMAN, THE(1959); BLUEPRINT FOR ROBBERY(1961); LOVELY WAY TO DIE, A(1968)
1984
KILLING FIELDS, THE(1984, Brit.)

Jean Barney
CATHERINE & CO.(1976, Fr.)

Lem Barney
BLACK SIX, THE(1974)

Marion Barney
Silents
DUST OF DESIRE(1919)
Misc. Silents
HEART OF GOLD(1919); POISON PEN, THE(1919); STEEL KING, THE(1919)

Pamela Barney
DURING ONE NIGHT(1962, Brit.)

Paul Barney
TEXAN MEETS CALAMITY JANE, THE(1950)

Barney Wilem's Orchestra
LES LIAISONS DANGEREUSES(1961, Fr./Ital.), m

Faith Barnhardt
STUDENT BODY, THE(1976)

Michael Barnicle
CANDIDATE, THE(1972)

Luc Barnier
1984
AVE MARIA(1984, Fr.), ed

Philip Barnikel
NIGHT MUST FALL(1964, Brit.), ed; ROMEO AND JULIET(1966, Brit.), ed; 1,000 CONVICTS AND A WOMAN(1971, Brit.), ed

Philip Barnikey
BLOOD BEAST FROM OUTER SPACE(1965, Brit.), ed

Baby Michael Barnitz
BUTCH MINDS THE BABY(1942)

Elizabeth Barnitz
TERROR EYES(1981)

H. Michael Barnitz
MAN FROM FRISCO(1944)

Harold Barnitz
YOUTH RUNS WILD(1944)

Pierre Barnley
VERY HAPPY ALEXANDER(1969, Fr.)

Lucille Barns
Misc. Silents
WHITE SLAVE, THE(1929)

Bill Barnsley
SORCERERS, THE(1967, Brit.)

Bill Barnum
THEY WERE EXPENDABLE(1945); TILL THE END OF TIME(1946)

George Barnum
Silents
SHERLOCK BROWN(1921); WILD OATS LANE(1926)
Misc. Silents
MOUNTAIN WOMAN, THE(1921); MINNIE(1922); MAN ALONE, THE(1923)

H.B. Barnum
HIT MAN(1972), m; FIVE ON THE BLACK HAND SIDE(1973), m; EMMA MAE(1976), m

Tony Barnum
TARGET: HARRY(1980)

H. B. Barnum III
MR. RICCO(1975)

John Barnwell
FIVE AGAINST THE HOUSE(1955), w; HUK(1956), d; SURRENDER–HELL!(1959), d, w

Amparo Baro
NEST, THE(1982, Span.)

Adriano Barocco
ARABELLA(1969, U.S./Ital.), w

Valerio Baroleschi
RED DESERT(1965, Fr./Ital.)

Boris Baromykin
FANTASTIC PLANET(1973, Fr./Czech.), ph

Baron, Jr.
MYSTERY OF THE PINK VILLA, THE(1930, Fr.)

Alexander Baron
ROBBERY UNDER ARMS(1958, Brit.), w; SIEGE OF SIDNEY STREET, THE(1960, Brit.), w; VICTORS, THE(1963), w

Allen Baron
BLAST OF SILENCE(1961), a, d&w; PIE IN THE SKY(1964), p, d&w; OUTSIDE IN(1972), d, w

Billy Baron
Silents
SISTER TO ASSIST 'ER, A(1922, Brit.)

Bob Baron
HOUSE OF ERRORS(1942); COTTONPICKIN' CHICKENPICKERS(1967), w

Bruce Baron
POWERFORCE(1983)

Cash Baron
PORKY'S(1982)

Charles Baron
FABULOUS DORSEYS, THE(1947), ch

D. W. Baron
FACE OF THE SCREAMING WEREWOLF(1959, Mex.)

David Baron
REPTILE, THE(1966, Brit.); TAMARIND SEED, THE(1974, Brit.)

Dick Baron
BABES ON BROADWAY(1941); HENRY ALDRICH GETS GLAMOUR(1942); SEA OF GRASS, THE(1947)

Elizabeth Baron
SALUTE JOHN CITIZEN(1942, Brit.), w; LAMP STILL BURNS, THE(1943, Brit.), w; STRAWBERRY ROAN(1945, Brit.), w; GAY INTRUDERS, THE(1946, Brit.), w

Emma Baron
FOUR WAYS OUT(1954, Ital.); DAVID AND GOLIATH(1961, Ital.); TWO WOMEN(1961, Ital./Fr.); LA VIACCIA(1962, Fr./Ital.); PRISONER OF THE IRON MASK(1962, Fr./Ital.); DISORDER(1964, Fr./Ital.); ARIZONA COLT(1965, It./Fr./Span.); SECRET SEVEN, THE(1966, Ital./Span.); PONTIUS PILATE(1967, Fr./Ital.); LONG RIDE FROM HELL, A(1970, Ital.)

George Baron
HELLO LONDON(1958, Brit.), ch

Geraldine Baron
MY BODY HUNGERS(1967); TARGETS(1968); WILD PARTY, THE(1975); TIME AFTER TIME(1979, Brit.); HUMAN HIGHWAY(1982)
1984
CITY GIRL, THE(1984)

Geralding Baron
CUTTER AND BONE(1981)

Helen Baron
RETURN OF COUNT YORGA, THE(1971); POLTERGEIST(1982)

J. D. Baron
HUMAN TORNADO, THE(1976)

Janie Baron
ADDING MACHINE, THE(1969)

Joan Baron
NEOPOLITAN CAROUSEL(1961, Ital.)

Joanne Baron
VALLEY GIRL(1983)
1984
JOY OF SEX(1984)

John Baron
HELL'S PLAYGROUND(1967), p

John L. Baron
Silents
SISTER TO ASSIST 'ER, A(1922, Brit.), p

Leon Baron
FOLIES DERGERE(1935)

Lily Baron
ROYAL AFFAIRS IN VERSAILLES(1957, Fr.)

Lita Baron
JUNGLE JIM(1948); BOMBA ON PANTHER ISLAND(1949); SAVAGE DRUMS(1951); JESSE JAMES' WOMEN(1954); BROKEN STAR, THE(1956); RED SUNDOWN(1956)

Louis Baron
Misc. Silents
CINDERS(1926, Brit.)

Lynda Baron
SMALL WORLD OF SAMMY LEE, THE(1963, Brit.); HOT MILLIONS(1968, Brit.); MRS. BROWN, YOU'VE GOT A LOVELY DAUGHTER(1968, Brit.); HANDS OF THE RIPPER(1971, Brit.)

Maksymilian Baron
BEADS OF ONE ROSARY, THE(1982, Pol.)

Margaret Hall Baron
TELEFON(1977)

Maurice Baron
RIVER, THE(1928), m
Norm Baron
LONE WOLF McQUADE(1983), prod d
Norman Baron
FAST BREAK(1979), art d; FORCE OF ONE, A(1979), art d; HERO AT LARGE(1980), art d
Paul Baron
TOWARD THE UNKNOWN(1956), m
Ruth Baron
WIRE SERVICE(1942)
Samuel Baron
OPEN THE DOOR AND SEE ALL THE PEOPLE(1964), md
Sandy Baron
SWEET NOVEMBER(1968); TARGETS(1968); IF IT'S TUESDAY, THIS MUST BE BELGIUM(1969); OUT OF TOWNERS, THE(1970)
1984
BIRDY(1984); BROADWAY DANNY ROSE(1984)
Sh. Baron
MARRIAGE OF BALZAMINOV, THE(1966, USSR)
Simone Baron
CATHERINE & CO.(1976, Fr.), cos
Steven Baron
TRAIN TO ALCATRAZ(1948)
Suzanne Baron
MR. HULOT'S HOLIDAY(1954, Fr.), ed; MY UNCLE(1958, Fr.), ed; FIRE WITHIN, THE(1964, Fr./Ital.), ed; VIVA MARIA(1965, Fr./Ital.), ed; ONE NIGHT... A TRAIN(1968, Fr./Bel.), ed; MURMUR OF THE HEART(1971, Fr./Ital./Ger.), ed; LACOMBE, LUCIEN(1974), ed; BLACK MOON(1975, Fr.), ed; PRETTY BABY(1978), ed; TIN DRUM, THE(1979, Ger./Fr./Yugo./Pol.), ed; ATLANTIC CITY(1981, U.S./Can.), ed; MY DINNER WITH ANDRE(1981), ed; CIRCLE OF DECEIT(1982, Fr./Ger.), ed
1984
CRACKERS(1984), ed
Todd Baron
SECRET LIFE OF AN AMERICAN WIFE, THE(1968); I LOVE MY WIFE(1970)
Tony Baron
ARRIVEDERCI, BABY!(1966, Brit.)
Vivian Baron
Silents
FURTHER ADVENTURES OF THE FLAG LIEUTENANT(1927, Brit.); PASSING OF MR. QUIN, THE(1928, Brit.)
Joseph Baroncini
VICE SQUAD(1982)
Barbara Barondess
DEVIL'S MATE(1933); HOLD YOUR MAN(1933); QUEEN CHRISTINA(1933); SOLDIERS OF THE STORM(1933); WHEN STRANGERS MARRY(1933); CHANGE OF HEART(1934); EIGHT GIRLS IN A BOAT(1934); FOUNTAIN, THE(1934); MERRY WIDOW, THE(1934); PURSUIT OF HAPPINESS, THE(1934); UNKNOWN BLONDE(1934); DIAMOND JIM(1935); LIFE BEGINS AT 40(1935); EASY MONEY(1936); PLOT THICKENS, THE(1936); MAKE A WISH(1937); EMERGENCY SQUAD(1940)
Misc. Talkies
BEGGAR'S HOLIDAY(1934)
Daniel Barone
ARABIAN NIGHTS(1942)
Frank Barone
MR. BILLION(1977)
Maria Barone
NAKED MAJA, THE(1959, Ital./U.S.), cos
Michael Baronne
WALK WITH LOVE AND DEATH, A(1969)
Philippe Baronnet
MATTER OF DAYS, A(1969, Fr./Czech.); SICILIAN CLAN, THE(1970, Fr.)
Boris Baronoff
Silents
FREEDOM OF THE PRESS(1928)
Irina Baronova
FLORIAN(1940); TOAST TO LOVE(1951, Mex.); TRAIN OF EVENTS(1952, Brit.)
John Barons
1984
FEAR CITY(1984)
Luciano Barontino
LIGHT IN THE PIAZZA(1962)
Dorothee Baroone
IT'S A WONDERFUL DAY(1949, Brit.)
Dominique Barouh
1984
AVE MARIA(1984, Fr.), art d
Pierre Barouh
GENDARME OF ST. TROPEZ, THE(1966, Fr./Ital.); MAN AND A WOMAN, A(1966, Fr.)
Pierre Barouth
TO BE A CROOK(1967, Fr.)
Lucien Baroux
DRAGNET NIGHT(1931, Fr.); FIRE IN THE STRAW(1943); MOULIN ROUGE(1944, Fr.); FATHER'S DILEMMA(1952, Ital.); FRENCH WAY, THE(1952, Fr.); DEVIL AND THE TEN COMMANDMENTS, THE(1962, Fr.)
A. Barov
Misc. Silents
TEARS(1914, USSR)
Miguel Barquero
FINGER ON THE TRIGGER(1965, US/Span.), ph
Alistair Barr
MAN IN THE MIDDLE(1964, U.S./Brit.)
Andrea Barr
JUST FOR THE HELL OF IT(1968)
Anthony Barr
MOZART STORY, THE(1948, Aust.)

Byron Barr [Gig Young]
MISBEHAVING HUSBANDS(1941); ONE FOOT IN HEAVEN(1941); CAPTAINS OF THE CLOUDS(1942); MAD MARTINDALES, THE(1942); DOUBLE INDEMNITY(1944); PRACTICALLY YOURS(1944); AFFAIRS OF SUSAN(1945); FOLLOW THAT WOMAN(1945); LOVE LETTERS(1945); TOKYO ROSE(1945); OUR HEARTS WERE GROWING UP(1946); THEY MADE ME A KILLER(1946); BIG TOWN(1947); SEVEN WERE SAVED(1947); PITFALL(1948); DOWN DAKOTA WAY(1949); COVERED WAGON RAID(1950); FILE ON THELMA JORDAN, THE(1950); PAID IN FULL(1950); TARNISHED(1950)
Byron S. Barr
MAIN STREET KID, THE(1947)
C.C. Barr
RIP ROARING RILEY(1935), p
Doug Barr
DEADLY BLESSING(1981); UNSEEN, THE(1981)
Douglas Barr
FORTUNE LANE(1947, Brit.); LAST LOAD, THE(1948, Brit.); DANCE HALL(1950, Brit.); HUE AND CRY(1950, Brit.); MADELEINE(1950, Brit.)
Edna Barr
DRUMS O' VOODOO(1934)
George Barr
UP FROM THE BEACH(1965), w; OCTAMAN(1971), spec eff & makeup
Howard Barr
TURNING POINT, THE(1977)
Ida Barr
HAPPY DAYS ARE HERE AGAIN(1936, Brit.); LAUGH IT OFF(1940, Brit.); LET THE PEOPLE SING(1942, Brit.)
Jaime Barr
MISSIONARY, THE(1982)
Janice Barr
GLASS HOUSES(1972)
Jeanne Barr
LONG DAY'S JOURNEY INTO NIGHT(1962); LILITH(1964)
John Barr
SCALPS(1983), ed
Julia Barr
I, THE JURY(1982)
Karen Barr
Misc. Talkies
SPITTIN' IMAGE(1983)
Kathy Barr
FORCE OF IMPULSE(1961)
Leonard Barr
DIAMONDS ARE FOREVER(1971, Brit.); STING, THE(1973); RECORD CITY(1978); SKATETOWN, U.S.A.(1979); UNDER THE RAINBOW(1981)
Matthew Barr
DEADLY BLESSING(1981), w
Mel Barr
MURDER, INC.(1960), w
Muriel Barr
NO, NO NANETTE(1940); MANPOWER(1941); I MARRIED AN ANGEL(1942); REUNION IN FRANCE(1942)
Patrick Barr
MEET MY SISTER(1933, Brit.); NORAH O'NEALE(1934, Brit.); EAST MEETS WEST(1936, Brit.); GAY OLD DOG(1936, Brit.); MIDNIGHT AT THE WAX MUSEUM(1936, Brit.); THINGS TO COME(1936, Brit.); WEDNESDAY'S LUCK(1936, Brit.); CAVALIER OF THE STREETS(1937, Brit.); INCIDENT IN SHANGHAI(1937, Brit.); SHOW GOES ON, THE(1937, Brit.); MARIGOLD(1938, Brit.); MEET MR. PENNY(1938, Brit.); RETURN OF THE SCARLET PIMPERNEL(1938, Brit.); SAILING ALONG(1938, Brit.); YELLOW SANDS(1938, Brit.); LET'S BE FAMOUS(1939, Brit.); PHANTOM STRIKES, THE(1939, Brit.); CASE OF THE FRIGHTENED LADY, THE(1940. Brit.); HIDDEN MENACE, THE(1940, Brit.); BLUE LAGOON, THE(1949, Brit.); MAN ON THE RUN(1949, Brit.); LAVENDER HILL MOB, THE(1951, Brit.); TO HAVE AND TO HOLD(1951, Brit.); DEATH OF AN ANGEL(1952, Brit.); KING OF THE UNDERWORLD(1952, Brit.); STORY OF ROBIN HOOD, THE(1952, Brit.); YOU'RE ONLY YOUNG TWICE(1952, Brit.); GAY ADVENTURE, THE(1953, Brit.); SAILOR OF THE KING(1953, Brit.); BLACK 13(1954, Brit.); CREST OF THE WAVE(1954, Brit.); DUEL IN THE JUNGLE(1954, Brit.); ESCAPE BY NIGHT(1954, Brit.); BRAIN MACHINE, THE(1955, Brit.); DAM BUSTERS, THE(1955, Brit.); INTRUDER, THE(1955, Brit.); ROOM IN THE HOUSE(1955, Brit.); AT THE STROKE OF NINE(1957, Brit.); LADY OF VENGEANCE(1957, Brit); SAINT JOAN(1957); TIME IS MY ENEMY(1957, Brit.); IT'S NEVER TOO LATE(1958, Brit.); NEXT TO NO TIME(1960, Brit.); URGE TO KILL(1960, Brit.); LONGEST DAY, THE(1962); VALIANT, THE(1962, Brit./Ital.); BILLY LIAR(1963, Brit.); RING OF SPIES(1964, Brit.); ON THE RUN(1967, Brit.); GREAT PONY RAID, THE(1968, Brit.); GUNS IN THE HEATHER(1968, Brit.); BLACK WINDMILL, THE(1974, Brit.); FLESH AND BLOOD SHOW, THE(1974, Brit.); HOUSE OF WHIPCORD(1974, Brit.); COUNT DRACULA AND HIS VAMPIRE BRIDE(1978, Brit.); GREAT TRAIN ROBBERY, THE(1979, Brit.); GODSEND, THE(1980, Can.); OCTOPUSSY(1983, Brit.)
Misc. Talkies
BLACK ORCHID(1952); MURDER AT SCOTLAND YARD(1952)
Robert Barr
HORSE'S MOUTH, THE(1953, Brit.), w; THIRD KEY, THE(1957, Brit.), w
Sharon Barr
Misc. Talkies
SPITTIN' IMAGE(1983)
Shimon Barr
BIG RED ONE, THE(1980)
Theda Barr
KNOCK ON ANY DOOR(1949)
Tim Barr
DINOSAURUS(1960), spec eff; MASTER OF THE WORLD(1961), spec eff; HORSE IN THE GRAY FLANNEL SUIT, THE(1968), spec eff
Tondi Barr
PULP(1972, Brit.)
Tony Barr
DAUGHTER OF THE WEST(1949); BETWEEN MIDNIGHT AND DAWN(1950); WHERE THE SIDEWALK ENDS(1950); CUBAN FIREBALL(1951); FLAME OF ARABY(1951); PEOPLE AGAINST O'HARA, THE(1951); TURNING POINT, THE(1952); WAIT 'TIL THE SUN SHINES, NELLIE(1952); SCARED STIFF(1953)

Warren Barr
SINCE YOU WENT AWAY(1944)

A. Barr-Carson
DANNY BOY(1941, Brit.), w

H. Barr-Carson
DANNY BOY(1934, Brit.), w

A. Barr-Smith
WELL DONE, HENRY(1936, Brit.), w; HATE IN PARADISE(1938, Brit.), p; HANGMAN WAITS, THE(1947, Brit.), p, d&w

Gianfranco Barra
AVANTI!(1972); BREAD AND CHOCOLATE(1978, Ital.); LION OF THE DESERT(1981, Libya/Brit.)

Vanda Barra
HERO AT LARGE(1980)

Vittoria Barracaracciolo
NEOPOLITAN CAROUSEL(1961, Ital.)

Roy Barraclough
SLIPPER AND THE ROSE, THE(1976, Brit.)

John Barracudo
PARRISH(1961)

John Barradino
SEVEN MEN FROM NOW(1956)

Nate Barrager
TOUCHDOWN!(1931)

Bob Barran
TIME MACHINE, THE(1960; Brit./U.S.)

George Barran
Misc. Silents
DAUGHTER OF ENGLAND, A(1915, Brit.)

Luis Barrancos
RUMBA(1935)

Olga Barrancos
RUMBA(1935)

Eloise Barrangon
SPRING MADNESS(1938, w

Martine Barraque
DAY FOR NIGHT(1973, Fr.), ed; LOVE ON THE RUN(1980, Fr.), ed; LAST METRO, THE(1981, Fr.), ed; WOMAN NEXT DOOR, THE(1981, Fr.), ed; CONFIDENTIALLY YOURS(1983, Fr.), ed

Martine Barraque-Curie
MAN WHO LOVED WOMEN, THE(1977, Fr.), ed; GREEN ROOM, THE(1979, Fr.), ed

John Barrard
MAN WHO KNEW TOO MUCH, THE(1956); THERE WAS A CROOKED MAN(1962, Brit.); WE JOINED THE NAVY(1962, Brit.); DON'T RAISE THE BRIDGE, LOWER THE RIVER(1968, Brit.); TALES FROM THE CRYPT(1972, Brit.)

Ann Barrass
OBLONG BOX, THE(1969, Brit.); CRY OF THE BANSHEE(1970, Brit.)

Martin Barrass
REMEMBRANCE(1982, Brit.)

Donald Barrat
REBELLION(1938), ed

Maxine Barrat
THOUSANDS CHEER(1943)

Michael Barrat
MAGIC CHRISTIAN, THE(1970, Brit.)

Pierre Barrat
RISE OF LOUIS XIV, THE(1970, Fr.)

Robert Barrat
ANN CARVER'S PROFESSION(1933); BABY FACE(1933); CAPTURED(1933); DEVIL'S IN LOVE, THE(1933); FROM HEADQUARTERS(1933); HEROES FOR SALE(1933); I LOVED A WOMAN(1933); KENNEL MURDER CASE, THE(1933); KING OF THE JUNGLE(1933); LILLY TURNER(1933); MAYOR OF HELL, THE(1933); PICTURE SNATCHER(1933); SECRET OF THE BLUE ROOM(1933); SILK EXPRESS, THE(1933); TUGBOAT ANNIE(1933); WILD BOYS OF THE ROAD(1933); BIG HEARTED HERBERT(1934); DARK HAZARD(1934); DRAGON MURDER CASE, THE(1934); FIREBIRD, THE(1934); FOG OVER FRISCO(1934); FRIENDS OF MR. SWEENEY(1934); GAMBLING LADY(1934); HERE COMES THE NAVY(1934); HI, NELLIE!(1934); HOUSEWIFE(1934); I SELL ANYTHING(1934); MASSACRE(1934); MIDNIGHT ALIBI(1934); RETURN OF THE TERROR(1934); ST. LOUIS KID, THE(1934); UPPER WORLD(1934); VERY HONORABLE GUY, A(1934); WONDER BAR(1934); BORDERTOWN(1935); CAPTAIN BLOOD(1935); DEVIL DOGS OF THE AIR(1935); DR. SOCRATES(1935); FLORENTINE DAGGER, THE(1935); I AM A THIEF(1935); MURDER MAN(1935); SPECIAL AGENT(1935); STRANDED(1935); VILLAGE TALE(1935); WHILE THE PATIENT SLEPT(1935); CHARGE OF THE LIGHT BRIGADE, THE(1936); COUNTRY DOCTOR, THE(1936); EXCLUSIVE STORY(1936); I MARRIED A DOCTOR(1936); LAST OF THE MOHICANS, THE(1936); MARY OF SCOTLAND(1936); MOONLIGHT ON THE PRAIRIE(1936); SONS O' GUNS(1936); TRAIL OF THE LONESOME PINE, THE(1936); TRAILIN' WEST(1936); BARRIER, THE(1937); BLACK LEGION, THE(1937); CONFESSION(1937); DRAEGERMAN COURAGE(1937); GOD'S COUNTRY AND THE WOMAN(1937); LIFE OF EMILE ZOLA, THE(1937); LOVE IS ON THE AIR(1937); MOUNTAIN JUSTICE(1937); SOULS AT SEA(1937); BAD MAN OF BRIMSTONE(1938); BREAKING THE ICE(1938); BUCCANEER, THE(1938); CHARLIE CHAN IN HONOLULU(1938); MARIE ANTOINETTE(1938); PENITENTIARY(1938); SHADOWS OVER SHANGHAI(1938); TEXANS, THE(1938); ALLEGHENY UPRISING(1939); BAD LANDS(1939); CISCO KID AND THE LADY, THE(1939); COLORADO SUNSET(1939); CONSPIRACY(1939); HERITAGE OF THE DESERT(1939); MAN OF CONQUEST(1939); RETURN OF THE CISCO KID(1939); UNION PACIFIC(1939); CAPTAIN CAUTION(1940); FUGITIVE FROM A PRISON CAMP(1940); GO WEST(1940); LADDIE(1940); MAN FROM DAKOTA, THE(1940); NORTHWEST PASSAGE(1940); PARACHUTE BATTALION(1941); RIDERS OF THE PURPLE SAGE(1941); THEY MET IN ARGENTINA(1941); BOMBER'S MOON(1943); JOHNNY COME LATELY(1943); STRANGER IN TOWN, A(1943); THEY CAME TO BLOW UP AMERICA(1943); ADVENTURES OF MARK TWAIN, THE(1944); ENEMY OF WOMEN(1944); GREAT JOHN L. THE(1945); ROAD TO UTOPIA(1945); SAN ANTONIO(1945); STRANGLER OF THE SWAMP(1945); THEY WERE EXPENDABLE(1945); WANDERER OF THE WASTELAND(1945); DANGEROUS MILLIONS(1946); JUST BEFORE DAWN(1946); SUNSET PASS(1946); TIME OF THEIR LIVES, THE(1946); ROAD TO RIO(1947); SEA OF GRASS, THE(1947); JOAN OF ARC(1948); RELENTLESS(1948); CANADIAN PACIFIC(1949); RIDERS OF THE RANGE(1949); BARON OF ARIZONA, THE(1950); DAVY CROCKETT, INDIAN SCOUT(1950); DOUBLE CROSSBONES(1950); DARLING, HOW COULD YOU!(1951); DISTANT DRUMS(1951); DENVER AND RIO GRANDE(1952); SON OF ALI BABA(1952); TALL MAN RIDING(1955)
Misc. Silents
HER OWN WAY(1915); WHISPERING SHADOWS(1922)

Robert H. Barrat
AMERICAN EMPIRE(1942); GIRL FROM ALASKA(1942); DAKOTA(1945); GRISSLY'S MILLIONS(1945); MAGNIFICENT DOLL(1946); FABULOUS TEXAN, THE(1947); I LOVE TROUBLE(1947); BAD MEN OF TOMBSTONE(1949); DOOLINS OF OKLAHOMA, THE(1949); LONE WOLF AND HIS LADY, THE(1949); SONG OF INDIA(1949); KID FROM TEXAS, THE(1950); FLIGHT TO MARS(1951); PRIDE OF MARYLAND(1951); COW COUNTRY(1953)

Chick Barratt
GAMEKEEPER, THE(1980, Brit.)

Donald Barratt
HARD ROCK HARRIGAN(1935), ed; COUNTY FAIR(1937), ed; RAW TIMBER(1937), ed; OLD LOUISIANA(1938), ed

George Barratt
PEG OF OLD DRURY(1936, Brit.)

Lawrence Barratt
SUPREME SECRET, THE(1958, Brit.), w; CROWNING GIFT, THE(1967, Brit.), w

Reginald Barratt
TASTE THE BLOOD OF DRACULA(1970, Brit.)

Daniele Barraud
SEVEN CAPITAL SINS(1962, Fr./Ital.)

George Barraud
BELLAMY TRIAL, THE(1929); LAST OF MRS. CHEYNEY, THE(1929); STRANGE CARGO(1929); WOMAN TO WOMAN(1929); PEACOCK ALLEY(1930); ROAD TO PARADISE(1930); HAPPY ENDING, THE(1931, Brit.); EBB TIDE(1932, Brit.); RETURN OF RAFFLES, THE(1932, Brit.); WOMEN WHO PLAY(1932, Brit.); DAUGHTERS OF TODAY(1933, Brit.); CHARLIE CHAN IN LONDON(1934); CHEATING CHEATERS(1934); STINGAREE(1934); MYSTERY WOMAN(1935); ACCUSED(1936, Brit.), w; SHOW FLAT(1936, Brit.), w; TWO ON A DOORSTEP(1936, Brit.), w; CAVALIER OF THE STREETS(1937, Brit.), w; TALK OF THE DEVIL(1937, Brit.), w; DARK SANDS(1938, Brit.), a, w; SONS OF THE SEA(1939, Brit.), w; STOLEN LIFE(1939, Brit.), w; HIDEOUT(1948, Brit.), w
Silents
NED MCCOBB'S DAUGHTER(1929)
Misc. Silents
WOLF MAN, THE(1924); TROPIC MADNESS(1928)

Jean Louis Barrault
PEARLS OF THE CROWN(1938, Fr.); BIZARRE BIZARRE(1939, Fr.)

Jean-Louis Barrault
LIFE AND LOVES OF BEETHOVEN, THE(1937, Fr.); CHILDREN OF PARADISE(1945, Fr.); SYMPHONIE FANTASTIQUE(1947, Fr.); BLIND DESIRE(1948, Fr.), LA RONDE(1954, Fr.); ROYAL AFFAIRS IN VERSAILLES(1957, Fr.); LONGEST DAY, THE(1962); CHAPPAQUA(1967); LA NUIT DE VARENNES(1983, Fr./Ital.)

Maria-Christine Barrault
DAYDREAMER, THE(1975, Fr.)

Marie Christine Barrault
TABLE FOR FIVE(1983)

Marie-Christine Barrault
MY NIGHT AT MAUD'S(1970, Fr.); CHLOE IN THE AFTERNOON(1972, Fr.); COUSIN, COUSINE(1976, Fr.); MEDUSA TOUCH, THE(1978, Brit.); STARDUST MEMORIES(1980)
1984
LOVE IN GERMANY, A(1984, Fr./Ger.); SWANN IN LOVE(1984, Fr.Ger.)

Victor Barravalle
VAGABOND LOVER(1929), md

Gerald Barray
ADVENTURES OF SCARAMOUCHE, THE(1964, Fr.)

Gerard Barray
GAME FOR SIX LOVERS, A(1962, Fr.); SCHEHERAZADE(1965, Fr./Ital./Span.); SEA PIRATE, THE(1967, Fr./Span./Ital.)

Harry Barrdollar
WINTER MEETING(1948), spec eff

Gabriel Barre
LUGGAGE OF THE GODS(1983)

Pamela Barreaux
BACHELOR OF HEARTS(1958, Brit.)

Anthony Barredo
SAIGON(1948)

Bessie Barredo
IMPASSE(1969)

Giovanni Barreila
LOYALTY OF LOVE(1937, Ital.)

Joseph Barrell
Misc. Silents
BRAWN OF THE NORTH(1922)

Rene Barrera
MAGNIFICENT ONE, THE(1974, Fr./Ital.); HIGH RISK(1981)
1984
ERENDIRA(1984, Mex./Fr./Ger.)

Michael Barrere
NAKED KISS, THE(1964)

Michel Barrere
HEART LIKE A WHEEL(1983)

Robert Barrere
MALIBU BEACH(1978), ed

Tino Barrero
KING OF KINGS(1961)

Andre Barret
DAY AND THE HOUR, THE(1963, Fr./ Ital.), w

Carolina Barret
LIVING COFFIN, THE(1965, Mex.)

Michael Barret
CARIBOO TRAIL, THE(1950)

Robert Barret
AMERICAN GUERRILLA IN THE PHILIPPINES, AN(1950)
Susan Barret
Misc. Talkies
SEX DU JOUR(1976)
Gil Barreta
HOW COME NOBODY'S ON OUR SIDE?(1975)
Bruno Barreto
KISS ME GOODBYE(1982), w
1984
GABRIELA(1984, Braz.), d, w
Gil Barreto
JOE KIDD(1972); SCARFACE(1983)
Guillermo Barreto
HELL'S ISLAND(1955)
Lucy Barreto
BYE-BYE BRASIL(1980, Braz.), p
1984
MEMOIRS OF PRISON(1984, Braz.), p
Luis Carlos Barreto
DONA FLOR AND HER TWO HUSHANDS(1977, Braz.), p
Luiz Carlos Barreto
TRAIN ROBBERY CONFIDENTIAL(1965, Braz.), w; EARTH ENTRANCED(1970, Braz.), ph
1984
MEMOIRS OF PRISON(1984, Braz.), p
Pedro Barreto
CARMEN(1949, Span.)
Adrienne Barrett
DEMENTIA(1955)
Alan Barrett
FAR FROM THE MADDING CROWD(1967, Brit.), cos; LOCK UP YOUR DAUGH-TERS(1969, Brit.), cos; START THE REVOLUTION WITHOUT ME(1970), cos; SEVEN-PER-CENT SOLUTION, THE(1977, Brit.), cos; NIJINSKY(1980, Brit.), cos
Albert Barrett
Misc. Silents
HALF AN HOUR(1920)
Albert L. Barrett
Silents
CURSE OF DRINK, THE(1922)
Misc. Silents
HIS BROTHER'S KEEPER(1921)
Alice Barrett
Misc. Talkies
MISSION HILL(1982)
Amy Barrett
HUMANOIDS FROM THE DEEP(1980); HOUSE WHERE EVIL DWELLS, THE(1982)
Ann Barrett
NIGHT OF THE STRANGLER(1975)
Anne Barrett
FOLLIES GIRL(1943)
Beatrice Barrett
FLESH AND FANTASY(1943)
Bernice Barrett
NOTORIOUS(1946)
Bill Barrett
THIN RED LINE, THE(1964)
Brandy Barrett
SCREAMS OF A WINTER NIGHT(1979)
Capt. W. Barrett
COLONEL BLIMP(1945, Brit.)
Caroline Barrett
DREAMS OF GLASS(1969)
Charles Barrett
GET YOUR MAN(1934, Brit.); POT LUCK(1936, Brit.)
Christopher Barrett
SUMMER SCHOOL TEACHERS(1977)
Claudia Barrett
WHITE HEAT(1949); HAPPY YEARS, THE(1950); OLD FRONTIER, THE(1950); RUSTLERS ON HORSEBACK(1950); NIGHT RIDERS OF MONTANA(1951); DE-SPERADOES OUTPOST(1952); ROBOT MONSTER(1953); CHAIN OF EVIDEN-CE(1957); SEVEN WAYS FROM SUNDOWN(1960); LAST TIME I SAW ARCHIE, THE(1961); YOU HAVE TO RUN FAST(1961); TAGGART(1964)
Clyde Barrett
DOCTOR DETROIT(1983)
Clyde J. Barrett
WIZ, THE(1978)
Covington Barrett
Silents
AS A WOMAN SOWS(1916)
Curt Barrett
SHADOWS OF THE WEST(1949)
Don Barrett
GLORY TRAIL, THE(1937), ed
Donald Barrett
BATTLE OF GREED(1934), ed; LAW COMMANDS, THE(1938), ed
Dorothy Barrett
O.S.S.(1946); WHERE THERE'S LIFE(1947)
Misc. Silents
PULSE OF LIFE, THE(1917)
Edith Barrett
LADIES IN RETIREMENT(1941); LADY FOR A NIGHT(1941); GET HEP TO LOVE(1942); YOU CAN'T ESCAPE FOREVER(1942); ALWAYS A BRIDESMAID(1943); GHOST SHIP, THE(1943); I WALKED WITH A ZOMBIE(1943); SONG OF BER-NADETTE, THE(1943); JANE EYRE(1944); KEYS OF THE KINGDOM, THE(1944); STORY OF DR. WASSELL, THE(1944); STRANGERS IN THE NIGHT(1944); MOLLY AND ME(1945); THAT'S THE SPIRIT(1945); RUTHLESS(1948); LADY GAMBLES, THE(1949); HOLIDAY FOR SINNERS(1952); SWAN, THE(1956); IN LOVE AND WAR(1958)

Ernestine Barrett
NIGHT THEY RAIDED MINSKY'S, THE(1968)
Ethel Barrett
FLAMING TEEN-AGE, THE(1956), a, w
George Barrett
BLARNEY KISS(1933, Brit.)
Gertrude Barrett
Silents
WITHOUT HOPE(1914)
Hoyle Barrett
READY FOR THE PEOPLE(1964), set d; HALLELUJAH TRAIL, THE(1965), set d; GENERATION(1969), set d
Hurd Barrett
PARDON MY RHYTHM(1944), w
James Barrett
RACERS, THE(1955)
James Lee Barrett
D.I., THE(1957), w; ON THE BEACH(1959), w; GREATEST STORY EVER TOLD, THE(1965), w; SHENANDOAH(1965), w; TRUTH ABOUT SPRING, THE(1965, Brit.), w; BANDOLERO!(1968), w; GREEN BERETS, THE(1968), w; UNDEFEATED, THE(1969), w; CHEYENNE SOCIAL CLUB, THE(1970), w; ...TICK...TICK...TICK...(1970), p, w; FOOLS' PARADE(1971), a, w; SMOKEY AND THE BANDIT(1977), w; WILD HORSE HANK(1979, Can.), w
Jane Barrett
CAPTIVE HEART, THE(1948, Brit.); COLONEL BOGEY(1948, Brit.); MASSACRE HILL(1949, Brit.); SWORD AND THE ROSE, THE(1953); TIME GENTLEMEN PLEASE!(1953, Brit.); BOND OF FEAR(1956, Brit.); CHANGE PARTNERS(1965, Brit.)
Janet Barrett
THANK YOUR LUCKY STARS(1943); MR. SKEFFINGTON(1944); MAN I LOVE, THE(1946); STORM WARNING(1950); I WAS A COMMUNIST FOR THE F.B.I.(1951)
Jerry Barrett
UNDER A TEXAS MOON(1930)
1984
HARRY AND SON(1984)
Jim Barrett
ON THE BEACH(1959)
John Barrett
FAR FROM THE MADDING CROWD(1967, Brit.); TRYGON FACTOR, THE(1969, Brit.); O LUCKY MAN!(1973, Brit.); EAGLE HAS LANDED, THE(1976, Brit.); ROBIN AND MARIAN(1976, Brit.); ALL THINGS BRIGHT AND BEAUTIFUL(1979, Brit.); FRENCH LIEUTENANT'S WOMAN, THE(1981); MISSIONARY, THE(1982); REMEM-BRANCE(1982, Brit.); SILENT RAGE(1982)
John P. Barrett
JOHNNY O'CLOCK(1947)
Judith Barrett
FLYING HOSTESS(1936); YELLOWSTONE(1936); ARMORED CAR(1937); BEHIND THE MIKE(1937); GOOD OLD SOAK, THE(1937); LET THEM LIVE(1937); ILLEGAL TRAFFIC(1938); DISPUTED PASSAGE(1939); GRACIE ALLEN MURDER CA-SE(1939); GREAT VICTOR HERBERT, THE(1939); I'M FROM MISSOURI(1939); PERSONS IN HIDING(1939); TELEVISION SPY(1939); ROAD TO SINGAPORE(1940); THOSE WERE THE DAYS(1940); WOMEN WITHOUT NAMES(1940)
June Barrett
FIRST LOVE(1977); CONCRETE JUNGLE, THE(1982)
Katharine Barrett
WAYWARD GIRL, THE(1957)
Katherine Barrett
EIGHTEEN AND ANXIOUS(1957)
Laurinda Barrett
WRONG MAN, THE(1956); HEART IS A LONELY HUNTER, THE(1968)
Lawrence Barrett
JOHN WESLEY(1954, Brit.), w; SHIELD OF FAITH, THE(1956, Brit.), w
Leslie Barrett
1984
PREPPIES(1984)
Liz Barrett
DEVIL'S MAN, THE(1967, Ital.); SUPERARGO(1968, Ital./Span.)
Louise Barrett
BLOODY PIT OF HORROR, THE(1965, Ital.); PAYMENT IN BLOOD(1968, Ital.)
Majel Barrett
AS YOUNG AS WE ARE(1958); LOVE IN A GOLDFISH BOWL(1961); QUICK AND THE DEAD, THE(1963); SYLVIA(1965); COUNTRY BOY(1966); GUIDE FOR THE MARRIED MAN, A(1967); TRACK OF THUNDER(1967); WESTWORLD(1973); DOMI-NO PRINCIPLE, THE(1977); STAR TREK: THE MOTION PICTURE(1979)
Michael Ann Barrett
FILE ON THELMA JORDAN, THE(1950); WRONG MAN, THE(1956)
Michael Barrett
SCENE OF THE CRIME(1949); HELL SHIP MUTINY(1957); ESCAPE FROM ZAH-RAIN(1962), w; REWARD, THE(1965), w; INVINCIBLE SIX, THE(1970, U.S./Iran), w
Monte Barrett
ADVENTURES OF JANE ARDEN(1939), w
Nancy Barrett
HOUSE OF DARK SHADOWS(1970); NIGHT OF DARK SHADOWS(1971)
Nitchie Barrett
1984
PREPPIES(1984)
Pat Barrett
COMIN' ROUND THE MOUNTAIN(1940)
Patrick Barrett
WAR AND PEACE(1956, Ital./U.S.)
Paul Barrett
BORDER FLIGHT(1936); MURDER WITH PICTURES(1936); THEODORA GOES WILD(1936); NAVY BLUE AND GOLD(1937); UNDER STRANGE FLAGS(1937); HERO FOR A DAY(1939); SINGING COWGIRL, THE(1939); TO BE OR NOT TO BE(1942); O.S.S.(1946)
Raina Barrett
FEMALE RESPONSE, THE(1972); OH! CALCUTTA!(1972); STIGMA(1972); BLA-DE(1973)

Ray Barrett
SUNDOWNERS, THE(1960); MIX ME A PERSON(1962, Brit.); TIME TO REMEMBER(1962, Brit.); TOUCH OF DEATH(1962, Brit.); TO HAVE AND TO HOLD(1963, Brit.); 80,000 SUSPECTS(1963, Brit.); JIG SAW(1965, Brit.); REPTILE, THE(1966, Brit.); JUST LIKE A WOMAN(1967, Brit.); THUNDERBIRDS ARE GO(1968, Brit.); TERROR FROM UNDER THE HOUSE(1971, Brit.); DON'S PARTY(1976, Aus.); LET THE BALLOON GO(1977, Aus.); CHANT OF JIMMIE BLACKSMITH, THE(1980, Aus.)

Raymond Barrett
DESPERATE WOMEN, THE(?)

Reginald Barrett
STOCK CAR(1955, Brit.)

Richard Barrett
STORY OF DR. WASSELL, THE(1944); BEYOND THE DOOR(1975, Ital./U.S.), w

Rita Barrett
PAL JOEY(1957)

Roger Barrett
DAYS OF WINE AND ROSES(1962)

Rona Barrett
DO NOT THROW CUSHIONS INTO THE RING(1970); PHYNX, THE(1970); SEXTETTE(1978)

Ross Barrett
MADELEINE IS(1971, Can.), m

Ruth Barrett
Silents
TILLIE WAKES UP(1917)

Sean Barrett
FOUR SIDED TRIANGLE(1953, Brit.); GENIE, THE(1953, Brit.); BANG! YOU'RE DEAD(1954, Brit.); ESCAPADE(1955, Brit.); WAR AND PEACE(1956, Ital./U.S.); DUNKIRK(1958, Brit.); CRY FROM THE STREET, A(1959, Brit.); SONS AND LOVERS(1960, Brit.); CAST A GIANT SHADOW(1966); ATTACK ON THE IRON COAST(1968, U.S./Brit.); GREAT CATHERINE(1968, Brit.); HELL BOATS(1970, Brit.); DARK CRYSTAL, THE(1982, Brit.)

Sheila Barrett
TWO HEARTS IN HARMONY(1935, Brit.)

Stan Barrett
LIFE AND TIMES OF JUDGE ROY BEAN, THE(1972); AIRPORT '77(1977), stunts
1984
HARRY AND SON(1984), stunts

Stanley W. Barrett
SUPPOSE THEY GAVE A WAR AND NOBODY CAME?(1970)

Susan Barrett
APRIL FOOLS, THE(1969)

Tim Barrett
BOY CRIED MURDER, THE(1966, Ger./Brit./Yugo.); PSYCHOPATH, THE(1966, Brit.); TRAITOR'S GATE(1966, Brit./Ger.); WHERE THE BULLETS FLY(1966, Brit.); DEADLY BEES,THE(1967, Brit.); MUMMY'S SHROUD, THE(1967, Brit.); FLYING SORCERER, THE(1974, Brit.); SLIPPER AND THE ROSE, THE(1976, Brit.)
1984
BLOODBATH AT THE HOUSE OF DEATH(1984, Brit.)

Tomi Barrett
Misc. Talkies
PYRAMID, THE(1976)

Tony Barrett
FALCON'S ADVENTURE, THE(1946); SAN QUENTIN(1946); BORN TO KILL(1947); DICK TRACY MEETS GRUESOME(1947); DICK TRACY'S DILEMMA(1947); SEVEN KEYS TO BALDPATE(1947); UNDER THE TONTO RIM(1947); WILD HORSE MESA(1947); GUNS OF HATE(1948); MYSTERY IN MEXICO(1948); WESTERN HERITAGE(1948); FLAME OF YOUTH(1949); IMPACT(1949); PRISONERS IN PETTICOATS(1950); GOOD TIMES(1967), w

William E. Barrett
LEFT HAND OF GOD, THE(1955), w; LILIES OF THE FIELD(1963), w; PIECES OF DREAMS(1970), w

Wilson Barrett
SIGN OF THE CROSS, THE(1932), w; CONCERNING MR. MARTIN(1937, Brit.)

Troy Barrett.
PUFNSTUF(1970), puppeter

Yvon Barrette
SLAP SHOT(1977)

Larry Barretto
THE CRASH(1932), w

Fern Barrey
SUBMARINE D-1(1937)

Jean Barrez
THUNDER IN THE BLOOD(1962, Fr.)

Barta Barri
BOY WHO STOLE A MILLION, THE(1960, Brit.); HAPPY THIEVES, THE(1962); CEREMONY, THE(1963, U.S./Span.); SECRET SEVEN, THE(1966, Ital./Span.); SON OF A GUNFIGHTER(1966, U.S./Span.); DRUMS OF TABU, THE(1967, Ital./Span.); FEW BULLETS MORE, A(1968, Ital./Span.); MAN CALLED NOON, THE(1973, Brit.)

Mario Barri
HUK(1956); STEEL CLAW, THE(1961); NO MAN IS AN ISLAND(1962); OUT OF THE TIGER'S MOUTH(1962); SAMAR(1962); YANK IN VIET-NAM, A(1964)

Babriele Barriale
DUEL OF THE TITANS(1963, Ital.), ed

John Barrick
WALK THE ANGRY BEACH(1961)

Amanda Barrie
CARRY ON CABBIE(1963, Brit.); DOCTOR IN DISTRESS(1963, Brit.); OPERATION BULLSHINE(1963, Brit.); PAIR OF BRIEFS, A(1963, Brit.); CARRY ON CLEO(1964, Brit.); I'VE GOTTA HORSE(1965, Brit.)

Angela Barrie
MUSIC HALL PARADE(1939, Brit.); OLD MOTHER RILEY AT HOME(1945, Brit.)

Barbara Barrie
GIANT(1956); CARETAKERS, THE(1963); ONE POTATO, TWO POTATO(1964); BELL JAR, THE(1979); BREAKING AWAY(1979); PRIVATE BENJAMIN(1980)

Brian Barrie
TIM(1981, Aus.)

Clive Barrie
SCARS OF DRACULA, THE(1970, Brit.)

Colin Barrie
MELODY(1971, Brit.); UNMAN, WITTERING AND ZIGO(1971, Brit.)

Craig Barrie
THIEVES(1977)

Elaine Barrie
MIDNIGHT(1939)
Misc. Talkies
HOW TO UNDRESS IN FRONT OF YOUR HUSBAND(1937)

Ellen Barrie
PASSIONATE SUMMER(1959, Brit.)

Evelyn Barrie
EVERYTHING OKAY(1936, Brit.), w; BOYS WILL BE GIRLS(1937, Brit.), w

George Barrie
JUKE BOX RACKET(1960), p; WHIFFS(1975), p; I WILL ...I WILL ...FOR NOW(1976), p; THIEVES(1977), p; FINGERS(1978), p

Gina Barrie
ROCKY HORROR PICTURE SHOW, THE(1975, Brit.)

Godfrey Barrie
HIDEOUT(1948, Brit.)

H. E. Barrie
SHE DEMONS(1958), w; MISSILE TO THE MOON(1959), w; CAREER GIRL(1960), w; GIRL IN ROOM 13(1961, U.S./Braz.), w

J.M. Barrie
AS YOU LIKE IT(1936, Brit.), w

James Barrie
DOCTOR'S SECRET(1929), w

James M. Barrie
DARLING, HOW COULD YOU!(1951), w; ADMIRABLE CRICHTON, THE(1957, Brit.), w
Silents
WHAT EVERY WOMAN KNOWS(1917, Brit.), w; ADMIRABLE CRICHTON, THE(1918, Brit.), w; PETER PAN(1924), w; QUALITY STREET(1927), w

James Matthew Barrie
Silents
WHAT EVERY WOMAN KNOWS(1921), w; KISS FOR CINDERELLA, A(1926), w

John Barrie
VICTIM(1961, Brit.); SWORD OF LANCELOT(1963, Brit.); YOUNG AND WILLING(1964, Brit.); WALK IN THE SHADOW(1966, Brit.); FILE OF THE GOLDEN GOOSE, THE(1969, Brit.); OBLONG BOX, THE(1969, Brit.); PATTON(1970); SONG OF NORWAY(1970)

Judith Barrie
PARTY GIRL(1930); EX-FLAME(1931); HIDDEN GOLD(1933)

Julie Barrie
THEY DRIVE BY NIGHT(1938, Brit.)

Keith Barrie
HOMER(1970), set d

Leslie Barrie
13 RUE MADELEINE(1946); IRON CURTAIN, THE(1948)
Misc. Silents
GREATER LOVE, THE(1919, Brit.)

Lina Barrie
PASTOR HALL(1940, Brit.)

Lisa Barrie
CAREER GIRL(1960)

M.E. Barrie
FRANKENSTEIN'S DAUGHTER(1958), w

Mona Barrie
ALL MEN ARE ENEMIES(1934); CAROLINA(1934); CHARLIE CHAN IN LONDON(1934); I'LL FIX IT(1934); ONE NIGHT OF LOVE(1934); SLEEPERS EAST(1934); SUCH WOMEN ARE DANGEROUS(1934); LADIES LOVE DANGER(1935); MELODY LINGERS ON, THE(1935); MYSTERY WOMAN(1935); STORM OVER THE ANDES(1935); UNWELCOME STRANGER(1935); HERE COMES TROUBLE(1936); KING OF BURLESQUE(1936); MESSAGE TO GARCIA, A(1936); I MET HIM IN PARIS(1937); MOUNTAIN JUSTICE(1937); SOMETHING TO SING ABOUT(1937); LOVE, HONOR AND BEHAVE(1938); MEN ARE SUCH FOOLS(1938); SAY IT IN FRENCH(1938); I TAKE THIS WOMAN(1940); LADY WITH RED HAIR(1940); LOVE, HONOR AND OH, BABY(1940); WHO KILLED AUNT MAGGIE?(1940); ELLERY QUEEN AND THE MURDER RING(1941); MURDER AMONG FRIENDS(1941); NEVER GIVE A SUCKER AN EVEN BREAK(1941); SKYLARK(1941); WHEN LADIES MEET(1941); CAIRO(1942); DAWN ON THE GREAT DIVIDE(1942); LADY IN A JAM(1942); ROAD TO HAPPINESS(1942); STRANGE CASE OF DR. RX, THE(1942); SYNCOPATION(1942); TODAY I HANG(1942); TRAGEDY AT MIDNIGHT, A(1942); ONE DANGEROUS NIGHT(1943); STORM OVER LISBON(1944); DEVIL'S MASK, THE(1946); JUST BEFORE DAWN(1946); SECRET OF THE WHISTLER(1946); CASS TIMBERLANE(1947); I COVER BIG TOWN(1947); WHEN A GIRL'S BEAUTIFUL(1947); MY DOG RUSTY(1948); FIRST TIME, THE(1952); STRANGE FASCINATION(1952)

Nigel Barrie
PLAYTHING, THE(1929, Brit.); GREENWOOD TREE, THE(1930, Brit.); UNDER THE GREENWOOD TREE(1930, Brit.); DREYFUS CASE, THE(1931, Brit.); OLD SOLDIERS NEVER DIE(1931, Brit.); PASSENGER TO LONDON(1937, Brit.)
Silents
BAB'S DIARY(1917); NOTORIOUS MISS LISLE, THE(1920); CHARGE IT(1921); PRINCE THERE WAS, A(1921); EAST IS WEST(1922); STRANGER'S BANQUET(1922); FIRES OF FATE(1923, Brit.); MUTINY(1925, Brit.); AMATEUR GENTLEMAN, THE(1926); HOME STRUCK(1927); HUSBAND HUNTERS(1927); LONE EAGLE, THE(1927); SHIELD OF HONOR, THE(1927); RINGER, THE(1928, Brit.)
Misc. Silents
BAB'S MATINEE IDOL(1917); MARIONETTES, THE(1918); BETTER WIFE, THE(1919); DIANE OF THE GREEN VAN(1919); JOSSELYN'S WIFE(1919); WHEN MY SHIP COMES IN(1919); CINEMA MURDER, THE(1920); GIRL IN THE WEB, THE(1920); HONEY BEE, THE(1920); SLAVE OF VANITY, A(1920); THEIR MUTUAL CHILD(1920); TURNING POINT, THE(1920); LITTLE FOOL, THE(1921); LITTLE MINISTER, THE(1921); HEROES AND HUSBANDS(1922); BOLTED DOOR, THE(1923); CLAUDE DUVAL(1924, Brit.); DESERT SHEIK, THE(1924); SUNSHINE OF PARADISE ALLEY(1926); COCTAILS(1928, Brit.); FORGER, THE(1928, Brit.)

Nuala Barrie
WE'LL SMILE AGAIN(1942, Brit.)
Pamela Barrie
MOON-SPINNERS, THE(1964)
Rita Barrie
OLGA'S GIRLS(1964)
Scott Barrie
GANJA AND HESS(1973), cos
Sir James M. Barrie
SEVEN DAYS LEAVE(1930), w; LITTLE MINISTER, THE(1934), w; QUALITY STREET(1937), w; FOREVER FEMALE(1953); PETER PAN(1953), w
Silents
MALE AND FEMALE(1919), w
Sir James Matthew Barrie
WHAT EVERY WOMAN KNOWS(1934), w
Suzanne Barrie
LOVESICK(1983)
Wendy Barrie
BARTON MYSTERY, THE(1932, Brit.); CALLBOX MYSTERY, THE(1932, Brit.); COLLISION(1932, Brit.); THREADS(1932, Brit.); WEDDING REHEARSAL(1932, Brit.); WHERE IS THIS LADY?(1932, Brit.); HOUSE OF TRENT, THE(1933, Brit.); PRIVATE LIFE OF HENRY VIII, THE(1933); THIS ACTING BUSINESS(1933, Brit.); FOR LOVE OR MONEY(1934, Brit.); FREEDOM OF THE SEAS(1934, Brit.); IT'S A BOY(1934, Brit.); MAN I WANT, THE(1934, Brit.); MURDER AT THE INN(1934, Brit.); WITHOUT YOU(1934, Brit.); BIG BROADCAST OF 1936, THE(1935); COLLEGE SCANDAL(1935); FEATHER IN HER HAT, A(1935); IT'S A SMALL WORLD(1935); MILLIONS IN THE AIR(1935); SCANDALS OF PARIS(1935, Brit.); GIVE HER A RING(1936, Brit.); LOVE ON A BET(1936); SPEED(1936); TICKET TO PARADISE(1936); UNDER YOUR SPELL(1936); BREEZING HOME(1937); DEAD END(1937); GIRL WITH IDEAS, A(1937); PRESCRIPTION FOR ROMANCE(1937); WHAT PRICE VENGEANCE?(1937); WINGS OVER HONOLULU(1937); I AM THE LAW(1938); DAY-TIME WIFE(1939); FIVE CAME BACK(1939); HOUND OF THE BASKERVILLES, THE(1939); NEWSBOY'S HOME(1939); PACIFIC LINER(1939); SAINT STRIKES BACK, THE(1939); WITNESS VANISHES, THE(1939); CROSS COUNTRY ROMANCE(1940); MEN AGAINST THE SKY(1940); SAINT TAKES OVER, THE(1940); WHO KILLED AUNT MAGGIE?(1940); WOMEN IN WAR(1940); DATE WITH THE FALCON, A(1941); GAY FALCON, THE(1941); PUBLIC ENEMIES(1941); REPENT AT LEISURE(1941); SAINT IN PALM SPRINGS, THE(1941); EYES OF THE UNDERWORLD(1943); FOLLIES GIRL(1943); FOREVER AND A DAY(1943); SUBMARINE ALERT(1943); IT SHOULD HAPPEN TO YOU(1954); MOVING FINGER, THE(1963)
Edgar Barrier
COMRADE X(1940); ESCAPE(1940); PENALTY, THE(1941); THEY DARE NOT LOVE(1941); ARABIAN NIGHTS(1942); DANGER IN THE PACIFIC(1942); EAGLE SQUADRON(1942); JOURNEY INTO FEAR(1942); PRIDE OF THE YANKEES, THE(1942); SHERLOCK HOLMES AND THE VOICE OF TERROR(1942); FLESH AND FANTASY(1943); PHANTOM OF THE OPERA(1943); WE'VE NEVER BEEN LICKED(1943); COBRA WOMAN(1944); SECRETS OF SCOTLAND YARD(1944); CORNERED(1945); GAME OF DEATH, A(1945); NOB HILL(1945); SONG OF MEXICO(1945); TARZAN AND THE LEOPARD WOMAN(1946); MACBETH(1948); PORT SAID(1948); ROCKY(1948); ROGUES' REGIMENT(1948); TO THE ENDS OF THE EARTH(1948); SECRET OF ST. IVES, THE(1949); CYRANO DE BERGERAC(1950); JOE PALOOKA IN THE SQUARED CIRCLE(1950); LAST OF THE BUCCANEERS(1950); HURRICANE ISLAND(1951); WHIP HAND, THE(1951); COUNT THE HOURS(1953); DESTINATION GOBI(1953); GOLDEN BLADE, THE(1953); PRINCE OF PIRATES(1953); STAND AT APACHE RIVER, THE(1953); WAR OF THE WORLDS, THE(1953); PRINCESS OF THE NILE(1954); SARACEN BLADE, THE(1954); SILVER LODE(1954); RUMBLE ON THE DOCKS(1956); GIANT CLAW, THE(1957); JUKE BOX RHYTHM(1959); ON THE DOUBLE(1961); PIRATES OF TORTUGA(1961); SNOW WHITE AND THE THREE STOOGES(1961); IRMA LA DOUCE(1963)
Misc. Talkies
EYES OF THE JUNGLE(1953)
Ernestine Barrier
PROJECT MOONBASE(1953); SLAVES OF BABYLON(1953); VANQUISHED, THE(1953); DRAGON'S GOLD(1954); BOTTOM OF THE BOTTLE, THE(1956); LUST FOR LIFE(1956); GNOME-MOBILE, THE(1967)
Francois Barrier
1984
L'ARGENT(1984, Fr./Switz.)
Maurice Barrier
RISE OF LOUIS XIV, THE(1970, Fr.); BLACK AND WHITE IN COLOR(1976, Fr.); AND THE SHIP SAILS ON(1983, Ital./Fr.); RETURN OF MARTIN GUERRE, THE(1983, Fr.)
1984
LES COMPERES(1984, Fr.)
Michael Barrier
ANGEL IN MY POCKET(1969)
Alicia Jorge Barriga
VIRIDIANA(1962, Mex./Span.)
Dania Barrigo
BORROW A MILLION(1934, Brit.)
A. B. Barringer
Silents
HEADS UP(1925), w; SMILIN' AT TROUBLE(1925), w; HAZARDOUS VALLEY(1927), w
Misc. Silents
VENGEANCE OF THE DEEP(1923), d; RIDING TO FAME(1927), d
B. B. Barringer
SIXTEEN FATHOMS DEEP(1934), w
Barry Barringer
GRAFT(1931), w; LIGHTNING FLYER(1931), w; DYNAMITE RANCH(1932), w; FACE ON THE BARROOM FLOOR, THE(1932), w; MIDNIGHT PATROL, THE(1932), w; DARING DAUGHTERS(1933), w; DEATH KISS(1933), w; DUDE RANGER, THE(1934), w; WAY OF THE WEST, THE(1934), w; WHAT'S YOUR RACKET?(1934), w; NORTHERN FRONTIER(1935), w; RED BLOOD OF COURAGE(1935), w; FEDERAL AGENT(1936), w; SONG OF THE TRAIL(1936), w; HELD FOR RANSOM(1938), w
Dale Barringer
DO YOU LOVE ME?(1946)

Emily Dunning Barringer
GIRL IN WHITE, THE(1952), w
Michael Barringer
BLOCKADE(1928, Brit.), d, w; INQUEST(1931, Brit.), w; FRAIL WOMEN(1932, Brit.), w; MURDER AT COVENT GARDEN(1932, Brit.), d, w; CLEANING UP(1933, Brit.), w; DAUGHTERS OF TODAY(1933, Brit.), w; GREAT STUFF(1933, Brit.), w; I'LL STICK TO YOU(1933, Brit.), w; MAROONED(1933, Brit.), w; MEDICINE MAN, THE(1933, Brit.), w; RIGHT TO LIVE, THE(1933, Brit.), w; STRIKE IT RICH(1933, Brit.), w; THAT'S MY WIFE(1933, Brit.), w; CRAZY PEOPLE(1934, Brit.), w; GLIMPSE OF PARADISE, A(1934, Brit.), w; KEEP IT QUIET(1934, Brit.), w; MAN I WANT, THE(1934, Brit.), w; ON THE AIR(1934, Brit.), w; PASSING SHADOWS(1934, Brit.), w; PERFECT FLAW, THE(1934, Brit.), w; SOMETIMES GOOD(1934, Brit.), w; THIRD CLUE, THE(1934, Brit.), w; WITHOUT YOU(1934, Brit.), w; ANNIE, LEAVE THE ROOM(1935, Brit.), w; BIG SPLASH, THE(1935, Brit.), w; BLACK MASK(1935, Brit.), w; FIRE HAS BEEN ARRANGED, A(1935, Brit.), w; FULL CIRCLE(1935, Brit.), w; IN A MONASTERY GARDEN(1935), w; MURDER AT MONTE CARLO(1935, Brit.), w; SEXTON BLAKE AND THE MADEMOISELLE(1935, Brit.), w; THAT'S MY UNCLE(1935, Brit.), w; THREE WITNESSES(1935, Brit.), w; CHEER UP!(1936, Brit.), w; DON'T RUSH ME(1936, Brit.), w; FAME(1936, Brit.), w; GAOL BREAK(1936, Brit.), w; INTERRUPTED HONEYMOON, THE(1936, Brit.), w; MILLIONS(1936, Brit.), w; MURDER ON THE SET(1936, Brit.), w; RHODES(1936, Brit.), w; FINE FEATHERS(1937, Brit.), w; MAN WHO MADE DIAMONDS, THE(1937, Brit.), w; SILENT BARRIERS(1937, Brit.), w; WHO KILLED FEN MARKHAM?(1937, Brit.), w; DOUBLE OR QUITS(1938, Brit.), w; SONG OF FREEDOM(1938, Brit.), w; YELLOW SANDS(1938, Brit.), w; INQUEST(1939, Brit.), w; SEVENTH SURVIVOR, THE(1941, Brit.), w; LADY FROM LISBON(1942, Brit.), w; SABOTAGE AT SEA(1942, Brit.), w; BUTLER'S DILEMMA, THE(1943, Brit.), w; DUMMY TALKS, THE(1943, Brit.), w; CURSE OF THE WRAYDONS, THE(1946, Brit.), w; LITTLE BALLERINA, THE(1951, Brit.), w
Misc. Silents
INFAMOUS LADY, THE(1928, Brit.), d; DOWN CHANNEL(1929, Brit.), d
Pat Barringer
ORGY OF THE DEAD(1965); ON HER BED OF ROSES(1966)
William Barringer
FIRST TIME, THE(1969)
DeDe Barrington
SALUTE FOR THREE(1943)
Derek Barrington
THREE WORLDS OF GULLIVER, THE(1960, Brit.), art d; MURDER ON THE CAMPUS(1963, Brit.), art d; LITTLE ONES, THE(1965, Brit.), art d; CRIMSON CULT, THE(1970, Brit.), art d
Diana Barrington
LOST AND FOUND(1979)
Herbert Barrington
Silents
BROKEN CHAINS(1916); MAN HUNT, THE(1918); EASY TO GET(1920)
Misc. Silents
HOODMAN BLIND(1913)
Jonah Barrington
BAND WAGGON(1940, Brit.)
Josephine Barrington
NOW THAT APRIL'S HERE(1958, Can.)
Lowell Barrington
VALLEY OF MYSTERY(1967), w; ADAM'S WOMAN(1972, Austral.), w
Michael Barrington
PAYROLL(1962, Brit.); PRIVILEGE(1967, Brit.); UP THE JUNCTION(1968, Brit.); RISE AND RISE OF MICHAEL RIMMER, THE(1970, Brit.); PUBLIC EYE, THE(1972, Brit.); STUD, THE(1979, Brit.)
Mr. Barrington
Silents
LOVE IN A HURRY(1919)
Pamela Barrington
ACCOUNT RENDERED(1957, Brit.), w; BIG CHANCE, THE(1957, Brit.), d&w
Pat Barrington
MANTIS IN LACE(1968)
Phillis Barrington
SUCKER MONEY(1933)
Phyllis Barrington
LAW OF THE TONG(1931); TEN NIGHTS IN A BARROOM(1931); DRIFTER, THE(1932); SCARLET WEEKEND, A(1932); SINISTER HANDS(1932); RACING STRAIN, THE(1933); UNDER SECRET ORDERS(1933); MURDER IN THE MUSEUM(1934)
Misc. Talkies
PLAYTHINGS OF HOLLYWOOD(1931); RECKLESS RIDER, THE(1932)
Rutland Barrington
Silents
GREAT ADVENTURE, THE(1915, Brit.); GIRL WHO LOVES A SOLDIER, THE(1916, Brit.); STILL WATERS RUN DEEP(1916, Brit.)
Brad Barrios
DOCTOR DETROIT(1983)
Elena Barrios
FLAME OVER VIETNAM(1967, Span./Ger.)
Miriam Barrios
DEVIL'S WEDDING NIGHT, THE(1973, Ital.)
Chuck Barris
GONG SHOW MOVIE, THE(1980), a, d, w
George Barris
JUNKMAN, THE(1982)
Misc. Talkies
DISCO FEVER(1978)
Harris Barris
COHENS, AND KELLYS IN HOLLYWOOD, THE(1932)
Harry Barris
SPIRIT OF NOTRE DAME, THE(1931); HOLLYWOOD PARTY(1934); AFTER THE DANCE(1935); EVERY NIGHT AT EIGHT(1935); LOVE ME FOREVER(1935); MAN I MARRY, THE(1936); SHOW BOAT(1936); DOUBLE OR NOTHING(1937); SOMETHING TO SING ABOUT(1937); COWBOY FROM BROOKLYN(1938); SHINING HOUR, THE(1938); TRADE WINDS(1938); SOME LIKE IT HOT(1939); RHYTHM ON THE RIVER(1940); BLONDIE GOES LATIN(1941); KISS THE BOYS GOODBYE(1941); SING FOR YOUR SUPPER(1941); WEST POINT WIDOW(1941); FLEET'S IN,

THE(1942); FOOTLIGHT SERENADE(1942); HOLIDAY INN(1942); PRIORITIES ON PARADE(1942); TRUE TO THE ARMY(1942); DIXIE(1943); HAPPY GO LUCKY(1943); IS EVERYBODY HAPPY?(1943); SALUTE FOR THREE(1943); YOUNGEST PROFESSION, THE(1943); AND THE ANGELS SING(1944); HERE COME THE WAVES(1944); SAN DIEGO, I LOVE YOU(1944); ANCHORS AWEIGH(1945); LOST WEEKEND, THE(1945); PENTHOUSE RHYTHM(1945); STEPPIN' IN SOCIETY(1945); WEEKEND AT THE WALDORF(1945); BLUE DAHLIA, THE(1946); YOUNG WIDOW(1946); YOU WERE MEANT FOR ME(1948); LIFE OF HER OWN, A(1950); THREE LITTLE WORDS(1950)

Marti Barris
GET YOURSELF A COLLEGE GIRL(1964)

Richard Barris
KRAMER VS. KRAMER(1979)

Bessie Barriscale
SHOW FOLKS(1928); SECRETS(1933); ABOVE THE CLOUDS(1934); BELOVED(1934); MAN WHO RECLAIMED HIS HEAD, THE(1935)
Silents
READY MONEY(1914); ROSE OF THE RANCHO(1914); PAINTED SOUL, THE(1915); REWARD, THE(1915); CORNER IN COLLEENS, A(1916); HOME(1916); NOT MY SISTER(1916); HATER OF MEN(1917); WOODEN SHOES(1917); ALL OF A SUDDEN NORMA(1919); NOTORIOUS MRS. SANDS, THE(1920); BREAKING POINT, THE(1921)
Misc. Silents
MAKING OF BOBBY BURNIT, THE(1914); GOLDEN CLAW, THE(1915); MATING, THE(1915); BAWBS O' BLUE RIDGE(1916); BULLETS AND BROWN EYES(1916); GREEN SWAMP, THE(1916); HONOR'S ALTAR(1916); LAST ACT, THE(1916); PAYMENT, THE(1916); PLAIN JANE(1916); SORROWS OF LOVE, THE(1916); BORROWED PLUMAGE(1917); MADAM WHO?(1917); SNARL, THE(1917); BLINDFOLDED(1918); HEART OF RACHAEL, THE(1918); ROSE O' PARADISE(1918); THOSE WHO PAY(1918); TWO-GUN BETTY(1918); WITHIN THE CUP(1918); BROKEN THREADS(1919); HEARTS ASLEEP(1919); HER PURCHASE PRICE(1919); JOSSELYN'S WIFE(1919); KITTY KELLY, M.D.(1919); TRICK OF FATE, A(1919); WOMAN MICHAEL MARRIED, THE(1919); BROKEN GATE, THE(1920); LIFE'S TWIST(1920); LUCK OF GERALDINE LAIRD, THE(1920); WOMAN WHO UNDERSTOOD, A(1920)

Bessie Barriscle
Misc. Silents
BECKONING ROADS(1920)

Jerry R. Barrish
DAN'S MOTEL(1982), p,d,w&ph, ed

Lloyd Barrista
Misc. Talkies
SILENT STRANGER, THE(1975)

Barrister
OTHER PEOPLE'S SINS(1931, Brit.)

Susan Barrister
NIGHT MOVES(1975)

Desmond Barritt
1984
LASSITER(1984)

Tony Barro
PUFNSTUF(1970)

Salvadore Barroga
PERFECT SNOB, THE(1941); T-MEN(1947)

Claude Barrois
MAN AND A WOMAN, A(1966, Fr.), ed; TO BE A CROOK(1967, Fr.), ed; LIFE LOVE DEATH(1969, Fr./Ital.), ed; LOVE IS A FUNNY THING(1970, Fr./Ital.), ed; WITHOUT APPARENT MOTIVE(1972, Fr.), ed

Charles Barromel
Misc. Talkies
ATOR, THE INVINCIBLE(1984)

Arthur Barron
JEREMY(1973), d,w; BROTHERS(1977), d

Baynes Barron
CALIFORNIA CONQUEST(1952); OPERATION SECRET(1952); BIG COMBO, THE(1955); DUEL ON THE MISSISSIPPI(1955); LEATHER SAINT, THE(1956); FROM HELL IT CAME(1957); AMBUSH AT CIMARRON PASS(1958); NORTH BY NORTHWEST(1959); SPEED CRAZY(1959); HOUSE IS NOT A HOME, A(1964); STRANGLER, THE(1964); WAR IS HELL(1964); SPACE MONSTER(1965); FIREBALL 590(1966); THUNDER ALLEY(1967); MARYJANE(1968); DEVIL'S 8, THE(1969)

Bebe Barron
FORBIDDEN PLANET(1956), m

Bob Barron
SONG OF OLD WYOMING(1945); SUDAN(1945); DON'T GAMBLE WITH STRANGERS(1946); SONG OF SCHEHERAZADE(1947); BALLAD OF A GUNFIGHTER(1964)

Claudia Barron
GUESS WHAT HAPPENED TO COUNT DRACULA(1970)

Dana Barron
HE KNOWS YOU'RE ALONE(1980); NATIONAL LAMPOON'S VACATION(1983)

Dick Barron
DIXIE DUGAN(1943); YUKON MANHUNT(1951)

Frank Barron
MAN WITH BOGART'S FACE, THE(1980)

Fred Barron
BETWEEN THE LINES(1977), w; SOMETHING SHORT OF PARADISE(1979), w

Jack Barron
WESTERN HERITAGE(1948), make up; STAGECOACH KID(1949), makeup; MARNIE(1964), makeup; RAIDERS, THE(1964), makeup; TORN CURTAIN(1966), makeup

James Barron
LAST GUNFIGHTER, THE(1961, Can.); FORTUNE AND MEN'S EYES(1971, U.S./Can.)

Jim Barron
SUNDAY IN THE COUNTRY(1975, Can.)

John Barron
DAY THE EARTH CAUGHT FIRE, THE(1961, Brit.); JIG SAW(1965, Brit.); HITLER: THE LAST TEN DAYS(1973, Brit./Ital.)

Keith Barron
BABY LOVE(1969, Brit.); FIRECHASERS, THE(1970, Brit.); MAN WHO HAD POWER OVER WOMEN, THE(1970, Brit.); LAND THAT TIME FORGOT, THE(1975, Brit.); NOTHING BUT THE NIGHT(1975, Brit.); AT THE EARTH'S CORE(1976, Brit.)

Misc. Talkies
SHE'LL FOLLOW YOU ANYWHERE(1971)

Kirk Barron
JANIE(1944); LAW OF THE VALLEY(1944); SINCE YOU WENT AWAY(1944)

Louis Barron
FORBIDDEN PLANET(1956), m

Lynda Barron
HIDE AND SEEK(1964, Brit.); YENTL(1983)

Marcus Barron
LOYALTIES(1934, Brit.); STRAUSS' GREAT WALTZ(1934, Brit.); TWO OF US, THE(1938, Brit.)

Paul Barron
BUSH CHRISTMAS(1983, Aus.), p

Ray Barron
POOR COW(1968, Brit.); 10 RILLINGTON PLACE(1971, Brit.)

Richard Barron
UNION STATION(1950); HOODLUM, THE(1951); KOREA PATROL(1951); SOMETHING TO LIVE FOR(1952); DEMENTIA(1955)

Robert Barron
BACK IN THE SADDLE(1941); PITTSBURGH KID, THE(1941); ARABIAN NIGHTS(1942); BOSS OF HANGTOWN MESA(1942); ROAD TO MOROCCO(1942); CHEYENNE ROUNDUP(1943); MAN FROM THUNDER RIVER, THE(1943); RETURN OF THE RANGERS, THE(1943); WEST OF TEXAS(1943); COBRA WOMAN(1944); GUNS OF THE LAW(1944); GUNSMOKE MESA(1944); SPOOK TOWN(1944); WILSON(1944); ONE EXCITING NIGHT(1945); SARATOGA TRUNK(1945); SONG OF THE SARONG(1945); CARAVAN TRAIL, THE(1946); TARZAN AND THE LEOPARD WOMAN(1946); SONG OF MY HEART(1947); TANK COMMANDOS(1959); ROAD HUSTLERS, THE(1968), w; YOUNG GIANTS(1983)

Robert V. Barron
PRIVATE EYES, THE(1980); HONKYTONK MAN(1982)

Ronnie Barron
STONY ISLAND(1978)
1984
ANGEL(1984)

Sandy Barron
STRAIGHT TIME(1978)

Steve Barron
1984
ELECTRIC DREAMS(1984), d

Zelda Barron
1984
SECRET PLACES(1984, Brit.), d, w

Cecil Barror
BROTH OF A BOY(1959, Brit.)

Mario Barros
VALDEZ IS COMING(1971)

Sylvia Barrouillet
EGLANTINE(1972, Fr.)

Baynes Barrow
TANK BATTALION(1958)

Bernard Barrow
RACHEL, RACHEL(1968); GLASS HOUSES(1972); SERPICO(1973); JANE AUSTEN IN MANHATTAN(1980); SURVIVORS, THE(1983)

Bernie Barrow
CLAUDINE(1974)

Carlotta Barrow
STOP THE WORLD-I WANT TO GET OFF(1966, Brit.); BLACK PANTHER, THE(1977, Brit.), art d

Ernest Barrow
STRAWBERRY ROAN(1945, Brit.)

Henry Barrow
CHU CHU AND THE PHILLY FLASH(1981), w

Janet Barrow
TROUBLE IN THE GLEN(1954, Brit.); NOT WANTED ON VOYAGE(1957, Brit.); CURSE OF THE DEMON(1958)

John Barrow
ROLLING IN MONEY(1934, Brit.), p; BLUE SMOKE(1935, Brit.), p; TONS OF TROUBLE(1956, Brit.), w; JUNKET 89(1970, Brit.)

Dan Barrows
STEELYARD BLUES(1973); ANY WHICH WAY YOU CAN(1980); USED CARS(1980); BEACH GIRLS(1982); EATING RAOUL(1982); JEKYLL AND HYDE...TOGETHER AGAIN(1982)

Don Barrows
PRIVATE LESSONS(1981)

George Barrows
MAGNIFICENT DOLL(1946); JOAN OF ARC(1948); DREAMBOAT(1952); JALOPY(1953); ROBOT MONSTER(1953); OUTLAW'S DAUGHTER, THE(1954); SON OF SINBAD(1955); BEHIND THE HIGH WALL(1956); FIRST TRAVELING SALESLADY, THE(1956); FLIGHT TO HONG KONG(1956); KETTLES ON OLD MACDONALD'S FARM, THE(1957); NIGHT RUNNER, THE(1957); FRANKENSTEIN'S DAUGHTER(1958); IMITATION OF LIFE(1959); GHOST IN THE INVISIBLE BIKINI(1966); HILLBILLYS IN A HAUNTED HOUSE(1967); PANIC IN THE CITY(1968)

Geroge Barrows
MESA OF LOST WOMEN, THE(1956)

H. A. Barrows
Silents
END OF THE TRAIL, THE(1916); FIRES OF CONSCIENCE(1916); CAPTAIN OF THE GRAY HORSE TROOP, THE(1917)

H.A. Barrows
Misc. Silents
STAINLESS BARRIER, THE(1917); MAGIC EYE, THE(1918)

H.J. Barrows
Silents
ARE YOU LEGALLY MARRIED?(1919)

Harry A. Barrows
Misc. Silents
HER COUNTRY'S CALL(1917)

Harry Barrows
Silents
KAISER, BEAST OF BERLIN, THE(1918)
Henry A. Barrows
KIBITZER, THE(1929)
Silents
BRIDE'S SILENCE, THE(1917); ON RECORD(1917); GIRL WHO WOULDN'T QUIT, THE(1918); QUICKSANDS(1918); PURPLE CIPHER, THE(1920); RECKLESS AGE, THE(1924); ATTA BOY!(1926)
Misc. Silents
SUNSET TRAIL(1917); COME AGAIN SMITH(1919); CRACK O'DAWN(1925)
Henry Barrows
GUILTY HANDS(1931)
Silents
AMAZING IMPOSTER, THE(1919); GAMBLING IN SOULS(1919); MASTER STROKE, A(1920); IT CAN BE DONE(1921); GREAT NIGHT, THE(1922); PUTTING IT OVER(1922); TAILOR MADE MAN, A(1922); JAZZMANIA(1923); LONG LIVE THE KING(1923); SHOCK, THE(1923); COBRA(1925); MAN ON THE BOX, THE(1925); LITTLE IRISH GIRL, THE(1926); OH, WHAT A NURSE!(1926); SKINNER'S DRESS SUIT(1926); ALL ABOARD(1927); LOST LIMITED, THE(1927); SUNSET DERBY, THE(1927); THREE'S A CROWD(1927); WHITE PANTS WILLIE(1927)
Misc. Silents
HOBBS IN A HURRY(1918); HELLION, THE(1919); RIGHT TO HAPPINESS, THE(1919); TREMBLING HOUR, THE(1919); PHANTOM MELODY, THE(1920); RENT FREE(1922); WOMAN'S SIDE, THE(1922); YELLOW MEN AND GOLD(1922); DRUSILLA WITH A MILLION(1925); LOST EXPRESS, THE(1926); MISTAKEN ORDERS(1926); HORSE SHOES(1927); PERFECT GENTLEMAN, A(1928)
James Barrows
Silents
DANGEROUS TO MEN(1920); PRIDE OF PALOMAR, THE(1922); SEA BEAST, THE(1926)
Misc. Silents
OLD FOOL, THE(1923); TOMBOY, THE(1924)
James O. Barrows
Silents
LORD LOVES THE IRISH, THE(1919); INFERIOR SEX, THE(1920); STEPHEN STEPS OUT(1923); SIGNAL TOWER, THE(1924); GOOSE WOMAN, THE(1925)
Misc. Silents
DOWN HOME(1920); WHEN DAWN CAME(1920); WHITE DOVE, THE(1920); HURRICANE'S GAL(1922); GAIETY GIRL, THE(1924); YOUNG IDEAS(1924)
Leslie S. Barrows
SINGING FOOL, THE(1928), w; HONKY TONK(1929), w; MADONNA OF AVENUE A(1929), w
Nicholas Barrows
GRIDIRON FLASH(1935), w; DANGEROUS HOLIDAY(1937), d&w; THAT'S MY BABY(1944), w
Nicholas H. Barrows
SWING IT, PROFESSOR(1937), w
Nicholas T. Barrows
I'M FROM THE CITY(1938), w
Nick Barrows
MILLION DOLLAR LEGS(1932), w; DELINQUENT PARENTS(1938), w
Silents
MAN ON THE BOX, THE(1925), ph
Thomas Barrows
TWO WEEKS OFF(1929), w
Norman Barrs
HOSTILE WITNESS(1968, Brit.)
A. Barry
Silents
MUMSIE(1927, Brit.)
Alan Barry
LADIES OF THE CHORUS(1948); DEAD MAN'S EVIDENCE(1962, Brit.); CAPTAIN NEMO AND THE UNDERWATER CITY(1969, Brit.); LIMBO LINE, THE(1969, Brit.)
1984
SECRET PLACES(1984, Brit.)
Ann Barry
MAIDSTONE(1970)
B. Constance Barry
FAT ANGELS(1980, U.S./Span.); ARTHUR(1981); EASY MONEY(1983); TRADING PLACES(1983)
Baby Charlene Barry
Misc. Talkies
TRAIL'S END(1935)
Bart Barry
RED SUN(1972, Fr./Ital./Span.)
Barta Barry
SAIL INTO DANGER(1957, Brit.); GLADIATORS 7(1964, Span./Ital.); MAN WHO KILLED BILLY THE KID, THE(1967, Span./Ital.); SAVAGE PAMPAS(1967, Span./Arg.)
Bruce Barry
NED KELLY(1970, Brit.); PATRICK(1979, Aus.)
Misc. Talkies
PLUNGE INTO DARKNESS(1977)
Cecil A. Barry
Misc. Silents
BELONGING(1922, Brit.)
Cecil Barry
AMERICAN PRISONER, THE(1929 Brit.); ROMANCE OF SEVILLE, A(1929, Brit.)
Silents
ONE OF THE BEST(1927, Brit.); AFTERWARDS(1928, Brit.); BOLIBAR(1928, Brit.); DAWN(1928, Brit.)
Misc. Silents
SECOND MATE, THE(1929, Brit.)
Charline Barry
Misc. Talkies
RIDDLE RANCH(1936)

Christiane Barry
PERFECTIONIST, THE(1952, Fr.)
Christopher Barry
NAKED KISS, THE(1964); SOMETHING'S ROTTEN(1979, Can.)
Curly Pat Barry
ROCK YOU SINNERS(1957, Brit.)
D. F. Barry
WHY RUSSIANS ARE REVOLTING(1970)
Dave Barry
DEAD END(1937); THERE'S THAT WOMAN AGAIN(1938); SAILOR'S LADY(1940); LADIES OF THE CHORUS(1948); DALTON GANG, THE(1949); RED DESERT(1949); RINGSIDE(1949); SQUARE DANCE JUBILEE(1949); TOUGH ASSIGNMENT(1949); BORDER RANGERS(1950); GUNFIRE(1950); I SHOT BILLY THE KID(1950); TRAIN TO TOMBSTONE(1950), a, w; JESSE JAMES' WOMEN(1954), a, d; PLAYGIRL(1954); HIGH SOCIETY(1955); I'LL CRY TOMORROW(1955); TWINKLE IN GOD'S EYE, THE(1955); FOUR GIRLS IN TOWN(1956); CHINA DOLL(1958); VOICE IN THE MIRROR(1958); SOME LIKE IT HOT(1959); SPINOUT(1966); HOW TO SEDUCE A WOMAN(1974); SEABO(1978)
David Barry
LILITH(1964); KING OF THE MOUNTAIN(1981), w
Don "Red" Barry [Donald Barry]
LETTER OF INTRODUCTION(1938); FRONTIER VENGEANCE(1939); ONLY ANGELS HAVE WINGS(1939); WYOMING OUTLAW(1939); ONE MAN'S LAW(1940); TEXAS TERRORS(1940); TULSA KID, THE(1940); APACHE KID, THE(1941); DEATH VALLEY OUTLAWS(1941); DESERT BANDIT(1941); KANSAS CYCLONE(1941); PHANTOM COWBOY, THE(1941); TWO GUN SHERIFF(1941); WYOMING WILDCAT(1941); ARIZONA TERRORS(1942); CYCLONE KID, THE(1942); JESSE JAMES, JR.(1942); MISSOURI OUTLAW, A(1942); OUTLAWS OF PINE RIDGE(1942); SOMBRERO KID, THE(1942); STAGECOACH EXPRESS(1942); SUNDOWN KID, THE(1942); BLACK HILLS EXPRESS(1943); CANYON CITY(1943); CARSON CITY CYCLONE(1943); DAYS OF OLD CHEYENNE(1943); DEAD MAN'S GULCH(1943); FUGITIVE FROM SONORA(1943); MAN FROM THE RIO GRANDE, THE(1943); WEST SIDE KID(1943); CALIFORNIA JOE(1944); OUTLAWS OF SANTA FE(1944); BELLS OF ROSARITA(1945); OCEAN'S ELEVEN(1960); BUFFALO GUN(1961); WALK ON THE WILD SIDE(1962); LAW OF THE LAWLESS(1964); SHAKIEST GUN IN THE WEST, THE(1968); RIO LOBO(1970); JUNIOR BONNER(1972); HUSTLE(1975); FROM NOON TO THREE(1976); ORCA(1977); HOOPER(1978); HOT LEAD AND COLD FEET(1978); ONE MAN JURY(1978); SWARM, THE(1978); BACK ROADS(1981)
Misc. Talkies
BLAZING STEWARDESSES(1975)
Donald Barry [Don "Red" Barry]
THIS DAY AND AGE(1933); BELOVED ENEMY(1936); NIGHT WAITRESS(1936); LAST GANGSTER, THE(1937); NAVY BLUE AND GOLD(1937); WOMAN I LOVE, THE(1937); CROWD ROARS, THE(1938); DUKE OF WEST POINT, THE(1938); SINNERS IN PARADISE(1938); CALLING ALL MARINES(1939); CALLING DR. KILDARE(1939); DAYS OF JESSE JAMES(1939); FIRST OFFENDERS(1939); PANAMA PATROL(1939); SAGA OF DEATH VALLEY(1939); SECRET OF DR. KILDARE, THE(1939); S.O.S. TIDAL WAVE(1939); GHOST VALLEY RAIDERS(1940); MY BUDDY(1944); PURPLE HEART, THE(1944); CHICAGO KID, THE(1945); LAST CROOKED MILE, THE(1946); OUT CALIFORNIA WAY(1946); PLAINSMAN AND THE LADY(1946); THAT'S MY GAL(1947); LIGHTNIN' IN THE FOREST(1948); MADONNA OF THE DESERT(1948); SLIPPY MCGEE(1948); TRAIN TO ALCATRAZ(1948); UNTAMED HEIRESS(1954); SEVEN MEN FROM NOW(1956); GUN DUEL IN DURANGO(1957); FRANKENSTEIN 1970(1958); BORN RECKLESS(1959); LAST MILE, THE(1959); WARLOCK(1959); WALK LIKE A DRAGON(1960); ERRAND BOY, THE(1961); TWILIGHT OF HONOR(1963); CARPETBAGGERS, THE(1964); IRON ANGEL(1964); CONVICT STAGE(1965), a, w; FORT COURAGEOUS(1965); TOWN TAMER(1965); WAR PARTY(1965); ALVAREZ KELLY(1966); APACHE UPRISING(1966); FORT UTAH(1967); HOSTILE GUNS(1967); RED TOMAHAWK(1967); BANDOLERO!(1968); SHALAKO(1968, Brit.); COCKEYED COWBOYS OF CALICO COUNTY, THE(1970); DIRTY DINGUS MAGEE(1970); JOHNNY GOT HIS GUN(1971); WHIFFS(1975)
Donald M. Barry
REMEMBER PEARL HARBOR(1942); TRAITOR WITHIN, THE(1942)
Duece Barry
WEREWOLVES ON WHEELS(1971)
Ed Barry
CONVICTED(1931), w
Eddie Barry
Misc. Silents
SAGEBRUSH LADY, THE(1925); LOST EXPRESS, THE(1926); RED BLOOD(1926)
Eleanor Barry
Silents
CLIMBERS, THE(1915); NATION'S PERIL, THE(1915); NO TRESPASSING(1922)
Misc. Silents
GREAT RUBY, THE(1915); FLAMES OF JOHANNIS, THE(1916); FLAMING CLUE, THE(1920)
Eugene Barry
MILKY WAY, THE(1936)
Fern Barry
EVER SINCE EVE(1937); ACCIDENTS WILL HAPPEN(1938); COMET OVER BROADWAY(1938); GIRLS ON PROBATION(1938); EACH DAWN I DIE(1939); ESPIONAGE AGENT(1939); OFF THE RECORD(1939); LUCY GALLANT(1955); FUNNY FACE(1957); THREE BRAVE MEN(1957); SUNRISE AT CAMPOBELLO(1960); ATTIC, THE(1979)
Frank Barry
DR. TERROR'S HOUSE OF HORRORS(1965, Brit.); TERRORNAUTS, THE(1967, Brit.)
Gene Barry
ATOMIC CITY, THE(1952); GIRLS OF PLEASURE ISLAND, THE(1953); THOSE REDHEADS FROM SEATTLE(1953); WAR OF THE WORLDS, THE(1953); ALASKA SEAS(1954); NAKED ALIBI(1954); RED GARTERS(1954); PURPLE MASK, THE(1955); SOLDIER OF FORTUNE(1955); BACK FROM ETERNITY(1956); HOUSTON STORY, THE(1956); CHINA GATE(1957); FORTY GUNS(1957); 27TH DAY, THE(1957); HONG KONG CONFIDENTIAL(1958); THUNDER ROAD(1958); MAROC 7(1967, Brit.); SUBTERFUGE(1969, US/Brit.); SECOND COMING OF SUZANNE, THE(1974), a, p; GUYANA, CULT OF THE DAMNED(1980, Mex./Span./Panama)

George Barry
1984
FALLING IN LOVE(1984)
Gerald Barry
HIS GLORIOUS NIGHT(1929); UNHOLY NIGHT, THE(1929); GIRL OF THE PORT(1930); CHANNEL CROSSING(1934, Brit.); LAD, THE(1935, Brit.); ONCE IN A NEW MOON(1935, Brit.); RIGHT AGE TO MARRY, THE(1935, Brit.); CHEER UP!(1936, Brit.); CRIMES OF STEPHEN HAWKE, THE(1936, Brit.); EVERYTHING IN LIFE(1936, Brit.); IMPROPER DUCHESS, THE(1936, Brit.); IT'S YOU I WANT(1936, Brit.); LAST WALTZ, THE(1936, Brit.), a, d; RADIO LOVER(1936, Brit.); TROPICAL TROUBLE(1936, Brit.); KNIGHTS FOR A DAY(1937, Brit.); SCHOONER GANG, THE(1937, Brit.); EVERYTHING IS RHYTHM(1940, Brit.)
Gertrude Barry
Silents
HER GREAT CHANCE(1918)
Guerin Barry
DIFFERENT STORY, A(1978)
Henrietta Barry
LONG DARK HALL, THE(1951, Brit.)
Herbert Barry
Silents
KENNEDY SQUARE(1916)
Hilda Barry
TIGER IN THE SMOKE(1956, Brit.); SCOTLAND YARD DRAGNET(1957, Brit.); HORRORS OF THE BLACK MUSEUM(1959, U.S./Brit.); JOHN OF THE FAIR(1962, Brit.); NEVER BACK LOSERS(1967, Brit.); POOR COW(1968, Brit.); GOODBYE GEMINI(1970, Brit.); FRAGMENT OF FEAR(1971, Brit.); MELODY(1971, Brit.); CONFESSIONAL, THE(1977, Brit.)
Hilde Barry
ONE MILLION DOLLARS(1965, Ital.)
Ian Barry
STONE(1974, Aus.), ed; CHAIN REACTION(1980, Aus.), d&w
Ivor Barry
NOBODY WAVED GOODBYE(1965, Can.); KING'S PIRATE(1967); IN ENEMY COUNTRY(1968); LAWYER, THE(1969); DOVE, THE(1974, Brit.); HERBIE RIDES AGAIN(1974); ISLAND AT THE TOP OF THE WORLD, THE(1974); LOST IN THE STARS(1974); TO BE OR NOT TO BE(1983)
J. A. Barry
Silents
STRANGER THAN FICTION(1921), d
J. J. Barry
LAST OF THE RED HOT LOVERS(1972)
1984
THIS IS SPINAL TAP(1984)
J.A. Barry
Misc. Silents
PASSION'S PLAYGROUND(1920), d; TURNING POINT, THE(1920), d; TRUST YOUR WIFE(1921), d; WOMAN'S SIDE, THE(1922), d
J.J. Barry
HARPER VALLEY, P.T.A.(1978); HISTORY OF THE WORLD, PART 1(1981)
Jack Barry
EVERYTHING YOU ALWAYS WANTED TO KNOW ABOUT SEX, BUT WE'RE AFRAID TO ASK(1972)
Jean Barry
WHY LEAVE HOME?(1929); STRICTLY PERSONAL(1933)
Jeff Barry
IDOLMAKER, THE(1980), m
Jerry Barry
HELLO DOWN THERE(1969), m
Jimmie Barry
THESE THIRTY YEARS(1934)
Joan Barry
ATLANTIC(1929 Brit.); MAN OF MAYFAIR(1931, Brit.); EBB TIDE(1932, Brit.); FIRST MRS. FRASER, THE(1932, Brit.); RICH AND STRANGE(1932, Brit.); SALLY BISHOP(1932, Brit.); WOMEN WHO PLAY(1932, Brit.); MRS. DANE'S DEFENCE(1933, Brit.); OUTSIDER, THE(1933, Brit.); ROME EXPRESS(1933, Brit.); SERGEANT WAS A LADY, THE(1961)
Silents
HUTCH STIRS 'EM UP(1923, Brit.)
Misc. Silents
CARD, THE(1922, Brit.); HAPPY ENDING, THE(1925, Brit.)
Joan Nixon Barry
SPACE MASTER X-7(1958)
Joe Barry
MAN WITH THE GUN(1955); BELL, BOOK AND CANDLE(1958)
John A. Barry
Misc. Silents
FEAR WOMAN, THE(1919), d
John Barry
MATTER OF MURDER, A(1949, Brit.); DARK INTERVAL(1950, Brit.); SOMETHING MONEY CAN'T BUY(1952, Brit.); HOLLY AND THE IVY, THE(1954, Brit.); STREET OF SINNERS(1957); NEVER LET GO(1960, Brit.), m&md; DR. NO(1962, Brit.), m; L-SHAPED ROOM, THE(1962, Brit.), m; DREAM MAKER, THE(1963, Brit.); FROM RUSSIA WITH LOVE(1963, Brit.), m; GOLDFINGER(1964, Brit.), m; JOLLY BAD FELLOW, A(1964, Brit.), m; MAN IN THE MIDDLE(1964, U.S./Brit.), m, md; SEANCE ON A WET AFTERNOON(1964 Brit.), m, md; ZULU(1964, Brit.), m; AMOROUS MR. PRAWN, THE(1965, Brit.), m; IPCRESS FILE, THE(1965, Brit.), m, md; KING RAT(1965), m, md; KNACK ... AND HOW TO GET IT, THE(1965, Brit.), m; MISTER MOSES(1965), m, md; THUNDERBALL(1965, Brit.), m, md; BORN FREE(1966), m; CHASE, THE(1966), m; DUTCHMAN(1966, Brit.), m; PARTY'S OVER, THE(1966, Brit.), m; QUILLER MEMORANDUM, THE(1966, Brit.), m, md; WRONG BOX, THE(1966, Brit.), m&md; WHISPERERS, THE(1967, Brit.), m&md; YOU ONLY LIVE TWICE(1967, Brit.), m; BOOM!(1968), m; DEADFALL(1968, Brit.), a, m; LION IN WINTER, THE(1968, Brit.), m, md; PETULIA(1968, U.S./Brit.), m, md; APPOINTMENT, THE(1969), m; MIDNIGHT COWBOY(1969), m; ON HER MAJESTY'S SECRET SERVICE(1969, Brit.), m; MONTE WALSH(1970); CLOCKWORK ORANGE, A(1971, Brit.), prod d; DIAMONDS ARE FOREVER(1971, Brit.), m; LAST VALLEY, THE(1971, Brit.), m, md; MARY, QUEEN OF SCOTS(1971, Brit.), m; MURPHY'S WAR(1971, Brit.), m, md; THEY MIGHT BE GIANTS(1971), m; WALKABOUT(1971, Aus./U.S.), m, md; ALICE'S ADVENTURES IN WONDERLAND(1972, Brit.), m; PUB-

LIC EYE, THE(1972, Brit.), m, md; DOLL'S HOUSE, A(1973), m; DOVE, THE(1974, Brit.), m; LITTLE PRINCE, THE(1974, Brit.), prod d; MAN WITH THE GOLDEN GUN, THE(1974, Brit.), m; PHASE IV(1974), art d; TAMARIND SEED, THE(1974, Brit.), m; DAY OF THE LOCUST, THE(1975), m; LUCKY LADY(1975), prod d; KING KONG(1976), m; ROBIN AND MARIAN(1976, Brit.), m; DEEP, THE(1977), m; STAR WARS(1977), prod d; WHITE BUFFALO, THE(1977), m; BETSY, THE(1978), m; SUPERMAN(1978), prod d; BLACK HOLE, THE(1979), m; GAME OF DEATH, THE(1979), m; HANOVER STREET(1979, Brit.), m; MOONRAKER(1979, Brit.), m; STARCRASH(1979), m; INSIDE MOVES(1980), m; NIGHT GAMES(1980), m; RAISE THE TITANIC(1980, Brit.), m; SATURN 3(1980), w; SOMEWHERE IN TIME(1980), m; SUPERMAN II(1980), prod d; TOUCHED BY LOVE(1980), m; BODY HEAT(1981), m; LEGEND OF THE LONE RANGER, THE(1981), m; FRANCES(1982), m; HAMMETT(1982), m; HIGH ROAD TO CHINA(1983), m; OCTOPUSSY(1983, Brit.), m
1984
COTTON CLUB, THE(1984), m; MIKE'S MURDER(1984), m; UNTIL SEPTEMBER(1984), m
John G. Barry
SAN FERRY ANN(1965, Brit.), p
Johnathan Barry
DECLINE AND FALL... OF A BIRD WATCHER(1969, Brit.), art d
Jonathan Barry
KELLY'S HEROES(1970, U.S./Yugo.), prod d, art d; SITTING TARGET(1972, Brit.), prod d
Julian Barry
SECRET AGENT FIREBALL(1965, Fr./Ital.), w; LENNY(1974), w; RHINOCEROS(1974), w
1984
RIVER, THE(1984), w
Kenneth Barry
SPLIT IMAGE(1982)
Kevin Barry
SAINTLY SINNERS(1962), w
Leila Barry
LOST LAGOON(1958)
Leon Barry
Silents
THREE MUSKETEERS, THE(1921); JUNE MADNESS(1922); WHITE FLOWER, THE(1923)
Misc. Silents
GEORGE(; CALL OF HOME, THE(1922)
Leonard Barry
PATRICIA GETS HER MAN(1937, Brit.)
Margaret Barry
Misc. Silents
RESPECTABLE BY PROXY(1920)
Matthew Barry
LUNA(1979, Ital.)
Maurice Barry
CAROLINE CHERIE(1951, Fr.), ph; FRENCH, THEY ARE A FUNNY RACE, THE(1956, Fr.), ph; GIVE ME MY CHANCE(1958, Fr.), ph; LOVE IN A HOT CLIMATE(1958, Fr./Span.), ph; WOMAN OF SIN(1961, Fr.), ph; L'IMMORTELLE(1969, Fr./Ital./Turkey), ph
Michael Barry
STOP PRESS GIRL(1949, Brit.), d; SECOND COMING OF SUZANNE, THE(1974), d&w
Mona Barry
DETOUR(1945), cos
Neill Barry
HERO AT LARGE(1980)
1984
OLD ENOUGH(1984)
Patricia Barry
SHOW BOAT(1936); HUMORESQUE(1946); SLIGHTLY FRENCH(1949); SAFE AT HOME(1962); DEAR HEART(1964); KITTEN WITH A WHIP(1964); SEND ME NO FLOWERS(1964); MARRIAGE OF A YOUNG STOCKBROKER, THE(1971); END OF AUGUST, THE(1982); TWILIGHT ZONE-THE MOVIE(1983)
Patrick Barry
SONG OF THE FORGE(1937, Brit.)
Paul Barry
Misc. Talkies
BODY IS A SHELL, THE(1957); LEGACY OF SATAN(1973)
Paula Barry
EXPRESSO BONGO(1959, Brit.)
Philip Barry
PARIS BOUND(1929), w; HOLIDAY(1930), w; BARGAIN, THE(1931), w; ANIMAL KINGDOM, THE(1932), w; TOMORROW AND TOMORROW(1932), w; HOLIDAY(1938), w; PHILADELPHIA STORY, THE(1940), w; WITHOUT LOVE(1945), w; ONE MORE TOMORROW(1946), w; HIGH SOCIETY(1956), w
Philip Barry, Jr.
MATING GAME, THE(1959), p; SAIL A CROOKED SHIP(1961), p
Phillip Barry
SPRING MADNESS(1938), w
Phyllis Barry
CYNARA(1932); BLIND ADVENTURE(1933); DIPLOMANIACS(1933); WHAT! NO BEER?(1933); GOODBYE LOVE(1934); LONG LOST FATHER(1934); LOVE PAST THIRTY(1934); MARRIAGE ON APPROVAL(1934); MOONSTONE, THE(1934); WHERE SINNERS MEET(1934); FORBIDDEN HEAVEN(1936); ONE RAINY AFTERNOON(1936); AFFAIRS OF CAPPY RICKS(1937); BULLDOG DRUMMOND COMES BACK(1937); DAMAGED GOODS(1937); PRINCE AND THE PAUPER, THE(1937); INVISIBLE MENACE, THE(1938); TRADE WINDS(1938); WE ARE NOT ALONE(1939); SECRETS OF A MODEL(1940); CASE OF THE BLACK PARROT, THE(1941); GENTLEMAN FROM DIXIE(1941); SHADOWS ON THE STAIRS(1941); UNFINISHED BUSINESS(1941); MYSTERIOUS DOCTOR, THE(1943); FRENCHMAN'S CREEK(1944); LOVE FROM A STRANGER(1947)
Ray Barry
BETWEEN THE LINES(1977); GOODBYE GIRL, THE(1977); YOU BETTER WATCH OUT(1980)

Raymond Barry
LONG HAUL, THE(1957, Brit.)
Raymond J. Barry
UNMARRIED WOMAN, AN(1978)
Richard Barry
Silents
LAST ROSE OF SUMMER, THE(1920, Brit.)
Rocky Barry
ESCAPE TO BURMA(1955)
Ron Barry
MEATBALLS(1979, Can.)
Roque Barry
SALOME(1953)
Russell Barry
WHILE THE SUN SHINES(1950, Brit.)
Tom Barry
IN OLD ARIZONA(1929), w; THRU DIFFERENT EYES(1929), w; VALIANT, THE(1929), w; COURAGE(1930), w; SONG O' MY HEART(1930), w; EAST LYNNE(1931), w; OVER THE HILL(1931), w; UNDER SUSPICION(1931), w; MY BILL(1938), w
Tony Barry
BREAK OF DAY(1977, Aus.); IRISHMAN, THE(1978, Aus.); NEWSFRONT(1979, Aus.); ODD ANGRY SHOT, THE(1979, Aus.); EARTHLING, THE(1980); HARD KNOCKS(1980, Aus.); GOODBYE PORK PIE(1981, New Zealand); WE OF THE NEVER NEVER(1983, Aus.)
1984
PALLET ON THE FLOOR(1984, New Zealand)
Viola Barry
Silents
SEA-WOLF, THE(1913); JOHN BARLEYCORN(1914); FLYING TORPEDO, THE(1916)
Wendy Barry
SUMMER HOLIDAY(1963, Brit.); YOUNG GIRLS OF ROCHEFORT, THE(1968, Fr.)
Weslesy E. Barry
CREATION OF THE HUMANOIDS(1962), d
Wesley Barry
BORDER ROMANCE(1930); SUNNY SKIES(1930); THOROUGHBRED, THE(1930); HELL BENT FOR 'FRISCO(1931); ENLIGHTEN THY DAUGHTER(1934); LIFE OF VERGIE WINTERS, THE(1934); LET 'EM HAVE IT(1935); MEN OF THE HOUR(1935); PLOUGH AND THE STARS, THE(1936); PICK A STAR(1937); WILD MONEY(1937); HAVING WONDERFUL TIME(1938); MEXICALI KID, THE(1938); MR. DOODLE KICKS OFF(1938); STUNT PILOT(1939); LADIES' DAY(1943); ROCKY(1948), d; STEEL FIST, THE(1952), p&d; OUTLAW'S DAUGHTER, THE(1954), p&d; RACING BLOOD(1954), p&d, w
Misc. Talkies
TRAIL BLAZERS(1953), d
Silents
AMARILLY OF CLOTHESLINE ALLEY(1918); DADDY LONG LEGS(1919); MALE AND FEMALE(1919); DINTY(1920); BOB HAMPTON OF PLACER(1921); SCHOOL DAYS(1921); STRANGER THAN FICTION(1921); PENROD(1922); RAGS TO RICHES(1922); COUNTRY KID, THE(1923); FIGHTING CUB, THE(1925); IN OLD KENTUCKY(1927)
Misc. Silents
GEORGE(; COUNTY FAIR, THE(1920); GO AND GET IT(1920); BITS OF LIFE(1921); HEROES OF THE STREET(1922); PRINTER'S DEVIL, THE(1923); HIS OWN LAW(1924); BATTLING BUNYON(1925); MIDSHIPMAN, THE(1925); MY HOME TOWN(1925); TOP SERGEANT MULLIGAN(1928)
Wesley E. Barry
SEA TIGER(1952), p; CREATION OF THE HUMANOIDS(1962), p
Misc. Talkies
JOLLY GENIE, THE(1964), d
Wesley Barry, Jr.
NIGHT LIFE OF THE GODS(1935)
Winifred Barry
Silents
IRON MAN, THE(1925)
Yane Barry
HEAT OF THE SUMMER(1961, Fr.); MAN AND A WOMAN, A(1966, Fr.); TO BE A CROOK(1967, Fr.)
Zena Barry
GOOD DIE YOUNG, THE(1954, Brit.)
Barry Twins
DODGING THE DOLE(1936, Brit.)
Wesley Barry, Jr.
NIGHT LIFE OF THE GODS(1935)
Emily Barrye
GODLESS GIRL, THE(1929)
Silents
VOLCANO(1926); KING OF KINGS, THE(1927)
Misc. Silents
FAST FIGHTIN'(1925)
Diana Barrymore
BETWEEN US GIRLS(1942); EAGLE SQUADRON(1942); NIGHTMARE(1942); FIRED WIFE(1943); FRONTIER BADMEN(1943); LADIES COURAGEOUS(1944); TOO MUCH, TOO SOON(1958), w
Dolores Costello Barrymore
LITTLE LORD FAUNTLEROY(1936); YOURS FOR THE ASKING(1936)
Drew Barrymore
ALTERED STATES(1980); E.T. THE EXTRA-TERRESTRIAL(1982)
1984
FIRESTARTER(1984); IRRECONCILABLE DIFFERENCES(1984)
Ethel Barrymore
RASPUTIN AND THE EMPRESS(1932); NONE BUT THE LONELY HEART(1944); SPIRAL STAIRCASE, THE(1946); FARMER'S DAUGHTER, THE(1947); MOSS ROSE(1947); NIGHT SONG(1947); PARADINE CASE, THE(1947); MOONRISE(1948); GREAT SINNER, THE(1949); PINKY(1949); PORTRAIT OF JENNIE(1949); RED DANUBE, THE(1949); THAT MIDNIGHT KISS(1949); IT'S A BIG COUNTRY(1951); KIND LADY(1951); SECRET OF CONVICT LAKE, THE(1951); DEADLINE-U.S.A.(1952); JUST FOR YOU(1952); MAIN STREET TO BROADWAY(1953); STORY OF THREE LOVES, THE(1953); YOUNG AT HEART(1955); JOHNNY TROUBLE(1957)

Silents
NIGHTINGALE, THE(1914); AMERICAN WIDOW, AN(1917); LIFE'S WHIRLPOOL(1917); OUR MRS. McCHESNEY(1918)
Misc. Silents
FINAL JUDGEMENT, THE(1915); AWAKENING OF HELENA RICHIE, THE(1916); KISS OF HATE, THE(1916); CALL OF HER PEOPLE, THE(1917); ETERNAL MOTHER, THE(1917); GREATEST POWER, THE(1917); LIFTED VEIL, THE(1917); DIVORCEE, THE(1919)
John Barrymore
GENERAL CRACK(1929); MAN FROM BLANKLEY'S, THE(1930); MOBY DICK(1930); MAD GENIUS, THE(1931); SVENGALI(1931); ARSENE LUPIN(1932); BILL OF DIVORCEMENT, A(1932); GRAND HOTEL(1932); RASPUTIN AND THE EMPRESS(1932); STATE'S ATTORNEY(1932); COUNSELLOR-AT-LAW(1933); DINNER AT EIGHT(1933); NIGHT FLIGHT(1933); REUNION IN VIENNA(1933); TOPAZE(1933); LONG LOST FATHER(1934); TWENTIETH CENTURY(1934); ROMEO AND JULIET(1936); BULLDOG DRUMMOND COMES BACK(1937); BULLDOG DRUMMOND'S REVENGE(1937); MAYTIME(1937); NIGHT CLUB SCANDAL(1937); TRUE CONFESSION(1937); BULLDOG DRUMMOND'S PERIL(1938); HOLD THAT CO-ED(1938); MARIE ANTOINETTE(1938); ROMANCE IN THE DARK(1938); SPAWN OF THE NORTH(1938); GREAT MAN VOTES, THE(1939); MIDNIGHT(1939); GREAT PROFILE, THE(1940); INVISIBLE WOMAN, THE(1941); PLAYMATES(1941); WORLD PREMIERE(1941)
Silents
ARE YOU A MASON?(1915); INCORRIGIBLE DUKANE, THE(1915); LOST BRIDEGROOM, THE(1916); NEARLY A KING(1916); RED WIDOW, THE(1916); ON THE QUIET(1918); DR. JEKYLL AND MR. HYDE(1920); SHERLOCK HOLMES(1922), a, art d; BEAU BRUMMEL(1924); DON JUAN(1926); SEA BEAST, THE(1926); BELOVED ROGUE, THE(1927); TEMPEST(1928); ETERNAL LOVE(1929)
Misc. Silents
MAN FROM MEXICO, THE(1914); RAFFLES, THE AMATEUR CRACKSMAN(1917); TEST OF HONOR, THE(1919); LOTUS EATER, THE(1921); WHEN A MAN LOVES(1927)
John Barrymore, Jr.
HIGH LONESOME(1950); SUNDOWNERS, THE(1950); BIG NIGHT, THE(1951); QUEBEC(1951); THUNDERBIRDS(1952); WHILE THE CITY SLEEPS(1956); SHADOW ON THE WINDOW, THE(1957); CLONES, THE(1973)
John Blyth Barrymore
NOCTURNA(1979); SMOKEY BITES THE DUST(1981); TRICK OR TREATS(1982)
1984
HARD TO HOLD(1984)
John Blythe Barrymore
BABY BLUE MARINE(1976); ONE MAN JURY(1978); FULL MOON HIGH(1982)
John Drew Barrymore
ER LOVE A STRANGER(1958); HIGH SCHOOL CONFIDENTIAL(1958); NIGHT OF THE QUARTER MOON(1959); COSSACKS, THE(1960, It.); PHAROAH'S WOMAN, THE(1961, Ital.); CENTURION, THE(1962, Fr./Ital.); NIGHT THEY KILLED RASPUTIN, THE(1962, Fr./Ital.); TROJAN HORSE, THE(1962, Fr./Ital.); CHRISTINE KEELER AFFAIR, THE(1964, Brit.); INVASION 1700(1965, Fr./Ital./Yugo.); WAR OF THE ZOMBIES, THE(1965 Ital.); PONTIUS PILATE(1967, Fr./Ital.); THIS SAVAGE LAND(1969)
Katherine Harris Barrymore
Misc. Silents
HOUSE OF MIRTH, THE(1918)
Lionel Barrymore
ALIAS JIMMY VALENTINE(1928); LION AND THE MOUSE, THE(1928); RIVER WOMAN, THE(1928); HIS GLORIOUS NIGHT(1929), d, m; MADAME X(1929), d; MYSTERIOUS ISLAND(1929); UNHOLY NIGHT, THE(1929), d; FREE AND EASY(1930); ROGUE SONG, THE(1930), p&d; FREE SOUL, A(1931); GUILTY HANDS(1931); MATA HARI(1931); TEN CENTS A DANCE(1931), d; YELLOW TICKET, THE(1931); ARSENE LUPIN(1932); BROKEN LULLABY(1932); GRAND HOTEL(1932); RASPUTIN AND THE EMPRESS(1932); WASHINGTON MASQUERADE(1932); BERKELEY SQUARE(1933); CHRISTOPHER BEAN(1933); DINNER AT EIGHT(1933); LOOKING FORWARD(1933); NIGHT FLIGHT(1933); ONE MAN'S JOURNEY(1933); SHOULD LADIES BEHAVE?(1933); STRANGER'S RETURN(1933); SWEEPINGS(1933); CAROLINA(1934); GIRL FROM MISSOURI, THE(1934); THIS SIDE OF HEAVEN(1934); TREASURE ISLAND(1934); AH, WILDERNESS!(1935); DAVID COPPERFIELD(1935); LITTLE COLONEL, THE(1935); MARK OF THE VAMPIRE(1935); PUBLIC HERO NO. 1(1935); RETURN OF PETER GRIMM, THE(1935); DEVIL DOLL, THE(1936); GORGEOUS HUSSY, THE(1936); ROAD TO GLORY, THE(1936); VOICE OF BUGLE ANN(1936); CAMILLE(1937); CAPTAINS COURAGEOUS(1937); FAMILY AFFAIR, A(1937); NAVY BLUE AND GOLD(1937); SARATOGA(1937); TEST PILOT(1938); YANK AT OXFORD, A(1938); YOU CAN'T TAKE IT WITH YOU(1938); YOUNG DR. KILDARE(1938); CALLING DR. KILDARE(1939); LET FREEDOM RING(1939); ON BORROWED TIME(1939); SECRET OF DR. KILDARE, THE(1939); DR. KILDARE GOES HOME(1940); DR. KILDARE'S CRISIS(1940); DR. KILDARE'S STRANGE CASE(1940); BAD MAN, THE(1941); DR. KILDARE'S VICTORY(1941); DR. KILDARE'S WEDDING DAY(1941); LADY BE GOOD(1941); PENALTY, THE(1941); PEOPLE VS. DR. KILDARE, THE(1941); CALLING DR. GILLESPIE(1942); DR. GILLESPIE'S NEW ASSISTANT(1942); TENNESSEE JOHNSON(1942); DR. GILLESPIE'S CRIMINAL CASE(1943); GUY NAMED JOE, A(1943); THOUSANDS CHEER(1943); BETWEEN TWO WOMEN(1944); DRAGON SEED(1944); SINCE YOU WENT AWAY(1944); THREE MEN IN WHITE(1944); VALLEY OF DECISION, THE(1945); DUEL IN THE SUN(1946); IT'S A WONDERFUL LIFE(1946); THREE WISE FOOLS(1946); DARK DELUSION(1947); KEY LARGO(1948); DOWN TO THE SEA IN SHIPS(1949); MALAYA(1950); RIGHT CROSS(1950); BANNERLINE(1951); LONE STAR(1952); MAIN STREET TO BROADWAY(1953)
Silents
CLASSMATES(1914); SEATS OF THE MIGHTY, THE(1914); BRAND OF COWARDICE, THE(1916); HIS FATHER'S SON(1917); LIFE'S WHIRLPOOL(1917), d&w; MASTER MIND, THE(1920); JIM THE PENMAN(1921); ENEMIES OF WOMEN, THE(1923); AMERICA(1924); DECAMERON NIGHTS(1924, Brit.); GIRL WHO WOULDN'T WORK, THE(1925); IRON MAN, THE(1925); SPLENDID ROAD, THE(1925); BARRIER, THE(1926); TEMPTRESS, THE(1926); ROAD HOUSE(1928); SADIE THOMPSON(1928); WEST OF ZANZIBAR(1928)
Misc. Silents
POWER OF THE PRESS, THE(1914); SPAN OF LIFE, THE(1914); WOMAN IN BLACK, THE(1914); DORA THORNE(1915); MODERN MAGDALEN, A(1915); WILDFIRE(1915); YELLOW STREAK, A(1915); DORIAN'S DIVORCE(1916); QUITTER, THE(1916); UPHEAVAL, THE(1916); END OF THE TOUR, THE(1917); MILLIONAIRE'S DOUBLE, THE(1917); COPPERHEAD, THE(1920); DEVIL'S GARDEN,

THE(1920); GREAT ADVENTURE, THE(1921); BOOMERANG BILL(1922); FACE IN THE FOG, THE(1922); ETERNAL CITY, THE(1923); UNSEEING EYES(1923); I AM THE MAN(1924); MEDDLING WOMEN(1924); CHILDREN OF THE WHIRL-WIND(1925); FIFTY-FIFTY(1925); WRONG DOERS, THE(1925); BELLS, THE(1926); BROODING EYES(1926); LUCKY LADY, THE(1926); PARIS AT MIDNIGHT(1926); BODY AND SOUL(1927); SHOW, THE(1927); THIRTEENTH HOUR, THE(1927); WOMEN LOVE DIAMONDS(1927); DRUMS OF LOVE(1928); RIVER WOMAN(1929)

Romeo Barrymore
RAT PFINK AND BOO BOO(1966)

William Barrymore
Misc. Talkies
RAWHIDE TERROR, THE(1934)
Misc. Silents
MILLIONAIRE ORPHAN, THE(1926); SECLUDED ROADHOUSE, THE(1926); GREY STREAK, THE(1927); RACING ROMANCE(1927); BATTLING BOOKWORM(1928); TRIPLE PASS(1928); MIDNIGHT ON THE BARBARY COAST(1929)

A. Barsacq
CHILDREN OF PARADISE(1945, Fr.), art d

Leom Barsacq
THREE FABLES OF LOVE(1963, Fr./Ital./Span.), art d

Leon Barsacq
CROSS OF THE LIVING(, art d; LA MARSEILLAISE(1938, Fr.), set d; LE MONDE TREMBLERA(1939, Fr.), art d; LUMIERE D'ETE(1943, Fr.), art d; ANGEL AND SINNER(1947, Fr.), art d; LES DERNIERES VACANCES(1947, Fr.), art d; MAN ABOUT TOWN(1947, Fr.), art d; BEAUTY AND THE DEVIL(1952, Fr./Ital.), art d; LES BELLES-DE-NUIT(1952, Fr.), prod d; GRAND MANEUVER, THE(1956, Fr.), art d; GATES OF PARIS(1958, Fr./Ital.), art d; LONGEST DAY, THE(1962), art d; VISIT, THE(1964, Ger./Fr./Ital./U.S.), art d; SYMPHONY FOR A MASSACRE(1965, Fr./Ital.), art d

Yves Barsacq
LOVE ON A PILLOW(1963, Fr./Ital.); MAGNIFICENT SINNER(1963, Fr.); SEVENTH JUROR, THE(1964, Fr.); SWEET SKIN(1965, Fr./Ital.); TWO FOR THE ROAD(1967, Brit.); UPPER HAND, THE(1967, Fr./Ital./Ger.); HIT(1973); LOVE AND DEATH(1975)

Leon Barsacqu
AMBASSADOR'S DAUGHTER, THE(1956), art d

Alberto Barsanti
GIANT OF MARATHON, THE(1960, Ital.), w

Monique Barscha
EVERY MAN FOR HIMSELF(1980, Fr.)

Dieter Barsche
AFFAIRS OF DR. HOLL(1954, Ger.)

Leon Barsche
BABY FACE NELSON(1957), ed

Paul Barselou
YOUR THREE MINUTES ARE UP(1973); BALTIMORE BULLET, THE(1980)

Paul Barselow
DON'T MAKE WAVES(1967)

Leon Barsha
BROADWAY SCANDALS(1929), ed; MEXICALI ROSE(1929), ed; GUILTY?(1930), ed; FIGHTING RANGER, THE(1934), ed; ONE MAN JUSTICE(1937), d; TRAP-PED(1937), d; TWO-FISTED SHERIFF(1937), d; TWO GUN LAW(1937), d; CONVICT-ED(1938), d; WHO KILLED GAIL PRESTON?(1938), d; MANHATTAN SHAKEDOWN(1939), d; MURDER IS NEWS(1939), d; SPECIAL INSPECTOR(1939), d; TAMING OF THE WEST, THE(1939), p; MAN FROM TUMBLEWEEDS, THE(1940), p; PIONEERS OF THE FRONTIER(1940), p; RETURN OF WILD BILL, THE(1940), p; TEXAS STAGECOACH(1940), p; TWO-FISTED RANGERS(1940), p; WEST OF ABI-LENE(1940), p; BEYOND THE SACRAMENTO(1941), p; KING OF DODGE CI-TY(1941), p; NORTH FROM LONE STAR(1941), p; OFFICER AND THE LADY, THE(1941), p; RETURN OF DANIEL BOONE, THE(1941), p; SING FOR YOUR SUPPER(1941), p; SON OF DAVY CROCKETT, THE(1941), p; WILDCAT OF TUC-SON(1941), p; DEVIL'S TRAIL, THE(1942), p; LONE PRAIRIE, THE(1942), p; LONE STAR VIGILANTES, THE(1942), p; POWER OF THE PRESS(1943), p; RIDERS OF THE NORTHWEST MOUNTED(1943), p; SILVER CITY RAIDERS(1943), p; LAST HORSEMAN, THE(1944), p; SING WHILE YOU DANCE(1946), p; PACE THAT THRILLS, THE(1952), d; SUDDEN FEAR(1952), ed; TARZAN AND THE SHE-DE-VIL(1953), ed; BULLET FOR JOEY, A(1955), ed; TARZAN'S HIDDEN JUNGLE(1955), ed; HIDDEN GUNS(1956), ed; HOT ROD GIRL(1956), ed; WALK THE DARK STREET(1956), ed; CARELESS YEARS, THE(1957), ed; LIZZIE(1957), ed; RIDE OUT FOR REVENGE(1957), ed; SIERRA STRANGER(1957), ed; SPRING REUNION(1957), ed; GIRLS' TOWN(1959), ed; MIDNIGHT LACE(1960), ed; LONELY ARE THE BRAVE(1962), ed; LADY IN A CAGE(1964), ed

Bela Barsi
ROUND UP, THE(1969, Hung.)

Bud Barskey
Silents
PRIDE OF SUNSHINE ALLEY(1924), sup

Odile Barski
VIOLETTE(1978, Fr.), w

Aaron Barsky
I, THE JURY(1982)

Bud Barsky
WALLABY JIM OF THE ISLANDS(1937), p
Misc. Silents
COAST PATROL, THE(1925), d

Georges Barsky
MADLY(1970, Fr.), ph; WE'LL GROW THIN TOGETHER(1979, Fr.), ph

V. Barsky
SEEDS OF FREEDOM(1943, USSR)

Vladimir Barsky
Silents
BATTLESHIP POTEMKIN, THE(1925, USSR)

Elsie Benjamin Barsoe
HIGH WIND IN JAMAICA, A(1965)

Paul Barsolow
COMEDY OF TERRORS, THE(1964)

Andor Sarnes Istvan Barsony
HIPPOLYT, THE LACKEY(1932, Hung.)

Sacha Barsov
THREE TALES OF CHEKHOV(1961, USSR)

Margaret Barstow
FROM HERE TO ETERNITY(1953)

Richard Barstow
GREATEST SHOW ON EARTH, THE(1952), ch; GIRL NEXT DOOR, THE(1953), ch; STAR IS BORN, A(1954), ch

Stan Barstow
KIND OF LOVING, A(1962, Brit.), w

Lester Barstow [Ben Hecht]
WHIRLPOOL(1949), w

Beata Barszczewska
YELLOW SLIPPERS, THE(1965, Pol.)

Bart
DUKE WORE JEANS, THE(1958, Brit.), m

Daniel Bart
MADE IN U.S.A.(1966, Fr.); OLDEST PROFESSION, THE(1968, Fr./Ital./Ger.)

Jacques Bart
NO EXIT(1962, U.S./Arg.), ed

Jan Bart
CATSKILL HONEYMOON(1950)

Jean Bart
SQUALL, THE(1929), w; MAN WHO RECLAIMED HIS HEAD, THE(1935), w; MAD EMPRESS, THE(1940), w; STRANGE CONFESSION(1945), w

Lionel Bart
DUKE WORE JEANS, THE(1958, Brit.), w; MAN IN THE MIDDLE(1964, U.S./Brit.), m; OLIVER!(1968, Brit.), w, m; LOCK UP YOUR DAUGHTERS(1969, Brit.), w; BLACK BEAUTY(1971, Brit./Ger./Span.), m; OPTIMISTS, THE(1973, Brit.), m

Norman Bart
CLOPORTES(1966, Fr., Ital.)

Peter Bart
MAKING IT(1971), w; FUN WITH DICK AND JANE(1977), p; ISLANDS IN THE STREAM(1977), p

Una Bart
NICHOLAS NICKLEBY(1947, Brit.)

Jindrick Barta
FANTASTIC PLANET(1973, Fr./Czech.), anim

John Barta
WAR BETWEEN THE PLANETS(1971, Ital.)

Gino Bartali
LOVE, THE ITALIAN WAY(1964, Ital.)

K. Bartashevich
CLEAR SKIES(1963, USSR)

Konstantin Bartashevich
SKY CALLS, THE(1959, USSR)

Barbara Bartay
NEVER SAY GOODBYE(1956)

Josef Bartczak
BEADS OF ONE ROSARY, THE(1982, Pol.), ed

Morton Barteaux
SIX HOURS TO LIVE(1932), w; TILL WE MEET AGAIN(1936), w

Eddie Bartel
EVERY NIGHT AT EIGHT(1935); LADY ON A TRAIN(1945)

Jean Bartel
SANCTUARY(1961); OSCAR, THE(1966)

Jose Bartel
YOUNG GIRLS OF ROCHEFORT, THE(1968, Fr.)

Paul Bartel
PRIVATE PARTS(1972), d; DEATH RACE 2000(1975), d; CANNONBALL(1976, U.S./Hong Kong), a, d, w; EAT MY DUST!(1976); HOLLYWOOD BOULEVARD(1976); GRAND THEFT AUTO(1977); MR. BILLION(1977); PIRANHA(1978); ROCK 'N' ROLL HIGH SCHOOL(1979); HEARTBEEPS(1981); EATING RAOUL(1982), a, d, w; TRICK OR TREATS(1982); WHITE DOG(1982); GET CRAZY(1983); HEART LIKE A WHEEL(1983)
1984
NOT FOR PUBLICATION(1984), d, w

Wendy Bartel
CANNONBALL(1976, U.S./Hong Kong)

Buster Bartell
THIRTEEN WOMEN(1932)

Dick Bartell
DESIGN FOR SCANDAL(1941); PHANTOM OF THE OPERA(1943); THOROUGH-BREDS(1945); NIGHT AND DAY(1946); POSSESSED(1947); VOICE OF THE TURTLE, THE(1947); GIRL FROM JONES BEACH, THE(1949); KNOCK ON ANY DOOR(1949); THIS WOMAN IS DANGEROUS(1952)

Eddie Bartell
LOUISIANA HAYRIDE(1944); TROCADERO(1944); BLONDE FROM BROOK-LYN(1945); PAL JOEY(1957)

Harry Bartell
DESTINATION TOKYO(1944); MONKEY BUSINESS(1952); GIRL WHO HAD EV-ERYTHING, THE(1953); DRAGNET(1954); BLACK TUESDAY(1955); SIX BRIDGES TO CROSS(1955); JOHNNY CONCHO(1956); AFFAIR IN RENO(1957); DECKS RAN RED, THE(1958); VOICE IN THE MIRROR(1958)

Phill Bartell
WILD WHEELS(1969)

R.D. Bartell
HATS OFF(1937)

Richard Bartell
SABOTAGE SQUAD(1942); GILDERSLEEVE'S BAD DAY(1943); I ACCUSE MY PARENTS(1945); SPELLBOUND(1945); UNDERCOVER MAN, THE(1949); BATTLING MARSHAL(1950); PERFECT STRANGERS(1950); TWO LOST WORLDS(1950); WOM-AN OF DISTINCTION, A(1950); ABBOTT AND COSTELLO MEET THE INVISIBLE MAN(1951); ENFORCER, THE(1951); VANQUISHED, THE(1953); JIVARO(1954)

Tim Bartell
1984
MEATBALLS PART II(1984)

Victor Bartell
HELL'S ISLAND(1955)

Barbara Bartelme
CAT ATE THE PARAKEET, THE(1972)
Dieter Bartels
QUESTION 7(1961, U.S./Ger.), art d; ESCAPE FROM EAST BERLIN(1962), art d; CITY OF SECRETS(1963, Ger.), ph; STOP TRAIN 349(1964, Fr./Ital./Ger.), set d
Erich Bartels
FINAL CHORD, THE(1936, Ger.)
Kay Bartels
CHARTROOSE CABOOSE(1960)
Louis J. Bartels
NOTHING BUT THE TRUTH(1929)
Louis John Bartels
CANARY MURDER CASE, THE(1929); FLORODORA GIRL, THE(1930); SIN TAKES A HOLIDAY(1930); BIG SHOT, THE(1931); PRODIGAL, THE(1931)
Misc. Silents
BROADWAY NIGHTS(1927)
Louis Jordan Bartels
Misc. Silents
DANCE MAGIC(1927)
John Barten
WINDSPLITTER, THE(1971)
George Bartenieff
DOUBLE-BARRELLED DETECTIVE STORY, THE(1965); ZERO IN THE UNIVERSE(1966); HERCULES IN NEW YORK(1970); HOT ROCK, THE(1972)
Jeffery Barter
GEORGE(1973, U.S./Switz.), a, animal t
John Barter
BIRDS OF A FEATHER(1935, Brit.), p; JIMMY BOY(1935, Brit.), p; REAL BLOKE, A(1935, Brit.), p; SMALL MAN, THE(1935, Brit.), p; MEN OF YESTERDAY(1936, Brit.), p; SONG OF THE ROAD(1937, Brit.), p; TALKING FEET(1937, Brit.), p; STEPPING TOES(1938, Brit.), p
Charles Bartfield
PASSION HOLIDAY(1963)
Eva Bartfield
PASSION HOLIDAY(1963)
David Barth
REVENGE OF THE NINJA(1983)
Ed Barth
BANANAS(1971); MADE FOR EACH OTHER(1971); SHAFT(1971); THUNDER AND LIGHTNING(1977)
Eddie Barth
BOARDWALK(1979); FAME(1980)
Isolde Barth
DESPAIR(1978, Ger.); MARRIAGE OF MARIA BRAUN, THE(1979, Ger.); IN A YEAR OF THIRTEEN MOONS(1980, Ger.); LOLA(1982, Ger.); QUERELLE(1983, Ger./Fr.)
Joseph Barth
MISTRESS OF ATLANTIS, THE(1932, Ger.), ph
Julie Barth
OCTOPUSSY(1983, Brit.)
Roger Barth
DAS BOOT(1982)
Janos Bartha
MISSION STARDUST(1968, Ital./Span./Ger.); SABATA(1969, Ital.); RETURN OF SABATA(1972, Ital./Fr./Ger.)
John Bartha
KILL THEM ALL AND COME BACK ALONE(1970, Ital./Span.); THIS MAN CAN'T DIE(1970, Ital.); DIRTY OUTLAWS, THE(1971, Ital.); JOHNNY HAMLET(1972, Ital.); DAISY MILLER(1974)
Richard Barthelmess
DRAG(1929); WEARY RIVER(1929); YOUNG NOWHERES(1929); DAWN PATROL, THE(1930); LASH, THE(1930); SON OF THE GODS(1930); FINGER POINTS, THE(1931); LAST FLIGHT, THE(1931); ALIAS THE DOCTOR(1932); CABIN IN THE COTTON(1932); CENTRAL AIRPORT(1933); HEROES FOR SALE(1933); MASSACRE(1934); MIDNIGHT ALIBI(1934); MODERN HERO, A(1934); FOUR HOURS TO KILL(1935); ONLY ANGELS HAVE WINGS(1939); SPY OF NAPOLEON(1939, Brit.); MAN WHO TALKED TOO MUCH, THE(1940); MAYOR OF 44TH STREET, THE(1942); SPOILERS, THE(1942)
Silents
BAB'S BURGLAR(1917); BAB'S DIARY(1917); ETERNAL SIN, THE(1917); BROKEN BLOSSOMS(1919); GIRL WHO STAYED AT HOME, THE(1919); I'LL GET HIM YET(1919); SCARLET DAYS(1919); IDOL DANCER, THE(1920); LOVE FLOWER, THE(1920); WAY DOWN EAST(1920); TOL'ABLE DAVID(1921); JUST A SONG AT TWILIGHT(1922); SEVENTH DAY, THE(1922); SONNY(1922); CLASSMATES(1924); ENCHANTED COTTAGE, THE(1924); SHORE LEAVE(1925); AMATEUR GENTLEMAN, THE(1926); JUST SUPPOSE(1926); RANSON'S FOLLY(1926); WHITE BLACK SHEEP, THE(1926); DROPKICK, THE(1927); NOOSE, THE(1928); SCARLET SEAS(1929)
Misc. Silents
FOR VALOUR(1917); MORAL CODE, THE(1917); STREETS OF ILLUSION, THE(1917); VALENTINE GIRL, THE(1917); HOPE CHEST, THE(1918); RICH MAN, POOR MAN(1918); SEVEN SWANS, THE(1918); SUNSHINE NAN(1918); WILD PRIMROSE(1918); BOOTS(1919); PEPPY POLLY(1919); THREE MEN AND A GIRL(1919); EXPERIENCE(1921); BOND BOY, THE(1922); FURY(1922); BRIGHT SHAWL, THE(1923); FIGHTING BLADE, THE(1923); TWENTY-ONE(1923); BEAUTIFUL CITY, THE(1925); NEW TOYS(1925); SOUL-FIRE(1925); PATENT LEATHER KID, THE(1927); LITTLE SHEPHERD OF KINGDOM COME(1928); OUT OF THE RUINS(1928); WHEEL OF CHANCE(1928)
Nikki Barthen
REDEEMER, THE(1978)
Jean Barthet
YESTERDAY, TODAY, AND TOMORROW(1964, Ital./Fr.), cos; YOUNG GIRLS OF ROCHEFORT, THE(1968, Fr.), cos; DELUSIONS OF GRANDEUR(1971 Fr.), cos
Philip Bartholomae
BARNUM WAS RIGHT(1929), w
Silents
SERPENT, THE(1916), w; OUTSIDE WOMAN, THE(1921), w
Phillip Bartholomae
Silents
LITTLE MISS BROWN(1915), w

Agnes Bartholomew
MAN CALLED PETER, THE(1955)
Freddie Bartholomew
FASCINATION(1931, Brit.); ANNA KARENINA(1935); DAVID COPPERFIELD(1935); DEVIL IS A SISSY, THE(1936); LITTLE LORD FAUNTLEROY(1936); PROFESSIONAL SOLDIER(1936); CAPTAINS COURAGEOUS(1937); KIDNAPPED(1938); LISTEN, DARLING(1938); LORD JEFF(1938); SPIRIT OF CULVER, THE(1939); TWO BRIGHT BOYS(1939); SWISS FAMILY ROBINSON(1940); TOM BROWN'S SCHOOL DAYS(1940); NAVAL ACADEMY(1941); YANK AT ETON, A(1942); JUNIOR ARMY(1943); TOWN WENT WILD, THE(1945); SEPIA CINDERELLA(1947); ST. BENNY THE DIP(1951)
Misc. Talkies
CADETS ON PARADE(1942)
Ian Bartholomew
1984
BREAKOUT(1984, Brit.)
John Bartholomew
NATURAL ENEMIES(1979)
Miss Bartholomew
Silents
BREWSTER'S MILLIONS(1914)
Ron Bartholomew
TAKE DOWN(1979)
Sunny Bartholomew
Misc. Talkies
FROZEN SCREAM(1980)
Collette Barthrop
CROOKED SKY, THE(1957, Brit.)
Roland Barthrop
CAST A GIANT SHADOW(1966)
Marina Barti
DEPORTED(1950)
Stefan Bartik
EVE WANTS TO SLEEP(1961, Pol.)
Elizabeth Bartilet
MISS SADIE THOMPSON(1953)
"Bartimeus"
FULL SPEED AHEAD(1939, Brit.), w
Eva Bartis
CONFIDENCE(1980, Hung.)
Georges Bartis
APOLLO GOES ON HOLIDAY(1968, Ger./Swed.)
Andrzei Bartkowiak
DANIEL(1983), ph
Andrzej Bartkowiak
DEADLY HERO(1976), ph; PRINCE OF THE CITY(1981), ph; DEATHTRAP(1982), ph; VERDICT, THE(1982), ph; TERMS OF ENDEARMENT(1983), ph
1984
GARBO TALKS(1984), ph
Pavel Bartl
SWEET LIGHT IN A DARK ROOM(1966, Czech.)
Dorothy Bartlam
BIRDS OF A FEATHER(1931, Brit.); FASCINATION(1931, Brit.); LOVE RACE, THE(1931, Brit.); STRANGLEHOLD(1931, Brit.); FIRES OF FATE(1932, Brit.); HER NIGHT OUT(1932, Brit.); RINGER, THE(1932, Brit.); TIN GODS(1932, Brit.); WATCH BEVERLY(1932, Brit.); CALL ME MAME(1933, Brit.); FEAR SHIP, THE(1933, Brit.); ON THIN ICE(1933, Brit.); UP FOR THE DERBY(1933, Brit.)
Silents
NOT QUITE A LADY(1928, Brit.)
Misc. Silents
FLYING SQUAD, THE(1929)
Barry Bartle
LIGHT FANTASTIC(1964); DARING GAME(1968)
James Bartle
1984
HEART OF THE STAG(1984, New Zealand), ph
Jim Bartle
SCARECROW, THE(1982, New Zealand), ph
Bennie Bartleit
HOLD THAT BABY!(1949)
Randolph Bartlet
Silents
ANY WOMAN(1925), t
Alice Bartlett
SNIPER, THE(1952)
Annabel Bartlett
SCAPEGOAT, THE(1959, Brit.)
Basil Bartlett
NEXT OF KIN(1942, Brit.), w; SECRET MISSION(1944, Brit.), w; THEY MET IN THE DARK(1945, Brit.), w
Bennie Bartlett
MILLIONS IN THE AIR(1935); PRINCESS COMES ACROSS, THE(1936); SKY PARADE(1936); TEXAS RANGERS, THE(1936); THIRTEEN HOURS BY AIR(1936); THREE MARRIED MEN(1936); TIMOTHY'S QUEST(1936); DANGER–LOVE AT WORK(1937); EASY LIVING(1937); EXCLUSIVE(1937); LET THEM LIVE(1937); MAID OF SALEM(1937); TIME OUT FOR ROMANCE(1937); JUST AROUND THE CORNER(1938); PENROD AND HIS TWIN BROTHER(1938); FAMILY NEXT DOOR, THE(1939); GREAT MAN VOTES, THE(1939); HONEYMOON IN BALI(1939); OUR NEIGHBORS–THE CARTERS(1939); WHAT A LIFE(1939); ALIAS THE DEACON(1940); LET'S MAKE MUSIC(1940); MEET JOHN DOE(1941); TILLIE THE TOILER(1941); CLANCY STREET BOYS(1943); FOLLOW THE BAND(1943); HE HIRED THE BOSS(1943); KID DYNAMITE(1943); NOBODY'S DARLING(1943); THANK YOUR LUCKY STARS(1943); HER ADVENTUROUS NIGHT(1946); GAS HOUSE KIDS GO WEST(1947); ANGELS ALLEY(1948); HEART OF VIRGINIA(1948); JINX MONEY(1948); TROUBLE MAKERS(1948); MASTER MINDS(1949); CRAZY OVER HORSES(1951); FEUDIN' FOOLS(1952); HERE COME THE MARINES(1952); HOLD THAT LINE(1952); NO HOLDS BARRED(1952); CLIPPED WINGS(1953); JALOPY(1953); LOOSE IN LONDON(1953); PRIVATE EYES(1953); BOWERY BOYS MEET THE MONSTERS, THE(1954); JUNGLE GENTS(1954); PARIS PLAYBOYS(1954); BOWERY TO BAGDAD(1955); HIGH SOCIETY(1955); JAIL BUS-

TERS(1955); DIG THAT URANIUM(1956); SPY CHASERS(1956)

Benny Bartlett
GANG BULLETS(1938); SONS OF THE LEGION(1938); ADVENTURES OF DON COYOTE(1947); GAS HOUSE KIDS IN HOLLYWOOD(1947); SMUGGLERS' COVE(1948); ANGELS IN DISGUISE(1949); FIGHTING FOOLS(1949); CHEAPER BY THE DOZEN(1950); REAR WINDOW(1954)

Bonnie Bartlett
LAST TYCOON, THE(1976); LAST WORD, THE(1979); PROMISES IN THE DARK(1979); SEED OF INNOCENCE(1980); FRANCES(1982); LOVE LETTERS(1983)

Cal Bartlett
COUNTERFEIT KILLER, THE(1968); PETE'S DRAGON(1977)

Calvin Bartlett
SEVEN MINUTES, THE(1971); JOSHUA(1976); MOUNTAIN FAMILY ROBINSON(1979)

Capt. Bob Bartlett
VIKING, THE(1931)

Charles Bartlett
LADY LIBERTY(1972, Ital./Fr.); METEOR(1979)
Misc. Silents
BRUISER, THE(1916), d; CRAVING, THE(1916), d; THOROUGHBRED, THE(1916), d; HEADIN' NORTH(1921), d; TANGLED TRAILS(1921), d; DON DESPERADO(1927)

Charles E. Bartlett
Misc. Silents
HELL HATH NO FURY(1917), d

Charles Earl Bartlett
Misc. Silents
GIRL WHO DOESN'T KNOW, THE(1917), d

Clifford Bartlett
EVERYTHING IS THUNDER(1936, Brit.)

Cy Bartlett
MAN WHO CRIED WOLF, THE(1937), w

Dick Bartlett
RUBY(1971), p&d, w, ph, ed

Don Bartlett
Silents
WHITE SISTER, THE(1923), t; WILDERNESS WOMAN, THE(1926), t

Dorothy Bartlett
1984
REPO MAN(1984)

Elise Bartlett
Silents
ANGEL OF BROADWAY, THE(1927)

Elsie Bartlett
SHOW BOAT(1929); OH! SAILOR, BEHAVE!(1930)

Frederick Orin Bartlett
Silents
ALIAS MIKE MORAN(1919), w

Gene Bartlett
WELCOME TO HARD TIMES(1967), makeup

George Bartlett
RUBY(1971)

Hal Bartlett
ISN'T IT ROMANTIC?(1948); BREAKDOWN(1953)

Hall Bartlett
PALEFACE, THE(1948); NAVAJO(1952), a, p; WILD BLUE YONDER, THE(1952); CRAZYLEGS, ALL AMERICAN(1953), p&w; UNCHAINED(1955), p,d&w; DRANGO(1957), p, d, w; ZERO HOUR!(1957), d, w; ALL THE YOUNG MEN(1960), p,d&w; CARETAKERS, THE(1963), p&d; GLOBAL AFFAIR, A(1964), p; SOL MADRID(1968), p; CHANGES(1969), p&d, w; WILD PACK, THE(1972), p,d&w; JONATHAN LIVINGSTON SEAGULL(1973), p&d, w; CHILDREN OF SANCHEZ, THE(1978, U. S./Mex.), p&d, w

Harry Bartlett
Silents
ANNE OF GREEN GABLES(1919)

Hedda Bartlett
Silents
LADY OF THE LAKE, THE(1928, Brit.)

Jack Bartlett
CATALINA CAPER, THE(1967), p

Jeanne Bartlett
WEREWOLF OF LONDON, THE(1935); SON OF LASSIE(1945), w; GALLANT BESS(1946), w; MAN-EATER OF KUMAON(1948), w

Lanier Bartlett
Silents
JIM GRIMSBY'S BOY(1916), w; MAN ABOVE THE LAW(1918), w

Lanier Stivers Bartlett
LASH, THE(1930), w

Lisabeth Bartlett
1984
AMADEUS(1984)

Lucy Bartlett
KNACK ... AND HOW TO GET IT, THE(1965, Brit.)

Martine Bartlett
SPLENDOR IN THE GRASS(1961); PRIZE, THE(1963); LORD LOVE A DUCK(1966); NO WAY TO TREAT A LADY(1968); FUZZ(1972); KANSAS CITY BOMBER(1972); ALOHA, BOBBY AND ROSE(1975); I NEVER PROMISED YOU A ROSE GARDEN(1977)

Michael Bartlett
LOVE ME FOREVER(1935); SHE MARRIED HER BOSS(1935); FOLLOW YOUR HEART(1936); MUSIC GOES ROUND, THE(1936); LILAC DOMINO, THE(1940, Brit.)

Parker Bartlett
NO DRUMS, NO BUGLES(1971), ph

Paul Bartlett
BOYS OF PAUL STREET, THE(1969, Hung./US)

Peter Bartlett
COUNTESS FROM HONG KONG, A(1967, Brit.)

Randolph Bartlett
CIRCUS KID, THE(1928), w; PERFECT CRIME, THE(1928), w; JAZZ AGE, THE(1929); LOVE IN THE DESERT(1929), w

Silents
ALEX THE GREAT(1928), t; AVENGING RIDER, THE(1928), t; BREED OF THE SUNSETS(1928), t; CAPTAIN CARELESS(1928), t; DEAD MAN'S CURVE(1928), t; FANGS OF THE WILD(1928), t; HEY RUBE!(1928), t; MAN IN THE ROUGH(1928), t; PHANTOM OF THE RANGE(1928), t; SALLY OF THE SCANDALS(1928), t; SINNERS IN LOVE(1928), t; SKINNER'S BIG IDEA(1928), t; STOCKS AND BLONDES(1928), t; AIR LEGION, THE(1929), t; LITTLE SAVAGE, THE(1929), t

Richard Bartlett
I WAS AN AMERICAN SPY(1951); NO QUESTIONS ASKED(1951); PEOPLE AGAINST O'HARA, THE(1951); STREET BANDITS(1951); HIAWATHA(1952); SILENT RAIDERS(1954), a, d, w; LONESOME TRAIL, THE(1955), a, d, w; SILVER STAR, THE(1955), a, d, w; I'VE LIVED BEFORE(1956), d; JOE DAKOTA(1957), d; MONEY, WOMEN AND GUNS(1958), d; CARRY ON ENGLAND(1976, Brit.)

Richard H. Bartlett
ROCK, PRETTY BABY(1956), d; TWO-GUN LADY(1956), p&d, w; SLIM CARTER(1957), d; GENTLE PEOPLE AND THE QUIET LAND, THE(1972), p,d&w

Robert Bartlett
OLIVER!(1968, Brit.)

Robin Bartlett
HEAVEN'S GATE(1980); SOPHIE'S CHOICE(1982)

Ronnie Bartlett
CODE OF THE OUTLAW(1942)

Sy Bartlett
BIG BRAIN, THE(1933), w; KANSAS CITY PRINCESS(1934), w; GOING HIGHBROW(1935), w; BOULDER DAM(1936), w; MURDER OF DR. HARRIGAN, THE(1936), w; UNDER YOUR SPELL(1936), w; DANGER PATROL(1937), w; COCOANUT GROVE(1938), w; SERGEANT MURPHY(1938), w; AMAZING MR. WILLIAMS(1939), w; SANDY GETS HER MAN(1940), w; ROAD TO ZANZIBAR(1941), w; BULLET SCARS(1942), w; TWO YANKS IN TRINIDAD(1942), w; PRINCESS AND THE PIRATE, THE(1944), w; 13 RUE MADELEINE(1946), w; DOWN TO THE SEA IN SHIPS(1949), w; TWELVE O'CLOCK HIGH(1949), w; PARATROOPER(1954, Brit.), w; LAST COMMAND, THE(1955), w; THAT LADY(1955, Brit.), p, w; BIG COUNTRY, THE(1958), w; BELOVED INFIDEL(1959), w; PORK CHOP HILL(1959), p; CAPE FEAR(1962), p; OUTSIDER, THE(1962), p; GATHERING OF EAGLES, A(1963), p, w; IN ENEMY COUNTRY(1968), w; CHE!(1969), p

T. Bartlett
HAPPY ROAD, THE(1957)

Tim Bartlett
HAPPY BIRTHDAY, DAVY(1970)

Vernon Bartlett
DEATH AT A BROADCAST(1934, Brit.)

Virginia Stivers Bartlett
LASH, THE(1930), w

William Bartlett
MORE THAN A SECRETARY(1936); CALL OF THE YUKON(1938), w

Betty Bartley
LAUGHING LADY, THE(1930)

James Bartley
ULYSSES(1967, U.S./Brit.); UNDERGROUND(1970, Brit.)

Janet Bartley
HARDER THEY COME, THE(1973, Jamaica)

Nalbro Bartley
DEVIL'S LOTTERY(1932), w
Silents
AMATEUR WIFE, THE(1920), w

Penelope Bartley
BIG CHANCE, THE(1957, Brit.)

Gabriela Bartlova
DO YOU KEEP A LION AT HOME?(1966, Czech.)

Beth Bartman
RESCUE SQUAD(1935)

Frederick Bartman
LIFE IN EMERGENCY WARD 10(1959, Brit.); DEVIL'S DAFFODIL, THE(1961, Brit./Ger.); MRS. GIBBONS' BOYS(1962, Brit.)

William Bartman
ANOTHER MAN, ANOTHER CHANCE(1977 Fr/US); CARNY(1980)

William S. Bartman
O'HARA'S WIFE(1983), d, w

C. O. Bartning
LOST ONE, THE(1951, Ger.), ed; BRIDGE, THE(1961, Ger.), ed; MARTYR, THE(1976, Ger./Israel), ed

Dominic Barto
LAST REBEL, THE(1971); SHAFT(1971); MAN OF LA MANCHA(1972); SUPERFLY T.N.T.(1973); MAN FROM THE EAST, A(1974, Ital./Fr.); COUNT OF MONTE CRISTO(1976, Brit.); HEARSE, THE(1980)
1984
LONELY GUY, THE(1984)

Dominic T. Barto
STILETTO(1969); OWL AND THE PUSSYCAT, THE(1970)

Pat Barto
DIAMOND HEAD(1962), cos; BYE BYE BIRDIE(1963), cos; GIDGET GOES TO ROME(1963), cos; MAN FROM THE DINERS' CLUB, THE(1963), cos; SOYLENT GREEN(1973), cos

Robyn Barto
BLUE SKIES AGAIN(1983)

Francesca Bartoccini
SLUMBER PARTY MASSACRE, THE(1982), art d

Bela Bartok
ILLIAC PASSION, THE(1968), m; NOT RECONCILED, OR "ONLY VIOLENCE HELPS WHERE IT RULES"(1969, Ger.), m; SHINING, THE(1980), m

Eva Bartok
MADELEINE(1950, Brit.); TALE OF FIVE WOMEN, A(1951, Brit.); CRIMSON PIRATE, THE(1952); ASSASSIN, THE(1953, Brit.); NORMAN CONQUEST(1953); SPACEWAYS(1953, Brit.); FRONT PAGE STORY(1954, Brit.); SPECIAL DELIVERY(1955, Ger.); GAMMA PEOPLE, THE(1956); BREAK IN THE CIRCLE, THE(1957, Brit.); TEN THOUSAND BEDROOMS(1957); CIRCUS OF LOVE(1958, Ger.); BEYOND THE CURTAIN(1960, Brit.); OPERATION AMSTERDAM(1960, Brit.); S.O.S. PACIFIC(1960, Brit.); BLOOD AND BLACK LACE(1965, Ital.)

Misc. Talkies
ORIENT EXPRESS(1952)
Norman Bartold
SHE'S WORKING HER WAY THROUGH COLLEGE(1952); LITTLEST HOBO, THE(1958); BUSYBODY, THE(1967); LADY SINGS THE BLUES(1972); BREEZY(1973); LEGACY OF BLOOD(1973); SUPERCHICK(1973); WESTWORLD(1973); DARKTOWN STRUTTERS(1975); SUMMER SCHOOL TEACHERS(1977); REAL LIFE(1979); IN GOD WE TRUST(1980); RAISE THE TITANIC(1980, Brit.)
Sheila Bartold
PROJECT X(1968)
Walter Bartoletti
TOO BAD SHE'S BAD(1954, Ital.)
Elio Bartolini
L'AVVENTURA(1960, Ital.), w; ECLIPSE(1962, Fr./Ital.), w; IL GRIDO(1962, U.S./ Ital.), w; VERY HANDY MAN, A(1966, Fr./Ital.), w
Luigi Bartolini
BICYCLE THIEF, THE(1949, Ital.), w
Giancarlo Bartolini-Salimbene
CONSTANTINE AND THE CROSS(1962, Ital.), cos
Ann Barton
DESTINATION 60,000(1957)
Anne Barton
GREEN-EYED BLONDE, THE(1957); PAWNEE(1957); LEFT-HANDED GUN, THE(1958); PRESSURE POINT(1962); WHATEVER HAPPENED TO BABY JANE?(1962); WAY WEST, THE(1967); GREAT NORTHFIELD, MINNESOTA RAID, THE(1972)
Beth Barton
ENLIGHTEN THY DAUGHTER(1934)
Betty Barton
PEER GYNT(1965)
Buddy Barton
Silents
SOULS AFLAME(1928)
Buzz Barton
CANYON HAWKS(1930); CYCLONE KID(1931); RIDERS OF THE CACTUS(1931); WILD WEST WHOOPEE(1931); HUMAN TARGETS(1932); FIGHTING PIONEERS(1935); POWDERSMOKE RANGE(1935); FEUD OF THE WEST(1936); RIDING AVENGER, THE(1936); ROMANCE RIDES THE RANGE(1936); IN EARLY ARIZONA(1938); PHANTOM GOLD(1938); ROLLING CARAVANS(1938); LONE STAR PIONEERS(1939); SILVER ON THE SAGE(1939); KID FROM SANTA FE, THE(1940); WILD HORSE VALLEY(1940); IN THE HEAT OF THE NIGHT(1967)
Misc. Talkies
FLYING LARIATS(1931); TANGLED FORTUNES(1932); GUNFIRE(1935); RECKLESS BUCKAROO, THE(1935); SADDLE ACES(1935); TONTO KID, THE(1935)
Silents
BOY RIDER, THE(1927); BANTAM COWBOY, THE(1928); ORPHAN OF THE SAGE(1928); YOUNG WHIRLWIND(1928); FRECKLED RASCAL, THE(1929); LITTLE SAVAGE, THE(1929); PALS OF THE PRAIRIE(1929)
Misc. Silents
SLINGSHOT KID, THE(1927); FIGHTIN' REDHEAD, THE(1928); LITTLE BUCKAROO, THE(1928); PINTO KID, THE(1928); ROUGH RIDIN' RED(1928); WIZARD OF THE SADDLE(1928); VAGABOND CUB, THE(1929)
"Buzz" Barton
STORY OF VERNON AND IRENE CASTLE, THE(1939)
Charles Barton
WAGON WHEELS(1934), d; CAR 99(1935), d; LAST OUTPOST, THE(1935), d; ROCKY MOUNTAIN MYSTERY(1935), d; AND SUDDEN DEATH(1936), d; MURDER WITH PICTURES(1936), d; NEVADA(1936), d; ROSE BOWL(1936), d; TIMOTHY'S QUEST(1936), d; BORN TO THE WEST(1937), d; CRIME NOBOBY SAW, THE(1937), d; FORLORN RIVER(1937), d; THUNDER TRAIL(1937), d; BEAU GESTE(1939), BEHIND PRISON GATES(1939), d; FIVE LITTLE PEPPERS AND HOW THEY GREW(1939), d; BABIES FOR SALE(1940), d; FIVE LITTLE PEPPERS AT HOME(1940), d; FIVE LITTLE PEPPERS IN TROUBLE(1940), d; ISLAND OF DOOMED MEN(1940), d; MY SON IS GUILTY(1940), d; NOBODY'S CHILDREN(1940), d; OUT WEST WITH THE PEPPERS(1940), d; BIG BOSS, THE(1941), d; HARMON OF MICHIGAN(1941), d; HONOLULU LU(1941), d; PHANTOM SUBMARINE, THE(1941), d; RICHEST MAN IN TOWN(1941), d; SING FOR YOUR SUPPER(1941), d; TWO LATINS FROM MANHATTAN(1941), d; HELLO ANNAPOLIS(1942), d; MAN'S WORLD, A(1942), d; PARACHUTE NURSE(1942), d; SHUT MY BIG MOUTH(1942), d; SPIRIT OF STANFORD, THE(1942), d; SWEETHEART OF THE FLEET(1942), d; TRAMP, TRAMP, TRAMP(1942), d; IS EVERYBODY HAPPY?(1943), d; LAUGH YOUR BLUES AWAY(1943), d; REVEILLE WITH BEVERLY(1943), d; SHE HAS WHAT IT TAKES(1943), d; WHAT'S BUZZIN COUSIN?(1943), d; BEAUTIFUL BUT BROKE(1944), d; HEY, ROOKIE(1944), d; JAM SESSION(1944), d; LOUISIANA HAYRIDE(1944), p&d; MEN IN HER DIARY(1945), d; BEAUTIFUL CHEAT, THE(1946), p&d; SMOOTH AS SILK(1946), d; TIME OF THEIR LIVES, THE(1946), d; BUCK PRIVATES COME HOME(1947), d; NOOSE HANGS HIGH, THE(1948), p&d; AFRICA SCREAMS(1949), d; MA AND PA KETTLE AT THE FAIR(1952), d; DANCE WITH ME, HENRY(1956), d; SHAGGY DOG, THE(1959), d; TOBY TYLER(1960), d; SWINGIN' ALONG(1962), d
Misc. Talkies
LET'S HAVE FUN(1943), d
Silents
WINGS(1927)
Charles T. Barton
WHITE TIE AND TAILS(1946), d; WISTFUL WIDOW OF WAGON GAP, THE(1947), d; ABBOTT AND COSTELLO MEET FRANKENSTEIN(1948), d; MEXICAN HAYRIDE(1948), d; ABBOTT AND COSTELLO MEET THE KILLER, BORIS KARLOFF(1949), d; FREE FOR ALL(1949), d; DOUBLE CROSSBONES(1950), d; MILKMAN, THE(1950), d
Dan Barton
I'LL SEE YOU IN MY DREAMS(1951); SAILOR BEWARE(1951); DREAM WIFE(1953); NO TIME FOR SERGEANTS(1958); ONIONHEAD(1958)
Dana Barton
WACKY WORLD OF DR. MORGUS, THE(1962)
Dee Barton
PLAY MISTY FOR ME(1971), m; HIGH PLAINS DRIFTER(1973), m; THUNDERBOLT AND LIGHTFOOT(1974), m

Dennis Barton
DEAD AND BURIED(1981), set d
Derek Barton
COACH(1978); I WANNA HOLD YOUR HAND(1978)
Don Barton
BLOOD WATERS OF DOCTOR Z(1982), p&d
Dora Barton
PRICE OF A SONG, THE(1935, Brit.)
Silents
ANSWER, THE(1916, Brit.)
Misc. Silents
GREEN ORCHARD, THE(1916, Brit.)
Earl Barton
SEVEN BRIDES FOR SEVEN BROTHERS(1954); CHA-CHA-CHA BOOM(1956), ch; DON'T KNOCK THE ROCK(1956), ch; ROCK AROUND THE CLOCK(1956), a, ch; TWIST AROUND THE CLOCK(1961), ch; ROUSTABOUT(1964), ch; HARUM SCARUM(1965), ch; WHEN THE BOYS MEET THE GIRLS(1965), ch; FRANKIE AND JOHNNY(1966), ch; DOCTOR, YOU'VE GOT TO BE KIDDING(1967), ch
Misc. Talkies
TRIP WITH THE TEACHER(1975), d
Ed Barton
LOVE BEFORE BREAKFAST(1936)
Eddie Barton
BELLBOY, THE(1960)
Eileen Barton
PROMISES, PROMISES(1963)
Finis Barton
MY PAL, THE KING(1932); SENSATION HUNTERS(1934); BECKY SHARP(1935); GET THAT MAN(1935); SECRET PATROL(1936); STAMPEDE(1936)
Gary Barton
COMA(1978)
George Barton
$1,000 A TOUCHDOWN(1939); BALL OF FIRE(1941); HONOLULU LU(1941); PHANTOM SUBMARINE, THE(1941); FRENCHMAN'S CREEK(1944); BLUE DAHLIA, THE(1946); O.S.S.(1946); ABBOTT AND COSTELLO MEET FRANKENSTEIN(1948); STATE OF THE UNION(1948); HURRICANE SMITH(1952); LOST IN ALASKA(1952)
Grace Barton
Silents
GREAT EXPECTATIONS(1917); INNER CHAMBER, THE(1921); SEVENTH DAY, THE(1922)
Misc. Silents
RAGGEDY QUEEN, THE(1917); HEART OF GOLD(1919)
Greg Barton
MICHAEL O'HALLORAN(1948); NOT WANTED(1949); TEXAS DYNAMO(1950); APACHE COUNTRY(1952); OPERATION SECRET(1952); DRUMS ACROSS THE RIVER(1954); JET PILOT(1957); GOOD DAY FOR A HANGING(1958); GUN HAWK, THE(1963)
Gregg Barton
FLYING TIGERS(1942); SONG OF THE THIN MAN(1947); WEST TO GLORY(1947); HOMECOMING(1948); JOAN OF ARC(1948); TAP ROOTS(1948); JOHNNY STOOL PIGEON(1949); MASSACRE RIVER(1949); SCENE OF THE CRIME(1949); TOO LATE FOR TEARS(1949); BEYOND THE PURPLE HILLS(1950); BLAZING SUN, THE(1950); MULE TRAIN(1950); TRIPOLI(1950); DISTANT DRUMS(1951); GENE AUTRY AND THE MOUNTIES(1951); SILVER CITY BONANZA(1951); VALLEY OF FIRE(1951); WHIRLWIND(1951); DEAD MAN'S TRAIL(1952); MAVERICK, THE(1952); MONTANA BELLE(1952); WAGON TEAM(1952); WORLD IN HIS ARMS, THE(1952); LAST OF THE PONY RIDERS(1953); LAW AND ORDER(1953); MOONLIGHTER, THE(1953); SAGINAW TRAIL(1953); WINNING OF THE WEST(1953); COMMAND, THE(1954); JIVARO(1954); MASTERSON OF KANSAS(1954); TWO GUNS AND A BADGE(1954); FAR COUNTRY, THE(1955); MAN FROM LARAMIE, THE(1955); BACKLASH(1956); RAW EDGE(1956); JOE DAKOTA(1957); MAN FROM GOD'S COUNTRY(1958); TOUGHEST GUN IN TOMBSTONE(1958); LONE TEXAN(1959); NEVER STEAL ANYTHING SMALL(1959); MORITURI(1965)
James Barton
TIME OF YOUR LIFE, THE(1948); CAPTAIN HURRICANE(1935); HIS FAMILY TREE(1936); HIDEAWAY GIRL(1937); SHEPHERD OF THE HILLS, THE(1941); YELLOW SKY(1948); DAUGHTER OF ROSIE O'GRADY, THE(1950); WABASH AVENUE(1950); GOLDEN GIRL(1951); HERE COMES THE GROOM(1951); SCARF, THE(1951); NAKED HILLS, THE(1956); QUANTEZ(1957); MISFITS, THE(1961)
Jeannie Dimter Barton
NATIONAL LAMPOON'S VACATION(1983)
Joan Barton
ROMANCE OF THE WEST(1946); CIGARETTE GIRL(1947); MARY LOU(1948); STRANGE GAMBLE(1948); TWO TICKETS TO BROADWAY(1951)
Misc. Talkies
LONE STAR MOONLIGHT(1946)
Joe Barton
TENDERFOOT, THE(1932); LONE COWBOY(1934); MC FADDEN'S FLATS(1935); LADY LUCK(1936)
John Barton
SCARLET STREET(1945); DEADLINE AT DAWN(1946); ANGEL AND THE BADMAN(1947); THERE WAS A CROOKED MAN(1970), spec eff
Julien Barton
Silents
NIGHT WORKERS, THE(1917)
Misc. Silents
BURNING THE CANDLE(1917)
Ken Barton
TEST PILOT(1938)
Larry Barton
TREASURE OF MONTE CRISTO(1949); WOMAN OF DISTINCTION, A(1950); TWO TICKETS TO BROADWAY(1951); BLACK LASH, THE(1952); FRONTIER PHANTOM, THE(1952); HOUSE IS NOT A HOME, A(1964); RAIDERS FROM BENEATH THE SEA(1964); FUZZ(1972); I OUGHT TO BE IN PICTURES(1982)
Lorna Barton
PINK FLOYD–THE WALL(1982, Brit.)
Lynn Barton
KITCHEN, THE(1961, Brit.)

Margaret Barton
BRIEF ENCOUNTER(1945, Brit.); FLY AWAY PETER(1948, Brit.); TEMPTATION HARBOR(1949, Brit.); GOOD TIME GIRL(1950, Brit.); NAUGHTY ARLETTE(1951, Brit.); MR. LORD SAYS NO(1952, Brit.); LANDFALL(1953, Brit.); GAY DOG, THE(1954, Brit.)

Mary Barton
MARIGOLD(1938, Brit.)

May Barton
WHISTLE DOWN THE WIND(1961, Brit.)

Michael Barton
BLACK HILLS AMBUSH(1952); SOUTH PACIFIC TRAIL(1952); LADY WANTS MINK, THE(1953)

Michele Barton
HOW TO STUFF A WILD BIKINI(1965)

Mickey Barton
TOP BANANA(1954)

Pat Barton
RECKLESS MOMENTS, THE(1949); IN A LONELY PLACE(1950); SECRET FURY, THE(1950)

Patrick Barton
JOHN WESLEY(1954, Brit.)

Peggy Barton
MISFITS, THE(1961)

Peter Barton
STIR(1980, Aus.); HELL NIGHT(1981)
1984
FRIDAY THE 13TH–THE FINAL CHAPTER(1984)

Peter J. Barton
CUBA CROSSING(1980), p

Phil Barton
I KILLED WILD BILL HICKOK(1956)

Ralph Barton
Silents
CONQUERING POWER, THE(1921), tech d

Rayner Barton
CARDINAL, THE(1936, Brit.); KILLER WALKS, A(1952, Brit.), w

Richard Barton
RED SNOW(1952)

Robert Barton
E.T. THE EXTRA-TERRESTRIAL(1982)

Rodger Barton
1984
MRS. SOFFEL(1984)

Sam Barton
VARIETY(1935, Brit.)

Sean Barton
EYE OF THE NEEDLE(1981), ed; RETURN OF THE JEDI(1983), ed
1984
UNTIL SEPTEMBER(1984), ed

Shirley Barton
SENTIMENTAL JOURNEY(1946)

Steve Barton
LOVE MERCHANT, THE(1966)
Misc. Talkies
RED ROSES OF PASSION(1967)

Sue Barton
NASHVILLE(1975)

Suzanne Barton
THAT TOUCH OF MINK(1962)

Travis Barton
YANK IN THE R.A.F., A(1941), cos

Rai Bartonious
FUNNY MONEY(1983, Brit.)

Zdena Bartova
FANTASTIC PLANET(1973, Fr./Czech.), anim

W. Bartowna
LAST STOP, THE(1949, Pol.)

Laurie Bartram
FRIDAY THE 13TH(1980)

Colette Bartrop
FACES IN THE DARK(1960, Brit.)

Roland Bartrop
MIDDLE COURSE, THE(1961, Brit.); MAKE MINE A DOUBLE(1962, Brit.); SLAVE, THE(1963, Ital.); TWO COLONELS, THE(1963, Ital.); JUDITH(1965); KISS THE GIRLS AND KILL THEM DIE(1967, U.S./Ital.)

Rowland Bartrop
NIGHT AMBUSH(1958, Brit.); FACES IN THE DARK(1960, Brit.)

Edward P. Bartsch
FLYING MATCHMAKER, THE(1970, Israel), ed

Eric Bartsch
1984
STRANGERS KISS(1984)

Joachim Bartsch
DESPERADO TRAIL, THE(1965, Ger./Yugo.), w; LAST TOMAHAWK, THE(1965, Ger./Ital./Span.), w; U-47 LT. COMMANDER PRIEN(1967, Ger.), w

Rudolph Hans Bartsch
Silents
LOVE ME AND THE WORLD IS MINE(1928), w

Ted Bartsch
ABSENCE OF MALICE(1981)

Josef Bartunek
MOST BEAUTIFUL AGE, THE(1970, Czech.)

Billy Barty
FOOTLIGHT PARADE(1933); GOLD DIGGERS OF 1933(1933); OUT ALL NIGHT(1933); ROMAN SCANDALS(1933); GIFT OF GAB(1934); MIDSUMMER'S NIGHT'S DREAM, A(1935); NOTHING SACRED(1937); PYGMY ISLAND(1950); CLOWN, THE(1953); UNDEAD, THE(1957); JUMBO(1962); ROUSTABOUT(1964); HARUM SCARUM(1965); PUFNSTUF(1970); DAY OF THE LOCUST, THE(1975); AMAZING DOBERMANS, THE(1976); W.C. FIELDS AND ME(1976); WON TON TON, THE DOG WHO SAVED HOLLYWOOD(1976); FOUL PLAY(1978); FIREPOWER(1979,

Brit.); SKATETOWN, U.S.A.(1979); HARDLY WORKING(1981); UNDER THE RAINBOW(1981)
1984
NIGHT PATROL(1984)

Jack Barty
THIS IS THE LIFE(1933, Brit.); MY SONG GOES ROUND THE WORLD(1934, Brit.); ALL IN(1936, Brit.); IT'S IN THE BAG(1936, Brit.); FEATHER YOUR NEST(1937, Brit.); TAKE A CHANCE(1937, Brit.); TALKING FEET(1937, Brit.); STEPPING TOES(1938, Brit.); WHAT WOULD YOU DO, CHUMS?(1939, Brit.); GASLIGHT(1940)

A. Barushnoy
GARNET BRACELET, THE(1966, USSR); WAR AND PEACE(1968, USSR)

Max Barvyn
CHOCOLATE SOLDIER, THE(1941)

Peggy Barwell
MRS. PYM OF SCOTLAND YARD(1939, Brit.), w; NAUGHTY ARLETTE(1951, Brit.), w

Muni Barwick
CALL OF THE JUNGLE(1944)

Ray D. Barwick
POLICE DOG STORY, THE(1961)

Patrick Barwise
DOCTOR FAUSTUS(1967, Brit.)

Hal Barwood
SUGARLAND EXPRESS, THE(1974), w; BINGO LONG TRAVELING ALL-STARS AND MOTOR KINGS, THE(1976), w; MAC ARTHUR(1977), w; CORVETTE SUMMER(1978), p, w; DRAGONSLAYER(1981), p, w

Max Barwym
PHANTOM SUBMARINE, THE(1941)

Max Barwyn
STAMBOUL QUEST(1934); FOLIES DERGERE(1935); YOURS FOR THE ASKING(1936); SAY IT IN FRENCH(1938); YOU AND ME(1938)
Silents
BEVERLY OF GRAUSTARK(1926)
Misc. Silents
VALENCIA(1926); FIGHTING EAGLE, THE(1927)

Jean Bary
COCK-EYED WORLD, THE(1929); LILIES OF THE FIELD(1930); MOTHERS CRY(1930); SCARLET PAGES(1930); BRIGHT LIGHTS(1931); JUNE MOON(1931); FLORIDA SPECIAL(1936)
Misc. Silents
TANGLED TRAILS(1921)

Leon Bary
IRON MASK, THE(1929); ROAD IS FINE, THE(1930, Fr.)
Silents
KISMET(1920); GALLOPING KID, THE(1922); SUZANNA(1922); KING OF THE WILD HORSES, THE(1924)
Misc. Silents
IN THE GRIP OF THE SULTAN(1915, Brit.), d; MARRIED FOR MONEY(1915, Brit.), d; LURE OF JADE, THE(1921); BUCKING THE BARRIER(1923); MIDNIGHT MOLLY(1925)

Rudolf Bary
SALZBURG CONNECTION, THE(1972)

Solange Bary
INNOCENTS IN PARIS(1955, Brit.)

Helen Barys
Misc. Talkies
SWANEE SHOWBOAT(1939)

G. Barysheva
LADY WITH THE DOG, THE(1962, USSR)

T. Barysheva
WELCOME KOSTYA!(1965, USSR); JACK FROST(1966, USSR)

Mikhail Baryshnikov
TURNING POINT, THE(1977)

Vajra Ky Barzaghi
1984
BREAKIN' 2: ELECTRIC BOOGALOO(1984)

Baronessa Barzani
GENERALE DELLA ROVERE(1960, Ital./Fr.)

Wolf Barzell
STREET OF SINNERS(1957)

Wolfe Barzell
BELL, BOOK AND CANDLE(1958); FRANKENSTEIN'S DAUGHTER(1958); BLUE ANGEL, THE(1959); ATLANTIS, THE LOST CONTINENT(1961); HOMICIDAL(1961); SCARFACE MOB, THE(1962); LOVE WITH THE PROPER STRANGER(1963); REBELS AGAINST THE LIGHT(1964); SANDS OF BEERSHEBA(1966, U.S./Israel)

Itzhak Barzilai
CLOUDS OVER ISRAEL(1966, Israel)

Yoram Barzilai
1984
AMBASSADOR, THE(1984), prod d; BLACK ROOM, THE(1984), prod d

Luigi Barzini
FAREWELL TO ARMS, A(1957)

Isa Barzizza
CARTOUCHE(1957, Ital./US)

Pippo Barzizza
LOVE AND LARCENY(1963, Fr./Ital.), m

Alan Barzman
MOUSE AND HIS CHILD, THE(1977)

Ben Barzman
TRUE TO LIFE(1943), w; YOU'RE A LUCKY FELLOW, MR. SMITH(1943), w; BACK TO BATAAN(1945), w; NEVER SAY GOODBYE(1946), w; BOY WITH THE GREEN HAIR, THE(1949), w; SALT TO THE DEVIL(1949, Brit.), w; TIME WITHOUT PITY(1957, Brit.), w; CHANCE MEETING(1960, Brit.), w; CEREMONY, THE(1963, U.S./Span.), w; FALL OF THE ROMAN EMPIRE, THE(1964), w; VISIT, THE(1964, Ger./Fr./Ital./U.S.), w; HEROES OF TELEMARK, THE(1965, Brit.), w; FRENCH CONSPIRACY, THE(1973, Fr.), w

Norma Barzman
NEVER SAY GOODBYE(1946), w

Sol Barzman
TRUE TO LIFE(1943), w; MEET THE PEOPLE(1944), w

Shaul Barzoweski
FLYING MATCHMAKER, THE(1970, Israel), m

Therese Bas
MANDABI(1970, Fr./Senegal)

Luigi Basagalupi
WHITE VOICES(1965, Fr./Ital.)

Emilio Basaldua
1984
DEATHSTALKER, THE(1984), art d

Emiolio Basaldua
DEATHSTALKER(1983, Arg./U.S.), art d

Ralph Basalla
ON THE YARD(1978)

Pedro Basanta
1984
DEMONS IN THE GARDEN(1984, Span.)

Pedro Basauri
MOMENT OF TRUTH, THE(1965, Ital./Span.)

Felix Basch
DESPERATE JOURNEY(1942); ENEMY AGENTS MEET ELLERY QUEEN(1942); HITLER—DEAD OR ALIVE(1942); ONCE UPON A HONEYMOON(1942); PACIFIC RENDEZVOUS(1942); REUNION IN FRANCE(1942); ABOVE SUSPICION(1943); CHETNIKS(1943); DESERT SONG, THE(1943); FALCON IN DANGER, THE(1943); HOSTAGES(1943); MISSION TO MOSCOW(1943); WOMEN IN BONDAGE(1943); MASK OF DIMITRIOS, THE(1944); UNCERTAIN GLORY(1944)

Harry Basch
MAN CALLED GANNON, A(1969); WINNING(1969); GANG THAT COULDN'T SHOOT STRAIGHT, THE(1971); THEY ONLY KILL THEIR MASTERS(1972); STONE KILLER, THE(1973); SWASHBUCKLER(1976); ROLLERCOASTER(1977); COMA(1978)

Helmut Basch
I LOVE YOU, I KILL YOU(1972, Ger.)

Franz Baschelin
STALAG 17(1953), art d

Bruno Baschiera
ROMAN HOLIDAY(1953)

Sauro Baschieri
NIGHT OF THE SHOOTING STARS, THE(1982, Ital.)

Wally Bascoe
RICHARD III(1956, Brit.)

Rose Bascom
LAWLESS RIDER, THE(1954)

Weldon Bascom
LAWLESS RIDER, THE(1954)

Purmendu Base
ADVERSARY, THE(1973, Ind.), ph

Rainer Basedow
1984
LOVE IN GERMANY, A(1984, Fr./Ger.)

Cesco Baseggio
WHITE LINE, THE(1952, Ital.)

Jackie Basehart
COUNTERFEIT COMMANDOS(1981, Ital.)

Richard Basehart
CRY WOLF(1947); REPEAT PERFORMANCE(1947); HE WALKED BY NIGHT(1948); BLACK BOOK, THE(1949); ROSEANNA McCOY(1949); TENSION(1949); OUTSIDE THE WALL(1950); DECISION BEFORE DAWN(1951); FIXED BAYONETS(1951); FOURTEEN HOURS(1951); HOUSE ON TELEGRAPH HILL(1951); TITANIC(1953); GOOD DIE YOUNG, THE(1954, Brit.); CANYON CROSSROADS(1955); STRANGER'S HAND, THE(1955, Brit.); EXTRA DAY, THE(1956, Brit.); FINGER OF GUILT(1956, Brit.); LA STRADA(1956, Ital.); MOBY DICK(1956, Brit.); CARTOUCHE(1957, Ital./US); TIME LIMIT(1957); BROTHERS KARAMAZOV, THE(1958); FIVE BRANDED WOMEN(1960); FOR THE LOVE OF MIKE(1960); PORTRAIT IN BLACK(1960); PASSPORT TO CHINA(1961, Brit.); HITLER(1962); SAVAGE GUNS, THE(1962, U.S./Span.); SWINDLE, THE(1962, Fr./Ital.); KINGS OF THE SUN(1963); SATAN BUG, THE(1965); CHATO'S LAND(1972); RAGE(1972); AND MILLIONS WILL DIE(1973); MANSION OF THE DOOMED(1976); GREAT BANK HOAX, THE(1977); ISLAND OF DR. MOREAU, THE(1977); BEING THERE(1979)
Misc. Talkies
HANS BRINKER AND THE SILVER SKATES(1969); SAGITTARIUS MINE, THE(1972)

Kevin Basel
MY WAY(1974, South Africa); KILLER FORCE(1975, Switz./Ireland)

Michael Baseleon
UPTIGHT(1968); CHILDRENS GAMES(1969); MAN CALLED HORSE, A(1970); GRISSOM GANG, THE(1971); PASSOVER PLOT, THE(1976, Israel)

James Basen
THEY CAME TO BLOW UP AMERICA(1943), art d

James Baseri
HOME IN INDIANA(1944), art d

James Baseui
MY MAN AND I(1952), art d

James Basevich
MYSTERIOUS ISLAND(1929), spec eff; SAN FRANCISCO(1936), spec eff; DEAD END(1937), spec eff; HURRICANE, THE(1937), spec eff; ADVENTURES OF MARCO POLO, THE(1938), spec eff; BLOCKADE(1938), spec eff; COWBOY AND THE LADY, THE(1938), art d; RAFFLES(1939), art d; REAL GLORY, THE(1939), art d; THEY SHALL HAVE MUSIC(1939), art d; LONG VOYAGE HOME, THE(1940), art d; WESTERNER, THE(1940), art d; TOBACCO ROAD(1941), art d; YANK IN THE R.A.F., A(1941), art d; BLACK SWAN, THE(1942), art d; MOONTIDE(1942), art d; SON OF FURY(1942), art d; THUNDER BIRDS(1942), art d; DANCING MASTERS, THE(1943), art d; GANG'S ALL HERE, THE(1943), art d; GUADALCANAL DIARY(1943), art d; HAPPY LAND(1943), art d; HEAVEN CAN WAIT(1943), art d; HELLO, FRISCO, HELLO(1943), art d; HOLY MATRIMONY(1943), art d; JITTERBUGS(1943), art d; MOON IS DOWN, THE(1943), art d; OX-BOW INCIDENT, THE(1943), art d; PARIS AFTER DARK(1943), art d; SONG OF BERNADETTE, THE(1943), art d; STORMY

WEATHER(1943), art d; SWEET ROSIE O'GRADY(1943), art d; WINTERTIME(1943), art d; BUFFALO BILL(1944), art d; EVE OF ST. MARK, THE(1944), art d; FOUR JILLS IN A JEEP(1944), art d; GREENWICH VILLAGE(1944), art d; IN THE MEANTIME, DARLING(1944), art d; JANE EYRE(1944), art d; KEYS OF THE KINGDOM, THE(1944), art d; LADIES OF WASHINGTON(1944), art d; LIFEBOAT(1944), art d; LODGER, THE(1944), art d; PIN UP GIRL(1944), art d; PURPLE HEART, THE(1944), art d; ROGER TOUHY, GANGSTER!(1944), art d; SULLIVANS, THE(1944), art d; TAMPICO(1944), art d; WILSON(1944), art d; SPELLBOUND(1945), prod d; DARK CORNER, THE(1946), art d; DUEL IN THE SUN(1946), art d; HOME SWEET HOMICIDE(1946), art d; IT SHOULDN'T HAPPEN TO A DOG(1946), art d; JOHNNY COMES FLYING HOME(1946), art d; MARGIE(1946), art d; MY DARLING CLEMENTINE(1946), art d; SOMEWHERE IN THE NIGHT(1946), art d; STRANGE TRIANGLE(1946), art d; 13 RUE MADELEINE(1946), art d; BRASHER DOUBLOON, THE(1947), art d; CAPTAIN FROM CASTILE(1947), art d; HOMESTRETCH, THE(1947), art d; LATE GEORGE APLEY, THE(1947), art d; SHOCKING MISS PILGRIM, THE(1947), art d; FORT APACHE(1948), art d; THREE GODFATHERS, THE(1948), art d; SHE WORE A YELLOW RIBBON(1949), art d; TO PLEASE A LADY(1950), art d; WAGONMASTER(1950), art d; ACROSS THE WIDE MISSOURI(1951), art d; NIGHT INTO MORNING(1951), art d; PEOPLE AGAINST O'HARA, THE(1951), art d; JUST THIS ONCE(1952), art d; ISLAND IN THE SKY(1953), art d; EAST OF EDEN(1955), art d; SEARCHERS, THE(1956), art d
Silents
BIG PARADE, THE(1925), art d; SOUL MATES(1925), set d; TOWER OF LIES, THE(1925), set d; LOVE'S BLINDNESS(1926), set d; TEMPTRESS, THE(1926), set d

Danny Basevitch
JESUS CHRIST, SUPERSTAR(1973)

Ed Bash
SLUMBER PARTY '57(1977), art d, set d

Edward Bash
WILD PARTY, THE(1975), spec eff

Felix Bash
DESTINATION UNKNOWN(1942)

John Bash
ROOGIE'S BUMP(1954), p; WOMAN'S DEVOTION, A(1956), p; MISSILE FROM HELL(1960, Brit.), p

Tom Basham
COLOSSUS: THE FORBIN PROJECT(1969); COCKEYED COWBOYS OF CALICO COUNTY, THE(1970); SQUARES(1972); PSYCHOPATH, THE(1973)
Misc. Talkies
PINK ANGELS, THE(1971); EYE FOR AN EYE, AN(1975)

Bud Bashaw
SOLDIER IN THE RAIN(1963), makeup; ROBINSON CRUSOE ON MARS(1964), makeup

Ernie Bashaw
RETURN OF THE SECAUCUS SEVEN(1980)

Haim Bashi
JESUS CHRIST, SUPERSTAR(1973)

Yosef Bashi
THEY WERE TEN(1961, Israel)

Yoseph Bashi
RABBI AND THE SHIKSE, THE(1976, Israel)

Philip Basi
Silents
FRUITS OF DESIRE, THE(1916)

Relja Basic
GAMBLERS, THE(1969); OPERATION CROSS EAGLES(1969, U.S./Yugo.); RAT SAVIOUR, THE(1977, Yugo.)
1984
MEMED MY HAWK(1984, Brit.)

Count Basie
CINDERFELLA(1960); BLAZING SADDLES(1974)

Toni Basil
PAJAMA PARTY(1964); VILLAGE OF THE GIANTS(1965), a, ch; COOL ONES, THE(1967), ch; HEAD(1968), ch; EASY RIDER(1969); SWEET CHARITY(1969); FIVE EASY PIECES(1970); LAST MOVIE, THE(1971); GREASER'S PALACE(1972); MOTHER, JUGS & SPEED(1976); ROSE, THE(1979), ch; HEY, GOOD LOOKIN'(1982)
Misc. Talkies
CITIZEN SOLDIER(1984)

Pierluigi Basila
1984
DUNE(1984), art d

O. Basilashvili
GARNET BRACELET, THE(1966, USSR)

Oleg Basilashvili
AUTUMN MARATHON(1982, USSR)

Costy Basile
1984
POWER, THE(1984)

Louis Basile
NO WAY TO TREAT A LADY(1968); LITTLE MISS MARKER(1980); TRUE CONFESSIONS(1981)

Missy Basile
HEART LIKE A WHEEL(1983)

Nadine Basile
CRAZY FOR LOVE(1960, Fr.)

Pier Luigi Basile
1984
CONAN THE DESTROYER(1984), prod d

Pierluigi Basile
SUPERARGO VERSUS DIABOLICUS(1966, Ital./Span.), set d; DIRTY HEROES(1971, Ital./Fr./Ger.), set d; MOSES(1976, Brit./Ital.), prod d, set d; AMITYVILLE II: THE POSSESSION(1982), prod d; CONAN THE BARBARIAN(1982), art d

Salvo Basile
LAST MERCENARY, THE(1969, Ital./Span./Ger.); ONCE UPON A TIME IN THE WEST(1969, U.S./Ital.)

Tony Basilicato
MUPPET MOVIE, THE(1979)

Barna Basilides
WINTER WIND(1970, Fr./Hung.)
Zoltan Basilides
ROUND UP, THE(1969, Hung.)
Basin Street Boys
DUKE IS THE TOPS, THE(1938)
Kim Basinger
HARD COUNTRY(1981); MOTHER LODE(1982); MAN WHO LOVED WOMEN, THE(1983); NEVER SAY NEVER AGAIN(1983)
1984
NATURAL, THE(1984)
L. Baskakova
MY NAME IS IVAN(1963, USSR), makeup
A. W. Baskcomb
MIDSHIPMAID GOB(1932, Brit.)
A.W. Baskcomb
GOOD COMPANIONS(1933, Brit.); PHANTOM FIEND, THE(1935, Brit.)
Batty Baskcomb
TREAD SOFTLY(1952, Brit.)
Betty Baskcomb
IT ALWAYS RAINS ON SUNDAY(1949, Brit.); DETECTIVE, THE(1954, Qit.); MAN WHO KNEW TOO MUCH, THE(1956)
John Baskcomb
CHITTY CHITTY BANG BANG(1968, Brit.); FINAL CONFLICT, THE(1981)
Lawrence Baskcomb
ESCAPE(1930, Brit.); EXTRAVAGANCE(1930); KNIGHT WITHOUT ARMOR(1937, Brit.); DRUMS(1938, Brit.); CHALLENGE, THE(1939, Brit.); HISTORY OF MR. POLLY, THE(1949, Brit.); MAN IN BLACK, THE(1950, Brit.)
Betty Baskomb
DR. CRIPPEN(1963, Brit.); YOUR MONEY OR YOUR WIFE(1965, Brit.)
John Baskcombe
OLIVER!(1968, Brit.); I WANT WHAT I WANT(1972, Brit.)
Denise Baske
MY BODYGUARD(1980)
1984
WINDY CITY(1984)
Norvin Baskerville
ROBBY(1968)
Ernest Baskett
STANLEY AND LIVINGSTONE(1939)
James Baskett
STRAIGHT TO HEAVEN(1939); REVENGE OF THE ZOMBIES(1943); SONG OF THE SOUTH(1946)
Misc. Talkies
COMES MIDNIGHT(1940)
Jimmy Baskette
HARLEM IS HEAVEN(1932)
Edie Baskin
LIVE A LITTLE, LOVE A LITTLE(1968)
Elya Baskin
BEING THERE(1979); BUTCH AND SUNDANCE: THE EARLY DAYS(1979); RAISE THE TITANIC(1980, Brit.)
1984
MOSCOW ON THE HUDSON(1984); 2010(1984)
Richard Baskin
NASHVILLE(1975), a, m, md; BUFFALO BILL AND THE INDIANS, OR SITTING BULL'S HISTORY LESSON(1976), m; WELCOME TO L.A.(1976), a, m; HONEYSUCKLE ROSE(1980), m
"Tiny Tim" Baskin
WIZARD OF BAGHDAD, THE(1960)
William Baskin
ZOMBIES OF MORA TAU(1957); RAVEN, THE(1963); DR. GOLDFOOT AND THE BIKINI MACHINE(1965)
William "Tiny" Baskin
GOOD DAY FOR A HANGING(1958)
Weems Oliver Baskin III
MIDNIGHT MAN, THE(1974)
Ron Baskins
1984
TANK(1984)
Bill Baskiville
ENGLANO MADE ME(1973, Brit.)
John Baskomb
DARWIN ADVENTURE, THE(1972, Brit.)
Tina Basle
SPRING FEVER(1983, Can.)
Molly Basler
HISTORY OF THE WORLD, PART 1(1981)
1984
KARATE KID, THE(1984)
V. Basner
IMMORTAL GARRISON, THE(1957, USSR), m; GIRL AND THE BUGLER, THE(1967, USSR), m
Veniamin Basner
DESTINY OF A MAN(1961, USSR), m; SUN SHINES FOR ALL, THE(1961, USSR), m
Alain Basnier
AND NOW MY LOVE(1975, Fr.)
Luigi Basogaluppi
CAFE EXPRESS(1980, Ital.)
Jack Bason
GOLDEN BLADE, THE(1953)
V. Basov
MEET ME IN MOSCOW(1966, USSR)
Volodya Basov
MOSCOW–CASSIOPEIA(1974, USSR); TEENAGERS IN SPACE(1975, USSR)
James Basquette
HEAVENLY BODY, THE(1943)

Lina Basquette
SHOW FOLKS(1928); COME ACROSS(1929); GODLESS GIRL, THE(1929); YOUNGER GENERATION(1929); DUDE WRANGLER, THE(1930); ARIZONA TERROR(1931); GOLDIE(1931); HARD HOMBRE(1931); MORALS FOR WOMEN(1931); MOUNTED FURY(1931); HELLO TROUBLE(1932); MIDNIGHT LADY(1932); PHANTOM EXPRESS, THE(1932); PLEASURE(1933); FINAL HOUR, THE(1936); EBB TIDE(1937); SOULS AT SEA(1937); FOUR MEN AND A PRAYER(1938); ROSE OF THE RIO GRANDE(1938); NIGHT FOR CRIME, A(1942)
Silents
PENROD(1922); RANGER OF THE NORTH(1927); NOOSE, THE(1928)
Misc. Silents
SERENADE(1927)
Linda Basquette
ARM OF THE LAW(1932)
Salvador Basquez
LOVE IS A MANY-SPLENDORED THING(1955)
Alfie Bass
HELL, HEAVEN OR HOBOKEN(1958, Brit.); JOHNNY FRENCHMAN(1946, Brit.); HOLIDAY CAMP(1947, Brit.); MONKEY'S PAW, THE(1948, Brit.); BOYS IN BROWN(1949, Brit.); HASTY HEART, THE(1949); IT ALWAYS RAINS ON SUNDAY(1949, Brit.); MAN ON THE RUN(1949, Brit.); GALLOPING MAJOR, THE(1951, Brit.); HIGH TREASON(1951, Brit.); LAVENDER HILL MOB, THE(1951, Brit.); POOL OF LONDON(1951, Brit.); BRANDY FOR THE PARSON(1952, Brit.); FOUR AGAINST FATE(1952, Brit.); MADE IN HEAVEN(1952, Brit.); OUTPOST IN MALAYA(1952, Brit.); TREASURE HUNT(1952, Brit.); YOU CAN'T BEAT THE IRISH(1952, Brit.); TOP OF THE FORM(1953, Brit.); BLACKOUT(1954, Brit.); MAKE ME AN OFFER(1954, Brit.); PASSING STRANGER, THE(1954, Brit.); NIGHT MY NUMBER CAME UP, THE(1955, Brit.); SQUARE RING, THE(1955, Brit.); SVENGALI(1955, Brit.); ANGEL WHO PAWNED HER HARP, THE(1956, Brit.); BEHIND THE HEADLINES(1956, Brit.); CASH ON DELIVERY(1956, Brit.); CHILD IN THE HOUSE(1956, Brit.); JUMPING FOR JOY(1956, Brit.); KID FOR TWO FARTHINGS, A(1956, Brit.); TOUCH OF THE SUN, A(1956, Brit.); CARRY ON ADMIRAL(1957, Brit.); NO ROAD BACK(1957, Brit.); TIME IS MY ENEMY(1957, Brit.); HELL DRIVERS(1958, Brit.); I ONLY ASKED!(1958, Brit.); TALE OF TWO CITIES, A(1958, Brit.); MILLIONAIRESS, THE(1960, Brit.); HELP!(1965, Brit.); ALFIE(1966, Brit.); FUNNY THING HAPPENED ON THE WAY TO THE FORUM, A(1966); SANDWICH MAN, THE(1966, Brit.); CARNABY, M.D.(1967, Brit.); FEARLESS VAMPIRE KILLERS, OR PARDON ME BUT YOUR TEETH ARE IN MY NECK, THE(1967); CHALLENGE FOR ROBIN HOOD, A(1968, Brit.); FIXER, THE(1968); UP THE JUNCTION(1968, Brit.); MAGNIFICENT SEVEN DEADLY SINS, THE(1971, Brit.); REVENGE OF THE PINK PANTHER(1978); MOONRAKER(1979, Brit.)
Alfred [Alfie] Bass
VICE VERSA(1948, Brit.)
Billy Bass
CARWASH(1976)
Bobby Bass
CORVETTE SUMMER(1978), stunts; HOOPER(1978), stunts; HUNTER, THE(1980); TOM HORN(1980); MEGAFORCE(1982); STAR 80(1983)
Cyril Bass
FIDDLER ON THE ROOF(1971)
David Bass
1984
PURPLE HEARTS(1984)
Emory Bass
1776(1972); CHEAP DETECTIVE, THE(1978); SCAVENGER HUNT(1979)
Fred Bass
WOMAN AGAINST THE WORLD(1938); SPECIAL INSPECTOR(1939)
G.V. Bass
UP FROM THE DEPTHS(1979, Phil.), ed
Harriet Bass
MADMAN(1982)
Jules Bass
DAYDREAMER, THE(1966), d; MAD MONSTER PARTY(1967), d; WACKY WORLD OF MOTHER GOOSE, THE,(1967), d; MARCO(1973), p; LAST UNICORN, THE(1982), p&d
Linda Bass
ONE DARK NIGHT(1983), cos
1984
BAD MANNERS(1984), cos
Linda M. Bass
1984
DREAMSCAPE(1984), cos; FEAR CITY(1984), cos
Mike Bass
Misc. Talkies
BROTHERHOOD OF DEATH(1976)
Milton R. Bass
JORY(1972), w
Saul Bass
PHASE IV(1974), d
Todd Bass
MITCHELL(1975)
Robert Bassac
BAKER'S WIFE, THE(1940, Fr.)
Dmitri Bassaligo
Misc. Silents
FIGHT FOR THE 'ULTIMATUM' FACTORY(1923, USSR), d
Giuseppe Bassan
DEAD OF SUMMER(1970 Ital./Fr.), art d; SUPERFLY T.N.T.(1973), prod d; DEEP RED(1976, Ital.), w; SUSPIRIA(1977, Ital.), art d; FROM HELL TO VICTORY(1979, Fr./Ital./Span.), set d; INFERNO(1980, Ital.), art d
Georgio Bassani
STRANGER'S HAND, THE(1955, Brit.), w
Giorgio Bassani
WOMAN OF THE RIVER(1954, Fr./Ital.), w; WOMAN OF ROME(1956, Ital.), w; SENSO(1968, Ital.), w

Giorgio Bassani(based on the novel by Bassani)
GARDEN OF THE FINZI-CONTINIS, THE(1976, Ital./Ger.), w
John Bassberger
DIVINE MR. J., THE(1974)
John Basscomb
BATTLE OF BRITAIN, THE(1969, Brit.)
Albert Basserman
1914(1932, Ger.); DISPATCH FROM REUTERS, A(1940); DR. EHRLICH'S MAGIC BULLET(1940); FOREIGN CORRESPONDENT(1940); KNUTE ROCKNE–ALL AMERICAN(1940); NEW WINE(1941); SHANGHAI GESTURE, THE(1941); WOMAN'S FACE(1941); DESPERATE JOURNEY(1942); FLY BY NIGHT(1942); INVISIBLE AGENT(1942); MOON AND SIXPENCE, THE(1942); ONCE UPON A HONEY-MOON(1942); REUNION IN FRANCE(1942); GOOD LUCK, MR. YATES(1943); MADAME CURIE(1943); SINCE YOU WENT AWAY(1944); RHAPSODY IN BLUE(1945); SEARCHING WIND, THE(1946); ESCAPE ME NEVER(1947); PRIVATE AFFAIRS OF BEL AMI, THE(1947); RED SHOES, THE(1948, Brit.)
Misc. Silents
OTHER, THE(1912, Ger.)
Elsa Basserman
ESCAPE(1940); DESPERATE JOURNEY(1942); MADAME CURIE(1943)
George Basserman
WHISTLING IN BROOKLYN(1943), m
Albert Bassermann
DAUGHTER OF EVIL(1930, Ger.); DREYFUS CASE, THE(1940, Ger.); MOON OVER BURMA(1940)
Misc. Talkies
PASSPORT TO HEAVEN(1943)
Gaby Basset
RECORD 413(1936, Fr.); FIRE IN THE STRAW(1943); MY SEVEN LITTLE SINS(1956, Fr./Ital.); DEADLIER THAN THE MALE(1957, Fr.); MAGNIFICENT TRAMP, THE(1962, Fr./Ital.); BEAR, THE(1963, Fr.)
Richard Basset
COCAINE COWBOYS(1979)
Basia Bassett
EVERY DAY'S A HOLIDAY(1938), cos
Betty Bassett
KID FROM SPAIN, THE(1932)
Bill Bassett
MURDER, INC.(1960)
Carling Bassett
SPRING FEVER(1983, Can.)
Grant Bassett
DEMON SEED(1977), anim
Heidi Bassett
SPRING FEVER(1983, Can.)
James Bassett
IN HARM'S WAY(1965), w
Joe Bassett
REDHEAD FROM WYOMING, THE(1953); CRIME WAVE(1954); DOWN THREE DARK STREETS(1954); SECURITY RISK(1954); ROBBER'S ROOST(1955); TALL MAN RIDING(1955); JOHNNY CONCHO(1956); SHORT CUT TO HELL(1957)
John F. Bassett
PAPERBACK HERO(1973, Can.), p; SPRING FEVER(1983, Can.), p
Ned Bassett
Silents
RUSTLER'S RANCH(1926)
R. H. Bassett
PILGRIMAGE(1933), m
R.H. Bassett
FACE IN THE SKY(1933), m; WORLD MOVES ON, THE(1934), m; DANTE'S INFERNO(1935), m; STANLEY AND LIVINGSTONE(1939), m
Reginald H. Bassett
WOMEN OF ALL NATIONS(1931), m
Richard Bassett
1984
ALPHABET CITY(1984)
Ronald Bassett
CONQUEROR WORM, THE(1968, Brit.), w
Roy Bassett
Silents
TERROR OF BAR X, THE(1927)
Russell Bassett
Silents
EAGLE'S MATE, THE(1914); SUCH A LITTLE QUEEN(1914); COMMANDING OFFICER, THE(1915); DAVID HARUM(1915); LITTLE PAL(1915); MASQUERADERS, THE(1915); MAY BLOSSOM(1915); SOLD(1915); NEARLY A KING(1916); QUEST OF LIFE, THE(1916)
Misc. Silents
BEHIND THE SCENES(1914); HEART OF JENNIFER, THE(1915); JIM, THE PENMAN(1915); DIPLOMACY(1916); HULDA FROM HOLLAND(1916); BROADWAY JONES(1917); HONEYMOON, THE(1917)
Sara Ware Bassett
CAPTAIN HURRICANE(1935), w
Steve Bassett
SPRING BREAK(1983)
Virginia Bassett
WITHOUT REGRET(1935); MRS. MINIVER(1942)
William Bassett
STRATTON STORY, THE(1949); OLD BOYFRIENDS(1979)
William H. Bassett
GRASSHOPPER, THE(1970); 1776(1972); TOWERING INFERNO, THE(1974); LUCKY LADY(1975)
1984
KARATE KID, THE(1984); SAM'S SON(1984)
Bernard Bassey
FIRST TIME, THE(1969), w
Hogan "Kid" Bassey
HEART OF A MAN, THE(1959, Brit.)

Parsifal Bassi
ROSSINI(1948, Ital.), w
Pier Emilio Bassi
SOUND OF TRUMPETS, THE(1963, Ital.), m
Boris Bassiak
JULES AND JIM(1962, Fr.)
Danielle Bassiak
JULES AND JIM(1962, Fr.)
Frank Bassill
BOY, A GIRL AND A BIKE, A(1949 Brit.), ph; MY BROTHER'S KEEPER(1949, Brit.), ph
Eileen Bassing
HOME BEFORE DARK(1958), w
Robert Bassing
HOME BEFORE DARK(1958), w
John Bassler
APPLAUSE(1929), ed
Robert Bassler
SHOPWORN ANGEL, THE(1928), ed; NOTHING BUT THE TRUTH(1929), ed; WOLF OF WALL STREET, THE(1929), ed; MAN FROM WYOMING, A(1930), ed; SAFETY IN NUMBERS(1930), ed; SHADOW OF THE LAW(1930), ed; CAROLINA(1934), ed; BLACK SWAN, THE(1942), p; GIRL TROUBLE(1942), p; MY GAL SAL(1942), p; LODGER, THE(1944), p; TAMPICO(1944), p; HANGOVER SQUARE(1945), p; MOLLY AND ME(1945), p; THUNDERHEAD-SON OF FLICKA(1945), p; BEHIND GREEN LIGHTS(1946), p; SMOKY(1946), p; BRASHER DOUBLOON, THE(1947), p; HOMES-TRETCH, THE(1947), p; GREEN GRASS OF WYOMING(1948), p; SNAKE PIT, THE(1948), p; SAND(1949), p; THIEVES' HIGHWAY(1949), p; TICKET TO TOMA-HAWK(1950), p; HALLS OF MONTEZUMA(1951), p; HOUSE ON TELEGRAPH HILL(1951), p; LET'S MAKE IT LEGAL(1951), p; KANGAROO(1952), p; MY WIFE'S BEST FRIEND(1952), p; NIGHT WITHOUT SLEEP(1952), p; BENEATH THE 12-MILE REEF(1953), p; DANGEROUS CROSSING(1953), p; GIRL NEXT DOOR, THE(1953), p; SILVER WHIP, THE(1953), p; SUDDENLY(1954), p; GUNSIGHT RIDGE(1957), p
Silents
SECRET HOUR, THE(1928), ed
George Bassman
SHIP AHOY(1942), m; YOUNG IDEAS(1943), m; CANTERVILLE GHOST, THE(1944), m; MAIN STREET AFTER DARK(1944), m; CLOCK, THE(1945), m; LET-TER FOR EVIE, A(1945), m; LITTLE MISTER JIM(1946), m; POSTMAN ALWAYS RINGS TWICE, THE(1946), m; TWO SMART PEOPLE(1946), m; ROMANCE OF ROSY RIDGE, THE(1947), m; JOE LOUIS STORY, THE(1953), m; LOUISIANA TER-RITORY(1953), m; CANYON CROSSROADS(1955), m; MIDDLE OF THE NIGHT(1959), m, md; RIDE THE HIGH COUNTRY(1962), m; MAIL ORDER BRI-DE(1964), m
Bob Basso
LOVE AT FIRST BITE(1979); ZOOT SUIT(1981)
Frank Basso
MANCHURIAN CANDIDATE, THE(1962)
Giorgio Basso
SUNFLOWER(1970, Fr./Ital.)
Hamilton Basso
HOLIDAY FOR SINNERS(1952), w; VIEW FROM POMPEY'S HEAD, THE(1955), p,d&w
Patrizia Basso
SPECIAL DAY, A(1977, Ital./Can.)
Renato Basso
LA CAGE AUX FOLLES II(1981, Ital./Fr.)
Lawrence Bassoff
1984
WEEKEND PASS(1984), d&w
Francesca Bassurini
TREE OF WOODEN CLOGS, THE(1979, Ital.)
Iselin Bast
EDVARD MUNCH(1976, Norway/Swed.)
William Bast
HAMMERHEAD(1968), w; BETSY, THE(1978), w
William E. Bast
VALLEY OF GWANGI, THE(1969), w
Bart Bastable
BROTH OF A BOY(1959, Brit.); SIEGE OF SIDNEY STREET, THE(1960, Brit.); DEVIL'S AGENT, THE(1962, Brit.)
Alexander Bastedo
MY LOVER, MY SON(1970, Brit.)
Alexandra Bastedo
THIS, THAT AND THE OTHER(1970, Brit.); WEDDING NIGHT(1970, Ireland); BLOOD SPATTERED BRIDE, THE(1974, Span.); GHOUL, THE(1975, Brit.); I HATE MY BODY(1975, Span./Switz.)
Misc. Talkies
LEGEND OF CHAMPIONS(1983)
Alexandra L. Bastedo
THIRTEEN FRIGHTENED GIRLS(1963)
Lajos Basthy
AZURE EXPRESS(1938, Hung.)
Jean Bastia
DYNAMITE JACK(1961, Fr.), d, w
Charles Bastian
36 HOURS(1965)
Denis Bastian
TARZAN GOES TO INDIA(1962, U.S./Brit./Switz.)
George Bastian
ESCAPE FROM EAST BERLIN(1962)
Giancarlo Bastianoni
GOD FORGIVES–I DON'T!(1969, Ital./Span.)
Alain Bastien-Thiry
1984
FIRST NAME: CARMEN(1984, Fr.)
Charles A. Bastin
CHEAP DETECTIVE, THE(1978)

Charles Bastin
WORLD MOVES ON, THE(1934); ARISE, MY LOVE(1940); ADAM'S RIB(1949)

J. Thornton Baston
Silents
BEYOND PRICE(1921); SPLENDID LIE, THE(1922); AS A MAN LIVES(1923); DOWN TO THE SEA IN SHIPS(1923); BY WHOSE HAND?(1927)
Misc. Silents
TIGER'S CUB(1920); VIRGIN PARADISE, A(1921); WHITE HELL(1922)

Jack Baston
DESERT FOX, THE(1951); LES MISERABLES(1952)
Silents
CIRCUS ACE, THE(1927)
Misc. Silents
CHAIN LIGHTING(1927); BRANDED SOMBRERO, THE(1928); HELLO CHEYE-NE(1928)

Jack Thornton Baston
Misc. Silents
WHITE MOLL, THE(1920)

Thornton Baston
Misc. Silents
FIGHTING KENTUCKIANS, THE(1920)

Ron Bastone
Misc. Talkies
SCREAM BLOODY MURDER(1973)

Augusto Roa Bastos
PUT UP OR SHUT UP(1968, Arg.), w

Othon Bastos
GIVEN WORD, THE(1964, Braz.); ANTONIO DAS MORTES(1970, Braz.)

Michael Bastow
NEITHER THE SEA NOR THE SAND(1974, Brit.), art d; STUD, THE(1979, Brit.), art d

Ganga Pada Basu
MUSIC ROOM, THE(1963, India)

Joe Basulto
TOUCH OF EVIL(1958)

C. Basurko
DULCINEA(1962, Span.), m

Roman Baszkiewicz
LOTNA(1966, Pol.), makeup

Michael Bat-Adam
HANNAH K.(1983, Fr.)
1984
AMBASSADOR, THE(1984)

Umberto Batacca
CHOSEN, THE(1978, Brit./Ital.), art d

Rick Bataglia
MYSTERIOUS ISLAND OF CAPTAIN NEMO, THE(1973, Fr./Ital. 87m Span./Cameroon)

Henri Bataille
L'ENIGMATIQUE MONSIEUR PARKES(1930), w, ed; PRIVATE LIFE OF DON JUAN, THE(1934, Brit.), w

Henry Bataille
NAKED WOMAN, THE(1950, Fr.), w

Laurence Bataille
FRENCH CANCAN(1956, Fr.)

Michel Bataille
CHRISTMAS TREE, THE(1969, Fr.), w

Nicholas Bataille
ZAZIE(1961, Fr.)

Nicolas Bataille
MY UNCLE(1958, Fr.); VERY PRIVATE AFFAIR, A(1962, Fr./Ital.)

Sylvia Bataille
CRIME OF MONSIEUR LANGE, THE(1936, Fr.); COURIER OF LYONS(1938, Fr.); CONFESSIONS OF A NEWLYWED(1941, Fr.); GATES OF THE NIGHT(1950, Fr.)

Lucien Batalle
Misc. Silents
LA CIQUILLE ET LE CLERGYMAN(1928, Fr.)

Aleksey Batalov
OVERCOAT, THE(1965, USSR), d

Alesksi Batalov
LADY WITH THE DOG, THE(1962, USSR)

Alexei Batalov
CRANES ARE FLYING, THE(1960, USSR); MOSCOW DOES NOT BELIEVE IN TEARS(1980, USSR)

Nikolai Batalov
ROAD TO LIFE(1932, USSR)
Misc. Silents
BED AND SOFA(1926, USSR); MOTHER(1926, USSR)

S. Batalova
DON QUIXOTE(1961, USSR)

Arthur Batanides
UNEARTHLY, THE(1957); VIOLENT ROAD(1958); CRY TOUGH(1959); LEECH WOMAN, THE(1960); SPARTACUS(1960); MAN-TRAP(1961); MALTESE BIPPY, THE(1969); CAT ATE THE PARAKEET, THE(1972); BRANNIGAN(1975, Brit.)
Misc. Talkies
POT! PARENTS! POLICE!(1975)

B. Batashov
WAR AND PEACE(1968, USSR)

Pierre Batcheff
LOVE IN MOROCCO(1933, Fr.); AMOUR, AMOUR(1937, Fr.), w
Silents
NAPOLEON(1927, Fr.)
Misc. Silents
LA SIRENE DES TROPIQUES(1928, Fr.); LES DEUX TIMIDES(1929, Fr.); MONTE-CRISTO(1929, Fr.)

Denise Batcheff-Tual
LA CHIENNE(1975, Fr.), ed

Gina Batchelder
HILDUR AND THE MAGICIAN(1969)

Mark Batchelder
HILDUR AND THE MAGICIAN(1969)

Warren Batchelder
BUGS BUNNY'S THIRD MOVIE–1001 RABBIT TALES(1982), anim

George R. Batcheleir
THRILL OF YOUTH(1932), p

George R. Batcheller
JAZZ CINDERELLA(1930), p; LADY FROM NOWHERE(1931), p; BEAUTY PAR-LOR(1932), p; ESCAPADE(1932), p; SECRETS OF WU SIN(1932), p; FORGOT-TEN(1933), p; STRANGE PEOPLE(1933), p; CITY PARK(1934), p; GREEN EYES(1934), p; MURDER ON THE CAMPUS(1934), p; CIRCUMSTANTIAL EVI-DENCE(1935), p; CURTAIN FALLS, THE(1935), p; FALSE PRETENSES(1935), p; GIRL WHO CAME BACK, THE(1935), p; HAPPINESS C.O.D.(1935), p; LADY IN SCARLET, THE(1935), p; SHOT IN THE DARK, A(1935), p; AUGUST WEEK-END(1936, Brit.), p; BELOW THE DEADLINE(1936), p; DARK HOUR, THE(1936), p; LADY LUCK(1936), p; LITTLE RED SCHOOLHOUSE(1936), p; MISSING GIRLS(1936), p; RING AROUND THE MOON(1936), p; HOUSE OF SECRETS, THE(1937), p; FEDERAL FUGITIVES(1941), p; TODAY I HANG(1942), p

Richard Batcheller
FOR PETE'S SAKE!(1966), ph

George R. Batchellor
BLONDE COMET(1941), p

Amelia Batchelor
JEALOUSY(1934)

George R. Batchelor
MIDNIGHT SPECIAL(1931), p

Ian "Iron Man" Batchelor
MIGHTY JOE YOUNG(1949)

Joy Batchelor
ANIMAL FARM(1955, Brit.), p&d, w; MONSTER OF HIGHGATE PONDS, THE(1961, Brit.), w
Misc. Talkies
RUDDIGORE(1967, Brit.), d

Luke Batchelor
DARWIN ADVENTURE, THE(1972, Brit.)
Misc. Talkies
ZOO ROBBERY(1973, Brit.); CHIFFY KIDS GANG, THE(1983)

Rev. Dr. Batchelor
Silents
ROAD TO LONDON, THE(1921, Brit.)

Ruth Batchelor
STRANGERS WHEN WE MEET(1960); LOVE MACHINE, THE,(1971), m/l $oqHe's Moving On,$cq Brian Wells

Pierre Batchoff
Misc. Silents
CHESS PLAYER, THE(1930, Fr.)

Anthony Bate
HIGH TIDE AT NOON(1957, Brit.); PRIZE OF ARMS, A(1962, Brit.); SET-UP, THE(1963, Brit.); STOPOVER FOREVER(1964, Brit.); ACT OF MURDER(1965, Brit.); GHOST STORY(1974, Brit.); NELLY'S VERSION(1983, Brit.)

Cherise Bate
XANADU(1980)

Natalie Bate
DIMBOOLA(1979, Aus.)

Ernest G. Bately
Misc. Silents
WHEN LONDON SLEEPS(1914, Brit.), d

Anthony Bateman
HATTER'S CASTLE(1948, Brit.)

Bill Bateman
1984
STREETS OF FIRE(1984)

Charles Bateman
BROTHERHOOD OF SATAN, THE(1971); INTERVAL(1973, Mex./U.S.)

Fred Bateman
LOVES OF JOANNA GODDEN, THE(1947, Brit.)

Geoffrey Bateman
1984
ANOTHER COUNTRY(1984, Brit.)

Gwen Bateman
MAN FROM MOROCCO, THE(1946, Brit.)

Helen Bateman
Misc. Silents
PLANTER, THE(1917)

Kent Bateman
LAND OF NO RETURN, THE(1981), p&d, w
Misc. Talkies
DEATH ON CREDIT(1976); HEADLESS EYES, THE(1983), d

Stephen Bateman
CONFESSIONS OF AMANS, THE(1977)

Victory Bateman
Silents
ROMEO AND JULIET(1916); IDLE RICH, THE(1921); KEEPING UP WITH LIZ-ZIE(1921); IF I WERE QUEEN(1922); ETERNAL THREE, THE(1923); TESS OF THE D'URBERVILLES(1924)
Misc. Silents
POWER OF EVIL, THE(1916)

Zillah Bateman
FATHER STEPS OUT(1937, Brit.); TAKE IT FROM ME(1937, Brit.); IF I WERE BOSS(1938, Brit.); NIGHT JOURNEY(1938, Brit.); HIS LORDSHIP GOES TO PRESS(1939, Brit.); MURDER IN THE NIGHT(1940, Brit.); OUTSIDER, THE(1940, Brit.)

Saskia Ten Batenburg
SPETTERS(1983, Holland)

A. Bates
MR. COHEN TAKES A WALK(1936, Brit.), ed

A. E. Bates
FIRES OF FATE(1932, Brit.), ed

A. S. Bates
GIRLS WILL BE BOYS(1934, Brit.), ed; YOU MADE ME LOVE YOU(1934, Brit.), ed; IDOL OF PARIS(1948, Brit.), ed; UNDER CAPRICORN(1949), ed; MAN BETWEEN, THE(1953, Brit.), ed; FIRE OVER AFRICA(1954, Brit.), ed; DEEP BLUE SEA, THE(1955, Brit.), ed; KID FOR TWO FARTHINGS, A(1956, Brit.), ed

Alan Bates
ENTERTAINER, THE(1960, Brit.); WHISTLE DOWN THE WIND(1961, Brit.); KIND OF LOVING, A(1962, Brit.); GUEST, THE(1963, Brit.); RUNNING MAN, THE(1963, Brit.); NOTHING BUT THE BEST(1964, Brit.); ZORBA THE GREEK(1964, U.S./Gr.); GEORGY GIRL(1966, Brit.); FAR FROM THE MADDING CROWD(1967, Brit.); KING OF HEARTS(1967, Fr./Ital.); FIXER, THE(1968); WOMEN IN LOVE(1969, Brit.); GO-BETWEEN, THE(1971, Brit.); DAY IN THE DEATH OF JOE EGG, A(1972, Brit.); IMPOSSIBLE OBJECT(1973, Fr.); BUTLEY(1974, Brit.); THREE SISTERS(1974, Brit.); IN CELEBRATION(1975, Brit.); ROYAL FLASH(1975, Brit.); SHOUT, THE(1978, Brit.); UNMARRIED WOMAN, AN(1978); ROSE, THE(1979); NIJINSKY(1980, Brit.); QUARTET(1981, Brit./Fr.); BRITTANIA HOSPITAL(1982, Brit.); RETURN OF THE SOLDIER, THE(1983, Brit.); WICKED LADY, THE(1983, Brit.)

Albert Bates
GOODBYE AGAIN(1961), ed

Amie Bates
G.I. JANE(1951)

Andrew Bates, Jr.
GEORGIA, GEORGIA(1972)

Anthony Bates
1984
GIVE MY REGARDS TO BROAD STREET(1984, Brit.)

Arthur Bates
Misc. Silents
UNEASY MONEY(1918)

Arthur W. Bates
Silents
ALSTER CASE, THE(1915); NIGHT WORKERS, THE(1917)

Barbara Bates
LADY ON A TRAIN(1945); SALOME, WHERE SHE DANCED(1945); STRANGE HOLIDAY(1945); THIS LOVE OF OURS(1945); NIGHT IN PARADISE, A(1946); JOHNNY BELINDA(1948); JUNE BRIDE(1948); ROMANCE ON THE HIGH SEAS(1948); HOUSE ACROSS THE STREET, THE(1949); INSPECTOR GENERAL, THE(1949); ONE LAST FLING(1949); ALL ABOUT EVE(1950); CHEAPER BY THE DOZEN(1950); QUICKSAND(1950); I'D CLIMB THE HIGHEST MOUNTAIN(1951); LET'S MAKE IT LEGAL(1951); SECRET OF CONVICT LAKE, THE(1951); BELLES ON THEIR TOES(1952); OUTCASTS OF POKER FLAT, THE(1952); ALL ASHORE(1953); CADDY, THE(1953); RHAPSODY(1954); TOWN ON TRIAL(1957, Brit.); TRIPLE DECEPTION(1957, Brit.); APACHE TERRITORY(1958)

Ben Bates
PIPE DREAMS(1976); LEGEND OF THE LONE RANGER, THE(1981); SWAMP THING(1982)

Bert Bates
SOMETHING ALWAYS HAPPENS(1934, Brit.), ed; SOME DAY(1935, Brit.), ed; HIGH FURY(1947, Brit.), ed; CURE FOR LOVE, THE(1950, Brit.), ed; HAPPY GO LOVELY(1951, Brit.), ed; OUTCAST OF THE ISLANDS(1952, Brit.), ed; MURDER ON MONDAY(1953, Brit.), ed; RINGER, THE(1953, Brit.), ed; HOLLY AND THE IVY, THE(1954, Brit.), ed; MAN WHO LOVED REDHEADS, THE(1955, Brit.), ed; ANASTASIA(1956), ed; TRAPEZE(1956), ed; LEGEND OF THE LOST(1957, U.S./Panama/ Ital.), ed; KEY, THE(1958, Brit.), ed; OUR MAN IN HAVANA(1960, Brit.), ed; WORLD OF SUZIE WONG, THE(1960), ed; FIVE MILES TO MIDNIGHT(1963, U.S./Fr./Ital.), ed; RUNNING MAN, THE(1963, Brit.), ed; SHOT IN THE DARK, A(1964), ed; SQUADRON 633(1964, U.S./Brit.), ed; 633 SQUADRON(1964), ed; BATTLE OF THE VILLA FIORITA, THE(1965, Brit.), ed; HEROES OF TELEMARK, THE(1965, Brit.), ed; CAST A GIANT SHADOW(1966), ed; RETURN OF THE SEVEN(1966, Span.), ed; LONG DUEL, THE(1967, Brit.), ed; INTERLUDE(1968, Brit.), ed; BATTLE OF BRITAIN, THE(1969, Brit.), ed; DIAMONDS ARE FOREVER(1971, Brit.), ed; LIGHT AT THE EDGE OF THE WORLD, THE(1971, U.S./Span./Lichtenstein), ed; TOWN CALLED HELL, A(1971, Span./Brit.), ed; LIVE AND LET DIE(1973, Brit.), ed

Bill Bates
GHOSTS ON THE LOOSE(1943)

Billy Bates
1984
ICE PIRATES, THE(1984)

Blanche Bates
Misc. Silents
BORDER LEGION, THE(1919)

Bobo Bates
TAKING OFF(1971)

Brigid Eric Bates
THEATRE OF BLOOD(1973, Brit.)

Brigid Erin Bates
TESS(1980, Fr./Brit.)

Buri Bates
BEST OF ENEMIES, THE(1962), ed

Caroline Bates
Misc. Talkies
GRAD NIGHT(1980)

Charles Bates
I MARRIED A WITCH(1942); NORTH STAR, THE(1943); SHADOW OF A DOUBT(1943); SON OF DRACULA(1943); SONG OF BERNADETTE, THE(1943); STRANGE DEATH OF ADOLF HITLER, THE(1943); LADY IN THE DARK(1944); ONCE UPON A TIME(1944); SAN DIEGO, I LOVE YOU(1944); DANNY BOY(1946); HOODLUM SAINT, THE(1946); NIGHT IN PARADISE, A(1946); HER HUSBAND'S AFFAIRS(1947); PURSUED(1947); SHOCKPROOF(1949); SNOWS OF KILIMANJARO, THE(1952)

Florence Bates
MAN IN BLUE, THE(1937); CALLING ALL HUSBANDS(1940); HUDSON'S BAY(1940); KITTY FOYLE(1940); REBECCA(1940); SON OF MONTE CRISTO(1940); CHOCOLATE SOLDIER, THE(1941); DEVIL AND MISS JONES, THE(1941); LOVE CRAZY(1941); ROAD SHOW(1941); STRANGE ALIBI(1941); MEXICAN SPITFIRE AT SEA(1942); MOON AND SIXPENCE, THE(1942); MY HEART BELONGS TO DADDY(1942); TUTTLES OF TAHITI(1942); WE WERE DANCING(1942); HEAVEN CAN WAIT(1943); HIS BUTLER'S SISTER(1943); MR. BIG(1943); MR. LUCKY(1943);

SLIGHTLY DANGEROUS(1943); THEY GOT ME COVERED(1943); BELLE OF THE YUKON(1944); KISMET(1944); MASK OF DIMITRIOS, THE(1944); SINCE YOU WENT AWAY(1944); OUT OF THIS WORLD(1945); SAN ANTONIO(1945); SARATOGA TRUNK(1945); SOUTHERNER, THE(1945); TAHITI NIGHTS(1945); TONIGHT AND EVERY NIGHT(1945); CLAUDIA AND DAVID(1946); CLUNY BROWN(1946); DIARY OF A CHAMBERMAID(1946); MAN I LOVE, THE(1946); TIME, THE PLACE AND THE GIRL, THE(1946); WHISTLE STOP(1946); BRASHER DOUBLOON, THE(1947); DESIRE ME(1947); LOVE AND LEARN(1947); SECRET LIFE OF WALTER MITTY, THE(1947); I REMEMBER MAMA(1948); INSIDE STORY, THE(1948); LETTER TO THREE WIVES, A(1948); MY DEAR SECRETARY(1948); RIVER LADY(1948); TEXAS, BROOKLYN AND HEAVEN(1948); WINTER MEETING(1948); GIRL FROM JONES BEACH, THE(1949); JUDGE STEPS OUT, THE(1949); ON THE TOWN(1949); PORTRAIT OF JENNIE(1949); BELLE OF OLD MEXICO(1950); COUNTY FAIR(1950); FATHER TAKES THE AIR(1951); HAVANA ROSE(1951); LULLABY OF BROADWAY, THE(1951); SECOND CHANCE, THE(1951); TALL TARGET, THE(1951); LES MISERABLES(1952); SAN FRANCISCO STORY, THE(1952); MAIN STREET TO BROADWAY(1953); PARIS MODEL(1953)

George Bates
Misc. Talkies
GALLOPING KID, THE(1932)

Granville Bates
JEALOUSY(1929); SAP FROM SYRACUSE, THE(1930); HONOR AMONG LOVERS(1931); SMILING LIEUTENANT, THE(1931); WISER SEX, THE(1932); MIDNIGHT(1934); WOMAN IN THE DARK(1934); PURSUIT(1935); WOMAN WANTED(1935); BELOVED ENEMY(1936); CHATTERBOX(1936); HERE COMES TROUBLE(1936); POPPY(1936); SING ME A LOVE SONG(1936); THIRTEEN HOURS BY AIR(1936); TIMES SQUARE PLAYBOY(1936); BACK IN CIRCULATION(1937); GREEN LIGHT(1937); IT HAPPENED IN HOLLYWOOD(1937); LARCENY ON THE AIR(1937); LET'S GET MARRIED(1937); MAKE WAY FOR TOMORROW(1937); MOUNTAIN JUSTICE(1937); NANCY STEELE IS MISSING(1937); PERFECT SPECIMEN, THE(1937); PLAINSMAN, THE(1937); THEY WON'T FORGET(1937); UNDER SUSPICION(1937); WAIKIKI WEDDING(1937); WELLS FARGO(1937); WHEN'S YOUR BIRTHDAY?(1937); WINGS OVER HONOLULU(1937); ADVENTURES OF MARCO POLO, THE(1938); AFFAIRS OF ANNABEL(1938); COWBOY FROM BROOKLYN(1938); GARDEN OF THE MOON(1938); GO CHASE YOURSELF(1938); GOLD IS WHERE YOU FIND IT(1938); HARD TO GET(1938); JURY'S SECRET, THE(1938); MAN TO REMEMBER, A(1938); MR. CHUMP(1938); NEXT TIME I MARRY(1938); ROMANCE ON THE RUN(1938); SHINING HOUR, THE(1938); SISTERS, THE(1938); YOUTH TAKES A FLING(1938); BLACKWELL'S ISLAND(1939); EACH DAWN I DIE(1939); ETERNALLY YOURS(1939); FAST AND FURIOUS(1939); GREAT MAN VOTES, THE(1939); INDIANAPOLIS SPEEDWAY(1939); NAUGHTY BUT NICE(1939); OF MICE AND MEN(1939); OUR NEIGHBORS–THE CARTERS(1939); PRIDE OF THE BLUEGRASS(1939); SWEEPSTAKES WINNER(1939); THOU SHALT NOT KILL(1939); TWELVE CROWDED HOURS(1939); BROTHER ORCHID(1940); BROTHER RAT AND A BABY(1940); FLOWING GOLD(1940); GRANNY GET YOUR GUN(1940); MEN AGAINST THE SKY(1940); MILLIONAIRE PLAYBOY(1940); MORTAL STORM, THE(1940); MY FAVORITE WIFE(1940); PRIVATE AFFAIRS(1940)
Misc. Silents
KILL-JOY, THE(1917); YOUNG MOTHER HUBBARD(1917)

H. E. Bates
LOVES OF JOANNA GODDEN, THE(1947, Brit.), w; MATING GAME, THE(1959), w; TRIPLE ECHO, THE(1973, Brit.), w

H.E. Bates
PURPLE PLAIN, THE(1954, Brit.), w; SUMMERTIME(1955), w; DULCIMA(1971, Brit.), d&w

Harry Bates
GIRL OF THE OZARKS(1936); DAY THE EARTH STOOD STILL, THE(1951), w

Ira Bates
MASTER GUNFIGHTER, THE(1975), set d; CITIZENS BAND(1977), set d; GAUNTLET, THE(1977), set d; HOOPER(1978), set d; SIX WEEKS(1982), set d

Jack Bates
Silents
IVANHOE(1913)

James Bates
SPRING BREAK(1983), stunts

Jane Bates
POPDOWN(1968, Brit.)

Jeanne Bates
CHANCE OF A LIFETIME, THE(1943); BLACK PARACHUTE, THE(1944); RACKET MAN, THE(1944); RETURN OF THE VAMPIRE, THE(1944); SHADOWS IN THE NIGHT(1944); SHE'S A SOLDIER TOO(1944); SOUL OF A MONSTER, THE(1944); SUNDOWN VALLEY(1944); SERGEANT MIKE(1945); TONIGHT AND EVERY NIGHT(1945); MASK OF DIIJON, THE(1946); PAULA(1952); HINDU, THE(1953, Brit.); BACK FROM THE DEAD(1957); TROOPER HOOK(1957); BLOOD ARROW(1958); VICE RAID(1959); STRANGLER, THE(1964); SUPPOSE THEY GAVE A WAR AND NOBODY CAME?(1970); ERASERHEAD(1978)

Jim Bates
SMILE(1975), ch

Jimmie Bates
WISTFUL WIDOW OF WAGON GAP, THE(1947); RUN SILENT, RUN DEEP(1958)

Jimmy Bates
EASTER PARADE(1948); ANDY HARDY COMES HOME(1958)

John Bates
PROVIDENCE(1977, Fr.), cos

Kathryn Bates
TEXAS RANGERS, THE(1936)

Kathy Bates
STRAIGHT TIME(1978); COME BACK TO THE 5 & DIME, JIMMY DEAN, JIMMY DEAN(1982); TWO OF A KIND(1983)

Kirk Bates
WICKED, WICKED(1973)

Kirsten Bates
OFFENDERS, THE(1980)

Les Bates
FIGHTING LEGION, THE(1930); MOUNTAIN JUSTICE(1930)
Silents
BROKEN DOLL, A(1921); DESERTED AT THE ALTAR(1922); MY DAD(1922); IRISH HEARTS(1927)

Misc. Silents
  BIG STAKES(1922); MARTYR SEX, THE(1924); SHACKLES OF FEAR(1924); LURE OF THE WEST(1925); GLORIOUS TRAIL, THE(1928)
Louise Bates
  DARK ANGEL, THE(1935); GIVE ME YOUR HEART(1936); POLO JOE(1936); LAUGH IT OFF(1939); MRS. MINIVER(1942); CASBAH(1948); GAL WHO TOOK THE WEST, THE(1949); TOAST OF NEW ORLEANS, THE(1950); PROWLER, THE(1951)
Silents
  ARMS AND THE GIRL(1917)
Misc. Silents
  EASIEST WAY, THE(1917); WRATH OF LOVE(1917)
Louise E. Bates
Misc. Silents
  SILAS MARNER(1916)
Louise Emerald Bates
Misc. Silents
  HER FATHER'S GOLD(1916)
Louise M. Bates
Silents
  MEN SHE MARRIED, THE(1916)
Mae Bates
Silents
  RISE OF JENNIE CUSHING, THE(1917)
Michael Bates
  COURT MARTIAL(1954, Brit.); DUNKIRK(1958, Brit.); I'M ALL RIGHT, JACK(1959, Brit.); BEDAZZLED(1967, Brit.); DON'T RAISE THE BRIDGE, LOWER THE RIVER(1968, Brit.); HAMMERHEAD(1968); HERE WE GO ROUND THE MULBERRY BUSH(1968, Brit.); SALT & PEPPER(1968, Brit.); BATTLE OF BRITAIN, THE(1969, Brit.); OH! WHAT A LOVELY WAR(1969, Brit.); PATTON(1970); RISE AND RISE OF MICHAEL RIMMER, THE(1970, Brit.); THINK DIRTY(1970, Brit.); CLOCKWORK ORANGE, A(1971, Brit.); FRENZY(1972, Brit.); BAWDY ADVENTURES OF TOM JONES, THE(1976, Brit.); GULLIVER'S TRAVELS(1977, Brit., Bel.); NO SEX PLEASE–WE'RE BRITISH(1979, Brit.)
Nan Bates
  PRIDE OF THE FORCE, THE(1933, Brit.)
Noel Bates
  THEODORA GOES WILD(1936)
Paul Bates
1984
  EXTERMINATOR 2(1984)
Peggy Bates
  WINE, WOMEN AND HORSES(1937)
Ralph Bates
  HORROR OF FRANKENSTEIN, THE(1970, Brit.); TASTE THE BLOOD OF DRACULA(1970, Brit.); DR. JEKYLL AND SISTER HYDE(1971, Brit.); LUST FOR A VAMPIRE(1971, Brit.); FEAR IN THE NIGHT(1972, Brit.); PERSECUTION(1974, Brit.); DEVIL WITHIN HER, THE(1976, Brit.)
Reginald Bates
  RIGHT AGE TO MARRY, THE(1935, Brit.)
Rhonda Bates
  FAST BREAK(1979); ROADIE(1980)
Richard Bates
Misc. Talkies
  MIDNIGHT SHADOW(1939)
Russell Bates
  PORKY'S II: THE NEXT DAY(1983)
Scotty Bates
  VARSITY SHOW(1937)
Stanley Bates
  THEATRE OF BLOOD(1973, Brit.)
Suxanne Creese Bates
  NEST OF VIPERS(1979, Ital.)
Thorpe Bates
  SMALL MAN, THE(1935, Brit.)
Tom Bates
Silents
  PARSON OF PANAMINT, THE(1916); HUCK AND TOM(1918); DON MIKE(1927)
Misc. Silents
  JUNGLE LOVERS, THE(1915)
Tom D. Bates
Silents
  ABABIAN KNIGHT, AN(1920); HUCKLEBERRY FINN(1920)
Virginia Bates
  TAKE ME OUT TO THE BALL GAME(1949); FRENCH LINE, THE(1954); SON OF SINBAD(1955)
William Bates
  ORGY OF THE DEAD(1965); HARRY IN YOUR POCKET(1973), art d & set d
Garrie Bateson
  TRAVELING EXECUTIONER, THE(1970), w
Timothy [Tim] Bateson
  VICE VERSA(1948, Brit.)
Timothy Bateson
  YESTERDAY'S ENEMY(1959, Brit.); NICHOLAS NICKLEBY(1947, Brit.); OUTSIDER, THE(1949, Brit.); WHITE CORRIDORS(1952, Brit.); RICHARD III(1956, Brit.); DEVIL'S BAIT(1959, Brit.); MOUSE THAT ROARED, THE(1959, Brit.); TREAD SOFTLY STRANGER(1959, Brit.); OUR MAN IN HAVANA(1960, Brit.); SHAKEDOWN, THE(1960, Brit.); UNSTOPPABLE MAN, THE(1961, Brit.); GIRL ON THE BOAT, THE(1962, Brit.); GOLDEN RABBIT, THE(1962, Brit.); RING-A-DING RHYTHM(1962, Brit. 73m Amicus/COL bw (G.B: IT'S TRAD, DAD!); THERE WAS A CROOKED MAN(1962, Brit.); WHAT A CARVE UP!(1962, Brit.); CROOKS ANONYMOUS(1963, Brit.); DOCTOR IN DISTRESS(1963, Brit.); NIGHTMARE(1963, Brit.); EVIL OF FRANKENSTEIN, THE(1964, Brit.); FATHER CAME TOO(1964, Brit.); SEVENTY DEADLY PILLS(1964, Brit.); JIG SAW(1965, Brit.); KNACK ... AND HOW TO GET IT, THE(1965, Brit.); WRONG BOX, THE(1966, Brit.); ANNIVERSARY, THE(1968, Brit.); DANGER ROUTE(1968, Brit.); TORTURE GARDEN(1968, Brit.); ITALIAN JOB, THE(1969, Brit.); TWISTED NERVE(1969, Brit.); HIGH ROAD TO CHINA(1983)

Hubert Bath
  BLACKMAIL(1929, Brit.), m; SILENT BARRIERS(1937, Brit.), m; YANK AT OXFORD, A(1938), m; ADVENTURES OF TARTU(1943, Brit.), m; PLACE OF ONE'S OWN, A(1945, Brit.), m; LADY SURRENDERS, A(1947, Brit.), m
John Bath
  FLAMING FRONTIER(1958, Can.), m, md; STRANGE CASE OF DR. MANNING, THE(1958, Brit.), md; WOLF DOG(1958, Can.), m; ONE PLUS ONE(1961, Can.), m; PARADISIO(1962, Brit.), m; RIGHT HAND OF THE DEVIL, THE(1963), m; SKYDIVERS, THE(1963), md; ADULTEROUS AFFAIR(1966), ed&md; NIGHT TRAIN TO MUNDO FINE(1966), m; TAKE HER BY SURPRISE(1967, Can.), m
John Hubert Bath
  NOW THAT APRIL'S HERE(1958, Can.), m
Larry Bathin
  ARM OF THE LAW(1932)
1p: Serafina Bathrick
Misc. Talkies
  11 X 14(1977)
Bathsheba
  HALLELUJAH THE HILLS(1963), cos; DOUBLE-BARRELLED DETECTIVE STORY, THE(1965), cos
Peter Bathurst
  BABES IN BAGDAD(1952); GLORY AT SEA(1952, Brit.); FINAL APPOINTMENT(1954, Brit.); TERROR SHIP(1954, Brit.); PACIFIC DESTINY(1956, Brit.); BETRAYAL, THE(1958, Brit.); DIPLOMATIC CORPSE, THE(1958, Brit.); LINKS OF JUSTICE(1958); THREE CROOKED MEN(1958, Brit.); MY SON, THE VAMPIRE(1963, Brit.); TWO LIVING, ONE DEAD(1964, Brit./Swed.); CHANGE PARTNERS(1965, Brit.); MURDER GAME, THE(1966, Brit.)
Franklin Batie
  BIG BOY(1930)
John Batis
  TEENAGE GANG DEBS(1966); FOREST, THE(1983)
Henry Batista
  MY NAME IS JULIA ROSS(1945), ed; BETTY CO-ED(1946), ed; BLONDIE IN THE DOUGH(1947), ed; KING OF THE WILD HORSES(1947), ed; LONE WOLF IN LONDON(1947), ed; ADVENTURES IN SILVERADO(1948), ed; GENTLEMAN FROM NOWHERE, THE(1948), ed; RACING LUCK(1948), ed; STRAWBERRY ROAN, THE(1948), ed; BIG SOMBRERO, THE(1949), ed; BLONDIE HITS THE JACKPOT(1949), ed; BLONDIE'S BIG DEAL(1949), ed; COWBOY AND THE INDIANS, THE(1949), ed; HOLIDAY IN HAVANA(1949), ed; LAW OF THE BARBARY COAST(1949), ed; RIDERS IN THE SKY(1949), ed; SONS OF NEW MEXICO(1949), ed; BLONDIE'S HERO(1950), ed; CAPTIVE GIRL(1950), ed; COW TOWN(1950), ed; DAVID HARDING, COUNTERSPY(1950), ed; LAST OF THE BUCCANEERS(1950), ed; MARK OF THE GORILLA(1950), ed; BRAVE BULLS, THE(1951), ed; JUNGLE MANHUNT(1951), ed; PURPLE HEART DIARY(1951), ed; FOUR POSTER, THE(1952), ed; JUNGLE JIM IN THE FORBIDDEN LAND(1952), ed; CHARGE OF THE LANCERS(1953), ed; MISSION OVER KOREA(1953), ed; SAVAGE MUTINY(1953), ed; CAINE MUTINY, THE(1954), ed; MASTERSON OF KANSAS(1954), ed; THEY RODE WEST(1954), ed; BAMBOO PRISON, THE(1955), ed; CELL 2455, DEATH ROW(1955), ed; JUNGLE MOON MEN(1955), ed; WOMEN'S PRISON(1955), ed; 1,000 PLANE RAID, THE(1969), ed; VENUS IN FURS(1970, Ital./Brit./Ger.), ed
Lloyd Batista
  BLINDMAN(1972, Ital.)
Miriam Batista
Silents
  EYE FOR EYE(1918)
Moises Batista
  SECRET DOOR, THE(1964)
Gina Batiste
1984
  OLD ENOUGH(1984)
John Batiste
  PEOPLE NEXT DOOR, THE(1970); LAST OF THE RED HOT LOVERS(1972)
Antonio Batistella
  WARRIOR EMPRESS, THE(1961, Ital./Fr.)
Joseph Batistich
  LUM AND ABNER ABROAD(1956)
Bedich Batka
  MARKETA LAZAROVA(1968, Czech.), ph
Bedrich Batka
  90 DEGREES IN THE SHADE(1966, Czech./Brit.), ph
Fred Batka
  LITTLE DARLINGS(1980), ph; NIGHT THE LIGHTS WENT OUT IN GEORGIA, THE(1981), ph
Dorothy Batley
  ANGEL WITH THE TRUMPET, THE(1950, Brit.); ROSSITER CASE, THE(1950, Brit.)
Misc. Silents
  SINS OF YOUTH, THE(1919, Brit.)
Ernest G. Batley
Misc. Silents
  BATTLE OF WATERLOO, THE(1913, Brit.); REVOLUTIONIST, THE(1914, Brit.), d; BOYS OF THE OLD BRIGADE, THE(1916, Brit.), d; SINS OF YOUTH, THE(1919, Brit.), a, d
Aleksey Batlov
  NINE DAYS OF ONE YEAR(1964, USSR)
Joseph Bato
  BONNIE PRINCE CHARLIE(1948, Brit.), prod d; FIGHTING PIMPERNEL, THE(1950, Brit.), set d; HAPPIEST DAYS OF YOUR LIFE(1950, Brit.), prod d; THIRD MAN, THE(1950, Brit.), prod d; WONDER BOY(1951, Brit./Aust.), prod d; BREAKING THE SOUND BARRIER(1952), art d; RINGER, THE(1953, Brit.), prod d; HEART OF THE MATTER, THE(1954, Brit.), prod d; INTRUDER, THE(1955, Brit.), art d; LADY GODIVA RIDES AGAIN(1955, Brit.), art d; RAISING A RIOT(1957, Brit.), art d
Bato-Ochir
  SON OF MONGOLIA(1936, USSR)
Stiv Bators
  POLYESTER(1981)
Sara Batsford
  DEADLY EYES(1982)

J. Hastings Batson
Silents
IN THE HANDS OF THE LONDON CROOKS(1913, Brit.); JACK TAR(1915, Brit.); JUST A GIRL(1916, Brit.); LOVE(1916, Brit.); ON THE BANKS OF ALLAN WATER(1916, Brit.)
Misc. Silents
STRANGE CASE OF PHILIP KENT, THE(1916, Brit.); WITH ALL HER HEART(1920, Brit.)

Susan Batson
WUSA(1970); CHOIRBOYS, THE(1977); HOUSE CALLS(1978); LOVE CHILD(1982)

Bert Batt
FRANKENSTEIN MUST BE DESTROYED!(1969, Brit.), w; QUEST FOR LOVE(1971, Brit.), w

Mike Batt
WOMBLING FREE(1977, Brit.), m; CARAVANS(1978, U.S./Iranian), m

Shelley Batt
HONKY TONK FREEWAY(1981)

Shelly Batt
SATURDAY NIGHT FEVER(1977); LOVING COUPLES(1980); TRUE CONFESSIONS(1981); SOME KIND OF HERO(1982)

Anthony Battaglia
ONE AND ONLY, THE(1978); SERIAL(1980)

Aurelius Battaglia
PINOCCHIO(1940), w

Guillermo Battaglia
END OF INNOCENCE(1960, Arg.); GAMES MEN PLAY, THE(1968, Arg.)

Joe Battaglia
1984
NIGHT PATROL(1984)

Luigi Battaglia
FELLINI SATYRICON(1969, Fr./Ital.); DEATH IN VENICE(1971, Ital./Fr.)

Rick Battaglia
ESTHER AND THE KING(1960, U.S./Ital.); MINOTAUR, THE(1961, Ital.); CAESAR THE CONQUEROR(1963, Ital.); LION OF ST. MARK(1967, Ital.); 'TIS A PITY SHE'S A WHORE(1973, Ital.)

Rik Battaglia
WOMAN OF THE RIVER(1954, Fr./Ital.); RAW WIND IN EDEN(1958); HANNIBAL(1960, Ital.); PRISONER OF THE VOLGA(1960, Fr./Ital.); FROM A ROMAN BALCONY(1961, Fr./Ital.); MIGHTY CRUSADERS, THE(1961, Ital.); SODOM AND GOMORRAH(1962, U.S./Fr./Ital.); RICE GIRL(1963, Fr./Ital.); SANDOKAN THE GREAT(1964, Fr./Ital./Span.); WHY BOTHER TO KNOCK(1964, Brit.); DESPERADO TRAIL, THE(1965, Ger./Yugo.); NIGHTMARE CASTLE(1966, Ital.); OLD SHATTERHAND(1968, Ger./Yugo./Ital.); THIS MAN CAN'T DIE(1970, Ital.); CALL OF THE WILD(1972, Ger./ Span./Ital./Fr.); DUCK, YOU SUCKER!(1972, Ital.); TREASURE ISLAND(1972, Brit./Span./Fr./Ger.)

Rudy Battaglia
ANGEL, ANGEL, DOWN WE GO(1969)

Augusto Battagliotti
Silents
CABIRIA(1914, Ital.), ph

Henri Bataille
Silents
SCANDAL, THE(1923, Brit.), w

Gerard Battaz
EVERY MAN FOR HIMSELF(1980, Fr.)

Gregory Battcock
ILLIAC PASSION, THE(1968)
Misc. Talkies
HORSE(1965)

Ivo Batteli
HEART AND SOUL(1950, Ital.), ed

Ivo Battelli
PSYCOSISSIMO(1962, Ital.), art d

John Batten
GREAT GAME, THE(1930); GREENWOOD TREE, THE(1930, Brit.); LOVE WALTZ, THE(1930, Ger.); UNDER THE GREENWOOD TREE(1930, Brit.); TRAPPED IN A SUBMARINE(1931, Brit.); WONDERFUL STORY, THE(1932, Brit.); CALL ME MAME(1933, Brit.); HIGH FINANCE(1933, Brit.); CHURCH MOUSE, THE(1934, Brit.); FOR THOSE IN PERIL(1944, Brit.)
Silents
BACKSTAGE(1927); BATTLE OF THE SEXES, THE(1928)

Paul Batten
1984
ICEMAN(1984); RUNAWAY(1984)

Peter Batten
YELLOW SUBMARINE(1958, Brit.)

Tom Batten
JUST TELL ME WHAT YOU WANT(1980)
Misc. Talkies
SWEET GENEVIEVE(1947)

Tommy Batten
RATIONING(1944)

Joe Battenberg
1984
SUBURBIA(1984)

Ter Battenburg
1984
SUPERGIRL(1984)

Roy Battersby
1984
WINTER FLIGHT(1984, Brit.), d

Jeanette Batti
HOLIDAY FOR HENRIETTA(1955, Fr.); FOUR BAGS FULL(1957, Fr./Ital.)

Nino Battieferri
MYSTERY OF THUG ISLAND, THE(1966, Ital./Ger.), p

Bob Battier
RETURN OF FRANK JAMES, THE(1940); ROLLIN' HOME TO TEXAS(1941)

Robert Battier
LOVE AND HISSES(1937)

Giulio Battiferri
MONSTER OF THE ISLAND(1953, Ital.); QUEEN OF THE PIRATES(1961, Ital./Ger.); RED SHEIK, THE(1963, Ital.); WHITE VOICES(1965, Fr./Ital.); SUPERARGO VERSUS DIABOLICUS(1966, Ital./Span.); SWEPT AWAY...BY AN UNUSUAL DESTINY IN THE BLUE SEA OF AUGUST(1975, Ital.), ph

Nino Battiferri
TIGER OF THE SEVEN SEAS(1964, Fr./Ital.), w

Giorgio Battilana
MAGIC WORLD OF TOPO GIGIO, THE(1961, Ital.), ph

Mary Battilana
1984
FLETCH(1984)

Skip Battin
CIAO MANHATTAN(1973), m

Marjorie Battis
STEPPING TOES(1938, Brit.)

Lloyd Battista
FLIPPER'S NEW ADVENTURE(1964); CHISUM(1970); LOVE AND DEATH(1975); GET MEAN(1976, Ital.), a, w; COMIN' AT YA!(1981), w; TREASURE OF THE FOUR CROWNS(1983, Span./U.S.), w

Miriam Battista
ENLIGHTEN THY DAUGHTER(1934)
Silents
SIN THAT WAS HIS, THE(1920); AT THE STAGE DOOR(1921); CURSE OF DRINK, THE(1922); MAN WHO PLAYED GOD, THE(1922); STEADFAST HEART, THE(1923)
Misc. Silents
BLONDE VAMPIRE, THE(1922); GOOD PROVIDER, THE(1922); CUSTARD CUP, THE(1923)

Antonio Battistella
THIEF OF BAGHDAD, THE(1961, Ital./Fr.)

Sandrine Battistella
NUMBER TWO(1975, Fr.)

C. Battistelli
MERCENARY, THE(1970, Ital./Span.), spec eff

Walter Battistelli
1990: THE BRONX WARRIORS(1983, Ital.), spec eff

Carlo Battisti
UMBERTO D(1955, Ital.)

Silvio Battistini
MAN WHO KILLED BILLY THE KID, THE(1967, Span./Ital.), p; FEW BULLETS MORE, A(1968, Ital./Span.), p

Mario Battistoni
RATATAPLAN(1979, Ital.), ph

Lucio Battistrada
DEAD ARE ALIVE, THE(1972, Yugo./Ger./Ital.), w

Ed Battle
MOTHER'S DAY(1980)

Hannah Battle
LANDLORD, THE(1970)

John Tucker Battle
IRISH EYES ARE SMILING(1944), w; CAPTAIN EDDIE(1945), w; MAN ALIVE(1949), w; SO DEAR TO MY HEART(1949), w; FROGMEN, THE(1951), w; INVADERS FROM MARS(1953), w; MAN ALONE, A(1955), w; LISBON(1956), w; SHOOT-OUT AT MEDICINE BEND(1957), w

Lavonne Battle
SOMETHING TO LIVE FOR(1952)

Lois Battle
MY FAIR LADY(1964)

Mike Battle
C. C. AND COMPANY(1971)

Norman Battle
MIDNIGHT WARNING, THE(1932), w; WIDOW IN SCARLET(1932), w

Rosemary Battle
FOLLOW THE BOYS(1944)

Dan Battles
WARRIORS, THE(1979)

Marjorie Battles
LUCKY LADY(1975)

David Battley
HOTEL PARADISO(1966, U.S./Brit.); WILLY WONKA AND THE CHOCOLATE FACTORY(1971); PUBLIC EYE, THE(1972, Brit.); MR. QUILP(1975, Brit.); KRULL(1983)
Misc. Talkies
THAT'S YOUR FUNERAL(1974, Brit.)

Marjorie Battress
Misc. Silents
FLOTSAM(1921)

Reggie Batts
SWAMP THING(1982)

Archibald Batty
DISCORD(1933, Brit.); WIVES BEWARE(1933, Brit.); OVER SHE GOES(1937, Brit.); VULTURE, THE(1937, Brit.); DRUMS(1938, Brit.); I SEE ICE(1938); FOUR FEATHERS, THE(1939, Brit.); LION HAS WINGS, THE(1940, Brit.); WINSLOW BOY, THE(1950)

Skip Battyn
COOGAN'S BLUFF(1968)

Boy Baty
HONEYSUCKLE ROSE(1980)

Zofia Batycka
Misc. Silents
10 CONDEMNED(1932, Pol.)

N. Batyroyova
NINE DAYS OF ONE YEAR(1964, USSR)

Brian Batytis
STUDENT BODIES(1981)

Jean-Claude Batz
BENVENUTA(1983, Fr.), p

George Bau
TRACK OF THE CAT(1954), makeup
Gordon Bau
THEY WON'T BELIEVE ME(1947), makeup; MR. WONG, DETECTIVE(1938), make-up; MR. WONG IN CHINATOWN(1939), makeup; MYSTERY OF MR. WONG, THE(1939), makeup; DOOMED TO DIE(1940), makeup; TO BE OR NOT TO BE(1942), makeup; CROSSFIRE(1947), makeup; OUT OF THE PAST(1947), makeup; I REMEMBER MAMA(1948), makeup; RACHEL AND THE STRANGER(1948), makeup; RETURN OF THE BADMEN(1948), makeup; STATION WEST(1948), makeup; FOLLOW ME QUIETLY(1949), makeup; GIRL FROM JONES BEACH, THE(1949), makeup; OCEAN BREAKERS(1949, Swed.), makeup; SET-UP, THE(1949), makeup; THEY LIVE BY NIGHT(1949), makeup; WOMAN'S SECRET, A(1949), makeup; COME FILL THE CUP(1951), makeup; DISTANT DRUMS(1951), makeup; I WAS A COMMUNIST FOR THE F.B.I.(1951), makeup; ON MOONLIGHT BAY(1951), makeup; STARLIFT(1951), makeup; STRANGERS ON A TRAIN(1951), makeup; MARA MARU(1952), makeup; ROOM FOR ONE MORE(1952), makeup; SPRINGFIELD RIFLE(1952), makeup; WINNING TEAM, THE(1952), makeup; SOUTH SEA WOMAN(1953), makeup; PHANTOM OF THE RUE MORGUE(1954), makeup; THEM!(1954), makeup; TRACK OF THE CAT(1954), makeup; COURT-MARTIAL OF BILLY MITCHELL, THE(1955), makeup; I DIED A THOUSAND TIMES(1955), makeup; MISTER ROBERTS(1955), makeup; PETE KELLY'S BLUES(1955), makeup; SEA CHASE, THE(1955), makeup; TALL MAN RIDING(1955), makeup; YOUNG AT HEART(1955), makeup; PAJAMA GAME, THE(1957), makeup; TOP SECRET AFFAIR(1957), makeup; FRANKENSTEIN 1970(1958), makeup; LAFAYETTE ESCADRILLE(1958), makeup; TOO MUCH, TOO SOON(1958), makeup; FBI STORY, THE(1959), makeup; RIO BRAVO(1959), makeup; WESTBOUND(1959), makeup; YELLOWSTONE KELLY(1959), makeup; YOUNG PHILADELPHIANS, THE(1959), makeup; OCEAN'S ELEVEN(1960), makeup; RISE AND FALL OF LEGS DIAMOND, THE(1960), makeup; SINS OF RACHEL CADE, THE(1960), makeup; PARRISH(1961), makeup; PORTRAIT OF A MOBSTER(1961), makeup; SUSAN SLADE(1961), makeup; GYPSY(1962), makeup; HOUSE OF WOMEN(1962), makeup; LAD: A DOG(1962), makeup; MERRILL'S MARAUDERS(1962), makeup; MUSIC MAN, THE(1962), makeup; ROME ADVENTURE(1962), makeup; MARY, MARY(1963), makeup; PALM SPRINGS WEEKEND(1963), makeup; SPENCER'S MOUNTAIN(1963), makeup; WALL OF NOISE(1963), makeup; KISSES FOR MY PRESIDENT(1964), makeup; MY FAIR LADY(1964), makeup; READY FOR THE PEOPLE(1964), makeup; ROBIN AND THE SEVEN HOODS(1964), makeup; SEX AND THE SINGLE GIRL(1964), makeup; YOUNGBLOOD HAWKE(1964), makeup; MARRIAGE ON THE ROCKS(1965), makeup; MY BLOOD RUNS COLD(1965), makeup; NEVER TOO LATE(1965), makeup; THIRD DAY, THE(1965), makeup; TWO ON A GUILLOTINE(1965), makeup; CHAMBER OF HORRORS(1966), makeup; NOT WITH MY WIFE, YOU DON'T!(1966), makeup; WHO'S AFRAID OF VIRGINIA WOOLF?(1966), makeup; COOL HAND LUKE(1967), makeup; FIRST TO FIGHT(1967), makeup; HOTEL(1967), makeup; WAIT UNTIL DARK(1967), makeup; FINIAN'S RAINBOW(1968), makeup; SWEET NOVEMBER(1968), makeup; ILLUSTRATED MAN, THE(1969), makeup; RABBIT, RUN(1970), makeup; DIRTY HARRY(1971), makeup; OMEGA MAN, THE(1971), makeup; SKIN GAME(1971), makeup
Robert Bau
SUPPOSE THEY GAVE A WAR AND NOBODY CAME?(1970), makeup
Georges Bauban
TRAIN, THE(1965, Fr./Ital./U.S.), makeup
Patrick Bauchau
LA COLLECTIONNEUSE(1971, Fr.), a, w; GUNS(1980, Fr.); STATE OF THINGS, THE(1983)
1984
CHOOSE ME(1984)
Anna Bauchens
THIS WAY PLEASE(1937), ed
Anne Bauchens
GODLESS GIRL, THE(1929), ed; NOISY NEIGHBORS(1929), ed; LORD BYRON OF BROADWAY(1930), ed; MADAME SATAN(1930), ed; THIS MAD WORLD(1930), ed; GUILTY HANDS(1931), ed; SQUAW MAN, THE(1931), ed; BEAST OF THE CITY, THE(1932), ed; SIGN OF THE CROSS, THE(1932), ed; WET PARADE, THE(1932), ed; THIS DAY AND AGE(1933), ed; CLEOPATRA(1934), ed; FOUR FRIGHTENED PEOPLE(1934), ed; MRS. WIGGS OF THE CABBAGE PATCH(1934), ed; CRUSADES, THE(1935), ed; PLAINSMAN, THE(1937), ed; BUCCANEER, THE(1938), ed; BULLDOG DRUMMOND IN AFRICA(1938), ed; HUNTED MEN(1938), ed; SONS OF THE LEGION(1938), ed; TELEVISION SPY(1939), ed; UNION PACIFIC(1939), ed; NORTHWEST MOUNTED POLICE(1940), ed; WOMEN WITHOUT NAMES(1940), ed; COMMANDOS STRIKE AT DAWN, THE(1942), ed; MRS. WIGGS OF THE CABBAGE PATCH(1942), ed; REAP THE WILD WIND(1942), ed; STORY OF DR. WASSELL, THE(1944), ed; TOMORROW THE WORLD(1944), ed; LOVE LETTERS(1945), ed; UNCONQUERED(1947), ed; SAMSON AND DELILAH(1949), ed; GREATEST SHOW ON EARTH, THE(1952), ed; TEN COMMANDMENTS, THE(1956), ed
Silents
AFFAIRS OF ANATOL, THE(1921), ed; ADAM'S RIB(1923), ph; TEN COMMANDMENTS, THE(1923), ed; VOLGA BOATMAN, THE(1926), ed; KING OF KINGS, THE(1927), ed; CHICAGO(1928), ed; CRAIG'S WIFE(1928), ed; NED MCCOBB'S DAUGHTER(1929), ed
Escolastico Baucin
TEXAS TO BATAAN(1942); I WAS AN AMERICAN SPY(1951)
Bill Baucon
LADY AND THE TRAMP(1955)
Antoine Baud
JUDGE AND THE ASSASSIN, THE(1979, Fr.)
Anna-Lisa Baude
AFFAIRS OF A MODEL(1952, Swed.)
Dr. Francois Baudet
PERMISSION TO KILL(1975, U.S./Aust.)
Henri Baudin
Silents
NAPOLEON(1927, Fr.)
Mabel Baudine
Silents
SPLENDID LIE, THE(1922)
Yvies Baudirier
DAMNED, THE(1948, Fr.), m

Serge Baudo
MAIN STREET(1956, Span.), md
Colette Baudot
SECRET WORLD(1969, Fr.), cos; JULIA(1977), cos
Yves Baudrier
BATTLE OF THE RAILS(1949, Fr.), m
Anne Baudry
BIRD WATCH, THE(1983, Fr.), ed
Jacques Baudry
LES BICHES(1968, Fr.), md; LES GAULOISES BLEUES(1969, Fr.)
Ray Bauduc
FABULOUS DORSEYS, THE(1947)
Arthur Bauer
Silents
NET, THE(1916); OVAL DIAMOND, THE(1916)
Misc. Silents
GOD'S WITNESS(1915); PRICE OF HER SILENCE, THE(1915); HIDDEN VALLEY, THE(1916); WOMAN IN POLITICS, THE(1916); IMAGE MAKER, THE(1917)
Axel Bauer
QUERELLE(1983, Ger./Fr.)
Belinda Bauer
WINTER KILLS(1979); AMERICAN SUCCESS COMPANY, THE(1980); FLASHDANCE(1983); TIMERIDER(1983)
Misc. Talkies
SINS OF DORIAN GRAY(1982)
Bruce Bauer
MY TUTOR(1983)
Cate Bauer
ONE HUNDRED AND ONE DALMATIANS(1961)
Charles Bauer
SECRET DOCUMENT – VIENNA(1954, Fr.), ph
David Bauer
FLAT TWO(1962, Brit.); MAN IN THE MIDDLE(1964, U.S./Brit.); SING AND SWING(1964, Brit.); WALK A TIGHTROPE(1964, U.S./Brit.); SPY WHO CAME IN FROM THE COLD, THE(1965, Brit.); DOUBLE MAN, THE(1967); DANGER ROUTE(1968, Brit.); DARK OF THE SUN(1968, Brit.); INSPECTOR CLOUSEAU(1968, Brit.); TORTURE GARDEN(1968, Brit.); ROYAL HUNT OF THE SUN, THE(1969, Brit.); PATTON(1970); SOPHIE'S PLACE(1970); DIAMONDS ARE FOREVER(1971, Brit.); 1,000 CONVICTS AND A WOMAN(1971, Brit.); EMBASSY(1972, Brit.); ROAD MOVIE(1974)
Dodie Bauer
SKY LINER(1949)
Dorothy Bauer
Misc. Talkies
SHERIFF'S SECRET, THE(1931)
Earl Bauer
Misc. Talkies
HIDEOUT IN THE SUN(1960)
Eddie Bauer
O.S.S.(1946)
Ellen Bauer
MAN WHO LOVED WOMEN, THE(1983)
Emma Bauer
Misc. Silents
CHILD OF THE BIG CITY(1914, USSR)
Fred Bauer
BUDDY HOLLY STORY, THE(1978), p; UNDER THE RAINBOW(1981), p, w
Gabriel Bauer
24-HOUR LOVER(1970, Ger.), art d
Grace Bauer
TAKE THE MONEY AND RUN(1969)
Harry Bauer
Misc. Silents
L'AME DU BRONZE(1918, Fr.)
Irv Bauer
SWEET BEAT(1962, Brit.)
Jamie Lyn Bauer
YOUNG DOCTORS IN LOVE(1982)
Jean Bauer
PASSION(1983, Fr./Switz.), art d
John W. Bauer
SATURDAY'S HERO(1951)
Margaret Bauer
LORDS OF FLATBUSH, THE(1974)
Mary Bauer
SQUARE ROOT OF ZERO, THE(1964); GUN RUNNER(1969); SUBSTITUTION(1970)
1984
OASIS, THE(1984), ed
Robert Bauer
DESPERATE CHARACTERS(1971)
1984
THIS IS SPINAL TAP(1984)
Rolf Bauer
SINAI COMMANDOS: THE STORY OF THE SIX DAY WAR(1968, Israel/Ger.), m
Rollin Bauer
KISS OF DEATH(1947)
Steven Bauer
SCARFACE(1983)
1984
THIEF OF HEARTS(1984)
Tom Bauer
LORDS OF FLATBUSH, THE(1974)
Warren Bauer
DARKER THAN AMBER(1970)
Wayne Bauer
DARKER THAN AMBER(1970)
Yevgeni Bauer
Misc. Silents
CHILD OF THE BIG CITY(1914, USSR), d; LIFE IN DEATH(1914, USSR), d; TEARS(1914, USSR), d; SONG OF TRIUMPHANT LOVE(1915, USSR), d; GRIFFON

OF AN OLD WARRIOR(1916, USSR), d; LIFE FOR A LIFE, A(1916, USSR), d; QUEEN OF THE SCREEN(1916, USSR), d; ALARM, THE(1917, USSR), d; REVOLUTIONIST(1917, USSR), d

Yevgeny Bauer
Misc. Silents
SINGED WINGS(1915, USSR), d

Monika Bauert
ODESSA FILE, THE(1974, Brit./Ger.), cos; BRASS TARGET(1978), cos; DAS BOOT(1982), cos

Andre Bauge
ROAD IS FINE, THE(1930, Fr.)

Michael Baugh
1984
WHERE THE BOYS ARE '84(1984), prod d

Sammy Baugh
TRIPLE THREAT(1948)

Stanley Baugh
MIDAS RUN(1969)

E. A. Baughan
Silents
ADVENTURES OF MR. PICKWICK, THE(1921, Brit.), w

Lysa Baugher
STORY OF THREE LOVES, THE(1953)

David Baughn
BEYOND EVIL(1980), p, w; GRADUATION DAY(1981), p

Bauhaus
HUNGER, THE(1983)

Alan Baulch
STRICTLY FOR THE BIRDS(1963, Brit.)

Jerry Baulch
NORA PRENTISS(1947)

Richard Bauleo
CURIOUS DR. HUMPP(1967, Arg.)

Barbara Baum
EFFI BRIEST(1974, Ger.), cos; MARRIAGE OF MARIA BRAUN, THE(1979, Ger.), cos; LILI MARLEEN(1981, Ger.), cos; LOLA(1982, Ger.), cos; QUERELLE(1983, Ger./Fr.), cos

Cliff Baum
CASE OF THE BLACK PARROT, THE(1941)

Fred Baum
1984
UP THE CREEK(1984), p

Ginger Baum
SORCERESS(1983)

L. Frank Baum
WIZ, THE(1978), w; WIZARD OF OZ, THE(1939), w; 20TH CENTURY OZ(1977, Aus.), d&w
Silents
LAST EGYPTIAN, THE(1914), d&w; PATCHWORK GIRL OF OZ, THE(1914), w

Lal Baum
CHANDLER(1971)

Lyman Frank Baum
WONDERFUL LAND OF OZ, THE(1969), p,d&w

Lyman Frank Baum, Jr.
Silents
WIZARD OF OZ, THE(1925), w

Martin Baum
BRING ME THE HEAD OF ALFREDO GARCIA(1974), p; KILLER ELITE, THE(1975), p; WILBY CONSPIRACY, THE(1975, Brit.), p

Ralph Baum
BIG CHIEF, THE(1960, Fr.), p; MODIGLIANI OF MONTPARNASSE(1961, Fr./Ital.), p; HEIST, THE(1979, Ital.), p

Sharon Baum
FEVER HEAT(1968)

Thomas Baum
CARNY(1980), w; SENDER, THE(1982, Brit.), w

Tom Baum
HUGO THE HIPPO(1976, Hung./U.S.), w

Vicki Baum
GRAND HOTEL(1932), w; WOMAN ACCUSED(1933), w; I GIVE MY LOVE(1934), w; NIGHT IS YOUNG, THE(1935), w; GIRL TROUBLE(1942), w; POWDER TOWN(1942), w; GREAT FLAMARION, THE(1945), w; HOTEL BERLIN(1945), w; WEEKEND AT THE WALDORF(1945), w; WOMAN'S SECRET, A(1949), w

Vickie Baum
HONEYMOON(1947), w

Vicky Baum
DANCE, GIRL, DANCE(1940), w

Anne-Marie Bauman
SEASON FOR LOVE, THE(1963, Fr.)

Bill Bauman
WESTERNER, THE(1940)

Erna Martha Bauman
LOS ASTRONAUTAS(1960, Mex.); INVASION OF THE VAMPIRES, THE(1961, Mex.)

Joanne Bauman
PURPLE HAZE(1982)

Sandrew Bauman
CHILDREN, THE(1949, Swed.), p

Anne Marie Baumann
LAST DAYS OF POMPEII, THE(1960, Ital.)

Christoph Baumann
KAMIKAZE '89(1983, Ger.)

Erik Baumann
JOHANSSON GETS SCOLDED(1945, Swed.), m

Joachim Baumann
ALL-AROUND REDUCED PERSONALITY–OUTTAKES, THE(1978, Ger.)

Katherine Baumann
99 AND 44/100% DEAD(1974)

Kathrine Baumann
Misc. Talkies
SUNBURST(1975)

Kathy Baumann
CHROME AND HOT LEATHER(1971); EVEL KNIEVEL(1971); THING WITH TWO HEADS, THE(1972)

Ray Baumel
LADY IN CEMENT(1968); GOODBYE COLUMBUS(1969)

Rey Baumel
STANLEY(1973)

Jacques Baumer
CAFE DE PARIS(1938, Fr.); THEY WERE FIVE(1938, Fr.); DOUBLE CRIME IN THE MAGINOT LINE(1939, Fr.); ENTENTE CORDIALE(1939, Fr.); HEART OF PARIS(1939, Fr.); RASPUTIN(1939, Fr.); DAYBREAK(1940, Fr.); STRANGERS IN THE HOUSE(1949, Fr.); CHEAT, THE(1950, Fr.); JUST ME(1950, Fr.); SIMPLE CASE OF MONEY, A(1952, Fr.)

Marie Baumer
SINNER'S HOLIDAY(1930), w; MEN IN EXILE(1937), w; FAMILY SECRET, THE(1951), w

Lt. Earl G. Baumgardner, USN
BACK TO BATAAN(1945)

Adam Baumgarten
1984
IMPULSE(1984)

Charlotte Baumgartner
VIRGIN PRESIDENT, THE(1968)

Karl Baumgartner
LONGEST DAY, THE(1962), spec eff; LADY L(1965, Fr./Ital.), spec eff; UP FROM THE BEACH(1965), spec eff; BLUE MAX, THE(1966), spec eff; I DEAL IN DANGER(1966), spec eff; WEEKEND AT DUNKIRK(1966, Fr./Ital.), spec eff; CHRISTMAS TREE, THE(1969, Fr.), spec eff; LAST ESCAPE, THE(1970, Brit.), spec eff; RED SUN(1972, Fr./Ital./Span.), spec eff; DAS BOOT(1982), spec eff

Karli Baumgartner
CARAVANS(1978, U.S./Iranian), spec eff

Ken Baumgartner
ON THE BEACH(1959)

Michele Baumgartner
WOMAN NEXT DOOR, THE(1981, Fr.)

Roland Baumgartner
1984
JUNGLE WARRIORS(1984, U.S./Ger./Mex.), m

Hans-Jurgen Baumler
FOUNTAIN OF LOVE, THE(1968, Aust.)

Cecile Baun
RAW FORCE(1982), makeup

Chris Baur
METEOR(1979)

Elizabeth Baur
THE BOSTON STRANGLER, THE(1968)

Esperanza Baur
GUADALAJARA(1943, Mex.)

Harry Baur
POIL DE CAROTTE(1932, Fr.); CRIME AND PUNISHMENT(1935, Fr.); I STAND CONDEMNED(1936, Brit.); LES MISERABLES(1936, Fr.); GOLEM, THE(1937, Czech./Fr.); GOLGOTHA(1937, Fr.); LIFE AND LOVES OF BEETHOVEN, THE(1937, Fr.); DARK EYES(1938, Fr.); ROTHSCHILD(1938, Fr.); UN CARNET DE BAL(1938, Fr.); RASPUTIN(1939, Fr.); REBEL SON, THE ½(1939, Brit.); HATRED(1941, Fr.); VOLPONE(1947, Fr.)

Lisa Baur
NATIONAL LAMPOON'S ANIMAL HOUSE(1978)

Sebastian Baur
AMERICAN SUCCESS COMPANY, THE(1980)

Pina Bausch
AND THE SHIP SAILS ON(1983, Ital./Fr.)

Didier Baussy
1984
L'ARGENT(1984, Fr./Switz.)

Aurora Bautista
MAD QUEEN, THE(1950, Span.)

Bobby Bautista
BEAST OF BLOOD(1970, U.S./Phil.), set d

Conchita Bautista
THUNDERSTORM(1956)

F. P. Bautista
CURSE OF THE VAMPIRES(1970, Phil., U.S.), cos

Jay Bautista
1984
BREAKIN' 2: ELECTRIC BOOGALOO(1984)

Joe Bautista
GIRL FROM MANDALAY(1936); HONOLULU LU(1941); IN THE NAVY(1941); STORY OF DR. WASSELL, THE(1944); LETTER TO THREE WIVES, A(1948); DANCING IN THE DARK(1949)

Joe R. Bautista
SAIGON(1948)

Jean Pierre Baux
ZIG-ZAG(1975, Fr/Ital.), ph

Marion Bauza
VIOLATED LOVE(1966, Arg.)

Liselotte Bav
HOUSE OF THE THREE GIRLS, THE(1961, Aust.)

Lamberto Bava
BEYOND THE DOOR II(1979, Ital.), w

Mario Bava
THIS WINE OF LOVE(1948, Ital.), ph; TAMING OF DOROTHY, THE(1950, Brit.), ph; DEVIL'S COMMANDMENT, THE zero(1956, Ital.), ph; DAY THE SKY EXPLODED, THE(1958, Fr./Ital.), ph; CALTIKI, THE IMMORTAL MONSTER(1959, Ital.), d; HERCULES(1959, Ital.), ph; ESTHER AND THE KING(1960, U.S./Ital.), ph; GIANT OF MARATHON, THE(1960, Ital.), ph; HERCULES UNCHAINED(1960, Ital./Fr.), ph; ATOM AGE VAMPIRE(1961, Ital.), p; BLACK SUNDAY(1961, Ital.), d, ph; WHITE WARRIOR, THE(1961, Ital./Yugo.), ph; NERO'S MISTRESS(1962, Ital.), ph; BLACK

SABBATH(1963, Ital.), d, w; ERIK THE CONQUEROR(1963, Fr./Ital.), d, w, ph; EVIL EYE(1964 Ital.), d, w, ph; HERCULES IN THE HAUNTED WORLD(1964, Ital.), d, w, ph; BLOOD AND BLACK LACE(1965, Ital.), d, w; PLANET OF THE VAMPIRES(1965, U.S./Ital./Span.), d, w; DR. GOLDFOOT AND THE GIRL BOMBS(1966, Ital.), d; KILL BABY KILL(1966, Ital.), d, w; KNIVES OF THE AVENGER(1967, Ital.), w; DANGER: DIABOLIK(1968, Ital./Fr.), d, w; HATCHET FOR A HONEYMOON(1969, Span./Ital.), d, w; BARON BLOOD(1972, Ital.), d; TWITCH OF THE DEATH NERVE(1973, Ital.), d, w, ph; MOSES(1976, Brit./Ital.), spec eff; BEYOND THE DOOR II(1979, Ital.), d&ph; INFERNO(1980, Ital.), spec eff

Chrester Bavhi
FORTY GUNS(1957), set d

Frances Bavier
DAY THE EARTH STOOD STILL, THE(1951); LADY SAYS NO, THE(1951); BEND OF THE RIVER(1952); HORIZONS WEST(1952); MY WIFE'S BEST FRIEND(1952); SALLY AND SAINT ANNE(1952); NICE LITTLE BANK THAT SHOULD BE ROBBED, A(1958); BENJI(1974)

Francis Bavier
STOOGE, THE(1952); IT STARTED WITH A KISS(1959)

Jose Baviera
VIVA MARIA(1965, Fr./Ital.); EXTERMINATING ANGEL, THE(1967, Mex.)

James Bawden
UNCANNY, THE(1977, Brit./Can.), ph

Nina Bawden
SOLITARY CHILD, THE(1958, Brit.), w; ON THE RUN(1969, Brit.), w

Arthur Bawtree
OTHER PEOPLE'S SINS(1931, Brit.)

Bax
SAVAGE SISTERS(1974), m

Clifford Bax
Silents
GATEWAY OF THE MOON, THE(1928), w

Roger Bax
NEVER LET ME GO(1953, U.S./Brit.), w

Sir Arnold Bax
OLIVER TWIST(1951, Brit.), m

Maria Baxa
VALACHI PAPERS, THE(1972, Ital./Fr.)

Charikila Baxevanos
MONSTER OF LONDON CITY, THE(1967, Ger.)

Chariklia Baxevanos
FOREVER MY LOVE(1962)

Barbara Baxley
SAVAGE EYE, THE(1960); ALL FALL DOWN(1962); COUNTDOWN(1968); NO WAY TO TREAT A LADY(1968); NASHVILLE(1975); NORMA RAE(1979); STRANGER IS WATCHING, A(1982)

Craig Baxley
WHAT'S UP, DOC?(1972); CHARLEY VARRICK(1973); ROLLERBALL(1975); FOUL PLAY(1978); NIGHTWING(1979); WARRIORS, THE(1979), a, stunts

Gary Baxley
ISLAND OF DR. MOREAU, THE(1977); HEART BEAT(1979); WARRIORS, THE(1979)

Jack Baxley
TRUE TO LIFE(1943); DANCING LADY(1933); GAY BRIDE, THE(1934); GOOD DAME(1934); MAN ON THE FLYING TRAPEZE, THE(1935); O'SHAUGHNESSY'S BOY(1935); OUR LITTLE GIRL(1935); GREAT ZIEGFELD, THE(1936); POPPY(1936); SAN FRANCISCO(1936); DOUBLE WEDDING(1937); LOVE IS NEWS(1937); MY DEAR MISS ALDRICH(1937); WOMAN CHASES MAN(1937); COWBOY AND THE LADY, THE(1938); INTERNATIONAL CRIME(1938); TRADE WINDS(1938); STRIKE UP THE BAND(1940); HONKY TONK(1941); CITY OF SILENT MEN(1942); GALLANT LADY(1942); LUCKY JORDAN(1942); MAGNIFICENT AMBERSONS, THE(1942); MR. CELEBRITY(1942); POWERS GIRL, THE(1942); PRISON GIRL(1942); MY BUDDY(1944); ALONG CAME JONES(1945); RIDERS OF THE DAWN(1945); THRILL OF A ROMANCE(1945); SONG OF THE SIERRAS(1946); DESPERATE(1947); EGG AND I, THE(1947); FRAMED(1947); HIGH WALL(1947); LAST ROUND-UP, THE(1947); LADY FROM SHANGHAI, THE(1948); KID FROM GOWER GULCH, THE(1949)

John Baxley
RAINBOW OVER THE ROCKIES(1947)

Margo Baxley
OMEGA MAN, THE(1971), cos; FUN WITH DICK AND JANE(1977), cos

Paul Baxley
WHIPLASH(1948); KNOCK ON ANY DOOR(1949); ALL THE YOUNG MEN(1960); DESIRE IN THE DUST(1960); MORITURI(1965); COOGAN'S BLUFF(1968), stunts; JOURNEY TO SHILOH(1968), stunts; SUPPOSE THEY GAVE A WAR AND NOBODY CAME?(1970), stunts; DIAMONDS ARE FOREVER(1971, Brit.), stunts; GODFATHER, THE(1972), stunts; WHAT'S UP, DOC?(1972); BOY WHO CRIED WEREWOLF, THE(1973); REPORT TO THE COMMISSIONER(1975), stunts; FUN WITH DICK AND JANE(1977), stunts; LATE SHOW, THE(1977), stunts; TELEFON(1977), stunts; IN GOD WE TRUST(1980)

David Baxt
TWILIGHT'S LAST GLEAMING(1977, U.S./Ger.); YANKS(1979); SHINING, THE(1980); HORROR PLANET(1982, Brit.); SILVER DREAM RACER(1982, Brit.); ENIGMA(1983)
1984
SCREAM FOR HELP(1984)

George Baxt
CIRCUS OF HORRORS(1960, Brit.), w; HORROR HOTEL(1960, Brit.), w; SHADOW OF THE CAT, THE(1961, Brit.), w; BURN WITCH BURN(1962), w; PAYROLL(1962, Brit.), w; THUNDER IN DIXIE(1965), w; STRANGLER'S WEB(1966, Brit.), w; VAMPIRE CIRCUS(1972, Brit.), w; BEYOND THE FOG(1981, Brit.), d&w

Adelaide Baxter
Silents
PENROD(1922)

Alan Baxter
MARY BURNS, FUGITIVE(1935); BIG BROWN EYES(1936); CASE AGAINST MRS. AMES, THE(1936); PAROLE(1936); THIRTEEN HOURS BY AIR(1936); TRAIL OF THE LONESOME PINE, THE(1936); BIG TOWN GIRL(1937); BREEZING HOME(1937); IT COULD HAPPEN TO YOU(1937); LAST GANGSTER, THE(1937); MEN IN EXILE(1937); NIGHT KEY(1937); BOY SLAVES(1938); GANGS OF NEW YORK(1938); I MET MY LOVE AGAIN(1938); WIDE OPEN FACES(1938); EACH DAWN I DIE(1939); IN NAME ONLY(1939); LET US LIVE(1939); MY SON IS A CRIMINAL(1939); OFF THE RECORD(1939); ABE LINCOLN IN ILLINOIS(1940); ESCAPE TO GLORY(1940);

FREE, BLONDE AND 21(1940); LONE WOLF STRIKES, THE(1940); MAN WHO TALKED TOO MUCH, THE(1940); SANTA FE TRAIL(1940); BAD MEN OF MISSOURI(1941); BORROWED HERO(1941); PITTSBURGH KID, THE(1941); RAGS TO RICHES(1941); SHADOW OF THE THIN MAN(1941); UNDER AGE(1941); CHINA GIRL(1942); PRISONER OF JAPAN(1942); SABOTEUR(1942); BEHIND PRISON WALLS(1943); HUMAN COMEDY, THE(1943); PILOT NO. 5(1943); SUBMARINE BASE(1943); WOMEN IN BONDAGE(1943); CLOSE-UP(1948); PRAIRIE, THE(1948); SET-UP, THE(1949); WILD WEED(1949); TRUE STORY OF JESSE JAMES, THE(1957); RESTLESS YEARS, THE(1958); END OF THE LINE, THE(1959, Brit.); FACE OF A FUGITIVE(1959); MOUNTAIN ROAD, THE(1960); JUDGMENT AT NUREMBERG(1961); THIS PROPERTY IS CONDEMNED(1966); WELCOME TO HARD TIMES(1967); PAINT YOUR WAGON(1969); CHISUM(1970); WILLARD(1971)
Misc. Talkies
STAND BY ALL NETWORKS(1942)

Ann Baxter
TEN COMMANDMENTS, THE(1956)

Anne Baxter
GREAT PROFILE, THE(1940); TWENTY MULE TEAM(1940); CHARLEY'S AUNT(1941); SWAMP WATER(1941); MAGNIFICENT AMBERSONS, THE(1942); PIED PIPER, THE(1942); CRASH DIVE(1943); FIVE GRAVES TO CAIRO(1943); NORTH STAR, THE(1943); EVE OF ST. MARK, THE(1944); GUEST IN THE HOUSE(1944); SULLIVANS, THE(1944); SUNDAY DINNER FOR A SOLDIER(1944); ROYAL SCANDAL, A(1945); ANGEL ON MY SHOULDER(1946); RAZOR'S EDGE, THE(1946); SMOKY(1946); BLAZE OF NOON(1947); MOTHER WORE TIGHTS(1947); HOMECOMING(1948); LUCK OF THE IRISH(1948); WALLS OF JERICHO(1948); YELLOW SKY(1948); YOU'RE MY EVERYTHING(1949); ALL ABOUT EVE(1950); TICKET TO TOMAHAWK(1950); FOLLOW THE SUN(1951); MY WIFE'S BEST FRIEND(1952); O. HENRY'S FULL HOUSE(1952); OUTCASTS OF POKER FLAT, THE(1952); BLUE GARDENIA, THE(1953); I CONFESS(1953); CARNIVAL STORY(1954); BEDEVILLED(1955); ONE DESIRE(1955); SPOILERS, THE(1955); COME ON, THE(1956); THREE VIOLENT PEOPLE(1956); CHASE A CROOKED SHADOW(1958, Brit.); CIMARRON(1960); SEASON OF PASSION(1961, Aus./Brit.); MIX ME A PERSON(1962, Brit.); WALK ON THE WILD SIDE(1962); FAMILY JEWELS, THE(1965); BUSYBODY, THE(1967); TALL WOMEN, THE(1967, Aust./Ital./Span.); FOOLS' PARADE(1971); LATE LIZ, THE(1971); JANE AUSTEN IN MANHATTAN(1980)

Arnold Baxter
Misc. Talkies
CYNTHIA'S SISTER(1975), d

Beryl Baxter
UNDERCOVER AGENT(1935, Brit.); IDOL OF PARIS(1948, Brit.)

Bill Baxter
LIFE BEGINS AT 40(1935)

Billy Baxter
LOVE AND ANARCHY(1974, Ital.), p

Bruce Baxter
LOST BATTALION(1961, U.S./Phil.)

Bud Baxter
FIGHTING COWBOY(1933)

Cash Baxter
DIARY OF A MAD HOUSEWIFE(1970)

Charles Baxter
LOVE AND PAIN AND THE WHOLE DAMN THING(1973)
Misc. Talkies
CURSE OF KILIMANJARO(1978)

Cherleen Baxter
TERROR IN THE JUNGLE(1968)

Clive Baxter
YOUNG AND INNOCENT(1938, Brit.); FOUR FEATHERS, THE(1939, Brit.); OUTSIDER, THE(1949, Brit.); LADY GODIVA RIDES AGAIN(1955, Brit.)

Cpl. Alan Baxter
WINGED VICTORY(1944)

Cynthia Baxter
ASSIGNMENT TO KILL(1968)

David Baxter
TOO MANY HUSBANDS(1938, Brit.); MR. EMMANUEL(1945, Brit.); MAN FROM MOROCCO, THE(1946, Brit.); NICHOLAS AND ALEXANDRA(1971, Brit.)

Deborah Baxter
HIGH WIND IN JAMAICA, A(1965); WIND AND THE LION, THE(1975)

Dorothy Baxter
1984
MUPPETS TAKE MANHATTAN, THE(1984)

Dr. Frank Baxter
MOLE PEOPLE, THE(1956)

Edward Baxter
NIGHT TRAIN(1940, Brit.)

Elizabeth Baxter
Misc. Silents
CITY OF SHADOWS(1929, Brit.)

Eugene Baxter
CIMARRON KID, THE(1951); RAINBOW 'ROUND MY SHOULDER(1952); SCANDAL SHEET(1952)

Farnham Baxter
DICK BARTON-SPECIAL AGENT(1948, Brit.); MEET THE DUKE(1949, Brit.), a, w

Frank Baxter
SLEEPING CITY, THE(1950)

George Baxter
CARELESS AGE(1929); MARIANNE(1929); RIGHT TO LOVE, THE(1931); WOMAN COMMANDS, A(1932); DINNER AT EIGHT(1933); GREAT FLIRTATION, THE(1934); MERRY WIDOW, THE(1934); THIRTY-DAY PRINCESS(1934); I LIVE MY LIFE(1935); SING SING NIGHTS(1935); SPANISH CAPE MYSTERY(1935); SOFIA(1948); SON OF BILLY THE KID(1949); CAGED(1950); TEA FOR TWO(1950); FOURTEEN HOURS(1951); IRON MAN, THE(1951); LADY AND THE BANDIT(1951); PRAIRIE ROUNDUP(1951); SWORD OF MONTE CRISTO, THE(1951); UNKNOWN WORLD(1951); ACTORS AND SIN(1952); LILI(1953); FIRST TRAVELING SALESLADY, THE(1956); TEN COMMANDMENTS, THE(1956); GUN BATTLE AT MONTEREY(1957); SHE DEVIL(1957); LEGION OF THE DOOMED(1958); PURPLE GANG, THE(1960)

Jane Baxter

BED AND BREAKFAST(1930, Brit.); DOWN RIVER(1931, Brit.); CONSTANT NYMPH, THE(1933, Brit.); WIVES BEWARE(1933, Brit.); DOUBLE EVENT, THE(1934, Brit.); GIRLS PLEASE!(1934, Brit.); NIGHT OF THE PARTY, THE(1934, Brit.); WE LIVE AGAIN(1934); CLAIRVOYANT, THE(1935, Brit.); DRAKE THE PIRATE(1935, Brit.); ENCHANTED APRIL(1935); LINE ENGAGED(1935, Brit.); REGAL CAVALCADE(1935, Brit.); MAN BEHIND THE MASK, THE(1936, Brit.); APRIL BLOSSOMS(1937, Brit.); MAN WHO COULD WORK MIRACLES, THE(1937, Brit.); SECOND BEST BED(1937, Brit.); CONFIDENTIAL LADY(1939, Brit.); MURDER WILL OUT(1939, Brit.); WARE CASE, THE(1939, Brit.); BRIGGS FAMILY, THE(1940, Brit.); CHINESE DEN, THE(1940, Brit.); SHIPS WITH WINGS(1942, Brit.); FLEMISH FARM, THE(1943, Brit.); DEATH OF AN ANGEL(1952, Brit.)

Misc. Talkies

ALL HALLOWE'EN(1952)

Jerry M. Baxter

JAWS II(1978)

Jimmy Baxter

DARK ANGEL, THE(1935)

Joan Baxter

KNOCK ON ANY DOOR(1949)

John Baxter

COUNTY FAIR(1933, Brit.), d; DOSS HOUSE(1933, Brit.), d; KENTUCKY MINSTRELS(1934, Brit.), d; LEST WE FORGET(1934, Brit.), d; MUSIC HALL(1934, Brit.), d&w; SAY IT WITH FLOWERS(1934, Brit.), d, w; BIRDS OF A FEATHER(1935, Brit.), d; FLOOD TIDE(1935, Brit.), d; JIMMY BOY(1935, Brit.), d; REAL BLOKE, A(1935, Brit.), d; SMALL MAN, THE(1935, Brit.), d; HEARTS OF HUMANITY(1936, Brit.), p&d; MEN OF YESTERDAY(1936, Brit.), p; SUNSHINE AHEAD(1936, Brit.), d; SONG OF THE ROAD(1937, Brit.), d&w; TALKING FEET(1937, Brit.), d; STEPPING TOES(1938, Brit.), d; WHAT WOULD YOU DO, CHUMS?(1939, Brit.), d; AMONG HUMAN WOLVES(1940 Brit.), d; CROOKS TOUR(1940, Brit.), d; LAUGH IT OFF(1940, Brit.), d; OLD MOTHER RILEY IN BUSINESS(1940, Brit.), d; OLD MOTHER RILEY IN SOCIETY(1940, Brit.), d; COMMON TOUCH, THE(1941, Brit.), p&d; OLD MOTHER RILEY'S GHOSTS(1941, Brit.), p&d; LET THE PEOPLE SING(1942, Brit.), p&d, w; WE'LL SMILE AGAIN(1942, Brit.), p&d; OLD MOTHER RILEY, DETECTIVE(1943, Brit.), p&d; SHIPBUILDERS, THE(1943, Brit.), p&d; THEATRE ROYAL(1943, Brit.), p&d; WHEN WE ARE MARRIED(1943, Brit.), p; DREAMING(1944, Brit.), p&d; HERE COMES THE SUN(1945, Brit.), p&d; LOVE ON THE DOLE(1945, Brit.), p&d; GRAND ESCAPADE, THE(1946, Brit.), p&d; FORTUNE LANE(1947, Brit.), p&d; WHEN YOU COME HOME(1947, Brit.), p&d; LAST LOAD, THE(1948, Brit.), p&d; NOTHING VENTURE(1948, Brit.), p&d; DRAGON OF PENDRAGON CASTLE, THE(1950, Brit.), p&d; SECOND MATE, THE(1950, Brit.), p&d; BRAVE DON'T CRY, THE(1952, Brit.), p; JUDGMENT DEFERRED(1952, Brit.), p, d; YOU'RE ONLY YOUNG TWICE(1952, Brit.), p. John Grierson; LOVE MATCH, THE(1955, Brit.), p; RAMSBOTTOM RIDES AGAIN(1956, Brit.), p&d, w; HEART WITHIN, THE(1957, Brit.), w; MAKE MINE A MILLION(1965, Brit.), p

June Baxter

HIDEOUT IN THE ALPS(1938, Brit.)

Keith Baxter

BARRETTS OF WIMPOLE STREET, THE(1957); CHIMES AT MIDNIGHT(1967, Span.,Switz.); ASH WEDNESDAY(1973); GOLDEN RENDEZVOUS(1977)

Les Baxter

TANGA-TIKA(1953), m; YELLOW TOMAHAWK, THE(1954), m; BLACK SLEEP, THE(1956), m; HOT BLOOD(1956), a, m; HOT CARS(1956), m, md; QUINCANNON, FRONTIER SCOUT(1956), m; REBEL IN TOWN(1956), m; BOP GIRL GOES CALYPSO(1957), m; GIRL IN BLACK STOCKINGS(1957), m; HELL BOUND(1957), m; INVISIBLE BOY, THE(1957), m; JUNGLE HEAT(1957), m; OUTLAW'S SON(1957), m; PHARAOH'S CURSE(1957), m; REVOLT AT FORT LARAMIE(1957), m; STORM RIDER, THE(1957), m; TOMAHAWK TRAIL(1957), m; UNTAMED YOUTH(1957), m; VOODOO ISLAND(1957), m; WAR DRUMS(1957), m; BRIDE AND THE BEAST, THE(1958), m; ESCAPE FROM RED ROCK(1958), m; FORT BOWIE(1958), m; LONE RANGER AND THE LOST CITY OF GOLD, THE(1958), m; MACABRE(1958), m; GOLIATH AND THE BARBARIANS(1960, Ital.), m; HOUSE OF USHER(1960), m; ALAKAZAM THE GREAT!(1961, Jap.), m; BLACK SUNDAY(1961, Ital.), m; GOLIATH AND THE DRAGON(1961, Ital./Fr.), m; LISETTE(1961), m; MASTER OF THE WORLD(1961), m; PIT AND THE PENDULUM, THE(1961), m; DAUGHTER OF THE SUN GOD(1962), ph; MARCO POLO(1962, Fr./Ital.), m; PANIC IN YEAR ZERO!(1962), m; TALES OF TERROR(1962), m; WHITE SLAVE SHIP(1962, Fr./Ital.), m; "X"-THE MAN WITH THE X-RAY EYES(1963), m; BEACH PARTY(1963), m; BLACK SABBATH(1963, Ital.), m; OPERATION BIKINI(1963), m; RAVEN, THE(1963), m; SAMSON AND THE SEVEN MIRACLES OF THE WORLD(1963, Fr./Ital.), m; YOUNG RACERS, THE(1963), m; BIKINI BEACH(1964), m; COMEDY OF TERRORS, THE(1964), m; EVIL EYE(1964 Ital.), m; MUSCLE BEACH PARTY(1964), m; PAJAMA PARTY(1964), m; BEACH BLANKET BINGO(1965), m; DR. GOLDFOOT AND THE BIKINI MACHINE(1965), m; HOW TO STUFF A WILD BIKINI(1965), m; MIGHTY JUNGLE, THE(1965, U.S./Mex.), m; SERGEANT DEADHEAD(1965), m; DR. GOLDFOOT AND THE GIRL BOMBS(1966, Ital.), m; FIREBALL 590(1966), m; GHOST IN THE INVISIBLE BIKINI(1966), m; GLASS SPHINX, THE(1968, Egypt/Ital./Span.), m; MINI-SKIRT MOB, THE(1968), m; TERROR IN THE JUNGLE(1968), m; WILD IN THE STREETS(1968), m; CRY OF THE BANSHEE(1970, Brit.), m; DUNWICH HORROR, THE(1970), m; BARON BLOOD(1972, Ital.), m; FROGS(1972), m, md; I ESCAPED FROM DEVIL'S ISLAND(1973), m; BORN AGAIN(1978), m; TARGET: HARRY(1980), m; BEAST WITHIN, THE(1982), m

Les Jim Baxter

DALTON GIRLS, THE(1957), m

Lex Baxter

WETBACKS(1956), m; WOMAN'S DEVOTION, A(1956), m; FLAREUP(1969), m, md; HELL'S BELLES(1969), m

Lora Baxter

BEFORE MORNING(1933)

Lynsey Baxter

FRENCH LIEUTENANT'S WOMAN, THE(1981)

1984

REAL LIFE(1984, Brit.)

May Baxter

Silents

PENROD(1922)

Meredith Baxter

BEN(1972); STAND UP AND BE COUNTED(1972); ALL THE PRESIDENT'S MEN(1976)

Ray Baxter

SHOCK CORRIDOR(1963); RUSSIANS ARE COMING, THE RUSSIANS ARE COMING, THE(1966)

Raymond Baxter

FAST LADY, THE(1963, Brit.); GRAND PRIX(1966)

Miss S. Baxter

Silents

SUMMER BACHELORS(1926), set d

Stanley Baxter

COMING-OUT PARTY, A(; WEE GEORDIE(1956, Brit.); CROOKS ANONYMOUS(1963, Brit.); FAST LADY, THE(1963, Brit.); FATHER CAME TOO(1964, Brit.); JOEY BOY(1965, Brit.)

Teresa Baxter

IT'S MY TURN(1980); DEATH WISH II(1982)

Trevor Baxter

NUTCRACKER(1982, Brit.)

Warner Baxter

BEHIND THAT CURTAIN(1929); IN OLD ARIZONA(1929); ROMANCE OF THE RIO GRANDE(1929); THRU DIFFERENT EYES(1929); ARIZONA KID, THE(1930); HAPPY DAYS(1930); RENEGADES(1930); SUCH MEN ARE DANGEROUS(1930); CISCO KID(1931); DADDY LONG LEGS(1931); DOCTORS' WIVES(1931); SQUAW MAN, THE(1931); SURRENDER(1931); AMATEUR DADDY(1932); MAN ABOUT TOWN(1932); SIX HOURS TO LIVE(1932); DANGEROUSLY YOURS(1933); I LOVED YOU WEDNESDAY(1933); PADDY, THE NEXT BEST THING(1933); PENTHOUSE(1933); 42ND STREET(1933); AS HUSBANDS GO(1934); BROADWAY BILL(1934); GRAND CANARY(1934); HELL IN THE HEAVENS(1934); STAND UP AND CHEER(1934 80m FOX bw); SUCH WOMEN ARE DANGEROUS(1934); ONE MORE SPRING(1935); UNDER THE PAMPAS MOON(1935); KING OF BURLESQUE(1936); PRISONER OF SHARK ISLAND, THE(1936); ROAD TO GLORY, THE(1936); ROBIN HOOD OF EL DORADO(1936); TO MARY-WITH LOVE(1936); WHITE HUNTER(1936); SLAVE SHIP(1937); VOGUES OF 1938(1937); WIFE, DOCTOR AND NURSE(1937); I'LL GIVE A MILLION(1938); KIDNAPPED(1938); BARRICADE(1939); RETURN OF THE CISCO KID(1939); WIFE, HUSBAND AND FRIEND(1939); EARTHBOUND(1940); ADAM HAD FOUR SONS(1941); CRIME DOCTOR(1943); CRIME DOCTOR'S STRANGEST CASE(1943); LADY IN THE DARK(1944); SHADOWS IN THE NIGHT(1944); CRIME DOCTOR'S COURAGE, THE(1945); CRIME DOCTOR'S WARNING(1945); CRIME DOCTOR'S MAN HUNT(1946); JUST BEFORE DAWN(1946); CRIME DOCTOR'S GAMBLE(1947); MILLERSON CASE, THE(1947); GENTLEMAN FROM NOWHERE, THE(1948); DEVIL'S HENCHMEN, THE(1949); PRISON WARDEN(1949); STATE PENITENTIARY(1950)

Silents

ALL WOMAN(1918); CHEATED HEARTS(1921); LOVE CHARM, THE(1921); IF I WERE QUEEN(1922); NINETY AND NINE, THE(1922); IN SEARCH OF A THRILL(1923); ST. ELMO(1923); ALIMONY(1924); AIR MAIL, THE(1925); AWFUL TRUTH, THE(1925); RUGGED WATER(1925); ALOMA OF THE SOUTH SEAS(1926); GREAT GATSBY, THE(1926); MISS BREWSTER'S MILLIONS(1926); RUNAWAY, THE(1926); COWARD, THE(1927); SINGED(1927); TELEPHONE GIRL, THE(1927); CRAIG'S WIFE(1928); RAMONA(1928); THREE SINNERS(1928); TRAGEDY OF YOUTH, THE(1928); WEST OF ZANZIBAR(1928); LINDA(1929)

Misc. Silents

FIRST LOVE(1921); SHELTERED DAUGHTERS(1921); GIRL IN HIS ROOM, THE(1922); GIRL'S DESIRE, A(1922); HER OWN MONEY(1922); BLOW YOUR OWN HORN(1923); CHRISTINE OF THE HUNGRY HEART(1924); FEMALE, THE(1924); GARDEN OF WEEDS, THE(1924); HIS FORGOTTEN WIFE(1924); THOSE WHO DANCE(1924); BEST PEOPLE, THE(1925); SON OF HIS FATHER, A(1925); WELCOME HOME(1925); MANNEQUIN(1926); MISMATES(1926); DRUMS OF THE DESERT(1927); DANGER STREET(1928); WOMAN'S WAY, A(1928)

Jerry Baxter-Worman

KING OF COMEDY, THE(1983)

Aldo Bay

VIOLENT ONES, THE(1967)

Dorothy Bay

SUBWAY EXPRESS(1931); DISGRACED(1933); OUT ALL NIGHT(1933); LONE WOLF RETURNS, THE(1936)

Dorothy Vernon Bay

YOU'RE TELLING ME(1934)

Frances Bay

FOUL PLAY(1978); BUDDY BUDDY(1981); CHILLY SCENES OF WINTER(1982); PRIVATE SCHOOL(1983)

1984

KARATE KID, THE(1984)

Francis Bay

ATTIC, THE(1979); AMY(1981); HONKY TONK FREEWAY(1981)

Howard Bay

EXILE, THE(1947), set d; UP IN CENTRAL PARK(1948), prod d

John Bay

GOLD(1974, Brit.)

Richard Bay

BROTHER JOHN(1971)

Sara Bay

ARENA, THE(1973)

Sarah Bay

LADY FRANKENSTEIN(1971, Ital.); DEVIL'S WEDDING NIGHT, THE(1973, Ital.)

Tom Bay

FIGHTING SHERIFF, THE(1931); FREIGHTERS OF DESTINY(1932)

Silents

FIGHTING BOOB, THE(1926); VALLEY OF BRAVERY, THE(1926); FIGHTING TERROR, THE(1929); LONE HORSEMAN, THE(1929)

Misc. Silents

DEAD LINE, THE(1926); DRIFTING ON(1927); TEARIN' INTO TROUBLE(1927); WHITE PEBBLES(1927); DESPERATE COURAGE(1928); FIGHTERS OF THE SADDLE(1929)

Tommy Bay

FIGHTING THRU(1931)

Silents

DEVIL'S TOWER(1929); OKLAHOMA KID, THE(1929)

Misc. Silents

MYSTERY VALLEY(1928)

Gabriel Bayman
HELLIONS, THE(1962, Brit.); COAST OF SKELETONS(1965, Brit.); SANDY THE SEAL(1969, Brit.)

Al Bayne
HOLLYWOOD STADIUM MYSTERY(1938); FIGHTING FOOLS(1949); LADY GAMBLES, THE(1949); RECKLESS MOMENTS, THE(1949)

Beverly Bayne
NAKED CITY, THE(1948)
Silents
PENNINGTON'S CHOICE(1915); ADOPTED SON, THE(1917); PAIR OF CUPIDS, A(1918); GOD'S OUTLAW(1919); MODERN MARRIAGE(1923); PASSIONATE YOUTH(1925)
Misc. Silents
CRIMSON WING, THE(1915); GRAUSTARK(1915); IN THE DIPLOMATIC SERVICE(1916); MAN AND HIS SOUL(1916); MILLION A MINUTE, A(1916); ROMEO AND JULIET(1916); THEIR COMPACT(1917); VOICE OF CONSCIENCE, THE(1917); BRASS CHECK, THE(1918); POOR RICH MAN, THE(1918); RED, WHITE AND BLUE BLOOD(1918); SOCIAL QUICKSANDS(1918); UNDER SUSPICION(1918); WITH NEATNESS AND DISPATCH(1918); DARING HEARTS(1919); HER MARRIAGE VOW(1924); TENTH WOMAN, THE(1924); WHO CARES(1925)

Harold Bayne
SLEEPING CITY, THE(1950)

Gay Baynes
1984
SUPERGIRL(1984)

Henrietta Baynes
NIJINSKY(1980, Brit.)

Henry Baynton
Silents
AULD LANG SYNE(1917, Brit.)

Aelia Bayntun
CARRY ON LOVING(1970, Brit.)

Victor Bayo
SAVAGE GUNS, THE(1962, U.S./Span.)

Delfina Bayon
CONFESSIONS OF AMANS, THE(1977)

Tanya Bayona
FIDDLER ON THE ROOF(1971)

Jose Luis Bayonas
MADIGAN'S MILLIONS(1970, Span./Ital), w; CAULDRON OF BLOOD(1971, Span.), w

Dene Bays
WEDNESDAY CHILDREN, THE(1973), m

Jimmy Bays
MOVE OVER, DARLING(1963)

Tim Bays
SIX PACK(1982)

Arthur Baysting
SLEEPING DOGS(1977, New Zealand), w

Carlos Baz
SHE-DEVIL ISLAND(1936, Mex.)

Michael Bazalgette
BEDTIME STORY(1938, Brit.); ROMANCE A LA CARTE(1938, Brit.); TEMPTRESS, THE(1949, Brit.); WARNING TO WANTONS, A(1949, Brit.)

Michel Bazalgette
HANGMAN WAITS, THE(1947, Brit.); RED SHOES, THE(1948, Brit.)

O. Bazarova
CAPTAIN GRANT'S CHILDREN(1939, USSR)

Rene Bazart
YOUNG GIRLS OF ROCHEFORT, THE(1968, Fr.); JE T'AIME, JE T'AIME(1972, Fr./Swed.)

Anthony Bazell
GENTLE SEX, THE(1943, Brit.); FOR THOSE IN PERIL(1944, Brit.)

Tony Bazell
ADVENTURE IN BLACKMAIL(1943, Brit.); NED KELLY(1970, Brit.); TRUE STORY OF ESKIMO NELL, THE(1975, Aus.)

Sally Bazely
WHAT'S GOOD FOR THE GOOSE(1969, Brit.)

Yakov Bazelyan
HOUSE WITH AN ATTIC, THE(1964, USSR), d

Irina Bazhenova
SLEEPING BEAUTY, THE(1966, USSR)

Y. Bazhenova
LADY WITH THE DOG, THE(1962, USSR), ed

Baziga
KING SOLOMON'S MINES(1950)

Robert Bazil
DAY AND THE HOUR, THE(1963, Fr./ Ital.); WEEKEND AT DUNKIRK(1966, Fr./Ital.)

Brenda Bazinet
SIEGE(1983, Can.)

Brigid Bazlen
HONEYMOON MACHINE, THE(1961); KING OF KINGS(1961); HOW THE WEST WAS WON(1962)

Sam Bazley
OUR HEARTS WERE GROWING UP(1946)

Loris Bazoki
LION OF THE DESERT(1981, Libya/Brit.)

Bazooka the Dog
STEP BY STEP(1946)

Maurice Bazuet
LOWER DEPTHS, THE(1937, Fr.)

John Bazz
1984
STREETS OF FIRE(1984)

Sergio Bazzini
DILLINGER IS DEAD(1969, Ital.), w; THANK YOU, AUNT(1969, Ital.), w; SEED OF MAN, THE(1970, Ital.), w; DRAMA OF THE RICH(1975, Ital./Fr.), w; INHERITANCE, THE(1978, Ital.), w

Loris Bazzocchi
STORY OF JOSEPH AND HIS BRETHREN THE(1962, Ital.); EIGHTEEN IN THE SUN(1964, Ital.); STRANGER IN TOWN, A(1968, U.S./Ital.); BLACK VEIL FOR LISA, A(1969 Ital./Ger.)

Camillio Bazzoni
1984
JOKE OF DESTINY LYING IN WAIT AROUND THE CORNER LIKE A STREET-BANDIT, A(1984, Ital.), ph

Camillo Bazzoni
ERNESTO(1979, Ital.), ph

Luigi Bazzoni
Misc. Talkies
EVIL FINGERS(1975), d

The BBC Dance Band
SAY IT WITH MUSIC(1932, Brit.)

BBC Dance Orchestra
MUSIC HATH CHARMS(1935, Brit.)

Could Be
HORSE IN THE GRAY FLANNEL SUIT, THE(1968)

Eduardo Bea
WIND AND THE LION, THE(1975)

A. Scott Beach
ONE IS A LONELY NUMBER(1972)

Ann Beach
HORROR HOTEL(1960, Brit.); OPERATION SNAFU(1965, Brit.); HOTEL PARADISO(1966, U.S./Brit.); SEBASTIAN(1968, Brit.); RISE AND RISE OF MICHAEL RIMMER, THE(1970, Brit.); UNDER MILK WOOD(1973, Brit.)

Bob Beach
FOR PETE'S SAKE!(1966)

Brandon Beach
UNDER WESTERN STARS(1938); OKLAHOMA TERROR(1939); ONCE UPON A HONEYMOON(1942); GANGWAY FOR TOMORROW(1943); IRON MAJOR, THE(1943); HEAVENLY DAYS(1944); WOMAN IN THE WINDOW, THE(1945); RETURN OF THE BADMEN(1948); STATE OF THE UNION(1948); PAULA(1952); PERILOUS JOURNEY, A(1953); VICKI(1953)

Colonel Beach
SHARKY'S MACHINE(1982)

Comdr. Edward L. Beach
RUN SILENT, RUN DEEP(1958), w

Corra Beach
Misc. Silents
WHAT BECOMES OF THE CHILDREN?(1918)

Guy Beach
COLONEL EFFINGHAM'S RAID(1945); CRACK-UP(1946); LEAVE HER TO HEAVEN(1946); SINGIN' IN THE CORN(1946); SMOKY(1946); BRUTE FORCE(1947); CASS TIMBERLANE(1947); HIGH WALL, THE(1947); TRAIL STREET(1947); SCUDDA-HOO! SCUDDA-HAY!(1948); WALLS OF JERICHO(1948); MISSISSIPPI RHYTHM(1949); THEY LIVE BY NIGHT(1949); TRAIL OF THE YUKON(1949); WOMAN'S SECRET, A(1949); ABBOTT AND COSTELLO IN THE FOREIGN LEGION(1950); CAGED(1950); IN A LONELY PLACE(1950); CRIMINAL LAWYER(1951); WELL, THE(1951); HIGH NOON(1952)

Guy L. Beach
PLAINSMAN AND THE LADY(1946)

James Beach
HARRAD SUMMER, THE(1974); MAN, WOMAN AND CHILD(1983)
1984
HOTEL NEW HAMPSHIRE, THE(1984), p

Jennifer Beach
MYSTERY ON BIRD ISLAND(1954, Brit.)

Jim Beach
BUDDY HOLLY STORY, THE(1978)

John Beach
TRAIL DUST(1936); HILLS OF OLD WYOMING(1937); HOPALONG RIDES AGAIN(1937); NORTH OF THE RIO GRANDE(1937); RUSTLER'S VALLEY(1937); TEXAS TRAIL(1937); BAR 20 JUSTICE(1938); FRONTIERSMAN, THE(1938); HEART OF ARIZONA(1938); HEROES OF THE HILLS(1938); OVERLAND STAGE RAIDERS(1938); PARTNERS OF THE PLAINS(1938); BLUE MONTANA SKIES(1939); CISCO KID AND THE LADY, THE(1939); HOME ON THE PRAIRIE(1939); MEXICALI ROSE(1939); OF MICE AND MEN(1939); GHOST VALLEY RAIDERS(1940)

Lewis Beach
THIS RECKLESS AGE(1932), w; HANDY ANDY(1934), w; YOUNG AS YOU FEEL(1940), w

Neva Beach
THX 1138(1971)

Peter Beach
CHILDRENS GAMES(1969), w

Rex Beach
SILVER HORDE, THE(1930), w; SON OF THE GODS(1930), w; SPOILERS, THE(1930), w; WHITE SHOULDERS(1931), w; YOUNG DONOVAN'S KID(1931), w; PAST OF MARY HOLMES, THE(1933), w; BARRIER, THE(1937), w; FLOWING GOLD(1940), w; SPOILERS, THE(1942), w; MICHIGAN KID, THE(1947), w; WORLD IN HIS ARMS, THE(1952), w; SPOILERS, THE(1955), w
Silents
SPOILERS, THE(1914), w; NE'ER-DO-WELL, THE(1916), w; AUCTION BLOCK, THE(1917), w; NORTH WIND'S MALICE, THE(1920), w; RECOIL, THE(1924), w; SAINTED DEVIL, A(1924), w; GOOSE WOMAN, THE(1925), w; AUCTION BLOCK, THE(1926), w; BARRIER, THE(1926), w; MICHIGAN KID, THE(1928), w

Richard Beach
JOIN THE MARINES(1937); MANDARIN MYSTERY, THE(1937); DOUBLE CROSS(1941); NAKED ALIBI(1954)

Sarah Beach
OLIVER'S STORY(1978)

Scott Beach
BON VOYAGE, CHARLIE BROWN(AND DON'T COME BACK)*** (1980); THX 1138(1971); AMERICAN GRAFFITI(1973); CHU CHU AND THE PHILLY FLASH(1981); OUT(1982); RIGHT STUFF, THE(1983); TO BE OR NOT TO BE(1983)

William Beach
SEEDS OF FREEDOM(1943, USSR); HOUSE ON 92ND STREET, THE(1945)

The Beach Bums
PHANTOM OF THE PARADISE(1974)
Jeannie Beacham
D.I., THE(1957)
Stephanie Beacham
GAMES, THE(1970); NIGHT COMERS, THE(1971, Brit.); DEVIL'S WIDOW, THE(1972, Brit.); DRACULA A.D. 1972(1972, Brit.); AND NOW THE SCREAMING STARTS(1973, Brit.); CONFESSIONAL, THE(1977, Brit.); SCHIZO(1977, Brit.); HORROR PLANET(1982, Brit.)
Misc. Talkies
MAFIA JUNCTION(1977); INSEMINOID(1980)
D.D. Beachamp
FATHER'S WILD GAME(1950), w
Francois Beachemin
TI-CUL TOUGAS(1977, Can.), ph
Janet Beacher
REAP THE WILD WIND(1942)
Susan Beacher
BIONIC BOY, THE(1977, Hong Kong/Phil.)
Ma Beachie
PHENIX CITY STORY, THE(1955)
Louis Beachner
ALICE'S RESTAURANT(1969)
The Bead Game
PEOPLE NEXT DOOR, THE(1970)
Bernard Beaden
ALL NIGHT LONG(1961, Brit.)
Phyllis Beadon
Silents
KILTIES THREE(1918, Brit.)
E. Hampton Beagle
NICKELODEON(1976); DEMON SEED(1977); CHINA SYNDROME, THE(1979); 1941(1979); MOTEL HELL(1980); YOUNG GIANTS(1983)
Peter Beagle
DOVE, THE(1974, Brit.), w
Peter S. Beagle
LORD OF THE RINGS, THE(1978), w; LAST UNICORN, THE(1982), w
Stephen Beagley
NUTCRACKER(1982, Brit.)
Charles Beahan
DANGEROUS NAN McGREW(1930), w; LADIES IN LOVE(1930), w; MURDER BY THE CLOCK(1931), w; NIGHT COURT(1932), w; ONE NIGHT OF LOVE(1934), w; SWEET SURRENDER(1935), w; DYNAMITE DELANEY(1938), w; WHITE TIE AND TAILS(1946), w
Silents
NAUGHTY BABY(1929), w
Barbara Beaird
MAN IN THE NET, THE(1959); FLAMING STAR(1960); TOBY TYLER(1960); ONE HUNDRED AND ONE DALMATIANS(1961)
John Beaird
MY BLOODY VALENTINE(1981, Can.), w
Pamela Beaird
GOOD MORNING, MISS DOVE(1955)
Etienne Beaker
SIX IN PARIS(1968, Fr.), ph
Jeanne Beakhurst
REAL GLORY, THE(1939), cos
Bobby Beakman
DARK AT THE TOP OF THE STAIRS, THE(1960)
Burgess Beal
Silents
NAMELESS MEN(1928), set d
Dorothy Beal
GREAT GUY(1936), cos
Eddie Beal
KISS ME DEADLY(1955)
Ethel Beal
KISS THE BRIDE GOODBYE(1944, Brit.); THREE WEIRD SISTERS, THE(1948, Brit.)
Frank Beal
SENOR AMERICANO(1929); WIDE OPEN(1930); CIMARRON(1931); EVERYTHING'S ROSIE(1931); YOUNG DONOVAN'S KID(1931); MADAME RACKETEER(1932); PHANTOM THUNDERBOLT, THE(1933); SUNSET PASS(1933)
Silents
DIVORCE TRAP, THE(1919), d; QUESTION OF HONOR, A(1922); PLAYING IT WILD(1923); WHEN ODDS ARE EVEN(1923); ARIZONA EXPRESS, THE(1924); HOOK AND LADDER(1924); MAN FOUR-SQUARE, A(1926); STOLEN BRIDE, THE(1927)
Misc. Silents
I'M GLAD MY BOY GREW TO BE A SOLDIER(1915), d; DEVIL, THE SERVANT AND THE MAN, THE(1916), d; DANGER ZONE, THE(1918), d; HER MOMENT(1918), d; MOTHER, I NEED YOU(1918), d; BROKEN COMMANDMENTS(1919), d; CHASING RAINBOWS(1919), d; THIEVES(1919), d; TIN PAN ALLEY(1920), d; WORLD OF FOLLY, A(1920), d; SOUL AND BODY(1921), d; MARRIAGE IN TRANSIT(1925); FINAL EXTRA, THE(1927); GALLOPING FURY(1927); BROKEN BARRIERS(1928); WOMEN WHO DARE(1928); BIG DIAMOND ROBBERY, THE(1929)
John Beal
ANOTHER LANGUAGE(1933); HAT, COAT AND GLOVE(1934); LITTLE MINISTER, THE(1934); BREAK OF HEARTS(1935); LADDIE(1935); LES MISERABLES(1935); M'LISS(1936); BEG, BORROW OR STEAL(1937); BORDER CAFE(1937); DANGER PATROL(1937); DOUBLE WEDDING(1937); MADAME X(1937); MAN WHO FOUND HIMSELF, THE(1937); WE WHO ARE ABOUT TO DIE(1937); ARKANSAS TRAVELER, THE(1938); I AM THE LAW(1938); PORT OF SEVEN SEAS(1938); CAT AND THE CANARY, THE(1939); DOCTORS DON'T TELL(1941); ELLERY QUEEN AND THE PERFECT CRIME(1941); GREAT COMMANDMENT, THE(1941); ATLANTIC CONVOY(1942); ONE THRILLING NIGHT(1942); EDGE OF DARKNESS(1943); KEY WITNESS(1947); ALIMONY(1949); CHICAGO DEADLINE(1949); SO DEAR TO MY HEART(1949); SONG OF SURRENDER(1949); MESSENGER OF PEACE(1950); MY SIX CONVICTS(1952); REMAINS TO BE SEEN(1953); THAT NIGHT(1957); VAMPIRE, THE(1957); SOUND AND THE FURY, THE(1959); TEN WHO DARED(1960); BRIDE, THE(1973); FUNHOUSE, THE(1981), m

Misc. Talkies
STAND BY ALL NETWORKS(1942); LET'S HAVE FUN(1943)
Kay Beal
NEW HOUSE ON THE LEFT, THE(1978, Brit.)
Misc. Talkies
LAST STOP ON THE NIGHT TRAIN(1976)
Raymond Beal
TAGGART(1964), art d
Royal Beal
BOOMERANG(1947); LOST BOUNDARIES(1949); DEATH OF A SALESMAN(1952); JOE LOUIS STORY, THE(1953); ANATOMY OF A MURDER(1959)
Scott E. Beal
CONVICTS AT LARGE(1938), d, w
Scott R. Beal
STRAIGHT FROM THE HEART(1935), d
Silents
JEALOUS HUSBANDS(1923), ph; JUST LIKE A WOMAN(1923), d
George Bealby
LAST HOUR, THE(1930, Brit.)
Alveda King Beale
SHARKY'S MACHINE(1982)
Barbara Beale
GIRLS! GIRLS! GIRLS!(1962)
Basil Beale
CIRCLE OF DECEPTON(1961, Brit.); DR. CRIPPEN(1963, Brit.); SILENT PLAYGROUND, THE(1964, Brit.)
Charlie Beale
NEW ORLEANS(1947)
Eddie Beale
HANDLE WITH CARE(1964)
Erica Beale
LUST FOR A VAMPIRE(1971, Brit.)
Frank Beale
NIGHT WORLD(1932)
Jack Beale
CARRY ON NURSE(1959, Brit.), w; TWICE AROUND THE DAFFODILS(1962, Brit.), w
Nada Beale
TWO-HEADED SPY, THE(1959, Brit.)
Richard Beale
WHERE EAGLES DARE(1968, Brit.); YOUNG WINSTON(1972, Brit.)
Will Beale
PARTNERS OF THE TRAIL(1931), w
The Beale Street Boys
GIFT OF GAB(1934)
Barbara Beall
FOLIES DERGERE(1935)
Betty Beall
GIRLS! GIRLS! GIRLS!(1962); DAY MARS INVADED EARTH, THE(1963)
Burgess Beall
IRON MASK, THE(1929), art d
Silents
NIGHT LIFE(1927), set d; TRAGEDY OF YOUTH, THE(1928), set d
Charles Beall
TERMS OF ENDEARMENT(1983)
1984
CLOAK AND DAGGER(1984)
Nada Beall
TELL-TALE HEART, THE(1962, Brit.)
Sandra Beall
NIGHT IN HEAVEN, A(1983)
1984
BIRDY(1984); COTTON CLUB, THE(1984)
Robart Bealmer
1984
CENSUS TAKER, THE(1984), p
Frank Beals
AIR MAIL(1932)
Jennifer Beals
FLASHDANCE(1983)
Richard Beals
SNOW QUEEN, THE(1959, USSR)
John Bealy
ORGY OF THE DEAD(1965)
Barbara Beaman
1984
BODY ROCK(1984)
David Beames
RADIO ON(1980, Brit./Ger.); GIRO CITY(1982, Brit.); MC VICAR(1982, Brit.)
Frank Beamish
Silents
AWAKENING, THE(1917); TILLIE WAKES UP(1917); LEAP TO FAME(1918); NEIGHBORS(1918)
Misc. Silents
MISS INNOCENCE(1918); WHIMS OF SOCIETY, THE(1918); PUTTING ONE OVER(1919)
May Beamish
DON'T RUSH ME(1936, Brit.)
Silents
IF YOUTH BUT KNEW(1926, Brit.)
Harry Beamont
Misc. Silents
GAY LORD QUEX, THE(1920), d
Lucy Beamont
Misc. Silents
STOOL PIGEON(1928)
Dovie Beams
WILD WHEELS(1969); GUNS OF A STRANGER(1973)

David Bean
WEST SIDE STORY(1961)
Henry Bean
RUNNING BRAVE(1983, Can.), w
Orson Bean
HOW TO BE VERY, VERY, POPULAR(1955); ANATOMY OF A MURDER(1959); LOLA(1971, Brit./Ital.); SKATEBOARD(1978); FORTY DEUCE(1982)
Reathal Bean
GOING IN STYLE(1979)
Reathel Bean
WINDFLOWERS(1968)
Richard Bean
GIGI(1958)
1984
PURPLE HEARTS(1984)
Robert B. Bean
MADE FOR EACH OTHER(1971), d
Robert Bean
WILD RIDE, THE(1960); CREATURE FROM THE HAUNTED SEA(1961)
Hilary Beane
THANK GOD IT'S FRIDAY(1978); ZAPPED!(1982); MR. MOM(1983)
Reginald Beane
TIME OF YOUR LIFE, THE(1948), a, m
Beans
Silents
CYCLONE OF THE RANGE(1927)
Beans The Dog
Silents
TOM AND HIS PALS(1926); PHANTOM OF THE RANGE(1928)
Beans, a Dog
Silents
SONORA KID, THE(1927)
Buddy Bear
DREAM WIFE(1953)
Jack Bear
WHAT DID YOU DO IN THE WAR, DADDY?(1966), cos; GUNN(1967), cos; PRESIDENT'S ANALYST, THE(1967), cos; WATERHOLE NO. 3(1967), cos; ODD COUPLE, THE(1968), cos; PARTY, THE(1968), cos; DARLING LILI(1970), cos; PLAZA SUITE(1971), cos; WILD ROVERS(1971), cos; SKYJACKED(1972), cos
Mary Bear
THAT LADY IN ERMINE(1948); BRIDE FOR SALE(1949); JOHNNY ALLEGRO(1949); TROUBLE PREFERRED(1949); MOTHER DIDN'T TELL ME(1950); SINGING GUNS(1950); STELLA(1950); I'LL CRY TOMORROW(1955)
Roger Bear
BEST FRIENDS(1975)
David Beard
STRANGE BREW(1983)
Dr. Charles Beard
SAINT JOAN(1957), cons
James Beard
TELL ME THAT YOU LOVE ME, JUNIE MOON(1970); SUCH GOOD FRIENDS(1971)
John Beard
UNSUITABLE JOB FOR A WOMAN, AN(1982, Brit.), art d; EUREKA(1983, Brit.), art d
Mathew Beard
KID MILLIONS(1934)
Nancy Beard
Silents
LITTLE DOOR INTO THE WORLD, THE(1923, Brit.)
Peter H. Beard
HALLELUJAH THE HILLS(1963)
Red Beard
RED BEARD(1966, Jap.)
Rene Beard
PINKY(1949); PRESIDENT'S LADY, THE(1953)
Renee Beard
FOXES OF HARROW, THE(1947); WHO KILLED "DOC" ROBBIN?(1948); BRIGHT ROAD(1953)
Robert Beard
DEER HUNTER, THE(1978)
Roy Beard
Misc. Silents
HEARTS THAT ARE HUMAN(1915, Brit.)
Stanley Beard
DULCIMER STREET(1948, Brit.); IDOL ON PARADE(1959, Brit.)
Stymie Beard
RAINBOW ON THE RIVER(1936); SLAVE SHIP(1937); BELOVED BRAT(1938); JEZEBEL(1938); KENTUCKY(1938); WAY DOWN SOUTH(1939); RETURN OF FRANK JAMES, THE(1940); SHOW BUSINESS(1944); FALLEN ANGEL(1945); DEAD RECKONING(1947); TRUCK TURNER(1974); BUDDY HOLLY STORY, THE(1978)
Misc. Talkies
TWO-GUN MAN FROM HARLEM(1938); BROKEN STRINGS(1940)
Tommy Beard
HIS BROTHER'S WIFE(1936)
William Beard II
1984
STREETS OF FIRE(1984)
Amanda H. Bearde
HYSTERICAL(1983)
Chris Bearde
HYSTERICAL(1983), d
Eugene Bearden
STRATTON STORY, THE(1949)
Gene Bearden
KID FROM CLEVELAND, THE(1949)
Jim Bearden
DEAD ZONE, THE(1983)
1984
POLICE ACADEMY(1984)

W.S. Bearden
GREAT LOCOMOTIVE CHASE, THE(1956)
John Beardmore
WARM DECEMBER, A(1973, Brit.)
Alice Beardsley
TIGER MAKES OUT, THE(1967); WHERE THE LILIES BLOOM(1974); PROMISES IN THE DARK(1979); HONKY TONK FREEWAY(1981); ZELIG(1983)
Helen Beardsley
YOURS, MINE AND OURS(1968), w
Cody Bearpaw
OKLAHOMA CRUDE(1973)
Misc. Talkies
DEVIL AND LEROY BASSETT, THE(1973)
Tom Bears
TWO-MINUTE WARNING(1976)
Amanda Bearse
1984
PROTOCOL(1984)
Barney Bearsley
DESERT VENGEANCE(1931)
Matt Bearson
1984
RIVER, THE(1984)
Frank Beascoechea
BUCK ROGERS IN THE 25TH CENTURY(1979), ph
1984
NADIA(1984, U.S./Yugo.), ph
Frank P Beascoechea
CONQUEST OF THE EARTH(1980), ph
Barney Beasley
GUN PLAY(1936)
Misc. Talkies
SUNDOWN TRAIL, THE(1975)
Bob Beasley
SPLENDOR(1935)
Charles E. Beasley
1984
RIVER RAT, THE(1984)
Cheryl Beasley
JOYRIDE(1977), cos; LINCOLN CONSPIRACY, THE(1977), cos
Harry Beasley
VARIETY PARADE(1936, Brit.)
Howard Beasley
MR. MAJESTYK(1974)
James Beasley
WOMAN IN THE WINDOW, THE(1945)
Jennifer Beasley
COAL MINER'S DAUGHTER(1980)
Kenyatta Beasley
1984
RIVER RAT, THE(1984)
Ted Beasley
Silents
BURN 'EM UP BARNES(1921), ph
Terrence Beasor
WHITE DOG(1982)
Alvah Beassie
HOTEL BERLIN(1945), w
Richard Beat
POT CARRIERS, THE(1962, Brit.), ed
Britannia Beatey
MY FAIR LADY(1964)
The Beatles
I WANNA HOLD YOUR HAND(1978), m
Affonso Beato
HOT TIMES(1974), ph
Alfonso Beato
ANTONIO DAS MORTES(1970, Braz.), ph; BOSS'S SON, THE(1978), ph
Alex Beaton
STRANGE LOVERS(1963), w; DAY OF THE EVIL GUN(1968), ed; SOLDIER BLUE(1970), ed; ...TICK...TICK...TICK...(1970), ed; J.W. COOP(1971), ed
Betsy Beaton
BOY WITH THE GREEN HAIR, THE(1949), w
Betzi Beaton
MORE THE MERRIER, THE(1943); ANGEL COMES TO BROOKLYN, AN(1945)
Cecil Beaton
ANNA KARENINA(1948, Brit.), cos; IDEAL HUSBAND, AN(1948, Brit.), cos; DOCTOR'S DILEMMA, THE(1958, Brit.), cos; GIGI(1958), prod d, cos; TRUTH ABOUT WOMEN, THE(1958, Brit.), cos; MY FAIR LADY(1964), prod d, cos; ON A CLEAR DAY YOU CAN SEE FOREVER(1970), cos
Kenneth Beaton
SONG OF THE CABELLERO(1930), w
Mary Louise Beaton
Silents
MAN WHO, THE(1921)
Norman Beaton
PRESSURE(1976, Brit.); BLACK JOY(1977, Brit.); EUREKA(1983, Brit.)
1984
REAL LIFE(1984, Brit.)
Timothy Beaton
RETURN OF A STRANGER(1962, Brit.); MIND BENDERS, THE(1963, Brit.)
Cynthia Beatt
JOURNEYS FROM BERLIN–1971(1980)
Alan Beattie
1984
HOUSE WHERE DEATH LIVES, THE(1984), p, d, w
Misc. Talkies
HOUSE WHERE DEATH LIVES, THE(1982), d

Ann Beattie
CHILLY SCENES OF WINTER(1982), a, w
Aubrey Beattie
Misc. Silents
DAZZLING MISS DAVISON, THE(1917); GREATER WOMAN, THE(1917); HEDDA
GABLER(1917)
Jim Beattie
GREAT WHITE HOPE, THE(1970)
John Beattie
OPERATION SECRET(1952)
Mrs. Charles Beattie
Silents
DAUGHTER OF LOVE, A(1925, Brit.)
Babs Beatty
FIREBALL JUNGLE(1968)
Belinda Beatty
EXORCIST II: THE HERETIC(1977)
Belinha Beatty
DELIVERANCE(1972)
Bernice Beatty
TREASURE ISLAND(1934)
Bunny Beatty
BECKY SHARP(1935); FATHER BROWN, DETECTIVE(1935); SYLVIA SCAR-
LETT(1936); FOREIGN CORRESPONDENT(1940)
Bunny Lauri Beatty
LIBELED LADY(1936)
Clarence Beatty
MOVIE MOVIE(1978)
Clyde Beatty
BIG CAGE, THE(1933), a, w; LOST JUNGLE, THE(1934); DARKEST AFRICA(1936);
AFRICA SCREAMS(1949); RING OF FEAR(1954)
Ethel Beatty
1984
GARBO TALKS(1984)
George Beatty
YOU'RE IN THE ARMY NOW(1941), w; HI' YA, SAILOR(1943)
Lauri Beatty
NANA(1934); WEE WILLIE WINKIE(1937); BILL OF DIVORCEMENT(1940)
May Beatty
BENSON MURDER CASE, THE(1930); EX-FLAME(1931); DINNER AT EIGHT(1933);
HORSEPLAY(1933); LOVE IS LIKE THAT(1933); RAINBOW OVER BROAD-
WAY(1933); LITTLE MINISTER, THE(1934); BECKY SHARP(1935); GIRL WHO CAME
BACK, THE(1935); LIVING ON VELVET(1935); MAD LOVE(1935); LITTLE LORD
FAUNTLEROY(1936); LLOYDS OF LONDON(1936); PRIVATE NUMBER(1936); SA-
TAN MET A LADY(1936); SHOW BOAT(1936); SYLVIA SCARLETT(1936); WHITE
ANGEL, THE(1936); WIDOW FROM MONTE CARLO, THE(1936); CALL IT A
DAY(1937); SHE LOVED A FIREMAN(1937); IF I WERE KING(1938); MAN-
PROOF(1938); ADVENTURES OF SHERLOCK HOLMES, THE(1939); ETERNALLY
YOURS(1939); I AM A CRIMINAL(1939); UNION PACIFIC(1939); WE ARE NOT
ALONE(1939); WOMEN, THE(1939); MY SON, MY SON!(1940); PRIDE AND PREJU-
DICE(1940); QUEEN OF THE MOB(1940); DRESSED TO KILL(1941); I WAKE UP
SCREAMING(1942); THIS ABOVE ALL(1942); CRYSTAL BALL, THE(1943); FOREV-
ER AND A DAY(1943); LASSIE, COME HOME(1943)
Ned Beatty
DELIVERANCE(1972); LIFE AND TIMES OF JUDGE ROY BEAN, THE(1972); LAST
AMERICAN HERO, THE(1973); THIEF WHO CAME TO DINNER, THE(1973); WHITE
LIGHTNING(1973); NASHVILLE(1975); W. W. AND THE DIXIE DANCEKINGS(1975);
ALL THE PRESIDENT'S MEN(1976); BIG BUS, THE(1976); MIKEY AND NICK-
Y(1976); NETWORK(1976); SILVER STREAK(1976); ALAMBRISTA!(1977); EXORCIST
II: THE HERETIC(1977); GREAT BANK HOAX, THE(1977); GRAY LADY
DOWN(1978); SUPERMAN(1978); PROMISES IN THE DARK(1979); WISE
BLOOD(1979, U.S./Ger.); 1941(1979); AMERICAN SUCCESS COMPANY, THE(1980);
HOPSCOTCH(1980); SUPERMAN II(1980); INCREDIBLE SHRINKING WOMAN,
THE(1981); TOY, THE(1982); STROKER ACE(1983); TOUCHED(1983)
Robert Beatty
MEIN KAMPF-MY CRIMES(1940, Brit.); MURDER IN THE NIGHT(1940, Brit.);
FLYING FORTRESS(1942, Brit.); ONE OF OUR AIRCRAFT IS MISSING(1942, Brit.);
SUICIDE SQUADRON(1942, Brit.); SPITFIRE(1943, Brit.); SUSPECTED PER-
SON(1943, Brit.); IT HAPPENED ONE SUNDAY(1944, Brit.); APPOINTMENT WITH
CRIME(1945, Brit.); GREEN FINGERS(1947); ODD MAN OUT(1947, Brit.); SAN
DEMETRIO, LONDON(1947, Brit.); AGAINST THE WIND(1948, Brit.); ANOTHER
SHORE(1948, Brit.); COUNTER BLAST(1948, Brit.); DEVIL'S PLOT, THE(1948, Brit.);
GIRL IN THE PAINTING, THE(1948, Brit.); TAMING OF DOROTHY, THE(1950, Brit.);
TWENTY QUESTIONS MURDER MYSTERY, THE(1950, Brit.); CALLING BULLDOG
DRUMMOND(1951, Brit.); CAPTAIN HORATIO HORNBLOWER(1951, Brit.); DEAD
ON COURSE(1952, Brit.); GENTLE GUNMAN, THE(1952, Brit.); MAGIC BOX,
THE(1952, Brit.); ALBERT, R.N.(1953, Brit.); BROKEN HORSESHOE, THE(1953, Brit.);
HORSE'S MOUTH, THE(1953, Brit.); MAN ON A TIGHTROPE(1953); PROJECT
M7(1953, Brit.); LOVES OF THREE QUEENS, THE(1954, Ital./Fr.); SQUARE RING,
THE(1955, Brit.); POSTMARK FOR DANGER(1956, Brit.); OUT OF THE CLOUDS(1957,
Brit.); SOMETHING OF VALUE(1957); TARZAN AND THE LOST SAFARI(1957, Brit.);
TIME LOCK(1959, Brit.); SHAKEDOWN, THE(1960, Brit.); INVITATION TO MUR-
DER(1962, Brit.); DR. MABUSE'S RAYS OF DEATH(1964, Ger./Fr./Ital.); AMOROUS
MR. PRAWN, THE(1965, Brit.); WHERE EAGLES DARE(1968, Brit.); 2001: A SPACE
ODYSSEY(1968, U.S./Brit.); POPE JOAN(1972, Brit.); SITTING TARGET(1972, Brit.);
SPIKES GANG, THE(1974); PINK PANTHER STRIKES AGAIN, THE(1976, Brit.);
UNIDENTIFIED FLYING ODDBALL, THE(1979, Brit.); SUPERMAN III(1983)
Roberta Beatty
HONOR AMONG LOVERS(1931)
Roger Beatty
BILLION DOLLAR HOBO, THE(1977), w
Warren Beatty
$(DOLLARS)**1/2 (1971); ROMAN SPRING OF MRS. STONE, THE(1961, U.S./Brit.);
SPLENDOR IN THE GRASS(1961); ALL FALL DOWN(1962); LILITH(1964); MICKEY
ONE(1965); KALEIDOSCOPE(1966, Brit.); PROMISE HER ANYTHING(1966, Brit.);
BONNIE AND CLYDE(1967), a, p; ONLY GAME IN TOWN, THE(1970); MC CABE
AND MRS. MILLER(1971); PARALLAX VIEW, THE(1974); FORTUNE, THE(1975);
SHAMPOO(1975), a, p, w; HEAVEN CAN WAIT(1978), a, p, d, w; REDS(1981), a,
p&d, w

David Beaty
TROUBLE IN THE SKY(1961, Brit.), w
May Beaty
VANITY STREET(1932)
Garrie Beau
MOVE(1970)
Marie Beau
1984
LE DERNIER COMBAT(1984, Fr.), cos
The Beau Brummels
VILLAGE OF THE GIANTS(1965); WILD, WILD WINTER(1966)
Beau the Dog
SCALAWAG(1973, Yugo.)
Julian Beaubien
Misc. Silents
BRAND'S DAUGHTER(1917)
Julien Beaubien
Silents
WINNING STROKE, THE(1919)
Cora Beaucaire
IT'S IN THE BAG(1936, Brit.)
Beauchamp
LOUISE(1940, Fr.)
Anthony Beauchamp
FABIAN OF THE YARD(1954, Brit.), p, d
Catherine Beauchamp
DESPERATE DECISION(1954, Fr.), w
Clem Beauchamp
STORY OF TEMPLE DRAKE, THE(1933); TERROR ABOARD(1933); NO MORE
LADIES(1935)
D D. Beauchamp
MAN WITHOUT A STAR(1955), w
D. D. Beauchamp
SAN FRANCISCO STORY, THE(1952), w; ALL-AMERICAN, THE(1953), w; MAN
FROM THE ALAMO, THE(1953), w; SON OF BELLE STARR(1953), w; MASSAC-
RE(1956), w; YAQUI DRUMS(1956), w; SHOOT-OUT AT MEDICINE BEND(1957), w;
NATCHEZ TRACE(1960), w
D.D. Beauchamp
WISTFUL WIDOW OF WAGON GAP, THE(1947), w; FEUDIN', FUSSIN' AND
A-FIGHTIN'(1948), w; RIVER LADY(1948), w; HENRY, THE RAINMAKER(1949), w;
LEAVE IT TO HENRY(1949), w; ABBOTT AND COSTELLO IN THE FOREIGN
LEGION(1950), w; FATHER MAKES GOOD(1950), w; GOLDEN GLOVES STORY,
THE(1950), w; BELLE LE GRAND(1951), w; FATHER TAKES THE AIR(1951), w;
ABBOTT AND COSTELLO GO TO MARS(1953), w; GUNSMOKE(1953), w; LAW AND
ORDER(1953), w; DESTRY(1954), w; JESSE JAMES' WOMEN(1954), w; RAILS INTO
LARAMIE(1954), w; RIDE CLEAR OF DIABLO(1954), w; SHE COULDN'T SAY
NO(1954), w; PORT OF HELL(1955), w; TENNESSEE'S PARTNER(1955), w; RAW-
HIDE YEARS, THE(1956), w; FOR THE LOVE OF MIKE(1960), w; MAN CALLED
GANNON, A(1969), w
Daniel D. Beauchamp
ALIAS JESSE JAMES(1959), w
Edmond Beauchamp
CRIME OF MONSIEUR LANGE, THE(1936, Fr.); LA MARSEILLAISE(1938, Fr.);
DEVIL IN THE FLESH, THE(1949, Fr.); LE BEAU SERGE(1959, Fr.)
Guy Beauchamp
YOU'RE THE DOCTOR(1938, Brit.), w
James W. Beauchamp
1984
FOOTLOOSE(1984), spec eff
Lane Beauchamp
HENRY, THE RAINMAKER(1949), w
Lary Beauchamp
NIGHT OF EVIL(1962)
Linsey Beauchamp
1984
SUPERGIRL(1984)
Richard Beauchamp
SUNNYSIDE(1979); GORP(1980)
Clem Beauchamps
STAGE DOOR CANTEEN(1943), prod d
Sarah Beauchesne
PASSION(1983, Fr./Switz.)
Alexandra Beauclerc
NIGHT TRAIN TO PARIS(1964, Brit.)
Eleanor Beaucour
HIGH INFIDELITY(1965, Fr./Ital.)
Deborah Beaudet
PARADISE ALLEY(1978), art d
Louise Beaudet
Silents
MAN BEHIND THE DOOR, THE(1914); BATTLE CRY OF PEACE, THE(1915); ON
HER WEDDING NIGHT(1915); PRICE FOR FOLLY, A(1915); WHEELS OF JUS-
TICE(1915); BABBLING TONGUES(1917); GOLD DIGGERS, THE(1923); SALLY(1925)
Misc. Silents
GREEN STOCKINGS(1916); PRICE SHE PAID, THE(1917); SLAVES OF PRIDE(1920)
Marc Beaudet
MY UNCLE ANTOINE(1971, Can.), p
Rolland Joseph Beaudet
QUEBEC(1951)
Jean Beaudin
CORDELIA(1980, Fr., Can.), d, w, ed
Helen Beaudine
PENROD AND SAM(1931)
Jean Beaudine
DEAD MEN DON'T WEAR PLAID(1982)
Kathy Beaudine
J.W. COOP(1971)

William Beaudine
GIRL FROM WOOLWORTH'S, THE(1929), d; GIVE AND TARE(1929), d; HARD TO GET(1929), d; TWO WEEKS OFF(1929), d; ROAD TO PARADISE(1930), d; THOSE WHO DANCE(1930), d; WEDDING RINGS(1930), d; FATHER'S SON(1931), d; LADY WHO DARED, THE(1931), d; MAD PARADE, THE(1931), d; MEN IN HER LIFE(1931), d; MISBEHAVING LADIES(1931), d; PENROD AND SAM(1931), d; MAKE ME A STAR(1932), d; THREE WISE GIRLS(1932), d; CRIME OF THE CENTURY, THE(1933), d; HER BODYGUARD(1933), d; OLD-FASHIONED WAY, THE(1934), d; DANDY DICK(1935, Brit.), d&w, w; GET OFF MY FOOT(1935, Brit.), d; TWO HEARTS IN HARMONY(1935, Brit.), d; BOYS WILL BE BOYS(1935, Brit.), d; EDUCATED EVANS(1936, Brit.), d; IT'S IN THE BAG(1936, Brit.), d; MR. COHEN TAKES A WALK(1936, Brit.), d; WHERE THERE'S A WILL(1936, Brit), d, w; FEATHER YOUR NEST(1937, Brit.), d; TAKE IT FROM ME(1937, Brit.), d; WINDBAG THE SAILOR(1937, Brit.), d; SEZ O'REILLY TO MACNAB(1938, Brit.), d; TORCHY BLANE IN CHINATOWN(1938), d; TORCHY GETS HER MAN(1938), d; BLONDE COMET(1941), d; DESPERATE CARGO(1941), w; EMERGENCY LANDING(1941), d; FEDERAL FUGITIVES(1941), d; MISBEHAVING HUSBANDS(1941), d; BROADWAY BIG SHOT(1942), d; DUKE OF THE NAVY(1942), d, w; FOREIGN AGENT(1942), d; GALLANT LADY(1942), d; LIVING GHOST, THE(1942), d; MEN OF SAN QUENTIN(1942), d; MIRACLE KID(1942), d; MR. CELEBRITY(1942), d; ONE THRILLING NIGHT(1942), d; PANTHER'S CLAW, THE(1942), d; PHANTOM KILLER(1942), d; PRISON GIRL(1942), d; APE MAN, THE(1943), d; CLANCY STREET BOYS(1943), d; GHOSTS ON THE LOOSE(1943), d; HERE COMES KELLY(1943), d; MR. MUGGS STEPS OUT(1943), d; MYSTERY OF THE 13TH GUEST, THE(1943), d; SPOTLIGHT SCANDALS(1943), d; ADVENTURES OF KITTY O'DAY(1944), d; BOWERY CHAMPS(1944), d; CRAZY KNIGHTS(1944), d; DETECTIVE KITTY O'DAY(1944), d; FOLLOW THE LEADER(1944), d; HOT RHYTHM(1944), d; LEAVE IT TO THE IRISH(1944), d; OH, WHAT A NIGHT(1944), d; SHADOW OF SUSPICION(1944), d; VOODOO MAN(1944), d; WHAT A MAN!(1944), d; BLONDE RANSOM(1945), d; COME OUT FIGHTING(1945), d; FASHION MODEL(1945), d; SWINGIN' ON A RAINBOW(1945), d; BELOW THE DEADLINE(1946), d; BLACK MARKET BABIES(1946), d; DON'T GAMBLE WITH STRANGERS(1946), d; FACE OF MARBLE, THE(1946), d; GIRL ON THE SPOT(1946), d; MR. HEX(1946), d; ONE EXCITING WEEK(1946), d; SPOOK BUSTERS(1946), d; BOWERY BUCKAROOS(1947), d; CHINESE RING, THE(1947), d; GAS HOUSE KIDS GO WEST(1947), d; HARD BOILED MAHONEY(1947), d; KILLER AT LARGE(1947), d; NEWS HOUNDS(1947), d; PHILO VANCE RETURNS(1947), d; TOO MANY WINNERS(1947), d; ANGELS ALLEY(1948), d; FEATHERED SERPENT, THE(1948), d; INCIDENT(1948), d; JINX MONEY(1948), d; KIDNAPPED(1948), d; MOM AND DAD(1948), d; MYSTERY OF THE GOLDEN EYE, THE(1948), d; SHANGHAI CHEST, THE(1948), d; SMUGGLERS' COVE(1948), d; FORGOTTEN WOMEN(1949), d; LAWTON STORY, THE(1949), d; TOUGH ASSIGNMENT(1949), d; TUNA CLIPPER(1949), d; BLONDE DYNAMITE(1950), d; BLUE GRASS OF KENTUCKY(1950), d; BLUES BUSTERS(1950), d; COUNTY FAIR(1950), d; LUCKY LOSERS(1950), d; BOWERY BATTALION(1951), d; CRAZY OVER HORSES(1951), d; CUBAN FIREBALL(1951), d; GHOST CHASERS(1951), d; HAVANA ROSE(1951), d; LET'S GO NAVY(1951), d; PRINCE OF PEACE, THE(1951), d; BELA LUGOSI MEETS A BROOKLYN GORILLA(1952), d; FEUDIN' FOOLS(1952), d; HERE COME THE MARINES(1952), d; HOLD THAT LINE(1952), d; JET JOB(1952), d; NO HOLDS BARRED(1952), d; RODEO(1952), d; ROSE BOWL STORY, THE(1952), d; BORN TO THE SADDLE(1953), d; JALOPY(1953), d; ROAR OF THE CROWD(1953), d; CITY STORY(1954), d; PARIS PLAYBOYS(1954), d; PRIDE OF THE BLUE GRASS(1954), d; YUKON VENGEANCE(1954), d; HIGH SOCIETY(1955), d; JAIL BUSTERS(1955), d; WESTWARD HO THE WAGONS!(1956), d; UP IN SMOKE(1957), d; IN THE MONEY(1958), d; TEN WHO DARED(1960), d; BILLY THE KID VS. DRACULA(1966), d; JESSE JAMES MEETS FRANKENSTEIN'S DAUGHTER(1966), d
Misc. Talkies
CONDEMNED MEN(1940), d; PROFESSOR CREEPS(1942), d; JIGGS AND MAGGIE IN COURT(1948), d; JIGGS AND MAGGIE IN JACKPOT JITTERS(1949), d; SECOND CHANCE(1950), d; BEYOND THE MOON(1964), d
Silents
WATCH YOUR STEP(1922), d; BOY OF MINE(1923), d; COUNTRY KID, THE(1923), d; HER FATAL MILLIONS(1923), d; PENROD AND SAM(1923), d; DARING YOUTH(1924), d; NARROW STREET, THE(1924), d; LITTLE ANNIE ROONEY(1925), d; SOCIAL HIGHWAYMAN, THE(1926), d; SPARROWS(1926), d; THAT'S MY BABY(1926), d; IRRESISTIBLE LOVER, THE(1927), d; COHENS AND THE KELLYS IN PARIS, THE(1928), d; DO YOUR DUTY(1928), d; FUGITIVES(1929), d
Misc. Silents
CATCH MY SMOKE(1922), d; HEROES OF THE STREET(1922), d; PRINTER'S DEVIL, THE(1923), d; CORNERED(1924), d; DAUGHTERS OF PLEASURE(1924), d; SELF-MADE FAILURE, A(1924), d; WANDERING HUSBANDS(1924), d; BROADWAY BUTTERFLY, A(1925), d; HOW BAXTER BUTTED IN(1925), d; CANADIAN, THE(1926), d; HOLD THAT LION(1926), d; FRISCO SALLY LEVY(1927), d; LIFE OF RILEY, THE(1927), d; HEART TO HEART(1928), d; HOME JAMES(1928), d

William Beaudine, Jr.
DUKE OF THE NAVY(1942); GIRL CRAZY(1943); SWEETHEART OF SIGMA CHI(1946); MAGIC OF LASSIE, THE(1978), p
1984
COUNTRY(1984), p

William Beaudine, Sr.
JIGGS AND MAGGIE OUT WEST(1950), d; MURDER WITHOUT TEARS(1953), d; LASSIE'S GREAT ADVENTURE(1963), d

Eugene Beaudino
Silents
SUPREME TEST, THE(1923)

Peter Beaudoin
HANK WILLIAMS: THE SHOW HE NEVER GAVE(1982, Can.)

Tonya Beauford
DESERT MESA(1935)

Dennis Beaufort
WOMAN ACCUSED(1933)

Max Beaufort
CLONUS HORROR, THE(1979), ph

Bruno Beauge
1984
THREE CROWNS OF THE SAILOR(1984, Fr.), set d

Marguerite Beauge
PEPE LE MOKO(1937, Fr.), ed

Silents
NAPOLEON(1927, Fr.), ed

Yvonne Beauge
HEART OF PARIS(1939, Fr.), ed

Andre Beaulieu
Silents
JO THE CROSSING SWEEPER(1918, Brit.); WAY OF AN EAGLE, THE(1918, Brit.)
Misc. Silents
MY LADY'S DRESS(1917, Brit.); NIGHT RIDERS, THE(1920, Brit.)

Harold Beaulieu
PUNISHMENT PARK(1971)

Marie-France Beaulieu
WHY ROCK THE BOAT?(1974, Can.)

Tony Beaulieu
CAMPUS SLEUTH(1948), m

Yolande Beaulieu
Misc. Silents
MENILMONTANT(1926, Fr.)

Nicholas Beauman
STARSTRUCK(1982, Aus.), ed
1984
MRS. SOFFEL(1984), ed

Nick Beauman
SINGER AND THE DANCER, THE(1977, Aus.), ed; EARTHLING, THE(1980), ed; MY BRILLIANT CAREER(1980, Aus.), ed; PICTURE SHOW MAN, THE(1980, Aus.), ed; HOODWINK(1981, Aus.), ed

Constance Beaumar
Silents
GETTING MARY MARRIED(1919)

Leon Beaumon
PIONEER TRAIL(1938); LAW COMES TO TEXAS, THE(1939)

Bobby Beaumont
TAKE A POWDER(1953, Brit.)

Charles Beaumont
QUEEN OF OUTER SPACE(1958), w; BURN WITCH BURN(1962), w; INTRUDER, THE(1962), a, w; PREMATURE BURIAL, THE(1962), w; WONDERFUL WORLD OF THE BROTHERS ERIMM, THE(1962), w; HAUNTED PALACE, THE(1963), w; MASQUE OF THE RED DEATH, THE(1964, U.S./Brit.), w; SEVEN FACES OF DR. LAO(1964), w; MISTER MOSES(1965), w

Dan Beaumont
FOR THOSE WHO THINK YOUNG(1964), w

Diana Beaumont
ALIBI(1931, Brit.); LUCKY SWEEP, A(1932, Brit.); OLD MAN, THE(1932, Brit.); WHEN LONDON SLEEPS(1932, Brit.); MANNEQUIN(1933, Brit.); AUTUMN CROCUS(1934, Brit.); BIRDS OF A FEATHER(1935, Brit.); REAL BLOKE, A(1935, Brit.); SECRET VOICE, THE(1936, Brit.); THEY DIDN'T KNOW(1936, Brit.); BLACK LIMELIGHT(1938, Brit.); MAKE IT THREE(1938, Brit.); NORTH SEA PATROL(1939, Brit.); LET GEORGE DO IT(1940, Brit.); MURDER IN THE NIGHT(1940, Brit.); OLD MOTHER RILEY IN SOCIETY(1940, Brit.); HI, GANG!(1941, Brit.); LET THE PEOPLE SING(1942, Brit.); STOLEN FACE(1952, Brit.); MURDER ON MONDAY(1953, Brit.); AUNT CLARA(1954, Brit.); FABIAN OF THE YARD(1954, Brit.)

Diane Beaumont
HELL, HEAVEN OR HOBOKEN(1958, Brit.)

Douglas Beaumont
ONE FAMILY(1930, Brit.); I LIVED WITH YOU(1933, Brit.)

Edna Beaumont
Silents
WATCHING EYES(1921)

Ena Beaumont
Silents
GIRL FROM DOWNING STREET, THE(1918, Brit.); PATRICIA BRENT, SPINSTER(1919, Brit.); ALL THE WINNERS(1920, Brit.)
Misc. Silents
GREATER LOVE, THE(1919, Brit.); GOLDEN WEB, THE(1920, Brit.); WATCHING EYES(1921, Brit.)

Evelyn Beaumont
Silents
MESSAGE FROM MARS, A(1913, Brit.)

Gabrielle Beaumont
CRUCIBLE OF HORROR(1971, Brit.), p; GODSEND, THE(1980, Can.), p&d
Misc. Talkies
CORVINI INHERITANCE(1984, Brit.), d

Geoffrey Beaumont
Misc. Silents
VARSITY(1930, Brit.)

Gerald Beaumont
FAST COMPANIONS(1932), w; GIRL OF THE RIO(1932), w; WINNER TAKE ALL(1932), w; FRISCO JENNY(1933), w; SILK HAT KID(1935), w; SWELLHEAD(1935), w; PRIDE OF THE MARINES(1936), w; GREAT O'MALLEY, THE(1937), w; RECKLESS LIVING(1938), w
Silents
REFEREE, THE(1922), w; JACK O' CLUBS(1924), w; HIGH AND HANDSOME(1925), w; RAINMAKER, THE(1926), w; BABE COMES HOME(1927), w; DOWN THE STRETCH(1927), w; JOHNNY GET YOUR HAIR CUT(1927), w; OUTLAWS OF RED RIVER(1927), w; SILKS AND SADDLES(1929), w

Grace Beaumont
Silents
CAPRICE OF THE MOUNTAINS(1916)

Harry Beaumont
BROADWAY MELODY, THE(1929), d; BLUSHING BRIDES(1930), d; CHILDREN OF PLEASURE(1930), d; FLORODORA GIRL, THE(1930), d; LORD BYRON OF BROADWAY(1930), d; OUR BLUSHING BRIDES(1930), d; THOSE THREE FRENCH GIRLS(1930), d; DANCE, FOOLS, DANCE(1931), d; GREAT LOVER, THE(1931), d; LAUGHING SINNERS(1931), d; WEST OF BROADWAY(1931), d; ARE YOU LISTENING?(1932), d; FAITHLESS(1932), d; UNASHAMED(1932), d; MADE ON BROADWAY(1933), d; SHOULD LADIES BEHAVE?(1933), d; WHEN LADIES MEET(1933), d; MURDER IN THE PRIVATE CAR(1934), d; ENCHANTED APRIL(1935), d; GIRL ON THE FRONT PAGE, THE(1936), d; WHEN'S YOUR BIRTHDAY?(1937), d; MAISIE GOES TO RENO(1944), d; TWICE BLESSED(1945), d; SHOWOFF, THE(1946), d; UP GOES MAISIE(1946), d; UNDERCOVER MAISIE(1947), d;

ALIAS A GENTLEMAN(1948), d

Silents

SKINNER'S DRESS SUIT(1917), d; GO WEST, YOUNG MAN(1919), d; DOLLARS AND SENSE(1920), d; STOP THIEF(1920), d; JUNE MADNESS(1922), d&w; LIGHTS OF THE DESERT(1922), d; RAGGED HEIRESS, THE(1922), d; SEEING'S BELIEVING(1922), d; CRINOLINE AND ROMANCE(1923), d; GOLD DIGGERS, THE(1923), d; NOISE IN NEWBORO, A(1923), d; BABBITT(1924), d; BEAU BRUMMEL(1924), d; LOST LADY, A(1924), d; RECOMPENSE(1925), d; ROSE OF THE WORLD(1925), d; SANDY(1926), d; WOMANPOWER(1926), d; OUR DANCING DAUGHTERS(1928), d; SINGLE MAN, A(1929), d

Misc. Silents

HER HAPPINESS(1915), d; DISCARD, THE(1916), d; BROWN IN HARVARD(1917), d; BURNING THE CANDLE(1917), d; FILLING HIS OWN SHOES(1917), d; SKINNER'S BABY(1917), d; SKINNER'S BUBBLE(1917), d; TRUANT SOUL, THE(1917), d; THIRTY A WEEK(1918), d; CITY OF COMRADES, THE(1919), d; HEARTSEASE(1919), d; LITTLE ROWDY, THE(1919), d; LORD AND LADY ALGY(1919), d; MAN AND HIS MONEY, A(1919), d; ONE OF THE FINEST(1919), d; TOBY'S BOW(1919), d; WILD GOOSE CHASE(1919), d; GOING SOME(1920), d; GREAT ACCIDENT, THE(1920), d; OFFICER 666(1920), d; FIVE DOLLAR BABY, THE(1922), d; FOURTEENTH LOVER, THE(1922), d; GLASS HOUSES(1922), d; LOVE IN THE DARK(1922), d; THEY LIKE 'EM ROUGH(1922), d; VERY TRULY YOURS(1922), d; MAIN STREET(1923), d; DON'T DOUBT YOUR HUSBAND(1924), d; LOVER OF CAMILLE, THE(1924), d; HIS MAJESTY BUNKER BEAN(1925), d; ONE INCREASING PURPOSE(1927), d; FORBIDDEN HOURS(1928), d; SPEEDWAY(1929), d

Helen Howard Beaumont

Silents

MERRY WIDOW, THE(1925)

Hugh Beaumont

SOUTH OF PANAMA(1941); UNFINISHED BUSINESS(1941); WEEKEND IN HAVANA(1941); FLIGHT LIEUTENANT(1942); RIGHT TO THE HEART(1942); TO THE SHORES OF TRIPOLI(1942); WAKE ISLAND(1942); WIFE TAKES A FLYER, THE(1942); DU BARRY WAS A LADY(1943); FALLEN SPARROW, THE(1943); FLIGHT FOR FREEDOM(1943); HE HIRED THE BOSS(1943); MEXICAN SPITFIRE'S BLESSED EVENT(1943); SALUTE TO THE MARINES(1943); SEVENTH VICTIM, THE(1943); THERE'S SOMETHING ABOUT A SOLDIER(1943); I LOVE A SOLDIER(1944); MR. WINKLE GOES TO WAR(1944); PRACTICALLY YOURS(1944); RACKET MAN, THE(1944); STORY OF DR. WASSELL, THE(1944); APOLOGY FOR MURDER(1945); BLOOD ON THE SUN(1945); LADY CONFESSES, THE(1945); OBJECTIVE, BURMA!(1945); YOU CAME ALONG(1945); BLONDE FOR A DAY(1946); BLUE DAHLIA, THE(1946); JOHNNY COMES FLYING HOME(1946); LARCENY IN HER HEART(1946); MURDER IS MY BUSINESS(1946); BURY ME DEAD(1947); GUILT OF JANET AMES, THE(1947); RAILROADED(1947); THREE ON A TICKET(1947); TOO MANY WINNERS(1947); COUNTERFEITERS, THE(1948); MONEY MADNESS(1948); CALLAWAY WENT THATAWAY(1951); DANGER ZONE(1951); LAST OUTPOST, THE(1951); LOST CONTINENT(1951); MR. BELVEDERE RINGS THE BELL(1951); OVERLAND TELEGRAPH(1951); PIER 23(1951); ROARING CITY(1951); BUGLES IN THE AFTERNOON(1952); NIGHT WITHOUT SLEEP(1952); PHONE CALL FROM A STRANGER(1952); WASHINGTON STORY(1952); WILD STALLION(1952); MISSISSIPPI GAMBLER, THE(1953); HELL'S HORIZON(1955); MOLE PEOPLE, THE(1956); NIGHT PASSAGE(1957); HUMAN DUPLICATORS, THE(1965)

Misc. Talkies

SECOND CHANCE(1950)

Joey Beaumont

HARDBOILED ROSE(1929)

Kathryn Beaumont

IT HAPPENED ONE SUNDAY(1944, Brit.); ON AN ISLAND WITH YOU(1948); ALICE IN WONDERLAND(1951); PETER PAN(1953)

L.C. Beaumont

TOILERS OF THE SEA(1936, Brit.), p

Leon Beaumont

FUGITIVE AT LARGE(1939)

Lucy Beaumont

GIRL IN THE SHOW, THE(1929); GREYHOUND LIMITED, THE(1929); SONNY BOY(1929); CAUGHT PLASTERED(1931); FREE SOUL, A(1931); NEW ADVENTURES OF GET-RICH-QUICK WALLINGFORD, THE(1931); MIDNIGHT LADY(1932); MOVIE CRAZY(1932); THREE WISE GIRLS(1932); THRILL OF YOUTH(1932); HIS DOUBLE LIFE(1933); BLIND JUSTICE(1934, Brit.); CONDEMNED TO LIVE(1935); FALSE PRETENSES(1935); TEMPTATION(1935, Brit.); DEVIL DOLL, THE(1936); MAID OF SALEM(1937)

Silents

ASHES OF VENGEANCE(1923); ENEMIES OF CHILDREN(1923); FAMILY SECRET, THE(1924); OLD SOAK, THE(1926); TORRENT, THE(1926); BELOVED ROGUE, THE(1927); HOOK AND LADDER NO. 9(1927); STRANDED(1927); CROWD, THE(1928); ONE SPLENDID HOUR(1929)

Misc. Silents

GOOD BAD BOY(1924); MAN WITHOUT A COUNTRY, THE(1925); FIGHTING FAILURE, THE(1926); MEN OF THE NIGHT(1926); CLOSED GATES(1927); LOVE WAGER, THE(1927); RESURRECTION(1927); SAVAGE PASSIONS(1927); BIT OF HEAVEN, A(1928); COMRADES(1928); LITTLE YELLOW HOUSE, THE(1928); OUTCAST SOULS(1928); RIDIN' DEMON, THE(1929)

Martin Beaumont

CRY WOLF(1968, Brit.); IF ...(1968, Brit.); BOYS OF PAUL STREET, THE(1969, Hung./US)

Misc. Talkies

LIONHEART(1970)

Richard Beaumont

SCROOGE(1970, Brit.); WHO SLEW AUNTIE ROO?(1971, U.S./Brit.); DIGBY, THE BIGGEST DOG IN THE WORLD(1974, Brit.); GREAT EXPECTATIONS(1975, Brit.)

Rober Beaumont

JUDITH(1965)

Robert Beaumont

GHOSTS OF BERKELEY SQUARE(1947, Brit.); LIVING FREE(1972, Brit.)

Roger Beaumont

Misc. Talkies

NO DIAMONDS FOR URSULA(1967)

Stephanie Beaumont

JOEY BOY(1965, Brit.); GIRL GETTERS, THE(1966, Brit.)

Susan Beaumont

MAN OF THE MOMENT(1955, Brit.); EYEWITNESS(1956, Brit.); JUMPING FOR JOY(1956, Brit.); SIMON AND LAURA(1956, Brit.); HIGH TIDE AT NOON(1957, Brit.); INNOCENT SINNERS(1958, Brit.); ON THE RUN(1958, Brit.); SPANIARD'S CURSE, THE(1958, Brit.); CARRY ON NURSE(1959, Brit.); MAN WHO LIKED FUNERALS, THE(1959, Brit.); NO SAFETY AHEAD(1959, Brit.); WEB OF SUSPICION(1959, Brit.)

Tom Beaumont

Silents

MUNITION GIRL'S ROMANCE, A(1917, Brit.); WHEN GREEK MEETS GREEK(1922, Brit.)

Victor Beaumont

HELL, HEAVEN OR HOBOKEN(1958, Brit.); SPITFIRE(1943, Brit.); THUNDER OVER TANGIER(1957, Brit.); MARK OF THE PHOENIX(1958, Brit.); SQUARE PEG, THE(1958, Brit.); SHOOT TO KILL(1961, Brit.); CONCRETE JUNGLE, THE(1962, Brit.); FREUD(1962); MAKE MINE A DOUBLE(1962, Brit.); BAY OF SAINT MICHEL, THE(1963, Brit.); MASTER SPY(1964, Brit.); HEROES OF TELEMARK, THE(1965, Brit.); TRAIN, THE(1965, Fr./Ital./U.S.); WHERE EAGLES DARE(1968, Brit.); KREMLIN LETTER, THE(1970)

Caroline Beaune

1984

JUST THE WAY YOU ARE(1984)

Michel Beaune

BACKFIRE(1965, Fr.); CONFESSION, THE(1970, Fr.); COUP DE TORCHON(1981, Fr.)

Marsa Beauplan

Silents

MADAME POMPADOUR(1927, Brit.)

Maurice Beaupre

LUCK OF GINGER COFFEY, THE(1964, U.S./Can.)

F. Beauregard

Silents

KAISER, BEAST OF BERLIN, THE(1918)

F. J. Beauregard

Silents

GOLD RUSH, THE(1925)

Georges Beauregard

LA COLLECTIONNEUSE(1971, Fr.), p

Bob Beausoleil

RAMRODDER, THE(1969)

Calude Beausoleil

ME(1970, Fr.), ph

Claude Beausoleil

LE BONHEUR(1966, Fr.), ph; SLOGAN(1970, Fr.), ph; WINTER WIND(1970, Fr./Hung.)

Venita Beautrice

GARBAGE MAN, THE(1963)

Beauty

Misc. Silents

MY PAL(1925)

Beauvais

JOUR DE FETE(1952, Fr.)

Fred K. Beauvais

Misc. Silents

LONELY TRAIL, THE(1922)

Paul Beauvais

LE PETIT SOLDAT(1965, Fr.)

Peter Beauvais

MAN ON A TIGHTROPE(1953); NIGHT PEOPLE(1954)

Richard Beauvais

ILLIAC PASSION, THE(1968)

Robert Beauvais

FOUR HUNDRED BLOWS, THE(1959); CHARLES AND LUCIE(1982, Fr.)

Georges Beauvilliers

WE ARE ALL NAKED(1970, Can./Fr.)

David Beauvis

ILLIAC PASSION, THE(1968)

Nicholas Beauvy

TOOLBOX MURDERS, THE(1978)

Nick Beauvy

TAKE DOWN(1979)

Nicolas Beauvy

CAMELOT(1967); SHOOT OUT(1971); COWBOYS, THE(1972); RAGE(1972)

Jenny Beavan

HULLABALOO OVER GEORGIE AND BONNIE'S PICTURES(1979, Brit.); JANE AUSTEN IN MANHATTAN(1980), cos

1984

BOSTONIANS, THE(1984), cos

Robert Beaven

FIGHTING BACK(1983, Brit.)

Chris Beaver

OFF THE WALL(1977), ph

Jack Beaver

SCANDALS OF PARIS(1935, Brit.), ph; WINGS OVER AFRICA(1939), m; CANDLELIGHT IN ALGERIA(1944, Brit.), md; SHOWTIME(1948, Brit.), md; HASTY HEART, THE(1949), m; CLUE OF THE MISSING APE, THE(1953, Brit.), m; STOLEN PLANS, THE(1962, Brit.), m; IT HAPPENED HERE(1966, Brit.), m

Lee W. Beaver [Carlo Lizzani]

HILLS RUN RED, THE(1967, Ital.), d

Paul Beaver

LAST DAYS OF MAN ON EARTH, THE(1975, Brit.), m

Terry Beaver

CARNY(1980); HOPSCOTCH(1980); NIGHT THE LIGHTS WENT OUT IN GEORGIA, THE(1981); STROKER ACE(1983)

1984

BEAR, THE(1984)

Terry L. Beaver

SIX PACK(1982)

Walter Beaver
PUSHOVER(1954); SEVEN BRIDES FOR SEVEN BROTHERS(1954); VIOLENT MEN, THE(1955)

Louise Beavers
YOU CAN'T RUN AWAY FROM IT(1956); COQUETTE(1929); GLAD RAG DOLL, THE(1929); NIX ON DAMES(1929); WALL STREET(1929); BACK PAY(1930); MANSLAUGHTER(1930); OUR BLUSHING BRIDES(1930); SAFETY IN NUMBERS(1930); SHE COULDN'T SAY NO(1930); TRUE TO THE NAVY(1930); WIDE OPEN(1930); ANNABELLE'S AFFAIRS(1931); DON'T BET ON WOMEN(1931); GIRLS ABOUT TOWN(1931); GOOD SPORT(1931); SUNDOWN TRAIL(1931); UP FOR MURDER(1931); DIVORCE IN THE FAMILY(1932); EXPERT, THE(1932); FREAKS(1932); IT'S TOUGH TO BE FAMOUS(1932); LADIES OF THE BIG HOUSE(1932); NIGHT WORLD(1932); STREET OF WOMEN(1932); TOO BUSY TO WORK(1932); UNASHAMED(1932); WHAT PRICE HOLLYWOOD?(1932); WILD GIRL(1932); YOUNG AMERICA(1932); BOMBSHELL(1933); GIRL MISSING(1933); HER BODYGUARD(1933); HER SPLENDID FOLLY(1933); HOLD YOUR MAN(1933); PICK-UP(1933); SHE DONE HIM WRONG(1933); SHRIEK IN THE NIGHT, A(1933); WHAT PRICE INNOCENCE?(1933); 42ND STREET(1933); CHEATERS(1934); DOCTOR MONICA(1934); GLAMOUR(1934); HAT, COAT AND GLOVE(1934); I GIVE MY LOVE(1934); IMITATION OF LIFE(1934); IN THE MONEY(1934); I'VE GOT YOUR NUMBER(1934); MERRY FRINKS, THE(1934); NOTORIOUS BUT NICE(1934); PALOOKA(1934); ANNAPOLIS FAREWELL(1935); WEST OF THE PECOS(1935); BULLETS OR BALLOTS(1936); GORGEOUS HUSSY, THE(1936); RAINBOW ON THE RIVER(1936); WIVES NEVER KNOW(1936); GENERAL SPANKY(1937); LAST GANGSTER, THE(1937); LOVE IN A BUNGALOW(1937); MAKE WAY FOR TOMORROW(1937); WINGS OVER HONOLULU(1937); BROTHER RAT(1938); PECK'S BAD BOY WITH THE CIRCUS(1938); SCANDAL STREET(1938); HEADLEYS AT HOME, THE(1939); LADY'S FROM KENTUCKY, THE(1939); MADE FOR EACH OTHER(1939); REFORM SCHOOL(1939); I WANT A DIVORCE(1940); NO TIME FOR COMEDY(1940); PAROLE FIXER(1940); WOMEN WITHOUT NAMES(1940); BELLE STARR(1941); KISSES FOR BREAKFAST(1941); SHADOW OF THE THIN MAN(1941); SIGN OF THE WOLF(1941); VANISHING VIRGINIAN, THE(1941); VIRGINIA(1941); HOLIDAY INN(1942); REAP THE WILD WIND(1942); SEVEN SWEETHEARTS(1942); TENNESSEE JOHNSON(1942); YOUNG AMERICA(1942); ALL BY MYSELF(1943); DU BARRY WAS A LADY(1943); GOOD MORNING, JUDGE(1943); JACK LONDON(1943); TOP MAN(1943); BARBARY COAST GENT(1944); FOLLOW THE BOYS(1944); SOUTH OF DIXIE(1944); DELIGHTFULLY DANGEROUS(1945); DIXIE JAMBOREE(1945); LOVER COME BACK(1946); BANJO(1947); FOR THE LOVE OF MARY(1948); GOOD SAM(1948); MR. BLANDINGS BUILDS HIS DREAM HOUSE(1948); TELL IT TO THE JUDGE(1949); GIRLS' SCHOOL(1950); JACKIE ROBINSON STORY, THE(1950); MY BLUE HEAVEN(1950); COLORADO SUNDOWN(1952); I DREAM OF JEANIE(1952); NEVER WAVE AT A WAC(1952); GOODBYE, MY LADY(1956); TEENAGE REBEL(1956); TAMMY AND THE BACHELOR(1957); GODDESS, THE(1958); ALL THE FINE YOUNG CANNIBALS(1960); FACTS OF LIFE, THE(1960)
Misc. Talkies
LIFE GOES ON(1938)

Richard Beavers
EASTER PARADE(1948); TAKE ME OUT TO THE BALL GAME(1949); DEEP IN MY HEART(1954)

Arthur Beavis
QUILLER MEMORANDUM, THE(1966, Brit.), spec eff; HORROR HOUSE(1970, Brit.), spec eff; YELLOWBEARD(1983), spec eff

E. F. Beavis
SPY IN THE SKY(1958)

Ivan Beavis
FRANKENSTEIN CREATED WOMAN(1965, Brit.)

Bob Beban
WILD BLUE YONDER, THE(1952)

George Beban
FABULOUS TEXAN, THE(1947); BAD BOY(1949); DUKE OF CHICAGO(1949)
Silents
ALIEN, THE(1915), a, w; ITALIAN, THE(1915); JULES OF THE STRONG HEART(1918); ONE MORE AMERICAN(1918); HEARTS OF MEN(1919), a, d; SIGN OF THE ROSE, THE(1922), a, sup, w; LOVES OF RICARDO, THE(1926), a, d&w
Misc. Silents
PASQUALE(1916); PAWN OF FATE, THE(1916); BOND BETWEEN, THE(1917); COOK OF CANYON CAMP, THE(1917); HIS SWEETHEART(1917); LOST IN TRANSIT(1917); MARCELLINI MILLIONS, THE(1917); ROADSIDE IMPRESARIO, A(1917); ONE MAN IN A MILLION(1921), a, d; GREATEST LOVE OF ALL, THE(1925), a, d

George Beban, Jr.
SWELL GUY(1946); BUCK PRIVATES COME HOME(1947)
Silents
HEARTS OF MEN(1919)

Richard Beban
1984
MASSIVE RETALIATION(1984), w

Velvet Beban
Silents
WOMAN'S MAN(1920)

Richard Bebb
FINAL TEST, THE(1953, Brit.); GUTTER GIRLS(1964, Brit.); POPE JOAN(1972, Brit.)

Ford Bebe
Silents
KING'S CREEK LAW(1923), w

Ford I. Bebe
Silents
NO MAN'S WOMAN(1921), w

Frances Bebe
Silents
KING'S CREEK LAW(1923), w

Marjorie Bebe
Silents
HOMESICK(1928)

Rolando Bebedetti
WHITE SHEIK, THE(1956, Ital.), ed

Pam Bebermeyer
HAROLD AND MAUDE(1971); NATIONAL LAMPOON'S ANIMAL HOUSE(1978)

M. Bebutova
BOUNTIFUL SUMMER(1951, USSR)

Henri Becae
BOYS FROM BRAZIL, THE(1978), ph

Gilbert Becaud
CASINO DE PARIS(1957, Fr./Ger.), a, m; BABETTE GOES TO WAR(1960, Fr.), m; DEVIL AND THE TEN COMMANDMENTS, THE(1962, Fr.), m; $100 A NIGHT(1968, Ger.), m; DEADLY TRAP, THE(1972, Fr./Ital.), m; AND NOW MY LOVE(1975, Fr.)

Mario Beccaria
LE BOUCHER(1971, Fr./Ital.)

Dr. Giuseppe Becce
REBEL, THE(1933, Ger.), m

Dr. Josef Becce
ECSTASY(1940, Czech.), m

Guiseppe Becce
BLUE LIGHT, THE(1932, Ger.), m; HANSEL AND GRETEL(1965, Ger.), m

Gino Becchi
SOHO CONSPIRACY(1951, Brit.)

Alberto Beccianti
HUNS, THE(1962, Fr./Ital.), art d

Pilar Becerra
1984
BIZET'S CARMEN(1984, Fr./Ital.)

John Becher
DIRTYMOUTH(1970)

John C. Becher
WRONG MAN, THE(1956); ODD COUPLE, THE(1968); UP THE SANDBOX(1972); NEXT STOP, GREENWICH VILLAGE(1976); BELOW THE BELT(1980); HONKY TONK FREEWAY(1981)
1984
GREMLINS(1984); MASS APPEAL(1984)

Lynden Bechervaise
ISABEL(1968, Can.)

Sidney Bechet
MURMUR OF THE HEART(1971, Fr./Ital./Ger.), m
Misc. Talkies
MOON OVER HARLEM(1939)

C.E. Bechhofer-Roberts
DON CHICAGO(1945, Brit.), w

Gino Becchi
VOICE IN YOUR HEART, A(1952, Ital.); LA TRAVIATA(1968, Ital.)

Robo Bechi
SIGN OF THE PAGAN(1954); VIOLENT MEN, THE(1955)

Gabriel Bechir
LONGEST DAY, THE(1962), set d; PARIS WHEN IT SIZZLES(1964), set d; START THE REVOLUTION WITHOUT ME(1970), set d

Erich Becht
DIE FLEDERMAUS(1964, Aust.), m

Fred Becht
PSYCHOTRONIC MAN, THE(1980), art d

Harry Bechtel
SNIPER, THE(1952)

Mrs. William Bechtel
Silents
EMBARRASSMENT OF RICHES, THE(1918)

William Bechtel
JAZZ AGE, THE(1929); SOCIAL LION, THE(1930)
Silents
ONE DAY(1916); SPITE MARRIAGE(1929)
Misc. Silents
VENGEANCE OF DURAND, THE(1919); IDLE HANDS(1920)

Hildegard Bechtler
1984
ADERYN PAPUR(1984, Brit.), art d

James E. Bechtold
MOTHER GOOSE A GO-GO(1966), art d

George Becinita
TEXAS STAGECOACH(1940)

Beck
HENRY V(1946, Brit.), ed; PINOCCHIO(1969, E. Ger.), w

Arthur F. Beck
JUNGLE BRIDE(1933), p
Silents
WHEN THE DEVIL DRIVES(1922), p

Billy Beck
THINGS ARE TOUGH ALL OVER(1982); IRMA LA DOUCE(1963); HOUSE IS NOT A HOME, A(1964); PATSY, THE(1964); FIREBALL 590(1966); FORTUNE COOKIE, THE(1966); VALLEY OF THE DOLLS(1967); NICKELODEON(1976); FIRST LOVE(1977); CHANGE OF SEASONS, A(1980)
1984
MICKI AND MAUDE(1984); WOMAN IN RED, THE(1984)

Bob Beck
WILD ROVERS(1971)

Brian Beck
DEALING: OR THE BERKELEY-TO-BOSTON FORTY-BRICK LOST-BAG BLUES(1971), set d; CLASS OF '44(1973), set d

Bro Beck
HELLCATS, THE(1968)

Christina Beck
1984
SUBURBIA(1984)

Christopher Beck
1984
GREYSTOKE: THE LEGEND OF TARZAN, LORD OF THE APES(1984)

Clara Beck
MONTE CARLO STORY, THE(1957, Ital.)

Cornish Beck
Misc. Silents
BROADWAY BILL(1918); POINT OF VIEW, THE(1920)

Danny Beck
SIX LESSONS FROM MADAME LA ZONGA(1941); LIVING GHOST, THE(1942); MUG TOWN(1943); MR. HEX(1946); HARD BOILED MAHONEY(1947); MAN OF A THOUSAND FACES(1957)

Deborah Beck
EYES OF LAURA MARS(1978); COLD RIVER(1982)

Eddie Beck
RED RUNS THE RIVER(1963)

Ellen Beck
LOVE CHILD(1982)

Ethel Beck
Misc. Talkies
GUN GRIT(1936)

Fred Beck
OPERATION DIAMOND(1948, Brit.)

George Beck
THERE GOES MY GIRL(1937), w; EVERYBODY'S DOING IT(1938), w; FORGOTTEN GIRLS(1940), w; HIRED WIFE(1940), w; TAKE A LETTER, DARLING(1942), w; BEHAVE YOURSELF(1951), d, w; BOY, DID I GET A WRONG NUMBER!(1966), w

Glenn Beck
DR. STRANGELOVE: OR HOW I LEARNED TO STOP WORRYING AND LOVE THE BOMB(1964); MAN IN THE MIDDLE(1964, U.S./Brit.); 2001: A SPACE ODYSSEY(1968, U.S./Brit.); TWILIGHT'S LAST GLEAMING(1977, U.S./Ger.); STRANGE BREW(1983)

Gregory Beck
1984
HOT DOG...THE MOVIE(1984)

Horst Beck
GREAT BRITISH TRAIN ROBBERY, THE(1967, Ger.); $100 A NIGHT(1968, Ger.)

J. E. Beck
BROADWAY MELODY, THE(1929)

Jackson Beck
TAKE THE MONEY AND RUN(1969)

James Beck
OUTSIDER, THE(1962); 40 GUNS TO APACHE PASS(1967); I AM A GROUPIE(1970, Brit.)

Jennifer Beck
1984
TIGHTROPE(1984)

Jill Beck
LONG SHOT(1981, Brit.)

Jim Beck
BONNIE PARKER STORY, THE(1958); HOUND-DOG MAN(1959); PARATROOP COMMAND(1959)
Misc. Talkies
SHANTYTOWN HONEYMOON(1972)

Joe Beck
GOODBYE, NORMA JEAN(1976), m

John Beck
SMILING IRISH EYES(1929); COCK O' THE WALK(1930); SPOILERS, THE(1930); DYNAMITE RANCH(1932); LADY AND GENT(1932); WET PARADE, THE(1932); JEALOUSY(1934); SPITFIRE(1934); PORT OF LOST DREAMS(1935); EVERYMAN'S LAW(1936); FARMER IN THE DELL, THE(1936); HOPALONG CASSIDY RETURNS(1936); KING OF THE PECOS(1936); TRAIL OF THE LONESOME PINE, THE(1936); ISLAND CAPTIVES(1937); REMEMBER THE NIGHT(1940); TWENTY MULE TEAM(1940); WHEN THE DALTONS RODE(1940); THEY RAID BY NIGHT(1942); HIGH WALL, THE(1947); LIFE WITH FATHER(1947); SUN COMES UP, THE(1949)
Silents
SHOCK, THE(1923); LITTLE BIG HORN(1927)
Misc. Silents
DEVIL'S BOWL, THE(1923); GENERAL CUSTER AT LITTLE BIG HORN(1926)

John Beck
CYBORG 2087(1966); THREE IN THE ATTIC(1968); LAWMAN(1971); MRS. POLLIFAX-SPY(1971); NIGHTMARE HONEYMOON(1973); PAPERBACK HERO(1973, Can.); PAT GARRETT AND BILLY THE KID(1973); SLEEPER(1973); ONLY GOD KNOWS(1974, Can.); ROLLERBALL(1975); BIG BUS, THE(1976); SKY RIDERS(1976, U.S./Gr.); AUDREY ROSE(1977); OTHER SIDE OF MIDNIGHT, THE(1977)
Misc. Talkies
DEADLY HONEYMOON(1974)

John Beck
COUNTESS OF MONTE CRISTO(1948), p; FAMILY HONEYMOON(1948), p; HARVEY(1950), p; KILL THE UMPIRE(1950), p; KING KONG VERSUS GODZILLA(1963$ Jap.), p; PRIVATE NAVY OF CHARLES O'FARRELL, THE(1968), p

Jorgen Beck
WEEKEND(1964, Den.); CRAZY PARADISE(1965, Den.)

Julian Beck
1984
COTTON CLUB, THE(1984)

Kimberly Beck
YOURS, MINE AND OURS(1968); MASSACRE AT CENTRAL HIGH(1976); ROLLER BOOGIE(1979)
1984
FRIDAY THE 13TH–THE FINAL CHAPTER(1984)

Lillian Beck
Silents
NUMBER 17(1920)

Lottie Beck
TAKE ME TO PARIS(1951, Brit.)

Mabel Beck
Silents
ADVENTUROUS SEX, THE(1925)

Marcus Beck
ADVENTURERS, THE(1970)

Marilyn Beck
MAN WITH BOGART'S FACE, THE(1980)

Martin Beck
CHALLENGE(1974), d; COAST TO COAST(1980)
Misc. Talkies
BRASS RING, THE(1975), d; LAST GAME, THE(1983), d; MANHUNTER(1983), d

Misc. Silents
ANY NIGHT(1922), d

Marvin Beck
VERDICT, THE(1982)

Maureen Beck
GOLDEN RABBIT, THE(1962, Brit.)

Michael Beck
WARRIORS, THE(1979); XANADU(1980); BATTLETRUCK(1982); MEGAFORCE(1982); GOLDEN SEAL, THE(1983); TRIUMPHS OF A MAN CALLED HORSE(1983, US/Mex.)

Nanci Beck
DIRT GANG, THE(1972)

Pierre-Michel Beck
GAME OF LOVE, THE(1954, Fr.)

Reggie Beck
OVER THE ODDS(1961, Brit.), ed; ASSASSINATION OF TROTSKY, THE(1972 Fr./Ital.), ed; SOMETHING TO HIDE(1972, Brit.), ed; DOLL'S HOUSE, A(1973, Brit.), ed

Reginald Beck
THIS MAN IS NEWS(1939, Brit.), ed; STARS LOOK DOWN, THE(1940, Brit.), ed; QUIET WEDDING(1941, Brit.), ed; VOICE IN THE NIGHT, A(1941, Brit.), ed; HENRY V(1946, Brit.), d; ANGEL WITH THE TRUMPET, THE(1950, Brit.), ed; LONG DARK HALL, THE(1951, Brit.), d; WONDER BOY(1951, Brit./Aust.), ed; BEGGAR'S OPERA, THE(1953), ed; BIG FRAME, THE(1953, Brit.), ed; TWICE UPON A TIME(1953, Brit.), ed; TROUBLE IN THE GLEN(1954, Brit.), ed; KING'S RHAPSODY(1955, Brit.), ed; LET'S MAKE UP(1955, Brit.), ed; ISLAND IN THE SUN(1957), ed; GYPSY AND THE GENTLEMAN, THE(1958, Brit.), ed; HARRY BLACK AND THE TIGER(1958, Brit.), ed; DESERT MICE(1960, Brit.), ed; TRUNK, THE(1961, Brit.), ed; EVA(1962, Fr./Ital.), ed; IMMORAL CHARGE(1962, Brit.), ed; LEATHER BOYS, THE(1965, Brit.), ed; MODESTY BLAISE(1966, Brit.), ed; ACCIDENT(1967, Brit.), ed; ROBBERY(1967, Brit.), ed; BOOM!(1968), ed; SECRET CEREMONY(1968, Brit.), ed; FIGURES IN A LANDSCAPE(1970, Brit.), ed; GO-BETWEEN, THE(1971, Brit.), ed; GALILEO(1975, Brit.), ed; ROMANTIC ENGLISHWOMAN, THE(1975, Brit./Fr.), ed; DON GIOVANNI(1979, Fr./Ital./Ger.), ed

Rob Beck
BIG SLEEP, THE½(1978, Brit.), cos

Robert Beck
CHARRO(1969), spec eff; IS THIS TRIP REALLY NECESSARY?(1970), spec eff

Ron Beck
CONCRETE JUNGLE, THE(1962, Brit.), cos; HELLFIRE CLUB, THE(1963, Brit.), cos; LAWMAN(1971), cos; LAST REMAKE OF BEAU GESTE, THE(1977), cos; STAR WARS(1977), cos

Stanley Beck
WHO KILLED TEDDY BEAR?(1965); JOHN AND MARY(1969); LENNY(1974); STRAIGHT TIME(1978), p; DEATH VALLEY(1982), p

Sylvie Beck
24-HOUR LOVER(1970, Ger.)

Thomas Beck
UNDER TWO FLAGS(1936); CHARLIE CHAN IN EGYPT(1935); CHARLIE CHAN IN PARIS(1935); LIFE BEGINS AT 40(1935); MUSIC IS MAGIC(1935); CAN THIS BE DIXIE?(1936); CHAMPAGNE CHARLIE(1936); CHARLIE CHAN AT THE OPERA(1936); CHARLIE CHAN AT THE RACE TRACK(1936); EVERY SATURDAY NIGHT(1936); MY MARRIAGE(1936); WHITE FANG(1936); CRACK-UP, THE(1937); GREAT HOSPITAL MYSTERY, THE(1937); HEIDI(1937); SEVENTH HEAVEN(1937); THANK YOU, MR. MOTO(1937); THINK FAST, MR. MOTO(1937); THIRTEENTH CHAIR, THE(1937); WOMAN-WISE(1937); 45 FATHERS(1937); I STAND ACCUSED(1938); ROAD DEMON(1938); WALKING DOWN BROADWAY(1938); THEY ASKED FOR IT(1939)

Tom Beck
FAMILY NEXT DOOR, THE(1939)

Vincent Beck
SANTA CLAUS CONQUERS THE MARTIANS(1964); SPY IN THE GREEN HAT, THE(1966); BAMBOO SAUCER, THE(1968); DON'T JUST STAND THERE(1968); PINK JUNGLE, THE(1968); ...AND JUSTICE FOR ALL(1979); FIREPOWER(1979, Brit.); VIGILANTE(1983)

Virgil Beck
POINT BLANK(1967), spec eff; SPLIT, THE(1968), spec eff; MARLOWE(1969), spec eff

Zoe Beck [Zoe Rae]
Silents
NAKED HEARTS(1916)

Rick Beck-Myer
WILD ANGELS, THE(1966), prod d

Eva Becke
SAY IT WITH DIAMONDS(1935, Brit.)

Eve Becke
HOME, SWEET HOME(1933, Brit.); DEATH AT A BROADCAST(1934, Brit.); ON THE AIR(1934, Brit.); RADIO FOLLIES(1935, Brit.)

Graham Beckel
HAPPY AS THE GRASS WAS GREEN(1973); PAPER CHASE, THE(1973); MONEY, THE(1975); HAZEL'S PEOPLE(1978)
1984
C.H.U.D.(1984)

Albrecht Becker
CAPTAIN FROM KOEPENICK, THE(1956, Ger.), set d; GLASS OF WATER, A(1962, Cgr.), art d

Antoine Becker
CARWASH(1976)

Antonie Becker
TIME AFTER TIME(1979, Brit.)
1984
STREETS OF FIRE(1984)

Arnold Becker
GO, MAN, GO!(1954), w

Auge Becker
Silents
PECK'S BAD GIRL(1918)

Ben Becker
1984
LOVE IN GERMANY, A(1984, Fr./Ger.)
Bruce Becker
THREE(1969, Brit.), p
Charles Becker
TERROR OF TINY TOWN, THE(1938)
Claus Becker
AFFAIR BLUM, THE(1949, Ger.)
David Becker
PANDEMONIUM(1982)
Etienne Becker
CHAPPAQUA(1967), ph; THREE(1969, Brit.), ph; MAN WITH THE TRANSPLANTED BRAIN, THE(1972, Fr./Ital./Ger.), ph; DON'T TOUCH WHITE WOMEN!(1974, Fr.), ph; POLICE PYTHON 357(1976, Fr.), ph; CASE AGAINST FERRO, THE(1980, Fr.), ph
1984
ONE DEADLY SUMMER(1984, Fr.), ph
Frawley Becker
UP FROM THE BEACH(1965)
Fred Becker
Silents
BLOOD AND SAND(1922); BLACK PIRATE, THE(1926); KING OF KINGS, THE(1927)
Fred G. Becker
Misc. Silents
GIRL FROM ROCKY POINT, THE(1922), d
George Becker
VAGABOND LADY(1935)
George E. Becker
YOUNG GIRLS OF ROCHEFORT, THE(1968, Fr.)
Gerhard Becker
JOURNEY TO THE LOST CITY(1960, Ger./Fr./Ital.), m; THOUSAND EYES OF DR. MABUSE, THE(1960, Fr./Ital./Ger.), m; ORDERED TO LOVE(1963, Ger.), m
Gunther Becker
NOT RECONCILED, OR "ONLY VIOLENCE HELPS WHERE IT RULES"(1969, Ger.)
Harold Becker
RAGMAN'S DAUGHTER, THE(1974, Brit.), p, d; ONION FIELD, THE(1979), d; BLACK MARBLE, THE(1980), d; TAPS(1981), d
Hazel Lee Becker
LAWTON STORY, THE(1949); PRINCE OF PEACE, THE(1951)
Horst Becker
CELESTE(1982, Ger.), ph
Israel Becker
LONG IS THE ROAD(1948, Ger.), a, w; TWO KOUNEY LEMELS(1966, Israel), d, w; FLYING MATCHMAKER, THE(1970, Israel), d, w
Jacques Becker
GRAND ILLUSION(1938, Fr.); IT HAPPENED AT THE INN(1945, Fr.), d; ANTOINE ET ANTOINETTE(1947 Fr.), d, w; EDWARD AND CAROLINE(1952, Fr.), d, w; ALI BABA(1954, Fr.), d, w; ADVENTURES OF ARSENE LUPIN(1956, Fr./Ital.), d, w; CASQUE D'OR(1956, Fr.), d, w; MODIGLIANI OF MONTPARNASSE(1961, Fr./Ital.), d, w; NIGHT WATCH, THE(1964, Fr./Ital.), d, w; BOUDU SAVED FROM DROWNING(1967, Fr.)
Jean Becker
BACKFIRE(1965, Fr.), d, w; TENDER SCOUNDREL(1967, Fr./Ital.), d, w
1984
ONE DEADLY SUMMER(1984, Fr.), d, w
Joe Becker
ESCAPE FROM RED ROCK(1958)
Joerg Becker
SPECIAL DELIVERY(1955, Ger.)
John Becker
JULIUS CAESAR(1952), m
John Richard Becker
Silents
NO BABIES WANTED(1928)
Jonathan Becker
WILD PARTY, THE(1975)
Joseph Becker
SPACE MASTER X-7(1958)
Joshua M. Becker
EVIL DEAD, THE(1983), ph
Jurek Becker
DAVID(1979, Ger.), w
Ken Becker
RAINMAKER, THE(1956); LOVING YOU(1957); ATOMIC SUBMARINE, THE(1960)
Kenneth Becker
TRUE GRIT(1969)
Kenneth M. Becker
ROUSTABOUT(1964)
Klaus Becker
ONE, TWO, THREE(1961)
Konrad Becker
DAS BOOT(1982)
Maria Becker
VOR SONNENUNTERGANG(1961, Ger)
Marie Becker
MY NIGHT AT MAUD'S(1970, Fr.)
Marie de Becker
RANDOM HARVEST(1942)
Martin Becker
MAN WHO WASN'T THERE, THE(1983), spec eff
1984
FRIDAY THE 13TH-THE FINAL CHAPTER(1984), spec eff
Neville Becker
CALL ME GENIUS(1961, Brit.); MALAGA(1962, Brit.); MODEL MURDER CASE, THE(1964, Brit.)

Pat Becker
GUIDE FOR THE MARRIED MAN, A(1967); IN LIKE FLINT(1967); VALLEY OF THE DOLLS(1967)
Pauline Becker
Silents
ARIZONA CATCLAW, THE(1919)
Rolf Becker
I LOVE YOU, I KILL YOU(1972, Ger.); LOST HONOR OF KATHARINA BLUM, THE(1975, Ger.)
1984
LITTLE DRUMMER GIRL, THE(1984)
Stephen Becker
COVENANT WITH DEATH, A(1966), w
Susan Becker
BLACK MARBLE, THE(1980), cos; KING OF THE MOUNTAIN(1981), cos
Tania Becker
LES GAULOISES BLEUES(1969, Fr.)
Terry Becker
TEACHER'S PET(1958); COMPULSION(1959); CODE OF SILENCE(1960); THIRSTY DEAD, THE(1975), d
Theodor Becker
Misc. Silents
MIDSUMMER NIGHT'S DREAM, A(1928, Ger.)
Tom Becker
DEER HUNTER, THE(1978)
Tony Becker
OTHER SIDE OF THE MOUNTAIN, THE(1975)
Misc. Talkies
CODY(1977)
Vernon Becker
NOCTURNA(1979), p
Vernon P. Becker
Misc. Talkies
GROOVE ROOM, THE(1974, Brit.), d
Walter Becker
YOU'VE GOT TO WALK IT LIKE YOU TALK IT OR YOU'LL LOSE THAT BEAT(1971), m
Wendy Becker
PORKY'S II: THE NEXT DAY(1983)
Barry Beckerman
SHAMUS(1973), w; ST. IVES(1976), w
1984
RED DAWN(1984), p
Henry Beckerman
BROOD, THE(1979, Can.)
Sidney Beckerman
LAST SUMMER(1969), p; MARLOWE(1969), p; KELLY'S HEROES(1970, U.S./Yugo.), p; JOE KIDD(1972), p; PORTNOY'S COMPLAINT(1972), p; MARATHON MAN(1976), p; RIVER NIGER, THE(1976), p; BLOODLINE(1979), p; SERIAL(1980), p; STRANGER IS WATCHING, A(1982), p
Teri Beckerman
XANADU(1980)
Betty Beckers
THINGS OF LIFE, THE(1970, Fr./Ital./Switz.)
Paul Beckers
PILLARS OF SOCIETY(1936, Ger.)
Albert Becket
COME FLY WITH ME(1963), prod d
George Becket
1984
NADIA(1984, U.S./Yugo.), prod d
Pat Becket
OPTIMISTS, THE(1973, Brit.)
Adam Beckett
STAR WARS(1977), anim
Elaine Beckett
EASY COME, EASY GO(1967); PANIC IN THE CITY(1968)
Hugh Beckett
PRIME MINISTER, THE(1941, Brit.)
Jack Beckett
LEGACY OF BLOOD(1973), ph; PSYCHOPATH, THE(1973), ph; HOW COME NOBODY'S ON OUR SIDE?(1975), ph
James Beckett
ROTTEN TO THE CORE(1956, Brit.); POOR COW(1968, Brit.)
John P. Beckett
LOOSE SHOES(1980), ph
Kay Beckett
TAKING OFF(1971)
Majorie Beckett
STORK BITES MAN(1947)
Michael Beckett
PRINCE OF THE CITY(1981)
Nuel Beckett
TAKE HER BY SURPRISE(1967, Can.)
Ruth Beckett
STAND UP AND CHEER(1934 80m FOX bw)
ESCAPE, THE(1939)
Scotty Beckett
STAND UP AND CHEER(1934 80m FOX bw); WHOM THE GODS DESTROY(1934); DANTE'S INFERNO(1935); I DREAM TOO MUCH(1935); PURSUIT(1935); ANTHONY ADVERSE(1936); CASE AGAINST MRS. AMES, THE(1936); CHARGE OF THE LIGHT BRIGADE, THE(1936); OLD HUTCH(1936); CONQUEST(1937); LIFE BEGINS WITH LOVE(1937); WHEN YOU'RE IN LOVE(1937); DEVIL'S PARTY, THE(1938); LISTEN, DARLING(1938); MARIE ANTOINETTE(1938); BLIND ALLEY(1939); DAYS OF JESSE JAMES(1939); FLYING IRISHMAN, THE(1939); LOVE AFFAIR(1939); MICKEY, THE KID(1939); OUR NEIGHBORS-THE CARTERS(1939); GOLD RUSH MAISIE(1940); MY FAVORITE WIFE(1940); MY SON, MY SON!(1940); STREET OF MEMORIES(1940); ALOMA OF THE SOUTH SEAS(1941); FATHER'S SON(1941); VANISHING VIRGINIAN, THE(1941); BETWEEN US GIRLS(1942); IT HAPPENED

IN FLATBUSH(1942); KING'S ROW(1942); GOOD LUCK, MR. YATES(1943); HEAVEN CAN WAIT(1943); YOUNGEST PROFESSION, THE(1943); ALI BABA AND THE FORTY THIEVES(1944); CLIMAX, THE(1944); CIRCUMSTANTIAL EVIDENCE(1945); JUNIOR MISS(1945); HER ADVENTUROUS NIGHT(1946); JOLSON STORY, THE(1946); MY REPUTATION(1946); WHITE TIE AND TAILS(1946); CYNTHIA(1947); DANGEROUS YEARS(1947); DATE WITH JUDY, A(1948); MICHAEL O'HAL-LORAN(1948); BATTLEGROUND(1949); HAPPY YEARS, THE(1950); LOUISA(1950); NANCY GOES TO RIO(1950); CORKY OF GASOLINE ALLEY(1951); GASOLINE ALLEY(1951); HOT NEWS(1953); THREE FOR JAMIE DAWN(1956); OKLAHOMAN, THE(1957)
Misc. Talkies
BOY FROM STALINGRAD, THE(1943)
Bill Beckford
RIDERS OF THE DEADLINE(1943)
Theophilus Beckford
ROCKERS(1980)
Rodric Beckham
STALAG 17(1953)
Arthur Beckhard
CURLY TOP(1935), w; SKY PARADE(1936), w
Arthur J. Beckhard
WEST POINT OF THE AIR(1935), w; BORDER FLIGHT(1936), w; POP ALWAYS PAYS(1940), w; GIRL ON THE RUN(1961), d, w
Israel Beckhardt
VIOLATORS, THE(1957), w
F.C. Beckhaus
FAUST(1963, Ger.)
Friedrich G. Beckhaus
1984
LOVE IN GERMANY, A(1984, Fr./Ger.)
Richard Beckinsale
LOVERS, THE(1972, Brit.); DOING TIME(1979, Brit.)
Gordon Beckles
STRANGLER, THE(1941, Brit.), w
Tony Beckley
CHIMES AT MIDNIGHT(1967, Span.,Switz.); PENTHOUSE, THE(1967, Brit.); LONG DAY'S DYING, THE(1968, Brit.); LOST CONTINENT, THE(1968, Brit.); ITALIAN JOB, THE(1969, Brit.); ASSAULT(1971, Brit.); GET CARTER(1971, Brit.); SITTING TAR-GET(1972, Brit.); DIAGNOSIS: MURDER(1974, Brit.); GOLD(1974, Brit.); REVENGE OF THE PINK PANTHER(1978); WHEN A STRANGER CALLS(1979)
Misc. Talkies
FIEND, THE(1971, Brit.); BEWARE MY BRETHREN(1972, Brit.)
William Beckley
MY FAIR LADY(1964); COLLECTOR, THE(1965); PRESIDENT'S ANALYST, THE(1967); TOO LATE THE HERO(1970)
C.A. Beckman
SHE COULDN'T TAKE IT(1935)
Harry Beckman
WRONG MAN, THE(1956)
Henry Beckman
NIAGARA(1953); THIRTEEN WEST STREET(1962); KISS ME, STUPID(1964); MAR-NIE(1964); GLORY GUYS, THE(1965); MC HALE'S NAVY JOINS THE AIR FOR-CE(1965); SATAN BUG, THE(1965); CAPER OF THE GOLDEN BULLS, THE(1967); MADIGAN(1968); STALKING MOON, THE(1969); SWEET CHARITY(1969); UN-DEFEATED, THE(1969); MERRY WIVES OF TOBIAS ROUKE, THE(1972, Can.); GET BACK(1973, Can.); WHY ROCK THE BOAT?(1974, Can.); SILVER STREAK(1976); BLOOD AND GUTS(1978, Can.); DEATH HUNT(1981)
Herb Beckman
FUNNYMAN(1967)
John Beckman
MONSIEUR VERDOUX(1947), art d; IRON MISTRESS, THE(1952), art d; SPRING-FIELD RIFLE(1952), art d; SO BIG(1953), art d; SYSTEM, THE(1953), art d; LUCKY ME(1954), art; MC CONNELL STORY, THE(1955), art d; YOUNG AT HEART(1955), art d; HELL ON FRISCO BAY(1956), art d; TOWARD THE UNKNOWN(1956), art d; LAFAYETTE ESCADRILLE(1958), art d; TOO MUCH, TOO SOON(1958), art d; FBI STORY, THE(1959), art d; HELEN MORGAN STORY, THE(1959), art d; GUNS OF THE TIMBERLAND(1960), art d; WAKE ME WHEN IT'S OVER(1960), art d; DEVIL AT FOUR O'CLOCK, THE(1961), art d; MAJORITY OF ONE, A(1961), art d; GYP-SY(1962), art d; MARY, MARY(1963), art d; TROUBLE WITH ANGELS, THE(1966), art d; WHO'S MINDING THE MINT?(1967), art d; ASSIGNMENT TO KILL(1968), art d; IN ENEMY COUNTRY(1968), art d; HOOK, LINE AND SINKER(1969), art d; WHICH WAY TO THE FRONT?(1970), art d
Lannie Beckman
Misc. Talkies
CARESSED(1965)
Lanny Beckman
SWEET SUBSTITUTE(1964, Can.); HIGH(1968, Can.)
Margit Beckman
PIMPERNEL SVENSSON(1953, Swed.), w
Ron Beckman
CHALLENGE, THE(1982), p. Robert L. Rosen
Rick Beckmeyer
HOW COME NOBODY'S ON OUR SIDE?(1975), ed
Fred Beckner
GUY NAMED JOE, A(1943); THEY WERE EXPENDABLE(1945)
Fred Beckner, Jr.
GIRL CRAZY(1943)
Fred G. Beckner
TWO GIRLS AND A SAILOR(1944)
Rick Beckner
UP IN SMOKE(1978); SSSSSSSS(1973); MODERN ROMANCE(1981)
Joan Beckstead
PAN-AMERICANA(1945)
Eric Beckstrom
TEX(1982)
Mark Beckstrom
STRANGERS WHEN WE MEET(1960)

William Beckway
SECRETS OF CHINATOWN(1935), ph; SECRET PATROL(1936), ph; STAM-PEDE(1936), ph; WHAT PRICE VENGEANCE?(1937), ph; WOMAN AGAINST THE WORLD(1938), ph
William J. Beckway
FIGHTING PLAYBOY(1937), ph
Alan Beckwith
CHINA SYNDROME, THE(1979)
Mildred Beckwith
Silents
CRIMSON DOVE, THE(1917)
Reginald Beckwith
VOICE IN THE NIGHT, A(1941, Brit.); THIS MAN IS MINE(1946 Brit.), w; BOYS IN BROWN(1949, Brit.), w; MY BROTHER'S KEEPER(1949, Brit.); SCOTT OF THE ANTARCTIC(1949, Brit.); BODY SAID NO!, THE(1950, Brit.); MISS PILGRIM'S PROGRESS(1950, Brit.); CIRCLE OF DANGER(1951, Brit.); MR. DRAKE'S DUCK(1951, Brit.); ANOTHER MAN'S POISON(1952, Brit.); BRANDY FOR THE PARSON(1952, Brit.); WHISPERING SMITH VERSUS SCOTLAND YARD(1952, Brit.); YOU'RE ONLY YOUNG TWICE(1952, Brit.), a, w; GENEVIEVE(1953, Brit.); PENNY PRINCESS(1953, Brit.); TITFIELD THUNDERBOLT, THE(1953, Brit.); AUNT CLARA(1954, Brit.); DANCE LITTLE LADY(1954, Brit.); DON'T BLAME THE STORK(1954, Brit.); FAST AND LOOSE(1954, Brit.); LEASE OF LIFE(1954, Brit.); MAN WITH A MILLION(1954, Brit.); RUNAWAY BUS, THE(1954, Brit.); INNOCENTS IN PARIS(1955, Brit.); LYONS IN PARIS, THE(1955, Brit.); THEY CAN'T HANG ME(1955, Brit.); YANK IN ERMINE, A(1955, Brit.); CHARLEY MOON(1956, Brit.); IT'S A WONDERFUL WORLD(1956, Brit.); JUMPING FOR JOY(1956, Brit.); MARCH HARE, THE(1956, Brit.); TOUCH OF THE SUN, A(1956, Brit.); BREAK IN THE CIRCLE, THE(1957, Brit.); CARRY ON ADMIRAL(1957, Brit.); LIGHT FINGERS(1957, Brit.); LUCKY JIM(1957, Brit.); MEN OF SHERWOOD FOREST(1957, Brit.); CURSE OF THE DEMON(1958); DANGEROUS YOUTH(1958, Brit.); HORSE'S MOUTH, THE(1958, Brit.); LAW AND DISORDER(1958, Brit.); MAD LITTLE ISLAND(1958, Brit.); UP THE CREEK(1958, Brit.); EXPRESSO BONGO(1959, Brit.); NAVY LARK, THE(1959, Brit.); UGLY DUCKLING, THE(1959, Brit.); BOTTOMS UP(1960, Brit.); CAPTAIN'S TABLE, THE(1960, Brit.); DENTIST IN THE CHAIR(1960, Brit.); DESERT MICE(1960, Brit.); DOCTOR IN LOVE(1960, Brit.); NEXT TO NO TIME(1960, Brit.); THIRTY NINE STEPS, THE(1960, Brit.); DAY THE EARTH CAUGHT FIRE, THE(1961, Brit.); DOUBLE BUNK(1961, Brit.); FIVE GOLD-EN HOURS(1961, Brit.); NIGHT WE GOT THE BIRD, THE(1961, Brit.); UPSTAIRS AND DOWNSTAIRS(1961, Brit.); BURN WITCH BURN(1962); GIRL ON THE BOAT, THE(1962, Brit.); HAIR OF THE DOG(1962, Brit.); PASSWORD IS COURAGE, THE(1962, Brit.); THERE WAS A CROOKED MAN(1962, Brit.); DOCTOR IN DIS-TRESS(1963, Brit.); FRIENDS AND NEIGHBORS(1963, Brit.); GET ON WITH IT(1963, Brit.); JUST FOR FUN(1963, Brit.); SWORD OF LANCELOT(1963, Brit.); V.I.P.s, THE(1963, Brit.); NEVER PUT IT IN WRITING(1964); SHOT IN THE DARK, A(1964); AMOROUS ADVENTURES OF MOLL FLANDERS, THE(1965); BIG JOB, THE(1965, Brit.); GONKS GO BEAT(1965, Brit.); MISTER MOSES(1965); SECRET OF MY SUCCESS, THE(1965, Brit.); THUNDERBALL(1965, Brit.); WHERE THE SPIES ARE(1965, Brit.); YELLOW ROLLS-ROYCE, THE(1965, Brit.)
Walter Beckwith
Misc. Silents
IT MIGHT HAPPEN TO YOU(1920)
Lloyd Beckworth
ETERNAL SUMMER(1961), ph
John Becleman
DECISION OF CHRISTOPHER BLAKE, THE(1948), art d
Alain Becourt
MY UNCLE(1958, Fr.)
Olivier Becquaert
WOMAN NEXT DOOR, THE(1981, Fr.)
Trmand Becque
GOHA(1958, Tunisia), ed
George Becwar
IT SHOULD HAPPEN TO YOU(1954); BRIDE OF THE MONSTER(1955); SLAUGH-TER ON TENTH AVENUE(1957); WAR OF THE COLOSSAL BEAST(1958)
Beda
STUDENT'S ROMANCE, THE(1936, Brit.), w
Art Bedard
COUNTERPLOT(1959); HARBOR LIGHTS(1963); THUNDER ISLAND(1963)
David Bedard
HOT MILLIONS(1968, Brit.)
Roland Bedard
BIG RED(1962)
Rolland Bedard
CORDELIA(1980, Fr., Can.)
Virginia Bedard
HELL IS SOLD OUT(1951, Brit.); BEYOND MOMBASA(1957); V.I.P.s, THE(1963, Brit.)
Eugene Beday
FOLIES DERGERE(1935); EBB TIDE(1937); ESPIONAGE(1937); ARTISTS AND MODELS ABROAD(1938); ROYAL SCANDAL, A(1945)
Rod Beddall
PINK FLOYD–THE WALL(1982, Brit.)
Perry Bedden
SHOCK TREATMENT(1981)
Carol Beddington
1984
LASSITER(1984)
Don Beddoe
THEY WON'T BELIEVE ME(1947); THERE'S THAT WOMAN AGAIN(1938); AMAZ-ING MR. WILLIAMS(1939); BEWARE SPOOKS(1939); BLONDIE MEETS THE BOSS(1939); GOLDEN BOY(1939); GOOD GIRLS GO TO PARIS(1939); KONGA, THE WILD STALLION(1939); LONE WOLF SPY HUNT, THE(1939); MAN THEY COULD NOT HANG, THE(1939); MISSING DAUGHTERS(1939); OUTSIDE THESE WALLS(1939); ROMANCE OF THE REDWOODS(1939); TAMING OF THE WEST, THE(1939); THOSE HIGH GREY WALLS(1939); BEFORE I HANG(1940); BLONDIE ON A BUDGET(1940); CHARLIE CHAN'S MURDER CRUISE(1940); DOCTOR TAKES A WIFE(1940); ESCAPE TO GLORY(1940); GIRLS OF THE ROAD(1940); GLAMOUR FOR SALE(1940); ISLAND OF DOOMED MEN(1940); LONE WOLF KEEPS A DATE, THE(1940); LONE WOLF STRIKES, THE(1940); MAN FROM TUMBLEWEEDS, THE(1940); MANHATTAN HEARTBEAT(1940); MEN WITHOUT SOULS(1940); MILI-TARY ACADEMY(1940); MY SON IS GUILTY(1940); SCANDAL SHEET(1940); SE-

CRET SEVEN, THE(1940); TEXAS STAGECOACH(1940); THIS THING CALLED LOVE(1940); BEYOND THE SACRAMENTO(1941); BIG BOSS, THE(1941); BLONDE FROM SINGAPORE, THE(1941); FACE BEHIND THE MASK, THE(1941); HONOLULU LU(1941); LONE WOLF TAKES A CHANCE, THE(1941); PHANTOM SUBMARINE, THE(1941); SHE KNEW ALL THE ANSWERS(1941); SING FOR YOUR SUPPER(1941); SWEETHEART OF THE CAMPUS(1941); TEXAS(1941); TWO LATINS FROM MANHATTAN(1941); UNDER AGE(1941); UNHOLY PARTNERS(1941); BOOGIE MAN WILL GET YOU, THE(1942); HARVARD, HERE I COME(1942); LUCKY LEGS(1942); MEET THE STEWARTS(1942); SABOTAGE SQUAD(1942); SHUT MY BIG MOUTH(1942); TALK OF THE TOWN, THE(1942); JUNIOR ARMY(1943); POWER OF THE PRESS(1943); WINGED VICTORY(1944); CRIME, INC.(1945); ONE EXCITING NIGHT(1945); BEHIND GREEN LIGHTS(1946); BEST YEARS OF OUR LIVES, THE(1946); NOTORIOUS LONE WOLF, THE(1946); O.S.S.(1946); BACHELOR AND THE BOBBY-SOXER, THE(1947); BUCK PRIVATES COME HOME(1947); CALCUTTA(1947); FARMER'S DAUGHTER, THE(1947); WELCOME STRANGER(1947); ACT OF MURDER, AN(1948); ANOTHER PART OF THE FOREST(1948); BLACK BART(1948); IF YOU KNEW SUSIE(1948); CRIME DOCTOR'S DIARY, THE(1949); DANCING IN THE DARK(1949); DEAR WIFE(1949); EASY LIVING(1949); FLAME OF YOUTH(1949); GUN CRAZY(1949); HIDEOUT(1949); LADY GAMBLES, THE(1949); ONCE MORE, MY DARLING(1949); WOMAN IN HIDING(1949); BEYOND THE PURPLE HILLS(1950); CAGED(1950); COMPANY SHE KEEPS, THE(1950); CYRANO DE BERGERAC(1950); EMERGENCY WEDDING(1950); TARNISHED(1950); YOUNG DANIEL BOONE(1950); CORKY OF GASOLINE ALLEY(1951); ENFORCER, THE(1951); FRANCIS GOES TO THE RACES(1951); GASOLINE ALLEY(1951); MAN IN THE SADDLE(1951); MILLION DOLLAR PURSUIT(1951); RACKET, THE(1951); RODEO KING AND THE SENORITA(1951); STARLIFT(1951); UNKNOWN MAN, THE(1951); BIG SKY, THE(1952); BLUE CANADIAN ROCKIES(1952); CARRIE(1952); CARSON CITY(1952); DON'T BOTHER TO KNOCK(1952); HOODLUM EMPIRE(1952); NARROW MARGIN, THE(1952); ROOM FOR ONE MORE(1952); SCANDAL SHEET(1952); STOP, YOU'RE KILLING ME(1952); WASHINGTON STORY(1952); BLADES OF THE MUSKETEERS(1953); CLOWN, THE(1953); COW COUNTRY(1953); SYSTEM, THE(1953); JUBILEE TRAIL(1954); LOOPHOLE(1954); RIVER OF NO RETURN(1954); STEEL CAGE, THE(1954); NIGHT OF THE HUNTER, THE(1955); TARZAN'S HIDDEN JUNGLE(1955); WYOMING RENEGADES(1955); BEHIND THE HIGH WALL(1956); RAWHIDE YEARS, THE(1956); JOKER IS WILD, THE(1957); SHOOT-OUT AT MEDICINE BEND(1957); BULLWHIP(1958); TOUGHEST GUN IN TOMBSTONE(1958); PILLOW TALK(1959); WARLOCK(1959); WIZARD OF BAGHDAD, THE(1960); BOY WHO CAUGHT A CROOK(1961); JACK THE GIANT KILLER(1962); SAINTLY SINNERS(1962); FOR LOVE OR MONEY(1963); PAPA'S DELICATE CONDITION(1963); VERY SPECIAL FAVOR, A(1965); TEXAS ACROSS THE RIVER(1966); IMPOSSIBLE YEARS, THE(1968); GENERATION(1969); HOW DO I LOVE THEE?(1970)

Donald Beddoe
WELL-GROOMED BRIDE, THE(1946); IRON MISTRESS, THE(1952)

Donald T. Beddoe
GETTING GERTIE'S GARTER(1945); GREAT RUPERT, THE(1950)

Ivor Beddoes
ATTILA(1958, Ital.), spec eff; PEEPING TOM(1960, Brit.), set d; CASINO ROYALE(1967, Brit.), art d

Margaret Beddon
COLLEGE HOLIDAY(1936)

Maurice Bedel
ALONG CAME YOUTH(1931), w

Bonnie Bedelia
GYPSY MOTHS, THE(1969); THEY SHOOT HORSES, DON'T THEY?(1969); LOVERS AND OTHER STRANGERS(1970); STRANGE VENEGEANCE OF ROSALIE, THE(1972); GET BACK(1973, Can.); BIG FIX, THE(1978); HEART LIKE A WHEEL(1983)

Austin Bedell
WOMAN IN THE WINDOW, THE(1945)

Charles Bedell
ARE YOU WITH IT?(1948)

Chick Bedell
CUBAN PETE(1946)

David Bedell
BIGGER THAN LIFE(1956); WAKE ME WHEN IT'S OVER(1960); FATE IS THE HUNTER(1964)

Lew Bedell
SLAUGHTER TRAIL(1951)

Patsy Bedell
JOAN OF OZARK(1942)

Rodney Bedell
GRUESOME TWOSOME(1968); JUST FOR THE HELL OF IT(1968); SHE-DEVILS ON WHEELS(1968)
Misc. Talkies
JUST FOR THE HELL OF IT(1968)

Dennis Beden
PAPER MOON(1973)

Max Beden
Misc. Talkies
GREATER ADVISOR, THE(1940)

Henry Bederski
GLEN OR GLENDA(1953)

Michel Bedetti
PIAF-THE EARLY YEARS(1982, U.S./Fr.)

Aaron Bedford
Misc. Talkies
FRIDAY ON MY MIND(1970); FIRST TIME ROUND(1972)

Barbara Bedford
CAVALIER, THE(1928); HAUNTED HOUSE, THE(1928); LASH, THE(1930); LOVE TRADER(1930); SUNNY(1930); TOL'ABLE DAVID(1930); DESERT VENGEANCE(1931); LADY FROM NOWHERE(1931); DEATH KISS, THE(1933); FOUND ALIVE(1934); GIRL OF THE LIMBERLOST(1934); FORCED LANDING(1935); KEEPER OF THE BEES(1935); ON PROBATION(1935); SONS OF STEEL(1935); SPANISH CAPE MYSTERY(1935); TOMORROW'S YOUTH(1935); WORLD ACCUSES, THE(1935); BRILLIANT MARRIAGE(1936); EASY MONEY(1936); HIS BROTHER'S WIFE(1936); MINE WITH THE IRON DOOR, THE(1936); RING AROUND THE MOON(1936); TANGO(1936); CHASER, THE(1938); FAST COMPANY(1938); FIRST 100 YEARS, THE(1938); RICH MAN, POOR GIRL(1938); THREE COMRADES(1938); TOY WIFE,

THE(1938); YOUNG DR. KILDARE(1938); DANCING CO-ED(1939); SERGEANT MADDEN(1939); STRONGER THAN DESIRE(1939); EARL OF CHICAGO, THE(1940); I LOVE YOU AGAIN(1940); THIRD FINGER, LEFT HAND(1940); LOVE CRAZY(1941); WHEN LADIES MEET(1941); WHISTLING IN THE DARK(1941); NAZI AGENT(1942); REUNION IN FRANCE(1942); SHIP AHOY(1942); GIRL CRAZY(1943); MEET THE PEOPLE(1944)
Misc. Talkies
MIDNIGHT PHANTOM, THE(1935); SENOR JIM(1936)
Silents
LAST OF THE MOHICANS, THE(1920); BIG PUNCH, THE(1921); ALIAS JULIUS CAESAR(1922); ANOTHER MAN'S SHOES(1922); GLEAM O'DAWN(1922); OUT OF THE SILENT NORTH(1922); STEP ON IT!(1922); ACQUITTAL, THE(1923); ROMANCE LAND(1923); SOULS FOR SALE(1923); TIE THAT BINDS, THE(1923); CHAMPION OF LOST CAUSES(1925); TUMBLEWEEDS(1925); WHAT FOOLS MEN(1925); OLD LOVES AND NEW(1926); BACKSTAGE(1927); MOCKERY(1927); NOTORIOUS LADY, THE(1927); MANHATTAN KNIGHTS(1928); MARRY THE GIRL(1928); HEROIC LOVER, THE(1929); SMOKE BELLEW(1929)
Misc. Silents
DEEP WATERS(1920); CINDERELLA OF THE HILLS(1921); FACE OF THE WORLD(1921); ANOTHER MAN'S SHOES(1922); ARABIA(1922); POWER OF LOVE, THE(1922); UNFOLDMENT, THE(1922); WINNING WITH WITS(1922); FORBIDDEN LOVER(1923); SPOILERS, THE(1923); PAGAN PASSIONS(1924); WOMEN WHO GIVE(1924); BEFORE MIDNIGHT(1925); BUSINESS OF LOVE, THE(1925); MAD WHIRL, THE(1925); MANSION OF ACHING HEARTS, THE(1925); DEVIL'S DICE(1926); SPORTING LOVER, THE(1926); SUNSHINE OF PARADISE ALLEY(1926); GIRL FROM GAY PAREE, THE(1927); LIFE OF AN ACTRESS(1927); MAN'S PAST, A(1927); BITTER SWEETS(1928); BROKEN MASK, THE(1928); CAVALIER, THE(1928); CITY OF PURPLE DREAMS(1928); DANGER TRAIL(1928); PORT OF MISSING GIRLS, THE(1928); BROTHERS(1929)

Brian Bedford
PAD, THE(AND HOW TO USE IT)* (1966, Brit.); MIRACLE IN SOHO(1957, Brit.); ANGRY SILENCE, THE(1960, Brit.); NUMBER SIX(1962, Brit.); PUNCH AND JUDY MAN, THE(1963, Brit.); GRAND PRIX(1966); ROBIN HOOD(1973)

Harry Bedford
THOSE WERE THE DAYS(1934, Brit.)

Hazel Bedford
Misc. Silents
DESERTER, THE(1916)

Paddy Bedford
CHIMES AT MIDNIGHT(1967, Span.,Switz.)

Patrick Bedford
UP THE DOWN STAIRCASE(1967); NEXT MAN, THE(1976)

Richard Bedford
SHOCK TREATMENT(1981), ed

Terry Bedford
MONTY PYTHON AND THE HOLY GRAIL(1975, Brit.), ph; JABBERWOCKY(1977, Brit.), ph
1984
SLAYGROUND(1984, Brit.), d

H. Bedford-Jones
GARDEN OF THE MOON(1938), w

John Bedford-Lloyd
TRADING PLACES(1983)

Kabir Bedi
ASHANTI(1979); SATAN'S MISTRESS(1982); OCTOPUSSY(1983, Brit.)
Misc. Talkies
DARK EYES(1980)

Mohinder Bedi
KING OF THE KHYBER RIFLES(1953)

Barry Bedig
EVEL KNIEVEL(1971), spec eff

Sam Bedig
THUNDERBOLT AND LIGHTFOOT(1974), spec eff

Sass Bedig
FOUR FOR TEXAS(1963), spec eff; LIVELY SET, THE(1964), spec eff; CAST A GIANT SHADOW(1966), spec eff; FORTUNE COOKIE, THE(1966), spec eff; HOUR OF THE GUN(1967), spec eff; GREEN BERETS, THE(1968), spec eff; GAILY, GAILY(1969), spec eff; HAWAIIANS, THE(1970), spec eff; FRENCH CONNECTION, THE(1971), spec eff; LE MANS(1971), spec eff; ORGANIZATION, THE(1971), spec eff; GODFATHER, THE(1972), spec eff; WALKING TALL(1973), spec eff; ROLLERBALL(1975), spec eff

Louis Bednarcik
THIS IS THE ARMY(1943)

Stefan Bednarcyzk
PRIVILEGED(1982, Brit.)

Odette Bedogni
DIFFICULT YEARS(1950, Ital.)

Guy Bedos
ELUSIVE CORPORAL, THE(1963, Fr.); SWEET AND SOUR(1964, Fr./Ital.), a, w; TASTE FOR WOMEN, A(1966, Fr./Ital.); MAN WITH CONNECTIONS, THE(1970, Fr.)

Leslie Bedos
YOU ONLY LIVE ONCE(1969, Fr.)

Becky Bedoy
MORE AMERICAN GRAFFITI(1979)

Alfonso Bedoya
ANGEL IN EXILE(1948); ANGEL ON THE AMAZON(1948); PEARL, THE(1948, U.S./Mex.); TREASURE OF THE SIERRA MADRE, THE(1948); BORDER INCIDENT(1949); STREETS OF LAREDO(1949); BLACK ROSE, THE(1950); FORTUNES OF CAPTAIN BLOOD(1950); MAN IN THE SADDLE(1951); CALIFORNIA CONQUEST(1952); STRONGHOLD(1952, Mex.); SOMBRERO(1953); STRANGER WORE A GUN, THE(1953); BLACK PIRATES, THE(1954, Mex.); BORDER RIVER(1954); RICOCHET ROMANCE(1954); TEN WANTED MEN(1955); BIG COUNTRY, THE(1958)

Alfredo Bedoya
MALE AND FEMALE SINCE ADAM AND EVE(1961, Arg.), p

Ingrid Bedoya
DEVIL'S MESSENGER, THE(1962 U.S./Swed.)

Anthony Bedrich
LIES MY FATHER TOLD ME(1975, Can.), p

Lilly Bo Beep
Misc. Talkies
BLUE SUMMER(1973)

Erica Beer
THEY WERE SO YOUNG(1955); DAS LETZTE GEHEIMNIS(1959, Ger.); COUNTERFEIT TRAITOR, THE(1962); YOUNG GO WILD, THE(1962, Ger.); DEEP END(1970 Ger./U.S.); KING, QUEEN, KNAVE(1972, Ger./U.S.)

Harry Beer
1984
PHILADELPHIA EXPERIMENT, THE(1984); STREETS OF FIRE(1984)

Jack Beer
NOBODY WAVED GOODBYE(1965, Can.)

Jacqueline Beer
SCREAMING EAGLES(1956); THAT CERTAIN FEELING(1956); SHORT CUT TO HELL(1957); PILLOW TALK(1959); PRIZE, THE(1963); MADE IN PARIS(1966)

Jakob Christoph Beer
Silents
ETERNAL LOVE(1929), w

Robert Beer
AMERICATHON(1979); RIGHT STUFF, THE(1983)

Sydney Beer
LADY SURRENDERS, A(1947, Brit.), a, md

Thomas Beer
Silents
LITTLE EVA ASCENDS(1922), w

Maurice Beerblock
MAN ESCAPED, A(1957, Fr.)

Claude Beerbohm
Silents
HIS HOUSE IN ORDER(1928, Brit.)

Elizabeth Beerbohm
Silents
GLORIOUS ADVENTURE, THE(1922, U.S./Brit.)

Bobby Beers
SOUTH OF SANTA FE(1942); LADY IN THE DARK(1944)

Francine Beers
1984
OVER THE BROOKLYN BRIDGE(1984)

Isabel Beers
SHADES OF SILK(1979, Can.)

John Beers
Misc. Talkies
FORBID THEM NOT(1961)

Bucklind Beery
MACHO CALLAHAN(1970)

Buckline Beery
BREAKFAST IN BED(1978)

Carol Ann Beery
CHINA SEAS(1935); RATIONING(1944)

Harry Beery
WAY OF THE WEST, THE(1934); TIMBER TERRORS(1935)

Lee Beery
HOSPITAL, THE(1971)

Noah Beery
CAREERS(1929); GODLESS GIRL, THE(1929); LOVE IN THE DESERT(1929); FEET FIRST(1930); GLORIFYING THE AMERICAN GIRL(1930); GOLDEN DAWN(1930); ISLE OF ESCAPE(1930); HONEYMOON LANE(1931); IN THE LINE OF DUTY(1931); RIDERS OF THE PURPLE SAGE(1931); BIG STAMPEDE, THE(1932); DRIFTER, THE(1932); KID FROM SPAIN, THE(1932); OUT OF SINGAPORE(1932); EASY MILLIONS(1933); FLAMING SIGNAL(1933); LAUGHING AT LIFE(1933); CARAVAN(1934); DAVID HARUM(1934); HAPPY LANDING(1934); AVENGING HAND, THE(1936, Brit.); CRIMSON CIRCLE, THE(1936, Brit.); FROG, THE(1937, Brit.); BAD MAN OF BRIMSTONE(1938); MEXICALI ROSE(1939); GRANDPA GOES TO TOWN(1940); MISSOURI OUTLAW, A(1942); CIMARRON KID, THE(1951); DECISION AT SUNDOWN(1957); HEAVEN WITH A GUN(1969); BEST LITTLE WHOREHOUSE IN TEXAS, THE(1982)
Silents
CLEVER MRS. CARFAX, THE(1917); MOLLY ENTANGLED(1917); HIS ROBE OF HONOR(1918); JOHNNY GET YOUR GUN(1919); LOUISIANA(1919); DINTY(1920); MARK OF ZORRO(1920); BOB HAMPTON OF PLACER(1921); EBB TIDE(1922); LYING TRUTH, THE(1922); TILLIE(1922); WILD HONEY(1922); YOUTH TO YOUTH(1922); SOUL OF THE BEAST(1923); SPIDER AND THE ROSE, THE(1923); STEPHEN STEPS OUT(1923); STORMSWEPT(1923); TO THE LAST MAN(1923); FIGHTING COWARD, THE(1924); NORTH OF 36(1924); WELCOME STRANGER(1924); COMING OF AMOS, THE(1925); EAST OF SUEZ(1925); LORD JIM(1925); BEAU GESTE(1926); ENCHANTED HILL, THE(1926); PARADISE(1926); EVENING CLOTHES(1927); OLD SHOES(1927); ROUGH RIDERS(1927); BEAU SABREUR(1928); TWO LOVERS(1928); FALSE FATHERS(1929); FOUR FEATHERS(1929); LINDA(1929)
Misc. Silents
SACRIFICE(1917); SOCIAL AMBITION(1918); VICKY VAN(1919); FIGHTING SHEPHERDESS, THE(1920); LOVE MADNESS(1920); MUTINY OF THE ELSINORE, THE(1920); SAGEBRUSHER, THE(1920); SEA WOLF, THE(1920); BITS OF LIFE(1921); CALL OF THE NORTH, THE(1921); LOTUS BLOSSOM(1921); BELLE OF ALASKA(1922); CROSSROADS OF NEW YORK, THE(1922); FLESH AND BLOOD(1922); GOOD MEN AND TRUE(1922); POWER OF LOVE, THE(1922); CALL OF THE CANYON, THE(1923); DANGEROUS TRAILS(1923); DESTROYING ANGEL, THE(1923); FORBIDDEN LOVER(1923); QUICKSANDS(1923); WHEN LAW COMES TO HADES(1923); FEMALE, THE(1924); HERITAGE OF THE DESERT, THE(1924); LILY OF THE DUST(1924); WANDERER OF THE WASTELAND(1924); CONTRABAND(1925); LIGHT OF THE WESTERN STARS, THE(1925); SPANIARD, THE(1925); THUNDERING HERD, THE(1925); VANISHING AMERICAN, THE(1925); WILD HORSE MESA(1925); PADLOCKED(1926); DOVE, THE(1927); LOVE MART, THE(1927); HELLSHIP BRONSON(1928)

Noah Beery, Sr.
NOAH'S ARK(1928); ISLE OF LOST SHIPS(1929); MURDER WILL OUT(1930); OH! SAILOR, BEHAVE!(1930); RENEGADES(1930); SONG OF THE FLAME(1930); TOL'ABLE DAVID(1930); UNDER A TEXAS MOON(1930); WAY OF ALL MEN, THE(1930); BRIGHT LIGHTS(1931); HOMICIDE SQUAD(1931); MILLIONAIRE, THE(1931); SHANGHAIED LOVE(1931); SOLDIER'S PLAYTHING, A(1931); CORNERED(1932);

NO LIVING WITNESS(1932); STOKER, THE(1932); STRANGER IN TOWN(1932); MAN OF THE FOREST(1933); SHE DONE HIM WRONG(1933); TO THE LAST MAN(1933); WOMAN I STOLE, THE(1933); COCKEYED CAVALIERS(1934); MADAME SPY(1934); MYSTERY LINER(1934); THUNDERING HERD, THE(1934); TRAIL BEYOND, THE(1934); KENTUCKY KERNELS(1935); SWEET ADELINE(1935); KING OF THE DAMNED(1936, Brit.); LIVE AGAIN(1936, Brit.); SOMEONE AT THE DOOR(1936, Brit.); STRANGERS ON A HONEYMOON(1937, Brit.); GIRL OF THE GOLDEN WEST, THE(1938); PANAMINT'S BAD MAN(1938); MUTINY ON THE BLACKHAWK(1939); PRISONER OF CORBAL(1939, Brit.); TORPEDOED!(1939); LITTLE BIT OF HEAVEN, A(1940); PIONEERS OF THE WEST(1940); TULSA KID, THE(1940); DEVIL'S TRAIL, THE(1942); OUTLAWS OF PINE RIDGE(1942); PARDON MY GUN(1942); TENNESSEE JOHNSON(1942); CARSON CITY CYCLONE(1943); CLANCY STREET BOYS(1943); MR. MUGGS STEPS OUT(1943); SALUTE TO THE MARINES(1943); BARBARY COAST GENT(1944); BLOCK BUSTERS(1944); GENTLE ANNIE(1944); MILLION DOLLAR KID(1944); THIS MAN'S NAVY(1945)
Misc. Silents
BEACH OF DREAMS(1921)

Noah Beery, Jr.
SERGEANT YORK(; LOVE TRADER(1930); RENEGADES(1930); RUSTLERS' ROUNDUP(1933); SUNSET PASS(1933); TRAIL BEYOND, THE(1934); STORMY(1935); PAROLE(1936); MIGHTY TREVE, THE(1937); ROAD BACK,THE(1937); SOME BLONDES ARE DANGEROUS(1937); TROUBLE AT MIDNIGHT(1937); FORBIDDEN VALLEY(1938); BAD LANDS(1939); FLIGHT AT MIDNIGHT(1939); OF MICE AND MEN(1939); ONLY ANGELS HAVE WINGS(1939); PARENTS ON TRIAL(1939); STRANGE CASE OF DR. MEADE(1939); CARSON CITY KID(1940); LIGHT OF WESTERN STARS, THE(1940); PASSPORT TO ALCATRAZ(1940); TWENTY MULE TEAM(1940); ALL-AMERICAN CO-ED(1941); TANKS A MILLION(1941); TWO IN A TAXI(1941); DUDES ARE PRETTY PEOPLE(1942); HAY FOOT(1942); 'NEATH BROOKLYN BRIDGE(1942); ALLERGIC TO LOVE(1943); CORVETTE K-225(1943); FRONTIER BADMEN(1943); GUNG HO!(1943); TOP MAN(1943); WE'VE NEVER BEEN LICKED(1943); FOLLOW THE BOYS(1944); HI BEAUTIFUL(1944); WEEKEND PASS(1944); CRIMSON CANARY(1945); DALTONS RIDE AGAIN, THE(1945); HER LUCKY NIGHT(1945); SEE MY LAWYER(1945); UNDER WESTERN SKIES(1945); BEAUTIFUL CHEAT, THE(1946); CAT CREEPS, THE(1946); INDIAN AGENT(1948); RED RIVER(1948); DOOLINS OF OKLAHOMA, THE(1949); DAVY CROCKETT, INDIAN SCOUT(1950); ROCKETSHIP X-M(1950); SAVAGE HORDE, THE(1950); TWO FLAGS WEST(1950); LAST OUTPOST, THE(1951); TEXAS RANGERS, THE(1951); STORY OF WILL ROGERS, THE(1952); WAGONS WEST(1952); TROPIC ZONE(1953); WAR ARROW(1953); WINGS OF THE HAWK(1953); BLACK DAKOTAS, THE(1954); YELLOW TOMAHAWK, THE(1954); WHITE FEATHER(1955); FASTEST GUN ALIVE(1956); JUBAL(1956); ESCORT WEST(1959); GUNS OF THE TIMBERLAND(1960); INHERIT THE WIND(1960); SEVEN FACES OF DR. LAO(1964); INCIDENT AT PHANTOM HILL(1966); JOURNEY TO SHILOH(1968); COCKEYED COWBOYS OF CALICO COUNTY, THE(1970); LITTLE FAUSS AND BIG HALSY(1970); WALKING TALL(1973); SPIKES GANG, THE(1974); WALKING TALL, PART II(1975); WALTZ ACROSS TEXAS(1982)
Misc. Talkies
DEVIL'S CANYON(1935); FIVE BAD MEN(1935); OUTSIDE THE LAW(1938); PETTY STORY, THE(1974)
Silents
MARK OF ZORRO(1920); PENROD(1922)

Rita Beery
DARK WATERS(1944)

Wallace Beery
BEGGARS OF LIFE(1928); CHINATOWN NIGHTS(1929); RIVER OF ROMANCE(1929); BIG HOUSE, THE(1930); BILLY THE KID(1930); LADY'S MORALS, A(1930); MIN AND BILL(1930); WAY FOR A SAILOR(1930); CHAMP, THE(1931); SECRET SIX, THE(1931); FLESH(1932); GRAND HOTEL(1932); HELL DIVERS(1932); BOWERY, THE(1933); DINNER AT EIGHT(1933); TUGBOAT ANNIE(1933); MIGHTY BARNUM, THE(1934); TREASURE ISLAND(1934); VIVA VILLA!(1934); AH, WILDERNESS!(1935); CHINA SEAS(1935); O'SHAUGHNESSY'S BOY(1935); WEST POINT OF THE AIR(1935); MESSAGE TO GARCIA, A(1936); OLD HUTCH(1936); GOOD OLD SOAR, THE(1937); SLAVE SHIP(1937); BAD MAN OF BRIMSTONE(1938); PORT OF SEVEN SEAS(1938); STABLEMATES(1938); SERGEANT MADDEN(1939); STAND UP AND FIGHT(1939); THUNDER AFLOAT(1939); MAN FROM DAKOTA, THE(1940); TWENTY MULE TEAM(1940); WYOMING(1940); BAD MAN, THE(1941); BARNACLE BILL(1941); JACKASS MAIL(1942); SALUTE TO THE MARINES(1943); BARBARY COAST GENT(1944); RATIONING(1944); THIS MAN'S NAVY(1945); BAD BASCOMB(1946); MIGHTY MCGURK, THE(1946); ALIAS A GENTLEMAN(1948); DATE WITH JUDY, A(1948); BIG JACK(1949)
Silents
SLIM PRINCESS, THE(1915); LAST OF THE MOHICANS, THE(1920); MOLLYCODDLE, THE(1920); ROUND UP, THE(1920); FOUR HORSEMEN OF THE APOCALYPSE, THE(1921); LAST TRAIL(1921); PATSY(1921); ROOKIE'S RETURN(1921); TALE OF TWO WORLDS, A(1921); ONLY A SHOP GIRL(1922); ROBIN HOOD(1922); TROUBLE(1922); WILD HONEY(1922); ASHES OF VENGEANCE(1923); ETERNAL STRUGGLE, THE(1923); STORMSWEPT(1923); THREE AGES, THE(1923); ANOTHER MAN'S WIFE(1924); SIGNAL TOWER, THE(1924); SO BIG(1924); ADVENTURE(1925); DEVIL'S CARGO, THE(1925); IN THE NAME OF LOVE(1925); LOST WORLD, THE(1925); NIGHT CLUB, THE(1925); PONY EXPRESS, THE(1925); RUGGED WATER(1925); BEHIND THE FRONT(1926); OLD IRONSIDES(1926); VOLCANO(1926); CASEY AT THE BAT(1927); FIREMAN, SAVE MY CHILD(1927); NOW WE'RE IN THE AIR(1927); PARTNERS IN CRIME(1928); WIFE SAVERS(1928); STAIRS OF SAND(1929)
Misc. Silents
LOVE BURGLAR, THE(1919); UNPARDONABLE SIN, THE(1919); VICTORY(1919); BEHIND THE DOOR(1920); VIRGIN OF STAMBOUL, THE(1920); GOLDEN SNARE, THE(1921); HURRICANE'S GAL(1922); MAN FROM HELL'S RIVER, THE(1922); ROSARY, THE(1922); SAGEBRUSH TRAIL, THE(1922); BAVU(1923); DRIFTING(1923); DRUMS OF JEOPARDY, THE(1923); FLAME OF LIFE, THE(1923); RICHARD, THE LION-HEARTED(1923); SPANISH DANCER, THE(1923); WHITE TIGER(1923); DYNAMITE SMITH(1924); RED LILY, THE(1924); UNSEEN HANDS(1924); COMING THROUGH(1925); GREAT DIVIDE, THE(1925); LET WOMEN ALONE(1925); WANDERER, THE(1926); WE'RE IN THE NAVY NOW(1926); BIG KILLING, THE(1928)

William Beery
VANQUISHED, THE(1953)

Beery & Hatton
Silents
TWO FLAMING YOUTHS(1927)
Paul Beesen
MUTATIONS, THE(1974, Brit.), ph
Ann Elizabeth Beesley
MEMORY OF US(1974)
Anne Beesley
YOUNG FRANKENSTEIN(1974)
Brad Beesley
MAGIC(1978)
Brent Beesley
OUTSIDERS, THE(1983)
David Beesley
MUTATIONS, THE(1974, Brit.), ed
Paul Beeson
AGAINST THE WIND(1948, Brit.), ph; UNDER CAPRICORN(1949), ph; IVORY HUNTER(1952, Brit.), ph; TRAIN OF EVENTS(1952, Brit.), ph; WEST OF ZANZIBAR(1954, Brit.), ph; GENTLE TOUCH, THE(1956, Brit.), ph; OUT OF THE CLOUDS(1957, Brit.), ph; SHIRALEE, THE(1957, Brit.), ph; DUNKIRK(1958, Brit.), ph; NOWHERE TO GO(1959, Brit.), ph; SCAPEGOAT, THE(1959, Brit.), ph; KIDNAPPED(1960), ph; GREYFRIARS BOBBY(1961, Brit.), ph; SEASON OF PASSION(1961, Aus./Brit.), ph; SPARE THE ROD(1961, Brit.), ph; HAPPY THIEVES, THE(1962), ph; IN SEARCH OF THE CASTAWAYS(1962, Brit.), ph; NEARLY A NASTY ACCIDENT(1962, Brit.), ph; TARZAN GOES TO INDIA(1962, U.S./Brit./ Switz.), ph; THREE LIVES OF THOMASINA, THE(1963, U.S./Brit.), ph; MOONSPINNERS, THE(1964), ph; DIE, MONSTER, DIE(1965), ph; NOT WITH MY WIFE, YOU DON'T(1966), ph; AFRICA–TEXAS STYLE!(1967 U.S./Brit.), ph; TO SIR, WITH LOVE(1967, Brit.), ph; ATTACK ON THE IRON COAST(1968, U.S./Brit.), ph; SUMARINE X-1(1969, Brit.), ph; HELL BOATS(1970, Brit.), ph; MOON ZERO TWO(1970, Brit.), ph; MOSQUITO SQUADRON(1970, Brit.), ph; JANE EYRE(1971, Brit.), ph; KIDNAPPED(1971, Brit.), ph; CRESCENDO(1972, Brit.), ph; WARM DECEMBER, A(1973, Brit.), ph; DR. SYN, ALIAS THE SCARECROW(1975), ph; ONE OF OUR DINOSAURS IS MISSING(1975, Brit.), ph; LITTLEST HORSE THIEVES, THE(1977, ph; CANDLESHOE(1978), ph; STARCRASH(1979), ph; UNIDENTIFIED FLYING ODDBALL, THE(1979, Brit.), ph; HAWK THE SLAYER(1980, Brit.), ph; RAIDERS OF THE LOST ARK(1981), ph; SILVER DREAM RACER(1982, Brit.), ph
Beethoven
INVITATION TO THE WALTZ(1935, Brit.), m; L'AGE D'OR(1979, Fr.), m; CONDUCTOR, THE(1981, Pol.), m
Sam Beetley
BROTHERS IN THE SADDLE(1949), ed
Sam E. Beetley
RACE STREET(1948), ed
Samuel Beetley
TOAST OF NEW YORK, THE(1937), ed; LONGEST DAY, THE(1962), ed
Samuel E. Beetley
ARMY SURGEON(1942), ed; NAVY COMES THROUGH, THE(1942), ed; POWDER TOWN(1942), ed; CHILD OF DIVORCE(1946), ed; SUNSET PASS(1946), ed; BEAT THE BAND(1947), ed; OUT OF THE PAST(1947), ed; BLOOD ON THE MOON(1948), ed; MYSTERY IN MEXICO(1948), ed; RETURN OF THE BADMEN(1948), ed; BIG STEAL, THE(1949), ed; THREAT, THE(1949), ed; HUNT THE MAN DOWN(1950), ed; WHITE TOWER, THE(1950), ed; AT SWORD'S POINT(1951), ed; OVERLAND TELEGRAPH(1951), ed; HALF-BREED, THE(1952), ed; MACAO(1952), ed; PACE THAT THRILLS, THE(1952), ed; TRAIL GUIDE(1952), ed; VISIT, THE(1964, Ger./Fr./Ital./ U.S.), ed; AGONY AND THE ECSTASY, THE(1965), ed; UP FROM THE BEACH(1965), ed; DOCTOR DOLITTLE(1967), ed; SOYLENT GREEN(1973), ed; FIVE DAYS FROM HOME(1978), ed; SAFARI 3000(1982), ed
Frank Beetson
NO HOLDS BARRED(1952), cos; JALOPY(1953), cos; MAN FROM DEL RIO(1956), cos; SEARCHERS, THE(1956), cos; MISSOURI TRAVELER, THE(1958), cos; YOUNG LAND, THE(1959), cos; ALAMO, THE(1960), tech adv; TWO RODE TOGETHER(1961), cos; CHEYENNE AUTUMN(1964), cos; STUNT MAN, THE(1980)
1984
LOVE STREAMS(1984)
Frank Beetson, Jr.
MC LINTOCK!(1963), cos; NEVADA SMITH(1966), cos
Frank C. Beetson, Jr.
GLORY GUYS, THE(1965), cos
Diana Beevers
CARRY ON TEACHER(1962, Brit.); SUMARINE X-1(1969, Brit.); FOURTEEN, THE(1973, Brit.)
Geoffrey Beevers
VICTOR/VICTORIA(1982); CURSE OF THE PINK PANTHER(1983)
Larry Beezer
KING OF THE MOUNTAIN(1981)
Eric Befche
NO TRACE(1950, Brit.), ph
Alberto Befilacqua
ATOM AGE VAMPIRE(1961, Ital.), w
Shama Beg
HOUSEHOLDER, THE(1963, US/India)
A. Begak
WAR AND PEACE(1968, USSR)
D. Begak
WAR AND PEACE(1968, USSR)
Wilson Bege
HER WEDDING NIGHT(1930)
Dr. Charles F. Begg
YOUNG DOCTORS, THE(1961), tech adv
Gordon Begg
OFFICER'S MESS, THE(1931, Brit.); OUT OF THE BLUE(1931, Brit.); SHERLOCK HOLMES' FATAL HOUR(1931, Brit.); PICCADILLY(1932, Brit.); DANGEROUS GROUND(1934, Brit.); SWORD OF HONOUR(1938, Brit.); PRISONER OF CORBAL(1939, Brit.); SONS OF THE SEA(1939, Brit.); SALUTE JOHN CITIZEN(1942, Brit.); LAMP STILL BURNS, THE(1943, Brit.); MY AIN FOLK(1944, Brit.); WELCOME, MR. WASHINGTON(1944, Brit.); STRAWBERRY ROAN(1945, Brit.); THEY KNEW MR. KNIGHT(1945, Brit.); GREAT EXPECTATIONS(1946, Brit.); QUEEN OF SPADES(1948, Brit.); WHILE THE SUN SHINES(1950, Brit.)

Misc. Silents
PORT OF MISSING WOMEN, THE(1915, Brit.); BANDOLERO, THE(1924); HIS BUDDY'S WIFE(1925)
James Begg
GHOST AND MR. CHICKEN, THE(1966); DEATH WISH II(1982)
Jim Begg
VILLAGE OF THE GIANTS(1965); COOL ONES THE(1967); IT'S A BIKINI WORLD(1967); LOVE GOD?, THE(1969); GRAND THEFT AUTO(1977); CAT FROM OUTER SPACE, THE(1978); LEO AND LOREE(1980), p
William Begg
GILDED LILY, THE(1935)
William J. Begg
WHOOPEE(1930)
Francis Beggins
ZELIG(1983)
Bill Beggs
DEVIL DOGS OF THE AIR(1935)
Hagan Beggs
LAST GUNFIGHTER, THE(1961, Can.); RUSSIAN ROULETTE(1975); SALLY FIELDGOOD & CO.(1975, Can.)
Hagen Beggs
GROUNDSTAR CONSPIRACY, THE(1972, Can.); WOLFPEN PRINCIPLE, THE(1974, Can.), art d; BEAR ISLAND(1980, Brit.-Can.); STAR 80(1983)
Lee Beggs
LOST LADY, A(1934)
Silents
AMERICA(1924); JANICE MEREDITH(1924); PLAYTHINGS OF DESIRE(1924); STEPPING ALONG(1926)
Misc. Silents
FOLKS FROM WAY DOWN EAST(1924), d
Malcolm Lee Beggs
IT GROWS ON TREES(1952); LOVE ISLAND(1952); BOTANY BAY(1953); HOUDINI(1953); EDGE OF FURY(1958)
Pat Beggs
Misc. Silents
DEVIL'S GULCH, THE(1926)
Luisella Beghi
ETERNAL MELODIES(1948, Ital.); DISILLUSION(1949, Ital.); ANGELO IN THE CROWD(1952, Ital.)
Catharine Begin
UNCANNY, THE(1977, Brit./Can.)
Orthrud Beginnen
JIMMY ORPHEUS(1966, Ger.)
Bert Begley
FIREBALL, THE(1950)
Ed Begley
BOOMERANG(1947); WEB, THE(1947); DEEP WATERS(1948); SITTING PRETTY(1948); SORRY, WRONG NUMBER(1948); STREET WITH NO NAME(1948); GREAT GATSBY, THE(1949); IT HAPPENS EVERY SPRING(1949); TULSA(1949); BACKFIRE(1950); CONVICTED(1950); DARK CITY(1950); SADDLE TRAMP(1950); WYOMING MAIL(1950); LADY FROM TEXAS, THE(1951); ON DANGEROUS GROUND(1951); YOU'RE IN THE NAVY NOW(1951); BOOTS MALONE(1952); DEADLINE–U.S.A.(1952); LONE STAR(1952); TURNING POINT, THE(1952); PATTERNS(1956); 12 ANGRY MEN(1957); ODDS AGAINST TOMORROW(1959); GREEN HELMET, THE(1961, Brit.); SWEET BIRD OF YOUTH(1962); UNSINKABLE MOLLY BROWN, THE(1964); OSCAR, THE(1966); BILLION DOLLAR BRAIN(1967, Brit.); WARNING SHOT(1967); FIRECREEK(1968); HANG'EM HIGH(1968); TIME TO SING, A(1968); WILD IN THE STREETS(1968); MONITORS, THE(1969); VIOLENT ENEMY, THE(1969, Brit.); DUNWICH HORROR, THE(1970); ROAD TO SALINA(1971, Fr./Ital.)
Ed Begley, Jr.
CONCORDE, THE–AIRPORT '79(; NOW YOU SEE HIM, NOW YOU DON'T(1972); CHARLEY AND THE ANGEL(1973); SHOWDOWN(1973); SUPERDAD(1974); STAY HUNGRY(1976); CITIZENS BAND(1977); BLUE COLLAR(1978); GOIN' SOUTH(1978); ONE AND ONLY, THE(1978); RECORD CITY(1978); HARDCORE(1979); IN-LAWS, THE(1979); BUDDY BUDDY(1981); PRIVATE LESSONS(1981); CAT PEOPLE(1982); EATING RAOUL(1982); GET CRAZY(1983)
1984
PROTOCOL(1984); STREETS OF FIRE(1984); THIS IS SPINAL TAP(1984)
Elizabeth Begley
SONS AND LOVERS(1960, Brit.); FACE OF A STRANGER(1964, Brit.); LEATHER BOYS, THE(1965, Brit.); OUTSIDER, THE(1980)
Jean Begley
GREENWICH VILLAGE STORY(1963), ed
Martin Begley
CRY OF THE CITY(1948); LENNY(1974)
Mary Jo Begley
WHERE ANGELS GO...TROUBLE FOLLOWS(1968)
Rita Begley
JACQUELINE(1956, Brit.)
Sally Beglin
WHAT'S GOOD FOR THE GOOSE(1969, Brit.)
Maud Begon
VERY PRIVATE AFFAIR, A(1962, Fr./Ital.), makeup
Jeff Begun
JACKSON COUNTY JAIL(1976), p; SATURDAY THE 14TH(1981), p, w
1984
HARDBODIES(1984), p
Behal
M(1933, Ger.)
Brendan Behan
QUARE FELLOW, THE(1962, Brit.), w
Dominic Behan
JOHNNY NOBODY(1965, Brit.)
Roscoe Behan
RED, HOT AND BLUE(1949)
Roscoe J. Behan
TASK FORCE(1949)

Gert Behanna
LATE LIZ, THE(1971), w
Henri Behar
SUMMER LOVERS(1982)
Kip Behar
Misc. Talkies
BEAUTY AND THE BODY(1963)
Julia Beharano
MEXICALI ROSE(1929)
Clayton Behee
THIRTEEN WOMEN(1932)
Ed Beheler
CAYMAN TRIANGLE, THE(1977)
1984
LONELY GUY, THE(1984)
Arthur Beherns
Misc. Silents
WHERE BONDS ARE LOOSED(1919)
Brionny Behets
ALVIN RIDES AGAIN(1974, Aus.)
Briony Behets
TRESPASSERS, THE(1976, Aus.); INSIDE LOOKING OUT(1977, Aus.); LONG WEEK-END(1978, Aus.)
Bob Behling
LAND OF THE MINOTAUR(1976, Gr.)
Robert A. Behling
OVER-UNDER, SIDEWAYS-DOWN(1977)
Robert Behling
NORTHERN LIGHTS(1978); EYE FOR AN EYE, AN(1981); CUJO(1983)
Eleanor Behm
SENSATIONS OF 1945(1944), cos; BRASHER DOUBLOON, THE(1947), cos
Joseph Behm
LAST SUNSET, THE(1961), prod d
Marc Behm
RETURN OF DR. MABUSE, THE(1961, Ger./Fr./Ital.), w; CHARADE(1963), w; HELP!(1965, Brit.), w; PARTY'S OVER, THE(1966, Brit.), w; TRUNK TO CAIRO(1966, Israel/Ger.), w; BLONDE FROM PEKING, THE(1968, Fr.), w; SOMEONE BEHIND THE DOOR(1971, Fr./Brit.), w; MAD BOMBER, THE(1973), w; LADY CHATTER-LEY'S LOVER(1981, Fr./Brit.), w; HOSPITAL MASSACRE(1982), w; PIAF–THE EAR-LY YEARS(1982, U.S./Fr.), w; NANA(1983, Ital.), w
1984
HOSPITAL MASSACRE(1984), w
Ernst Behmer
BLONDE NIGHTINGALE(1931, Ger.); SHOT AT DAWN, A(1934, Ger.); WORLD WITHOUT A MASK, THE(1934, Ger.); MASTER OF THE WORLD(1935, Ger.)
Harry Behn
HELL'S ANGELS(1930), w; SECRET OF THE CHATEAU(1935), w
Silents
BIG PARADE, THE(1925), w; PROUD FLESH(1925), w; CROWD, THE(1928), w; RACKET, THE(1928), w; SIN SISTER, THE(1929), w
Noel Behn
KREMLIN LETTER, THE(1970), w; BRINK'S JOB, THE(1978), w
Peter Behn
BAMBI(1942)
Friedel Behn-Grun
EMPRESS AND I, THE(1933, Ger.), ph
Friedl Behn-Grun
BARBERINA(1932, Ger.), ph
Fr. Behn-Grund
EIGHT GIRLS IN A BOAT(1932, Ger.), ph
Freidl Behn-Grund
ALRAUNE(1952, Ger.), ph
Fridl Behn-Grund
KARAMAZOV(1931, Ger.), ph
Friedel Behn-Grund
TRAPEZE(1932, Ger.), ph; MARRIAGE IN THE SHADOWS(1948, Ger.), ph; TALE OF FIVE WOMEN, A(1951, Brit.), ph
Friedl Behn-Grund
MURDERERS AMONG US(1948, Ger.), ph; RESTLESS NIGHT, THE(1964, Ger.), ph
Lorrain Behnan
1984
ISAAC LITTLEFEATHERS(1984, Can.)
F. BehnGrund
HEART SONG(1933, Brit.), ph
Albert Behnitz
REBEL, THE(1933, Ger.), ph
Dietmar Behnke
COUNT DRACULA(1971, Sp., Ital., Ger., Brit.), w
Edward Behr
ROSEBUD(1975)
Jack Behr
1984
BIRDY(1984), w
Jacques Behr
1984
L'ARGENT(1984, Fr./Switz.)
Johnny Behr
GOLDEN GLOVES STORY, THE(1950)
Roger Behr
Misc. Talkies
CAN I DO IT 'TIL I NEED GLASSES?(1977)
Behrend
BARBERINA(1932, Ger.), w
Arthur Behrend
HOUSE OF THE SPANIARD, THE(1936, Brit.), w
Bonnie Behrend
TRADING PLACES(1983)

Hans Behrendt
DANTON(1931, Ger.), d
Misc. Silents
ROYAL SCANDAL(1929, Ger.), d
Klaus Behrendt
WILLY(1963, U.S./Ger.)
Maria Behrendt
1984
ELEMENT OF CRIME, THE(1984, Den.)
Olive Behrendt
TRAVELS WITH MY AUNT(1972, Brit.)
Bernard Behrens
SWASHBUCKLER(1976); ANOTHER MAN, ANOTHER CHANCE(1977 Fr/US); LOV-ING COUPLES(1980); RESURRECTION(1980); GALAXY OF TERROR(1981); FIRE-FOX(1982); MAN WITH TWO BRAINS, THE(1983)
1984
UNFAITHFULLY YOURS(1984)
Berrand Behrens
CHANGELING, THE(1980, Can.)
Frank Behrens
WAKE ME WHEN IT'S OVER(1960)
Inge Behrens
1984
CLASS ENEMY(1984, Ger.), ed
Josef Behrens
LEPKE(1975, U.S./Israel)
Marla Behrens
REPTILICUS(1962, U.S./Den.)
Marlene Behrens
LOUISIANA TERRITORY(1953)
Marlies Behrens
48 HOURS TO LIVE(1960, Brit./Swed.); FREDDY UNTER FREMDEN STER-NEN(1962, Ger.)
Herbert Behrent
TIN DRUM, THE(1979, Ger./Fr./Yugo./Pol.)
Joseph Behrens
MAN OF THE MOMENT(1955, Brit.); CURSE OF FRANKENSTEIN, THE(1957, Brit.); KITCHEN, THE(1961, Brit.); WRONG BOX, THE(1966, Brit.)
S. H. Behrman
TWO-FACED WOMAN(1941), w
S. N. Behrman
BRAT, THE(1931), w; BRIEF MOMENT(1933), w; CONQUEST(1937), w; ME AND THE COLONEL(1958), w; STOWAWAY IN THE SKY(1962, Fr.), d&w
S.N. Behrman
HE KNEW WOMEN(1930), w; LIGHTNIN'(1930), w; LILIOM(1930), w; SEA WOLF, THE(1930), w; DADDY LONG LEGS(1931), w; SURRENDER(1931), w; REBECCA OF SUNNYBROOK FARM(1932), w; TESS OF THE STORM COUNTRY(1932), w; HAL-LELUJAH, I'M A BUM(1933), w; MY LIPS BETRAY(1933), w; QUEEN CHRIS-TINA(1933), w; BIOGRAPHY OF A BACHELOR GIRL(1935), w; SCARLET PIMPERNEL, THE(1935, Brit.), w; TALE OF TWO CITIES, A(1935), w; PAR-NELL(1937), w; COWBOY AND THE LADY, THE(1938), w; NO TIME FOR COME-DY(1940), w; WATERLOO BRIDGE(1940), w; PIRATE, THE(1948), w; GABY(1956), w; FANNY(1961), w
Joseph Behrmann
IPCRESS FILE, THE(1965, Brit.)
Roscoe C. Behrmann
SEVEN AGAINST THE SUN(1968, South Africa), p
Don P. Behrns
UNSEEN, THE(1981), p; LIAR'S MOON(1982), p
Pati Behrs
FOREVER AMBER(1947); APARTMENT FOR PEGGY(1948); UNFAITHFULLY YOURS(1948); WHEN MY BABY SMILES AT ME(1948); BEAUTIFUL BLONDE FROM BASHFUL BEND, THE(1949); COME TO THE STABLE(1949)
Patti Behrs
RAZOR'S EDGE, THE(1946)
Roger Behrstock
POSSE(1975); FORCED VENGEANCE(1982)
Ella Bei
BREATH OF SCANDAL, A(1960), cos
Leo Bei
SECRET WAYS, THE(1961), cos; FOREVER MY LOVE(1962), cos; MIRACLE OF THE WHITE STALLIONS(1963), cos; EMIL AND THE DETECTIVES(1964), cos
Al Beich
CAMPUS RHYTHM(1943), w
Albert Beich
WEST SIDE KID(1943), w; GANGS OF THE WATERFRONT(1945), w; BRIDE GOES WILD, THE(1948), w, w; KEY TO THE CITY(1950), w; MILKMAN, THE(1950), w; YELLOW CAB MAN, THE(1950), w; LIEUTENANT WORE SKIRTS, THE(1956), w; DEAD RINGER(1964), w; DISTANT TRUMPET, A(1964), w; PERILS OF PAULINE, THE(1967), w
Margot Beichler
PINOCCHIO(1969, E. Ger.), w
Charles Beiden
FIFTEEN WIVES(1934), w
Jurgen Beier
NOT RECONCILED, OR "ONLY VIOLENCE HELPS WHERE IT RULES"(1969, Ger.)
Alfred Beierle
CAPTAIN FROM KOEPENICK(1933, Ger.)
John Beifer
HEADIN' FOR GOD'S COUNTRY(1943)
Ulrich Beiger
WHITE HORSE INN, THE(1959, Ger.); GREAT ESCAPE, THE(1963)
Walter Beilbey
STATE FAIR(1962)
Vangie Beilby
DR. SOCRATES(1935); MAID OF SALEM(1937); CAPTAIN IS A LADY, THE(1940); EARL OF CHICAGO, THE(1940); FOREVER AND A DAY(1943); GIRL CRAZY(1943); YOUNGEST PROFESSION, THE(1943); THIS LOVE OF OURS(1945); EGG AND I, THE(1947); FAMILY HONEYMOON(1948); STRATTON STORY, THE(1949); SECRET FURY, THE(1950)

Leon Beileres
CONFLICT(1939, Fr.)
Bangie Beilly
FUGITIVE ROAD(1934)
Kurt Beimel
NED KELLY(1970, Brit.); TRUE STORY OF ESKIMO NELL, THE(1975, Aus.)
Albert Bein
BOY SLAVES(1938), w; TOUGH AS THEY COME(1942), w; JUNIOR ARMY(1943), w
Jean-Jacques Beineix
DIVA(1982, Fr.), d, w; MOON IN THE GUTTER, THE(1983, Fr./Ital.), d, w
Alf Beinell
SALZBURG CONNECTION, THE(1972)
Larry Beinhart
NO PLACE TO HIDE(1975), w
T. Beinikevich
VOW, THE(1947, USSR.)
Michael Beint
BATTLEAXE, THE(1962, Brit.); FAR FROM THE MADDING CROWD(1967, Brit.); CONQUEROR WORM, THE(1968, Brit.)
Fred Beir
VIOLATORS, THE(1957); FORT COURAGEOUS(1965); ORGANIZATION, THE(1971)
Michael Beirne
MINX, THE(1969)
Yerye Beirut
FEAR CHAMBER, THE(1968, US/Mex.)
Jorge Beirute
TARZAN AND THE VALLEY OF GOLD(1966 U.S./Switz.)
Yerye Beirute
SEVEN CITIES OF GOLD(1955); WOMAN'S DEVOTION, A(1956); VAMPIRE'S COFFIN, THE(1958, Mex.); FACE OF THE SCREAMING WEREWOLF(1959, Mex.); INCREDIBLE INVASION, THE(1971, Mex./U.S.)
Klaus Beiser
1984
CHINESE BOXES(1984, Ger./Brit.), art d
Maggie Beistle
1984
FLASH OF GREEN, A(1984)
Dorothy Beitel
Silents
WOMAN, THE(1915)
Emmett Bejano
CARNY(1980)
Percilla Bejano
CARNY(1980)
Hernan Bejar
MIRAGE(1972, Peru)
Julia Bejarano
COWBOY HOLIDAY(1934)
Maurice Bejart
BOLERO(1982, Fr.), ch
Vladimir Bejval
JOURNEY TO THE BEGINNING OF TIME(1966, Czech)
Amo Bek-Nazarov
Misc. Silents
EVA(1918, USSR); IN THE PILLORY(1924, USSR), d; NAMUS(1926, USSR), d
Stephen Bekassy
CALYPSO JOE(1957)
Stephan Bekassy
FAIR WIND TO JAVA(1953)
Stephen Bekassy
SONG TO REMEMBER, A(1945); ARCH OF TRIUMPH(1948); BLACK MAGIC(1949); SECRETS OF MONTE CARLO(1951); TEN TALL MEN(1951); PATHFINDER, THE(1952); WOMAN OF THE NORTH COUNTRY(1952); HELL AND HIGH WATER(1954); PRISONER OF WAR(1954); INTERRUPTED MELODY(1955); PURPLE MASK, THE(1955); RACERS, THE(1955); SERENADE(1956); LIGHT IN THE FOREST, THE(1958); YOUNG LIONS, THE(1958); BEYOND THE TIME BARRIER(1960); PEPE(1960); BACHELOR FLAT(1962); FOUR HORSEMEN OF THE APOCALYPSE, THE(1962)
Istvan Bekeffi
MAN WHO WAGGED HIS TAIL, THE(1961, Ital./Span.), w; SHADOWS GROW LONGER, THE(1962, Switz./Ger.), w; JUDGE AND THE SINNER, THE(1964, Ger.), w; MAN WHO WALKED THROUGH THE WALL, THE(1964, Ger.), w
Stephen Bekeffi
KISS AND MAKE UP(1934), w
Istvan Bekeffy
MISS PRESIDENT(1935, Hung.), w
Rita Bekes
FATHER(1967, Hung.)
Apostolis Bekiaros
BAREFOOT BATTALION, THE(1954, Gr.)
Mohammed Bekireche
INQUISITOR, THE(1982, Fr.)
Ronald Bekker
DON QUIXOTE(1973, Aus.)
Sadao Bekku
WHITE ROSE OF HONG KONG(1965, Jap.), m
Frank Bekum
Silents
MADAME BUTTERFLY(1915)
Franca Bel
HANDS OF ORLAC, THE(1964, Brit./Fr.)
Barbara Bel Geddes
LONG NIGHT, THE(1947); BLOOD ON THE MOON(1948); I REMEMBER MAMA(1948); PANIC IN THE STREETS(1950); FOURTEEN HOURS(1951); VERTIGO(1958); FIVE PENNIES, THE(1959); FIVE BRANDED WOMEN(1960); BY LOVE POSSESSED(1961); TODD KILLINGS, THE(1971)

Nicholas Bela
LADY IN QUESTION, THE(1940)
Silents
ADORATION(1928); NIGHT WATCH, THE(1928)
Nick Bela
LITTLE CAESAR(1931)
Bela Berkes and his Gypsy Orchestra
IT'S A KING(1933, Brit.)
Doris Belack
LOOKING UP(1977); BLACK MARBLE, THE(1980); HANKY-PANKY(1982); TOOTSIE(1982)
Constantine Beladames
FANTASIES(1981)
Gina Belafonte
1984
BEAT STREET(1984)
Harry Belafonte
BRIGHT ROAD(1953); CARMEN JONES(1954); ISLAND IN THE SUN(1957); ODDS AGAINST TOMORROW(1959); WORLD, THE FLESH, AND THE DEVIL, THE(1959); ANGEL LEVINE, THE(1970); BUCK AND THE PREACHER(1972); UPTOWN SATURDAY NIGHT(1974)
1984
BEAT STREET(1984), p, m
Shari Belafonte-Harper
TIME WALKER(1982)
Betty Belairs
Misc. Silents
SPANISH JADE, THE(1915)
Adrian Belanger
QUEBEC(1951)
George Belanger
SUNBURN(1979)
Roland Belanger
13 RUE MADELEINE(1946)
Heinrich Belasch
SONG OF LIFE, THE(1931, Ger.), ph
Art Belasco
THIRD FINGER, LEFT HAND(1940); HONKY TONK(1941); SHADOW OF THE THIN MAN(1941); JACKASS MAIL(1942); JOHNNY EAGER(1942); THREE HEARTS FOR JULIA(1943)
Arthur Belasco
PENTHOUSE(1933); STORY OF TEMPLE DRAKE, THE(1933); FIGHTING ROOKIE, THE(1934); HIDE-OUT(1934); THIN MAN, THE(1934); NAUGHTY MARIETTA(1935); MY DEAR MISS ALDRICH(1937); NEW MOON(1940); NAZI AGENT(1942)
David Belasco
DU BARRY, WOMAN OF PASSION(1930), d&w; GIRL OF THE GOLDEN WEST(1930), w; SWEET KITTY BELLAIRS(1930), w; KIKI(1931), w; HATCHET MAN, THE(1932), w; MADAME BUTTERFLY(1932), w; SON-DAUGHTER, THE(1932), w; RETURN OF PETER GRIMM, THE(1935), w; ROSE OF THE RANCHO(1936), w; GIRL OF THE GOLDEN WEST, THE(1938), w; UNA SIGNORA DELL'OVEST(1942, Ital), w
Silents
GOOD LITTLE DEVIL, A(1914), a, sup; ROSE OF THE RANCHO(1914), w; GIRL OF THE GOLDEN WEST, THE(1915), w; MAY BLOSSOM(1915), w; WOMAN, THE(1915), w; HEART OF MARYLAND, THE(1921), w; PAWN TICKET 210(1922), w; GIRL OF THE GOLDEN WEST, THE(1923), w; GOLD DIGGERS, THE(1923), p; FORTY WINKS(1925), w; RETURN OF PETER GRIMM, THE(1926), w; LAUGH, CLOWN, LAUGH(1928), w
Jacques Belasco
MAGIC FOUNTAIN, THE(1961), m
Jay Belasco
WOMAN ACCUSED(1933); WEDDING NIGHT, THE(1935); MILKY WAY, THE(1936); OUR RELATIONS(1936)
Silents
GILDED SPIDER, THE(1916); HELP WANTED–MALE!(1920); JENNY BE GOOD(1920)
Misc. Silents
BOBBIE OF THE BALLET(1916); GRASP OF GREED, THE(1916); GRIP OF JEALOUSY, THE(1916); LORELEI OF THE SEA(1917); LIFE'S A FUNNY PROPOSITION(1919); PALACE OF THE DARKENED WINDOWS, THE(1920); SMOULDERING EMBERS(1920)
Leon Belasco
BROADWAY SERENADE(1939); FISHERMAN'S WHARF(1939); GOOD GIRLS GO TO PARIS(1939); LEGION OF LOST FLYERS(1939); TOPPER TAKES A TRIP(1939); I TAKE THIS WOMAN(1940); IT'S A DATE(1940); LADY IN QUESTION, THE(1940); LUCKY PARTNERS(1940); MUMMY'S HAND, THE(1940); MY FAVORITE WIFE(1940); TUGBOAT ANNIE SAILS AGAIN(1940); CHOCOLATE SOLDIER, THE(1941); DESIGN FOR SCANDAL(1941); GIRL, A GUY AND A GOB, A(1941); I'LL WAIT FOR YOU(1941); KISSES FOR BREAKFAST(1941); NEVER GIVE A SUCKER AN EVEN BREAK(1941); NOTHING BUT THE TRUTH(1941); PLAYMATES(1941); SKYLARK(1941); TALL, DARK AND HANDSOME(1941); WHERE DID YOU GET THAT GIRL?(1941); CASABLANCA(1942); GIVE OUT, SISTERS(1942); HOLIDAY INN(1942); NIGHT BEFORE THE DIVORCE, THE(1942); OVER MY DEAD BODY(1942); ROAD TO MOROCCO(1942); ROXIE HART(1942); THAT OTHER WOMAN(1942); YANKEE DOODLE DANDY(1942); GANG'S ALL HERE, THE(1943); HEAT'S ON, THE(1943); HERS TO HOLD(1943); IT COMES UP LOVE(1943); SHE'S FOR ME(1943); AND THE ANGELS SING(1944); CONSPIRATORS, THE(1944); MEET THE PEOPLE(1944); NIGHT CLUB GIRL(1944); PIN UP GIRL(1944); SAN DIEGO, I LOVE YOU(1944); STORM OVER LISBON(1944); EARL CARROLL'S VANITIES(1945); EASY TO LOOK AT(1945); HOLLYWOOD AND VINE(1945); OUT OF THIS WORLD(1945); WONDER MAN(1945); YOLANDA AND THE THIEF(1945); LITTLE IODINE(1946); SUSPENSE(1946); SWING PARADE OF 1946(1946); IT HAPPENED ON 5TH AVENUE(1947); PHILO VANCE RETURNS(1947); EVERY GIRL SHOULD BE MARRIED(1948); FOR THE LOVE OF MARY(1948); I, JANE DOE(1948); THREE DARING DAUGHTERS(1948); ADVENTURES OF DON JUAN(1949); BAGDAD(1949); EVERYBODY DOES IT(1949); HOLIDAY IN HAVANA(1949); LOVE HAPPY(1949); ABBOTT AND COSTELLO IN THE FOREIGN LEGION(1950); BOMBA AND THE HIDDEN CITY(1950); LOVE THAT BRUTE(1950); NANCY GOES TO RIO(1950); PLEASE BELIEVE ME(1950); TOAST OF NEW ORLEANS, THE(1950); CUBAN FIREBALL(1951); GOLDEN HORDE, THE(1951); HAVANA ROSE(1951); LITTLE

EGYPT(1951); FABULOUS SENORITA, THE(1952); GOBS AND GALS(1952); SON OF ALI BABA(1952); CALL ME MADAM(1953); GERALDINE(1953); JALOPY(1953); CAN-CAN(1960); MY SIX LOVES(1963); ART OF LOVE, THE(1965); SUPERDAD(1974)

Ruby Belasco
Silents
JUSTICE(1914, Brit.); RAGGED MESSENGER, THE(1917, Brit.)

Walter Belasco
Silents
JUDGE NOT OR THE WOMAN OF MONA DIGGINGS(1915); JOHN NEEDHAM'S DOUBLE(1916); ALIAS MARY BROWN(1918); KAISER, BEAST OF BERLIN, THE(1918)
Misc. Silents
FROM A BROADWAY TO A THRONE(1916); JEWEL IN PAWN, A(1917)

William Belasco
CAREY TREATMENT, THE(1972), p; THEY ONLY KILL THEIR MASTERS(1972), p; SUPER COPS, THE(1974), p

Anik Belaubre
CONFIDENTIALLY YOURS(1983, Fr.)

N. Belayev
Misc. Silents
BEAUTY AND THE BOLSHEVIK(1923, USSR)

Michel Belber
COURIER OF LYONS(1938, Fr.), ph

George Belbin
FRANKENSTEIN MUST BE DESTROYED!(1969, Brit.); SOME GIRLS DO(1969, Brit.); MAN OF VIOLENCE(1970, Brit.); GAMES THAT LOVERS PLAY(1971, Brit.); SUNDAY BLOODY SUNDAY(1971, Brit.); EYE OF THE NEEDLE(1981)

Berry Belchamber
RECOMMENDATION FOR MERCY(1975, Can.)

Alice Belcher
Silents
SECOND HAND ROSE(1922)
Misc. Silents
COWBOY KID, THE(1928)

Charles Belcher
Silents
MARK OF ZORRO(1920); THREE MUSKETEERS, THE(1921); BLOOD AND SAND(1922); ROSITA(1923); THIEF OF BAGDAD, THE(1924); BEN-HUR(1925); BLACK PIRATE, THE(1926); KING OF KINGS, THE(1927)
Misc. Silents
FOOLS IN THE DARK(1924); DEVIL'S GULCH, THE(1926)

David Belcher
THREE SISTERS(1974, Brit.); CONFESSIONS OF A POP PERFORMER(1975, Brit.)

Frank Belcher
Silents
DANGER SIGNAL, THE(1915); KEEP MOVING(1915); SENTIMENTAL LADY, THE(1915); FINAL CURTAIN, THE(1916)
Misc. Silents
DEVIL'S PRAYER-BOOK, THE(1916); MRS. BALFANE(1917); RECOIL, THE(1917); DOCTOR AND THE BRICKLAYER, THE(1918)

Frank H. Belcher
Silents
ON THE QUIET(1918)

Harry Belcher
THIRD MAN, THE(1950, Brit.)

Joe Belcher
DRACULA(1979); DRESSER, THE(1983)

Leo Belcher
Silents
LOVE'S OLD SWEET SONG(1917, Brit.)
Misc. Silents
IN ANOTHER GIRL'S SHOES(1917, Brit.)

Leon Belcher
Misc. Silents
BONNIE MARY(1918, Brit.)

Lionel Belcher
Misc. Silents
HER CROSS(1919, Brit.)

Majorie Belcher [Marge Champion]
STORY OF VERNON AND IRENE CASTLE, THE(1939)

Pat Belcher
CIRCUS FRIENDS(1962, Brit.)

Paul Belcher
TARGETS(1968)

Robeit Belcher
HEX(1973), ed

Robert A. Belcher
FRIENDLY PERSUASION(1956), ed

Robert Belcher
ONE MINUTE TO ZERO(1952), ed; BIG COUNTRY, THE(1958), ed; ACE ELI AND RODGER OF THE SKIES(1973), ed

Jose Belchior
VOYAGE OF SILENCE(1968, Fr.)

Teresa Belczynska
WALKOVER(1969, Pol.)

Lia Beldam
SHINING, THE(1980)

Barbara Belden
WHEN THE LIGHTS GO ON AGAIN(1944)

Charles Belden
PORT OF LOST DREAMS(1935), w; SHOT IN THE DARK, A(1935), w; SONS OF STEEL(1935), w; WORLD ACCUSES, THE(1935), w; MURDER OF DR. HARRIGAN, THE(1936), w; WIDOW FROM MONTE CARLO, THE(1936), w; CHARLIE CHAN AT MONTE CARLO(1937), w; CHARLIE CHAN ON BROADWAY(1937), w; GOD'S COUNTRY AND THE WOMAN(1937), w; CHARLIE CHAN IN HONOLULU(1938), w; MR. MOTO'S GAMBLE(1938), w; ONE WILD NIGHT(1938), w; DEAD END KIDS ON DRESS PARADE(1939), w; KID NIGHTINGALE(1939), w; TORCHY PLAYS WITH DYNAMITE(1939), w; TEAR GAS SQUAD(1940), w; BEAUTY AND THE BANDIT(1946), w; MARAUDERS, THE(1947), w; BORROWED TROUBLE(1948), w; SILENT CONFLICT(1948), w

Charles F. Belden
WE HAVE OUR MOMENTS(1937), w

Charles S. Belden
MYSTERY OF THE WAX MUSEUM, THE(1933), w; FUGITIVE ROAD(1934), w; GHOST WALKS, THE(1935), w; CHARLIE CHAN AT THE OPERA(1936), w; STRANGE MR. GREGORY, THE(1945), w; MILLION DOLLAR WEEKEND(1948), w; DOUBLE DEAL(1950), w

Charles Spencer Belden
SYMPHONY OF LIVING(1935), w

Eileen Belden
PYGMALION(1938, Brit.)

John Belden
HANGMAN'S WHARF(1950, Brit.), w

Dale Beldin
THOMASINE AND BUSHROD(1974), prod d; HIT AND RUN(1982), ed

Dale Belding
INNER SANCTUM(1948); WHO KILLED "DOC" ROBBIN?(1948); MA AND PA KETTLE(1949); MA AND PA KETTLE GO TO TOWN(1950)

Richard Belding
MAGIC TOWN(1947); KILLERS, THE(1964), ed; THIS SAVAGE LAND(1969), ed; TAKE THIS JOB AND SHOVE IT(1981), ed

Charles Beldon
BULLET SCARS(1942), w

Eileen Beldon
POISON PEN(1941, Brit.)

Marguerite Belefonte
NIGHT OF THE QUARTER MOON(1959)

Christian Belegue
CONFORMIST, THE(1971, Ital., Fr)

Belen
CHARLES AND LUCIE(1982, Fr.)

Ana Belen
1984
DEMONS IN THE GARDEN(1984, Span.)

Lucas Belevaux
DEATH OF MARIO RICCI, THE(1983, Ital.)

N. Belevtzeva
ANNA CROSS, THE(1954, USSR)

Belew Twins
ROCK BABY, ROCK IT(1957)

Lucia Belfadel
VOLCANO(1953, Ital.)

Harold Belfaer
SAN FRANCISCO STORY, THE(1952), ch

Hal Belfer
MEET DANNY WILSON(1952), ch; GIRLS IN THE NIGHT(1953), ch; TAKE ME TO TOWN(1953), ch; JUKE BOX RHYTHM(1959), ch; COMANCHEROS, THE(1961), ch; PIRATES OF TORTUGA(1961), ch; DON'T KNOCK THE TWIST(1962), ch; HOOTENANNY HOOT(1963), ch; GET YOURSELF A COLLEGE GIRL(1964), ch; I'D RATHER BE RICH(1964), ch; KISSIN' COUSINS(1964), ch; LOVE-INS, THE(1967), ch; RIDE TO HANGMAN'S TREE, THE(1967), ch; RIOT ON SUNSET STRIP(1967), ch

Harold Belfer
BUCCANEER'S GIRL(1950), ch; LITTLE EGYPT(1951), ch; HAS ANYBODY SEEN MY GAL?(1952), ch; LOST IN ALASKA(1952), ch; SCARLET ANGEL(1952), ch; SON OF ALI BABA(1952), ch; WORLD IN HIS ARMS, THE(1952), ch

Maurice Belfer
CIRCLE OF DECEPTON(1961, Brit.)

Richard Belfield
Silents
JAZZLAND(1928)

Frank Belfin
FABULOUS WORLD OF JULES VERNE, THE(1961, Czech.), md

Frantisek Belfin
VOYAGE TO THE END OF THE UNIVERSE(1963, Czech.), md; DIVINE EMMA, THE(1983, Czech.), md

Gianni Belfiore
DEAD OF SUMMER(1970 Ital./Fr.)

Guy Belfond
STORY OF A THREE DAY PASS, THE(1968, Fr.), p; MISTER FREEDOM(1970, Fr.), p

Christine Belford
GROUNDSTAR CONSPIRACY, THE(1972, Can.); POCKET MONEY(1972); CHRISTINE(1983)

Marta Belfort
Silents
GOLD RUSH, THE(1925)

Bruce Belfrage
C.O.D.(1932, Brit.); TOO MANY MILLIONS(1934, Brit.); FULL CIRCLE(1935, Brit.); SCARLET PIMPERNEL, THE(1935, Brit.); CORRIDOR OF MIRRORS(1948, Brit.); BLACK MAGIC(1949); CASE OF CHARLES PEACE, THE(1949, Brit.); MAN ON THE RUN(1949, Brit.); WARNING TO WANTONS, A(1949, Brit.); HUE AND CRY(1950, Brit.); MISS PILGRIM'S PROGRESS(1950, Brit.); GALLOPING MAJOR, THE(1951, Brit.); HOME TO DANGER(1951, Brit.); NEVER LOOK BACK(1952, Brit.)

Cecil Belfrage
INVISIBLE MAN RETURNS, THE(1940), w

Arnold Belgard
BAR 20 JUSTICE(1938), w; BLOCKHEADS(1938), w; ZENOBIA(1939), w; TRIPLE JUSTICE(1940), w; WOLF OF NEW YORK(1940), w; MY LIFE WITH CAROLINE(1941), w; ROAD SHOW(1941), w; THAT NIGHT WITH YOU(1945), w; DANGEROUS YEARS(1947), w; INVISIBLE WALL, THE(1947), w; SECOND CHANCE(1947), w; HALF PAST MIDNIGHT(1948), w; NIGHT WIND(1948), w; MISS MINK OF 1949(1949), w; TROUBLE PREFERRED(1949), w; TUCSON(1949), w; TARZAN AND THE SLAVE GIRL(1950), w; BOP GIRL GOES CALYPSO(1957), w; PANAMA SAL(1957), w; EAST OF KILIMANJARO(1962, Brit./Ital.), d, w; MIGHTY JUNGLE, THE(1965, U.S./Mex.), d, w

Harold Belgard
TENDER YEARS, THE(1947), w

Cynthia Belgrave
TAKING OF PELHAM ONE, TWO, THREE, THE(1974); HOSPITAL, THE(1971)
1984
DESIREE(1984, Neth.)
Andre Belhomme
CAESAR AND CLEOPATRA(1946, Brit.); LAUGHING LADY, THE(1950, Brit.)
Andrew Belhomme
MAN WITH THE MAGNETIC EYES, THE(1945, Brit.)
Carmen Beliaeff
DOUBLE CONFESSION(1953, Brit.), ed; OPERATION CONSPIRACY(1957, Brit.), ed
Carmen Beliaoff
GOLDEN MADONNA, THE(1949, Brit.), ed
N. Beliava
ANDREI ROUBLOV(1973, USSR), ed
Radu Beligan
STEPS TO THE MOON(1963, Rum.)
Wolfgang Beliharz
ILLUMINATIONS(1976, Aus.), ph
Belin
SELLERS OF GIRLS(1967, Fr.), set d
Graham Belin
UNION CITY(1980), p
L. Belinskaya
Silents
STORM OVER ASIA(1929, USSR)
Bo Belinsky
C'MON, LET'S LIVE A LITTLE(1967)
Monique Belisle
RABID(1976, Can.)
Belita
ICE-CAPADES(1941); SILVER SKATES(1943); LADY, LET'S DANCE(1944); SUSPENSE(1946); GANGSTER, THE(1947); HUNTED, THE(1948); MAN ON THE EIFFEL TOWER, THE(1949); NEVER LET ME GO(1953, U.S./Brit.); INVITATION TO THE DANCE(1956); SILK STOCKINGS(1957); TERRACE, THE(1964, Arg.)
Alan Belkin
DIFFERENT STORY, A(1978), p; FORCE OF ONE, A(1979), p
Bell
MAGIC FACE, THE(1951, Aust.)
Ada Bell
Silents
AFTER A MILLION(1924)
Alfred Bell
CRY WOLF(1968, Brit.); LE MANS(1971); RIDE A WILD PONY(1976, U.S./Aus.); BLUE FIN(1978, Aus.)
Alistair Bell
MOONRAKER, THE(1958, Brit.), w
Anita Bell
NOT RECONCILED, OR "ONLY VIOLENCE HELPS WHERE IT RULES"(1969, Ger.)
Ann Bell
MIDSUMMERS NIGHT'S DREAM, A(1961, Czech); FLAT TWO(1962, Brit.); STOPOVER FOREVER(1964, Brit.); DR. TERROR'S HOUSE OF HORRORS(1965, Brit.); DEVIL'S OWN, THE(1967, Brit.); TO SIR, WITH LOVE(1967, Brit.); RECKONING, THE(1971, Brit.); STATUE, THE(1971, Brit.)
1984
CHAMPIONS(1984)
Anne Bell
FAHRENHEIT 451(1966, Brit.); STUDENT BODIES(1981)
Annie Bell
LA NUIT DE VARENNES(1983, Fr./Ital.)
Aran Bell
1984
LAUGHTER HOUSE(1984, Brit.)
Arnita Bell
SCREAM BLACULA SCREAM(1973)
Arnold Bell
DR. JOSSER KC(1931, Brit.); JOSSER IN THE ARMY(1932, Brit.); DOSS HOUSE(1933, Brit.); SABOTAGE(1937, Brit.); STRANGE EXPERIMENT(1937, Brit.); YOU'RE IN THE ARMY NOW(1937, Brit.); TWO OF US, THE(1938, Brit.); GREED OF WILLIAM HART, THE(1948, Brit.); TEMPTRESS, THE(1949, Brit.); NO PLACE FOR JENNIFER(1950, Brit.); FAKE, THE(1953, Brit.); MURDER AT 3 A.M.(1953, Brit.); SHOOT FIRST(1953, Brit.); TWILIGHT WOMEN(1953, Brit.); GOLDEN LINK, THE(1954, Brit.); PROFILE(1954, Brit.); CONTRABAND SPAIN(1955, Brit.); MASTER PLAN, THE(1955, Brit.); ONE JUMP AHEAD(1955, Brit.); PRIZE OF GOLD, A(1955); SVENGALI(1955, Brit.); STAR OF INDIA(1956, Brit.); AS LONG AS THEY'RE HAPPY(1957, Brit.); MOMENT OF INDISCRETION(1958, Brit.); SAFECRACKER, THE(1958, Brit.); SQUARE PEG, THE(1958, Brit.); THREE CROOKED MEN(1958, Brit.); HIGH JUMP(1959, Brit.); HONOURABLE MURDER, AN(1959, Brit.); INNOCENT MEETING(1959, Brit.); TOP FLOOR GIRL(1959, Brit.); NIGHT TRAIN FOR INVERNESS(1960, Brit.); SENTENCED FOR LIFE(1960, Brit.); VIRGIN ISLAND(1960, Brit.); NOTHING BARRED(1961, Brit.); MAKE MINE A DOUBLE(1962, Brit.); RUNAWAY, THE(1964, Brit.); SEANCE ON A WET AFTERNOON(1964 Brit.); CURSE OF THE FLY(1965, Brit.)
Arthur H. Bell
NAVAJO TRAIL, THE(1945), ed
Barry Bell
REUBEN, REUBEN(1983)
Misc. Talkies
ELECTRIC CHAIR, THE(1977)
Betsy Bell
CLEOPATRA'S DAUGHTER(1963, Fr., Ital.)
Bill Bell
RECESS(1967), art d
Bob Bell
THUNDERBIRD 6(1968, Brit.), art d; THUNDERBIRDS ARE GO(1968, Brit.), art d; JOURNEY TO THE FAR SIDE OF THE SUN(1969, Brit.), art d; WILD GEESE, THE(1978, Brit.), art d; LION OF THE DESERT(1981, Libya/Brit.), art d
Bobbie Bell
RETURN OF THE JEDI(1983)

Bogue Bell
MYSTERY LAKE(1953)
Brand Bell
HELL'S BLOODY DEVILS(1970); SANTEE(1973), w
Brian Bell
1984
RENO AND THE DOC(1984, Can.), m
Carl Bell
PHANTOM TOLLBOOTH, THE(1970), anim; HEY, GOOD LOOKIN'(1982), anim
Charles Bell
I'D RATHER BE RICH(1964)
Misc. Silents
WYOMING(1928)
Charles SchneeThomas Bell
FROM THIS DAY FORWARD(1946), w
Charles W. Bell
PARLOR, BEDROOM AND BATH(1931), w
Christopher Bell
IT HAPPENED HERE(1966, Brit.)
Chuck Bell
WEREWOLVES ON WHEELS(1971), stunts
Clark Bell
NO RETURN ADDRESS(1961), w
Cliff Bell
DUKE OF CHICAGO(1949), ed; DOUBLE JEOPARDY(1955), ed; JAGUAR(1956), ed; SATAN'S SATELLITES(1958), ed; GHOST OF ZORRO(1959), ed
Cliff Bell, Jr.
SKULLDUGGERY(1970)
Colin Bell
RESCUE SQUAD, THE(1963, Brit.), d
Crissie Bell
Silents
MESSAGE FROM MARS, A(1913, Brit.)
Cynthia Bell
THOSE REDHEADS FROM SEATTLE(1953)
Daniel Bell
FANNY AND ALEXANDER(1983, Swed./Fr./Ger.), m
Derrick Bell
WIZ, THE(1978)
Digby Bell
Misc. Silents
FATHER AND THE BOYS(1915)
Don Bell
DISC JOCKEY(1951); BOYS IN COMPANY C, THE(1978, U.S./Hong Kong)
Dorothy Bell
FOREVER AND A DAY(1943)
Doug Bell
CHANGES(1969)
Douglas Bell
LIEUTENANT DARING, RN(1935, Brit.)
Earl Bell
PERSONAL BEST(1982)
Ed Bell
PASSION HOLIDAY(1963)
Eda Bell
OLD MOTHER RILEY OVERSEAS(1943, Brit.)
Edith Bell
LOVE HUNGER(1965, Arg.), makeup; THE CRAZIES(1973)
Edward Bell
TERROR-CREATURES FROM THE GRAVE(1967, U.S./Ital.); PREMONITION, THE(1976)
Eileen Bell
FROZEN LIMITS, THE(1939, Brit.); INSPECTOR HORNLEIGH ON HOLIDAY(1939, Brit.)
Emily Bell
NIGHT THEY ROBBED BIG BERTHA'S, THE(1975)
Enid Bell
Misc. Silents
MOTHER OF DARTMOOR, THE(1916, Brit.)
Freddie Bell
RUMBLE ON THE DOCKS(1956), m/l Jimmy DeKnight
Frederic Bell
PATHS OF GLORY(1957)
Gaston Bell
Silents
FORTUNE HUNTER, THE(1914); HOUSE NEXT DOOR, THE(1914); DESTRUCTION(1915)
Misc. Silents
GAMBLERS, THE(1914); LION AND THE MOUSE, THE(1914); THIRD DEGREE, THE(1914); WOLF, THE(1914)
Gene Bell
DAYS OF HEAVEN(1978)
Genevieve Bell
SO'S YOUR UNCLE(1943); FOLLOW THE BOYS(1944); DON JUAN QUILLIGAN(1945); HER LUCKY NIGHT(1945); MACAO(1952); PHONE CALL FROM A STRANGER(1952); SOMETHING TO LIVE FOR(1952)
George Bell
LOVES OF CARMEN, THE(1948); SHOOT-OUT AT MEDICINE BEND(1957)
Gladys Bell
Misc. Silents
STRIPPED FOR A MILLION(1919)
Gordon Bell
GIRL IN THE PAINTING, THE(1948, Brit.); DECAMERON NIGHTS(1953, Brit.); GHOST SHIP(1953, Brit.); FRONT PAGE STORY(1954, Brit.); MAN WHO NEVER WAS, THE(1956, Brit.)
Gurney Bell
IRISH EYES ARE SMILING(1944)

Hank Bell
ABRAHAM LINCOLN(1930); MIN AND BILL(1930); NEAR THE RAINBOW'S END(1930); SHADOW RANCH(1930); TRAILS OF DANGER(1930); MAN FROM DEATH VALLEY, THE(1931); BEYOND THE ROCKIES(1932); BIG STAMPEDE, THE(1932); RIDING TORNADO, THE(1932); SINGLE-HANDED SANDERS(1932); SOUTH OF SANTA FE(1932); TEXAS PIONEERS(1932); WHISTLIN' DAN(1932); YOUNG BLOOD(1932); COME ON TARZAN(1933); DUDE BANDIT, THE(1933); FARGO EXPRESS(1933); FIGHTING CHAMP(1933); TERROR TRAIL(1933); BLUE STEEL(1934); DUDE RANGER, THE(1934); FIDDLIN' BUCKAROO, THE(1934); GUN JUSTICE(1934); HONOR OF THE RANGE(1934); SAGEBRUSH TRAIL(1934); SMOKING GUNS(1934); THUNDER OVER TEXAS(1934); TRAIL DRIVE, THE(1934); WHEELS OF DESTINY(1934); CHEYENNE TORNADO(1935); CIRCLE OF DEATH(1935); OUTLAW DEPUTY, THE(1935); END OF THE TRAIL(1936); LAWLESS RIDERS(1936); LUCKY TERROR(1936); MAN FROM GUN TOWN, THE(1936); RED RIVER VALLEY(1936); TEXAS RANGERS, THE(1936); THUNDERBOLT(1936); TRAIL OF THE LONESOME PINE, THE(1936); WESTWARD HO(1936); DODGE CITY TRAIL(1937); ONE MAN JUSTICE(1937); PLAINSMAN, THE(1937); THUNDER TRAIL(1937); TWO GUN LAW(1937); COLORADO TRAIL(1938); GIRL OF THE GOLDEN WEST, THE(1938); GUN LAW(1938); OUTLAWS OF THE PRAIRIE(1938); RENEGADE RANGER(1938); SOUTH OF ARIZONA(1938); WEST OF SANTA FE(1938); FIGHTING GRINGO, THE(1939); FRONTIER PONY EXPRESS(1939); LET FREEDOM RING(1939); OKLAHOMA FRONTIER(1939); RIO GRANDE(1939); ROUGH RIDERS' ROUNDUP(1939); SILVER ON THE SAGE(1939); SPOILERS OF THE RANGE(1939); TAMING OF THE WEST, THE(1939); TEXAS STAMPEDE(1939); THUNDERING WEST, THE(1939); WESTERN CARAVANS(1939); CARSON CITY KID(1940); CHIP OF THE FLYING U(1940); MY LITTLE CHICKADEE(1940); RIDERS OF PASCO BASIN(1940); ROCKY MOUNTAIN RANGERS(1940); TRAIL OF THE VIGILANTES(1940); WESTBOUND STAGE(1940); WESTERNER, THE(1940); YOUNG BILL HICKOK(1940); YOUNG BUFFALO BILL(1940); BORDER VIGILANTES(1941); DOWN MEXICO WAY(1941); JESSE JAMES AT BAY(1941); NEVADA CITY(1941); NORTH FROM LONE STAR(1941); PINTO KID, THE(1941); RETURN OF DANIEL BOONE, THE(1941); RIDERS OF THE TIMBERLINE(1941); SHEPHERD OF THE HILLS, THE(1941); TONTO BASIN OUTLAWS(1941); WRANGLER'S ROOST(1941); BILLY THE KID TRAPPED(1942); GREAT MAN'S LADY, THE(1942); HEART OF THE GOLDEN WEST(1942); ROCK RIVER RENEGADES(1942); SHUT MY BIG MOUTH(1942); SILVER BULLET, THE(1942); SOMBRERO KID, THE(1942); SOUTH OF SANTA FE(1942); STAGECOACH BUCKAROO(1942); VALLEY OF THE SUN(1942); CATTLE STAMPEDE(1943); HAUNTED RANCH, THE(1943); LAW RIDES AGAIN, THE(1943); MAN FROM MUSIC MOUNTAIN(1943); OVERLAND MAIL ROBBERY(1943); OX-BOW INCIDENT, THE(1943); RAIDERS OF SUNSET PASS(1943); WAGON TRACKS WEST(1943); CODE OF THE PRAIRIE(1944); FIREBRANDS OF ARIZONA(1944); JAM SESSION(1944); MYSTERY MAN(1944); SAN FERNANDO VALLEY(1944); ALONG CAME JONES(1945); CHEROKEE FLASH, THE(1945); EVE KNEW HER APPLES(1945); FLAME OF THE BARBARY COAST(1945); GREAT STAGECOACH ROBBERY(1945); ROUGH RIDERS OF CHEYENNE(1945); SALOME, WHERE SHE DANCED(1945); SARATOGA TRUNK(1945); SHE GETS HER MAN(1945); STAGECOACH OUTLAWS(1945); SUNSET IN EL DORADO(1945); TOPEKA TERROR, THE(1945); PLAINSMAN AND THE LADY(1946); RUSTLER'S ROUNDUP(1946); CHEYENNE TAKES OVER(1947); GALLANT LEGION, THE(1948); LOADED PISTOLS(1948); PLUNDERERS, THE(1948); TORNADO RANGE(1948); LAST BANDIT, THE(1949); RED DESERT(1949); COPPER CANYON(1950); FANCY PANTS(1950); GUNSLINGERS(1950); OVER THE BORDER(1950); MONTANA BELLE(1952)
Misc. Talkies
PUEBLO TERROR(1931); LAW OF THE WEST(1932); BORDER VENGEANCE(1935)
Silents
LAST STRAW, THE(1920); PONY EXPRESS, THE(1925); ACE OF ACTION(1926); FIGHTING TERROR, THE(1929); LAST ROUNDUP, THE(1929)
Misc. Silents
DOUBLE DARING(1926); CODE OF THE COW COUNTRY(1927); SADDLE MATES(1928); 'NEATH WESTERN SKIES(1929)

Hermione Bell
GIDEON OF SCOTLAND YARD(1959, Brit.)

High Bell
BLACK RODEO(1972), ph

Howard Bell
VENOM(1982, Brit.)
Silents
ISLE OF HOPE, THE(1925)

Hugh Bell
THEY SHOOT HORSES, DON'T THEY?(1969)

Ivery Bell
NOCTURNA(1979)

J. Eric Bell
HONEYBABY, HONEYBABY(1974)

J. Ford Bell
Misc. Talkies
DANGEROUS RELATIONS(1973), d

J. J. Bell
Silents
THOU FOOL(1926, Brit.), w

Jack Bell
SUGAR HILL(1974)
Misc. Talkies
RIM OF HELL(1970)

James Bell
I AM A FUGITIVE FROM A CHAIN GANG(1932); DAY OF RECKONING(1933); INFERNAL MACHINE(1933); KING'S VACATION, THE(1933); MONKEY'S PAW, THE(1933); PRIVATE DETECTIVE 62(1933); WHITE WOMAN(1933); STUDENT TOUR(1934); LIVES OF A BENGAL LANCER(1935); HOLIDAY INN(1942); GANGWAY FOR TOMORROW(1943); I WALKED WITH A ZOMBIE(1943); LEOPARD MAN, THE(1943); MY FRIEND FLICKA(1943); SO PROUDLY WE HAIL(1943); I LOVE A SOLDIER(1944); BLOOD ON THE SUN(1945); GIRL OF THE LIMBERLOST, THE(1945); THUNDERHEAD-SON OF FLICKA(1945); SPIRAL STAIRCASE, THE(1946); UNKNOWN, THE(1946); BRUTE FORCE(1947); DEAD RECKONING(1947); DRIFTWOOD(1947); KILLER McCOY(1947); MILLERSON CASE, THE(1947); PHILO VANCE'S SECRET MISSION(1947); ROMANCE OF ROSY RIDGE, THE(1947); SEA OF GRASS, THE(1947); BLACK EAGLE(1948); I, JANE DOE(1948); SEALED VERDICT(1948); ROUGHSHOD(1949); STREETS OF LAREDO(1949); COMPANY SHE KEEPS, THE(1950); DIAL 1119(1950); ARIZONA MANHUNT(1951);

BUCKAROO SHERIFF OF TEXAS(1951); DAKOTA KID, THE(1951); RED MOUNTAIN(1951); JAPANESE WAR BRIDE(1952); MILLION DOLLAR MERMAID(1952); RIDE THE MAN DOWN(1952); WILD HORSE AMBUSH(1952); ALL THE BROTHERS WERE VALIANT(1953); DEVIL'S CANYON(1953); GLENN MILLER STORY, THE(1953); LAST POSSE, THE(1953); ABOUT MRS. LESLIE(1954); CRIME WAVE(1954); RIDING SHOTGUN(1954); BLACK TUESDAY(1955); LAWLESS STREET, A(1955); LAY THAT RIFLE DOWN(1955); SINCERELY YOURS(1955); STRANGER ON HORSEBACK(1955); STRATEGIC AIR COMMAND(1955); TEEN-AGE CRIME WAVE(1955); TEXAS LADY(1955); DAY OF FURY, A(1956); FOUR GIRLS IN TOWN(1956); HUK(1956); SEARCH FOR BRIDEY MURPHY, THE(1956); TRIBUTE TO A BADMAN(1956); BACK FROM THE DEAD(1957); JOHNNY TROUBLE(1957); LONELY MAN, THE(1957); TIN STAR, THE(1957); IN LOVE AND WAR(1958); –30–(1959); OREGON TRAIL, THE(1959); CLAUDELLE INGLISH(1961); POSSE FROM HELL(1961); TWILIGHT OF HONOR(1963)
Misc. Talkies
BLIND SPOT(1947)

Jeanie Bell
MELINDA(1972); THREE THE HARD WAY(1974); CHOIRBOYS, THE(1977)
Misc. Talkies
MUTHERS, THE(1976); DISCO 9000(1977)

Jeann Bell
GLAMOUR GIRL(1947)

Jeanne Bell
BLACK GUNN(1972); TNT JACKSON(1975)

Jeannie Bell
MEAN STREETS(1973); KLANSMAN, THE(1974); POLICEWOMAN(1974)

Jeffrey Bell
FRENCH MISTRESS(1960, Brit.), w

Jerry Bell
EDUCATION OF SONNY CARSON, THE(1974)

Jimmy Bell
2001: A SPACE ODYSSEY(1968, U.S./Brit.)

Joanie Bell
THIS LOVE OF OURS(1945)

Joe Bell
HAPPY BIRTHDAY, DAVY(1970)

John Bell
RELUCTANT WIDOW, THE(1951, Brit.); BREAK OF DAY(1977, Aus.)

Johnny Bell
CONRACK(1974)

Jonn Bell
CHELSEA STORY(1951, Brit.)

Judith Bell
SERPENTS OF THE PIRATE MOON, THE(1973), m

Kathey Bell
HERE COME THE TIGERS(1978)

Kay Bell
EVERYBODY DOES IT(1949); THOSE REDHEADS FROM SEATTLE(1953)

Keith Bell
ISLAND OF TERROR(1967, Brit.); FIRST LOVE(1970, Ger./Switz.); HANDS OF THE RIPPER(1971, Brit.); MACKINTOSH MAN, THE(1973, Brit.); MOMENTS(1974, Brit.)

Kenneth Bell
TOGETHER BROTHERS(1974)

Kenny Bell
MR. MAJESTYK(1974)

Leonard Bell
I WANT TO LIVE!(1958)

Marjorie Bell [Marge Chapion]
HONOR OF THE WEST(1939)

Marie Bell
NIGHT IS OURS(1930, Fr.); UN CARNET DE BAL(1938, Fr.); COLONEL CHABERT(1947, Fr.); LA BONNE SOUPE(1964, Fr./Ital.); HOTEL PARADISO(1966, U.S./Brit.); SANDRA(1966, Ital.)
Misc. Silents
LE VALSE DE L'ADIEU(1928, Fr.); MADAME RECAMIER(1928, Fr.)

Marion Bell
ZIEGFELD FOLLIES(1945)

Marshall Bell
1984
BIRDY(1984)

Martin Bell
TIGER MAKES OUT, THE(1967), makeup; LOVE STORY(1970), makeup; SHAFT(1971), makeup; SHAFT'S BIG SCORE(1972), makeup; SIR HENRY AT RAWLINSON END(1980, Brit.), ph

Mary Bell
SHRIKE, THE(1955)

Mary Beth Bell
NICKELODEON(1976)

[Mary] Hayley Bell
VINTAGE WINE(1935, Brit.)

Mary Hayley Bell
SCOTT OF THE ANTARCTIC(1949, Brit.), w; WHISTLE DOWN THE WIND(1961, Brit.), w; GYPSY GIRL(1966, Brit.), w

Melita Bell
GIRL IN THE CROWD, THE(1934, Brit.)

Melodie Bell
10 VIOLENT WOMEN(1982)

Michael Bell
HELL, HEAVEN OR HOBOKEN(1958, Brit.); FIRST MAN INTO SPACE(1959, Brit.); IDOL ON PARADE(1959, Brit.); SUBWAY IN THE SKY(1959, Brit.); TOO YOUNG TO LOVE(1960, Brit.); V.D.(1961); GREAT VAN ROBBERY, THE(1963, Brit.); WAR IS HELL(1964); POINT BLANK(1967); THUNDER ALLEY(1967); BROTHER JOHN(1971); PROUD RIDER, THE(1971, Can.); ROLLERCOASTER(1977); HOW TO BEAT THE HIGH COST OF LIVING(1980); HEIDI'S SONG(1982)

Monta Bell
APPLAUSE(1929), p; BELLAMY TRIAL, THE(1929), d; COCOANUTS, THE(1929), p; HOLE IN THE WALL(1929), p; LETTER, THE(1929), p, w, ed; EAST IS WEST(1930), d; YOUNG MAN OF MANHATTAN(1930), d; PERSONAL MAID(1931), d; UP FOR MURDER(1931), d, w; DOWNSTAIRS(1932), d; WORST WOMAN IN PARIS(1933), d, w; MEN IN WHITE(1934), p; STUDENT TOUR(1934), p; WEST POINT OF THE

AIR(1935), p; BEYOND THE BLUE HORIZON(1942), p; CHINA'S LITTLE DE-VILS(1945), d
Silents
PILGRIM, THE(1923); WOMAN OF PARIS, A(1923), ed; BROADWAY AFTER DARK(1924), d; SNOB, THE(1924), d&w; LADY OF THE NIGHT(1925), d; PRETTY LADIES(1925), d; TORRENT, THE(1926), d; AFTER MIDNIGHT(1927), d&w
Misc. Silents
HOW TO EDUCATE A WIFE(1924), d; KING ON MAIN STREET, THE(1925), d; LIGHTS OF OLD BROADWAY(1925), d; BOY FRIEND, THE(1926), d; UP-STAGE(1926), d; MAN, WOMAN AND SIN(1927), d

Nancy Bell
TAKING OFF(1971); FUTUREWORLD(1976)

Neil Bell
QUERELLE(1983, Ger./Fr.)
1984
LOVE STREAMS(1984)

Olive Bell
Silents
HOLY ORDERS(1917, Brit.)

Patty Bell
RETURN OF THE JEDI(1983)

Pearl Doles Bell
Silents
HER ELEPHANT MAN(1920), w; WING TOY(1921), w

Peter Bell
NATE AND HAYES(1983, U.S./New Zealand)

R. J. Bell
SUPERMAN III(1983)

Rachel Bell
SWEET WILLIAM(1980, Brit.)

Ralph Bell
CLANCY IN WALL STREET(1930), w; COCK O' THE WALK(1930), w; EDGE OF THE CITY(1957); WOLFEN(1981); ZELIG(1983)
Misc. Silents
FOUR FLUSHER, THE(1919)

Rex Bell
PLEASURE CRAZED(1929); SALUTE(1929); THEY HAD TO SEE PARIS(1929); COURAGE(1930); HAPPY DAYS(1930); HARMONY AT HOME(1930); LIGHT-NIN'(1930); TRUE TO THE NAVY(1930); ARM OF THE LAW(1932); BROADWAY TO CHEYENNE(1932); FORGOTTEN WOMEN(1932); LAW OF THE SEA(1932); CRASH-ING BROADWAY(1933); DIAMOND TRAIL(1933); FIGHTING TEXANS(1933); FUGI-TIVE, THE(1933); LUCKY LARRIGAN(1933); RAINBOW RANCH(1933); FIGHTING PIONEERS(1935); MEN OF THE PLAINS(1936); STORMY TRAILS(1936); TOO MUCH BEEF(1936); WEST OF NEVADA(1936); IDAHO KID, THE(1937); LAW AND LEAD(1937); DAWN ON THE GREAT DIVIDE(1942); TOMBSTONE, THE TOWN TOO TOUGH TO DIE(1942); LONE STAR(1952)
Misc. Talkies
MAN FROM ARIZONA, THE(1932); GUNFIRE(1935); SADDLE ACES(1935); TONTO KID, THE(1935)
Silents
JOY STREET(1929)
Misc. Silents
COWBOY KID, THE(1928); GIRL-SHY COWBOY, THE(1928); TAKING A CHAN-CE(1928); WILD WEST ROMANCE(1928)

Rex Bell, Jr.
STAGE TO THUNDER ROCK(1964); YOUNG FURY(1965)

Rickey Bell
OLGA'S GIRLS(1964); MY BODY HUNGERS(1967)

Robert Bell
GOD'S COUNTRY AND THE WOMAN(1937); WHILE I LIVE(1947, Brit.), w; LIVING VENUS(1961); NORSEMAN, THE(1978), ed

Rod Bell
LITTLE MISS BIG(1946)

Rodney Bell
UNCLE HARRY(1945); ANGEL COMES TO BROOKLYN, AN(1945); SCARLET STREET(1945); CENTENNIAL SUMMER(1946); DARK MIRROR, THE(1946); LIVE WIRES(1946); BLONDIE'S HOLIDAY(1947); MY WILD IRISH ROSE(1947); SENATOR WAS INDISCREET, THE(1947); FATHER WAS A FULLBACK(1949); JOHN LOVES MARY(1949); FILE ON THELMA JORDAN, THE(1950); CLOSE TO MY HEART(1951); GUY WHO CAME BACK, THE(1951); MEET ME AFTER THE SHOW(1951); MON-TANA BELLE(1952); SOMETHING FOR THE BIRDS(1952); HITCH-HIKER, THE(1953); LADY WANTS MINK, THE(1953); WOMAN'S WORLD(1954); TRIAL(1955); FOUR GIRLS IN TOWN(1956); PHANTOM FROM 10,000 LEAGUES(1956); MISSOURI TRAVELER, THE(1958); WINK OF AN EYE(1958); ROOKIE, THE(1959); GO NAKED IN THE WORLD(1961)

Ronnie Bell
FIREBALL JUNGLE(1968); MY BROTHER'S WEDDING(1983)

Russ Bellak
FATAL LADY(1936)

Sam Bell
Misc. Talkies
DANGEROUS RELATIONS(1973)

Sharon Bell
SECOND GREATEST SEX, THE(1955)

Sonny Bell
DEMON LOVER, THE(1977)

Spencer Bell
MIDNIGHT TAXI, THE(1928); SMART MONEY(1931)
Silents
OUTLAW DOG, THE(1927); PEACOCK FAN(1929)
Misc. Silents
TENDERFEET(1928), d

Stephanie A. Bell
EMMA MAE(1976), cos

Steve Bell
DEAR HEART(1964)

Susan Bell
WHO IS HARRY KELLERMAN AND WHY IS HE SAYING THOSE TERRIBLE THINGS ABOUT ME?(1971)

Temple Bell
Silents
AMAZING PARTNERSHIP, THE(1921, Brit.)
Misc. Silents
COLONEL NEWCOME THE PERFECT GENTLEMAN(1920, Brit.)

Thom Bell
FISH THAT SAVED PITTSBURGH, THE(1979), m; STRANGE BREW(1983)

Tita Bell
BABY BLUE MARINE(1976)

Tom Bell
KELLY THE SECOND(1936), w; ECHO OF BARBARA(1961, Brit.); KITCHEN, THE(1961, Brit.); DAMN THE DEFIANT!(1962, Brit.); L-SHAPED ROOM, THE(1962, Brit.); PAYROLL(1962, Brit.); PRIZE OF ARMS, A(1962, Brit.); REBELS AGAINST THE LIGHT(1964); BLUES FOR LOVERS(1966, Brit.); HE WHO RIDES A TIGER(1966, Brit.); SANDS OF BEERSHEBA(1966, U.S./Israel); IN ENEMY COUNTRY(1968); LONG DAY'S DYING, THE(1968, Brit.); LOCK UP YOUR DAUGHTERS(1969, Brit.); VIOLENT ENEMY, THE(1969, Brit.); QUEST FOR LOVE(1971, Brit.); ALL THE RIGHT NOISES(1973, Brit.); STRAIGHT ON TILL MORNING(1974, Brit.); ROYAL FLASH(1975, Brit.); SAILOR'S RETURN, THE(1978, Brit.); STRONGER THAN THE SUN(1980, Brit.)

Vereen Bell
SWAMP WATER(1941), w; LURE OF THE WILDERNESS(1952), w

Vinnie Bell
IF EVER I SEE YOU AGAIN(1978)

Virginia Bell
FRAULEIN DOKTOR(1969, Ital./Yugo.)
Misc. Talkies
LARIATS AND SIXSHOOTERS(1931)

W.R. Bell
Misc. Silents
HARP KING, THE(1920, Brit.)

Wayne Bell
TEXAS CHAIN SAW MASSACRE, THE(1974), m
1984
LAST NIGHT AT THE ALAMO(1984), m

William Bell
Silents
GOLD RUSH, THE(1925)

Bell Sisters
CRUISIN' DOWN THE RIVER(1953)

Blanche Bella
Misc. Silents
BILLY'S SPANISH LOVE SPASM(1915, Brit.); MAN IN POSSESSION, THE(1915, Brit.); ONLY MAN, THE(1915, Brit.)

Frank Bella
LOOKIN' TO GET OUT(1982)

Giuseppe Bella
QUIET PLACE IN THE COUNTRY, A(1970, Ital./Fr.); ANONYMOUS VENETIAN, THE(1971)

Max Bella
DARWIN ADVENTURE, THE(1972, Brit.), w

Nicholas Bella
HEADLEYS AT HOME, THE(1939), w

Carmen Bellaeff
CALL OF THE BLOOD(1948, Brit.), ed

James Bellah
MAN BEHIND THE GUN, THE(1952)

James Warner Bellah
DANCING LADY(1933), w; FORT APACHE(1948), w; SHE WORE A YELLOW RIBBON(1949), w; RIO GRANDE(1950), w; TEN TALL MEN(1951), w; COMMAND, THE(1954), w; SEA CHASE, THE(1955), w; TARGET ZERO(1955), w; SERGEANT RUTLEDGE(1960), w; THUNDER OF DRUMS, A(1961), w; X-15(1961), w; MAN WHO SHOT LIBERTY VALANCE, THE(1962), w; LEGEND OF NIGGER CHARLEY, THE(1972), w

John Bellah
LIMIT, THE(1972)

Ross Bellah
NINE GIRLS(1944), art d; HER FIRST ROMANCE(1951), art d; LAST OF THE COMANCHES(1952), art d; PAULA(1952), art d; TARGET HONG KONG(1952), art d; GUN FURY(1953), art d; LAST OF THE PONY RIDERS(1953), art d; SAGINAW TRAIL(1953), art d; QUEEN BEE(1955), art d; VIOLENT MEN, THE(1955), art d; NIGHTFALL(1956), art d; SOLID GOLD CADILLAC, THE(1956), art d; WHITE SQUAW, THE(1956), art d; JEANNE EAGELS(1957), art d; PHANTOM STAGE-COACH, THE(1957), art d; LINEUP, THE(1958), art d; TRUE STORY OF LYNN STUART, THE(1958), art d; GIDGET(1959), art d; HEY BOY! HEY GIRL!(1959), art d; STRANGERS WHEN WE MEET(1960), art d; LADIES MAN, THE(1961), art d

George Bellak
INVISIBLE AVENGER, THE(1958), w; TOO MANY THIEVES(1968), w

Marcia Bellak
DR. COPPELIUS(1968, U.S./Span.)

Henry Bellamann
KING'S ROW(1942), w

Ann Bellamy
BORN LOSERS(1967)
Misc. Talkies
BABYSITTER, THE(1969)

Anne Bellamy
WESTWORLD(1973)

Diana Bellamy
D.C. CAB(1983)

Earl Bellamy
SEMINOLE UPRISING(1955), d; BLACKJACK KETCHUM, DESPERADO(1956), d; TOUGHEST GUN IN TOMBSTONE(1958), d; STAGECOACH TO DANCER'S PARK(1962), p&d; FLUFFY(1965), d; GUNPOINT(1966), d; INCIDENT AT PHAN-TOM HILL(1966), d; MUNSTER, GO HOME(1966), d; THREE GUNS FOR TEX-AS(1968), d; BACKTRACK(1969), d; AGAINST A CROOKED SKY(1975), d; SEVEN ALONE(1975), d; SIDECAR RACERS(1975, Aus.), d; WALKING TALL, PART II(1975), d; SIDEWINDER ONE(1977), d; SPEEDTRAP(1978), d

Eileen Bellamy
Silents
FATHER O'FLYNN(1919, Brit.)
Franklin Bellamy
YELLOW STOCKINGS(1930, Brit.); LET'S BE FAMOUS(1939, Brit.)
Franklyn Bellamy
WOLVES(1930, Brit.); NIGHT BIRDS(1931, Brit.); BARTON MYSTERY, THE(1932, Brit.); LEAP YEAR(1932, Brit.); MURDER ON THE SECOND FLOOR(1932, Brit.); IT'S A KING(1933, Brit.); LITTLE DAMOZEL, THE(1933, Brit.); UP FOR THE DERBY(1933, Brit.); EXPERT'S OPINION(1935, Brit.); LAST CHANCE, THE(1937, Brit.); MEMBER OF THE JURY(1937, Brit.); MR. SMITH CARRIES ON(1937, Brit.); SPLINTERS IN THE AIR(1937, Brit.)
Silents
POWER OVER MEN(1929, Brit.)
Misc. Silents
FOR HER PEOPLE(1914, Brit.); GOD'S CLAY(1928, Brit.)

George Bellamy
OFFICER'S MESS, THE(1931, Brit.); MIXED DOUBLES(1933, Brit.)
Silents
PRISONER OF ZENDA, THE(1915, Brit.); RUPERT OF HENTZAU(1915, Brit.); ANSWER, THE(1916, Brit.); FATAL FINGERS(1916. Brit.); HARD WAY, THE(1916, Brit.); AULD LANG SYNE(1917, Brit.); ENCHANTMENT(1920, Brit.); ERNEST MALTRAVERS(1920, Brit.); JUDGE NOT(1920, Brit.); TRUE TILDA(1920, Brit.); IN HIS GRIP(1921, Brit.); OLD COUNTRY, THE(1921, Brit.); OPEN COUNTRY(1922, Brit.); MATING OF MARCUS, THE(1924, Brit.); NOT FOR SALE(1924, Brit.); MR. NOBODY(1927, Brit.); NOT QUITE A LADY(1928, Brit.); LADY NOGGS-PEERESS(1929, Brit.)
Misc. Silents
CALLED BACK(1914, Brit.); SCORPION'S STING, THE(1915, Brit.); HONOUR IN PAWN(1916, Brit.); MOTHER OF DARTMOOR, THE(1916, Brit.); LAUGHING CAVALIER, THE(1917, Brit.); QUICKSANDS(1917, a, d); BLACK SHEEP, THE(1920, Brit.); LORNA DOONE(1920, Brit.); UNCLE DICK'S DARLING(1920, Brit.); WOMAN OF THE IRON BRACELETS, THE(1920, Brit.); PRINCESS OF NEW YORK, THE(1921 US/Brit.)

Madge Bellamy
MOTHER KNOWS BEST(1928); TONIGHT AT TWELVE(1929); WHITE ZOMBIE(1932); GIGOLETTES OF PARIS(1933); CHARLIE CHAN IN LONDON(1934); DARING YOUNG MAN, THE(1935); GREAT HOTEL MURDER(1935); UNDER YOUR SPELL(1936); NORTHWEST TRAIL(1945)
Misc. Talkies
RIOT SQUAD(1933)
Silents
RIDDLE: WOMAN, THE(1920); BLIND HEARTS(1921); ARE YOU A FAILURE?(1923); GARRISON'S FINISH(1923); SOUL OF THE BEAST(1923); IRON HORSE, THE(1924); NO MORE WOMEN(1924); ON THE STROKE OF THREE(1924); LAZYBONES(1925); RECKLESS SEX, THE(1925); SANDY(1926); SUMMER BACHELORS(1926); ANKLES PREFERRED(1927); BERTHA, THE SEWING MACHINE GIRL(1927); LORNA DOONE(1927); SILK LEGS(1927); TELEPHONE GIRL, THE(1927); PLAY GIRL, THE(1928); FUGITIVES(1929)
Misc. Silents
CALL OF THE NORTH, THE(1921); CUP OF LIFE, THE(1921); LOVE NEVER DIES(1921); PASSING THRU(1921); HOTTENTOT, THE(1922); DO IT NOW(1924); HIS FORGOTTEN WIFE(1924); LOVE AND GLORY(1924); WHITE SIN, THE(1924); DANCERS, THE(1925); FOOL AND HIS MONEY, A(1925); GOLDEN STRAIN, THE(1925); HAVOC(1925); LIGHTNIN'(1925); MAN IN BLUE, THE(1925); PARASITE, THE(1925); SECRETS OF THE NIGHT(1925); THUNDER MOUNTAIN(1925); WINGS OF YOUTH(1925); BLACK PARADISE(1926); DIXIE MERCHANT, THE(1926); COLLEEN(1927); VERY CONFIDENTIAL(1927); SOFT LIVING(1928)

Mark Bellamy
BRAIN MACHINE, THE(1955, Brit.); COUNTERFEIT PLAN, THE(1957, Brit.)
Patsy Bellamy
LIGHTNING RANGE(1934); MURDER WITH PICTURES(1936)
Ralph Bellamy
MAGNIFICENT LIE(1931); SECRET SIX, THE(1931); SURRENDER(1931); WEST OF BROADWAY(1931); AIR MAIL(1932); ALMOST MARRIED(1932); DISORDERLY CONDUCT(1932); FORBIDDEN(1932); REBECCA OF SUNNYBROOK FARM(1932); WILD GIRL(1932); WOMAN IN ROOM 13, THE(1932); YOUNG AMERICA(1932); ACE OF ACES(1933); BELOW THE SEA(1933); BLIND ADVENTURE(1933); DESTINATION UNKNOWN(1933); EVER IN MY HEART(1933); FLYING DEVILS(1933); HEADLINE SHOOTER(1933); NARROW CORNER, THE(1933); PAROLE GIRL(1933); PICTURE SNATCHER(1933); SECOND HAND WIFE(1933); BEFORE MIDNIGHT(1934); CRIME OF HELEN STANLEY(1934); GIRL IN DANGER(1934); ONCE TO EVERY WOMAN(1934); ONE IS GUILTY(1934); SPITFIRE(1934); THIS MAN IS MINE(1934); WOMAN IN THE DARK(1934); AIR HAWKS(1935); EIGHT BELLS(1935); GIGOLETTE(1935); HANDS ACROSS THE TABLE(1935); HEALER, THE(1935); HELLDORADO(1935); RENDEZVOUS AT MIDNIGHT(1935); WEDDING NIGHT, THE(1935); DANGEROUS INTRIGUE(1936); FINAL HOUR, THE(1936); MAN WHO LIVED TWICE(1936); NAVY WIFE(1936); ROAMING LADY(1936); STRAIGHT FROM THE SHOULDER(1936); WILD BRIAN KENT(1936); AWFUL TRUTH, THE(1937); COUNTERFEIT LADY(1937); IT CAN'T LAST FOREVER(1937); LET'S GET MARRIED(1937); BOY MEETS GIRL(1938); CAREFREE(1938); CRIME OF DR. HALLET(1938); FOOLS FOR SCANDAL(1938); GIRLS' SCHOOL(1938); TRADE WINDS(1938); BLIND ALLEY(1939); COAST GUARD(1939); LET US LIVE(1939); SMASHING THE SPY RING(1939); BROTHER ORCHID(1940); DANCE, GIRL, DANCE(1940); ELLERY QUEEN. MASTER DETECTIVE(1940); FLIGHT ANGELS(1940); HIS GIRL FRIDAY(1940); MEET THE WILDCAT(1940); PUBLIC DEB NO. 1(1940); QUEEN OF THE MOB(1940); AFFECTIONATELY YOURS(1941); DIVE BOMBER(1941); ELLERY QUEEN AND THE MURDER RING(1941); ELLERY QUEEN AND THE PERFECT CRIME(1941); ELLERY QUEEN'S PENTHOUSE MYSTERY(1941); FOOTSTEPS IN THE DARK(1941); WOLF MAN, THE(1941); GHOST OF FRANKENSTEIN, THE(1942); GREAT IMPERSONATION, THE(1942); LADY IN A JAM(1942); MEN OF TEXAS(1942); STAGE DOOR CANTEEN(1943); GUEST IN THE HOUSE(1944); DELIGHTFULLY DANGEROUS(1945); LADY ON A TRAIN(1945); COURT-MARTIAL OF BILLY MITCHELL, THE(1955); SUNRISE AT CAMPOBELLO(1960); PROFESSIONALS, THE(1966); ROSEMARY'S BABY(1968); DOCTORS' WIVES(1971); CANCEL MY RESERVATION(1972); OH, GOD!(1977); TRADING PLACES(1983)
Misc. Talkies
BEAUTY'S DAUGHTER(1935); BILLION DOLLAR THREAT, THE(1979, Brit.)

Richard Bellamy
SWEET SUBSTITUTE(1964, Can.), ph
Somers Bellamy
Silents
IF FOUR WALLS TOLD(1922, Brit.)
Misc. Silents
HEARTS THAT ARE HUMAN(1915, Brit.)
Ferdinand Bellan
DARK JOURNEY(1937, Brit.), prod d
Jana Bellan
AMERICAN GRAFFITI(1973); SIX PACK ANNIE(1975)
Misc. Talkies
BLACK HEAT(1976); KINGS OF THE HILL(1976)
Joe Bellan
FOUL PLAY(1978); DIE LAUGHING(1980); CHARLIE CHAN AND THE CURSE OF THE DRAGON QUEEN(1981); EYE FOR AN EYE, AN(1981); SUDDEN IMPACT(1983)
1984
CRACKERS(1984)
Piero Bellanova
LA FUGA(1966, Ital.), w
Adriana Bellanti
GIANT OF METROPOLIS, THE(1963, Ital.), ed
Ivor Bellas
SHIPMATES O' MINE(1936, Brit.), w
Harry Bellaver
ANOTHER THIN MAN(1939); HOUSE ON 92ND STREET, THE(1945); NO WAY OUT(1950); PERFECT STRANGERS(1950); SIDE STREET(1950); STAGE TO TUCSON(1950); LEMON DROP KID, THE(1951); TANKS ARE COMING, THE(1951); SOMETHING TO LIVE FOR(1952); FROM HERE TO ETERNITY(1953); GREAT DIAMOND ROBBERY(1953); MISS SADIE THOMPSON(1953); LOVE ME OR LEAVE ME(1955); SERENADE(1956); BROTHERS RICO, THE(1957); SLAUGHTER ON TENTH AVENUE(1957); OLD MAN AND THE SEA, THE(1958); ONE POTATO, TWO POTATO(1964); BIRDS AND THE BEES, THE(1965); FINE MADNESS, A(1966); MADIGAN(1968); HOT ROCK, THE(1972); GOD TOLD ME TO(1976); BLUE COLLAR(1978); HERO AT LARGE(1980)
Annie Belle
WIFEMISTRESS(1979, Ital.)
Annier Belle
NANA(1983, Ital.)
Ida Belle
Misc. Talkies
WHILE THOUSANDS CHEER(1940)
Lena Belle
LET'S FACE IT(1943); RAINBOW ISLAND(1944)
Nick Belle
SLAUGHTERHOUSE-FIVE(1972)
Theresa Belle
1984
BODY ROCK(1984)
Tula Belle
Silents
BRAND OF COWARDICE, THE(1916); MIRACLE MAN, THE(1919)
Misc. Silents
BLUEBIRD, THE(1918)
Yva Belle
PORTRAIT OF A WOMAN(1946, Fr.)
Belle the Dog
MIRACLE WORKER, THE(1962)
Georges Bellec
PLAYMATES(1969, Fr./Ital.)
Robert Leslie Bellen
BLACKMAIL(1947), w
Benno Bellenbaum
SINAI COMMANDOS: THE STORY OF THE SIX DAY WAR(1968, Israel/Ger.), ph
Natino Bellentino
1984
RUNAWAY(1984)
Georges Beller
LEGEND OF FRENCHIE KING, THE(1971, Fr./Ital./Span./Brit.); DESTRUCTORS, THE(1974, Brit.); PAUL AND MICHELLE(1974, Fr./Brit.); ROSEBUD(1975); MOONRAKER(1979, Brit.)
Kathleen Beller
BETSY, THE(1978); MOVIE MOVIE(1978); PROMISES IN THE DARK(1979); FORT APACHE, THE BRONX(1981); SWORD AND THE SORCERER, THE(1982); TOUCHED(1983)
Kathy Beller
GODFATHER, THE, PART II(1974)
Michael Belleran
STARTING OVER(1979)
Leon Belleres
AFFAIR LAFONT, THE(1939, Fr.)
Carlo Bellero
ANGELO(1951, Ital.), ph; ANGELO IN THE CROWD(1952, Ital.), ph; GUNS OF THE BLACK WITCH(1961, Fr./Ital.), ph; REBEL GLADIATORS, THE(1963, Ital.), ph
Louris Bellero
MYSTERY OF THE BLACK JUNGLE(1955), ed
Mario Bellero
RAGE OF THE BUCCANEERS(1963, Ital.), ph
Herbert Belles
RED MOUNTAIN(1951)
Ken Bellet
HIDE IN PLAIN SIGHT(1980)
Tony Belletier
SEEDS OF EVIL(1981), p
Dorene Belleus
NUNZIO(1978)
Anita Bellew
LUMMOX(1930)

Cosmo Kryle Bellew
LOVE CONTRACT, THE(1932, Brit.)
Cosmo Kyrle Bellew
DISRAELI(1929); STRANGE CARGO(1929); LUMMOX(1930); LADY WHO DARED, THE(1931); MERRY WIDOW, THE(1934); RIP TIDE(1934); SPLENDOR(1935)
Silents
SUMMER BACHELORS(1926); MIDNIGHT LIFE(1928); DEVIL'S APPLE TREE(1929)
Dorothy Bellew
Silents
KING CHARLES(1913, Brit.); HARD TIMES(1915, Brit.); LOST CHORD, THE(1917, Brit.); PROFLIGATE, THE(1917, Brit.); LEAD, KINDLY LIGHT(1918, Brit.)
Misc. Silents
LOVE OF AN ACTRESS, THE(1914, Brit.); AVENGING HAND, THE(1915, Brit.); WHEN EAST MEETS WEST(1915, Brit.); DISRAELI(1916, Brit.); MASTER OF MEN, A(1917, Brit.)
Frank Bellew
DATE WITH DEATH, A(1959)
Kyrle Bellew
NORAH O'NEALE(1934, Brit.); IT HAPPENED IN PARIS(1935, Brit.)
Nellie Bellflower
TUNNELVISION(1976); AMERICATHON(1979)
Bellfontevro
ERRAND BOY, THE(1961)
Agostina Belli
BLUEBEARD(1972); BLOOD IN THE STREETS(1975, Ital./Fr.); SCENT OF A WOMAN(1976, Ital.); PURPLE TAXI, THE(1977, Fr./Ital./Ireland)
Misc. Talkies
FAMILY KILLER(1975)
Agostine Belli
CHOSEN, THE(1978, Brit./Ital.)
Guiseppe Belli
BLACK VEIL FOR LISA, A(1969 Ital./Ger.), w
Laura Belli
LADY OF MONZA, THE(1970, Ital.); ALMOST HUMAN(1974,Ital.)
Lia Belli
GROUND ZERO(1973)
Marisa Belli
DISORDER(1964, Fr./Ital.); HERCULES IN THE HAUNTED WORLD(1964, Ital.)
Melvin Belli
WILD IN THE STREETS(1968); GROUND ZERO(1973)
Pino Belli
TORPEDO BAY(1964, Ital./Fr.), w
Angelo Bellia
WHITE SISTER(1973, Ital./Span./Fr.)
Gunther Bellier
COURT CONCERT, THE(1936, Ger.)
Leon Bellieres
ROAD IS FINE, THE(1930, Fr.); SIMPLE CASE OF MONEY, A(1952, Fr.)
Harvey Bellin
SALLY'S HOUNDS(1968)
Mike Bellin
JAZZ SINGER, THE(1980)
Olga Bellin
TOMORROW(1972)
Andrew Belling
KILLING KIND, THE(1973), m; CRASH(1977), m; WIZARDS(1977), m, md; DRACULA'S DOG(1978), m
Davina Belling
SCUM(1979, Brit.), p; THAT SUMMER(1979, Brit.), p; BREAKING GLASS(1980, Brit.), p; BRITTANIA HOSPITAL(1982, Brit.), p; GREGORY'S GIRL(1982, Brit.), p; PARTY PARTY(1983, Brit.), p
1984
COMFORT AND JOY(1984, Brit.), p
Capt. P.N.L. Bellinger
WINGS OVER HONOLULU(1937)
Ted Bellinger
FIGHTING TROOPER, THE(1935), ed
Theodore Bellinger
GREAT JOHN L. THE(1945), ed
Lynda Bellingham
STAND UP VIRGIN SOLDIERS(1977, Brit.); SWEENEY(1977, Brit.)
Bellings' Dogs
ON VELVET(1938, Brit.)
Anne-Marie Bellini
LIARS, THE(1964, Fr.)
Cal Bellini
LITTLE BIG MAN(1970); FUZZ(1972); MOUNTAIN MEN, THE(1980)
Carlo Bellini
GREAT HOPE, THE(1954, Ital.); HELL RAIDERS OF THE DEEP(1954, Ital.)
Francesca Bellini
LADIES MAN, THE(1961); BACHELOR FLAT(1962); IT'S ONLY MONEY(1962); WHO'S MINDING THE STORE?(1963); CARPETBAGGERS, THE(1964); GRAVY TRAIN, THE(1974)
Giacomo Bellini
INVESTIGATION OF A CITIZEN ABOVE SUSPICION(1970, Ital.)
Luigi Bellini
PLAYMATES(1969, Fr./Ital.)
Mario Bellini
VAN NUYS BLVD.(1979)
Mino Bellini
MISSION TO MOSCOW(1943)
Nino Bellini
THIN ICE(1937); THRILL OF BRAZIL, THE(1946)
Rino Bellini
WATERLOO(1970, Ital./USSR)
Roxana Bellini
SANTO EN EL MUSEO DE CERA(1963, Mex.)

Vincenzo Bellini
VOICE IN YOUR HEART, A(1952, Ital.), m
Andreas Bellis
GEORGIA, GEORGIA(1972), ph; HONEYBABY, HONEYBABY(1974), ph
Andrew Bellis
1984
BLIND DATE(1984), ph
Dickie Bellis
PORTLAND EXPOSE(1957); SHOOT-OUT AT MEDICINE BEND(1957)
Guy Bellis
MARK OF THE VAMPIRE(1935); LITTLE PRINCESS, THE(1939); PRIVATE LIVES OF ELIZABETH AND ESSEX, THE(1939); ADVENTURE IN DIAMONDS(1940); KATHLEEN(1941); I MARRIED AN ANGEL(1942); MRS. MINIVER(1942); MRS. PARKINGTON(1944); TWO LOST WORLDS(1950); PRIDE OF MARYLAND(1951); PRISONER OF ZENDA, THE(1952)
Richard Bellis
THEM!(1954)
Goffredo Bellisario
KAPO(1964, Ital./Fr./Yugo.), ph
Al Bello
DAUGHTER OF THE SUN GOD(1962)
Frank Bello
BLACK GUNN(1972)
Lisa Dal Bello
MELANIE(1982, Can.)
Teodorina Bello
POSSESSION OF JOEL DELANEY, THE(1972)
Teodorino Bello
SEEDS OF EVIL(1981)
Theodorina Bello
LAW AND DISORDER(1974)
Mrs. Belloc-Lowndes
Silents
LODGER, THE(1926, Brit.), w
Mrs. Marie Belloc-Lowndes
PHANTOM FIEND, THE(1935, Brit.), w
Celestina Bellocchio
FIST IN HIS POCKET(1968, Ital.)
Marco Bellocchio
CHINA IS NEAR(1968, Ital.), d, w; FIST IN HIS POCKET(1968, Ital.), d&w; EYES, THE MOUTH, THE(1982, Ital./Fr.), d, w; LEAP INTO THE VOID(1982, Ital.), d, w
Piergiorgio Bellocchio
LEAP INTO THE VOID(1982, Ital.)
Steve Belloise
REQUIEM FOR A HEAVYWEIGHT(1962)
Andre Bellon
Silents
AMAZONS, THE(1917)
Fernand Bellon
LA MARSEILLAISE(1938, Fr.)
Loleh Bellon
CASQUE D'OR(1956, Fr.)
Yannick Bellon
SEASON FOR LOVE, THE(1963, Fr.), ed
Adriana Bellone
LONELY LADY, THE(1983), art d
Gabria Belloni
GODFATHER, THE, PART II(1974)
Nanda Belloni
NIGHT AFFAIR(1961, Fr.), cos
Saul Bellow
ZELIG(1983)
Louis Bellson
SONG IS BORN, A(1948)
John Belluci
LOVE AND BULLETS(1979, Brit.)
Rocco Bellusci
CHRISTMAS STORY, A(1983)
Pamela Bellwood
TWO-MINUTE WARNING(1976); AIRPORT '77(1977); HANGAR 18(1980); SERIAL(1980); INCREDIBLE SHRINKING WOMAN, THE(1981)
Peter Bellwood
PHOBIA(1980, Can.), w; ST. HELENS(1981), w
Henry Belmar
Misc. Silents
LIFE'S SHOP WINDOW(1914), a, d; RAIDERS, THE(1916)
Maria Belmar
NIGHTFALL(1956)
Jean Paul Belmondo
ACE OF ACES(1982, Fr./Ger.)
Jean-Paul Belmondo
BREATHLESS(1959, Fr.); CHEATERS, THE(1961, Fr.); LOVE AND THE FRENCH-WOMAN(1961, Fr.); TWO WOMEN(1961, Ital./Fr.); WEB OF PASSION(1961, Fr.); WOMAN IS A WOMAN, A(1961, Fr./Ital.); CARTOUCHE(1962, Fr./Ital.); LA VIAC-CIA(1962, Fr./Ital.); MONKEY IN WINTER, A(1962, Fr.); FINGERMAN, THE(1963, Fr.); RITA(1963, Fr./Ital.); DOULOS–THE FINGER MAN(1964, Fr./Ital.); MODERATO CANTABILE(1964, Fr./Ital.); SWEET AND SOUR(1964, Fr./Ital.); THAT MAN FROM RIO(1964, Fr./Ital.); BACKFIRE(1965, Fr.); BANANA PEEL(1965, Fr.); GREED IN THE SUN(1965, Fr./ Ital.); MALE HUNT(1965, Fr./Ital.); IS PARIS BURNING?(1966, U.S./Fr.); UP TO HIS EARS(1966, Fr./Ital.); WEEKEND AT DUNKIRK(1966, Fr./Ital.); CASINO ROYALE(1967, Brit.); TENDER SCOUNDREL(1967, Fr./Ital.); THIEF OF PARIS, THE(1967, Fr./Ital.); HO(1968, Fr.); PIERROT LE FOU(1968, Fr./Ital.); BRAIN, THE(1969, Fr./US); LOVE IS A FUNNY THING(1970, Fr./Ital.); MISSISSIPPI MERMAID(1970, Fr./Ital.); BURGLARS, THE(1972, Fr./Ital.); DOCTEUR POPAUL(1972, Fr.); MAGNIFICENT ONE, THE(1974, Fr./Ital.); STA-VISKY(1974, Fr.); INCORRIGIBLE(1980, Fr.)
Baldy Belmont
PAINTED FACES(1929); STAGE STRUCK(1936)

Jerry Belson
HOW SWEET IT IS(1968), p, w; GRASSHOPPER, THE(1970), p, w; SMILE(1975), w; FUN WITH DICK AND JANE(1977), w; END, THE(1978), w; SMOKEY AND THE BANDIT II(1980), w; MODERN ROMANCE(1981); JEKYLL AND HYDE...TOGETHER AGAIN(1982), d, w

Jordan Belson
RIGHT STUFF, THE(1983), spec eff

Frank Belt
LIMIT, THE(1972)

Cesare Beltarini
DESTINY(1938)

Robert Beltcher
TANGA-TIKA(1953), ed

Jean Pierre Beltoise
GRAND PRIX(1966)

Eve Belton
TIME LOST AND TIME REMEMBERED(1966, Brit.); SMASHING TIME(1967 Brit.)

Ray Beltram
THIS WOMAN IS MINE(1941); MASQUERADE IN MEXICO(1945); SALOME(1953); TREASURE OF THE GOLDEN CONDOR(1953)

Alma Beltran
PAN-AMERICANA(1945); HE WALKED BY NIGHT(1948); LOVES OF CARMEN, THE(1948); SOMBRERO(1953); JUBILEE TRAIL(1954); DRAGON WELLS MASSACRE(1957); MARRIAGE OF A YOUNG STOCKBROKER, THE(1971); RED SKY AT MORNING(1971); GLASS HOUSES(1972); MARATHON MAN(1976); HOUSE CALLS(1978); HERBIE GOES BANANAS(1980); OH GOD! BOOK II(1980); ZOOT SUIT(1981)

Alma Lenor Beltran
THEY ONLY KILL THEIR MASTERS(1972)

Guillermo Beltran
PANDORA AND THE FLYING DUTCHMAN(1951, Brit.)

Henry Beltran
HIGH WIND IN JAMAICA, A(1965); MAGNIFICENT TWO, THE(1967, Brit.)

Jose Maria Beltran
DARK RIVER(1956, Arg.), ph

Orlando Beltran
CRISIS(1950); KANSAS CITY CONFIDENTIAL(1952); SECOND CHANCE(1953); SOMBRERO(1953); NIGHTFALL(1956)

Pedro Beltran
MOMENT OF TRUTH, THE(1965, Ital./Span.), w

Ray Beltran
FLAMING STAR(1960)

Robert Beltran
ZOOT SUIT(1981); EATING RAOUL(1982); LONE WOLF McQUADE(1983)
1984
NIGHT OF THE COMET(1984)

Susan Beltran
CURIOUS DR. HUMPP(1967, Arg.)

Annibale Beltrone
ISLAND OF PROCIDA, THE(1952, Ital.)

Harry Belts
TIME FOR DYING, A(1971), m

Frank Belty
CASTLE OF BLOOD(1964, Fr./Ital.), p

James Belushi
THIEF(1981); TRADING PLACES(1983)

John Belushi
GOIN' SOUTH(1978); NATIONAL LAMPOON'S ANIMAL HOUSE(1978); OLD BOYFRIENDS(1979); 1941(1979); BLUES BROTHERS, THE(1980); CONTINENTAL DIVIDE(1981); NEIGHBORS(1981)
Misc. Talkies
SHAME OF THE JUNGLE(1980, Fr./Bel.)

Antonietta Beluzzi
AMARCORD(1974, Ital.)

Maria Antonietta Beluzzi
8 ½(1963, Ital.); TAKE ALL OF ME(1978, Ital.)

Malcolm Belvins
Misc. Silents
TERROR, THE(1917)

Antonio Belviso
BEHIND CLOSED SHUTTERS(1952, Ital.), ph

Alma Belwin
Silents
IVORY SNUFF BOX, THE(1915)

Alexander Belyavsky
YOLANTA(1964, USSR)

V. Belyayeva
NINE DAYS OF ONE YEAR(1964, USSR)

Jon G. Belyeu
HALLOWEEN III: SEASON OF THE WITCH(1982), spec eff

Jon Belyou
DEAD ZONE, THE(1983), sp eff

Ihor Belza
Silents
ARSENAL(1929, USSR), m

Richard Belzer
GROOVE TUBE, THE(1974); FAME(1980); AUTHOR! AUTHOR!(1982); NIGHT SHIFT(1982); SCARFACE(1983)

Steve Belzer
VISITOR, THE(1980, Ital./U.S.)

Judy Bember
YOUNG AND DANGEROUS(1957)

Maggie Bemby
Misc. Talkies
ANGELS' WILD WOMEN(1972)

Ludwig Bemelmans
YOLANDA AND THE THIEF(1945), w

Stephen A. Bement
DREAMER(1979)

Bill Bemiller
1984
PLAGUE DOGS, THE(1984, U.S./Brit.), ph

Bob Bemiller
SHINBONE ALLEY(1971), anim

Ted Bemiller
HEY THERE, IT'S YOGI BEAR(1964), ph; SHINBONE ALLEY(1971), ph

Ted Bemiller, Jr.
1984
PLAGUE DOGS, THE(1984, U.S./Brit.), ph

Ted C. Bemiller
COONSKIN(1975), anim; WIZARDS(1977), ph; HEY, GOOD LOOKIN'(1982), ph

George E. Bemis
PICNIC(1955)

Franco Bemporad
DOLL THAT TOOK THE TOWN, THE(1965, Ital.), w

"Ben"
LIFE AND TIMES OF GRIZZLY ADAMS, THE(1974)

Jorge Ben
XICA(1982, Braz.), m

Robert Ben Ali
HOLLOW TRIUMPH(1948)

Ben Bernie and Band
WAKE UP AND LIVE(1937)

Ben Carter Choir
DIXIE JAMBOREE(1945)

The Ben Carter Choir
STARS ON PARADE(1944)

Ben the Bear
GENTLE GIANT(1967)

The Ben Tyber Ballet Troupe
ANY NUMBER CAN WIN(1963 Fr.)

Aron Ben-Ami
GREEN FIELDS(1937)

Jacob Ben-Ami
WANDERING JEW, THE(1933); GREEN FIELDS(1937), d

Yoram Ben-Ami
LONE WOLF McQUADE(1983), p

Dan Ben-Amotz
NOT MINE TO LOVE(1969, Israel), w

Gaddi Ben-Artzi
PEDESTRIAN, THE(1974, Ger.)

Albert Ben-Astar
QUEEN FOR A DAY(1951)

Moshe Ben-Ephraim
SIMCHON FAMILY, THE(1969, Israel), w

Avi Ben-Haim
JESUS CHRIST, SUPERSTAR(1973)

Kador Ben-Selim
Misc. Silents
RED IMPS(1923, USSR)

Avraham Ben-Yosef
SANDS OF BEERSHEBA(1966, U.S./Israel)

Rosine Bena
SHE DANCES ALONE(1981, Aust./U.S.)

Andre Benaben
BIQUEFARRE(1983, Fr.)

Francine Benaben
BIQUEFARRE(1983, Fr.)

Helene Benaben
BIQUEFARRE(1983, Fr.)

Marie-Helene Benaben
BIQUEFARRE(1983, Fr.)

Marius Benaben
BIQUEFARRE(1983, Fr.)

Gabriela Benackova
DIVINE EMMA, THE(1983, Czech,)

Bea Benadaret
TENDER IS THE NIGHT(1961)

Bea Benaderet
NOTORIOUS(1946); ON THE TOWN(1949); FIRST TIME, THE(1952); PLUNDERERS OF PAINTED FLATS(1959)

Steven Benally, Jr.
LEGEND OF COUGAR CANYON(1974)
Misc. Talkies
SECRET OF NAVAJO CAVE(1976)

Tamar Benamy
SCAVENGERS, THE(1959, U.S./Phil.)

Christian Benard
QUEST FOR FIRE(1982, Fr./Can.)

Ray Benard
DARKEST AFRICA(1936)

Raymond Benard
NIGHT LIFE OF THE GODS(1935)

Pasquino Benassati
1990: THE BRONX WARRIORS(1983, Ital.), spec eff

Memo Benassi
DEFEAT OF HANNIBAL, THE(1937, Ital.); FEDORA(1946, Ital.); ROSSINI(1948, Ital.); AFFAIRS OF MESSALINA, THE(1954, Ital.)

Pat Benatar
UNION CITY(1980)

Ralph Benatsky
IMMORTAL VAGABOND(1931, Ger.), m; LOVE CONTRACT, THE(1932, Brit.), m

Ralph Benatzky
WHITE HORSE INN, THE(1959, Ger.), m

Al Benault
UP IN ARMS(1944)
Sauto Benavente
ALIAS BIG SHOT(1962, Argen.), ed
Jorge Benavides
DOCTOR CRIMEN(1953, Mex.), spec eff
Paul Benay
SHADOWS ON THE STAIRS(1941)
Jose Benazeraf
PORT OF DESIRE(1960, Fr.), p, w; NO TIME FOR ECSTASY(1963, Fr.), p; PARIS OOH-LA-LA!(1963, U.S./Fr.), p,d&w; SIN ON THE BEACH(1964, Fr.), p&d; NIGHT OF LUST(1965, Fr.), p&d, w
June Benbow
SECRET FURY, THE(1950)
Amelia Bence
GAMES MEN PLAY, THE(1968, Arg.)
Nat Benchley
DINER(1982)
Nathaniel Benchley
GREAT AMERICAN PASTIME, THE(1956), a, w; SAIL A CROOKED SHIP(1961), w; RUSSIANS ARE COMING, THE RUSSIANS ARE COMING, THE(1966), w; SPIRIT IS WILLING, THE(1967), w
Peter Benchley
JAWS(1975), a, w; DEEP, THE(1977), a, w; JAWS II(1978), w; ISLAND, THE(1980), w; JAWS 3-D(1983), w
Robert Benchley
SKY DEVILS(1932), w; SPORT PARADE, THE(1932), a, w; DANCING LADY(1933); HEADLINE SHOOTER(1933); RAFTER ROMANCE(1934); SOCIAL REGISTER(1934); CHINA SEAS(1935); MURDER ON A HONEYMOON(1935), w; PICCADILLY JIM(1936); BROADWAY MELODY OF '38(1937); LIVE, LOVE AND LEARN(1937); FOREIGN CORRESPONDENT(1940), a, w; HIRED WIFE(1940); NICE GIRL?(1941); RELUCTANT DRAGON, THE(1941); THREE GIRLS ABOUT TOWN(1941); YOU'LL NEVER GET RICH(1941); BEDTIME STORY(1942); I MARRIED A WITCH(1942); MAJOR AND THE MINOR, THE(1942); TAKE A LETTER, DARLING(1942); FLESH AND FANTASY(1943); SKY'S THE LIMIT, THE(1943); SONG OF RUSSIA(1943); YOUNG AND WILLING(1943); HER PRIMITIVE MAN(1944); JANIE(1944); NATIONAL BARN DANCE(1944); PRACTICALLY YOURS(1944); SEE HERE, PRIVATE HARGROVE(1944); IT'S IN THE BAG(1945); KISS AND TELL(1945); PAN-AMERICANA(1945); ROAD TO UTOPIA(1945); SNAFU(1945); STORK CLUB, THE(1945); WEEK-END AT THE WALDORF(1945); BRIDE WORE BOOTS, THE(1946); JANIE GETS MARRIED(1946)
Alfred Bencic
DESERTER AND THE NOMADS, THE(1969, Czech./Ital.), ed
Edoardo Bencivenga
Misc. Silents
LA DUBARRY(1914, Ital.), d
Margaret Benczak
HEAVEN'S GATE(1980)
G. K. Benda
CARNIVAL IN FLANDERS(1936, Fr.), cos
G.K. Benda
MAN ABOUT THE HOUSE, A(1947, Brit.), cos
George Benda
KNIGHT WITHOUT ARMOR(1937, Brit.), cos
Georges Benda
SARABAND(1949, Brit.), cos; THIEF OF BAGHDAD, THE(1961, Ital./Fr.), cos
Helena Benda
HEAVENLY DAYS(1944)
Kenneth Benda
THANK YOU ALL VERY MUCH(1969, Brit.); PRIVATE LIFE OF SHERLOCK HOLMES, THE(1970, Brit.); SCREAM AND SCREAM AGAIN(1970, Brit.); SECRETS OF SEX(1970, Brit.); RULING CLASS, THE(1972, Brit.)
W. T. Benda
Silents
AMERICAN VENUS, THE(1926)
Robert Bendall
SOMEWHERE IN FRANCE(1943, Brit.)
Poldo Bendandi
VIVA MARIA(1965, Fr./Ital.); 00-2 MOST SECRET AGENTS(1965, Ital.); MAN OF LA MANCHA(1972)
Bruce Bendell
Misc. Talkies
INSTRUCTOR, THE(1983)
Don Bendell
Misc. Talkies
INSTRUCTOR, THE(1983), d
Ada Mae Bender
KID MILLIONS(1934)
Dawn Bender
UNCLE HARRY(1945); CONFESSION(1937); 'TILL WE MEET AGAIN(1944); SONG TO REMEMBER, A(1945); ACTRESS, THE(1953); ISLAND IN THE SKY(1953)
Eleanor Bender
SON OF SINBAD(1955)
Henry Bender
DAUGHTER OF EVIL(1930, Ger.)
Misc. Silents
IMAGINARY BARON, THE(1927, Ger.)
Jack Bender
BAREFOOT EXECUTIVE, THE(1971); $1,000,000 DUCK(1971); NOW YOU SEE HIM, NOW YOU DON'T(1972)
Joel Bender
RETURNING, THE(1983), d
Misc. Talkies
GAS PUMP GIRLS(1979), d
Lawrence E. Bender
GOING HOME(1971)
Richard Bender
LEATHER SAINT, THE(1956)

Russ Bender
IT CONQUERED THE WORLD(1956); AMAZING COLOSSAL MAN, THE(1957); BADLANDS OF MONTANA(1957); DRAGSTRIP GIRL(1957); INVASION OF THE SAUCER MEN(1957); MOTORCYCLE GANG(1957); HOT ROD GANG(1958); I BURY THE LIVING(1958); SUICIDE BATTALION(1958); WAR OF THE COLOSSAL BEAST(1958); COMPULSION(1959); GHOST OF DRAGSTRIP HOLLOW(1959); NO NAME ON THE BULLET(1959); VICE RAID(1959); WALK TALL(1960); ANATOMY OF A PSYCHO(1961); LITTLE SHEPHERD OF KINGDOM COME(1961); PURPLE HILLS, THE(1961), a, w; AIR PATROL(1962); BROKEN LAND, THE(1962), w; PANIC IN YEAR ZERO!(1962); THAT TOUCH OF MINK(1962); WOMAN HUNT(1962), w; GATHERING OF EAGLES, A(1963); RAIDERS FROM BENEATH THE SEA(1964); STRANGLER, THE(1964); SATAN BUG, THE(1965); SPACE MONSTER(1965); WILD ON THE BEACH(1965); NAVY VS. THE NIGHT MONSTERS, THE(1966); DEVIL'S ANGELS(1967); BORN WILD(1968); MARYJANE(1968)
Russell Bender
WAR OF THE WORLDS, THE(1953); JOKER IS WILD, THE(1957); VOODOO WOMAN(1957), w; STINGRAY(1978)
Sherrie Bender
SOUP FOR ONE(1982)
Bender and Daum
IT ALL CAME TRUE(1940)
Kathy Bendett
PATERNITY(1981); GOING BERSERK(1983)
Mary Bendetta
BAIT(1950, Brit.), w
Nora Bendich
TELL ME A RIDDLE(1980)
Silvia D'Amico Bendico
1984
JOKE OF DESTINY LYING IN WAIT AROUND THE CORNER LIKE A STREET-BANDIT, A(1984, Ital.), w
Doreen Bendix
ONE EMBARRASSING NIGHT(1930, Brit.); PLUNDER(1931, Brit.)
Lorraine Bendix
LAW OF THE LAWLESS(1964)
William Bendix
TIME OF YOUR LIFE, THE(1948); BROOKLYN ORCHID(1942); GLASS KEY, THE(1942); STAR SPANGLED RHYTHM(1942); WAKE ISLAND(1942); WHO DONE IT?(1942); WOMAN OF THE YEAR(1942); CHINA(1943); CRYSTAL BALL, THE(1943); GUADALCANAL DIARY(1943); HOSTAGES(1943); ABROAD WITH TWO YANKS(1944); GREENWICH VILLAGE(1944); HAIRY APE, THE(1944); LIFEBOAT(1944); BELL FOR ADANO, A(1945); DON JUAN QUILLIGAN(1945); DUFFY'S TAVERN(1945); IT'S IN THE BAG(1945); BLUE DAHLIA, THE(1946); DARK CORNER, THE(1946); SENTIMENTAL JOURNEY(1946); TWO YEARS BEFORE THE MAST(1946); WHITE TIE AND TAILS(1946); BLAZE OF NOON(1947); CALCUTTA(1947); I'LL BE YOURS(1947); VARIETY GIRL(1947); WEB, THE(1947); WHERE THERE'S LIFE(1947); BABE RUTH STORY, THE(1948); RACE STREET(1948); BIG STEAL, THE(1949); CONNECTICUT YANKEE IN KING ARTHUR'S COURT, A(1949); COVER-UP(1949); JOHNNY HOLIDAY(1949); LIFE OF RILEY, THE(1949); STREETS OF LAREDO(1949); GAMBLING HOUSE(1950); KILL THE UMPIRE(1950); DETECTIVE STORY(1951); SUBMARINE COMMAND(1951); BLACKBEARD THE PIRATE(1952); GIRL IN EVERY PORT, A(1952); MACAO(1952); DANGEROUS MISSION(1954); CRASHOUT(1955); BATTLE STATIONS(1956); DEEP SIX, THE(1958); IDOL ON PARADE(1959, Brit.); PORTRAIT OF A SINNER(1961, Brit.); BOYS' NIGHT OUT(1962); FOR LOVE OR MONEY(1963); YOUNG AND THE BRAVE, THE(1963); LAW OF THE LAWLESS(1964); PHONY AMERICAN, THE(1964, Ger.); JOHNNY NOBODY(1965, Brit.); YOUNG FURY(1965)
Misc. Talkies
TWO MUGS FROM BROOKLYN(1942)
Holder Bendixen
O.S.S.(1946)
Holger Bendixen
MAN'S FAVORITE SPORT(?)**1/2 (1964); TALK OF THE TOWN(1942); RECKLESS MOMENTS, THE(1949); 80 STEPS TO JONAH(1969)
Mia Bendixsen
FUZZ(1972); ALICE DOESN'T LIVE HERE ANYMORE(1975); PROPHECY(1979); WHY WOULD I LIE(1980)
Christian Bendomir
DAS BOOT(1982)
Jitka Bendova
CLOSELY WATCHED TRAINS(1967, Czech.)
Wilhelm Bendow
BLONDE NIGHTINGALE(1931, Ger.)
Hans Bendrik
GLADIATORS, THE(1970, Swed.)
Henning Bendsten
HAGBARD AND SIGNE(1968, Den./Iceland/Swed.), ph
Henning Bendtsen
ORDET(1957, Den.), ph; CRAZY PARADISE(1965, Den.), ph; GERTRUD(1966, Den.), ph; SUDDENLY, A WOMAN!(1967, Den.), ph; LURE OF THE JUNGLE, THE(1970, Den.), ph
Richard Bendy
SCOTT OF THE ANTARCTIC(1949, Brit.), spec eff
Carmelo Bene
CATCH AS CATCH CAN(1968, Ital.)
Eli Beneche
10 NORTH FREDERICK(1958), set d
Barbara Benedek
BIG CHILL, THE(1983), w
Laslo Benedek
LITTLE BIT OF HEAVEN, A(1940), ed; KISSING BANDIT, THE(1948), d; PORT OF NEW YORK(1949), d; DEATH OF A SALESMAN(1952), d; STORM OVER TIBET(1952), p; WILD ONE, THE(1953), d; BENGAL BRIGADE(1954), d; AFFAIR IN HAVANA(1957), d; MALAGA(1962, Brit.), d; NAMU, THE KILLER WHALE(1966), p&d; DARING GAME(1968), d; NIGHT VISITOR, THE(1970, Swed./U.S.), d; ASSAULT ON AGATHON(1976, Brit./Gr.), d
Marie Benedetta
Silents
ROSE OF THE WORLD(1918)

Adriana Benedetti
DOCTOR BEWARE(1951, Ital.)
Benedetto Benedetti
CONFORMIST, THE(1971, Ital., Fr)
Francesca Benedetti
DEAF SMITH AND JOHNNY EARS(1973, Ital.)
Nelly Benedetti
SOFT SKIN, THE(1964, Fr.)
Pierre Benedetti
BEAST, THE(1975, Fr.)
Rolando Benedetti
BEHIND CLOSED SHUTTERS(1952, Ital.), ed; FATAL DESIRE(1953), ed; VITEL-LONI(1956, Ital./Fr.), ed
Wanda Benedetti
TOO BAD SHE'S BAD(1954, Ital.)
Pat Benedetto
UNSINKABLE MOLLY BROWN, THE(1964)
Jule Benedic
GO, MAN, GO!(1954)
Max Benedica
VERY EDGE, THE(1963, Brit.), ed
Augustino Benedico
SANTO CONTRA EL CEREBRO DIABOLICO zero(1962, Mex.)
Augusto Benedico
INVISIBLE MAN, THE(1958, Mex.); EXTERMINATING ANGEL, THE(1967, Mex.); BIG CUBE, THE(1969)
Benedict
Misc. Silents
COEUR FIDELE(1923, Fr.)
Bill Benedict
MAGNETIC MONSTER, THE(1953)
Billy [William] Benedict
WILDCAT(1942)
Billy Benedict
FARMER TAKES A WIFE, THE(1935); AFTER THE THIN MAN(1936); HOLD THAT CO-ED(1938); SAY IT IN FRENCH(1938); THERE'S ALWAYS A WOMAN(1938); GIVE US WINGS(1940); LUCKY PARTNERS(1940); MY LITTLE CHICKADEE(1940); RHYTHM ON THE RIVER(1940); SECOND CHORUS(1940); YOUNG PEOPLE(1940); CONFESSIONS OF BOSTON BLACKIE(1941); IN OLD CHEYENNE(1941); JESSE JAMES AT BAY(1941); MAD DOCTOR, THE(1941); MAN WHO LOST HIMSELF, THE(1941); RICHEST MAN IN TOWN(1941); TUXEDO JUNCTION(1941); GET HEP TO LOVE(1942); HOME IN WYOMIN'(1942); LADY IN A JAM(1942); NIGHT TO REMEMBER, A(1942); ON THE SUNNY SIDE(1942); RINGS ON HER FINGERS(1942); TALK OF THE TOWN(1942); VALLEY OF HUNTED MEN(1942); AERIAL GUN-NER(1943); CLANCY STREET BOYS(1943); GHOSTS ON THE LOOSE(1943); HANG-MEN ALSO DIE(1943); MOONLIGHT IN VERMONT(1943); MR. MUGGS STEPS OUT(1943); OX-BOW INCIDENT, THE(1943); THANK YOUR LUCKY STARS(1943); WHISPERING FOOTSTEPS(1943); BLOCK BUSTERS(1944); BOWERY CHAMPS(1944); COVER GIRL(1944); FOLLOW THE BOYS(1944); FOLLOW THE LEADER(1944); GOODNIGHT SWEETHEART(1944); LADY AND THE MONSTER, THE(1944); MILLION DOLLAR KID(1944); THAT'S MY BABY(1944); THEY LIVE IN FEAR(1944); COME OUT FIGHTING(1945); DOCKS OF NEW YORK(1945); HOLLY-WOOD AND VINE(1945); MR. MUGGS RIDES AGAIN(1945); PATRICK THE GREAT(1945); STORY OF G.I. JOE, THE(1945); BOWERY BOMBSHELL(1946); IN FAST COMPANY(1946); KID FROM BOOKLYN, THE(1946); LIVE WIRES(1946); MR. HEX(1946); SPOOK BUSTERS(1946); BOWERY BUCKAROOS(1947); HARD BOILED MAHONEY(1947); HUCKSTERS, THE(1947); NEWS HOUNDS(1947); ANGELS AL-LEY(1948); JINX MONEY(1948); SECRET SERVICE INVESTIGATOR(1948); SMUG-GLERS' COVE(1948); TROUBLE MAKERS(1948); ANGELS IN DISGUISE(1949); FIGHTING FOOLS(1949); HOLD THAT BABY!(1949); MASTER MINDS(1949); TRIPLE TROUBLE(1950); LET'S GO NAVY(1951); HALLELUJAH TRAIL, THE(1965); WHAT AM I BID?(1967); BIG DADDY(1969)
Misc. Talkies
RIDERS OF THE PONY EXPRESS(1949)
Brooks Benedict
CLEAR THE DECKS(1929); SOPHOMORE, THE(1929); TRESPASSER, THE(1929); DERELICT(1930); OFFICE WIFE, THE(1930); RECAPTURED LOVE(1930); STREET OF CHANCE(1930); WIDOW FROM CHICAGO, THE(1930); GUN SMOKE(1931); RECKLESS LIVING(1931); GIRL CRAZY(1932); WHAT PRICE HOLLYWOOD?(1932); DON'T BET ON LOVE(1933); NO OTHER WOMAN(1933); PICK-UP(1933); TILLIE AND GUS(1933); CAT'S PAW, THE(1934); GAMBLING LADY(1934); PICTURE BRIDES(1934); G-MEN(1935); GIRL FROM TENTH AVENUE, THE(1935); MURDER ON A HONEYMOON(1935); NO MORE LADIES(1935); RUMBA(1935); EARLY TO BED(1936); FOLLOW THE FLEET(1936); SHOW BOAT(1936); LAST GANGSTER, THE(1937); LOVE TAKES FLIGHT(1937); MIDNIGHT MADONNA(1937); PICK A STAR(1937); CITY GIRL(1938); SWEETHEARTS(1938); TRADE WINDS(1938); LAUGH IT OFF(1939); ENEMY AGENT(1940); I TAKE THIS OATH(1940); KITTY FOY-LE(1940); QUEEN OF THE MOB(1940); REMEMBER THE NIGHT(1940); I WAKE UP SCREAMING(1942); RINGS ON HER FINGERS(1942); HERS TO HOLD(1943); HI'YA, CHUM(1943); IRON MAJOR, THE(1943); JACK LONDON(1943); GYPSY WILD-CAT(1944); MAN WHO DARED, THE(1946); MURDER IN THE MUSIC HALL(1946); OUT CALIFORNIA WAY(1946); JOHNNY O'CLOCK(1947); KILLER AT LARGE(1947); OUT OF THE PAST(1947); THREE ON A TICKET(1947); PEOPLE AGAINST O'HARA, THE(1951); LAS VEGAS STORY, THE(1952); HOUSEBOAT(1958)
Silents
ONLY WOMAN, THE(1924); FRESHMAN, THE(1925); HIS MASTER'S VOICE(1925); COLLEGE DAYS(1926); RANSON'S FOLLY(1926); TRAMP, TRAMP, TRAMP(1926); BACKSTAGE(1927); DROPKICK, THE(1927); KID SISTER, THE(1927); THREE'S A CROWD(1927); WHITE FLANNELS(1927); SPEEDY(1928)
Misc. Silents
CUPID'S FIREMAN(1923); GOING THE LIMIT(1926); COWBOY KID, THE(1928); MORAN OF THE MARINES(1928)
David Benedict
GOODBYE COLUMBUS(1969)
Dick Benedict
BIG TIP OFF, THE(1955); SHRIKE, THE(1955)
Dirk Benedict
GEORGIA, GEORGIA(1972); SSSSSSSS(1973); W(1974); BATTLESTAR GALAC-TICA(1979); MISSION GALACTICA: THE CYLON ATTACK(1979); SCAVENGER HUNT(1979); RUCKUS(1981)

Misc. Talkies
UNDERGROUND ACES(1981)
Gail Benedict
FAN, THE(1981)
Greg Benedict
ISLAND OF LOVE(1963); PALM SPRINGS WEEKEND(1963); GREAT RACE, THE(1965)
Harold Benedict
DEVIL MAKES THREE, THE(1952); NIGHT PEOPLE(1954); PATHS OF GLO-RY(1957)
Howard Benedict
CURTAIN CALL(1940), p; LET'S MAKE MUSIC(1940), p; MEN AGAINST THE SKY(1940), p; MILLIONAIRES IN PRISON(1940), p; SAINT TAKES OVER, THE(1940), p; DATE WITH THE FALCON, A(1941), p; FOOTLIGHT FEVER(1941), p; GAY FALCON, THE(1941), p; HURRY, CHARLIE, HURRY(1941), p; OBLIGING YOUNG LADY(1941), p; PARACHUTE BATTALION(1941), p; SAINT IN PALM SPRINGS, THE(1941), p; BEHIND THE EIGHT BALL(1942), p; CALL OUT THE MARINES(1942), p; FALCON TAKES OVER, THE(1942), p; SHERLOCK HOLMES AND THE SECRET WEAPON(1942), p; SHERLOCK HOLMES AND THE VOICE OF TERROR(1942), p; HI'YA, CHUM(1943), p; LARCENY WITH MUSIC(1943), p; NEV-ER A DULL MOMENT(1943), p; SHERLOCK HOLMES IN WASHINGTON(1943), p; DESTINY(1944), p; PATRICK THE GREAT(1945), p; THIS LOVE OF OURS(1945), p; WHITE TIE AND TAILS(1946), p
Jay Benedict
HANOVER STREET(1979, Brit.); VICTOR/VICTORIA(1982); LONELY LADY, THE(1983)
Jean Benedict
BLONDES AT WORK(1938); FOOLS FOR SCANDAL(1938); LITTLE MISS THOROUGHBRED(1938); MYSTERY HOUSE(1938); PATIENT IN ROOM 18, THE(1938); SLIGHT CASE OF MURDER, A(1938)
Joan Benedict
SATURDAY NIGHT IN APPLE VALLEY(1965)
Kenneth Benedict
Silents
FIGHTER'S PARADISE(1924)
Kingsley Benedict
Silents
JUDGE NOT OR THE WOMAN OF MONA DIGGINGS(1915); LOVE GIRL, THE(1916); SECRET OF THE HILLS, THE(1921); GAY AND DEVILISH(1922); KEN-TUCKY DERBY, THE(1922)
Misc. Silents
BUGLER OF ALGIERS, THE(1916); MAN AND BEAST(1917)
Laura Benedict
THRILL KILLERS, THE(1965)
Lawrence Benedict
FAR SHORE, THE(1976, Can.)
Linda Benedict
SMOKEY AND THE BANDIT–PART 3(1983), cos
Max Benedict
HELL, HEAVEN OR HOBOKEN(1958, Brit.), ed; HIGH TREASON(1951, Brit.), ed; CREST OF THE WAVE(1954, Brit.), ed; WILL ANY GENTLEMAN?(1955, Brit.), ed; IT'S GREAT TO BE YOUNG(1956, Brit.), ed; LUCKY JIM(1957, Brit.), ed; PORTRAIT IN SMOKE(1957, Brit.), ed; TOWN ON TRIAL(1957, Brit.), ed; HIS AND HERS(1961, Brit.), ed; TROUBLE IN THE SKY(1961, Brit.), ed; WHISTLE DOWN THE WIND(1961, Brit.), ed; TARZAN GOES TO INDIA(1962, U.S./Brit./Switz.), ed; WHAT A CRAZY WORLD(1963, Brit.), ed; GUNS AT BATASI(1964, Brit.), ed; PSYCHE 59(1964, Brit.), ed; RAPTURE(1965), ed; BLUE MAX, THE(1966), ed; FATHOM(1967), ed; MAGUS, THE(1968, Brit.), ed; OBLONG BOX, THE(1969, Brit.), ed; EAGLE IN A CAGE(1971, U.S./Yugo.), ed; MURDERS IN THE RUE MORGUE(1971), ed; SHAFT IN AFRICA(1973), ed; CLASS OF MISS MAC MICHAEL, THE(1978, Brit./U.S.), ed; MR. PATMAN(1980, Can.), ed; NUTCRACKER(1982, Brit.), ed
Maxwell Benedict
JOSEPHINE AND MEN(1955, Brit.), ed
Paul Benedict
DOUBLE-BARRELLED DETECTIVE STORY, THE(1965); VIRGIN PRESIDENT, THE(1968); COLD TURKEY(1971); GANG THAT COULDN'T SHOOT STRAIGHT, THE(1971); TAKING OFF(1971); THEY MIGHT BE GIANTS(1971); JEREMIAH JOHN-SON(1972); UP THE SANDBOX(1972); FRONT PAGE, THE(1974); MANDINGO(1975); SMILE(1975); GOODBYE GIRL, THE(1977); BILLY IN THE LOWLANDS(1979); DEADHEAD MILES(1982); MAN WITH TWO BRAINS, THE(1983)
1984
THIS IS SPINAL TAP(1984)
Pippa Benedict
DON'T RAISE THE BRIDGE, LOWER THE RIVER(1968, Brit.)
Richard Benedict
SEE MY LAWYER(1945); WALK IN THE SUN, A(1945); O.S.S.(1946); SOMEWHERE IN THE NIGHT(1946); TILL THE END OF TIME(1946); BACKLASH(1947); CROSS-FIRE(1947); GUILT OF JANET AMES, THE(1947); ARIZONA RANGER, THE(1948); RACE STREET(1948); SMART GIRLS DON'T TALK(1948); ANGELS IN DIS-GUISE(1949); CITY ACROSS THE RIVER(1949); HOMICIDE(1949); OMOO OMOO, THE SHARK GOD(1949); POST OFFICE INVESTIGATOR(1949); SCENE OF THE CRIME(1949); SHOCKPROOF(1949); STREETS OF SAN FRANCISCO(1949); WIN-DOW, THE(1949); DESTINATION BIG HOUSE(1950); ROOKIE FIREMAN(1950); STATE PENITENTIARY(1950); TRIPLE TROUBLE(1950); BIG CARNIVAL, THE(1951); LET'S GO NAVY(1951); HOODLUM EMPIRE(1952); OKINAWA(1952); WOMAN IN THE DARK(1952); ACT OF LOVE(1953); BREAKDOWN(1953); JALO-PY(1953); JUGGLER, THE(1953); MURDER WITHOUT TEARS(1953); RUN FOR THE HILLS(1953); HE LAUGHED LAST(1956); MAN IS ARMED, THE(1956); SPY CHAS-ERS(1956); WIRETAPPERS(1956); BEGINNING OF THE END(1957); MONKEY ON MY BACK(1957); SPRING REUNION(1957); IT! THE TERROR FROM BEYOND SPACE(1958); I'LL GIVE MY LIFE(1959); OCEAN'S ELEVEN(1960); SCARFACE MOB, THE(1962); WINTER A GO-GO(1965), d; IMPASSE(1969), d
Steve Benedict
COWBOYS, THE(1972)
Tony Benedict
SANTA AND THE THREE BEARS(1970), p,d&w
Val Benedict
BERNARDINE(1957); WILD AND THE INNOCENT, THE(1959)

Vicki Benedict
THIS LOVE OF OURS(1945)

William Benedict
WITHOUT RESERVATIONS(l946); COLLEGE SCANDAL(1935); DOUBTING THOMAS(1935); SHOW THEM NO MERCY(1935); SILK HAT KID(1935); STEAMBOAT ROUND THE BEND(1935); WAY DOWN EAST(1935); $10 RAISE(1935); COUNTRY DOCTOR, THE(1936); LIBELED LADY(1936); MEET NERO WOLFE(1936); M'LISS(1936); RAMONA(1936); LAST GANGSTER, THE(1937); LAUGHING AT TROUBLE(1937); LOVE IN A BUNGALOW(1937); THAT I MAY LIVE(1937); KING OF THE NEWSBOYS(1938); LITTLE TOUGH GUYS IN SOCIETY(1938); CALL A MESSENGER(1939); CODE OF THE STREETS(1939); NEWSBOY'S HOME(1939); TIMBER STAMPEDE(1939); LEGION OF THE LAWLESS(1940); MELODY RANCH(1940); CITADEL OF CRIME(1941); GREAT MR. NOBODY, THE(1941); SHE KNEW ALL THE ANSWERS(1941); UNHOLY PARTNERS(1941); GLASS KEY, THE(1942); JANIE(1944); ROAD TO UTOPIA(1945); DO YOU LOVE ME?(1946); NEVER SAY GOODBYE(1946); ONE MORE TOMORROW(1946); PILGRIM LADY, THE(1947); BLONDE DYNAMITE(1950); BLUES BUSTERS(1950); LUCKY LOSERS(1950); BOWERY BATTALION(1951); CRAZY OVER HORSES(1951); GHOST CHASERS(1951); BRIDE OF THE MONSTER(1955); LOVER COME BACK(1961); DIRT GANG, THE(1972); STING, THE(1973); HOMEBODIES(1974); WON TON TON, THE DOG WHO SAVED HOLLYWOOD(1976); BORN AGAIN(1978)

William "Billy" Benedict
THREE KIDS AND A QUEEN(1935); YOUR UNCLE DUDLEY(1935); THEODORA GOES WILD(1936); WITNESS CHAIR, THE(1936); THEY WANTED TO MARRY(1937); BRINGING UP BABY(1938); WALKING DOWN BROADWAY(1938); YOUNG FUGITIVES(1938); KILLING, THE(1956)

David Benedictius
YOU'RE A BIG BOY NOW(1966), d&w

Barry Benefield
VALIANT IS THE WORD FOR CARRIE(1936), w; CHICKEN WAGON FAMILY(1939), w; TEXAS, BROOKLYN AND HEAVEN(1948), w

Paul Benefield
Misc. Talkies
POLK COUNTY POT PLANE(1977)

Tex Beneke
SUN VALLEY SERENADE(1941); ORCHESTRA WIVES(1942)

Sennuccio Benelli
SALVATORE GIULIANO(1966, Ital.)

Benempinga
KING SOLOMON'S MINES(1950)

Bill Benenson
BOULEVARD NIGHTS(1979), p

Susan Benenson
VERDICT, THE(1982)

Karel J. Benes
STOLEN LIFE(1939, Brit.), w; STOLEN LIFE, A(1946), w

Pasquino Benesanti
MAN CALLED SLEDGE, A(1971, Ital.), spec eff

Lynn Benesch
GREAT BRAIN, THE(1978)

Natalie Benesh
BABES IN BAGDAD(1952)

Glenn M. Benest
DEADLY BLESSING(1981), w

Brenda Benet
BEACH BALL(1965); HARUM SCARUM(1965); TRACK OF THUNDER(1967); WALKING TALL(1973)

Joile Benet
RIDING SPEED(1934)

Marianne Benet
SHAKE HANDS WITH THE DEVIL(1959, Ireland); BOY WHO STOLE A MILLION, THE(1960, Brit.); NIGHT FIGHTERS, THE(1960)

Michael Benet
Misc. Talkies
RIP OFF(1977)

Sheri Benet
THUNDER IN DIXIE(1965)

Stephen Vincent Benet
ABRAHAM LINCOLN(1930), w; LOVE, HONOR AND BEHAVE(1938), w; CHEERS FOR MISS BISHOP(1941), w; DEVIL AND DANIEL WEBSTER, THE(1941), w; JUST FOR YOU(1952), w; SEVEN BRIDES FOR SEVEN BROTHERS(1954), w
Silents
NECESSARY EVIL, THE(1925), w

Vicki Benet
LADIES MAN, THE(1961)

Adriana Benetti
DARK RIVER(1956, Arg.)

Armando Benetti
MAGIC WORLD OF TOPO GIGIO, THE(1961, Ital.)

Luciano Benetti
AVENGER, THE(1962, Fr./Ital.); REVOLT OF THE MERCENARIES(1964, Ital./Span.)

Bob Beneveds
MONSTER THAT CHALLENGED THE WORLD, THE(1957)

Frank Benevenuto
IT HAPPENED IN CANADA(1962, Can.)

Yves Beneyton
WEEKEND(1968, Fr./Ital.); TWO OR THREE THINGS I KNOW ABOUT HER(1970, Fr.); LACEMAKER, THE(1977, Fr.); CHARRIOTS OF FIRE(1981, Brit.)

Betty Benfield
NORMAN LOVES ROSE(1982, Aus.)

Derek Benfield
ROOM AT THE TOP(1959, Brit.); DEVIL WITHIN HER, THE(1976, Brit.); REMEMBRANCE(1982, Brit.)

Feral Benga
BLOOD OF A POET, THE(1930, Fr.)

Ben Bengal
CRACK-UP(1946), w; ILLEGAL ENTRY(1949), w; MUTINEERS, THE(1949), w

Wilson Benge
BULLDOG DRUMMOND(1929); MOST IMMORAL LADY, A(1929); THIS THING CALLED LOVE(1929); UNTAMED(1929); BAT WHISPERS, THE(1930); CHARLEY'S AUNT(1930); RAFFLES(1930); MEN IN HER LIFE(1931); PLATINUM BLONDE(1931); CYNARA(1932); BY APPOINTMENT ONLY(1933); DEATH KISS, THE(1933); SONG OF SONGS(1933); BULLDOG DRUMMOND STRIKES BACK(1934); CITY PARK(1934); FUGITIVE LADY(1934); GLAMOUR(1934); NANA(1934); TREASURE ISLAND(1934); TWIN HUSBANDS(1934); FALSE PRETENSES(1935); FEATHER IN HER HAT, A(1935); GHOST WALKS, THE(1935); DODSWORTH(1936); MURDER AT GLEN ATHOL(1936); BANK ALARM(1937); EASY LIVING(1937); LAST OF MRS. CHEYNEY, THE(1937); MAID OF SALEM(1937); MAN WHO CRIED WOLF, THE(1937); OH DOCTOR(1937); ROSALIE(1937); SOULS AT SEA(1937); WALLABY JIM OF THE ISLANDS(1937); MR. BOGGS STEPS OUT(1938); SWEETHEARTS(1938); TRADE WINDS(1938); ONLY ANGELS HAVE WINGS(1939); RULERS OF THE SEA(1939); GREEN HELL(1940); LADY EVE, THE(1941); MAN WHO LOST HIMSELF, THE(1941); NOTHING BUT THE TRUTH(1941); VIRGINIA(1941); MISS ANNIE ROONEY(1942); PALM BEACH STORY, THE(1942); PIED PIPER, THE(1942); YOU'RE TELLING ME(1942); IMMORTAL SERGEANT, THE(1943); LODGER, THE(1944); MAN IN HALF-MOON STREET, THE(1944); PEARL OF DEATH, THE(1944); WHITE CLIFFS OF DOVER, THE(1944); HOUSE OF FEAR, THE(1945); MINISTRY OF FEAR(1945); PURSUIT TO ALGIERS(1945); TONIGHT AND EVERY NIGHT(1945); QUEEN OF THE AMAZONS(1947); MY OWN TRUE LOVE(1948); THREE MUSKETEERS, THE(1948); EMERGENCY WEDDING(1950); MILLION DOLLAR MERMAID(1952); SCARLET COAT, THE(1955)
Silents
ROBIN HOOD(1922); MIDNIGHT MESSAGE, THE(1926); LONE EAGLE, THE(1927); FREEDOM OF THE PRESS(1928); QUEEN KELLY(1929)

Norma Bengell
MAFIOSO(1962, Ital.); GIVEN WORD, THE(1964, Braz.); MYTH, THE(1965, Ital.); PLANET OF THE VAMPIRES(1965, U.S./Ital./Span.); HELLBENDERS, THE(1967, U.S./Ital./Span.)

Habib Benglia
CHILDREN OF PARADISE(1945, Fr.); ROOTS OF HEAVEN, THE(1958)

Carl Bengs
GREEN SLIME, THE(1969)

Hubertus Bengsch
DAS BOOT(1982)

Bengt
DEAR JOHN(1966, Swed.), m

Bengt-Ake Bengtsson
DREAMS(1960, Swed.)

Eric Bengtsson
ON THE SUNNYSIDE(1936, Swed.), md; DOLLAR(1938, Swed.), m

Frans T. Bengtsson
LONG SHIPS, THE(1964, Brit./Yugo.), w

Jean Benguigui
AFRICAN, THE(1983, Fr.)

Barbara Benham
1984
SUBURBIA(1984)

Dorothy Benham
Misc. Silents
FUGITIVE, THE(1916)

Elsa Benham
Silents
WESTERN COURAGE(1927); AIR PATROL, THE(1928)
Misc. Silents
ROUGH RIDIN'(1924); CODE OF THE COW COUNTRY(1927)

Ernest Benham
Misc. Silents
GREATHEART(1921, Brit.)

Grace Benham
Silents
ALIEN SOULS(1916)
Misc. Silents
FLIRT, THE(1916)

Harry Benham
Silents
MISCHIEF MAKER, THE(1916); DANCER'S PERIL, THE(1917); HUSH MONEY(1921)
Misc. Silents
MOTHS(1913); FROU FROU(1914); PAMELA'S PAST(1916); PATH OF HAPPINESS, THE(1916); PUTTING THE BEE IN HERBERT(1917); VICTIM, THE(1917); CECILIA OF THE PINK ROSES(1918); CONVICT 993(1918); WHEN YOU AND I WERE YOUNG(1918); DANGEROUS PARADISE, THE(1920); POLLY WITH A PAST(1920); PREY, THE(1920); ROAD TO ARCADY, THE(1922); TOWN THAT FORGOT GOD, THE(1922); YOUR BEST FRIEND(1922)

Joan Benham
PICKWICK PAPERS, THE(1952, Brit.); INNOCENTS IN PARIS(1955, Brit.); KING'S RHAPSODY(1955, Brit.); MAN WHO LOVED REDHEADS(1955, Brit.); CHILD IN THE HOUSE(1956, Brit.); LOSER TAKES ALL(1956, Brit.); WHOLE TRUTH, THE(1958, Brit.); BRIDAL PATH, THE(1959, Brit.); DESERT MICE(1960, Brit.); I THANK A FOOL(1962, Brit.); V.I.P.s, THE(1963, Brit.); LADIES WHO DO(1964, Brit.); MURDER AHOY(1964, Brit.); TAMAHINE(1964, Brit.); WILD AFFAIR, THE(1966, Brit.); LIMBO LINE, THE(1969, Brit.); MAGIC CHRISTIAN, THE(1970, Brit.); PERFECT FRIDAY(1970, Brit.); PETER RABBIT AND TALES OF BEATRIX POTTER(1971, Brit.); GREEK TYCOON, THE(1978)

Marc Benham
TWELVE PLUS ONE(1970, Fr./Ital.), w

W.H. Benham
Misc. Silents
DOWN UNDER DONOVAN(1922, Brit.)

June Benhow
JOAN OF ARC(1948)

Ted Beniades
MAN CALLED ADAM, A(1966); REFLECTIONS IN A GOLDEN EYE(1967); DETECTIVE, THE(1968); GANG THAT COULDN'T SHOOT STRAIGHT, THE(1971); PURSUIT OF HAPPINESS, THE(1971); THEY MIGHT BE GIANTS(1971); SERPICO(1973); NEXT MAN, THE(1976); SCARFACE(1983)

A. Beniaminov
DON QUIXOTE(1961, USSR)

Alexander Beniaminov
1984
MOSCOW ON THE HUDSON(1984)

Guy Benier
ME(1970, Fr.), p

Roberto Benigni
LUNA(1979, Ital.)

Y. Benin
HUNTING IN SIBERIA(1962, USSR), art d

Peter Benison
TERROR TRAIN(1980, Can.), ph

Andres Benitez
CURSE OF THE VAMPIRES(1970, Phil., U.S.)

Leila Benitez
WONDER WOMEN(1973, Phil.)

Albert Benitz
PRODIGAL SON, THE(1935), ph; CHALLENGE, THE(1939, Brit.), ph; THEY MET ON SKIS(1940, Fr.), ph; CAPTAIN FROM KOEPENICK, THE(1956, Ger.), ph; DEVIL'S GENERAL, THE(1957, Ger.), ph; MAN ON A STRING(1960), ph; MRS. WARREN'S PROFESSION(1960, Ger.), ph; GIRL OF THE MOORS, THE(1961, Ger.), ph; CITY OF SECRETS(1963, Ger.), ph; TERROR OF DR. MABUSE, THE(1965, Ger.), ph

Teddy Benivedes
HUK(1956)

Yoko Benizawa
Misc. Silents
LASCIVIOUSNESS OF THE VIPER, THE(1920, Jap.)

Adrian Benjamin
DOCTOR FAUSTUS(1967, Brit.)

Arthur Benjamin
MAN WHO KNEW TOO MUCH, THE(1935, Brit.), m; SCARLET PIMPERNEL, THE(1935, Brit.), m; MISTER HOBO(1936, Brit.), m; UNDER THE RED ROBE(1937, Brit.), m; WINGS OF THE MORNING(1937, Brit.), m&md; RETURN OF THE SCARLET PIMPERNEL(1938, Brit.), m; MASTER OF BANKDAM, THE(1947, Brit.), m; IDEAL HUSBAND, AN(1948, Brit.), m; ABOVE US THE WAVES(1956, Brit.), m; NAKED EARTH, THE(1958, Brit.), m

Bob Benjamin
STRAWBERRY STATEMENT, THE(1970)

Christopher Benjamin
RING OF BRIGHT WATER(1969, Brit.); HAWK THE SLAYER(1980, Brit.)
1984
PLAGUE DOGS, THE(1984, U.S./Brit.)

Don Benjamin
1984
IRRECONCILABLE DIFFERENCES(1984)

Floella Benjamin
BLACK JOY(1977, Brit.)

Harry Benjamin
WANDERERS, THE(1979)

Janis Benjamin
SUMMER LOVERS(1982)

Paul Benjamin
MIDNIGHT COWBOY(1969); ANDERSON TAPES, THE(1971); ACROSS 110TH STREET(1972); DEADLY TRACKERS(1973); EDUCATION OF SONNY CARSON, THE(1974); DISTANCE(1975); FRIDAY FOSTER(1975); LEADBELLY(1976); ESCAPE FROM ALCATRAZ(1979); SOME KIND OF HERO(1982)

Philip Benjamin
QUICK, BEFORE IT MELTS(1964), a, w

Richard Benjamin [Richard Lightner]
HOUSE OF WAX(1953); STRANGER WORE A GUN, THE(1953); THUNDER OVER THE PLAINS(1953); CRIME WAVE(1954); RIDING SHOTGUN(1954)

Richard Benjamin
GOODBYE COLUMBUS(1969); CATCH-22(1970); DIARY OF A MAD HOUSEWIFE(1970); MARRIAGE OF A YOUNG STOCKBROKER, THE(1971); STEAGLE, THE(1971); PORTNOY'S COMPLAINT(1972); LAST OF SHEILA, THE(1973); WESTWORLD(1973); SUNSHINE BOYS, THE(1975); HOUSE CALLS(1978); LOVE AT FIRST BITE(1979); SCAVENGER HUNT(1979); FIRST FAMILY(1980); HOW TO BEAT THE HIGH COST OF LIVING(1980); LAST MARRIED COUPLE IN AMERICA, THE(1980); SATURDAY THE 14TH(1981); MY FAVORITE YEAR(1982), d
1984
CITY HEAT(1984), d; RACING WITH THE MOON(1984), d
Misc. Talkies
WITCHES' BREW(1980)

Rita Benjamin
SUDAN(1945)

Sonyia Benjamin
RETURN OF MR. MOTO, THE(1965, Brit.)

William Benjamin
CHAMPAGNE MURDERS, THE(1968, Fr.), w

Benji
OH, HEAVENLY DOG!(1980)

Fita Benkhoff
BOCCACCIO(1936, Ger.); INHERITANCE IN PRETORIA(1936, Ger.); HELP I'M INVISIBLE(1952, Ger.); BEGGAR STUDENT, THE(1958, Ger.)

Tom Benko
YOUNG GRADUATES, THE(1971); LADIES AND GENTLEMEN, THE FABULOUS STAINS(1982), ed

Benkt-Ake Benktsson
SEVENTH SEAL, THE(1958, Swed.)

Ralph Benmurgie
BY DESIGN(1982)

Simone Benmuse
LEFT-HANDED WOMAN, THE(1980, Ger.)

Harry Benn
DATELINE DIAMONDS(1966, Brit.), p
1984
RAZOR'S EDGE, THE(1984), p

Jon T. Benn
RETURN OF THE DRAGON(1974, Chin.)

Sean Benn
1984
WINTER FLIGHT(1984, Brit.)

Susann Benn
TOUGH ENOUGH(1983)

Heather Benna
SCARFACE(1983)

Giuseppe Bennati
GIRL WITH A SUITCASE(1961, Fr./Ital.), w; RED LIPS(1964, Fr./Ital.), d, w

Eli Benneche
THREE FACES OF EVE, THE(1957), set d; SAY ONE FOR ME(1959), set d; ADVISE AND CONSENT(1962), set d

Katja Bennefeld
EIGHT GIRLS IN A BOAT(1932, Ger.)

Ann Bennent
1984
SWANN IN LOVE(1984, Fr.Ger.)

Anne Bennent
WILD DUCK, THE(1977, Ger./Aust.)

David Bennent
TIN DRUM, THE(1979, Ger./Fr./Yugo./Pol.)
1984
DOG DAY(1984, Fr.)

Heinz Bennent
LOST HONOR OF KATHARINA BLUM, THE(1975, Ger.); SERPENT'S EGG, THE(1977, Ger./U.S.); WILD DUCK, THE(1977, Ger./Aust.); GERMANY IN AUTUMN(1978, Ger.); TIN DRUM, THE(1979, Ger./Fr./Yugo./Pol.); WOMANLIGHT(1979, Fr./Ger./Ital.); CLAIR DE FEMME(1980,Fr.); FROM THE LIFE OF THE MARIONETTES(1980, Ger.); LAST METRO, THE(1981, Fr.); POSSESSION(1981, Fr./Ger.); SISTERS, OR THE BALANCE OF HAPPINESS(1982, Ger.); DEATH OF MARIO RICCI, THE(1983, Ital.)

Richard Benner
OUTRAGEOUS!(1977, Can.), d&w; HAPPY BIRTHDAY, GEMINI(1980), d, w

Yale Benner
Silents
MAN FROM BEYOND, THE(1922)
Misc. Silents
FAITH AND FORTUNE(1915); VANITY FAIR(1915); WAY BACK, THE(1915); CATSPAW, THE(1916); OTHER PEOPLE'S MONEY(1916)

Gay Bennes
JOURNEY FOR MARGARET(1942)

Andrew Bennet
BLACK JACK(1979, Brit.)

Carol Bennet
GHOST, THE(1965, Ital.)

Dorothea Bennet
1984
JIGSAW MAN, THE(1984, Brit.), w

Harriet Bennet
ROLLIN' PLAINS(1938)

High Bennet
WHITE RAT(1972)

Hywel Bennet
ENDLESS NIGHT(1971, Brit.)

Jill Bennet
ANATOMIST, THE(1961, Brit.)

John Bennet
TRUE STORY OF ESKIMO NELL, THE(1975, Aus.)
1984
PLAGUE DOGS, THE(1984, U.S./Brit.)

Larry Bennet
PASSION HOLIDAY(1963), ed

Linda Bennet
1,000 SHAPES OF A FEMALE(1963); VICE GIRLS, LTD.(1964)

Louise Bennet
CALYPSO(1959, Fr./It.)

Richard Bennet
ANGRY HILLS, THE(1959, Brit.), m

Sarah Bennet
SUMMERFIELD(1977, Aus.), ed

Spencer Bennet
ARIZONA BOUND(1941), d; CALLING WILD BILL ELLIOTT(1943), d; CANYON CITY(1943), d; BENEATH WESTERN SKIES(1944), d; CALIFORNIA JOE(1944), d; CODE OF THE PRAIRIE(1944), d; PHANTOM OF THE JUNGLE(1955), d

Spencer G. Bennet
AVENGING WATERS(1936), d; COWBOY FROM SUNDOWN(1940), d; GUN MAN FROM BODIE, THE(1941), d; BRAVE WARRIOR(1952), d; DEVIL GODDESS(1955), d; SUBMARINE SEAHAWK(1959), d; ATOMIC SUBMARINE, THE(1960), d; BOUNTY KILLER, THE(1965), d
Misc. Talkies
CALLING ALL CARS(1935), d

Spencer Gordon Bennet
JAWS OF JUSTICE(1933), d; BADGE OF HONOR(1934), d; HEIR TO TROUBLE(1936), d; LAWLESS RIDERS(1936), d; VOODOO TIGER(1952), d; KILLER APE(1953), d
Misc. Talkies
OIL RAIDER, THE(1934), d

Spenser Gordon Bennet
MIDNIGHT WARNING, THE(1932), d

Alan Bennett
LONG SHOT(1981, Brit.); RETURN OF THE JEDI(1983)

Alex Bennett
PLEASE STAND BY(1972)

Alma Bennett
MIDNIGHT DADDIES(1929); NEW ORLEANS(1929); PAINTED FACES(1929); TWO MEN AND A MAID(1929)

Silents

AFFAIRS OF ANATOL, THE(1921); LOST WORLD, THE(1925); SILENT LOVER, THE(1926); LONG PANTS(1927); GOOD-BYE KISS, THE(1928); GRAIN OF DUST, THE(1928); HEAD OF THE FAMILY, THE(1928)

Misc. Silents

FLAMING HEARTS(1922); SMILING JIM(1922); MAN'S SIZE(1923); THREE JUMPS AHEAD(1923); CYCLONE RIDER, THE(1924); LILLIES OF THE FIELD(1924); FOOL AND HIS MONEY, A(1925); LIGHT OF THE WESTERN STARS, THE(1925); THRILL HUNTER, THE(1926); COMPASSION(1927)

Ann Bennett

OPERATION DIPLOMAT(1953, Brit.); WEDDING OF LILLI MARLENE, THE(1953, Brit.)

Anne Bennett

THEY MEET AGAIN(1941)

Arnold Bennett

PICCADILLY(1932, Brit.), w; HIS DOUBLE LIFE(1933), w; HOLY MATRIMONY(1943), w; PROMOTER, THE(1952, Brit.), w

Silents

GREAT ADVENTURE, THE(1915, Brit.), w; OLD WIVES' TALE, THE(1921, Brit.), w

Audrey Bennett

SOMEWHERE IN TIME(1980)

Barbara Bennett

MOTHER'S BOY(1929); SYNCOPATION(1929); LOVE AMONG THE MILLIONAIRES(1930)

Misc. Silents

BLACK JACK(1927)

Belle Bennett

IRON MASK, THE(1929); MOLLY AND ME(1929); THEIR OWN DESIRE(1929); COURAGE(1930); RECAPTURED LOVE(1930); BIG SHOT, THE(1931)

Silents

ASHES OF HOPE(1917); DEVIL DODGER, THE(1917); ATOM, THE(1918); RECKONING DAY, THE(1918); IN HOLLYWOOD WITH POTASH AND PERLMUTTER(1924); STELLA DALLAS(1925); RECKLESS LADY, THE(1926); WAY OF ALL FLESH, THE(1927); BATTLE OF THE SEXES, THE(1928)

Misc. Silents

SWEET KITTY BELLAIRS(1916); BECAUSE OF THE WOMAN(1917); BOND OF FEAR, THE(1917); CHARMER, THE(1917); FIRES OF REBELLION(1917); FUEL OF LIFE(1917); LAST REBEL, THE(1918); LONELY WOMAN, THE(1918); SOUL IN TRUST, A(1918); MAYOR OF FILBERT, THE(1919); FLESH AND SPIRIT(1922); YOUR BEST FRIEND(1922); HIS SUPREME MOMENT(1925); IF MARRIAGE FAILS(1925); PLAYING WITH SOULS(1925); LILY, THE(1926); FOURTH COMMANDMENT, THE(1927); MOTHER(1927); WILD GEESE(1927); DEVIL'S SKIPPER, THE(1928); DEVIL'S TRADEMARK, THE(1928); MOTHER MACHREE(1928); POWER OF SILENCE, THE(1928); SPORTING AGE, THE(1928); WOMAN WHO WAS FORGOTTEN, THE(1930)

Ben Bennett

OPERATION BOTTLENECK(1961); IT HAPPENED IN ATHENS(1962)

Beverly Bennett

MOUSE ON THE MOON, THE(1963, Brit.)

Misc. Talkies

MORALS SQUAD(1960)

Bill Bennett

LIVE AND LET DIE(1973, Brit.), stunts; PETERSEN(1974, Aus.)

Billie Bennett

FASHIONS IN LOVE(1929); NIGHT WORK(1930); ONE ROMANTIC NIGHT(1930)

Silents

CROSSING TRAILS(1921); PENROD(1922); ROBIN HOOD(1922); ETERNAL THREE, THE(1923); FIGHTING SMILE, THE(1925); LADY WINDERMERE'S FAN(1925); AMATEUR GENTLEMAN, THE(1926); MEMORY LANE(1926); RANSON'S FOLLY(1926); SONORA KID, THE(1927); TRAGEDY OF YOUTH, THE(1928)

Misc. Silents

CALL OF THE MATE(1924); MARTYR SEX, THE(1924); WYOMING WILDCAT, THE(1925)

Billy Bennett

RADIO FOLLIES(1935, Brit.); ALMOST A GENTLEMAN(1938, Brit.); YOUNG MAN'S FANCY(1943, Brit.)

Silents

TILLIE'S PUNCTURED ROMANCE(1914)

Bob Bennett

NUMBER ONE(1969); OUT OF TOWNERS, THE(1970)

Bonnie Bennett

GLAMOUR FOR SALE(1940)

Boyd Bennett

YOUTH ON TRIAL(1945)

Brenda Bennett

1984

PURPLE RAIN(1984)

Brian Bennett

SWINGER'S PARADISE(1965, Brit.)

Britan Bennett

FINDERS KEEPERS(1966, Brit.)

Bruce Bennett [Herman Brix]

RIP TIDE(1934); AMATEUR CROOK(1937); BLONDIE BRINGS UP BABY(1939); FIVE LITTLE PEPPERS AND HOW THEY GREW(1939); BEFORE I HANG(1940); BLAZING SIX SHOOTERS(1940); CAFE HOSTESS(1940); ESCAPE TO GLORY(1940); FIVE LITTLE PEPPERS AT HOME(1940); GIRLS OF THE ROAD(1940); INVISIBLE STRIPES(1940); ISLAND OF DOOMED MEN(1940); LONE WOLF KEEPS A DATE, THE(1940); LONE WOLF MEETS A LADY, THE(1940); MAN WITH NINE LIVES, THE(1940); MY SON IS GUILTY(1940); SECRET SEVEN, THE(1940); WEST OF ABILENE(1940); HONOLULU LU(1941); OFFICER AND THE LADY, THE(1941); PHANTOM SUBMARINE, THE(1941); THREE GIRLS ABOUT TOWN(1941); TWO LATINS FROM MANHATTAN(1941); ATLANTIC CONVOY(1942); SABOTAGE SQUAD(1942); SUBMARINE RAIDER(1942); TRAMP, TRAMP, TRAMP(1942); UNDERGROUND AGENT(1942); MORE THE MERRIER, THE(1943); MURDER IN TIMES SQUARE(1943); SAHARA(1943); THERE'S SOMETHING ABOUT A SOLDIER(1943); I'M FROM ARKANSAS(1944); U-BOAT PRISONER(1944); DANGER SIGNAL(1945); MILDRED PIERCE(1945); MAN I LOVE, THE(1946); STOLEN LIFE, A(1946); CHEYENNE(1947); DARK PASSAGE(1947); NORA PRENTISS(1947); SILVER RIVER(1948); SMART GIRLS DON'T TALK(1948); TO THE VICTOR(1948); TREASURE OF THE SIERRA MADRE, THE(1948); DOCTOR AND THE GIRL, THE(1949);

HOUSE ACROSS THE STREET, THE(1949); TASK FORCE(1949); UNDERTOW(1949); WITHOUT HONOR(1949); YOUNGER BROTHERS, THE(1949); GREAT MISSOURI RAID, THE(1950); MYSTERY STREET(1950); SECOND FACE, THE(1950); SHAKEDOWN(1950); ANGELS IN THE OUTFIELD(1951); LAST OUTPOST, THE(1951); SUDDEN FEAR(1952); DRAGONFLY SQUADRON(1953); BIG TIP OFF, THE(1955); ROBBER'S ROOST(1955); STRATEGIC AIR COMMAND(1955); BOTTOM OF THE BOTTLE, THE(1956); HIDDEN GUNS(1956); LOVE ME TENDER(1956); THREE OUTLAWS, THE(1956); THREE VIOLENT PEOPLE(1956); DANIEL BOONE, TRAIL BLAZER(1957); FLAMING FRONTIER(1958, Can.); ALLIGATOR PEOPLE, THE(1959); COSMIC MAN, THE(1959); FIEND OF DOPE ISLAND(1961), a, w; OUTSIDER, THE(1962); CLONES, THE(1973); DEADHEAD MILES(1982)

Brunetta Bennett

SHAMPOO(1975)

Carl Bennett

EGG AND I, THE(1947)

Catherine Bennett

Silents

DANGEROUS HOUR(1923); SOUL MATES(1925)

Misc. Silents

DEVIL'S BOWL, THE(1923); WILD BULL'S LAIR, THE(1925)

Charles Bennett

BLACKMAIL(1929, Brit.), w; LAST HOUR, THE(1930, Brit.), w; DEADLOCK(1931, Brit.), w; HAWLEY'S OF HIGH STREET(1933, Brit.), w; HOUSE OF TRENT, THE(1933, Brit.), w; MANNEQUIN(1933, Brit.), w; MATINEE IDOL(1933, Brit.), w; PARIS PLANE(1933, Brit.), w; SECRET OF THE LOCH, THE(1934, Brit.), w; TREASURE ISLAND(1934); WARN LONDON!(1934, Brit.), w; BLUE SMOKE(1935, Brit.), w; CLAIRVOYANT, THE(1935, Brit.), w; MAN WHO KNEW TOO MUCH, THE(1935, Brit.), w; NIGHT MAIL(1935, Brit.), w; 39 STEPS, THE(1935, Brit.), w; GAY LOVE(1936, Brit.), w; KING OF THE DAMNED(1936, Brit.), w; SECRET AGENT, THE(1936, Brit.), w; KING SOLOMON'S MINES(1937, Brit.), w; MAN WHO CRIED WOLF, THE(1937); SABOTAGE(1937, Brit.), w; YOUNG AND INNOCENT(1938, Brit.), w; YOUNG IN HEART, THE(1938), w; BALALAIKA(1939), w; GUNGA DIN(1939); FOREIGN CORRESPONDENT(1940), w; MAN HUNT(1941); THEY DARE NOT LOVE(1941), w; JOAN OF PARIS(1942), w; MRS. MINIVER(1942); REAP THE WILD WIND(1942), w; FOREVER AND A DAY(1943), w; IT AIN'T HAY(1943); STORY OF DR. WASSELL, THE(1944), w; IVY(1947), w; UNCONQUERED(1947), w; SIGN OF THE RAM, THE(1948), w; BLACK MAGIC(1949), w; MADNESS OF THE HEART(1949, Brit.), d&w; WHERE DANGER LIVES(1950), w; KIND LADY(1951), w; GREEN GLOVE, THE(1952), w; NO ESCAPE(1953), d&w; DANGEROUS MISSION(1954), w; MAN WHO KNEW TOO MUCH, THE(1956), w; STORY OF MANKIND, THE(1957), w; 27TH DAY, THE(1957); CURSE OF THE DEMON(1958), w; BIG CIRCUS, THE(1959), w; LOST WORLD, THE(1960), w; VOYAGE TO THE BOTTOM OF THE SEA(1961), w; FIVE WEEKS IN A BALLOON(1962), w; CITY UNDER THE SEA(1965, Brit.), w; LINCOLN CONSPIRACY, THE(1977), set d; ROLLERCOASTER(1977); BEYOND AND BACK(1978), art d

1984

GO TELL IT ON THE MOUNTAIN(1984), prod d

Silents

TILLIE'S PUNCTURED ROMANCE(1914); JOHN HALIFAX, GENTLEMAN(1915, Brit.); BRIDE OF FEAR, THE(1918); ALL WRONG(1919); ALWAYS AUDACIOUS(1920); AMERICA(1924); TOP OF NEW YORK, THE(1925)

Misc. Silents

RAINBOW GIRL, THE(1917)

Chester Bennett

Silents

MASTER STROKE, A(1920), d; PURPLE CIPHER, THE(1920), d; DIAMONDS ADRIFT(1921), d; SECRET OF THE HILLS, THE(1921), d; THELMA(1922), d; DIVORCE(1923), d; LULLABY, THE(1924), d; ANCIENT MARINER, THE(1925), d; CHAMPION OF LOST CAUSES(1925), d

Misc. Silents

LAIR OF THE WOLF, THE(1917); ROMANCE PROMOTORS, THE(1920), d; WHEN A MAN LOVES(1920), d; THREE SEVENS(1921), d; BELLE OF ALASKA(1922), d; COLLEEN OF THE PINES(1922), d; SNOWSHOE TRAIL, THE(1922), d; PAINTED LADY, THE(1924), d; HONESTY-THE BEST POLICY(1926), d

Colin Bennett

1984

SUCCESS IS THE BEST REVENGE(1984, Brit.)

Compton Bennett

SEVENTH VEIL, THE(1946, Brit.), d; YEARS BETWEEN, THE(1947, Brit.), d; DAYDREAK(1948, Brit.), d; MY OWN TRUE LOVE(1948), d; THAT FORSYTE WOMAN(1949), d; KING SOLOMON'S MINES(1950), d; GLORY AT SEA(1952, Brit.), d; IT STARTED IN PARADISE(1952, Brit.), d; DESPERATE MOMENT(1953, Brit.), d; SO LITTLE TIME(1953, Brit.), d; AFTER THE BALL(1957, Brit.), d; CITY AFTER MIDNIGHT(1957, Brit.), d&w; MAILBAG ROBBERY(1957, Brit.), p&d; BEYOND THE CURTAIN(1960, Brit.), d, w

Connie Lee Bennett

LADY FROM TEXAS, THE(1951), w; LAST POSSE, THE(1953), w; MA AND PA KETTLE AT WAIKIKI(1955), w

Constance Bennett

RICH PEOPLE(1929); THIS THING CALLED LOVE(1929); COMMON CLAY(1930); SIN TAKES A HOLIDAY(1930); SON OF THE GODS(1930); THREE FACES EAST(1930); BORN TO LOVE(1931); BOUGHT(1931); COMMON LAW, THE(1931); EASIEST WAY, THE(1931); LADY WITH A PAST(1932); ROCKABYE(1932); TWO AGAINST THE WORLD(1932); WHAT PRICE HOLLYWOOD?(1932); AFTER TONIGHT(1933); BED OF ROSES(1933); OUR BETTERS(1933); AFFAIRS OF CELLINI, THE(1934); MOULIN ROUGE(1934); OUTCAST LADY(1934); AFTER OFFICE HOURS(1935); EVERYTHING IS THUNDER(1936, Brit.); LADIES IN LOVE(1936); TOPPER(1937); MERRILY WE LIVE(1938); SERVICE DE LUXE(1938); TAIL SPIN(1939); TOPPER TAKES A TRIP(1939); ESCAPE TO GLORY(1940); LAW OF THE TROPICS(1941); TWO-FACED WOMAN(1941); MADAME SPY(1942); SIN TOWN(1942); WILD BILL HICKOK RIDES(1942); PARIS UNDERGROUND(1945), a, p; CENTENNIAL SUMMER(1946); UNSUSPECTED, THE(1947); ANGEL ON THE AMAZON(1948); SMART WOMAN(1948); AS YOUNG AS YOU FEEL(1951); IT SHOULD HAPPEN TO YOU(1954); MADAME X(1966)

Silents

RECKLESS YOUTH(1922); CYTHEREA(1924); GOOSE WOMAN, THE(1925); MY SON(1925)

Misc. Silents

FIGHTING DEATH(1914); EVIDENCE(1922); CYTHEREA(1924); CODE OF THE WEST(1925); GOOSE HANGS HIGH, THE(1925); PINCH HITTER, THE(1925); SALLY,

IRENE AND MARY(1925); WANDERING FIRES(1925); MARRIED?(1926)

Cora Bennett
TIME GENTLEMEN PLEASE!(1953, Brit.); RETURN OF THE SECAUCUS SEVEN(1980)

Darlene Bennett
OLGA'S GIRLS(1964); "RENT-A-GIRL"(1965); TASTE OF FLESH, A(1967)

Dave Bennett
FOLLOW THRU(1930), ch; SONS OF THE DESERT(1933), ch

David Bennett
HONEY(1930), ch; LET'S GO NATIVE(1930), ch; SAFETY IN NUMBERS(1930), ch; LAST MARRIED COUPLE IN AMERICA, THE(1980); LEGEND OF THE LONE RANGER, THE(1981)

Dean Bennett
BLOW OUT(1981)

Diana Bennett
NO HIGHWAY IN THE SKY(1951, Brit.)

Dickie Bennett
ROCK YOU SINNERS(1957, Brit.)

Don Bennett
SMALL CIRCLE OF FRIENDS, A(1980)

Dorothy Bennett
LIFE BEGINS WITH LOVE(1937), w; DAUGHTERS COURAGEOUS(1939), w; ALWAYS IN MY HEART(1942), w; ALL BY MYSELF(1943), w; FOLLOW THE BAND(1943), w; IT COMES UP LOVE(1943), w; MR. BIG(1943), w; WHEN JOHNNY COMES MARCHING HOME(1943), w; SENSATIONS OF 1945(1944), w; SHOW BUSINESS(1944), w; PATRICK THE GREAT(1945), w; DO YOU LOVE ME?(1946), w
Misc. Talkies
HITCHHIKE TO HELL(1978)

Douglas Bennett
ANNE OF THE INDIES(1951)

Duane Bennett
HARRY IN YOUR POCKET(1973)

Earl Bennett
EGG AND I, THE(1947); SARGE GOES TO COLLEGE(1947); 1001 ARABIAN NIGHTS(1959), ed; GAY PURR-EE(1962), ed; MR. MAGOO'S HOLIDAY FESTIVAL(1970), ed

Ed Bennett
CHILDISH THINGS(1969)

Edith Barker Bennett
WATCH BEVERLY(1932, Brit.)

Edmond Bennett
CLUE OF THE TWISTED CANDLE(1968, Brit.)

Edna Bennett
TRUE TO LIFE(1943); LADIES OF THE BIG HOUSE(1932); ST. LOUIS KID, THE(1934); CASINO MURDER CASE, THE(1935); KLONDIKE ANNIE(1936); SMALL TOWN GIRL(1936); COWBOY COMMANDOS(1943); SALUTE FOR THREE(1943); THAT TOUCH OF MINK(1962)

Edward Bennett
SECRET EVIDENCE(1941), w; FINGER ON THE TRIGGER(1965, US/Span.), set d; ASCENDANCY(1983, Brit.), d, w

Edward Knoblock Arnold Bennett
DEAR MR. PROHACK(1949, Brit.), w

Eileen Bennett
DESIGN FOR MURDER(1940, Brit.); MUCH TOO SHY(1942, Brit.); THURSDAY'S CHILD(1943, Brit.)

Elaine Bennett
GODLESS GIRL, THE(1929)
Silents
KING OF KINGS, THE(1927)

Elizabeth Bennett
BROTHERS AND SISTERS(1980, Brit.)

Enid Bennett
WATERLOO BRIDGE(1931); SKIPPY(1931); SOOKY(1931); INTERMEZZO: A LOVE STORY(1939); MEET DR. CHRISTIAN(1939); STRIKE UP THE BAND(1940)
Silents
BATTLE OF GETTYSBURG(1914); LITTLE BROTHER, THE(1917); NAUGHTY, NAUGHTY!(1918); WHEN DO WE EAT?(1918); HAIRPINS(1920); KEEPING UP WITH LIZZIE(1921); ROBIN HOOD(1922); COURTSHIP OF MILES STANDISH, THE(1923); STRANGERS OF THE NIGHT(1923)
Misc. Silents
GIRL GLORY, THE(1917); HAPPINESS(1917); MOTHER INSTINCT, THE(1917); PRINCESS OF THE DARK, A(1917); THEY'RE OFF(1917); BIGGEST SHOW ON EARTH, THE(1918); COALS OF FIRE(1918); DESERT WOOING, A(1918); FUSS AND FEATHERS(1918); KEYS OF THE RIGHTEOUS, THE(1918); MARRIAGE RING, THE(1918); VAMP, THE(1918); HAPPY THOUGH MARRIED(1919); HAUNTED BEDROOM, THE(1919); LAW OF MEN, THE(1919); PARTNERS THREE(1919); STEPPING OUT(1919); VIRTUOUS THIEF, THE(1919); WHAT EVERY WOMAN LEARNS(1919); FALSE ROAD, THE(1920); HER HUSBAND'S FRIEND(1920); SILK HOSIERY(1920); WOMAN IN THE SUITCASE(1920); BOOTLEGGER'S DAUGHTER, THE(1922); SCANDALOUS TONGUES(1922); BAD MAN, THE(1923); YOUR FRIEND AND MINE(1923); FOOL'S AWAKENING, A(1924); RED LILY, THE(1924); SEA HAWK, THE(1924); WOMAN'S HEART, A(1926); WRONG MR. WRIGHT, THE(1927)

Evelyn Bennett
HIRED WIFE(1934)

Faith Bennett
OFFICER'S MESS, THE(1931, Brit.); EYES OF FATE(1933, Brit.); HAWLEY'S OF HIGH STREET(1933, Brit.); MANNEQUIN(1933, Brit.); PRIDE OF THE FORCE, THE(1933, Brit.); MASTER AND MAN(1934, Brit.); SEEING IS BELIEVING(1934, Brit.); ONE GOOD TURN(1936, Brit.)

Fran Bennett
ANNAPOLIS STORY, AN(1955); FAR HORIZONS, THE(1955); GIANT(1956); PROMISES IN THE DARK(1979); ROMANTIC COMEDY(1983)

Frances Bennett
HAND, THE(1960, Brit.); MARY HAD A LITTLE(1961, Brit.); SNAKE WOMAN, THE(1961, Brit.); BAXTER(1973, Brit.)

Frank Bennett
IT HAPPENED HERE(1966, Brit.)
Silents
DISHONORED MEDAL, THE(1914); GRETCHEN, THE GREENHORN(1916); INTOLERANCE(1916); REGGIE MIXES IN(1916)

Misc. Silents
SISTER OF SIX, A(1916); SOLD FOR MARRIAGE(1916); STRANDED(1916); HEIRESS AT "COFFEE DAN'S", THE(1917); HER OFFICAL FATHERS(1917); LITTLE YANK, THE(1917); LOST IN TRANSIT(1917); STAGE STRUCK(1917)

Frank Fisher Bennett
Misc. Silents
JURY OF FATE, THE(1917)

Franklin Bennett
IT'S THAT MAN AGAIN(1943, Brit.); WE DIVE AT DAWN(1943, Brit.); JOHNNY FRENCHMAN(1946, Brit.)

Franklyn Bennett
HERITAGE(1935, Aus.)
CHAMPAGNE WALTZ(1937)

Gertrude Bennett
IDIOT'S DELIGHT(1939); WESTERNER, THE(1940); UNHOLY PARTNERS(1941)
Misc. Talkies
TEMPTATION(1930)
Silents
MERRY WIDOW, THE(1925)

Gordona Bennett
DANCE OF LIFE, THE(1929)

Gregory Bennett
YOUNG WARRIORS(1983)

Harriet Bennett
ZIEGFELD GIRL(1941)

Harriett Bennett
ONE TOUCH OF VENUS(1948)

Harve Bennett
STAR TREK II: THE WRATH OF KHAN(1982), w
1984
STAR TREK III: THE SEARCH FOR SPOCK(1984), a, p, w

Heather Bennett
MISSING NOTE, THE(1961, Brit.)

Heinz Bennett
WAR AND PEACE(1983, Ger.)

Helen Bennett
MIDDLETON FAMILY AT THE N.Y. WORLD'S FAIR(1939); ON THE THRESHOLD OF SPACE(1956); RETURN TO PEYTON PLACE(1961)

Hope Bennett
Misc. Talkies
LIFE GOES ON(1938)

Howard Bennett
DUTCHMAN(1966, Brit.)

Hugh Bennett
SATURDAY'S CHILDREN(1929), ed; ARROWSMITH(1931), ed; STREET SCENE(1931), ed; CYNARA(1932), ed; SECRETS(1933), ed; BOLERO(1934), ed; SHE LOVES ME NOT(1934), ed; CORONADO(1935), ed; GLASS KEY, THE(1935), ed; RUMBA(1935), ed; ROSE OF THE RANCHO(1936), ed; MAID OF SALEM(1937), ed; WELLS FARGO(1937), ed; COCOANUT GROVE(1938), ed; HER JUNGLE LOVE(1938), ed; IF I WERE KING(1938), ed; GRAND JURY SECRETS(1939), ed; OUR LEADING CITIZEN(1939), ed; PERSONS IN HIDING(1939), ed; GREAT McGINTY, THE(1940), ed; RHYTHM ON THE RIVER(1940), ed; HENRY ALDRICH FOR PRESIDENT(1941), d; I WANTED WINGS(1941), ed; HENRY ALDRICH, EDITOR(1942), d; HENRY ALDRICH GETS GLAMOUR(1942), d; HENRY AND DIZZY(1942), d; HENRY ALDRICH HAUNTS A HOUSE(1943), d; HENRY ALDRICH SWINGS IT(1943), d; HENRY ALDRICH, BOY SCOUT(1944), d; HENRY ALDRICH PLAYS CUPID(1944), d; HENRY ALDRICH'S LITTLE SECRET(1944), d; NATIONAL BARN DANCE(1944), d; CHAMPAGNE FOR CAESAR(1950), ed
Silents
AFFAIR OF THE FOLLIES, AN(1927), ed; OUTCAST(1928), ed

Hywel Bennett
FAMILY WAY, THE(1966, Brit.); DROP DEAD, MY LOVE(1968, Italy); TWISTED NERVE(1969, Brit.); VIRGIN SOLDIERS, THE(1970, Brit.); BUTTERCUP CHAIN, THE(1971, Brit.); LOOT(1971, Brit.); PERCY(1971, Brit.); IT'S A 2"6" ABOVE THE GROUND WORLD(1972, Brit.)

J. Moy Bennett
Silents
IRON MAN, THE(1925); UNGUARDED HOUR, THE(1925)
Misc. Silents
FIFTY-FIFTY(1925)

Jack Bennett
IN THE YEAR 2889(1966), spec eff; IT'S ALIVE(1968), spec eff; DON'T LOOK IN THE BASEMENT(1973), spec eff; FOR THE LOVE OF BENJI(1977), art d, spec eff; SILENT RAGE(1982), spec eff; SPLIT IMAGE(1982), spec eff
1984
INITIATION, THE(1984), spec eff

Jay Bennett
WOMAN WHO WOULDN'T DIE, THE(1965, Brit.), w

Jean Bennett
FARMER'S OTHER DAUGHTER, THE(1965)

Jesse Bennett
HANGAR 18(1980)

Jill Bennett
GOOD DAME(1934); HEAT LIGHTNING(1934); TREASURE ISLAND(1934); ONE MORE SPRING(1935); MANHATTAN HEARTBEAT(1940); LONG DARK HALL, THE(1951, Brit.); MOULIN ROUGE(1952); AUNT CLARA(1954, Brit.); HELL BELOW ZERO(1954, Brit.); EXTRA DAY, THE(1956, Brit.); LUST FOR LIFE(1956); CONCRETE JUNGLE, THE(1962, Brit.); NANNY, THE(1965, Brit.); SKULL, THE(1965, Brit.); CHARGE OF THE LIGHT BRIGADE, THE(1968, Brit.); INADMISSIBLE EVIDENCE(1968, Brit.); JULIUS CAESAR(1970, Brit.); I WANT WHAT I WANT(1972, Brit.); MR. QUILP(1975, Brit.); FULL CIRCLE(1977, Brit./Can.); FOR YOUR EYES ONLY(1981); HAUNTING OF JULIA, THE(1981, Brit./Can.); BRITTANIA HOSPITAL(1982, Brit.)
Misc. Talkies
AERODROME, THE(1983, Brit.)

Joan Bennett
BULLDOG DRUMMOND(1929); DISRAELI(1929); MISSISSIPPI GAMBLER(1929); THREE LIVE GHOSTS(1929); CRAZY THAT WAY(1930); MAYBE IT'S LOVE(1930); MOBY DICK(1930); PUTTIN' ON THE RITZ(1930); SCOTLAND YARD(1930); DOC-

TORS' WIVES(1931); HUSH MONEY(1931); MANY A SLIP(1931); CARELESS LADY(1932); ME AND MY GAL(1932); SHE WANTED A MILLIONAIRE(1932); TRIAL OF VIVIENNE WARE, THE(1932); WEEK-ENDS ONLY(1932); WILD GIRL(1932); ARIZONA TO BROADWAY(1933); LITTLE WOMEN(1933); PURSUIT OF HAPPINESS, THE(1934); MAN WHO BROKE THE BANK AT MONTE CARLO, THE(1935); MAN WHO RECLAIMED HIS HEAD, THE(1935); MISSISSIPPI(1935); PRIVATE WORLDS(1935); SHE COULDN'T TAKE IT(1935); TWO FOR TONIGHT(1935); BIG BROWN EYES(1936); THIRTEEN HOURS BY AIR(1936); TWO IN A CROWD(1936); WEDDING PRESENT(1936); VOGUES OF 1938(1937); ARTISTS AND MODELS ABROAD(1938); I MET MY LOVE AGAIN(1938); TEXANS, THE(1938); TRADE WINDS(1938); HOUSEKEEPER'S DAUGHTER(1939); MAN IN THE IRON MASK, THE(1939); GREEN HELL(1940); HOUSE ACROSS THE BAY, THE(1940); MAN I MARRIED, THE(1940); SON OF MONTE CRISTO(1940); CONFIRM OR DENY(1941); MAN HUNT(1941); SHE KNEW ALL THE ANSWERS(1941); WILD GEESE CALLING(1941); GIRL TROUBLE(1942); TWIN BEDS(1942); WIFE TAKES A FLYER, THE(1942); MARGIN FOR ERROR(1943); COLONEL EFFINGHAM'S RAID(1945); NOB HILL(1945); SCARLET STREET(1945); WOMAN IN THE WINDOW, THE(1945); MACOMBER AFFAIR, THE(1947); WOMAN ON THE BEACH, THE(1947); HOLLOW TRIUMPH(1948); SECRET BEYOND THE DOOR, THE(1948); RECKLESS MOMENTS, THE(1949); FATHER OF THE BRIDE(1950); FOR HEAVEN'S SAKE(1950); FATHER'S LITTLE DIVIDEND(1951); GUY WHO CAME BACK, THE(1951); HIGHWAY DRAGNET(1954); WE'RE NO ANGELS(1955); NAVY WIFE(1956); THERE'S ALWAYS TOMORROW(1956); DESIRE IN THE DUST(1960); HOUSE OF DARK SHADOWS(1970); SUSPIRIA(1977, Ital.)

Joan Sterndale Bennett
SAN FERRY ANN(1965, Brit.)

Joe Bennett
SOMETHING TO SING ABOUT(1937)
1984
NADIA(1984, U.S./Yugo.)
Silents
SOMEWHERE IN SONORA(1927); LARIAT KID, THE(1929)
Misc. Silents
CROWN JEWELS(1918); FAITH AND ENDURIN'(1918); GOLDEN FLEECE, THE(1918); GREY PARASOL, THE(1918); LIMOUSINE LIFE(1918); LOVE NEVER DIES(1921); BARBARA FRIETCHIE(1924); FLASHING SPURS(1924); COLD NERVE(1925); SIGN OF THE CLAW, THE(1926); STRAIGHT SHOOTIN'(1927); WOLF'S TRAIL(1927)

John B. Bennett
WATERMELON MAN(1970), p; MAN, A WOMAN, AND A BANK, A(1979, Can.), p; FORCED VENGEANCE(1982), p

John Bennett
IT TAKES A THIEF(1960, Brit.); PIRATES OF BLOOD RIVER, THE(1962, Brit.); POSTMAN'S KNOCK(1962, Brit.); BARBER OF STAMFORD HILL, THE(1963, Brit.); CROOKS ANONYMOUS(1963, Brit.); KALEIDOSCOPE(1966, Brit.); SYNDICATE, THE(1968, Brit.); HOUSE THAT DRIPPED BLOOD, THE(1971, Brit.); HENRY VIII AND HIS SIX WIVES(1972, Brit.); HITLER: THE LAST TEN DAYS(1973, Brit./Ital.); MOHAMMAD, MESSENGER OF GOD(1976, Lebanon/Brit.); GREEK TYCOON, THE(1978); WATERSHIP DOWN(1978, Brit.); MIRROR CRACK'D, THE(1980, Brit.); EYE OF THE NEEDLE(1981)
1984
GIVE MY REGARDS TO BROAD STREET(1984, Brit.); STRANGERS KISS(1984)

John D. Bennett
Misc. Silents
BLUE ENVELOPE MYSTERY, THE(1916)

John Drew Bennett
Misc. Silents
ONE TOUCH OF NATURE(1917)

Jordan Bennett
1984
NINJA III–THE DOMINATION(1984)

Joseph Bennett
AFTER THE FOG(1930)
Silents
NIGHT HORSEMAN, THE(1921); ELOPE IF YOU MUST(1922)
Misc. Silents
INDISCREET CORINNE(1917); YOUTH'S DESIRE(1920); MAN IN THE SHADOW, THE(1926); GOD'S GREAT WILDERNESS(1927)

Josephine Bennett
THIEVES LIKE US(1974)

Judge William Thomas Bennett
SOUNDER(1972)

Julie Bennett
ILLEGAL(1955); GAY PURR-EE(1962); HEY THERE, IT'S YOGI BEAR(1964); WHAT'S UP, TIGER LILY?(1966), a, w; MR. MAGOO'S HOLIDAY FESTIVAL(1970)

June Bennett
WOMEN WON'T TELL(1933)

Kathy Bennett
ISLAND OF LOVE(1963); SPENCER'S MOUNTAIN(1963)

Kem Bennett
TERROR ON A TRAIN(1953), w; DOUBLE CROSS(1956, Brit.), w

Ken Bennett
SMALL TOWN STORY(1953, Brit.), p

Kevin Bennett
PAYROLL(1962, Brit.); RUNAWAY RAILWAY(1965, Brit.); OPERATION THIRD FORM(1966, Brit.); OTLEY(1969, Brit.)

Lee Bennett
WITHOUT RESERVATIONS(1946); THRILL OF A LIFETIME(1937); VIVACIOUS LADY(1938); THESE GLAMOUR GIRLS(1939); GIRL TROUBLE(1942); GANG'S ALL HERE, THE(1943); FOLLOW THE BOYS(1944); HAT CHECK HONEY(1944); IN THE MEANTIME, DARLING(1944); SLIGHTLY TERRIFIC(1944); TWO GIRLS AND A SAILOR(1944); SONG OF OLD WYOMING(1945); CARAVAN TRAIL, THE(1946); COLORADO SERENADE(1946); DRIFTIN' RIVER(1946); LARCENY IN HER HEART(1946); STARS OVER TEXAS(1946); TILL THE CLOUDS ROLL BY(1946); WILD WEST(1946); LAST ROUND-UP, THE(1947); SCARED TO DEATH(1947); SPIRIT OF WEST POINT, THE(1947); CORONER CREEK(1948); PRAIRIE OUTLAWS(1948); TIOGA KID, THE(1948); STATE DEPARTMENT–FILE 649(1949); DALTON'S WOMEN, THE(1950); DAKOTA KID, THE(1951); MY FAVORITE SPY(1951); THREE DESPERATE MEN(1951)

Leila Bennett
DOCTOR X(1932); EMMA(1932); FIRST YEAR, THE(1932); PURCHASE PRICE, THE(1932); TAXI!(1932); TIGER SHARK(1932); TWO AGAINST THE WORLD(1932); STUDY IN SCARLET, A(1933); SUNSET PASS(1933); TERROR ABOARD(1933); DAMES(1934); HOUSEWIFE(1934); JOURNAL OF A CRIME(1934); ONCE TO EVERY WOMAN(1934); STRICTLY DYNAMITE(1934); UNKNOWN BLONDE(1934); WAGON WHEELS(1935); MARK OF THE VAMPIRE(1935); FURY(1936)

Lelia Bennett
NO OTHER WOMAN(1933); STUDY IN SCARLET, A(1933)

Les Bennett
HOLD'EM NAVY!(1937)

Lesley Bennett
SWALLOWS AND AMAZONS(1977, Brit.)

Leslie Bennett
ON DANGEROUS GROUND(1951)

Libby Bennett
TOO MANY GIRLS(1940)

Linda Bennett
BIG HEAT, THE(1953); CLOWN, THE(1953); CREATURE WITH THE ATOM BRAIN(1955); GOOD MORNING, MISS DOVE(1955); QUEEN BEE(1955); SEVEN LITTLE FOYS, THE(1955); SPY CHASERS(1956); NAKED FLAME, THE(1970, Can.)

Lou Bennett
TWO ARE GUILTY(1964, Fr.)

Louise Bennett
HIGH WIND IN JAMAICA, A(1965); DARK OF THE SUN(1968, Brit.)

Luke Bennett
NOTHING BUT A MAN(1964), ed; FEARLESS FRANK(1967), ed; MADELEINE IS(1971, Can.), ed

Majorie Bennett
36 HOURS(1965)

Margaret Bennett
Silents
AMERICAN LIVE WIRE, AN(1918)

Margery Bennett
Misc. Silents
GIRL GLORY, THE(1917); HUGON THE MIGHTY(1918)

Margot Bennett
CROWNING TOUCH, THE(1959, Brit.), w; MAN WHO LIKED FUNERALS, THE(1959, Brit.), w; WHO KILLED TEDDY BEAR?(1965); O LUCKY MAN!(1973, Brit.)

Marjorie Bennett
MONSIEUR VERDOUX(1947); JUNE BRIDE(1948); SILVER RIVER(1948); ABBOTT AND COSTELLO MEET THE KILLER, BORIS KARLOFF(1949); FLAXY MARTIN(1949); TAKE ONE FALSE STEP(1949); UNDERTOW(1949); PEGGY(1950); PERFECT STRANGERS(1950); TWO FLAGS WEST(1950); MAN WHO CHEATED HIMSELF, THE(1951); LIMELIGHT(1952); SO BIG(1953); ABBOTT AND COSTELLO MEET DR. JEKYLL AND MR. HYDE(1954); RICOCHET ROMANCE(1954); SABRINA(1954); ABBOTT AND COSTELLO MEET THE KEYSTONE KOPS(1955); COBWEB, THE(1955); FEMALE ON THE BEACH(1955); GIRL RUSH, THE(1955); KISS ME DEADLY(1955); LAY THAT RIFLE DOWN(1955); YOUNG AT HEART(1955); AUTUMN LEAVES(1956); OUR MISS BROOKS(1956); STRANGE INTRUDER(1956); MAN OF A THOUSAND FACES(1957); SHOOT-OUT AT MEDICINE BEND(1957); HOME BEFORE DARK(1958); CAREER(1959); OCEAN'S ELEVEN(1960); RAT RACE, THE(1960); ONE HUNDRED AND ONE DALMATIANS(1961); SAIL A CROOKED SHIP(1961); SUMMER AND SMOKE(1961); THUNDER OF DRUMS, A(1961); NOTORIOUS LANDLADY, THE(1962); SAINTLY SINNERS(1962); WHATEVER HAPPENED TO BABY JANE?(1962); FOUR FOR TEXAS(1963); PROMISES, PROMISES(1963); MAN FROM GALVESTON, THE(1964); MARY POPPINS(1964); MY FAIR LADY(1964); NIGHT WALKER, THE(1964); QUICK, BEFORE IT MELTS(1964); THREE NUTS IN SEARCH OF A BOLT(1964); WHAT A WAY TO GO(1964); FAMILY JEWELS, THE(1965); BILLY THE KID VS. DRACULA(1966); GAMES(1967); COOGAN'S BLUFF(1968); LOVE GOD?, THE(1969); CHARLEY VARRICK(1973); STACEY!(1973); NORTH AVENUE IRREGULARS, THE(1979)
Silents
MIDNIGHT PATROL, THE(1918); NAUGHTY, NAUGHTY!(1918)

Mark Bennett
GIRL IN BLACK STOCKINGS(1957); TOY, THE(1982)

Matt Bennett
HICKEY AND BOGGS(1972); UNHOLY ROLLERS(1972)

Maureen Bennett
MIRROR CRACK'D, THE(1980, Brit.)
1984
JIGSAW MAN, THE(1984, Brit.); SCANDALOUS(1984); SUCCESS IS THE BEST REVENGE(1984, Brit.)

Michael Bennett
NAVY HEROES(1959, Brit.); PICTURES(1982, New Zealand)
1984
REPO MAN(1984)

Mickey Bennett
DUMMY, THE(1929); FOOTLIGHTS AND FOOLS(1929); GHOST TALKS, THE(1929); STRICTLY MODERN(1930); SWING HIGH(1930); BIG BUSINESS GIRL(1931); FATHER'S SON(1931); FINGER POINTS, THE(1931); LAUGHTER IN HELL(1933); MAYOR OF HELL, THE(1933); MAN ON THE FLYING TRAPEZE, THE(1935)
Silents
MAN WHO PLAYED GOD, THE(1922); LOYAL LIVES(1923); SECOND YOUTH(1924); BIG PAL(1925); COHENS AND KELLYS, THE(1926); IT'S THE OLD ARMY GAME(1926); BABE COMES HOME(1927); SLAVES OF BEAUTY(1927); HEAD OF THE FAMILY, THE(1928); TILLIE'S PUNCTURED ROMANCE(1928)
Misc. Silents
EMPTY CRADLE, THE(1923); NEW SCHOOL TEACHER, THE(1924); BOY OF THE STREETS, A(1927); UNITED STATES SMITH(1928)

Micky Bennett
Silents
REPORTED MISSING(1922)

Mike Bennett
MACHISMO–40 GRAVES FOR 40 GUNS(1970), ed; STUDENT BODY, THE(1976), art d

Mrs. Bennett
Silents
PLEYDELL MYSTERY, THE(1916, Brit.)

Nan Bennett
THIS TIME FOR KEEPS(1947); THREE DARING DAUGHTERS(1948)
Nicholas Bennett
KONGA(1961, Brit.)
Norman Bennett
TENDER MERCIES(1982); TERMS OF ENDEARMENT(1983)
1984
CLOAK AND DAGGER(1984); COUNTRY(1984); RIVER RAT, THE(1984)
Pamela Bennett
O'HARA'S WIFE(1983), set d
Peter Bennett
LADY CHATTERLEY'S LOVER(1981, Fr./Brit.)
Phil Bennett
TINGLER, THE(1959), art d
Phillip Bennett
UPTIGHT(1968), art d; CHEAP DETECTIVE, THE(1978), art d; ORDINARY PEOPLE(1980), art d
Rafael [Ray] Bennett
PUBLIC COWBOY NO. 1(1937); RAW TIMBER(1937); TEXAS TRAIL(1937)
Rafael Bennett
DRUMS OF DESTINY(1937); FEMALE FUGITIVE(1938)
Ralph Bennett
BORDER BADMEN(1945)
Randall Bennett
MORGAN'S MARAUDERS(1929)
Randy Bennett
BEST LITTLE WHOREHOUSE IN TEXAS, THE(1982); PANDEMONIUM(1982)
Raphael [Ray] Bennett
KNIGHTS OF THE RANGE(1940); KANSAN, THE(1943)
Raphael [Ray] Bennett
OLD BARN DANCE, THE(1938); PRAIRIE MOON(1938); RANGE WAR(1939); TEXAS STAMPEDE(1939); THUNDERING FRONTIER(1940); ROMANCE OF THE RIO GRANDE(1941); RAIDERS OF THE BORDER(1944)
Raphael Bennett
DEVIL'S SADDLE LEGION, THE(1937); FORLORN RIVER(1937); FRAME-UP THE(1937); ADVENTURE IN SAHARA(1938); HI-YO SILVER(1940); HIDDEN GOLD(1940); MAN FROM TUMBLEWEEDS, THE(1940); DOOMED CARAVAN(1941); GAUCHOS OF EL DORADO(1941); LAWLESS PLAINSMEN(1942); FLAME OF THE WEST(1945); MESSENGER OF PEACE(1950)
Misc. Talkies
HAUNTED MINE, THE(1946)
Ray [Raphael] Bennett
OLD LOUISIANA(1938); SCENE OF THE CRIME(1949); SONG OF SURRENDER(1949)
Ray Bennett
BATTLE OF GREED(1934); FIREFLY, THE(1937); UNDERCOVER AGENT(1939); MEDICO OF PAINTED SPRINGS, THE(1941); RETURN OF DANIEL BOONE, THE(1941); ROBBERS OF THE RANGE(1941); MISSOURI OUTLAW, A(1942); PRISONER OF JAPAN(1942); SPOILERS, THE(1942); CATTLE STAMPEDE(1943); CYCLONE PRAIRIE RANGERS(1944); DEAD OR ALIVE(1944); DEATH RIDES THE PLAINS(1944); DRIFTER, THE(1944); MARSHAL OF GUNSMOKE(1944); TRAIL TO GUNSIGHT(1944); NAVAJO TRAIL, THE(1945); BETTY CO-ED(1946); GUN TOWN(1946); UNDER ARIZONA SKIES(1946); HEAVEN ONLY KNOWS(1947); CANON CITY(1948); FRONTIER REVENGE(1948); HOLLOW TRIUMPH(1948); NORTHWEST STAMPEDE(1948); DALTON GANG, THE(1949); MA AND PA KETTLE(1949); RED CANYON(1949); RIMFIRE(1949); SAMSON AND DELILAH(1949); STATE DEPARTMENT–FILE 649(1949); TENSION(1949); WHITE HEAT(1949); FANCY PANTS(1950); WINCHESTER '73(1950); APACHE DRUMS(1951); THUNDERING TRAIL, THE(1951); BLACK LASH, THE(1952); KANSAS CITY CONFIDENTIAL(1952); MAN FROM BLACK HILLS, THE(1952); SPRINGFIELD RIFLE(1952); UNTAMED FRONTIER(1952); WACO(1952); GREAT SIOUX UPRISING, THE(1953); POWDER RIVER(1953); REDHEAD FROM WYOMING, THE(1953); FRENCH LINE, THE(1954); AFRICAN MANHUNT(1955); GIANT(1956); WRONG MAN, THE(1956); STONE(1974, Aus.); FIGHTING BACK(1983, Brit.)
Misc. Talkies
RENEGADE, THE(1943); CODE OF THE PLAINS(1947)
Reggie Bennett
SPACEHUNTER: ADVENTURES IN THE FORBIDDEN ZONE(1983)
Richard Bennett
HOME TOWNERS, THE(1928); ARROWSMITH(1931); BOUGHT(1931); FIVE AND TEN(1931); IF I HAD A MILLION(1932); MADAME RACKETEER(1932); NO GREATER LOVE(1932); STRANGE JUSTICE(1932); THIS RECKLESS AGE(1932); BIG EXECUTIVE(1933); SONG OF SONGS(1933); NANA(1934); 18 MINUTES(1935, Brit.); JOURNEY INTO FEAR(1942); MAGNIFICENT AMBERSONS, THE(1942); RICHARD III(1956, Brit.); HIGH FLIGHT(1957, Brit.); PICKUP ALLEY(1957, Brit.), m; INDISCREET(1958), m; MAN INSIDE, THE(1958, Brit.), m; MENACE IN THE NIGHT(1958, Brit.), m; MAN WHO COULD CHEAT DEATH, THE(1959, Brit.), m; CHANCE MEETING(1960, Brit.), m; WATCH YOUR STERN(1961, Brit.), m; PIRATES OF BLOOD RIVER, THE(1962, Brit.); TELL-TALE HEART, THE(1962, Brit.); HARPER VALLEY, P.T.A.(1978), d
Silents
DAMAGED GOODS(1915); YOUTH FOR SALE(1924)
Misc. Silents
AND THE LAW SAYS(1916); PHILIP HOLDEN - WASTER(1916); SABLE BLESSING, THE(1916); VALLEY OF DECISION, THE(1916); DAMAGED GOODS(1917); GILDED YOUTH, A(1917); ETERNAL CITY, THE(1923); LYING WIVES(1925)
Richard Rodney Bennett
SAFECRACKER, THE(1958, Brit.), m; DEVIL'S DISCIPLE, THE(1959), m; MARK, THE(1961, Brit.), m; ONLY TWO CAN PLAY(1962, Brit.), m; SATAN NEVER SLEEPS(1962), m; BILLY LIAR(1963, Brit.), m; HEAVENS ABOVE!(1963, Brit.), m; WRONG ARM OF THE LAW, THE(1963, Brit.), m; NANNY, THE(1965, Brit.), m; ONE WAY PENDULUM(1965, Brit.), m; BILLION DOLLAR BRAIN(1967, Brit.), m; DEVIL'S OWN, THE(1967, Brit.), m; FAR FROM THE MADDING CROWD(1967, Brit.), m; SECRET CEREMONY(1968, Brit.), m; FIGURES IN A LANDSCAPE(1970, Brit.), m; BUTTERCUP CHAIN, THE(1971, Brit.), m; NICHOLAS AND ALEXANDRA(1971, Brit.), m; LADY CAROLINE LAMB(1972, Brit./Ital.), m; VOICES(1973, Brit.), m; MURDER ON THE ORIENT EXPRESS(1974, Brit.), m; PERMISSION TO KILL(1975, U.S./Aust.), m; "EQUUS"(1977), m; BRINK'S JOB, THE(1978), m; YANKS(1979), m; RETURN OF THE SOLDIER, THE(1983, Brit.), m

Rita Bennett
SHAME, SHAME, EVERYBODY KNOWS HER NAME(1969); RAGING BULL(1980)
Robert Bennett
CHANCES(1931); LOCAL BOY MAKES GOOD(1931)
Robert C. Bennett
WHEN G-MEN STEP IN(1938), w
Robert R. Bennett
STANLEY AND LIVINGSTONE(1939), m
Robert Russell Bennett
FIFTH AVENUE GIRL(1939), m; OKLAHOMA(1955), md
Rod Bennett
QUEST FOR FIRE(1982, Fr./Can.)
Ronald Bennett
GASLIGHT(1944)
Roph Bennett
BACHELOR'S BABY(1932, Brit.), w
Roy Bennett
NUREMBERG(1961)
Ruffin Barron Bennett
CATAMOUNT KILLING, THE(1975, Ger.), prod d
Rus Bennett
DAYS OF WINE AND ROSES(1962)
Russell Bennett
PACIFIC LINER(1939), md; CARNEGIE HALL(1947), md
Ruth Bennett
KILLERS FROM SPACE(1954)
Samaki Bennett
SOLOMON KING(1974)
Sara Bennett
TOUCH AND GO(1955), ed
Sarah Bennett
RETURN OF THE JEDI(1983)
Sedal Bennett
GOOD SAM(1948)
Seldon Bennett
SHADOW OF THE THIN MAN(1941)
Seymour Bennett
MACOMBER AFFAIR, THE(1947), w; LAST POSSE, THE(1953), w
Sheldon Bennett
JOHNNY EAGER(1942)
Spencer Bennett
NIGHT ALARM(1935), d; ACROSS THE PLAINS(1939), d; OKLAHOMA TERROR(1939), d; RIDERS OF THE FRONTIER(1939), d
Spencer G. Bennett
FUGITIVE SHERIFF, THE(1936), d; HEROES OF THE RANGE(1936), d; RANGER COURAGE(1937), d; RANGERS STEP IN, THE(1937), d; RECKLESS RANGER(1937), d; RIO GRANDE RANGER(1937), d; RIDING THE CHEROKEE TRAIL(1941), d; MOJAVE FIREBRAND(1944), d; TUCSON RAIDERS(1944), d; REQUIEM FOR A GUNFIGHTER(1965), d
Spencer Gordon Bennett
ROGUE OF THE RIO GRANDE(1930), d; 99 WOUNDS(1931), d; JUSTICE TAKES A HOLIDAY(1933), d; FEROCIOUS PAL(1934), d; FIGHTING ROOKIE, THE(1934), d; GET THAT MAN(1935), d; RESCUE SQUAD(1935), d; WESTERN COURAGE(1935), d; CATTLE THIEF, THE(1936), d; UNKNOWN RANGER, THE(1936), d; LAW OF THE RANGER(1937), d; WESTBOUND STAGE(1940), d; THEY RAID BY NIGHT(1942), d; LONE TEXAS RANGER(1945), d; SAVAGE MUTINY(1953), d
Silents
MARKED MONEY(1928), d
Misc. Silents
BEHOLD THE MAN(1921, US/Fr.), d; FIGHTING MARINE, THE(1926), d; HAWK OF THE HILLS(1929), d
Stephen Bennett
HER HUSBAND'S AFFAIRS(1947)
Steve Bennett
SOUTHERN YANKEE, A(1948); THEY SAVED HITLER'S BRAIN(1964), w
Terrell Bennett
NIGHT THEY ROBBED BIG BERTHA'S, THE(1975)
Tony Bennett
OSCAR, THE(1966); LAST PICTURE SHOW, THE(1971), m
Vaea Bennett
NUDE ODYSSEY(1962, Fr./Ital.)
Van Bennett
HUCKLEBERRY FINN(1974)
Vivienne Bennett
ALMOST A HONEYMOON(1938, Brit.); DEVIL'S BAIT(1959, Brit.)
Wallace Bennett
GEORGE(1973, U.S./Switz.)
1984
PHILADELPHIA EXPERIMENT, THE(1984), w
Wallace C. Bennett
GEORGE(1973, U.S./Switz.), d&w; TENDER FLESH(1976), w; SILENT SCREAM(1980), w
Whitman Bennett
Silents
JIM THE PENMAN(1921), p; SALVATION NELL(1921), sup; WIFE AGAINST WIFE(1921), d; SECRETS OF PARIS, THE(1922), p; LOYAL LIVES(1923), p; MODERN MARRIAGE(1923), sup
Misc. Silents
LOVE OF WOMEN(1924), d; TWO SHALL BE BORN(1924), d; VIRTUOUS LIARS(1924), d; BACK TO LIFE(1925), d; CHILDREN OF THE WHIRLWIND(1925), d; LENA RIVERS(1925), d; SCANDAL STREET(1925), d; SHARE AND SHARE ALIKE(1925), d
Wilda Bennett
DARK VICTORY(1939); WHAT A LIFE(1939); THOSE WERE THE DAYS(1940); LADY EVE, THE(1941)
Silents
GOOD LITTLE DEVIL, A(1914); LOVE, HONOR AND OBEY(1920)

William Bennett
Silents
IRON MAN, THE(1925), d
Bennett & Williams
SATURDAY NIGHT REVUE(1937, Brit.)
Lillian Bennett-Thompson
Silents
LOVE GAMBLER, THE(1922), w
Rich Bennette
DAY TIME ENDED, THE(1980, Span.), David Allen
Adriana Bennetti
FURIA(1947, Ital.)
James Benning
Misc. Talkies
11 X 14(1977), d
Russ Benning
1984
STARMAN(1984)
Willim Benninger
LOST HONOR OF KATHARINA BLUM, THE(1975, Ger.), p
John Bennings
LEGEND OF NIGGER CHARLEY, THE(1972), m
Clive Bennington
GALLIPOLI(1981, Aus.)
F. Bennington
Silents
HOUSE OF TEMPERLEY, THE(1913, Brit.)
Andrew Bennison
AIR CIRCUS, THE(1928), w; WORDS AND MUSIC(1929), w, w; LET'S GO PLACES(1930), w; ON THE LEVEL(1930), w; AFFAIR OF SUSAN(1935), w; UNDERCOVER MAN(1936), w; LAWLESS LAND(1937), w; DESPERATE TRAILS(1939), w; CHIP OF THE FLYING U(1940), w; YOU'LL FIND OUT(1940), w; POT O' GOLD(1941), w
Silents
DIVORCE(1923), w; WOMAN WISE(1928), w; SIN SISTER, THE(1929), w; STRONG BOY(1929), w
Andrew W. Bennison
THIS SPORTING AGE(1932), d
Silents
RED WINE(1928), w
Ishia Bennison
AWAKENING, THE(1980)
Lewis Bennison
Silents
DAMAGED GOODS(1915)
Louis Bennison
Silents
PRETTY MRS. SMITH(1915); OH, JOHNNY(1919); LAVENDER AND OLD LACE(1921)
Misc. Silents
HIGH POCKETS(1919); MISFIT EARL, A(1919); ROAD CALLED STRAIGHT, THE(1919); SANDY BURKE OF THE U-BAR-U(1919); SPEEDY MEADE(1919)
Carolyn Bennitt
DOCTOR FAUSTUS(1967, Brit.)
Mohamed Bennour
OLIVE TREES OF JUSTICE, THE(1967, Fr.)
Bill Benny
HIGH JINKS IN SOCIETY(1949, Brit.)
Jack Benny
WITHOUT RESERVATIONS(1946); CHASING RAINBOWS(1930); MEDICINE MAN, THE(1930); TRANSATLANTIC MERRY-GO-ROUND(1934); BROADWAY MELODY OF 1936(1935); IT'S IN THE AIR(1935); BIG BROADCAST OF 1937, THE(1936); COLLEGE HOLIDAY(1936); ARTISTS AND MODELS(1937); ARTISTS AND MODELS ABROAD(1938); MAN ABOUT TOWN(1939); BUCK BENNY RIDES AGAIN(1940); LOVE THY NEIGHBOR(1940); CHARLEY'S AUNT(1941); GEORGE WASHINGTON SLEPT HERE(1942); TO BE OR NOT TO BE(1942); MEANEST MAN IN THE WORLD, THE(1943); HOLLYWOOD CANTEEN(1944); HORN BLOWS AT MIDNIGHT, THE(1945); IT'S IN THE BAG(1945); LUCKY STIFF, THE(1949), p; SOMEBODY LOVES ME(1952); GYPSY(1962); IT'S A MAD, MAD, MAD, MAD WORLD(1963); GUIDE FOR THE MARRIED MAN, A(1967); MAN, THE(1972)
Jim Benny
1984
CALIFORNIA GIRLS(1984)
Prudence Benny
REMEDY FOR RICHES(1941)
Benny & McNulty
Silents
TWO FLAMING YOUTHS(1927)
Benny Carter and Orchestra
THOUSANDS CHEER(1943)
Benny Diggs
EDUCATION OF SONNY CARSON, THE(1974)
Benny Goodman and His Band
SWEET AND LOWDOWN(1944)
Benny Goodman and his orchestra
BIG BROADCAST OF 1937, THE(1936); HOLLYWOOD HOTEL(1937); POWERS GIRL, THE(1942); GANG'S ALL HERE, THE(1943); MAKE MINE MUSIC(1946)
Benny The Gouge
BULLETS OR BALLOTS(1936)
Mac Benoff
LOVE HAPPY(1949), w; BLESS THE BEASTS AND CHILDREN(1971), w
Alexandre Benois
Silents
NAPOLEON(1927, Fr.), art d
Nadia Benois
VICE VERSA(1948, Brit.), cos; PRIVATE ANGELO(1949, Brit.), cos

Robert Benois
LES ABYSSES(1964, Fr.)
Michel Benoist
SEVEN CAPITAL SINS(1962, Fr./Ital.)
Ben Benoit
IS THIS TRIP REALLY NECESSARY?(1970), p&d
Misc. Talkies
BLOOD OF THE IRON MAIDEN(1969), d
G. Benoit
HEART OF PARIS(1939, Fr.), ph
George Benoit
Silents
SERPENT, THE(1916), ph; IDLE HANDS(1921), ph; WELCOME STRANGER(1924), ph; LOVER'S OATH, A(1925), ph
George S. Benoit
Silents
HONOR SYSTEM, THE(1917), ph
Georges Benoit
FANNY(1948, Fr.), ph
Silents
LITTLE 'FRAID LADY, THE(1920), ph; WHAT'S A WIFE WORTH?(1921), ph; JEWELS OF DESIRE(1927), ph; NO CONTROL(1927), ph
Glenn Benoit
WOLFEN(1981)
Ludwik Benoit
EVE WANTS TO SLEEP(1961, Pol.); PORTRAIT OF LENIN(1967, Pol./USSR); SARAGOSSA MANUSCRIPT, THE(1972, Pol.)
Mary Benoit
MEET JOHN DOE(1941); THREE HEARTS FOR JULIA(1943); PICTURE OF DORIAN GRAY, THE(1945); THAT NIGHT WITH YOU(1945); ONE TOUCH OF VENUS(1948); TOAST OF NEW ORLEANS, THE(1950); IT GROWS ON TREES(1952); I DIED A THOUSAND TIMES(1955); LONG GRAY LINE, THE(1955); AUTUMN LEAVES(1956); LEATHER SAINT, THE(1956); MAN IN THE GREY FLANNEL SUIT, THE(1956); FEAR STRIKES OUT(1957); ROCKABILLY BABY(1957); SUNRISE AT CAMPOBELLO(1960); CASE OF PATTY SMITH, THE(1962); DAYS OF WINE AND ROSES(1962); FIVE FINGER EXERCISE(1962); MANCHURIAN CANDIDATE, THE(1962); GATHERING OF EAGLES, A(1963); SANDPIPER, THE(1965)
Pierre Benoit
SURRENDER(1931), w; MISTRESS OF ATLANTIS, THE(1932, Ger.), w; KOENIGSMARK(1935, Fr.), w; I STAND CONDEMNED(1936, Brit.), w; COLONEL CHABERT(1947, Fr.), w; SIREN OF ATLANTIS(1948), w; JOURNEY BENEATH THE DESERT(1967, Fr./Ital.), w
Robert Benoit
DISCREET CHARM OF THE BOURGEOISIE, THE(1972, Fr.)
Ronald Benoit
CASEY'S SHADOW(1978)
Sally Benoit
ON THE RIGHT TRACK(1981)
Victor Benoit
Silents
GREYHOUND, THE(1914); FOOL THERE WAS, A(1915)
Misc. Silents
DEVIL'S DAUGHTER, THE(1915); FOURTH ESTATE, THE(1916)
Jean Benoit-Levy
LA MATERNELLE(1933, Fr.), d&w; FIRE IN THE STRAW(1943), p&d, w
Misc. Silents
AMES D'ENFANTS(1929, Fr.), d; PEAU DE PECHE(1929, Fr.), d
The Benoits
ICE-CAPADES(1941); ICE-CAPADES REVUE(1942)
Mario Benotti
LITTLE MARTYR, THE(1947, Ital.), ph
Pat Benoye
HAIR(1979)
Martin Benrath
MORITURI(1965); FROM THE LIFE OF THE MARIONETTES(1980, Ger.)
Dee Dee Benrey
WARRIORS, THE(1979)
Tony Benroy
RED SNOW(1952)
Al Bensalt
WOMAN IN THE WINDOW, THE(1945)
Eliane Bensdorp
I SPIT ON YOUR GRAVE(1962, Fr.), ed
Jacques Bense
1984
LE BAL(1984, Fr./Ital./Algeria), ch
Bob Bensen
1,000 SHAPES OF A FEMALE(1963)
Carl Bensen
Misc. Talkies
DISCIPLES OF DEATH(1975)
Carle Bensen
Misc. Talkies
ENTER THE DEVIL(1975)
Greg Bensen
1984
BOLERO(1984)
Lucille Bensen
1941(1979); HALLOWEEN II(1981)
Deborah Benso
1941(1979)
Annette Benson
DEADLOCK(1931, Brit.)
Silents
LOVE AT THE WHEEL(1921, Brit.); SQUIBS(1921, Brit.); NONENTITY, THE(1922, Brit.); SQUIBS WINS THE CALCUTTA SWEEP(1922, Brit.); MONEY HABIT, THE(1924, Brit.); RINGER, THE(1928, Brit.); WEEKEND WIVES(1928, Brit.); WHEN BOYS LEAVE HOME(1928, Brit.); INSEPARABLES, THE(1929, Brit.)

Misc. Silents
LOVERS IN ARABY(1924, Brit.); CONFETTI(1927, Brit.); SHOOTING STARS(1928); SIR OR MADAM(1928, Brit.); SOUTH SEA BUBBLE, A(1928, Brit.)

Anthony Benson
1984
1984(1984, Brit.)

Ben Benson
RUNNING WILD(1955), w

Bernadette Benson
THIS SPORTING LIFE(1963, Brit.)

Carl Benson
HOUSE ON 92ND STREET, THE(1945); FLOOD TIDE(1958)

Christopher Benson
STRANGE BREW(1983)

Clyde Benson
Silents
FLASHLIGHT, THE(1917); GIRL WHO WOULDN'T QUIT, THE(1918); MORE TROUBLE(1918); ROMANCE OF TARZAN, THE(1918); JANE GOES A' WOOING(1919); GENTLE JULIA(1923)
Misc. Silents
FALSE CODE, THE(1919); GATES OF BRASS(1919); SHERIFF'S SON, THE(1919)

Court Benson
NO, MY DARLING DAUGHTER(1964, Brit.); DIRTYMOUTH(1970)

Danny Benson
THAT SINKING FEELING(1979, Brit.)

Deborah Benson
9/30/55(1977); OUR WINNING SEASON(1978); NORTH DALLAS FORTY(1979); JUST BEFORE DAWN(1980)

E. Benson
TOWER OF TERROR, THE(1942, Brit.), m

E.F. Benson
DEAD OF NIGHT(1946, Brit.), w

Elaine Benson
OLD CURIOSITY SHOP, THE(1935, Brit.); REGAL CAVALCADE(1935, Brit.)

Esther Benson
FAN, THE(1981)

Flo Benson
MRS. MINIVER(1942)

Frank Benson
BARBARY COAST(1935); GREAT IMPERSONATION, THE(1935); RETURN OF SOPHIE LANG, THE(1936); WUTHERING HEIGHTS(1939); EARL OF CHICAGO, THE(1940); FOREIGN CORRESPONDENT(1940); MAN HUNT(1941); SCOTLAND YARD(1941); LUCKY JORDAN(1942); NATIONAL VELVET(1944)

George Benson
KEEP FIT(1937, Brit.); CONVOY(1940); YOUNG MAN'S FANCY(1943, Brit.); OCTOBER MAN, THE(1948, Brit.); HELTER SKELTER(1949, Brit.); HAPPIEST DAYS OF YOUR LIFE(1950, Brit.); HIGHLY DANGEROUS(1950, Brit.); LOST PEOPLE, THE(1950, Brit.); POOL OF LONDON(1951, Brit.); ISLAND RESCUE(1952, Brit.); MAN IN THE WHITE SUIT, THE(1952); BROKEN HORSESHOE, THE(1953, Brit.); CAPTAIN'S PARADISE, THE(1953, Brit.); THREE'S COMPANY(1953, Brit.); DOCTOR IN THE HOUSE(1954, Brit.); VALUE FOR MONEY(1957, Brit.); HORROR OF DRACULA, THE(1958, Brit.); YOUR PAST IS SHOWING(1958, Brit.); LEFT, RIGHT AND CENTRE(1959); MODEL FOR MURDER(1960, Brit.); PURE HELL OF ST. TRINIAN'S, THE(1961, Brit.); MY SON, THE VAMPIRE(1963, Brit.); JOLLY BAD FELLOW, A(1964, Brit.); GREAT ST. TRINIAN'S TRAIN ROBBERY, THE(1966, Brit.); STRANGE AFFAIR, THE(1968, Brit.); PRIVATE LIFE OF SHERLOCK HOLMES, THE(1970, Brit.); WHAT BECAME OF JACK AND JILL?(1972, Brit.); CREEPING FLESH, THE(1973, Brit.); SGT. PEPPER'S LONELY HEARTS CLUB BAND(1978)

Graham Benson
RED MONARCH(1983, Brit.), p

Hamlyn Benson
I'LL NEVER FORGET YOU(1951); TREASURE HUNT(1952, Brit.); TROUBLE IN STORE(1955, Brit.)

Hugh Benson
SPELL OF AMY NUGENT, THE(1945, Brit.), w; FOR THOSE WHO THINK YOUNG(1964), p; NIGHTMARE HONEYMOON(1973), p; CASTAWAY COWBOY, THE(1974), w

Ivy Benson
DUMMY TALKS, THE(1943, Brit.)

James Benson
ABOVE US THE WAVES(1956, Brit.), w; BOYS IN COMPANY C, THE(1978, U.S./Hong Kong), ed; GIRO CITY(1982, Brit.)

Jim Benson
HONKY(1971), ed; COUNT YOUR BULLETS(1972), ed; ELECTRA GLIDE IN BLUE(1973), ed

Joey Benson
PSYCHO A GO-GO!(1965); DR. TERROR'S GALLERY OF HORRORS(1967); HORROR OF THE BLOOD MONSTERS(1970, U.S./Phil.)

John Benson
HEAVENLY DAYS(1944); STORY OF DR. WASSELL, THE(1944); CALCUTTA(1947); RAINMAKER, THE(1956); DEVIL'S HAIRPIN, THE(1957); FEAR STRIKES OUT(1957); GUNFIGHT AT THE O.K. CORRAL(1957); JOKER IS WILD, THE(1957); BLOB, THE(1958); VERTIGO(1958); ERRAND BOY, THE(1961); BIRDS AND THE BEES, THE(1965); SLENDER THREAD, THE(1965)

John D. Benson
JOKER IS WILD, THE(1957)

Jon Benson
FOXES(1980)

Jonathan Benson
LISZTOMANIA(1975, Brit.), m

Larry Benson
STRANGE INVADERS(1983), spec eff

Leon Benson
FLIPPER'S NEW ADVENTURE(1964), d; TARZAN'S DEADLY SILENCE(1970), p; CHOSEN SURVIVORS(1974 U.S.-Mex.), p

Linda Benson
MUSCLE BEACH PARTY(1964); PAJAMA PARTY(1964)

Lindy Benson
TO THE DEVIL A DAUGHTER(1976, Brit./Ger.)

Lucille Benson
FUGITIVE KIND, THE(1960); LITTLE FAUSS AND BIG HALSY(1970); WUSA(1970); CACTUS IN THE SNOW(1972); PRIVATE PARTS(1972); SLAUGHTERHOUSE-FIVE(1972); TOM SAWYER(1973); HUCKLEBERRY FINN(1974); SILVER STREAK(1976); GREATEST, THE(1977, U.S./Brit.); AMY(1981)

Marjorie Benson
Silents
WHEN GREEK MEETS GREEK(1922, Brit.)
Misc. Silents
WHAT PRICE LOVING CUP?(1923, Brit.); GREAT TURF MYSTERY, THE(1924, Brit.)

Martin Benson
BLIND GODDESS, THE(1948, Brit.); BUT NOT IN VAIN(1948, Brit.); ADVENTURES OF PC 49, THE(1949, Brit.); TRAPPED BY THE TERROR(1949, Brit.); ASSASSIN FOR HIRE(1951, Brit.); DARK LIGHT, THE(1951, Brit.); LUCKY NICK CAIN(1951); MYSTERY JUNCTION(1951, Brit.); FRIGHTENED MAN, THE(1952, Brit.); GAMBLER AND THE LADY, THE(1952, Brit.); JUDGMENT DEFERRED(1952, Brit.); WIDE BOY(1952, Brit.); NIGHT WITHOUT STARS(1953, Brit.); RECOIL(1953); TOP OF THE FORM(1953, Brit.); WHEEL OF FATE(1953, Brit.); BLACK 13(1954, Brit.); DEATH OF MICHAEL TURBIN, THE(1954, Brit.); ESCAPE BY NIGHT(1954, Brit.); WEST OF ZANZIBAR(1954, Brit.); DOCTOR AT SEA(1955, Brit.); LOVERS, HAPPY LOVERS!(1955, Brit.); PASSAGE HOME(1955, Brit.); KING AND I, THE(1956); SPIN A DARK WEB(1956, Brit.); 23 PACES TO BAKER STREET(1956); DOCTOR AT LARGE(1957, Brit.); FLESH IS WEAK, THE(1957, Brit.); ISTANBUL(1957); PICKUP ALLEY(1957, Brit.); THUNDER OVER TANGIER(1957, Brit.); COSMIC MONSTERS(1958, Brit.); WINDOM'S WAY(1958, Brit.); TWO-HEADED SPY, THE(1959, Brit.); EXODUS(1960); GENTLE TRAP, THE(1960, Brit.); KILLERS OF KILIMANJARO(1960, Brit.); ONCE MORE, WITH FEELING(1960); OSCAR WILDE(1960, Brit.); SANDS OF THE DESERT(1960, Brit.); THREE WORLDS OF GULLIVER, THE(1960, Brit.); FIVE GOLDEN HOURS(1961, Brit.); GORGO(1961, Brit.); FUR COLLAR, THE(1962, Brit.); MATTER OF WHO, A(1962, Brit.); NIGHT CREATURES(1962, Brit.); SATAN NEVER SLEEPS(1962); SILENT INVASION, THE(1962, Brit.); VILLAGE OF DAUGHTERS(1962, Brit.); CLEOPATRA(1963); BEHOLD A PALE HORSE(1964); SECRET DOOR, THE(1964, Brit.); SHOT IN THE DARK, A(1964); MAKE MINE A MILLION(1965, Brit.); SECRET OF MY SUCCESS, THE(1965, Brit.); MAN COULD GET KILLED, A(1966); MOZAMBIQUE(1966, Brit.); MAGNIFICENT TWO, THE(1967, Brit.); BATTLE BENEATH THE EARTH(1968, Brit.); POPE JOAN(1972, Brit.); MOHAMMAD, MESSENGER OF GOD(1976, Lebanon/Brit.); OMEN, THE(1976); TIFFANY JONES(1976); HUMAN FACTOR, THE(1979, Brit.); MEETINGS WITH REMARKABLE MEN(1979, Brit.); SEA WOLVES, THE(1981, Brit.); SPHINX(1981)
Misc. Talkies
CRAWLING TERROR, THE(1958, Brit.)

Millard Benson
Silents
RED WIDOW, THE(1916)

Norland Benson
HOT LEAD AND COLD FEET(1978)

Paul Benson
LOST CONTINENT, THE(1968, Brit.), ph

Perry Benson
WHAT'S NEXT?(1975, Brit.); CLASS OF MISS MAC MICHAEL, THE(1978, Brit./U.S.)

Peter Benson
SPIN A DARK WEB(1956, Brit.); PUTNEY SWOPE(1969); CRY OF THE BANSHEE(1970, Brit.); GREAT TRAIN ROBBERY, THE(1979, Brit.); HAWK THE SLAYER(1980, Brit.); TESS(1980, Fr./Brit.)

Phyllis Benson
MALIBU HIGH(1979)

R. Benson
CAR OF DREAMS(1935, Brit.), w

Ray Benson
FLESH EATERS, THE(1964), spec eff; ROADIE(1980)

Richard Benson
DIVINE SPARK, THE(1935, Brit./Ital.), w; MY HEART IS CALLING(1935, Brit.), w; MY SONG FOR YOU(1935, Brit.), w; WEREWOLF IN A GIRL'S DORMITORY(1961, Ital./Aust.), d

Robby Benson
TRIBUTE(1980, Can.); JORY(1972); JEREMY(1973); LUCKY LADY(1975); ODE TO BILLY JOE(1976); ONE ON ONE(1977), a, w; END, THE(1978); ICE CASTLES(1978); WALK PROUD(1979), a, m; DIE LAUGHING(1980), a, p, w, m; CHOSEN, THE(1982); RUNNING BRAVE(1983, Can.)
1984
HARRY AND SON(1984)

Robert Benson
NOTHING PERSONAL(1980, Can.); BY DESIGN(1982)

Roy Benson
LADY OBJECTS, THE(1938); SWEET AND LOWDOWN(1944); DIAMOND HORSESHOE(1945)

Sally Benson
SHADOW OF A DOUBT(1943), w; MEET ME IN ST. LOUIS(1944), w; JUNIOR MISS(1945), w; ANNA AND THE KING OF SIAM(1946), w; COME TO THE STABLE(1949), w; CONSPIRATOR(1949, Brit.), w; NO MAN OF HER OWN(1950), w; FARMER TAKES A WIFE, THE(1953), w; SUMMER MAGIC(1963), w; SIGNPOST TO MURDER(1964), w; VIVA LAS VEGAS(1964), w; JOY IN THE MORNING(1965), w; SINGING NUN, THE(1966), w

Sidney Benson
HIDEOUT(1948, Brit.)

Sir Frank Benson
Misc. Silents
BECKET(1923, Brit.)

Steven Benson
Misc. Talkies
ENDGAME(1984), d

Sydney Benson
MEN OF STEEL(1932, Brit.); SONG OF FREEDOM(1938, Brit.); JOHNNY IN THE CLOUDS(1945, Brit.); SO WELL REMEMBERED(1947, Brit.); TAWNY PIPIT(1947, Brit.); OPERATION DIAMOND(1948, Brit.)

Toni Benson
Misc. Talkies
CLOSE SHAVE(1981)
Tony Benson
RIOT ON SUNSET STRIP(1967); DREAMS OF GLASS(1969); WITCHMAKER, THE(1969)
Wilfred Benson
FLOOD TIDE(1935, Brit.)
Misc. Silents
TICKET-OF-LEAVE MAN, THE(1918, Brit.)
Fabbie Benstead
Silents
REPENTANCE(1922, Brit.)
Geoffrey Benstead
Silents
REPENTANCE(1922, Brit.), a, p
Misc. Silents
NAUGHTY HUSBANDS(1930, Brit.), d
Inez Bensusan
Silents
GRIT OF A JEW, THE(1917, Brit.); ADAM BEDE(1918, Brit.)
Buena Bent
ROMANCE AND RICHES(1937, Brit.)
Silents
PIPES OF PAN, THE(1923, Brit.)
Linda Bent
HOW TO STUFF A WILD BIKINI(1965); FIREBALL 590(1966)
Stephen Bent
MC VICAR(1982, Brit.); FINAL OPTION, THE(1983, Brit.)
Paul Bentall
FLASH GORDON(1980)
Bruno Bentegeac
RETURN OF MARTIN GUERRE, THE(1983, Fr.)
Dwinelle Benthall
Silents
GOOSE WOMAN, THE(1925), t; MAN CRAZY(1927), t; SMILE, BROTHER, SMILE(1927), t; HEART OF A FOLLIES GIRL, THE(1928), t; NIGHT WATCH, THE(1928), t
Josephine Bentham
BRIDE FOR HENRY, A(1937), w; JANIE(1944), w; JANIE GETS MARRIED(1946), w
Galeazzo Benti
ANGELA(1955, Ital.)
Gleazzo Benti
NEOPOLITAN CAROUSEL(1961, Ital.)
Joseph Benti
S.O.B.(1981)
Anna Bentinck
TO THE DEVIL A DAUGHTER(1976, Brit./Ger.)
Tim Bentinck
FFOLKES(1980, Brit.); PIRATES OF PENZANCE, THE(1983)
1984
WINTER FLIGHT(1984, Brit.)
Fusty Bentine
RAISING A RIOT(1957, Brit.)
Michael Bentine
DOWN AMONG THE Z MEN(1952, Brit.); FORCES' SWEETHEART(1953, Brit.), a, w; RAISING A RIOT(1957, Brit.); I ONLY ASKED!(1958, Brit.); WE JOINED THE NAVY(1962, Brit.); SANDWICH MAN, THE(1966, Brit.), a, w; RENTADICK(1972, Brit.)
Bentinho
MARGIN, THE,(1969, Braz.)
Warner Bentivegna
TROJAN HORSE, THE(1962, Fr./Ital.)
Fabrizio Bentivoglio
MASOCH(1980, Ital.)
Leonetta Bentivoglio
CITY OF WOMEN(1980, Ital./Fr.), ch
Adriana Bentley
PRETTY MAIDS ALL IN A ROW(1971)
Arthur Bentley
SECRET VENTURE(1955, Brit.)
Babette Bentley
COURAGEOUS DR. CHRISTIAN, THE(1940)
Beatrice Bentley
Misc. Silents
TOLL OF THE SEA, THE(1922)
Ben Bentley
EVEL KNIEVEL(1971)
Beverly Bentley
SCENT OF MYSTERY(1960); BEYOND THE LAW(1968); WILD 90(1968); MAIDSTONE(1970)
1984
C.H.U.D.(1984)
Bob Bentley
FOOL'S GOLD(1946); JOAN OF ARC(1948)
Bobette Bentley
FRENCH LINE, THE(1954); PRINCESS OF THE NILE(1954); SON OF SINBAD(1955)
Dick Bentley
AND THE SAME TO YOU(1960, Brit.); DESERT MICE(1960, Brit.); SUNDOWNERS, THE(1960); GIRL ON THE BOAT, THE(1962, Brit.); GOLDEN RABBIT, THE(1962, Brit.); IN THE DOGHOUSE(1964, Brit.); TAMAHINE(1964, Brit.); GUNFIGHTERS OF CASA GRANDE(1965, U.S./Span.); ADVENTURES OF BARRY McKENZIE(1972, Austral.); BARRY MC KENZIE HOLDS HIS OWN(1975, Aus.)
E.C. Bentley
TRENT'S LAST CASE(1953, Brit.), w
Frederick Bentley
SPLINTERS IN THE NAVY(1931, Brit.)

Grendon Bentley
Silents
HAMLET(1913, Brit.)
Helen Bentley
MR. BILLION(1977)
Irene Bentley
MY WEAKNESS(1933); SMOKY(1933); FRONTIER MARSHAL(1934); KID MILLIONS(1934); FOLIES DERGERE(1935)
Jack Bentley
JUST FOR FUN(1963, Brit.)
John Bentley
NIGHT INVADER, THE(1943, Brit.), w; HILLS OF DONEGAL, THE(1947, Brit.); CALLING PAUL TEMPLE(1948, Brit.); BAIT(1950, Brit.); HAPPIEST DAYS OF YOUR LIFE(1950, Brit.); PAPER GALLOWS(1950, Brit.); SHE SHALL HAVE MURDER(1950, Brit.); PAUL TEMPLE'S TRIUMPH(1951, Brit.); HAMMER THE TOFF(1952, Brit.); PAUL TEMPLE RETURNS(1952, Brit.); SALUTE THE TOFF(1952, Brit.); TREAD SOFTLY(1952, Brit.); BIG FRAME, THE(1953, Brit.); MEN AGAINST THE SUN(1953, Brit.); DOUBLE EXPOSURE(1954, Brit.); FINAL APPOINTMENT(1954, Brit.); PROFILE(1954, Brit.); RIVER BEAT(1954); SCARLET SPEAR, THE(1954, Brit.); WOMAN'S ANGLE, THE(1954, Brit.); COUNT OF TWELVE(1955, Brit.); FLAW, THE(1955, Brit.); STOLEN ASSIGNMENT(1955, Brit.); DEADLIEST SIN, THE(1956, Brit.); ESCAPE IN THE SUN(1956, Brit.); FLIGHT FROM VIENNA(1956, Brit.); WAY OUT, THE(1956, Brit.); ISTANBUL(1957); WHITE HUNTRESS(1957, Brit.); SUBMARINE SEA-HAWK(1959); MARY HAD A LITTLE(1961, Brit.); SINGER NOT THE SONG, THE(1961, Brit.); FUR COLLAR, THE(1962, Brit.); SINISTER MAN, THE(1965, Brit.); FRONT, THE(1976); ARTHUR(1981); SO FINE(1981); STILL OF THE NIGHT(1982)
1984
MUPPETS TAKE MANHATTAN, THE(1984); POPE OF GREENWICH VILLAGE, THE(1984)
Misc. Talkies
BRIGHTHAVEN EXPRESS(1950); BLACK ORCHID(1952); BOMBAY WATERFRONT(1952, Brit.)
Marc Bentley
SEPARATE WAYS(1981)
Mark Bentley
1984
HAMBONE AND HILLIE(1984)
Max Bentley
PAPERBACK HERO(1973, Can.)
Nicolas Bentley
FLOATING DUTCHMAN, THE(1953, Brit.), a, w; DEADLY GAME, THE(1955, Brit.), d&w
Paul Bentley
LAST ESCAPE, THE(1970, Brit.)
Rick Bentley
WILD SCENE, THE(1970)
Savannah Bentley
HOW TO FRAME A FIGG(1971)
Thomas Bentley
AMERICAN PRISONER, THE(1929 Brit.), d; HARMONY HEAVEN(1930, Brit.), d; IT'S A DEAL(1930), p&d; YOUNG WOODLEY(1930, Brit.), d; COMPROMISED!(1931, Brit.), d; HOBSON'S CHOICE(1931, Brit.), d; KEEPERS OF YOUTH(1931, Brit.), d, w; AFTER OFFICE HOURS(1932, Brit.), d, w; LAST COUPON, THE(1932, Brit.), d; HAWLEY'S OF HIGH STREET(1933, Brit.), d; LOVE NEST, THE(1933, Brit.), d; SLEEPLESS NIGHTS(1933, Brit.), d; GREAT DEFENDER, THE(1934, Brit.), d; THOSE WERE THE DAYS(1934, Brit.), d; MUSIC HATH CHARMS(1935, Brit.), d; OLD CURIOSITY SHOP, THE(1935, Brit.), d; REGAL CAVALCADE(1935, Brit.), d; LIVING DEAD, THE(1936, Brit.), d; SHE KNEW WHAT SHE WANTED(1936, Brit.), p&d; LAST CHANCE, THE(1937, Brit.), d; WHO KILLED FEN MARKHAM?(1937, Brit.), d; MARIGOLD(1938, Brit.), d; NIGHT ALONE(1938, Brit.), d; DEAD MAN'S SHOES(1939, Brit.), d; LUCKY TO ME(1939, Brit.), d; ME AND MY PAL(1939, Brit.), d; MIDDLE WATCH, THE(1939, Brit.), d; MURDER AT THE BASKERVILLES(1941, Brit.), d; OLD MOTHER RILEY'S CIRCUS(1941, Brit.), d
Silents
OLD CURIOSITY SHOP, THE(1913, Brit.), d&w; HARD TIMES(1915, Brit.), d&w; LABOUR LEADER, THE(1917, Brit.), d; ONCE UPON A TIME(1918, Brit.), d; GENERAL POST(1920, Brit.), d; ADVENTURES OF MR. PICKWICK, THE(1921, Brit.), d; OLD CURIOSITY SHOP, THE(1921, Brit.), d; MASTER OF CRAFT, A(1922, Brit.), d; OLD BILL THROUGH THE AGES(1924, Brit.), d; MONEY ISN'T EVERYTHING(1925, Brit.), d; NOT QUITE A LADY(1928, Brit.), d
Misc. Silents
DAVID COPPERFIELD(1913, Brit.), d; BARNABY RUDGE(1915), d; SOUL FOR SALE, A(1915, Brit.), d; BEAU BROCADE(1916, Brit.), d; MILESTONES(1916, Brit.), d; DADDY(1917, Brit.), d; LES CLOCHES DE CORNEVILLE(1917, Brit.), d; DIVINE GIFT, THE(1918, Brit.), d; LACKEY AND THE LADY, THE(1919, Brit.), d; BEYOND THE DREAMS OF AVARICE(1920, Brit.), d; THROUGH FIRE AND WATER(1923, Brit.), d; CHAPPY - THAT'S ALL(1924, Brit.), d; ROMANCE OF THE MAYFAIR, A(1925, Brit.), d; WHITE HEAT(1926, Brit.), d; SILVER LINING, THE(1927, Brit.), d; YOUNG WOODLEY(1929, Brit.), d
Yvette Bentley
PARIS CALLING(1941)
Serge Bento
SEVEN CAPITAL SINS(1962, Fr./Ital.); LANDRU(1963, Fr./Ital); OPHELIA(1964, Fr.); LES BICHES(1968, Fr.); LA FEMME INFIDELE(1969, Fr./Ital.)
Ann Benton
MARRIAGE-GO-ROUND, THE(1960)
Anne Benton
FLAMING STAR(1960)
Barbi Benton
HOSPITAL MASSACRE(1982); DEATHSTALKER(1983, Arg./U.S.)
1984
DEATHSTALKER, THE(1984); HOSPITAL MASSACRE(1984)
Misc. Talkies
AND THE WALL CAME TUMBLING DOWN(1984)
Bob Benton
CHEECH AND CHONG'S NEXT MOVIE(1980), set d
Brook Benton
MISTER ROCK AND ROLL(1957)

Charles Benton
PURSUIT OF D.B. COOPER, THE(1981)

Curtis Benton
FIREMAN, SAVE MY CHILD(1932); MANHATTAN MELODRAMA(1934); KID GALAHAD(1937)
Silents
20,000 LEAGUES UNDER THE SEA(1916); IT IS THE LAW(1924), w; CLANCY'S KOSHER WEDDING(1927), w; DOWN THE STRETCH(1927), w; SUNSET DERBY, THE(1927), w; BACHELOR'S PARADISE(1928), w; FREEDOM OF THE PRESS(1928), w
Misc. Silents
STRENGTH OF THE WEAK, THE(1916); SIREN, THE(1917)

Dean Benton
COWBOY MILLIONAIRE(1935); HARD ROCK HARRIGAN(1935); THUNDER MOUNTAIN(1935); LIFE RETURNS(1939); DESTROYER(1943); IRON MAJOR, THE(1943); WE'VE NEVER BEEN LICKED(1943)

Eddie Benton
SHAPE OF THINGS TO COME, THE(1979, Can.); PROM NIGHT(1980)

Garth Benton
THIRTEEN FRIGHTENED GIRLS(1963); RAIDERS FROM BENEATH THE SEA(1964)

Jack Benton [Cheney]
SATAN'S CRADLE(1949), w

James Benton
FINAL RECKONING, THE(1932, Brit.); THOROUGHBRED(1932, Brit.)
Misc. Silents
LAST TIDE, THE(1931, Brit.)

Jerome Benton
1984
PURPLE RAIN(1984)

John Benton
TOO MANY GIRLS(1940)

Joseph Benton
STARK FEAR(1963)

Marie Benton
Silents
QUESTION, THE(1916)

Robert Benton
IRON MAJOR, THE(1943); GEISHA BOY, THE(1958), set d; ROCK-A-BYE BA-BY(1958), set d; TEACHER'S PET(1958), set d; HUD(1963), set d; BONNIE AND CLYDE(1967), w; EL DORADO(1967), set d; THERE WAS A CROOKED MAN(1970), w; WILD ROVERS(1971), set d; BAD COMPANY(1972), d, w; HAMMERSMITH IS OUT(1972), set d; LIFE AND TIMES OF JUDGE ROY BEAN, THE(1972), set d; OH! CALCUTTA!(1972), w; WAR BETWEEN MEN AND WOMEN, THE(1972), set d; WHAT'S UP, DOC?(1972), w; SOYLENT GREEN(1973), set d; FREAKY FRI-DAY(1976), set d; SHAGGY D.A., THE(1976), set d; LATE SHOW, THE(1977), d&w; TELEFON(1977), set d; SUPERMAN(1978), w; BEING THERE(1979), set d; KRAMER VS. KRAMER(1979), d&w; JINXED!(1982), set d; STILL OF THE NIGHT(1982), d&w
1984
PLACES IN THE HEART(1984), d&w; STARMAN(1984), set d

Robert R. Benton
NO TIME FOR SERGEANTS(1958), set d; ONE-EYED JACKS(1961), set d; HELL IS FOR HEROES(1962), set d; FUN IN ACAPULCO(1963), set d; NUTTY PROFESSOR, THE(1963), set d; OUTRAGE, THE(1964), set d; ROUSTABOUT(1964), set d; FAMILY JEWELS, THE(1965), set d; SLENDER THREAD, THE(1965), set d; VILLAGE OF THE GIANTS(1965), set d; JOHNNY RENO(1966), set d; LAST OF THE SECRET AGENTS?, THE(1966), set d; MONEY TRAP, THE(1966), set d; NEVADA SMITH(1966), set d; NIGHT OF THE GRIZZLY, THE(1966), set d; OSCAR, THE(1966), set d; PICTURE MOMMY DEAD(1966), set d; SPY WITH MY FACE, THE(1966), set d; SWINGER, THE(1966), set d; WACO(1966), set d; EASY COME, EASY GO(1967), set d; FORT UTAH(1967), set d; HOSTILE GUNS(1967), set d; PRESIDENT'S ANALYST, THE(1967), set d; RED TOMAHAWK(1967), set d; SPIRIT IS WILLING, THE(1967), set d; WARNING SHOT(1967), set d; ODD COUPLE, THE(1968), set d; PROJECT X(1968), set d; WILL PENNY(1968), set d; MALTESE BIPPY, THE(1969), set d; DIRTY DINGUS MAGEE(1970), set d; MOONSHINE WAR, THE(1970), set d; STRAWBERRY STATEMENT, THE(1970), set d; ...TICK...TICK...TICK...(1970), set d; TRAVELING EXECUTIONER, THE(1970), set d; ZIGZAG(1970), set d; PRETTY MAIDS ALL IN A ROW(1971), set d; FOUL PLAY(1978), set d

Stanley Susanne Benton
1984
LAST HORROR FILM, THE(1984)

Steve Benton
YOU CAN'T RUN AWAY FROM IT(1956); LIFE WITH BLONDIE(1946); GUILT OF JANET AMES, THE(1947); LADY FROM SHANGHAI, THE(1948); JOLSON SINGS AGAIN(1949); RIDERS OF THE WHISTLING PINES(1949); PAL JOEY(1957); WALK ON THE WILD SIDE(1962)

Steven Benton
PICNIC(1955)

Susanne Benton
JIGSAW(1968); THAT COLD DAY IN THE PARK(1969, U.S./Can.); CATCH-22(1970); BOY AND HIS DOG, A(1975)
Misc. Talkies
BEST FRIENDS(1975)

Suzanne Benton
COVER ME BABE(1970); BEST FRIENDS(1975); SURVIVAL(1976)

Dean Richmond Bentor
ROMEO AND JULIET(1936)

Sara Bentz
VAMPIRES, THE(1969, Mex.)

Jayne Bentzen
1984
BREED APART, A(1984)

Paul Bentzen
DEVONSVILLE TERROR, THE(1983)
Misc. Talkies
INVASION FROM INNER EARTH(1977)

Niels Viggo Bentzon
VENOM(1968, Den.), m

Viggo Bentzon
NIGHT VISITOR, THE(1970, Swed./U.S.), art d

Pippe "Palsa" Benucci
GOLDEN MADONNA, THE(1949, Brit.)

Femi Benussi
HAWKS AND THE SPARROWS, THE(1967, Ital.); BIGGEST BUNDLE OF THEM ALL, THE(1968); HATCHET FOR A HONEYMOON(1969, Span./Ital.); ITALIAN CONNECTION, THE(1973, U.S./Ital./Ger.)

Leonardo Benvenut
IMPERIAL VENUS(1963, Ital./Fr.), w

Iolanda Benvenuti
MONSTER OF THE ISLAND(1953, Ital.), ed; GUNS OF THE BLACK WITCH(1961, Fr./Ital.), ed; PIRATE AND THE SLAVE GIRL, THE(1961, Fr./Ital.), ed; SAMSON AND THE SLAVE QUEEN(1963, Ital.), ed; SANDOKAN THE GREAT(1964, Fr./Ital./Span.), ed; GIRL AND THE GENERAL, THE(1967, Fr./Ital.), ed; THREE NIGHTS OF LOVE(1969, Ital.), ed; AUGUSTINE OF HIPPO(1973, Ital.), ed

Jolanda Benvenuti
STROMBOLI(1950, Ital.), ed; GREATEST LOVE, THE(1954, Ital.), ed; JOAN AT THE STAKE(1954, Ital./Fr.), ed; STRANGERS, THE(1955, Ital.), ed; BANDITS OF OR-GOSOLO(1964, Ital.), ed; MORE THAN A MIRACLE(1967, Ital./Fr.), ed; AGE OF THE MEDICI, THE(1979, Ital.), ed

Jolande Benvenuti
GHOSTS, ITALIAN STYLE(1969, Ital./Fr.), ed

Leo Benvenuti
GIRL WITH A SUITCASE(1961, Fr./Ital.), w; FRIENDS FOR LIFE(1964, Ital.), w; MARRIAGE–ITALIAN STYLE(1964, Fr./Ital.), w; ITALIAN SECRET SERVICE(1968, Ital.), w; GHOSTS, ITALIAN STYLE(1969, Ital./Fr.), w; SERAFINO(1970, Fr./Ital.), w; ALFREDO, ALFREDO(1973, Ital.), w; GOODNIGHT, LADIES AND GENT-LEMEN(1977, Ital.), d&w; CLARETTA AND BEN(1983, Ital., Fr.), w
1984
MISUNDERSTOOD(1984), w

Leonardo Benvenuti
CALYPSO(1959, Fr./It.), d
1984
ONCE UPON A TIME IN AMERICA(1984), w

Mario Benvenuti
MARGIN, THE,(1969, Braz.)

Iolanda Benvenuto
YEAR ONE(1974, Ital.), ed

Henry Benvenutti
SUBWAY RIDERS(1981)

Itzhak Benyamini
CLOUDS OVER ISRAEL(1966, Israel)

Eva Benyon
IT'S A WONDERFUL DAY(1949, Brit.)

Nancy Benyon
Silents
ODDS AGAINST HER, THE(1919, Brit.)
Misc. Silents
BEETLE, THE(1919, Brit.)

Barbara Benz
1984
NIGHT PATROL(1984), set d

Donna Benz
LOOKER(1981)

Donna Kei Benz
CHALLENGE, THE(1982)

Hamilton Benz
HOUSE ON 92ND STREET, THE(1945)

Inge Benz
BRIDGE, THE(1961, Ger.); PHONY AMERICAN, THE(1964, Ger.)

Simon Benzakein
LOST COMMAND, THE(1966)

Daniel Benzalli
1984
HOME FREE ALL(1984)

Peter Benzencenet
JACK THE RIPPER(1959, Brit.), ed

Vangie Beolby
SEA OF GRASS, THE(1947)

Bepy
AUGUSTINE OF HIPPO(1973, Ital.)

John Beradino
THEM!(1954); BEHIND THE HIGH WALL(1956); KILLER IS LOOSE, THE(1956); WILD HERITAGE(1958); NORTH BY NORTHWEST(1959); SCARFACE MOB, THE(1962); YOUNG DOCTORS IN LOVE(1982)

Bertolt Beraht
HANGMEN ALSO DIE(1943), w

Beram
THINGS OF LIFE, THE(1970, Fr./Ital./Switz.)

Cecil Beran
NIGHT WAS OUR FRIEND(1951, Brit.)

Mario Berandrei
MAN FROM CAIRO, THE(1953), ed

Andre Beranger
GLAD RAG DOLL, THE(1929); STARK MAD(1929); STRANGE CARGO(1929); BOU-DOIR DIPLOMAT(1930); LILIES OF THE FIELD(1930); AGE FOR LOVE, THE(1931); MAMA LOVES PAPA(1933); YOUNG AND BEAUTIFUL(1934); PAYOFF, THE(1935); BIG NOISE, THE(1936); DOWN THE STRETCH(1936); HOT MONEY(1936); KING OF HOCKEY(1936); LOVE BEFORE BREAKFAST(1936); WAKE UP AND LIVE(1937)
Misc. Talkies
BEWARE OF BACHELORS(1928)
Silents
DULCY(1923); EXTRA GIRL, THE(1923); BEAU BRUMMEL(1924); ARE PARENTS PEOPLE?(1925); GRAND DUCHESS AND THE WAITER, THE(1926); ALTARS OF DESIRE(1927); IF I WERE SINGLE(1927); POWDER MY BACK(1928)
Misc. Silents
BRIGHT SHAWL, THE(1923); PARADISE FOR TWO(1927); SMALL BACHELOR, THE(1927)

Clara Beranger
IDLE RICH, THE(1929), w; THIS MAD WORLD(1930), w; HIS DOUBLE LIFE(1933), w; SOCIAL REGISTER(1934), w
Silents
ONLY SON, THE(1914), w; DUST OF DESIRE(1919), w; PRAISE AGENT, THE(1919), w; WHITE YOUTH(1920), w; EXIT THE VAMP(1921), w; GILDED LILY, THE(1921), w; NICE PEOPLE(1922), w; ONLY 38(1923), w; BEDROOM WINDOW, THE(1924), w; ICEBOUND(1924), w; NEW BROOMS(1925), w; NOBODY'S WIDOW(1927), w; CRAIG'S WIFE(1928), w

Clara S. Beranger
Silents
COST, THE(1920), w; DR. JEKYLL AND MR. HYDE(1920), w; FLAMES OF THE FLESH(1920), w; JUDY OF ROGUES' HARBOUR(1920), w

George A. Beranger
HOLLYWOOD ROUNDUP(1938)
Silents
NUMBER 17(1920), d; BURN 'EM UP BARNES(1921), d
Misc. Silents
BRED IN THE BONE(1915); MANHATTAN KNIGHT, A(1920), d

George Andre Beranger
ANNABELLE'S AFFAIRS(1931); SURRENDER(1931); LADIES OF THE JURY(1932); KISS AND MAKE UP(1934); COLLEEN(1936); DANGEROUS(1936); GOLDEN AR-ROW, THE(1936); SNOWED UNDER(1936); STORY OF LOUIS PASTEUR, THE(1936); WALKING ON AIR(1936); CAFE METROPOLE(1937); I'LL TAKE ROMANCE(1937); SOULS AT SEA(1937); BEAUTY FOR THE ASKING(1939); HE STAYED FOR BREAKFAST(1940); OVER MY DEAD BODY(1942)
Silents
BIRTH OF A NATION, THE(1915); WESTERN LUCK(1924), d
Misc. Silents
SINISTER STREET(1922, Brit.), d; WAS SHE GUILTY?(1922, Brit.), d

George Beranger
MAN WHO BROKE THE BANK AT MONTE CARLO, THE(1935); SHE KNEW ALL THE ANSWERS(1941); SARATOGA TRUNK(1945); NIGHTMARE ALLEY(1947); CRY OF THE CITY(1948); ROAD HOUSE(1948); UNFAITHFULLY YOURS(1948); DANC-ING IN THE DARK(1949); FAN, THE(1949); WABASH AVENUE(1950)
Silents
FLIRTING WITH FATE(1916); GOOD BAD MAN, THE(1916); MANHATTAN MAD-NESS(1916); THOSE WITHOUT SIN(1917); BROKEN BLOSSOMS(1919)
Misc. Silents
MIXED BLOOD(1916); PILLARS OF SOCIETY(1916)

Lee Beranger
FIVE AND TEN(1931)

Andres Beranguer
MONSTER ISLAND(1981, Span./U.S.), ph

Jarmila Berankova
ECSTACY OF YOUNG LOVE(1936, Czech.)

Christian Berard
BEAUTY AND THE BEAST(1947, Fr.), art d; LES PARENTS TERRIBLES(1950, Fr.), art d

Jack Berard
MAGNIFICENT ONE, THE(1974, Fr./Ital.); PAUL AND MICHELLE(1974, Fr./Brit.); LOVE AND DEATH(1975)

Davida Berardi
1984
FIRST TURN-ON!, THE(1984)

John Berardino
WINNER'S CIRCLE, THE(1948); KID FROM LEFT FIELD, THE(1953); NAKED AND THE DEAD, THE(1958); WORLD WAS HIS JURY, THE(1958); SEVEN THIEVES(1960)

Johnny Berardino
KID FROM CLEVELAND, THE(1949)

Judy Berares
SINISTER URGE, THE(1961)

Luc Beraud
BEST WAY, THE(1978, Fr.), w; LIKE A TURTLE ON ITS BACK(1981, Fr.), p, d, w
1984
HEAT OF DESIRE(1984, Fr.), d, w

Enrique Beraza
UNDER FIRE(1983)

Evangelus Berbas
ISLAND OF LOST SOULS(1933)

Howard Berbeck
Silents
ALIAS JULIUS CAESAR(1922), art d

Marcel Berbeet
WILD CHILD, THE(1970, Fr.), p

Marcel Berbeit
GREEN ROOM, THE(1979, Fr.)

Iris Berben
COMPANEROS(1970 Ital./Span./Ger.)

Adi Berber
CARNIVAL STORY(1954); CIRCUS OF LOVE(1958, Ger.); BEN HUR(1959); RETURN OF DR. MABUSE, THE(1961, Ger./Fr./Ital.); SECRET WAYS, THE(1961)

Ady Berber
DARK EYES OF LONDON(1961, Ger.)

Anita Berber
Misc. Silents
FIVE SINISTER STORIES(1919, Ger.); CAGLIOSTRO(1920, Ger.)

Cathy Berberian
1984
LIFE IS A BED OF ROSES(1984, Fr.)

Marcel Berbert
JULES AND JIM(1962, Fr.), p; MATA HARI(1965, Fr./Ital.); STOLEN KISSES(1969, Fr.), p; MISSISSIPPI MERMAID(1970, Fr./Ital.), a, p; TWO ENGLISH GIRLS(1972, Fr.), p; DAY FOR NIGHT(1973, Fr.), a, p; SUCH A GORGEOUS KID LIKE ME(1973, Fr.), p; STORY OF ADELE H., THE(1975, Fr.), p; LAST METRO, THE(1981, Fr.)

Marty Bercaw
SUMMER SCHOOL TEACHERS(1977), art d

Aleksandar Bercek
FRAGRANCE OF WILD FLOWERS, THE(1979, Yugo.)

Joseph Bercholtz
STEPPIN' IN SOCIETY(1945), p

Joseph Bercholz
BEHIND LILY LIGHTS(1945), p

Jean-Claude Berck
BEHOLD A PALE HORSE(1964)

Nicole Berckmans
MAN WITH THE TRANSPLANTED BRAIN, THE(1972, Fr./Ital./Ger.), ed

Eric Bercovici
COMMANDO(1962, Ital., Span., Bel., Ger.), w; CAPTIVE CITY, THE(1963, Ital.), w; SQUARE OF VIOLENCE(1963, U.S./Yugo.), w; CONQUERED CITY(1966, Ital.), w; DAY OF THE EVIL GUN(1968), w; HELL IN THE PACIFIC(1968), w; CHANGE OF HABIT(1969), w; CULPEPPER CATTLE COMPANY, THE(1972), w; THREE THE HARD WAY(1974), w; OUT OF SEASON(1975, Brit.), p, w; TAKE A HARD RIDE(1975, U.S./Ital.), w

Karen Bercovici
THIEF(1981)

Konrad Bercovici
Silents
LAW OF THE LAWLESS, THE(1923), w; VOLGA BOATMAN, THE(1926), w

Leonardo Bercovici
RACKET BUSTERS(1938), w; CHASING DANGER(1939), w; BISHOP'S WIFE, THE(1947), w; LOST MOMENT, THE(1947), w; KISS THE BLOOD OFF MY HANDS(1948), w; PORTRAIT OF JENNIE(1949), w; MONSOON(1953), w; SQUARE OF VIOLENCE(1963, U.S./Yugo.), p, d, w; STORY OF A WOMAN(1970, U.S./Ital.), p,d&w

Luca Bercovici
PARASITE(1982); FRIGHTMARE(1983); SPACE RAIDERS(1983)

Marie M. Bercovici
STRANGERS ALL(1935), w

Reuben Bercovitch
FRANKENSTEIN CONQUERS THE WORLD(1964, Jap./US), w; HELL IN THE PACIFIC(1968), p, w; OUT OF SEASON(1975, Brit.), w

Jean-Claude Bercq
TRAIN, THE(1965, Fr./Ital./U.S.); LOST COMMAND, THE(1966); TRIPLE CROSS(1967, Fr./Brit.); UPPER HAND, THE(1967, Fr./Ital./Ger.); MAYERLING(1968, Brit./Fr.); PLAYMATES(1969, Fr./Ital.); LE MANS(1971); HIT(1973)

Sharon Bercutt
FLAMING STAR(1960)

Geza Berczy
Misc. Silents
PAUL STREET BOYS(1929)

Francoise Berd
SPECIAL DAY, A(1977, Ital./Can.); QUINTET(1979)

Lili Berde
SMALL WORLD OF SAMMY LEE, THE(1963, Brit.), ch

Eugene Berden
GOIN' TO TOWN(1935)

Janine Berdin
DEVIL BY THE TAIL, THE(1969, Fr./Ital.)

Alexander Berdink
DREAM COME TRUE, A(1963, USSR), w

Jean-Louis Berdot
1984
L'ARGENT(1984, Fr./Switz.)

A. Berdovskiy
TRAIN GOES TO KIEV, THE(1961, USSR), ch

Gheorghe Berechet
1984
NADIA(1984, U.S./Yugo.)

Oscar Beregi
BLUE IDOL, THE(1931, Hung.); ANYTHING CAN HAPPEN(1952); CALL ME MADAM(1953); DESERT LEGION(1953); TONIGHT WE SING(1953); OREGON TRAIL, THE(1959); LET'S MAKE LOVE(1960); NORTH TO ALASKA(1960); FIERCEST HEART, THE(1961); OPERATION EICHMANN(1961); POLICE NURSE(1963); IN-CREDIBLE MR. LIMPET, THE(1964); MY FAIR LADY(1964); MORITURI(1965); SHIP OF FOOLS(1965); 36 HOURS(1965); PANIC IN THE CITY(1968); CHRISTINE JOR-GENSEN STORY, THE(1970); GREAT WHITE HOPE, THE(1970); CACTUS IN THE SNOW(1972); EVERYTHING YOU ALWAYS WANTED TO KNOW ABOUT SEX, BUT WE'RE AFRAID TO ASK(1972); YOUNG FRANKENSTEIN(1974)
Silents
CAMILLE(1927)
Misc. Silents
MOON OF ISRAEL(1927, Aust.)

Oskar Beregi
TESTAMENT OF DR. MABUSE, THE(1943, Ger.)

Katalin Berek
DIALOGUE(1967, Hung.)

Allan Berendt
BLOOD(1974, Brit.)

Lars Eric Berenett
GEORGIA, GEORGIA(1972)

George Andre Berenger
LOVE ON THE RUN(1936)

Manuel Berenger
55 DAYS AT PEKING(1963), ph

Tom Berenger
LOOKING FOR MR. GOODBAR(1977); SENTINEL, THE(1977); IN PRAISE OF OLDER WOMEN(1978, Can.); BUTCH AND SUNDANCE: THE EARLY DAYS(1979); DOGS OF WAR, THE(1980, Brit.); BIG CHILL, THE(1983); EDDIE AND THE CRUISERS(1983)
1984
FEAR CITY(1984)

Barry Berenges
TIMBER WAR(1936), w

Manuel Berenguer
THUNDERSTORM(1956), ph; KING OF KINGS(1961), ph; LAZARILLO(1963, Span.), ph; PYRO(1964, U.S./Span.), ph; THIN RED LINE, THE(1964), ph; SON OF A GUNFIGHTER(1966, U.S./Span.), ph; SOUND OF HORROR(1966, Span.), ph; WEB OF FEAR(1966, Fr./Span.), ph; SAVAGE PAMPAS(1967, Span./Arg.), ph; DAY THE HOTLINE GOT HOT, THE(1968, Fr./Span.), ph; KRAKATOA, EAST OF JAVA(1969), ph; MURDERS IN THE RUE MORGUE(1971), ph; RAIN FOR A DUSTY SUMMER(1971, U.S./Span.), ph; TOWN CALLED HELL, A(1971, Span./Brit.), ph

Manuel Berengues
CRACK IN THE WORLD(1965), ph

Manuel Berengver
HOUSE THAT SCREAMED, THE(1970, Span.), ph

Harold Berens
CANDLELIGHT IN ALGERIA(1944, Brit.); MAN FROM MOROCCO, THE(1946, Brit.); DUAL ALIBI(1947, Brit.); THIRD TIME LUCKY(1950, Brit.); UP FOR THE CUP(1950, Brit.); SECRET, THE(1955, Brit.); KID FOR TWO FARTHINGS, A(1956, Brit.); NOT SO DUSTY(1956, Brit.); THUNDER OVER TANGIER(1957, Brit.); BLUEBEARD'S TEN HONEYMOONS(1960, Brit.); PURE HELL OF ST. TRINIAN'S, THE(1961, Brit.); WEEKEND WITH LULU, A(1961, Brit.); WHAT A WHOPPER(1961, Brit.); BIG MONEY, THE(1962, Brit.); LIVE NOW–PAY LATER(1962, Brit.); MURDER CAN BE DEADLY(1963, Brit.); STRAIGHT ON TILL MORNING(1974, Brit.); TRAIL OF THE PINK PANTHER, THE(1982)

Leslie Berens
TOUCH OF THE OTHER, A(1970, Brit.), p

Norman Berens
PENTHOUSE RHYTHM(1945), m

Ammon Berenson
SINAI COMMANDOS: THE STORY OF THE SIX DAY WAR(1968, Israel/Ger.)

Berry Berenson
REMEMBER MY NAME(1978); WINTER KILLS(1979); CAT PEOPLE(1982)

Marisa Berenson
DEATH IN VENICE(1971, Ital./Fr.); CABARET(1972); BARRY LYNDON(1975, Brit.); KILLER FISH(1979, Ital./Braz.); SOME LIKE IT COOL(1979, Ger./Aust./Ital./Fr.); S.O.B.(1981)
1984
SECRET DIARY OF SIGMUND FREUD, THE(1984)

Ilona Beres
AGE OF ILLUSIONS(1967, Hung.); DIALOGUE(1967, Hung.)

Al Beresford
SOLDIER, SAILOR(1944, Brit.)
Misc. Talkies
SCREAMTIME(1983, Brit.), d

Andrew Beresford
FLYING DOCTOR, THE(1936, Aus.)

Bruce Beresford
ADVENTURES OF BARRY McKENZIE(1972, Austral.), d, w; BARRY MC KENZIE HOLDS HIS OWN(1975, Aus.), p&d, w; DON'S PARTY(1976, Aus.), d; GETTING OF WISDOM, THE(1977, Aus.), d; MONEY MOVERS(1978, Aus.), d&w; BREAKER MORANT(1980, Aus.), d, w; CLUB, THE(1980, Aus.), d; TENDER MERCIES(1982), d; PUBERTY BLUES(1983, Aus.), d

Elizabeth Beresford
WOMBLING FREE(1977, Brit.), w

Evelyn Beresford
PRISONER OF ZENDA, THE(1937); YOUNG PEOPLE(1940); LADY EVE, THE(1941); FOREVER AND A DAY(1943); BUFFALO BILL(1944); MINISTRY OF FEAR(1945); UNFAITHFULLY YOURS(1948); THAT FORSYTE WOMAN(1949); ANNIE GET YOUR GUN(1950)

Frank Beresford
Silents
DEVIL'S TRAIL, THE(1919), w; ANNE OF LITTLE SMOKY(1921), w; PAINTED PONIES(1927), w

Frank S. Beresford
Silents
CAROLYN OF THE CORNERS(1919), w; IMPOSSIBLE CATHERINE(1919), w; IDOL OF THE NORTH, THE(1921), w

Harry Beresford
CHARLIE CHAN CARRIES ON(1931); FINN AND HATTIE(1931); HEAVEN ON EARTH(1931); SCANDAL SHEET(1931); SECRET CALL, THE(1931); SOB SISTER(1931); SOOKY(1931); UP POPS THE DEVIL(1931); DANCE TEAM(1932); DOCTOR X(1932); FORGOTTEN COMMANDMENTS(1932); HIGH PRESSURE(1932); MATCH KING, THE(1932); SCANDAL FOR SALE(1932); SIGN OF THE CROSS, THE(1932); SO BIG(1932); STRANGE LOVE OF MOLLY LOUVAIN, THE(1932); TWO SECONDS(1932); COLLEGE COACH(1933); DINNER AT EIGHT(1933); EVER IN MY HEART(1933); I COVER THE WATERFRONT(1933); LADY KILLER(1933); LITTLE WOMEN(1933); MIND READER, THE(1933); MURDERS IN THE ZOO(1933); NIGHT FLIGHT(1933); CLEOPATRA(1934); FASHIONS OF 1934(1934); FRIENDS OF MR. SWEENEY(1934); LITTLE MINISTER, THE(1934); MERRY FRINKS, THE(1934); ANNA KARENINA(1935); DAVID COPPERFIELD(1935); DOG OF FLANDERS, A(1935); I FOUND STELLA PARISH(1935); I'LL LOVE YOU ALWAYS(1935); PAGE MISS GLORY(1935); SEVEN KEYS TO BALDPATE(1935); FOLLOW THE FLEET(1936); GRAND JURY(1936); IN HIS STEPS(1936); KLONDIKE ANNIE(1936); POSTAL INSPECTOR(1936); GO-GETTER, THE(1937); PRINCE AND THE PAUPER, THE(1937); SHE ASKED FOR IT(1937); SHE'S NO LADY(1937); THEY WON'T FORGET(1937); LONG SHOT, THE(1939), w; NEWSBOY'S HOME(1939)
Silents
QUARTERBACK, THE(1926)

Marcus Beresford
NANA(1983, Ital.)

Maurice Beresford
WHY SAPS LEAVE HOME(1932, Brit.)

Miss Beresford
Silents
MISS BREWSTER'S MILLIONS(1926)

Nadine Beresford
SCARLET EMPRESS, THE(1934); MUTINY ON THE BOUNTY(1935)
Silents
TOWN SCANDAL, THE(1923)
Misc. Silents
PARDON MY FRENCH(1921)

Pearl Beresford
MELODY OF MY HEART(1936, Brit.)

Vera Beresford
Misc. Silents
DAUGHTER OF THE OLD SOUTH, A(1918)

David Beresh
1984
MELVIN, SON OF ALVIN(1984, Aus.)

Nicolai Beresnyev
ENEMIES OF PROGRESS(1934, USSR), d&w

Fred Berest
SCARLET ANGEL(1952); SALOME(1953)

Frederic Berest
FLAME OF ARABY(1951); JUNGLE JIM IN THE FORBIDDEN LAND(1952); LAST TRAIN FROM BOMBAY(1952); VOODOO TIGER(1952)

Fredric Berest
SERPENT OF THE NILE(1953)

Dawn Beret
DEVIL'S DAFFODIL, THE(1961, Brit./Ger.); PURE HELL OF ST. TRINIAN'S, THE(1961, Brit.); VICTIM(1961, Brit.); SWITCH, THE(1963, Brit.); WHY BOTHER TO KNOCK(1964, Brit.)

Tasma Bereton
CRIMSON CULT, THE(1970, Brit.)

Carmen Beretta
SYLVIA SCARLETT(1936); PASSAGE TO MARSEILLE(1944); O.S.S.(1946); CALCUTTA(1947); GOLDEN EARRINGS(1947)

Tatyana Berezantseva
DUEL, THE(1964, USSR), d, w

Tania Berezin
GIRLFRIENDS(1978)

Tanya Berezin
LITTLE SEX, A(1982)

V. Berezko
DESTINY OF A MAN(1961, USSR); ITALIANO BRAVA GENTE(1965, Ital./USSR)

Piotr Berezov
WINGS OF VICTORY(1941, USSR)

Lydia Berezovska
GIRL FROM POLTAVA(1937)

N. Berezovskaya
ON HIS OWN(1939, USSR)

Teresa Berezowska
KANAL(1961, Pol.)

Vera Berezutskaya
RED AND THE WHITE, THE(1969, Hung./USSR)

A. Scott Berg
MAKING LOVE(1982), w

Alban Berg
LULU(1978), m

Alex Berg
CREATURE WITH THE BLUE HAND(1971, Ger.), w

Almut Berg
VIKINGS, THE(1958); LOVE FEAST, THE(1966, Ger.)

Alphonse Berg
DOUBLE OR NOTHING(1937)

Ann Lonn Berg
LOVE AND DEATH(1975)

Bernard Berg
RENDEZVOUS 24(1946)

Catherine Berg
MADWOMAN OF CHAILLOT, THE(1969)

Cherney Berg
COME SPY WITH ME(1967), w

Claudine Berg
MILKY WAY, THE(1969, Fr./Ital.)

Dave Berg
LAST OF THE LONE WOLF(1930), ed; STRANGERS OF THE EVENING(1932), ed; SATURDAY'S MILLIONS(1933), ed

David Berg
ACQUITTED(1929), ed; PERSONALITY(1930), ed; PRINCE OF DIAMONDS(1930), ed

Dick Berg
BANNING(1967), p; COUNTERPOINT(1967), p; HOUSE OF CARDS(1969), p; SHOOT(1976, Can.), w

Dr. Louis Berg
PRISON NURSE(1938), w

Francine Berg
CIRCLE OF LOVE(1965, Fr.)

Gene Berg
THIS IS THE ARMY(1943)

George Berg
DAN'S MOTEL(1982)

Gertrude Berg
GOLDBERGS, THE(1950), a, w; MAIN STREET TO BROADWAY(1953)

Gertude Berg
MAKE A WISH(1937), w

Heinrich Berg
DECISION BEFORE DAWN(1951)

Jon Berg
STAR WARS(1977), anim; PIRANHA(1978), spec eff

Judita Berg
DYBBUK THE(1938, Pol.), ch

Judith Berg
ALMOST SUMMER(1978), w

Kid Berg
MONEY TALKS(1933, Brit.); SQUARE RING, THE(1955, Brit.)

Lorena Berg
PAISAN(1948, Ital.)

Marc Berg
MERRY CHRISTMAS MR. LAWRENCE(1983, Jap./Brit.)
Marvin Berg
HEARTLAND(1980)
Nancy Berg
FAIL SAFE(1964); THUNDER IN DIXIE(1965)
Perry Berg
WHIP'S WOMEN(1968), w
Peter Berg
RIVERRUN(1968), m; DE SADE(1969), w; DEMONSTRATOR(1971, Aus.)
Richard Berg
JUMBO(1962); SPECIAL DELIVERY(1976), p
Sandra Berg
ALMOST SUMMER(1978), w
Sonia Berg
STORM BOY(1976, Aus.), w
Stina Berg
Misc. Silents
LOVE AND JOURNALISM(1916, Swed.); GUNNAR HEDE'S SAGA(1922, Swed.)
Tony Berg
PERFECT COUPLE, A(1979); KING OF THE MOUNTAIN(1981)
Tracy Berg
PIRANHA II: THE SPAWNING(1981, Neth.)
Velma Berg
MY HEART BELONGS TO DADDY(1942)
Wayne Berg
GREAT WALDO PEPPER, THE(1975), stunts
Jose Bergamin
EXTERMINATING ANGEL, THE(1967, Mex.), w
Gianfranco Bergamini
COUNTERFEIT COMMANDOS(1981, Ital.), ph
Gianni Bergamini
OPERATION KID BROTHER(1967, Ital.), ph; DIRTY HEROES(1971, Ital./Fr./Ger.), ph
Giovanni Bergamini
LOVES AND TIMES OF SCARAMOUCHE, THE(1976, Ital.), ph
Sandra Bergamini
FIST IN HIS POCKET(1968, Ital.)
Eduardo Bergamo
THIEF OF BAGHDAD, THE(1961, Ital./Fr.)
Rosella Bergamonti
PAYMENT IN BLOOD(1968, Ital.)
Rossella Bergamonti
SEA PIRATE, THE(1967, Fr./Span./Ital.); STRANGER IN TOWN, A(1968, U.S./Ital.); THEY CAME TO ROB LAS VEGAS(1969, Fr./Ital./Span./Ger.)
Judith Marie Bergan
ABDUCTION(1975)
Charles Bergansky
GORDON'S WAR(1973)
Chuck Bergansky
ONE MAN JURY(1978)
Teresa Berganza
BARBER OF SEVILLE, THE(1973, Ger./Fr.); DON GIOVANNI(1979, Fr./Ital./Ger.)
Tamara Bergdall
PREMONITION, THE(1976)
Alphonse Berge
THAT'S MY BABY(1944)
Amund Berge
EDVARD MUNCH(1976, Norway/Swed.)
Colette Berge
LES ABYSSES(1964, Fr.); DAY OF THE JACKAL, THE(1973, Brit./Fr.)
Francine Berge
LES ABYSSES(1964, Fr.); JUDEX(1966, Fr./Ital.); BENJAMIN(1968, Fr.); NUN, THE(1971, Fr.); MR. KLEIN(1976, Fr.)
Pieter Bergema
SAFE PLACE, A(1971), ed
Avril Bergen
PETER RABBIT AND TALES OF BEATRIX POTTER(1971, Brit.)
Birgitt Bergen
ORDERED TO LOVE(1963, Ger.)
Candice Bergen
END OF THE WORLD(in Our Usual Bed in a Night Full of Rain), THE*1/2 (1978, Ital.); GROUP, THE(1966); SAND PEBBLES, THE(1966); DAY THE FISH CAME OUT, THE(1967. Brit./Gr.); LIVE FOR LIFE(1967, Fr./Ital.); MAGUS, THE(1968, Brit.); ADVENTURERS, THE(1970); GETTING STRAIGHT(1970); SOLDIER BLUE(1970); CARNAL KNOWLEDGE(1971); T.R. BASKIN(1971); 11 HARROWHOUSE(1974, Brit.); BITE THE BULLET(1975); WIND AND THE LION, THE(1975); DOMINO PRINCIPLE, THE(1977); HUNTING PARTY, THE(1977, Brit.); OLIVER'S STORY(1978); STARTING OVER(1979); RICH AND FAMOUS(1981); GANDHI(1982)
Connie Bergen
TOO MUCH BEEF(1936); MAN MADE MONSTER(1941)
Misc. Talkies
BIG BOY RIDES AGAIN(1935)
Constance Bergen
SHE GETS HER MAN(1935); PETRIFIED FOREST, THE(1936); WIVES NEVER KNOW(1936); HIGH, WIDE AND HANDSOME(1937); TURN OFF THE MOON(1937); FOOLS OF DESIRE(1941)
Misc. Talkies
IT'S ALL IN YOUR MIND(1938)
Edgar Bergen
GOLDWYN FOLLIES, THE(1938); LETTER OF INTRODUCTION(1938); CHARLIE MC CARTHY, DETECTIVE(1939); YOU CAN'T CHEAT AN HONEST MAN(1939); LOOK WHO'S LAUGHING(1941); HERE WE GO AGAIN(1942); STAGE DOOR CANTEEN(1943); SONG OF THE OPEN ROAD(1944); FUN AND FANCY FREE(1947); I REMEMBER MAMA(1948); CAPTAIN CHINA(1949); MYSTERY LAKE(1953); ONE WAY WAHINI(1965); DON'T MAKE WAVES(1967); PHYNX, THE(1970); WON TON TON, THE DOG WHO SAVED HOLLYWOOD(1976); MUPPET MOVIE, THE(1979)
Misc. Talkies
ROGUE'S GALLERY(1968)

Frances Bergen
TITANIC(1953); HER TWELVE MEN(1954); INTERLUDE(1957); AMERICAN GIGOLO(1980); RICH AND FAMOUS(1981); STAR CHAMBER, THE(1983); STING II, THE(1983)
Francis Bergen
1984
MUPPETS TAKE MANHATTAN, THE(1984)
Jerry Bergen
POPPY(1936); ARTISTS AND MODELS(1937); THIS WAY PLEASE(1937); WITH LOVE AND KISSES(1937); COLLEGE SWING(1938); FLYING WITH MUSIC(1942); LET'S GET TOUGH(1942); PIRATE, THE(1948); LUST FOR LIFE(1956)
Polly Bergen
AT WAR WITH THE ARMY(1950); THAT'S MY BOY(1951); WARPATH(1951); STOOGE, THE(1952); ARENA(1953); CRY OF THE HUNTED(1953); ESCAPE FROM FORT BRAVO(1953); FAST COMPANY(1953); HALF A HERO(1953); CAPE FEAR(1962); CARETAKERS, THE(1963); MOVE OVER, DARLING(1963); KISSES FOR MY PRESIDENT(1964); GUIDE FOR THE MARRIED MAN, A(1967)
Misc. Talkies
BELLE SOMMERS(1962)
Ted Bergen
MY SIX LOVES(1963)
Thurlow Bergen
Silents
PRINCE OF INDIA, A(1914); STAIN, THE(1914); PROHIBITION(1915); RUNNING FIGHT, THE(1915); LOVE AUCTION, THE(1919)
Misc. Silents
LITTLE GYPSY, THE(1915); CITY, THE(1916); LOTTERY MAN, THE(1916); WOMAN'S FIGHT, A(1916); LURE OF AMBITION(1919); BLIND LOVE, THE(1920)
Alan Berger
SMOKEY AND THE BANDIT–PART 3(1983)
Anna Berger
TAKING OF PELHAM ONE, TWO, THREE, THE(1974); MIDDLE OF THE NIGHT(1959); ENDLESS LOVE(1981); LOVESICK(1983)
Belle Berger
1984
BROADWAY DANNY ROSE(1984)
Bror Berger
Misc. Silents
SIR ARNE'S TREASURE(1920, Swed.)
Burt Berger
PEACE FOR A GUNFIGHTER(1967)
Carin Berger
DR. HECKYL AND MR. HYPE(1980)
1984
SURF II(1984), cos
Carl Berger
OUANGA(1936, Brit.), ph; BOOLOO(1938), ph; RETURN OF RIN TIN TIN, THE(1947), ph; HIGHWAY 13(1948), ph; JUNGLE GODDESS(1948), ph; LOOK OUT SISTER(1948), ph; ARSON, INC.(1949), ph; DEPUTY MARSHAL(1949), ph; SKY LINER(1949), ph; THUNDER IN THE PINES(1949), ph; ONE TOO MANY(1950), ph; STOP THAT CAB(1951), ph; PORTLAND EXPOSE(1957), ph; YOUNG JESSE JAMES(1960), ph; C'MON, LET'S LIVE A LITTLE(1967), ph
Charly Berger
JOHNNY STEALS EUROPE(1932, Ger.)
Debra Berger
ROSEBUD(1975); COUNTERFEIT COMMANDOS(1981, Ital.); NANA(1983, Ital.)
Dinah Berger
ORDERED TO LOVE(1963, Ger.)
Erna Berger
DON GIOVANNI(1955, Brit.)
Fred Berger
FALSE COLORS(1943), ed; RIDERS OF THE DEADLINE(1943), ed; PERFECT WOMAN, THE(1950, Brit.); ONE WILD OAT(1951, Brit.); MR. POTTS GOES TO MOSCOW(1953, Brit.); LADY GODIVA RIDES AGAIN(1955, Brit.); CASH ON DELIVERY(1956, Brit.); TROOPER HOOK(1957), ed; RESURRECTION OF ZACHARY WHEELER, THE(1971), ed
Fred W. Berger
DEVIL'S PLAYGROUND, THE(1946), ed; FOOL'S GOLD(1946), ed; UNEXPECTED GUEST(1946), ed; DANGEROUS VENTURE(1947), ed; HOPPY'S HOLIDAY(1947), ed; MARAUDERS, THE(1947), ed; BORROWED TROUBLE(1948), ed; DEAD DON'T DREAM, THE(1948), ed; DON'T TRUST YOUR HUSBAND(1948), ed; FALSE PARADISE(1948), ed; SILENT CONFLICT(1948), ed; SINISTER JOURNEY(1948), ed; STRANGE GAMBLE(1948), ed; COVER-UP(1949), ed; GREAT DAN PATCH, THE(1949), ed; BLACK WHIP, THE(1956), ed; BACK FROM THE DEAD(1957), ed; COPPER SKY(1957), ed; RIDE A VIOLENT MILE(1957), ed; UNKNOWN TERROR, THE(1957), ed; DESERT HELL(1958), ed; VIOLENT ONES, THE(1967), ed; DAYTON'S DEVILS(1968), ed; HOT ROCK, THE(1972), ed
Frederick Berger
MYSTERY MAN(1944), ed; NO TIME FOR FLOWERS(1952); WOMAN'S ANGLE, THE(1954, Brit.)
Fritz Berger
FIDELIO(1961, Aust.); VIENNA WALTZES(1961, Aust.)
Gregg Berger
STUNT MAN, THE(1980)
1984
LOVE STREAMS(1984)
Greta Berger
Silents
SPIES(1929, Ger.)
Grete Berger
Silents
KRIEMHILD'S REVENGE(1924, Ger.); METROPOLIS(1927, Ger.)
Misc. Silents
STUDENT OF PRAGUE, THE(1913, Ger.)
Gustav Berger
Misc. Talkies
LIVING ORPHAN, THE(1939); GOD, MAN AND DEVIL(1949)

Hal Berger
KING OF THE ARENA(1933), w

Hans Berger
GLADIATORS, THE(1970, Swed.)

Harris Berger
ANGELS WITH DIRTY FACES(1938); LITTLE TOUGH GUYS IN SOCIETY(1938); CALL A MESSENGER(1939); CODE OF THE STREETS(1939); NEWSBOY'S HOME(1939); EAST SIDE KIDS(1940); GIVE US WINGS(1940); OH JOHNNY, HOW YOU CAN LOVE!(1940); YOU'RE NOT SO TOUGH(1940); MOB TOWN(1941)

Helmut Berger
DORIAN GRAY(1970, Ital./Brit./Ger./Liechtenstein); ASH WEDNESDAY(1973); LUDWIG(1973, Ital./Ger./Fr.); ROMANTIC ENGLISHWOMAN, THE(1975, Brit./Fr.); CONVERSATION PIECE(1976, Ital., Fr.); GARDEN OF THE FINZI-CONTINIS, THE(1976, Ital./Ger.); SLAVE OF THE CANNIBAL GOD(1979, Ital.)
Misc. Talkies
ORDER TO KILL(1974)

Henning Berger
WAY OF ALL MEN, THE(1930), w

Jason Berger
1984
FIRSTBORN(1984)

Jean Phillipe Berger
SECOND WIND, A(1978, Fr.), ed

Jean-Philippe Berger
TUSK(1980, Fr.), ed

John Berger
JONAH–WHO WILL BE 25 IN THE YEAR 2000(1976, Switz.), w

Katherine Berger
TENDER IS THE NIGHT(1961)

Katia Berger
MOON IN THE GUTTER, THE(1983, Fr./Ital.); TALES OF ORDINARY MADNESS(1983, Ital.)

Katya Berger
NANA(1983, Ital.)

Keith Berger
Misc. Talkies
ANGELS(1976)

Kerstin Berger
PINOCCHIO(1969, E. Ger.)

Lauree Berger
FAT SPY(1966)

Laurel Berger
MILESTONES(1975)

Ludwig Berger
SINS OF THE FATHERS(1928), d; PLAYBOY OF PARIS(1930), p&d; VAGABOND KING, THE(1930), d; EARLY TO BED(1933, Brit./Ger.), d; THIEF OF BAGHDAD, THE(1940, Brit.), d; TALE OF FIVE WOMEN, A(1951, Brit.), ph; WILLY(1963, U.S./Ger.), ph
Misc. Silents
CINDERELLA(1926, Ger.), d; WALTZ DREAM, A(1926, Ger.), d; SINS OF THE FATHER(1928), d; WOMAN FROM MOSCOW, THE(1928), d

Maria Berger
MR. EMMANUEL(1945, Brit.)

Marilyn Berger
ROLLOVER(1981)

Martin Berger
ECHO OF A DREAM(1930, Ger.), d
Misc. Silents
RASPUTIN(1930), d

Mel Berger
SAVAGE SEVEN, THE(1968); HAMMERSMITH IS OUT(1972); BAD CHARLESTON CHARLIE(1973); DEADLY HERO(1976)

Michel Berger
IS PARIS BURNING?(1966, U.S./Fr.)

Monika Berger
MY SON, THE HERO(1963, Ital./Fr.); TURKISH CUCUMBER, THE(1963, Ger.)

Nicole Berger
GAME OF LOVE, THE(1954, Fr.); JULIETTA(1957, Fr.); LOVE IS MY PROFESSION(1959, Fr.); SIEGE OF SIDNEY STREET, THE(1960, Brit.); SHOOT THE PIANO PLAYER(1962, Fr.); HIGHWAY PICKUP(1965, Fr./Ital.); IMMORAL MOMENT, THE(1967, Fr.); STORY OF A THREE DAY PASS, THE(1968, Fr.)

Peter Berger
NOT RECONCILED, OR "ONLY VIOLENCE HELPS WHERE IT RULES"(1969, Ger.); HOT POTATO(1976), ed

Peter E. Berger
PACK, THE(1977), ed; PROMISE, THE(1979), ed; LAST MARRIED COUPLE IN AMERICA, THE(1980), ed; OH GOD! BOOK II(1980), ed; MOMMIE DEAREST(1981), ed; MONSIGNOR(1982), ed

Ralph Berger
WITHOUT RESERVATIONS(1946), art d; WHITE ZOMBIE(1932), set d; FLASH GORDON(1936), art d; WESTLAND CASE, THE(1937), art d; I COVER CHINATOWN(1938), art d; INTERNATIONAL CRIME(1938), art d; SHADOWS OVER SHANGHAI(1938), art d; EXILE EXPRESS(1939), art d; PANAMA PATROL(1939), art d; OUTLAWS OF THE DESERT(1941), art d; PARSON OF PANAMINT, THE(1941), art d; WIDE OPEN TOWN(1941), art d; SILVER QUEEN(1942), art d; UNDERCOVER MAN(1942), art d; BAR 20(1943), art d; COLT COMRADES(1943), art d; FALSE COLORS(1943), art d; HOPPY SERVES A WRIT(1943), art d; LEATHER BURNERS, THE(1943), art d; LOST CANYON(1943), art d; RIDERS OF THE DEADLINE(1943), art d; TARZAN'S DESERT MYSTERY(1943), art d; WOMAN OF THE TOWN, THE(1943), art d; HEAVENLY DAYS(1944), art d; NIGHT OF ADVENTURE, A(1944), art d; TALL IN THE SADDLE(1944), art d; TEXAS MASQUERADE(1944), art d; BACK TO BATAAN(1945), art d; CHINA SKY(1945), art d; DICK TRACY(1945), art d; STRANGE VOYAGE(1945), art d; GEORGE WHITE'S SCANDALS(1945), art d; GENIUS AT WORK(1946), art d; PARTNERS IN TIME(1946), art d; HONEYMOON(1947), art d; TRAIL STREET(1947), art d; IF YOU KNEW SUSIE(1948), art d; MIRACLE OF THE BELLS, THE(1948), art d; RETURN OF THE BADMEN(1948), art d; WHERE DANGER LIVES(1950), art d; WHITE TOWER, THE(1950), art d; ON DANGEROUS GROUND(1951), art d; HALF-BREED, THE(1952), art d; MACAO(1952), art d; MAN OF CONFLICT(1953), art d; FOREVER DARLING(1956), art d; SCARFACE MOB, THE(1962), art d

Rea Berger
Misc. Silents
CRAVING, THE(1916); MILLION FOR MARY, A(1916), d; OVERCOAT, THE(1916), d; PURITY(1916), d; THREE PALS(1916), d; VALLEY OF DECISION, THE(1916), d; VOICE OF LOVE, THE(1916), d; DANGER WITHIN(1918), d; MAGIC EYE, THE(1918), d

Red Berger
STUDENT TOUR(1934)

Richard Berger
HARRY AND WALTER GO TO NEW YORK(1976), art d; NICKELODEON(1976), art d; MR. BILLION(1977), art d; ROCKY II(1979), art d; SCAVENGER HUNT(1979), art d

Richard H. Berger
LIKELY STORY, A(1947), p; RACHEL AND THE STRANGER(1948), p; ADVENTURE IN BALTIMORE(1949), p; ROUGHSHOD(1949), p

Ricky Berger
FIGHTING FATHER DUNNE(1948)

Rob Berger
BIG BAD MAMA(1974)

Robert Berger
IT SHOULD HAPPEN TO YOU(1954); THEM!(1954); DOGS OF WAR, THE(1980, Brit.); ZELIG(1983)

Robert Brian Berger
TILT(1979)

Roy Berger
HILDUR AND THE MAGICIAN(1969), a, set d

Sally Berger
HILDUR AND THE MAGICIAN(1969)

Senta Berger
SECRET WAYS, THE(1961); SHERLOCK HOLMES AND THE DEADLY NECKLACE(1962, Ger.); GOOD SOLDIER SCHWEIK, THE(1963, Ger.); VICTORS, THE(1963); GLORY GUYS, THE(1965); MAJOR DUNDEE(1965); TERROR OF DR. MABUSE, THE(1965, Ger.); BANG, BANG, YOU'RE DEAD(1966); CAST A GIANT SHADOW(1966); POPPY IS ALSO A FLOWER, THE(1966); QUILLER MEMORANDUM, THE(1966, Brit.); SPY WITH MY FACE, THE(1966); AMBUSHERS, THE(1967); DIABOLICALLY YOURS(1968, Fr.); TREASURE OF SAN GENNARO(1968, Fr./Ital./Ger.); DE SADE(1969); IF IT'S TUESDAY, THIS MUST BE BELGIUM(1969); TO COMMIT A MURDER(1970, Fr./Ital./Ger.); WHEN WOMEN HAD TAILS(1970, Ital.); SWISS CONSPIRACY, THE(1976, U.S./Ger.); CROSS OF IRON(1977, Brit., Ger.); GOODNIGHT, LADIES AND GENTLEMEN(1977, Ital.); NEST OF VIPERS(1979, Ital.)

Sidney Berger
CARNIVAL OF SOULS(1962)

Stephen Berger
MISSOURI BREAKS, THE(1976), art d

Stephen M. Berger
NORMAN...IS THAT YOU?(1976), art d

Steve Berger
BAD NEWS BEARS IN BREAKING TRAINING, THE(1977), art d; ROLLING THUNDER(1977), art d

Ted Berger
WHERE THE BOYS ARE(1960)

Thomas Berger
LITTLE BIG MAN(1970), w; NEIGHBORS(1981), w

Toni Berger
SERPENT'S EGG, THE(1977, Ger./U.S.); FROM THE LIFE OF THE MARIONETTES(1980, Ger.)

Tres Berger
HILDUR AND THE MAGICIAN(1969)

William Berger
DAY THE FISH CAME OUT, THE(1967. Brit./Gr.); FACE TO FACE(1967, Ital.); MURDER CLINIC, THE(1967, Ital./Fr.); EVERY BASTARD A KING(1968, Israel); MAN WITH THE BALLOONS, THE(1968, Ital./Fr.); TODAY IT'S ME...TOMORROW YOU!(1968, Ital.); NO ROOM TO DIE(1969, Ital.); SABATA(1969, Ital.); SUPERFLY T.N.T.(1973); THREE TOUGH GUYS(1974, U.S./Ital.); WIFEMISTRESS(1979, Ital.); GIRL FROM TRIESTE, THE(1983, Ital.); HANNAH K.(1983, Fr.); HERCULES(1983)
Misc. Talkies
TODAY WE KILL...TOMORROW WE DIE(1971); OIL(1977, Ital.); SLAUGHTERDAY(1981)

Zachary Berger
SEALED CARGO(1951)

Jacques Bergerac
BEAUTIFUL STRANGER(1954, Brit.); STRANGE INTRUDER(1956); LES GIRLS(1957); GIGI(1958); THUNDER IN THE SUN(1959); THE HYPNOTIC EYE(1960); FEAR NO MORE(1961); GLOBAL AFFAIR, A(1964); ONE MILLION DOLLARS(1965, Ital.); TAFFY AND THE JUNGLE HUNTER(1965); MOTHER GOOSE A GO-GO(1966)
Misc. Talkies
UNKISSED BRIDE(1966)

Lee Bergere
SULLIVAN'S EMPIRE(1967); IN ENEMY COUNTRY(1968); BOB AND CAROL AND TED AND ALICE(1969)

Ouida Bergere
Silents
ARMS AND THE WOMAN(1916), w; NEW YORK(1916), w; MORE TROUBLE(1918), w; NARROW PATH, THE(1918), w; AVALANCHE, THE(1919), w; COUNTERFEIT(1919), w; ON WITH THE DANCE(1920), w; KICK IN(1922), w; PEACOCK ALLEY(1922), w; TO HAVE AND TO HOLD(1922), w; SIX DAYS(1923), w

Valerie Bergere
IT'S LOVE I'M AFTER(1937); MEET THE MISSUS(1937); SINGING MARINE, THE(1937)

Stanley Bergerman
DESTRY RIDES AGAIN(1932), p; RIDER OF DEATH VALLEY(1932), w; UNEXPECTED FATHER(1932), p; MANHATTAN MOON(1935), p; STRANGE WIVES(1935), p; WEREWOLF OF LONDON, THE(1935), p

Bergeron
BETRAYAL(1939, Fr.)

Elizabeth Bergeron
WOMAN UNDER THE INFLUENCE, A(1974), ed

Jean-Pierre Bergeron
ONE MAN(1979, Can.)
Rene Bergeron
MAYERLING(1937, Fr.); PEPE LE MOKO(1937, Fr.); HEART OF PARIS(1939, Fr.); DAYBREAK(1940, Fr.)
Theodora Bergery
HIRED KILLER, THE(1967, Fr./Ital.); EDGE, THE(1968)
Joanne Berges
Misc. Talkies
NOT TONIGHT HENRY(1961)
Garrett Bergfeld
DELIRIUM(1979)
Johannes Bergfeld
COURT CONCERT, THE(1936, Ger.); FINAL CHORD, THE(1936, Ger.)
Ulrich Bergfelder
NOSFERATU, THE VAMPIRE(1979, Fr./Ger.), prod d; FITZCARRALDO(1982), art d
Richard Berggren
HIS KIND OF WOMAN(1951); SUBMARINE COMMAND(1951)
Thommy Berggren
ELVIRA MADIGAN(1967, Swed.); ADVENTURERS, THE(1970); RAVEN'S END(1970, Swed.); JOE HILL(1971, Swed./U.S.)
Ulf Berggren
CHILDREN, THE(1949, Swed.)
Eva Bergh
LONG MEMORY, THE(1953, Brit.)
Jerry Bergh
HITTIN' THE TRAIL(1937); MYSTERY RANGE(1937)
Johnny Bergh
1984
KAMILLA(1984, Norway)
Pat Bergh
SAFARI 3000(1982), set d
Hiroko Berghauer
BED AND BOARD(1971, Fr.)
Jose Berghmans
WAR OF THE BUTTONS(1963 Fr.), m; TO COMMIT A MURDER(1970, Fr./Ital./Ger.), m
Fritz Berghof
COURT CONCERT, THE(1936, Ger.)
Herbert Berghof
ASSIGNMENT–PARIS(1952); DIPLOMATIC COURIER(1952); FIVE FINGERS(1952); RED PLANET MARS(1952); FRAULEIN(1958); CLEOPATRA(1963); AFFAIR OF THE SKIN, AN(1964); HARRY AND TONTO(1974); MASTERMIND(1977); VOICES(1979); THOSE LIPS, THOSE EYES(1980); TIMES SQUARE(1980)
Diane Berghoff
Misc. Talkies
HILARY'S BLUES(1983)
Kalle Bergholm
PIPPI IN THE SOUTH SEAS(1974, Swed./Ger.), ph
Richard Bergholtz
CANDIDATE, THE(1972)
Emmett Bergholz
YOUNG AND THE BRAVE, THE(1963), ph
Joseph Bergholz
OLDEST PROFESSION, THE(1968, Fr./Ital./Ger.), p
Enrico Bergier
LEAP INTO THE VOID(1982, Ital.); LA NUIT DE VARENNES(1983, Fr./Ital.)
Dan Bergin
BUTTERFIELD 8(1960)
Emmet Bergin
MC KENZIE BREAK, THE(1970); RYAN'S DAUGHTER(1970, Brit.); CRIMINAL CONVERSATION(1980, Ireland); EXCALIBUR(1981)
Emmett Bergin
FLIGHT OF THE DOVES(1971)
Eric Bergland
WHALERS, THE(1942, Swed.)
Sverre Bergli
SNOW TREASURE(1968), ph
Bjorn Berglund
SWEDENHIELMS(1935, Swed.)
Bullen Berglund
ON THE SUNNYSIDE(1936, Swed.)
Erik Berglund
INTERMEZZO(1937, Swed.); WOMAN'S FACE, A(1939, Swed.); WALPURGIS NIGHT(1941, Swed.)
Erik "Bullen" Berglund
ONLY ONE NIGHT(1942, Swed.)
Per Berglund
SHAME(1968, Swed.)
Alan Bergman
STOP THE WORLD–I WANT TO GET OFF(1966, Brit.), w; FROM NOON TO THREE(1976)
Andrew Bergman
BLAZING SADDLES(1974), w; IN-LAWS, THE(1979), w; SO FINE(1981), d&w
1984
FLETCH(1984), w; OH GOD! YOU DEVIL(1984), w
Anna Bergman
FANNY AND ALEXANDER(1983, Swed./Fr./Ger.)
Brenda Bergman
GEEK MAGGOT BINGO(1983)
Edward Bergman
CONFESSOR(1973), p,d,ph&ed
Gene Bergman
GHOST OF THE CHINA SEA(1958)
Harold Bergman
FINAL COUNTDOWN, THE(1980); NOBODY'S PERFEKT(1981); NIGHT IN HEAVEN, A(1983)
1984
HARRY AND SON(1984)

Helmer Bergman
SENOR AMERICANO(1929), w
Helmer Walton Bergman
Silents
ALADDIN FROM BROADWAY(1917), w
Henri Bergman
Misc. Silents
IN THE DIPLOMATIC SERVICE(1916)
Henry Bergman
MODERN TIMES(1936)
Silents
ONE MILLION DOLLARS(1915); KID, THE(1921); PILGRIM, THE(1923); WOMAN OF PARIS, A(1923); GOLD RUSH, THE(1925); CIRCUS, THE(1928); CITY LIGHTS(1931)
Misc. Silents
ENEMY TO SOCIETY, AN(1915); HOUSE OF TEARS, THE(1915); ONE MILLION DOLLARS(1915); BLACK STORK, THE(1917)
Hjalmar Bergman
SWEDENHIELMS(1935, Swed.), w; DOLLAR(1938, Swed.), w
Ingmar Bergman
TORMENT(1947, Swed.), w; ILLICIT INTERLUDE(1954, Swed.), d, w; NAKED NIGHT, THE(1956, Swed.), d&w; SMILES OF A SUMMER NIGHT(1957, Swed.), d&w; SEVENTH SEAL, THE(1958, Swed.), d, w; MAGICIAN, THE(1959, Swed.), d&w; WILD STRAWBERRIES(1959, Swed.), d&w; BRINK OF LIFE(1960, Swed.), d&w; DEVIL'S EYE, THE(1960, Swed.), d, w; DREAMS(1960, Swed.), p,d&w; LESSON IN LOVE, A(1960, Swed.), p,d&w; VIRGIN SPRING, THE(1960, Swed.), p, d; SECRETS OF WOMEN(1961, Swed.), a, d&w; DEVIL'S WANTON, THE(1962, Swed.), d&w; NIGHT IS MY FUTURE(1962, Swed.), d; THROUGH A GLASS DARKLY(1962, Swed.), d&w; PORT OF CALL(1963, Swed.), d&w; WINTER LIGHT, THE(1963, Swed.), p,d&w; ALL THESE WOMEN(1964, Swed.), p&d, w; SILENCE, THE(1964, Swed.), d&w; PERSONA(1967, Swed.), p,d&w; HOUR OF THE WOLF, THE(1968, Swed.), d&w; SHAME(1968, Swed.), d&w; PASSION OF ANNA, THE(1970, Swed.), d&w; RITUAL, THE(1970, Swed.), a, d&w; TOUCH, THE(1971, U.S./Swed.), p,d&w; CRIES AND WHISPERS(1972, Swed.), p,d&w; SCENES FROM A MARRIAGE(1974, Swed.), p,d&w; FACE TO FACE(1976, Swed.), pd&w; SERPENT'S EGG, THE(1977, Ger./Fr./Ital./U.S.), d&w; AUTUMN SONATA(1978, Swed.), d&w; FROM THE LIFE OF THE MARIONETTES(1980, Ger.), d&w; FANNY AND ALEXANDER(1983, Swed./Fr./Ger.), d&w
1984
AFTER THE REHEARSAL(1984, Swed.), d&w
Ingrid Bergman
COUNT OF THE MONK'S BRIDGE, THE(1934, Swed.); SWEDENHIELMS(1935, Swed.); ON THE SUNNYSIDE(1936, Swed.); INTERMEZZO(1937, Swed.); DOLLAR(1938, Swed.); FOUR COMPANIONS, THE(1938, Ger.); INTERMEZZO: A LOVE STORY(1939); WOMAN'S FACE, A(1939, Swed.); NIGHT IN JUNE, A(1940, Swed.); ADAM HAD FOUR SONS(1941); DR. JEKYLL AND MR. HYDE(1941); RAGE IN HEAVEN(1941); WALPURGIS NIGHT(1941, Swed.); CASABLANCA(1942); ONLY ONE NIGHT(1942, Swed.); FOR WHOM THE BELL TOLLS(1943); GASLIGHT(1944); BELLS OF ST. MARY'S, THE(1945); SARATOGA TRUNK(1945); SPELLBOUND(1945); NOTORIOUS(1946); ARCH OF TRIUMPH(1948); JOAN OF ARC(1948); OCEAN BREAKERS(1949, Swed.); UNDER CAPRICORN(1949); STROMBOLI(1950, Ital.); GREATEST LOVE, THE(1954, Ital./Fr.); JOAN AT THE STAKE(1954, Ital./Fr.); STRANGERS, THE(1955, Ital.); ANASTASIA(1956); FEAR(1956, Ger.); PARIS DOES STRANGE THINGS(1957, Fr./Ital.); INDISCREET(1958); INN OF THE SIXTH HAPPINESS, THE(1958); GOODBYE AGAIN(1961); VISIT, THE(1964, Ger./Fr./Ital./U.S.); YELLOW ROLLS-ROYCE, THE(1965, Brit.); CACTUS FLOWER(1969); WALK IN THE SPRING RAIN, A(1970); FROM THE MIXED-UP FILES OF MRS. BASIL E. FRANKWEILER(1973); MURDER ON THE ORIENT EXPRESS(1974, Brit.); MATTER OF TIME, A(1976, Ital./U.S.); AUTUMN SONATA(1978, Swed.)
Jan Bergman
SHAME(1968, Swed.)
Joel Bergman
RUNNING(1979, Can.)
Jonathan Bergman
FLOOD, THE(1963, Brit.)
Jos Bergman
LITTLE ARK, THE(1972)
Joseph Bergman
WARRIORS, THE(1979); VERDICT, THE(1982)
Karl-Arne Bergman
SILENCE, THE(1964, Swed.); SHAME(1968, Swed.)
Lena Bergman
WILD STRAWBERRIES(1959, Swed.)
Lillevi Bergman
JUST ONCE MORE(1963, Swed.)
Marilyn and Alan Bergman
LIFE AND TIMES OF JUDGE ROY BEAN, THE(1972), m/1
Marilyn Bergman
STOP THE WORLD–I WANT TO GET OFF(1966, Brit.), w
Mats Bergman
FANNY AND ALEXANDER(1983, Swed./Fr./Ger.)
Peter Bergman
LOVE IS A FUNNY THING(1970, Fr./Ital.); ZACHARIAH(1971), w; CRACKING UP(1977); AMERICATHON(1979), w; J-MEN FOREVER(1980), a, w
Sandahl Bergman
XANADU(1980); AIRPLANE II: THE SEQUEL(1982); CONAN THE BARBARIAN(1982)
Misc. Talkies
SHE(1983)
Stanley Bergman
CHINATOWN SQUAD(1935), p
Stina Bergman
SWEDENHIELMS(1935, Swed.), w; DOLLAR(1938, Swed.), w
Giovanni Bergmanini
1984
RUSH(1984, Ital.), ph
Alan Bergmann
LIGHT FANTASTIC(1964)

Christa Bergmann
WHO WAS MADDOX?(1964, Brit.)
Erik Bergmann
RIGHT STUFF, THE(1983)
Erika Bergmann
COME BACK PETER(1971, Brit.)
Alan Bergnan
COP HATER(1958)
Elisabeth Bergner
ARIANE(1931, Ger.); CATHERINE THE GREAT(1934, Brit.); ESCAPE ME NE-VER(1935, Brit.); AS YOU LIKE IT(1936, Brit.); STOLEN LIFE(1939, Brit.); CRY OF THE BANSHEE(1970, Brit.); PEDESTRIAN, THE(1974, Ger.)
Elizabeth Bergner
DREAMING LIPS(1937, Brit.); PARIS CALLING(1941)
Aino Bergo
THISTLEDOWN(1938, Brit.)
Serge Bergon
JOY(1983, Fr./Can.), d, w
Sergio Bergonzelli
SEA PIRATE, THE(1967, Fr./Span./Ital.), d
Jose Bergosa
MILKY WAY, THE(1969, Fr./Ital.)
Lyn Bergquist
1984
PALLET ON THE FLOOR(1984, New Zealand), prod d
R. J. Bergquist
Silents
PAIR OF CUPIDS, A(1918), ph
Rudolph Bergquist
Silents
HUNCH, THE(1921), ph; SANDY(1926), ph; SILK LEGS(1927), ph
Jacob Bergreen
Misc. Talkies
JEWISH KING LEAR(1935)
Eric Bergren
ELEPHANT MAN, THE(1980, Brit.), w; FRANCES(1982), w
1984
DUNE(1984), w
Ulla Bergryd
BIBLE...IN THE BEGINNING, THE(1966); APOLLO GOES ON HOLIDAY(1968, Ger./Swed.)
Conrad Bergschneider
LUGGAGE OF THE GODS(1983)
Deanne Bergsma
ROMEO AND JULIET(1966, Brit.)
Eleanor Bergstein
IT'S MY TURN(1980), w
Miriam Bergstein-Cohen
TEL AVIV TAXI(1957, Israel)
Carmelle Bergstrom
OUR HEARTS WERE YOUNG AND GAY(1944); OUT OF THIS WORLD(1945)
Catherine Bergstrom
HALLOWEEN 11(1981)
Christine Bergstrom
MEDIUM COOL(1969)
Jonas Bergstrom
ADALEN 31(1969, Swed.); LADY OSCAR(1979, Fr./Jap.)
Olof Bergstrom
ADALEN 31(1969, Swed.); VICTOR FRANKENSTEIN(1975, Swed./Ireland)
Jacques Berguine
VERY CURIOUS GIRL, A(1970, Fr.), w
Adolph Bergunker
FATHERS AND SONS(1960, USSR), p&d
Max Bergunker
SHOPWORN ANGEL, THE(1928), m; FIGHTING CARAVANS(1931), m
Sven Bergvali
AFFAIRS OF A MODEL(1952, Swed.)
Sven Bergvall
RAILROAD WORKERS(1948, Swed.)
Ed Berhard
BLUE THUNDER(1983)
Guy Berhille
BUCK AND THE PREACHER(1972), cos
Fred Berhle
RIDE 'EM COWGIRL(1939)
Lori Berhon
DANIEL(1983)
John Berhosky
ON THE YARD(1978)
Audrey Berindy
PROMISE AT DAWN(1970, U.S./Fr.)
Esme Beringer
OCTOBER MAN, THE(1948, Brit.); DARK SECRET(1949, Brit.); SOMETHING IN THE CITY(1950, Brit.); CASTLE IN THE AIR(1952, Brit.)
Silents
ALL THE WORLD'S A STAGE(1917, Brit.)
Mario Berini
DAMSEL IN DISTRESS, A(1937)
Paul Berini
MR. SYCAMORE(1975)
Berinoff and Charlot
STRAUSS' GREAT WALTZ(1934, Brit.)
Svetlana Beriosova
SOLDIER'S TALE, THE(1964, Brit.)
Siegfried Berisch
BLONDE NIGHTINGALE(1931, Ger.); HIS MAJESTY, KING BALLYHOO(1931, Ger.)
Luis Beristain
MADCAP OF THE HOUSE(1950, Mex.); EL(1955, Mex.); EXTERMINATING ANGEL, THE(1967, Mex.)

Ailsa Berk
1984
GREYSTOKE: THE LEGEND OF TARZAN, LORD OF THE APES(1984)
Howard Berk
WITCH WITHOUT A BROOM, A(1967, U.S./Span.), w; BANG BANG KID, THE(1968 U.S./Span./Ital.), w; LAST DAY OF THE WAR, THE(1969, U.S./Ital./Span.), w; NAR-CO MEN, THE(1969, Span./Ital.), w
Irma Berk
THIS REBEL BREED(1960), w
Kathy Berk
SPOOK WHO SAT BY THE DOOR, THE(1973)
Lara Berk
ANNIE(1982)
1984
PREPPIES(1984)
Michael Berk
PEACE KILLERS, THE(1971), w
Ray Berk
ONE EXCITING NIGHT(1945), set d
Richard Alan Berk
NEW YORK, NEW YORK(1977)
Robert Berk
BAT PEOPLE, THE(1974)
Sara Berk
LIGHT FANTASTIC(1964)
Wayne Berk
SON OF SINBAD(1955)
Dary Berkani
AUGUSTINE OF HIPPO(1973, Ital.)
Alfred Berke
STEEL HELMET, THE(1951), cos
Ed Berke
1984
LAST STARFIGHTER, THE(1984)
Irwin Berke
FRANKENSTEIN 1970(1958); HIGH SCHOOL CONFIDENTIAL(1958); SEX KIT-TENS GO TO COLLEGE(1960)
Jody Berke
1984
SPLASH(1984), cos
Johnny Berke
DANCING IN THE DARK(1949)
Lester William Berke
LOST MISSILE, THE(1958, U.S./Can.), d, w; WILD YOUTH(1961), w
Sandra Berke
PARADISE ALLEY(1978), cos; ROCKY II(1979), cos
Sandy Berke
TABLE FOR FIVE(1983), cos
Stephen Berke
YOU'VE GOT TO WALK IT LIKE YOU TALK IT OR YOU'LL LOSE THAT BEAT(1971)
William Berke
CORRUPTION(1933), p; FLAMING SIGNAL(1933), p; LAST OF THE CLINTONS, THE(1935), p; ROARING ROADS(1935), p; RUSTLER'S PARADISE(1935), p; WAGON TRAIL(1935), p; WILD MUSTANG(1935), p; DESERT JUSTICE(1936), p; TOLL OF THE DESERT(1936), p; ACES WILD(1937), p; ATLANTIC FLIGHT(1937), p; DAN-GEROUS HOLIDAY(1937), p; GHOST TOWN(1937), p; GHOST TOWN GOLD(1937), p; MAN BETRAYED, A(1937), p; YOUNG DYNAMITE(1937), p; CALL THE MES-QUITEERS(1938), p; HEROES OF THE HILLS(1938), p; OUTLAWS OF SONO-RA(1938), p; OVERLAND STAGE RAIDERS(1938), p; PALS OF THE SADDLE(1938), p; RED RIVER RANGE(1938), p; RIDERS OF THE BLACK HILLS(1938), p; SANTA FE STAMPEDE(1938), p; COLORADO SUNSET(1939), p; NEW FRONTIER(1939), p; NIGHT RIDERS, THE(1939), p; ROVIN' TUM-BLEWEEDS(1939), p; SOUTH OF THE BORDER(1939), p; THREE TEXAS STEERS(1939), p; WYOMING OUTLAW(1939), p; CAROLINA MOON(1940), p; GAU-CHO SERENADE(1940), p; RANCHO GRANDE(1940), p; RIDE, TENDERFOOT, RIDE(1940), p; CONFESSIONS OF BOSTON BLACKIE(1941), p; PRAIRIE STRAN-GER(1941), p; RIDERS OF THE BADLANDS(1941), p; ROYAL MOUNTED PATROL, THE(1941), p; THUNDER OVER THE PRAIRIE(1941), p; BAD MEN OF THE HILLS(1942), d; DOWN RIO GRANDE WAY(1942), d; LAWLESS PLAINSMEN(1942), d; LONE PRAIRIE, THE(1942), d; PARDON MY GUN(1942), d; RIDERS OF THE NORTHLAND(1942), d; WEST OF TOMBSTONE(1942), p; FIGHTING BUCKAROO, THE(1943), d; HAIL TO THE RANGERS(1943), d; LAW OF THE NORTHWEST(1943), d; MINESWEEPER(1943), d; RIDERS OF THE NORTHWEST MOUNTED(1943), d; ROBIN HOOD OF THE RANGE(1943), d; SILVER CITY RAIDERS(1943), d; TOR-NADO(1943), d; DARK MOUNTAIN(1944), d; FAL-CON IN MEXICO, THE(1944), d; GIRL IN THE CASE(1944), d; LAST HORSEMAN, THE(1944), d; NAVY WAY, THE(1944), d; RIDING WEST(1944), d; SAILOR'S HOLI-DAY(1944), d; THAT'S MY BABY(1944), d; BETRAYAL FROM THE EAST(1945), d; DICK TRACY(1945), d; HIGH POWERED(1945), d; WHY GIRLS LEAVE HOME(1945), d; DING DONG WILLIAMS(1946), d; FALCON'S ADVENTURE, THE(1946), d; FAL-CON'S ALIBI, THE(1946), d; RENEGADE GIRL(1946), p&d; SUNSET PASS(1946), d; CODE OF THE WEST(1947), d; SHOOT TO KILL(1947), p&d; CAGED FURY(1948), d; HIGHWAY 13(1948), d; JUNGLE JIM(1948), d; RACING LUCK(1948), d; SPEED TO SPARE(1948), d; WATERFRONT AT MIDNIGHT(1948), d; ARSON, INC.(1949), d; DEPUTY MARSHAL(1949), d, w; LOST TRIBE, THE(1949), d; SKY LINER(1949), d; TREASURE OF MONTE CRISTO(1949), d; ZAMBA(1949), d; BANDIT QUEEN(1950), p&d; BORDER RANGERS(1950), p&d, w; CAPTIVE GIRL(1950), d; GUNFIRE(1950), p&d, w; I SHOT BILLY THE KID(1950), p&d; MARK OF THE GORILLA(1950), d; ON THE ISLE OF SAMOA(1950), d; OPERATION HAYLIFT(1950), d; PYGMY IS-LAND(1950), d; TRAIN TO TOMBSTONE(1950), d; BANDIT QUEEN(1951), p&d; FURY OF THE CONGO(1951), d; PIER 23(1951), p&d; ROARING CITY(1951), p&d; SAVAGE DRUMS(1951), p&d; SMUGGLER'S GOLD(1951), d; JUNGLE, THE(1952), p&d; MARSHAL'S DAUGHTER, THE(1953), d; VALLEY OF THE HEADHUN-TERS(1953), d; FOUR BOYS AND A GUN(1957), p&d; STREET OF SINNERS(1957), p&d; ISLAND WOMEN(1958), p&d; MUGGER, THE(1958), p&d
Misc. Talkies
PECOS KID, THE(1935), d; OVERLAND TO DEADWOOD(1942), d; RIDING THROUGH NEVADA(1942), d; TORNADO IN THE SADDLE, A(1942), d; SADDLES AND SAGEBRUSH(1943), d; VIGILANTES RIDE, THE(1944), d; WYOMING HURRI-

CANE(1944), d; ROLLING HOME(1948), d

Christian Berkel
SERPENT'S EGG, THE(1977, Ger./U.S.)

Anthony Berkeley
FLIGHT FROM DESTINY(1941), w

Arthur Berkeley
TEENAGE MONSTER(1958)

Ballard Berkeley
CHINESE BUNGALOW, THE(1930, Brit.); LONDON MELODY(1930, Brit.); TROUBLE(1933, Brit.); WHITE ENSIGN(1934, Brit.); EAST MEETS WEST(1936, Brit.); JENIFER HALE(1937, Brit.); LAST ADVENTURERS, THE(1937, Brit); SAINT IN LONDON, THE(1939, Brit.); IN WHICH WE SERVE(1942, Brit.); I BECAME A CRIMINAL(1947); QUIET WEEKEND(1948, Brit.); STAGE FRIGHT(1950, Brit.); THIRD TIME LUCKY(1950, Brit.); LONG DARK HALL, THE(1951, Brit.); NIGHT WON'T TALK, THE(1952, Brit.); BLUE PARROT, THE(1953, Brit.); OPERATION DIPLOMAT(1953, Brit.); WHITE FIRE(1953, Brit.); CHILD'S PLAY(1954, Brit.); CIRCUMSTANIAL EVIDENCE(1954, Brit.); DANGEROUS CARGO(1954, Brit.); DELAYED ACTION(1954, Brit.); SEE HOW THEY RUN(1955, Brit.); PASSPORT TO TREASON(1956, Brit.); AFTER THE BALL(1957, Brit.); MEN OF SHERWOOD FOREST(1957, Brit.); BETRAYAL, THE(1958, Brit.); CHAIN OF EVENTS(1958, Brit.); FURTHER UP THE CREEK(1958, Brit.); MAN WHO WOULDN'T TALK, THE(1958, Brit.); TEENAGE BAD GIRL(1959, Brit.); TROUBLE IN THE SKY(1961, Brit.); STOLEN AIRLINER, THE(1962, Brit.); IMPACT(1963, Brit.); MATTER OF CHOICE, A(1963, Brit.); MURDER GAME, THE(1966, Brit.); HOSTILE WITNESS(1968, Brit.); WEEKEND MURDERS, THE(1972, Ital.)

Bert Berkeley
Misc. Silents
ROARING FIRES(1927)

Bonnie Berkeley
INCREDIBLY STRANGE CREATURES WHO STOPPED LIVING AND BECAME CRAZY MIXED-UP ZOMBIES, THE(1965)

Busby Berkeley
WHOOPEE(1930), ch; FLYING HIGH(1931), ch; PALMY DAYS(1931), ch; BIRD OF PARADISE(1932), ch; KID FROM SPAIN, THE(1932), ch; NIGHT WORLD(1932), ch; SKY DEVILS(1932), ch; FOOTLIGHT PARADE(1933), d; GOLD DIGGERS OF 1933(1933), a, ch; ROMAN SCANDALS(1933), ch; SHE HAD TO SAY YES(1933), d; 42ND STREET(1933), ch; DAMES(1934), ch; FASHIONS OF 1934(1934), ch; WONDER BAR(1934), ch; BRIGHT LIGHTS(1935), ch; GOLD DIGGERS OF 1935(1935), d; I LIVE FOR LOVE(1935), d; IN CALIENTE(1935), ch; STARS OVER BROADWAY(1935), ch; GOLD DIGGERS OF 1937(1936), ch; STAGE STRUCK(1936), d; GO-GETTER, THE(1937), d; HOLLYWOOD HOTEL(1937), d; SINGING MARINE, THE(1937), ch; VARSITY SHOW(1937), ch; COMET OVER BROADWAY(1938), d; GARDEN OF THE MOON(1938), d; MEN ARE SUCH FOOLS(1938), d; BABES IN ARMS(1939), d; BROADWAY SERENADE(1939), ch; FAST AND FURIOUS(1939), d; THEY MADE ME A CRIMINAL(1939), d; FORTY LITTLE MOTHERS(1940), d; STRIKE UP THE BAND(1940), d; BABES ON BROADWAY(1941), d; BLONDE INSPIRATION(1941), d; LADY BE GOOD(1941), ch; ZIEGFELD GIRL(1941), ch; FOR ME AND MY GAL(1942), d; GANG'S ALL HERE, THE(1943), d, ch; GIRL CRAZY(1943), ch; CINDERELLA JONES(1946), d; ROMANCE ON THE HIGH SEAS(1948), ch; TAKE ME OUT TO THE BALL GAME(1949), d; TWO WEEKS WITH LOVE(1950), ch; CALL ME MISTER(1951), ch; TWO TICKETS TO BROADWAY(1951), ch; MILLION DOLLAR MERMAID(1952), ch; EASY TO LOVE(1953), md, m; SMALL TOWN GIRL(1953), ch; ROSE MARIE(1954), ch; PHYNX, THE(1970)

Capt. Reginald Berkeley
NURSE EDITH CAVELL(1939), w

Claude Berkeley
SAILORS' HOLIDAY(1929), ed; SAL OF SINGAPORE(1929), ed; JOURNEY'S END(1930), ed; BAD COMPANY(1931), ed; BORN TO LOVE(1931), ed
Silents
ANNAPOLIS(1928), ed; LEOPARD LADY, THE(1928), ed; WALKING BACK(1928), ed

George Berkeley
PICKUP ON SOUTH STREET(1953); LAW VS. BILLY THE KID, THE(1954)

Gertrude Berkeley
Silents
SOUL OF BROADWAY, THE(1915); JUST SYLVIA(1918); WAY OF A WOMAN(1919)
Misc. Silents
IRON HEART, THE(1917); OVER THERE(1917); BREAK THE NEWS TO MOTHER(1919)

Lennox Berkeley
HOTEL RESERVE(1946, Brit.), m; AFFAIRS OF A ROGUE, THE(1949, Brit.), m

Lynne Berkeley
CAREER WOMAN(1936); GIRLS' DORMITORY(1936); LOVE AND HISSES(1937); YOU CAN'T HAVE EVERYTHING(1937); GOLDWYN FOLLIES, THE(1938)
Misc. Talkies
SONGS AND SADDLES(1938)

Martin Berkeley
PENALTY, THE(1941), w; CITY WITHOUT MEN(1943), w; DR. GILLESPIE'S CRIMINAL CASE(1943), w; HARRIGAN'S KID(1943), w; THREE MEN IN WHITE(1944), w; NOTORIOUS LONE WOLF, THE(1946), w; OUT OF THE DEPTHS(1946), w; SHOCK(1946), w; SO DARK THE NIGHT(1946), w; GREEN GRASS OF WYOMING(1948), w; SAND(1949), w; KANGAROO(1952), w; MEET ME AT THE FAIR(1952), w; STOLEN FACE(1952, Brit.), w; NEBRASKAN, THE(1953), w; WAR PAINT(1953), w; GYPSY COLT(1954), w; REVENGE OF THE CREATURE(1955), w; TARANTULA(1955), w; RED SUNDOWN(1956), w; BIG CAPER, THE(1957), w; DEADLY MANTIS, THE(1957), w

Mowbray Berkeley
ESCORT WEST(1959), set d

Reginald Berkeley
BRAT, THE(1930, Brit.), w; LOVES OF ROBERT BURNS, THE(1930, Brit.), w; WOLVES(1930, Brit.), w; DREYFUS CASE, THE(1931, Brit.), w; FRENCH LEAVE(1931, Brit.), w; MAN FROM CHICAGO, THE(1931, Brit.), w; 77 PARK LANE(1931, Brit.), w; BROKEN LULLABY(1932), w; LUCKY GIRL(1932, Brit.), w; CAVALCADE(1933), w; CAROLINA(1934), w; MARIE GALANTE(1934), w; FRENCH LEAVE(1937, Brit.), w; LADY WITH A LAMP, THE(1951, Brit.), w
Silents
DAWN(1928, Brit.), w

Reginald C. Berkeley
WORLD MOVES ON, THE(1934), w

Robert Berkeley
EYES THAT KILL(1947, Brit.)

Ron Berkeley
MANCHURIAN CANDIDATE, THE(1962), makeup; TWILIGHT OF HONOR(1963), makeup; OUTRAGE, THE(1964), makeup; GIRL HAPPY(1965), makeup; WHO'S AFRAID OF VIRGINIA WOOLF?(1966), makeup; TAMING OF THE SHREW, THE(1967, U.S./Ital.), makeup; IF IT'S TUESDAY, THIS MUST BE BELGIUM(1969), makeup; STAIRCASE(1969 U.S./Brit./Fr.), makeup; HAMMERSMITH IS OUT(1972), makeup

Xander Berkeley
MOMMIE DEAREST(1981)

George Berkely
DEVIL GODDESS(1955)

John Berkes
CORPSE CAME C.O.D., THE(; I STOLE A MILLION(1939); WINTER CARNIVAL(1939); BOWERY AT MIDNIGHT(1942); PRIDE OF THE ARMY(1942); HONEYMOON AHEAD(1945); INSIDE JOB(1946); KILLERS, THE(1946); NIGHT IN PARADISE, A(1946); SUSIE STEPS OUT(1946); EGG AND I, THE(1947); GUILT OF JANET AMES, THE(1947); JOHNNY O'CLOCK(1947); STATION WEST(1948); MY DREAM IS YOURS(1949); BRANDED(1951); JOURNEY INTO LIGHT(1951)

Johnnie Berkes
SHADOW OF THE THIN MAN(1941); ARABIAN NIGHTS(1942); BEHIND THE EIGHT BALL(1942); SHINE ON, HARVEST MOON(1944); TREE GROWS IN BROOKLYN, A(1945)

Johnny Berkes
COWBOY SERENADE(1942); MADAME SPY(1942); MR. CELEBRITY(1942); WOMAN OF THE YEAR(1942); MRS. PARKINGTON(1944); OUR VINES HAVE TENDER GRAPES(1945); ROMANCE ON THE HIGH SEAS(1948)

James Berkey
LOVE-INS, THE(1967), set d; WITH SIX YOU GET EGGROLL(1968), set d; HAWAIIANS, THE(1970), set d; LAST AMERICAN HERO, THE(1973), set d; THUNDERBOLT AND LIGHTFOOT(1974), set d; ISLAND OF DR. MOREAU, THE(1977), set d; GREASE(1978), set d

James I. Berkey
PAINT YOUR WAGON(1969), set d; EVERY LITTLE CROOK AND NANNY(1972), set d; MAN, THE(1972), set d; OUTFIT, THE(1973), set d; GREASED LIGHTNING(1977), set d; WHITE BUFFALO, THE(1977), set d

Jim Berkey
W. W. AND THE DIXIE DANCEKINGS(1975), set d; PRETTY BABY(1978), set d; KISS ME GOODBYE(1982), set d

Ralph Berkey
TIME LIMIT(1957), w

Denis Berkfeldt
ESCAPE FROM ALCATRAZ(1979)

James Berkin
Misc. Talkies
MAY MORNING(1970)

Sandra Berkin
1984
1919(1984, Brit.)

George Berkley
GLASS HOUSES(1972)

Martin Berkley
TROOPER HOOK(1957), w

Edward O. Berkman
MURDER ON DIAMOND ROW(1937, Brit.), w; GREEN COCKATOO, THE(1947, Brit.), w

Ted Berkman
BEDTIME FOR BONZO(1951), w; FEAR STRIKES OUT(1957), w; SHORT CUT TO HELL(1957), w; EDGE OF FURY(1958), w; GIRL OF THE NIGHT(1960), w; CAST A GIANT SHADOW(1966), w

Rafael Berko
1984
FEAR CITY(1984)

Louis Berkoff
STRANGE MR. GREGORY, THE(1945), p

Stephen Berkoff
PASSENGER, THE(1975, Ital.)

Steven Berkoff
PREHISTORIC WOMEN(1967, Brit.); CLOCKWORK ORANGE, A(1971, Brit.); NICHOLAS AND ALEXANDRA(1971, Brit.); BARRY LYNDON(1975, Brit.); OUTLAND(1981); MC VICAR(1982, Brit.); OCTOPUSSY(1983, Brit.)
1984
BEVERLY HILLS COP(1984)

Peter Berkos
GREAT WALDO PEPPER, THE(1975), ed

Saundra Berkova
CAPTAIN TUGBOAT ANNIE(1945); OLD-FASHIONED GIRL, AN(1948)

Myles Berkowitz
1984
NO SMALL AFFAIR(1984)

Zilla Berkowitz
DREAM NO MORE(1950, Palestine)

Peter Berkrot
CADDY SHACK(1980)

John Berks
BIG CARNIVAL, THE(1951)

David Berkson
E.T. THE EXTRA-TERRESTRIAL(1982)

Ross Berkson
1984
SIXTEEN CANDLES(1984)

Yu Berkum
HAMLET(1966, USSR)

Lily Berky
SUN SHINES, THE(1939, Hung.)

David Berlackie
JESUS TRIP, THE(1971), ed
Terri Berland
PINK MOTEL(1983)
Terry Berland
STING II, THE(1983)
Luis G. Berlanga
CALABUCH(1956, Span./Ital.), d, w
Luis Garcia Berlanga
NOT ON YOUR LIFE(1965, Ital./Span.), d, w
Juliette Berlanger
Silents
DON Q, SON OF ZORRO(1925)
David Berlatsky
VIVA MAX!(1969), ed; LAST MOVIE, THE(1971), ed; HICKEY AND BOGGS(1972), ed; KANSAS CITY BOMBER(1972), ed; PAT GARRETT AND BILLY THE KID(1973), ed; SHANKS(1974), ed; WILD McCULLOCHS, THE(1975), ed; DEEP, THE(1977), ed; FARMER, THE(1977), d
Frank Berle
TAKING OFF(1971)
Milton Berle
NEW FACES OF 1937(1937); RADIO CITY REVELS(1938); RISE AND SHINE(1941); SUN VALLEY SERENADE(1941); TALL, DARK AND HANDSOME(1941); GENTLEMAN AT HEART, A(1942); OVER MY DEAD BODY(1942); WHISPERING GHOSTS(1942); MARGIN FOR ERROR(1943); ALWAYS LEAVE THEM LAUGHING(1949); BELLBOY, THE(1960); LET'S MAKE LOVE(1960); IT'S A MAD, MAD, MAD, MAD WORLD(1963); LOVED ONE, THE(1965); DON'T WORRY, WE'LL THINK OF A TITLE(1966); OSCAR, THE(1966); HAPPENING, THE(1967); WHO'S MINDING THE MINT?(1967); FOR SINGLES ONLY(1968); WHERE ANGELS GO...TROUBLE FOLLOWS(1968); JOURNEY BACK TO OZ(1974); LEPKE(1975, U.S./Israel); WON TON TON, THE DOG WHO SAVED HOLLYWOOD(1976); MUPPET MOVIE, THE(1979); SMORGASBORD(1983)
1984
BROADWAY DANNY ROSE(1984)
Misc. Talkies
CAN HIERONYMUS MERKIN EVER FORGET MERCY HUMPPE AND FIND TRUE HAPPINESS?(1969); OFF YOUR ROCKER(1980)
Francois Berleand
LA BALANCE(1983, Fr.)
Andre Berley
Silents
PASSION OF JOAN OF ARC, THE(1928, Fr.)
Abby Berlin
LEAVE IT TO BLONDIE(1945), d; BLONDIE KNOWS BEST(1946), d; BLONDIE'S LUCKY DAY(1946), d; LIFE WITH BLONDIE(1946), d; BLONDIE IN THE DOUGH(1947), d; BLONDIE'S ANNIVERSARY(1947), d; BLONDIE'S BIG MOMENT(1947), d; BLONDIE'S HOLIDAY(1947), d; BLONDIE'S REWARD(1948), d; MARY RYAN, DETECTIVE(1949), d; DOUBLE DEAL(1950), d; FATHER IS A BACHELOR(1950), d
Alexandra Berlin
REVOLUTIONARY, THE(1970, Brit.)
Carl Berlin
Misc. Silents
SECRETS OF THE RANGE(1928)
Francoise Berlin
PEPPERMINT SODA(1979, Fr.)
Hilary Berlin
PRIME OF MISS JEAN BRODIE, THE(1969, Brit.)
Ida Berlin
NEW LEAF, A(1971)
Irving Berlin
COCOANUTS, THE(1929), w; HALLELUJAH(1929), m; GLORIFYING THE AMERICAN GIRL(1930); MAMMY(1930), w, m; REACHING FOR THE MOON(1931), w, m; ON THE AVENUE(1937), m; HOLIDAY INN(1942), w; THIS IS THE ARMY(1943), w; BLUE SKIES(1946), w; CALL ME MADAM(1953), m; RUN FOR THE HILLS(1953), ed; THERE'S NO BUSINESS LIKE SHOW BUSINESS(1954), m; SPEED CRAZY(1959), ed; CLOWN AND THE KID, THE(1961), ed; WINTER A GO-GO(1965), ed
Jeannie Berlin
BABY MAKER, THE(1970); GETTING STRAIGHT(1970); STRAWBERRY STATEMENT, THE(1970); HEARTBREAK KID, THE(1972); PORTNOY'S COMPLAINT(1972); SHEILA LEVINE IS DEAD AND LIVING IN NEW YORK(1975)
Misc. Talkies
BONE(1972)
Judy Berlin
1984
ICEMAN(1984)
Milton Berlin
BURN 'EM UP O'CONNER(1939), w
Minnie Berlin
Misc. Silents
LAST CONCERT, THE(1915)
Patsy Berlin
CRIME OF DR. CRESPI, THE(1936)
Peter Berlin
BLOOD IN THE STREETS(1975, Ital./Fr.)
Steve Berlin
1984
STREETS OF FIRE(1984)
Susan Berlin
THOSE LIPS, THOSE EYES(1980); DREAM ON(1981); SOME KIND OF HERO(1982)
Berlin Brats
UP IN SMOKE(1978)
Chamber Choir of Berlin Radio
CITY OF TORMENT(1950, Ger.), m
Boyd Berlind
ICE STATION ZEBRA(1968)

Byron Berline
STAY HUNGRY(1976), m
Alan Berliner
RICH AND FAMOUS(1981)
Brin Berliner
1984
WILD LIFE, THE(1984)
George Berliner
LONESOME TRAIL, THE(1930); GOOD BAD GIRL, THE(1931)
Martin Berliner
VOICE IN THE WIND(1944); COUNTERFEIT TRAITOR, THE(1962); THREE PENNY OPERA(1963, Fr./Ger.)
Norman Berliner [Jerry Burke]
SATAN'S BED(1965)
Rudolph Berliner
Silents
GREAT SHADOW, THE(1920), w
Trude Berliner
BECAUSE I LOVED YOU(1930, Ger.); STRANGE DEATH OF ADOLF HITLER, THE(1943)
Trudy Berliner
DOLLY SISTERS, THE(1945)
Peter Berling
BLACK AND WHITE IN COLOR(1976, Fr.); AGUIRRE, THE WRATH OF GOD(1977, W. Ger.); MARRIAGE OF MARIA BRAUN, THE(1979, Ger.); FITZCARRALDO(1982); VERONIKA VOSS(1982, Ger.)
Warren Berlinger
TEENAGE REBEL(1956); THREE BRAVE MEN(1957); BLUE DENIM(1959); BECAUSE THEY'RE YOUNG(1960); PLATINUM HIGH SCHOOL(1960); ALL HANDS ON DECK(1961); WACKIEST SHIP IN THE ARMY, THE(1961); BILLIE(1965); SPINOUT(1966); THUNDER ALLEY(1967); LONG GOODBYE, THE(1973); LEPKE(1975, U.S./Israel); FOUR DEUCES, THE(1976); HARRY AND WALTER GO TO NEW YORK(1976); I WILL ...I WILL ...FOR NOW(1976); SHAGGY D.A., THE(1976); MAGICIAN OF LUBLIN, THE(1979, Israel/Ger.); CANNONBALL RUN, THE(1981); WORLD ACCORDING TO GARP, The(1982)
Ricardo Berlingeri
LA CAGE AUX FOLLES II(1981, Ital./Fr.)
Zeev Berlinski
RETURN OF DR. MABUSE, THE(1961, Ger./Fr./Ital.); TERROR OF DR. MABUSE, THE(1965, Ger.); TRUNK TO CAIRO(1966, Israel/Ger.)
Zeev Berlinsky
RABBI AND THE SHIKSE, THE(1976, Israel)
Zev Berlinsky
BILLY TWO HATS(1973, Brit.)
J. Berlinz
RUY BLAS(1948, Fr.)
Hector Berlioz
WEB OF PASSION(1961, Fr.), m; WOMAN OF STRAW(1964, Brit.), m; SHADOWMAN(1974, Fr./Ital.), m
Jacques Berlioz
LA BETE HUMAINE(1938, Fr.); DOUBLE CRIME IN THE MAGINOT LINE(1939, Fr.)
Charles Berlitz
1984
PHILADELPHIA EXPERIMENT, THE(1984), w
Jerry Berloshan
LEGEND OF THE LONE RANGER, THE(1981), w
Sonja Berlovitz
1984
PURPLE RAIN(1984), cos
Ivan Berlyn
IMMORTAL GENTLEMAN(1935, Brit.)
Silents
PHANTOM PICTURE, THE(1916, Brit.)
Misc. Silents
HONOUR IN PAWN(1916, Brit.)
Berman
RECOIL(1953), ph
Anita Berman
CITY LOVERS(1982, S. African), art d
Dave Berman
WITNESS TO MURDER(1954), cos
David Berman
JACK THE GIANT KILLER(1962), cos; ON THE YARD(1978)
Francis Berman
WEREWOLF IN A GIRL'S DORMITORY(1961, Ital./Aust.), m
Fred Berman
PUNCH AND JUDY MAN, THE(1963, Brit.)
Gerald Berman
GUEST AT STEENKAMPSKRAAL, THE(1977, South Africa), p
1984
GUEST, THE(1984, Brit.), p
Harold Berman
WRONG MAN, THE(1956)
Harvey Berman
WILD RIDE, THE(1960), p&d
Henry Berman
FOLLOW THE FLEET(1936), ed; SWING TIME(1936), ed; DAMSEL IN DISTRESS, A(1937), ed; HIDEAWAY(1937), m; QUALITY STREET(1937), ed; VIVACIOUS LADY(1938), ed; BACHELOR MOTHER(1939), ed; FIXER DUGAN(1939), ed; GUNGA DIN(1939), ed; KITTY FOYLE(1940), ed; LUCKY PARTNERS(1940), ed; VIGIL IN THE NIGHT(1940), ed; OBLIGING YOUNG LADY(1941), ed; SCATTERGOOD BAINES(1941), ed; SCATTERGOOD RIDES HIGH(1942), ed; SING YOUR WORRIES AWAY(1942), ed; BANNERLINE(1951), p; JUST THIS ONCE(1952), p; YOU FOR ME(1952), p; FAST COMPANY(1953), p; SLIGHT CASE OF LARCENY, A(1953), p; TORCH SONG(1953), p; MEN OF THE FIGHTING LADY(1954), p; PRISONER OF WAR(1954), p; BAR SINISTER, THE(1955), p; BEDEVILLED(1955), p; GREAT AMERICAN PASTIME, THE(1956), p; SWEET BIRD OF YOUTH(1962), ed; ONE OF OUR SPIES IS MISSING(1966), ed; ONE SPY TOO MANY(1966), ed; TO TRAP A SPY(1966), ed; POINT BLANK(1967), ed; VENETIAN AFFAIR, THE(1967), ed; FIX-

ER, THE(1968), ed; GYPSY MOTHS, THE(1969), ed; I WALK THE LINE(1970), ed; TELL ME THAT YOU LOVE ME, JUNIE MOON(1970), ed; EVERY LITTLE CROOK AND NANNY(1972), ed

Herbert Berman
GILDERSLEEVE'S BAD DAY(1943)

Israel M. Berman
JET ATTACK(1958), p

Jane Berman
LOVELESS, THE(1982)

Lee Berman
DOUBLE DEAL(1950), w

Len Berman
MUSIC HATH CHARMS(1935, Brit.)

Lester Berman
SOMETHING SHORT OF PARADISE(1979), p

Marc Berman
1984
LE BAL(1984, Fr./Ital./Algeria)

Martin Berman
MAN IN THE GLASS BOOTH, THE(1975)

Michael Berman
BOYS IN COMPANY C, THE(1978, U.S./Hong Kong), ed

Monte Berman
BLOOD OF THE VAMPIRE(1958, Brit.), p

Monty Berman
SOME DAY(1935, Brit.), ph; EDGE OF THE WORLD, THE(1937, Brit.), ph; DATE WITH A DREAM, A(1948, Brit.), p, w, ph; MELODY CLUB(1949, Brit.), p, d; BLACK-OUT(1950, Brit.), p, ph; NO TRACE(1950, Brit.), p; QUIET WOMAN, THE(1951, Brit.), p, ph; FRIGHTENED MAN, THE(1952, Brit.), p, ph; 13 EAST STREET(1952, Brit.), p, ph; BIG FRAME, THE(1953, Brit.), p, ph; DEADLY NIGHTSHADE(1953, Brit.), p, ph; LOVE IN PAWN(1953, Brit.), p, ph; MURDER WILL OUT(1953, Brit.), p, ph; RECOIL(1953), p; STEEL KEY, THE(1953, Brit.), p; WHITE FIRE(1953, Brit.), p, ph; DELAYED ACTION(1954, Brit.), p, ph; DOUBLE EXPOSURE(1954, Brit.), p, ph; EMBEZZLER, THE(1954, Brit.), p; ESCAPE BY NIGHT(1954, Brit.), p, ph; GILDED CAGE, THE(1954, Brit.), p, ph; IMPULSE(1955, Brit.), p; NO SMOKING(1955, Brit.), p, ph; WINDFALL(1955 Brit.), p, ph; BOND OF FEAR(1956, Brit.), p, ph; BREAKA-WAY(1956, Brit.), p, ph; MURDER ON APPROVAL(1956, Brit.), p, ph; PASSPORT TO TREASON(1956, Brit.), p, ph; HIGH TERRACE(1957, Brit.), p; HOUR OF DECI-SION(1957, Brit.), p; PROFESSOR TIM(1957, Ireland), p; TWO GROOMS FOR A BRIDE(1957), p, ph; BLIND SPOT(1958, Brit.), p; CRAWLING EYE, THE(1958, Brit.), p; CROSS-UP(1958), p; STORMY CROSSING(1958, Brit.), p; HOME IS THE HE-RO(1959, Ireland), p; JACK THE RIPPER(1959, Brit.), p; BOYD'S SHOP(1960, Brit.), p; SIEGE OF SIDNEY STREET, THE(1960, Brit.), p&d, ph, ed; MANIA(1961, Brit.), p, ph; SECRET OF MONTE CRISTO, THE(1961, Brit.), p&d, ph; DESERT PATROL(1962, Brit.), p; WHAT A CARVE UP!(1962, Brit.), p, ph; HELLFIRE CLUB, THE(1963, Brit.), p&d, ph

Pandro S. Berman
TAXI 13(1928), ed; SYMPHONY OF SIX MILLION(1932), p; WAY BACK HO-ME(1932), p; AGGIE APPLEBY, MAKER OF MEN(1933), p; CHRISTOPHER STRONG(1933), p; MORNING GLORY(1933), p; ONE MAN'S JOURNEY(1933), p; SILVER CORD(1933), p; SWEEPINGS(1933), p; FOUNTAIN, THE(1934), p; GAY DIVORCEE, THE(1934), p; LIFE OF VERGIE WINTERS, THE(1934), p; LITTLE MINISTER, THE(1934), p; MAN OF TWO WORLDS(1934), p; OF HUMAN BON-DAGE(1934), p; RICHEST GIRL IN THE WORLD, THE(1934), p; STINGAREE(1934), p; STRICTLY DYNAMITE(1934), p; THIS MAN IS MINE(1934), p; ALICE ADAMS(1935), p; BY YOUR LEAVE(1935), p; FRECKLES(1935), p; I DREAM TOO MUCH(1935), p; IN PERSON(1935), p; LADDIE(1935), p; ROBERTA(1935), p; RO-MANCE IN MANHATTAN(1935), p; STAR OF MIDNIGHT(1935), p; TOP HAT(1935), p; BIG GAME, THE(1936), p; FOLLOW THE FLEET(1936), p; MARY OF SCOT-LAND(1936), p; MUSS 'EM UP(1936), p; SWING TIME(1936), p; SYLVIA SCAR-LETT(1936), p; WINTERSET(1936), p; WOMAN REBELS, A(1936), p; DAMSEL IN DISTRESS, A(1937), p; QUALITY STREET(1937), p; SHALL WE DANCE(1937), p; SOLDIER AND THE LADY, THE(1937), p; STAGE DOOR(1937), p; THAT GIRL FROM PARIS(1937), p; CAREFREE(1938), p; HAVING WONDERFUL TIME(1938), p; MAD MISS MANTON, THE(1938), p; MOTHER CAREY'S CHICKENS(1938), p; ROOM SERVICE(1938), p; BACHELOR MOTHER(1939), p; FLYING IRISHMAN, THE(1939), p; GUNGA DIN(1939), p; HUNCHBACK OF NOTRE DAME, THE(1939), p; STORY OF VERNON AND IRENE CASTLE, THE(1939), p; HONKY TONK(1941), p; LOVE CRAZY(1941), p; ZIEGFELD GIRL(1941), p; RIO RITA(1942), p; SOMEWHERE I'LL FIND YOU(1942), p; SLIGHTLY DANGEROUS(1943), p; DRAGON SEED(1944), p; MARRIAGE IS A PRIVATE AFFAIR(1944), p; NATIONAL VELVET(1944), p; SEV-ENTH CROSS, THE(1944), p; PICTURE OF DORIAN GRAY, THE(1945), p; UNDER-CURRENT(1946), p; IF WINTER COMES(1947), p; LIVING IN A BIG WAY(1947), p; SEA OF GRASS, THE(1947), p; THREE MUSKETEERS, THE(1948), p; BRIBE, THE(1949), p; DOCTOR AND THE GIRL, THE(1949), p; MADAME BOVARY(1949), p; FATHER OF THE BRIDE(1950), p; FATHER'S LITTLE DIVIDEND(1951), p; LIGHT TOUCH, THE(1951), p; SOLDIERS THREE(1951), p; IVANHOE(1952, Brit.), p; PRIS-ONER OF ZENDA, THE(1952), p; ALL THE BROTHERS WERE VALIANT(1953), p; BATTLE CIRCUS(1953), p; KNIGHTS OF THE ROUND TABLE(1953), p; LONG, LONG TRAILER, THE(1954), p; BLACKBOARD JUNGLE, THE(1955), p; QUENTIN DURWARD(1955), p; BHOWANI JUNCTION(1956), p; TEA AND SYMPATHY(1956), p; JAILHOUSE ROCK(1957), p; BROTHERS KARAMAZOV, THE(1958), p; RELUCTANT DEBUTANTE, THE(1958), p; ALL THE FINE YOUNG CANNIBALS(1960), p; BUTTERFIELD 8(1960), p; SWEET BIRD OF YOUTH(1962), p; PRIZE, THE(1963), p; HONEYMOON HOTEL(1964), p; PATCH OF BLUE, A(1965), p; JUSTINE(1969), p; MOVE(1970), p
Silents
FANGS OF THE WILD(1928), ed; PHANTOM OF THE RANGE(1928), ed; STOCKS AND BLONDES(1928), ed

Sandy Berman
SCREAMERS(1978, Ital.), m

Shelley Berman
BEST MAN, THE(1964); DIVORCE AMERICAN STYLE(1967); THINK DIRTY(1970, Brit.); BEWARE! THE BLOB(1972)
Misc. Talkies
KEEP OFF! KEEP OFF!(1975), d

Sonia Berman
CRAZY QUILT, THE(1966)

Sonya Berman
HOT TOMORROWS(1978)

Susan Berman
SMITHEREENS(1982)

Ted Berman
ONE HUNDRED AND ONE DALMATIANS(1961), anim; RESCUERS, THE(1977), w; FOX AND THE HOUND, THE(1981), d, w

Tom Berman
CRY DR. CHICAGO(1971), ed

Berman's
GUESS WHAT HAPPENED TO COUNT DRACULA(1970), cos

Pandro S. Bermand
SPITFIRE(1934), p

Bermans
FIRE DOWN BELOW(1957, U.S./Brit.), cos

Anthony Bermans
KRULL(1983), cos

Bermans and Nathans
DRESSER, THE(1983), cos

Bermans of London
30 IS A DANGEROUS AGE, CYNTHIA(1968, Brit.), cos

Chiro Bermejo
DOS COSMONAUTAS A LA FUERZA(1967, Span./*Ital.); UGLY ONES, THE(1968, Ital./Span.)

Janoz Bermez
IN A YEAR OF THIRTEEN MOONS(1980, Ger.)

Pedro Bermudez
RETURN OF THE SEVEN(1966, Span.)

Britt Bern
BEFORE WINTER COMES(1969, Brit.)

Paul Bern
GERALDINE(1929), p; RED HEADED WOMAN(1932), p
Silents
NORTH WIND'S MALICE, THE(1920), d; WANTERS, THE(1923), w; MARRIAGE CIRCLE, THE(1924), w; OPEN ALL NIGHT(1924), d; BELOVED ROGUE, THE(1927), w
Misc. Silents
MAN WITH TWO MOTHERS, THE(1922), d; WORLDLY GOODS(1924), d; DRESS-MAKER FROM PARIS, THE(1925), d; FLOWER OF NIGHT(1925), d; GROUNDS FOR DIVORCE(1925), d; TOMORROW'S LOVE(1925), d

Svenolof Bern
EMIGRANTS, THE(1972, Swed.)

Tonia Bern
GLASS TOMB, THE(1955, Brit.); KEEP IT CLEAN(1956, Brit.)

Elsa Berna
Silents
PASSION(1920, Ger.)

Emil Berna
LAST CHANCE, THE(1945, Switz.), ph; SEARCH, THE(1948), ph; FOUR DAYS LEAVE(1950, Switz.), ph; FOUR IN A JEEP(1951, Switz.), ph; VILLAGE, THE(1953, Brit./Switz.), ph; HEIDI(1954, Switz.), ph; HEIDI AND PETER(1955, Switz.), ph

Bernabe
NEST, THE(1982, Span.)

Joby Bernabe
1984
SUGAR CANE ALLEY(1984, Fr.)

Harold Bernadi
MISS SUSIE SLAGLE'S(1945)

Peter Bernados
NO. 96(1974, Aus.), d

Prince Sigvard Bernadotte
PRISONER OF ZENDA, THE(1937), tech adv

Dan Bernaducci
CLASH BY NIGHT(1952); SECOND CHANCE(1953); FRENCH LINE, THE(1954); UNDERWATER!(1955)

Francisco Bernal
SPANISH AFFAIR(1958, Span.); BOY WHO STOLE A MILLION, THE(1960, Brit.)

Robert Bernal
CAPTAIN LIGHTFOOT(1955); QUARE FELLOW, THE(1962, Brit.); GUNS IN THE HEATHER(1968, Brit.); TWELVE CHAIRS, THE(1970)

George Bernanos
DIARY OF A COUNTRY PRIEST(1954, Fr.), d&w

Georges Bernanos
MOUCHETTE(1970, Fr.), w

Carmelo Bernaola
HUNCHBACK OF THE MORGUE, THE(1972, Span.), m; ERNESTO(1979, Ital.), m; THAT HOUSE IN THE OUTSKIRTS(1980, Span.), m

Francisco Bernar
GOLIATH AGAINST THE GIANTS(1963, Ital./Span.)

Bernard
CRY TERROR(1958), cos

Alec Bernard
UNEASY TERMS(1948, Brit.)

Alex Bernard
LA MATERNELLE(1933, Fr.)
Silents
CABIRIA(1914, Ital.)

Alexandre Bernard
Silents
NAPOLEON(1927, Fr.)

Anna Bernard
DOCTOR DEATH: SEEKER OF SOULS(1973)

Armand Bernard
UNDER THE ROOFS OF PARIS(1930, Fr.), md; MILLION, THE(1931, Fr.), m; AFFAIR LAFONT, THE(1939, Fr.); CONFLICT(1939, Fr.); LE MONDE TREM-BLERA(1939, Fr.)

Armond Bernard
AMPHYTRYON(1937, Ger.)

Arthur Bernard
$1,000 A TOUCHDOWN(1939)
Barney Bernard
Silents
INTOLERANCE(1916); PRINCE IN A PAWNSHOP, A(1916)
Misc. Silents
PHANTOM FORTUNES, THE(1916); POTASH AND PERLMUTTER(1923)
Barry Bernard
FOREIGN CORRESPONDENT(1940); DESPERATE JOURNEY(1942); PANTHER'S
CLAW, THE(1942); ADVENTURES IN IRAQ(1943); FATAL WITNESS, THE(1945); I'LL
TELL THE WORLD(1945); PRISON SHIP(1945); CRY WOLF(1947); TWO MRS.
CARROLLS, THE(1947); CASBAH(1948); WOMAN IN WHITE, THE(1948); KIND
LADY(1951); ROGUE'S MARCH(1952); FORBIDDEN(1953); GIRLS OF PLEASURE
ISLAND, THE(1953); HOUDINI(1953); ROYAL AFRICAN RIFLES, THE(1953); TITAN-
IC(1953); ELEPHANT WALK(1954); KILLER LEOPARD(1954); SOLDIER OF FOR-
TUNE(1955); VIRGIN QUEEN, THE(1955); PAL JOEY(1957); SOMETHING OF
VALUE(1957); MY WORLD DIES SCREAMING(1958); RETURN OF THE FLY(1959);
NOTORIOUS LANDLADY, THE(1962); BIRDS AND THE BEES, THE(1965); ONE OF
OUR SPIES IS MISSING(1966)
Misc. Silents
GOD'S GOOD MAN(1921, Brit.)
Bert Bernard
GOBS AND GALS(1952); DECAMERON NIGHTS(1953, Brit.)
Bob Bernard
WEEKEND WITH THE BABYSITTER(1970)
Butch Bernard
SEVEN YEAR ITCH, THE(1955); TOY TIGER(1956); ALL MINE TO GIVE(1957);
MAN AFRAID(1957)
Camille Bernard
KAMOURASKA(1973, Can./Fr.)
Carl Bernard
SILVER DARLINGS, THE(1947, Brit.); LARGE ROPE, THE(1953, Brit.); LOSER
TAKES ALL(1956, Brit.); ACCOUNT RENDERED(1957, Brit.); HIGH TERRACE(1957,
Brit.); HOUR OF DECISION(1957, Brit.); THREE MEN IN A BOAT(1958, Brit.);
HEADLESS GHOST, THE(1959, Brit.); CORRIDORS OF BLOOD(1962, Brit.); THIS IS
MY STREET(1964, Brit.); DARWIN ADVENTURE, THE(1972, Brit.); POPE JOAN(1972,
Brit.); TALES FROM THE CRYPT(1972, Brit.)
Cheril Bernard
PHONY AMERICAN, THE(1964, Ger.)
Christian Bernard
EAGLE WITH TWO HEADS(1948, Fr.), art d
Crystal Bernard
YOUNG DOCTORS IN LOVE(1982)
Denis Bernard
MASQUERADE(1965, Brit.)
Diane Bernard
DARK VICTORY(1939)
Dick Bernard
Silents
BLUEBEARD'S SEVEN WIVES(1926)
Misc. Silents
POOR SCHMALTZ(1915)
Dodo Bernard
KITTY(1945)
Dorothy Bernard
Silents
CLASSMATES(1914); SONG OF HATE, THE(1915); LES MISERABLES(1918);
GREAT SHADOW, THE(1920); WILD GOOSE, THE(1921)
Misc. Silents
BROKEN LAW, THE(1915); DISTRICT ATTORNEY, THE(1915); DR. RA-
MEAU(1915); LITTLE GYPSY, THE(1915); MAN OF SORROW, A(1916); SINS OF
MEN(1916); SPORTING BLOOD(1916); ACCOMPLICE, THE(1917); RAINBOW,
THE(1917); LITTLE WOMEN(1919)
Ed Bernard
SHAFT(1971); ACROSS 110TH STREET(1972); HOT ROCK, THE(1972); TRADER
HORN(1973); TOGETHER BROTHERS(1974)
Edmond Bernard
JULIA(1977)
Edwige Bernard
LES ABYSSES(1964, Fr.), ed
Elsie Bernard
DULCIMER STREET(1948, Brit.)
Evelyn Bernard
SON OF SINBAD(1955)
Francois Bernard
RISE OF LOUIS XIV, THE(1970, Fr.)
George Bernard
GOBS AND GALS(1952); DECAMERON NIGHTS(1953, Brit.)
Guy Bernard
LES DERNIERES VACANCES(1947, Fr.), m; PARDON MY FRENCH(1951, U.S./Fr.),
m; NAKED HEART, THE(1955, Brit.), m
Harry Bernard
LET'S GO NATIVE(1930); ROGUE SONG, THE(1930); PARDON US(1931); DEVIL'S
BROTHER, THE(1933); SONS OF THE DESERT(1933); SIX OF A KIND(1934);
RUGGLES OF RED GAP(1935); STOLEN HARMONY(1935); MILKY WAY, THE(1936);
OUR RELATIONS(1936); SWING TIME(1936); NEW FACES OF 1937(1937); SHADOW,
THE(1937); WAY OUT WEST(1937); JUVENILE COURT(1938); ROLL ALONG, COW-
BOY(1938); TRADE WINDS(1938); FIVE LITTLE PEPPERS AND HOW THEY
GREW(1939); HOMICIDE BUREAU(1939); OUT WEST WITH THE PEPPERS(1940);
SAPS AT SEA(1940)
Harvey Bernard
LIKE A CROW ON A JUNE BUG(1972), p
Heinz Bernard
TRAITOR'S GATE(1966, Brit./Ger.); CIRCLE OF IRON(1979, Brit.)
Herb Bernard
ACTORS AND SIN(1952)
Ian Bernard
I'LL TELL THE WORLD(1945); THIS LOVE OF OURS(1945); BACHELOR AND THE
BOBBY-SOXER, THE(1947); SYNANON(1965), w; OH DAD, POOR DAD, MAMA'S
HUNG YOU IN THE CLOSET AND I'M FEELIN' SO SAD(1967), w

Ivor Bernard
DON'T TAKE IT TO HEART(1944, Brit.)
Jack Bernard
MAN MADE MONSTER(1941), p; PERILOUS WATERS(1948), d
Jacques Bernard
LES ENFANTS TERRIBLES(1952, Fr.)
James Bernard
SEVEN DAYS TO NOON(1950, Brit.), w; PACIFIC DESTINY(1956, Brit.), m;
ACROSS THE BRIDGE(1957, Brit.), m; ENEMY FROM SPACE(1957, Brit.), m; X THE
UNKNOWN(1957, Brit.), m; HORROR OF DRACULA, THE(1958, Brit.), m; WIN-
DOM'S WAY(1958, Brit.), m; ELEPHANT GUN(1959, Brit.), m; HOUND OF THE
BASKERVILLES, THE(1959, Brit.), m; STRANGLERS OF BOMBAY, THE(1960, Brit.),
m; TERROR OF THE TONGS, THE(1961, Brit.), m; KISS OF EVIL(1963, Brit.), m;
GORGON, THE(1964, Brit.), m; FRANKENSTEIN CREATED WOMAN(1965, Brit.), m;
SECRET OF BLOOD ISLAND, THE(1965, Brit.), m; SHE(1965, Brit.), m; THESE ARE
THE DAMNED(1965, Brit.), m; DRACULA–PRINCE OF DARKNESS(1966, Brit.), m;
PLAGUE OF THE ZOMBIES, THE(1966, Brit.), m; DEVIL'S BRIDE, THE(1968,
Brit.), m; DRACULA HAS RISEN FROM HIS GRAVE(1968, Brit.), m; TORTURE
GARDEN(1968, Brit.), m; FRANKENSTEIN MUST BE DESTROYED!(1969, Brit.), m;
HORROR OF FRANKENSTEIN, THE(1970, Brit.), m; SCARS OF DRACULA,
THE(1970, Brit.), m; TASTE THE BLOOD OF DRACULA(1970, Brit.), m; FRANKEN-
STEIN AND THE MONSTER FROM HELL(1974, Brit.), m
Jason Bernard
GOING HOME(1971); THOMASINE AND BUSHROD(1974); CARWASH(1976); UN-
CLE JOE SHANNON(1978); BLUE THUNDER(1983); STAR CHAMBER, THE(1983);
WARGAMES(1983)
1984
ALL OF ME(1984)
Jay Bernard
HARRY'S WAR(1981)
1984
FOOTLOOSE(1984); PHILADELPHIA EXPERIMENT, THE(1984)
Jean-Pierre Bernard
FINO A FARTI MALE(1969, Fr./Ital.); EIGER SANCTION, THE(1975)
Jeffrey Bernard
WHERE ARE YOUR CHILDREN?(1943), p; BLACK MARKET BABIES(1946), p;
DON'T GAMBLE WITH STRANGERS(1946), p; BLACK GOLD(1947), p
Joe Bernard
LILIES OF THE FIELD(1930); HOT HEIRESS(1931); YOU CAN'T TAKE IT WITH
YOU(1938); BEAU GESTE(1939); DANGER FLIGHT(1939); CAPTAIN IS A LADY,
THE(1940); I LOVE YOU AGAIN(1940); KITTY FOYLE(1940); THEY KNEW WHAT
THEY WANTED(1940); FOUR JACKS AND A JILL(1941); GIRL, A GUY AND A GOB,
A(1941); PLAYMATES(1941); THUNDERING HOOFS(1941); TOM, DICK AND HAR-
RY(1941); WILD GEESE CALLING(1941); MY GAL SAL(1942); MYSTERY OF MARIE
ROGET, THE(1942); FOLLOW THE BAND(1943); GOVERNMENT GIRL(1943); HAPPY
LAND(1943); SKY'S THE LIMIT, THE(1943); WATCH ON THE RHINE(1943); NOB
HILL(1945); SUDAN(1945); WHERE DO WE GO FROM HERE?(1945); NIGHT IN
PARADISE, A(1946); TANGIER(1946); DOUBLE LIFE, A(1947); EGG AND I,
THE(1947); LIFE WITH FATHER(1947); PIRATES OF MONTEREY(1947); SEA OF
GRASS, THE(1947); I WOULDN'T BE IN YOUR SHOES(1948); SILVER RIVER(1948);
ADAM'S RIB(1949); DON'T JUST STAND THERE(1968); STEAGLE, THE(1971);
LAUGHING POLICEMAN, THE(1973)
Joe E. Bernard
HOOSIER SCHOOLMASTER(1935)
Joelle Bernard
DIARY OF A BAD GIRL(1958, Fr.); DIARY OF A CHAMBERMAID(1964, Fr./Ital.);
FINO A FARTI MALE(1969, Fr./Ital.)
Joseph Bernard
SWEET ADELINE(1935); SIGN OF THE WOLF(1941); TALES OF MANHAT-
TAN(1942); MOONLIGHT IN VERMONT(1943); RAIDERS OF SAN JOAQUIN(1943);
HONEYMOON AHEAD(1945); WITHIN THESE WALLS(1945); MURDER, INC.(1960);
JUDGMENT AT NUREMBERG(1961); ICE STATION ZEBRA(1968); MAN WHO
LOVED WOMEN, THE(1983)
Joseph E. Bernard
NO OTHER WOMAN(1933); FOLIES DERGERE(1935); GOING HIGHBROW(1935);
SARATOGA(1937); TELL NO TALES(1939); FRONTIER GAL(1945); HOUSE OF
DRACULA(1945); PAT AND MIKE(1952)
Josephine Bernard
Silents
WAY DOWN EAST(1920)
Judd Bernard
DOUBLE TROUBLE(1967), p; POINT BLANK(1967), p; BLUE(1968), p; NEGA-
TIVES(1968, Brit.), p; DESTRUCTORS, THE(1974, Brit.), p, w; INSIDE OUT(1975,
Brit.), p, w; CLASS OF MISS MAC MICHAEL, THE(1978, Brit./U.S.), p, w; ENTER
THE NINJA(1982), p, w
Kathy Bernard
ENDLESS LOVE(1981)
Len Bernard
GOODBYE PORK PIE(1981, New Zealand)
Lester Bernard
Silents
PRINCE IN A PAWNSHOP, A(1916); FLYING ROMEOS(1928)
Misc. Silents
PHANTOM FORTUNES, THE(1916)
Maurice Bernard
INCREDIBLE PETRIFIED WORLD, THE(1959)
Napoleon Bernard
GOLDEN MISTRESS, THE(1954)
Nicolette Bernard
END OF THE RIVER, THE(1947, Brit.); IT HAPPENED HERE(1966, Brit.)
Paul Bernard
LUMIERE D'ETE(1943, Fr.); PANIQUE(1947, Fr.); DAMNED, THE(1948, Fr.);
FRIEND WILL COME TONIGHT, A(1948, Fr.); LADIES OF THE PARK(1964, Fr.)
Peta Bernard
CLASS OF MISS MAC MICHAEL, THE(1978, Brit./U.S.)
Peter Bernard
WHY SAPS LEAVE HOME(1932, Brit.); SO YOU WON'T TALK?(1935, Brit.);
DREAMING(1944, Brit.); DEVIL'S HARBOR(1954, Brit.)

Pierre Bernard
TAKE IT ALL(1966, Can.), ed
R. Bernard
NO WAY TO TREAT A LADY(1968)
Ray Bernard
SINGING VAGABOND, THE(1935)
Misc. Talkies
MYSTERY RANCH(1934), d
Raymond Bernard
ANNE-MARIE(1936, Fr.), d; LES MISERABLES(1936, Fr.), d, w; FRIEND WILL COME TONIGHT, A(1948, Fr.), d, w
Misc. Silents
LE RAVIN SANS FOND(1917, Fr.), d; LE GENTILHOMME COMMERCANT(1918, Fr.), d; LE TRAITEMENT DU HOQUET(1918, Fr.), d; LE PETIT CAFE(1919, Fr.), d; LE SECRET DE ROSETTE LAMBERT(1920, Fr.), d; LA MAISON VIDE(1921, Fr.), d; TRIPLEPATTE(1922, Fr.), d; GRANDEUR ET DECADENCE(1923, Fr.), d; LE COSTAUD DES EPINETTES(1923, Fr.), d; L'HOMME INUSABLE(1923, Fr.), d; MIRACLE OF WOLVES, THE(1925, Fr.), d; TARAKANOVA(1930, Fr.), d
Roger Bernard
MY WIFE'S HUSBAND(1965, Fr./Ital.)
Sam Bernard
PRISON TRAIN(1938); WANTED BY THE POLICE(1938); PUBLIC ENEMIES(1941); SHADOW OF THE THIN MAN(1941); TUMBLEDOWN RANCH IN ARIZONA(1941); ICE-CAPADES REVUE(1942); LET'S GET TOUGH(1942); SMART ALECKS(1942); TODAY I HANG(1942); MAN FROM FRISCO(1944); MY BUDDY(1944); THOROUGHBREDS(1945); WHERE DO WE GO FROM HERE?(1945); DEVIL SHIP(1947); VICIOUS CIRCLE, THE(1948); WHEN MY BABY SMILES AT ME(1948)
Sam Bernard
Misc. Silents
POOR SCHMALTZ(1915)
Sue Bernard
STRANGER IN HOLLYWOOD(1968); THAT TENDER TOUCH(1969); WITCHMAKER, THE(1969); MACHISMO-40 GRAVES FOR 40 GUNS(1970); PHYNX, THE(1970); NECROMANCY(1972); KILLING KIND, THE(1973)
Misc. Talkies
TEENAGER(1975)
Sylvia Bernard
Silents
SPARROWS(1926)
Thelonious Bernard
LITTLE ROMANCE, A(1979, U.S./Fr.)
Tom Bernard
HELL'S ISLAND(1955); REBEL WITHOUT A CAUSE(1955)
Tommy Bernard
YANKEE FAKIR(1947); FATHER WAS A FULLBACK(1949)
Tristan Bernard
PLAYBOY OF PARIS(1930), w; SLIPPER EPISODE, THE(1938, Fr), w
Tristram Bernard
RUNAWAY LADIES(1935, Brit.), w
Yannick Bernard
MYSTERIES(1979, Neth.), p
Claude Bernard-Aubert
MY BABY IS BLACK!(1965, Fr.), p&d, w, ed; POSTMAN GOES TO WAR, THE(1968, Fr.), d, w; CHECKERBOARD(1969, Fr.), d, w
Dominique Bernard-Deschamps
Misc. Silents
48, AVENUE DE L'OPERA(1917, Fr.), d; HIER ET AUJOURD'HUI(1918, Fr.), d; L'AGONIE DES AIGLES(1921, Fr.), d; LA NUIT DU 11 SEPTEMBRE(1922, Fr.), d
Iolanda Bernardes
Misc. Silents
LIMITE(1930, Braz.)
Bernardi
DISHONOR BRIGHT(1936, Brit.); MURDER AT THE CABARET(1936, Brit.)
Donald Bernardi
1984
GRANDVIEW, U.S.A.(1984)
Fay Bernardi
JENNY(1969)
Fernand Bernardi
LOVE IS A BALL(1963), set d; CHRISTMAS TREE, THE(1969, Fr.), set d
Herschel Bernardi
GREEN FIELDS(1937); MURDER BY CONTRACT(1958); STAKEOUT ON DOPE STREET(1958); 1001 ARABIAN NIGHTS(1959); SAVAGE EYE, THE(1960); COLD WIND IN AUGUST(1961); GEORGE RAFT STORY, THE(1961); IRMA LA DOUCE(1963); LOVE WITH THE PROPER STRANGER(1963); MAN FROM BUTTON WILLOW, THE(1965); HONEY POT, THE(1967, Brit.); JOURNEY BACK TO OZ(1974); FRONT, THE(1976); NO DEPOSIT, NO RETURN(1976)
Hershel Bernardi
SINGING BLACKSMITH(1938)
Jack Bernardi
MC HALE'S NAVY JOINS THE AIR FORCE(1965); IT'S A BIKINI WORLD(1967); STEAGLE, THE(1971); WILLIE DYNAMITE(1973); FAREWELL, MY LOVELY(1975); SHAMPOO(1975); SHEILA LEVINE IS DEAD AND LIVING IN NEW YORK(1975); SUNSHINE BOYS, THE(1975); WON TON TON, THE DOG WHO SAVED HOLLYWOOD(1976); GONG SHOW MOVIE, THE(1980)
James Bernardi
SHINBONE ALLEY(1971), prod d
Nerio Bernardi
LOYALTY OF LOVE(1937, Ital.); HEART AND SOUL(1950, Ital.); FANFAN THE TULIP(1952, Fr.); NEVER TAKE NO FOR AN ANSWER(1952, Brit./Ital.); COUNTERFEITERS, THE(1953, Ital.); CARTOUCHE(1957, Ital./US); NANA(1957, Fr./Ital.); PRISONER OF THE VOLGA(1960, Fr./Ital.); MINOTAUR, THE(1961, Ital.); PHAROAH'S WOMAN, THE(1961, Ital.); AVENGER, THE(1962, Fr./Ital.); NIGHT THEY KILLED RASPUTIN, THE(1962, Fr./Ital.); TOMORROW IS MY TURN(1962, Fr./Ital./Ger.); TROJAN HORSE, THE(1962, Fr./Ital.); CAESAR THE CONQUEROR(1963, Ital.); CONQUEST OF MYCENE(1965, Ital., Fr./Ital./Yugo.); INVASION 1700(1965, Fr./Ital./Yugo.); KISS THE GIRLS AND MAKE THEM DIE(1967, U.S./Ital.)

Nero Bernardi
Silents
NERO(1922, U.S./Ital.)
Misc. Silents
SHEPHERD KING, THE(1923)
Roberto Bernardi
1984
COMFORT AND JOY(1984, Brit.)
John Bernardino
SUDDENLY(1954)
Al Bernardo
HOUSE BY THE LAKE, THE(1977, Can.)
Albert Bernardo
ONLY GOD KNOWS(1974, Can.); HEARTACHES(1981, Can.)
Carlos Bernardo
LAW FOR TOMBSTONE(1937)
Claudio Bernardo
PIXOTE(1981, Braz.)
Mario Bernardo
HAWKS AND THE SPARROWS, THE(1967, Ital.), ph
Carlo Bernari
CLIMAX, THE(1967, Fr., Ital.), w
Michele Bernath
CHEAP DETECTIVE, THE(1978)
Paul Bernath
TOMBOY AND THE CHAMP(1961)
Shari Lee Bernath
FIEND WHO WALKED THE WEST, THE(1958); JAYHAWKERS, THE(1959)
A. Hilarius Bernauer
GIVE ME THE STARS(1944, Brit.), w
R. Bernauer
HER MAJESTY LOVE(1931), w
Rudolf Bernauer
ONCE A LADY(1931), w; LILAC DOMINO, THE(1940, Brit.), w; GIVE ME THE STARS(1944, Brit.), w
Rudolph Bernauer
FORBIDDEN MUSIC(1936, Brit.), w; SOUTHERN ROSES(1936, Brit.), w
Lynn Bernay
GHOST OF THE CHINA SEA(1958); I BURY THE LIVING(1958); VALLEY OF THE REDWOODS(1960); NIGHT OF EVIL(1962); DRIVE, HE SAID(1971); DEATHMASTER, THE(1972), cos; STEELYARD BLUES(1973); HOMEBODIES(1974), cos; FIRE SALE(1977), cos; PACK, THE(1977), cos
Lynne Bernay
PIT AND THE PENDULUM, THE(1961)
Paul Bernd
TESTAMENT OF DR. MABUSE, THE(1943, Ger.)
Edward Bernds
BLONDIE KNOWS BEST(1946), w; BLONDIE'S REWARD(1948), w; BLONDIE'S SECRET(1948), d; BLONDIE HITS THE JACKPOT(1949), d; BLONDIE'S BIG DEAL(1949), d; BEWARE OF BLONDIE(1950), d; BLONDIE'S HERO(1950), d; CORKY OF GASOLINE ALLEY(1951), d, w; GASOLINE ALLEY(1951), d; GOLD RAIDERS, THE(1952), d; HAREM GIRL(1952), d, w; CLIPPED WINGS(1953), d; HOT NEWS(1953), d; LOOSE IN LONDON(1953), d, w; PRIVATE EYES(1953), d, w; WHITE LIGHTNING(1953), d; BOWERY BOYS MEET THE MONSTERS, THE(1954), d, w; JUNGLE GENTS(1954), d, w; PARIS PLAYBOYS(1954), w; BOWERY TO BAGDAD(1955), d, w; HIGH SOCIETY(1955), w; JAIL BUSTERS(1955), w; CALLING HOMICIDE(1956), d&w; DIG THAT URANIUM(1956), d; SPY CHASERS(1956), w; WORLD WITHOUT END(1956), d&w; LOOKING FOR DANGER(1957), w; REFORM SCHOOL GIRL(1957), d&w; STORM RIDER, THE(1957), d, w; ESCAPE FROM RED ROCK(1958), d&w; HIGH SCHOOL HELLCATS(1958), d; JOY RIDE(1958), d; QUANTRILL'S RAIDERS(1958), d; QUEEN OF OUTER SPACE(1958), d; SPACE MASTER X-7(1958), d; ALASKA PASSAGE(1959), d, w; RETURN OF THE FLY(1959), d&w; VALLEY OF THE DRAGONS(1961), d&w; THREE STOOGES IN ORBIT, THE(1962), d; THREE STOOGES MEET HERCULES, THE(1962), d; GUNFIGHT AT COMANCHE CREEK(1964), w; TICKLE ME(1965), w
Misc. Talkies
FEUDIN' RHYTHM(1949), d
Edward L. Bernds
NAVY WIFE(1956), d
George Berndt
HEARSE, THE(1980), ed; ST. HELENS(1981), ed; O'HARA'S WIFE(1983), ed
1984
MEATBALLS PART II(1984), ed
Gustave Berne
BLOOD MONEY(1974, U.S./Hong Kong/Ital./Span.), p
I.R. Berne
PRETENDER, THE(1947), cos
Israel Berne
THIRTEEN WEST STREET(1962), cos
Joe Berne
CATSKILL HONEYMOON(1950), d
Josef Berne
THEY LIVE IN FEAR(1944), d; DOWN MISSOURI WAY(1946), p&d
Joseph Berne
Misc. Talkies
MIRELE EFROS(1939), d
Stefan Berne
DOCTOR CRIMEN(1953, Mex.)
Tonia Berne
FLAW, THE(1955, Brit.)
Arthur Bernede
JUDEX(1966, Fr./Ital.), w
Peter Berneis
PORTRAIT OF JENNIE(1949), w; GLASS MENAGERIE, THE(1950), w; CHICAGO CALLING(1951), p, w; MY MAN GODFREY(1957), w; STRANGER IN MY ARMS(1959), w; ESCAPE FROM EAST BERLIN(1962), w; NO SURVIVORS, PLEASE(1963, Ger.), d, w

John Bernek
 I AM THE CHEESE(1983)
Agnes Bernelle
 CAESAR AND CLEOPATRA(1946, Brit.); WOMAN TO WOMAN(1946, Brit.); BUT NOT IN VAIN(1948, Brit.); STRANGER AT MY DOOR(1950, Brit.); GOOD COMPANIONS, THE(1957, Brit.); QUARE FELLOW, THE(1962, Brit.); GREAT TRAIN ROBBERY, THE(1979, Brit.)
Bernice Berner
 Misc. Silents
 WHAT HAPPENED TO FATHER(1915)
Charles Berner
 CORRUPTION(1933), w; INSIDE INFORMATION(1934); FORBIDDEN TRAIL(1936)
Sara Berner
 LUCKY JORDAN(1942); ROAD TO MOROCCO(1942); WIFE WANTED(1946); BACKLASH(1947); GAY INTRUDERS, THE(1948); CITY ACROSS THE RIVER(1949); STORY OF MOLLY X, THE(1949); CARRIE(1952); REAR WINDOW(1954); NAKED STREET, THE(1955); SPRING REUNION(1957); NORTH BY NORTHWEST(1959)
Sarah Berner
 SCENE OF THE CRIME(1949)
Jeffrey Bernerd
 ARE THESE OUR PARENTS?(1944), p; ALLOTMENT WIVES, INC.(1945), p; DIVORCE(1945), p; FOREVER YOURS(1945), p; FACE OF MARBLE, THE(1946), p; SWEETHEART OF SIGMA CHI(1946), p; WIFE WANTED(1946), p; KING OF THE BANDITS(1948), p; STAGE STRUCK(1948), p; FORGOTTEN WOMEN(1949), p, w; BLUE GRASS OF KENTUCKY(1950), p
Lord Berners
 HALF-WAY HOUSE, THE(1945, Brit.), m; NICHOLAS NICKLEBY(1947, Brit.), m
M. Bernes
 DIARY OF A NAZI(1943, USSR)
Mark Bernes
 GIRL AND THE BUGLER, THE(1967, USSR)
Jack Bernett
 COVER GIRL(1944)
Sheila Bernette
 SONS AND LOVERS(1960, Brit.); WILD AFFAIR, THE(1966, Brit.); LITTLE OF WHAT YOU FANCY, A(1968, Brit.)
Fred Berney
 ONCE UPON A COFFEE HOUSE(1965), p
Goran Bernhard
 WOMAN'S FACE, A(1939, Swed.)
Harvey Bernhard
 MACK, THE(1973), p; THOMASINE AND BUSHROD(1974), p; OMEN, THE(1976), p; DAMIEN-OMEN II(1978), p; FINAL CONFLICT, THE(1981), p; BEAST WITHIN, THE(1982), p
Jack Bernhard
 WEST OF CARSON CITY(1940), w; SEALED LIPS(1941), p; STRANGE CASE OF DR. RX, THE(1942), p; DECOY(1946), p, d; SMOOTH AS SILK(1946), p; SWEETHEART OF SIGMA CHI(1946), d; VIOLENCE(1947), p, d; APPOINTMENT WITH MURDER(1948), p&d; HUNTED, THE(1948), d; UNKNOWN ISLAND(1948), d; ALASKA PATROL(1949), d; BLONDE ICE(1949), d; SEARCH FOR DANGER(1949), p&d; SECOND FACE, THE(1950), d
 Misc. Talkies
 IN SELF DEFENSE(1947), d
Joachim Bernhard
 DAS BOOT(1982)
Joseph Bernhard
 JOURNEY INTO LIGHT(1951), p; JAPANESE WAR BRIDE(1952), p; RUBY GENTRY(1952), p; MOONLIGHTER, THE(1953), p
Karl Bernhard
 Misc. Silents
 PEST IN FLORENZ(1919, Ger.)
Patrick Bernhard
 LANCELOT OF THE LAKE(1975, Fr.)
Sandra Bernhard
 KING OF COMEDY, THE(1983)
Werner Bernhardl
 Misc. Silents
 DEVIL'S PAWN, THE(1922, Ger.)
Lena-Pia Bernhardsson
 ELVIS! ELVIS!(1977, Swed.)
Curtis Bernhardt
 MY LOVE CAME BACK(1940), d; MILLION DOLLAR BABY(1941), d; JUKE GIRL(1942), d; HAPPY GO LUCKY(1943), d; CONFLICT(1945), d; DEVOTION(1946), d; MY REPUTATION(1946), d; HIGH WALL, THE(1947), d; STOLEN LIFE, A(1946), d; POSSESSED(1947), d; DOCTOR AND THE GIRL, THE(1949), d; BLUE VEIL, THE(1951), d; PAYMENT ON DEMAND(1951), d, w; SIROCCO(1951), d; MERRY WIDOW, THE(1952), d; MISS SADIE THOMPSON(1953), d; BEAU BRUMMELL(1954), d; INTERRUPTED MELODY(1955), d; GABY(1956), d; DAMON AND PYTHIAS(1962), d; KISSES FOR MY PRESIDENT(1964), p&d
 Misc. Talkies
 STEFANIE IN RIO(1963), d
Eve Bernhardt
 WIZARD OF MARS(1964)
Francis Bernhardt
 Silents
 GOLD RUSH, THE(1925)
Kurt Bernhardt
 GIRL IN THE TAXI(1937, Brit.), p; CROSSROADS(1938, Fr.), d; LADY WITH RED HAIR(1940), d
 Misc. Silents
 THREE LOVES(1931, Ger.), d
Kurt "Curtis" Bernhardt
 BELOVED VAGABOND, THE(1936, Brit.), d
Sarah Bernhardt
 Silents
 QUEEN ELIZABETH(1912, Fr.)
 Misc. Silents
 JEANNE DORE(1916, Fr.); MERES FRANCAISES(1917, Fr.)

Steve Bernhardt
 GET TO KNOW YOUR RABBIT(1972), p
Steven Bernhardt
 FUNHOUSE, THE(1981), p
Alain Bernheim
 1984
 RACING WITH THE MOON(1984), p
Francois Bernheim
 1984
 LES COMPERES(1984, Fr.)
Julian Bernheim
 CRASH DONOVAN(1936), p
Julius Bernheim
 KING SOLOMON OF BROADWAY(1935), p; TRANSIENT LADY(1935), p
Michel Bernheim
 PARIS PICK-UP(1963, Fr./Ital.), p
Mara Berni
 FURY OF HERCULES, THE(1961, Ital.); SAMSON(1961, Ital.); MORALIST, THE(1964, Ital.); HOURS OF LOVE, THE(1965, Ital.); CHECKERBOARD(1969, Fr.)
Ugo Scotti Berni
 ADVENTURE OF SALVATOR ROSA, AN(1940, Ital.), w, ph
Ben Bernie
 SHOOT THE WORKS(1934); STOLEN HARMONY(1935); LOVE AND HISSES(1937)
Dick Bernie
 THIS IS THE ARMY(1943)
Jason Bernie
 DECOY(1946), ed; BELLE STARR'S DAUGHTER(1947), ed; BURNING CROSS, THE(1947), ed; FOR YOU I DIE(1947), ed; ROAD TO THE BIG HOUSE(1947), ed; SARGE GOES TO COLLEGE(1947), ed; VIOLENCE(1947), ed; OPEN SECRET(1948), ed; KID MONK BARONI(1952), ed; I DEAL IN DANGER(1966), ed
Jason H. Bernie
 KID FROM CLEVELAND, THE(1949), ed
Jean-Paul Bernier
 CAT IN THE SACK, THE(1967, Can.)
Marcel Bernier
 VERY HAPPY ALEXANDER(1969, Fr.)
Irwin Jay Berniker
 HERE COME THE NELSONS(1952)
Jay Berniker
 NIGHT RUNNER, THE(1957)
Jeff Bernini
 HOLLYWOOD BOULEVARD(1976), set d
Jeffrey Bernini
 TAKE THIS JOB AND SHOVE IT(1981), w
Blanche Bernis
 Silents
 MOULIN ROUGE(1928, Brit.)
Michael Bernosky
 THAT CHAMPIONSHIP SEASON(1982)
Jane Bernoudy
 Misc. Silents
 GIRL IN THE CHECKERED COAT, THE(1917)
Gerald Berns
 PENITENTIARY II(1982); TRON(1982)
 1984
 BEVERLY HILLS COP(1984)
Hal Berns
 EASY TO LOVE(1953)
Irving Berns
 JOHNNY ALLEGRO(1949), makeup; D.O.A.(1950), makeup
Jack Berns
 Misc. Talkies
 BROAD COALITION, THE(1972); WHAT DO I TELL THE BOYS AT THE STATION(1972)
Larry Berns
 PUBLIC PIGEON NO. 1(1957), w
Lester Berns
 M(1970), makeup
Mel Berns
 PORTRAIT OF JENNIE(1949), makeup; WHERE DANGER LIVES(1950), makeup; TWO TICKETS TO BROADWAY(1951), makeup; MACAO(1952), makeup; GIDGET GOES TO ROME(1963), makeup
Norman Berns
 HOSPITAL, THE(1971)
Waldo K. Berns
 WILD PARTY, THE(1975)
Wally Berns
 RUN, ANGEL, RUN(1969); MAURIE(1973), art d; BIG BAD MAMA(1974); APPLE DUMPLING GANG, THE(1975); DAY OF THE LOCUST, THE(1975); FAREWELL, MY LOVELY(1975); CHEAP DETECTIVE, THE(1978)
William A. Berns
 GAMBLERS, THE(1969), p
Caren Bernsen
 TRIP, THE(1967)
Corbin Bernsen
 THREE THE HARD WAY(1974); S.O.B.(1981)
Harry Bernsen
 TAKE A HARD RIDE(1975, U.S./Ital.), p
Herry Bernsen
 THREE THE HARD WAY(1974), p
Bernstein
 TERRIFIED!(1963), w
Alexander Bernstein
 DANIEL(1983)
Andrew Bernstein
 FRONT, THE(1976)
Armyan Bernstein
 ONE FROM THE HEART(1982), p, w; WINDY CITY(1984), d, w

Barry Armyan Bernstein
THANK GOD IT'S FRIDAY(1978), w
Blanche Bernstein
WHERE IS MY CHILD?(1937)
Brunetta Bernstein
MAN CALLED ADAM, A(1966)
Carl Bernstein
ALL THE PRESIDENT'S MEN(1976), w
Charles Bernstein
MAN FROM O.R.G.Y., THE(1970), m; AROUSERS, THE(1973), m; HEX(1973), m; THAT MAN BOLT(1973), m; WHITE LIGHTNING(1973), m; MR. MAJESTYK(1974), m; GATOR(1976), m; SMALL TOWN IN TEXAS, A(1976), m; TRACKDOWN(1976), m; OUTLAW BLUES(1977), m; VIVA KNIEVEL!(1977), m; LOVE AT FIRST BITE(1979), m; COAST TO COAST(1980), m; FOOLIN' AROUND(1980), m; ENTITY, THE(1982), m; CUJO(1983), m; INDEPENDENCE DAY(1983), m
1984
DADDY'S DEADLY DARLING(1984), m; NIGHTMARE ON ELM STREET, A(1984), m
Chuck Bernstein
INVASION OF THE BEE GIRLS(1973), m
Davis Bernstein
MAKE A FACE(1971)
Dr. Maurice Bernstein
NOT WANTED(1949)
Elmer Bernstein
SILENCERS, THE(, m; THOROUGHLY MODERN MILLIE(1967), m; SATURDAY'S HERO(1951), m; BATTLES OF CHIEF PONTIAC(1952), m; BOOTS MALONE(1952), m; NEVER WAVE AT A WAC(1952), m&md; SUDDEN FEAR(1952), m; CAT WOMEN OF THE MOON(1953), m; ROBOT MONSTER(1953), m; MAKE HASTE TO LIVE(1954), m; MISS ROBIN CRUSOE(1954), m; SILENT RAIDERS(1954), m; BAR SINISTER, THE(1955), m; ETERNAL SEA, THE(1955), m; MAN WITH THE GOLDEN ARM, THE(1955), m, md; VIEW FROM POMPEY'S HEAD, THE(1955), m; STORM FEAR(1956), m; TEN COMMANDMENTS, THE(1956), m; DRANGO(1957), m; FEAR STRIKES OUT(1957), m; MEN IN WAR(1957), m, md; SWEET SMELL OF SUCCESS(1957), m, md; TIN STAR, THE(1957), m; ANNA LUCASTA(1958), m; BUCCANEER, THE(1958), m; GOD'S LITTLE ACRE(1958), m; KINGS GO FORTH(1958), m, md; MIRACLE, THE(1959), m; SOME CAME RUNNING(1959), m, md; STORY ON PAGE ONE, THE(1959), m; FROM THE TERRACE(1960), m; MAGNIFICENT SEVEN, THE(1960), m; RAT RACE, THE(1960), m; BY LOVE POSSESSED(1961), m; COMANCHEROS, THE(1961), m; SUMMER AND SMOKE(1961), m; YOUNG DOCTORS, THE(1961), m; BIRDMAN OF ALCATRAZ(1962), m; GIRL NAMED TAMIRO, A(1962), m; TO KILL A MOCKINGBIRD(1962), m, md; WALK ON THE WILD SIDE(1962), m; CARETAKERS, THE(1963), m; GREAT ESCAPE, THE(1963), m; HUD(1963), m; KINGS OF THE SUN(1963), m; LOVE WITH THE PROPER STRANGER(1963), m; RAMPAGE(1963), m; CARPETBAGGERS, THE(1964), m; WORLD OF HENRY ORIENT, THE(1964), m; BABY, THE RAIN MUST FALL(1965), m; HALLELUJAH TRAIL, THE(1965), m; REWARD, THE(1965), m; SONS OF KATIE ELDER, THE(1965), m; CAST A GIANT SHADOW(1966), m; HAWAII(1966), m; RETURN OF THE SEVEN(1966, Span.), m; SEVEN WOMEN(1966), m; I LOVE YOU, ALICE B. TOKLAS!(1968), m; SCALPHUNTERS, THE(1968), m; BRIDGE AT REMAGEN, THE(1969), m; GUNS OF THE MAGNIFICENT SEVEN(1969), m&md; GYPSY MOTHS, THE(1969), m; MIDAS RUN(1969), m; TRUE GRIT(1969), m; WHERE'S JACK?(1969, Brit.), m; CANNON FOR CORDOBA(1970), m; LIBERATION OF L.B. JONES, THE(1970), m; WALK IN THE SPRING RAIN, A(1970), m; BIG JAKE(1971), m; DOCTORS' WIVES(1971), m; SEE NO EVIL(1971, Brit.), m; MAGNIFICENT SEVEN RIDE, THE(1972), m, md; AMAZING MR. BLUNDEN, THE(1973, Brit.), m; CAHILL, UNITED STATES MARSHAL(1973), m; NIGHTMARE HONEYMOON(1973), m; GOLD(1974, Brit.), m; MC Q(1974), m; TRIAL OF BILLY JACK, THE(1974), m; REPORT TO THE COMMISSIONER(1975), m; FROM NOON TO THREE(1976), a, m; INCREDIBLE SARAH, THE(1976, Brit.), m; SHOOTIST, THE(1976), m; BILLY JACK GOES TO WASHINGTON(1977), m; SLAP SHOT(1977), m; BLOODBROTHERS(1978), m; NATIONAL LAMPOON'S ANIMAL HOUSE(1978), m; MEATBALLS(1979, Can.), m; AIRPLANE!(1980), m; SATURN 3(1980), m; ZULU DAWN(1980, Brit.), m; AMERICAN WEREWOLF IN LONDON, AN(1981), m; GOING APE!(1981), m; HEAVY METAL(1981, Can.), m; HONKY TONK FREEWAY(1981), m; STRIPES(1981), m; AIRPLANE II: THE SEQUEL(1982), m; CHOSEN, THE(1982), m; FIVE DAYS ONE SUMMER(1982), m; CLASS(1983), m; SPACEHUNTER: ADVENTURES IN THE FORBIDDEN ZONE(1983), m; TRADING PLACES(1983), m
1984
BOLERO(1984), m; GHOSTBUSTERS(1984), m
G. W. Bernstein
WHEN HELL BROKE LOOSE(1958), set d
G.W. Bernstein
THEM!(1954), set d
Harvey Bernstein
MARCH OF THE SPRING HARE(1969), p; ROOMMATES(1971), p
Henri Bernstein
WASHINGTON MASQUERADE(1932), w; DREAMING LIPS(1937, Brit.), w; DREADING LIPS(1958, Ger.), w
Silents
SOLD(1915), w; THIEF, THE(1915), w; SHACKLES OF GOLD(1922), w
Herman Bernstein
HER PRIVATE AFFAIR(1930), w
I. Bernstein
CITY STREETS(1938), w
Isadore Bernstein
BY WHOSE HAND?(1932), w; DESTRY RIDES AGAIN(1932), w; NO GREATER LOVE(1932), w; FOR THE SERVICE(1936), w
Silents
PURE GRIT(1923), w; BACK-TRAIL, THE(1924), w; DARING CHANCES(1924), w; GALLOPING ACE, THE(1924), w; MAN FROM WYOMING, THE(1924), w; MEASURE OF A MAN, THE(1924), w; RIDGEWAY OF MONTANA(1924), w; WHITE OUTLAW, THE(1925), w; ARIZONA SWEEPSTAKES(1926), w; MASKED ANGEL(1928), t; RAWHIDE KID, THE(1928), w; DREAM MELODY, THE(1929), w, t; ONE SPLENDID HOUR(1929), w
Jacob Bernstein
FRONT, THE(1976)

Jamie Bernstein
ENDLESS LOVE(1981)
Jonathan Bernstein
TESTAMENT(1983), p
Leonard Bernstein
ON THE TOWN(1949), m; ON THE WATERFRONT(1954), m; WEST SIDE STORY(1961), m
Linda Bernstein
MAGICIAN OF LUBLIN, THE(1979, Israel/Ger.)
Milton Bernstein
LAST OF THE FAST GUNS, THE(1958); TEN DAYS TO TULARA(1958)
Morey Bernstein
SEARCH FOR BRIDEY MURPHY, THE(1956), d&w
Peter Bernstein
BRIDE, THE(1973), m; SILENT RAGE(1982), m
1984
BOLERO(1984), m; HOT DOG...THE MOVIE(1984), m; SURF II(1984), m
Richard Bernstein
FROM HELL IT CAME(1957), w; TANK BATTALION(1958), p, w; SPEED CRAZY(1959), p, w; WHY MUST I DIE?(1960), p, w; FORCE OF IMPULSE(1961), w; GUN HAWK, THE(1963), p, w; TERRIFIED!(1963), p
Sheryl Bernstein
1984
EL NORTE(1984)
Sidney Bernstein
ROPE(1948), p; UNDER CAPRICORN(1949), p
Stan Bernstein
Misc. Talkies
YUM-YUM GIRLS(1976)
Sylvia Bernstein
Silents
ONE SPLENDID HOUR(1929), w
Thelma Bernstein
REAL LIFE(1979)
Walter Bernstein
KISS THE BLOOD OFF MY HANDS(1948), w; THAT KIND OF WOMAN(1959), w; BREATH OF SCANDAL, A(1960), w; HELLER IN PINK TIGHTS(1960), w; MAGNIFICENT SEVEN, THE(1960), w; FAIL SAFE(1964), w; TRAIN, THE(1965, Fr./Ital./U.S.), w; MONEY TRAP, THE(1966), w; MOLLY MAGUIRES, THE(1970), p, w; FRONT, THE(1976), w; ANNIE HALL(1977); SEMI-TOUGH(1977), w; BETSY, THE(1978), w; ALMOST PERFECT AFFAIR, AN(1979), w; YANKS(1979), w; LITTLE MISS MARKER(1980), d&w
G. W. Bernsten
WALLFLOWER(1948), set d
G.W. Bernsten
TALL MAN RIDING(1955), set d
Gustav Bernsten
JOHNNY CONCHO(1956), set d
Elmer Bernstien
GREAT SANTINI, THE(1979), m
Reinhold Bernt
BLUE ANGEL, THE(1930, Ger.); TRAPEZE(1932, Ger.); REBEL, THE(1933, Ger.)
G. W. Berntsen
NIGHT UNTO NIGHT(1949), set d; CAGED(1950), set d; MONTANA(1950), set d; STARLIFT(1951), set d; MIRACLE OF OUR LADY OF FATIMA, THE(1952), set d; SPRINGFIELD RIFLE(1952), set d; TARGET ZERO(1955), set d; STORY ON PAGE ONE, THE(1959), set d
G.W. Berntsen
STORM WARNING(1950), set d
Gustav Berntsen
FLAMING STAR(1960), set d
Rolf Berntzen
SONG OF NORWAY(1970)
Mary Ann Berold
SAFARI 3000(1982)
Chester L. Berolund
SWEETHEARTS(1938)
Leo Berolund
SWEETHEARTS(1938)
Bobby Berosini
GOING APE!(1981), animal t
Olinka Berova
VENGEANCE OF SHE, THE(1968, Brit.)
Misc. Talkies
TOGETHERNESS(1970)
Harold Berquest
TIMBER TERRORS(1935)
Harold Berquist
BLONDE VENUS(1932); GUILTY AS HELL(1932); LADY BY CHOICE(1934); YOU'RE TELLING ME(1934); ENTER MADAME(1935); PORT OF LOST DREAMS(1935)
Rudolph Berquist
Silents
LITTLE EVA ASCENDS(1922), ph; RED LIGHTS(1923), ph; WOMANPOWER(1926), ph; GIRL IN EVERY PORT, A(1928), ph; PLAY GIRL, THE(1928), ph
George Berr
CROSS MY HEART(1946), w
Georges Berr
AZAIS(1931, Fr.), d; MILLION, THE(1931, Fr.), w; TRUE CONFESSION(1937), w; MY LIFE WITH CAROLINE(1941), w
Ulrich Berr
1984
MIXED BLOOD(1984)
Yogi Berra
THAT TOUCH OF MINK(1962)
Clara S. Berranger
Silents
APPEARANCE OF EVIL(1918), w

George Berrell
Silents
FLASHLIGHT, THE(1917); MAN FROM MONTANA, THE(1917); IN FOR THIRTY DAYS(1919); POLLYANNA(1920)
Misc. Silents
DRUGGED WATERS(1916); THREE GODFATHERS, THE(1916); STRAIGHT SHOOTING(1917); HELL ROARIN' REFORM(1919); GIRL FROM GOD'S COUNTRY, THE(1921); TRACKS(1922); GRUB STAKE, THE(1923); EVERLASTING WHISPER, THE(1925); BLACK JACK(1927)

George W. Berrell
Silents
AS THE SUN WENT DOWN(1919)

Lloyd Berrell
HIS MAJESTY O'KEEFE(1953); LONG JOHN SILVER(1954, Aus.); KING OF THE CORAL SEA(1956, Aus.)

Jane Berretta
MADEMOISELLE(1966, Fr./Brit.)

Joka Berretty
SCANDAL IN SORRENTO(1957, Ital./Fr.)

Claude Berri
TRUTH, THE(1961, Fr./Ital.); I SPIT ON YOUR GRAVE(1962, Fr.); SEVEN CAPITAL SINS(1962, Fr./Ital.); PLEASE, NOT NOW!(1963, Fr./Ital.); BEHOLD A PALE HORSE(1964); MY BABY IS BLACK!(1965, Fr.); TWO OF US, THE(1968, Fr.), d, w; MARRY ME! MARRY ME!(1969, Fr.), a, p,d&w; MAN WITH CONNECTIONS, THE(1970, Fr.), p,d&w; ME(1970, Fr.), p; FIRST TIME, THE(1978, Fr.), d&w; TESS(1980, Fr./Brit.), p; AFRICAN, THE(1983, Fr.), p; BANZAI(1983, Fr.), p
1984
BLAME IT ON RIO(1984), w

Robert Berri
GAME OF LOVE, THE(1954, Fr.); RED AND THE BLACK, THE(1954, Fr./Ital.); MAIDEN, THE(1961, Fr.); NIGHT AFFAIR(1961, Fr.); PALACE OF NUDES(1961, Fr./Ital.)

Simone Berriau
CAFE DE PARIS(1938, Fr.); MOULIN ROUGE(1944, Fr.)

Gina Berriault
1984
STONE BOY, THE(1984), w

Beth Berridge
NATURAL ENEMIES(1979)

Elizabeth Berridge
FUNHOUSE, THE(1981)
1984
AMADEUS(1984)

Janice Elaine Berridge
STUDENT BODIES(1981)

Daniel Berrigan
TRIAL OF THE CATONSVILLE NINE, THE(1972), w

George Berrill
Misc. Silents
BETTINA LOVED A SOLDIER(1916)

Douglas Berring
WIZ, THE(1978)

H. Douglas Berring
HAIR(1979)

Betty George Berringer
Silents
HOME SWEET HOME(1914)

Dawn Berrington
HIGHWAY TO BATTLE(1961, Brit.)

Jennifer Berrington
FATHER GOOSE(1964)

Stephanie Berrington
FATHER GOOSE(1964)

Carlos Berriochea
GUNS FOR SAN SEBASTIAN(1968, U.S./Fr./Mex./Ital.)

Carlos Berriochoa
SHARK(1970, U.S./Mex.)

Louis "Sonny" Berrios
Misc. Talkies
SKEZAG(1971)

Mario Berroatua
LAST DAYS OF POMPEII, THE(1960, Ital.)

Paul Berrones
ALAMBRISTA!(1977)

Odette Berroyer
LOVE AT NIGHT(1961, Fr.), makeup; LOVE ON A PILLOW(1963, Fr./Ital.), makeup; VICE AND VIRTUE(1965, Fr./Ital.), makeup; VIVA MARIA(1965, Fr./Ital.), makeup; HOTEL PARADISO(1966, U.S./Brit.), make up; RAVISHING IDIOT, A(1966, Ital./Fr.), makeup; TWO WEEKS IN SEPTEMBER(1967, Fr./Brit.), makeup

Pierre Berroyer
LOVE ON A PILLOW(1963, Fr./Ital.), makeup; DAY OF THE JACKAL, THE(1973, Brit./Fr.), makeup

Joseph Berrutti
GREEN TREE, THE(1965, Ital.), w

Al Berry
HALLOWEEN III: SEASON OF THE WITCH(1982)
1984
LAST STARFIGHTER, THE(1984)

Alex Berry
ILLUMINATIONS(1976, Aus.), m

Amanda Berry
PALM BEACH(1979, Aus.)

Art Berry, Sr.
CAPTAINS COURAGEOUS(1937); EARL OF CHICAGO, THE(1940); THIRD FINGER, LEFT HAND(1940); MRS. MINIVER(1942)

Audrey Berry
Silents
JAVA HEAD(1923)

Bill Berry
HIGH COUNTRY, THE(1981, Can.)
Misc. Talkies
BROTHERHOOD OF DEATH(1976), d

Carol Berry
THRESHOLD(1983, Can.)

Chuck Berry
ROCK, ROCK, ROCK!(1956); MISTER ROCK AND ROLL(1957); GO, JOHNNY, GO!(1959); AMERICAN HOT WAX(1978); NATIONAL LAMPOON'S CLASS REUNION(1982)

Dale Berry
PASSION IN THE SUN(1964), a, p&d

David Berry
1984
FLAMINGO KID, THE(1984)

Denis Berry
SINGAPORE, SINGAPORE(1969, Fr./Ital.); PROMISE AT DAWN(1970, U.S./Fr.); LA COLLECTIONNEUSE(1971, Fr.)

Dennis Berry
BORSALINO(1970, Fr.)

Don Berry
KNIGHTRIDERS(1981); VISITING HOURS(1982, Can.), spec eff

Eric Berry
EDGE OF THE WORLD, THE(1937, Brit.); RED SHOES, THE(1948, Brit.); MISS ROBIN HOOD(1952, Brit.); GREAT GILBERT AND SULLIVAN, THE(1953, Brit.); OPERATION DIPLOMAT(1953, Brit.); DIAMOND WIZARD, THE(1954, Brit.); ESCAPE BY NIGHT(1954, Brit.); CONSTANT HUSBAND, THE(1955, Brit.); INTRUDER, THE(1955, Brit.); TO TRAP A SPY(1966)

Etienne Berry
OBJECTIVE 500 MILLION(1966, Fr.)

Fern Berry
LOVE IS ON THE AIR(1937); STORM WARNING(1950)

Frank Berry
DR. STRANGELOVE: OR HOW I LEARNED TO STOP WORRYING AND LOVE THE BOMB(1964)

Fred A. Berry
VICE SQUAD(1982)

Hazel Berry
RUNNERS(1983, Brit.)

James Berry
LADY BE GOOD(1941); PILGRIMAGE(1972), w

Jody Berry
SCAVENGERS, THE(1969); BUDDY HOLLY STORY, THE(1978)

John Berry
SEEDS OF FREEDOM(1943, USSR); MISS SUSIE SLAGLE'S(1945), d; CROSS MY HEART(1946), d; FROM THIS DAY FORWARD(1946), d; CASBAH(1948), d; TENSION(1949), d; HE RAN ALL THE WAY(1951), d; UTOPIA(1952, Fr./Ital.), d; TAMANGO(1959, Fr.), d, w; MAYA(1966), d; CLAUDINE(1974), d; THIEVES(1977), d; BAD NEWS BEARS GO TO JAPAN, THE(1978), d

Jules Berry
CRIME OF MONSIEUR LANGE, THE(1936, Fr.); RECORD 413(1936, Fr.); CAFE DE PARIS(1938, Fr.); CROSSROADS(1938, Fr.); DAYBREAK(1940, Fr.); DEVIL'S ENVOYS, THE(1947, Fr.); SYMPHONIE FANTASTIQUE(1947, Fr.)

Julian Berry
WEREWOLF IN A GIRL'S DORMITORY(1961, Ital./Aust.), w; WHAT!(1965, Fr./Brit./Ital.), w; MURDER CLINIC, THE(1967, Ital./Fr.), w
1984
AFTER THE FALL OF NEW YORK(1984, Ital./Fr.), w

June Berry
LOOKING UP(1977); NATURAL ENEMIES(1979); NESTING, THE(1981)

Ken Berry
HELLO DOWN THERE(1969); HERBIE RIDES AGAIN(1974); GUARDIAN OF THE WILDERNESS(1977); CAT FROM OUTER SPACE, THE(1978)

Kerry Berry
HOW TO STUFF A WILD BIKINI(1965)

Lloyd Berry
THAT COLD DAY IN THE PARK(1969, U.S./Can.); SALLY FIELDGOOD & CO.(1975, Can.); EUREKA(1983, Brit.)
1984
RUNAWAY(1984)

Mady Berry
LA MATERNELLE(1933, Fr.); LE MONDE TREMBLERA(1939, Fr.); PERSONAL COLUMN(1939, Fr.); DAYBREAK(1940, Fr.); GATES OF THE NIGHT(1950, Fr.)

Maria Berry
SILK NOOSE, THE(1950, Brit.)

Michael Berry
TOUCH OF SATAN, THE(1971)
Misc. Talkies
TOUCH OF SATAN, THE(1974)

Mimi Berry
MY FAVORITE SPY(1951)

Nady Berry
ROAD IS FINE, THE(1930, Fr.)

Nick Berry
PARTY PARTY(1983, Brit.)

Noah Berry
Silents
TIPPED OFF(1923)
Misc. Silents
OMAR THE TENTMAKER(1922); CROWN OF LIES, THE(1926); PASSION SONG, THE(1928)

Nyas Berry
SAN FRANCISCO(1936); LADY BE GOOD(1941); YOU'RE MY EVERYTHING(1949)

Oliver Berry
OUT OF IT(1969)

Owen Berry
FIRE MAIDENS FROM OUTER SPACE(1956, Brit.); MAN WHO COULDN'T WALK, THE(1964, Brit.); FAR FROM THE MADDING CROWD(1967, Brit.)

Ralph W. Berry
SWEETHEARTS(1938)
Ramon Berry
Misc. Talkies
NICOLE(1972)
Rex Berry
MANOLIS(1962, Brit.), w
Richard Berry
MY FIRST LOVE(1978, Fr.); LA BALANCE(1983, Fr.)
Robert Berry
Misc. Talkies
HOUSE OF DREAMS(1963), d
Rollin B. Berry
SWEETHEARTS(1938)
Sam Berry
1984
PARIS, TEXAS(1984, Ger./Fr.)
Serge Berry
1984
AMERICAN DREAMER(1984); UNTIL SEPTEMBER(1984)
Sheila Berry
TERROR STREET(1953)
W.H. Berry
MISTER CINDERS(1934, Brit.); HONOURS EASY(1935, Brit.); MUSIC HATH CHARMS(1935, Brit.); REGAL CAVALCADE(1935, Brit.); SHE KNEW WHAT SHE WANTED(1936, Brit.); STAR FELL FROM HEAVEN, A(1936, Brit.); STUDENT'S ROMANCE, THE(1936, Brit.); WEEKEND MILLIONAIRE(1937, Brit.)
Wallace Berry
BUGLE SOUNDS, THE(1941)
Walter Berry
DON GIOVANNI(1955, Brit.); DON JUAN(1956, Aust.); OH ROSALINDA(1956, Brit.)
Warren Berry
LADY BE GOOD(1941); YOU'RE MY EVERYTHING(1949)
Wild Red Berry
MY WIFE'S BEST FRIEND(1952)
William Berry
RUNNING BRAVE(1983, Can.)
Winston Berry
YOICKS!(1932, Brit.), m, md
The Berry Brothers
PANAMA HATTIE(1942)
Sharon Berryhill
SIMON, KING OF THE WITCHES(1971)
Jackie Berryman
1984
SCARRED(1984)
Leslie Berryman
LITTLE JUNGLE BOY(1969, Aus.)
Michael Berryman
DOC SAVAGE... THE MAN OF BRONZE(1975); ONE FLEW OVER THE CUCKOO'S NEST(1975); HILLS HAVE EYES, THE(1978); DEADLY BLESSING(1981)
Ross Berryman
BUSH CHRISTMAS(1983, Aus.), ph; FIRE IN THE STONE, THE(1983, Aus.), ph
1984
MELVIN, SON OF ALVIN(1984, Aus.), ph
Arrigo Berschi
MASSACRE IN ROME(1973, Ital.), art d
Bob Bersell
BIRDS DO IT(1966)
Kevin Bersell
UP THE SANDBOX(1972)
Michael Bersell
LIMBO(1972)
Sean Bersell
SIDELONG GLANCES OF A PIGEON KICKER, THE(1970)
Adriana Berselli
DAMON AND PYTHIAS(1962), cos; PRISONER OF THE IRON MASK(1962, Fr./Ital.), cos; BOBO, THE(1967, Brit.), cos; BETTER A WIDOW(1969, Ital.), cos; PUSSYCAT, PUSSYCAT, I LOVE YOU(1970), cos; KILLER FISH(1979, Ital./Braz.), cos
Adrianna Berselli
SQUEEZE, THE(1980, Ital.), cos
Andriana Berselli
CASSANDRA CROSSING, THE(1977), cos
Ican Bersenev
Misc. Silents
YEKATERINA IVANOVNA(1915, USSR)
Ivan Bersenev
Misc. Silents
TEARS(1914, USSR); MOTHER(1920, USSR)
I. Bersenov
GREAT CITIZEN, THE(1939, USSR)
Fernand Berset
VERY CURIOUS GIRL, A(1970, Fr.)
James Bershad
FAST TIMES AT RIDGEMONT HIGH(1982)
Charles Bershatsky
HOSPITAL, THE(1971)
Elmer Berstein
DESIRE UNDER THE ELMS(1958), m
Walter Berstein
PARIS BLUES(1961), w
Miriam Berstein-Cohen
NEITHER BY DAY NOR BY NIGHT(1972, U.S./Israel)
Lisette Bersy
LIFE LOVE DEATH(1969, Fr./Ital.)
Bert
WANDA NEVADA(1979)

Camille Bert
ACCUSED–STAND UP(1930, Fr.); DAVID GOLDER(1932, Fr.); LOWER DEPTHS, THE(1937, Fr.)
Flo Bert
HAPPY DAYS(1930); I'M FROM ARKANSAS(1944); SHE-CREATURE, THE(1956)
Genevieve Bert
Silents
STRUGGLE, THE(1921); SO THIS IS ARIZONA(1922); TRAIL'S END(1922)
Misc. Silents
CROSS ROADS(1922)
Kirk Bert
ROAD TO FORT ALAMO, THE(1966, Fr./Ital.)
Liliane Bert
DEADLIER THAN THE MALE(1957, Fr.); ROYAL AFFAIRS IN VERSAILLES(1957, Fr.)
Mabel Bert
Silents
STRAIGHT IS THE WAY(1921)
Malcolm Bert
STAR IS BORN, A(1954), art d; COURT-MARTIAL OF BILLY MITCHELL, THE(1955), art d; EAST OF EDEN(1955), art d; GIRL RUSH, THE(1955), art d; REBEL WITHOUT A CAUSE(1955), art d; PAJAMA GAME, THE(1957), art d; TOP SECRET AFFAIR(1957), art d; AUNTIE MAME(1958), art d; MARJORIE MORNING-STAR(1958), art d; YOUNG PHILADELPHIANS, THE(1959), art d; FEVER IN THE BLOOD, A(1961), art d; DIRTY LITTLE BILLY(1972), art d
Malcolm C. Bert
CLAUDELLE INGLISH(1961), art d; FOLLOW THAT DREAM(1962), art d; ARRANGEMENT, THE(1969), art d; WATERMELON MAN(1970), art d
Margaret Bert
MIRACLES FOR SALE(1939); STRONGER THAN DESIRE(1939); KATHLEEN(1941); NAZI AGENT(1942); TISH(1942); YOUNGEST PROFESSION, THE(1943); I'LL BE SEEING YOU(1944); MRS. PARKINGTON(1944); ON STAGE EVERYBODY(1945); HOODLUM SAINT, THE(1946); TILL THE CLOUDS ROLL BY(1946); SEA OF GRASS, THE(1947); CAMPUS SLEUTH(1948); FORCE OF EVIL(1948); SUMMER HOLIDAY(1948); BARKLEYS OF BROADWAY, THE(1949); PREJUDICE(1949); SCENE OF THE CRIME(1949); VENGEANCE VALLEY(1951); SINGIN' IN THE RAIN(1952); TALK ABOUT A STRANGER(1952); EASY TO LOVE(1953); PARTY GIRL(1958)
Renato Berta
CHARLES, DEAD OR ALIVE(1972, Switz.), ph; MOSES AND AARON(1975, Ger./Fr./Ital.), ph; JONAH–WHO WILL BE 25 IN THE YEAR 2000(1976, Switz.), ph; EVERY MAN FOR HIMSELF(1980, Fr.), ph
1984
FULL MOON IN PARIS(1984, Fr.), ph
Roberto Berta
ATOM AGE VAMPIRE(1961, Ital.)
Uberta Bertacca
ROME WANTS ANOTHER CAESAR(1974, Ital.), m, cos
Umberto Bertacca
TEMPTER, THE(1978, Ital.), art d
Lella Bertante
FIST IN HIS POCKET(1968, Ital.)
Julien Bertau
CARMEN(1946, Ital.)
Riccardo Bertazzolo
MIRACLE IN MILAN(1951, Ital.)
Genevieve Berte
Misc. Silents
GOLD GRABBERS(1922)
Simone Berteaut
PIAF–THE EARLY YEARS(1982, U.S./Fr.), w
Adele Bertei
OFFENDERS, THE(1980), a, m; VORTEX(1982), m; BORN IN FLAMES(1983)
Erich Bertel
FIDELIO(1961, Aust.), md
Fred Bertelmann
HIPPODROME(1961, Aust./Ger.)
Burt Bertez
PHONY AMERICAN, THE(1964, Ger.)
Merline Berth
PAISAN(1948, Ital.)
Bertha
80 STEPS TO JONAH(1969)
Gabi Bertha
FATHER(1967, Hung.)
Jackie Berthe
KINGS GO FORTH(1958)
Julien Bertheau
LOVE IS MY PROFESSION(1959, Fr.); MADAME(1963, Fr./Ital./Span.); MILKY WAY, THE(1969, Fr./Ital.); DISCREET CHARM OF THE BOURGEOISIE, THE(1972, Fr.); PHANTOM OF LIBERTY, THE(1974, Fr.); VERDICT(1975, Fr./Ital.); THAT OBSCURE OBJECT OF DESIRE(1977, Fr./Span.)
Hans Berthel
I AIM AT THE STARS(1960), art d; ARMORED COMMAND(1961), art d; TWO IN A SLEEPING BAG(1964, Ger.), art d; GIRL FROM HONG KONG(1966, Ger.), art d
Arthur Berthelet
Silents
ENEMIES OF YOUTH(1925), d
Misc. Silents
CHAPERON, THE(1916), d; HAVOC, THE(1916), d; MISLEADING LADY, THE(1916), d; RETURN OF EVE, THE(1916), d; SHERLOCK HOLMES(1916), d; GOLDEN IDIOT, THE(1917), d; LITTLE SHOES(1917), d; PANTS(1917), d; SAINT'S ADVENTURE, THE(1917), d; YOUNG MOTHER HUBBARD(1917), d; MEN WHO HAVE MADE LOVE TO ME(1918), d; YOUNG AMERICA(1918), d; PENNY OF TOP HILL TRAIL(1921), d
Greta Berthels
WALPURGIS NIGHT(1941, Swed.)
Maud Berthelsen
EPILOGUE(1967, Den.)

Francois Berthet
DEATH OF MARIO RICCI, THE(1983, Ital.)
Berthier
ACCUSED–STAND UP(1930, Fr.)
Eugene Berthier
DIVA(1982, Fr.)
Jacques Berthier
MASTER OF BALLANTRAE, THE(1953, U.S./Brit.); RASPOUTINE(1954, Fr.); ROY-AL AFFAIRS IN VERSAILLES(1957, Fr.); NATHALIE, AGENT SECRET(1960, Fr.); MAYERLING(1968, Brit./Fr.); EAGLE OVER LONDON(1973, Ital.)
Rene Berthier
PARIS DOES STRANGE THINGS(1957, Fr./Ital.)
Simone Berthier
NIGHTS OF SHAME(1961, Fr.); VICE DOLLS(1961, Fr.)
Will Berthold
COURT MARTIAL(1962, Ger.), w; ORDERED TO LOVE(1963, Ger.), w
George C. Bertholen
CRY IN THE NIGHT, A(1956), p
George Bertholon
SILVER LINING(1932), p; KING KELLY OF THE U.S.A(1934), p, w; FLIRTING WITH DANGER(1935), w
George Bertholon, Jr.
Silents
LITTLE 'FRAID LADY, THE(1920)
George C. Bertholon
HELL ON FRISCO BAY(1956), p; BIG LAND, THE(1957), p
Marcel Berthomier
1984
LE DERNIER COMBAT(1984, Fr.)
Andre Berthomieu
BARRANCO(1932, Fr.), d; GIRL IN THE TAXI(1937, Brit.), d
J. Berthomieu
NAKED WOMAN, THE(1950, Fr.), d
Aldo Berti
MYTH, THE(1965, Ital.); STRANGER IN TOWN, A(1968, U.S./Ital.); ONCE UPON A TIME IN THE WEST(1969, U.S./Ital.); DIRTY OUTLAWS, THE(1971, Ital.)
Misc. Talkies
ANGEL FOR SATAN, AN(1966, Ital.)
Dehl Berti
TOUGHEST MAN ALIVE(1955); APACHE WARRIOR(1957); HELL BOUND(1957); UNDER FIRE(1957); UNDERSEA GIRL(1957); SEVEN ALONE(1975); WOLFEN(1981); SECOND THOUGHTS(1983)
Marina Berti
EARTH CRIES OUT, THE(1949, Ital.); PRINCE OF FOXES(1949); QUO VADIS(1951); UP FRONT(1951); SKY IS RED, THE(1952, Ital.); QUEEN OF SHEBA(1953, Ital.); ABDULLAH'S HAREM(1956, Brit./Egypt.); BEN HUR(1959); DAMON AND PY-THIAS(1962); JESSICA(1962, U.S./Ital./Fr.); SWORDSMAN OF SIENA, THE(1962, Fr./Ital.); CLEOPATRA(1963); FACE IN THE RAIN, A(1963); MADAME(1963, Fr./Ital./Span.); MADE IN ITALY(1967, Fr./Ital.); SHOOT FIRST, LAUGH LAST(1967, Ital./Ger./U.S.); STRANGER RETURNS, THE(1968, U.S./Ital./Ger./Span.); IF IT'S TUES-DAY, THIS MUST BE BELGIUM(1969); MOSES(1976, Brit./Ital.); DIVINE NYMPH, THE(1979, Ital.)
Orietta Berti
VIVA ITALIA(1978, Ital.)
Sahn Berti
NAKED ANGELS(1969)
Sanh Berti
CATTLE ANNIE AND LITTLE BRITCHES(1981), m
Sean Berti
Misc. Talkies
HILARY'S BLUES(1983)
Thane Berti
1984
PLAGUE DOGS, THE(1984, U.S./Brit.), ph
Guy Bertil
DIARY OF A BAD GIRL(1958, Fr.); GREEN MARE, THE(1961, Fr./Ital.)
Annie Bertin
JE T'AIME, JE T'AIME(1972, Fr./Swed.)
Francoise Bertin
LAST YEAR AT MARIENBAD(1962, Fr./Ital.); MURIEL(1963, Fr./Ital.); DIARY OF A CHAMBERMAID(1964, Fr./Ital.); LA GUERRE EST FINIE(1967, Fr./Swed.)
Pierre Bertin
ORPHEUS(1950, Fr.); AMAZING MONSIEUR FABRE, THE(1952, Fr.); KNOCK(1955, Fr.); PARIS DOES STRANGE THINGS(1957, Fr./Ital.); BABETTE GOES TO WAR(1960, Fr.); STRANGER, THE(1967, Algeria/Fr./Ital.); DON'T LOOK NOW(1969, Brit./Fr.)
Roland Bertin
BRONTE SISTERS, THE(1979, Fr.); DIVA(1982, Fr.); TROUT, THE(1982, Fr.)
Yori Bertin
FRANTIC(1961, Fr.); NUN, THE(1971, Fr.)
Valerie Bertinelli
C.H.O.M.P.S.(1979)
Francesca Bertini
1900(1976, Ital.)
Gari Bertini
THEY WERE TEN(1961, Israel), m
Bertini and the Tower Blackpool Band
DODGING THE DOLE(1936, Brit.)
Al Bertino
MAKE MINE MUSIC(1946), anim
Max Bertisch
WALK IN THE SUN, A(1945), art d
Suzanne Bertish
HANOVER STREET(1979, Brit.); HUNGER, THE(1983)
Giuseppe Berto
ANNA(1951, Ital.), d; EYE OF THE NEEDLE, THE(1965, Ital./Fr.), w
Guiseppe Berto
ANONYMOUS VENETIAN, THE(1971), w

Juliet Berto
LA CHINOISE(1967, Fr.); LE GAI SAVOIR(1968, Fr.); CELINE AND JULIE GO BOATING(1974, Fr.), a, w; SUMMER RUN(1974); MR. KLEIN(1976, Fr.); GUNS(1980, Fr.); SNOW(1983, Fr.), a, d, w
Juliette Berto
WEEKEND(1968, Fr./Ital.); SLOGAN(1970, Fr.); TWO OR THREE THINGS I KNOW ABOUT HER(1970, Fr.)
Max Berto
MAIS OU ET DONC ORNICAR(1979, Fr.), art d; LOULOU(1980, Fr.), set d
Michel Berto
ZIG-ZAG(1975, Fr./Ital.); BEAU PERE(1981, Fr.)
Antonio Bertocchi
AND THERE CAME A MAN(1968, Ital.)
Rita Bertocchi
AND THERE CAME A MAN(1968, Ital.)
Christian Bertola
THEY ARE NOT ANGELS(1948, Fr.); THINGS OF LIFE, THE(1970, Fr./Ital./Switz.)
Pierangelo Bertoli
TREE OF WOODEN CLOGS, THE(1979, Ital.)
Angelo Bertolini
WRONG IS RIGHT(1982)
Vittorio Bertolini
LA NOTTE(1961, Fr./Ital.)
George Bertolis
AFTER YOU, COMRADE(1967, S. Afr.)
Pietro Bertolissi
ONE MAN(1979, Can.)
Sergio Bertolli
BON VOYAGE, CHARLIE BROWN(AND DON'T COME BACK)*** (1980), anim
A. Bertolotto
MAN WHO LAUGHS, THE(1966, Ital.), w
Bernardo Bertolucc
ONCE UPON A TIME IN THE WEST(1969, U.S./Ital.), w
Bernardo Bertolucci
BEFORE THE REVOLUTION(1964, Ital.), d&w; CONFORMIST, THE(1971, Ital., Fr), d, w; 1900(1976, Ital.), d, w; LUNA(1979, Ital.), d, w; TRAGEDY OF A RIDICU-LOUS MAN, THE(1982, Ital.), d&w
Giovanni Bertolucci
INNOCENT, THE(1979, Ital.), p; LUNA(1979, Ital.), p; TRAGEDY OF A RIDICU-LOUS MAN, THE(1982, Ital.), p
Giuseppe Bertolucci
1900(1976, Ital.), w; LUNA(1979, Ital.), w
Peter Berton
ROOMMATES(1962, Brit.)
Stuart I. Berton
STRAIGHT TIME(1978)
Daniel Bertona
Silents
FORGIVEN, OR THE JACK O'DIAMONDS(1914)
Alfredo Bertone
Silents
WHITE SISTER, THE(1923); ROMOLA(1925)
Guido Bertone
WARRIORS FIVE(1962)
Guido Bertoni
SHADOWMAN(1974, Fr./Ital.), ph
Nick Bertoni
CRY DR. CHICAGO(1971)
Riccardo Bertoni
THEY ALL LAUGHED(1981)
Francesca Bertorelli
WINGS OF MYSTERY(1963, Brit.)
Lorain Bertorelli
POPE JOAN(1972, Brit.)
Maria Julia Bertott
1984
DEATHSTALKER, THE(1984), cos
M.J. Bertotto
DEATHSTALKER(1983, Arg./U.S.), art d
Paul Bertoya
COP-OUT(1967, Brit.); HOT RODS TO HELL(1967); ANGELS FROM HELL(1968); CHE!(1969); ONLY GOD KNOWS(1974, Can.)
Bert Bertram
HOW TO STEAL A MILLION(1966); SIDELONG GLANCES OF A PIGEON KICKER, THE(1970); SHAMUS(1973)
Frank Bertram
STRANGLEHOLD(1931, Brit.); LORD OF THE MANOR(1933, Brit.); THREE MEN IN A BOAT(1933, Brit.); JUBILEE WINDOW(1935, Brit.)
Gustav Bertram
SLEEPING BEAUTY(1965, Ger.)
Helen Bertram
CAPTAIN IS A LADY, THE(1940); RHYTHM ON THE RIVER(1940)
Paul Bertram
ADVENTURES OF BARRY McKENZIE(1972, Austral.); SIDECAR RACERS(1975, Aus.)
William Bertram
SPURS(1930)
Silents
DAMAGED GOODS(1915); LITTLE PATRIOT, A(1917), d; CUPID BY PROXY(1918), d; DOLLY'S VACATION(1918), d; ARIZONA CATCLAW, THE(1919), d; OLD MAID'S BABY, THE(1919), d; WOLVERINE, THE(1921), d; LONG CHANCE, THE(1922); WESTERN MUSKETEER, THE(1922), d&w; ACE OF ACTION(1926), d; UNDER FIRE(1926); WANTED–A COWARD(1927)
Misc. Silents
TEARS AND SMILES(1917), d; UNDERSTUDY, THE(1917), d; DADDY'S GIRL(1918), d; DAUGHTER OF THE WEST, A(1918), d; DOLLY DOES HER BIT(1918), d; MILADY O' THE BEAN STALK(1918), d; VOICE OF DESTINY, THE(1918), d; WINNING GRANDMA(1918), d; SAWDUST DOLL, THE(1919), d; GHOST CITY(1921), d; ALIAS PHIL KENNEDY(1922), d; TEXAS(1922), d; SMOKING TRAIL, THE(1924), a, d; HOODOO RANCH(1926), d; TANGLED HERDS(1926), d; GOLD FROM WEE-

PAH(1927), d; PHANTOM BUSTER, THE(1927), d; SWIFT SHADOW, THE(1927)

Bertram Mills' Circus
CIRCUS BOY(1947, Brit.)

Aline Bertrand
DIARY OF A CHAMBERMAID(1964, Fr./Ital.); TWO OF US, THE(1968, Fr.)

Claude Bertrand
AND SOON THE DARKNESS(1970, Brit.); CHLOE IN THE AFTERNOON(1972, Fr.)

Cliff Bertrand
CAPTURE THAT CAPSULE(1961), art d

Eva Bertrand
LOVE AND DEATH(1975)

Guy Bertrand
RETURN OF MARTIN GUERRE, THE(1983, Fr.)

J.P. Bertrand
DYNAMITE JACK(1961, Fr.), p

Jacqueline Bertrand
HELL WITH HEROES, THE(1968)

Jacques Bertrand
HIGHWAY PICKUP(1965, Fr./Ital.)

Jacques-Paul Bertrand
TRIPLE CROSS(1967, Fr./Brit.), p

Janette Bertrand
BIG RED(1962)

Jean Bertrand
CANDIDE(1962, Fr.), set d; TRIPLE CROSS(1967, Fr./Brit.)

Jean-Paul Bertrand
GENDARME OF ST. TROPEZ, THE(1966, Fr./Ital.)

Marcheline Bertrand
LOOKIN' TO GET OUT(1982)

Mary Bertrand
WIFE TAKES A FLYER, THE(1942)

Paul Bertrand
DAMNED, THE(1948, Fr.), prod d; FORBIDDEN GAMES(1953, Fr.), art d; CHEATERS, THE(1961, Fr.), art d; PURPLE NOON(1961, Fr./Ital.), art d; END OF DESIRE(1962 Fr./Ital.), art d

Rafael Bertrand
PROFESSIONALS, THE(1966)

Ralph [Rafael] Bertrand
SNAKE PEOPLE, THE(1968, Mex./U.S.)

Raphael Bertrand
BLACK PIT OF DOCTOR M(1958, Mex.)

Robert Bertrand
RIVERRUN(1968)

Rosemary Bertrand
DECOY(1946); TARZAN AND THE SLAVE GIRL(1950)

Maj. Gen. Victor Bertrandias, USAF/ret.
SPIRIT OF ST. LOUIS, THE(1957), tech adv

Marguerite Bertsch
Silents

FLORIDA ENCHANTMENT, A(1914), w
Misc. Silents
DEVIL'S PRIZE, THE(1916), d; GLORY OF YOLANDA, THE(1917), d; SOUL MASTER, THE(1917), d

Jean-Louis Bertucelli
DESERT OF THE TARTARS, THE(1976 Fr./Ital./Iranian), w; NO TIME FOR BREAKFAST(1978, Fr.), d, w

Gary Bertz
HEROES(1977)

Magdelaine Berubet
CRIME AND PUNISHMENT(1935, Fr.); SEVEN CAPITAL SINS(1962, Fr./Ital.); LA CHIENNE(1975, Fr.)

Overlau Beruta
PACIFIC DESTINY(1956, Brit.)

Jean-Claude Berva
UP FROM THE BEACH(1965)

Berval
ARTHUR(1931, Fr.); LIGHT ACROSSS THE STREET, THE(1957, Fr.)

Annie Berval
DAY THE SKY EXPLODED, THE(1958, Fr./Ital.)

Bervil
OF FLESH AND BLOOD(1964, Fr./Ital.)

Andre Bervil
DEVIL IN THE FLESH, THE(1949, Fr.); FERNANDEL THE DRESSMAKER(1957, Fr.); NIGHT WATCH, THE(1964, Fr./Ital.)

Jay Berwanger
BIG GAME, THE(1936)

Brad David Berwick
WARGAMES(1983)

Irv Berwick
MALIBU HIGH(1979), d
Misc. Talkies
HITCHHIKE TO HELL(1978), d

Irvin Berwick
MONSTER OF PIEDRAS BLANCAS, THE(1959), d; 7TH COMMANDMENT, THE(1961), p&d, w; STREET IS MY BEAT, THE(1966), p, d, w

James Berwick
WUTHERING HEIGHTS(1970, Brit.); VALENTINO(1977, Brit.); OUTLAND(1981)

Ray Berwick
BIRDS, THE(1963), animal t; EYE OF THE CAT(1969), animal t

Wayne Berwick
MONSTER OF PIEDRAS BLANCAS, THE(1959); MICROWAVE MASSACRE(1983), d

Isabel Berwin
Silents

PRUNELLA(1918)
Misc. Silents
STRONG WAY, THE(1918)

Isabelle Berwin
Misc. Silents
WOMAN BENEATH, THE(1917); BELOVED BLACKMAILER, THE(1918); INTERLOPER, THE(1918)

Isobel Berwin
Misc. Silents
MISS PETTICOATS(1916)

Tania Beryl
SPY IN YOUR EYE(1966, Ital.)

Beryl & Bobo
ENTERTAINER, THE(1960, Brit.)

Eddie Beryll
Silents
OPEN YOUR EYES(1919)

The Beryozka Dance Ensemble
SPRINGTIME ON THE VOLGA(1961, USSR)

Pierre Besancon
WHEEL OF ASHES(1970, Fr.)

Sir Walter Besant
Silents
ALL SORTS AND CONDITIONS OF MEN(1921, Brit.), w

Anne Besault
ANGEL IN MY POCKET(1969)

Peter Besbas
GIRL IN THE KREMLIN, THE(1957); MASTER OF THE WORLD(1961)

Peter E. Besbas
JOURNEY TO FREEDOM(1957)

Bibi Besch
DISTANCE(1975); PACK, THE(1977); HARDCORE(1979); METEOR(1979); PROMISE, THE(1979); BEAST WITHIN, THE(1982); STAR TREK II: THE WRATH OF KHAN(1982); LONELY LADY, THE(1983)

Herb Beschanner
HEAD, THE(1961, Ger.)

E. Besche
QUIET WOMAN, THE(1951, Brit.), ph

Eric Besche
INTERRUPTED JOURNEY, THE(1949, Brit.), ph; WEAKER SEX, THE(1949, Brit.), ph

S. Besedina
MEET ME IN MOSCOW(1966, USSR)

Sam Besekow
WHILE THE ATTORNEY IS ASLEEP(1945, Den.)

Anna-Maria Besendahl
TINDER BOX, THE(1968, E. Ger.)

Ben Besenko
Misc. Talkies
JEWISH DAUGHTER(1933)

Camillo Besenzon
QUIET PLACE IN THE COUNTRY, A(1970, Ital./Fr.)

James Beshears
HOMEWORK(1982), p&d; HUMAN HIGHWAY(1982), w

Chuk Besher
1984
RED DAWN(1984)

Annabella Besi
KAPO(1964, Ital./Fr./Yugo.)

Rudolf Besier
SECRETS(1933), w
Silents
PRUDES FALL, THE(1924, Brit.), w

Rudolph Besier
BARRETTS OF WIMPOLE STREET, THE(1934), w; BARRETTS OF WIMPOLE STREET, THE(1957), w

Greg Besnak
MIDNIGHT(1983)

Jacques Besnard
MADMAN OF LAB 4, THE(1967, Fr.), p&d

Jean-Pierre Besnard
1984
LIFE IS A BED OF ROSES(1984, Fr.), ed

Nicole Besnard
BEAUTY AND THE DEVIL(1952, Fr./Ital.)

Jose Garcia Besne
VENGEANCE OF THE VAMPIRE WOMEN, THE(1969, Mex.), p, w

Dominique Besnehard
1984
A NOS AMOURS(1984, Fr.)

Mario Besozzi
LAW IS THE LAW, THE(1959, Fr.)

Nino Besozzi
ROSSINI(1948, Ital.); LUCKY TO BE A WOMAN(1955, Ital.)

Bess
ADVENTURES OF GALLANT BESS(1948)

Ardon Bess
PROM NIGHT(1980)
1984
HIGHPOINT(1984, Can.)

Arods Bess
SHAPE OF THINGS TO COME, THE(1979, Can.)

Big Jeff Bess
FACE IN THE CROWD, A(1957); WILD RIVER(1960)

Milad Bessada
QUIET DAY IN BELFAST, A(1974, Can.), p&d

Memo Bessami
MESSALINE(1952, Fr./Ital.)

Ariel Besse
BEAU PERE(1981, Fr.)

Jacques Besse
DEDEE(1949, Fr.), m
Claribel Bessel
LUCK OF THE IRISH(1948)
Eric Besseling
1984
QUESTION OF SILENCE(1984, Neth.)
Ted Bessell
LOVER COME BACK(1961); OUTSIDER, THE(1962); CAPTAIN NEWMAN,
M.D.(1963); BILLIE(1965); MC HALE'S NAVY JOINS THE AIR FORCE(1965); DON'T
DRINK THE WATER(1969)
Albert Besser
MAD EXECUTIONERS, THE(1965, Ger.)
Joe Besser
HOT STEEL(1940); HEY, ROOKIE(1944); EADIE WAS A LADY(1945); TALK ABOUT
A LADY(1946); FEUDIN', FUSSIN' AND A-FIGHTIN'(1948); AFRICA
SCREAMS(1949); WOMAN IN HIDING(1949); DESERT HAWK, THE(1950); JOE
PALOOKA MEETS HUMPHREY(1950); SINS OF JEZEBEL(1953); ABBOTT AND
COSTELLO MEET THE KEYSTONE KOPS(1955); HEADLINE HUNTERS(1955);
TWO-GUN LADY(1956); PLUNDERERS OF PAINTED FLATS(1959); ROOKIE,
THE(1959); SAY ONE FOR ME(1959); STORY ON PAGE ONE, THE(1959); LET'S
MAKE LOVE(1960); ERRAND BOY, THE(1961); SILENT CALL, THE(1961); HAND OF
DEATH(1962); WHICH WAY TO THE FRONT?(1970)
Eugenie Besserer
JAZZ SINGER, THE(1927); LADY OF CHANCE, A(1928); BRIDGE OF SAN LUIS
REY, THE(1929); FAST COMPANY(1929); ILLUSION(1929); MADAME X(1929); MIS-
TER ANTONIO(1929); SEVEN FACES(1929); THUNDERBOLT(1929); WHISPERING
WINDS(1929); IN GAY MADRID(1930); TO THE LAST MAN(1933)
Silents
CARPET FROM BAGDAD, THE(1915); CITY OF PURPLE DREAMS, THE(1918);
EYES OF JULIA DEEP, THE(1918); SCARLET DAYS(1919); FICKLE WOMEN(1920);
GREATEST QUESTION, THE(1920); BREAKING POINT, THE(1921); MOLLY O'(1921);
SIN OF MARTHA QUEED, THE(1921); WHAT HAPPENED TO ROSA?(1921); JUNE
MADNESS(1922); KINDRED OF THE DUST(1922); PENROD(1922); STRANGER'S
BANQUET(1922); ANNA CHRISTIE(1923); ENEMIES OF CHILDREN(1923); LONELY
ROAD, THE(1923); RENDEZVOUS, THE(1923); BRIGHT LIGHTS(1925); FLESH AND
THE DEVIL(1926); SKYROCKET, THE(1926); CAPTAIN SALVATION(1927); SLIGHT-
LY USED(1927); WANDERING GIRLS(1927); LILAC TIME(1928); TWO LOVERS(1928)
Misc. Silents
MONTE CRISTO(1912); STORY OF THE BLOOD RED ROSE, THE(1914); CIRCULAR
STAIRCASE, THE(1915); I'M GLAD MY BOY GREW TO BE A SOLDIER(1915);
GARDEN OF ALLAH, THE(1916); THOU SHALT NOT COVET(1916); LITTLE LOST
SISTER(1917); LITTLE ORPHANT ANNIE(1919); FOR THE SOUL OF RAFAEL(1920);
GIFT SUPREME, THE(1920); SEEDS OF VENGEANCE(1920); 45 MINUTES FROM
BROADWAY(1920); LIGHT IN THE CLEARING, THE(1921); AUCTION OF
SOULS(1922); PRICE SHE PAID, THE(1924); CIRCLE, THE(1925); CONFESSIONS OF
A QUEEN(1925); WANDERING FOOTSTEPS(1925); MILLIONAIRE POLICEMAN,
THE(1926)
Roberto Bessi
TO KILL OR TO DIE(1973, Ital.), p
Alvah Bessie
NORTHERN PURSUIT(1943), w; VERY THOUGHT OF YOU, THE(1944), w; OBJEC-
TIVE, BURMA!(1945), w; SMART WOMAN(1948), w
Bessie the Bear
Silents
IT'S A BEAR(1919)
Claudette Bessing
THX 1138(1971)
Wag Bessing
ESCAPE TO BURMA(1955)
Sonia Bessis
LE MONDE TREMBLERA(1939, Fr.)
Albert Bessler
THOUSAND EYES OF DR. MABUSE, THE(1960, Fr./Ital./Ger.); BRAINWA-
SHED(1961, Ger.); RETURN OF DR. MABUSE, THE(1961, Ger./Fr./Ital.); DIE FAST-
NACHTSBEICHTE(1962, Ger.); RESTLESS NIGHT, THE(1964, Ger.); TERROR OF DR.
MABUSE, THE(1965, Ger.); FROZEN ALIVE(1966, Brit./Ger.); SUNSCORCHED(1966,
Span./Ger.)
Luc Besson
1984
LE DERNIER COMBAT(1984, Fr.), p, d, w
Claude Bessy
INVITATION TO THE DANCE(1956)
M. Bessy
CHILDREN OF CHAOS(1950, Fr.), w
Maurice Bessy
DEADLIER THAN THE MALE(1957, Fr.), w; DEVIL AND THE TEN COMMAND-
MENTS, THE(1962, Fr.), w
Alyson Best
1984
BROTHERS(1984, Aus.); MAN OF FLOWERS(1984, Aus.)
Anya Best
BY DESIGN(1982)
Bettie Best
TRAP, THE(1947)
Bill Best
NORA PRENTISS(1947)
Deannie Best
WONDER MAN(1945); BIG SLEEP, THE(1946); SHANGHAI CHEST, THE(1948)
Dick Best
LAMBETH WALK, THE(1940, Brit.), ed
Edna Best
BEYOND THE CITIES(1930, Brit.); ESCAPE(1930, Brit.); LOOSE ENDS(1930, Brit.);
SLEEPING PARTNERS(1930, Brit.); CALENDAR, THE(1931, Brit.); MICHAEL AND
MARY(1932, Brit.); FAITHFUL HEART(1933, Brit.); KEY, THE(1934); MAN WHO
KNEW TOO MUCH, THE(1935, Brit.); SOUTH RIDING(1938, Brit.); INTERMEZZO: A
LOVE STORY(1939, Brit.); PRISON WITHOUT BARS(1939, Brit.); DISPATCH FROM REU-
TERS, A(1940); SWISS FAMILY ROBINSON(1940); GHOST AND MRS. MUIR,
THE(1947); LATE GEORGE APLEY, THE(1947); IRON CURTAIN, THE(1948)

Misc. Silents
TILLY OF BLOOMSBURY(1921, Brit.); COUPLE OF DOWN AND OUTS, A(1923,
Brit.)
Eric Best
STERILE CUCKOO, THE(1969)
Geoffrey Best
BORN FREE(1966)
George Best
Misc. Silents
LAND JUST OVER YONDER, THE(1916)
H.M. Best
Silents
RAMONA(1916)
Misc. Silents
YEARS OF THE LOCUST, THE(1916)
Howard Best
MARJORIE MORNINGSTAR(1958)
Iain Best
1984
BIG MEAT EATER(1984, Can.), spec eff
Jack Best
PIGSKIN PARADE(1936)
James Best
COMMANCHE TERRITORY(1950); KANSAS RAIDERS(1950); PEGGY(1950); WIN-
CHESTER '73(1950); AIR CADET(1951); APACHE DRUMS(1951); CIMARRON KID,
THE(1951); TARGET UNKNOWN(1951); FRANCIS GOES TO WEST POINT(1952); MA
AND PA KETTLE AT THE FAIR(1952); STEEL TOWN(1952); CITY OF BAD
MEN(1953); COLUMN SOUTH(1953); PRESIDENT'S LADY, THE(1953); SEMINO-
LE(1953); CAINE MUTINY, THE(1954); RAID, THE(1954); RETURN FROM THE
SEA(1954); THEY RODE WEST(1954); SEVEN ANGRY MEN(1955); CALLING HOMI-
CIDE(1956); COME NEXT SPRING(1956); GABY(1956); RACK, THE(1956); WHEN
GANGLAND STRIKES(1956); HOT SUMMER NIGHT(1957); LAST OF THE BAD-
MEN(1957); MAN ON THE PROWL(1957); COLE YOUNGER, GUNFIGHTER(1958);
LEFT-HANDED GUN, THE(1958); NAKED AND THE DEAD, THE(1958); CAST A
LONG SHADOW(1959); KILLER SHREWS, THE(1959); RIDE LONESOME(1959);
VERBOTEN!(1959); MOUNTAIN ROAD, THE(1960); BLACK GOLD(1963); SHOCK
CORRIDOR(1963); QUICK GUN, THE(1964); BLACK SPURS(1965); SHENAN-
DOAH(1965); THREE ON A COUCH(1966); FIRST TO FIGHT(1967); FIRE-
CREEK(1968); SOUNDER(1972); NICKELODEON(1976); ODE TO BILLY JOE(1976);
ROLLING THUNDER(1977); END, THE(1978); HOOPER(1978)
Misc. Talkies
BRAIN MACHINE, THE(1972)
James K. Best
RIDERS TO THE STARS(1954)
Jimmy Best
MYSTERY SUBMARINE(1950); BATTLE AT APACHE PASS, THE(1952)
Johnny Best
SUN VALLEY SERENADE(1941)
Jonathon Best
1984
SILENT NIGHT, DEADLY NIGHT(1984)
Katherine Best
XTRO(1983, Brit.)
Larry Best
BELLBOY, THE(1960); MARCO POLO JUNIOR(1973, Aus.)
Marjorie Best
SILVER RIVER(1948), cos; DALLAS(1950), cos; ROCKY MOUNTAIN(1950), cos;
WEST POINT STORY, THE(1950), cos; DISTANT DRUMS(1951), cos; I'LL SEE YOU
IN MY DREAMS(1951), cos; ON MOONLIGHT BAY(1951), cos; ROOM FOR ONE
MORE(1952), cos; BURNING HILLS, THE(1956), cos; GIANT(1956), cos; SAN-
TIAGO(1956), cos; BAND OF ANGELS(1957), cos; SHOOT-OUT AT MEDICINE
BEND(1957), cos; STORY OF MANKIND, THE(1957), cos; DARBY'S RANGERS(1958),
cos; FORT DOBBS(1958), cos; LAFAYETTE ESCADRILLE(1958), cos; LEFT-HAND-
ED GUN, THE(1958), cos; HANGING TREE, THE(1959), cos; MIRACLE, THE(1959),
cos; NUN'S STORY, THE(1959), cos; RIO BRAVO(1959), cos; YELLOWSTONE KEL-
LY(1959), cos; DARK AT THE TOP OF THE STAIRS, THE(1960), cos; SERGEANT
RUTLEDGE(1960), cos; SINS OF RACHEL CADE, THE(1960), cos; SUNRISE AT
CAMPOBELLO(1960), cos; COMANCHEROS, THE(1961), cos; TENDER IS THE
NIGHT(1961), cos; STATE FAIR(1962), cos; SPENCER'S MOUNTAIN(1963), cos;
GREATEST STORY EVER TOLD, THE(1965), cos
Marjorie O. Best
BORN RECKLESS(1959), cos
Martin Best
Silents
CHORUS GIRL'S ROMANCE, A(1920)
Misc. Silents
HOTTENTOT, THE(1922)
Michael Best
LA TRAVIATA(1982)
Patricia Best
BY DESIGN(1982)
Peggy Best
Silents
BLACK BIRD, THE(1926)
Peter Best
CITY OF FEAR(1965, Brit.), art d; ADVENTURES OF BARRY McKENZIE(1972,
Austral.), m; PETERSEN(1974, Aus.), m; BARRY MC KENZIE HOLDS HIS
OWN(1975, Aus.), m; PICTURE SHOW MAN, THE(1980, Aus.), m; WE OF THE
NEVER NEVER(1983, Aus.), m
Richard Best
FAME IS THE SPUR(1947, Brit.), ed; MINE OWN EXECUTIONER(1948, Brit.), ed;
AFFAIRS OF ADELAIDE(1949, U. S/Brit.), ed; OUTSIDER, THE(1949, Brit.), ed;
DANCING YEARS, THE(1950, Brit.), ed; MAGIC BOX, THE(1952, Brit.), ed; MEN ARE
CHILDREN TWICE(1953, Brit.), ed; YELLOW BALLOON, THE(1953, Brit.), ed;
WEAK AND THE WICKED, THE(1954, Brit.), ed; DAM BUSTERS, THE(1955, Brit.),
ed; NOW AND FOREVER(1956, Brit.), ed; PICKUP ALLEY(1957, Brit.), ed; SILKEN
AFFAIR, THE(1957, Brit.), ed; WOMEN IN A DRESSING GOWN(1957, Brit.), ed;
DESERT ATTACK(1958, Brit.), ed; MOONRAKER, THE(1958, Brit.), ed; LOOK BACK
IN ANGER(1959, Brit.), ed; BOTTOMS UP(1960, Brit.), ed; SANDS OF THE DESERT(1960,
Brit.), ed; SCHOOL FOR SCOUNDRELS(1960, Brit.), ed; CALL ME GENIUS(1961,

Brit.), ed; GO TO BLAZES(1962, Brit.), ed; WE JOINED THE NAVY(1962, Brit.), ed; CRACKSMAN, THE(1963, Brit.), ed; BARGEE, THE(1964, Brit.), ed; NO TREE IN THE STREET(1964, Brit.), ed; DOUBLE MAN, THE(1967), ed; CHAIRMAN, THE(1969), ed; OTLEY(1969, Brit.), ed

Ulla Best
DECISION BEFORE DAWN(1951)

Warden Roy Best
CANON CITY(1948)

William Best
DOWN THE STRETCH(1936); BREEZING HOME(1937); GENERAL SPANKY(1937)

Willie Best [Sleep 'n'
LITTLE MISS MARKER(1934); LITTLEST REBEL, THE(1935); MURDER ON A HONEYMOON(1935); NITWITS, THE(1935); BRIDE WALKS OUT, THE(1936); LADY CONSENTS, THE(1936); MAKE WAY FOR A LADY(1936); MUMMY'S BOYS(1936); MURDER ON A BRIDLE PATH(1936); THANK YOU, JEEVES(1936); LADY FIGHTS BACK(1937); MEET THE MISSUS(1937); RACING LADY(1937); SATURDAY'S HEROES(1937); SUPER SLEUTH(1937); GOLD IS WHERE YOU FIND IT(1938); GOODBYE BROADWAY(1938); MERRILY WE LIVE(1938); MR. MOTO TAKES A VACATION(1938); VIVACIOUS LADY(1938); YOUTH TAKES A FLING(1938); BLACKMAIL(1939); COVERED TRAILER, THE(1939); NANCY DREW, TROUBLE SHOOTER(1939); PRIVATE DETECTIVE(1939); SAINT STRIKES BACK, THE(1939); BLONDIE ON A BUDGET(1940); GHOST BREAKERS, THE(1940); I TAKE THIS WOMAN(1940); MONEY AND THE WOMAN(1940); SLIGHTLY HONORABLE(1940); WHO KILLED AUNT MAGGIE?(1940); BODY DISAPPEARS, THE(1941); FLIGHT FROM DESTINY(1941); HIGH SIERRA(1941); HIGHWAY WEST(1941); KISSES FOR BREAKFAST(1941); LADY FROM CHEYENNE(1941); NOTHING BUT THE TRUTH(1941); ROAD SHOW(1941); SCATTERGOOD BAINES(1941); SMILING GHOST, THE(1941); A-HAUNTING WE WILL GO(1942); BUSSES ROAR(1942); HIDDEN HAND, THE(1942); JUKE GIRL(1942); POWERS GIRL, THE(1942); SCATTERGOOD SURVIVES A MURDER(1942); WHISPERING GHOSTS(1942); CABIN IN THE SKY(1943); DIXIE(1943); KANSAN, THE(1943); THANK YOUR LUCKY STARS(1943); ADVENTURES OF MARK TWAIN, THE(1944); GIRL WHO DARED, THE(1944); HOME IN INDIANA(1944); HOLD THAT BLONDE(1945); PILLOW TO POST(1945); SHE WOULDN'T SAY YES(1945); BRIDE WORE BOOTS, THE(1946); DANGEROUS MONEY(1946); FACE OF MARBLE, THE(1946); RED DRAGON, THE(1946); RED STALLION, THE(1947); SUDDENLY IT'S SPRING(1947); HALF PAST MIDNIGHT(1948); SHANGHAI CHEST, THE(1948); SMART WOMAN(1948); SOUTH OF CALIENTE(1951)

Willy Best
CINDERELLA SWINGS IT(1942)

Barbara Bestar
NAVAJO TRAIL RAIDERS(1949); SAFARI DRUMS(1953); WHITE LIGHTNING(1953); KILLERS FROM SPACE(1954)

Tatyana Bestayeva
SANDU FOLLOWS THE SUN(1965, USSR); SHADOWS OF FORGOTTEN ANCESTORS(1967, USSR)

Billy Bester
FOREIGN CORRESPONDENT(1940); SHOW BUSINESS(1944)

Diane Bester
MODEL FOR MURDER(1960, Brit.); MAROC 7(1967, Brit.)

Paul Besterman
BUGSY MALONE(1976, Brit.)

Chuck Beston
THEY SAVED HITLER'S BRAIN(1964)

Peter Beston
1984
GIVE MY REGARDS TO BROAD STREET(1984, Brit.), ed

Barbara Bestor
TWO DOLLAR BETTOR(1951)

Doug Bestwick
OCTAMAN(1971), spec eff & makeup

Douglas Beswick
STAR WARS(1977), makeup

Martine Beswick
FROM RUSSIA WITH LOVE(1963, Brit.); THUNDERBALL(1965, Brit.); BULLET FOR THE GENERAL, A(1967, Ital.); ONE MILLION YEARS B.C.(1967, Brit./U.S.); PENTHOUSE, THE(1967, Brit.); PREHISTORIC WOMEN(1967, Brit.); DR. JEKYLL AND SISTER HYDE(1971, Brit.); SEIZURE(1974); MELVIN AND HOWARD(1980)

Martine Beswicke
HAPPY HOOKER GOES TO HOLLYWOOD, THE(1980)

J. Betancourt
MESSAGE TO GARCIA, A(1936)

Mariano Betancourt
UNDER THE PAMPAS MOON(1935)

Mrs. William Betchel
Silents
QUEST OF LIFE, THE(1916)

William Betchel
Silents
LOVE IN A HURRY(1919); IDLE HANDS(1921)

William Betchell
Misc. Silents
NECKLACE OF RAMESES, THE(1914)

Eric Bethancourt
ROLLOVER(1981)

Francis Bethancourt
ROYAL WEDDING(1951); ROGUE'S MARCH(1952)

Bob Bethard
PLAY DEAD(1981), ph

Robert Bethard
NORSEMAN, THE(1978), ph

Robert E. Bethard
STARK FEAR(1963), ph; MARK OF THE WITCH(1970), ph

Dale Ellen Bethea
MIRACLE WORKER, THE(1962)

David Bethea
GREEN PASTURES(1936); HI-DE-HO(1947)

Barry Bethel
WHAT A CRAZY WORLD(1963, Brit.)

Dell Bethel
BANG THE DRUM SLOWLY(1973)

Len Bethel
Misc. Silents
DAVID COPPERFIELD(1913, Brit.)

Francis Bethencourt
THIS EARTH IS MINE(1959)

Herbert Bethew
Misc. Silents
UNDER NORTHERN LIGHTS(1920); CHEROKEE STRIP, THE(1925)

Jeanette Bethge
GIRL FROM THE MARSH CROFT, THE(1935, Ger.)

Veite Bethke
VICTORS, THE(1963)

Sabine Bethmann
JOURNEY TO THE LOST CITY(1960, Ger./Fr./Ital.); SCOTLAND YARD HUNTS DR. MABUSE(1963, Ger.)

Siegfried Bethmann
TINDER BOX, THE(1968, E. Ger.), m

Betty Bethune
MURDER AT THE VANITIES(1934)

Ivey Bethune
GOODBYE, NORMA JEAN(1976)

Ivy Bethune
LEGACY OF BLOOD(1973); I WANNA HOLD YOUR HAND(1978); WRONG IS RIGHT(1982)

Zina Bethune
SUNRISE AT CAMPOBELLO(1960); WHO'S THAT KNOCKING AT MY DOOR?(1968)

Edward G. Betlow
NIGHT SHIFT(1982)

Victor Betral
JOURNEY TO THE BEGINNING OF TIME(1966, Czech)

Annibale Betrone
FEDORA(1946, Ital.); DUEL WITHOUT HONOR(1953, Ital.)

Anneliese Betschart
IT HAPPENED IN BROAD DAYLIGHT(1960, Ger./Switz.); SHADOWS GROW LONGER, THE(1962, Switz./Ger.)

John Bett
GREAT TRAIN ROBBERY, THE(1979, Brit.); TESS(1980, Fr./Brit.); BRITTANIA HOSPITAL(1982, Brit.); GREGORY'S GIRL(1982, Brit.); PIRATES OF PENZANCE, THE(1983)
1984
SACRED HEARTS(1984, Brit.)

Ulrich Bettac
APRIL 1, 2000(1953, Aust.); ETERNAL WALTZ, THE(1959, Ger.)

Clemence Bettany
Misc. Talkies
OUR MAN IN THE CARIBBEAN(1962)

Thane Bettany
FFOLKES(1980, Brit.)

Steve Bettcher
VISITING HOURS(1982, Can.)

Karl Bette
IT'S HOT IN PARADISE(1962, Ger./Yugo.), m; SEVEN DARING GIRLS(1962, Ger.), m; ISLE OF SIN(1963, Ger.), m

Dr. Bruno Bettelheim
ZELIG(1983)

Mary Betten
LITTLE DARLINGS(1980); SOME KIND OF HERO(1982)

Gary Bettenhausen
GONE IN 60 SECONDS(1974)

Sidney Bettex
DANIELLA BY NIGHT(1962, Fr/Ger.), set d; NUDE IN HIS POCKET(1962, Fr.), art d; GENDARME OF ST. TROPEZ, THE(1966, Fr./Ital.), art d; ASSOCIATE, THE(1982 Fr./Ger.), art d

Lyle Bettger
NO MAN OF HER OWN(1950); UNION STATION(1950); DEAR BRAT(1951); FIRST LEGION, THE(1951); DENVER AND RIO GRANDE(1952); GREATEST SHOW ON EARTH, THE(1952); HURRICANE SMITH(1952); ALL I DESIRE(1953); FORBIDDEN(1953); GREAT SIOUX UPRISING, THE(1953); VANQUISHED, THE(1953); CARNIVAL STORY(1954); DESTRY(1954); DRUMS ACROSS THE RIVER(1954); LONE RANGER, THE(1955); SEA CHASE, THE(1955); SHOWDOWN AT ABILENE(1956); GUNFIGHT AT THE O.K. CORRAL(1957); GUNS OF THE TIMBERLAND(1960); TOWN TAMER(1965); JOHNNY RENO(1966); NEVADA SMITH(1966); FASTEST GUITAR ALIVE, THE(1967); IMPASSE(1969); HAWAIIANS, THE(1970); SEVEN MINUTES, THE(1971)

Giuliano Betti
UNDER THE SUN OF ROME(1949, Ital.), ed

Laura Betti
LA DOLCE VITA(1961, Ital./Fr.); RED LIPS(1964, Fr./Ital.); HATCHET FOR A HONEYMOON(1969, Span./Ital.); TEOREMA(1969, Ital.); WITCHES, THE(1969, Fr./Ital.); MAN CALLED SLEDGE, A(1971, Ital.); TWITCH OF THE DEATH NERVE(1973, Ital.); SONNY AND JED(1974, Ital.); DRAMA OF THE RICH(1975, Ital./Fr.); 1900(1976, Ital.); WOMAN WITH RED BOOTS, THE(1977, Fr./Span.); BUTTERFLY ON THE SHOULDER, A(1978, Fr.); LOVERS AND LIARS(1981, Ital.); LA NUIT DE VARENNES(1983, Fr./Ital.)
1984
TO CATCH A COP(1984, Fr.)

Sandra Gale Bettin
WONDERFUL WORLD OF THE BROTHERS ERIMM, THE(1962); SWINGIN' AFFAIR, A(1963); ONE MAN'S WAY(1964)

Val Bettin
SOMEWHERE IN TIME(1980)

Bianca Maria Bettinali
FRIENDS FOR LIFE(1964, Ital.)

Silla Bettini
EVERYBODY GO HOME!(1962, Fr./Ital.); FACTS OF MURDER, THE(1965, Ital.); ENGAGEMENT ITALIANO(1966, Fr./Ital.); TRAMPLERS, THE(1966, Ital.); MINUTE TO PRAY, A SECOND TO DIE, A(1968, Ital.)
R. Bettinson
GIRL FROM MAXIM'S, THE(1936, Brit.), ed
Ralph Bettinson
ROSE OF THE RIO GRANDE(1938), w; SOUTH OF THE RIO GRANDE(1945), w; ROGUES OF SHERWOOD FOREST(1950), w; MASK OF THE AVENGER(1951), w
Ralph G. Bettinson
DOOMED TO DIE(1940), w
Ralph Gilbert Bettinson
GREAT GAME, THE(1930), w; LATIN LOVE(1930, Brit.), w; DOWN RIVER(1931, Brit.), w; NIGHT RIDE(1937, Brit.), w; YOU'RE IN THE ARMY NOW(1937, Brit.), w; TORSO MURDER MYSTERY, THE(1940, Brit.), w; 1984(1956, Brit.), w
John Bettis
1984
OH GOD! YOU DEVIL(1984), m/l "If It Was Only Up to Me," "Dangerous Eyes," Mike Post
Larry Bettis
SECOND-HAND HEARTS(1981)
Valerie Bettis
AFFAIR IN TRINIDAD(1952); LET'S DO IT AGAIN(1953), a, ch; SALOME(1953), ch; ATHENA(1954), ch
Ralph Gilbert Bettison
HEADLINE(1943, Brit.), w
Robert Bettles
RIDE A WILD PONY(1976, U.S./Aus.); LET THE BALLOON GO(1977, Aus.)
Otto Bettman
LOVESICK(1983)
Franca Bettoia
LAST MAN ON EARTH, THE(1964, U.S./Ital.)
Franca Bettoja
DESERT WARRIOR(1961 Ital./Span.); DUEL OF CHAMPIONS(1964 Ital./Span.); LION OF ST. MARK(1967, Ital.); DON'T TOUCH WHITE WOMEN!(1974, Fr.)
George Betton
LITTLE ONES, THE(1965, Brit.)
Roberto Bettoni
AVENGER, THE(1962, Fr./Ital.); FALL OF ROME, THE(1963, Ital.); LOVE IS A BALL(1963)
David Betts
TOTO AND THE POACHERS(1958, Brit.)
Ernest Betts
CLOWN MUST LAUGH, A(1936, Brit.), w; LOVE IN EXILE(1936, Brit.), w; UNDER SECRET ORDERS(1943, Brit.), w
Fred Betts
RUNNING WILD(1973)
Harry Betts
SWINGIN' SUMMER, A(1965), m; WINTER A GO-GO(1965), m; BIG MOUTH, THE(1967), m; BLACK MAMA, WHITE MAMA(1973), m; LITTLE CIGARS(1973), m; CHEECH AND CHONG'S NICE DREAMS(1981), m
Jack Betts
BLOODY BROOD, THE(1959, Can.); ONE PLUS ONE(1961, Can.)
Jane Betts
UP THE SANDBOX(1972)
Kirsten Betts
VAMPIRE LOVERS, THE(1970, Brit.); CRESCENDO(1972, Brit.)
Matthew Betts
Silents
BURN 'EM UP BARNES(1921); SINGLE TRACK, THE(1921); LUCK(1923)
Pamela Betts
RETURN OF THE JEDI(1983)
William Betts
Silents
SAINTED DEVIL, A(1924)
Eve Betts, Ltd.
POET'S PUB(1949, Brit.), cos
Lauri Betty
FRENCHMAN'S CREEK(1944)
Betty and Beverly
CASA MANANA(1951)
Jonathan Betuel
1984
LAST STARFIGHTER, THE(1984), w
Audrey Betz
LEAVE HER TO HEAVEN(1946); MONSIEUR VERDOUX(1947); CRISIS(1950); MILKMAN, THE(1950); NEW KIND OF LOVE, A(1963); OUTLAWS IS COMING, THE(1965)
Byron Betz
TARGETS(1968)
Carl Betz
CITY OF BAD MEN(1953); DANGEROUS CROSSING(1953); INFERNO(1953); POWDER RIVER(1953); PRESIDENT'S LADY, THE(1953); VICKI(1953); SPINOUT(1966); MEAL, THE(1975)
Misc. Talkies
DEADLY ENCOUNTER(1979)
Edward Betz
I'M DANCING AS FAST AS I CAN(1982); HANNAH K.(1983, Fr.)
Mathew Betz
BIG HOUSE, THE(1930); HER MAN(1930); SINGLE SIN(1931); BROADWAY TO CHEYENNE(1932); GOLD(1932); TARZAN THE FEARLESS(1933); VIA PONY EXPRESS(1933); GIRL WHO CAME BACK, THE(1935); LAW COMMANDS, THE(1938)
Misc. Talkies
FROM BROADWAY TO CHEYENNE(1932)
Silents
BIG CITY, THE(1928)
Misc. Silents
LOVE'S WHIRLPOOL(1924); WAY OF A GIRL, THE(1925)

Matther Betz
Silents
EXQUISITE SINNER, THE(1926)
Matthew Betz
SINS OF THE FATHERS(1928); TERROR, THE(1928); GIRL IN THE GLASS CAGE, THE(1929); SEE AMERICA THIRST(1930); SHOOTING STRAIGHT(1930); SQUEALER, THE(1930); SALVATION NELL(1931); SIDE SHOW(1931); ALIAS MARY SMITH(1932); DYNAMITE DENNY(1932); FIGHTING MARSHAL, THE(1932); SPEED MADNESS(1932); BIG CHANCE, THE(1933); I HAVE LIVED(1933); MYSTERY OF THE WAX MUSEUM, THE(1933); STATE TROOPER(1933); UNDER SECRET ORDERS(1933); FIGHTING ROOKIE, THE(1934); MEN OF THE NIGHT(1934); LET 'EM HAVE IT(1935); MISSISSIPPI(1935); MUTINY AHEAD(1935); ON PROBATION(1935); RECKLESS ROADS(1935); TRAILS OF THE WILD(1935); FLORIDA SPECIAL(1936); LITTLE RED SCHOOLHOUSE(1936); OUTCAST(1937); FURY BELOW(1938); RACING BLOOD(1938)
Misc. Talkies
WESTERN CODE(1932); WHIRLWIND, THE(1933)
Silents
SALVATION NELL(1921); SAWDUST(1923); LIGHTHOUSE BY THE SEA, THE(1924); ONLY WOMAN, THE(1924); UNHOLY THREE, THE(1925); LITTLE IRISH GIRL, THE(1926); OH, WHAT A NURSE!(1926); WEDDING MARCH, THE(1927); CRIMSON CITY, THE(1928); TELLING THE WORLD(1928); FUGITIVES(1929); GIRLS GONE WILD(1929)
Misc. Silents
WHITE FANG(1925); FLAME OF THE YUKON, THE(1926); SHIPWRECKED(1926); BROADWAY AFTER MIDNIGHT(1927); PATENT LEATHER KID, THE(1927); SHEPHERD OF THE HILL, THE(1928)
Marion Betzold
ELEPHANT MAN, THE(1980, Brit.)
Philippe Beuans
WORLD OF HENRY ORIENT, THE(1964)
Roland Beubner
TIN DRUM, THE(1979, Ger./Fr./Yugo./Pol.)
Lt. Raphael G. Beugnon, AUS
O.S.S.(1946), tech adv
Francois Beukelaers
ONE NIGHT... A TRAIN(1968, Fr./Bel.)
Billie Beurne
ZAZA(1939)
Chris Beute
HEADLEYS AT HOME, THE(1939), d
Bill Beutel
HANKY-PANKY(1982)
Jack Beutel
OUTLAW, THE(1943); JESSE JAMES' WOMEN(1954); MUSTANG(1959)
Jiggs Beutler
WHEN THE LEGENDS DIE(1972)
Beuve
PASTEUR(1936, Fr.)
Alfred Bevan
ON OUR SELECTION(1930, Aus.)
Bill Bevan
CAPTAIN FURY(1939)
Billy Bevan
WATERLOO BRIDGE(1931); HIGH VOLTAGE(1929); SKY HAWK(1929); TRESPASSER, THE(1929); FOR THE DEFENSE(1930); FOR THE LOVE O'LIL(1930); JOURNEY'S END(1930); MONTE CARLO(1930); PEACOCK ALLEY(1930); BORN TO LOVE(1931); TRANSATLANTIC(1931); ME AND MY GAL(1932); PAYMENT DEFERRED(1932); SILENT WITNESS, THE(1932); SKY DEVILS(1932); VANITY FAIR(1932); CAVALCADE(1933); LOOKING FORWARD(1933); LUXURY LINER(1933); MIDNIGHT CLUB(1933); PEG O' MY HEART(1933); STUDY IN SCARLET, A(1933); TOO MUCH HARMONY(1933); WAY TO LOVE, THE(1933); CARAVAN(1934); LIMEHOUSE BLUES(1934); LOST PATROL, THE,(1934); PAINTED VEIL, THE(1934); SHOCK(1934); STINGAREE(1934); LAST OUTPOST, THE(1935); MYSTERY WOMAN(1935); TALE OF TWO CITIES, A(1935); DRACULA'S DAUGHTER(1936); MR. DEEDS GOES TO TOWN(1936); PICCADILLY JIM(1936); PRIVATE NUMBER(1936); SONG AND DANCE MAN, THE(1936); WIDOW FROM MONTE CARLO, THE(1936); ANOTHER DAWN(1937); GOD'S COUNTRY AND THE WOMAN(1937); PERSONAL PROPERTY(1937); SHEIK STEPS OUT, THE(1937); SLAVE SHIP(1937); WRONG ROAD, THE(1937); BRINGING UP BABY(1938); CHRISTMAS CAROL, A(1938); GIRL OF THE GOLDEN WEST, THE(1938); SHADOWS OVER SHANGHAI(1938); YOUNG IN HEART, THE(1938); LET FREEDOM RING(1939); WE ARE NOT ALONE(1939); EARL OF CHICAGO, THE(1940); LONG VOYAGE HOME, THE(1940); REBECCA(1940); TIN PAN ALLEY(1940); CONFIRM OR DENY(1941); DR. JEKYLL AND MR. HYDE(1941); ONE NIGHT IN LISBON(1941); PENNY SERENADE(1941); SCOTLAND YARD(1941); SHINING VICTORY(1941); SUSPICION(1941); COUNTER-ESPIONAGE(1942); I MARRIED A WITCH(1942); LONDON BLACKOUT MURDERS(1942); MAN WHO WOULDN'T DIE, THE(1942); MRS. MINIVER(1942); THIS ABOVE ALL(1942); YANK AT ETON, A(1942); FOREVER AND A DAY(1943); YOUNG AND WILLING(1943); INVISIBLE MAN'S REVENGE(1944); JANE EYRE(1944); LODGER, THE(1944); NATIONAL VELVET(1944); ONCE UPON A TIME(1944); PEARL OF DEATH, THE(1944); RETURN OF THE VAMPIRE, THE(1944); SOUTH OF DIXIE(1944); PICTURE OF DORIAN GRAY, THE(1945); WOMAN IN GREEN, THE(1945); CLUNY BROWN(1946); DEVOTION(1946); TERROR BY NIGHT(1946); LOVE FROM A STRANGER(1947); MOSS ROSE(1947); LET'S LIVE A LITTLE(1948); SECRET GARDEN, THE(1949); SECRET OF ST. IVES, THE(1949); THAT FORSYTE WOMAN(1949)
Misc. Talkies
TEMPTATION(1930)
Silents
SMALL TOWN IDOL, A(1921); EXTRA GIRL, THE(1923); EASY PICKINGS(1927); RILEY THE COP(1928)
Cecil Bevan
KING OF THE CASTLE(1936, Brit.); ELDER BROTHER, THE(1937, Brit.); GAIETY GIRLS, THE(1938, Brit.); TWILIGHT HOUR(1944, Brit.); WALTZ TIME(1946, Brit.); BLIND GODDESS, THE(1948, Brit.); ONCE UPON A DREAM(1949, Brit.); WINSLOW BOY, THE(1950); RELUCTANT WIDOW, THE(1951, Brit.)
Silents
OLD CURIOSITY SHOP, THE(1921, Brit.)

David Bevan
CARAVAN TO VACCARES(1974, Brit./Fr), ph
Donald Bevan
STALAG 17(1953), w
Faith Bevan
Misc. Silents
MONEY(1921); RIVER OF STARS, THE(1921, Brit.)
Isla Bevan
FACE AT THE WINDOW, THE(1932, Brit.); NINE TILL SIX(1932, Brit.); SIGN OF FOUR, THE(1932, Brit.); WORLD, THE FLESH, AND THE DEVIL, THE(1932, Brit.); WOLVES OF THE UNDERWORLD(1935, Brit.); FAIR EXCHANGE(1936, Brit.)
Pamela Bevan
DARBY AND JOAN(1937, Brit.); SABOTAGE(1937, Brit.); YOUNG AND IN-NOCENT(1938, Brit.); TWO SMART MEN(1940, Brit.)
Stewart Bevan
TO SIR, WITH LOVE(1967, Brit.); BRANNIGAN(1975, Brit.); GHOUL, THE(1975, Brit.)
William [Billy] Bevan
SWORDSMAN, THE(1947); ROGUES OF SHERWOOD FOREST(1950)
William Bevan
IT HAD TO BE YOU(1947); TELL IT TO THE JUDGE(1949); FORTUNES OF CAPTAIN BLOOD(1950)
Alexander Bevani
PHANTOM OF THE OPERA, THE(1929)
Silents
PHANTOM OF THE OPERA, THE(1925)
Clem Bevans
SERGEANT YORK(; WAY DOWN EAST(1935); COME AND GET IT(1936); RHYTHM ON THE RANGE(1936); BIG CITY(1937); IDOL OF THE CROWDS(1937); RIDING ON AIR(1937); TOAST OF NEW YORK, THE(1937); COMET OVER BROADWAY(1938); MR. CHUMP(1938); OF HUMAN HEARTS(1938); YOUNG FUGITIVES(1938); AM-BUSH(1939); COWBOY QUARTERBACK(1939); DODGE CITY(1939); HELL'S KITCH-EN(1939); IDIOT'S DELIGHT(1939); KID FROM KOKOMO, THE(1939); KING OF THE UNDERWORLD(1939); MAIN STREET LAWYER(1939); NIGHT WORK(1939); OK-LAHOMA KID, THE(1939); STAND UP AND FIGHT(1939); THEY MADE ME A CRIMINAL(1939); THUNDER AFLOAT(1939); TOM SAWYER, DETECTIVE(1939); ZENOBIA(1939); ABE LINCOLN IN ILLINOIS(1940); CALLING ALL HUS-BANDS(1940); CAPTAIN IS A LADY, THE(1940); GIRL FROM GOD'S COUN-TRY(1940); GO WEST(1940); GOLD RUSH MAISIE(1940); GRANNY GET YOUR GUN(1940); HALF A SINNER(1940); TWENTY MULE TEAM(1940); UNTAMED(1940); WYOMING(1940); YOUNG TOM EDISON(1940); MIDNIGHT ANGEL(1941); PARSON OF PANAMINT, THE(1941); SHE COULDN'T SAY NO(1941); SMILING GHOST, THE(1941); CAPTAINS OF THE CLOUDS(1942); FOREST RANGERS, THE(1942); LADY BODYGUARD(1942); LUCKY JORDAN(1942); MRS. WIGGS OF THE CAB-BAGE PATCH(1942); SABOTEUR(1942); THIS GUN FOR HIRE(1942); TOMBSTONE, THE TOWN TOO TOUGH TO DIE(1942); HAPPY GO LUCKY(1943); HUMAN COME-DY, THE(1943); KANSAN, THE(1943); WOMAN OF THE TOWN, THE(1943); NIGHT CLUB GIRL(1944); TALL IN THE SADDLE(1944); CAPTAIN EDDIE(1945); GRISSLY'S MILLIONS(1945); GALLANT BESS(1946); WAKE UP AND DREAM(1946); YEAR-LING, THE(1946); MILLERSON CASE, THE(1947); MOURNING BECOMES ELEC-TRA(1947); YANKEE FAKIR(1947); HIGHWAY 13(1948); LOADED PISTOLS(1948); MOONRISE(1948); PALEFACE, THE(1948); RELENTLESS(1948); TEXAS, BROOK-LYN AND HEAVEN(1948); BIG JACK(1949); DEPUTY MARSHAL(1949); GAL WHO TOOK THE WEST, THE(1949); PORTRAIT OF JENNIE(1949); RIM OF THE CA-NYON(1949); STREETS OF LAREDO(1949); TELL IT TO THE JUDGE(1949); HAR-VEY(1950); JOE PALOOKA MEETS HUMPHREY(1950); MAN IN THE SADDLE(1951); SILVER CITY BONANZA(1951); CAPTIVE OF BILLY THE KID(1952); HANGMAN'S KNOT(1952); STRANGER WORE A GUN, THE(1953); BOY FROM OKLAHOMA, THE(1954); KENTUCKIAN, THE(1955); TEN WANTED MEN(1955); TWINKLE IN GOD'S EYE, THE(1955); DAVY CROCKETT AND THE RIVER PI-RATES(1956)
Philippa Bevans
NOTORIOUS LANDLADY, THE(1962); GROUP, THE(1966); MADIGAN(1968)
Carol Bevar
WAITRESS(1982)
Stewart Beven
CONFESSIONAL, THE(1977, Brit.)
Bever
BACK STREETS OF PARIS(1962, Fr.)
Georges Bever
GATES OF PARIS(1958, Fr./Ital.); HELLO–GOODBYE(1970)
Hortense Beveridge
HONEYBABY, HONEYBABY(1974), ed
Phyllis Beveridge
Misc. Silents
TRIUMPH OF VENUS, THE(1918)
Stewart H. Beveridge
JOE PANTHER(1976), p
Guido Beverini
VOICE IN YOUR HEART, A(1952, Ital.), titles
Helen Beverley
GREEN FIELDS(1937); CHARLIE CHAN IN BLACK MAGIC(1944)
Joan Beverley
Silents
AT THE VILLA ROSE(1920, Brit.)
Trazana Beverley
RESURRECTION(1980)
The Beverley Sisters
MAN OF THE MOMENT(1955, Brit.)
Beverly
DUSTY AND SWEETS McGEE(1971)
Eddie Beverly, Jr.
Misc. Talkies
MODERN DAY HOUDINI(1983), d
Helen Beverly
OVERTURE TO GLORY(1940); MASTER RACE, THE(1944); ROBE, THE(1953); PLAYGIRL(1954)
Misc. Talkies
DOBBIN, THE(1939); STAIRWAY FOR A STAR(1947)

James Steven Beverly
SECOND-HAND HEARTS(1981)
John Beverly
NORTH STAR, THE(1943); PARIS AFTER DARK(1943)
Sharon Beverly
GUESS WHAT HAPPENED TO COUNT DRACULA(1970)
Beverly Hillbillies
MEET THE BOY FRIEND(1937)
The Beverly Hillbillies
ROLLIN' PLAINS(1938)
Alberto Bevilacqua
BLACK SABBATH(1963, Ital.), w; EYE OF THE NEEDLE, THE(1965, Ital./Fr.), w; PLANET OF THE VAMPIRES(1965, U.S./Ital./Span.), w
Amerigo Bevilacqua
GOSPEL ACCORDING TO ST. MATTHEW, THE(1966, Fr., Ital.)
Angelo Bevilacqua
MASOCH(1980, Ital.), ph
M. Bevilacqua
MAN COULD GET KILLED, A(1966)
Marcella Bevilacqua
LOVE PROBLEMS(1970, Ital.), ed
Umberto Bevilacqua
ACCATTONE!(1961, Ital.); HAWKS AND THE SPARROWS, THE(1967, Ital.)
Ettore Bevilaqua
SWINDLE, THE(1962, Fr./Ital.)
Victor Bevine
SEPARATE PEACE, A(1972)
Nancy Bevington
Silents
REBECCA THE JEWESS(1913, Brit.)
Misc. Silents
SINS OF YOUTH, THE(1919, Brit.)
Frank Bevis
SCARLET WEB, THE(1954, Brit.), p; NARROWING CIRCLE, THE(1956, Brit.), p; SECRET TENT, THE(1956, Brit.), p; WEAPON, THE(1957, Brit.), p; DEATH OVER MY SHOULDER(1958, Brit.), p; LIMBO LINE, THE(1969, Brit.), p
Rodney Bewes
PRIZE OF ARMS, A(1962, Brit.); BILLY LIAR(1963, Brit.); SAN FERRY ANN(1965, Brit.); DECLINE AND FALL... OF A BIRD WATCHER(1969, Brit.); SPRING AND PORT WINE(1970, Brit.); THREE MUSKETEERS, THE(1974, Panama); LIKELY LADS, THE(1976, Brit.); JABBERWOCKY(1977, Brit.); SAINT JACK(1979); UNIDENTIFIED FLYING ODDBALL, THE(1979, Brit.); WILDCATS OF ST. TRINIAN'S, THE(1980, Brit.)
Charles Bewley
SILVER CHALICE, THE(1954)
Don Bexley
SPARKLE(1976); LITTLE MISS MARKER(1980)
Donald T. Bexley
WHAT'S UP, DOC?(1972)
Ahmed Bey
STREET FIGHTER(1959)
Erik Bey
MONTE CARLO(1930)
Marki Bey
LANDLORD, THE(1970); ROOMMATES, THE(1973); HANGUP(1974); SUGAR HILL(1974)
Misc. Talkies
CLASS OF '74(1972)
Rouhia Bey
TEMPTATION(1946)
Tema Bey
TWELVE TO THE MOON(1960)
Turhan Bey
BURMA CONVOY(1941); FOOTSTEPS IN THE DARK(1941); GAY FALCON, THE(1941); RAIDERS OF THE DESERT(1941); SHADOWS ON THE STAIRS(1941); ARABIAN NIGHTS(1942); BOMBAY CLIPPER(1942); DANGER IN THE PACI-FIC(1942); DESTINATION UNKNOWN(1942); DRUMS OF THE CONGO(1942); FAL-CON TAKES OVER, THE(1942); MUMMY'S TOMB, THE(1942); UNSEEN ENEMY(1942); BACKGROUND TO DANGER(1943); MAD GHOUL, THE(1943); WHITE SAVAGE(1943); ALI BABA AND THE FORTY THIEVES(1944); BOWERY TO BROADWAY(1944); CLIMAX, THE(1944); DRAGON SEED(1944); FOLLOW THE BOYS(1944); FRISCO SAL(1945); SUDAN(1945); NIGHT IN PARADISE, A(1946); OUT OF THE BLUE(1947); ADVENTURES OF CASANOVA(1948); SPIRITUALIST, THE(1948); PAROLE, INC.(1949); SONG OF INDIA(1949); PRISONERS OF THE CASBAH(1953); STOLEN IDENTITY(1953), p
Kent Beyda
SATURDAY THE 14TH(1981), ed; GET CRAZY(1983), ed
1984
THIS IS SPINAL TAP(1984), ed
Louis Beydts
CARNIVAL IN FLANDERS(1936, Fr.), m; COURIER OF LYONS(1938, Fr.), m; COLONEL CHABERT(1947, Fr.), m
Dr. Henry K. Beye
TAHITIAN, THE(1956)
Charles Beyer
Silents
YOUTH FOR SALE(1924); PACE THAT THRILLS, THE(1925); UNGUARDED HOUR, THE(1925); SO'S YOUR OLD MAN(1926)
Misc. Silents
LOST IN A BIG CITY(1923)
Ed Beyer
ALAMBRISTA!(1977), ed
Edward Beyer
LIES MY FATHER TOLD ME(1975, Can.), ed; SHORT EYES(1977), ed; RICH KIDS(1979), ed; ONE-TRICK PONY(1980), ed
Frank Beyer
NAKED AMONG THE WOLVES(1967, Ger.), d

Harold A. Beyer
PICNIC(1955)
J. W. Beyer
ELUSIVE CORPORAL, THE(1963, Fr.), p
J.W. Beyer
TRIAL, THE(1948, Aust.), p
Jim Beyer
TOY, THE(1982)
Ted Beyer
GAMEKEEPER, THE(1980, Brit.); LOOKS AND SMILES(1982, Brit.)
Tot Beyer
TOY, THE(1982)
Bert Beyers
OPERATION PETTICOAT(1959)
Bobby Beyers
SUN COMES UP, THE(1949)
Clara Beyers
Misc. Silents
MIGNON(1915); BLACK BAG, THE(1922)
Robert Beyers
EGG AND I, THE(1947)
C.F. Beyers-Boshoff
KILL OR BE KILLED(1980), w
Christoph Beyertt
1984
LOVE IN GERMANY, A(1984, Fr./Ger.)
Alex Beyfuss
Misc. Silents
MIGNON(1915), d
Alex E. Beyfuss
Silents
SALOMY JANE(1914), d
Thomas Beyl
ENEMY BELOW, THE(1957)
Jean Beylieu
LIVE FOR LIFE(1967, Fr./Ital.), spec eff
Dick [Richard] Beymer
JOHNNY TREMAIN(1957)
Richard Beymer
SO BIG(1953); INDISCRETION OF AN AMERICAN WIFE(1954, U.S./Ital.); DIARY OF ANNE FRANK, THE(1959); HIGH TIME(1960); WEST SIDE STORY(1961); ADVENTURES OF A YOUNG MAN(1962); BACHELOR FLAT(1962); FIVE FINGER EXERCISE(1962); LONGEST DAY, THE(1962); STRIPPER, THE(1963); FREE GRASS(1969); INNERVIEW, THE(1974), a, p,d,w,ph,&ed; CROSS COUNTRY(1983, Can.)
Richard Beynon
RUNAWAY BUS, THE(1954, Brit.)
Bolot Beyshenaliyev
RED AND THE WHITE, THE(1969, Hung./USSR)
Bibisara Beyshenaliyeva
MORNING STAR(1962, USSR)
Mike Beytagh
SMASH PALACE(1982, New Zealand)
Gustavo Beytelman
MAFIA, THE(1972, Arg.), m
Christine Beytout
1984
ONE DEADLY SUMMER(1984, Fr.), p
Gerard Beytout
GENDARME OF ST. TROPEZ, THE(1966, Fr./Ital.), p; LAST ADVENTURE, THE(1968, Fr./Ital.), p; ZITA(1968, Fr.), p
Josef Beyvl
DEATH OF TARZAN, THE(1968, Czech)
Khalil Bezaleel
IN THE HEAT OF THE NIGHT(1967); WHO'S MINDING THE MINT?(1967); MELINDA(1972)
Jacques Bezard
JOY HOUSE(1964, Fr.); CHECKERBOARD(1969, Fr.)
Peter Bezbaz
EDGE OF HELL(1956)
Mary Bezemes
DARK HORSE, THE(1946)
Peter Bezencenet
CONQUEST OF THE AIR(1940), w, ed; DISOBEDIENT(1953, Brit.), ed; WEST OF ZANZIBAR(1954, Brit.), ed; DIVIDED HEART, THE(1955, Brit.), ed; SQUARE RING, THE(1955, Brit.), ed; GENTLE TOUCH, THE(1956, Brit.), ed; SHIP THAT DIED OF SHAME, THE(1956, Brit.), ed; DANGEROUS EXILE(1958, Brit.), ed; FLOODS OF FEAR(1958, Brit.), ed; ROONEY(1958, Brit.), ed; SECRET PLACE, THE(1958, Brit.), ed; BOY WHO STOLE A MILLION, THE(1960, Brit.), ed; SIEGE OF SIDNEY STREET, THE(1960, Brit.), ed; TOMMY THE TOREADOR(1960, Brit.), ed; BOMB IN THE HIGH STREET(1961, Brit.), d; JUNGLE STREET GIRLS(1963, Brit.), ed; CITY OF FEAR(1965, Brit.), d; 24 HOURS TO KILL(1966, Brit.), d
Zoltan Bezeredi
CONFIDENCE(1980, Hung.)
Fred Bezerril
Misc. Silents
LONELY TRAIL, THE(1922)
Boris Bezgin
COUNTRY BRIDE(1938, USSR)
Danilo Bezlay
ISLE OF SIN(1963, Ger.)
Zdenek Bezusek
INTIMATE LIGHTING(1969, Czech.)
Igor Bezyayev
MUMU(1961, USSR)
A. I. Bezzerides
KISS ME DEADLY(1955), w

A.I. Bezzerides
THEY DRIVE BY NIGHT(1940), w; JUKE GIRL(1942), w; THIEVES' HIGHWAY(1949), w; ON DANGEROUS GROUND(1951), a, w; SIROCCO(1951), w; HOLIDAY FOR SINNERS(1952), w; BENEATH THE 12-MILE REEF(1953), w; TRACK OF THE CAT(1954), w; BULLET FOR JOEY, A(1955), w; ANGRY HILLS, THE(1959, Brit.), w; JAYHAWKERS, THE(1959), w
Jaya Bhaduri
BIG CITY, THE(1963, India)
P. Bhalchander
TIGER AND THE FLAME, THE(1955, India), ed
Bhanu
SIDDHARTHA(1972), cos
Bhaskar
I DRINK YOUR BLOOD(1971)
Jugat Bhatia
RAINS OF RANCHIPUR, THE(1955)
Vanraj Bhatia
1984
MOHAN JOSHI HAAZIR HO(1984, India), m
Shukla Bhattercharjee
PRIVATE ENTERPRISE, A(1975, Brit.)
Sophie Bhaud
LE VIOL(1968, Fr./Swed.), ed; BOLERO(1982, Fr.), ed
Souare Bhime
LIKE A TURTLE ON ITS BACK(1981, Fr.)
Sudha Bhuchar
1984
MAJDHAR(1984, Brit.)
Franz Bi
HOUSE OF LIFE(1953, Ger.), set d; COW AND I, THE(1961, Fr., Ital., Ger.), art d; RESTLESS NIGHT, THE(1964, Ger.), set d; UNWILLING AGENT(1968, Ger.), art d
Ambroise Bia
PASSENGER, THE(1975, Ital.)
Edward Biaganti
LADY ICE(1973)
Edy Biagetti
EAGLE OVER LONDON(1973, Ital.)
Giuliano Biagetti
LOVE PROBLEMS(1970, Ital.), d, w
Paolo Biagetti
VOYAGE, THE(1974, Ital.), art d
E. Biagi
ANITA GARIBALDI(1954, Ital.), w
Nina Biagio
MISSION TO MOSCOW(1943)
Betty Bialis
TWO SISTERS(1938)
Rosetta Bialis
Misc. Talkies
AMERICAN MATCHMAKER(1940); DOBBIN, THE(1939)
Elisa Bialk
SAINTED SISTERS, THE(1948), w
Tadeusz Bialoszczynski
KNIGHTS OF THE TEUTONIC ORDER, THE(1962, Pol.); YELLOW SLIPPERS, THE(1965, Pol.); YOUNG GIRLS OF WILKO, THE(1979, Pol./Fr.)
Ermanno Biamonte
YETI(1977, Ital.), spec eff; HUMANOID, THE(1979, Ital.), spec eff
Suzanne Bianchetti
Silents
NAPOLEON(1927, Fr.)
Misc. Silents
VIOLETTES IMPERIALES(1924, Fr.); CASANOVA(1927, Fr.)
Adelchi Bianchi
LOST SOULS(1961, Ital.), d&w
Christian Bianchi
1984
LES COMPERES(1984, Fr.)
Daniela Bianchi
FROM RUSSIA WITH LOVE(1963, Brit.); SWORD OF EL CID, THE(1965, Span./Ital.); REQUIEM FOR A SECRET AGENT(1966, Ital.); OPERATION KID BROTHER(1967, Ital.); WEEKEND, ITALIAN STYLE(1967, Fr./Ital./Span.); DIRTY HEROES(1971, Ital./Fr./Ger.)
Edward Bianchi
FAN, THE(1981), d
Eleanora Bianchi
GOLIATH AND THE SINS OF BABYLON(1964, Ital.)
Erik Bianchi
MISSION BLOODY MARY(1967, Fr./Ital./Span.)
Giorgio Bianchi
MORALIST, THE(1964, Ital.), d; CLIMAX, THE(1967, Fr., Ital.)
Guillermo Alvarez Bianchi
LITTLE RED RIDING HOOD(1963, Mex.); LITTLE RED RIDING HOOD AND HER FRIENDS(1964, Mex.); LIVING COFFIN, THE(1965, Mex.); EXTERMINATING ANGEL, THE(1967, Mex.)
Guillermo Bianchi
VILLA!(1958)
Nadia Bianchi
GIRL WITH A SUITCASE(1961, Fr./Ital.)
R. Bianchi
CARNIVAL(1953, Fr.), ed
Regina Bianchi
FOUR DAYS OF NAPLES, THE(1963, US/Ital.); SHOOT LOUD, LOUDER... I DON'T UNDERSTAND(1966, Ital.)
Richard Bianchi
PUZZLE OF A DOWNFALL CHILD(1970), art d; LADY LIBERTY(1972, Ital./Fr.), art d; VOICES(1979), art d
Tino Bianchi
BLACK SUNDAY(1961, Ital.); SPY IN YOUR EYE(1966, Ital.); SENSO(1968, Ital.)

Alfred Bianchini
TAMING OF THE SHREW, THE(1967, U.S./Ital.)
Alfredo Bianchini
WHITE VOICES(1965, Fr./Ital.); MAIDEN FOR A PRINCE, A(1967, Fr./Ital.)
Paolo Bianchini
GRAND SLAM(1968, Ital., Span., Ger.), w
Misc. Talkies
OUR MEN IN BAGHDAD(1967, Ital.), d
Biancini
UGLY ONES, THE(1968, Ital./Span.), w
Larry Bianco
FIDDLER ON THE ROOF(1971)
Marco Bianco
1984
POLICE ACADEMY(1984)
Peggy Lou Bianco
WHY GIRLS LEAVE HOME(1945)
Sally V. Bianco
BANDIDOS(1967, Ital.), p
Solly Bianco
BUFFALO BILL, HERO OF THE FAR WEST(1962, Ital.), p
Solly V. Bianco
SANDOKAN THE GREAT(1964, Fr./Ital./Span.), p
Tomas Bianco
HOUSE THAT SCREAMED, THE(1970, Span.)
Tony Lo Bianco
F.I.S.T.(1978)
O. Biancoli
ATLAS AGAINST THE CYCLOPS(1963, Ital.), w
Oreste Biancoli
BALL AT THE CASTLE(1939, Ital.), w; DISILLUSION(1949, Ital.), w; HEART AND SOUL(1950, Ital.), w; CENTO ANNI D'AMORE(1954, Ital.), w; GRAN VARIETA(1955, Ital.), w; MARCO POLO(1962, Fr./Ital.), w; SON OF SAMSON(1962, Fr./Ital./Yugo.), w; STORY OF JOSEPH AND HIS BRETHREN THE(1962, Ital.), w; ERIK THE CONQUEROR(1963, Fr./Ital.), w; SAMSON AND THE SEVEN MIRACLES OF THE WORLD(1963, Fr./Ital.), w; WITCH'S CURSE, THE(1963, Ital.), w; LOVE, THE ITALIAN WAY(1964, Ital.), w; MORALIST, THE(1964, Ital.), w; LOVE AND MARRIAGE(1966, Ital.), w
O. Biancolo
PONTIUS PILATE(1967, Fr./Ital.), w
Harry Biard
HAPPY DEATHDAY(1969, Brit.)
Jade Biarese
MOON IN THE GUTTER, THE(1983, Fr./Ital.)
Bridget Biargi
1984
GREYSTOKE: THE LEGEND OF TARZAN, LORD OF THE APES(1984)
Michael Bias
LITTLE SEX, A(1982)
Ricardo Biasco
NO TIME FOR ECSTASY(1963, Fr.), m
Alessandro Biasetti
ADVENTURE OF SALVATOR ROSA, AN(1940, Ital.), m
Zeudi Biasolo
ARABIAN NIGHTS(1980, Ital./Fr.)
Bruno Biassibetti
WHITE SISTER(1973, Ital./Span./Fr.)
Claudio Biava
LA VIACCIA(1962, Fr./Ital.); MACHINE GUN McCAIN(1970, Ital.)
F. Biazhevich
VOW, THE(1947, USSR.)
Robert Bibal
DOUBLE CRIME IN THE MAGINOT LINE(1939, Fr.), w
Bibas
I'LL NEVER FORGET WHAT'S 'IS NAME(1967, Brit.), cos
Leon Bibb
STAGE STRUCK(1958); FOR LOVE OF IVY(1968); UPTIGHT(1968); LOST MAN, THE(1969)
Otto Bibber
Misc. Silents
RIDIN' DEMON, THE(1929)
Ann Bibby
TRUE AND THE FALSE, THE(1955, Swed.)
Edward Bibby
ONE RAINY AFTERNOON(1936)
Gertrude Bibby
LIVE AGAIN(1936, Brit.)
Ken Bibeau
WRONG IS RIGHT(1982)
Wilda Biber
WOMAN OF DISTINCTION, A(1950)
Prof. L. Biberavich
COSSACKS IN EXILE(1939, Ukrainian), tech adv
Abner Biberman
ANOTHER THIN MAN(1939); BALALAIKA(1939); EACH DAWN I DIE(1939); GUNGA DIN(1939); MAGNIFICENT FRAUD, THE(1939); PANAMA LADY(1939); PANAMA PATROL(1939); RAINS CAME, THE(1939); ROARING TWENTIES, THE(1939); ENEMY AGENT(1940); GIRL FROM HAVANA(1940); HIS GIRL FRIDAY(1940); SOUTH OF PAGO PAGO(1940); SOUTH TO KARANGA(1940); ZANZIBAR(1940); DEVIL PAYS OFF, THE(1941); GAY VAGABOND, THE(1941); MONSTER AND THE GIRL, THE(1941); SINGAPORE WOMAN(1941); SOUTH OF TAHITI(1941); THIS WOMAN IS MINE(1941); BEYOND THE BLUE HORIZON(1942); BROADWAY(1942); LITTLE TOKYO, U.S.A.(1942); WHISPERING GHOSTS(1942); BEHIND THE RISING SUN(1943); BOMBARDIER(1943); LEOPARD MAN, THE(1943); SUBMARINE ALERT(1943); BRIDGE OF SAN LUIS REY, THE(1944); DRAGON SEED(1944); KEYS OF THE KINGDOM, THE(1944); TWO-MAN SUBMARINE(1944); BACK TO BATAAN(1945); BETRAYAL FROM THE EAST(1945); CAPTAIN KIDD(1945); SALOME, WHERE SHE DANCED(1945); STRANGE CONQUEST(1946); WINCHESTER '73(1950); ROARING CITY(1951); VIVA ZAPATA!(1952); ELEPHANT WALK(1954); GOLDEN MISTRESS, THE(1954); KNOCK ON WOOD(1954); LOOTERS, THE(1955), d; RUN-

NING WILD(1955), d; BEHIND THE HIGH WALL(1956), d; PRICE OF FEAR, THE(1956), d; GUN FOR A COWARD(1957), d; NIGHT RUNNER, THE(1957), d; FLOOD TIDE(1958), d; TOO MANY THIEVES(1968), d
Herbert Biberman
ONE-WAY TICKET(1935), d; MEET NERO WOLFE(1936), d; KING OF CHINATOWN(1939), w; ACTION IN ARABIA(1944), w; TOGETHER AGAIN(1944), w
Herbert J. Biberman
MASTER RACE, THE(1944), d; SALT OF THE EARTH(1954), d; SLAVES(1969), d, w
J. Biberman
NEW ORLEANS(1947), w
Michael Wilson Biberman
SALT OF THE EARTH(1954), w
Sonja Dahl Biberman
SALT OF THE EARTH(1954), p
Leopold Biberti
LAST CHANCE, THE(1945, Switz.); FOUR DAYS LEAVE(1950, Switz.); SINS OF ROSE BERND, THE(1959, Ger.)
A. Bibikoff
Misc. Silents
SNOW MAIDEN, THE(1914, USSR)
Maria Bibikoff
GIRL ON THE BRIDGE, THE(1951); STRANGE FASCINATION(1952)
A. Bibikov
Misc. Silents
CHILD OF THE BIG CITY(1914, USSR); RUSLAN I LUDMILA(1915, USSR)
Maria Bibikov
DAYS OF GLORY(1944)
Walter Bibo
GARDEN OF EDEN(1954), p; UNTOUCHED(1956), p
Ed Biby
SECRETS OF SCOTLAND YARD(1944); NIGHT AND DAY(1946); JOAN OF ARC(1948)
Edward Biby
STRANGE WOMAN, THE(1946); DEAR WIFE(1949)
Bob [Robert] Bice
SPACE MASTER X-7(1958)
Bob Bice
HE WALKED BY NIGHT(1948); HOLLOW TRIUMPH(1948); RACKET, THE(1951); GOOD DAY FOR A HANGING(1958)
Hi Bice
1984
LAST NIGHT AT THE ALAMO(1984)
Robert Bice
FIGHTING VALLEY(1943); GANGWAY FOR TOMORROW(1943); GHOST AND THE GUEST(1943); GHOST SHIP, THE(1943); IRON MAJOR, THE(1943); DRAGON SEED(1944); THIRTY SECONDS OVER TOKYO(1944); MYSTERIOUS MR. VALENTINE, THE(1946); RED STALLION, THE(1947); SEA OF GRASS, THE(1947); ASSIGNED TO DANGER(1948); CANON CITY(1948); IN THIS CORNER(1948); JOAN OF ARC(1948); BANDIT KING OF TEXAS(1949); SUSANNA PASS(1949); THIEVES' HIGHWAY(1949); TOO LATE FOR TEARS(1949); BELLS OF CORONADO(1950); BUNCO SQUAD(1950); JACKPOT, THE(1950); UNDER MEXICALI STARS(1950); AL JENNINGS OF OKLAHOMA(1951); GUNPLAY(1951); MILLIONAIRE FOR CHRISTY, A(1951); TALES OF ROBIN HOOD(1951); CAPTAIN PIRATE(1952); CAPTIVE WOMEN(1952); CRIPPLE CREEK(1952); DESERT PURSUIT(1952); HIAWATHA(1952); HORIZONS WEST(1952); INVASION U.S.A.(1952); JUNCTION CITY(1952); LOAN SHARK(1952); NIGHT STAGE TO GALVESTON(1952); RED SNOW(1952); BANDITS OF THE WEST(1953); MARKSMAN, THE(1953); MOONLIGHTER, THE(1953); ON TOP OF OLD SMOKY(1953); PARIS MODEL(1953); PORT SINISTER(1953); STAR OF TEXAS(1953); TARZAN AND THE SHE-DEVIL(1953); WILD ONE, THE(1953); ADVENTURES OF HAJJI BABA(1954); JOHNNY DARK(1954); SNOW CREATURE, THE,(1954); STEEL CAGE, THE(1954); BIG BLUFF, THE(1955); BOWERY TO BAGDAD(1955); DIAL RED O(1955); FAR COUNTRY, THE(1955); FOXFIRE(1955); GANG BUSTERS(1955); GUN THAT WON THE WEST, THE(1955); TEEN-AGE CRIME WAVE(1955); THREE FOR THE SHOW(1955); TRIAL(1955); VIOLENT MEN, THE(1955); TEN COMMANDMENTS, THE(1956); JAILHOUSE ROCK(1957); DIAMOND SAFARI(1958); IT! THE TERROR FROM BEYOND SPACE(1958)
Marcelle Bichette
Misc. Talkies
MISS LESLIE'S DOLLS(1972)
Bruno Bichir
UNDER FIRE(1983)
Stan Bichman
HIGH SCHOOL BIG SHOT(1959), p
Jerry Bick
LONG GOODBYE, THE(1973), p; THIEVES LIKE US(1974), p; RUSSIAN ROULETTE(1975), p
1984
SWING SHIFT(1984), p
Aaron Bickel
Misc. Silents
POLITICIANS, THE(1915)
George Bickel
MAYBE IT'S LOVE(1930); RECAPTURED LOVE(1930); SOUP TO NUTS(1930); ONE HEAVENLY NIGHT(1931); BROKEN LULLABY(1932); DANCERS IN THE DARK(1932)
Silents
KEEP MOVING(1915)
Misc. Silents
HELLO BILL!(1915)
Mary Bickel
45 FATHERS(1937), w
Ray Bickel
VILLAIN, THE(1979); HUNTER, THE(1980)
Derek Bickerton
PAYROLL(1962, Brit.), w
F. H. Bickerton
MUTINY OF THE ELSINORE, THE(1939, Brit.), ed; LITTLE MISS MOLLY(1940), ed

F.H. Bickerton
HAPPY DAYS ARE HERE AGAIN(1936, Brit.), w
Richard Bickerton
GREAT BRAIN, THE(1978), p
Hugh Bickett
JOHN HALIFAX–GENTLEMAN(1938, Brit.)
Allen Bickford
IT TAKES ALL KINDS(1969, U.S./Aus.); NED KELLY(1970, Brit.); KILLING OF ANGEL STREET, THE(1983, Aus.)
Charles Bickford
YOU CAN'T RUN AWAY FROM IT(1956); SOUTH SEA ROSE(1929); ANNA CHRISTIE(1930); DYNAMITE(1930); HELL'S HEROES(1930); PASSION FLOWER(1930); SEA BAT, THE(1930); EAST OF BORNEO(1931); MEN IN HER LIFE(1931); PAGAN LADY(1931); RIVER'S END(1931); SQUAW MAN, THE(1931); LAST MAN(1932); PANAMA FLO(1932); SCANDAL FOR SALE(1932); THUNDER BELOW(1932); VANITY STREET(1932); NO OTHER WOMAN(1933); SONG OF THE EAGLE(1933); THIS DAY AND AGE(1933); WHITE WOMAN(1933); LITTLE MISS MARKER(1934); WICKED WOMAN, A(1934); EAST OF JAVA(1935); FARMER TAKES A WIFE, THE(1935); NOTORIOUS GENTLEMAN, A(1935); UNDER PRESSURE(1935); PRIDE OF THE MARINES(1936); RED WAGON(1936); ROSE OF THE RANCHO(1936); DAUGHTER OF SHANGHAI(1937); HIGH, WIDE AND HANDSOME(1937); NIGHT CLUB SCANDAL(1937); PLAINSMAN, THE(1937); THUNDER TRAIL(1937); GANGS OF NEW YORK(1938); STORM, THE(1938); VALLEY OF THE GIANTS(1938); MUTINY IN THE BIG HOUSE(1939); OF MICE AND MEN(1939); ONE HOUR TO LIVE(1939); OUR LEADING CITIZEN(1939); ROMANCE OF THE REDWOODS(1939); STAND UP AND FIGHT(1939); STREET OF MISSING MEN(1939); THOU SHALT NOT KILL(1939); GIRL FROM GOD'S COUNTRY(1940); QUEEN OF THE YUKON(1940); SOUTH TO KARANGA(1940); BURMA CONVOY(1941); REAP THE WILD WIND(1942); TARZAN'S NEW YORK ADVENTURE(1942); MR. LUCKY(1943); SONG OF BERNADETTE, THE(1943); WING AND A PRAYER(1944); CAPTAIN EDDIE(1945); FALLEN ANGEL(1945); DUEL IN THE SUN(1946); BRUTE FORCE(1947); FARMER'S DAUGHTER, THE(1947); WOMAN ON THE BEACH, THE(1947); BABE RUTH STORY, THE(1948); COMMAND DECISION(1948); FOUR FACES WEST(1948); JOHNNY BELINDA(1948); ROSEANNA McCOY(1949); WHIRLPOOL(1949); GUILTY OF TREASON(1950); RIDING HIGH(1950); BRANDED(1951); ELOPEMENT(1951); JIM THORPE–ALL AMERICAN(1951); RAGING TIDE, THE(1951); LAST POSSE, THE(1953); STAR IS BORN, A(1954); COURT-MARTIAL OF BILLY MITCHELL, THE(1955); NOT AS A STRANGER(1955); PRINCE OF PLAYERS(1955); MISTER CORY(1957); BIG COUNTRY, THE(1958); UNFORGIVEN, THE(1960); DAYS OF WINE AND ROSES(1962); BIG HAND FOR THE LITTLE LADY, A(1966)
John Bickford
BEAST WITH A MILLION EYES, THE(1956), m
Steve Bickford
STAYING ALIVE(1983)
Imogen Bickford-Smith
MONTY PYTHON'S THE MEANING OF LIFE(1983, Brit.)
Jack Bickham
BAKER'S HAWK(1976), w
Jack M. Bickham
APPLE DUMPLING GANG, THE(1975), w; APPLE DUMPLING GANG RIDES AGAIN, THE(1979), w
Tony Bickley
SWIMMER, THE(1968)
William Bickley
HAWMPS!(1976), w
Eugene Bicknell
WARRIORS, THE(1979)
Gene Bicknell
1984
THEY'RE PLAYING WITH FIRE(1984)
Heather Bicknell
HIDE IN PLAIN SIGHT(1980)
Karoly Bicskei
WITNESS, THE(1982, Hung.)
Karoly Bicskey
DIALOGUE(1967, Hung.)
Jan Paulus Biczyzcki
NIGHT CROSSING(1982)
Sidney Biddell
ESCAPE TO GLORY(1940), w; NIGHT PLANE FROM CHUNGKING(1942), w; THRILL OF BRAZIL, THE(1946), p; DEAD RECKONING(1947), p, w
Carl Biddiscombe
GAILY, GAILY(1969), set d; TERROR IN THE WAX MUSEUM(1973), set d
Baldy Biddle
CONDEMNED(1929)
Cordelia Drexel Biddle
HAPPIEST MILLIONAIRE, THE(1967), w
Craig Biddle, Jr.
Silents
THREE WISE FOOLS(1923)
Charles Biddles, Jr.
GAS(1981, Can.)
Earl Biddle
MIGHTY MOUSE IN THE GREAT SPACE CHASE(1983), ed
Francis Biddle
MAGNIFICENT YANKEE, THE(1950), w
Mary Ann Biddle
CONCORDE, THE–AIRPORT '79(, set d; BIG FIX, THE(1978), set d; SOMEWHERE IN TIME(1980), set d; ALL THE RIGHT MOVES(1983), art d
Biddu
STUD, THE(1979, Brit.), md
Jean Luc Bideau
STATE OF SIEGE(1973, Fr./U.S./Ital./Ger.)
Jean-Luc Bideau
INVITATION, THE(1975, Fr./Switz.); JONAH–WHO WILL BE 25 IN THE YEAR 2000(1976, Switz.); SORCERER(1977); ASHANTI(1979)
Ann Biderman
1984
AMERICAN DREAMER(1984), w

Claus Biderstaedt
ETERNAL WALTZ, THE(1959, Ger.)
Harry Bidgood
YOU CAN'T DO WITHOUT LOVE(1946, Brit.), md
Richard Bidlake
PRIZE OF ARMS, A(1962, Brit.); GUNS AT BATASI(1964, Brit.); DARLING(1965, Brit.); ISLAND OF TERROR(1967, Brit.)
Stephanie Bidmead
RUNNING SCARED(1972, Brit.)
Sylvia Bidmead
GENTLE TOUCH, THE(1956, Brit.); MOONRAKER, THE(1958, Brit.)
Henri Bidon
DOC(1971)
Capt. Ray Bidwell
WINGED VICTORY(1944)
Richard Bidwell
1984
SUPERGIRL(1984)
Francis Bieber
GHOST SHIP(1953, Brit.), ed; BANG! YOU'RE DEAD(1954, Brit.), ed; EIGHT O'CLOCK WALK(1954, Brit.), ed
Leo Bieber
TAKE MY LIFE(1948, Brit.); THIRD MAN, THE(1950, Brit.); GREAT MANHUNT, THE(1951, Brit.); QUESTION 7(1961, U.S./Ger.)
Linda Ann Bieber
GOOD MORNING, JUDGE(1943); THIS LAND IS MINE(1943)
Linda Bieber
EAGLE SQUADRON(1942); AMAZING MRS. HOLLIDAY(1943); HIGH BARBAREE(1947)
Nita Bieber
NEWS HOUNDS(1947); LADY WITHOUT PASSPORT, A(1950); SUMMER STOCK(1950); PRINCE WHO WAS A THIEF, THE(1951)
Rodney Bieber
REUNION IN FRANCE(1942)
Wilda Bieber
REUNION IN FRANCE(1942)
Rudolf Biebrach
EMIL AND THE DETECTIVE(1931, Ger.)
Rudolph Biebrach
Misc. Silents
FOOLS OF PASSION(1926, Ger.), d
Julia Biedermann
GERMAN SISTERS, THE(1982, Ger.)
Claus Biederstaedt
VOR SONNENUNTERGANG(1961, Ger); TWO IN A SLEEPING BAG(1964, Ger.)
Leon Biedryski
HAPPY GO LOVELY(1951, Brit.)
Erwin Biegel
DANCING HEART, THE(1959, Ger.)
Genadii Biegouloff
SKYJACKED(1972)
Michael Biehn
COACH(1978); HOG WILD(1980, Can.); FAN, THE(1981); LORDS OF DISCIPLINE, THE(1983)
1984
TERMINATOR, THE(1984)
Dick Biel
1984
SPLATTER UNIVERSITY(1984)
Zygmunt Bielawski
1984
SHIVERS(1984, Pol.)
Vangle Bielby
CAT'S PAW, THE(1934)
Georges Bielec
LONG ABSENCE, THE(1962, Fr./Ital.)
Mara Inken Bielenberg
HANSEL AND GRETEL(1965, Ger.)
Helena Bielicic
TWO OR THREE THINGS I KNOW ABOUT HER(1970, Fr.)
Linda Bielima
BEAST OF YUCCA FLATS, THE(1961)
Marie-Louise Bielke
THIRTEEN FRIGHTENED GIRLS(1963)
Nella Bielski
LES GAULOISES BLEUES(1969, Fr.)
Stanislas Bielski
RAZOR'S EDGE, THE(1946)
Max A. Bienek
MOONWOLF(1966, Fin./Ger.), art d
Virginia Bieneman
1984
TREASURE OF THE YANKEE ZEPHYR(1984), art d
Dagmar Biener
FREDDY UNTER FREMDEN STERNEN(1962, Ger.)
Gerhard Bienert
BLUE ANGEL, THE(1930, Ger.); M(1933, Ger.); TESTAMENT OF DR. MABUSE, THE(1943, Ger.)
Paul Biensfeld
TREMENDOUSLY RICH MAN, A(1932, Ger.)
Paul Biensfeldt
CASE VAN GELDERN(1932, Ger.)
Silents
PASSION(1920, Ger.); ONE ARABIAN NIGHT(1921, Ger.)
Misc. Silents
HARAKIRI(1919, Ger.)
Henri Bienvenu
GREEN ROOM, THE(1979, Fr.)

Mrs. E. Bienvenu
LOUISIANA STORY(1948)
Fred Bier
PERFECT COUPLE, A(1979)
Bill Bierd
TO THE SHORES OF HELL(1966)
Ramon Bieri
GRASSHOPPER, THE(1970); R.P.M.(1970); ANDROMEDA STRAIN, THE(1971); BROTHER JOHN(1971); HONKERS, THE(1972); BADLANDS(1974); SORCERER(1977); FRISCO KID, THE(1979); REDS(1981)
1984
GRANDVIEW, U.S.A.(1984)
Arthur Bierman
HI, MOM!(1970)
Emil Bierman
FIGHTING CARAVANS(1931), m
Wolf Biermann
GERMANY IN AUTUMN(1978, Ger.)
Etienne Bierry
SHAMELESS OLD LADY, THE(1966, Fr.)
Stephane Bierry
1984
LES COMPERES(1984, Fr.)
Edward A. Biery
DAUGHTER OF THE SUN GOD(1962), p; JIGSAW(1968), ed; WINNING(1969), ed; GANG THAT COULDN'T SHOOT STRAIGHT, THE(1971), ed; RED SKY AT MORNING(1971), ed; THEY ONLY KILL THEIR MASTERS(1972), ed; DON IS DEAD, THE(1973), ed; SWASHBUCKLER(1976), ed; ROLLERCOASTER(1977), ed
Edward A. Biery, Jr.
SIX GUN SERENADE(1947), ed; FRIENDLY PERSUASION(1956), ed
Edward Biery
WHEN TIME RAN OUT(1980), ed
Edward Biery, Jr.
YOUNG STRANGER, THE(1957), ed
Jean-Pierre Biesse
MADE IN U.S.A.(1966, Fr.)
John Biezard
ASSIGNMENT K(1968, Brit.), art d
Baby Biffle
PENNY SERENADE(1941)
Big Brother and the Holding Company
PETULIA(1968, U.S./Brit.)
Big Mack and the Truckstoppers
TRUCK STOP WOMEN(1974), m
Big Red the Horse
RED STALLION, THE(1947)
Dolly Big Soldier
HARRY'S WAR(1981)
"Big Ted"
KING OF THE GRIZZLIES(1970)
Claudio Bigagli
NIGHT OF THE SHOOTING STARS, THE(1982, Ital.)
Barney Bigard
NEW ORLEANS(1947); ST. LOUIS BLUES(1958)
Gianpaolo Bigazzi
GODDESS OF LOVE, THE(1960, Ital./Fr.), p; TROJAN HORSE, THE(1962, Fr./Ital.), p; MILL OF THE STONE WOMEN(1963, Fr./Ital.), p; INVASION 1700(1965, Fr./Ital./Yugo.), prod d
North Bigbee
WILDCAT(1942), w
Ben Bigelow
HELL SQUAD(1958)
Bob Bigelow
PARTNERS(1982)
Charles J. Bigelow
UNDER THE BIG TOP(1938), p; GHOST GUNS(1944), p; LAND OF THE OUTLAWS(1944), p; LAW MEN(1944), p; LAW OF THE VALLEY(1944), p; RANGE LAW(1944), p; FRONTIER FEUD(1945), p; LOST TRAIL, THE(1945), p; NAVAJO TRAIL, THE(1945), p
Diane Bigelow
I, MAUREEN(1978, Can.); STONE COLD DEAD(1980, Can.)
Jane Bigelow
ROAR OF THE DRAGON(1932), w
Joe Bigelow
ANNABEL TAKES A TOUR(1938), w; WIDE OPEN FACES(1938), w; HERE WE GO AGAIN(1942), w; TAKE IT BIG(1944), w
Kathryn Bigelow
LOVELESS, THE(1982), d&w; BORN IN FLAMES(1983)
Ven Bigelow
Misc. Talkies
WELCOME HOME, BROTHER CHARLES(1975)
Pietro Bigerna
MONTE CASSINO(1948, Ital.)
Barbara Biggart
ANGEL BABY(1961)
Barbara G. Biggart
RACING FEVER(1964)
Brad Biggart
1984
NIGHT PATROL(1984)
Clarence Bigge
SO EVIL MY LOVE(1948, Brit.)
Allison Bigger
SIX PACK(1982)
Hal Bigger
HOT LEAD AND COLD FEET(1978), spec eff
Michael Bigger
1984
ULTIMATE SOLUTION OF GRACE QUIGLEY, THE(1984), makeup

Earl Derr Biggers
BEHIND THAT CURTAIN(1929), w; INSIDE THE LINES(1930), w; SECOND FLOOR MYSTERY, THE(1930), w; SEVEN KEYS TO BALDPATE(1930), w; BLACK CAMEL, THE(1931), w; MILLIONAIRE, THE(1931), w; CHARLIE CHAN'S CHANCE(1932), w; CHARLIE CHAN'S GREATEST CASE(1933), w; CHARLIE CHAN'S COURAGE(1934), w; TAKE THE STAND(1934), w; SEVEN KEYS TO BALDPATE(1935), w; CHARLIE CHAN'S MURDER CRUISE(1940), w; ONE NIGHT IN THE TROPICS(1940), w; DEAD MEN TELL(1941), w; PASSAGE FROM HONG KONG(1941), w; SCARLET CLUE, THE(1945), w; DANGEROUS MONEY(1946), w; DARK ALIBI(1946), w; SHADOWS OVER CHINATOWN(1946), w; SEVEN KEYS TO BALDPATE(1947), w; THAT WAY WITH WOMEN(1947), w; DOCKS OF NEW ORLEANS(1948), w; HOUSE OF LONG SHADOWS, THE(1983, Brit.), m
Silents
INSIDE THE LINES(1918), w; FIFTY CANDLES(1921), w; RULING PASSION, THE(1922), w; TOO MUCH BUSINESS(1922), w; RECKLESS AGE, THE(1924), w; HONEYMOON FLATS(1928), w
Robert Biggers
GET OUTTA TOWN(1960)
Antoinette Biggerstaff
PRIME OF MISS JEAN BRODIE, THE(1969, Brit.)
Caroline Biggerstaff
1984
SOLDIER'S STORY, A(1984), ed
Bob Biggert
1984
NIGHT PATROL(1984)
Paola Biggio
SEDUCED AND ABANDONED(1964, Fr./Ital.)
Eliot Biggons
CODE OF THE SADDLE(1947), w
Chris Biggs
SCALPS(1983), makeup
Douglas Biggs
HELL'S ANGELS(1930), ed; REVOLT OF THE ZOMBIES(1936), ed; I DEMAND PAYMENT(1938), ed; PURPLE HEART, THE(1944), ed; TWICE BLESSED(1945), ed; SHOW-OFF, THE(1946), ed; TWO SISTERS FROM BOSTON(1946), ed; ON AN ISLAND WITH YOU(1948), ed; GUNPLAY(1951), ed; PISTOL HARVEST(1951), ed
Douglass Biggs
MUSIC FOR MILLIONS(1944), ed; THEY WERE EXPENDABLE(1945), ed
Jerry Biggs
TENDER MERCIES(1982)
Julie Biggs
NOBODY WAVED GOODBYE(1965, Can.)
Mike Biggs
ROCK BABY, ROCK IT(1957)
Morris"Tex" Biggs
1984
SWING SHIFT(1984)
Tex Biggs
9/30/55(1977)
James Bigham
CINDERELLA LIBERTY(1973)
Jack Bighead
TEN WHO DARED(1960); LAST CHALLENGE, THE(1967)
Seth Bigman
TAZA, SON OF COCHISE(1954)
Nino Bignamini
NIGHT PORTER, THE(1974, Ital./U.S.); ALL SCREWED UP(1976, Ital.)
John Bignell
LADIES WHO DO(1964, Brit.), w
Rodolfo Bigotti
LION OF THE DESERT(1981, Libya/Brit.)
Joseph Bigwood
Misc. Talkies
BLOODRAGE(1979), d
Paul Bihaudo
HERCULES' PILLS(1960, Ital.), w
Bob Biheller
YOUNG SAVAGES, THE(1961); DEAR BRIGETTE(1965); YOUNG FURY(1965); MADIGAN(1968)
Louis Bihi
GUNS(1980, Fr.), ph
Severin Bijelic
I EVEN MET HAPPY GYPSIES(1968, Yugo.)
Leon Bijou
FOXES(1980), ph
Miss Bijou
Misc. Silents
TALE OF A SHIRT(1916, Brit.)
Frederick Bijuerenda
MAN OF AFRICA(1956, Brit.)
Theodore Bikel
AFRICAN QUEEN, THE(1951, U.S./Brit.); MOULIN ROUGE(1952); DAY TO REMEMBER, A(1953, Brit.); MELBA(1953, Brit.); NEVER LET ME GO(1953, U.S./Brit.); CHANCE MEETING(1954, Brit.); FORBIDDEN CARGO(1954, Brit.); LITTLE KIDNAPPERS, THE(1954, Brit.); LOVE LOTTERY, THE(1954, Brit.); COLDITZ STORY, THE(1955, Brit.); DIVIDED HEART, THE(1955, Brit.); ABOVE US THE WAVES(1956, Brit.); FLIGHT FROM VIENNA(1956, Brit.); ENEMY BELOW, THE(1957); PRIDE AND THE PASSION, THE(1957); VINTAGE, THE(1957); DEFIANT ONES, THE(1958); FRAULEIN(1958); I BURY THE LIVING(1958); I WANT TO LIVE!(1958); ANGRY HILLS, THE(1959, Brit.); BLUE ANGEL, THE(1959); DOG OF FLANDERS, A(1959); WOMAN OBSESSED(1959); MY FAIR LADY(1964); SANDS OF THE KALAHARI(1965, Brit.); RUSSIANS ARE COMING, THE RUSSIANS ARE COMING, THE(1966); DESPERATE ONES, THE(1968 U.S./Span.); SWEET NOVEMBER(1968); MY SIDE OF THE MOUNTAIN(1969); DARKER THAN AMBER(1970); TWO HUNDRED MOTELS(1971, Brit.); LITTLE ARK, THE(1972)
Jirina Bila
DEVIL'S TRAP, THE(1964, Czech.)

Barbara Bilabel
CASTLE, THE(1969, Ger.), cos
Davy Biladeau
ANGEL BABY(1961)
Enki Bilal
1984
LIFE IS A BED OF ROSES(1984, Fr.), art d
Piero Bilancioni
GOLD OF NAPLES(1957, Ital.)
Bernard Bilaoul
1984
MY NEW PARTNER(1984, Fr.)
Celia Bilar
ROSE FOR EVERYONE, A(1967, Ital.)
Robert Bilbal
AMOUR, AMOUR(1937, Fr.), d
Carlota Bilbao
REDEEMER, THE(1965, Span.)
Fernando Bilbao
FINGER ON THE TRIGGER(1965, US/Span.); DRACULA VERSUS FRANKEN-STEIN(1972, Span.); MALENKA, THE VAMPIRE(1972, Span./Ital.); ANTONY AND CLEOPATRA(1973, Brit.)
A. C. Bilbrew
FOXES OF HARROW, THE(1947)
Felicity Bilbrook
NATIONAL VELVET(1944)
Lydia Bilbrook
MEXICAN SPITFIRE'S BABY(1941); MEXICAN SPITFIRE AT SEA(1942); MEXI-CAN SPITFIRE'S ELEPHANT(1942); NIGHTMARE(1942); FOREVER AND A DAY(1943); MEXICAN SPITFIRE'S BLESSED EVENT(1943); PISTOL PACKIN' MAMA(1943); PASSPORT TO DESTINY(1944); SHERLOCK HOLMES AND THE SPIDER WOMAN(1944); BRIGHTON STRANGLER, THE(1945); PICTURE OF DORI-AN GRAY, THE(1945); WHAT A BLONDE(1945); IVY(1947); MR. PEABODY AND THE MERMAID(1948)
Lydia Bilbrooke
Silents
PLACE IN THE SUN, A(1916, Brit.)
Bangy Bilby
IF I HAD A MILLION(1932)
Edward Allen Bilby
Misc. Talkies
RACKETEER ROUND-UP(1934)
David Bilcock
ALVIN RIDES AGAIN(1974, Aus.), d; PETERSEN(1974, Aus.), ed; END PLAY(1975, Aus.), ed
Jill Bilcock
1984
STRIKEBOUND(1984, Aus.), ed
David Bilcock, Jr.
2,000 WEEKS(1970, Aus.), ed
David Bilcock, Sr.
2,000 WEEKS(1970, Aus.), p
Robert Bilder
OUT OF THE BLUE(1947)
Paul Bildt
REBEL, THE(1933, Ger.); MOSCOW SHANGHAI(1936, Ger.); LA HABANERA(1937, Ger.); MAN WHO WAS SHERLOCK HOLMES, THE(1937, Ger.); DREYFUS CASE, THE(1940, Ger.); AFFAIR BLUM, THE(1949, Ger.); SOMEWHERE IN BERLIN(1949, E. Ger.); OUR DAILY BREAD(1950, Ger.); TOXI(1952, Ger.); AS LONG AS YOU'RE NEAR ME(1956, Ger.); DEVIL IN SILK(1968, Ger.)
Misc. Silents
HAUNTED CASTLE, THE(1921, Ger.)
Fred Biletnikoff
NORSEMAN, THE(1978)
B. Bilewski
GREAT BIG WORLD AND LITTLE CHILDREN, THE(1962, Pol.)
C.C. Bilham
FIDDLER ON THE ROOF(1971)
Florence Bilings
Misc. Silents
WHO ARE MY PARENTS?(1922)
Jef Bilings
1984
CHATTANOOGA CHOO CHOO(1984), cos
Boris Bilinsky
ENTENTE CORDIALE(1939, Fr.), cos; DAYBREAK(1940, Fr.), cos
Enze Biliotti
SPIRIT AND THE FLESH, THE(1948, Ital.)
Enzo Biliotti
DIFFICULT YEARS(1950, Ital.)
Teddy Bilis
GATES OF PARIS(1958, Fr./Ital.); IMPOSSIBLE ON SATURDAY(1966, Fr./Israel)
Acker Bilk
BAND OF THIEVES(1962, Brit.)
Helen S. Bilkie
NAKED HILLS, THE(1956), w
Bill
GENGHIS KHAN(U.S./Brit./Ger./Yugo), spec eff; ESCAPE BY NIGHT(1937)
Cheyenne Bill
Misc. Silents
DON JUAN OF THE WEST(1928); SHEIK OF MOJAVE, THE(1928); WEST OF PARADISE(1928); RAINBOW RANGE(1929); THUNDERING THOMPSON(1929); BRANDING FIRE(1930); COWBOY PRINCE, THE(1930)
David Bill
DOUBLE MAN, THE(1967), set d
Harmonica Bill
ACROSS THE BADLANDS(1950); PECOS RIVER(1951)

John Bill
OUTSIDE IN(1972)
Montana Bill
Misc. Silents
RIDERS OF VENGEANCE(1928); SECRETS OF THE RANGE(1928); TRAILS OF TREACHERY(1928); COWBOY CAVALIER(1929); LURE OF THE MINE(1929); ROUGH AND READY(1930)
Rene Bill
BLACK SPIDER, THE(1983, Swit.)
Richard Bill
GIRL WHO COULDN'T SAY NO, THE(1969, Ital.)
Tony Bill
COME BLOW YOUR HORN(1963); SOLDIER IN THE RAIN(1963); MARRIAGE ON THE ROCKS(1965); NONE BUT THE BRAVE(1965, U.S./Jap.); YOU'RE A BIG BOY NOW(1966); ICE STATION ZEBRA(1968); FLAP(1970); STEELYARD BLUES(1973), p; STING, THE(1973), p; HEARTS OF THE WEST(1975), p; SHAMPOO(1975); LAS VEGAS LADY(1976); GOING IN STYLE(1979), p; HEART BEAT(1979); LITTLE DRAGONS, THE(1980); MY BODYGUARD(1980), d; DEADHEAD MILES(1982), p; SIX WEEKS(1982), d
Tory Bill
CASTLE KEEP(1969)
Bill Black's Combo
TEENAGE MILLIONAIRE(1961)
Bill Burns and Birds
HOLIDAY RHYTHM(1950)
Bill Haley and the Comets
ROCK AROUND THE CLOCK(1956)
Bill Nolan Quintet Minus Two
DELINQUENTS, THE(1957), m
Buffalo Bill, Jr.
BAR L RANCH(1930); BEYOND THE RIO GRANDE(1930); CHEYENNE KID, THE(1930); SOUTH OF SONORA(1930); WESTWARD BOUND(1931); RIDERS OF THE GOLDEN GULCH(1932); DEADWOOD PASS(1933); FIGHTING COWBOY(1933); RID-ING SPEED(1934); POWDERSMOKE RANGE(1935); RAINBOW VALLEY(1935); TEX-AS TERROR(1935)
Silents
COMING AN' GOING(1926)
Misc. Silents
BRINGIN' HOME THE BACON(1924); FAST AND FEARLESS(1924); HARD HITTIN' HAMILTON(1924); RARIN' TO GO(1924); THUNDERING ROMANCE(1924); DESERT DEMON, THE(1925); DOUBLE ACTION DANIELS(1925); FULL SPEED(1925); SAD-DLE CYCLONE(1925); STREAK OF LUCK, A(1925); BONANZA BUCKAROO, THE(1926); DEUCE HIGH(1926); RAWHIDE(1926); SPEEDY SPURS(1926); TRUMPIN' TROUBLE(1926); INTERFERIN' GENT, THE(1927); OBLIGIN' BUCKAROO, THE(1927); PALS IN PERIL(1927); RIDIN' ROWDY, THE(1927); ROARIN' BRONCS(1927); VALLEY OF HUNTED MEN, THE(1928)
Pawnee Bill, Jr.
Misc. Silents
FORBIDDEN TRAILS(1928); MYSTERY RIDER(1928); TEXAS FLASH(1928); THRILL CHASER, THE(1928); WHERE THE WEST BEGINS(1928)
Salvatore Billa
ADIOS SABATA(1971, Ital./Span.)
Reg Billado
RACE STREET(1948)
Reginald Billado
DOUBLE LIFE, A(1947); INTRIGUE(1947)
A.C.H. Billbrew
HEARTS IN DIXIE(1929)
The Billbrew Chorus
HEARTS IN DIXIE(1929); SHOW BOAT(1929)
Lydia Billbrook
MEXICAN SPITFIRE OUT WEST(1940)
Pam Bille
UP IN SMOKE(1978)
Svend Bille
LURE OF THE JUNGLE, THE(1970, Den.)
Anna Biller
PERSONAL BEST(1982)
Dan Biller
FRANCHETTE; LES INTRIGUES(1969)
G.B. Biller
MORGAN'S MARAUDERS(1929), stunts
Hal Biller
DOMINO KID(1957), w; PANIC BUTTON(1964), w
Irene Biller
MAN WHO DARED, THE(1933)
Raoul Billery
ME(1970, Fr.)
Don Billett
SERPICO(1973); HUSTLE(1975); PRINCE OF THE CITY(1981)
Donald Billett
LADY LIBERTY(1972, Ital./Fr.)
Stewart C. Billett
BAREFOOT EXECUTIVE, THE(1971), w
Mimo Billi
CROSSED SWORDS(1954); MONTE CARLO STORY, THE(1957, Ital.); STORY OF JOSEPH AND HIS BRETHREN THE(1962, Ital.); GIDGET GOES TO ROME(1963); MANDRAGOLA(1966 Fr./Ital.)
Mino Billi
NEVER TAKE NO FOR AN ANSWER(1952, Brit./Ital.)
Nino Billi
WHITE SHEIK, THE(1956, Ital.)
Riccardo Billi
VOICE IN YOUR HEART, A(1952, Ital.); PINK PANTHER, THE(1964); CLIMAX, THE(1967, Fr.); BATTLE OF THE AMAZONS(1973, Ital./Span.), p
Catherine Billich
GOING IN STYLE(1979)

Billie
NORA PRENTISS(1947)
Silents
MATING OF MARCUS, THE(1924, Brit.)
Billie and Blue
WILD WHEELS(1969)
Lydia Billiet
GERMAN SISTERS, THE(1982, Ger.)
Graham Billing
CRY OF THE PENGUINS(1972, Brit.), w
John Billing
VOYAGE OF THE DAMNED(1976, Brit.), cos
Roy Billing
SCARECROW, THE(1982, New Zealand); NATE AND HAYES(1983, U.S./New Zealand)
Sheila Billing
NOW THAT APRIL'S HERE(1958, Can.)
Tanya Billing
CARRY ON CLEO(1964, Brit.)
Richard Billinger
MOZART STORY, THE(1948, Aust.), w
Al Billings
BUCK PRIVATES(1941)
Bennie Billings
Silents
PENROD(1922)
Billie Billings
Silents
APARTMENT 29(1917); ARSENE LUPIN(1917)
Misc. Silents
REDEMPTION OF DAVE DARCEY, THE(1916); SOUL MASTER, THE(1917)
Earl Billings
SOUNDER, PART 2(1976); BUSTIN' LOOSE(1981)
Elmo Billings
FLAMING FEATHER(1951), ed; SILVER CITY(1951), ed
Silents
TUMBLING RIVER(1927)
Florence Billings
Silents
SPREADING DAWN, THE(1917); FAIR PRETENDER, THE(1918); ROMANCE OF THE AIR, A(1919); NOBODY(1921); DESTINY'S ISLE(1922); WHAT FOOLS MEN ARE(1922); SINNERS IN HEAVEN(1924); MISS BLUEBEARD(1925)
Misc. Silents
GREAT VICTORY, WILSON OR THE KAISER?, THE(1918); LOADED DICE(1918); CROOK OF DREAMS(1919); DANGEROUS AFFAIR, A(1919); FALSE GODS(1919); HEART OF A GYPSY, THE(1919); HER GAME(1919); PROBATION WIFE, THE(1919); WHY GERMANY MUST PAY(1919); WOMAN(1919); BLUE PEARL, THE(1920); ROAD OF AMBITION, THE(1920); WIT WINS(1920); WOMAN GAME, THE(1920); WONDER MAN, THE(1920); WORLDS APART(1921); LOVE'S MASQUERADE(1922); FOR ANOTHER WOMAN(1924)
Florence K. Billings
Misc. Silents
REASON WHY, THE(1918)
Gail Billings
THEY SHOOT HORSES, DON'T THEY?(1969)
Gary Billings
RAISING A RIOT(1957, Brit.)
George Billings
NIGHT WORK(1930); KING FOR A NIGHT(1933); WICKED WOMAN, A(1934); GALLANT DEFENDER(1935); DANGEROUS INTRIGUE(1936); LOVE IS ON THE AIR(1937); PENROD AND SAM(1937); JUVENILE COURT(1938); LITTLE TOUGH GUY(1938); RECKLESS LIVING(1938); KNUTE ROCKNE–ALL AMERICAN(1940); MY LITTLE CHICKADEE(1940); NICE GIRL?(1941); O.S.S.(1946)
Silents
HANDS UP(1926)
Georgie Billings
WOMAN TO WOMAN(1929); THIRD ALARM, THE(1930); OLD-FASHIONED WAY, THE(1934); PURSUIT OF HAPPINESS, THE(1934)
Jack Billings
SPRINGTIME(1948, Brit.); BODY SAID NO!, THE(1950, Brit.); MYSTERY AT THE BURLESQUE(1950, Brit.), ch; HAPPY GO LOVELY(1951, Brit.), a, ch; WEDDING OF LILLI MARLENE, THE(1953, Brit.)
Joe Billings
FLAREUP(1969); GREAT WALDO PEPPER, THE(1975)
Richard Billings
FIERCEST HEART, THE(1961), ed
Silents
GENTLE JULIA(1923)
Ted Billings
MAN WHO RECLAIMED HIS HEAD, THE(1935); REMEMBER LAST NIGHT(1935); RECKLESS LIVING(1938); MRS. MINIVER(1942); THANK YOUR LUCKY STARS(1943); NONE BUT THE LONELY HEART(1944); PRINCESS AND THE PIRATE, THE(1944); IMPERFECT LADY, THE(1947)
Teddy Billings
STAGECOACH(1939)
Beau Billingslea
NIGHT SHIFT(1982); 10 TO MIDNIGHT(1983)
Barbara Billingsley
ADVENTURE(1945); SECRET HEART, THE(1946); UNDERCURRENT(1946); ARGYLE SECRETS, THE(1948); SAXON CHARM, THE(1948); VALIANT HOMBRE, THE(1948); AIR HOSTESS(1949); I CHEATED THE LAW(1949); PREJUDICE(1949); SUN COMES UP, THE(1949); PRETTY BABY(1950); SHADOW ON THE WALL(1950); TRIAL WITHOUT JURY(1950); INSIDE STRAIGHT(1951); TALL TARGET, THE(1951); THREE GUYS NAMED MIKE(1951); TWO DOLLAR BETTOR(1951); WOMAN IN THE DARK(1952); LADY WANTS MINK, THE(1953); CARELESS YEARS, THE(1957); AIRPLANE!(1980)
Hugh Billingsley
BEN HUR(1959)

Jennifer Billingsley
LADY IN A CAGE(1964); YOUNG LOVERS, THE(1964); SPY WITH MY FACE, THE(1966); C. C. AND COMPANY(1971); WELCOME HOME, SOLDIER BOYS(1972); WHITE LIGHTNING(1973); THIRSTY DEAD, THE(1975)
Misc. Talkies
BRUTE CORPS(1972); HOLLYWOOD MAN, THE(1976)
Michael Billingsley
WAR AND PEACE(1956, Ital./U.S.); THEN THERE WERE THREE(1961); CAPTIVE CITY, THE(1963, Ital.), ed; CONQUERED CITY(1966, Ital.), ed; REASON TO LIVE, A REASON TO DIE, A(1974, Ital./Fr./Ger./Span.), p; GUNS AND THE FURY, THE(1983), ed
Patrick Billingsley
FURY, THE(1978); MY BODYGUARD(1980); SOMEWHERE IN TIME(1980)
Peter Billingsley
IF EVER I SEE YOU AGAIN(1978); HONKY TONK FREEWAY(1981); PATERNITY(1981); DEATH VALLEY(1982); CHRISTMAS STORY, A(1983)
Bill Billington
I AM A CAMERA(1955, Brit.)
Francelia Billington
MOUNTED STRANGER, THE(1930)
Silents
NAKED HEARTS(1916); IN BAD(1918); BLIND HUSBANDS(1919)
Misc. Silents
CHILD OF GOD, A(1915); STRATHMORE(1915); BETTINA LOVED A SOLDIER(1916); BLACK SHEEP OF THE FAMILY, THE(1916); EVIL WOMEN DO, THE(1916); MAINSPRING, THE(1916); HIGH PLAY(1917); MASKED HEART, THE(1917); MY FIGHTING GENTLEMAN(1917); NEW YORK LUCK(1917); PRIDE AND THE MAN(1917); RIGHT TO BE HAPPY, THE(1917); SANDS OF SACRIFICE(1917); SEA MASTER, THE(1917); SHACKLES OF TRUTH(1917); SNAP JUDGEMENT(1917); MIDNIGHT TRAIL, THE(1918); DAY SHE PAID, THE(1919); DESERT LOVE(1920); GREAT AIR ROBBERY, THE(1920); HEARTS ARE TRUMPS(1920); TERROR, THE(1920); HIGH GEAR JEFFREY(1921); RANGER AND THE LAW, THE(1921); TRUANT HUSBAND, THE(1921); BLAZING ARROWS(1922); BLUE BLAZES(1922); RESTLESS SOULS(1922); WHITE SIN, THE(1924); TEX(1926); ROUGH SHOD FIGHTER, A(1927)
Francelina Billington
Misc. Silents
HEART STRINGS(1917)
Francella Billington
Silents
FRAME UP, THE(1917)
Kevin Billington
INTERLUDE(1968, Brit.), d; RISE AND RISE OF MICHAEL RIMMER, THE(1970, Brit.), d, w; LIGHT AT THE EDGE OF THE WORLD, THE(1971, U.S./Span./Lichtenstein), d; VOICES(1973, Brit.), d
1984
REFLECTIONS(1984, Brit.), p, d
Misc. Talkies
RISE AND RISE OF MICHAEL RIMMER, THE(1970, Brit.), d
Michael Billington
ALFRED THE GREAT(1969, Brit.); SPY WHO LOVED ME, THE(1977, Brit.)
Rachel Billington
LIGHT AT THE EDGE OF THE WORLD, THE(1971, U.S./Span./Lichtenstein), w
Teddy Billis
WHERE THE HOT WIND BLOWS(1960, Fr., Ital.)
Salvatore Billitteri
ALAKAZAM THE GREAT!(1961, Jap.), ed; GUNS OF THE BLACK WITCH(1961, Fr./Ital.), p; TRAPP FAMILY, THE(1961, Ger.), ed; PRISONER OF THE IRON MASK(1962, Fr./Ital.), p; BLACK SABBATH(1963, Ital.), p
Salvatore F. Billitteri
BURIED ALIVE(1951, Ital.), titles
Beverly Billman
NATIONAL VELVET(1944)
Larry Billman
MIRACLE OF THE WHITE STALLIONS(1963); FIVE THE HARD WAY(1969), w; SWEET CHARITY(1969)
David C. Billodeau
EASY RIDER(1969)
Pierre Billon
SECOND BUREAU(1936, Fr.), d; COURRIER SUD(1937, Fr.), d; ETERNAL HUSBAND, THE(1946, Fr.), d, w; RUY BLAS(1948, Fr.), d
Enzo Billotti
ADVENTURE OF SALVATOR ROSA, AN(1940, Ital.)
William Billowit
SLEEPAWAY CAMP(1983), prod d
Trillot Billquist
VALLEY OF EAGLES(1952, Brit.)
Michael Bills
DEVIL'S WIDOW, THE(1972, Brit.)
Little Billy
SWING HIGH(1930); POLLY OF THE CIRCUS(1932); THEY NEVER COME BACK(1932); TERROR OF TINY TOWN, THE(1938)
Misc. Silents
OH, BABY!(1926); SIDESHOW, THE(1928)
Michele Ameen Billy
STAR TREK: THE MOTION PICTURE(1979)
Billy Cotton and His Band
FIRST MRS. FRASER, THE(1932, Brit.); VARIETY(1935, Brit.); MUSIC HALL PARADE(1939, Brit.)
Billy Lee's Band
REG'LAR FELLERS(1941)
Billy Merrin and His Commanders
DANCE OF DEATH, THE(1938, Brit.)
Billy Reid and His Band
SATURDAY NIGHT REVUE(1937, Brit.)
The Billy Smart Circus
BERSERK(1967)

Billy Yellow
SEARCHERS, THE(1956)

Vera Biloshisky
JESUS CHRIST, SUPERSTAR(1973)

Enzo Bilotti
MATA HARI'S DAUGHTER(1954, Fr./Ital)

Edward Bilous
SLEEPAWAY CAMP(1983), m

William Bilowit
1984
C.H.U.D.(1984), prod d

Bruce Bilson
CONFLICT(1945); NORTH AVENUE IRREGULARS, THE(1979), d
1984
CHATTANOOGA CHOO CHOO(1984), d

George Bilson
TALENT SCOUT(1937), w; EXPOSED(1938), w; FRESHMAN YEAR(1938), p; ADVENTURES IN IRAQ(1943), w; HELL SHIP MUTINY(1957), p

George R. Bilson
WE'RE IN THE MONEY(1935), w; BUSSES ROAR(1942), w

Michael Bilton
SING ALONG WITH ME(1952, Brit.); EARLY BIRD, THE(1965, Brit.); THIRTY NINE STEPS, THE(1978, Brit.)

Asher Bilu
1984
MAN OF FLOWERS(1984, Aus.), art d

Lirit Bilu
1984
MAN OF FLOWERS(1984, Aus.), a, set d, cos

Luba Bilu
1984
MAN OF FLOWERS(1984, Aus.), set d

Chick Bilyeu
HEROES DIE YOUNG(1960)

John Bilyeu
SANTA'S CHRISTMAS CIRCUS(1966)

Bimbo
Silents
CHANG(1927)

Charles Bimbo
THERE'S MAGIC IN MUSIC(1941)

Kate Bimchy
MIND OF MR. SOAMES, THE(1970, Brit.)

Roger Bimpage
UNKNOWN MAN OF SHANDIGOR, THE(1967, Switz.), ph

Joseph Bimstone
INNOCENTS IN PARIS(1955, Brit.)

Bin
RANGO(1931)

Ibrahim Bin
SEVENTH DAWN, THE(1964)

Soly Bina
WORM EATERS, THE(1981), ed

Angelo Binarelli
SENSUALITA(1954, Ital.)

Kate Binchy
SMASHING TIME(1967 Brit.); EAGLE HAS LANDED, THE(1976, Brit.)

Jerome Binder
SO FINE(1981)

John Binder
HONEYSUCKLE ROSE(1980), w; ENDANGERED SPECIES(1982), w

Lou Binder
HORROR OF PARTY BEACH, THE(1964), w

Maurice Binder
PASSAGE, THE(1979, Brit.), p

Steve Binder
GIVE'EM HELL, HARRY!(1975), d&e

Sybilla Binder
NIGHT INVADER, THE(1943, Brit); THUNDER ROCK(1944, Brit.); FRENZY(1946, Brit.); MAN FROM MOROCCO, THE(1946, Brit.); AGAINST THE WIND(1948, Brit.); BLANCHE FURY(1948, Brit.); BROKEN JOURNEY(1948, Brit.); COUNTER BLAST(1948, Brit.); DEVIL'S PLOT, THE(1948, Brit.); GIRL IN THE PAINTING, THE(1948, Brit.); IDOL OF PARIS(1948, Brit.); GOLDEN SALAMANDER(1950, Brit.)

Clara Bindi
BLACK SUNDAY(1961, Ital.)

Sarah Bindley
Misc. Silents
HEART OF A TEXAN, THE(1922); WEST OF THE PECOS(1922)

John Bindon
INSPECTOR CLOUSEAU(1968, Brit.); POOR COW(1968, Brit.); GET CARTER(1971, Brit.); MAN IN THE WILDERNESS(1971, U.S./Span.); MACKINTOSH MAN, THE(1973, Brit.); 11 HARROWHOUSE(1974, Brit.); BARRY LYNDON(1975, Brit.); DIRTY KNIGHT'S WORK(1976, Brit.)
Misc. Talkies
PERFORMANCE(1970, Brit.)

Isabelle Binet
CONFIDENTIALLY YOURS(1983, Fr.)

G. Binevskaya
WHEN THE TREES WERE TALL(1965, USSR)

Herman Bing
MARRIED IN HOLLYWOOD(1929); SONG OF KENTUCKY(1929); SHOW GIRL IN HOLLYWOOD(1930); THREE SISTERS, THE(1930); GREAT LOVER, THE(1931); GUARDSMAN, THE(1931); BIG CITY BLUES(1932) 65m WB bw; FLESH(1932); JEWEL ROBBERY(1932); MURDERS IN THE RUE MORGUE(1932); SILVER DOLLAR(1932); THREE ON A MATCH(1932); WESTWARD PASSAGE(1932); BOWERY, THE(1933); CHANCE AT HEAVEN(1933); COLLEGE COACH(1933); DINNER AT EIGHT(1933); FOOTLIGHT PARADE(1933); HYPNOTIZED(1933); LADY KILLER(1933); MY LIPS BETRAY(1933); NUISANCE, THE(1933); BLACK CAT, THE(1934); CAT'S PAW, THE(1934); CRIMSON ROMANCE(1934); EMBARRASSING MOMENTS(1934); EVELYN PRENTICE(1934); HIDE-OUT(1934); I'LL TELL THE WORLD(1934); LOVE TIME(1934); MANDALAY(1934); MANHATTAN LOVE SONG(1934); MANHATTAN MELODRAMA(1934); MELODY IN SPRING(1934); MERRY WIDOW, THE(1934); MIGHTY BARNUM, THE(1934); ONE NIGHT OF LOVE(1934); TWENTIETH CENTURY(1934); WHEN STRANGERS MEET(1934); BARBARY COAST(1935); CALL OF THE WILD(1935); CALM YOURSELF(1935); DON'T BET ON BLONDES(1935); EVERY NIGHT AT EIGHT(1935); FIGHTING YOUTH(1935); FLORENTINE DAGGER, THE(1935); GREAT HOTEL MURDER(1935); IN CALIENTE(1935); IT HAPPENED IN NEW YORK(1935); NIGHT IS YOUNG, THE(1935); REDHEADS ON PARADE(1935); THREE KIDS AND A QUEEN(1935); THUNDER IN THE NIGHT(1935); VAGABOND LADY(1935); $1,000 A MINUTE(1935); ADVENTURE IN MANHATTAN(1936); COME CLOSER, FOLKS(1936); DIMPLES(1936); GREAT ZIEGFELD, THE(1936); HIS FAMILY TREE(1936); HUMAN CARGO(1936); KING STEPS OUT, THE(1936); LAUGHING IRISH EYES(1936); MUSIC GOES ROUND, THE(1936); ROSE MARIE(1936); TANGO(1936); THREE WISE GUYS, THE(1936); BEG, BORROW OR STEAL(1937); CHAMPAGNE WALTZ(1937); MAYTIME(1937); THAT GIRL FROM PARIS(1937); BLUEBEARD'S EIGHTH WIFE(1938); EVERY DAY'S A HOLIDAY(1938); FOUR'S A CROWD(1938); GREAT WALTZ, THE(1938); PARADISE FOR THREE(1938); SWEETHEARTS(1938); VACATION FROM LOVE(1938); PUBLIC DEB NO. 1(1940); DUMBO(1941); DEVIL WITH HITLER, THE(1942); WHERE DO WE GO FROM HERE?(1945); NIGHT AND DAY(1946); RENDEZVOUS 24(1946)
Misc. Talkies
PASSPORT TO HEAVEN(1943)

Leon Bing
SWEET CHARITY(1969)

Mack Bing
HARD COUNTRY(1981), p
Misc. Talkies
CLASS OF '74(1972), d

Ronald Binge
ONCE A SINNER(1952, Brit.), m; DESPERATE MOMENT(1953, Brit.), m; DANCE LITTLE LADY(1954, Brit.), m; RUNAWAY BUS, THE(1954, Brit.), m; ADVENTURES OF SADIE, THE(1955, Brit.), m

Rodney Bingenheimer
UP IN SMOKE(1978)
1984
REPO MAN(1984)

Maurits Binger
Silents
AS GOD MADE HER(1920, Brit.), p; FATE'S PLAYTHING(1920, Brit.), p; JOHN HERIOT'S WIFE(1920, Brit.), p; SHEER BLUFF(1921), p; BULLDOG DRUMMOND(1923, Brit.), p

Maurtis H. Binger
Misc. Silents
CARMEN OF THE NORTH(1920), d

R.O. Binger
FALSE FACES(1932), ph; REAL GLORY, THE(1939), spec eff; NORTH STAR, THE(1943), spec eff; PRINCESS AND THE PIRATE, THE(1944), spec eff; UP IN ARMS(1944), spec eff; WHISTLE STOP(1946), spec eff; NORTHWEST STAMPEDE(1948), spec eff

Ray Binger
MEN OF THE NORTH(1930), ph; PRIVATE LIVES(1931), ph; COME AND GET IT(1936), spec eff; DODSWORTH(1936), spec eff; STRIKE ME PINK(1936), ph; ETERNALLY YOURS(1939), ph; STAGECOACH(1939), spec eff; LONG VOYAGE HOME, THE(1940), spec eff; THEY GOT ME COVERED(1943), spec eff; HEAVEN ONLY KNOWS(1947), spec eff
Silents
GOLDFISH, THE(1924), ph

Ray O. Binger
SUNDOWN(1941), spec eff; CHASE, THE(1946), spec eff

Barbara M. Bingham
1984
SPLITZ(1984)

Bob Bingham
JESUS CHRIST, SUPERSTAR(1973)

Daryl Bingham
EARTHBOUND(1981)

David Bingham
PINK FLOYD–THE WALL(1982, Brit.)

Dawn Bingham
TROJAN BROTHERS, THE(1946); WALTZ TIME(1946, Brit.)

E. Douglas Bingham
Silents
NO TRESPASSING(1922), art d

Edfrid A. Bingham
Silents
GUILE OF WOMEN(1921), w; SINGED WINGS(1922), w

Edfrid Bingham
Silents
LAW OF THE LAWLESS, THE(1923), w; STEPHEN STEPS OUT(1923), w; BREAKING POINT, THE(1924), w; STRANGER, THE(1924), w; PORTS OF CALL(1925), w; RIDERS OF THE PURPLE SAGE(1925), w; JOHNSTOWN FLOOD, THE(1926), w; TONY RUNS WILD(1926), w; COWARD, THE(1927), w

Howard Bingham
GREATEST, THE(1977, U.S./Brit.)

John Bingham
FRAGMENT OF FEAR(1971, Brit.), w; STUCK ON YOU(1983)

Joseph Bingham
Silents
RANSON'S FOLLY(1915)

S. J. Bingham
Silents
ALIAS JULIUS CAESAR(1922); TAILOR MADE MAN, A(1922)

S.J. Bingham
Misc. Silents
THREE WORD BRAND(1921); THRU THE FLAMES(1923)

Stanley Bingham
Silents
AFTER A MILLION(1924)

Misc. Silents
ROBIN HOOD, JR.(1923)
Virginia P. Bingham
GHOST STORY(1981)
Bingo and the Rest of the Beasts
Silents
POLLY OF THE CIRCUS(1917)
Alfred Bini
MANDRAGOLA(1966 Fr./Ital.), p
Alfredo Bini
ACCATTONE!(1961, Ital.), p; LA VIACCIA(1962, Fr./Ital.), p; MAMMA ROMA(1962, Ital.), p; GOSPEL ACCORDING TO ST. MATTHEW, THE(1966, Fr., Ital.), p; HAWKS AND THE SPARROWS, THE(1967, Ital.), p; ROVER, THE(1967, Ital.), p; WITCH, THE(1969, Ital.), p
Carlo Bini
SHE AND HE(1969, Ital.), art d
Gikas Biniaris
NAKED BRIGADE, THE(1965, U.S./Gr.)
Crawford Binion
1984
OH GOD! YOU DEVIL(1984)
George Binkey
LOVE MERCHANT, THE(1966), ed
Allan Binkley
NEW ORLEANS AFTER DARK(1958)
Hans Binner
CONFESS DR. CORDA(1960, Ger.)
Margery Binner
GLAMOUR(1931, Brit.); OFFICER'S MESS, THE(1931, Brit.); FOOTSTEPS IN THE NIGHT(1932, Brit.); LOVE ON THE SPOT(1932, Brit.); GOOD COMPANIONS(1933, Brit.)
Marjorie Binner
ALMOST A DIVORCE(1931, Brit.)
John Binnet
KANSAS CITY PRINCESS(1934)
Amy C. Binney
DANCE OF DEATH, THE(1971, Brit.), cos
Claire Binney
DON'S PARTY(1976, Aus.); DIMBOOLA(1979, Aus.)
Constance Binney
Silents
ERSTWHILE SUSAN(1919); SUCH A LITTLE QUEEN(1921); SLEEPWALKER, THE(1922)
Misc. Silents
SPORTING LIFE(1918); TEST OF HONOR, THE(1919); SOMETHING DIFFERENT(1920); STOLEN KISS, THE(1920); 39 EAST(1920); CASE OF BECKY, THE(1921); FIRST LOVE(1921); MAGIC CUP, THE(1921); ROOM AND BOARD(1921); BILL FOR DIVORCEMENT, A(1922); MIDNIGHT(1922); THREE O'CLOCK IN THE MORNING(1923)
Faire Binney
LOVE NEST(1951); MONKEY BUSINESS(1952); DREAM WIFE(1953)
Silents
OPEN YOUR EYES(1919); MADONNAS AND MEN(1920); MAN'S HOME, A(1921); WHAT FOOLS MEN ARE(1922); WIDE-OPEN TOWN, A(1922); LOYAL LIVES(1923); SECOND YOUTH(1924)
Misc. Silents
BLUE PEARL, THE(1920); WONDER MAN, THE(1920); FRONTIER OF THE STARS, THE(1921); GIRL FROM PORCUPINE, THE(1921); MAN WITHOUT A HEART, THE(1924); SPEED SPOOK, THE(1924)
Geoff Binney
RAW FORCE(1982)
Geoffrey Binney
HOT POTATO(1976); BATTLESTAR GALACTICA(1979)
Josh Binney
HI-DE-HO(1947), d; MERRY-GO-ROUND(1948, Brit.), d
Misc. Talkies
BOARDING HOUSE BLUES(1948), d; KILLER DILLER(1948), d
Nixon Binney
JUST OUT OF REACH(1979, Aus.), ph
Col. Percy Binns
IT HAPPENED HERE(1966, Brit.)
Ed Binns
PILOT, THE(1979)
Eddie [Edward] Binns
YOUNG AND DANGEROUS(1957)
Edward Binns
TERESA(1951); WITHOUT WARNING(1952); VICE SQUAD(1953); BEYOND A REASONABLE DOUBT(1956); SCARLET HOUR, THE(1956); PORTLAND EXPOSE(1957); 12 ANGRY MEN(1957); COMPULSION(1959); CURSE OF THE UNDEAD(1959); MAN IN THE NET, THE(1959); NORTH BY NORTHWEST(1959); DESIRE IN THE DUST(1960); HELLER IN PINK TIGHTS(1960); JUDGMENT AT NUREMBERG(1961); ADVENTURES OF A YOUNG MAN(1962); PUBLIC AFFAIR, A(1962); AMERICANIZATION OF EMILY, THE(1964); FAIL SAFE(1964); PLAINSMAN, THE(1966); CHUBASCO(1968); PATTON(1970); LOVIN' MOLLY(1974); NIGHT MOVES(1975); OLIVER'S STORY(1978); VERDICT, THE(1982)
Leslie Binns
ELIZA FRASER(1976, Aus.), art d; HIGH ROLLING(1977, Aus.), art d; PATRICK(1979, Aus.), art d; LAST OF THE KNUCKLEMEN, THE(1981, Aus.), art d; MANGO TREE, THE(1981, Aus.), art d; MAN FROM SNOWY RIVER, THE(1983, Aus.), art d
Jerzy Binycki
1984
SHIVERS(1984, Pol.)
Claude Binyon
YOU CAN'T RUN AWAY FROM IT(1956), w; IF I HAD A MILLION(1932), w; COLLEGE HUMOR(1933), w; GAMBLING SHIP(1933), w; GIRL WITHOUT A ROOM(1933), w; WAY TO LOVE(1933), w; LADIES SHOULD LISTEN(1934), w; MANY HAPPY RETURNS(1934), w; SEARCH FOR BEAUTY(1934), w; SHOOT THE WORKS(1934), w; ACCENT ON YOUTH(1935), w; DARING YOUNG MAN, THE(1935), w; GILDED LILY, THE(1935), w; MISSISSIPPI(1935), w; STOLEN HAR-

MONY(1935), w; BRIDE COMES HOME(1936), w; VALIANT IS THE WORD FOR CARRIE(1936), w; I MET HIM IN PARIS(1937), w; TRUE CONFESSION(1937), w; SING YOU SINNERS(1938), w; INVITATION TO HAPPINESS(1939), w; ARIZONA(1940), w; TOO MANY HUSBANDS(1940), w; YOU BELONG TO ME(1941), w; HOLIDAY INN(1942), w; TAKE A LETTER, DARLING(1942), w; DIXIE(1943), w; NO TIME FOR LOVE(1943), w; THIS IS THE ARMY(1943), w; AND THE ANGELS SING(1944), d; INCENDIARY BLONDE(1945), w; CROSS MY HEART(1946), w; WELL-GROOMED BRIDE, THE(1946), w; SUDDENLY IT'S SPRING(1947), w; FAMILY HONEYMOON(1948), d; SAXON CHARM, THE(1948), d&w; EMERGENCY WEDDING(1950), w; MOTHER DIDN'T TELL ME(1950), d&w; MY BLUE HEAVEN(1950), w; STELLA(1950), d&w; AARON SLICK FROM PUNKIN CRICK(1952), d&w; DREAMBOAT(1952), d&w; DOWN AMONG THE SHELTERING PALMS(1953), w; HERE COME THE GIRLS(1953), d; WOMAN'S WORLD(1954), w; RALLY 'ROUND THE FLAG, BOYS!(1958), w; SING, BOY, SING(1958), w; NORTH TO ALASKA(1960), w; PEPE(1960), w; SATAN NEVER SLEEPS(1962), w; KISSES FOR MY PRESIDENT(1964), w
Conrad Binyon
GLASS KEY, THE(1942); FIRST COMES COURAGE(1943); GOOD LUCK, MR. YATES(1943); UNDERDOG, THE(1943); SINCE YOU WENT AWAY(1944); LOVE LETTERS(1945); BLUE SIERRA(1946); GALLANT JOURNEY(1946); TROUBLE WITH WOMEN, THE(1947); WOMAN'S SECRET, A(1949); I WAS A SHOPLIFTER(1950); MILITARY ACADEMY WITH THAT TENTH AVENUE GANG(1950); MY BLUE HEAVEN(1950)
Misc. Talkies
BOY FROM STALINGRAD, THE(1943)
Hugh Binyon
PRACTICALLY YOURS(1944)
Biographic Cartoon Films
HAND OF NIGHT, THE(1968, Brit.), art d
Lidia Biondi
COBRA, THE(1968); DANGER: DIABOLIK(1968, Ital./Fr.); GLASS SPHINX, THE(1968, Egypt/Ital./Span.); RATATAPLAN(1979, Ital.)
Pietro Biondi
THREE BROTHERS(1982, Ital.)
Frank Biondo
OH! CALCUTTA!(1972), ph
Theo Bipolet
CHECKERBOARD(1969, Fr.)
Thelma Biral
MAFIA, THE(1972, Arg.)
Jeanne Biras
TESS(1980, Fr./Brit.)
Jean-Jacques Biraud
MAIS OU ET DONC ORNICAR(1979, Fr.)
Maurice Biraud
COUNTERFEITERS OF PARIS, THE(1962, Fr., Ital.); DEVIL AND THE TEN COMMANDMENTS, THE(1962, Fr.); ANY NUMBER CAN WIN(1963 Fr.); PARIS PICK-UP(1963, Fr./Ital.); SEVENTH JUROR, THE(1964, Fr.); TAXI FOR TOBRUK(1965, Fr./Span./Ger.); CLOPORTES(1966, Fr., Ital.); FEMMINA(1968 Fr./Ital./Ger.)
Enrico Birbichi
GRIM REAPER, THE(1981, Ital.), ph
A.F. Birch
YOUNG WOODLEY(1930, Brit.), ph
Carolyn Birch
Silents
ON HER WEDDING NIGHT(1915); BABBLING TONGUES(1917)
Cecil Birch
Silents
PAULA(1915, Brit.), d
Derek Birch
HAUNTED STRANGLER, THE(1958, Brit.)
Dudley Birch
FLIGHT FROM SINGAPORE(1962, Brit.), d&w
Faul Birch
CATTLE QUEEN OF MONTANA(1954)
Frank Birch
VICTORIA THE GREAT(1937, Brit.); CROSS CURRENTS(1935, Brit.); JUBILEE WINDOW(1935, Brit.); SCHOOL FOR STARS(1935, Brit.); LOVE AT SEA(1936, Brit.); SUCH IS LIFE(1936, Brit.); WOLF'S CLOTHING(1936, Brit.); DOUBLE EXPOSURES(1937, Brit.); JENIFER HALE(1937, Brit.); TWIN FACES(1937, Brit.); WHEN THIEF MEETS THIEF(1937, Brit.); VILLIERS DIAMOND, THE(1938, Brit.); WHO GOES NEXT?(1938, Brit.); CHALLENGE, THE(1939, Brit.); SCOTLAND YARD INSPECTOR(1952, Brit.); WILL ANY GENTLEMAN?(1955, Brit.); DRACULA(1979)
Harry Birch
DELINQUENTS, THE(1957), ph; COOL AND THE CRAZY, THE(1958), ph; HIGH SCHOOL CAESAR(1960), ph
Jack Birch
Misc. Talkies
ROAD OF DEATH(1977)
Patricia Birch
WILD PARTY, THE(1975), ch; LITTLE NIGHT MUSIC, A(1977, Aust./U.S./Ger.), ch; ROSELAND(1977), ch; GREASE(1978), ch; SGT. PEPPER'S LONELY HEARTS CLUB BAND(1978), ch; ZOOT SUIT(1981), ch; GREASE 2(1982), d&ch
Paul Birch
TILL THE END OF TIME(1946); WAR OF THE WORLDS, THE(1953); RIDE CLEAR OF DIABLO(1954); SILVER LODE(1954); APACHE WOMAN(1955); FIGHTING CHANCE, THE(1955); FIVE GUNS WEST(1955); MAN WITHOUT A STAR(1955); REBEL WITHOUT A CAUSE(1955); BEAST WITH A MILLION EYES, THE(1956); DAY THE WORLD ENDED, THE(1956); EVERYTHING BUT THE TRUTH(1956); FASTEST GUN ALIVE(1956); WHEN GANGLAND STRIKES(1956); WHITE SQUAW, THE(1956); GUN FOR A COWARD(1957); JOE DAKOTA(1957); NOT OF THIS EARTH(1957); SPIRIT OF ST. LOUIS, THE(1957); TATTERED DRESS, THE(1957); 27TH DAY, THE(1957); GUN RUNNERS(1958); GUNMAN'S WALK(1958); QUEEN OF OUTER SPACE(1958); WILD HERITAGE(1958); WORLD WAS HIS JURY, THE(1958); GUNMEN FROM LAREDO(1959); DARK AT THE TOP OF THE STAIRS, THE(1960); PAY OR DIE(1960); PORTRAIT IN BLACK(1960); TWO RODE TOGETHER(1961); MAN WHO SHOT LIBERTY VALANCE, THE(1962); PUBLIC AFFAIR, A(1962); IT'S A MAD, MAD, MAD, MAD WORLD(1963); RAIDERS, THE(1964); COVENANT WITH DEATH, A(1966); WELCOME TO HARD TIMES(1967)

Peter Birch
1984
PLOUGHMAN'S LUNCH, THE(1984, Brit.)
Rod Birch
1984
PURPLE HEARTS(1984)
William Birch
ROLLERCOASTER(1977), ph; FAST CHARLIE... THE MOONBEAM RIDER(1979), ph
Wryley Birch
MR. DEEDS GOES TO TOWN(1936); LOST HORIZON(1937)
Wyrley Birch
AFTER THE DANCE(1935); AIR HAWKS(1935); AWAKENING OF JIM BURKE, THE(1935); GRAND EXIT(1935); GUARD THAT GIRL(1935); LAST DAYS OF POMPEII, THE(1935); SHE COULDN'T TAKE IT(1935); BLACKMAILER(1936); LONE WOLF RETURNS, THE(1936); MUSIC GOES ROUND, THE(1936); TRAPPED BY TELEVISION(1936); BOOMERANG(1947)
Robert Birchall
SPECTRE OF EDGAR ALLAN POE, THE(1974), ph
Cheryl Birchfield
1984
GHOSTBUSTERS(1984)
Robert Birchler
FOUR DAYS LEAVE(1950, Switz.)
Allison Bird
GRENDEL GRENDEL GRENDEL(1981, Aus.)
Anthony Bird
WINSLOW BOY, THE(1950)
Billie Bird
DALLAS(1950); JOURNEY INTO LIGHT(1951); MATING SEASON, THE(1951); JUST ACROSS THE STREET(1952); MY WIFE'S BEST FRIEND(1952); SOMEBODY LOVES ME(1952); HALF A HERO(1953); WOMAN'S WORLD(1954); JOKER IS WILD, THE(1957); PANAMA SAL(1957); UNWED MOTHER(1958); BORN TO BE LOVED(1959); TOO SOON TO LOVE(1960); CAT BURGLAR, THE(1961); SECRET OF DEEP HARBOR(1961); LAS VEGAS HILLBILLYS(1966); GETTING STRAIGHT(1970); MAX DUGAN RETURNS(1983)
1984
SIXTEEN CANDLES(1984)
Carol Bird
BUREAU OF MISSING PERSONS(1933), w
Charles Bird
WRONG BOX, THE(1966, Brit.)
Charlie Bird
VIOLENT STRANGER(1957, Brit.); NIGHTWING(1979)
Chris Willow Bird
BROKEN ARROW(1950)
Colin Bird
ULYSSES(1967, U.S./Brit.)
Dick Bird
MEN OF IRELAND(1938, Ireland), d
Getty Bird
SATURDAY NIGHT KID, THE(1929)
Joe "Peppy" Bird
THEY ALL LAUGHED(1981), set d
John Bird
DANDY IN ASPIC, A(1968, Brit.); 30 IS A DANGEROUS AGE, CYNTHIA(1968, Brit.); BEST HOUSE IN LONDON, THE(1969, Brit.); TAKE A GIRL LIKE YOU(1970, Brit.); THIS, THAT AND THE OTHER(1970, Brit.), w; JABBERWOCKY(1977, Brit.); SEVEN-PER-CENT SOLUTION, THE(1977, Brit.)
Julian Bird
PORKY'S(1982)
Kristi Bird
PHANTOM OF THE PARADISE(1974)
Lauri Bird
ANNIE HALL(1977)
Laurie Bird
TWO-LANE BLACKTOP(1971); BORN TO KILL(1975)
Michael Bird
HELL, HEAVEN OR HOBOKEN(1958, Brit.); END OF THE ROAD, THE(1954, Brit.); MAN WHO LIKED FUNERALS, THE(1959, Brit.); WRONG BOX, THE(1966, Brit.)
Minah Bird
ALFIE DARLING(1975, Brit.); OLD DRACULA(1975, Brit.); STUD, THE(1979, Brit.)
Nicholas Bird
LEAVE IT TO ME(1937, Brit.)
Norman Bird
COMING-OUT PARTY, A(; INSPECTOR CALLS, AN(1954, Brit.); ANGRY SILENCE, THE(1960, Brit.); LEAGUE OF GENTLEMEN, THE(1961, Brit.); MAN IN THE MOON(1961, Brit.); SECRET PARTNER, THE(1961, Brit.); VICTIM(1961, Brit.); WHISTLE DOWN THE WIND(1961, Brit.); BURN WITCH BURN(1962, Brit.); CASH ON DEMAND(1962, Brit.); IN SEARCH OF THE CASTAWAYS(1962, Brit.); TERM OF TRIAL(1962, Brit.); AGENT 8 3/4(1963, Brit.); BITTER HARVEST(1963, Brit.); CRACKSMAN, THE(1963, Brit.); MANIAC(1963, Brit.); MIND BENDERS, THE(1963, Brit.); PUNCH AND JUDY MAN, THE(1963, Brit.); 80,000 SUSPECTS(1963, Brit.); BARGEE, THE(1964, Brit.); BLACK TORMENT, THE(1965, Brit.); HILL, THE(1965, Brit.); BEAUTY JUNGLE(1966, Brit.); GYPSY GIRL(1966, Brit.); WRONG BOX, THE(1966, Brit.); DANDY IN ASPIC, A(1968, Brit.); LIMBO LINE, THE(1969, Brit.); ALL AT SEA(1970, Brit.); RISE AND RISE OF MICHAEL RIMMER, THE(1970, Brit.); VIRGIN AND THE GYPSY, THE(1970, Brit.); HANDS OF THE RIPPER(1971, Brit.); LONG AGO, TOMORROW(1971, Brit.); YOUNG WINSTON(1972, Brit.); GET CHARLIE TULLY(1976, Brit.); SLIPPER AND THE ROSE, THE(1976, Brit.); MEDUSA TOUCH, THE(1978, Brit.); FINAL CONFLICT, THE(1981)
Misc. Talkies
BLACK CARRION(1984)
Penny Bird
INADMISSIBLE EVIDENCE(1968, Brit.)
Richard Bird
TILLY OF BLOOMSBURY(1931, Brit.); NINE TILL SIX(1932, Brit.); WATER GYPSIES, THE(1932, Brit.); RIGHT TO LIVE, THE(1933, Brit.); WHITE FACE(1933, Brit.); GREAT DEFENDER, THE(1934, Brit.); WARREN CASE, THE(1934, Brit.); WHAT HAPPENED THEN?(1934, Brit.); INVITATION TO THE WALTZ(1935, Brit.); MI-

MI(1935, Brit.); NIGHT MAIL(1935, Brit.); CROUCHING BEAST, THE(1936, U. S./Brit.); SENSATION(1936, Brit.); BULLDOG DRUMMOND AT BAY(1937, Brit.); CHAMBER OF HORRORS(1941, Brit.); TERROR, THE(1941, Brit.), d; I'LL WALK BESIDE YOU(1943, Brit.); DON'T TAKE IT TO HEART(1944, Brit.); HALF-WAY HOUSE, THE(1945, Brit.); FORBIDDEN(1949, Brit.); DEATH TRAP(1962, Brit.); RETURN TO SENDER(1963, Brit.)
Misc. Talkies
BUTTERFLY AFFAIR, THE(1934, Brit.)
Scott Bird
1984
REVENGE OF THE NERDS(1984)
Sheila Bird
TENDER MERCIES(1982)
Stewart Bird
HOME FREE ALL(1983), p, d&w
1984
HOME FREE ALL(1984), p, d&w
T. H. Bird
MARCH HARE, THE(1956, Brit.), w
Tom Bird
1984
KILLING FIELDS, THE(1984, Brit.)
Violet Bird
JAZZ SINGER, THE(1927); LOCKED DOOR, THE(1929)
Silents
JAZZLAND(1928)
Misc. Silents
CYCLONE COWBOY, THE(1927)
Willow Bird
KING OF THE STALLIONS(1942); DAUGHTER OF THE WEST(1949)
Jesse Birdsall
REMEMBRANCE(1982, Brit.)
Amy Birdsong
Misc. Silents
MARCUS GARLAND(1925)
Sally Birdsong
TOY, THE(1982)
Marvin Birdt
CAR, THE(1977), p
The Birdwatchers
WILD REBELS, THE(1967)
Russell Birdwell
FLYING DEVILS(1933), d; I RING DOORBELLS(1946), w; COME ON, THE(1956), d; GIRL IN THE KREMLIN, THE(1957), d
Russell J. Birdwell
MASQUERADE(1929), d; JIM THORPE–ALL AMERICAN(1951), w
Tala Birell
DOOMED BATTALION, THE(1932); NAGANA(1933); CAPTAIN HATES THE SEA, THE(1934); LET'S FALL IN LOVE(1934); AIR HAWKS(1935); CRIME AND PUNISHMENT(1935); LET'S LIVE TONIGHT(1935); SPRING TONIC(1935); LONE WOLF RETURNS, THE(1936); WHITE LEGION, THE(1936); AS GOOD AS MARRIED(1937); SHE'S DANGEROUS(1937); BRINGING UP BABY(1938); INVISIBLE ENEMY(1938); JOSETTE(1938); SEVEN MILES FROM ALCATRAZ(1942); CHINA(1943); ISLE OF FORGOTTEN SINS(1943); ONE DANGEROUS NIGHT(1943); SONG OF BERNADETTE, THE(1943); WOMEN IN BONDAGE(1943); MAKE YOUR OWN BED(1944); MONSTER MAKER, THE(1944); MRS. PARKINGTON(1944); PURPLE HEART, THE(1944); TILL WE MEET AGAIN(1944); FROZEN GHOST, THE(1945); GIRLS OF THE BIG HOUSE(1945); POWER OF THE WHISTLER, THE(1945); DANGEROUS MILLIONS(1946); PHILO VANCE'S GAMBLE(1947); PHILO VANCE'S SECRET MISSION(1947); SONG OF LOVE(1947); HOMICIDE FOR THREE(1948); WOMEN IN THE NIGHT(1948)
Bireno
ROMA(1972, Ital./Fr.)
Willy Birgel
BARCAROLE(1935, Ger.); FINAL CHORD, THE(1936, Ger.); DEAD MELODY(1938, Ger.); LIFE BEGINS ANEW(1938, Ger.); HEIDI(1954, Switz.); HEIDI AND PETER(1955, Switz.); BETWEEN TIME AND ETERNITY(1960, Ger.); HIPPODROME(1961, Aust./Ger.); END OF MRS. CHENEY(1963, Ger.)
Leo Birinski
MATA HARI(1931), w; SONG OF SONGS(1933), w; STAMBOUL QUEST(1934), w; GAY DESPERADO, THE(1936), w; FULL CONFESSION(1939), w; LADY HAS PLANS, THE(1942), w
Raye Birk
1984
ADVENTURES OF BUCKAROO BANZAI: ACROSS THE 8TH DIMENSION, THE(1984); BEST DEFENSE(1984)
Bobby Birkenfeld
PHANTOM OF THE PARADISE(1974)
Fanny Birkenmaier
SAFE PLACE, A(1971)
Bernadette Birkett
JEKYLL AND HYDE...TOGETHER AGAIN(1982); KISS ME GOODBYE(1982); MR. MOM(1983)
Michael Birkett
GUEST, THE(1963, Brit.), p; SOLDIER'S TALE, THE(1964, Brit.), d&w; PERSECUTION AND ASSASSINATION OF JEAN-PAUL MARAT AS PERFORMED BY THE INMATES OF THE ASYLUM OF CHARENTON UNDER THE DIRECTION OF THE MARQUIS DE SADE, THE(1967, Brit.), p; MIDSUMMER NIGHT'S DREAM, A(1969, Brit.), p; KING LEAR(1971, Brit./Den.), p
Viva Birkett
Misc. Silents
TRILBY(1914, Brit.)
Sally Birkhead
WHO KILLED MARY WHAT'SER NAME?(1971)
1984
VAMPING(1984)
Allen Birkin
YOUR UNCLE DUDLEY(1935), w

Andrew Birkin
MELODY(1971, Brit.), d; PIED PIPER, THE(1972, Brit.); w; FLAME(1975, Brit.), w; FINAL CONFLICT, THE(1981), w

Jane Birkin
BLOW-UP(1966, Brit.); KALEIDOSCOPE(1966, Brit.); WONDERWALL(1969, Brit.); CANNABIS(1970, Fr.); SLOGAN(1970, Fr.); ROMANCE OF A HORSE THIEF(1971); DARK PLACES(1974, Brit.); FRENCH WAY, THE(1975, Fr.); CATHERINE & CO.(1976, Fr.); DEATH ON THE NILE(1978, Brit.); EGON SCHIELE–EXCESS AND PUNISHMENT(1981, Ger.); EVIL UNDER THE SUN(1982, Brit.)
1984
LOVE ON THE GROUND(1984,Fr.)

Alan Birkinshaw
Misc. Talkies
KILLER'S MOON(1978), d

Phillip Birkinshaw
IVORY HUNTER(1952, Brit.)

Prof. Birkmeyer
DON JUAN(1956, Aust.), md

Dave Birks
HOUND OF THE BASKERVILLES, THE(1959, Brit.); TRAITOR'S GATE(1966, Brit./Ger.)

U. Birkukov
TAXI TO HEAVEN(1944, USSR), m

Len Birman
LIES MY FATHER TOLD ME(1975, Can.); SILVER STREAK(1976); GREAT BRAIN, THE(1978)

Matt Birman
QUEST FOR FIRE(1982, Fr./Can.)

Sefafima Birman
Misc. Silents
GIRL WITH THE HAT-BOX(1927, USSR)

Serafima Birman
IVAN THE TERRIBLE(Part I, 1947, USSR); DON QUIXOTE(1961, USSR)

Matt Birman-Feldman
HOG WILD(1980, Can.)

Alan Birmingham
GREAT POWER, THE(1929); MASQUERADE(1929); FURIES, THE(1930); KING'S VACATION, THE(1933); ARTISTS AND MODELS(1937); SHE ASKED FOR IT(1937)

Allen Birmingham
GREAT GAMBINI, THE(1937)

George A. Birmingham
GENERAL JOHN REGAN(1933, Brit.), w
Silents
GENERAL JOHN REGAN(1921, Brit.), w

Birnbach Circus
MAN ON A TIGHTROPE(1953)

Bettina Birnbaum
FLASHDANCE(1983)

Harvey Birnbaum
DEADLY SPAWN, THE(1983), ph

Irving Birnbaum
RED-HAIRED ALIBI, THE(1932), ed; DARING DAUGHTERS(1933), ed; MOLE PEOPLE, THE(1956), ed; OUTSIDE THE LAW(1956), ed

Jesse Birnbaum
CANDIDATE, THE(1972)

Stuart Birnbaum
SMOKEY AND THE BANDIT–PART 3(1983), w

Carol Birner
SWEET CHARITY(1969)

David Birney
CARAVAN TO VACCARES(1974, Brit./Fr); DIRTY KNIGHT'S WORK(1976, Brit.); OH GOD! BOOK II(1980)

Frank Birney
FEAR NO EVIL(1981); MODERN PROBLEMS(1981); MR. MOM(1983)

Hoffman Birney
GLORY GUYS, THE(1965), w

Meredith Baxter Birney
BITTERSWEET LOVE(1976)

Reed Birney
FOUR FRIENDS(1981)

Arthur Birnkrant
LIFE STUDY(1973), w

Don Birnkrant
CURIOUS FEMALE, THE(1969), ph; ZERO TO SIXTY(1978), ph
1984
TANK(1984), ph

Joseph Birns
Misc. Silents
PRETENDERS, THE(1915)

Barney Biro
DIARY OF A HIGH SCHOOL BRIDE(1959); CASE OF PATTY SMITH, THE(1962)

Frank Biro
FRASIER, THE SENSUOUS LION(1973)

Hajni Biro
SEANCE ON A WET AFTERNOON(1964 Brit.)

Lajos Biro
WOMEN EVERYWHERE(1930), w; MICHAEL AND MARY(1932, Brit.), w; RESERVED FOR LADIES(1932, Brit.), w; WEDDING REHEARSAL(1932, Brit.), w; FAITHFUL HEART(1933, Brit.), w; GHOST TRAIN, THE(1933, Brit.), w; PRIVATE LIFE OF HENRY VIII, THE(1933), w; STRANGE EVIDENCE(1933, Brit.), w; CATHERINE THE GREAT(1934, Brit.), w; PRIVATE LIFE OF DON JUAN, THE(1934, Brit.), w; SANDERS OF THE RIVER(1935, Brit.), w; SCARLET PIMPERNEL, THE(1935, Brit.), w; REMBRANDT(1936, Brit.), w; THINGS TO COME(1936, Brit.), w; DARK JOURNEY(1937, Brit.), w; KNIGHT WITHOUT ARMOR(1937, Brit.), w; MAN WHO COULD WORK MIRACLES, THE(1937, Brit.), w; UNDER THE RED ROBE(1937, Brit.), w; DIVORCE OF LADY X, THE(1938, Brit.), w; DRUMS(1938, Brit.), w; RETURN OF THE SCARLET PIMPERNEL(1938, Brit.), w; FOUR FEATHERS, THE(1939, Brit.), w; HOTEL IMPERIAL(1939), w; OVER THE MOON(1940, Brit.), w; THIEF OF BAGHDAD, THE(1940, Brit.), w; WAY OF ALL FLESH, THE(1940), w; FIVE GRAVES TO CAIRO(1943), w; ROYAL SCANDAL, A(1945), w; IDEAL HUSBAND, AN(1948,

Brit.), w; STORM OVER THE NILE(1955, Brit.), w
Silents
FORBIDDEN PARADISE(1924), w; EVE'S SECRET(1925), w; SILENT LOVER, THE(1926), w; WAY OF ALL FLESH, THE(1927), w; ADORATION(1928), w; LAST COMMAND, THE(1928), w; NIGHT WATCH, THE(1928), w

Miklos Biro
FORTRESS, THE(1979, Hung.), ph

Joe Biroc
NIGHTMARE(1956), ph; BULLET FOR A BADMAN(1964), ph; DETECTIVE, THE(1968), ph

Joseph Biroc
TOWERING INFERNO, THE(1974), ph

Joseph Biroc
IT'S A WONDERFUL LIFE(1946), ph; MY DEAR SECRETARY(1948), ph; ON OUR MERRY WAY(1948), ph; JOHNNY ALLEGRO(1949), ph; MRS. MIKE(1949), ph; KILLER THAT STALKED NEW YORK, THE(1950), ph; BUSHWHACKERS, THE(1952), ph; LOAN SHARK(1952), ph; RED PLANET MARS(1952), ph; APPOINTMENT IN HONDURAS(1953), ph; BWANA DEVIL(1953), ph; DONOVAN'S BRAIN(1953), ph; TALL TEXAN, THE(1953), ph; TWONKY, THE(1953), ph; DOWN THREE DARK STREETS(1954), ph; STEEL CAGE, THE(1954), ph; BENGAZI(1955), ph; ATTACK!(1956), ph; BLACK WHIP, THE(1956), ph; TENSION AT TABLE ROCK(1956), ph; AMAZING COLOSSAL MAN, THE(1957), ph; CHINA GATE(1957), ph; FORTY GUNS(1957), ph; GARMENT JUNGLE, THE(1957), ph; RIDE BACK, THE(1957), ph; RUN OF THE ARROW(1957), ph; UNKNOWN TERROR, THE(1957), ph; UNDERWATER WARRIOR(1958), ph; BAT, THE(1959), ph; FBI STORY, THE(1959), ph; VERBOTEN!(1959), ph; ICE PALACE(1960), ph; THIRTEEN GHOSTS(1960), ph; DEVIL AT FOUR O'CLOCK, THE(1961), ph; GOLD OF THE SEVEN SAINTS(1961), ph; OPERATION EICHMANN(1961), ph; SAIL A CROOKED SHIP(1961), ph; CONFESSIONS OF AN OPIUM EATER(1962), ph; CONVICTS FOUR(1962), ph; HITLER(1962), ph; BYE BYE BIRDIE(1963), ph; PROMISES, PROMISES(1963), ph; UNDER THE YUM-YUM TREE(1963), ph; HUSH... HUSH, SWEET CHARLOTTE(1964), ph; KITTEN WITH A WHIP(1964), ph; RIDE THE WILD SURF(1964), ph; VIVA LAS VEGAS(1964), ph; YOUNG LOVERS, THE(1964), ph; FLIGHT OF THE PHOENIX, THE(1965), ph; I SAW WHAT YOU DID(1965), ph; RUSSIANS ARE COMING, THE RUSSIANS ARE COMING, THE(1966), ph; SWINGER, THE(1966), ph; TO TRAP A SPY(1966), ph; ENTER LAUGHING(1967), ph; FITZWILLY(1967), ph; TONY ROME(1967), ph; WARNING SHOT(1967), ph; WHO'S MINDING THE MINT?(1967), ph; LADY IN CEMENT(1968), ph; LEGEND OF LYLAH CLARE, THE(1968), ph; WHAT EVER HAPPENED TO AUNT ALICE?(1969), ph; TOO LATE THE HERO(1970), ph; ESCAPE FROM THE PLANET OF THE APES(1971), ph; GRISSOM GANG, THE(1971), ph; MRS. POLLIFAX-SPY(1971), ph; ORGANIZATION, THE(1971), ph; ULZANA'S RAID(1972), ph; CAHILL, UNITED STATES MARSHAL(1973), ph; EMPEROR OF THE NORTH POLE(1973), ph; BLAZING SADDLES(1974), ph; LONGEST YARD, THE(1974), ph; SHANKS(1974), ph; HUSTLE(1975), ph; DUCHESS AND THE DIRTWATER FOX, THE(1976), ph; CHOIRBOYS, THE(1977), ph; BEYOND THE POSEIDON ADVENTURE(1979), ph; AIRPLANE!(1980), ph; ...ALL THE MARBLES(1981), ph; AIRPLANE II: THE SEQUEL(1982), ph; HAMMETT(1982), ph

Joseph C. Biroc
VICE SQUAD(1953), ph

Joseph F Biroc
CRY DANGER(1951), ph

Joseph F. Biroc
TOYS IN THE ATTIC(1963), ph; MAGIC TOWN(1947), ph; ROUGHSHOD(1949), ph; WITHOUT WARNING(1952), ph; GLASS WALL, THE(1953), ph; WORLD FOR RANSOM(1954), ph; GHOST TOWN(1956), ph; QUINCANNON, FRONTIER SCOUT(1956), ph; HOME BEFORE DARK(1958), ph; BORN RECKLESS(1959), ph; GUNFIGHT AT COMANCHE CREEK(1964), ph

Lillian Biron
Misc. Silents
BELOW THE DEAD LINE(1921)

James Birrie
THIS MAN IS NEWS(1939, Brit.)

Felippe Birriel
FLIGHT OF THE LOST BALLOON(1961)

Dan Birt
LUCKY NUMBER, THE(1933, Brit.), ed; HAPPY DAYS ARE HERE AGAIN(1936, Brit.), w; OLD SPANISH CUSTOM, AN(1936, Brit.), ed; WOMAN TO WOMAN(1946, Brit.), ed; THREE WEIRD SISTERS, THE(1948, Brit.), d; NO ROOM AT THE INN(1950, Brit.), d; LAUGHING IN THE SUNSHINE(1953, Brit./Swed.), d; BURNT EVIDENCE(1954, Brit.), d; CIRCUMSTANIAL EVIDENCE(1954, Brit.), d

Daniel Birt
GIRL WHO FORGOT, THE(1939, Brit.), p; THREE SILENT MEN(1940, Brit.), d; INTERRUPTED JOURNEY, THE(1949, Brit.), d; SHE SHALL HAVE MURDER(1950, Brit.), d; NIGHT WON'T TALK, THE(1952, Brit.), d; BACKGROUND(1953, Brit.), d; THREE STEPS IN THE DARK(1953, Brit.), d; ANGELS ONE FIVE(1954, Brit.), ed; MEET MR. MALCOLM(1954, Brit.), d; DEADLY GAME, THE(1955, Brit.), d&w

George Birt
LOVE AND DEATH(1975); MOONRAKER(1979, Brit.)

Louise Birt
GIRL WHO FORGOT, THE(1939, Brit.), p; THREE WEIRD SISTERS, THE(1948, Brit.), w

Celia Birtwell
1984
BIGGER SPLASH, A(1984)

P. Biryukov
Misc. Silents
DEFENCE OF SEVASTOPOL(1911, USSR); LIFE IN DEATH(1914, USSR)

Yu. Biryukov
HOME FOR TANYA, A(1961, USSR), m

V. Biryukova
DIMKA(1964, USSR), w

L. Biryulin
LAST GAME, THE(1964, USSR)

Roberto Bisacca
STAVISKY(1974, Fr.)

Robert Bisacco
TORSO(1974, Ital.)

Roberto Bisacco
MODESTY BLAISE(1966, Brit.); ROMEO AND JULIET(1968, Brit./Ital.); CAMILLE 2000(1969); FRAULEIN DOKTOR(1969, Ital./Yugo.); DETECTIVE BELLI(1970, Ital.); LA CAGE AUX FOLLES II(1981, Ital./Fr.)

Michael Bisaroff
DU BARRY WAS A LADY(1943)

Mary Jo Bisby
GUN RUNNER(1969)

Mimma Biscardi
CHINA IS NEAR(1968, Ital.)

Frank Bischell
LITTLE TOUGH GUY(1938); YOU'RE NOT SO TOUGH(1940)

August Bischof
DIAMONDS OF THE NIGHT(1968, Czech.)

Larry Bischof
HOT SUMMER WEEK(1973, Can.), w; SHAMPOO(1975); ULTIMATE WARRIOR, THE(1975)

R.W. Bischoff
ADORABLE(1933), ed; STATE FAIR(1933), ed

Robert Bischoff
RACKETY RAX(1932), ed; WAY DOWN EAST(1935), ed; TRAIL OF THE LONESOME PINE, THE(1936), ed; WEDDING PRESENT(1936), ed; GREAT GAMBINI, THE(1937), ed; HER HUSBAND LIES(1937), ed; JOHN MEADE'S WOMAN(1937), ed; SHE ASKED FOR IT(1937), ed; LITTLE ORPHAN ANNIE(1938), ed; ADVENTURES OF SHERLOCK HOLMES, THE(1939), ed; FRONTIER MARSHAL(1939), ed; SUSANNAH OF THE MOUNTIES(1939), ed; BLUE BIRD, THE(1940), ed; BRIGHAM YOUNG–FRONTIERSMAN(1940), ed; JOHNNY APOLLO(1940), ed; MARK OF ZORRO, THE(1940), ed; BLOOD AND SAND(1941), ed; CHARLEY'S AUNT(1941), ed; CONFIRM OR DENY(1941), ed; WESTERN UNION(1941), ed; ORCHESTRA WIVES(1942), ed; TALES OF MANHATTAN(1942), ed; MEANEST MAN IN THE WORLD, THE(1943), ed

Sam Bischoff
BETWEEN FIGHTING MEN(1932), p; DYNAMITE RANCH(1932), p; LAST MILE, THE(1932), d; STRANGERS OF THE EVENING(1932), p; COME ON TARZAN(1933), p; DRUM TAPS(1933), p; FARGO EXPRESS(1933), p; FROM HEADQUARTERS(1933), p; LONE AVENGER, THE(1933), p; PHANTOM THUNDERBOLT, THE(1933), p; BABBITT(1934), p; BEDSIDE(1934), p; CASE OF THE HOWLING DOG, THE(1934), p; FRIENDS OF MR. SWEENEY(1934), p; HEAT LIGHTNING(1934), p; I'VE GOT YOUR NUMBER(1934), p; MURDER IN THE CLOUDS(1934), p; REGISTERED NURSE(1934), p; RETURN OF THE TERROR(1934), p; SIDE STREETS(1934), p; SIX-DAY BIKE RIDER(1934), p; TWENTY MILLION SWEETHEARTS(1934), p; FRONT PAGE WOMAN(1935), p; GO INTO YOUR DANCE(1935), p; LITTLE BIG SHOT(1935), p; RED HOT TIRES(1935), p; STARS OVER BROADWAY(1935), p; SWEET MUSIC(1935), p; TRAVELING SALESLADY, THE(1935), p; CAIN AND MABEL(1936), p; CHINA CLIPPER(1936), p; EARTHWORM TRACTORS(1936), p; PUBLIC ENEMY'S WIFE(1936), p; SING ME A LOVE SONG(1936), p; THREE MEN ON A HORSE(1936), p; READY, WILLING AND ABLE(1937), p; SLIM(1937), p; ANGELS WITH DIRTY FACES(1938), p; BOY MEETS GIRL(1938), p; GOLD DIGGERS IN PARIS(1938), p; KID FROM KOKOMO, THE(1939), p; NAUGHTY BUT NICE(1939), p; CHILD IS BORN, A(1940), p; ESCAPE TO GLORY(1940), p; TEXAS(1941), p; SOUTH SEA WOMAN(1953), p; SYSTEM, THE(1953), p; BOUNTY HUNTER, THE(1954), p
Silents
CATCH AS CATCH CAN(1927), sup; GIRL FROM RIO, THE(1927), p; WOMAN WHO DID NOT CARE, THE(1927), sup

Samuel Bischoff
CORPSE CAME C.O.D., THE(, p; HOMICIDE SQUAD(1931), p; X MARKS THE SPOT(1931), p; DARK HORSE, THE(1932), p; RICH ARE ALWAYS WITH US, THE(1932), p; THREE ON A MATCH(1932), p; DELUGE(1933), p; STUDY IN SCARLET, A(1933), p; BIG SHAKEDOWN, THE(1934), p; ST. LOUIS KID, THE(1934), p; DON'T BET ON BLONDES(1935), p; FRISCO KID(1935), p; IRISH IN US, THE(1935), p; CHARGE OF THE LIGHT BRIGADE, THE(1936), p; GOLDEN ARROW, THE(1936), p; SAN QUENTIN(1937), p; OKLAHOMA KID, THE(1939), p; YOU CAN'T GET AWAY WITH MURDER(1939), p; CASTLE ON THE HUDSON(1940), p; THREE CHEERS FOR THE IRISH(1940), p; THEY DARE NOT LOVE(1941), p; THREE GIRLS ABOUT TOWN(1941), p; YOU'LL NEVER GET RICH(1941), p; NIGHT TO REMEMBER, A(1942), p; TWO YANKS IN TRINIDAD(1942), p; APPOINTMENT IN BERLIN(1943), p; DANGEROUS BLONDES(1943), p; THERE'S SOMETHING ABOUT A SOLDIER(1943), p; CAROLINA BLUES(1944), p; NONE SHALL ESCAPE(1944), p; THOUSAND AND ONE NIGHTS, A(1945), p; MR. DISTRICT ATTORNEY(1946), p; INTRIGUE(1947), p; PITFALL(1948), p; MRS. MIKE(1949), p; OUTPOST IN MOROCCO(1949), p; BULLET FOR JOEY, A(1955), p; PHENIX CITY STORY, THE(1955), p; SCREAMING EAGLES(1956), p; KING OF THE ROARING TWENTIES-THE STORY OF ARNOLD ROTHSTEIN(1961), p; OPERATION EICHMANN(1961), p; STRANGLER, THE(1964), p

Smauel Bischoff
RACKET BUSTERS(1938), p

Ilse Bischofova
DIAMONDS OF THE NIGHT(1968, Czech.)

Paul Bisciglia
PARIS BELONGS TO US(1962, Fr.); CHECKERBOARD(1969, Fr.)

Biscot
HEART OF A NATION, THE(1943, Fr.)

George Biscot
CAGE OF NIGHTINGALES, A(1947, Fr.)

Cesare Biseo
1984
BURIED ALIVE(1984, Ital.), makeup

Vittorio Biseo
HAWKS AND THE SPARROWS, THE(1967, Ital.), set d; IF IT'S TUESDAY, THIS MUST BE BELGIUM(1969), makeup

Olga Bisera
SUPERFLY T.N.T.(1973); SPY WHO LOVED ME, THE(1977, Brit.); WOMEN IN CELL BLOCK 7(1977, Ital./U.S.)

Ernie Biship
FIRST MONDAY IN OCTOBER(1981), set d

Larry Bishoff
DREAMER(1979), w

Robert Bishoff
EXILE EXPRESS(1939), ed

Alfred Bishop
Misc. Silents
BRASS BOTTLE, THE(1914, Brit.); LIFEGUARDSMAN, THE(1916, Brit.); WANTED - A WIDOW(1916, Brit.); HIS LAST DEFENCE(1919, Brit.)

Amanda Bishop
1984
SONGWRITER(1984)

Andrew S. Bishop
TEMPTATION(1936)
Misc. Silents
SON OF SATAN, A(1924); HOUSE BEHIND THE CEDARS, THE(1927)

Brian J. Bishop
YELLOW SUBMARINE(1958, Brit.), ed

Bunny Bishop
MODEL AND THE MARRIAGE BROKER, THE(1951)

Cecil Bishop
WHEN LONDON SLEEPS(1934, Brit.); FIND THE LADY(1936, Brit.)

Charles Bishop
NEARLY A NASTY ACCIDENT(1962, Brit.), art d; THERE WAS A CROOKED MAN(1962, Brit.), art d; MYSTERY SUBMARINE(1963, Brit.), art d; EAGLE HAS LANDED, THE(1976, Brit.), art d; MOONRAKER(1979, Brit.), art d; GREAT MUPPET CAPER, THE(1981), art d; SENDER, THE(1982, Brit.), art d; SUPERMAN III(1983), art d

Curtis Bishop
COW COUNTRY(1953), w

David Bishop
GIANT(1956)

Debbie Bishop
MISSIONARY, THE(1982); PARTY PARTY(1983, Brit.)
1984
SCRUBBERS(1984, Brit.)

Debby Bishop
1984
SLAYGROUND(1984, Brit.)

Denise Bishop
GOIN' DOWN THE ROAD(1970, Can.)

DeWitt Bishop
WEST POINT STORY, THE(1950)

Dolly Bishop
Silents
ACE OF HEARTS, THE(1916, Brit.)

Donald Bishop
I NEVER PROMISED YOU A ROSE GARDEN(1977); CHINA SYNDROME, THE(1979); WRONG IS RIGHT(1982)

Ed Bishop
PETS(1974); TWILIGHT'S LAST GLEAMING(1977, U.S./Ger.); BRASS TARGET(1978); SATURN 3(1980); NUTCRACKER(1982, Brit.); SILVER DREAM RACER(1982, Brit.); LONELY LADY, THE(1983); LORDS OF DISCIPLINE, THE(1983)

Edith Bishop
Silents
LONG ODDS(1922, Brit.); HEARTSTRINGS(1923, Brit.); PRODIGAL SON, THE(1923, Brit.)

Edward Bishop
WAR LOVER, THE(1962, U.S./Brit.); MOUSE ON THE MOON, THE(1963, Brit.); MAN IN THE MIDDLE(1964, U.S./Brit.); BEDFORD INCIDENT, THE(1965, Brit.); BATTLE BENEATH THE EARTH(1968, Brit.); 2001: A SPACE ODYSSEY(1968, U.S./Brit.); JOURNEY TO THE FAR SIDE OF THE SUN(1969, Brit.); DIAMONDS ARE FOREVER(1971, Brit.)

Elsie Bishop
WIFE TAKES A FLYER, THE(1942)
Silents
GIRLS DON'T GAMBLE(1921)

Ernie Bishop
ANY WHICH WAY YOU CAN(1980), set d; WILLIE AND PHIL(1980), set d; FIREFOX(1982), set d; ALL THE RIGHT MOVES(1983), set d; SUDDEN IMPACT(1983), set d
1984
TIGHTROPE(1984), set d

George Bishop
REUNION(1932, Brit.); MYSTERIOUS MR. NICHOLSON, THE(1947, Brit.); WHAT THE BUTLER SAW(1950, Brit.); WINSLOW BOY, THE(1950); TAKE ME TO PARIS(1951, Brit.); MADE IN HEAVEN(1952, Brit.); JOHN WESLEY(1954, Brit.); VIOLENT STRANGER(1957, Brit.); MANIA(1961, Brit.)
Silents
GAMBLE WITH HEARTS, A(1923, Brit.); HEARTSTRINGS(1923, Brit.); REST CURE, THE(1923, Brit.)

Jenifer Bishop
FEMALE BUNCH, THE(1969); MAD ROOM, THE(1969); MALTESE BIPPY, THE(1969)

Jennifer Bishop
HORROR OF THE BLOOD MONSTERS(1970, U.S./Phil.); IMPULSE(1975); JESSIE'S GIRLS(1976); MAKO: THE JAWS OF DEATH(1976)

Jim Bishop
SANTA CLAUS CONQUERS THE MARTIANS(1964)

Jimmy Bishop
GOOD COMPANIONS(1933, Brit.)

Joey Bishop
DEEP SIX, THE(1958); NAKED AND THE DEAD, THE(1958); ONIONHEAD(1958); OCEAN'S ELEVEN(1960); PEPE(1960); SERGEANTS 3(1962); JOHNNY COOL(1963); TEXAS ACROSS THE RIVER(1966); GUIDE FOR THE MARRIED MAN, A(1967); VALLEY OF THE DOLLS(1967); WHO'S MINDING THE MINT?(1967)

John Bishop
I WALK ALONE(1948); DARK CITY(1950); JET PILOT(1957); NEXT OF KIN(1983, Aus.)
1984
FOOTLOOSE(1984)

Silents
LET'S GET MARRIED(1926), t
Joseph E. Bishop
DIRT GANG, THE(1972), p
Julie Bishop
INTERNATIONAL SQUADRON(1941); NURSE'S SECRET, THE(1941); STEEL AGAINST THE SKY(1941); BUSSES ROAR(1942); ESCAPE FROM CRIME(1942); HARD WAY, THE(1942); HIDDEN HAND, THE(1942); I WAS FRAMED(1942); LADY GANGSTER(1942); WILD BILL HICKOK RIDES(1942); ACTION IN THE NORTH ATLANTIC(1943); NORTHERN PURSUIT(1943); PRINCESS O'ROURKE(1943); RHAPSODY IN BLUE(1945); YOU CAME ALONG(1945); CINDERELLA JONES(1946); IDEA GIRL(1946); MURDER IN THE MUSIC HALL(1946); STRANGE CONQUEST(1946); HIGH TIDE(1947); LAST OF THE REDMEN(1947); DEPUTY MARSHAL(1949); SANDS OF IWO JIMA(1949); THREAT, THE(1949); WESTWARD THE WOMEN(1951); SABRE JET(1953); HIGH AND THE MIGHTY, THE(1954); HEADLINE HUNTERS(1955); BIG LAND, THE(1957)
Justin Bishop
NIGHTMARE IN BLOOD(1978)
Kelly Bishop
UNMARRIED WOMAN, AN(1978); O'HARA'S WIFE(1983)
Kenneth Bishop
DEATH GOES NORTH(1939), p
Kenneth J. Bishop
SECRETS OF CHINATOWN(1935), p; FIGHTING PLAYBOY(1937), p; FURY AND THE WOMAN(1937), p; WHAT PRICE VENGEANCE?(1937), p; CONVICTED(1938), p; MANHATTAN SHAKEDOWN(1939), p; MURDER IS NEWS(1939), p; SPECIAL INSPECTOR(1939), p
Kim Bishop
PLEASURE PLANTATION(1970)
Larry Bishop
SAVAGE SEVEN, THE(1968); WILD IN THE STREETS(1968); DEVIL'S 8, THE(1969); ANGEL UNCHAINED(1970); CHROME AND HOT LEATHER(1971); SHANKS(1974); HOW COME NOBODY'S ON OUR SIDE?(1975); BIG FIX, THE(1978); C.H.O.M.P.S.(1979); HEY, GOOD LOOKIN'(1982); STING II, THE(1983)
Misc. Talkies
DAY THE LORD GOT BUSTED, THE(1976)
Linda Bishop
BEYOND AND BACK(1978)
Lindsay Bishop
1984
MYSTERY MANSION(1984)
Lt. Cmdr. H. T. Bishop
TORPEDOED!(1939), w
Melanie Bishop
PERFECT COUPLE, A(1979)
Molly Bishop
Silents
JOYOUS TROUBLEMAKERS, THE(1920)
Neal Bishop
Misc. Talkies
TOY BOX, THE(1971)
Norman Bishop
TALES OF ROBIN HOOD(1951); BOWERY BOYS MEET THE MONSTERS, THE(1954)
Pat Bishop
DON'S PARTY(1976, Aus.)
Phillan Bishop
DEAD PEOPLE(1974), m; KISS OF THE TARANTULA(1975), m
Piers Bishop
TOMORROW AT TEN(1964, Brit.); BLUES FOR LOVERS(1966, Brit.)
R.C. Bishop
GUNFIGHT, A(1971)
Richard Bishop
NATIVE LAND(1942); CALL NORTHSIDE 777(1948); TERESA(1951); GIANT(1956)
Richard E. Bishop
WAKAMBA!(1955), ph
Robert Bishop
COURT MARTIAL(1954, Brit.); RICHARD III(1956, Brit.)
Ron Bishop
UNDERGROUND(1970, Brit.), w
Rummy Bishop
TRIBUTE(1980, Can.); OCEAN'S ELEVEN(1960); NOTHING PERSONAL(1980, Can.)
Shawn Bishop
CLOSE ENCOUNTERS OF THE THIRD KIND(1977)
Stark Bishop
SHE COULDN'T TAKE IT(1935)
Stephan Bishop
NATIONAL LAMPOON'S ANIMAL HOUSE(1978)
Stephen Bishop
SGT. PEPPER'S LONELY HEARTS CLUB BAND(1978); TWILIGHT ZONE–THE MOVIE(1983)
Terence Bishop
BOMB IN THE HIGH STREET(1961, Brit.), d
Terry Bishop
YOU'RE ONLY YOUNG TWICE(1952, Brit.), d, w; TIM DRISCOLL'S DONKEY(1955, Brit.), d, w; LIGHT FINGERS(1957, Brit.), d; COVER GIRL KILLER(1960, Brit.), d&w; DANGER TOMORROW(1960, Brit.), d; MODEL FOR MURDER(1960, Brit.), d, w; UNSTOPPABLE MAN, THE(1961, Brit.), d, w; HAIR OF THE DOG(1962, Brit.), d; LIFE IN DANGER(1964, Brit.), d; HAMILE(1965, Ghana), d
Tony Bishop
FRIDAY THE 13TH PART III(1982), p
1984
FRIDAY THE 13TH–THE FINAL CHAPTER(1984), p; MEATBALLS PART II(1984), p
Troy Bishop
TERMS OF ENDEARMENT(1983)
Wes Bishop
HOT SPUR(1968); SCAVENGERS, THE(1969); CHROME AND HOT LEATHER(1971), a, p; THING WITH TWO HEADS, THE(1972), a, p, w; POLICEWOMAN(1974), a, p, w; BLACK GESTAPO, THE(1975), a, p, w; RACE WITH THE DEVIL(1975), a, p, w;

DIXIE DYNAMITE(1976), a, p, w
William Bishop
GIRL CRAZY(1943); GUY NAMED JOE, A(1943); PILOT NO. 5(1943); SALUTE TO THE MARINES(1943); SWING FEVER(1943); SWING SHIFT MAISIE(1943); LOST ANGEL(1944); DEVIL SHIP(1947); ROMANCE OF ROSY RIDGE, THE(1947); SONG OF THE THIN MAN(1947); ADVENTURES IN SILVERADO(1948); BLACK EAGLE(1948); CORONER CREEK(1948); PORT SAID(1948); THUNDERHOOF(1948); UNTAMED BREED, THE(1948); ANNA LUCASTA(1949); SLIGHTLY FRENCH(1949); WALKING HILLS, THE(1949); HARRIET CRAIG(1950); KILLER THAT STALKED NEW YORK, THE(1950); TOUGHER THEY COME, THE(1950); BASKETBALL FIX, THE(1951); FROGMEN, THE(1951); LORNA DOONE(1951); TEXAS RANGERS, THE(1951); CRIPPLE CREEK(1952); RAIDERS, THE(1952); BREAKDOWN(1953); GUN BELT(1953); REDHEAD FROM WYOMING, THE(1953); OVERLAND PACIFIC(1954); TOP GUN(1955); WYOMING RENEGADES(1955); BOSS, THE(1956); WHITE SQUAW, THE(1956); PHANTOM STAGECOACH, THE(1957); SHORT CUT TO HELL(1957); OREGON TRAIL, THE(1959)
Shelton H. Bishop III
1984
FRIDAY THE 13TH–THE FINAL CHAPTER(1984), prod d
Kirsten Bishopric
GAS(1981, Can.); VISITING HOURS(1982, Can.)
Thor Bishopric
JACOB TWO-TWO MEETS THE HOODED FANG(1979, Can.)
Ilarrio Bisi-Pedro
DOGS OF WAR, THE(1980, Brit.)
Gary Bisig
NINE TO FIVE(1980); WARGAMES(1983)
1984
ADVENTURES OF BUCKAROO BANZAI: ACROSS THE 8TH DIMENSION, THE(1984)
Jeannine Bisignano
1984
BODY ROCK(1984)
Fernando Bislani
LAND OF THE MINOTAUR(1976, Gr.)
Dimitrios Bislanis
STEFANIA(1968, Gr.)
Stephen Bisley
LAST OF THE KNUCKLEMEN, THE(1981, Aus.)
Steve Bisley
MAD MAX(1979, Aus.); CHAIN REACTION(1980, Aus.)
1984
SQUIZZY TAYLOR(1984, Aus.)
Misc. Talkies
LITTLE FELLER, THE(1979)
Tom Bismark
1984
ALLEY CAT(1984)
Val Bisoglio
COOL WORLD, THE(1963); HOT ROD HULLABALOO(1966); BROTHERHOOD, THE(1968); NO WAY TO TREAT A LADY(1968); DON IS DEAD, THE(1973); HINDENBURG, THE(1975); ST. IVES(1976); SATURDAY NIGHT FEVER(1977); FRISCO KID, THE(1979)
Misc. Talkies
LINDA LOVELACE FOR PRESIDENT(1975)
Evelyn Bispham
BUSHWHACKERS, THE(1952)
Louis Bispo
FLIGHT(1960), d
Alan Biss
BEYOND AND BACK(1978), stunts
Toto Bissainthe
GUTS IN THE SUN(1959, Fr.); CHECKERBOARD(1969, Fr.)
Whit Bissel
DOUBLE LIFE, A(1947); RED BADGE OF COURAGE, THE(1951); COVENANT WITH DEATH, A(1966)
James D. Bissell
E.T. THE EXTRA-TERRESTRIAL(1982), prod d; TWILIGHT ZONE–THE MOVIE(1983), prod d
1984
LAST STARFIGHTER, THE(1984), art d
Jim Bissell
GOOD LUCK, MISS WYCKOFF(1979), art d
Nina Bissell
ZIEGFELD GIRL(1941)
Richard Bissell
PAJAMA GAME, THE(1957), w
Whit Bissell
HOLY MATRIMONY(1943); DESTINATION TOKYO(1944); BRUTE FORCE(1947); NIGHT SONG(1947); ANOTHER PART OF THE FOREST(1948); CANON CITY(1948); CHICKEN EVERY SUNDAY(1948); HE WALKED BY NIGHT(1948); THAT LADY IN ERMINE(1948); ANNA LUCASTA(1949); CRIME DOCTOR'S DIARY, THE(1949); CONVICTED(1950); FOR HEAVEN'S SAKE(1950); GREAT MISSOURI RAID, THE(1950); KILLER THAT STALKED NEW YORK, THE(1950); LIFE OF HER OWN, A(1950); PERFECT STRANGERS(1950); SIDE STREET(1950); WHEN WILLIE COMES MARCHING HOME(1950); WYOMING MAIL(1950); FAMILY SECRET, THE(1951); LOST CONTINENT(1951); NIGHT INTO MORNING(1951); RED MOUNTAIN(1951); SEALED CARGO(1951); SELLOUT, THE(1951); TALES OF ROBIN HOOD(1951); BOOTS MALONE(1952); HOODLUM EMPIRE(1952); SKIRTS AHOY!(1952); TURNING POINT, THE(1952); DEVIL'S CANYON(1953); ATOMIC KID, THE(1954); CAINE MUTINY, THE(1954); CREATURE FROM THE BLACK LAGOON(1954); IT SHOULD HAPPEN TO YOU(1954); RIOT IN CELL BLOCK 11(1954); SHANGHAI STORY, THE(1954); TARGET EARTH(1954); THREE HOURS TO KILL(1954); AT GUNPOINT(1955); BIG COMBO, THE(1955); DESPERATE HOURS, THE(1955); NAKED STREET, THE(1955); NOT AS A STRANGER(1955); SHACK OUT ON 101(1955); TRIAL(1955); DAKOTA INCIDENT(1956); INVASION OF THE BODY SNATCHERS(1956); MAN FROM DEL RIO(1956); PROUD ONES, THE(1956); GUNFIGHT AT THE O.K. CORRAL(1957); I WAS A TEENAGE WEREWOLF(1957); JOHNNY TREMAIN(1957); TALL STRANGER, THE(1957); WAYWARD GIRL, THE(1957); YOUNG STRANGER, THE(1957); DEFIANT ONES, THE(1958); GANG WAR(1958); I WAS A

TEENAGE FRANKENSTEIN(1958); MONSTER ON THE CAMPUS(1958); NEVER SO FEW(1959); NO NAME ON THE BULLET(1959); WARLOCK(1959); MAGNIFICENT SEVEN, THE(1960); TIME MACHINE, THE(1960; Brit./U.S.); ADVENTURES OF A YOUNG MAN(1962); MANCHURIAN CANDIDATE, THE(1962); THIRD OF A MAN(1962); HUD(1963); SPENCER'S MOUNTAIN(1963); ADVANCE TO THE REAR(1964); SEVEN DAYS IN MAY(1964); WHERE LOVE HAS GONE(1964); FLUFFY(1965); HALLELUJAH TRAIL, THE(1965); FIVE CARD STUD(1968); ONCE YOU KISS A STRANGER(1969); AIRPORT(1970); PETE 'N' TILLIE(1972); SALZBURG CONNECTION, THE(1972); SOYLENT GREEN(1973); PSYCHIC KILLER(1975); LINCOLN CONSPIRACY, THE(1977); CASEY'S SHADOW(1978)

Whitner [Whit] Bissell
IT SHOULDN'T HAPPEN TO A DOG(1946); SENATOR WAS INDISCREET, THE(1947)

Whitner Bissell
CLUNY BROWN(1946); SOMEWHERE IN THE NIGHT(1946); RAW DEAL(1948)

William Bissell
TRAUMA(1962)

Donald Bisset
MURDER IN THE CATHEDRAL(1952, Brit.); CASE OF THE RED MONKEY(1955, Brit.); UP THE CREEK(1958, Brit.); FRIENDS AND NEIGHBORS(1963, Brit.); EYE OF THE DEVIL(1967, Brit.); TWO A PENNY(1968, Brit.); SEE NO EVIL(1971, Brit.); LITTLEST HORSE THIEVES, THE(1977); THIRTY NINE STEPS, THE(1978, Brit.); WARLORDS OF ATLANTIS(1978, Brit.)

Jacqueline Bisset
KNACK ... AND HOW TO GET IT, THE(1965, Brit.); CAPETOWN AFFAIR(1967, U.S./South Afr.); CASINO ROYALE(1967, Brit.); TWO FOR THE ROAD(1967, Brit.); BULLITT(1968); DETECTIVE, THE(1968); SWEET RIDE, THE(1968); FIRST TIME, THE(1969); SECRET WORLD(1969, Fr.); AIRPORT(1970); GRASSHOPPER, THE(1970); BELIEVE IN ME(1971); MEPHISTO WALTZ, THE(1971); SECRETS(1971); LIFE AND TIMES OF JUDGE ROY BEAN, THE(1972); STAND UP AND BE COUNTED(1972); THIEF WHO CAME TO DINNER, THE(1973); MAGNIFICENT ONE, THE(1974, Fr./Ital.); MURDER ON THE ORIENT EXPRESS(1974, Brit.); SPIRAL STAIRCASE, THE(1975, Brit.); END OF THE GAME(1976, Ger./Ital.); ST. IVES(1976); DEEP, THE(1977); GREEK TYCOON, THE(1978); WHO IS KILLING THE GREAT CHEFS OF EUROPE?(1978, US/Ger.); WHEN TIME RAN OUT(1980); INCHON(1981); RICH AND FAMOUS(1981); CLASS(1983)
1984
UNDER THE VOLCANO(1984)

Donald Bissett
BRAIN MACHINE, THE(1955, Brit.); HEADLESS GHOST, THE(1959, Brit.); BATTLE OF THE SEXES, THE(1960, Brit.); HIDE AND SEEK(1964, Brit.)

Jackie Bissett
CUL-DE-SAC(1966, Brit.)

Jacqueline Bissett
DAY FOR NIGHT(1973, Fr.)

Louis Bissiner
FOREVER AND A DAY(1943)

Karl Bissinger
DOUBLE-BARRELLED DETECTIVE STORY, THE(1965), ph; WINDFLOWERS(1968)

Marsha Bissler
WHERE THE BUFFALO ROAM(1980)

Joachim Bissmeyer
GERMANY IN AUTUMN(1978, Ger.)

Alexandre Bisson
MADAME X(1929), w; MADAME X(1937), w; TRIAL OF MADAM X, THE(1948, Brit.), w; MADAME X(1966), w

Bruce Bissonette
GETAWAY, THE(1972)

Lilly Bistrattin
MAFIOSO(1962, Ital.)

A. Bistritzky
Misc. Silents
ROMANCE OF A RUSSIAN BALLERINA(1913, USSR), d

Erwin Biswanger
Silents
SIEGFRIED(1924, Ger.); METROPOLIS(1927, Ger.)

Chabi Biswas
MUSIC ROOM, THE(1963, India)

Chhabi Biswas
GODDESS, THE(1962, India); KANCHENJUNGHA(1966, India)

Maria Bisztrai
MEPHISTO(1981, Ger.)

Demeter Bitenc
CROOKED ROAD, THE(; SEVEN DARING GIRLS(1962, Ger.); ISLE OF SIN(1963, Ger.); APACHE GOLD(1965, Ger.); SEVENTH CONTINENT, THE(1968, Czech./Yugo.); ENGLANO MADE ME(1973, Brit.)

Charles Bitsch
PARIS BELONGS TO US(1962, Fr.), ph; MADE IN U.S.A.(1966, Fr.); LAST MAN, THE(1968, Fr.), d&w

Tibor Bitskei
LOVE(1972, Hung.)

Tibor Bitskey
DIALOGUE(1967, Hung.)

Albert Bitterling
Misc. Talkies
VERNON, FLORIDA(1982)

Michael Bittins
DAS BOOT(1982), p

Hans Bittmann
VAMPYR(1932, Fr./Ger.), art d

Bonnie Bittner
JUD(1971)

Jack Bittner
DREAMS THAT MONEY CAN BUY(1948)

W.W. Bittner
Misc. Silents
WORLD FOR SALE, THE(1918)

William Bittner
Silents
MY FOUR YEARS IN GERMANY(1918)

B. Bityukov
MEET ME IN MOSCOW(1966, USSR)

Olya Bityukova
TEENAGERS IN SPACE(1975, USSR)

Billy Bitzer
Silents
AVENGING CONSCIENCE, THE(1914), ph; HOME SWEET HOME(1914), ph; HEARTS OF THE WORLD(1918), ph; BROKEN BLOSSOMS(1919), ph; ROMANCE OF HAPPY VALLEY, A(1919), ph; TRUE HEART SUSIE(1919), ph; LOVE FLOWER, THE(1920), ph; SURE FIRE FLINT(1922), ph

G. W. "Billy" Bitzer
Silents
SCARLET DAYS(1919), ph

G. W. Bitzer
Silents
ESCAPE, THE(1914), ph; JUDITH OF BETHULIA(1914), ph; BIRTH OF A NATION, THE(1915), ph; INTOLERANCE(1916), ph; GREAT LOVE, THE(1918), ph; GREATEST THING IN LIFE, THE(1918), ph; GIRL WHO STAYED AT HOME, THE(1919), ph; GREATEST QUESTION, THE(1920), ph; IDOL DANCER, THE(1920), ph; WAY DOWN EAST(1920), ph; ORPHANS OF THE STORM(1922), ph; WHITE ROSE, THE(1923), ph; AMERICA(1924), ph

G.W. Bitzer
Silents
BATTLE OF THE SEXES, THE(1914), ph; BATTLE OF THE SEXES, THE(1928), ph

John Bitzer
Silents
KING TUT-ANKH-AMEN'S EIGHTH WIFE(1923), ph

William Bitzer
HOTEL VARIETY(1933), ph

Yip Chin Biu
EXIT THE DRAGON, ENTER THE TIGER(1977, Hong Kong), ph

Hector Biuchet
CURIOUS DR. HUMPP(1967, Arg.)

Jose Maria Biurrun
1984
HOLY INNOCENTS, THE(1984, Span.), ed

Loren Bivens
1984
BLOOD SIMPLE(1984), a, spec eff

John Bix
VOYAGE TO THE PREHISTORIC PLANET(1965)

Bill Bixby
IRMA LA DOUCE(1963); UNDER THE YUM-YUM TREE(1963); RIDE BEYOND VENGEANCE(1966); CLAMBAKE(1967); DOCTOR, YOU'VE GOT TO BE KIDDING(1967); SPEEDWAY(1968); APPLE DUMPLING GANG, THE(1975); KENTUCKY FRIED MOVIE, THE(1977)

Gail Bixby
ROADIE(1980), cos

Jay Lewis Bixby
FANTASTIC VOYAGE(1966), w

Jerome Bixby
CURSE OF THE FACELESS MAN(1958), w; IT! THE TERROR FROM BEYOND SPACE(1958), w; LOST MISSILE, THE(1958, U.S./Can.), w; TWILIGHT ZONE–THE MOVIE(1983), w

Dammico Bixio
LOVES AND TIMES OF SCARAMOUCHE, THE(1976, Ital.), m

Giorgio Bixio
TWO COLONELS, THE(1963, Ital.)

S. A. M. Bixio
LOYALTY OF LOVE(1937, Ital.), m

Georges Bizet
CARMEN(1931, Brit.), w; MELODY LINGERS ON, THE(1935), m; CARMEN(1946, Ital.), m; CARMEN JONES(1954), m; DEVIL MADE A WOMAN, THE(1962, Span.), w
1984
BIZET'S CARMEN(1984, Fr./Ital.), m

Jacques Bizeul
Silents
MARRIAGE PRICE(1919), ph; OUT OF THE SHADOW(1919), ph; BOB HAMPTON OF PLACER(1921), ph; CHARGE IT(1921), ph

Peter Biziou
SECRET WORLD(1969, Fr.), ph; BUGSY MALONE(1976, Brit.), ph; MONTY PYTHON'S LIFE OF BRIAN(1979, Brit.), ph; TIME BANDITS(1981, Brit.), ph; PINK FLOYD–THE WALL(1982, Brit.), ph
1984
ANOTHER COUNTRY(1984, Brit.), ph

Andrew Bizub
RAMPARTS WE WATCH, THE(1940)

Jacques Bizuel
Silents
NEW YORK IDEA, THE(1920), ph

Carla Bizzari
RED LIPS(1964, Fr./Ital.)

Anchise Bizzi
IF THIS BE SIN(1950, Brit.), ph

Harold Bizzy
NASTY RABBIT, THE(1964); DEADWOOD'76(1965)

Frithiof Bjarne
SWEDISH WEDDING NIGHT(1965, Swed.)

Bjorn Bjelvenstam
SMILES OF A SUMMER NIGHT(1957, Swed.); SECRETS OF WOMEN(1961, Swed.)

Bjorn Bjelvenstram
WILD STRAWBERRIES(1959, Swed.)

Vojislav Bjenjas
BATTLE OF THE NERETVA(1971, Yugo./Ital./Ger.), ed
Birgitta Bjerke
1984
PARIS, TEXAS(1984, Ger./Fr.), cos
Gunnar Bjoernstrand
FANNY AND ALEXANDER(1983, Swed./Fr./Ger.)
Anita Bjork
NIGHT PEOPLE(1954); SECRETS OF WOMEN(1961, Swed.); SQUARE OF VIO-
LENCE(1963, U.S./Yugo.); LOVING COUPLES(1966, Swed.); ADALEN 31(1969, Swed.)
Misc. Talkies
MEMORY OF LOVE(1949)
Erik Bjork
THOSE DARING YOUNG MEN IN THEIR JAUNTY JALOPIES(1969, Fr./Brit./
Ital.), art d
Halvar Bjork
EMIGRANTS, THE(1972, Swed.); NEW LAND, THE(1973, Swed.); AUTUMN SONA-
TA(1978, Swed.)
Millgard Bjorklund
HERE'S YOUR LIFE(1968, Swed.)
Stig Bjorkman
GEORGIA, GEORGIA(1972), d
Ulf Bjorlin
GUILT(1967, Swed.), m
Ulf Bjorlin
ELVIRA MADIGAN(1967, Swed.), m
Olle Bjorling
ADALEN 31(1969, Swed.)
Renee Bjorling
LESSON IN LOVE, A(1960, Swed.)
Susan Bjorman
ZONTAR, THE THING FROM VENUS(1966)
Anna Bjorn
MORE AMERICAN GRAFFITI(1979); SWORD AND THE SORCERER, THE(1982);
GET CRAZY(1983)
Hugo Bjorne
INTERMEZZO(1937, Swed.); TORMENT(1947, Swed.); CRIME AND PUNISH-
MENT(1948, Swed.)
Lars Bjorne
SWEDISH MISTRESS, THE(1964, Swed.), ph; WOMAN OF DARKNESS(1968, Swed.),
ph; MY FATHER'S MISTRESS(1970, Swed.), ph
Lars Goran Bjorne
GUILT(1967, Swed.), ph
Lars-Goran Bjorne
SABINA, THE(1979, Span./Swed.), ph
Erle Bjornstad
NIGHTHAWKS(1981)
Roy Bjornstad
HUNGER(1968, Den./Norway/Swed.); ONE DAY IN THE LIFE OF IVAN DENISO-
VICH(1971, U.S./Brit./Norway)
Gunnar Bjornstrand
NAKED NIGHT, THE(1956, Swed.); SMILES OF A SUMMER NIGHT(1957, Swed.);
SEVENTH SEAL, THE(1958, Swed.); MAGICIAN, THE(1959, Swed.); WILD STRAWB-
ERRIES(1959, Swed.); DEVIL'S EYE, THE(1960, Swed.); DREAMS(1960, Swed.);
LESSON IN LOVE, A(1960, Swed.); SECRETS OF WOMEN(1961, Swed.); NIGHT IS MY
FUTURE(1962, Swed.); THROUGH A GLASS DARKLY(1962, Swed.); WINTER LIGHT,
THE(1963, Swed.); LOVING COUPLES(1966, Swed.); PERSONA(1967, Swed.); HAG-
BARD AND SIGNE(1968, Den./Iceland/Swed.); HERE'S YOUR LIFE(1968, Swed.);
SHAME(1968, Swed.); RITUAL, THE(1970, Swed.); GIRLS, THE(1972, Swed.); FACE TO
FACE(1976, Swed.); AUTUMN SONATA(1978, Swed.)
Louis Blaazar
DR. NO(1962, Brit.)
"Pietro" Blacaman
YOU CAN'T CHEAT AN HONEST MAN(1939)
David K. Blace
BREAKING AWAY(1979)
A. Blach
OTHELLO(1960, U.S.S.R.)
Leonard Blach
CASEY'S SHADOW(1978)
Albert Blache
Misc. Silents
TEMPTATIONS OF SATAN, THE(1914), d
Alice Blache
Silents
LURE, THE(1914), p,d&w; TIGRESS, THE(1914), w; WOMAN OF MYSTERY,
THE(1914), d&w
Misc. Silents
ROGUES OF PARIS(1913), d; BENEATH THE CZAR(1914), d; DREAM WOMAN,
THE(1914), d; SHADOWS OF THE MOULIN ROUGE, THE(1914), d; WHAT WILL
PEOPLE SAY(1915), d; MY MADONNA(1916), d; OCEAN WAIF, THE(1916), d; AD-
VENTURER, THE(1917), d; BEHIND THE MASK(1917), d; WHEN YOU AND I WERE
YOUNG(1918), d
Herbert Blache
Silents
SHOOTING OF DAN MCGREW, THE(1915), d; BRAT, THE(1919), d; NEW YORK
IDEA, THE(1920), d; SAPHEAD, THE(1921), d; NEAR LADY, THE(1923), d; NO-
BODY'S BRIDE(1923), d
Misc. Silents
FIGHT FOR MILLIONS, THE(1913), d; BURGLAR AND THE LADY, THE(1914), d;
FIGHT FOR FREEDOM, A OR EXILED TO SIBERIA(1914), d; HER OWN WAY(1915),
d; LADY AND THE BURGLAR, THE(1915), d; GIRL WITH THE GREEN EYES,
THE(1916), d; WOMAN'S FIGHT, A(1916), d; ADVENTURER, THE(1917), d; AUC-
TION OF VIRTUE, THE(1917), d; PEDDLER, THE(1917), d; THINK IT OVER(1917), d;
LOADED DICE(1918), d; MAN'S WORLD, A(1918), d; SILENT WOMAN, THE(1918),
d; DIVORCEE, THE(1919), d; FOOLS AND THEIR MONEY(1919), d; JEANNE OF
THE GUTTER(1919), d; MAN WHO STAYED AT HOME, THE(1919), d; PARISIAN
TIGRESS, THE(1919), d; SATAN JUNIOR(1919), d; UPLIFTERS, THE(1919), d;
HOPE, THE(1920), d; STRONGER THAN DEATH(1920), d; WALK-OFFS, THE(1920),
d; OUT OF THE CHORUS(1921), d; FOOLS AND RICHES(1923), d; UNTAMEABLE,

THE(1923), d; WILD PARTY, THE(1923), d; HIGH SPEED(1924), d; CALGARY STAM-
PEDE, THE(1925), d; HEAD WINDS(1925), d; SECRETS OF THE NIGHT(1925), d;
MYSTERY CLUB, THE(1926), d; BURNING THE WIND(1929), d
Mme. Blache [Alice Guy]
Silents
MAN AND THE WOMAN, A(1917), d&w
Misc. Silents
EMPRESS, THE(1917), d; TARNISHED REPUTATIONS(1920), d
Tatjana Blacher
1984
FLIGHT TO BERLIN(1984, Ger./Brit.)
Melinda Blachley
ME, NATALIE(1969)
Alfred Black
LOVE IN EXILE(1936, Brit.), ph; TROUBLE IN THE AIR(1948, Brit.), p, w; PER-
FECT WOMAN, THE(1950, Brit.), p
Amanda Black
MARK, THE(1961, Brit.)
Anita Rowe Black
LOVE AND KISSES(1965), w
Art Black
BLIND DATE(1934), w
Arthur Black
PLAYTHING, THE(1929, Brit.), w
Arthur Jarvis Black
VILLAGE SQUIRE, THE(1935, Brit.), w
Bill Black
FOLLOW THE LEADER(1930); PLAYBOY, THE(1942, Brit.)
Bob Black
FAMILY AFFAIR(1954, Brit.), w
Bret Black
UNKNOWN VALLEY(1933)
Buck Black
PERSONALITY(1930)
Silents
REGULAR SCOUT, A(1926)
Misc. Silents
HILLS OF PERIL(1927)
C. Howe Black
Silents
BLUE BLOOD(1925)
Cathal Black
1984
PIGS(1984, Ireland), d
Cilla Black
FERRY ACROSS THE MERSEY(1964, Brit.); WORK IS A FOUR LETTER
WORD(1968, Brit.)
Dalla Black
YOUNG MR. PITT, THE(1942, Brit.)
Dan Black
SWEET JESUS, PREACHER MAN(1973)
Danny Big Black
TOGETHER BROTHERS(1974)
Danny "Big" Black
HANGUP(1974)
Danny Black
UP THE SANDBOX(1972)
Diane Black
NATIONAL LAMPOON'S CLASS REUNION(1982)
Don Black
DEAD MARCH, THE(1937); GULLIVER'S TRAVELS(1977, Brit., Bel.), w
Dorothy Black
CAPTIVATION(1931, Brit); HER REPUTATION(1931, Brit.); ADMIRAL'S SECRET,
THE(1934, Brit.); IMITATION OF LIFE(1934); TERROR HOUSE(1942, Brit.)
Eazy Black
BOYS IN COMPANY C, THE(1978, U.S./Hong Kong)
Edward Black
CHARLEY'S(BIG-HEARTED) AUNT*1/2 (1940), p; DOCTOR SYN(1937, Brit.), p;
OH, MR. PORTER!(1937, Brit.), p; OKAY FOR SOUND(1937, Brit.), p; WHERE
THERE'S A WILL(1937, Brit.), p; ALF'S BUTTON AFLOAT(1938, Brit.), p; BANK
HOLIDAY(1938, Brit.), p; CONVICT 99(1938, Brit.), p; HEY! HEY! U.S.A.(1938, Brit.),
p; LADY VANISHES, THE(1938, Brit.), p; MAN WITH 100 FACES, THE(1938, Brit.), p;
OLD BONES OF THE RIVER(1938, Brit.), p; SEZ O'REILLY TO MACNAB(1938,
Brit.), p; STRANGE BOARDERS(1938, Brit.), p; TO THE VICTOR(1938, Brit.), p;
YOUNG AND INNOCENT(1938, Brit.), p; ASK A POLICEMAN(1939, Brit.), p; FROZ-
EN LIMITS, THE(1939, Brit.), p; INSPECTOR HORNLEIGH ON HOLIDAY(1939,
Brit.), p; WHERE'S THAT FIRE?(1939, Brit.), p; BAND WAGGON(1940, Brit.), p; FOR
FREEDOM(1940, Brit.), p; GASBAGS(1940, Brit.), p; NIGHT TRAIN(1940, Brit.), p;
THEY CAME BY NIGHT(1940, Brit.), p; BOMBSIGHT STOLEN(1941, Brit.), p; GHOST
TRAIN, THE(1941, Brit.), p; GIRL IN THE NEWS, THE(1941, Brit.), p; GIRL MUST
LIVE, A(1941, Brit.), p; HI, GANG!(1941, Brit.), p; I THANK YOU(1941, Brit.), p; MAIL
TRAIN(1941, Brit.), p; NEUTRAL PORT(1941, Brit.), p; ONCE A CROOK(1941, Brit.),
p; BACK ROOM BOY(1942, Brit.), p; KING ARTHUR WAS A GENTLEMAN(1942,
Brit.), p; REMARKABLE MR. KIPPS(1942, Brit.), p; YOUNG MR. PITT, THE(1942,
Brit.), p; IT'S THAT MAN AGAIN(1943, Brit.), p; MAN IN GREY, THE(1943, Brit.), p;
MILLIONS LIKE US(1943, Brit.), p; MISS LONDON LTD.(1943, Brit.), p; WE DIVE AT
DAWN(1943, Brit.), p; BEES IN PARADISE(1944, Brit.), p; GIVE US THE MOON(1944,
Brit.), p; TIME FLIES(1944, Brit.), p; UNCENSORED(1944, Brit.), p; 2,000 WO-
MEN(1944, Brit.), p; RANDOLPH FAMILY, THE(1945, Brit.), p; MAN ABOUT THE
HOUSE, A(1947, Brit.), p; BONNIE PRINCE CHARLIE(1948, Brit.), p; MAN OF
EVIL(1948, Brit.), p; WATERLOO ROAD(1949, Brit.), p
Eleanor Black
Misc. Silents
IGNORANCE(1916)
Elinore Black
Misc. Silents
MARK OF CAIN, THE(1917)

Elizabeth Black
MIDNIGHT MAN, THE(1974)
Esther Black
RANCHO DELUXE(1975)
Eunice Black
TASTE OF HONEY, A(1962, Brit.); ARRIVEDERCI, BABY!(1966, Brit.)
G. Howe Black
Silents
WIZARD OF OZ, THE(1925)
Gabriel Black
1984
INITIATION, THE(1984), m
George Black
PENNY POOL, THE(1937, Brit.), d; CALLING ALL CROOKS(1938, Brit.), d; TROUBLE IN THE AIR(1948, Brit.), p, w; PERFECT WOMAN, THE(1950, Brit.), p, w
George R. Black
WILD WOMEN OF WONGO, THE(1959), p
Gerry Black
HERO AT LARGE(1980); NATIONAL LAMPOON'S VACATION(1983)
Ian Stuart Black
SHADOW OF THE PAST(1950, Brit.), w; SPIN A DARK WEB(1956, Brit.), w; LONG KNIFE, THE(1958, Brit.), w; IN THE WAKE OF A STRANGER(1960, Brit.), w; MAID FOR MURDER(1963, Brit.), w; MC GUIRE, GO HOME!(1966, Brit.), w
Imprid Black
ON HER MAJESTY'S SECRET SERVICE(1969, Brit.)
Isobel Black
KISS OF EVIL(1963, Brit.); MAGNIFICENT TWO, THE(1967, Brit.); DAVID COPPERFIELD(1970, Brit.); TWINS OF EVIL(1971, Brit.); 10 RILLINGTON PLACE(1971, Brit.)
Jack Black
JAZZ BABIES(1932)
James Black
Misc. Silents
I'LL SAY SO(1918)
Jean Ann Black
1984
BLOOD SIMPLE(1984), makeup
Jean Black
OLD MOTHER RILEY'S CIRCUS(1941, Brit.)
Jennifer Black
LOCAL HERO(1983, Brit.)
Jeremy Black
BOYS FROM BRAZIL, THE(1978)
Jessica Black
TOMORROW WE LIVE(1936, Brit.)
Jim Black
JAZZ BABIES(1932)
Jimmy Carl Black
TWO HUNDRED MOTELS(1971, Brit.)
Jody Black
KID FROM BOOKLYN, THE(1946)
Joe Black
SHILLINGBURY BLOWERS, THE(1980, Brit.)
John Black
Misc. Talkies
ZOO ROBBERY(1973, Brit.), d
John D.F. Black
GUNFIGHT IN ABILENE(1967), w; NOBODY'S PERFECT(1968), w; THREE GUNS FOR TEXAS(1968), w; SHAFT(1971), w; CAREY TREATMENT, THE(1972), w; TROUBLE MAN(1972), w
John F.F. Black
SURVIVAL(1976), w
Jonathan Black
SONG OF THE SIERRAS(1946)
Joseph Black
SISTERS UNDER THE SKIN(1934), ph
June Black
CAESAR AND CLEOPATRA(1946, Brit.)
Karen Black
PRIME TIME, THE(1960); YOU'RE A BIG BOY NOW(1966); EASY RIDER(1969); HARD CONTRACT(1969); FIVE EASY PIECES(1970); BORN TO WIN(1971); CISCO PIKE(1971); DRIVE, HE SAID(1971); GUNFIGHT, A(1971); PORTNOY'S COMPLAINT(1972); LITTLE LAURA AND BIG JOHN(1973); OUTFIT, THE(1973); PYX, THE(1973, Can.); AIRPORT 1975(1974); GREAT GATSBY, THE(1974); LAW AND DISORDER(1974); RHINOCEROS(1974); DAY OF THE LOCUST, THE(1975); NASHVILLE(1975); BURNT OFFERINGS(1976); CRIME AND PASSION(1976, U.S., Ger.); FAMILY PLOT(1976); CAPRICORN ONE(1978); IN PRAISE OF OLDER WOMEN(1978, Can.); KILLER FISH(1979, Ital./Braz.); LAST WORD, THE(1979); SQUEEZE, THE(1980, Ital.); CHANEL SOLITAIRE(1981); SEPARATE WAYS(1981); COME BACK TO THE 5 & DIME, JIMMY DEAN, JIMMY DEAN(1982); GRASS IS SINGING, THE(1982, Brit./Swed.); CAN SHE BAKE A CHERRY PIE?(1983)
1984
BAD MANNERS(1984); KILLING HEAT(1984); SAVAGE DAWN(1984)
Katherine Black
EASY TO WED(1946)
Katy Black
1984
COMFORT AND JOY(1984, Brit.)
Kelly Black
LOOKER(1981)
King Black
UP THE MACGREGORS(1967, Ital./Span.)
Lindsay Armstrong Black
WORM EATERS, THE(1981)
Lizzy Temple Black
MONDO TRASHO(1970)
Louise Black
OCEAN'S ELEVEN(1960)

Lydia Black
Misc. Talkies
BIJOU(1972)
Martin Black
GUADALCANAL DIARY(1943); FOUR JILLS IN A JEEP(1944); TAMPICO(1944)
Mary Black
GOIN' DOWN THE ROAD(1970, Can.)
Maurice Black
BROADWAY BABIES(1929); CARNATION KID(1929); DARK STREETS(1929); BROTHERS(1930); FRAMED(1930); NUMBERED MEN(1930); PLAYING AROUND(1930); RUNAWAY BRIDE(1930); SEA GOD, THE(1930); STREET OF CHANCE(1930); TRUE TO THE NAVY(1930); FRONT PAGE, THE(1931); LITTLE CAESAR(1931); LONELY WIVES(1931); NO LIMIT(1931); SMART MONEY(1931); SOB SISTER(1931); WOMEN GO ON FOREVER(1931); DANCERS IN THE DARK(1932); FACE ON THE BARROOM FLOOR, THE(1932); HIGH PRESSURE(1932); KING MURDER, THE(1932); RASPUTIN AND THE EMPRESS(1932); SCARFACE(1932); SCARLET DAWN(1932); STEADY COMPANY(1932); STOWAWAY(1932); STRANGE LOVE OF MOLLY LOUVAIN, THE(1932); WHILE PARIS SLEEPS(1932); FLYING DOWN TO RIO(1933); GRAND SLAM(1933); I COVER THE WATERFRONT(1933); KEYHOLE, THE(1933); PICTURE SNATCHER(1933); SHIP OF WANTED MEN(1933); SHRIEK IN THE NIGHT, A(1933); TILLIE AND GUS(1933); DOWN TO THEIR LAST YACHT(1934); MURDER ON THE CAMPUS(1934); SIXTEEN FATHOMS DEEP(1934); TWIN HUSBANDS(1934); WAKE UP AND DREAM(1934); BONNIE SCOTLAND(1935); CRUSADES, THE(1935); STARS OVER BROADWAY(1935); WEST OF THE PECOS(1935); LAUGHING IRISH EYES(1936); ADVENTURE'S END(1937); CALIFORNIAN, THE(1937); FIREFLY, THE(1937); GAME THAT KILLS, THE(1937); THREE LEGIONNAIRES, THE(1937); UNDER STRANGE FLAGS(1937); VIVACIOUS LADY(1938)
Silents
MARKED MONEY(1928)
Michael Black
PICTURES(1982, New Zealand), d
Nicole Black
Misc. Talkies
SIMPLY IRRESISTIBLE(1983)
Noel Black
PRETTY POISON(1968), p, d; COVER ME BABE(1970), d; JENNIFER ON MY MIND(1971), d; MAN, A WOMAN, AND A BANK, A(1979, Can.), d; PRIVATE SCHOOL(1983), d
1984
MIRRORS(1984), d
Misc. Talkies
MIRRORS(1978), d
Phyllis Black
SAM'S SONG(1971)
R. Black
PRISONER OF CORBAL(1939, Brit.), ph
Ralph Black
MONSTER WALKS, THE(1932), set d
Ricardo Adalid Black
SEVEN CITIES OF GOLD(1955)
Robert J. Black, Jr.
WILD YOUTH(1961), w
Robin Black
1984
COMFORT AND JOY(1984, Brit.)
Roger Black
REUBEN, REUBEN(1983)
Stanley Black
FATAL NIGHT, THE(1948, Brit.), m; HIDEOUT(1948, Brit.), m; MONKEY'S PAW, THE(1948, Brit.), md; IT ALWAYS RAINS ON SUNDAY(1949, Brit.), m; MRS. FITZHERBERT(1950, Brit.), m; THIRD TIME LUCKY(1950, Brit.), m; LAUGHTER IN PARADISE(1951, Brit.), m; LILLI MARLENE(1951, Brit.), m; ONE WILD OAT(1951, Brit.), m; MR. POTTS GOES TO MOSCOW(1953, Brit.), m; WHITE FIRE(1953, Brit.), m; TONIGHT'S THE NIGHT(1954, Brit.), m; NOW AND FOREVER(1956, Brit.), m; PASSPORT TO TREASON(1956, Brit.), m; AS LONG AS THEY'RE HAPPY(1957, Brit.), m; CITY AFTER MIDNIGHT(1957, Brit.), m; HIGH TERRACE(1957, Brit.), m, md; MAILBAG ROBBERY(1957, Brit.), md; PROFESSOR TIM(1957, Ireland), m; TWO GROOMS FOR A BRIDE(1957, Brit.), m; BLOOD OF THE VAMPIRE(1958, Brit.), m; CROSS-UP(1958), m; DANGEROUS YOUTH(1958, Brit.), m; FURTHER UP THE CREEK!(1958, Brit.), m; MAN WHO WOULDN'T TALK, THE(1958, Brit.), m; STORMY CROSSING(1958, Brit.), m; YOUR PAST IS SHOWING(1958, Brit.), m; BROTH OF A BOY(1959, Brit.), m; CIRCLE, THE(1959, Brit.), m; JACK THE RIPPER(1959, Brit.), m; TEENAGE BAD GIRL(1959, Brit.), m; TIME LOCK(1959, Brit.), m; TOO MANY CROOKS(1959, Brit.), m; BATTLE OF THE SEXES, THE(1960, Brit.), m; BOTTOMS UP(1960, Brit.), m; FOLLOW THAT HORSE!(1960, Brit.), m; HAND IN HAND(1960, Brit.), m; HELL IS A CITY(1960, Brit.), m; SANDS OF THE DESERT(1960, Brit.), m; SIEGE OF SIDNEY STREET, THE(1960, Brit.), m, md; TOMMY THE TOREADOR(1960, Brit.), m; CALL ME GENIUS(1961, Brit.), m; DAY THE EARTH CAUGHT FIRE, THE(1961, Brit.), m; DOUBLE BUNK(1961, Brit.), m; FIVE GOLDEN HOURS(1961, Brit.), m; LONG AND THE SHORT AND THE TALL, THE(1961, Brit.), m, md; MANIA(1961, Brit.), m; STOP ME BEFORE I KILL!(1961, Brit.), m; POT CARRIERS, THE(1962, Brit.), m; WONDERFUL TO BE YOUNG!(1962, Brit.), m; MANIAC(1963, Brit.), m, md; SPARROWS CAN'T SING(1963, Brit.), md; SUMMER HOLIDAY(1963, Brit.), m, md; WEST 11(1963, Brit.), m; 80,000 SUSPECTS(1963, Brit.), m; RATTLE OF A SIMPLE MAN(1964, Brit.), m; CITY UNDER THE SEA(1965, Brit.), m; MAKE MINE A MILLION(1965, Brit.), md; SWINGER'S PARADISE(1965, Brit.), m; BLUES FOR LOVERS(1966, Brit.), m; GIRL GETTERS, THE(1966, Brit.), m; VIOLENT MOMENT(1966, Brit.), m; CROSSPLOT(1969, Brit.), m; VALENTINO(1977, Brit.), m
Stephen Black
BELLS GO DOWN, THE(1943, Brit.), w; HE SNOOPS TO CONQUER(1944, Brit.), w; IT HAPPENED ONE SUNDAY(1944, Brit.), w; I DIDN'T DO IT(1945, Brit.), w; GIRL ON THE CANAL, THE(1947, Brit.), w; QUIET WEEKEND(1948, Brit.), w; SAILOR WHO FELL FROM GRACE WITH THE SEA, THE(1976, Brit.)
Stewart Black
DORIAN GRAY(1970, Ital./Brit./Ger./Liechtenstein)

Stu Black
1984
ALL OF ME(1984)
Thurman Black
DIMPLES(1936)
Trevor Black
HAUNTING OF M, THE(1979), ed
Valerie Black
BEWARE(1946)
W.W. Black
Silents
AMBITION(1916); GREAT EXPECTATIONS(1917); NEW YORK PEACOCK, THE(1917)
Misc. Silents
SECRET OF THE STORM COUNTRY, THE(1917)
William Black
Silents
AMATEUR WIDOW, AN(1919); FLYING PAT(1920); STEADFAST HEART, THE(1923); RAMSHACKLE HOUSE(1924)
Misc. Silents
GUARDIAN, THE(1917); THAT WOMAN(1922)
William J. Black
Silents
MAN'S HOME, A(1921), ph; WET GOLD(1921), ph; SUCCESS(1923), ph
William W. Black
Misc. Silents
HELL CAT, THE(1918); HIGH POCKETS(1919)
Black and Blue
UP THE RIVER(1930)
Ben Black Bear
MAN CALLED HORSE, A(1970)
Black Beauty the Horse
Silents
BLACK BEAUTY(1921); WILD GIRL, THE(1925)
The Black Brothers
MEET ME AT THE FAIR(1952)
Black Diamond
Silents
WHEN KNIGHTHOOD WAS IN FLOWER(1922)
Harry Black Horse
SEARCHERS, THE(1956)
Black Jack
BOLD FRONTIERSMAN, THE(1948); DENVER KID, THE(1948); GUNMEN OF ABILENE(1950); CAPTIVE OF BILLY THE KID(1952); LEADVILLE GUNSLINGER(1952)
Black Jack the Horse
SILVER STALLION(1941); WILD FRONTIER, THE(1947); MARSHAL OF AMARILLO(1948); OKLAHOMA BADLANDS(1948); RENEGADES OF SONORA(1948); NAVAJO TRAIL RAIDERS(1949); POWDER RIVER RUSTLERS(1949); WYOMING BANDIT, THE(1949); FRISCO TORNADO(1950); RUSTLERS ON HORSEBACK(1950); VIGILANTE HIDEOUT(1950); ROUGH RIDERS OF DURANGO(1951); WELLS FARGO GUNMASTER(1951); MARSHAL OF CEDAR ROCK(1953)
Black Jack the Stallion
THUNDERING CARAVANS(1952)
Black Jack, a horse
BLACK HILLS AMBUSH(1952)
The Black Knights
FERRY ACROSS THE MERSEY(1964, Brit.)
Black Pearls
GORKY PARK(1983)
Black Spades
EDUCATION OF SONNY CARSON, THE(1974)
Arline Blackburn
Silents
ANNABEL LEE(1921); SCHOOL DAYS(1921)
Clarice Blackburn
VIOLATORS, THE(1957); PRETTY POISON(1968); MAN ON A SWING(1974)
Clarisse Blackburn
NIGHT OF DARK SHADOWS(1971)
Col. Donald D. Blackburn
SURRENDER–HELL!(1959), w
Dick Blackburn
EATING RAOUL(1982)
Greta Blackburn
48 HOURS(1982); YELLOWBEARD(1983)
Jane Blackburn
SUBTERFUGE(1969, US/Brit.)
John Blackburn
SCARLET COAT, THE(1955); NOTHING BUT THE NIGHT(1975, Brit.), w
Julia Blackburn
GUN RUNNER(1969); RAMRODDER, THE(1969)
Ken Blackburn
SKIN DEEP(1978, New Zealand); PICTURES(1982, New Zealand)
Mary Blackburn
Silents
SCALES OF JUSTICE, THE(1914)
Maurice Blackburn
TAKE IT ALL(1966, Can.), m; CORDELIA(1980, Fr., Can.), m
Michael Blackburn
SATAN'S MISTRESS(1982)
Richard Blackburn
THE LADY DRACULA(1974), a, d, w; IMPROPER CHANNELS(1981, Can.); EATING RAOUL(1982), w; THRESHOLD(1983, Can.)
1984
NOT FOR PUBLICATION(1984)
Thomas Blackburn
COLT .45(1950), w; CAVALRY SCOUT(1951), w; CATTLE QUEEN OF MONTANA(1954), w; JOHNNY TIGER(1966), w

Thomas W. Blackburn
WILD DAKOTAS, THE(1956), w
Thomas Wakefield Blackburn
SIERRA BARON(1958), w
Tom Blackburn
KILLER AT LARGE(1947), w; CATTLE TOWN(1952), w; RIDING SHOTGUN(1954), w; DAVY CROCKETT, KING OF THE WILD FRONTIER(1955), w; DAVY CROCKETT AND THE RIVER PIRATES(1956), w; WESTWARD HO THE WAGONS!(1956), w; JOHNNY TREMAIN(1957), w; REDEEMER, THE(1965, Span.), w; MARA OF THE WILDERNESS(1966), w; SANTEE(1973), w
Tom W. Blackburn
SHORT GRASS(1950), w; RATON PASS(1951), w; SIERRA PASSAGE(1951), w
Vivian Blackburn
Misc. Silents
EXCUSE ME(1916)
Robert E. Blackburn III
TENDER MERCIES(1982)
The Blackburn Twins
TAKE ME OUT TO THE BALL GAME(1949); SHE'S WORKING HER WAY THROUGH COLLEGE(1952)
The Blackbyrds
CORNBREAD, EARL AND ME(1975)
Irwin Blacker
BRUSHFIRE(1962), w
Vera Blacker
1984
GODS MUST BE CRAZY, THE(1984, Botswana)
Andrew Blackett
SCHOOL FOR SECRETS(1946, Brit.); TURNERS OF PROSPECT ROAD, THE(1947, Brit.); AGAINST THE WIND(1948, Brit.); VICE VERSA(1948, Brit.); TREASURE ISLAND(1950, Brit.)
Annabel Blackett
SMASH PALACE(1982, New Zealand), cos
Anthony Blackett
MEDUSA TOUCH, THE(1978, Brit.)
Jeanne Blackford
HOLLOW TRIUMPH(1948); HIGH NOON(1952); IT GROWS ON TREES(1952)
Lottie Blackford
Silents
KNAVE OF HEARTS, THE(1919, Brit.); NARROW VALLEY, THE(1921, Brit.)
Mary Blackford
SWEETHEART OF SIGMA CHI(1933); LOVE TIME(1934)
Nessie Blackford
Silents
KNAVE OF HEARTS, THE(1919, Brit.); PATRICIA BRENT, SPINSTER(1919, Brit.); NARROW VALLEY, THE(1921, Brit.)
Blackhawk
NORTH OF NOME(1937)
Barbara Blackhorse
RUNNING BRAVE(1983, Can.)
Michael Blackie
CAYMAN TRIANGLE, THE(1977)
Blackjack
FORT DODGE STAMPEDE(1951)
Blackjack the Horse
SAVAGE FRONTIER(1953)
Calon Blackledge
1984
REVENGE OF THE NERDS(1984)
Betty Blackler
HAPPIEST DAYS OF YOUR LIFE(1950, Brit.); NO ROOM AT THE INN(1950, Brit.)
George Blackler
HOTEL SAHARA(1951, Brit.), makeup; MAN WITH A MILLION(1954, Brit.), makeup; CARRY ON CONSTABLE(1960, Brit.), makeup; SINGER NOT THE SONG, THE(1961, Brit.), makeup; MOUSE ON THE MOON, THE(1963, Brit.), makeup; SWORD OF LANCELOT(1963, Brit.), makeup; IN THE DOGHOUSE(1964, Brit.), makeup; SING AND SWING(1964, Brit.), makeup; TOMB OF LIGEIA, THE(1965, Brit.), makeup; STITCH IN TIME, A(1967, Brit.), makeup; STRANGE AFFAIR, THE(1968, Brit.), makeup; SUMARINE X-1(1969, Brit.), makeup; NO BLADE OF GRASS(1970, Brit.), makeup; FRIGHT(1971, Brit.), makeup; LUST FOR A VAMPIRE(1971, Brit.), makeup; TWINS OF EVIL(1971, Brit.), makeup; MADHOUSE(1974, Brit.), makeup; TOMMY(1975, Brit.), makeup; TO THE DEVIL A DAUGHTER(1976, Brit./Ger.), makeup
Doug Blackley
WILD WEED(1949)
Douglas Blackley
CAR 99(1935); COLLEGE SCANDAL(1935); FOUR HOURS TO KILL(1935); LOVE IN BLOOM(1935); LOVE BEFORE BREAKFAST(1936); BIG TOWN AFTER DARK(1947); JUNGLE FLIGHT(1947); SHOOT TO KILL(1947); COUNTERFEITERS, THE(1948); DRAGNET(1974)
Bertha Blackman
SUBWAY EXPRESS(1931)
Bond Blackman
TRAUMA(1962); CATALINA CAPER, THE(1967), p
Charles Blackman
HOUR OF THE GUN(1967), makeup; WILL PENNY(1968), makeup
Cheryl Blackman
1984
MUPPETS TAKE MANHATTAN, THE(1984)
Don Blackman
TWO TICKETS TO BROADWAY(1951); AFFAIR IN TRINIDAD(1952); BOMBA AND THE JUNGLE GIRL(1952); DESERT LEGION(1953); VALLEY OF THE HEADHUNTERS(1953); EGYPTIAN. THE(1954); ON THE WATERFRONT(1954); BLACK TUESDAY(1955); SANTIAGO(1956); OLD MAN AND THE SEA, THE(1958); SCREAM BLACULA SCREAM(1973)
Fig Blackman
SCAVENGERS, THE(1969)

Gordon Blackman
Misc. Talkies
CAXAMBU(1968)
Honor Blackman
DAUGHTER OF DARKNESS(1948, Brit.); BOY, A GIRL AND A BIKE, A(1949 Brit.); CONSPIRATOR(1949, Brit.); DIAMOND CITY(1949, Brit.); QUARTET(1949, Brit.); GREEN GROW THE RUSHES(1951, Brit.); SO LONG AT THE FAIR(1951, Brit.); DELAVINE AFFAIR, THE(1954, Brit.); DIPLOMATIC PASSPORT(1954, Brit.); RAINBOW JACKET, THE(1954, Brit.); YELLOW ROBE, THE(1954, Brit.); GLASS TOMB, THE(1955, Brit.); BREAKAWAY(1956, Brit.); ACCOUNT RENDERED(1957, Brit.); SUSPENDED ALIBI(1957, Brit.); YOU PAY YOUR MONEY(1957, Brit.); NIGHT TO REMEMBER, A(1958, Brit.); SQUARE PEG, THE(1958, Brit.); MATTER OF WHO, A(1962, Brit.); SERENA(1962, Brit.); JASON AND THE ARGONAUTS(1963, Brit.); GOLDFINGER(1964, Brit.); LIFE AT THE TOP(1965, Brit.); SECRET OF MY SUCCESS, THE(1965, Brit.); MOMENT TO MOMENT(1966); SHALAKO(1968, Brit.); TWIST OF SAND, A(1968, Brit.); FIGHT FOR ROME, A(1969, Ger./Rum.); LAST GRENADE, THE(1970, Brit.); VIRGIN AND THE GYPSY, THE(1970, Brit.); FRIGHT(1971, Brit.); LOLA(1971, Brit./Ital.); SOMETHING BIG(1971); TO THE DEVIL A DAUGHTER(1976, Brit./Ger.); AGE OF INNOCENCE(1977, Can.); CAT AND THE CANARY, THE(1979, Brit.)
Jack Blackman
1984
ULTIMATE SOLUTION OF GRACE QUIGLEY, THE(1984), art d
Joan Blackman
GOOD DAY FOR A HANGING(1958); CAREER(1959); GREAT IMPOSTOR, THE(1960); VISIT TO A SMALL PLANET(1960); BLUE HAWAII(1961); KID GALAHAD(1962); TWILIGHT OF HONOR(1963); INTIMACY(1966); DARING GAME(1968); DESTRUCTORS, THE(1968); MACON COUNTY LINE(1974); PETS(1974); MOONRUNNERS(1975); ONE MAN(1979, Can.)
Misc. Talkies
VENGEANCE OF VIRGO(1972)
Lonnie Blackman
SERGEANT WAS A LADY, THE(1961)
Ronald Blackman
PIRATES OF BLOOD RIVER, THE(1962, Brit.)
Tommy Blackman
HALF PINT, THE(1960)
Wanda Blackman
OBSESSION(1976)
Ron Blackmer
IS THIS TRIP REALLY NECESSARY?(1970), m
Sidney Blackmer
LOVE RACKET, THE(1929); BAD MAN, THE(1930); KISMET(1930); MOTHERS CRY(1930); STRICTLY MODERN(1930); SWEETHEARTS AND WIVES(1930); IT'S A WISE CHILD(1931); LADY WHO DARED, THE(1931); LITTLE CAESAR(1931); WOMAN HUNGRY(1931); COCKTAIL HOUR(1933); DELUGE(1933); FROM HELL TO HEAVEN(1933); WRECKER, THE(1933); COUNT OF MONTE CRISTO, THE(1934); DOWN TO THEIR LAST YACHT(1934); GOODBYE LOVE(1934); PRESIDENT VANISHES, THE(1934); THIS MAN IS MINE(1934); TRANSATLANTIC MERRY-GO-ROUND(1934); BEHIND GREEN LIGHTS(1935); FALSE PRETENSES(1935); FIRE-TRAP, THE(1935); FORCED LANDING(1935); GIRL WHO CAME BACK, THE(1935); GREAT GOD GOLD(1935); LITTLE COLONEL, THE(1935); NOTORIOUS GENTLEMAN, A(1935); SMART GIRL(1935); STREAMLINE EXPRESS(1935); ANY MAN'S WIFE(1936); EARLY TO BED(1936); FLORIDA SPECIAL(1936); MISSING GIRLS(1936); PRESIDENT'S MYSTERY, THE(1936); WOMAN TRAP(1936); CHARLIE CHAN AT MONTE CARLO(1937); DOCTOR'S DIARY, A(1937); GIRL OVERBOARD(1937); HEART OF THE WEST(1937); HEIDI(1937); HOUSE OF SECRETS, THE(1937); JOHN MEADE'S WOMAN(1937); LAST GANGSTER, THE(1937); MICHAEL O'HALLORAN(1937); SHADOWS OF THE ORIENT(1937); THANK YOU, MR. MOTO(1937); THIS IS MY AFFAIR(1937); WIFE, DOCTOR AND NURSE(1937); WOMEN MEN MARRY, THE(1937); IN OLD CHICAGO(1938); SHARP-SHOOTERS(1938); SPEED TO BURN(1938); STRAIGHT, PLACE AND SHOW(1938); SUEZ(1938); TRADE WINDS(1938); WHILE NEW YORK SLEEPS(1938); CONVICT'S CODE(1939); FAST AND LOOSE(1939); HOTEL FOR WOMEN(1939); IT'S A WONDERFUL WORLD(1939); LAW OF THE PAMPAS(1939); ORPHANS OF THE STREET(1939); TRAPPED IN THE SKY(1939); UNMARRIED(1939); WITHIN THE LAW(1939); DANCE, GIRL, DANCE(1940); FRAMED(1940); I WANT A DIVORCE(1940); MARYLAND(1940); THIRD FINGER, LEFT HAND(1940); ANGELS WITH BROKEN WINGS(1941); CHEERS FOR MISS BISHOP(1941); DOWN MEXICO WAY(1941); ELLERY QUEEN AND THE PERFECT CRIME(1941); FEMININE TOUCH, THE(1941); GREAT SWINDLE, THE(1941); LOVE CRAZY(1941); MURDER AMONG FRIENDS(1941); OBLIGING YOUNG LADY(1941); OFFICER AND THE LADY, THE(1941); ROOKIES ON PARADE(1941); ALWAYS IN MY HEART(1942); GALLANT LADY(1942); NAZI AGENT(1942); PANTHER'S CLAW, THE(1942); PRISON GIRL(1942); QUIET PLEASE, MURDER(1942); SABOTAGE SQUAD(1942); I ESCAPED FROM THE GESTAPO(1943); IN OLD OKLAHOMA(1943); MURDER IN TIMES SQUARE(1943); BUFFALO BILL(1944); LADY AND THE MONSTER, THE(1944); WILSON(1944); DUEL IN THE SUN(1946); MY GIRL TISA(1948); SONG IS BORN, A(1948); PEOPLE WILL TALK(1951); SATURDAY'S HERO(1951); SAN FRANCISCO STORY, THE(1952); WASHINGTON STORY(1952); HIGH AND THE MIGHTY, THE(1954); JOHNNY DARK(1954); VIEW FROM POMPEY'S HEAD, THE(1955); ACCUSED OF MURDER(1956); BEYOND A REASONABLE DOUBT(1956); HIGH SOCIETY(1956); TAMMY AND THE BACHELOR(1957); HOW TO MURDER YOUR WIFE(1965); JOY IN THE MORNING(1965); COVENANT WITH DEATH, A(1966); ROSEMARY'S BABY(1968)
Misc. Talkies
REVENGE IS MY DESTINY(1971)
Sydney Blackmer
MOST IMMORAL LADY, A(1929)
Esther Blackmon
MUTATIONS, THE(1974, Brit.)
Sam Blackmon
HUCKLEBERRY FINN(1974)
Barry Blackmore
ANGEL(1982, Irish), p
H. B. Blackmore
Silents
RIP VAN WINKLE(1914)

Jackie Blackmore
CONFESSIONS OF A POP PERFORMER(1975, Brit.)
Peter Blackmore
MIRANDA(1949, Brit.), w; TIME GENTLEMEN PLEASE!(1953, Brit.), w; CHILD'S PLAY(1954, Brit.), w; MAD ABOUT MEN(1954, Brit.), w; ALL FOR MARY(1956, Brit.), w; SIMON AND LAURA(1956, Brit.), w; AFTER THE BALL(1957, Brit.), w; JUST MY LUCK(1957, Brit.), w; UP IN THE WORLD(1957, Brit.), w; MAKE MINE MINK(1960, Brit.), w; MRS. GIBBONS' BOYS(1962, Brit.), w; MAKE MINE A MILLION(1965, Brit.), w; SPYLARKS(1965, Brit.), w; MAGNIFICENT TWO, THE(1967, Brit.), w; THAT RIVIERA TOUCH(1968, Brit.), w
R. D. Blackmore
LORNA DOONE(1935, Brit.), w
Richard D. Blackmore
LORNA DOONE(1951), w
Richard Doddridge Blackmore
Silents
LORNA DOONE(1927), w
Stephen Blackmore
...AND JUSTICE FOR ALL(1979)
Dan Blackner
RETURN OF THE JEDI(1983)
Taurean Blackque
HUNTER, THE(1980)
Anthony Blackshaw
EVIL OF FRANKENSTEIN, THE(1964, Brit.); IPCRESS FILE, THE(1965, Brit.)
John Merton Blacksmith
WESTERN RENEGADES(1949)
Cliff Blackston
Silents
WINGS(1927), ph
Harry Blackstone, Jr.
GET TO KNOW YOUR RABBIT(1972), tech adv
Lisbeth Blackstone
Misc. Silents
JANE EYRE(1914); TOLL OF LOVE, THE(1914)
Susan Blackstone
1984
STONE BOY, THE(1984); WILD LIFE, THE(1984)
Charles Blackton
Misc. Silents
LITTLEST SCOUT(1919)
E. Blackton
Silents
PEEP BEHIND THE SCENES, A(1918, Brit.)
J. Stuart Blackton
Silents
CHRISTIAN, THE(1914), sup; MR. BARNES OF NEW YORK(1914), sup; BATTLE CRY OF PEACE, THE(1915), p, w; MAN AND HIS WOMAN(1920), p&d; GLORIOUS ADVENTURE, THE(1922, U.S./Brit.), p&d&w; ON THE BANKS OF THE WABASH(1923), d; REDEEMING SIN, THE(1925), d; BRIDE OF THE STORM(1926), d; GILDED HIGHWAY, THE(1926), d
Misc. Silents
LIFE OF MOSES(1909), d; WHOM THE GODS DESTROY(1916), d; JUDGEMENT HOUSE, THE(1917), d; MESSAGE OF THE MOUSE, THE(1917), d; WOMANHOOD(1917), d; COMMON CAUSE, THE(1918), d; WORLD FOR SALE, THE(1918), d; DAWN(1919), d; HOUSE DIVIDED, A(1919), d; LIFE'S GREATEST PROBLEM(1919), d; MOONSHINE TRAIL, THE(1919), d; MY HUSBAND'S OTHER WIFE(1919), d; BLOOD BARRIER, THE(1920), d; FORBIDDEN VALLEY(1920), d; HOUSE OF THE TOLLING BELLS, THE(1920), d; PASSERS-BY(1920), d; RESPECTABLE BY PROXY(1920), d; GIPSY CAVALIER, A(1922, Brit.), d; VIRGIN QUEEN, THE(1923, Brit.), d; BEHOLD THIS WOMAN(1924), d; BELOVED BRUTE, THE(1924), d; BETWEEN FRIENDS(1924), d; CLEAN HEART, THE(1924), d; LET NO MAN PUT ASUNDER(1924), d; HAPPY WARRIOR, THE(1925), d; TIDES OF PASSION(1925), d; HELL-BENT FOR HEAVEN(1926), d; PASSIONATE QUEST, THE(1926), d
Jay Blackton
MERRY WIDOW, THE(1952), md; GUYS AND DOLLS(1955), md; OKLAHOMA(1955), md
Marion Blackton
MANIAC(1934)
Paula Blackton
Misc. Silents
LITTLEST SCOUT(1919), d
Violet Blackton
Silents
GLORIOUS ADVENTURE, THE(1922, U.S./Brit.)
Misc. Silents
LITTLEST SCOUT(1919)
Leslie Blackwater
WICKER MAN, THE(1974, Brit.)
Bill Blackwell
INDIAN PAINT(1965)
Carlyle Blackwell
BEYOND THE CITIES(1930, Brit.), a, p&d, w; CROOKED BILLET, THE(1930, Brit.); DESTINATION TOKYO(1944); FOLLOW THE BOYS(1944); STORY OF DR. WASSELL, THE(1944)
Silents
MAN WHO COULD NOT LOSE, THE(1914); SUCH A LITTLE QUEEN(1914); LAST CHAPTER, THE(1915); PUPPET CROWN, THE(1915); SECRET ORCHARD(1915); BROKEN CHAINS(1916); CLARION, THE(1916); CRIMSON DOVE, THE(1917); CABARET, THE(1918); LEAP TO FAME(1918), a, d; LOVE IN A HURRY(1919); BULLDOG DRUMMOND(1923, Brit.); SHADOW OF EGYPT, THE(1924, Brit.); ONE OF THE BEST(1927, Brit.)
Misc. Silents
(; BOER WAR, THE(1914); KEY TO YESTERDAY, THE(1914); SPITFIRE, THE(1914); HIGH HAND, THE(1915); MR. GREX OF MONTE CARLO(1915); UNCANNY ROOM, THE(1915, Ger.); HIS BROTHER'S WIFE(1916); MADNESS OF HELEN(1916); OCEAN WAIF, THE(1916); SALLY IN OUR ALLEY(1916); SHADOW OF DOUBT, THE(1916); WOMAN'S WAY, A(1916); BURGLAR, THE(1917); GOOD FOR NOTHING, THE(1917), a, d; MARRIAGE MARKET, THE(1917); ON DANGEROUS GROUND(1917); PAGE MYSTERY, THE(1917); PRICE OF PRIDE, THE(1917); SOCIAL

LEPER, THE(1917); SQUARE DEAL, A(1917); YOUTH(1917); BEAUTIFUL MRS. REYNOLDS, THE(1918); BELOVED BLACKMAILER, THE(1918); BY HOOK OR CROOK(1918); HIS ROYAL HIGHNESS(1918), a, d; HITTING THE TRAIL(1918); ROAD TO FRANCE, THE(1918); STOLEN ORDERS(1918); WAY OUT, THE(1918); HIT OR MISS(1919); THREE GREEN EYES(1919); RESTLESS SEX, THE(1920); THIRD WOMAN, THE(1920); BELOVED VAGABOND, THE(1923, Brit.); VIRGIN QUEEN, THE(1923, Brit.); ROLLING ROAD, THE(1927); WRECKER, THE(1928, Brit.); HOUND OF THE BASKERVILLES, THE(1929, Ger.)

Charles Blackwell
PLACE TO GO, A(1964, Brit.), m; SINISTER MAN, THE(1965, Brit.), md; WHAT'S NEW, PUSSYCAT?(1965, U.S./Fr.), md; CANDIDATE FOR MURDER(1966, Brit.), m; SOME GIRLS DO(1969, Brit.), m; PIECE OF THE ACTION, A(1977, w; TIMES SQUARE(1980); FAN, THE(1981)

Chris Blackwell
COUNTRYMAN(1982, Jamaica), p

David Blackwell
CLAUDINE(1974)

Debra Blackwell
MANDINGO(1975)

Douglas Blackwell
HELL, HEAVEN OR HOBOKEN(1958, Brit.); IT'S A WONDERFUL WORLD(1956, Brit.); PANIC IN THE PARLOUR(1957, Brit.); PRIZE OF ARMS, A(1962, Brit.); CRIMSON BLADE, THE(1964, Brit.); IPCRESS FILE, THE(1965, Brit.); BIG SWITCH, THE(1970, Brit.); 10 RILLINGTON PLACE(1971, Brit.)

Evelyn Blackwell
Misc. Talkies
ASHES AND EMBERS(1982)

G. Blackwell
1984(1956, Brit.), spec eff

George Blackwell
ONE NIGHT WITH YOU(1948, Brit), spec eff; LONG AND THE SHORT AND THE TALL, THE(1961, Brit.), spec eff; SUMMER HOLIDAY(1963, Brit.), spec eff; MASQUE OF THE RED DEATH, THE(1964, U.S./Brit.), spec eff; SECRET INVASION, THE(1964), spec eff; SHE(1965, Brit.), spec eff; PREHISTORIC WOMEN(1967, Brit.), spec eff

George Blackwell, Jr.
TWO-HEADED SPY, THE(1959, Brit.), spec eff

Greg Blackwell
TAKE THIS JOB AND SHOVE IT(1981), p

Irene Blackwell
Silents
BLIND HEARTS(1921)
Misc. Silents
EMPTY ARMS(1920); GOOD WOMEN(1921)

James Blackwell
Silents
ONLY SON, THE(1914)

Jim Blackwell
Silents
WITCHING HOUR, THE(1921); ABRAHAM LINCOLN(1924); LOVE'S WILDERNESS(1924)
Misc. Silents
DANCING CHEAT, THE(1924)

John Blackwell
NICKELODEON(1976); OTHER SIDE OF MIDNIGHT, THE(1977)

Ken Blackwell
TRIUMPHS OF A MAN CALLED HORSE(1983, US/Mex.), w

Mary Blackwell
PICK A STAR(1937)

Monika Blackwell
WIZARD OF GORE, THE(1970)

Mr. Blackwell
PROMISES, PROMISES(1963), cos

Nell Blackwell
MAN FROM YESTERDAY, THE(1932), w

Otis Blackwell
JAMBOREE(1957), m

Perry Blackwell
PILLOW TALK(1959)

Tamu Blackwell
1984
STREETS OF FIRE(1984)

Carlyle Blackwell, Jr.
FLIRTATION WALK(1934); STUDENT TOUR(1934); DEVIL DOGS OF THE AIR(1935); GOOSE AND THE GANDER, THE(1935); OLD MAN RHYTHM(1935); DAN MATTHEWS(1936); ROMEO AND JULIET(1936); THRILL OF A LIFETIME(1937); ALL-AMERICAN CO-ED(1941); DOUGHGIRLS, THE(1944); DOCKS OF NEW YORK(1945); THIS MAN'S NAVY(1945); PILGRIM LADY, THE(1947)

The Blackwells
FERRY ACROSS THE MERSEY(1964, Brit.)

Adam Blackwood
1984
PASSAGE TO INDIA, A(1984, Brit.)

George Blackwood
I LOVED A WOMAN(1933); LADY KILLER(1933); SON OF A SAILOR(1933); MASSACRE(1934)

Hope Blackwood
ARIZONA ROUNDUP(1942)

John H. Blackwood
Silents
EASY TO MAKE MONEY(1919), w

Kael Blackwood
CHARLIE CHAN AND THE CURSE OF THE DRAGON QUEEN(1981)

Mary Blackwood
COME ON, MARINES(1934)

Nina Blackwood
VICE SQUAD(1982)

Peggy Blackwood
Silents
ARE ALL MEN ALIKE?(1920)

Carlyle Blackwood, Jr.
OBJECTIVE, BURMA!(1945)

Judi Blacque
KEEP YOUR POWDER DRY(1945)

Taurean Blacque
HOUSE CALLS(1978); ROCKY II(1979)

Madge Blade
GLORY(1955)

Rawyn Blade
HUMAN FACTOR, THE(1979, Brit.)

Brian Blades
FIRE DOWN BELOW(1957, U.S./Brit.)

Kelcie Blades
1984
CHATTANOOGA CHOO CHOO(1984)

Kelsie Blades
HONKYTONK MAN(1982)

Peter Blades
MISSION BLOODY MARY(1967, Fr./Ital./Span.)

Ruben Blades
LAST FIGHT, THE(1983)
Misc. Talkies
LAST FIGHT, THE(1983)

Hilding Bladh
NAKED NIGHT, THE(1956, Swed.), ph; INVASION OF THE ANIMAL PEOPLE(1962, U.S./Swed.), ph

Regine Blaess
PICNIC ON THE GRASS(1960, Fr.)

Michael Blagdon
SEVEN-PER-CENT SOLUTION, THE(1977, Brit.)

Linda Blagg
JUST OUT OF REACH(1979, Aus.), d&w

George Blagoi
NAVY COMES THROUGH, THE(1942); NOB HILL(1945); NORTHWEST OUTPOST(1947)

Lt. George Blagoi
IT HAPPENED ON 5TH AVENUE(1947)
Silents
FOUR SONS(1928)

Tina Blagoi
LITTLE BOY LOST(1953)

Alexander Blagovestov
AND QUIET FLOWS THE DON(1960 USSR)

Rudolf Blahacek
EGON SCHIELE–EXCESS AND PUNISHMENT(1981, Ger.), ph

Hilding Blahd
DREAMS(1960, Swed.), ph

Laszlo Blaho
WITNESS, THE(1982, Hung.), art d

Brian Blain
TOUCH AND GO(1955); PRIVATE COLLECTION(1972, Aus.)

Estella Blain
ROAD TO SHAME, THE(1962, Fr.); THUNDER IN THE BLOOD(1962, Fr.); DIABOLICAL DR. Z, THE(1966 Span./Fr.); FLEA IN HER EAR, A(1968, Fr.)

Gerard Blain
DEADLIER THAN THE MALE(1957, Fr.); YOUNG HUSBANDS(1958, Ital./Fr.); COUSINS, THE(1959, Fr.); LE BEAU SERGE(1959, Fr.); HATARI!(1962); HUNCHBACK OF ROME, THE(1963, Ital.); RUN WITH THE DEVIL(1963, Fr./Ital.); LA BONNE SOUPE(1964, Fr./Ital.); EYE OF THE NEEDLE, THE(1965, Ital./Fr.); SHOCK TROOPS(1968, Ital./Fr.); AMERICAN FRIEND, THE(1977, Ger.); SECOND WIND, A(1978, Fr.), d, w

Howard Blain
LOVE ISLAND(1952)

James Blain
MURDER GOES TO COLLEGE(1937); JOHNNY APOLLO(1940)

Louise Blain
NIGHT OF THE WITCHES(1970)

Luci Blain
DINOSAURUS(1960)

Lucita Blain
FIVE BOLD WOMEN(1960)

Manon Blain
CAT IN THE SACK, THE(1967, Can.)

Pierre Blain
GOLDEN MISTRESS, THE(1954)

Tats Blain
NAVY WIFE(1956), w

Barbara Blaine
SITTING PRETTY(1948); LUSTY MEN, THE(1952)

Doris Blaine
Misc. Talkies
STOLEN PARADISE(1941)

Frank Blaine
INN OF THE SIXTH HAPPINESS, THE(1958); KARATE, THE HAND OF DEATH(1961)

James Blaine
RETURN OF SOPHIE LANG, THE(1936); RHYTHM ON THE RANGE(1936); MAN WHO CRIED WOLF, THE(1937); EXPOSED(1938); JUVENILE COURT(1938); LONE WOLF SPY HUNT, THE(1939); OKLAHOMA FRONTIER(1939); ROARING TWENTIES, THE(1939); GHOST BREAKERS, THE(1940); MAN WHO TALKED TOO MUCH, THE(1940); MAN FROM MONTANA(1941); NOTHING BUT THE TRUTH(1941); REMEMBER THE DAY(1941); FIGHTING BILL FARGO(1942)

James G. Blaine
TELL NO TALES(1939)

Jerry Blaine
BLOOD OF DRACULA(1957); I WAS A TEENAGE WEREWOLF(1957), m/l

Jim Blaine
LET US LIVE(1939)

Lois Blaine
Silents
CRADLE BUSTER, THE(1922)

Marla Blaine
Misc. Talkies
BULLET FOR BILLY THE KID(1963)

Martin Blaine
GLOBAL AFFAIR, A(1964); LIVELY SET, THE(1964); SATAN BUG, THE(1965); FORTUNE COOKIE, THE(1966)

Nancy Lee Blaine
ROYAL BED, THE(1931)

Robert Blaine
Silents
WATCHING EYES(1921), w

Ruby Blaine
Silents
BLUEBEARD'S SEVEN WIVES(1926); LIGHTNING LARIATS(1927); TERROR OF BAR X, THE(1927)
Misc. Silents
GUN-HAND GARRISON(1927); RIDIN' LUCK(1927); WILD BORN(1927)

Sally Blaine
CROSS-EXAMINATION(1932); ANGEL'S HOLIDAY(1937)
Silents
DEAD MAN'S CURVE(1928)

Sparky Blaine
UNHOLY ROLLERS(1972), a, tech adv

Vivian Blaine
GIRL TROUBLE(1942); THRU DIFFERENT EYES(1942); HE HIRED THE BOSS(1943); JITTERBUGS(1943); GREENWICH VILLAGE(1944); SOMETHING FOR THE BOYS(1944); DOLL FACE(1945); NOB HILL(1945); STATE FAIR(1945); IF I'M LUCKY(1946); THREE LITTLE GIRLS IN BLUE(1946); SKIRTS AHOY!(1952); GUYS AND DOLLS(1955); PUBLIC PIGEON NO. 1(1957); RICHARD(1972); DARK, THE(1979); PARASITE(1982)
Misc. Talkies
I'M GOING TO BE FAMOUS(1981)

Alan Blair
HOUR OF THE WOLF, THE(1968, Swed.), subtitles

Alison Blair
DAVID COPPERFIELD(1970, Brit.)

Anthony Blair
ARABIAN NIGHTS(1942); I MARRIED AN ANGEL(1942); FOLLIES GIRL(1943)

Barbara Blair
HOLD MY HAND(1938, Brit.); LUCKY TO ME(1939, Brit.); HIDDEN MENACE, THE(1940, Brit.); OUTSIDER, THE(1940, Brit.); WHO IS GUILTY?(1940, Brit.); FRIGHTENED BRIDE, THE(1952, Brit.)

Bernard Blair
GREAT SPY CHASE, THE(1966, Fr.)

Betsy Blair
DOUBLE LIFE, A(1947); GUILT OF JANET AMES, THE(1947); ANOTHER PART OF THE FOREST(1948); SNAKE PIT, THE(1948); MYSTERY STREET(1950); KIND LADY(1951); MARTY(1955); MAIN STREET(1956, Span.); HALLIDAY BRAND, THE(1957); LIES MY FATHER TOLD ME(1960, Brit.); ALL NIGHT LONG(1961, Brit.); IL GRIDO(1962, U.S./Ital.); MARRY ME! MARRY ME!(1969, Fr.); DELICATE BALANCE, A(1973)

Betty Blair
SPLENDOR(1935); NIGHT AND DAY(1946)

Bill Blair
NEW YEAR'S EVIL(1980)

Bob Blair
LAST FRONTIER UPRISING(1947)

Bonnie Blair
CRACK-UP(1946); FALCON'S ALIBI, THE(1946); RIFFRAFF(1947); WOMAN ON THE BEACH, THE(1947)

Charles Blair
RETURN FROM THE ASHES(1965, U.S./Brit.), w

Charles F. Blair
BEYOND THE CURTAIN(1960, Brit.), w

Clay Blair, Jr.
SURVIVE!(1977, Mex.), w

Collin Blair
WIFE TAKES A FLYER, THE(1942)

David Blair
CLOWN, THE(1953); RACK, THE(1956); ENEMY BELOW, THE(1957); ROMEO AND JULIET(1966, Brit.); PRIVATE LIFE OF SHERLOCK HOLMES, THE(1970, Brit.), ch

Dennis Blair
EASY MONEY(1983), a, w

Dick Blair
NIGHT WALKER, THE(1964), makeup; JOURNEY TO SHILOH(1968), makeup

Don Blair
SANTA CLAUS CONQUERS THE MARTIANS(1964); NO WAY TO TREAT A LADY(1968)

Eleanor Blair
VIOLENT WOMEN(1960)

Frank Blair
SWARM, THE(1978); MARVIN AND TIGE(1983), art d

George Blair
WHISPERING FOOTSTEPS(1943), p; END OF THE ROAD(1944), p&d; SECRETS OF SCOTLAND YARD(1944), p&d; SILENT PARTNER(1944), p&d; GANGS OF THE WATERFRONT(1945), p&d; SCOTLAND YARD INVESTIGATOR(1945, Brit.), p&d; SPORTING CHANCE, A(1945), d; THOROUGHBREDS(1945), d; AFFAIRS OF GERALDINE(1946), d; GAY BLADES(1946), p&d; G.I. WAR BRIDES(1946), d; EXPOSED(1947), d; GHOST GOES WILD, THE(1947), d; THAT'S MY GAL(1947), d; TRESPASSER, THE(1947), d; DAREDEVILS OF THE CLOUDS(1948), d; HOMICIDE FOR THREE(1948), d; KING OF THE GAMBLERS(1948), d; LIGHTNIN' IN THE FOREST(1948), d; MADONNA OF THE DESERT(1948), d; ALIAS THE CHAMP(1949), d; DAUGHTER OF THE JUNGLE(1949), d; DUKE OF CHICAGO(1949), d; FLAMING

FURY(1949), d; POST OFFICE INVESTIGATOR(1949), d; ROSE OF THE YUKON(1949), d; STREETS OF SAN FRANCISCO(1949), d; DESTINATION BIG HOUSE(1950), d; FEDERAL AGENT AT LARGE(1950), d; LONELY HEARTS BANDITS(1950), d; MISSOURIANS, THE(1950), d; UNDER MEXICALI STARS(1950), d; UNMASKED(1950), d; WOMAN FROM HEADQUARTERS(1950), d; INSURANCE INVESTIGATOR(1951), d; SECRETS OF MONTE CARLO(1951), d; SILVER CITY BONANZA(1951), d; THUNDER IN GOD'S COUNTRY(1951), d; DESERT PURSUIT(1952), d; TWINKLE IN GOD'S EYE, THE(1955), d; FIGHTING TROUBLE(1956), d; JAGUAR(1956), d; SABU AND THE MAGIC RING(1957), d; SPOOK CHASERS(1957), d; THE HYPNOTIC EYE(1960), d

Helen Blair
Silents
SPREADING DAWN, THE(1917)

Henry Blair
PRIVATE DETECTIVE(1939); EMERGENCY SQUAD(1940); FOREIGN CORRESPONDENT(1940); AFFECTIONATELY YOURS(1941); KING'S ROW(1942); YANKEE DOODLE DANDY(1942); AIR FORCE(1943); TENTH AVENUE ANGEL(1948); COME FILL THE CUP(1951); WINNING TEAM, THE(1952); SAGINAW TRAIL(1953); DEVIL'S HAIRPIN, THE(1957)
Misc. Talkies
TRAIL BLAZERS(1953)

Isla Blair
DR. TERROR'S HOUSE OF HORRORS(1965, Brit.); FLEA IN HER EAR, A(1968, Fr.); BATTLE OF BRITAIN, THE(1969, Brit.); TASTE THE BLOOD OF DRACULA(1970, Brit.)
1984
REAL LIFE(1984, Brit.)

Janet Blair
THREE GIRLS ABOUT TOWN(1941); BLONDIE GOES TO COLLEGE(1942); BROADWAY(1942); MY SISTER EILEEN(1942); TWO YANKS IN TRINIDAD(1942); SOMETHING TO SHOUT ABOUT(1943); ONCE UPON A TIME(1944); TONIGHT AND EVERY NIGHT(1945); GALLANT JOURNEY(1946); TARS AND SPARS(1946); FABULOUS DORSEYS, THE(1947); I LOVE TROUBLE(1947); BLACK ARROW(1948); FULLER BRUSH MAN(1948); PUBLIC PIGEON NO. 1(1957); BOYS' NIGHT OUT(1962); BURN WITCH BURN(1962); ONE AND ONLY GENUINE ORIGINAL FAMILY BAND, THE(1968); WON TON TON, THE DOG WHO SAVED HOLLYWOOD(1976)

Joan Blair
HIS WOMAN(1931); MURDER OF DR. HARRIGAN, THE(1936); NO, NO NANETTE(1940); SHOP AROUND THE CORNER, THE(1940); MR. DISTRICT ATTORNEY(1941); RAGS TO RICHES(1941); CONSTANT NYMPH, THE(1943); LADY TAKES A CHANCE, A(1943); MY SON, THE HERO(1943); SON OF DRACULA(1943); STRANGE DEATH OF ADOLF HITLER, THE(1943); WHISPERING FOOTSTEPS(1943); SILENT PARTNER(1944); GRISSLY'S MILLIONS(1945); ANGEL ON MY SHOULDER(1946); DEADLINE FOR MURDER(1946); ARTHUR TAKES OVER(1948); SONS OF ADVENTURE(1948); STREET WITH NO NAME, THE(1948); NEVER WAVE AT A WAC(1952)

Joe Blair
SUNSET IN WYOMING(1941), w

John Blair
SYNDICATE, THE(1968, Brit.), ed

Joyce Blair
TROJAN BROTHERS, THE(1946); JAZZ BOAT(1960, Brit.); KILLERS OF KILIMANJARO(1960, Brit.); NUMBER SIX(1962, Brit.); CROOKS ANONYMOUS(1963, Brit.); BE MY GUEST(1965, Brit.); WILD AFFAIR, THE(1966, Brit.); MISTER TEN PERCENT(1967, Brit.)

June Blair
OUR MISS BROOKS(1956); HELL BOUND(1957); THIS COULD BE THE NIGHT(1957); ISLAND OF LOST WOMEN(1959); LONE TEXAN(1959); RABBIT TRAP, THE(1959); WARLOCK(1959); FEVER IN THE BLOOD, A(1961)

Katherine Blair
Misc. Silents
PAUPER MILLIONAIRE, THE(1922, Brit.)

Leonel Blair
WORLD OF SUZIE WONG, THE(1960)

Les Blair
1984
NUMBER ONE(1984, Brit.), d

Leslie Blair
BLEAK MOMENTS(1972, Brit.), p, ed

Linda Blair
WAY WE LIVE NOW, THE(1970); SPORTING CLUB, THE(1971); EXORCIST, THE(1973); AIRPORT 1975(1974); EXORCIST II: THE HERETIC(1977); ROLLER BOOGIE(1979); WILD HORSE HANK(1979, Can.); HELL NIGHT(1981); RUCKUS(1981); CHAINED HEAT(1983 U.S./Ger.)
1984
NIGHT PATROL(1984); SAVAGE STREETS(1984)

Lionel Blair
LIMPING MAN, THE(1953, Brit.); KING'S RHAPSODY(1955, Brit.); WORLD OF SUZIE WONG, THE(1960); MAIN ATTRACTION, THE(1962, Brit.), a, ch; COOL MIKADO, THE(1963, Brit.); HARD DAY'S NIGHT, A(1964, Brit.); PROMISE HER ANYTHING(1966, Brit.), ch; MAROC 7(1967, Brit.); SALT & PEPPER(1968, Brit.), ch; MAGIC CHRISTIAN, THE(1970, Brit.), ch

Mary Blair
MAKE MINE MUSIC(1946), art d

Nancy Blair
ROLLERBALL(1975)

Nickey Blair
HELL TO ETERNITY(1960)

Nicky Blair
UNTIL THEY SAIL(1957); ROGUE COP(1954); BEHIND THE HIGH WALL(1956); CRASHING LAS VEGAS(1956); HOLD BACK THE NIGHT(1956); RUNAWAY DAUGHTERS(1957); JET ATTACK(1958); OPERATION PETTICOAT(1959); SUBMARINE SEAHAWK(1959); OCEAN'S ELEVEN(1960); SECOND TIME AROUND, THE(1961); FORTY POUNDS OF TROUBLE(1962); MANCHURIAN CANDIDATE, THE(1962); VIVA LAS VEGAS(1964); DIAMONDS ARE FOREVER(1971, Brit.); HARRY AND WALTER GO TO NEW YORK(1976); NEW YORK, NEW YORK(1977)

Pam Blair
ANNIE(1982)

Pat Blair
  CAGE OF EVIL(1960)
Patricia Blair
  CITY OF FEAR(1959); LADIES MAN, THE(1961)
Misc. Talkies
  LEFT HAND OF GEMINI, THE(1972)
Preston Blair
  FANTASIA(1940), anim, anim; PINOCCHIO(1940), anim
Reno Blair [Browne]
  GENTLEMAN FROM TEXAS(1946); UNDER ARIZONA SKIES(1946); RAIDERS OF
  THE SOUTH(1947); FRONTIER AGENT(1948)
Misc. Talkies
  LAW COMES TO GUNSIGHT, THE(1947)
Rhio H. Blair
  COMPETITION, THE(1980); ONE DARK NIGHT(1983)
Robert Blair
  ROCKY MOUNTAIN RANGERS(1940); TRAIL BLAZERS, THE(1940); UNDER-
  GROUND RUSTLERS(1941); SWINGIN' SUMMER, A(1965); WILD ONES ON
  WHEELS(1967)
Ruth Blair
Misc. Silents
  FOURTH ESTATE, THE(1916)
Sally Blair
  GUN RUNNER(1969)
Susan Blair
  SALT & PEPPER(1968, Brit.)
Thomas A. Blair
  PEER GYNT(1965)
Violet Blair
Silents
  SIGN OF THE ROSE, THE(1922), ed
Virginia Blair
  MANNEQUIN(1937)
William Blair
Silents
  GARRISON'S FINISH(1923), w
William E. "Red" Blair
  STANLEY AND LIVINGSTONE(1939)
Hal Blaire
  ROLLIN' HOME TO TEXAS(1941)
Linda Blais
1984
  BLAME IT ON THE NIGHT(1984)
Robert Blais
  GAS(1981, Can.)
Yvette Blais
  MIGHTY MOUSE IN THE GREAT SPACE CHASE(1983), m
Audrey A. Blaisdel
  BLUME IN LOVE(1973), set d
Audrey Blaisdel
  GOING HOME(1971), set d; BAD COMPANY(1972), set d
Anne Blaisdell
  DIE, DIE, MY DARLING(1965, Brit.), w
Brad Blaisdell
  TOGETHER FOR DAYS(1972)
Charles Blaisdell
Misc. Silents
  MAINSPRING, THE(1917)
Makee K. Blaisdell
  LAST OF THE SECRET AGENTS?, THE(1966)
Nesbitt Blaisdell
  EDDIE MACON'S RUN(1983)
Paul Blaisdell
  DAY THE WORLD ENDED, THE(1956), a, spec eff; IT CONQUERED THE
  WORLD(1956), a, spec eff; SHE-CREATURE, THE(1956); FROM HELL IT CA-
  ME(1957), spec eff; INVASION OF THE SAUCER MEN(1957), spec eff; MOTORCYCLE
  GANG(1957); NOT OF THIS EARTH(1957), spec eff; VOODOO WOMAN(1957); IT! THE
  TERROR FROM BEYOND SPACE(1958), cos; GHOST OF DRAGSTRIP HOLLOW
  zero(1959)
William Blaisdell
Silents
  YANKEE CLIPPER, THE(1927)
Jean Blaise
  WANDERER, THE(1969, Fr.)
Pierre Blaise
  LACOMBE, LUCIEN(1974); DOWN THE ANCIENT STAIRCASE(1975, Ital.)
Harry Blaising
Misc. Silents
  LONG CHANCE, THE(1915)
A. Blajaev
  AMPHIBIOUS MAN, THE(1961, USSR), w
A. D. Blake
Silents
  KNIGHT OF THE RANGE, A(1916)
Alfonso Corona Blake
  SANTO EN EL MUSEO DE CERA(1963, Mex.), d
Amanda Blake
  COUNTERSPY MEETS SCOTLAND YARD(1950); DUCHESS OF IDAHO, THE(1950);
  STARS IN MY CROWN(1950); SMUGGLER'S GOLD(1951); SUNNY SIDE OF THE
  STREET(1951); CATTLE TOWN(1952); SCARLET ANGEL(1952); LILI(1953); SABRE
  JET(1953); ABOUT MRS. LESLIE(1954); ADVENTURES OF HAJJI BABA(1954); MISS
  ROBIN CRUSOE(1954); STAR IS BORN, A(1954); GLASS SLIPPER, THE(1955); HIGH
  SOCIETY(1955)
Angela Blake
  I WAS A TEENAGE FRANKENSTEIN(1958)
Ann Blake
  ADVANCE TO THE REAR(1964); DIAMONDS FOR BREAKFAST(1968, Brit.)

Anne Blake
  DRAGON OF PENDRAGON CASTLE, THE(1950, Brit.); SECOND MATE, THE(1950,
  Brit.); HOSTAGE, THE(1956, Brit.); CURSE OF FRANKENSTEIN, THE(1957, Brit.);
  PANIC IN THE PARLOUR(1957, Brit.); DUBLIN NIGHTMARE(1958, Brit.); MURDER
  REPORTED(1958, Brit.); ORDERS TO KILL(1958, Brit.); SECRET PLACE, THE(1958,
  Brit.); CURSE OF THE WEREWOLF, THE(1961, Brit.); SATURDAY NIGHT AND SUNDAY
  MORNING(1961, Brit.); SCREAM OF FEAR(1961, Brit.); SPY WHO CAME IN FROM
  THE COLD, THE(1965, Brit.); GYPSY GIRL(1966, Brit.); PRIVATE LIFE OF SHER-
  LOCK HOLMES, THE(1970, Brit.)
Anthony Blake
  PICKUP ON 101(1972), w
Arthur Blake
  SHERLOCK HOLMES AND THE VOICE OF TERROR(1942); GASLIGHT(1944);
  MAN IN HALF-MOON STREET, THE(1944); MINISTRY OF FEAR(1945); DOWN TO
  EARTH(1947); PORT OF NEW YORK(1949); CYRANO DE BERGERAC(1950); DI-
  PLOMATIC COURIER(1952); HAREM GIRL(1952); ENEMY FROM SPACE(1957, Brit.)
B.K. Blake
Misc. Silents
  DELIVERANCE(1928), d
Barbara Blake
  SURVIVAL(1976)
Barry Edward Blake
  GAS(1981, Can.)
Ben Blake
Misc. Silents
  PORCELAIN LAMP, THE(1921), d
Ben K. Blake
  TWO SISTERS(1938), d
Benjamin Blake
1984
  COLD FEET(1984), ph
Betty Blake
  MADNESS OF THE HEART(1949, Brit.)
Misc. Silents
  CLEAN-UP, THE(1929)
Beverly Blake
  CREATURES THE WORLD FORGOT(1971, Brit.)
Bill Blake
1984
  RHINESTONE(1984), p
Bobby [Robert] Blake
  I LOVE YOU AGAIN(1940); ANDY HARDY'S DOUBLE LIFE(1942); CHINA
  GIRL(1942); MOKEY(1942); SALUTE TO THE MARINES(1943); SLIGHTLY DANGER-
  OUS(1943); BIG NOISE, THE(1944); CHEYENNE WILDCAT(1944); LOST AN-
  GEL(1944); MARSHAL OF RENO(1944); MEET THE PEOPLE(1944); SAN ANTONIO
  KID, THE(1944); SHERIFF OF LAS VEGAS(1944); VIGILANTES OF DODGE CI-
  TY(1944); COLORADO PIONEERS(1945); DAKOTA(1945); GREAT STAGECOACH
  ROBBERY(1945); HORN BLOWS AT MIDNIGHT, THE(1945); LONE TEXAS RANG-
  ER(1945); MARSHAL OF LAREDO(1945); PHANTOM OF THE PLAINS(1945); PIL-
  LOW TO POST(1945); WOMAN IN THE WINDOW, THE(1945); CONQUEST OF
  CHEYENNE(1946); GUY COULD CHANGE, A(1946); HOME ON THE RANGE(1946);
  HUMORESQUE(1946); IN OLD SACRAMENTO(1946); OUT CALIFORNIA WAY(1946);
  SANTA FE UPRISING(1946); SHERIFF OF REDWOOD VALLEY(1946); STAGE-
  COACH TO DENVER(1946); SUN VALLEY CYCLONE(1946); HOMESTEADERS OF
  PARADISE VALLEY(1947); LAST ROUND-UP, THE(1947); MARSHAL OF CRIPPLE
  CREEK, THE(1947); OREGON TRAIL SCOUTS(1947); RETURN OF RIN TIN TIN,
  THE(1947); RUSTLERS OF DEVIL'S CANYON(1947); VIGILANTES OF BOOM-
  TOWN(1947); TREASURE OF THE SIERRA MADRE, THE(1948); BLACK ROSE,
  THE(1950); APACHE WAR SMOKE(1952); TREASURE OF THE GOLDEN CON-
  DOR(1953); VEILS OF BAGDAD, THE(1953); RACK, THE(1956); SCREAMING EA-
  GLES(1956); THREE VIOLENT PEOPLE(1956); WAGON WHEELS WESTWARD(1956)
Misc. Talkies
  CALIFORNIA GOLD RUSH(1946)
Carole Blake
  SECOND BEST SECRET AGENT IN THE WHOLE WIDE WORLD, THE(1965, Brit.)
Catherine Blake
  DARK LIGHT, THE(1951, Brit.)
Charles E. Blake
  COUNTRY DOCTOR, THE(1936), w
Denis Blake
  CARRY ON SCREAMING(1966, Brit.)
Douglas Blake
  MY THIRD WIFE GEORGE(1968)
Edmund Blake
Misc. Silents
  FLOTSAM(1921), d
Elizabeth Blake
  DON'T EVER LEAVE ME(1949, Brit.)
Ellen Blake
  HARRY AND WALTER GO TO NEW YORK(1976); CHAMELEON(1978); CANNERY
  ROW(1982)
1984
  LAST STARFIGHTER, THE(1984)
Ellsworth Blake
  MY REPUTATION(1946); TAKE ME OUT TO THE BALL GAME(1949)
Eubie Blake
  SCOTT JOPLIN(1977)
Frank Blake
  KID FOR TWO FARTHINGS, A(1956, Brit.)
Geoffrey Blake
1984
  LAST STARFIGHTER, THE(1984)
George Blake
  KID GALAHAD(1937); SHIPBUILDERS, THE(1943, Brit.), w; GIRL ON THE
  SPOT(1946), w; FLOODTIDE(1949, Brit.), w
Gerald Blake
  DANCE OF DEATH, THE(1938, Brit.), p&d

Gilliam Blake
ROGUES OF SHERWOOD FOREST(1950)

Gisella Blake
GRAND THEFT AUTO(1977)

Gladys Blake
TIME OF YOUR LIFE, THE(1948); BY APPOINTMENT ONLY(1933); I HAVE LIVED(1933); MY WEAKNESS(1933); RAINBOW OVER BROADWAY(1933); SING SINNER, SING(1933); MARRYING WIDOWS(1934); SERVANTS' ENTRANCE(1934); RACING BLOOD(1938); THERE'S THAT WOMAN AGAIN(1938); YOU CAN'T TAKE IT WITH YOU(1938); FAST AND FURIOUS(1939); LUCKY NIGHT(1939); TELL NO TALES(1939); THESE GLAMOUR GIRLS(1939); WHEN TOMORROW COMES(1939); DR. KILDARE'S CRISIS(1940); EARL OF CHICAGO, THE(1940); I LOVE YOU AGAIN(1940); MONEY TO BURN(1940); SAILOR'S LADY(1940); YOUNG AS YOU FEEL(1940); LADY FROM CHEYENNE(1941); LUCKY DEVILS(1941); WEST POINT WIDOW(1941); JOHNNY EAGER(1942); MAGNIFICENT DOPE, THE(1942); SHIP AHOY(1942); STAR SPANGLED RHYTHM(1942); WHO DONE IT?(1942); WOMAN OF THE YEAR(1942); MORE THE MERRIER, THE(1943); PHANTOM OF THE OPERA(1943); STRANGER IN TOWN, A(1943); CAREER GIRL(1944); Hl BEAUTIFUL(1944); IN SOCIETY(1944); JOHNNY DOESN'T LIVE HERE ANY MORE(1944); PRACTICALLY YOURS(1944); RECKLESS AGE(1944); BEWITCHED(1945); HER HIGHNESS AND THE BELLBOY(1945); HER LUCKY NIGHT(1945); LET'S GO STEADY(1945); NAUGHTY NINETIES, THE(1945); OVER 21(1945); ROCKIN' IN THE ROCKIES(1945); THERE GOES KELLY(1945); UNDER WESTERN SKIES(1945); LIVE WIRES(1946); NOCTURNE(1946); SHADOWS OVER CHINATOWN(1946); STRANGE TRIANGLE(1946); TO EACH HIS OWN(1946); FEAR IN THE NIGHT(1947); SCARED TO DEATH(1947); LADIES OF THE CHORUS(1948); MICHAEL O'HALLORAN(1948); NIGHT HAS A THOUSAND EYES(1948); SMART WOMAN(1948); PAID IN FULL(1950); THIS WOMAN IS DANGEROUS(1952)

Grey Blake
YOUTHFUL FOLLY(1934, Brit.); JAVA HEAD(1935, Brit.); SOMEWHERE IN CIVVIES(1943, Brit.); TWILIGHT HOUR(1944, Brit.); TAWNY PIPIT(1947, Brit.); BROKEN JOURNEY(1948, Brit.); EASY MONEY(1948, Brit.); JASSY(1948, Brit.); DANCING YEARS, THE(1950, Brit.); LOST PEOPLE, THE(1950, Brit.); NIGHT WON'T TALK, THE(1952, Brit.); PAUL TEMPLE RETURNS(1952, Brit.)

Guy Blake
WHEN THE LIGHTS GO ON AGAIN(1944)

Harold Blake
FOLLOW THE SUN(1951)

Henry Blake
OPERATION SECRET(1952), p

Honor Blake
WINSLOW BOY, THE(1950)

Howard Blake
ALL THE WAY UP(1970, Brit.), m; ELEPHANT CALLED SLOWLY, AN(1970, Brit.), m, md; SOME WILL, SOME WON'T(1970, Brit.), m; RAINBOW BOYS, THE(1973, Can.), m; DUELLISTS, THE(1977, Brit.), m; ODD JOB, THE(1978, Brit.), m; FLASH GORDON(1980), m; STRONGER THAN THE SUN(1980, Brit.), m; AMITYVILLE 3-D(1983), m; LORDS OF DISCIPLINE, THE(1983), m
1984
RIDDLE OF THE SANDS, THE(1984, Brit.), m

Jean Blake
THIS EARTH IS MINE(1959)

Jeremy Blake
MC VICAR(1982, Brit.)

John Blake
FEAR SHIP, THE(1933, Brit.); PROFILE(1954, Brit.)

Jon Blake
Misc. Talkies
CHILL, THE(1981)

Jonathan Blake
FORCE 10 FROM NAVARONE(1978, Brit.)

Joseph Blake
Misc. Silents
BROKEN VIOLIN, THE(1923)

Josephine Blake
HEADLESS GHOST, THE(1959, Brit.); THREE HATS FOR LISA(1965, Brit.)

Jovanhy Blake
UNDERGROUND AGENT(1942)

Judith Blake
WANTED: JANE TURNER(1936)

Julia Blake
GETTING OF WISDOM, THE(1977, Aus.); PATRICK(1979, Aus.); MY BRILLIANT CAREER(1980, Aus.); DAY AFTER HALLOWEEN, THE(1981, Aus.); LONELY HEARTS(1983, Aus.)
1984
MAN OF FLOWERS(1984, Aus.)

Julie Blake
WORDS AND MUSIC(1929)

Karen Blake
Misc. Talkies
SUNDANCE CASSIDY AND BUTCH THE KID(1975); CONVOY BUDDIES(1977)

Karin Blake
GNOME-MOBILE, THE(1967)

Katharine Blake
TO HAVE AND TO HOLD(1963, Brit.); ANNE OF THE THOUSAND DAYS(1969, Brit.)

Katherine Blake
HAMMER THE TOFF(1952, Brit.); STRANGER IN BETWEEN, THE(1952, Brit.); NOW THAT APRIL'S HERE(1958, Can.)

Kathleen Blake
Silents
NEW CLOWN, THE(1916, Brit.)

Kathryn Blake
ASSASSIN FOR HIRE(1951, Brit.)

Larry Blake
YOU CAN'T RUN AWAY FROM IT(1956); ROAD BACK,THE(1937); TROUBLE AT MIDNIGHT(1937); AIR DEVILS(1938); JURY'S SECRET, THE(1938); NURSE FROM BROOKLYN(1938); STATE POLICE(1938); YOUNG FUGITIVES(1938); THEY MADE HER A SPY(1939); DEADLINE FOR MURDER(1946); MAGNIFICENT DOLL(1946); UNDERCOVER WOMAN, THE(1946); BACKLASH(1947); SECOND CHANCE(1947);

SMASH-UP, THE STORY OF A WOMAN(1947); TRAP, THE(1947); CALL NORTHSIDE 777(1948); FORCE OF EVIL(1948); FRENCH LEAVE(1948); HUNTED, THE(1948); LUCKY STIFF, THE(1949); SUNSET BOULEVARD(1950); MARRYING KIND, THE(1952); WINNING TEAM, THE(1952); CRUISIN' DOWN THE RIVER(1953); DEVIL'S CANYON(1953); REMAINS TO BE SEEN(1953); SEVEN BRIDES FOR SEVEN BROTHERS(1954); CREATURE WITH THE ATOM BRAIN(1955); I DIED A THOUSAND TIMES(1955); INSIDE DETROIT(1955); SON OF SINBAD(1955); TEENAGE CRIME WAVE(1955); EARTH VS. THE FLYING SAUCERS(1956); RUMBLE ON THE DOCKS(1956); WHILE THE CITY SLEEPS(1956); BADLANDS OF MONTANA(1957); BAND OF ANGELS(1957); ESCAPE FROM SAN QUENTIN(1957); JEANNE EAGELS(1957); OUTCASTS OF THE CITY(1958); TOO MUCH, TOO SOON(1958); PORTRAIT OF A MOBSTER(1961); THAT FUNNY FEELING(1965); RARE BREED, THE(1966); HANG'EM HIGH(1968); DIAMONDS ARE FOREVER(1971, Brit.)

Larry J. Blake
HOLIDAY AFFAIR(1949); BLONDE BANDIT, THE(1950); DESTINATION BIG HOUSE(1950); ONE TOO MANY(1950); IRON MAN, THE(1951); HIGH NOON(1952); MAN IS ARMED, THE(1956); WEREWOLF, THE(1956); BEGINNING OF THE END(1957); THAT DARN CAT(1965); DEMON SEED(1977); TIME AFTER TIME(1979, Brit.)

Loretta Blake
Silents
SABLE LORCHA, THE(1915); JUST OUT OF COLLEGE(1921)
Misc. Silents
HIS PICTURE IN THE PAPERS(1916)

Lorette Blake
Silents
ETERNAL GRIND, THE(1916)

Lucius Blake
POISONED DIAMOND, THE(1934, Brit.); POWER(1934, Brit.)

Lucy Blake
Silents
SOLD AT AUCTION(1917)
Misc. Silents
STOLEN PLAY, THE(1917)

Madge Blake
ADAM'S RIB(1949); BETWEEN MIDNIGHT AND DAWN(1950); FINDERS KEEPERS(1951); PROWLER, THE(1951); QUEEN FOR A DAY(1951); BAD AND THE BEAUTIFUL, THE(1952); IRON MISTRESS, THE(1952); IT GROWS ON TREES(1952); SINGIN' IN THE RAIN(1952); SKIRTS AHOY!(1952); SOMETHING FOR THE BIRDS(1952); DANGEROUS CROSSING(1953); IT HAPPENS EVERY THURSDAY(1953); FIREMAN SAVE MY CHILD(1954); LONG, LONG TRAILER, THE(1954); RHAPSODY(1954); IT'S ALWAYS FAIR WEATHER(1955); TENDER TRAP, THE(1955); PLEASE MURDER ME(1956); SOLID GOLD CADILLAC, THE(1956); LOVING YOU(1957); PLEASE DON'T EAT THE DAISIES(1960); SERGEANTS 3(1962); BATMAN(1966); FOLLOW ME, BOYS!(1966); LAST OF THE SECRET AGENTS?, THE(1966)

Marian Blake
PLAYGROUND, THE(1965)

Marie Blake
MANNEQUIN(1937); MY DEAR MISS ALDRICH(1937); DRAMATIC SCHOOL(1938); LOVE FINDS ANDY HARDY(1938); MAN-PROOF(1938); RICH MAN, POOR GIRL(1938); THREE LOVES HAS NANCY(1938); YOUNG DR. KILDARE(1938); BLIND ALLEY(1939); CALLING DR. KILDARE(1939); DAY-TIME WIFE(1939); ICE FOLLIES OF 1939(1939); JUDGE HARDY AND SON(1939); SECRET OF DR. KILDARE, THE(1939); WOMEN, THE(1939); CHILD IS BORN, A(1940); DR. KILDARE GOES HOME(1940); DR. KILDARE'S CRISIS(1940); DR. KILDARE'S STRANGE CASE(1940); SAILOR'S LADY(1940); THEY DRIVE BY NIGHT(1940); THEY KNEW WHAT THEY WANTED(1940); BLUE, WHITE, AND PERFECT(1941); CAUGHT IN THE DRAFT(1941); DR. KILDARE'S VICTORY(1941); DR. KILDARE'S WEDDING DAY(1941); HERE COMES HAPPINESS(1941); PEOPLE VS. DR. KILDARE, THE(1941); REMEMBER THE DAY(1941); SMALL TOWN DEB(1941); CALLING DR. GILLESPIE(1942); DR. GILLESPIE'S NEW ASSISTANT(1942); GIVE OUT, SISTERS(1942); I MARRIED A WITCH(1942); MAJOR AND THE MINOR, THE(1942); WIFE TAKES A FLYER, THE(1942); CAMPUS RYTHM(1943); DR. GILLESPIE'S CRIMINAL CASE(1943); DU BARRY WAS A LADY(1943); GOOD MORNING, JUDGE(1943); WHISPERING FOOTSTEPS(1943); BETWEEN TWO WOMEN(1944); GILDERSLEEVE'S GHOST(1944); MAKE YOUR OWN BED(1944); SENSATIONS OF 1945(1944); SOUTH OF DIXIE(1944); ABBOTT AND COSTELLO IN HOLLYWOOD(1945); CHRISTMAS IN CONNECTICUT(1945); KEEP YOUR POWDER DRY(1945); PILLOW TO POST(1945); ROUGHLY SPEAKING(1945); CHRISTMAS EVE(1947); DARK DELUSION(1947); GANGSTER, THE(1947); MOURNING BECOMES ELECTRA(1947); GIRL FROM MANHATTAN(1948); SNAKE PIT, THE(1948); ALIMONY(1949); ANGELS IN DISGUISE(1949); CHICAGO DEADLINE(1949); SONS OF NEW MEXICO(1949); PAID IN FULL(1950); WOMAN OF DISTINCTION, A(1950); FBI GIRL(1951); LOVE NEST(1951); SMALL TOWN GIRL(1953)

Marle Blake
DON'T TRUST YOUR HUSBAND(1948)

Mary Blake
CODE OF THE RANGE(1937)

Michael Blake
STACY'S KNIGHTS(1983), w

Miriam Blake
HAPPY ENDING, THE(1969)

Mitzi Blake
LUST FOR LIFE(1956)

Morris Blake
KIMBERLEY JIM(1965, South Africa)

Nicholas Blake
THIS MAN MUST DIE(1970, Fr./Ital.), w

Nina Blake
Misc. Silents
PRIMROSE PATH, THE(1915)

Noble Blake
FRENCHMAN'S CREEK(1944); KISMET(1944)

Oliver B. Blake
REUNION IN FRANCE(1942)

Oliver Blake

NEW YORK TOWN(1941); SHADOW OF THE THIN MAN(1941); MISSION TO MOSCOW(1943); SWEET ROSIE O'GRADY(1943); DOUGHGIRLS, THE(1944); THIN MAN GOES HOME, THE(1944); UP IN ARMS(1944); COLONEL EFFINGHAM'S RAID(1945); MEDAL FOR BENNY, A(1945); BLONDE ALIBI(1946); MY REPUTATION(1946); GINGER(1947); GUILTY, THE(1947); NIGHTMARE ALLEY(1947); OUT OF THE PAST(1947); SENATOR WAS INDISCREET, THE(1947); CHALLENGE, THE(1948); CRY OF THE CITY(1948); LET'S LIVE A LITTLE(1948); MIRACLE OF THE BELLS, THE(1948); MOONRISE(1948); PALEFACE, THE(1948); SUMMER HOLIDAY(1948); WALLS OF JERICHO(1948); COLORADO TERRITORY(1949); WOMAN'S SECRET, A(1949); FANCY PANTS(1950); FATHER OF THE BRIDE(1950); MA AND PA KETTLE GO TO TOWN(1950); CHAIN OF CIRCUMSTANCE(1951); MA AND PA KETTLE BACK ON THE FARM(1951); RHUBARB(1951); FEUDIN' FOOLS(1952); MA AND PA KETTLE AT THE FAIR(1952); ROOM FOR ONE MORE(1952); SON OF PALEFACE(1952); HOUDINI(1953); HOUSE OF WAX(1953); JULIUS CAESAR(1953); MA AND PA KETTLE ON VACATION(1953); SO BIG(1953); CASANOVA'S BIG NIGHT(1954); LONG, LONG TRAILER, THE(1954); MA AND PA KETTLE AT HOME(1954); SUSAN SLEPT HERE(1954); COBWEB, THE(1955); HELL'S OUTPOST(1955); MA AND PA KETTLE AT WAIKIKI(1955); SEVEN LITTLE FOYS, THE(1955); RAINTREE COUNTY(1957)

Pamela Blake [Adele Pearce]

SORORITY HOUSE(1939); MEN AGAINST THE SKY(1940); TOO MANY GIRLS(1940); DR. GILLESPIE'S NEW ASSISTANT(1942); MAISIE GETS HER MAN(1942); OMAHA TRAIL, THE(1942); THIS GUN FOR HIRE(1942); KID DYNAMITE(1943); SLIGHTLY DANGEROUS(1943); SWING FEVER(1943); SWING SHIFT MAISIE(1943); UNKNOWN GUEST, THE(1943); CAPTAIN TUGBOAT ANNIE(1945); THREE'S A CROWD(1945); WHY GIRLS LEAVE HOME(1945); LIVE WIRES(1946); MYSTERIOUS INTRUDER(1946); PARTNERS IN TIME(1946); WAKE UP AND DREAM(1946); HIGHWAY 13(1948); SON OF GOD'S COUNTRY(1948); STAGE STRUCK(1948); SKY LINER(1949); BORDER RANGERS(1950); DALTON'S WOMEN, THE(1950); FEDERAL MAN(1950); GUNFIRE(1950); JOE PALOOKA MEETS HUMPHREY(1950); DANGER ZONE(1951); WACO(1952); GHOST OF ZORRO(1959)

Misc. Talkies

ROLLING HOME(1948)

Pat Blake

JUMP INTO HELL(1955)

Patricia Blake

BLACK SLEEP, THE(1956); CRIME AGAINST JOE(1956)

Paul Blake

JOY RIDE(1935, Brit.); LAZYBONES(1935, Brit.); CRIMSON CIRCLE, THE(1936, Brit.); KING OF THE CASTLE(1936, Brit.); TWICE BRANDED(1936, Brit.); CAFE COLETTE(1937, Brit.); CATCH AS CATCH CAN(1937, Brit.); FIVE POUND MAN, THE(1937, Brit.); JENIFER HALE(1937, Brit.); DARTS ARE TRUMPS(1938, Brit.); YOU'RE THE DOCTOR(1938, Brit.); LILAC DOMINO, THE(1940, Brit.); WELCOME, MR. WASHINGTON(1944, Brit.); GREEN FINGERS(1947); NOTHING VENTURE(1948, Brit.); SHOWTIME(1948, Brit.); MY BROTHER JONATHAN(1949, Brit.); CASTLE IN THE AIR(1952, Brit.); SOME OF MY BEST FRIENDS ARE...(1971)

Richard Blake

DEVIL IS DRIVING, THE(1937), w; CROOKED ROAD, THE(1940), w; INVADERS FROM MARS(1953), w; COUNTERPLOT(1959), w; GIRL ON A MOTORCYCLE, THE(1968, Fr./Brit.)

Robby [Robert] Blake

TUCSON RAIDERS(1944)

Robert Blake

BLACKOUT(1950, Brit.), p; RUMBLE ON THE DOCKS(1956); TIJUANA STORY, THE(1957); BEAST OF BUDAPEST, THE(1958); REVOLT IN THE BIG HOUSE(1958); BATTLE CRY(1959); PORK CHOP HILL(1959); PURPLE GANG, THE(1960); TOWN WITHOUT PITY(1961, Ger./Switz./U.S.); PT 109(1963); GREATEST STORY EVER TOLD, THE(1965); THIS PROPERTY IS CONDEMNED(1966); IN COLD BLOOD(1967); TELL THEM WILLIE BOY IS HERE(1969); RIPPED-OFF(1971, Ital.); CORKY(1972); ELECTRA GLIDE IN BLUE(1973); BUSTING(1974); COAST TO COAST(1980); SECOND-HAND HEARTS(1981)

Robin Blake

PATERNITY(1981)

Roger Blake

WHITE HUNTER(1965)

Rosemary Blake

DEVIL'S WIDOW, THE(1972, Brit.)

Sally Blake

MATCHLESS(1974, Aus.), a, w

Sam Blake

M'BLIMEY(1931, Brit.); DOUBLE OR QUITS(1938, Brit.); DREAMING(1944, Brit.); KISENGA, MAN OF AFRICA(1952, Brit.)

Sarah Blake

MOM AND DAD(1948)

Seon Blake

POWERFORCE(1983)

Sondra Blake

KILLER ELITE, THE(1975); SECOND-HAND HEARTS(1981); MAX DUGAN RETURNS(1983)

Steven Blake

1984

AMERICAN NIGHTMARE(1984), w

Stuart Blake

FLASH GORDON(1980)

Sue Ellen Blake

SWINDLE, THE(1962, Fr./Ital.)

Terry Blake

CARNIVAL ROCK(1957)

Thomas Blake

Silents

PAIR OF CUPIDS, A(1918)

Misc. Silents

CHILDREN OF EVE, THE(1915)

Timothy Blake

DIRTY DINGUS MAGEE(1970); LOVE IS A FUNNY THING(1970, Fr./Ital.); PETE 'N' TILLIE(1972); HANGUP(1974); SPECIAL DELIVERY(1976); NEW YORK, NEW YORK(1977); THEY WENT THAT-A-WAY AND THAT-A-WAY(1978)

1984

DREAMSCAPE(1984); FINDERS KEEPERS(1984)

Tom Blake

Silents

AVENGING TRAIL, THE(1918); FLYING PAT(1920); EXCITERS, THE(1923); LOYAL LIVES(1923); YOUTH FOR SALE(1924)

Misc. Silents

MAROONED HEARTS(1920); WONDERFUL CHANCE, THE(1920)

Whitney Blake

MY GUN IS QUICK(1957); –30–(1959); BETSY, THE(1978)

William Blake

FBI GIRL(1951), p&d

William Dorsey Blake

SHAME, SHAME, EVERYBODY KNOWS HER NAME(1969), w

Yvonne Blake

JUDITH(1965), cos; FAHRENHEIT 451(1966, Brit.); IDOL, THE(1966, Brit.), cos; SPY WITH A COLD NOSE, THE(1966, Brit.), cos; ASSIGNMENT K(1968, Brit.), cos; CHARLIE BUBBLES(1968, Brit.), cos; DUFFY(1968, Brit.), cos; BEST HOUSE IN LONDON, THE(1969, Brit.), cos; BROTHERLY LOVE(1970, Brit.), cos; LAST VALLEY, THE(1971, Brit.), cos; NICHOLAS AND ALEXANDRA(1971, Brit.), cos; PUPPET ON A CHAIN(1971, Brit.), cos; JESUS CHRIST, SUPERSTAR(1973), cos; THREE MUSKETEERS, THE(1974, Panama), cos; CRIME AND PASSION(1976, U.S., Ger.), cos; EAGLE HAS LANDED, THE(1976, Brit.), cos; ROBIN AND MARIAN(1976, Brit.), cos; SUPERMAN(1978), cos; ESCAPE TO ATHENA(1979, Brit.), cos; SUPERMAN II(1980), cos; GREEN ICE(1981, Brit.), cos

1984

FINDERS KEEPERS(1984), cos

Colin Blakeley

MEETINGS WITH REMARKABLE MEN(1979, Brit.)

James Blakeley

PARIS IN SPRING(1935); SHE COULDN'T TAKE IT(1935); TWO FOR TONIGHT(1935); GAY DESPERADO, THE(1936); MUSIC BOX KID, THE(1960), ed

John E. Blakeley

DODGING THE DOLE(1936, Brit.), p&d; PENNY POOL, THE(1937, Brit.), p; SOMEWHERE IN ENGLAND(1940, Brit.), p&d; SOMEWHERE IN CAMP(1942, Brit.), p&d; SOMEWHERE ON LEAVE(1942, Brit.), p&d; DEMOBBED(1944, Brit.), p&d; HOME SWEET HOME(1945, Brit.), p&d; HONEYMOON HOTEL(1946, Brit.), p&d; CUP-TIE HONEYMOON(1948, Brit.), p&d; SCHOOL FOR RANDLE(1949, Brit.), p&d, w; SOMEWHERE IN POLITICS(1949, Brit.), p&d; WHAT A CARRY ON!(1949, Brit.), p&d; OVER THE GARDEN WALL(1950, Brit.), p&d; STICK 'EM UP(1950, Brit.), p&d

Tom Blakeley

CARETAKERS DAUGHTER, THE(1952, Brit.), p; THOSE PEOPLE NEXT DOOR(1952, Brit.), p; BREAK, THE(1962, Brit.), p; YOUNG, WILLING AND EAGER(1962, Brit.), p; MAN IN THE DARK(1963, Brit.), p; MARKED ONE, THE(1963, Brit.), p; IN TROUBLE WITH EVE(1964, Brit.), p; TOMORROW AT TEN(1964, Brit.), p; DEVILS OF DARKNESS, THE(1965, Brit.), p; ISLAND OF TERROR(1967, Brit.), p; ISLAND OF THE BURNING DAMNED(1971, Brit.), p

W. Blakeley

NO FUNNY BUSINESS(1934, Brit.), ph

Walter Blakeley

NORAH O'NEALE(1934, Brit.), ph

Alban Blakelock

DISTANT TRUMPET(1952, Brit.); MURDER IN THE CATHEDRAL(1952, Brit.)

Denys Blakelock

MARRIAGE BOND, THE(1932, Brit.); LAZYBONES(1935, Brit.)

Art Blakely

ROAD TO SHAME, THE(1962, Fr.), m

Colin Blakely

SATURDAY NIGHT AND SUNDAY MORNING(1961, Brit.); HELLIONS, THE(1962, Brit.); PASSWORD IS COURAGE, THE(1962, Brit.); THIS SPORTING LIFE(1963, Brit.); LONG SHIPS, THE(1964, Brit./Yugo.); NEVER PUT IT IN WRITING(1964); UNDERWORLD INFORMERS(1965, Brit.); COUNTERFEIT CONSTABLE, THE(1966, Fr.); MAN FOR ALL SEASONS, A(1966, Brit.); SPY WITH A COLD NOSE, THE(1966, Brit.); DAY THE FISH CAME OUT, THE(1967. Brit./Gr.); CHARLIE BUBBLES(1968, Brit.); VENGEANCE OF SHE, THE(1968, Brit.); ALFRED THE GREAT(1969, Brit.); DECLINE AND FALL... OF A BIRD WATCHER(1969, Brit.); PRIVATE LIFE OF SHERLOCK HOLMES, THE(1970, Brit.); SOMETHING TO HIDE(1972, Brit.); YOUNG WINSTON(1972, Brit.); NATIONAL HEALTH, OR NURSE NORTON'S AFFAIR, THE(1973, Brit.); MURDER ON THE ORIENT EXPRESS(1974, Brit.); GALILEO(1975, Brit.); PINK PANTHER STRIKES AGAIN, THE(1976, Brit.); "EQUUS"(1977); BIG SLEEP, THE½(1978, Brit.); ALL THINGS BRIGHT AND BEAUTIFUL(1979, Brit.); DOGS OF WAR, THE(1980, Brit.); NIJINSKY(1980, Brit.); LOOPHOLE(1981, Brit.); EVIL UNDER THE SUN(1982, Brit.); RED MONARCH(1983, Brit.)

Dennis Blakely

PSYCHO-CIRCUS(1967, Brit.)

Don Blakely

CROSS AND THE SWITCHBLADE, THE(1970); PARADES(1972); SHAFT'S BIG SCORE(1972); SPOOK WHO SAT BY THE DOOR, THE(1973); SHORT EYES(1977); ON THE YARD(1978); DEFIANCE(1980); LINE, THE(1982); VIGILANTE(1983)

Gene Blakely

BATTLE OF THE CORAL SEA(1959); EVERYTHING'S DUCKY(1961); THAT DARN CAT(1965); BEACH RED(1967); PRISONER OF SECOND AVENUE, THE(1975); USED CARS(1980)

James Blakely

FUGITIVE LADY(1934); MILLS OF THE GODS(1935); EXCLUSIVE(1937); SHADOW STRIKES, THE(1937); SMALL TOWN BOY(1937); PRISON TRAIN(1938)

John E. Blakely

BOOTS! BOOTS!(1934, Brit.), p; OFF THE DOLE(1935, Brit.), p; CALLING ALL CROOKS(1938, Brit.), p; HOLIDAYS WITH PAY(1948, Brit.), p&d; IT'S A GRAND LIFE(1953, Brit.), p&d

Ronee Blakely

RENALDO AND CLARA(1978); GOOD LUCK, MISS WYCKOFF(1979)

Susan Blakely

CONCORDE, THE–AIRPORT '79(; TOWERING INFERNO, THE(1974); CAPONE(1975); REPORT TO THE COMMISSIONER(1975); DREAMER(1979)

Susie Blakely

WAY WE WERE, THE(1973); SAVAGES(1972)

Susie [Susan] Blakely
LORDS OF FLATBUSH, THE(1974)
Tom Blakely
MURDER CAN BE DEADLY(1963, Brit.), p
Walter Blakely
LOVE STORM, THE(1931, Brit.), ph
Susan Blakeman
PERFECT COUPLE, A(1979)
Donald Blakemore
Misc. Silents
FIRST WOMAN, THE(1922)
Eric Blakemore
GREAT VAN ROBBERY, THE(1963, Brit.), art d
Erik Blakemore
SATELLITE IN THE SKY(1956), art d
H.D. Blakemore
Misc. Silents
IN MIZZOURA(1914)
Michael Blakemore
HAVING A WILD WEEKEND(1965, Brit.); PRIVATES ON PARADE(1982), d
1984
PRIVATES ON PARADE(1984, Brit.), d
Ben Blakeney
NED KELLY(1970, Brit.)
Don Blakeney
1984
UTU(1984, New Zealand), p
Olive Blakeney
THAT UNCERTAIN FEELING(1941); HER IMAGINARY LOVER(1933, Brit.); LEAVE IT TO BLANCHE(1934, Brit.); COME OUT OF THE PANTRY(1935, Brit.); HELLO SWEETHEART(1935, Brit.); MR. WHAT'S-HIS-NAME(1935, Brit.); EXCUSE MY GLOVE(1936, Brit.); GIVE HER A RING(1936, Brit.); DON'T GET ME WRONG(1937, Brit.); GANGWAY(1937, Brit.); SHOW GOES ON, THE(1938, Brit.); TWO'S COMPANY(1939, Brit.); THIRD FINGER, LEFT HAND(1940); BILLY THE KID(1941); GLAMOUR BOY(1941); TWO-FACED WOMAN(1941); ARE HUSBANDS NECESSARY?(1942); HENRY ALDRICH, EDITOR(1942); HENRY ALDRICH GETS GLAMOUR(1942); HENRY AND DIZZY(1942); RANDOM HARVEST(1942); ALLERGIC TO LOVE(1943); HENRY ALDRICH HAUNTS A HOUSE(1943); HENRY ALDRICH SWINGS IT(1943); EXPERIMENT PERILOUS(1944); HENRY ALDRICH, BOY SCOUT(1944); HENRY ALDRICH PLAYS CUPID(1944); HENRY ALDRICH'S LITTLE SECRET(1944); PORT OF 40 THIEVES, THE(1944); DAKOTA(1945); NOB HILL(1945); LEAVE HER TO HEAVEN(1946); SENTIMENTAL JOURNEY(1946); STRANGE WOMAN, THE(1946); TIME OUT OF MIND(1947); SEALED VERDICT(1948); ROOGIE'S BUMP(1954); GREEN-EYED BLONDE, THE(1957); THREE BRAVE MEN(1957); I WANT TO LIVE!(1958)
Richard Blakeslee
UNHINGED(1982), ph
Oswell Blakeston
ESCAPE DANGEROUS(1947, Brit.), w
William Blakewell
Silents
BATTLE OF THE SEXES, THE(1928); LATEST FROM PARIS, THE(1928)
Ruble Blakey
SEPIA CINDERELLA(1947); MIRACLE IN HARLEM(1948)
Caroline Blakiston
IDOL, THE(1966, Brit.); TRYGON FACTOR, THE(1969, Brit.); MAGIC CHRISTIAN, THE(1970, Brit.); SUNDAY BLOODY SUNDAY(1971, Brit.); RETURN OF THE JEDI(1983)
Clarence Blakiston
GIRL IN THE CROWD, THE(1934, Brit.); LOVE UP THE POLE(1936, Brit.)
Silents
PEEP BEHIND THE SCENES, A(1929, Brit.)
Michael Blakley
STRAIGHT TIME(1978)
Ronee Blakley
NASHVILLE(1975); DRIVER, THE(1978); PRIVATE FILES OF J. EDGAR HOOVER, THE(1978); BALTIMORE BULLET, THE(1980)
1984
NIGHTMARE ON ELM STREET, A(1984)
Jorgen Blaksted
REPTILICUS(1962, U.S./Den.); OPERATION LOVEBIRDS(1968, Den.)
Jacques Blal
ENTRE NOUS(1983, Fr.)
Robert Blalack
STAR WARS(1977), ph; WOLFEN(1981), spec eff; ZAPPED!(1982), spec eff
Leslie Blalock
Misc. Talkies
INCOMING FRESHMEN(1979)
Norman Blalock
Misc. Talkies
ASHES AND EMBERS(1982)
Steve Blalock
1984
STAR TREK III: THE SEARCH FOR SPOCK(1984)
Emilie Blameble
1984
SUGAR CANE ALLEY(1984, Fr.)
Norita Blameble
1984
SUGAR CANE ALLEY(1984, Fr.)
John Blamy
LOVES OF SALAMMBO, THE(1962, Fr./Ital.), w
Anne Marie Blanc
HIGH FURY(1947, Brit.)
Erica Blanc
DEVIL'S NIGHTMARE, THE(1971 Bel./Ital.); NIGHT EVELYN CAME OUT OF THE GRAVE, THE(1973, Ital.); MARK OF THE DEVIL II(1975, Ger./Brit.)

Erika Blanc
HE WHO SHOOTS FIRST(1966, Ital.); KILL BABY KILL(1966, Ital.)
Francoise Blanc
$(DOLLARS)**1/2 (1971)
Julia Blanc
Misc. Silents
M. LECOQ(1915)
Lee Le Blanc
TWO LOVES(1961), spec eff
Margaret Blanc
Misc. Silents
SCARLET TRAIL, THE(1919)
Mel Blanc
NEPTUNE'S DAUGHTER(1949); CHAMPAGNE FOR CAESAR(1950); GAY PURR-EE(1962); HEY THERE, IT'S YOGI BEAR(1964); KISS ME, STUPID(1964); MAN CALLED FLINTSTONE, THE(1966); PHANTOM TOLLBOOTH, THE(1970); SCALAWAG(1973, Yugo.); JOURNEY BACK TO OZ(1974); BUGS BUNNY, SUPERSTAR(1975); BUCK ROGERS IN THE 25TH CENTURY(1979); GREAT AMERICAN BUGS BUNNY-ROAD RUNNER CHASE(1979); BUGS BUNNY'S THIRD MOVIE-1001 RABBIT TALES(1982); DAFFY DUCK'S MOVIE: FANTASTIC ISLAND(1983); STRANGE BREW(1983)
Misc. Talkies
LOONEY, LOONEY, LOONEY BUGS BUNNY MOVIE, THE(1981)
Michel Blanc
TENANT, THE(1976, Fr.); LIKE A TURTLE ON ITS BACK(1981, Fr.)
1984
DREAM ONE(1984, Brit./Fr.); TO CATCH A COP(1984, Fr.)
Rene Blancard
CAGE OF NIGHTINGALES, A(1947, Fr.); CARNIVAL OF SINNERS(1947, Fr.); JENNY LAMOUR(1948, Fr.); TO CATCH A THIEF(1955); MAIN STREET(1956, Span.); DIARY OF A BAD GIRL(1958, Fr.); NIGHTS OF SHAME(1961, Fr.), a, w; TRUTH, THE(1961, Fr./Ital.); JULIE THE REDHEAD(1963, Fr.)
Eumenio Blance
MACHINE GUN MAMA(1944)
Anita Blanch
PEARL OF TLAYUCAN, THE(1964, Mex.); MAN AND THE MONSTER, THE(1965, Mex.)
Dennis Blanch
PERMISSION TO KILL(1975, U.S./Aust.); SPY WHO LOVED ME, THE(1977, Brit.)
Jewel Blanch
AGAINST A CROOKED SKY(1975)
Jose Blanch
TRISTANA(1970, Span./Ital./Fr.)
Dominique Blanchar
DECISION BEFORE DAWN(1951); L'AVVENTURA(1960, Ital.)
Pierre Blanchar
CRIME AND PUNISHMENT(1935, Fr.); COURIER OF LYONS(1938, Fr.); ROYAL DIVORCE, A(1938, Brit.); UN CARNET DE BAL(1938, Fr.); TWO WOMEN(1940, Fr.); APRES L'AMOUR(1948, Fr.); SYMPHONIE PASTORALE(1948, Fr.); THEY ARE NOT ANGELS(1948, Fr.); DOCTEUR LAENNEC(1949, Fr.); RIFF RAFF GIRLS(1962, Fr./Ital.); MAGNIFICENT SINNER(1963, Fr.)
Misc. Silents
LE VALSE DE L'ADIEU(1928, Fr.); LA MARCHE NUPTIALE(1929, Fr.)
Alan Blanchard
FOES(1977); SLITHIS(1978)
Claude Blanchard
FANTASTICA(1980, Can./Fr.)
Dale Blanchard
APACHE CHIEF(1949)
Dave Blanchard
RACING FEVER(1964)
Elenore Blanchard
Silents
LIFE'S WHIRLPOOL(1916)
Felix "Doc" Blanchard
SPIRIT OF WEST POINT, THE(1947)
Frederic Blanchard
MAN HUNT(1936)
Howard Blanchard
Silents
LONE EAGLE, THE(1927), w
Jacqueline Blanchard
EDDY DUCHIN STORY, THE(1956)
Jerry Blanchard
FOLLIES GIRL(1943)
Mari Blanchard
NO QUESTIONS ASKED(1951); ON THE RIVERA(1951); OVERLAND TELEGRAPH(1951); TEN TALL MEN(1951); UNKNOWN MAN, THE(1951); ASSIGNMENT-PARIS(1952); BACK AT THE FRONT(1952); BRIGAND, THE(1952); SOMETHING TO LIVE FOR(1952); ABBOTT AND COSTELLO GO TO MARS(1953); VEILS OF BAGDAD, THE(1953); BLACK HORSE CANYON(1954); DESTRY(1954); RAILS INTO LARAMIE(1954); CROOKED WEB, THE(1955); RETURN OF JACK SLADE, THE(1955); SON OF SINBAD(1955); CRUEL TOWER, THE(1956); STAGECOACH TO FURY(1956); JUNGLE HEAT(1957); SHE DEVIL(1957); MACHETE(1958); NO PLACE TO LAND(1958); DON'T KNOCK THE TWIST(1962); MC LINTOCK!(1963); TWICE TOLD TALES(1963)
Moody Blanchard
LONELY MAN, THE(1957)
Pierre Blanchard
Misc. Silents
CHESS PLAYER, THE(1930, Fr.)
Rene Blanchard
LE PLAISIR(1954, Fr.)
Richard Blanchard
COMING HOME(1978)
Rick Blanchard
HEROES(1977)

Ron Blanchard
CADDIE(1976, Aus.)
Saga Blanchard
ENTRE NOUS(1983, Fr.)
Toby Blanchard
1984
CAREFUL, HE MIGHT HEAR YOU(1984, Aus.)
Cosette Blanche
PARIS OOH-LA-LA!(1963, U.S./Fr.)
Francis Blanche
BABETTE GOES TO WAR(1960, Fr.); GREEN MARE, THE(1961, Fr./Ital.); LOVE AND THE FRENCHWOMAN(1961, Fr.); PEEK-A-BOO(1961, Fr.), a, w; BEAR, THE(1963, Fr.); LIARS, THE(1964, Fr.); SEVENTH JUROR, THE(1964, Fr.); SWEET AND SOUR(1964, Fr./Ital.); MALE HUNT(1965, Fr./Ital.); THANK HEAVEN FOR SMALL FAVORS(1965, Fr.); GREAT SPY CHASE, THE(1966, Fr.); BEAUTIFUL SWINDLERS, THE(1967, Fr./Ital./Jap./Neth.); BELLE DE JOUR(1968, Fr.); FEMMINA(1968 Fr./Ital./Ger.); OLDEST PROFESSION, THE(1968, Fr./Ital./Ger.)
Herbert Blanche
Misc. Silents
FIGHTING DEATH(1914), d
Jeanne Blanche
ZAZA(1939)
Margaret Blanche
Silents
PLACE IN THE SUN, A(1916, Brit.); GRIT OF A JEW, THE(1917, Brit.)
Misc. Silents
COMIN' THRO' THE RYE(1916, Brit.); GRAND BABYLON HOTEL, THE(1916, Brit.); MY SWEETHEART(1918, Brit.); WOMAN OF THE IRON BRACELETS, THE(1920, Brit.)
Marguerite Blanche
Misc. Silents
BLACK SHEEP, THE(1920, Brit.); SCARLET WOOING, THE(1920, Brit.)
Marguertie Blanche
Misc. Silents
SWEET AND TWENTY(1919, Brit.)
Marie Blanche
Silents
ELUSIVE PIMPERNEL, THE(1919, Brit.); DON QUIXOTE(1923, Brit.); PREHISTORIC MAN, THE(1924, Brit.)
Misc. Silents
GREAT IMPOSTER, THE(1918, Brit.)
Roland Blanche
HOW NOT TO ROB A DEPARTMENT STORE(1965, Fr./Ital.); FIRST TIME, THE(1978, Fr.); DANTON(1983)
1984
LES COMPERES(1984, Fr.)
William "Shorty" Blanche
Silents
"THAT ROYLE GIRL"(1925); SALLY OF THE SAWDUST(1925); SO'S YOUR OLD MAN(1926)
Jacky Blanchot
THE DIRTY GAME(1966, Fr./Ital./Ger.); KING OF HEARTS(1967, Fr./Ital.)
Dorothee Blanck
CLEO FROM 5 TO 7(1961, Fr.)
E.G.S. Blanckart
WAKAMBA!(1955), ph
Kate Blancke
Silents
BRAND OF COWARDICE, THE(1916); PRETENDERS, THE(1916); TIGER WOMAN, THE(1917); TRAIL OF THE SHADOW, THE(1917); WITHOUT LIMIT(1921); AS A MAN LIVES(1923); SILENT COMMAND, THE(1923)
Misc. Silents
LEST WE FORGET(1918)
Carlos Blanco
MAD QUEEN, THE(1950, Span.), w
Emilio Blanco
SECRET SERVICE OF THE AIR(1939)
Eumenco Blanco
SUNSET OF POWER(1936)
Eumenio Blanco
SWING HIGH, SWING LOW(1937); GREEN HELL(1940); ESCAPE FROM RED ROCK(1958)
Euminio Blanco
OUT OF THE PAST(1947)
Hugo Blanco
UP THE MACGREGORS(1967, Ital./Span.); UGLY ONES, THE(1968, Ital./Span.)
Miguel Angel Blanco
AFFAIR IN HAVANA(1957)
Rafael Blanco
DESIRE(1936)
Tomas Blanco
LEGIONS OF THE NILE(1960, Ital.); CASTILIAN, THE(1963, Span./U.S.); REVOLT OF THE MERCENARIES(1964, Ital./Span.); SECRET SEVEN, THE(1966, Ital./Span.); FOR A FEW DOLLARS MORE(1967, Ital./Ger./Span.); MISSION BLOODY MARY(1967, Fr./Ital./Span.); SEA PIRATE, THE(1967, Fr./Span./Ital.); FEW BULLETS MORE, A(1968, Ital./Span.); LAST DAY OF THE WAR, THE(1969, U.S./Ital./Span.)
Valerie Blanco
THAT OBSCURE OBJECT OF DESIRE(1977, Fr./Span.)
Enrico Blancocello
STRANGE FETISHES, THE(1967), p&d
A. Trevor Bland
MAN WHO BROKE THE BANK AT MONTE CARLO, THE(1935)
Henderson Bland
Silents
GENERAL POST(1920, Brit.)
Misc. Silents
CIGARETTE MAKER'S ROMANCE, A(1920, Brit.)

Joyce Bland
BARTON MYSTERY, THE(1932, Brit.); FLAG LIEUTENANT, THE(1932, Brit.); MAGIC NIGHT(1932, Brit.); CRIME AT BLOSSOMS, THE(1933, Brit.); RIGHT AGE TO MARRY, THE(1935, Brit.); TOUCH OF THE MOON, A(1936, Brit.); DREAMING LIPS(1937, Brit.); CHIPS(1938. Brit.); CITADEL, THE(1938); SIXTY GLORIOUS YEARS(1938, Brit.); SPY OF NAPOLEON(1939, Brit.)
Peter Bland
DON'T JUST LIE THERE, SAY SOMETHING!(1973, Brit.)
R. Henderson Bland
Misc. Silents
MR. GILFIL'S LOVE STORY(1920, Brit.); GWYNETH OF THE WELSH HILLS(1921, Brit.)
Sidney Bland
JOHN OF THE FAIR(1962, Brit.)
Silents
KENT, THE FIGHTING MAN(1916, Brit.)
Sydney Bland
Silents
PICTURE OF DORIAN GRAY, THE(1916, Brit.)
Misc. Silents
UNDER THE RED ROBE(1915, Brit.); SHE(1916, Brit.)
Trever Bland
Silents
SNARE, THE(1918, Brit.)
Trevor Bland
BELOW THE SEA(1933); PADDY, THE NEXT BEST THING(1933)
Douglas Blandford
BOAT FROM SHANGHAI(1931, Brit.)
Clara Blandick
GIRL SAID NO, THE(1930); MEN ARE LIKE THAT(1930); ROMANCE(1930); SINS OF THE CHILDREN(1930); TOM SAWYER(1930); WISE GIRLS(1930); BOUGHT(1931); DAYBREAK(1931); DRUMS OF JEOPARDY(1931); EASIEST WAY, THE(1931); HUCKLEBERRY FINN(1931); I TAKE THIS WOMAN(1931); IT'S A WISE CHILD(1931); MURDER AT MIDNIGHT(1931); NEW ADVENTURES OF GET-RICH-QUICK WALLINGFORD, THE(1931); ONCE A SINNER(1931); POSSESSED(1931); CASE OF CLARA DEANE, THE(1932); EXPERT, THE(1932); LIFE BEGINS(1932); ROCKABYE(1932); SHOPWORN(1932); STRANGE CASE OF CLARA DEANE, THE(1932); THREE ON A MATCH(1932); TWO AGAINST THE WORLD(1932); WET PARADE, THE(1932); BITTER TEA OF GENERAL YEN, THE(1933); CHARLIE CHAN'S GREATEST CASE(1933); CHILD OF MANHATTAN(1933); EVER IN MY HEART(1933); MIND READER, THE(1933); ONE SUNDAY AFTERNOON(1933); THREE-CORNERED MOON(1933); TURN BACK THE CLOCK(1933); FUGITIVE LADY(1934); GIRL FROM MISSOURI, THE(1934); HAROLD TEEN(1934); JEALOUSY(1934); PRESIDENT VANISHES, THE(1934); SHOW-OFF, THE(1934); SISTERS UNDER THE SKIN(1934); PARTY WIRE(1935); PRINCESS O'HARA(1935); STRAIGHT FROM THE HEART(1935); TRANSIENT LADY(1935); ANTHONY ADVERSE(1936); FURY(1936); GORGEOUS HUSSY, THE(1936); HEARTS DIVIDED(1936); IN HIS STEPS(1936); MAKE WAY FOR A LADY(1936); TRAIL OF THE LONESOME PINE, THE(1936); HER HUSBAND'S SECRETARY(1937); ROAD BACK, THE(1937); SMALL TOWN BOY(1937); STAR IS BORN, A(1937); WINGS OVER HONOLULU(1937); YOU CAN'T HAVE EVERYTHING(1937); CRIME RING(1938); MY OLD KENTUCKY HOME(1938); PROFESSOR BEWARE(1938); SWING, SISTER, SWING(1938); DRUMS ALONG THE MOHAWK(1939); HUCKLEBERRY FINN(1939); STAR MAKER, THE(1939); SWANEE RIVER(1939); TOM SAWYER, DETECTIVE(1939); WIZARD OF OZ, THE(1939); ANNE OF WINDY POPLARS(1940); DREAMING OUT LOUD(1940); NORTHWEST MOUNTED POLICE(1940); TOMBOY(1940); YOUTH WILL BE SERVED(1940); IT STARTED WITH EVE(1941); NURSE'S SECRET, THE(1941); ONE FOOT IN HEAVEN(1941); PRIVATE NURSE(1941); WAGONS ROLL AT NIGHT, THE(1941); LADY IN A JAM(1942); RINGS ON HER FINGERS(1942); DIXIE(1943); DU BARRY WAS A LADY(1943); HEAVEN CAN WAIT(1943); CAN'T HELP SINGING(1944); SHADOW OF SUSPICION(1944); FRONTIER GAL(1945); PEOPLE ARE FUNNY(1945); PILLOW OF DEATH(1945); CLAUDIA AND DAVID(1946); SHE-WOLF OF LONDON(1946); SO GOES MY LOVE(1946); STOLEN LIFE, A(1946); LIFE WITH FATHER(1947); PHILO VANCE RETURNS(1947); BRIDE GOES WILD, THE(1948); MR. SOFT TOUCH(1949); KEY TO THE CITY(1950); LOVE THAT BRUTE(1950)
Silents
MRS. BLACK IS BACK(1914)
Misc. Silents
STOLEN TRIUMPH, THE(1916)
Don Blanding
HAWAII CALLS(1938), w
Oscar Blando
UNDER THE SUN OF ROME(1949, Ital.)
Barbara Blane
MY MARRIAGE(1936); SATAN MET A LADY(1936)
Ralph Blane
ZIEGFELD FOLLIES(1945), w
Sallie Blane
HALF A SINNER(1934)
Sally Blane
HALF-MARRIAGE(1929); TANNED LEGS(1929); VAGABOND LOVER(1929); VERY IDEA, THE(1929); LITTLE ACCIDENT(1930); ANNABELLE'S AFFAIRS(1931); DANGEROUS AFFAIR, A(1931); GOOD SPORT(1931); ONCE A SINNER(1931); SHANGHAIED LOVE(1931); SPIRIT OF NOTRE DAME, THE(1931); STAR WITNESS(1931); TEN CENTS A DANCE(1931); WOMEN MEN MARRY(1931); X MARKS THE SPOT(1931); DISORDERLY CONDUCT(1932); ESCAPADE(1932); FORBIDDEN COMPANY(1932); I AM A FUGITIVE FROM A CHAIN GANG(1932); LAW OF THE SEA(1932); LOCAL BAD MAN(1932); PHANTOM EXPRESS, THE(1932); PRIDE OF THE LEGION, THE(1932); PROBATION(1932); RECKONING, THE(1932); WILD HORSE MESA(1932); ADVICE TO THE LOVELORN(1933); BIG PAYOFF, THE(1933); CRIME ON THE HILL(1933, Brit.); HELLO, EVERYBODY(1933); HERITAGE OF THE DESERT(1933); MAYFAIR GIRL(1933, Brit.); NIGHT OF TERROR(1933); TRICK FOR TRICK(1933); AGAINST THE LAW(1934); CITY LIMITS(1934); CITY PARK(1934); NO MORE WOMEN(1934); SHE HAD TO CHOOSE(1934); STOLEN SWEETS(1934); SILVER STREAK, THE(1935); THIS IS THE LIFE(1935); GREAT HOSPITAL MYSTERY, THE(1937); ONE MILE FROM HEAVEN(1937); CRASHIN' THRU DANGER(1938); CHARLIE CHAN AT TREASURE ISLAND(1939); FIGHTING MAD(1939); STORY OF ALEXANDER GRAHAM BELL, THE(1939); WAY DOWN SOUTH(1939); BULLET FOR JOEY, A(1955)

Misc. Talkies
NUMBERED WOMAN(1938)
Silents
CASEY AT THE BAT(1927); SHOOTIN' IRONS(1927); WIFE SAVERS(1928); EYES OF THE UNDERWORLD(1929); OUTLAWED(1929)
Misc. Silents
FOOLS FOR LUCK(1928); HORSEMAN OF THE PLAINS, A(1928); KING COWBOY(1928); VANISHING PIONEER, THE(1928); WOLVES OF THE CITY(1929)
Sue Blane
ROCKY HORROR PICTURE SHOW, THE(1975, Brit.), cos; SHOCK TREATMENT(1981), cos; DRAUGHTSMAN'S CONTRACT, THE(1983, Brit.), cos
Tony Blane
LAST RHINO, THE(1961, Brit.)
George Blaness
YOUNG GIRLS OF ROCHEFORT, THE(1968, Fr.)
Georges Blaness
CLOPORTES(1966, Fr., Ital.)
Charles E. Blaney
PICTURE BRIDES(1934), w
Silents
CURSE OF DRINK, THE(1922), w; ONE LAW FOR THE WOMAN(1924), p, w; ACROSS THE PACIFIC(1926), w
Harry Clay Blaney
PICTURE BRIDES(1934), w
Silents
WHAT FOOLS MEN ARE(1922)
May Blaney
Misc. Silents
OLD WOOD CARVER, THE(1913, Brit.)
Norah Blaney
WHO DONE IT?(1956, Brit.)
Robert Blanford
NASHVILLE REBEL(1966), m
Ace Blangsted
TARAS BULBA(1962), ed
David Blangsted
CREATURE WASN'T NICE,THE(1981), ed
Folmar Blangsted
NEVER SAY GOODBYE(1946), ed; CRY WOLF(1947), ed; TO THE VICTOR(1948), ed; WALLFLOWER(1948), ed; FLAMINGO ROAD(1949), ed; MY DREAM IS YOURS(1949), ed; BREAKTHROUGH(1950), ed; PRETTY BABY(1950), ed; I WAS A COMMUNIST FOR THE F.B.I.(1951), ed; JIM THORPE–ALL AMERICAN(1951), ed; STORY OF WILL ROGERS, THE(1952), ed; CHARGE AT FEATHER RIVER, THE(1953), ed; SHE'S BACK ON BROADWAY(1953), ed; SO THIS IS LOVE(1953), ed; STAR IS BORN, A(1954), ed; COURT-MARTIAL OF BILLY MITCHELL, THE(1955), ed; STRANGE LADY IN TOWN(1955), ed; CRY IN THE NIGHT, A(1956), ed; HELL ON FRISCO BAY(1956), ed; STEEL JUNGLE, THE(1956), ed; BAND OF ANGELS(1957), ed; TOP SECRET AFFAIR(1957), ed; LEFT-HANDED GUN, THE(1958), ed; MARJORIE MORNINGSTAR(1958), ed; RIO BRAVO(1959), ed; BRAMBLE BUSH, THE(1960), ed; DARK AT THE TOP OF THE STAIRS, THE(1960), ed; RISE AND FALL OF LEGS DIAMOND, THE(1960), ed; CLAUDELLE INGLISH(1961), ed; GOLD OF THE SEVEN SAINTS(1961), ed; MERRILL'S MARAUDERS(1962), ed; TARAS BULBA(1962), ed; PALM SPRINGS WEEKEND(1963), ed; PT 109(1963), ed; DEAD RINGER(1964), ed; DEAR HEART(1964), ed; BUS RILEY'S BACK IN TOWN(1965), ed; WAR LORD, THE(1965), ed; CAMELOT(1967), ed; UP THE DOWN STAIRCASE(1967), ed; BANDOLERO!(1968), ed; HELLFIGHTERS(1968), ed; COLOSSUS: THE FORBIN PROJECT(1969), ed; PURSUIT OF HAPPINESS, THE(1971), ed; SUMMER OF '42(1971), ed; MAN OF LA MANCHA(1972), ed; OTHER, THE(1972), ed; OKLAHOMA CRUDE(1973), ed
Folmer Blangsted
OLD WYOMING TRAIL, THE(1937), d; WESTBOUND MAIL(1937), d; CATTLE RAIDERS(1938), w; DOUGHGIRLS, THE(1944), ed; RHAPSODY IN BLUE(1945), ed; TOO YOUNG TO KNOW(1945), ed; ALWAYS TOGETHER(1947), ed; THAT WAY WITH WOMEN(1947), ed; DISTANT DRUMS(1951), ed
Karen Blanguernon
NO SURVIVORS, PLEASE(1963, Ger.); CASTLE KEEP(1969); YOU ONLY LIVE ONCE(1969, Fr.); SICILIAN CLAN, THE(1970, Fr.)
B. Blank
WELCOME KOSTYA!(1965, USSR), art d
Dorothee Blank
LOLA(1961, Fr./Ital.); UMBRELLAS OF CHERBOURG, THE(1964, Fr./Ger.); VICE AND VIRTUE(1965, Fr./Ital.); CLOPORTES(1966, Fr., Ital.); YOUNG GIRLS OF ROCHEFORT, THE(1968, Fr.); MATTER OF DAYS, A(1969, Fr./Czech.)
Dorothy Ann Blank
SNOW WHITE AND THE SEVEN DWARFS(1937), w
Thomas Blank [Blanco]
SUPERARGO(1968, Ital./Span.)
Hanry Blanke
MIRACLE, THE(1959), p
Henry Blanke
HER MAJESTY LOVE(1931), w; BUREAU OF MISSING PERSONS(1933), p; CONVENTION CITY(1933), p; I LOVED A WOMAN(1933), p; LADY KILLER(1933), p; MYSTERY OF THE WAX MUSEUM, THE(1933), p; SHE HAD TO SAY YES(1933), p; SILK EXPRESS, THE(1933), p; DRAGON MURDER CASE, THE(1934), p; EASY TO LOVE(1934), p; FASHIONS OF 1934(1934), p; JOURNAL OF A CRIME(1934), p; MADAME DU BARRY(1934), p; CASE OF THE LUCKY LEGS, THE(1935), p; GIRL FROM TENTH AVENUE, THE(1935), p; I AM A THIEF(1935), p; SECRET BRIDE, THE(1935), p; WHITE COCKATOO(1935), p; ANTHONY ADVERSE(1936), p; GREEN PASTURES(1936), p; PETRIFIED FOREST, THE(1936), p; SATAN MET A LADY(1936), p; STORY OF LOUIS PASTEUR, THE(1936), p; WHITE ANGEL, THE(1936), p; LIFE OF EMILE ZOLA, THE(1937), p; ADVENTURES OF ROBIN HOOD, THE(1938), p; JEZEBEL(1938), p; WHITE BANNERS(1938), p; OLD MAID, THE(1939), p; WE ARE NOT ALONE(1939), p; SEA HAWK, THE(1940), p; BLUES IN THE NIGHT(1941), p; HONEYMOON FOR THREE(1941), p; MALTESE FALCON, THE(1941), p; GAY SISTERS, THE(1942), p; CONSTANT NYMPH, THE(1943), p; EDGE OF DARKNESS(1943), p; OLD ACQUAINTANCE(1943), p; MASK OF DIMITRIOS, THE(1944), p; ROUGHLY SPEAKING(1945), p; DECEPTION(1946), p; MY REPUTATION(1946), p; OF HUMAN BONDAGE(1946), p; ONE MORE TOMORROW(1946), p; CRY WOLF(1947), p; DEEP VALLEY(1947), p; ESCAPE ME NEVER(1947), p; JUNE BRIDE(1948), p; TREASURE OF THE SIERRA MADRE,

THE(1948), p; WINTER MEETING(1948), p; WOMAN IN WHITE, THE(1948), p; BEYOND THE FOREST(1949), p; FOUNTAINHEAD, THE(1949), p; BRIGHT LEAF(1950), p; COME FILL THE CUP(1951), p; GOODBYE, MY FANCY(1951), p; LIGHTNING STRIKES TWICE(1951), p; TOMORROW IS ANOTHER DAY(1951), p; IRON MISTRESS, THE(1952), p; ROOM FOR ONE MORE(1952), p; SHE'S BACK ON BROADWAY(1953), p; SO BIG(1953), p; SO THIS IS LOVE(1953), p; KING RICHARD AND THE CRUSADERS(1954), p; LUCKY ME(1954), p; PHANTOM OF THE RUE MORGUE(1954), p; MC CONNELL STORY, THE(1955), p; SINCERELY YOURS(1955), p; YOUNG AT HEART(1955), p; SERENADE(1956), p; TOO MUCH, TOO SOON(1958), p; NUN'S STORY, THE(1959), p; WESTBOUND(1959), p; CASH McCALL(1960), p; ICE PALACE(1960), p; SINS OF RACHEL CADE, THE(1960), p; HELL IS FOR HEROES(1962), p
Kate Blanke
Silents
STREETS OF NEW YORK, THE(1922)
Oscar Blanke
THEM!(1954)
Heinz Blankenburg
MARRIAGE OF FIGARO, THE(1970, Ger.)
Toni Blankenheim
DER FREISCHUTZ(1970, Ger.)
Harold Blankenship
MEDIUM COOL(1969)
Norm Blankenship
ZORRO, THE GAY BLADE(1981); I, THE JURY(1982)
Norman Blankenship
GONG SHOW MOVIE, THE(1980)
Robert Blankenship
MEDIUM COOL(1969)
Betsy Blankett
PENITENTIARY(1979), ed
1984
EL NORTE(1984), ed
Enrica Blankey
SCHLOCK(1973)
Mark Blankfield
INCREDIBLE SHRINKING WOMAN, THE(1981); JEKYLL AND HYDE...TOGETHER AGAIN(1982)
Henry Blankfort
KLONDIKE FURY(1942), w; RUBBER RACKETEERS(1942), w; TALES OF MANHATTAN(1942), w; HARRIGAN'S KID(1943), w; I ESCAPED FROM THE GESTAPO(1943), w; SHE'S FOR ME(1943), w; NIGHT CLUB GIRL(1944), w; RECKLESS AGE(1944), w; SINGING SHERIFF, THE(1944), w; CRIMSON CANARY(1945), w; DALTONS RIDE AGAIN, THE(1945), w; EASY TO LOOK AT(1945), p, w; I'LL TELL THE WORLD(1945), w; SWING OUT, SISTER(1945), w; OPEN SECRET(1948), w; JOE PALOOKA IN THE COUNTERPUNCH(1949), w; HUMPHREY TAKES A CHANCE(1950), w; JOE PALOOKA MEETS HUMPHREY(1950), w; WHIPPED, THE(1950), w
Henry Blankfort, Jr.
YOUTH ON PAROLE(1937), w
Michael Blankfort
BLIND ALLEY(1939), w; ADAM HAD FOUR SONS(1941), w; TEXAS(1941), w; FLIGHT LIEUTENANT(1942), w; ACT OF MURDER, AN(1948), w; DARK PAST, THE(1948), w; BROKEN ARROW(1950), w; HALLS OF MONTEZUMA(1951), w; LYDIA BAILEY(1952), w; MY SIX CONVICTS(1952), w; JUGGLER, THE(1953), w; UNTAMED(1955), w; TRIBUTE TO A BADMAN(1956), w; VINTAGE, THE(1957), w; PLAINSMAN, THE(1966), w
Anthony Blankley
HARDER THEY FALL, THE(1956)
George Blankley
CAPTAIN LIGHTFOOT(1955)
Hedi Blankner
GERMANY, YEAR ZERO(1949, Ger.)
Polan Blanks
GREAT LIE, THE(1941), w
Folmer Blanksted
GOD IS MY CO-PILOT(1945), ed
Joby Blanshard
PASSING STRANGER, THE(1954, Brit.); HELL IS A CITY(1960, Brit.); MOON ZERO TWO(1969, Brit.); RECKONING, THE(1971, Brit.)
Arell Blanton
WILD RIDERS(1971); BLACK GUNN(1972); SWARM, THE(1978); WHEN A STRANGER CALLS(1979); PENNIES FROM HEAVEN(1981)
Emily Blas
1984
CAGED FURY(1984, Phil.), p
Joe Blasco
RABID(1976, Can.), makeup; THEY CAME FROM WITHIN(1976, Can.), spec eff & makeup; TRACK OF THE MOONBEAST(1976), a, makeup
Maite Blasco
1984
IT'S NEVER TOO LATE(1984, Span.)
Ricardo Blasco
GRINGO(1963, Span./Ital.), d, w
Teresa Blasco
GAMES MEN PLAY, THE(1968, Arg.)
Vicente Blasco-Ibanez
Silents
FOUR HORSEMEN OF THE APOCALYPSE, THE(1921), w; BLOOD AND SAND(1922), w; ENEMIES OF WOMEN(1923), w; MARE NOSTRUM(1926), w; TEMPTRESS, THE(1926), w; TORRENT, THE(1926), w
Evanne Blasdale
Silents
BULLDOG PLUCK(1927), w
Audrey A. Blasdel
MARRIAGE OF A YOUNG STOCKBROKER, THE(1971), set d; THIEF WHO CAME TO DINNER, THE(1973), set d

Audrey Blasdel
OUT OF SIGHT(1966), set d; TAMMY AND THE MILLIONAIRE(1967), set d; I LOVE YOU, ALICE B. TOKLAS!(1968), set d; PETULIA(1968, U.S./Brit.), set d; LAWYER, THE(1969), set d; ALEX IN WONDERLAND(1970), set d; LITTLE FAUSS AND BIG HALSY(1970), set d; FUNNY LADY(1975), set d

Audrey Blasdel-Goddard
FURY, THE(1978), set d

Herman Blaser
BLUES FOR LOVERS(1966, Brit.), p

Alessandro Blasetti
ADVENTURE OF SALVATOR ROSA, AN(1940, Ital.), d; BELLISSIMA(1952, Ital.); FATHER'S DILEMMA(1952, Ital.), d; TIMES GONE BY(1953, Ital.), d; LUCKY TO BE A WOMAN(1955, Ital.), d, w; THREE FABLES OF LOVE(1963, Fr./Ital./Span.), a, w, d; VERY HANDY MAN, A(1966, Fr./Ital.), d, w

Allessandro Blasetti
FABIOLA(1951, Ital.), d, w; TOO BAD SHE'S BAD(1954, Ital.), d

S. Blasetti
ANATOMY OF LOVE(1959, Ital.), d

Ralph Blasi
CHAFED ELBOWS(1967)

Silvana Blasi
BED AND BOARD(1971, Fr.)

Silverio Blasi
MONTE CASSINO(1948, Ital.); RE: LUCKY LUCIANO(1974, Fr./Ital.)

Dan Blasko
JAWS 3-D(1983)

Mira Blaskovic
ROMANCE OF A HORSE THIEF(1971)

Adelaide Blasquez
BELLE DE JOUR(1968, Fr.)

Herman Blass
COPPER, THE(1930, Brit.); DOLLY GETS AHEAD(1931, Ger.)

Hermann Blass
JOHNNY STEALS EUROPE(1932, Ger.)

Freddie Blassie
MY BREAKFAST WITH BLASSIE(1983)

Helen Blatch
DOLL'S HOUSE, A(1973)

Frederick Blatchford
Silents
ELUSIVE PIMPERNEL, THE(1919, Brit.), w; MR. WU(1919, Brit.), w

William Blatchford
OLD-FASHIONED WAY, THE(1934)

Joseph Blatchley
STORY OF ADELE H., THE(1975, Fr.)

Raymond Blathwayt
Silents
BEYOND THE ROCKS(1922); WILD HONEY(1922)

Christian Blatt
NIGHT GAMES(1966, Swed.)

Daniel H. Blatt
I NEVER PROMISED YOU A ROSE GARDEN(1977), p; AMERICAN SUCCESS COMPANY, THE(1980), p; CUJO(1983), a, p; INDEPENDENCE DAY(1983), p

Edward A. Blatt
BETWEEN TWO WORLDS(1944), d; ESCAPE IN THE DESERT(1945), d; SMART WOMAN(1948), d

Jerry Blatt
TIKI TIKI(1971, Can.), m

Betty Blattner
IF ...(1968, Brit.), makeup; MELODY(1971, Brit.), makeup

Gerry Blattner
SUNDOWNERS, THE(1960), p

Louis Blattner
MY LUCKY STAR(1933, Brit.), p, d

Ludwig Blattner
KNIGHT IN LONDON, A(1930, Brit./Ger.), p

Bill Blatty
NO PLACE TO LAND(1958); MAN FROM THE DINERS' CLUB, THE(1963), w

William Peter Blatty
JOHN GOLDFARB, PLEASE COME HOME(1964), w; SHOT IN THE DARK, A(1964), w; PROMISE HER ANYTHING(1966, Brit.), w; WHAT DID YOU DO IN THE WAR, DADDY?(1966), w; GUNN(1967), w; GREAT BANK ROBBERY, THE(1969), w; DARLING LILI(1970), w; EXORCIST, THE(1973), p&w, d; EXORCIST II: THE HERETIC(1977), w; NINTH CONFIGURATION, THE(1980), p,d&w

Andrew Blau
THAT'S THE WAY OF THE WORLD(1975)

Bea Blau
BANG THE DRUM SLOWLY(1973)

Eric Blau
JACQUES BREL IS ALIVE AND WELL AND LIVING IN PARIS(1975), w

Eugene Blau
Z.P.G.(1972)

Fred Blau
HAPPY ENDING, THE(1969), makeup; SEPARATE PEACE, A(1972), makeup

Fred C. Blau, Jr.
SUPERBEAST(1972), makeup

Raphael Blau
MOTHER IS A FRESHMAN(1949), w; FEAR STRIKES OUT(1957), w; SHORT CUT TO HELL(1957), w; GIRL OF THE NIGHT(1960), w

Raphael David Blau
BEDTIME FOR BONZO(1951), w

Karen Blaugueron
DEADLY TRAP, THE(1972, Fr./Ital.)

Steve Blauner
DRIVE, HE SAID(1971), p

Brian Blauser
MISS JESSICA IS PREGNANT(1970), ph

Julian Blaustein
NOOSE HANGS HIGH, THE(1948), w

Julian Blaustein
FOR LOVE OR MONEY(1939), w; BROKEN ARROW(1950), p; MISTER 880(1950), p; DAY THE EARTH STOOD STILL, THE(1951), p; GUY WHO CAME BACK, THE(1951), p; HALF ANGEL(1951), p; TAKE CARE OF MY LITTLE GIRL(1951), p; DON'T BOTHER TO KNOCK(1952), p; OUTCASTS OF POKER FLAT, THE(1952), p; DESIREE(1954), p; RACERS, THE(1955), p; STORM CENTER(1956), p; BELL, BOOK AND CANDLE(1958), p; COWBOY(1958), p; TWO LOVES(1961), p; KHARTOUM(1966, Brit.), p; THREE INTO TWO WON'T GO(1969, Brit.), p

Marc Blavet
JONAH–WHO WILL BE 25 IN THE YEAR 2000(1976, Switz.), ed

Blavette
STORMY WATERS(1946, Fr.)

Aimos Blavette
LUMIERE D'ETE(1943, Fr.)

Charles Blavette
WAYS OF LOVE(1950, Ital./Fr.); PICNIC ON THE GRASS(1960, Fr.); LONG ABSENCE, THE(1962, Fr./Ital.); TONI(1968, Fr.)

Jacek Blawut
ECHO, THE(1964, Pol.)

Peter William Blaxill
GROOVE TUBE, THE(1974)

Helen Blay
Misc. Talkies
JEWISH DAUGHTER(1933)

Margaret Blay
SCARECROW, THE(1982, New Zealand)

Roger Blay
1984
HOTEL NEW HAMPSHIRE, THE(1984)

William Warren Blaylock
1984
GRANDVIEW, U.S.A.(1984), p

Andrea Blayne
PLAYGROUND, THE(1965)

Antonin Blazejovsky
LOVES OF A BLONDE(1966, Czech.); FIREMAN'S BALL, THE(1968, Czech.)

Jiri Blazek
WISHING MACHINE(1971, Czech.), w

Karel Blazek
INTIMATE LIGHTING(1969, Czech.)

Vratislav Blazek
LADY ON THE TRACKS, THE(1968, Czech.), w

F.L. Blazhevich
HEROES OF THE SEA(1941)

F.B. Blazhevitch
DIARY OF A REVOLUTIONIST(1932, USSR)

Manolo Blazquez
TOMMY THE TOREADOR(1960, Brit.)

Annie Bleakley
LAST WAVE, THE(1978, Aus.), cos

Jose Bleakley
1984
WILD HORSES(1984, New Zealand), prod d

Lord James Blears
WRESTLER, THE(1974)

Hans C. Blech
LONGEST DAY, THE(1962)

Hans Christian Blech
AFFAIR BLUM(1949, Ger.); DECISION BEFORE DAWN(1951); LONGEST DAY, THE(1962); BATTLE OF THE BULGE(1965); MORITURI(1965); BRIDGE AT REMAGEN, THE(1969); GIORDANO BRUNO(1973, Ital.); DIRTY HANDS(1976, Fr/Ital./Ger.)

Hans-Christian Blech
VISIT, THE(1964, Ger./Fr./Ital./U.S.)

Rene Bleck
L'ATALANTE(1947, Fr.)

Douglas Bleckley
GREAT LOCOMOTIVE CHASE, THE(1956)

Morris Bleckman
MEDIUM COOL(1969)

Vaslav Bledis
WATERLOO(1970, Ital./USSR)

Doug Bledsoe
COAL MINER'S DAUGHTER(1980)

Jules Bledsoe
SHOW BOAT(1929); DRUMS OF THE CONGO(1942)

Muriel Bledsoe
LYDIA BAILEY(1952)

Will Bledsoe
1984
UP THE CREEK(1984)

Debra Blee
BEACH GIRLS(1982)
1984
SAVAGE STREETS(1984)

William F. Bleecher
TEN LAPS TO GO(1938), w

Oliver Bleeck
ST. IVES(1976), w

Henry "Hank" Bleeker
1984
FLETCH(1984)

Robert Blees
SWEATER GIRL(1942), w; PAID IN FULL(1950), w; ALL I DESIRE(1953), w; GLASS WEB, THE(1953), w; CATTLE QUEEN OF MONTANA(1954), w; MAGNIFICENT OBSESSION(1954), w; PLAYGIRL(1954), w; YELLOW MOUNTAIN, THE(1954), w; FIGHTING CHANCE, THE(1955), w; ONE DESIRE(1955), w; AUTUMN LEAVES(1956), w; SLIGHTLY SCARLET(1956), w; BLACK SCORPION, THE(1957), w;

FROM THE EARTH TO THE MOON(1958), w; HIGH SCHOOL CONFIDENTIAL(1958), w; SCREAMING MIMI(1958), w; WHO SLEW AUNTIE ROO?(1971, U.S./Brit.), w; DOCTOR PHIBES RISES AGAIN(1972, Brit.), w; FROGS(1972), w; SAVAGE HARVEST(1981), w

William Blees
FOUR JACKS AND A JILL(1941); NAVAL ACADEMY(1941); HELLO ANNAPOLIS(1942); HENRY ALDRICH GETS GLAMOUR(1942); MAGNIFICENT AMBERSONS, THE(1942); JUNIOR ARMY(1943); WE'VE NEVER BEEN LICKED(1943)

Yasmine Bleeth
1984
HEY BABE!(1984, Can.)

Dr. Leo Blei
GOOD SOLDIER SCHWEIK, THE(1963, Ger.), cos

Leon Bleiberg
DAY OF THE NIGHTMARE(1965), p

Hedwig Bleibtreu
THIRD MAN, THE(1950, Brit.)

Bill Bleich
HEARSE, THE(1980), w

Juda Bleich
VICTIMS OF PERSECUTION(1933)

Judah Bleich
CANTOR'S SON, THE(1937)

Jill Bleidner
FAT SPY(1966)

Otto Bleidner
1984
LOOSE CONNECTIONS(1984, Brit.)

Nancy Bleier
FIRST NUDIE MUSICAL, THE(1976); GREAT TEXAS DYNAMITE CHASE, THE(1976); HERO AT LARGE(1980)

John Bleifer
WITHOUT RESERVATIONS(1946); BOWERY, THE(1933); CAPTURED(1933); BLACK ROOM, THE(1935); CRIMSON TRAIL, THE(1935); LES MISERABLES(1935); NIGHT ALARM(1935); LADIES IN LOVE(1936); SUTTER'S GOLD(1936); CHARLIE CHAN AT MONTE CARLO(1937); SEVENTH HEAVEN(1937); SLAVE SHIP(1937); THANK YOU, MR. MOTO(1937); MR. MOTO TAKES A VACATION(1938); RIDE A CROOKED MILE(1938); EVERYTHING HAPPENS AT NIGHT(1939); FRONTIER MARSHAL(1939); PACIFIC LINER(1939); GIRL FROM GOD'S COUNTRY(1940); MARK OF ZORRO, THE(1940); MONSTER AND THE GIRL, THE(1941); PARIS CALLING(1941); LURE OF THE ISLANDS(1942); FOR WHOM THE BELL TOLLS(1943); MR. LUCKY(1943); MASK OF DIMITRIOS, THE(1944); WATERFRONT(1944); TONIGHT AND EVERY NIGHT(1945); RENDEZVOUS 24(1946); WIFE OF MONTE CRISTO, THE(1946); FALL GUY(1947); HIGH CONQUEST(1947); NORTHWEST OUTPOST(1947); CALL NORTHSIDE 777(1948); ENCHANTED VALLEY, THE(1948); FRENCH LEAVE(1948); SIXTEEN FATHOMS DEEP(1948); SMUGGLERS' COVE(1948); JACKPOT, THE(1950); STATE PENITENTIARY(1950); BOWERY BATTALION(1951); RED SNOW(1952); JUGGLER, THE(1953); WHITE LIGHTNING(1953); CRASHING LAS VEGAS(1956); FIGHTING TROUBLE(1956); SPY CHASERS(1956); CHAIN OF EVIDENCE(1957); 27TH DAY, THE(1957); GENE KRUPA STORY, THE(1959); ICE PALACE(1960); GEORGE RAFT STORY, THE(1961); HOOK, THE(1962); IF A MAN ANSWERS(1962); LOVED ONE, THE(1965)

John M. Bleifer
MANHATTAN MELODRAMA(1934)

John Melvin Bleifer
CLEAR ALL WIRES(1933)

John Bleiffer
IN OUR TIME(1944)

M. Bleiman
GREAT CITIZEN, THE(1939, USSR), w; NO GREATER LOVE(1944, USSR), w

A. Blek
MORNING STAR(1962, USSR), art d

M. Bleman
SECRET MISSION(1949, USSR), w

The Blenders
IT CAN'T LAST FOREVER(1937)

James Blendick
SHOOT(1976, Can.); CORDELIA(1980, Fr., Can.); RESURRECTION(1980); STAR 80(1983); UTILITIES(1983, Can.)

Adele Bleneau
Silents
ADELE(1919), w

Gerhard Blenert
AFFAIR BLUM, THE(1949, Ger.)

Brian Blessed
CHRISTMAS TREE, THE(1966, Brit.); ALF 'N' FAMILY(1968, Brit.); BROTHERLY LOVE(1970, Brit.); LAST VALLEY, THE(1971, Brit.); TROJAN WOMEN, THE(1971); HENRY VIII AND HIS SIX WIVES(1972, Brit.); MAN OF LA MANCHA(1972); FLASH GORDON(1980); HIGH ROAD TO CHINA(1983); HOUND OF THE BASKERVILLES, THE(1983, Brit.)

Bert Blessing
JINXED!(1982), w

Jack Blessing
HEAVEN'S GATE(1980); GALAXY OF TERROR(1981)

Ed Blessington
HARDLY WORKING(1981)

Barbara Bletcher
SHOW BOAT(1936); TOMORROW IS FOREVER(1946)

Bill Bletcher
TRUE TO LIFE(1943)

Billy Bletcher
DANCING SWEETIES(1930); MAN HUNTER, THE(1930); TOP SPEED(1930); BRANDED MEN(1931); TEXAS RANGER, THE(1931); BOILING POINT, THE(1932); MAKE ME A STAR(1932); DIPLOMANIACS(1933); LADY'S PROFESSION, A(1933); BABES IN TOYLAND(1934); CAT'S PAW, THE(1934); HOLLYWOOD PARTY(1934); OLD-FASHIONED WAY, THE(1934); LIFE BEGINS AT 40(1935); MAN ON THE FLYING TRAPEZE, THE(1935); ONE HOUR LATE(1935); CAN THIS BE DIXIE?(1936); SATAN MET A LADY(1936); GIRL WITH IDEAS, A(1937); GOD'S COUNTRY AND THE MAN(1937); HIGH, WIDE AND HANDSOME(1937); MEN WITH WINGS(1938); PROFESSOR BEWARE(1938); DESTRY RIDES AGAIN(1939); MELODY

RANCH(1940); CRACKED NUTS(1941); SULLIVAN'S TRAVELS(1941); WHISTLING IN THE DARK(1941); I MARRIED A WITCH(1942); CHATTERBOX(1943); GOOD MORNING, JUDGE(1943); IS EVERYBODY HAPPY?(1943); BOSS OF THE RAWHIDE(1944); MRS. PARKINGTON(1944); SHINE ON, HARVEST MOON(1944); DEADLINE AT DAWN(1946); KID FROM BOOKLYN, THE(1946); DOWN TO EARTH(1947); SECRET LIFE OF WALTER MITTY, THE(1947); SENATOR WAS INDISCREET, THE(1947); SINBAD THE SAILOR(1947); NIGHT UNTO NIGHT(1949); FATHER TAKES THE AIR(1951); NAVY BOUND(1951); HOUDINI(1953); PATSY, THE(1964)
Silents
ROMANCE ROAD(1925); DUDE COWBOY, THE(1926); ONE HOUR OF LOVE(1927); DAREDEVIL'S REWARD(1928)

William Bletcher
Silents
BILLY JIM(1922); WILD GIRL, THE(1925), d
Misc. Silents
SILENT GUARDIAN, THE(1926), d

Joele Bleton
WHEEL OF ASHES(1970, Fr.), ed

Russell R. Bletzer
GHOST STORY(1981)

Jean-Claude Bleuze
ICE CASTLES(1978)

Eleanor Blevins
Misc. Silents
DEAD SOUL, THE(1915)

Gaines Blevins
Misc. Talkies
TRAIL OF THE HAWK(1935)

Malcolm Blevins
Silents
AMERICAN LIVE WIRE, AN(1918)
Misc. Silents
REFORM CANDIDATE, THE(1915)

Bill Blewett
NINE MEN(1943, Brit.); SOMEWHERE IN FRANCE(1943, Brit.); GIRL ON THE CANAL, THE(1947, Brit.)

Kitty Blewett
WHAT A CARRY ON!(1949, Brit.); STICK 'EM UP(1950, Brit.)

Mrs. Blewett
SOMEWHERE IN FRANCE(1943, Brit.)

Bill Blewitt
JOHNNY FRENCHMAN(1946, Brit.)

David Blewitt
LOVE MACHINE, THE,(1971), ed; BUTTERFLIES ARE FREE(1972), ed; HAMMERSMITH IS OUT(1972), ed; FORTY CARATS(1973), ed; REPORT TO THE COMMISSIONER(1975), ed; BUDDY HOLLY STORY, THE(1978), ed; COMPETITION, THE(1980), ed; IN GOD WE TRUST(1980), ed; UNDER THE RAINBOW(1981), ed; D.C. CAB(1983), ed; SMOKEY AND THE BANDIT–PART 3(1983), ed
1984
GHOSTBUSTERS(1984), ed

Risa Martha Blewitt
1984
LOVE STREAMS(1984)

Jack Blezard
CARRY ON AGAIN, DOCTOR(1969, Brit.), art d

John Blezard
HORROR HOTEL(1960, Brit.), art d; MARY HAD A LITTLE(1961, Brit.), art d; THREE ON A SPREE(1961, Brit.), art d; REACH FOR GLORY(1963, Brit.), art d; HANDS OF ORLAC, THE(1964, Brit./Fr.), art d; OPERATION SNAFU(1965, Brit.), art d; LIQUIDATOR, THE(1966, Brit.), art d; JOKERS, THE(1967, Brit.), art d; ONLY WHEN I LARF(1968, Brit.), art d; THAT RIVIERA TOUCH(1968, Brit.), art d; BEFORE WINTER COMES(1969, Brit.), art d; HOFFMAN(1970, Brit.), art d; WHEN DINOSAURS RULED THE EARTH(1971, Brit.), art d; HIDING PLACE, THE(1975), prod d; AMSTERDAM KILL, THE(1978, Hong Kong), art d; NIJINSKY(1980, Brit.), prod d; WICKED LADY, THE(1983, Brit.), art d

John Blick
SOLO(1978, New Zealand/Aus.), ph

Newton Blick
COURT MARTIAL(1954, Brit.); CHARLEY MOON(1956, Brit.); GENTLE TOUCH, THE(1956, Brit.); THIRD KEY, THE(1957, Brit.); TOWN ON TRIAL(1957, Brit.); ALL AT SEA(1958, Brit.); BACHELOR OF HEARTS(1958, Brit.); GYPSY AND THE GENTLEMAN, THE(1958, Brit.); FLAME IN THE STREETS(1961, Brit.); MAN IN THE MOON(1961, Brit.); TERM OF TRIAL(1962, Brit.); RING OF SPIES(1964, Brit.); SEVENTY DEADLY PILLS(1964, Brit.); LORD JIM(1965, Brit.); MORGAN!(1966, Brit.)

Georg Blickingberg
WALPURGIS NIGHT(1941, Swed.)

John Blieffer
FULL CONFESSION(1939)

Bernard Blier
DAYBREAK(1940, Fr.); CARMEN(1946, Ital.); SYMPHONIE FANTASTIQUE(1947, Fr.); JENNY LAMOUR(1948, Fr.); DEDEE(1949, Fr.); CHEAT(1950, Fr.); MONSEIGNEUR(1950, Fr.); PASSION FOR LIFE(1951, Fr.); SECRETS D'ALCOVE(1954, Fr./Ital.); SPICE OF LIFE(1954, Fr.); GAMBLER, THE(1958, Fr.); CAT, THE(1959, Fr.); GREAT WAR, THE(1961, Fr., Ital.); COUNTERFEITERS OF PARIS, THE(1962, Fr., Ital.); MAGNIFICENT TRAMP, THE(1962, Fr./Ital.); GERMINAL(1963, Fr.); HUNCHBACK OF ROME, THE(1963, Ital.); MATHIAS SANDORF(1963, Fr.); AND SUDDENLY IT'S MURDER!(1964, Ital.); LA BONNE SOUPE(1964, Fr./Ital.); ORGANIZER, THE(1964, Fr./Ital./Yugo.); SEVENTH JUROR, THE(1964, Fr.); CASANOVA '70(1965, Ital.); GREED IN THE SUN(1965, Fr./ Ital.); HIGH INFIDELITY(1965, Fr./Ital.); MAGNIFICENT CUCKOLD, THE(1965, Fr./Ital.); MALE HUNT(1965, Fr./Ital.); WOMEN AND WAR(1965, Fr.); MADMAN OF LAB 4, THE(1967, Fr.); STRANGER, THE(1967, Algeria/Fr./Ital.); CAROLINE CHERIE(1968, Fr.); HOW TO SEDUCE A PLAYBOY(1968, Aust./Fr./Ital.); TO COMMIT A MURDER(1970, Fr./Ital./Ger.); ATCH ME A SPY(1971, Fr./Fr.); TALL BLOND MAN WITH ONE BLACK SHOE, THE(1973, Fr.); DAYDREAMER, THE(1975, Fr.); PASSION OF LOVE(1982, Ital./Fr.)

Bertrand Blier
GOING PLACES(1974, Fr.), d, w; GET OUT YOUR HANDKERCHIEFS(1978, Fr.), d&w

1984
MY BEST FRIEND'S GIRL(1984, Fr.), d, w
Henry Bligh
BULLDOG BREED, THE(1960, Brit.), w
Jack Bligh
HORROR OF IT ALL, THE(1964, Brit.); GYPSY GIRL(1966, Brit.); ISLAND OF THE BURNING DAMNED(1971, Brit.)
Jasmine Bligh
BAND WAGGON(1940, Brit.)
Sheila Bligh
MISS LONDON LTD.(1943, Brit.)
Susan Bligh
SECRET VOICE, THE(1936, Brit.); WEDNESDAY'S LUCK(1936, Brit.)
Roger Blin
LIFE AND LOVES OF BEETHOVEN, THE(1937, Fr.); ALIBI, THE(1939, Fr.); CURTAIN RISES, THE(1939, Fr.); COLONEL CHABERT(1947, Fr.); ORPHEUS(1950, Fr.); ADVENTURES OF CAPTAIN FABIAN(1951); HUNCHBACK OF NOTRE DAME, THE(1957, Fr.); GUTS IN THE SUN(1959, Fr.); PARIS BLUES(1961); TASTE FOR WOMEN, A(1966, Fr./Ital.); CHECKERBOARD(1969, Fr.); MAIN THING IS TO LOVE, THE(1975, Ital./Fr.); ADOLESCENT, THE(1978, Fr./W.Ger.)
Anna Maria Blind
HERE'S YOUR LIFE(1968, Swed.)
Eric Blind
Misc. Silents
THEN I'LL COME BACK TO YOU(1916)
Johannes Blind
OBSESSION(1968, Swed.)
B. F. Blinn
Silents
QUICKER'N LIGHTNIN'(1925)
Beatrice Blinn
AND SO THEY WERE MARRIED(1936); MR. DEEDS GOES TO TOWN(1936); GIRLS CAN PLAY(1937); LOST HORIZON(1937); PAID TO DANCE(1937); SHADOW, THE(1937); YOU CAN'T TAKE IT WITH YOU(1938); GOLDEN BOY(1939); GOOD GIRLS GO TO PARIS(1939); HOMICIDE BUREAU(1939); CAFE HOSTESS(1940); CONVICTED WOMAN(1940); MY SON IS GUILTY(1940)
F. Blinn
Silents
KID, THE(1921)
Genevieve Blinn
COMMON CLAY(1930)
Silents
AMERICAN METHODS(1917); KINGDOM OF LOVE, THE(1918); WHEN A WOMAN SINS(1918); CRAZY TO MARRY(1921); DON'T TELL EVERYTHING(1921); QUEEN OF SHEBA, THE(1921); WITCHING HOUR, THE(1921); IF I WERE QUEEN(1922); ABRAHAM LINCOLN(1924)
Holbrook Blinn
Silents
WISHING RING, THE(1914); FAMILY CUPBOARD, THE(1915); IVORY SNUFF BOX, THE(1915); BALLET GIRL, THE(1916); HIDDEN SCAR, THE(1916); LIFE'S WHIRLPOOL(1916); ROSITA(1923); JANICE MEREDITH(1924); NEW COMMANDMENT, THE(1925); ZANDER THE GREAT(1925); TELEPHONE GIRL, THE(1927)
Misc. Silents
BOSS, THE(1915); HUSBAND AND WIFE(1916); PRIMA DONNA'S HUSBAND, THE(1916); UNPARDONABLE SIN, THE(1916); WEAKNESS OF MAN, THE(1916); EMPRESS, THE(1917); PRIDE(1917); SEVENTH SIN, THE(1917); BAD MAN, THE(1923); YOLANDA(1924); UNFAIR SEX, THE(1926); MASKED WOMAN, THE(1927)
William Blinn
1984
PURPLE RAIN(1984), w
S. Blinnikov
1812(1944, USSR); VOW, THE(1947, USSR.); SOUND OF LIFE, THE(1962, USSR); NINE DAYS OF ONE YEAR(1964, USSR)
S.K. Blinnikov
ALEXANDER NEVSKY(1939)
Boris Blinoff
DEFENSE OF VOLOTCHAYEVSK, THE(1938, USSR)
Boris Blinov
TAXI TO HEAVEN(1944, USSR)
K. Blinova
NIGHT BEFORE CHRISTMAS, A(1963, USSR), ed; SANDU FOLLOWS THE SUN(1965, USSR), ed
Jacob Bliokh
Silents
BATTLESHIP POTEMKIN, THE(1925, USSR), p
Arthur Bliss
CHRISTOPHER COLUMBUS(1949, Brit.), m; KISENGA, MAN OF AFRICA(1952, Brit.), m
Bradley Bliss
FIRST TIME, THE(1983)
Debby Bliss
PIE IN THE SKY(1964)
Imogene Bliss
KING OF MARVIN GARDENS, THE(1972); RICHARD(1972); CHAPTER TWO(1979)
John Bliss
VENGEANCE(1964); SCAVENGERS, THE(1969); THING WITH TWO HEADS, THE(1972)
Leila Bliss
Silents
PRETTY MRS. SMITH(1915)
Lela Bliss
WITHOUT RESERVATIONS(1946); HITCH HIKE TO HEAVEN(1936); SINCE YOU WENT AWAY(1944); DARK MIRROR, THE(1946); GAS HOUSE KIDS GO WEST(1947); MIRACLE ON 34TH STREET, THE(1947); SONG OF LOVE(1947); WHEN A GIRL'S BEAUTIFUL(1947); GIVE MY REGARDS TO BROADWAY(1948); I REMEMBER MAMA(1948); SNAKE PIT, THE(1948); WHEN MY BABY SMILES AT ME(1948); INTRUDER IN THE DUST(1949); NEVER A DULL MOMENT(1950); TO PLEASE A LADY(1950); GHOST CHASERS(1951); ON THE LOOSE(1951); PAYMENT ON DEMAND(1951); ARMY BOUND(1952); BIG TIP OFF, THE(1955); PEPE(1960)

Lucille Bliss
CINDERELLA(1950); FUNNYMAN(1967); SECRET OF NIMH, THE(1982)
Roy Bliss
MEET NERO WOLFE(1936)
Sally Bliss
MEET MISS BOBBY SOCKS(1944); SWING IN THE SADDLE(1944); DANCING IN MANHATTAN(1945)
Misc. Talkies
RUSTLERS OF THE BADLANDS(1945)
Sir Arthur Bliss
BEGGAR'S OPERA, THE(1953), m; ABANDON SHIP(1957, Brit.), m
Ted Bliss
THREE MEN ON A HORSE(1936)
Gerda Blisse
ESCAPE TO BERLIN(1962, U.S./Switz./Ger.); MONSTER OF LONDON CITY, THE(1967, Ger.); TIN DRUM, THE(1979, Ger./Fr./Yugo./Pol.)
Catherine Blisson
L'IMMORTELLE(1969, Fr./Ital./Turkey)
Marcel Blistene
PLEASURES AND VICES(1962, Fr.), d&w
Donald Blitner
WE OF THE NEVER NEVER(1983, Aus.)
Peter Blitz
VALLEY OF EAGLES(1952, Brit.)
Rusty Blitz
PRODUCERS, THE(1967); YOUNG FRANKENSTEIN(1974); NICKELODEON(1976)
Marc Blitzstein
THREE PENNY OPERA(1963, Fr./Ger.), w
Helen Blizard
LAS VEGAS STORY, THE(1952)
Andrew Bloch
ABDUCTION(1975); HANGAR 18(1980); IN SEARCH OF HISTORIC JESUS(1980)
Arthur Bloch
STUDENT TOUR(1934), w
Bert Bloch
LUDWIG(1973, Ital./Ger./Fr.)
Bertram Bloch
GABRIEL OVER THE WHITE HOUSE(1933), w; DARK VICTORY(1939), w
Silents
OH, WHAT A NURSE!(1926), w
Charles B. Bloch
THE HYPNOTIC EYE(1960), p, w
Eric Bloch
MONTREAL MAIN(1974, Can.), ph
Ivan Bloch
1984
STONE BOY, THE(1984), p
John W. Bloch
ONE MAN'S WAY(1964), w
Lars Bloch
STRANGER IN TOWN, A(1968, U.S./Ital.); WILD EYE, THE(1968, Ital.)
Robert Bloch
PSYCHO(1960), w; CABINET OF CALIGARI, THE(1962), w; COUCH, THE(1962), w; NIGHT WALKER, THE(1964), w; STRAIT-JACKET(1964), w; SKULL, THE(1965, Brit.), w; PSYCHOPATH, THE(1966, Brit.), w; DEADLY BEES, THE(1967, Brit.), w; JOURNEY INTO MIDNIGHT(1968, Brit.), w; TORTURE GARDEN(1968, Brit.), w; HOUSE THAT DRIPPED BLOOD, THE(1971, Brit.), w; ASYLUM(1972, Brit.), w; PSYCHO II(1983), w
Timothy J. Bloch
FIRST NUDIE MUSICAL, THE(1976), set d
L. G. Blochman
BOMBAY MAIL(1934), w; CHINATOWN SQUAD(1935), w
Lawrence G. Blochman
PURSUIT(1935), w; SECRET OF THE CHATEAU(1935), w; QUIET PLEASE, MURDER(1942), w
Aleck Block
EMBRACEABLE YOU(1948), w
Alfred Block
IT'S A GREAT LIFE(1930), w; WAY OUT WEST(1930), w; ROAR OF THE PRESS(1941), w
Andrew Block
BIG FIX, THE(1978)
Arthur Block
CANTOR'S SON, THE(1937), p
Bernice Block
DINO(1957), p
Bertram Block
STOLEN HOURS(1963), w
Bob Block
LYONS IN PARIS, THE(1955, Brit.), w
Bruce Block
OSTERMAN WEEKEND, THE(1983)
Carolyn Block
LAS VEGAS STORY, THE(1952)
Chad Dee Block
COURT JESTER, THE(1956)
Edwin Block
711 OCEAN DRIVE(1950), tech adv
Frederick Block
PATRICK THE GREAT(1945), w
Hal Block
I'M NOBODY'S SWEETHEART NOW(1940), w
Hunt Block
1984
LONELY GUY, THE(1984)
Irving Block
FLIGHT TO MARS(1951), spec eff; INVADERS FROM MARS(1953), spec eff; FORBIDDEN PLANET(1956), spec eff; WORLD WITHOUT END(1956), spec eff; INVISIBLE BOY, THE(1957), spec eff; KRONOS(1957), p, w, spec eff; SAGA OF THE VIKING WOMEN AND THEIR VOYAGE TO THE WATERS OF THE GREAT SEA SERPENT, THE(1957),

w; MACABRE(1958), spec eff; WAR OF THE SATELLITES(1958), p, w, spec eff; THIRTY FOOT BRIDE OF CANDY ROCK, THE(1959), w, spec eff; ATOMIC SUBMARINE, THE(1960), spec eff

Irving A. Block
ROCKETSHIP X-M(1950), spec eff

Irwin A. Block
UNKNOWN WORLD(1951), p, spec eff

Jesse Block
KID MILLIONS(1934)

Jim Block
SCARAB(1982, U.S./Span.), Ned Miller

Katherine Block
Silents
ADVENTURER, THE(1928)

Kimberly Block
BABY, THE RAIN MUST FALL(1965)

Larry Block
SHAMUS(1973); SLAP SHOT(1977); HEAVEN CAN WAIT(1978); HARDCORE(1979); FUNHOUSE, THE(1981), w

Lawrence Block
NIGHTMARE HONEYMOON(1973), w

Libbie Block
ONE HOUR LATE(1935), w; PIN UP GIRL(1944), w; CAUGHT(1949), w

Martin Block
MAKE BELIEVE BALLROOM(1949), w; DISC JOCKEY(1951)

Maurice Block
GIFT OF GAB(1934)

Paul Block
SHADY LADY, THE(1929), p

Ralph Block
SHOW FOLKS(1928), p; LEATHERNECK, THE(1929), p; RACKETEER, THE(1929), p; RICH PEOPLE(1929), p; THIS THING CALLED LOVE(1929), p; SCOTLAND YARD(1930), p; SEA WOLF, THE(1930), w; HOLY TERROR, A(1931), w; BEFORE DAWN(1933), w; DARK HAZARD(1934), w; GAMBLING LADY(1934), w; MASSACRE(1934), w; I AM A THIEF(1935), w; IN CALIENTE(1935), w; MELODY LINGERS ON, THE(1935), w; NOBODY'S FOOL(1936), w; SPY FOR A DAY(1939, Brit.), w; IT'S A DATE(1940), w; PATRICK THE GREAT(1945), w; NANCY GOES TO RIO(1950), w
Silents
QUARTERBACK, THE(1926), p; MAN-MADE WOMEN(1928), p

Scotty Block
KING OF COMEDY, THE(1983)

Sheridan Block
Silents
SOUL OF BROADWAY, THE(1915)

Tom Block
THIRD TIME LUCKY(1950, Brit.)

Walter Block
BORN AGAIN(1978), w

The Blockbusters
CARNIVAL ROCK(1957); ROCK ALL NIGHT(1957)

Dan Blocker
YOUNG CAPTIVES, THE(1959); ERRAND BOY, THE(1961); COME BLOW YOUR HORN(1963); LADY IN CEMENT(1968); COCKEYED COWBOYS OF CALICO COUNTY, THE(1970)

David Blocker
1984
CHOOSE ME(1984), p

Dirk Blocker
RAISE THE TITANIC(1980, Brit.); BORDER, THE(1982); POLTERGEIST(1982)
1984
STARMAN(1984)

Mike Blodget
TRIP, THE(1967)

Carol Blodgett
RACE WITH THE DEVIL(1975)

James Blodgett
MIGHTY MOUSE IN THE GREAT SPACE CHASE(1983), ed

Michael Blodgett
SWINGIN' SUMMER, A(1965), ch; CATALINA CAPER, THE(1967), ch; 40 GUNS TO APACHE PASS(1967); THERE WAS A CROOKED MAN(1970); VELVET VAMPIRE, THE(1971); CAREY TREATMENT, THE(1972); ULTIMATE THRILL, THE(1974)
Misc. Talkies
DISCO FEVER(1978)

Mike Blodgett
CATALINA CAPER, THE(1967)

William Bloecher
HOLLYWOOD MYSTERY(1934), w

Jerry Bloedow
DARK END OF THE STREET, THE(1981), ed

David Blok
DARK IS THE NIGHT(1946, USSR), m

Jerzy Blok
SALTO(1966, Pol.)

Walter J. Blokesch
GIRL AND THE LEGEND, THE(1966, Ger.), set d

Klavdia Blokhina
THREE TALES OF CHEKHOV(1961, USSR)

August Blom
Misc. Silents
ATLANTIS(1913, Ger./Den.), d

Magda Blom
DANCE OF LIFE, THE(1929)

Anne Blomberg
MAKE WAY FOR LILA(1962, Swed./Ger.)

Arvid Blomberg
1984
SUBURBIA(1984)

Jan Blomberg
DEVIL'S MESSENGER, THE(1962 U.S./Swed.)

Karl-Birger Blomdahl
NAKED NIGHT, THE(1956, Swed.), m

Mme. Blome
THINGS OF LIFE, THE(1970, Fr./Ital./Switz.)

Derek Blomfield
SHIPMATES O' MINE(1936, Brit.); WRATH OF JEALOUSY(1936, Brit.); EMIL(1938, Brit.); GHOST OF ST. MICHAEL'S. THE(1941, Brit.); ALIBI, THE(1943, Brit.); NIGHT AND THE CITY(1950, Brit.); ISLAND RESCUE(1952, Brit.); FLOATING DUTCHMAN, THE(1953, Brit.); GAY ADVENTURE, THE(1953, Brit.); RECOIL(1953); HOBSON'S CHOICE(1954, Brit.); IT'S A WONDERFUL WORLD(1956, Brit.); IT'S GREAT TO BE YOUNG(1956, Brit.); CARRY ON ADMIRAL(1957, Brit.); REACH FOR THE SKY(1957, Brit.); SMALL HOTEL(1957, Brit.); ESCORT FOR HIRE(1960, Brit.)

Bengt Blomgren
INVASION OF THE ANIMAL PEOPLE(1962, U.S./Swed.); MAKE WAY FOR LILA(1962, Swed./Ger.)

Lennart Blomkvist
SHAME(1968, Swed.), art d; PASSION OF ANNA, THE(1970, Swed.); RITUAL, THE(1970, Swed.), art d

Paul Blomley
MAN IN THE MIDDLE(1964, U.S./Brit.)

Marianne Blomquist
I LOVE YOU, I KILL YOU(1972, Ger.)

Anssi Blomstedt
TIME OF ROSES(1970, Fin.), spec eff

Ulla Blomstrand
HERE'S YOUR LIFE(1968, Swed.)

Susan Blond
1984
MIXED BLOOD(1984)

Michele Blondel
JE T'AIME, JE T'AIME(1972, Fr./Swed.)

Patrick Blondel
1984
LES COMPERES(1984, Fr.)

Roger Blondel
FRENCH WAY, THE(1975, Fr.), w

Gloria Blondell
ACCIDENTS WILL HAPPEN(1938); DAREDEVIL DRIVERS(1938); FOUR'S A CROWD(1938); JUVENILE COURT(1938); MODEL WIFE(1941); DON'T BOTHER TO KNOCK(1952); TWONKY, THE(1953); WHITE LIGHTNING(1953)

Joan Blondell
CORPSE CAME C.O.D., THE(; OFFICE WIFE, THE(1930); SINNER'S HOLIDAY(1930); BIG BUSINESS GIRL(1931); BLONDE CRAZY(1931); GOD'S GIFT TO WOMEN(1931); ILLICIT(1931); MILLIE(1931); MY PAST(1931); NIGHT NURSE(1931); OTHER MEN'S WOMEN(1931); PUBLIC ENEMY, THE(1931); RECKLESS HOUR, THE(1931); BIG CITY BLUES(1932); CENTRAL PARK(1932); CROWD ROARS, THE(1932); FAMOUS FERGUSON CASE, THE(1932); GREEKS HAD A WORD FOR THEM(1932); MAKE ME A STAR(1932); MISS PINKERTON(1932); THREE ON A MATCH(1932); UNION DEPOT(1932); BLONDIE JOHNSON(1933); BROADWAY BAD(1933); CONVENTION CITY(1933); FOOTLIGHT PARADE(1933); GOLD DIGGERS OF 1933(1933); GOODBYE AGAIN(1933); HAVANA WIDOWS(1933); LAWYER MAN(1933); DAMES(1934); HE WAS HER MAN(1934); I'VE GOT YOUR NUMBER(1934); KANSAS CITY PRINCESS(1934); SMARTY(1934); BROADWAY GONDOLIER(1935); MISS PACIFIC FLEET(1935); TRAVELING SALESLADY, THE(1935); WE'RE IN THE MONEY(1935); BULLETS OR BALLOTS(1936); COLLEEN(1936); GOLD DIGGERS OF 1937(1936); SONS O' GUNS(1936); STAGE STRUCK(1936); THREE MEN ON A HORSE(1936); BACK IN CIRCULATION(1937); KING AND THE CHORUS GIRL, THE(1937); PERFECT SPECIMEN, THE(1937); STAND-IN(1937); THERE'S ALWAYS A WOMAN(1938); AMAZING MR. WILLIAMS(1939); EAST SIDE OF HEAVEN(1939); GOOD GIRLS GO TO PARIS(1939); KID FROM KOKOMO, THE(1939); OFF THE RECORD(1939); I WANT A DIVORCE(1940); TWO GIRLS ON BROADWAY(1940); LADY FOR A NIGHT(1941); MODEL WIFE(1941); THREE GIRLS ABOUT TOWN(1941); TOPPER RETURNS(1941); CRY HAVOC(1943); ADVENTURE(1945); DON JUAN QUILLIGAN(1945); TREE GROWS IN BROOKLYN, A(1945); CHRISTMAS EVE(1947); NIGHTMARE ALLEY(1947); FOR HEAVEN'S SAKE(1950); BLUE VEIL, THE(1951); OPPOSITE SEX, THE(1956); DESK SET(1957); LIZZIE(1957); THIS COULD BE THE NIGHT(1957); WILL SUCCESS SPOIL ROCK HUNTER?(1957); ANGEL BABY(1961); ADVANCE TO THE REAR(1964); CINCINNATI KID, THE(1965); RIDE BEYOND VENGEANCE(1966); SPY IN THE GREEN HAT, THE(1966); WATERHOLE NO. 3(1967); KONA COAST(1968); STAY AWAY, JOE(1968); BIG DADDY(1969); PHYNX, THE(1970); SUPPORT YOUR LOCAL GUNFIGHTER(1971); WON TON TON, THE DOG WHO SAVED HOLLYWOOD(1976); OPENING NIGHT(1977); GREASE(1978); CHAMP, THE(1979); GLOVE, THE(1980); WOMAN INSIDE, THE(1981)
Misc. Talkies
GLOVE, THE(1979)

Leopold Blonder
BLUE LIGHT, THE(1932, Ger.), set d

Antoine Blondin
OBSESSION(1954, Fr./Ital.), w; SECRETS D'ALCOVE(1954, Fr./Ital.), w; MONKEY IN WINTER, A(1962, Fr.), w

Rosemary Blong
NONE BUT THE LONELY HEART(1944)

Colette Blonigan
DINER(1982)

Alex Blonksteiner
CANNIBALS IN THE STREETS(1982, Ital./Span.), m

Adele Blood
Silents
RIDDLE: WOMAN, THE(1920)
Misc. Silents
DEVIL'S TOY, THE(1916)

Captain John Blood
LLOYDS OF LONDON(1936)

John Blood
DRACULA'S DAUGHTER(1936); TERROR EYES(1981); HANKY-PANKY(1982); VERDICT, THE(1982)

Stephen Blood
PURSUIT OF D.B. COOPER, THE(1981)
William Blood
CURSE OF THE LIVING CORPSE, THE(1964)
Blood and Thunder Boys
HUE AND CRY(1950, Brit.)
Margaret Bloodgood
CASE AGAINST MRS. AMES, THE(1936)
Herman Bloodsworth
LADY GREY(1980)
Robert C. Bloodwell
HURRY SUNDOWN(1967)
Anne Bloom
LOVING COUPLES(1980)
Bill Bloom
MAN FROM THE DINERS' CLUB, THE(1963), p
Brian Bloom
1984
ONCE UPON A TIME IN AMERICA(1984)
Claire Bloom
BLIND GODDESS, THE(1948, Brit.); LIMELIGHT(1952); MAN BETWEEN, THE(1953, Brit.); INNOCENTS IN PARIS(1955, Brit.); ALEXANDER THE GREAT(1956); RICHARD III(1956, Brit.); BROTHERS KARAMAZOV, THE(1958); BUCCANEER, THE(1958); LOOK BACK IN ANGER(1959); THREE MOVES TO FREEDOM(1960, Ger.); BRAINWASHED(1961, Ger.); CHAPMAN REPORT, THE(1962); WONDERFUL WORLD OF THE BROTHERS ERIMM, THE(1962); HAUNTING, THE(1963); 80,000 SUSPECTS(1963, Brit.); OUTRAGE, THE(1964); HIGH INFIDELITY(1965, Fr./Ital.); SPY WHO CAME IN FROM THE COLD, THE(1965, Brit.); CHARLY(1968); ILLUSTRATED MAN, THE(1969); THREE INTO TWO WON'T GO(1969, Brit.); RED SKY AT MORNING(1971); SEVERED HEAD, A(1971, Brit.); DOLL'S HOUSE, A(1973); ISLANDS IN THE STREAM(1977); CLASH OF THE TITANS(1981)
Doris Bloom
GREEN FINGERS(1947)
Eric L. Bloom
EYES OF A STRANGER(1980), w
Fred Bloom
Misc. Silents
MAN OF COURAGE(1922)
Gaetan Bloom
1984
DREAM ONE(1984, Brit./Fr.)
George Arthur Bloom
LAST FLIGHT OF NOAH'S ARK, THE(1980), w
Harold Jack Bloom
ARENA(1953), w; NAKED SPUR, THE(1953), w; YELLOW TOMAHAWK, THE(1954), w; LAND OF THE PHARAOHS(1955), w; BEHIND THE HIGH WALL(1956), w; GUNFIGHT, A(1971), p, w
Harry Jack Bloom
FOREIGN INTRIGUE(1956), w; YOU ONLY LIVE TWICE(1967, Brit.), w
Jeffrey Bloom
SNOW JOB(1972), w; 11 HARROWHOUSE(1974, Brit.), w; DOGPOUND SHUF-FLE(1975, Can.), d; SWASHBUCKLER(1976), w; STICK UP, THE(1978, Brit.), d&w; BLOOD BEACH(1981), d, w; NIGHTMARES(1983), w
Jim Bloom
RETURN OF THE JEDI(1983), p
Joe Bloom
GOOD DIE YOUNG, THE(1954, Brit.); SQUARE RING, THE(1955, Brit.)
John Bloom
IMPERSONATOR, THE(1962, Brit.), ed; MAN IN THE MIDDLE(1964, U.S./Brit.), ed; FUNERAL IN BERLIN(1966, Brit.), ed; GEORGY GIRL(1966, Brit.), ed; PARTY'S OVER, THE(1966, Brit.), ed; LAST SAFARI, THE(1967, Brit.), ed; LION IN WINTER, THE(1968, Brit.), ed; HARD TRAIL(1969); BLOOD OF FRANKENSTEIN(1970); IN SEARCH OF GREGORY(1970, Brit./Ital.), ed; BRAIN OF BLOOD(1971, Phil.); CATCH ME A SPY(1971, Brit./Fr./Fr.), ed; INCREDIBLE TWO-HEADED TRANSPLANT, THE(1971); LAST VALLEY, THE(1971, Brit.), ed; NIGHT DIGGER, THE(1971, Brit.), ed; HENRY VIII AND HIS SIX WIVES(1972, Brit.), ed; TRAVELS WITH MY AUNT(1972, Brit.), ed; ABDICATION, THE(1974, Brit.), ed; MOHAMMAD, MESSEN-GER OF GOD(1976, Lebanon/Brit.), ed; RITZ, THE(1976), ed; ORCA(1977), ed; MAG-IC(1978), ed; WHO'LL STOP THE RAIN?(1978), ed; DARK, THE(1979); DRACULA(1979), ed; FRENCH LIEUTENANT'S WOMAN, THE(1981), ed; GAND-HI(1982), ed; BETRAYAL(1983, Brit.), ed; UNDER FIRE(1983), ed
Judi Bloom
BARBER OF STAMFORD HILL, THE(1963, Brit.); SCREAM AND SCREAM AGAIN(1970, Brit.)
Leo Bloom
PRETTY BOY FLOYD(1960)
Les Bloom
WINDOWS(1980), set d; SO FINE(1981), set d; ZELIG(1983), set d
1984
BROADWAY DANNY ROSE(1984), set d; COTTON CLUB, THE(1984), set d
Leslie Bloom
SOMEBODY KILLED HER HUSBAND(1978), set d; TIMES SQUARE(1980), set d
Lindsay Bloom
SIX PACK ANNIE(1975); FRENCH QUARTER(1978); H.O.T.S.(1979); MAIN EVENT, THE(1979)
Misc. Talkies
COVER GIRL MODELS(1975); HUGHES AND HARLOW: ANGELS IN HELL(1978); TEXAS DETOUR(1978), a ADD 15666
Murray Teigh Bloom
LAST EMBRACE(1979), w
Phil Bloom
BOWERY, THE(1933)
Roberts Bloom
CRY DR. CHICAGO(1971)
Verna Bloom
CHILDRENS GAMES(1969); MEDIUM COOL(1969); HIRED HAND, THE(1971); BADGE 373(1973); HIGH PLAINS DRIFTER(1973); NATIONAL LAMPOON'S ANI-MAL HOUSE(1978); HONKYTONK MAN(1982)

William Bloom
FLIGHT INTO NOWHERE(1938), w; CIGARETTE GIRL(1947), p; MILLIE'S DAUGHTER(1947), p; SPORT OF KINGS(1947), p; GLORY BRIGADE, THE(1953), p; INFERNO(1953), p; ON THE THRESHOLD OF SPACE(1956), p; I MARRIED A WOMAN(1958), p; THIRTEEN WEST STREET(1962), p
William [Willi] Bloom
NOCTURNE(1946)
Bernard Bloomer
YOUNG WARRIORS(1983)
Ray Bloomer
Silents
BROADWAY ROSE(1922)
Raymond Bloomer
Silents
KENNEDY SQUARE(1916); OUT OF A CLEAR SKY(1918); PRODIGAL WIFE, THE(1918); LOVE LIGHT, THE(1921); NET, THE(1923); SENSATION SEEKERS(1927)
Misc. Silents
MARRIAGE BOND, THE(1916); WOMAN OF IMPULSE, A(1918); BELLE OF NEW YORK, THE(1919); BREAK THE NEWS TO MOTHER(1919); VICE OF FOOLS, THE(1920); OTHER WOMEN'S CLOTHES(1922); FOOL, THE(1925)
Bess Bloomfield
CHILD UNDER A LEAF(1975, Can.)
Derek Bloomfield
EAST OF SUDAN(1964, Brit.)
George Bloomfield
JENNY(1969), d, w; TO KILL A CLOWN(1972), d, w; CHILD UNDER A LEAF(1975, Can.), d&w, ed; DOUBLE NEGATIVE(1980, Can.), d; NOTHING PERSONAL(1980, Can.), d; SPASMS(1983, Can.)
Misc. Talkies
RIEL(1979), d
John Bloomfield
NEVER TAKE CANDY FROM A STRANGER(1961, Brit.); DURING ONE NIGHT(1962, Brit.); ADDING MACHINE, THE(1969); HENRY VIII AND HIS SIX WIVES(1972, Brit.), cos; FIENDISH PLOT OF DR. FU MANCHU, THE(1980), cos; EYE OF THE NEEDLE(1981), cos; CONAN THE BARBARIAN(1982), cos; WICKED LADY, THE(1983, Brit.), cos
1984
BOUNTY, THE(1984), cos; CONAN THE DESTROYER(1984), cos
Mike Bloomfield
MEDIUM COOL(1969), m
Pamela Bloomfield
THIS STUFF'LL KILL YA!(1971)
Patrick Bloomfield
WHILE THE SUN SHINES(1950, Brit.)
Philip Bloomfield
KEEP, THE(1983)
Robert Bloomfield
FEAR NO MORE(1961), w; DOG EAT DOG(1963, U.S./Ger./Ital.), w
Jonny Bloor
THREE COCKEYED SAILORS(1940, Brit.)
Clara Blore
SWING, SISTER, SWING(1938); LITTLE ACCIDENT(1939); I'M NOBODY'S SWEET-HEART NOW(1940); MOB TOWN(1941); MUG TOWN(1943)
Clara M. Blore
LIGHT THAT FAILED, THE(1939)
Clara Mackin Blore
SAY IT IN FRENCH(1938)
Clara Macklin Blore
LITTLE TOUGH GUY(1938)
Eric Blore
TARNISHED LADY(1931); FLYING DOWN TO RIO(1933); GAY DIVORCEE, THE(1934); LIMEHOUSE BLUES(1934); BEHOLD MY WIFE(1935); CASINO MUR-DER CASE, THE(1935); DIAMOND JIM(1935); FOLIES DERGERE(1935); GOOD FAIRY, THE(1935); I DREAM TOO MUCH(1935); I LIVE MY LIFE(1935); OLD MAN RHYTHM(1935); SEVEN KEYS TO BALDPATE(1935); TO BEAT THE BAND(1935); TOP HAT(1935); EX-MRS. BRADFORD, THE(1936); PICCADILLY JIM(1936); SMART-EST GIRL IN TOWN(1936); SONS O' GUNS(1936); SWING TIME(1936); TWO IN THE DARK(1936); BREAKFAST FOR TWO(1937); HITTING A NEW HIGH(1937); IT'S LOVE I'M AFTER(1937); QUALITY STREET(1937); SHALL WE DANCE(1937); SOL-DIER AND THE LADY, THE(1937); DESPERATE ADVENTURE, A(1938); JOY OF LIVING(1938); SWISS MISS(1938); GENTLEMAN'S GENTLEMAN, A(1939, Brit.); ISLAND OF LOST MEN(1939); $1,000 A TOUCHDOWN(1939); BOYS FROM SYRA-CUSE(1940); EARL OF PUDDLESTONE(1940); LONE WOLF KEEPS A DATE, THE(1940); LONE WOLF MEETS A LADY, THE(1940); LONE WOLF STRIKES, THE(1940); MAN WHO WOULDN'T TALK, THE(1940); MUSIC IN MY HEART(1940); SOUTH OF SUEZ(1940); 'TIL WE MEET AGAIN(1940); CONFIRM OR DENY(1941); LADY EVE, THE(1941); LADY SCARFACE(1941); LONE WOLF TAKES A CHANCE, THE(1941); NEW YORK TOWN(1941); REDHEAD(1941); ROAD TO ZANZIBAR(1941); SECRETS OF THE LONE WOLF(1941); SHANGHAI GESTURE, THE(1941); SUL-LIVAN'S TRAVELS(1941); THREE GIRLS ABOUT TOWN(1941); COUNTER-ESPION-AGE(1942); MOON AND SIXPENCE, THE(1942); FOREVER AND A DAY(1943); HAPPY GO LUCKY(1943); HOLY MATRIMONY(1943); ONE DANGEROUS NIGHT(1943); PASSPORT TO SUEZ(1943); SKY'S THE LIMIT, THE(1943); SUBMA-RINE BASE(1943); SAN DIEGO, I LOVE YOU(1944); EASY TO LOOK AT(1944); KITTY(1945); MEN IN HER DIARY(1945); PENTHOUSE RHYTHM(1945); ABIE'S IRISH ROSE(1946); NOTORIOUS LONE WOLF, THE(1946); LONE WOLF IN LON-DON(1947); LONE WOLF IN MEXICO(1947); WINTER WONDERLAND(1947); ROMANCE ON THE HIGH SEAS(1948); ADVENTURES OF ICHABOD AND MR. TOAD(1949); LOVE HAPPY(1949); FANCY PANTS(1950); BOWERY TO BAG-DAD(1955)
Misc. Talkies
PASSPORT TO HEAVEN(1943)
Silents
GREAT GATSBY, THE(1926)
Henry Blossom
KISS ME AGAIN(1931), w

Henry Martyn Blossom
Silents
RED MILL, THE(1927), w
Jack Blossom
Silents
CATCH AS CATCH CAN(1927)
Nathalie Blossom
POPEYE(1980)
Roberts Blossom
HOSPITAL, THE(1971); PLEASE STAND BY(1972); SLAUGHTERHOUSE-FI-VE(1972); DERANGED(1974, Can.); GREAT GATSBY, THE(1974); CITIZENS BAND(1977); CLOSE ENCOUNTERS OF THE THIRD KIND(1977); ESCAPE FROM ALCATRAZ(1979); RESURRECTION(1980); CHRISTINE(1983); REUBEN, REU-BEN(1983)
1984
FLASHPOINT(1984)
Rose Blossom
Silents
NIGHT PATROL, THE(1926); SPEED COP(1926); CATCH AS CATCH CAN(1927); WHITE FLANNELS(1927); LADDIE BE GOOD(1928)
Misc. Silents
GENTLE CYCLONE, THE(1926)
Winter Blossom
Silents
THIEF OF BAGDAD, THE(1924)
Blossom Toes
POPDOWN(1968, Brit.)
Henry M. Blosson, Jr.
Silents
CHECKERS(1913), w
Florence Blot
BIG CHIEF, THE(1960, Fr.); SUNDAYS AND CYBELE(1962, Fr.); TENANT, THE(1976, Fr.)
Jacques Blot
TRAIN, THE(1965, Fr./Ital./U.S.)
Adrian Blount
NIGHT TRAIN FOR INVERNESS(1960, Brit.)
Frank Blount
Silents
GRIM GAME, THE(1919), ph
Gabriel Blount
NOOSE FOR A LADY(1953, Brit.)
Jim Blount
EXORCIST II: THE HERETIC(1977), spec eff; TIME AFTER TIME(1979, Brit.), spec eff
Lisa Blount
SAM'S SONG(1971); 9/30/55(1977); OFFICER AND A GENTLEMAN, AN(1982)
Marguerite Blount
SAN FERNANDO VALLEY(1944)
Sheraton Blount
THIS IS MY STREET(1964, Brit.); DEADLY AFFAIR, THE(1967, Brit.)
Lisa Blout
DEAD AND BURIED(1981)
Leila Blow
Silents
LIGHTS OF NEW YORK, THE(1916)
Peggy Blow
PENITENTIARY II(1982)
Sidney Blow
LORD RICHARD IN THE PANTRY(1930, Brit.), w; OFFICER'S MESS, THE(1931, Brit.), w; WEDDINGS ARE WONDERFUL(1938, Brit.), w
Sydney Blow
WHERE IS THIS LADY?(1932, Brit.), w
W. Molesworth Blow
77 PARK LANE(1931, Brit.)
Laurie Blower
1984
SAM'S SON(1984)
Patsy Blower
THAT'LL BE THE DAY(1974, Brit.)
Alan Blowey
FAKE'S PROGRESS(1950, Brit.), ph
Jason S. Blown
BIG BLUFF, THE(1933), art d
Wiggie Blowne
STAGECOACH(1939)
Alana Blue
Misc. Talkies
FORBIDDEN UNDER THE CENSORSHIP OF THE KING(1973)
Angela Blue
FOLIES DERGERE(1935); PIN UP GIRL(1944)
Arkey Blue
RACE WITH THE DEVIL(1975)
Arlana Blue
Misc. Talkies
HOW TO SCORE WITH GIRLS(1980)
Ben Blue
COLLEGE HOLIDAY(1936); FOLLOW YOUR HEART(1936); ARTISTS AND MOD-ELS(1937); BIG BROADCAST OF 1938, THE(1937); HIGH, WIDE AND HAND-SOME(1937); THRILL OF A LIFETIME(1937); TURN OFF THE MOON(1937); COCOANUT GROVE(1938); COLLEGE SWING(1938); PARIS HONEYMOON(1939); FOR ME AND MY GAL(1942); PANAMA HATTIE(1942); THOUSANDS CHEER(1943); BROADWAY RHYTHM(1944); TWO GIRLS AND A SAILOR(1944); EASY TO WED(1946); TWO SISTERS FROM BOSTON(1946); MY WILD IRISH ROSE(1947); ONE SUNDAY AFTERNOON(1948); IT'S A MAD, MAD, MAD, MAD WORLD(1963); RUSSIANS ARE COMING, THE RUSSIANS ARE COMING, THE(1966); BUSYBODY, THE(1967); GUIDE FOR THE MARRIED MAN, A(1967); WHERE WERE YOU WHEN THE LIGHTS WENT OUT?(1968)

Silents
ARCADIANS, THE(1927, Brit.)
Betty Blue
Misc. Talkies
NOT TONIGHT HENRY(1961)
Brother Blue
KNIGHTRIDERS(1981)
Corine Blue
CHANEL SOLITAIRE(1981)
David Blue
RENALDO AND CLARA(1978)
Edgar Washington Blue
Silents
BY WHOSE HAND?(1927)
Misc. Silents
PASSION SONG, THE(1928)
Harry Blue
REUNION(1932, Brit.)
Hedi Blue
SANTO Y BLUE DEMON CONTRA LOS MONSTRUOS(1968, Mex.)
James Blue
OLIVE TREES OF JUSTICE, THE(1967, Fr.), d, w
Jean Blue
OVERLANDERS, THE(1946, Brit./Aus.); BITTER SPRINGS(1950, Aus.)
Monte Blue
WHITE SHADOWS IN THE SOUTH SEAS(1928); CONQUEST(1929); FROM HEAD-QUARTERS(1929); GREYHOUND LIMITED, THE(1929); NO DEFENSE(1929); SKIN DEEP(1929); ISLE OF ESCAPE(1930); THOSE WHO DANCE(1930); TIGER RO-SE(1930); FLOOD, THE(1931); INTRUDER, THE(1932); STOKER, THE(1932); HER FORGOTTEN PAST(1933); OFFICER 13(1933); COME ON, MARINES(1934); LAST ROUND-UP, THE(1934); STUDENT TOUR(1934); THUNDERING HERD, THE(1934); WAGON WHEELS(1934); G-MEN(1935); LIVES OF A BENGAL LANCER(1935); ON PROBATION(1935); TRAILS OF THE WILD(1935); WANDERER OF THE WASTE-LAND(1935); DESERT GOLD(1936); LAWLESS NINETIES, THE(1936); MARY OF SCOTLAND(1936); NEVADA(1936); PRISON SHADOWS(1936); RIDE, RANGER, RIDE(1936); SONG OF THE GRINGO(1936); TREACHERY RIDES THE RANGE(1936); AMATEUR CROOK(1937); BORN TO THE WEST(1937); OUTCASTS OF POKER FLAT, THE(1937); ROOTIN' TOOTIN' RHYTHM(1937); SOULS AT SEA(1937); THUNDER TRAIL(1937); ILLEGAL TRAFFIC(1938); KING OF ALCATRAZ(1938); MILLION TO ONE, A(1938); MYSTERIOUS RIDER, THE(1938); REBELLIOUS DAUGHTERS(1938); SPAWN OF THE NORTH(1938); DAYS OF JESSE JAMES(1939); DODGE CITY(1939); FRONTIER PONY EXPRESS(1939); GERONIMO(1939); JUAREZ(1939); OUR LEAD-ING CITIZEN(1939); PORT OF HATE(1939); TOM SAWYER, DETECTIVE(1939); UNION PACIFIC(1939); LITTLE BIT OF HEAVEN, A(1940); MYSTERY SEA RAI-DER(1940); NORTHWEST MOUNTED POLICE(1940); ROAD TO SINGAPORE(1940); TEXAS RANGERS RIDE AGAIN(1940); YOUNG BILL HICKOK(1940); ARKANSAS JUDGE(1941); BAD MAN OF DEADWOOD(1941); GREAT TRAIN ROBBERY, THE(1941); LAW OF THE TIMBER(1941); NEW YORK TOWN(1941); SCATTERGOOD PULLS THE STRINGS(1941); SULLIVAN'S TRAVELS(1941); SUNSET IN WYO-MING(1941); ACROSS THE PACIFIC(1942); CASABLANCA(1942); GENTLEMAN JIM(1942); GREAT MAN'S LADY, THE(1942); HIDDEN HAND, THE(1942); I MAR-RIED A WITCH(1942); KLONDIKE FURY(1942); MY FAVORITE BLONDE(1942); NORTH TO THE KLONDIKE(1942); PALM BEACH STORY, THE(1942); REAP THE WILD WIND(1942); REMARKABLE ANDREW, THE(1942); ROAD TO MOROC-CO(1942); SECRET ENEMIES(1942); TREAT EM' ROUGH(1942); EDGE OF DARK-NESS(1943); MISSION TO MOSCOW(1943); NORTHERN PURSUIT(1943); THANK YOUR LUCKY STARS(1943); TRUCK BUSTERS(1943); ADVENTURES OF MARK TWAIN, THE(1944); CONSPIRATORS, THE(1944); JANIE(1944); MASK OF DI-MITRIOS, THE(1944); PASSAGE TO MARSEILLE(1944); DANGER SIGNAL(1945); HORN BLOWS AT MIDNIGHT, THE(1945); SAN ANTONIO(1945); SARATOGA TRUNK(1945); CINDERELLA JONES(1946); HUMORESQUE(1946); JANIE GETS MARRIED(1946); MAN I LOVE, THE(1946); NEVER SAY GOODBYE(1946); SHADOW OF A WOMAN(1946); STOLEN LIFE, A(1946); BELLS OF SAN FERNANDO(1947); CHEYENNE(1947); LIFE WITH FATHER(1947); MY WILD IRISH ROSE(1947); POS-SESSED(1947); STALLION ROAD(1947); THAT WAY WITH WOMEN(1947); UN-FAITHFUL, THE(1947); JOHNNY BELINDA(1948); KEY LARGO(1948); SILVER RIVER(1948); TWO GUYS FROM TEXAS(1948); FLAXY MARTIN(1949); HOMICI-DE(1949); LOOK FOR THE SILVER LINING(1949); RANGER OF CHEROKEE STRIP(1949); SOUTH OF ST. LOUIS(1949); YOUNGER BROTHERS, THE(1949); BACKFIRE(1950); BLONDE BANDIT, THE(1950); DALLAS(1950); IROQUOIS TRAIL, THE(1950); MONTANA(1950); THIS SIDE OF THE LAW(1950); SEA HORNET, THE(1951); SNAKE RIVER DESPERADOES(1951); THREE DESPERATE MEN(1951); WARPATH(1951); GOLD RAIDERS, THE(1952); HANGMAN'S KNOT(1952); ROSE OF CIMARRON(1952); STORY OF WILL ROGERS, THE(1952); LAST POSSE, THE(1953); RIDE, VAQUERO!(1953); APACHE(1954)
Misc. Talkies
AFRICAN INCIDENT(1934); HOT OFF THE PRESS(1935)
Silents
BIRTH OF A NATION, THE(1915); HELL-TO-PAY AUSTIN(1916); INTOLERAN-CE(1916); MAN FROM PAINTED POST, THE(1917); WILD AND WOOLLY(1917); M'LISS(1918); RED, RED HEART, THE(1918); ROMANCE OF TARZAN, THE(1918); ROMANCE AND ARABELLA(1919); CUMBERLAND ROMANCE, A(1920); SOME-THING TO THINK ABOUT(1920); AFFAIRS OF ANATOL, THE(1921); BIG GA-ME(1921); BROKEN DOLL, A(1921); KENTUCKIANS, THE(1921); PERFECT CRIME, A(1921); BROADWAY ROSE(1922); ORPHANS OF THE STORM(1922); PEACOCK ALLEY(1922); MARRIAGE CIRCLE, THE(1924); REVELATION(1924); KISS ME AGAIN(1925); RECOMPENSE(1925); ACROSS THE PACIFIC(1926); SO THIS IS PARIS(1926); BRUTE, THE(1927); ONE-ROUND HOGAN(1927); WOLF'S CLO-THING(1927)
Misc. Silents
BETRAYED(1917); HANDS UP(1917); SHIP OF DOOM, THE(1917); EVERYWO-MAN(1919); IN MIZZOURA(1919); PETTIGREW'S GIRL(1919); RUSTLING A BRI-DE(1919); JUCKLINS, THE(1920); 13TH COMMANDMENT, THE(1920); MOONLIGHT AND HONEYSUCKLE(1921); MY OLD KENTUCKY HOME(1922); BRASS(1923); DEFYING DESTINY(1923); LUCRETIA LOMBARD(1923); MAIN STREET(1923); PUR-PLE HIGHWAY, THE(1923); TENTS OF ALLAH, THE(1923); BEING RESPECTA-BLE(1924); DARK SWAN, THE(1924); DAUGHTERS OF PLEASURE(1924); HER MARRIAGE VOW(1924); HOW TO EDUCATE A WIFE(1924); LOVER OF CAMILLE, THE(1924); LOVING LIES(1924); MADEMOISELLE MIDNIGHT(1924); HOGAN'S ALLEY(1925); LIMITED MAIL, THE(1925); RED HOT TIRES(1925); MAN UPSTAIRS,

THE(1926); OTHER WOMEN'S HUSBANDS(1926); BITTER APPLES(1927); BLACK DIAMOND EXPRESS, THE(1927); BRASS KNUCKLES(1927); BUSH LEAGUER, THE(1927); ACROSS THE ATLANTIC(1928); NO DEFENSE(1929)

Simone Blue
1984
NADIA(1984, U.S./Yugo.)

Vicki Blue
1984
THIS IS SPINAL TAP(1984)

Vida Blue
BLACK GUNN(1972)

Virginia Blue
FINNEGANS WAKE(1965)

Blue Boy the Hog
STATE FAIR(1933)

The Blue Boys
KIMBERLEY JIM(1965, South Africa)

BLUE CLOUD
SANTA FE TRIAL, THE(1930)

The Blue Keys
SWEETHEART OF SIGMA CHI(1933)

The Blue Mountain Boys
STRANGE AFFAIR, THE(1968, Brit.)

The Bluebell Girls
PEEK-A-BOO(1961, Fr.)

Richard Bluel
RAID ON ROMMEL(1971), w; CASTAWAY COWBOY, THE(1974), w

Walter Bluemel
TWO-GUN TROUBADOR(1939), ph

Ralph C. Bluemke
ROBBY(1968), a, p, d&w

Billy Blueriver
FIREBALL JUNGLE(1968)

Steve Bluestein
CRACKING UP(1977)

Abby Bluestone
LITTLE DARLINGS(1980); NIGHT OF THE JUGGLER(1980)

George Bluestone
WALKING STICK, THE(1970, Brit.), w

Harry Bluestone
KILLER SHREWS, THE(1959), m; MARA OF THE WILDERNESS(1966), m

Betty Bluett
BOOTLEGGERS(1974)

The Bluettes
OKAY AMERICA(1932)

Carl Bluhm
MOZART STORY, THE(1948, Aust.)

Walter Bluhm
SOMEWHERE IN BERLIN(1949, E. Ger.); SLEEPING BEAUTY(1965, Ger.)

Ben Blum
SECRET OF THE PURPLE REEF, THE(1960)

Daniel Blum
Misc. Talkies
SWEET SOUND OF DEATH(1965, U.S./Span.)

Edwin Blum
KIDNAPPED(1938), w; ADVENTURES OF SHERLOCK HOLMES, THE(1939), w; YOUNG PEOPLE(1940), w; GREAT AMERICAN BROADCAST, THE(1941), w; BOOGIE MAN WILL GET YOU, THE(1942), w; HENRY ALDRICH GETS GLAMOUR(1942), w; DOWN TO EARTH(1947), w; SOUTH SEA WOMAN(1953), w; STALAG 17(1953), w; BAMBOO PRISON, THE(1955), w; MIDNIGHT STORY, THE(1957), w

Edwin H. Blum
NEW ADVENTURES OF TARZAN(1935), w; TARZAN AND THE GREEN GODDESS(1938), w

Edwin Harvey Blum
CANTERVILLE GHOST, THE(1944), w; MAN ALIVE(1945), w

Harry N. Blum
OBSESSION(1976), p; SKATEBOARD(1978), p

Jack Blum
MEATBALLS(1979, Can.); HOG WILD(1980, Can.); HAPPY BIRTHDAY TO ME(1981); FUNNY FARM, THE(1982, Can.)

Jeff Blum
CHAMP, THE(1979)

Joe Blum
FIRST NUDIE MUSICAL, THE(1976)

Katherine Blum
1984
STAR TREK III: THE SEARCH FOR SPOCK(1984)

Len Blum
MEATBALLS(1979, Can.), w; HEAVY METAL(1981, Can.), w; STRIPES(1981), w; SPACEHUNTER: ADVENTURES IN THE FORBIDDEN ZONE(1983), w

Lillian Blum
Misc. Talkies
PEOPLE THAT SHALL NOT DIE, A(1939)

Mark Blum
LOVESICK(1983)

Max Blum
TORRID ZONE(1940); MEET JOHN DOE(1941)

Prof. John Morton Blum
ZELIG(1983)

R. Blum
LOVE CONTRACT, THE(1932, Brit.), w

Richard Blum
PENNIES FROM HEAVEN(1981)

Robert Blum
LAST CHANCE, THE(1945, Switz.), m; SEARCH, THE(1948), m; FOUR DAYS LEAVE(1950, Switz.), m; FOUR IN A JEEP(1951, Switz.), ed; VILLAGE, THE(1953, Brit./Switz.), m; HEIDI(1954, Switz.), m; HEIDI AND PETER(1955, Switz.), m; SHADOWS GROW LONGER, THE(1962, Switz./Ger.), m

Roger Blum
Silents
NAPOLEON(1927, Fr.)

Sam Blum
RIO RITA(1929); GRAND PARADE, THE(1930); IRON MAN, THE(1931); UNDER YOUR SPELL(1936)
Silents
WINNING OF BARBARA WORTH, THE(1926); SMILE, BROTHER, SMILE(1927)

Sammy Blum
PARTY GIRL(1930); NIGHT WORLD(1932); JEALOUSY(1934); CRIMINALS OF THE AIR(1937); DEVIL'S PLAYGROUND(1937); MONSTER AND THE GIRL, THE(1941); FALCON IN HOLLYWOOD, THE(1944); NEVADA(1944); NONE BUT THE LONELY HEART(1944); GEORGE WHITE'S SCANDALS(1945); WEST OF THE PECOS(1945); DEADLINE AT DAWN(1946)
Silents
WHEEL OF DESTINY, THE(1927)

Samuel Blum
DELIGHTFUL HOGUE(1929)
Silents
SIBERIA(1926)

Stanford Blum
TWO-MINUTE WARNING(1976)

Lewis F. Blumberg
BIG BOODLE, THE(1957), p

A.J. Blume
Misc. Silents
GREATER SINNER, THE(1919), d

Dave Blume
WINDFLOWERS(1968), md; TAXI DRIVER(1976), md

Jochen Blume
JOURNEY TO THE LOST CITY(1960, Ger./Fr./Ital.); COUNTERFEIT TRAITOR, THE(1962)

Richardo Blume
POLITICAL ASYLUM(1975, Mex./Guatemalan)

Alan Blumenfeld
WARGAMES(1983)

Mort Blumenstock
MORALS FOR WOMEN(1931), d
Silents
CRYSTAL CUP, THE(1927), t; SUNSET DERBY, THE(1927), t

Morton Blumenstock
GENTLEMEN OF THE PRESS(1929), ed; HOLE IN THE WALL(1929), ed; NOTHING BUT THE TRUTH(1929), ed
Silents
HONEYMOON FLATS(1928), w; RUNAWAY GIRLS(1928), t

Herman A. Blumentahl
TWO-MINUTE WARNING(1976), art d

Andy Blumenthal
1984
HARDBODIES(1984), ed; HIGHWAY TO HELL(1984), ed; RUNNING HOT(1984), ed

E. Blumenthal
Silents
GOLD RUSH, THE(1925)

George Blumenthal
1984
FLAMINGO KID, THE(1984)

Henry Blumenthal
CRY, THE BELOVED COUNTRY(1952, Brit.)

Herman A. Blumenthal
NO DOWN PAYMENT(1957), art d; THREE FACES OF EVE, THE(1957), art d; SING, BOY, SING(1958), art d; HOLIDAY FOR LOVERS(1959), ait d; JOURNEY TO THE CENTER OF THE EARTH(1959), art d; THESE THOUSAND HILLS(1959), art d; HIGH TIME(1960), art d; WILD RIVER(1960), art d; RIGHT APPROACH, THE(1961), art d; VOYAGE TO THE BOTTOM OF THE SEA(1961), art d; MORITURI(1965), art d; STAGECOACH(1966), art d; PIECES OF DREAMS(1970), art d; WHAT'S UP, DOC?(1972), art d; MR. RICCO(1975), art d; BETSY, THE(1978), prod d; ZORRO, THE GAY BLADE(1981), prod d

Herman Blumenthal
WARLOCK(1959), art d; CLEOPATRA(1963), art d; RAMPAGE(1963), art d; KISSES FOR MY PRESIDENT(1964), art d; SATAN BUG, THE(1965), art d; ONE AND ONLY GENUINE ORIGINAL FAMILY BAND, THE(1968), art d; HELLO, DOLLY!(1969), art d; ONLY GAME IN TOWN, THE(1970), art d; SKIN GAME(1971), art d; LOLLY-MADONNA XXX(1973), art d; WESTWORLD(1973), art d; 99 AND 44/100% DEAD(1974), art d; BALTIMORE BULLET, THE(1980), prod d; FORMULA, THE(1980), prod d

Oskar Blumenthal
WHITE HORSE INN, THE(1959, Ger.), w

Richard Blumenthal
REMARKABLE ANDREW, THE(1942), p; CHINA(1943), p; CRYSTAL BALL, THE(1943), p; LADY IN THE DARK(1944), p

Richard M. Blumenthal
THIS GUN FOR HIRE(1942), p

Maria Blumenthal-Tamarina
Misc. Silents
BEAUTY AND THE BOLSHEVIK(1923, USSR); BROKEN CHAINS(1925, USSR)

Baby Blumfield
Silents
LITTLE MISS SMILES(1922)

James Blumgarten
MISTER ROCK AND ROLL(1957), w

Dudone Blumier
KID MILLIONS(1934)

Jon Bluming
MODESTY BLAISE(1966, Brit.)

Rudolf Blumner
M(1933, Ger.)

Robert F. Blumofe
YOURS, MINE AND OURS(1968), p; PIECES OF DREAMS(1970), p; BOUND FOR GLORY(1976), p

Ute Blunck
SILENCE OF THE NORTH(1981, Can.)
Dick Blundell
MAN CALLED FLINTSTONE, THE(1966), ph; CHARLOTTE'S WEB(1973), ph
Graeme Blundell
STORK(1971, Aus.); ALVIN PURPLE(1974, Aus.); ALVIN RIDES AGAIN(1974, Aus.); DON'S PARTY(1976, Aus.); WEEKEND OF SHADOWS(1978, Aus.); ODD ANGRY SHOT, THE(1979, Aus.)
1984
MELVIN, SON OF ALVIN(1984, Aus.)
Misc. Talkies
DOCTORS AND NURSES(1983)
John Blundell
JUNKET 89(1970, Brit.); SCUM(1979, Brit.)
1984
SECRET PLACES(1984, Brit.)
Bill Blunden
SHALAKO(1968, Brit.), ed; 30 IS A DANGEROUS AGE, CYNTHIA(1968, Brit.), ed; THANK YOU ALL VERY MUCH(1969, Brit.), ed; MIND OF MR. SOAMES, THE(1970, Brit.), ed; NIGHT VISITOR, THE(1970, Swed./U.S.), ed; QUACKSER FORTUNE HAS A COUSIN IN THE BRONX(1970), ed; BAWDY ADVENTURES OF TOM JONES, THE(1976, Brit.), ed; GET CHARLIE TULLY(1976, Brit.), ed; WARLORDS OF ATLANTIS(1978, Brit.), ed
De Don Blunier
DAMES(1934)
John Blunk
WOLF LARSEN(1958), ed
Charlotte Blunt
FAR SHORE, THE(1976, Can.); SOMETHING'S ROTTEN(1979, Can.)
Erin Blunt
BAD NEWS BEARS, THE(1976); CARWASH(1976); BAD NEWS BEARS IN BREAKING TRAINING, THE(1977); HERO AIN'T NOTHIN' BUT A SANDWICH, A(1977); BAD NEWS BEARS GO TO JAPAN, THE(1978)
Gabrielle Blunt
TIGHT LITTLE ISLAND(1949, Brit.); CLOUDED YELLOW, THE(1950, Brit.); ROSSITER CASE, THE(1950, Brit.); TONY DRAWS A HORSE(1951, Brit.); CRASH OF SILENCE(1952, Brit.); TERROR STREET(1953); LOVE LOTTERY, THE(1954, Brit.); MAD LITTLE ISLAND(1958, Brit.); BREATH OF LIFE(1962, Brit.)
Joyce Blunt
GIRL MOST LIKELY, THE(1957)
Robert Blunt
FRANCIS(1949)
Vicki Lee Blunt
MY BLUE HEAVEN(1950)
Howard Blustein
HERCULES IN NEW YORK(1970)
Don Bluth
ROBIN HOOD(1973), anim; PETE'S DRAGON(1977), anim; RESCUERS, THE(1977), anim d; XANADU(1980), anim; SECRET OF NIMH, THE(1982), p, d, w
Hans Jung Bluth
THREE TOUGH GUYS(1974, U.S./Ital.)
Joseph E. Bluth
GIVE'EM HELL, HARRY!(1975), p
John Bluthal
TOUCH AND GO(1955); MOUSE ON THE MOON, THE(1963, Brit.); CARRY ON SPYING(1964, Brit.); FATHER CAME TOO(1964, Brit.); HARD DAY'S NIGHT, A(1964, Brit.); THIS IS MY STREET(1964, Brit.); HELP!(1965, Brit.); KNACK ... AND HOW TO GET IT, THE(1965, Brit.); FOLLOW THAT CAMEL(1967, Brit.); BLISS OF MRS. BLOSSOM, THE(1968, Brit.); DON'T RAISE THE BRIDGE, LOWER THE RIVER(1968, Brit.); CARRY ON HENRY VIII(1970, Brit.); DOCTOR IN TROUBLE(1970, Brit.); DIGBY, THE BIGGEST DOG IN THE WORLD(1974, Brit.); FLYING SORCERER, THE(1974, Brit.); GREAT MCGONAGALL, THE(1975, Brit.); RETURN OF THE PINK PANTHER, THE(1975, Brit.); FANTASM(1976, Aus.); REVENGE OF THE PINK PANTHER(1978); SUPERMAN III(1983)
Marcel Bluwal
PARIS PICK-UP(1963, Fr./Ital.), d, w
Hans Bluwe
BECAUSE I LOVED YOU(1930, Ger.)
Bernard Bly
TOMB OF TORTURE(1966, Ital.)
Norman Bly
CROSS AND THE SWITCHBLADE, THE(1970)
Wesley Bly
OUT OF THE PAST(1947); EAST SIDE, WEST SIDE(1949); AFRICAN TREASURE(1952)
Wesly Bly
SOMETHING OF VALUE(1957)
Larry Blyden
BACHELOR PARTY, THE(1957); KISS THEM FOR ME(1957); ON A CLEAR DAY YOU CAN SEE FOREVER(1970)
Sal Blydenburgh
MELINDA(1972), set d
Maggie Blye
DIAMONDS FOR BREAKFAST(1968, Brit.); ITALIAN JOB, THE(1969, Brit.); SPORTING CLUB, THE(1971); HARD TIMES(1975); LITTLE DARLINGS(1980); LIAR'S MOON(1982)
1984
KIDCO(1984)
Margaret Blye
HOMBRE(1967); WATERHOLE NO. 3(1967); ASH WEDNESDAY(1973); FINAL CHAPTER-WALKING TALL zero(1977); ENTITY, THE(1982)
Margaret Jane Blye
SUMMER AND SMOKE(1961)
Richard Blye
Misc. Talkies
THREE WAY WEEKEND(1979)
Charles J. Blynn
HOUSE OF STRANGERS(1949)

Yakov Blyokh
Misc. Silents
SHANGHAI DOCUMENT, A(1929, USSR), d
J.G. Blystone
Silents
OH, YOU TONY!(1924), d; LUCKY HORSESHOE, THE(1925), d; WINGS OF THE STORM(1926), d; ANKLES PREFERRED(1927), d, w; PAJAMAS(1927), d; SLAVES OF BEAUTY(1927), d; SHARP SHOOTERS(1928), d
Misc. Silents
SOFT BOILED(1923), d; LAST MAN ON EARTH, THE(1924), d; BEST BAD MAN, THE(1925), d; EVERLASTING WHISPER, THE(1925), d; FAMILY UPSTAIRS, THE(1926), d; HARD BOILED(1926), d; MY OWN PAL(1926), d
Jasper Blystone
RELUCTANT DRAGON, THE(1941), cartoon d
John Blystone
MOTHER KNOWS BEST(1928), d; SKY HAWK(1929), d; THRU DIFFERENT EYES(1929), d; BIG PARTY, THE(1930), d; PRINCESS AND THE PLUMBER, THE(1930), d; TOL'ABLE DAVID(1930), d; MEN ON CALL(1931), d; YOUNG SINNERS(1931), d; AMATEUR DADDY(1932), d; CHARLIE CHAN'S CHANCE(1932), d; PAINTED WOMAN(1932), d; SHE WANTED A MILLIONAIRE(1932), d; HOT PEPPER(1933), d; MY LIPS BETRAY(1933), d; SHANGHAI MADNESS(1933), d; COMING OUT PARTY(1934), d; HELL IN THE HEAVENS(1934), d; BAD BOY(1935), d; COUNTY CHAIRMAN, THE(1935), d; GENTLE JULIA(1936), d; LITTLE MISS NOBODY(1936), d; MUSIC FOR MADAME(1937), d; WOMAN CHASES MAN(1937), d
Silents
FRIENDLY HUSBAND, A(1923), d, w; OUR HOSPITALITY(1923), d; CAPTAIN LASH(1929), d
Misc. Silents
TEETH(1924), d
John G. Blystone
SO THIS IS LONDON(1930), d; MR. LEMON OF ORANGE(1931), d; TOO BUSY TO WORK(1932), d; CHANGE OF HEART(1934), d; GREAT GUY(1936), d; MAGNIFICENT BRUTE, THE(1936), d; 23 ½ HOURS LEAVE(1937), d; BLOCKHEADS(1938), d; SWISS MISS(1938), d
Silents
LADIES TO BOARD(1924), d; DICK TURPIN(1925), d
Stan Blystone
HEADIN' EAST(1937); PHANTOM OF THE OPERA(1943)
Stanley Blystone
THRU DIFFERENT EYES(1929); FIGHTING LEGION, THE(1930); PARADE OF THE WEST(1930); YOUNG EAGLES(1930); DANCING DYNAMITE(1931); MAN FROM DEATH VALLEY, THE(1931); SUNDOWN TRAIL(1931); GALLOPING THRU(1932); GOLDEN WEST, THE(1932); HONOR OF THE MOUNTED(1932); TRIAL OF VIVIENNE WARE, THE(1932); WILD GIRL(1932); CROSSFIRE(1933); DANCING LADY(1933); FIGHTING PARSON, THE(1933); INFERNAL MACHINE(1933); LUCKY LARRIGAN(1933); PICTURE SNATCHER(1933); ROMAN SCANDALS(1933); SONS OF THE DESERT(1933); LEMON DROP KID, THE(1934); MANHATTAN MELODRAMA(1934); MURDER AT THE VANITIES(1934); WE LIVE AGAIN(1934); WE'RE NOT DRESSING(1934); CODE OF THE MOUNTED(1935); FARMER TAKES A WIFE, THE(1935); FIGHTING PIONEERS(1935); G-MEN(1935); GALLANT DEFENDER(1935); IVORY-HANDLED GUN(1935); JUSTICE OF THE RANGE(1935); LADIES CRAVE EXCITEMENT(1935); RAINBOW'S END(1935); SHOW THEM NO MERCY(1935); SMART GIRL(1935); THREE MUSKETEERS, THE(1935); EX-MRS. BRADFORD, THE(1936); HERE COMES TROUBLE(1936); HUMAN CARGO(1936); MODERN TIMES(1936); RIDING AVENGER, THE(1936); STRIKE ME PINK(1936); THREE MESQUITEERS, THE(1936); ARMORED CAR(1937); BOOTS AND SADDLES(1937); GALLOPING DYNAMITE(1937); LOVE IN A BUNGALOW(1937); MUSIC FOR MADAME(1937); SECOND HONEYMOON(1937); SHE'S DANGEROUS(1937); TOAST OF NEW YORK, THE(1937); TWO WISE MAIDS(1937); WINDJAMMER(1937); BRINGING UP BABY(1938); CALIFORNIA FRONTIER(1938); CIPHER BUREAU(1938); DANGEROUS TO KNOW(1938); KING OF ALCATRAZ(1938); RED RIVER RANGE(1938); STRANGER FROM ARIZONA, THE(1938); VIVACIOUS LADY(1938); CRASHING THRU(1939); DISBARRED(1939); DRIFTING WESTWARD(1939); THEY SHALL HAVE MUSIC(1939); THREE TEXAS STEERS(1939); TORTURE SHIP(1939); TRIGGER PALS(1939); CAPTAIN CAUTION(1940); CHARLIE CHAN AT THE WAX MUSEUM(1940); CHUMP AT OXFORD, A(1940); EMERGENCY SQUAD(1940); JOHNNY APOLLO(1940); LITTLE MEN(1940); MA, HE'S MAKING EYES AT ME(1940); PONY POST(1940); TULSA KID, THE(1940); SUNSET IN WYOMING(1941); TALL, DARK AND HANDSOME(1941); WEST OF CIMARRON(1941); I WAKE UP SCREAMING(1942); ICE-CAPADES REVUE(1942); IN OLD CALIFORNIA(1942); JESSE JAMES, JR.(1942); LADY BODYGUARD(1942); MY FAVORITE SPY(1942); ROXIE HART(1942); TRUE TO THE ARMY(1942); ROGER TOUHY, GANGSTER!(1944); HOODLUM SAINT, THE(1946); MAGNIFICENT DOLL(1946); NAVAJO KID, THE(1946); SIX GUN MAN(1946); HER HUSBAND'S AFFAIRS(1947); KILLER AT LARGE(1947); PERILS OF PAULINE, THE(1947); ROAD TO RIO(1947); SUDDENLY IT'S SPRING(1947); EYES OF TEXAS(1948); I, JANE DOE(1948); I WOULDN'T BE IN YOUR SHOES(1948); LOADED PISTOLS(1948); PALEFACE, THE(1948); SMART WOMAN(1948); STATION WEST(1948); DEPUTY MARSHAL(1949); EL DORADO PASS(1949); MASTER MINDS(1949); POWDER RIVER RUSTLERS(1949); RANGE LAND(1949); RIDE, RYDER, RIDE!(1949); RUSTLERS(1949); SAMSON AND DELILAH(1949); COUNTY FAIR(1950); MRS. O'MALLEY AND MR. MALONE(1950); SQUARE DANCE KATY(1950); HONEYCHILE(1951); MY FAVORITE SPY(1951); SANTA FE(1951); SILVER CANYON(1951); LAWLESS BREED, THE(1952); ROAD AGENT(1952); JACK MCCALL, DESPERADO(1953); PERILOUS JOURNEY, A(1953); LIVING IT UP(1954); LAWLESS STREET, A(1955); YOU'RE NEVER TOO YOUNG(1955); PARDNERS(1956)
Misc. Talkies
MAN OF ACTION(1933); SADDLE ACES(1935)
Silents
EXCITEMENT(1924); CIRCUS ACE, THE(1927); FOUR SONS(1928)
Misc. Silents
DARWIN WAS RIGHT(1924)
Stanley G. Blystone
STRANGE PEOPLE(1933)
Ann Blyth
BABES ON SWING STREET(1944); BOWERY TO BROADWAY(1944); CHIP OFF THE OLD BLOCK(1944); MERRY MONAHANS, THE(1944); MILDRED PIERCE(1945); SWELL GUY(1946); BRUTE FORCE(1947); KILLER MCCOY(1947); WOMAN'S VENGEANCE, A(1947); ANOTHER PART OF THE FOREST(1948); MR. PEABODY AND THE MERMAID(1948); FREE FOR ALL(1949); ONCE MORE, MY DARLING(1949);

RED CANYON(1949); TOP O' THE MORNING(1949); OUR VERY OWN(1950); GOLD-EN HORDE, THE(1951); GREAT CARUSO, THE(1951); I'LL NEVER FORGET YOU(1951); KATIE DID IT(1951); THUNDER ON THE HILL(1951); ONE MINUTE TO ZERO(1952); SALLY AND SAINT ANNE(1952); WORLD IN HIS ARMS, THE(1952); ALL THE BROTHERS WERE VALIANT(1953); ROSE MARIE(1954); STUDENT PRINCE, THE(1954); KING'S THIEF, THE(1955); KISMET(1955); SLANDER(1956); BUSTER KEATON STORY, THE(1957); HELEN MORGAN STORY, THE(1959)

Billy Blyth
GREAT GAME, THE(1930)

Eric Blyth
MASQUERADE(1965, Brit.)

Harry Blyth
MEET SEXTON BLAKE(1944, Brit.), w; ECHO MURDERS, THE(1945, Brit.), d&w

Henry Blyth
COMING-OUT PARTY, A(, w; FOLLOW A STAR(1959, Brit.), w; SEVEN KEYS(1962, Brit.), w; CROOKS ANONYMOUS(1963, Brit.), w; FAST LADY, THE(1963, Brit.), w; FATHER CAME TOO(1964, Brit.), w; EARLY BIRD, THE(1965, Brit.), w; STITCH IN TIME, A(1967, Brit.), w

Henry E. Blyth
UP IN THE WORLD(1957, Brit.), w; SQUARE PEG, THE(1958, Brit.), w

Janus Blyth
BLACK OAK CONSPIRACY(1977)

Lize Bechtold Blyth
STAR IS BORN, A(1954), ph

Sidney Blyth
BRIDE OF THE LAKE(1934, Brit.), ph; LOST CHORD, THE(1937, Brit.), ph

Astrid Blythe
Misc. Talkies
SWINGING COEDS, THE(1976)

Betty Blythe
LENA RIVERS(1932); TOM BROWN OF CULVER(1932); ONLY YESTERDAY(1933); PILGRIMAGE(1933); BADGE OF HONOR(1934); BEFORE MIDNIGHT(1934); EVER SINCE EVE(1934); GIRL OF THE LIMBERLOST(1934); MONEY MEANS NO-THING(1934); SCARLET LETTER, THE(1934); TWO HEADS ON A PILLOW(1934); I'VE BEEN AROUND(1935); NIGHT ALARM(1935); PERFECT CLUE, THE(1935); SPANISH CAPE MYSTERY(1935); WESTERN COURAGE(1935); CHEERS OF THE CROWD(1936); GORGEOUS HUSSY, THE(1936); MURDER AT GLEN ATHOL(1936); RAINBOW ON THE RIVER(1936); YOURS FOR THE ASKING(1936); CON-QUEST(1937); ESPIONAGE(1937); TOPPER(1937); DELINQUENT PARENTS(1938); GANGSTER'S BOY(1938); MAN-PROOF(1938); ROMANCE OF THE LIMBER-LOST(1938); WOMEN, THE(1939); EARL OF PUDDLESTONE(1940); FEDERAL FUGI-TIVES(1941); HONKY TONK(1941); MISBEHAVING HUSBANDS(1941); SIS HOPKINS(1941); TOP SERGEANT MULLIGAN(1941); TUXEDO JUNCTION(1941); DAWN ON THE GREAT DIVIDE(1942); FRECKLES COMES HOME(1942); HOUSE OF ERRORS(1942); MIRACLE KID(1942); YOKEL BOY(1942); GIRLS IN CHAINS(1943); MR. MUGGS STEPS OUT(1943); SARONG GIRL(1943); SPOTLIGHT SCANDALS(1943); WHERE ARE YOUR CHILDREN?(1943); CHINESE CAT, THE(1944); DOCKS OF NEW YORK(1945); HER HIGHNESS AND THE BELL-BOY(1945); THEY WERE EXPENDABLE(1945); HOODLUM SAINT, THE(1946); JOE PALOOKA, CHAMP(1946); KID FROM BOOKLYN, THE(1946); POSTMAN ALWAYS RINGS TWICE, THE(1946); UNDERCOVER WOMAN(1946); UNDERCUR-RENT(1946); SECRET LIFE OF WALTER MITTY, THE(1947); SONG OF LOVE(1947); JIGGS AND MAGGIE IN SOCIETY(1948); LETTER FROM AN UNKNOWN WO-MAN(1948); LUXURY LINER(1948); MADONNA OF THE DESERT(1948); HOLLY-WOOD STORY(1951); LONESOME TRAIL, THE(1955); MY FAIR LADY(1964)
Silents
ALL MAN(1918); KING OF DIAMONDS, THE(1918); DUST OF DESIRE(1919); NOMADS OF THE NORTH(1920); OCCASIONALLY YOURS(1920); CHARGE IT(1921); QUEEN OF SHEBA, THE(1921); DARLING OF THE RICH, THE(1923); IN HOLLY-WOOD WITH POTASH AND PERLMUTTER(1924); RECOIL, THE(1924); SPITFIRE, THE(1924); WOMAN'S SECRET, A(1924, Brit.); EAGER LIPS(1927); INTO NO MAN'S LAND(1928)
Misc. Silents
BUSINESS OF LIFE, THE(1918); GAME WITH FATE, A(1918); GREEN GOD, THE(1918); HOARDED ASSETS(1918); MISS AMBITION(1918); TANGLED LI-VES(1918); BEATING THE ODDS(1919); BEAUTY PROOF(1919); FIGHTING DESTI-NY(1919); MAN WHO WON, THE(1919); SILENT STRENGTH(1919); UNDERCURRENT, THE(1919); BURNT WINGS(1920); SILVER HORDE, THE(1920); THIRD GENERATION, THE(1920); JUST OUTSIDE THE DOOR(1921); MOTHER O' MINE(1921); TRUANT HUSBAND, THE(1921); FAIR LADY(1922); HIS WIFE'S HUS-BAND(1922); HOW WOMEN LOVE(1922); CHU CHIN CHOW(1923, Brit.); SINNER OR SAINT(1923); TRUTH ABOUT WIVES, THE(1923); BREATH OF A SCANDAL, THE(1924); SHE(1925, Brit.); SPEED(1925); GIRL FROM GAY PAREE, THE(1927); MILLION BID, A(1927); SNOWBOUND(1927); DOMESTIC TROUBLES(1928); SIS-TERS OF EVE(1928)

Bob Blythe
GIRO CITY(1982, Brit.)

Domini Blythe
VAMPIRE CIRCUS(1972, Brit.)

Dorothy Blythe
LOVE MATCH, THE(1955, Brit.)

Erik Blythe
INVASION U.S.A.(1952); KING RICHARD AND THE CRUSADERS(1954)

Henry E. Blythe
JUMPING FOR JOY(1956, Brit.), w

Janus Blythe
HILLS HAVE EYES, THE(1978); INCREDIBLE MELTING MAN, THE(1978)

John Blythe
THIS HAPPY BREED(1944, Brit.); DEAR MURDERER(1947, Brit.); HOLIDAY CAMP(1947, Brit.); EASY MONEY(1948, Brit.); GIRL IN THE PAINTING, THE(1948, Brit.); HERE COME THE HUGGETTS(1948, Brit.); VOTE FOR HUGGETT(1948, Brit.); BOY, A GIRL AND A BIKE, A(1949 Brit.); BOYS IN BROWN(1949, Brit.); DIAMOND CITY(1949, Brit.); HUGGETTS ABROAD, THE(1949, Brit.); IT'S A WONDERFUL DAY(1949, Brit.); GOOD TIME GIRL(1950, Brit.); LILLI MARLENE(1951, Brit.); WORM'S EYE VIEW(1951, Brit.); FRIGHTENED MAN, THE(1952, Brit.); IT'S A GRAND LIFE(1953, Brit.); WEDDING OF LILLI MARLENE, THE(1953, Brit.); WHITE FIRE(1953, Brit.); GAY DOG, THE(1954, Brit.); MEET MR. MALCOLM(1954, Brit.); DOUBLE CROSS(1956, Brit.); FOXHOLE IN CAIRO(1960, Brit.); GAOLBREAK(1962, Brit.); ON THE BEAT(1962, Brit.); V.I.P.s, THE(1963, Brit.); STITCH IN TIME, A(1967, Brit.)

Peggy Blythe
CONSTANT NYMPH, THE(1933, Brit.); LASH, THE(1934, Brit.); SCOOP, THE(1934, Brit.); LORNA DOONE(1935, Brit.)

Peter Blythe
FRANKENSTEIN CREATED WOMAN(1965, Brit.); KALEIDOSCOPE(1966, Brit.); CHALLENGE FOR ROBIN HOOD, A(1968, Brit.); JANE EYRE(1971, Brit.)

Robert Blythe
MOUSE AND THE WOMAN, THE(1981, Brit.); EXPERIENCE PREFERRED... BUT NOT ESSENTIAL(1983, Brit.)

Samuel Blythe
WASHINGTON MASQUERADE(1932), w

Sidney Blythe
MYSTERY AT THE VILLA ROSE(1930, Brit.), ph; SHERLOCK HOLMES' FATAL HOUR(1931, Brit.), ph; FOUR MASKED MEN(1934, Brit.), ph; PHANTOM FIEND, THE(1935, Brit.), ph; SHE SHALL HAVE MUSIC(1935, Brit.), ph; MORALS OF MARCUS, THE(1936, Brit.), ph; HIGH TREASON(1937, Brit.), ph

Sydney Blythe
BLOCKADE(1928, Brit.), ph; ALIBI(1931, Brit.), ph; CONDEMNED TO DEATH(1932, Brit.), ph; MISSING REMBRANDT, THE(1932, Brit.), ph; EXCESS BAGGAGE(1933, Brit.), ph; I LIVED WITH YOU(1933, Brit.), ph; THIS WEEK OF GRACE(1933, Brit.), ph; BELLA DONNA(1934, Brit.), ph; BLIND JUSTICE(1934, Brit.), ph; BROK-EN MELODY, THE(1934, Brit.), ph; LORD EDGEWARE DIES(1934, Brit.), ph; MAN WHO CHANGED HIS NAME, THE(1934, Brit.), ph; SAY IT WITH FLOWERS(1934, Brit.), ph; FIRE HAS BEEN ARRANGED, A(1935, Brit.), ph; LAD, THE(1935, Brit.), ph; PRIVATE SECRETARY, THE(1935, Brit.), ph; SCROOGE(1935, Brit.), ph; SQUIBS(1935, Brit.), ph; VINTAGE WINE(1935, Brit.), ph; WANDERING JEW, THE(1935, Brit.), ph; ELIZA COMES TO STAY(1936, Brit.), ph; IN THE SOUP(1936, Brit.), ph; SHADOW, THE(1936, Brit.), ph; BEAUTY AND THE BARGE(1937, Brit.), ph; JUGGERNAUT(1937, Brit.), ph; UNDERNEATH THE ARCHES(1937, Brit.), ph; CAPTAIN MOONLIGHT(1940, Brit.), ph; MURDER AT THE BASKERVILLES(1941, Brit.), ph

Thomas C. Blythe
SCARLET EMPRESS, THE(1934)

Enid Blyton
NOBODY IN TOYLAND(1958, Brit.), w

Angela Bo
Misc. Talkies
DEATH SMILES ON A MURDER(1974)

Armando Bo
PUT UP OR SHUT UP(1968, Arg.), a, p,d&w; HEAT(1970, Arg.), a, p,d&w

Facundo Bo
1984
LOVE ON THE GROUND(1984,Fr.)

Katinka Bo
WHEEL OF ASHES(1970, Fr.)

Victor Bo
DEATHSTALKER(1983, Arg./U.S.)
1984
DEATHSTALKER, THE(1984)

Bo-Ching
INTERNATIONAL HOUSE(1933)

Bo-Ling
INTERNATIONAL HOUSE(1933)

Sun Bo-yang
Misc. Silents
BLUE EXPRESS(1929, USSR)

Bruce Boa
MAN IN THE MOON(1961, Brit.); STOPOVER FOREVER(1964, Brit.); ADDING MACHINE, THE(1969); REVOLUTIONARY, THE(1970, Brit.); WHO?(1975, Brit./Ger.); SILVER BEARS(1978); EMPIRE STRIKES BACK, THE(1980); RAGTIME(1981); OCTO-PUSSY(1983, Brit.)
1984
RAZOR'S EDGE, THE(1984); SCREAM FOR HELP(1984)

Wally Boag
THRILL OF A ROMANCE(1945); ABSENT-MINDED PROFESSOR, THE(1961); SON OF FLUBBER(1963); LOVE BUG, THE(1968)

Jeffery Boam
STRAIGHT TIME(1978), w

Jeffrey Boam
DEAD ZONE, THE(1983), w

Boarang
WAJAN(1938, South Bali)

Bob Board
GILDA(1946)

John Board
MERRY WIVES OF TOBIAS ROUKE, THE(1972, Can.), p, d

Paul Board
HAPPY BIRTHDAY TO ME(1981)

Robert Board
MAGNIFICENT YANKEE, THE(1950); SKIRTS AHOY!(1952)

Eleanor Boardman
SHE GOES TO WAR(1929); MAMBA(1930); REDEMPTION(1930); FLOOD, THE(1931); GREAT, MEADOW, THE(1931); SQUAW MAN, THE(1931); WOMEN LOVE ONCE(1931)
Silents
STRANGER'S BANQUET(1922); GIMMIE(1923); SOULS FOR SALE(1923); THREE WISE FOOLS(1923); PROUD FLESH(1925); AUCTION BLOCK, THE(1926); MEMORY LANE(1926); TELL IT TO THE MARINES(1926); CROWD, THE(1928)
Misc. Silents
DAY OF FAITH, THE(1923); SILENT ACCUSER, THE(1924); SINNERS IN SILK(1924); SO THIS IS MARRIAGE(1924); TRUE AS STEEL(1924); WIFE OF THE CENTAUR(1924); WINE OF YOUTH(1924); CIRCLE, THE(1925); EXCHANGE OF WIVES(1925); ONLY THING, THE(1925); WAY OF A GIRL, THE(1925); BARDELYS THE MAGNIFICENT(1926)

Eleanor True Boardman
BIG CHANCE, THE(1933)

Nan Boardman
JULIA MISBEHAVES(1948); VICIOUS CIRCLE, THE(1948); COME TO THE STA-BLE(1949); MRS. MIKE(1949); CLOSE TO MY HEART(1951); I CONFESS(1953); FEMALE ON THE BEACH(1955); TO HELL AND BACK(1955)

True Boardman
SON OF THE NAVY(1940), w; KEEP 'EM FLYING(1941), w; ARABIAN NIGHTS(1942), w; BETWEEN US GIRLS(1942), w; PARDON MY SARONG(1942), w; RIDE 'EM COWBOY(1942), w; HIT THE ICE(1943), w; PAINTED HILLS, THE(1951), w
Silents
ROMANCE OF TARZAN, THE(1918); TARZAN OF THE APES(1918)
Misc. Silents
DANGER WITHIN(1918); DOCTOR AND THE WOMAN, THE(1918); MOLLY, GO GET 'EM(1918)

Virginia Boardman
Silents
TOWN SCANDAL, THE(1923)

Virginia True Boardman
LADY LIES, THE(1929); SCAREHEADS(1931); ONE YEAR LATER(1933); PENAL CODE, THE(1933); ROAD TO RUIN(1934); CRIME PATROL, THE(1936); FUGITIVE SHERIFF, THE(1936)
Misc. Talkies
BRAND OF THE OUTLAWS(1936)
Silents
BLIND BARGAIN, A(1922); PENROD(1922); THIRD ALARM, THE(1922); MAIL-MAN, THE(1923); DOWN THE STRETCH(1927)
Misc. Silents
VILLAGE BLACKSMITH, THE(1922); WHERE IS MY WANDERING BOY TO-NIGHT?(1922); MICHAEL O'HALLORAN(1923); SPEEDY SMITH(1927)

Al Boasberg
SO THIS IS COLLEGE(1929), w; DOUGH BOYS(1930), w; FLORODORA GIRL, THE(1930), w; FREE AND EASY(1930), w; IT'S A GREAT LIFE(1930), w; WAY FOR A SAILOR(1930), w; EVERYTHING'S ROSIE(1931), w; FIFTY MILLION FRENCH-MEN(1931), w; FREAKS(1932), w; BACHELOR MOTHER(1933), w; MURDER IN THE PRIVATE CAR(1934), w; MYRT AND MARGE(1934), d&w; NIGHT AT THE OPERA, A(1935), w; NITWITS, THE(1935), w; SILLY BILLIES(1936), w; MAKE A WISH(1937), w
Silents
CALIFORNIA OR BUST(1927), t; CLANCY'S KOSHER WEDDING(1927), w; GEN-ERAL, THE(1927), w; SMILE, BROTHER, SMILE(1927), w

Albert Boasberg
Silents
BATTLING BUTLER(1926), w

Ralph Spence Boasberg
CRACKED NUTS(1931), w

Gladys Boat
HANDCUFFS, LONDON(1955, Brit.)

Bob Boatman
RESURRECTION OF ZACHARY WHEELER, THE(1971), ph

Colostine Boatwright
SPOOK WHO SAT BY THE DOOR, THE(1973)

Helen Boatwright
HANSEL AND GRETEL(1954)

Charles Boaz
SEARCH FOR BRIDEY MURPHY, THE(1956); MY GUN IS QUICK(1957); SAGA OF HEMP BROWN, THE(1958)

The Bob Chester Orchestra
TROCADERO(1944)

Bob Crosby and His Orchestra
PRESENTING LILY MARS(1943); REVEILLE WITH BEVERLY(1943); THOU-SANDS CHEER(1943); PARDON MY RHYTHM(1944)

The Bob Crosby Orchestra with the Bobcats
SIS HOPKINS(1941)

Bob Crosby's Orchestra with The Bobcats
LET'S MAKE MUSIC(1940)

Bob Mitchell and the St. Brendan's Choristers
COLLEGE SWING(1938)

Bob Mitchell Boy Choir
GREAT BANK ROBBERY, THE(1969)

The Bob Mitchell Boy Choir
GOOD LUCK, MR. YATES(1943)

Bob Nolan and Sons of the Pioneers
UTAH(1945)

Bob Nolan and The Sons of the Pioneers
OUTLAWS OF THE PRAIRIE(1938); HEART OF THE GOLDEN WEST(1942); RIDIN' DOWN THE CANYON(1942); ROMANCE ON THE RANGE(1942); SUNSET SERE-NADE(1942); HANDS ACROSS THE BORDER(1943); IDAHO(1943); MAN FROM MUSIC MOUNTAIN(1943); SILVER SPURS(1943); SONG OF TEXAS(1943); COWBOY AND THE SENORITA(1944); LIGHTS OF OLD SANTA FE(1944); SAN FERNANDO VALLEY(1944); SONG OF NEVADA(1944); YELLOW ROSE OF TEXAS, THE(1944); ALONG THE NAVAJO TRAIL(1945); DON'T FENCE ME IN(1945); MAN FROM OKLAHOMA, THE(1945); SUNSET IN EL DORADO(1945); DING DONG WIL-LIAMS(1946); HOME IN OKLAHOMA(1946); HOME ON THE RANGE(1946); MY PAL TRIGGER(1946); RAINBOW OVER TEXAS(1946); ROLL ON TEXAS MOON(1946); SONG OF ARIZONA(1946); UNDER NEVADA SKIES(1946); APACHE ROSE(1947); ON THE OLD SPANISH TRAIL(1947); SPRINGTIME IN THE SIERRAS(1947); EYES OF TEXAS(1948); GAY RANCHERO, THE(1948); NIGHT TIME IN NEVADA(1948); UNDER CALIFORNIA STARS(1948)

The Bob Pusilo Studio
1984
DELIVERY BOYS(1984), cos

Bob Scobey and His Band
LIVING VENUS(1961)

Bob Scott and Louis Jordan's Tymphany 6
LOOK OUT SISTER(1948)

Bob Wallis and His Storyville Jazzmen
RING-A-DING RHYTHM(1962, Brit. 73m Amicus/COL bw (G.B: IT'S TRAD, DAD!); TWO LEFT FEET(1965, Brit.)

Bob Wills and His Texas Playboys
GO WEST, YOUNG LADY(1941); LONE PRAIRIE, THE(1942); LAWLESS EM-PIRE(1946)
Misc. Talkies
WYOMING HURRICANE(1944)

Bob Wills and the Texas Playboys
MELODY RANCH(1940); RIDERS OF THE NORTHWEST MOUNTED(1943); LAST PICTURE SHOW, THE(1971), m
Misc. Talkies
TORNADO IN THE SADDLE, A(1942); SADDLES AND SAGEBRUSH(1943)

Bob Woodward and The Rodeoliers
HOME ON THE PRAIRIE(1939)

Sudana Bobatoon
VICE SQUAD(1982)

Nina Bobbie
SERENITY(1962)

Betty Bobbitt
CLINIC, THE(1983, Aus.)

Elizabeth Bobbs
Misc. Silents
HER WAYWARD SISTER(1916)

Bobby Breen Quintet
CURSE OF THE VOODOO(1965, Brit.)

Bobby Brooks and His Quartet
HONEYMOON LODGE(1943)

Bobby Brooks and Quartet
SOUTH OF DIXIE(1944)

Bobby Brooks Quartet
TOP MAN(1943); THIS IS THE LIFE(1944)

Bobby Byrne and Band
FOLLIES GIRL(1943)

The Bobby Fuller Four
GHOST IN THE INVISIBLE BIKINI(1966)

Bobby Hargreaves and His Kit Kat Club Orchestra
TEMPTATION(1936)

Bobby Ramos Band
HIT PARADE OF 1951(1950)

Members of the Bobby Ramos Band
SUSPENSE(1946)

Bobby Sherwood and his Orchestra
CAMPUS SLEUTH(1948)

Bobby Z
1984
PURPLE RAIN(1984)

Pura Bobe
1984
HOME FREE ALL(1984)

Mike Bobenko
LASERBLAST(1978)

Browyn Bober
1984
LOVE STREAMS(1984)

Elen Bober
JULES AND JIM(1962, Fr.)

Jacques Bobet
CAT IN THE SACK, THE(1967, Can.), p

Charles Bobett
MAD EMPRESS, THE(1940)

Lea Bobey
UNSTRAP ME(1968)

Petit Bobo
SUITOR, THE(1963, Fr.)

Bobo the Clown
INVISIBLE DR. MABUSE, THE(1965, Ger.)

Sam Bobrick
NORMAN...IS THAT YOU?(1976), w; LAST REMAKE OF BEAU GESTE, THE(1977), w; JIMMY THE KID(1982), w

Alexis Bobrinskoy
I AM A CAMERA(1955, Brit.); WEEKEND WITH LULU, A(1961, Brit.)

Alexis Bobrinsky
MAN WHO KNEW TOO MUCH, THE(1956)

Neal Bobrofsky
BRONCO BILLY(1980), p

I. Bobrov
Silents
BATTLESHIP POTEMKIN, THE(1925, USSR)

Anatoli Bobrovsky
MUMU(1961, USSR), d

Fred Boby
CRIME WAVE(1954)

G. Bobynin
Misc. Silents
WOMEN OF RYAZAN(1927, USSR)

Poupee Bocar
LAST MOVIE, THE(1971); POCKET MONEY(1972)

Al Bocca
MILLION DOLLAR MANHUNT(1962, Brit.), d&w

Christine Bocca
FLAW, THE(1955, Brit.); JIG SAW(1965, Brit.)

Antonio Boccacci
REVOLT OF THE MERCENARIES(1964, Ital./Span.), w; TOMB OF TORTURE(1966, Ital.)

Giovanni Boccaccio
BAMBOLE!(1965, Ital.), w
Silents
DECAMERON NIGHTS(1924, Brit.), w

Vera Boccadoro
LOVE IN THE AFTERNOON(1957)

Delia Boccardo
INSPECTOR CLOUSEAU(1968, Brit.); WILD EYE, THE(1968, Ital.); ADVENTURERS, THE(1970); CANNIBALS, THE(1970, Ital.); DETECTIVE BELLI(1970, Ital.); SNOW JOB(1972); WOMAN AT HER WINDOW, A(1978, Fr./Ital./Ger.); HERCULES(1983)
1984
NOSTALGHIA(1984, USSR/Ital.)

Della Boccardo
MASSACRE IN ROME(1973, Ital.)
Dick Boccelli
TRICK BABY(1973); EXTERMINATOR, THE(1980); SO FINE(1981)
Arrigo Bocchi
Silents
ORA PRO NOBIS(1917, Brit.), p; MAN AND THE MOMENT, THE(1918, Brit.), d;
NOT GUILTY(1919, Brit.), d; POLAR STAR, THE(1919, Brit.), d
Misc. Silents
SLAVE, THE(1918, Brit.), d; TOP DOG, THE(1918, Brit.), d; WAGES OF SIN,
THE(1918, Brit.), d; FETTERED(1919, Brit.), d; SPLENDID FOLLY(1919, Brit.), d;
WHEN IT WAS DARK(1919, Brit.), d; WHOSOEVER SHALL OFFEND(1919, Brit.), d
Luigi Bocchi
ROMAN HOLIDAY(1953)
Alfeo Bocchicchio
SNOWFIRE(1958), art d; LITTLE CIGARS(1973), art d; SCREAM BLACULA
SCREAM(1973), art d; SLAUGHTER'S BIG RIP-OFF(1973), art d
Alfreo Bocchicchio
RING OF TERROR(1962), p
Gildo Bocci
ROMAN HOLIDAY(1953)
Piero Boccia
AWAKENING, THE(1958, Ital.)
Alberto Boccianti
APPOINTMENT FOR MURDER(1954, Ital.), art d; SWORDSMAN OF SIENA,
THE(1962, Fr./Ital.), art d; ATLAS AGAINST THE CYCLOPS(1963, Ital.), art d;
GRAND SLAM(1968, Ital., Span., Ger.), art d; ARABELLA(1969, U.S./Ital.), art d
Vitezslav Bocek
SKELETON ON HORSEBACK(1940, Czech.)
Edward Boch
CRIME DOCTOR'S GAMBLE(1947), w
Larry Boch
GALAXY OF TERROR(1981), ed
Pierre Bochart
SECRET OF MAGIC ISLAND, THE(1964, Fr./Ital.), p
Joanna Bochco
INNERVIEW, THE(1974)
Steve Bochco
SILENT RUNNING(1972), w
Steven Bochco
COUNTERFEIT KILLER, THE(1968), w
Arthur Somers Boche
SOCIETY LAWYER(1939), w
Irka Bochenko
MOONRAKER(1979, Brit.)
Los Bocheros
FIESTA(1947)
Hart Bochner
ISLANDS IN THE STREAM(1977); BREAKING AWAY(1979); TERROR TRAIN(1980,
Can.); RICH AND FAMOUS(1981)
1984
SUPERGIRL(1984); WILD LIFE, THE(1984)
Lloyd Bochner
DRUMS OF AFRICA(1963); NIGHT WALKER, THE(1964); HARLOW(1965); SYL-
VIA(1965); POINT BLANK(1967); TONY ROME(1967); DETECTIVE, THE(1968);
HORSE IN THE GRAY FLANNEL SUIT, THE(1968); YOUNG RUNAWAYS,
THE(1968); DUNWICH HORROR, THE(1970); TIGER BY THE TAIL(1970); ULZANA'S
RAID(1972); IT SEEMED LIKE A GOOD IDEA AT THE TIME(1975, Can.); MAN IN
THE GLASS BOOTH, THE(1975); LONELY LADY, THE(1983)
1984
LOUISIANE(1984, Fr./Can.)
Stanley Bochner
STOOLIE, THE(1972), ed
Keto Bochorishvili
FATHER OF A SOLDIER(1966, USSR)
Curt Bock
SKI FEVER(1969, U.S./Aust./Czech.)
Edward Bock
MAN WHO DARED, THE(1946), w; KEY WITNESS(1947), w; 13TH HOUR,
THE(1947), w; RETURN OF THE WHISTLER, THE(1948), w; TRAPPED BY BOSTON
BLACKIE(1948), w
Frederick Bock
Silents
PORT OF MISSING MEN(1914)
Larry Bock
AVALANCHE(1978), ed; DEATHSPORT(1978), ed; LADY IN RED, THE(1979), ed;
ROCK 'N' ROLL HIGH SCHOOL(1979), ed; GALAXINA(1980), ed; SMOKEY BITES
THE DUST(1981), ed; HEARTBREAKER(1983), ed; JOYSTICKS(1983), ed; SORCER-
ESS(1983), ed
1984
BREAKIN'(1984), ed
Mitchell Bock
HISTORY OF THE WORLD, PART 1(1981)
Richard C. Bock
MAUSOLEUM(1983), ed
Robert Bock
OCEAN'S ELEVEN(1960)
Steven Bock
PROWLER, THE(1981)
Basil Bockasta
REUNION IN FRANCE(1942)
Bill Bocket
UNDER THE ROOFS OF PARIS(1930, Fr.)
Michael Bockman
NURSE SHERRI(1978), w; HAUNTING OF M, THE(1979), ed
Walter Bockmayer
IN A YEAR OF THIRTEEN MOONS(1980, Ger.)

V Bockris
COCAINE COWBOYS(1979), w
Peter Bocour
HI, MOM!(1970), art d; JEREMY(1973), art d
Ruth Bocour
HI, MOM!(1970)
Roland Bocquet
LA BALANCE(1983, Fr.), m
Benjamin Boda
JUDEX(1966, Fr./Ital.)
Jose Bodalo
DJANGO(1966 Ital./Span.); SOUND OF HORROR(1966, Span.); NARCO MEN,
THE(1969, Span./Ital.); CAPTAIN APACHE(1971, Brit.); TO BEGIN AGAIN(1982,
Span.)
Robert Bodansky
ROGUE SONG, THE(1930), w
Lucien Bodard
LES CREATURES(1969, Fr./Swed.)
Mag Bodard
UMBRELLAS OF CHERBOURG, THE(1964, Fr./Ger.), p; LE BONHEUR(1966, Fr.),
p; BENJAMIN(1968, Fr.), p; LE VIOL(1968, Fr./Swed.), p; ONE NIGHT... A
TRAIN(1968, Fr./Bel.), p; LES CREATURES(1969, Fr./Swed.), p; AU HASARD, BAL-
THAZAR(1970, Fr.), p; ME(1970, Fr.), p; GENTLE CREATURE, A(1971, Fr.), p; JE
T'AIME, JE T'AIME(1972, Fr./Swed.), p; DONKEY SKIN(1975, Fr.), p
Ada Bodart
Silents
DAWN(1928, Brit.)
Martin Boddey
SONG FOR TOMORROW, A(1948, Brit.); CAIRO ROAD(1950, Brit.); SEVEN DAYS TO
NOON(1950, Brit.); THIRD MAN, THE(1950, Brit.); ADVENTURERS, THE(1951, Brit.);
GREAT MANHUNT, THE(1951, Brit.); LAUGHTER IN PARADISE(1951, Brit.);
CLOUDBURST(1952, Brit.); FRANCHISE AFFAIR, THE(1952, Brit.); ISLAND RES-
CUE(1952, Brit.); MAGIC BOX, THE(1952, Brit.); VALLEY OF EAGLES(1952, Brit.);
ASSASSIN, THE(1953, Brit.); FOLLY TO BE WISE(1953); MR. POTTS GOES TO
MOSCOW(1953, Brit.); NORMAN CONQUEST(1953, Brit.); SAILOR OF THE
KING(1953, Brit.); BLACK GLOVE(1954, Brit.); DOCTOR IN THE HOUSE(1954, Brit.);
FORBIDDEN CARGO(1954, Brit.); MAD ABOUT MEN(1954, Brit.); PERSONAL AF-
FAIR(1954, Brit.); UP TO HIS NECK(1954, Brit.); YELLOW ROBE, THE(1954, Brit.);
SECRET VENTURE(1955, Brit.); SVENGALI(1955, Brit.); YOU CAN'T ESCAPE(1955,
Brit.); ESCAPE IN THE SUN(1956, Brit.); EYEWITNESS(1956, Brit.); IRON PET-
TICOAT, THE(1956, Brit.); LAST MAN TO HANG, THE(1956, Brit.); HOW TO
MURDER A RICH UNCLE(1957, Brit.); NOT WANTED ON VOYAGE(1957, Brit.);
SILKEN AFFAIR, THE(1957, Brit.); THERE'S ALWAYS A THURSDAY(1957, Brit.);
VIOLENT STRANGER(1957, Brit.); CHAIN OF EVENTS(1958, Brit.); DANGEROUS
YOUTH(1958, Brit.); I ONLY ASKED!(1958, Brit.); SQUARE PEG, THE(1958, Brit.);
TANK FORCE(1958, Brit.); CARRY ON SERGEANT(1959, Brit.); IDOL ON PARA-
DE(1959, Brit.); I'M ALL RIGHT, JACK(1959, Brit.); TWO-HEADED SPY, THE(1959,
Brit.); FOUR DESPERATE MEN(1960, Brit.); KILLERS OF KILIMANJARO(1960,
Brit.); OSCAR WILDE(1960, Brit.); CIRCLE OF DECEPTON(1961, Brit.); KITCHEN,
THE(1961, Brit.); NAKED EDGE, THE(1961); TOO HOT TO HANDLE(1961, Brit.);
MALAGA(1962, Brit.); WRONG ARM OF THE LAW, THE(1963, Brit.); MODEL
MURDER CASE, THE(1964, Brit.); MAN FOR ALL SEASONS, A(1966, Brit.); VIOLENT
MOMENT(1966, Brit.); DARK PLACES(1974, Brit.)
Michael Boddicker
JEKYLL AND HYDE...TOGETHER AGAIN(1982), spec eff; GET CRAZY(1983), m
1984
ADVENTURES OF BUCKAROO BANZAI: ACROSS THE 8TH DIMENSION,
THE(1984), m
Aaron Boddie
WIZ, THE(1978)
E.F. Boddington
Silents
AUDREY(1916), w
Allan F. Boddoh
GO TELL THE SPARTANS(1978), p
Manchester Boddy
MALAYA(1950), w
Martin Boddy
ROB ROY, THE HIGHLAND ROGUE(1954, Brit.); CAT GIRL(1957)
Michael Boddy
AGE OF CONSENT(1969, Austral.); NED KELLY(1970, Brit.)
Philip L. Boddy
CITY THAT NEVER SLEEPS(1953)
Terence Boddy
Silents
HOLY ORDERS(1917, Brit.)
Heinrich Bode
TO LIVE IN PEACE(1947, Ital.)
Homi Bode
FLAME OVER INDIA(1960, Brit.); TROUBLE IN THE SKY(1961, Brit.)
Homi D. Bode
TWENTY QUESTIONS MURDER MYSTERY, THE(1950, Brit.)
Ralf Bode
FOREPLAY(1975), ph; SATURDAY NIGHT AT THE BATHS(1975), ph; THERE IS
NO 13(1977), ph; SLOW DANCING IN THE BIG CITY(1978), ph; DRESSED TO
KILL(1980), ph; RAGGEDY MAN(1981), ph
Ralf D. Bode
SATURDAY NIGHT FEVER(1977), ph; SOMEBODY KILLED HER HUS-
BAND(1978), ph; COAL MINER'S DAUGHTER(1980), ph; LITTLE SEX, A(1982), ph;
GORKY PARK(1983), ph
1984
FIRSTBORN(1984), ph
Ralph D. Bode
RICH KIDS(1979), ph
De Witt Bodeen
ENCHANTED COTTAGE, THE(1945), w
Dewitt Bodeen
CAT PEOPLE(1942), w; SEVENTH VICTIM, THE(1943), w; CURSE OF THE CAT
PEOPLE, THE(1944), w; YELLOW CANARY, THE(1944, Brit.), w; NIGHT
SONG(1947), w; I REMEMBER MAMA(1948), w; MIRACLE OF THE BELLS,

Roberto Bodegas-

THE(1948), w; MRS. MIKE(1949), w; GIRL IN THE KREMLIN, THE(1957), w; TWELVE TO THE MOON(1960), w; CAT PEOPLE(1982), w

Roberto Bodegas
VOYAGE OF SILENCE(1968, Fr.), w

Herman Bodel
SET-UP, THE(1949)

Anders Bodelson
SILENT PARTNER, THE(1979, Can.), w

Herman Boden
SIREN OF ATLANTIS(1948); MONEY TRAP, THE(1966); SWEET CHARITY(1969)

Meb Boden
TERROR EYES(1981)

Karl Bodenschatz
NOT RECONCILED, OR "ONLY VIOLENCE HELPS WHERE IT RULES"(1969, Ger.)

Luciano Bodi
ROMEO AND JULIET(1954, Brit.)

Esther Bodie
COOL WORLD, THE(1963)

Burman Bodil
IT GROWS ON TREES(1952)

John Bodimeade
KHARTOUM(1966, Brit.), set d

Ivor Bodin
SANTA CLAUS CONQUERS THE MARTIANS(1964)

Mark Bodin
GRIM REAPER, THE(1981, Ital.); LA CAGE AUX FOLLES II(1981, Ital./Fr.)

Martin Bodin
WALPURGIS NIGHT(1941, Swed.), ph; TORMENT(1947, Swed.), ph; RAILROAD WORKERS(1948, Swed.), ph; LESSON IN LOVE, A(1960, Swed.), ph; JUST ONCE MORE(1963, Swed.), ph

Luba Bodine
HUNCHBACK OF ROME, THE(1963, Ital.)

Norbert Bodine
GOOD FAIRY, THE(1935), ph

Carsten Bodinus
NOSFERATU, THE VAMPIRE(1979, Fr./Ger.)

Geoffrey Bodkin
MAILBAG ROBBERY(1957, Brit.)

Jeremy Bodkin
DECISION AGAINST TIME(1957, Brit.); MAILBAG ROBBERY(1957, Brit.)

Perry Bodkin
PETE KELLY'S BLUES(1955)

Dick Bodkins
Silents
WALLOPING WALLACE(1924)

Theodor Bodnar
ONE MAN JURY(1978), p

John Bodne
WHISTLE DOWN THE WIND(1961, Brit.)

Jacob Bodo
IMPOSSIBLE ON SATURDAY(1966, Fr./Israel)

Ya'acoy Bodo
MY MARGO(1969, Israel)

Allan F. Bodoh
DOGS(1976), p; ACAPULCO GOLD(1978), p; GOOD GUYS WEAR BLACK(1978), p; GREAT SMOKEY ROADBLOCK, THE(1978), p

James Bodrero
WHITE HEAT(1934), w; FANTASIA(1940), art d, anim; DUMBO(1941), art d; THREE CABALLEROS, THE(1944), w; MAKE MINE MUSIC(1946), w

John Bodrero
MYSTERY LAKE(1953), w

Rosalie Bodrero
MYSTERY LAKE(1953), w

Jack Body
1984
VIGIL(1984, New Zealand), m

Peter Body
XTRO(1983, Brit.), art d

Ariane Boeglin
QUESTION, THE(1977, Fr.), ed

Frank Boeheim
WONDER BOY(1951, Brit./Aust.)

George Boehler
FAST COMPANY(1929)

Mabel Boehlke
KID FROM BOOKLYN, THE(1946)

Carla Boehm
HITLER'S CHILDREN(1942); KISMET(1944); STORY OF DR. WASSELL, THE(1944)

David Boehm
EMPLOYEE'S ENTRANCE(1933), w; EX-LADY(1933), w; GOLD DIGGERS OF 1933(1933), w; GRAND SLAM(1933), w; LIFE OF JIMMY DOLAN, THE(1933), w; EASY TO LOVE(1934), w; PERSONALITY KID, THE(1934), w; SEARCH FOR BEAUTY(1934), w; RAVEN, THE(1935), w; FLORIDA SPECIAL(1936), w; DOCTOR'S DIARY, A(1937), w; MIDNIGHT MADONNA(1937), w; PECK'S BAD BOY WITH THE CIRCUS(1938), w; POWDER TOWN(1942), w; GUY NAMED JOE, A(1943), w; KNICKERBOCKER HOLIDAY(1944), w

Endre Boehm
HOUSE OF A THOUSAND CANDLES, THE(1936), w; MONSTER FROM THE GREEN HELL(1958), w

Friedhelm Boehm
TOWN WITHOUT PITY(1961, Ger./Switz./U.S.), set d

Karl Boehm
PEEPING TOM(1960, Brit.); TOO HOT TO HANDLE(1961, Brit.); FOREVER MY LOVE(1962); FOUR HORSEMEN OF THE APOCALYPSE, THE(1962); WONDERFUL WORLD OF THE BROTHERS GRIMM, THE(1962); COME FLY WITH ME(1963); GOLDEN PLAGUE, THE(1963, Ger.); RIFIFI IN TOKYO(1963, Fr./Ital.); VENETIAN AFFAIR, THE(1967)

Karl Heinz Boehm
EFFI BRIEST(1974, Ger.)

Karlheinz Boehm
ALRAUNE(1952, Ger.); HOUSE OF THE THREE GIRLS, THE(1961, Aust.)

Michele Boehm
1984
PERILS OF GWENDOLINE, THE(1984, Fr.), ed

Sidney Boehm
SIX BRIDGES TO CROSS(1955), w; BOTTOM OF THE BOTTLE, THE(1956), w; HARRY BLACK AND THE TIGER(1958, Brit.), w; ONE FOOT IN HELL(1960), p, w; ROUGH NIGHT IN JERICHO(1967), w

Sydney Boehm
HIGH WALL, THE(1947), w; UNDERCOVER MAN, THE(1949), w; MYSTERY STREET(1950), w; SIDE STREET(1950), w; UNION STATION(1950), w; BRANDED(1951), w; WHEN WORLDS COLLIDE(1951), w; ATOMIC CITY, THE(1952), w; BIG HEAT, THE(1953), w; SAVAGE, THE(1953), w; SECOND CHANCE(1953), w; RAID, THE(1954), w; ROGUE COP(1954), w; SECRET OF THE INCAS(1954), w; SIEGE AT RED RIVER, THE(1954), w; BLACK TUESDAY(1955); TALL MEN, THE(1955), w; VIOLENT SATURDAY(1955), w; HELL ON FRISCO BAY(1956), w; REVOLT OF MAMIE STOVER, THE(1956), w; NICE LITTLE BANK THAT SHOULD BE ROBBED, A(1958), w; WOMAN OBSESSED(1959), p, w; SEVEN THIEVES(1960), p, w; SHOCK TREATMENT(1964), w; SYLVIA(1965), w

Werner Boehm
GLASS OF WATER, A(1962, Cgr.), cos

Herbert Boehme
MILL OF THE STONE WOMEN(1963, Fr./Ital.)

Michael Boehme
MALOU(1983)

William Boehnel
FORCED LANDING(1935), w

James F. Boeke
NORTH DALLAS FORTY(1979)

Jim Boeke
HEAVEN CAN WAIT(1978); PENNIES FROM HEAVEN(1981); PANDEMONIUM(1982)
1984
FEAR CITY(1984)

Todd Boekelheide
LULU(1978), ed

Bill Boelk
STRAWBERRY STATEMENT, THE(1970)

Heinrich Boell
GERMANY IN AUTUMN(1978, Ger.), w

Willard Boelner
Silents
LITTLE SAVAGE, THE(1929)

Jim Boelsen
HAZING, THE(1978); HONKYTONK MAN(1982)

George Boemier
HOLLYWOOD PARTY(1934), ed; ESCAPE(1940), ed

George Boemler
GIRL SAID NO, THE(1930), ed; PERFECT GENTLEMAN, THE(1935), ed; PURSUIT(1935), ed; MAD HOLIDAY(1936), ed; SUZY(1936), ed; VOICE OF BUGLE ANN(1936), ed; FAMILY AFFAIR, A(1937), ed; LONDON BY NIGHT(1937), ed; MAMA STEPS OUT(1937), ed; WOMEN MEN MARRY, THE(1937), ed; CHASER, THE(1938), ed; CHRISTMAS CAROL, A(1938), ed; WOMAN AGAINST WOMAN(1938), ed; BALALAIKA(1939), ed; FOUR GIRLS IN WHITE(1939), ed; ON BORROWED TIME(1939), ed; WITHIN THE LAW(1939), ed; I TAKE THIS WOMAN(1940), ed; WATERLOO BRIDGE(1940), ed; BLOSSOMS IN THE DUST(1941), ed; TRIAL OF MARY DUGAN, THE(1941), ed; TWO-FACED WOMAN(1941), ed; CROSSROADS(1942), ed; FINGERS AT THE WINDOW(1942), ed; STAND BY FOR ACTION(1942), ed; WE WERE DANCING(1942), ed; THOUSANDS CHEER(1943), ed; MRS. PARKINGTON(1944), ed; TWO GIRLS AND A SAILOR(1944), ed; HER HIGHNESS AND THE BELLBOY(1945), ed; THRILL OF A ROMANCE(1945), ed; BRIDE GOES WILD, THE(1948), ed, ed; TENTH AVENUE ANGEL(1948), ed; THREE MUSKETEERS, THE(1948), ed; ADAM'S RIB(1949), ed; BIG JACK(1949), ed; ASPHALT JUNGLE, THE(1950), ed; KIM(1950), ed; LIGHT TOUCH, THE(1951), ed; INVITATION(1952), ed; LOVE IS BETTER THAN EVER(1952), ed; PAT AND MIKE(1952), ed; PRISONER OF ZENDA, THE(1952), ed; ACTRESS, THE(1953), ed; BATTLE CIRCUS(1953), ed; ESCAPE FROM FORT BRAVO(1953), ed; HER TWELVE MEN(1954), ed; BHOWANI JUNCTION(1956), ed; POWER AND THE PRIZE, THE(1956), ed; SLANDER(1956), ed; THIS COULD BE THE NIGHT(1957), ed; DESIRE UNDER THE ELMS(1958), ed; RUN SILENT, RUN DEEP(1958), ed; PORK CHOP HILL(1959), ed; SUNRISE AT CAMPOBELLO(1960), ed; VOYAGE TO THE BOTTOM OF THE SEA(1961), ed; FIVE WEEKS IN A BALLOON(1962), ed

Earl Boen
MR. BILLION(1977); MAIN EVENT, THE(1979); BATTLE BEYOND THE STARS(1980); NINE TO FIVE(1980); MAN WITH TWO BRAINS, THE(1983); TO BE OR NOT TO BE(1983)
1984
TERMINATOR, THE(1984)

Lyman Boening
Silents
BROKEN DOLL, A(1921), ph

Paul Boensch III
THIS IS ELVIS(1982)

Steve Boergadine
SASQUATCH(1978)

Charles Boerner
RED, HOT AND BLUE(1949), makeup

Charlotte Boerner
ROSEMARY'S BABY(1968)

Frank Boers, Jr.
EQUINOX(1970)

Richard Boes
PERMANENT VACATION(1982)
1984
STRANGER THAN PARADISE(1984, U.S./Ger.)

Carl Boese
RENDEZ-VOUS(1932, Ger.), d
Silents
GOLEM: HOW HE CAME INTO THE WORLD, THE(1920, Ger.), d
Misc. Silents
SIR OR MADAM(1928, Brit.), d
Karl Boese
HIS MAJESTY, KING BALLYHOO(1931, Ger.), d
William H. Boesen
PUTNEY SWOPE(1969); GANG THAT COULDN'T SHOOT STRAIGHT, THE(1971)
Fritz Boetiger
BEGGAR STUDENT, THE(1958, Ger.), w
Bill Boeton
UTILITIES(1983, Can.), prod d
Herbert Boettcher
DREAM TOWN(1973, Ger.)
Martin Boettcher
FRONTIER HELLCAT(1966, Fr./Ital./Ger./Yugo.), m; FLAMING FRONTIER(1968, Ger./Yugo.), m; DUCK RINGS AT HALF PAST SEVEN, THE(1969, Ger./Ital.), m
Budd Boetticher
BLOOD AND SAND(1941), ch; BULLFIGHTER AND THE LADY(1951), d, w; CIMARRON KID, THE(1951), d; BRONCO BUSTER(1952), d; HORIZONS WEST(1952), d; RED BALL EXPRESS(1952), d; BLADES OF THE MUSKETEERS(1953), d; CITY BENEATH THE SEA(1953), d; EAST OF SUMATRA(1953), d; MAN FROM THE ALAMO, THE(1953), d; SEMINOLE(1953), d; WINGS OF THE HAWK(1953), d; MAGNIFICENT MATADOR, THE(1955), d, w; KILLER IS LOOSE, THE(1956), d; SEVEN MEN FROM NOW(1956), d; DECISION AT SUNDOWN(1957), d; TALL T, THE(1957), d; BUCHANAN RIDES ALONE(1958), d; RIDE LONESOME(1959), p&d; WESTBOUND(1959), d; COMANCHE STATION(1960), p, d; RISE AND FALL OF LEGS DIAMOND, THE(1960), d; TWO MULES FOR SISTER SARA(1970), w; TIME FOR DYING, A(1971), d&w
Oscar "Bud" Boetticher
ASSIGNED TO DANGER(1948), d; BLACK MIDNIGHT(1949), d; WOLF HUNTERS, THE(1949), d; KILLER SHARK(1950), d
Oscar Boetticher, Jr.
GUY, A GAL AND A PAL, A(1945), d
Oscar "Budd" Boetticher, Jr.
MISSING JUROR, THE(1944), d; ONE MYSTERIOUS NIGHT(1944), d; ESCAPE IN THE FOG(1945), d; YOUTH ON TRIAL(1945), d; BEHIND LOCKED DOORS(1948), d
Ed Bofas
LOVE AND THE MIDNIGHT AUTO SUPPLY(1978), m
Jean Bofferty
JE T'AIME, JE T'AIME(1972, Fr./Swed.), ph
Jean Boffety
YOUNG WORLD, A(1966, Fr./Ital.), ph; YO YO(1967, Fr.), ph; HO(1968, Fr.), ph; LAST ADVENTURE, THE(1968, Fr./Ital.), ph; ZITA(1968, Fr.), ph; WISE GUYS(1969, Fr./Ital.), ph; ACT OF THE HEART(1970, Can.), ph; THANOS AND DESPINA(1970, Fr./Gr.), ph; THINGS OF LIFE, THE(1970, Fr./Ital./Switz.), ph; CESAR AND ROSALIE(1972, Fr.), ph; THIEVES LIKE US(1974), ph; ELIZA'S HOROSCOPE(1975, Can.), ph; JOURNEY(1977, Can.), ph; LACEMAKER, THE(1977, Fr.), ph; BUTTERFLY ON THE SHOULDER, A(1978, Fr.), ph; ANGRY MAN, THE(1979 Fr./Can.), ph; QUINTET(1979), ph; BY DESIGN(1982), ph
1984
DOG DAY(1984, Fr.), ph; EDITH AND MARCEL(1984, Fr.), ph
John Boffety
BOLERO(1982, Fr.), ph
Aurelio Bogado
DR. COPPELIUS(1968, U.S./Span.)
Gustav Bogaert
Misc. Silents
VISAGES VIOLES...AMES CLOSES(1921, Fr.)
Lucien Bogaert
LEATHER AND NYLON(1969, Fr./Ital.)
Lucienne Bogaert
DEADLIER THAN THE MALE(1957, Fr.); MAIGRET LAYS A TRAP(1958, Fr.); CRIME DOES NOT PAY(1962, Fr.); LADIES OF THE PARK(1964, Fr.)
Emmett Bogan
ESPIONAGE AGENT(1939)
C. Boganny
BLESS 'EM ALL(1949, Brit.), w
Dick Bogarde
PASSWORD IS COURAGE, THE(1962, Brit.)
Dirk Bogarde
DANCING WITH CRIME(1947, Brit.); ESTHER WATERS(1948, Brit.); BOYS IN BROWN(1949, Brit.); DEAR MR. PROHACK(1949, Brit.); QUARTET(1949, Brit.); BLUE LAMP, THE(1950, Brit.); FIVE ANGLES ON MURDER(1950, Brit.); BLACKMAILED(1951, Brit.); MANIACS ON WHEELS(1951, Brit.); SO LONG AT THE FAIR(1951, Brit.); GENTLE GUNMAN, THE(1952, Brit.); STRANGER IN BETWEEN, THE(1952, Brit.); APPOINTMENT IN LONDON(1953, Brit.); DESPERATE MOMENT(1953, Brit.); PENNY PRINCESS(1953, Brit.); DOCTOR IN THE HOUSE(1954, Brit.); FOR BETTER FOR WORSE(1954, Brit.); SLEEPING TIGER, THE(1954, Brit.); THEY WHO DARE(1954, Brit.); DOCTOR AT SEA(1955, Brit.); SEA SHALL NOT HAVE THEM, THE(1955, Brit.); SIMBA(1955, Brit.); CAMPBELL'S KINGDOM(1957, Brit.); DOCTOR AT LARGE(1957, Brit.); SPANISH GARDENER, THE(1957, Span.); CAST A DARK SHADOW(1958, Brit.); DOCTOR'S DILEMMA, THE(1958, Brit.); NIGHT AMBUSH(1958, Brit.); TALE OF TWO CITIES, A(1958, Brit.); WIND CANNOT READ, THE(1958, Brit.); LIBEL(1959, Brit.); ANGEL WORE RED, THE(1960); SONG WITHOUT END(1960); SINGER NOT THE SONG, THE(1961, Brit.); VICTIM(1961, Brit.); DAMN THE DEFIANT!(1962, Brit.); WE JOINED THE NAVY(1962, Brit.); AGENT 8 3/4(1963, Brit.); DOCTOR IN DISTRESS(1963, Brit.); I COULD GO ON SINGING(1963); MIND BENDERS, THE(1963, Brit.); KING AND COUNTRY(1964, Brit.); SERVANT, THE(1964, Brit.); DARLING(1965, Brit.); MC GUIRE, GO HOME!(1966, Brit.); MODESTY BLAISE(1966, Brit.); ACCIDENT(1967, Brit.); OUR MOTHER'S HOUSE(1967, Brit.); FIXER, THE(1968, Brit.); SEBASTIAN(1968, Brit.); JUSTINE(1969, Brit.); OH! WHAT A LOVELY WAR(1969, Brit.); DEATH IN VENICE(1971, Ital./Fr.); SERPENT, THE(1973, Fr./Ital./Ger.); NIGHT PORTER, THE(1974, Ital./U.S.); PERMISSION TO KILL(1975, U.S./Aust.); BRIDGE TOO FAR, A(1977, Brit.); PROVIDENCE(1977, Fr.); DESPAIR(1978, Ger.)

Bud Bogart
SUMMER CAMP(1979)
Eleanor Bogart
PAPER MOON(1973)
Frank Bogart
HORROR CASTLE(1965, Ital.), w
Hal Bogart
MOTORCYCLE GANG(1957); ATTACK OF THE PUPPET PEOPLE(1958); JET ATTACK(1958); SUBMARINE SEAHAWK(1959)
Humphrey Bogart
DEVIL WITH WOMEN, A(1930); UP THE RIVER(1930); BAD SISTER(1931); BODY AND SOUL(1931); HOLY TERROR, A(1931); WOMEN OF ALL NATIONS(1931); BIG CITY BLUES(1932); LOVE AFFAIR(1932); THREE ON A MATCH(1932); MIDNIGHT(1934); BULLETS OR BALLOTS(1936); CHINA CLIPPER(1936); ISLE OF FURY(1936); PETRIFIED FOREST, THE(1936); TWO AGAINST THE WORLD(1936); BLACK LEGION, THE(1937); DEAD END(1937); GREAT O'MALLEY, THE(1937); KID GALAHAD(1937); MARKED WOMAN(1937); SAN QUENTIN(1937); STAND-IN(1937); AMAZING DR. CLITTERHOUSE, THE(1938); ANGELS WITH DIRTY FACES(1938); CRIME SCHOOL(1938); MEN ARE SUCH FOOLS(1938); RACKET BUSTERS(1938); SWING YOUR LADY(1938); DARK VICTORY(1939); KING OF THE UNDERWORLD(1939); OKLAHOMA KID, THE(1939); RETURN OF DR. X, THE(1939); ROARING TWENTIES, THE(1939); YOU CAN'T GET AWAY WITH MURDER(1939); BROTHER ORCHID(1940); INVISIBLE STRIPES(1940); IT ALL CAME TRUE(1940); THEY DRIVE BY NIGHT(1940); VIRGINIA CITY(1940); HIGH SIERRA(1941); MALTESE FALCON, THE(1941); WAGONS ROLL AT NIGHT, THE(1941); ACROSS THE PACIFIC(1942); ALL THROUGH THE NIGHT(1942); BIG SHOT, THE(1942); CASABLANCA(1942); IN THIS OUR LIFE(1942); ACTION IN THE NORTH ATLANTIC(1943); SAHARA(1943); THANK YOUR LUCKY STARS(1943); PASSAGE TO MARSEILLE(1944); TO HAVE AND HAVE NOT(1944); CONFLICT(1945); BIG SLEEP, THE(1946); DARK PASSAGE(1947); DEAD RECKONING(1947); TWO MRS. CARROLLS, THE(1947); KEY LARGO(1948); TREASURE OF THE SIERRA MADRE, THE(1948); KNOCK ON ANY DOOR(1949); TOKYO JOE(1949); CHAIN LIGHTNING(1950); IN A LONELY PLACE(1950); AFRICAN QUEEN, THE(1951, U.S./Brit.); ENFORCER, THE(1951); SIROCCO(1951); DEADLINE-U.S.A.(1952); ROAD TO BALI(1952); BATTLE CIRCUS(1953); BEAT THE DEVIL(1953); BAREFOOT CONTESSA, THE(1954); CAINE MUTINY, THE(1954); LOVE LOTTERY, THE(1954, Brit.); SABRINA(1954); DESPERATE HOURS, THE(1955); LEFT HAND OF GOD, THE(1955); WE'RE NO ANGELS(1955); HARDER THEY FALL, THE(1956)
Jane Bogart
1984
IRRECONCILABLE DIFFERENCES(1984), art d; RIVER, THE(1984), set d
Jean Paul Bogart
1984
BIZET'S CARMEN(1984, Fr./Ital.)
Jill Barrie Bogart
FOXES(1980)
Paul Bogart
MARLOWE(1969), d; HALLS OF ANGER(1970), d; SKIN GAME(1971), d; CANCEL MY RESERVATION(1972), d; CLASS OF '44(1973), p&d; MR. RICCO(1975), d; THREE SISTERS, THE(1977), d
1984
OH GOD! YOU DEVIL(1984), d
Tiffany Bogart
KING OF THE GYPSIES(1978)
Tracy Bogart
SKIN GAME(1971); STUDENT TEACHERS, THE(1973)
1984
OH GOD! YOU DEVIL(1984)
Harry Bogarth
Silents
BULLDOG DRUMMOND(1923, Brit.)
Ed Bogas
BON VOYAGE, CHARLIE BROWN(AND DON'T COME BACK)*** (1980), m; BLACK GIRL(1972), m; MEMORY OF US(1974), m; RACE FOR YOUR LIFE, CHARLIE BROWN(1977), m
A. Bogatyrov
SECRET BRIGADE, THE(1951 USSR), m
V. Bogatyy
SANDU FOLLOWS THE SUN(1965, USSR)
Vasili Bogazianos
...AND JUSTICE FOR ALL(1979)
Adriana Bogdan
ONE NIGHT... A TRAIN(1968, Fr./Bel.)
Paul Bogdan
MAN WHO LIKED FUNERALS, THE(1959, Brit.); STRICTLY CONFIDENTIAL(1959, Brit.); MAKE MINE A DOUBLE(1962, Brit.); BAY OF SAINT MICHEL, THE(1963, Brit.); FRIENDS AND NEIGHBORS(1963, Brit.)
Bogdanov
HOUSE OF GREED(1934, USSR)
Fyodor Bogdanov
WINGS OF VICTORY(1941, USSR)
Mikhail Bogdanov
WAR AND PEACE(1968, USSR), art d
A. Bogdanova
CRANES ARE FLYING, THE(1960, USSR)
Anna Bogdanova
SPRINGTIME ON THE VOLGA(1961, USSR)
Z. Bogdanova
Misc. Silents
REVOLUTIONIST(1917, USSR)
G. Bogdanova-Chestnokova
TIGER GIRL(1955, USSR)
Alexandra Bogdanovich
THEY ALL LAUGHED(1981)
Antonia Bogdanovich
THEY ALL LAUGHED(1981)
Josef Bogdanovich
BOXOFFICE(1982), p, d

Peter Bogdanovich
WILD ANGELS, THE(1966); TRIP, THE(1967); TARGETS(1968), a, w, p,d, ed; LIONS LOVE(1969); LAST PICTURE SHOW, THE(1971), d, w; WHAT'S UP, DOC?(1972), p&d, w; PAPER MOON(1973), p&d; DAISY MILLER(1974), p&d; AT LONG LAST LOVE(1975), p,d&w; NICKELODEON(1976), d, w; SAINT JACK(1979), a, d, w; THEY ALL LAUGHED(1981), d&w

Alexei Bogdanovsky
Misc. Silents
NINTH OF JANUARY(1925, USSR)

John Bogden
MAJOR AND THE MINOR, THE(1942); STORY OF DR. WASSELL, THE(1944); O.S.S.(1946)

Geraldine Bogdonovich
EGYPTIAN. THE(1954)

Gustaf Boge
JUNGLE OF CHANG(1951), ph

Benedict Bogeaus
BRIDGE OF SAN LUIS REY, THE(1944), p; DARK WATERS(1944), p; CAPTAIN KIDD(1945), p; DIARY OF A CHAMBERMAID(1946), p; MR. ACE(1946), p; CHRISTMAS EVE(1947), p; MACOMBER AFFAIR, THE(1947), p; GIRL FROM MANHATTAN(1948), p; LULU BELLE(1948), p; ON OUR MERRY WAY(1948), p; CROOKED WAY, THE(1949), p; JOHNNY ONE-EYE(1950), p; MY BROTHER, THE OUTLAW(1951), p; ONE BIG AFFAIR(1952), P; APPOINTMENT IN HONDURAS(1953), p; COUNT THE HOURS(1953), p; CATTLE QUEEN OF MONTANA(1954), p; PASSION(1954), p; SILVER LODE(1954), p; PEARL OF THE SOUTH PACIFIC(1955), p; TENNESSEE'S PARTNER(1955), p; SLIGHTLY SCARLET(1956), p; RIVER'S EDGE, THE(1957), p; ENCHANTED ISLAND(1958), p; FROM THE EARTH TO THE MOON(1958), p; MOST DANGEROUS MAN ALIVE, THE(1961), p

Benedict E. Bogeaus
ESCAPE TO BURMA(1955), p; JET OVER THE ATLANTIC(1960), p

John Bogen
GUY NAMED JOE, A(1943)

Bill Bogert
FIRE SALE(1977)

William Bogert
DOG DAY AFTERNOON(1975); FRONT, THE(1976); HEAVEN CAN WAIT(1978); HERO AT LARGE(1980); LAST MARRIED COUPLE IN AMERICA, THE(1980); WARGAMES(1983)

Sal Bogese
Misc. Talkies
SUPER BUG(1975)

Vera Bogetti
BORROW A MILLION(1934, Brit.); CRAZY PEOPLE(1934, Brit.); GENTLEMAN'S AGREEMENT(1935, Brit.); GET OFF MY FOOT(1935, Brit.); HANDLE WITH CARE(1935, Brit.); INSIDE THE ROOM(1935, Brit.); MAD HATTERS, THE(1935, Brit.); SAY IT WITH DIAMONDS(1935, Brit.); ELIZA COMES TO STAY(1936, Brit.); EVERYTHING IN LIFE(1936, Brit.); EXCUSE MY GLOVE(1936, Brit.); INTIMATE RELATIONS(1937, Brit.); SINGING COP, THE(1938, Brit.); SPECIAL EDITION(1938, Brit.); THISTLEDOWN(1938, Brit.); CONFIDENTIAL LADY(1939, Brit.); TWO FOR DANGER(1940, Brit.); PRIME MINISTER, THE(1941, Brit.); THIS WAS PARIS(1942, Brit.); IT'S IN THE BAG(1943, Brit.); THURSDAY'S CHILD(1943, Brit.); CANDLES AT NINE(1944, Brit.); NO ROOM AT THE INN(1950, Brit.)

Bogey
MS. 45(1981)

Bill Boggess
MILLION DOLLAR LEGS(1939)

Vera Boggetti
MANNEQUIN(1933, Brit.); GIRL IN THE FLAT, THE(1934, Brit.); LIFE OF THE PARTY(1934, Brit.); SEEING IS BELIEVING(1934, Brit.); TO BE A LADY(1934, Brit.)

Victor Boggetti
Silents
MOTHERHOOD(1915, Brit.)

Jean-Francois Boggi
STATE OF SIEGE(1973, Fr./U.S./Ital./Ger.)

Bill Boggs
EYES OF LAURA MARS(1978); TRADING PLACES(1983)

Haskell B. Boggs
LEATHER SAINT, THE(1956), ph

Haskell Boggs
DELICATE DELINQUENT, THE(1957), ph; FEAR STRIKES OUT(1957), ph; HEAR ME GOOD(1957), ph; SHORT CUT TO HELL(1957), ph; AS YOUNG AS WE ARE(1958), ph; GEISHA BOY, THE(1958), ph; I MARRIED A MONSTER FROM OUTER SPACE(1958), ph; ROCK-A-BYE BABY(1958), ph; ST. LOUIS BLUES(1958), ph; TEACHER'S PET(1958), ph; DON'T GIVE UP THE SHIP(1959), ph; BELLBOY, THE(1960), ph; CINDERFELLA(1960), ph; RED LINE 7000(1965), ph; YOUNG FURY(1965), ph

Peter Boggs
9/30/55(1977)

Robert Boggs
THERE IS NO 13(1977), p

Russell A. Boggs
Silents
SAND(1920), w

Jack D. Boghaossian
TEARS OF HAPPINESS(1974)

Duane Bogie
ALL CREATURES GREAT AND SMALL(1975, Brit.), p

Mikhail Bogin
EYEWITNESS(1981)

Charles Bogle [W.C. Fields]
OLD-FASHIONED WAY, THE(1934), w; YOU CAN'T CHEAT AN HONEST MAN(1939), w

Marco Bogliani
WAR BETWEEN THE PLANETS(1971, Ital.)

Ludvik Bogner
1984
RENO AND THE DOC(1984, Can.), ph

Norman Bogner
PRIVILEGE(1967, Brit.), w

Willy Bogner
SNOW JOB(1972), ph; BENJAMIN(1973, Ger.), p&d, w, ph

Willy Bogner, Jr.
ON HER MAJESTY'S SECRET SERVICE(1969, Brit.), ph

Bogo the Chimp
JUNGLE PRINCESS, THE(1936)

N. Bogoliubov
GREAT CITIZEN, THE(1939, USSR); VOW, THE(1947, USSR.)

Nikolai Bogoliubov
LAD FROM OUR TOWN(1941, USSR)

S. Bogoliubova
VOW, THE(1947, USSR.)

A. Bogolyubov
MEET ME IN MOSCOW(1966, USSR)

I. Bogolyubov
KATERINA IZMAILOVA(1969, USSR)

Vladimir Osipovich Bogomolov
MY NAME IS IVAN(1963, USSR), w

Nelly Bogor
PILLAR OF FIRE, THE(1963, Israel), ed; FLYING MATCHMAKER, THE(1970, Israel), ed

Eric Bogosian
1984
SPECIAL EFFECTS(1984)

Andrey Bogoslovskiy
SONS AND MOTHERS(1967, USSR)

Axel Bogousslavsky
RETURN OF MARTIN GUERRE, THE(1983, Fr.)

N. Bogoyavlenskaya
RESURRECTION(1963, USSR)

Julius Bogua
LAUGHING BOY(1934)

M A. Bogue
CAROLINA BLUES(1944)

N. Boguliubov
SEVEN BRAVE MEN(1936, USSR)

Nikolai Boguliubov
NO GREATER LOVE(1944, USSR)

Ed Bogus
SILENCE(1974), m; STREET MUSIC(1982), m

Peter Bogyo
FAT ANGELS(1980, U.S./Span.)
1984
BOSTONIANS, THE(1984)

Ladislav Bohac
SKELETON ON HORSEBACK(1940, Czech.)

Dennis Bohan
KISS OF DEATH(1947)

Jim Bohan
PUNISHMENT PARK(1971); AMERICAN GRAFFITI(1973); BUCKTOWN(1975); HOMETOWN U.S.A.(1979)
Misc. Talkies
KINGS OF THE HILL(1976)

Marc Bohan
PHAEDRA(1962, U.S./Gr./Fr.); SECRET CEREMONY(1968, Brit.), cos

Fred Bohanan
GIANT(1956), ed

Kelley Bohanan
IDAHO TRANSFER(1975)

Rebecca Bohannen
FOREIGN CORRESPONDENT(1940)

Becky Bohannon
GUY NAMED JOE, A(1943)

Heidi Bohay
VOICES(1979)

Charles Bohbot
HELL ON DEVIL'S ISLAND(1957)

Jirina Bohdalova
LADY ON THE TRACKS, THE(1968, Czech.)

Blanka Bohdanova
SWEET LIGHT IN A DARK ROOM(1966, Czech.)

Franz Boheim
GOOD SOLDIER SCHWEIK, THE(1963, Ger.)

Olly Boheim
Silents
METROPOLIS(1927, Ger.)

Endre Bohem
GIRL FROM MANDALAY(1936), w; HAPPY-GO-LUCKY(1937), w; LARCENY ON THE AIR(1937), w; TWO WISE MAIDS(1937), w; LITTLE ORPHAN ANNIE(1938), w; LORD JEFF(1938), w; BLACKMAIL(1939), w; FOUR GIRLS IN WHITE(1939), w; TELEVISION SPY(1939), w; NIGHT HAS A THOUSAND EYES(1948), p; ALIAS NICK BEAL(1949), w; BENGAZI(1955), w; PAWNEE(1957), w; CATTLE EMPIRE(1958), w; DESERT HELL(1958), w; BOYS OF PAUL STREET, THE(1969, Hung./US), p, w

Carl Boheme
Silents
FOUR SONS(1928)

Heide Bohlen
CORRUPT ONES, THE(1967, Ger.)

Allan Bohlin
WHALERS, THE(1942, Swed.)

Therese Bohlin
FANTASIES(1981)

Peter Bohlke
HANNIBAL BROOKS(1969, Brit.)

Adolph Bohm
MEN IN HER LIFE, THE(1941), ch

Alfred Bohm
$100 A NIGHT(1968, Ger.)
Christina Bohm
LADY OSCAR(1979, Fr./Jap.)
Ernest Bohm
ALICE IN THE CITIES(1974, W. Ger.)
Hark Bohm
AMERICAN SOLDIER, THE(1970 Ger.); EFFI BRIEST(1974, Ger.); DESPAIR(1978, Ger.); MARRIAGE OF MARIA BRAUN, THE(1979, Ger.); LILI MARLEEN(1981, Ger.); LOLA(1982, Ger.)
Karlheinz Bohm
COURT MARTIAL(1962, Ger.); FOUR HORSEMEN OF THE APOCALYPSE, THE(1962); CROSS OF THE LIVING(1963, Fr.); FOX AND HIS FRIENDS(1976, Ger.); MOTHER KUSTERS GOES TO HEAVEN(1976, Ger.)
Marquand Bohm
AMERICAN SOLDIER, THE(1970 Ger.)
Marquard Bohm
FEAR EATS THE SOUL(1974, Ger.); KINGS OF THE ROAD(1976, Ger.); JAIL BAIT(1977, Ger.)
Rolf Bohman
SWEDISH WEDDING NIGHT(1965, Swed.), art d
Chris Bohn
SPELL OF THE HYPNOTIST(1956); JEREMY(1973)
Jack Lionel Bohn
Silents
ASHAMED OF PARENTS(1921)
John Bohn
CRIME OF DR. CRESPI, THE(1936); HOUSE ACROSS THE BAY, THE(1940); MRS. PARKINGTON(1944); DEAD RECKONING(1947); JOAN OF ARC(1948)
Misc. Silents
INSIDE OF THE CUP, THE(1921); SIXTH COMMANDMENT, THE(1924)
Marquard Bohn
FOX AND HIS FRIENDS(1976, Ger.)
Merritt Bohn
MANCHURIAN CANDIDATE, THE(1962); WILD SEED(1965); ZEBRA IN THE KITCHEN(1965); NEVADA SMITH(1966); SOL MADRID(1968)
Walter Bohn
CIPHER BUREAU(1938)
Richard Bohne
MAN WHO WALKED THROUGH THE WALL, THE(1964, Ger.)
Werner Bohne
GOLD(1934, Ger.), ph; SHOT AT DAWN, A(1934, Ger.), ph
Marina Bohnen
NONE BUT THE LONELY HEART(1944)
Michael Bohnen
GOLD(1934, Ger.); PRIVATE LIFE OF LOUIS XIV(1936, Ger.)
Misc. Silents
HEADS UP, CHARLIE(1926, Ger.); SAJENKO THE SOVIET(1929, Ger.)
Roman Bohnen
VOGUES OF 1938(1937); 52ND STREET(1937); OF MICE AND MEN(1939); APPOINTMENT FOR LOVE(1941); BUGLE SOUNDS, THE(1941); SO ENDS OUR NIGHT(1941); THEY DARE NOT LOVE(1941); GRAND CENTRAL MURDER(1942); HARD WAY, THE(1942); YOUNG AMERICA(1942); EDGE OF DARKNESS(1943); MISSION TO MOSCOW(1943); SONG OF BERNADETTE, THE(1943); HAIRY APE, THE(1944); HITLER GANG, THE(1944); NONE BUT THE LONELY HEART(1944); BELL FOR ADANO, A(1945); COUNTER-ATTACK(1945); MISS SUSIE SLAGLE'S(1945); BEST YEARS OF OUR LIVES, THE(1946); CALIFORNIA(1946); DEADLINE AT DAWN(1946); HOODLUM SAINT, THE(1946); MR. ACE(1946); STRANGE LOVE OF MARTHA IVERS, THE(1946); TWO YEARS BEFORE THE MAST(1946); BRUTE FORCE(1947); FOR YOU I DIE(1947); SONG OF LOVE(1947); WINTER WONDERLAND(1947); ARCH OF TRIUMPH(1948); JOAN OF ARC(1948); NIGHT HAS A THOUSAND EYES(1948); OPEN SECRET(1948); KAZAN(1949); MR. SOFT TOUCH(1949)
Folker Bohnet
LUDWIG(1973, Ital./Ger./Fr.)
Volker Bohnet
BRIDGE, THE(1961, Ger.)
Huerequeque Enrique Bohorquez
FITZCARRALDO(1982)
Jose Bohr
ROGUE OF THE RIO GRANDE(1930); EX-FLAME(1931)
Corinne Bohrer
MY FAVORITE YEAR(1982); JOYSTICKS(1983)
1984
SURF II(1984)
Corrinne Bohrer
I, THE JURY(1982)
Jack Bohrer
UNHOLY ROLLERS(1972), p
Richard Bohringer
LAST METRO, THE(1981, Fr.); BOLERO(1982, Fr.); DIVA(1982, Fr.)
Lula Mae Bohrman
PLACE IN THE SUN, A(1951)
Lulu Mae Bohrman
HOLLOW TRIUMPH(1948); LOVES OF CARMEN, THE(1948); SOLID GOLD CADILLAC, THE(1956)
Lulu May Bohrman
SWEETHEARTS(1938)
Lulumae Bohrman
TEST PILOT(1938); DEEP IN MY HEART(1954)
Stan Bohrman
CHINA SYNDROME, THE(1979)
Gerhard Bohrmann
TO COMMIT A MURDER(1970, Fr./Ital./Ger.)
Margot Boht
SCARS OF DRACULA, THE(1970, Brit.)
Carl Bohun
BEAST MUST DIE, THE(1974, Brit.)

Ted Bohus
DEADLY SPAWN, THE(1983), p
Samanta Boi
NIGHT OF THE SHOOTING STARS, THE(1982, Ital.)
Helen Boice
ZIEGFELD FOLLIES(1945); ABILENE TOWN(1946)
Rico Boido
PLANET OF THE VAMPIRES(1965, U.S./Ital./Span.)
Elaine Boies
LEGACY OF BLOOD(1978)
Misc. Talkies
LEGACY OF HORROR(1978)
Marius Beugre Boignan
BLACK AND WHITE IN COLOR(1976, Fr.)
Pierre Boileau
DIABOLIQUE(1955, Fr.), w; DEMONIAQUE(1958, Fr.), w; VERTIGO(1958), w; FACES IN THE DARK(1960, Brit.), w; CRIME DOES NOT PAY(1962, Fr.), w; HORROR CHAMBER OF DR. FAUSTUS, THE(1962, Fr./Ital.), w; WHERE THE TRUTH LIES(1962, Fr.), w; DOUBLE DECEPTION(1963, Fr.), w
Curt Bois
TREMENDOUSLY RICH MAN, A(1932, Ger.); HOLLYWOOD HOTEL(1937); TOVARICH(1937); AMAZING DR. CLITTERHOUSE, THE(1938); BOY MEETS GIRL(1938); GARDEN OF THE MOON(1938); GOLD DIGGERS IN PARIS(1938); GREAT WALTZ, THE(1938); ROMANCE IN THE DARK(1938); HOTEL IMPERIAL(1939); BITTER SWEET(1940); BOOM TOWN(1940); HE STAYED FOR BREAKFAST(1940); HULLABALOO(1940); LADY IN QUESTION, THE(1940); BLUE, WHITE, AND PERFECT(1941); HOLD BACK THE DAWN(1941); THAT NIGHT IN RIO(1941); CASABLANCA(1942); MY GAL SAL(1942); PACIFIC RENDEZVOUS(1942); TUTTLES OF TAHITI(1942); DESERT SONG, THE(1943); DESTROYER(1943); PARIS AFTER DARK(1943); PRINCESS O'ROURKE(1943); SWING FEVER(1943); BLONDE FEVER(1944); COVER GIRL(1944); GYPSY WILDCAT(1944); SARATOGA TRUNK(1945); SPANISH MAIN, THE(1945); JUNGLE FLIGHT(1947); ARCH OF TRIUMPH(1948); FRENCH LEAVE(1948); LET'S LIVE A LITTLE(1948); UP IN CENTRAL PARK(1948); WOMAN FROM TANGIER, THE(1948); WOMAN IN WHITE, THE(1948); CAUGHT(1949); GREAT SINNER(1949); KISS IN THE DARK, A(1949); LOVABLE CHEAT, THE(1949); OH, YOU BEAUTIFUL DOLL(1949); FORTUNES OF CAPTAIN BLOOD(1950); JOE PALOOKA MEETS HUMPHREY(1950)
Ilse Bois
Misc. Silents
GHOST TRAIN, THE(1927, Brit.)
Lise Bois
Silents
GHOST TRAIN, THE(1927, Brit.)
Robert Boisey
JUPITER(1952, Fr.), w
Michel Boisrond
LA PARISIENNE(1958, Fr./Ital.), d, w; COME DANCE WITH ME(1960, Fr.), d; LOVE AND THE FRENCHWOMAN(1961, Fr.), d; TALES OF PARIS(1962, Fr./Ital.), d, w; GODSON, THE(1972, Ital./Fr.); CATHERINE & CO.(1976, Fr.), d
Christian Boisseau
I SPIT ON YOUR GRAVE(1962, Fr.)
Guillaume Boisseau
MON ONCLE D'AMERIQUE(1980, Fr.)
1984
LIFE IS A BED OF ROSES(1984, Fr.)
Jocelyne Boisseau
SPERMULA(1976, Fr.)
Jean Boissemond
LA MARSEILLAISE(1938, Fr.)
G. Boisser
MAN AND A WOMAN, A(1966, Fr.), ed
Yves Boisset
FRENCH CONSPIRACY, THE(1973, Fr.), d; PURPLE TAXI, THE(1977, Fr./Ital./Ireland), d, w
1984
DOG DAY(1984, Fr.), d, w
Claude Boissol
RASPOUTINE(1954, Fr.), w; JULIE THE REDHEAD(1963, Fr.), d, w
Christine Boisson
IDENTIFICATION OF A WOMAN(1983, Ital.)
Noelle Boisson
VERY CURIOUS GIRL, A(1970, Fr.), ed; MEN PREFER FAT GIRLS(1981, Fr.), ed
John Boister
FAST LADY, THE(1963, Brit.)
Dominique Boisvert
HOG WILD(1980, Can.), ed
Huguette Boisvert
WE ARE ALL NAKED(1970, Can./Fr.), w
Nicole Boisvert
CATHY'S CURSE(1977, Can.), p; BLACKOUT(1978, Fr./Can.), p
Peter Boita
AFTER THE BALL(1957, Brit.), ed; DUKE WORE JEANS, THE(1958, Brit.), ed; SOLITARY CHILD, THE(1958, Brit.), ed; CARRY ON SERGEANT(1959, Brit.), ed; THIRD MAN ON THE MOUNTAIN(1959), ed; SWISS FAMILY ROBINSON(1960), ed; CIRCUS FRIENDS(1962, Brit.), ed; TRAITORS, THE(1963, Brit.), ed; CITY OF FEAR(1965, Brit.), ed; TEN LITTLE INDIANS(1965, Brit.), ed; FIGHTING PRINCE OF DONEGAL, THE(1966, Brit.), ed; VIKING QUEEN, THE(1967, Brit.), ed; GUNS IN THE HEATHER(1968, Brit.), ed; DAVID COPPERFIELD(1970, Brit.), ed; DOCTOR IN TROUBLE(1970, Brit.), ed; JANE EYRE(1971, Brit.), ed; KIDNAPPED(1971, Brit.), ed; LITTLE PRINCE, THE(1974, Brit.), ed; LUCKY LADY(1975), ed; CANDLESHOE(1978), ed; CARRY ON EMANUELLE(1978, Brit.), ed; UNIDENTIFIED FLYING ODDBALL, THE(1979, Brit.), ed; HEARTACHES(1981, Can.), ed
Cyr Boitard
1984
A NOS AMOURS(1984, Fr.)
Jeanne Boitel
AMPHYTRYON(1937, Ger.); NAPOLEON(1955, Fr.); IF PARIS WERE TOLD TO US(1956, Fr.); ROYAL AFFAIRS IN VERSAILLES(1957, Fr.); MAIGRET LAYS A TRAP(1958, Fr.)

Camillo Boito
TIMES GONE BY(1953, Ital.), w; SENSO(1968, Ital.), w
Federico Boito
DANGER: DIABOLIK(1968, Ital./Fr.)
Lucie Boitres
THIRTEENTH LETTER, THE(1951)
Jay Boivin
PICK-UP SUMMER(1981), m
Sandra Boize
HYSTERIA(1965, Brit.)
Leon Boje
MR. H. C. ANDERSEN(1950, Brit.), anim d
Francisco Bojorquez
1984
TOY SOLDIERS(1984), ph
Yolanda Bojorquez
TOUCH OF EVIL(1958)
Gilbert Boka
IF PARIS WERE TOLD TO US(1956, Fr.); ROYAL AFFAIRS IN VERSAILLES(1957, Fr.)
V. Bokadoro
PEACE TO HIM WHO ENTERS(1963, USSR)
Gilbert Bokanowski
CRIME DOES NOT PAY(1962, Fr.), p
Hal Bokar
NASTY RABBIT, THE(1964); MORITURI(1965); RAT FINK(1965)
V. Bokaryov
RESURRECTION(1963, USSR)
John Bokers
Silents
ETERNAL GRIND, THE(1916)
Attila Bokor
PASSION(1983, Fr./Switz.)
Colette Boky
MERRY WIVES OF WINDSOR, THE(1966, Aust.)
James Bolam
KITCHEN, THE(1961, Brit.); KIND OF LOVING, A(1962, Brit.); LONELINESS OF THE LONG DISTANCE RUNNER, THE(1962, Brit.); MURDER MOST FOUL(1964, Brit.); HALF A SIXPENCE(1967, Brit.); OTLEY(1969, Brit.); CRUCIBLE OF TERROR(1971, Brit.); O LUCKY MAN!(1973, Brit.); STRAIGHT ON TILL MORNING(1974, Brit.); IN CELEBRATION(1975, Brit.); LIKELY LADS, THE(1976, Brit.)
1984
PLAGUE DOGS, THE(1984, U.S./Brit.)
Bridget Boland
GASLIGHT(1940), w; LAUGH IT OFF(1940, Brit.), w; OLD MOTHER RILEY IN SOCIETY(1940, Brit.), w; SPIES OF THE AIR(1940, Brit.), w; HE FOUND A STAR(1941, Brit.), w; THIS ENGLAND(1941, Brit.), w; VOICE IN THE NIGHT, A(1941, Brit.), w; LOST PEOPLE, THE(1950, Brit.), w; FAKE, THE(1953, Brit.), w; PRISONER, THE(1955, Brit.), w; WAR AND PEACE(1956, Ital./U.S.), w; DAMON AND PYTHIAS(1962), w; ANNE OF THE THOUSAND DAYS(1969, Brit.), w
Brona Boland
VIOLENT PLAYGROUND(1958, Brit.)
Ed Boland
HIT THE SADDLE(1937)
Eddie Boland
WINGS OF ADVENTURE(1930); LIGHTNING FLYER(1931); MIRACLE WOMAN, THE(1931); MURDER AT DAWN(1932); SECRETS OF WU SIN(1932); VANITY STREET(1932); DEATH KISS, THE(1933); FLYING DOWN TO RIO(1933); I HAVE LIVED(1933); CAT'S PAW, THE(1934); RIDERS OF THE WHISTLING SKULL(1937)
Silents
OLIVER TWIST(1922); LONG LIVE THE KING(1923); KID BROTHER, THE(1927); SUNRISE–A SONG OF TWO HUMANS(1927); MANHATTAN KNIGHTS(1928)
Misc. Silents
UNKNOWN DANGERS(1926)
Eily Boland
FIDDLERS THREE(1944, Brit.), ed; UNDERGROUND GUERRILLAS(1944, Brit.), ed; DANCING WITH CRIME(1947, Brit.), ed; SAN DEMETRIO, LONDON(1947, Brit.), ed; THINGS HAPPEN AT NIGHT(1948, Brit.), ed; INBETWEEN AGE, THE(1958, Brit.), ed; STOLEN AIRLINER, THE(1962, Brit.), ed
Fergal Boland
VIOLENT PLAYGROUND(1958, Brit.)
Gene Boland
PENDULUM(1969)
Herbert Boland
WHY RUSSIANS ARE REVOLTING(1970)
John Boland
LEAGUE OF GENTLEMEN, THE(1961, Brit.), w
John J. Boland
TE QUIERO CON LOCURA(1935), d
Mary Boland
PERSONAL MAID(1931); SECRETS OF A SECRETARY(1931); EVENINGS FOR SALE(1932); IF I HAD A MILLION(1932); NIGHT OF JUNE 13(1932); MAMA LOVES PAPA(1933); SOLITAIRE MAN, THE(1933); THREE-CORNERED MOON(1933); DOWN TO THEIR LAST YACHT(1934); FOUR FRIGHTENED PEOPLE(1934); HERE COMES THE GROOM(1934); MELODY IN SPRING(1934); PURSUIT OF HAPPINESS, THE(1934); SIX OF A KIND(1934); STINGAREE(1934); BIG BROADCAST OF 1936, THE(1935); PEOPLE WILL TALK(1935); RUGGLES OF RED GAP(1935); TWO FOR TONIGHT(1935); COLLEGE HOLIDAY(1936); EARLY TO BED(1936); SON COMES HOME, A(1936); WIVES NEVER KNOW(1936); DANGER–LOVE AT WORK(1937); MARRY THE GIRL(1937); THERE GOES THE GROOM(1937); ARTISTS AND MODELS ABROAD(1938); LITTLE TOUGH GUYS IN SOCIETY(1938); MAMA RUNS WILD(1938); BOY TROUBLE(1939); MAGNIFICENT FRAUD, THE(1939); NIGHT WORK(1939); WOMEN, THE(1939); HE MARRIED HIS WIFE(1940); HIT PARADE OF 1941(1940); NEW MOON(1940); ONE NIGHT IN THE TROPICS(1940); PRIDE AND PREJUDICE(1940); IN OUR TIME(1944); NOTHING BUT TROUBLE(1944); FOREVER YOURS(1945); JULIA MISBEHAVES(1948); GUILTY BYSTANDER(1950)
Silents
EDGE OF THE ABYSS, THE(1915); PRODIGAL WIFE, THE(1918); PERFECT LOVER, THE(1919)

Misc. Silents
PRICE OF HAPPINESS, THE(1916); STEPPING STONE, THE(1916); WOMAN'S EXPERIENCE, A(1918); HIS TEMPORARY WIFE(1920)
Nora Boland
CALIFORNIA SUITE(1978)
Patrick Boland
PUNISHMENT PARK(1971)
Millan Bolander
INTERMEZZO(1937, Swed.); DOLLAR(1938, Swed.)
Ana Eliza Perez Bolanos
ZORRO, THE GAY BLADE(1981)
Roberto Gomez Bolanos
LOS ASTRONAUTAS(1960, Mex.), w; LOS INVISIBLES(1961, Mex.), w
Jean Bolary
MADAME ROSA(1977, Fr.), p
Xan Das Bolas
BOY WHO STOLE A MILLION, THE(1960, Brit.); CEREMONY, THE(1963, U.S./Span.); GUNMEN OF THE RIO GRANDE(1965, Fr./Ital./Span.); MURDERS IN THE RUE MORGUE(1971)
Xan Des Bolas
NOT ON YOUR LIFE(1965, Ital./Span.)
S. Bolchi
ANITA GARIBALDI(1954, Ital.), w
William Bolcom
HESTER STREET(1975), m
Eva-Maria Bold
NOT RECONCILED, OR "ONLY VIOLENCE HELPS WHERE IT RULES"(1969, Ger.)
Gottfried Bold
NOT RECONCILED, OR "ONLY VIOLENCE HELPS WHERE IT RULES"(1969, Ger.)
Kathrin Bold
NOT RECONCILED, OR "ONLY VIOLENCE HELPS WHERE IT RULES"(1969, Ger.)
Bold Venture
WINNER'S CIRCLE, THE(1948)
Harry Bolden
MEMBER OF THE WEDDING, THE(1952)
Ronald Bolden
SOUNDER, PART 2(1976); FRENCH QUARTER(1978)
Bobbie Bolder
RIP TIDE(1934)
Misc. Silents
FOOLS FOR LUCK(1917)
Bobby Bolder
TREASURE ISLAND(1934); CASE AGAINST MRS. AMES, THE(1936); MOON'S OUR HOME, THE(1936)
Misc. Silents
DREAM DOLL, THE(1917)
Cal Bolder
HELLER IN PINK TIGHTS(1960); JESSE JAMES MEETS FRANKENSTEIN'S DAUGHTER(1966); ONE OF OUR SPIES IS MISSING(1966); ONE SPY TOO MANY(1966)
Robert Bolder
FLORODORA GIRL, THE(1930); GRUMPY(1930); LADY OF SCANDAL, THE(1930); BARRETTS OF WIMPOLE STREET, THE(1934); GREAT IMPERSONATION, THE(1935); WEDDING NIGHT, THE(1935); WHITE ANGEL, THE(1936)
Silents
BLACK BEAUTY(1921); MARRIAGE OF WILLIAM ASHE, THE(1921); SILENT CALL, THE(1921); BEYOND THE ROCKS(1922); ABRAHAM LINCOLN(1924); BLUE BLOOD(1925); HANDSOME BRUTE, THE(1925); RAFFLES, THE AMATEUR CRACKSMAN(1925); STELLA MARIS(1925)
Misc. Silents
GOLDEN IDIOT, THE(1917); STRICTLY CONFIDENTIAL(1919); WORDS AND MUSIC BY...(1919)
Eric Bolderson
KES(1970, Brit.)
Bonnie Bolding
GARMENT JUNGLE, THE(1957); NO TIME TO BE YOUNG(1957)
Janko Boldis
ADRIFT(1971, Czech.)
Ivan Boldizsar
GOLDEN HEAD, THE(1965, Hung., U.S.), w
Rolf Boldrewood
ROBBERY UNDER ARMS(1958, Brit.), w
Pina Boldrini
IL GRIDO(1962, U.S./Ital.)
Gerhard Boldt
HITLER: THE LAST TEN DAYS(1973, Brit./Ital.), w
M. Bolduman
SILVER DUST(1953, USSR)
A. Boldyrev
WAR AND PEACE(1968, USSR)
Billy Bolen
UTAH KID, THE(1930), ed
Charles Bolender
DARK INTRUDER(1965)
Robert Boler
DEAD AND BURIED(1981)
Jess Bolero
EDUCATION OF SONNY CARSON, THE(1974)
Barbara Boles
DOCTOR DEATH: SEEKER OF SOULS(1973)
Buddy Boles
REG'LAR FELLERS(1941)
Eric Boles
WAY WE WERE, THE(1973); COLD TURKEY(1971); DOCTOR DEATH: SEEKER OF SOULS(1973); GREAT TEXAS DYNAMITE CHASE, THE(1976); DREAM ON(1981)
1984
HADLEY'S REBELLION(1984)

Florence C. Boles
Silents
AMERICAN WAY, THE(1919), w
Glen Boles
RAINBOW OVER BROADWAY(1933); BABBITT(1934); FLIRTATION WALK(1934);
GUILTY PARENTS(1934); QUITTERS, THE(1934); ROAD TO RUIN(1934); $10 RAI-
SE(1935); CLIPPED WINGS(1938)
Glenn Boles
FIGHTING YOUTH(1935)
Col. J.K. Boles
WE'VE NEVER BEEN LICKED(1943), tech adv
Jennifer Boles
STRANGE LOVERS(1963)
Jim Boles
TATTOOED STRANGER, THE(1950); MAN WITH MY FACE, THE(1951); NAKED IN
THE SUN(1957); PUSHER, THE(1960); FATE IS THE HUNTER(1964); FLUFFY(1965);
BIG HAND FOR THE LITTLE LADY, A(1966); GHOST AND MR. CHICKEN,
THE(1966); TROUBLE WITH ANGELS, THE(1966); KARATE KILLERS, THE(1967);
WATERHOLE NO. 3(1967); P.J.(1968); ANGEL IN MY POCKET(1969); LOVE GOD?,
THE(1969); WUSA(1970); SKIN GAME(1971); ACE ELI AND RODGER OF THE
SKIES(1973); DOCTOR DEATH: SEEKER OF SOULS(1973); APPLE DUMPLING
GANG, THE(1975); ONCE IS NOT ENOUGH(1975)
John Boles
DESERT SONG, THE(1929); LAST WARNING, THE(1929); RIO RITA(1929); SCAN-
DAL(1929); CAPTAIN OF THE GUARD(1930); SONG OF THE WEST(1930); FRAN-
KENSTEIN(1931); GOOD SPORT(1931); ONE HEAVENLY NIGHT(1931);
RESURRECTION(1931); SEED(1931); BACK STREET(1932); CARELESS LADY(1932);
SIX HOURS TO LIVE(1932); CHILD OF MANHATTAN(1933); MY LIPS BE-
TRAY(1933); ONLY YESTERDAY(1933); AGE OF INNOCENCE(1934); BELO-
VED(1934); BOTTOMS UP(1934); I BELIEVED IN YOU(1934); LIFE OF VERGIE
WINTERS, THE(1934); MUSIC IN THE AIR(1934); STAND UP AND CHEER(1934 80m
FOX bw); WHITE PARADE, THE(1934); WILD GOLD(1934); CURLY TOP(1935);
LITTLEST REBEL, THE(1935); ORCHIDS TO YOU(1935); REDHEADS ON PARA-
DE(1935); CRAIG'S WIFE(1936); MESSAGE TO GARCIA, A(1936); ROSE OF THE
RANCHO(1936); AS GOOD AS MARRIED(1937); FIGHT FOR YOUR LADY(1937);
STELLA DALLAS(1937); ROMANCE IN THE DARK(1938); SHE MARRIED AN
ARTIST(1938); SINNERS IN PARADISE(1938); BETWEEN US GIRLS(1942); ROAD TO
HAPPINESS(1942); THOUSANDS CHEER(1943); BABES IN BAGDAD(1952)
Silents
MAN-MADE WOMEN(1928)
Misc. Silents
LOVE OF SUNYA, THE(1927); ROMANCE OF THE UNDERWORLD(1928); SHE-
PHERD OF THE HILL, THE(1928); VIRGIN LIPS(1928); WATER HOLE, THE(1928)
Steve Boles
1984
FIRESTARTER(1984)
Richard Boleslavsky
GRAND PARADE, THE(1930), ch; GAY DIPLOMAT, THE(1931), d; STORM AT
DAYBREAK(1933), d; OPERATOR 13(1934), d
Misc. Talkies
WOMAN PURSUED(1931), d
Jan Boleslaw
TO LOVE(1964, Swed.), art d; DEAR JOHN(1966, Swed.), art d; LOVING COU-
PLES(1966, Swed.), art d; LOVE MATES(1967, Swed.), art d; LE VIOL(1968, Fr./Swed.),
art d; SHORT IS THE SUMMER(1968, Swed.), set d
Richard Boleslawski
BEAUTY FOR SALE(1933), d; FUGITIVE LOVERS(1934), d; HOLLYWOOD PAR-
TY(1934), d; MEN IN WHITE(1934), d; PAINTED VEIL, THE(1934), d; CLIVE OF
INDIA(1935), d; LES MISERABLES(1935), d; METROPOLITAN(1935), d; O'SHAU-
GHNESSY'S BOY(1935), d; GARDEN OF ALLAH, THE(1936), d; THEODORA GOES
WILD(1936), d; THREE GODFATHERS(1936), d; LAST OF MRS. CHEYNEY,
THE(1937), d
Misc. Silents
TSAR IVAN VASILYEVICH GROZNY(1915, USSR); BREAD(1918, USSR), d; LOVE
ONE ANOTHER(1922, Den.)
Richard Boleslawsky
LAST OF THE LONE WOLF(1930), d; RASPUTIN AND THE EMPRESS(1932), d
Misc. Silents
LOVE - HATE - DEATH(1918, USSR)
Joseph Boley
BUTTERFIELD 8(1960); ALICE'S RESTAURANT(1969); HUSBANDS(1970)
May Boley
DANCE OF LIFE, THE(1929); DANGEROUS CURVES(1929); CHILDREN OF PLEAS-
URE(1930); LILIES OF THE FIELD(1930); MOBY DICK(1930); FIGHTING CARA-
VANS(1931); GOING WILD(1931); EXPERT, THE(1932); WOMAN COMMANDS,
A(1932); ADVICE TO THE LOVELORN(1933); KISS BEFORE THE MIRROR,
THE(1933); MIGHTY BARNUM, THE(1934); INFORMER, THE(1935); WITHOUT
ORDERS(1936); READY, WILLING AND ABLE(1937); TOVARICH(1937); COWBOY
FROM BROOKLYN(1938); LETTER OF INTRODUCTION(1938); PRISON
FARM(1938); RECKLESS LIVING(1938); DEATH OF A CHAMPION(1939); PERSONS
IN HIDING(1939); SKYLARK(1941)
Raymond Boley
PEACE FOR A GUNFIGHTER(1967), d
Benjie Bolgar
LITTLEST HORSE THIEVES, THE(1977)
Frank Bolger
ROPE OF FLESH(1965)
Michael Lee Bolger
OFFICER AND A GENTLEMAN, AN(1982)
Ray Bolger
GREAT ZIEGFELD, THE(1936); ROSALIE(1937); SWEETHEARTS(1938); WIZARD
OF OZ, THE(1939); FOUR JACKS AND A JILL(1941); SUNNY(1941); FOREVER AND
A DAY(1943); STAGE DOOR CANTEEN(1943); HARVEY GIRLS, THE(1946); LOOK
FOR THE SILVER LINING(1949); WHERE'S CHARLEY?(1952, Brit.); APRIL IN
PARIS(1953); BABES IN TOYLAND(1961); DAYDREAMER, THE(1966); ENTERTAIN-
ER, THE(1975); JUST YOU AND ME, KID(1979); THE RUNNER STUMBLES(1979)
Mikael Bolin
TWO LIVING, ONE DEAD(1964, Brit./Swed.)

Nick Bolin
MANCHURIAN CANDIDATE, THE(1962); BLACKENSTEIN(1973)
Shannon Bolin
DAMN YANKEES(1958); IF EVER I SEE YOU AGAIN(1978); CHILDREN, THE(1980)
Inga Boling
GO, JOHNNY, GO!(1959)
Robert Boling
Silents
COLLEGE(1927)
Jorge Bolio
ZORRO, THE GAY BLADE(1981)
David Boliver
TASTE OF HONEY, A(1962, Brit.)
Florinda Bolkan
CANDY(1968, Ital./Fr.); DETECTIVE BELLI(1970, Ital.); INVESTIGATION OF A
CITIZEN ABOVE SUSPICION(1970, Ital.); MACHINE GUN McCAIN(1970, Ital.);
ANONYMOUS VENETIAN, THE(1971); LAST VALLEY, THE(1971, Brit.); MASTER
TOUCH, THE(1974, Ital./Ger.); BRIEF VACATION, A(1975, Ital.); FRENCH WAY,
THE(1975, Fr.); ROYAL FLASH(1975, Brit.); DAY THAT SHOOK THE WORLD,
THE(1977, Yugo./Czech.)
Misc. Talkies
FOOTSTEPS ON THE MOON(1973)
Bradley Bolke
DIARY OF A BACHELOR(1964)
Heinrich Boll
NOT RECONCILED, OR "ONLY VIOLENCE HELPS WHERE IT RULES"(1969,
Ger.), w; LOST HONOR OF KATHARINA BLUM, THE(1975, Ger.), w; WAR AND
PEACE(1983, Ger.), d&w, titles
Helen Boll
TILT(1979)
Peter Bollag
MOTHER KUSTERS GOES TO HEAVEN(1976, Ger.)
Margaret Bolland
GREYFRIARS BOBBY(1961, Brit.), cos
Michael Bolland
TRIAL OF BILLY JACK, THE(1974)
T. Bolland
LAST BLITZKRIEG, THE(1958)
Letitia Bollante
WHITE SLAVE SHIP(1962, Fr./Ital.)
Philip Bollard
LAST REMAKE OF BEAU GESTE, THE(1977)
Charles Bollender
GIRL ON THE RUN(1961)
Florence C. Bolles
Silents
FALSE FRIEND, THE(1917), w; FAIR PRETENDER, THE(1918), w
Andre Bollet
BORSALINO(1970, Fr.)
Danielle Bollettieri
SPRING FEVER(1983, Can.)
Angie Bolling
1984
RIVER RAT, THE(1984)
Claude Bolling
WORLD IN MY POCKET, THE(1962, Fr./Ital./Ger.), m, md; DAY AND THE HOUR,
THE(1963, Fr./ Ital.), m; HANDS OF ORLAC, THE(1964, Brit./Fr.), m; WEB OF
FEAR(1966, Fr./Span.), m; BORSALINO(1970, Fr.), m; CATCH ME A SPY(1971,
Brit./Fr.), m; BORSALINO AND CO.(1974, Fr.), m; MAGNIFICENT ONE, THE(1974,
Fr./Ital.), m; CALIFORNIA SUITE(1978), m; SILVER BEARS(1978), m; ANGRY
MAN, THE(1979 Fr./Can.), m; AWAKENING, THE(1980), m; THREE MEN TO DE-
STROY(1980, Fr.), m; WILLIE AND PHIL(1980), m, md
1984
BAY BOY(1984, Can.), m; LOUISIANE(1984, Fr./Can.), m
Gary Bolling
TAKING OF PELHAM ONE, TWO, THREE, THE(1974); COOL WORLD, THE(1963);
AMAZING GRACE(1974)
Misc. Talkies
LOSING GROUND(1982)
Jens Bolling
SHORT IS THE SUMMER(1968, Swed.)
Tiffany Bolling
TONY ROME(1967); MARRIAGE OF A YOUNG STOCKBROKER, THE(1971);
WICKED, WICKED(1973); WILD PARTY, THE(1975); KINGDOM OF THE SPI-
DERS(1977)
Misc. Talkies
TRIANGLE(1971); BONNIE'S KIDS(1973); CANDY SNATCHERS, THE(1974); CEN-
TERFOLD GIRLS, THE(1974)
Alan Bollinger
BEYOND REASONABLE DOUBT(1980, New Zeal.), ph
Alaun Bollinger
GOODBYE PORK PIE(1981, New Zealand), ph
Alun Bollinger
MIDDLE AGE SPREAD(1979, New Zealand), ph
1984
VIGIL(1984, New Zealand), ph
Henri Bollinger
JOHNNY FRENCHMAN(1946, Brit.); FOOLS(1970), p; MARY, MARY, BLOODY
MARY(1975, U.S./Mex.), p
Hannelore Bollmann
CONGRESS DANCES(1957, Ger.)
Michael Bollner
WILLY WONKA AND THE CHOCOLATE FACTORY(1971)
Filip Bolluyt
1984
FOURTH MAN, THE(1984, Neth.)
Adolph Bolm
MAD GENIUS, THE(1931), ch

Jean Bolo
LA GUERRE EST FINIE(1967, Fr./Swed.)

Bela Bologh
AZURE EXPRESS(1938, Hung.), d

Mauro Bologini
YOUNG HUSBANDS(1958, Ital./Fr.), w

Carmine Bologna
RED LIPS(1964, Fr./Ital.), p

Enrico Bologna
L'AVVENTURA(1960, Ital.)

Joe Bologna
COPS AND ROBBERS(1973)

Joseph Bologna
LOVERS AND OTHER STRANGERS(1970), w; MADE FOR EACH OTHER(1971), a, w; MIXED COMPANY(1974); BIG BUS, THE(1976); CHAPTER TWO(1979); MY FAVORITE YEAR(1982)
1984
BLAME IT ON RIO(1984); WOMAN IN RED, THE(1984)

Dino Bolognese
SEPTEMBER AFFAIR(1950); TOAST OF NEW ORLEANS, THE(1950); THREE COINS IN THE FOUNTAIN(1954)

Bruno Bolognesi
VAMPIRE AND THE BALLERINA, THE(1962, Ital.), p

Manola Bolognini
DJANGO(1966 Ital./Span.), p

Manolo Bolognini
TEOREMA(1969, Ital.), p; UNHOLY FOUR, THE(1969, Ital.), p; STREET PEOPLE(1976, U.S./Ital.), p

Maura Bolognini
DRAMA OF THE RICH(1975, Ital./Fr.), d, w

Mauro Bolognini
YOUNG HUSBANDS(1958, Ital./Fr.), d; FROM A ROMAN BALCONY(1961, Fr./Ital.), d; AGOSTINO(1962, Ital.), d; BELL' ANTONIO(1962, Ital.), d; LA NOTTE BRAVA(1962, Fr./Ital.), d; LA VIACCIA(1962, Fr./Ital.), d; BAMBOLE!(1965, Ital.), d; THREE FACES OF A WOMAN(1965, Ital./Fr.), d; QUEENS, THE(1968, Ital./Fr.), d; ARABELLA(1969, U.S./Ital.), d; SHE AND HE(1969, Ital.), d, w; WITCHES, THE(1969, Fr./Ital.), d; THAT SPLENDID NOVEMBER(1971, Ital./Fr.), p&d; DOWN THE ANCIENT STAIRCASE(1975, Ital.), d; LA GRANDE BOURGEOISE(1977, Ital.), d; INHERITANCE, THE(1978, Ital.), d

Patricia Bolomet
SWAMP THING(1982), cos

Massimo Bolongaro
SAMSON AND THE SEVEN MIRACLES OF THE WORLD(1963, Fr./Ital.), cos

Zhanna Bolotova
SILENCE OF DR. EVANS, THE(1973, USSR)

Piet Bolscher
BEAUTIFUL PRISONER, THE(1983, Fr.), cos

M. Bolshintsov
GREAT CITIZEN, THE(1939, USSR), w

Corps de Ballet of the Bolshoi Theater
SPRING(1948, USSR)

Bolshoi Theater Ballet
LITTLE HUMPBACKED HORSE, THE(1962, USSR)

Bolshoi Theater Chorus
TSAR'S BRIDE, THE(1966, USSR)

Alice Bolster
SILVER TOP(1938, Brit.)

Anita Bolster
GOLD MINE IN THE SKY(1938); I MARRIED AN ANGEL(1942); JOURNEY FOR MARGARET(1942); LONDON BLACKOUT MURDERS(1942); NIGHTMARE(1942); PRIDE OF THE YANKEES, THE(1942); THIS ABOVE ALL(1942); FOREVER AND A DAY(1943); HEAVEN CAN WAIT(1943); HENRY ALDRICH HAUNTS A HOUSE(1943); DOUGHGIRLS, THE(1944); GOING MY WAY(1944); LODGER, THE(1944); PASSPORT TO DESTINY(1944); THIN MAN GOES HOME, THE(1944); WHITE CLIFFS OF DOVER, THE(1944); KITTY(1945); LOST WEEKEND, THE(1945); MY NAME IS JULIA ROSS(1945); NOB HILL(1945); SCARLET STREET(1945); TWO MRS. CARROLLS, THE(1947); JUDGE STEPS OUT, THE(1949); YOU CAN'T BEAT THE IRISH(1952, Brit.); BOTANY BAY(1953)

Anita Sharp Bolster
WOULD YOU BELIEVE IT!(1930, Brit.); FLESH AND FANTASY(1943); MADAME LOUISE(1951, Brit.); HORNET'S NEST, THE(1955, Brit.); RAISING A RIOT(1957, Brit.); RISING OF THE MOON, THE(1957, Ireland); TEARS FOR SIMON(1957, Brit.); TWO GROOMS FOR A BRIDE(1957); MAN WHO LIKED FUNERALS, THE(1959, Brit.); HOUSE IN MARSH ROAD, THE(1960, Brit.); ALIVE AND KICKING(1962, Brit.); MACBETH(1963); FATHER CAME TOO(1964, Brit.); HANDS OF ORLAC, THE(1964, Brit./Fr.); PROMISE HER ANYTHING(1966, Brit.)

Joe Bolster
1984
GIRLS NIGHT OUT(1984), w

Anne Bolt
IMMORTAL GENTLEMAN(1935, Brit.)

Ben Bolt
Misc. Talkies
BLACK ISLAND(1979, Brit.), d
Silents
GAY CORINTHIAN, THE(1924), w; MUTINY(1925, Brit.), w

Charles Bolt
1984
NO SMALL AFFAIR(1984), w

David Bolt
LOST AND FOUND(1979); PHOBIA(1980, Can.); PROM NIGHT(1980); VIDEODROME(1983, Can.)

Eunice Bolt
SCREAMERS(1978, Ital.)

John Bolt
GREEK TYCOON, THE(1978)

Jonathan Bolt
EYES OF THE AMARYLLIS, THE(1982)

Patricia Bolt
1984
CANNONBALL RUN II(1984)

Robert Bolt
LAWRENCE OF ARABIA(1962, Brit.), w; DOCTOR ZHIVAGO(1965), w; MAN FOR ALL SEASONS, A(1966, Brit.), w; RYAN'S DAUGHTER(1970, Brit.), w; LADY CAROLINE LAMB(1972, Brit./Ital.), d&w
1984
BOUNTY, THE(1984), w

Stanley Bolt
HARRY IN YOUR POCKET(1973)

Peter Bolta
MOSES(1976, Brit./Ital.), ed

Murray Boltinoff
BUY ME THAT TOWN(1941), w

Lt. Comdr. A. J. Bolton
MARINES FLY HIGH, THE(1940), w

Arthur Bolton
JOURNEY TOGETHER(1946, Brit.)

Betty Bolton
WOLVES(1930, Brit.)

Clint Bolton
FOUR FOR THE MORGUE(1962)

Delle Bolton
JEREMIAH JOHNSON(1972)

Elaine Bolton
GOING BERSERK(1983)

Emily Bolton
MOONRAKER(1979, Brit.)

Fredric Bolton
WIFE TAKES A FLYER, THE(1942)

George Bolton
BOB'S YOUR UNCLE(1941, Brit.)

Gregory Bolton
WITHOUT A TRACE(1983), art d
1984
COTTON CLUB, THE(1984), art d

Guy Bolton
LOVE DOCTOR, THE(1929), w; LOVE PARADE, THE(1929), w; RIO RITA(1929), w; SALLY(1929), w; CUCKOOS, THE(1930), w; TOP SPEED(1930), w; DELICIOUS(1931), w; LADY REFUSES, THE(1931), w; TRANSATLANTIC(1931), w; YELLOW TICKET, THE(1931), w; ALMOST MARRIED(1932), w; CARELESS LADY(1932), w; DEVIL'S LOTTERY(1932), w; GIRL CRAZY(1932), w; PAINTED WOMAN(1932), w; WOMAN IN ROOM 13, THE(1932), w; PLEASURE CRUISE(1933), w; ALONG CAME SALLY(1934, Brit.), w; CAMELS ARE COMING, THE(1934, Brit.), w; LADIES SHOULD LISTEN(1934), w; LADY IS WILLING, THE(1934, Brit.), w; STRAUSS' GREAT WALTZ(1934, Brit.), w; DARK ANGEL, THE(1935), w; MAN OF THE MOMENT(1935, Brit.), w; MURDER MAN(1935), w; ANYTHING GOES(1936), w; MORALS OF MARCUS, THE(1936, Brit.), w; ANGEL(1937), w; ROSALIE(1937), w; THIS'LL MAKE YOU WHISTLE(1938, Brit.), w; GIRL CRAZY(1943), w; WEEKEND AT THE WALDORF(1945), w; ZIEGFELD FOLLIES(1945), w; TILL THE CLOUDS ROLL BY(1946), w; EASTER PARADE(1948), w; ANASTASIA(1956), w; ANYTHING GOES(1956), w; ADORABLE JULIA(1964, Fr./Aust.), w; WHEN THE BOYS MEET THE GIRLS(1965), w
Silents
OH, BOY!(1919), w; OH, LADY, LADY(1920), w; ADAM AND EVA(1923), w; SALLY(1925), w; WAGES FOR WIVES(1925), w; LADY BE GOOD(1928), w; OH, KAY(1928), w

Guy Pelham Bolton
TOO MANY HUSBANDS(1938, Brit.), w

Henry Bolton
Misc. Silents
GIRL ALASKA, THE(1919)

Irene Bolton
DRIVE A CROOKED ROAD(1954); SON OF SINBAD(1955); REVOLT OF MAMIE STOVER, THE(1956)

Joe Bolton
OUTLAWS IS COMING, THE(1965)

June Bolton
VALENTINO(1977, Brit.)

Lois Bolton
ONE, TWO, THREE(1961); LAFAYETTE(1963, Fr.)

Lyn Bolton
BLOOD FEAST(1963)

Matthew Bolton
TARZAN AND THE MERMAIDS(1948)

Michael Bolton
MOTHER LODE(1982), art d; STAR 80(1983), art d
1984
RUNAWAY(1984), art d

Muriel Ross Bolton
SPIRITUALIST, THE(1948), w

Muriel Roy Bolton
HENRY ALDRICH, EDITOR(1942), w; THIS TIME FOR KEEPS(1942), w; HENRY ALDRICH HAUNTS A HOUSE(1943), w; HENRY ALDRICH SWINGS IT(1943), w; HENRY ALDRICH, BOY SCOUT(1944), w; HENRY ALDRICH PLAYS CUPID(1944), w; MEET MISS BOBBY SOCKS(1944), w; PASSPORT TO DESTINY(1944), w; SHE'S A SWEETHEART(1944), w; YOU CAN'T RATION LOVE(1944), w; GRISSLY'S MILLIONS(1945), w; MY NAME IS JULIA ROSS(1945), w; MICKEY(1948), w; MYSTERY IN MEXICO(1948), w

Patsy Bolton
SHAMROCK HILL(1949)

Reg Bolton
SATURDAY NIGHT REVUE(1937, Brit.)

Roy Bolton
MONTE WALSH(1970), spec eff

Ruth Bolton
PERMANENT VACATION(1982)

Tim Bolton
STAGECOACH TO DANCER'S PARK(1962)

Walter Bolton
IN PRAISE OF OLDER WOMEN(1978, Can.)

Whitney Bolton
IF I HAD A MILLION(1932), w; SPIRIT OF CULVER, THE(1939), w

Ray Boltz
SKY DRAGON(1949), set d; TUNA CLIPPER(1949), set d; RING, THE(1952), set d; HE RIDES TALL(1964), set d; NIGHTMARE IN THE SUN(1964), set d; HUMAN DUPLICATORS, THE(1965), set d; RAGE TO LIVE, A(1965), set d; CURIOUS FEMALE, THE(1969), set d; GAY DECEIVERS, THE(1969), set d; RUN, ANGEL, RUN(1969), set d; DUNWICH HORROR, THE(1970), set d

Ray Boltz, Jr.
SMART WOMAN(1948), set d

Raymond G. Boltz
MODERN MARRIAGE, A(1962), set d; BALLAD OF A GUNFIGHTER(1964), set d; HAWAII(1966), set d; DESTRUCTORS, THE(1968), set d; MONEY JUNGLE, THE(1968), set d

Raymond Boltz, Jr.
MR. HEX(1946), set d; SONG OF MY HEART(1947), set d; FIGHTING MAD(1948), set d; I WOULDN'T BE IN YOUR SHOES(1948), set d; JINX MONEY(1948), set d; MYSTERY OF THE GOLDEN EYE, THE(1948), set d; SHANGHAI CHEST, THE(1948), set d; SMUGGLERS' COVE(1948), set d; STAGE STRUCK(1948), set d; TROUBLE MAKERS(1948), set d; GUN CRAZY(1949), set d; HOLD THAT BABY!(1949), set d; JOE PALOOKA IN THE BIG FIGHT(1949), set d; JOE PALOOKA IN THE COUNTER-PUNCH(1949), set d; MASTER MINDS(1949), set d; LUCKY LOSERS(1950), set d; SOUTHSIDE 1-1000(1950), set d; TRIPLE TROUBLE(1950), set d; DESERT HELL(1958), set d

Geza M. Bolvary
NUMBER SEVENTEEN(1928, Brit./Ger.), d&w

Silents
GHOST TRAIN, THE(1927, Brit.), d

Misc. Silents
GHOST TRAIN, THE(1927, Brit.), d; WRECKER, THE(1928, Brit.), d

Jean Bolvary
THINGS OF LIFE, THE(1970, Fr./Ital./Switz.), p

June Bolyn
NIGHTMARE ALLEY(1947)

Ray Bolz
CASE OF PATTY SMITH, THE(1962), set d

Adrian Bolzoni
COBRA, THE(1968), w

Adriano Bolzoni
SLAVE, THE(1963, Ital.), w; MINNESOTA CLAY(1966, Ital./Fr./Span.), w; RINGO AND HIS GOLDEN PISTOL(1966, Ital.), w; SPY IN YOUR EYE(1966, Ital.), w; VERY HANDY MAN, A(1966, Fr./Ital.), w; GLASS SPHINX, THE(1968, Egypt/Ital./Span.), w; SONNY AND JED(1974, Ital.), w; HUMANOID, THE(1979, Ital.), w

Andriano Bolzoni
BRIEF RAPTURE(1952, Ital.), w

Anja Boman
LOVING COUPLES(1966, Swed.)

Barbara Boman
WHERE ANGELS GO...TROUBLE FOLLOWS(1968)

Herry Boman
MAN WHO CRIED WOLF, THE(1937)

Mirko Boman
TREASURE OF SILVER LAKE(1965, Fr./Ger./Yugo.); LAST OF THE RENEGA-DES(1966, Fr./Ital./Ger./Yugo.)

Rolf Boman
HERE'S YOUR LIFE(1968, Swed.), art d

Renato Bomarsi
TARTARS, THE(1962, Ital./Yugo.), makeup

Jack Bomay
SOLOMON KING(1974), d

Enrico Bomba
YOUNG REBEL, THE(1969, Fr./Ital./Span.), w

The Bombardiers
FOLLOW THE BAND(1943)

Bombolo
CRIME AT PORTA ROMANA(1980, Ital.)

Angela Bomford
HOT STUFF(1979); HARDLY WORKING(1981)

Jean Bommart
CONTINENTAL EXPRESS(1939, Brit.), w

Valentino Bompiani
LA NOTTE(1961, Fr./Ital.)

Ulla Bomser
TELL ME THAT YOU LOVE ME, JUNIE MOON(1970)

Jean-Marie Bon
SUCKER, THE(1966, Fr./Ital.)

Lillian Bon
SNIPER, THE(1952)

Richard Bon
ANGELS OVER BROADWAY(1940)

Sheila Bon
CURSE OF THE STONE HAND(1965, Mex/Chile)

Nick Bon Tempi
MAGIC SWORD, THE(1962)

Paul Bon Tempi
MAGIC SWORD, THE(1962)

Giampiero Bona
LADY OF MONZA, THE(1970, Ital.), w

Micheline Bona
MURMUR OF THE HEART(1971, Fr./Ital./Ger.)

Ronaldo Bonacchi
LUNA(1979, Ital.)

Anna Bonacci
KISS ME, STUPID(1964), w

Carmen Bonacci
WHAT'S UP FRONT(1964)

Paolo Bonacelli
MIDNIGHT EXPRESS(1978, Brit.); NEST OF VIPERS(1979, Ital.)

Paoloa Bonacelli
INHERITANCE, THE(1978, Ital.)

Senta Bonacker
TINDER BOX, THE(1968, E. Ger.)

Enrico Bonacorti
CAGLIOSTRO(1975, Ital.), w

Elio Bonadonna
MONSIGNOR(1982)

Giovanni Bonadonna
MONSIGNOR(1982)

Danny Bonaduce
CHARLOTTE'S WEB(1973); BAKER'S HAWK(1976); CORVETTE SUMMER(1978); H.O.T.S.(1979)

Jay Bonafield
TATTOOED STRANGER, THE(1950), p; LOUISIANA TERRITORY(1953), p

Gianni Bonagura
DAMON AND PYTHIAS(1962); FIASCO IN MILAN(1963, Fr./Ital.); PASSIONATE THIEF, THE(1963, Ital.)

Catalina Bonaki
BYE-BYE BRASIL(1980, Braz.)

Denis Bonan
DAUGHTERS OF DARKNESS(1971, Bel./ Fr./ Ger./ Ital.), ed

Luciano Bonanni
KISS THE OTHER SHEIK(1968, Fr./Ital.)

Roberto Bonanni
INVESTIGATION OF A CITIZEN ABOVE SUSPICION(1970, Ital.)

Leslie Bonano
HARD TIMES(1975)

Fortunio Bonanova
CARELESS LADY(1932); SUCCESSFUL CALAMITY, A(1932); ROMANCE IN THE DARK(1938); TROPIC HOLIDAY(1938); DOWN ARGENTINE WAY(1940); I WAS AN ADVENTURESS(1940); MARK OF ZORRO, THE(1940); BLOOD AND SAND(1941); CITIZEN KANE(1941); FOUR JACKS AND A JILL(1941); MOON OVER MIAMI(1941); MR. AND MRS. NORTH(1941); OBLIGING YOUNG LADY(1941); THAT NIGHT IN RIO(1941); THEY MET IN ARGENTINA(1941); TWO LATINS FROM MANHAT-TAN(1941); UNFINISHED BUSINESS(1941); YANK IN THE R.A.F., A(1941); BLACK SWAN, THE(1942); GIRL TROUBLE(1942); LARCENY, INC.(1942); SING YOUR WORRIES AWAY(1942); DIXIE(1943); FIVE GRAVES TO CAIRO(1943); FOR WHOM THE BELL TOLLS(1943); HELLO, FRISCO, HELLO(1943); SULTAN'S DAUGHTER, THE(1943); ALI BABA AND THE FORTY THIEVES(1944); BRAZIL(1944); DOUBLE INDEMNITY(1944); GOING MY WAY(1944); MRS. PARKINGTON(1944); MY BEST GAL(1944); BELL FOR ADANO, A(1945); HIT THE HAY(1945); MAN ALIVE(1945); WHERE DO WE GO FROM HERE?(1945); MONSIEUR BEAUCAIRE(1946); RED DRAGON, THE(1946); FIESTA(1947); FUGITIVE, THE(1947); ANGEL ON THE AMA-ZON(1948); ROMANCE ON THE HIGH SEAS(1948); ADVENTURES OF DON JUAN(1949); BAD MEN OF TOMBSTONE(1949); WHIRLPOOL(1949); NANCY GOES TO RIO(1950); SEPTEMBER AFFAIR(1950); HAVANA ROSE(1951); CONQUEST OF COCHISE(1953); MOON IS BLUE, THE(1953); SECOND CHANCE(1953); SO THIS IS LOVE(1953); THUNDER BAY(1953); KISS ME DEADLY(1955); NEW YORK CONFI-DENTIAL(1955); JAGUAR(1956); AFFAIR TO REMEMBER, AN(1957); SAGA OF HEMP BROWN, THE(1958); THUNDER IN THE SUN(1959); RUNNING MAN, THE(1963, Brit.)

Misc. Talkies
ROSE OF SANTA ROSA(1947)

Ivan Bonar
AIR PATROL(1962); WOMAN HUNT(1962); POLICE NURSE(1963); LOVE AND KISSES(1965); MARYJANE(1968); PROJECT X(1968); MAC ARTHUR(1977); SAME TIME, NEXT YEAR(1978); T.A.G.: THE ASSASSINATION GAME(1982)

Jack Bonar
NOTHING BUT TROUBLE(1944), set d; WEEKEND AT THE WALDORF(1945), set d; EASY TO WED(1946), set d; TO PLEASE A LADY(1950), set d

Augusto Bonardi
WAKE UP AND DIE(1967, Fr./Ital.)

Carla Bonavera
DAMON AND PYTHIAS(1962)

Mike Bonavia
IT FELL FROM THE SKY(1980)

Tracy Bonbrest
MONSIGNOR(1982)

M. Bonch-Tomashevsky
Misc. Silents
THIEF(1916, USSR), d

Claude Boncompain
BELLMAN, THE(1947, Fr.), w

Alicia Bond
1984
BREAKIN' 2: ELECTRIC BOOGALOO(1984)

Anson Bond
JUDGE, THE(1949), p, w; NOT WANTED(1949), p; VICIOUS YEARS, THE(1950), p; JOURNEY INTO LIGHT(1951), p, w; JAPANESE WAR BRIDE(1952), w; CHINA VENTURE(1953), p, w; UNWED MOTHER(1958), w

Betsy Bond
VALLEY GIRL(1983)

Bill Bond
WHITE LIGHTNING(1973)

Brenda Bond
Misc. Silents
RAINBOW RILEY(1926)

Bryce Bond
WINDOWS(1980)

David Bond
SILENCERS, THE(; CIGARETTE GIRL(1947); DOUBLE LIFE, A(1947); LATE GEORGE APLEY, THE(1947); PRIVATE AFFAIRS OF BEL AMI, THE(1947); JOAN OF ARC(1948); THAT LADY IN ERMINE(1948); SONG OF INDIA(1949); TARZAN'S MAGIC FOUNTAIN(1949); WE WERE STRANGERS(1949); IN A LONELY PLA-CE(1950); GREAT CARUSO, THE(1951); MASK OF THE AVENGER(1951); SIROC-

CO(1951); SWORD OF MONTE CRISTO, THE(1951); GOLDEN HAWK, THE(1952); MY SON, JOHN(1952); FIGHTER ATTACK(1953); JULIUS CAESAR(1953); THREE SAILORS AND A GIRL(1953); SILVER CHALICE, THE(1954); LUST FOR LIFE(1956); RUMBLE ON THE DOCKS(1956); ISTANBUL(1957); STORY OF MANKIND, THE(1957); 27TH DAY, THE(1957); GUN FEVER(1958); MARRIED TOO YOUNG(1962); HOUSE CALLS(1978); IN GOD WE TRUST(1980)

Denville Bond
CONQUEST OF THE AIR(1940)

Derek Bond
LOVES OF JOANNA GODDEN, THE(1947, Brit.); NICHOLAS NICKLEBY(1947, Brit.); BROKEN JOURNEY(1948, Brit.); CAPTIVE HEART, THE(1948, Brit.); CHRISTOPHER COLUMBUS(1949, Brit.); MARRY ME!(1949, Brit.); POET'S PUB(1949, Brit.); SCOTT OF THE ANTARCTIC(1949, Brit.); WEAKER SEX, THE(1949, Brit.); INHERITANCE, THE(1951, Brit.); QUIET WOMAN, THE(1951, Brit.); TONY DRAWS A HORSE(1951, Brit.); CARETAKERS DAUGHTER, THE(1952, Brit.); DISTANT TRUMPET(1952, Brit.); HOUR OF THIRTEEN, THE(1952); STRANGER FROM VENUS, THE(1954, Brit.); TALE OF THREE WOMEN, A(1954, Brit.); THREE CORNERED FATE(1954, Brit.); SVENGALI(1955, Brit.); TROUBLE IN STORE(1955, Brit.); ROGUE'S YARN(1956, Brit.); HIGH TERRACE(1957, Brit.); STORMY CROSSING(1958, Brit.); GIDEON OF SCOTLAND YARD(1959, Brit.); HAND, THE(1960, Brit.); SATURDAY NIGHT OUT(1964, Brit.); SWINGER'S PARADISE(1965, Brit.); PRESS FOR TIME(1966, Brit.); SECRETS OF A WINDMILL GIRL(1966, Brit.); WHEN EIGHT BELLS TOLL(1971, Brit.)
Misc. Talkies
BLACK TIDE(1958)

Diane Bond
PAJAMA PARTY(1964); SWINGIN' SUMMER, A(1965); HOUSE OF 1,000 DOLLS(1967, Ger./Span./Brit.); IN LIKE FLINT(1967)

Edward Bond
BLOW-UP(1966, Brit.), w; NICHOLAS AND ALEXANDRA(1971, Brit.), w; WALKABOUT(1971, Aus./U.S.), w

Eric Bond
BATTLE STATIONS(1956)

Fred Bond
Silents
FICKLE WOMEN(1920)

Fred C. Bond
SAMURAI(1945)

Frederick Bond
Misc. Silents
SHE DEVIL, THE(1918)

Gary Bond
ZULU(1964, Brit.); ANNE OF THE THOUSAND DAYS(1969, Brit.); OUTBACK(1971, Aus.)

Geoffrey Bond
DARK MAN, THE(1951, Brit.); BLOW YOUR OWN TRUMPET(1958, Brit.), w; HEADLINE HUNTERS(1968, Brit.), w

Graham Bond
PRIVATE COLLECTION(1972, Aus.); FATTY FINN(1980, Aus.), m

Grahame Bond
THREE TO GO(1971, Aus.), a, m; TRUE STORY OF ESKIMO NELL, THE(1975, Aus.)

Guy Bond
BETWEEN THE LINES(1977); TICKET TO HEAVEN(1981)

Jack Bond
SEPARATION(1968, Brit.), p&d; OTHER SIDE OF THE UNDERNEATH, THE(1972, Brit.), p, ph; ANTI-CLOCK(1980), p, d

James Bond
TRICK BABY(1973), m

James Bond III
FISH THAT SAVED PITTSBURGH, THE(1979)
1984
GO TELL IT ON THE MOUNTAIN(1984)

Jane Bond
1984
PRIVATES ON PARADE(1984, Brit.), cos

Janice Bond
KENNER(1969), cos

John Bond
SIX LESSONS FROM MADAME LA ZONGA(1941); KANSAS CITY KITTY(1944)

Johnny Bond
SAGA OF DEATH VALLEY(1939); STICK TO YOUR GUNS(1941); COWBOY COMMANDOS(1943); OLD CHISHOLM TRAIL(1943); ROBIN HOOD OF THE RANGE(1943); RIDING WEST(1944); SINCE YOU WENT AWAY(1944); GALLANT BESS(1946)

Joy Bond
IF EVER I SEE YOU AGAIN(1978)

Julian Bond
WITNESS, THE(1959, Brit.), w; MAN OUTSIDE, THE(1968, Brit.), w; DIRTY KNIGHT'S WORK(1976, Brit.), w; GREASED LIGHTNING(1977)

Lee Bond
LAND OF THE OPEN RANGE(1941), w

Leland Bond
1984
TOY SOLDIERS(1984), m

Lenore Bond
INVASION OF THE STAR CREATURES(1962)

Lilian Bond
JUST A GIGOLO(1931); HIGH PRESSURE(1932); DOUBLE HARNESS(1933); PICKUP(1933); HOUSEKEEPER'S DAUGHTER(1939); SCOTLAND YARD(1941); THAT FORSYTE WOMAN(1949)

Lillian Bond
SAGEBRUSH POLITICS(1930); RIDER OF THE PLAINS(1931); SQUAW MAN, THE(1931); AIR MAIL(1932); BEAUTY AND THE BOSS(1932); FIREMAN, SAVE MY CHILD(1932); HOT SATURDAY(1932); IT'S TOUGH TO BE FAMOUS(1932); MAN ABOUT TOWN(1932); OLD DARK HOUSE, THE(1932); TRIAL OF VIVIENNE WARE, THE(1932); UNION DEPOT(1932); BIG BRAIN, THE(1933); BISHOP MISBEHAVES, THE(1933); HER SPLENDID FOLLY(1933); HOT PEPPER(1933); TAKE A CHANCE(1933); WHEN STRANGERS MARRY(1933); AFFAIRS OF A GENTLEMAN(1934); DIRTY WORK(1934, Brit.); HELL BENT FOR LOVE(1934); CHINA SEAS(1935); BLOND CHEAT(1938); WOMEN, THE(1939); SUED FOR LIBEL(1940); WESTERNER,

THE(1940); DESPERATE CHANCE FOR ELLERY QUEEN, A(1942); TRAGEDY AT MIDNIGHT, A(1942); PICTURE OF DORIAN GRAY, THE(1945); JOLSON STORY, THE(1946); NOCTURNE(1946); MAN IN THE ATTIC(1953); MAZE, THE(1953); PIRATES OF TRIPOLI(1955)
Misc. Talkies
STEPPING OUT(1931)

Margery Bond
WEDDING, A(1978); PERFECT COUPLE, A(1979); ENDANGERED SPECIES(1982)
1984
CHOOSE ME(1984)

Michael Bond
WINTER KILLS(1979); SILKWOOD(1983)

Philip Bond
COUNT FIVE AND DIE(1958, Brit.); ORDERS TO KILL(1958, Brit.); I WANT WHAT I WANT(1972, Brit.)

Raleigh Bond
ONION FIELD, THE(1979); BLACK MARBLE, THE(1980); ALL NIGHT LONG(1981); PENNIES FROM HEAVEN(1981); POSTMAN ALWAYS RINGS TWICE, THE(1981); BEST LITTLE WHOREHOUSE IN TEXAS, THE(1982); NIGHTMARES(1983)

Ralph Bond
DON'T PANIC CHAPS!(1959, Brit.), p; DEAD LUCKY(1960, Brit.), p

Ray Bond
RHYTHM IN THE CLOUDS(1937), w

Raymond Bond
BURNING CROSS, THE(1947); CANON CITY(1948); FOREIGN AFFAIR, A(1948); JOAN OF ARC(1948); JUNE BRIDE(1948); IMPACT(1949); SO DEAR TO MY HEART(1949); SPECIAL AGENT(1949); STATE DEPARTMENT-FILE 649(1949); WOMAN'S SECRET, A(1949); LIGHTNING GUNS(1950); OUTRAGE(1950); RETURN OF THE FRONTIERSMAN(1950); TICKET TO TOMAHAWK(1950); JOURNEY INTO LIGHT(1951); MAN FROM PLANET X, THE(1951); SOMETHING TO LIVE FOR(1952)
Misc. Silents
IN MIZZOURA(1914)

Rene Bond
INSIDE AMY(1975); FANTASM(1976, Aus.)
Misc. Talkies
COUNTRY CUZZINS(1972); PLEASE DON'T EAT MY MOTHER(1972); FUGITIVE GIRLS(1975); COCKTAIL HOSTESSES, THE(1976); PANAMA RED(1976)

Richard Bond
SCOUNDREL, THE(1935); CONDEMNED WOMEN(1938); DOUBLE DANGER(1938); LAW OF THE UNDERWORLD(1938); SISTERS, THE(1938); TORCHY BLANE IN CHINATOWN(1938); BOY FRIEND(1939); DARK VICTORY(1939); HERE I AM A STRANGER(1939); KING OF THE UNDERWORLD(1939); SECRET SERVICE OF THE AIR(1939); THEY MADE ME A CRIMINAL(1939); WOMEN IN THE WIND(1939); DEVIL'S ISLAND(1940); I'LL SELL MY LIFE(1941); YOU'RE OUT OF LUCK(1941); SAINTED SISTERS, THE(1948); CRY OF THE PENGUINS(1972, Brit.)

Rudy Bond
TAKING OF PELHAM ONE, TWO, THREE, THE(1974); STREETCAR NAMED DESIRE, A(1951); MISS SADIE THOMPSON(1953); ON THE WATERFRONT(1954); NIGHTFALL(1956); BROTHERS RICO, THE(1957); HARD MAN, THE(1957); 12 ANGRY MEN(1957); RUN SILENT, RUN DEEP(1958); MIDDLE OF THE NIGHT(1959); BECAUSE THEY'RE YOUNG(1960); BUTTERFIELD 8(1960); MOUNTAIN ROAD, THE(1960); MOVE(1970); WHO IS HARRY KELLERMAN AND WHY IS HE SAYING THOSE TERRIBLE THINGS ABOUT ME?(1971); GODFATHER, THE(1972); ROSE, THE(1979)

Sheila Bond
MARRYING KIND, THE(1952); SPIRIT OF ST. LOUIS, THE(1957)
1984
BROADWAY DANNY ROSE(1984)

Sidonie Bond
DARLING(1965, Brit.); WILD AFFAIR, THE(1966, Brit.); SUBURBAN WIVES(1973, Brit.)

Steve Bond
CAT MURKIL AND THE SILKS(1976); MASSACRE AT CENTRAL HIGH(1976); H.O.T.S.(1979)
1984
PREY, THE(1984)
Misc. Talkies
GAS PUMP GIRLS(1979)

Steven Bond
TARZAN AND THE JUNGLE BOY(1968, US/Switz.)

Sudie Bond
GUNS OF THE TREES(1964); DOUBLE-BARRELLED DETECTIVE STORY, THE(1965); TIGER MAKES OUT, THE(1967); VIRGIN PRESIDENT, THE(1968); LOVE STORY(1970); COLD TURKEY(1971); JUMP(1971); THEY MIGHT BE GIANTS(1971); TOMORROW(1972); WHERE THE LILIES BLOOM(1974); COME BACK TO THE 5 & DIME, JIMMY DEAN, JIMMY DEAN(1982); I AM THE CHEESE(1983); SILKWOOD(1983)
1984
JOHNNY DANGEROUSLY(1984); SWING SHIFT(1984)

Sue Bond
SECRETS OF SEX(1970, Brit.); O LUCKY MAN!(1973, Brit.)

Timothy Bond
HAPPY BIRTHDAY TO ME(1981), w
Misc. Talkies
DEADLY HARVEST(1972), d

Tommy Bond
KID MILLIONS(1934); HIDEAWAY(1937); MARRIED BEFORE BREAKFAST(1937); ROSALIE(1937); CITY STREETS(1938); FIVE LITTLE PEPPERS AND HOW THEY GREW(1939); FIVE LITTLE PEPPERS AT HOME(1940); FIVE LITTLE PEPPERS IN TROUBLE(1940); LITTLE BIT OF HEAVEN, A(1940); OUT WEST WITH THE PEPPERS(1940); ADVENTURE IN WASHINGTON(1941); NEW YORK TOWN(1941); THIS LAND IS MINE(1943); MAN FROM FRISCO(1944); BEAUTIFUL CHEAT, THE(1946); GAS HOUSE KIDS GO WEST(1947); GAS HOUSE KIDS IN HOLLYWOOD(1947); HOT ROD(1950); CALL ME MISTER(1951)

Trevor Bond
MOUSE ON THE MOON, THE(1963, Brit.), anim

Ward Bond
TIME OF YOUR LIFE, THE(1948); SALUTE(1929); WORDS AND MUSIC(1929); BIG TRAIL, THE(1930); BORN RECKLESS(1930); QUICK MILLIONS(1931); FLESH(1932); HELLO TROUBLE(1932); HIGH SPEED(1932); RACKETY RAX(1932); TRIAL OF

VIVIENNE WARE, THE(1932); VIRTUE(1932); WHITE EAGLE(1932); HEROES FOR SALE(1933); LUCKY DEVILS(1933); OBEY THE LAW(1933); POLICE CAR 17(1933); SUNDOWN RIDER, THE(1933); UNKNOWN VALLEY(1933); WHEN STRANGERS MARRY(1933); WILD BOYS OF THE ROAD(1933); WRECKER, THE(1933); AGAINST THE LAW(1934); CHAINED(1934); CRIME OF HELEN STANLEY(1934); FIGHTING CODE, THE(1934); FIGHTING RANGER, THE(1934); FRONTIER MARSHAL(1934); GIRL IN DANGER(1934); HERE COMES THE GROOM(1934); HUMAN SIDE, THE(1934); IT HAPPENED ONE NIGHT(1934); MAN'S GAME, A(1934); MEN OF THE NIGHT(1934); MOST PRECIOUS THING IN LIFE(1934); POOR RICH, THE(1934); STRAIGHTAWAY(1934); VOICE IN THE NIGHT(1934); WHIRLPOOL(1934); BLACK FURY(1935); CRIMSON TRAIL, THE(1935); DEVIL DOGS OF THE AIR(1935); FIGHTING SHADOWS(1935); G-MEN(1935); GUARD THAT GIRL(1935); HEADLINE WOMAN, THE(1935); HIS NIGHT OUT(1935); JUSTICE OF THE RANGE(1935); LAST DAYS OF POMPEII, THE(1935); LITTLE BIG SHOT(1935); MURDER IN THE FLEET(1935); SHE GETS HER MAN(1935); TOO TOUGH TO KILL(1935); WATERFRONT LADY(1935); WESTERN COURAGE(1935); AVENGING WATERS(1936); BRIDE WALKS OUT, THE(1936); CATTLE THIEF, THE(1936); COLLEEN(1936); CRASH DONOVAN(1936); FATAL LADY(1936); FURY(1936); GORGEOUS HUSSY, THE(1936); LEATHERNECKS HAVE LANDED, THE(1936); LEGION OF TERROR(1936); MAN WHO LIVED TWICE(1936); MUSS 'EM UP(1936); PRIDE OF THE MARINES(1936); SECOND WIFE(1936); THEY MET IN A TAXI(1936); WE'RE ONLY HUMAN(1936); WITHOUT ORDERS(1936); CONFLICT(1937); DEAD END(1937); DEVIL'S PLAYGROUND(1937); ESCAPE BY NIGHT(1937); FIGHT FOR YOUR LADY(1937); FIGHT TO THE FINISH, A(1937); GO-GETTER, THE(1937); MOUNTAIN MUSIC(1937); MUSIC FOR MADAME(1937); NIGHT KEY(1937); PARK AVENUE LOGGER(1937); SINGING MARINE, THE(1937); WILDCATTER, THE(1937); YOU ONLY LIVE ONCE(1937); 23 ½ HOURS LEAVE(1937); ADVENTURES OF MARCO POLO, THE(1938); AMAZING DR. CLITTERHOUSE, THE(1938); BORN TO BE WILD(1938); BRINGING UP BABY(1938); GUN LAW(1938); HAWAII CALLS(1938); LAW WEST OF TOMBSTONE, THE(1938); MR. MOTO'S GAMBLE(1938); OF HUMAN HEARTS(1938); OVER THE WALL(1938); PENITENTIARY(1938); PRISON BREAK(1938); PROFESSOR BEWARE(1938); REFORMATORY(1938); SUBMARINE PATROL(1938); YOU CAN'T TAKE IT WITH YOU(1938); CISCO KID AND THE LADY, THE(1939); CONFESSIONS OF A NAZI SPY(1939); DODGE CITY(1939); DRUMS ALONG THE MOHAWK(1939); FRONTIER MARSHAL(1939); GIRL FROM MEXICO, THE(1939); GOING PLACES(1939); GONE WITH THE WIND(1939); HEAVEN WITH A BARBED WIRE FENCE(1939); KID FROM KOKOMO, THE(1939); MADE FOR EACH OTHER(1939); MR. MOTO IN DANGER ISLAND(1939); OKLAHOMA KID, THE(1939); PARDON OUR NERVE(1939); RETURN OF THE CISCO KID(1939); SON OF FRANKENSTEIN(1939); THEY MADE ME A CRIMINAL(1939); TROUBLE IN SUNDOWN(1939); WATERFRONT(1939); YOUNG MR. LINCOLN(1939); BUCK BENNY RIDES AGAIN(1940); GRAPES OF WRATH(1940); KIT CARSON(1940); LITTLE OLD NEW YORK(1940); LONG VOYAGE HOME, THE(1940); MORTAL STORM, THE(1940); SAILOR'S LADY(1940); SANTA FE TRAIL(1940); VIRGINIA CITY(1940); DOCTORS DON'T TELL(1941); MALTESE FALCON, THE(1941); MAN BETRAYED, A(1941); MANPOWER(1941); SERGEANT YORK(1941); SHEPHERD OF THE HILLS, THE(1941); SWAMP WATER(1941); TOBACCO ROAD(1941); FALCON TAKES OVER, THE(1942); GENTLEMAN JIM(1942); HITLER—DEAD OR ALIVE(1942); IN THIS OUR LIFE(1942); SIN TOWN(1942); TEN GENTLEMEN FROM WEST POINT(1942); WILD BILL HICKOK RIDES(1942); GUY NAMED JOE, A(1943); HELLO, FRISCO, HELLO(1943); SLIGHTLY DANGEROUS(1943); THEY CAME TO BLOW UP AMERICA(1943); HOME IN INDIANA(1944); SULLIVANS, THE(1944); TALL IN THE SADDLE(1944); DAKOTA(1945); THEY WERE EXPENDABLE(1945); CANYON PASSAGE(1946); IT'S A WONDERFUL LIFE(1946); MY DARLING CLEMENTINE(1946); FUGITIVE, THE(1947); UNCONQUERED(1947); FORT APACHE(1948); JOAN OF ARC(1948); TAP ROOTS(1948); THREE GODFATHERS, THE(1948); GREAT MISSOURI RAID, THE(1950); KISS TOMORROW GOODBYE(1950); RIDING HIGH(1950); SINGING GUNS(1950); WAGONMASTER(1950); ON DANGEROUS GROUND(1951); ONLY THE VALIANT(1951); OPERATION PACIFIC(1951); HELLGATE(1952); QUIET MAN, THE(1952); THUNDERBIRDS(1952); BLOWING WILD(1953); HONDO(1953); MOONLIGHTER, THE(1953); BOB MATHIAS STORY, THE(1954); GYPSY COLT(1954); JOHNNY GUITAR(1954); LONG GRAY LINE, THE(1955); MAN ALONE, A(1955); MISTER ROBERTS(1955); DAKOTA INCIDENT(1956); PILLARS OF THE SKY(1956); SEARCHERS, THE(1956); HALLIDAY BRAND, THE(1957); WINGS OF EAGLES, THE(1957); CHINA DOLL(1958); ALIAS JESSE JAMES(1959); RIO BRAVO(1959)

Misc. Talkies
NUMBERED WOMAN(1938)

Nicholas Bond-Owen
1984
LASSITER(1984)

I. Bondar
TRAIN GOES TO KIEV, THE(1961, USSR); OPTIMISTIC TRAGEDY, THE(1964, USSR)

Bondarchuk
MEXICO IN FLAMES(1982, USSR/Mex./Ital.), w

Nathalie Bondarchuk
SOLARIS(1972, USSR)

Semyon Bondarchuk
DREAM OF A COSSACK(1982, USSR)

Sergei Bondarchuk
OTHELLO(1960, U.S.S.R.); WAR AND PEACE(1968, USSR), a, p&d, w; WATERLOO(1970, Ital./USSR), d, w; BATTLE OF THE NERETVA(1971, Yugo./Ital./Ger.); UNCLE VANYA(1972, USSR); SILENCE OF DR. EVANS, THE(1973, USSR); MEXICO IN FLAMES(1982, USSR/Mex./Ital.), d

Sergey Bondarchuk
DESTINY OF A MAN(1961, USSR), a, d; SUMMER TO REMEMBER, A(1961, USSR)

Wally Bondarenko
DEAD ZONE, THE(1983)
1984
POLICE ACADEMY(1984)

Yura Bondarenko
WELCOME KOSTYA!(1965, USSR)

Vitalik Bondarev
CLEAR SKIES(1963, USSR)

Vladimir Bondarev
SILENCE OF DR. EVANS, THE(1973, USSR), ph

Yu. Bondarev
FORTY-NINE DAYS(1964, USSR), w

Gertrude Bondhill
Misc. Silents
SINS THAT YE SIN, THE(1915); AWAKENING OF BESS MORTON, THE(1916); MISS ARIZONA(1919)

Alex Bondi
Silents
ITALIAN STRAW HAT, AN(1927, Fr.)

Beulah Bondi
ARROWSMITH(1931); STREET SCENE(1931); RAIN(1932); CHRISTOPHER BEAN(1933); STRANGER'S RETURN(1933); FINISHING SCHOOL(1934); PAINTED VEIL, THE(1934); READY FOR LOVE(1934); REGISTERED NURSE(1934); TWO ALONE(1934); BAD BOY(1935); GOOD FAIRY, THE(1935); CASE AGAINST MRS. AMES, THE(1936); GORGEOUS HUSSY, THE(1936); HEARTS DIVIDED(1936); MOON'S OUR HOME, THE(1936); THE INVISIBLE RAY(1936); TRAIL OF THE LONESOME PINE, THE(1936); MAID OF SALEM(1937); MAKE WAY FOR TOMORROW(1937); BUCCANEER, THE(1938); OF HUMAN HEARTS(1938); SISTERS, THE(1938); VIVACIOUS LADY(1938); MR. SMITH GOES TO WASHINGTON(1939); UNDER-PUP, THE(1939); CAPTAIN IS A LADY, THE(1940); OUR TOWN(1940); REMEMBER THE NIGHT(1940); ONE FOOT IN HEAVEN(1941); PENNY SERENADE(1941); SHEPHERD OF THE HILLS, THE(1941); TONIGHT WE RAID CALAIS(1943); WATCH ON THE RHINE(1943); AND NOW TOMORROW(1944); I LOVE A SOLDIER(1944); OUR HEARTS WERE YOUNG AND GAY(1944); SHE'S A SOLDIER TOO(1944); VERY THOUGHT OF YOU, THE(1944); BACK TO BATAAN(1945); SOUTHERNER, THE(1945); BREAKFAST IN HOLLYWOOD(1946); IT'S A WONDERFUL LIFE(1946); SISTER KENNY(1946); HIGH CONQUEST(1947); SAINTED SISTERS, THE(1948); SNAKE PIT, THE(1948); LIFE OF RILEY, THE(1949); MR. SOFT TOUCH(1949); SO DEAR TO MY HEART(1949); FURIES, THE(1950); LONE STAR(1952); LATIN LOVERS(1953); TRACK OF THE CAT(1954); BACK FROM ETERNITY(1956); UNHOLY WIFE, THE(1957); BIG FISHERMAN, THE(1959); SUMMER PLACE, A(1959); TAMMY, TELL ME TRUE(1961); WONDERFUL WORLD OF THE BROTHERS ERIMM, THE(1962); TAMMY AND THE DOCTOR(1963)

Francesca Bondi
GOLDEN MADONNA, THE(1949, Brit.)

I. Bondin
NO GREATER LOVE(1944, USSR), w

Ivan Bondin
DREAM COME TRUE, A(1963, USSR), w

V. Bondina
KIEV COMEDY, A(1963, USSR), ed

Rikke Bondo
1984
ZAPPA(1984, Den.)

Robert Bondrioz
Misc. Silents
IN THE SPIDER'S WEB(1924), d

Bill Bonds
ESCAPE FROM THE PLANET OF THE APES(1971)

Gary "U.S." Bonds
RING-A-DING RHYTHM(1962, Brit.)

Gigi Bonds
MARCH OR DIE(1977, Brit.)

Dave Bondu
TELL ME IN THE SUNLIGHT(1967)

Bob Bondurant
GRAND PRIX(1966)

Luc Bondy
GERMAN SISTERS, THE(1982, Ger.)

Selda Bondy
FRIENDS AND HUSBANDS(1983, Ger.)

Ben Bone
BRIGHT LEAF(1950), set d; MEXICAN MANHUNT(1953), set d; LOOPHOLE(1954), set d

Ben S. Bone
BIG CAT, THE(1949), set d

Benjamin S. Bone
RIDING SHOTGUN(1954), set d

Stephen Bone
KADOYNG(1974, Brit.)

Richard Bonehill
1984
TOP SECRET!(1984)

Richard Bonelli
ENTER MADAME(1935); THERE'S MAGIC IN MUSIC(1941)

William Bonelli
Misc. Silents
AMERICAN GENTLEMAN, AN(1915)

Samuel Bonello
STRICTLY DISHONORABLE(1931)

Peter Bonerz
FUNNYMAN(1967), a, w; MEDIUM COOL(1969); WHAT EVER HAPPENED TO AUNT ALICE?(1969); CATCH-22(1970); JENNIFER ON MY MIND(1971); FUZZ(1972); SERIAL(1980); NOBODY'S PERFEKT(1981), a, d

Brother Bones
YES SIR, MR. BONES(1951)

Chesley Bonestell
WAR OF THE WORLDS, THE(1953), spec eff; CONQUEST OF SPACE(1955), w, art d

Charles Bonet
Misc. Talkies
SUPER WEAPON, THE(1976)

Charlie Bonet
DON'T GO IN THE HOUSE(1980)

Nai Bonet
DIARY OF A BACHELOR(1964); JOHN GOLDFARB, PLEASE COME HOME(1964); SPY WITH A COLD NOSE, THE(1966, Brit.); DEVIL'S ANGELS(1967); SOUL OF NIGGER CHARLEY, THE(1973); GREATEST, THE(1977, U.S./Brit.); NOCTURNA(1979)

Emery Bonett
GIRL MUST LIVE, A(1941, Brit.), w
Eddie Bonette
MAIDSTONE(1970)
Massimo Bonetti
NIGHT OF THE SHOOTING STARS, THE(1982, Ital.)
Luis Bonfa
BLACK ORPHEUS(1959 Fr./Ital./Braz.), m
Luiz Bonfa
HOURS OF LOVE, THE(1965, Ital.), m; GENTLE RAIN, THE(1966, Braz.), m
Agnes Bonfanti
8 ½(1963, Ital.)
Marina Bonfigli
RED LIPS(1964, Fr./Ital.)
Jean Pascal Bongard
DAISY MILLER(1974)
Susan Bongard
EDDIE MACON'S RUN(1983)
Mary Bongfeld
PHANTOM OF THE PARADISE(1974)
Giulio Bongini
WARRIOR EMPRESS, THE(1961, Ital./Fr.), art d; JESSICA(1962, U.S./Ital./Fr.), art d; DUEL OF CHAMPIONS(1964 Ital./Span.), art d
Guilio Bongini
QUEEN OF SHEBA(1953, Ital.), art d
Rafael Bongini
Silents
LIFTING SHADOWS(1920); SAINTED DEVIL, A(1924)
Gianni Bongioanni
WILD EYE, THE(1968, Ital.)
Frank Bongiorno
NATURAL ENEMIES(1979); FAME(1980); PATERNITY(1981)
Fred Bongusto
TIGER AND THE PUSSYCAT, THE(1967, U.S., Ital.), m; DETECTIVE BELLI(1970, Ital.), m; MAN WHO CAME FOR COFFEE, THE(1970, Ital.), m; WHITE SISTER(1973, Ital./Span./Fr.), m; MALICIOUS(1974, Ital.), m
Frank Bonham
STAGE TO TUCSON(1950), w
Guy Bonham
BADLANDS OF DAKOTA(1941); DOUGHBOYS IN IRELAND(1943)
John Bonham
SON OF DRACULA(1974, Brit.)
Olive Bonham-Carter
LADY WITH A LAMP, THE(1951, Brit.)
Gaston Bonheur
LADY CHATTERLEY'S LOVER(1959, Fr.), d&w
Stella Bonheur
RED WAGON(1936); TERROR ON TIPTOE(1936, Brit.); BEHIND YOUR BACK(1937, Brit.); ELDER BROTHER, THE(1937, Brit.); WANTED(1937, Brit.); HIGH TIDE AT NOON(1957, Brit.); VIOLENT STRANGER(1957, Brit.); INTENT TO KILL(1958, Brit.); END OF THE LINE, THE(1959, Brit.); ROMAN SPRING OF MRS. STONE, THE(1961, U.S./Brit.); HOT MONEY GIRL(1962, Brit./Ger.)
Ludovice Bonhomme
NUN'S STORY, THE(1959)
Carmen Boni
Misc. Silents
ART OF LOVE, THE(1928, Ger.)
Franca Boni
SUMMERSKIN(1962, Arg.)
Louisella Boni
NANA(1957, Fr./Ital.)
Luisa Boni
LAND OF THE PHARAOHS(1955)
Paolo Bonicelli
LA GRANDE BOURGEOISE(1977, Ital.)
Victorio Bonicelli
MOSES(1976, Brit./Ital.), w
Vittorio Bonicelli
BIBLE...IN THE BEGINNING, THE(1966), w; BARBARELLA(1968, Fr./Ital.), w; WATERLOO(1970, Ital./USSR), w; GARDEN OF THE FINZI-CONTINIS, THE(1976, Ital./Ger.), w
Etienne Bonichon
UNEASY TERMS(1948, Brit.)
Boniface
WE ARE ALL NAKED(1970, Can./Fr.)
Isabel Boniface
WALK, DON'T RUN(1966); TRUE GRIT(1969)
Paul Boniface
AMAZING MONSIEUR FABRE, THE(1952, Fr.)
Symona Boniface
GIRLS' DORMITORY(1936); CONFESSION(1937); IN EARLY ARIZONA(1938); NINOTCHKA(1939); ONE DANGEROUS NIGHT(1943); LOST IN A HAREM(1944); MRS. PARKINGTON(1944); JOAN OF ARC(1948); MAN FROM COLORADO, THE(1948); ROGUES OF SHERWOOD FOREST(1950)
Symonia Boniface
TARZAN THE FEARLESS(1933); MURDER IN THE MUSEUM(1934)
Carmen Bonifant
EASY MONEY(1983)
Bonifas
LOVE IN THE AFTERNOON(1957)
Paul Bonifas
SOMEWHERE IN FRANCE(1943, Brit.); CANDLELIGHT IN ALGERIA(1944, Brit.); HEAVEN IS ROUND THE CORNER(1944, Brit.); JOHNNY FRENCHMAN(1946, Brit.); LISBON STORY, THE(1946, Brit.); PARDON MY FRENCH(1951, U.S./Fr.); TAKE ME TO PARIS(1951, Brit.); GREEN GLOVE, THE(1952); HUNCHBACK OF NOTRE DAME, THE(1957, Fr.); ENEMY GENERAL, THE(1960); LOVE AND THE FRENCHWOMAN(1961, Fr.); SUNDAYS AND CYBELE(1962, Fr.); CHARADE(1963); LES ABYSSES(1964, Fr.); TRAIN, THE(1965, Fr./Ital./U.S.); SECRET WORLD(1969, Fr.)

Luce Bonifassy
TENTH VICTIM, THE(1965, Fr./Ital.)
Jack Bonigul
SCANDAL AT SCOURIE(1953)
Chichi Bonilla
WHO SAYS I CAN'T RIDE A RAINBOW!(1971)
Dennis Bonilla
KING AND I, THE(1956)
Roxanna Bonilla
UNHOLY ROLLERS(1972)
Thomas Bonilla
KING AND I, THE(1956)
Roxanna Bonilla-Giannini
NINE TO FIVE(1980)
Myrta Bonillas
LUMMOX(1930)
Misc. Silents
CUSTARD CUP, THE(1923)
Myrtle Bonillas
Silents
SHACKLES OF GOLD(1922)
John D. Bonin
SARUMBA(1950)
Madeleine Bonin
CHILDREN OF PARADISE(1945, Fr.), ed
Sharon Bonin
NOBODY WAVED GOODBYE(1965, Can.)
Julio Bonini
CALCUTTA(1947)
Steve Bonino
THREE DAYS OF THE CONDOR(1975)
Jean Bernard Bonis
BEST WAY, THE(1978, Fr.), ed
Jean-Bernard Bonis
COUSINS IN LOVE(1982), ed
Franco Bonisolli
LA TRAVIATA(1968, Ital.)
Bonita
MILKY WAY, THE(1936)
Mme. Bonita
VIRGINIA JUDGE, THE(1935)
Paul Bonitas
MAN FROM MOROCCO, THE(1946, Brit.)
Mario Bonitti
CAPTIVE CITY, THE(1963, Ital.), ed
Marion Bonitti
CONQUERED CITY(1966, Ital.), ed
Pascal Bonitzer
BRONTE SISTERS, THE(1979, Fr.), w
1984
LOVE ON THE GROUND(1984,Fr.), w
Peter Bonke
CONTRACT, THE(1982, Pol.)
Ferdinand Bonn
GREAT YEARNING, THE(1930, Ger.)
Frank Bonn
Misc. Silents
DAVID GARRICK(1916)
Issy Bonn
DISCOVERIES(1939, Brit.); I THANK YOU(1941, Brit.)
Walter Bonn
MAN WHO BROKE THE BANK AT MONTE CARLO, THE(1935); ESPIONAGE(1937); LANCER SPY(1937); THIN ICE(1937); GIRL OF THE GOLDEN WEST, THE(1938); INTERNATIONAL CRIME(1938); THREE COMRADES(1938); FLORIAN(1940); MAN I MARRIED, THE(1940); DEADLY GAME, THE(1941); MAN HUNT(1941); UNDERGROUND(1941); ONCE UPON A HONEYMOON(1942); PARIS AFTER DARK(1943); WE'VE NEVER BEEN LICKED(1943); PASSAGE TO MARSEILLE(1944); SONG TO REMEMBER, A(1945); WHERE DO WE GO FROM HERE?(1945); RAZOR'S EDGE, THE(1946); PROBLEM GIRLS(1953)
Pierre Bonnafet
QUARTET(1981, Brit./Fr.)
Jacques Bonnaffe
1984
FIRST NAME: CARMEN(1984, Fr.)
Sandrine Bonnaire
1984
A NOS AMOURS(1984, Fr.)
Roberto Bonnanni
PRIEST OF LOVE(1981, Brit.)
Arlette Bonnard
JUDGE AND THE ASSASSIN, THE(1979, Fr.); PEPPERMINT SODA(1979, Fr.)
Keith Bonnard
SOME MAY LIVE(1967, Brit.); HIGH COMMISSIONER, THE(1968, U.S./Brit.); CHAIRMAN, THE(1969); MOON ZERO TWO(1970, Brit.)
Mario Bonnard
KING'S JESTER, THE(1947, Ital.), d; ROSSINI(1948, Ital.), d, w; DISILLUSION(1949, Ital.), d, w; CITY OF PAIN(1951, Ital.), d; LAST DAYS OF POMPEII, THE(1960, Ital.), d
Misc. Silents
RUSSIA(1929, Ger.), d
Yvette Bonnay
TIME BOMB(1961, Fr./Ital.), cos
Shirley Bonne
SANDPIPER, THE(1965); IT'S ALIVE(1968)
the Bonne Ski Ballet
BENJAMIN(1973, Ger.)
Eliane Bonneau
SIX IN PARIS(1968, Fr.), art d

Francoise Bonneau
NAKED HEARTS(1970, Fr.)
Paul Bonneau
FIRE IN THE FLESH(1964, Fr.), m
Paul Bonnecarrere
ROSEBUD(1975), w
Jean Pierre Bonnefous
DIABOLIQUE(1955, Fr.)
Madame Bonnefoux
MARRIAGE OF FIGARO, THE(1963, Fr.)
Patrick Bonnel
PASSION(1983, Fr./Switz.)
Bonnie Bonnell
MYRT AND MARGE(1934)
Dan Bonnell
WARRIORS, THE(1979)
Lee Bonnell
FOOTLIGHT FEVER(1941); GAY FALCON, THE(1941); LADY SCARFACE(1941); LAND OF THE OPEN RANGE(1941); LOOK WHO'S LAUGHING(1941); PARACHUTE BATTALION(1941); SAINT IN PALM SPRINGS, THE(1941); MAYOR OF 44TH STREET, THE(1942); NAVY COMES THROUGH, THE(1942); CRIMINAL COURT(1946); SAN QUENTIN(1946); CHECKERED COAT, THE(1948); JIGGS AND MAGGIE IN SOCIETY(1948); SMART WOMAN(1948); NUREMBERG(1961)
Leo Bonnell
SISTER KENNY(1946)
Virginia Bonnell
1984
TEACHERS(1984)
Vivian Bonnell
LEADBELLY(1976); FOR PETE'S SAKE(1977)
Louis Bonnemaison
WEB OF PASSION(1961, Fr.), makeup; PLEASURES AND VICES(1962, Fr.), makeup; HOTEL PARADISO(1966, U.S./Brit.), make up
Ricardo Bonnemaison
GALLANT ONE, THE(1964, U.S./Peru)
Beverly Bonner
BASKET CASE(1982)
Bill Bonner
PSYCHIC KILLER(1975)
Misc. Talkies
OUTLAW RIDERS(1971)
Charles Bonner
ADAM HAD FOUR SONS(1941), w
Ed Bonner
JAMBOREE(1957)
Frank Bonner
HOAX, THE(1972); LAS VEGAS LADY(1976)
Silents
HAWTHORNE OF THE U.S.A.(1919); OLD IRONSIDES(1926)
Geraldine Bonner
Silents
SHAM(1921), w
Hal Bonner
Misc. Talkies
DAY THE LORD GOT BUSTED, THE(1976)
Hilton Bonner
HARD KNOCKS(1980, Aus.), a, p&w
Isabel Bonner
SHRIKE, THE(1955)
James P. Bonner [Irving Ravetch
CAREY TREATMENT, THE(1972), w
Joe Bonner
Silents
IS YOUR DAUGHTER SAFE?(1927)
Misc. Silents
AFFINITIES(1922); MAN WHO WAITED, THE(1922); WESTERN GRIT(1924)
Ken Bonner
DISCOVERIES(1939, Brit.)
Marjorie Bonner
Silents
MASTER CRACKSMAN, THE(1914); SEATS OF THE MIGHTY, THE(1914); RENO(1923); DAUGHTERS OF TODAY(1924); ANCIENT HIGHWAY, THE(1925); HIGH AND HANDSOME(1925); SINNER'S PARADE(1928)
Misc. Silents
BROADWAY LADY(1925); RAPID FIRE ROMANCE(1926); RIDING ROMANCE(1926); PAYING THE PRICE(1927); FOUR-FOOTED RANGER, THE(1928); MADE-TO-ORDER HERO, A(1928); TRAIL OF COURAGE, THE(1928)
Miriam Bonner
RED RUNS THE RIVER(1963)
Priscilla Bonner
Silents
BOB HAMPTON OF PLACER(1921); HOME STUFF(1921); SHADOWS(1922); APRIL SHOWERS(1923); PROUD FLESH(1925); RED KIMONO(1925); STRONG MAN, THE(1926); IT(1927); LONG PANTS(1927); GIRLS WHO DARE(1929)
Misc. Silents
HOMER COMES HOME(1920); HONEST HUTCH(1920); MAN WHO HAD EVERYTHING, THE(1920); DESPERATE ADVENTURE, A(1924); DRUSILLA WITH A MILLION(1925); EYES OF HOLLYWOOD(1925); MANSION OF ACHING HEARTS, THE(1925); EARTH WOMAN, THE(1926); BROADWAY AFTER MIDNIGHT(1927); PAYING THE PRICE(1927); PRINCE OF HEADWAITERS, THE(1927); GOLDEN SHACKLES(1928); OUTCAST SOULS(1928)
Roy Bonner
LEGEND OF THE LONE RANGER, THE(1981)
Tom Bonner
9/30/55(1977)
Tony Bonner
THEY'RE A WEIRD MOB(1966, Aus.); SUDDEN TERROR(1970, Brit.); YOU CAN'T WIN 'EM ALL(1970, Brit.); CREATURES THE WORLD FORGOT(1971, Brit.); INN OF THE DAMNED(1974, Aus.); MONEY MOVERS(1978, Aus.); MANGO TREE, THE(1981, Aus.); MAN FROM SNOWY RIVER, THE(1983, Aus.)

Misc. Talkies
CHOPPER SQUAD(1971); ALTERNATIVE(1976); IMAGE OF DEATH(1977, Brit.)
William Bonner
HELL'S CHOSEN FEW(1968); FEMALE BUNCH, THE(1969); RUN, ANGEL, RUN(1969); SATAN'S SADISTS(1969); ANGELS DIE HARD(1970); HARD ROAD, THE(1970); HELL'S BLOODY DEVILS(1970); HARD RIDE, THE(1971)
Beatrice Bonnesen
WHILE THE ATTORNEY IS ASLEEP(1945, Den.)
Emery Bonnet
MY SISTER AND I(1948, Brit.), w; GLASS MOUNTAIN, THE(1950, Brit), w; CHILDREN GALORE(1954, Brit.), w
Frank Oliver Bonnet
QUEST FOR FIRE(1982, Fr./Can.)
Frank Olivier Bonnet
1984
AMERICAN DREAMER(1984)
James Bonnet
CROSS AND THE SWITCHBLADE, THE(1970), w
John Bonnet
CHILDREN GALORE(1954, Brit.), w
Theordore Bonnet
MUDLARK, THE(1950, Brit.), w
Harold Bonnett
SATAN IN HIGH HEELS(1962), w
Neil Bonnett
STROKER ACE(1983)
Oliver Bonnett
YOUNG GIRLS OF ROCHEFORT, THE(1968, Fr.)
Edward Bonnetti
BEYOND THE LAW(1968)
Bob Bonney
NIGHT THE LIGHTS WENT OUT IN GEORGIA, THE(1981), w
Gail Bonney
ONE SUNDAY AFTERNOON(1948); FOUNTAINHEAD, THE(1949); RECKLESS MOMENTS, THE(1949); CAGED(1950); FULLER BRUSH GIRL, THE(1950); SECRET FURY, THE(1950); SIDE STREET(1950); WOMAN OF DISTINCTION, A(1950); PEOPLE WILL TALK(1951); CARRIE(1952); LOVE IS BETTER THAN EVER(1952); MILLION DOLLAR MERMAID(1952); MY SON, JOHN(1952); SNIPER, THE(1952); DREAM WIFE(1953); LADY WANTS MINK, THE(1953); DEEP IN MY HEART(1954); MAGNIFICENT OBSESSION(1954); OPPOSITE SEX, THE(1956); PAL JOEY(1957); BELL, BOOK AND CANDLE(1958); PERFECT FURLOUGH, THE(1958); TOO MUCH, TOO SOON(1958); PLEASE DON'T EAT THE DAISIES(1960); DAYS OF WINE AND ROSES(1962); CAT BALLOU(1965); ROSEMARY'S BABY(1968); PIECES OF DREAMS(1970); LATE LIZ, THE(1971)
Jim Bonney
1984
PREPPIES(1984)
John Bonney
PARANOIAC(1963, Brit.); GUTTER GIRLS(1964, Brit.); SATURDAY NIGHT OUT(1964, Brit.); SQUADRON 633(1964, U.S./Brit.); 633 SQUADRON(1964)
Marilyn Bonney
SON OF SINBAD(1955)
Therese Bonney
SEARCH, THE(1948), tech adv
Bruce Bonnheim
NATIONAL LAMPOON'S ANIMAL HOUSE(1978)
Joakim Bonnier
GRAND PRIX(1966), a, tech adv
Johan Bonnier
HAGBARD AND SIGNE(1968, Den./Iceland/Swed.), p
Valerie Bonnier
MAN WHO LOVED WOMEN, THE(1977, Fr.)
Claude Bonniere
LUCK OF GINGER COFFEY, THE(1964, U.S./Can.), set d; IT SEEMED LIKE A GOOD IDEA AT THE TIME(1975, Can.), art d; CIRCLE OF TWO(1980, Can.), set d; LOVE(1982, Can.), prod d; PARADISE(1982), prod d
Paul Bonniere
HIGH-BALLIN'(1978), art d
Rene Bonniere
Misc. Talkies
AMANITA PESTILENS(1963), d
Nancy Bonniwell
LOVE GOD?, THE(1969); HUSTLE(1975)
Dick Bonnor-Moris
WEEKEND WITH LULU, A(1961, Brit.), makeup; THERE WAS A CROOKED MAN(1962, Brit.), makeup
Francoise Bonnot
L'ARMEE DES OMBRES(1969, Fr./Ital.), ed
Francois Bonnot
CASSANDRA CROSSING, THE(1977), ed
Francoise Bonnot
MONKEY IN WINTER, A(1962, Fr.), ed; 25TH HOUR, THE(1967, Fr./Ital./Yugo.), ed; GUNS FOR SAN SEBASTIAN(1968, U.S./Fr./Mex./Ital.), ed; Z(1969, Fr./Algeria), ed; CONFESSION, THE(1970, Fr.), ed; MASSACRE IN ROME(1973, Ital.), ed; STATE OF SIEGE(1973, Fr./U.S./Ital./Ger.), ed; 1★2?(1975, Fr.), ed; BLACK AND WHITE IN COLOR(1976, Fr.), ed; TENANT, THE(1976, Fr.), ed; WOMANLIGHT(1979, Fr./Ger./Ital.), ed; CLAIR DE FEMME(1980,Fr.), ed; I SENT A LETTER TO MY LOVE(1981, Fr.), ed; MISSING(1982), ed; HANNAH K.(1983, Fr.), ed
1984
SWANN IN LOVE(1984, Fr.Ger.), ed
Monique Bonnot
LES ENFANTS TERRIBLES(1952, Fr.), ed; MONKEY IN WINTER, A(1962, Fr.), ed; FINGERMAN, THE(1963, Fr.), ed; DOULOS–THE FINGER MAN(1964, Fr./Ital.), ed; POPPY IS ALSO A FLOWER, THE(1966), ed; GODSON, THE(1972, Ital./Fr.), ed
M.I. Bonns
Misc. Talkies
NIGHT OF THE HOWLING BEAST(1977), d

Fred Bonny
DRUMS O' VOODOO(1934)
Joseph Bono
RAGING BULL(1980)
Sonny Bono
GOOD TIMES(1967), m; CHASTITY(1969), p, w&m; ESCAPE TO ATHENA(1979, Brit.); AIRPLANE II: THE SEQUEL(1982)
Steve Bono
LAST PORNO FLICK, THE(1974), p; LORD SHANGO(1975), p; ONE MAN JURY(1978), p
Susie Bono
1984
BREAKIN' 2: ELECTRIC BOOGALOO(1984)
Joe Bonomo
NOAH'S ARK(1928); COURTIN' WILDCATS(1929); LONE TRAIL, THE(1932); SIGN OF THE CROSS, THE(1932); ISLAND OF LOST SOULS(1933)
Silents
KING OF KINGS, THE(1927); SEA TIGER, THE(1927); VAMPING VENUS(1928); PHANTOM OF THE NORTH(1929)
Gigi Bonos
SECRET OF SANTA VITTORIA, THE(1969)
Luigi Bonos
DAMON AND PYTHIAS(1962)
Vittorio Bonos
WONDERS OF ALADDIN, THE(1961, Fr./Ital.); DAMON AND PYTHIAS(1962); HILLS RUN RED, THE(1967, Ital.); WILD, WILD PLANET, THE(1967, Ital.)
Mario Bonotti
REVOLT OF THE SLAVES, THE(1961, Ital./Span./Ger.), makeup; VARIETY LIGHTS(1965, Ital.), ed
Michele Bonpart
EASY LIFE, THE(1971, Fr.)
Marc Bonseignour
FIVE WILD GIRLS(1966, Fr.); CONFESSION, THE(1970, Fr.)
Claude Bonser
END OF THE ROAD, THE(1954, Brit.); GOOD COMPANIONS, THE(1957, Brit.)
Umberto Bonsignori
MAEVA(1961), p&d, ed
Claude Bonsor
WILLIAM COMES TO TOWN(1948, Brit.)
Candy Bonstein
FIDDLER ON THE ROOF(1971)
Nick Bontempo
WILD REBELS, THE(1967)
Roger Bontemps
LAFAYETTE(1963, Fr.)
Gerard Bonthuys
CREATURES THE WORLD FORGOT(1971, Brit.)
Thomas Bontross
HIDEOUS SUN DEMON, THE(1959), d, ed
Alberto Bonucci
BLOOD AND ROSES(1961, Fr./Ital.); NEOPOLITAN CAROUSEL(1961, Ital.); LOVE AND LARCENY(1963, Fr./Ital.); OF WAYWARD LOVE(1964, Ital./Ger.), d; LITTLE NUNS, THE(1965, Ital.); LOVE IN 4 DIMENSIONS(1965 Fr./Ital.); VARIETY LIGHTS(1965, Ital.); TAMING OF THE SHREW, THE(1967, U.S./Ital.); SEVEN GOLDEN MEN(1969, Fr./Ital./Span.)
Maurizio Bonuglia
DETECTIVE BELLI(1970, Ital.); LUDWIG(1973, Ital./Ger./Fr.)
Shelley R. Bonus
MOMENT BY MOMENT(1978)
Vicente Bonus
TERROR IS A MAN(1959, U.S./Phil.), art d
Vincente Bonus
LOST BATTALION(1961, U.S./Phil.), art d; MORO WITCH DOCTOR(1964, U.S./Phil.), art d
Bonvallet
PASTEUR(1936, Fr.); SECOND BUREAU(1936, Fr.)
Robert Bonvento
IN SEARCH OF HISTORIC JESUS(1980)
Andorjan Bonyi
BLUE IDOL, THE(1931, Hung.), w
Leta Bonynge
GROUP, THE(1966)
Bonzo
BONZO GOES TO COLLEGE(1952)
Luis Bar Boo
GOD FORGIVES–I DON'T!(1969, Ital./Span.)
Sigrid Boo
SERVANTS' ENTRANCE(1934), w
Boochie
HEROES DIE YOUNG(1960)
Steve Boockvor
JESUS CHRIST, SUPERSTAR(1973)
Bill Bood
RED, HOT AND BLUE(1949), makeup
Celia Boodkin
GO, MAN, GO!(1954)
George Book-Asta
HELL HARBOR(1930)
George Bookasta
IT HAD TO HAPPEN(1936); THAT NIGHT IN RIO(1941)
Jane Booke
HAIR(1979)
Sorrel Booke
BLACK LIKE ME(1964); MANCHU EAGLE MURDER CAPER MYSTERY, THE(1975)
Sorrell Booke
GONE ARE THE DAYS(1963); FAIL SAFE(1964); JOY HOUSE(1964, Fr.); FINE MADNESS, A(1966); MATCHLESS(1967, Ital.); UP THE DOWN STAIRCASE(1967); BYE BYE BRAVERMAN(1968); WHAT'S UP, DOC?(1972); ICEMAN COMETH, THE(1973); BANK SHOT(1974); DEVIL TIMES FIVE(1974); TAKE, THE(1974);

FREAKY FRIDAY(1976); SPECIAL DELIVERY(1976); MASTERMIND(1977); OTHER SIDE OF MIDNIGHT, THE(1977); RECORD CITY(1978)
Beulah Booker
Silents
SAPHEAD, THE(1921)
Bob Booker
PHYNX, THE(1970), p, w
Fred Booker
1984
MRS. SOFFEL(1984)
Gladys Booker
DRUMS O' VOODOO(1934)
Jane Booker
HULLABALOO OVER GEORGIE AND BONNIE'S PICTURES(1979, Brit.); PRIEST OF LOVE(1981, Brit.)
Jessica Booker
IMPROPER CHANNELS(1981, Can.)
Rosemary Lee Booker
MOUNTAIN, THE(1935, Brit.)
William Booker
RETURN OF THE SOLDIER, THE(1983, Brit.)
"Buzzy" Bookman
ONE TOO MANY(1950)
Ivan Bookman
LAUGHING POLICEMAN, THE(1973)
DeVeren Bookwalter
OMEGA MAN, THE(1971); ENFORCER, THE(1976)
Van Boolen
DECAMERON NIGHTS(1953, Brit.); DATE WITH DISASTER(1957, Brit.); LONG HAUL, THE(1957, Brit.); PICKUP ALLEY(1957, Brit.); NAVY LARK, THE(1959, Brit.); QUESTION OF ADULTERY, A(1959, Brit.)
Bill Booley
TREASURE ISLAND(1934)
Bjorn Watt Boolsen
NIGHT VISITOR, THE(1970, Swed./U.S.)
Steve Boomer
SOMEWHERE IN TIME(1980)
Sue Boomer
PAL JOEY(1957)
Boomsie the Dog
STOLEN LIFE(1939, Brit.)
Eric Boon
CHAMPAGNE CHARLIE(1944, Brit.); GAMBLER AND THE LADY, THE(1952, Brit.)
Frank Boon
Silents
CODE OF MARCIA GRAY(1916)
Kurt Boon
WILD RACERS, THE(1968)
Robert Boon
TREASURE OF MONTE CRISTO(1949); FLYING SAUCER, THE(1950); MISTER 880(1950); SEALED CARGO(1951); TANKS ARE COMING, THE(1951); AFFAIR IN TRINIDAD(1952); FORT ALGIERS(1953); FOUR GIRLS IN TOWN(1956); MAN IN THE GREY FLANNEL SUIT, THE(1956); SCREAMING EAGLES(1956); ENEMY BELOW, THE(1957); LAST BLITZKRIEG, THE(1958); DIARY OF ANNE FRANK, THE(1959); VERBOTEN!(1959); QUEEN OF BLOOD(1966)
Walter Boon
ALL MY SONS(1948)
Bernice Boone
MIDSTREAM(1929), w; LETTER OF INTRODUCTION(1938), w
Brendon Boone
BIG GAME, THE(1972)
Collin Boone
SECOND-HAND HEARTS(1981)
David Boone
TAKING TIGER MOUNTAIN(1983, U.S./Welsh), m
Dell Boone
Silents
ON THE QUIET(1918)
Misc. Silents
OTHER MEN'S WIVES(1919)
Libby Boone
FINAL CHAPTER–WALKING TALL zero(1977); SOUP FOR ONE(1982)
Mark Boone, Jr.
1984
VARIETY(1984)
Pat Boone
APRIL LOVE(1957); BERNARDINE(1957); MARDI GRAS(1958); JOURNEY TO THE CENTER OF THE EARTH(1959); ALL HANDS ON DECK(1961); MAIN ATTRACTION, THE(1962, Brit.); STATE FAIR(1962); YELLOW CANARY, THE(1963); GOODBYE CHARLIE(1964); HORROR OF IT ALL, THE(1964, Brit.); NEVER PUT IT IN WRITING(1964), m/l; GREATEST STORY EVER TOLD, THE(1965); PERILS OF PAULINE, THE(1967); CROSS AND THE SWITCHBLADE, THE(1970)
Randy Boone
COUNTRY BOY(1966); BACKTRACK(1969); TERMINAL ISLAND(1973); DR. MINX(1975)
Ray Boone
KID FROM CLEVELAND, THE(1949)
Richard Boone
CALL ME MISTER(1951); DESERT FOX, THE(1951); HALLS OF MONTEZUMA(1951); KANGAROO(1952); RED SKIES OF MONTANA(1952); RETURN OF THE TEXAN(1952); WAY OF A GAUCHO(1952); BENEATH THE 12-MILE REEF(1953); CITY OF BAD MEN(1953); MAN ON A TIGHTROPE(1953); ROBE, THE(1953); VICKI(1953); DRAGNET(1954); RAID, THE(1954); SIEGE AT RED RIVER, THE(1954); MAN WITHOUT A STAR(1955); ROBBER'S ROOST(1955); TEN WANTED MEN(1955); AWAY ALL BOATS(1956); BATTLE STATIONS(1956); STAR IN THE DUST(1956); GARMENT JUNGLE, THE(1957); LIZZIE(1957); TALL T, THE(1957); I BURY THE LIVING(1958); ALAMO, THE(1960); THUNDER OF DRUMS, A(1961); RIO CONCHOS(1964); WAR LORD, THE(1965); HOMBRE(1967); KONA COAST(1968); ARRANGEMENT, THE(1969); NIGHT OF THE FOLLOWING DAY, THE(1969, Brit.); KREMLIN LETTER, THE(1970); MADRON(1970, U.S./Israel); BIG JAKE(1971);

AGAINST A CROOKED SKY(1975); SHOOTIST, THE(1976); GOD'S GUN(1977); BIG SLEEP, THE½(1978, Brit.); WINTER KILLS(1979); BUSHIDO BLADE, THE(1982 Brit./U.S.)

Walker Boone
GAS(1981, Can.); VISITING HOURS(1982, Can.)

Jose Sukhum Boonive
COUNTESS FROM HONG KONG, A(1967, Brit.)

Jose Sukhum Boonlive
KALEIDOSCOPE(1966, Brit.)

Abigail Booraem
1984
IMPULSE(1984)

Charley Boorman
1984
DREAM ONE(1984, Brit./Fr.)

Charlie Boorman
DELIVERANCE(1972)

Christel Kruse Boorman
ZARDOZ(, cos

Joanne Boorman
GODSEND, THE(1980, Can.)

John Boorman
ZARDOZ(, p,d&w; HAVING A WILD WEEKEND(1965, Brit.), d; POINT BLANK(1967), d; HELL IN THE PACIFIC(1968), d; LEO THE LAST(1970, Brit.), d, w; DELIVERANCE(1972), p&d; EXORCIST II: THE HERETIC(1977), p, d; EXCALIBUR(1981), p&d, w; LONG SHOT(1981, Brit.)
1984
DREAM ONE(1984, Brit./Fr.), p

Joyce Boorman
SCARLET THREAD(1951, Brit.)

Katrine Boorman
EXCALIBUR(1981)
1984
DREAM ONE(1984, Brit./Fr.)

Telshe Boorman
1984
DREAM ONE(1984, Brit./Fr.), w

Walter Boos
TOWN WITHOUT PITY(1961, Ger./Switz./U.S.), ed; FAUST(1963, Ger.), ed; SITUATION HOPELESS–BUT NOT SERIOUS(1965), ed

Elayne Boosler
1984
MEATBALLS PART II(1984)

Gladys Boot
GYPSY AND THE GENTLEMAN, THE(1958, Brit.); HARRY BLACK AND THE TIGER(1958, Brit.); MURDER REPORTED(1958, Brit.); VIRGIN ISLAND(1960, Brit.); YOUR MONEY OR YOUR WIFE(1965, Brit.)

Clifford Boote
PORTRAIT OF CLARE(1951, Brit.), ed; FRANCHISE AFFAIR, THE(1952, Brit.), ed

Clifton Boote
DESIGN FOR MURDER(1940, Brit.), ed

Maurice Bootes
FOUR SIDED TRIANGLE(1953, Brit.), ed

Adrian Booth
GOOD GIRLS GO TO PARIS(1939); LONE WOLF SPY HUNT, THE(1939); MR. SMITH GOES TO WASHINGTON(1939); DAKOTA(1945); TELL IT TO A STAR(1945); HOME ON THE RANGE(1946); MAN FROM RAINBOW VALLEY, THE(1946); OUT CALIFORNIA WAY(1946); VALLEY OF THE ZOMBIES(1946); ALONG THE OREGON TRAIL(1947); EXPOSED(1947); LAST FRONTIER UPRISING(1947); SPOILERS OF THE NORTH(1947); UNDER COLORADO SKIES(1947); CALIFORNIA FIREBRAND(1948); GALLANT LEGION, THE(1948); LIGHTNIN' IN THE FOREST(1948); PLUNDERERS, THE(1948); BRIMSTONE(1949); HIDEOUT(1949); LAST BANDIT, THE(1949); ROCK ISLAND TRAIL(1950); SAVAGE HORDE, THE(1950); OH! SUSANNA(1951); SEA HORNET, THE(1951); YELLOW FIN(1951)

Al Booth
BITER BIT, THE(1937, Brit.), w

Alfred Booth
Silents
FARMER'S WIFE, THE(1928, Brit.), ed

Alison Booth
UNDERNEATH THE ARCHES(1937, Brit.), w; WISE GUYS(1937, Brit.), w

Anita Booth
Misc. Silents
SHADOW OF ROSALIE BYRNES, THE(1920)

Anthony Booth
PIT OF DARKNESS(1961, Brit.); RISK, THE(1961, Brit.); L-SHAPED ROOM, THE(1962, Brit.); MIX ME A PERSON(1962, Brit.); HI-JACKERS(1963, Brit.); OF HUMAN BONDAGE(1964, Brit.); RETURN OF MR. MOTO(1965, Brit.); PARTNER, THE(1966, Brit.); ALF 'N' FAMILY(1968, Brit.); CORRUPTION(1968, Brit.); GIRL WITH A PISTOL, THE(1968, Ital.); CONFESSIONS OF A WINDOW CLEANER(1974, Brit.); NEITHER THE SEA NOR THE SAND(1974, Brit.); BRANNIGAN(1975, Brit.); CONFESSIONS OF A POP PERFORMER(1975, Brit.); CONFESSIONS FROM A HOLIDAY CAMP(1977, Brit.)

Barbara Booth
LADIES OF WASHINGTON(1944)

Benita Booth
SON OF DR. JEKYLL, THE(1951)

Bill Booth
FOLLOW ME, BOYS!(1966)

Billy Booth
SNOW QUEEN, THE(1959, USSR)

Calvin Booth
INVASION OF THE SAUCER MEN(1957); UNDER FIRE(1957)

Carol Booth
LOVE-INS, THE(1967)

Charles G. Booth
GENERAL DIED AT DAWN, THE(1936), w; MAGNIFICENT FRAUD, THE(1939), w; SUNDOWN(1941), w; HURRICANE SMITH(1942), w; TRAITOR WITHIN, THE(1942), w; HOUSE ON 92ND STREET, THE(1945), w; BEHIND GREEN LIGHTS(1946), w; STRANGE TRIANGLE(1946), w; FURY AT FURNACE CREEK(1948), w

Charles Gordon Booth
JOHNNY ANGEL(1945), w

Connie Booth
AND NOW FOR SOMETHING COMPLETELY DIFFERENT(1972, Brit.); MONTY PYTHON AND THE HOLY GRAIL(1975, Brit.)

Craig Booth
INSPECTOR CLOUSEAU(1968, Brit.)

Delores Booth
DESERT MESA(1935)

Dolores Booth
RIDING SPEED(1934), w

Duncan Booth
COUNTRYMAN(1982, Jamaica)

Edwina Booth
TRADER HORN(1931); MIDNIGHT PATROL, THE(1932)

Elmer Booth
Silents
MRS. BLACK IS BACK(1914)

Emma Booth
CONFESSIONS OF A POP PERFORMER(1975, Brit.)

Ernest Booth
LADIES OF THE BIG HOUSE(1932), w; PENROD'S DOUBLE TROUBLE(1938), w; WOMEN WITHOUT NAMES(1940), w; MEN OF SAN QUENTIN(1942), w
Silents
LADIES OF THE MOB(1928), w

Frank H. Booth
ALL QUIET ON THE WESTERN FRONT(1930), spec eff; EAST IS WEST(1930), spec eff

Grant H. Booth
BROADWAY(1929), spec eff

Hal Booth
WINDJAMMER, THE(1931, Brit.); FEAR SHIP, THE(1933, Brit.); RADIO PIRATES(1935, Brit.)

Harry Booth
AT THE STROKE OF NINE(1957, Brit.), w; ON THE BUSES(1972, Brit.), d; FLYING SORCERER, THE(1974, Brit.), d, w
Misc. Talkies
DOUBLE TAKE(1972, Brit.), d; GO FOR A TAKE(1972, Brit.), d

Helen Booth
FAMILY WAY, THE(1966, Brit.); VIRGIN AND THE GYPSY, THE(1970, Brit.)

James Booth
IN THE NICK(1960, Brit.); JAZZ BOAT(1960, Brit.); LET'S GET MARRIED(1960, Brit.); MAN WITH THE GREEN CARNATION, THE(1960, Brit.); HELLIONS, THE(1962, Brit.); SPARROWS CAN'T SING(1963, Brit.); FRENCH DRESSING(1964, Brit.); IN THE DOGHOUSE(1964, Brit.); ZULU(1964, Brit.); SECRET OF MY SUCCESS, THE(1965, Brit.); 90 DEGREES IN THE SHADE(1966, Czech./Brit.); ROBBERY(1967, Brit.); BLISS OF MRS. BLOSSOM, THE(1968, Brit.); FRAULEIN DOKTOR(1969, Ital./Yugo.); DARKER THAN AMBER(1970); MACHO CALLAHAN(1970); MAN WHO HAD POWER OVER WOMEN, THE(1970, Brit.); TERROR FROM UNDER THE HOUSE(1971, Brit.); ADAM'S WOMAN(1972, Austral.); RENTADICK(1972, Brit.); THAT'LL BE THE DAY(1974, Brit.); BRANNIGAN(1975, Brit.); AIRPORT '77(1977); SUNBURN(1979), w; JAZZ SINGER, THE(1980); ZORRO, THE GAY BLADE(1981)
Misc. Talkies
PLAY IT COOLER(1961)

James Hunter Booth
VALIANT, THE(1929), w

Janie Booth
OTHELLO(1965, Brit.)

John Hunter Booth
FOUR DEVILS(1929), w; LUCKY STAR(1929), w; LONE STAR RANGER, THE(1930), w; MASQUERADER, THE(1933), w
Silents
ROLLING HOME(1926), w

Jolyan Booth
GEORGY GIRL(1966, Brit.)

Joylan Booth
PLAGUE OF THE ZOMBIES, THE(1966, Brit.)

June Booth
GOVERNMENT GIRL(1943); MEXICAN SPITFIRE'S BLESSED EVENT(1943); GREAT SINNER, THE(1949)

Karen Booth
AFRICAN MANHUNT(1955); TOP GUN(1955)

Karin Booth
STAR SPANGLED RHYTHM(1942); UNFINISHED DANCE,THE(1947); BIG CITY(1948); MY FOOLISH HEART(1949); CARIBOO TRAIL, THE(1950); LAST OF THE BUCCANEERS(1950); STATE PENITENTIARY(1950); CRIPPLE CREEK(1952); CHARGE OF THE LANCERS(1953); LET'S DO IT AGAIN(1953); JUNGLE MANEATERS(1954); TOBOR THE GREAT(1954); SEMINOLE UPRISING(1955); CROOKED SKY, THE(1957, Brit.); BADMAN'S COUNTRY(1958); WORLD WAS HIS JURY, THE(1958); BELOVED INFIDEL(1959); JUKE BOX RHYTHM(1959)

Katharine Booth
HOLIDAY INN(1942); GIRL CRAZY(1943); SWING SHIFT MAISIE(1943); LOST IN A HAREM(1944); MEET THE PEOPLE(1944); ABBOTT AND COSTELLO IN HOLLYWOOD(1945); DANGEROUS PARTNERS(1945)

Katharine "Karin" Booth
TAKE A LETTER, DARLING(1942); SWING FEVER(1943); MAISIE GOES TO RENO(1944); MARRIAGE IS A PRIVATE AFFAIR(1944); WONDER MAN(1945); EASY TO WED(1946)

Katherine Booth
GLAMOUR BOY(1941); LOUISIANA PURCHASE(1941); FLEET'S IN, THE(1942); THIS GUN FOR HIRE(1942); ZIEGFELD FOLLIES(1945); HOODLUM SAINT, THE(1946)

M. Haworth Booth
RUNAWAY LADIES(1935, Brit.), p

Margaret Booth
WAY WE WERE, THE(1973), ed; LADY OF CHANCE, A(1928), ed; BRIDGE OF SAN LUIS REY, THE(1929), ed; LADY OF SCANDAL, THE(1930), ed; LADY'S MORALS, A(1930), ed; NEW MOON(1930), ed; REDEMPTION(1930), ed; ROGUE SONG, THE(1930), ed; STRICTLY UNCONVENTIONAL(1930), ed; WISE GIRLS(1930), ed; CUBAN LOVE SONG,THE(1931), ed; FIVE AND TEN(1931), ed; IT'S A WISE

CHILD(1931), ed; PRODIGAL, THE(1931), ed; SUSAN LENOX–HER FALL AND RISE(1931), ed; LOVERS COURAGEOUS(1932), ed; SMILIN' THROUGH(1932), ed; SON-DAUGHTER, THE(1932), ed; STRANGE INTERLUDE(1932), ed; BOMB-SHELL(1933), ed; DANCING LADY(1933), ed; PEG O' MY HEART(1933), ed; STORM AT DAYBREAK(1933), ed; BARRETTS OF WIMPOLE STREET, THE(1934), ed; RIP TIDE(1934), ed; MUTINY ON THE BOUNTY(1935), ed; RECKLESS(1935), ed; ROMEO AND JULIET(1936), ed; CAMILLE(1937), ed; YANK AT OXFORD, A(1938), ed; OWL AND THE PUSSYCAT, THE(1970), ed; BLACK BIRD, THE(1975), ed; SUNSHINE BOYS, THE(1975), ed; MURDER BY DEATH(1976), ed; CHAPTER TWO(1979), ed
Silents
HUSBANDS AND LOVERS(1924), ed; MEMORY LANE(1926), ed; ENEMY, THE(1927), ed; IN OLD KENTUCKY(1927), ed; MYSTERIOUS LADY, THE(1928), ed; TELLING THE WORLD(1928), ed
Marguerite Booth
FAT CITY(1972), ed
Mary Booth
GIRLS OF THE ROAD(1940)
Matthew Booth
MAN WHO HAD POWER OVER WOMEN, THE(1970, Brit.)
May Booth
PALM SPRINGS WEEKEND(1963), cos
Mike Booth
GOODBYE PORK PIE(1981, New Zealand)
Mildred Booth
SPLENDOR(1935)
Ned Booth
GLASS WALL, THE(1953)
Nesdon Booth
ROGUE COP(1954); I DIED A THOUSAND TIMES(1955); PETE KELLY'S BLUES(1955); THESE WILDER YEARS(1956); FUNNY FACE(1957); RAINTREE COUNTY(1957); REFORM SCHOOL GIRL(1957); SHADOW ON THE WINDOW, THE(1957); CATTLE EMPIRE(1958); ESCAPE FROM RED ROCK(1958); SPACE MASTER X-7(1958); TOO MUCH, TOO SOON(1958); RIO BRAVO(1959); LET NO MAN WRITE MY EPITAPH(1960); RISE AND FALL OF LEGS DIAMOND, THE(1960); ONE-EYED JACKS(1961); GUN STREET(1962); WALK ON THE WILD SIDE(1962)
Paul Booth
TICKET TO HEAVEN(1981)
Richard Booth
Misc. Talkies
ONE PAGE OF LOVE(1979)
Robert Booth
DAVY CROCKETT, KING OF THE WILD FRONTIER(1955); NATCHEZ TRACE(1960); STAND UP VIRGIN SOLDIERS(1977, Brit.)
Roger Booth
ROBBERY(1967, Brit.); WORK IS A FOUR LETTER WORD(1968, Brit.); KIDNAPPED(1971, Brit.); BARRY LYNDON(1975, Brit.); REMEMBRANCE(1982, Brit.)
Sara Booth
MAN WHO HAD POWER OVER WOMEN, THE(1970, Brit.)
Shelagh Booth
SECOND BEST SECRET AGENT IN THE WHOLE WIDE WORLD, THE(1965, Brit.)
Shirley Booth
COME BACK LITTLE SHEBA(1952); MAIN STREET TO BROADWAY(1953); ABOUT MRS. LESLIE(1954); HOT SPELL(1958); MATCHMAKER, THE(1958)
Sidney Booth
Misc. Silents
YOUR GIRL AND MINE(1914)
Stephen F. Booth
BRIGHTY OF THE GRAND CANYON(1967), p
Tim Booth
PADDY(1970, Irish), set d
Walter Booth
Silents
ROULETTE(1924)
Webster Booth
OLD SPANISH CUSTOM, AN(1936, Brit.); SUNSHINE AHEAD(1936, Brit.); ROBBER SYMPHONY, THE(1937, Brit.); SATURDAY NIGHT REVUE(1937, Brit.); DEMOB-BED(1944, Brit.); WALTZ TIME(1946, Brit.); LAUGHING LADY, THE(1950, Brit.); GREAT GILBERT AND SULLIVAN, THE(1953, Brit.); KIMBERLEY JIM(1965, South Africa)
Guy Boothby
Silents
BID FOR FORTUNE, A(1917, Brit.), w
Robert Boothby
MAD LITTLE ISLAND(1958, Brit.)
Victoria Boothby
GOODBYE GIRL, THE(1977); TOUCHED(1983)
Clare Boothe
WOMEN, THE(1939), w; KISS THE BOYS GOODBYE(1941), w; MARGIN FOR ERROR(1943), w; OPPOSITE SEX, THE(1956), w
Jon Boothe
PURSUIT OF HAPPINESS, THE(1971), w
Mildred Boothe
ENTER MADAME(1935)
Powers Boothe
CRUISING(1980); SOUTHERN COMFORT(1981)
1984
BREED APART, A(1984); RED DAWN(1984)
Derrick Boothroyd
VALUE FOR MONEY(1957, Brit.), w
J. B. Boothroyd
PERFECT WOMAN, THE(1950, Brit.), w; RELUCTANT WIDOW, THE(1951, Brit.), w
Gypsy Boots
CHILDISH THINGS(1969)
Boots the Cat
YOU NEVER CAN TELL(1951)
Boots the Dog
Silents
OCCASIONALLY YOURS(1920)

David Booze
1984
VAMPING(1984)
Steve Boozer
CARNIVAL OF SOULS(1962)
Joe Boppo
TOO YOUNG, TOO IMMORAL!(1962), m
Hanus Bor
ROCKET TO NOWHERE(1962, Czech.); STOLEN DIRIGIBLE, THE(1966, Czech.)
Vladimir Bor
DAY THAT SHOOK THE WORLD, THE(1977, Yugo./Czech.), w
Juliette Bora
ONE MORE TIME(1970, Brit.)
Renato Boracherro
JACK AND THE BEANSTALK(1970)
Carl Borack
BIG FIX, THE(1978), p
Charles Borah
Silents
COLLEGE(1927)
Boralta
OLIVE TREES OF JUSTICE, THE(1967, Fr.)
Mikho Borashvili
STEPCHILDREN(1962, USSR)
Frank Borass
MANTIS IN LACE(1968), set d
Caterina Boratto
8 ½(1963, Ital.); JULIET OF THE SPIRITS(1965, Fr./Ital./W.Ger.); TIGER AND THE PUSSYCAT, THE(1967, U.S., Ital.); DANGER: DIABOLIK(1968, Ital./Fr.); CASTLE KEEP(1969); LADY OF MONZA, THE(1970, Ital.); LA NUIT DE VARENNES(1983, Fr./Ital.)
Jose Luis Borau
SABINA, THE(1979, Span./Swed.), p,d&w
1984
ON THE LINE(1984, Span.), d&w
Eduardo Borbolla
1984
UNDER THE VOLCANO(1984)
Paola Borboni
HIS LAST TWELVE HOURS(1953, Ital.); VITELLONI(1956, Ital./Fr.); MAIDEN FOR A PRINCE, A(1967, Fr./Ital.); BIGGEST BUNDLE OF THEM ALL, THE(1968); LA CAGE AUX FOLLES II(1981, Ital./Fr.); YES, GIORGIO(1982)
Paolo Borboni
ROMAN HOLIDAY(1953); WHEN WOMEN HAD TAILS(1970, Ital.)
James Borby
STRANGE LOVE OF MOLLY LOUVAIN, THE(1932), ed
Gaston Borch
WHITE ZOMBIE(1932), m
Randi Borch
SNOW TREASURE(1968)
Adolph Borchard
STORY OF A CHEAT, THE(1938, Fr.), m
Adolphe Borchard
ULTIMATUM(1940, Fr.), m
Cornell Borchers
BIG LIFT, THE(1950); HOUSE OF LIFE(1953, Ger.); DIVIDED HEART, THE(1955, Brit.); NEVER SAY GOODBYE(1956); ISTANBUL(1957); FLOOD TIDE(1958); DAS LETZTE GEHEIMNIS(1959, Ger.)
Donald P. Borchers
1984
ANGEL(1984), p; CHILDREN OF THE CORN(1984), p; CRIMES OF PASSION(1984), p
Brigitte Borchert
Misc. Silents
PEOPLE ON SUNDAY(1929, Ger.)
Ernst Borchert
MURDERERS AMONG US(1948, Ger.)
Rudolph Borchert
LITTLE DRAGONS, THE(1980), w
Sali Borchman
1984
AMERICAN TABOO(1984), p
Hanne Borchsenius
SCANDAL IN DENMARK(1970, Den.)
Jose Borcia
JEKYLL AND HYDE...TOGETHER AGAIN(1982)
Carlos Borcosque
Misc. Talkies
FIGHTING LADY(1935), d
Bordan
WAYS OF LOVE(1950, Ital./Fr.)
Gyorgy Bordas
WINTER WIND(1970, Fr./Hung.)
Mark Borde
SUMMER CAMP(1979), p
1984
HOLLYWOOD HOT TUBS(1984), p, w; SCARRED(1984), p
Marke Borde
LUNCH WAGON(1981), p
Francine Bordeau
HOMECOMING(1948)
Francine Bordeaux
I MARRIED AN ANGEL(1942); WOMEN IN BONDAGE(1943); SO DARK THE NIGHT(1946)
Jeanette Bordeaux
SILENT RAIDERS(1954)
Joe Bordeaux
MAN HUNTER, THE(1930); HIGH SPEED(1932); MISS PACIFIC FLEET(1935); OUR RELATIONS(1936); YOU CAN'T TAKE IT WITH YOU(1938); STORY OF VERNON AND IRENE CASTLE, THE(1939); MEN AGAINST THE SKY(1940)

Silents
TILLIE'S PUNCTURED ROMANCE(1914)
Cleo Louise Borden
WOMAN COMMANDS, A(1932)
Cope Borden
Misc. Talkies
TEXAS JACK(1935)
Eddie Borden
TIME OF YOUR LIFE, THE(1948); RAMPANT AGE, THE(1930); ROUGH ROMAN-CE(1930); FLYING DOWN TO RIO(1933); JUNGLE BRIDE(1933); BELLE OF THE NINETIES(1934); DEVIL IS A WOMAN, THE(1935); BOHEMIAN GIRL, THE(1936); EARLY TO BED(1936); WEDDING PRESENT(1936); CONFLICT(1937); WAY OUT WEST(1937); MEET THE MAYOR(1938); CAFE SOCIETY(1939); FLYING DEUCES, THE(1939); ST. LOUIS BLUES(1939); CHUMP AT OXFORD, A(1940); SAPS AT SEA(1940); SECRETS OF A MODEL(1940); OBLIGING YOUNG LADY(1941); MEXI-CAN SPITFIRE'S ELEPHANT(1942); GHOST SHIP, THE(1943); GILDERSLEEVE'S BAD DAY(1943); GUY NAMED JOE, A(1943); HERS TO HOLD(1943); LADIES' DAY(1943); LADY OF BURLESQUE(1943); MEXICAN SPITFIRE'S BLESSED EVENT(1943); EVER SINCE VENUS(1944); FRONTIER GAL(1945); FALCON'S ALIBI, THE(1946); LIVE WIRES(1946); LOCKET, THE(1946); RIFFRAFF(1947); TROUBLE WITH WOMEN, THE(1947); KNOCK ON ANY DOOR(1949); RED PONY, THE(1949); WOMAN'S SECRET, A(1949); ON DANGEROUS GROUND(1951)
Silents
BACK HOME AND BROKE(1922); BATTLING BUTLER(1926); ONE CHANCE IN A MILLION(1927); SHOW GIRL, THE(1927)
Misc. Silents
DOVE, THE(1927)
Ethel B. Borden
I LIVE MY LIFE(1935), w
Ethel Borden
THEY WANTED TO MARRY(1937), w
Eugene Borden
UNDER TWO FLAGS(1936); HOLD YOUR MAN(1929); WOMAN RACKET, THE(1930); WIFE VERSUS SECRETARY(1936); CAFE METROPOLE(1937); CHARLIE CHAN ON BROADWAY(1937); ESPIONAGE(1937); FIREFLY, THE(1937); I MET HIM IN PARIS(1937); SEVENTH HEAVEN(1937); SOULS AT SEA(1937); THIN ICE(1937); ARTISTS AND MODELS ABROAD(1938); CHARLIE CHAN IN THE CITY OF DARKNESS(1939); EVERYTHING HAPPENS AT NIGHT(1939); MIDNIGHT(1939); STORY OF VERNON AND IRENE CASTLE, THE(1939); ARISE, MY LOVE(1940); HUDSON'S BAY(1940); MAN I MARRIED, THE(1940); MARK OF ZORRO, THE(1940); CHARLIE CHAN IN RIO(1941); PARIS CALLING(1941); SCOTLAND YARD(1941); THAT NIGHT IN RIO(1941); DR. RENAULT'S SECRET(1942); LADY IS WILLING, THE(1942); SLEEPYTIME GAL(1942); ADVENTURES IN IRAQ(1943); MISSION TO MOSCOW(1943); PARIS AFTER DARK(1943); SONG OF BERNADETTE, THE(1943); WINTERTIME(1943); DARK WATERS(1944); MRS. PARKINGTON(1944); OUR HEARTS WERE YOUNG AND GAY(1944); 'TILL WE MEET AGAIN(1944); TO HAVE AND HAVE NOT(1944); DAKOTA(1945); DOLLY SISTERS(1945); DO YOU LOVE ME?(1946); GILDA(1946); JOLSON STORY, THE(1946); RAZOR'S EDGE, THE(1946); RETURN OF MONTE CRISTO, THE(1946); SEARCHING WIND, THE(1946); SO DARK THE NIGHT(1946); THRILL OF BRAZIL, THE(1946); CIGARETTE GIRL(1947); FOXES OF HARROW, THE(1947); GLAMOUR GIRL(1947); JEWELS OF BRANDEN-BURG(1947); LOST MOMENT, THE(1947); PERILS OF PAULINE, THE(1947); ROGUES' REGIMENT(1948); SAIGON(1948); ON THE TOWN(1949); ALL ABOUT EVE(1950); LAST OF THE BUCCANEERS(1950); UNDER MY SKIN(1950); AMERI-CAN IN PARIS, AN(1951); MY FAVORITE SPY(1951); ON THE RIVERA(1951); SILVER CANYON(1951); HAPPY TIME, THE(1952); IRON MISTRESS, THE(1952); BLUEPRINT FOR MURDER, A(1953); DANGEROUS WHEN WET(1953); SAGINAW TRAIL(1953); SCANDAL AT SCOURIE(1953); TITANIC(1953); JUBILEE TRAIL(1954); PHFFFT!(1954); FAR COUNTRY, THE(1955); IT'S ALWAYS FAIR WEATHER(1955); THREE FOR THE SHOW(1955); TO CATCH A THIEF(1955); BEST THINGS IN LIFE ARE FREE, THE(1956); SPIRIT OF ST. LOUIS, THE(1957); TARNISHED ANGELS, THE(1957); FLY, THE(1958); ME AND THE COLONEL(1958); NEW KIND OF LOVE, A(1963); WHAT A WAY TO GO(1964)
Silents
BLUE BLOOD(1925); GENTLEMEN PREFER BLONDES(1928)
Misc. Silents
DRAFT 258(1917); THINK IT OVER(1917); BARRICADE, THE(1921); PORCELAIN LAMP, THE(1921); JADE CUP, THE(1926)
Gene Borden
PIRATES OF TRIPOLI(1955)
Jack Borden
DOZENS, THE(1981)
James Borden
HORROR CASTLE(1965, Ital.)
Lawrence Borden
WAR OF THE WIZARDS(1983, Taiwan), m
Leo Borden
DOCKS OF NEW YORK(1945); JOAN OF ARC(1948)
Lizzie Borden
BORN IN FLAMES(1983), p&d, w
Lynn Borden
CARPETBAGGERS, THE(1964); ROUSTABOUT(1964); WHAT A WAY TO GO(1964); FROGS(1972); BLACK MAMA, WHITE MAMA(1973); BREEZY(1973); THIS IS A HIJACK(1973); WALKING TALL(1973); DIRTY MARY, CRAZY LARRY(1974); ST. IVES(1976)
Marshall Borden
CLOUD DANCER(1980), ed
Marshall M. Borden
TOYS IN THE ATTIC(1963), ed; PINK PANTHER, THE(1964), ed; HAWAII(1966), spec eff; TOGETHER FOR DAYS(1972), ed; WILD PACK, THE(1972), ed; SUR-VIVE!(1977, Mex.), ed; WOLFEN(1981), ed
Mary Borden
ACTION FOR SLANDER(1937, Brit.), w; WOMAN I LOVE, THE(1937), w
Mathew Borden
PRISON TRAIN(1938), w
Olive Borden
GANG WAR(1928); DANCE HALL(1929); HALF-MARRIAGE(1929); LOVE IN THE DESERT(1929); HELLO SISTER(1930); SOCIAL LION, THE(1930); WEDDING RINGS(1930); HOTEL VARIETY(1933); LEAVE IT TO ME(1933, Brit.)

Silents
OVERLAND LIMITED, THE(1925); YANKEE SENOR, THE(1926); YELLOW FIN-GERS(1926); JOY GIRL, THE(1927); MONKEY TALKS, THE(1927); PAJAMAS(1927); ALBANY NIGHT BOAT, THE(1928); SINNERS IN LOVE(1928); ETERNAL WOMAN, THE(1929)
Misc. Silents
COUNTRY BEYOND, THE(1926); FIG LEAVES(1926); MY OWN PAL(1926); THREE BAD MEN(1926); COME TO MY HOUSE(1927); SECRET STUDIO, THE(1927); STOOL PIGEON(1928); VIRGIN LIPS(1928)
Phillip Borden
Misc. Talkies
TAKE ONE(1977)
Rene Borden
CANYON HAWKS(1930); RIDIN' LAW(1930)
Renee Borden
FIGHTING HERO(1934); KID COURAGEOUS(1935)
Roger Borden
LOGAN'S RUN(1976)
Viola Borden
1984
MUPPETS TAKE MANHATTAN, THE(1984)
Robert Bordenave
MURIEL(1963, Fr./Ital.)
Bernard Borderie
GORILLA GREETS YOU, THE(1958, Fr.), d, w; YOUR TURN, DARLING(1963, Fr.), d, w
Raymond Borderie
LOVERS OF VERONA, THE(1951, Fr.), p
Laurencio Bordero
REVENGERS, THE(1972, U.S./Mex.), spec eff
James Borders
1984
TIGHTROPE(1984)
Bob Bordiga
JETLAG(1981, U.S./Span.), p
Al Bordighi
MURPH THE SURF(1974)
Edwin Bordo
1984
BROADWAY DANNY ROSE(1984)
Trudy Bordoff
HARVEY MIDDLEMAN, FIREMAN(1965)
Giuseppe Bordogni
ROCCO AND HIS BROTHERS(1961, Fr./Ital.), p; DISORDER(1964, Fr./Ital.), p
Eugene Bordon
SONG TO REMEMBER, A(1945); PERFECT FURLOUGH, THE(1958)
Renee Bordon
WESTERN JUSTICE(1935)
Irene Bordoni
PARIS(1929); LOUISIANA PURCHASE(1941)
Vova Bordukov
WELCOME KOSTYA!(1965, USSR)
The Bored
NIGHT OF BLOODY HORROR zero(1969)
Annik Borel
WEEKEND WITH THE BABYSITTER(1970); TRUCK TURNER(1974); LEGEND OF THE WOLF WOMAN, THE(1977, Span.)
Jacques Borel
WAYS OF LOVE(1950, Ital./Fr.)
June Borel
SOUTHERN COMFORT(1981)
Matt Borel
SCREAMS OF A WINTER NIGHT(1979)
Raymond Borel
SHADOW OF EVIL(1967, Fr./Ital.), w
Louis Borell
AVENGING HAND, THE(1936, Brit.); HOUSE BROKEN(1936, Brit.); HEAD OVER HEELS IN LOVE(1937, Brit.); OVER THE MOON(1940, Brit.); PIRATES OF THE SEVEN SEAS(1941, Brit.); LONDON BLACKOUT MURDERS(1942); IRON MAJOR, THE(1943); PARIS AFTER DARK(1943); NIGHT OF ADVENTURE, A(1944); DE-SIREE(1954)
Wilmut Borell
DEVIL STRIKES AT NIGHT, THE(1959, Ger.)
Buzz Borelli
MORE AMERICAN GRAFFITI(1979)
Carla Borelli
GNOME-MOBILE, THE(1967); LOVE GOD?, THE(1969); DO NOT THROW CUSH-IONS INTO THE RING(1970)
Misc. Talkies
ASYLUM OF SATAN(1972)
Carlo Borelli
MAN WITH A GUN(1958, Brit.); ELECTRONIC MONSTER. THE(1960, Brit.)
Charles Borelli
NEVER TAKE NO FOR AN ANSWER(1952, Brit./Ital.)
Colette Borelli
LA CHIENNE(1975, Fr.)
Franco Borelli
VALACHI PAPERS, THE(1972, Ital./Fr.); WEEKEND MURDERS, THE(1972, Ital.)
M. Borelli
EAST LYNNE ON THE WESTERN FRONT(1931, Brit.)
Rosario Borelli
THIEF OF BAGHDAD, THE(1961, Ital./Fr.); GOLDEN ARROW, THE(1964, Ital.)
Sergio Borelli
1984
AFTER THE FALL OF NEW YORK(1984, Ital./Fr.), prod d
Evelyn Boren
THUNDERBALL(1965, Brit.)

Lamar Boren
UNDERWATER!(1955), ph; OLD MAN AND THE SEA, THE(1958), ph; UNDERWATER WARRIOR(1958), ph; FORBIDDEN ISLAND(1959), ph; SEPTEMBER STORM(1960), ph; FLIPPER(1963), ph; FLIPPER'S NEW ADVENTURE(1964), ph; RHINO(1964), ph; CLARENCE, THE CROSS-EYED LION(1965), ph; THUNDERBALL(1965, Brit.), ph; ZEBRA IN THE KITCHEN(1965), ph; AROUND THE WORLD UNDER THE SEA(1966), ph; NAMU, THE KILLER WHALE(1966), ph; HELLO DOWN THERE(1969), ph; BREWSTER McCLOUD(1970), ph; NEPTUNE FACTOR, THE(1973, Can.), ph; SPY WHO LOVED ME, THE(1977, Brit.), ph

Jackie Borene
ONCE IN A BLUE MOON(1936)

Dan Borenstein
DREAM ON(1981), ed

Emile Boreo
STREET SINGER, THE(1937, Brit.); LADY VANISHES, THE(1938, Brit.); CARNEGIE HALL(1947)

Mary Cathcard Borer
CIRCUS BOY(1947, Brit.), w

Mary Cathcart Borer
OLD MOTHER RILEY IN SOCIETY(1940, Brit.), w; FORTUNE LANE(1947, Brit.), w; LAST LOAD, THE(1948, Brit.), w; TRAPPED BY THE TERROR(1949, Brit.), w; DRAGON OF PENDRAGON CASTLE, THE(1950, Brit.); LITTLE BALLERINA, THE(1951, Brit.), w; MYSTERY ON BIRD ISLAND(1954, Brit.), w; TIM DRISCOLL'S DONKEY(1955, Brit.), w; ONE WISH TOO MANY(1956, Brit.), w; SECOND FIDDLE(1957, Brit.), w; TREASURE AT THE MILL(1957, Brit.), w; BLOW YOUR OWN TRUMPET(1958, Brit.), w; SALVAGE GANG, THE(1958, Brit.), w; MISSING NOTE, THE(1961, Brit.), w; MONSTER OF HIGHGATE PONDS, THE(1961, Brit.), w; DOG AND THE DIAMONDS, THE(1962, Brit.), w; RESCUE SQUAD, THE(1963, Brit.), w; EAGLE ROCK(1964, Brit.), p,d&w; WHO KILLED THE CAT?(1966, Brit.), w

Paul Boretski
SPACEHUNTER: ADVENTURES IN THE FORBIDDEN ZONE(1983)

Alan Boretz
COPACABANA(1947), w

Allen Boretz
ROOM SERVICE(1938), w; IT AIN'T HAY(1943), w; BATHING BEAUTY(1944), w; PRINCESS AND THE PIRATE, THE(1944), w; STEP LIVELY(1944), w; UP IN ARMS(1944), w; ZIEGFELD FOLLIES(1945), w; IT HAD TO BE YOU(1947), w; WHERE THERE'S LIFE(1947), w; MY GIRL TISA(1948), w; TWO GUYS FROM TEXAS(1948), w; GIRL FROM JONES BEACH, THE(1949), w

Alvin Boretz
BRASS TARGET(1978), w

Nick Boretz
STRANGE LOVERS(1963), w

Bjorn Borg
RACQUET(1979)

Brita Borg
INVASION OF THE ANIMAL PEOPLE(1962, U.S./Swed.)

Carl Oscar Borg
Silents
BLACK PIRATE, THE(1926), art d; GAUCHO, THE(1928), art d; TWO LOVERS(1928), art d

Karl Oscar Borg
Silents
WINNING OF BARBARA WORTH, THE(1926), art d; NIGHT OF LOVE, THE(1927), art d

Mr. Borg
LEFT-HANDED WOMAN, THE(1980, Ger.)

Mrs. Borg
LEFT-HANDED WOMAN, THE(1980, Ger.)

Odd Borg
PASSIONATE DEMONS, THE(1962, Norway)

Sonia Borg
BLUE FIN(1978, Aus.), w

Sven Borg
LET'S FALL IN LOVE(1934); THEODORA GOES WILD(1936); ESPIONAGE(1937); MAN HUNT(1941); THIS LAND IS MINE(1943)

Sven Hugo Borg
CRUSADES, THE(1935); SLAVE SHIP(1937); DEATH RIDES THE RANGE(1940); MYSTERY SEA RAIDER(1940); DANGEROUSLY THEY LIVE(1942); DESPERATE JOURNEY(1942); THEY RAID BY NIGHT(1942); TO BE OR NOT TO BE(1942); FIRST COMES COURAGE(1943); JACK LONDON(1943); MOON IS DOWN, THE(1943); TARZAN TRIUMPHS(1943); THEY CAME TO BLOW UP AMERICA(1943); KNICKERBOCKER HOLIDAY(1944); MY BUDDY(1944); SECRETS OF SCOTLAND YARD(1944); STORY OF DR. WASSELL, THE(1944); U-BOAT PRISONER(1944); NOB HILL(1945); PURSUIT TO ALGIERS(1945); FARMER'S DAUGHTER, THE(1947); SENATOR WAS INDISCREET, THE(1947); FORTUNES OF CAPTAIN BLOOD(1950); SANTA FE(1951); CAPTAIN PIRATE(1952); DESIREE(1954); PRIZE, THE(1963)
Misc. Talkies
BUZZY AND THE PHANTOM PINTO(1941)

Veda Ann Borg
THREE CHEERS FOR LOVE(1936); ALCATRAZ ISLAND(1937); CASE OF THE STUTTERING BISHOP, THE(1937); CONFESSION(1937); IT'S LOVE I'M AFTER(1937); KID GALAHAD(1937); MEN IN EXILE(1937); PUBLIC WEDDING(1937); SAN QUENTIN(1937); SHE LOVED A FIREMAN(1937); SINGING MARINE, THE(1937); SUBMARINE D-1(1937); OVER THE WALL(1938); LAW COMES TO TEXAS, THE(1939); DR. CHRISTIAN MEETS THE WOMEN(1940); GLAMOUR FOR SALE(1940); I TAKE THIS OATH(1940); LAUGHING AT DANGER(1940); MELODY RANCH(1940); MIRACLE ON MAIN STREET, A(1940); ARKANSAS JUDGE(1941); BEHIND THE NEWS(1941); CORSICAN BROTHERS, THE(1941); DOWN IN SAN DIEGO(1941); HONKY TONK(1941); PENALTY, THE(1941); PITTSBURGH KID, THE(1941); ABOUT FACE(1942); DUKE OF THE NAVY(1942); I MARRIED AN ANGEL(1942); LADY IN A JAM(1942); SHE'S IN THE ARMY(1942); TWO YANKS IN TRINIDAD(1942); FALSE FACES(1943); GIRL FROM MONTEREY, THE(1943); ISLE OF FORGOTTEN SINS(1943); MURDER IN TIMES SQUARE(1943); REVENGE OF THE ZOMBIES(1943); SMART GUY(1943); SOMETHING TO SHOUT ABOUT(1943); UNKNOWN GUEST, THE(1943); BIG NOISE, THE(1944); DETECTIVE KITTY O'-DAY(1944); FALCON IN HOLLYWOOD, THE(1944); GIRL WHO DARED, THE(1944); IRISH EYES ARE SMILING(1944); MARKED TRAILS(1944); STANDING ROOM ONLY(1944); DANGEROUS INTRUDER(1945); DON JUAN QUILLIGAN(1945); FOG ISLAND(1945); LOVE, HONOR AND GOODBYE(1945); NOB HILL(1945); ROUGH,

TOUGH AND READY(1945); SCARED STIFF(1945); WHAT A BLONDE(1945); ACCOMPLICE(1946); AVALANCHE(1946); FABULOUS SUZANNE, THE(1946); LIFE WITH BLONDIE(1946); WIFE WANTED(1946); BACHELOR AND THE BOBBY-SOXER, THE(1947); BIG TOWN(1947); BLONDE SAVAGE(1947); MOTHER WORE TIGHTS(1947); PILGRIM LADY, THE(1947); CHICKEN EVERY SUNDAY(1948); JULIA MISBEHAVES(1948); FORGOTTEN WOMEN(1949); MISSISSIPPI RHYTHM(1949); ONE LAST FLING(1949); KANGAROO KID, THE(1950, Aus./U.S.); RIDER FROM TUCSON(1950); AARON SLICK FROM PUNKIN CRICK(1952); BIG JIM McLAIN(1952); HOLD THAT LINE(1952); HOT NEWS(1953); MR. SCOUTMASTER(1953); PERILOUS JOURNEY, A(1953); THREE SAILORS AND A GIRL(1953); BITTER CREEK(1954); GUYS AND DOLLS(1955); I'LL CRY TOMORROW(1955); LOVE ME OR LEAVE ME(1955); YOU'RE NEVER TOO YOUNG(1955); FRONTIER GAMBLER(1956); NAKED GUN, THE(1956); WINGS OF EAGLES, THE(1957); FEARMAKERS, THE(1958); THUNDER IN THE SUN(1959); ALAMO, THE(1960)

Nick Borgaini
ST. VALENTINE'S DAY MASSACRE, THE(1967)

Nick Borgani
CASBAH(1948); SEPTEMBER AFFAIR(1950)

James A. Borgardt
O'HARA'S WIFE(1983), ed

Agostino Borgat
LOVE ON THE RUN(1936); FIREFLY, THE(1937)

Agostino Borgato
ROMANCE OF THE RIO GRANDE(1929); BEHIND THE MAKEUP(1930); HOT FOR PARIS(1930); FAREWELL TO ARMS, A(1932); WHITE SISTER, THE(1933); ROSE MARIE(1936); DAUGHTER OF SHANGHAI(1937); EMPEROR'S CANDLESTICKS, THE(1937); INTERNES CAN'T TAKE MONEY(1937); MAYTIME(1937); SWISS MISS(1938); HOTEL IMPERIAL(1939)

Augostino Borgato
MALTESE FALCON, THE(1931)

Augustino Borgato
SHE GOES TO WAR(1929); REDEMPTION(1930); TRANSGRESSION(1931)
Misc. Silents
MAGIC FLAME, THE(1927)

Agostino Borgator
BIRD OF PARADISE(1932)

Maria Borge
LIGHT AT THE EDGE OF THE WORLD, THE(1971, U.S./Span./Lichtenstein)

Rikke Borge
TATTOO(1981); STILL OF THE NIGHT(1982)

Vebe Borge
EDDIE AND THE CRUISERS(1983)

1984
FIRSTBORN(1984)

Victor Borge
HIGHER AND HIGHER(1943); DAYDREAMER, THE(1966); KING OF COMEDY, THE(1983)

Nelly Borgeaud
MISSISSIPPI MERMAID(1970, Fr./Ital.); MAN WHO LOVED WOMEN, THE(1977, Fr.); MON ONCLE D'AMERIQUE(1980, Fr.)

Chris Borgen
HERO AT LARGE(1980)

Nancy Borgenicht
1984
SILENT NIGHT, DEADLY NIGHT(1984)

Graciela Borges
SUMMERSKIN(1962, Arg.); TERRACE, THE(1964, Arg.); MONDAY'S CHILD(1967, U.S., Arg.)

Jose Borges
VOYAGE OF SILENCE(1968, Fr.)

Sal Borgese
BOUNTY HUNTERS, THE(1970, Ital.); ADIOS SABATA(1971, Ital./Span.); MADDEST CAR IN THE WORLD, THE(1974, Ger.)

Salvatore Borgese
OPIATE '67(1967, Fr./Ital.)

Linda Borgeson
Misc. Talkies
WHISKEY MOUNTAIN(1977)

Diane Borget
TWENTY MILLION SWEETHEARTS(1934)

Mina Borget
PARIS UNDERGROUND(1945)

Mme. Borget
THEY WON'T BELIEVE ME(1947); SYLVIA SCARLETT(1936)

Nina Borget
'TILL WE MEET AGAIN(1944); LOVE LETTERS(1945); BLUE DAHLIA, THE(1946); MONSIEUR BEAUCAIRE(1946); TO CATCH A THIEF(1955); FUNNY FACE(1957)

Olga Borget
FOLIES DERGERE(1935); KISS OF DEATH(1947); HOMECOMING(1948)

Olga Nina Borget
THAT FORSYTE WOMAN(1949); THIS EARTH IS MINE(1959)

Luigi Borghese
STREET PEOPLE(1976, U.S./Ital.), p

Sal Borghese
SUPER FUZZ(1981)

Antonio Borghesi
LOVE PROBLEMS(1970, Ital.), ph

Bruno Borghi
RED DESERT(1965, Fr./Ital.)

Gene Borghi
MAN CALLED FLINTSTONE, THE(1966), ph; SHINBONE ALLEY(1971), ph

Mario Borghi
ANGELO IN THE CROWD(1952, Ital.), p

Ake Borglund
STRANGER KNOCKS, A(1963, Den.), ph

Frank Borgman
FUGITIVE KIND, THE(1960)

Hans Otto Borgmann
MOSCOW SHANGHAI(1936, Ger.), m
Hans-Otto Borgmann
WHITE DEMON, THE(1932, Ger.), m; BARCAROLE(1935, Ger.), m; GIRL FROM THE MARSH CROFT, THE(1935, Ger.), m
Ernest Borgnine
CHINA CORSAIR(1951); MOB, THE(1951); WHISTLE AT EATON FALLS(1951); FROM HERE TO ETERNITY(1953); STRANGER WORE A GUN, THE(1953); BOUNTY HUNTER, THE(1954); DEMETRIUS AND THE GLADIATORS(1954); JOHNNY GUITAR(1954); VERA CRUZ(1954); BAD DAY AT BLACK ROCK(1955); LAST COMMAND, THE(1955); MARTY(1955); RUN FOR COVER(1955); SQUARE JUNGLE, THE(1955); VIOLENT SATURDAY(1955); BEST THINGS IN LIFE ARE FREE, THE(1956); CATERED AFFAIR, THE(1956); JUBAL(1956); THREE BRAVE MEN(1957); BADLANDERS, THE(1958); TORPEDO RUN(1958); VIKINGS, THE(1958); RABBIT TRAP, THE(1959); MAN ON A STRING(1960); PAY OR DIE(1960); GO NAKED IN THE WORLD(1961); SEASON OF PASSION(1961, Aus./Brit.); BARABBAS(1962, Ital.); MC HALE'S NAVY(1964); FLIGHT OF THE PHOENIX, THE(1965); OSCAR, THE(1966); CHUKA(1967); DIRTY DOZEN, THE(1967, Brit.); ICE STATION ZEBRA(1968); LEGEND OF LYLAH CLARE, THE(1968); SPLIT, THE(1968); VENGEANCE IS MINE(1969, Ital./Span.); WILD BUNCH, THE(1969); ADVENTURERS, THE(1970); BULLET FOR SANDOVAL, A(1970, Ital./Span.); SUPPOSE THEY GAVE A WAR AND NOBODY CAME?(1970); BUNNY O'HARE(1971); HANNIE CALDER(1971, Brit.); RAIN FOR A DUSTY SUMMER(1971, U.S./Span.); RIPPED-OFF(1971, Ital.); WILLARD(1971); POSEIDON ADVENTURE, THE(1972); REVENGERS, THE(1972, U.S./Mex.); EMPEROR OF THE NORTH POLE(1973); NEPTUNE FACTOR, THE(1973, Can.); LAW AND DISORDER(1974); DEVIL'S RAIN, THE(1975, U.S./Mex.); HUSTLE(1975); SUNDAY IN THE COUNTRY(1975, Can.); SHOOT(1976, Can.); GREATEST, THE(1977, U.S./Brit.); CONVOY(1978); CROSSED SWORDS(1978); BLACK HOLE, THE(1979); RAVAGERS, THE(1979); THE DOUBLE McGUFFIN(1979); WHEN TIME RAN OUT(1980); DEADLY BLESSING(1981); ESCAPE FROM NEW YORK(1981); HIGH RISK(1981); SUPER FUZZ(1981); YOUNG WARRIORS(1983)
Fred Borgognoni
ORGANIZER, THE(1964, Fr./Ital./Yugo.)
Enrico Borgstrom
GOLD OF NAPLES(1957, Ital.)
Hilda Borgstrom
WOMAN'S FACE, A(1939, Swed.); NIGHT IS MY FUTURE(1962, Swed.)
Misc. Silents
GIVE US THIS DAY(1913, Swed.); INGEBORG HOLM(1913, Swed.); PHANTOM CARRIAGE, THE(1921, Swed.)
Corine Borher
ZAPPED!(1982)
Diana Bori
ANN CARVER'S PROFESSION(1933)
Diane Bori
BIG TOWN(1932)
Gene Bori
MARATHON MAN(1976)
Jean Bori
TENDER IS THE NIGHT(1961)
Rita Bori
Misc. Silents
SMUGGLERS, THE(1916)
Yuri Borienko
SMASHING TIME(1967 Brit.); GREAT CATHERINE(1968, Brit.); ON HER MAJESTY'S SECRET SERVICE(1969, Brit.); TRYGON FACTOR, THE(1969, Brit.); DOCTOR IN TROUBLE(1970, Brit.); INNOCENT BYSTANDERS(1973, Brit.); S(1974)
Alcide Borik
SECRET AGENT FIREBALL(1965, Fr./Ital.)
Ingvar Borild
TIME OF DESIRE, THE(1957, Swed.), ph
Edward Boring
Silents
NEPTUNE'S DAUGHTER(1914)
Josephine Borio
Silents
SCARLET DOVE, THE(1928); WOMAN WISE(1928)
Misc. Silents
SPORTING AGE, THE(1928); TYRANT OF RED GULCH(1928)
Joe Boris
HUCKLEBERRY FINN(1974)
Robert Boris
ELECTRA GLIDE IN BLUE(1973), w; SOME KIND OF HERO(1982), w; DOCTOR DETROIT(1983), w
1984
OXFORD BLUES(1984), d&w
V. Boris
1984
SECRET DIARY OF SIGMUND FREUD, THE(1984), m
Boris Borisenko
DREAM COME TRUE, A(1963, USSR)
Don Borisenko
GENGHIS KHAN(U.S./Brit./Ger./Yugo); NOW THAT APRIL'S HERE(1958, Can.); LAST GUNFIGHTER, THE(1961, Can.); DURING ONE NIGHT(1962, Brit.); NINE HOURS TO RAMA(1963, U.S./Brit.); PSYCHOPATH, THE(1966, Brit.)
Misc. Talkies
IVY LEAGUE KILLERS(1962, Can.)
L. Borisenko
SKY CALLS, THE(1959, USSR); WAR AND PEACE(1968, USSR)
B. Borisenok
MOTHER AND DAUGHTER(1965, USSR)
Pavilk Boriskin
DESTINY OF A MAN(1961, USSR)
V. Boriskin
DAY THE EARTH FROZE, THE(1959, Fin./USSR); HUNTING IN SIBERIA(1962, USSR); RESURRECTION(1963, USSR)
Norman Borisoff
STOP TRAIN 349(1964, Fr./Ital./Ger.), w

Albert Borisov
KIEV COMEDY, A(1963, USSR)
Aleksandr Borisov
MUMU(1961, USSR), art d; WAR AND PEACE(1968, USSR)
I. Borisov
LAST GAME, THE(1964, USSR)
L. Borisov
DESTINY OF A MAN(1961, USSR)
Slava Borisov
VIOLIN AND ROLLER(1962, USSR)
G. Borisova
JACK FROST(1966, USSR)
Natalie Borisova
PARTY, THE(1968)
Nina Borisova
MOTHER AND DAUGHTER(1965, USSR)
Yulia Borisova
IDIOT, THE(1960, USSR)
Etan Boritzer
1984
FIRESTARTER(1984)
Josephine Borjo
Misc. Silents
SWIFT SHADOW, THE(1927)
Hanne Bork
NIGHT VISITOR, THE(1970, Swed./U.S.)
Gene Borkan
DEALING: OR THE BERKELEY-TO-BOSTON FORTY-BRICK LOST-BAG BLUES(1971); ALL-AMERICAN BOY, THE(1973); TERMINAL MAN, THE(1974); SHARK'S TREASURE(1975); MELVIN AND HOWARD(1980); AMERICAN POP(1981)
1984
BEVERLY HILLS COP(1984); SWING SHIFT(1984)
Misc. Talkies
AMERICAN RASPBERRY(1980)
Jules Borkon
WICKED GO TO HELL, THE(1961, Fr.), p; HORROR CHAMBER OF DR. FAUSTUS, THE(1962, Fr./Ital.), p; SWEET SKIN(1965, Fr./Ital.), p; MARRIAGE CAME TUMBLING DOWN, THE(1968, Fr.), p
Leopold Borkowski
SEARCH, THE(1948)
Shelley Borkum
1984
FOREVER YOUNG(1984, Brit.)
Barlow Borland
STAMBOUL QUEST(1934); MURDER GOES TO COLLEGE(1937); KING OF THE TURF(1939)
Barlowe Borland
LITTLE MINISTER, THE(1934); MYSTERY OF MR. X, THE(1934); RIP TIDE(1934); FOLIES DERGERE(1935); INFORMER, THE(1935); TALE OF TWO CITIES, A(1935); LLOYDS OF LONDON(1936); MARY OF SCOTLAND(1936); WITNESS CHAIR, THE(1936); BLONDE TROUBLE(1937); EASY LIVING(1937); FORLORN RIVER(1937); KING OF GAMBLERS(1937); MAYTIME(1937); NIGHT CLUB SCANDAL(1937); NIGHT OF MYSTERY(1937); SOPHIE LANG GOES WEST(1937); THUNDER TRAIL(1937); BLUEBEARD'S EIGHTH WIFE(1938); COLLEGE SWING(1938); DANGEROUS TO KNOW(1938); GUN PACKER(1938); TIP-OFF GIRLS(1938); GOOD GIRLS GO TO PARIS(1939); HOUND OF THE BASKERVILLES, THE(1939); WE ARE NOT ALONE(1939); WITNESS VANISHES, THE(1939); EARL OF CHICAGO, THE(1940); TOM BROWN'S SCHOOL DAYS(1940); WE WERE DANCING(1942)
Carol Borland
MARK OF THE VAMPIRE(1935)
Carroll Borland
SCALPS(1983)
Misc. Talkies
BIO-HAZARD(1984)
Drew Borland
PARALLELS(1980, Can.), art d
Hal Borland
WHEN THE LEGENDS DIE(1972), w
Scott Borland
HEROES DIE YOUNG(1960)
Orel Borle
SOUTHERN COMFORT(1981)
Jean Borlin
Misc. Silents
LE VOYAGE IMAGINAIRE(1926, Fr.)
Rose Bormacher
MEDIUM COOL(1969)
Bibs Borman
PARIS MODEL(1953)
E. W. Borman
LIFE BEGINS AT 40(1935)
Edward W. Borman
Silents
STRANGER'S BANQUET(1922)
Misc. Silents
WHEN LAW COMES TO HADES(1923)
Gehrard Borman
IS PARIS BURNING?(1966, U.S./Fr.)
M. Borman
HAROLD AND MAUDE(1971)
Moritz Borman
1984
UNDER THE VOLCANO(1984), p
Jurgen Born
1984
LOVE IN GERMANY, A(1984, Fr./Ger.)
Max Born
FELLINI SATYRICON(1969, Fr./Ital.)

Nicolas Born
CIRCLE OF DECEIT(1982, Fr./Ger.), w
Clovis Bornay
EARTH ENTRANCED(1970, Braz.)
Zoubeir Bornaz
1984
MISUNDERSTOOD(1984)
Hal Borne
HOW DO YOU DO?(1946), m; SUSIE STEPS OUT(1946), md; HEADING FOR HEAVEN(1947), m; EXPLOSIVE GENERATION, THE(1961), m; FLIGHT OF THE LOST BALLOON(1961), m; PROMISES, PROMISES(1963), m; HILLBILLYS IN A HAUNTED HOUSE(1967), m
Ernest Borneman
BANG! YOU'RE DEAD(1954, Brit.), w
Mick Borneman
COLOR ME DEAD(1969, Aus.), ph
Ernest Bornemann
BLACK GLOVE(1954, Brit.), w; LONG DUEL, THE(1967, Brit.), w
Mick Bornemann
IT TAKES ALL KINDS(1969, U.S./Aus.), ph
Phil Borneo
GAS-S-S-S!(1970)
Ruby Borner
TRAUMA(1962)
Gabriella Borni
LA TRAVIATA(1982)
Lawrence Bornman
LAST HOUSE ON DEAD END STREET(1977)
Misc. Talkies
FUN HOUSE, THE(1977)
Charles Bornstein
FOG, THE(1980), ed
1984
ANGEL(1984), ed
Claus Boro
AS LONG AS YOU'RE NEAR ME(1956, Ger.), ed
Aleksandr Porfiryevich Borodin
ISADORA(1968, Brit.), m
Alexander Porphyrievich Borodin
FIRE MAIDENS FROM OUTER SPACE(1956, Brit.), m
Doris Borodin
REUNION IN FRANCE(1942)
Alexander Borodyansky
1984
JAZZMAN(1984, USSR), w
Marvin Borofsky
GAMBLING HOUSE(1950), w
Paul Borofsky
GIRL IN THE CASE(1944), ed; MISSING JUROR, THE(1944), ed; RACKET MAN, THE(1944), ed; RETURN OF THE VAMPIRE, THE(1944), ed; SAILOR'S HOLIDAY(1944), ed; SOUL OF A MONSTER, THE(1944), ed; U-BOAT PRISONER(1944), ed; DESERT HORSEMAN, THE(1946), ed; LAWLESS EMPIRE(1946), ed; OUT OF THE DEPTHS(1946), ed; LAST DAYS OF BOOT HILL(1947), ed; LONE HAND TEXAN, THE(1947), ed; BUCKAROO FROM POWDER RIVER(1948), ed; PHANTOM VALLEY(1948), ed; WHIRLWIND RAIDERS(1948), ed; BLAZING TRAIL, THE(1949), ed; CHALLENGE OF THE RANGE(1949), ed; LARAMIE(1949), ed; QUICK ON THE TRIGGER(1949), ed; RENEGADES OF THE SAGE(1949), ed; SMOKY MOUNTAIN MELODY(1949), ed; SOUTH OF DEATH VALLEY(1949), ed; ACROSS THE BADLANDS(1950), ed; FRONTIER OUTPOST(1950), ed; HOEDOWN(1950), ed; HORSEMEN OF THE SIERRAS(1950), ed; LIGHTNING GUNS(1950), ed; OUTCAST OF BLACK MESA(1950), ed; RAIDERS OF TOMAHAWK CREEK(1950), ed; STREETS OF GHOST TOWN(1950), ed; TEXAS DYNAMO(1950), ed; BANDITS OF EL DORADO(1951), ed; BONANZA TOWN(1951), ed; CYCLONE FURY(1951), ed; FORT SAVAGE RAIDERS(1951), ed; KID FROM AMARILLO, THE(1951), ed; PECOS RIVER(1951), ed; PRAIRIE ROUNDUP(1951), ed; RIDIN' THE OUTLAW TRAIL(1951), ed; SNAKE RIVER DESPERADOES(1951), ed; WHIRLWIND(1951), ed; HAWK OF WILD RIVER, THE(1952), ed; JUNCTION CITY(1952), ed; KID FROM BROKEN GUN, THE(1952), ed; LARAMIE MOUNTAINS(1952), ed; MONTANA TERRITORY(1952), ed; ROUGH, TOUGH WEST(1952), ed; SMOKY CANYON(1952), ed; DON'T KNOCK THE ROCK(1956), ed; NIGHT THE WORLD EXPLODED, THE(1957), ed; RAWHIDE TRAIL, THE(1958), ed
Joaquin Garcia Vargas Borolas
FRANKENSTEIN, THE VAMPIRE AND CO.(1961, Mex.)
Tor Borong
ONLY ONE NIGHT(1942, Swed.); VIRGIN SPRING, THE(1960, Swed.); WINTER LIGHT, THE(1963, Swed.)
Y. Boronikhin
Misc. Silents
PALACE AND FORTRESS(1924, USSR)
Yevgeni Boronikhin
Misc. Silents
NINTH OF JANUARY(1925, USSR)
Sandor Boronkay
WITNESS, THE(1982, Hung.), ed
Ferike Boros
BORN RECKLESS(1930); LADIES LOVE BRUTES(1930); GENTLEMAN'S FATE(1931); HUDDLE(1932); NO LIVING WITNESS(1932); WORLD AND THE FLESH, THE(1932); HUMANITY(1933); EIGHT GIRLS IN A BOAT(1934); FOUNTAIN, THE(1934); RAFTER ROMANCE(1934); SYMPHONY OF LIVING(1935); HI GAUCHO!(1936); MAKE WAY FOR TOMORROW(1937); BACHELOR MOTHER(1939); DUST BE MY DESTINY(1939); FIFTH AVENUE GIRL(1939); LIGHT THAT FAILED, THE(1939); LOVE AFFAIR(1939); RIO(1939); STRONGER THAN DESIRE(1939); ARGENTINE NIGHTS(1940); CHRISTMAS IN JULY(1940); GALLANT SONS(1940); GIRL FROM GOD'S COUNTRY(1940); LA CONGA NIGHTS(1940); LILLIAN RUSSELL(1940); CAUGHT IN THE DRAFT(1941); PRIVATE NURSE(1941); SLEEPERS WEST(1941); ONCE UPON A HONEYMOON(1942); PIED PIPER, THE(1942); TALK OF THE TOWN(1942); MARGIN FOR ERROR(1943); PRINCESS O'ROURKE(1943); THEY GOT ME COVERED(1943); THIS LOVE OF OURS(1945); TREE GROWS IN BROOKLYN, A(1945); SPECTER OF THE ROSE(1946); EAST SIDE, WEST SIDE(1949)

Frank Boros
1984
NEW YORK NIGHTS(1984), art d
Julius Boros
CADDY, THE(1953)
Paul Borosky
DESERT VIGILANTE(1949), ed
Tadeusz Borowczyk
JOAN OF THE ANGELS(1962, Pol.), art d
Walerian Borowczyk
BLANCHE(1971, Fr.), d&w; BEAST, THE(1975, Fr.), w&d, ed
Katherine Borowitz
WORLD ACCORDING TO GARP, The(1982)
1984
HARRY AND SON(1984)
Henryk Borowski
KNIGHTS OF THE TEUTONIC ORDER, THE(1962, Pol.)
Marvin Borowsky
FREE AND EASY(1941), w; REUNION IN FRANCE(1942), w; ESCAPE IN THE DESERT(1945), w; PRIDE OF THE MARINES(1945), w; SOMEWHERE IN THE NIGHT(1946), w; BIG JACK(1949), w
Apastimo Borpato
NOW AND FOREVER(1934)
Ralph Borque
TEXICAN, THE(1966, U.S./Span.), cos
O. H. Borradaile
MACOMBER AFFAIR, THE(1947), ph; I WAS A MALE WAR BRIDE(1949), ph
Osmond Borradaile
ELEPHANT BOY(1937, Brit.), ph; FOUR FEATHERS, THE(1939, Brit.), ph; LION HAS WINGS, THE(1940, Brit.), ph; OVERLANDERS, THE(1946, Brit./Aus.), ph; SAINTS AND SINNERS(1949, Brit.), ph; SCOTT OF THE ANTARCTIC(1949, Brit.), ph; WINSLOW BOY, THE(1950), ph
Osmund Borradaile
SANDERS OF THE RIVER(1935, Brit.), ph
Borrah Minevich and His Gang
LOVE UNDER FIRE(1937)
Borrah Minevitch and his Harmonica Rascals
ONE IN A MILLION(1936); HIT PARADE OF 1941(1940)
Borrah Minevitch and His Rascals
ALWAYS IN MY HEART(1942)
Borrah Minnevitch and His Harmonica Rascals
TOP MAN(1943)
Ernest Borrand
HOWARD CASE, THE(1936, Brit.)
Eduardo Borras
DARK RIVER(1956, Arg.), w; ROSE FOR EVERYONE, A(1967, Ital.), w; GAMES MEN PLAY, THE(1968, Arg.), p, w
Mimi Borrel
PRISONERS OF THE CASBAH(1953)
Louis Borrell
FOREIGN CORRESPONDENT(1940)
Carlo Borrelli
WHEN IN ROME(1952)
Jim Borrelli
1984
BEAT STREET(1984); WINDY CITY(1984)
Charles Borrett
MURDER BY ROPE(1936, Brit.)
Osmond Borrodaile
DRUMS(1938, Brit.), ph; THIEF OF BAGHDAD, THE(1940, Brit.), ph
Charles Borromel
STORY OF JOSEPH AND HIS BRETHREN THE(1962, Ital.); WHITE SLAVE SHIP(1962, Fr./Ital.); GIDGET GOES TO ROME(1963); WATERLOO(1970, Ital./USSR)
Christian Borromeo
NEST OF VIPERS(1979, Ital.)
Claudio Borroni
NIGHT OF THE ZOMBIES(1983, Span./Ital.), ed
Ernest Borrow
TROUBLED WATERS(1936, Brit.); WEDNESDAY'S LUCK(1936, Brit.); I SEE ICE(1938); DICK BARTON–SPECIAL AGENT(1948, Brit.); THINGS HAPPEN AT NIGHT(1948, Brit.); MY BROTHER JONATHAN(1949, Brit.)
Dieter Borsche
ALI BABA(1954, Fr.); TIME TO LOVE AND A TIME TO DIE, A(1958); DAY WILL COME, A(1960, Ger.); DARK EYES OF LONDON(1961, Ger.); SCOTLAND YARD HUNTS DR. MABUSE(1963, Ger.); MAD EXECUTIONERS, THE(1965, Ger.); PHANTOM OF SOHO, THE(1967, Ger.); U-47 LT. COMMANDER PRIEN(1967, Ger.); DOCTOR OF ST. PAUL, THE(1969, Ger.); LADY HAMILTON(1969, Ger./Ital./Fr.); PRIEST OF ST. PAULI, THE(1970, Ger.)
Randy Borscheidt
CHELSEA GIRLS, THE(1967)
Bill Borsella
LOOKIN' TO GET OUT(1982)
Guilio Borsetti
REQUIEM FOR A SECRET AGENT(1966, Ital.)
A. Borshchagovskiy
LAST GAME, THE(1964, USSR), w
Natasha Borskaya
MILITARY SECRET(1945, USSR)
Haal Borske
NAKED WITCH, THE(1964); GHASTLY ONES, THE(1968); TORTURE DUNGEON(1970)
John Borske
BLOODTHIRSTY BUTCHERS(1970), w; TORTURE DUNGEON(1970), w
Ursula Borsodi
GOOD SOLDIER SCHWEIK, THE(1963, Ger.)
Hans Borsody
CANDIDATE FOR MURDER(1966, Brit.)

Philip Borsos
GREY FOX, THE(1983, Can.), d
Jarl Borssen
PIPPI IN THE SOUTH SEAS(1974, Swed./Ger.)
Margrit Borstel
NOT RECONCILED, OR "ONLY VIOLENCE HELPS WHERE IT RULES"(1969, Ger.)
Orin Borsten
ANGEL BABY(1961), w
Pete Borsz
STACY'S KNIGHTS(1983)
Ingrid Borthen
RAILROAD WORKERS(1948, Swed.)
Andrew Borthwick
ELEPHANT CALLED SLOWLY, AN(1970, Brit.), ed; CHRISTIAN THE LION(1976, Brit.), ed
James Borthwick
GUEST AT STEENKAMPSKRAAL, THE(1977, South Africa)
1984
GUEST, THE(1984, Brit.)
Richard Borthwick
FUNNY MONEY(1983, Brit.)
1984
JIGSAW MAN, THE(1984, Brit.)
Ruth Borthwick
TRENCHCOAT(1983)
Grigoriy Bortnikov
GROWN-UP CHILDREN(1963, USSR); SONG OVER MOSCOW(1964, USSR)
Annalisa Bortolin
BON VOYAGE, CHARLIE BROWN(AND DON'T COME BACK)*** (1980)
Gianni Bortolotti
VIOLENT FOUR, THE(1968, Ital.); SUNFLOWER(1970, Fr./Ital.)
Steve Borton
MAIDSTONE(1970)
Neal Bortz
VISITOR, THE(1980, Ital./U.S.)
Paul Borum
PEOPLE MEET AND SWEET MUSIC FILLS THE HEART(1969, Den./Swed.), w
Wlodzimierz Borunski
SALTO(1966, Pol.)
Radu Borusescu
MONTENEGRO(1981, Brit./Swed.), art d
Jean-Marc Bory
LOVERS, THE(1959, Fr.); ADORABLE LIAR(1962, Fr.); WHERE THE TRUTH LIES(1962, Fr.); LOVE ON A PILLOW(1963, Fr./Ital.); SWEET AND SOUR(1964, Fr./Ital.); TRIPLE CROSS(1967, Fr./Brit.)
Maria Bory
QUEEN OF BABYLON, THE(1956, Ital.), w
Peppi Borza
MAN OF LA MANCHA(1972); PIRATES OF PENZANCE, THE(1983)
Dan Borzabe
WESTERNER, THE(1940); WHAT PRICE GLORY?(1952)
Bill Borzage
NORTH STAR, THE(1943); MOONRISE(1948); HOUSE OF USHER(1960)
Dan Borzage
TRUE TO LIFE(1943); LONG VOYAGE HOME, THE(1940); DESTINATION TOKYO(1944); THEY WERE EXPENDABLE(1945); MY DARLING CLEMENTINE(1946); SEARCHERS, THE(1956); WINGS OF EAGLES, THE(1957); LAST HURRAH, THE(1958); HORSE SOLDIERS, THE(1959); TWO RODE TOGETHER(1961); MC LINTOCK!(1963); CHEYENNE AUTUMN(1964)
Silents
IRON HORSE, THE(1924)
Daniel Borzage
MAN WHO SHOT LIBERTY VALANCE, THE(1962)
Danny Borzage
MISTER ROBERTS(1955)
Frank Borzage
RIVER, THE(1928), d; STREET ANGEL(1928), d; LUCKY STAR(1929), d; THEY HAD TO SEE PARIS(1929), d; LILIOM(1930), d; SONG O' MY HEART(1930), d; BAD GIRL(1931), d; DOCTORS' WIVES(1931), d; YOUNG AS YOU FEEL(1931), d; AFTER TOMORROW(1932), d; FAREWELL TO ARMS, A(1932), d; YOUNG AMERICA(1932), d; MAN'S CASTLE, A(1933), d; SECRETS(1933), d; FLIRTATION WALK(1934), d; NO GREATER GLORY(1934), d; LIVING ON VELVET(1935), d; SHIPMATES FOREVER(1935), d; STRANDED(1935), d; DESIRE(1936), d; HEARTS DIVIDED(1936), d; BIG CITY(1937), d; GREEN LIGHT(1937), d; HISTORY IS MADE AT NIGHT(1937), d; MANNEQUIN(1937), d; SHINING HOUR, THE(1938), d; THREE COMRADES(1938), d; DISPUTED PASSAGE(1939), d; I TAKE THIS WOMAN(1940), d; MORTAL STORM, THE(1940), d; STRANGE CARGO(1940), d; SMILIN' THROUGH(1941), d; VANISHING VIRGINIAN, THE(1941), d; SEVEN SWEETHEARTS(1942), d; HIS BUTLER'S SISTER(1943), d; STAGE DOOR CANTEEN(1943), d; 'TILL WE MEET AGAIN(1944), d; SPANISH MAIN, THE(1945), d; I'VE ALWAYS LOVED YOU(1946), p&d; MAGNIFICENT DOLL(1946), d; THAT'S MY MAN(1947), p&d; MOONRISE(1948), d; JEANNE EAGELS(1957); CHINA DOLL(1958), p&d; BIG FISHERMAN, THE(1959), d; JOURNEY BENEATH THE DESERT(1967, Fr./Ital.)
Silents
BATTLE OF GETTYSBURG(1914); TYPHOON, THE(1914); WRATH OF THE GODS, THE or THE DESTRUCTION OF SAKURA JIMA(1914); IMMEDIATE LEE(1916), a, d; BILLY JIM(1922), d; PRIDE OF PALOMAR, THE(1922), d; VALLEY OF SILENT MEN, THE(1922), d; NTH COMMANDMENT, THE(1923), d; LAZYBONES(1925), d; WAGES FOR WIVES(1925), d; EARLY TO WED(1926), d; FIRST YEAR, THE(1926), d; 'MARRIAGE LICENSE?'(1926), d; SEVENTH HEAVEN(1927), d
Misc. Silents
ALOHA OE(1915); LAND O' LIZARDS(1916), a, d; FLYING COLORS(1917), d; MORMON MAID, A(1917); WEE LADY BETTY(1917); CURSE OF IKU, THE(1918), a, d; GHOST FLOWER, THE(1918), d; GUN WOMAN, THE(1918), d; HONEST MAN, AN(1918), d; INNOCENT'S PROGRESS(1918), d; SHOES THAT DANCED, THE(1918), d; SOCIETY FOR SALE(1918), d; UNTIL THEY GET ME(1918), d; WHO IS TO BLAME?(1918), d; ASHES OF DESIRE(1919), d; PRUDENCE ON BROADWAY(1919), d; TOTON(1919), d; WHOM THE GODS WOULD DESTROY(1919), d; HUMORESQUE(1920), d; DUKE OF CHIMNEY BUTTE, THE(1921), d; GET-RICH-QUICK WALLINGFORD(1921), d; BACK PAY(1922), d; GOOD PROVIDER, THE(1922), d;

HAIR TRIGGER CASEY(1922), a, d; AGE OF DESIRE, THE(1923), d; CHILDREN OF DUST(1923), d; SECRETS(1924), d; CIRCLE, THE(1925), d; DADDY'S GONE A-HUNTING(1925), d; LADY, THE(1925), d; DIXIE MERCHANT, THE(1926), d; STREET ANGEL(1928), d
Franz Borzage
LITTLE MAN, WHAT NOW?(1934), d
Lou Borzage
JEANNE EAGELS(1957)
Raymond Borzage
YOUNG AMERICA(1932); MAYOR OF HELL, THE(1933); MEET NERO WOLFE(1936)
William Borzage
WAY DOWN EAST(1935)
Samantha Borzaui
HIGH RISK(1981)
V. Borzho
OTHELLO(1960, U.S.S.R.)
Anna Bos
Misc. Silents
CARMEN OF THE NORTH(1920)
Ery Bos
SHOT AT DAWN, A(1934, Ger.)
Gerry Bos
RIDE THE HIGH IRON(1956), cos
Jane Bos
DIE MANNER UM LUCIE(1931), m; GLORY OF FAITH, THE(1938, Fr.), m
Jenny Bos
HENRY VIII AND HIS SIX WIVES(1972, Brit.)
Jerry Bos
DESTINATION MURDER(1950), cos; MAN WITH THE GUN(1955), cos; NIGHT OF THE HUNTER, THE(1955), cos; FLIGHT THAT DISAPPEARED, THE(1961), cos
John Bos
TWO-WAY STRETCH(1961, Brit.), art d
Paul Bos
ONE, TWO, THREE(1961)
Beth Bosacker
FOOLIN' AROUND(1980)
Oldrich Bosak
CLOSELY WATCHED TRAINS(1967, Czech.), art d; DIAMONDS OF THE NIGHT(1968, Czech.), art d; REPORT ON THE PARTY AND THE GUESTS, A(1968, Czech.), art d
Olin Bosak
LADY ON THE TRACKS, THE(1968, Czech.), art d; MARTYRS OF LOVE(1968, Czech.), art d
Henri Bosc
Silents
MADAME POMPADOUR(1927, Brit.)
Thierry Bosc
CONFESSION, THE(1970, Fr.)
Peter Bosch
MISSION BLOODY MARY(1967, Fr./Ital./Span.)
Ricardo Ferrer Bosch
LAST MERCENARY, THE(1969, Ital./Span./Ger.), w
Angelo Boschariol
BIBLE...IN THE BEGINNING, THE(1966)
Peter Bosche
LILITH(1964)
Jeff Boschee
HEARTLAND(1980)
Ada Boschell
Misc. Silents
SALAMANDER, THE(1916)
Dominique Boschero
TALE OF TWO CITIES, A(1958, Brit.); ROAD TO SHAME, THE(1962, Fr.); GOLDEN ARROW, THE(1964, Ital.); PARIS WHEN IT SIZZLES(1964); DOUBLE BED, THE(1965, Fr./Ital.); SECRET AGENT FIREBALL(1965, Fr./Ital.)
Tony Boschetti
KING OF COMEDY, THE(1983)
Eliseo Boschi
GOSPEL ACCORDING TO ST. MATTHEW, THE(1966, Fr., Ital.)
Philip Bosco
LOVELY WAY TO DIE, A(1968); TRADING PLACES(1983)
1984
POPE OF GREENWICH VILLAGE, THE(1984)
Robert Bosco
Misc. Talkies
FOX AFFAIR, THE(1978)
W. Bosco
Silents
POTTER'S CLAY(1922, Brit.)
Wallace Bosco
SCHOOL FOR SCANDAL, THE(1930, Brit.); TIME FLIES(1944, Brit.); 2,000 WOMEN(1944, Brit.); GREAT PONY RAID, THE(1968, Brit.), w
Silents
IVANHOE(1913); FLAG LIEUTENANT, THE(1919, Brit.); DEAD CERTAINTY, A(1920, Brit.); JUDGE NOT(1920, Brit.); WON BY A HEAD(1920, Brit.); GREEN CARAVAN, THE(1922, Brit.); ROB ROY(1922, Brit.); MAN WHO CHANGED HIS NAME, THE(1928, Brit.)
Misc. Silents
SAVED FROM THE SEA(1920, Brit.); VALLEY OF THE GHOSTS(1928, Brit.); DIZZY LIMIT, THE(1930, Brit.)
Wally Bosco
DANGEROUS SEAS(1931, Brit.); WICKHAM MYSTERY, THE(1931, Brit.); REGAL CAVALCADE(1935, Brit.); BRIEF ENCOUNTER(1945, Brit.); LOVE IS A WOMAN(1967, Brit.), w; UP IN THE AIR(1969, Brit.), w
Silents
HANDY ANDY(1921, Brit.); OLD BILL THROUGH THE AGES(1924, Brit.)

Boscoe Holder Dancers
HAND OF NIGHT, THE(1968, Brit.)
Tania Boscoli
1984
GABRIELA(1984, Braz.)
Amit Bose
SHAKESPEARE WALLAH(1966, India), ed
Ashoke Bose
1984
HOME AND THE WORLD, THE(1984, India), art d
Lucia Bose
AGE OF INFIDELITY(1958, Span.); TESTAMENT OF ORPHEUS, THE(1962, Fr.);
FELLINI SATYRICON(1969, Fr./Ital.); FEMALE BUTCHER, THE(1972, Ital./Span.);
NATHALIE GRANGER(1972, Fr.); DOWN THE ANCIENT STAIRCASE(1975, Ital.);
LUMIERE(1976, Fr.); LADY WITHOUT CAMELLIAS, THE(1981, Ital.)
Misc. Talkies
SOMETHING CREEPING IN THE DARK(1972, Ital.)
Miguel Bose
SUSPIRIA(1977, Ital.)
Monish Bose
LONG DUEL, THE(1967, Brit.)
Phyllis Bose
1984
PASSAGE TO INDIA, A(1984, Brit.)
Promotha Bose
Silents
EMERALD OF THE EAST(1928, Brit.)
Ursula V. Bose
TOXI(1952, Ger.)
Pavel Bosek
REPORT ON THE PARTY AND THE GUESTS, A(1968, Czech.)
Emy Boselli
JUKE BOX RACKET(1960)
Bosenko
VILNA LEGEND, A(1949, U.S./Pol.)
F. Bosetti
MAN WHO LAUGHS, THE(1966, Ital.), w
Giulio Bosetti
MORGAN THE PIRATE(1961, Fr./Ital.); RELUCTANT SAINT, THE(1962, U.S./Ital.);
CAPTIVE CITY, THE(1963, Ital.); IMPERIAL VENUS(1963, Ital./Fr.); GOLD FOR THE
CAESARS(1964); ORGANIZER, THE(1964, Fr./Ital./Yugo.); CONQUERED CITY(1966,
Ital.); MADE IN ITALY(1967, Fr./Ital.)
Ada Boshell
Misc. Silents
NOT GUILTY(1915); BEAUTIFUL ADVENTURE, THE(1917)
William Boshell
Silents
IN SEARCH OF A SINNER(1920)
Dennis Bosher
1984
SLAYGROUND(1984, Brit.), art d
Kate Langley Bosher
Silents
NOBODY'S KID(1921), w
Beyer Boshoff
SPOTS ON MY LEOPARD, THE(1974, S. Africa), w
John Boshoff
1984
GODS MUST BE CRAZY, THE(1984, Botswana), m
Andrea Bosic
DAMON AND PYTHIAS(1962); SWORD OF THE CONQUEROR(1962, Ital.); DUEL
OF THE TITANS(1963, Ital.); WITCH'S CURSE, THE(1963, Ital.); SANDOKAN THE
GREAT(1964, Fr./Ital./Span.); ARIZONA COLT(1965, It./Fr./Span.); EL GRECO(1966,
Ital., Fr.); KILL OR BE KILLED(1967, Ital.); DANGER: DIABOLIK(1968, Ital./Fr.);
ROMEO AND JULIET(1968, Ital./Span.); DAY OF ANGER(1970, Ital./Ger.); HOR-
NET'S NEST(1970)
Andrea J. Bosic
APPOINTMENT FOR MURDER(1954, Ital.)
Anita Bosic
RENT CONTROL(1981)
Andrea Bosie
PRISONER OF THE IRON MASK(1962, Fr./Ital.)
Ray Bosier
STEPPENWOLF(1974), ch
Roy Bosier
BETTER A WIDOW(1969, Ital.); DUCK, YOU SUCKER!(1972, Ital.); STEPPEN-
WOLF(1974)
Virginia Bosier
BRIGADOON(1954)
Paul Bosiger
DEVIL IN SILK(1968, Ger.)
Milan Bosiljcic
STEPPE, THE(1963, Fr./Ital.)
Anna Bosilova
Silents
JOHN HERIOT'S WIFE(1920, Brit.)
Roy Bosler
SUPERFLY T.N.T.(1973)
Virginia Bosler
OKLAHOMA(1955)
Bosley
WHO'S MINDING THE STORE?(1963)
Tom Bosley
LOVE WITH THE PROPER STRANGER(1963); WORLD OF HENRY ORIENT,
THE(1964); DIVORCE AMERICAN STYLE(1967); BANG BANG KID, THE(1968
U.S./Span./Ital.); SECRET WAR OF HARRY FRIGG, THE(1968); YOURS, MINE AND
OURS(1968); TO FIND A MAN(1972); MIXED COMPANY(1974); GUS(1976); O'HARA'S
WIFE(1983)

Ned Bosnic
Misc. Talkies
IMAGO(1970), d
Ned Bosnick
TO BE FREE(1972), p,d&w
Vladimir Bosnjak
APACHE GOLD(1965, Ger.)
Alfred G. Bosnos
LIFE AND TIMES OF JUDGE ROY BEAN, THE(1972)
Mme. Bosocki
SMILING IRISH EYES(1929)
Clay Boss
LEGEND OF THE LONE RANGER, THE(1981)
May Boss
WESTBOUND(1959); DRUM(1976)
May R. Boss
GOIN' SOUTH(1978)
Yale Boss
Silents
EMBARRASSMENT OF RICHES, THE(1918); SOULS FOR SALE(1923)
Misc. Silents
KNIGHTS OF THE SQUARE TABLE(1917)
Paola Bossalino
ROVER, THE(1967, Ital.)
Peter Bosse
FINAL CHORD, THE(1936, Ger.)
Gordon Bosserman
STAR SPANGLED GIRL(1971)
Renaud Bossert
1984
ONE DEADLY SUMMER(1984, Fr.)
Bernard Bossick
GUERRILLA GIRL(1953), m; GOLDEN BOX, THE(1970)
Roy Bossier
UP THE MACGREGORS(1967, Ital./Span.)
Robert Bossis
EDWARD AND CAROLINE(1952, Fr.), p
Giorgio Bosso
STUD, THE(1979, Brit.)
Barbara Bosson
1984
LAST STARFIGHTER, THE(1984)
Jacques Bost
LES MAINS SALES(1954, Fr.), w
Jacques Laurent Bost
LES JEUX SONT FAITS(1947, Fr.), w
Jacques-Laurent Bost
TIME BOMB(1961, Fr./Ital.), w; LA NOTTE BRAVA(1962, Fr./Ital.), w
Pierre Bost
CROISIERES SIDERALES(1941, Fr.), w; SYMPHONIE PASTORALE(1948, Fr.), w;
DEVIL IN THE FLESH, THE(1949, Fr.), w; LOVE STORY(1949, Fr.), w; WALLS OF
MALAPAGA, THE(1950, Fr./Ital.), w; FORBIDDEN GAMES(1953, Fr.), w; SEVEN
DEADLY SINS, THE(1953, Fr./Ital.), w; DAUGHTERS OF DESTINY(1954, Fr./Ital.),
w; GAME OF LOVE, THE(1954, Fr.), w; RED AND THE BLACK, THE(1954, Fr./Ital.),
w; RED, INN, THE(1954, Fr.), w; GERVAISE(1956, Fr.), w; FOUR BAGS FULL(1957,
Fr./Ital.), w; GAMBLER, THE(1958, Fr.), w; LOVE IS MY PROFESSION(1959, Fr.), w;
GREEN MARE, THE(1961, Fr./Ital.), w; CRIME DOES NOT PAY(1962, Fr.), w;
ENOUGH ROPE(1966, Fr./Ital./Ger.), w; IS PARIS BURNING?(1966, U.S./Fr.), w;
THIS SPECIAL FRIENDSHIP(1967, Fr.), w; CLOCKMAKER, THE(1976, Fr.), w;
JUDGE AND THE ASSASSIN, THE(1979, Fr.), w
1984
SUNDAY IN THE COUNTRY, A(1984, Fr.), w
Alfonzo Rivas Bostamente
RANCHO GRANDE(1938, Mex.), p
Honore Bostel
TRAFFIC(1972, Fr.)
Cynthia Bostick
THAT'S THE WAY OF THE WORLD(1975)
Floyd Bostick
SALT OF THE EARTH(1954)
Barbara Bostock
GIRLS ON THE LOOSE(1958); SENIOR PROM(1958)
Evalyn Bostock
COWBOY MILLIONAIRE(1935)
Evelyn Bostock
THARK(1932, Brit.); PERFECT UNDERSTANDING(1933, Brit.); MOONSTONE,
THE(1934)
Bernard Boston
ONE PLUS ONE(1969, Brit.); LEO THE LAST(1970, Brit.); SWEET SUZY(1973)
J.L. Boston
Silents
AT THE VILLA ROSE(1920, Brit.)
Joan Boston
MAN'S FAVORITE SPORT [?](1964)
Matt Boston
1984
HIGHWAY TO HELL(1984)
Misc. Talkies
GHOSTS THAT STILL WALK(1977)
Sarah Boston
LONG SHOT(1981, Brit.)
Ingrid Bostrom
HUGS AND KISSES(1968, Swed.)
Barry Bostwick
JENNIFER ON MY MIND(1971); ROAD MOVIE(1974); ROCKY HORROR PICTURE
SHOW, THE(1975, Brit.); WRONG DAMN FILM, THE zero(1975); MOVIE MO-
VIE(1978); MEGAFORCE(1982)

E.F. Bostwick
KITTY(1929, Brit.)
Edith Bostwick
Silents
PILGRIM, THE(1923)
Elwood Bostwick
Silents
FACTORY MAGDALEN, A(1914), d
Harold Bostwick
WOMAN HUNT(1962)
Jackson Bostwick
LATE LIZ, THE(1971); PSYCHOPATH, THE(1973); TRON(1982)
1984
PREY, THE(1984)
Phyllis Bostwick
Misc. Silents
FROU FROU(1914)
Stephen Bosustow
1001 ARABIAN NIGHTS(1959), p
C. Bosvier
THIRTEENTH LETTER, THE(1951)
John Boswall
1984
1984(1984, Brit.)
Charles Boswell
WHEN A STRANGER CALLS(1979); DREAM ON(1981)
Connee Boswell
KISS THE BOYS GOODBYE(1941); SYNCOPATION(1942); SENIOR PROM(1958)
Connie Boswell
ARTISTS AND MODELS(1937); IT'S ALL YOURS(1937); SWING PARADE OF 1946(1946)
David Boswell
HALF A SIXPENCE(1967, Brit.)
Donna Boswell
FULLER BRUSH GIRL, THE(1950)
Hugh Boswell
HUMAN JUNGLE, THE(1954); HIGH SOCIETY(1956)
Peter Boswell
1984
RAZORBACK(1984, Aus.)
Tailor Boswell
DEEP IN MY HEART(1954)
The Boswell Sisters
TRANSATLANTIC MERRY-GO-ROUND(1934)
The Boswell Twins
I DIDN'T DO IT(1945, Brit.)
Allan R. Bosworth
NOBODY'S PERFECT(1968), w
Hobard Bosworth
Silents
RUPERT OF HENTZAU(1923)
Hobart Bosworth
GENERAL CRACK(1929); HURRICANE(1929); ABRAHAM LINCOLN(1930); DEVIL'S HOLIDAY, THE(1930); DU BARRY, WOMAN OF PASSION(1930); JUST IMAGINE(1930); MAMMY(1930); OFFICE WIFE, THE(1930); THIRD ALARM, THE(1930); DIRIGIBLE(1931); FANNY FOLEY HERSELF(1931); SHIPMATES(1931); SIT TIGHT(1931); THIS MODERN AGE(1931); CARNIVAL BOAT(1932); JAZZ BABIES(1932); MILLION DOLLAR LEGS(1932); MIRACLE MAN, THE(1932); NO GREATER LOVE(1932); PHANTOM EXPRESS, THE(1932); LADY FOR A DAY(1933); MUSIC IN THE AIR(1934); WHOM THE GODS DESTROY(1934); CRUSADES, THE(1935); KEEPER OF THE BEES(1935); STEAMBOAT ROUND THE BEND(1935); TOGETHER WE LIVE(1935); DARK HOUR, THE(1936); WILDCAT TROOPER(1936); GENERAL SPANKY(1937); PORTIA ON TRIAL(1937); KING OF THE SIERRAS(1938); ROLLIN' PLAINS(1938); WOLVES OF THE SEA(1938); BULLETS FOR O'HARA(1941); LAW OF THE TROPICS(1941); ONE FOOT IN HEAVEN(1941); BULLET SCARS(1942); GAY SISTERS, THE(1942); I WAS FRAMED(1942); SIN TOWN(1942); THEY DIED WITH THEIR BOOTS ON(1942)
Silents
SEA-WOLF, THE(1913), a, d; COUNTRY MOUSE, THE(1914), a, w; JOHN BARLEYCORN(1914), a, d; ODYSSEY OF THE NORTH, AN(1914), a, d; PURSUIT OF THE PHANTOM, THE(1914), a, d&w; CAPTAIN COURTESY(1915), d; PRETTY MRS. SMITH(1915); d; SCARLET SIN, THE(1915), a, d; JOAN THE WOMAN(1916); OLIVER TWIST(1916); TARGET, THE(1916); BLIND HEARTS(1921), a, p; SEA LION, THE(1921); STRANGER'S BANQUET(1922); WHITE HANDS(1922); COMMON LAW, THE(1923); ETERNAL THREE, THE(1923); LITTLE CHURCH AROUND THE CORNER(1923); SOULS FOR SALE(1923); CAPTAIN JANUARY(1924); HEARTS OF OAK(1924); NELLIE, THE BEAUTIFUL CLOAK MODEL(1924); BIG PARADE, THE(1925); IF I MARRY AGAIN(1925); MY SON(1925); ZANDER THE GREAT(1925); FAR CRY, THE(1926); NERVOUS WRECK, THE(1926); ANNIE LAURIE(1927); MY BEST GIRL(1927); AFTER THE STORM(1928); ANNAPOLIS(1928); SMART SET, THE(1928); WOMAN OF AFFAIRS, A(1928); ETERNAL LOVE(1929)
Misc. Silents
(; MONTE CRISTO(1912); BURNING DAYLIGHT(1914), a, d; VALLEY OF THE MOON, THE(1914), a, d; BUCKSHOT JOHN(1915), a, d; FATHERHOOD(1915), a, d; HELP WANTED(1915); LITTLE BROTHER OF THE RICH, A(1915), a, d; LITTLE SUNSET(1915); TWAS EVER THUS(1915); WHITE SCAR, THE(1915), a, d; DR. NEIGHBOR(1916); IRON HAND, THE(1916); TWO MEN OF SANDY BAR(1916); WAY OF THE WORLD, THE(1916); YAQUI, THE(1916); BETRAYED(1917); DEVIL STONE, THE(1917); FRECKLES(1917); INNER SHRINE, THE(1917); LITTLE AMERICAN, THE(1917); MORMON MAID, A(1917); UNCONQUERED(1917); WHAT MONEY CAN'T BUY(1917); WOMAN GOD FORGOT, THE(1917); BORDER LEGION, THE(1919); BEHIND THE DOOR(1920); BELOW THE SURFACE(1920); BRUTE MASTER, THE(1920); HIS OWN LAW(1920); THOUSAND TO ONE, A(1920); CUP OF LIFE, THE(1921); FOOLISH MATRONS, THE(1921); IN THE PALACE OF THE KING(1923); MAN ALONE, THE(1923); VANITY FAIR(1923); NAME THE MAN(1924); SILENT WATCHER, THE(1924); SUNDOWN(1924); THROUGH THE DARK(1924); CHICKIE(1925); GOLDEN STRAIN, THE(1925); HALF-WAY GIRL, THE(1925); WINDS OF CHANCE(1925); SPANGLES(1926); STEEL PREFERRED(1926); BLOOD SHIP, THE(1927); CHINESE PARROT, THE(1927); THREE HOURS(1927); FRECKLES(1928); SAWDUST PARADISE, THE(1928)

Hobert Bosworth
COUNTY FAIR, THE(1932)
Maria Bosworth
MY WAY(1974, South Africa)
Pam Bosworth
JEDDA, THE UNCIVILIZED(1956, Aus.), ed
Patricia Bosworth
FOUR BOYS AND A GUN(1957); NUN'S STORY, THE(1959)
Geza Boszormenyi
FATHER(1967, Hung.)
Edouard Botcharov
THREE TALES OF CHEKHOV(1961, USSR), d
Grit Botcher
Misc. Talkies
BEYOND CONTROL(1971)
Victor Botel
HARD ROCK HARRIGAN(1935)
Wade Boteleo
DEAD END(1937)
Wade Boteler
BIG NEWS(1929); CLOSE HARMONY(1929); GODLESS GIRL, THE(1929); LEATHERNECK, THE(1929); COLLEGE LOVERS(1930); DERELICT(1930); DEVIL'S HOLIDAY, THE(1930); NAVY BLUES(1930); SOLDIERS AND WOMEN(1930); TOP SPEED(1930); WAY OF ALL MEN, THE(1930); BAD COMPANY(1931); BLONDE CRAZY(1931); IRON MAN, THE(1931); KICK IN(1931); LOCAL BOY MAKES GOOD(1931); PAINTED DESERT, THE(1931); PENROD AND SAM(1931); SILENCE(1931); 24 HOURS(1931); CENTRAL PARK(1932); COME ON DANGER!(1932); END OF THE TRAIL(1932); MAN WHO PLAYED GOD, THE(1932); MANHATTAN TOWER(1932); NIGHT MAYOR, THE(1932); PAINTED WOMAN(1932); SILVER DOLLAR(1932); SPEED MADNESS(1932); DEATH KISS, THE(1933); HELLO SISTER!(1933); HUMANITY(1933); KENNEL MURDER CASE, THE(1933); KING FOR A NIGHT(1933); LAWYER MAN(1933); QUEEN CHRISTINA(1933); SHE DONE HIM WRONG(1933); SITTING PRETTY(1933); AMONG THE MISSING(1934); BELLE OF THE NINETIES(1934); BORN TO BE BAD(1934); CHAINED(1934); CROSBY CASE, THE(1934); FUGITIVE LADY(1934); GAMBLING LADY(1934); MAN WITH TWO FACES, THE(1934); MANHATTAN MELODRAMA(1934); MAN'S GAME, A(1934); MELODY IN SPRING(1934); OPERATOR 13(1934); RICHEST GIRL IN THE WORLD, THE(1934); ST. LOUIS KID, THE(1934); BLACK FURY(1935); FARMER TAKES A WIFE, THE(1935); FRECKLES(1935); FRONT PAGE WOMAN(1935); GOIN' TO TOWN(1935); GOOSE AND THE GANDER, THE(1935); HEADLINE WOMAN, THE(1935); LIVING ON VELVET(1935); LOVE IN BLOOM(1935); MELODY TRAIL(1935); O'SHAUGHNESSY'S BOY(1935); RECKLESS(1935); REMEMBER LAST NIGHT(1935); SECRET BRIDE, THE(1935); STREAMLINE EXPRESS(1935); THREE MUSKETEERS, THE(1935); ALIBI FOR MURDER(1936); AND SO THEY WERE MARRIED(1936); BRIDE WALKS OUT, THE(1936); CHARLIE CHAN AT THE CIRCUS(1936); CHEERS OF THE CROWD(1936); EXCLUSIVE STORY(1936); GORGEOUS HUSSY, THE(1936); HERE COMES TROUBLE(1936); HUMAN CARGO(1936); POPPY(1936); PRESIDENT'S MYSTERY, THE(1936); RETURN OF JIMMY VALENTINE, THE(1936); RIFF-RAFF(1936); STRIKE ME PINK(1936); WALKING DEAD, THE(1936); WHIPSAW(1936); BORROWING TROUBLE(1937); CAPTAINS COURAGEOUS(1937); COUNTRY GENTLEMEN(1937); DANGEROUS HOLIDAY(1937); FIGHT TO THE FINISH, A(1937); FIND THE WITNESS(1937); FRAME-UP THE(1937); GREAT HOSPITAL MYSTERY, THE(1937); GREEN LIGHT(1937); HOLD'EM NAVY!(1937); IT CAN'T LAST FOREVER(1937); JIM HANVEY, DETECTIVE(1937); LAST GANGSTER, THE(1937); LOVE IS NEWS(1937); MANDARIN MYSTERY, THE(1937); SECOND HONEYMOON(1937); SLIM(1937); STAR IS BORN, A(1937); THREE SMART GIRLS(1937); YOU ONLY LIVE ONCE(1937); YOUTH ON PAROLE(1937); 52ND STREET(1937); AMAZING DR. CLITTERHOUSE, THE(1938); BILLY THE KID RETURNS(1938); CITY GIRL(1938); IN OLD CHICAGO(1938); LETTER OF INTRODUCTION(1938); LITTLE MISS ROUGHNECK(1938); MARINES ARE HERE, THE(1938); PECK'S BAD BOY WITH THE CIRCUS(1938); SHOPWORN ANGEL(1938); SLIGHT CASE OF MURDER, A(1938); SPAWN OF THE NORTH(1938); THERE'S ALWAYS A WOMAN(1938); TIP-OFF GIRLS(1938); VALLEY OF THE GIANTS(1938); AMBUSH(1939); DAYS OF JESSE JAMES(1939); EAST SIDE OF HEAVEN(1939); EVERYTHING'S ON ICE(1939); ICE FOLLIES OF 1939(1939); MISSING DAUGHTERS(1939); MYSTERIOUS MISS X, THE(1939); OFF THE RECORD(1939); OKLAHOMA KID, THE(1939); SABOTAGE(1939); SERGEANT MADDEN(1939); SOUTHWARD HO!(1939); ST. LOUIS BLUES(1939); TELEVISION SPY(1939); THEY SHALL HAVE MUSIC(1939); THUNDER AFLOAT(1939); WHEN TOMORROW COMES(1939); CASTLE ON THE HUDSON(1940); CHARLIE CHAN'S MURDER CRUISE(1940); DANCE, GIRL, DANCE(1940); DOUBLE ALIBI(1940); FRAMED(1940); GAUCHO SERENADE(1940); HIS GIRL FRIDAY(1940); HOT STEEL(1940); HOWARDS OF VIRGINIA, THE(1940); INVISIBLE STRIPES(1940); LEATHER-PUSHERS, THE(1940); MA, HE'S MAKING EYES AT ME(1940); MY LITTLE CHICKADEE(1940); THREE CHEERS FOR THE IRISH(1940); THREE FACES WEST(1940); 'TIL WE MEET AGAIN(1940); UNDER TEXAS SKIES(1940); YOUNG BUFFALO BILL(1940); BLUE, WHITE, AND PERFECT(1941); BODY DISAPPEARS, THE(1941); GIRL, A GUY AND A GOB, A(1941); HIGH SIERRA(1941); IT STARTED WITH EVE(1941); KATHLEEN(1941); KID FROM KANSAS, THE(1941); LOVE CRAZY(1941); SINGING HILL, THE(1941); SIX LESSONS FROM MADAME LA ZONGA(1941); STRANGE ALIBI(1941); STRAWBERRY BLONDE, THE(1941); UNEXPECTED UNCLE(1941); WHERE DID YOU GET THAT GIRL?(1941); BOMBAY CLIPPER(1942); ESCAPE FROM CRIME(1942); GENTLEMAN JIM(1942); GET HEP TO LOVE(1942); I MARRIED A WITCH(1942); I WAKE UP SCREAMING(1942); I WAS FRAMED(1942); JACKASS MAIL(1942); MISSISSIPPI GAMBLER(1942); MOONLIGHT IN HAVANA(1942); MY FAVORITE BLONDE(1942); PITTSBURGH(1942); RIDE 'EM COWBOY(1942); TIMBER(1942); EYES OF THE UNDERWORLD(1943); FIND THE BLACKMAILER(1943); GOOD FELLOWS, THE(1943); HI, BUDDY(1943); HIT THE ICE(1943); IT AIN'T HAY(1943); KEEP 'EM SLUGGING(1943); RIDING HIGH(1943); LAST RIDE, THE(1944)
Silents
OLD FASHIONED BOY, AN(1920); BLIND HEARTS(1921); DUCKS AND DRAKES(1921); FIFTY CANDLES(1921); STRANGER THAN FICTION(1921); AFRAID TO FIGHT(1922); DESERTED AT THE ALTAR(1922); GREAT NIGHT, THE(1922); LYING TRUTH, THE(1922); RIDIN' WILD(1922); SECOND HAND ROSE(1922); WHILE SATAN SLEEPS(1922); ALIAS THE NIGHT WIND(1923); NEVER SAY DIE(1924), a, w; INTRODUCE ME(1925), a, w; JIMMIE'S MILLIONS(1925); LAST EDITION, THE(1925); THAT'S MY BABY(1926), a, w; LET IT RAIN(1927), a, w; SOFT CUSHIONS(1927), a, w; JUST MARRIED(1928); LET 'ER GO GALLEGHER(1928); SPORTING GOODS(1928); TOILERS, THE(1928)

Misc. Silents
FALSE ROAD, THE(1920); LAHOMA(1920); LET'S BE FASHIONABLE(1920); WATER, WATER, EVERYWHERE(1920); SHE COULDN'T HELP IT(1921); AT THE SIGN OF THE JACK O'LANTERN(1922); DON'T SHOOT(1922); MAN OF ACTION, THE(1923); PHANTOM HORSEMAN, THE(1924); WHIPPING BOSS, THE(1924); CRASH, THE(1928)

Wede Boteler
PROFESSOR BEWARE(1938)

Erlynn Mary Botelho
MISS SADIE THOMPSON(1953)

Wade Botelor
UNKNOWN VALLEY(1933)

Alvaro Botero
PROUD AND THE DAMNED, THE(1972), art d

Bela Both
WITNESS, THE(1982, Hung.)

Emsie Botha
RIDER IN THE NIGHT, THE(1968, South Africa)

Manie Botha
DINGAKA(1965, South Africa), ph; AFTER YOU, COMRADE(1967, S. Afr.), ph

Willem Botha
DINGAKA(1965, South Africa)

Bud Botham
WINTERHAWK(1976), stunts

Art Bothum
SAVAGE WILD, THE(1970), ph

Dick Botiller
GUN LAW(1933); HOUSE OF MYSTERY(1934); MAN TRAILER, THE(1934); THUNDER OVER TEXAS(1934); CHEYENNE TORNADO(1935); CIRCLE OF DEATH(1935); JUSTICE OF THE RANGE(1935); WAGON TRAIL(1935); WILD MUSTANG(1935); CHARGE OF THE LIGHT BRIGADE, THE(1936); GUN PLAY(1936); GUN SMOKE(1936); MYSTERIOUS AVENGER, THE(1936); TREACHERY RIDES THE RANGE(1936); WEST OF NEVADA(1936); DEVIL'S SADDLE LEGION, THE(1937); IDAHO KID, THE(1937); OLD WYOMING TRAIL, THE(1937); RIO GRANDE RANGER(1937); TWO-FISTED SHERIFF(1937); WHEN YOU'RE IN LOVE(1937); FLIRTING WITH FATE(1938); PIONEER TRAIL(1938); STAGECOACH DAYS(1938); TRADE WINDS(1938); CODE OF THE SECRET SERVICE(1939); FIGHTING GRINGO, THE(1939); MEXICALI ROSE(1939); ONLY ANGELS HAVE WINGS(1939); SOUTH OF THE BORDER(1939); DARK STREETS OF CAIRO(1940); TORRID ZONE(1940); WYOMING(1940); MASKED RIDER, THE(1941); NORTH FROM LONE STAR(1941); SON OF DAVY CROCKETT, THE(1941); WYOMING WILDCAT(1941); ACROSS THE PACIFIC(1942); BAD MEN OF THE HILLS(1942); ROAD TO MOROCCO(1942); WILD BILL HICKOK RIDES(1942); ADVENTURES IN IRAQ(1943); FOR WHOM THE BELL TOLLS(1943); HAIL TO THE RANGERS(1943); RHYTHM OF THE ISLANDS(1943); KISMET(1944); THIN MAN GOES HOME, THE(1944); YELLOW ROSE OF TEXAS, THE(1944); THOUSAND AND ONE NIGHTS, A(1945)
Misc. Talkies
GUNSMOKE ON THE GUADALUPE(1935); RIDING WILD(1935)

Richard Botiller
CRIMINALS OF THE AIR(1937); GOLD IS WHERE YOU FIND IT(1938); MAN FROM SUNDOWN, THE(1939); NORTH OF THE YUKON(1939); PINTO KID, THE(1941)

Richard "Dick" Botiller
SOUTH OF ARIZONA(1938); WEST OF SANTA FE(1938)

Perry Botkin
MURDER BY CONTRACT(1958), m; TARZAN, THE APE MAN(1981), m; DANCE OF THE DWARFS(1983, U.S., Phil.), m
1984
SILENT NIGHT, DEADLY NIGHT(1984), m

Perry Botkin, Jr.
R.P.M.(1970), m; BLESS THE BEASTS AND CHILDREN(1971), m; SKYJACKED(1972), m; THEY ONLY KILL THEIR MASTERS(1972), m; YOUR THREE MINUTES ARE UP(1973), m, m/l; GOIN' SOUTH(1978), m

Pierre Botkin, Jr.
LADY ICE(1973), m

Betty Botley
PORTRAIT OF THE ARTIST AS A YOUNG MAN, A(1979, Ireland), p

A.M. Botsford
ACCUSING FINGER, THE(1936), p; AND SUDDEN DEATH(1936), p; ARIZONA MAHONEY(1936), p; ARIZONA RAIDERS, THE(1936), p; BORDER FLIGHT(1936), p; FORGOTTEN FACES(1936), p; GIRL OF THE OZARKS(1936), p; HOLLYWOOD BOULEVARD(1936), p; MURDER WITH PICTURES(1936), p; RETURN OF SOPHIE LANG, THE(1936), p; ROSE BOWL(1936), p; STRAIGHT FROM THE SHOULDER(1936), p; THREE CHEERS FOR LOVE(1936), p; TOO MANY PARENTS(1936), p; HIDEAWAY GIRL(1937), p; ADVENTURE IN DIAMONDS(1940), p; DANCING ON A DIME(1940), p

Sara Botsford
BELLS(1981, Can.); BY DESIGN(1982); STILL OF THE NIGHT(1982)

Emil Botta
STEPS TO THE MOON(1963, Rum.)

Leonardo Botta
NAKED MAJA, THE(1959, Ital./U.S.); HEAD OF A TYRANT(1960, Fr./Ital.); LA DOLCE VITA(1961, Ital./Fr.); GIDGET GOES TO ROME(1963); PLAYGIRLS AND THE VAMPIRE(1964, Ital.)

Frank Bottar [Franco Bottari]
YOUNG, THE EVIL AND THE SAVAGE, THE(1968, Ital.), w

Franco Bottari
SEATED AT HIS RIGHT(1968, Ital.), art d & cos; DEATH RIDES A HORSE(1969, Ital.), art d; RUTHLESS FOUR, THE(1969, Ital./Ger.), prod d; LOVE PROBLEMS(1970, Ital.), art d; DIARY OF AN ITALIAN(1972, Ital.), art d

Pamela Bottaro
PLANET OF DINOSAURS(1978)

Christian Bottcher
ESCAPE FROM EAST BERLIN(1962)

Grit Bottcher
DIE FASTNACHTSBEICHTE(1962, Ger.); GREAT BRITISH TRAIN ROBBERY, THE(1967, Ger.)

Hermann Bottcher
Misc. Silents
ART OF LOVE, THE(1928, Ger.)

Martin Bottcher
APACHE GOLD(1965, Ger.), m; DESPERADO TRAIL, THE(1965, Ger./Yugo.), m; TREASURE OF SILVER LAKE(1965, Fr./Ger./Yugo.), m; LAST OF THE RENEGADES(1966, Fr./Ital./Ger./Yugo.), m; RAMPAGE AT APACHE WELLS(1966, Ger./Yugo.), m; MONSTER OF LONDON CITY, THE(1967, Ger.), m; PHANTOM OF SOHO, THE(1967, Ger.), m; 24-HOUR LOVER(1970, Ger.), m

May Botterill
WE OF THE NEVER NEVER(1983, Aus.), cos

Alain Bottet
L'ARMEE DES OMBRES(1969, Fr./Ital.)

Fritz Bottger [Jamie Nolan]
IT'S HOT IN PARADISE(1962, Ger./Yugo.), d

Herbert Botticher
HAMLET(1962, Ger.); 24-HOUR LOVER(1970, Ger.)

Dick Bottiler
FIGHTING HERO(1934); RENEGADES OF THE RIO GRANDE(1945)

Dick Bottilier
TRAITOR, THE(1936)

Armando Bottin
WITCHES, THE(1969, Fr./Ital.); WATERLOO(1970, Ital./USSR)

Pina Bottin
NAKED MAJA, THE(1959, Ital./U.S.); PIRATE OF THE BLACK HAWK, THE(1961, Fr./Ital.)

Rob Bottin
FOG, THE(1980); HUMANOIDS FROM THE DEEP(1980), spec eff; HOWLING, THE(1981), makeup eff; TANYA'S ISLAND(1981, Can.), spec eff, makeup; THING, THE(1982), makeup; TWILIGHT ZONE–THE MOVIE(1983), makeup

Anna Maria Bottini
LEOPARD, THE(1963, Ital.)

Anna-Maria Bottini
WHERE THE HOT WIND BLOWS(1960, Fr., Ital.)

Mariano Bottino
WOMAN OF ROME(1956, Ital.)

Phyllis Bottome
PRIVATE WORLDS(1935), w; MORTAL STORM, THE(1940), w; DANGER SIGNAL(1945), w

Horatio Bottomley
Misc. Silents
TRUTH AND JUSTICE(1916, Brit.)

Roland Bottomley
Silents
MAN'S HOME, A(1921); MODERN MARRIAGE(1923)
Misc. Silents
DAWN OF A TOMORROW, THE(1924)

Rolland Bottomley
Silents
RAFFLES, THE AMATEUR CRACKSMAN(1925)

Chris Bottomly
THUNDER IN DIXIE(1965), art d

Ben Bottoms
MORE AMERICAN GRAFFITI(1979)

James A. Bottoms
OTHER SIDE OF THE MOUNTAIN–PART 2, THE(1978)

John Bottoms
TRAVELING EXECUTIONER, THE(1970); DOC(1971); PLEASANTVILLE(1976); GOOD DISSONANCE LIKE A MAN, A(1977); NORTH DALLAS FORTY(1979); HE KNOWS YOU'RE ALONE(1980); LONG RIDERS, THE(1980)

Joseph Bottoms
DOVE, THE(1974, Brit.); CRIME AND PASSION(1976, U.S., Ger.); HIGH ROLLING(1977, Aus.); BLACK HOLE, THE(1979); CLOUD DANCER(1980); KING OF THE MOUNTAIN(1981)
1984
BLIND DATE(1984)
Misc. Talkies
SINS OF DORIAN GRAY(1982)

Sam Bottoms
CLASS OF '44(1973); ZANDY'S BRIDE(1974); OUTLAW JOSEY WALES, THE(1976); APOCALYPSE NOW(1979); UP FROM THE DEPTHS(1979, Phil.); BRONCO BILLY(1980)

Timothy Bottoms
JOHNNY GOT HIS GUN(1971); LAST PICTURE SHOW, THE(1971); LOVE AND PAIN AND THE WHOLE DAMN THING(1973); PAPER CHASE, THE(1973); CRAZY WORLD OF JULIUS VROODER, THE(1974); WHITE DAWN, THE(1974); OPERATION DAYBREAK(1976, U.S./Brit./Czech.); SMALL TOWN IN TEXAS, A(1976); ROLLERCOASTER(1977); OTHER SIDE OF THE MOUNTAIN–PART 2, THE(1978); HURRICANE(1979); HIGH COUNTRY, THE(1981, Can.); TIN MAN(1983)
1984
CENSUS TAKER, THE(1984); HAMBONE AND HILLIE(1984)

Charles Bottrill
LIMPING MAN, THE(1953, Brit.)

John Botvid
NIGHT IN JUNE, A(1940, Swed.); ILLICIT INTERLUDE(1954, Swed.)

Pauline Boty
STRANGLER'S WEB(1966, Brit.)

Gustav Botz
Silents
NOSFERATU, THE VAMPIRE(1922, Ger.)

Bouake
1984
HERE COMES SANTA CLAUS(1984)

Georges Bouban
GOODBYE AGAIN(1961), makeup; TWO FOR THE ROAD(1967, Brit.), makeup; HELLO–GOODBYE(1970), makeup; WITHOUT APPARENT MOTIVE(1972, Fr.), makeup

Jacky Bouban
RETURN OF MARTIN GUERRE, THE(1983, Fr.), makeup

Gerard Boucaron
GOING PLACES(1974, Fr.)

Corinne Boucart
SMALL CHANGE(1976, Fr.)
Ray Bouchard
SMOKEY AND THE BANDIT-PART 3(1983); SPRING FEVER(1983, Can.)
Jean Bouchaud
TRAIN, THE(1965, Fr./Ital./U.S.); DESTRUCTORS, THE(1974, Brit.)
Claudine Bouche
LA PARISIENNE(1958, Fr./Ital.), ed; END OF DESIRE(1962 Fr./Ital.), ed; JULES AND JIM(1962, Fr.), ed; SHOOT THE PIANO PLAYER(1962, Fr.), ed; ARMY GAME, THE(1963, Fr.), ed; LOVE AT TWENTY(1963, Fr./Ital./Jap./Pol./Ger.), ed; NO TIME FOR ECSTASY(1963, Fr.), ed; SOFT SKIN, THE(1964, Fr.), ed; BRIDE WORE BLACK, THE(1968, Fr./Ital.), ed
Tessa Bouche
ARABIAN NIGHTS(1980, Ital./Fr.)
Anthony Boucher
MACABRE(1958), w
Christian Boucher
LOULOU(1980, Fr.)
David E. Boucher
MAN, WOMAN AND CHILD(1983)
Denis Boucher
MY UNCLE ANTOINE(1971, Can.), art d; WHY ROCK THE BOAT?(1974, Can.), art d, set d; COLD JOURNEY(1975, Can.), art d; ONE MAN(1979, Can.), art d; CORDELIA(1980, Fr., Can.), art d
Donald Boucher
ARTISTS AND MODELS ABROAD(1938)
Evelyn Boucher
Silents
IF THOU WERT BLIND(1917, Brit.); LOVE'S OLD SWEET SONG(1917, Brit.); KNAVE OF HEARTS, THE(1919, Brit.); POWER OF RIGHT, THE(1919, Brit.)
Misc. Silents
FAITH OF A CHILD, THE(1915, Brit.); DIANA AND DESTINY(1916, Brit.); MAN WHO BOUGHT LONDON, THE(1916, Brit.); TOM BROWN'S SCHOOLDAYS(1916, Brit.); HAPPY WARRIOR, THE(1917, Brit.); MAN WHO FORGOT, THE(1919, Brit.); WARRIOR STRAIN, THE(1919, Brit.); FLAME, THE(1920, Brit.); MY LORD CONCEIT(1921, Brit.); MEN WHO FORGET(1923)
Mark E. Boucher
MAN, WOMAN AND CHILD(1983)
Pegi Boucher
PRIVATE DUTY NURSES(1972)
Sherry Boucher
WHITE LIGHTNING(1973); FIVE DAYS FROM HOME(1978)
Misc. Talkies
SISTERS OF DEATH(1976)
Barbara Bouchet
GLOBAL AFFAIR, A(1964); GOOD NEIGHBOR SAM(1964); JOHN GOLDFARB, PLEASE COME HOME(1964); SEX AND THE SINGLE GIRL(1964); WHAT A WAY TO GO(1964); IN HARM'S WAY(1965); AGENT FOR H.A.R.M.(1966); CASINO ROYALE(1967, Brit.); DANGER ROUTE(1968, Brit.); SWEET CHARITY(1969); BLACK BELLY OF THE TARANTULA, THE(1972, Ital.); DOWN THE ANCIENT STAIRCASE(1975, Ital.); BLOOD FEAST(1976, Ital.); DUCH IN ORANGE SAUCE(1976, Ital.); DEATH RACE(1978, Ital.); MANIAC MANSION(1978, Ital.); CAULDRON OF DEATH, THE(1979, Ital.)
Misc. Talkies
DEADLY GAME, THE(1974); SURABAYA CONSPIRACY(1975); ROGUE, THE(1976)
Guy Bouchet
FRENCH POSTCARDS(1979)
Pierre Bouchet
RETURN OF MARTIN GUERRE, THE(1983, Fr.)
Lilieba Bouchette
WHALERS, THE(1942, Swed.)
Jean Bouchety
GAME IS OVER, THE(1967, Fr.), m
William Bouchey
ELOPEMENT(1951)
Willis B. Bouchey
DEADLINE-U.S.A.(1952); DON'T BOTHER TO KNOCK(1952); PICKUP ON SOUTH STREET(1953); BRIDGES AT TOKO-RI, THE(1954); BIG HOUSE, U.S.A.(1955); FOREVER DARLING(1956)
Willis Bouchey
ASSIGNMENT-PARIS(1952); CARBINE WILLIAMS(1952); JUST FOR YOU(1952); MILLION DOLLAR MERMAID(1952); RED PLANET MARS(1952); WASHINGTON STORY(1952); BIG HEAT, THE(1953); DANGEROUS CROSSING(1953); FROM HERE TO ETERNITY(1953); GUN BELT(1953); PRESIDENT'S LADY, THE(1953); BATTLE OF ROGUE RIVER(1954); DRUM BEAT(1954); EXECUTIVE SUITE(1954); FIREMAN SAVE MY CHILD(1954); STAR IS BORN, A(1954); SUDDENLY(1954); THEM!(1954); BATTLE FLAME(1955); I COVER THE UNDERWORLD(1955); LONG GRAY LINE, THE(1955); MC CONNELL STORY, THE(1955); SPOILERS, THE(1955); VIOLENT MEN, THE(1955); HELL ON FRISCO BAY(1956); JOHNNY CONCHO(1956); MAGNIFICENT ROUGHNECKS(1956); PILLARS OF THE SKY(1956); BEAU JAMES(1957); GARMENT JUNGLE, THE(1957); LAST OF THE BADMEN(1957); LAST STAGECOACH WEST, THE(1957); MISTER CORY(1957); NIGHT RUNNER, THE(1957); WINGS OF EAGLES, THE(1957); ZERO HOUR!(1957); DARBY'S RANGERS(1958); LAST HURRAH, THE(1958); SHEEPMAN, THE(1958); HORSE SOLDIERS, THE(1959); NO NAME ON THE BULLET(1959); SERGEANT RUTLEDGE(1960); FIVE GUNS TO TOMBSTONE(1961); POCKETFUL OF MIRACLES(1961); TWO RODE TOGETHER(1961); YOU HAVE TO RUN FAST(1961); HOW THE WEST WAS WON(1962); INCIDENT IN AN ALLEY(1962); MAN WHO SHOT LIBERTY VALANCE, THE(1962); PANIC IN YEAR ZERO!(1962); SAINTLY SINNERS(1962); WHERE LOVE HAS GONE(1964); MC HALE'S NAVY JOINS THE AIR FORCE(1965); FOLLOW ME, BOYS!(1966); LOVE GOD?, THE(1969); SUPPORT YOUR LOCAL SHERIFF(1969); YOUNG BILLY YOUNG(1969); DIRTY DINGUS MAGEE(1970); SUPPORT YOUR LOCAL GUNFIGHTER(1971)
Chili Bouchier [Dorothy Bouchier]
CITY OF PLAY(1929, Brit.); CALL OF THE SEA, THE(1930, Brit.); KISSING CUP'S RACE(1930, Brit.); BROWN SUGAR(1931, Brit.); HONOURS EASY(1935, Brit.); LUCKY DAYS(1935, Brit.); MAD HATTERS, THE(1935, Brit.); REGAL CAVALCADE(1935, Brit.); GHOST GOES WEST, THE(1936, Brit.); MR. COHEN TAKES A WALK(1936, Brit.); SOUTHERN ROSES(1936, Brit.); WHERE'S SALLY?(1936, Brit.); CHANGE FOR A SOVEREIGN(1937, Brit.); GYPSY(1937, Brit.); MAYFAIR MELODY(1937, Brit.); MIN-

STREL BOY, THE(1937, Brit.); DARK STAIRWAY, THE(1938, Brit.); MR. SATAN(1938, Brit.); RETURN OF CAROL DEANE, THE(1938, Brit.); SINGING COP, THE(1938, Brit.); MYSTERIOUS MR. REEDER, THE(1940, Brit.); MY WIFE'S FAMILY(1941, Brit.); QUERY(1945, Brit.); MURDER IN REVERSE(1946, Brit.); CASE OF CHARLES PEACE, THE(1949, Brit.); LAUGHING LADY, THE(1950, Brit.); MRS. FITZHERBERT(1950, Brit.); OLD MOTHER RILEY(1952, Brit.); WALLET, THE(1952, Brit.); COUNTERFEIT PLAN, THE(1957, Brit.); BOY AND THE BRIDGE, THE(1959, Brit.); DEAD LUCKY(1960, Brit.)
Silents
PALAIS DE DANSE(1928, Brit.)
Misc. Silents
WOMAN IN PAWN, A(1927, Brit.); CHICK(1928, Brit.); WARNED OFF(1928, Brit.); YOU KNOW WHAT SAILORS ARE(1928, Brit.); DOWNSTREAM(1929, Brit.); SILVER KING, THE(1929, Brit.)
Dorothy Bouchier [Chili Bouchier]
CARNIVAL(1931, Brit.); BLUE DANUBE(1932, Brit.); EBB TIDE(1932, Brit.); KING'S CUP, THE(1933, Brit.); PURSE STRINGS(1933, Brit.); SUMMER LIGHTNING(1933, Brit.); IT'S A COP(1934, Brit.); TO BE A LADY(1934, Brit.); DEATH DRIVES THROUGH(1935, Brit.); GET OFF MY FOOT(1935, Brit.); FAITHFUL(1936, Brit.); EVERYTHING HAPPENS TO ME(1938, Brit.); FACING THE MUSIC(1941, Brit.)
Patrick Bouchitey
BEST WAY, THE(1978, Fr.)
Dion Boucicault
KATHLEEN MAVOURNEEN(1930), w; BRIDE OF THE LAKE(1934, Brit.), w
Silents
RIP VAN WINKLE(1914), w; KATHLEEN MAVOURNEEN(1919), w; RIP VAN WINKLE(1921), w
Nina Boucicault
THIS WEEK OF GRACE(1933, Brit.); OH, WHAT A NIGHT(1935); JUGGERNAUT(1937, Brit.); FOLLOW YOUR STAR(1938, Brit.); STRANGE BOARDERS(1938, Brit.)
Silents
PADDY, THE NEXT BEST THING(1923, Brit.); MIRIAM ROZELLA(1924, Brit.)
Rene Boucicault
Misc. Silents
HIS PICTURE IN THE PAPERS(1916)
Boucot
ARTHUR(1931, Fr.)
Fathia Boudabous
1984
MISUNDERSTOOD(1984)
Alphonse Boudard
CLOPORTES(1966, Fr., Ital.), w; UPPER HAND, THE(1967, Fr./Ital./Ger.), w; LEATHER AND NYLON(1969, Fr./Ital.), w
Jacques Boudet
1984
SWANN IN LOVE(1984, Fr.Ger.)
Micheline Boudet
ETERNAL HUSBAND, THE(1946, Fr.); WOULD-BE GENTLEMAN, THE(1960, Fr.); MARRIAGE OF FIGARO, THE(1963, Fr.)
Peter Boudoures
BAREFOOT BATTALION, THE(1954, Gr.), p
Lou Boudreau
KID FROM CLEVELAND, THE(1949)
Jerry Boudreaux
OPEN SEASON(1974, U.S./Span.)
Joseph Boudreaux
LOUISIANA STORY(1948)
Robert Boudrioz
Misc. Silents
L'APRE LUTTE(1917, Fr.), d; LA DISTANCE(1918, Fr.), d; UN SOIR(1919, Fr.), d; TEMPETES(1922, Fr.), d; L'ATRE(1923, Fr.), d; L'EPERVIER(1924, Fr.), d; LES LOUVES(1925, Fr.), d; LA CHAUSSEE DES GEANTS(1926, Fr.), d; TROIS JEUNES FILLES(1928, Fr.), d; VIVRE(1928, Fr.), d
David Boudrot
SHE FREAK(1967)
Barbara Boudwin
FOREIGN CORRESPONDENT(1940)
Jimmy Boudwin
ONE MILLION B.C.(1940)
Jimsy Boudwin
Silents
UNKNOWN CAVALIER, THE(1926); ONE WOMAN TO ANOTHER(1927)
Misc. Silents
SCRAPPIN' KID, THE(1926)
Richard Boue
PIRATE MOVIE, THE(1982, Aus.)
John Bouer
GIRL FROM MANDALAY(1936)
Jane Bough
MAGNET, THE(1950, Brit.)
Patrice Bough
WINTER KILLS(1979)
Abbas El Boughdadly
TEN COMMANDMENTS, THE(1956)
Paul Bougie
HOUNDS... OF NOTRE DAME, THE(1980, Can.)
Simpion Bouglione
TRAPEZE(1956)
Karroum Ben Bouih
MAN WHO WOULD BE KING, THE(1975, Brit.)
Charles Bouillard
LOVE IN THE AFTERNOON(1957)
Charles Bouillaud
WE ARE ALL MURDERERS(1957, Fr.); GATES OF PARIS(1958, Fr./Ital.); COUNTERFEITERS OF PARIS, THE(1962, Fr., Ital.); LONG ABSENCE, THE(1962, Fr./Ital.); MONKEY IN WINTER, A(1962, Fr.); UP FROM THE BEACH(1965); WEEKEND AT DUNKIRK(1966, Fr./Ital.)

George Bouillet
GREASED LIGHTNING(1977), ph
Jean-Claude Bouillon
MADE IN U.S.A.(1966, Fr.); LAST MAN, THE(1968, Fr.)
Jean Nicolas Bouilly
FIDELIO(1961, Aust.), w; FIDELIO(1970, Ger.), w
Jean Bouise
SHAMELESS OLD LADY, THE(1966, Fr.); LA GUERRE EST FINIE(1967, Fr./Swed.); Z(1969, Fr./Algeria); CONFESSION, THE(1970, Fr.); THINGS OF LIFE, THE(1970, Fr./Ital./Switz.); MR. KLEIN(1976, Fr.); BUTTERFLY ON THE SHOULDER, A(1978, Fr.)
1984
EDITH AND MARCEL(1984, Fr.); LE DERNIER COMBAT(1984, Fr.)
Bernard Bouix
BEAUTIFUL PRISONER, THE(1983, Fr.), p
Evelyn Bouix
BOLERO(1982, Fr.)
Evelyne Bouix
LES MISERABLES(1982, Fr.)
1984
EDITH AND MARCEL(1984, Fr.)
Lucien Boujema
UNSTRAP ME(1968)
Ray Bouk
KING OF THE ARENA(1933), w
Robert Bouladoux
MAIDEN, THE(1961, Fr.), art d; NIGHT AFFAIR(1961, Fr.), art d; I SPIT ON YOUR GRAVE(1962, Fr.), set d; SEVENTH JUROR, THE(1964, Fr.), art d
Daniel Boulanger
BREATHLESS(1959, Fr.); JOKER, THE(1961, Fr.), w; CARTOUCHE(1962, Fr./Ital.), w; SEVEN CAPITAL SINS(1962, Fr./Ital.), w; SHOOT THE PIANO PLAYER(1962, Fr.); PLAYTIME(1963, Fr.), w; THIRD LOVER, THE(1963, Fr.), w; THAT MAN FROM RIO(1964, Fr./Ital.), w; UP TO HIS EARS(1966, Fr./Ital.), w; KING OF HEARTS(1967, Fr./Ital.), a, w; LA VIE DE CHATEAU(1967, Fr.), w; TENDER SCOUNDREL(1967, Fr./Ital.), w; BRIDE WORE BLACK, THE(1968, Fr./Ital.), w; DEVIL BY THE TAIL, THE(1969, Fr./Ital.), w; SPIRITS OF THE DEAD(1969, Fr./Ital.), w; GIVE HER THE MOON(1970, Fr./Ital.), w; WHO'S GOT THE BLACK BOX?(1970, Fr./Gr./Ital.), w; BED AND BOARD(1971, Fr.); LEGEND OF FRENCHIE KING, THE(1971, Fr./Ital./Span./Brit.), w; AND NOW MY LOVE(1975, Fr.); POLICE PYTHON 357(1976, Fr.), w; CASE AGAINST FERRO, THE(1980, Fr.), w; HORSE OF PRIDE(1980, Fr.), w
Patti Boulaye
MUSIC MACHINE, THE(1979, Brit.)
Beckett Bould
OLD MOTHER RILEY'S CIRCUS(1941, Brit.); SHIPBUILDERS, THE(1943, Brit.); LOYAL HEART(1946, Brit.); ANNA KARENINA(1948, Brit.); POOL OF LONDON(1951, Brit.); PORTRAIT OF CLARE(1951, Brit.); LEASE OF LIFE(1954, Brit.); WHAT EVERY WOMAN WANTS(1954, Brit.); RAMSBOTTOM RIDES AGAIN(1956, Brit.); FIGHTING MAD(1957, Brit.); LET'S BE HAPPY(1957, Brit.); ROCK YOU SINNERS(1957, Brit.); SECOND FIDDLE(1957, Brit.); NOWHERE TO GO(1959, Brit.); ANGRY SILENCE, THE(1960, Brit.); MANIA(1961, Brit.)
Robert Boulder
Silents
ARIZONA(1918)
Edward Bouldin
Silents
HALDANE OF THE SECRET SERVICE(1923)
Pierre Boule
BRIDGE ON THE RIVER KWAI, THE(1957), w
George Boulet
MEDIUM COOL(1969)
Jean Boulet
NIGHT OF THE FOLLOWING DAY, THE(1969, Brit.), art d
S. Boulface
DRAGNET PATROL(1932)
Hella Boulila
1984
MISUNDERSTOOD(1984)
Fred Boulk
Misc. Silents
ME UND GOTT(1918)
Pierre Boulle
PLANET OF THE APES(1968), w; ESCAPE FROM THE PLANET OF THE APES(1971), w; CONQUEST OF THE PLANET OF THE APES(1972), w
Rene Bouloc
MURMUR OF THE HEART(1971, Fr./Ital./Ger.); LACOMBE, LUCIEN(1974); RETURN OF MARTIN GUERRE, THE(1983, Fr.)
Afif Boulos
EMBASSY(1972, Brit.)
John Boulter
DREAM MAKER, THE(1963, Brit.)
Rosalyn Boulter
LOVE AT SEA(1936, Brit.); HOLIDAY'S END(1937, Brit.); ROYAL DIVORCE, A(1938, Brit.); FACE BEHIND THE SCAR(1940, Brit.); GENTLE SEX, THE(1943, Brit.); RHYTHM SERENADE(1943, Brit.); SPITFIRE(1943, Brit.); GAY INTRUDERS, THE(1946, Brit.); GEORGE IN CIVVY STREET(1946, Brit.); THIS MAN IS MINE(1946 Brit.); FOR THEM THAT TRESPASS(1949, Brit.); ALL MINE TO GIVE(1957)
David Boultin
PASSWORD IS COURAGE, THE(1962, Brit.), ph
Gideon Boulting
1984
ANOTHER COUNTRY(1984, Brit.)
Ingrid Boulting
LAST TYCOON, THE(1976)
John Boulting
INQUEST(1939, Brit.), p; DESIGN FOR MURDER(1940, Brit.), p; PASTOR HALL(1940, Brit.), p; THUNDER ROCK(1944, Brit.), p; JOURNEY TOGETHER(1946, Brit.), d, w; BRIGHTON ROCK(1947, Brit.), d; FAME IS THE SPUR(1947, Brit.), p; OUTSIDER, THE(1949, Brit.), p; SEVEN DAYS TO NOON(1950, Brit.), p; MAGIC BOX, THE(1952, Brit.), d; CREST OF THE WAVE(1954, Brit.), p&d; JOSEPHINE AND MEN(1955, Brit.), p; PRIVATE'S PROGRESS(1956, Brit.), d, w; ROTTEN TO THE

CORE(1956, Brit.), d; BROTHERS IN LAW(1957, Brit.), p; LUCKY JIM(1957, Brit.), d; I'M ALL RIGHT, JACK(1959, Brit.), d, w; FRENCH MISTRESS(1960, Brit.), p; MAN IN A COCKED HAT(1960, Brit.), p; RISK, THE(1961, Brit.), p&d; HEAVENS ABOVE!(1963, Brit.), d, w; FAMILY WAY, THE(1966, Brit.), p; TWISTED NERVE(1969, Brit.), p; THERE'S A GIRL IN MY SOUP(1970, Brit.), p; UNDERCOVERS HERO(1975, Brit.), p
R. Boulting
JOSEPHINE AND MEN(1955, Brit.), w
Roy Boulting
INQUEST(1939, Brit.), d; DESIGN FOR MURDER(1940, Brit.), d; PASTOR HALL(1940, Brit.), d; THUNDER ROCK(1944, Brit.), d, ed; BRIGHTON ROCK(1947, Brit.), p; FAME IS THE SPUR(1947, Brit.), d; OUTSIDER, THE(1949, Brit.), d, w; SEVEN DAYS TO NOON(1950, Brit.), p, w, ed; HIGH TREASON(1951, Brit.), d, w; SAILOR OF THE KING(1953, Brit.), d; CREST OF THE WAVE(1954, Brit.), p&d, w; JOSEPHINE AND MEN(1955, Brit.), d; PRIVATE'S PROGRESS(1956, Brit.), d; ROTTEN TO THE CORE(1956, Brit.), p, w; RUN FOR THE SUN(1956), d, w; BROTHERS IN LAW(1957, Brit.), d, w; LUCKY JIM(1957, Brit.), p; HAPPY IS THE BRIDE(1958, Brit.), d, w; I'M ALL RIGHT, JACK(1959, Brit.), p; FRENCH MISTRESS(1960, Brit.), d, w; MAN IN A COCKED HAT(1960, Bri.), d&w; RISK, THE(1961, Brit.), p&d, w; HEAVENS ABOVE!(1963, Brit.), p; FAMILY WAY, THE(1966, Brit.), d, w; TWISTED NERVE(1969, Brit.), d, w; THERE'S A GIRL IN MY SOUP(1970, Brit.), d; UNDERCOVERS HERO(1975, Brit.), d, w, m; KINGFISH CAPER, THE(1976, South Africa), w; LAST WORD, THE(1979), d
The Boulting Twins
NO TIME FOR TEARS(1957, Brit.)
Betty Boulton
Silents
MOLLYCODDLE, THE(1920)
Dave Boulton
GREAT WALTZ, THE(1972), ph
David Boulton
CHILDREN OF THE DAMNED(1963, Brit.), ph
Davis Boulton
HAUNTING, THE(1963), ph; SECRET OF MY SUCCESS, THE(1965, Brit.), ph; FROZEN DEAD, THE(1967, Brit.), ph; IT!(1967, Brit.), ph; BUSHBABY, THE(1970), ph; SONG OF NORWAY(1970), ph
Matthew Boulton
TO WHAT RED HELL(1929, Brit.); BED AND BREAKFAST(1930, Brit.); HER STRANGE DESIRE(1931, Brit.); KEEPERS OF YOUTH(1931, Brit.); LIMPING MAN, THE(1931, Brit.); MAN FROM CHICAGO(1931, Brit.); THIRD TIME LUCKY(1931, Brit.); KING OF HEARTS(1936, Brit.), w; FIREFLY, THE(1937); NIGHT MUST FALL(1937); SABOTAGE(1937, Brit.); THIRTEENTH CHAIR, THE(1937); BULLDOG DRUMMOND IN AFRICA(1938); BULLDOG DRUMMOND'S PERIL(1938); LORD JEFF(1938); ADVENTURE IN DIAMONDS(1940); EARL OF CHICAGO, THE(1940); INVISIBLE MAN RETURNS, THE(1940); MYSTERY SEA RAIDER(1940); RAGE IN HEAVEN(1941); THEY MET IN BOMBAY(1941); COUNTER-ESPIONAGE(1942); DANGEROUSLY THEY LIVE(1942); JOURNEY FOR MARGARET(1942); MY FAVORITE BLONDE(1942); TARZAN'S NEW YORK ADVENTURE(1942); UNDYING MONSTER, THE(1942); YANK ON THE BURMA ROAD, A(1942); ABOVE SUSPICION(1943); TWO TICKETS TO LONDON(1943); MAN IN HALF-MOON STREET, THE(1944); NATIONAL VELVET(1944); NONE BUT THE LONELY HEART(1944); NOTHING BUT TROUBLE(1944); SECRETS OF SCOTLAND YARD(1944); WHITE CLIFFS OF DOVER, THE(1944); BRIGHTON STRANGLER, THE(1945); LOVE LETTERS(1945); MINISTRY OF FEAR(1945); MOLLY AND ME(1945); WOMAN IN GREEN, THE(1945); IVY(1947); STALLION ROAD(1947); ENCHANTMENT(1948); IRON CURTAIN, THE(1948); WOMAN IN WHITE, THE(1948); BARBARY PIRATE(1949); SECRET GARDEN, THE(1949); ROGUES OF SHERWOOD FOREST(1950); RACKET, THE(1951); SON OF DR. JEKYLL, THE(1951); LAST TRAIN FROM BOMBAY(1952); LOOSE IN LONDON(1953)
Matthew Boulton, Sr.
PHANTOM RAIDERS(1940)
Milo Boulton
ME, NATALIE(1969); SOME KIND OF A NUT(1969); LOVE STORY(1970)
Ralf Boumans
SPLITTING UP(1981, Neth.), ph
Bouncer the Dog
THERE WAS A YOUNG MAN(1937, Brit.)
Carole Bouquet
THAT OBSCURE OBJECT OF DESIRE(1977, Fr./Span.); FOR YOUR EYES ONLY(1981); BINGO BONGO(1983, Ital.)
1984
DREAM ONE(1984, Brit./Fr.)
Michel Bouquet
MONSIEUR VINCENT(1949, Fr.); MAGNIFICENT SINNER(1963, Fr.); THIS SPECIAL FRIENDSHIP(1967, Fr.); BRIDE WORE BLACK, THE(1968, Fr./Ital.); LA FEMME INFIDELE(1969, Fr./Ital.); BORSALINO(1970, Fr.); MISSISSIPPI MERMAID(1970, Fr./Ital.); WHO'S GOT THE BLACK BOX?(1970, Fr./Gr./Ital.); MALPERTIUS(1972, Bel./Fr.); FRENCH CONSPIRACY, THE(1973, Fr./Ital./Ger.); SERPENT, THE(1973, Fr./Ital./Ger.); TWO MEN IN TOWN(1973, Fr.); JUST BEFORE NIGHTFALL(1975, Fr./Ital.); BEYOND FEAR(1977, Fr.); LES MISERABLES(1982, Fr.)
Regis Bouquet
1984
LE BAL(1984, Fr./Ital./Algeria)
Romain Bouquet
AMERICAN LOVE(1932, Fr.); LA CHIENNE(1975, Fr.)
Armand Bour
Misc. Silents
LA TERRE(1921, Fr.); AU BONHEUR DES DAMES(1929, Fr.)
Marguerite Bour
DIARY OF A CHAMBERMAID(1964, Fr./Ital.)
Georges Bourban
WOMAN TIMES SEVEN(1967, U.S./Fr./Ital.), makeup
Jean-Claude Bourbault
BIRD WATCH, THE(1983, Fr.)
Adrienne Bourbeau
WILD WOMEN OF WONGO, THE(1959)
Barbara Bourbon
Misc. Talkies
RIP OFF(1977)

Diana Bourbon
ATLANTIC ADVENTURE(1935), w; ROAMING LADY(1936), w; BORN THAT WAY(1937, Brit.), w; MY FAIR LADY(1964)

Maurice Bourbotte
MODIGLIANI OF MONTPARNASSE(1961, Fr./Ital.), set d; WEB OF PASSION(1961, Fr.), set d

Arthur Bourchier
Misc. Silents
MACBETH(1916, Ger.); GREAT DAY, THE(1921, Brit.)

Micheline Bourdax
1984
AMERICAN DREAMER(1984)

Tommy Bourdel
Misc. Silents
EN RADE(1927, Fr.)

Joan Bourdelle
LOVE KISS, THE(1930)

Thomy Bourdelle
UNDER THE ROOFS OF PARIS(1930, Fr.); DOMMED CARGO(1936, Brit.); TESTAMENT OF DR. MABUSE, THE(1943, Ger.)

Jean Bourdelon
FAR FROM DALLAS(1972, Fr.), ph

Edouard Bourdet
FRIC FRAC(1939, FR.), w

Lise Bourdin
WOMAN OF THE RIVER(1954, Fr./Ital.); LOVE IN THE AFTERNOON(1957); LAST BLITZKRIEG, THE(1958)

Roger Bourdin
BARBER OF SEVILLE(1949, Fr.); CHRISTINE KEELER AFFAIR, THE(1964, Brit.), m

Roland Bourdin
ROYAL AFFAIRS IN VERSAILLES(1957, Fr.)

Jacques Bourdon
SCHEHERAZADE(1965, Fr./Ital./Span.), d

Maurice Bourdon
RISE OF LOUIS XIV, THE(1970, Fr.)

Pierre Bourdon
TO BE A CROOK(1967, Fr.)

Leon Bourelly
TONI(1968, Fr.), set d

Wilson Bourg
NEW ORLEANS AFTER DARK(1958); FOUR FOR THE MORGUE(1962)

Wilson Bourg, Jr.
PANIC IN THE STREETS(1950)

F. Bourgas
LOWER DEPTHS, THE(1937, Fr.), ph; SLIPPER EPISODE, THE(1938, Fr), ph

Richard Pierre Bourgeade
DIANE'S BODY(1969, Fr./Czech.), w

Gerard Bourgeois
Misc. Silents
CHRISTOPHE COLOMB(1919, Fr.), d; LES MYSTERES SU CIEL(1920, Fr.), d; UN DRAME SOUS NAPOLEON(1921, Fr.), d; FAUST(1922, Fr.), d; LA DETTE DE SANG(1923, Fr.), d

Nathalie Bourgeois
NATHALIE GRANGER(1972, Fr.)

Jean Bourgin
GIGOT(1962), ph

Jean Bourgoin
DEDEE(1949, Fr.), ph; WAYS OF LOVE(1950, Ital./Fr.), ph; IT HAPPENED IN PARIS(1953, Fr.), ph; GOHA(1958, Tunisia), ph; MY UNCLE(1958, Fr.), ph; BLACK ORPHEUS(1959 Fr./Ital./Braz.), ph; COUNTERFEIT TRAITOR, THE(1962), ph; LONGEST DAY, THE(1962), ph; MR. ARKADIN(1962, Brit./Fr./Span.), ph; GERMINAL(1963, Fr.), ph; MISTRESS FOR THE SUMMER, A(1964, Fr./Ital.), ph; IMPOSSIBLE ON SATURDAY(1966, Fr./Israel), ph

Jean-Serge Bourgoin
LA MARSEILLAISE(1938, Fr.), ph; WE ARE ALL MURDERERS(1957, Fr.), ph

Alain Bourguignon
1984
L'ARGENT(1984, Fr./Switz.)

Serge Bourguignon
SUNDAYS AND CYBELE(1962, Fr.), a, d, w; REWARD, THE(1965), d, w; TWO WEEKS IN SEPTEMBER(1967, Fr./Brit.), d, w

Richard Bourin
DETROIT 9000(1973)

Anthony Bourke
CHRISTIAN THE LION(1976, Brit.)

Fan Bourke
LUMMOX(1930)

Jimmy Bourke
RISING OF THE MOON, THE(1957, Ireland), cos

Peter Bourke
STAND UP VIRGIN SOLDIERS(1977, Brit.); MISSIONARY, THE(1982)

Terry Bourke
INN OF THE DAMNED(1974, Aus.), p, d&w
1984
BROTHERS(1984, Aus.), p,d&w

A.I. Bourkova
Misc. Silents
BREAK-UP, THE(1930, USSR)

Carolyn Lee Bourland
THEODORA GOES WILD(1936)

Nikolai Bourliaiev
ANDREI ROUBLOV(1973, USSR)

Claudie Bourlon
SEASON FOR LOVE, THE(1963, Fr.)

Einar Bourman
INSIDE THE MAFIA(1959), cos; GUN FIGHT(1961), cos; SECRET OF DEEP HARBOR(1961), cos; YOU HAVE TO RUN FAST(1961), cos; DEADLY DUO(1962), cos; GUN STREET(1962), cos; INCIDENT IN AN ALLEY(1962), cos

Einar H. Bourman
SHOCK CORRIDOR(1963), cos; NAKED KISS, THE(1964), cos

Adeleine Bourne
Silents
HAMLET(1913, Brit.)

Ernie Bourne
TRUE STORY OF ESKIMO NELL, THE(1975, Aus.); GRENDEL GRENDEL GRENDEL(1981, Aus.); LONELY HEARTS(1983, Aus.)
1984
SQUIZZY TAYLOR(1984, Aus.)

Helen Whitney Bourne
HEAD OVER HEELS IN LOVE(1937, Brit.)

Margaret Bourne
Silents
SOULS FOR SALE(1923)

Max Bourne
CITY OF FEAR(1965, Brit.), w

Mel Bourne
THAT NIGHT(1957), art d; MIRACLE WORKER, THE(1962), art d; ANNIE HALL(1977), art d; GREEK TYCOON, THE(1978), art d; INTERIORS(1978), prod d; NUNZIO(1978), prod d; MANHATTAN(1979), prod d; THIEF(1981), prod d; MIDSUMMER NIGHT'S SEX COMEDY, A(1982), prod d; STILL OF THE NIGHT(1982), prod d; ZELIG(1983), prod d
1984
BROADWAY DANNY ROSE(1984), prod d; NATURAL, THE(1984), prod d

Melvin Bourne
WINDOWS(1980), prod d

Neva Bourne
DRANGO(1957), cos

Peter Bourne
SEALED CARGO(1951); DESIREE(1954); DESERT SANDS(1955); JUMP INTO HELL(1955); TOP OF THE WORLD(1955); PARTY GIRL(1958); NORTH TO ALASKA(1960); 48 HOURS TO LIVE(1960, Brit./Swed.), a, d&w; PRIZE, THE(1963); I'LL TAKE SWEDEN(1965); TORN CURTAIN(1966); CHRISTINE JORGENSEN STORY, THE(1970); METEOR(1979)

St. Claire Bourne
LONG NIGHT, THE(1976), p

Steve Bourne
SKATETOWN, U.S.A.(1979)

Steven Bourne
WHOSE LIFE IS IT ANYWAY?(1981)

Tammy Bourne
PROM NIGHT(1980)

Whitney Bourne
CRIME WITHOUT PASSION(1934); ONCE IN A BLUE MOON(1936); PRISONER OF SHARK ISLAND, THE(1936); FLIGHT FROM GLORY(1937); LIVING ON LOVE(1937); BLIND ALIBI(1938); DOUBLE DANGER(1938); MAD MISS MANTON, THE(1938); BEAUTY FOR THE ASKING(1939)

Cpl. Phillip Bourneuf
WINGED VICTORY(1944)

Philip Bourneuf
JOAN OF ARC(1948); BIG NIGHT, THE(1951); THUNDER IN THE EAST(1953); BEYOND A REASONABLE DOUBT(1956); EVERYTHING BUT THE TRUTH(1956); ADVENTURES OF A YOUNG MAN(1962); CHAMBER OF HORRORS(1966); ARRANGEMENT, THE(1969); MOLLY MAGUIRES, THE(1970); MAN, THE(1972); PETE 'N' TILLIE(1972)

Maher Bouros
JEKYLL AND HYDE...TOGETHER AGAIN(1982)

Antoine Bourseiller
CLEO FROM 5 TO 7(1961, Fr.); MASCULINE FEMININE(1966, Fr./Swed.); LA GUERRE EST FINIE(1967, Fr./Swed.)

Christophe Bourseiller
TWO OR THREE THINGS I KNOW ABOUT HER(1970, Fr.); FRENCH POSTCARDS(1979)

Marie Bourseiller
TWO OR THREE THINGS I KNOW ABOUT HER(1970, Fr.)

Helen Boursnell
TIME GENTLEMEN PLEASE!(1953, Brit.)

Evelyne Boursotti
FRUSTRATIONS(1967, Fr./Ital.)

Mike Bourstein
TWO KOUNEY LEMELS(1966, Israel)

Jean-Pierre Bourtayre
GAME IS OVER, THE(1967, Fr.), m; WANDERER, THE(1969, Fr.), m

Rayner Bourton
OUTLAND(1981)

Bourvil
MR. PEEK-A-BOO(1951, Fr.); PRIZE, THE(1952, Fr.); CADET-ROUSSELLE(1954, Fr.); FOUR BAGS FULL(1957, Fr./Ital.); ROYAL AFFAIRS IN VERSAILLES(1957, Fr.); MIRROR HAS TWO FACES, THE(1959, Fr.); CRAZY FOR LOVE(1960, Fr.); GREEN MARE, THE(1961, Fr./Ital.); DON'T TEMPT THE DEVIL(1964, Fr./Ital.); MY WIFE'S HUSBAND(1965, Fr.); THANK HEAVEN FOR SMALL FAVORS(1965, Fr.); SUCKER, THE(1966, Fr./Ital.); THE DIRTY GAME(1966, Fr./Ital./Ger.); BRAIN, THE(1969, Fr./US); DON'T LOOK NOW(1969, Brit./Fr.); THOSE DARING YOUNG MEN IN THEIR JAUNTY JALOPIES(1969, Fr./Brit./ Ital.); WISE GUYS(1969, Fr./Ital.)

Andre Bourvil
CHRISTMAS TREE, THE(1969, Fr.)

Morris Bousel
KILLER'S KISS(1955), p

Joy Boushel
TERROR TRAIN(1980, Can.); HUMONGOUS(1982, Can.)

Joy Boushell
QUEST FOR FIRE(1982, Fr./Can.)

Liz Bousman
SIDEWINDER ONE(1977), art d

Terry Bousman
SMORGASBORD(1983), art d

Tracy Bousman
NORMA RAE(1979), art d; YOUNG DOCTORS IN LOVE(1982), art d
1984
PROTOCOL(1984), art d
Jacques Bousquet
RENDEZ-VOUS(1932, Ger.), w
Robert Bousquet
LIFE UPSIDE DOWN(1965, Fr.); SHAMELESS OLD LADY, THE(1966, Fr.)
Jean-Michel Boussaguet
LES ABYSSES(1964, Fr.), ph; MICHELLE(1970, Fr.), ph
Alan Boustead
THEY'RE A WEIRD MOB(1966, Aus.), m
Gabriel Boustiani
DEATHWATCH(1980, Fr./Ger.), p
Mariette Bout
STILL SMOKIN'(1983)
Kathleen Boutall
GIRL MUST LIVE, A(1941, Brit.); MAN IN GREY, THE(1943, Brit.); UNCENSORED(1944, Brit.); 2,000 WOMEN(1944, Brit.); ADVENTURESS, THE(1946, Brit.); SO WELL REMEMBERED(1947, Brit.); FLY AWAY PETER(1948, Brit.); OCTOBER MAN, THE(1948, Brit.); MY BROTHER JONATHAN(1949, Brit.); TEMPTATION HARBOR(1949, Brit.); WEAKER SEX, THE(1949, Brit.); GOLDEN SALAMANDER(1950, Brit.); HER PANELLED DOOR(1951, Brit.); COME BACK PETER(1952, Brit.)
Roy Boutcher
BROTHERLY LOVE(1970, Brit.)
Romain Bouteille
FIRE WITHIN, THE(1964, Fr./Ital.); JOHNNY BANCO(1969, Fr./Ital./Ger.); TENANT, THE(1976, Fr.)
Maurice Boutel
PROSTITUTION(1965, Fr.), p&d, w
Phil Boutelje
GREAT VICTOR HERBERT, THE(1939), md; THERE'S MAGIC IN MUSIC(1941), md; HI DIDDLE DIDDLE(1943), md; WHERE DANGER LIVES(1950)
Genee Boutell
FIGHTING COWBOY(1933); LIGHTNING RANGE(1934)
Misc. Talkies
RAWHIDE ROMANCE(1934)
Jeanne Boutell
Misc. Talkies
WHIRLWIND RIDER, THE(1935)
Andre Boutie
ROYAL AFFAIR, A(1950), set d
Paul-Louis Boutie
WHERE THE TRUTH LIES(1962, Fr.), set d; TAXI FOR TOBRUK(1965, Fr./Span./Ger.), art d; FANTOMAS(1966, Fr./Ital.), art d; OSS 117–MISSION FOR A KILLER(1966, Fr./Ital.), art d
Andre Boutilier
1984
SUBURBIA(1984)
Dennis Boutin
JOHNNY THE GIANT KILLER(1953, Fr.), anim
Tony Armstrong Boutique
NO BLADE OF GRASS(1970, Brit.), cos
Betty Bouton
Silents
DADDY LONG LEGS(1919); NO TRESPASSING(1922); ENEMIES OF WOMEN, THE(1923); EXILES, THE(1923); CYTHEREA(1924)
Misc. Silents
FINAL CLOSEUP, THE(1919); HELL SHIP, THE(1920); YOU CAN'T GET AWAY WITH IT(1923); NOT A DRUM WAS HEARD(1924)
Jim Bouton
LONG GOODBYE, THE(1973)
Thomas F. Boutress
LEGEND OF BOGGY CREEK, THE(1973), ed
Thomas Boutross
FEVER HEAT(1968), ed
Tom Boutross
RAT FINK(1965), ed; MAN CALLED DAGGER, A(1967), ed; SAVAGE WILD, THE(1970), ed; BOOTLEGGERS(1974), ed; TOWN THAT DREADED SUNDOWN, THE(1977), ed; WISHBONE CUTTER(1978), ed
Tom Boutrouss
WINTERHAWK(1976), ed
Dennis Boutsikaris
EXTERMINATOR, THE(1980)
Jean-Claude Bouttier
BOLERO(1982, Fr.)
Philippe Bouvard
THE DIRTY GAME(1966, Fr./Ital./Ger.), w
Rene Bouve
Misc. Talkies
CURSE OF KILIMANJARO(1978)
Winston Bouve
Silents
GIRL ON THE STAIRS, THE(1924), w
Bouvette
INNOCENTS IN PARIS(1955, Brit.)
Alain Bouvette
GATES OF PARIS(1958, Fr./Ital.); ME AND THE COLONEL(1958); SUNDAYS AND CYBELE(1962, Fr.)
Charles Bouvier
1984
CRACKERS(1984)
George Bouvier
BIG RED(1962)
Jean-Pierre Bouvier
GOODBYE EMMANUELLE(1980, Fr.)
Jean-Yves Bouvier
ZAZIE(1961, Fr.)

Bouvril
LONGEST DAY, THE(1962)
Ada Bouwman
GIRL WITH THE RED HAIR, THE(1983, Neth.)
Claude Bouxin
PASSION FOR LIFE(1951, Fr.), art d; WOMAN OF SIN(1961, Fr.), art d; PRICE OF FLESH, THE(1962, Fr.), art d; FIRE IN THE FLESH(1964, Fr.), art d; SIN ON THE BEACH(1964, Fr.), art d
Stephane Bouy
MILKY WAY, THE(1969, Fr./Ital.); LACOMBE, LUCIEN(1974)
Zina Bouzaiane
GOHA(1958, Tunisia)
Bouzauquet
GENERALS WITHOUT BUTTONS(1938, Fr.)
Joe Bova
SERPICO(1973); WHO?(1975, Brit./Ger.)
Joseph Bova
YOUNG DOCTORS, THE(1961); PRETTY POISON(1968); UP THE SANDBOX(1972)
Perri Bova
OCEAN'S ELEVEN(1960)
Jacques Bovanich
ONCE IN PARIS(1978)
Mary Bovard
MAN BETRAYED, A(1937); STAGE DOOR(1937); HAVING WONDERFUL TIME(1938); LADY IN QUESTION, THE(1940); FLYING WILD(1941); HONOLULU LU(1941); PENNY SERENADE(1941); DELINQUENT DAUGHTERS(1944)
Julie Bovasso
TELL ME THAT YOU LOVE ME, JUNIE MOON(1970); SATURDAY NIGHT FEVER(1977); WILLIE AND PHIL(1980); VERDICT, THE(1982); DANIEL(1983); STAYING ALIVE(1983)
Hans Dieter Bove
LOVE FEAST, THE(1966, Ger.), d
Melodie Bovee
STING II, THE(1983)
Brian Bovell
BABYLON(1980, Brit.)
Denis Bovell
BABYLON(1980, Brit.), m
Bover
BIG CHIEF, THE(1960, Fr.)
Auguste Boverio
CHILDREN OF PARADISE(1945, Fr.)
Pasquali-Aug. Boverio
CALL, THE(1938, Fr.)
Auguste Boverlo
CROSSROADS(1938, Fr.)
Crag Bovia
COME BACK BABY(1968)
Craig Bovia
JOHNNY GOT HIS GUN(1971); DIRTY LITTLE BILLY(1972)
Mario Boviello
LAUGH PAGLIACCI(1948, Ital.)
Don Bovingloh
THINGS ARE TOUGH ALL OVER(1982)
Brunella Bovo
MIRACLE IN MILAN(1951, Ital.); LUXURY GIRLS(1953, Ital.); ALONE IN THE STREETS(1956, Ital.); WHITE SHEIK, THE(1956, Ital.); LOVES OF SALAMMBO, THE(1962, Fr./Ital.)
Bertha Bovy
ANGEL AND SINNER(1947, Fr.)
Berthe Bovy
LES DERNIERES VACANCES(1947, Fr.)
Betty Bovy
THREE HOURS(1944, Fr.)
Clara Bow
WILD PARTY, THE(1929); DANGEROUS CURVES(1929); SATURDAY NIGHT KID, THE(1929); HER WEDDING NIGHT(1930); LOVE AMONG THE MILLIONAIRES(1930); TRUE TO THE NAVY(1930); KICK IN(1931); NO LIMIT(1931); CALL HER SAVAGE(1932); HOOPLA(1933)
Silents
DOWN TO THE SEA IN SHIPS(1923); GRIT(1924); HELEN'S BABIES(1924); ADVENTUROUS SEX, THE(1925); ANCIENT MARINER, THE(1925); EVE'S LOVER(1925); KISS ME AGAIN(1925); LAWFUL CHEATERS(1925); PLASTIC AGE, THE(1925); DANCING MOTHERS(1926); KID BOOTS(1926); RUNAWAY, THE(1926); CHILDREN OF DIVORCE(1927); IT(1927); ROUGH HOUSE ROSIE(1927); WINGS(1927); LADIES OF THE MOB(1928); RED HAIR(1928)
Misc. Silents
DARING YEARS, THE(1923); MAYTIME(1923); BLACK LIGHTING(1924); DAUGHTERS OF PLEASURE(1924); EMPTY HEARTS(1924); POISONED PARADISE: THE FORBIDDEN STORY OF MONTE CARLO(1924); WINE(1924); BEST BAD MAN, THE(1925); KEEPER OF THE BEES, THE(1925); MY LADY OF WHIMS(1925); MY LADY'S LIPS(1925); PARISIAN LOVE(1925); PRIMROSE PATH, THE(1925); SCARLET WEST, THE(1925); MANTRAP(1926); SHADOW OF THE LAW, THE(1926); TWO CAN PLAY(1926); GET YOUR MAN(1927); HULA(1927); FLEET'S IN, THE(1928); THREE WEEK-ENDS(1928)
Simmy Bow
HOT ROD GANG(1958); DOBERMAN GANG, THE(1972); LEPKE(1975, U.S./Israel); ROCKY(1976); TRACKDOWN(1976); YOU LIGHT UP MY LIFE(1977); DRACULA'S DOG(1978); LITTLE MISS MARKER(1980); SWORD AND THE SORCERER, THE(1982)
Tui Bow
HEATWAVE(1983, Aus.)
Tui Lorraine Bow
IRISHMAN, THE(1978, Aus.)
Bow Wow Wow
1984
SCANDALOUS(1984)

Arthur Bowan
Silents
SHATTERED REPUTATIONS(1923)
J. E. Bowan
Silents
SUPREME TEST, THE(1923), p
Rolf Bowan
GUILT(1967, Swed.), set d
Sybil Bowan
HARRY AND TONTO(1974)
Ann Bowden
DOUBLES(1978)
Beth Bowden
HI, MOM!(1970)
David Bowden
1984
PHAR LAP(1984, Aus.), art d
George Bowden
CORPSE GRINDERS, THE(1972)
Layte Bowden
BILLIE(1965)
Richard Bowden
SWEET CREEK COUNTY WAR, THE(1979), m
Tom Bowden, Jr.
SCAVENGERS, THE(1969)
Dorris Bowdon
DOWN ON THE FARM(1938); DRUMS ALONG THE MOHAWK(1939); YOUNG MR. LINCOLN(1939); GRAPES OF WRATH(1940); JENNIE(1941); MOON IS DOWN, THE(1943)
Cornelius Bowe
MEDUSA TOUCH, THE(1978, Brit.)
Harry Bowe
NEXT TIME WE LOVE(1936)
Rosemarie Bowe
MILLION DOLLAR MERMAID(1952); ADVENTURES OF HAJJI BABA(1954); GOLDEN MISTRESS, THE(1954); BIG BLUFF, THE(1955); VIEW FROM POMPEY'S HEAD, THE(1955); PEACEMAKER, THE(1956)
Roy Bowe
NEVER SAY NEVER AGAIN(1983)
Charles Bowell
Misc. Silents
PROFITEER, THE(1919)
Adam Bowen
Misc. Talkies
SWEET DREAMERS(1981)
Ann Bowen
DIRTY HARRY(1971)
Beryl Bowen
COMIN' THRU' THE RYE(1947, Brit.)
Catherine Drinker Bowen
MUSIC LOVERS, THE(1971, Brit.), w
Dennis Bowen
RECORD CITY(1978); VAN NUYS BLVD.(1979)
Misc. Talkies
GAS PUMP GIRLS(1979)
Edward Bowen
WHITE DEATH(1936, Aus.), d
Frank Bowen
Silents
BATTLES OF THE CORONEL AND FALKLAND ISLANDS, THE(1928, Brit.), w
Frederick Bowen
NAUGHTY FLIRT, THE(1931), w
Harry Bowen
FOURTH ALARM, THE(1930); NIGHT WORK(1930); RED HOT RHYTHM(1930); GHOST VALLEY(1932); SADDLE BUSTER, THE(1932); CHANCE AT HEAVEN(1933); CRASHING BROADWAY(1933); FLYING DOWN TO RIO(1933); MURDER ON THE CAMPUS(1934); ANNIE OAKLEY(1935); HEADLINE WOMAN, THE(1935); RED SALUTE(1935); RUGGLES OF RED GAP(1935); BOHEMIAN GIRL, THE(1936); HAR-VESTER, THE(1936); HEIR TO TROUBLE(1936); MILKY WAY, THE(1936); MOON'S OUR HOME, THE(1936); RETURN OF JIMMY VALENTINE, THE(1936); SWING TIME(1936); STELLA DALLAS(1937)
Jenny Bowen
STREET MUSIC(1982), d
Jimmy Bowen
JAMBOREE(1957); VANISHING POINT(1971), m
Marjorie Bowen
Silents
NELL GWYNNE(1926, Brit.), w
Michael Bowen
FORBIDDEN WORLD(1982); VALLEY GIRL(1983)
1984
NIGHT OF THE COMET(1984); WILD LIFE, THE(1984)
Richard Bowen
STREET MUSIC(1982), p, ph
Rodger Bowen
FUNNYMAN(1967)
Roger Bowen
PETULIA(1968, U.S./Brit.); M(1970); MOVE(1970); STEELYARD BLUES(1973); WICKED, WICKED(1973); TUNNELVISION(1976); HEAVEN CAN WAIT(1978); MAIN EVENT, THE(1979); FOXES(1980); ZAPPED!(1982)
Susan Bowen
Misc. Talkies
CYNTHIA'S SISTER(1975)
Terry Bowen
LASERBLAST(1978), ph
Trevor Bowen
DARLING(1965, Brit.)

A. Bower
Silents
ARMS AND THE GIRL(1917)
Anjanette Bower
Misc. Talkies
COMPANION, THE(1976)
Anthony Bower
LAST ACT OF MARTIN WESTON, THE(1970, Can./Czech.), ed
Antoinette Bower
SUPERBEAST(1972); PROM NIGHT(1980); TIME WALKER(1982)
1984
EVIL THAT MEN DO, THE(1984)
Misc. Talkies
DIE SISTER, DIE!(1978); BLOOD SONG(1982)
Arthur Bower
Misc. Silents
WOMAN IN WHITE, THE(1917)
Aubrey Bower
ADVENTURES OF CAPTAIN FABIAN(1951)
B. M. Bower
CHIP OF THE FLYING U(1940), w
Silents
WOLVERINE, THE(1921), w; KING OF THE RODEO(1929), w, t; POINTS WEST(1929), w
D.M. [Pamela] Bower
YELLOW CANARY, THE(1944, Brit.), w
Dallas Bower
PATH OF GLORY, THE(1934, Brit.), p&d; ALICE IN WONDERLAND(1951, Fr.), d; SECOND MRS. TANQUERAY, THE(1952, Brit.), d
Edward Bower
BIG TOWN(1932)
Elsie Bower
PICCADILLY NIGHTS(1930, Brit.)
Hugo Bower
OCTOPUSSY(1983, Brit.)
1984
RAZOR'S EDGE, THE(1984)
Ingrid Bower
SHUTTERED ROOM, THE(1968, Brit.)
Lulu May Bower
Misc. Silents
WHEN A MAN SEES RED(1917)
Pamela Bower
KING'S RHAPSODY(1955, Brit.), w; HEART OF A MAN, THE(1959, Brit.), w; LADY IS A SQUARE, THE(1959, Brit.), w
Pamela Wilcox Bower
TRENT'S LAST CASE(1953, Brit.), w; LAUGHING ANNE(1954, Brit./U.S.), w
Sharon Bower
1984
BOUNTY, THE(1984)
Stephen Bower
EVENTS(1970), ph; YOU'VE GOT TO WALK IT LIKE YOU TALK IT OR YOU'LL LOSE THAT BEAT(1971), ph
Stone Bower
1984
AGAINST ALL ODDS(1984)
Sue Bower
NORWOOD(1970), makeup
Tom Bower
COMMITMENT, THE(1976); BALLAD OF GREGORIO CORTEZ, THE(1983)
1984
MASSIVE RETALIATION(1984)
Barbara Bowers
WEEKEND AT THE WALDORF(1945)
Bob Bowers
COME SPY WITH ME(1967), m
Cookie Bowers
CATSKILL HONEYMOON(1950)
Dawnell Bowers
SCARFACE(1983)
Ellen Bowers
VIOLENT SATURDAY(1955)
George Bowers
FABLE, A(1971), ed; COME BACK CIHARLESTON BLUE(1972), ed; POM POM GIRLS, THE(1976), ed; VAN NUYS BLVD.(1979), ed; HEARSE, THE(1980), d; BODY AND SOUL(1981), d; BEACH GIRLS(1982), ed; MY TUTOR(1983), d
1984
ADVENTURES OF BUCKAROO BANZAI: ACROSS THE 8TH DIMENSION, THE(1984), ed
Jess Bowers [Adele Buffington]
ARIZONA BOUND(1941), w; FORBIDDEN TRAILS(1941), w; GUN MAN FROM BODIE, THE(1941), w; BELOW THE BORDER(1942), w; DAWN ON THE GREAT DIVIDE(1942), w; DOWN TEXAS WAY(1942), w; GHOST TOWN LAW(1942), w; RIDERS OF THE WEST(1942), w; WEST OF THE LAW(1942), w; OUTLAWS OF STAMPEDE PASS(1943), w; SIX GUN GOSPEL(1943), w; STRANGER FROM PECOS, THE(1943), w; RAIDERS OF THE BORDER(1944), w; TEXAS KID, THE(1944), w; FRONTIER FEUD(1945), w; LOST TRAIL, THE(1945), w; NAVAJO TRAIL, THE(1945), w; RIDERS OF THE DUSK(1949), w
John Bowers
SAY IT WITH SONGS(1929); SKIN DEEP(1929); MOUNTED FURY(1931)
Silents
DIVORCE GAME, THE(1917); CABARET, THE(1918); JOAN OF THE WOODS(1918); JOURNEY'S END(1918); OLDEST LAW, THE(1918); DAUGHTER OF MINE(1919); PEST, THE(1919); CUMBERLAND ROMANCE, A(1920); OUT OF THE STORM(1920); ACE OF HEARTS, THE(1921); POVERTY OF RICHES, THE(1921); SILENT CALL, THE(1921); SKY PILOT, THE(1921); GOLDEN GIFT, THE(1922); SOUTH OF SU-VA(1922); CRINOLINE AND ROMANCE(1923); DIVORCE(1923); SO BIG(1924); DAUGHTERS WHO PAY(1925); FLATTERY(1925); OFF THE HIGHWAY(1925); HEARTS AND FISTS(1926); WHISPERING SMITH(1926); JEWELS OF DESIRE(1927); LORNA DOONE(1927); RAGTIME(1927)

John E. Bowers-

Misc. Silents
DESTINY'S TOY(1916); HULDA FROM HOLLAND(1916); MADAME X(1916); REWARD OF PATIENCE, THE(1916); BETSY ROSS(1917); BONDAGE OF FEAR, THE(1917); DARKEST RUSSIA(1917); EASY MONEY(1917); MATERNITY(1917); SELF MADE WIDOW(1917); SHALL WE FORGIVE HER?(1917); TENTH CASE, THE(1917); HEREDITY(1918); SEA WAIF, THE(1918); SPURS OF SYBIL, THE(1918); STOLEN HOURS(1918); STRONG WAY, THE(1918); T'OTHER DEAR CHARMER(1918); WAY OUT, THE(1918); WOMAN OF REDEMPTION, A(1918); DAY DREAMS(1919); SIS HOPKINS(1919); STRICTLY CONFIDENTIAL(1919); THROUGH THE WRONG DOOR(1919); WHAT LOVE FORGIVES(1919); LOVES OF LETTY, THE(1920); WOMAN IN ROOM 13, THE(1920); GODLESS MEN(1921); NIGHT ROSE, THE(1921); ROADS OF DESTINY(1921); UNWILLING HERO, AN(1921); AFFINITIES(1922); BONDED WOMAN, THE(1922); QUINCY ADAMS SAWYER(1922); BAREFOOT BOY, THE(1923); DESIRE(1923); DESTROYING ANGEL, THE(1923); WHAT A WIFE LEARNED(1923); WOMAN OF BRONZE, THE(1923); CODE OF THE WILDERNESS(1924); EMPTY HEARTS(1924); THOSE WHO DARE(1924); WHEN A MAN'S A MAN(1924); WHITE SIN, THE(1924); CHICKIE(1925); CONFESSIONS OF A QUEEN(1925); FLATTERY(1925); PEOPLE VS. NANCY PRESTON, THE(1925); DANGER GIRL, THE(1926); LADDIE(1926); PALS IN PARADISE(1926); ROCKING MOON(1926); DICE WOMAN, THE(1927); FOR LADIES ONLY(1927); HEART OF THE YUKON, THE(1927); HEROES IN BLUE(1927); OPENING NIGHT, THE(1927); THREE HOURS(1927)

John E. Bowers
Misc. Silents
WOMAN PAYS, THE(1915)

Kenny Bowers
BEST FOOT FORWARD(1943); BROADWAY RHYTHM(1944); I'LL BE SEEING YOU(1944)

Lally Bowers
WE JOINED THE NAVY(1962, Brit.); CHALK GARDEN, THE(1964, Brit.); TAMAHINE(1964, Brit.); ALL THE WAY UP(1970, Brit.); I START COUNTING(1970, Brit.); DRACULA A.D. 1972(1972, Brit.); OUR MISS FRED(1972, Brit.); SLIPPER AND THE ROSE, THE(1976, Brit.)

Marge Bowers
OUTSIDERS, THE(1983), cos; RUMBLE FISH(1983), cos

Raymond Bowers
SCHIZO(1977, Brit.)

Richard Bowers
MISSION OVER KOREA(1953)

Tanya Bowers
HEARSE, THE(1980)

William Bowers
MY FAVORITE SPY(1942), w; SEVEN DAYS LEAVE(1942), w; ADVENTURES OF A ROOKIE(1943), w; HIGHER AND HIGHER(1943), w; SING YOUR WAY HOME(1945), w; FABULOUS SUZANNE, THE(1946), w; NIGHT AND DAY(1946), w; LADIES' MAN(1947), w; SOMETHING IN THE WIND(1947), w; WEB, THE(1947), w; WISTFUL WIDOW OF WAGON GAP, THE(1947), w; BLACK BART(1948), w; COUNTESS OF MONTE CRISTO, THE(1948), w; JUNGLE PATROL(1948), w; LARCENY(1948), w; RIVER LADY(1948), w; GAL WHO TOOK THE WEST, THE(1949), w; CONVICTED(1950), w; GUNFIGHTER, THE(1950), w; MRS. O'MALLEY AND MR. MALONE(1950), w; CRY DANGER(1951), w; MOB, THE(1951), w; ASSIGNMENT-PARIS(1952), w; SPLIT SECOND(1953), w; SHE COULDN'T SAY NO(1954), w; FIVE AGAINST THE HOUSE(1955), w; TIGHT SPOT(1955), w; BEST THINGS IN LIFE ARE FREE, THE(1956), w; MY MAN GODFREY(1957), w; IMITATION GENERAL(1958), w; LAW AND JAKE WADE, THE(1958), w; SHEEPMAN, THE(1958), w; –30–(1959), w; ALIAS JESSE JAMES(1959), w; LAST TIME I SAW ARCHIE, THE(1961), w; ADVANCE TO THE REAR(1964), w; WAY...WAY OUT(1966), w; RIDE TO HANGMAN'S TREE, THE(1967), w; SUPPORT YOUR LOCAL SHERIFF(1969), p, w; GODFATHER, THE, PART II(1974)

William J. Bowers
NOTORIOUS LONE WOLF, THE(1946), w

Bob Bowes
KES(1970, Brit.)

Bobby Bowes
Silents
LAW FORBIDS, THE(1924)

Brian Bowes
TIME BANDITS(1981, Brit.)

Donnie Bowes
SCREWBALLS(1983)

Ed Bowes
BORN IN FLAMES(1983), ph

Geoffrey Bowes
SOMETHING'S ROTTEN(1979, Can.); MIDDLE AGE CRAZY(1980, Can.); FISH HAWK(1981, Can.)
Misc. Talkies
SOLDIER'S STORY, THE(1981)

Larry Bowes
Silents
BIG TOWN IDEAS(1921)

Margie Bowes
GOLD GUITAR, THE(1966); COTTONPICKIN' CHICKENPICKERS(1967)

Hon. David Bowes-Lyon
BIG BLOCKADE, THE(1942, Brit.)

Bowie
ONE WISH TOO MANY(1956, Brit.), spec eff

David Bowie
MAN WHO FELL TO EARTH, THE(1976, Brit.); JUST A GIGOLO(1979, Ger.); RADIO ON(1980, Brit./Ger.), m; HUNGER, THE(1983); MERRY CHRISTMAS MR. LAWRENCE(1983, Jap./Brit.); YELLOWBEARD(1983)

Douglas Bowie
U-TURN(1973, Can.), w

James Bowie
INCREDIBLY STRANGE CREATURES WHO STOPPED LIVING AND BECAME CRAZY MIXED-UP ZOMBIES, THE(1965); RAT PFINK AND BOO BOO(1966); TARGETS(1968)

Les Bowie
ENEMY FROM SPACE(1957, Brit.), spec eff; X THE UNKNOWN(1957, Brit.), spec eff; HAUNTED STRANGLER, THE(1958, Brit.), spec eff; CURSE OF THE WEREWOLF, THE(1961, Brit.), spec eff; DAY THE EARTH CAUGHT FIRE, THE(1961, Brit.), spec eff; DR. BLOOD'S COFFIN(1961), spec eff; SHADOW OF THE CAT, THE(1961, Brit.), spec eff; NIGHT CREATURES(1962, Brit.), spec eff; PIRATES OF BLOOD RIVER, THE(1962, Brit.), spec eff; KISS OF EVIL(1963, Brit.), spec eff; NIGHTMARE(1963, Brit.), spec eff; OLD DARK HOUSE, THE(1963, Brit.), spec eff; PARANOIAC(1963, Brit.), spec eff; CRIMSON BLADE, THE(1964, Brit.), spec eff; DEVIL-SHIP PIRATES, THE(1964, Brit.), spec eff; EVIL OF FRANKENSTEIN, THE(1964, Brit.), spec eff; CITY UNDER THE SEA(1965, Brit.), spec eff; FRANKENSTEIN CREATED WOMAN(1965, Brit.), spec eff; QUILLER MEMORANDUM, THE(1966, Brit.), spec eff; THOSE FANTASTIC FLYING FOOLS(1967, Brit), spec eff; MOON ZERO TWO(1970, Brit.), spec eff; MOSQUITO SQUADRON(1970, Brit.), spec eff; DRACULA A.D. 1972(1972, Brit.), spec eff; VAMPIRE CIRCUS(1972, Brit.), spec eff; NOTHING BUT THE NIGHT(1975, Brit.), spec eff; TO THE DEVIL A DAUGHTER(1976, Brit./Ger.), Spec eff; DRACULA AND THE SEVEN GOLDEN VAMPIRES(1978, Brit./Chi.), spec eff; SUPERMAN(1978), spec eff

Leslie Bowie
SO LONG AT THE FAIR(1951, Brit.), spec eff

Bowie Films
DRACULA–PRINCE OF DARKNESS(1966, Brit.), spec eff; PLAGUE OF THE ZOMBIES, THE(1966, Brit.), spec eff

Aldrich Bowker
ANGELS WASH THEIR FACES(1939); DEAD END KIDS ON DRESS PARADE(1939); EVERYBODY'S HOBBY(1939); JOE AND ETHEL TURP CALL ON THE PRESIDENT(1939); NANCY DREW, TROUBLE SHOOTER(1939); NO PLACE TO GO(1939); PRIDE OF THE BLUEGRASS(1939); TORCHY PLAYS WITH DYNAMITE(1939); WATERFRONT(1939); ABE LINCOLN IN ILLINOIS(1940); SUSAN AND GOD(1940); THOSE WERE THE DAYS(1940); BALL OF FIRE(1941); JENNIE(1941); LOVE CRAZY(1941); MEET JOHN DOE(1941); POT O' GOLD(1941); ROMANCE OF THE RIO GRANDE(1941); SHADOW OF THE THIN MAN(1941); WAGONS ROLL AT NIGHT, THE(1941); I MARRIED A WITCH(1942); I WAS FRAMED(1942); MAJOR AND THE MINOR, THE(1942); MISSISSIPPI GAMBLER(1942)

Fanny Bowker
SHE WAS ONLY A VILLAGE MAIDEN(1933, Brit.), w

Judi Bowker
BROTHER SUN, SISTER MOON(1973, Brit./Ital.); EAST OF ELEPHANT ROCK(1976, Brit.); CLASH OF THE TITANS(1981)

Ryall Bowker
MISFITS, THE(1961)

Virginia Bowker
Silents
PAIR OF SIXES, A(1918)

Sydney Bowkett
Silents
AUDACIOUS MR. SQUIRE, THE(1923, Brit.), w

Clive Colin Bowler
TERM OF TRIAL(1962, Brit.); SMALL WORLD OF SAMMY LEE, THE(1963, Brit.); GIRL GETTERS, THE(1966, Brit.)

Jean Bowler
MARK OF CAIN, THE(1948, Brit.)

John Bowler
1984
BREAKOUT(1984, Brit.)

Norman Bowler
SUMARINE X-1(1969, Brit.); JULIUS CAESAR(1970, Brit.)

Richard Bowler
LOVE WITH THE PROPER STRANGER(1963); I DRINK YOUR BLOOD(1971)

Billy Bowles
TODD KILLINGS, THE(1971); $1,000,000 DUCK(1971)

Buddy Bowles
FOREST RANGERS, THE(1942)

Donald Bowles
Misc. Silents
SQUAW MAN'S SON, THE(1917)

James H. Bowles
STONE(1974, Aus.)

Jim Bowles
GREAT MACARTHY, THE(1975, Aus.)

Paul Bowles
DREAMS THAT MONEY CAN BUY(1948), m; SENSO(1968, Ital.), w

Peter Bowles
DEAD MAN'S CHEST(1965, Brit.); THREE HATS FOR LISA(1965, Brit.); BLOW-UP(1966, Brit.); CHARGE OF THE LIGHT BRIGADE, THE(1968, Brit.); ASSASSINATION BUREAU, THE(1969, Brit.); TASTE OF EXCITEMENT(1969, Brit.); SUDDEN TERROR(1970, Brit.); ENDLESS NIGHT(1971, Brit.); DAY IN THE DEATH OF JOE EGG, A(1972, Brit.); LEGEND OF HELL HOUSE, THE(1973, Brit.); OFFENSE, THE(1973, Brit.); FOR THE LOVE OF BENJI(1977); DISAPPEARANCE, THE(1981, Brit./Can.)

Linda Bowley
RETURN OF THE JEDI(1983)

Al Bowlly
MAYOR'S NEST, THE(1932, Brit.)

Amanda Bowman
MODEL MURDER CASE, THE(1964, Brit.)

Bob Bowman
HONEYMOON MERRY-GO-ROUND(1939, Brit.); LOUISA(1950)

Cal Bowman
WAVELENGTH(1983)

David Bowman
THREE DAYS OF THE CONDOR(1975)

Don Bowman
LAS VEGAS HILLBILLYS(1966); HILLBILLYS IN A HAUNTED HOUSE(1967)

Dulcie Bowman
LOVE IS A WOMAN(1967, Brit.); HOSTILE WITNESS(1968, Brit.)

Earl Wayland Bowman
LONG, LONG TRAIL, THE(1929), w
Silents
WHEN SECONDS COUNT(1927)

Empsie Bowman
POISON PEN(1941, Brit.); VOTE FOR HUGGETT(1948, Brit.)

Isa Bowman
VOTE FOR HUGGETT(1948, Brit.)
James Bowman
LEGEND OF THE LONE RANGER, THE(1981)
John Bowman
TRESPASSERS, THE(1976, Aus.)
Silents
FIELD OF HONOR, THE(1922, Brit.), p
Laura Bowman
DRUMS O' VOODOO(1934); SON OF INGAGI(1940)
Misc. Talkies
BRAND OF CAIN, THE(1935); BIRTHRIGHT(1939); SHE DEVIL(1940)
Lee Bowman
EASY LIVING(1937); I MET HIM IN PARIS(1937); INTERNES CAN'T TAKE MONEY(1937); LAST TRAIN FROM MADRID, THE(1937); SOPHIE LANG GOES WEST(1937); SWING HIGH, SWING LOW(1937); THIS WAY PLEASE(1937); FIRST 100 YEARS, THE(1938); HAVING WONDERFUL TIME(1938); MAN TO REMEMBER, A(1938); NEXT TIME I MARRY(1938); TARNISHED ANGEL(1938); DANCING CO-ED(1939); FAST AND FURIOUS(1939); GREAT VICTOR HERBERT, THE(1939); LADY AND THE MOB, THE(1939); LOVE AFFAIR(1939); MIRACLES FOR SALE(1939); SOCIETY LAWYER(1939); STRONGER THAN DESIRE(1939); FLORIAN(1940); GOLD RUSH MAISIE(1940); THIRD FINGER, LEFT HAND(1940); WYOMING(1940); BUCK PRIVATES(1941); DESIGN FOR SCANDAL(1941); MARRIED BACHELOR(1941); MODEL WIFE(1941); WASHINGTON MELODRAMA(1941); KID GLOVE KIL-LER(1942); PACIFIC RENDEZVOUS(1942); TISH(1942); WE WERE DANCING(1942); BATAAN(1943); THREE HEARTS FOR JULIA(1943); COVER GIRL(1944); IMPA-TIENT YEARS, THE(1944); UP IN MABEL'S ROOM(1944); SHE WOULDN'T SAY YES(1945); TONIGHT AND EVERY NIGHT(1945); WALLS CAME TUMBLING DOWN, THE(1946); SMASH-UP, THE STORY OF A WOMAN(1947); MY DREAM IS YOURS(1949); THERE'S A GIRL IN MY HEART(1949); HOUSE BY THE RIVER(1950); YOUNGBLOOD HAWKE(1964)
Leslie Bowman
Misc. Talkies
RAPE KILLER, THE(1976)
Marcia Bowman
EASY RIDER(1969)
Nellie Bowman
EYES OF FATE(1933, Brit.); BYPASS TO HAPPINESS(1934, Brit.); OLD MOTHER RILEY, DETECTIVE(1943, Brit.); VOTE FOR HUGGETT(1948, Brit.); WATERLOO ROAD(1949, Brit.)
Pam Bowman
TWO OF A KIND(1983)
Pamela Bowman
SCARED TO DEATH(1981); STRIPES(1981); HYSTERICAL(1983)
Patricia Bowman
OKAY FOR SOUND(1937, Brit.)
Peter Bowman
BEACH RED(1967), w
Ralph Bowman [John Archer]
OVERLAND STAGE RAIDERS(1938); BARNYARD FOLLIES(1940); CHEERS FOR MISS BISHOP(1941)
Ralph D. Bowman
DON'T GO IN THE HOUSE(1980)
Rudy Bowman
SOUTHWARD HO!(1939); CHEYENNE WILDCAT(1944); WEST OF THE ALA-MO(1946); ROARING WESTWARD(1949); SHE WORE A YELLOW RIBBON(1949)
Tina Bowman
WIZARDS(1977); HEY, GOOD LOOKIN'(1982)
Tom Bowman
MEN OF SHERWOOD FOREST(1957, Brit.); SURGEON'S KNIFE, THE(1957, Brit.); HARRY BLACK AND THE TIGER(1958, Brit.); SECRET MAN, THE(1958, Brit.); STEEL BAYONET, THE(1958, Brit.); IDOL ON PARADE(1959, Brit.); WITNESS, THE(1959, Brit.); IN THE WAKE OF A STRANGER(1960, Brit.); S.O.S. PACIFIC(1960, Brit.); FRIGHTENED CITY, THE(1961, Brit.); TOO HOT TO HANDLE(1961, Brit.); HOT MONEY GIRL(1962, Brit./Ger.); CHILDREN OF THE DAMNED(1963, Brit.); ESCAPE BY NIGHT(1965, Brit.); I'VE GOTTA HORSE(1965, Brit.); WHERE THE BULLETS FLY(1966, Brit.); PSYCHO-CIRCUS(1967, Brit.); TRYGON FACTOR, THE(1969, Brit.); INNOCENT BYSTANDERS(1973, Brit.)
William Bowman
Silents
SILENT VOICE, THE(1915), d, w; FALSE FACES(1919)
Misc. Silents
ROSEMARY(1915), d; FROM A BROADWAY TO A THRONE(1916), d
William J. Bowman
Silents
PENNINGTON'S CHOICE(1915), d; SECOND IN COMMAND, THE(1915), d
Misc. Silents
BAIT, THE(1916), d; HEART OF TARA, THE(1916), d
Hal Bown
ROBERTA(1935)
Harry Joe Bown
SONS O' GUNS(1936), p
John Bown
TUNES OF GLORY(1960, Brit.)
Anne Bownen
FUNNYMAN(1967)
Richard Bowser
YOICKS!(1932, Brit.), art d
Sue Bowser
STRIPES(1981); DOCTOR DETROIT(1983)
Willard Bowsky
GULLIVER'S TRAVELS(1939), anim d
Stephen Bowson
NATIONAL VELVET(1944)
Ivor Bowyer
LAST LOAD, THE(1948, Brit.)
1984
STRIKEBOUND(1984, Aus.)

Jim Bowyer
DAN'S MOTEL(1982)
Betty Box
DEAR MURDERER(1947, Brit.), p; HERE COME THE HUGGETTS(1948, Brit.), p; VOTE FOR HUGGETT(1948, Brit.), p; HUGGETTS ABROAD, THE(1949, Brit.), p; IT'S NOT CRICKET(1949, Brit.), p; MARRY ME!(1949, Brit.), p; DEADLIER THAN THE MALE(1967, Brit.), p; DOCTOR IN TROUBLE(1970, Brit.), p
Betty E. Box
WHEN THE BOUGH BREAKS(1947, Brit.), p; DON'T EVER LEAVE ME(1949, Brit.), p; MIRANDA(1949, Brit.), p; CLOUDED YELLOW, THE(1950, Brit.), p; SO LONG AT THE FAIR(1951, Brit.), p; ISLAND RESCUE(1952, Brit.), p; ASSASSIN, THE(1953, Brit.), p; DAY TO REMEMBER, A(1953, Brit.), p; DOCTOR IN THE HOUSE(1954, Brit.), p; MAD ABOUT MEN(1954, Brit.), p; DOCTOR AT SEA(1955, Brit.), p; IRON PETTICOAT, THE(1956, Brit.), p; CAMPBELL'S KINGDOM(1957, Brit.), p; CHECKPOINT(1957, Brit.), p; DOCTOR AT LARGE(1957, Brit.), p; TALE OF TWO CITIES, A(1958, Brit.), p; WIND CANNOT READ, THE(1958, Brit.), p; CON-SPIRACY OF HEARTS(1960, Brit.), p; DOCTOR IN LOVE(1960, Brit.), p; THIRTY NINE STEPS, THE(1960, Brit.), p; NO LOVE FOR JOHNNIE(1961, Brit.), p; UP-STAIRS AND DOWNSTAIRS(1961, Brit.), p; AGENT 8 3/4(1963, Brit.), p; DOCTOR IN DISTRESS(1963, Brit.), p; PAIR OF BRIEFS, A(1963, Brit.), p; NO, MY DARLING DAUGHTER!(1964, Brit.), p; YOUNG AND WILLING(1964, Brit.), p; MC GUIRE, GO HOME!(1966, Brit.), p; CARNABY, M.D.(1967, Brit.), p; HIGH COMMISSIONER, THE(1968, U.S./Brit.), p; SOME GIRLS DO(1969, Brit.), p; PERCY(1971, Brit.), p; IT'S A 2'6" ABOVE THE GROUND WORLD(1972, Brit.), p; IT'S NOT THE SIZE THAT COUNTS(1979, Brit.), p
Brian Box
VAMPIRE LOVERS, THE(1970, Brit.), cos
Euel Box
BENJI(1974), m; HAWMPS!(1976), m; FOR THE LOVE OF BENJI(1977), m; CHARGE OF THE MODEL-T'S(1979), m; THE DOUBLE McGUFFIN(1979), m
Evel Box
OH, HEAVENLY DOG!(1980), m
George Box
TORTURE DUNGEON(1970)
John Box
GAMMA PEOPLE, THE(1956), art d; ZARAK(1956, Brit.), art d; FIRE DOWN BELOW(1957, U.S./Brit.), set d; HIGH FLIGHT(1957, Brit.), art d; INN OF THE SIXTH HAPPINESS, THE(1958, Brit.), art d; TANK FORCE(1958, Brit.), art d; OUR MAN IN HAVANA(1960, Brit.), art d; WORLD OF SUZIE WONG, THE(1960), art d; LAW-RENCE OF ARABIA(1962, Brit.), prod d; OF HUMAN BONDAGE(1964, Brit.), prod d; DOCTOR ZHIVAGO(1965), prod d; MAN FOR ALL SEASONS, A(1966, Brit.), prod d; WILD AFFAIR, THE(1966, Brit.), prod d; OLIVER!(1968, Brit.), prod d; LOOKING GLASS WAR, THE(1970, Brit.), p; NICHOLAS AND ALEXANDRA(1971, Brit.), prod d; TRAVELS WITH MY AUNT(1972, Brit.), prod d; ROLLERBALL(1975), prod d; SOR-CERER(1977), prod d; KEEP, THE(1983), prod d
1984
PASSAGE TO INDIA, A(1984, Brit.), prod d
M. Box
NOVEL AFFAIR, A(1957, Brit.), w
Martyn Box
GARRISON FOLLIES(1940, Brit.)
Muriel Box
ALIBI INN(1935, Brit.), w; GIRL IN A MILLION, A(1946, Brit.), w; HOLIDAY CAMP(1947, Brit.), w; WHEN THE BOUGH BREAKS(1947, Brit.), w; YEARS BE-TWEEN, THE(1947, Brit.), w; BLIND GODDESS, THE(1948, Brit.), w; BROTHERS, THE(1948, Brit.), w; DAYDREAK(1948, Brit.), w; EASY MONEY(1948, Brit.), w; GIRL IN THE PAINTING, THE(1948, Brit.), w; HERE COME THE HUGGETTS(1948, Brit.), w; SMUGGLERS, THE(1948, Brit.), w; CHRISTOPHER COLUMBUS(1949, Brit.), w; FACTS OF LOVE(1949, Brit.), w; GOOD TIME GIRL(1950, Brit.), w; LOST PEOPLE, THE(1950, Brit.), w; MR. LORD SAYS NO(1952, Brit.), d, w; BOTH SIDES OF THE LAW(1953, Brit.), d, w; THE BEACHCOMBER(1955, Brit.), d; CASH ON DELIVERY(1956, Brit.), d; EYEWITNESS(1956, Brit.), d; SIMON AND LAURA(1956, Brit.), d; NOVEL AFFAIR, A(1957, Brit.), d; TRUTH ABOUT WOMEN, THE(1958, Brit.), d; SUBWAY IN THE SKY(1959, Brit.), d; THIS OTHER EDEN(1959, Brit.), d; TOO YOUNG TO LOVE(1960, Brit.), d, w; PIPER'S TUNE(1962, Brit.), d; RATTLE OF A SIMPLE MAN(1964, Brit.), d
Muriel Box
DEAR MURDERER(1947, Brit.), w
Sidney Box
BROKEN JOURNEY(1948, Brit.), p; BROTHERS, THE(1948, Brit.), p; GIRL IN THE PAINTING, THE(1948, Brit.), w; BAD LORD BYRON, THE(1949, Brit.), p; ASTON-ISHED HEART, THE(1950, Brit.), p
Sydney Box [Aubrey Baring]
ALIBI INN(1935, Brit.), w; FLEMISH FARM, THE(1943, Brit.), p; DON'T TAKE IT TO HEART(1944, Brit.), p; ON APPROVAL(1944, Brit.), p; GIRL IN A MILLION, A(1946, Brit.), p, w; SEVENTH VEIL, THE(1946, Brit.), p, w; DEAR MUR-DERER(1947, Brit.), w; HOLIDAY CAMP(1947, Brit.), p, w; UPTURNED GLASS, THE(1947, Brit.), p; WHEN THE BOUGH BREAKS(1947, Brit.), w; YEARS BE-TWEEN, THE(1947, Brit.), p, w; BLIND GODDESS, THE(1948, Brit.), w; BROTHERS, THE(1948, Brit.), w; DAYDREAK(1948, Brit.), p, w; EASY MONEY(1948, Brit.), w; HERE COME THE HUGGETTS(1948, Brit.), w; JASSY(1948, Brit.), p; SMUGGLERS, THE(1948, Brit.), p, w; CHRISTOPHER COLUMBUS(1949, Brit.), w; FACTS OF LOVE(1949, Brit.), p, w; HER MAN GILBEY(1949, Brit.), p; MY BROTHER'S KEEP-ER(1949, Brit.), p; GOOD TIME GIRL(1950, Brit.), p, w; MR. LORD SAYS NO(1952, Brit.), p, w; BOTH SIDES OF THE LAW(1953, Brit.), p, w; FORBIDDEN CARGO(1954, Brit.), p, w; THE BEACHCOMBER(1955, Brit.), w; EYEWITNESS(1956, Brit.), p; NOVEL AFFAIR, A(1957, Brit.), w; FLOODS OF FEAR(1958, Brit.), p; TRUTH ABOUT WOMEN, THE(1958, Brit.), p, w; SUBWAY IN THE SKY(1959, Brit.), p; TOO YOUNG TO LOVE(1960, Brit.), w; DEADLIER THAN THE MALE(1967, Brit.), p
Tillman Box
WHEN THE LEGENDS DIE(1972)
Harold Boxall
OLD BILL AND SON(1940, Brit.), p; HAPPIDROME(1943, Brit.), p
Rosalind Boxall
KID FOR TWO FARTHINGS, A(1956, Brit.)
David Boxer
TULIPS(1981, Can)

Herman Boxer
CALIFORNIA STRAIGHT AHEAD(1937), w

John Boxer
GEORGE AND MARGARET(1940, Brit.); FLYING FORTRESS(1942, Brit.); IN WHICH WE SERVE(1942, Brit.); MILLIONS LIKE US(1943, Brit.); SOMEWHERE IN FRANCE(1943, Brit.); ADVENTURE FOR TWO(1945, Brit.); HALF-WAY HOUSE, THE(1945, Brit.); DULCIMER STREET(1948, Brit.); OCTOBER MAN, THE(1948, Brit.); BLUE LAGOON, THE(1949, Brit.); IT'S NOT CRICKET(1949, Brit.); MAN ON THE RUN(1949, Brit.); MARRY ME!(1949, Brit.); MY BROTHER'S KEEPER(1949, Brit.); STOP PRESS GIRL(1949, Brit.); WATERLOO ROAD(1949, Brit.); FIVE ANGLES ON MURDER(1950, Brit.); HAPPIEST DAYS OF YOUR LIFE(1950, Brit.); ENCORE(1951, Brit.); MR. DRAKE'S DUCK(1951, Brit.); PARATROOPER(1954, Brit.); SECRET VENTURE(1955, Brit.); BRIDGE ON THE RIVER KWAI, THE(1957); ROCK AROUND THE WORLD(1957, Brit.); UNDERCOVER GIRL(1957, Brit.); HEART OF A CHILD(1958, Brit.); REQUIEM FOR A HEAVYWEIGHT(1962), cos; HIDE AND SEEK(1964, Brit.); STARTING OVER(1979), cos; VOICES(1979), cos; FORT APACHE, THE BRONX(1981), cos; NEIGHBORS(1981), cos; WOLFEN(1981), cos; REUBEN, REUBEN(1983), cos

Patrick Boxil
BROTHERS, THE(1948, Brit.)

Patrick Boxill
CLUE OF THE MISSING APE, THE(1953, Brit.); GOLD EXPRESS, THE(1955, Brit.); STOLEN PLANS, THE(1962, Brit.); FOXY LADY(1971, Can.)

Bruce Boxleitner
SIX PACK ANNIE(1975); BALTIMORE BULLET, THE(1980); TRON(1982)

David Boxwell
TOUCH OF HER FLESH, THE(1967)

Billy Boy
MOUNTAIN RHYTHM(1942)

Grey Boy
Silents
AVENGING SHADOW, THE(1928)

Lola Boy
ONCE BEFORE I DIE(1967, U.S./Phil.); SECRET OF THE SACRED FOREST, THE(1970)

Mildred Boy
Silents
GENTLEMEN PREFER BLONDES(1928)

The Boy Choristers
OFF THE DOLE(1935, Brit.)

Boy Scout Troop 107 of Los Angeles
DRUM TAPS(1933)

Boy Scouts of America
MIND YOUR OWN BUSINESS(1937)

Troop 536 Boy Scouts of Los Angeles
THAT CERTAIN AGE(1938)

Billy Boya
PRISONER OF JAPAN(1942)

Tom Boya
PUTNEY SWOPE(1969)

Aram Boyaian
FEARLESS FRANK(1967), ed

Sully Boyar
ME AND MY BROTHER(1969); GANG THAT COULDN'T SHOOT STRAIGHT, THE(1971); MADE FOR EACH OTHER(1971); PANIC IN NEEDLE PARK(1971); KING OF MARVIN GARDENS, THE(1972); LAST OF THE RED HOT LOVERS(1972); GAMBLER, THE(1974); DOG DAY AFTERNOON(1975); CARWASH(1976); OLIVER'S STORY(1978); JAZZ SINGER, THE(1980); NIGHT OF THE JUGGLER(1980); FORT APACHE, THE BRONX(1981); ENTITY, THE(1982)

Nikolay Boyarskiy
KATERINA IZMAILOVA(1969, USSR)

Alanna Boyce
LAVENDER HILL MOB, THE(1951, Brit.); TWICE UPON A TIME(1953, Brit.)

Donna Jo Boyce
BREAKING POINT, THE(1950)

Eddie Boyce
THERE WAS A CROOKED MAN(1962, Brit.)

George Boyce
NIGHT AND DAY(1946); CLOWN, THE(1953); TITANIC(1953); THREE RING CIRCUS(1954); SEVEN LITTLE FOYS, THE(1955); TEN WANTED MEN(1955); HOW TO STUFF A WILD BIKINI(1965)

Helen Boyce
HOLLYWOOD BARN DANCE(1947)

Jim Boyce
SLUMBER PARTY MASSACRE, THE(1982)

Linda Boyce
GIRL GRABBERS, THE(1968); TORTURE ME KISS ME(1970)
Misc. Talkies
DEATH ON CREDIT(1976)

William Boyce
SLIME PEOPLE, THE(1963)

Boyce and Evans
YES SIR, MR. BONES(1951)

Boyd
BAR 20 RIDES AGAIN(1936)

Alan Boyd
TENTACLES(1977, Ital.)
Misc. Talkies
ENCOUNTERS OF THE DEEP(1984)

Alex Boyd
YOU CAN'T BEAT THE IRISH(1952, Brit.), p

Anne Boyd
AREN'T MEN BEASTS?(1937, Brit.)

Betty Boyd
GODLESS GIRL, THE(1929); GREEN GODDESS, THE(1930); LILIES OF THE FIELD(1930); PARADISE ISLAND(1930); UNDER A TEXAS MOON(1930); ALONG CAME YOUTH(1931); MAID TO ORDER(1932); GUN LAW(1933); SAMSON AND DELILAH(1949)

Beverly Boyd
GIRLS IN CHAINS(1943); NOBODY'S DARLING(1943); YOUNGEST PROFESSION, THE(1943); JIVE JUNCTION(1944)
Misc. Talkies
GHOST RIDER, THE(1943)

Bill Boyd
BEYOND VICTORY(1931); BIG GAMBLE, THE(1931); SUICIDE FLEET(1931); CARNIVAL BOAT(1932); GHOST CITY(1932); EMERGENCY CALL(1933); LUCKY DEVILS(1933); CHEATERS(1934); FLAMING GOLD(1934); RACING LUCK(1935); BURNING GOLD(1936)

Bill "Cowboy Rambler" Boyd
PRAIRIE PALS(1942); RAIDERS OF THE WEST(1942); ROLLING DOWN THE GREAT DIVIDE(1942); TEXAS MAN HUNT(1942)
Misc. Talkies
TUMBLEWEED TRAIL(1942)

Bill [William] Boyd
MEN OF AMERICA(1933)

Bill [William "Stage"] Boyd
PORT OF LOST DREAMS(1935)

Centa Boyd
HONEYSUCKLE ROSE(1980)

Clement Boyd
Silents
KAISER'S SHADOW, THE(1918)

Dallas Boyd
LONG, LONG TRAILER, THE(1954); ROGUE COP(1954); HOLD BACK TOMORROW(1955)

David Boyd
MAGNET, THE(1950, Brit.)

Don Boyd
EAST OF ELEPHANT ROCK(1976, Brit.), p,d&w; HONKY TONK FREEWAY(1981), p
1984
SCRUBBERS(1984, Brit.), p

Dorothy Boyd
AULD LANG SYNE(1929, Brit.); GIRL IN THE NIGHT, THE(1931, Brit.); HOUSE OF UNREST, THE(1931, Brit.); LOVE LIES(1931, Brit.); LOVE RACE, THE(1931, Brit.); PERFECT ALIBI, THE(1931, Brit.); SPORT OF KINGS, THE(1931, Brit.); THIRD TIME LUCKY(1931, Brit.); CALLED BACK(1933, Brit.); IRON STAIR, THE(1933, Brit.); SHOT IN THE DARK, A(1933, Brit.); BRIDE OF THE LAKE(1934, Brit.); GET YOUR MAN(1934, Brit.); OH NO DOCTOR!(1934, Brit.); VIRGINIA'S HUSBAND(1934, Brit.); ACE OF SPADES, THE(1935, Brit.); INSIDE THE ROOM(1935, Brit.); IT HAPPENED IN PARIS(1935, Brit.); EVERYTHING IN LIFE(1936, Brit.); TICKET OF LEAVE(1936, Brit.); TOUCH OF THE MOON, A(1936, Brit.); PEARLS BRING TEARS(1937, Brit.); ROMANCE A LA CARTE(1938, Brit.); SHADOWED EYES(1939, Brit.); EVERYTHING IS RHYTHM(1940, Brit.)
Silents
EASY VIRTUE(1927, Brit.); SOMEHOW GOOD(1927, Brit.)
Misc. Silents
LOVE'S OPTION(1928, Brit.); TONI(1928, Brit.)

Edward Boyd
ROBBERY(1967, Brit.), w

Ernest Boyd
TOGETHER BROTHERS(1974)

Eunice Mays Boyd
MACABRE(1958), w

Franklyn Boyd
JUST FOR FUN(1963, Brit.), md

Gordon Boyd
SIEGE OF THE SAXONS(1963, Brit.)
Misc. Talkies
PARTNERS IN CRIME(1961, Brit.)

Guy Boyd
GHOST STORY(1981); ONLY WHEN I LAUGH(1981); EYES OF THE AMARYLLIS, THE(1982); STREAMERS(1983)
1984
BODY DOUBLE(1984); EYES OF FIRE(1984); FLASHPOINT(1984); TANK(1984)

Hutchinson Boyd
BARNUM WAS RIGHT(1929), w

Jack Boyd
MAKE MINE MUSIC(1946), anim; MARY POPPINS(1964), anim

James Boyd
MEAN DOG BLUES(1978)

Jane Boyd
1984
REFLECTIONS(1984, Brit.), cos

Jerold Hayden Boyd
PLACE CALLED GLORY, A(1966, Span./Ger.), w

Jimmy Boyd
RACING BLOOD(1954); SECOND GREATEST SEX, THE(1955); HIGH TIME(1960); INHERIT THE WIND(1960); PLATINUM HIGH SCHOOL(1960); TWO LITTLE BEARS, THE(1961); NORWOOD(1970); THAT'S THE WAY OF THE WORLD(1975)

John Boyd
SEEDS OF FREEDOM(1943, USSR); BAD COMPANY(1972)

Karin Boyd
MEPHISTO(1981, Ger.)

Kathryn Boyd
Misc. Silents
BLACK GOLD(1928); FLYING ACE(1928)

Lois Boyd
Silents
THUMBS DOWN(1927)
Misc. Silents
WOLVES OF THE AIR(1927)

Margaret Boyd
TWICE UPON A TIME(1953, Brit.); FABIAN OF THE YARD(1954, Brit.); SCOTCH ON THE ROCKS(1954, Brit.); WEE GEORDIE(1956, Brit.); HOT MONEY GIRL(1962, Brit./Ger.); DOCTOR IN DISTRESS(1963, Brit.); LADIES WHO DO(1964, Brit.); THIS IS MY STREET(1964, Brit.); 10 RILLINGTON PLACE(1971, Brit.)

Marie Boyd
Misc. Silents
IN THE SHADOW(1915)
Mary Boyd
LUCY GALLANT(1955)
Michael Boyd
1984
BREAKIN'(1984), m
Mildred Boyd
MERRILY WE GO TO HELL(1932); RED DRAGON, THE(1946); OUT OF THE PAST(1947); VARIETY GIRL(1947); FORCE OF EVIL(1948); I WAS A COMMUNIST FOR THE F.B.I.(1951); LYDIA BAILEY(1952)
Misc. Talkies
SUN TAN RANCH(1948)
Silents
RILEY THE COP(1928)
Neil Boyd
WHEN LONDON SLEEPS(1934, Brit.)
Pattie Boyd
HARD DAY'S NIGHT, A(1964, Brit.)
Priscilla Boyd
POINT BLANK(1967)
Rex Boyd
CHARLIE BUBBLES(1968, Brit.)
Rick Boyd
PAYMENT IN BLOOD(1968, Ital.); RUTHLESS FOUR, THE(1969, Ital./Ger.); SPIRITS OF THE DEAD(1969, Fr.); WIND FROM THE EAST(1970, Fr./Ital./Ger.)
Rik Boyd
SUPERFLY T.N.T.(1973)
Rita Ascot Boyd
DREAMER(1979)
Robert Boyd
RAGTIME(1981)
Roy Boyd
WICKER MAN, THE(1974, Brit.); OMEN, THE(1976)
Russell Boyd
MATCHLESS(1974, Aus.), ph; MAN FROM HONG KONG(1975), ph; PICNIC AT HANGING ROCK(1975, Aus.), ph; SUMMER OF SECRETS(1976, Aus.), ph; BREAK OF DAY(1977, Aus.), ph; SINGER AND THE DANCER, THE(1977, Aus.), ph; LAST WAVE, THE(1978, Aus.), ph; DAWN(1979, Aus.), ph; JUST OUT OF REACH(1979, Aus.), ph; CHAIN REACTION(1980, Aus.), ph; GALLIPOLI(1981, Aus.), ph; STARSTRUCK(1982, Aus.), ph; TENDER MERCIES(1982), ph; YEAR OF LIVING DANGEROUSLY, THE(1982, Aus.), ph
1984
MRS. SOFFEL(1984), ph; PHAR LAP(1984, Aus.), ph; SOLDIER'S STORY, A(1984), ph
Ruth Boyd
Silents
MADNESS OF YOUTH(1923); GALLANT FOOL, THE(1926)
Sarah Boyd
1984
OLD ENOUGH(1984)
Stan Boyd
HOW TO BEAT THE HIGH COST OF LIVING(1980)
Stepha Boyd
FALL OF THE ROMAN EMPIRE, THE(1964)
Stephen Boyd
GENGHIS KHAN(U.S./Brit./Ger./Yugo); HELL IN KOREA(1956, Brit.); MAN WHO NEVER WAS, THE(1956, Brit.); ABANDON SHIP(1957, Brit.); ALLIGATOR NAMED DAISY, AN(1957, Brit.); ISLAND IN THE SUN(1957); BRAVADOS, THE(1958); NIGHT HEAVEN FELL, THE(1958, Fr.); BEASTS OF MARSEILLES, THE(1959, Brit.); BEN HUR(1959); BEST OF EVERYTHING, THE(1959); WOMAN OBSESSED(1959); BIG GAMBLE, THE(1961); JUMBO(1962); LISA(1962, Brit.); IMPERIAL VENUS(1963, Ital./Fr.); THIRD SECRET, THE(1964, Brit.); BIBLE...IN THE BEGINNING, THE(1966); FANTASTIC VOYAGE(1966); OSCAR, THE(1966); POPPY IS ALSO A FLOWER, THE(1966); CAPER OF THE GOLDEN BULLS, THE(1967); ASSIGNMENT K(1968, Brit.); SHALAKO(1968, Brit.); SLAVES(1969); HANNIE CALDER(1971, Brit.); BIG GAME, THE(1972); KILL! KILL! KILL!(1972, Fr./Ger./Ital./Span.); MAN CALLED NOON, THE(1973, Brit.); THOSE DIRTY DOGS(1974, U.S./Ital./Span.); TREASURE OF JAMAICA REEF, THE(1976); SQUEEZE, THE(1977, Brit.)
Misc. Talkies
BORN FOR TROUBLE(1955); MANIPULATOR, THE(1972); DEVIL HAS SEVEN FACES, THE(1977); ONE MAN AGAINST THE ORGANIZATION(1977)
Tanya Boyd
BLACK SHAMPOO(1976); WHOLLY MOSES(1980)
Thomas Boyd
BLAZE O' GLORY(1930), w
1984
REPO MAN(1984)
Tom Boyd
NIGHT PEOPLE(1954)
Tony Boyd
MIDNIGHT EXPRESS(1978, Brit.)
William Boyd
FLYING FOOL(1929); HIGH VOLTAGE(1929); HIS FIRST COMMAND(1929); LADY OF THE PAVEMENTS(1929); LEATHERNECK, THE(1929); BENSON MURDER CASE, THE(1930); DERELICT(1930); OFFICER O'BRIEN(1930); THOSE WHO DANCE(1930); MURDER BY THE CLOCK(1931); PAINTED DESERT, THE(1931); ROAD TO RENO(1931); WISER SEX, THE(1932); CHIEF, THE(1933); HOPALONG CASSIDY(1935); CALL OF THE PRAIRIE(1936); EAGLE'S BROOD, THE(1936); FEDERAL AGENT(1936); HOPALONG CASSIDY RETURNS(1936); THREE ON THE TRAIL(1936); TRAIL DUST(1936); BORDERLAND(1937); HEART OF THE WEST(1937); HILLS OF OLD WYOMING(1937); HOPALONG RIDES AGAIN(1937); NORTH OF THE RIO GRANDE(1937); RUSTLER'S VALLEY(1937); TEXAS TRAIL(1937); BAR 20 JUSTICE(1938); CASSIDY OF BAR 20(1938); FRONTIERSMAN, THE(1938); HEART OF ARIZONA(1938); IN OLD MEXICO(1938); PARTNERS OF THE PLAINS(1938); PRIDE OF THE WEST(1938); SUNSET TRAIL(1938); LAW OF THE PAMPAS(1939); RANGE WAR(1939); RENEGADE TRAIL(1939); SILVER ON THE SAGE(1939); HIDDEN GOLD(1940); SANTA FE MARSHAL(1940); SHOWDOWN, THE(1940); STAGECOACH WAR(1940); THREE MEN FROM TEXAS(1940); BORDER

VIGILANTES(1941); DOOMED CARAVAN(1941); IN OLD COLORADO(1941); OUTLAWS OF THE DESERT(1941); PIRATES ON HORSEBACK(1941); RIDERS OF THE TIMBERLINE(1941); SECRETS OF THE WASTELANDS(1941); STICK TO YOUR GUNS(1941); TWILIGHT ON THE TRAIL(1941); WIDE OPEN TOWN(1941); UNDERCOVER MAN(1942); BAR 20(1943); BORDER PATROL(1943); COLT COMRADES(1943); FALSE COLORS(1943); HOPPY SERVES A WRIT(1943); LEATHER BURNERS, THE(1943); LOST CANYON(1943); RIDERS OF THE DEADLINE(1943); FORTY THIEVES(1944); LUMBERJACK(1944); MYSTERY MAN(1944); TEXAS MASQUERADE(1944); DEVIL'S PLAYGROUND, THE(1946); FOOL'S GOLD(1946); UNEXPECTED GUEST(1946); DANGEROUS VENTURE(1947); HOPPY'S HOLIDAY(1947); MARAUDERS, THE(1947); BORROWED TROUBLE(1948); DEAD DON'T DREAM, THE(1948); FALSE PARADISE(1948); SILENT CONFLICT(1948); SINISTER JOURNEY(1948); STRANGE GAMBLE(1948); GREATEST SHOW ON EARTH, THE(1952)
Misc. Talkies
GO-GET-'EM HAINES(1936); ALONG THE SUNDOWN TRAIL(1942)
Silents
OLD WIVES FOR NEW(1918); AFFAIRS OF ANATOL, THE(1921); BIG GAME(1921); BREWSTER'S MILLIONS(1921); EXIT THE VAMP(1921); WISE FOOL, A(1921); NICE PEOPLE(1922); ON THE HIGH SEAS(1922); ENEMIES OF CHILDREN(1923); FORTY WINKS(1925); VOLGA BOATMAN, THE(1926); DRESS PARADE(1927); JIM THE CONQUEROR(1927); KING OF KINGS, THE(1927); YANKEE CLIPPER, THE(1927); NIGHT FLYER, THE(1928)
Misc. Silents
BLACKBIRDS(1920); BOBBED HAIR(1922); ROAD TO YESTERDAY, THE(1925); EVE'S LEAVES(1926); HER MAN O'WAR(1926); LAST FRONTIER, THE(1926); STEEL PREFERRED(1926); TWO ARABIAN KNIGHTS(1927); WAS HE GUILTY?(1927); COP, THE(1928); POWER(1928); SKYSCRAPER(1928)
William ["Stage"] Boyd
LOCKED DOOR, THE(1929); SPOILERS, THE(1930); STORM, THE(1930); CITY STREETS(1931); GANG BUSTER, THE(1931); GUN SMOKE(1931); FALSE MADONNA(1932); MIDNIGHT WARNING, THE(1932); PAINTED WOMAN(1932); SKY DEVILS(1932); STATE'S ATTORNEY(1932); HOUSE ON 56TH STREET, THE(1933); LAUGHING AT LIFE(1933); OLIVER TWIST(1933); GIRL FROM MISSOURI, THE(1934); TRANSATLANTIC MERRY-GO-ROUND(1934); NIGHT LIFE OF THE GODS(1935)
Eric Boyd-Perkins
LADY OF VENGEANCE(1957, Brit), ed; BACHELOR OF HEARTS(1958, Brit.), ed; HIGH HELL(1958), ed; GORGO(1961, Brit.), ed; HOUSE OF FRIGHT(1961), ed; SCREAM OF FEAR(1961, Brit.), ed; TERROR OF THE TONGS, THE(1961, Brit.), ed; CASH ON DEMAND(1962, Brit.), ed; NIGHT CREATURES(1962, Brit.), ed; PIRATES OF BLOOD RIVER, THE(1962, Brit.), ed; IN TROUBLE WITH EVE(1964, Brit.), ed; MASTER SPY(1964, Brit.), ed; SHE(1965, Brit.), ed; NO BLADE OF GRASS(1970, Brit.), ed; ANTONY AND CLEOPATRA(1973, Brit.), ed; WICKER MAN, THE(1974, Brit.), ed; HENNESSY(1975, Brit.), ed; CALL HIM MR. SHATTER(1976, Hong Kong), ed; THIRTY NINE STEPS, THE(1978, Brit.), ed
1984
SECRETS(1984, Brit.), ed
Chuck Boyde
SLAUGHTER IN SAN FRANCISCO(1981)
Peter Boyden
BLOW OUT(1981); HANKY-PANKY(1982)
1984
COLD FEET(1984)
Sally Boyden
DEAD MAN'S FLOAT(1980, Aus.); LITTLE DRAGONS, THE(1980)
Dan Boydston
SHOWDOWN(1973)
Bill Boydstun
1984
KILLERS, THE(1984), m
Hans-Peter Boye
CHRONICLE OF ANNA MAGDALENA BACH(1968, Ital., Ger.)
Robert Boye
NEVER SAY GOODBYE(1956), art d
Jacqueline Boyen
PEPPERMINT SODA(1979, Fr.)
Phyllis Boyens
COAL MINER'S DAUGHTER(1980)
Boyer
MONTE CARLO BABY(1953, Fr.), w
Andrew Boyer
1984
DREAMSCAPE(1984); NIGHT OF THE COMET(1984)
Anise Boyer
HARLEM IS HEAVEN(1932)
Arne Boyer
DEGREE OF MURDER, A(1969, Ger.), w
Chance Boyer
1984
NIGHT OF THE COMET(1984)
Charles Boyer
MAGNIFICENT LIE(1931); MAN FROM YESTERDAY, THE(1932); RED HEADED WOMAN(1932); EMPRESS AND I, THE(1933, Ger.); HEART SONG(1933, Brit.); BATTLE, THE(1934, Fr.); CARAVAN(1934); BREAK OF HEARTS(1935); LILIOM(1935, Fr.); PRIVATE WORLDS(1935); SHANGHAI(1935); GARDEN OF ALLAH, THE(1936); CONQUEST(1937); HISTORY IS MADE AT NIGHT(1937); MAYERLING(1937, Fr.); TOVARICH(1937); ALGIERS(1938); LOVE AFFAIR(1939); WHEN TOMORROW COMES(1939); ALL THIS AND HEAVEN TOO(1940); APPOINTMENT FOR LOVE(1941); BACK STREET(1941); HOLD BACK THE DAWN(1941); TALES OF MANHATTAN(1942); CONSTANT NYMPH, THE(1943); FLESH AND FANTASY(1943), a, p; HEART OF A NATION, THE(1943, Fr.); GASLIGHT(1944); TOGETHER AGAIN(1944); CONFIDENTIAL AGENT(1945); CLUNY BROWN(1946); WOMAN'S VENGEANCE, A(1947); ARCH OF TRIUMPH(1948); BATTLE OF THE RAILS(1949, Fr.); FIRST LEGION, THE(1951); THIRTEENTH LETTER, THE(1951); HAPPY TIME, THE(1952); THUNDER IN THE EAST(1953); EARRINGS OF MADAME DE..., THE(1954, Fr.); COBWEB, THE(1955); LUCKY TO BE A WOMAN(1955, Ital.); AROUND THE WORLD IN 80 DAYS(1956); NANA(1957, Fr./Ital.); BUCCANEER, THE(1958); LA PARISIENNE(1958, Fr./Ital.); FANNY(1961); FOUR HORSEMEN OF THE APOCALYPSE, THE(1962); MAXIME(1962, Fr.); MIDNIGHT FOLLY(1962, Fr.); LOVE IS A BALL(1963); ADORABLE JULIA(1964, Fr./Aust.); VERY SPECIAL

FAVOR, A(1965); HOW TO STEAL A MILLION(1966); IS PARIS BURNING?(1966, U.S./Fr.); BAREFOOT IN THE PARK(1967); CASINO ROYALE(1967, Brit.); DAY THE HOTLINE GOT HOT, THE(1968, Fr./Span.); MADWOMAN OF CHAILLOT, THE(1969); LOST HORIZON(1973); STAVISKY(1974, Fr.); MATTER OF TIME, A(1976, Ital./U.S.)
Misc. Silents
L'HOMME DU LARGE(1920, Fr.)

Claire Boyer
MY UNCLE ANTOINE(1971, Can.), ed

David Boyer
SIDELONG GLANCES OF A PIGEON KICKER, THE(1970), w

Eileen Boyer
NO WAY OUT(1950)

Elizabeth Boyer
Misc. Silents
SPORT OF THE GODS, THE(1921)

Francois Boyer
FORBIDDEN GAMES(1953, Fr.), w; GAMBLER, THE(1958, Fr.), w; MONKEY IN WINTER, A(1962, Fr.), w; DOUBLE DECEPTION(1963, Fr.), w; WAR OF THE BUTTONS(1963 Fr.), w; WEEKEND AT DUNKIRK(1966, Fr./Ital.), w

Francoise Boyer
25TH HOUR, THE(1967, Fr./Ital./Yugo.), w

Hal Boyer
DANTE'S INFERNO(1935)

Jack Boyer
ON THE BEACH(1959)

Jay Boyer
SCARLET EMPRESS, THE(1934)

Jean Boyer
ABUSED CONFIDENCE(1938, Fr. ABUS DE CONFIANCE), w; COUNSEL FOR ROMANCE(1938, Fr.), w; NOUS IRONS A PARIS(1949, Fr.), d, w; MR. PEEK-A-BOO(1951, Fr.), d, w; PRIZE, THE(1952, Fr.), d; MONTE CARLO BABY(1953, Fr.), d; FRENCH TOUCH, THE(1954, Fr.), d, w; MY SEVEN LITTLE SINS(1956, Fr./Ital.), d, w; FERNANDEL THE DRESSMAKER(1957, Fr.), d, w; CRAZY FOR LOVE(1960, Fr.), d

John Boyer
SKI PARTY(1965)

Ken Boyer
ODD COUPLE, THE(1968)

Lyle Boyer
ISLE OF THE DEAD(1945), ed; BEDLAM(1946), ed; TRAIL STREET(1947), ed; UNDER THE TONTO RIM(1947), ed; WOMAN ON THE BEACH, THE(1947), ed

Marianne Boyer
SPETTERS(1983, Holland)

Marie-France Boyer
LE BONHEUR(1966, Fr.); WEEKEND AT DUNKIRK(1966, Fr./Ital.); UNKNOWN MAN OF SHANDIGOR, THE(1967, Switz.); MAN WHO HAD POWER OVER WOMEN, THE(1970, Brit.)

Myriam Boyer
JONAH-WHO WILL BE 25 IN THE YEAR 2000(1976, Switz.)

Pat Boyer
GENTLE PEOPLE AND THE QUIET LAND, THE(1972)

Pia Boyer
OFFICER AND A GENTLEMAN, AN(1982)

Ronald Boyer
SILK NOOSE, THE(1950, Brit.)

Sully Boyer
UP THE SANDBOX(1972)

Volta Boyer
SPIRIT OF STANFORD, THE(1942)

Linda Boyers
PLEASURE PLANTATION(1970)

Adrian Boyes
END OF AUGUST, THE(1982)

Karen Boyes
Misc. Talkies
THREE DIMENSIONS OF GRETA(1973)

Jorge Boyet
SONG WITHOUT END(1960), m

William Boyet
EMERGENCY HOSPITAL(1956)

Bill Boyett
TARAWA BEACHHEAD(1958); WHEN A STRANGER CALLS(1979); SPACE RAIDERS(1983)

Bill [William] Boyett
YOUNG AND DANGEROUS(1957)

Robert Boyett
BEST LITTLE WHOREHOUSE IN TEXAS, THE(1982), p

William Boyett
UNTIL THEY SAIL(1957); SO THIS IS LOVE(1953); FIGHTING TROUBLE(1956); SAM WHISKEY(1969)
1984
SAM'S SON(1984)

Pat Boyette
WEIRD ONES, THE(1962), p,d&w; DUNGEONS OF HARROW(1964), a, d; GIRLS FROM THUNDER STRIP, THE(1966), w

Charles Boyilland
DOULOS-THE FINGER MAN(1964, Fr./Ital.)

Melvina Boykin
OPEN THE DOOR AND SEE ALL THE PEOPLE(1964)

Nancy Boykin
KIRLIAN WITNESS, THE(1978)

Catherine Boyl
FRENCH, THEY ARE A FUNNY RACE, THE(1956, Fr.)

Buddy Boylan
LENNY(1974)

John Boylan
RABID(1976, Can.); ONE MAN(1979, Can.)
1984
PRODIGAL, THE(1984)

M.S. Boylan
CHEATERS AT PLAY(1932), w

Malcolm Boylan
MAN WHO DARED, THE(1946), w
Silents
PREP AND PEP(1928), t; WOMAN WISE(1928), t

Malcolm Stuart Boylan
MAKING THE GRADE(1929), w; MASQUERADE(1929), w; NOT QUITE DECENT(1929), titles; WHY LEAVE HOME?(1929), p; SHIPMATES(1931), w; HELL DIVERS(1932), w; MADAME RACKETEER(1932), w; LADY'S PROFESSION, A(1933), w; FLAMING GOLD(1934), w; DEVIL DOGS OF THE AIR(1935), w; O'SHAUGHNESSY'S BOY(1935), w; DANGEROUS WATERS(1936), w; WHEN'S YOUR BIRTHDAY?(1937), w; YANK AT OXFORD, A(1938), w; LADY'S FROM KENTUCKY, THE(1939), w; ST. LOUIS BLUES(1939), w; GIRL FROM GOD'S COUNTRY(1940), w; DEVIL PAYS OFF, THE(1941), w; MERCY ISLAND(1941), w; MR. DISTRICT ATTORNEY(1941), w; RED RIVER VALLEY(1941), w; SAILORS ON LEAVE(1941), w; REMEMBER PEARL HARBOR(1942), w; ALASKA(1944), w; BEDSIDE MANNER(1945), w; UNKNOWN, THE(1946), w; FOR THE LOVE OF RUSTY(1947), w; KEEPER OF THE BEES(1947), w; LONE WOLF AND HIS LADY, THE(1949), w; CUSTOMS AGENT(1950), w; ONE TOO MANY(1950), w; SOLDIERS THREE(1951), w
Silents
SPEED MAD(1925), t; HANDS ACROSS THE BORDER(1926), t; WHAT PRICE GLORY(1926), t; GAY RETREAT, THE(1927), t; JOY GIRL, THE(1927), t; LADIES MUST DRESS(1927), t; OUTLAWS OF RED RIVER(1927), t; PAJAMAS(1927), t; SILVER VALLEY(1927), t; GIRL IN EVERY PORT, A(1928), t; NEWS PARADE, THE(1928), t; SHARP SHOOTERS(1928), t; CAPTAIN LASH(1929), t; FUGITIVES(1929), t; GIRLS GONE WILD(1929), t; JOY STREET(1929), t; STRONG BOY(1929), t

Malcom Stuart Boylan
POLITICS(1931), w; BOSTON BLACKIE BOOKED ON SUSPICION(1945), w

Mary Boylan
WRONG MAN, THE(1956); ODDS AGAINST TOMORROW(1959); NIGHT OF THE IGUANA, THE(1964)

Mary Elizabeth Boylan
EDGE OF FURY(1958)

May Boylan
ANNIE HALL(1977)

Patrick Boylan
1984
CHILDREN OF THE CORN(1984)

Robert Boylan
WHAT AM I BID?(1967)

Linda Boyland
CHARRIOTS OF FIRE(1981, Brit.)

Malcolm Stuart Boyland
IF I HAD A MILLION(1932), w; GIRL FROM HAVANA(1940), w

Mary Boyland
HEARTLAND(1980)

Alan Boyle
MOHAMMAD, MESSENGER OF GOD(1976, Lebanon/Brit.), makeup

Billy Boyle
I AM A GROUPIE(1970, Brit.); BARRY LYNDON(1975, Brit.)

Catherine Boyle
NOT WANTED ON VOYAGE(1957, Brit.); INTENT TO KILL(1958, Brit.); TRUTH ABOUT WOMEN, THE(1958, Brit.)

Charles B. Boyle
FOLLOW THRU(1930), ph

Charles Boyle
IN OLD CALIFORNIA(1929), ph; AFTER THE FOG(1930), ph; MAMBA(1930), ph; BEYOND THE BLUE HORIZON(1942), ph; ANCHORS AWEIGH(1945), ph; BATTLE AT APACHE PASS, THE(1952), ph; DAVY CROCKETT, KING OF THE WILD FRONTIER(1955), ph; GREAT LOCOMOTIVE CHASE, THE(1956), ph; WESTWARD HO THE WAGONS!(1956), ph
Silents
REGULAR FELLOW, A(1925), ph; BEHIND THE FRONT(1926), ph; OLD IRONSIDES(1926), ph; RUNAWAY, THE(1926), ph; CLANCY'S KOSHER WEDDING(1927), ph; RANGER OF THE NORTH(1927), ph; TILLIE'S PUNCTURED ROMANCE(1928), ph

Charles P. Boyle
GREAT COMMANDMENT, THE(1941), ph; FRONTIER GAL(1945), ph; DUEL IN THE SUN(1946), ph; FUN AND FANCY FREE(1947), ph; SHE WORE A YELLOW RIBBON(1949), ph; SADDLE TRAMP(1950), ph; APACHE DRUMS(1951), ph; CIMARRON KID, THE(1951), ph; LADY FROM TEXAS, THE(1951), ph; MARK OF THE RENEGADE(1951), ph; TOMAHAWK(1951), ph; HORIZONS WEST(1952), ph; STEEL TOWN(1952), ph; UNTAMED FRONTIER(1952), ph; CITY BENEATH THE SEA(1953), ph; GUNSMOKE(1953), ph; STAND AT APACHE RIVER, THE(1953), ph; JOHNNY TREMAIN(1957), ph; OLD YELLER(1957), ph

Consolata Boyle
1984
ANNE DEVLIN(1984, Ireland), cos

David Boyle
HOLLYWOOD BOULEVARD(1976)

E.G. Boyle
Misc. Silents
FIGHTING FAILURE, THE(1926), d

Ed Boyle
RUBY GENTRY(1952), set d; MAN OF THE WEST(1958), set d

Eddie Boyle
TOMBSTONE CANYON(1932), set d

Edward Boyle
GARDEN OF ALLAH, THE(1936), art d; STAR IS BORN, A(1937), set d; FORCE OF EVIL(1948), set d; PRIVATE HELL 36(1954), set d; NIGHTMARE(1956), set d

Edward C. Boyle
PARDON MY PAST(1945), set d

Edward G. Boyle
NOTHING SACRED(1937), set d; GONE WITH THE WIND(1939), set d; MADE FOR EACH OTHER(1939), set d; STORY OF G.I. JOE, THE(1945), set d; OTHER LOVE, THE(1947), set d; NO MINOR VICES(1948), set d; SO THIS IS NEW YORK(1948), set d; CAUGHT(1949), set d; KISS FOR CORLISS, A(1949), set d; SUDDEN FEAR(1952), set d; MOON IS BLUE, THE(1953), set d; JOHNNY GUITAR(1954), prod d; GREAT

AMERICAN PASTIME, THE(1956), set d; THESE WILDER YEARS(1956), set d; SEPARATE TABLES(1958), set d; SOME LIKE IT HOT(1959), set d; BY LOVE POSSESSED(1961), set d; CHILDREN'S HOUR, THE(1961), set d; JACK THE GIANT KILLER(1962), set d; KID GALAHAD(1962), set d; TWO FOR THE SEESAW(1962), set d; IRMA LA DOUCE(1963), set d; KISS ME, STUPID(1964), set d; SEVEN DAYS IN MAY(1964), set d; SEX AND THE SINGLE GIRL(1964), set d; FORTUNE COOKIE, THE(1966), set d; THOMAS CROWN AFFAIR, THE(1968), set d; GAILY, GAILY(1969), set d; THEY CALL ME MISTER TIBBS(1970), set d; HOW TO SUCCEED IN BUSINESS WITHOUT REALLY TRYING(1976), set d

Edward J. Boyle
BODY AND SOUL(1947), set d

Edwin G. Boyle
HAWAII(1966), set d

Gary Boyle
DEATH WISH II(1982)

George Boyle
CONVENTION GIRL(1935), w

Hal Boyle
STORY OF G.I. JOE, THE(1945)

Irene Boyle
Misc. Silents
DEAD LINE, THE(1920); OTHER MEN'S SHOES(1920); RIDER OF THE KING LOG, THE(1921)

Jack Boyle
CONFESSIONS OF BOSTON BLACKIE(1941), w; MEET BOSTON BLACKIE(1941), w; AFTER MIDNIGHT WITH BOSTON BLACKIE(1943), w; MELODY PARADE(1943), ch; SPOTLIGHT SCANDALS(1943), a, ch; YOUTH ON PARADE(1943); COVER GIRL(1944); EVER SINCE VENUS(1944), ch; MY BEST GAL(1944); ONE MYSTERIOUS NIGHT(1944), w; SHINE ON, HARVEST MOON(1944); SUNBONNET SUE(1945), ch; FREDDIE STEPS OUT(1946), ch; HIGH SCHOOL HERO(1946), ch; SWING PARADE OF 1946(1946), ch; LADIES OF THE CHORUS(1948), ch; STATE OF THE UNION(1948); TRAPPED BY BOSTON BLACKIE(1948), w; BOSTON BLACKIE'S CHINESE VENTURE(1949), w; LADY TAKES A SAILOR, THE(1949); TAKE ME OUT TO THE BALL GAME(1949); FRENCH LINE, THE(1954); TENDER TRAP, THE(1955); JUMBO(1962)
Silents
POPPY GIRL'S HUSBAND, THE(1919), w; MISSING MILLIONS(1922), w; CROOKED ALLEY(1923), w

Jack Boyle, Jr.
FIGHTING 69TH, THE(1940)

Jeri Boyle
1984
MAKING THE GRADE(1984)

John Boyle
DANGER LIGHTS(1930), ph; SUNDOWN RIDER, THE(1933), ph; LADY BY CHOICE(1934); STRANGERS ALL(1935), ph; FORBIDDEN MUSIC(1936, Brit.), ph; CATTLE RAIDERS(1938), ph; OUTLAWS OF THE PRAIRIE(1938), ph; MUTINY ON THE BLACKHAWK(1939), ph; MYSTERY OF THE WHITE ROOM(1939), ph; DEVIL'S PIPELINE, THE(1940), ph; GENTLEMAN FROM ARIZONA, THE(1940), ph; GIVE US WINGS(1940), ph; DOUBLE DATE(1941), ph; MR. DYNAMITE(1941), ph; RAIDERS OF THE DESERT(1941), ph; WHERE DID YOU GET THAT GIRL?(1941), ph; UNSEEN ENEMY(1942), ph; YANKEE DOODLE DANDY(1942), ch; HE'S MY GUY(1943), ph; BOWERY TO BROADWAY(1944), ch; BRIDGE OF SAN LUIS REY, THE(1944), ph; CARSON CITY(1952), ph; NIGHT SHIFT(1982)
Silents
KICK IN(1917); GOLDEN GIFT, THE(1922), ph; SLAVE OF DESIRE(1923), ph; FAR CRY, THE(1926), ph; MISS NOBODY(1926), ph; GOOD-BYE KISS, THE(1928), ph
Misc. Silents
YELLOW PASSPORT, THE(1916)

John Boyle, Jr.
YOUTH ON PARADE(1943)

John W. Boyle
MIDNIGHT DADDIES(1929), ph; HYPNOTIZED(1933), ph; GRIDIRON FLASH(1935), ph; KEEP YOUR SEATS PLEASE(1936, Brit.), ph; LABURNUM GROVE(1936, Brit.), ph; QUEEN OF HEARTS(1936, Brit.), ph; TAKE A CHANCE(1937, Brit.), ph; HERO FOR A DAY(1939), ph; SOCIETY SMUGGLERS(1939), ph; BURMA CONVOY(1941), ph; FLYING CADETS(1941), ph; KID FROM KANSAS, THE(1941), ph; MEN OF THE TIMBERLAND(1941), ph; MUTINY IN THE ARCTIC(1941), ph; SIX LESSONS FROM MADAME LA ZONGA(1941), ph; DESTINATION UNKNOWN(1942), ph; HALF WAY TO SHANGHAI(1942), ph; JUKE BOX JENNY(1942), ph; MISSISSIPPI GAMBLER(1942), ph; RIDE 'EM COWBOY(1942), ph; STRICTLY IN THE GROOVE(1942), ph; THERE'S ONE BORN EVERY MINUTE(1942), ph; GOOD MORNING, JUDGE(1943), ph; HI, BUDDY(1943), ph; JACK LONDON(1943), ph; SONG OF THE OPEN ROAD(1944), ph; GALLANT BESS(1946), ph; HERE COMES TROUBLE(1948), ph; MICKEY(1948), ph; NORTHWEST STAMPEDE(1948), ph; WHO KILLED "DOC" ROBBIN?(1948), ph; MEN OF THE SEA(1951, Brit.), ph; RESTLESS BREED, THE(1957), ph
Silents
WHEN A WOMAN SINS(1918), ph; JOYOUS TROUBLEMAKERS, THE(1920), ph; QUEEN OF SHEBA, THE(1921), ph

John W.W. Boyle
DARK SANDS(1938, Brit.), ph

Johnny Boyle
BORN TO THE WEST(1937); SOMETHING TO SING ABOUT(1937); MINSTREL MAN(1944), ch

Johnny Boyle, Jr.
WEST POINT STORY, THE(1950), ch

Joseph C. Boyle
TIMES SQUARE(1929), d
Silents
CONVOY(1927), d; HEAD OF THE FAMILY, THE(1928), d; WHIP WOMAN, THE(1928), d
Misc. Silents
BROADWAY NIGHTS(1927), d; MAD HOUR(1928), d; THROUGH THE BREAKERS(1928), d

Kay Boyle
FIVE DAYS ONE SUMMER(1982), w

Marc Boyle
MACKINTOSH MAN, THE(1973, Brit.); SUPERMAN II(1980); FINAL CONFLICT, THE(1981); OUTLAND(1981); HIGH ROAD TO CHINA(1983)
1984
LASSITER(1984), stunts

Marie Boyle
BIG TRAIL, THE(1930), w

Mark Boyle
THOSE DARING YOUNG MEN IN THEIR JAUNTY JALOPIES(1969, Fr./Brit./ Ital.)

Mary Boyle
CAESAR AND CLEOPATRA(1946, Brit.)

Michael Boyle
CALIFORNIA SUITE(1978)

Nancy Boyle
Misc. Talkies
BARBARA(1970)

Paul Boyle
MEATBALLS(1979, Can.)

Peter Boyle
VIRGIN PRESIDENT, THE(1968); MEDIUM COOL(1969); DIARY OF A MAD HOUSEWIFE(1970); JOE(1970); T.R. BASKIN(1971); CANDIDATE, THE(1972); FRIENDS OF EDDIE COYLE, THE(1973); KID BLUE(1973); SLITHER(1973); STEELYARD BLUES(1973); CRAZY JOE(1974); YOUNG FRANKENSTEIN(1974); SWASHBUCKLER(1976); TAXI DRIVER(1976); BRINK'S JOB, THE(1978); F.I.S.T.(1978); BEYOND THE POSEIDON ADVENTURE(1979); HARDCORE(1979); IN GOD WE TRUST(1980); WHERE THE BUFFALO ROAM(1980); OUTLAND(1981); COUNTRYMAN(1982, Jamaica), ed; HAMMETT(1982); HORROR PLANET(1982, Brit.), ed; MC VICAR(1982), ed; YELLOWBEARD(1983)
1984
JOHNNY DANGEROUSLY(1984); RAZOR'S EDGE, THE(1984), ed
Misc. Talkies
GHOST IN THE NOONDAY SUN(1974)

Ray Boyle
SATAN'S SATELLITES(1958)

Richard Charles Boyle
1984
TIGHTROPE(1984)

Robert Boyle
THEY WON'T BELIEVE ME(1947), art d; FLESH AND FANTASY(1943), art d; GOOD MORNING, JUDGE(1943), art d; SHADOW OF A DOUBT(1943), art d; WHITE SAVAGE(1943), art d; NOCTURNE(1946), prod d, art d; RIDE THE PINK HORSE(1947), art d; ABANDONED(1949), art d; GAL WHO TOOK THE WEST, THE(1949), art d; LOUISA(1950), art d; MILKMAN, THE(1950), art d; MYSTERY SUBMARINE(1950), art d; IRON MAN, THE(1951), art d; LADY PAYS OFF, THE(1951), art d; MARK OF THE RENEGADE(1951), art d; WEEKEND WITH FATHER(1951), art d; LOST IN ALASKA(1952), art d; YANKEE BUCCANEER(1952), art d; EAST OF SUMATRA(1953), art d; GIRLS IN THE NIGHT(1953), art d; IT CAME FROM OUTER SPACE(1953), art d; MA AND PA KETTLE ON VACATION(1953), art d; JOHNNY DARK(1954), art d; MA AND PA KETTLE AT HOME(1954), art d; CHIEF CRAZY HORSE(1955), art d; KISS OF FIRE(1955), art d; LADY GODIVA(1955), art d; PRIVATE WAR OF MAJOR BENSON, THE(1955), art d; RUNNING WILD(1955), art d; CONGO CROSSING(1956), art d; DAY OF FURY, A(1956), art d; BROTHERS RICO, THE(1957), art d; NIGHT RUNNER, THE(1957), art d; OPERATION MAD BALL(1957), art d; WILD HERITAGE(1958), art d; CRIMSON KIMONO, THE(1959), art d; NORTH BY NORTHWEST(1959), prod d, set d; CAPE FEAR(1962), art d; BIRDS, THE(1963), set d; THRILL OF IT ALL, THE(1963), art d; MARNIE(1964), prod d; DO NOT DISTURB(1965), art d; REWARD, THE(1965), art d; RUSSIANS ARE COMING, THE RUSSIANS ARE COMING, THE(1966), art d; IN COLD BLOOD(1967), art d; THOMAS CROWN AFFAIR, THE(1968), art d; GAILY, GAILY(1969), prod d; LANDLORD, THE(1970), prod d; BITE THE BULLET(1975), art d; HOW TO SUCCEED IN BUSINESS WITHOUT REALLY TRYING(1976), art d; LEADBELLY(1976), prod d; SHOOTIST, THE(1976), prod d; W.C. FIELDS AND ME(1976), prod d; WINTER KILLS(1979), a, prod d; PRIVATE BENJAMIN(1980), prod d; LOOKIN' TO GET OUT(1982), prod d
1984
ANNE DEVLIN(1984, Ireland), m; NO SMALL AFFAIR(1984), prod d; RHINESTONE(1984), prod d

Robert F. Boyle
BUCCANEER'S GIRL(1950), art d; SIERRA(1950), art d; GUNSMOKE(1953), art d; FITZWILLY(1967), art d; PORTNOY'S COMPLAINT(1972), prod d; BIG FIX, THE(1978), prod d; STAYING ALIVE(1983), prod d

Robert Ott Boyle
WITHOUT A TRACE(1983)

Robert R. Boyle
TABLE FOR FIVE(1983), prod d

Roy Boyle
PRISONER OF WAR(1954)

Tom Boyle
MAGIC CHRISTIAN, THE(1970, Brit.)

Tommy Boyle
CHARIOTS OF FIRE(1981, Brit.)

Walden Boyle
DECOY(1946); SHE WROTE THE BOOK(1946); BURNING CROSS, THE(1947); ROAD TO THE BIG HOUSE(1947); TRAP, THE(1947); I, JANE DOE(1948); I WOULDN'T BE IN YOUR SHOES(1948); FOLLOW ME QUIETLY(1949)

Waldon Boyle
ILLEGAL ENTRY(1949)

Waldron Boyle
THEM!(1954)

Wally Boyle
PALEFACE, THE(1948); SON OF PALEFACE(1952)

Wilfred Boyle
THREE WEIRD SISTERS, THE(1948, Brit.); WILL ANY GENTLEMAN?(1955, Brit.)

William Boyle
CONVICTS AT LARGE(1938)

William N. Boyle
COMPANIONS IN CRIME(1954, Brit.), p; GREEN BUDDHA, THE(1954, Brit.), p; CROSS CHANNEL(1955, Brit.), p; SECRET VENTURE(1955, Brit.), p; TRACK THE MAN DOWN(1956, Brit.), p; LADY OF VENGEANCE(1957, Brit), p; HIGH HELL(1958), p

Edward G. Boyler
PORK CHOP HILL(1959), set d
John Boyles
NAUGHTY NINETIES, THE(1945), ch
Marc Boyman
INCUBUS, THE(1982, Can.), p
Clifton Boyne
OTHER PEOPLE'S SINS(1931, Brit.); HARD STEEL(1941, Brit.)
Silents
CRIMSON CIRCLE, THE(1922, Brit.); MUTINY(1925, Brit.)
Misc. Silents
CRIMSON CIRCLE, THE(1922, Brit.)
Eva Lernard Boyne
NONE BUT THE LONELY HEART(1944)
Hazel Boyne
KNOCK ON ANY DOOR(1949); BORN TO BE BAD(1950); IN A LONELY PLA-
CE(1950); WHERE DANGER LIVES(1950); SON OF PALEFACE(1952); TURNING
POINT, THE(1952); WAR OF THE WORLDS, THE(1953)
Hazel "Sonny" Boyne
LUSTY MEN, THE(1952); KING CREOLE(1958)
Sonny Boyne
SECRET FURY, THE(1950)
Sunny Boyne
DISPATCH FROM REUTERS, A(1940); DEVIL AND DANIEL WEBSTER, THE(1941)
Brad Boynton
RED RUNS THE RIVER(1963)
Arthur Boys
QUEEN OF SPADES(1948, Brit.), w
Heather Boys
HER MAN GILBEY(1949, Brit.)
Boys' Choir of St. Joseph's School
RANCHO GRANDE(1940)
Rolf Boysen
HAMLET(1962, Ger.)
John Boyt
COPS AND ROBBERS(1973), cos
Stephen Boyum
ROLLERBALL(1975)
Steve Boyum
HERBIE GOES BANANAS(1980)
Aghul Rain Bozan
SPY IN YOUR EYE(1966, Ital.)
Alonzo Bozan
VIRGIN ISLAND(1960, Brit.)
George Bozanic
ALL-AMERICAN, THE(1953)
Max Bozhky
CATSKILL HONEYMOON(1950)
Rose Bozhky
CATSKILL HONEYMOON(1950)
Bozo
Silents
WHITE PANTS WILLIE(1927)
Petar Bozovic
TWILIGHT TIME(1983, U.S./Yugo.)
Marcel Bozuffi
CARAVAN TO VACCARES(1974, Brit./Fr)
M. Bozyk
YIDDLE WITH HIS FIDDLE(1937, Pol.); DYBBUK THE(1938, Pol.)
Max Bozyk
Misc. Talkies
GOD, MAN AND DEVIL(1949)
Gianni Bozzacchi
CHINA 9, LIBERTY 37(1978, Ital.), p
Bruno Bozzetto
ALLEGRO NON TROPPO(1977, Ital.), d, w, anim
Marie Anita Bozzi
Silents
PRISONER OF ZENDA, THE(1915, Brit.)
Paul Bozzi
TONI(1968, Fr.), a, m
Dale Bozzio
LUNCH WAGON(1981)
Terry Bozzio
LUNCH WAGON(1981)
Marcel Bozzuffi
LADY IN THE CAR WITH GLASSES AND A GUN, THE(1970, U.S./Fr.); TIME OF
THE WOLVES(1970, Fr.); FRENCH CONNECTION, THE(1971); IMAGES(1972, Ire-
land); DESTRUCTORS, THE(1974, Brit.); DRAMA OF THE RICH(1975, Ital./Fr.);
CHINO(1976, Ital., Span., Fr.); LA GRANDE BOURGEOISE(1977, Ital.); MARCH OR
DIE(1977, Brit.); BLOODLINE(1979); PASSAGE, THE(1979, Brit.); LA CAGE AUX
FOLLES II(1981, Ital./Fr.); IDENTIFICATION OF A WOMAN(1983, Ital.)
Marcel Bozzufi
DAY AND THE HOUR, THE(1963, Fr./Ital.); SKY ABOVE HEAVEN(1964, Fr./Ital.);
SLEEPING CAR MURDER THE(1966, Fr.); UPPER HAND, THE(1967, Fr./Ital./Ger.);
LIFE LOVE DEATH(1969, Fr./Ital.); Z(1969, Fr./Algeria); LOVE IS A FUNNY
THING(1970, Fr./Ital.)
Ernst Braasch
SPESSART INN, THE(1961, Ger.)
Harvey Braban
BLACKMAIL(1929, Brit.); ALIBI(1931, Brit.); GIRL IN THE NIGHT, THE(1931, Brit.);
SHOULD A DOCTOR TELL?(1931, Brit.); BROTHER ALFRED(1932, Brit.); CALLBOX
MYSTERY, THE(1932, Brit.); BOOMERANG(1934, Brit.); EASY MONEY(1934, Brit.);
PATH OF GLORY, THE(1934, Brit.); DARBY AND JOAN(1937, Brit.); SIXTY GLORI-
OUS YEARS(1938, Brit.); THANK EVANS(1938, Brit.); VIPER, THE(1938, Brit.)
Silents
QUESTION OF TRUST, A(1920, Brit.); PRINCE AND THE BEGGARMAID,
THE(1921, Brit.); GIRL OF LONDON, A(1925, Brit.)

Misc. Silents
YELLOW CLAW, THE(1920, Brit.); PREY OF THE DRAGON, THE(1921, Brit.);
BENTLEY'S CONSCIENCE(1922, Brit.); LITTLE MOTHER, THE(1922, Brit.); SHIR-
LEY(1922, Brit.); ROMANY, THE(1923, Brit.)
Andree Brabant
Misc. Silents
LA ZOME DE LA MORT(1917, Fr.); LE DROIT A LA VIE(1917, Fr.); LE REVE(1921,
Fr.); LES OMBRES QUI PASSANT(1924, Fr.)
Eddie Braben
UP THE FRONT(1972, Brit.), w
Jaroslav Brabenec
TRANSPORT FROM PARADISE(1967, Czech.), art d
Jack Brabham
GREEN HELMET, THE(1961, Brit.); GRAND PRIX(1966)
Philip Brabham
Silents
BATTLING BUTLER(1926), w
Charles Brabin
BRIDGE OF SAN LUIS REY, THE(1929), d; CALL OF THE FLESH(1930), d; SHIP
FROM SHANGHAI, THE(1930), d; SPORTING BLOOD(1931), d; BEAST OF THE
CITY, THE(1932), d; MASK OF FU MANCHU, THE(1932), d; RASPUTIN AND THE
EMPRESS(1932), d; WASHINGTON MASQUERADE(1932), d; DAY OF RECK-
ONING(1933), d; SECRET OF MADAME BLANCHE, THE(1933), d; WICKED WOM-
AN, A(1934), d; I MARRIED AN ANGEL(1942)
Silents
HOUSE OF THE LOST CORD, THE(1915), d; ADOPTED SON, THE(1917), d; PAIR
OF CUPIDS, A(1918), d; SIX DAYS(1923), d; SO BIG(1924), d; TWINKLETOES(1926),
d
Misc. Silents
NECKLACE OF RAMESES, THE(1914), d; RAVEN, THE(1915), d; VANITY
FAIR(1915), d; BABETTE(1917), d; SIXTEENTH WIFE, THE(1917), d; BLIND WI-
VES(1920), d; MISMATES(1926), d; HARD BOILED HAGGERTY(1927), d
Charles F. Brabin
NEW MORALS FOR OLD(1932), d
Charles J. Brabin
Silents
PERSUASIVE PEGGY(1917), d&w; KATHLEEN MAVOURNEEN(1919), d&w;
WHILE NEW YORK SLEEPS(1920), d, w; STELLA MARIS(1925), d, w
Misc. Silents
PRICE OF FAME, THE(1916), d; THAT SORT(1916), d; BREAKERS AHEAD(1918),
d; BUCHANAN'S WIFE(1918), d; HIS BONDED WIFE(1918), d; POOR RICH MAN,
THE(1918), d; RED, WHITE AND BLUE BLOOD(1918), d; SOCIAL QUICK-
SANDS(1918), d; LA BELLE RUSSE(1919), d; THOU SHALT NOT(1919), d; FOOT-
FALLS(1921), d; LIGHTS OF NEW YORK, THE(1922), d; DRIVEN(1923), d;
FRAMED(1927), d; VALLEY OF THE GIANTS, THE(1927), d; BURNING DAY-
LIGHT(1928), d; WHIP, THE(1928), d
Charles R. Brabin
STAGE MOTHER(1933), d
Michele Brabo
MR. HULOT'S HOLIDAY(1954, Fr.)
John Brabourne
HARRY BLACK AND THE TIGER(1958, Brit.), p; SINK THE BISMARCK!(1960,
Brit.), p; DAMN THE DEFIANT!(1962, Brit.), p; OTHELLO(1965, Brit.), p; MIKADO,
THE(1967, Brit.), p; ROMEO AND JULIET(1968, Brit./Ital.), p; UP THE JUNC-
TION(1968, Brit.), p; DANCE OF DEATH, THE(1971, Brit.), p; MURDER ON THE
ORIENT EXPRESS(1974, Brit.), p; DEATH ON THE NILE(1978, Brit.), p; STORIES
FROM A FLYING TRUNK(1979, Brit.), p; MIRROR CRACK'D, THE(1980, Brit.), p;
EVIL UNDER THE SUN(1982, Brit.), p
1984
PASSAGE TO INDIA, A(1984, Brit.), p
John Bracci
AMERICAN GRAFFITI(1973); DIE LAUGHING(1980)
Teda Bracci
R.P.M.(1970); C. C. AND COMPANY(1971); BIG BIRD CAGE, THE(1972); TRIAL OF
BILLY JACK, THE(1974); WORLD'S GREATEST LOVER, THE(1977)
Lola Braccini
LEOPARD, THE(1963, Ital.); SEDUCED AND ABANDONED(1964, Fr./Ital.)
Blanche Brace
LETTER FOR EVIE, A(1945), w
Linda Brace
GOOD MORNING, MISS DOVE(1955); BEST THINGS IN LIFE ARE FREE,
THE(1956); BUS STOP(1956)
Peter Brace
GORGO(1961, Brit.); PSYCHO-CIRCUS(1967, Brit.); PINK PANTHER STRIKES
AGAIN, THE(1976, Brit.); FLASH GORDON(1980); RAIDERS OF THE LOST
ARK(1981)
Allan Bracewell
ROOM AT THE TOP(1959, Brit.)
Edith Bracewell
Silents
REBECCA THE JEWESS(1913, Brit.)
Ethel Bracewell
Misc. Silents
REVOLUTIONIST, THE(1914, Brit.); BEGGAR GIRL'S WEDDING, THE(1915, Brit.)
Joyanne Bracewell
CUP-TIE HONEYMOON(1948, Brit.); HOLIDAYS WITH PAY(1948, Brit.)
Sidney Bracey [Sidney Bracy]
HAUNTED HOUSE, THE(1928); HIS CAPTIVE WOMAN(1929); ANYBODY'S WOM-
AN(1930); BISHOP MURDER CASE, THE(1930); FREE LOVE(1930); MONTE CAR-
LO(1930); OUTSIDE THE LAW(1930); SECOND FLOOR MYSTERY, THE(1930);
AVENGER, THE(1931); LION AND THE LAMB(1931); RULING VOICE, THE(1931);
SHANGHAIED LOVE(1931); SUBWAY EXPRESS(1931); TEN CENTS A DANCE(1931);
GREEKS HAD A WORD FOR THEM(1932); LITTLE ORPHAN ANNIE(1932); TAN-
GLED DESTINIES(1932); FLYING DOWN TO RIO(1933); LITTLE GIANT, THE(1933);
NO MORE ORCHIDS(1933); SATURDAY'S MILLIONS(1933); SITTING PRET-
TY(1933); HE WAS HER MAN(1934); HOLLYWOOD PARTY(1934); NINTH GUEST,
THE(1934); POOR RICH, THE(1934); ANNA KARENINA(1935); MAGNIFICENT
OBSESSION(1935); CHARLIE CHAN AT THE RACE TRACK(1936); MURDER AT
GLEN ATHOL(1936); SUTTER'S GOLD(1936); TROUBLE FOR TWO(1936); BREAK-
FAST FOR TWO(1937); PRINCE AND THE PAUPER, THE(1937); WRONG ROAD,

THE(1937); ANGELS WITH DIRTY FACES(1938); HARD TO GET(1938); MERRILY WE LIVE(1938); GOING PLACES(1939); ON TRIAL(1939); SECRET SERVICE OF THE AIR(1939); SMASHING THE MONEY RING(1939); SWEEPSTAKES WINNER(1939); WE ARE NOT ALONE(1939); DEVIL'S ISLAND(1940); SOUTH OF SUEZ(1940); TUGBOAT ANNIE SAILS AGAIN(1940); BULLETS FOR O'HARA(1941); SCOTLAND YARD(1941); SHADOWS ON THE STAIRS(1941)

Silents
ELUSIVE ISABEL(1916); FOOD FOR SCANDAL(1920); AMATEUR DEVIL, AN(1921); CRAZY TO MARRY(1921); MORALS(1921); OUTSIDE WOMAN, THE(1921); DICTATOR, THE(1922); MERRY-GO-ROUND(1923); NOBODY'S BRIDE(1923); RUGGLES OF RED GAP(1923); MERRY WIDOW, THE(1925); MAN FOUR-SQUARE, A(1926); MY BEST GIRL(1927); PAINTING THE TOWN(1927); SUNRISE–A SONG OF TWO HUMANS(1927); WEDDING MARCH, THE(1927); WOMAN ON TRIAL, THE(1927); MAN-MADE WOMEN(1928); QUEEN KELLY(1929)

Misc. Silents
HUNTRESS OF MEN, THE(1916); TEMPTATION AND THE MAN(1916); DEEMSTER, THE(1917); PASSION FRUIT(1921); MIDNIGHT(1922); BY DIVINE RIGHT(1924)

Bill Brach
ECHOES OF SILENCE(1966)

Gerald Brach
BYE BYE MONKEY(1978, Ital/Fr.), w

Gerard Brach
REPULSION(1965, Brit.), w; CUL-DE-SAC(1966, Brit.), w; TASTE FOR WOMEN, A(1966, Fr./Ital.), w; BEAUTIFUL SWINDLERS, THE(1967, Fr./Ital./Jap./Neth.), w; FEARLESS VAMPIRE KILLERS, OR PARDON ME BUT YOUR TEETH ARE IN MY NECK, THE(1967), w; TWO OF US, THE(1968, Fr.), w; SECRET WORLD(1969, Fr.), w; WONDERWALL(1969, Brit.), w; CHE?(1973, Ital./Fr./Ger.), w; TENANT, THE(1976, Fr.), w; TESS(1980, Fr./Brit.), w; I SENT A LETTER TO MY LOVE(1981, Fr.), w; QUEST FOR FIRE(1982, Fr./Can.), w; AFRICAN, THE(1983, Fr.), w; IDENTIFICATION OF A WOMAN(1983, Ital.), w

1984
MY BEST FRIEND'S GIRL(1984, Fr.), w

Jimmy Brachen
WITH SIX YOU GET EGGROLL(1968)

Diana Bracho
DOGS OF WAR, THE(1980, Brit.)

Jesu's Bracho
EMPTY STAR, THE(1962, Mex.), art d

Jesus Bracho
SONG OF MEXICO(1945), art d; YOUNG ONE, THE(1961, Mex.), art d; CRIMINAL LIFE OF ARCHIBALDO DE LA CRUZ, THE(1962, Mex.), art d; PEARL OF TLAYUCAN, THE(1964, Mex.), art d; EXTERMINATING ANGEL, THE(1967, Mex.), art d

Frank Bracht
MATING SEASON, THE(1951), ed; MY FAVORITE SPY(1951), ed; HURRICANE SMITH(1952), ed; SOMEBODY LOVES ME(1952), ed; ARROWHEAD(1953), ed; FLIGHT TO TANGIER(1953), ed; VANQUISHED, THE(1953), ed; WHITE CHRISTMAS(1954), ed; FAR HORIZONS, THE(1955), ed; ANYTHING GOES(1956), ed; MOUNTAIN, THE(1956), ed; FUNNY FACE(1957), ed; DAMN YANKEES(1958), ed; HELEN MORGAN STORY, THE(1959), ed; MIRACLE, THE(1959), ed; FACTS OF LIFE, THE(1960), ed; IT STARTED IN NAPLES(1960), ed; VISIT TO A SMALL PLANET(1960), ed; ON THE DOUBLE(1961), ed; PIGEON THAT TOOK ROME, THE(1962), ed; TOO LATE BLUES(1962), ed; HUD(1963), ed; NEW KIND OF LOVE, A(1963), ed; CARPETBAGGERS, THE(1964), ed; WHERE LOVE HAS GONE(1964), ed; HARLOW(1965), ed; SYLVIA(1965), ed; NEVADA SMITH(1966), ed; HOMBRE(1967), ed; BROTHERHOOD, THE(1968), ed; ODD COUPLE, THE(1968), ed; FLAP(1970), ed; MOLLY MAGUIRES, THE(1970), ed; PLAZA SUITE(1971), ed; STAR SPANGLED GIRL(1971), ed; PETE 'N' TILLIE(1972), ed; WAR BETWEEN MEN AND WOMEN, THE(1972), ed; CONRACK(1974), ed; MANDINGO(1975), ed; DUCHESS AND THE DIRTWATER FOX, THE(1976), ed; SIDEWINDER ONE(1977), ed; GOIN' COCONUTS(1978), ed; SOMETHING SHORT OF PARADISE(1979), ed

Claudia Brack
COME SEPTEMBER(1961); BLACK ZOO(1963); FOR LOVE OR MONEY(1963)

Philip Brack
MAN FOR ALL SEASONS, A(1966, Brit.); DARWIN ADVENTURE, THE(1972, Brit.)

Lotte Brackebusch
TOXI(1952, Ger.); ETERNAL LOVE(1960, Ger.)

Andrew Bracken
1984
PHILADELPHIA EXPERIMENT, THE(1984)

Bert Bracken
FACE ON THE BARROOM FLOOR, THE(1932), d, w

Misc. Silents
MARTINACHE MARRIAGE, THE(1917), d

Bertram Bracken
Silents
EAST LYNNE(1916), d; ETERNAL SAPHO, THE(1916), d; AND A STILL, SMALL VOICE(1918), d&w; MASK, THE(1921), d; DAME CHANCE(1926), d

Misc. Silents
SHRINE OF HAPPINESS, THE(1916), d; SPORTING BLOOD(1916), d; BEST MAN, THE(1917), d; BRANDED SOUL, A(1917), d; CONSCIENCE(1917), d; INSPIRATIONS OF HARRY LARRABEE(1917), d; PRIMITIVE CALL, THE(1917), d; FOR LIBERTY(1918), d; MORAL LAW, THE(1918), d; BOOMERANG, THE(1919), d; CODE OF THE YUKON(1919), d; IN SEARCH OF ARCADY(1919), d; LONG ARM OF MANNISTER, THE(1919), d; CONFESSION, THE(1920), d; HARRIET AND THE PIPER(1920), d; KAZAN(1921), d; DEFYING THE LAW(1924), d; PASSION'S PATHWAY(1924), d; HEARTLESS HUSBANDS(1925), d; SPEEDING THROUGH(1926), d; DUTY'S REWARD(1927), d; FIRE AND STEEL(1927), d; ROSE OF THE BOWERY(1927), d

Eddie Bracken
TOO MANY GIRLS(1940); CAUGHT IN THE DRAFT(1941); LIFE WITH HENRY(1941); REACHING FOR THE SUN(1941); FLEET'S IN, THE(1942); STAR SPANGLED RHYTHM(1942); SWEATER GIRL(1942); HAPPY GO LUCKY(1943); YOUNG AND WILLING(1943); HAIL THE CONQUERING HERO(1944); MIRACLE OF MORGAN'S CREEK, THE(1944); RAINBOW ISLAND(1944); BRING ON THE GIRLS(1945); DUFFY'S TAVERN(1945); HOLD THAT BLONDE(1945); OUT OF THIS WORLD(1945); LADIES' MAN(1947); GIRL FROM JONES BEACH, THE(1949); SUMMER STOCK(1950); TWO TICKETS TO BROADWAY(1951); ABOUT FACE(1952); WE'RE NOT MARRIED(1952); SLIGHT CASE OF LARCENY, A(1953); SHINBONE ALLEY(1971); FUN ON A WEEKEND(1979); NATIONAL LAMPOON'S VACATION(1983)

Eversley Bracken
NIGHT OF MAGIC, A(1944, Brit.), w

John Bracken
Misc. Silents
PARTED CURTAINS(1921), d

Kathleen Bracken
MAN WITH BOGART'S FACE, THE(1980)

Mary Bracken
MIRACLE WOMAN, THE(1931)

Richard Bracken
DON'T JUST STAND THERE(1968), ed; GAMBLERS, THE(1969), ed; WRATH OF GOD, THE(1972), ed; DEADLY BLESSING(1981), ed; SWAMP THING(1982), ed

Susan Bracken
Misc. Talkies
DON'T OPEN THE DOOR(1974)

Pat Brackenbury
DR. JEKYLL AND SISTER HYDE(1971, Brit.)

Bracket
NIAGARA(1953), w

Charles Brackett
POINTED HEELS(1930), w; SECRETS OF A SECRETARY(1931), w; COLLEGE SCANDAL(1935), w; ENTER MADAME(1935), w; LAST OUTPOST, THE(1935), w; WITHOUT REGRET(1935), w; PICCADILLY JIM(1936), w; ROSE OF THE RANCHO(1936), w; WOMAN TRAP(1936), w; LIVE, LOVE AND LEARN(1937), w; BLUEBEARD'S EIGHTH WIFE(1938), w; THAT CERTAIN AGE(1938), w; MIDNIGHT(1939), w; NINOTCHKA(1939), w; WHAT A LIFE(1939), w; ARISE, MY LOVE(1940), w; BALL OF FIRE(1941), w; HOLD BACK THE DAWN(1941), w; MAJOR AND THE MINOR, THE(1942), w; FIVE GRAVES TO CAIRO(1943), w; UNINVITED, THE(1944), p; LOST WEEKEND, THE(1945), p, w; TO EACH HIS OWN(1946), p, w; EMPEROR WALTZ, THE(1948), p, w; FOREIGN AFFAIR, A(1948), p, w; MISS TATLOCK'S MILLIONS(1948), p, w; SUNSET BOULEVARD(1950), p, w; MATING SEASON, THE(1951), p, w; MODEL AND THE MARRIAGE BROKER, THE(1951), p, w; NIAGARA(1953), p; TITANIC(1953), p, w; GARDEN OF EVIL(1954), p; WOMAN'S WORLD(1954), p; GIRL IN THE RED VELVET SWING, THE(1955), p, w; VIRGIN QUEEN, THE(1955), p; D-DAY, THE SIXTH OF JUNE(1956), p; KING AND I, THE(1956), p; TEENAGE REBEL(1956), p, w; SILK STOCKINGS(1957), w; WAYWARD BUS, THE(1957), p; GIFT OF LOVE, THE(1958), p; 10 NORTH FREDERICK(1958), p; BLUE DENIM(1959), p; JOURNEY TO THE CENTER OF THE EARTH(1959), p, w; REMARKABLE MR. PENNYPACKER, THE(1959), p; HIGH TIME(1960), p; STATE FAIR(1962), p

Christian Brackett
1984
MEATBALLS PART II(1984)

Dick Brackett
COUNTRY BOY(1966)

Leigh Brackett
VAMPIRE'S GHOST, THE(1945), w; BIG SLEEP, THE(1946), w; CRIME DOCTOR'S MAN HUNT(1946), w; RIO BRAVO(1959), w; GOLD OF THE SEVEN SAINTS(1961), w; HATARI!(1962), w; THIRTEEN WEST STREET(1962), w; EL DORADO(1967), w; RIO LOBO(1970), w; LONG GOODBYE, THE(1973), w; EMPIRE STRIKES BACK, THE(1980), w

Sarah Brackett
MASQUE OF THE RED DEATH, THE(1964, U.S./Brit.); THIRD SECRET, THE(1964, Brit.); BATTLE BENEATH THE EARTH(1968, Brit.); EMILY(1976, Brit.); PRIEST OF LOVE(1981, Brit.); LORDS OF DISCIPLINE, THE(1983)
1984
SCREAM FOR HELP(1984)

Jacob Brackman
KING OF MARVIN GARDENS, THE(1972), w; TIMES SQUARE(1980), p, w

David Bracknell
CUP FEVER(1965, Brit.), d&w; BATTLE OF BRITAIN, THE(1969, Brit.), ph

David Bracks
STONE(1974, Aus.); DEATHCHEATERS(1976, Aus.); MAD MAX(1979, Aus.)

Elizabeth Braconnier
LES GAULOISES BLEUES(1969, Fr.)

Lisa Braconnier
JOY(1983, Fr./Can.)

Liza Braconnier
JUDGE AND THE ASSASSIN, THE(1979, Fr.)

Clair Bracy
IF I HAD A MILLION(1932)

Sidney Bracy [Sidney Bracey]
DOUGH BOYS(1930); DANGEROUS AFFAIR, A(1931); DECEIVER, THE(1931); PARLOR, BEDROOM AND BATH(1931); INTRUDER, THE(1932); MONSTER WALKS, THE(1932); MONKEY'S PAW, THE(1933); CAT'S PAW, THE(1934); FIFTEEN WIVES(1934); LET 'EM HAVE IT(1935); RENDEZVOUS(1935); ISLE OF FURY(1936); SAN FRANCISCO(1936); CALL IT A DAY(1937); EASY LIVING(1937); FIGHT FOR YOUR LADY(1937); FIREFLY, THE(1937); GIRL WITH IDEAS, A(1937); MAID OF SALEM(1937); ROSALIE(1937); TOAST OF NEW YORK, THE(1937); AMAZING DR. CLITTERHOUSE, THE(1938); BARONESS AND THE BUTLER, THE(1938); COMET OVER BROADWAY(1938); DAWN PATROL, THE(1938); MR. CHUMP(1938); MY BILL(1938); DARK VICTORY(1939); ESPIONAGE AGENT(1939); EVERYBODY'S HOBBY(1939); KING OF THE UNDERWORLD(1939); NAUGHTY BUT NICE(1939); SUN NEVER SETS, THE(1939); BRITISH INTELLIGENCE(1940); CHILD IS BORN, A(1940); MY LOVE CAME BACK(1940); BODY DISAPPEARS, THE(1941); MEET JOHN DOE(1941); YOU BELONG TO ME(1941)

Silents
CAPRICE OF THE MOUNTAINS(1916); CRIME AND PUNISHMENT(1917); BLACK BIRD, THE(1926); CAMERAMAN, THE(1928); SHOW PEOPLE(1928); SIOUX BLOOD(1929)

Misc. Silents
MERELY MARY ANN(1916); PATH OF HAPPINESS, THE(1916); SPORTING BLOOD(1916); HAUNTED HOUSE, THE(1928)

Jaroslav Bradac
STEPPENWOLF(1974), anim

Nurven Bradangen
ONE DAY IN THE LIFE OF IVAN DENISOVICH(1971, U.S./Brit./Norway), makeup

Donald Bradburn
SWEET CHARITY(1969)
Basil Bradbury
HONEYMOON OF TERROR(1961), p; INVASION OF THE STAR CREATU-
RES(1962), ph; TASTE OF HELL, A(1973), d
Misc. Talkies
KING MONSTER(1977)
Basil C. Bradbury
DO NOT THROW CUSHIONS INTO THE RING(1970), ph
James Bradbury, Jr.
ALIBI(1929); HALF-MARRIAGE(1929); IN OLD ARIZONA(1929); LAST OF THE
DUANES(1930); MAN TROUBLE(1930); PUTTIN' ON THE RITZ(1930); ROGUE SONG,
THE(1930); CISCO KID(1931); NIGHT NURSE(1931); SOUL OF THE SLUMS(1931);
BETWEEN FIGHTING MEN(1932); DANCERS IN THE DARK(1932); GORILLA SHIP,
THE(1932); JEALOUSY(1934); MARK OF THE VAMPIRE(1935); SILVER STREAK,
THE(1935)
Silents
PEST, THE(1919); CLASSMATES(1924); MANHATTAN(1924); KENTUCKY HAND-
ICAP(1926); BABE COMES HOME(1927); CIRCUS ACE, THE(1927); DROPKICK,
THE(1927); LET IT RAIN(1927); SHE'S A SHEIK(1927); FLYING ROMEOS(1928);
MIDNIGHT MADNESS(1928); SPEEDY(1928); ANNE AGAINST THE WORLD(1929);
SCARLET SEAS(1929)
Misc. Silents
BLACK SHEEP, A(1915); HIGH FLYER, THE(1926); LITTLE GIANT, THE(1926);
ROMANTIC ROGUE(1927); WRECK, THE(1927); CHEYENNE(1929)
James Bradbury, Sr.
BLOCKADE(1929); ABRAHAM LINCOLN(1930); MATRIMONIAL BED, THE(1930);
TOL'ABLE DAVID(1930)
Silents
LEOPARD LADY, THE(1928); SKINNER'S BIG IDEA(1928); WALKING BACK(1928)
Misc. Silents
HOT HEELS(1928); WATERFRONT(1928)
Jane Bradbury
JOANNA(1968, Brit.)
John Bradbury
FANTASIA(1940), anim
Kitty Bradbury
Silents
KID, THE(1921); OUR HOSPITALITY(1923); PILGRIM, THE(1923)
Lane Bradbury
ALICE DOESN'T LIVE HERE ANYMORE(1975); ULTIMATE WARRIOR, THE(1975)
Mrs. Bradbury
Silents
CAPTAIN OF THE GRAY HORSE TROOP, THE(1917)
R. Bradbury
Misc. Silents
WHEN MEN ARE TEMPTED(1918)
R. N. Bradbury
SON OF THE PLAINS(1931), d&w; BREED OF THE BORDER(1933), d; HAPPY
LANDING(1934), d; DAWN RIDER(1935), d&w; GOD'S COUNTRY AND THE
MAN(1937), p&d; GUN RANGER, THE(1937), d; HITTIN' THE TRAIL(1937), d; RID-
ERS OF THE DAWN(1937), p&d; STARS OVER ARIZONA(1937), p&d; TROUBLE IN
TEXAS(1937), d; TRUSTED OUTLAW, THE(1937), d; WHERE TRAILS DIVIDE(1937),
p&d; DANGER VALLEY(1938), p&d; ROMANCE OF THE ROCKIES(1938), p&d
Silents
NOBODY'S WIFE(1918), w
R. S. Bradbury
Silents
BY THE WORLD FORGOT(1918)
Ray Bradbury
BEAST FROM 20,000 FATHOMS, THE(1953), w; IT CAME FROM OUTER SPA-
CE(1953), w; MOBY DICK(1956, Brit.), w; FAHRENHEIT 451(1966, Brit.), w; RICH
AND FAMOUS(1981); SOMETHING WICKED THIS WAY COMES(1983), w
Robert Bradbury
Silents
RACE, THE(1916)
Robert N. Bradbury
DUGAN OF THE BAD LANDS(1931), d&w; HIDDEN VALLEY(1932), d; MAN
FROM HELL'S EDGES(1932), d, w; RIDERS OF THE DESERT(1932), d; SON OF
OKLAHOMA(1932), d; TEXAS BUDDIES(1932), d&w; GALLANT FOOL, THE(1933),
d, w; GALLOPING ROMEO(1933), d, w; RANGER'S CODE, THE(1933), d; BLUE
STEEL(1934), d, w; LUCKY TEXAN, THE(1934), d&w; MAN FROM UTAH,
THE(1934), d; STAR PACKER, THE(1934), d&w; TRAIL BEYOND, THE(1934), d;
WEST OF THE DIVIDE(1934), d&w; ALIAS JOHN LAW(1935), d; BETWEEN
MEN(1935), d&w; COURAGEOUS AVENGER, THE(1935), d; KID COURA-
GEOUS(1935), d&w; LAWLESS FRONTIER, THE(1935), d&w; LAWLESS RAN-
GE(1935), d, w; NO MAN'S RANGE(1935), d, w; RAINBOW VALLEY(1935), d; RIDER
OF THE LAW, THE(1935), d; SMOKEY SMITH(1935), d&w; TEXAS TERROR(1935),
d&w; TOMBSTONE TERROR(1935), d&w; TRAIL OF TERROR(1935), d&w; WEST-
ERN JUSTICE(1935), d&w; CAVALRY(1936), d, w; KID RANGER, THE(1936), d&w;
LAST OF THE WARRENS, THE(1936), d&w; LAW RIDES, THE(1936), d; VALLEY OF
THE LAWLESS(1936), d&w; WESTWARD HO(1936), d; HEADIN' FOR THE RIO
GRANDE(1937), d; SING, COWBOY, SING(1937), d; SUNDOWN SAUNDERS(1937),
d&w
Misc. Talkies
LAW OF THE WEST(1932), d; BIG CALIBRE(1935), d; BRAND OF THE OUT-
LAWS(1936), d
Silents
BANTAM COWBOY, THE(1928), sup, w
Misc. Silents
BEHIND TWO GUNS(1924), d; WANTED BY THE LAW(1924), d; YANKEE
SPEED(1924), d; BATTLER, THE(1925), d; DANGER ZONE, THE(1925), d; NORTH
OF NOME(1925); SPEED DEMON, THE(1925), d; DANIEL BOONE THRU THE
WILDERNESS(1926), d
Robert North Bradbury
RIDERS OF DESTINY(1933), d&w; RIDERS OF THE ROCKIES(1937), d; FORBID-
DEN TRAILS(1941), d
Silents
GALLOPING THRU(1923), d; GALLOPING ACE, THE(1924), d; IN HIGH
GEAR(1924), d, w; MAN FROM WYOMING, THE(1924), d; RIDERS OF MYS-

TERY(1925), d; LOOKING FOR TROUBLE(1926), d
Misc. Silents
FAITH OF THE STRONG(1919), d; LAST OF HIS PEOPLE, THE(1919), d; THINGS
MEN DO(1921), d; RIDERS OF THE LAW(1922), d; DESERT RIDER(1923), d; FORB-
IDDEN TRAIL, THE(1923), d; RED WARNING, THE(1923), d; WHAT LOVE WILL
DO(1923), d; PHANTOM HORSEMAN, THE(1924), d; HIDDEN LOOT(1925), d; JUST
PLAIN FOLKS(1925), d; MOCCASINS(1925), d; BORDER SHERIFF, THE(1926), d;
DAVY CROCKETT AT THE FALL OF THE ALAMO(1926), d; FIGHTING DOCTOR,
THE(1926), d; MOJAVE KID, THE(1927), d; SITTING BULL AT THE "SPIRIT LAKE
MASSACRE"(1927), d; HEADIN' FOR DANGER(1928), d; LIGHTING SPEED(1928), d
Ronald Bradbury
Silents
TARGET, THE(1916), a, w
Misc. Silents
TO HAVE AND TO HOLD(1916)
Ronnie Bradbury
I AM THE CHEESE(1983)
Saax Bradbury
TURNING POINT, THE(1977)
Scott Bradbury
SEPARATE PEACE, A(1972)
Stephen C. Bradbury
HARD COUNTRY(1981)
William Bradbury
Silents
TENNESSEE'S PARDNER(1916)
Maurice Braddell
SCHOOL FOR SCANDAL, THE(1930, Brit.); HER REPUTATION(1931, Brit.); THIS
WEEK OF GRACE(1933, Brit.), w; LOVE, LIFE AND LAUGHTER(1934, Brit.), w; IT'S
YOU I WANT(1936, Brit.), w; THINGS TO COME(1936, Brit.); WHERE'S THAT
FIRE?(1939, Brit.), w
Silents
DAWN(1928, Brit.); NOT QUITE A LADY(1928, Brit.)
Misc. Silents
MASTER AND MAN(1929, Brit.)
Mac Bradden
GAS(1981, Can.)
Claudia Braddock
LADY'S PROFESSION, A(1933)
Jack Braddock
SHOCK TREATMENT(1964)
Martin Braddock
HIGH SCHOOL HELLCATS(1958); GHOST OF DRAGSTRIP HOLLOW(1959)
John D. Braddon
Silents
NERO(1922, U.S./Ital.), art d
Mary Elizabeth Braddon
Silents
EAST LYNNE(1916), w
Russell Braddon
NIGHT OF THE LEPUS(1972), w; END PLAY(1975, Aus.), p,d&w
Tadeusz Bradecki
CONSTANT FACTOR, THE(1980, Pol.); CAMERA BUFF(1983, Pol.)
Maurice Bradell
MEN OF TOMORROW(1935, Brit.)
Bernard Braden
LOVE IN PAWN(1953, Brit.); KID FROM CANADA, THE(1957, Brit.); DAY THE
EARTH CAUGHT FIRE, THE(1961, Brit.); JET STORM(1961, Brit.); STOP ME BEFORE
I KILL!(1961, Brit.); TWO AND TWO MAKE SIX(1962, Brit.); WAR LOVER, THE(1962,
U.S./Brit.)
Christopher Braden
KID FROM CANADA, THE(1957, Brit.)
Clay Braden
MR. BILLION(1977)
Edwin Braden
MAKE MINE A DOUBLE(1962, Brit.), m
Harry Braden
PRETTY BABY(1978)
Hub Braden
1984
MIKE'S MURDER(1984), art d
John Braden
ANDERSON TAPES, THE(1971); BANANAS(1971)
Kim Braden
TROG(1970, Brit.); THAT'LL BE THE DAY(1974, Brit.)
Mike Braden
WEIRD ONES, THE(1962)
Ronald Braden
SKY RAIDERS, THE(1938, Brit.)
Alicia Bradet
BAMBOLE!(1965, Ital.)
Jac Bradette
STONE COLD DEAD(1980, Can.), set d
Jacques Bradette
1984
MRS. SOFFEL(1984), set d
Bobby Bradfield
RANDOLPH FAMILY, THE(1945, Brit.)
Keith Bradfield
GLADIATORS, THE(1970, Swed.)
Louis Bradfield
DIRTY WORK(1934, Brit.); STORMY WEATHER(1935, Brit.); POT LUCK(1936, Brit.);
WE DIVE AT DAWN(1943, Brit.); VARIETY JUBILEE(1945, Brit.)
Robert Bradfield
MAN WITH THE MAGNETIC EYES, THE(1945, Brit.); SECRET OF THE WHIS-
TLER(1946), set d; TRACKDOWN(1976), set d
Robert C. Bradfield
RAIDERS, THE(1964), set d; COUNTERFEIT KILLER, THE(1968), set d; NOBODY'S
PERFECT(1968), set d; THREE GUNS FOR TEXAS(1968), set d

Andrew Bradford
OTHELLO(1965, Brit.); FAMILY WAY, THE(1966, Brit.); ALFRED THE GREAT(1969, Brit.); FIGURES IN A LANDSCAPE(1970, Brit.); JUGGERNAUT(1974, Brit.); FLASH GORDON(1980)

Andy Bradford
KRULL(1983); OCTOPUSSY(1983, Brit.)

Art Bradford
SEED OF INNOCENCE(1980)

Big Jim Bradford
FROM NASHVILLE WITH MUSIC(1969)

Cathy Bradford
DRIVE, HE SAID(1971)

David Bradford
STRANGE HOLIDAY(1945)

Delia Bradford
GOIN' HOME(1976)

Ernie Bradford
ROGUE'S YARN(1956, Brit.), w; BURKE AND HARE(1972, Brit.), w

Gardner Bradford
Silents
DESERT'S TOLL, THE(1926), t; ONE GLORIOUS SCRAP(1927), t; SKY-HIGH SAUNDERS(1927), t; WEB OF FATE(1927), t; AIR PATROL, THE(1928), t; ARIZONA CYCLONE(1928), t; HEART TROUBLE(1928), t; HARVEST OF HATE, THE(1929), t; HOOFBEATS OF VENGEANCE(1929), t; PLUNGING HOOFS(1929), t; SKY SKIDDER, THE(1929), t; WILD BLOOD(1929), t

George Bradford
PRIVATE ANGELO(1949, Brit.); WEAPON, THE(1957, Brit.)

Greg Bradford
SKATETOWN, U.S.A.(1979); ZAPPED!(1982)
1984
LOVELINES(1984)

J.E. Bradford
WILD BOY(1934, Brit.), w

Jack Bradford
NAVY WIFE(1956)

James Bradford
SHEPHERD OF THE HILLS, THE(1964)
1984
MRS. SOFFEL(1984)

James C. Bradford
MAMBA(1930), m; SAVAGE GOLD(1933), md

Jesse Bradford
1984
FALLING IN LOVE(1984)

Jim Bradford
SASQUATCH(1978)

John Bradford
365 NIGHTS IN HOLLYWOOD(1934); LIFE BEGINS AT 40(1935); OLD CORRAL, THE(1937)

John C. Bradford
FROM NASHVILLE WITH MUSIC(1969)

Johnny Bradford
I WAS A COMMUNIST FOR THE F.B.I.(1951)

Lane Bradford
FRONTIER CRUSADER(1940); LONE RIDER IN GHOST TOWN, THE(1941); FIGHTING BUCKAROO, THE(1943); THUNDERING TRAILS(1943); MARSHAL OF LAREDO(1945); OVERLAND RIDERS(1946); TERRORS ON HORSEBACK(1946); GHOST TOWN RENEGADES(1947); PIONEER JUSTICE(1947); RETURN OF THE LASH(1947); SHADOW VALLEY(1947); BLACK HILLS(1948); CHECK YOUR GUNS(1948); DEAD MAN'S GOLD(1948); FRONTIER AGENT(1948); HAWK OF POWDER RIVER, THE(1948); SUNDOWN IN SANTA FE(1948); TORNADO RANGE(1948); BANDIT KING OF TEXAS(1949); DEATH VALLEY GUNFIGHTER(1949); FAR FRONTIER, THE(1949); LAW OF THE GOLDEN WEST(1949); OUTCASTS OF THE TRAIL(1949); PRINCE OF THE PLAINS(1949); RANGER OF CHEROKEE STRIP(1949); ROLL, THUNDER, ROLL(1949); SAN ANTONE AMBUSH(1949); SHERIFF OF WICHITA(1949); SOUTH OF RIO(1949); WESTERN RENEGADES(1949); WYOMING BANDIT, THE(1949); ARIZONA COWBOY, THE(1950); BELLS OF CORONADO(1950); CODE OF THE SILVER SAGE(1950); DESERT HAWK, THE(1950); FIGHTING REDHEAD, THE(1950); FRISCO TORNADO(1950); HILLS OF OKLAHOMA(1950); MISSOURIANS, THE(1950); OLD FRONTIER, THE(1950); TEXAS DYNAMO(1950); I WAS AN AMERICAN SPY(1951); LADY FROM TEXAS, THE(1951); LONGHORN(1951); OKLAHOMA JUSTICE(1951); STAGE TO BLUE RIVER(1951); TEXAS LAWMEN(1951); WHISTLING HILLS(1951); AFRICAN TREASURE(1952); DEAD MAN'S TRAIL(1952); DESERT PASSAGE(1952); DESPERADOES OUTPOST(1952); FORT OSAGE(1952); KANSAS TERRITORY(1952); LAWLESS COWBOYS(1952); LUSTY MEN, THE(1952); MAN FROM BLACK HILLS, THE(1952); NIGHT RAIDERS(1952); RAIDERS, THE(1952); ROSE OF CIMARRON(1952); TARGET(1952); TEXAS CITY(1952); WACO(1952); GREAT SIOUX UPRISING, THE(1953); SAVAGE FRONTIER(1953); SON OF BELLE STARR(1953); DRUMS ACROSS THE RIVER(1954); FORTYNINERS, THE(1954); FRENCH LINE, THE(1954); GOLDEN IDOL, THE(1954); RIDE CLEAR OF DIABLO(1954); SPOILERS, THE(1955); RAWHIDE YEARS, THE(1956); SHOWDOWN AT ABILENE(1956); STEEL JUNGLE, THE(1956); APACHE WARRIOR(1957); GUN GLORY(1957); PHANTOM STAGECOACH, THE(1957); SHOOT-OUT AT MEDICINE BEND(1957); LONE RANGER AND THE LOST CITY OF GOLD, THE(1958); SATAN'S SATELLITES(1958); TOUGHEST GUN IN TOMBSTONE(1958); GUN HAWK, THE(1963); DISTANT TRUMPET, A(1964); SHENANDOAH(1965); SLENDER THREAD, THE(1965); JOURNEY TO SHILOH(1968)
Misc. Talkies
STAGECOACH DRIVER(1951); WANTED DEAD OR ALIVE(1951); MAN FROM THE BLACK HILLS(1952)

Maj. J.S. Bradford
DUNKIRK(1958, Brit.), w

Mark Bradford
1984
ALLEY CAT(1984)

Marshall Bradford
WESTERN RENEGADES(1949); WHITE HEAT(1949); CONVICTED(1950); MAGNIFICENT YANKEE, THE(1950); COLORADO AMBUSH(1951); GHOST CHASERS(1951); LONGHORN, THE(1951); NIGHT RIDERS OF MONTANA(1951); CARBINE WILLIAMS(1952); HELLGATE(1952); FAST AND THE FURIOUS,

THE(1954); THEM!(1954); YUKON VENGEANCE(1954); STRANGE LADY IN TOWN(1955); BAND OF ANGELS(1957); NIGHT RUNNER, THE(1957); SHOOT-OUT AT MEDICINE BEND(1957); I WAS A TEENAGE FRANKENSTEIN(1958); PARTY GIRL(1958); TEENAGE CAVEMAN(1958); SUMMER PLACE, A(1959); TERROR AT BLACK FALLS(1962)

Mike Bradford
THUNDER IN DIXIE(1965)

Perry Bradford
Misc. Talkies
PARADISE IN HARLEM(1939)

Peter Bradford
HEIGHTS OF DANGER(1962, Brit.), d

Raymond Bradford
UNDER AGE(1964)

Richard Bradford
CHASE, THE(1966); RED SKY AT MORNING(1971), w; MISSOURI BREAKS, THE(1976); ENEMY OF THE PEOPLE, AN(1978); GOIN' SOUTH(1978); MORE AMERICAN GRAFFITI(1979); HAMMETT(1982); LOOKIN' TO GET OUT(1982); MISSING(1982)
1984
HIGHWAY TO HELL(1984); RUNNING HOT(1984)
Misc. Talkies
TO CHASE A MILLION(1967)

Roark Bradford
GREEN PASTURES(1936), w

Robert C. Bradford
RAID ON ROMMEL(1971), set d

Roy Bradford
DEEP BLUE SEA, THE(1955, Brit.), m/l

Spencer Bradford
SOUNDER(1972)

Sue Bradford
INDESTRUCTIBLE MAN, THE(1956), w

Tom Bradford
Misc. Talkies
BIJOU(1972)

Virginia Bradford
PRIVATE LIFE OF DON JUAN, THE(1934, Brit.)
Silents
ATTA BOY!(1926); STAGE MADNESS(1927); CHICAGO(1928); CRAIG'S WIFE(1928); MARKED MONEY(1928); TWO LOVERS(1928); ONE MAN DOG, THE(1929)
Misc. Silents
COUNTRY DOCTOR, THE(1927); WRECK OF THE HESPERUS, THE(1927)

Walter Bradford
SPIELER, THE(1929), set d; MEDIUM COOL(1969)

William Bradford
ADVENTURES OF GALLANT BESS(1948), ph; SOMBRERO KID, THE(1942), ph; CARSON CITY CYCLONE(1943), ph; FALSE FACES(1943), ph; FUGITIVE FROM SONORA(1943), ph; MAN FROM MUSIC MOUNTAIN(1943), ph; MANTRAP, THE(1943), ph; MYSTERY BROADCAST(1943), ph; CALL OF THE SOUTH SEAS(1944), ph; END OF THE ROAD(1944), ph; FIGHTING SEABEES, THE(1944), ph; JAMBOREE(1944), ph; SAN ANTONIO KID, THE(1944), ph; SAN FERNANDO VALLEY(1944), ph; SECRETS OF SCOTLAND YARD(1944), ph; SILENT PARTNER(1944), ph; STAGECOACH TO MONTEREY(1944), ph; VIGILANTES OF DODGE CITY(1944), ph; ALONG THE NAVAJO TRAIL(1945), ph; BEHIND CITY LIGHTS(1945), ph; CHICAGO KID, THE(1945), ph; DON'T FENCE ME IN(1945), ph; GRISSLY'S MILLIONS(1945), ph; MAN FROM OKLAHOMA, THE(1945), ph; PHANTOM OF THE PLAINS(1945), ph; PHANTOM SPEAKS, THE(1945), ph; ROUGH RIDERS OF CHEYENNE(1945), ph; SANTA FE SADDLEMATES(1945), ph; SCOTLAND YARD INVESTIGATOR(1945, Brit.), ph; SUNSET IN EL DORADO(1945), ph; THOROUGHBREDS(1945), ph; THREE'S A CROWD(1945), ph; UTAH(1945), ph; CONQUEST OF CHEYENNE(1946), ph; GAY BLADES(1946), ph; HELLDORADO(1946), ph; HOME IN OKLAHOMA(1946), ph; INVISIBLE INFORMER(1946), ph; MY PAL TRIGGER(1946), ph; NIGHT TRAIN TO MEMPHIS(1946), ph; PASSKEY TO DANGER(1946), ph; RED RIVER RENEGADES(1946), ph; ROLL ON TEXAS MOON(1946), ph; UNDER NEVADA SKIES(1946), ph; EXPOSED(1947), ph; LAST ROUND-UP, THE(1947), ph; MARSHAL OF CRIPPLE CREEK, THE(1947), ph; ROBIN OF TEXAS(1947), ph; RUSTLERS OF DEVIL'S CANYON(1947), ph; TRAIL TO SAN ANTONE(1947), ph; TWILIGHT ON THE RIO GRANDE(1947), ph; CARSON CITY RAIDERS(1948), ph; LOADED PISTOLS(1948), ph; MACBETH(1948), ph; OLD LOS ANGELES(1948), ph; BIG SOMBRERO, THE(1949), ph; COWBOY AND THE INDIANS, THE(1949), ph; RIDERS IN THE SKY(1949), ph; RIDERS OF THE WHISTLING PINES(1949), ph; RIM OF THE CANYON(1949), ph; SONS OF NEW MEXICO(1949), ph; ARIZONA COWBOY, THE(1950), ph; BEYOND THE PURPLE HILLS(1950), ph; BLAZING SUN, THE(1950), ph; COW TOWN(1950), ph; INDIAN TERRITORY(1950), ph; MILITARY ACADEMY WITH THAT TENTH AVENUE GANG(1950), ph; MULE TRAIN(1950), ph; ON THE ISLE OF SAMOA(1950), ph; GENE AUTRY AND THE MOUNTIES(1951), ph; HILLS OF UTAH(1951), ph; SILVER CANYON(1951), ph; TEXANS NEVER CRY(1951), ph; VALLEY OF FIRE(1951), ph; WHIRLWIND(1951), ph; APACHE COUNTRY(1952), ph; BARBED WIRE(1952), ph; BLUE CANADIAN ROCKIES(1952), ph; NIGHT STAGE TO GALVESTON(1952), ph; OLD WEST, THE(1952), ph; WAGON TEAM(1952), ph; GOLDTOWN GHOST RIDERS(1953), ph; LAST OF THE PONY RIDERS(1953), ph; ON TOP OF OLD SMOKY(1953), ph; PACK TRAIN(1953), ph; PARIS MODEL(1953), ph; PORT SINISTER(1953), ph; SAGINAW TRAIL(1953), ph; WINNING OF THE WEST(1953), ph; RETURN TO TREASURE ISLAND(1954), ph; TOP BANANA(1954), ph; WAGON WHEELS WESTWARD(1956), ph
Silents
GOLD RUSH, THE(1925)

Bradford and Amoro
VAMPIRE CIRCUS(1972, Brit.)

John Bradford-Lloyd
1984
C.H.U.D.(1984)

Jean Bradin
DAVID GOLDER(1932, Fr.)
Silents
CHAMPAGNE(1928, Brit.); MOULIN ROUGE(1928, Brit.)

Misc. Silents
ISLAND OF DESPAIR, THE(1926, Brit.)

Barbara Bradish
SIX WEEKS(1982)

Bradjose
R.P.M.(1970)

Bradley
PEER GYNT(1965), ph

Al Bradley
BATTLE OF THE AMAZONS(1973, Ital./Span.), d; THREE STOOGES VS. THE WONDER WOMEN(1975, Ital./Chi.), d&w

Alma Bradley
Misc. Silents
ARIZONA(1913)

Art Bradley
1984
IRRECONCILABLE DIFFERENCES(1984)

Bart Bradley
CELL 2455, DEATH ROW(1955); DOMINO KID(1957); 20 MILLION MILES TO EARTH(1957); VOICE IN THE MIRROR(1958); PAY OR DIE(1960)

Bea Bradley
HOW SWEET IT IS(1968); NOBODY'S PERFECT(1968)

Betty Bradley
FOREIGN CORRESPONDENT(1940); TROCADERO(1944)

Bill Bradley
LOST MISSILE, THE(1958, U.S./Can.); THUNDERING JETS(1958); ALLIGATOR PEOPLE, THE(1959); RETURN TO PEYTON PLACE(1961); TIME AFTER TIME(1979, Brit.)

Buddy Bradley
RADIO FOLLIES(1935, Brit.), ch; IT'S LOVE AGAIN(1936, Brit.), ch; GANGWAY(1937, Brit.), ch; HEAD OVER HEELS IN LOVE(1937, Brit.), a, ch; SPIDER, THE(1940, Brit.), ch

Catherine Bradley
Misc. Silents
FALSE WOMEN(1921)

Chief Bradley
HE WALKED BY NIGHT(1948)

Christopher Bradley
1984
INITIATION, THE(1984)

Chuckie Bradley
IMITATION OF LIFE(1959); MISTER BROWN(1972); HARRAD SUMMER, THE(1974)

Dai Bradley
MALACHI'S COVE(1973, Brit.); ZULU DAWN(1980, Brit.); ABSOLUTION(1981, Brit.)

Dan Bradley
1984
EXECUTIONER PART II, THE(1984)

David Bradley
JULIUS CAESAR(1952), a, p&d; TALK ABOUT A STRANGER(1952), d; DRAG-STRIP RIOT(1958), d; TWELVE TO THE MOON(1960), d; THEY SAVED HITLER'S BRAIN(1964), d; PEER GYNT(1965), a, p&d; KES(1970, Brit.); HARD RIDE, THE(1971)

Donna Bradley
HARD TRAIL(1969)

Dorothy Bradley
GETTING OF WISDOM, THE(1977, Aus.)

Estelle Bradley
ONCE A GENTLEMAN(1930)
Misc. Silents
STICK TO YOUR STORY(1926)

Frank Bradley
SPLENDID FELLOWS(1934, Aus.); TWO MINUTES' SILENCE(1934, Brit.)

Grace Bradley
GIRL WITHOUT A ROOM(1933); TOO MUCH HARMONY(1933); WAY TO LOVE, THE(1933); CAT'S PAW, THE(1934); COME ON, MARINES(1934); RED HEAD(1934); SHE MADE HER BED(1934); SIX OF A KIND(1934); GILDED LILY, THE(1935); OLD MAN RHYTHM(1935); STOLEN HARMONY(1935); TWO FISTED(1935); ANYTHING GOES(1936); DANGEROUS WATERS(1936); DON'T TURN'EM LOOSE(1936); F MAN(1936); ROSE OF THE RANCHO(1936); SITTING ON THE MOON(1936); THIRTEEN HOURS BY AIR(1936); THREE CHEERS FOR LOVE(1936); BIG BROADCAST OF 1938, THE(1937); IT'S ALL YOURS(1937); LARCENY ON THE AIR(1937); ROARING TIMBER(1937); WAKE UP AND LIVE(1937); YOU'RE IN THE ARMY NOW(1937, Brit.); ROMANCE ON THE RUN(1938); INVISIBLE KILLER, THE(1940); SIGN OF THE WOLF(1941); THERE'S MAGIC IN MUSIC(1941); BROOKLYN ORCHID(1942)
Misc. Talkies
TWO MUGS FROM BROOKLYN(1942)

H.C. Bradley
EMPLOYEE'S ENTRANCE(1933); LADY KILLER(1933); SING WHILE YOU'RE ABLE(1937)

Harold Bradley
UNCLE TOM'S CABIN(1969, Fr./Ital./Ger./Yugo.)

Harry Bradley
SMILING LIEUTENANT, THE(1931); DANCING LADY(1933); BEYOND THE LAW(1934); FIFTEEN WIVES(1934); SADIE MCKEE(1934); I LIVE MY LIFE(1935); LIVING ON VELVET(1935); LOVE IN BLOOM(1935); COME AND GET IT(1936); GOLD DIGGERS OF 1937(1936); I AM THE LAW(1938); I STOLE A MILLION(1939); LET US LIVE(1939); PANAMA PATROL(1939); SHOULD HUSBANDS WORK?(1939); STAR MAKER, THE(1939); QUEEN OF THE MOB(1940); THOSE WERE THE DAYS(1940); NEW YORK TOWN(1941); HENRY ALDRICH GETS GLAMOUR(1942); MORE THE MERRIER, THE(1943); PAYOFF, THE(1943); PRINCESS O'ROURKE(1943); SOMEONE TO REMEMBER(1943); HENRY ALDRICH PLAYS CUPID(1944); HENRY ALDRICH'S LITTLE SECRET(1944); MAKE YOUR OWN BED(1944); MR. SKEFFINGTON(1944)

Harry C. Bradley
KID FROM SPAIN, THE(1932); GRAND SLAM(1933); LADIES THEY TALK ABOUT(1933); PRIZEFIGHTER AND THE LADY, THE(1933); SITTING PRETTY(1933); THIS DAY AND AGE(1933); AMONG THE MISSING(1934); HEAT LIGHTNING(1934); HELL BENT FOR LOVE(1934); HOUSE OF MYSTERY(1934); IT HAPPENED ONE NIGHT(1934); KID MILLIONS(1934); LADY BY CHOICE(1934);

LAST GENTLEMAN, THE(1934); MANDALAY(1934); MERRY FRINKS, THE(1934); MAN ON THE FLYING TRAPEZE, THE(1935); MILLIONS IN THE AIR(1935); PRIVATE WORLDS(1935); RENDEZVOUS(1935); STRANDED(1935); THIS IS THE LIFE(1935); TOMORROW'S YOUTH(1935); WAY DOWN EAST(1935); $1,000 A MINUTE(1935); DON'T GET PERSONAL(1936); FLORIDA SPECIAL(1936); LIBELED LADY(1936); MR. DEEDS GOES TO TOWN(1936); MURDER WITH PICTURES(1936); NEXT TIME WE LOVE(1936); PAROLE(1936); RHYTHM ON THE RANGE(1936); STRIKE ME PINK(1936); THREE OF A KIND(1936); WEDDING PRESENT(1936); YOURS FOR THE ASKING(1936); EVER SINCE EVE(1937); NEW FACES OF 1937(1937); TROUBLE AT MIDNIGHT(1937); JURY'S SECRET, THE(1938); LITTLE ADVENTURESS, THE(1938); OUR LEADING CITIZEN(1939); WHEN TOMORROW COMES(1939); DANGER ON WHEELS(1940); ROAD TO SINGAPORE(1940); SLIGHTLY TEMPTED(1940); STRANGER ON THE THIRD FLOOR(1940); INVISIBLE WOMAN, THE(1941); MONSTER AND THE GIRL, THE(1941); BUSSES ROAR(1942); GAY SISTERS, THE(1942); DIXIE(1943); GIRL CRAZY(1943); THEY GOT ME COVERED(1943); KNICKERBOCKER HOLIDAY(1944)

Henry C. Bradley
IF I HAD A MILLION(1932); LONE COWBOY(1934); ROARING TWENTIES, THE(1939)

James Bradley, Jr.
COOL HAND LUKE(1967)

Jan Bradley
LEATHER SAINT, THE(1956); THAT CERTAIN FEELING(1956); FUNNY FACE(1957); ERRAND BOY, THE(1961); SOYLENT GREEN(1973)

Joan Bradley
JIGSAW(1968)

John Bradley
SNIPER, THE(1952)

John H. Bradley
SANDS OF IWO JIMA(1949)

Josephine Bradley
LET'S MAKE A NIGHT OF IT(1937, Brit.)

Josie Bradley
MYSTERIOUS MR. NICHOLSON, THE(1947, Brit.)

Karl Bradley
NATE AND HAYES(1983, U.S./New Zealand)

Katharine Bradley
PEER GYNT(1965)

Lee Bradley
SHE WORE A YELLOW RIBBON(1949); GUN HAWK, THE(1963); TERRIFIED!(1963)

Les Bradley
CAT, THE(1966)

Leslie Bradley
WAY OF YOUTH, THE(1934, Brit.); PLAY UP THE BAND(1935, Brit.); STOKER, THE(1935, Brit.); EVERYTHING OKAY(1936, Brit.); HOLIDAY'S END(1937, Brit.); ON VELVET(1938, Brit.); YOUNG MR. PITT, THE(1942, Brit.); DUMMY TALKS, THE(1943, Brit.); I'LL WALK BESIDE YOU(1943, Brit.); CANDLELIGHT IN ALGERIA(1944, Brit.); TIME FLIES(1944, Brit.); WELCOME, MR. WASHINGTON(1944, Brit.); FLIGHT FROM FOLLY(1945, Brit.); ANNA KARENINA(1948, Brit.); JUST WILLIAM'S LUCK(1948, Brit.); NO ORCHIDS FOR MISS BLANDISH(1948, Brit.); PRINCE OF FOXES(1949); WATERLOO ROAD(1949, Brit.); DRAGON OF PENDRAGON CASTLE, THE(1950, Brit.); SILK NOOSE, THE(1950, Brit.); CASE FOR PC 49, A(1951, Brit.); CRIMSON PIRATE, THE(1952); MAN IN THE ATTIC(1953); SLAVES OF BABYLON(1953); HELL AND HIGH WATER(1954); IRON GLOVE, THE(1954); KING RICHARD AND THE CRUSADERS(1954); GOOD MORNING, MISS DOVE(1955); KISS OF FIRE(1955); LADY GODIVA(1955); SEVEN CITIES OF GOLD(1955); CONQUEROR, THE(1956); WESTWARD HO THE WAGONS!(1956); ATTACK OF THE CRAB MONSTERS(1957); NAKED PARADISE(1957); FRONTIER GUN(1958); JOHNNY ROCCO(1958); MARJORIE MORNINGSTAR(1958); TEENAGE CAVEMAN(1958); ALASKA PASSAGE(1959); SAD HORSE, THE(1959); YOUNG JESSE JAMES(1960); SPIRAL ROAD, THE(1962); GIT!(1965); 36 HOURS(1965); ASSAULT ON A QUEEN(1966)

Leslie E. Bradley
BUCCANEER, THE(1958)

Lilian Trimbler Bradley
WHAT HAPPENED THEN?(1934, Brit.), w

Lovyss Bradley
THEY WON'T BELIEVE ME(1947); CAGED(1950); OUTRAGE(1950); GOLDEN GIRL(1951); MEET ME AFTER THE SHOW(1951); MAN OF CONFLICT(1953); FIRST TRAVELING SALESLADY, THE(1956)

Lynne Bradley
Misc. Talkies
TRUCKIN' MAN(1975)

Malcolm Bradley
Misc. Silents
ROOM AND BOARD(1921)

Mark Bradley
STRANGE LOVERS(1963)

Mary Bradley
SINBAD THE SAILOR(1947)

Mary Hastings Bradley
I PASSED FOR WHITE(1960), w

Michael Bradley
PROMISE HER ANYTHING(1966, Brit.)

Omar Bradley
NEVER WAVE AT A WAC(1952)

Gen. Omar N. Bradley
PATTON(1970), w

Oscar Bradley
CURLY TOP(1935), md; FARMER TAKES A WIFE, THE(1935), md; MAN WHO BROKE THE BANK AT MONTE CARLO, THE(1935), md; OUR LITTLE GIRL(1935), md; WAY DOWN EAST(1935), m; WELCOME HOME(1935), md

Owen Bradley
COAL MINER'S DAUGHTER(1980), m

Pat Bradley
LITTLEST HOBO, THE(1958); CAPTURE THAT CAPSULE(1961); UNDER THE RAINBOW(1981), w

Paul Bradley
KISMET(1944); CORNERED(1945); WOMAN IN THE WINDOW, THE(1945); GILDA(1946); POSTMAN ALWAYS RINGS TWICE, THE(1946); DEAD RECKONING(1947); JOHNNY O'CLOCK(1947); POSSESSED(1947); UNFAITHFUL,

THE(1947); DATE WITH JUDY, A(1948); LOVES OF CARMEN, THE(1948); MUSIC MAN(1948); EMERGENCY WEDDING(1950); MISTER 880(1950); ROGUES OF SHERWOOD FOREST(1950); I WAS A COMMUNIST FOR THE F.B.I.(1951); MILLION DOLLAR MERMAID(1952); BAND WAGON, THE(1953); MISSISSIPPI GAMBLER, THE(1953); AUTUMN LEAVES(1956); FIRST TRAVELING SALESLADY, THE(1956); WRITTEN ON THE WIND(1956); IMITATION OF LIFE(1959); GAMBIT(1966); MADAME X(1966); GOIN' DOWN THE ROAD(1970, Can.); MERRY WIVES OF TOBIAS ROUKE, THE(1972, Can.); WEDDING IN WHITE(1972, Can.); HARD PART BEGINS, THE(1973, Can.); HOW TO SUCCEED IN BUSINESS WITHOUT REALLY TRYING(1976); CROSS COUNTRY(1983, Can.)

1984
AMERICAN NIGHTMARE(1984)
Misc. Talkies
LIONS FOR BREAKFAST(1977)

Richard Bradley
MY BODYGUARD(1980)

Robin Bradley
SCREAMS OF A WINTER NIGHT(1979)

Samuel Bradley
Misc. Silents
DANGEROUS TOYS(1921), d; SUPREME PASSION, THE(1921), d

Samuel R. Bradley
Misc. Silents
WOMEN MEN LOVE(1921), d; FALSE FRONTS(1922), d

Scott Bradley
COURAGE OF LASSIE(1946), m; KISSING BANDIT, THE(1948), m; YELLOW CAB MAN, THE(1950), m

Stephan Bradley
DISCIPLE OF DEATH(1972, Brit.)

Stephen Bradley
ESCAPE FROM ALCATRAZ(1979)
1984
BEST DEFENSE(1984)

Steve Bradley
GET OUTTA TOWN(1960)

Stewart Bradley
BURGLAR, THE(1956); COOL BREEZE(1972)

Tomi-Lee Bradley
PERFECT COUPLE, A(1979)

Tony Bradley
LITTLE BIG SHOT(1952, Brit.)

Truman Bradley
SPRING MADNESS(1938); VACATION FROM LOVE(1938); YOUNG DR. KILDARE(1938); HARDYS RIDE HIGH, THE(1939); ICE FOLLIES OF 1939(1939); MIRACLES FOR SALE(1939); ON BORROWED TIME(1939); MILLIONAIRES IN PRISON(1940); NIGHT AT EARL CARROLL'S, A(1940); NORTHWEST PASSAGE(1940); WE WHO ARE YOUNG(1940); YESTERDAY'S HEROES(1940); BURMA CONVOY(1941); CHARLIE CHAN IN RIO(1941); DEAD MEN TELL(1941); KEEP 'EM FLYING(1941); LAST OF THE DUANES(1941); MOB TOWN(1941); MURDER AMONG FRIENDS(1941); BOMBAY CLIPPER(1942); LONE STAR RANGER(1942); NIGHT BEFORE THE DIVORCE, THE(1942); TREAT EM' ROUGH(1942); HORN BLOWS AT MIDNIGHT, THE(1945); I WONDER WHO'S KISSING HER NOW(1947); CALL NORTHSIDE 777(1948); SPECIAL AGENT(1949)

Vera Bradley
NIGHT OF MAGIC, A(1944, Brit.)

Virginia Bradley
LIFE OF RILEY, THE(1949)

Wilbert Bradley
SAMSON AND THE SEVEN MIRACLES OF THE WORLD(1963, Fr./Ital.), ch; HERCULES, SAMSON & ULYSSES(1964, Ital.), ch; QUEEN OF THE NILE(1964, Ital.), ch; SANDOKAN THE GREAT(1964, Fr./Ital./Span.); SNOW DEVILS, THE(1965, Ital.)
1984
TEACHERS(1984); WINDY CITY(1984)

Willard King Bradley
Silents
IDLE HANDS(1921), w; WEB OF FATE(1927), w

William Bradley
Misc. Silents
TAME CAT, THE(1921), d

Douglas Bradley-Smith
PROJECT M7(1953, Brit.); SWORD AND THE ROSE, THE(1953); IT'S A WONDERFUL WORLD(1956, Brit.); SHAKEDOWN, THE(1960, Brit.); DR. CRIPPEN(1963, Brit.); NEVER BACK LOSERS(1967, Brit.)

Erich Bradly
THIS STUFF'LL KILL YA!(1971)

Don Bradman
FLYING DOCTOR, THE(1936, Aus.)

Olympe Bradna
COLLEGE HOLIDAY(1936); THREE CHEERS FOR LOVE(1936); LAST TRAIN FROM MADRID, THE(1937); SOULS AT SEA(1937); SAY IT IN FRENCH(1938); STOLEN HEAVEN(1938); NIGHT OF NIGHTS, THE(1939); SOUTH OF PAGO PAGO(1940); HIGHWAY WEST(1941); INTERNATIONAL SQUADRON(1941); KNOCKOUT(1941)

Harold Bradow
STRANGE ILLUSION(1945), cos

Michael Bradsell
WOMEN IN LOVE(1969, Brit.), ed; BOY FRIEND, THE(1971, Brit.), ed; MUSIC LOVERS, THE(1971, Brit.), ed; SAVAGE MESSIAH(1972, Brit.), ed; MAHLER(1974, Brit.), ed; THAT'LL BE THE DAY(1974, Brit.), ed; JABBERWOCKY(1977, Brit.), ed; SWALLOWS AND AMAZONS(1977, Brit.), ed; THAT SUMMER(1979, Brit.), ed; I'M DANCING AS FAST AS I CAN(1982), ed; VENOM(1982, Brit.), ed; LOCAL HERO(1983, Brit.), ed
1984
CAL(1984, Ireland), ed; SCANDALOUS(1984), ed

Mike Bradsell
STARDUST(1974, Brit.), ed; FLAME(1975, Brit.), ed; SCUM(1979, Brit.), ed

Bobbie Bradshaw
Misc. Silents
SCRAGS(1930, Brit.)

Booker Bradshaw
SKULLDUGGERY(1970); STRAWBERRY STATEMENT, THE(1970); COFFY(1973); GALAXY EXPRESS(1982, Jap.)

Carl Bradshaw
HARDER THEY COME, THE(1973, Jamaica); SMILE ORANGE(1976, Jamaican); COUNTRYMAN(1982, Jamaica)

Catherine Bradshaw
NAKED HEART, THE(1955, Brit.)

Charles Bradshaw
TRAIL DUST(1936), m; SULLIVAN'S TRAVELS(1941), m; MIRACLE OF MORGAN'S CREEK, THE(1944), m

David Bradshaw
KITTY AND THE BAGMAN(1983, Aus.); MAN FROM SNOWY RIVER, THE(1983, Aus.)

Dean Bradshaw
FOLLOW ME, BOYS!(1966)

Dorothy Bradshaw
UNDER SUSPICION(1937); DEATH GOES NORTH(1939); SWEETHEARTS OF THE U.S.A.(1944)

Frederick Bradshaw
ALIBI INN(1935, Brit.); BELLES OF ST. CLEMENTS, THE(1936, Brit.); DREAMS COME TRUE(1936, Brit.); HIGHLAND FLING(1936, Brit.); IF I WERE RICH(1936); WHAT A MAN!(1937, Brit.); IDOL OF PARIS(1948, Brit.); MISS PILGRIM'S PROGRESS(1950, Brit.); OVER THE GARDEN WALL(1950, Brit.)

George Bradshaw
NEW FACES OF 1937(1937), w; LADY AND THE MOB, THE(1939), w; SECOND FIDDLE(1939), w; BAD AND THE BEAUTIFUL, THE(1952), w; HOW TO STEAL A MILLION(1966), w

Irene Bradshaw
DR. JEKYLL AND SISTER HYDE(1971, Brit.)

Joan Bradshaw
LOOKING FOR DANGER(1957); SHE DEVIL(1957); YOUNG AND DANGEROUS(1957)

Jon Bradshaw
SHE DANCES ALONE(1981, Aust./U.S.), w

Melanie Bradshaw
1984
HOME FREE ALL(1984)

Terry Bradshaw
HOOPER(1978); SMOKEY AND THE BANDIT II(1980); CANNONBALL RUN, THE(1981)

Charles Bradstreet
LADY IN THE LAKE(1947); ABBOTT AND COSTELLO MEET FRANKENSTEIN(1948); PAROLE, INC.(1949); PAID IN FULL(1950)

Charles Bradswell
PRETTY BOY FLOYD(1960)

Mike Bradwell
BLEAK MOMENTS(1972, Brit.)

Al Brady
Silents
ALL FOR A GIRL(1915)

Alice Brady
BEAUTY FOR SALE(1933); BROADWAY TO HOLLYWOOD(1933); SHOULD LADIES BEHAVE?(1933); STAGE MOTHER(1933); WHEN LADIES MEET(1933); GAY DIVORCEE, THE(1934); MISS FANE'S BABY IS STOLEN(1934); GOLD DIGGERS OF 1935(1935); LADY TUBBS(1935); LET 'EM HAVE IT(1935); METROPOLITAN(1935); GO WEST, YOUNG MAN(1936); HARVESTER, THE(1936); MY MAN GODFREY(1936); CALL IT A DAY(1937); MAMA STEPS OUT(1937); MERRY-GO-ROUND OF 1938(1937); MIND YOUR OWN BUSINESS(1937); MR. DODD TAKES THE AIR(1937); THREE SMART GIRLS(1937); 100 MEN AND A GIRL(1937); GOODBYE BROADWAY(1938); IN OLD CHICAGO(1938); JOY OF LIVING(1938); YOUNG MR. LINCOLN(1939); ZENOBIA(1939)
Silents
AS YE SOW(1914); BALLET GIRL, THE(1916); GILDED CAGE, THE(1916); TANGLED FATES(1916); DANCER'S PERIL, THE(1917); DIVORCE GAME, THE(1917); HER GREAT CHANCE(1918); KNIFE, THE(1918); NEW YORK IDEA, THE(1920); DAWN OF THE EAST(1921); HUSH MONEY(1921); ANNA ASCENDS(1922); MISSING MILLIONS(1922)
Misc. Silents
BOSS, THE(1915); BOUGHT AND PAID FOR(1916); LA VIE DE BOHEME(1916); MISS PETTICOATS(1916); THEN I'LL COME BACK TO YOU(1916); WOMAN IN 47, THE(1916); BETSY ROSS(1917); DARKEST RUSSIA(1917); HER SILENT SACRIFICE(1917); HUNGRY HEART, A(1917); MAID OF BELGIUM, THE(1917); MATERNITY(1917); SELF MADE WIDOW(1917); WOMAN ALONE, A(1917); AT THE MERCY OF MEN(1918); BETTER HALF, THE(1918); DEATH DANCE, THE(1918); IN THE HOLLOW OF HER HAND(1918); ORDEAL OF ROSETTA, THE(1918); SPURS OF SYBIL, THE(1918); TRAP, THE(1918); WHIRLPOOL, THE(1918); WOMAN AND WIFE(1918); HIS BRIDAL NIGHT(1919); INDESTRUCTIBLE WIFE, THE(1919); MARIE, LTD.(1919); REDHEAD(1919); WORLD TO LIVE IN, THE(1919); DARK LANTERN, A(1920); FEAR MARKET, THE(1920); SINNERS(1920); LAND OF HOPE, THE(1921); LITTLE ITALY(1921); OUT OF THE CHORUS(1921); LEOPARDESS, THE(1923); SNOW BRIDE, THE(1923)

Ann Brady
TIMES SQUARE(1929)

Bernadette Brady
WHERE'S JACK?(1969, Brit.)
1984
HARDBODIES(1984), cos

Bob Brady
OKAY BILL(1971); SUPERFLY(1972), ed; SUPERFLY T.N.T.(1973), ed; SHOOT IT: BLACK, SHOOT IT: BLUE(1974), ed; LIQUID SKY(1982)

Brandon Brady
MYSTERY SUBMARINE(1963, Brit.); DOUBLE MAN, THE(1967)

Buff Brady
RODEO KING AND THE SENORITA(1951); BIG COUNTRY, THE(1958); SPARTACUS(1960); RARE BREED, THE(1966); BLACK OAK CONSPIRACY(1977)

Connie Brady
Misc. Talkies
BRANCHES(1971)
Cyrus Townsend Brady
Silents
HEARTS ADRIFT(1914), w; LITTLE ANGEL OF CANYON CREEK, THE(1914), w; RING AND THE MAN, THE(1914), w; ISLAND OF REGENERATION, THE(1915), w; BY THE WORLD FORGOT(1918), w
Don Brady
TALES OF MANHATTAN(1942)
Dorothy Brady
DOWN TO EARTH(1947)
Ed Brady
DELIGHTFUL HOGUE(1929); TRESPASSER, THE(1929); VIRGINIAN, THE(1929); CITY GIRL(1930); MADONNA OF THE STREETS(1930); DESERT VENGEANCE(1931); OKLAHOMA JIM(1931); SQUAW MAN, THE(1931); TEXAS RANGER, THE(1931); HAT CHECK GIRL(1932); MADAME RACKETEER(1932); NIGHT CLUB LADY(1932); WITHOUT HONORS(1932); GALLOPING ROMEO(1933); LONE AVENGER, THE(1933); RANGER'S CODE, THE(1933); SON OF KONG(1933); SUNDOWN RIDER, THE(1933); TILLIE AND GUS(1933); RED HEAD(1934); IT'S A SMALL WORLD(1935); NAUGHTY MARIETTA(1935); FORBIDDEN TRAIL(1936); RIDERS OF THE DAWN(1937); IN OLD CHICAGO(1938); MYSTERIOUS RIDER, THE(1938); THUNDER IN THE DESERT(1938); MESQUITE BUCKAROO(1939); NORTH OF THE YUKON(1939); OKLAHOMA KID, THE(1939); SAGA OF DEATH VALLEY(1939); STAGECOACH(1939); HOUSE OF THE SEVEN GABLES, THE(1940); SAPS AT SEA(1940); SHOOTING HIGH(1940); WHEN THE DALTONS RODE(1940); FUGITIVE VALLEY(1941); HONKY TONK(1941); SIGN OF THE WOLF(1941); WYOMING WILDCAT(1941); IN OLD CALIFORNIA(1942); VALLEY OF THE SUN(1942); OUTLAW, THE(1943)
Misc. Talkies
NEVADA BUCKAROO, THE(1931); LAW OF THE WEST(1932)
Silents
SPINDLE OF LIFE, THE(1917); IF YOU BELIEVE IT, IT'S SO(1922); QUESTION OF HONOR, A(1922); CLANCY'S KOSHER WEDDING(1927); KING OF KINGS, THE(1927); HAROLD TEEN(1928); NOOSE, THE(1928)
Misc. Silents
LEARNIN' OF JIM BENTON, THE(1917); BEYOND THE SHADOWS(1918); DEUCE DUNCAN(1918); GUN WOMAN, THE(1918); WILD LIFE(1918); CHILD OF THE PRAIRIE, A(1925); CODE OF THE SCARLET, THE(1928)
Ed J. Brady
CAPTAIN IS A LADY, THE(1940)
Silents
ALMOST A HUSBAND(1919)
Edward Brady
THEIR BIG MOMENT(1934); VIRGIN WITCH, THE(1973, Brit.), p
Silents
PRIDE OF PALOMAR, THE(1922); TO THE LAST MAN(1923); DO YOUR DUTY(1928)
Misc. Silents
DOUBLE-ROOM MYSTERY, THE(1917); HIGH SIGN, THE(1917); HOOF MARKS(1927)
Edward J. Brady
Silents
OVER THE BORDER(1922); SIREN CALL, THE(1922); ETERNAL STRUGGLE, THE(1923)
Misc. Silents
SPELLBOUND(1916); DEVIL'S BAIT, THE(1917); STOLEN PLAY, THE(1917)
Edwin Brady
KLONDIKE ANNIE(1936); SOUTHWARD HO!(1939)
Misc. Silents
WHO KILLED WALTON?(1918)
Edwin J. Brady
TEXAN, THE(1930); CONQUERING HORDE, THE(1931); SHANGHAIED LOVE(1931); DEADLINE, THE(1932); UNDER THE TONTO RIM(1933); TREASURE ISLAND(1934); FURY(1936); FOREST RANGERS, THE(1942)
Silents
SILENT CALL, THE(1921); RACING HEARTS(1923); FIGHTING AMERICAN, THE(1924); ROSE OF PARIS, THE(1924)
Misc. Silents
WILD SUMAC(1917); ROUGH DIAMOND, THE(1921); TRAIL OF THE LONESOME, THE(1923)
Edwin John Brady
TEXANS, THE(1938)
Francis J. Brady
REQUIEM FOR A HEAVYWEIGHT(1962), set d
Fred Brady
STAGE DOOR CANTEEN(1943); SWING SHIFT MAISIE(1943); 3 IS A FAMILY(1944); DANCING IN MANHATTAN(1945); CAT CREEPS, THE(1946); LITTLE MISS BIG(1946); MEET ME ON BROADWAY(1946); SLIGHTLY SCANDALOUS(1946); CHAMPAGNE FOR CAESAR(1950), w; MRS. O'MALLEY AND MR. MALONE(1950); HOLLYWOOD STORY(1951), w; NEVER WAVE AT A WAC(1952), w; TAXI(1953), w
Gary Brady
WILD REBELS, THE(1967)
George Brady
CRISIS(1950)
Gloria Brady
BLOOD WATERS OF DOCTOR Z(1982)
H.G. Brady
RAMPARTS WE WATCH, THE(1940)
Jack Brady
INCREDIBLY STRANGE CREATURES WHO STOPPED LIVING AND BECAME CRAZY MIXED-UP ZOMBIES, THE(1965)
Jasper Ewing Brady
Silents
TANGLE, THE(1914), w; DIVORCE TRAP, THE(1919), w
Jerry Brady
BALTIMORE BULLET, THE(1980), ed

John Brady
MAN AT LARGE(1941), ed; CASTLE IN THE DESERT(1942), ed
Joseph Brady
FATHER CAME TOO(1964, Brit.)
June Brady
ON STAGE EVERYBODY(1945)
Leo Brady
EDGE OF DOOM(1950), w
Leslie Brady
BLACK LIMELIGHT(1938, Brit.)
Lisa Brady
SPRING FEVER(1983, Can.)
Marie E. Brady
DREAMER(1979)
Martin Brady
SHELL SHOCK(1964)
Mary Brady
JOURNEY TO THE CENTER OF THE EARTH(1959)
Mike Brady
CLUB, THE(1980, Aus.), m
Nicholas Brady
YESTERDAY'S ENEMY(1959, Brit.); JOHN PAUL JONES(1959)
Nick Brady
SHERIFF OF FRACTURED JAW, THE(1958, Brit.)
Pat Brady
SOUTH OF ARIZONA(1938); WEST OF CHEYENNE(1938); MAN FROM SUNDOWN, THE(1939); RIO GRANDE(1939); DURANGO KID, THE(1940); TEXAS STAGECOACH(1940); THUNDERING FRONTIER(1940); TWO-FISTED RANGERS(1940); OUTLAWS OF THE PANHANDLE(1941); PINTO KID, THE(1941); RED RIVER VALLEY(1941); MAN FROM CHEYENNE(1942); ROMANCE ON THE RANGE(1942); SUNSET ON THE DESERT(1942); MAN FROM MUSIC MOUNTAIN(1943); SILVER SPURS(1943); SONG OF TEXAS(1943); DOWN DAKOTA WAY(1949); GOLDEN STALLION, THE(1949); BELLS OF CORONADO(1950); TRIGGER, JR.(1950); TWILIGHT IN THE SIERRAS(1950); SOUTH OF CALIENTE(1951)
Patrick Brady
STAYING ALIVE(1983)
Patti Brady
NEVER SAY GOODBYE(1946); KING OF THE WILD HORSES(1947); STALLION ROAD(1947); LETTER TO THREE WIVES, A(1948); STATE OF THE UNION(1948); ADVENTURE IN BALTIMORE(1949); CORKY OF GASOLINE ALLEY(1951); GASOLINE ALLEY(1951)
Phil Brady
RUNAWAY BRIDE(1930)
Randall Brady
SKATETOWN, U.S.A.(1979)
Ruth Brady
THEY CAME TO BLOW UP AMERICA(1943); MRS. PARKINGTON(1944); CLOCK, THE(1945); HARVEY GIRLS, THE(1946); LITTLE MISTER JIM(1946); SECRET HEART, THE(1946); ARNELO AFFAIR, THE(1947); HIGH BARBAREE(1947); UNFINISHED DANCE,THE(1947); STRANGE MRS. CRANE, THE(1948); SUMMER HOLIDAY(1948); CAUGHT(1949); MILKMAN, THE(1950); TRUE AND THE FALSE, THE(1955, Swed.); FOREVER DARLING(1956)
Ruthe Brady
JANE EYRE(1944)
Scott Brady
$(DOLLARS) (1971); CANON CITY(1948); HE WALKED BY NIGHT(1948); IN THIS CORNER(1948); GAL WHO TOOK THE WEST, THE(1949); PORT OF NEW YORK(1949); UNDERTOW(1949); I WAS A SHOPLIFTER(1950); KANSAS RAIDERS(1950); UNDERCOVER GIRL(1950); MODEL AND THE MARRIAGE BROKER, THE(1951); BLOODHOUNDS OF BROADWAY(1952); BRONCO BUSTER(1952); MONTANA BELLE(1952); UNTAMED FRONTIER(1952); YANKEE BUCCANEER(1952); PERILOUS JOURNEY, A(1953); WHITE FIRE(1953, Brit.); EL ALAMEIN(1954); JOHNNY GUITAR(1954); LAW VS. BILLY THE KID, THE(1954); GENTLEMEN MARRY BRUNETTES(1955); THEY WERE SO YOUNG(1955); VANISHING AMERICAN, THE(1955); MAVERICK QUEEN, THE(1956); MOHAWK(1956); TERROR AT MIDNIGHT(1956); RESTLESS BREED, THE(1957); STORM RIDER, THE(1957); AMBUSH AT CIMARRON PASS(1958); BLOOD ARROW(1958); OPERATION BIKINI(1963); JOHN GOLDFARB, PLEASE COME HOME(1964); STAGE TO THUNDER ROCK(1964); BLACK SPURS(1965); DESTINATION INNER SPACE(1966); CASTLE OF EVIL(1967); FORT UTAH(1967); JOURNEY TO THE CENTER OF TIME(1967); RED TOMAHAWK(1967); ARIZONA BUSHWHACKERS(1968); ROAD HUSTLERS, THE(1968); THEY RAN FOR THEIR LIVES(1968); CAIN'S WAY(1969); CYCLE SAVAGES(1969); GUN RIDERS, THE(1969); ICE HOUSE, THE(1969); MAROONED(1969); MIGHTY GORGA, THE(1969); NIGHTMARE IN WAX(1969); SATAN'S SADISTS(1969); HELL'S BLOODY DEVILS(1970); DOCTORS' WIVES(1971); LONERS, THE(1972); WICKED, WICKED(1973); CHINA SYNDROME, THE(1979); DEAD KIDS(1981 Aus./New Zealand)
1984
GREMLINS(1984)
Misc. Talkies
NIGHTMARE BLOOD BATH(1971); LEO CHRONICLES, THE(1972); BONNIE'S KIDS(1973)
Sue Brady
LIBIDO(1973, Aus.)
Terence Brady
FORT APACHE, THE BRONX(1981)
Tete Brady
RIDERS OF THE CACTUS(1931)
Veronica Brady
LOVE, LIFE AND LAUGHTER(1934, Brit.); PRIVATE LIFE OF DON JUAN, THE(1934, Brit.); WHAT HAPPENED TO HARKNESS(1934, Brit.); BIRDS OF A FEATHER(1935, Brit.)
Vincent Brady
LAST MILE, THE(1959), spec eff
W.J. Brady
Misc. Silents
ACCOMPLICE, THE(1917)

William Brady
NEW FACES OF 1937(1937); EARL OF PUDDLESTONE(1940)
Silents
BALLET GIRL, THE(1916), p
Eric Braeden
ESCAPE FROM THE PLANET OF THE APES(1971); ULTIMATE THRILL, THE(1974); HERBIE GOES TO MONTE CARLO(1977)
Misc. Talkies
ADULTERESS, THE(1976)
Eric [Hans Gudegast] Braeden
LADY ICE(1973)
Angela Braemar
IT'S A WONDERFUL WORLD(1956, Brit.)
Paula Braend
PHONY AMERICAN, THE(1964, Ger.); SERPENT'S EGG, THE(1977, Ger./U.S.)
Ian Braested
MEN OF STEEL(1932, Brit.)
Karen Braga
TAPS(1981)
Sonia Braga
DONA FLOR AND HER TWO HUSBANDS(1977, Braz.)
1984
GABRIELA(1984, Braz.)
A. Bragadin
HELL RAIDERS OF THE DEEP(1954, Ital.), w
Marc Antonio Bragadin
GREAT HOPE, THE(1954, Ital.), w
Anna Bragaglia
LUCIANO(1963, Ital.)
Arturo Bragaglia
MIRACLE IN MILAN(1951, Ital.); BELLISSIMA(1952, Ital.); PRISONER OF THE VOLGA(1960, Fr./Ital.); MOST WANTED MAN, THE(1962, Fr./Ital.)
Carlo Bragaglia
ONE NIGHT WITH YOU(1948, Brit), w
Carlo L. Bragaglia
MY WIDOW AND I(1950, Ital.), d
Carlo Ludovicio Bragaglia
MIGHTY CRUSADERS, THE(1961, Ital.), d
Carlo Ludovico Bragaglia
QUEEN OF BABYLON, THE(1956, Ital.), d, w
Ludovico Bragaglia
HANNIBAL(1960, Ital.), d
Carlo Ludnico Bragalia
LOVES OF HERCULES, THE(1960), d
Cliff Bragdon
SAINT IN NEW YORK, THE(1938); FATHER TAKES A WIFE(1941)
Helen Bragdon
WHERE THE LILIES BLOOM(1974)
Melvyn Bragg
ISADORA(1968, Brit.), w; PLAY DIRTY(1969, Brit.), w; MUSIC LOVERS, THE(1971, Brit.), w; JESUS CHRIST, SUPERSTAR(1973), w
Suzanne Bragg
WILD SCENE, THE(1970)
Herbert Braggioti
FLYING HIGH(1931)
Francesca Braggiotti
DEFEAT OF HANNIBAL, THE(1937, Ital.)
Herbert Braggiotti
WHAT A WIDOW(1930)
Krystina Bragiel
VILLAGE, THE(1953, Brit./Switz.)
Emil Veniaminovich Braginskiy
UNCOMMON THIEF, AN(1967, USSR), w
Ace Bragunier
ONCE UPON A HONEYMOON(1942)
Herb Braha
OLIVER'S STORY(1978); HOWLING, THE(1981); BEACH GIRLS(1982); SOME KIND OF HERO(1982)
Herbie Braha
ROCK 'N' ROLL HIGH SCHOOL(1979)
Hal Braham
TRAMP, TRAMP, TRAMP(1942), w
Lionel Braham
PERSONAL PROPERTY(1937); PRINCE AND THE PAUPER, THE(1937); WEE WILLIE WINKIE(1937); CHRISTMAS CAROL, A(1938); LITTLE PRINCESS, THE(1939); SONG OF BERNADETTE, THE(1943); ONCE UPON A TIME(1944); MACBETH(1948)
Silents
DON JUAN(1926); SKINNER'S DRESS SUIT(1926); NIGHT LIFE(1927); OUT ALL NIGHT(1927)
Misc. Silents
SNOW WHITE(1917)
Johannes Brahams
LOVERS, THE(1959, Fr.), m
Mahjoub Ben Brahim
SAADIA(1953)
Himmoud Brahimi
DAUGHTER OF THE SANDS(1952, Fr.)
Hans [John] Brahm
SCROOGE(1935, Brit.), ed, p
Hans Brahm
BROKEN BLOSSOMS(1936, Brit.), d
John Brahm
COUNSEL FOR CRIME(1937), d; GIRLS' SCHOOL(1938), d; PENITENTIARY(1938), d; LET US LIVE(1939), d; RIO(1939), d; ESCAPE TO GLORY(1940), d; WILD GEESE CALLING(1941), d; UNDYING MONSTER, THE(1942), d; TONIGHT WE RAID CALAIS(1943), d; WINTERTIME(1943), d; GUEST IN THE HOUSE(1944), d; LODGER, THE(1944), d; HANGOVER SQUARE(1945), d; LOCKET, THE(1946), d; BRASHER DOUBLOON, THE(1947), d; SINGAPORE(1947), d; FACE TO FACE(1952), d; MIRACLE OF OUR LADY OF FATIMA, THE(1952), d; THIEF OF VENICE,

THE(1952), d; DIAMOND QUEEN, THE(1953), d; MAD MAGICIAN, THE(1954), d; BENGAZI(1955), d; SPECIAL DELIVERY(1955, Ger.), d; GOLDEN PLAGUE, THE(1963, Ger.), d; HOT RODS TO HELL(1967), d
Brahms
PEOPLE WILL TALK(1951), m
Caryl Brahms
GIVE US THE MOON(1944, Brit.), w; GHOSTS OF BERKELEY SQUARE(1947, Brit.), w; ONE NIGHT WITH YOU(1948, Brit), w; GAY LADY, THE(1949, Brit.), w; GIRL STROKE BOY(1971, Brit.), w
Johannes Brahms
SONG OF LOVE(1947), m; PEOPLE WILL TALK(1951), m; TWICE UPON A TIME(1953, Brit.), m; INTERLUDE(1957), m; RIVERRUN(1968), m; 24 HOURS IN A WOMAN'S LIFE(1968, Fr./Ger.), m
Penny Brahms
WRONG BOX, THE(1966, Brit.); HAMMERHEAD(1968); 2001: A SPACE ODYSSEY(1968, U.S./Brit.); PRIVATE LIFE OF SHERLOCK HOLMES, THE(1970, Brit.); GAMES THAT LOVERS PLAY(1971, Brit.)
Misc. Talkies
SHE'LL FOLLOW YOU ANYWHERE(1971); LADY CHATTERLY VS. FANNY HILL(1980)
Eric Braiden
MORITURI(1965)
Thomas A. Braiden
LLOYDS OF LONDON(1936)
Rina Braido
BARABBAS(1962, Ital.)
Thomas A. Braidon
SYLVIA SCARLETT(1936)
Thomas Braidon
DESIGN FOR LIVING(1933); BRITISH AGENT(1934); GIRL WITH IDEAS, A(1937); LAST OF MRS. CHEYNEY, THE(1937); MARIE ANTOINETTE(1938)
Misc. Silents
GREAT ADVENTURE, THE(1921)
Frank Braidwood
Misc. Silents
SMART SEX, THE(1921); MAN WHO WAITED, THE(1922)
Jill Braidwood
BELLES OF ST. TRINIAN'S, THE(1954, Brit.)
Tom Braidwood
DESERTERS(1983, Can.), p
Mark Brailsford
1984
KIPPERBANG(1984, Brit.)
Jonas Braimer
MAN COULD GET KILLED, A(1966)
Dave Brain
MOUSE AND HIS CHILD, THE(1977), anim
Karl Brainard
HOODLUM PRIEST, THE(1961), set d; DIME WITH A HALO(1963), set d
Wendy Brainard
1984
BLAME IT ON THE NIGHT(1984)
John Braine
ROOM AT THE TOP(1959, Brit.), w; LIFE AT THE TOP(1965, Brit.), w; MAN AT THE TOP(1973, Brit.), w
Danny Brainin
XTRO(1983, Brit.); YENTL(1983)
Ives Brainville
PARIS HOLIDAY(1958)
Yves Brainville
MAN WHO KNEW TOO MUCH, THE(1956); MOUNTAIN, THE(1956); DIARY OF A BAD GIRL(1958, Fr.); CRACK IN THE MIRROR(1960); FIVE MILES TO MIDNIGHT(1963, U.S./Fr./Ital.); SKY ABOVE HEAVEN(1964, Fr./Ital.); NIGHT OF THE GENERALS, THE(1967, Brit./Fr.); SICILIAN CLAN, THE(1970, Fr.); LOVE AND DEATH(1975); CHANEL SOLITAIRE(1981)
Michael Braisford
OUTSIDER, THE(1949, Brit.)
John Braislin
KENTUCKY JUBILEE(1951)
Carla Brait
TORSO(1974, Ital.)
B. Braithwaite
WOLF DOG(1958, Can.)
E.R. Braithwaite
TO SIR, WITH LOVE(1967, Brit.), p,d&w
Lilian Braithwaite
CARNIVAL(1931, Brit.); MAN OF MAYFAIR(1931, Brit.); CHINESE PUZZLE, THE(1932, Brit.); MAN ABOUT THE HOUSE, A(1947, Brit.)
Silents
MOTHERHOOD(1915, Brit.); GAY LORD QUEX, THE(1917, Brit.); GENERAL POST(1920, Brit.)
Misc. Silents
WORLD'S DESIRE, THE(1915, Brit.); DOMBEY AND SON(1917, Brit.); JUSTICE(1917, Brit.); WOMAN WHO WAS NOTHING, THE(1917, Brit.); BECAUSE(1918, Brit.); CHINESE PUZZLE, THE(1919, Brit.); CASTLES IN SPAIN(1920, Brit.)
Lillian Braithwaite
Silents
WHEN BOYS LEAVE HOME(1928, Brit.)
Max Braithwaite
WHY SHOOT THE TEACHER(1977, Can.), w
Nicola Braithwaite
STOLEN AIRLINER, THE(1962, Brit.)
David Brake
TWO-LANE BLACKTOP(1971)
Patricia Brake
MY LOVER, MY SON(1970, Brit.); OPTIMISTS, THE(1973, Brit.)
Anndorthe Braker
EFFI BRIEST(1974, Ger.)

Barbara Brand
SEVENTH JUROR, THE(1964, Fr.)
Bill Brand
SWING TIME(1936)
Chris Brand
WEDDING, A(1978)
Christianna Brand
GREEN FOR DANGER(1946, Brit.), w; MARK OF CAIN, THE(1948, Brit.), w; SECRET PEOPLE(1952, Brit.), w
Christopher Brand
VOYAGE TO THE PREHISTORIC PLANET(1965)
Cliff Brand
PONY EXPRESS RIDER(1976)
David Brand
WEDDING, A(1978); FRIDAY THE 13TH PART II(1981)
Frank Brand
SECRETS OF SCOTLAND YARD(1944)
George Brand
MYSTERY STREET(1950); MILLION DOLLAR PURSUIT(1951); GIRL WHO HAD EVERYTHING, THE(1953); DESIREE(1954); CHICAGO SYNDICATE(1955); FIVE AGAINST THE HOUSE(1955); RAINS OF RANCHIPUR, THE(1955); TEXAS LADY(1955); FIRST TRAVELING SALESLADY, THE(1956); FRONTIER GUN(1958); ISLAND OF LOST WOMEN(1959)
Harry Brand
MAKING THE GRADE(1929), w
Silents
COLLEGE(1927), sup; MASKED EMOTIONS(1929), w
James Brand
NOTORIOUS CLEOPATRA, THE(1970)
Jenny Brand
WEDDING, A(1978)
Jerome R. Brand
SLENDER THREAD, THE(1965)
Joline Brand
GIANT FROM THE UNKNOWN(1958)
Max Brand
CAVALIER, THE(1928), w; FAIR WARNING(1931), w; HOLY TERROR, A(1931), w; DESTRY RIDES AGAIN(1932), w; INTERNES CAN'T TAKE MONEY(1937), w; YOUNG DR. KILDARE(1938), w; CALLING DR. KILDARE(1939), w; DESTRY RIDES AGAIN(1939), w; SECRET OF DR. KILDARE, THE(1939), w; DR. KILDARE GOES HOME(1940), w; DR. KILDARE'S CRISIS(1940), w; DR. KILDARE'S STRANGE CASE(1940), w; DR. KILDARE'S VICTORY(1941), w; DR. KILDARE'S WEDDING DAY(1941), w; PEOPLE VS. DR. KILDARE, THE(1941), w; CALLING DR. GILLESPIE(1942), w; DR. GILLESPIE'S NEW ASSISTANT(1942), w; POWDER TOWN(1942), w; DESPERADOES, THE(1943), w; DR. GILLESPIE'S CRIMINAL CASE(1943), w; THREE MEN IN WHITE(1944), w; UNCERTAIN GLORY(1944), w; RAINBOW OVER TEXAS(1946), w; SINGING GUNS(1950), w; MY BROTHER, THE OUTLAW(1951), w; DESTRY(1954), w
Silents
ADOPTED SON, THE(1917), w; CHILDREN OF THE NIGHT(1921), w; NIGHT HORSEMAN, THE(1921), w; SHAME(1921), w; JUST TONY(1922), w; AGAINST ALL ODDS(1924), w; CHAMPION OF LOST CAUSES(1925), w
Mike Brand
TEXAS TORNADO(1934)
Millen Brand
SNAKE PIT, THE(1948), w
Neville Brand
PORT OF NEW YORK(1949); D.O.A.(1950); KISS TOMORROW GOODBYE(1950); WHERE THE SIDEWALK ENDS(1950); FLAME OF ARABY(1951); HALLS OF MONTEZUMA(1951); MOB, THE(1951); ONLY THE VALIANT(1951); RED MOUNTAIN(1951); KANSAS CITY CONFIDENTIAL(1952); TURNING POINT, THE(1952); CHARGE AT FEATHER RIVER(1953); GUN FURY(1953); MAN CRAZY(1953); MAN FROM THE ALAMO, THE(1953); STALAG 17(1953); LONE GUN, THE(1954); PRINCE VALIANT(1954); RETURN FROM THE SEA(1954); RIOT IN CELL BLOCK 11(1954); BOBBY WARE IS MISSING(1955); PRODIGAL, THE(1955); RETURN OF JACK SLADE, THE(1955); FURY AT GUNSIGHT PASS(1956); GUN BROTHERS(1956); LOVE ME TENDER(1956); MOHAWK(1956); RAW EDGE(1956); THREE OUTLAWS, THE(1956); LONELY MAN, THE(1957); TIN STAR, THE(1957); WAY TO THE GOLD, THE(1957); BADMAN'S COUNTRY(1958); CRY TERROR(1958); FIVE GATES TO HELL(1959); ADVENTURES OF HUCKLEBERRY FINN, THE(1960); GEORGE RAFT STORY, THE(1961); LAST SUNSET, THE(1961); BIRDMAN OF ALCATRAZ(1962); HERO'S ISLAND(1962); SCARFACE MOB, THE(1962); THAT DARN CAT(1965); THREE GUNS FOR TEXAS(1968); BACKTRACK(1969); DESPERADOS, THE(1969); TORA! TORA! TORA!(1970, U.S./Jap.); CAHILL, UNITED STATES MARSHAL(1973); DEADLY TRACKERS(1973); MAD BOMBER, THE(1973); SCALAWAG(1973, Yugo.); THIS IS A HIJACK(1973); PSYCHIC KILLER(1975); EATEN ALIVE(1976); MOUSE AND HIS CHILD, THE(1977); FIVE DAYS FROM HOME(1978); HI-RIDERS(1978); ANGELS BRIGADE(1980); NINTH CONFIGURATION, THE(1980); RETURN, THE(1980); WITHOUT WARNING(1980)
Misc. Talkies
EVILS OF THE NIGHT(1983)
Nils Brand
FANNY AND ALEXANDER(1983, Swed./Fr./Ger.)
Oscar Brand
ONCE UPON A COFFEE HOUSE(1965)
Peter Brand
NO TIME FOR FLOWERS(1952)
Roland Brand
CAMPBELL'S KINGDOM(1957, Brit.); LONG HAUL, THE(1957, Brit.); WEAPON, THE(1957, Brit.); TIME LOCK(1959, Brit.); CIRCLE OF DECEPTON(1961, Brit.); LOLITA(1962); FEAR IS THE KEY(1973)
Ronald Brand
THEM NICE AMERICANS(1958, Brit.)
Rowland Brand
FIRST MAN INTO SPACE(1959, Brit.)
Richard Branda
TWO-MINUTE WARNING(1976)

Rick Branda
LILITH(1964)
Klaus Maria Brandauer
MEPHISTO(1981, Ger.); NEVER SAY NEVER AGAIN(1983)
Klaus-Maria Brandauer
SALZBURG CONNECTION, THE(1972)
Dorothea Brande
WAKE UP AND LIVE(1937), w
Ruth Brande
LADY CONFESSES, THE(1945); STRANGER IN HOLLYWOOD(1968), art d
Tony Brande
LET'S ROCK(1958); SAM'S SONG(1971); PORTNOY'S COMPLAINT(1972); AUDREY ROSE(1977); CAR, THE(1977); THEY CALL ME BRUCE(1982)
Alaine Brandeis
HOLD THAT WOMAN(1940); ZIEGFELD GIRL(1941)
Marc Brandel
CAPTIVE CITY, THE(1963, Ital.), w; CONQUERED CITY(1966, Ital.), w; DOUBLE TROUBLE(1967), w; HAND, THE(1981), w
Michael Branden
MISSING CORPSE, THE(1945); ACCOMPLICE(1946); AFFAIRS OF GERALDINE(1946); OUT OF THE PAST(1947); ROBIN OF TEXAS(1947); WEB OF DANGER, THE(1947); MOONRISE(1948); GUNFIGHTER, THE(1950); SUNSET BOULEVARD(1950)
Chet Brandenberg
PACK UP YOUR TROUBLES(1932); SONS OF THE DESERT(1933); DESERT HAWK, THE(1950); LOVE ME OR LEAVE ME(1955)
Ed Brandenberg
OUR RELATIONS(1936); LONE WOLF SPY HUNT, THE(1939)
Chet Brandenburg
HITLER'S MADMAN(1943); WING AND A PRAYER(1944); VICKI(1953)
Ed Brandenburg
SWISS MISS(1938)
Larry Brandenburg
1984
GRANDVIEW, U.S.A.(1984)
Rosemary Brandenburg
1984
THEY'RE PLAYING WITH FIRE(1984), art d
Arthur Brander
LIEUTENANT DARING, RN(1935, Brit.); DREAMS COME TRUE(1936, Brit.); FULL SPEED AHEAD(1936, Brit.); LIMPING MAN, THE(1936, Brit.); KATE PLUS TEN(1938, Brit.); NICHOLAS NICKLEBY(1947, Brit.); NIGHT COMES TOO SOON(1948, Brit.); VENGEANCE IS MINE(1948, Brit.); ADVENTURES OF PC 49, THE(1949, Brit.); SWORD AND THE ROSE, THE(1955, Brit.); LADY GODIVA RIDES AGAIN(1955, Brit.); MY SON, THE VAMPIRE(1963, Brit.)
Richard Brander
HELL'S BLOODY DEVILS(1970)
Alaine Brandes
LONE RIDER IN GHOST TOWN, THE(1941); LOUISIANA PURCHASE(1941); ARABIAN NIGHTS(1942); FLEET'S IN, THE(1942)
Elliott Brandes
COMMITMENT, THE(1976), p
Janet Brandes
GIRL WITH A PISTOL, THE(1968, Ital.)
Werner Brandes
INFORMER, THE(1929, Brit.), ph; TESHA(1929, Brit.), ph; LOVE WALTZ, THE(1930, Ger.), ph; TEMPORARY WIDOW, THE(1930, Ger./Brit.), ph; "W" PLAN, THE(1931, Brit.), ph; BLONDE NIGHTINGALE(1931, Ger.), ph; EMIL AND THE DETECTIVE(1931, Ger.), ph; PICCADILLY(1932, Brit.), ph
Wulf Gunther Brandes
MARCH ON PARIS 1914–OF GENERALOBERST ALEXANDER VON KLUCK–AND HIS MEMORY OF JESSIE HOLLADAY(1977)
Alicia Brandet
CHRISTINE KEELER AFFAIR, THE(1964, Brit.); WEEKEND, ITALIAN STYLE(1967, Fr./Ital./Span.)
Walter Brandi
VAMPIRE AND THE BALLERINA, THE(1962, Ital.); PLAYGIRLS AND THE VAMPIRE(1964, Ital.); CURSE OF THE BLOOD GHOULS(1969, Ital.)
Bob Brandin
ST. VALENTINE'S DAY MASSACRE, THE(1967)
Gilbert Brandini
STATE OF SIEGE(1973, Fr./U.S./Ital./Ger.)
Mrs. O Brandini
Silents
QUO VADIS?(1913, Ital.)
Helmut Brandis
EIGHT GIRLS IN A BOAT(1932, Ger.), w; EIGHT GIRLS IN A BOAT(1934), w
Patricia Brandkamp
1984
SOLDIER'S STORY, A(1984)
Candyce Jane Brandl
OPTIMISTS, THE(1973, Brit.)
Majo Brandley
TEMPTATION(1962, Fr.), cos
Gary Brandner
HOWLING, THE(1981), w
Uwe Brandner
I LOVE YOU, I KILL YOU(1972, Ger.), p,d,&w, m
Jocelyn Brando
BIG HEAT, THE(1953); CHINA VENTURE(1953); TEN WANTED MEN(1955); NIGHTFALL(1956); STEP DOWN TO TERROR(1958); EXPLOSIVE GENERATION, THE(1961); UGLY AMERICAN, THE(1963); BUS RILEY'S BACK IN TOWN(1965); CHASE, THE(1966); MOVIE MOVIE(1978); GOOD LUCK, MISS WYCKOFF(1979); WHY WOULD I LIE(1980); MOMMIE DEAREST(1981)
Kevin Brando
SATURDAY THE 14TH(1981); UNCOMMON VALOR(1983)
Marlon Brando
MEN, THE(1950); STREETCAR NAMED DESIRE, A(1951); VIVA ZAPATA!(1952); JULIUS CAESAR(1953); WILD ONE, THE(1953); DESIREE(1954); ON THE WATERFRONT(1954); GUYS AND DOLLS(1955); TEAHOUSE OF THE AUGUST MOON,

THE(1956); SAYONARA(1957); YOUNG LIONS, THE(1958); FUGITIVE KIND, THE(1960); ONE-EYED JACKS(1961), a, d; MUTINY ON THE BOUNTY(1962); UGLY AMERICAN, THE(1963); BEDTIME STORY(1964); MORITURI(1965); APPALOOSA, THE(1966); CHASE, THE(1966); COUNTESS FROM HONG KONG, A(1967, Brit.); REFLECTIONS IN A GOLDEN EYE(1967); CANDY(1968, Ital./Fr.); NIGHT OF THE FOLLOWING DAY, THE(1969, Brit.); BURN(1970); NIGHT COMERS, THE(1971, Brit.); GODFATHER, THE(1972); MISSOURI BREAKS, THE(1976); SUPERMAN(1978); APOCALYPSE NOW(1979); FORMULA, THE(1980)

Richard Brando
STUDENT BODIES(1981)

Thom Brandolino
ON THE RIGHT TRACK(1981)

Beverly Brandon
DISTANT DRUMS(1951)

Bill Brandon
I AM A CAMERA(1955, Brit.); CROOKED SKY, THE(1957, Brit.)

Bob Brandon
STALLION CANYON(1949)

Casey Brandon
POINT BLANK(1967)

Catherine Brandon
PERSECUTION(1974, Brit.)

Clark Brandon
SERIAL(1980); MY TUTOR(1983)

Curt Brandon
SEMINOLE UPRISING(1955), w

David Brandon
ALL HANDS ON DECK(1961); MARINES, LET'S GO(1961); STATE FAIR(1962); BOYS FROM BRAZIL, THE(1978)

Dick Brandon
THREE ON A MATCH(1932)

Dickey Brandon
Misc. Silents
LIFE'S GREATEST GAME(1924)

Dicky Brandon
Silents
WOMAN WHO SINNED, A(1925); TOM AND HIS PALS(1926)

Dorothy Brandon
OUTSIDER, THE(1933, Brit.), w; OUTSIDER, THE(1940, Brit.), w
Silents
OUTSIDER, THE(1926), w

Edward Brandon
HARLEM ON THE PRAIRIE(1938)

Ella Brandon
Misc. Silents
FORGOTTEN(1914, Brit.)

Eric Brandon
COLOSSUS: THE FORBIN PROJECT(1969)

H.R. Brandon
STALLION CANYON(1949), art d

Harriet Brandon
NEW FACES OF 1937(1937); STAGE DOOR(1937)

Harriette Brandon
KITTY FOYLE(1940)

Harry Brandon
HURRICANE SMITH(1942)

Henry Brandon
GARDEN OF ALLAH, THE(1936); KILLER AT LARGE(1936); TRAIL OF THE LONESOME PINE, THE(1936); BLACK LEGION, THE(1937); I PROMISE TO PAY(1937); ISLAND CAPTIVES(1937); LAST TRAIN FROM MADRID, THE(1937); WESTBOUND LIMITED(1937); IF I WERE KING(1938); SPAWN OF THE NORTH(1938); THREE COMRADES(1938); BEAU GESTE(1939); CONSPIRACY(1939); MARSHAL OF MESA CITY, THE(1939); NURSE EDITH CAVELL(1939); PIRATES OF THE SKIES(1939); DARK STREETS OF CAIRO(1940); DOOMED TO DIE(1940); FLORIAN(1940); HALF A SINNER(1940); RANGER AND THE LADY, THE(1940); SKI PATROL(1940); SON OF MONTE CRISTO(1940); UNDER TEXAS SKIES(1940); BAD MAN OF DEADWOOD(1941); SHEPHERD OF THE HILLS, THE(1941); TWO IN A TAXI(1941); UNDERGROUND(1941); NIGHT IN NEW ORLEANS, A(1942); DRUMS OF FU MANCHU(1943); EDGE OF DARKNESS(1943); NORTHWEST OUTPOST(1947); CANON CITY(1948); HOLLOW TRIUMPH(1948); JOAN OF ARC(1948); OLD LOS ANGELES(1948); PALEFACE, THE(1948); FIGHTING O'FLYNN, THE(1949); TARZAN'S MAGIC FOUNTAIN(1949); WAKE OF THE RED WITCH(1949); CATTLE DRIVE(1951); FLAME OF ARABY(1951); GOLDEN HORDE, THE(1951); HAREM GIRL(1952); HURRICANE SMITH(1952); SCARLET ANGEL(1952); WAGONS WEST(1952); CADDY, THE(1953); PONY EXPRESS(1953); RAIDERS OF THE SEVEN SEAS(1953); SCARED STIFF(1953); TARZAN AND THE SHE-DEVIL(1953); WAR ARROW(1953); WAR OF THE WORLDS, THE(1953); CASANOVA'S BIG NIGHT(1954); KNOCK ON WOOD(1954); VERA CRUZ(1954); LADY GODIVA(1955); BANDIDO(1956); COMANCHE(1956); SEARCHERS, THE(1956); TEN COMMANDMENTS, THE(1956); HELL'S CROSSROADS(1957); LAND UNKNOWN, THE(1957); OMAR KHAYYAM(1957); AUNTIE MAME(1958); BIG FISHERMAN, THE(1959); OKEFE-NOKEE(1960); TWO RODE TOGETHER(1961); CAPTAIN SINDBAD(1963); SO LONG, BLUE BOY(1973); ASSAULT ON PRECINCT 13(1976); TO BE OR NOT TO BE(1983)
Misc. Talkies
SEARCH FOR THE EVIL ONE(1967); WHEN THE NORTH WIND BLOWS(1974); MANHANDLERS, THE(1975)

Jennifer Brandon
1984
EXTERMINATOR 2(1984)

John Brandon
ARRIVEDERCI, BABY!(1966, Brit.); ISADORA(1968, Brit.); ADDING MACHINE, THE(1969); FUN WITH DICK AND JANE(1977); BRINK'S JOB, THE(1978); SCAR-FACE(1983)
1984
RACING WITH THE MOON(1984)

Johnny Brandon
FUN AT ST. FANNY'S(1956, Brit.)

Michael Brandon
FRENCH KEY, THE(1946); ARNELO AFFAIR, THE(1947); SECOND CHANCE(1947); BRIDE FOR SALE(1949); CHICAGO DEADLINE(1949); FOLLOW ME QUIETLY(1949); MOTHER DIDN'T TELL ME(1950); CHANGE OF STRANGERS(1970); JENNIFER ON MY MIND(1971); FOUR FLIES ON GREY VELVET(1972, Ital.); FM(1978); PROMISES IN THE DARK(1979); CHANGE OF SEASONS, A(1980); RICH AND FAMOUS(1981)

Peter Brandon
WHAT EVER HAPPENED TO AUNT ALICE?(1969); CATAMOUNT KILLING, THE(1975, Ger.); HUSTLE(1975); WINTER KILLS(1979); ALTERED STATES(1980)

Phil Brandon
MISSING MILLION, THE(1942, Brit.), d; WE'LL MEET AGAIN(1942, Brit.), d; HAPPIDROME(1943, Brit.), d; UP WITH THE LARK(1943, Brit.), d; TARZAN'S PERIL(1951), d; HOLIDAY WEEK(1952, Brit.), d; HOUSE OF BLACKMAIL(1953, Brit.), p; CIRCUMSTANIAL EVIDENCE(1954, Brit.), p

Philip Brandon
CAPTAIN'S TABLE, THE(1936, Brit.); OUANGA(1936, Brit.)

Richard Brandon
SUDDENLY IT'S SPRING(1947)
1984
FIRSTBORN(1984)

William Brandon
Silents
AUTOCRAT, THE(1919, Brit.)
Misc. Silents
ESTHER REDEEMED(1915, Brit.)

Una Brandon-Jones
DIRTY KNIGHT'S WORK(1976, Brit.)

Amy Brandon-Thomas
Silents
GREATER NEED, THE(1916, Brit.)
Misc. Silents
PARTNERS AT LAST(1916, Brit.)

Jevan Brandon-Thomas
HER REPUTATION(1931, Brit.), p,d&w, w

Bill Brandor
BLACK KNIGHT, THE(1954)

Jerry Brandow
MEET ME AFTER THE SHOW(1951)

X Brands
NAKED GUN, THE(1956); YOUNG AND DANGEROUS(1957); BEAU GESTE(1966)

X. Brands
ESCORT WEST(1959); GUNMEN FROM LAREDO(1959); SANTEE(1973)

Michael Brandsell
BREAKING GLASS(1980, Brit.), ed

Gil Brandsen
SIN OF MONA KENT, THE(1961)

Jutta Brandstadter
OUTSIDER IN AMSTERDAM(1983, Neth.), ed

Jutta Brandstaedter
OUR HITLER, A FILM FROM GERMANY(1980, Ger.), ed; PARSIFAL(1983, Fr.), ed

Jutta Brandstaetter
WILD DUCK, THE(1977, Ger./Aust.), ed

Greta Brandstedt
ON OUR MERRY WAY(1948)

Frank Brandstetter
TARZAN AND THE VALLEY OF GOLD(1966 U.S./Switz.)

Brandt
SEVEN ANGRY MEN(1955), md

Bernard Brandt
DECOY(1946), p; VIOLENCE(1947), p

Bert Brandt
DECISION BEFORE DAWN(1951); RIVER CHANGES, THE(1956)

Bettina Brandt
PRIME TIME, THE(1960)

Bill Brandt
JOLSON STORY, THE(1946)

Brian Brandt
9/30/55(1977)

Bryan Brandt
ACROSS 110TH STREET(1972), ed

Buzz Brandt
BREAKHEART PASS(1976), ed

Byron Brandt
THOMAS CROWN AFFAIR, THE(1968), ed; FOOLS(1970), ed; HAWAIIANS, THE(1970), ed; GREATEST, THE(1977, U.S./Brit.), ed; TIME TO DIE, A(1983), ed

Byron ["Buzz"] Brandt
SHARK'S TREASURE(1975), ed; PRISONER OF ZENDA, THE(1979), ed; ROLLER BOOGIE(1979), ed; IT'S MY TURN(1980), ed; SMOKEY AND THE BANDIT–PART 3(1983), ed

Carl Brandt
BOBBY WARE IS MISSING(1955), m; SEVEN ANGRY MEN(1955), m; SHOT-GUN(1955), m, md; MR. MAGOO'S HOLIDAY FESTIVAL(1970), m; CLEOPATRA JONES(1973), m

Carolyn Brandt
EEGAH!(1962); INCREDIBLY STRANGE CREATURES WHO STOPPED LIVING AND BECAME CRAZY MIXED-UP ZOMBIES, THE(1965); THRILL KILLERS, THE(1965); LEMON GROVE KIDS MEET THE MONSTERS, THE(1966); RAT PFINK AND BOO BOO(1966)
Misc. Talkies
BLOOD MONSTER(1972)

Charles Brandt
Silents
FORTUNE HUNTER, THE(1914); CLIMBERS, THE(1915); FRIDAY THE 13TH(1916); NANETTE OF THE WILDS(1916); MASTER MIND, THE(1920)
Misc. Silents
MISFIT EARL, A(1919)

Charles C. Brandt
Misc. Silents
AS A MAN THINKS(1919)
Dan Brandt
1984
AMERICAN TABOO(1984), m
Edwin Brandt
Silents
MILLION DOLLAR ROBBERY, THE(1914)
Frances Brandt
MR. BELVEDERE RINGS THE BELL(1951); DRUMS OF TAHITI(1954)
George Brandt
HOUSE ON 92ND STREET, THE(1945)
Hank Brandt
FOLLOW ME, BOYS!(1966); PANIC IN THE CITY(1968); MAD BOMBER, THE(1973); TELEFON(1977)
Heidrun Brandt
1984
WOMAN IN FLAMES, A(1984, Ger.), prod d
Ivan Brandt
FIRST MRS. FRASER, THE(1932, Brit.); REASONABLE DOUBT(1936, Brit.); THINGS TO COME(1936, Brit.); FOREVER YOURS(1937, Brit.); MAN WHO COULD WORK MIRACLES, THE(1937, Brit.); BLONDES FOR DANGER(1938, Brit.); FUGITIVE, THE(1940, Brit.); LION HAS WINGS, THE(1940, Brit.); IT HAPPENED TO ONE MAN(1941, Brit.); MISSING MILLION, THE(1942, Brit.); OLD MOTHER RILEY, DETECTIVE(1943, Brit.)
Janet Brandt
GOOD MORNING, MISS DOVE(1955); MURDER BY CONTRACT(1958); COLD WIND IN AUGUST(1961); UP THE SANDBOX(1972); ADVENTURES OF RABBI JACOB, THE(1973, Fr.); HIT(1973); SHEILA LEVINE IS DEAD AND LIVING IN NEW YORK(1975); SEMI-TOUGH(1977); FM(1978); HOT TOMORROWS(1978); JAZZ SINGER, THE(1980)
1984
OH GOD! YOU DEVIL(1984)
Jerrold T. Brandt
SCATTERGOOD BAINES(1941), p; SCATTERGOOD MEETS BROADWAY(1941), p; SCATTERGOOD PULLS THE STRINGS(1941), p; CINDERELLA SWINGS IT(1942), p; SCATTERGOOD RIDES HIGH(1942), p; SCATTERGOOD SURVIVES A MURDER(1942), p
Jerrold Brandt, Jr.
BELL JAR, THE(1979), p
Jim Brandt
MAN IN THE GREY FLANNEL SUIT, THE(1956); PEYTON PLACE(1957); LONG, HOT SUMMER, THE(1958)
Jimmy Brandt
CRASHING LAS VEGAS(1956)
John Brandt
WILD GYPSIES(1969), cos
Kurt Brandt
VERY NATURAL THING, A(1974)
Lee Brandt
VIVA MAX!(1969)
Lois Brandt
FLYING MATCHMAKER, THE(1970, Israel); FAST TIMES AT RIDGEMONT HIGH(1982)
Lou Brandt
CACTUS IN THE SNOW(1972), p
Margit Brandt
Z.P.G.(1972), cos
Martin Brandt
13 RUE MADELEINE(1946); DEVIL AT FOUR O'CLOCK, THE(1961); JUDGMENT AT NUREMBERG(1961); HITLER(1962); SPIRAL ROAD, THE(1962); PRIZE, THE(1963); MORITURI(1965); ODESSA FILE, THE(1974, Brit./Ger.)
Mathilde Brandt
Misc. Silents
HAMLET(1921, Ger.)
Mcgens Brandt
HIDDEN FEAR(1957)
Michael Brandt
THEY CAN'T HANG ME(1955, Brit.), ph; MISSING NOTE, THE(1961, Brit.), d
Mogens Brandt
OPERATION CAMEL(1961, Den.); REPTILICUS(1962, U.S./Den.)
Nils Brandt
MAKE LIKE A THIEF(1966, Fin.)
Rainer Brandt
DIE FASTNACHTSBEICHTE(1962, Ger.); IT'S HOT IN PARADISE(1962, Ger./Yugo.); JUDGE AND THE SINNER, THE(1964, Ger.); FUNERAL IN BERLIN(1966, Brit.)
Raymond A. Brandt
INCREDIBLE SHRINKING WOMAN, THE(1981), prod d
Raymond Brandt
BIG FIX, THE(1978), art d
Ruth Brandt
DECISION BEFORE DAWN(1951)
Thordis Brandt
IN LIKE FLINT(1967); FUNNY GIRL(1968); LIVE A LITTLE, LOVE A LITTLE(1968); SPLIT, THE(1968); WITCHMAKER, THE(1969); UP YOUR TEDDY BEAR(1970)
Thordis I. Brandt
LAST OF THE SECRET AGENTS?, THE(1966)
Victor Brandt
THREE THE HARD WAY(1974); I WANNA HOLD YOUR HAND(1978); WACKO(1983)
Walter Brandt
BLOODY PIT OF HORROR, THE(1965, Ital.); TERROR-CREATURES FROM THE GRAVE(1967, U.S./Ital.)
Howard Brandy
BLOOD FROM THE MUMMY'S TOMB(1972, Brit.), p; TAKE, THE(1974), p
Roland Branel
MATTER OF WHO, A(1962, Brit.)

George Brangier
MISTER ROBERTS(1955)
Antonio Branioni
Silents
CABIRIA(1914, Ital.)
Lidija Branis
NINTH CIRCLE, THE(1961, Yugo.), ed; SEVENTH CONTINENT, THE(1968, Czech./Yugo.), ed
Charles Branklyn
INDEPENDENCE DAY(1976)
Thom Brann
LILITH(1964)
Thomas Brann
SHAFT'S BIG SCORE(1972)
Carol Brannan
CYNTHIA(1947); ADVENTURE IN BALTIMORE(1949); LIFE OF HER OWN, A(1950)
Ralph Brannen
GO TELL THE SPARTANS(1978); EATING RAOUL(1982)
Terry Brannen
YOU LIGHT UP MY LIFE(1977)
Owen Brannigan
GREAT GILBERT AND SULLIVAN, THE(1953, Brit.)
Paddy Brannigan
TREASURE ISLAND(1950, Brit.); YOU CAN'T ESCAPE(1955, Brit.)
Roy Brannigan
THIS, THAT AND THE OTHER(1970, Brit.)
Thomas Brannigan
Silents
NIGHT OF LOVE, THE(1927), ph
Tom Brannigan
THRILL OF A ROMANCE(1945)
Ben F. Brannon III
URBAN COWBOY(1980)
Carol Brannon
FLAME OF YOUTH(1949); TAKE CARE OF MY LITTLE GIRL(1951); GIRL IN WHITE, THE(1952)
Fred Brannon
BANDIT KING OF TEXAS(1949), d
Fred C. Brannon
CYCLOTRODE X(1946), d; FRONTIER INVESTIGATOR(1949), d; CODE OF THE SILVER SAGE(1950), d; GUNMEN OF ABILENE(1950), d; RUSTLERS ON HORSEBACK(1950), d; SALT LAKE RAIDERS(1950), d; VIGILANTE HIDEOUT(1950), d; ARIZONA MANHUNT(1951), d; ROUGH RIDERS OF DURANGO(1951), d; CAPTIVE OF BILLY THE KID(1952), d; WILD HORSE AMBUSH(1952), d; SATAN'S SATELLITES(1958), d; GHOST OF ZORRO(1959), d
Gavin Brannon
Misc. Talkies
UPS AND DOWNS(1981)
Terry Brannon
LOST LAGOON(1958), m
Janya Brannt
KOTCH(1971); WAR BETWEEN MEN AND WOMEN, THE(1972)
Tom Brannum
JOHN PAUL JONES(1959)
Leopold Branover
DANIELLA BY NIGHT(1962, Fr./Ger.), p
Arthur Branscombe
Silents
FOUNDATIONS OF FREEDOM, THE(1918, Brit.), d&w
Bob Bransford
SHINBONE ALLEY(1971), anim; BUGS BUNNY'S THIRD MOVIE–1001 RABBIT TALES(1982), anim
Doris Bransgrove
Silents
ARCADIANS, THE(1927, Brit.)
Chimmo Branson
IN WHICH WE SERVE(1942, Brit.)
Truck Branss
SWAN LAKE, THE(1967), d
Richard Bransten
SAN DIEGO, I LOVE YOU(1944), w; MARGIE(1946), w; TROUBLE WITH WOMEN, THE(1947), w; SONG OF SURRENDER(1949), w
S/Sgt. Sascha Branstoff
WINGED VICTORY(1944)
Henry Brant
MY FATHER'S HOUSE(1947, Palestine), m
Lynton Brant
OUR DAILY BREAD(1934)
Michael Brant
EVERY BASTARD A KING(1968, Israel)
Neil Brant
INTERNATIONAL HOUSE(1933), w
Peggy Brant
MOONLIGHT IN VERMONT(1943); PATRICK THE GREAT(1945)
Roy Brant
CRIME BY NIGHT(1944)
Ward Brant
IT HAPPENS EVERY SPRING(1949)
Aggie Brantford
LAST POST, THE(1929, Brit.)
Agnes Brantford
EVERYTHING IS RHYTHM(1940, Brit.)
Albert Brantford
Misc. Silents
DICK'S FAIRY(1921, Brit.)
Michael Brantford
Silents
MARE NOSTRUM(1926)

Mickey Brantford
TESHA(1929, Brit.); SUSPENSE(1930, Brit.); NEW HOTEL, THE(1932, Brit.); MY OLD DUTCH(1934, Brit.); POWER(1934, Brit.); ME AND MARLBOROUGH(1935, Brit.); MY HEART IS CALLING(1935, Brit.); PHANTOM LIGHT, THE(1935, Brit.); STRICTLY ILLEGAL(1935, Brit.); TEMPTATION(1935, Brit.); LAST JOURNEY, THE(1936, Brit.); MR. COHEN TAKES A WALK(1936, Brit.); TWICE BRANDED(1936, Brit.); WHERE THERE'S A WILL(1936, Brit); DARBY AND JOAN(1937, Brit.); REVERSE BE MY LOT, THE(1938, Brit.)
Silents
GAME OF LIFE, THE(1922, Brit.); GAMBLE WITH HEARTS, A(1923, Brit.); REST CURE, THE(1923, Brit.); NOT FOR SALE(1924, Brit.); AFRAID OF LOVE(1925, Brit.); THOU FOOL(1926, Brit.); DAWN(1928, Brit.)
Misc. Silents
SPORTING INSTINCT, THE(1922, Brit.)
Micky Brantford
Silents
MAN THE ARMY MADE, A(1917, Brit.); KNOCKOUT, THE(1923, Brit.)
Misc. Silents
SECOND TO NONE(1926, Brit.)
Betsy Brantley
SHOCK TREATMENT(1981); FIVE DAYS ONE SUMMER(1982)
1984
ANOTHER COUNTRY(1984, Brit.)
Cherie Brantley
BACK ROADS(1981)
Nell Brantley
Misc. Silents
DARWIN WAS RIGHT(1924); FAST FIGHTIN'(1925); SADDLE CYCLONE(1925)
Alban Branton
AMY(1981)
William Branton
Silents
MAN WHO COULD NOT LOSE, THE(1914)
Patrick Braoude
1984
UNTIL SEPTEMBER(1984)
Willy Braque
NIGHT OF LUST(1965, Fr.)
Albert Bras
VAMPYR(1932, Fr./Ger.)
Misc. Silents
VISAGES VIOLES...AMES CLOSES(1921, Fr.)
Jean-Pierre Bras
LOVERS OF TERUEL, THE(1962, Fr.)
Helmut Brasch
UNWILLING AGENT(1968, Ger.)
Vittorio Braschi
TOO BAD SHE'S BAD(1954, Ital.)
Dominick Brascia
1984
THEY'RE PLAYING WITH FIRE(1984)
John Brascia
WHITE CHRISTMAS(1954); MEET ME IN LAS VEGAS(1956); AMBUSHERS, THE(1967); WRECKING CREW, THE(1968); EXECUTIVE ACTION(1973); WALKING TALL(1973)
John F. Brascia
BALTIMORE BULLET, THE(1980), p, w
Tybee Brascia
LOST HORIZON(1973)
Rod Brasfield
FACE IN THE CROWD, A(1957); COUNTRY MUSIC HOLIDAY(1958)
Henry Brash
HER SISTER'S SECRET(1946), p
Marion Brash
GROUP, THE(1966); DETECTIVE, THE(1968); MC MASTERS, THE(1970); SLAUGHTER(1972)
Peter Brash
WITHOUT A TRACE(1983)
Alan Brasington
TATTOO(1981)
Stanley H. Brasloff
TOYS ARE NOT FOR CHILDREN(1972), p, d, w; BEHIND LOCKED DOORS(1976, S. Africa), w
George Brasno
SITTING PRETTY(1933); MIGHTY BARNUM, THE(1934); CHARLIE CHAN AT THE CIRCUS(1936); LITTLE MISS BROADWAY(1938); GREAT JOHN L. THE(1945)
Olive Brasno
SITTING PRETTY(1933); MIGHTY BARNUM, THE(1934); CHARLIE CHAN AT THE CIRCUS(1936); LITTLE MISS BROADWAY(1938)
Richard Brasno
MIGHTY BARNUM, THE(1934)
John Brason
WALK A CROOKED PATH(1969, Brit.), p&d
Arthur Brass
CARMEN, BABY(1967, Yugo./Ger.)
Kenneth Brass
STONY ISLAND(1978)
Tinto Brass
FLYING SAUCER, THE(1964, Ital.), d; VACATION, THE(1971, Ital.), p, w, ed
Robert Brassac
CESAR(1936, Fr.)
Jean Brassat
LES CARABINIERS(1968, Fr./Ital.)
Keefe Brasselle
JANIE(1944); RIVER GANG(1945); RAILROADED(1947); T-MEN(1947); NOT WANTED(1949); DIAL 1119(1950); NEVER FEAR(1950); BANNERLINE(1951); IT'S A BIG COUNTRY(1951); PLACE IN THE SUN, A(1951); UNKNOWN MAN, THE(1951); SKIRTS AHOY!(1952); EDDIE CANTOR STORY, THE(1953); THREE YOUNG TEXANS(1954); BRING YOUR SMILE ALONG(1955); MAD AT THE WORLD(1955); BATTLE STATIONS(1956); FIGHTING WILDCATS, THE(1957, Brit.); DEATH OVER

MY SHOULDER(1958, Brit.); BLACK GUNN(1972)
Misc. Talkies
IF YOU DON'T STOP IT, YOU'LL GO BLIND(1977), d
George Brassens
GATES OF PARIS(1958, Fr./Ital.), a, m
Stephen Brassett
JUNKET 89(1970, Brit.)
Claude Brasseur
HORROR CHAMBER OF DR. FAUSTUS, THE(1962, Fr./Ital.); SEVEN CAPITAL SINS(1962, Fr./Ital.); ELUSIVE CORPORAL, THE(1963, Fr.); GERMINAL(1963, Fr.); PLEASE, NOT NOW!(1963, Fr./Ital.); LIARS, THE(1964, Fr.); SWEET AND SOUR(1964, Fr./Ital.); BANANA PEEL(1965, Fr.); BAND OF OUTSIDERS(1966, Fr.); UPPER HAND, THE(1967, Fr./Ital./Ger.); SHOCK TROOPS(1968, Fr.); SUCH A GORGEOUS KID LIKE ME(1973, Fr.); BAROCCO(1976, Fr.); LA BOUM(1983, Fr.)
Pierre Brasseur
CAFE DE PARIS(1938, Fr.); PORT OF SHADOWS(1938, Fr.); CONFESSIONS OF A NEWLYWED(1941, Fr.); LUMIERE D'ETE(1943, Fr.); CHILDREN OF PARADISE(1945, Fr.); GATES OF THE NIGHT(1950, Fr.); LOVERS OF VERONA, THE(1951, Fr.); LE PLAISIR(1954, Fr.); LES MAINS SALES(1954, Fr.); RASPOUTINE(1954, Fr.); NAPOLEON(1955, Fr.); GATES OF PARIS(1958, Fr./Ital.); WHERE THE HOT WIND BLOWS(1960, Fr., Ital.); CARTHAGE IN FLAMES(1961, Fr./Ital.); BELL' ANTONIO(1962, Ital.); CANDIDE(1962, Fr.); CRIME DOES NOT PAY(1962, Fr.); HORROR CHAMBER OF DR. FAUSTUS, THE(1962, Fr./Ital.); DON'T TEMPT THE DEVIL(1964, Fr./Ital.); CLOPORTES(1966, Fr., Ital.); VERY HANDY MAN, A(1966, Fr./Ital.); YOUNG WORLD, A(1966, Fr./Ital.); KING OF HEARTS(1967, Fr./Ital.); LA VIE DE CHATEAU(1967, Fr.); MADMAN OF LAB 4, THE(1967, Fr.); BIRDS COME TO DIE IN PERU(1968, Fr.); MOST WONDERFUL EVENING OF MY LIFE, THE(1972, Ital./Fr.)
Robert Brassler
Silents
THREE SINNERS(1928), ed
Charles Braswell
ONLY GAME IN TOWN, THE(1970)
John Braswell
WEDDING PARTY, THE(1969)
Joe Bratcher
SKATEBOARD(1978); HOWLING, THE(1981); MODERN ROMANCE(1981)
Nikolai Bratersky
RAINBOW, THE(1944, USSR)
N. Bratorsky
DIARY OF A NAZI(1943, USSR)
Anatol Bratt
HOW TO SEDUCE A PLAYBOY(1968, Aust./Fr./Ital.), w
Barbara Bratt
LITTLE SEX, A(1982)
Harold Bratt
MASTER PLAN, THE(1955, Brit.), w
Paul Bratti
FRONTIER GAL(1945); SLAVE GIRL(1947)
The Brattle Street East
FEELIN' GOOD(1966)
Creed Bratton
HEART LIKE A WHEEL(1983)
Marla Bratton
WAY OF THE WEST, THE(1934); TIMBER TERRORS(1935)
Misc. Talkies
LONE RIDER, THE(1934)
Myra Bratton
WILD GOLD(1934)
Eva Brauer
PRINCE OF FOXES(1949)
Peter Paul Brauer
GIRL FROM THE MARSH CROFT, THE(1935, Ger.), p
Robert Brauer
Silents
LYING TRUTH, THE(1922)
Tiny Brauer
OUTLAWS IS COMING, THE(1965)
Carl Braugner
VIVA MAX!(1969), art d
Michael Brault
ORDERS, THE(1977, Can.), d, w, ph; THRESHOLD(1983, Can.), ph
Michel Brault
TAKE IT ALL(1966, Can.), ph, ed; ADOLESCENTS, THE(1967, Can.), d; MY UNCLE ANTOINE(1971, Can.), ph; KAMOURASKA(1973, Can./Fr.), ph; ELIZA'S HOROSCOPE(1975, Can.), ph
1984
LOUISIANE(1984, Fr./Can.), ph
Pierre Brault
RED(1970, Can.), m
Pierre F. Brault
1984
KINGS AND DESPERATE MEN(1984, Brit.), m
Vladimir Braum
HEROES OF THE SEA(1941), d
Alfred Braun
KOLBERG(1945, Ger.), w
Annemarie Braun
QUESTION 7(1961, U.S./Ger.)
Curt Braun
BLACK ROSES(1936, Ger.), w
Curt Johannes Braun
CITY OF SECRETS(1963, Ger.), w
Eddie Braun
1984
LIES(1984, Brit.)
Gertrude Braun
Misc. Silents
NECKLACE OF RAMESES, THE(1914)

Gunther Braun
TERROR BENEATH THE SEA(1966, Jap.)
Harald Braun
AS LONG AS YOU'RE NEAR ME(1956, Ger.), d; KING IN SHADOW(1961, Ger.), d
Harold Braun
GLASS TOWER, THE(1959, Ger.), d; KING IN SHADOW(1961, Ger.), w
Heiner Braun
NOT RECONCILED, OR "ONLY VIOLENCE HELPS WHERE IT RULES"(1969, Ger.)
Heinz Braun
YOUNG MONK, THE(1978, Ger.)
Jo. Braun
MOTHER KUSTERS GOES TO HEAVEN(1976, Ger.), cos
Jonathan Braun
UNSEEN, THE(1981), ed
Judith Braun
FLAME OF ARABY(1951); HORIZONS WEST(1952); RED BALL EXPRESS(1952)
Kh. Braun
DAY THE WAR ENDED, THE(1961, USSR)
Kurt Braun
DIPLOMATIC LOVER, THE(1934, Brit.), w
Lillian Braun
PIRATE, THE(1948), w
Lotte Braun
FOUR COMPANIONS, THE(1938, Ger.)
Lucio Braun
GIRL IN ROOM 13(1961, U.S./Braz.), ed
Marianne Braun
END OF THE LINE, THE(1959, Brit.)
Pinkas Braun
DOG EAT DOG(1963, U.S./Ger./Ital.); CITY OF FEAR(1965, Brit.); SECRET AGENT SUPER DRAGON(1966, Fr./Ital./Ger./Monaco); MAN OUTSIDE, THE(1968, Brit.); MISSION STARDUST(1968, Ital./Span./Ger.); LAST ESCAPE, THE(1970, Brit.); BLOODLINE(1979); PRAYING MANTIS(1982, Brit.)
Robert Braun
LAFAYETTE(1963, Fr.), titles
Toni Braun
NO TIME FOR FLOWERS(1952), ph
Tony Braun
HIGH CONQUEST(1947), ph; MAGIC FACE, THE(1951, Aust.), ph; PAPER TIGER(1975, Brit.), ph
Viktor Braun
STORY OF VICKIE, THE(1958, Aust.)
Vladimir Braun
DIARY OF A NAZI(1943, USSR), d
Zev Braun
GOLDSTEIN(1964), p; PEDESTRIAN, THE(1974, Ger.), p; LITTLE GIRL WHO LIVES DOWN THE LANE, THE(1977, Can.), p; FIENDISH PLOT OF DR. FU MANCHU, THE(1980), p
Pierre Braunberger
ROAD IS FINE, THE(1930, Fr.), p; WAYS OF LOVE(1950, Ital./Fr.), p; GAME FOR SIX LOVERS, A(1962, Fr.), p; SHOOT THE PIANO PLAYER(1962, Fr.), p; MY LIFE TO LIVE(1963, Fr.), p; IMMORAL MOMENT, THE(1967, Fr.), p; DE L'AMOUR(1968, Fr./Ital.), p; CATCH ME A SPY(1971, Brit./Fr.), p
Arthur Brauner
RETURN OF DR. MABUSE, THE(1961, Ger./Fr./Ital.), p; SHERLOCK HOLMES AND THE DEADLY NECKLACE(1962, Ger.), p; INVISIBLE DR. MABUSE, THE(1965, Ger.), p; MAD EXECUTIONERS, THE(1965, Ger.), p; CORRUPT ONES, THE(1967, Ger.), p; PHANTOM OF SOHO, THE(1967, Ger.), p; OLD SHATTERHAND(1968, Ger./Yugo./Fr./Ital.), p; FIGHT FOR ROME(1969, Ger./Rum.), p
1984
LOVE IN GERMANY, A(1984, Fr./Ger.), p
Artur Brauner
CONFESS DR. CORDA(1960, Ger.), p; VOR SONNENUNTERGANG(1961, Ger), p; SHADOWS GROW LONGER, THE(1962, Switz./Ger.), p; SCOTLAND YARD HUNTS DR. MABUSE(1963, Ger.), p; DR. MABUSE'S RAYS OF DEATH(1964, Ger./Fr./Ital.), p; TERROR OF DR. MABUSE, THE(1965, Ger.), p; FROZEN ALIVE(1966, Brit./Ger.), p; MONSTER OF LONDON CITY, THE(1967, Ger.), p; MARTYR, THE(1976, Ger./Israel), p
Asher Brauner
BOSS'S SON, THE(1978); MAKING LOVE(1982)
1984
WHERE THE BOYS ARE '84(1984)
Isolde Brauner
24-HOUR LOVER(1970, Ger.)
Wolf Brauner
ORDERED TO LOVE(1963, Ger.), p; MOONWOLF(1966, Fin./Ger.), p
Bonnie Braunger
IRON MAJOR, THE(1943)
Carl Braunger
PAINT YOUR WAGON(1969), art d
Tom Braunger
WAGONS ROLL AT NIGHT, THE(1941)
Rudolf Braungraber
TRIAL, THE(1948, Aust.), w
Marianne Brauns
X THE UNKNOWN(1957, Brit.); BLUE MURDER AT ST. TRINIAN'S(1958, Brit.); KILL HER GENTLY(1958, Brit.); NAKED FURY(1959, Brit.); PLEASURE LOVERS, THE(1964, Brit.)
Andrew Braunsberg
WONDERWALL(1969, Brit.), p; MACBETH(1971, Brit.), p; TENANT, THE(1976, Fr.), p; BEING THERE(1979), p
1984
ALPHABET CITY(1984), p
Zdenek Braunschlager
TRANSPORT FROM PARADISE(1967, Czech.)
Daniel Braunschweig
UP FROM THE BEACH(1965), spec eff

Alan Braunstein
GAS-S-S-S!(1970); WANDERERS, THE(1979); CARNY(1980)
George Braunstein
FADE TO BLACK(1980), p
George G. Braunstein
1984
SURF II(1984), p
Nathan Cy Braunstein
SPIRIT AND THE FLESH, THE(1948, Ital.), ed
Eric Braunsteiner
NORTH STAR, THE(1943)
Nan Braunton
WILL ANY GENTLEMAN?(1955, Brit.); IT'S A GREAT DAY(1956, Brit.)
Marius Brauquier
TONI(1968, Fr.), set d
Katharina Brauren
TOXI(1952, Ger.)
Mort Braus
THREE LOVES HAS NANCY(1938), w; LAUGH IT OFF(1939), w
Mortimer Braus
WOMEN IN PRISON(1938), w; POSTMAN DIDN'T RING, THE(1942), w; WING AND A PRAYER(1944), w; STRANGE TRIANGLE(1946), w; DESTINATION BIG HOUSE(1950), w; LET'S MAKE IT LEGAL(1951), w; SON OF DR. JEKYLL, THE(1951), w; FIVE BOLD WOMEN(1960), w; HANNIBAL(1960, Ital.), w
Hans Brausaewetter
BARBERINA(1932, Ger.)
Marlena Brause
1984
SUBURBIA(1984)
Hans Brausewetter
DREAMER, THE(1936, Ger.)
Misc. Silents
VERDUN, VISIONS D'HISTOIRE(1929, Fr.)
Art Brauss
STOP TRAIN 349(1964, Fr./Ital./Ger.); TRAIN, THE(1965, Fr./Ital./U.S.); SLAVERS(1977, Ger.)
Arthur Brauss
$(DOLLARS)**1/2 (1971); SWISS CONSPIRACY, THE(1976, U.S./Ger.); CROSS OF IRON(1977, Brit., Ger.); AVALANCHE EXPRESS(1979); VICTORY(1981)
Otto Brautigan
Silents
BIG TOWN IDEAS(1921), ph; BLUSHING BRIDE, THE(1921), ph; MAID OF THE WEST(1921), ph; WHATEVER SHE WANTS(1921), ph; ELOPE IF YOU MUST(1922), ph
R. Douglas Brautigham
SATURDAY NIGHT AT THE BATHS(1975)
Hal Brav
STORY OF A THREE DAY PASS, THE(1968, Fr.)
Bravado
GERONIMO(1962)
"Braveheart"
DESERT JUSTICE(1936)
Braveheart
Misc. Silents
FLASH OF THE FOREST(1928)
Bart Braverman
GREAT TEXAS DYNAMITE CHASE, THE(1976); ALLIGATOR(1980); HIT AND RUN(1982)
Charles Braverman
HIT AND RUN(1982), p&d
Marvin Braverman
RICHARD(1972)
Patti Braverman
HOW SWEET IT IS(1968)
Bravo
THEY RAN FOR THEIR LIVES(1968)
Antonio Bravo
PASSION ISLAND(1943, Mex.); FRANKENSTEIN, THE VAMPIRE AND CO.(1961, Mex.); PEARL OF TLAYUCAN, THE(1964, Mex.); SPIRITISM(1965, Mex.); EXTERMINATING ANGEL, THE(1967, Mex.); NAZARIN(1968, Mex.)
Ben Bravo
BADLANDS(1974)
Carlos Bravo
100 RIFLES(1969); EL CONDOR(1970); HUNTING PARTY, THE(1977, Brit.); ZORRO, THE GAY BLADE(1981)
Charley Bravo
MAN CALLED NOON, THE(1973, Brit.); WIND AND THE LION, THE(1975)
Charlie Bravo
CAPTAIN APACHE(1971, Brit.); TOWN CALLED HELL, A(1971, Span./Brit.); TRAVELS WITH MY AUNT(1972, Brit.)
Charly Bravo
BOLDEST JOB IN THE WEST, THE(1971, Ital.)
Misc. Talkies
TO LOVE, PERHAPS TO DIE(1975)
Danny Bravo
FOR THE LOVE OF MIKE(1960); FOR PETE'S SAKE!(1966)
Feliciano Ituero Bravo
CONFESSIONS OF AMANS, THE(1977)
Jaime Bravo
LOVE HAS MANY FACES(1965)
Ninette Bravo
ACT OF VENGEANCE(1974)
Ramon Bravo
TINTORERA...BLOODY WATERS(1977, Brit./Mex.), w
Peter Bravos
FLIGHT OF THE PHOENIX, THE(1965); LEGEND OF LYLAH CLARE, THE(1968)
Tasso Bravos
HUSTLE(1975)

Rose Brawd
INCREDIBLE MR. LIMPET, THE(1964), cos
Alan Brawer
SPACED OUT(1981, Brit.), m
Sol Brawerman
PUTNEY SWOPE(1969)
Ernest Brawley
FAST-WALKING(1982), w
Peter Brawley
RUBBER GUN, THE(1977, Can.)
Charles Brawn
Misc. Silents
C.O.D.(1915)
Jack Brawn
Silents
ISLAND OF REGENERATION, THE(1915); JUGGERNAUT, THE(1915)
Patrick Brawn
CHAIN OF EVENTS(1958, Brit.), w
Hilda Brawner
ONE PLUS ONE(1961, Can.)
Kenny Brawner
HAIR(1979)
Frank Braxton
BOY NAMED CHARLIE BROWN, A(1969), anim
Harry Braxton
Silents
NIGHT LIFE(1927), t; BACHELOR'S PARADISE(1928), t; NAMELESS MEN(1928), t; SCARLET DOVE, THE(1928), t; TOILERS, THE(1928), t; MORGAN'S LAST RAID(1929), t
Steve Braxton [Sam Robbins]
LONE RIDER AND THE BANDIT, THE(1942), w; MYSTERIOUS RIDER, THE(1942), w; OVERLAND STAGECOACH(1942), w
Barbara Bray
GALILEO(1975, Brit.), w
Bernard B. Bray
FIGHTING HERO(1934), p
Bill Bray
KANGAROO(1952)
Billy Bray
PLAY UP THE BAND(1935, Brit.); LOVE AT SEA(1936, Brit.); SHOW FLAT(1936, Brit.); KNIGHTS FOR A DAY(1937, Brit.); RIDING HIGH(1937, Brit.); TAKE A CHANCE(1937, Brit.); THUNDER IN THE CITY(1937, Brit.); WANTED(1937, Brit.); JOHN HALIFAX–GENTLEMAN(1938, Brit.); MURDER TOMORROW(1938, Brit.); FLYING FIFTY-FIVE(1939, Brit.)
Bob Bray
GREAT MISSOURI RAID, THE(1950); FEUDIN' FOOLS(1952); LUSTY MEN, THE(1952)
Bob [Robert] Bray
WARPATH(1951); MARSHAL'S DAUGHTER, THE(1953)
Catherine Bray
TIM(1981, Aus.)
Charles Bray
KNIGHTS FOR A DAY(1937, Brit.), a, w
David K. Bray
BIRD OF PARADISE(1951)
Dawson Bray
1984
UNDER THE VOLCANO(1984)
Gill Bray
DEATH TOOK PLACE LAST NIGHT(1970, Ital./Ger.)
Gillian Bray
Misc. Talkies
BOD SQUAD, THE(1976)
Hazel Bray
HUNDRED POUND WINDOW, THE(1943, Brit.); 2,000 WOMEN(1944, Brit.)
Jim Bray
ROLLER BOOGIE(1979)
Peter Bray
POPEYE(1980)
Richard Bray
PIE IN THE SKY(1964)
Robert Bray
CRACK-UP(1946); SUNSET PASS(1946); CROSSFIRE(1947); DESPERATE(1947); WILD HORSE MESA(1947); ARIZONA RANGER, THE(1948); BLOOD ON THE MOON(1948); FIGHTING FATHER DUNNE(1948); GUN SMUGGLERS(1948); GUNS OF HATE(1948); INDIAN AGENT(1948); MR. BLANDINGS BUILDS HIS DREAM HOUSE(1948); RETURN OF THE BADMEN(1948); WESTERN HERITAGE(1948); BROTHERS IN THE SADDLE(1949); CLAY PIGEON, THE(1949); RUSTLERS(1949); STAGECOACH KID(1949); STRANGE BARGAIN(1949); LAW OF THE BADLANDS(1950); OVERLAND TELEGRAPH(1951); THING, THE(1951); FARGO(1952); MAN FROM BLACK HILLS, THE(1952); MAVERICK, THE(1952); ONE MINUTE TO ZERO(1952); VOODOO TIGER(1952); MAIN STREET TO BROADWAY(1953); SEMINOLE(1953); VIGILANTE TERROR(1953); BUS STOP(1956); STEEL JUNGLE, THE(1956); MY GUN IS QUICK(1957); WAYWARD BUS, THE(1957); ACCURSED, THE(1958, Brit.); ER LOVE A STRANGER(1958); NEVER SO FEW(1959); FIEND OF DOPE ISLAND(1961); GATHERING OF EAGLES, A(1963)
Silents
SPITFIRE OF SEVILLE, THE(1919)
Roger Bray
DIAMOND CITY(1949, Brit.), w
Thom Bray
PROWLER, THE(1981)
Vicki Bray
ELIZA FRASER(1976, Aus.)
Will H. Bray
Silents
WOODEN SHOES(1917)

Master William Bray
Silents
MY COUSIN(1918)
Peter Brayham
FROM RUSSIA WITH LOVE(1963, Brit.); LISZTOMANIA(1975, Brit.); SKY RIDERS(1976, U.S./Gr.), stunts; HORROR PLANET(1982, Brit.), stunts
William Brayne
WHAT'S GOOD FOR THE GOOSE(1969, Brit.), ph
Edward Brayshaw
SQUADRON 633(1964, U.S./Brit.); 633 SQUADRON(1964)
Margaret Brayton
GREAT HOSPITAL MYSTERY, THE(1937); FRONTIER MARSHAL(1939); HERO FOR A DAY(1939); LITTLE ACCIDENT(1939); HIGH SCHOOL(1940); QUIET PLEASE, MURDER(1942); WHO DONE IT?(1942); SPIDER, THE(1945); SHOCK(1946); SARGE GOES TO COLLEGE(1947); TRAP, THE(1947); WHIRLPOOL(1949); FATHER MAKES GOOD(1950); SIDE STREET(1950); UNKNOWN MAN, THE(1951); TREASURE OF THE GOLDEN CONDOR(1953); GREEN-EYED BLONDE, THE(1957); GODDESS, THE(1958); VERTIGO(1958)
Hal Brazeal
LAW OF THE TIMBER(1941)
Hal Brazeale
DAWN PATROL, THE(1938); DEATH OF A CHAMPION(1939); I WANTED WINGS(1941)
Hal Brazealeo
'TIL WE MEET AGAIN(1940)
A. Laurie Brazee
AND SO THEY WERE MARRIED(1936), w
Laurie Brazee
OUTER GATE, THE(1937), w
Sharon Brazell
PERSONAL BEST(1982)
Conni Marie Brazelton
1984
JOY OF SEX(1984)
Jake Braziel
PURPLE HAZE(1982)
Edward Brazier
DARK ODYSSEY(1961)
Lt. Thomas Brazil
THREE STRIPES IN THE SUN(1955)
The Brazilian Turunas
FLYING DOWN TO RIO(1933)
Fedir Braznick
GIRL FROM POLTAVA(1937)
Greg Brazzell
1984
PLACES IN THE HEART(1984)
Lidia Brazzi
AFTER THE FOX(1966, U.S./Brit./Ital.)
Lydia Brazzi
CHRISMAS THAT ALMOST WASN'T. THE(1966, Ital.)
Oscar Brazzi
PSYCHOUT FOR MURDER(1971, Arg./Ital.), p
Rossano Brazzi
UNA SIGNORA DELL'OVEST(1942, Ital); FURIA(1947, Ital.); GREAT DAWN, THE(1947, Ital.); KING'S JESTER, THE(1947, Ital.); WHITE DEVIL, THE(1948, Ital.); LITTLE WOMEN(1949, Ital.); RETURN OF THE BLACK EAGLE(1949, Ital.); BULLET FOR STEFANO(1950, Ital.); VOLCANO(1953, Ital.); BAREFOOT CONTESSA, THE(1954); THREE COINS IN THE FOUNTAIN(1954); ANGELA(1955, Ital.); SUMMERTIME(1955); LOSER TAKES ALL(1956, Brit.); INTERLUDE(1957); LEGEND OF THE LOST(1957, U.S./Panama/Ital.); STORY OF ESTHER COSTELLO, THE(1957, Brit.); CERTAIN SMILE, A(1958); SOUTH PACIFIC(1958); COUNT YOUR BLESSINGS(1959); AUSTERLITZ(1960, Fr./Ital./Yugo.); LIGHT IN THE PIAZZA(1962); ROME ADVENTURE(1962); SIEGE OF SYRACUSE(1962, Fr./Ital.); THREE FABLES OF LOVE(1963, Fr./Ital./Span.); DARK PURPOSE(1964); BATTLE OF THE VILLA FIORITA, THE(1965, Brit.); CHRISMAS THAT ALMOST WASN'T. THE(1966, Ital.), a, d; ENGAGEMENT ITALIANO(1966, Fr./Ital.); BOBO, THE(1967, Brit.); WOMAN TIMES SEVEN(1967, U.S./Fr./Ital.); GUILT IS NOT MINE(1968, Ital.); ITALIAN JOB, THE(1969, Brit.); KRAKATOA, EAST OF JAVA(1969); ONE STEP TO HELL(1969, U.S./Ital./Span.); ADVENTURERS, THE(1970); PSYCHOUT FOR MURDER(1971, Arg./Ital.); GREAT WALTZ, THE(1972); HOUSE OF FREAKS(1973, Ital.); DRUMMER OF VENGEANCE(1974, Brit.); POLITICAL ASYLUM(1975, Mex./Guatemalan); FINAL CONFLICT, THE(1981)
1984
FEAR CITY(1984)
Misc. Talkies
MR. KINGSTREET'S WAR(1973)
Jiri Brdecka
EMPEROR AND THE NIGHTINGALE, THE(1949, Czech.), w; EMPEROR AND THE GOLEM, THE(1955, Czech.), w; MIDSUMMERS NIGHT'S DREAM, A(1961, Czech), w; NIGHTS OF PRAGUE, THE(1968, Czech.), d, w; ADELE HASN'T HAD HER SUPPER YET(1978, Czech.), w
Pierre Richard Bre
LA COLLECTIONNEUSE(1971, Fr.)
Freddie William Breach
OLD MOTHER RILEY OVERSEAS(1943, Brit.)
Bernice Breacher
Silents
IS YOUR DAUGHTER SAFE?(1927)
Sebastian Breaks
HEROES OF TELEMARK, THE(1965, Brit.); BIG SWITCH, THE(1970, Brit.); UNDERGROUND(1970, Brit.); NIGHT DIGGER, THE(1971, Brit.)
Bernard Breakston
PHANTOM SUBMARINE, THE(1941)
Bernie Breakston
ISLAND OF DOOMED MEN(1940)
George Breakston
GREAT EXPECTATIONS(1934); IT HAPPENED ONE NIGHT(1934); MRS. WIGGS OF THE CABBAGE PATCH(1934); NO GREATER GLORY(1934); SUCCESSFUL FAILURE, A(1934); DARK ANGEL, THE(1935); RETURN OF PETER GRIMM,

THE(1935); BOULDER DAM(1936); SECOND WIFE(1936); SMALL TOWN GIRL(1936); LOVE FINDS ANDY HARDY(1938); ANDY HARDY GETS SPRING FEVER(1939); JESSE JAMES(1939); JUDGE HARDY AND SON(1939); LIFE RETURNS(1939); ANDY HARDY MEETS DEBUTANTE(1940); ANDY HARDY'S PRIVATE SECRETARY(1941); LIFE BEGINS FOR ANDY HARDY(1941); COURTSHIP OF ANDY HARDY, THE(1942); MEN OF SAN QUENTIN(1942); TOKYO FILE 212(1951), p, d&w; GEISHA GIRL(1952), p&d; SCARLET SPEAR, THE(1954, Brit.), d&w; ESCAPE IN THE SUN(1956, Brit.), d&w, p; WHITE HUNTRESS(1957, Brit.), p, d; WOMAN AND THE HUNTER, THE(1957), d; BOY CRIED MURDER, THE(1966, Ger./Brit./Yugo.), d
Misc. Talkies
URUBU(1948), d

George P. Breakston
MANSTER, THE(1962, Jap.), p, d, w

George Breakstone
SWANEE RIVER(1939); GRAPES OF WRATH(1940)

P.A. Breal
DEADLIER THAN THE MALE(1957, Fr.), w

Sylvie Breal
MAN WHO LIES, THE(1970, Czech./Fr.); SOLO(1970, Fr.)

Gil Brealey
THREE TO GO(1971, Aus.), p

Toney Brealond
COME BACK CIHARLESTON BLUE(1972)

Tony Brealond
WIZ, THE(1978)

Julian Bream
SEA FURY(1959, Brit.)

Sylvia Breamer
TOO MANY PARENTS(1936)
Silents
PINCH HITTER, THE(1917); DOUBLING FOR ROMEO(1921); NOT GUILTY(1921); SHERLOCK BROWN(1921); WOLF LAW(1922); GIRL OF THE GOLDEN WEST, THE(1923); RECKLESS ROMANCE(1924); LIGHTNING REPORTER(1926)
Misc. Silents
COLD DECK, THE(1917); NARROW TRAIL, THE(1917); COMMON CAUSE, THE(1918); DAWN(1919); MOONSHINE(1918); HOUSE DIVIDED, A(1919); MOONSHINE TRAIL, THE(1919); MY HUSBAND'S OTHER WIFE(1919); BLOOD BARRIER, THE(1920); MY LADY'S GARTER(1920); RESPECTABLE BY PROXY(1920); UNSEEN FORCES(1920); DEVIL, THE(1921); POOR RELATION, A(1921); ROOF TREE, THE(1921); CALVERT'S VALLEY(1922); FACE BETWEEN, THE(1922); MAN UNCONQUERABLE, THE(1922); MAN WHO MARRIED HIS OWN WIFE, THE(1922); MAN WITH TWO MOTHERS, THE(1922); MONEY TO BURN(1922); BAREFOOT BOY, THE(1923); BAVU(1923); FIRST DEGREE, THE(1923); FLAMING YOUTH(1923); HER TEMPORARY HUSBAND(1923); THUNDERGATE(1923); LILLIES OF THE FIELD(1924); ROBES OF SIN(1924); WOMAN ON THE JURY, THE(1924); TOO MUCH YOUTH(1925); WOMEN AND GOLD(1925)

Francois Breant
SNOW(1983, Fr.), m

Bill Breashears
RECORD CITY(1978), ed

Christiane Breaud
SEASON FOR LOVE, THE(1963, Fr.)

Marc Breaux
MARY POPPINS(1964), ch; SOUND OF MUSIC, THE(1965), ch; HAPPIEST MILLIONAIRE, THE(1967), ch; CHITTY CHITTY BANG BANG(1968, Brit.), ch; HUCKLEBERRY FINN(1974), ch; SLIPPER AND THE ROSE, THE(1976, Brit.), ch; SEXTETTE(1978), ch

Walter Breaux
SOUNDER, PART 2(1976)

Bob Brebor
FARMER'S OTHER DAUGHTER, THE(1965), ed

Egon Brecher
ROYAL BOX, THE(1930); TO THE LAST MAN(1933); BLACK CAT, THE(1934); MANY HAPPY RETURNS(1934); NO GREATER GLORY(1934); NOW AND FOREVER(1934); BLACK FURY(1935); BLACK ROOM, THE(1935); FLORENTINE DAGGER, THE(1935); MARK OF THE VAMPIRE(1935); PADDY O'DAY(1935); WEREWOLF OF LONDON, THE(1935); ALIBI FOR MURDER(1936); BOULDER DAM(1936); CHARLIE CHAN'S SECRET(1936); DEVIL DOLL, THE(1936); LADIES IN LOVE(1936); LOVE ON THE RUN(1936); ONE IN A MILLION(1936); SINS OF MAN(1936); TILL WE MEET AGAIN(1936); WHITE ANGEL, THE(1936); BLACK LEGION, THE(1937); EMPEROR'S CANDLESTICKS, THE(1937); ESPIONAGE(1937); HEIDI(1937); I MET HIM IN PARIS(1937); LANCER SPY(1937); LIFE OF EMILE ZOLA, THE(1937); LOVE UNDER FIRE(1937); STOLEN HOLIDAY(1937); THIN ICE(1937); ARSENE LUPIN RETURNS(1938); COCOANUT GROVE(1938); INVISIBLE ENEMY(1938); SPAWN OF THE NORTH(1938); SPY RING, THE(1938); SUEZ(1938); YOU AND ME(1938); ANGELS WASH THEIR FACES(1939); CONFESSIONS OF A NAZI SPY(1939); ESPIONAGE AGENT(1939); JUAREZ(1939); JUDGE HARDY AND SON(1939); NURSE EDITH CAVELL(1939); THREE MUSKETEERS, THE(1939); WE ARE NOT ALONE(1939); ALL THIS AND HEAVEN TOO(1940); DEVIL'S ISLAND(1940); DISPATCH FROM REUTERS, A(1940); DR. EHRLICH'S MAGIC BULLET(1940); FOUR SONS(1940); I WAS AN ADVENTURESS(1940); KNUTE ROCKNE–ALL AMERICAN(1940); MAN I MARRIED, THE(1940); MAN HUNT(1941); MANPOWER(1941); THEY DARE NOT LOVE(1941); UNDERGROUND(1941); HITLER'S CHILDREN(1942); ISLE OF MISSING MEN(1942); KING'S ROW(1942); ABOVE SUSPICION(1943); DESERT SONG, THE(1943); MISSION TO MOSCOW(1943); THEY CAME TO BLOW UP AMERICA(1943); HAIRY APE, THE(1944); U-BOAT PRISONER(1944); CORNERED(1945); ROYAL SCANDAL, A(1945); VOICE OF THE WHISTLER(1945); WHITE PONGO(1945); O.S.S.(1946); SISTER KENNY(1946); SO DARK THE NIGHT(1946); TEMPTATION(1946); WIFE OF MONTE CRISTO, THE(1946)

Irving Brecher
FOOLS FOR SCANDAL(1938), w; AT THE CIRCUS(1939), w; GO WEST(1940), w; SHADOW OF THE THIN MAN(1941), w; FOR ME AND MY GAL(1942), w; SHIP AHOY(1942), w; BEST FOOT FORWARD(1943), w; DU BARRY WAS A LADY(1943), w; MEET ME IN ST. LOUIS(1944), w; YOLANDA AND THE THIEF(1945), w; ZIEGFELD FOLLIES(1945), w; SUMMER HOLIDAY(1948), w; LIFE OF RILEY, THE(1949), p,d&w; SOMEBODY LOVES ME(1952), d&w; CRY FOR HAPPY(1961), w; SAIL A CROOKED SHIP(1961), d; BYE BYE BIRDIE(1963), w

Irving S. Brecher
NEW FACES OF 1937(1937), w

Kenneth Brecher
ZOOT SUIT(1981), p

Bertolt Brecht
THREEPENNY OPERA, THE(1931, Ger./U.S.), w; THREE PENNY OPERA(1963, Fr./Ger.), w; SHAMELESS OLD LADY, THE(1966, Fr.), w; GALILEO(1975, Brit.), w

S. Brecht
FREUD(1962)

Gavin Breck
ATTACK ON THE IRON COAST(1968, U.S./Brit.)

Kathleen Breck
WEST 11(1963, Brit.); SPACEFLIGHT IC-1(1965, Brit.); FROZEN DEAD, THE(1967, Brit.)

Peter Breck
DEADLINE AT DAWN(1946); I WANT TO LIVE!(1958); THUNDER ROAD(1958); WILD AND THE INNOCENT, THE(1959); BEATNIKS, THE(1960); PORTRAIT OF A MOBSTER(1961); LAD: A DOG(1962); CRAWLING HAND, THE(1963); HOOTENANNY HOOT(1963); SHOCK CORRIDOR(1963); GLORY GUYS, THE(1965); BENJI(1974); SWORD AND THE SORCERER, THE(1982)
Misc. Talkies
MAN FOR HANGING, A(1972)

Betty Breckenridge
TOM, DICK AND HARRY(1941)

John Breckinridge
PLAN 9 FROM OUTER SPACE(1959)

Gary Breckner
LOVE AND HISSES(1937); WAKE UP AND LIVE(1937); REBECCA OF SUNNYBROOK FARM(1938); THANKS FOR EVERYTHING(1938); JOHNNY APOLLO(1940); STAR DUST(1940); GREAT AMERICAN BROADCAST, THE(1941); STRANGE CASE OF DR. RX, THE(1942); SUBMARINE RAIDER(1942); SWEETHEART OF THE FLEET(1942); MARGIN FOR ERROR(1943)

Ragna Breda
ONLY ONE NIGHT(1942, Swed.)

Jiri Bredecka
LEMONADE JOE(1966, Czech.), w, cos

Ellwood Bredell
BIG TOWN CZAR(1939), ph

Elwood Bredell
BEHIND THE MIKE(1937), ph; THAT'S MY STORY(1937), ph; WESTBOUND LIMITED(1937), ph; FORBIDDEN VALLEY(1938), ph; FRESHMAN YEAR(1938), ph; LITTLE TOUGH GUY(1938), ph; RECKLESS LIVING(1938), ph; SECRETS OF A NURSE(1938), ph; STRANGE FACES(1938), ph; SWING, SISTER, SWING(1938), ph; SWING THAT CHEER(1938), ph; CALL A MESSENGER(1939), ph; EX-CHAMP(1939), ph; SPIRIT OF CULVER, THE(1939), ph; TWO BRIGHT BOYS(1939), ph; ARGENTINE NIGHTS(1940), ph; BLACK FRIDAY(1940), ph; DANGER ON WHEELS(1940), ph; DARK STREETS OF CAIRO(1940), ph; DOUBLE ALIBI(1940), ph; GANGS OF CHICAGO(1940), ph; HONEYMOON DEFERRED(1940), ph; I CAN'T GIVE YOU ANYTHING BUT LOVE, BABY(1940), ph; I'M NOBODY'S SWEETHEART NOW(1940), ph; LA CONGA NIGHTS(1940), ph; MA, HE'S MAKING EYES AT ME(1940), ph; MUMMY'S HAND, THE(1940), ph; SANDY GETS HER MAN(1940), ph; YOU'RE NOT SO TOUGH(1940), ph; HOLD THAT GHOST(1941), ph; HORROR ISLAND(1941), ph; INVISIBLE WOMAN, THE(1941), ph; MAN MADE MONSTER(1941), ph; MEET THE CHUMP(1941), ph; MOB TOWN(1941), ph; SOUTH OF TAHITI(1941), ph; SWING IT SOLDIER(1941), ph; TIGHT SHOES(1941), ph; JAIL HOUSE BLUES(1942), ph; TOUGH AS THEY COME(1942), ph; HERS TO HOLD(1943), ph; SO'S YOUR UNCLE(1943), ph; ROMANCE ON THE HIGH SEAS(1948), ph; ADVENTURES OF DON JUAN(1949), ph; INSPECTOR GENERAL, THE(1949), ph; JOURNEY INTO LIGHT(1951), ph; FEMALE JUNGLE, THE(1955), ph
Misc. Silents
UP OR DOWN(1917)

Elwood "Woody" Bredell
MYSTERY OF MARIE ROGET, THE(1942), ph

Woody Bredell
HELLZAPOPPIN'(1941), ph; BUTCH MINDS THE BABY(1942), ph; ESCAPE FROM HONG KONG(1942), ph; GHOST OF FRANKENSTEIN, THE(1942), ph; PRIVATE BUCKAROO(1942), ph; SHERLOCK HOLMES AND THE VOICE OF TERROR(1942), ph; STRANGE CASE OF DR. RX, THE(1942), ph; AMAZING MRS. HOLLIDAY(1943), ph; COWBOY IN MANHATTTAN(1943), ph; FOLLOW THE BAND(1943), ph; HIS BUTLER'S SISTER(1943), ph; HOW'S ABOUT IT?(1943), ph; CAN'T HELP SINGING(1944), ph; CHRISTMAS HOLIDAY(1944), ph; PHANTOM LADY(1944), ph; LADY ON A TRAIN(1945), ph; BEAUTIFUL CHEAT, THE(1946), ph; KILLERS, THE(1946), ph; SMOOTH AS SILK(1946), ph; TANGIER(1946), ph; UNSUSPECTED, THE(1947), ph

Guillermo Bredeston
GAMES MEN PLAY, THE(1968, Arg.)

Susan Bredhoff
HEROES(1977); FRENCH POSTCARDS(1979); ISLAND, THE(1980)

Asta Bredigand
HANDS OF DESTINY(1954, Brit.)

Patricia Bredin
BRIDAL PATH, THE(1959, Brit.); LEFT, RIGHT AND CENTRE(1959); DESERT MICE(1960, Brit.); SECRET OF MONTE CRISTO, THE(1961, Brit.); TO HAVE AND TO HOLD(1963, Brit.); MAKE MINE A MILLION(1965, Brit.)

Jim Bredouw
DOUBLES(1978), m

James Bree
JUST MY LUCK(1957, Brit.); MATTER OF CHOICE, A(1963, Brit.); WHO WAS MADDOX?(1964, Brit.); ON HER MAJESTY'S SECRET SERVICE(1969, Brit.); SATAN'S SLAVE(1976, Brit.)

Jack Breed
BIG CHASE, THE(1954)

John Breeden
FOX MOVIETONE FOLLIES(1929); MASQUERADE(1929); SALUTE(1929); SHANNONS OF BROADWAY, THE(1929); BELOVED BACHELOR, THE(1931); FALSE MADONNA(1932); MADAME RACKETEER(1932)
Silents
JOY STREET(1929)

Larry Breeding
STREET MUSIC(1982)
Richard Breeding
COUNT YOUR BULLETS(1972); MAN WHO FELL TO EARTH, THE(1976, Brit.)
Joe Breedlove
EYEWITNESS(1981)
Norman Breedlove
FORTY GUNS(1957), spec eff; VERBOTEN!(1959), spec eff; NUN AND THE SERGEANT, THE(1962), spec eff; DIARY OF A MADMAN(1963), spec eff; RAGE TO LIVE, A(1965), spec eff; PARTY, THE(1968), spec eff
Phillip Breedlove
REPRISAL(1956)
Agness Breen
HAIR(1979)
Bob Breen
HARPER VALLEY, P.T.A.(1978), set d
Bobby Breen
LET'S SING AGAIN(1936); RAINBOW ON THE RIVER(1936); MAKE A WISH(1937); BREAKING THE ICE(1938); HAWAII CALLS(1938); ESCAPE TO PARADISE(1939); FISHERMAN'S WHARF(1939); WAY DOWN SOUTH(1939); JOHNNY DOUGHBOY(1943)
Charles Breen
BATTLE BEYOND THE STARS(1980), art d
Elizabeth Breen
Silents
COUNTERFEIT(1919)
George Breen
JIGSAW(1949)
Hurley Breen
BOOTS MALONE(1952)
Joe Breen
SCANDAL INCORPORATED(1956)
Joe Breen, Jr.
PRODIGAL, THE(1955), w
John Breen
RHUBARB(1951); MAN IN THE GREY FLANNEL SUIT, THE(1956)
Joseph Breen
REDEEMER, THE(1965, Span.), d
Joseph I. Breen, Jr.
BREAKTHROUGH(1950), w
Margaret Breen
HEADS UP(1930)
Mary Breen
HONEYMOON KILLERS, THE(1969)
Michael Breen
GIRLS CAN PLAY(1937)
Paulette Breen
CLONUS HORROR, THE(1979)
Philip Breen
GAWAIN AND THE GREEN KNIGHT(1973, Brit.), w
Philip M. Breen
1984
SWORD OF THE VALIANT(1984, Brit.), w
Phillip Breen
BEST HOUSE IN LONDON, THE(1969, Brit.), p
Richard Breen
FOREIGN AFFAIR, A(1948), w; TOP O' THE MORNING(1949), w; APPOINTMENT WITH DANGER(1951), w; MATING SEASON(1951), w; MODEL AND THE MARRIAGE BROKER, THE(1951), w; O. HENRY'S FULL HOUSE(1952), w; NIAGARA(1953), w; TITANIC(1953), w; WAKE ME WHEN IT'S OVER(1960), w; STATE FAIR(1962), w; CAPTAIN NEWMAN, M.D.(1963), w; MARY, MARY(1963), w; DO NOT DISTURB(1965), w; MAN COULD GET KILLED, A(1966), w; TONY ROME(1967), w
Richard L. Breen
ISN'T IT ROMANTIC?(1948), w; MISS TATLOCK'S MILLIONS(1948), w; DRAGNET(1954), w; PETE KELLY'S BLUES(1955), w; SEVEN CITIES OF GOLD(1955), w; STOPOVER TOKYO(1957), d, w; FBI STORY, THE(1959), w; PT 109(1963), w
Robert Breen
NAKED ALIBI(1954), w
Thomas E. Breen
B. F.'S DAUGHTER(1948); HOMECOMING(1948); LUXURY LINER(1948); THREE DARING DAUGHTERS(1948); BATTLEGROUND(1949); SCENE OF THE CRIME(1949); RIVER, THE(1951)
William Breen
SPENCER'S MOUNTAIN(1963)
Art Breese
FEVER HEAT(1968)
Carlotta Breese
Misc. Silents
SHIRLEY(1922, Brit.)
Edmond Breese
PERFECT CRIME, THE(1928)
Edmund Breese
HAUNTED HOUSE, THE(1928); ON TRIAL(1928); CONQUEST(1929); FANCY BAGGAGE(1929); GIRL OVERBOARD(1929); HOTTENTOT, THE(1929); IN THE HEADLINES(1929); SONNY BOY(1929); ALL QUIET ON THE WESTERN FRONT(1930); CZAR OF BRODWAY, THE(1930); HOLD EVERYTHING(1930); KISMET(1930); PLAYBOY OF PARIS(1930); ROUGH WATERS(1930); SEA BAT, THE(1930); TOL'ABLE DAVID(1930); TOP SPEED(1930); BRIGHT LIGHTS(1931); CHINATOWN AFTER DARK(1931); DEFENDERS OF THE LAW(1931); GOOD BAD GIRL, THE(1931); LAST PARADE, THE(1931); MATA HARI(1931); MILLIE(1931); PAINTED DESERT, THE(1931); PLATINUM BLONDE(1931); PUBLIC DEFENDER, THE(1931); SHE-WOLF, THE(1931); WICKED(1931); ALIAS MARY SMITH(1932); CABIN IN THE COTTON(1932); CROSS-EXAMINATION(1932); DRIFTING(1932); GOLDEN WEST, THE(1932); HATCHET MAN, THE(1932); LOVE BOUND(1932); MADAME BUTTERFLY(1932); MATCH KING, THE(1932); DUCK SOUP(1933); INTERNATIONAL HOUSE(1933); LADIES MUST LOVE(1933); LAUGHING AT LIFE(1933); MAN OF SENTIMENT, A(1933); WOMEN WON'T TELL(1933); ABOVE THE CLOUDS(1934); BELOVED(1934); COME ON, MARINES(1934); DANCING MAN(1934); RETURN OF THE TERROR(1934); TREASURE ISLAND(1934); LOST IN THE STRATOS-

PHERE(1935)
Misc. Talkies
PLAYTHINGS OF HOLLYWOOD(1931); MARRIAGE BARGAIN, THE(1935)
Silents
MASTER MIND, THE(1914); SHOOTING OF DAN MCGREW, THE(1915); SONG OF THE WAGE SLAVE, THE(1915); MAN'S HOME, A(1921), w; CURSE OF DRINK, THE(1922); SURE FIRE FLINT(1922); JACQUELINE, OR BLAZING BARRIERS(1923); LUCK(1923); PLAYTHINGS OF DESIRE(1924); EARLY BIRD, THE(1925); POLICE PATROL, THE(1925); WOMANHANDLED(1925); STEPPING ALONG(1926); GIRLS GONE WILD(1929)
Misc. Silents
WALLS OF JERICHO, THE(1914); LURE OF HEART'S DESIRE, THE(1916); SPELL OF THE YUKON, THE(1916); WEAKNESS OF STRENGTH, THE(1916); SOMEONE MUST PAY(1919); CHAINS OF EVIDENCE(1920); COMMON LEVEL, A(1920); HIS TEMPORARY WIFE(1920); BRIGHT LIGHTS OF BROADWAY(1923); FAIR CHEAT, THE(1923); THREE O'CLOCK IN THE MORNING(1923); RESTLESS WIVES(1924); SPEED SPOOK, THE(1924); WILDFIRE(1925); BACK TO LIBERTY(1927); PARADISE FOR TWO(1927); FINDERS KEEPERS(1928); HAUNTED HOUSE, THE(1928); WRIGHT IDEA, THE(1928)
Elias Breeskin
PANCHO VILLA RETURNS(1950, Mex.), m; CAPTAIN SCARLETT(1953), m
Stella Breeton
Misc. Silents
BOYS OF THE OLD BRIGADE, THE(1916, Brit.)
Edmund Breeze
YOUNG SINNERS(1931)
Silents
BURN 'EM UP BARNES(1921)
Michelle Breeze
HARRY AND WALTER GO TO NEW YORK(1976)
Alexandre Breffort
IRMA LA DOUCE(1963), w
Mario Brega
BUFFALO BILL, HERO OF THE FAR WEST(1962, Ital.); FOR A FEW DOLLARS MORE(1967, Ital./Ger./Span.); GOOD, THE BAD, AND THE UGLY, THE(1967, Ital./Span.); OPIATE '67(1967, Fr./Ital.); MINUTE TO PRAY, A SECOND TO DIE, A(1968, Ital.); UGLY ONES, THE(1968, Ital./Span.); DEATH RIDES A HORSE(1969, Ital.); GIRL WHO COULDN'T SAY NO, THE(1969, Ital.); NO ROOM TO DIE(1969, Ital.)
1984
ONCE UPON A TIME IN AMERICA(1984)
Moira Breggni
Silents
KNOCKNAGOW(1918, Ireland)
Buddy Bregman
FIVE GUNS WEST(1955), md; FIGHTING TROUBLE(1956), md; WILD PARTY, THE(1956), m; DELICATE DELINQUENT, THE(1957), m; GUNS, GIRLS AND GANGSTERS(1958), m; STEP DOWN TO TERROR(1958), m; BORN RECKLESS(1959), m; SECRET OF THE PURPLE REEF, THE(1960), m; VALLEY OF THE REDWOODS(1960), m; CAT BURGLAR, THE(1961), m
Martin Bregman
SERPICO(1973), p; DOG DAY AFTERNOON(1975), p; NEXT MAN, THE(1976), a, p, w; SEDUCTION OF JOE TYNAN, THE(1979), p; SIMON(1980), p; FOUR SEASONS, THE(1981), p; VENOM(1982, Brit.), p; SCARFACE(1983), p
Tracy Bregman
HAPPY BIRTHDAY TO ME(1981); CONCRETE JUNGLE, THE(1982); FUNNY FARM, THE(1982, Can.)
Alex Bregonzi
RICOCHET(1966, Brit.)
Lionel Brehan
Silents
BATTLE CRY OF PEACE, THE(1915)
George Brehat
WAR AND PEACE(1956, Ital./U.S.)
Georges Brehat
FAREWELL TO ARMS, A(1957); ATTILA(1958, Ital.); QUIET AMERICAN, THE(1958)
Richard Brehm
COLT .45(1950)
Richard J. Brehm
AND NOW MIGUEL(1966)
Anja Breien
HUNGER(1968, Den./Norway/Swed.), ed
Mitch Breif
WOMAN UNDER THE INFLUENCE, A(1974), ph
Joseph Carl Breil
Silents
BIRTH OF A NATION, THE(1915), m; INTOLERANCE(1916), m; AMERICA(1924), m
Paulette Breil
DOULOS-THE FINGER MAN(1964, Fr./Ital.)
Catherine Breillat
CATHERINE & CO.(1976, Fr.), w; DRACULA AND SON(1976, Fr.)
Marie-Helene Breillat
DRACULA AND SON(1976, Fr.)
Stephen Breimer
BUTCHER BAKER(NIGHTMARE MAKER)* (1982), p, w
Wilfred Breistrand
HUNGER(1968, Den./Norway/Swed.); SNOW TREASURE(1968)
Mitchell Breit
BREAKFAST IN BED(1978)
Earl Breitbard
BETWEEN MIDNIGHT AND DAWN(1950)
Rick Breitenfeld
POLYESTER(1981)
Jochen Breitenstein
COCAINE COWBOYS(1979), ph; TASTE OF SIN, A(1983), ph
Gerald Breitigam
OLD SWIMMIN' HOLE, THE(1941), w

Donahl Breitman
PUTNEY SWOPE(1969)
Trudy Breitschopf
BRIDGE, THE(1961, Ger.)
Hana Brejchova
LOVES OF A BLONDE(1966, Czech.); MATTER OF DAYS, A(1969, Fr./Czech.); MOST BEAUTIFUL AGE, THE(1970, Czech.)
Jana Brejchova
BARON MUNCHAUSEN(1962, Czech.); END OF A PRIEST(1970, Czech.)
Kristin M. Brekke
TENTACLES(1977, Ital.)
Jacques Brel
DEVIL AND THE TEN COMMANDMENTS, THE(1962, Fr.), m; JACQUES BREL IS ALIVE AND WELL AND LIVING IN PARIS(1975), a, m
Mark Breland
LORDS OF DISCIPLINE, THE(1983)
Beppo Brem
TONIO KROGER(1968, Fr./Ger.)
Rudolph Waldemar Brem
JAIL BAIT(1977, Ger.)
Lennie Breman
TROPICAL HEAT WAVE(1952)
Leonard Breman
FRONT PAGE, THE(1974)
Jean Bremaud
CRIME OF MONSIEUR LANGE, THE(1936, Fr.)
Ferruccio Brembilla
AMARCORD(1974, Ital.)
Lennie Bremen
PRIDE OF THE MARINES(1945); WITHIN THESE WALLS(1945); BUCK PRIVATES COME HOME(1947); DARK PASSAGE(1947); DEEP VALLEY(1947); GANGSTER, THE(1947); IT HAPPENED IN BROOKLYN(1947); NIGHT SONG(1947); SONG OF THE THIN MAN(1947); GIRL FROM JONES BEACH, THE(1949); HENRY, THE RAINMAKER(1949); INSPECTOR GENERAL, THE(1949); MY DREAM IS YOURS(1949); TAKE ONE FALSE STEP(1949); M(1951); PEOPLE AGAINST O'HARA, THE(1951); CLOWN, THE(1953); IT SHOULD HAPPEN TO YOU(1954); NEW YORK CONFIDENTIAL(1955); TENDER TRAP, THE(1955); ICE PALACE(1960); SWINGIN' ALONG(1962); LOVE WITH THE PROPER STRANGER(1963); WHO'S MINDING THE MINT?(1967); P.J.(1968); LITTLE MISS MARKER(1980)
Lenny Bremen
LINDA BE GOOD(1947)
Leonard Bremen
TURNING POINT, THE(1952); MAN WITH THE GOLDEN ARM, THE(1955)
Karin Bremer
GERMAN SISTERS, THE(1982, Ger.)
Lucille Bremer
MEET ME IN ST. LOUIS(1944); YOLANDA AND THE THIEF(1945); ZIEGFELD FOLLIES(1945); TILL THE CLOUDS ROLL BY(1946); DARK DELUSION(1947); ADVENTURES OF CASANOVA(1948); BEHIND LOCKED DOORS(1948); RUTHLESS(1948)
Sylvia Bremer
Silents
FAMILY SKELETON, THE(1918)
Misc. Silents
MILLIONAIRE VAGRANT, THE(1917); SUDDEN JIM(1917); TEMPLE OF DUSK, THE(1918)
Belinda Bremner
ON THE RIGHT TRACK(1981)
Lola Bremon
MAN WHO WAGGED HIS TAIL, THE(1961, Ital./Span.)
Romain Bremond
QUARTET(1981, Brit./Fr.)
1984
SWANN IN LOVE(1984, Fr.Ger.)
J. R. Bren
LOOKING FOR TROUBLE(1934), w
J. Robert Bren
BAND PLAYS ON, THE(1934), w; HIGH TENSION(1936), w; WITHOUT ORDERS(1936), w; BAD GUY(1937), w; BEHIND THE HEADLINES(1937), w; CHINA PASSAGE(1937), w; HIDEAWAY(1937), w; MAN WHO FOUND HIMSELF, THE(1937), w; RACING LADY(1937), w; CRIME RING(1938), w; DOUBLE DANGER(1938), w; EVERYBODY'S DOING IT(1938), w; THIS MARRIAGE BUSINESS(1938), w; PARENTS ON TRIAL(1939), w; ARGENTINE NIGHTS(1940), w; CHARTER PILOT(1940), w; AMERICAN EMPIRE(1942), w; IN OLD CALIFORNIA(1942), w; UNDERGROUND AGENT(1942), w; FIRST YANK INTO TOKYO(1945), p, w; GAY SENORITA, THE(1945), w; EL PASO(1949), w; GREAT SIOUX UPRISING, THE(1953), w; OVERLAND PACIFIC(1954), w; SIEGE AT RED RIVER, THE(1954), w; TREASURE OF PANCHO VILLA, THE(1955), w
Milton Bren
REMEMBER?(1939), p; WYOMING(1940), p; BARNACLE BILL(1941), p; FREE AND EASY(1941), p
Silents
DESERT RIDER, THE(1929), w
Milton H. Bren
TARS AND SPARS(1946), p; BORDERLINE(1950), p; THREE FOR BEDROOM C(1952), d&w
Ernest Brenck
LOST IN A HAREM(1944)
Baby Brenda
KATHLEEN(1938, Ireland)
Brenda & Cobina
TIME OUT FOR RHYTHM(1941)
Mike Brendall
FIRE OVER AFRICA(1954, Brit.)
Ed Brendel
SPIRIT OF CULVER, THE(1939)
El Brendel
COCK-EYED WORLD, THE(1929); FROZEN JUSTICE(1929); SUNNY SIDE UP(1929); BIG TRAIL, THE(1930); FOX MOVIETONE FOLLIES OF 1930(1930); GOLDEN CALF, THE(1930); HAPPY DAYS(1930); HOT FOR PARIS(1930); JUST IMAGINE(1930);

DELICIOUS(1931); MR. LEMON OF ORANGE(1931); SIX CYLINDER LOVE(1931); SPIDER, THE(1931); WEST OF BROADWAY(1931); WOMEN OF ALL NATIONS(1931); DISORDERLY CONDUCT(1932); HANDLE WITH CARE(1932); HOT PEPPER(1933); MY LIPS BETRAY(1933); LAST TRAIL, THE(1934); MEANEST GAL IN TOWN, THE(1934); OLSEN'S BIG MOMENT(1934); CAREER WOMAN(1936); BLONDE TROUBLE(1937); GOD'S COUNTRY AND THE WOMAN(1937); HOLY TERROR, THE(1937); HAPPY LANDING(1938); LITTLE MISS BROADWAY(1938); VALLEY OF THE GIANTS(1938); CALL A MESSENGER(1939); CODE OF THE STREETS(1939); HOUSE OF FEAR, THE(1939); RISKY BUSINESS(1939); CAPTAIN CAUTION(1940); GALLANT SONS(1940); IF I HAD MY WAY(1940); I'M FROM ARKANSAS(1944); MACHINE GUN MAMA(1944); BEAUTIFUL BLONDE FROM BASHFUL BEND, THE(1949); PARIS MODEL(1953); SHE-CREATURE, THE(1956)
Silents
CAMPUS FLIRT, THE(1926); ARIZONA BOUND(1927); ROLLED STOCKINGS(1927); WINGS(1927)
Misc. Silents
MAN OF THE FOREST(1926); YOU NEVER KNOW WOMEN(1926); TOO MANY CROOKS(1927)
Elwood Brendel
CODE OF THE STREETS(1939), ph
Frank Brendel
WINNING(1969), spec eff; TWO MULES FOR SISTER SARA(1970), spec eff; MAGNIFICENT SEVEN RIDE, THE(1972), spec eff; EARTHQUAKE(1974), spec eff; SUGARLAND EXPRESS, THE(1974), spec eff; FAMILY PLOT(1976), spec eff
Mike Brendel
BOY WHO STOLE A MILLION, THE(1960, Brit.); GUNFIGHTERS OF CASA GRANDE(1965, U.S./Span.); MURIETA(1965, Span.); KID RODELO(1966, U.S./Span.); ISLAND OF THE DOOMED(1968, Span./Ger.); RUN LIKE A THIEF(1968, Span.)
Frank Brendell
REVENGERS, THE(1972, U.S./Mex.), spec eff
Robert Brendlin
DOWNHILL RACER(1969)
Ann Brendon
DIANE(1955)
Smadar Brener
1984
LITTLE DRUMMER GIRL, THE(1984)
Martha Brenes
RIDE THE PINK HORSE(1947)
Ulises Brenes
COUNTERPLOT(1959)
George Brengel
SOME CAME RUNNING(1959); ON THE RIGHT TRACK(1981); ESCAPE ARTIST, THE(1982)
Dominique Brenguier
MOON IN THE GUTTER THE(1983, Fr./Ital.), ph
1984
AVE MARIA(1984, Fr.), ph
George Brenholtz
THUNDER IN DIXIE(1965)
Bill Brenie
LIFE AND TIMES OF CHESTER-ANGUS RAMSGOOD, THE(1971, Can.)
George Brenlin
PROUD AND THE PROFANE, THE(1956); YOUNG AND DANGEROUS(1957); RIOT IN JUVENILE PRISON(1959); CIMARRON(1960)
Doris Brenn
BELOVED BRAT(1938); FOLLOW THE BOYS(1944)
Bettina Brenna
FUNNY GIRL(1968)
Sheila Brenna
CAPTAIN LIGHTFOOT(1955)
Brennan
WORDS AND MUSIC(1929), w
Andrew Brennan
SAN ANTONE(1953)
Andy Brennan
HOODLUM EMPIRE(1952); WILD BLUE YONDER, THE(1952); FAR COUNTRY, THE(1955); SHOOT OUT AT BIG SAG(1962)
Arthur Brennan
GRIEF STREET(1931)
Brian Brennan
NUNZIO(1978)
Brid Brennan
EXCALIBUR(1981)
1984
ANNE DEVLIN(1984, Ireland); FOUR DAYS IN JULY(1984)
Claire Brennan
DOMINO PRINCIPLE, THE(1977)
Connor Brennan
Misc. Talkies
JOHNSTOWN MONSTER, THE(1971)
Dennis Brennan
RISING OF THE MOON, THE(1957, Ireland); BROTH OF A BOY(1959, Brit.); PLAY DIRTY(1969, Brit.)
Eamonn Brennan
QUARE FELLOW, THE(1962, Brit.)
Ed Brennan
DARK PLACES(1974, Brit.), w
Edward Brennan
Misc. Silents
BLACK FEAR(1915); RIGHT OF WAY, THE(1915); WOMAN PAYS, THE(1915); MAN AND HIS SOUL(1916)
Eileen Brennan
DIVORCE AMERICAN STYLE(1967); LAST PICTURE SHOW, THE(1971); SCARECROW(1973); STING, THE(1973); DAISY MILLER(1974); AT LONG LAST LOVE(1975); HUSTLE(1975); MURDER BY DEATH(1976); CHEAP DETECTIVE, THE(1978); FM(1978); GREAT SMOKEY ROADBLOCK, THE(1978); PRIVATE BENJAMIN(1980); FUNNY FARM, THE(1982, Can.)

Fred Hazlitt Brennan
GREENWICH VILLAGE(1944), w
Frederick Brennan
GHOST TALKS, THE(1929), w
Frederick H. Brennan
GUY NAMED JOE, A(1943), w
Frederick Hazlett Brennan
WIVES NEVER KNOW(1936), w; SAILOR'S LADY(1940), w; GIRL IN EVERY PORT, A(1952), w
Frederick Hazlitt Brennan
MASQUERADE(1929), w; SONG OF KENTUCKY(1929), w; SPEAKEASY(1929), w; WORDS AND MUSIC(1929), w; ONE NIGHT AT SUSIE'S(1930), w; SWEET MA-MA(1930), w; SPORTING BLOOD(1931), w; PLAY GIRL(1932), w; MAN OF SENTI-MENT, A(1933), w; SHANGHAI MADNESS(1933), w; ST. LOUIS KID, THE(1934), w; MISS PACIFIC FLEET(1935), w; LITTLE MISS NOBODY(1936), w; BIG BROADCAST OF 1938, THE(1937), w; ST. LOUIS BLUES(1939), w; UNTAMED(1940), w; MY PAL, WOLF(1944), w; ADVENTURE(1945), w; KILLER McCOY(1947), w; FOLLOW THE SUN(1951), w; DEVIL'S CANYON(1953), w; THUNDER IN THE EAST(1953), w
Silents
PROTECTION(1929), w; SIN SISTER, THE(1929), w; STRONG BOY(1929), w
Godfrey Brennan
FOUR FEATHERS, THE(1939, Brit.), cos
Hazel Brennan
Misc. Silents
PALISER CASE, THE(1920)
J. Brennan
Misc. Silents
HIDDEN LIGHT(1920)
Jack Brennan
Silents
GREED(1925), m
James Brennan
NEVER LOOK BACK(1952, Brit.), p
Silents
GREED(1925), m
Jay Brennan
EXPENSIVE HUSBANDS(1937), w; FOLLIES GIRL(1943)
Jimmy Brennan
1984
PIGS(1984, Ireland), a, w
John Brennan
SOME CAME RUNNING(1959); PLEASE DON'T EAT THE DAISIES(1960); WHERE THE BOYS ARE(1960)
Kevin Brennan
MASSACRE HILL(1949, Brit.); ON THE BEACH(1959); LIVE NOW-PAY LA-TER(1962, Brit.); PUSSYCAT ALLEY(1965, Brit.); GET CARTER(1971, Brit.); LOOT(1971, Brit.); UNIDENTIFIED FLYING ODDBALL, THE(1979, Brit.); MAN WITH TWO BRAINS, THE(1983), cos
Kirk Brennan
TRUE CONFESSIONS(1981)
Marguerite Brennan
SCOTLAND YARD INSPECTOR(1952, Brit.); TREASURE HUNT(1952, Brit.); RE-COIL(1953); TWILIGHT WOMEN(1953, Brit.); LADY IS A SQUARE, THE(1959, Brit.); I THANK A FOOL(1962, Brit.)
Matthew Brennan
LUCKY LOSER(1934, Brit.), w
Michael Brennan
I BECAME A CRIMINAL(1947); CARDBOARD CAVALIER, THE(1949, Brit.); FOR THEM THAT TRESPASS(1949, Brit.); BLACKOUT(1950, Brit.); CLOUDED YELLOW, THE(1950, Brit.); NO TRACE(1950, Brit.); SILK NOOSE, THE(1950, Brit.); CIRCLE OF DANGER(1951, Brit.); LADY WITH A LAMP, THE(1951, Brit.); OPERATION DISAS-TER(1951, Brit.); PAUL TEMPLE'S TRIUMPH(1951, Brit.); THEY WERE NOT DIVID-ED(1951, Brit.); TOM BROWN'S SCHOOLDAYS(1951, Brit.); IVANHOE(1952, Brit.); MADE IN HEAVEN(1952, Brit.); SOMETHING MONEY CAN'T BUY(1952, Brit.); WATERFRONT WOMEN(1952, Brit.); 13 EAST STREET(1952, Brit.); IT'S A GRAND LIFE(1953, Brit.); UP TO HIS NECK(1954, Brit.); SEE HOW THEY RUN(1955, Brit.); TROUBLE IN STORE(1955, Brit.); JUST MY LUCK(1957, Brit.); NOT WANTED ON VOYAGE(1957, Brit.); LAW AND DISORDER(1958, Brit.); DAY THEY ROBBED THE BANK OF ENGLAND, THE(1960, Brit.); THIRTY NINE STEPS, THE(1960, Brit.); WATCH YOUR STERN(1961, Brit.); AMBUSH IN LEOPARD STREET(1962, Brit.); DEVIL'S AGENT, THE(1962, Brit.); LIVE NOW-PAY LATER(1962, Brit.); GIRL HUNTERS, THE(1963, Brit.); TOM JONES(1963, Brit.); ACT OF MURDER(1965, Brit.); AMOROUS ADVENTURES OF MOLL FLANDERS, THE(1965); CUCKOO PA-TROL(1965, Brit.); JOHNNY NOBODY(1965, Brit.); THREE HATS FOR LISA(1965, Brit.); THUNDERBALL(1965, Brit.); DEADLY AFFAIR, THE(1967, Brit.); JUST LIKE A WOMAN(1967, Brit.); LOVE IS A WOMAN(1967, Brit.); GREAT PONY RAID, THE(1968, Brit.); FRIGHT(1971, Brit.); LUST FOR A VAMPIRE(1971, Brit.); NOTHING BUT THE NIGHT(1975, Brit.)
Mick Brennan
DOUBLE NICKELS(1977), a, ed
Nell Brennan
MAN AT THE TOP(1973, Brit.)
Patrick Brennan
ATTIC, THE(1979); FAST TIMES AT RIDGEMONT HIGH(1982)
Paul Brennan
HENNESSY(1975, Brit.); BELOW THE BELT(1980); STAR CHAMBER, THE(1983)
Peggy Lee Brennan
MESSAGE FROM SPACE(1978, Jap.)
Peter Brennan
1984
RAZORBACK(1984, Aus.), w
Richard Brennan
LONG WEEKEND(1978, Aus.), p; STIR(1980, Aus.), p; STARSTRUCK(1982, Aus.), p
Robert Brennan
HIGH TREASON(1951, Brit.)
Ruth Brennan
THIS LOVE OF OURS(1945); SET-UP, THE(1949); CALIFORNIA PASSAGE(1950); OH! SUSANNA(1951); HELL'S OUTPOST(1955)

Sean Brennan
NOBODY'S PERFEKT(1981)
Sheila Brennan
CURSE OF THE WEREWOLF, THE(1961); CAT ATE THE PARAKEET, THE(1972); SPIRAL STAIRCASE, THE(1975, Brit.)
Steven Brennan
1984
STARMAN(1984)
Sunday Brennan
CHAPTER TWO(1979)
Tom Brennan
RECOMMENDATION FOR MERCY(1975, Can.); WILLIE AND PHIL(1980)
Walter Brennan
LONG, LONG TRAIL, THE(1929); SHANNONS OF BROADWAY, THE(1929); ONE HYSTERICAL NIGHT(1930); NECK AND NECK(1931); ALL-AMERICAN, THE(1932); LAW AND ORDER(1932); MISS PINKERTON(1932); TEXAS CYCLONE(1932); TWO-FISTED LAW(1932); FOURTH HORSEMAN, THE(1933); INVISIBLE MAN, THE(1933); KISS BEFORE THE MIRROR, THE(1933); ONE YEAR LATER(1933); RUSTLERS' ROUNDUP(1933); SATURDAY'S MILLIONS(1933); SING SINNER, SING(1933); STRANGE PEOPLE(1933); DEATH OF THE DIAMOND(1934); GOOD DAME(1934); HALF A SINNER(1934); LIFE OF VERGIE WINTERS, THE(1934); RIP TIDE(1934); WHOM THE GODS DESTROY(1934); BARBARY COAST(1935); LADY TUBBS(1935); LAW BEYOND THE RANGE(1935); MAN ON THE FLYING TRAPEZE, THE(1935); NORTHERN FRONTIER(1935); PUBLIC HERO NO. 1(1935); SEVEN KEYS TO BALDPATE(1935); WEDDING NIGHT, THE(1935); WE'RE IN THE MONEY(1935); BANJO ON MY KNEE(1936); COME AND GET IT(1936); FURY(1936); MOON'S OUR HOME, THE(1936); PRESCOTT KID, THE(1936); THESE THREE(1936); THREE GODFATHERS(1936); AFFAIRS OF CAPPY RICKS(1937); SHE'S DANGEROUS(1937); WHEN LOVE IS YOUNG(1937); WILD AND WOOLLY(1937); ADVENTURES OF TOM SAWYER, THE(1938); BUCCANEER, THE(1938); COWBOY AND THE LADY, THE(1938); KENTUCKY(1938); MOTHER CAREY'S CHICKENS(1938); TEXANS, THE(1938); JOE AND ETHEL TURP CALL ON THE PRESIDENT(1939); STANLEY AND LIVINGSTONE(1939); STORY OF VERNON AND IRENE CASTLE, THE(1939); THEY SHALL HAVE MUSIC(1939); MARYLAND(1940); NORTHWEST PASS-AGE(1940); WESTERNER, THE(1940); MEET JOHN DOE(1941); NICE GIRL?(1941); RISE AND SHINE(1941); SERGEANT YORK(1941); SWAMP WATER(1941); THIS WOMAN IS MINE(1941); PRIDE OF THE YANKEES, THE(1942); STAND BY FOR ACTION(1942); HANGMEN ALSO DIE(1943); NORTH STAR, THE(1943); SLIGHTLY DANGEROUS(1943); HOME IN INDIANA(1944); PRINCESS AND THE PIRATE, THE(1944); TO HAVE AND HAVE NOT(1944); DAKOTA(1945); CENTENNIAL SUM-MER(1946); MY DARLING CLEMENTINE(1946); NOBODY LIVES FOREVER(1946); STOLEN LIFE, A(1946); DRIFTWOOD(1947); BLOOD ON THE MOON(1948); RED RIVER(1948); SCUDDA-HOO! SCUDDA-HAY!(1948); BRIMSTONE(1949); GREEN PROMISE, THE(1949); TASK FORCE(1949); CURTAIN CALL AT CACTUS CREEK(1950); SHOWDOWN, THE(1950); SINGING GUNS(1950); SURRENDER(1950); TICKET TO TOMAHAWK(1950); ALONG THE GREAT DIVIDE(1951); BEST OF THE BADMEN(1951); LURE OF THE WILDERNESS(1952); RETURN OF THE TEX-AN(1952); WILD BLUE YONDER, THE(1952); SEA OF LOST SHIPS(1953); DRUMS ACROSS THE RIVER(1954); FOUR GUNS TO THE BORDER(1954); AT GUN-POINT(1955); BAD DAY AT BLACK ROCK(1955); FAR COUNTRY, THE(1955); GLORY(1955); COME NEXT SPRING(1956); GOODBYE, MY LADY(1956); PROUD ONES, THE(1956); GOD IS MY PARTNER(1957); TAMMY AND THE BA-CHELOR(1957); WAY TO THE GOLD(1957); RIO BRAVO(1959); HOW THE WEST WAS WON(1962); SHOOT OUT AT BIG SAG(1962); THOSE CALLOWAYS(1964); OSCAR, THE(1966); GNOME-MOBILE, THE(1967); WHO'S MINDING THE MINT?(1967); ONE AND ONLY GENUINE ORIGINAL FAMILY BAND, THE(1968); SUPPORT YOUR LOCAL SHERIFF(1969); SMOKE IN THE WIND(1975)
Misc. Talkies
FIGHTING FOR JUSTICE(1932); MAN OF ACTION(1933); SILENT MEN(1933)
Silents
LARIAT KID, THE(1929)
Misc. Silents
TEARIN' INTO TROUBLE(1927)
Walter Brennan, Jr.
STARLIFT(1951)
Walter A. Brennan, Jr.
SHOOT OUT AT BIG SAG(1962), p
Joachim Brennecke
YOU ARE THE WORLD FOR ME(1964, Aust.)
Tom Brenneman
BREAKFAST IN HOLLYWOOD(1946)
Claire Brennen
SHE FREAK(1967); TRAVELING EXECUTIONER, THE(1970); HERO AIN'T NO-THIN' BUT A SANDWICH, A(1977)
Al Brenner
BROTHER JOHN(1971), art d; SCARECROW(1973), prod d; ZANDY'S BRIDE(1974), prod d; SILENT MOVIE(1976), prod d
Albert Brenner
HEY, LET'S TWIST!(1961), art d; HUSTLER, THE(1961), art d; CONNECTION, THE(1962), art d; TWO TICKETS TO PARIS(1962), art d; LADYBUG, LADY-BUG(1963), art d; FAIL SAFE(1964), art d; LIGHT FANTASTIC(1964), set d; LUCK OF GINGER COFFEY, THE(1964, U.S./Can.), art d; MIDSUMMER NIGHT'S DREAM, A(1966), art d; HAPPENING, THE(1967), art d; LUV(1967), prod d; POINT BLANK(1967), art d; BULLITT(1968), art d; SOME KIND OF A NUT(1969), art d; WHERE IT'S AT(1969), art d; I WALK THE LINE(1970), art d; MONTE WALSH(1970), prod d, cos; SUMMER OF '42(1971), prod d; T.R. BASKIN(1971), prod d&art d; OTHER, THE(1972), prod d; TROUBLE MAN(1972), art d; BANK SHOT(1974), art d; MASTER GUNFIGHTER, THE(1975), prod d; PEEPER(1975), prod d; SUNSHINE BOYS, THE(1975), prod d; MISSOURI BREAKS, THE(1976), prod d; GOODBYE GIRL, THE(1977), prod d; TURNING POINT, THE(1977), prod d; COMA(1978), prod d; HERO AT LARGE(1980), prod d; LEGEND OF THE LONE RANGER, THE(1981), prod d; ONLY WHEN I LAUGH(1981), prod d; I OUGHT TO BE IN PICTURES(1982), prod d; MAX DUGAN RETURNS(1983), prod d; TWO OF A KIND(1983), prod d
1984
UNFAITHFULLY YOURS(1984), prod d; 2010(1984), prod d
Alfred Brenner
KEY WITNESS(1960), w

Dori Brenner
SCARECROW IN A GARDEN OF CUCUMBERS(1972); SUMMER WISHES, WINTER DREAMS(1973); OTHER SIDE OF THE MOUNTAIN, THE(1975); NEXT STOP, GREENWICH VILLAGE(1976); ALTERED STATES(1980)
1984
OASIS, THE(1984)

Eve Brenner
RAT FINK(1965); MARCH OR DIE(1977, Brit.)

Gordon D. Brenner
PETE'S DRAGON(1977, ed; APPLE DUMPLING GANG RIDES AGAIN, THE(1979), ed; NORTH AVENUE IRREGULARS, THE(1979), ed; HERBIE GOES BANANAS(1980), ed; LAST FLIGHT OF NOAH'S ARK, THE(1980), ed; CONDORMAN(1981), ed; NIGHT CROSSING(1982), ed

Joseph Brenner
EYEBALL(1978, Ital.), p

Jules Brenner
WHEN YOU COMIN' BACK, RED RYDER?(1979), ph; JOHNNY GOT HIS GUN(1971), ph; DILLINGER(1973), ph; OUR TIME(1974), ph; CORNBREAD, EARL AND ME(1975), ph; OUTLAW BLUES(1977), ph; LAST WORD, THE(1979), ph

Maurice Brenner
LILITH(1964)

Max Brenner
SILVER DARLINGS, THE(1947, Brit.), ed

Paul Brenner
DISC JOCKEY(1951)

Sylvia Brenner
STRANGE LOVERS(1963)

Walter Brenner
NOT RECONCILED, OR "ONLY VIOLENCE HELPS WHERE IT RULES"(1969, Ger.)

Rachel Brennock
DARWIN ADVENTURE, THE(1972, Brit.)
Misc. Talkies
MR. HORATIO KNIBBLES(1971)

C.H. Brennon
Misc. Silents
HIGH ROAD, THE(1915)

Claire Brennon
CHOIRBOYS, THE(1977)

Herbert Brennon
Misc. Silents
FORBIDDEN PARADISE(1922, Ital.), d

Donald Brenon
OUR NEIGHBORS–THE CARTERS(1939)

Elizabeth Brenon
LUMMOX(1930), w

Herbert Brenon
CASE OF SERGEANT GRISCHA, THE(1930), d; LUMMOX(1930), d; BEAU IDEAL(1931), d; TRANSGRESSION(1931), d; GIRL OF THE RIO(1932), d; WINE, WOMEN, AND SONG(1934), d; HONOURS EASY(1935, Brit.), d; REGAL CAVALCADE(1935, Brit.), d; LIVING DANGEROUSLY(1936, Brit.), d; SOMEONE AT THE DOOR(1936, Brit.), d; DOMINANT SEX, THE(1937, Brit.), d; LIVE WIRE, THE(1937, Brit.), d; SPRING HANDICAP(1937, Brit.), d; HOUSEMASTER(1938, Brit.), d; YELLOW SANDS(1938, Brit.), d; BLACK EYES(1939, Brit.), d; FLYING SQUAD, THE(1940, Brit.), d; FALSE RAPTURE(1941), d
Silents
IVANHOE(1913), a, d&w; NEPTUNE'S DAUGHTER(1914), a, d; CLEMENCEAU CASE, THE(1915), d&w; SIN(1915), d&w; SOUL OF BROADWAY, THE(1915), d&w; ETERNAL SIN, THE(1917), d, w; 12-10(1919, Brit.), d; ANY WIFE(1922), d; MOONSHINE VALLEY(1922), d, w; SHACKLES OF GOLD(1922), d; ALASKAN, THE(1924), d; BREAKING POINT, THE(1924), d; PETER PAN(1924), d; SIDESHOW OF LIFE, THE(1924), p&d; BEAU GESTE(1926), d; DANCING MOTHERS(1926), d; GREAT GATSBY, THE(1926), d; KISS FOR CINDERELLA, A(1926), d; TELEPHONE GIRL, THE(1927), p&d; LAUGH, CLOWN, LAUGH(1928), d; RESCUE, THE(1929), d
Misc. Silents
IVANHOE(1913, Brit.), a, d; ABSINTHE(1914), d; LIFE'S SHOP WINDOW(1914), d; HEART OF MARYLAND, THE(1915), a, d; KREUTZER SONATA, THE(1915), d; TWO ORPHANS, THE(1915), a, d; DAUGHTER OF THE GODS, A(1916), d; RULING PASSION, THE(1916), d; WAR BRIDES(1916), d; FALL OF THE ROMANOFFS, THE(1917), d; LONE WOLF, THE(1917), d; EMPTY POCKETS(1918), d; PASSING OF THE THIRD FLOOR BACK, THE(1918, Brit.), d; VICTORY AND PEACE(1918, Brit.), d; PASSION FLOWER, THE(1921), d; SIGN ON THE DOOR, THE(1921), d; WONDERFUL THING, THE(1921), d; STAGE ROMANCE, A(1922), d; CUSTARD CUP, THE(1923), d; RUSTLE OF SILK, THE(1923), d; SPANISH DANCER, THE(1923), d; WOMAN WITH FOUR FACES(1924), d; SHADOWS OF PARIS(1924), d; LITTLE FRENCH GIRL, THE(1925), d; STREET OF FORGOTTEN MEN, THE(1925), d; GOD GAVE ME TWENTY CENTS(1926), d; SONG AND DANCE MAN, THE(1926), d; SORRELL AND SON(1927), d

Juliet Brenon
Silents
ETERNAL SIN, THE(1917); KISS FOR CINDERELLA, A(1926)

Nora Brenon
ENEMY OF THE POLICE(1933, Brit.)

Robert Brenon
SECRET, THE(1955, Brit.), d&w

Peter Brensing
AMERICAN SUCCESS COMPANY, THE(1980)

Angela Brent
BLACK GESTAPO, THE(1975)

Barbara Brent
GUYS AND DOLLS(1955)

Catherine Brent
NEW FACES OF 1937(1937)

Charles Brent
SECRET INVASION, THE(1964)

Dennis Brent
Misc. Talkies
STAIRWAY FOR A STAR(1947)

Doris Brent
BRAIN THAT WOULDN'T DIE, THE(1959)

Earl Brent
JACKASS MAIL(1942), m

Earl K. Brent
CALL ME MISTER(1951), m/l Rome

Eva Brent
TARZAN'S FIGHT FOR LIFE(1958); CAGE OF EVIL(1960)

Eve Brent
FORTY GUNS(1957); SAD HORSE, THE(1959); STAKEOUT!(1962); MARA OF THE WILDERNESS(1966); GUIDE FOR THE MARRIED MAN, A(1967); HAPPY ENDING, THE(1969); BAREFOOT EXECUTIVE, THE(1971); TODD KILLINGS, THE(1971); HOW TO SEDUCE A WOMAN(1974); WHITE BUFFALO, THE(1977)
Misc. Talkies
TIMBER TRAMPS(1975)

Evelyn Brent [Betty Riggs]
INTERFERENCE(1928); BROADWAY(1929); DARKENED ROOMS(1929); FAST COMPANY(1929); WHY BRING THAT UP?(1929); WOMAN TRAP(1929); DARKENED SKIES(1930); FRAMED(1930); MADONNA OF THE STREETS(1930); SILVER HORDE, THE(1930); SLIGHTLY SCARLET(1930); MAD PARADE, THE(1931); PAGAN LADY(1931); TRAVELING HUSBANDS(1931); ATTORNEY FOR THE DEFENSE(1932); CRUSADER, THE(1932); HIGH PRESSURE(1932); WORLD GONE MAD, THE(1933); HOME ON THE RANGE(1935); NITWITS, THE(1935); SYMPHONY OF LIVING(1935); HOPALONG CASSIDY RETURNS(1936); IT COULDN'T HAVE HAPPENED–BUT IT DID(1936); PENTHOUSE PARTY(1936); PRESIDENT'S MYSTERY, THE(1936); SONG OF THE TRAIL(1936); DAUGHTER OF SHANGHAI(1937); KING OF GAMBLERS(1937); LAST TRAIN FROM MADRID, THE(1937); NIGHT CLUB SCANDAL(1937); LAW WEST OF TOMBSTONE, THE(1938); MR. WONG, DETECTIVE(1938); SUDDEN BILL DORN(1938); TIP-OFF GIRLS(1938); DAUGHTER OF THE TONG(1939); PANAMA LADY(1939); MAD EMPRESS, THE(1940); SPEED LIMITED(1940); DANGEROUS LADY(1941); EMERGENCY LANDING(1941); FORCED LANDING(1941); WIDE OPEN TOWN(1941); WESTWARD HO(1942); WRECKING CREW(1942); PAYOFF, THE(1943); SEVENTH VICTIM, THE(1943); SPY TRAIN(1943); BOWERY CHAMPS(1944); RAIDERS OF THE SOUTH(1947); MYSTERY OF THE GOLDEN EYE, THE(1948); STAGE STRUCK(1948)
Misc. Talkies
ROBIN HOOD OF MONTEREY(1947)
Silents
OTHER MAN'S WIFE, THE(1919); LAUGHTER AND TEARS(1921, Brit.); EXPERIMENT, THE(1922, Brit.); MARRIED TO A MORMAN(1922, Brit.); PAGES OF LIFE(1922, Brit.); TRAPPED BY THE MORMONS(1922, Brit.); HELD TO ANSWER(1923); ARIZONA EXPRESS, THE(1924); MY HUSBAND'S WIVES(1924); LADY ROBINHOOD(1925); QUEEN O' DIAMONDS(1926); BLIND ALLEYS(1927); UNDERWORLD(1927); BEAU SABREUR(1928); DRAGNET, THE(1928); LAST COMMAND, THE(1928); NIGHT OF MYSTERY, A(1928)
Misc. Silents
IRON WOMAN, THE(1916); PLAYING WITH FIRE(1916); SPELL OF THE YUKON, THE(1916); WEAKNESS OF STRENGTH, THE(1916); MILLIONAIRE'S DOUBLE, THE(1917); WHO'S YOUR NEIGHBOR?(1917); FOOL'S GOLD(1919); GLORIOUS LADY, THE(1919); LAW DIVINE, THE(1920, Brit.); SHUTTLE OF LIFE, THE(1920, Brit.); CIRCUS JIM(1921, Brit.); DOOR THAT HAS NO KEY, THE(1921, Brit.); SONIA(1921, Brit.); SYBIL(1921, Brit.); WHY MEN FORGET(1921, Brit.); SPANISH JADE(1922, Brit.); DANGEROUS FLIRT, THE(1924); DESERT OUTLAW, THE(1924); LONE CHANCE, THE(1924); LOVING LIES(1924); PLUNDERER, THE(1924); SILK STOCKING SAL(1924); ALIAS MARY FLYNN(1925); BROADWAY LADY(1925); FORBIDDEN CARGO(1925); MIDNIGHT MOLLY(1925); SMOOTH AS SATIN(1925); THREE WISE CROOKS(1925); FLAME OF THE ARGENTINE(1926); IMPOSTER, THE(1926); JADE CUP, THE(1926); LOVE 'EM AND LEAVE 'EM(1926); SECRET ORDERS(1926); LOVE'S GREATEST MISTAKE(1927); WOMEN'S WARES(1927); HIS TIGER LADY(1928); MATING CALL, THE(1928); SHOWDOWN, THE(1928)

George Brent
CORPSE CAME C.O.D., THE(; CHARLIE CHAN CARRIES ON(1931); EX-BAD BOY(1931); FAIR WARNING(1931); HOMICIDE SQUAD(1931); ONCE A SINNER(1931); UNDER SUSPICION(1931); MISS PINKERTON(1932); PURCHASE PRICE, THE(1932); RICH ARE ALWAYS WITH US, THE(1932); SO BIG(1932); THE CRASH(1932); THEY CALL IT SIN(1932); WEEK-END MARRIAGE(1932); BABY FACE(1933); FEMALE(1933); FROM HEADQUARTERS(1933); KEYHOLE, THE(1933); LILLY TURNER(1933); LUXURY LINER(1933); PRIVATE DETECTIVE 62(1933); 42ND STREET(1933); DESIRABLE(1934); HOUSEWIFE(1934); PAINTED VEIL, THE(1934); STAMBOUL QUEST(1934); FRONT PAGE WOMAN(1935); GOOSE AND THE GANDER, THE(1935); IN PERSON(1935); LIVING ON VELVET(1935); RIGHT TO LIVE, THE(1935); SPECIAL AGENT(1935); STRANDED(1935); CASE AGAINST MRS. AMES, THE(1936); GIVE ME YOUR HEART(1936); GOLDEN ARROW, THE(1936); MORE THAN A SECRETARY(1936); SNOWED UNDER(1936); GO-GETTER, THE(1937); GOD'S COUNTRY AND THE WOMAN(1937); MOUNTAIN JUSTICE(1937); SUBMARINE D-1(1937); GOLD IS WHERE YOU FIND IT(1938); JEZEBEL(1938); RACKET BUSTERS(1938); SECRETS OF AN ACTRESS(1938); DARK VICTORY(1939); OLD MAID, THE(1939); RAINS CAME, THE(1939); WINGS OF THE NAVY(1939); ADVENTURE IN DIAMONDS(1940); FIGHTING 69TH, THE(1940); MAN WHO TALKED TOO MUCH, THE(1940); SOUTH OF SUEZ(1940); 'TIL WE MEET AGAIN(1940); GREAT LIE, THE(1941); HONEYMOON FOR THREE(1941); INTERNATIONAL LADY(1941); THEY DARE NOT LOVE(1941); GAY SISTERS, THE(1942); IN THIS OUR LIFE(1942); SILVER QUEEN(1942); TWIN BEDS(1942); YOU CAN'T ESCAPE FOREVER(1942); EXPERIMENT PERILOUS(1944); LOVER COME BACK(1946); MY REPUTATION(1946); SPIRAL STAIRCASE, THE(1946); TEMPTATION(1946); TOMORROW IS FOREVER(1946); OUT OF THE BLUE(1947); SLAVE GIRL(1947); ANGEL ON THE AMAZON(1948); LUXURY LINER(1948); BRIDE FOR SALE(1949); ILLEGAL ENTRY(1949); KID FROM CLEVELAND, THE(1949); RED CANYON(1949); FBI GIRL(1951); MAN BAIT(1952, Brit.); MONTANA BELLE(1952); MEXICAN MANHUNT(1953); TANGIER INCIDENT(1953); DEATH OF A SCOUNDREL(1956); BORN AGAIN(1978)

Gloria Brent
WHAT DO WE DO NOW?(1945, Brit.)

John Brent
GREENWICH VILLAGE STORY(1963); CATCH-22(1970); STEELYARD BLUES(1973); MORE AMERICAN GRAFFITI(1979)

L.W. "Lynton" Brent
SIX GUN GOSPEL(1943)

Linda Brent
$1,000 A TOUCHDOWN(1939); BELOW THE BORDER(1942); BROADWAY(1942); MOONLIGHT IN HAVANA(1942); OLD HOMESTEAD, THE(1942); RIDE 'EM COWBOY(1942); YOU'RE TELLING ME(1942); SALUTE FOR THREE(1943); SCREAM IN THE DARK, A(1943); SO PROUDLY WE HAIL(1943); CAREER GIRL(1944); DEATH VALLEY RANGERS(1944); FOLLOW THE BOYS(1944); LARAMIE TRAIL, THE(1944); CHICAGO CONFIDENTIAL(1957); ROBIN AND THE SEVEN HOODS(1964)

Lynton Brent
LAST DANCE, THE(1930); EASIEST WAY, THE(1931); VICE SQUAD, THE(1931); INTRUDER, THE(1932); TEXAS BAD MAN(1932); THIRTEENTH GUEST, THE(1932); KING KONG(1933); FIFTEEN WIVES(1934); GUILTY PARENTS(1934); MURDER IN THE MUSEUM(1934); TWENTIETH CENTURY(1934); EVERY NIGHT AT EIGHT(1935); LADIES CRAVE EXCITEMENT(1935); RENDEZVOUS(1935); SHE MARRIED HER BOSS(1935); BRILLIANT MARRIAGE(1936); DEATH FROM A DISTANCE(1936); GREAT GUY(1936); IT COULDN'T HAVE HAPPENED–BUT IT DID(1936); GIT ALONG, LITTLE DOGIES(1937); MYSTERY OF THE HOODED HORSEMEN, THE(1937); OLD CORRAL, THE(1937); STAGE DOOR(1937); TEX RIDES WITH THE BOY SCOUTS(1937); TOAST OF NEW YORK, THE(1937); FRONTIER TOWN(1938); GO CHASE YOURSELF(1938); MR. WONG, DETECTIVE(1938); ROLLIN' PLAINS(1938); UTAH TRAIL(1938); DAYS OF JESSE JAMES(1939); PIONEERS OF THE FRONTIER(1940); STRANGER ON THE THIRD FLOOR(1940); FOOLS OF DESIRE(1941); FORBIDDEN TRAILS(1941); GUN MAN FROM BODIE, THE(1941); PENNY SERENADE(1941); PIONEERS, THE(1941); RED RIVER VALLEY(1941); LONE RIDER IN CHEYENNE, THE(1942); ONE THRILLING NIGHT(1942); RAIDERS OF THE WEST(1942); RANGERS TAKE OVER, THE(1942); RIDERS OF THE WEST(1942); SHERIFF OF SAGE VALLEY(1942); SOUTH OF SANTA FE(1942); TRAIL RIDERS(1942); UNDERGROUND AGENT(1942); WEST OF THE LAW(1942); CALLING WILD BILL ELLIOTT(1943); STRANGER FROM PECOS, THE(1943); TENTING TONIGHT ON THE OLD CAMP GROUND(1943); TWO FISTED JUSTICE(1943); MARKED TRAILS(1944); MY BUDDY(1944); PARTNERS OF THE TRAIL(1944); RAIDERS OF THE BORDER(1944); RANGE LAW(1944); TEXAS KID, THE(1944); VALLEY OF VENGEANCE(1944); LOST TRAIL, THE(1945); DRIFTING ALONG(1946); GENTLEMAN FROM TEXAS(1946); RIDERS IN THE SKY(1949); REDHEAD FROM MANHATTAN(1954)
Misc. Talkies
IT'S ALL IN YOUR MIND(1938)

Lynton W. Brent
TEXAS KID, THE(1944), w

Mauryne Brent
Misc. Talkies
COME ON, COWBOY!(1948)

Max Brent
HAMMER THE TOFF(1952, Brit.)

Maya Brent
BATTLE OF THE WORLDS(1961, Ital.)

Milarde Brent
FOUR FACES WEST(1948), w

Nancy Brent
WOMEN OF DESIRE(1968)

Ray Brent
HIS BROTHER'S GHOST(1945)

Romney Brent
EAST MEETS WEST(1936, Brit.); DINNER AT THE RITZ(1937, Brit.), a, w; DOMINANT SEX, THE(1937, Brit.); DREAMING LIPS(1937, Brit.); HEAD OVER HEELS IN LOVE(1937, Brit.); UNDER THE RED ROBE(1937, Brit.); WHO'S YOUR LADY FRIEND?(1937, Brit.); RAT, THE(1938, Brit.), w; HIS LORDSHIP GOES TO PRESS(1939, Brit.); MIDDLE WATCH, THE(1939, Brit.); SCHOOL FOR HUSBANDS(1939, Brit.); FUGITIVE, THE(1940, Brit.); LET GEORGE DO IT(1940, Brit.); ADVENTURES OF DON JUAN(1949); BALLERINA(1950, Fr.); GYPSY FURY(1950, Fr.), a, d&w; VIRGIN QUEEN, THE(1955); SCREAMING MIMI(1958); SIGN OF ZORRO, THE(1960); DON'T GO NEAR THE WATER(1975)

Roy Brent
PIRATES OF THE SKIES(1939); ONE MAN'S LAW(1940); DEEP IN THE HEART OF TEXAS(1942); OUTLAWS OF PINE RIDGE(1942); CATTLE STAMPEDE(1943); KEEP 'EM SLUGGING(1943); MAN FROM THUNDER RIVER, THE(1943); RAIDERS OF SAN JOAQUIN(1943); DRIFTER, THE(1944); GUNSMOKE MESA(1944); MARSHAL OF GUNSMOKE(1944); PRACTICALLY YOURS(1944); RAIDERS OF RED GAP(1944); WESTWARD BOUND(1944); CODE OF THE LAWLESS(1945); LIGHTNING RAIDERS(1945); TRAIL TO VENGEANCE(1945); OUTLAW OF THE PLAINS(1946); RUSTLER'S ROUNDUP(1946); SIX GUN MAN(1946); WILD BEAUTY(1946)

Rudolph Brent
STRANGE WORLD(1952), ed

Simon Brent
LOVE IS A SPLENDID ILLUSION(1970, Brit.); LEGEND OF SPIDER FOREST, THE(1976, Brit.)

Steve Brent
MR. SCOUTMASTER(1953)

Timothy Brent
CON MEN, THE(1973, Ital.,Span.); GREAT WHITE, THE(1982, Ital.); NEW BARBARIANS, THE(1983, Ital.)

Timothy Brent [Giancarlo Prete]
1984
WARRIORS OF THE WASTELAND(1984, Ital.)

Tom Brent
VICE SQUAD(1982)

Wesley Brent
COVER GIRL(1944); GEORGE WHITE'S SCANDALS(1945); TILL THE CLOUDS ROLL BY(1946)

William Brent
COWBOY AND THE BLONDE, THE(1941), w; SPIRIT OF STANFORD, THE(1942), w; FOUR FACES WEST(1948), w

Lowell Brentano
SPIDER, THE(1931), w; PENGUIN POOL MURDER, THE(1932), w; I'M NO ANGEL(1933), w; MELODY LINGERS ON, THE(1935), w; CRIME NOBOBY SAW, THE(1937), w; SPIDER, THE(1945), w

Brentford Football Club
GREAT GAME, THE(1953, Brit.)

Breols
LETTERS FROM MY WINDMILL(1955, Fr.)

Edmond Breon
ON APPROVAL(1930, Brit.); UNEASY VIRTUE(1931, Brit.); LEAP YEAR(1932, Brit.); WOMEN WHO PLAY(1932, Brit.); THREE MEN IN A BOAT(1933, Brit.); MISTER CINDERS(1934, Brit.); NO FUNNY BUSINESS(1934, Brit.); NIGHT MAIL(1935, Brit.); SHE SHALL HAVE MUSIC(1935, Brit.); FRENCH LEAVE(1937, Brit.); ALMOST A HONEYMOON(1938, Brit.); DANGEROUS MEDICINE(1938, Brit.); MAN WITH 100 FACES, THE(1938, Brit.); MANY TANKS MR. ATKINS(1938, Brit.); ANYTHING TO DECLARE?(1939, Brit.); ONE NIGHT IN PARIS(1940, Brit.); OUTSIDER, THE(1940, Brit.); IT HAPPENED TO ONE MAN(1941, Brit.); CASANOVA BROWN(1944); HOUR BEFORE THE DAWN, THE(1944); MAN IN HALF-MOON STREET, THE(1944); OUR HEARTS WERE YOUNG AND GAY(1944); SARATOGA TRUNK(1945); WOMAN IN THE WINDOW, THE(1945); DEVOTION(1946); DRESSED TO KILL(1946); FOREVER AMBER(1947); IMPERFECT LADY, THE(1947); ENCHANTMENT(1948); HILLS OF HOME(1948); JULIA MISBEHAVES(1948); CHALLENGE TO LASSIE(1949); ROPE OF SAND(1949)
Misc. Silents
SKIRTS(1928, Brit.)

Edmund Breon
DAWN PATROL, THE(1930); BORN TO LOVE(1931); I LIKE YOUR NERVE(1931); LOVE HABIT, THE(1931, Brit.); WEDDING REHEARSAL(1932, Brit.); WALTZ TIME(1933, Brit.); PRIVATE LIFE OF DON JUAN, THE(1934, Brit.); DIVINE SPARK, THE(1935, Brit./Ital.); SCARLET PIMPERNEL, THE(1935, Brit.); LOVE IN EXILE(1936, Brit.); KEEP FIT(1937, Brit.); STRANGERS ON A HONEYMOON(1937, Brit.); RETURN OF THE SCARLET PIMPERNEL(1938, Brit.); TO THE VICTOR(1938, Brit.); YANK AT OXFORD, A(1938); GOODBYE MR. CHIPS(1939, Brit.); NORTH SEA PATROL(1939, Brit.); GASLIGHT(1944); LODGER, THE(1944); WHITE CLIFFS OF DOVER, THE(1944); AT SWORD'S POINT(1951); THING, THE(1951)

Tasma Brereton
CONQUEROR WORM, THE(1968, Brit.)

Tyrone Brereton
CIMARRON(1931); ANOTHER DAWN(1937); TOAST OF NEW YORK, THE(1937); DAWN PATROL, THE(1938)

Arrigo Breschi
GOLD FOR THE CAESARS(1964), set d; LET'S TALK ABOUT WOMEN(1964, Fr./Ital.), art d; PINK PANTHER, THE(1964), set d; THREE BITES OF THE APPLE(1967), set d; SHOES OF THE FISHERMAN, THE(1968), set d; PUSSYCAT, PUSSYCAT, I LOVE YOU(1970), set d; MAN OF LA MANCHA(1972), set d; MATTER OF TIME, A(1976, Ital./U.S.), set d

Teresa Brescianini
TREE OF WOODEN CLOGS, THE(1979, Ital.)

Bobbie Bresee
MAUSOLEUM(1983)

Mr. Bresee
Silents
STORK'S NEST, THE(1915)

Frank Bresford
Silents
ENTER MADAME(1922), w

Joan Breslau
IN PERSON(1935); SMALL TOWN GIRL(1936); LOVE IN A BUNGALOW(1937)

Susan Breslau
1984
TOP SECRET!(1984)

Joan Breslaw
AMATEUR DADDY(1932); MAYTIME(1937); DOUGHGIRLS, THE(1944)

Betty Bresler
NOT WITH MY WIFE, YOU DON'T!(1966); SHAFT(1971)

Jerry Bresler
MAIN STREET AFTER DARK(1944), p; BEWITCHED(1945), p; ARNELO AFFAIR, THE(1947), p; SINGAPORE(1947), p; WEB, THE(1947), p; ACT OF MURDER, AN(1948), p; ANOTHER PART OF THE FOREST(1948), p; ABANDONED(1949), p; CONVICTED(1950), p; FLYING MISSILE(1950), p; MOB, THE(1951), p; ASSIGNMENT–PARIS(1952), p; LIZZIE(1957), p; SPRING REUNION(1957), p; VIKINGS, THE(1958), p; BECAUSE THEY'RE YOUNG(1960), p; GIDGET GOES HAWAIIAN(1961), p; DIAMOND HEAD(1962), p; GIDGET GOES TO ROME(1963), p; LOVE HAS MANY FACES(1965), p; MAJOR DUNDEE(1965), p; CASINO ROYALE(1967, Brit.), p; PUSSYCAT, PUSSYCAT, I LOVE YOU(1970), p

Howard Breslin
BAD DAY AT BLACK ROCK(1955), w; PLATINUM HIGH SCHOOL(1960), w

Jerry Breslin
OUR RELATIONS(1936)

Jimmy Breslin
GANG THAT COULDN'T SHOOT STRAIGHT, THE(1971), w; IF EVER I SEE YOU AGAIN(1978)

John Breslin
DANGEROUS YOUTH(1958, Brit.); SHAKE HANDS WITH THE DEVIL(1959, Ireland)

Kevin Breslin
TRUE CONFESSIONS(1981)
1984
POPE OF GREENWICH VILLAGE, THE(1984)

Pat Breslin
GO, MAN, GO!(1954)

Patricia Breslin
ANDY HARDY COMES HOME(1958); HOMICIDAL(1961); I SAW WHAT YOU DID(1965)

Lou Breslow
NO GREATER LOVE(1932), w; RACKETY RAX(1932), w; SITTING PRETTY(1933), w; GIFT OF GAB(1934), w; NO MORE WOMEN(1934), w; MUSIC IS MAGIC(1935), w; PADDY O'DAY(1935), w; SILK HAT KID(1935), w; THIS IS THE LIFE(1935), w; CHARLIE CHAN AT THE RACE TRACK(1936), w; FIFTEEN MAIDEN LANE(1936), w; HIGH TENSION(1936), w; LITTLE MISS NOBODY(1936), w; THIRTY SIX HOURS TO KILL(1936), w; BIG TOWN GIRL(1937), w; DANGEROUSLY YOURS(1937), w; HOLY TERROR, THE(1937), w; MIDNIGHT TAXI(1937), w; ONE MILE FROM HEAVEN(1937), w; SING AND BE HAPPY(1937), w; TIME OUT FOR ROMANCE(1937), w; BATTLE OF BROADWAY(1938), w; CITY STREETS(1938), w; FIVE OF A KIND(1938), w; INTERNATIONAL SETTLEMENT(1938), w; MR. MOTO TAKES A CHANCE(1938), w; UP THE RIVER(1938), w; HOLLYWOOD CAVALCADE(1939), w; IT

COULD HAPPEN TO YOU(1939), w; PACK UP YOUR TROUBLES(1939), w; 20,000 MEN A YEAR(1939), w; SAILOR'S LADY(1940), w; SHOOTING HIGH(1940), w; GREAT GUNS(1941), w; SLEEPERS WEST(1941), w; A-HAUNTING WE WILL GO(1942), w; BLONDIE GOES TO COLLEGE(1942), w; WHISPERING GHOSTS(1942), w; GOOD LUCK, MR. YATES(1943), w; HEAT'S ON, THE(1943), w; SOMETHING TO SHOUT ABOUT(1943), w; FOLLOW THE BOYS(1944), w; ABBOTT AND COSTELLO IN HOLLYWOOD(1945), w; MURDER, HE SAYS(1945), w; MERTON OF THE MOVIES(1947), w; SECOND CHANCE(1947), w; DON'T TRUST YOUR HUSBAND(1948), w; ON OUR MERRY WAY(1948), w; AND BABY MAKES THREE(1949), w; NEVER A DULL MOMENT(1950), w; BEDTIME FOR BONZO(1951), w; MY FAVORITE SPY(1951), w; REUNION IN RENO(1951), w; YOU NEVER CAN TELL(1951), d, w; BACK AT THE FRONT(1952), w; STEEL TOWN(1952), w; CROOKED WEB, THE(1955), w

Louis Breslow
$10 RAISE(1935), w

Herb Bress
RICH AND FAMOUS(1981)

Bill Bressant
CLAUDINE(1974)

William Bressant
GOD TOLD ME TO(1976)

Felix Bressart
BRIDAL SUITE(1939); NINOTCHKA(1939); SWANEE RIVER(1939); THREE SMART GIRLS GROW UP(1939); BITTER SWEET(1940); COMRADE X(1940); EDISON, THE MAN(1940); ESCAPE(1940); IT ALL CAME TRUE(1940); SHOP AROUND THE CORNER, THE(1940); THIRD FINGER, LEFT HAND(1940); BLOSSOMS IN THE DUST(1941); KATHLEEN(1941); MARRIED BACHELOR(1941); MR. AND MRS. NORTH(1941); ZIEGFELD GIRL(1941); CROSSROADS(1942); ICELAND(1942); TO BE OR NOT TO BE(1942); ABOVE SUSPICION(1943); SONG OF RUSSIA(1943); THREE HEARTS FOR JULIA(1943); BLONDE FEVER(1944); GREENWICH VILLAGE(1944); SEVENTH CROSS, THE(1944); DANGEROUS PARTNERS(1945); WITHOUT LOVE(1945); DING DONG WILLIAMS(1946); HER SISTER'S SECRET(1946); I'VE ALWAYS LOVED YOU(1946); THRILL OF BRAZIL, THE(1946); SONG IS BORN, A(1948); PORTRAIT OF JENNIE(1949); TAKE ONE FALSE STEP(1949)

Edmund Bresse
MORALS FOR WOMEN(1931)
Misc. Silents
LIVE WIRE, THE(1925)

Bernard Bresslaw
HIGH TIDE AT NOON(1957, Brit.); MEN OF SHERWOOD FOREST(1957, Brit.); UP IN THE WORLD(1957, Brit.); BLOOD OF THE VAMPIRE(1958, Brit.); I ONLY ASKED!(1958, Brit.); TOO MANY CROOKS(1959, Brit.); UGLY DUCKLING, THE(1959, Brit.); DREAM MAKER, THE(1963, Brit.); CARRY ON COWBOY(1966, Brit.); CARRY ON SCREAMING(1966, Brit.); MORGAN!(1966, Brit.); FOLLOW THAT CAMEL(1967, Brit.); CARRY ON DOCTOR(1968, Brit.); CARRY ON, UP THE KHYBER(1968, Brit.); CARRY ON CAMPING(1969, Brit.); CARRY ON LOVING(1970, Brit.); CARRY ON UP THE JUNGLE(1970, Brit.); MOON ZERO TWO(1970, Brit.); SPRING AND PORT WINE(1970, Brit.); UP POMPEII(1971, Brit.); OLD DRACULA(1975, Brit.); ONE OF OUR DINOSAURS IS MISSING(1975, Brit.); JABBERWOCKY(1977, Brit.); HAWK THE SLAYER(1980, Brit.); KRULL(1983)

Albert Bressler
THREE MOVES TO FREEDOM(1960, Ger.)

Angela Bressler
STUDENT BODIES(1981)

Sophie Bressler
SINGING BLACKSMITH(1938)

Bresson
ANGELS OF THE STREETS(1950, Fr.), w

Robert Bresson
ANGELS OF THE STREETS(1950, Fr.), d; DIARY OF A COUNTRY PRIEST(1954, Fr.), d&w; MAN ESCAPED, A(1957, Fr.), d&w; PICKPOCKET(1963, Fr.), d&w; LADIES OF THE PARK(1964, Fr.), d, w; TRIAL OF JOAN OF ARC(1965, Fr.), d&w; AU HASARD, BALTHAZAR(1970, Fr.), d&w; MOUCHETTE(1970, Fr.), a, d&w; GENTLE CREATURE, A(1971, Fr.), d&w; FOUR NIGHTS OF A DREAMER(1972, Fr.), d&w; LANCELOT OF THE LAKE(1975, Fr.), d&w; DEVIL PROBABLY, THE(1977, FR.), d&w
1984
L'ARGENT(1984, Fr./Switz.), d&w

George Brest
ASSIGNMENT IN BRITTANY(1943)

Harriett Brest
EASY TO LOVE(1953)

Harry Brest
BLOOD AND BLACK LACE(1965, Ital.), art d

Martin Brest
HOT TOMORROWS(1978), p,d&w, ed; GOING IN STYLE(1979), d, w; FAST TIMES AT RIDGEMONT HIGH(1982)
1984
BEVERLY HILLS COP(1984), d

Richard Brestoff
CARWASH(1976); FAST BREAK(1979); ENTITY, THE(1982); MAN WITH TWO BRAINS, THE(1983)

Tom Bret
Silents
REPORTED MISSING(1922), t

B. Bretherton
CROONER(1932), ed

Bud Bretherton
HOUSE ON 56TH STREET, THE(1933), ed

David Bretherton
BOTTOM OF THE BOTTLE, THE(1956), ed; HILDA CRANE(1956), ed; BERNARDINE(1957), ed; PEYTON PLACE(1957), ed; VALERIE(1957), ed; 10 NORTH FREDERICK(1958), ed; LET'S MAKE LOVE(1960), ed; RETURN TO PEYTON PLACE(1961), ed; STATE FAIR(1962), ed; SANDPIPER, THE(1965), ed; TRAIN, THE(1965, Fr./Ital./U.S.), ed; HONEY POT, THE(1967, Brit.), ed; VILLA RIDES(1968), ed; LOVERS AND OTHER STRANGERS(1970), ed; ON A CLEAR DAY YOU CAN SEE FOREVER(1970), ed; FOOLS' PARADE(1971), ed; NO DRUMS, NO BUGLES(1971), ed; CABARET(1972), ed; SAVE THE TIGER(1973), ed; SLITHER(1973), ed; WESTWORLD(1973), ed; BANK SHOT(1974), ed; MAN IN THE GLASS BOOTH, THE(1975), ed; HARRY AND WALTER GO TO NEW YORK(1976), ed; SILVER

STREAK(1976), ed; COMA(1978), ed; GREAT TRAIN ROBBERY, THE(1979, Brit.), ed; WINTER KILLS(1979), ed; FORMULA, THE(1980), ed; BEST LITTLE WHOREHOUSE IN TEXAS, THE(1982), ed; CANNERY ROW(1982), ed; MAN, WOMAN AND CHILD(1983), ed
1984
LOVELINES(1984), ed

H.P. Bretherton
Silents
ONE WEEK OF LOVE(1922), ed
Misc. Silents
WHILE LONDON SLEEPS(1926), d

Haward Bretherton
MIDNIGHT LIMITED(1940), d

Howard Bretherton
CAUGHT IN THE FOG(1928), d; ARGYLE CASE, THE(1929), d; FROM HEADQUARTERS(1929), p; GREYHOUND LIMITED, THE(1929), p; REDEEMING SIN, THE(1929), d; TIME, THE PLACE AND THE GIRL, THE(1929), d; ISLE OF ESCAPE(1930), d; SECOND CHOICE(1930), d; FAMOUS FERGUSON CASE, THE(1932), ed; MATCH KING, THE(1932), d; SUCCESSFUL CALAMITY, A(1932), ed; BABY FACE(1933), ed; LADIES THEY TALK ABOUT(1933), d; HEAT LIGHTNING(1934), ed; RETURN OF THE TERROR(1934), d; DINKY(1935), d; HOPALONG CASSIDY(1935), d; BAR 20 RIDES AGAIN(1936), d; CALL OF THE PRAIRIE(1936), d; EAGLE'S BROOD, THE(1936), d; GIRL FROM MANDALAY(1936), d; KING OF THE ROYAL MOUNTED(1936), d; LEATHERNECKS HAVE LANDED, THE(1936), d; THREE ON THE TRAIL(1936), d; WILD BRIAN KENT(1936), d; COUNTY FAIR(1937), d; HEART OF THE WEST(1937), d; IT HAPPENED OUT WEST(1937), d; SECRET VALLEY(1937), d; WESTERN GOLD(1937), d; WANTED BY THE POLICE(1938), d; BOY'S REFORMATORY(1939), d; DANGER FLIGHT(1939), d; IRISH LUCK(1939), d; NAVY SECRETS(1939), d; SKY PATROL(1939), d; STAR REPORTER(1939), d; TOUGH KID(1939), d; UNDERCOVER AGENT(1939), d; CHASING TROUBLE(1940), d; HIDDEN ENEMY(1940), d; LAUGHING AT DANGER(1940), d; ON THE SPOT(1940), d; SHOWDOWN, THE(1940), d; UP IN THE AIR(1940), d; IN OLD COLORADO(1941), d; OUTLAWS OF THE DESERT(1941), d; RIDERS OF THE BADLANDS(1941), d; SIGN OF THE WOLF(1941), d; TWILIGHT ON THE TRAIL(1941), d; YOU'RE OUT OF LUCK(1941), d; DAWN ON THE GREAT DIVIDE(1942), d; DOWN TEXAS WAY(1942), d; GHOST TOWN LAW(1942), d; PIRATES OF THE PRAIRIE(1942), d; RIDERS OF THE WEST(1942), d; WEST OF THE LAW(1942), d; WEST OF TOMBSTONE(1942), d; BEYOND THE LAST FRONTIER(1943), d; BORDERTOWN GUNFIGHTERS(1943), d; CARSON CITY CYCLONE(1943), d; FUGITIVE FROM SONORA(1943), d; MAN FROM THE RIO GRANDE, THE(1943), d; RHYTHM PARADE(1943), d; RIDERS OF THE RIO GRANDE(1943), d; SANTA FE SCOUTS(1943), d; WAGON TRACKS WEST(1943), d; WHISPERING FOOTSTEPS(1943), d; GIRL WHO DARED, THE(1944), d; HIDDEN VALLEY OUTLAWS(1944), d; LAW OF THE VALLEY(1944), d; OUTLAWS OF SANTA FE(1944), d; SAN ANTONIO KID, THE(1944), d; BIG SHOW-OFF, THE(1945), d; IDENTITY UNKNOWN(1945), p; NAVAJO TRAIL, THE(1945), d; RENEGADES OF THE RIO GRANDE(1945), d; TOPEKA TERROR, THE(1945), d; RIDIN' DOWN THE TRAIL(1947), d; TRAP, THE(1947), d; BECAUSE OF EVE(1948), d; PRINCE OF THIEVES, THE(1948), d; NIGHT RAIDERS(1952), d
Misc. Talkies
GUN SMOKE(1945), d; TRIGGERMAN(1948), d
Silents
LIGHTHOUSE BY THE SEA, THE(1924), ed; HILLS OF KENTUCKY(1927), d; ONE-ROUND HOGAN(1927), d; SILVER SLAVE, THE(1927), d
Misc. Silents
BLACK DIAMOND EXPRESS, THE(1927), d; BUSH LEAGUER, THE(1927), d; ACROSS THE ATLANTIC(1928), d; CHORUS KID, THE(1928), d; TURN BACK THE HOURS(1928), d

Howard P. Bretherton
BELOW THE BORDER(1942), d

Vivian B. Bretherton
LOVE FINDS ANDY HARDY(1938), w

Daniel Breton
AND HOPE TO DIE(1972 Fr/US)

Flora le Breton
Misc. Silents
LOVE'S INFLUENCE(1922, Brit.); GOD'S PRODIGAL(1923, Brit.)

Hernandez Breton
EL(1955, Mex.), m

L. Hernandez Breton
ONE BIG AFFAIR(1952), m

Luis Hernandez Breton
FACE OF THE SCREAMING WEREWOLF(1959, Mex.), m; ILLUSION TRAVELS BY STREETCAR, THE(1977, Mex.), m

Maestro Breton
DOLORES(1949, Span.), m

Marie-Claude Breton
ANATOMY OF A MARRIAGE(MY DAYS WITH JEAN-MARC AND MY NIGHTS WITH FRANCOISE)**1/2 (1964 Fr.)

Michele Breton
Misc. Talkies
PERFORMANCE(1970, Brit.)

Pierre Breton
ZAZA(1939), w

Raphael Breton
RAISE THE TITANIC(1980, Brit.), set d

Charles Bretoneiche
MR. HULOT'S HOLIDAY(1954, Fr.), ed; BLANCHE(1971, Fr.), ed

Bretonneche
DEVIL'S DAUGHTER(1949, Fr.), ed

Jean Bretonniere
JUDGE AND THE ASSASSIN, THE(1979, Fr.)

Jean Bretonniers
GREEN GLOVE, THE(1952)

Constance Bretrand
BEFORE MORNING(1933)

Frank Bretson
HORSE SOLDIERS, THE(1959), cos

Alan Brett
SCHIZO(1977, Brit.), ed; COMEBACK, THE(1982, Brit.), ed
Allan Brett
SO ENDS OUR NIGHT(1941)
Anna Brett
DR. JEKYLL AND SISTER HYDE(1971, Brit.)
Bredon Brett
HORROR CASTLE(1965, Ital.)
Christopher Brett
RESCUE SQUAD, THE(1963, Brit.)
Harry Brett
Silents
MY OLD DUTCH(1915, Brit.)
Misc. Silents
BOTTLE, THE(1915, Brit.); FALLEN STAR, A(1916, Brit.)
Hon. Angela Brett
KNIGHT IN LONDON, A(1930, Brit./Ger.)
Ingred Brett
INADMISSIBLE EVIDENCE(1968, Brit.)
Ingrid Brett
DEVIL'S OWN, THE(1967, Brit.); JOKERS, THE(1967, Brit.); FIGHT FOR RO-
ME(1969, Ger./Rum.)
Jackie Brett
HOW TO SEDUCE A WOMAN(1974)
Jeremy Brett
WAR AND PEACE(1956, Ital./U.S.); MACBETH(1963); VERY EDGE, THE(1963,
Brit.); MODEL MURDER CASE, THE(1964, Brit.); MY FAIR LADY(1964); YOUNG
AND WILLING(1964, Brit.); MEDUSA TOUCH, THE(1978, Brit.)
Misc. Talkies
ACT OF REPRISAL(1965)
Leander Brett
PUBERTY BLUES(1983, Aus.)
Leonard Brett
DANCE PRETTY LADY(1932, Brit.)
Peter Brett
FRENCH DRESSING(1964, Brit.), w
Tommy Brett
Silents
APARTMENT 29(1917)
Colette Brettel
Misc. Silents
WUTHERING HEIGHTS(1920, Brit.)
Colette Brettell
Misc. Silents
LOVES OF COLLEEN BAWN, THE(1924, Brit.)
Colette Brettelle
Silents
PRODIGAL SON, THE(1923, Brit.)
Raphael Bretton
FOUR FOR TEXAS(1963), set d; HUSH... HUSH, SWEET CHARLOTTE(1964), set d;
ROBIN AND THE SEVEN HOODS(1964), set d; VON RYAN'S EXPRESS(1965), set d;
LORD LOVE A DUCK(1966), set d; OUR MAN FLINT(1966), set d; GUIDE FOR THE
MARRIED MAN, A(1967), set d; HOMBRE(1967), set d; VALLEY OF THE
DOLLS(1967), set d; SECRET LIFE OF AN AMERICAN WIFE, THE(1968), set d; THE
BOSTON STRANGLER, THE(1968), set d; HELLO, DOLLY!(1969), set d; JUS-
TINE(1969), set d; GREAT WHITE HOPE, THE(1970), set d; MEPHISTO WALTZ,
THE(1971), set d; SEVEN MINUTES, THE(1971), set d; POSEIDON ADVENTURE,
THE(1972), set d; ICEMAN COMETH, THE(1973), set d; TOWERING INFERNO,
THE(1974), set d; HUSTLE(1975), set d; CHOIRBOYS, THE(1977), set d; DOMINO
PRINCIPLE, THE(1977), set d; ISLANDS IN THE STREAM(1977), set d; OTHER SIDE
OF MIDNIGHT, THE(1977), set d
Raphel Bretton
MIXED COMPANY(1974), set d
Beatrice Bretty
WOMEN AND WAR(1965, Fr.)
Siegfried Breuer
THIRD MAN, THE(1950, Brit.)
Beta Breuil
Silents
WHEN A WOMAN SINS(1918), w
Marcel Breuil
JOHNNY THE GIANT KILLER(1953, Fr.), anim
R. Breuil
LES DERNIERES VACANCES(1947, Fr.), w
Bob Breuler
PURPLE HAZE(1982)
Siegfried Breuner
OPERETTA(1949, Ger.)
Sorrel Breuning
NICE GIRL LIKE ME, A(1969, Brit.)
Clem Brevans
GOLD RAIDERS, THE(1952)
A'Leisha Brevard
HARD COUNTRY(1981)
A'Leshia Brevard
MAN WITH BOGART'S FACE, THE(1980)
David Brevick
STACY'S KNIGHTS(1983)
John Brevick
STACY'S KNIGHTS(1983)
Alex Brewer
MUSIC LOVERS, THE(1971, Brit.)
Art Brewer
SMOKEY AND THE BANDIT(1977), spec eff; OTHER SIDE OF THE MOUNTAIN-
PART 2, THE(1978), spec eff
Bessie Brewer
IN NAME ONLY(1939), w

Betty Brewer
RANGERS OF FORTUNE(1940); LAS VEGAS NIGHTS(1941); ROUNDUP,
THE(1941); JUKE GIRL(1942); MRS. WIGGS OF THE CABBAGE PATCH(1942); WILD
BILL HICKOK RIDES(1942); MY KINGDOM FOR A COOK(1943)
Bill Brewer
HELLIONS, THE(1962, Brit.); SANDERS(1963, Brit.); AFTER YOU, COMRADE(1967,
S. Afr.); JACKALS, THE(1967, South Africa); SANDY THE SEAL(1969, Brit.)
Capt. Kidd Brewer, Jr.
PIRANHA II: THE SPAWNING(1981, Neth.)
Charles Brewer
MARRYING KIND, THE(1952); SWEET CHARITY(1969); AIRPORT(1970)
Dave Brewer
MOONSHINE COUNTY EXPRESS(1977)
Dorothy Brewer
PICKUP ON 101(1972)
Ed Brewer
MR. SMITH GOES TO WASHINGTON(1939)
George Emerson Brewer, Jr.
DARK VICTORY(1939), w; STOLEN HOURS(1963), w
Gil Brewer
LURE OF THE SWAMP(1957), w
Griffith Brewer
IN PRAISE OF OLDER WOMEN(1978, Can.); HAPPY BIRTHDAY TO ME(1981)
Harold Brewer
DEPUTY DRUMMER, THE(1935, Brit.)
Ilene Brewer
DEVIL AND MISS JONES, THE(1941); RIDERS OF THE BADLANDS(1941); COVER
GIRL(1944)
James Brewer
1984
FEAR CITY(1984)
Jameson Brewer
TWO BLONDES AND A REDHEAD(1947), w; FRENCH LEAVE(1948), w; OKINA-
WA(1952), w; GHOST TOWN(1956), w; JUNGLE HEAT(1957), w; MARY HAD A
LITTLE(1961, Brit.), w; SWINGIN' ALONG(1962), w; INCREDIBLE MR. LIMPET,
THE(1964), w; LADY HAMILTON(1969, Ger./Ital./Fr.), w; ARNOLD(1973), w; TER-
ROR IN THE WAX MUSEUM(1973), w; HEIDI'S SONG(1982), w
Jim Brewer
Misc. Talkies
MISSION TO DEATH(1966)
Kim Brewer
LOVE BUG, THE(1968)
Leslie Brewer
PHANTOM OF THE PARADISE(1974)
Logan Brewer
1984
SQUIZZY TAYLOR(1984, Aus.), prod d
Mary Brewer
RAZOR'S EDGE, THE(1946); SECRET LIFE OF WALTER MITTY, THE(1947);
MEXICAN HAYRIDE(1948); HIS KIND OF WOMAN(1951)
Monte "Sonny" Brewer
MR. DYNAMITE(1941)
Richard Brewer
VILLAIN, THE(1979)
Roy M. Brewer, Jr.
SLEEPING BEAUTY(1959), ed; ONE HUNDRED AND ONE DALMATIANS(1961),
ed
Sherri Brewer
SHAFT(1971)
Solomon Brewer
GREATEST, THE(1977, U.S./Brit.), set d
Tammy Brewer
TWO OF A KIND(1983)
1984
WOMAN IN RED, THE(1984)
Teresa Brewer
THOSE REDHEADS FROM SEATTLE(1953)
Thomas Brewer
FIGHTING ROOKIE, THE(1934)
Thurlow Brewer
Misc. Silents
PHANTOM BUCCANEER, THE(1916)
Tom Brewer
PERFECT SPECIMEN, THE(1937); TOAST OF NEW YORK, THE(1937)
Brewer Kids
RANCHO GRANDE(1940)
Linda Brewerton
ROSEMARY'S BABY(1968)
Peter Brewis
WICKER MAN, THE(1974, Brit.)
Bruce Brewster
WITHOUT RESERVATIONS(1946)
Carol Brewster
BARKLEYS OF BROADWAY, THE(1949); FLAMINGO ROAD(1949); GIRL FROM
JONES BEACH, THE(1949); IT'S A GREAT FEELING(1949); LIFE OF HER OWN,
A(1950); CASA MANANA(1951); TWO TICKETS TO BROADWAY(1951); BELLE OF
NEW YORK, THE(1952); UNTAMED WOMEN(1952); CAT WOMEN OF THE
MOON(1953); SON OF SINBAD(1955); MAVERICK QUEEN, THE(1956); POLICE
NURSE(1963); ROSEMARY'S BABY(1968); HELL'S BLOODY DEVILS(1970)
Diane Brewster
BLACK PATCH(1957); COURAGE OF BLACK BEAUTY(1957); INVISIBLE BOY,
THE(1957); OKLAHOMAN, THE(1957); PHARAOH'S CURSE(1957); QUANTRILL'S
RAIDERS(1958); TORPEDO RUN(1958); KING OF THE WILD STALLIONS(1959);
MAN IN THE NET, THE(1959); YOUNG PHILADELPHIANS, THE(1959)
Dorothy Brewster
LONG KNIFE, THE(1958, Brit.)
E. V. Brewster
Silents
TWO-EDGED SWORD, THE(1916), w

Derrick Brice
DOCTOR DETROIT(1983)

Fannie Brice
MY MAN(1928); BE YOURSELF(1930); GREAT ZIEGFELD, THE(1936); ZIEGFELD FOLLIES(1945)

Fanny Brice
CRIME WITHOUT PASSION(1934); EVERYBODY SING(1938)

Lew Brice
HAPPY DAYS(1930); TWO SECONDS(1932)
Silents
PARTNERS AGAIN(1926)

Monte Brice
MOONLIGHT AND PRETZELS(1933), d, w; TAKE A CHANCE(1933), d; SWEET SURRENDER(1935), p, d; MERRY-GO-ROUND OF 1938(1937), w; YOU'RE A SWEET-HEART(1937), w; BOY TROUBLE(1939), w; NIGHT WORK(1939), w; YOU'LL FIND OUT(1940), w; FOUR JACKS AND A JILL(1941), w; POT O' GOLD(1941), w; FLEET'S IN, THE(1942), w; JOAN OF OZARK(1942), w; MEXICAN SPITFIRE SEES A GHOST(1942), w; SING YOUR WORRIES AWAY(1942), w; DOUGHBOYS IN IRE-LAND(1943), w; IS EVERYBODY HAPPY?(1943), w; BEAUTIFUL BUT BROKE(1944), w; STARS ON PARADE(1944), w; EADIE WAS A LADY(1945), w; GUY, A GAL AND A PAL, A(1945), w; MAMA LOVES PAPA(1945), w; GENIUS AT WORK(1946), w; SINGIN' IN THE CORN(1946), w; VARIETY GIRL(1947), w
Silents
BEHIND THE FRONT(1926), w; CASEY AT THE BAT(1927), d, w; FIREMAN, SAVE MY CHILD(1927), w; NOW WE'RE IN THE AIR(1927), w; HOT NEWS(1928), w; TILLIE'S PUNCTURED ROMANCE(1928), w

Monty Brice
RADIO STARS ON PARADE(1945), w
Silents
HANDS UP(1926), w; MISS BREWSTER'S MILLIONS(1926), w

Pierre Brice
COSSACKS, THE(1960, It.); CHEATERS, THE(1961, Fr.); PHAROAH'S WOMAN, THE(1961, Ital.); SWEET ECSTASY(1962, Fr.); BACCHANTES, THE(1963, Fr./Ital.); MILL OF THE STONE WOMEN(1963, Fr./Ital.); SAMSON AND THE SLAVE QUEEN(1963, Ital.); AMONG VULTURES(1964, Ger./Ital./Fr./Yugo.); APACHE GOLD(1965, Ger.); DESPERADO TRAIL(1965, Ger./Yugo.); INVASION 1700(1965, Fr./Ital./Yugo.); LIPSTICK(1965, Fr./Ital.); TREASURE OF SILVER LA-KE(1965, Fr./Ger./Yugo.); FRONTIER HELLCAT(1966, Fr./Ital./Ger./Yugo.); LAST OF THE RENEGADES(1966, Fr./Ital./Ger./Yugo.); PLACE CALLED GLORY, A(1966, Span./Ger.); RAMPAGE AT APACHE WELLS(1966, Ger./Yugo.); THUNDER AT THE BORDER(1966, Ger./Yugo.); TERROR OF THE BLACK MASK(1967, Fr./Ital.); FLAM-ING FRONTIER(1968, Ger./Yugo.); OLD SHATTERHAND(1968, Ger./Yugo./Fr./Ital.)
Misc. Talkies
KILLER'S CARNIVAL(1965)

Rosetta Brice
Silents
FORTUNE HUNTER, THE(1914); CLIMBERS, THE(1915); LOVE'S TOLL(1916)
Misc. Silents
COLLEGE WIDOW, THE(1915); MAN'S MAKING, THE(1915); ONLY WAY OUT, THE(1915); RIGHTS OF MAN, THE(1915); SPORTING DUCHESS, THE(1915); GODS OF FATE, THE(1916); HER BLEEDING HEART(1916)

Bice Brichetto
DISORDER(1964, Fr./Ital.), cos; SANDRA(1966, Ital.), cos

Al Brick
SEVEN FACES(1929), ph; THEY HAD TO SEE PARIS(1929), ph; THRU DIFFER-ENT EYES(1929), ph; DEVIL WITH WOMEN, A(1930), ph; SONG O' MY HEART(1930), ph

Jean Porter Brick
THRILL OF A ROMANCE(1945)

Beth Brickell
ONLY WAY HOME, THE(1972); POSSE(1975); DEATH GAME(1977)

Alene Bricken
EXPLOSION(1969, Can.), w

Jules Bricken
DRANGO(1957), d; TRAIN, THE(1965, Fr./Ital./U.S.), p; EXPLOSION(1969, Can.), d, w

Barbara Bricker
NIGHT OF EVIL(1962)
Misc. Talkies
IVY LEAGUE KILLERS(1962, Can.)

Betty Bricker
MRS. PARKINGTON(1944)

Clarence Bricker
HELD FOR RANSOM(1938), d; HEROES OF THE ALAMO(1938), art d
Misc. Silents
ROBIN HOOD, JR.(1923), d

Elsie Bricker
GAS HOUSE KIDS(1946), w

George Bricker
CORPSE CAME C.O.D., THE(, w; BROADWAY HOSTESS(1935), w; PAYOFF, THE(1935), w; BIG NOISE, THE(1936), w; FRESHMAN LOVE(1936), w; KING OF HOCKEY(1936), w; LAW IN HER HANDS, THE(1936), w; WIDOW FROM MONTE CARLO, THE(1936), w; FUGITIVE IN THE SKY(1937), w; KID COMES BACK, THE(1937), w; MELODY FOR TWO(1937), w; SH! THE OCTOPUS(1937), w; ACCI-DENTS WILL HAPPEN(1938), w; LITTLE MISS THOROUGHBRED(1938), w; MR. CHUMP(1938), w; OVER THE WALL(1938), w; TORCHY BLANE IN CHINA-TOWN(1938), w; TORCHY BLANE IN PANAMA(1938), w; BURIED ALIVE(1939), w; KING OF THE UNDERWORLD(1939), w; MISSING DAUGHTERS(1939), w; MR. MOTO IN DANGER ISLAND(1939), w; THEY MADE HER A SPY(1939), w; HOLD THAT WOMAN(1940), w; I TAKE THIS OATH(1940), w; MARKED MEN(1940), w; BLONDE FROM SINGAPORE, THE(1941), w; DEVIL BAT, THE(1941), w; MURDER BY INVITATION(1941), w; FRISCO LILL(1942), w; LAW OF THE JUNGLE(1942), w; LITTLE TOKYO, U.S.A.(1942), w; LURE OF THE ISLANDS(1942), w; MEET THE MOB(1942), w; NORTH TO THE KLONDIKE(1942), w; DANCING MASTERS, THE(1943), w; MARK OF THE WHISTLER, THE(1944), w; PILLOW OF DEATH(1945), w; BLONDE ALIBI(1946), w; BRUTE MAN, THE(1946), w; GAS HOUSE KIDS(1946), w; HOUSE OF HORRORS(1946), w; IF I'M LUCKY(1946), w; INSIDE JOB(1946), w; JOHNNY COMES FLYING HOME(1946), w; MEET ME ON BROADWAY(1946), w; SHE-WOLF OF LONDON(1946), w; BIG FIX, THE(1947), w; HEARTACHES(1947), w; ALIMONY(1949), w; MARY RYAN, DETECTIVE(1949), w; BEAUTY ON PARA-

DE(1950), w; BODYHOLD(1950), w; TOUGHER THEY COME, THE(1950), w; AL JENNINGS OF OKLAHOMA(1951), w; ROADBLOCK(1951), w; WHIP HAND, THE(1951), w; ARCTIC FLIGHT(1952), w; ONE BIG AFFAIR(1952), w; MAN IN THE DARK(1953), w; MEXICAN MANHUNT(1953), w; TANGIER INCIDENT(1953), w; CRY VENGEANCE(1954), w; LOOPHOLE(1954), w

Kurt Bricker
SECRET INVASION, THE(1964)

Mary Ann Bricker
SENTIMENTAL JOURNEY(1946)

Sammy Bricker
DARKENED ROOMS(1929)

Carl Brickert
Silents
EMBARRASSMENT OF RICHES, THE(1918)
Misc. Silents
HALF MILLION BRIBE, THE(1916)

Carl Brickett
Misc. Silents
DAUGHTER OF MARYLAND, A(1917)

Joan Brickhill
ELEPHANT GUN(1959, Brit.)

Paul Brickhill
DAM BUSTERS, THE(1955, Brit.), w; REACH FOR THE SKY(1957, Brit.), w; GREAT ESCAPE, THE(1963), w

Jack Brickhouse
GOLDEN GLOVES STORY, THE(1950)

The Bricklayers
SOMETHING TO SHOUT ABOUT(1943)

Marshall Brickman
SLEEPER(1973), w; ANNIE HALL(1977), w; MANHATTAN(1979), w; SIMON(1980), d&w; LOVESICK(1983), d&w

Paul Brickman
BAD NEWS BEARS IN BREAKING TRAINING, THE(1977), w; CITIZENS BAND(1977), w; DEAL OF THE CENTURY(1983), w; RISKY BUSINESS(1983), d&w

Richard Brickman
TASTE OF BLOOD, A(1967), ed

Bricktop
HONEYBABY, HONEYBABY(1974); ZELIG(1983)

Wendy Greene Bricmont
ANNIE HALL(1977), ed; ON THE NICKEL(1980), ed

Leslie Bricusse
CHARLEY MOON(1956, Brit.), w; BACHELOR OF HEARTS(1958, Brit.), w; SWIN-GIN' MAIDEN, THE(1963, Brit.), w; VERY EDGE, THE(1963, Brit.), w; THREE HATS FOR LISA(1965, Brit.), w, m; STOP THE WORLD-I WANT TO GET OFF(1966, Brit.), w; SCROOGE(1970, Brit.), w, m; SAMMY STOPS THE WORLD zero(1978), w; SUNDAY LOVERS(1980, Ital./Fr.), w

W. Leslie Bricusse
DOCTOR DOLITTLE(1967), d

Edith Briden
COWARDS(1970)

Milton Bridenbecker
PHANTOM OF THE OPERA, THE(1929), ph
Silents
PHANTOM OF THE OPERA, THE(1925), ph

Adam Bridge
VOICES(1973, Brit.)

Al Bridge
GOD'S COUNTRY AND THE MAN(1931); BLONDE VENUS(1932); BROADWAY TO CHEYENNE(1932); FORTY-NINERS, THE(1932); GALLOPING THRU(1932); MAN'S LAND, A(1932); MILLION DOLLAR LEGS(1932); SPIRIT OF THE WEST(1932); CHEYENNE KID, THE(1933); COWBOY COUNSELOR(1933); DRUM TAPS(1933); FIGHTING TEXANS(1933); LONE AVENGER, THE(1933); SON OF THE BOR-DER(1933); SUCKER MONEY(1933); SUNSET PASS(1933); WHEN A MAN RIDES ALONE(1933); FIDDLIN' BUCKAROO, THE(1934); HONOR OF THE RANGE(1934); THUNDERING HERD, THE(1934); TRUMPET BLOWS, THE(1934); GALLANT DE-FENDER(1935); MELODY TRAIL(1935); NEW FRONTIER(1935); PUBLIC STE-NOGRAPHER(1935); RENDEZVOUS(1935); CALL OF THE PRAIRIE(1936); FAST BULLETS(1936); LAWLESS NINETIES, THE(1936); THREE MESQUITEERS, THE(1936); TRAIL DUST(1936); BORDERLAND(1937); DEAD END(1937); DODGE CITY TRAIL(1937); TWO-FISTED SHERIFF(1937); COLORADO TRAIL(1938); CRIME SCHOOL(1938); GUNSMOKE TRAIL(1938); LITTLE MISS ROUGHNECK(1938); PARTNERS OF THE PLAINS(1938); BLUE MONTANA SKIES(1939); OKLAHOMA FRONTIER(1939); OKLAHOMA KID, THE(1939); BLAZING SIX SHOOTERS(1940); DEVIL'S ISLAND(1940); MY SON IS GUILTY(1940); PIONEERS OF THE FRON-TIER(1940); STRANGER FROM TEXAS(1940); WEST OF ABILENE(1940); WEST OF CARSON CITY(1940); FACE BEHIND THE MASK, THE(1941); HONOLULU LU(1941); KID'S LAST RIDE, THE(1941); LAW OF THE RANGE(1941); RAWHIDE RANGERS(1941); BELLS OF CAPISTRANO(1942); FIGHTING BILL FARGO(1942); LADY IN A JAM(1942); MAN FROM THUNDER RIVER, THE(1943); TREE GROWS IN BROOKLYN, A(1945); DEADLINE AT DAWN(1946); FALCON'S ALIBI, THE(1946); VIRGINIAN, THE(1946); DICK TRACY'S DILEMMA(1947); T-MEN(1947); SMART WOMAN(1948); THAT WONDERFUL URGE(1948); MAD WEDNESDAY(1950); MESS-ENGER OF PEACE(1950)
Misc. Talkies
NORTH OF ARIZONA(1935); OUTLAW RULE(1935)

Alan [Al] Bridge
TRAIL DRIVE, THE(1934); TWO GUN LAW(1937); WESTERN GOLD(1937); SABO-TEUR(1942); UNWRITTEN CODE, THE(1944); TRAIL OF THE YUKON(1949); TOUGHER THEY COME, THE(1950); TRAVELING SALESWOMAN(1950)

Alan Bridge
RIDER OF THE PLAINS(1931); THIRTEENTH GUEST, THE(1932); DIAMOND JIM(1935); NIGHT AT THE OPERA, A(1935); AND SO THEY WERE MARRIED(1936); PUBLIC ENEMY'S WIFE(1936); AWFUL TRUTH, THE(1937); GO-GETTER, THE(1937); ONE MAN JUSTICE(1937); SPRINGTIME IN THE ROCKIES(1937); WOMAN CHASES MAN(1937); ADVENTURE IN SAHARA(1938); DOWN IN ARKAN-SAW(1938); HIGHWAY PATROL(1938); JEZEBEL(1938); MARIE ANTOINETTE(1938); MAN FROM SUNDOWN, THE(1939); MR. SMITH GOES TO WASHINGTON(1939); NO PLACE TO GO(1939); ROARING TWENTIES, THE(1939); ROMANCE OF THE RED-WOODS(1939); CHRISTMAS IN JULY(1940); COURAGEOUS DR. CHRISTIAN, THE(1940); DARK COMMAND, THE(1940); MY LITTLE CHICKADEE(1940); SANTA

FE TRAIL(1940); HONKY TONK(1941); LADY EVE, THE(1941); LADY FROM CHEYENNE(1941); LITTLE FOXES, THE(1941); ROAD TO ZANZIBAR(1941); SULLIVAN'S TRAVELS(1941); WILD GEESE CALLING(1941); BAD MEN OF THE HILLS(1942); I MARRIED A WITCH(1942); IN THIS OUR LIFE(1942); JUKE GIRL(1942); MAD DOCTOR OF MARKET STREET, THE(1942); PALM BEACH STORY, THE(1942); REAP THE WILD WIND(1942); TALK OF THE TOWN(1942); TENTING TONIGHT ON THE OLD CAMP GROUND(1943); DOUBLE INDEMNITY(1944); HAIL THE CONQUERING HERO(1944); MIRACLE OF MORGAN'S CREEK, THE(1944); PRINCESS AND THE PIRATE, THE(1944); GUY, A GAL AND A PAL, A(1945); JADE MASK, THE(1945); MISS SUSIE SLAGLE'S(1945); ROAD TO UTOPIA(1945); SARATOGA TRUNK(1945); THEY WERE EXPENDABLE(1945); THUNDERHEAD-SON OF FLICKA(1945); BELOW THE DEADLINE(1946); CROSS MY HEART(1946); MY PAL TRIGGER(1946); SHADOWS OVER CHINATOWN(1946); SINGIN' IN THE CORN(1946); BLACK GOLD(1947); DOWN TO EARTH(1947); FRAMED(1947); LAST DAYS OF BOOT HILL(1947); NORA PRENTISS(1947); ROAD TO RIO(1947); ROBIN OF TEXAS(1947); SONG OF THE THIN MAN(1947); FURY AT FURNACE CREEK(1948); PALEFACE, THE(1948); SILVER RIVER(1948); UNFAITHFULLY YOURS(1948); BEAUTIFUL BLONDE FROM BASHFUL BEND, THE(1949); DEVIL'S HENCHMEN, THE(1949); QUICK ON THE TRIGGER(1949); ROSEANNA McCOY(1949); CALIFORNIA PASSAGE(1950); IN OLD AMARILLO(1951); OH! SUSANNA(1951); LAST MUSKETEER, THE(1952); WE'RE NOT MARRIED(1952); IRON MOUNTAIN TRAIL(1953); JUBILEE TRAIL(1954); HELL'S OUTPOST(1955)
Misc. Talkies
BLAZING THE WESTERN TRAIL(1945); BOTH BARRELS BLAZING(1945); ALIAS MR. TWILIGHT(1946)

Bekki Bridge
LAST REMAKE OF BEAU GESTE, THE(1977)

Hugh Broad Bridge
ETERNAL FEMININE, THE(1931, Brit.), w

Jim Bridge
1984
BIG MEAT EATER(1984, Can.), spec eff

Joan Bridge
AMOROUS ADVENTURES OF MOLL FLANDERS, THE(1965), cos; LIQUIDATOR, THE(1966, Brit.), cos; MAN FOR ALL SEASONS, A(1966, Brit.), cos; HALF A SIXPENCE(1967, Brit.), cos; CHITTY CHITTY BANG BANG(1968, Brit.), cos; PRIME OF MISS JEAN BRODIE, THE(1969, Brit.), cos; FIDDLER ON THE ROOF(1971), cos; POPE JOAN(1972, Brit.), cos; DAY OF THE JACKAL, THE(1973, Brit./Fr.), cos; HOMECOMING, THE(1973), cos; LUTHER(1974), cos; CONDUCT UNBECOMING(1975, Brit.), cos; JULIA(1977), cos; HANOVER STREET(1979, Brit.), cos

Loie Bridge
RODEO RHYTHM(1941); LIFE WITH FATHER(1947); RIDERS IN THE SKY(1949); RIDERS OF THE WHISTLING PINES(1949)
Misc. Talkies
WYOMING WHIRLWIND(1932)

Lois Bridge
SINGLE-HANDED SANDERS(1932); O, MY DARLING CLEMENTINE(1943)

Nicholas Bridge
LAST REMAKE OF BEAU GESTE, THE(1977)

Rebecca Bridge
NICE GIRL LIKE ME, A(1969, Brit.)

Bridgehouse
COURAGEOUS DR. CHRISTIAN, THE(1940), cos

Bonita Bridgeman
ROOM AT THE TOP(1959, Brit.)

Ken Bridgeman
SMASHING TIME(1967 Brit.), art d; NICE GIRL LIKE ME, A(1969, Brit.), art d; TWO GENTLEMEN SHARING(1969, Brit.), art d; STRAW DOGS(1971, Brit.), art d; VAMPYRES, DAUGHTERS OF DRACULA(1977, Brit.), art d
1984
ORDEAL BY INNOCENCE(1984, Brit.), prod d

Peter Bridgemen
NIGHT THE LIGHTS WENT OUT IN GEORGIA, THE(1981)

Grant Bridger
MERRY CHRISTMAS MR. LAWRENCE(1983, Jap./Brit.)

William Bridger
UNEASY TERMS(1948, Brit.)

Aaron Bridgers
PARIS BLUES(1961)

Penny Bridgers
WEDDING PARTY, THE(1969)

Raymond Bridgers
1984
NADIA(1984, U.S./Yugo.), ed

Adam Bridges
MEDUSA TOUCH, THE(1978, Brit.)

Al Bridges
GOOD FAIRY, THE(1935); WESTBOUND MAIL(1937); TWO-GUN JUSTICE(1938)

Alan Bridges
MAN'S WORLD, A(1942); COWBOY BLUES(1946); ACT OF MURDER(1965, Brit.), d; INVASION(1965, Brit.), d; HIRELING, THE(1973, Brit.), d; OUT OF SEASON(1975, Brit.), d; AGE OF INNOCENCE(1977, Can.), d; RETURN OF THE SOLDIER, THE(1983, Brit.), d

Beau Bridges
FORCE OF EVIL(1948); NO MINOR VICES(1948); RED PONY, THE(1949); ZAMBA(1949); EXPLOSIVE GENERATION, THE(1961); VILLAGE OF THE GIANTS(1965); INCIDENT, THE(1967); FOR LOVE OF IVY(1968); GAILY, GAILY(1969); LANDLORD, THE(1970); CHRISTIAN LICORICE STORE, THE(1971); ADAM'S WOMAN(1972, Austral.); CHILD'S PLAY(1972); HAMMERSMITH IS OUT(1972); YOUR THREE MINUTES ARE UP(1973); LOVIN' MOLLY(1974); OTHER SIDE OF THE MOUNTAIN, THE(1975); ONE SUMMER LOVE(1976); SWASHBUCKLER(1976); TWO-MINUTE WARNING(1976); BEHIND THE IRON MASK(1977); GREASED LIGHTNING(1977); NORMA RAE(1979); THE RUNNER STUMBLES(1979); HONKY TONK FREEWAY(1981); LOVE CHILD(1982); NIGHT CROSSING(1982); SILVER DREAM RACER(1982, Brit.); HEART LIKE A WHEEL(1983)
1984
HOTEL NEW HAMPSHIRE, THE(1984)

Bob Bridges
TERROR IN THE JUNGLE(1968)

Darlene Bridges
LAWTON STORY, THE(1949); PRINCE OF PEACE, THE(1951)

J. Bridges
TO ALL A GOODNIGHT(1980)

James Bridges
APPALOOSA, THE(1966), w; FACES(1968); COLOSSUS: THE FORBIN PROJECT(1969), w; BABY MAKER, THE(1970), d&w; LIMBO(1972), w; PAPER CHASE, THE(1973), d; 9/30/55(1977), d&w; CHINA SYNDROME, THE(1979), d, w; URBAN COWBOY(1980), d, w; FIRE AND ICE(1983)
1984
MIKE'S MURDER(1984), d&w

Jeff Bridges
HALLS OF ANGER(1970); LAST PICTURE SHOW, THE(1971); BAD COMPANY(1972); FAT CITY(1972); ICEMAN COMETH, THE(1973); LAST AMERICAN HERO, THE(1973); LOLLY-MADONNA XXX(1973); THUNDERBOLT AND LIGHTFOOT(1974); HEARTS OF THE WEST(1975); RANCHO DELUXE(1975); KING KONG(1976); STAY HUNGRY(1976); SOMEBODY KILLED HER HUSBAND(1978); WINTER KILLS(1979); AMERICAN SUCCESS COMPANY, THE(1980); HEAVEN'S GATE(1980); CUTTER AND BONE(1981); KISS ME GOODBYE(1982); LAST UNICORN, THE(1982); TRON(1982)
1984
AGAINST ALL ODDS(1984); STARMAN(1984)
Misc. Talkies
YIN AND YANG OF DR. GO, THE(1972)

Jenny Bridges
COUNTESS FROM HONG KONG, A(1967, Brit.)

Jim Bridges
INVASION OF THE SAUCER MEN(1957); JOHNNY TROUBLE(1957); JOY RIDE(1958)

John Bridges
LAW RIDES AGAIN, THE(1943); WILD HORSE STAMPEDE(1943); DEATH VALLEY RANGERS(1944); OUTLAW TRAIL(1944); SONORA STAGECOACH(1944); WESTWARD BOUND(1944); LOST TRAIL, THE(1945); WILD WEST(1946); WHITE STALLION(1947); PRAIRIE OUTLAWS(1948)

Juli Bridges
TWO-MINUTE WARNING(1976)

Lloyd Bridges
HARMON OF MICHIGAN(1941); HERE COMES MR. JORDAN(1941); HONOLULU LU(1941); LONE WOLF TAKES A CHANCE, THE(1941); MEDICO OF PAINTED SPRINGS, THE(1941); ROYAL MOUNTED PATROL, THE(1941); SING FOR YOUR SUPPER(1941); SON OF DAVY CROCKETT, THE(1941); THREE GIRLS ABOUT TOWN(1941); TWO LATINS FROM MANHATTAN(1941); YOU BELONG TO ME(1941); ALIAS BOSTON BLACKIE(1942); ATLANTIC CONVOY(1942); BLONDIE GOES TO COLLEGE(1942); CANAL ZONE(1942); COMMANDOS STRIKE AT DAWN, THE(1942); DARING YOUNG MAN, THE(1942); FLIGHT LIEUTENANT(1942); HARVARD, HERE I COME(1942); MAN'S WORLD, A(1942); PARDON MY GUN(1942); RIDERS OF THE NORTHLAND(1942); SHUT MY BIG MOUTH(1942); SPIRIT OF STANFORD, THE(1942); SWEETHEART OF THE FLEET(1942); TALK OF THE TOWN(1942); TRAMP, TRAMP, TRAMP(1942); UNDERGROUND AGENT(1942); WEST OF TOMBSTONE(1942); WIFE TAKES A FLYER, THE(1942); CRIME DOCTOR'S STRANGEST CASE(1943); DESTROYER(1943); HAIL TO THE RANGERS(1943); HEAT'S ON, THE(1943); PASSPORT TO SUEZ(1943); SAHARA(1943); LOUISIANA HAYRIDE(1944); MASTER RACE, THE(1944); SHE'S A SOLDIER TOO(1944); MISS SUSIE SLAGLE'S(1945); STRANGE CONFESSION(1945); WALK IN THE SUN, A(1945); ABILENE TOWN(1946); CANYON PASSAGE(1946); RAMROD(1947); TROUBLE WITH WOMEN, THE(1947); UNCONQUERED(1947); MOONRISE(1948); SECRET SERVICE INVESTIGATOR(1948); SIXTEEN FATHOMS DEEP(1948); CALAMITY JANE AND SAM BASS(1949); HIDEOUT(1949); HOME OF THE BRAVE(1949); RED CANYON(1949); TRAPPED(1949); COLT .45(1950); ROCKETSHIP X-M(1950); SOUND OF FURY, THE(1950); WHITE TOWER, THE(1950); LITTLE BIG HORN(1951); THREE STEPS NORTH(1951); WHISTLE AT EATON FALLS(1951); HIGH NOON(1952); LAST OF THE COMANCHES(1952); PLYMOUTH ADVENTURE(1952); CITY OF BAD MEN(1953); KID FROM LEFT FIELD, THE(1953); LIMPING MAN, THE(1953, Brit.); TALL TEXAN, THE(1953); PRIDE OF THE BLUE GRASS(1954); APACHE WOMAN(1955); DEADLY GAME, THE(1955, Brit.); WICHITA(1955); RAINMAKER, THE(1956); RIDE OUT FOR REVENGE(1957); GODDESS, THE(1958); AROUND THE WORLD UNDER THE SEA(1966); ATTACK ON THE IRON COAST(1968, U.S./Brit.); DARING GAME(1968); HAPPY ENDING, THE(1969); TO FIND A MAN(1972); RUNNING WILD(1973); BEHIND THE IRON MASK(1977); MISSION GALACTICA: THE CYLON ATTACK(1979); AIRPLANE!(1980); BEAR ISLAND(1980, Brit.-Can.); AIRPLANE II: THE SEQUEL(1982)
Misc. Talkies
SADDLE LEATHER LAW(1944); DELIVER US FROM EVIL(1975)

Lorraine Bridges
NIGHT AT THE OPERA, A(1935)

Robert Bridges
MORGAN!(1966, Brit.); VIRGIN SOLDIERS, THE(1970, Brit.); PINK FLOYD–THE WALL(1982, Brit.); NANA(1983, Ital.)

Ron Bridges
WHERE THE BULLETS FLY(1966, Brit.), m/l

Ronald Bridges
DATELINE DIAMONDS(1966, Brit.); EXORCISM AT MIDNIGHT(1966, Brit. revised 1973, U.S.)

Tom Bridges
GANG'S ALL HERE, THE(1943), w

Matla Bridgestone
SATIN MUSHROOM, THE(1969)

Billy Bridget
TAWNY PIPIT(1947, Brit.)

Blockbuster Bridget
OPERATION BULLSHINE(1963, Brit.)

Dee Dee Bridgewater
FISH THAT SAVED PITTSBURGH, THE(1979)
1984
BROTHER FROM ANOTHER PLANET, THE(1984)

Leslie Bridgewater
BELOVED VAGABOND, THE(1936, Brit.), md; AGAINST THE WIND(1948, Brit.), m; TRAIN OF EVENTS(1952, Brit.), m

Robert Bridgewood
GET THAT MAN(1935), w

James Bridie
PARADINE CASE, THE(1947), w; UNDER CAPRICORN(1949), w; STAGE FRIGHT(1950, Brit.), w; FLESH AND BLOOD(1951, Brit.), w; YOU'RE ONLY YOUNG TWICE(1952, Brit.), w; FOLLY TO BE WISE(1953), w; ANATOMIST, THE(1961, Brit.), w; THERE WAS A CROOKED MAN(1962, Brit.), w

Lucienne Bridou
FUNNY THING HAPPENED ON THE WAY TO THE FORUM, A(1966); COME SPY WITH ME(1967); THIS MAN CAN'T DIE(1970, Ital.)

V. Bridzinksy
Misc. Silents
SLAVE OF PASSION, SLAVE OF VICE(1914, USSR)

Sheryl Briedel
URBAN COWBOY(1980); TEX(1982)

Frederique Briel
TROUT, THE(1982, Fr.)

Ken Briell
COLD RIVER(1982)

Johanna Briem
1984
PRODIGAL, THE(1984)

Ernst Briemle
WILD GEESE, THE(1978, Brit.)

Edwin Brien
MYSTERIOUS RIDER, THE(1942)

Louise Brien
SMART GIRL(1935); TOWER OF LONDON(1939); BRITISH INTELLIGENCE(1940); FOREIGN CORRESPONDENT(1940); INVISIBLE MAN RETURNS, THE(1940)

A. J. Brier
DOWN THE WYOMING TRAIL(1939)

Adrien Brier
GOLD DIGGERS OF 1933(1933)

Audrene Brier
DARBY AND JOAN(1937, Brit.); WISE GUYS(1937, Brit.); REVERSE BE MY LOT, THE(1938, Brit.); DOWN IN SAN DIEGO(1941); PARACHUTE NURSE(1942); MILLION DOLLAR MERMAID(1952), ch

Audreno Brier
JOAN OF OZARK(1942)

Barbara Brier
MANHATTAN ANGEL(1948); OLD-FASHIONED GIRL, AN(1948); SHAMROCK HILL(1949), a, cos; HARD, FAST, AND BEAUTIFUL(1951)

Joann Brier
VICE GIRLS, LTD.(1964)

Margot Brier
ILLIAC PASSION, THE(1968)

Shorty Brier
STARLIGHT OVER TEXAS(1938)

J. F. Briere
BREAKING AWAY(1979)

Maurice Briere
MRS. PARKINGTON(1944)

Richard Briere
VISITING HOURS(1982, Can.)

Yveline Briere
HERBIE GOES TO MONTE CARLO(1977)

Con Brierley
OLD ROSES(1935, Brit.)

Joan Brierley
LEAP YEAR(1932, Brit.); NIGHT LIKE THIS, A(1932, Brit.); THARK(1932, Brit.); CUCKOO IN THE NEST, THE(1933, Brit.)

Roger Brierley
SUPERMAN II(1980); WICKED LADY, THE(1983, Brit.)

Suzanne M. Brierley
1984
HARRY AND SON(1984)

Thomas A. Brierley
Silents
SAND(1920), art d

David Brierly
CALCULATED RISK(1963, Brit.)

Maurice Brierre
GAMBLING LADY(1934); PARIS INTERLUDE(1934); HEARTS IN BONDAGE(1936); THEODORA GOES WILD(1936); CONFESSION(1937); ARTISTS AND MODELS ABROAD(1938); HOLIDAY(1938); JEZEBEL(1938); TOM, DICK AND HARRY(1941); NIGHT AND DAY(1946); JOAN OF ARC(1948); UNDER MY SKIN(1950); THREE COINS IN THE FOUNTAIN(1954)

Jane Briers
1984
SECRETS(1984, Brit.)

Richard Briers
GIRLS AT SEA(1958, Brit.); BOTTOMS UP(1960, Brit.); MURDER SHE SAID(1961, Brit.); GIRL ON THE BOAT, THE(1962, Brit.); MATTER OF WHO, A(1962, Brit.); V.I.P.s, THE(1963, Brit.); BARGEE, THE(1964, Brit.); FATHOM(1967); ALL THE WAY UP(1970, Brit.); RENTADICK(1972, Brit.); WATERSHIP DOWN(1978, Brit.)
Misc. Talkies
AERODROME, THE(1983, Brit.)

Eugene Brieux
DAMAGED GOODS(1937), w
Silents
DAMAGED GOODS(1915), w; CRADLE, THE(1922), w

Jeanne Briey
Misc. Silents
LA TERRE(1921, Fr.)

Louis Brigante
GUNS OF THE TREES(1964)

Elisa Livia Briganti
1984
HOUSE BY THE CEMETERY, THE(1984, Ital.), w

Elsia Briganti
ZOMBIE(1980, Ital.), w

Philippe Brigaud
1984
LES COMPERES(1984, Fr.)

Stephen Brigden
FLASH GORDON(1980)

Barry Briggs
WINSLOW BOY, THE(1950)

Carol Briggs
LIFE AND TIMES OF CHESTER-ANGUS RAMSGOOD, THE(1971, Can.)

Charles Briggs
HOW THE WEST WAS WON(1962); MERRILL'S MARAUDERS(1962); CAPTAIN NEWMAN, M.D.(1963); KLANSMAN, THE(1974)

Charlie Briggs
HOME FROM THE HILL(1960); ABSENT-MINDED PROFESSOR, THE(1961); THIRTEEN FRIGHTENED GIRLS(1963); TIME FOR KILLING, A(1967); TRAVELING EXECUTIONER, THE(1970); CHARLEY VARRICK(1973); LINCOLN CONSPIRACY, THE(1977); NORMA RAE(1979); SIX PACK(1982)

Daniel Briggs
SEXTETTE(1978), p

Derek Briggs
HELL, HEAVEN OR HOBOKEN(1958, Brit.)

Don Briggs
LOVE BEFORE BREAKFAST(1936); SUTTER'S GOLD(1936); SUBMARINE D-1(1937); WHEELER DEALERS, THE(1963)

Donald Briggs
SHOW BOAT(1936); ALL-AMERICAN SWEETHEART(1937); CAPTAINS COURAGEOUS(1937); FIT FOR A KING(1937); MAN OF THE PEOPLE(1937); THEY WON'T FORGET(1937); BELOVED BRAT(1938); BLONDES AT WORK(1938); COWBOY FROM BROOKLYN(1938); CRIME SCHOOL(1938); DAREDEVIL DRIVERS(1938); FIRST 100 YEARS, THE(1938); LOVE, HONOR AND BEHAVE(1938); MEN ARE SUCH FOOLS(1938); MR. CHUMP(1938); EX-CHAMP(1939); FORGOTTEN WOMAN, THE(1939); HARDYS RIDE HIGH, THE(1939); MADE FOR EACH OTHER(1939); PANAMA LADY(1939); UNEXPECTED FATHER(1939); WHISPERING ENEMIES(1939); WINGS OF THE NAVY(1939); DR. KILDARE GOES HOME(1940); DREAMING OUT LOUD(1940); HOT STEEL(1940); MEN AGAINST THE SKY(1940); OUTSIDE THE 3-MILE LIMIT(1940)

Douglas Briggs
UNFINISHED DANCE,THE(1947), ed

Fran Briggs
SUBSTITUTION(1970)

Geoff Briggs
CIAO MANHATTAN(1973)

Harian Briggs
ABE LINCOLN IN ILLINOIS(1940)

Harlan Briggs
UNCLE HARRY(1945); I FOUND STELLA PARISH(1935); WE'RE IN THE MONEY(1935); DODSWORTH(1936); GARDEN OF ALLAH, THE(1936); MAD HOLIDAY(1936); BEG, BORROW OR STEAL(1937); BEHIND THE MIKE(1937); EASY LIVING(1937); EXCLUSIVE(1937); FAMILY AFFAIR, A(1937); HAPPY-GO-LUCKY(1937); LIVE, LOVE AND LEARN(1937); MARKED WOMAN(1937); MARRIED BEFORE BREAKFAST(1937); MAYTIME(1937); RIDING ON AIR(1937); STELLA DALLAS(1937); THAT'S MY STORY(1937); TROUBLE AT MIDNIGHT(1937); DYNAMITE DELANEY(1938); HAVING WONDERFUL TIME(1938); MAN TO REMEMBER, A(1938); MEET THE GIRLS(1938); MISSING GUEST, THE(1938); ONE WILD NIGHT(1938); QUICK MONEY(1938); RECKLESS LIVING(1938); YOU AND ME(1938); ALMOST A GENTLEMAN(1939); BLONDIE TAKES A VACATION(1939); BOY TROUBLE(1939); CAFE SOCIETY(1939); CALLING DR. KILDARE(1939); FIFTH AVENUE GIRL(1939); FLIGHT AT MIDNIGHT(1939); MADE FOR EACH OTHER(1939); MAISIE(1939); MYSTERIOUS MISS X, THE(1939); TELL NO TALES(1939); BANK DICK, THE(1940); CHARLIE CHAN'S MURDER CRUISE(1940); EDISON, THE MAN(1940); I LOVE YOU AGAIN(1940); LUCKY PARTNERS(1940); MAN WHO WOULDN'T TALK, THE(1940); MY LITTLE CHICKADEE(1940); STRIKE UP THE BAND(1940); YOUNG AS YOU FEEL(1940); AMONG THE LIVING(1941); JENNIE(1941); LOOK WHO'S LAUGHING(1941); ONE FOOT IN HEAVEN(1941); PARIS CALLING(1941); VANISHING VIRGINIAN, THE(1941); LADY BODYGUARD(1942); REMARKABLE ANDREW, THE(1942); TENNESSEE JOHNSON(1942); THERE'S ONE BORN EVERY MINUTE(1942); CONFLICT(1945); STATE FAIR(1945); DO YOU LOVE ME?(1946); MAGNIFICENT DOLL(1946); MY PAL TRIGGER(1946); MYSTERIOUS INTRUDER(1946); NIGHT AND DAY(1946); PERSONALITY KID(1946); STOLEN LIFE, A(1946); TO EACH HIS OWN(1946); CYNTHIA(1947); DOUBLE LIFE, A(1947); SPOILERS OF THE NORTH(1947); VIGILANTES OF BOOMTOWN(1947); FURY AT FURNACE CREEK(1948); LITTLE WOMEN(1949); RUSTY SAVES A LIFE(1949); CARRIE(1952)

Hedley Briggs
MY BROTHER'S KEEPER(1949, Brit.)

Jack Briggs
FOUR JACKS AND A JILL(1941); MEXICAN SPITFIRE'S BABY(1941); PARACHUTE BATTALION(1941); REPENT AT LEISURE(1941); TOM, DICK AND HARRY(1941); ARMY SURGEON(1942); JOAN OF PARIS(1942); MEXICAN SPITFIRE'S ELEPHANT(1942); LADIES' DAY(1943); MY FORBIDDEN PAST(1951); NEW MEXICO(1951); PRINCE WHO WAS A THIEF, THE(1951)

John Briggs
SLASHER, THE(1953, Brit.); SECOND FIDDLE(1957, Brit.)

Johnny Briggs
DIPLOMATIC CORPSE, THE(1958, Brit.); LIGHT UP THE SKY(1960, Brit.); WIND OF CHANGE, THE(1961, Brit.); DAMN THE DEFIANT!(1962, Brit.); INFORMATION RECEIVED(1962, Brit.); DEVIL-SHIP PIRATES, THE(1964, Brit.); SQUADRON 633(1964, U.S./Brit.); YOUNG AND WILLING(1964, Brit.); 633 SQUADRON(1964); LEATHER BOYS, THE(1965, Brit.); SPYLARKS(1965, Brit.); STITCH IN TIME, A(1967, Brit.); LAST ESCAPE, THE(1970, Brit.); PERFECT FRIDAY(1970, Brit.); CARRY ON ENGLAND(1976, Brit.)

Julie Briggs
BOWERY BUCKAROOS(1947)
Lillian Briggs
LADIES MAN, THE(1961)
M. J. Briggs
Silents
ETERNAL SIN, THE(1917)
Matt Briggs
ADVICE TO THE LOVELORN(1933); BORN TO BE BAD(1934); HIPS, HIPS, HOORAY(1934); CONEY ISLAND(1943); DANCING MASTERS, THE(1943); MEANEST MAN IN THE WORLD, THE(1943); OX-BOW INCIDENT, THE(1943); WINTERTIME(1943); BUFFALO BILL(1944); ROGER TOUHY, GANGSTER!(1944); BABE RUTH STORY, THE(1948)
Michael Briggs
RUN FOR YOUR WIFE(1966, Fr./Ital.)
Samuel Briggs
STRIPES(1981)
Walter Briggs
ALL THE RIGHT MOVES(1983)
Wellington Briggs
OLD SOLDIERS NEVER DIE(1931, Brit.)
Misc. Silents
WHEN KNIGHTS WERE BOLD(1929, Brit.)
Constance Brigham
HANSEL AND GRETEL(1954)
Fred Brigham
1984
POLICE ACADEMY(1984)
Leslie Brigham
MIDSTREAM(1929)
Elisa Livia Brighanti
1990: THE BRONX WARRIORS(1983, Ital.), d
Harold Brighouse
HOBSON'S CHOICE(1931, Brit.), w; HOBSON'S CHOICE(1954, Brit.), w
Silents
WINNING GOAL, THE(1929, Brit.), w
Bebe Bright
1984
SLOW MOVES(1984)
Bernard Bright
CAESAR AND CLEOPATRA(1946, Brit.)
Bobby Bright
GRENDEL GRENDEL GRENDEL(1981, Aus.)
Dick "Richard" Bright
1984
ONCE UPON A TIME IN AMERICA(1984)
John Bright
BLONDE CRAZY(1931), w; PUBLIC ENEMY, THE(1931), w; SMART MONEY(1931), w; CROWD ROARS, THE(1932), w; IF I HAD A MILLION(1932), w; TAXI!(1932), w; THREE ON A MATCH(1932), w; UNION DEPOT(1932), w; SHE DONE HIM WRONG(1933), w; ACCUSING FINGER, THE(1936), w; GIRL OF THE OZARKS(1936), w; HERE COMES TROUBLE(1936), w; JOHN MEADE'S WOMAN(1937), w; SAN QUENTIN(1937), w; BACK DOOR TO HEAVEN(1939), w; GLAMOUR FOR SALE(1940), w; BROADWAY(1942), w; SHERLOCK HOLMES AND THE VOICE OF TERROR(1942), w; CLOSE-UP(1948), w; FIGHTING MAD(1948), w; I WALK ALONE(1948), w; OPEN SECRET(1948), w; KID FROM CLEVELAND, THE(1949), w; BRAVE BULLS, THE(1951), w
1984
BOSTONIANS, THE(1984), cos
June Bright
EASY LIVING(1949)
M. Bright
FORBIDDEN ZONE(1980), w
Mildred Bright
Misc. Silents
PARTNERS OF THE SUNSET(1922)
Paul Bright
1984
MICKI AND MAUDE(1984)
Richard Bright
ODDS AGAINST TOMORROW(1959); LIONS LOVE(1969); PANIC IN NEEDLE PARK(1971); GETAWAY, THE(1972); GODFATHER, THE(1972); PAT GARRETT AND BILLY THE KID(1973); GODFATHER, THE, PART II(1974); RANCHO DELUXE(1975); MARATHON MAN(1976); CITIZENS BAND(1977); LOOKING FOR MR. GOODBAR(1977); ON THE YARD(1978); HAIR(1979); IDOLMAKER, THE(1980); TWO OF A KIND(1983); VIGILANTE(1983)
1984
CRACKERS(1984); GIRLS NIGHT OUT(1984)
Robert Bright
ANGEL WORE RED, THE(1960)
Robert E. Bright
GREAT CARUSO, THE(1951)
Ronnell Bright
THEY SHOOT HORSES, DON'T THEY?(1969)
Sol Bright
FLIRTATION WALK(1934)
Homer Brightman
THREE CABALLEROS, THE(1944), w; MAKE MINE MUSIC(1946), w; FUN AND FANCY FREE(1947), w; MELODY TIME(1948), w; ADVENTURES OF ICHABOD AND MR. TOAD(1949), w; CINDERELLA(1950), w
Stanley Brightman
Silents
BATTLING BUTLER(1926), w
Ernest Brightmore
GUNMAN HAS ESCAPED, A(1948, Brit.); STRANGER'S MEETING(1957, Brit.)
Bruce Brighton
BRAIN THAT WOULDN'T DIE, THE(1959)

Connie Brighton
SMOKEY AND THE BANDIT–PART 3(1983)
Dick Brighton
SIN OF MONA KENT, THE(1961), w
Brigitte
MARGIN, THE,(1969, Braz.)
Giuseppe Brignoli
TREE OF WOODEN CLOGS, THE(1979, Ital.)
Mario Brignoli
TREE OF WOODEN CLOGS, THE(1979, Ital.)
Omar Brignoli
TREE OF WOODEN CLOGS, THE(1979, Ital.)
Guido Brignone
LOYALTY OF LOVE(1937, Ital.), d; BROKEN LOVE(1946, Ital.), d; DISHONORED(1950, Ital.), d; BURIED ALIVE(1951, Ital.), d; DEAD WOMAN'S KISS, A(1951, Ital.), d; SIGN OF THE GLADIATOR(1959, Fr./Ger./Ital.), p; WITCH'S CURSE, THE(1963, Ital.), w
Misc. Silents
MACISTE IN HELL(1926, Ital.), d
Guy Brignone
Misc. Silents
HERO OF THE CIRCUS, THE(1928, Ital.), d
Lilla Brignone
ANGELS OF DARKNESS(1956, Ital.); VIOLENT SUMMER(1961, Fr./Ital.); ECLIPSE(1962, Fr./Ital.); RICE GIRL(1963, Fr./Ital.); RITA(1963, Fr./Ital.); MALICIOUS(1974, Ital.)
Philippe Briguad
LITTLE ROMANCE, A(1979, U.S./Fr.)
Michel Briguet
1984
L'ARGENT(1984, Fr./Switz.)
Lily Brik
Misc. Silents
SHACKLED BY FILM(1918, USSR)
O. Brik
Silents
STORM OVER ASIA(1929, USSR), w
Arthur M. Brilant
CASE OF CLARA DEANE, THE(1932), w; STRANGE CASE OF CLARA DEANE, THE(1932), w
Chuck Briles
TROUBLE WITH GIRLS(AND HOW TO GET INTO IT), THE*1/2 (1969)
Alex Briley
CAN'T STOP THE MUSIC(1980)
Anne Briley
SUMMER HOLIDAY(1963, Brit.)
John Briley
INVASION QUARTET(1961, Brit.), w; POSTMAN'S KNOCK(1962, Brit.), w; CHILDREN OF THE DAMNED(1963, Brit.), w; SITUATION HOPELESS–BUT NOT SERIOUS(1965); POPE JOAN(1972, Brit.), w; THAT LUCKY TOUCH(1975, Brit.), w; MEDUSA TOUCH, THE(1978, Brit.), w; EAGLE'S WING(1979, Brit.), w; GANDHI(1982), w; ENIGMA(1983), w
Patti Brilhante
HENRY ALDRICH GETS GLAMOUR(1942); SALUTE FOR THREE(1943)
Charles Brill
PASTOR HALL(1940, Brit.), m, md; BEAST OF BUDAPEST, THE(1958)
Charlie Brill
MAN WHO WASN'T THERE, THE(1983)
Corinne Brill
LAST MAN, THE(1968, Fr.)
Eddie Brill
STUCK ON YOU(1983)
1984
STUCK ON YOU(1984)
Ellen Brill
RICH AND FAMOUS(1981)
Fran Brill
BEING THERE(1979)
1984
OLD ENOUGH(1984)
Francesca Brill
1984
CHAMPIONS(1984)
Hubert Brill
OUT OF THE PAST(1947)
Joseph Carl Brill
Silents
WHITE SISTER, THE(1923), m
Leighton Brill
SONG FOR MISS JULIE, A(1945), w
Marty Brill
ANGEL, ANGEL, DOWN WE GO(1969); RAGGEDY ANN AND ANDY(1977)
1984
POPE OF GREENWICH VILLAGE, THE(1984)
Michael Brill
BATTLE HELL(1956, Brit.); MAN WHO NEVER WAS, THE(1956, Brit.); ABOMINABLE SNOWMAN OF THE HIMALAYAS, THE(1957, Brit.); BARRETTS OF WIMPOLE STREET, THE(1957); SILENT ENEMY, THE(1959, Brit.)
Patti Brill
ADVENTURES OF A ROOKIE(1943); FALCON AND THE CO-EDS, THE(1943); FALLEN SPARROW, THE(1943); GILDERSLEEVE'S BAD DAY(1943); GOVERNMENT GIRL(1943); MEXICAN SPITFIRE'S BLESSED EVENT(1943); TENDER COMRADE(1943); FALCON IN HOLLYWOOD, THE(1944); FALCON OUT WEST, THE(1944); GIRL RUSH(1944); MUSIC IN MANHATTAN(1944); NEVADA(1944); SEVEN DAYS ASHORE(1944); PAN-AMERICANA(1945); LIVE WIRES(1946); HARD BOILED MAHONEY(1947); KILROY WAS HERE(1947); INCIDENT(1948)
Pattie Brill
SING YOUR WAY HOME(1945)

Richard Brill
THAT TENNESSEE BEAT(1966), p&d; LOVE BUG, THE(1968)
Dinorah Brillanti
DONA FLOR AND HER TWO HUSBANDS(1977, Braz.)
Alfredda Brilliant
PROUD VALLEY, THE(1941, Brit.), w; TINKER(1949, Brit.), p&w
Arthur Brilliant
Silents
ANNABEL LEE(1921), w
E. Brilling
1812(1944, USSR)
N. Brilling
OTHELLO(1960, U.S.S.R.)
Jacques Brillouin
CARNIVAL IN FLANDERS(1936, Fr.), ed
Ian Brimble
VENOM(1982, Brit.)
Nick Brimble
SWEENEY(1977, Brit.); SILVER DREAM RACER(1982, Brit.)
1984
SHEENA(1984)
Lloyd Brimhall
LOVE AND PAIN AND THE WHOLE DAMN THING(1973)
A. Wilford Brimley
BORDERLINE(1980); DEATH VALLEY(1982); THING, THE(1982)
Bill Brimley
LAWMAN(1971)
Lynne Brimley
1984
STONE BOY, THE(1984)
Wilford Brimley
CHINA SYNDROME, THE(1979); ELECTRIC HORSEMAN, THE(1979); BRUBA-KER(1980); ABSENCE OF MALICE(1981); TENDER MERCIES(1982); HIGH ROAD TO CHINA(1983); TOUGH ENOUGH(1983); 10 TO MIDNIGHT(1983)
1984
COUNTRY(1984); HARRY AND SON(1984); HOTEL NEW HAMPSHIRE, THE(1984); NATURAL, THE(1984); STONE BOY, THE(1984)
Max Brimmel
QUESTION OF ADULTERY, A(1959, Brit.)
Max Brimmell
HANGMAN'S WHARF(1950, Brit.); EIGHT O'CLOCK WALK(1954, Brit.); SOLUTION BY PHONE(1954, Brit.); HORNET'S NEST, THE(1955, Brit.)
J.A. Brimstone
HER MAN GILBEY(1949, Brit.)
Harisse Brin
SUSPENSE(1946)
M. Brin
YIDDLE WITH HIS FIDDLE(1937, Pol.)
Rolf Brin
1984
SAHARA(1984)
Paul Brinazar
I DIED A THOUSAND TIMES(1955)
Bruce Brinckerhoff
DOGS(1976), d
Burt Brinckerhoff
GODDESS, THE(1958); GREATEST STORY EVER TOLD, THE(1965); ACAPULCO GOLD(1978), d
Nancy Brinckman
FOLLOW THE BOYS(1944); SLAVE GIRL(1947)
Tessa Brind
YOUTH RUNS WILD(1944)
Yvette Brind'Amour
PYX, THE(1973, Can.)
Jean Brindeau
Silents
ENEMIES OF WOMEN, THE(1923)
Jeanne Brindeau
END OF THE WORLD, THE(1930, Fr.); DARK EYES(1938, Fr.)
Eugene Brindel
DAVY CROCKETT, KING OF THE WILD FRONTIER(1955)
Lloyd Brinder
YOICKS!(1932, Brit.), d
Daisy Brindley
SMITH'S WIVES(1935, Brit.)
Madge Brindley
KENTUCKY MINSTRELS(1934, Brit.); GHOSTS OF BERKELEY SQUARE(1947, Brit.); PICCADILLY INCIDENT(1948, Brit.); OLD MOTHER RILEY, HEADMIS-TRESS(1950, Brit.); MOULIN ROUGE(1952); SPIDER AND THE FLY, THE(1952, Brit.); HOBSON'S CHOICE(1954, Brit.); GENTLE TOUCH, THE(1956, Brit.); KID FOR TWO FARTHINGS, A(1956, Brit.); LADYKILLERS, THE(1956, Brit.); LONG HAUL, THE(1957, Brit.); ALF 'N' FAMILY(1968, Brit.); NICE GIRL LIKE ME, A(1969, Brit.)
Adrian Brine
WATERLOO(1970, Ital./USSR); MYSTERIES(1979, Neth.); GIRL WITH THE RED HAIR, THE(1983, Neth.)
Paul Brinegar
LARCENY(1948); GAL WHO TOOK THE WEST, THE(1949); SWORD IN THE DESERT(1949); TAKE ONE FALSE STEP(1949); STORM WARNING(1950); JOURNEY INTO LIGHT(1951); CAPTIVE CITY(1952); HERE COME THE NELSONS(1952); PAT AND MIKE(1952); FAST COMPANY(1953); SO BIG(1953); DAWN AT SOCORRO(1954); HUMAN DESIRE(1954); ROGUE COP(1954); FLIGHT TO HONG KONG(1956); WORLD WITHOUT END(1957); COPPER SKY(1957); HELL ON DEVIL'S IS-LAND(1957); SPIRIT OF ST. LOUIS, THE(1957); VAMPIRE, THE(1957); CATTLE EMPIRE(1958); HOW TO MAKE A MONSTER(1958); COUNTRY BOY(1966); CHAR-RO(1969); HIGH PLAINS DRIFTER(1973)
1984
CHATTANOOGA CHOO CHOO(1984)

Bob Bring
CHARLEY AND THE ANGEL(1973), ed; WHERE THE RED FERN GROWS(1974), ed; SHAGGY D.A., THE(1976), ed; RETURN FROM WITCH MOUNTAIN(1978), ed; FORCE: FIVE(1981), ed; ZAPPED!(1982), ed
Lou Bring
LADY, LET'S DANCE(1944)
Christopher Bringard
YOUNG GIANTS(1983)
Erik Bringard
YOUNG GIANTS(1983)
Mark Bringelson
GOING BERSERK(1983)
Dominique Bringuier
GIRL FROM LORRAINE, A(1982, Fr./Switz.), ph
Myron Brinig
SISTERS, THE(1938), w
Carol Brink
ALL I DESIRE(1953), w
Connie Brink
STRANGER IS WATCHING, A(1982), spec eff
Conrad Brink
1984
COTTON CLUB, THE(1984), spec eff
Elga Brink
CASE VAN GELDERN(1932, Ger.)
Silents
FAKE, THE(1927, Brit.); PHYSICIAN, THE(1928, Brit.)
Misc. Silents
QUO VADIS?(1925, Ital.)
Gary Brink
DRESSED TO KILL(1980), set d; SOUP FOR ONE(1982), set d; LOVESICK(1983), set d
Jan Brinker
Misc. Talkies
MONEY IN MY POCKET(1962)
Lynn Brinker
ROSEMARY'S BABY(1968)
Kate Brinkler
DESERT GUNS(1936)
Charles Brinkley
FIGHTING CODE, THE(1934)
Christie Brinkley
NATIONAL LAMPOON'S VACATION(1983)
Gordon Brinkley
Silents
DEVIL'S MASTERPIECE, THE(1927)
John Brinkley
HOT ROD RUMBLE(1957); TEENAGE DOLL(1957); HOT CAR GIRL(1958); WAR OF THE SATELLITES(1958); BLOOD AND STEEL(1959); BUCKET OF BLOOD, A(1959); I, MOBSTER(1959); T-BIRD GANG(1959), a, w; TOKYO AFTER DARK(1959); VAL-LEY OF THE REDWOODS(1960)
Nan Brinkley
HER LUCKY NIGHT(1945); SHE GETS HER MAN(1945)
Ritch Brinkley
1984
RHINESTONE(1984)
William Brinkley
DON'T GO NEAR THE WATER(1975), w
Dolores Brinkman
MYSTERIOUS ISLAND(1929); SO IT'S SUNDAY(1932)
Silents
JAKE THE PLUMBER(1927)
Nancy Brinkman
MR. MUGGS RIDES AGAIN(1945); BEHIND THE MASK(1946); LIVE WIRES(1946)
Misc. Talkies
SADDLE SERENADE(1945)
Paul Brinkman
THOSE ENDEARING YOUNG CHARMS(1945)
Richard Brinkman
GIRL, THE BODY, AND THE PILL, THE(1967), ed; JUST FOR THE HELL OF IT(1968), ed; SHE-DEVILS ON WHEELS(1968), ed
Ruth Brinkman
LITTLE NIGHT MUSIC, A(1977, Aust./U.S./Ger.)
Heinz Brinkmann
MORITURI(1965)
Angela Brinkworth
UNDER MILK WOOD(1973, Brit.)
Charles Brinley
LOVE IN THE DESERT(1929); COVERED WAGON TRAILS(1930); DAWN TRAIL, THE(1931); SPIRIT OF THE WEST(1932); DUDE BANDIT, THE(1933); WHARF ANGEL(1934); CRIMSON TRAIL, THE(1935); IT HAPPENED IN HOLLYWOOD(1937); OLD WYOMING TRAIL, THE(1937); YOU CAN'T TAKE IT WITH YOU(1938); SPOILERS OF THE RANGE(1939); TEXAS STAMPEDE(1939); WESTERN CARA-VANS(1939)
Silents
BEAUTIFUL GAMBLER, THE(1921); IF ONLY JIM(1921); HILLS OF MISSING MEN(1922); MORAN OF THE LADY LETTY(1922); FIGHTING SMILE, THE(1925); WHITE OUTLAW, THE(1925)
Misc. Silents
CALIFORNIA IN '49(1924); WESTERN WALLOP, THE(1924); COVERED WAGON TRAILS(1930)
Harvey Brinton
ROSE OF TRALEE(1938, Ireland)
Helena Brinton
LET'S FACE IT(1943)
Jasper Brinton
WAY OUT(1966), art d

Ralph Brinton
WINGS OF THE MORNING(1937, Brit.), art d; LADY IN DISTRESS(1942, Brit.), art d; ODD MAN OUT(1947, Brit.), art d; GAY LADY, THE(1949, Brit.), art d; SLEEPING CAR TO TRIESTE(1949, Brit.), art d; EYE WITNESS(1950, Brit.), art d; HOTEL SAHARA(1951, Brit.), art d; INHERITANCE, THE(1951, Brit.), art d; LUCKY NICK CAIN(1951), art d; OUTPOST IN MALAYA(1952, Brit.), art d; MASTER OF BALLANTRAE, THE(1953, U.S./Brit.), art d; MOBY DICK(1956, Brit.), art d; GYPSY AND THE GENTLEMAN, THE(1958, Brit.), prod d, art d; ROOM AT THE TOP(1959, Brit.), art d; ENTERTAINER, THE(1960, Brit.), art d; LONELINESS OF THE LONG DISTANCE RUNNER, THE(1962, Brit.), prod d; TASTE OF HONEY, A(1962, Brit.), art d; TOM JONES(1963, Brit.), prod d

Tim Brinton
INFORMATION RECEIVED(1962, Brit.); HEAVENS ABOVE!(1963, Brit.); BUNNY LAKE IS MISSING(1965); COUNTERFEIT CONSTABLE, THE(1966, Fr.); MAN AT THE TOP(1973, Brit.)

W. Ralph Brinton
BLIND MAN'S BLUFF(1936, Brit.), art d

Francoise Brion
GAME FOR SIX LOVERS, A(1962, Fr.); TALES OF PARIS(1962, Fr./Ital.); FRENCH GAME, THE(1963, Fr.); MAGNIFICENT SINNER(1963, Fr.); SWEET AND SOUR(1964, Fr./Ital.); YOUNG WORLD, A(1966, Fr./Ital.); IMMORAL MOMENT, THE(1967, Fr.); BLONDE FROM PEKING, THE(1968, Fr./Ital./Turkey); L'IMMORTELLE(1969, Fr./Ital./Turkey); VERY HAPPY ALEXANDER(1969, Fr.); CARAVAN TO VACCARES(1974, Brit./Fr); ROSEBUD(1975); ATTENTION, THE KIDS ARE WATCHING(1978, Fr.)

Mildred Brion
HANKY-PANKY(1982)

Romy Brion
W.I.A.(WOUNDED IN ACTION)*1/2 (1966)

Felix Briones
MAGNIFICENT MATADOR, THE(1955)

Sacha Briquet
SEVEN CAPITAL SINS(1962, Fr./Ital.); ELUSIVE CORPORAL, THE(1963, Fr.); LANDRU(1963, Fr./Ital); OPHELIA(1964, Fr.); MALE COMPANION(1965, Fr./Ital.); BEAUTIFUL SWINDLERS, THE(1967, Fr./Ital./Jap./Neth.)

Jane Brisbane
ROAD TO FORT ALAMO, THE(1966, Fr./Ital.), w

William Brisbane
LADIES IN LOVE(1936); MEET THE MISSUS(1937); SHALL WE DANCE(1937); THERE GOES THE GROOM(1937); YOU CAN'T BEAT LOVE(1937); EVERYBODY'S DOING IT(1938); MAID'S NIGHT OUT(1938); SHE'S GOT EVERYTHING(1938); VIVACIOUS LADY(1938); SHOULD HUSBANDS WORK?(1939); BLONDIE ON A BUDGET(1940); TOO MANY HUSBANDS(1940)

Gwen Brisco
GETTING OVER(1981)

Donald Briscoe
HOUSE OF DARK SHADOWS(1970)

J. F. Briscoe
Silents
FIGHTING FOR LOVE(1917)

Marion Briscoe
LITTLE OLD NEW YORK(1940)

Danielle Brisebois
PREMONITION, THE(1976); IF EVER I SEE YOU AGAIN(1978); KING OF THE GYPSIES(1978)

Michele Brisigotti
AMERICAN WEREWOLF IN LONDON, AN(1981)

Barney Briskin
ESCAPE TO PARADISE(1939), p

Irving Briskin
BORDER LAW(1931), p; ONE WAY TRAIL, THE(1931), p; RANGE FEUD, THE(1931), p; DARING DANGER(1932), p; END OF THE TRAIL(1932), p; RIDIN' FOR JUSTICE(1932), p; RIDING TORNADO, THE(1932), p; SOUTH OF THE RIO GRANDE(1932), p; TEXAS CYCLONE(1932), p; TWO-FISTED LAW(1932), p; THRILL HUNTER, THE(1933), p; FIGHTING RANGER, THE(1934), p; MAN TRAILER, THE(1934), p; JUSTICE OF THE RANGE(1935), p; END OF THE TRAIL(1936), p; HELL-SHIP MORGAN(1936), p; TWO IN A TAXI(1941), p; IS EVERYBODY HAPPY?(1943), p; BEAUTIFUL BUT BROKE(1944), p; HEY, ROOKIE(1944), p; JAM SESSION(1944), p; KLONDIKE KATE(1944), p

Joel Briskin
FRAMED(1975), p

Mort Briskin
BIG WHEEL, THE(1949), p; JACKIE ROBINSON STORY, THE(1950), p; QUICKSAND(1950), p; MAGIC FACE, THE(1951, Aust.), p, w; SECOND WOMAN, THE(1951), p, w; NO TIME FOR FLOWERS(1952), p; MAN ALONE, A(1955), w; WILLARD(1971), p; BEN(1972), p; YOU'LL LIKE MY MOTHER(1972), p; WALKING TALL(1973), p, w; FRAMED(1975), p, w

Samuel Briskin
GIRL FRIEND, THE(1935), p

Samuel J. Briskin
STRATEGIC AIR COMMAND(1955), p; JOKER IS WILD, THE(1957), p
Silents
WASTED LIVES(1925), p

Jack Brisko
CROWD ROARS, THE(1932)

Norman Brisky
JETLAG(1981, U.S./Span.)

Stuart Brisley
1984
GHOST DANCE(1984, Brit.)

Jean Brismee
DEVIL'S NIGHTMARE, THE(1971 Bel./Ital.), d

Gilles Brissac
LAFAYETTE(1963, Fr.)

Virginia Brissac
BIG NOISE, THE(1936); DOWN THE STRETCH(1936); LOVE LETTERS OF A STAR(1936); MURDER BY AN ARISTOCRAT(1936); THREE GODFATHERS(1936); TWO AGAINST THE WORLD(1936); ADVENTUROUS BLONDE(1937); ARTISTS AND MODELS(1937); IDOL OF THE CROWDS(1937); MOUNTAIN JUSTICE(1937); WHITE BONDAGE(1937); DELINQUENT PARENTS(1938); SECRETS OF A NURSE(1938); YOUNG DR. KILDARE(1938); DARK VICTORY(1939); DESTRY RIDES AGAIN(1939);

FORGOTTEN WOMAN, THE(1939); HOTEL FOR WOMEN(1939); I STOLE A MILLION(1939); INVITATION TO HAPPINESS(1939); JESSE JAMES(1939); PARENTS ON TRIAL(1939); RETURN OF DR. X, THE(1939); THEY SHALL HAVE MUSIC(1939); WOMAN DOCTOR(1939); YOUNG MR. LINCOLN(1939); ALIAS THE DEACON(1940); ALL THIS AND HEAVEN TOO(1940); ALWAYS A BRIDE(1940); BLACK FRIDAY(1940); CHAD HANNA(1940); CHILD IS BORN, A(1940); GHOST BREAKERS, THE(1940); HIRED WIFE(1940); HOUSE ACROSS THE BAY, THE(1940); IT'S A DATE(1940); LADY WITH RED HAIR(1940); LITTLE OLD NEW YORK(1940); LITTLE ORVIE(1940); REMEMBER THE NIGHT(1940); STRIKE UP THE BAND(1940); WAGONS WESTWARD(1940); APPOINTMENT FOR LOVE(1941); BAD MAN OF MISSOURI(1941); DRESSED TO KILL(1941); GREAT LIE, THE(1941); LITTLE FOXES, THE(1941); NURSE'S SECRET, THE(1941); ONE FOOT IN HEAVEN(1941); REMEMBER THE DAY(1941); UNFINISHED BUSINESS(1941); WASHINGTON MELODRAMA(1941); BIG SHOT, THE(1942); GET HEP TO LOVE(1942); LADY GANGSTER(1942); LUCKY JORDAN(1942); MUMMY'S TOMB, THE(1942); STAR SPANGLED RHYTHM(1942); TAKE A LETTER, DARLING(1942); THEY DIED WITH THEIR BOOTS ON(1942); TOUGH AS THEY COME(1942); CRIME DOCTOR'S STRANGEST CASE(1943); IRON MAJOR, THE(1943); MOONLIGHT IN VERMONT(1943); MUG TOWN(1943); SHADOW OF A DOUBT(1943); SOMEONE TO REMEMBER(1943); MARRIAGE IS A PRIVATE AFFAIR(1944); NIGHT CLUB GIRL(1944); PHANTOM LADY(1944); SING, NEIGHBOR, SING(1944); THIS IS THE LIFE(1944); TOGETHER AGAIN(1944); BEWITCHED(1945); CAPTAIN EDDIE(1945); DALTONS RIDE AGAIN, THE(1945); DOLLY SISTERS, THE(1945); G.I. HONEYMOON(1945); SCARLET CLUE, THE(1945); STATE FAIR(1945); THREE'S A CROWD(1945); THRILL OF A ROMANCE(1945); TREE GROWS IN BROOKLYN, A(1945); WHY GIRLS LEAVE HOME(1945); HOT CARGO(1946); MYSTERIOUS MR. VALENTINE, THE(1946); RENEGADES(1946); SISTER KENNY(1946); CAPTAIN FROM CASTILE(1947); MONSIEUR VERDOUX(1947); PURSUED(1947); ACT OF MURDER, AN(1948); MATING OF MILLIE, THE(1948); OLD LOS ANGELES(1948); SECRET BEYOND THE DOOR, THE(1948); SNAKE PIT, THE(1948); SUMMER HOLIDAY(1948); THREE DARING DAUGHTERS(1948); UNTAMED BREED, THE(1948); DOOLINS OF OKLAHOMA, THE(1949); LAST BANDIT, THE(1949); MOTHER IS A FRESHMAN(1949); TENSION(1949); CHEAPER BY THE DOZEN(1950); EDGE OF DOOM(1950); HARRIET CRAIG(1950); NO MAN OF HER OWN(1950); FLAME OF ARABY(1951); OPERATION PACIFIC(1951); TWO OF A KIND(1951); BUGLES IN THE AFTERNOON(1952); MEET ME AT THE FAIR(1952); WOMAN OF THE NORTH COUNTRY(1952); BANDITS OF CORSICA, THE(1953); FAIR WIND TO JAVA(1953); ABOUT MRS. LESLIE(1954); EXECUTIVE SUITE(1954); MA AND PA KETTLE AT HOME(1954); REBEL WITHOUT A CAUSE(1955)
Misc. Talkies
IN OLD LOS ANGELES(1948)

Tiffany Brissette
HEART LIKE A WHEEL(1983)

Carl Brisson
AMERICAN PRISONER, THE(1929 Brit.); KNOWING MEN(1930, Brit.); SONG OF SOHO(1930, Brit.); PRINCE OF ARCADIA(1933, Brit.); MURDER AT THE VANITIES(1934); TWO HEARTS IN WALTZ TIME(1934, Brit.); ALL THE KING'S HORSES(1935); SHIP CAFE(1935)
Silents
RING, THE(1927, Brit.); MANXMAN, THE(1929, Brit.)

Frederick Brisebois
VELVET TOUCH, THE(1948), p; NEVER WAVE AT A WAC(1952), p; GIRL RUSH, THE(1955), p; UNDER THE YUM-YUM TREE(1963), p; GENERATION(1969), p; MRS. POLLIFAX-SPY(1971), p

Fredrick Brisson
FIVE FINGER EXERCISE(1962), p

Anne-Marie Brissoniere
QUARTET(1981, Brit./Fr.)

Robert Brister
NIGHT CLUB SCANDAL(1937); TOAST OF NEW YORK, THE(1937); DANGEROUS TO KNOW(1938); PRISON FARM(1938); SUDDEN MONEY(1939)

Frank Bristol
Silents
PATCHWORK GIRL OF OZ, THE(1914)

Howard Bristol
THOROUGHLY MODERN MILLIE(1967), set d; HOWARDS OF VIRGINIA, THE(1940), set d; LITTLE FOXES, THE(1941), set d; SHANGHAI GESTURE, THE(1941), set d; PRIDE OF THE YANKEES, THE(1942), set d; NORTH STAR, THE(1943), set d; PRINCESS AND THE PIRATE, THE(1944), set d; UP IN ARMS(1944), set d; WONDER MAN(1945), set d; ROPE(1948), set d; SLEEP, MY LOVE(1948), set d; WALK A CROOKED MILE(1948), set d; OCEAN BREAKERS(1949, Swed.), set d; 711 OCEAN DRIVE(1950), set d; ACTORS AND SIN(1952), set d; HANS CHRISTIAN ANDERSEN(1952), set d; NEVER WAVE AT A WAC(1952), set d; SUDDENLY(1954), set d; GUYS AND DOLLS(1955), set d; WITNESS FOR THE PROSECUTION(1957), set d; ANATOMY OF A MURDER(1959), set d; PORGY AND BESS(1959), set d; OCEAN'S ELEVEN(1960), set d; TAMMY, TELL ME TRUE(1961), set d; IF A MAN ANSWERS(1962), set d; CAPTAIN NEWMAN, M.D.(1963), set d; TAMMY AND THE DOCTOR(1963), set d; THRILL OF IT ALL, THE(1963), set d; DEAR HEART(1964), set d; I'D RATHER BE RICH(1964), set d; MADAME X(1966), set d; THREE ON A COUCH(1966), set d; ROSIE!(1967), set d; STAR!(1968), set d

Iris Bristol
NOTORIOUS LANDLADY, THE(1962)

John Bristol
POPEYE(1980)

John E. Bristol
1984
TERMINATOR, THE(1984)

Robert Bristol
HANGAR 18(1980)

Iris Briston
MY FAIR LADY(1964)

Sam "Birmingham" Briston
BINGO LONG TRAVELING ALL-STARS AND MOTOR KINGS, THE(1976)

Billie Bristow
DEADLOCK(1931, Brit.), w; MEN OF STEEL(1932, Brit.), w; SELF-MADE LADY(1932, Brit.), w; HOUSE OF TRENT, THE(1933, Brit.), w; SECRET OF THE LOCH, THE(1934, Brit.), w; WARN LONDON!(1934, Brit.), w; NIGHT MAIL(1935, Brit.), w; GAY LOVE(1936, Brit.), w

Cyril Bristow
GENERAL JOHN REGAN(1933, Brit.), ph; SECRET AGENT(1933, Brit.), ph; UP TO THE NECK(1933, Brit.), ph; DANGEROUS GROUND(1934, Brit.), ph; LILIES OF THE FIELD(1934, Brit.), ph; SORRELL AND SON(1934, Brit.), ph; HYDE PARK CORNER(1935, Brit.), ph; RADIO FOLLIES(1935, Brit.), ph; CARDINAL, THE(1936, Brit.), ph; GAY ADVENTURE, THE(1936, Brit.), ph; LIMPING MAN, THE(1936, Brit.), ph; ONE GOOD TURN(1936, Brit.), ph; BIG FELLA(1937, Brit.), ph; BOMBS OVER LONDON(1937, Brit.), ph; BOYS WILL BE GIRLS(1937, Brit.), ph; COMMAND PERFORMANCE(1937, Brit.), ph; COTTON QUEEN(1937, Brit.), ph; FOLLOW YOUR STAR(1938, Brit.), ph; HOUSE OF DARKNESS(1948, Brit.), ph; BOYS IN BROWN(1949, Brit.), ph; MAN FROM YESTERDAY, THE(1949, Brit.), ph; STOP PRESS GIRL(1949, Brit.), ph

Daryl Bristow
PEOPLE THAT TIME FORGOT, THE(1977, Brit.), cos

Frank Bristow
HOLLYWOOD BARN DANCE(1947)

Gwen Bristow
TOMORROW IS FOREVER(1946), w; JUBILEE TRAIL(1954), w

Jimmy Bristow
LADY'S FROM KENTUCKY, THE(1939)

Norman Bristow
TERRORISTS, THE(1975, Brit.)

Owen Davis Gwen Bristow
NINTH GUEST, THE(1934), w

Tania Bristowe
1984
HEART OF THE STAG(1984, New Zealand); UTU(1984, New Zealand)

Donald Britain
Misc. Talkies
ACCIDENT(1983), d

Britgitta
PUTNEY SWOPE(1969)

Maria Britneva
MOULIN ROUGE(1952); SCAPEGOAT, THE(1959, Brit.); SUDDENLY, LAST SUMMER(1959, Brit.)

Maria Britnewa
TOO BAD SHE'S BAD(1954, Ital.)

Phil Brito
SWEETHEART OF SIGMA CHI(1946); MUSIC MAN(1948); SQUARE DANCE KATY(1950)

Elton Britt
LARAMIE(1949)

Hector Britt
ROADIE(1980)

Kelly Britt
PIPE DREAMS(1976)

Leo Britt
MONKEY'S PAW, THE(1933); ROOF, THE(1933, Brit.); THEY CAME BY NIGHT(1940, Brit.); TAKE MY LIFE(1948, Brit.); MAGNETIC MONSTER, THE(1953); DIAL M FOR MURDER(1954); ELEPHANT WALK(1954); COURT JESTER, THE(1956); CHARGE OF THE LIGHT BRIGADE, THE(1968, Brit.); GOODBYE MR. CHIPS(1969, U.S./Brit.); MOON ZERO TWO(1970, Brit.)

Lisa Britt
SUDDEN IMPACT(1983)

May Britt
FATAL DESIRE(1953); WAR AND PEACE(1956, Ital./U.S.); HUNTERS, THE(1958); YOUNG LIONS, THE(1958); BLUE ANGEL, THE(1959); MURDER, INC.(1960); UNFAITHFULS, THE(1960, Ital.); SHIP OF CONDEMNED WOMEN, THE(1963, ITAL.); HAUNTS(1977)

Melendy Britt
LAWYER, THE(1969); GRAY LADY DOWN(1978)

Olin Britt
MUSIC MAN, THE(1962)

Rod Britt
1984
RIVER RAT, THE(1984)

Ron Britt
NORSEMAN, THE(1978)

Scott Britt
THOMASINE AND BUSHROD(1974)

Sheila Britt
SEDUCERS, THE(1962)

Steven Britt
UP THE SANDBOX(1972)

Regimental Sergeant Major Brittain
THEY WERE NOT DIVIDED(1951, Brit.); MISSING NOTE, THE(1961, Brit.)

Aileen Brittain
MY BRILLIANT CAREER(1980, Aus.)

Dianne Brittain
SET, THE(1970, Aus.), w

Frank Brittain
SET, THE(1970, Aus.), p&d

Ronald Brittain
CONCRETE JUNGLE, THE(1962, Brit.); 55 DAYS AT PEKING(1963); AMOROUS MR. PRAWN, THE(1965, Brit.); SPY WITH A COLD NOSE, THE(1966, Brit.)

RSM Brittain
YOU LUCKY PEOPLE(1955, Brit.); JOEY BOY(1965, Brit.)

Tibby Brittain
LISA(1962, Brit.)

Sheba Brittan
PLEASURE PLANTATION(1970)

John Brittany
ASPHYX, THE(1972, Brit.), p

Morgan Brittany
GABLE AND LOMBARD(1976); IN SEARCH OF HISTORIC JESUS(1980)
1984
PRODIGAL, THE(1984)

Alleen Britten
TALL TIMBERS(1937, Aus.)

Benjamin Britten
FANNY AND ALEXANDER(1983, Swed./Fr./Ger.), m

Bill Britten
FAME(1980)

Hal Britten
THIS WAS A WOMAN(1949, Brit.), ph

Lawrence Britten
Misc. Talkies
WHOSE CHILD AM I?(1976), d

Aileen Britton
NOW AND FOREVER(1983, Aus.)

Barbara Britton
LOUISIANA PURCHASE(1941); SECRETS OF THE WASTELANDS(1941); BEYOND THE BLUE HORIZON(1942); FLEET'S IN, THE(1942); MRS. WIGGS OF THE CABBAGE PATCH(1942); REAP THE WILD WIND(1942); WAKE ISLAND(1942); SO PROUDLY WE HAIL(1943); YOUNG AND WILLING(1943); STORY OF DR. WASSELL, THE(1944); 'TILL WE MEET AGAIN(1944); CAPTAIN KIDD(1945); GREAT JOHN L. THE(1945); FABULOUS SUZANNE, THE(1946); RETURN OF MONTE CRISTO, THE(1946); THEY MADE ME A KILLER(1946); VIRGINIAN, THE(1946); GUNFIGHTERS, THE(1947); ALBUQUERQUE(1948); LOADED PISTOLS(1948); MR. RECKLESS(1948); UNTAMED BREED, THE(1948); COVER-UP(1949); I SHOT JESSE JAMES(1949); BANDIT QUEEN(1950); CHAMPAGNE FOR CAESAR(1950); RAIDERS, THE(1952); RIDE THE MAN DOWN(1952); BWANA DEVIL(1953); DRAGONFLY SQUADRON(1953); AIN'T MISBEHAVIN'(1955); NIGHT FREIGHT(1955); SPOILERS, THE(1955)

Bill Britton
HUSBANDS(1970)

Burt Britton
FRONT, THE(1976)

Christopher Britton
TICKET TO HEAVEN(1981)

Devon Britton
1984
HIGHPOINT(1984, Can.)

Edna Britton
Misc. Silents
SCREAM IN THE NIGHT, A(1919)

Florence Britton
DEVIL TO PAY, THE(1930); ARROWSMITH(1931); CHANCES(1931); CONFESSIONS OF A CO-ED(1931); DEVIL PAYS, THE(1932); MERRILY WE GO TO HELL(1932); STRANGE CASE OF CLARA DEANE, THE(1932); BRIEF MOMENT(1933); KING OF THE JUNGLE(1933)
Misc. Talkies
SILENT MEN(1933)

George B. Britton
Misc. Talkies
EVERYDAY(1976), d

Hutin Britton
Misc. Silents
WANDERING JEW, THE(1923, Brit.)

Jill Britton
UNDER MILK WOOD(1973, Brit.)

Jocelyn Britton
BOY AND THE BRIDGE, THE(1959, Brit.); SAPPHIRE(1959, Brit.); SO EVIL SO YOUNG(1961, Brit.)

Keith Britton
STORM FEAR(1956)

Kenneth Britton
ROMANCE ON THE HIGH SEAS(1948); LADY TAKES A SAILOR, THE(1949); MY DREAM IS YOURS(1949)

Layne Britton
PORGY AND BESS(1959), makeup; TIMBUKTU(1959), makeup; BY LOVE POSSESSED(1961), makeup; GLOBAL AFFAIR, A(1964), makeup; LADY IN CEMENT(1968), makeup

Marty Britton
CLASS(1983)

Mike Britton
SECRETS OF SEX(1970, Brit.)

Nellie Hutin Britton
Silents
MERCHANT OF VENICE, THE(1916, Brit.)

Pam Britton
WATCH THE BIRDIE(1950)

Pamela Britton
ANCHORS AWEIGH(1945); LETTER FOR EVIE, A(1945); D.O.A.(1950); KEY TO THE CITY(1950); IF IT'S TUESDAY, THIS MUST BE BELGIUM(1969); SUPPOSE THEY GAVE A WAR AND NOBODY CAME?(1970)

Sheilla Britton
MURDER IN MISSISSIPPI(1965)

Susanna Britton
Misc. Talkies
BLONDE GODDESS(1982)

Tony Britton
SALUTE THE TOFF(1952, Brit.); LOSER TAKES ALL(1956, Brit.); BIRTHDAY PRESENT, THE(1957, Brit.); BEHIND THE MASK(1958, Brit.); HEART OF A MAN, THE(1959, Brit.); OPERATION AMSTERDAM(1960, Brit.); PORTRAIT OF A SINNER(1961, Brit.); RISK, THE(1961, Brit.); BREAK, THE(1962, Brit.); STORK TALK(1964, Brit.); THERE'S A GIRL IN MY SOUP(1970, Brit.); SUNDAY BLOODY SUNDAY(1971, Brit.); CRY OF THE PENGUINS(1972, Brit.); DAY OF THE JACKAL, THE(1973, Brit./Fr.); NIGHT WATCH(1973, Brit.); DR. SYN, ALIAS THE SCARECROW(1975); PEOPLE THAT TIME FORGOT, THE(1977, Brit.); AGATHA(1979, Brit.)

Mozelle Brittone
FIGHTING RANGER, THE(1934)

Pierre Brive
ETERNAL HUSBAND, THE(1946, Fr.), w

Nadia Brivio
PHAROAH'S WOMAN, THE(1961, Ital.); PIRATE AND THE SLAVE GIRL, THE(1961, Fr./Ital.)
Herman Brix
AMATEUR CROOK(1937)
Misc. Talkies
FIGHTING DEVIL DOGS(1938)
Herman Brix [Bruce Bennett]
TOUCHDOWN!(1931); MILLION DOLLAR LEGS(1932); DEATH OF THE DIAMOND(1934); STUDENT TOUR(1934); NEW ADVENTURES OF TARZAN(1935); DANGER PATROL(1937); TWO MINUTES TO PLAY(1937); $1,000,000 RACKET(1937); FLYING FISTS, THE(1938); LAND OF FIGHTING MEN(1938); MILLION TO ONE, A(1938); TARZAN AND THE GREEN GODDESS(1938); HI-YO SILVER(1940)
Misc. Talkies
SILKS AND SADDLES(1938)
William Brix
SINGAPORE, SINGAPORE(1969, Fr./Ital.)
Len Brixton
GAY DESPERADO, THE(1936)
Philippe Brizard
HOW NOT TO ROB A DEPARTMENT STORE(1965, Fr./Ital.)
Luciano Brizi
LA TRAVIATA(1982)
Brizzi
ETERNAL MELODIES(1948, Ital.), ph
Anchise Brizzi
DEFEAT OF HANNIBAL, THE(1937, Ital.), ph; LOYALTY OF LOVE(1937, Ital.), ph; BEFORE HIM ALL ROME TREMBLED(1947, Ital.), ph; SHOE SHINE(1947, Ital.), ph; BLACK MAGIC(1949), ph; GOLDEN MADONNA, THE(1949, Brit.), ph; PIRATES OF CAPRI, THE(1949), ph; RIGOLETTO(1949), ph; THIEF OF VENICE, THE(1952), ph; OTHELLO(1955, U.S./Fr./Ital.), ph; ANGELS OF DARKNESS(1956, Ital.), ph; CLEOPATRA'S DAUGHTER(1963, Fr., Ital.), ph
Anchiso Brizzi
SPIRIT AND THE FLESH, THE(1948, Ital.), ph
Andre Brizzi
MESSALINE(1952, Fr./Ital.), ph
Jacques Brizzio
DIE GANS VON SEDAN(1962, Fr/Ger.), art d; VIOLETTE(1978, Fr.), artd; THREE MEN TO DESTROY(1980, Fr.), art d
Anthony Broad
SILVER BEARS(1978)
Kid Broad
BOWERY, THE(1933)
Silents
LOVE IN A HURRY(1919); EASY TO GET(1920); MAN WORTH WHILE, THE(1921)
Lois Broad
NIGHT OF EVIL(1962)
Ada Broadbent
SIS HOPKINS(1941), ch
Aida Broadbent
MELODY AND MOONLIGHT(1940), art d; COWBOY IN MANHATTTAN(1943), ch; TELL IT TO A STAR(1945), ch
Alda Broadbent
IRENE(1940), ch
Basil Broadbent
SCHOONER GANG, THE(1937, Brit.); DANCE OF DEATH, THE(1938, Brit.)
James Broadbent
PASSAGE, THE(1979, Brit.)
Jim Broadbent
DOGS OF WAR, THE(1980, Brit.); TIME BANDITS(1981, Brit.)
Hugh Broadbridge
ROAD TO FORTUNE, THE(1930, Brit.), w
Tom Broadbridge
DEAD MAN'S FLOAT(1980), p; BMX BANDITS(1983), p
Charles Broaddus
SHEBA BABY(1975)
Roger Broaddus
PLYMOUTH ADVENTURE(1952)
J. Paul Broadhead
1984
FOOTLOOSE(1984)
Meghan Broadhead
1984
FOOTLOOSE(1984)
Mimi Broadhead
1984
FOOTLOOSE(1984)
Alan Broadhurst
HAPPIEST DAYS OF YOUR LIFE(1950, Brit.)
Cece Broadhurst
SUSAN AND GOD(1940)
Cecil Broadhurst
CROWNING EXPERIENCE, THE(1960)
George Broadhurst
TODAY(1930), w; PRIVATE SECRETARY, THE(1935, Brit.), w
Silents
CALL OF THE NORTH, THE(1914), w; DOLLAR MARK, THE(1914), w; LAW OF THE LAND, THE(1917), w; TODAY(1917), w; INNOCENT(1918), w
George H. Broadhurst
Silents
WIFE AGAINST WIFE(1921), w; WHAT HAPPENED TO JONES(1926), w; WILD OATS LANE(1926), w
Kent Broadhurst
VERDICT, THE(1982); LOVESICK(1983); SILKWOOD(1983)
Thomas Broadhurst
GENERAL CRACK(1929), w
Thomas W. Broadhurst
DAMAGED LOVE(1931), w

Colin Broadley
ABANDON SHIP(1957, Brit.)
Edward Broadley
JURY'S SECRET, THE(1938); WOMEN ARE LIKE THAT(1938)
David Broadnax
Misc. Talkies
ZOMBIE ISLAND MASSACRE(1984)
Ted Broadribb
EXCUSE MY GLOVE(1936, Brit.)
William Broadus
SUNDOWN(1941)
Nicky Broadway
ESCAPE FROM THE SEA(1968, Brit.)
The Broadway Boys
NIGHT OF MAGIC, A(1944, Brit.)
Robert R. Broadwell
Misc. Silents
VENGEANCE IS MINE!(1916), d
J.K. Broady
ASSIGNMENT OUTER SPACE(1960, Ital.), m
Linda Broan
INN OF THE DAMNED(1974, Aus.)
Lily Broberg
CRAZY PARADISE(1965, Den.); ERIC SOYA'S "17"(1967, Den.)
Marcelle Broc
LOVE IN THE AFTERNOON(1957)
Nic Broca
GULLIVER'S TRAVELS(1977, Brit., Bel.), anim
1984
SMURFS AND THE MAGIC FLUTE, THE(1984, Fr./Belg.), anim
Fred Brocco
APPOINTMENT WITH MURDER(1948)
Peter Brocco
DEVIL AND THE DEEP(1932); LONE WOLF IN MEXICO, THE(1947); ARGYLE SECRETS, THE(1948); GALLANT BLADE, THE(1948); SAXON CHARM, THE(1948); VICIOUS CIRCLE, THE(1948); BOSTON BLACKIE'S CHINESE VENTURE(1949); FLAMING FURY(1949); JOLSON SINGS AGAIN(1949); LADY GAMBLES, THE(1949); MISS GRANT TAKES RICHMOND(1949); POST OFFICE INVESTIGATOR(1949); RECKLESS MOMENTS, THE(1949); SEARCH FOR DANGER(1949); TENSION(1949); UNDERCOVER MAN, THE(1949); BLACK HAND, THE(1950); BREAKING POINT, THE(1950); CHAMPAGNE FOR CAESAR(1950); GUNMEN OF ABILENE(1950); HOUSE BY THE RIVER(1950); KILLER THAT STALKED NEW YORK, THE(1950); PEGGY(1950); DRUMS IN THE DEEP SOUTH(1951); FAT MAN, THE(1951); FRANCIS GOES TO THE RACES(1951); GREAT CARUSO, THE(1951); ROADBLOCK(1951); SIROCCO(1951); TALL TARGET, THE(1951); TOO YOUNG TO KISS(1951); WHIP HAND, THE(1951); ACTORS AND SIN(1952); CRIPPLE CREEK(1952); HAREM GIRL(1952); MUTINY(1952); PRISONER OF ZENDA, THE(1952); WOMAN IN THE DARK(1952); BANDITS OF CORSICA, THE(1953); MA AND PA KETTLE ON VACATION(1953); STORY OF THREE LOVES, THE(1953); DUFFY OF SAN QUENTIN(1954); EL ALAMEIN(1954); ROGUE COP(1954); TOBOR THE GREAT(1954); I'LL CRY TOMORROW(1955); RACERS, THE(1955); HE LAUGHED LAST(1956); HOT BLOOD(1956); BLACK PATCH(1957); FLAME OF STAMBOUL(1957); SPARTACUS(1960); FEAR NO MORE(1961); UNDERWORLD U.S.A.(1961); INTERNS, THE(1962); PUBLIC AFFAIR, A(1962); THREE STOOGES IN ORBIT, THE(1962); BALCONY, THE(1963); PLEASURE SEEKERS, THE(1964); DARK INTRUDER(1965); OUR MAN FLINT(1966); RUSSIANS ARE COMING, THE RUSSIANS ARE COMING, THE(1966); ENTER LAUGHING(1967); GAMES(1967); GAILY, GAILY(1969); HAIL, HERO!(1969); SOME KIND OF A NUT(1969); JOHNNY GOT HIS GUN(1971); TIME FOR DYING, A(1971); WHAT'S THE MATTER WITH HELEN?(1971); FUZZ(1972); HOMEBODIES(1974); ONE FLEW OVER THE CUCKOO'S NEST(1975); BUTCH AND SUNDANCE: THE EARLY DAYS(1979); JEKYLL AND HYDE...TOGETHER AGAIN(1982); TWILIGHT ZONE–THE MOVIE(1983)
Albert Broccoli
MAN INSIDE, THE(1958, Brit.), p; TANK FORCE(1958, Brit.), p; BANDIT OF ZHOBE, THE(1959), p
Albert J. Broccoli
ZARAK(1956, Brit.), p
Albert R. Broccoli
BLACK KNIGHT, THE(1954), p; HELL BELOW ZERO(1954, Brit.), p; PARATROOPER(1954, Brit.), p; COCKLESHELL HEROES, THE(1955), p; PRIZE OF GOLD, A(1955), p; FIRE DOWN BELOW(1957, U.S./Brit.), p; HIGH FLIGHT(1957, Brit.), p; PICKUP ALLEY(1957, Brit.), p; DR. NO(1962, Brit.), p; CALL ME BWANA(1963, Brit.), p; FROM RUSSIA WITH LOVE(1963, Brit.), p; GOLDFINGER(1964, Brit.), p; YOU ONLY LIVE TWICE(1967, Brit.), p; CHITTY CHITTY BANG BANG(1968, Brit.), p; ON HER MAJESTY'S SECRET SERVICE(1969, Brit.), p; DIAMONDS ARE FOREVER(1971, Brit.), p; LIVE AND LET DIE(1973, Brit.), p; MAN WITH THE GOLDEN GUN, THE(1974, Brit.), p; SPY WHO LOVED ME, THE(1977, Brit.), p; MOONRAKER(1979, Brit.), p; FOR YOUR EYES ONLY(1981), p; OCTOPUSSY(1983, Brit.), p
Brochard
ENTENTE CORDIALE(1939, Fr.)
Jean Brochard
ANGEL AND SINNER(1947, Fr.); RAVEN, THE(1948, Fr.); SIMPLE CASE OF MONEY, A(1952, Fr.); DIABOLIQUE(1955, Fr.); KNOCK(1955, Fr.); VITELLONI(1956, Ital./Fr.); LAW IS THE LAW, THE(1959, Fr.); MAIDEN, THE(1961, Fr.)
Martine Brochard
STOLEN KISSES(1969, Fr.); EYEBALL(1978, Ital.)
Eduardo M. Brochero
ONE STEP TO HELL(1969, U.S./Ital./Span.), w; NEXT!(1971, Ital./Span.), w
Alan Brock
SHRIEK OF THE MUTILATED(1974)
Baby Dorothy Brock
Silents
GAMBLING WIVES(1924); WOMAN ON TRIAL, THE(1927)
Cecil Brock
MY HANDS ARE CLAY(1948, Irish); LILLI MARLENE(1951, Brit.); POLICE DOG(1955, Brit.)
Dorothy Brock
Silents
LULLABY, THE(1924); SO BIG(1924); IF I MARRY AGAIN(1925); JUST A WOMAN(1925)

George Brock
Silents
GOLD RUSH, THE(1925)
Gerald Brock
SPY TRAIN(1943)
Hal Brock
KILLERS, THE(1964); LOVE BUG, THE(1968)
Hall Brock
MR. SYCAMORE(1975)
Harold Brock
ALL FOR MARY(1956, Brit.), w
Jules Brock
CLOWN, THE(1953)
Lou Brock
FLYING DOWN TO RIO(1933), p, w; DOWN TO THEIR LAST YACHT(1934), p, w; BEHIND THE MIKE(1937), p; TOP OF THE TOWN(1937), p, w; THEY MET IN ARGENTINA(1941), p, w; GIRLS' TOWN(1942), p; ENCHANTED FOREST, THE(1945), w; SLIPPY MCGEE(1948), p; TRAIN TO ALCATRAZ(1948), p; FLAME OF YOUTH(1949), p; PRISONERS IN PETTICOATS(1950), p
Nancy Brock
SINGLE ROOM FURNISHED(1968); WILD WHEELS(1969); LAST AMERICAN VIRGIN, THE(1982)
Patrick Brock
WICKED LADY, THE(1983, Brit.)
Phil Brock
TEX(1982); BABY, IT'S YOU(1983)
Ralph Brock
ARIZONA KID, THE(1930), w
Stanley Brock
MARCH OF THE SPRING HARE(1969); ROOMMATES(1971); NICKELODEON(1976); ST. IVES(1976); AUDREY ROSE(1977); HERBIE GOES TO MONTE CARLO(1977); WORLD'S GREATEST LOVER, THE(1977); LOVE AT FIRST BITE(1979); DEVIL AND MAX DEVLIN, THE(1981)
1984
EXTERMINATOR 2(1984); NIGHT OF THE COMET(1984)
Lino Brocka
JAGUAR(1980, Phil.), d
1984
BONA(1984, Phil.), d
Maria Brockerhoff
HANNIBAL BROOKS(1969, Brit.)
Don Brockett
FLASHDANCE(1983)
Gary Brockette
MARK OF THE WITCH(1970); LAST PICTURE SHOW, THE(1971); ENCOUNTER WITH THE UNKNOWN(1973)
1984
ICE PIRATES, THE(1984); PHILADELPHIA EXPERIMENT, THE(1984)
David Brockhurst
ALL NEAT IN BLACK STOCKINGS(1969, Brit.), art d; VIRGIN AND THE GYPSY, THE(1970, Brit.), art d; DELICATE BALANCE, A(1973), art d; PRIEST OF LOVE(1981, Brit.), prod d
Eric Brockington
FAME(1980)
James Brockington
SUPERMAN(1978)
Bill Brocklehurst
1984
VIGIL(1984, New Zealand)
J. A. Brocklehurst
Silents
SIGN OF THE ROSE, THE(1922), w
Tony Brockliss
1984
STREETS OF FIRE(1984), art d
Camilla Brockman
ROAD TO HONG KONG, THE(1962, U.S./Brit.)
David Brockman
FRANKENSTEIN(1931), m; CROWDED PARADISE(1956), m
James Brockman
FOX MOVIETONE FOLLIES OF 1930(1930), m
Joe Brockman
SEA OF GRASS, THE(1947); TRAIL STREET(1947); KNOCK ON ANY DOOR(1949); RIDING SHOTGUN(1954)
Michael Brockman
ANY WHICH WAY YOU CAN(1980)
1984
HARRY AND SON(1984)
Robert Brockman
LAST MILE, THE(1959), ed
Susan Brockman
MADE FOR EACH OTHER(1971)
Jochen Brockmann
JOURNEY TO THE LOST CITY(1960, Ger./Fr./Ital.); SECRET WAYS, THE(1961)
Joscen Brockmann
FANTASTIC THREE, THE(1967, Ital./Ger./Fr./Yugo.)
John Brockmeyer
IMPOSTORS(1979)
Blake Brocksmith
1984
FLAMINGO KID, THE(1984)
Ray Brocksmith
WOLFEN(1981)
Roy Brocksmith
KING OF THE GYPSIES(1978); KILLER FISH(1979, Ital./Braz.); RENT CONTROL(1981); TALES OF ORDINARY MADNESS(1983, Ital.)
Gordon Brockway
1984
BEST DEFENSE(1984), cos

Richard Brockway
HERO'S ISLAND(1962), ed; IF HE HOLLERS, LET HIM GO(1968), ed; NUMBER ONE(1969), ed; LOSERS, THE(1970), ed; MONTE WALSH(1970), ed; MEPHISTO WALTZ, THE(1971), ed; REFLECTION OF FEAR, A(1973), ed
Richard K. Brockway
EVERYTHING'S DUCKY(1961), ed; INCUBUS(1966), ed
William W. Brockway
EVERYBODY'S HOBBY(1939), w
Brian Brockwell
GUMSHOE(1972, Brit.), set d
Gladys Brockwell
HOME TOWNERS, THE(1928); LIGHTS OF NEW YORK(1928); ARGYLE CASE, THE(1929); DRAKE CASE, THE(1929); FROM HEADQUARTERS(1929); HARD-BOILED ROSE(1929); HOTTENTOT, THE(1929)
Silents
TYPHOON, THE(1914); WRATH OF THE GODS, THE or THE DESTRUCTION OF SAKURA JIMA(1914); MAN AND HIS MATE, A(1915); END OF THE TRAIL, THE(1916); FIRES OF CONSCIENCE(1916); HONOR SYSTEM, THE(1917); DIVORCE TRAP, THE(1919); FLAMES OF THE FLESH(1920); OLIVER TWIST(1922); PAID BACK(1922); DRUG TRAFFIC, THE(1923); HUNCHBACK OF NOTRE DAME, THE(1923); PENROD AND SAM(1923); SO BIG(1924); ANCIENT MARINER, THE(1925); NECESSARY EVIL, THE(1925); RECKLESS SEX, THE(1925); SPLENDID ROAD, THE(1925); STELLA MARIS(1925); CARNIVAL GIRL, THE(1926); SKYROCKET, THE(1926); TWINKLETOES(1926); LONG PANTS(1927); SEVENTH HEAVEN(1927); MY HOME TOWN(1928)
Misc. Silents
UP FROM THE DEPTHS(1915); CRIPPLED HAND, THE(1916); SINS OF HER PARENT(1916); BRANDED SOUL, A(1917); CONSCIENCE(1917); HER TEMPTATION(1917); ONE TOUCH OF SIN(1917); PRICE OF HER SOUL, THE(1917); SOUL OF SATAN, THE(1917); TO HONOR AND OBEY(1917); BIRD OF PREY, THE(1918); DEVIL'S WHEEL, THE(1918); FOR LIBERTY(1918); HER ONE MISTAKE(1918); KULTUR(1918); MORAL LAW, THE(1918); SCARLET ROAD, THE(1918); STRANGE WOMAN, THE(1918); BROKEN COMMANDMENTS(1919); CALL OF THE SOUL, THE(1919); CHASING RAINBOWS(1919); FORBIDDEN ROOM, THE(1919); PITFALLS OF A BIG CITY(1919); SNEAK, THE(1919); THIEVES(1919); MOTHER OF HIS CHILDREN, THE(1920); ROSE OF NOME(1920); SISTER TO SALOME, A(1920); WHITE LIES(1920); SAGE HEN, THE(1921); DARLING OF NEW YORK, THE(1923); HIS LAST RACE(1923); FOOLISH VIRGIN, THE(1924); UNMARRIED WIVES(1924); CHICKIE(1925); HER SACRIFICE(1926); SPANGLES(1926); MAN, WOMAN AND SIN(1927); LAW AND THE MAN(1928)
Leonard Brockwell
RUNAWAY RAILWAY(1965, Brit.); HEADLINE HUNTERS(1968, Brit.); MELODY(1971, Brit.)
Robert Brockwell
Misc. Silents
LAW UNTO HIMSELF, A(1916), d
Sid Brod
THIS IS THE LIFE(1935), w
Frank M. Broda
SILENT ENEMY, THE(1930), ph
Al Brodax
YELLOW SUBMARINE(1958, Brit.), p, w
Rachel Brodbrar
FRENZY(1946, Brit.)
Lutz Brode
RUNNING(1979, Can.)
Robert Stephen Brode
SING WHILE YOU DANCE(1946), w; DICK TRACY'S DILEMMA(1947), w
Betty Brodel
COVER GIRL(1944); HOLLYWOOD CANTEEN(1944); SWING HOSTESS(1944); TOO YOUNG TO KNOW(1945)
Joan Brodel
CAMILLE(1937)
Joan [Leslie] Brodel
LADDIE(1940)
Mary Brodel
I AM THE LAW(1938); MEN WITH WINGS(1938); RECKLESS LIVING(1938); DOWN THE WYOMING TRAIL(1939); SUNSET MURDER CASE(1941)
Esther Brodelet
GEORGE WHITE'S 1935 SCANDALS(1935); YOUNG AS YOU FEEL(1940); DO YOU LOVE ME?(1946)
Edith Broder
BIG TOWN(1932)
Jack Broder
BRIDE OF THE GORILLA(1951), p; BATTLES OF CHIEF PONTIAC(1952), p; BELA LUGOSI MEETS A BROOKLYN GORILLA(1952), p; KID MONK BARONI(1952), p
Martin Broder
Silents
GRIT(1924)
Bob Broderick
Misc. Silents
OPEN DOOR, THE(1919)
Chris Broderick
LEGACY OF BLOOD(1978)
Misc. Talkies
LEGACY OF HORROR(1978)
Helen Broderick
FIFTY MILLION FRENCHMEN(1931); TO BEAT THE BAND(1935); TOP HAT(1935); BRIDE WALKS OUT, THE(1936); LOVE ON A BET(1936); MURDER ON A BRIDLE PATH(1936); SMARTEST GIRL IN TOWN(1936); SWING TIME(1936); LIFE OF THE PARTY, THE(1937); MEET THE MISSUS(1937); WE'RE ON THE JURY(1937); RADIO CITY REVELS(1938); RAGE OF PARIS, THE(1938); ROAD TO RENO, THE(1938); SERVICE DE LUXE(1938); SHE'S GOT EVERYTHING(1938); HONEYMOON IN BALI(1939); NAUGHTY BUT NICE(1939); STAND UP AND FIGHT(1939); CAPTAIN IS A LADY, THE(1940); NO, NO NANETTE(1940); FATHER TAKES A WIFE(1941); NICE GIRL?(1941); VIRGINIA(1941); STAGE DOOR CANTEEN(1943); CHIP OFF THE OLD BLOCK(1944); HER PRIMITIVE MAN(1944); 3 IS A FAMILY(1944); LOVE, HONOR AND GOODBYE(1945); BECAUSE OF HIM(1946)

James Broderick
TAKING OF PELHAM ONE, TWO, THREE, THE(1974); GIRL OF THE NIGHT(1960); YOUNG DOCTORS, THE(1961); GROUP, THE(1966); ALICE'S RESTAURANT(1969); TREE, THE(1969); TODD KILLINGS, THE(1971); DOG DAY AFTERNOON(1975)
Misc. Talkies
KEEPING ON(1981)
John Broderick
SUMMER RUN(1974)
John C. Broderick
SAM'S SONG(1971), d; DIRTY O'NEIL(1974), p; SIX PACK ANNIE(1975), p; MANIAC!(1977), w
Misc. Talkies
BAD GEORGIA ROAD(1977), d
Matthew Broderick
MAX DUGAN RETURNS(1983); WARGAMES(1983)
Oneida Broderick
RANCHO DELUXE(1975)
Robert Broderick
Silents
EAGLE'S MATE, THE(1914); LAST VOLUNTEER, THE(1914); RING AND THE MAN, THE(1914); PRINCE AND THE PAUPER, THE(1915); STILL WATERS(1915); ARMS AND THE WOMAN(1916); ONE DAY(1916); JUST FOR TONIGHT(1918)
Misc. Silents
BETTER MAN, THE(1914); DAUGHTER OF THE PEOPLE, A(1915); GAMBLER'S ADVOCATE(1915); POOR SCHMALTZ(1915); DAUGHTER OF DESTINY(1917); HIT-THE-TRAIL HOLLIDAY(1918); BISHOP'S EMERALDS, THE(1919); ROUGHNECK, THE(1919); SHARK, THE(1920); CALL OF THE HILLS, THE(1923)
Susan Broderick
BLOW-UP(1966, Brit.)
Virginia Broderick
WILD GUITAR(1962)
Paul Brodeur
STUNT MAN, THE(1980), w
James Brodhead
FRANCES(1982)
James E. Brodhead
KOTCH(1971); APPLE DUMPLING GANG, THE(1975); LEADBELLY(1976); WON TON TON, THE DOG WHO SAVED HOLLYWOOD(1976); FIRST MONDAY IN OCTOBER(1981)
Ann Brodie
1984
SUPERGIRL(1984), makeup
Bill Brodie
SILENCE OF THE NORTH(1981, Can.), prod d; GREY FOX, THE(1983, Can.), art d
Buster Brodie
TALES OF MANHATTAN(1942); CRAZY KNIGHTS(1944); LADY IN THE DARK(1944); GEORGE WHITE'S SCANDALS(1945); HIT THE HAY(1945); PATRICK THE GREAT(1945)
Charles Brodie
IT'S A WONDERFUL WORLD(1956, Brit.); DATE WITH DISASTER(1957, Brit.); INVASION QUARTET(1961, Brit.)
Don Brodie
YOU SAID A MOUTHFUL(1932); KENNEL MURDER CASE, THE(1933); PICTURE SNATCHER(1933); SATURDAY'S MILLIONS(1933); SONS OF THE DESERT(1933); DEATH OF THE DIAMOND(1934); LITTLE MISS MARKER(1934); MANHATTAN MELODRAMA(1934); GIRL WHO CAME BACK, THE(1935); RECKLESS(1935); RUMBA(1935); FATAL LADY(1936); GOLDEN ARROW, THE(1936); LITTLE RED SCHOOLHOUSE(1936); NAVY BORN(1936); SPEED(1936); SPENDTHRIFT(1936); STRIKE ME PINK(1936); THEODORA GOES WILD(1936); CAPTAINS COURAGEOUS(1937); CHARLIE CHAN AT THE OLYMPICS(1937); EASY LIVING(1937); GIRL FROM SCOTLAND YARD, THE(1937); HOTEL HAYWIRE(1937); KID GALAHAD(1937); MAKE WAY FOR TOMORROW(1937); PARTNERS IN CRIME(1937); TOAST OF NEW YORK, THE(1937); LADY IN THE MORGUE(1938); LAST EXPRESS, THE(1938); LETTER OF INTRODUCTION(1938); SHOPWORN ANGEL(1938); EXILE EXPRESS(1939); GOLDEN BOY(1939); ROOKIE COP, THE(1939); STORY OF VERNON AND IRENE CASTLE, THE(1939); MAN FROM MONTREAL, THE(1940); MUSIC IN MY HEART(1940); PINOCCHIO(1940); ROAD TO SINGAPORE(1940); SECOND CHORUS(1940); HELLZAPOPPIN'(1941); LIFE BEGINS FOR ANDY HARDY(1941); TWO LATINS FROM MANHATTAN(1941); MR. LUCKY(1943); THEY GOT ME COVERED(1943); JOHNNY ANGEL(1945); MAN WHO WALKED ALONE, THE(1945); WOMAN IN THE WINDOW, THE(1945); LUCK OF THE IRISH(1948); MR. BLANDINGS BUILDS HIS DREAM HOUSE(1948); STREET CORNER(1948); MY DREAM IS YOURS(1949); ON THE TOWN(1949); COUNTERSPY MEETS SCOTLAND YARD(1950); HARVEY(1950); WOMAN ON PIER 13, THE(1950); ON THE LOOSE(1951); HELL'S OUTPOST(1955); PROUD ONES, THE(1956); FEAR STRIKES OUT(1957); DIARY OF A MADMAN(1963); PATSY, THE(1964); BUSYBODY, THE(1967); LITTLE BIG MAN(1970); ESCAPE TO WITCH MOUNTAIN(1975); EAT MY DUST!(1976); HOT LEAD AND COLD FEET(1978); HEART BEAT(1979)
Donald Brodie
JEWEL ROBBERY(1932); STRANGE FACES(1938); SCATTERGOOD MEETS BROADWAY(1941); DETOUR(1945)
Julian Brodie
LOVE ON THE RUN(1936), w
Kevin Brodie
BATTLE AT BLOODY BEACH(1961); SHOWDOWN(1963); NIGHT OF THE GRIZZLY, THE(1966); GIANT SPIDER INVASION, THE(1975)
Lea Brodie
WARLORDS OF ATLANTIS(1978, Brit.); FFOLKES(1980, Brit.)
Lutz Brodie
SHAPE OF THINGS TO COME, THE(1979, Can.)
Richard Brodie
1984
EVIL THAT MEN DO, THE(1984)
Ronnie Brodie
FINDERS KEEPERS(1966, Brit.)
Steve Brodie
FOLLOW THE BOYS(1944); LADIES COURAGEOUS(1944); THIRTY SECONDS OVER TOKYO(1944); ANCHORS AWEIGH(1945); CRIMSON CANARY(1945); THIS MAN'S NAVY(1945); WALK IN THE SUN, A(1945); BADMAN'S TERRITORY(1946); CRIMINAL COURT(1946); FALCON'S ADVENTURE, THE(1946); SUNSET PASS(1946); YOUNG WIDOW(1946); CODE OF THE WEST(1947); CROSSFIRE(1947); DESPERATE(1947); OUT OF THE PAST(1947); THUNDER MOUNTAIN(1947); TRAIL STREET(1947); ARIZONA RANGER, THE(1948); BODYGUARD(1948); GUNS OF HATE(1948); RETURN OF THE BADMEN(1948); STATION WEST(1948); BIG WHEEL, THE(1949); BROTHERS IN THE SADDLE(1949); HOME OF THE BRAVE(1949); I CHEATED THE LAW(1949); MASSACRE RIVER(1949); ROSE OF THE YUKON(1949); RUSTLERS(1949); TOUGH ASSIGNMENT(1949); TREASURE OF MONTE CRISTO(1949); ADMIRAL WAS A LADY, THE(1950); ARMORED CAR ROBBERY(1950); GREAT PLANE ROBBERY(1950); IT'S A SMALL WORLD(1950); KISS TOMORROW GOODBYE(1950); WINCHESTER '73(1950); FIGHTING COAST GUARD(1951); JOE PALOOKA IN TRIPLE CROSS(1951); M(1951); ONLY THE VALIANT(1951); STEEL HELMET, THE(1951); SWORD OF MONTE CRISTO, THE(1951); TWO DOLLAR BETTOR(1951); ARMY BOUND(1952); BAL TABARIN(1952); LADY IN THE IRON MASK(1952); STORY OF WILL ROGERS, THE(1952); THREE FOR BEDROOM C(1952); BEAST FROM 20,000 FATHOMS, THE(1953); CHARGE AT FEATHER RIVER, THE(1953); DONOVAN'S BRAIN(1953); SEA OF LOST SHIPS(1953); WHITE LIGHTNING(1953); CAINE MUTINY, THE(1954); FAR COUNTRY, THE(1955); CRUEL TOWER, THE(1956); GUN DUEL IN DURANGO(1957); UNDER FIRE(1957); CROOKED CIRCLE, THE(1958); SIERRA BARON(1958); SPY IN THE SKY(1958); ARSON FOR HIRE(1959); HERE COME THE JETS(1959); THREE CAME TO KILL(1960); BLUE HAWAII(1961); GIRL NAMED TAMIRO, A(1962); OF LOVE AND DESIRE(1963); ROUSTABOUT(1964); WILD WORLD OF BATWOMAN, THE(1966); CYCLE SAVAGES(1969); GIANT SPIDER INVASION, THE(1975)
Misc. Talkies
BULLET FOR BILLY THE KID(1963)
William Brodie
THAT KIND OF GIRL(1963, Brit.), art d; PRIVILEGE(1967, Brit.), art d; GLADIATORS, THE(1970, Swed.), art d
Helena Brodin
GUILT(1967, Swed.)
Norbert Brodine
LION AND THE MOUSE, THE(1928), ph; PARIS BOUND(1929), ph; RICH PEOPLE(1929), ph; THIS THING CALLED LOVE(1929), ph; DIVORCEE, THE(1930), ph; HER PRIVATE AFFAIR(1930), ph; HOLIDAY(1930), ph; LET US BE GAY(1930), ph; GUARDSMAN, THE(1931), ph; PAGAN LADY(1931), ph; REBOUND(1931), ph; BACHELOR'S AFFAIRS(1932), ph; BEAST OF THE CITY, THE(1932), ph; NIGHT COURT(1932), ph; UNASHAMED(1932), ph; UPTOWN NEW YORK(1932), ph; WILD GIRL(1932), ph; BROADWAY TO HOLLYWOOD(1933), ph; COUNSELLOR-AT-LAW(1933), ph; DEATH KISS, THE(1933), ph; DELUGE(1933), ph; MADE ON BROADWAY(1933), ph; WHISTLING IN THE DARK(1933), ph; CROSBY CASE, THE(1934), ph; HUMAN SIDE, THE(1934), ph; LITTLE MAN, WHAT NOW?(1934), ph; LOVE BIRDS(1934), ph; MADAME SPY(1934), ph; AFFAIR OF SUSAN(1935), ph; EAST OF JAVA(1935), ph; LADY TUBBS(1935), ph; ONE EXCITING ADVENTURE(1935), ph; PRINCESS O'HARA(1935), ph; SHE GETS HER MAN(1935), ph; DON'T GET PERSONAL(1936), ph; LIBELED LADY(1936), ph; NOBODY'S FOOL(1936), ph; NOBODY'S BABY(1937), ph; PICK A STAR(1937), ph; TOPPER(1937), ph; MERRILY WE LIVE(1938), ph; SWISS MISS(1938), ph; THERE GOES MY HEART(1938), ph; CAPTAIN FURY(1939), ph; HOUSEKEEPER'S DAUGHTER(1939), ph; OF MICE AND MEN(1939), ph; TOPPER TAKES A TRIP(1939), ph; CAPTAIN CAUTION(1940), ph; ONE MILLION B.C.(1940), ph; TURNABOUT(1940), ph; LADY FOR A NIGHT(1941), ph; MODEL WIFE(1941), ph; ROAD SHOW(1941), ph; TOPPER RETURNS(1941), ph; DANCING MASTERS, THE(1943), ph; DR. GILLESPIE'S CRIMINAL CASE(1943), ph; BULLFIGHTERS, THE(1945), ph; DON JUAN QUILLIGAN(1945), ph; HOUSE ON 92ND STREET, THE(1945), ph; SENTIMENTAL JOURNEY(1946), ph; SOMEWHERE IN THE NIGHT(1946), ph; 13 RUE MADELEINE(1946), ph; BOOMERANG(1947), ph; KISS OF DEATH(1947), ph; SITTING PRETTY(1948), ph; I WAS A MALE WAR BRIDE(1949), ph; THIEVES' HIGHWAY(1949), ph; RIGHT CROSS(1950), ph; DESERT FOX, THE(1951), ph; FROGMEN, THE(1951), ph; FIVE FINGERS(1952), ph
Silents
ALMOST A HUSBAND(1919), ph; DOLLARS AND SENSE(1920), ph; STOP THIEF(1920), ph; INVISIBLE POWER, THE(1921), ph; TALE OF TWO WORLDS, A(1921), ph; BLIND BARGAIN, A(1922), ph; DULCY(1923), ph; PLEASURE MAD(1923), ph; SPLENDID ROAD, THE(1925), ph; WHAT FOOLS MEN(1925), ph; CLOWN, THE(1927), ph; ONE-ROUND HOGAN(1927), ph
R. Brodis-Turner
QUIET WEDDING(1941, Brit.)
Harold Brodkey
FIRST LOVE(1977), w
Temmie Brodkey
LOCAL COLOR(1978)
Herbert Brodkin
SEBASTIAN(1968, Brit.), p; PEOPLE NEXT DOOR, THE(1970), p
Oscar Brodney
BABY FACE MORGAN(1942), w; MOONLIGHT IN HAVANA(1942), w; ALWAYS A BRIDESMAID(1943), w; RHYTHM OF THE ISLANDS(1943), w; WHEN JOHNNY COMES MARCHING HOME(1943), w; YOU'RE A LUCKY FELLOW, MR. SMITH(1943), w; ON STAGE EVERYBODY(1945), w; WHAT A BLONDE(1945), w; SHE WROTE THE BOOK(1946), w; ARE YOU WITH IT?(1948), w; FOR THE LOVE OF MARY(1948), w; IF YOU KNEW SUSIE(1948), w; MEXICAN HAYRIDE(1948), w; ARCTIC MANHUNT(1949), w; GAL WHO TOOK THE WEST, THE(1949), w; YES SIR, THAT'S MY BABY(1949), w; COMMANCHE TERRITORY(1950), w; DOUBLE CROSSBONES(1950), w; FRENCHIE(1950), w; HARVEY(1950), w; SOUTH SEA SINNER(1950), w; FRANCIS GOES TO THE RACES(1951), w; KATIE DID IT(1951), w; LITTLE EGYPT(1951), w; BACK AT THE FRONT(1952), w; FRANCIS GOES TO WEST POINT(1952), w; SCARLET ANGEL(1952), w; FRANCIS COVERS THE BIG TOWN(1953), w; GLENN MILLER STORY, THE(1953), w; WALKING MY BABY BACK HOME(1953), w; BLACK SHIELD OF FALWORTH, THE(1954), w; SIGN OF THE PAGAN(1954), w; CAPTAIN LIGHTFOOT(1955), w; LADY GODIVA(1955), w; PURPLE MASK, THE(1955), w; SPOILERS, THE(1955), w; DAY OF FURY, A(1956), w; STAR IN THE DUST(1956), w; TAMMY AND THE BACHELOR(1957), w; WHEN HELL BROKE LOOSE(1958), p, w; BOBBIKINS(1959, Brit.), p, w; ALL HANDS ON DECK(1961), w; RIGHT APPROACH, THE(1961), p; TAMMY, TELL ME TRUE(1961), w; TAMMY AND THE DOCTOR(1963), w; BRASS BOTTLE, THE(1964), w; I'D RATHER BE RICH(1964), w; SWORD OF ALI BABA, THE(1965), w; 1,000 CONVICTS AND A WOMAN(1971, Brit.), w
Bill Brodrick
STROKER ACE(1983)

Malcolm Brodrick
MAN ON FIRE(1957); THAT NIGHT(1957)
Susan Brodrick
DR. JEKYLL AND SISTER HYDE(1971, Brit.)
Brodsky
RECORD 413(1936, Fr.), m
Silents
BATTLESHIP POTEMKIN, THE(1925, USSR)
Jack Brodsky
LITTLE MURDERS(1971), p; SUMMER WISHES, WINTER DREAMS(1973), p; HARRY AND WALTER GO TO NEW YORK(1976); TWO-MINUTE WARNING(1976)
Nicholas Brodsky
FRENCH WITHOUT TEARS(1939, Brit.), m; QUIET WEDDING(1941, Brit.), m; MAN ABOUT THE HOUSE, A(1947, Brit.), m; HER MAN GILBEY(1949, Brit.), m; WHILE THE SUN SHINES(1950, Brit.), m
Samuel Brodsky
Misc. Silents
HOUSE WITHOUT CHILDREN, THE(1919), d
Vlastimil Brodsky
LOST FACE, THE(1965, Czech.); CLOSELY WATCHED TRAINS(1967, Czech.); TRANSPORT FROM PARADISE(1967, Czech.); CAPRICIOUS SUMMER(1968, Czech.); END OF A PRIEST(1970, Czech.)
Edward Brodsky-Schuster
PIRATE MOVIE, THE(1982, Aus.)
Nicholas Brodszky
VOICE IN THE NIGHT, A(1941, Brit.), m; ADVENTURE FOR TWO(1945, Brit.), m; TURNERS OF PROSPECT ROAD, THE(1947, Brit.), m; LATIN LOVERS(1953), m; FLAME AND THE FLESH(1954), m; OPPOSITE SEX, THE(1956), m; LET'S BE HAPPY(1957, Brit.), m
Nicolaus Brodszky
GUILTY MELODY(1936, Brit.), m
Tex Brodus
PACIFIC RENDEZVOUS(1942); GIRL MOST LIKELY, THE(1957)
Tex Brodux
MATING SEASON, THE(1951)
Ann Brody
MY MAN(1928); SO THIS IS COLLEGE(1929); WOLF SONG(1929); FALL GUY, THE(1930); PLAYING AROUND(1930); DRUMS OF JEOPARDY(1931); DRIFTER, THE(1932); HEART OF NEW YORK(1932); THREE ON A MATCH(1932); HIGH GEAR(1933); LAWYER MAN(1933); MONEY MEANS NOTHING(1934)
Silents
PERFECT LOVER, THE(1919); SHAMS OF SOCIETY(1921); SAINTED DEVIL, A(1924); ALIAS THE LONE WOLF(1927); CLANCY'S KOSHER WEDDING(1927); JAKE THE PLUMBER(1927)
Misc. Silents
HEROES IN BLUE(1927)
Anna Brody
Misc. Silents
INDIAN SUMMER OF DRY VALLEY JOHNSON, THE(1917)
Bruce Brody
DINER(1982), m
Buster Brody
KNICKERBOCKER HOLIDAY(1944)
Dale Brody
DEMENTED(1980), spec eff
David Brody
DON'T GO IN THE HOUSE(1980)
Don Brody
MAN WHO BROKE THE BANK AT MONTE CARLO, THE(1935); BEDSIDE MANNER(1945)
Donald Brody
INCREDIBLE TWO-HEADED TRANSPLANT, THE(1971)
Ed Brody
UNION DEPOT(1932)
Estelle Brody
KITTY(1929, Brit.); PLAYTHING, THE(1929, Brit.); LILLI MARLENE(1951, Brit.); THEY WERE NOT DIVIDED(1951, Brit.); LUXURY GIRLS(1953, Ital.); STORY OF ESTHER COSTELLO, THE(1957, Brit.); NEVER TAKE CANDY FROM A STRANGER(1961, Brit.)
Silents
THIS MARRIAGE BUSINESS(1927, Brit.); WEEKEND WIVES(1928, Brit.)
Misc. Silents
FANNY HAWTHORNE(1927, Brit.); FLIGHT COMMANDER, THE(1927); GLAD EYE, THE(1927, Brit.); SAILORS DON'T CARE(1928, Brit.); KITTY(1929, Brit.)
Fiona Brody
OUT OF THE BLUE(1982)
Hugh Brody
1984
1919(1984, Brit.), d, w
Jo Ann Brody
LONG GOODBYE, THE(1973)
Kevin Brody
EIGHT ON THE LAM(1967)
Marvin Brody
GUIDE FOR THE MARRIED MAN, A(1967)
Merrill Brody
BLAST OF SILENCE(1961), p; PIE IN THE SKY(1964), p
Michael Brody
FOREST, THE(1983)
Raymond Brody
KING AND COUNTRY(1964, Brit.); FINAL OPTION, THE(1983, Brit.)
Ron Brody
BED SITTING ROOM, THE(1969, Brit.)
Ronnie Brody
HELP!(1965, Brit.); PERCY(1971, Brit.); 1,000 CONVICTS AND A WOMAN(1971, Brit.); RITZ, THE(1976); HITCH IN TIME, A(1978, Brit.); SUPERMAN III(1983)
Sally Brody
WIZARD OF GORE, THE(1970)

Todd Brody
CUBAN REBEL GIRLS(1960)
K. Brodzikowski
YOUNG GIRLS OF WILKO, THE(1979, Pol./Fr.)
Nicholas Brodzsky
JOHNNY IN THE CLOUDS(1945, Brit.), m
Terry Ten Broeck
DELIRIUM(1979)
Ken Broeker
FIGHTING COWBOY(1933); LIGHTNING RANGE(1934); FEAR(1946)
David Broekman
SKINNER STEPS OUT(1929), m; ALL QUIET ON THE WESTERN FRONT(1930), m
Robert Broekman
JAMBOREE(1957), ed
H. Lyman Broening
Silents
CALIFORNIA OR BUST(1927), ph; HOOK AND LADDER NO. 9(1927), ph
Henry Broening
Silents
STILL WATERS(1915), ph
Lyman Broening
Silents
RAINBOW PRINCESS, THE(1916), ph; GETTING MARY MARRIED(1919), ph; PERFECT CRIME, A(1921), ph; KINDRED OF THE DUST(1922), ph; ABRAHAM LINCOLN(1924), ph; LIGHTHOUSE BY THE SEA, THE(1924), ph; LITTLE IRISH GIRL, THE(1926), ph; DEVIL'S MASTERPIECE, THE(1927), ph; SALVATION JANE(1927), ph
Paul Broesse
TRIBUTE TO A BADMAN(1956), art d
Helga Brofeldt
OCEAN BREAKERS(1949, Swed.)
Ferdinando Brofferio
LA DOLCE VITA(1961, Ital./Fr.)
Walter Brofferio
RUN WITH THE DEVIL(1963, Fr./Ital.)
Arturo Brogaglia
RING AROUND THE CLOCK(1953, Ital.)
Angela Brogan
CLASS OF MISS MAC MICHAEL, THE(1978, Brit./U.S.)
Anne Brogan
PLAYBOY OF THE WESTERN WORLD, THE(1963, Ireland)
Harry Brogan
GENTLE GUNMAN, THE(1952, Brit.); BROTH OF A BOY(1959, Brit.); HOME IS THE HERO(1959, Ireland); SHAKE HANDS WITH THE DEVIL(1959, Ireland); THIS OTHER EDEN(1959, Brit.); LIES MY FATHER TOLD ME(1960, Brit.); NIGHT FIGHTERS, THE(1960); POACHER'S DAUGHTER, THE(1960, Brit.); SIEGE OF SIDNEY STREET, THE(1960, Brit.); QUARE FELLOW, THE(1962, Brit.); WEBSTER BOY, THE(1962, Brit.); GIRL WITH GREEN EYES(1964, Brit.); NEVER PUT IT IN WRITING(1964); YOUNG CASSIDY(1965, U.S./Brit.); VICTOR FRANKENSTEIN(1975, Swed./Ireland)
John Brogan
PRIVATE RIGHT, THE(1967, Brit.)
Pete Brogan
Silents
GOLD RUSH, THE(1925)
Ron Brogan
CAPTAIN NEWMAN, M.D.(1963); DR. TERROR'S GALLERY OF HORRORS(1967)
Ronald Brogan
UNKNOWN MAN, THE(1951)
Teddy Brogden
LOVE UP THE POLE(1936, Brit.)
Shirley Ann Broger
SUNSET COVE(1978)
Shirley Anne Broger
HOMETOWN U.S.A.(1979)
Frederick Brogger
JANE EYRE(1971, Brit.), p
Frederick H. Brogger
DAVID COPPERFIELD(1970, Brit.), p; KIDNAPPED(1971, Brit.), p
Ivar Brogger
1984
C.H.U.D.(1984)
Isidoro Broggi
CRAZY DESIRE(1964, Ital.), p; EIGHTEEN IN THE SUN(1964, Ital.), p; FASCIST, THE(1965, Ital.), p; HOURS OF LOVE, THE(1965, Ital.), p
Giulio Brogi
SUBVERSIVES, THE(1967, Ital.)
Peter Brogle
SIGNS OF LIFE(1981, Ger.)
Arthur M. Broidy
B.S. I LOVE YOU(1971), p
William F. Broidy
SIDESHOW(1950), p, w; NAVY BOUND(1951), p; YUKON GOLD(1952), p; MURDER WITHOUT TEARS(1953), p; HIGHWAY DRAGNET(1954), p; SECURITY RISK(1954), p; YUKON VENGEANCE(1954), p; BETRAYED WOMEN(1955), p; BIG TIP OFF, THE(1955), p; LAS VEGAS SHAKEDOWN(1955), p; PORT OF HELL(1955), p; TOUGHEST MAN ALIVE(1955), p; TREASURE OF RUBY HILLS(1955), p; YAQUI DRUMS(1956), p; CALYPSO JOE(1957), p; LEGION OF THE DOOMED(1958), p; SEVEN GUNS TO MESA(1958), p; ARSON FOR HIRE(1959), p
Rusinek B. Brok
FIRST START(1953, Pol.), m
Charles Brokaw
BEHIND THE MIKE(1937); I COVER THE WAR(1937); IDOL OF THE CROWDS(1937); LUCK OF ROARING CAMP, THE(1937); OUTER GATE, THE(1937); AIR DEVILS(1938); CONVICTS AT LARGE(1938); SECOND FIDDLE(1939); MURDER IN THE AIR(1940); TO THE SHORES OF TRIPOLI(1942)
Misc. Talkies
BEHIND PRISON BARS(1937)

Jack Brokensha
QUADROON(1972), m
Norman Brokenshire
GLORIFYING THE AMERICAN GIRL(1930)
Lee Broker
PYX, THE(1973, Can.); SALLY FIELDGOOD & CO.(1975, Can.); PARTNERS(1976, Can.); UTILITIES(1983, Can.)
Iona Brokski
Misc. Silents
SON OF THE LAND(1931, USSR)
Colette Broldo
AMOUR, AMOUR(1937, Fr.)
James Brolin
DEAR BRIGETTE(1965); VON RYAN'S EXPRESS(1965); FANTASTIC VOYAGE(1966); OUR MAN FLINT(1966); WAY...WAY OUT(1966); CAPETOWN AFFAIR(1967, U.S./South Afr.); THE BOSTON STRANGLER, THE(1968); SKYJACKED(1972); WESTWORLD(1973); GABLE AND LOMBARD(1976); CAR, THE(1977); CAPRICORN ONE(1978); AMITYVILLE HORROR, THE(1979); NIGHT OF THE JUGGLER(1980); HIGH RISK(1981)
Pasqualina Brolis
TREE OF WOODEN CLOGS, THE(1979, Ital.)
Eleanor Brom
WOMEN IN LOVE(1969, Brit.)
Betz Bromberg
WOLFEN(1981), spec eff
Erich Bromberg
TEENAGE ZOMBIES(1960), md
J. Edward Bromberg
UNDER TWO FLAGS(1936); CRIME OF DR. FORBES(1936); GIRLS' DORMITORY(1936); LADIES IN LOVE(1936); REUNION(1936); SINS OF MAN(1936); STAR FOR A NIGHT(1936); STOWAWAY(1936); CHARLIE CHAN ON BROADWAY(1937); FAIR WARNING(1937); SECOND HONEYMOON(1937); SEVENTH HEAVEN(1937); THAT I MAY LIVE(1937); BARONESS AND THE BUTLER, THE(1938); FOUR MEN AND A PRAYER(1938); I'LL GIVE A MILLION(1938); MR. MOTO TAKES A CHANCE(1938); ONE WILD NIGHT(1938); REBECCA OF SUNNYBROOK FARM(1938); SALLY, IRENE AND MARY(1938); SUEZ(1938); HOLLYWOOD CAVALCADE(1939); JESSE JAMES(1939); THREE SONS(1939); WIFE, HUSBAND AND FRIEND(1939); MARK OF ZORRO, THE(1940); RETURN OF FRANK JAMES, THE(1940); STRANGE CARGO(1940); DANCE HALL(1941); DEVIL PAYS OFF, THE(1941); MIDNIGHT ANGEL(1941); HALF WAY TO SHANGHAI(1942); HURRICANE SMITH(1942); INVISIBLE AGENT(1942); LIFE BEGINS AT 8:30(1942); PACIFIC BLACKOUT(1942); REUNION IN FRANCE(1942); TENNESSEE JOHNSON(1942); LADY OF BURLESQUE(1943); PHANTOM OF THE OPERA(1943); SON OF DRACULA(1943); CHIP OFF THE OLD BLOCK(1944); VOICE IN THE WIND(1944); EASY TO LOOK AT(1945); MISSING CORPSE, THE(1945); PILLOW OF DEATH(1945); SALOME, WHERE SHE DANCED(1945); CLOAK AND DAGGER(1946); TANGIER(1946); WALLS CAME TUMBLING DOWN, THE(1946); QUEEN OF THE AMAZONS(1947); ARCH OF TRIUMPH(1948); SONG IS BORN, A(1948); I SHOT JESSE JAMES(1949); GUILTY BYSTANDER(1950)
Herve Bromberger
VIOLETTE(1978, Fr.), w
Frans Bromet
1984
QUESTION OF SILENCE(1984, Neth.), ph
Chris Bromfield
NAKED WORLD OF HARRISON MARKS, THE(1967, Brit.)
John Bromfield
HARPOON(1948); SORRY, WRONG NUMBER(1948); ROPE OF SAND(1949); FURIES, THE(1950); PAID IN FULL(1950); CIMARRON KID, THE(1951); FLAT TOP(1952); HOLD THAT LINE(1952); EASY TO LOVE(1953); BLACK DAKOTAS, THE(1954); RING OF FEAR(1954); BIG BLUFF, THE(1955); REVENGE OF THE CREATURE(1955); CRIME AGAINST JOE(1956); CURUCU, BEAST OF THE AMAZON(1956); FRONTIER GAMBLER(1956); HOT CARS(1956); MANFISH(1956); QUINCANNON, FRONTIER SCOUT(1956); THREE BAD SISTERS(1956)
Louis Bromfield
ONE HEAVENLY NIGHT(1931), w; 24 HOURS(1931), w; NIGHT AFTER NIGHT(1932), w; LIFE OF VERGIE WINTERS, THE(1934), w; MODERN HERO, A(1934), w; RAINS CAME, THE(1939), w; BRIGHAM YOUNG–FRONTIERSMAN(1940), w; IT ALL CAME TRUE(1940), w; JOHNNY COME LATELY(1943), w; MRS. PARKINGTON(1944), w; RAINS OF RANCHIPUR, THE(1955), w
Rex Bromfield
LOVE AT FIRST SIGHT(1977, Can.), d&w; TULIPS(1981, Can), d; MELANIE(1982, Can.), d
Valri Bromfield
MR. MOM(1983)
Dorothy Bromiley
GIRLS OF PLEASURE ISLAND, THE(1953); IT'S GREAT TO BE YOUNG(1956, Brit.); TOUCH OF THE SUN, A(1956, Brit.); ZOO BABY(1957, Brit.); CONCRETE JUNGLE, THE(1962, Brit.); SERVANT, THE(1964, Brit.)
Peter Bromilow
CAMELOT(1967); RAILWAY CHILDREN, THE(1971, Brit.); NASTY HABITS(1976, Brit.); SEMI-TOUGH(1977)
1984
BREAKIN'(1984)
Dorothy Bromily
SMALL HOTEL(1957, Brit.)
Elaine Bromka
WITHOUT A TRACE(1983)
A. Bromley
LOST IN THE LEGION(1934, Brit.)
Harold Bromley
COUNT OF MONTE CRISTO(1976, Brit.)
Haworth Bromley
EAST MEETS WEST(1936, Brit.), p; STRANGERS ON A HONEYMOON(1937, Brit.), p; PASTOR HALL(1940, Brit.), w; WHAT'S COOKIN'?(1942), w
Karen Bromley
BLACK CHRISTMAS(1974, Can.), art d; OUTRAGEOUS!(1977, Can.), art d; WHY SHOOT THE TEACHER(1977, Can.), art d; STARSHIP INVASIONS(1978, Can.), art d; MIDDLE AGE CRAZY(1980, Can.), art d; HARRY TRACY–DESPERADO(1982, Can.), prod d; TITLE SHOT(1982, Can.), art d

Sheila Bromley
GOLD DIGGERS OF 1937(1936); KELLY OF THE SECRET SERVICE(1936); IDOL OF THE CROWDS(1937); MISSING WITNESSES(1937); WEST OF SHANGHAI(1937); ACCIDENTS WILL HAPPEN(1938); GIRLS ON PROBATION(1938); KING OF THE NEWSBOYS(1938); MAKING THE HEADLINES(1938); MIDNIGHT INTRUDER(1938); MYSTERY HOUSE(1938); REBELLIOUS DAUGHTERS(1938); REFORMATORY(1938); DEATH GOES NORTH(1939); NANCY DREW–REPORTER(1939); THOU SHALT NOT KILL(1939); TORCHY PLAYS WITH DYNAMITE(1939); TORTURE SHIP(1939); WATERFRONT(1939); WOMEN IN THE WIND(1939); CALLING PHILO VANCE(1940); TIME TO KILL(1942); HOUSE ON 92ND STREET, THE(1945); SILVER LODE(1954); DAY OF FURY, A(1956); THERE'S ALWAYS TOMORROW(1956); WORLD IN MY CORNER(1956); LAWLESS EIGHTIES, THE(1957); SPOILERS OF THE FOREST(1957); YOUNG JESSE JAMES(1960); JUDGMENT AT NUREMBERG(1961); FOR THOSE WHO THINK YOUNG(1964); GIRLS ON THE BEACH(1965); HOTEL(1967)
Shiela Bromley
FUGITIVE FROM JUSTICE, A(1940)
Sidney Bromley
MARK OF CAIN, THE(1948, Brit.); DEVIL'S HARBOR(1954, Brit.); BLONDE BLACKMAILER(1955, Brit.); OPERATION THIRD FORM(1966, Brit.); LITTLE OF WHAT YOU FANCY, A(1968, Brit.); ISLAND OF THE BURNING DAMNED(1971, Brit.)
Sydney Bromley
DEMOBBED(1944, Brit.); BRIEF ENCOUNTER(1945, Brit.); LOYAL HEART(1946, Brit.); DARK ROAD, THE(1948, Brit.); LOVE MATCH, THE(1955, Brit.); SAINT JOAN(1957); CONCRETE JUNGLE, THE(1962, Brit.); NIGHT CREATURES(1962, Brit.); PARANOIAC(1963, Brit.); FATHER CAME TOO(1964, Brit.); DIE, MONSTER, DIE(1965, Brit.); CARRY ON COWBOY(1966, Brit.); CHRISTMAS TREE, THE(1966, Brit.); FEARLESS VAMPIRE KILLERS, OR PARDON ME BUT YOUR TEETH ARE IN MY NECK, THE(1967); HALF A SIXPENCE(1967, Brit.); PREHISTORIC WOMEN(1967, Brit.); SMASHING TIME(1967 Brit.); MACBETH(1971, Brit.); FRANKENSTEIN AND THE MONSTER FROM HELL(1974, Brit.); CANDLESHOE(1978); DRAGONSLAYER(1981)
1984
NEVERENDING STORY, THE(1984, Ger.)
Karen Bromley-Watkins
WEDDING IN WHITE(1972, Can.), art d
Alan Bromly
ANGEL WHO PAWNED HER HARP, THE(1956, Brit.), d; FOLLOW THAT HORSE!(1960, Brit.), d
Eleanor Bron
HELP!(1965, Brit.); ALFIE(1966, Brit.); BEDAZZLED(1967, Brit.); TWO FOR THE ROAD(1967, Brit.); THANK YOU ALL VERY MUCH(1969, Brit.); NATIONAL HEALTH, OR NURSE NORTON'S AFFAIR, THE(1973, Brit.); HOUND OF THE BASKERVILLES, THE(1983, Brit.)
Marcelle Ginette Bron
ROMA(1972, Ital./Fr.)
Lucia Bronder
ROCKABYE(1932), w
William Bronder
CANNERY ROW(1982)
Misc. Talkies
FLUSH(1981, Brit.)
Jerome Brondfield
LOUISIANA TERRITORY(1953), w
Helen Broneau
Silents
MERRY-GO-ROUND(1923)
S. Bronecki
DYBBUK THE(1938, Pol.)
Robert Broner
HORIZONTAL LIEUTENANT, THE(1962), ph
Leonid Bronevoy
ARMED AND DANGEROUS(1977, USSR)
Edgar Bronfman
BORDER, THE(1982), p
Edgar M. Bronfman, Jr.
BLOCKHOUSE, THE(1974, Brit.), p
M. Broniewska
BORDER STREET(1950, Pol.)
James Bronis
Silents
INTO THE NIGHT(1928), w
Robert Bronnen
IT'S ALWAYS FAIR WEATHER(1955), ph
Robert Bronner
MEET ME IN LAS VEGAS(1956), ph; OPPOSITE SEX, THE(1956), ph; JAILHOUSE ROCK(1957), ph; SILK STOCKINGS(1957), ph; TEN THOUSAND BEDROOMS(1957), ph; PARTY GIRL(1958), ph; SHEEPMAN, THE(1958), ph; TUNNEL OF LOVE, THE(1958), ph; ASK ANY GIRL(1959), ph; IT STARTED WITH A KISS(1959), ph; MATING GAME, THE(1959), ph; PLEASE DON'T EAT THE DAISIES(1960), ph; WHERE THE BOYS ARE(1960), ph; POCKETFUL OF MIRACLES(1961), ph; SEVEN FACES OF DR. LAO(1964), ph; QUICK, LET'S GET MARRIED(1965), ph; THREE ON A COUCH(1966), ph; DON'T GO NEAR THE WATER(1975), ph
Robert J. Bronner
GIDGET GOES HAWAIIAN(1961), ph; GIDGET GOES TO ROME(1963), ph
Ego Bronnum-Jacobsen
LURE OF THE JUNGLE, THE(1970, Den.)
Annett Bronson
FIST OF FEAR, TOUCH OF DEATH(1980)
Betty Bronson
SINGING FOOL, THE(1928); BELLAMY TRIAL, THE(1929); LOCKED DOOR, THE(1929); ONE STOLEN NIGHT(1929); SONNY BOY(1929); MEDICINE MAN, THE(1930); LOVER COME BACK(1931); MIDNIGHT PATROL, THE(1932); YODELIN' KID FROM PINE RIDGE(1937); POCKETFUL OF MIRACLES(1961); NAKED KISS, THE(1964); EVEL KNIEVEL(1971)
Silents
JAVA HEAD(1923); PETER PAN(1924); ARE PARENTS PEOPLE?(1925); BEN-HUR(1925); NOT SO LONG AGO(1925); CAT'S PAJAMAS, THE(1926); KISS FOR CINDERELLA, A(1926); PARADISE(1926)

Misc. Silents
GOLDEN PRINCESS, THE(1925); EVERYBODY'S ACTING(1926); BRASS KNUCK-LES(1927); OPEN RANGE(1927); PARADISE FOR TWO(1927); RITZY(1927); COMPAN-IONATE MARRIAGE, THE(1928)

Bunny Bronson
OUR RELATIONS(1936); HEADLINE CRASHER(1937); WITH LOVE AND KIS-SES(1937)

Charles Bronson [Charles Buchinsky]
MISS SADIE THOMPSON(1953); DRUM BEAT(1954); BIG HOUSE, U.S.A.(1955); TARGET ZERO(1955); JUBAL(1956); RUN OF THE ARROW(1957); GANG WAR(1958); MACHINE GUN KELLY(1958); SHOWDOWN AT BOOT HILL(1958); WHEN HELL BROKE LOOSE(1958); 10 NORTH FREDERICK(1958); NEVER SO FEW(1959); MAG-NIFICENT SEVEN, THE(1960); MASTER OF THE WORLD(1961); THUNDER OF DRUMS, A(1961); X-15(1961); KID GALAHAD(1962); FOUR FOR TEXAS(1963); GREAT ESCAPE, THE(1963); GUNS OF DIABLO(1964); BATTLE OF THE BULGE(1965); SANDPIPER, THE(1965); THIS PROPERTY IS CONDEMNED(1966); DIRTY DOZEN, THE(1967, Brit.); FAREWELL, FRIEND(1968, Fr./Ital.); GUNS FOR SAN SEBAS-TIAN(1968, U.S./Fr./Mex./Ital.); VILLA RIDES(1968); ONCE UPON A TIME IN THE WEST(1969, U.S./Ital.); RIDER ON THE RAIN(1970, Fr./Ital.); YOU CAN'T WIN 'EM ALL(1970, Brit.); LOLA(1971, Brit./Ital.); SOMEONE BEHIND THE DOOR(1971, Fr./Brit.); CHATO'S LAND(1972); MECHANIC, THE(1972); RED SUN(1972, Fr./Ital./Span.); VALACHI PAPERS, THE(1972, Ital./Fr.); STONE KILLER, THE(1973); COLD SWEAT(1974, Ital., Fr.); DEATH WISH(1974); FAMILY, THE(1974, Fr./Ital.); MR. MAJESTYK(1974); BREAKOUT(1975); HARD TIMES(1975); BREAKHEART PASS(1976); CHINO(1976, Ital., Span., Fr.); FROM NOON TO THREE(1976); ST. IVES(1976); TELEFON(1977); WHITE BUFFALO, THE(1977); LOVE AND BUL-LETS(1979, Brit.); BORDERLINE(1980); CABOBLANCO(1981); DEATH HUNT(1981); DEATH WISH II(1982); 10 TO MIDNIGHT(1983)
1984
EVIL THAT MEN DO, THE(1984)

Emerick Bronson
PUZZLE OF A DOWNFALL CHILD(1970)

George Bronson
STORY OF DR. WASSELL, THE(1944)

Harry Bronson
CROOKED WAY, THE(1949); JOHNNY ONE-EYE(1950); THIEF, THE(1952)

Lilliam Bronson
ROOM FOR ONE MORE(1952)

Lillian Bronson
THEY WON'T BELIEVE ME(1947); HAPPY LAND(1943); ENTER ARSENE LU-PIN(1944); GASLIGHT(1944); HERE COME THE WAVES(1944); IN THE MEANTIME, DARLING(1944); MADEMOISELLE FIFI(1944); PEARL OF DEATH, THE(1944); WHAT A MAN!(1944); CHRISTMAS IN CONNECTICUT(1945); GIRL OF THE LIM-BERLOST, THE(1945); HOLLYWOOD AND VINE(1945); JUNIOR MISS(1945); MOLLY AND ME(1945); OVER 21(1945); ROAD TO ALCATRAZ(1945); TREE GROWS IN BROOKLYN, A(1945); DRESSED TO KILL(1946); MURDER IN THE MUSIC HALL(1946); NOCTURNE(1946); SENTIMENTAL JOURNEY(1946); DEAD RECKON-ING(1947); HUCKSTERS, THE(1947); SHOCKING MISS PILGRIM, THE(1947); WEL-COME STRANGER(1947); FAMILY HONEYMOON(1948); SLEEP, MY LOVE(1948); IN THE GOOD OLD SUMMERTIME(1949); RUSTY'S BIRTHDAY(1949); DAKOTA LIL(1950); FATHER OF THE BRIDE(1950); JOE PALOOKA MEETS HUM-PHREY(1950); EXCUSE MY DUST(1951); PASSAGE WEST(1951); SWORD OF MONTE CRISTO, THE(1951); HERE COME THE NELSONS(1952); NO ROOM FOR THE GROOM(1952); ROSE OF CIMARRON(1952); AFFAIR WITH A STRANGER(1953); SO THIS IS LOVE(1953); FOXFIRE(1955); BATTLE AT BLOODY BEACH(1961); WALK ON THE WILD SIDE(1962); SPENCER'S MOUNTAIN(1963)

Milly Bronson
LITTLE GIANT(1946)

Milt Bronson
IN SOCIETY(1944); HERE COME THE CO-EDS(1945); NAUGHTY NINETIES, THE(1945); ABBOTT AND COSTELLO MEET THE INVISIBLE MAN(1951); ABBOTT AND COSTELLO GO TO MARS(1953)

Mrs. Owen Bronson
Silents
HIDDEN SCAR, THE(1916), w

Rose Bronson
Misc. Silents
CHILD OF THE PRAIRIE, A(1925)

Sue Bronson
MY FAIR LADY(1964)

Thomas Bronson
ROCKY II(1979), cos

Thomas M. Bronson
STAYING ALIVE(1983), cos

Tom Bronson
DEEP, THE(1977), cos; SLAP SHOT(1977), cos; VICTORY(1981), cos; FIRST BLOOD(1982), cos
1984
BEVERLY HILLS COP(1984), cos

Aude Bronson-Howard
EXPOSED(1983), cos

N.A. "Nat" Bronsten
I BECAME A CRIMINAL(1947), p

Nat Bronsten
MASTER OF BANKDAM, THE(1947, Brit.), p

Nat A. Bronsten
HIDDEN ROOM, THE(1949, Brit.), p; SALT TO THE DEVIL(1949, Brit.), p; SILENT DUST(1949, Brit.), p; LUCKY MASCOT, THE(1951, Brit.), p; VALLEY OF EA-GLES(1952, Brit.), p, d&w

Michael Bronstien
DEATHSTALKER(1983, Arg./U.S.), spec eff

Ann Bronston
GOING BERSERK(1983)

Douglas Bronston
Silents
AMATEUR DEVIL, AN(1921), w; OUTSIDE WOMAN, THE(1921), w; ENEMY OF MEN, AN(1925), w; REDHEADS PREFERRED(1926), w; WHEN THE WIFE'S AWAY(1926), w; HUSBAND HUNTERS(1927), w

Jack Bronston
FIGHTING COWBOY(1933); LIGHTNING RANGE(1934)

Samual Bronston
FALL OF THE ROMAN EMPIRE, THE(1964), p

Samuel Bronston
CITY WITHOUT MEN(1943), p; JACK LONDON(1943), p; JOHN PAUL JO-NES(1959), p; EL CID(1961, U.S./Ital.), p; KING OF KINGS(1961), p; 55 DAYS AT PEKING(1963), p; CIRCUS WORLD(1964), p

Charlotte Bronte
JANE EYRE(1935), w; JANE EYRE(1944), w; JANE EYRE(1971, Brit.), w
Silents
JANE EYRE(1921), w

Emily Bronte
WUTHERING HEIGHTS(1939), w; WUTHERING HEIGHTS(1970, Brit.), w

James Bronte
WILD PARTY, THE(1956)

Jean Bronte
Silents
MOONSHINE VALLEY(1922)

Peter Bronte
GREEN HELL(1940)

Roger Bronte
INTERNS, THE(1962)

Adelaide Bronti
Misc. Silents
SAVED FROM THE HAREM(1915); EMBODIED THOUGHT, THE(1916)

Francesco Bronzi
FAMILY, THE(1974, Fr./Ital.), art d; MASTER TOUCH, THE(1974, Ital./Ger.), art d; THREE TOUGH GUYS(1974, U.S./Ital.), art d; GENIUS, THE(1976, Ital./Fr./Ger.), art d; KILLER FISH(1979, Ital./Braz.), art d; SQUEEZE, THE(1980, Ital.), art d

Alfred Brook
UNDER TEXAS SKIES(1931), ed

Allen Brook
ALL-AMERICAN SWEETHEART(1937); LEAGUE OF FRIGHTENED MEN(1937); MOTOR MADNESS(1937); CATTLE RAIDERS(1938); WHO KILLED GAIL PRES-TON?(1938)

Apple Brook
HALF A SIXPENCE(1967, Brit.)

Arthur A. Brook
RUSTLER'S PARADISE(1935), ed

Barry Brook
FLIGHT TO HONG KONG(1956)

Charles Brook
Silents
PARADISE(1926)
Misc. Silents
FIFTH HORSEMAN, THE(1924)

Claude Brook
DANIEL BOONE, TRAIL BLAZER(1957); DR. TARR'S TORTURE DUNGEON(1972, Mex.)
Silents
SILVER WINGS(1922)

Claudio Brook
WONDERFUL COUNTRY, THE(1959); LAST REBEL, THE(1961, Mex.); YOUNG ONE, THE(1961, Mex.); NEUTRON EL ENMASCARADO NEGRO(1962, Mex.); SANTO EN EL MUSEO DE CERA(1963, Mex.); VIVA MARIA(1965, Fr./Ital.); EXTERMINAT-ING ANGEL, THE(1967, Mex.); UPPER HAND, THE(1967, Fr./Ital./Ger.); BLONDE FROM PEKING, THE(1968, Fr.); DON'T LOOK NOW(1969, Brit./Fr.); MILKY WAY, THE(1969, Fr./Ital.); ASSASSINATION OF TROTSKY, THE(1972 Fr./Ital.); JO-RY(1972); INTERVAL(1973, Mex./U.S.); CASTLE OF PURITY(1974, Mex.); RETURN OF A MAN CALLED HORSE, THE(1976); FOXTROT(1977, Mex./Swiss); BEES, THE(1978); EAGLE'S WING(1979, Brit.); ONLY ONCE IN A LIFETIME(1979)

Clive Brook
TARNISHED LADY(1931); INTERFERENCE(1928); PERFECT CRIME, THE(1928); CHARMING SINNERS(1929); DANGEROUS WOMAN(1929); ANYBODY'S WO-MAN(1930); LAUGHING LADY, THE(1930); SLIGHTLY SCARLET(1930); SWEET-HEARTS AND WIVES(1930); EAST LYNNE(1931); HUSBAND'S HOLIDAY(1931); LAWYER'S SECRET, THE(1931); SCANDAL SHEET(1931); SILENCE(1931); 24 HOURS(1931); MAKE ME A STAR(1932); MAN FROM YESTERDAY, THE(1932); NIGHT OF JUNE 13(1932); SHANGHAI EXPRESS(1932); SHERLOCK HOLMES(1932); CAVALCADE(1933); IF I WERE FREE(1933); MIDNIGHT CLUB(1933); GALLANT LADY(1934); LET'S TRY AGAIN(1934); WHERE SINNERS MEET(1934); DICTATOR, THE(1935, Brit./Ger.); DRESSED TO THRILL(1935); LOVE IN EXILE(1936, Brit.); RETURN OF SHERLOCK HOLMES(1936); ACTION FOR SLANDER(1937, Brit.); SCOTLAND YARD COMMANDS(1937, Brit.); WARE CASE, THE(1939, Brit.); CON-VOY(1940); RETURN TO YESTERDAY(1940, Brit.); VOICE IN THE NIGHT, A(1941, Brit.); ADVENTURE IN BLACKMAIL(1943, Brit.); FLEMISH FARM, THE(1943, Brit.); SHIPBUILDERS, THE(1943, Brit.); ON APPROVAL(1944, Brit.), a, p, d, w; LIST OF ADRIAN MESSENGER, THE(1963)
Silents
KISSING CUP'S RACE(1920, Brit.); DEBT OF HONOR(1922, Brit.); EXPERIMENT, THE(1922, Brit.); MARRIED TO A MORMAN(1922, Brit.); OUT TO WIN(1923, Brit.); ROYAL OAK, THE(1923, Brit.); HUMAN DESIRES(1924, Brit.); MONEY HABIT, THE(1924, Brit.); PASSIONATE ADVENTURE, THE(1924, Brit.); RECOIL, THE(1924); COMPROMISE(1925); AFRAID TO LOVE(1927); BARBED WIRE(1927); FRENCH DRESSING(1927); UNDERWORLD(1927); MIDNIGHT MADNESS(1928); FOUR FEATHERS(1929)
Misc. Silents
KISSING CUP'S RACE(1920, Brit.); TRENT'S LAST CASE(1920, Brit.); CHRISTIE JOHNSTONE(1921, Brit.); DANIEL DERONDA(1921, Brit.); HER PENALTY(1921, Brit.); LOUDWATER MYSTERY, THE(1921, Brit.); SONIA(1921, Brit.); SPORTSMAN'S WIFE, A(1921, Brit.); SHIRLEY(1922, Brit.); STABLE COMPANIONS(1922, Brit.); THIS FREEDOM(1923, Brit.); THROUGH FIRE AND WATER(1923, Brit.); WOMAN TO WOMAN(1923, Brit.); CHRISTINE OF THE HUNGRY HEART(1924); MIRAGE, THE(1924); WHITE SHADOWS(1924, Brit.); WINE OF LIFE, THE(1924, Brit.); DE-CLASSE(1925); ENTICEMENT(1925); HOME MAKER, THE(1925); IF MARRIAGE FAILS(1925); PLAYING WITH SOULS(1925); PLEASURE BUYERS, THE(1925); SEV-EN SINNERS(1925); WHEN LOVE GROWS COLD(1925); FOR ALIMONY ONLY(1925); POPULAR SIN, THE(1926); WHY GIRLS GO BACK HOME(1926); YOU NEVER KNOW WOMEN(1926); DEVIL DANCER, THE(1927); HULA(1927); FORGOTTEN

FACES(1928); YELLOW LILY, THE(1928)

Croftt Brook
FORTY POUNDS OF TROUBLE(1962)

Doris Brook
WILDERNESS MAIL(1935)
Misc. Talkies
LONE BANDIT, THE(1934); BEAST OF BORNEO(1935)

Faith Brook
SUSPICION(1941); JUNGLE BOOK(1942); NO TIME FOR LOVE(1943); UNEASY TERMS(1948, Brit.); FINGER OF GUILT(1956, Brit.); ACROSS THE BRIDGE(1957, Brit.); PORTRAIT IN SMOKE(1957, Brit.); VIOLENT STRANGER(1957, Brit.); CHASE A CROOKED SHADOW(1958, Brit.); THIRTY NINE STEPS, THE(1960, Brit.); WE SHALL SEE(1964, Brit.); HEROES OF TELEMARK, THE(1965, Brit.); TO SIR, WITH LOVE(1967, Brit.); FINO A FARTI MALE(1969, Fr./Ital.); WALK A CROOKED PATH(1969, Brit.); SCHOOL FOR UNCLAIMED GIRLS(1973, Brit.); FFOLKES(1980, Brit.); EYE OF THE NEEDLE(1981); SEA WOLVES, THE(1981, Brit.); WEATHER IN THE STREETS, THE(1983, Brit.)
1984
RAZOR'S EDGE, THE(1984)

Fay Brook
SEPARATION(1968, Brit.)

Hugh Brook
Silents
RAT, THE(1925, Brit.)

Joseph Brook
JEREMY(1973), m

Kathryn Brook
Misc. Silents
GREEN CLOAK, THE(1915)

Lesley Brook
MAN WHO MADE DIAMONDS, THE(1937, Brit.); PATRICIA GETS HER MAN(1937, Brit.); SIDE STREET ANGEL(1937, Brit.); VULTURE, THE(1937, Brit.); DARK STAIRWAY, THE(1938, Brit.); GLAMOUR GIRL(1938, Brit.); IT'S IN THE BLOOD(1938, Brit.); NIGHT ALONE(1938, Brit.); QUIET PLEASE(1938, Brit.); RETURN OF CAROL DEANE, THE(1938, Brit.); VIPER, THE(1938, Brit.); DEAD MEN TELL NO TALES(1939, Brit.); NURSEMAID WHO DISAPPEARED, THE(1939, Brit.); BRIGGS FAMILY, THE(1940, Brit.); ROSE OF TRALEE(1942, Brit.); BELLS GO DOWN, THE(1943, Brit.); I'LL WALK BESIDE YOU(1943, Brit.); WHEN WE ARE MARRIED(1943, Brit.); TWILIGHT HOUR(1944, Brit.); FOR YOU ALONE(1945, Brit.); VARIETY JUBILEE(1945, Brit.); TROJAN BROTHERS, THE(1946); FOOL AND THE PRINCESS, THE(1948, Brit.); HOUSE OF DARKNESS(1948, Brit.)

Lyndon Brook
TRAIN OF EVENTS(1952, Brit.); PASSING STRANGER, THE(1954, Brit.); PURPLE PLAIN, THE(1954, Brit.); ONE WAY OUT(1955, Brit.); ABOVE US THE WAVES(1956, Brit.); REACH FOR THE SKY(1957, Brit.); SPANISH GARDENER, THE(1957, Span.); SURGEON'S KNIFE, THE(1957, Brit.); GYPSY AND THE GENTLEMAN, THE(1958, Brit.); INNOCENT SINNERS(1958, Brit.); SONG WITHOUT END(1960); SURPRISE PACKAGE(1960); CLUE OF THE SILVER KEY, THE(1961, Brit.); INVASION(1965, Brit.); VIOLENT MOMENT(1966, Brit.); HIRELING, THE(1973, Brit.); WHO?(1975, Brit./Ger.)

Michael Brook
X THE UNKNOWN(1957, Brit.)

Neville Brook
SHADOW OF MIKE EMERALD, THE(1935, Brit.); PRISON BREAKER(1936, Brit.); TWICE BRANDED(1936, Brit.); GARRISON FOLLIES(1940, Brit.); HEAVEN IS ROUND THE CORNER(1944, Brit.)

Patrick Brook
JOHNNY DOUGHBOY(1943)

Peter Brook
BEGGAR'S OPERA, THE(1953), d; LORD OF THE FLIES(1963, Brit.), d&w, ed; MODERATO CANTABILE(1964, Fr./Ital.), d, w; PERSECUTION AND ASSASSINATION OF JEAN-PAUL MARAT AS PERFORMED BY THE INMATES OF THE ASYLUM OF CHARENTON UNDER THE DIRECTION OF THE MARQUIS DE SADE, THE(1967, Brit.), d; TELL ME LIES(1968, Brit.), p&d; KING LEAR(1971, Brit./Den.), d&w; MEETINGS WITH REMARKABLE MEN(1979, Brit.), d
1984
SWANN IN LOVE(1984, Fr.Ger.), w

Sebastian Brook
CURIOUS FEMALE, THE(1969); GAY DECEIVERS, THE(1969); MOVIE MOVIE(1978)
Misc. Talkies
JEKYLL AND HYDE PORTFOLIO, THE(1972)

Terence Brook
SECRET VENTURE(1955, Brit.); MODEL MURDER CASE, THE(1964, Brit.)

Walter Brook
GRADUATE, THE(1967); ST. IVES(1976)

The Brook Brothers
RING-A-DING RHYTHM(1962, Brit. 73m Amicus/COL bw (G.B: IT'S TRAD, DAD!)

Elwyn Brook-Jones
DUKE WORE JEANS, THE(1958, Brit.)

Elwyn Brook-Jones
ODD MAN OUT(1947, Brit.); BONNIE PRINCE CHARLIE(1948, Brit.); THREE WEIRD SISTERS, THE(1948, Brit.); HOUR OF GLORY(1949, Brit.); GOOD TIME GIRL(1950, Brit.); IT'S HARD TO BE GOOD(1950, Brit.); LIFE IN HER HANDS(1951, Brit.); LUCKY NICK CAIN(1951); WONDER BOY(1951, Brit./Aust.); JUDGMENT DEFERRED(1952, Brit.); NIGHT WON'T TALK, THE(1952, Brit.); THREE STEPS IN THE DARK(1953, Brit.); BEAU BRUMMELL(1954); GILDED CAGE, THE(1954, Brit.); HARASSED HERO, THE(1954, Brit.); ROGUE'S YARN(1956, Brit.); ROOM 43(1959, Brit.); UGLY DUCKLING, THE(1959, Brit.); PURE HELL OF ST. TRINIAN'S, THE(1961, Brit.); MILLION DOLLAR MANHUNT(1962, Brit.)

Loma Lee Brookbank
1984
HOLLYWOOD HOT TUBS(1984), art d

Anne Brooke
DISTANT TRUMPET(1952, Brit.)

Ashley Brooke
Misc. Talkies
SHANTYTOWN HONEYMOON(1972)

Bunney Brooke
NO. 96(1974, Aus.); DAWN(1979, Aus.); DEAD MAN'S FLOAT(1980, Aus.)
Misc. Talkies
ALISON'S BIRTHDAY(1979, Aus.)

Claude Brooke
Silents
CLASSMATES(1924)

Clifford Brooke
SEA HAWK, THE(1940); WOMAN'S FACE(1941); KEEPER OF THE FLAME(1942); SUSPECT, THE(1944); WHITE CLIFFS OF DOVER, THE(1944); WILSON(1944); HANGOVER SQUARE(1945); LOVE LETTERS(1945); MOLLY AND ME(1945); BLACK BEAUTY(1946); MADONNA'S SECRET, THE(1946); THREE STRANGERS(1946); LATE GEORGE APLEY, THE(1947); MOSS ROSE(1947); MISS TATLOCK'S MILLIONS(1948); MY OWN TRUE LOVE(1948); WOMAN IN WHITE, THE(1948); WHERE DANGER LIVES(1950); FIRST LEGION, THE(1951)

E. H. Brooke
Silents
GREAT ADVENTURE, THE(1915, Brit.); STILL WATERS RUN DEEP(1916, Brit.)

Edgar Brooke
IT'S A BIG COUNTRY(1951), w

Eleanor Brooke
THAT CERTAIN FEELING(1956), w

Eva Brooke
Silents
HER LONELY SOLDIER(1919, Brit.)

Graham Brooke
CHARRIOTS OF FIRE(1981, Brit.)

Harold Brooke
PAIR OF BRIEFS, A(1963, Brit.), w; NO, MY DARLING DAUGHTER(1964, Brit.), w

Hilary Brooke
HEATWAVE(1954, Brit.)

Hillary Brooke
ETERNALLY YOURS(1939); FLORIAN(1940); NEW MOON(1940); PHILADELPHIA STORY, THE(1940); TWO GIRLS ON BROADWAY(1940); DR. JEKYLL AND MR. HYDE(1941); MAISIE WAS A LADY(1941); MARRIED BACHELOR(1941); UNFINISHED BUSINESS(1941); CALLING DR. GILLESPIE(1942); COUNTER-ESPIONAGE(1942); SHERLOCK HOLMES AND THE VOICE OF TERROR(1942); SHIP AHOY(1942); SLEEPYTIME GAL(1942); TO THE SHORES OF TRIPOLI(1942); WAKE ISLAND(1942); CRYSTAL BALL, THE(1943); HAPPY GO LUCKY(1943); SHERLOCK HOLMES FACES DEATH(1943); AND THE ANGELS SING(1944); JANE EYRE(1944); LADY IN THE DARK(1944); STANDING ROOM ONLY(1944); CRIME DOCTOR'S COURAGE, THE(1945); ENCHANTED COTTAGE, THE(1945); MINISTRY OF FEAR(1945); ROAD TO UTOPIA(1945); WOMAN IN GREEN, THE(1945); EARL CARROLL SKETCHBOOK(1946); GENTLEMAN MISBEHAVES, THE(1946); MONSIEUR BEAUCAIRE(1946); STRANGE IMPERSONATION(1946); STRANGE JOURNEY(1946); STRANGE WOMAN, THE(1946); UP GOES MAISIE(1946); BIG TOWN(1947); BIG TOWN AFTER DARK(1947); I COVER BIG TOWN(1947); BIG TOWN SCANDAL(1948); FULLER BRUSH MAN(1948); LET'S LIVE AGAIN(1948); AFRICA SCREAMS(1949); ALIMONY(1949); ADMIRAL WAS A LADY, THE(1950); BEAUTY ON PARADE(1950); BODYHOLD(1950); LUCKY LOSERS(1950); UNMASKED(1950); VENDETTA(1950); INSURANCE INVESTIGATOR(1951); LOST CONTINENT(1951); SKIPALONG ROSENBLOOM(1951); ABBOTT AND COSTELLO MEET CAPTAIN KIDD(1952); CONFIDENCE GIRL(1952); NEVER WAVE AT A WAC(1952); INVADERS FROM MARS(1953); LADY WANTS MINK, THE(1953); MAZE, THE(1953); MEXICAN MANHUNT(1953); DRAGON'S GOLD(1954); BENGAZI(1955); MAN WHO KNEW TOO MUCH, THE(1956); SPOILERS OF THE FOREST(1957)
Misc. Talkies
LONE RIDER IN FRONTIER FURY, THE(1941); LONE RIDER RIDES ON, THE(1941)

Holly Brooke
RIDING SHOTGUN(1954)

Hugh Brooke
DARK WORLD(1935, Brit.), a, w; WRATH OF JEALOUSY(1936, Brit.), w; GLAMOROUS NIGHT(1937, Brit.), w; LET'S MAKE A NIGHT OF IT(1937, Brit.), w; OVER SHE GOES(1937, Brit.), w; ISLAND OF DESIRE(1952, Brit.), w; THIS IS MY LOVE(1954), p, w

Jerry Brooke
EXPERIENCE PREFERRED... BUT NOT ESSENTIAL(1983, Brit.)

Ken Brooke
NIKKI, WILD DOG OF THE NORTH(1961, U.S./Can.), makeup; DEALING: OR THE BERKELEY-TO-BOSTON FORTY-BRICK LOST-BAG BLUES(1971), makeup; STRANGE INVADERS(1983), makeup

Lawrence Brooke
Silents
IS MONEY EVERYTHING?(1923)

Michael Brooke
BULLDOG DRUMMOND IN AFRICA(1938); BULLDOG DRUMMOND'S PERIL(1938); DAWN PATROL, THE(1938); ZAZA(1939); ADVENTURE IN BLACKMAIL(1943, Brit.), p; MUDLARK, THE(1950, Brit.); SECRET PLACE, THE(1958, Brit.)

Michael Brooke, Jr.
MAGNET, THE(1950, Brit.); THIRD KEY, THE(1957, Brit.)

Noni Brooke
MISS LONDON LTD.(1943, Brit.)

Paul Brooke
HOLLYWOOD CANTEEN(1944); GOD IS MY CO-PILOT(1945); AGATHA(1979, Brit.); FOR YOUR EYES ONLY(1981)
1984
GREYSTOKE: THE LEGEND OF TARZAN, LORD OF THE APES(1984)

Peter R. Brooke
BASKETBALL FIX, THE(1951), w; OUTSIDE THE LAW(1956), w

Ralph Brooke
MYSTERY SUBMARINE(1950); CHARGE AT FEATHER RIVER, THE(1953); GIANT FROM THE UNKNOWN(1958), w; BLOODLUST(1959), p,d&w; RIGHT HAND OF THE DEVIL, THE(1963), w

Rebecca Brooke
Misc. Talkies
LITTLE GIRL, BIG TEASE(1977); NAUGHTY SCHOOL GIRLS(1977)

Sorrell Brooke
SLAUGHTERHOUSE-FIVE(1972)

Sybil Brooke
TROUBLED WATERS(1936, Brit.); WHERE THERE'S A WILL(1936, Brit); PASSENGER TO LONDON(1937, Brit.); MOONLIGHT SONATA(1938, Brit.); VILLIERS DIAMOND, THE(1938, Brit.)

Tom Brooke
Silents
KENNEDY SQUARE(1916); MODERN CINDERELLA, A(1917); SACRED SILENCE(1919)
Misc. Silents
SLAVE, THE(1917); WAR AND THE WOMAN(1917)

Tyler Brooke
DIVORCEE, THE(1930); DYNAMITE(1930); FURIES, THE(1930); LILIES OF THE FIELD(1930); MADAME SATAN(1930); MONTE CARLO(1930); PLAYBOY OF PARIS(1930); DANGEROUS AFFAIR, A(1931); MAGNIFICENT LIE(1931); LOVE ME TONIGHT(1932); MILLION DOLLAR LEGS(1932); TROUBLE IN PARADISE(1932); CHILD OF MANHATTAN(1933); DON'T BET ON LOVE(1933); HALLELUJAH, I'M A BUM(1933); MORNING GLORY(1933); BELLE OF THE NINETIES(1934); IMITATION OF LIFE(1934); MERRY WIDOW, THE(1934); 365 NIGHTS IN HOLLYWOOD(1934); NEXT TIME WE LOVE(1936); POOR LITTLE RICH GIRL(1936); SUZY(1936); TWO IN A CROWD(1936); THIS IS MY AFFAIR(1937); IN OLD CHICAGO(1938); STORY OF ALEXANDER GRAHAM BELL, THE(1939); KITTY FOYLE(1940); LITTLE OLD NEW YORK(1940); ONE NIGHT IN THE TROPICS(1940); TIN PAN ALLEY(1940); TWO LATINS FROM MANHATTAN(1941); I MARRIED AN ANGEL(1942); LUCKY LEGS(1942); SHE HAS WHAT IT TAKES(1943)
Silents
STAGE MADNESS(1927); NONE BUT THE BRAVE(1928)

Valerie Brooke
CHILDISH THINGS(1969)

Van Dyke Brooke
Silents
LIGHTS OF NEW YORK, THE(1916), d
Misc. Silents
CROWN PRINCE'S DOUBLE, THE(1916), d; AMATEUR ORPHAN, AN(1917), d; IT HAPPENED TO ADELE(1917), d; MOONSHINE TRAIL, THE(1919); FORTUNE HUNTER, THE(1920); SEA RIDER, THE(1920); WHAT WOMEN WANT(1920); MIDNIGHT BELL, A(1921)

Walter Brooke
BULLET SCARS(1942); DESPERATE JOURNEY(1942); GAY SISTERS, THE(1942); MALE ANIMAL, THE(1942); THEY DIED WITH THEIR BOOTS ON(1942); YANKEE DOODLE DANDY(1942); IRON MAJOR, THE(1943); C-MAN(1949); CONQUEST OF SPACE(1955); PARTY CRASHERS, THE(1958); WONDERFUL WORLD OF THE BROTHERS ERIMM, THE(1962); HOW SWEET IT IS(1968); SERGEANT RYKER(1968); MAROONED(1969); LANDLORD, THE(1970); TORA! TORA! TORA!(1970, U.S./Jap.); ZIGZAG(1970); LAWMAN(1971); RETURN OF COUNT YORGA, THE(1971); EXECUTIVE ACTION(1973); ONE LITTLE INDIAN(1973); HARRAD SUMMER, THE(1974); FRAMED(1975); OTHER SIDE OF THE MOUNTAIN, THE(1975); BIG BUS, THE(1976); BLACK SUNDAY(1977); FUN WITH DICK AND JANE(1977); NORTH DALLAS FORTY(1979); IN SEARCH OF HISTORIC JESUS(1980); NUDE BOMB, THE(1980); SEPARATE WAYS(1981)
Misc. Talkies
BEYOND REASON(1977)

Tim Brooke-Taylor
STATUE, THE(1971, Brit.)

Bob Brooker
TRICK BABY(1973)

Richard Brooker
FRIDAY THE 13TH PART III(1982); DEATHSTALKER(1983, Arg./U.S.)
1984
DEATHSTALKER, THE(1984); FRIDAY THE 13TH–THE FINAL CHAPTER(1984)

Robert Brooker
MANHUNT IN THE JUNGLE(1958), ph

Tom Brooker
Silents
GUN LAW(1929)

Trevor Brooker
SWAPPERS, THE(1970, Brit.), ph

William Brooker
SOMETHING WEIRD(1967)

Arthur A. Brookes
LAST OF THE CLINTONS, THE(1935), ed

Jacqueline Brookes
HOSPITAL, THE(1971); GAMBLER, THE(1974); LOOKING UP(1977); LAST EMBRACE(1979); GHOST STORY(1981); PATERNITY(1981); LINE, THE(1982); WITHOUT A TRACE(1983)

Olwen Brookes
THIS MAN IS MINE(1946 Brit.); MARK OF CAIN, THE(1948, Brit.); MY SISTER AND I(1948, Brit.); POET'S PUB(1949, Brit.); STOP PRESS GIRL(1949, Brit.); WARNING TO WANTONS, A(1949, Brit.); HAPPIEST DAYS OF YOUR LIFE(1950, Brit.); ISLAND RESCUE(1952, Brit.); SOMETHING MONEY CAN'T BUY(1952, Brit.); MEN ARE CHILDREN TWICE(1953, Brit.); BLACK KNIGHT, THE(1954); INSPECTOR CALLS, AN(1954, Brit.); GENTLE TOUCH, THE(1956, Brit.); GOOD COMPANIONS, THE(1957, Brit.); HIGH TERRACE(1957, Brit.); LEFT, RIGHT AND CENTRE(1959)

Victor Brookes
MAN UPSTAIRS, THE(1959, Brit.)

Fred Brookfield
LIFE AND TIMES OF JUDGE ROY BEAN, THE(1972); ULZANA'S RAID(1972)

John Brooking
GLORY AT SEA(1952, Brit.); STORY OF ROBIN HOOD, THE(1952, Brit.); BAD BLONDE(1953, Brit.); KNIGHTS OF THE ROUND TABLE(1953); INNOCENTS IN PARIS(1955, Brit.); HONOURABLE MURDER, AN(1959, Brit.); NO SAFETY AHEAD(1959, Brit.); TWO-HEADED SPY, THE(1959, Brit.); WEB OF SUSPICION(1959, Brit.); LONELINESS OF THE LONG DISTANCE RUNNER, THE(1962, Brit.)

Don Brookins
WAY OUT WEST(1937)

Brookins and Van
SAM SMALL LEAVES TOWN(1937, Brit.)

The Brooklyn Bridge
DAREDEVIL, THE(1971), m

The Brooklyn Dodgers
WHISTLING IN BROOKLYN(1943); ROOGIE'S BUMP(1954)

A. Brooks
TERMS OF ENDEARMENT(1983)

Adam Brooks
1984
ALMOST YOU(1984), d, w

Alan Brooks
HOLE IN THE WALL(1929); ENEMIES OF THE LAW(1931); BIG TOWN(1932); HOTEL VARIETY(1933); CONVENTION GIRL(1935); GOING IN STYLE(1979)
Silents
RED DICE(1926); HOME STRUCK(1927); KING OF KINGS, THE(1927)
Misc. Silents
SHANGHAIED(1927); SOUTH SEA LOVE(1927)

Albert Brooks
TAXI DRIVER(1976); REAL LIFE(1979), a, d, w; PRIVATE BENJAMIN(1980); MODERN ROMANCE(1981), a, d, w; TWILIGHT ZONE–THE MOVIE(1983)
1984
UNFAITHFULLY YOURS(1984)

Alden Brooks
Silents
EXQUISITE SINNER, THE(1926), w

Arthur A. Brooks
WILD WEST WHOOPEE(1931), ed; WAGON TRAIL(1935), ed; WILD MUSTANG(1935), ed; TOLL OF THE DESERT(1936), ed; ACES WILD(1937), ed; HEROES OF THE ALAMO(1938), ed; RENEGADE GIRL(1946), ed; SHOOT TO KILL(1947), ed; OLD-FASHIONED GIRL, AN(1948), ed; SHAMROCK HILL(1949), ed

Arthur Brooks
CODE OF HONOR(1930), ed; SECRET MENACE(1931), ed; CAVALCADE OF THE WEST(1936), ed; DOUGHNUTS AND SOCIETY(1936), ed; GHOST TOWN(1937), ed; FURY BELOW(1938), ed

Barbara Brooks
LET'S FACE IT(1943)

Barry Brooks
RACE STREET(1948); DANGEROUS PROFESSION, A(1949); ROOKIE FIREMAN(1950); WOMAN ON PIER 13, THE(1950); COMIN' ROUND THE MOUNTAIN(1951); FLAME OF ARABY(1951); HIS KIND OF WOMAN(1951); MY FORBIDDEN PAST(1951); RACKET, THE(1951); ROADBLOCK(1951); KANSAS CITY CONFIDENTIAL(1952); LAST TRAIN FROM BOMBAY(1952); SNIPER, THE(1952); SALOME(1953); STRANGER WORE A GUN, THE(1953); SHE COULDN'T SAY NO(1954); LAWLESS STREET, A(1955); ESCAPE FROM SAN QUENTIN(1957)

Betty Brooks
SING FOR YOUR SUPPER(1941)

Beverley Brooks
FIND THE LADY(1956, Brit.); TEARS FOR SIMON(1957, Brit.)

Beverly Brooks
MAN OF THE MOMENT(1955, Brit.); SIMON AND LAURA(1956, Brit.); REACH FOR THE SKY(1957, Brit.)

Bob Brooks
TATTOO(1981), d, w

Bobby Brooks
TOMORROW IS FOREVER(1946)

Bonnie Brooks
NOTHING PERSONAL(1980, Can.)

Carolyn Brooks
RETURN OF THE SECAUCUS SEVEN(1980)

Charlene Brooks
TWO LITTLE BEARS, THE(1961)

Charles Brooks
Silents
KING LEAR(1916)

Charles David Brooks III
EMMA MAE(1976)

Chris Brooks
JACK AND THE BEANSTALK(1970)

Christopher Brooks
ONE IS A LONELY NUMBER(1972); MACK, THE(1973)
Misc. Talkies
ALABAMA'S GHOST(1972)

Clarence Brooks
ARROWSMITH(1931); DARK MANHATTAN(1937); BRONZE BUCKAROO, THE(1939); HARLEM RIDES THE RANGE(1939); AM I GUILTY?(1940)
Misc. Talkies
GEORGIA ROSE(1930); BRAND OF CAIN, THE(1935); UP JUMPED THE DEVIL(1941)
Silents
ABSENT(1928)
Misc. Silents
BY RIGHT OF BIRTH(1921)

Claud Brooks
FURY IN PARADISE(1955, U.S./Mex.)

Claude Brooks
WIZ, THE(1978)
Silents
WIDE-OPEN TOWN, A(1922)

Rand Brooks, Jr.
OLD MAID, THE(1939)

Claudio Brooks
DEVIL'S RAIN, THE(1975, U.S./Mex.)

Clive Brooks
Misc. Silents
THREE FACES EAST(1926)

Conrad Brooks
CLIPPED WINGS(1953); GLEN OR GLENDA(1953); JALOPY(1953); PLAN 9 FROM OUTER SPACE(1959)

Cyrus Brooks
EMIL(1938, Brit.), w
David Brooks
AMERICAN SUCCESS COMPANY, THE(1980)
1984
SCREAM FOR HELP(1984)
Dawn Brooks
GENTLE TRAP, THE(1960, Brit.)
Dean Brooks
BORN AGAIN(1978)
Dean R. Brooks
ONE FLEW OVER THE CUCKOO'S NEST(1975)
Donald Brooks
CARDINAL, THE(1963), cos; THIRD DAY, THE(1965), cos; STAR!(1968), cos; DAR-LING LILI(1970), cos; DROWNING POOL, THE(1975), cos; BELL JAR, THE(1979), cos
Donnie Brooks
GET YOURSELF A COLLEGE GIRL(1964); SWINGIN' SUMMER, A(1965); LOVE-INS, THE(1967)
Douglas Brooks
DEMETRIUS AND THE GLADIATORS(1954)
Dwight Brooks
POCO...LITTLE DOG LOST(1977), p&d
Edward Brooks
WHERE'S POPPA?(1970)
Edwart Brooks
REASONABLE DOUBT(1936, Brit.), w
Elisabeth Brooks
HOWLING, THE(1981)
Eric Brooks
MIND OF MR. SOAMES, THE(1970, Brit.)
Eunice Brooks
EXILE, THE(1931)
Foster Brooks
VILLAIN, THE(1979); SMORGASBORD(1983)
1984
CANNONBALL RUN II(1984)
Misc. Talkies
SUPER SEAL(1976)
George Brooks
CORPSE CAME C.O.D., THE(, art d; DOUBLE CROSS ROADS(1930), w; THREE SISTERS, THE(1930), w; MISSING JUROR, THE(1944), art d; ONE MYSTERIOUS NIGHT(1944), art d; SHE'S A SOLDIER TOO(1944), art d; SOUL OF A MONSTER, THE(1944), art d; DANCING IN MANHATTAN(1945), art d; I LOVE A MYS-TERY(1945), art d; TAHITI NIGHTS(1945), art d; TEN CENTS A DANCE(1945), art d; MAN WHO DARED, THE(1946), art d; MR. DISTRICT ATTORNEY(1946), art d; ONE WAY TO LOVE(1946), art d; TALK ABOUT A LADY(1946), art d; UNKNOWN, THE(1946), art d; BLONDIE'S ANNIVERSARY(1947), art d; BLONDIE'S BIG MO-MENT(1947), art d; CIGARETTE GIRL(1947), art d; CRIME DOCTOR'S GAM-BLE(1947), art d; BLONDIE'S SECRET(1948), art d; MY DOG RUSTY(1948), art d; RETURN OF THE WHISTLER, THE(1948), art d; RUSTY LEADS THE WAY(1948), art d; TRAPPED BY BOSTON BLACKIE(1948), art d; UNTAMED BREED, THE(1948), art d; DOOLINS OF OKLAHOMA, THE(1949), art d; MARY RYAN, DETEC-TIVE(1949), art d; MR. SOFT TOUCH(1949), art d; FLYING MISSILE(1950), art d; FORTUNES OF CAPTAIN BLOOD(1950), art d; NEVADAN, THE(1950), art d; STAGE TO TUCSON(1950), art d; FAMILY SECRET, THE(1951), art d; LADY AND THE BANDIT, THE(1951), art d; MAN IN THE SADDLE(1951), art d; OKINAWA(1952), art d; RAINBOW 'ROUND MY SHOULDER(1952), art d; GOLDTOWN GHOST RI-DERS(1953), art d; LAST POSSE, THE(1953), art d; MISSION OVER KOREA(1953), art d; ON TOP OF OLD SMOKY(1953), art d; PACK TRAIN(1953), art d; STRANGER WORE A GUN, THE(1953), art d; THREE HOURS TO KILL(1954), art d; LAWLESS STREET, A(1955), art d; FURY AT GUNSIGHT PASS(1956), art d; SEVENTH CAVAL-RY(1956), art d; GUNS OF FORT PETTICOAT, THE(1957), art d; TALL T, THE(1957), art d
George S. Brooks
BIG NEWS(1929), w; WINNING OF THE WEST(1953), art d
George W. Brooks
TROUBLE WITH GIRLS(AND HOW TO GET INTO IT), THE*1/2 (1969), ed; STAY AWAY, JOE(1968), ed; SUPPORT YOUR LOCAL SHERIFF(1969), ed; SANTEE(1973), ed
Geraldine Brooks
CRY WOLF(1947); POSSESSED(1947); ACT OF MURDER, AN(1948); EMBRACEA-BLE YOU(1948); CHALLENGE TO LASSIE(1949); RECKLESS MOMENTS, THE(1949); YOUNGER BROTHERS, THE(1949); GREEN GLOVE, THE(1952); VOLCANO(1953, Ital.); STREET OF SINNERS(1957); JOHNNY TIGER(1966); MR. RICCO(1975)
Gigi Brooks
SHADOWS(1960)
Glynis Brooks
WICKED LADY, THE(1983, Brit.)
Hadda Brooks
OUT OF THE BLUE(1947); IN A LONELY PLACE(1950)
Harold Brooks
SWINGIN' MAIDEN, THE(1963, Brit.), w
Harry Brooks
UNEASY TERMS(1948, Brit.); WHERE THE SIDEWALK ENDS(1950); LAS VEGAS STORY, THE(1952)
Harry Brooks, Jr.
UNDERGROUND(1970, Brit.); HANOVER STREET(1979, Brit.)
Harvey Brooks
I'M NO ANGEL(1933), m; MR. WASHINGTON GOES TO TOWN(1941), m
Hazel Brooks
DU BARRY WAS A LADY(1943); GIRL CRAZY(1943); MARRIAGE IS A PRIVATE AFFAIR(1944); MEET THE PEOPLE(1944); RATIONING(1944); THIRTY SECONDS OVER TOKYO(1944); WITHOUT LOVE(1945); HARVEY GIRLS, THE(1946); BODY AND SOUL(1947); ARCH OF TRIUMPH(1948); SLEEP, MY LOVE(1948); BASKET-BALL FIX, THE(1951); I DON'T CARE GIRL, THE(1952)
Hildy Brooks
ANDERSON TAPES, THE(1971); FABLE, A(1971); ICEMAN COMETH, THE(1973); ISLANDS IN THE STREAM(1977); ROSE, THE(1979); CHOSEN, THE(1982)

1984
WILD LIFE, THE(1984)
Howard Brooks
TRUMPET BLOWS, THE(1934); AFFAIRS OF CAPPY RICKS(1937); PICK A STAR(1937); MAN IN THE IRON MASK, THE(1939); BELLBOY, THE(1960)
Ida Brooks
Misc. Silents
WHOSO TAKETH A WIFE(1916)
Ina Brooks
Misc. Silents
ONE HOUR(1917)
Irene Brooks
GANGSTER, THE(1947)
Iris Brooks
I DRINK YOUR BLOOD(1971); UP THE SANDBOX(1972)
Irving Brooks
Silents
NIGHTINGALE, THE(1914); MISS CRUSOE(1919); HALDANE OF THE SECRET SERVICE(1923)
Jack Brooks
PENTHOUSE RHYTHM(1945), m; CANYON PASSAGE(1946), m/l; SLIGHTLY SCANDALOUS(1946), m
Jackie Brooks
DOZENS, THE(1981)
Jacqueline Brooks
ENTITY, THE(1982); LOVE AND MONEY(1982)
Jacquiline Brooks
WEREWOLF OF WASHINGTON(1973)
James Brooks
PRIME TIME, THE(1960)
James L. Brooks
REAL LIFE(1979); STARTING OVER(1979), p, w; MODERN ROMANCE(1981); TERMS OF ENDEARMENT(1983), p, w
Jan Brooks
HIGH FLIGHT(1957, Brit.); SUBMARINE SEAHAWK(1959); WILD YOUTH(1961); GOOD NEIGHBOR SAM(1964)
Jay Brooks
PAYMENT ON DEMAND(1951); COOL WORLD, THE(1963); NOTHING BUT A MAN(1964); BIG BAD MAMA(1974)
Jean Brooks
CONFESSIONS OF A NAZI SPY(1939); FOR BEAUTY'S SAKE(1941); KLONDIKE FURY(1942); BOSS OF BIG TOWN(1943); FALCON AND THE CO-EDS, THE(1943); FALCON IN DANGER, THE(1943); LEOPARD MAN, THE(1943); SEVENTH VICTIM, THE(1943); FALCON IN HOLLYWOOD, THE(1944); NIGHT OF ADVENTURE, A(1944); YOUTH RUNS WILD(1944); TWO O'CLOCK COURAGE(1945); BAMBOO BLONDE, THE(1946); FALCON'S ALIBI, THE(1946)
Misc. Talkies
BOOT HILL BANDITS(1942)
Jeff Lee Brooks
DARK MANHATTAN(1937)
Jennifer Brooks
Misc. Talkies
ABDUCTORS, THE(1972)
Jeremy Brooks
OUR MOTHER'S HOUSE(1967, Brit.), w; WORK IS A FOUR LETTER WORD(1968, Brit.), w; TORTURE DUNGEON(1970); GURU, THE MAD MONK(1971)
Jerry Brooks
SIMON, KING OF THE WITCHES(1971)
Jess Brooks
JUNGLE SIREN(1942)
Jess Lee Brooks
SANTA FE TRAIL(1940); HIT THE ROAD(1941); SULLIVAN'S TRAVELS(1941); DRUMS OF THE CONGO(1942); GIRL CRAZY(1943); SON OF DRACULA(1943); THANK YOUR LUCKY STARS(1943); WILSON(1944)
Jesse Brooks
AM I GUILTY?(1940)
Jesse C. Brooks
GANG WAR(1940)
Jesse Lee Brooks
Misc. Talkies
CONDEMNED MEN(1940)
Joe Brooks
TALL MAN RIDING(1955); ENEMY BELOW, THE(1957); YOUNG LIONS, THE(1958); FLAMING STAR(1960); ADVANCE TO THE REAR(1964); ROBIN AND THE SEVEN HOODS(1964); LORDS OF FLATBUSH, THE(1974), m; BAD NEWS BEARS, THE(1976); YOU LIGHT UP MY LIFE(1977); IF EVER I SEE YOU AGAIN(1978), a, p&d, w, m
1984
GREMLINS(1984)
Silents
REACHING FOR THE MOON(1917); MR. FIX-IT(1918)
Joel Brooks
STIR CRAZY(1980)
1984
PROTOCOL(1984)
Jose Brooks
Misc. Silents
WHEN WOMAN HATES(1916, Brit.)
Joseph Brooks
YOU LIGHT UP MY LIFE(1977), p,d&w, m; HEADIN' FOR BROADWAY(1980), p&d, w, m; EDDIE AND THE CRUISERS(1983), p
Julian Brooks
STORY OF JOSEPH AND HIS BRETHREN THE(1962, Ital.)
Kimberly Brooks
SCREWBALLS(1983)
Laura Brooks
DREAMBOAT(1952); STEEL ARENA(1973)

Laura K. Brooks
IN A LONELY PLACE(1950)
Laura Kasley Brooks
DOUBLE LIFE, A(1947); SAXON CHARM, THE(1948)
Laurence Brooks
SILENT ENEMY, THE(1959, Brit.)
Leslie Brooks
CORPSE CAME C.O.D., THE(; NAVY BLUES(1941); YOU'RE IN THE ARMY NOW(1941); LUCKY LEGS(1942); TALK OF THE TOWN(1942); UNDERGROUND AGENT(1942); YANKEE DOODLE DANDY(1942); YOU WERE NEVER LOVELIER(1942); CITY WITHOUT MEN(1943); TWO SENORITAS FROM CHICAGO(1943); WHAT'S BUZZIN COUSIN?(1943); COVER GIRL(1944); NINE GIRLS(1944); I LOVE A BANDLEADER(1945); TONIGHT AND EVERY NIGHT(1945); IT'S GREAT TO BE YOUNG(1946); MAN WHO DARED, THE(1946); SECRET OF THE WHISTLER(1946); CIGARETTE GIRL(1947); COBRA STRIKES, THE(1948); HOLLOW TRIUMPH(1948); ROMANCE ON THE HIGH SEAS(1948); BLONDE ICE(1949)
Misc. Talkies
OVERLAND TO DEADWOOD(1942)
Lois Brooks
MONSTER A GO-GO(1965)
Lola Brooks
ON THE BEACH(1959); SUNDOWNERS, THE(1960)
Louis Brooks
VINTAGE WINE(1935, Brit.), cos; MORALS OF MARCUS, THE(1936, Brit.), set d
Louise Brooks
BEGGARS OF LIFE(1928); CANARY MURDER CASE, THE(1929); GOD'S GIFT TO WOMEN(1931); IT PAYS TO ADVERTISE(1931); EMPTY SADDLES(1937); KING OF GAMBLERS(1937); WHEN YOU'RE IN LOVE(1937); OVERLAND STAGE RAIDERS(1938)
Silents
AMERICAN VENUS, THE(1926); IT'S THE OLD ARMY GAME(1926); SOCIAL CELEBRITY, A(1926); CITY GONE WILD, THE(1927); EVENING CLOTHES(1927); NOW WE'RE IN THE AIR(1927); ROLLED STOCKINGS(1927); GIRL IN EVERY PORT, A(1928); PANDORA'S BOX(1929, Ger.)
Misc. Silents
LOVE 'EM AND LEAVE 'EM(1926); SHOW OFF, THE(1926); DIARY OF A LOST GIRL(1929, Ger.)
Lucius Brooks
HARLEM RIDES THE RANGE(1939); YOU'LL NEVER GET RICH(1941)
Lynn Brooks
MARK OF THE WITCH(1970), makeup; NATIONAL LAMPOON'S ANIMAL HOUSE(1978), makeup
Maggie Brooks
1984
LOOSE CONNECTIONS(1984, Brit.), w
Margaret Brooks
OUR MOTHER'S HOUSE(1967, Brit.); BUSHBABY, THE(1970)
Marion Brooks
Silents
DO AND DARE(1922), w
Marjorie Brooks
HER STRANGE DESIRE(1931, Brit.); NIGHT OF THE GARTER(1933, Brit.); THIS WEEK OF GRACE(1933, Brit.); EVERGREEN(1934, Brit.); SHE SHALL HAVE MUSIC(1935, Brit.); THIS'LL MAKE YOU WHISTLE(1938, Brit.)
Martin Brooks
COLOSSUS: THE FORBIN PROJECT(1969); MAN, THE(1972)
Matt Brooks
TWENTY MILLION SWEETHEARTS(1934); DOUGHNUTS AND SOCIETY(1936), w; RADIO CITY REVELS(1938), w; SHIP AHOY(1942), w; SWING FEVER(1943), w
Max Brooks
TO BE OR NOT TO BE(1983)
Mel Brooks
PRODUCERS, THE(1967), d&w; PUTNEY SWOPE(1969); TWELVE CHAIRS, THE(1970), a, d&w; SHINBONE ALLEY(1971), w; BLAZING SADDLES(1974), a, d, w; YOUNG FRANKENSTEIN(1974), d, w; SILENT MOVIE(1976), a, d, w; HIGH ANXIETY(1977), a, p&d, w; MUPPET MOVIE, THE(1979); HISTORY OF THE WORLD, PART 1(1981), a, p,d&w; TO BE OR NOT TO BE(1983), a, p
Melvin Brooks
NEW FACES(1954), w
Myra Brooks
Silents
KNIFE, THE(1918)
Misc. Silents
FIGHTING KENTUCKIANS, THE(1920); FATHER TOM(1921)
Nicky Brooks
WHO SAYS I CAN'T RIDE A RAINBOW!(1971)
Norma Brooks
OVER-EXPOSED(1956)
Norman Brooks
ATTACK!(1956), w; BEST THINGS IN LIFE ARE FREE, THE(1956)
Norville Brooks
EQUINOX(1970)
Olwen Brooks
JACK THE RIPPER(1959, Brit.); ON THE RUN(1969, Brit.)
Olwyn Brooks
CAESAR AND CLEOPATRA(1946, Brit.)
Oscar J. Brooks
LOS PLATILLOS VOLADORES(1955, Mex.), p
Pat Brooks
TONIGHT FOR SURE(1962)
Patti Brooks
FIFTH FLOOR, THE(1980)
Paul Brooks
FALCON'S ALIBI, THE(1946); ROARING CITY(1951); PLEDGEMASTERS, THE(1971), ed
Pauline Brooks
STUDENT TOUR(1934); MAKE A MILLION(1935)

Perry Brooks
SPY WITH A COLD NOSE, THE(1966, Brit.)
Peter Brooks
GIDGET GOES TO ROME(1963); HUD(1963); GIRL HAPPY(1965); GIRLS ON THE BEACH(1965)
Phyllis Brooks
ANOTHER FACE(1935); I'VE BEEN AROUND(1935); LADY TUBBS(1935); MAN WHO RECLAIMED HIS HEAD, THE(1935); MC FADDEN'S FLATS(1935); STRANGE WIVES(1935); TO BEAT THE BAND(1935); DANGEROUSLY YOURS(1937); YOU CAN'T HAVE EVERYTHING(1937); CHARLIE CHAN IN HONOLULU(1938); CITY GIRL(1938); IN OLD CHICAGO(1938); LITTLE MISS BROADWAY(1938); REBECCA OF SUNNYBROOK FARM(1938); STRAIGHT, PLACE AND SHOW(1938); UP THE RIVER(1938); WALKING DOWN BROADWAY(1938); CHARLIE CHAN IN RENO(1939); LUCKY TO ME(1939, Brit.); FLYING SQUAD, THE(1940, Brit.); SLIGHTLY HONORABLE(1940); SHANGHAI GESTURE, THE(1941); HI' YA, SAILOR(1943); NO PLACE FOR A LADY(1943); SILVER SPURS(1943); DANGEROUS PASSAGE(1944); LADY IN THE DARK(1944); HIGH POWERED(1945); UNSEEN, THE(1945)
Ralph Brooks
SATURDAY'S MILLIONS(1933); FOG OVER FRISCO(1934); GAMBLING LADY(1934); NAUGHTY MARIETTA(1935); SHOT IN THE DARK, A(1935); STRANGE WIVES(1935); DEATH FROM A DISTANCE(1936); LIBELED LADY(1936); LOVE BEFORE BREAKFAST(1936); SWING TIME(1936); CHAMPAGNE WALTZ(1937); DAMSEL IN DISTRESS, A(1937); MAKE WAY FOR TOMORROW(1937); MUSIC FOR MADAME(1937); SWEETHEARTS(1938); GONE WITH THE WIND(1939); SECOND FIDDLE(1939); YOU CAN'T CHEAT AN HONEST MAN(1939); LOVE, HONOR AND OH, BABY(1940); GIRL, A GUY AND A GOB, A(1941); MR. AND MRS. SMITH(1941); MAGNIFICENT DOPE, THE(1942); MEXICAN SPITFIRE'S ELEPHANT(1942); SABOTEUR(1942); SPIRIT OF STANFORD, THE(1942); THERE'S ONE BORN EVERY MINUTE(1942); YOU'RE TELLING ME(1942); THIN MAN GOES HOME, THE(1944); WITHOUT LOVE(1945); HER ADVENTUROUS NIGHT(1946); SMOOTH AS SILK(1946); WHITE TIE AND TAILS(1946); SONG OF SCHEHERAZADE(1947); T-MEN(1947); FORCE OF EVIL(1948); LETTER TO THREE WIVES, A(1948); MICHAEL O'HALLORAN(1948); ONE TOUCH OF VENUS(1948); MYSTERY STREET(1950); SHAKEDOWN(1950); HE RAN ALL THE WAY(1951); I WANT YOU(1951); JUBILEE TRAIL(1954); THIRD VOICE, THE(1960)
Rand Brooks
DRAMATIC SCHOOL(1938); LOVE FINDS ANDY HARDY(1938); BABES IN ARMS(1939); GONE WITH THE WIND(1939); AND ONE WAS BEAUTIFUL(1940); FLORIAN(1940); GIRL FROM AVENUE A(1940); LADDIE(1940); NORTHWEST PASSAGE(1940); SON OF MONTE CRISTO(1940); CHEERS FOR MISS BISHOP(1941); DOUBLE DATE(1941); JENNIE(1941); LADY SCARFACE(1941); LIFE WITH HENRY(1941); SOMBRERO KID, THE(1942); VALLEY OF HUNTED MEN(1942); AIR FORCE(1943); HIGH EXPLOSIVE(1943); LADY IN THE DARK(1944); DEVIL'S PLAYGROUND, THE(1946); FOOL'S GOLD(1946); UNEXPECTED GUEST(1946); DANGEROUS VENTURE(1947); HOPPY'S HOLIDAY(1947); KILROY WAS HERE(1947); MARAUDERS, THE(1947); BORROWED TROUBLE(1948); DEAD DON'T DREAM, THE(1948); FALSE PARADISE(1948); JOAN OF ARC(1948); LADIES OF THE CHORUS(1948); SILENT CONFLICT(1948); SINISTER JOURNEY(1948); STRANGE GAMBLE(1948); SUNDOWN IN SANTA FE(1948); BLACK MIDNIGHT(1949); WYOMING BANDIT, THE(1949); RIDING HIGH(1950); VANISHING WESTERNER, THE(1950); CIMARRON KID, THE(1951); HEART OF THE ROCKIES(1951); YUKON MANHUNT(1951); MAVERICK, THE(1952); STEEL FIST, THE(1952); WACO(1952); BORN TO THE SADDLE(1953); TO HELL AND BACK(1955); LAST HURRAH, THE(1958); COMANCHE STATION(1960); STAGECOACH TO DANCER'S PARK(1962); REQUIEM FOR A GUNFIGHTER(1965)
Misc. Talkies
BEHIND SOUTHERN LINES(1952); GUNMAN, THE(1952); MAN FROM THE BLACK HILLS(1952); MONTANA INCIDENT(1952)
Randi Brooks
LOOKER(1981); DEAL OF THE CENTURY(1983); MAN WITH TWO BRAINS, THE(1983)
1984
TIGHTROPE(1984)
Randy Brooks
COWBOY SERENADE(1942); MAN FROM BLACK HILLS, THE(1952); MONKEY HUSTLE, THE(1976)
Ranee Brooks
Misc. Silents
LIBERTY HALL(1914, Brit.)
Ray Brooks
DAMN THE DEFIANT!(1962, Brit.); PLAY IT COOL(1963, Brit.); SOME PEOPLE(1964, Brit.); KNACK ... AND HOW TO GET IT, THE(1965, Brit.); DALEKS-INVASION EARTH 2155 A.D.(1966, Brit.); LAST GRENADE, THE(1970, Brit.); MELINDA(1972), makeup; ASSASSIN(1973, Brit.); FLESH AND BLOOD SHOW, THE(1974, Brit.); HOUSE OF WHIPCORD(1974, Brit.); RIVER NIGER, THE(1976), makeup; TIFFANY JONES(1976)
Rebecca Brooks
ROLLOVER(1981)
Richard Brooks
$(DOLLARS)**1/2 (1971), d&w; MEN OF TEXAS(1942), w; SIN TOWN(1942), w; WHITE SAVAGE(1943), w; COBRA WOMAN(1944), w; MY BEST GAL(1944), w; SWELL GUY(1946), w; BRUTE FORCE(1947), w; CROSSFIRE(1947), w; KEY LARGO(1948), w; TO THE VICTOR(1948), w; ANY NUMBER CAN PLAY(1949), w; MYSTERY STREET(1950), w; STORM WARNING(1950), w; LIGHT TOUCH, THE(1951), d&w; DEADLINE-U.S.A.(1952), d&w; BATTLE CIRCUS(1953), d&w; TAKE THE HIGH GROUND(1953), d; FLAME AND THE FLESH(1954), d; LAST TIME I SAW PARIS, THE(1954), d; BLACKBOARD JUNGLE, THE(1955), d&w; CATERED AFFAIR, THE(1956), d; LAST HUNT, THE(1956), d&w; SOMETHING OF VALUE(1957), d&w; BROTHERS KARAMAZOV, THE(1958), d&w; CAT ON A HOT TIN ROOF(1958), d, w; ELMER GANTRY(1960), d&w; SWEET BIRD OF YOUTH(1962), d&w; LORD JIM(1965, Brit.), p,d&w; PROFESSIONALS, THE(1966), p,d&w; IN COLD BLOOD(1967), p,d&w; HAPPY ENDING, THE(1969), p,d&w; BITE THE BULLET(1975), p,d&w; LOOKING FOR MR. GOODBAR(1977), d&w; WRONG IS RIGHT(1982), p,d&w
Richard C. Brooks
BELIEVE IN ME(1971), ph
Richard E. Brooks
TEENAGE MOTHER(1967), ph; NATURAL ENEMIES(1979), ph

Robert Brooks
HEARTS IN DIXIE(1929)
Rolland Brooks
MAN AND BOY(1972), art d
Rolland M. Brooks
TEENAGE MILLIONAIRE(1961), art d; X-15(1961), art d; CARETAKERS, THE(1963), art d; BEN(1972), art d; CANCEL MY RESERVATION(1972), art d
Sammy Brooks
Silents
GRANDMA'S BOY(1922)
Sebastian Brooks
ROSEMARY'S BABY(1968)
Shelton Brooks
HARLEM IS HEAVEN(1932), m; ADVENTURES OF KITTY O'DAY(1944)
Misc. Talkies
UP JUMPED THE DEVIL(1941)
Ted Brooks
Misc. Silents
MARKED MEN(1920); TWO KINDS OF LOVE(1920); BLACK SHEEP(1921)
Teri Brooks
HOMICIDAL(1961)
Terri Foster Brooks
HARD COUNTRY(1981)
Theodore Brooks
Misc. Silents
RIDER OF THE LAW(1919)
Thomas Brooks
Silents
RIGHT WAY, THE(1921)
Thor Brooks
CALYPSO JOE(1957), ed; BULLWHIP(1958), ed; LEGION OF THE DOOMED(1958), d; SEVEN GUNS TO MESA(1958), ed; ARSON FOR HIRE(1959), d; THEY RAN FOR THEIR LIVES(1968), ed; REBEL ROUSERS(1970), ed
Tom Brooks
Silents
MISCHIEF MAKER, THE(1916)
Misc. Silents
CHILD OF THE WILD, A(1917)
Tony Brooks
KILL, THE(1968)
Tyler Brooks
MRS. WIGGS OF THE CABBAGE PATCH(1934); TO MARY–WITH LOVE(1936); ALEXANDER'S RAGTIME BAND(1938)
Van Brooks
1984
BLOOD SIMPLE(1984)
Van Dyke Brooks
Silents
STRAIGHT IS THE WAY(1921)
Misc. Silents
CRIMSON CROSS, THE(1921)
Victor Brooks
HOSTAGE, THE(1956, Brit.); NO TIME FOR TEARS(1957, Brit.); DANGEROUS YOUTH(1958, Brit.); FURTHER UP THE CREEK!(1958, Brit.); LONG KNIFE, THE(1958, Brit.); MOONRAKER, THE(1958, Brit.); STRANGE AFFECTION(1959, Brit.); WHIRLPOOL(1959, Brit.); BRIDES OF DRACULA, THE(1960, Brit.); COVER GIRL KILLER(1960, Brit.); FOLLOW THAT HORSE!(1960, Brit.); IN THE NICK(1960, Brit.); IT TAKES A THIEF(1960, Brit.); JACKPOT(1960, Brit.); PRICE OF SILENCE, THE(1960, Brit.); OFFBEAT(1961, Brit.); LISA(1962, Brit.); ROAD TO HONG KONG, THE(1962, U.S./Brit.); DAY OF THE TRIFFIDS, THE(1963); EYES OF ANNIE JONES, THE(1963, Brit.); FAST LADY, THE(1963, Brit.); DOWNFALL(1964, Brit.); GUTTER GIRLS(1964, Brit.); LIFE IN DANGER(1964, Brit.); NO, MY DARLING DAUGHTER(1964, Brit.); NO TREE IN THE STREET(1964, Brit.); WITCHCRAFT(1964, Brit.); YOUNG AND WILLING(1964, Brit.); BRAIN, THE(1965, Ger./Brit.); DEVILS OF DARKNESS, THE(1965, Brit.); MURDER GAME, THE(1966, Brit.)
Wallace Brooks
COWBOYS, THE(1972)
Wally Brooks
APPLE DUMPLING GANG RIDES AGAIN, THE(1979)
Wayne Brooks
FOURTEEN, THE(1973, Brit.)
William Brooks
I'LL BE YOURS(1947); MICHIGAN KID, THE(1947); SONG OF SCHEHERAZA-DE(1947)
Brooks-Carrington
IT'S A WONDERFUL DAY(1949, Brit.), ph
Robert Brooks-Turner
POOR OLD BILL(1931, Brit.)
Tom Brookshier
BLACK SUNDAY(1977)
Bill Brookshire
ROCK BABY, ROCK IT(1957)
Marianne Broom
ALFIE DARLING(1975, Brit.)
Alfred Broome
WOMAN FOR JOE, THE(1955, Brit.), ed
Marianne Broome
SLIPPER AND THE ROSE, THE(1976, Brit.); LEGACY, THE(1979, Brit.)
Ray Broome
THUNDERING TRAIL, THE(1951); VANISHING OUTPOST, THE(1951)
Broome Bros
SQUARE DANCE JUBILEE(1949)
Broome Brothers
KENTUCKY JUBILEE(1951)
LeRoy Broomfield
VIRGINIA JUDGE, THE(1935)
Dorothy Broomham
ROOT OF ALL EVIL, THE(1947, Brit.), cos

Martin Broones
MYSTERIOUS ISLAND(1929), m; SO THIS IS COLLEGE(1929), m
Huib Broos
LIFT, THE(1983, Neth.)
Ed Brophy
FLESH(1932); WOMAN TRAP(1936); VARSITY SHOW(1937); GOLD DIGGERS IN PARIS(1938); GAMBLING SHIP(1939); KID FROM KOKOMO, THE(1939); KID NIGHTINGALE(1939); BUY ME THAT TOWN(1941); LADY BODYGUARD(1942); DESTROYER(1943); COVER GIRL(1944)
Edward Brophy
BLUSHING BRIDES(1930); DOUGH BOYS(1930); OUR BLUSHING BRIDES(1930); REMOTE CONTROL(1930); THOSE THREE FRENCH GIRLS(1930); CHAMP, THE(1931); DANGEROUS AFFAIR, A(1931); FREE SOUL, A(1931); PARLOR, BED-ROOM AND BATH(1931); FREAKS(1932); SPEAK EASILY(1932); BROADWAY TO HOLLYWOOD(1933); WHAT! NO BEER?(1933); DEATH OF THE DIAMOND(1934); EVELYN PRENTICE(1934); HIDE-OUT(1934); I'LL FIX IT(1934); PARIS INTER-LUDE(1934); POOR RICH, THE(1934); THIN MAN, THE(1934); CHINA SEAS(1935); I LIVE MY LIFE(1935); MAD LOVE(1935); NAUGHTY MARIETTA(1935); PEOPLE WILL TALK(1935); REMEMBER LAST NIGHT(1935); SHADOW OF A DOUBT(1935); SHE GETS HER MAN(1935); SHOW THEM NO MERCY(1935); WHOLE TOWN'S TALKING, THE(1935); $1,000 A MINUTE(1935); ALL-AMERICAN CHUMP(1936); CASE AGAINST MRS. AMES, THE(1936); GREAT GUY(1936); HERE COMES TROU-BLE(1936); KELLY THE SECOND(1936); MISTER CINDERELLA(1936); SPEND-THRIFT(1936); STRIKE ME PINK(1936); WEDDING PRESENT(1936); BLOSSOMS ON BROADWAY(1937); GREAT GAMBINI, THE(1937); HIDEAWAY GIRL(1937); HIT PARADE, THE(1937); JIM HANVEY, DETECTIVE(1937); LAST GANGSTER, THE(1937); OH DOCTOR(1937); SOLDIER AND THE LADY, THE(1937); TRAPPED BY G-MEN(1937); COME ON, LEATHERNECKS(1938); ROMANCE ON THE RUN(1938); SLIGHT CASE OF MURDER, A(1938); AMAZING MR. WILLIAMS(1939); BIG GUY, THE(1939); FOR LOVE OR MONEY(1939); PARDON OUR NERVE(1939); YOU CAN'T CHEAT AN HONEST MAN(1939); ALIAS THE DEACON(1940); CALLING PHILO VANCE(1940); DANCE, GIRL, DANCE(1940); GREAT PROFILE, THE(1940); SANDY GETS HER MAN(1940); BRIDE CAME C.O.D., THE(1941); DANGEROUS GAME, A(1941); DUMBO(1941); INVISIBLE WOMAN, THE(1941); NINE LIVES ARE NOT ENOUGH(1941); SLEEPERS WEST(1941); STEEL AGAINST THE SKY(1941); THIEVES FALL OUT(1941); ALL THROUGH THE NIGHT(1942); MADAME SPY(1942); AIR FORCE(1943); IT HAPPENED TOMORROW(1944); NIGHT OF AD-VENTURE, A(1944); THIN MAN GOES HOME, THE(1944); RENEGADE GIRL(1946); SWEETHEART OF SIGMA CHI(1946); SWING PARADE OF 1946(1946); IT HAP-PENED ON 5TH AVENUE(1947); ARSON, INC.(1949); DANGER ZONE(1951); PIER 23(1951); ROARING CITY(1951); LAST HURRAH, THE(1958); TWO RODE TOGETH-ER(1961)
Silents
CAMERAMAN, THE(1928)
Edward J. Brophy
GIRL SAID NO, THE(1937)
Edward S. Brophy
CAREER WOMAN(1936); HOLD THAT KISS(1938); PASSPORT HUSBAND(1938); VACATION FROM LOVE(1938); GOLDEN BOY(1939); SOCIETY LAWYER(1939); GOLDEN GLOVES(1940); GAY FALCON, THE(1941); BROADWAY(1942); LARCENY, INC.(1942); SCREAM IN THE DARK, A(1943); FALCON IN SAN FRANCISCO, THE(1945); I'LL REMEMBER APRIL(1945); PENTHOUSE RHYTHM(1945); SEE MY LAWYER(1945); WONDER MAN(1945); FALCON'S ADVENTURE, THE(1946); GIRL ON THE SPOT(1946); BUNDLE OF JOY(1956)
John Brophy
IMMORTAL SERGEANT, THE(1943), w; FIXED BAYONETS(1951), w; WATER-FRONT WOMEN(1952, Brit.), w; DAY THEY ROBBED THE BANK OF ENGLAND, THE(1960, Brit.), w
Kevin Brophy
LONG RIDERS, THE(1980); HELL NIGHT(1981); SEDUCTION, THE(1982); TIME WALKER(1982)
Lee John Brophy
TURN THE KEY SOFTLY(1954, Brit.), w
Noel Brophy
THEY'RE A WEIRD MOB(1966, Aus.)
Richard Brophy
HONEYMOON KILLERS, THE(1969), ed
Sallie Brophy
STORM CENTER(1956); GREEN-EYED BLONDE, THE(1957)
Peter Brosco
RING, THE(1952)
Gunter Brosda
JOURNEY TO THE LOST CITY(1960, Ger./Fr./Ital.), cos
Bill Brosie
JOSEPH ANDREWS(1977, Brit.), art d
Eugen Brosig
TREMENDOUSLY RICH MAN, A(1932, Ger.)
Gino Brosio
SPIRIT AND THE FLESH, THE(1948, Ital.), ed; NAKED MAJA, THE(1959, Ital./U.S.), set d; SODOM AND GOMORRAH(1962, U.S./Fr./Ital.), set d; SENSO(1968, Ital.), set d
Valentino Brosio
SPIRIT AND THE FLESH, THE(1948, Ital.), d; DISILLUSION(1949, Ital.), p
Octavia Broske
Silents
SHE LOVES AND LIES(1920)
Misc. Silents
GREAT ADVENTURE, THE(1921)
Gerald Brosnan
MOUNTAINS O'MOURNE(1938, Brit.), w
Pierce Brosnan
LONG GOOD FRIDAY, THE(1982, Brit.)
Claude Brosset
SHOCK TROOPS(1968, Ital./Fr.); LITTLE ROMANCE, A(1979, U.S./Fr.)
1984
MY NEW PARTNER(1984, Fr.)
Colette Brosset
LA BELLE AMERICAINE(1961, Fr.); PEEK-A-BOO(1961, Fr.), a, ch; COUNTERFEIT CONSTABLE, THE(1966, Fr.), a, w; DON'T LOOK NOW(1969, Brit./Fr.)

Yvonne Brosset
LESSON IN LOVE, A(1960, Swed.)

Gudrun Brost
NIGHT IN JUNE, A(1940, Swed.); NAKED NIGHT, THE(1956, Swed.); SEVENTH SEAL, THE(1958, Swed.); VIRGIN SPRING, THE(1960, Swed.); JUST ONCE MORE(1963, Swed.); HERE'S YOUR LIFE(1968, Swed.); HOUR OF THE WOLF, THE(1968, Swed.)

Gunnel Brostrom
RAILROAD WORKERS(1948, Swed.); WILD STRAWBERRIES(1959, Swed.); DEVIL'S MESSENGER, THE(1962 U.S./Swed.)

Jerzy Broszkiewicz
GREAT BIG WORLD AND LITTLE CHILDREN, THE(1962, Pol.), w

Dr. Joyce Brothers
STAND UP AND BE COUNTED(1972); WAR BETWEEN MEN AND WOMEN, THE(1972); EMBRYO(1976); HERO AT LARGE(1980); OH GOD! BOOK II(1980); KING OF COMEDY, THE(1983)
1984
LONELY GUY, THE(1984)

John Brothers
POLYESTER(1981)

Robert Brothers
TIN PAN ALLEY(1940)

Arnaut Brothers
TILL THE CLOUDS ROLL BY(1946)

Condos Brothers
IN THE NAVY(1941)

Cromwell Brothers
DUAL ALIBI(1947, Brit.)

Glaser Brothers
COUNTRY BOY(1966)

Hakim Brothers
BAKER'S WIFE, THE(1940, Fr.), p

Hudson Brothers
ZERO TO SIXTY(1978)

Nicholas Brothers
DOWN ARGENTINE WAY(1940); SUN VALLEY SERENADE(1941)

Rios Brothers
MAIN ATTRACTION, THE(1962, Brit.)

Ritz Brothers
ONE IN A MILLION(1936); SING, BABY, SING(1936)

The Seven Imeson Brothers
IT'S A WONDERFUL DAY(1949, Brit.)

The Tur brothers
DEVOTION(1955, USSR), w

Wilburn Brothers
NASHVILLE REBEL(1966)

Williams Brothers
JANIE(1944)

The Brothers and Sisters of Local 890, International Union of Mine, Mill and Smelter Workers, Bayard, New Mexico
SALT OF THE EARTH(1954)

The Brothers Candoli
BELL, BOOK AND CANDLE(1958)

The Brothers Four
HOOTENANNY HOOT(1963)

The Brothers Grimm
HANSEL AND GRETEL(1954), w; TOM THUMB(1958, Brit./U.S.), w

Eric Brotherson
BLACULA(1972); WHAT'S UP, DOC?(1972)

David Brotherton
KING AND FOUR QUEENS, THE(1956), ed; THREE BRAVE MEN(1957), ed; DIARY OF ANNE FRANK, THE(1959), ed

Joe Brotherton
TARZAN THE FEARLESS(1933), ph

Joseph Brotherton
MELODY LANE(1929), ph
Silents
ANGEL CHILD(1918), ph; NOTORIOUS MISS LISLE, THE(1920), ph; BEAUTIFUL LIAR, THE(1921), ph; STRANGER THAN FICTION(1921), ph; LONELY ROAD, THE(1923), ph; MONEY! MONEY! MONEY!(1923), ph; SCARLET LILY, THE(1923), ph; WHEN ODDS ARE EVEN(1923), ph; AGAINST ALL ODDS(1924), ph; WESTERN LUCK(1924), ph; BEAUTY AND BULLETS(1928), ph; SILKS AND SADDLES(1929), ph

Walt Brotherton
1984
PRODIGAL, THE(1984)

Stuart Brotman
RACE FOR YOUR LIFE, CHARLIE BROWN(1977)

Hubert Brotten
ACE ELI AND RODGER OF THE SKIES(1973)

Alba Brotto
EMBALMER, THE(1966, Ital.)

Jerry Brouer
SERGEANT, THE(1968); THINGS OF LIFE, THE(1970, Fr./Ital./Switz.); STATE OF SIEGE(1973, Fr./U.S./Ital./Ger.); DESTRUCTORS, THE(1974, Brit.)

Albert Brouett
WOULD YOU BELIEVE IT!(1930, Brit.)
Silents
ROGUE IN LOVE, A(1922, Brit.), d; PARADISE(1928, Brit.); BROKEN MELODY, THE(1929, Brit.)
Misc. Silents
WOULD YOU BELIEVE IT!(1929, Brit.)

Max Brouggy
SUNSTRUCK(1973, Aus.)

Antonia Brough
SONG OF SOHO(1930, Brit.); SPANISH EYES(1930, Brit.); UNDER THE GREENWOOD TREE(1930, Brit.); MURDER IN THE OLD RED BARN(1936, Brit.)
Silents
FARMER'S WIFE, THE(1928, Brit.)

Arthur Brough
GREEN MAN, THE(1957, Brit.); IT TAKES A THIEF(1960, Brit.); MAKE MINE A DOUBLE(1962, Brit.); DEAD MAN'S CHEST(1965, Brit.)

Candi Brough
DR. HECKYL AND MR. HYPE(1980); PANDEMONIUM(1982)
1984
CHATTANOOGA CHOO CHOO(1984); LONELY GUY, THE(1984)

Jean Webster Brough
CHEER BOYS CHEER(1939, Brit.)

Mary Brough
ON APPROVAL(1930, Brit.); ONE EMBARRASSING NIGHT(1930, Brit.); TONS OF MONEY(1931, Brit.); NIGHT LIKE THIS, A(1932, Brit.); THARK(1932, Brit.); CUCKOO IN THE NEST, THE(1933, Brit.); TURKEY TIME(1933, Brit.); UP TO THE NECK(1933, Brit.)
Silents
ENCHANTMENT(1920, Brit.); JUDGE NOT(1920, Brit.); LONDON PRIDE(1920, Brit.); ADVENTURES OF MR. PICKWICK, THE(1921, Brit.); ALL SORTS AND CONDITIONS OF MEN(1921, Brit.); BACHELORS' CLUB, THE(1921, Brit.); DIAMOND NECKLACE, THE(1921, Brit.); OLD WIVES' TALE, THE(1921, Brit.); SQUIBS(1921, Brit.); SISTER TO ASSIST 'ER, A(1922, Brit.); SQUIBS WINS THE CALCUTTA SWEEP(1922, Brit.); LILY OF THE ALLEY(1923, Brit.); ALLEY OF GOLDEN HEARTS, THE(1924, Brit.); MIRIAM ROZELLA(1924, Brit.); NOT FOR SALE(1924, Brit.); PASSIONATE ADVENTURE, THE(1924, Brit.); ONLY WAY, THE(1926, Brit.); SAFETY FIRST(1926, Brit.); SISTER TO ASSIST 'ER, A(1927, Brit.); DAWN(1928, Brit.); PASSING OF MR. QUIN, THE(1928, Brit.); PHYSICIAN, THE(1928, Brit.); BROKEN MELODY, THE(1929, Brit.)
Misc. Silents
FORDINGTON TWINS, THE(1920, Brit.); LAW DIVINE, THE(1920, Brit.); TONS OF MONEY(1924, Brit.)

Randi Brough
DR. HECKYL AND MR. HYPE(1980); PANDEMONIUM(1982)
1984
CHATTANOOGA CHOO CHOO(1984); LONELY GUY, THE(1984)

Walter Brough
DESPERADOS, THE(1969), w; FUNERAL FOR AN ASSASSIN(1977), p, w

Bob Broughton
WATCHER IN THE WOODS, THE(1980, Brit.), spec eff

Bruce Broughton
1984
ICE PIRATES, THE(1984), m; PRODIGAL, THE(1984), m

Cliff Broughton
DUDE WRANGLER, THE(1930), p; MIDNIGHT MORALS(1932), p; MONSTER WALKS, THE(1932), p; NO LIVING WITNESS(1932), p

George Broughton
LASSIE, COME HOME(1943); MAN IN HALF-MOON STREET, THE(1944); MINISTRY OF FEAR(1945); CALCUTTA(1947)

Jayne Broughton
1984
POLICE ACADEMY(1984)

Lewis Broughton
REMBRANDT(1936, Brit.)

Louis Broughton
MR. WHAT'S-HIS-NAME(1935, Brit.)
Misc. Silents
WOMAN GAME, THE(1920)

Pascale Brouillard
PARIS PICK-UP(1963, Fr./Ital.)

Alexander Broun
Misc. Silents
HELL DIGGERS, THE(1921)

Heywood Hale Broun
IT SHOULD HAPPEN TO YOU(1954); ODD COUPLE, THE(1968); SOME KIND OF A NUT(1969); FOR PETE'S SAKE(1977)

H. H. Brounell
WEST OF THE ROCKIES(1931), ph

Ella Brouner
SUNDOWN RIDERS(1948), ed

Eddie Broussard
PRIVATE LIVES OF ADAM AND EVE, THE(1961), ed

Everett H. Broussard
INCREDIBLE SHRINKING MAN, THE(1957), spec eff

Liliane Brousse
IMMORAL CHARGE(1962, Brit.); THUNDER IN THE BLOOD(1962, Fr.); HOT HOURS(1963, Fr.); MANIAC(1963, Brit.); PARANOIAC(1963, Brit.)

Paul Brousse
TOWN ON TRIAL(1957, Brit.), m

Pierre Brousseau
TANYA'S ISLAND(1981, Can.), p, w; FUNNY FARM, THE(1982, Can.), m

Jean-Louis Broust
MILKY WAY, THE(1969, Fr./Ital.)

Alexandra Brouwer
SHADES OF SILK(1979, Can.)

Chris Brouwer
GIRL WITH THE RED HAIR, THE(1983, Neth.), p

Jerry Brouwer
FIVE DAYS ONE SUMMER(1982)

Leo Brouwer
DEATH OF A BUREAUCRAT(1979, Cuba), m

Peter Brouwer
FRIDAY THE 13TH(1980)
1984
FRIDAY THE 13TH-THE FINAL CHAPTER(1984)

Angelo Brovelli
LOVE AND KISSES(1965)

V. Brovkin
SUMMER TO REMEMBER, A(1961, USSR)

Billy Brow
HITLER'S CHILDREN(1942)

Harry Joe Brow
DESPERADOES, THE(1943), p
Carl Browallius
ON THE SUNNYSIDE(1936, Swed.); OCEAN BREAKERS(1949, Swed.)
Hollywood Browde
FIST OF FEAR, TOUCH OF DEATH(1980)
Barbara Brower
Silents
SALOMY JANE(1923)
Bart Brower
WHEN THE LEGENDS DIE(1972)
Dorcas Brower
ICE PALACE(1960)
Leo Brower
ALSINO AND THE CONDOR(1983, Nicaragua), m
Mitchell Brower
MC CABE AND MRS. MILLER(1971), p; GETAWAY, THE(1972), p
Otto Brower
UNDER TWO FLAGS(1936), d; BORDER LEGION, THE(1930), d; LIGHT OF WESTERN STARS, THE(1930), d; SANTA FE TRAIL, THE(1930), d; CLEARING THE RANGE(1931), d; FIGHTING CARAVANS(1931), d; HARD HOMBRE(1931), d; GOLD(1932), d; LAW OF THE SEA(1932), d; LOCAL BAD MAN(1932), d; SPIRIT OF THE WEST(1932), d; CROSSFIRE(1933), d; HEADLINE SHOOTER(1933), d; PLEASURE(1933), d; SCARLET RIVER(1933), d; I CAN'T ESCAPE(1934), d; SPEED WINGS(1934), d; STRAIGHTAWAY(1934), d; OUTLAW DEPUTY, THE(1935), d; POSTAL INSPECTOR(1936), d; SINS OF MAN(1936), d; ROAD DEMON(1938), d; SPEED TO BURN(1938), d; SUEZ(1938), d; STANLEY AND LIVINGSTONE(1939), ph; STOP, LOOK, AND LOVE(1939), d; TOO BUSY TO WORK(1939), d; WINNER TAKE ALL(1939), d; GAY CABALLERO, THE(1940), d; GIRL FROM AVENUE A(1940), d; ON THEIR OWN(1940), d; YOUTH WILL BE SERVED(1940), d; LITTLE TOKYO, U.S.A.(1942), d; DIXIE DUGAN(1943), d; BEHIND GREEN LIGHTS(1946), d
Misc. Talkies
FIGHTING FOR JUSTICE(1932), d
Silents
EXCUSE MY DUST(1920); ON THE HIGH SEAS(1922); ALL THE BROTHERS WERE VALIANT(1923); AVALANCHE(1928), d; STAIRS OF SAND(1929), d; SUNSET PASS(1929), d
Misc. Silents
SUNSET PASS(1929), d
Robert Brower
BEGGARS OF LIFE(1928); ABRAHAM LINCOLN(1930)
Silents
QUEST OF LIFE, THE(1916); HAWTHORNE OF THE U.S.A.(1919); CUMBERLAND ROMANCE, A(1920); JACK STRAW(1920); FAITH HEALER, THE(1921); WHAT EVERY WOMAN KNOWS(1921); MAN WHO SAW TOMORROW, THE(1922); SINGED WINGS(1922); THIRTY DAYS(1922); ADAM'S RIB(1923); LONG LIVE THE KING(1923); RACING HEARTS(1923); WILD OATS LANE(1926); LAST TRAIL, THE(1927)
Misc. Silents
GREAT PHYSICIAN, THE(1913); NECKLACE OF RAMESES, THE(1914); FRIEND WILSON'S DAUGHTER(1915); MATCH-MAKERS, THE(1916); BUILDERS OF CASTLES(1917); ROSE OF THE RIVER(1919); SOMETHING TO DO(1919); RIDERS UP(1924)
Thomas Brower
Silents
HOOK AND LADDER NO. 9(1927)
Thomas L. Brower
MAID OF SALEM(1937)
Tom Brower
SINGING VAGABOND, THE(1935); LAWLESS NINETIES, THE(1936); LOVE BEGINS AT TWENTY(1936); CALIFORNIA MAIL, THE(1937); CHEROKEE STRIP(1937); EMPTY HOLSTERS(1937); LAND BEYOND THE LAW(1937); THEY WON'T FORGET(1937)
Fred Browett
POISONED DIAMOND, THE(1934, Brit.), p; SOMETIMES GOOD(1934, Brit.), p; LEND ME YOUR WIFE(1935, Brit.), p; LUCKY JADE(1937, Brit.), p
Ricou Browning
REVENGE OF THE CREATURE(1955)
Tod Browing
Misc. Silents
LOVE SUBLIME, A(1917), d; DECIDING KISS, THE(1918), d; DOLLAR DOWN(1925), d
Brown
TRAP, THE(1967, Can./Brit.), p
A. J. Brown
MAN WITH THE GREEN CARNATION, THE(1960, Brit.); CLUE OF THE TWISTED CANDLE(1968, Brit.); CLEGG(1969, Brit.)
A.J. Brown
CIRCLE OF DECEPTON(1961, Brit.); TRAITORS, THE(1963, Brit.); WALK A TIGHTROPE(1964, U.S./Brit.); WOMAN OF STRAW(1964, Brit.); LAST GRENADE, THE(1970, Brit.); HANDS OF THE RIPPER(1971, Brit.); FLAME(1975, Brit.)
Ada Brown
STORMY WEATHER(1943)
Al Brown
JOHN PAUL JONES(1959); CUBAN REBEL GIRLS(1960); SOLOMON KING(1974), art d
Alan Brown
RACE FOR LIFE, A(1955, Brit.); TRUTH ABOUT SPRING, THE(1965, Brit.), p
Albert Brown, Jr.
MARDI GRAS MASSACRE(1978), makeup
Alex A. Brown
DIRTY HARRY(1971); EARTHQUAKE(1974); BRUBAKER(1980); WHITE DOG(1982)
Alex Brown
BLACK BELT JONES(1974); SHEBA BABY(1975), m; UNDER FIRE(1983)
1984
NIGHT OF THE COMET(1984)
Alfred Brown
SEVENTH VOYAGE OF SINBAD, THE(1958); CRACK IN THE WORLD(1965)

Alfredine Brown
BEING THERE(1979)
Alfredine P. Brown
D.C. CAB(1983)
Alonzo Brown
ONE FLEW OVER THE CUCKOO'S NEST(1975)
Alton Brown
Silents
ALIMONY(1924)
Amelda Brown
BIDDY(1983, Brit.)
Andrea Brown
GOLDENGIRL(1979)
Andrew Brown
MY FAIR LADY(1964)
Anita Brown
TWENTIETH CENTURY(1934); CHARLIE CHAN IN EGYPT(1935); SLAVE SHIP(1937); SONG OF THE SOUTH(1946)
Silents
EYE FOR EYE(1918)
Anna Lynn Brown
LAST MOVIE, THE(1971); WEREWOLVES ON WHEELS(1971)
Anne Brown
RHAPSODY IN BLUE(1945)
Anthony Brown
SOPHOMORE, THE(1929), w; LITTLE ACCIDENT(1930), w; SWEENEY(1977, Brit.)
1984
GIVE MY REGARDS TO BROAD STREET(1984, Brit.)
Arnold Brown
1984
COMFORT AND JOY(1984, Brit.)
Arnolda Brown
EVERY GIRL SHOULD BE MARRIED(1948)
Arthur Brown
TOMMY(1975, Brit.)
Arthur Brown, Jr.
CLAMBAKE(1967), w
Arthur William Brown
ARTISTS AND MODELS(1937)
Barbara Brown
MELODY LANE(1941); THREE GIRLS ABOUT TOWN(1941); YOU BELONG TO ME(1941); MEET THE STEWARTS(1942); PARACHUTE NURSE(1942); THERE'S ONE BORN EVERY MINUTE(1942); WIFE TAKES A FLYER, THE(1942); YOU WERE NEVER LOVELIER(1942); FALCON AND THE CO-EDS, THE(1943); LAUGH YOUR BLUES AWAY(1943); MISSION TO MOSCOW(1943); MOONLIGHT IN VERMONT(1943); NEVER A DULL MOMENT(1943); REVEILLE WITH BEVERLY(1943); SHE HAS WHAT IT TAKES(1943); TOP MAN(1943); WHAT A WOMAN!(1943); DOUGHGIRLS, THE(1944); GHOST THAT WALKS ALONE, THE(1944); HEY, ROOKIE(1944); HOLLYWOOD CANTEEN(1944); JANIE(1944); SULLIVANS, THE(1944); MILDRED PIERCE(1945); PILLOW TO POST(1945); ROUGHLY SPEAKING(1945); TOO YOUNG TO KNOW(1945); BEAST WITH FIVE FINGERS, THE(1946); JANIE GETS MARRIED(1946); MAN I LOVE, THE(1946); PERSONALITY KID(1946); WHITE TIE AND TAILS(1946); HIGH BARBAREE(1947); LOVE AND LEARN(1947); THAT HAGEN GIRL(1947); THAT WAY WITH WOMEN(1947); ARTHUR TAKES OVER(1948); WALLFLOWER(1948); HENRY, THE RAINMAKER(1949); LEAVE IT TO HENRY(1949); MISS MINK OF 1949(1949); YES SIR, THAT'S MY BABY(1949); FATHER MAKES GOOD(1950); FATHER'S WILD GAME(1950); MA AND PA KETTLE GO TO TOWN(1950); BORN YESTERDAY(1951); FATHER TAKES THE AIR(1951); HOME TOWN STORY(1951); LADY AND THE BANDIT, THE(1951); MA AND PA KETTLE BACK ON THE FARM(1951); BRIGAND, THE(1952); JACK AND THE BEANSTALK(1952); YOU FOR ME(1952); MA AND PA KETTLE ON VACATION(1953); ANNAPOLIS STORY, AN(1955); MY SISTER EILEEN(1955); SINCERELY YOURS(1955); TWO GROOMS FOR A BRIDE(1957); TERROR OF THE TONGS, THE(1961, Brit.); DOG AND THE DIAMONDS, THE(1962, Brit.); GONKS GO BEAT(1965, Brit.); RED, WHITE AND BLACK, THE(1970)
Barbara Ann Brown
WICKER MAN, THE(1974, Brit.)
Barry Brown
HALLS OF ANGER(1970); WAY WE LIVE NOW, THE(1970), p&d, w, ph, ed; BAD COMPANY(1972); GREAT NORTHFIELD, MINNESOTA RAID, THE(1972); DAISY MILLER(1974); ULTIMATE THRILL, THE(1974); PIRANHA(1978); CLOUD DANCER(1980), p&d, w
Becky Brown
SHADOW OF A WOMAN(1946); ODE TO BILLY JOE(1976)
Ben Brown
TERROR IN THE WAX MUSEUM(1973)
Bernard B. Brown
MR. MUGGS RIDES AGAIN(1945)
Bernard Brown
SCREAM OF FEAR(1961, Brit.); RED, WHITE AND BLACK, THE(1970); BATTLE OF LOVE'S RETURN(1971)
Milton M. Raison Bert C. Brown
SOUTHSIDE 1-1000(1950), w
Beth Brown
APPLAUSE(1929), w; INSURANCE INVESTIGATOR(1951), w
Bette Rae Brown
CLUNY BROWN(1946)
Betty Brown
Misc. Silents
CALL OF THE SEA, THE(1915); VILLAGE HOMESTEAD, THE(1915); DISCARD, THE(1916); HELL'S OASIS(1920)
Betty Jane Brown
LET'S MAKE IT LEGAL(1951)
Beverly Brown
1984
PREPPIES(1984)
Beverly C. Brown
PANIC IN THE STREETS(1950)

Bill D. Brown
STROKER ACE(1983)
Billy Brown
HARLEM GLOBETROTTERS, THE(1951)
Blair Brown
CHOIRBOYS, THE(1977); ALTERED STATES(1980); ONE-TRICK PONY(1980); CONTINENTAL DIVIDE(1981)
1984
FLASH OF GREEN, A(1984)
Bob Brown
HIGH YELLOW(1965); STREET IS MY BEAT, THE(1966); DAY AFTER HALLOWEEN, THE(1981, Aus.)
Bobbie Brown
FLASH GORDON(1980)
Boots Brown
MY BUDDY(1944); TOMORROW THE WORLD(1944)
Brendon Brown
LITTLE JUNGLE BOY(1969, Aus.), ph
Brian Brown
SALLY FIELDGOOD & CO.(1975, Can.)
Bridget Brown
LADY TAKES A SAILOR, THE(1949); YOUNG MAN WITH A HORN(1950)
Bruce Brown
PASSION HOLIDAY(1963)
Bryan Brown
IRISHMAN, THE(1978, Aus.); MONEY MOVERS(1978, Aus.); CATHY'S CHILD(1979, Aus.); NEWSFRONT(1979, Aus.); ODD ANGRY SHOT, THE(1979, Aus.); PALM BEACH(1979, Aus.); BREAKER MORANT(1980, Aus.); CHANT OF JIMMIE BLACKSMITH, THE(1980, Aus.); STIR(1980, Aus.); WINTER OF OUR DREAMS(1982, Aus.)
1984
GIVE MY REGARDS TO BROAD STREET(1984, Brit.)
Misc. Talkies
LOVELETTERS FROM TERALBA ROAD(1977)
Bubbles Brown
Silents
POSSESSION(1919, Brit.)
Bud Brown
SIERRA SUE(1941)
Buff Brown
DALTON'S WOMEN, THE(1950)
Burton Brown
WHAT DO WE DO NOW?(1945, Brit.)
C. Harding Brown
ON THE BEACH(1959)
Cal Brown
SPLIT, THE(1968)
Calvin Brown
...TICK...TICK...TICK...(1970); MIXED COMPANY(1974)
Calvin Brown, Jr.
Misc. Talkies
DUNCAN'S WORLD(1977)
Campbell Brown
DAVY CROCKETT, KING OF THE WILD FRONTIER(1955)
Campbell Rae Brown
KISSING CUP'S RACE(1930, Brit.), w
Silents
KISSING CUP'S RACE(1920, Brit.), w
Candy Ann Brown
UP THE ACADEMY(1980)
Candy Brown
HEART BEAT(1979)
Carlos Brown
NO EXIT(1962, U.S./Arg.); REMEMBER MY NAME(1978); NORTH DALLAS FORTY(1979); POPEYE(1980); SOUTHERN COMFORT(1981)
Carmen Brown
STRANGE WORLD(1952)
Carol Brown [Bruno Carotentuto]
FISTFUL OF DOLLARS, A(1964, Ital./Ger./Span.); SECRET AGENT FIREBALL(1965, Fr./Ital.)
Carol Curtis Brown
ICELAND(1942)
Cecil Brown
WHICH WAY IS UP?(1977), w
Charles Brown
ICE FOLLIES OF 1939(1939); FLORIAN(1940); OLD SWIMMIN' HOLE, THE(1941); TRADING PLACES(1983); WITHOUT A TRACE(1983)
Silents
NIGHT OUT, A(1916)
Misc. Silents
DUST OF EGYPT, THE(1915)
Charles D. Brown
DANCE OF LIFE, THE(1929); DANGEROUS CURVES(1929); MURDER BY THE CLOCK(1931); SECRET CALL, THE(1931); TOUCHDOWN!(1931); FALSE MADONNA(1932); GOLD DIGGERS OF 1937(1936); THOROUGHBREDS DON'T CRY(1937); ALGIERS(1938); BAREFOOT BOY(1938); CROWD ROARS, THE(1938); DUKE OF WEST POINT, THE(1938); EXPOSED(1938); FIVE OF A KIND(1938); FLIGHT TO FAME(1938); ISLAND IN THE SKY(1938); MR. MOTO'S GAMBLE(1938); SHOPWORN ANGEL(1938); SPEED TO BURN(1938); UP THE RIVER(1938); CHARLIE CHAN IN RENO(1939); DISBARRED(1939); INSIDE STORY(1939); KID NIGHTINGALE(1939); LITTLE ACCIDENT(1939); MR. MOTO IN DANGER ISLAND(1939); SMASHING THE MONEY RING(1939); TELL NO TALES(1939); BROTHER ORCHID(1940); FORGOTTEN GIRLS(1940); GRAPES OF WRATH(1940); HE MARRIED HIS WIFE(1940); I TAKE THIS WOMAN(1940); JOHNNY APOLLO(1940); LEATHER-PUSHERS, THE(1940); PIER 13(1940); SAILOR'S LADY(1940); SANTA FE TRAIL(1940); WOLF OF NEW YORK(1940); WOMEN IN WAR(1940); DEVIL PAYS OFF, THE(1941); INTERNATIONAL LADY(1941); MAISIE WAS A LADY(1941); REACHING FOR THE SUN(1941); RIDE, KELLY, RIDE(1941); TALL, DARK AND HANDSOME(1941); FINGERS AT THE WINDOW(1942); RIGHT TO THE HEART(1942); ROXIE HART(1942); SWEATER GIRL(1942); BOMBARDIER(1943); IRON MAJOR, THE(1943); LADY TAKES A CHANCE, A(1943); MINESWEEPER(1943); FOLLOW THE BOYS(1944); HERE COME

THE WAVES(1944); JAM SESSION(1944); LADIES OF WASHINGTON(1944); SECRET COMMAND(1944); UP IN ARMS(1944); APOLOGY FOR MURDER(1945); DON JUAN QUILLIGAN(1945); EVE KNEW HER APPLES(1945); HAVING WONDERFUL CRIME(1945); SUNBONNET SUE(1945); BIG SLEEP, THE(1946); BRIDE WORE BOOTS, THE(1946); DANGER WOMAN(1946); HOODLUM SAINT, THE(1946); IN FAST COMPANY(1946); JUST BEFORE DAWN(1946); KILLERS, THE(1946); LAST CROOKED MILE, THE(1946); MAN WHO DARED, THE(1946); NIGHT EDITOR(1946); NOTORIOUS(1946); SEARCHING WIND, THE(1946); STRANGE LOVE OF MARTHA IVERS, THE(1946); TOMORROW IS FOREVER(1946); WAKE UP AND DREAM(1946); MERTON OF THE MOVIES(1947); RAILROADED(1947); SENATOR WAS INDISCREET, THE(1947); SMASH-UP, THE STORY OF A WOMAN(1947); UNDERCOVER MAISIE(1947); I WALK ALONE(1948); I WOULDN'T BE IN YOUR SHOES(1948); IN THIS CORNER(1948); LET'S LIVE AGAIN(1948); ON OUR MERRY WAY(1948); FOLLOW ME QUIETLY(1949)
Silents
WAY OF A MAID, THE(1921)
Charles E. Brown
STROKER ACE(1983)
Charles K. Brown
SPOTLIGHT SCANDALS(1943)
Charles M. Brown
BLONDIE PLAYS CUPID(1940), w
Charles Molyneaux Brown
IRISH LUCK(1939), w; BLONDIE ON A BUDGET(1940), w
Charles W. Brown, Jr.
SHE MAN, THE(1967), p
Charlie Brown
WILD 90(1968), m
Chelsea Brown
SWEET CHARITY(1969); THING WITH TWO HEADS, THE(1972)
Chris Brown
MERRY CHRISTMAS MR. LAWRENCE(1983, Jap./Brit.)
Christopher Brown
1984
BAD MANNERS(1984)
Christopher J. Brown
RITZ, THE(1976)
Christy Brown
LITTLE SEX, A(1982)
Claire P. Brown
THREE GUNS FOR TEXAS(1968), set d; SSSSSSSS(1973), set d; WILLIE DYNAMITE(1973), set d
Clancy Brown
BAD BOYS(1983)
1984
ADVENTURES OF BUCKAROO BANZAI: ACROSS THE 8TH DIMENSION, THE(1984)
Clarence Brown
WONDER OF WOMEN(1929), d; ANNA CHRISTIE(1930), d; NAVY BLUES(1930), d; ROMANCE(1930), d; FREE SOUL, A(1931), d; INSPIRATION(1931), p&d; POSSESSED(1931), d; EMMA(1932), d; LETTY LYNTON(1932), d; SON-DAUGHTER, THE(1932), d; LOOKING FORWARD(1933), p&d; NIGHT FLIGHT(1933), d; CHAINED(1934), d; FIFTEEN WIVES(1934); SADIE MCKEE(1934), d; AH, WILDERNESS!(1935), d; ANNA KARENINA(1935), d; GORGEOUS HUSSY, THE(1936), d; WIFE VERSUS SECRETARY(1936), d; CONQUEST(1937), d; OF HUMAN HEARTS(1938), d; IDIOT'S DELIGHT(1939), d; RAINS CAME, THE(1939), d; EDISON, THE MAN(1940), d; COME LIVE WITH ME(1941), p&d; THEY MET IN BOMBAY(1941), d; HUMAN COMEDY, THE(1943), p&d; NATIONAL VELVET(1944), d; WHITE CLIFFS OF DOVER, THE(1944), d; YEARLING, THE(1946), d; SONG OF LOVE(1947), p&d; INTRUDER IN THE DUST(1949), p&d; SECRET GARDEN, THE(1949), p; TO PLEASE A LADY(1950), p&d; ANGELS IN THE OUTFIELD(1951), p&d; PLYMOUTH ADVENTURE(1952), d; WHEN IN ROME(1952), p&d; NEVER LET ME GO(1953, U.S./Brit.), p
Silents
LAST OF THE MOHICANS, THE(1920), d; ACQUITTAL, THE(1923), d; SIGNAL TOWER, THE(1924); EAGLE, THE(1925), d; GOOSE WOMAN, THE(1925), d; FLESH AND THE DEVIL(1926), d; KIKI(1926), d; WOMAN OF AFFAIRS, A(1928), d; TRAIL OF '98, THE(1929), d
Misc. Silents
GREAT REDEEMER, THE(1920), d; BUTTERFLY(1924), d; SMOULDERING FIRES(1925), d
Clarence L. Brown
Silents
LIGHT IN THE DARK, THE(1922), d, w; DON'T MARRY FOR MONEY(1923), d; SIGNAL TOWER, THE(1924), d
Clarence Brown, Jr.
HAPPY DAYS(1930)
Clifton Brown
Misc. Talkies
MEAN MOTHER(1974)
Coral Brown
GUILTY MELODY(1936, Brit.)
Courtney Brown
FLIPPER'S NEW ADVENTURE(1964); BIRDS DO IT(1966); SPEEDWAY(1968); JOE PANTHER(1976), stunts; SPRING BREAK(1983), stunts
1984
WHERE THE BOYS ARE '84(1984)
D.W. Brown
FAST TIMES AT RIDGEMONT HIGH(1982)
1984
JOY OF SEX(1984); WEEKEND PASS(1984)
Misc. Talkies
SECTOR 13(1982)
Dale Brown
MURDERERS' ROW(1966)
Dana Brown
SPEEDWAY(1968)

Daniel Brown
HEADING FOR HEAVEN(1947), w
Darcy Brown
SHRIEK OF THE MUTILATED(1974)
Misc. Talkies
BACCHANALE(1970)
Darren Brown
CLARENCE AND ANGEL(1981)
David Brown
WILLIE DYNAMITE(1973), p; GIRL FROM PETROVKA, THE(1974), p; SUGAR-LAND EXPRESS, THE(1974), p; JAWS(1975), p; JAWS II(1978), p; ISLAND, THE(1980), p; NEIGHBORS(1981), p; VERDICT, THE(1982), p
Misc. Talkies
DEADLY HARVEST(1972)
David Gavin Brown
PHANTASM(1979), art d
Dayton Brown
CLASS OF MISS MAC MICHAEL, THE(1978, Brit./U.S.)
Dee Brown
Misc. Talkies
DYNAMITE(1972)
Denis Brown
SALTY O'ROURKE(1945)
Dolores Brown
CIMARRON(1931)
Don Brown
PERFECT CLUE, THE(1935), w; SATIN MUSHROOM, THE(1969), d
Don Evan Brown
$1,000 A TOUCHDOWN(1939)
Donald Brown
OLD-FASHIONED WAY, THE(1934)
Donald H. Brown
SING, NEIGHBOR, SING(1944), p; DON'T FENCE ME IN(1945), p; HITCHHIKE TO HAPPINESS(1945), p; UTAH(1945), p; MYSTERIOUS MR. VALENTINE, THE(1946), p; ONE EXCITING WEEK(1946), p; TRAFFIC IN CRIME(1946), p; SPOILERS OF THE NORTH(1947), p; WEB OF DANGER, THE(1947), p
Dorian Brown
TICKLE ME(1965)
Dorothy Brown
GIRL FROM HAVANA, THE(1929)
Dottye Brown
LOUISIANA(1947); SONG OF THE WASTELAND(1947)
Dottye D. Brown
CAMPUS SLEUTH(1948)
Douggie Brown
KES(1970, Brit.)
Drew Bundi Brown
SHAFT'S BIG SCORE(1972)
Drew Bundini Brown
SHAFT(1971)
Drew "Bundini" Brown
GREATEST, THE(1977, U.S./Brit.)
Earl Brown
SALOME(1953); PICKUP ON 101(1972); BLACK BELT JONES(1974)
Earl Brown, Jr.
AMERICATHON(1979), m
Earl Jolly Brown
LIVE AND LET DIE(1973, Brit.)
Earle Brown
LOCKED DOOR, THE(1929), w
Ed Brown
DEALING: OR THE BERKELEY-TO-BOSTON FORTY-BRICK LOST-BAG BLUES(1971), ph; HOT ROCK, THE(1972), ph
Silents
SCARLET SIN, THE(1915)
Misc. Silents
PAY ME(1917)
Edith Brown
TRAPPED(1931), w
Edmond Brown
Misc. Silents
LITTLE BROTHER OF THE RICH, A(1915)
Edward Brown
LOVIN' MOLLY(1974), ph; LORD SHANGO(1975), ph
Misc. Silents
(
Ed Brown, Sr.
AMAZING GRACE(1974), ph; GREAT SMOKEY ROADBLOCK, THE(1978), ph
Edward R. Brown
NUNZIO(1978), ph
Edwin Brown
TWO-WAY STRETCH(1961, Brit.); 10 RILLINGTON PLACE(1971, Brit.); PIED PIPER, THE(1972, Brit.)
Misc. Talkies
SIMPLY IRRESISTIBLE(1983), d
Silents
JENNY BE GOOD(1920)
Edwin Scott Brown
1984
PREY, THE(1984), d, w
Eleanor Brown
ANNIE GET YOUR GUN(1950); SAILOR FROM GIBRALTAR, THE(1967, Brit.)
Eleanora Brown
YOUNG, THE EVIL AND THE SAVAGE, THE(1968, Ital.)
Eleonor Brown
TWO WOMEN(1961, Ital./Fr.)
Eleonora Brown
TIGER AND THE PUSSYCAT, THE(1967, U.S., Ital.)

Elizabeth Brown
BELIEVE IN ME(1971)
Ella Mae Brown
REIVERS, THE(1969)
Elmer Brown
COUNSELLOR-AT-LAW(1933); HOUSE ON 92ND STREET, THE(1945)
Elyse Brown
MILDRED PIERCE(1945); PICTURE OF DORIAN GRAY, THE(1945)
Emmett Brown
HARRY AND WALTER GO TO NEW YORK(1976); RUMBLE FISH(1983)
1984
BODY DOUBLE(1984)
Eric Brown
PRIVATE LESSONS(1981)
1984
THEY'RE PLAYING WITH FIRE(1984)
Errol Brown
ROCKERS(1980)
Esther Brown
TEN COMMANDMENTS, THE(1956)
Everett Brown
HELL'S HEADQUARTERS(1932); I AM A FUGITIVE FROM A CHAIN GANG(1932); NAGANA(1933); KID MILLIONS(1934); NOTHING SACRED(1937); DUKE IS THE TOPS, THE(1938); TEXANS, THE(1938); BLACKMAIL(1939); GONE WITH THE WIND(1939); STANLEY AND LIVINGSTONE(1939); TELL NO TALES(1939); CONGO MAISIE(1940); ZANZIBAR(1940); WHITE WITCH DOCTOR(1953); BOY NAMED CHARLIE BROWN, A(1969), anim
Everett G. Brown
ROPE OF SAND(1949)
Ewing Brown
SHANE(1953); SON OF THE RENEGADE(1953); FRONTIER GAMBLER(1956); WALK THE DARK STREET(1956); ASTOUNDING SHE-MONSTER, THE(1958), ed; VEN-GEANCE(1964), ed; HELL'S CHOSEN FEW(1968), ph; HORROR OF THE BLOOD MONSTERS(1970, U.S./Phil.), ed
Ewing M. Brown
WHALE OF A TALE, A(1977), p&d
Fayte Brown
ARIZONA(1940), ph; HOEDOWN(1950), ph
Fayte M. Brown
CYCLONE PRAIRIE RANGERS(1944), ph; JUNGLE JIM IN THE FORBIDDEN LAND(1952), ph; LARAMIE MOUNTAINS(1952), ph
Floyce Brown
ELMER AND ELSIE(1934)
Forrest Brown
BOSS OF LONELY VALLEY(1937), w
Fred Brown
IS THIS TRIP REALLY NECESSARY?(1970), ed
Frederic Brown
SCREAMING MIMI(1958), w
Frederika Brown
ZAZA(1939)
Fredric Brown
CRACK-UP(1946), w
G. Carleton Brown
MC HALE'S NAVY(1964), w
Gail Brown
THING WITH TWO HEADS, THE(1972), makeup
Garrett Brown
ROCKY(1976), spec eff; ZELIG(1983)
Gary Brown
I LOVE YOU, ALICE B. TOKLAS!(1968); SECRET LIFE OF AN AMERICAN WIFE, THE(1968); YENTL(1983)
Gaye Brown
MASQUE OF THE RED DEATH, THE(1964, U.S./Brit.); CLOCKWORK ORANGE, A(1971, Brit.); TOUCH OF CLASS, A(1973, Brit.)
Gene Brown
SECRET FURY, THE(1950)
Geoff Brown
I WANT WHAT I WANT(1972, Brit.), w
Geoff R. Brown
VAMPYRES, DAUGHTERS OF DRACULA(1977, Brit.), ed
Georg Stanford Brown
COMEDIANS, THE(1967); BULLITT(1968); DAYTON'S DEVILS(1968); COLOSSUS: THE FORBIN PROJECT(1969); MAN, THE(1972); BLACK JACK(1973); STIR CRA-ZY(1980)
George Brown
SELF-MADE LADY(1932, Brit.), d; IT'S A PLEASURE(1945); SEARCHERS, THE(1956), spec eff; GUNS AT BATASI(1964, Brit.), p; GIRL, THE BODY, AND THE PILL, THE(1967); RELUCTANT ASTRONAUT, THE(1967), spec eff
1984
DELIVERY BOYS(1984), art d
George C. Brown
1984
PREPPIES(1984), art d
George Carleton Brown
GAMBLING SHIP(1939), w; THOU SHALT NOT KILL(1939), w; BORDER LEGION, THE(1940), w; ANGELS WITH BROKEN WINGS(1941), w; CHATTERBOX(1943), w; SLEEPY LAGOON(1943), w; YOUTH ON PARADE(1943), w; ATLANTIC CITY(1944), w; MAN FROM FRISCO(1944), w; TIGER WOMAN, THE(1945), w; BIG PUNCH, THE(1948), w; HERE COMES TROUBLE(1948), w; HALF ANGEL(1951), w; MR. WALKIE TALKIE(1952), w
George Edward Brown
WEST OF THE ROCKIES(1929)
Misc. Silents
SECRET SORROW(1921); SPORT OF THE GODS, THE(1921); CALL OF HIS PEOPLE, THE(1922)
George H. Brown
SCHOOL FOR SECRETS(1946, Brit.), p; VICE VERSA(1948, Brit.), p; AMAZING MR. BEECHAM, THE(1949, Brit.), p; SLEEPING CAR TO TRIESTE(1949, Brit.), p; HOTEL SAHARA(1951, Brit.), p, w; MADE IN HEAVEN(1952, Brit.), p, w; DESPERATE

MOMENT(1953, Brit.), p, w; LAND OF FURY(1955 Brit.), p; JACQUELINE(1956, Brit.), p; DANGEROUS EXILE(1958, Brit.), p; ROONEY(1958, Brit.), p; BOY WHO STOLE A MILLION, THE(1960, Brit.), p; TOMMY THE TOREADOR(1960, Brit.), p, w; DOUBLE BUNK(1961, Brit.), p; KILL OR CURE(1962, Brit.), p; VILLAGE OF DAUGHTERS(1962, Brit.), p; MURDER AT THE GALLOP(1963, Brit.), p; GO KART GO(1964, Brit.), p; LADIES WHO DO(1964, Brit.), p; RUNAWAY RAILWAY(1965, Brit.), p; FINDERS KEEPERS(1966, Brit.), p, w; UP IN THE AIR(1969, Brit.), p; HOVERBUG(1970, Brit.), p; TERROR FROM UNDER THE HOUSE(1971, Brit.); INNOCENT BYSTANDERS(1973, Brit.), p

George N. Brown
MURDER SHE SAID(1961, Brit.), p

Georgia Brown
MURDER REPORTED(1958, Brit.); STUDY IN TERROR, A(1966, Brit./Ger.); FIXER, THE(1968); LOCK UP YOUR DAUGHTERS(1969, Brit.); LONG AGO, TOMORROW(1971, Brit.); RUNNING SCARED(1972, Brit.); TALES THAT WITNESS MADNESS(1973, Brit.); GALILEO(1975, Brit.); NOTHING BUT THE NIGHT(1975, Brit.); BAWDY ADVENTURES OF TOM JONES, THE(1976, Brit.); SEVEN-PER-CENT SOLUTION, THE(1977, Brit.)

Gibran Brown
MARVIN AND TIGE(1983)

Gilson Brown
BOY OF THE STREETS(1937), w; LITTLE TOUGH GUY(1938), w

Gina Brown
AMSTERDAM KILL, THE(1978, Hong Kong), ed

Grace Drew Brown
Silents
NANCY FROM NOWHERE(1922), w

Graham Brown
1984
MUPPETS TAKE MANHATTAN, THE(1984)

Gwendolyn Brown
1984
BREAKIN'(1984)

Hal Brown
Misc. Silents
PLEASE HELP EMILY(1917)

Halbert Brown
Silents
MY FOUR YEARS IN GERMANY(1918); OPEN YOUR EYES(1919); OTHER MAN'S WIFE, THE(1919)

Harold Brown
BENNY GOODMAN STORY, THE(1956), m

Harris Brown
CASBAH(1948); NAKED CITY, THE(1948); FREE FOR ALL(1949); SCENE OF THE CRIME(1949); GOLDEN GIRL(1951); HALF ANGEL(1951); MODEL AND THE MARRIAGE BROKER, THE(1951); MR. BELVEDERE RINGS THE BELL(1951); DEADLINE–U.S.A.(1952); PRIDE OF ST. LOUIS, THE(1952); PRESIDENT'S LADY, THE(1953); AIN'T MISBEHAVIN'(1955)

Harrison Brown
Misc. Silents
POSSESSION(1922, Brit.)

Harry Brown
H.M. PULHAM, ESQ.(1941); MARINE RAIDERS(1944); SPELLBOUND(1945); WALK IN THE SUN, A(1945), w; HER ADVENTUROUS NIGHT(1946); INSIDE JOB(1946); KILLERS, THE(1946); LAWLESS BREED, THE(1946); TIME OF THEIR LIVES, THE(1946); OTHER LOVE, THE(1947), w; SHOOT TO KILL(1947); ABBOTT AND COSTELLO MEET FRANKENSTEIN(1948); ARCH OF TRIUMPH(1948), w; FEUDIN', FUSSIN' AND A-FIGHTIN'(1948); MEXICAN HAYRIDE(1948); NOOSE HANGS HIGH, THE(1948); ABBOTT AND COSTELLO MEET THE KILLER, BORIS KARLOFF(1949); MAN ON THE EIFFEL TOWER, THE(1949), w; MASSACRE RIVER(1949); OCEAN BREAKERS(1949, Swed.); RINGSIDE(1949); SANDS OF IWO JIMA(1949), w; WAKE OF THE RED WITCH(1949), w; KISS TOMORROW GOODBYE(1950), w; APACHE DRUMS(1951), w; ONLY THE VALIANT(1951), w; PLACE IN THE SUN, A(1951), w; BUGLES IN THE AFTERNOON(1952), w; EIGHT IRON MEN(1952), w; SNIPER, THE(1952), w; ALL THE BROTHERS WERE VALIANT(1953), w; CITY OF BAD MEN(1953); MANY RIVERS TO CROSS(1955), w; VIRGIN QUEEN, THE(1955), w; BETWEEN HEAVEN AND HELL(1956), w; D-DAY, THE SIXTH OF JUNE(1956), w; DEEP SIX, THE(1958), w; FIEND WHO WALKED THE WEST, THE(1958), w; OCEAN'S ELEVEN(1960), w; THREE WEEKS OF LOVE(1965), w; EL DORADO(1967), w
Misc. Silents
HEART OF JENNIFER, THE(1915)

Harry C. Brown
Misc. Silents
FLOWER OF NO MAN'S LAND, THE(1916); BATTLER, THE(1919)

Harry D. Brown
WANDERER OF THE WASTELAND(1945)

Harry J. Brown
FIGHTING LEGION, THE(1930), d
Silents
NORTH OF NEVADA(1924), p; BASHFUL BUCCANEER(1925), d; FIGHTING SMILE, THE(1925), w, ph; BROADWAY BILLY(1926), d; KENTUCKY HANDICAP(1926), d; NIGHT OWL, THE(1926), d; ONE PUNCH O'DAY(1926), d; RACING ROMANCE(1926), d; SOMEWHERE IN SONORA(1927), sup; LAWLESS LEGION, THE(1929), d; ROYAL RIDER, THE(1929), d
Misc. Silents
DANGER QUEST(1926), d; DANGEROUS DUDE, THE(1926), d; FIGHTING THOROBREDS(1926), d; HIGH FLYER, THE(1926), d; MORAN OF THE MOUNTED(1926), d; RAPID FIRE ROMANCE(1926), d; SELF STARTER, THE(1926), d; STICK TO YOUR STORY(1926), d; WINDJAMMER, THE(1926), d; WINNER, THE(1926), d; GUN GOSPEL(1927), d; LAND BEYOND THE LAW(1927), d; RACING FOOL, THE(1927), d; ROMANTIC ROGUE(1927), d; ROYAL AMERICAN, THE(1927), d; SCORCHER, THE(1927), d; CODE OF THE SCARLET, THE(1928), d; WAGON SHOW, THE(1928), d; LUCKY LARKIN(1930), d

Harry Joe Brown
SENOR AMERICANO(1929), d; WAGON MASTER, THE(1929), d; MOUNTAIN JUSTICE(1930), p, d; PARADE OF THE WEST(1930), d; SONG OF THE CABELLERO(1930), d; SONS OF THE SADDLE(1930), d; SQUEALER, THE(1930), d; WOMAN OF EXPERIENCE, A(1931), d; BEYOND THE ROCKIES(1932), d; BILLION DOLLAR SCANDAL(1932), d; IS MY FACE RED?(1932), p; LADY WITH A PAST(1932), p; MADISON SQUARE GARDEN(1932), d; PANAMA FLO(1932), p; WESTWARD PASSAGE(1932), p; YOUNG BRIDE(1932), p; I LOVE THAT MAN(1933), d; SITTING PRETTY(1933), d; CASE OF THE CURIOUS BRIDE, THE(1935), p; CEILNG ZERO(1935), p; I FOUND STELLA PARISH(1935), p; MAYBE IT'S LOVE(1935), p; WE'RE IN THE MONEY(1935), p; WHILE THE PATIENT SLEPT(1935), p; WOMAN IN RED, THE(1935), p; DANGEROUS(1936), p; HEARTS DIVIDED(1936), p; I MARRIED A DOCTOR(1936), p; SNOWED UNDER(1936), p; GREAT O'MALLEY, THE(1937), p; PERFECT SPECIMEN, THE(1937), p; GORILLA, THE(1939), p; YOUNG PEOPLE(1940), p; MOON OVER MIAMI(1941), p; WILD GEESE CALLING(1941), p; FIRST COMES COURAGE(1943), p; SAHARA(1943), p; KNICKERBOCKER HOLIDAY(1944), p&d; GUNFIGHTERS, THE(1947), p; SPIRIT OF WEST POINT, THE(1947), p; UNTAMED BREED, THE(1948), p; DOOLINS OF OKLAHOMA, THE(1949), p; WALKING HILLS, THE(1949), p; FORTUNES OF CAPTAIN BLOOD(1950), p; NEVADAN, THE(1950), p; STAGE TO TUCSON(1950), p; LADY AND THE BANDIT, THE(1951), p; MAN IN THE SADDLE(1951), p; SANTA FE(1951), p; CAPTAIN PIRATE(1952), p; HANGMAN'S KNOT(1952), p; LAST POSSE, THE(1953), p; STRANGER WORE A GUN, THE(1953), p; THREE HOURS TO KILL(1954), p; LAWLESS STREET, A(1955), p; TEN WANTED MEN(1955), p; SEVENTH CAVALRY(1956), p; DECISION AT SUNDOWN(1957), p; GUNS OF FORT PETTICOAT, THE(1957), p; TALL T, THE(1957), p; BUCHANAN RIDES ALONE(1958), p; SCREAMING MIMI(1958), p; COMANCHE STATION(1960), p; SON OF CAPTAIN BLOOD, THE(1964, U.S./Ital./Span.), p; TIME FOR KILLING, A(1967), p

Harry Joe Brown, Jr.
DUFFY(1968, Brit.), w

Helen Brown
MAGNIFICENT OBSESSION(1935); MEN WITHOUT NAMES(1935); BIG BROWN EYES(1936); THREE GODFATHERS(1936); TO MARY–WITH LOVE(1936); INTERNES CAN'T TAKE MONEY(1937); SHOULD A GIRL MARRY?(1939); WHEN TOMORROW COMES(1939); BABIES FOR SALE(1940); FIVE LITTLE PEPPERS IN TROUBLE(1940); LITTLE BIT OF HEAVEN, A(1940); OUT WEST WITH THE PEPPERS(1940); UNTAMED(1940); MR. DISTRICT ATTORNEY(1941); SHE'S FOR ME(1943); TAMPICO(1944); DANNY BOY(1946); NORA PRENTISS(1947); ALL MY SONS(1948); EVERY GIRL SHOULD BE MARRIED(1948); WALLS OF JERICHO(1948); ARCTIC MANHUNT(1949); DANCING IN THE DARK(1949); HOLIDAY AFFAIR(1949); SET-UP, THE(1949); GOLDBERGS, THE(1950); KEY TO THE CITY(1950); SHADOW ON THE WALL(1950); WHERE DANGER LIVES(1950); AL JENNINGS OF OKLAHOMA(1951); DREAMBOAT(1952); SCANDAL SHEET(1952); SOMETHING TO LIVE FOR(1952); SHANE(1953); EXECUTIVE SUITE(1954); STRATEGIC AIR COMMAND(1955); TEEN-AGE CRIME WAVE(1955); HOUSEBOAT(1958); MISSOURI TRAVELER, THE(1958); DARK AT THE TOP OF THE STAIRS, THE(1960); THAT TOUCH OF MINK(1962); VERY SPECIAL FAVOR, A(1965)

Helen Gurley Brown
SEX AND THE SINGLE GIRL(1964), w

Hennie Brown
MISBEHAVING HUSBANDS(1941)

Henry Brown
MAN IN THE GLASS BOOTH, THE(1975); SKY RIDERS(1976, U.S./Gr.)

Henry Brown, Jr.
R.P.M.(1970)

Hilyard Brown
DON'T FENCE ME IN(1945), art d; GUY, A GAL AND A PAL, A(1945), art d; LOVE, HONOR AND GOODBYE(1945), art d; MARSHAL OF LAREDO(1945), art d; PHANTOM OF THE PLAINS(1945), art d; GUY COULD CHANGE, A(1946), art d; MADONNA'S SECRET, THE(1946), art d; MAN FROM RAINBOW VALLEY, THE(1946), art d; MYSTERIOUS MR. VALENTINE, THE(1946), art d; OUT CALIFORNIA WAY(1946), md; RAINBOW OVER TEXAS(1946), art d; RENDEZVOUS WITH ANNIE(1946), art d; UNDERCOVER WOMAN, THE(1946), art d; VALLEY OF THE ZOMBIES(1946), art d; EXILE, THE(1947), art d; GHOST GOES WILD, THE(1947), art d; NORTHWEST OUTPOST(1947), art d; ALL MY SONS(1948), art d; WYOMING MAIL(1950), art d; HOME TOWN STORY(1951), art d; RAGING TIDE, THE(1951), art d; TARGET UNKNOWN(1951), art d; HAS ANYBODY SEEN MY GAL?(1952), art d; HERE COME THE NELSONS(1952), art d; SALLY AND SAINT ANNE(1952), art d; REDHEAD FROM WYOMING, THE(1953), art d; STAND AT APACHE RIVER, THE(1953), art d; TAKE ME TO TOWN(1953), art d; MAN WITH THE GUN(1955), art d; NIGHT OF THE HUNTER, THE(1955), art d; HOLD BACK THE NIGHT(1956), art d; DEVIL'S HAIRPIN, THE(1957), art d; MAN OF THE WEST(1958), art d; AL CAPONE(1959), art d; MAN IN THE NET, THE(1959), art d; TEN WHO DARED(1960), art d; LOOK IN ANY WINDOW(1961), art d; CLEOPATRA(1963), art d; MOVE OVER, DARLING(1963), art d; WALL OF NOISE(1963), art d; FATE IS THE HUNTER(1964), art d; SHOCK TREATMENT(1964), art d; VON RYAN'S EXPRESS(1965), art d; WAY...WAY OUT(1966), art d; FINIAN'S RAINBOW(1968), prod d; BOATNIKS, THE(1970), art d; FUZZ(1972), art d; CRAZY WORLD OF JULIUS VROODER, THE(1974), art d; FREEBIE AND THE BEAN(1974), art d; HUSTLE(1975), art d; BILLY JACK GOES TO WASHINGTON(1977), art d; COAST TO COAST(1980), art d; SIX WEEKS(1982), art d

Hilyard John Brown
SIXTH AND MAIN(1977), ph

Hilyard M. Brown
SKULLDUGGERY(1970), prod d; WELCOME HOME, SOLDIER BOYS(1972), art d

Himan Brown
THAT NIGHT(1957), p; VIOLATORS, THE(1957), p

Hiram S. Brown, Jr.
DRUMS OF FU MANCHU(1943), p

Horace Brown
DESTRUCTORS, THE(1968)

Howard Brown
THINGS ARE TOUGH ALL OVER(1982), p; CHEECH AND CHONG'S NEXT MOVIE(1980), p; CHEECH AND CHONG'S NICE DREAMS(1981), p

Howard C. Brown
KANGAROO KID, THE(1950, Aus./U.S.), p

Hugh Brown
THREE VIOLENT PEOPLE(1956), p

Ilene Brown
BETWEEN HEAVEN AND HELL(1956)

Irene Brown
LETTER, THE(1929); PYGMALION(1938, Brit.)
Silents
AFTER MANY DAYS(1919, Brit.)

Iva Brown
Misc. Silents
DIAMOND CARLISLE(1922)
J. Bertram Brown
KISSING CUP'S RACE(1930, Brit.), w
Silents
WARE CASE, THE(1917, Brit.), w; KISSING CUP'S RACE(1920, Brit.), w; BEAUTI-FUL KITTY(1923, Brit.), w; IN THE BLOOD(1923, Brit.), w
J. Edwin Brown
Silents
SCARAMOUCHE(1923)
J. G. Brown
BOND STREET(1948, Brit.), w
J.P.S. Brown
POCKET MONEY(1972), w; DEATH VALLEY(1982)
J. S. Brown
MYSTERY TRAIN(1931), ph
Jack Brown
Silents
TILLIE WAKES UP(1917); ASHAMED OF PARENTS(1921), ph; SCHOOL DAYS(1921), ph; SOCIETY SNOBS(1921), ph; RECKLESS YOUTH(1922), ph; AVER-AGE WOMAN, THE(1924), ph; LEND ME YOUR HUSBAND(1924), ph; SPITFIRE, THE(1924), ph; YOUTH FOR SALE(1924), ph; POLICE PATROL, THE(1925), ph; NEST, THE(1927), ph
Jack W. Brown
Misc. Silents
SHADOW, THE(1921), d
Jackie Brown
THIS IS THE ARMY(1943); ADVENTURES OF MARK TWAIN, THE(1944); COVER GIRL(1944); FRONT PAGE STORY(1954, Brit.), md; ACCURSED, THE(1958, Brit.), m
Jacques Brown
HI, GANG!(1941, Brit.); SOUTH AMERICAN GEORGE(1941, Brit.); ALWAYS A BRIDE(1954, Brit.)
James B. Brown, Jr.
COUNTERFEITERS, THE(1948), ph
James Brown
FOREST RANGERS, THE(1942); WAKE ISLAND(1942); AIR FORCE(1943); COR-VETTE K-225(1943); GOOD FELLOWS, THE(1943); YOUNG AND WILLING(1943); GOING MY WAY(1944); OUR HEARTS WERE YOUNG AND GAY(1944); DUFFY'S TAVERN(1945); OBJECTIVE, BURMA!(1945); OUR HEARTS WERE GROWING UP(1946); BIG FIX, THE(1947); FABULOUS TEXAN, THE(1947); GALLANT LEGION, THE(1948); ANNA LUCASTA(1949); BRIMSTONE(1949); SANDS OF IWO JIMA(1949); YES SIR, THAT'S MY BABY(1949); YOUNGER BROTHERS, THE(1949); CHAIN LIGHTNING(1950); FIREBALL, THE(1950); MONTANA(1950); FATHER TAKES THE AIR(1951); GROOM WORE SPURS, THE(1951); MISSING WOMEN(1951); SEA HOR-NET, THE(1951); STARLIFT(1951); MAN BEHIND THE GUN, THE(1952); PRIDE OF ST. LOUIS, THE(1952); SPRINGFIELD RIFLE(1952); WILD BLUE YONDER, THE(1952); CHARGE AT FEATHER RIVER, THE(1953); CRAZYLEGS, ALL AMERI-CAN(1953); FLIGHT NURSE(1953); SEA OF LOST SHIPS(1953); THUNDER OVER THE PLAINS(1953); WOMAN THEY ALMOST LYNCHED, THE(1953); RUNAWAY BUS, THE(1954, Brit.); STAR IS BORN, A(1954); FIVE GUNS TO TOMBSTONE(1961); GUN FIGHT(1961); POLICE DOG STORY, THE(1961); WHEN THE CLOCK STRI-KES(1961); WINGS OF CHANCE(1961, Can.); 20,000 EYES(1961); GUN STREET(1962); CEREMONY, THE(1963, U.S./Span.); IRMA LA DOUCE(1963); BLACK SPURS(1965); TOWN TAMER(1965); TARGETS(1968); PHYNX, THE(1970); SAM'S SONG(1971); ADIOS AMIGO(1975); WHIFFS(1975); MEAN JOHNNY BARROWS(1976); BLUES BROTHERS, THE(1980); DOCTOR DETROIT(1983)
James Brown
Pennywhistle blues , The(1952, South Africa), w
James Brown
SLAUGHTER'S BIG RIP-OFF(; BLACK CAESARC(1973), m
James Brown, Jr.
DEFENDERS OF THE LAW(1931), ph; AIR EAGLES(1932), ph; RENEGADE GIRL(1946), ph; TORNADO RANGE(1948), ph
James Earl "Texas Blood" Brown
TROUBLE MAN(1972)
James S. Brown
VANISHING FRONTIER, THE(1932), ph; CHEATING BLONDES(1933), ph; RECK-LESS ROADS(1935), ph; ROLLING CARAVANS(1938), ph; FRONTIERS OF '49(1939), ph; LAW COMES TO TEXAS, THE(1939), ph; CRIME DOCTOR'S STRANGEST CASE(1943), ph; NO PLACE FOR A LADY(1943), ph; WHISTLER, THE(1944), ph; RIDIN' DOWN THE TRAIL(1947), ph; ZAMBA(1949), ph
James S. Brown, Jr.
HER FORGOTTEN PAST(1933), ph; SECRET SINNERS(1933), ph; DANCING MAN(1934), ph; FIGHTING ROOKIE, THE(1934), ph; SCARLET LETTER, THE(1934), ph; SHE HAD TO CHOOSE(1934), ph; WHAT'S YOUR RACKET?(1934), ph; GET THAT MAN(1935), ph; NIGHT ALARM(1935), ph; WESTERN FRONTIER(1935), ph; FUGITIVE SHERIFF, THE(1936), ph; HEROES OF THE RANGE(1936), ph; UN-KNOWN RANGER, THE(1936), ph; LAW OF THE RANGER(1937), ph; NORTH OF NOME(1937), ph; OUTLAWS OF THE ORIENT(1937), ph; RANGERS STEP IN, THE(1937), ph; RIO GRANDE RANGER(1937), ph; ROARING TIMBER(1937), ph; SHADOWS OF THE ORIENT(1937), ph; TRAPPED BY G-MEN(1937), ph; TROUBLE IN MOROCCO(1937), ph; UNDER SUSPICION(1937), ph; CRIME TAKES A HOLI-DAY(1938), ph; FLIGHT INTO NOWHERE(1938), ph; IN EARLY ARIZONA(1938), ph; MAKING THE HEADLINES(1938), ph; PHANTOM GOLD(1938), ph; PIONEER TRAIL(1938), ph; REFORMATORY(1938), ph; STAGECOACH DAYS(1938), ph; FUGI-TIVE AT LARGE(1939), ph; HIDDEN POWER(1939), ph; LONE STAR PIONEERS(1939), ph; STRANGE CASE OF DR. MEADE(1939), ph; TRAPPED IN THE SKY(1939), ph; WHISPERING ENEMIES(1939), ph; ELLERY QUEEN. MASTER DE-TECTIVE(1940), ph; FUGITIVE FROM A PRISON CAMP(1940), ph; OUTSIDE THE 3-MILE LIMIT(1940), ph; PASSPORT TO ALCATRAZ(1940), ph; ELLERY QUEEN AND THE MURDER RING(1941), ph; ELLERY QUEEN AND THE PERFECT CRI-ME(1941), ph; ELLERY QUEEN'S PENTHOUSE MYSTERY(1941), ph; GREAT SWIN-DLE, THE(1941), ph; CLOSE CALL FOR ELLERY QUEEN, A(1942), ph; DESPERATE CHANCE FOR ELLERY QUEEN, A(1942), ph; ENEMY AGENTS MEET ELLERY QUEEN(1942), ph; CRIME DOCTOR(1943), ph; STRANGLER OF THE SWAMP(1945), ph; DEVIL BAT'S DAUGHTER, THE(1946), ph; DEADLINE(1948), ph; FRONTIER REVENGE(1948), ph; PRAIRIE, THE(1948), ph; DRAGNET(1974), ph

James Brown, Sr.
STAGE TO MESA CITY(1947), ph
James Spencer Brown
GREAT FLAMARION, THE(1945), ph
Jamie Brown
SUPERMAN(1978), makeup; MOTHER LODE(1982), makeup
Jane Brown
LUCKY JADE(1937, Brit.), w
Janet Brown
FLOODTIDE(1949, Brit.); FOLLY TO BE WISE(1953); ADDING MACHINE, THE(1969); MY LOVER, MY SON(1970, Brit.); FOR YOUR EYES ONLY(1981)
Janice Brown
HEAVY METAL(1981, Can.), ed
Jeannine Brown
LEPKE(1975, U.S./Israel)
Jed Brown
TOUCH OF THE SUN, A(1956, Brit.)
Jeff Brown
ETERNAL SUMMER(1961)
Jeffrey Brown
FIST OF FEAR, TOUCH OF DEATH(1980), ed
Jerry Brown
BEN HUR(1959); SPARTACUS(1960); GREAT BANK ROBBERY, THE(1969); OK-LAHOMA CRUDE(1973)
Jesse Brown
ONE MAN(1979, Can.)
Jim Brown
HARD BOILED MAHONEY(1947), ph; RIO CONCHOS(1964); DIRTY DOZEN, THE(1967, Brit.); DARK OF THE SUN(1968, Brit.); ICE STATION ZEBRA(1968); SPLIT, THE(1968); KENNER(1969); RIOT(1969); 100 RIFLES(1969); EL CONDOR(1970); GRASSHOPPER, THE(1970); ...TICK...TICK...TICK...(1970); BLACK GUNN(1972); SLAUGHTER(1972); I ESCAPED FROM DEVIL'S ISLAND(1973); SLAMS, THE(1973); SLAUGHTER'S BIG RIP-OFF(1973); THREE THE HARD WAY(1974); TAKE A HARD RIDE(1975, U.S./Ital.); KID VENGEANCE(1977); FINGERS(1978); ONE DOWN TWO TO GO(1982)
Misc. Talkies
SUPERBUG, THE WILD ONE(1977)
Jim L. Brown
INSIDE THE MAFIA(1959)
Jimmy Brown
WALLET, THE(1952, Brit.); ROAD WARRIOR, THE(1982, Aus.)
Silents
AVENGING FANGS(1927), ph
Joan Winmill Brown
NO LONGER ALONE(1978), w
Joanne Brown
HOUSE OF WAX(1953); MUSIC LOVERS, THE(1971, Brit.)
Joe Brown
COCK-EYED WORLD, THE(1929); GHOST TALKS, THE(1929); IN OLD ARIZO-NA(1929); BORN RECKLESS(1930); UP THE RIVER(1930); MEN ON CALL(1931); SOB SISTER(1931); RACKETY RAX(1932); DANTE'S INFERNO(1935); OKLAHOMA WOM-AN, THE(1956); RAINMAKER, THE(1956); WHAT A CRAZY WORLD(1963, Brit.); THREE HATS FOR LISA(1965, Brit.); HOSTILE GUNS(1967); LIONHEART(1968, Brit.)
Silents
ROAD HOUSE(1928); PROTECTION(1929)
Misc. Silents
CROOKS CAN'T WIN(1928)
Joe Brown, Jr.
HIGH SCHOOL(1940); LA CONGA NIGHTS(1940); YOUTH WILL BE SERVED(1940); ALL-AMERICAN CO-ED(1941); NAVAL ACADEMY(1941); SING ANOTHER CHORUS(1941); WHERE DID YOU GET THAT GIRL?(1941); HENRY ALDRICH GETS GLAMOUR(1942); JUKE BOX JENNY(1942); TEN GENTLEMEN FROM WEST POINT(1942); FATHER OF THE BRIDE(1950); MESSENGER OF PEACE(1950); WILD BLUE YONDER, THE(1952); FUGITIVE KIND, THE(1960)
Joe David Brown
STARS IN MY CROWN(1950), w; KINGS GO FORTH(1958), w; PAPER MOON(1973), w
Joe E. Brown
CIRCUS KID, THE(1928); MOLLY AND ME(1929); ON WITH THE SHOW(1929); PAINTED FACES(1929); SALLY(1929); SUNNY SIDE UP(1929); HOLD EVERY-THING(1930); LOTTERY BRIDE, THE(1930); SONG OF THE WEST(1930); TOP SPEED(1930); BROADMINDED(1931); GOING WILD(1931); LOCAL BOY MAKES GOOD(1931); SIT TIGHT(1931); FIREMAN, SAVE MY CHILD(1932); TENDERFOOT, THE(1932); YOU SAID A MOUTHFUL(1932); ELMER THE GREAT(1933); SON OF A SAILOR(1933); CIRCUS CLOWN(1934); SIX-DAY BIKE RIDER(1934); VERY HONOR-ABLE GUY, A(1934); ALIBI IKE(1935); BRIGHT LIGHTS(1935); MIDSUMMER'S NIGHT'S DREAM, A(1935); EARTHWORM TRACTORS(1936); POLO JOE(1936); SONS O' GUNS(1936); FIT FOR A KING(1937); RIDING ON AIR(1937); WHEN'S YOUR BIRTHDAY?(1937); FLIRTING WITH FATE(1938); GLADIATOR, THE(1938); WIDE OPEN FACES(1938); BEWARE SPOOKS(1939); $1,000 A TOUCHDOWN(1939); SO YOU WON'T TALK(1940); DARING YOUNG MAN, THE(1942); JOAN OF OZARK(1942); SHUT MY BIG MOUTH(1942); CHATTERBOX(1943); CASANOVA IN BURLES-QUE(1944); HOLLYWOOD CANTEEN(1944); PIN UP GIRL(1944); TENDER YEARS, THE(1947); SHOW BOAT(1951); AROUND THE WORLD IN 80 DAYS(1956); SOME LIKE IT HOT(1959); IT'S A MAD, MAD, MAD, MAD WORLD(1963); COMEDY OF TERRORS, THE(1964)
Misc. Talkies
HIT OF THE SNOW(1928)
Silents
TAKE ME HOME(1928)
Joe L. Brown
SUNBURN(1979)
Joe. E. Brown
MAYBE IT'S LOVE(1930)
John Brown
CASANOVA BROWN(1944); HORN BLOWS AT MIDNIGHT, THE(1945); LIFE OF RILEY, THE(1949); DAY THE EARTH STOOD STILL(1951); STRANGERS ON A TRAIN(1951); THREE DESPERATE MEN(1951); HANS CHRISTIAN ANDER-SEN(1952); SNIPER, THE(1952); SOMETHING FOR THE BIRDS(1952); BIGAMIST,-THE(1953); CRAZYLEGS, ALL AMERICAN(1953); MAN CRAZY(1953); ROBOT

MONSTER(1953); WILD ONE, THE(1953); CONSCIENCE BAY(1960, Brit.); TRAITORS, THE(1963, Brit.); MASTER SPY(1964, Brit.); DR. WHO AND THE DALEKS(1965, Brit.); DEVIL'S BRIDE, THE(1968, Brit.); RIDER IN THE NIGHT, THE(1968, South Africa), ph; FEAR IN THE NIGHT(1972, Brit.); VAMPIRE CIRCUS(1972, Brit.)

John F. Brown
JABBERWOCKY(1977, Brit.), spec eff

John Mack Brown
LADY OF CHANCE, A(1928); JAZZ HEAVEN(1929); VALIANT, THE(1929); BILLY THE KID(1930); GREAT, MEADOW, THE(1931); SECRET SIX, THE(1931); BELLE OF THE NINETIES(1934); THREE ON A HONEYMOON(1934); WELLS FARGO(1937)
Silents
DIVINE WOMAN, THE(1928); OUR DANCING DAUGHTERS(1928); WOMAN OF AFFAIRS, A(1928); SINGLE STANDARD, THE(1929)

John Moulder Brown
NIGHT WITHOUT PITY(1962, Brit.); OPERATION THIRD FORM(1966, Brit.); FIRST LOVE(1970, Ger./Switz.); HOUSE THAT SCREAMED, THE(1970, Span.); LUDWIG(1973, Ital./Ger./Fr.)

John Neill Brown
GIRL THIEF, THE(1938), ed

John W. Brown
WHAT EVER HAPPENED TO AUNT ALICE?(1969), set d; TOO LATE THE HERO(1970), set d
Silents
OUTCASTS OF POKER FLAT, THE(1919), ph; RIDERS OF VENGEANCE(1919), ph; DAUGHTER PAYS, THE(1920), ph; FLAPPER, THE(1920), ph; PRINCE OF AVENUE A., THE(1920), ph

John-Pierre Brown
1984
KINGS AND DESPERATE MEN(1984, Brit.)

Johnnie Mack Brown
MALAY NIGHTS(1933)

Johnny Brown
WIZ, THE(1978); MAN CALLED ADAM, A(1966); OUT OF TOWNERS, THE(1970); HANKY-PANKY(1982)

Johnny Mack Brown
COQUETTE(1929); HURRICANE(1929); MONTANA MOON(1930); UNDERTOW(1930); LASCA OF THE RIO GRANDE(1931); LAST FLIGHT, THE(1931); FLAMES(1932); VANISHING FRONTIER, THE(1932); 70,000 WITNESSES(1932); FEMALE(1933); SATURDAY'S MILLIONS(1933); SON OF A SAILOR(1933); AGAINST THE LAW(1934); CROSS STREETS(1934); MARRYING WIDOWS(1934); BETWEEN MEN(1935); BRANDED A COWARD(1935); COURAGEOUS AVENGER, THE(1935); CROOKED TRAIL, THE(1936); EVERYMAN'S LAW(1936); UNDERCOVER MAN(1936); VALLEY OF THE LAWLESS(1936); BAR Z BAD MEN(1937); BOOTHILL BRIGADE(1937); BORN TO THE WEST(1937); DESERT PHANTOM(1937); GAMBLING TERROR, THE(1937); GUNS IN THE DARK(1937); LAWLESS LAND(1937); LAWMAN IS BORN, A(1937); ROGUE OF THE RANGE(1937); TRAIL OF VENGEANCE(1937); DESPERATE TRAILS(1939); OKLAHOMA FRONTIER(1939); BAD MAN FROM RED BUTTE(1940); CHIP OF THE FLYING U(1940); LAW AND ORDER(1940); PONY POST(1940); RAGTIME COWBOY JOE(1940); RIDERS OF PASCO BASIN(1940); SON OF ROARING DAN(1940); WEST OF CARSON CITY(1940); ARIZONA CYCLONE(1941); BOSS OF BULLION CITY(1941); BURY ME NOT ON THE LONE PRAIRIE(1941); LAW OF THE RANGE(1941); MAN FROM MONTANA(1941); MASKED RIDER, THE(1941); RAWHIDE RANGERS(1941); BOSS OF HANGTOWN MESA(1942); DEEP IN THE HEART OF TEXAS(1942); FIGHTING BILL FARGO(1942); LITTLE JOE, THE WRANGLER(1942); RIDE 'EM COWBOY(1942); SILVER BULLET, THE(1942); STAGECOACH BUCKAROO(1942); CHEYENNE ROUNDUP(1943); LONE STAR TRAIL, THE(1943); OLD CHISHOLM TRAIL(1943); OUTLAWS OF STAMPEDE PASS(1943); RAIDERS OF SAN JOAQUIN(1943); SIX GUN GOSPEL(1943); STRANGER FROM PECOS, THE(1943); TENTING TONIGHT ON THE OLD CAMP GROUND(1943); GHOST GUNS(1944); LAND OF THE OUTLAWS(1944); LAW MEN(1944); LAW OF THE VALLEY(1944); PARTNERS OF THE TRAIL(1944); RAIDERS OF THE BORDER(1944); RANGE LAW(1944); TEXAS KID, THE(1944); FLAME OF THE WEST(1945); FOREVER YOURS(1945); FRONTIER FEUD(1945); LOST TRAIL, THE(1945); NAVAJO TRAIL, THE(1945); BORDER BANDITS(1946); DRIFTING ALONG(1946); GENTLEMAN FROM TEXAS(1946); UNDER ARIZONA SKIES(1946); CODE OF THE SADDLE(1947); FLASHING GUNS(1947); LAND OF THE LAWLESS(1947); PRAIRIE EXPRESS(1947); RAIDERS OF THE SOUTH(1947); BACK TRAIL(1948); CROSSED TRAILS(1948); FIGHTING RANGER, THE(1948); FRONTIER AGENT(1948); GUN TALK(1948); GUNNING FOR JUSTICE(1948); HIDDEN DANGER(1949); LAW OF THE WEST(1949); RANGE JUSTICE(1949); STAMPEDE(1949); TRAIL'S END(1949); WEST OF EL DORADO(1949); WESTERN RENEGADES(1949); LAW OF THE PANHANDLE(1950); OUTLAW GOLD(1950); OVER THE BORDER(1950); SHORT GRASS(1950); WEST OF WYOMING(1950); COLORADO AMBUSH(1951); MONTANA DESPERADO(1951); OKLAHOMA JUSTICE(1951); TEXAS LAWMEN(1951); WHISTLING HILLS(1951); CANYON AMBUSH(1952); DEAD MAN'S TRAIL(1952); MAN FROM BLACK HILLS, THE(1952); TEXAS CITY(1952); MARSHAL'S DAUGHTER, THE(1953); BOUNTY KILLER, THE(1965); REQUIEM FOR A GUNFIGHTER(1965); APACHE UPRISING(1966)
Misc. Talkies
ST. LOUIS WOMAN(1935); GHOST RIDER, THE(1943); WEST OF THE RIO GRANDE(1944); GUN SMOKE(1945); STRANGER FROM SANTA FE(1945); HAUNTED MINE, THE(1946); SHADOWS ON THE RANGE(1946); SILVER RANGE(1946); TRIGGER FINGERS(1946); LAW COMES TO GUNSIGHT, THE(1947); TRAILING DANGER(1947); VALLEY OF FEAR(1947); OVERLAND TRAILS(1948); SHERIFF OF MEDICINE BOW, THE(1948); TRIGGERMAN(1948); SIX GUN MESA(1950); BLAZING BULLETS(1951); MAN FROM SONORA(1951); GUNS ALONG THE BORDER(1952); MAN FROM THE BLACK HILLS(1952)
Silents
FAIR CO-ED, THE(1927); ANNAPOLIS(1928); PLAY GIRL, THE(1928)
Misc. Silents
SOFT LIVING(1928); SQUARE CROOKS(1928)

Jophery Brown
BINGO LONG TRAVELING ALL-STARS AND MOTOR KINGS, THE(1976); FOUL PLAY(1978); SUDDEN IMPACT(1983)
1984
AGAINST ALL ODDS(1984)

Jophery Clifford Brown
MIXED COMPANY(1974)

Josephine Brown
STRANGE CARGO(1929); TONIGHT AT TWELVE(1929); MAN INSIDE, THE(1958, Brit.); ROMAN SPRING OF MRS. STONE, THE(1961, U.S./Brit.); STRANGLEHOLD(1962, Brit.)

Judith Brown
PSYCHIC KILLER(1975); HOT POTATO(1976); HOUSE CALLS(1978)
Misc. Talkies
WOMAN FOR ALL MEN, A(1975)

Judith Hannah Brown
CALIFORNIA SUITE(1978)

Julia Brown
GODLESS GIRL, THE(1929)
Silents
ABYSMAL BRUTE, THE(1923); GALLOPING ACE, THE(1924); THREE'S A CROWD(1927)

Julie Brown
ANY WHICH WAY YOU CAN(1980)

June Brown
IT STARTED IN PARADISE(1952, Brit.); INADMISSIBLE EVIDENCE(1968, Brit.); STRAW DOGS(1971, Brit.); SUNDAY BLOODY SUNDAY(1971, Brit.); SITTING TARGET(1972, Brit.); FOURTEEN, THE(1973, Brit.); NIJINSKY(1980, Brit.)
1984
MISUNDERSTOOD(1984)

Ka-Ron Sowell Brown
SUMMER SCHOOL TEACHERS(1977)

Karl Brown
MISSISSIPPI GAMBLER(1929), w; PRINCE OF DIAMONDS(1930), d; FLAMES(1932), d, w; CITY PARK(1934), w; STOLEN SWEETS(1934), w; CURTAIN FALLS, THE(1935), w; ONE IN A MILLION(1935), w; ANY MAN'S WIFE(1936), d; DAN MATTHEWS(1936), w; HEARTS IN BONDAGE(1936), w; IN HIS STEPS(1936), d, w; TARZAN ESCAPES(1936), w; WHITE LEGION, THE(1936), d&w; FEDERAL BULLETS(1937), d, w; GIRL LOVES BOY(1937), w; JOIN THE MARINES(1937), w; MICHAEL O'HALLORAN(1937), d; BAREFOOT BOY(1938), d; GANGSTER'S BOY(1938), w; PORT OF MISSING GIRLS(1938), d, w; UNDER THE BIG TOP(1938), d; MAN THEY COULD NOT HANG, THE(1939), w; WOMAN IS THE JUDGE, A(1939), w; GANGS OF CHICAGO(1940), w; GIRL FROM HAVANA(1940), w; MAN WITH NINE LIVES, THE(1940), w; MILITARY ACADEMY(1940), w; MY SON IS GUILTY(1940), w; I WAS A PRISONER ON DEVIL'S ISLAND(1941), w; MR. DISTRICT ATTORNEY(1941), w; ROOKIES ON PARADE(1941), w; UNDER FIESTA STARS(1941), w; HARVARD, HERE I COME(1942), w; HITLER—DEAD OR ALIVE(1942), w; PHANTOM KILLER(1942), w; CHICAGO KID, THE(1945), w; VANQUISHED, THE(1953), w
Misc. Talkies
NUMBERED WOMAN(1938), d; PORT OF MISSING GIRLS(1938), d
Silents
AVENGING CONSCIENCE, THE(1914), ph; HOME SWEET HOME(1914); INTOLERANCE(1916), ph; BROKEN BLOSSOMS(1919), ph; BREWSTER'S MILLIONS(1921), ph; CRAZY TO MARRY(1921), ph; DICTATOR, THE(1922), ph; THIRTY DAYS(1922), ph; COVERED WAGON, THE(1923), ph; RUGGLES OF RED GAP(1923), ph; ENEMY SEX, THE(1924), ph; FIGHTING COWARD, THE(1924), ph; MERTON OF THE MOVIES(1924), ph; BEGGAR ON HORSEBACK(1925), ph; PONY EXPRESS, THE(1925), ph
Misc. Silents
HIS DOG(1927), d; STARK LOVE(1927), d

Katherine Brown
ZERO TO SIXTY(1978), p

Katherine L. Brown
1984
RACING WITH THE MOON(1984)

Kathie Brown
BRAINSTORM(1965)
Misc. Talkies
PETTY STORY, THE(1974)

Kathy Jo Brown
DR. COPPELIUS(1968, U.S./Span.)

Kay Brown
STRIP, THE(1951)

Keith Jerome Brown
1984
TANK(1984)

Kelly Brown
SEVEN BRIDES FOR SEVEN BROTHERS(1954); DADDY LONG LEGS(1955); OKLAHOMA(1955); GIRL MOST LIKELY, THE(1957)

Ken Brown
PALM BEACH(1979, Aus.)

Kendal Carey Brown
1984
FEAR CITY(1984)

Kendall Carly Brown
1984
DREAMSCAPE(1984)

Kenneth Brown
UNDER-PUP, THE(1939); IN THE NAVY(1941); MAN FROM MONTANA(1941); MELODY LANE(1941); NEVER GIVE A SUCKER AN EVEN BREAK(1941); CINDERELLA SWINGS IT(1942); BOMBER'S MOON(1943); ARMY WIVES(1944); TERROR STREET(1953)

Kenneth G. Brown
KOREA PATROL(1951), w

Kerry Brown
THREE TO GO(1971, Aus.), ph

Kirke Brown
Misc. Silents
ADVENTURER, THE(1917); AUCTION OF VIRTUE, THE(1917); BEHIND THE MASK(1917)

Kitty Brown
Silents
OUT OF THE DRIFTS(1916)

L.R. Brown
MARRIAGE BY CONTRACT(1928), ed; EVERYMAN'S LAW(1936), ed; YANK IN LIBYA, A(1942), ed

Laidman Brown
WIDE BOY(1952, Brit.)

Larry Brown
PSYCHOPATH, THE(1973), p&d, w; MITCHELL(1975), m
Misc. Talkies
EYE FOR AN EYE, AN(1975), d

Laurence Brown
DARK SANDS(1938, Brit.)

Laurie Brown
SPASMS(1983, Can.)

Laverne Lucille Brown
1984
KILLPOINT(1984)

Lawrence Brown
BIG FELLA(1937, Brit.); MARYJANE(1968), m; WOLFPEN PRINCIPLE, THE(1974, Can.)

Lee R. Brown
GAY BUCKAROO, THE(1932), w

Leete Brown
OFFICER 13(1933), ed

Leete R. Brown
INTRUDER, THE(1932), ed; THIRTEENTH GUEST, THE(1932), ed; SHRIEK IN THE NIGHT, A(1933), ed

Leete Renick Brown
Silents
AFRAID TO FIGHT(1922), w; KINDLED COURAGE(1923), w; STORM DAUGHTER, THE(1924), w

Leigh Brown
CHRISTMAS STORY, A(1983), w

Leland Brown
HOSTAGE, THE(1966)

Lena Brown
LET'S BE FAMOUS(1939, Brit.)

Leon Brown
LAST PICTURE SHOW, THE(1971)

Les Brown
ROCKABILLY BABY(1957)

Les Brown, Jr.
WILD, WILD WINTER(1966)

Lew Brown
SUNNY SIDE UP(1929), w, m; FOLLOW THE LEADER(1930), w; FOLLOW THRU(1930), w; GOOD NEWS(1930), w; HOLD EVERYTHING(1930), m; JUST IMAGINE(1930), p, w; INDISCREET(1931), p, w; STAND UP AND CHEER(1934 80m FOX bw), a, w, m; STRAIGHT, PLACE AND SHOW(1938), w; YOKEL BOY(1942), w; GOOD NEWS(1947), w; CRIME AND PUNISHMENT, U.S.A.(1959); THREAT, THE(1960); FITZWILLY(1967); HELL WITH HEROES, THE(1968); COLOSSUS: THE FORBIN PROJECT(1969); TOPAZ(1969, Brit.); AIRPORT(1970); MAN, THE(1972); ACE ELI AND RODGER OF THE SKIES(1973); BREEZY(1973); GRAND THEFT AUTO(1977); TELEFON(1977)

Lewis Brown
I WALK THE LINE(1970), cos

Lionel Brown
PRICE OF WISDOM, THE(1935, Brit.), w; TO HAVE AND TO HOLD(1951, Brit.), w

Lizard Brown
RUDE BOY(1980, Brit.)

Lloyd Brown
Silents
RAMONA(1916), w

Loren Brown
DESTRY RIDES AGAIN(1939); PLYMOUTH ADVENTURE(1952)

Loren B. Brown
HURRICANE SMITH(1952); HERE COME THE GIRLS(1953)

Louis Brown
HUSBANDS(1970), cos; VALDEZ IS COMING(1971), cos; FINAL CUT, THE(1980, Aus.)

Louis Polliman Brown
WHITE WITCH DOCTOR(1953); UNTAMED(1955)

Louis Y. Brown
THREE ON A COUCH(1966), m; WHICH WAY TO THE FRONT?(1970), m&md

Lowell Brown
GHOST DIVER(1957); TOKYO AFTER DARK(1959); GIRL IN LOVER'S LANE, THE(1960); HIGH SCHOOL CAESAR(1960); TAMMY, TELL ME TRUE(1961); DAY MARS INVADED EARTH, THE(1963)

Lucile Brown
LAST OF THE DUANES(1930); TEXAS TERROR(1935); CROOKED TRAIL, THE(1936); DEAD END(1937)

Lucille Brown
GIRLS ABOUT TOWN(1931); HIDE-OUT(1934); SWEETHEARTS(1938); ONCE UPON A TIME(1944); THIN MAN GOES HOME, THE(1944); WOMAN OF DISTINCTION, A(1950)
Misc. Talkies
BRAND OF HATE(1934)
Silents
INTOLERANCE(1916); KING OF KINGS, THE(1927)

Lynn Brown
EAT MY DUST!(1976)

Maggi Brown
TENDER IS THE NIGHT(1961)

Malcolm Brown
YOUNG DR. KILDARE(1938), art d; MAISIE(1939), art d; MAN FROM DAKOTA, THE(1940), artd; NORTHWEST PASSAGE(1940), art d; H.M. PULHAM, ESQ.(1941), art d; SOMEWHERE I'LL FIND YOU(1942), art d; SLIGHTLY DANGEROUS(1943), art d; GREEN DOLPHIN STREET(1947), art d; THREE MUSKETEERS, THE(1948), art d; BRIBE, THE(1949), art d; DUCHESS OF IDAHO, THE(1950), art d; MALAYA(1950), art d; IT'S A BIG COUNTRY(1951), art d; SOLDIERS THREE(1951), art d; VENGEANCE VALLEY(1951), art d; GLORY ALLEY(1952), art d; ABOVE AND BEYOND(1953), art d; ESCAPE FROM FORT BRAVO(1953), art d; NAKED SPUR, THE(1953), art d; PRISONER OF WAR(1954), art d; BAD DAY AT BLACK ROCK(1955), art d; I'LL CRY TOMORROW(1955), art d; KING'S THIEF, THE(1955), art d; SOMEBODY UP THERE LIKES ME(1956), art d; WINGS OF EAGLES, THE(1957), art d; IMITATION GENERAL(1958), art d; NO TIME FOR SERGEANTS(1958), art d; SADDLE THE WIND(1958), art d; SHEEPMAN, THE(1958), art d; TORPEDO RUN(1958), art d; MATING GAME, THE(1959), art d; NIGHT OF THE QUARTER MOON(1959), art d; TARZAN, THE APE MAN(1959), art d; WATUSI(1959), art d; KEY WITNESS(1960), art d; BY LOVE POSSESSED(1961), art d; TENDER IS THE NIGHT(1961), art d; DIAMOND HEAD(1962), prod d; MR. HOBBS TAKES A VACATION(1962), art d; FOR LOVE OR MONEY(1963), art d; TAKE HER, SHE'S MINE(1963), art d; KITTEN WITH A WHIP(1964), art d; DEAR BRIGETTE(1965), art d; JOHNNY RENO(1966), art d; LORD LOVE A DUCK(1966), art d

Malcolm F. Brown
THEY WERE EXPENDABLE(1945), art d

Margaret Brown
MA AND PA KETTLE(1949); MA AND PA KETTLE GO TO TOWN(1950); MA AND PA KETTLE AT THE FAIR(1952); MA AND PA KETTLE ON VACATION(1953); MA AND PA KETTLE AT WAIKIKI(1955)

Marguerite Brown
RAMPARTS WE WATCH, THE(1940)

Marian Brown
PREACHERMAN(1971)

Marie Brown
HELLO, FRISCO, HELLO(1943); DREAM WIFE(1953); D-DAY, THE SIXTH OF JUNE(1956); SING, BOY, SING(1958); ENTERTAINER, THE(1975), cos

Marie M. Brown
MY PAL GUS(1952)

Marie V. Brown
PIECE OF THE ACTION, A(1977), cos

Mark Brown
HOMEWORK(1982)

Martin Brown
PARIS(1929), w; VIRTUOUS SIN, THE(1930), w; MAD GENIUS, THE(1931), w; SECRET OF MADAME BLANCHE, THE(1933), w; WORST WOMAN IN PARIS(1933), w; JAVA HEAD(1935, Brit.), w
Silents
EXCITERS, THE(1923), w

Mary Ellen Brown
COLLEGE SCANDAL(1935); MISSISSIPPI(1935)

Mathew Brown
SLEEPING DOGS(1977, New Zealand), m

Maureen Brown
EMBALMER, THE(1966, Ital.)

Max. M. Brown
WOLFEN(1981)

Maxine Brown
Silents
CAPTAIN SWIFT(1914)

Meg Brown
MY FAIR LADY(1964)

Mel Brown
PIE IN THE SKY(1964)

Melba Brown
JUDGE PRIEST(1934)

Melville Brown
DANCE HALL(1929), d; GERALDINE(1929), d; JAZZ HEAVEN(1929), d; LOVE DOCTOR, THE(1929), d; AMOS 'N' ANDY(1930), d; LOVIN' THE LADIES(1930), d; SHE'S MY WEAKNESS(1930), d; BEHIND OFFICE DOORS(1931), d; FANNY FOLEY HERSELF(1931), d; WHITE SHOULDERS(1931), d; RED HEAD(1934), d; CHAMPAGNE FOR BREAKFAST(1935), d; FORCED LANDING(1935), d; LOST IN THE STRATOSPHERE(1935), d; NUT FARM, THE(1935), d; HEAD OFFICE(1936, Brit.), d; HE LOVED AN ACTRESS(1938, Brit.), d
Silents
ROSE OF PARIS, THE(1924), w; GOOSE WOMAN, THE(1925), w; RED LIPS(1928), d, w
Misc. Silents
BUCK PRIVATES(1928), d

Melville W. Brown
Silents
PEST, THE(1919), w; WHAT HAPPENED TO JONES(1926), w; TAXI! TAXI!(1927), d, w; 13 WASHINGTON SQUARE(1928), d
Misc. Silents
HER BIG NIGHT(1926), d; FAST AND FURIOUS(1927), d

Mende Brown
CLOWN AND THE KIDS, THE(1968, U.S./Bulgaria), d&w; LITTLE JUNGLE BOY(1969, Aus.), p,d&w; STRANGE HOLIDAY(1969, Aus.), p,d&w; ON THE RUN(1983, Aus.), p&d

Michael Brown
PRIDE OF THE MARINES(1945); FRASIER, THE SENSUOUS LION(1973), ed; TOWN THAT DREADED SUNDOWN, THE(1977); NIGHTMARES(1983), ed; TOUGH ENOUGH(1983)

Miguel Brown
SUPERMAN(1978)

Mike Brown
PSYCHIC KILLER(1975), ed

Mildred Brown
Misc. Talkies
COUNTRY BLUE(1975)

Milt Brown
LOCAL BAD MAN(1932)
Silents
RUGGLES OF RED GAP(1923); BREAKING POINT, THE(1924); POINTS WEST(1929)

Milton A. Brown
Silents
CARMEN(1915)

Milton Brown
MOUNTED STRANGER, THE(1930); HIRED WIFE(1940), ed
Silents
CALL OF THE NORTH, THE(1914); ONLY SON, THE(1914); ARAB, THE(1915); WARRENS OF VIRGINIA, THE(1915); KING'S CREEK LAW(1923)

Morgan Brown
GILDERSLEEVE'S BAD DAY(1943); THANK YOUR LUCKY STARS(1943); RIDING SHOTGUN(1954); SHE COULDN'T SAY NO(1954)
Silents
GALLOPING GOBS, THE(1927)
Misc. Silents
TAMING OF THE WEST, THE(1925)
Munro Brown
I'LL SELL MY LIFE(1941)
Murray Brown
DEADLY AFFAIR, THE(1967, Brit.); BLACK WINDMILL, THE(1974, Brit.); VAMPYRES, DAUGHTERS OF DRACULA(1977, Brit.)
Naaman Brown
WHITE WITCH DOCTOR(1953); TANGANYIKA(1954); SOMETHING OF VALUE(1957); WACKIEST SHIP IN THE ARMY, THE(1961); CLARENCE, THE CROSS-EYED LION(1965)
Nacio Brown
TAKE A CHANCE(1933), w
Nacio Herb Brown
WOMAN COMMANDS, A(1932), m; SINGIN' IN THE RAIN(1952), m
Nancy Brown
MAID OF THE MOUNTAINS, THE(1932, Brit.); FACING THE MUSIC(1933, Brit.); SOUTHERN MAID, A(1933, Brit.); RED WAGON(1936); LIMIT, THE(1972), cos
Nannette Brown
SWAMP THING(1982)
Nick Brown
WHERE THE LILIES BLOOM(1974), ed
Nina G. Brown
I'D CLIMB THE HIGHEST MOUNTAIN(1951)
Noelene Brown
WALKABOUT(1971, Aus./U.S.)
Norma Brown
NOCTURNE(1946); THRILL OF BRAZIL, THE(1946); ROBIN OF TEXAS(1947); SINBAD THE SAILOR(1947); PALM SPRINGS WEEKEND(1963), cos
O. Nicholas Brown
OTHER, THE(1972), ed; NICKEL RIDE, THE(1974), ed; WHITE LINE FEVER(1975, Can.), ed; SHADOW OF THE HAWK(1976, Can.), ed; MARCH OR DIE(1977, Brit.), ed; MR. BILLION(1977), ed; HEART LIKE A WHEEL(1983), ed
Olga Hall Brown
OTHER WOMAN, THE(1931, Brit.), w
Olivia Brown
NORMAN LOVES ROSE(1982, Aus.)
1984
STREETS OF FIRE(1984)
Olivia M. Brown
48 HOURS(1982)
Ollie E. Brown
1984
BLAME IT ON THE NIGHT(1984)
P. L. Brown
NEIGHBORS(1981)
Pamela Brown
ONE OF OUR AIRCRAFT IS MISSING(1942, Brit.); I KNOW WHERE I'M GOING(1947, Brit.); ALICE IN WONDERLAND(1951, Fr.); TALES OF HOFFMANN, THE(1951, Brit.); SECOND MRS. TANQUERAY, THE(1952, Brit.); PERSONAL AFFAIR(1954, Brit.); LUST FOR LIFE(1956); NOW AND FOREVER(1956, Brit.); RICHARD III(1956, Brit.); SCAPEGOAT, THE(1959, Brit.); CLEOPATRA(1963); BECKET(1964, Brit.); FUNNY THING HAPPENED ON THE WAY TO THE FORUM, A(1966); HALF A SIXPENCE(1967, Brit.); SECRET CEREMONY(1968, Brit.); FIGURES IN A LANDSCAPE(1970, Brit.); ON A CLEAR DAY YOU CAN SEE FOREVER(1970); WUTHERING HEIGHTS(1970, Brit.); NIGHT DIGGER, THE(1971, Brit.); LADY CAROLINE LAMB(1972, Brit./Ital.)
Pat Carroll Brown
CURTAINS(1983, Can.)
Pat Mullins Brown
DREAMER(1979)
Patty Brown
WARRIORS, THE(1979)
Paul B. Brown
GODFATHER, THE, PART II(1974)
Paul Brown
LINCOLN CONSPIRACY, THE(1977)
Penny Brown
CHAPPAQUA(1967)
Pepe Brown
TROUBLE WITH GIRLS(AND HOW TO GET INTO IT), THE*1/2 (1969)
Peter Brown
DARBY'S RANGERS(1958); MARJORIE MORNINGSTAR(1958); ONION-HEAD(1958); MERRILL'S MARAUDERS(1962); SUMMER MAGIC(1963); KITTEN WITH A WHIP(1964); RIDE THE WILD SURF(1964); TIGER WALKS, A(1964); THREE GUNS FOR TEXAS(1968); BACKTRACK(1969); CHROME AND HOT LEATHER(1971); ACT OF VENGEANCE(1974); FOXY DROWN(1974); MEMORY OF US(1974); CONCRETE JUNGLE, THE(1982)
Misc. Talkies
PIRANHA, PIRANHA(1972); SUNBURST(1975); TEENAGE TEASE(1983)
Phil Brown
WITHOUT RESERVATIONS(1946); H.M. PULHAM, ESQ.(1941); I WANTED WINGS(1941); CALLING DR. GILLESPIE(1942); HELLO ANNAPOLIS(1942); PIERRE OF THE PLAINS(1942); IMPATIENT YEARS, THE(1944); WEIRD WOMAN(1944); JUNGLE CAPTIVE(1945); OVER 21(1945); STATE FAIR(1945); KILLERS, THE(1946); JOHNNY O'CLOCK(1947); IF YOU KNEW SUSIE(1948); LUCK OF THE IRISH(1948); MOONRISE(1948); HIDDEN ROOM, THE(1949, Brit.); HARLEM GLOBETROTTERS, THE(1951), d; GREEN SCARF, THE(1954, Brit.); KING IN NEW YORK, A(1957, Brit.); JOHN PAUL JONES(1959); COUNTERFEIT TRAITOR, THE(1962); BEDFORD INCIDENT, THE(1965, Brit.); BOY CRIED MURDER, THE(1966, Ger./Brit./Yugo.); ADDING MACHINE, THE(1969); LAND RAIDERS(1969); OPERATION CROSS EAGLES(1969, U.S./Yugo.); VALDEZ IS COMING(1971); SCALAWAG(1973, Yugo.); ROMANTIC ENGLISHWOMAN, THE(1975, Brit./Fr.); GET CHARLIE TULLY(1976, Brit.); PINK PANTHER STRIKES AGAIN, THE(1976, Brit.); STAR WARS(1977); TWILIGHT'S LAST GLEAMING(1977, U.S./Ger.); SILVER BEARS(1978); SUPER-

MAN(1978)
Philip Brown
PLAYGROUND, THE(1965)
Philip Martin Brown
EYE OF THE NEEDLE(1981); PARTY PARTY(1983, Brit.)
1984
BOUNTY, THE(1984)
Phillip Brown
PRETTY MAIDS ALL IN A ROW(1971)
Priscilla Brown
Silents
GALLOPING THRU(1923)
R. Hansel Brown
SEA GYPSIES, THE(1978), ed
Rae Brown
THAT COLD DAY IN THE PARK(1969, U.S./Can.)
Ralph Brown
FOREIGN INTRIGUE(1956); DEVIL'S MESSENGER, THE(1962 U.S./Swed.); NO TIME TO KILL(1963, Brit./Swed./Ger.); FICKLE FINGER OF FATE, THE(1967, Span./U.S.); VALDEZ IS COMING(1971); SPIKES GANG, THE(1974); HUNTING PARTY, THE(1977, Brit.); JAGUAR LIVES(1979); FINAL EXAM(1981)
Ralph L. Brown
FIREBALL JUNGLE(1968), set d
Randi Brown
1984
MYSTERY MANSION(1984)
Ray Brown
MYSTERY LINER(1934); SHE GETS HER MAN(1935); BULLETS OR BALLOTS(1936); CAREER WOMAN(1936); FURY(1936); GREAT ZIEGFELD, THE(1936); MAGNIFICENT BRUTE, THE(1936); STORY OF LOUIS PASTEUR, THE(1936); WE HAVE OUR MOMENTS(1937); THUNDERBIRD 6(1968, Brit.), art d; THUNDERBIRDS ARE GO(1968, Brit.), art d
Raymond Brown
MY WOMAN(1933); THIN MAN, THE(1934); DR. SOCRATES(1935); COMIN' ROUND THE MOUNTAIN(1936); DOWN THE STRETCH(1936); I MARRIED A DOCTOR(1936); MOONLIGHT ON THE PRAIRIE(1936); CARNIVAL QUEEN(1937); CHAMPAGNE WALTZ(1937); HIGH, WIDE AND HANDSOME(1937); HOLY TERROR, THE(1937); PAROLE RACKET(1937); THEY WON'T FORGET(1937); TWO WISE MAIDS(1937); COMET OVER BROADWAY(1938); GOLD IS WHERE YOU FIND IT(1938); SERGEANT MURPHY(1938); KING OF THE UNDERWORLD(1939); PRIDE OF THE BLUEGRASS(1939); THEY MADE ME A CRIMINAL(1939); TALISMAN, THE(1966)
Raymond H. Brown
TO PLEASE A LADY(1950)
Raymonda Brown
WORDS AND MUSIC(1929)
Reb Brown
SSSSSSSS(1973); BIG WEDNESDAY(1978); FAST BREAK(1979); HARDCORE(1979); SWORD AND THE SORCERER, THE(1982); UNCOMMON VALOR(1983); YOR, THE HUNTER FROM THE FUTURE(1983, Ital.)
Reed Brown, Jr.
WOMAN IN THE DARK(1934)
Reg Brown
MARK OF THE WHISTLER, THE(1944), ed; SON OF THE RENEGADE(1953), d
Reginald Brown
FOUR FAST GUNS(1959), ed
Ricardo Brown
SHAFT(1971)
Richard Brown
NORTHERN LIGHTS(1978), art d; NEW YEAR'S EVIL(1980); PURSUIT OF D.B. COOPER, THE(1981)
1984
UNFAITHFULLY YOURS(1984), stunts
Rita Mae Brown
SLUMBER PARTY MASSACRE, THE(1982), w
Ritchey Brown
SMOKEY AND THE BANDIT II(1980)
Ritza Brown
MONSIGNOR(1982)
Misc. Talkies
ATOR: THE FIGHTING EAGLE(1983)
Robert Alan Brown
SEED OF INNOCENCE(1980)
Robert Brown
CLOUDBURST(1952, Brit.); DEATH OF AN ANGEL(1952, Brit.); FOUR AGAINST FATE(1952, Brit.); GAMBLER AND THE LADY, THE(1952, Brit.); LARGE ROPE, THE(1953, Brit.); NOOSE FOR A LADY(1953, Brit.); TIME GENTLEMEN PLEASE!(1953, Brit.); PASSAGE HOME(1955, Brit.); WARRIORS, THE(1955); HELEN OF TROY(1956, Ital.); HELL IN KOREA(1956, Brit.); MAN WHO NEVER WAS, THE(1956, Brit.); ABOMINABLE SNOWMAN OF THE HIMALAYAS, THE(1957, Brit.); CAMPBELL'S KINGDOM(1957, Brit.); TEARS FOR SIMON(1957, Brit.); FLAME BARRIER, THE(1958); KILL ME TOMORROW(1958, Brit.); STEEL BAYONET, THE(1958, Brit.); BEN HUR(1959); ROOM 43(1959, Brit.); SHAKE HANDS WITH THE DEVIL(1959, Ireland); IT TAKES A THIEF(1960, Brit.); SANDS OF THE DESERT(1960, Brit.); STORY OF DAVID, A(1960, Brit.); BILLY BUDD(1962); TOWER OF LONDON(1962); 300 SPARTANS, THE(1962); DOUBLE, THE(1963, Brit); MACBETH(1963); MYSTERY SUBMARINE(1963, Brit.); MASQUE OF THE RED DEATH, THE(1964, U.S./Brit.); ESCAPE BY NIGHT(1965, Brit.); OPERATION CROSSBOW(1965, U.S./Ital.); ONE MILLION YEARS B.C.(1967, Brit./U.S.); 1,000 CONVICTS AND A WOMAN(1971, Brit.); TOM(1973), p; MOHAMMAD, MESSENGER OF GOD(1976, Lebanon/Brit.); SPY WHO LOVED ME, THE(1977, Brit.); DAMIEN–OMEN II(1978), ed; WARLORDS OF ATLANTIS(1978, Brit.); AMITYVILLE HORROR, THE(1979), ed; BRUBAKER(1980), ed; PILGRIM, FAREWELL(1980); LION OF THE DESERT(1981, Libya/Brit.); BEAST WITHIN, THE(1982), ed; OCTOPUSSY(1983, Brit.)
1984
POLICE ACADEMY(1984), ed; POPE OF GREENWICH VILLAGE, THE(1984), ed
Misc. Talkies
FLIGHT FROM TREASON(1960, Brit.)

Robert W. Brown
LETTER FROM AN UNKNOWN WOMAN(1948)
Robin Brown
ALL FOR MARY(1956, Brit.); RAISING A RIOT(1957, Brit.)
Roger Aaron Brown
STAR TREK: THE MOTION PICTURE(1979); DON'T CRY, IT'S ONLY THUN-DER(1982)
Roger Brown
PAPER LION(1968)
Roland Brown
WHAT PRICE HOLLYWOOD?(1932), w; LEAVE IT TO BLANCHE(1934, Brit.), w; WHAT HAPPENED TO HARKNESS(1934, Brit.), w; WIDOW'S MIGHT(1934, Brit.), w
Ron Brown
CHARLIE, THE LONESOME COUGAR(1967)
Ronald Brown
FOREIGN CORRESPONDENT(1940)
Ross Brown
NOTORIOUS LANDLADY, THE(1962)
Rowland Brown
DOORWAY TO HELL(1930), w; QUICK MILLIONS(1931), d, w; HELL'S HIGH-WAY(1932), d, w; STATE'S ATTORNEY(1932), w; BLOOD MONEY(1933), d, w; DEVIL IS A SISSY, THE(1936), w; BOY OF THE STREETS(1937), w; ANGELS WITH DIRTY FACES(1938), w; LADY'S FROM KENTUCKY, THE(1939), w; JOHNNY APOLLO(1940), w; NOCTURNE(1946), w; NEVADAN, THE(1950), w; KANSAS CITY CONFIDENTIAL(1952), w
Silents
POINTS WEST(1929), w
Rowland V. Brown
SCARLET PIMPERNEL, THE(1935, Brit.), d
Roy Brown
MAGNIFICENT OBSESSION(1935)
Roy Lee Brown
TOWN THAT DREADED SUNDOWN, THE(1977)
Royal Brown
Silents
KISS IN TIME, A(1921), w
Russ Brown
LET'S TALK IT OVER(1934); LOVE CAPTIVE, THE(1934); MOULIN ROUGE(1934); SWEET SURRENDER(1935); MILLIONAIRE PLAYBOY(1940); DAMN YAN-KEES(1958); SOUTH PACIFIC(1958); ANATOMY OF A MURDER(1959); IT HAP-PENED TO JANE(1959); CARDINAL, THE(1963)
Sam Brown
HI, GANG!(1941, Brit.)
Sam O. Brown [Blake Edwards]
1984
CITY HEAT(1984), w
Samuel Gibson Brown
TWO HEARTS IN HARMONY(1935, Brit.), w
Samuel Gilson Brown
DINKY(1935), w
Sandra Brown
MACK, THE(1973)
Sarah Brown
Misc. Talkies
SUPER SEAL(1976)
Scott Brown
FRATERNITY ROW(1977)
Scotty Brown
TALES OF TERROR(1962)
Sedley Brown
Silents
MEDIATOR, THE(1916); JOYOUS TROUBLEMAKERS, THE(1920)
Misc. Silents
ONE TOUCH OF SIN(1917)
Sharon Brown
DOZENS, THE(1981)
Sidney Brown
SHOOT(1976, Can.)
Speedy Brown
BLUE COLLAR(1978)
Stanley Brown
ADVENTURE IN SAHARA(1938); HAVING WONDERFUL TIME(1938); BLIND ALLEY(1939); BLONDIE MEETS THE BOSS(1939); GOOD GIRLS GO TO PARIS(1939); HOMICIDE BUREAU(1939); LONE WOLF SPY HUNT, THE(1939); OUTPOST OF THE MOUNTIES(1939); RIDERS OF BLACK RIVER(1939); RIO GRANDE(1939); TAMING OF THE WEST, THE(1939); ANGELS OVER BROADWAY(1940); BLAZING SIX SHOOTERS(1940); ISLAND OF DOOMED MEN(1940); MAN FROM TUMBLEWEEDS, THE(1940); MAN WITH NINE LIVES, THE(1940); MY SON IS GUILTY(1940); NOBODY'S CHILDREN(1940); PIONEERS OF THE FRONTIER(1940); CONFESSIONS OF BOSTON BLACKIE(1941); FACE BEHIND THE MASK, THE(1941); OUTLAWS OF THE PANHANDLE(1941); PENNY SERENADE(1941); THUNDER OVER THE PRAI-RIE(1941); TILLIE THE TOILER(1941); TWO LATINS FROM MANHATTAN(1941); WILDCAT OF TUCSON(1941); YOU BELONG TO ME(1941); YOU'LL NEVER GET RICH(1941); ATLANTIC CONVOY(1942); BLONDIE'S BLESSED EVENT(1942); CA-NAL ZONE(1942); DEVIL'S TRAIL, THE(1942); HARVARD, HERE I COME(1942); HELLO ANNAPOLIS(1942); LAWLESS PLAINSMEN(1942); SABOTAGE SQUAD(1942); SPIRIT OF STANFORD, THE(1942); SUBMARINE RAIDER(1942); SWEETHEART OF THE FLEET(1942); YOU WERE NEVER LOVELIER(1942); DAN-GEROUS BLONDES(1943); FIGHTING BUCKAROO, THE(1943); LAW OF THE NORTHWEST(1943); MR. MUGGS STEPS OUT(1943); ROBIN HOOD OF THE RAN-GE(1943); TARZAN TRIUMPHS(1943); TWO SENORITAS FROM CHICAGO(1943); MILLION DOLLAR KID(1944); REDHEAD FROM MANHATTAN(1954)
Stanley Brown, Jr.
ONLY ANGELS HAVE WINGS(1939)
Stephen Brown
CALAMITY THE COW(1967, Brit.)
Steve Brown
I REMEMBER MAMA(1948); GOODBYE, NORMA JEAN(1976); SECOND THOUGHTS(1983), w

Steven Brown
SILENT RUNNING(1972)
Steven James Brown
1984
NO SMALL AFFAIR(1984)
Strelsa Brown
GHOSTS OF BERKELEY SQUARE(1947, Brit.); QUO VADIS(1951); ROMANOFF AND JULIET(1961); WARRIOR EMPRESS, THE(1961, Ital./Fr.)
Stuart Brown
KILLER FORCE(1975, Switz./Ireland)
Summer Brown
HUMAN EXPERIMENTS(1980), p
1984
PREY, THE(1984), p, w
Susan Brown
STRIPPER, THE(1963); KLANSMAN, THE(1974)
Syd Brown
WOLF DOG(1958, Can.)
Sydney Brown
ONE PLUS ONE(1961, Can.); LUCK OF GINGER COFFEY, THE(1964, U.S./Can.); CHANGE OF MIND(1969)
Tally Brown
ILLIAC PASSION, THE(1968); SCARECROW IN A GARDEN OF CUCUM-BERS(1972); SILENT NIGHT, BLOODY NIGHT(1974); NIGHT OF THE JUG-GLER(1980)
Misc. Talkies
BRAND X(1970)
Teddy Brown
INDISCRETIONS OF EVE(1932, Brit.); ON THE AIR(1934, Brit.); RADIO PIRA-TES(1935, Brit.); VARIETY PARADE(1936, Brit.); CONVICT 99(1938, Brit.)
Silents
ARCADIANS, THE(1927, Brit.)
Teri Brown
1984
RECKLESS(1984)
Thelma Brown
JUDGE PRIEST(1934)
Thomas Henry Brown
HOUSE OF STRANGERS(1949)
Thomas S. Brown
Silents
KENTUCKIANS, THE(1921)
Tim Brown
M(1970)
1984
SUCCESS IS THE BEST REVENGE(1984, Brit.)
Timothy Brown
BLACK GUNN(1972); SWEET SUGAR(1972); NASHVILLE(1975); LOSIN' IT(1983)
Misc. Talkies
GIRLS ARE FOR LOVING(1973); DYNAMITE BROTHERS, THE(1974); BLACK HEAT(1976)
Timothy Wayne Brown
TRACK OF THE MOONBEAST(1976)
Tina Paget Brown
GREAT PONY RAID, THE(1968, Brit.)
Toch Brown
WIND ACROSS THE EVERGLADES(1958)
Tod Brown
Silents
ARIZONA SWEEPSTAKES(1926)
Tom Brown
LADY LIES, THE(1929); QUEEN HIGH(1930); FAMOUS FERGUSON CASE, THE(1932); FAST COMPANIONS(1932); HELL'S HIGHWAY(1932); TOM BROWN OF CULVER(1932); CENTRAL AIRPORT(1933); CROSSFIRE(1933); DESTINATION UN-KNOWN(1933); LAUGHTER IN HELL(1933); THREE-CORNERED MOON(1933); ANNE OF GREEN GABLES(1934); HAT, COAT AND GLOVE(1934); JUDGE PRIEST(1934); THIS SIDE OF HEAVEN(1934); TWO ALONE(1934); WITCHING HOUR, THE(1934); ANNAPOLIS FAREWELL(1935); BACHELOR OF ARTS(1935); BLACK SHEEP(1935); FRECKLES(1935); MARY JANE'S PA(1935); SWEEPSTAKE ANNIE(1935); AND SUDDEN DEATH(1936); GENTLE JULIA(1936); I'D GIVE MY LIFE(1936); ROSE BOWL(1936); HER HUSBAND LIES(1937); JIM HANVEY, DETEC-TIVE(1937); MAN WHO CRIED WOLF, THE(1937); MAYTIME(1937); NAVY BLUE AND GOLD(1937); THAT MAN'S HERE AGAIN(1937); DUKE OF WEST POINT, THE(1938); GOODBYE BROADWAY(1938); IN OLD CHICAGO(1938); MERRILY WE LIVE(1938); STORM, THE(1938); SWING THAT CHEER(1938); BIG TOWN CZAR(1939); EX-CHAMP(1939); SERGEANT MADDEN(1939); THESE GLAMOUR GIRLS(1939); MA, HE'S MAKING EYES AT ME(1940); MARGIE(1940); OH JOHNNY, HOW YOU CAN LOVE!(1940); SANDY IS A LADY(1940); HELLO SUCKER(1941); THREE SONS O'GUNS(1941); HELLO ANNAPOLIS(1942); LET'S GET TOUGH(1942); SLEEPYTIME GAL(1942); THERE'S ONE BORN EVERY MINUTE(1942); PAYOFF, THE(1943); ONCE UPON A TIME(1944); HOUSE ON 92ND STREET, THE(1945); BUCK PRIVATES COME HOME(1947); SLIPPY MCGEE(1948); DUKE OF CHICAGO(1949); RINGSIDE(1949); OPERATION HAYLIFT(1950); FIREMAN SAVE MY CHILD(1954); I KILLED WILD BILL HICKOK(1956); NAKED GUN, THE(1956); QUIET GUN, THE(1957); NOTORIOUS MR. MONKS, THE(1958); CHOPPERS, THE(1961)
Tommy Brown
M(1970)
Misc. Silents
THAT OLD GANG OF MINE(1925)
Tony Brown
WOLF DOG(1958, Can.); POPPY IS ALSO A FLOWER, THE(1966), ph; MAN WHO LOVED WOMEN, THE(1983)
Treg Brown
GREAT AMERICAN BUGS BUNNY-ROAD RUNNER CHASE(1979), ed
Troy Brown
CAN THIS BE DIXIE?(1936); UNDER YOUR SPELL(1936); NOTHING SAC-RED(1937); SECOND HONEYMOON(1937)

Troy Brown, Jr.
DREAMING OUT LOUD(1940)
Vanessa Brown
GHOST AND MRS. MUIR, THE(1942); GIRL OF THE LIMBERLOST, THE(1945); I'VE ALWAYS LOVED YOU(1946); MARGIE(1946); FOXES OF HARROW, THE(1947); LATE GEORGE APLEY, THE(1947); MOTHER WORE TIGHTS(1947); BIG JACK(1949); HEIRESS, THE(1949); SECRET OF ST. IVES, THE(1949); TARZAN AND THE SLAVE GIRL(1950); THREE HUSBANDS(1950); BASKETBALL FIX, THE(1951); BAD AND THE BEAUTIFUL, THE(1952); FIGHTER, THE(1952); ROSIE!(1967); BLESS THE BEASTS AND CHILDREN(1971)
Misc. Talkies
WITCH WHO CAME FROM THE SEA, THE(1976)
Vera Brown
JUDGE PRIEST(1934); RED HEAD(1934), w; REDHEAD(1941), w
Vernon Brown
RODEO RHYTHM(1941)
Victoria Brown
DOCTOR DETROIT(1983); PSYCHO II(1983)
Virginia Brown
Silents
OLD FASHIONED BOY, AN(1920)
Vivian Brown
1984
PHILADELPHIA EXPERIMENT, THE(1984)
W. Earl Brown
YOUNG GIRLS OF ROCHEFORT, THE(1968, Fr.)
W. Graham Brown
ALL IN(1936, Brit.)
W. H. Brown
Silents
LITTLE EVA ASCENDS(1922)
W. L. Brown
MISS V FROM MOSCOW(1942), ed
W.J. Brown
MAD LITTLE ISLAND(1958, Brit.)
W.R. "Bill" Brown
THIEF(1981)
Wallace Brown
COME TO THE STABLE(1949)
Wally Brown
ADVENTURES OF A ROOKIE(1943); AROUND THE WORLD(1943); GANGWAY FOR TOMORROW(1943); MEXICAN SPITFIRE'S BLESSED EVENT(1943); PETTICOAT LARCENY(1943); ROOKIES IN BURMA(1943); SEVENTH VICTIM, THE(1943); GIRL RUSH(1944); SEVEN DAYS ASHORE(1944); STEP LIVELY(1944); RADIO STARS ON PARADE(1945); ZOMBIES ON BROADWAY(1945); FROM THIS DAY FORWARD(1946); GENIUS AT WORK(1946); NOTORIOUS(1946); VACATION IN RENO(1946); FAMILY HONEYMOON(1948); AS YOUNG AS YOU FEEL(1951); HIGH AND THE MIGHTY, THE(1954); WILD DAKOTAS, THE(1956); JOKER IS WILD, THE(1957); UNTAMED YOUTH(1957); LEFT-HANDED GUN, THE(1958); WINK OF AN EYE(1958); HOLIDAY FOR LOVERS(1959); WESTBOUND(1959); ABSENT-MINDED PROFESSOR, THE(1961)
Walter Brown
INFORMATION RECEIVED(1962, Brit.); LOCKER 69(1962, Brit.); MIX ME A PERSON(1962, Brit.); BRIGAND OF KANDAHAR, THE(1965, Brit.); DRACULA–PRINCE OF DARKNESS(1966, Brit.); SOME MAY LIVE(1967, Brit.); SHALAKO(1968, Brit.); BEST HOUSE IN LONDON, THE(1969, Brit.)
Walter C. Brown
HOUSE IN THE WOODS, THE(1957, Brit.), w
Warren Brown
V.D.(1961), ed; EXILES, THE(1966), ed
Wayne Brown
1984
FOOTLOOSE(1984)
Wendell Brown
UP THE ACADEMY(1980)
Wenzell Brown
VIOLATORS, THE(1957), w
Weona T. Brown
NORMA RAE(1979)
Will C. Brown
MAN OF THE WEST(1958), w
William Brown
LAST OUTPOST, THE(1935)
Silents
INTOLERANCE(1916)
William H. Brown
Silents
HELL-TO-PAY AUSTIN(1916); M'LISS(1918); HUNCH, THE(1921)
Misc. Silents
HOODOO ANN(1916); RUMMY, THE(1916); HOUSE BUILT UPON SAND, THE(1917)
William Lyon Brown
ONE MILLION YEARS B.C.(1967, Brit./U.S.); VENGEANCE OF SHE, THE(1968, Brit.)
William O. Brown
ONE WAY WAHINI(1965), p&d; WITCHMAKER, THE(1969), p,d&w
William F. Brown
WIZ, THE(1978), w
Winnie Brown
1984
WILD LIFE, THE(1984), cos
Winona Brown
Silents
CAPTAIN COURTESY(1915)
Wyndham Brown
INTERRUPTED HONEYMOON, THE(1936, Brit.), w
Wynne Brown
HOUSE IS NOT A HOME, A(1964)

Brown and Spencer
HEARTS OF HUMANITY(1932), m
Brown Eyes the Cow
Silents
GO WEST(1925)
The Brown Family
WINDFLOWERS(1968)
Kathryn Brown-Decker
Misc. Silents
BELOVED VAGABOND, THE(1912)
Deloris Brown-Harper
TRICK BABY(1973)
Al Browne
PUTNEY SWOPE(1969)
Alan Browne
FORTY DEUCE(1982), w
1984
MIXED BLOOD(1984), w
Alfred Browne
ROMAN HOLIDAY(1953); GREATEST LOVE, THE(1954, Ital.)
Angela Browne
STORY OF DAVID, A(1960, Brit.); PRESS FOR TIME(1966, Brit.); JUST LIKE A WOMAN(1967, Brit.)
Austin Browne
FOLIES DERGERE(1935)
Barton Browne
GARDEN OF THE MOON(1938), w
Bernard Browne
MEN OF TOMORROW(1935, Brit.), ph; SANDERS OF THE RIVER(1935, Brit.), ph; KNIGHT WITHOUT ARMOR(1937, Brit.), ph; CONTINENTAL EXPRESS(1939, Brit.), ph; REBEL SON, THE ½(1939, Brit.), ph; U-BOAT 29(1939, Brit.), ph; ROOM FOR TWO(1940, Brit.), ph; TILLY OF BLOOMSBURY(1940, Brit.), ph
Betty Browne
Misc. Silents
WHAT WOMEN WANT(1920)
Bill Browne
HEROES DIE YOUNG(1960); THIRTEEN FIGHTING MEN(1960); IT HAPPENED IN ATHENS(1962)
Brad Browne
BEDTIME FOR BONZO(1951)
Cathy Browne
MURDER BY CONTRACT(1958); CITY OF FEAR(1959)
Cecily Browne
BURN(1970)
Charles Browne
WOMAN I STOLE, THE(1933)
Charles A. Browne
FEDERAL AGENT(1936); SEALED CARGO(1951)
Charlie Browne
LINEUP, THE(1934)
Cicely Browne
FORT TI(1953); FORTY-NINTH MAN, THE(1953); DRUMS OF TAHITI(1954); CASANOVA(1976, Ital.)
Clarke Browne
GIANT GILA MONSTER, THE(1959)
Coral Browne
CHARING CROSS ROAD(1935, Brit.); LINE ENGAGED(1935, Brit.); AMATEUR GENTLEMAN(1936, Brit.); BLACK LIMELIGHT(1938, Brit.); WE'RE GOING TO BE RICH(1938, Brit.); YELLOW SANDS(1938, Brit.); NURSEMAID WHO DISAPPEARED, THE(1939, Brit.); LET GEORGE DO IT(1940, Brit.); COURTNEY AFFAIR, THE(1947, Brit.); PICCADILLY INCIDENT(1948, Brit.); AUNTIE MAME(1958); ROMAN SPRING OF MRS. STONE, THE(1961, U.S./Brit.); GO TO BLAZES(1962, Brit.); DR. CRIPPEN(1963, Brit.); TAMAHINE(1964, Brit.); NIGHT OF THE GENERALS, THE(1967, Brit./Fr.); LEGEND OF LYLAH CLARE, THE(1968); RULING CLASS, THE(1972, Brit.); THEATRE OF BLOOD(1973, Brit.); DROWNING POOL, THE(1975)
1984
AMERICAN DREAMER(1984)
Diana Browne
BASKET CASE(1982)
Earle Browne
LOCKED DOOR, THE(1929); MR. ROBINSON CRUSOE(1932)
Silents
SHERLOCK HOLMES(1922), w
Ed Browne
FOLLOW THE BOYS(1944)
Eleanor Browne
CROSS COUNTRY ROMANCE(1940), w
Elyse Browne
MY REPUTATION(1946)
Fayte Browne
RENEGADES OF THE SAGE(1949), ph; SOUTH OF DEATH VALLEY(1949), ph; ACROSS THE BADLANDS(1950), ph; FRONTIER OUTPOST(1950), ph; HORSEMEN OF THE SIERRAS(1950), ph; LIGHTNING GUNS(1950), ph; OUTCAST OF BLACK MESA(1950), ph; RAIDERS OF TOMAHAWK CREEK(1950), ph; STREETS OF GHOST TOWN(1950), ph; TEXAS DYNAMO(1950), ph; BANDITS OF EL DORADO(1951), ph; KID FROM AMARILLO, THE(1951), ph; PECOS RIVER(1951), ph; PRAIRIE ROUNDUP(1951), ph; RIDIN' THE OUTLAW TRAIL(1951), ph; SNAKE RIVER DESPERADOES(1951), ph; HAWK OF WILD RIVER, THE(1952), ph; KID FROM BROKEN GUN, THE(1952), ph; ROUGH, TOUGH WEST(1952), ph; SMOKY CANYON(1952), ph
Fred Browne
SMASH-UP, THE STORY OF A WOMAN(1947); CHECKERED COAT, THE(1948)
Fred M. Browne
NOOSE HANGS HIGH, THE(1948)
George Browne
NATIONAL HEALTH, OR NURSE NORTON'S AFFAIR, THE(1973, Brit.)
George "Calypso" Browne
ROCK YOU SINNERS(1957, Brit.)

Susan Brownell
PERSONAL BEST(1982)
Vincent Brownell
Silents
HAZARDOUS VALLEY(1927)
Bert Brownhill
KEEP IT CLEAN(1956, Brit.)
George Brownhill
Misc. Silents
PIONEERS OF THE WEST(1929)
Alan Brownie
MC KENZIE BREAK, THE(1970), makeup
Alan Browning
GUNS AT BATASI(1964, Brit.); JULIUS CAESAR(1970, Brit.)
Alice Browning
Misc. Silents
SILK STOCKING SAL(1924)
Alistair Browning
MERRY CHRISTMAS MR. LAWRENCE(1983, Jap./Brit.)
Colleen Browning
MY SISTER AND I(1948, Brit.), set d; GAY LADY, THE(1949, Brit.), set d
David Browning
HELL, HEAVEN OR HOBOKEN(1958, Brit.); MUMMY, THE(1959, Brit.); SWEET
BEAT(1962, Brit.)
Irving Browning
HOUSE OF SECRETS(1929), ph; UNMASKED(1929), ph
Ivan Browning
THEY WON'T BELIEVE ME(1947); SUNDOWN(1941); NO MAN OF HER OWN(1950);
AFFAIR IN TRINIDAD(1952); YOU FOR ME(1952); YOUNG AT HEART(1955);
SUNRISE AT CAMPOBELLO(1960)
Ivan H. Browning
MR. PEABODY AND THE MERMAID(1948); MY FRIEND IRMA GOES WEST(1950);
PEGGY(1950); NARROW MARGIN, THE(1952)
Ivy Ray Browning
DEAR MR. WONDERFUL(1983, Ger.)
Jill Browning
WHEN THE LIGHTS GO ON AGAIN(1944); TOWN WENT WILD, THE(1945);
UTAH(1945)
Kelly Browning
1984
WHERE THE BOYS ARE '84(1984)
Lynn Browning
KID FROM SPAIN, THE(1932); GOLD DIGGERS OF 1933(1933); LITTLE GIANT,
THE(1933); 42ND STREET(1933); SIDE STREETS(1934); GLAMOUR FOR SALE(1940)
Maurice Browning
LAST DAYS OF DOLWYN, THE(1949, Brit.); PICKUP ALLEY(1957, Brit.); COOL
MIKADO, THE(1963, Brit.), w; PARTY'S OVER, THE(1966, Brit.); WHERE THE
BULLETS FLY(1966, Brit.); ASSASSINATION BUREAU, THE(1969, Brit.)
Michael Browning
NIGHT WITHOUT PITY(1962, Brit.)
Natalie Browning
WANDERING JEW, THE(1933)
Norman Browning
STAR 80(1983)
Ricou Browning
CREATURE WALKS AMONG US, THE(1956); FLIPPER(1963), w; FLIPPER'S NEW
ADVENTURE(1964); LADY IN CEMENT(1968), ph; SALTY(1975), d, w; ISLAND
CLAWS(1981), w
Robert Browning
PIED PIPER, THE(1972, Brit.), w
Silents
CHILD OF M'SIEU(1919), w
Rod Browning
CATAMOUNT KILLING, THE(1975, Ger.); THE DOUBLE McGUFFIN(1979); OH,
HEAVENLY DOG!(1980), w
Misc. Talkies
HEROWORK(1977)
Susan Browning
WORLD ACCORDING TO GARP, The(1982)
Terry Browning
NIGHT THE LIGHTS WENT OUT IN GEORGIA, THE(1981)
Tod Browning
OUTSIDE THE LAW(1930), d, w; THIRTEENTH CHAIR, THE(1930), p&d; DRACU-
LA(1931), d; IRON MAN, THE(1931), d; FREAKS(1932), p&d; FAST WORKERS(1933),
d; MARK OF THE VAMPIRE(1935), d; DEVIL DOLL, THE(1936), d, w; MIRACLES
FOR SALE(1939), d; INSIDE JOB(1946), w
Silents
ATTA BOY'S LAST RACE(1916), w; INTOLERANCE(1916); BRAZEN BEAU-
TY(1918), d; PETAL ON THE CURRENT, THE(1919), d; NO WOMAN KNOWS(1921),
d, w; OUTSIDE THE LAW(1921), d, w; UNHOLY THREE, THE(1925), d; BLACK
BIRD, THE(1926), d, w; ROAD TO MANDALAY, THE(1926), d, w; LONDON AFTER
MIDNIGHT(1927), p&d, w; UNKNOWN, THE(1927), d, w; BIG CITY, THE(1928), d,
w; WEST OF ZANZIBAR(1928), d; WHERE EAST IS EAST(1929), d, w
Misc. Silents
HANDS UP(1917), d; JIM BLUDSO(1917), d; JURY OF FATE, THE(1917), d; PEGGY,
THE WILL O' THE WISP(1917), d; EYES OF MYSTERY, THE(1918), d; LEGION OF
DEATH, THE(1918), d; REVENGE(1918), d; SET FREE(1918), d; WHICH WO-
MAN?(1918), d; BONNIE, BONNIE LASSIE(1919), d; EXQUISIT THIEF, THE(1919),
d; UNPAINTED WOMAN, THE(1919), d; WICKED DARLING, THE(1919), d; VIRGIN
OF STAMBOUL, THE(1920), d; MAN UNDER COVER, THE(1922), d; UNDER TWO
FLAGS(1922), d; WISE KID, THE(1922), d; DAY OF FAITH, THE(1923), d; DRIFT-
ING(1923), d; WHITE TIGER(1923), d; DANGEROUS FLIRT, THE(1924), d; SILK
STOCKING SAL(1924), d; MYSTIC, THE(1925), d; SHOW, THE(1927), d
William Browning
Silents
BULLDOG DRUMMOND(1923, Brit.)
John Brownjohn
TESS(1980, Fr./Brit.), w

Robert Brownjohn
OTLEY(1969, Brit.)
Francis Brownlee
TERROR TRAIL(1933)
Frank Brownlee
BEGGARS OF LIFE(1928); LOTTERY BRIDE, THE(1930); PACK UP YOUR TROU-
BLES(1932); TOMBSTONE CANYON(1932); DESERT TRAIL(1935); LUCKY DE-
VILS(1941); SOUTH OF TAHITI(1941); ARIZONA TERRORS(1942); ICE-CAPADES
REVUE(1942); JESSE JAMES, JR.(1942); MAN FROM CHEYENNE(1942); MISSOURI
OUTLAW, A(1942); SHADOWS ON THE SAGE(1942); SOMBRERO KID, THE(1942);
STAGECOACH BUCKAROO(1942); DEAD MAN'S GULCH(1943)
Misc. Talkies
MAN'S BEST FRIEND(1935)
Silents
RIDERS OF THE DAWN(1920); FOOLS OF FORTUNE(1922); NOBODY'S BRI-
DE(1923); ROMANCE LAND(1923); SAWDUST(1923); DESERT FLOWER, THE(1925);
SOCIAL HIGHWAYMAN, THE(1926); WANTED–A COWARD(1927)
Misc. Silents
SHE LEFT WITHOUT HER TRUNKS(1916); DOUBLE STANDARD, THE(1917);
INSPIRATIONS OF HARRY LARRABEE(1917); LITTLE PIRATE, THE(1917); MEN-
TIONED IN CONFIDENCE(1917); PHANTOM SHOTGUN, THE(1917); WILD SU-
MAC(1917); EMPTY CAB, THE(1918); BRASS BUTTONS(1919); MISS
ADVENTURE(1919); HEARTS ARE TRUMPS(1920); HIS OWN LAW(1920); LINCOLN
HIGHWAYMAN, THE(1920); MAN WHO DARED, THE(1920); SHORE ACRES(1920);
HOLE IN THE WALL, THE(1921); SOUL AND BODY(1921); WHISTLE, THE(1921);
BOSTON BLACKIE(1923); RIDIN' STREAK, THE(1925)
Lark Brownlee
Misc. Silents
HOUSE OF DARKENED WINDOWS, THE(1925)
Lester Brownlee
MEDIUM COOL(1969)
Frank Brownley
GALLANT LADY(1942); PRISON GIRL(1942)
Kevin Brownlow
IT HAPPENED HERE(1966, Brit.), p,d&w, ph, ed; CHARGE OF THE LIGHT BRI-
GADE, THE(1968, Brit.), ed; WINSTANLEY(1979, Brit.), d&w
Lt. Gen. Sir Douglas Brownrigg
COLONEL BLIMP(1945, Brit.), tech adv
S.F. Brownrigg
DON'T LOOK IN THE BASEMENT(1973), p&d; SCUM OF THE EARTH(1976), d;
KEEP MY GRAVE OPEN(1980), p&d
Sandy Brownwyeth
JOHNNY GOT HIS GUN(1971)
Kelley Jean Browser
1984
LOVELINES(1984)
Guus Brox
BOEFJE(1939, Ger.)
Lorayne Brox
PROUD AND THE PROFANE, THE(1956)
The Brox Sisters
SPRING IS HERE(1930)
Dan Broyles
SQUARE ROOT OF ZERO, THE(1964)
Robert Broyles
FEVER HEAT(1968); EAT MY DUST!(1976); BORN AGAIN(1978); NORMA RA-
E(1979); RAISE THE TITANIC(1980, Brit.); POLTERGEIST(1982)
Irene Broza
MY FATHER'S HOUSE(1947, Palestine)
Remy Brozeck
YOUNG GIRLS OF ROCHEFORT, THE(1968, Fr.)
Martin Brozius
LITTLE ARK, THE(1972)
Miriam Bru
AND THE WILD, WILD WOMEN(1961, Ital.)
Shimon Bruan
KAZABLAN(1974, Israel), ch
Paul Bruar
VALENTINO(1951)
Anthony Brubaker
99 AND 44/100% DEAD(1974)
Bob Brubaker
BUS IS COMING, THE(1971)
Judy Brubaker
MR. BELVEDERE GOES TO COLLEGE(1949); CHICAGO CALLING(1951); UN-
TAMED WOMEN(1952)
Robert Brubaker
COURT-MARTIAL OF BILLY MITCHELL, THE(1955); PARDNERS(1956); WRITTEN
ON THE WIND(1956); MY MAN GODFREY(1957); WALKING TARGET, THE(1960);
MOON PILOT(1962); APACHE RIFLES(1964); SECONDS(1966); 40 GUNS TO APACHE
PASS(1967)
Tommy Brubaker
THREE TOUGH GUYS(1974, U.S./Ital.)
Tony Brubaker
BUCK AND THE PREACHER(1972); SLAUGHTER'S BIG RIP-OFF(1973); SOUL OF
NIGGER CHARLEY, THE(1973); SUGAR HILL(1974); TRON(1982); WHITE
DOG(1982); UNDER FIRE(1983)
1984
LOVE STREAMS(1984)
Dave Brubeck
ALL NIGHT LONG(1961, Brit.)
1984
ORDEAL BY INNOCENCE(1984, Brit.), m
Alan Bruce
MEET THE MISSUS(1937); MUSIC FOR MADAME(1937); ON AGAIN–OFF
AGAIN(1937); SATURDAY'S HEROES(1937); SUPER SLEUTH(1937); YOU CAN'T
BEAT LOVE(1937); GO CHASE YOURSELF(1938); I AM THE LAW(1938); MR.
DOODLE KICKS OFF(1938); SHE'S GOT EVERYTHING(1938)

Angela Bruce
MAN AT THE TOP(1973, Brit.)
Barbara Bruce
TWO A PENNY(1968, Brit.)
Belle Bruce
Silents
BATTLE CRY OF PEACE, THE(1915); NIGHT OUT, A(1916); GOD'S OUTLAW(1919)
Misc. Silents
MAKING OVER OF GEOFFREY MANNING, THE(1915); FOR A WOMAN'S FAIR NAME(1916); REDEMPTION OF DAVE DARCEY, THE(1916); SON OF THE HILLS, A(1917)
Betty Bruce
GYPSY(1962); ISLAND OF LOVE(1963)
Bill Bruce
STINGRAY(1978), p
Brenda Bruce
MILLIONS LIKE US(1943, Brit.); THEY CAME TO A CITY(1944, Brit.); CARNIVAL(1946, Brit.); NIGHT BOAT TO DUBLIN(1946, Brit.); YANK IN LONDON, A(1946, Brit.); WHEN THE BOUGH BREAKS(1947, Brit.); PICCADILLY INCIDENT(1948, Brit.); DON'T EVER LEAVE ME(1949, Brit.); MARRY ME!(1949, Brit.); MY BROTHER'S KEEPER(1949, Brit.); WHILE THE SUN SHINES(1950, Brit.); SCHOOL FOR BRIDES(1952, Brit.); FINAL TEST, THE(1953, Brit.); BEHIND THE MASK(1958, Brit.); LAW AND DISORDER(1958, Brit.); PEEPING TOM(1960, Brit.); NIGHTMARE(1963, Brit.); UNCLE, THE(1966, Brit.); VIRGIN SOLDIERS, THE(1970, Brit.); THAT'LL BE THE DAY(1974, Brit.); ALL CREATURES GREAT AND SMALL(1975, Brit.); SWALLOWS AND AMAZONS(1977, Brit.)
Carol Bruce
KEEP 'EM FLYING(1941); THIS WOMAN IS MINE(1941); BEHIND THE EIGHT BALL(1942); AMERICAN GIGOLO(1980)
Clifford Bruce
DEVIL MAY CARE(1929)
Silents
FOOL THERE WAS, A(1915)
Misc. Silents
DEVIL AT HIS ELBOW, THE(1916); FOURTH ESTATE, THE(1916); WEAKNESS OF STRENGTH, THE(1916); BLUE JEANS(1917); FINAL PAYMENT, THE(1917); PASSION(1917); SIN WOMAN, THE(1917); SIREN, THE(1917); BREAKERS AHEAD(1918); WINDING TRAIL, THE(1918); RACING STRAIN(1919); WOMAN! WOMAN!(1919)
Colin Bruce
CHARRIOTS OF FIRE(1981, Brit.); SENDER, THE(1982, Brit.)
David Bruce
DISPATCH FROM REUTERS, A(1940); KNUTE ROCKNE–ALL AMERICAN(1940); MAN WHO TALKED TOO MUCH, THE(1940); RIVER'S END(1940); SANTA FE TRAIL(1940); SEA HAWK, THE(1940); BODY DISAPPEARS, THE(1941); FLIGHT FROM DESTINY(1941); SEA WOLF, THE(1941); SERGEANT YORK(1941); SINGAPORE WOMAN(1941); SMILING GHOST, THE(1941); FLYING TIGERS(1942); ALLERGIC TO LOVE(1943); CALLING DR. DEATH(1943); CORVETTE K-225(1943); GUNG HO!(1943); HONEYMOON LODGE(1943); HOW'S ABOUT IT?(1943); MAD GHOUL, THE(1943); SHE'S FOR ME(1943); YOU'RE A LUCKY FELLOW, MR. SMITH(1943); CAN'T HELP SINGING(1944); CHRISTMAS HOLIDAY(1944); LADIES COURAGEOUS(1944); MOON OVER LAS VEGAS(1944); SOUTH OF DIXIE(1944); LADY ON A TRAIN(1945); SALOME, WHERE SHE DANCED(1945); THAT NIGHT WITH YOU(1945); SUSIE STEPS OUT(1946); RACING LUCK(1948); JOE PALOOKA IN THE BIG FIGHT(1949); PREJUDICE(1949); GREAT PLANE ROBBERY(1950); HIJACKED(1950); PYGMY ISLAND(1950); REVENUE AGENT(1950); TIMBER FURY(1950); YOUNG DANIEL BOONE(1950); PIER 23(1951); SEEDS OF DESTRUCTION(1952); CANNIBAL ATTACK(1954); IRON GLOVE, THE(1954); MASTERSON OF KANSAS(1954)
Misc. Talkies
JUNGLE HELL(1956)
Misc. Silents
CHILDREN OF THE GHETTO, THE(1915)
Dean Bruce
BUDDY BUDDY(1981)
Dorothy Bruce
MISSISSIPPI GAMBLER, THE(1953); THERE'S ALWAYS TOMORROW(1956); DRAGSTRIP GIRL(1957)
Douglas Bruce
PARTNERS(1982)
Earle Bruce
SWING HOSTESS(1944)
Ed Bruce
HERE COMES MR. JORDAN(1941); SING FOR YOUR SUPPER(1941); TWO LATINS FROM MANHATTAN(1941)
Eddie Bruce
LUCKY DEVILS(1941); NEVER GIVE A SUCKER AN EVEN BREAK(1941); SABOTAGE SQUAD(1942); TALK OF THE TOWN(1942); WHO DONE IT?(1942); IS EVERYBODY HAPPY?(1943); IT AIN'T HAY(1943); SHE'S FOR ME(1943); JAM SESSION(1944); JANIE(1944); LOUISIANA HAYRIDE(1944); ONCE UPON A TIME(1944); SHE'S A SWEETHEART(1944); SOUTH OF DIXIE(1944); EVE KNEW HER APPLES(1945); HER LUCKY NIGHT(1945); LADY ON A TRAIN(1945); LET'S GO STEADY(1945); TAHITI NIGHTS(1945); MAN I LOVE, THE(1946); NOTORIOUS(1946)
Edgar K. Bruce
SCHOOL FOR SCANDAL, THE(1930, Brit.); FIRST MRS. FRASER, THE(1932, Brit.); PHANTOM LIGHT, THE(1935, Brit.); MACUSHLA(1937, Brit.); STORM IN A TEACUP(1937, Brit.); MURDER IN THE FAMILY(1938, Brit.); MASTER OF BANKDAM, THE(1947, Brit.); SCHOOL FOR SEX(1969, Brit.)
Eve Bruce
JOHN GOLDFARB, PLEASE COME HOME(1964); TICKLE ME(1965); IN LIKE FLINT(1967); HOW SWEET IT IS(1968); ANGEL IN MY POCKET(1969); CACTUS FLOWER(1969); LOVE MACHINE, THE,(1971); UNHOLY ROLLERS(1972); WHERE DOES IT HURT?(1972)
Gary Bruce
CHATTERBOX(1943); FUGITIVE FROM SONORA(1943); ONCE UPON A TIME(1944); PRACTICALLY YOURS(1944); TONIGHT AND EVERY NIGHT(1945)
George Bruce
NAVY BLUE AND GOLD(1937), w; SHE'S NO LADY(1937), w; CROWD ROARS, THE(1938), w; DUKE OF WEST POINT, THE(1938), w; KING OF THE TURF(1939), w; MAN IN THE IRON MASK, THE(1939), w; KIT CARSON(1940), w; SON OF MONTE CRISTO(1940), w; SOUTH OF PAGO PAGO(1940), w; CORSICAN BROTHERS,

THE(1941), w; GENTLEMAN AFTER DARK, A(1942), w; MISS ANNIE ROONEY(1942), w; STAND BY FOR ACTION(1942), w; SALUTE TO THE MARINES(1943), w; KEEP YOUR POWDER DRY(1945), w; LITTLE MISTER JIM(1946), w; RETURN OF MONTE CRISTO, THE(1946), w; TWO YEARS BEFORE THE MAST(1946), w; FIESTA(1947), w; KILLER McCOY(1947), w; WALK A CROOKED MILE(1948), w; ROGUES OF SHERWOOD FOREST(1950), w; MASK OF THE AVENGER(1951), w; VALENTINO(1951), w; BRIGAND, THE(1952), w; KANSAS CITY CONFIDENTIAL(1952), w; FURY IN PARADISE(1955, U.S./Mex.), d&w; RIDE A CROOKED TRAIL(1958), w; FRONTIER UPRISING(1961), w; BEAUTY AND THE BEAST(1963), w; BEHIND THE IRON MASK(1977), w
Graeme Bruce
MYSTERY SUBMARINE(1963, Brit.)
Hunter Bruce
STROKER ACE(1983)
Ian Bruce
TO BE OR NOT TO BE(1983)
J. Campbell Bruce
ESCAPE FROM ALCATRAZ(1979), w
Jack Bruce
TAKE ME OUT TO THE BALL GAME(1949); SGT. PEPPER'S LONELY HEARTS CLUB BAND(1978)
Jane Bruce
CURSE OF THE LIVING CORPSE, THE(1964)
Janet Bruce
MAN WHO KNEW TOO MUCH, THE(1956); NOTHING BUT THE NIGHT(1975, Brit.)
Jean Bruce
OSS 117-MISSION FOR A KILLER(1966, Fr./Ital.), w; VISCOUNT, THE(1967, Fr./Span./Ital./Ger.), w; SINGAPORE, SINGAPORE(1969, Fr./Ital.), w
Jimmy Bruce
CHEER THE BRAVE(1951, Brit.)
Joan Bruce
1984
BROTHERS(1984, Aus.)
Misc. Talkies
NEWMAN SHAME, THE(1977)
John Bruce
WINGS OVER HONOLULU(1937)
Josette Bruce
NO ROSES FOR OSS 117(1968, Fr.), w
Judy Bruce
MOMENT OF INDISCRETION(1958, Brit.); TOO HOT TO HANDLE(1961, Brit.)
K. Edgar Bruce
CARDINAL, THE(1936, Brit.)
Kate Bruce
Silents
JUDITH OF BETHULIA(1914); GRETCHEN, THE GREENHORN(1916); INTOLERANCE(1916); GREATEST THING IN LIFE, THE(1918); HEARTS OF THE WORLD(1918); HUN WITHIN, THE(1918); GIRL WHO STAYED AT HOME, THE(1919); ROMANCE OF HAPPY VALLEY, A(1919); SCARLET DAYS(1919); TRUE HEART SUSIE(1919); FLYING PAT(1920); IDOL DANCER, THE(1920); WAY DOWN EAST(1920); CITY OF SILENT MEN(1921); ORPHANS OF THE STORM(1922); WHITE ROSE, THE(1923); HIS DARKER SELF(1924); BOWERY CINDERELLA(1927); RAGTIME(1927)
Misc. Silents
BETTY OF GRAYSTONE(1916); MARRIAGE OF MOLLY-O, THE(1916); BETSY'S BURGLAR(1917); WOMAN'S AWAKENING, A(1917); MARY ELLEN COMES TO TOWN(1920)
Kitty Bruce
SWITCHBLADE SISTERS(1975)
Lenny Bruce
ROCKET MAN, THE(1954), w
Misc. Talkies
DANCE HALL RACKET(1956)
Marie Bruce
Silents
CHARITY?(1916)
Millie Bruce
SKIRTS AHOY!(1952)
Misty Bruce
GLOVE, THE(1980)
Mona Bruce
TO SIR, WITH LOVE(1967, Brit.); CROSSPLOT(1969, Brit.)
Morris Bruce
GOODBYE PORK PIE(1981, New Zealand)
Nicholas Bruce
BLACK MAGIC(1949); CONSPIRATOR(1949, Brit.); IF THIS BE SIN(1950, Brit.); SAILOR OF THE KING(1953, Brit.); OTHELLO(1955, U.S./Fr./Ital.); TO PARIS WITH LOVE(1955, Brit.); OH ROSALINDA(1956, Brit.); PRIVATE'S PROGRESS(1956, Brit.); GOOD COMPANIONS, THE(1957, Brit.); DIPLOMATIC CORPSE, THE(1958, Brit.)
Nigel Bruce
UNDER TWO FLAGS(1936); ESCAPE(1930, Brit.); SQUEAKER, THE(1930, Brit.); PERFECT ALIBI, THE(1931, Brit.); LORD CAMBER'S LADIES(1932, Brit.); MIDSHIPMAID GOB(1932, Brit.); CHANNEL CROSSING(1934, Brit.); COMING OUT PARTY(1934); I WAS A SPY(1934, Brit.); LADY IS WILLING, THE(1934, Brit.); MURDER IN TRINIDAD(1934); SPRINGTIME FOR HENRY(1934); STAND UP AND CHEER(1934 80m FOX bw); TREASURE ISLAND(1934); BECKY SHARP(1935); JALNA(1935); MAN WHO BROKE THE BANK AT MONTE CARLO, THE(1935); SCARLET PIMPERNEL, THE(1935, Brit.); SHE(1935); CHARGE OF THE LIGHT BRIGADE, THE(1936); FOLLOW YOUR HEART(1936); MAN I MARRY, THE(1936); TRAIL OF THE LONESOME PINE, THE(1936); WHITE ANGEL, THE(1936); LAST OF MRS. CHEYNEY, THE(1937); THUNDER IN THE CITY(1937, Brit.); BARONESS AND THE BUTLER, THE(1938); KIDNAPPED(1938); ADVENTURES OF SHERLOCK HOLMES, THE(1939); HOUND OF THE BASKERVILLES, THE(1939); RAINS CAME, THE(1939); ADVENTURE IN DIAMONDS(1940); BLUE BIRD, THE(1940); DISPATCH FROM REUTERS, A(1940); HUDSON'S BAY(1940); LILLIAN RUSSELL(1940); PLAY GIRL(1940); REBECCA(1940); SUSAN AND GOD(1940); CHOCOLATE SOLDIER, THE(1941); FREE AND EASY(1941); SUSPICION(1941); THIS WOMAN IS MINE(1941); EAGLE SQUADRON(1942); JOURNEY FOR MARGARET(1942); ROXIE HART(1942); SHERLOCK HOLMES AND THE SECRET WEAPON(1942); SHERLOCK HOLMES AND THE VOICE OF TERROR(1942); THIS ABOVE

ALL(1942); CRAZY HOUSE(1943); FOREVER AND A DAY(1943); LASSIE, COME HOME(1943); SHERLOCK HOLMES FACES DEATH(1943); SHERLOCK HOLMES IN WASHINGTON(1943); FOLLOW THE BOYS(1944); FRENCHMAN'S CREEK(1944); GYPSY WILDCAT(1944); PEARL OF DEATH, THE(1944); SCARLET CLAW, THE(1944); SHERLOCK HOLMES AND THE SPIDER WOMAN(1944); CORN IS GREEN, THE(1945); HOUSE OF FEAR, THE(1945); PURSUIT TO ALGIERS(1945); SON OF LASSIE(1945); WOMAN IN GREEN, THE(1945); DRESSED TO KILL(1946); TERROR BY NIGHT(1946); EXILE, THE(1947); TWO MRS. CARROLLS, THE(1947); JULIA MISBEHAVES(1948); VENDETTA(1950); HONG KONG(1951); LIMELIGHT(1952); BWANA DEVIL(1953); WORLD FOR RANSOM(1954)

Olive Bruce
Silents
PARADISE GARDEN(1917)

Paul Bruce
WALK THE ANGRY BEACH(1961); BORN LOSERS(1967); HAREM BUNCH; OR WAR AND PIECE, THE(1969); BILLY JACK(1971)

Robert Bruce
NIGHT MY NUMBER CAME UP, THE(1955, Brit.); PORT OF ESCAPE(1955, Brit.); PRIVATE'S PROGRESS(1956, Brit.); ROTTEN TO THE CORE(1956, Brit.); NO ROAD BACK(1957, Brit.); BANK RAIDERS, THE(1958, Brit.); GIDEON OF SCOTLAND YARD(1959, Brit.); I'M ALL RIGHT, JACK(1959, Brit.); SON OF ROBIN HOOD(1959, Brit.); FRENCH MISTRESS(1960, Brit.); RISK, THE(1961, Brit.); NOTHING BUT THE BEST(1964, Brit.); THIS IS MY STREET(1964, Brit.); WOMAN OF STRAW(1964, Brit.); HEROES OF TELEMARK, THE(1965, Brit.); NATE AND HAYES(1983, U.S./New Zealand)
1984
TREASURE OF THE YANKEE ZEPHYR(1984)

Robert C. Bruce
TRAIL OF THE LONESOME PINE, THE(1936), ph

Rodman Bruce
UNTAMED FURY(1947)

Sally Jane Bruce
NIGHT OF THE HUNTER, THE(1955)

Shanco Bruce
HAMILE(1965, Ghana)

Timothy Bruce
KISS THE BLOOD OFF MY HANDS(1948)

Tommy Bruce
ONE WAY PENDULUM(1965, Brit.); YELLOW HAT, THE(1966, Brit.)

Toni Bruce
BLAME THE WOMAN(1932, Brit.)

Toni Edgar Bruce
WARM CORNER, A(1930, Brit.); BEHIND YOUR BACK(1937, Brit.); HEAVEN IS ROUND THE CORNER(1944, Brit.); WALTZ TIME(1946, Brit.)

Tonie Edgar Bruce
BROTHER ALFRED(1932, Brit.); LUCKY GIRL(1932, Brit.); CHARMING DECEIVER, THE(1933, Brit.); FALLING FOR YOU(1933, Brit.); LEAVE IT TO ME(1933, Brit.); LETTING IN THE SUNSHINE(1933, Brit.); MAN WHO WON, THE(1933, Brit.); MANNEQUIN(1933, Brit.); MELODY MAKER, THE(1933, Brit.); BROKEN MELODY, THE(1934, Brit.); LILIES OF THE FIELD(1934, Brit.); WHISPERING TONGUES(1934, Brit.); CAPTAIN BILL(1935, Brit.); HANDLE WITH CARE(1935, Brit.); MR. WHAT'S-HIS-NAME(1935, Brit.); NIGHT MAIL(1935, Brit.); LAST WALTZ, THE(1936, Brit.); BOYS WILL BE GIRLS(1937, Brit.); SCRUFFY(1938, Brit.); TOO DANGEROUS TO LIVE(1939, Brit.); GERT AND DAISY CLEAN UP(1942, Brit.); SOMEWHERE ON LEAVE(1942, Brit.); SPITFIRE(1943, Brit.); IT HAPPENED ONE SUNDAY(1944, Brit.); TWILIGHT HOUR(1944, Brit.)

Tony Bruce
BATTLE OF GALLIPOLI(1931, Brit.); WINDJAMMER, THE(1931, Brit.)

Virginia Bruce
YELLOW JACK(1938); LOVE PARADE, THE(1929); WOMAN TRAP(1929); LET'S GO NATIVE(1930); LILIES OF THE FIELD(1930); ONLY THE BRAVE(1930); RAFFLES(1930); SAFETY IN NUMBERS(1930); SLIGHTLY SCARLET(1930); WHOOPEE(1930); YOUNG EAGLES(1930); DOWNSTAIRS(1932); HELL DIVERS(1932); KONGO(1932); MIRACLE MAN, THE(1932); SCARLET WEEKEND, A(1932); SKY BRIDE(1932); WINNER TAKE ALL(1932); MIGHTY BARNUM, THE(1934); DANGEROUS CORNER(1935); ESCAPADE(1935); HERE COMES THE BAND(1935); JANE EYRE(1935); LET 'EM HAVE IT(1935); METROPOLITAN(1935); MURDER MAN(1935); SHADOW OF A DOUBT(1935); SOCIETY DOCTOR(1935); TIMES SQUARE LADY(1935); BORN TO DANCE(1936); GARDEN MURDER CASE, THE(1936); GREAT ZIEGFELD, THE(1936); BETWEEN TWO WOMEN(1937); WHEN LOVE IS YOUNG(1937); WIFE, DOCTOR AND NURSE(1937); WOMEN OF GLAMOUR(1937); ARSENE LUPIN RETURNS(1938); BAD MAN OF BRIMSTONE(1938); FIRST 100 YEARS, THE(1938); THERE GOES MY HEART(1938); THERE'S THAT WOMAN AGAIN(1938); WOMAN AGAINST WOMAN(1938); LET FREEDOM RING(1939); SOCIETY LAWYER(1939); STRONGER THAN DESIRE(1939); FLIGHT ANGELS(1940); HIRED WIFE(1940); MAN WHO TALKED TOO MUCH, THE(1940); ADVENTURE IN WASHINGTON(1941); INVISIBLE WOMAN, THE(1941); BUTCH MINDS THE BABY(1942); CAREFUL, SOFT SHOULDERS(1942); PARDON MY SARONG(1942); ACTION IN ARABIA(1944); BRAZIL(1944); LOVE, HONOR AND GOODBYE(1945); NIGHT HAS A THOUSAND EYES(1948); STATE DEPARTMENT-FILE 649(1949); TWO GROOMS FOR A BRIDE(1957); STRANGERS WHEN WE MEET(1960)

William Bruce
ALL THE KING'S MEN(1949)

Hilda Bruce-Potter
Silents
STILL WATERS RUN DEEP(1916, Brit.)

Max Bruch
CLINIC, THE(1983, Aus.)

Pascale Bruchon
SMALL CHANGE(1976, Fr.)

Bella Bruck
LOVED ONE, THE(1965); DIVORCE AMERICAN STYLE(1967); TAMMY AND THE MILLIONAIRE(1967); HOW SWEET IT IS(1968); LAST OF THE RED HOT LOVERS(1972); FOR PETE'S SAKE(1977); CHEAP DETECTIVE, THE(1978); VAN NUYS BLVD.(1979); GONG SHOW MOVIE, THE(1980)

Karl Bruck
PAINT YOUR WAGON(1969)

Ruth Bruck
1984
LOOSE CONNECTIONS(1984, Brit.)

Georg Bruckbauer
INVISIBLE OPPONENT(1933, Ger.), ph

R.L. Bruckberger
ANGELS OF THE STREETS(1950, Fr.), w

Jerry Bruckheimer
FAREWELL, MY LOVELY(1975), p; MARCH OR DIE(1977, Brit.), p; AMERICAN GIGOLO(1980), p; DEFIANCE(1980), p; THIEF(1981), p; YOUNG DOCTORS IN LOVE(1982), p; FLASHDANCE(1983), p
1984
BEVERLY HILLS COP(1984), p; THIEF OF HEARTS(1984), p

Clyde Bruckman
WELCOME DANGER(1929), d, w; FEET FIRST(1930), d, w; EVERYTHING'S ROSIE(1931), d; MOVIE CRAZY(1932), d; MAN ON THE FLYING TRAPEZE, THE(1935), d; SPRING TONIC(1935), d; PROFESSOR BEWARE(1938), w; BLONDIE GOES TO COLLEGE(1942), w; HONEYMOON LODGE(1943), w; SO'S YOUR UNCLE(1943), w; MOON OVER LAS VEGAS(1944), w; SOUTH OF DIXIE(1944), w; SWINGTIME JOHNNY(1944), w; TWILIGHT ON THE PRAIRIE(1944), w; WEEKEND PASS(1944), w; HER LUCKY NIGHT(1945), w; SHE GETS HER MAN(1945), w; UNDER WESTERN SKIES(1945), w; PROFESSIONALS, THE(1966), w
Silents
OUR HOSPITALITY(1923), w&t; THREE AGES, THE(1923), w; NAVIGATOR, THE(1924), w&t; SHERLOCK, JR.(1924), w; FRESHMAN, THE(1925), w; KEEP SMILING(1925), w; SEVEN CHANCES(1925), w; FOR HEAVEN'S SAKE(1926), w; GENERAL, THE(1927), w; CAMERAMAN, THE(1928), w
Misc. Silents
HORSE SHOES(1927), d; PERFECT GENTLEMAN, A(1928), d

Anton Bruckner
IT HAPPENED HERE(1966, Brit.), m; SENSO(1968, Ital.), m

Parris Bruckner
THEY ALL LAUGHED(1981)

Robert Bruckner
FOR THE LOVE O'LIL(1930), w

William Bruckner
RIDERS OF THE PURPLE SAGE(1941), w; DR. RENAULT'S SECRET(1942), w; SUNDOWN JIM(1942), w

Brian Bruderlin
Misc. Talkies
BOARDING HOUSE(1984)

Gerd Brudern
AFFAIRS OF DR. HOLL(1954, Ger.); GLASS TOWER, THE(1959, Ger.)

Annabelle Brudie
PALM SPRINGS(1936)

Marianne Brudie
PALM SPRINGS(1936)

Bo Brudnin
RUSSIAN ROULETTE(1975)

Betty Brueck
JESSE JAMES' WOMEN(1954)

Heidi Bruehl
ETERNAL LOVE(1960, Ger.)

Birgit Bruel
WEEKEND(1964, Den.)

Jed Bruell
MR. WASHINGTON GOES TO TOWN(1941), p&d

Joseph Bruelle
Misc. Silents
THAT WOMAN(1922)

Edna Bruenell
SERPENT'S EGG, THE(1977, Ger./U.S.)

George Bruggeman
I'M NO ANGEL(1933); SPLENDOR(1935); FOREST RANGERS, THE(1942); ONCE UPON A TIME(1944); SONG OF THE SARONG(1945); SPANISH MAIN, THE(1945); THEY WERE EXPENDABLE(1945); O.S.S.(1946); TWO YEARS BEFORE THE MAST(1946); WHERE THERE'S LIFE(1947); FATHER'S LITTLE DIVIDEND(1951); WHAT PRICE GLORY?(1952); DEMETRIUS AND THE GLADIATORS(1954); PURPLE MASK, THE(1955); NEW KIND OF LOVE, A(1963)

Guy Brugger
THUMBELINA(1970), set d

George Bruggerman
STUDENT TOUR(1934); OVER 21(1945); CRACK-UP(1946); DESERT HAWK, THE(1950); RIO BRAVO(1959); BACHELOR FLAT(1962)

Eddy Brugman
1984
QUESTION OF SILENCE(1984, Neth.)

Erika Bruhl
NOT RECONCILED, OR "ONLY VIOLENCE HELPS WHERE IT RULES"(1969, Ger.)

Heidi Bruhl
YOUNG GO WILD, THE(1962, Ger.); CAPTAIN SINDBAD(1963); HOW TO SEDUCE A WOMAN(1974); EIGER SANCTION, THE(1975)

Helga Bruhl
NOT RECONCILED, OR "ONLY VIOLENCE HELPS WHERE IT RULES"(1969, Ger.)

Linda Bruhl
PAPA'S DELICATE CONDITION(1963)

Walter Bruhl
NOT RECONCILED, OR "ONLY VIOLENCE HELPS WHERE IT RULES"(1969, Ger.)

Erik Bruhn
HANS CHRISTIAN ANDERSEN(1952)

Lothar Bruhne
LA HABANERA(1937, Ger.), m; LONG IS THE ROAD(1948, Ger.), m

Werner Bruhns
ODESSA FILE, THE(1974, Brit./Ger.); 1900(1976, Ital.)

The Bruiser
WRESTLER, THE(1974)

Claude Brule
BLOOD AND ROSES(1961, Fr./Ital.), d&w; LES LIAISONS DANGEREUSES(1961, Fr./Ital.), w; TALES OF PARIS(1962, Fr./Ital.), w; PLEASE, NOT NOW!(1963, Fr./Ital.), w; UP FROM THE BEACH(1965), w; IS PARIS BURNING?(1966, U.S./Fr.), w;

BARBARELLA(1968, Fr./Ital.), w; CHAMPAGNE MURDERS, THE(1968, Fr.), w; WHO'S GOT THE BLACK BOX?(1970, Fr./Gr./Ital.), w

Nigel de Brulier
Silents
ROMANCE OF TARZAN, THE(1918)
Misc. Silents
TESTING OF MILDRED VANE, THE(1918)

Pamela Brull
1984
PHILADELPHIA EXPERIMENT, THE(1984)

Mark A. Brum
COUNSEL FOR ROMANCE(1938, Fr.), titles; ROTHSCHILD(1938, Fr.), titles

Colette Brumaire
MAIDEN, THE(1961, Fr.)

Mme. Brumbach
MAN ON A TIGHTROPE(1953)

Thomas Brumberger
SEIZURE(1974), spec eff

Tom Brumberger
JACK AND THE BEANSTALK(1970), makeup; THUMBELINA(1970), makeup; DON'T GO IN THE HOUSE(1980); EXTERMINATOR, THE(1980), spec eff
1984
GIRLS NIGHT OUT(1984), makeup

Andre Brumer
MONSTER FROM THE OCEAN FLOOR, THE(1954), m

Harvey Brumfield
HAROLD AND MAUDE(1971)

John Brumfield
1984
BIRDY(1984)

Beau Brummell
Misc. Talkies
THREE BULLETS FOR A LONG GUN(1973)

Andre Brummer
AIR STRIKE(1955), m; JAILBREAKERS, THE(1960), m; DAY OF THE NIGHTMARE(1965), m

Andre S. Brummer
RAWHIDE TRAIL, THE(1958), m

Andrew Brummer
RAMPARTS WE WATCH, THE(1940)

Dick Brummer
SCHIZOID(1980), ed

Richard Brummer
MOTOR PSYCHO(1965); GOOD MORNING... AND GOODBYE(1967), ed; FINDERS KEEPERS, LOVERS WEEPERS(1968), ed; RETURN, THE(1980), ed; BRAINWAVES(1983), ed

Richard S. Brummer
REVENGE OF THE CHEERLEADERS(1976), ed

Charles Brummit
RECESS(1967)

Joseph Brun
WHISTLE AT EATON FALLS(1951), ph; WALK EAST ON BEACON(1952), ph; JOE LOUIS STORY, THE(1953), ph; SPECIAL DELIVERY(1955, Ger.), ph; EDGE OF THE CITY(1957), ph; WIND ACROSS THE EVERGLADES(1958), ph; LAST MILE, THE(1959), ph; MIDDLE OF THE NIGHT(1959), ph; ODDS AGAINST TOMORROW(1959), ph; GIRL OF THE NIGHT(1960), ph; THUNDER IN CAROLINA(1960), ph; LOVE AT NIGHT(1961, Fr.), ph; HATARI!(1962), ph; FLIPPER(1963), ph; WHO KILLED TEDDY BEAR?(1965), ph; FAT SPY(1966), ph; EXPLOSION(1969, Can.), ph; SLAVES(1969), ph; TRUMAN CAPOTE'S TRILOGY(1969), ph; 300 YEAR WEEKEND(1971), ph

Joseph C. Brun
MARTIN LUTHER(1953), ph

Philippe Brun
MADEMOISELLE(1966, Fr./Brit.), ph; STAIRCASE(1969 U.S./Brit./Fr.), ph

Sloca Bruna
Misc. Silents
PRIMITIVE LOVE(1927)

Tony Brunaker
ROLLERBALL(1975)

Mathilda Brundage
Silents
STORK'S NEST, THE(1915); OH, YOU TONY!(1924); MIDNIGHT MESSAGE, THE(1926); RACING ROMANCE(1926)
Misc. Silents
LIFE MASK, THE(1918); CAREER OF KATHERINE BUSH, THE(1919); HEART OF A GYPSY, THE(1919); BORDER INTRIGUE(1925); SPANIARD, THE(1925)

Mathilde Brundage
Silents
ROYAL FAMILY, A(1915); NEIGHBORS(1918); NEW MOON, THE(1919); RAGE OF PARIS, THE(1921); FRONT PAGE STORY, A(1922); MY BOY(1922); SHIRLEY OF THE CIRCUS(1922); STRANGERS OF THE NIGHT(1923); WESTBOUND(1924); ANYTHING ONCE(1925); CHARMER, THE(1925); COMING AN' GOING(1926); SILVER COMES THROUGH(1927); LOVE ME AND THE WORLD IS MINE(1928)
Misc. Silents
LITTLE TERROR, THE(1917); SOUL OF MAGDALEN, THE(1917); THOU SHALT NOT STEAL(1917); WAITING SOUL, THE(1917); WIFE NUMBER TWO(1917); SUSPICION(1918); WIVES OF MEN(1918); DANGEROUS BUSINESS(1920); LADY FROM LONGACRE, THE(1921); TOO MUCH MARRIED(1921); CONQUERING THE WOMAN(1922); DON'T DOUBT YOUR WIFE(1922); SELF-MADE MAN, A(1922); BLINKY(1923); FASHION ROW(1923); TONGUES OF SCANDAL(1927)

Sarah Brundage
Misc. Silents
LOVE'S PILGRIMAGE TO AMERICA(1916)

Bill Brundige
CRAZYLEGS, ALL AMERICAN(1953)

Bo Brundin
GREAT WALDO PEPPER, THE(1975); METEOR(1979); RAISE THE TITANIC(1980, Brit.)

Misc. Talkies
SHOOT THE SUN DOWN(1981); HEADLESS EYES, THE(1983)

Lena Brundin
NIGHT GAMES(1966, Swed.)

Gabrielle Brune
BAD BOY(1938, Brit.); WIFE OF GENERAL LING, THE(1938, Brit.); GARRISON FOLLIES(1940, Brit.); HE FOUND A STAR(1941, Brit.); AT DAWN WE DIE(1943, Brit.); RUN FOR YOUR MONEY, A(1950, Brit.); CRASH OF SILENCE(1952, Brit.); HOT ICE(1952, Brit.); TITFIELD THUNDERBOLT, THE(1953, Brit.); WEDDING OF LILLI MARLENE, THE(1953, Brit.); WHITE FIRE(1953, Brit.); HARASSED HERO, THE(1954, Brit.); LIGHT TOUCH, THE(1955, Brit.); FUN AT ST. FANNY'S(1956, Brit.); STARS IN YOUR EYES(1956, Brit.); TRUE AS A TURTLE(1957, Brit.); MODEL MURDER CASE, THE(1964, Brit.); PUBLIC EYE, THE(1972, Brit.)

Helen Bruneau
Silents
ALL DOLLED UP(1921); HUNCHBACK OF NOTRE DAME, THE(1923)
Misc. Silents
SCAR HANAN(1925)

Adrain Brunel
Misc. Silents
LOVERS IN ARABY(1924, Brit.)

Adrian Brunel
CROOKED BILLET, THE(1930, Brit.), d; I'M AN EXPLOSIVE(1933, Brit.), d&w; BADGER'S GREEN(1934, Brit.), d; WHEN LONDON SLEEPS(1934, Brit.), d; CITY OF BEAUTIFUL NONSENSE, THE(1935, Brit.), d; CROSS CURRENTS(1935, Brit.), d, w; VANITY(1935), d&w; VARIETY(1935, Brit.), d, w; WHILE PARENTS SLEEP(1935, Brit.), d; LOVE AT SEA(1936, Brit.), d; OLD SPANISH CUSTOM, AN(1936, Brit.), d; PRISON BREAKER(1936, Brit.), d; RETURN OF THE SCARLET PIMPERNEL(1938, Brit.), w; GIRL WHO FORGOT, THE(1939, Brit.), d; REBEL SON, THE ½(1939, Brit.), d, w; LION HAS WINGS(1940, Brit.), d, w; SPITFIRE(1943, Brit.), p
Silents
AUCTION MART, THE(1920, Brit.), w; FACE AT THE WINDOW, THE(1920, Brit.), w; MAN WITHOUT DESIRE, THE(1923, Brit.), a, d; LAND OF HOPE AND GLORY(1927, Brit.), w; VORTEX, THE(1927, Brit.), w
Misc. Silents
LOVERS IN ARABY(1924, Brit.), d; BLIGHTY(1927, Brit.), d

Bernard Brunel
CONDEMNED TO DEATH(1932, Brit.)

Jane Brunel-Cohen
Misc. Talkies
LUCIFER'S WOMEN(1978)

Andre Brunelin
DESERT OF THE TARTARS, THE(1976 Fr./Ital./Iranian), w

Andre G. Brunelin
NO TIME FOR BREAKFAST(1978, Fr.), w

Peter Brunelli
DEVIL WITH WOMEN, A(1930), m; MEN WITHOUT WOMEN(1930), m; BODY AND SOUL(1931), m; FACE IN THE SKY(1933), m; POWER AND THE GLORY, THE(1933), m; DANTE'S INFERNO(1935), m

Ugo Brunelli
PLAYGIRLS AND THE VAMPIRE(1964, Ital.), ph; CURSE OF THE BLOOD GHOULS(1969, Ital.), ph

Gus Bruneman
LAUGHING POLICEMAN, THE(1973)

Neil Brunenkant
BADLANDS OF MONTANA(1957), ed

Anne Bruner
HALLOWEEN II(1981); MAN, WOMAN AND CHILD(1983)

James Bruner
1984
MISSING IN ACTION(1984), w

Genevieve Brunet
FRENCH, THEY ARE A FUNNY RACE, THE(1956, Fr.); LOVERS ON A TIGHTROPE(1962, Fr.)

Nicolas Brunet
LE BEAU MARIAGE(1982, Fr.), ph

Fritzi Brunett
MAID OF SALEM(1937)

Fritzi Brunette
THIS IS THE LIFE(1935); SAN FRANCISCO(1936); SOULS AT SEA(1937); WAY OUT WEST(1937); HONEYMOON IN BALI(1939); STAGECOACH(1939); STAR MAKER, THE(1939); MEET JOHN DOE(1941)
Silents
AND A STILL, SMALL VOICE(1918); CITY OF PURPLE DREAMS, THE(1918); LORD LOVES THE IRISH, THE(1919); DEVIL TO PAY, THE(1920); GREEN FLAME, THE(1920); WIFE'S AWAKENING, A(1921); WHILE SATAN SLEEPS(1922); PACE THAT THRILLS, THE(1925)
Misc. Silents
AT PINEY RIDGE(1916); UNTO THOSE WHO SIN(1916); JAGUAR'S CLAWS(1917); BEWARE OF STRANGERS(1918); PLAYTHINGS(1918); VELVET HAND, THE(1918); WHO SHALL TAKE MY LIFE?(1918); JACQUES OF THE SILVER NORTH(1919); RAILROADER, THE(1919); SEALED ENVELOPE, THE(1919); SPORTING CHANCE, A(1919); WOMAN UNDER COVER, THE(1919); COAST OF OPPORTUNITY, THE(1920); HOUSE OF WHISPERS, THE(1920); LIVE SPARKS(1920); NO.99(1920); $30,000(1920); BUTTERFLY GIRL, THE(1921); DISCONTENTED WIVES(1921); MAN FROM LOST RIVER, THE(1921); TIGER TRUE(1921); BELLS OF SAN JUAN(1921); BOSS OF CAMP 4, THE(1922); CRUSADER, THE(1922); OTHER SIDE, THE(1922); CAUSE FOR DIVORCE(1923); FOOTLIGHT RANGER, THE(1923); CAMILLE OF THE BARBARY COAST(1925)

Fritzie Brunette
$1,000 A TOUCHDOWN(1939)
Silents
FORGIVEN, OR THE JACK O'DIAMONDS(1914)

Argentina Brunetti
CALIFORNIA(1946); GILDA(1946); IT'S A WONDERFUL LIFE(1946); HIGH TIDE(1947); TYCOON(1947); MAN-EATER OF KUMAON(1948); MEXICAN HAYRIDE(1948); HOLIDAY IN HAVANA(1949); HOUSE OF STRANGERS(1949); KNOCK ON ANY DOOR(1949); RED DANUBE, THE(1949); WE WERE STRANGERS(1949); BLONDE BANDIT, THE(1950); BROKEN ARROW(1950); LAWLESS, THE(1950); FORCE OF ARMS(1951); GHOST CHASERS(1951); GREAT CARUSO, THE(1951);

APACHE WAR SMOKE(1952); FIGHTER, THE(1952); MY COUSIN RACHEL(1952); ROSE OF CIMARRON(1952); WHEN IN ROME(1952); WOMAN IN THE DARK(1952); CADDY, THE(1953); KING OF THE KHYBER RIFLES(1953); SAN ANTONE(1953); STORY OF THREE LOVES, THE(1953); TROPIC ZONE(1953); FAR HORIZONS, THE(1955); HELL'S ISLAND(1955); PRODIGAL, THE(1955); RAINS OF RANCHIPUR, THE(1955); TALL MEN, THE(1955); ANYTHING GOES(1956); THREE VIOLENT PEOPLE(1956); BROTHERS RICO, THE(1957); DUEL AT APACHE WELLS(1957); MIDNIGHT STORY, THE(1957); UNHOLY WIFE, THE(1957); SHOWDOWN AT BOOT HILL(1958); JET OVER THE ATLANTIC(1960); GEORGE RAFT STORY, THE(1961); HORIZONTAL LIEUTENANT, THE(1962); SEVEN FACES OF DR. LAO(1964); STAGE TO THUNDER ROCK(1964); APPALOOSA, THE(1966); MONEY TRAP, THE(1966)

Susana Brunetti
TERRACE, THE(1964, Arg.)

Fernando Bruni
LOVE AND LARCENY(1963, Fr./Ital.)

Peter Bruni
ASSAULT ON PRECINCT 13(1976)

Romolo Bruni
PIRATES OF PENZANCE, THE(1983)

Sandro Bruni
LITTLE NUNS, THE(1965, Ital.)

Sergio Bruni
VOYAGE, THE(1974, Ital.)

Robert Bruning
NED KELLY(1970, Brit.); DAY AFTER HALLOWEEN, THE(1981, Aus.)

Britta Brunius
CHILDREN, THE(1949, Swed.); DUET FOR CANNIBALS(1969, Swed.); PASSION OF ANNA, THE(1970, Swed.)

Jacques B. Brunius
LA BETE HUMAINE(1938, Fr.)

Jacques Brunius
CRIME OF MONSIEUR LANGE, THE(1936, Fr.); LAVENDER HILL MOB, THE(1951, Brit.); WOODEN HORSE, THE(1951); AFFAIR IN MONTE CARLO(1953, Brit.); SEA DEVILS(1953); ALWAYS A BRIDE(1954, Brit.); FORBIDDEN CARGO(1954, Brit.); GOLDEN MASK, THE(1954, Brit.); LAUGHING ANNE(1954, Brit./U.S.); COCKLE-SHELL HEROES, THE(1955); TO PARIS WITH LOVE(1955, Brit.); PORTRAIT IN SMOKE(1957, Brit.); TRIPLE DECEPTION(1957, Brit.); TRUE AS A TURTLE(1957, Brit.); DANGEROUS EXILE(1958, Brit.); ORDERS TO KILL(1958, Brit.); LOSS OF INNOCENCE(1961, Brit.); RETURN FROM THE ASHES(1965, U.S./Brit.); YELLOW ROLLS-ROYCE, THE(1965, Brit.); L'AGE D'OR(1979, Fr.)

Pauline Brunius
Misc. Silents
GUNNAR HEDE'S SAGA(1922, Swed.)

David Brunjes
LORD OF THE FLIES(1963, Brit.)

Ralph Brunjes
TWO SOLITUDES(1978, Can.), ed; FUNERAL HOME(1982, Can.), ed; SPASMS(1983, Can.), ed

Nadja Brunkhorst
QUERELLE(1983, Ger./Fr.)

Ernst Brunman
NIGHT IN JUNE, A(1940, Swed.)

Brigitte Brunmuller
SECRET WAYS, THE(1961)

Frederic Brunn
WOMEN IN BONDAGE(1943); RENDEZVOUS 24(1946); 13 RUE MADELEINE(1946); DESIRE ME(1947); I, JANE DOE(1948)

Frederick Brunn
FIRST COMES COURAGE(1943); GANGWAY FOR TOMORROW(1943); NORTH STAR, THE(1943); THEY CAME TO BLOW UP AMERICA(1943); WHITE SAVAGE(1943)

Ulf Brunnberd
APOLLO GOES ON HOLIDAY(1968, Ger./Swed.)

Ulf Brunnberg
VIBRATION(1969, Swed.)

Marcia Brunne
THRESHOLD(1983, Can.)

Neil Brunnenkant
LORD OF THE JUNGLE(1955), ed; HOT SHOTS(1956), ed; FOOTSTEPS IN THE NIGHT(1957), ed; LOOKING FOR DANGER(1957), ed; SPOOK CHASERS(1957), ed; IN THE MONEY(1958), ed; UNWED MOTHER(1958), ed; ATOMIC SUBMARINE, THE(1960), m

Neil Brunnenkent
CHAIN OF EVIDENCE(1957), ed

Andre Brunner
WILD GYPSIES(1969), md

Angela Brunner
NAKED AMONG THE WOLVES(1967, Ger.)

Arthur Brunner
SNOWS OF KILIMANJARO, THE(1952)

Bernard Brunner
HANGUP(1974), w

Bob Brunner
TIGER WALKS, A(1964), md; THAT DARN CAT(1965), m; LT. ROBIN CRUSOE, U.S.N.(1966), m

Cecil Brunner
Silents
NOOSE, THE(1928)

Charles Brunner
KING OF THE STALLIONS(1942)

Cliff Brunner
1984
PLACES IN THE HEART(1984)

Ernest Brunner
SNOWS OF KILIMANJARO, THE(1952)

Howard Brunner
FROM NOON TO THREE(1976); LINCOLN CONSPIRACY, THE(1977)

John Brunner
TERRORNAUTS, THE(1967, Brit.), w

Kathrin Brunner
END OF THE GAME(1976, Ger./Ital.)

Phyllis Brunner
WE'RE NOT MARRIED(1952)

Robert F. Brunner
MONKEYS, GO HOME!(1967), m; BLACKBEARD'S GHOST(1968), m; NEVER A DULL MOMENT(1968), m; SMITH(1969), m; BOATNIKS, THE(1970), m; COMPUTER WORE TENNIS SHOES, THE(1970), m; BAREFOOT EXECUTIVE, THE(1971), m; WILD COUNTRY, THE(1971), m; BISCUIT EATER, THE(1972), m; NOW YOU SEE HIM, NOW YOU DON'T(1972), m; SNOWBALL EXPRESS(1972), m; CASTAWAY COWBOY, THE(1974), m; STRONGEST MAN IN THE WORLD, THE(1975), m; GUS(1976), m; NORTH AVENUE IRREGULARS, THE(1979), m; AMY(1981), m

Rudolf Brunngraber
ONE APRIL 2000(1952, Aust.), w; APRIL 1, 2000(1953, Aust.), w

Harry Brunning
VARIETY(1935, Brit.); TWILIGHT WOMEN(1953, Brit.); MIRACLE IN SOHO(1957, Brit.); TEARS FOR SIMON(1957, Brit.); JIG SAW(1965, Brit.)

Harry Brunnings
HEATWAVE(1954, Brit.)

Richard Brunno
DEADHEAD MILES(1982), cos

Alberico Bruno
LOLLIPOP(1966, Braz.)

Antonino Faa'Di Bruno
AVANTI!(1972)

Chic Bruno
SMART BLONDE(1937)

Cinzia Bruno
MAFIOSO(1962, Ital.); HERCULES, SAMSON & ULYSSES(1964, Ital.); GARDEN OF THE FINZI-CONTINIS, THE(1976, Ital./Ger.)

Dick Bruno
ENTERTAINER, THE(1975), cos

Fernando Bruno
TWO NIGHTS WITH CLEOPATRA(1953, Ital.); TIME OUT FOR LOVE(1963, Ital./Fr.)

Frank Bruno
KING OF HOCKEY(1936); TREACHERY RIDES THE RANGE(1936); EXCLUSIVE(1937); INTERNES CAN'T TAKE MONEY(1937); I AM THE LAW(1938); MR. WONG, DETECTIVE(1938); KING OF THE UNDERWORLD(1939); HOUSE ACROSS THE BAY, THE(1940); INVISIBLE STRIPES(1940); TALL, DARK AND HANDSOME(1941); DR. BROADWAY(1942); GLASS KEY, THE(1942); DRIVER, THE(1978)

George Bruno
VIOLATED LOVE(1966, Arg.), makeup

Jennie Bruno
STREET ANGEL(1928)

JoAnn Bruno
SWEET JESUS, PREACHER MAN(1973)

John Bruno
RAGGEDY ANN AND ANDY(1977), anim
1984
GHOSTBUSTERS(1984), spec eff

Juanne Bruno
PSYCHO FROM TEXAS(1982)

Leo Bruno
INVISIBLE AVENGER, THE(1958); FOUR FOR THE MORGUE(1962)

Mando Bruno
INDISCRETION OF AN AMERICAN WIFE(1954, U.S./Ital.)

Mauro Bruno
INDEPENDENCE DAY(1976), m

Nando Bruno
OPEN CITY(1946, Ital.); TO LIVE IN PEACE(1947, Ital.); ANGELINA(1948, Ital.); JOURNEY TO LOVE(1953, Ital.); STRANGER ON THE PROWL(1953, Ital.); HELLO, ELEPHANT(1954, Ital.); LOVE SPECIALIST, THE(1959, Ital.)

Pierrette Bruno
LETTERS FROM MY WINDMILL(1955, Fr.)

Richard Bruno
HOW TO STUFF A WILD BIKINI(1965), cos; SKI PARTY(1965), cos; FIREBALL 590(1966), cos; GHOST IN THE INVISIBLE BIKINI(1966), cos; THUNDER ALLEY(1967), cos; TRIP, THE(1967), cos; KILLERS THREE(1968), cos; WILD IN THE STREETS(1968), cos; HELL'S BELLES(1969), cos; HIRED HAND, THE(1971), cos; SOMETHING BIG(1971), cos; TWO-LANE BLACKTOP(1971), cos; HEAVEN CAN WAIT(1978), cos; ICE CASTLES(1978), cos; PLAYERS(1979), cos; STRIPES(1981), cos; GORKY PARK(1983), cos; KING OF COMEDY, THE(1983), cos
1984
FALLING IN LOVE(1984), cos; KARATE KID, THE(1984), cos

Tony Bruno
HELL'S ANGELS '69(1969), m

Danielle Brunon
1984
FIRST TURN-ON!, THE(1984), cos

Andre Brunot
CURTAIN RISES, THE(1939, Fr.); PERSONAL COLUMN(1939, Fr.); PORTRAIT OF INNOCENCE(1948, Fr.); RED AND THE BLACK, THE(1954, Fr./Ital.); PICNIC ON THE GRASS(1960, Fr.); MAXIME(1962, Fr.)

Blanchette Brunoy
LA BETE HUMAINE(1938, Fr.); TWO WOMEN(1940, Fr.); IT HAPPENED AT THE INN(1945, Fr.); LA MARIE DU PORT(1951, Fr.); FRENCH TOUCH, THE(1954, Fr.); BERNADETTE OF LOURDES(1962, Fr.); LA BONNE SOUPE(1964, Fr./Ital.)

George Bruns
DAVY CROCKETT, KING OF THE WILD FRONTIER(1955), m; DAVY CROCKETT AND THE RIVER PIRATES(1956), m; WESTWARD HO THE WAGONS!(1956), m; JOHNNY TREMAIN(1957), m; SLEEPING BEAUTY(1959), m; ABSENT-MINDED PROFESSOR, THE(1961), m; ONE HUNDRED AND ONE DALMATIANS(1961), m; SON OF FLUBBER(1963), m; SWORD IN THE STONE, THE(1963), m; FIGHTING PRINCE OF DONEGAL, THE(1966, Brit.), m; FOLLOW ME, BOYS!(1966), m; UGLY DACHSHUND, THE(1966), m; ADVENTURES OF BULLWHIP GRIFFIN, THE(1967), m; JUNGLE BOOK, THE(1967), m; DARING GAME(1968), m; HORSE IN THE GRAY FLANNEL SUIT, THE(1968), m; LOVE BUG, THE(1968), m; ARISTOCATS, THE(1970), m; ROBIN HOOD(1973), m; HERBIE RIDES AGAIN(1974), m

Jeanne Bruns
ONE HUNDRED AND ONE DALMATIANS(1961)
Julia Bruns
Misc. Silents
AT FIRST SIGHT(1917)
Mona Bruns
WEDNESDAY'S CHILD(1934)
Norbert W. Bruns
1984
COUNTRY(1984)
Phil Bruns
ALL WOMAN(1967); JENNY(1969); OUT OF TOWNERS, THE(1970); GANG THAT COULDN'T SHOOT STRAIGHT, THE(1971); FLASHDANCE(1983)
Philip Bruns
GREAT WALDO PEPPER, THE(1975); NICKELODEON(1976); CORVETTE SUMMER(1978); STUNT MAN, THE(1980)
Phillip Bruns
TAKING OFF(1971)
Henrietta Brunsch
MAGIC FACE, THE(1951, Aust.), ed; NO TIME FOR FLOWERS(1952), ed
John Brunskill
LONG JOHN SILVER(1954, Aus.)
Muriel Brunskill
GREAT GILBERT AND SULLIVAN, THE(1953, Brit.)
Bengt Brunskog
LOVING COUPLES(1966, Swed.)
Caroline Brunson
Misc. Silents
POWER DIVINE, THE(1923)
Glenda Brunson
LEGEND OF BLOOD MOUNTAIN, THE(1965); SPEED LOVERS(1968)
Misc. Talkies
LEGEND OF BLOOD MOUNTAIN, THE(1965)
Earle Brunswick
Misc. Silents
DRAFT 258(1917)
Eckart Bruntjen
CHRONICLE OF ANNA MAGDALENA BACH(1968, Ital., Ger.)
Paul Brunton
FANDANGO(1970)
Robert Brunton
Silents
PATRIOT, THE(1916), art d; TRUTHFUL TULLIVER(1917), art d
Will Brunton
Misc. Silents
VALLEY OF THE GIANTS, THE(1919)
William Brunton
Silents
JUDITH OF THE CUMBERLANDS(1916); AS THE SUN WENT DOWN(1919); MAD MARRIAGE, THE(1921)
Misc. Silents
BARNSTORMERS, THE(1915); HIGH HAND, THE(1915); CRUISE OF THE MAKE-BELIEVES, THE(1918)
Jose Bruquera
ADVENTURES OF SCARAMOUCHE, THE(1964, Fr.)
Ferruccio Brusarosco
LITTLE NUNS, THE(1965, Ital.), p
Ferrucio Brusarosco
SUPERFLY T.N.T.(1973)
Franco Brusati
ANNA(1951, Ital.), w; HONEYMOON DEFERRED(1951, Brit.), w; ULYSSES(1955, Ital.), w; UNFAITHFULS, THE(1960, Ital.), w; RUN WITH THE DEVIL(1963, Fr./Ital.), w; DISORDER(1964, Fr./Ital.), d; ROMEO AND JULIET(1968, Brit./Ital.), w; SEATED AT HIS RIGHT(1968, Ital.), w; GIRL WHO COULDN'T SAY NO, THE(1969, Ital.), d, w; BREAD AND CHOCOLATE(1978, Ital.), d, w
Margrit Brusendorf
PINOCCHIO(1969, E. Ger.), ed
Katharine Brush
RED HEADED WOMAN(1932), w; HONEYMOON IN BALI(1939), w
Katherine Brush
FOOTLIGHTS AND FOOLS(1929), w; YOUNG MAN OF MANHATTAN(1930), w; LADY OF SECRETS(1936), w; MANNEQUIN(1937), w; LISTEN, DARLING(1938), w
Silents
DROPKICK, THE(1927), w
Peter Brush
SEPARATE PEACE, A(1972)
Johanna Brushay
DON'T GO IN THE HOUSE(1980)
Kees Brusse
MYSTERIES(1979, Neth.)
M.J. Brusse
BOEFJE(1939, Ger.), w
William E. Brusseau
THREE WEEKS OF LOVE(1965), p&d, w
Yura Brusser
VIOLIN AND ROLLER(1962, USSR)
Alf Brustellin
GERMANY IN AUTUMN(1978, Ger.), d
Hans Brustellin
BATTLE OF BRITAIN, THE(1969, Brit.), tech adv
Andrew Brut
BLACK PANTHER, THE(1977, Brit.)
Giovanni Bruti
TREASURE OF SAN GENNARO(1968, Fr./Ital./Ger.)
Stephen Bruton
1984
SONGWRITER(1984)

Gerald Brutsche
WHAT'S UP, DOC?(1972); HERBIE GOES TO MONTE CARLO(1977)
Jerry Brutsche
PAJAMA PARTY(1964); HOW TO STUFF A WILD BIKINI(1965); SERGEANT DEADHEAD(1965); GHOST IN THE INVISIBLE BIKINI(1966); HELL'S BELLES(1969); ELECTRA GLIDE IN BLUE(1973); ST. IVES(1976)
1984
BODY DOUBLE(1984), a, stunts
Brutus the Dog
DEPUTY DRUMMER, THE(1935, Brit.)
Einar J. Bruun
Silents
ENCHANTMENT(1920, Brit.), d; JUDGE NOT(1920, Brit.), d; PENNILESS MILLIONAIRE, THE(1921, Brit.), d
Misc. Silents
CORNER MAN, THE(1921, Brit.), d; HER PENALTY(1921, Brit.), d
Einer J. Bruun
Misc. Silents
IN FULL CRY(1921, Brit.), d
The Bruvvers
WHAT A CRAZY WORLD(1963, Brit.)
Gaby Bruyere
LE PLAISIR(1954, Fr.); INNOCENTS IN PARIS(1955, Brit.)
Mme. Bruyere
END OF THE WORLD, THE(1930, Fr.), ed
Jan Bruyns
HELLIONS, THE(1962, Brit.)
Sergio Bruzzichinini
HERCULES(1983)
Henri Bry
PERSONAL COLUMN(1939, Fr.)
Al Bryan
BRIDE OF THE REGIMENT(1930), m
Arthur Q. Bryan
I STOLE A MILLION(1939); LITTLE ACCIDENT(1939); THESE GLAMOUR GIRLS(1939); MILLIONAIRE PLAYBOY(1940); ROAD TO SINGAPORE(1940); DEVIL BAT, THE(1941); LOOK WHO'S LAUGHING(1941); LARCENY, INC.(1942); SWING OUT THE BLUES(1943); I'M FROM ARKANSAS(1944); SHE WOULDN'T SAY YES(1945); DARK HORSE, THE(1946); IDEA GIRL(1946); ROAD TO RIO(1947); SAMSON AND DELILAH(1949); HERE COME THE NELSONS(1952); HELL'S OUTPOST(1955); LIEUTENANT WORE SKIRTS, THE(1956)
Blanche Bryan
Misc. Silents
HIS VINDICATION(1915, Brit.); MAN IN THE ATTIC, THE(1915, Brit.); SONS OF SATAN, THE(1915, Brit.)
Bob Bryan
SWORD OF LANCELOT(1963, Brit.)
Brandy Bryan
YOUNG AND DANGEROUS(1957)
Buddy Bryan
MY FAIR LADY(1964)
Darlene Bryan
ZOOT SUIT(1981)
David Bryan
RED RUNS THE RIVER(1963)
Diane Bryan
MIRACLE WORKER, THE(1962)
Donna Bryan
MIRACLE WORKER, THE(1962)
Dora Bryan
ODD MAN OUT(1947, Brit.); FALLEN IDOL, THE(1949, Brit.); INTERRUPTED JOURNEY, THE(1949, Brit.); NOW BARABBAS WAS A ROBBER(1949, Brit.); ONCE UPON A DREAM(1949, Brit.); CURE FOR LOVE, THE(1950, Brit.); NO ROOM AT THE INN(1950, Brit.); NO TRACE(1950, Brit.); SOMETHING IN THE CITY(1950, Brit.); CIRCLE OF DANGER(1951, Brit.); FILES FROM SCOTLAND YARD(1951, Brit.); HIGH TREASON(1951, Brit.); NO HIGHWAY IN THE SKY(1951, Brit.); QUIET WOMAN, THE(1951, Brit.); SCARLET THREAD(1951, Brit.); TRAVELLER'S JOY(1951, Brit.); GLORY AT SEA(1952, Brit.); MADE IN HEAVEN(1952, Brit.); MISS ROBIN HOOD(1952, Brit.); WHISPERING SMITH VERSUS SCOTLAND YARD(1952, Brit.); 13 EAST STREET(1952, Brit.); BOTH SIDES OF THE LAW(1953, Brit.); FAKE, THE(1953, Brit.); RINGER, THE(1953, Brit.); TIME GENTLEMEN PLEASE!(1953, Brit.); TWILIGHT WOMEN(1953, Brit.); CROWDED DAY, THE(1954, Brit.); FAST AND LOOSE(1954, Brit.); MAD ABOUT MEN(1954, Brit.); YOU KNOW WHAT SAILORS ARE(1954, Brit.); COCKLESHELL HEROES, THE(1955); INTRUDER, THE(1955, Brit.); LADY GODIVA RIDES AGAIN(1955, Brit.); SEE HOW THEY RUN(1955, Brit.); YOU LUCKY PEOPLE(1955, Brit.); CHILD IN THE HOUSE(1956, Brit.); AS LONG AS THEY'RE HAPPY(1957, Brit.); GREEN MAN, THE(1957, Brit.); SMALL HOTEL(1957, Brit.); HELLO LONDON(1958, Brit.); MAN WHO WOULDN'T TALK, THE(1958, Brit.); CARRY ON SERGEANT(1959, Brit.); DESERT MICE(1960, Brit.); FOLLOW THAT HORSE!(1960, Brit.); NIGHT WE GOT THE BIRD, THE(1961, Brit.); TASTE OF HONEY, A(1962, Brit.); MY SON, THE VAMPIRE(1963, Brit.); OPERATION BULLSHINE(1963, Brit.); GREAT ST. TRINIAN'S TRAIN ROBBERY, THE(1966, Brit.); SANDWICH MAN, THE(1966, Brit.); TWO A PENNY(1968, Brit.); HANDS OF THE RIPPER(1971, Brit.); UP THE FRONT(1972, Brit.)
Misc. Talkies
SCREAMTIME(1983, Brit.)
Eleanor Bryan
NEXT TO NO TIME(1960, Brit.)
Eleanore Bryan
ROSSITER CASE, THE(1950, Brit.)
Ernest E. Bryan
LAST COUPON, THE(1932, Brit.), w; SPRING HANDICAP(1937, Brit.), w
Jack Bryan
PORTRAIT IN BLACK(1960)
James Edward Bryan
1984
CRACKERS(1984)

Jane Bryan
CASE OF THE BLACK CAT, THE(1936); CAPTAIN'S KID, THE(1937); CHEROKEE STRIP(1937); CONFESSION(1937); KID GALAHAD(1937); MARKED WOMAN(1937); BROTHER RAT(1938); GIRLS ON PROBATION(1938); SISTERS, THE(1938); SLIGHT CASE OF MURDER, A(1938); EACH DAWN I DIE(1939); I AM NOT AFRAID(1939); MAN WHO DARED, THE(1939); OLD MAID, THE(1939); THESE GLAMOUR GIRLS(1939); WE ARE NOT ALONE(1939); INVISIBLE STRIPES(1940)

Janice Bryan
ONE MAN(1979, Can.)

Jay J. Bryan
FAST BULLETS(1936), w

Jim Bryan
Misc. Talkies
DON'T GO INTO THE WOODS(1980), d

John Bryan
GARDEN OF ALLAH, THE(1936); ROMEO AND JULIET(1936); SUICIDE SQUADRON(1942, Brit.), art d; RANDOLPH FAMILY, THE(1945, Brit.), art d; CAESAR AND CLEOPATRA(1946, Brit.), set d; CARAVAN(1946, Brit.), art d; GREAT EXPECTATIONS(1946, Brit.), prod d; WICKED LADY, THE(1946, Brit.), art d; ROOT OF ALL EVIL, THE(1947, Brit.), set d; MAN OF EVIL(1948, Brit.), art d; TAKE MY LIFE(1948, Brit.), prod d; ONE WOMAN'S STORY(1949, Brit.), set d; MADELEINE(1950, Brit.), set d; OLIVER TWIST(1951, Brit.), set d; PANDORA AND THE FLYING DUTCHMAN(1951, Brit.), art d; MAGIC BOX, THE(1952, Brit.), prod d; PROMOTER, THE(1952, Brit.), p; MAN WITH A MILLION(1954, Brit.), p; PURPLE PLAIN, THE(1954, Brit.), p; SPANISH GARDENER, THE(1957, Span.), p, w; HORSE'S MOUTH, THE(1958, Brit.), p; SECRET PLACE, THE(1958, Brit.), p; WINDOM'S WAY(1958, Brit.), p; GIRL ON THE BOAT, THE(1962, Brit.), p; THERE WAS A CROOKED MAN(1962, Brit.), p; BECKET(1964, Brit.), prod d; TAMAHINE(1964, Brit.), p; VERDICT, THE(1964, Brit.), p; AFTER THE FOX(1966, U.S./Brit./Ital.), p; GREAT CATHERINE(1968, Brit.), prod d

Michael Bryan
INTENT TO KILL(1958, Brit.), w

Paul Bryan
DUKE OF THE NAVY(1942); NOTORIOUS(1946)

Paul M. Bryan
Silents
ACCORDING TO LAW(1916), w; IDOL OF THE STAGE, THE(1916), w; DUDE COWBOY, THE(1926), w; HAIR TRIGGER BAXTER(1926), w

Peggy Bryan
MY WIFE'S FAMILY(1941, Brit.); TURNED OUT NICE AGAIN(1941, Brit.); DEAD OF NIGHT(1946, Brit.)

Peter Bryan
BOOBY TRAP(1957, Brit.), w; BRIDES OF DRACULA, THE(1960, Brit.), w; PLAGUE OF THE ZOMBIES, THE(1966, Brit.), w; BLOOD BEAST TERROR, THE(1967, Brit.), w; PROJECTED MAN, THE(1967, Brit.), w; CHALLENGE FOR ROBIN HOOD, A(1968, Brit.), w; TROG(1970, Brit.), w

R. Bryan
HELL, HEAVEN OR HOBOKEN(1958, Brit.)

Richard Bryan
PUSHOVER(1954); SECRET WORLD(1969, Fr.), ed; HELLO–GOODBYE(1970), ed

Ruth Bryan
Silents
FORTUNE HUNTER, THE(1914)

Trevor Bryan
OUTRAGEOUS!(1977, Can.)

William Bryan
CONFESSIONS OF AMANS, THE(1977); HAUNTING OF M, THE(1979)

Winifred Bryan
Misc. Talkies
QUEEN OF SHEBA MEETS THE ATOM MAN, THE(1963)

John Bryans
HOUSE THAT DRIPPED BLOOD, THE(1971, Brit.); HENRY VIII AND HIS SIX WIVES(1972, Brit.)

Baird Bryant
SEDUCERS, THE(1962), ph; COOL WORLD, THE(1963), ph; GREENWICH VILLAGE STORY(1963), ph

Betty Bryant
FORTY THOUSAND HORSEMEN(1941, Aus.); SAIGON(1948)

Bill Bryant
BATTLE OF ROGUE RIVER(1954); BULLET FOR JOEY, A(1955); KING DINOSAUR(1955)

Billy Bryant
MISSOURI TRAVELER, THE(1958)

Bob Bryant
CURSE OF THE FACELESS MAN(1958)

Buddy Bryant
GIRL MOST LIKELY, THE(1957)

Buel Bryant
OUTLAWS OF THE PRAIRIE(1938); MAN FROM TUMBLEWEEDS, THE(1940); RETURN OF WILD BILL, THE(1940); STRANGER FROM TEXAS, THE(1940); SIERRA SUE(1941)

Celeste Bryant
YOUNG AT HEART(1955)

Celia Bryant
GREASED LIGHTNING(1977), cos; I, THE JURY(1982), cos

Charles Bryant
Silents
MASQUERADERS, THE(1915); EYE FOR EYE(1918); BRAT, THE(1919), a, w; SALOME(1922), d
Misc. Silents
WAR BRIDES(1916); REVELATION(1918); TOYS OF FATE(1918); OUT OF THE FOG(1919); BILLIONS(1920); HEART OF A CHILD, THE(1920); STRONGER THAN DEATH(1920), a, d; DOLL'S HOUSE, A(1922), d

Chris Bryant
DON'T LOOK NOW(1973, Brit./Ital.), w; GIRL FROM PETROVKA, THE(1974), w; SPIRAL STAIRCASE, THE(1975, Brit.), w; JOSEPH ANDREWS(1977, Brit.), w; AWAKENING, THE(1980), w

Chuck Bryant
EVICTORS, THE(1979), ph

Cris Bryant
MAN WHO HAD POWER OVER WOMEN, THE(1970, Brit.), w

David Bryant
BLACK GESTAPO, THE(1975)
Misc. Talkies
ANGELS(1976)

Edward Bryant
ENEMY GENERAL, THE(1960), ed

Edwin Bryant
RETURN OF DANIEL BOONE, THE(1941); CHINATOWN AT MIDNIGHT(1949), ed; GIRLS' SCHOOL(1950), ed; REVENUE AGENT(1950), ed; TYRANT OF THE SEA(1950), ed; WHEN YOU'RE SMILING(1950), ed; MAGIC CARPET, THE(1951), ed; YANK IN KOREA, A(1951), ed; GOLDEN HAWK, THE(1952), ed; SKY COMMANDO(1953), ed; CANNIBAL ATTACK(1954), ed; CROOKED WEB, THE(1955), ed; DUEL ON THE MISSISSIPPI(1955), ed; PIRATES OF TRIPOLI(1955), ed; WYOMING RENEGADES(1955), ed; DON'T KNOCK THE ROCK(1956), ed; HOUSTON STORY, THE(1956), ed; OVER-EXPOSED(1956), ed; SECRET OF TREASURE MOUNTAIN(1956), ed; URANIUM BOOM(1956), ed; WHITE SQUAW, THE(1956), ed; CALYPSO HEAT WAVE(1957), ed; PHANTOM STAGECOACH, THE(1957), ed; TIJUANA STORY, THE(1957), ed; 20 MILLION MILES TO EARTH(1957), ed; CASE AGAINST BROOKLYN, THE(1958), ed; SEVENTH VOYAGE OF SINBAD, THE(1958), ed; WORLD WAS HIS JURY, THE(1958), ed; GENE KRUPA STORY, THE(1959), ed; COMANCHE STATION(1960), ed; THIRTEEN GHOSTS(1960), ed; HOMICIDAL(1961), ed; MR. SARDONICUS(1961), ed; VALLEY OF THE DRAGONS(1961), ed; THREE STOOGES IN ORBIT, THE(1962), ed; THREE STOOGES MEET HERCULES, THE(1962), ed; ZOTZ!(1962), ed; THIRTEEN FRIGHTENED GIRLS(1963), ed; THREE STOOGES GO AROUND THE WORLD IN A DAZE, THE(1963), ed; STRAIT-JACKET(1964), ed

Edwin H. Bryant
NIGHT WALKER, THE(1964), ed; I SAW WHAT YOU DID(1965), ed; LET'S KILL UNCLE(1966), ed; BUSYBODY, THE(1967), ed; SPIRIT IS WILLING, THE(1967), ed; PROJECT X(1968), ed; RIOT(1969), ed

Ethel Bryant
FILE ON THELMA JORDAN, THE(1950); VICKI(1953)

Fred Bryant
MATTER OF INNOCENCE, A(1968, Brit.); FOR YOUR EYES ONLY(1981)

Geoffrey Bryant
BIG TOWN(1932)
Misc. Talkies
SHADOW LAUGHS(1933)

George Bryant
RANGLE RIVER(1939, Aus.)

Gerard Bryant
HELTER SKELTER(1949, Brit.), w; IT'S NOT CRICKET(1949, Brit.), w; NO HAUNT FOR A GENTLEMAN(1952, Brit.), w; ROCK AROUND THE WORLD(1957, Brit.), d; ROCKETS IN THE DUNES(1960, Brit.), w

Gerry [Gerard] Bryant
SECRET OF THE FOREST, THE(1955, Brit.), w

Howard Bryant
LOST RANCH(1937); ORPHAN OF THE PECOS(1938)

James Bryant
1984
EXECUTIONER PART II, THE(1984), d

James W. Bryant
1984
SOLDIER'S STORY, A(1984)

Jan Bryant
LOST IN A HAREM(1944); UP IN ARMS(1944); KID FROM BROOKLYN, THE(1946); FLASHING GUNS(1947); GAS HOUSE KIDS IN HOLLYWOOD(1947); TRAP, THE(1947); COWBOY CAVALIER(1948); CRASHING THRU(1949)
Misc. Talkies
SHADOWS ON THE RANGE(1946); SILVER RANGE(1946)

Johanna Bryant
NAKED ANGELS(1969), ed

John Bryant
DARLING, HOW COULD YOU!(1951); MATING SEASON, THE(1951); RED SNOW(1952); FROM HERE TO ETERNITY(1953); TO HELL AND BACK(1955); FOUR GIRLS IN TOWN(1956); COURAGE OF BLACK BEAUTY(1957); 27TH DAY, THE(1957); RUN SILENT, RUN DEEP(1958); BAT, THE(1959); I'LL GIVE MY LIFE(1959); MARRIAGE-GO-ROUND, THE(1960); STRANGERS WHEN WE MEET(1960); FLIGHT THAT DISAPPEARED, THE(1961); TWIST AROUND THE CLOCK(1961); WALK ON THE WILD SIDE(1962); DEADWOOD'76(1965)

Josh Bryant
CURIOUS FEMALE, THE(1969)
Misc. Talkies
DISCIPLES OF DEATH(1975); ENTER THE DEVIL(1975)

Joshua Bryant
FRAMED(1975); FIRST MONDAY IN OCTOBER(1981)

Joyce Bryant
ACROSS THE PLAINS(1939); FIGHTING RENEGADE(1939); TRIGGER FINGERS ½(1939); TRIGGER SMITH(1939); EAST SIDE KIDS(1940); SAGEBRUSH FAMILY TRAILS WEST, THE(1940); THAT GANG OF MINE(1940); MANPOWER(1941); JOHNNY EAGER(1942); PACIFIC RENDEZVOUS(1942); MR. ACE(1946)

Judith Bryant
EGG AND I, THE(1947)

Kay Bryant
WILD PARTY, THE(1929)
Silents
ROAD HOUSE(1928)

Lee Bryant
CAPRICORN ONE(1978); AIRPLANE II: THE SEQUEL(1982)

Lynette Bryant
SOMEONE TO REMEMBER(1943); MAN WITH A CLOAK, THE(1951)

Lynn Bryant
DAY THE FISH CAME OUT, THE(1967. Brit./Gr.)

Margot Bryant
CURE FOR LOVE, THE(1950, Brit.)
Marguerite Bryant
Silents
RAILROADED(1923), w
Marie Bryant
THEY LIVE BY NIGHT(1949); WABASH AVENUE(1950); CROSS-UP(1958)
Michael Bryant
PASSAGE HOME(1955, Brit.); URANIUM BOOM(1956); NIGHT TO REMEMBER, A(1958, Brit.); MIND BENDERS, THE(1963, Brit.); WALK IN THE SHADOW(1966, Brit.); DEADLY AFFAIR, THE(1967, Brit.); TORTURE GARDEN(1968, Brit.); GOODBYE MR. CHIPS(1969, U.S./Brit.); MUMSY, NANNY, SONNY, AND GIRLY(1970, Brit.); NICHOLAS AND ALEXANDRA(1971, Brit.); RULING CLASS, THE(1972, Brit.); CARAVAN TO VACCARES(1974, Brit./Fr); GANDHI(1982)
Nana Bryant
ATLANTIC ADVENTURE(1935); FEATHER IN HER HAT, A(1935); GUARD THAT GIRL(1935); ONE-WAY TICKET(1935); UNKNOWN WOMAN(1935); BLACKMAILER(1936); KING STEPS OUT, THE(1936); LADY OF SECRETS(1936); LONE WOLF RETURNS, THE(1936); MAN WHO LIVED TWICE(1936); MEET NERO WOLFE(1936); PENNIES FROM HEAVEN(1936); THEODORA GOES WILD(1936); YOU MAY BE NEXT(1936); COUNSEL FOR CRIME(1937); DANGEROUS ADVENTURE, A(1937); DEVIL IS DRIVING, THE(1937); LEAGUE OF FRIGHTENED MEN(1937); LET'S GET MARRIED(1937); ADVENTURES OF TOM SAWYER, THE(1938); ALWAYS IN TROUBLE(1938); GIVE ME A SAILOR(1938); MAD ABOUT MUSIC(1938); MAN-PROOF(1938); MIDNIGHT INTRUDER(1938); OUT WEST WITH THE HARDYS(1938); PECK'S BAD BOY WITH THE CIRCUS(1938); SINNERS IN PARADISE(1938); SWING, SISTER, SWING(1938); ESPIONAGE AGENT(1939); OUR NEIGHBORS–THE CARTERS(1939); PARENTS ON TRIAL(1939); STREET OF MISSING MEN(1939); BROTHER RAT AND A BABY(1940); FATHER IS A PRINCE(1940); IF I HAD MY WAY(1940); LITTLE BIT OF HEAVEN, A(1940); CORSICAN BROTHERS, THE(1941); NICE GIRL?(1941); ONE FOOT IN HEAVEN(1941); PUBLIC ENEMIES(1941); RELUCTANT DRAGON, THE(1941); THIEVES FALL OUT(1941); CALLING DR. GILLESPIE(1942); GET HEP TO LOVE(1942); MADAME SPY(1942); THUNDER BIRDS(1942); BEST FOOT FORWARD(1943); GET GOING(1943); HANGMEN ALSO DIE(1943); PRINCESS O'ROURKE(1943); SONG OF BERNADETTE, THE(1943); WEST SIDE KID(1943); YOUTH ON PARADE(1943); ADVENTURES OF MARK TWAIN, THE(1944); BATHING BEAUTY(1944); JUNGLE WOMAN(1944); MARRIAGE IS A PRIVATE AFFAIR(1944); TAKE IT OR LEAVE IT(1944); BREWSTER'S MILLIONS(1945); WEEKEND AT THE WALDORF(1945); BLACK MARKET BABIES(1946); PERFECT MARRIAGE, THE(1946); RUNAROUND, THE(1946); VIRGINIAN, THE(1946); BIG FIX, THE(1947); BIG TOWN(1947); DANGEROUS YEARS(1947); HER HUSBAND'S AFFAIRS(1947); MILLIE'S DAUGHTER(1947); POSSESSED(1947); UNSUSPECTED, THE(1947); EYES OF TEXAS(1948); INNER SANCTUM(1948); LADIES OF THE CHORUS(1948); LADY AT MIDNIGHT(1948); ON OUR MERRY WAY(1948); RETURN OF OCTOBER, THE(1948); STAGE STRUCK(1948); HIDEOUT(1949); LADY GAMBLES, THE(1949); STATE DEPARTMENT–FILE 649(1949); BLONDE BANDIT, THE(1950); HARVEY(1950); I WAS A SHOPLIFTER(1950); KEY TO THE CITY(1950); LET'S DANCE(1950); BRIGHT VICTORY(1951); FOLLOW THE SUN(1951); ONLY THE VALIANT(1951); GERALDINE(1953); ABOUT MRS. LESLIE(1954); OUTCAST, THE(1954); PRIVATE WAR OF MAJOR BENSON, THE(1955); MODERN MARRIAGE, A(1962)
Pamela Bryant
DON'T ANSWER THE PHONE(1980); LUNCH WAGON(1981); PRIVATE LESSONS(1981); SEPARATE WAYS(1981)
Pamela Jean Bryant
H.O.T.S.(1979)
Patti Bryant
TOMCAT, THE(1968, Brit.); NASHVILLE(1975)
Paul Bryant
IS EVERYBODY HAPPY?(1943); SARATOGA TRUNK(1945)
Peter Bryant
MAN OF THE MOMENT(1955, Brit.); IT'S A GREAT DAY(1956, Brit.); SUPREME KID, THE(1976, Can.), d&w
Robert Henry Bryant
1984
TANK(1984)
Sally Bryant
BOY FRIEND, THE(1971, Brit.)
Sandra Bryant
WUTHERING HEIGHTS(1970, Brit.)
Shane Bryant
1984
CONSTANCE(1984, New Zealand)
Stan Bryant
OWL AND THE PUSSYCAT, THE(1970)
Theona Bryant
MIRACLE OF THE HILLS, THE(1959); COLLEGE CONFIDENTIAL(1960); LAST TIME I SAW ARCHIE, THE(1961); PRIVATE LIVES OF ADAM AND EVE, THE(1961)
Todd Bryant
1984
LOVELINES(1984)
William Bryant
ESCAPE FROM SAN QUENTIN(1957); OPERATION PETTICOAT(1959); EXPERIMENT IN TERROR(1962); GOOD NEIGHBOR SAM(1964); GREAT RACE, THE(1965); RIDE BEYOND VENGEANCE(1966); WHAT DID YOU DO IN THE WAR, DADDY?(1966); KARATE KILLERS, THE(1967); HEAVEN WITH A GUN(1969); CHISUM(1970); MACHO CALLAHAN(1970); ANIMALS, THE(1971); WILD ROVERS(1971); PICKUP ON 101(1972); DEADLY TRACKERS(1973); MC Q(1974); OTHER SIDE OF THE MOUNTAIN, THE(1975); WALKING TALL, PART II(1975); GABLE AND LOMBARD(1976); TWO-MINUTE WARNING(1976); CORVETTE SUMMER(1978); OTHER SIDE OF THE MOUNTAIN–PART 2, THE(1978); MOUNTAIN FAMILY ROBINSON(1979)
Bryant Washburn and FAmily
Silents
NIGHT LIFE IN HOLLYWOOD(1922)
Ursaline Bryant-King
...ALL THE MARBLES(1981)

Claudia Bryar
HOUSTON STORY, THE(1956); I WAS A TEENAGE FRANKENSTEIN(1958); TRUE STORY OF LYNN STUART, THE(1958); ANGEL IN MY POCKET(1969); BAD COMPANY(1972); ACE ELI AND RODGER OF THE SKIES(1973); PAT GARRETT AND BILLY THE KID(1973); PSYCHO II(1983)
Claudie Bryar
GAILY, GAILY(1969)
Paul Bryar
CORPSE CAME C.O.D., THE(; MAN'S FAVORITE SPORT(?)(1964); ARTISTS AND MODELS ABROAD(1938); PROFESSOR BEWARE(1938); TENTH AVENUE KID(1938); MIDNIGHT(1939); ARISE, MY LOVE(1940); HOLD THAT WOMAN(1940); MARKED MEN(1940); DESPERATE CARGO(1941); GANG'S ALL HERE(1941); MAN WHO LOST HIMSELF, THE(1941); PARIS CALLING(1941); SEALED LIPS(1941); INVISIBLE AGENT(1942); JUNGLE SIREN(1942); MAN FROM HEADQUARTERS(1942); MIRACLE KID(1942); MYSTERY OF MARIE ROGET, THE(1942); QUEEN OF BROADWAY(1942); SHERLOCK HOLMES AND THE SECRET WEAPON(1942); SIN TOWN(1942); STRANGE CASE OF DR. RX, THE(1942); FLESH AND FANTASY(1943); LADY FROM CHUNGKING(1943); BLONDE FOR A DAY(1946); GAS HOUSE KIDS(1946); LADY CHASER(1946); LARCENY IN HER HEART(1946); SHADOWS OVER CHINATOWN(1946); BRUTE FORCE(1947); CHINESE RING, THE(1947); RIDE THE PINK HORSE(1947); ROBIN OF TEXAS(1947); THREE ON A TICKET(1947); CAMPUS SLEUTH(1948); FIGHTING MAD(1948); I WOULDN'T BE IN YOUR SHOES(1948); ROGUES' REGIMENT(1948); SMART WOMAN(1948); WALK A CROOKED MILE(1948); ALASKA PATROL(1949); CHICAGO DEADLINE(1949); FOLLOW ME QUIETLY(1949); MADAME BOVARY(1949); MARY RYAN, DETECTIVE(1949); MISSISSIPPI RHYTHM(1949); PAROLE, INC.(1949); BLUES BUSTERS(1950); CALL OF THE KLONDIKE(1950); FULLER BRUSH GIRL, THE(1950); JOE PALOOKA IN THE SQUARED CIRCLE(1950); SQUARE DANCE KATY(1950); UNDER MY SKIN(1950); ACCORDING TO MRS. HOYLE(1951); CALLAWAY WENT THATAWAY(1951); GHOST CHASERS(1951); LEAVE IT TO THE MARINES(1951); LET'S GO NAVY(1951); MOB, THE(1951); NAVY BOUND(1951); PEOPLE AGAINST O'HARA, THE(1951); ARCTIC FLIGHT(1952); HAS ANYBODY SEEN MY GAL?(1952); HOLD THAT LINE(1952); SKY HIGH(1952); DANGEROUS WHEN WET(1953); EASY TO LOVE(1953); HOT NEWS(1953); ROAR OF THE CROWD(1953); SHE'S BACK ON BROADWAY(1953); SOUTH SEA WOMAN(1953); STORY OF THREE LOVES, THE(1953); TREASURE OF THE GOLDEN CONDOR(1953); WHITE LIGHTNING(1953); BOB MATHIAS STORY, THE(1954); BOWERY BOYS MEET THE MONSTERS, THE(1954); EXECUTIVE SUITE(1954); ROGUE COP(1954); FAR COUNTRY, THE(1955); INSIDE DETROIT(1955); MAD AT THE WORLD(1955); NIGHT OF THE HUNTER, THE(1955); PRODIGAL, THE(1955); REBEL WITHOUT A CAUSE(1955); KILLER IS LOOSE, THE(1956); TEA AND SYMPATHY(1956); WRONG MAN, THE(1956); JOKER IS WILD, THE(1957); LOOKING FOR DANGER(1957); MISTER CORY(1957); TEENAGE THUNDER(1957); YOUNG AND DANGEROUS(1957); GUNMAN'S WALK(1958); TOO MUCH, TOO SOON(1958); VERTIGO(1958); SQUAD CAR(1961); HOW THE WEST WAS WON(1962); SAINTLY SINNERS(1962); QUICK GUN, THE(1964); SEX AND THE SINGLE GIRL(1964); GREAT RACE, THE(1965); BUTCH CASSIDY AND THE SUNDANCE KID(1969); SPECTRE OF EDGAR ALLAN POE, THE(1974); FUNNY LADY(1975); CHANGE OF SEASONS, A(1980); HEART LIKE A WHEEL(1983)
Paul Bryarr
WRECK OF THE MARY DEAR, THE(1959)
Alan Bryce
FROM BEYOND THE GRAVE(1974, Brit.), spec eff
Alex Bryce
WARM CORNER, A(1930, Brit.), ph; SALLY IN OUR ALLEY(1931, Brit.), ph; SPORT OF KINGS, THE(1931, Brit.), ph; SALLY BISHOP(1932, Brit.), ph; CLEANING UP(1933, Brit.), ph; THERE GOES THE BRIDE(1933, Brit.), ph; WHITE FACE(1933, Brit.), ph; GREEN PACK, THE(1934, Brit.), ph; ON THE AIR(1934, Brit.), ph; PASSING SHADOWS(1934, Brit.), ph; THIRD CLUE, THE(1934, Brit.), ph; WARN LONDON!(1934, Brit.), ph; WITHOUT YOU(1934, Brit.), ph; BLUE SMOKE(1935, Brit.), ph; LATE EXTRA(1935, Brit.), ph; OLD ROSES(1935, Brit.), ph; RIVER HOUSE MYSTERY, THE(1935, Brit.), ph; SEXTON BLAKE AND THE MADEMOISELLE(1935, Brit.), d, ph; WHITE LILAC(1935, Brit.), ph; BIG NOISE, THE(1936, Brit.), d; END OF THE ROAD, THE(1936, Brit.), d; GAY LOVE(1936, Brit.), ph; WRATH OF JEALOUSY(1936, Brit.), d; AGAINST THE TIDE(1937, Brit.), d; BLACK TULIP, THE(1937, Brit.), d; MACUSHLA(1937, Brit.), d, w; LAST BARRICADE, THE(1938, Brit.), d&w; LITTLE MISS MOLLY(1940), d, w
Allan Bryce
VIKING QUEEN, THE(1967, Brit.), spec eff; OLIVER!(1968, Brit.), spec eff; WHEN DINOSAURS RULED THE EARTH(1971, Brit.), spec eff; SENDER, THE(1982, Brit.), spec eff
Ed Bryce
WRONG MAN, THE(1956)
Hope Bryce
EXODUS(1960), cos; ADVISE AND CONSENT(1962), cos; IN HARM'S WAY(1965), cos; HUMAN FACTOR, THE(1979, Brit.), cos
Jim Bryce
TREASURE OF THE FOUR CROWNS(1983, Span./U.S.), w
John Bryce
PACIFIC DESTINY(1956, Brit.)
Yvonne Bryceland
Misc. Talkies
BOESMAN AND LENA(1976)
Jan Brychta
DO YOU KEEP A LION AT HOME?(1966, Czech.), a, art d
Bill Bryden
LONG RIDERS, THE(1980), w
George Bryden
THINGS HAPPEN AT NIGHT(1948, Brit.); OUTSIDER, THE(1949, Brit.)
Jon Bryden
DESERTERS(1983, Can.)
1984
BIG MEAT EATER(1984, Can.)
Nellie Bryden
Silents
ALBANY NIGHT BOAT, THE(1928)
Sonia Bryden
LADY TAKES A SAILOR, THE(1949)

Sonja Bryden
LETTER FROM AN UNKNOWN WOMAN(1948)
William Bryden
MASK, THE(1961, Can.)
Barbara Brydenthal
MEDIUM COOL(1969)
Lars Brydesen
CRAZY PARADISE(1965, Den.), ed; HAGBARD AND SIGNE(1968, Den./Iceland/Swed.), ed
John Brydon
1984
RUNAWAY(1984)
W.B. Brydon
TRADING PLACES(1983)
William Brydon
BLOODY BROOD, THE(1959, Can.)
Chas Bryer
1984
TOP SECRET!(1984)
Denis Bryer
GULLIVER'S TRAVELS(1977, Brit., Bel.)
Paul Bryer
SARONG GIRL(1943)
Vera Bryer
SLEEPING CAR(1933, Brit.)
Silents
PEEP BEHIND THE SCENES, A(1918, Brit.)
Lubomir Bryg
LEMONADE JOE(1966, Czech.)
Larry Bryggman
...AND JUSTICE FOR ALL(1979); HANKY-PANKY(1982)
Kirsten Bryhni
CHILDREN OF GOD'S EARTH(1983, Norwegian), p
Valentin Bryleyev
DAY THE EARTH FROZE, THE(1959, Fin./USSR); SUMMER TO REMEMBER, A(1961, USSR); FAREWELL, DOVES(1962, USSR); MAGIC WEAVER, THE(1965, USSR); JACK FROST(1966, USSR); RED AND THE WHITE, THE(1969, Hung./USSR)
Patrick Brymar
KIDNAPPING OF THE PRESIDENT, THE(1980, Can.)
Brymer
MOONLIGHT AND PRETZELS(1933), cos; LOVE BEFORE BREAKFAST(1936), cos; MY MAN GODFREY(1936), cos
Patrick Brymer
"EQUUS"(1977); TICKET TO HEAVEN(1981)
Ruth Brynan
Silents
CLIMBERS, THE(1915)
Anne Bryne
WHY WOULD I LIE(1980)
Barbara Bryne
1984
AMADEUS(1984); BOSTONIANS, THE(1984)
John Bryne
ADOLF HITLER–MY PART IN HIS DOWNFALL(1973, Brit.), w
John Bryning
REMBRANDT(1936, Brit.); FLYING FIFTY-FIVE(1939, Brit.); CAESAR AND CLEOPATRA(1946, Brit.)
Roc Brynner
WHERE'S JACK?(1969, Brit.)
Yul Brynner
PORT OF NEW YORK(1949); ANASTASIA(1956); KING AND I, THE(1956); TEN COMMANDMENTS, THE(1956); BROTHERS KARAMAZOV, THE(1958); BUCCANEER, THE(1958); JOURNEY, THE(1959, U.S./Aust.); SOUND AND THE FURY, THE(1959); MAGNIFICENT SEVEN, THE(1960); ONCE MORE, WITH FEELING(1960); SURPRISE PACKAGE(1960); ESCAPE FROM ZAHRAIN(1962); TARAS BULBA(1962); TESTAMENT OF ORPHEUS, THE(1962, Fr.); KINGS OF THE SUN(1963); FLIGHT FROM ASHIYA(1964, U.S./Jap.); INVITATION TO A GUNFIGHTER(1964); MORITURI(1965); CAST A GIANT SHADOW(1966); POPPY IS ALSO A FLOWER, THE(1966); RETURN OF THE SEVEN(1966, Span.); DOUBLE MAN, THE(1967); LONG DUEL, THE(1967, Brit.); TRIPLE CROSS(1967, Fr./Brit.); VILLA RIDES(1968); FILE OF THE GOLDEN GOOSE, THE(1969, Brit.); MADWOMAN OF CHAILLOT, THE(1969); BOUNTY HUNTERS, THE(1970, Ital.); MAGIC CHRISTIAN, THE(1970, Brit.); ADIOS SABATA(1971, Ital./Span.); BATTLE OF THE NERETVA(1971, Yugo./Ital./Ger.); CATLOW(1971, Span.); LIGHT AT THE EDGE OF THE WORLD, THE(1971, U.S./Span./Lichtenstein); ROMANCE OF A HORSE THIEF(1971); FUZZ(1972); SERPENT, THE(1973, Fr./Ital./Ger.); WESTWORLD(1973); ULTIMATE WARRIOR, THE(1975); FUTUREWORLD(1976); DEATH RACE(1978, Ital.)
Misc. Talkies
HEROES, THE(1975)
Zbynek Brynych
TRANSPORT FROM PARADISE(1967, Czech.), d, w; FIFTH HORSEMAN IS FEAR, THE(1968, Czech.), d, w; SIGN OF THE VIRGIN(1969, Czech.), d, w
Kathleen Bryon
TWINS OF EVIL(1971, Brit.)
Peter Bryon
HOUND OF THE BASKERVILLES, THE(1959, Brit.), w
Betty Bryson
KISS AND MAKE UP(1934); YOUNG AND BEAUTIFUL(1934); SHINE ON, HARVEST MOON(1944)
Bill Bryson
LONG RIDERS, THE(1980)
Chere Bryson
LEGEND OF THE LONE RANGER, THE(1981)
1984
OH GOD! YOU DEVIL(1984)
J. J. Bryson
Silents
HANDSOME BRUTE, THE(1925)

James Bryson
FAN, THE(1981)
1984
MUPPETS TAKE MANHATTAN, THE(1984)
John Bryson
GRAND PRIX(1966); GETAWAY, THE(1972); OSTERMAN WEEKEND, THE(1983)
Kendall Bryson
WE'VE NEVER BEEN LICKED(1943)
Scott Bryson
WHITE BUFFALO, THE(1977)
Shirley Bryson
Silents
ONE OF MANY(1917)
Tom Bryson
MUSIC IN MANHATTAN(1944); TONIGHT AND EVERY NIGHT(1945); WOMAN IN GREEN, THE(1945)
Winifred Bryson
Silents
GREAT NIGHT, THE(1922); SOUTH OF SUVA(1922); SUZANNA(1922); HUNCHBACK OF NOTRE DAME, THE(1923); PLEASURE MAD(1923); LAW FORBIDS, THE(1924); AWFUL TRUTH, THE(1925); ADORATION(1928)
Misc. Silents
BEHIND THE CURTAIN(1924); DON'T DOUBT YOUR HUSBAND(1924); FLIRTING WITH LOVE(1924)
Yevgeniy Bryunchugin
MOTHER AND DAUGHTER(1965, USSR), d
Radoslav Brzobohaty
LADY ON THE TRACKS, THE(1968, Czech.)
Gene Bua
GAMERA THE INVINCIBLE(1966, Jap.); HOT ROD HULLABALOO(1966); PRINCE AND THE PAUPER, THE(1969)
Rosolino Bua
LEOPARD, THE(1963, Ital.); FACTS OF MURDER, THE(1965, Ital.)
Michael Buades
BIRDS COME TO DIE IN PERU(1968, Fr.)
Chico Buarque
DONA FLOR AND HER TWO HUSBANDS(1977, Braz.), m
Tino Buazzelli
STORMBOUND(1951, Ital.); MOST WANTED MAN, THE(1962, Fr./Ital.); AFTER THE FOX(1966, U.S./Brit./Ital.); MAIDEN FOR A PRINCE, A(1967, Fr./Ital.)
Pasquale Buba
EFFECTS(1980), ed, p; KNIGHTRIDERS(1981), ed; CREEPSHOW(1982), ed
Eva Bubat
ORDERED TO LOVE(1963, Ger.)
Joe Bubbico
BLAST OF SILENCE(1961)
Dwight Bubcock
DEVIL GODDESS(1955), w
Christopher Bubetz
NIGHTMARES(1983)
Nilgun Bubikoglu
YOR, THE HUNTER FROM THE FUTURE(1983, Ital.)
Alvis K. Bubis
DEVIL'S HAND, THE(1961), p
Countess Bubna
Misc. Silents
DEFINITE OBJECT, THE(1920, Brit.), d
N. Bubnov
WAR AND PEACE(1968, USSR)
V. Bubnov
DIARY OF A NAZI(1943, USSR); HEROES ARE MADE(1944, USSR)
V. Bubnova
NIGHT BEFORE CHRISTMAS, A(1963, USSR)
Art Bucaro
NIGHTFALL(1956)
Maria Grazia Buccela
THE DIRTY GAME(1966, Fr./Ital./Ger.)
Maria Grazia Buccella
DEAD RUN(1961, Fr./Ital./Ger.); NIGHT THEY KILLED RASPUTIN, THE(1962, Fr./Ital.); FALL OF ROME, THE(1963, Ital.); AFTER THE FOX(1966, U.S./Brit./Ital.); LOVE AND MARRIAGE(1966, Ital.); MAN FROM COCODY(1966, Fr./Ital.); WHITE, RED, YELLOW, PINK(1966, Ital.); MAIDEN FOR A PRINCE, A(1967, Fr./Ital.); VILLA RIDES(1968); LOVE FACTORY(1969, Ital.)
Franco Bucceri
YOUNG WORLD, A(1966, Fr./Ital.); MASTER TOUCH, THE(1974, Ital./Ger.), w
Gianfranco Bucceri
STREET PEOPLE(1976, U.S./Ital.), w
Valentino Bucchi
SKY IS RED, THE(1952, Ital.), m
Flavio Bucci
SUSPIRIA(1977, Ital.)
Marc Bucci
HUMAN EXPERIMENTS(1980), m
Valentino Bucci
BANDITS OF ORGOSOLO(1964, Ital.), m
Guy Buccola
STREET GIRL(1929)
Fred Buch
LINCOLN CONSPIRACY, THE(1977); SHOCK WAVES(1977); NIGHT IN HEAVEN, A(1983); PORKY'S II: THE NEXT DAY(1983); SPRING BREAK(1983)
Philip Buchal
ACCUSED(1936, Brit.), ch
John Buchan
39 STEPS, THE(1935, Brit.), w; THIRTY NINE STEPS, THE(1960, Brit.), w; THIRTY NINE STEPS, THE(1978, Brit.), w
Silents
HUNTINGTOWER(1927, Brit.), w

Muhammed Ygner Buchen
  ALGIERS(1938), m
Jane Buchenan
  WORLD OF HENRY ORIENT, THE(1964)
Cheryl Bucher
  LOVING(1970)
Raimondo Bucher
  ROMMEL'S TREASURE(1962, Ital.), ph
Raimund Bucher
  GEORGE(1973, U.S./Switz.)
Lothar-Guenther Buchheim
  DAS BOOT(1982), w
Horst Buchholz
  TIGER BAY(1959, Brit.); MAGNIFICENT SEVEN, THE(1960); FANNY(1961); KING IN SHADOW(1961, Ger.); ONE, TWO, THREE(1961); NINE HOURS TO RAMA(1963, U.S./Brit.); EMPTY CANVAS, THE(1964, Fr./Ital.); GIRL AND THE LEGEND, THE(1966, Ger.); MARCO THE MAGNIFICENT(1966, Ital./Fr./Yugo./Egypt/Afghanistan); THAT MAN IN ISTANBUL(1966, Fr./Ital./Span.); JOHNNY BANCO(1969, Fr./Ital./Ger.); YOUNG REBEL, THE(1969, Fr./Ital./Span.); GREAT WALTZ, THE(1972); FROM HELL TO VICTORY(1979, Fr./Ital./Span.)
1984
  SAHARA(1984)
Ella Buchi
  FAUST(1963, Ger.)
Victor Buchino
  VIOLATED LOVE(1966, Arg.), m; CURIOUS DR. HUMPP(1967, Arg.), m
Charles [Bronson] Buchinski
  MOB, THE(1951); BLOODHOUNDS OF BROADWAY(1952); DIPLOMATIC COURIER(1952); MARRYING KIND, THE(1952); PAT AND MIKE(1952)
Charles Buchinsky [Charles Bronson]
  PEOPLE AGAINST O'HARA, THE(1951); YOU'RE IN THE NAVY NOW(1951); MY SIX CONVICTS(1952); RED SKIES OF MONTANA(1952); CLOWN, THE(1953); HOUSE OF WAX(1953); APACHE(1954); CRIME WAVE(1954); RIDING SHOTGUN(1954); TENNESSEE CHAMP(1954); VERA CRUZ(1954)
Alexei Buchma
  IVAN THE TERRIBLE(Part I, 1947, USSR)
Ambrose Buchma
Misc. Silents
  SOLD APPETITE, THE(1928, USSR)
Ambrosi Buchma
  SECRET MISSION(1949, USSR)
Amvroziy Buchma
Silents
  ARSENAL(1929, USSR)
Harold Buchman
  CASE OF THE MISSING MAN, THE(1935), w; BLACKMAILER(1936), w; COME CLOSER, FOLKS(1936), w; DON'T GAMBLE WITH LOVE(1936), w; TRAPPED BY TELEVISION(1936), w; COUNSEL FOR CRIME(1937), w; DEVIL IS DRIVING, THE(1937), w; IT CAN'T LAST FOREVER(1937), w; SHALL WE DANCE(1937), w; FORGOTTEN WOMAN, THE(1939), w; HERO FOR A DAY(1939), w; NORTH OF SHANGHAI(1939), w; OUTSIDE THESE WALLS(1939), w; DOUBLE ALIBI(1940), w; MANHATTAN HEARTBEAT(1940), w; ON THEIR OWN(1940), w; JENNIE(1941), w; PERFECT SNOB, THE(1941), w; ROMANCE OF THE RIO GRANDE(1941), w; GENTLEMAN AT HEART, A(1942), w; IT HAPPENED IN FLATBUSH(1942), w; DIXIE DUGAN(1943), w; PARIS AFTER DARK(1943), w; SNAFU(1945), w; CYNTHIA(1947), w; OPERATION SNAFU(1965, Brit.), w; LAWYER, THE(1969), w
Harry Buchman
  FAIL SAFE(1964), makeup
Herman Buchman
  HAPPY ANNIVERSARY(1959), makeup; GONE ARE THE DAYS(1963), makeup; INCIDENT, THE(1967), makeup; PANIC IN NEEDLE PARK(1971), makeup
Irv Buchman
  92 IN THE SHADE(1975, U.S./Brit.), makeup
Irving Buchman
  LILITH(1964), makeup; THOUSAND CLOWNS, A(1965), makeup; PRODUCERS, THE(1967), makeup; UP THE DOWN STAIRCASE(1967), makeup; JOHN AND MARY(1969), makeup; MIDNIGHT COWBOY(1969), makeup; FRENCH CONNECTION, THE(1971), makeup; NEW LEAF, A(1971), makeup; HOT ROCK, THE(1972), makeup; TAXI DRIVER(1976), makeup; EXPOSED(1983)
1984
  FLAMINGO KID, THE(1984), makeup
Sidney Buchman
  DAUGHTER OF THE DRAGON(1931), w; NO ONE MAN(1932), w; SIGN OF THE CROSS, THE(1932), w; THUNDER BELOW(1932), w; FROM HELL TO HEAVEN(1933), w; RIGHT TO ROMANCE(1933), w; ALL OF ME(1934), w; HIS GREATEST GAMBLE(1934), w; WHOM THE GODS DESTROY(1934), w; I'LL LOVE YOU ALWAYS(1935), w; LOVE ME FOREVER(1935), w; SHE MARRIED HER BOSS(1935), w; ADVENTURE IN MANHATTAN(1936), w; KING STEPS OUT, THE(1936), w; MUSIC GOES ROUND, THE(1936), w; THEODORA GOES WILD(1936), w; HOLIDAY(1938), w; SHE MARRIED AN ARTIST(1938), p; MR. SMITH GOES TO WASHINGTON(1939), w; HOWARDS OF VIRGINIA, THE(1940), w; HERE COMES MR. JORDAN(1941), w; TALK OF THE TOWN(1942), w; OVER 21(1945), p, w; SONG TO REMEMBER, A(1945), w; TO THE ENDS OF THE EARTH(1948), p; JOLSON SINGS AGAIN(1949), p&w; SATURDAY'S HERO(1951), w; MARK, THE(1961, Brit.), w; CLEOPATRA(1963), w; GROUP, THE(1966), p, w; DEADLY TRAP, THE(1972, Fr./Ital.), w
John F. Buchmelter III
  DEER HUNTER, THE(1978)
Fern Buchner
  THEY MIGHT BE GIANTS(1971), cos; LADY LIBERTY(1972, Ital./Fr.), makeup; MANHATTAN(1979), makeup
Georg Buchner
  WOZZECK(1962, E. Ger.), w
"Butch" Bucholtz
  CHRISTIAN LICORICE STORE, THE(1971)
Horst Bucholz
  CONFESSIONS OF FELIX KRULL, THE(1957, Ger.); CATAMOUNT KILLING, THE(1975, Ger.); AVALANCHE EXPRESS(1979)

Dimitri Buchowetski
Misc. Silents
  ALL FOR A WOMAN(1921, Ger.), d; LILY OF THE DUST(1924), d; CROWN OF LIES, THE(1926), d; MIDNIGHT SUN, THE(1926), d
Dimitri Buchowetzki
Misc. Silents
  PETER THE GREAT(1923, Ger.), d; MEN(1924), d; GRAUSTARK(1925), d; SWAN, THE(1925), d; VALENCIA(1926), d
Dmitri Buchowetzki
  STAMBOUL(1931, Brit.), d
Dimitri Buchowtzki
Misc. Silents
  OTHELLO(1922, Ger.), d
Franz Buchriesser
  FRIENDS AND HUSBANDS(1983, Ger.)
Misc. Talkies
  UPPERCRUST, THE(1982)
Julio Buchs
  MAN WHO KILLED BILLY THE KID, THE(1967, Span./Ital.), d, w; FEW BULLETS MORE, A(1968, Ital./Span.), d, w; VENGEANCE IS MINE(1969, Ital./Span.), d, w; BULLET FOR SANDOVAL, A(1970, Ital./Span.), d; NUN AT THE CROSSROADS, A(1970, Ital./Span.), d, w
Max Buchsbaum
  ONE, TWO, THREE(1961); QUESTION 7(1961, U.S./Ger.); TRIAL, THE(1963, Fr./Ital./Ger.)
Art Buchwald
  SURPRISE PACKAGE(1960), w; PLAYTIME(1973, Fr.), w
Barbara Buchwald
  OUR HITLER, A FILM FROM GERMANY(1980, Ger.), puppets
Franz Buchwieser
  LILI MARLEEN(1981, Ger.)
Buck
  COUNTRY BEYOND, THE(1936)
Allen Buck
  ON THE NICKEL(1980)
Andrew Buck
  PARTY GIRL(1958)
Ashley Buck
  SKY RAIDERS(1931)
Silents
  STARDUST(1921)
Billie Joyce Buck
  NORMA RAE(1979)
Buckie Buck
Misc. Talkies
  ACID EATERS, THE(1968)
Charles Neville Buck
Silents
  LOVE, HONOR AND OBEY(1920), w; RUNAWAY, THE(1926), w
Connie Buck
  GUN FIGHT(1961)
David Buck
  MUMMY'S SHROUD, THE(1967, Brit.); DEADFALL(1968, Brit.); TASTE OF EXCITEMENT(1969, Brit.); MOSQUITO SQUADRON(1970, Brit.); DARK CRYSTAL, THE(1982, Brit.)
Donald Buck
  LITTLE MEN(1935)
Ed Buck
  SUBWAY RIDERS(1981)
Frank Buck
  TIGER FANGS(1943); AFRICA SCREAMS(1949)
Gene Buck
  NIGHT PARADE(1929, Brit.), w
George Buck
1984
  BIRDY(1984)
Harold Buck
  YOU CAN'T WIN 'EM ALL(1970, Brit.), p
Inez Buck
Silents
  LOVE'S TOLL(1916)
Misc. Silents
  HER BLEEDING HEART(1916); SORROWS OF HAPPINESS(1916)
Joan Buck
  GREYFRIARS BOBBY(1961, Brit.)
Jules Buck
  FIXED BAYONETS(1951), p; LOVE NEST(1951), p; TREASURE OF THE GOLDEN CONDOR(1953), p; DAY THEY ROBBED THE BANK OF ENGLAND, THE(1960, Brit.), p; OPERATION SNATCH(1962, Brit.), p; GREAT CATHERINE(1968, Brit.), p; RULING CLASS, THE(1972, Brit.), p; UNDER MILK WOOD(1973, Brit.), p; GREAT SCOUT AND CATHOUSE THURSDAY, THE(1976), p
Larry Buck
  THE RUNNER STUMBLES(1979)
Leon Buck
  YOU'LL NEVER GET RICH(1941)
Pamela Buck
  VILLAGE OF THE DAMNED(1960, Brit.)
Pearl Buck
  SATAN NEVER SLEEPS(1962), w
Pearl S. Buck
  GOOD EARTH, THE(1937), w; DRAGON SEED(1944), w; CHINA SKY(1945), w; GUIDE, THE(1965, U.S./India), w
Richard Buck
1984
  FLAMINGO KID, THE(1984)
Ronald Buck
  CLAY PIGEON(1971), w

Ronald L. Buck
1984
HARRY AND SON(1984), p, w
Buck & Bubbles
ATLANTIC CITY(1944)
Buck and Bubbles
VARSITY SHOW(1937); SONG IS BORN, A(1948)
Buck The Dog
Silents
CALL OF THE WILD, THE(1923)
Buck the Great Dane
TRIGGER TRIO, THE(1937)
Buck the Wonder Dog
MELODY TRAIL(1935); FANGS OF THE WILD(1954)
Buckalew
MACHISMO–40 GRAVES FOR 40 GUNS(1970)
Bethel Buckalew
MANTIS IN LACE(1968); SATIN MUSHROOM, THE(1969), a, prod d; MY BOYS ARE GOOD BOYS(1978), p, d, w
Misc. Talkies
MAG WHEELS(1978), d
Mark Buckalew
Misc. Talkies
COUNTRY CUZZINS(1972)
The Buckaroos
FROM NASHVILLE WITH MUSIC(1969)
The Buckaroos Band
RIDE 'EM COWBOY(1942)
Christine Buckegger
DISORDER AND EARLY TORMENT(1977, Ger.)
Robert Bucker
LIFE WITH FATHER(1947), p
Allan A. Buckhantz
WILLY(1963, U.S./Ger.), p&d
Misc. Talkies
PORTRAIT OF A HITMAN(1984), d
Jorgen Buckhoj
SUDDENLY, A WOMAN!(1967, Den.)
Per Buckhoj
VIKINGS, THE(1958)
Bob Buckingham
WILD PARTY, THE(1975); LOOKIN' TO GET OUT(1982)
Bruce Buckingham
SO LONG, BLUE BOY(1973), m
Jan Buckingham
GOOSE AND THE GANDER, THE(1935); WOMAN IN RED, THE(1935); LADY OBJECTS, THE(1938); MEN AGAINST THE SKY(1940); SULLIVAN'S TRAVELS(1941); VIRGINIA(1941); MISS ANNIE ROONEY(1942); AFTER MIDNIGHT WITH BOSTON BLACKIE(1943); LADY IN THE DARK(1944); MIRACLE OF MORGAN'S CREEK, THE(1944); PRACTICALLY YOURS(1944)
John Buckingham
1984
CHAMPIONS(1984)
Meg Buckingham
TOWN LIKE ALICE, A(1958, Brit.)
Naida Buckingham
MAN WHO KNEW TOO MUCH, THE(1956)
Ray Buckingham
OH ROSALINDA(1956, Brit.)
Robert Buckingham
NEW YORK, NEW YORK(1977)
Teresa Buckingham
SMASHING TIME(1967 Brit.)
Thomas Buckingham
BAD COMPANY(1931), w
Silents
ARIZONA EXPRESS, THE(1924), d; TONY RUNS WILD(1926), d
Misc. Silents
CYCLONE RIDER, THE(1924), d; TROUBLES OF A BRIDE(1924), d; FORBIDDEN CARGO(1925), d; LADIES OF LEISURE(1926), d; LAND OF THE LAWLESS(1927), d; LURE OF THE NIGHT CLUB, THE(1927), d; CRASHING THROUGH(1928), d; WHAT PRICE BEAUTY(1928), d
Tom Buckingham
HELL'S ISLAND(1930), w; HER MAN(1930), w; OFFICER O'BRIEN(1930), w; PAINTED DESERT, THE(1931), w; COCK OF THE AIR(1932), d; TOM BROWN OF CULVER(1932), w; DESTINATION UNKNOWN(1933), w; HE WAS HER MAN(1934), w; SECRET BRIDE, THE(1935), w; STAGE STRUCK(1936), w; SPIRIT OF CULVER, THE(1939), w
Silents
ATOM, THE(1918); RECKONING DAY, THE(1918)
Yvonne Buckingham
BLOOD OF THE VAMPIRE(1958, Brit.); ROBBERY UNDER ARMS(1958, Brit.); ROOM AT THE TOP(1959, Brit.); SAPPHIRE(1959, Brit.); NEXT TO NO TIME(1960, Brit.); OUR MAN IN HAVANA(1960, Brit.); URGE TO KILL(1960, Brit.); QUESTION OF SUSPENSE, A(1961, Brit.); MURDER IN EDEN(1962, Brit.); TELL-TALE HEART, THE(1962, Brit.); CHRISTINE KEELER AFFAIR, THE(1964, Brit.); SINISTER MAN, THE(1965, Brit.)
Fred Buckland
UNDERCOVER AGENT(1935, Brit.)
Frederick Buckland
HOME TO DANGER(1951, Brit.)
Jack Buckland
HERE COMES THE SUN(1945, Brit.)
Jane Buckland
SINGER AND THE DANCER, THE(1977, Aus.)
Mrs. Mildred Buckland
GREENE MURDER CASE, THE(1929)

Ved Buckland
WOMAN'S FACE(1941)
Veda Buckland
TEXAN, THE(1930); THIS MAD WORLD(1930); RIGHT TO LOVE, THE(1931); SINNERS IN THE SUN(1932); DR. BULL(1933); GLASS KEY, THE(1935); NO MORE LADIES(1935); STRAIGHT FROM THE HEART(1935); WOMEN, THE(1939); PHILADELPHIA STORY, THE(1940)
Vera Buckland
MYSTERY OF EDWIN DROOD, THE(1935)
Warwick Buckland
Silents
OLD CURIOSITY SHOP, THE(1913, Brit.)
Misc. Silents
VICAR OF WAKEFIELD, THE(1913, Brit.); AFTER DARK(1915, Brit.), d
Wilfred Buckland
Silents
JOAN THE WOMAN(1916), art d; ROBIN HOOD(1922), art d
Misc. Silents
MAN ON THE BOX, THE(1914), d
Ken Buckle
TREASURE ISLAND(1950, Brit.); SEE HOW THEY RUN(1955, Brit.); CAST A GIANT SHADOW(1966); YOU CAN'T WIN 'EM ALL(1970, Brit.); MOHAMMAD, MESSENGER OF GOD(1976, Lebanon/Brit.), stunts
Hugh Buckler
CRASH DONOVAN(1936); JUNGLE PRINCESS, THE(1936); LAST OF THE MOHICANS, THE(1936); LOST HORIZON(1937)
Silents
PLACE OF HONOUR, THE(1921, Brit.); NONENTITY, THE(1922, Brit.)
Misc. Silents
GENTLEMAN OF FRANCE, A(1921, Brit.); BELONGING(1922, Brit.); GUY FAWKES(1923, Brit.)
Hugh C. Buckler
Misc. Silents
LURE OF CROONING WATER, THE(1920, Brit.); SQUANDERED LIVES(1920, Brit.)
John Buckler
THAT'S GRATITUDE(1934); BLACK ROOM, THE(1935); DAVID COPPERFIELD(1935); EIGHT BELLS(1935); TARZAN ESCAPES(1936); UNGUARDED HOUR, THE(1936)
Robert Buckler
PRESSURE(1976, Brit.), p
Ann Buckles
CROWNING EXPERIENCE, THE(1960)
D. G. Buckles
LIAR'S DICE(1980)
Anthony Buckley
AGE OF CONSENT(1969, Austral.), ed; OUTBACK(1971, Aus.), ed; ADAM'S WOMAN(1972, Austral.), ed; DON QUIXOTE(1973, Aus.), ed; SUNSTRUCK(1973, Aus.), ed; REMOVALISTS, THE(1975, Aus.), ed; CADDIE(1976, Aus.), p; IRISHMAN, THE(1978, Aus.), p; NIGHT OF THE PROWLER, THE(1979, Aus.), p; KILLING OF ANGEL STREET, THE(1983, Aus.), p; KITTY AND THE BAGMAN(1983, Aus.), p
Betty Buckley
CARRIE(1976); TENDER MERCIES(1982)
Bill Buckley
ROBBY(1968), ed
Buz Buckley
SAGA OF DEATH VALLEY(1939); SOMEONE TO REMEMBER(1943); LADY IN THE DARK(1944); DARK HORSE, THE(1946); LITTLE MISTER JIM(1946); CASS TIMBERLANE(1947); FABULOUS DORSEYS, THE(1947); HER HUSBAND'S AFFAIRS(1947)
Buzz Buckley
CHILD IS BORN, A(1940)
Christine Buckley
ALL CREATURES GREAT AND SMALL(1975, Brit.)
David Buckley
SATURDAY NIGHT AT THE BATHS(1975), p, d, w
Emerson Buckley
YES, GIORGIO(1982)
Fred Buckley
Silents
OTHER MAN, THE(1918), w
Frederic R. Buckley
Silents
BY THE WORLD FORGOT(1918), w
Hal Buckley
KELLY'S HEROES(1970, U.S./Yugo.); SHAMPOO(1975)
Harold Buckley
PUBLIC ENEMY'S WIFE(1936), w; ROAD GANG(1936), w; CALIFORNIA MAIL, THE(1937), w; CARNIVAL QUEEN(1937), w; GUNS OF THE PECOS(1937), w; IDOL OF THE CROWDS(1937), w; AIR DEVILS(1938), w; BLACK DOLL, THE(1938), w; SINNERS IN PARADISE(1938), w; NICK CARTER, MASTER DETECTIVE(1939), w
Harry Buckley
Misc. Silents
RAPID FIRE ROMANCE(1926)
Jack Buckley
BROADWAY BIG SHOT(1942); MAN WITH TWO LIVES, THE(1942)
John Buckley
NO BLADE OF GRASS(1970, Brit.); FOREVER YOUNG, FOREVER FREE(1976, South Afr.), cos; MALIBU HIGH(1979), w
Joss Buckley
DRAUGHTSMAN'S CONTRACT, THE(1983, Brit.)
Kay Buckley
RAIDERS OF TOMAHAWK CREEK(1950); STAGE TO TUCSON(1950); TOUGHER THEY COME, THE(1950); MILLIONAIRE FOR CHRISTY, A(1951); I MARRIED A WOMAN(1958)
Keith Buckley
KING AND COUNTRY(1964, Brit.); ATTACK ON THE IRON COAST(1968, U.S./Brit.); SPRING AND PORT WINE(1970, Brit.); WUTHERING HEIGHTS(1970, Brit.); DOCTOR PHIBES RISES AGAIN(1972, Brit.); PIED PIPER, THE(1972, Brit.); FOURTEEN, THE(1973, Brit.); VIRGIN WITCH, THE(1973, Brit.); DIRTY KNIGHT'S WORK(1976, Brit.); EAGLE HAS LANDED, THE(1976, Brit.); SPY WHO LOVED ME, THE(1977, Brit.); HANOVER STREET(1979, Brit.); EXCALIBUR(1981); STAR CHAM-

BER, THE(1983)

Kenneth Buckley
WALTZ TIME(1933, Brit.); BEHIND YOUR BACK(1937, Brit.); HOLIDAY'S END(1937, Brit.); MINSTREL BOY, THE(1937, Brit.); NIGHT RIDE(1937, Brit.); STOLEN LIFE(1939, Brit.); THIS MAN IS NEWS(1939, Brit.); SECOND MR. BUSH, THE(1940, Brit.); ADVENTURESS, THE(1946, Brit.); SCHOOL FOR SECRETS(1946, Brit.); MASTER OF BANKDAM, THE(1947, Brit.); SILK NOOSE, THE(1950, Brit.)

Pamela Buckley
HAUNTING, THE(1963); V.I.P.s, THE(1963, Brit.)

R. Buckley
SUMMERTIME KILLER(1973), w

Ralph Buckley
1984
UNFAITHFULLY YOURS(1984)

Richard Buckley
WE'RE NOT MARRIED(1952)

Valerie Buckley
NEXT TO NO TIME(1960, Brit.)

William Buckley
EACH DAWN I DIE(1939), tech adv
Silents
ESMERALDA(1915); BAR NOTHIN'(1921); CHASING THE MOON(1922); SKY HIGH(1922); WANTERS, THE(1923); GOAT GETTER(1925)
Misc. Silents
WHAT'S YOUR HUSBAND DOING?(1919); DEVIL'S CLAIM, THE(1920); UNDER NORTHERN LIGHTS(1920); AFTER YOUR OWN HEART(1921); COLORADO PLUCK(1921); RATTLER, THE(1925)

Irving Buckman
KLUTE(1971), makeup; TAKING OFF(1971), makeup

Sidney R. Buckman
Silents
MATINEE LADIES(1927), w

Tara Buckman
ROLLERCOASTER(1977); HOOPER(1978); CANNONBALL RUN, THE(1981)
1984
SILENT NIGHT, DEADLY NIGHT(1984)

Charles Buckmaster
Misc. Silents
HER BENNY(1920, Brit.)

Col. Maurice Buckmaster
ODETTE(1951, Brit.)

Paul Buckmaster
FRIENDS(1971, Brit.), m

Nathalie Bucknall
FIVE LITTLE PEPPERS AND HOW THEY GREW(1939), w; FOUR GIRLS IN WHITE(1939), w

Robert Bucknell
MORE DEADLY THAN THE MALE(1961, Brit.), p&d, ph, ed

Bill Buckner
DEVIL'S BEDROOM, THE(1964)

Jack Buckner
MAN'S WORLD, A(1942), w

Parris Clifton Buckner
MALIBU BEACH(1978)

Robert Buckner
COMET OVER BROADWAY(1938), w; GOLD IS WHERE YOU FIND IT(1938), w; LOVE, HONOR AND BEHAVE(1938), w; ANGELS WASH THEIR FACES(1939), w; DODGE CITY(1939), w; OKLAHOMA KID, THE(1939), w; YOU CAN'T GET AWAY WITH MURDER(1939), w; KNUTE ROCKNE–ALL AMERICAN(1940), w; MY LOVE CAME BACK(1940), w; SANTA FE TRAIL(1940), w; VIRGINIA CITY(1940), w; DIVE BOMBER(1941), w; GENTLEMAN JIM(1942), p; YANKEE DOODLE DANDY(1942), w; DESERT SONG, THE(1943), p, w; MISSION TO MOSCOW(1943), p; UNCERTAIN GLORY(1944), p; CONFIDENTIAL AGENT(1945), p&w; GOD IS MY CO-PILOT(1945), p; SAN ANTONIO(1945), p; DEVOTION(1946), p; NOBODY LIVES FOREVER(1946), p; CHEYENNE(1947), p; ROGUES' REGIMENT(1948), p, w; FREE FOR ALL(1949), p, w; SWORD IN THE DESERT(1949), p, w; DEPORTED(1950), p, w; BRIGHT VICTORY(1951), p, w; MAN BEHIND THE GUN, THE(1952), w; WHEN IN ROME(1952), w; PRIZE OF GOLD, A(1955), w; TO PARIS WITH LOVE(1955, Brit.), w; LOVE ME TENDER(1956), w; SAFARI(1956), w; TRIPLE DECEPTION(1957, Brit.), w; FROM HELL TO TEXAS(1958), p, w; MOON PILOT(1962), w

Robert Henry Buckner
ESPIONAGE AGENT(1939), w

Robert L. Buckner
PRIMROSE PATH(1940), w

Susan Buckner
FIRST NUDIE MUSICAL, THE(1976); GREASE(1978); DEADLY BLESSING(1981)

Teddy Buckner
ST. LOUIS BLUES(1958); THEY SHOOT HORSES, DON'T THEY?(1969)

Buck Bucko
TWO GUN MAN, THE(1931); TEXAS GUN FIGHTER(1932); WHISTLIN' DAN(1932); KING OF THE ARENA(1933); LONE AVENGER, THE(1933); STRAWBERRY ROAN(1933); FIDDLIN' BUCKAROO, THE(1934); GUN JUSTICE(1934); HONOR OF THE RANGE(1934); SMOKING GUNS(1934); TRAIL DRIVE, THE(1934); WESTERN COURAGE(1935); FUGITIVE SHERIFF, THE(1936); GAUCHO SERENADE(1940); SKY'S THE LIMIT, THE(1943); DEVIL RIDERS(1944); CHEROKEE FLASH, THE(1945); SUNSET PASS(1946)

Ralph Bucko
MAN FROM BLACK HILLS, THE(1952)

Roy Bucko
TWO GUN MAN, THE(1931); TEXAS GUN FIGHTER(1932); WHISTLIN' DAN(1932); YOUNG BLOOD(1932); LONE AVENGER, THE(1933); STRAWBERRY ROAN(1933); FIDDLIN' BUCKAROO, THE(1934); GUN JUSTICE(1934); HONOR OF THE RANGE(1934); SMOKING GUNS(1934); TRAIL DRIVE, THE(1934); WHEELS OF DESTINY(1934); WESTERN COURAGE(1935); FUGITIVE SHERIFF, THE(1936); HEIR TO TROUBLE(1936); RIDERS OF THE DEADLINE(1943); SKY'S THE LIMIT, THE(1943); WOLVES OF THE RANGE(1943); DEVIL RIDERS(1944); CHEROKEE FLASH, THE(1945); RIO GRANDE RAIDERS(1946); SUNSET PASS(1946); DALLAS(1950); MAN FROM BLACK HILLS, THE(1952)

Friedel Buckow
PILLARS OF SOCIETY(1936, Ger.), ed

Friedl BuckowSchier
HEAD, THE(1961, Ger.), ed

Max Bucksbaum
COUNTERFEIT TRAITOR, THE(1962)

Colin Bucksey
RUDE BOY(1980, Brit.)

Ben Buckton
GLITTERBALL, THE(1977, Brit)
Misc. Talkies
BATTLE OF BILLY'S POND(1976)

C. Buckton
GUILTY MELODY(1936, Brit.)

Clifford Buckton
PRISON BREAKER(1936, Brit.); FATHER O'FLYNN(1938, Irish); KING ARTHUR WAS A GENTLEMAN(1942, Brit.); SOMEWHERE IN CAMP(1942, Brit.); GENTLE SEX, THE(1943, Brit.); YELLOW CANARY, THE(1944, Brit.); UNEASY TERMS(1948, Brit.); FAKE, THE(1953, Brit.); BRAIN MACHINE, THE(1955, Brit.); MAN WHO KNEW TOO MUCH, THE(1956); PACIFIC DESTINY(1956, Brit.); WAY OUT, THE(1956, Brit.); DOCTOR'S DILEMMA, THE(1958, Brit.)

John Buckwalter
ZELIG(1983)

Harold S. Bucquet
YOUNG DR. KILDARE(1938), d; CALLING DR. KILDARE(1939), d; ON BORROWED TIME(1939), d; SECRET OF DR. KILDARE, THE(1939), d; DR. KILDARE GOES HOME(1940), d; DR. KILDARE'S CRISIS(1940), d; DR. KILDARE'S STRANGE CASE(1940), d; WE WHO ARE YOUNG(1940), d; DR. KILDARE'S WEDDING DAY(1941), d; PENALTY, THE(1941), d; PEOPLE VS. DR. KILDARE, THE(1941), d; CALLING DR. GILLESPIE(1942), d; WAR AGAINST MRS. HADLEY, THE(1942), d; ADVENTURES OF TARTU(1943, Brit.), d; DRAGON SEED(1944), d; WITHOUT LOVE(1945), d

Thomas Bucson
LEO THE LAST(1970, Brit.)

James Bucton
OVERNIGHT(1933, Brit.)

Leonard Buczkowski
FIRST START(1953, Pol.), d

Bud Flanagan & Chesney Allen
FROZEN LIMITS, THE(1939, Brit.)

N. Budashkin
BRIDE WITH A DOWRY(1954, USSR), m

Nikolay Budashkin
JACK FROST(1966, USSR), m

Moura Budberg
ROMANOFF AND JULIET(1961); SEA GULL, THE(1968), w; THREE SISTERS(1974, Brit.), w

Frances Budd
JACKPOT, THE(1950)

Jackson Budd
I BECAME A CRIMINAL(1947), w; GOLD EXPRESS, THE(1955, Brit.), w

Julie Budd
DEVIL AND MAX DEVLIN, THE(1981)

Norman Budd
BURIED ALIVE(1939); ONE MILLION B.C.(1940); TURNABOUT(1940); JUDGE, THE(1949); RED MENACE, THE(1949); SURRENDER(1950); UNMASKED(1950); WOMAN FROM HEADQUARTERS(1950); MILLION DOLLAR PURSUIT(1951); OKINAWA(1952); THUNDERBIRDS(1952); PORT SINISTER(1953)

Roy Budd
SOLDIER BLUE(1970), m; CATLOW(1971, Span.), m; FLIGHT OF THE DOVES(1971), m; GET CARTER(1971, Brit.), m, md; KIDNAPPED(1971, Brit.), m, md; MAGNIFICENT SEVEN DEADLY SINS, THE(1971, Brit.), m; ZEPPELIN(1971, Brit.), m; CAREY TREATMENT, THE(1972), m; SOMETHING TO HIDE(1972, Brit.), m; STEPTOE AND SON(1972, Brit.), m; FEAR IS THE KEY(1973), m; MAN AT THE TOP(1973, Brit.), m; STONE KILLER, THE(1973), m; BLACK WINDMILL, THE(1974, Brit.), m; DESTRUCTORS, THE(1974, Brit.), m; INTERNECINE PROJECT, THE(1974, Brit.), m; DIAMONDS(1975, U.S./Israel), m; PAPER TIGER(1975, Brit.), m; SINBAD AND THE EYE OF THE TIGER(1977, U.S./Brit.), m; WELCOME TO BLOOD CITY(1977, Brit./Can.), m; WILD GEESE, THE(1978, Brit.), m; MAMMA DRACULA(1980, Bel./Fr.), m; SEA WOLVES, THE(1981, Brit.), m; FINAL OPTION, THE(1983, Brit.), m

Ruth Budd
Misc. Silents
SCREAM IN THE NIGHT, A(1919)

William H. Budd
Misc. Silents
MANHATTAN KNIGHT, A(1920)

William Budde
BRIDAL SUITE(1939), m

Adele Buddington
Silents
MIDNIGHT LIFE(1928), w

Buddy
SOUTH PACIFIC TRAIL(1952)

Avery Buddy
ON THE RIGHT TRACK(1981), w

Cousin Buddy
WORLD'S GREATEST LOVER, THE(1977)

Buddy Bradley Dancers
EVERGREEN(1934, Brit.)

Buddy Bradley Girls
RADIO FOLLIES(1935, Brit.)

The Buddy Bradley Girls
FIRE HAS BEEN ARRANGED, A(1935, Brit.)

Buddy Bradley Rhythm Girls
JOY RIDE(1935, Brit.)

Buddy Bradley's Rhythm Girls
ON THE AIR(1934, Brit.)

The Buddy DeFranco Quartet Combo
WILD PARTY, THE(1956)
Buddy the Dog
Silents
GAMBLING WIVES(1924); SPEED MAD(1925)
Steffen Bude-Wab
BEFORE HIM ALL ROME TREMBLED(1947, Ital.)
Don Budge
PAT AND MIKE(1952)
Irving Budham
FRIENDS OF EDDIE COYLE, THE(1973), makeup
A. Budin
Silents
HUNGRY HEARTS(1922)
Daniel Budin
1984
CHEECH AND CHONG'S THE CORSICAN BROTHERS(1984), art d
Beverly Budinger
1984
CANNONBALL RUN II(1984)
Jean Budinger
RIDE, RYDER, RIDE!(1949)
Slavka Budinova
DEATH OF TARZAN, THE(1968, Czech); FIFTH HORSEMAN IS FEAR, THE(1968, Czech.); GIRL WITH THREE CAMELS, THE(1968, Czech.)
Horst Budjuhn
WHITE HORSE INN, THE(1959, Ger.), w; RESTLESS NIGHT, THE(1964, Ger.), w
Celia Budkin
TWO SISTERS(1938)
Hal Budlong
MR. DEEDS GOES TO TOWN(1936); HOUSE OF THE SEVEN GABLES, THE(1940)
Marianne Budrow
GREAT SINNER, THE(1949)
Algis Budrys
TO KILL A CLOWN(1972), w; WHO?(1975, Brit./Ger.), w
Ronald R. Budsan
EVERY SPARROW MUST FALL(1964), d
Mette Budtz-Jorgensen
SUDDENLY, A WOMAN!(1967, Den.), w
Frank R. Budz
WAR PARTY(1965), cos
Bobby Buechler
MILESTONES(1975)
J.C. Buechler
FORBIDDEN WORLD(1982), spec eff
John Buechler
DEATHSTALKER(1983, Arg./U.S.), makeup
1984
DEATHSTALKER, THE(1984), spec eff
Art Buehler
THRILL OF A ROMANCE(1945)
Betty Buehler
MOB, THE(1951); TAXI(1953)
Jack Buehler
ROCK 'N' ROLL HIGH SCHOOL(1979), cos; TIMERIDER(1983), cos; WAVELENGTH(1983), cos
1984
BAD MANNERS(1984), cos
William Buehler
Misc. Silents
CROSSED TRAILS(1924)
John Buehre
OF STARS AND MEN(1961), ph
Kenean Buel
Silents
NEW YORK PEACOCK, THE(1917), d; AMERICAN BUDS(1918), d&w; DOING THEIR BIT(1918), d&w
Misc. Silents
SCHOOL FOR SCANDAL, THE(1914), d; BLAZING LOVE(1916), d; HYPOCRISY(1916), d; MARBLE HEART, THE(1916), d; WAR BRIDE'S SECRET, THE(1916), d; BITTER TRUTH(1917), d; SHE(1917), d; TROUBLEMAKERS(1917), d; TWO LITTLE IMPS(1917), d; WE SHOULD WORRY(1918), d; WOMAN WHO GAVE, THE(1918), d; FALLEN IDOL, A(1919), d; MY LITTLE SISTER(1919), d; WOMAN! WOMAN!(1919), d; PLACE OF THE HONEYMOONS, THE(1920), d; VEILED MARRIAGE, THE(1920), d
Kenean J. Buel
Misc. Silents
DAREDEVIL KATE(1916), d
Bill Buell
SUDDENLY(1954), makeup
Jed Buell
ROMANCE RIDES THE RANGE(1936), p; FIGHTING DEPUTY, THE(1937), p; MELODY OF THE PLAINS(1937), p; MOONLIGHT ON THE RANGE(1937), p; ROAMING COWBOY, THE(1937), p; SINGING BUCKAROO, THE(1937), p; HARLEM ON THE PRAIRIE(1938), p; RANGER'S ROUNDUP, THE(1938), p; SONGS AND BULLETS(1938), p; TERROR OF TINY TOWN, THE(1938), p; KNIGHT OF THE PLAINS(1939), p; EMERGENCY LANDING(1941), p; MISBEHAVING HUSBANDS(1941), p; BROADWAY BIG SHOT(1942), p
John Buell
PYX, THE(1973, Can.), w
Willard Buell
STAR!(1968), makeup; DARLING LILI(1970), makeup
Jose Buenagu
CASTILIAN, THE(1963, Span./U.S.), m; FACE OF TERROR(1964, Span.), m
Angel Buenaventura
WALLS OF HELL, THE(1964, U.S./Phil.); BEAST OF BLOOD(1970, U.S./Phil.); TASTE OF HELL, A(1973)

Col. Antonio Buenaventura
BEACH RED(1967), m
Francisco Buencamino, Jr.
SURRENDER–HELL!(1959), m
Clovis Bueno
PIXOTE(1981, Braz.), art d
Leoncio Bueno
FITZCARRALDO(1982)
Paul Buerks
SERPENT'S EGG, THE(1977, Ger./U.S.)
Jack Buetel
BEST OF THE BADMEN(1951); HALF-BREED, THE(1952); ROSE OF CIMARRON(1952)
Alf Buetow
SPECIAL DELIVERY(1955, Ger.), art d
John Buettner
HANDS ACROSS THE TABLE(1935)
Peter Bufa
Misc. Talkies
GHOST DANCE(1982), d
Louis Bufano
1984
GOODBYE PEOPLE, THE(1984)
Remo Bufano
YOLANDA AND THE THIEF(1945)
Vincent Bufano
TWO OF A KIND(1983)
Marilyn Buferd
LES BELLES-DE-NUIT(1952, Fr.); UNEARTHLY, THE(1957); QUEEN OF OUTER SPACE(1958)
Monica Buferd
SENDER, THE(1982, Brit.)
Norton Buffalo
HEAVEN'S GATE(1980); EDDIE MACON'S RUN(1983), m; STACY'S KNIGHTS(1983), m
Buffalo Bill, Jr. [Jay Wilsey]
SOUTH OF SONORA(1930); DEADWOOD PASS(1933); LAWLESS FRONTIER, THE(1935)
Misc. Talkies
PUEBLO TERROR(1931); TRAILS OF THE GOLDEN WEST(1931); TEXAN, THE(1932); RAWHIDE ROMANCE(1934); FIVE BAD MEN(1935); TRAILS OF ADVENTURE(1935), d; WHIRLWIND RIDER, THE(1935)
Silents
ON THE GO(1925); QUICKER'N LIGHTNIN'(1925); GALLOPING GOBS, THE(1927)
Misc. Silents
BAD MAN'S BLUFF(1926); BALLYHOO BUSTER, THE(1928)
Vincent Buffano
Misc. Talkies
HARD FEELINGS(1981)
Gianni Buffardi
TWO COLONELS, THE(1963, Ital.), p
Marilyn Bufferd
ADORABLE CREATURES(1956, Fr.)
Daisy Buffert
LOVE ON TOAST(1937)
Eugenie Buffet
Silents
NAPOLEON(1927, Fr.)
Jimmy Buffett
RANCHO DELUXE(1975), m; FM(1978)
1984
REPO MAN(1984)
Adele Buffington
RIVER WOMAN, THE(1928), w; TIMES SQUARE(1929), w; EXTRAVAGANCE(1930), w; JUST LIKE HEAVEN(1930), w; SWELLHEAD, THE(1930), w; FORGOTTEN WOMEN(1932), w; FREIGHTERS OF DESTINY(1932), w; GHOST VALLEY(1932), w; HAUNTED GOLD(1932), w; HIGH SPEED(1932), w; MAN'S LAND, A(1932), w; SINGLE-HANDED SANDERS(1932), w; ELEVENTH COMMANDMENT(1933), w; IRON MASTER, THE(1933), w; WEST OF SINGAPORE(1933), w; CHEATERS(1934), w; HELL CAT, THE(1934), w; MARRYING WIDOWS(1934), w; MOONSTONE, THE(1934), w; PICTURE BRIDES(1934), w; WHEN STRANGERS MEET(1934), w; KEEPER OF THE BEES(1935), w; POWDERSMOKE RANGE(1935), w; ANY MAN'S WIFE(1936), w; HI GAUCHO!(1936), w; CIRCUS GIRL(1937), w; DUKE COMES BACK, THE(1937), w; MICHAEL O'HALLORAN(1937), w; SHEIK STEPS OUT, THE(1937), w; TENTH AVENUE KID(1938), w; GHOST TOWN LAW(1942), w; BAD MEN OF THE BORDER(1945), w; FLAME OF THE WEST(1945), w; NAVAJO TRAIL, THE(1945), w; DRIFTING ALONG(1946), w; WILD BEAUTY(1946), w; VALIANT HOMBRE, THE(1948), w; CRASHING THRU(1949), w; RANGE LAND(1949), w; SHADOWS OF THE WEST(1949), w; STREETS OF SAN FRANCISCO(1949), w; WEST OF EL DORADO(1949), w; WESTERN RENEGADES(1949), w; ARIZONA TERRITORY(1950), w; GUNSLINGERS(1950), w; JIGGS AND MAGGIE OUT WEST(1950), w; WEST OF WYOMING(1950), w; OVERLAND TELEGRAPH(1951), w; BORN TO THE SADDLE(1953), w; COW COUNTRY(1953), w; BULLWHIP(1958), w
Silents
FIGHTING CUB, THE(1925), w; EAGER LIPS(1927), w; AVENGING RIDER, THE(1928), w; DEVIL DOGS(1928), w
Adele S. Buffington
PRISON NURSE(1938), w
Sam Buffington
INVASION OF THE SAUCER MEN(1957); DAMN CITIZEN(1958); LIGHT IN THE FOREST, THE(1958); RAWHIDE TRAIL, THE(1958); UNWED MOTHER(1958); THEY CAME TO CORDURA(1959)
Daisy Bufford
NEXT TIME WE LOVE(1936); TOAST OF NEW YORK, THE(1937); JEZEBEL(1938); STAR MAKER, THE(1939); SON OF INGAGI(1940); TWO GIRLS ON BROADWAY(1940); LADY GANGSTER(1942)

Charles Buffum
PUTNEY SWOPE(1969)
Ray Buffum
GIRLS IN THE NIGHT(1953), w; BLACK DAKOTAS, THE(1954), w; PLAY-GIRL(1954), w; SO THIS IS PARIS(1954), w; TEEN-AGE CRIME WAVE(1955), w; BRAIN FROM THE PLANET AROUS, THE(1958), w; TEENAGE MONSTER(1958), w; ISLAND OF LOST WOMEN(1959), w
Aldo Bufi-Landi
ATLAS AGAINST THE CYCLOPS(1963, Ital.); SEVEN SEAS TO CALAIS(1963, Ital.); MYSTERY OF THUG ISLAND, THE(1966, Ital./Ger.); MADE IN ITALY(1967, Fr./Ital.); TERROR OF THE BLACK MASK(1967, Fr./Ital.); MIDAS RUN(1969); ONE STEP TO HELL(1969, U.S./Ital./Span.)
Zeev Bufman
TEN COMMANDMENTS, THE(1956)
Zev Bufman
NAKED APE, THE(1973), p
Jacques Bufnoir
CIRCLE OF DECEIT(1982, Fr./Ger.), set d; ENTRE NOUS(1983, Fr.), prod d; LA BOUM(1983, Fr.), art d
1984
EDITH AND MARCEL(1984, Fr.), art d
Daisy Buford
THOUSANDS CHEER(1943)
Gordon Buford
LOVE BUG, THE(1968), w; HERBIE RIDES AGAIN(1974), w
Justin Buford
CASEY'S SHADOW(1978)
Marilyn Buford
WITHOUT RESERVATIONS(1946); GEORGE WHITE'S SCANDALS(1945)
Al Bugatti
CURIOUS DR. HUMPP(1967, Arg.)
Dominic Bugatti
WORLD IS FULL OF MARRIED MEN, THE(1980, Brit.), m
Chris Bugbee
STERILE CUCKOO, THE(1969)
Bugette
GATES OF PARIS(1958, Fr./Ital.)
Susan Bugg
SOMEWHERE IN TIME(1980)
Niall Buggy
ZARDOZ(; PORTRAIT OF THE ARTIST AS A YOUNG MAN, A(1979, Ireland)
Carlo Bugiani
ANYTHING FOR A SONG(1947, Ital.), d
Harry Bugin
LAST AMERICAN VIRGIN, THE(1982)
Bror Bugler
WOMAN'S FACE, A(1939, Swed.)
Alberto Bugli
SHOOT LOUD, LOUDER... I DON'T UNDERSTAND(1966, Ital.)
Piero Bugli
HUNCHBACK OF ROME, THE(1963, Ital.)
Bob Buguor
DON'T MAKE WAVES(1967), ph
Valerie Buhagiar
1984
MRS. SOFFEL(1984)
Jeff Buhai
1984
REVENGE OF THE NERDS(1984), w
Leila Buheiry
EMBASSY(1972, Brit.)
Rolf Buhl
NOT RECONCILED, OR "ONLY VIOLENCE HELPS WHERE IT RULES"(1969, Ger.)
Bully Buhlan
SCHLAGER-PARADE(1953)
Kitty Buhler
CHINA DOLL(1958), w
Richard Buhler
Silents
EVIDENCE(1915); THIEF, THE(1915); LOVE'S TOLL(1916)
Misc. Silents
MAN'S MAKING, THE(1915); RIGHTS OF MAN, THE(1915); GODS OF FATE, THE(1916); HER BLEEDING HEART(1916)
Walter Buhler
HOT MONEY GIRL(1962, Brit./Ger.)
Gerard Buhr
PARIS DOES STRANGE THINGS(1957, Fr./Ital.); GATES OF PARIS(1958, Fr./Ital.); ME AND THE COLONEL(1958); BACK TO THE WALL(1959, Fr.); MICHAEL STROG-OFF(1960, Fr./Ital./Yugo.); COUNTERFEITERS OF PARIS, THE(1962, Fr., Ital.); LOVERS ON A TIGHTROPE(1962, Fr.); TRAIN, THE(1965, Fr./Ital./U.S.); NIGHT OF THE GENERALS, THE(1967, Brit./Fr.); NIGHT OF THE FOLLOWING DAY, THE(1969, Brit.); SICILIAN CLAN, THE(1970, Fr.); DEADLY TRAP, THE(1972, Fr./Ital.); DAY OF THE JACKAL, THE(1973, Brit./Fr.); LOVE AND DEATH(1975); JULIA(1977); FIVE DAYS ONE SUMMER(1982)
Dorothy Buhrman
STARHOPS(1978)
Rolf Buhrmann
MARRIAGE OF MARIA BRAUN, THE(1979, Ger.)
Son Hoang Bui
TABLE FOR FIVE(1983)
Charles Buie
SUPER FUZZ(1981); SPRING BREAK(1983), stunts
Gregori Buimistre
BIG RED ONE, THE(1980)
Felicity Buirski
STUD, THE(1979, Brit.)
Paul Buissoneau
WAITING FOR CAROLINE(1969, Can.)

Genevieve Bujold
KING OF HEARTS(1967, Fr./Ital.); LA GUERRE EST FINIE(1967, Fr./Swed.); THIEF OF PARIS, THE(1967, Fr./Ital.); ISABEL(1968, Can.); ANNE OF THE THOUSAND DAYS(1969, Brit.); ACT OF THE HEART(1970, Can.); TROJAN WOMEN, THE(1971); KAMOURASKA(1973, Can./Fr.); EARTHQUAKE(1974); ALEX AND THE GYPSY(1976); OBSESSION(1976); SWASHBUCKLER(1976); ANOTHER MAN, ANOTHER CHANCE(1977 Fr./US); JOURNEY(1977, Can.); COMA(1978); MURDER BY DE-CREE(1979, Brit.); FINAL ASSIGNMENT(1980, Can.); INCORRIGIBLE(1980, Fr.); LAST FLIGHT OF NOAH'S ARK, THE(1980); MONSIGNOR(1982)
1984
CHOOSE ME(1984); TIGHTROPE(1984)
Misc. Talkies
AMANITA PESTILENS(1963)
Fernando Bujones
TURNING POINT, THE(1977)
Istvan Bujtor
WINTER WIND(1970, Fr./Hung.)
Donald Buka
WATCH ON THE RHINE(1943); STREET WITH NO NAME, THE(1948); BETWEEN MIDNIGHT AND DAWN(1950); VENDETTA(1950); NEW MEXICO(1951); STOLEN IDENTITY(1953); OPERATION EICHMANN(1961); SHOCK TREATMENT(1964)
Robert Buka
HANKY-PANKY(1982)
Sufi Bukhari
"EQUUS"(1977)
Yaacov Bukman
EVERY BASTARD A KING(1968, Israel)
Yanci Bukovec
STONE COLD DEAD(1980, Can.)
Anatoliy Bukovskiy
MOTHER AND DAUGHTER(1965, USSR), d
Wiliam Bukovy
DO YOU KEEP A LION AT HOME?(1966, Czech.), m
William Bukovy
WISHING MACHINE(1971, Czech.), m
Charles Bukowski
TALES OF ORDINARY MADNESS(1983, Ital.), w
1984
KILLERS, THE(1984), a, w
Julien Bukowsky
L'ETOILE DU NORD(1983, Fr.)
Kurt Bula
DEGREE OF MURDER, A(1969, Ger.)
Dusan Bulajic
FRONTIER HELLCAT(1966, Fr./Ital./Ger./Yugo.); FRAULEIN DOKTOR(1969, Ital./Yugo.)
Stephan Bulajic
DAY THAT SHOOK THE WORLD, THE(1977, Yugo./Czech.), w
Stevo Bulajic
BATTLE OF THE NERETVA(1971, Yugo./Ital./Ger.), w
Veljko Bulajic
BATTLE OF THE NERETVA(1971, Yugo./Ital./Ger.), p, w; DAY THAT SHOOK THE WORLD, THE(1977, Yugo./Czech.), d
Velko Bulajic
RAT(1960, Yugo.), d
Zozimo Bulbul
EARTH ENTRANCED(1970, Braz.)
Maurice Bulbulian
LONG SHOT(1981, Brit.)
Stefan Bulejko
TRANSPORT FROM PARADISE(1967, Czech.)
Euro Bulfoni
1984
BASILEUS QUARTET(1984, Ital.)
Leo Bulgakov
AFTER THE DANCE(1935), d; I'LL LOVE YOU ALWAYS(1935), d; WHITE LIES(1935), d; FOR WHOM THE BELL TOLLS(1943); SONG OF RUSSIA(1943); THIS LAND IS MINE(1943)
S. Bulgakov
LULLABY(1961, USSR), art d; SANDU FOLLOWS THE SUN(1965, USSR), art d
V. Bulgakov
Misc. Silents
POLIKUSHKA(1919, USSR)
Enzo Bulgarelli
MONGOLS, THE(1966, Fr./Ital.), cos; DEATH RIDES A HORSE(1969, Ital.), cos; FRAULEIN DOKTOR(1969, Ital./Yugo.), cos; FIVE MAN ARMY, THE(1970, Ital.), art d; KILL THEM ALL AND COME BACK ALONE(1970, Ital./Span.), art d; THEY CALL ME TRINITY(1971, Ital.), art d; TRINITY IS STILL MY NAME(1971, Ital.), art d; BARON BLOOD(1972, Ital.), art d; JOHNNY HAMLET(1972, Ital.), art d; MAN FROM THE EAST, A(1974, Ital./Fr.), art d; LOVES AND TIMES OF SCARAMOUCHE, THE(1976, Ital.), art d; LONELY LADY, THE(1983), prod d
Ruzena Bulickova
CLOSELY WATCHED TRAINS(1967, Czech.), cos
Joyce Bulifant
HAPPIEST MILLIONAIRE, THE(1967); AIRPLANE!(1980)
Fred Bulin
TRANSPORT FROM PARADISE(1967, Czech.)
Charles Edward Bull
Silents
IRON HORSE, THE(1924)
Donald Bull
DREAMS COME TRUE(1936, Brit.), w; STORM IN A TEACUP(1937, Brit.), w; SOUTH RIDING(1938, Brit.), w; ARSENAL STADIUM MYSTERY, THE(1939, Brit.), w; CHEER BOYS CHEER(1939, Brit.), w; DEAR MR. PROHACK(1949, Brit.), w; MASTER PLAN, THE(1955, Brit.), w; JUST JOE(1960, Brit.), w
Frank Bull
ST. LOUIS KID, THE(1934); CASE OF THE CURIOUS BRIDE, THE(1935); G-MEN(1935)

John Bull
CHEER THE BRAVE(1951, Brit.); STOLEN FACE(1952, Brit.); SAIL INTO DANGER(1957, Brit.); LONELINESS OF THE LONG DISTANCE RUNNER, THE(1962, Brit.); WEBSTER BOY, THE(1962, Brit.)

Margaret Bull
MARY HAD A LITTLE(1961, Brit.); HE WHO RIDES A TIGER(1966, Brit.)

Peter Bull
AS YOU LIKE IT(1936, Brit.); KNIGHT WITHOUT ARMOR(1937, Brit.); NON-STOP NEW YORK(1937, Brit.); SABOTAGE(1937, Brit.); MARIE ANTOINETTE(1938); DEAD MAN'S SHOES(1939, Brit.); WARE CASE, THE(1939, Brit.); BLACKOUT(1940, Brit.); QUIET WEDDING(1941, Brit.); YOUNG MAN'S FANCY(1943, Brit.); GRAND ESCAPADE, THE(1946, Brit.); TURNERS OF PROSPECT ROAD, THE(1947, Brit.); CARDBOARD CAVALIER, THE(1949, Brit.); SARABAND(1949, Brit.); LOST PEOPLE, THE(1950, Brit.); AFRICAN QUEEN, THE(1951, U.S./Brit.); CHRISTMAS CAROL, A(1951, Brit.); LAVENDER HILL MOB, THE(1951, Brit.); LUCKY NICK CAIN(1951); OLIVER TWIST(1951, Brit.); RELUCTANT WIDOW, THE(1951, Brit.); SIX MEN, THE(1951, Brit.); SECOND MRS. TANQUERAY, THE(1952, Brit.); CAPTAIN'S PARADISE, THE(1953, Brit.); SAADIA(1953); BEAU BRUMMELL(1954); MALTA STORY(1954, Brit.); FOOTSTEPS IN THE FOG(1955, Brit.); GREEN MAN, THE(1957, Brit.); TOM THUMB(1958, Brit./U.S.); SCAPEGOAT, THE(1959, Brit.); THREE WORLDS OF GULLIVER, THE(1960, Brit.); CALL ME GENIUS(1961, Brit.); FOLLOW THAT MAN(1961, Brit.); GOODBYE AGAIN(1961); GIRL ON THE BOAT, THE(1962, Brit.); OLD DARK HOUSE, THE(1963, Brit.); TOM JONES(1963, Brit.); DR. STRANGELOVE: OR HOW I LEARNED TO STOP WORRYING AND LOVE THE BOMB(1964); SECOND BEST SECRET AGENT IN THE WHOLE WIDE WORLD, THE(1965, Brit.); SPYLARKS(1965, Brit.); YOU MUST BE JOKING!(1965, Brit.); DOCTOR DOLITTLE(1967); LOCK UP YOUR DAUGHTERS(1969, Brit.); EXECUTIONER, THE(1970, Brit.); GIRL STROKE BOY(1971, Brit.); LADY CAROLINE LAMB(1972, Brit./Ital.); JOSEPH ANDREWS(1977, Brit.); YELLOWBEARD(1983)
Misc. Talkies
TEMPEST, THE(1980, Brit.)

Richard Bull
FEAR STRIKES OUT(1957); THEN THERE WERE THREE(1961); SATAN BUG, THE(1965); HOUR OF THE GUN(1967); SECRET LIFE OF AN AMERICAN WIFE, THE(1968); THOMAS CROWN AFFAIR, THE(1968); STALKING MOON, THE(1969); MOVE(1970); LAWMAN(1971); ULZANA'S RAID(1972); BREEZY(1973); EXECUTIVE ACTION(1973); HIGH PLAINS DRIFTER(1973); NEWMAN'S LAW(1974); MR. SYCAMORE(1975); DIFFERENT STORY, A(1978)

Bull and Buster
LOVE ON SKIS(1933, Brit.)

Elma Bulla
DIALOGUE(1967, Hung.)

Kim Bullard
NORTH AVENUE IRREGULARS, THE(1979)

Steve Bullard
ROLLOVER(1981)

James Bulleit
1984
POPE OF GREENWICH VILLAGE, THE(1984)

Leonard Bullen
NOT SO DUSTY(1936, Brit.)

Sarah Bullen
INTERNATIONAL VELVET(1978, Brit.)

Susan Bullen
DEMON LOVER, THE(1977)

Bullet
Misc. Silents
HUNTIN' TROUBLE(1924); PERFECT ALIBI, THE(1924)

Bullet the Dog
OVERLAND BOUND(1929); SPOILERS OF THE PLAINS(1951); PALS OF THE GOLDEN WEST(1952)
Silents
KING'S CREEK LAW(1923); LOSER'S END, THE(1924)

Bullet the Horse
Silents
THIRD ALARM, THE(1922)

Billy Bullet
YOUNG CYCLE GIRLS, THE(1979)

Gerald Bullett
LAST MAN TO HANG, THE(1956, Brit.), w

James Bullett
NEXT MAN, THE(1976)

Jeanne Louise Bulliard
SOUTHERN COMFORT(1981)

Ernest Bullingham
DEVIL DOLL(1964, Brit.), ed

Perry Bullington
Misc. Talkies
CHATTERBOX(1977)

Gertrude Bullman
Misc. Talkies
JEWISH FATHER(1934); BAR MITSVE(1935)

Jeremy Bulloch
CAUGHT IN THE NET(1960, Brit.); FRENCH MISTRESS(1960, Brit.); SPARE THE ROD(1961, Brit.); DEVIL'S AGENT, THE(1962, Brit.); PLAY IT COOL(1963, Brit.); SUMMER HOLIDAY(1963, Brit.); IDOL, THE(1966, Brit.); HOFFMAN(1970, Brit.); VIRGIN AND THE GYPSY, THE(1970, Brit.); MARY, QUEEN OF SCOTS(1971, Brit.); O LUCKY MAN!(1973, Brit.); LITTLEST HORSE THIEVES, THE(1977); SPY WHO LOVED ME, THE(1977, Brit.); EMPIRE STRIKES BACK, THE(1980); RETURN OF THE JEDI(1983)

Sally Bulloch
PURE HELL OF ST. TRINIAN'S, THE(1961, Brit.); ALFIE DARLING(1975, Brit.)

Wally Bulloch
MOUSE AND HIS CHILD, THE(1977), ph

Boris Bullock
FORGOTTEN COMMANDMENTS(1932); FIGHTING COWBOY(1933); LIGHTNING RANGE(1934)

Silents
DON X(1925)
Misc. Silents
RANGE TERROR, THE(1925); LAWLESS TRAILS(1926); PRINCE OF THE SADDLE(1926); BORDER CAVALIER, THE(1927); THRILL CHASER, THE(1928); WHERE THE WEST BEGINS(1928)

Burl Bullock
BUS IS COMING, THE(1971)

Dick Bullock
HELL'S BELLES(1969); MOLLY AND LAWLESS JOHN(1972)

Earl Houston Bullock
SMOKEY AND THE BANDIT–PART 3(1983)
1984
CLOAK AND DAGGER(1984)

Elias Bullock
Misc. Silents
IN THE WEST(1923); HORSE SENSE(1924)

Harry Bullock
WHO'S MINDING THE MINT?(1967), w

Harvey Bullock
HONEYMOON HOTEL(1964), w; GIRL HAPPY(1965), w; MAN CALLED FLINTSTONE, THE(1966), w; WITH SIX YOU GET EGGROLL(1968), w; DON'T DRINK THE WATER(1969), w

Jeremy Bullock
CAT GANG, THE(1959, Brit.); OCTOPUSSY(1983, Brit.)
Misc. Talkies
YOUNG JACOBITES(1959)

Julia Bullock
CHILD UNDER A LEAF(1975, Can.)

Wally Bullock
SHINBONE ALLEY(1971), ph

Walter Bullock
52ND STREET(1937), m; JUST AROUND THE CORNER(1938), m; LITTLE MISS BROADWAY(1938), m; LITTLE PRINCESS, THE(1939), m; BLUE BIRD, THE(1940), w; GAY CABALLERO, THE(1940), w; COWBOY AND THE BLONDE, THE(1941), w; FOR BEAUTY'S SAKE(1941), w; MOON OVER HER SHOULDER(1941), w; RIGHT TO THE HEART(1942), w; SPRINGTIME IN THE ROCKIES(1942), w; GANG'S ALL HERE, THE(1943), w; GREENWICH VILLAGE(1944), w; OUT OF THE BLUE(1947), w; REPEAT PERFORMANCE(1947), w; ADVENTURES OF CASANOVA(1948), w; GOLDEN GIRL(1951), w; I DON'T CARE GIRL, THE(1952), w; O. HENRY'S FULL HOUSE(1952), w; FARMER TAKES A WIFE, THE(1953), w

Lester Bullocks
ROCKERS(1980)

Michael Bulmer
HONG KONG AFFAIR(1958)

Quintin Bulnes
DALTON THAT GOT AWAY(1960); FRANKENSTEIN, THE VAMPIRE AND CO.(1961, Mex.); QUEEN'S SWORDSMEN, THE(1963, Mex.); LITTLE RED RIDING HOOD AND THE MONSTERS(1965, Mex.); LIVING COFFIN, THE(1965, Mex.); RAGE(1966, U.S./Mex.); CURSE OF THE DOLL PEOPLE, THE(1968, Mex.); JO-RY(1972)

Quinton Bulnes
SNAKE PEOPLE, THE(1968, Mex./U.S.); POR MIS PISTOLAS(1969, Mex.)

Gordon Buloe
MARS NEEDS WOMEN(1966)

Joseph Buloff
LET'S MAKE MUSIC(1940); THEY MET IN ARGENTINA(1941); CARNEGIE HALL(1947); LOVES OF CARMEN, THE(1948); TO THE VICTOR(1948); KISS IN THE DARK, A(1949); VILNA LEGEND, A(1949, U.S./Pol.); SOMEBODY UP THERE LIKES ME(1956); SILK STOCKINGS(1957); REDS(1981)
Misc. Talkies
LIVE AND LAUGH(1933)

Yusef Bulos
SIMON(1980)

Edward Bulwer-Lytton
CARDINAL RICHELIEU(1935), w
Silents
DAMON AND PYTHIAS(1914), w; IN THE NAME OF LOVE(1925), w

Kir Bulychev
CHEREZ TERNII K SVEZDAM(1981 USSR), w

Victor Bumbalo
CROSS AND THE SWITCHBLADE, THE(1970)

Karli Bumgartner
KELLY'S HEROES(1970, U.S./Yugo.), spec eff

Lori Bump
HOLLYWOOD HIGH(1977)

Bob Bumpas
BIG CARNIVAL, THE(1951)

Roger Bumpass
HEAVY METAL(1981, Can.)

Bumper
AMY(1981)

Wayne Bumpus
HEADLINE CRASHER(1937)

Edward Bumstead
MISSIONARY, THE(1982)

Harry Bumstead
DEAR BRAT(1951), art d

Henry Bumstead
CONCORDE, THE–AIRPORT '79(, prod d; MY OWN TRUE LOVE(1948), art d; SAIGON(1948), art d; SAINTED SISTERS, THE(1948), art d; MY FRIEND IRMA(1949), art d; SONG OF SURRENDER(1949), art d; STREETS OF LAREDO(1949), art d; TOP O' THE MORNING(1949), art d; FURIES, THE(1950), art d; GOLDBERGS, THE(1950), art d; MY FRIEND IRMA GOES WEST(1950), art d; NO MAN OF HER OWN(1950), art d; REDHEAD AND THE COWBOY, THE(1950), art d; RHUBARB(1951), art d; SAILOR BEWARE(1951), art d; SUBMARINE COMMAND(1951), art d; JUMPING JACKS(1952), art d; LITTLE BOY LOST(1953), art d; STARS ARE SINGING, THE(1953), art d; BRIDGES AT TOKO-RI, THE(1954), art d; LUCY GALLANT(1955), art d; RUN FOR COVER(1955), art d; HOLLYWOOD OR BUST(1956), art d; LEATHER SAINT, THE(1956), art d; MAN WHO KNEW TOO MUCH, THE(1956),

art d; THAT CERTAIN FEELING(1956), art d; VAGABOND KING, THE(1956), art d; I MARRIED A MONSTER FROM OUTER SPACE(1958), art d; VERTIGO(1958), art d; HANGMAN, THE(1959), art d; BELLBOY, THE(1960), art d; CINDERFELLA(1960), art d; COME SEPTEMBER(1961), art d; SPIRAL ROAD, THE(1962), art d; TO KILL A MOCKINGBIRD(1962), art d; GATHERING OF EAGLES, A(1963), art d; FATHER GOOSE(1964), art d; WAR LORD, THE(1965), art d; GUNPOINT(1966), art d; TO-BRUK(1966), art d; SECRET WAR OF HARRY FRIGG, THE(1968), art d; WHAT'S SO BAD ABOUT FEELING GOOD?(1968), art d; MAN CALLED GANNON, A(1969), art d; TELL THEM WILLIE BOY IS HERE(1969), art d; TOPAZ(1969, Brit.), prod d; ONE MORE TRAIN TO ROB(1971), art d; RAID ON ROMMEL(1971), art d; JOE KIDD(1972), art d; SLAUGHTERHOUSE-FIVE(1972), a, prod d; HIGH PLAINS DRIFTER(1973), art d; SHOWDOWN(1973), art d; STING, THE(1973), art d; FRONT PAGE, THE(1974), art d; GREAT WALDO PEPPER, THE(1975), art d; FAMILY PLOT(1976), art d; ROLLERCOASTER(1977), prod d; SLAP SHOT(1977), art d; HOUSE CALLS(1978), prod d; SAME TIME, NEXT YEAR(1978), prod d; LITTLE ROMANCE, A(1979, U.S./Fr.), prod d; SMOKEY AND THE BANDIT II(1980), prod d; WORLD ACCORDING TO GARP, The(1982), prod d
1984
HARRY AND SON(1984), prod d; LITTLE DRUMMER GIRL, THE(1984), prod d

J.P. Bumstead
PRIVATE BENJAMIN(1980)

Raymond Bun
FBI GIRL(1951)

Alan Bunce
SHE'S MY WEAKNESS(1930); LAST MILE, THE(1959); SUNRISE AT CAMPOBELLO(1960); HOMICIDAL(1961)

Betty Bunch
GOING IN STYLE(1979)
1984
OH GOD! YOU DEVIL(1984); STARMAN(1984)

Farah Bunch
RETURN, THE(1980)

Martha Bunch
WOMAN ON THE RUN(1950), cos

Sacha Bunchuk
LUCKY BOY(1929), md; LUCKY IN LOVE(1929), md

Yasha Bunchuk
HEAT'S ON, THE(1943), md

Poul Bundgaard
OPERATION LOVEBIRDS(1968, Den.); SCANDAL IN DENMARK(1970, Den.)

A. Frank Bundy
EASY MONEY(1948, Brit.), p; CHRISTOPHER COLUMBUS(1949, Brit.), p; DIAMOND CITY(1949, Brit.), p; CAUGHT IN THE NET(1960, Brit.), p; COUNTDOWN TO DANGER(1967, Brit.), p; ESCAPE FROM THE SEA(1968, Brit.), p

A.E. Bundy
CROSS ROADS(1930, Brit.), w
Silents
BATTLES OF THE CORONEL AND FALKLAND ISLANDS, THE(1928, Brit.), p

Brooke Bundy
FIRECREEK(1968); YOUNG RUNAWAYS, THE(1968); GAY DECEIVERS, THE(1969)
Misc. Talkies
MAN FOR HANGING, A(1972); DANGEROUS RELATIONS(1973)

E. Newton Bungey
Silents
AUTUMN OF PRIDE, THE(1921, Brit.), w

Florence Bunin
ZIEGFELD FOLLIES(1945), cos

Lou Bunin
ALICE IN WONDERLAND(1951, Fr.), p

Nicholas Bunin
FAME(1980)

Edward Bunker
STRAIGHT TIME(1978), a, w; LONG RIDERS, THE(1980)

Jill Bunker
1984
SAVAGE STREETS(1984)

Ralph Bunker
GHOST GOES WEST, THE(1936); HUCKSTERS, THE(1947); NAKED CITY, THE(1948)
Silents
IN SEARCH OF A SINNER(1920); ANOTHER SCANDAL(1924)
Misc. Silents
SCRAMBLED WIVES(1921)

Robert Bunker
JEREMIAH JOHNSON(1972), w

Billy Bunkley
MAD DOCTOR OF MARKET STREET, THE(1942)

Alfred Bunn
BOHEMIAN GIRL, THE(1936), w

Earl Bunn
HONOLULU LU(1941); MEET JOHN DOE(1941); SING FOR YOUR SUPPER(1941); TWO YANKS IN TRINIDAD(1942)

Earle D. Bunn
LAST PARADE, THE(1931)

Evelyn Hope Bunn
KRAMER VS. KRAMER(1979)

Graham Bunn
WAGNER(1983, Brit./Hung./Aust.), ed

Sharon Bunn
KEEP MY GRAVE OPEN(1980)

Rom Bunnag
1 2 3 MONSTER EXPRESS(1977, Thai.), w

Sasidhorn Bunnag
UGLY AMERICAN, THE(1963), tech adv

Avis Bunnage
ROTTEN TO THE CORE(1956, Brit.); EXPRESSO BONGO(1959, Brit.); SATURDAY NIGHT AND SUNDAY MORNING(1961, Brit.); L-SHAPED ROOM, THE(1962, Brit.); LONELINESS OF THE LONG DISTANCE RUNNER, THE(1962, Brit.); SPARROWS CAN'T SING(1963, Brit.); TOM JONES(1963, Brit.); WHAT A CRAZY WORLD(1963,

Brit.); STUDY IN TERROR, A(1966, Brit./Ger.); WRONG BOX, THE(1966, Brit.); WHISPERERS, THE(1967, Brit.); MRS. BROWN, YOU'VE GOT A LOVELY DAUGHTER(1968, Brit.); GANDHI(1982)

Bunny
HOME MOVIES(1979)

Frank Bunny
Silents
NIGHT OUT, A(1916)

George Bunny
LOCKED DOOR, THE(1929); MAN AND THE MOMENT, THE(1929); WILD HORSE(1931)
Silents
IF ONLY JIM(1921); SUPER-SEX, THE(1922); LOST WORLD, THE(1925); BREED OF THE SUNSETS(1928); LADDIE BE GOOD(1928)
Misc. Silents
CAMOUFLAGE KISS, A(1918); CAUGHT IN THE ACT(1918); FRIEND HUSBAND(1918); HEART OF ROMANCE, THE(1918); BROADWAY SAINT, A(1919); PICCADILLY JIM(1920); THRILLING YOUTH(1926)

George Bunny
YOU WERE NEVER LOVELIER(1942); KNICKERBOCKER HOLIDAY(1944); HOODLUM SAINT, THE(1946); SHE WROTE THE BOOK(1946); HIGH WALL, THE(1947); KISS THE BLOOD OFF MT HANDS(1948); SUMMER STOCK(1950)

Inga Bunsch
HAPPY HOOKER, THE(1975)

Herbert Bunsten
CHARLIE CHAN'S CHANCE(1932)

Carmen Bunster
ALSINO AND THE CONDOR(1983, Nicaragua)

Henry Bunston
I LIKE YOUR NERVE(1931)

Herbert Bunston
LAST OF MRS. CHEYNEY, THE(1929); LADY OF SCANDAL, THE(1930); ALWAYS GOODBYE(1931); AMBASSADOR BILL(1931); DRACULA(1931); ONCE A LADY(1931); UNDER SUSPICION(1931); ALMOST MARRIED(1932); FILE 113(1932); MASK OF FU MANCHU, THE(1932); VANITY FAIR(1932); DINNER AT EIGHT(1933); MONKEY'S PAW, THE(1933); TRICK FOR TRICK(1933); DOCTOR MONICA(1934); LITTLE MINISTER, THE(1934); LONG LOST FATHER(1934); MOONSTONE, THE(1934); RICHEST GIRL IN THE WORLD, THE(1934); RIP TIDE(1934); AFTER OFFICE HOURS(1935); CARDINAL RICHELIEU(1935); CLIVE OF INDIA(1935); SHOT IN THE DARK, A(1935)

James Bunting
RADIO FOLLIES(1935, Brit.), w

Yetim Buntsis
STRIPES(1981)

David Buntzman
1984
EXTERMINATOR 2(1984)

Mark Buntzman
EXTERMINATOR, THE(1980), p
1984
EXTERMINATOR 2(1984), p,d&w
Misc. Talkies
ASTROLOGER, THE(1979)

Joyce Bunuel
BLACK MOON(1975, Fr.), w; TATTOO(1981), w

Juan Bunuel
LEONOR(1977, Fr./Span./Ital.), d, w; WOMAN WITH RED BOOTS, THE(1977, Fr./Span.), d&w

Luis Bunuel
LOS OLVIDADOS(1950, Mex.), d, w; BRUTE, THE(1952, Mex.), d, w; ADVENTURES OF ROBINSON CRUSOE, THE(1954), d; EL(1955, Mex.), d, w; GINA(1961, Fr./Mex.), d, w; YOUNG ONE, THE(1961, Mex.), d, w; CRIMINAL LIFE OF ARCHIBALDO DE LA CRUZ, THE(1962, Mex.), d, w; VIRIDIANA(1962, Mex./Span.), d, w; DIARY OF A CHAMBERMAID(1964, Fr./Ital.), d, w; EXTERMINATING ANGEL, THE(1967, Mex.), d, w; BELLE DE JOUR(1968, Fr.), p, d, w; NAZARIN(1968, Mex.), d, w; MILKY WAY, THE(1969, Fr./Ital.), d, w, m; TRISTANA(1970, Span./Ital./Fr.), d, w; DISCREET CHARM OF THE BOURGEOISIE, THE(1972, Fr.), d, w; PHANTOM OF LIBERTY, THE(1974, Fr.), d, w; DAUGHTER OF DECEIT(1977, Mex.), d; DEATH IN THE GARDEN(1977, Fr./Mex.), d, w; ILLUSION TRAVELS BY STREETCAR, THE(1977, Mex.), d; THAT OBSCURE OBJECT OF DESIRE(1977, Fr./Span.), d, w; L'AGE D'OR(1979, Fr.), d, w, ed

Mabel Bunyea
Silents
BRAVE AND BOLD(1918)

Danny J. Bunz
NORTH DALLAS FORTY(1979)

Angelo Buono
THIS IS THE ARMY(1943)

Victor Buono
SILENCERS, THE(; WHATEVER HAPPENED TO BABY JANE?(1962); FOUR FOR TEXAS(1963); MY SIX LOVES(1963); HUSH... HUSH, SWEET CHARLOTTE(1964); ROBIN AND THE SEVEN HOODS(1964); STRANGLER, THE(1964); GREATEST STORY EVER TOLD, THE(1965); YOUNG DILLINGER(1965); WHO'S MINDING THE MINT?(1967); BIG DADDY(1969); BOOT HILL(1969, Ital.); BENEATH THE PLANET OF THE APES(1970); UP YOUR TEDDY BEAR(1970); MOONCHILD(1972); WRATH OF GOD, THE(1972); ARNOLD(1973); EVIL, THE(1978); MAN WITH BOGART'S FACE, THE(1980); TARGET: HARRY(1980)
Misc. Talkies
ASYLUM FOR A SPY(1967); SAVAGE SEASON(1970); MAN WITH THE ICY EYES, THE(1971); MAD BUTCHER, THE(1972); NORTHEAST TO SEOUL(1974)

Sonny Bupp
LOVE IS ON THE AIR(1937); MY DEAR MISS ALDRICH(1937); ANGELS WITH DIRTY FACES(1938); SWING YOUR LADY(1938); BOY TROUBLE(1939); NO PLACE TO GO(1939); RENEGADE TRAIL(1939); WHEN TOMORROW COMES(1939); HALF A SINNER(1940); PAROLE FIXER(1940); QUEEN OF THE MOB(1940); THREE FACES WEST(1940); CITIZEN KANE(1941); DEVIL AND DANIEL WEBSTER, THE(1941); FATHER'S SON(1941); SHE COULDN'T SAY NO(1941)

Tom Bupp
IT'S A GIFT(1934)
Tommy Bupp
GIRL OF THE LIMBERLOST(1934); MAN FROM HELL, THE(1934); ARIZONA BADMAN(1935); GINGER(1935); HOOSIER SCHOOLMASTER(1935); LITTLE MEN(1935); PADDY O'DAY(1935); IT HAD TO HAPPEN(1936); LONGEST NIGHT, THE(1936); PEPPER(1936); PICCADILLY JIM(1936); ROARIN' GUNS(1936); SAN FRANCISCO(1936); CAPTAINS COURAGEOUS(1937); CHEROKEE STRIP(1937); CONFLICT(1937); HIGH, WIDE AND HANDSOME(1937); HITTIN' THE TRAIL(1937); LOVE IS ON THE AIR(1937); MAKE WAY FOR TOMORROW(1937); ROARIN' LEAD(1937); TEX RIDES WITH THE BOY SCOUTS(1937); TOVARICH(1937); BLIND ALIBI(1938); DEVIL'S PARTY, THE(1938); HEY! HEY! U.S.A.(1938, Brit.); NANCY DREW-DETECTIVE(1938); OVER THE WALL(1938); REFORMATORY(1938); SWING YOUR LADY(1938); FISHERMAN'S WHARF(1939); HERO FOR A DAY(1939); INDIANAPOLIS SPEEDWAY(1939); MYSTERY PLANE(1939); OFF THE RECORD(1939); WHEN TOMORROW COMES(1939); BROTHER RAT AND A BABY(1940); WAY OF ALL FLESH, THE(1940); NAVAL ACADEMY(1941)
Jean Buquet
PORTRAIT OF INNOCENCE(1948, Fr.)
Dee Bura
MUTATIONS, THE(1974, Brit.)
Fay Bura
MUTATIONS, THE(1974, Brit.)
Madame Burani
Silents
ALOMA OF THE SOUTH SEAS(1926)
Micheletta Burani
EVERYBODY SING(1938)
Michelette Burani
ENTER MADAME(1935); GILDED LILY, THE(1935); GIVE US THIS NIGHT(1936)
Michellette Burani
FOOLS FOR SCANDAL(1938)
Barbara Burbank
IT CAN'T LAST FOREVER(1937)
Leon Burbank
NO ESCAPE(1953); BOWERY TO BAGDAD(1955)
Lynda Burbank
1984
REPO MAN(1984), art d
Zadee Burbank
Silents
MAN AND THE WOMAN, A(1917)
Misc. Silents
WASP, THE(1918)
Frank Burbeck
Misc. Silents
WHAT HAPPENED AT 22(1916); WHO'S YOUR BROTHER?(1919)
Betty Burbidge
ROVIN' TUMBLEWEEDS(1939), w
Ted Burbidge
TITFIELD THUNDERBOLT, THE(1953, Brit.)
Berry Burbridge
PHANTOM THUNDERBOLT, THE(1933), w
Betty Burbridge
CHINATOWN AFTER DARK(1931), w; IN OLD CHEYENNE(1931), w; IS THERE JUSTICE?(1931), w; LAW OF THE RIO GRANDE(1931), w; MOUNTED FURY(1931), w; NECK AND NECK(1931), w; BETWEEN FIGHTING MEN(1932), w; HELL FIRE AUSTIN(1932), w; LONE TRAIL, THE(1932), w; SIN'S PAYDAY(1932), w; DANCE MALL HOSTESS(1933), w; LONE AVENGER, THE(1933), w; RACING STRAIN, THE(1933), w; RED HEAD(1934), w; FALSE PRETENSES(1935), w; GET THAT MAN(1935), w; RECKLESS ROADS(1935), w; RESCUE SQUAD(1935), w; SINGING VAGABOND, THE(1935), w; CRIME PATROL, THE(1936), w; HONEYMOON LIMITED(1936), w; COME ON, COWBOYS(1937), w; PARADISE EXPRESS(1937), w; SPRINGTIME IN THE ROCKIES(1937), w; GOLD MINE IN THE SKY(1938), w; HEROES OF THE HILLS(1938), w; MAN FROM MUSIC MOUNTAIN(1938), w; OUTLAWS OF SONORA(1938), w; PALS OF THE SADDLE(1938), w; PURPLE VIGILANTES, THE(1938), w; RED RIVER RANGE(1938), w; RIDERS OF THE BLACK HILLS(1938), w; SANTA FE STAMPEDE(1938), w; UNDER WESTERN STARS(1938), w; WILD HORSE RODEO(1938), w; COLORADO SUNSET(1939), w; KANSAS TERRORS, THE(1939), w; NEW FRONTIER(1939), w; NIGHT RIDERS, THE(1939), w; SOUTH OF THE BORDER(1939), w; THREE TEXAS STEERS(1939), w; WYOMING OUTLAW(1939), w; GAUCHO SERENADE(1940), w; RANCHO GRANDE(1940), w; RIDE, TENDERFOOT, RIDE(1940), w; UNDER TEXAS SKIES(1940), w; RIDERS OF THE BADLANDS(1941), w; THUNDER OVER THE PRAIRIE(1941), w; STARDUST ON THE SAGE(1942), w; ROBIN HOOD OF THE RANGE(1943), w; SANTA FE SCOUTS(1943), w; OKLAHOMA RAIDERS(1944), w; CHEROKEE FLASH, THE(1945), w; CISCO KID RETURNS, THE(1945), w; IN OLD NEW MEXICO(1945), w; OREGON TRAIL(1945), w; UTAH(1945), w; ALIAS BILLY THE KID(1946), w; HOME ON THE RANGE(1946), w; MAN FROM RAINBOW VALLEY, THE(1946), w; OUT CALIFORNIA WAY(1946), w; RETURN OF WILDFIRE, THE(1948), w; DARING CABALLERO, THE(1949), w
Silents
QUICKER'N LIGHTNIN'(1925), w; ACE OF ACTION(1926), w; FIGHTING CHEAT, THE(1926), w; VANISHING HOOFS(1926), w
Charles Burbridge
Misc. Silents
MAN INSIDE, THE(1916)
Elizabeth Burbridge
MELODY TRAIL(1935), w
Silents
CHARITY?(1916); TONGUES OF MEN, THE(1916)
Misc. Silents
RUMPELSTILKIN(1915)
Oteil Burbridge
BEING THERE(1979)
William Burbridge
Silents
TRAFFIC IN SOULS(1913)

Curt Burch
IT LIVES AGAIN(1978), ed
Curtis Burch
RETURN, THE(1980), w; WITHOUT WARNING(1980), ed; JOYSTICKS(1983), w; WACKO(1983), ed
Dick Burch
Misc. Talkies
POSSE FROM HEAVEN(1975)
John Burch
GOOD COMPANIONS(1933, Brit.); GREAT EXPECTATIONS(1946, Brit.)
Silents
GUN LAW(1929), d
John E. Burch
FANNY FOLEY HERSELF(1931), p
Lee Burch
OLLY, OLLY, OXEN FREE(1978), ed
Lew Burch
ELECTRA GLIDE IN BLUE(1973)
Matthew Burch
HOT STUFF(1979)
Shelly Burch
SAMMY STOPS THE WORLD zero(1978)
Sydney Burchell
LAUGH IT OFF(1940, Brit.)
Kevin Burchett
BOY, DID I GET A WRONG NUMBER!(1966); FOLLOW ME, BOYS!(1966); YOURS, MINE AND OURS(1968)
Stephanie Burchfield
WHITE LIGHTNING(1973); GATOR(1976)
Giantito Burchiellaro
JULIET OF THE SPIRITS(1965, Fr./Ital./W.Ger.), set d; DETECTIVE BELLI(1970, Ital.), art d; DEAD ARE ALIVE, THE(1972, Yugo./Ger./Ital.), art d; SALAMANDER, THE(1983, U.S./Ital./Brit.), art d
1984
CORRUPT(1984, Ital.), art d
Brian J. Burchill
1984
STRANGER THAN PARADISE(1984, U.S./Ger.)
William Burchill
Silents
MANCHESTER MAN, THE(1920, Brit.)
Rhonda Burchmore
PIRATE MOVIE, THE(1982, Aus.)
Miguel Burciaga
SUNBURN(1979)
Barbara Burck
TAZA, SON OF COCHISE(1954)
Clark Burckhalter
PUZZLE OF A DOWNFALL CHILD(1970)
Frank Burckner
ALL-AROUND REDUCED PERSONALITY-OUTTAKES, THE(1978, Ger.)
Edgar Burcksen
SPLITTING UP(1981, Neth.), ed
1984
DESIREE(1984, Neth.), ed
Joan Burclay
AMATEUR CROOK(1937)
Marion Burdell
UNDER THE TONTO RIM(1933)
H. E. Burden
MURDER IN EDEN(1962, Brit.), w
High Burden
FAME IS THE SPUR(1947, Brit.)
Hugh Burden
DEATH CROONS THE BLUES(1937, Brit.); ONE OF OUR AIRCRAFT IS MISSING(1942, Brit.); SHIPS WITH WINGS(1942, Brit.); WAY AHEAD, THE(1945, Brit.); SLEEPING CAR TO TRIESTE(1949, Brit.); GHOST SHIP(1953, Brit.); MALTA STORY(1954, Brit.); NO LOVE FOR JOHNNIE(1961, Brit.); SECRET PARTNER, THE(1961, Brit.); FUNERAL IN BERLIN(1966, Brit.); BEST HOUSE IN LONDON, THE(1969, Brit.); STATUE, THE(1971, Brit.); BLOOD FROM THE MUMMY'S TOMB(1972, Brit.); RULING CLASS, THE(1972, Brit.)
W. Douglas Burden
SILENT ENEMY, THE(1930), p
Gammy Burdett
EMMA MAE(1976); INDEPENDENCE DAY(1976); SIXTH AND MAIN(1977); BOSS'S SON, THE(1978)
Laetitia Burdett
EMMA MAE(1976)
Jack Burdette
ISLAND OF LOST SOULS(1933)
John Burdette
Silents
STREET OF SIN, THE(1928)
Margo Burdichevsky
I NEVER PROMISED YOU A ROSE GARDEN(1977)
Eugene Burdick
UGLY AMERICAN, THE(1963), w; FAIL SAFE(1964), w
Laura Burdick
MY BREAKFAST WITH BLASSIE(1983)
Linda Burdick
MY BREAKFAST WITH BLASSIE(1983)
Ray Burdis
MUSIC MACHINE, THE(1979, Brit.); SCUM(1979, Brit.)
Albert Burdon
MAID OF THE MOUNTAINS, THE(1932, Brit.); LETTING IN THE SUNSHINE(1933, Brit.); IT'S A BOY(1934, Brit.); HEAT WAVE(1935, Brit.); SHE KNEW WHAT SHE WANTED(1936, Brit.); OH BOY!(1938, Brit.); JAILBIRDS(1939, Brit.); NORTH SEA PATROL(1939, Brit.)

Tom Burdon
GUY CALLED CAESAR, A(1962, Brit.), w
Vi Burdon
GRAND ESCAPADE, THE(1946, Brit.), ed; NOTHING VENTURE(1948, Brit.), ed
G. Burdzhalov
Misc. Silents
DOMESTIC-AGITATOR(1920, USSR)
L.H. Burel
LOVE IN MOROCCO(1933, Fr.), ph; ABUSED CONFIDENCE(1938, Fr. ABUS DE CONFIANCE), ph; SECRETS D'ALCOVE(1954, Fr./Ital.), ph; HIGHWAY PICK-UP(1965, Fr./Ital.), ph; THANK HEAVEN FOR SMALL FAVORS(1965, Fr.), ph
Leonce-Henri Burel
PICKPOCKET(1963, Fr.), ph; TRIAL OF JOAN OF ARC(1965, Fr.), ph
Leonce-Henry Burel
DIARY OF A COUNTRY PRIEST(1954, Fr.), ph; MAN ESCAPED, A(1957, Fr.), ph
Silents
NAPOLEON(1927, Fr.), ph
Louis Burel
SPICE OF LIFE(1954, Fr.), ph
Meredyth Burel
MOTHERS CRY(1930)
Catherine Van Buren
Misc. Silents
LAST OF HIS PEOPLE, THE(1919)
Yevgeniy Burenkov
SUN SHINES FOR ALL, THE(1961, USSR)
N. Burenkova
SUN SHINES FOR ALL, THE(1961, USSR)
L.H. Buret
CROSSROADS(1938, Fr.), ph
Susan Buret
DULCIMER STREET(1948, Brit.)
Kim Burfield
BLOOMFIELD(1971, Brit./Israel); TREASURE ISLAND(1972, Brit./Span./Fr./Ger.); FLYING SORCERER, THE(1974, Brit.)
Joan Burfield [Fontaine]
NO MORE LADIES(1935)
John Burford
GHOST SHIP, THE(1943); GALLANT BESS(1946)
Phyllis Burford
GALLIPOLI(1981, Aus.)
Robert Burford
LOVES OF MADAME DUBARRY, THE(1938, Brit.), w
Roger Burford
PICCADILLY NIGHTS(1930, Brit.), w; FREEDOM OF THE SEAS(1934, Brit.), w; GIRLS WILL BE BOYS(1934, Brit.), w; ABDUL THE DAMNED(1935, Brit.), w; DANCE BAND(1935, Brit.), w; INVITATION TO THE WALTZ(1935, Brit.), w; NO MONKEY BUSINESS(1935, Brit.), w; CLOWN MUST LAUGH, A(1936, Brit.), w; LOVE IN EXILE(1936, Brit.), w; PUBLIC NUISANCE NO. 1(1936, Brit.), w; RED WA-GON(1936), w; APRIL BLOSSOMS(1937, Brit.), w; DOCTOR SYN(1937, Brit.), w; HEART'S DESIRE(1937, Brit.), w; BANK HOLIDAY(1938, Brit.), w; ONCE A CROOK(1941, Brit.), w; MOLLY AND ME(1945), w; NIGHT WON'T TALK, THE(1952, Brit.), w
Alexy Burg
NEW LIFE STYLE, THE(1970, Ger.)
Emmy Burg
CONFESS DR. CORDA(1960, Ger.)
Eugen Burg
Misc. Silents
DARK CASTLE, THE(1915)
Michael Burg
LOCAL COLOR(1978); IMPOSTORS(1979)
Barbara Burgdorph
CLONES, THE(1973)
James Burge
ANNIE HALL(1977)
Stuart Burge
MALTA STORY(1954, Brit.); THERE WAS A CROOKED MAN(1962, Brit.), d; OTHELLO(1965, Brit.), d; MIKADO, THE(1967, Brit.), d; JULIUS CAESAR(1970, Brit.), d; UNCLE VANYA(1977, Brit.), d
Fairfax Burger
FEAR(1946)
Germain Burger
DOWN OUR ALLEY(1939, Brit.), p, ph; SHEEPDOG OF THE HILLS(1941, Brit.), d, ph; ROSE OF TRALEE(1942, Brit.), d
Germain Gerard Burger
DEVIL'S ROCK(1938, Brit.), p&d, ph
Germaine Burger
PENNY POOL, THE(1937, Brit.), ph; MY AIN FOLK(1944, Brit.), d
Gottfried Burger
BARON MUNCHAUSEN(1962, Czech.), w
Gotz Burger
PHONY AMERICAN, THE(1964, Ger.)
Hans Burger
SEEDS OF FREEDOM(1943, USSR), d
John Burger
IT HAPPENED IN FLATBUSH(1942)
John "Red" Burger
TAKE ME OUT TO THE BALL GAME(1949)
Julie Burger
ECHOES(1983)
Ludwig Burger
BALLERINA(1950, Fr.), d&w
Michael Burger
AMERICAN SUCCESS COMPANY, THE(1980)
Paul Burger
FIFTEEN MAIDEN LANE(1936), w; LITTLE MISS NOBODY(1936), w; CHARLIE CHAN AT THE OLYMPICS(1937), w

Peter E. Burger
FIRST MONDAY IN OCTOBER(1981), ed
Ralph Burger
TROUBLE IN TEXAS(1937), art d
Red Burger
TREASURE ISLAND(1934)
W. Burgermaster
Misc. Silents
PLAIN JANE(1916)
Adrienne Burgess
PRIEST OF LOVE(1981, Brit.)
Alan Burgess
INN OF THE SIXTH HAPPINESS, THE(1958), w; OPERATION DAYBREAK(1976, U.S./Brit./Czech.), w
Anthony Burgess
CLOCKWORK ORANGE, A(1971, Brit.), w; MOSES(1976, Brit./Ital.), w
Barbara Burgess
SILENCERS, THE(; MURDERERS' ROW(1966)
1984
LAUGHTER HOUSE(1984, Brit.)
Misc. Talkies
BRAIN MACHINE, THE(1972)
Betty Burgess
CORONADO(1935); I DEMAND PAYMENT(1938)
Misc. Talkies
ADVENTURES OF THE MASKED PHANTOM, THE(1939)
Cara Burgess
Misc. Talkies
MANHANDLERS, THE(1975)
Christopher Burgess
MEDUSA TOUCH, THE(1978, Brit.)
Deborah Burgess
CURTAINS(1983, Can.)
Deborah Templeton Burgess
RUNNING(1979, Can.)
Dennis Burgess
ELEPHANT MAN, THE(1980, Brit.)
Dorothy Burgess
IN OLD ARIZONA(1929); PLEASURE CRAZED(1929); SONG OF KENTUCKY(1929); RECAPTURED LOVE(1930); SWING HIGH(1930); LASCA OF THE RIO GRAN-DE(1931); OUT OF SINGAPORE(1932); PLAY GIRL(1932); STOKER, THE(1932); TAXI!(1932); EASY MILLIONS(1933); FROM HEADQUARTERS(1933); HEADLINE SHOOTER(1933); HOLD YOUR MAN(1933); I LOVE THAT MAN(1933); IMPORTANT WITNESS, THE(1933); IT'S GREAT TO BE ALIVE(1933); LADIES MUST LOVE(1933); LADIES THEY TALK ABOUT(1933); MALAY NIGHTS(1933); RUSTY RIDES ALO-NE(1933); STRICTLY PERSONAL(1933); WHAT PRICE DECENCY?(1933); AFFAIRS OF A GENTLEMAN(1934); BLACK MOON(1934); CIRCUS CLOWN(1934); FASHIONS OF 1934(1934); FRIENDS OF MR. SWEENEY(1934); GAMBLING(1934); HAT, COAT AND GLOVE(1934); MISS FANE'S BABY IS STOLEN(1934); MODERN HERO, A(1934); ORIENT EXPRESS(1934); VILLAGE TALE(1935); I WANT A DIVORCE(1940); LADY IN QUESTION, THE(1940); LADY FOR A NIGHT(1941); LONE STAR RANGER(1942); GIRLS IN CHAINS(1943); MAN OF COURAGE(1943)
Silents
PROTECTION(1929)
Elizabeth Burgess
TWO TICKETS TO BROADWAY(1951)
Gelett Burgess
TWO IN THE DARK(1936), w; TWO O'CLOCK COURAGE(1945), w
Gelette Burgess
Silents
CAVEMAN, THE(1926), w
Grover Burgess
SEEDS OF FREEDOM(1943, USSR); NAKED CITY, THE(1948)
Harry Burgess
MURDER BY THE CLOCK(1931)
Helen Burgess
DOCTOR'S DIARY, A(1937); KING OF GAMBLERS(1937); NIGHT OF MYS-TERY(1937); PLAINSMAN, THE(1937)
Hovey Burgess
POPEYE(1980), a, ch
Jane Burgess
KISS THEM FOR ME(1957); LOOKING FOR DANGER(1957)
John Burgess
1984
GIVE MY REGARDS TO BROAD STREET(1984, Brit.)
Kylie Burgess
1984
CAREFUL, HE MIGHT HEAR YOU(1984, Aus.)
Madalene Burgess
STRANGER AT MY DOOR(1950, Brit.)
Madeleine Burgess
HAND, THE(1960, Brit.)
Ray Burgess
TEXAS RANGERS, THE(1936)
Rick Burgess
JOHNNY DARK(1954)
Scot Burgess
Misc. Talkies
OUTBREAK OF HOSTILITIES(1979)
Susan Burgess
1984
GREMLINS(1984)
Vivienne Burgess
HAMMER THE TOFF(1952, Brit.); MAROC 7(1967, Brit.); NO LONGER ALONE(1978)
Wesley Burgess
BUTCH AND SUNDANCE: THE EARLY DAYS(1979)
William Burgess
WILD MONEY(1937)

Wilma Burgess
LAS VEGAS HILLBILLYS(1966)
Arthur Burghardt
NETWORK(1976)
George Burghardt
Misc. Silents
RICHTOFEN(1932, Ger.)
Sheila Burghart
GUIDE, THE(1965, U.S./India)
Gary Burghoff
M(1970); B.S. I LOVE YOU(1971)
Scott Burgi
TAKE DOWN(1979)
Polly Burgin
ACROSS THE RIO GRANDE(1949)
Geoffrey Burgon
MONTY PYTHON'S LIFE OF BRIAN(1979, Brit.), m; DOGS OF WAR, THE(1980, Brit.), m
Gabriel Burgos
VAMPIRE'S NIGHT ORGY, THE(1973, Span./Ital.), w
Gabriel Moreno Burgos
HYPNOSIS(1966, Ger./Sp./Ital.), w
Jose Burgos
MASQUERADE(1965, Brit.); VALLEY OF GWANGI, THE(1969)
Robert Burgos
NAKED WITCH, THE(1964)
Marcella Burgoyne
IRISHMAN, THE(1978, Aus.)
Ollie Burgoyne
LAUGHTER(1930)
Victoria Burgoyne
DEATH SHIP(1980, Can.)
William Burgress
AFTER THE THIN MAN(1936)
Betty Burgridge
PRAIRIE MOON(1938), w
L. Robert Burgs
PRIDE OF THE MARINES(1945), spec eff
Charles Burguet
Misc. Silents
LES DEUX AMOURS(1917, Fr.), d; POUR EPOUSER GABY(1917, Fr.), d; SON HEROS(1917, Fr.), d; AU PARADIS DES ENFANTS(1918, Fr.), d; L'AME DE PIER-RE(1918, Fr.), d; LA SULTANE DE L'AMOUR(1919, Fr.), d; LE CHEVALIER DE GABY(1920, Fr.), d; UN OURS(1921, Fr.), d; FAUBOURG MONTMARTE(1924, Fr.), d; BAROCCO(1925, Fr.), d; MARTYRE(1926, Fr.), d; LE MENEUR DE JOIES(1929, Fr.), d
Franz-Andre Burguet
CANNABIS(1970, Fr.), w
E.F. Burian
JOURNEY TO THE BEGINNING OF TIME(1966, Czech), m
Vlasia Burian
INSPECTOR GENERAL, THE(1937, Czech.)
Rose Burich
RAIDERS OF THE DESERT(1941)
Gisella Burinato
LEAP INTO THE VOID(1982, Ital.)
Rene Burjavel
HIGHWAY PICKUP(1965, Fr./Ital.), w
Alan Burk
THUNDER TRAIL(1937)
David Burk
DIRTY DINGUS MAGEE(1970)
Gene Burk
MY THIRD WIFE GEORGE(1968)
James Burk
GERONIMO(1962); WAY WEST, THE(1967)
James H. Burk
PROPHECY(1979)
Jim Burk
BIG COUNTRY, THE(1958); HALLELUJAH TRAIL, THE(1965); ONE MORE TRAIN TO ROB(1971); SOMETIMES A GREAT NOTION(1971); COWBOYS, THE(1972); LIFE AND TIMES OF JUDGE ROY BEAN, THE(1972); OKLAHOMA CRUDE(1973); HOOP-ER(1978)
Jimmy H. Burk
PONY EXPRESS(1953)
Michael Burk
MAN WHO WALKED THROUGH THE WALL, THE(1964, Ger.)
Aileen Burke
BLESS 'EM ALL(1949, Brit.), w; SKIMPY IN THE NAVY(1949, Brit.), w; FAREWELL PERFORMANCE(1963, Brit.), w
Al Burke
MILLIONS IN THE AIR(1935); LEGEND OF LYLAH CLARE, THE(1968), spec eff
Albert Burke
SURRENDER(1931)
Alfred Burke
KID FROM BOOKLYN, THE(1946); CONSTANT HUSBAND, THE(1955, Brit.); LIGHT TOUCH, THE(1955, Brit.); BATTLE HELL(1956, Brit.); HIGH FLIGHT(1957, Brit.); LET'S BE HAPPY(1957, Brit.); PICKUP ALLEY(1957, Brit.); BITTER VIC-TORY(1958, Fr.); LAW AND DISORDER(1958, Brit.); MAN INSIDE, THE(1958, Brit.); TANK FORCE(1958, Brit.); MAN UPSTAIRS, THE(1959, Brit.); ANGRY SILENCE, THE(1960, Brit.); DEAD LUCKY(1960, Brit.); MODEL FOR MURDER(1960, Brit.); BACKFIRE(1961, Brit.); MAN AT THE CARLTON TOWER(1961, Brit.); MALA-GA(1962, Brit.); MIX ME A PERSON(1962, Brit.); ON THE BEAT(1962, Brit.); POT CARRIERS, THE(1962, Brit.); CHILDREN OF THE DAMNED(1963, Brit.); CROOKS ANONYMOUS(1963, Brit.); FAREWELL PERFORMANCE(1963, Brit.); SMALL WORLD OF SAMMY LEE, THE(1963, Brit.); 20,000 POUNDS KISS(1964, Brit.); BLOOD BEAST FROM OUTER SPACE(1965, Brit.); NANNY, THE(1965, Brit.); MAN WHO FINALLY DIED, THE(1967, Brit.); GUNS IN THE HEATHER(1968, Brit.); ONE DAY IN THE LIFE OF IVAN DENISOVICH(1971, U.S./Brit./Norway)

Archie Burke
GODLESS GIRL, THE(1929)
Art Burke
HOT LEAD AND COLD FEET(1978)
Misc. Talkies
STREET GIRLS(1975)
Barbara Burke
REPENT AT LEISURE(1941); MAN WHO KNEW TOO MUCH, THE(1956); PASS-PORT TO TREASON(1956, Brit.); JACK THE RIPPER(1959, Brit.)
Becki Burke
FOREST, THE(1983)
Bernard Burke
FOURTEEN HOURS(1951)
Bill Burke
SALLY OF THE SUBWAY(1932); MALIBU HIGH(1979)
Billie Burke
BILL OF DIVORCEMENT, A(1932); CHRISTOPHER STRONG(1933); DINNER AT EIGHT(1933); ONLY YESTERDAY(1933); FINISHING SCHOOL(1934); WE'RE RICH AGAIN(1934); WHERE SINNERS MEET(1934); AFTER OFFICE HOURS(1935); BECKY SHARP(1935); DOUBTING THOMAS(1935); FEATHER IN HER HAT, A(1935); FORSAKING ALL OTHERS(1935); SHE COULDN'T TAKE IT(1935); SOCIETY DOC-TOR(1935); SPLENDOR(1935); CRAIG'S WIFE(1936); MY AMERICAN WIFE(1936); PICCADILLY JIM(1936); BRIDE WORE RED, THE(1937); NAVY BLUE AND GOLD(1937); PARNELL(1937); TOPPER(1937); EVERYBODY SING(1938); MERRILY WE LIVE(1938); YOUNG IN HEART, THE(1938); BRIDAL SUITE(1939); ETERNALLY YOURS(1939); REMEMBER?(1939); TOPPER TAKES A TRIP(1939); WIZARD OF OZ, THE(1939); ZENOBIA(1939); AND ONE WAS BEAUTIFUL(1940); CAPTAIN IS A LADY, THE(1940); DULCY(1940); GHOST COMES HOME, THE(1940); HUL-LABALOO(1940); IRENE(1940); ONE NIGHT IN LISBON(1941); TOPPER RE-TURNS(1941); WILD MAN OF BORNEO, THE(1941); GIRL TROUBLE(1942); IN THIS OUR LIFE(1942); MAN WHO CAME TO DINNER, THE(1942); THEY ALL KISSED THE BRIDE(1942); WHAT'S COOKIN'?(1942); GILDERSLEEVE ON BROAD-WAY(1943); HI DIDDLE DIDDLE(1943); SO'S YOUR UNCLE(1943); YOU'RE A LUCKY FELLOW, MR. SMITH(1943); SWING OUT, SISTER(1945); BACHELOR'S DAUGHTERS, THE(1946); BREAKFAST IN HOLLYWOOD(1946); AND BABY MAKES THREE(1949); BARKLEYS OF BROADWAY(1949); BOY FROM IN-DIANA(1950); FATHER OF THE BRIDE(1950); THREE HUSBANDS(1950); DARLING, HOW COULD YOU!(1951); FATHER'S LITTLE DIVIDEND(1951); SMALL TOWN GIRL(1953); YOUNG PHILADELPHIANS, THE(1959); PEPE(1960); SERGEANT RUT-LEDGE(1960)
Silents
PEGGY(1916); ARMS AND THE GIRL(1917); EVE'S DAUGHTER(1918); AWAY GOES PRUDENCE(1920); EDUCATION OF ELIZABETH, THE(1921)
Misc. Silents
LAND OF PROMISE, THE(1917); MYSTERIOUS MISS TERRY, THE(1917); IN PURSUIT OF POLLY(1918); LET'S GET A DIVORCE(1918); MAKE-BELIEVE WIFE, THE(1918); GOOD GRACIOUS ANNABELLE(1919); MISLEADING WIDOW, THE(1919); WANTED - A HUSBAND(1919); FRISKY MRS. JOHNSON, THE(1920); SADIE LOVE(1920)
Bobbie Jo Burke
1984
FLAMINGO KID, THE(1984)
Brandon Burke
ODD ANGRY SHOT, THE(1979, Aus.)
Brenda Burke
Silents
KNOCKNAGOW(1918, Ireland)
Brian Burke
ANGELS WITH DIRTY FACES(1938); LADY IN THE MORGUE(1938)
Misc. Talkies
MISSION HILL(1982)
Cameron Burke
HAIR(1979)
Caroline Burke
MYSTERIOUS RIDER, THE(1942)
Chris Burke
FRIGHTMARE(1974, Brit.), art d; DEATH SHIP(1980, Can.), art d; PINK FLOYD-THE WALL(1982, Brit.), art d
1984
SPLATTER UNIVERSITY(1984), m
Clem Burke
ROADIE(1980)
Coleman Burke
LIAR'S DICE(1980), m
Daniel Burke
Silents
QUEST OF LIFE, THE(1916)
David Burke
SATURDAY NIGHT OUT(1964, Brit.)
Denny Burke
WHISPERING SKULL, THE(1944); NIGHT IN PARADISE, A(1946)
Donald Burke
YOUNG GIRLS OF ROCHEFORT, THE(1968, Fr.)
Donny Burke
WITHOUT A TRACE(1983)
Edie Burke
SOFT SKIN ON BLACK SILK(1964, Fr./Span.)
Edmund Lawrence Burke
Silents
JOHNNY GET YOUR GUN(1919), w
Edwin Burke
LOVE, LIVE AND LAUGH(1929), w; NOT QUITE DECENT(1929), w; SPEAKEA-SY(1929), w; THIS THING CALLED LOVE(1929), w; WOMAN TRAP(1929), w; DANC-ERS, THE(1930), w; HAPPY DAYS(1930), w; HARMONY AT HOME(1930), w; MAN TROUBLE(1930), w; BAD GIRL(1931), w; MR. LEMON OF ORANGE(1931), w; SOB SISTER(1931), w; YOUNG AS YOU FEEL(1931), w; CALL HER SAVAGE(1932), w; DANCE TEAM(1932), w; DOWN TO EARTH(1932), w; PADDY, THE NEXT BEST THING(1933), w; BRIGHT EYES(1934), w; NOW I'LL TELL(1934), d&w; FARMER TAKES A WIFE, THE(1935), w; LITTLEST REBEL, THE(1935), w; ONE MORE SPRING(1935), w; THIS THING CALLED LOVE(1940), w

Edwin H. Burke
GIRL FROM HAVANA, THE(1929), w
Edwin J. Burke
MAN WHO CAME BACK, THE(1931), w
Eldon Burke
BREAKHEART PASS(1976)
Frank Burke
OUTSIDE THE LAW(1930); QUARTERBACK, THE(1940)
Silents
BATTLE OF GETTYSBURG(1914)
Misc. Silents
BAWBS O' BLUE RIDGE(1916)
Frankie Burke
ANGELS WITH DIRTY FACES(1938); HELL'S KITCHEN(1939); PRIDE OF THE BLUEGRASS(1939); SWEEPSTAKES WINNER(1939); WOMEN IN THE WIND(1939); BOYS OF THE CITY(1940); EAST SIDE KIDS(1940); FUGITIVE FROM A PRISON CAMP(1940); RIDE, KELLY, RIDE(1941)
George K. Burke
SEA WIFE(1957, Brit.), w
Georgia Burke
ANNA LUCASTA(1958); COOL WORLD, THE(1963)
Helen Burke
DEAR MURDERER(1947, Brit.)
Honoria Burke
ROOM AT THE TOP(1959, Brit.)
Hoolihan Burke
RAGTIME(1981)
J. Frank Burke
Silents
DESPOILER, THE(1915); ITALIAN, THE(1915); CIVILIZATION(1916); HELL'S HINGES(1916); ICED BULLET, THE(1917); WOODEN SHOES(1917)
Misc. Silents
BARGAIN, THE(1914); TOAST OF DEATH, THE(1915); DAWN MAKER, THE(1916)
Jack Burke
BENEATH THE 12-MILE REEF(1953)
James Burke
BOWERY, THE(1933); GIRL IN 419(1933); KENNEL MURDER CASE, THE(1933); LADY KILLER(1933); LADY'S PROFESSION, A(1933); TILLIE AND GUS(1933); TO THE LAST MAN(1933); CAT'S PAW, THE(1934); GAMBLING LADY(1934); GIRL FROM MISSOURI, THE(1934); GOOD DAME(1934); IT HAPPENED ONE NIGHT(1934); IT'S A GIFT(1934); LADY BY CHOICE(1934); LEMON DROP KID, THE(1934); LITTLE MISS MARKER(1934); LOVE TIME(1934); MERRY FRINKS, THE(1934); SCARLET EMPRESS, THE(1934); SIX OF A KIND(1934); TICKET TO CRIME(1934); TREASURE ISLAND(1934); TWENTIETH CENTURY(1934); WHARF ANGEL(1934); AFFAIR OF SUSAN(1935); BROADWAY GONDOLIER(1935); CALL OF THE WILD(1935); CASE OF THE MISSING MAN, THE(1935); CORONADO(1935); DINKY(1935); FRISCO WATERFRONT(1935); HERE COMES COOKIE(1935); MAKE A MILLION(1935); MAN ON THE FLYING TRAPEZE, THE(1935); MISSISSIPPI(1935); MYSTERY MAN, THE(1935); RUGGLES OF RED GAP(1935); RUMBA(1935); SECRET BRIDE, THE(1935); SO RED THE ROSE(1935); WELCOME HOME(1935); CAN THIS BE DIXIE?(1936); DANCING FEET(1936); FORGOTTEN FACES(1936); GREAT GUY(1936); IT HAD TO HAPPEN(1936); KLONDIKE ANNIE(1936); LEATHERNECKS HAVE LANDED, THE(1936); OLD HUTCH(1936); RHYTHM ON THE RANGE(1936); SONG AND DANCE MAN, THE(1936); THIRTY SIX HOURS TO KILL(1936); CHAMPAGNE WALTZ(1937); DEAD END(1937); HIGH, WIDE AND HANDSOME(1937); LAUGHING AT TROUBLE(1937); LIFE BEGINS WITH LOVE(1937); PERFECT SPECIMEN, THE(1937); PICK A STAR(1937); AFFAIRS OF ANNABEL(1938); DAWN PATROL, THE(1938); FLIGHT INTO NOWHERE(1938); JOY OF LIVING(1938); LITTLE ORPHAN ANNIE(1938); MAD MISS MANTON, THE(1938); MEN WITH WINGS(1938); YOU CAN'T TAKE IT WITH YOU(1938); AT THE CIRCUS(1939); BEAU GESTE(1939); CISCO KID AND THE LADY, THE(1939); DODGE CITY(1939); FAST AND FURIOUS(1939); I'M FROM MISSOURI(1939); ON BORROWED TIME(1939); ORPHANS OF THE STREET(1939); SAINT STRIKES BACK, THE(1939); SUDDEN MONEY(1939); WITHIN THE LAW(1939); BUCK BENNY RIDES AGAIN(1940); CHARLIE CHAN'S MURDER CRUISE(1940); DOUBLE ALIBI(1940); ELLERY QUEEN. MASTER DETECTIVE(1940); GOLDEN FLEECING, THE(1940); LITTLE NELLIE KELLY(1940); NO TIME FOR COMEDY(1940); OPENED BY MISTAKE(1940); SAINT TAKES OVER, THE(1940); WAY OF ALL FLESH, THE(1940); ELLERY QUEEN AND THE MURDER RING(1941); ELLERY QUEEN AND THE PERFECT CRIME(1941); ELLERY QUEEN'S PENTHOUSE MYSTERY(1941); MALTESE FALCON, THE(1941); MILLION DOLLAR BABY(1941); POT O' GOLD(1941); REACHING FOR THE SUN(1941); ALL THROUGH THE NIGHT(1942); ARMY SURGEON(1942); CLOSE CALL FOR ELLERY QUEEN, A(1942); DESPERATE CHANCE FOR ELLERY QUEEN, A(1942); ENEMY AGENTS MEET ELLERY QUEEN(1942); IT HAPPENED IN FLATBUSH(1942); MY FAVORITE BLONDE(1942); NIGHT TO REMEMBER, A(1942); DIXIE(1943); NO PLACE FOR A LADY(1943); RIDING HIGH(1943); THANK YOUR LUCKY STARS(1943); CASANOVA BROWN(1944); ANCHORS AWEIGH(1945); HORN BLOWS AT MIDNIGHT, THE(1945); I LOVE A BANDLEADER(1945); SHADY LADY(1945); BOWERY BOMBSHELL(1946); CALIFORNIA(1946); HOW DO YOU DO?(1946); TWO YEARS BEFORE THE MAST(1946); VIRGINIAN, THE(1946); YOUNG WIDOW(1946); BODY AND SOUL(1947); DOWN TO EARTH(1947); EASY COME, EASY GO(1947); GAS HOUSE KIDS IN HOLLYWOOD(1947); NIGHTMARE ALLEY(1947); PHILO VANCE'S GAMBLE(1947); SONG OF THE THIN MAN(1947); BIG CLOCK, THE(1948); JUNE BRIDE(1948); NIGHT WIND(1948); TEXAS, BROOKLYN AND HEAVEN(1948); TIMBER TRAIL, THE(1948); RED, HOT AND BLUE(1949); SHAMROCK HILL(1949); TAKE ME OUT TO THE BALL GAME(1949); COPPER CANYON(1950); MRS. O'MALLEY AND MR. MALONE(1950); HERE COMES THE GROOM(1951); LAST OUTPOST, THE(1951); RATON PASS(1951); WARPATH(1951); DENVER AND RIO GRANDE(1952); LONE STAR(1952); WE'RE NOT MARRIED(1952); LUCKY ME(1954); YOU'RE NEVER TOO YOUNG(1955); PUBLIC PIGEON NO. 1(1957); UNHOLY WIFE, THE(1957); ALIAS JESSE JAMES(1959)
Jerry Burke
SATAN'S BED(1965), p
Jim Burke
TRAIL OF THE LONESOME PINE, THE(1936); HIS KIND OF WOMAN(1951); BIG JAKE(1971); CHINATOWN(1974); MIDNIGHT MAN, THE(1974)
Joanne Burke
ANDERSON TAPES, THE(1971), ed; CHILD'S PLAY(1972), ed; LOVIN' MOLLY(1974), ed

Joe Burke
HOLD EVERYTHING(1930), m
Joe E. Burke
STARK FEAR(1963), p
John Burke
KING RAT(1965), spec eff; SHIP OF FOOLS(1965), spec eff; SORCERERS, THE(1967, Brit.), w; UNCLE SCAM(1981), ph
Johnny Burke
LITTLE MEN(1940); DIXIE(1943), m; MY HEART GOES CRAZY(1953, Brit.), m
Silents
GOOD-BYE KISS, THE(1928)
Jonathan Burke
ECHO OF BARBARA(1961, Brit.), w
Jonnie Burke
BATTLETRUCK(1982), spec eff; ENDANGERED SPECIES(1982), spec eff
Joseph Burke
Silents
SENATOR, THE(1915); CHRIS AND THE WONDERFUL LAMP(1917); KIDNAPPED(1917); OUTWITTED(1917); GOOD-BYE, BILL(1919); WHITE ROSE, THE(1923); ADVENTUROUS SEX, THE(1925); KICK-OFF, THE(1926); STRIVING FOR FORTUNE(1926); MANHATTAN KNIGHTS(1928); OBEY YOUR HUSBAND(1928); ROYAL RIDER, THE(1929)
Misc. Silents
IMMORTAL FLAME, THE(1916); AWAKENING OF RUTH, THE(1917); CUSTOMARY TWO WEEKS, THE(1917); COME ON IN(1918); OH, YOU WOMEN!(1919); HERITAGE(1920); PERFECT WOMAN, THE(1920)
Karen Burke
WIZARD OF GORE, THE(1970)
Katherine Burke [Virginia Field]
MERRY WIDOW, THE(1934)
Kathleen Burke
ISLAND OF LOST SOULS(1933); MAD GAME, THE(1933); MURDERS IN THE ZOO(1933); SUNSET PASS(1933); TORCH SINGER(1933); BULLDOG DRUMMOND STRIKES BACK(1934); GOOD DAME(1934); SIX OF A KIND(1934); AWAKENING OF JIM BURKE(1935); LAST OUTPOST, THE(1935); LIVES OF A BENGAL LANCER(1935); MUTINY AHEAD(1935); ROCKY MOUNTAIN MYSTERY(1935); SCHOOL FOR GIRLS(1935); CRAIG'S WIFE(1936); NAVY WIFE(1936); NEVADA(1936); BOY OF THE STREETS(1937); SHEIK STEPS OUT, THE(1937); RASCALS(1938)
Misc. Talkies
BEAUTY'S DAUGHTER(1935); LION MAN, THE(1936)
Kathy Burke
1984
FOREVER YOUNG(1984, Brit.); SACRED HEARTS(1984, Brit.); SCRUBBERS(1984, Brit.)
Larry Burke
MY BUDDY(1944); THOSE ENDEARING YOUNG CHARMS(1945)
Leland Burke
GOD IS MY WITNESS(1931), art d
Lew Burke
FOR PETE'S SAKE(1977)
Marcella Burke
MAD ABOUT MUSIC(1938), w; TOY TIGER(1956), w
Marie Burke
UNMASKED(1929); AFTER THE BALL(1932, Brit.); MADNESS OF THE HEART(1949, Brit.); MAN FROM YESTERDAY, THE(1949, Brit.); WARNING TO WANTONS, A(1949, Brit.); LAVENDER HILL MOB, THE(1951, Brit.); ODETTE(1951, Brit.); BAD BLONDE(1953, Brit.); CONSTANT HUSBAND, THE(1955, Brit.); GREEN MAN, THE(1957, Brit.); MIRACLE IN SOHO(1957, Brit.); MENACE IN THE NIGHT(1958, Brit.); SNORKEL, THE(1958, Brit.); MAN WHO COULD CHEAT DEATH, THE(1959, Brit.); CALL ME GENIUS(1961, Brit.); TERROR OF THE TONGS, THE(1961, Brit.); MODEL MURDER CASE, THE(1964, Brit.); RATTLE OF A SIMPLE MAN(1964, Brit.); DEVILS OF DARKNESS, THE(1965, Brit.); LOST COMMAND, THE(1966); SUNDAY BLOODY SUNDAY(1971, Brit.)
Silents
RISE OF JENNIE CUSHING, THE(1917); LITTLE MISS REBELLION(1920); SLIM SHOULDERS(1922); WITHOUT FEAR(1922); HEART RAIDER, THE(1923)
Misc. Silents
HELP! HELP! POLICE!(1919); REMODELING HER HUSBAND(1920); ISLE OF DOUBT(1922); YOUTHFUL CHEATERS(1923)
Mark Burke
NOTORIOUS LANDLADY, THE(1962)
Martin Burke
ONE SUMMER LOVE(1976)
Martyn Burke
CLOWN MURDERS, THE(1976, Can.), d&w; POWER PLAY(1978, Brit./Can.), d&w; LAST CHASE, THE(1981), p&d, w
1984
TOP SECRET!(1984), w
Mary Ellen Burke
CORPSE GRINDERS, THE(1972)
Michael Burke
PUBLIC ENEMIES(1941), w; CLOAK AND DAGGER(1946), a, tech adv
Michele Burke
1984
ICEMAN(1984), makeup
Mildred Burke
BELOW THE BELT(1980)
Min Burke
LEGEND OF THE LONE RANGER, THE(1981)
Olive Burke
Silents
BULLIN' THE BULLSHEVIKI(1919)
Orrin Burke
SHOW THEM NO MERCY(1935); HIS BROTHER'S WIFE(1936); SAN FRANCISCO(1936); NOBODY'S BABY(1937)
P. H. Burke
Silents
SUPER-SEX, THE(1922), p

Patricia Burke
LISBON STORY, THE(1946, Brit.); TROJAN BROTHERS, THE(1946); WHILE I LIVE(1947, Brit.); FORBIDDEN(1949, Brit.); HAPPINESS OF THREE WOMEN, THE(1954, Brit.); DESPERATE MAN, THE(1959, Brit.); IMPERSONATOR, THE(1962, Brit.); DAYLIGHT ROBBERY(1964, Brit.); STRANGLER'S WEB(1966, Brit.); MARRIAGE OF CONVENIENCE(1970, Brit.); UNDERCOVERS HERO(1975, Brit.)

Patrick Burke
DAY THE FISH CAME OUT, THE(1967. Brit./Gr.); EQUINOX(1970)

Patrick Sullivan Burke
CASTAWAY COWBOY, THE(1974)

Paul Burke
FRANCIS GOES TO WEST POINT(1952); SOUTH SEA WOMAN(1953); THREE SAILORS AND A GIRL(1953); FRANCIS IN THE NAVY(1955); SCREAMING EAGLES(1956); SPY CHASERS(1956); DISEMBODIED, THE(1957); VALLEY OF THE DOLLS(1967); THOMAS CROWN AFFAIR, THE(1968); DADDY'S GONE A-HUNTING(1969); ONCE YOU KISS A STRANGER(1969); PSYCHIC KILLER(1975)

Peggy Burke
MIRACLE WORKER, THE(1962)
Misc. Silents
IT HAPPENED TO ADELE(1917)

Peter Burke
Silents
THELMA(1922); LULLABY, THE(1924)

Phil Burke
Misc. Silents
WHITE PANTHER, THE(1924)

Richard Burke
DRESSED TO KILL(1941), w

Richard Frankie Burke
SHADOW OF THE THIN MAN(1941)

Rita Burke
EXPRESSO BONGO(1959, Brit.)

Robert Burke
DISPATCH FROM REUTERS, A(1940), spec eff; KEY LARGO(1948), spec eff; HONDO(1953), ph; VAGABOND KING, THE(1956), ph

Robert Easton Burke
RED BADGE OF COURAGE, THE(1951)

Rodney Burke
HIGH HELL(1958); QUESTION OF ADULTERY, A(1959, Brit.); SHADOW OF THE CAT, THE(1961, Brit.)

Ron Burke
DESTINATION INNER SPACE(1966); WELCOME TO HARD TIMES(1967); CUTTER AND BONE(1981)

Samson Burke
THREE STOOGES MEET HERCULES, THE(1962)

Sandra Burke
CHICKEN CHRONICLES, THE(1977), cos

Simon Burke
DEVIL'S PLAYGROUND, THE(1976, Aus.); IRISHMAN, THE(1978, Aus.); CLINIC, THE(1983, Aus.)

Solomon Burke
COOL BREEZE(1972), m; HAMMER(1972), m

Sonny Burke
HOLIDAYS WITH PAY(1948, Brit.); SOMEWHERE IN POLITICS(1949, Brit.); FLAME OF THE ISLANDS(1955), m; HAND OF DEATH(1962), m, md; RABBIT, RUN(1970), md

Susan Burke
ISLAND WOMEN(1958), cos

T. Frank Burke
Misc. Silents
BECKONING FLAME, THE(1916)

Thomas Burke
CARMEN(1931, Brit.); BROKEN BLOSSOMS(1936, Brit.), w; NO WAY BACK(1949, Brit.), w
Silents
BROKEN BLOSSOMS(1919), w; DREAM STREET(1921), w; LONDON(1926, Brit.), w; TWINKLETOES(1926), w

Tom Burke
FATHER O'FLYNN(1938, Irish); KATHLEEN(1938, Ireland); LITTLE MISS MOLLY(1940)
Silents
CLAY DOLLARS(1921)

Walter Burke
NAKED CITY, THE(1948); ALL THE KING'S MEN(1949); DARK CITY(1950); KILLER THAT STALKED NEW YORK, THE(1950); MYSTERY STREET(1950); GUY WHO CAME BACK, THE(1951); M(1951); ER LOVE A STRANGER(1958); CRIMSON KIMONO, THE(1959); LET NO MAN WRITE MY EPITAPH(1960); HOW THE WEST WAS WON(1962); JACK THE GIANT KILLER(1962); BEAUTY AND THE BEAST(1963); THREE STOOGES GO AROUND THE WORLD IN A DAZE, THE(1963); WHEELER DEALERS, THE(1963); MY FAIR LADY(1964); PLAINSMAN, THE(1966); DOUBLE TROUBLE(1967); PRESIDENT'S ANALYST, THE(1967); SUPPORT YOUR LOCAL SHERIFF(1969); CHANDLER(1971); SUPPORT YOUR LOCAL GUNFIGHTER(1971); STONE KILLER, THE(1973)

Warren Burke
Silents
ROAD HOUSE(1928)

William Burke
A NOUS LA LIBERTE(1931, Fr.); BILL CRACKS DOWN(1937), p; FALCON OUT WEST, THE(1944), p; COP HATER(1958), p&d

John Burkell
CONVICT'S CODE(1930)
Misc. Silents
WILL YOU BE STAYING FOR SUPPER?(1919)

Ilse Burkert
MR. SARDONICUS(1961); WILD WESTERNERS, THE(1962)

Bartine Burkett
Misc. Silents
DON'T WRITE LETTERS(1922); I CAN EXPLAIN(1922)

Eldon Burkett
WHITE CLIFFS OF DOVER, THE(1944)

Elton Burkett
WHITE CLIFFS OF DOVER, THE(1944)

Howard Burkett
FAST COMPANY(1929)

James B. Burkett
SCARLET CLUE, THE(1945), p; RED DRAGON, THE(1946), p

James Burkett
ALASKA PATROL(1949), p

James S. Burkett
SULTAN'S DAUGHTER, THE(1943), p; CALL OF THE JUNGLE(1944), p; CHARLIE CHAN IN BLACK MAGIC(1944), p; CHARLIE CHAN IN THE SECRET SERVICE(1944), p; CHINESE CAT, THE(1944), p; CAPTAIN TUGBOAT ANNIE(1945), p; JADE MASK, THE(1945), p; SHANGHAI COBRA, THE(1945), p; DANGEROUS MONEY(1946), p; DARK ALIBI(1946), p; DON RICARDO RETURNS(1946), p; SHADOWS OVER CHINATOWN(1946), p; BELLS OF SAN FERNANDO(1947), p; CHINESE RING, THE(1947), p; TRAP, THE(1947), p; DOCKS OF NEW ORLEANS(1948), p; FEATHERED SERPENT, THE(1948), p; MYSTERY OF THE GOLDEN EYE, THE(1948), p; SHANGHAI CHEST, THE(1948), p; SIXTEEN FATHOMS DEEP(1948), p; SKY DRAGON(1949), p; YOUNG DANIEL BOONE(1950), p

Jane Burkett
WHY WOULD I LIE(1980)

Eugenie Burkette
Silents
SEVEN CHANCES(1925)

Shukur Burkhanov
SWORD AND THE DRAGON, THE(1960, USSR)

Jack Burkhard
1984
PREPPIES(1984)

Harry Burkhardt
SECOND HONEYMOON(1937)
Misc. Silents
STOLEN TRIUMPH, THE(1916); LIFE OR HONOR?(1918); MILLIONAIRE FOR A DAY, A(1921)

Jay Burkhardt
1984
NIGHT PATROL(1984), art d

Robert Burkhardt
MURDER WITH PICTURES(1936)

Addison Burkhart
HOME TOWNERS, THE(1928), w; QUEEN OF THE NIGHTCLUBS(1929), w

Harry Burkhart
ARE WE CIVILIZED?(1934)

Jay Burkhart
WACKO(1983), art d

Jeff Burkhart
1984
WHERE THE BOYS ARE '84(1984), w

Monte Burkhart
FLAMING STAR(1960); GUN FIGHT(1961)

Elizabeth Burkland
1984
HOME FREE ALL(1984)

Dennis Burkley
HEROES(1977); LASERBLAST(1978)
Misc. Talkies
BUMMER(1973)

L. Burkova
SHE-WOLF, THE(1963, USSR)

Alex Burks [Camillo Bazzoni]
LONG RIDE FROM HELL, A(1970, Ital.), d

Donny Burks
SHAFT(1971); BANG THE DRUM SLOWLY(1973)

Hattie Burks
Misc. Silents
SINS OF MEN(1916)

Ivyl Burks
WAR OF THE WORLDS, THE(1953), spec eff; CONQUEST OF SPACE(1955), spec eff

Robert Burks
MARKED WOMAN(1937), spec eff; GREAT LIE, THE(1941), spec eff; INTERNATIONAL SQUADRON(1941), spec eff; IN THIS OUR LIFE(1942), spec eff; ARSENIC AND OLD LACE(1944), spec eff; MAKE YOUR OWN BED(1944), ph; ESCAPE IN THE DESERT(1945), ph; GOD IS MY CO-PILOT(1945), spec eff; NIGHT AND DAY(1946), spec eff; CRY WOLF(1947), spec eff; POSSESSED(1947), spec eff; TWO MRS. CARROLLS, THE(1947), spec eff; UNFAITHFUL, THE(1947), spec eff; UNSUSPECTED, THE(1947), spec eff; ROMANCE ON THE HIGH SEAS(1948), spec eff; SMART GIRLS DON'T TALK(1948), spec eff; TO THE VICTOR(1948), ph; BEYOND THE FOREST(1949), ph; FOUNTAINHEAD, THE(1949), ph; JOHN LOVES MARY(1949), spec eff; KISS IN THE DARK, A(1949), ph; TASK FORCE(1949), ph; GLASS MENAGERIE, THE(1950), ph; CLOSE TO MY HEART(1951), ph; COME FILL THE CUP(1951), ph; ENFORCER, THE(1951), ph; STRANGERS ON A TRAIN(1951), ph; TOMORROW IS ANOTHER DAY(1951), ph; MARA MARU(1952), ph; MIRACLE OF OUR LADY OF FATIMA, THE(1952), spec eff; ROOM FOR ONE MORE(1952), ph; DESERT SONG, THE(1953), ph; I CONFESS(1953), ph; SO THIS IS LOVE(1953), ph; BOY FROM OKLAHOMA, THE(1954), ph; DIAL M FOR MURDER(1954), ph; REAR WINDOW(1954), ph; TO CATCH A THIEF(1955), ph; TROUBLE WITH HARRY, THE(1955), ph; WRONG MAN, THE(1956), ph; SPIRIT OF ST. LOUIS, THE(1957), ph; VERTIGO(1958), ph; BLACK ORCHID(1959), ph; BUT NOT FOR ME(1959), ph; NORTH BY NORTHWEST(1959), ph; GREAT IMPOSTOR, THE(1960), ph; RAT RACE, THE(1960), ph; PLEASURE OF HIS COMPANY, THE(1961), ph; MUSIC MAN, THE(1962), ph; BIRDS, THE(1963), ph; MARNIE(1964), ph; ONCE A THIEF(1965), ph; PATCH OF BLUE, A(1965), ph; COVENANT WITH DEATH, A(1966), ph; WATERHOLE NO. 3(1967), ph

Stephen Burks
1984
GARBO TALKS(1984)

V. Burlakova
RESURRECTION(1963, USSR); DUEL, THE(1964, USSR)
Martin Burland
PLAY DIRTY(1969, Brit.)
Sascha Burland
DIRTY LITTLE BILLY(1972, m, md
Joseph Burlando
RAZOR'S EDGE, THE(1946)
Andrew Burleigh
AMERICAN SUCCESS COMPANY, THE(1980)
Bertram Burleigh
Silents
JOHN HALIFAX, GENTLEMAN(1915, Brit.); TRAPPED BY THE LONDON
SHARKS(1916, Brit.); MRS. THOMPSON(1919, Brit.); ALL ROADS LEAD TO CAL-
VARY(1921, Brit.); CRIMSON CIRCLE, THE(1922, Brit.); OPEN COUNTRY(1922, Brit.);
SQUIBS WINS THE CALCUTTA SWEEP(1922, Brit.); DON QUIXOTE(1923, Brit.)
Misc. Silents
INFELICE(1915, Brit.); LOVE TRAIL, THE(1916, Brit.); MEG OF THE SLUMS(1916,
Brit.); MOTHER OF DARTMOOR, THE(1916, Brit.); GATES OF DUTY(1919, Brit.);
SANDS OF TIME, THE(1919, Brit.); BLACK SPIDER, THE(1920, Brit.); BURNT
IN(1920, Brit.); GARRYOWEN(1920, Brit.); GREAT DAY, THE(1921, Brit.); HOW
KITCHENER WAS BETRAYED(1921, Brit.)
Mary Burleigh
CRY WOLF(1968, Brit.)
Misc. Talkies
LIONHEART(1970)
Patricia Burleigh
COMIN' THRU' THE RYE(1947, Brit.)
William Burleigh
CHRISTMAS TREE, THE(1966, Brit.); HOT MILLIONS(1968, Brit.); BOYS OF PAUL
STREET, THE(1969, Hung./US)
Dave Burleson
MOLLY AND LAWLESS JOHN(1972); THOMASINE AND BUSHROD(1974)
David Burleson
GUNFIGHT, A(1971)
Bill Burley
MUSIC HALL PARADE(1939, Brit.)
Douglas Burley
TALKING FEET(1937, Brit.)
Fred Burley
Silents
SILENT VOW, THE(1922)
Fulton Burley
THRILL OF A ROMANCE(1945)
Gary Burlingame
FRATERNITY ROW(1977), makeup
Michael Burlington
1984
TOP SECRET!(1984)
Tom Burlinson
MAN FROM SNOWY RIVER, THE(1983, Aus.)
1984
PHAR LAP(1984, Aus.)
Tommy Burlison
1984
RIVER RAT, THE(1984)
Helen Burls
QUIET WEEKEND(1948, Brit.); ONE WOMAN'S STORY(1949, Brit.); PICKWICK
PAPERS, THE(1952, Brit.); LADYKILLERS, THE(1956, Brit.)
Helene Burls
DEAR MURDERER(1947, Brit.); UPTURNED GLASS, THE(1947, Brit.); NEVER
LOOK BACK(1952, Brit.); GENTLE TOUCH, THE(1956, Brit.)
Kolya Burlyayev
MY NAME IS IVAN(1963, USSR)
Serafima Burlyuk
HUNTING IN SIBERIA(1962, USSR), w
Ben Lucien Burman
HEAVEN ON EARTH(1931), w; STEAMBOAT ROUND THE BEND(1935), w
Ellis Burman
FRANKENSTEIN MEETS THE WOLF MAN(1943), makeup; UNKNOWN IS-
LAND(1948), spec eff; ONE DARK NIGHT(1983), spec eff
Robert Burman
DEMENTED(1980), spec eff
S.D. Burman
GUIDE, THE(1965, U.S./India), m
Sigfrido Burman
DESERT WARRIOR(1961 Ital./Span.), art d; FACE OF TERROR(1964, Span.), art d;
SAUL AND DAVID(1968, Ital./Span.), art d
Thomas R. Burman
PROPHECY(1979), makeup; BEAST WITHIN, THE(1982), makeup eff; SPACE-
HUNTER: ADVENTURES IN THE FORBIDDEN ZONE(1983), makeup
Tom Burman
FROGS(1972), makeup; THING WITH TWO HEADS, THE(1972), makeup; ISLAND
OF DR. MOREAU, THE(1977), makeup; CAT PEOPLE(1982), makeup; HALLOWEEN
III: SEASON OF THE WITCH(1982), makeup; ONE DARK NIGHT(1983), spec eff
Wolfgang Burman
DRUMS OF TABU, THE(1967, Ital./Span.), art d; TREASURE OF MAKUBA,
THE(1967, U.S./Span.), art d
Hans Burmann
BOLDEST JOB IN THE WEST, THE(1971, Ital.), ph
1984
HOLY INNOCENTS, THE(1984, Span.), ph
Wolfgang Burmann
SABINA, THE(1979, Span./Swed.), set d
Augusta Burmeister
GREENE MURDER CASE, THE(1929)
Silents
DANCER'S PERIL, THE(1917)

Misc. Silents
MARY MORELAND(1917)
Leo Burmeister
DANIEL(1983)
Leo Burmester
CRUISING(1980); HONKY TONK FREEWAY(1981)
Vladimir Burmeyster
WAR AND PEACE(1968, USSR), cos
Jonathan Burn
PARTY'S OVER, THE(1966, Brit.); PERSECUTION AND ASSASSINATION OF
JEAN-PAUL MARAT AS PERFORMED BY THE INMATES OF THE ASYLUM OF
CHARENTON UNDER THE DIRECTION OF THE MARQUIS DE SADE, THE(1967,
Brit.); SUDDEN TERROR(1970, Brit.); BUTTERCUP CHAIN, THE(1971, Brit.); BLOOD
FROM THE MUMMY'S TOMB(1972, Brit.)
Tam Dean Burn
LOCAL HERO(1983, Brit.)
Ann Burnaby
YOUNG WIVES' TALE(1954, Brit.), w
Anne Burnaby
FATHER'S DOING FINE(1952, Brit.), w; YELLOW BALLOON, THE(1953, Brit.), w;
WEAK AND THE WICKED, THE(1954, Brit.), w; NO TIME FOR TEARS(1957,
Brit.), w; SANDS OF THE DESERT(1960, Brit.), w; OPERATION BULLSHINE(1963,
Brit.), w
Dave Burnaby
RIGHT TO LIVE, THE(1933, Brit.); PLAYBOY, THE(1942, Brit.)
Davy Burnaby
DEVIL'S MAZE, THE(1929, Brit.); CLEANING UP(1933, Brit.); JUST MY LUCK(1933,
Brit.); SHOT IN THE DARK, A(1933, Brit.); STRIKE IT RICH(1933, Brit.); THAT'S MY
WIFE(1933, Brit.); THREE MEN IN A BOAT(1933, Brit.); WISHBONE, THE(1933, Brit.);
DIPLOMATIC LOVER, THE(1934, Brit.); KEEP IT QUIET(1934, Brit.); MAN I WANT,
THE(1934, Brit.); MURDER AT THE INN(1934, Brit.); ON THE AIR(1934, Brit.);
DANDY DICK(1935, Brit.); RADIO FOLLIES(1935, Brit.); WHILE PARENTS
SLEEP(1935, Brit.); BOYS WILL BE BOYS(1936, Brit.); FEATHER YOUR NEST(1937,
Brit.); LEAVE IT TO ME(1937, Brit.); SECOND BEST BED(1937, Brit.); SONG OF THE
FORGE(1937, Brit.); SONG OF THE ROAD(1937, Brit.); TALKING FEET(1937, Brit.);
CHIPS(1938. Brit.); MANY TANKS MR. ATKINS(1938, Brit.); ANYTHING TO DE-
CLARE?(1939, Brit.); COME ON GEORGE(1939, Brit.); PRISONER OF CORBAL(1939,
Brit.)
Earl Burnam
CORPSE GRINDERS, THE(1972)
Grace Burnard
STRANGER IN HOLLYWOOD(1968)
Jenny Burnay
PORT OF SHADOWS(1938, Fr.)
Irving Burnbaum
LOVE IN A BUNGALOW(1937), ed
Arthur Burne
TAWNY PIPIT(1947, Brit.)
Silents
MONEY ISN'T EVERYTHING(1925, Brit.)
Nacy Burne
TRUST THE NAVY(1935, Brit.)
Nancy Burne
FACING THE MUSIC(1933, Brit.); LOVE NEST, THE(1933, Brit.); NORAH O'-
NEALE(1934, Brit.); SONG AT EVENTIDE(1934, Brit.); WARREN CASE, THE(1934,
Brit.); DANDY DICK(1935, Brit.); IT HAPPENED IN PARIS(1935, Brit.); LEND ME
YOUR HUSBAND(1935, Brit.); OLD ROSES(1935, Brit.); ONCE A THIEF(1935, Brit.);
WIFE OR TWO, A(1935, Brit.); REASONABLE DOUBT(1936, Brit.); ROYAL EA-
GLE(1936, Brit.); SKYLARKS(1936, Brit.); KNIGHTS FOR A DAY(1937, Brit.); THUN-
DER IN THE CITY(1937, Brit.); JOHN HALIFAX–GENTLEMAN(1938, Brit.); FLYING
FIFTY-FIVE(1939, Brit.)
Misc. Talkies
BUTTERFLY AFFAIR, THE(1934, Brit.)
Doris Burnell
Misc. Talkies
CAPTAIN CELLULOID VS THE FILM PIRATES(1974)
Janet Burnell
TROOPSHIP(1938, Brit.); HENRY V(1946, Brit.); UPTURNED GLASS, THE(1947,
Brit.); DEAR MR. PROHACK(1949, Brit.)
Janey Burnell
STOLEN FACE(1952, Brit.)
Peter Burnell
WITHOUT A TRACE(1983)
Robert Burnell
TWO GENTLEMEN SHARING(1969, Brit.)
Lise Burnelle
MY UNCLE ANTOINE(1971, Can.)
Eric Burnelli
SOLO(1970, Fr.); MURMUR OF THE HEART(1971, Fr./Ital./Ger.)
Cesar Burner
BLIND DEAD, THE(1972, Span.); MAN CALLED NOON, THE(1973, Brit.)
Misc. Talkies
TOMBS OF THE BLIND DEAD(1974)
James Burner
EYE FOR AN EYE, AN(1981), w
Pete Burness
1001 ARABIAN NIGHTS(1959), w
Dana Burnet
SHOPWORN ANGEL, THE(1928), w; LOVE, LIVE AND LAUGH(1929), w; HIGH
SOCIETY BLUES(1930), w; STOLEN HEAVEN(1931), w; STRAIGHT IS THE
WAY(1934), w; SHOPWORN ANGEL(1938), w; GREAT COMMANDMENT,
THE(1941), w
Silents
EYES OF THE HEART(1920), w; MR. BILLINGS SPENDS HIS DIME(1923), w;
MARRIAGE CLAUSE, THE(1926), w; FOUR WALLS(1928), w
Myno Burnet
NEW HOTEL, THE(1932, Brit.)

Susan Burnet
  EXPRESSO BONGO(1959, Brit.); LIGHT UP THE SKY(1960, Brit.); THIS IS MY STREET(1964, Brit.); GIRL GETTERS, THE(1966, Brit.)
Al Burnett
  KING ARTHUR WAS A GENTLEMAN(1942, Brit.); SWEET BEAT(1962, Brit.)
Angela Burnett
1984
  BLESS THEIR LITTLE HEARTS(1984)
Carol Burnett
  WHO'S BEEN SLEEPING IN MY BED?(1963); PETE 'N' TILLIE(1972); FRONT PAGE, THE(1974); WEDDING, A(1978); HEALTH(1980); CHU CHU AND THE PHILLY FLASH(1981); FOUR SEASONS, THE(1981); ANNIE(1982)
Charles Burnett
  MY BROTHER'S WEDDING(1983), p, d,w&ph
1984
  BLESS THEIR LITTLE HEARTS(1984), w&ph
Dana Burnett
  SEVEN FACES(1929), w
Don Burnett
  HELL'S HORIZON(1955); TEA AND SYMPATHY(1956); THESE WILDER YEARS(1956); JAILHOUSE ROCK(1957); RAINTREE COUNTY(1957); UNTAMED YOUTH(1957); DAMON AND PYTHIAS(1962)
Misc. Talkies
  TRIUMPH OF ROBIN HOOD, THE(1960)
Elsa Burnett
  DOLLAR(1938, Swed.)
Frances Hodgson Burnett
  LITTLE LORD FAUNTLEROY(1936), w; LITTLE PRINCESS, THE(1939), w; DARK COMMAND, THE(1940), w; SECRET GARDEN, THE(1949), w
Silents
  LITTLE LORD FAUNTLEROY(1914, Brit.), w; DAWN OF A TOMORROW, THE(1915), w; ESMERALDA(1915), w; PRETTY SISTER OF JOSE(1915), w; SECRET LOVE(1916), w; LOUISIANA(1919), w; LITTLE LORD FAUNTLEROY(1921), w; FAMILY SECRET, THE(1924), w
George Burnett
  TILL THE END OF TIME(1946)
John Burnett
  DOMINO PRINCIPLE, THE(1977), ed
John F Burnett
  CULPEPPER CATTLE COMPANY, THE(1972), ed; CAN'T STOP THE MUSIC(1980), ed
John F. Burnett
  HEART IS A LONELY HUNTER, THE(1968), ed; OWL AND THE PUSSYCAT, THE(1970), ed; SUPPOSE THEY GAVE A WAR AND NOBODY CAME?(1970), ed; WILD ROVERS(1971), ed; GIRL FROM PETROVKA, THE(1974), ed; SUNSHINE BOYS, THE(1975), ed; MURDER BY DEATH(1976), ed; GOODBYE GIRL, THE(1977), ed; GREASE(1978), ed; MOMENT BY MOMENT(1978), ed; ...AND JUSTICE FOR ALL(1979), ed; DEATH HUNT(1981), ed; RICH AND FAMOUS(1981), ed; GREASE 2(1982), ed
1984
  IRRECONCILABLE DIFFERENCES(1984), ed
Kimberly Burnett
1984
  BLESS THEIR LITTLE HEARTS(1984)
Louise Burnett
  PAN-AMERICANA(1945)
Marlene Burnett
  OLD MAID, THE(1939)
Mary Nancy Burnett
  IT'S ALIVE(1974)
Mina Burnett
  HOURS OF LONELINESS(1930, Brit.)
Murray Burnett
  CASABLANCA(1942), w
Nancy Burnett
  STRAWBERRY STATEMENT, THE(1970)
Rexford Burnett
Silents
  MASTER CRACKSMAN, THE(1914)
Ronald Burnett
1984
  BLESS THEIR LITTLE HEARTS(1984)
Steve Burnett
1984
  MUPPETS TAKE MANHATTAN, THE(1984)
Sue Ann Burnett
  FIVE LITTLE PEPPERS IN TROUBLE(1940)
Vera Burnett
  IT GROWS ON TREES(1952); BIRDS AND THE BEES, THE(1965)
W.R. Burnett
  FINGER POINTS, THE(1931), w; IRON MAN, THE(1931), w; LITTLE CAESAR(1931), w; BEAST OF THE CITY, THE(1932), w; LAW AND ORDER(1932), w; SCARFACE(1932), w; DARK HAZARD(1934), w; DR. SOCRATES(1935), w; THIRTY SIX HOURS TO KILL(1936), w; SOME BLONDES ARE DANGEROUS(1937), w; WINE, WOMEN AND HORSES(1937), w; KING OF THE UNDERWORLD(1939), w; LAW AND ORDER(1940), w; DANCE HALL(1941), w; GET-AWAY, THE(1941), w; HIGH SIERRA(1941), w; THIS GUN FOR HIRE(1942), w; WAKE ISLAND(1942), w; BACKGROUND TO DANGER(1943), w; CRASH DIVE(1943), w; SAN ANTONIO(1945), w; NOBODY LIVES FOREVER(1946), w; BELLE STARR'S DAUGHTER(1947), w; YELLOW SKY(1948), w; ASPHALT JUNGLE, THE(1950), w; VENDETTA(1950), w; RACKET, THE(1951), w; ARROWHEAD(1953), w; LAW AND ORDER(1953), w; DANGEROUS MISSION(1954), w; CAPTAIN LIGHTFOOT(1955), w; I DIED A THOUSAND TIMES(1955), w; ILLEGAL(1955), w; ACCUSED OF MURDER(1956), w; SHORT CUT TO HELL(1957), w; BADLANDERS, THE(1958), w; SEPTEMBER STORM(1960), w; SERGEANTS 3(1962), w; CAIRO(1963), w; GREAT ESCAPE, THE(1963), w; JACKALS, THE(1967, South Africa), w; COOL BREEZE(1972), d&w

William R. Burnett
  WHOLE TOWN'S TALKING, THE(1935), w; IRON MAN, THE(1951), w
Coral Burnette
Silents
  SIGN OF THE ROSE, THE(1922), t
Dorsey Burnette
  KINGDOM OF THE SPIDERS(1977), m
Fritzi Burnette
  YOU'RE TELLING ME(1942)
Jack Burnette
  STOLEN HARMONY(1935); STORY OF WILL ROGERS, THE(1952)
Lester "Smiley" Burnette
  IN OLD SANTA FE(1935); JUNCTION CITY(1952)
Louise Burnette
  I'LL REMEMBER APRIL(1945); EASY TO WED(1946)
Lynn Burnette
  JOURNEY THROUGH ROSEBUD(1972)
Smiley Burnette
  HARMONY LANE(1935); MELODY TRAIL(1935); SAGEBRUSH TROUBADOR(1935); SINGING VAGABOND, THE(1935); TUMBLING TUMBLEWEEDS(1935); WATERFRONT LADY(1935); BORDER PATROLMAN, THE(1936); COMIN' ROUND THE MOUNTAIN(1936); GUNS AND GUITARS(1936); HEARTS IN BONDAGE(1936); RED RIVER VALLEY(1936); RIDE, RANGER, RIDE(1936); SINGING COWBOY, THE(1936); BIG SHOW, THE(1937); BOOTS AND SADDLES(1937); GIT ALONG, LITTLE DOGIES(1937); LARCENY ON THE AIR(1937); MAN BETRAYED, A(1937); MANHATTAN MERRY-GO-ROUND(1937); MEET THE BOY FRIEND(1937); OH, SUSANNA(1937); OLD CORRAL, THE(1937); PUBLIC COWBOY NO. 1(1937); ROOTIN' TOOTIN' RHYTHM(1937); ROUNDUP TIME IN TEXAS(1937); SPRINGTIME IN THE ROCKIES(1937); YODELIN' KID FROM PINE RIDGE(1937), a, m/1; BILLY THE KID RETURNS(1938); GOLD MINE IN THE SKY(1938); HOLLYWOOD STADIUM MYSTERY(1938); MAN FROM MUSIC MOUNTAIN(1938); OLD BARN DANCE, THE(1938); PRAIRIE MOON(1938); RHYTHM OF THE SADDLE(1938); UNDER WESTERN STARS(1938); WESTERN JAMBOREE(1938); BLUE MONTANA SKIES(1939); COLORADO SUNSET(1939); HOME ON THE PRAIRIE(1939); IN OLD MONTEREY(1939); MEXICALI ROSE(1939); MOUNTAIN RHYTHM(1939); ROVIN' TUMBLEWEEDS(1939); SOUTH OF THE BORDER(1939); CAROLINA MOON(1940); GAUCHO SERENADE(1940); RANCHO GRANDE(1940); RIDE, TENDERFOOT, RIDE(1940); BACK IN THE SADDLE(1941); DOWN MEXICO WAY(1941); RIDIN' ON A RAINBOW(1941); SIERRA SUE(1941); SINGING HILL, THE(1941); SUNSET IN WYOMING(1941); UNDER FIESTA STARS(1941); BELLS OF CAPISTRANO(1942); CALL OF THE CANYON(1942); COWBOY SERENADE(1942); HEART OF THE GOLDEN WEST(1942); HEART OF THE RIO GRANDE(1942); HOME IN WYOMIN'(1942); STARDUST ON THE SAGE(1942); BEYOND THE LAST FRONTIER(1943); IDAHO(1943); KING OF THE COWBOYS(1943); RAIDERS OF SUNSET PASS(1943); SILVER SPURS(1943); BENEATH WESTERN SKIES(1944); CODE OF THE PRAIRIE(1944); FIREBRANDS OF ARIZONA(1944); LARAMIE TRAIL, THE(1944); PRIDE OF THE PLAINS(1944); DESERT HORSEMAN, THE(1946); LANDRUSH(1946); LAST DAYS OF BOOT HILL(1947); LONE HAND TEXAN, THE(1947); BUCKAROO FROM POWDER RIVER(1948); PHANTOM VALLEY(1948); SIX-GUN LAW(1948); WEST OF SONORA(1948); WHIRLWIND RAIDERS(1948); BLAZING TRAIL, THE(1949); CHALLENGE OF THE RANGE(1949); DESERT VIGILANTE(1949); EL DORADO PASS(1949); LARAMIE(1949); QUICK ON THE TRIGGER(1949); RENEGADES OF THE SAGE(1949); SOUTH OF DEATH VALLEY(1949); ACROSS THE BADLANDS(1950); FRONTIER OUTPOST(1950); HORSEMEN OF THE SIERRAS(1950); LIGHTNING GUNS(1950); OUTCAST OF BLACK MESA(1950); RAIDERS OF TOMAHAWK CREEK(1950); STREETS OF GHOST TOWN(1950); TEXAS DYNAMO(1950); BANDITS OF EL DORADO(1951); BONANZA TOWN(1951); CYCLONE FURY(1951); FORT SAVAGE RAIDERS(1951); KID FROM AMARILLO, THE(1951); PECOS RIVER(1951); PRAIRIE ROUNDUP(1951); RIDIN' THE OUTLAW TRAIL(1951); SNAKE RIVER DESPERADOES(1951); WHIRLWIND(1951); HAWK OF WILD RIVER, THE(1952); KID FROM BROKEN GUN, THE(1952); LARAMIE MOUNTAINS(1952); ROUGH, TOUGH WEST, THE(1952); SMOKY CANYON(1952); GOLDTOWN GHOST RIDERS(1953); LAST OF THE PONY RIDERS(1953); ON TOP OF OLD SMOKY(1953); PACK TRAIN(1953); SAGINAW TRAIL(1953); WINNING OF THE WEST(1953)
Misc. Talkies
  BORDERTOWN TRAIL(1944); CALL OF THE ROCKIES(1944); FIGHTING FRONTIERSMAN, THE(1946); GALLOPING THUNDER(1946); GUNNING FOR VENGEANCE(1946); HEADING WEST(1946); ROARING RANGERS(1946); TERROR TRAIL(1946); TWO-FISTED STRANGER(1946); LAW OF THE CANYON(1947); PRAIRIE RAIDERS(1947); RIDERS OF THE LONE STAR(1947); SOUTH OF THE CHISHOLM TRAIL(1947); STRANGER FROM PONCA CITY, THE(1947); WEST OF DODGE CITY(1947); BLAZING ACROSS THE PECOS(1948); TRAIL TO LAREDO(1948); TRAIL OF THE RUSTLERS(1950); WHIRLWIND(1951)
Vera Burnette
  YOU'RE TELLING ME(1942)
Hal Burney
  MAN'S LAND, A(1932)
John Burney
  KITTY AND THE BAGMAN(1983, Aus.), w
Myno Burney
  FOUR BAGS FULL(1957, Fr./Ital.)
Thomas S. Burney, Jr.
  RAMPARTS WE WATCH, THE(1940)
Paul Burnford
  ADVENTURES OF RUSTY(1945), d
Sheila Burnford
  INCREDIBLE JOURNEY, THE(1963), w
Jeremy Burngam
  HORROR OF FRANKENSTEIN, THE(1970, Brit.), w
Beatrice Burnham
Silents
  JACK AND JILL(1917); PETAL ON THE CURRENT, THE(1919); DIAMONDS ADRIFT(1921); GET YOUR MAN(1921); KINDLED COURAGE(1923); WESTERN LUCK(1924); RIDERS OF THE PURPLE SAGE(1925)
Misc. Silents
  HITCHIN' POSTS(1920); LAHOMA(1920); HOME STRETCH, THE(1921); ONE-MAN TRAIL, THE(1921); TRACKS(1922); TROOPER O'NEIL(1922); MILLION TO BURN, A(1923)

Clara Louise Burnham
Silents
OPENED SHUTTERS, THE(1914), w
Edward Burnham
TO SIR, WITH LOVE(1967, Brit.); ABOMINABLE DR. PHIBES, THE(1971, Brit.); WHEN EIGHT BELLS TOLL(1971, Brit.); 10 RILLINGTON PLACE(1971, Brit.); YOUNG WINSTON(1972, Brit.)
1984
MEMED MY HAWK(1984, Brit.)
Eunice Burnham
Silents
SHAM(1921)
Frances Burnham
Silents
AS THE SUN WENT DOWN(1919)
Misc. Silents
LOVE THIEF, THE(1916); LORELEI OF THE SEA(1917); ON THE JUMP(1918)
Janet Burnham
1984
HOME FREE ALL(1984)
Jeremy Burnham
GOOD COMPANIONS, THE(1957, Brit.); BACHELOR OF HEARTS(1958, Brit.); BONJOUR TRISTESSE(1958); LAW AND DISORDER(1958, Brit.); UPSTAIRS AND DOWNSTAIRS(1961, Brit.); I COULD GO ON SINGING(1963); TORPEDO BAY(1964, Ital./Fr.); BRIGAND OF KANDAHAR, THE(1965, Brit.); GIRL GETTERS, THE(1966, Brit.)
Julia Burnham
Silents
ADVENTURES OF CAROL, THE(1917), w; LOVE AUCTION, THE(1919), w
Leslie Burnham
FEELIN' GOOD(1966)
Louise Burnham
Misc. Silents
LAHOMA(1920)
Stephen C. Burnham
SOGGY BOTTOM U.S.A.(1982), w
Terry Burnham
IMITATION OF LIFE(1959); KEY WITNESS(1960); BOY, DID I GET A WRONG NUMBER!(1966)
Mr. Burnhett
SIGN OF FOUR, THE(1932, Brit.)
Jeannine Burnier
MUSIC MAN, THE(1962)
Robert Burnier
LA BELLE AMERICAINE(1961, Fr.); PRICE OF FLESH, THE(1962, Fr.); LANDRU(1963, Fr./Ital) OPHELIA(1964, Fr.); COUNTERFEIT CONSTABLE, THE(1966, Fr.)
Shirley Burniston
DOCTOR IN THE HOUSE(1954, Brit.); UP TO HIS NECK(1954, Brit.)
Fred Burnley
TARZAN'S THREE CHALLENGES(1963), ed; EL GRECO(1966, Ital., Fr.), ed; GIRL GETTERS, THE(1966, Brit.), ed; NEITHER THE SEA NOR THE SAND(1974, Brit.), d
Rick Burnley
DAN'S MOTEL(1982), m
Nando Burno
RING AROUND THE CLOCK(1953, Ital.)
Allan Burns
BUTCH AND SUNDANCE: THE EARLY DAYS(1979), w; LITTLE ROMANCE, A(1979, U.S./Fr.), w
1984
JUST THE WAY YOU ARE(1984), w
Ann Burns
ATLANTIC CITY(1981, U.S./Can.)
Barry Burns
LOOKING UP(1977)
Bart Burns
BETWEEN HEAVEN AND HELL(1956); FEAR STRIKES OUT(1957); TALL STORY(1960); SEVEN DAYS IN MAY(1964); NUMBER ONE(1969); THERE WAS A CROOKED MAN(1970); ICEMAN COMETH, THE(1973); NICKEL RIDE, THE(1974); SEED OF INNOCENCE(1980); FRANCES(1982)
Bernard K. Burns
LOVE RACKET, THE(1929), w
Beulah Burns
Silents
GRETCHEN, THE GREENHORN(1916)
Misc. Silents
CHILDREN OF THE FEUD(1916)
Bill Burns
LIPSTICK(1976)
Binnie Burns
Misc. Silents
TEMPTATIONS OF SATAN, THE(1914)
Blanche Burns
Misc. Silents
HER WAYWARD SISTER(1916)
Bob Burns
DAWN TRAIL, THE(1931); TEXAS GUN FIGHTER(1932); TOMBSTONE CANYON(1932); WHEN A MAN RIDES ALONE(1933); BIG BROADCAST OF 1937, THE(1936); FUGITIVE SHERIFF, THE(1936); GUNS AND GUITARS(1936); LONELY TRAIL, THE(1936); RHYTHM ON THE RANGE(1936); SONG OF THE GRINGO(1936); GHOST TOWN GOLD(1937); GIT ALONG, LITTLE DOGIES(1937); GUNS OF THE PECOS(1937); HIT THE SADDLE(1937); MOUNTAIN MUSIC(1937); PRAIRIE THUNDER(1937); PUBLIC COWBOY NO. 1(1937); WAIKIKI WEDDING(1937); WELLS FARGO(1937); YODELIN' KID FROM PINE RIDGE(1937); ARKANSAS TRAVELER, THE(1938); LAND OF FIGHTING MEN(1938); OUTLAWS OF THE PRAIRIE(1938); RADIO CITY REVELS(1938); TROPIC HOLIDAY(1938); WESTERN TRAILS(1938); I'M FROM MISSOURI(1939); KNIGHT OF THE PLAINS(1939); NEW FRONTIER(1939); OUR LEADING CITIZEN(1939); ALIAS THE DEACON(1940); COMIN' ROUND THE MOUNTAIN(1940); MY LITTLE CHICKADEE(1940); PIONEERS OF THE WEST(1940); PRAIRIE SCHOONERS(1940); PRAIRIE PALS(1942); RIDING THE WIND(1942); BELLE OF THE YUKON(1944); CHEYENNE WILDCAT(1944); FIREBRANDS OF

ARIZONA(1944); LUMBERJACK(1944); MOJAVE FIREBRAND(1944); MYSTERY MAN(1944); OUTLAWS OF SANTA FE(1944); RUSTLERS OF DEVIL'S CANYON(1947); SADDLE PALS(1947); TWILIGHT ON THE RIO GRANDE(1947); WILD FRONTIER, THE(1947); TWILIGHT IN THE SIERRAS(1950); ROUGH RIDERS OF DURANGO(1951); SPARTACUS(1960)
Silents
OUTLAW'S DAUGHTER, THE(1925)
Misc. Silents
GIRL FROM BEYOND, THE(1918); RIDING FOOL(1924); DESPERATE ODDS(1925); JUST TRAVELIN'(1927)
Bob Burns
DEMONOID(1981), spec eff
Bobbi Burns
I, THE JURY(1982); Q(1982)
1984
NEW YORK NIGHTS(1984)
Bobby Burns
COCK-EYED WORLD, THE(1929); FOX MOVIETONE FOLLIES(1929); THIRTEENTH GUEST, THE(1932); BORDER G-MAN(1938)
Brendan Burns
SSSSSSSS(1973); NICKEL RIDE, THE(1974); LAST TYCOON, THE(1976); RAISE THE TITANIC(1980, Brit.)
Burke Burns
THUMB TRIPPING(1972); METEOR(1979)
C. Stewart Burns
NIGHTMARES(1983)
Carol Burns
MANGO TREE, THE(1981, Aus.)
1984
STRIKEBOUND(1984, Aus.)
Catherine Burns
ME, NATALIE(1969); RED SKY AT MORNING(1971)
Cathy Burns
LAST SUMMER(1969)
Charles C. Burns
HUCKLEBERRY FINN(1974)
David Burns
PATH OF GLORY, THE(1934, Brit.); ROMANCE IN RHYTHM(1934, Brit.); RENDEZVOUS(1935); RUNAWAY QUEEN, THE(1935, Brit.); CRIME OVER LONDON(1936, Brit.); GREAT ZIEGFELD, THE(1936); LIVE WIRE, THE(1937, Brit.); SKY'S THE LIMIT, THE(1937, Brit.); SPRING HANDICAP(1937, Brit.); STRANGERS ON A HONEYMOON(1937, Brit.); HEY! HEY! U.S.A.(1938, Brit.); RETURN OF CAROL DEANE, THE(1938, Brit.); GENTLEMAN'S GENTLEMAN, A(1939, Brit.); JUST LIKE A WOMAN(1939, Brit.); SAINT IN LONDON, THE(1939, Brit.); SHE COULDN'T SAY NO(1939, Brit.); SIDEWALKS OF LONDON(1940, Brit.); SO THIS IS LONDON(1940, Brit.); WHO IS GUILTY?(1940, Brit.); GIRL MUST LIVE, A(1941, Brit.); LARCENY STREET(1941, Brit.); AMAZING MR. FORREST, THE(1943, Brit.); FOURTEEN HOURS(1951); DEEP IN MY HEART(1954); KNOCK ON WOOD(1954); IT'S ALWAYS FAIR WEATHER(1955); FOUR BOYS AND A GUN(1957); ONCE UPON A HORSE(1958); LET'S MAKE LOVE(1960); TIGER MAKES OUT, THE(1967); MOVE(1970); WHO IS HARRY KELLERMAN AND WHY IS HE SAYING THOSE TERRIBLE THINGS ABOUT ME?(1971)
Detective William J. Burns
Silents
ARGYLE CASE, THE(1917), w
Don Burns
BUTTERFIELD 8(1960)
Doug Burns
ELECTRA GLIDE IN BLUE(1973)
Duncan Burns
MARRIAGE OF CONVENIENCE(1970, Brit.)
Ed Burns
WHEN A MAN RIDES ALONE(1933)
Silents
INTOLERANCE(1916); CHILDREN OF THE NIGHT(1921); KNOCKOUT KID, THE(1925)
Misc. Silents
BLAZE AWAY(1922)
Eddie Burns
OUTLAWS OF STAMPEDE PASS(1943)
Silents
ABRAHAM LINCOLN(1924)
Edmund Burns
HARD TO GET(1929); LOVE RACKET, THE(1929); SHE GOES TO WAR(1929); TANNED LEGS(1929); SEA DEVILS(1931); AIR MAIL(1932); DEVIL PAYS, THE(1932); WESTERN LIMITED(1932); DANGEROUSLY YOURS(1933); DEATH KISS, THE(1933); RUSTY RIDES ALONE(1933); IT HAPPENED ONE NIGHT(1934); ONE NIGHT OF LOVE(1934); SHE MARRIED HER BOSS(1935); MURDER WITH PICTURES(1936)
Silents
LODGE IN THE WILDERNESS, THE(1926); PRINCESS FROM HOBOKEN, THE(1927); PHYLLIS OF THE FOLLIES(1928); RANSOM(1928)
Misc. Silents
HELL'S HIGHROAD(1925); MANICURE GIRL, THE(1925); MILLION DOLLAR HANDICAP, THE(1925); SIMON THE JESTER(1925); FORLORN RIVER(1926); MADE FOR LOVE(1926); OUT OF THE STORM(1926); PARIS AT MIDNIGHT(1926); SUNNYSIDE UP(1926); WHISPERING WIRES(1926); POOR GIRLS(1927); SHAMROCK AND THE ROSE, THE(1927)
Edward Burns
ANOTHER FACE(1935); FOLLOW THE FLEET(1936)
Silents
DANGER MARK, THE(1918); HEADIN' SOUTH(1918); MALE AND FEMALE(1919); EYES OF THE HEART(1920); FIFTY CANDLES(1921); DANGEROUS AGE, THE(1922); EAST IS WEST(1922); FRESHIE, THE(1922); LAVENDER BATH LADY, THE(1922); LIGHTS OF THE DESERT(1922); RULING PASSION, THE(1922); COUNTRY KID, THE(1923); JAZZMANIA(1923); SCARS OF JEALOUSY(1923); BROADWAY AFTER DARK(1924)
Misc. Silents
HER HOUR(1917); LOVE WATCHES(1918); MORGAN'S RAIDERS(1918); SOAP GIRL, THE(1918); UNDER THE GREENWOOD TREE(1918); MISS ADVEN-

TURE(1919); PEGEEN(1920); TO PLEASE ONE WOMAN(1920); GIRL FROM GOD'S COUNTRY, THE(1921); WOMAN'S SIDE, THE(1922); GUILTY ONE, THE(1924); HUMMING BIRD, THE(1924); CHINESE PARROT, THE(1927)

Edward J. Burns
Misc. Silents
QUEEN OF HEARTS, THE(1918)

Evelyn Burns
Silents
STRANGER THAN FICTION(1921); SUPER-SEX, THE(1922)

Fannetta Burns
Misc. Silents
HIS GREAT CHANCE(1923)

Forest Burns
UNTAMED(1955)

Forrest Burns
SANTA FE UPRISING(1946); SIOUX CITY SUE(1946); GAMBLING HOUSE(1950); RIO GRANDE PATROL(1950); HERE COME THE NELSONS(1952); ABBOTT AND COSTELLO MEET THE KEYSTONE KOPS(1955)

Francis Burns [Larry Gelbart]
ROUGH CUT(1980, Brit.), w

Fred Burns
RIO RITA(1929); VIRGINIAN, THE(1929); CHEYENNE KID, THE(1930); HEADIN' NORTH(1930); LAND OF MISSING MEN, THE(1930); MEN WITHOUT LAW(1930); MOUNTAIN JUSTICE(1930); MOUNTED STRANGER, THE(1930); OKLAHOMA CYCLONE(1930); PARADE OF THE WEST(1930); SHADOW RANCH(1930); BRANDED(1931); FIGHTING THRU(1931); NEAR THE TRAIL'S END(1931); SUNRISE TRAIL(1931); FREIGHTERS OF DESTINY(1932); LAW AND LAWLESS(1932); PARTNERS(1932); SADDLE BUSTER, THE(1932); DUDE BANDIT, THE(1933); FLAMING GUNS(1933); FOURTH HORSEMAN, THE(1933); HERITAGE OF THE DESERT(1933); WAR OF THE RANGE(1933); HONOR OF THE RANGE(1934); TEXAS TORNADO(1934); WHEELS OF DESTINY(1934); LAWLESS RANGE(1935); FUGITIVE SHERIFF, THE(1936); TOO MUCH BEEF(1936); TRAIL OF THE LONESOME PINE, THE(1936); CALIFORNIA MAIL, THE(1937); GUNSMOKE RANCH(1937); OH, SUSANNA(1937); OLD WYOMING TRAIL, THE(1937); SPRINGTIME IN THE ROCKIES(1937); TRAILING TROUBLE(1937); TWO-FISTED SHERIFF(1937); IN OLD MEXICO(1938); LAW COMMANDS, THE(1938); OUTLAWS OF THE PRAIRIE(1938); PIONEER TRAIL(1938); SUNSET TRAIL(1938); UNDER WESTERN STARS(1938); ARIZONA KID, THE(1939); COLORADO SUNSET(1939); DAYS OF JESSE JAMES(1939); FRONTIER PONY EXPRESS(1939); IN OLD MONTEREY(1939); RIO GRANDE(1939); ROVIN' TUMBLEWEEDS(1939); SAGA OF DEATH VALLEY(1939); SOUTHWARD HO!(1939); THUNDERING WEST, THE(1939); WALL STREET COWBOY(1939); COLORADO(1940); GAUCHO SERENADE(1940); GHOST VALLEY RAIDERS(1940); RIDE, TENDERFOOT, RIDE(1940); TEXAS STAGECOACH(1940); THUNDERING FRONTIER(1940); YOUNG BILL HICKOK(1940); DOWN MEXICO WAY(1941); IN OLD CHEYENNE(1941); JESSE JAMES AT BAY(1941); NEVADA CITY(1941); RAWHIDE RANGERS(1941); RIDING THE CHEROKEE TRAIL(1941); SINGING HILL, THE(1941); SUNSET IN WYOMING(1941); WYOMING WILDCAT(1941); HEART OF THE GOLDEN WEST(1942); MAN FROM CHEYENNE(1942); SONS OF THE PIONEERS(1942); STARDUST ON THE SAGE(1942); SUNSET ON THE DESERT(1942); SUNSET SERENADE(1942); RAIDERS OF SUNSET PASS(1943); SILVER SPURS(1943); MARSHAL OF RENO(1944); IN OLD SACRAMENTO(1946); RIO GRANDE RAIDERS(1946)
Misc. Talkies
TRAILING NORTH(1933)
Silents
HOME SWEET HOME(1914); JORDAN IS A HARD ROAD(1915); MARTYRS OF THE ALAMO, THE(1915); GOOD BAD MAN, THE(1916); SHADOWS OF CONSCIENCE(1921); HAUNTED RANGE, THE(1926); UNKNOWN CAVALIER, THE(1926); GALLOPING GOBS, THE(1927) .
Misc. Silents
SUNLIGHT'S LAST RAID(1917); DEMON RIDER, THE(1925); WILD TO GO(1926)

George Burns
BIG BROADCAST, THE(1932); COLLEGE HUMOR(1933); INTERNATIONAL HOUSE(1933); MANY HAPPY RETURNS(1934); SIX OF A KIND(1934); WE'RE NOT DRESSING(1934); BIG BROADCAST OF 1936, THE(1935); HERE COMES COOKIE(1935); LOVE IN BLOOM(1935); BIG BROADCAST OF 1937, THE(1936); COLLEGE HOLIDAY(1936); DAMSEL IN DISTRESS, A(1937); COLLEGE SWING(1938); HONOLULU(1939); SOLID GOLD CADILLAC, THE(1956); SUNSHINE BOYS, THE(1975); OH, GOD!(1977); SGT. PEPPER'S LONELY HEARTS CLUB BAND(1978); GOING IN STYLE(1979); JUST YOU AND ME, KID(1979); OH GOD! BOOK II(1980)
1984
OH GOD! YOU DEVIL(1984)

Grace Burns
EMERGENCY WEDDING(1950)

Harry Burns
HOT MONEY(1936); TWO WISE MAIDS(1937); THERE'S THAT WOMAN AGAIN(1938); KID NIGHTINGALE(1939); NORTHWEST MOUNTED POLICE(1940); BLOOD AND SAND(1941); LADY SCARFACE(1941); REDHEAD(1941); SHADOW OF THE THIN MAN(1941); YOU'LL NEVER GET RICH(1941); TORTILLA FLAT(1942); CALL OF THE JUNGLE(1944); SONG OF THE THIN MAN(1947)

Comdr. Harry A. Burns, USN
MEN OF THE FIGHTING LADY(1954), w

Helen Burns
CHANGELING, THE(1980, Can.); ZORRO, THE GAY BLADE(1981); IF YOU COULD SEE WHAT I HEAR(1982); UTILITIES(1983, Can.)

Helene Burns
NIGHT WON'T TALK, THE(1952, Brit.)

Hildy Burns
1984
SIGNAL 7(1984), art d

Jack Burns
NIGHT THEY RAIDED MINSKY'S, THE(1968); MUPPET MOVIE, THE(1979), w
Silents
MILLION DOLLAR ROBBERY, THE(1914)

Janine Burns
TEX(1982)

Jean Burns
ATLANTIC CITY(1981, U.S./Can.)

Jessie Burns
Silents
BRIGHT LIGHTS(1925), w; NO OTHER WOMAN(1928), w

John Burns
LIKE FATHER LIKE SON(1961); YOUNG SINNER, THE(1965); ATLANTIC CITY(1981, U.S./Can.)

John Charles Burns
DAMIEN–OMEN II(1978)

Larry Burns
SCOTT OF THE ANTARCTIC(1949, Brit.); KING OF THE UNDERWORLD(1952, Brit.); DIAMOND WIZARD, THE(1954, Brit.); MEET MR. CALLAGHAN(1954, Brit.); HORNET'S NEST, THE(1955, Brit.); COUNT FIVE AND DIE(1958, Brit.); STRICTLY CONFIDENTIAL(1959, Brit.); WITNESS IN THE DARK(1959, Brit.); CAUGHT IN THE NET(1960, Brit.); SHAKEDOWN, THE(1960, Brit.); STOLEN PLANS, THE(1962, Brit.); JUNGLE STREET GIRLS(1963, Brit.)
Misc. Talkies
LEFT-HANDED(1972)

Lee Burns
CODE OF THE CACTUS(1939)

Leonard Burns
1984
IMPULSE(1984)

Lillian Burns
Silents
FLORIDA ENCHANTMENT, A(1914)
Misc. Silents
CAVEMAN, THE(1915); WINIFRED THE SHOP GIRL(1916)

Lisa Burns
SHINING, THE(1980)

Louise Burns
SHINING, THE(1980)

Lt. William Burns
711 OCEAN DRIVE(1950), tech adv

Lydia Burns
Misc. Talkies
BACCHANALE(1970)

Marc Burns
EXODUS(1960)

Marie Burns
ATLANTIC CITY(1981, U.S./Can.)

Marilyn Burns
TEXAS CHAIN SAW MASSACRE, THE(1974); EATEN ALIVE(1976)
Misc. Talkies
KISS DADDY GOODBYE(1981)

Marion Burns
OKLAHOMA JIM(1931); GOLDEN WEST, THE(1932); ME AND MY GAL(1932); BORN TO BE BAD(1934); DEVIL TIGER(1934); SENSATION HUNTERS(1934); DAWN RIDER(1935); FLIRTING WITH DANGER(1935); PARADISE CANYON(1935); RIP ROARING RILEY(1935)

Mark Burns
PRIZE OF ARMS, A(1962, Brit.); DAY AND THE HOUR, THE(1963, Fr./ Ital.); TAKE ME OVER(1963, Brit.); GIRL GETTERS, THE(1966, Brit.); I'LL NEVER FORGET WHAT'S 'IS NAME(1967, Brit.); IT!(1967, Brit.); JOKERS, THE(1967, Brit.); LOVE IS A WOMAN(1967, Brit.); CHARGE OF THE LIGHT BRIGADE, THE(1968, Brit.); ADVENTURES OF GERARD, THE(1970, Brit.); DAY AT THE BEACH, A(1970); VIRGIN AND THE GYPSY, THE(1970, Brit.); DEATH IN VENICE(1971, Ital./Fr.); GIORDANO BRUNO(1973, Ital.); HOUSE OF THE LIVING DEAD(1973, S. Afr.); LUDWIG(1973, Ital./Ger./Fr.); JUGGERNAUT(1974, Brit.); MAIDS, THE(1975, Brit.); ROSEBUD(1975); STUD, THE(1979, Brit.); EYEWITNESS(1981); WICKED LADY, THE(1983, Brit.)
1984
ALMOST YOU(1984), ed; CHAMPIONS(1984); OLD ENOUGH(1984), ed

Matt Burns
DIMBOOLA(1979, Aus.); NEXT OF KIN(1983, Aus.)

Mel Burns
BILL OF DIVORCEMENT, A(1932), makeup; LITTLE WOMEN(1933), makeup; MORNING GLORY(1933), makeup; PROFESSIONAL SWEETHEART(1933), makeup; FINISHING SCHOOL(1934), makeup; LITTLE MINISTER, THE(1934), makeup; RAFTER ROMANCE(1934), makeup; SPITFIRE(1934), makeup; IN PERSON(1935), makeup; ROMANCE IN MANHATTAN(1935), makeup; STAR OF MIDNIGHT(1935), makeup; TOP HAT(1935), makeup; MARY OF SCOTLAND(1936), makeup; SWING TIME(1936), makeup; SYLVIA SCARLETT(1936), makeup; WOMAN REBELS, A(1936), makeup; QUALITY STREET(1937), makeup; SHALL WE DANCE(1937), makeup; STAGE DOOR(1937), makeup; VIVACIOUS LADY(1938), makeup; STORY OF VERNON AND IRENE CASTLE, THE(1939), makeup; KITTY FOYLE(1940), makeup; LUCKY PARTNERS(1940), makeup; TOM, DICK AND HARRY(1941), makeup; ONCE UPON A HONEYMOON(1942), makeup; TENDER COMRADE(1943), makeup; HEARTBEAT(1946), makeup; TEXAS, BROOKLYN AND HEAVEN(1948), makeup; HIS KIND OF WOMAN(1951), makeup; ON DANGEROUS GROUND(1951), makeup; RACKET, THE(1951), makeup; LAS VEGAS STORY, THE(1952), makeup

Michael Burns
WIZARD OF BAGHDAD, THE(1960); MR. HOBBS TAKES A VACATION(1962); RAIDERS, THE(1964); 40 GUNS TO APACHE PASS(1967); JOURNEY TO SHILOH(1968); PRIVATE NAVY OF SGT. O'FARRELL, THE(1968); MAD ROOM, THE(1969); THAT COLD DAY IN THE PARK(1969, U.S./Can.); TIME FOR LOVING, A(1971, Brit.); THUMB TRIPPING(1972); SANTEE(1973); THRESHOLD(1983, Can.), p

Millie Burns
JABBERWOCKY(1977, Brit.), art d; TIME BANDITS(1981, Brit.), prod d

Milly Burns
YANKS(1979), art d

Mrs. Jack W. Burns
OUR RELATIONS(1936)

Nancy Burns
MERMAIDS OF TIBURON, THE(1962)

Neal Burns
SOB SISTER(1931); SIX OF A KIND(1934); GUN LAW(1938); FACE OF MARBLE, THE(1946)
Misc. Silents
LION'S BREATH, THE(1916); MARY'S ANKLE(1920)

Neil Burns
STORY OF VERNON AND IRENE CASTLE, THE(1939)

Patrick Burns
DRIVER, THE(1978); MORE AMERICAN GRAFFITI(1979)

Paul Burns
JESSE JAMES(1939); ROSE OF WASHINGTON SQUARE(1939); YOUNG MR. LINCOLN(1939); CHAD HANNA(1940); DANCE, GIRL, DANCE(1940); LILLIAN RUSSELL(1940); LITTLE ORVIE(1940); BELLE STARR(1941); LAST OF THE DUANES(1941); SWAMP WATER(1941); WILD GEESE CALLING(1941); JUKE GIRL(1942); MY GAL SAL(1942); CRASH DIVE(1943); DIXIE DUGAN(1943); MEANEST MAN IN THE WORLD, THE(1943); OX-BOW INCIDENT, THE(1943); TOGETHER AGAIN(1944); COLONEL EFFINGHAM'S RAID(1945); FALLEN ANGEL(1945); MYSTERIOUS INTRUDER(1946); FRAMED(1947); BEST MAN WINS(1948); HOLLOW TRIUMPH(1948); FLAMING FEATHER(1951); SUPERMAN AND THE MOLE MEN(1951); WARPATH(1951); GLORY(1955); LOVE ME TENDER(1956); FACE OF A FUGITIVE(1959); SPARTACUS(1960)

Silents
MOLLYCODDLE, THE(1920); THREE MUSKETEERS, THE(1921), cos

Misc. Silents
WHAT THREE MEN WANTED(1924), d

Paul E. Burns
HELL HARBOR(1930); ANOTHER THIN MAN(1939); DAY THE BOOKIES WEPT, THE(1939); RETURN OF THE CISCO KID(1939); SAINT STRIKES BACK, THE(1939); SPELLBINDER, THE(1939); NEW MOON(1940); SEVENTEEN(1940); MEN OF THE TIMBERLAND(1941); WESTERN UNION(1941); MUMMY'S TOMB, THE(1942); MYSTERY OF MARIE ROGET, THE(1942); SABOTEUR(1942); TIMBER(1942); WILD BILL HICKOK RIDES(1942); BARBARY COAST GENT(1944); DRAGON SEED(1944); ALONG CAME JONES(1945); DAKOTA(1945); SOUTHERNER, THE(1945); STATE FAIR(1945); CRIME DOCTOR'S MAN HUNT(1946); DEVIL'S MASK, THE(1946); GALLANT JOURNEY(1946); HOODLUM SAINT, THE(1946); MY PAL TRIGGER(1946); NIGHT EDITOR(1946); RENEGADES(1946); SHADOWED(1946); SING WHILE YOU DANCE(1946); DESPERATE(1947); EXPOSED(1947); PILGRIM LADY, THE(1947); SADDLE PALS(1947); UNCONQUERED(1947); ACT OF MURDER, AN(1948); BLACK EAGLE(1948); LETTER FROM AN UNKNOWN WOMAN(1948); MADONNA OF THE DESERT(1948); ON OUR MERRY WAY(1948); PALEFACE, THE(1948); RELENTLESS(1948); ARCTIC MANHUNT(1949); COVER-UP(1949); DEAR WIFE(1949); HIDEOUT(1949); JOHNNY ALLEGRO(1949); LOOK FOR THE SILVER LINING(1949); LUST FOR GOLD(1949); RECKLESS MOMENTS, THE(1949); SUN COMES UP, THE(1949); TULSA(1949); DOUBLE DEAL(1950); FATHER MAKES GOOD(1950); FRENCHIE(1950); FULLER BRUSH GIRL, THE(1950); IT'S A SMALL WORLD(1950); MONTANA(1950); STORM WARNING(1950); SUMMER STOCK(1950); SUNSET IN THE WEST(1950); TARNISHED(1950); WOMAN ON PIER 13, THE(1950); YOUNG MAN WITH A HORN(1950); BIG GUSHER, THE(1951); HOT LEAD(1951); SANTA FE(1951); SILVER CITY(1951); VENGEANCE VALLEY(1951); CARRIE(1952); LUSTY MEN, THE(1952); SON OF PALEFACE(1952); THREE HOURS TO KILL(1954); LAY THAT RIFLE DOWN(1955); MAN WITH THE GOLDEN ARM, THE(1955); FURY AT GUNSIGHT PASS(1956); PROUD ONES, THE(1956); GUNMAN'S WALK(1958); GUNS OF THE TIMBERLAND(1960); POCKETFUL OF MIRACLES(1961); SUMMER MAGIC(1963); STAGE TO THUNDER ROCK(1964)

Peter Burns
VIXENS, THE(1969)

Phil Burns
HARRY AND TONTO(1974)

Philip Burns
SILENT NIGHT, BLOODY NIGHT(1974); FLASH AND THE FIRECAT(1976)

R.A. Burns
TIME WALKER(1982), art d

Ralph Burns
CABARET(1972), m; MAME(1974), md; LUCKY LADY(1975), m; NEW YORK, NEW YORK(1977), m, md; MOVIE MOVIE(1978), m; ALL THAT JAZZ(1979), m; URBAN COWBOY(1980), m; KISS ME GOODBYE(1982), m; MY FAVORITE YEAR(1982), m; NATIONAL LAMPOON'S VACATION(1983), m; STAR 80(1983), m
1984
MUPPETS TAKE MANHATTAN, THE(1984), m

Robert Burns
UP THE RIVER(1930); HARD HOMBRE(1931); HEAVEN ON EARTH(1931); QUICK MILLIONS(1931); LAW AND LAWLESS(1932); SOUTH OF SANTA FE(1932); FAST WORKERS(1933); GUN LAW(1933); KING OF THE ARENA(1933); SONS OF THE DESERT(1933); WHEELS OF DESTINY(1934); COURAGEOUS AVENGER, THE(1935); SINGING VAGABOND, THE(1935); WANDERER OF THE WASTELAND(1935); GALLOPING DYNAMITE(1937); GUN LAW(1938); ARIZONA LEGION(1939); FEUD OF THE RANGE(1939); ROVIN' TUMBLEWEEDS(1939); TROUBLE IN SUNDOWN(1939); RIDE, TENDERFOOT, RIDE(1940); THREE MEN FROM TEXAS(1940); TERROR IN THE JUNGLE(1968); HILLS HAVE EYES, THE(1978), art d; TOURIST TRAP, THE(1979), art d; PLAY DEAD(1981), art d; FULL MOON HIGH(1982), art d; MAUSOLEUM(1983), art d; MICROWAVE MASSACRE(1983), art d

Silents
CAPTAIN OF THE GRAY HORSE TROOP, THE(1917); APACHE RAIDER, THE(1928)

Misc. Silents
THOROBRED(1922); CHEROKEE KID, THE(1927); SKEDADDLE GOLD(1927); SON OF THE DESERT, A(1928)

Robert A. Burns
TEXAS CHAIN SAW MASSACRE, THE(1974), art d; HOWLING, THE(1981), art d; MONGREL(1982), d&w

Robert "Bob" Burns
TIMBER STAMPEDE(1939)

Robert [Bobby] Burns
PARDON US(1931)

Robert E. Burns
I AM A FUGITIVE FROM A CHAIN GANG(1932), w; SAGEBRUSH TRAIL(1934); JOAN OF ARC(1948); REDWOOD FOREST TRAIL(1950); DARLING, HOW COULD YOU!(1951)

Ron Burns
ALL-AMERICAN BOY, THE(1973)

Ronald Burns
APARTMENT FOR PEGGY(1948)

Ronnie Burns
BERNARDINE(1957); ANATOMY OF A PSYCHO(1961)

Ruth Burns
L-SHAPED ROOM, THE(1962, Brit.)

Sammy Burns
Misc. Silents
RUBE, THE(1925); FUN ON THE FARM(1926)

Sandy Burns
Misc. Silents
HIS GREAT CHANCE(1923)

Stan Burns
CHARLIE CHAN AND THE CURSE OF THE DRAGON QUEEN(1981), w

Stephan W. Burns
HERBIE GOES BANANAS(1980)

Stephen Burns
CASEY'S SHADOW(1978)

Steve Burns
LIFEGUARD(1976)
1984
SIGNAL 7(1984), art d

Tas Burns
MANGANINNIE(1982, Aus.)

Terry Burns
OFFENDERS, THE(1980), m; WAVELENGTH(1983)

Tim Burns
MAD MAX(1979, Aus.); MONKEY GRIP(1983, Aus.)

Timothy Burns
TARGETS(1968); DREAMS OF GLASS(1969)

Tommy Burns
RUGGED O'RIORDANS, THE(1949, Aus.)

Vinnie Burns
Silents
WOMAN OF MYSTERY, THE(1914); WILD HONEY(1919)
Misc. Silents
OLIVER TWIST(1912); ROGUES OF PARIS(1913); DESERT HONEYMOON, A(1915); WESTERN GOVERNOR'S HUMANITY, A(1915)

Walter Burns
Misc. Talkies
BARBARA(1970), d

Walter Noble Burns
BILLY THE KID(1930), w; ROBIN HOOD OF EL DORADO(1936), w; BILLY THE KID(1941), w; TOMBSTONE, THE TOWN TOO TOUGH TO DIE(1942), w

Wilfred Burns
FOOLS RUSH IN(1949, Brit.), m; FIGHTING WILDCATS, THE(1957, Brit.), md; OPERATION CONSPIRACY(1957, Brit.), m, md; THUNDER OVER TANGIER(1957, Brit.), md; HAND, THE(1960, Brit.), md; MILLION DOLLAR MANHUNT(1962, Brit.), m; MURDER IN EDEN(1962, Brit.), m; IN TROUBLE WITH EVE(1964, Brit.), m; MAN WHO COULDN'T WALK, THE(1964, Brit.), m; RUNAWAY, THE(1964, Brit.), m; ALF 'N' FAMILY(1968, Brit.), m; DAD'S ARMY(1971, Brit.), m; ADOLF HITLER–MY PART IN HIS DOWNFALL(1973, Brit.), m

William Burns
PASSOVER PLOT, THE(1976, Israel)
1984
MIRRORS(1984)
Misc. Talkies
MIRRORS(1978)

William G. Burns
Silents
$5,000,000 COUNTERFEITING PLOT, THE(1914)

William J. Burns
ARGYLE CASE, THE(1929), w

Wilred Burns
HUNDRED HOUR HUNT(1953, Brit.), m

Davy Burnsby
ARE YOU A MASON?(1934, Brit.)

Henrietta Burnside
LADIES SHOULD LISTEN(1934)

John Burnside
PEPE(1960)

Norman Burnside
DR. EHRLICH'S MAGIC BULLET(1940), w

R. H. Burnside
Silents
MANHATTAN(1924), d

William Burnside
KARATE KILLERS, THE(1967)

Charles Burnstein
HALLOWEEN(1978), ed

L. Burnstein
TIKI TIKI(1971, Can.), m

Norman Burnstine
SINS OF THE FATHERS(1928), w; ARSON GANG BUSTERS(1938), w; INVISIBLE ENEMY(1938), w

Drew Burnt
THAT SINKING FEELING(1979, Brit.)

Fred Burnworth
Silents
LADDIE BE GOOD(1928), ed
Misc. Silents
LEFT HAND BRAND, THE(1924)

Suzanne Buron
GIRL IN THE BIKINI, THE(1958, Fr.), ed

Alaistair Burr
GIRL GRABBERS, THE(1968)

Aleen Burr
Silents
WET GOLD(1921)
Misc. Silents
HIGHEST LAW, THE(1921)

Ann Burr
DEVIL ON WHEELS, THE(1947); NIGHT UNTO NIGHT(1949); MY BLUE HEAVEN(1950); FOLLOW THE SUN(1951)

C. C. Burr
KENTUCKY BLUE STREAK(1935), p; SPECIAL AGENT K-7(1937), p; CODE OF THE FEARLESS(1939), p; IN OLD MONTANA(1939), p; TWO-GUN TROUBADOR(1939), p
Silents
SURE FIRE FLINT(1922), p; LUCK(1923), p

Cynthia Burr
DEATH WISH II(1982)

Donald Burr
ELIZA COMES TO STAY(1936, Brit.)

Eugene Burr
Silents
ALIAS MARY BROWN(1918); NANCY COMES HOME(1918)
Misc. Silents
HEIRESS FOR A DAY(1918); OLD HARTWELL'S CUB(1918); VORTEX, THE(1918); BROADWAY MADONNA, THE(1922)

Fritzi Burr
HOW DO I LOVE THEE?(1970); FRASIER, THE SENSUOUS LION(1973); CHINATOWN(1974)

Gene Burr
Silents
ATOM, THE(1918)
Misc. Silents
MADAME SPHINX(1918); PRETENDER, THE(1918); GIRL WITH NO REGRETS, THE(1919)

Jane Burr
ARNELO AFFAIR, THE(1947), d&w

Lonnie Burr
SWEET CHARITY(1969)

Lonny Burr
QUEEN FOR A DAY(1951)

Raymond Burr
WITHOUT RESERVATIONS(1946); SAN QUENTIN(1946); CODE OF THE WEST(1947); DESPERATE(1947); I LOVE TROUBLE(1947); FIGHTING FATHER DUNNE(1948); PITFALL(1948); RAW DEAL(1948); RUTHLESS(1948); SLEEP, MY LOVE(1948); STATION WEST(1948); WALK A CROOKED MILE(1948); ABANDONED(1949); ADVENTURES OF DON JUAN(1949); BLACK MAGIC(1949); BRIDE OF VENGEANCE(1949); LOVE HAPPY(1949); RED LIGHT(1949); BORDERLINE(1950); KEY TO THE CITY(1950); UNMASKED(1950); BRIDE OF THE GORILLA(1951); HIS KIND OF WOMAN(1951); M(1951); MAGIC CARPET, THE(1951); NEW MEXICO(1951); PLACE IN THE SUN, A(1951); WHIP HAND, THE(1951); HORIZONS WEST(1952); MARA MARU(1952); MEET DANNY WILSON(1952); BANDITS OF CORSICA, THE(1953); BLUE GARDENIA, THE(1953); FORT ALGIERS(1953); SERPENT OF THE NILE(1953); TARZAN AND THE SHE-DEVIL(1953); CASANOVA'S BIG NIGHT(1954); GORILLA AT LARGE(1954); KHYBER PATROL(1954); PASSION(1954); REAR WINDOW(1954); THUNDER PASS(1954); COUNT THREE AND PRAY(1955); MAN ALONE, A(1955); THEY WERE SO YOUNG(1955); YOU'RE NEVER TOO YOUNG(1955); BRASS LEGEND, THE(1956); CRY IN THE NIGHT, A(1956); GODZILLA, KING OF THE MONSTERS(1956, Jap.); GREAT DAY IN THE MORNING(1956); PLEASE MURDER ME(1956); RIDE THE HIGH IRON(1956); SECRET OF TREASURE MOUNTAIN(1956); AFFAIR IN HAVANA(1957); CRIME OF PASSION(1957); DESIRE IN THE DUST(1960); P.J.(1968); TOMORROW NEVER COMES(1978, Brit./Can.); RETURN, THE(1980); AIRPLANE II: THE SEQUEL(1982); OUT OF THE BLUE(1982)
Misc. Talkies
BRIDE OF THE GORILLA(1951); ALIEN'S RETURN, THE(1980)

Robert Burr
POSSESSION OF JOEL DELANEY, THE(1972); SEVEN UPS, THE(1973); GHOST STORY(1981); TATTOO(1981); LITTLE SEX, A(1982)
Misc. Talkies
BLACK STREETFIGHTER(1976); BLACK FIST(1977)

Ron Burr
THRILL KILLERS, THE(1965)

Wally Burr
PROJECT X(1968), d

Warren Burr
JANIE(1944); YOUTH AFLAME(1945)

Wilfred Burr
DR. MORELLE–THE CASE OF THE MISSING HEIRESS(1949, Brit.), w

George R. Burrafato
DIRTY HARRY(1971); WHAT'S UP, DOC?(1972)

Daisy Burrell
WOMAN TO WOMAN(1946, Brit.); GREEN FINGERS(1947)
Silents
JUST A GIRL(1916, Brit.); ARTISTIC TEMPERAMENT, THE(1919, Brit.); BRIDAL CHAIR, THE(1919, Brit.); LAST ROSE OF SUMMER, THE(1920, Brit.); PRIDE OF THE FANCY, THE(1920, Brit.)
Misc. Silents
VALLEY OF FEAR, THE(1916, Brit.); LITTLE WOMEN(1917, Brit.); CONVICT 99(1919, Brit.)

Fred Burrell
KLUTE(1971); SHOOT IT: BLACK, SHOOT IT: BLUE(1974)

George Burrell
Silents
SEA BEAST, THE(1926)
Misc. Silents
BARBARIAN, THE(1921)

Gretchen Burrell
PRETTY MAIDS ALL IN A ROW(1971)

James Burrell
THIS IS THE ARMY(1943)

Jan Burrell
THAT TOUCH OF MINK(1962); CACTUS IN THE SNOW(1972); CULPEPPER CATTLE COMPANY, THE(1972); I NEVER PROMISED YOU A ROSE GARDEN(1977); RUBY(1977)

Johnnie Burrell
KILLER ELITE, THE(1975)

Maryedith Burrell
WHOLLY MOSES(1980); KISS ME GOODBYE(1982)

Michael Burrell
FIVE DAYS ONE SUMMER(1982)

Pamela Burrell
POPEYE(1980)

Peter Burrell
ZOOT SUIT(1981), p

Richard Burrell
HANDS OF DESTINY(1954, Brit.); MURDER AT SITE THREE(1959, Brit.); CALL ME BWANA(1963, Brit.); ACT OF MURDER(1965, Brit.); IPCRESS FILE, THE(1965, Brit.)

Rusty Burrell
FATE IS THE HUNTER(1964)

Sheila Burrell
MAN IN BLACK, THE(1950, Brit.); ROSSITER CASE, THE(1950, Brit.); CLOUDBURST(1952, Brit.); COLONEL MARCH INVESTIGATES(1952,Brit.); PARANOIAC(1963, Brit.); HELL IS EMPTY(1967, Brit./Ital)

Jimmy Burress
GREEN PASTURES(1936)

John Burress
MISSOURI TRAVELER, THE(1958), w

William Burress
BLONDE CRAZY(1931); LOCAL BOY MAKES GOOD(1931); LOVE IS A RACKET(1932); STRANGE LOVE OF MOLLY LOUVAIN, THE(1932); STREET OF WOMEN(1932); YOU SAID A MOUTHFUL(1932); BROADWAY THROUGH A KEYHOLE(1933); THEY JUST HAD TO GET MARRIED(1933); WORLD CHANGES, THE(1933); BABES IN TOYLAND(1934); FASHIONS OF 1934(1934); ONE NIGHT OF LOVE(1934); DR. SOCRATES(1935); GRAND OLD GIRL(1935); JANE EYRE(1935); LIFE BEGINS AT 40(1935); LITTLE COLONEL, THE(1935); NAUGHTY MARIETTA(1935); I'D GIVE MY LIFE(1936); STORY OF LOUIS PASTEUR, THE(1936); RACKETEERS IN EXILE(1937); SHALL WE DANCE(1937)
Silents
END OF THE TRAIL, THE(1916); FIRES OF CONSCIENCE(1916)
Misc. Silents
BUNCH OF KEYS, A(1915); MAN FROM BITTER ROOTS, THE(1916); BOOK AGENT, THE(1917); SCARLET PIMPERNEL, THE(1917); SOUL OF SATAN, THE(1917); RAINBOW TRAIL, THE(1918); YOURS TO COMMAND(1927)

Daniel Burret
Silents
NAPOLEON(1927, Fr.)

E. Burri
BOCCACCIO(1936, Ger.), w; ROYAL WALTZ, THE(1936), w

Emil Burri
WATER FOR CANITOGA(1939, Ger.), w; GIRL AND THE LEGEND, THE(1966, Ger.), w

Betty Burridge
ANYBODY'S BLONDE(1931), w

Geoffrey Burridge
INTERNECINE PROJECT, THE(1974, Brit.)

Ena Burrill
CAESAR AND CLEOPATRA(1946, Brit.)

Matthew Burrill
WHERE THE LILIES BLOOM(1974)

Robert L. Burrill
Misc. Talkies
MILPITAS MONSTER, THE(1980), d

Timothy Burrill
ALPHA BETA(1973, Brit.), p
1984
SUPERGIRL(1984), p

Ralph Burris
SECOND COMING OF SUZANNE, THE(1974), p

James Burross
TO HAVE AND HAVE NOT(1944)

Tom Burrough
Silents
CAPRICE OF THE MOUNTAINS(1916)
Misc. Silents
UNWELCOME MOTHER, THE(1916); MISS U.S.A.(1917); SHE(1917); UNKNOWN 274(1917)

Benjamin Burroughs
HOUSE ON 92ND STREET, THE(1945)

Buddy Burroughs
GOD IS MY CO-PILOT(1945); MILITARY ACADEMY WITH THAT TENTH AVENUE GANG(1950)

Clark Burroughs
PUBLIC ENEMY, THE(1931); SMART MONEY(1931)

Clark "Buddy" Burroughs
COW TOWN(1950)

Dale Burroughs
DEER HUNTER, THE(1978)

Edgar Rice Burroughs
TARZAN, THE APE MAN(1932), w; TARZAN THE FEARLESS(1933), p, w; TARZAN AND HIS MATE(1934), w; NEW ADVENTURES OF TARZAN(1935), p, w; TARZAN ESCAPES(1936), w; TARZAN AND THE GREEN GODDESS(1938), w; TARZAN'S REVENGE(1938), w; TARZAN FINDS A SON!(1939), w; TARZAN'S SECRET TREASURE(1941), w; TARZAN'S NEW YORK ADVENTURE(1942), w; TARZAN TRIUMPHS(1943), w; TARZAN'S DESERT MYSTERY(1943), w; TARZAN AND THE AMAZONS(1945), w; TARZAN AND THE LEOPARD WOMAN(1946), w; TARZAN AND THE HUNTRESS(1947), w; TARZAN AND THE MERMAIDS(1948), w; TARZAN'S MAGIC FOUNTAIN(1949), w; TARZAN AND THE SLAVE GIRL(1950), w; TARZAN'S PERIL(1951), w; TARZAN'S SAVAGE FURY(1952), w; TARZAN'S HIDDEN JUNGLE(1955), w; TARZAN AND THE LOST SAFARI(1957, Brit.), w; TARZAN'S FIGHT FOR LIFE(1958), w; TARZAN, THE APE MAN(1959), w; TARZAN'S GREATEST ADVENTURE(1959), w; TARZAN THE MAGNIFICENT(1960, Brit.), w; TARZAN GOES TO INDIA(1962, U.S./Brit./Switz.), w; TARZAN'S THREE CHALLENGES(1963), w; TARZAN AND THE VALLEY OF GOLD(1966 U.S./Switz.), w; TARZAN AND THE GREAT RIVER(1967, U.S./Switz.), w; TARZAN AND THE

JUNGLE BOY(1968, US/Switz.), w; TARZAN'S DEADLY SILENCE(1970), w; TARZAN'S JUNGLE REBELLION(1970), w; LAND THAT TIME FORGOT, THE(1975, Brit.), w; AT THE EARTH'S CORE(1976, Brit.), w; PEOPLE THAT TIME FORGOT, THE(1977, Brit.), w; TARZAN, THE APE MAN(1981), w
1984
GREYSTOKE: THE LEGEND OF TARZAN, LORD OF THE APES(1984), w
Silents
ROMANCE OF TARZAN, THE(1918), w; TARZAN OF THE APES(1918), w; OAKDALE AFFAIR, THE(1919), w
Jackie Burroughs
125 ROOMS OF COMFORT(1974, Can.); KIDNAPPING OF THE PRESIDENT, THE(1980, Can.); HEAVY METAL(1981, Can.); DEAD ZONE, THE(1983); GREY FOX, THE(1983, Can.)
1984
SURROGATE, THE(1984, Can.)
Julian Burroughs
LONESOME COWBOYS(1968)
Peter Burroughs
RETURN OF THE JEDI(1983)
Robin Burroughs
STUCK ON YOU(1983)
1984
STUCK ON YOU(1984)
Russell Burroughs
CHARLEY'S AUNT(1941); TONIGHT AND EVERY NIGHT(1945)
Tom Burroughs
Misc. Silents
FIGHTING KENTUCKIANS, THE(1920); HEEDLESS MOTHS(1921)
William S. Burroughs
CHAPPAQUA(1967); PROLOGUE(1970, Can.); TAKING TIGER MOUNTAIN(1983, U.S./Welsh), w
Geoff Burrowes
MAN FROM SNOWY RIVER, THE(1983, Aus.), p
Abe Burrows
GUYS AND DOLLS(1955), d&w; SOLID GOLD CADILLAC, THE(1956), w; SILK STOCKINGS(1957), w; CAN-CAN(1960), w; CACTUS FLOWER(1969), w; HOW TO SUCCEED IN BUSINESS WITHOUT REALLY TRYING(1976), w
Bill Burrows
NETWORK(1976)
Blair Burrows
WHICH WAY IS UP?(1977); ESCAPE FROM ALCATRAZ(1979); NIGHT OF THE JUGGLER(1980)
Bob Burrows
COLT .45(1950); CATTLE QUEEN OF MONTANA(1954); JUBILEE TRAIL(1954)
Cindy Burrows
HOFFMAN(1970, Brit.); SUNDAY BLOODY SUNDAY(1971, Brit.)
Dan Burrows
GOING BERSERK(1983)
Don Burrows
2,000 WEEKS(1970, Aus.), m, md
Harry A. Burrows
Silents
WHAT WIVES WANT(1923)
James Burrows
PARTNERS(1982), d
Jill Burrows
NAKED FURY(1959, Brit.)
John Burrows
WILD RIDERS(1971), p; SUPERCHICK(1973), p
John H. Burrows
AL CAPONE(1959), p
Ken Burrows
MURDER A LA MOD(1968), a, p
Martin Burrows
NUTCRACKER(1982, Brit.)
Peter Burrows
FLASH GORDON(1980)
Rosemary Burrows
PIRATES OF BLOOD RIVER, THE(1962, Brit.), cos; FRANKENSTEIN CREATED WOMAN(1965, Brit.), cos; NANNY, THE(1965, Brit.), cos; COUNTESS FROM HONG KONG, A(1967, Brit.), cos; FRANKENSTEIN MUST BE DESTROYED!(1969, Brit.), cos; WILBY CONSPIRACY, THE(1975, Brit.), cos
Thomas Burrows
Silents
ROMANCE OF THE AIR, A(1919)
William Burrows
Silents
PRINCE AND THE PAUPER, THE(1915)
Bill Burrud
HITLER'S CHILDREN(1942)
Misc. Talkies
CURSE OF THE MAYAN TEMPLE(1977), d
Billie Burrud
CAPTAINS COURAGEOUS(1937)
Billy Burrud
HIS NIGHT OUT(1935); THREE KIDS AND A QUEEN(1935); COWBOY AND THE KID,THE(1936); DEVIL'S SQUADRON(1936); MAGNIFICENT BRUTE, THE(1936); POSTAL INSPECTOR(1936); PRIDE OF THE MARINES(1936); TWO IN A CROWD(1936); FAIR WARNING(1937); GIRL OVERBOARD(1937); IDOL OF THE CROWDS(1937); IT HAPPENED IN HOLLYWOOD(1937); MAN IN BLUE, THE(1937); NIGHT HAWK, THE(1938)
John Tim Burrus
DIE LAUGHING(1980)
Tim Burrus
MORE AMERICAN GRAFFITI(1979)
Wayne Bursam
CATTLE QUEEN OF MONTANA(1954)

Tina Bursill
1984
MELVIN, SON OF ALVIN(1984, Aus.)
Harry Burslem
RANGERS OF FORTUNE(1940)
Polly Burson
ESCAPE TO BURMA(1955); KETTLES ON OLD MACDONALD'S FARM, THE(1957); NIGHT PASSAGE(1957)
Wayne Burson
RIDIN' DOWN THE TRAIL(1947); SONG OF THE DRIFTER(1948); WILD HORSE AMBUSH(1952)
Dan Burstall
ELIZA FRASER(1976, Aus.), ph; HIGH ROLLING(1977, Aus.), ph; 20TH CENTURY OZ(1977, Aus.), ph; LAST OF THE KNUCKLEMEN, THE(1981, Aus.), ph; DUET FOR FOUR(1982, Aus.), ph
1984
SQUIZZY TAYLOR(1984, Aus.), ph
Tim Burstall
2,000 WEEKS(1970, Aus.), d, w; LIBIDO(1973, Aus.), d; ALVIN PURPLE(1974, Aus.), p&d; ALVIN RIDES AGAIN(1974, Aus.), p, w; PETERSEN(1974, Aus.), p&d; END PLAY(1975, Aus.), p,d&w; ELIZA FRASER(1976, Aus.), p&d; HIGH ROLLING(1977, Aus.), p; LAST OF THE KNUCKLEMEN, THE(1981, Aus.), p,d&w; DUET FOR FOUR(1982, Aus.), p, d
Tom Burstall
STORK(1971, Aus.), d; DUET FOR FOUR(1982, Aus.), p
Jules Burstein
1984
SIGNAL 7(1984)
Mike Burstein
FLYING MATCHMAKER, THE(1970, Israel)
Pesach Burstein
FLYING MATCHMAKER, THE(1970, Israel)
Janet Burston
BLONDIE GOES LATIN(1941); IN THE MEANTIME, DARLING(1944)
Ellen Burstyn [Ellen McRae]
ALEX IN WONDERLAND(1970); LAST PICTURE SHOW, THE(1971); KING OF MARVIN GARDENS, THE(1972); EXORCIST, THE(1973); HARRY AND TONTO(1974); ALICE DOESN'T LIVE HERE ANYMORE(1975); PROVIDENCE(1977, Fr.); DREAM OF PASSION, A(1978, Gr.); SAME TIME, NEXT YEAR(1978); RESURRECTION(1980); SILENCE OF THE NORTH(1981, Can.)
1984
AMBASSADOR, THE(1984)
Joseph Burstyn
LOWER DEPTHS, THE(1937, Fr.), p
Mike Burstyn
RABBI AND THE SHIKSE, THE(1976, Israel)
Neil Burstyn
ALEX IN WONDERLAND(1970); REBEL ROUSERS(1970)
Ben Burt
LONG SHOT, THE(1939); LUCY GALLANT(1955)
Benny Burt
PICK A STAR(1937); SEA RACKETEERS(1937); SWEETHEART OF THE NAVY(1937); HAWAIIAN BUCKAROO(1938); NOCTURNE(1946); OUR HEARTS WERE GROWING UP(1946); THREE STRANGERS(1946); CONVICTED(1950); CRY DANGER(1951); DOUBLE DYNAMITE(1951); IT'S A BIG COUNTRY(1951); M(1951); PEOPLE AGAINST O'HARA, THE(1951); PROWLER, THE(1951); TEN TALL MEN(1951); MILLION DOLLAR MERMAID(1952); STEEL TRAP, THE(1952); FAST COMPANY(1953); HOW TO MARRY A MILLIONAIRE(1953); ROGUE COP(1954); LOVE ME OR LEAVE ME(1955); FIGHTING TROUBLE(1956); CHICAGO CONFIDENTIAL(1957); APARTMENT, THE(1960)
Bill Burt
MISSISSIPPI RHYTHM(1949)
Billy Burt
OH JOHNNY, HOW YOU CAN LOVE!(1940); O.S.S.(1946); STRANGE LOVE OF MARTHA IVERS, THE(1946); NIGHT HAS A THOUSAND EYES(1948)
Chris Burt
SWEENEY(1977, Brit.), ed; SWEENEY 2(1978, Brit.), ed
Clare Burt
1984
SCREAM FOR HELP(1984)
Daniel Burt
CHANNEL CROSSING(1934, Brit.), ed
Eddie Burt
THAT SINKING FEELING(1979, Brit.)
Frank Burt
OPERATOR 13(1934); STRANGE MRS. CRANE, THE(1948), w; AIR HOSTESS(1949), w; BARBARY PIRATE(1949), w; CHINATOWN AT MIDNIGHT(1949), w; FLAME OF YOUTH(1949), w; LAW OF THE BARBARY COAST(1949), w; FORTUNES OF CAPTAIN BLOOD(1950), w; STAGE TO TUCSON(1950), w; STATE PENITENTIARY(1950), w; TYRANT OF THE SEA(1950), w; GROOM WORE SPURS, THE(1951), w; LADY AND THE BANDIT, THE(1951), w; CAPTAIN PIRATE(1952), w; BANDITS OF CORSICA, THE(1953), w; MAN FROM LARAMIE, THE(1955), w
Frederic Burt
EYES OF THE WORLD, THE(1930); SHADOW OF THE LAW(1930)
Frederick Burt
UP FOR MURDER(1931)
George Burt
CRY DR. CHICAGO(1971), md
1984
SECRET HONOR(1984), m
Heinz Burt
SING AND SWING(1964, Brit.)
June Burt
YOUNG AND DANGEROUS(1957)
Katharine Newlin Burt
Silents
SNOWBLIND(1921), w; SINGED WINGS(1922), w; EAGLE'S FEATHER, THE(1923), w

Katherine Newlin Burt
Silents
BRANDING IRON, THE(1920), w
Keith Erik Burt
NIGHT OF THE WITCHES(1970), d&w, a, p
Kendal Burt
ONE THAT GOT AWAY, THE(1958, Brit.), w
Laura Burt
Misc. Silents
SOCIAL PIRATE, THE(1919)
Margaret Burt
SARGE GOES TO COLLEGE(1947)
Silents
NIGHT OF MYSTERY, A(1928)
Nellie Burt
GREAT NORTHFIELD, MINNESOTA RAID, THE(1972)
Silents
IDLE HANDS(1921)
Oliver Burt
STOP PRESS GIRL(1949, Brit.)
Willard Burt
Misc. Silents
DO THE DEAD TALK?(1920)
William Burt
GIRL OF THE PORT(1930); TANGLED DESTINIES(1932)
Misc. Talkies
PASSPORT TO PARADISE(1932)
Silents
LEOPARD LADY, THE(1928)
Misc. Silents
HER FATHER'S GOLD(1916)
William Fresley Burt
MIDNIGHT MYSTERY(1930)
William P. Burt
DANGER LIGHTS(1930); ROGUE OF THE RIO GRANDE(1930)
Misc. Silents
WOMAN IN CHAINS, THE(1923), d
Eddie Burtell
SPOTLIGHT SCANDALS(1943)
Billy Burtis
OUTLAWS OF THE CHEROKEE TRAIL(1941)
Eric Burtis
EAST SIDE KIDS(1940)
James Burtis
JAZZ CINDERELLA(1930); LADIES IN LOVE(1930); GRIEF STREET(1931); LADY FROM NOWHERE(1931); LAWLESS WOMAN, THE(1931); SUICIDE FLEET(1931); TIP-OFF, THE(1931); CROWD ROARS, THE(1932); IF I HAD A MILLION(1932); STRANGERS OF THE EVENING(1932); TEXAS BAD MAN(1932); WESTERN LIMITED(1932); ONE SUNDAY AFTERNOON(1933); SITTING PRETTY(1933); TRICK FOR TRICK(1933); CASE OF THE HOWLING DOG, THE(1934); HERE COMES THE GROOM(1934); HERE COMES THE NAVY(1934); HIPS, HIPS, HOORAY(1934); JEALOUSY(1934); ST. LOUIS KID, THE(1934); YOUNG AND BEAUTIFUL(1934); FARMER TAKES A WIFE, THE(1935); FRONT PAGE WOMAN(1935); KEEPER OF THE BEES(1935); MISS PACIFIC FLEET(1935); MR. DYNAMITE(1935); SECRET BRIDE, THE(1935); SHE COULDN'T TAKE IT(1935); WINGS IN THE DARK(1935); $1,000 A MINUTE(1935); RETURN OF JIMMY VALENTINE, THE(1936); GENERAL SPANKY(1937); PERFECT SPECIMEN, THE(1937); PUBLIC WEDDING(1937); MEN WITH WINGS(1938); TEXANS, THE(1938); WHO KILLED GAIL PRESTON?(1938); ST. LOUIS BLUES(1939)
James C. Burtis
READY FOR LOVE(1934)
James P. Burtis
TWENTIETH CENTURY(1934); UPPER WORLD(1934); ONE HOUR LATE(1935); RENDEZVOUS(1935); RUMBA(1935); STORMY(1935); GREAT ZIEGFELD, THE(1936); MURDER AT GLEN ATHOL(1936); POLO JOE(1936); SATAN MET A LADY(1936)
Janet Maria Burtis
SIDELONG GLANCES OF A PIGEON KICKER, THE(1970)
Jim Burtis
GHOST PATROL(1936)
Jimmie Burtis
MYSTERY MAN, THE(1935)
Jimmy Burtis
SINISTER HANDS(1932); RACING STRAIN, THE(1933); DANCING FEET(1936)
Marilyn Burtis
LAST TIME I SAW ARCHIE, THE(1961)
T. Burtis
IN OLD OKLAHOMA(1943), w
Thomas Burtis
MADISON SQUARE GARDEN(1932), w
Thomson Burtis
UNDER-COVER MAN(1932), w; SOLDIERS OF THE STORM(1933), w; IN OLD OKLAHOMA(1943), w; CROSSWINDS(1951), w
Burton
ROLLERCOASTER(1977), cos
Al Burton
YOUNG CAPTIVES, THE(1959), w
B. W. Burton
MELODY OF LOVE, THE(1928), ed; CLEAR THE DECKS(1929), ed
Basil Burton
MURDER IN THE CATHEDRAL(1952, Brit.)
Beatrice Burton
Silents
HIS JAZZ BRIDE(1926), w
Bernard Burton
WELCOME DANGER(1929), ed; CLIMAX, THE(1930), ed; FEET FIRST(1930), ed; MOVIE CRAZY(1932), ed; OUT ALL NIGHT(1933), ed; CAT'S PAW, THE(1934), ed; VAGABOND LADY(1935), ed; THE INVISIBLE RAY(1936), ed; LOVE IN A BUNGALOW(1937), ed; RAGE OF PARIS, THE(1938), ed; CHARLIE MC CARTHY, DETECTIVE(1939), ed; EX-CHAMP(1939), ed; FIRST LOVE(1939), ed; IT'S A DATE(1940), ed; SPRING PARADE(1940), ed; HIT THE ROAD(1941), ed

Bernard B. Burton
SOLOMON KING(1974)
Bernard W. Burton
SHE GETS HER MAN(1935), ed; MAN I MARRY, THE(1936), ed; SHOW BOAT(1936), ed; MYSTERIOUS CROSSING(1937), ed; OH DOCTOR(1937), ed; WHEN LOVE IS YOUNG(1937), ed; YOU'RE A SWEETHEART(1937), ed; 100 MEN AND A GIRL(1937), ed; LITTLE TOUGH GUYS IN SOCIETY(1938), ed; MIDNIGHT INTRUDER(1938), ed; THAT STARTED WITH EVE(1938), ed; IT STARTED WITH EVE(1941), ed; NICE GIRL?(1941), ed; SAN FRANCISCO DOCKS(1941), ed; TOO MANY BLONDES(1941), ed; GET HEP TO LOVE(1942), p; GIVE OUT, SISTERS(1942), p; MOONLIGHT IN HAVANA(1942), p; STRANGE CASE OF DR. RX, THE(1942), ed; TOUGH AS THEY COME(1942), ed; ALL BY MYSELF(1943), p; MOONLIGHT IN VERMONT(1943), p; RHYTHM OF THE ISLANDS(1943), p; TOP MAN(1943), p; WHEN JOHNNY COMES MARCHING HOME(1943), p; BABES ON SWING STREET(1944), p; CHIP OFF THE OLD BLOCK(1944), p; PARDON MY RHYTHM(1944), p; SINGING SHERIFF, THE(1944), p; THIS IS THE LIFE(1944), p; SWING OUT, SISTER(1945), p; BREAKFAST IN HOLLYWOOD(1946), ed; JOE PALOOKA, CHAMP(1946), ed; NEW ORLEANS(1947), ed; CRY DANGER(1951), ed; MODELS, INC.(1952), ed; BEAST FROM 20,000 FATHOMS, THE(1953), p, ed
Bill Burton
ULZANA'S RAID(1972); POSSE(1975); HEROES(1977); MOONSHINE COUNTY EXPRESS(1977), stunts; OCTOPUSSY(1983, Brit.), stunts
1984
AGAINST ALL ODDS(1984); ROMANCING THE STONE(1984)
Bob Burton
BRASS LEGEND, THE(1956)
Cecil Burton
SHOOT IT: BLACK, SHOOT IT: BLUE(1974)
Charlotte Burton
Silents
POLLY OF THE STORM COUNTRY(1920)
Misc. Silents
BRUISER, THE(1916); CRAVING, THE(1916); HIGHEST BID, THE(1916); LONE STAR(1916); LOVE HERMIT, THE(1916); MAN WHO WOULD NOT DIE, THE(1916); SEQUEL TO THE DIAMOND FROM THE SKY(1916); SOUL MATES(1916); STRENGTH OF DONALD MCKENZIE, THE(1916); THOROUGHBRED, THE(1916); TORCH BEARER, THE(1916); TWINKLER, THE(1916); FATE AND THE CHILD(1917); GYPSY'S TRUST, THE(1917); HEARTS OR DIAMONDS?(1918); UP ROMANCE ROAD(1918)
Clarence Burton
BARNUM WAS RIGHT(1929); GODLESS GIRL, THE(1929); LOCKED DOOR, THE(1929); LOVE RACKET, THE(1929); DYNAMITE(1930); LOVE TRADER(1930); ONLY SAPS WORK(1930); UNHOLY THREE, THE(1930); SIGN OF THE CROSS, THE(1932)
Silents
FRAME UP, THE(1917); FAME AND FORTUNE(1918); HAWTHORNE OF THE U.S.A.(1919); HEARTS OF MEN(1919); MALE AND FEMALE(1919); THOU ART THE MAN(1920); WHAT'S YOUR HURRY?(1920); CRAZY TO MARRY(1921); BEAUTIFUL AND DAMNED, THE(1922); CRIMSON CHALLENGE, THE(1922); IMPOSSIBLE MRS. BELLEW, THE(1922); ORDEAL, THE(1922); ADAM'S RIB(1923); GARRISON'S FINISH(1923); MR. BILLINGS SPENDS HIS DIME(1923); NOBODY'S MONEY(1923); SALOMY JANE(1923); SIXTY CENTS AN HOUR(1923); TEN COMMANDMENTS, THE(1923); BLUFF(1924); NAVIGATOR, THE(1924); NO MORE WOMEN(1924); COMING OF AMOS, THE(1925); WEDDING SONG, THE(1925); NERVOUS WRECK, THE(1926); RED DICE(1926); ANGEL OF BROADWAY, THE(1927); KING OF KINGS, THE(1927); RUBBER TIRES(1927); YANKEE CLIPPER, THE(1927); CHICAGO(1928); MIDNIGHT MADNESS(1928); STAND AND DELIVER(1928)
Misc. Silents
DREAM OR TWO AGO, A(1916); FAITH(1916); LYING LIPS(1916); OVERCOAT, THE(1916); RECLAMATION, THE(1916); TWINKLER, THE(1916); NEW YORK LUCK(1917); PERIWINKLE(1917); MYSTERY OF A GIRL, THE(1918); POWERS THAT PREY(1918); RETURN OF MARY, THE(1918); CASTLES IN THE AIR(1919); SPENDER, THE(1919); FIGHTING CHANCE, THE(1920); SIX BEST CELLARS, THE(1920); FORBIDDEN FRUIT(1921); HIGH GEAR JEFFREY(1921); HER OWN MONEY(1922); MAN UNCONQUERABLE, THE(1922); SATIN GIRL, THE(1923); SHIPWRECKED(1926); WARNING SIGNAL, THE(1926); SUBMARINE(1928)
Corey Burton
WOLFEN(1981); GALAXY EXPRESS(1982, Jap.)
David Burton
BISHOP MURDER CASE, THE(1930), d; FREE AND EASY(1930); STRICTLY UNCONVENTIONAL(1930), d; CONFESSIONS OF A CO-ED(1931), d; FIGHTING CARAVANS(1931), d; DANCERS IN THE DARK(1932), d; BRIEF MOMENT(1933), d; LADY BY CHOICE(1934), d; LET'S FALL IN LOVE(1934), d; SISTERS UNDER THE SKIN(1934), d; MELODY LINGERS ON, THE(1935), d; PRINCESS O'HARA(1935), d; MAKE WAY FOR A LADY(1936), d; MAN WHO WOULDN'T TALK, THE(1940), d; MANHATTAN HEARTBEAT(1940), d; JENNIE(1941), d; PRIVATE NURSE(1941), d; IN GOD WE TRUST(1980)
1984
AGAINST ALL ODDS(1984); STAR TREK III: THE SEARCH FOR SPOCK(1984)
Silents
MADAME BUTTERFLY(1915)
Debbie Burton
WHATEVER HAPPENED TO BABY JANE?(1962)
Devera Burton
OMOO OMOO, THE SHARK GOD(1949)
Donald Burton
MOHAMMAD, MESSENGER OF GOD(1976, Lebanon/Brit.)
Fred Burton
SWEEPSTAKES(1931); FAMOUS FERGUSON CASE, THE(1932); KENTUCKY(1938); TOWN WENT WILD, THE(1945)
Misc. Silents
HELIOTROPE(1920)
Frederick Burton
BIG TRAIL, THE(1930); AMERICAN TRAGEDY, AN(1931); CISCO KID(1931); ROYAL BED, THE(1931); SECRET SERVICE(1931); FREIGHTERS OF DESTINY(1932); I AM A FUGITIVE FROM A CHAIN GANG(1932); OKAY AMERICA(1932); ONE WAY PASSAGE(1932); SILVER DOLLAR(1932); STATE'S ATTORNEY(1932); TOO BUSY TO WORK(1932); TWO SECONDS(1932); WET PARADE, THE(1932); WOMAN FROM MONTE CARLO, THE(1932); BROADWAY BAD(1933); COUNSELLOR-AT-LAW(1933); GOLDEN HARVEST(1933); LAWYER

MAN(1933); NO OTHER WOMAN(1933); WORKING MAN, THE(1933); BELLE OF THE NINETIES(1934); FLIRTATION WALK(1934); LOVE BIRDS(1934); ONE NIGHT OF LOVE(1934); SMARTY(1934); FARMER TAKES A WIFE, THE(1935); MC FADDEN'S FLATS(1935); SHIPMATES FOREVER(1935); TRANSIENT LADY(1935); DAN MATTHEWS(1936); EVERYBODY'S OLD MAN(1936); FURY(1936); MUMMY'S BOYS(1936); THEODORA GOES WILD(1936); VOICE OF BUGLE ANN(1936); WIFE VERSUS SECRETARY(1936); DUKE COMES BACK, THE(1937); LAST GANGSTER, THE(1937); LOVE IS NEWS(1937); MAN IN BLUE, THE(1937); NANCY STEELE IS MISSING(1937); FLIGHT TO FAME(1938); I AM THE LAW(1938); JEZEBEL(1938); MY LUCKY STAR(1938); SAINT IN NEW YORK, THE(1938); CONFESSIONS OF A NAZI SPY(1939); INSIDE INFORMATION(1939); JOE AND ETHEL TURP CALL ON THE PRESIDENT(1939); MR. SMITH GOES TO WASHINGTON(1939); OLD MAID, THE(1939); SILVER ON THE SAGE(1939); BOWERY BOY(1940); BRIGHAM YOUNG–FRONTIERSMAN(1940); MAN FROM DAKOTA, THE(1940); THIRD FINGER, LEFT HAND(1940); BABES ON BROADWAY(1941); MAN WHO LOST HIMSELF, THE(1941); WASHINGTON MELODRAMA(1941); MAN WITH TWO LIVES, THE(1942); SILVER QUEEN(1942); TENNESSEE JOHNSON(1942); HANDS ACROSS THE BORDER(1943); CASANOVA BROWN(1944); MISS SUSIE SLAGLE'S(1945); FOXES OF HARROW, THE(1947)
Silents
FORGIVEN, OR THE JACK O'DIAMONDS(1914); ARIZONA(1918); ANNE OF GREEN GABLES(1919); GETTING MARY MARRIED(1919); EDUCATION OF ELIZABETH, THE(1921); IF WOMEN ONLY KNEW(1921); ANNA ASCENDS(1922); BACK HOME AND BROKE(1922); REJECTED WOMAN, THE(1924)
Misc. Silents
RUGGLES OF RED GAP(1918); FORTUNE TELLER, THE(1920); RUNNING WILD(1927)
G. Marion Burton
Silents
MISS DULCIE FROM DIXIE(1919), w; ANOTHER SCANDAL(1924), w; OUT WITH THE TIDE(1928), w
Geoff Burton
SUNDAY TOO FAR AWAY(1975, Aus.), ph; STORM BOY(1976, Aus.), ph; BLUE FIN(1978, Aus.), ph; PICTURE SHOW MAN, THE(1980, Aus.), ph
Geoffrey Burton
STIR(1980, Aus.), ph
George Burton
PAINTED DESERT, THE(1931); IN OLD SANTA FE(1935); RUGGLES OF RED GAP(1935); TUMBLING TUMBLEWEEDS(1935); COME ON, COWBOYS(1937); BILL AND COO(1947)
Humphrey Burton
INTERLUDE(1968, Brit.)
Iain Burton
MISCHIEF(1969, Brit.)
Iris Burton
TOP BANANA(1954)
James Burton
HEART LIKE A WHEEL(1983)
Janet Burton
GINGER(1947)
Jay Burton
TWO TICKETS TO PARIS(1962); YOUNG NURSES, THE(1973); HISTORY OF THE WORLD, PART 1(1981)
Jean Burton
BUCKET OF BLOOD, A(1959)
Jeff Burton
GIT!(1965); MADAME X(1966); PLANET OF THE APES(1968); SWEET CHARITY(1969)
Misc. Talkies
BLACK HOOKER(1974)
Jennifer Burton
TRUCK STOP WOMEN(1974)
Jhean Burton
PLEASE DON'T EAT THE DAISIES(1960); WHY MUST I DIE?(1960)
John Burton
BELOVED ENEMY(1936); LLOYDS OF LONDON(1936); LANCER SPY(1937); LOST HORIZON(1937); KIDNAPPED(1938); LORD JEFF(1938); MARIE ANTOINETTE(1938); STORM OVER BENGAL(1938); HOUND OF THE BASKERVILLES, THE(1939); SUN NEVER SETS, THE(1939); EARL OF CHICAGO, THE(1940); FOREIGN CORRESPONDENT(1940); RAGE IN HEAVEN(1941); BLACK SWAN, THE(1942); EAGLE SQUADRON(1942); INVISIBLE AGENT(1942); JOURNEY FOR MARGARET(1942); MRS. MINIVER(1942); SHERLOCK HOLMES AND THE SECRET WEAPON(1942); TWO TICKETS TO LONDON(1943); SHERLOCK HOLMES AND THE SPIDER WOMAN(1944); BLACK BEAUTY(1946); CAPTAIN FROM CASTILE(1947); DARK DELUSION(1947); EVERYBODY DOES IT(1949); FAN, THE(1949); THREE CAME HOME(1950); DAVID AND BATHSHEBA(1951); DAY THE EARTH STOOD STILL, THE(1951); HOUSE ON TELEGRAPH HILL(1951); TWELVE TO THE MOON(1960), set d; ATTACK OF THE MAYAN MUMMY(1963, U.S./Mex.); TRUE GRIT(1969), set d; WATERMELON MAN(1970), set d; BLACK STALLION, THE(1979)
Silents
HUCK AND TOM(1918); M'LISS(1918); SIN THAT WAS HIS, THE(1920)
Misc. Silents
MAKING OF MADDALENA, THE(1916); BIG TIMBER(1917); BOND BETWEEN, THE(1917); HEIR OF THE AGES, THE(1917); LONESOME CHAP, THE(1917); WORLD APART, THE(1917); UP ROMANCE ROAD(1918); SCOFFER, THE(1920); FLAMES OF WRATH(1923)
John Burton, Jr.
Silents
KISS FOR SUSIE, A(1917)
John Nelson Burton
NEVER MENTION MURDER(1964, Brit.), d
Julian Burton
MAN OR GUN(1958); YOUNG LIONS, THE(1958); BUCKET OF BLOOD, A(1959); MAN IN THE MIDDLE(1964, U.S./Brit.); MASQUE OF THE RED DEATH, THE(1964, U.S./Brit.)
Langhorne Burton
CROSS ROADS(1930, Brit.)
Silents
AULD ROBIN GRAY(1917, Brit.); PROFLIGATE, THE(1917, Brit.); GOD AND THE MAN(1918, Brit.); IMPOSSIBLE WOMAN, THE(1919, Brit.); AMATEUR GENTLE-

MAN, THE(1920, Brit.); AT THE VILLA ROSE(1920, Brit.); MAN'S SHADOW, A(1920, Brit.); APPEARANCES(1921); 'MARRIAGE LICENSE?'(1926)
Misc. Silents
BOOTLE'S BABY(1914, Brit.); TREASURE OF HEAVEN, THE(1916, Brit.); AULD ROBIN GRAY(1917, Brit.); DADDY(1917, Brit.); TOM JONES(1917, Brit.); SWEET AND TWENTY(1919, Brit.); BY BERWIN BANKS(1920, Brit.); CHILDREN OF GIBEON, THE(1920, Brit.); LITTLE DORRIT(1920, Brit.); TEMPTRESS, THE(1920, Brit.); TWO LITTLE WOODEN SHOES(1920, Brit.); MOTH AND RUST(1921, Brit.); WHO IS THE MAN?(1924, Brit.)
Laurie Burton
TICKLE ME(1965); BLACK MAMA, WHITE MAMA(1973)
Lee Burton [Guido Lollobrigida]
HE WHO SHOOTS FIRST(1966, Ital.); LONG RIDE FROM HELL, A(1970, Ital.); RED SUN(1972, Fr./Ital./Span.)
Leonard M. Burton
SATAN IN HIGH HEELS(1962), p
Lesley Margret Burton
MELVIN AND HOWARD(1980)
Levar Burton
LOOKING FOR MR. GOODBAR(1977); HUNTER, THE(1980)
Linda Burton
RED SKY AT MORNING(1971)
Lionel Burton
SURPRISE PACKAGE(1960)
Loftus Burton
ROLLERBALL(1975)
Louise Burton
CARRY ON ENGLAND(1976, Brit.)
Maggi Burton
Misc. Talkies
KEEP IT UP, JACK!(1975)
Mal Burton
WIRE SERVICE(1942)
Marie Burton
DAUGHTER OF SHANGHAI(1937); HOLD'EM NAVY!(1937); THRILL OF A LIFETIME(1937); ARTISTS AND MODELS ABROAD(1938); SAY IT IN FRENCH(1938); TROPIC HOLIDAY(1938); YOU AND ME(1938)
Martin Burton
CAUGHT(1931); LADIES' MAN(1931); HOTEL VARIETY(1933); WHEN LADIES MEET(1933)
Mary Burton
UNDER YOUR HAT(1940, Brit.)
Matthew Burton
THREE TO GO(1971, Aus.)
Ned Burton
Silents
AUCTION BLOCK, THE(1917); JIM THE PENMAN(1921); BACK HOME AND BROKE(1922)
Misc. Silents
HER GREAT MATCH(1915); VELVET PAW, THE(1916); DANGER GAME, THE(1918); MORAL DEADLINE, THE(1919); THOU SHALT NOT(1919); THUNDERBOLTS OF FATE(1919); TARNISHED REPUTATIONS(1920)
Nelson Burton, Jr.
DREAMER(1979)
Norman Burton
SPELL OF THE HYPNOTIST(1956); PRETTY BOY FLOYD(1960); HAND OF DEATH(1962); WOMAN HUNT(1962); WILD SEED(1965); VALLEY OF THE DOLLS(1967); PLANET OF THE APES(1968); R.P.M.(1970); DIAMONDS ARE FOREVER(1971, Brit.); ESCAPE FROM THE PLANET OF THE APES(1971); JUD(1971); SIMON, KING OF THE WITCHES(1971); FUZZ(1972); HIT(1973); SAVE THE TIGER(1973); GUMBALL RALLY, THE(1976); FADE TO BLACK(1980); AMY(1981); MAUSOLEUM(1983)
1984
CRIMES OF PASSION(1984)
Normann Burton
TERMINAL MAN, THE(1974); TOWERING INFERNO, THE(1974); REINCARNATION OF PETER PROUD, THE(1975); SCORCHY(1976)
Peter Burton
WHAT THE BUTLER SAW(1950, Brit.); THEY WERE NOT DIVIDED(1951, Brit.); WOODEN HORSE, THE(1951); FRIGHTENED BRIDE, THE(1952, Brit.); GREEN SCARF, THE(1954, Brit.); HEART OF THE MATTER, THE(1954, Brit.); PARATROOPER(1954, Brit.); THEY WHO DARE(1954, Brit.); THREE CASES OF MURDER(1955, Brit.); CHILD IN THE HOUSE(1956, Brit.); JOHNNY, YOU'RE WANTED(1956, Brit.); SPIN A DARK WEB(1956, Brit.); BETRAYAL, THE(1958, Brit.); SINK THE BISMARCK!(1960, Brit.); DR. NO(1962, Brit.); MAKE MINE A DOUBLE(1962, Brit.); STOLEN PLANS, THE(1962, Brit.); SWINGIN' MAIDEN, THE(1963, Brit.); THAT KIND OF GIRL(1963, Brit.); JUDITH(1965); BERSERK(1967); CLOCKWORK ORANGE, A(1971, Brit.); INCHON(1981); RICHARD'S THINGS(1981, Brit.)
1984
JIGSAW MAN, THE(1984, Brit.)
Ray Burton
RABBIT, RUN(1970), m
Richard Burton
LAST DAYS OF DOLWYN, THE(1949, Brit.); NOW BARABBAS WAS A ROBBER(1949, Brit.); GREEN GROW THE RUSHES(1951, Brit.); HER PANELLED DOOR(1951, Brit.); MY COUSIN RACHEL(1952, Brit.); WATERFRONT WOMEN(1952, Brit.); DESERT RATS, THE(1953); ROBE, THE(1953); DEMETRIUS AND THE GLADIATORS(1954); PRINCE OF PLAYERS(1955); RAINS OF RANCHIPUR, THE(1955); ALEXANDER THE GREAT(1956); SEA WIFE(1957, Brit.); BITTER VICTORY(1958, Fr.); LOOK BACK IN ANGER(1959); BRAMBLE BUSH, THE(1960); ICE PALACE(1960); MIDSUMMERS NIGHT'S DREAM, A(1961, Czech); LONGEST DAY, THE(1962); CLEOPATRA(1963); V.I.P.s(1963, Brit.); BECKET(1964, Brit.); HAMLET(1964); NIGHT OF THE IGUANA, THE(1964); ZULU(1964, Brit.); SANDPIPER, THE(1965); SPY WHO CAME IN FROM THE COLD, THE(1965, Brit.); WHAT'S NEW, PUSSYCAT?(1965, U.S./Fr.); WHO'S AFRAID OF VIRGINIA WOOLF?(1966); COMEDIANS, THE(1967); DOCTOR FAUSTUS(1967, Brit.), a, p, d; TAMING OF THE SHREW, THE(1967, U.S./Ital.), a, p; BOOM!(1968); CANDY(1968, Ital./Fr.); WHERE EAGLES DARE(1968, Brit.); ANNE OF THE THOUSAND DAYS(1969, Brit.); STAIRCASE(1969 U.S./Brit./Fr.); RAID ON ROMMEL(1971); VILLAIN(1971, Brit.); ASSASSINATION OF TROTSKY, THE(1972 Fr./Ital.); BLUEBEARD(1972); HAMMERSMITH

IS OUT(1972); MASSACRE IN ROME(1973, Ital.); UNDER MILK WOOD(1973, Brit.); KLANSMAN, THE(1974); VOYAGE, THE(1974, Ital.); "EQUUS"(1977); EXORCIST II: THE HERETIC(1977); BREAKTHROUGH(1978, Ger.); MEDUSA TOUCH, THE(1978, Brit.); WILD GEESE, THE(1978, Brit.); CIRCLE OF TWO(1980, Can.); ABSOLUTION(1981, Brit.); WAGNER(1983, Brit./Hung./Aust.)
1984
   1984(1984, Brit.)

Robert Burton
BAD AND THE BEAUTIFUL, THE(1952); DESPERATE SEARCH(1952); EVERYTHING I HAVE IS YOURS(1952); FEARLESS FAGAN(1952); MY MAN AND I(1952); SKY FULL OF MOON(1952); ABOVE AND BEYOND(1953); ALL THE BROTHERS WERE VALIANT(1953); BIG HEAT, THE(1953); CODE TWO(1953); CONFIDENTIAL CONNIE(1953); CRY OF THE HUNTED(1953); FAST COMPANY(1953); GIRL WHO HAD EVERYTHING, THE(1953); INFERNO(1953); LATIN LOVERS(1953); SLIGHT CASE OF LARCENY, A(1953); BROKEN LANCE(1954); RIOT IN CELL BLOCK 11(1954); ROGUE COP(1954); SIEGE AT RED RIVER, THE(1954); TAZA, SON OF COCHISE(1954); COUNT THREE AND PRAY(1955); LAY THAT RIFLE DOWN(1955); LEFT HAND OF GOD, THE(1955); MAN CALLED PETER, THE(1955); ROAD TO DENVER, THE(1955); SOLDIER OF FORTUNE(1955); JUBAL(1956); RACK, THE(1956); RANSOM(1956); REPRISAL(1956); DOMINO KID(1957); HARD MAN, THE(1957); HIRED GUN, THE(1957); SPIRIT OF ST. LOUIS, THE(1957); TALL T, THE(1957); THREE BRAVE MEN(1957); I WAS A TEENAGE FRANKENSTEIN(1958); MAN OR GUN(1958); MARDI GRAS(1958); YOUNG LIONS, THE(1958); COMPULSION(1959); PRIVATE'S AFFAIR, A(1959); STORY ON PAGE ONE, THE(1959); THIRTY FOOT BRIDE OF CANDY ROCK, THE(1959); GALLANT HOURS, THE(1960); SEVEN WAYS FROM SUNDOWN(1960); WAKE ME WHEN IT'S OVER(1960); YOUNG SAVAGES, THE(1961); INVASION OF THE ANIMAL PEOPLE(1962, U.S./Swed.); JUMBO(1962); MANCHURIAN CANDIDATE, THE(1962); SWEET BIRD OF YOUTH(1962); SLIME PEOPLE, THE(1963); REASON TO LIVE, A REASON TO DIE, A(1974, Ital./Fr./Ger./Span.); BUCKTOWN(1975)
Misc. Talkies
   KINGS OF THE HILL(1976)

Rosamund Burton
EDUCATING RITA(1983)

Sam Burton
CHEYENNE WILDCAT(1944)

Sarah Burton
GROUP, THE(1966)

Shelley Burton
THE BOSTON STRANGLER, THE(1968)

Shelly Burton
ELECTRIC HORSEMAN, THE(1979), w

Simone Burton
CANNONBALL RUN, THE(1981)

Sybil Burton
KITTY(1945)

Terry Burton
NEXT TO NO TIME(1960, Brit.)

Therese Burton
NOT WANTED ON VOYAGE(1957, Brit.)

Tom Burton
GHOST SHIP, THE(1943); GOVERNMENT GIRL(1943); FALCON OUT WEST, THE(1944); MADEMOISELLE FIFI(1944); MY PAL, WOLF(1944); YOUTH RUNS WILD(1944); HAVING WONDERFUL CRIME(1945)

Tony Burton
ASSAULT ON PRECINCT 13(1976); BINGO LONG TRAVELING ALL-STARS AND MOTOR KINGS, THE(1976); RIVER NIGER, THE(1976); ROCKY(1976); TRACKDOWN(1976); HEROES(1977); ROCKY II(1979); HUNTER, THE(1980); INSIDE MOVES(1980); SHINING, THE(1980); ROCKY III(1982)
Misc. Talkies
   BLACKJACK(1978)

Torrance Burton
Silents
   SHATTERED REPUTATIONS(1923)

Val Burton
DRUMS OF JEOPARDY(1931), md; MURDER AT MIDNIGHT(1931), md; LAST MILE, THE(1932), md; STRANGERS OF THE EVENING(1932), md; THOSE WE LOVE(1932), m; TOMBSTONE CANYON(1932), md; DEATH KISS, THE(1933), md; DELUGE(1933), m, md; STUDY IN SCARLET, A(1933), md; LORD JEFF(1938), w; TWO BRIGHT BOYS(1939), w; EARL OF PUDDLESTONE(1940), w; HULLABALOO(1940), w; MEET THE MISSUS(1940), w; ON THEIR OWN(1940), w; SCATTERBRAIN(1940), w; GLAMOUR BOY(1941), w; HENRY ALDRICH FOR PRESIDENT(1941), w; HENRY ALDRICH, EDITOR(1942), w; HENRY AND DIZZY(1942), w; HENRY ALDRICH HAUNTS A HOUSE(1943), w; HENRY ALDRICH SWINGS IT(1943), w; HENRY ALDRICH PLAYS CUPID(1944), w; HENRY ALDRICH'S LITTLE SECRET(1944), w; PARDON MY RHYTHM(1944), w; PASSPORT TO DESTINY(1944), w; YOU CAN'T RATION LOVE(1944), w; HONEYMOON AHEAD(1945), w; TIME OF THEIR LIVES, THE(1946), p, w; SMART POLITICS(1948), m/l; BEDTIME FOR BONZO(1951), w

Velera Burton
PAN-AMERICANA(1945)

W.C. "Mutt" Burton
BEING THERE(1979)

W.H. Burton
Misc. Silents
   RADIO-MANIA(1923)

Warren Burton
BABY BLUE MARINE(1976); WORLD'S GREATEST LOVER, THE(1977)

Wendell Burton
STERILE CUCKOO, THE(1969); FORTUNE AND MEN'S EYES(1971, U.S./Can.)

William A. Burton
Silents
   FIGHTING SMILE, THE(1925), w; EASY PICKINGS(1927), w

William Burton
Misc. Silents
   CY WHITTAKER'S WARD(1917); MAKERS OF MEN(1925)

Clee Burtonya
SHAFT(1971)

Robert M. Burtt
SKY PARADE(1936), w

Frederick Burtt
GENTLEMAN OF PARIS, A(1931); DOWN OUR STREET(1932, Brit.); JUST MY LUCK(1933, Brit.); PATH OF GLORY, THE(1934, Brit.); INSIDE THE ROOM(1935, Brit.); SILENT PASSENGER, THE(1935, Brit.); EDUCATED EVANS(1936, Brit.); IT'S IN THE BAG(1936, Brit.); LABURNUM GROVE(1936, Brit.); REMBRANDT(1936, Brit.); TWELVE GOOD MEN(1936, Brit.); DOCTOR SYN(1937, Brit.); FEATHER YOUR NEST(1937, Brit.); GYPSY(1937, Brit.); IT'S NOT CRICKET(1937, Brit.); VULTURE, THE(1937, Brit.); ALMOST A HONEYMOON(1938, Brit.); DANGEROUS MEDICINE(1938, Brit.); EVERYTHING HAPPENS TO ME(1938, Brit.); I SEE ICE(1938); MANY TANKS MR. ATKINS(1938, Brit.); SIMPLY TERRIFIC(1938, Brit.); SINGING COP, THE(1938, Brit.); ANYTHING TO DECLARE?(1939, Brit.); CONFIDENTIAL LADY(1939, Brit.); HIS BROTHER'S KEEPER(1939, Brit.); MURDER WILL OUT(1939, Brit.); GIRL MUST LIVE, A(1941, Brit.); MUCH TOO SHY(1942, Brit.); THIS WAS PARIS(1942, Brit.); DARK TOWER, THE(1943, Brit.); WE DIVE AT DAWN(1943, Brit.); I'LL BE YOUR SWEETHEART(1945, Brit.); NOTORIOUS GENTLEMAN(1945, Brit.); SILVER FLEET, THE(1945, Brit.); THEY KNEW MR. KNIGHT(1945, Brit.); NICHOLAS NICKLEBY(1947, Brit.); SHOWTIME(1948, Brit.); LAUGHING LADY, THE(1950, Brit.); INHERITANCE, THE(1951, Brit.); MEN OF THE SEA(1951, Brit.)

Fredrick Burtwell
FRENCH LEAVE(1937, Brit.)

Stephen H. Burum
DEATH VALLEY(1982), ph; ENTITY, THE(1982), ph; ESCAPE ARTIST, THE(1982), ph; OUTSIDERS, THE(1983), ph; RUMBLE FISH(1983), ph; SOMETHING WICKED THIS WAY COMES(1983), ph; UNCOMMON VALOR(1983), ph
1984
   BODY DOUBLE(1984), ph

Steve Burum
WILD GYPSIES(1969), ph

Sandra Burville
STOP THE WORLD–I WANT TO GET OFF(1966, Brit.)

Gordon Burwash
SINS OF THE FATHERS(1948, Can.), w

Carter Burwell
1984
   BLOOD SIMPLE(1984), m

Faith Burwell
NEW FACES(1954); ONE POTATO, TWO POTATO(1964)

Myra Burwell
Misc. Silents
   TEN NIGHTS IN A BARROOM(1926)

John Bury
CASTLE OF EVIL(1967), set d; HOMECOMING, THE(1973), prod d

Jonathan Bury
SPY WHO LOVED ME, THE(1977, Brit.)

Sean Bury
IF ...(1968, Brit.); ABOMINABLE DR. PHIBES, THE(1971, Brit.); FRIENDS(1971, Brit.); PAUL AND MICHELLE(1974, Fr./Brit.); SPY WHO LOVED ME, THE(1977, Brit.)

Norman Burza
SUPPORT YOUR LOCAL SHERIFF(1969), cos; STRAWBERRY STATEMENT, THE(1970), cos; FIRE SALE(1977), cos
1984
   GREMLINS(1984), cos; TEACHERS(1984), cos

S. Burzynski
BEADS OF ONE ROSARY, THE(1982, Pol.), art d

Zenon Burzynski
GUESTS ARE COMING(1965, Pol.)

L. Bus-Fekete
CASBAH(1948), w

Ladislas Bus-Fekete
REUNION IN FRANCE(1942), w

Ladislaus Bus-Fekete
LADIES IN LOVE(1936), w; BARONESS AND THE BUTLER, THE(1938), w; PERFECT STRANGERS(1950), w

Lazlo Bus-Fekete
HEAVEN CAN WAIT(1943), w

Ladislaus Bus-Fekets
APPOINTMENT FOR LOVE(1941), w

Jean Busada
VOICES(1979)

Ivan Busatt
OVERTURE TO GLORY(1940)

Mary Beth Busbee
SHARKY'S MACHINE(1982)

The Busboys
48 HOURS(1982)

Bert Busby
Misc. Silents
   RIVER OF ROMANCE, THE(1916); PARENTAGE(1918)

Bob Busby
HOLIDAY CAMP(1947, Brit.), m; WATERLOO ROAD(1949, Brit.), m

Gerald Busby
THREE WOMEN(1977), m; WEDDING, A(1978)

Jane Busby
RETURN OF THE JEDI(1983)

John Busby
NIGHT TRAIN TO PARIS(1964, Brit.)

Matt Busby
CUP FEVER(1965, Brit.)

Tom Busby
NEVER TAKE CANDY FROM A STRANGER(1961, Brit.); DURING ONE NIGHT(1962, Brit.); WAR LOVER, THE(1962, U.S./Brit.); VICTORS, THE(1963); DIRTY DOZEN, THE(1967, Brit.)

Zane Busby
SMORGASBORD(1983)

Angelo Buscaglia
MY BODYGUARD(1980)
G.B. Buscemi
RAIN FOR A DUSTY SUMMER(1971, U.S./Span.), p, w
Bettina Busch
FANTASTIC THREE, THE(1967, Ital./Ger./Fr./Yugo.)
Dick Busch
HOUND OF THE BASKERVILLES, THE(1980, Brit.), ph
Ernest Busch
HELL ON EARTH(1934, Ger.)
Ernst Busch
THREEPENNY OPERA, THE(1931, Ger./U.S.); CASE VAN GELDERN(1932, Ger.)
Gustel Busch
TOXI(1952, Ger.)
Gustl Busch
FAUST(1963, Ger.)
Judy Busch
ROCKABILLY BABY(1957)
Mae Busch
ALIBI(1929); YOUNG DESIRE(1930); DEFENDERS OF THE LAW(1931); WICKED(1931); DOCTOR X(1932); HEART PUNCH(1932); MAN CALLED BACK, THE(1932); RIDER OF DEATH VALLEY(1932); SCARLET DAWN(1932); WITHOUT HONORS(1932); BLONDIE JOHNSON(1933); CHEATING BLONDES(1933); DANCE, GIRL, DANCE(1933); LILLY TURNER(1933); OUT ALL NIGHT(1933); RACING STRAIN, THE(1933); SONS OF THE DESERT(1933); SUCKER MONEY(1933); WOMEN WON'T TELL(1933); BELOVED(1934); I LIKE IT THAT WAY(1934); PICTURE BRIDES(1934); ROAD TO RUIN(1934); AFFAIR OF SUSAN(1935); STRANDED(1935); BOHEMIAN GIRL, THE(1936); DAUGHTER OF SHANGHAI(1937); MARIE ANTOINETTE(1938); NANCY DREW–DETECTIVE(1938); PRISON FARM(1938); WOMEN WITHOUT NAMES(1940); ZIEGFELD GIRL(1941); HELLO ANNAPOLIS(1942); MAD MONSTER, THE(1942); STORK CLUB, THE(1945); BLUE DAHLIA, THE(1946); CROSS MY HEART(1946)
Misc. Talkies
SECRETS OF HOLLYWOOD(1933)
Silents
GRIM GAME, THE(1919); DEVIL'S PASSKEY, THE(1920); FOOLISH WIVES(1920); LOVE CHARM, THE(1921); ONLY A SHOP GIRL(1922); PARDON MY NERVE!(1922); SOULS FOR SALE(1923); MARRIED FLIRTS(1924); NELLIE, THE BEAUTIFUL CLOAK MODEL(1924); UNHOLY THREE, THE(1925); WOMAN WHO SINNED, A(1925); NUT-CRACKER, THE(1926); HUSBAND HUNTERS(1927); WHILE THE CITY SLEEPS(1928); MAN'S MAN, A(1929)
Misc. Silents
HER HUSBAND'S FRIEND(1920); BROTHERS UNDER THE SKIN(1922); CHRISTIAN, THE(1923); BREAD(1924); BROKEN BARRIERS(1924); NAME THE MAN(1924); SHOOTING OF DAN MCGREW, THE(1924); TRIFLERS, THE(1924); CAMILLE OF THE BARBARY COAST(1925); FRIVOLOUS SAL(1925); TIME, THE COMEDIAN(1925); FOOLS OF FASHION(1926); MIRACLE OF LIFE, THE(1926); TRUTHFUL SEX, THE(1926); BEAUTY SHOPPERS(1927); PERCH OF THE DEVIL(1927); TONGUES OF SCANDAL(1927); BLACK BUTTERFLIES(1928); FAZIL(1928); SAN FRANCISCO NIGHTS(1928)
Marie Busch
MY FAIR LADY(1964)
Nevin Busch
MISS PINKERTON(1932), w
Niven Busch
CROWD ROARS, THE(1932), w; SCARLET DAWN(1932), w; COLLEGE COACH(1933), w; BABBITT(1934), w; BIG SHAKEDOWN, THE(1934), w; HE WAS HER MAN(1934), w; MAN WITH TWO FACES, THE(1934), w; IN OLD CHICAGO(1938), w; ANGELS WASH THEIR FACES(1939), w; OFF THE RECORD(1939), w; WESTERNER, THE(1940), w; BELLE STARR(1941), w; DUEL IN THE SUN(1946), w; POSTMAN ALWAYS RINGS TWICE, THE(1946), w; TILL THE END OF TIME(1946), w; MOSS ROSE(1947), w; PURSUED(1947), w; CAPTURE, THE(1950), p, w; FURIES, THE(1950), w; DISTANT DRUMS(1951), w; MAN FROM THE ALAMO, THE(1953), w; MOONLIGHTER, THE(1953), w; TREASURE OF PANCHO VILLA, THE(1955), w
Paul Busch
FANTASIA(1940), anim; CHINA GATE(1957); PARATROOP COMMAND(1959); VERBOTEN!(1959); JUDGMENT AT NUREMBERG(1961); PRIZE, THE(1963); 36 HOURS(1965); DEVIL'S BRIGADE, THE(1968); IN ENEMY COUNTRY(1968)
Rickey Busch
SNOW QUEEN, THE(1959, USSR)
Robert Busch
GREATEST STORY EVER TOLD, THE(1965)
Walther Busch
1984
WOMAN IN FLAMES, A(1984, Ger.)
Eda Buschatzky
"RENT-A-GIRL"(1965), set d
Brian Buschel
SPY OF NAPOLEON(1939, Brit.)
Joey Buschmann
GERMANY IN AUTUMN(1978, Ger.)
Walter Buschoff
FOUNTAIN OF LOVE, THE(1968, Aust.)
Renata Buser
YENTL(1983)
Giovanna Busetti
LA DOLCE VITA(1961, Ital./Fr.)
Massimo Busetti
LA DOLCE VITA(1961, Ital./Fr.)
Gary Busey
ANGELS HARD AS THEY COME(1971); DIRTY LITTLE BILLY(1972); MAGNIFICENT SEVEN RIDE, THE(1972); HEX(1973); LAST AMERICAN HERO, THE(1973); LOLLY-MADONNA XXX(1973); THUNDERBOLT AND LIGHTFOOT(1974); GUMBALL RALLY, THE(1976); STAR IS BORN, A(1976); BIG WEDNESDAY(1978); BUDDY HOLLY STORY, THE(1978); STRAIGHT TIME(1978); CARNY(1980); FOOLIN' AROUND(1980); BARBAROSA(1982); D.C. CAB(1983)
1984
BEAR, THE(1984)

Misc. Talkies
DIDN'T YOU HEAR(1983)
Jacob Busey
STRAIGHT TIME(1978)
Tim Busfield
1984
REVENGE OF THE NERDS(1984)
Timothy Busfield
STRIPES(1981)
Howard Busgang
TERROR TRAIN(1980, Can.)
Anita Bush
Misc. Silents
CRIMSON SKULL, THE(1921)
Arthur Bush
DICK BARTON–SPECIAL AGENT(1948, Brit.)
Billy Green Bush
FIVE EASY PIECES(1970); MONTE WALSH(1970); JESUS TRIP, THE(1971); ORGANIZATION, THE(1971); CULPEPPER CATTLE COMPANY, THE(1972); MISTER BROWN(1972); WELCOME HOME, SOLDIER BOYS(1972); ELECTRA GLIDE IN BLUE(1973); FORTY CARATS(1973); ALICE DOESN'T LIVE HERE ANYMORE(1975); MACKINTOSH & T.J.(1975); TOM HORN(1980)
1984
RIVER, THE(1984)
Clark Bush
Misc. Talkies
GUNSMOKE(1947)
David Bush
DAISY MILLER(1974)
Dick Bush
OKLAHOMA FRONTIER(1939); ALL THE WAY UP(1970, Brit.), ph; BLOOD ON SATAN'S CLAW, THE(1970, Brit.), ph; TAKE A GIRL LIKE YOU(1970, Brit.), ph; TOOMORROW(1970, Brit.), ph; TWINS OF EVIL(1971, Brit.), ph; WHEN DINOSAURS RULED THE EARTH(1971, Brit.), ph; DRACULA A.D. 1972(1972, Brit.), ph; OUR MISS FRED(1972, Brit.), ph; SAVAGE MESSIAH(1972, Brit.), ph; MAHLER(1974, Brit.), ph; PHASE IV(1974), ph; IN CELEBRATION(1975, Brit.), ph; TOMMY(1975, Brit.), ph; SORCERER(1977), ph; LEGACY, THE(1979, Brit.), ph; YANKS(1979), ph; FALLING IN LOVE AGAIN(1980), ph; ONE-TRICK PONY(1980), ph; FAN, THE(1981), ph; TRAIL OF THE PINK PANTHER, THE(1982), ph; VICTOR/VICTORIA(1982), ph; CURSE OF THE PINK PANTHER(1983), ph
1984
CRIMES OF PASSION(1984), ph; PHILADELPHIA EXPERIMENT, THE(1984), ph
Dorothy Bush
MERRY COMES TO STAY(1937, Brit.)
Doug Bush
MARRIED COUPLE, A(1969, Can.), m
Eddie Bush
WORDS AND MUSIC(1929)
Gilmore Bush
FIRST TRAVELING SALESLADY, THE(1956); SCARLET HOUR, THE(1956)
Grand Bush
NIGHT SHIFT(1982); VICE SQUAD(1982)
Misc. Talkies
HARD FEELINGS(1981)
Grand L. Bush
1984
STREETS OF FIRE(1984); WEEKEND PASS(1984)
James Bush
IF I HAD A MILLION(1932); WILD HORSE MESA(1932); GREAT JASPER, THE(1933); ONE MAN'S JOURNEY(1933); WORKING MAN, THE(1933); AGAINST THE LAW(1934); BATTLE OF GREED(1934); BEGGARS IN ERMINE(1934); CRIMSON ROMANCE(1934); EIGHT GIRLS IN A BOAT(1934); HOUSE OF DANGER(1934); MERRY FRINKS, THE(1934); YOUNG AND BEAUTIFUL(1934); ARIZONIAN, THE(1935); FRECKLES(1935); HARMONY LANE(1935); LADY IN SCARLET, THE(1935); RENDEZVOUS AT MIDNIGHT(1935); RETURN OF PETER GRIMM, THE(1935); SHOT IN THE DARK, A(1935); STRANGERS ALL(1935); M'LISS(1936); O'MALLEY OF THE MOUNTED(1936); GLORY TRAIL, THE(1937); GOOD OLD SOAK, THE(1937); I COVER THE WAR(1937); INTERNES CAN'T TAKE MONEY(1937); OUTLAWS OF THE ORIENT(1937); 100 MEN AND A GIRL(1937); COME ON, LEATHERNECKS(1938); CRASHIN' THRU DANGER(1938); I AM THE LAW(1938); SKY GIANT(1938); FAMILY NEXT DOOR, THE(1939); GONE WITH THE WIND(1939); JOE AND ETHEL TURP CALL ON THE PRESIDENT(1939); THEY ASKED FOR IT(1939); YOU CAN'T CHEAT AN HONEST MAN(1939); BEYOND TOMORROW(1940); KILLERS OF THE WILD(1940); SO ENDS OUR NIGHT(1941); WEST OF CIMARRON(1941); A-HAUNTING WE WILL GO(1942); ICELAND(1942); SUNDOWN JIM(1942); AIR FORCE(1943); HANGMEN ALSO DIE(1943); HE HIRED THE BOSS(1943); HERS TO HOLD(1943); IDAHO(1943); KING OF THE COWBOYS(1943); SPOTLIGHT SCANDALS(1943); BIG NOISE, THE(1944); CALL OF THE JUNGLE(1944); SHINE ON, HARVEST MOON(1944); THEY MADE ME A KILLER(1946); OUT OF THE PAST(1947); HOMECOMING(1948); MAN FROM COLORADO, THE(1948); RACE STREET(1948); MASSACRE RIVER(1949); CONVICTED(1950); LAWLESS, THE(1950); SADDLE LEGION(1951)
Misc. Talkies
TOPA TOPA(1938)
James H. Bush
CEILNG ZERO(1935); NIGHT OF MYSTERY(1937)
Jimmy Bush
GIRL, A GUY AND A GOB, A(1941)
Josef Bush
NAKED WITCH, THE(1964)
Jovita Bush
Misc. Talkies
CHEERLEADERS, THE(1973); FOX STYLE(1973)
Karla Bush
PENNIES FROM HEAVEN(1981)
Lucy Bush
ENTER THE NINJA(1982)

Mae Bush
MASQUERADE IN MEXICO(1945)
Maurice Bush
LAUGHING ANNE(1954, Brit./U.S.)
Mike Bush
STALAG 17(1953)
Morris Bush
SCARS OF DRACULA, THE(1970, Brit.)
Nora Bush
VALLEY OF VENGEANCE(1944); FIRST TRAVELING SALESLADY, THE(1956)
Norman Bush
SUPER COPS, THE(1974); THREE DAYS OF THE CONDOR(1975)
1984
MUPPETS TAKE MANHATTAN, THE(1984)
Owen Bush
CAGE OF EVIL(1960); MA BARKER'S KILLER BROOD(1960); ROUSTABOUT(1964);
VANISHING POINT(1971); MAN WHO LOVED CAT DANCING, THE(1973); SKATE-
BOARD(1978); DREAMER(1979)
1984
LAST STARFIGHTER, THE(1984)
Pauline Bush
Silents
ENEMY SEX, THE(1924)
Misc. Silents
FORBIDDEN ROOM, THE(1914); RICHELIEU(1914)
Robert Bush
ELEPHANT MAN, THE(1980, Brit.); URBAN COWBOY(1980)
Robin Michel Bush
1984
STARMAN(1984), cos
Roger Bush
FARMER'S OTHER DAUGHTER, THE(1965)
Roy Bush
DRAMATIC SCHOOL(1938)
Terry Bush
MERRY WIVES OF TOBIAS ROUKE, THE(1972, Can.), m
Tom Bush
GETAWAY, THE(1972)
L. Bush-Fekete
GIRL NEXT DOOR, THE(1953), w
Ladislas Bush-Fekete
PEPE(1960), w
Laslo Bush-Fekete
LYDIA(1941), w
Jack Bushanman
HAPPIDROME(1943, Brit.), p
Bert Bushby
Misc. Silents
TEMPTATION AND THE MAN(1916)
Beverly Bushe
CORNERED(1945)
Anthony Bushell
DISRAELI(1929); FLIRTING WIDOW, THE(1930); JOURNEY'S END(1930); LOVIN'
THE LADIES(1930); THREE FACES EAST(1930); BORN TO LOVE(1931); CHAN-
CES(1931); EXPENSIVE WOMEN(1931); FIVE STAR FINAL(1931); ROYAL BED,
THE(1931); ESCAPADE(1932); MIDSHIPMAID GOB(1932, Brit.); SALLY BISH-
OP(1932, Brit.); SHOP ANGEL(1932); VANITY FAIR(1932); WOMAN COMMANDS,
A(1932); CRIME ON THE HILL(1933, Brit.); CHANNEL CROSSING(1934, Brit.);
GHOUL, THE(1934, Brit.); I WAS A SPY(1934, Brit.); LILIES OF THE FIELD(1934,
Brit.); WOMAN IN COMMAND, THE(1934 Brit.); ADMIRALS ALL(1935, Brit.);
SCARLET PIMPERNEL, THE(1935, Brit.); DARK JOURNEY(1937, Brit.); WHO
KILLED FEN MARKHAM?(1937, Brit.); FORBIDDEN TERRITORY(1938, Brit.); GIRL
THIEF, THE(1938); HIDEOUT IN THE ALPS(1938, Brit.); RETURN OF THE SCARLET
PIMPERNEL(1938, Brit.); TROOPSHIP(1938, Brit.); ARSENAL STADIUM MYSTERY,
THE(1939, Brit.); REBEL SON, THE ½(1939, Brit.); LION HAS WINGS, THE(1940,
Brit.); FOR THOSE IN PERIL(1944, Brit.); HAMLET(1948, Brit.); HOUR OF GLO-
RY(1949, Brit.); ANGEL WITH THE TRUMPET, THE(1950, Brit.), a, d; MINIVER
STORY, THE(1950, Brit./U.S.); HIGH TREASON(1951, Brit.); LONG DARK HALL,
THE(1951, Brit.), a, d; PASSIONATE SENTRY, THE(1952, Brit.); BLACK KNIGHT,
THE(1954); PARATROOPER(1954, Brit.); PURPLE PLAIN, THE(1954, Brit.); BLACK
TENT, THE(1956, Brit.); RICHARD III(1956, Brit.), d; PURSUIT OF THE GRAF
SPEE(1957, Brit.); BITTER VICTORY(1958, Fr.); NIGHT TO REMEMBER, A(1958,
Brit.); WIND CANNOT READ, THE(1958, Brit.); DESERT MICE(1960, Brit.); TERROR
OF THE TONGS, THE(1961, Brit.), d; QUEEN'S GUARDS, THE(1963, Brit.)
David Bushell
CRY FROM THE STREET, A(1959, Brit.)
Gordon Bushell
DARTS ARE TRUMPS(1938, Brit.), w
Ted Bushell
INFORMATION RECEIVED(1962, Brit.)
Jeff Bushelman
CAT MURKIL AND THE SILKS(1976), ed
John A. Bushelman
HELL BOUND(1957), ed; JUNGLE HEAT(1957), ed; TOMAHAWK TRAIL(1957), ed;
WAR DRUMS(1957), ed; DRAGSTRIP RIOT(1958), ed; FORT BOWIE(1958), ed;
FRANKENSTEIN 1970(1958), ed; DINOSAURUS(1960), ed; THIRD VOICE,
THE(1960), ed
John Bushelman
CAT WOMEN OF THE MOON(1953), ed; KING DINOSAUR(1955), ed; THIRTEEN
FIGHTING MEN(1960), ed; FEAR NO MORE(1961), ed; SILENT CALL, THE(1961), ed;
SNIPER'S RIDGE(1961), p&d; WILD YOUTH(1961), p; BROKEN LAND, THE(1962),
d; DAY OF THE NIGHTMARE(1965), d; VILLAGE OF THE GIANTS(1965), ed;
PICTURE MOMMY DEAD(1966), ed; WAY OUT(1966), ed; DAUGHTERS OF SA-
TAN(1972), w; CAT MURKIL AND THE SILKS(1976), d
Piero Bushin
HURRICANE(1979)
Joe Bushkin
RAT RACE, THE(1960)

Bruce Bushman
GENTLE GIANT(1967), art d
Francis X. Bushman
CALL OF THE CIRCUS(1930); DUDE WRANGLER, THE(1930); GIRL SAID NO,
THE(1930); ONCE A GENTLEMAN(1930); WATCH BEVERLY(1932, Brit.); HOLLY-
WOOD BOULEVARD(1936); MR. CELEBRITY(1942); SILVER QUEEN(1942); WIL-
SON(1944); DAVID AND BATHSHEBA(1951); HOLLYWOOD STORY(1951); APACHE
COUNTRY(1952); BAD AND THE BEAUTIFUL, THE(1952); SABRINA(1954); STORY
OF MANKIND, THE(1957); TWELVE TO THE MOON(1960); PHANTOM PLANET,
THE(1961); PEER GYNT(1965); GHOST IN THE INVISIBLE BIKINI(1966)
Silents
PENNINGTON'S CHOICE(1915); SECOND IN COMMAND, THE(1915); SILENT
VOICE, THE(1915); SLIM PRINCESS, THE(1915); ADOPTED SON, THE(1917); PAIR
OF CUPIDS, A(1918); GOD'S OUTLAW(1919); MODERN MARRIAGE(1923); BEN-
HUR(1925); MARRIAGE CLAUSE, THE(1926); MIDNIGHT LIFE(1928)
Misc. Silents
ONE WONDERFUL NIGHT(1914); GRAUSTARK(1915); IN THE DIPLOMATIC
SERVICE(1916), a, d; MAN AND HIS SOUL(1916); MILLION A MINUTE, A(1916);
ROMEO AND JULIET(1916), a, d; WALL BETWEEN, THE(1916); THEIR COM-
PACT(1917); VOICE OF CONSCIENCE, THE(1917); BRASS CHECK, THE(1918);
CYCLONE HIGGINS, D.D.(1918); POOR RICH MAN, THE(1918); RED, WHITE AND
BLUE BLOOD(1918); SOCIAL QUICKSANDS(1918); UNDER SUSPICION(1918); WITH
NEATNESS AND DISPATCH(1918); DARING HEARTS(1919); MASKED BRIDE,
THE(1925); WHO'S YOUR FRIEND(1925); LADY IN ERMINE, THE(1927); THIR-
TEENTH JUROR, THE(1927); CHARGE OF THE GAUCHOS, THE(1928); GRIP OF
THE YUKON, THE(1928); SAY IT WITH SABLES(1928)
Francis X. Bushman, Jr.
SINS OF THE CHILDREN(1930); THEY LEARNED ABOUT WOMEN(1930); WAY
OUT WEST(1930); CYCLONE KID(1931); HUMAN TARGETS(1932); DEATH OF THE
DIAMOND(1934); MURDER MAN(1935); CARYL OF THE MOUNTAINS(1936); MAN-
PROOF(1938); SHINING HOUR, THE(1938); HONKY TONK(1941); CROSS-
ROADS(1942)
Misc. Talkies
TANGLED FORTUNES(1932)
Silents
PRIDE OF THE FORCE, THE(1925); BROWN OF HARVARD(1926); EYES
RIGHT(1926); FOUR SONS(1928)
Misc. Silents
AWAY IN THE LEAD(1925); NEVER TOO LATE(1925); DANGEROUS TRAF-
FIC(1926); MIDNIGHT FACES(1926); UNDERSTANDING HEART, THE(1927); MARL-
IE THE KILLER(1928)
Lenore Bushman
JUST A GIGOLO(1931); RED RIVER RANGE(1938)
Misc. Silents
LOVE WAGER, THE(1927)
Ralph Bushman [Francis X. Bushman, Jr.]
VIVA VILLA!(1934); I FOUND STELLA PARISH(1935); THREE COMRADES(1938);
LOVE CRAZY(1941)
Silents
OUR HOSPITALITY(1923)
Susan Bushman
PSYCH-OUT(1968)
Adelyn Bushnell
LAUGHING AT TROUBLE(1937), w
Anthony Bushnell
RED WAGON(1936)
Scott Bushnell
THIEVES LIKE US(1974), cons; QUINTET(1979), cos; POPEYE(1980), cos; COME
BACK TO THE 5 & DIME, JIMMY DEAN, JIMMY DEAN(1982), p; STREA-
MERS(1983), cos
William H. Bushnell, Jr.
FOUR DEUCES, THE(1976), d
Misc. Talkies
PRISONERS(1975), d
Bert Bushy
Misc. Silents
UNDER SOUTHERN SKIES(1915)
Akosua Busia
FINAL TERROR, THE(1983)
Marion Busia
GONE IN 60 SECONDS(1974)
Lori Busk
MAURIE(1973)
Speirs Buskell
DARK VICTORY(1939)
Bessie Buskirk
Misc. Silents
HOUSE BUILT UPON SAND, THE(1917)
Hattie Buskirk
Misc. Silents
GIRL FROM BEYOND, THE(1918)
Hattis Buskirk
Silents
MAID OF THE WEST(1921)
Jessie Busley
PERSONAL MAID(1931); BROTHER RAT(1938); KING OF THE UNDER-
WORLD(1939); BROTHER RAT AND A BABY(1940); ESCAPE TO GLORY(1940); IT
ALL CAME TRUE(1940)
Gail Busman
TAKING OFF(1971)
Thomas Buson
DIAMOND SAFARI(1958)
Manlio Busoni
TOO BAD SHE'S BAD(1954, Ital.); DIARY OF A SCHIZOPHRENIC GIRL(1970, Ital.)
Narciso Busquets
DEMONOID(1981)
Carl A. Buss
WAGON WHEELS(1934), w

Jodi Buss
1984
CHOOSE ME(1984)
Livio Bussa
MONTE CASSINO(1948, Ital.)
Mark Bussan
DEATHMASTER, THE(1972), spec eff; JEKYLL AND HYDE...TOGETHER AGAIN(1982), makeup
Henry Busse
LADY, LET'S DANCE(1944); FABULOUS DORSEYS, THE(1947)
Joe Busse
Misc. Talkies
WOMEN FOR SALE(1975)
Norma Busse
NEVER WAVE AT A WAC(1952)
Reinout Bussemaker
1984
FOURTH MAN, THE(1984, Neth.)
Susan Busset
BABY, IT'S YOU(1983)
C. V. Bussey
MAN FROM NEW MEXICO, THE(1932)
Donia Bussey
TIGER WOMAN, THE(1945); INVISIBLE INFORMER(1946); MAGNIFICENT ROGUE, THE(1946); PASSKEY TO DANGER(1946); HONEYCHILE(1951)
Fargo Bussey
HELL FIRE AUSTIN(1932); GHOST PATROL(1936); LUCKY TERROR(1936)
Solange Bussi
THREEPENNY OPERA, THE(1931, Ger./U.S.), w
Bussieres
PORTRAIT OF INNOCENCE(1948, Fr.)
Raymond Bussieres
THEY ARE NOT ANGELS(1948, Fr.); CHILDREN OF CHAOS(1950, Fr.); GATES OF THE NIGHT(1950, Fr.); JUST ME(1950, Fr.); ALICE IN WONDERLAND(1951, Fr.); LES BELLES-DE-NUIT(1952, Fr.); BEDEVILLED(1955); CASQUE D'OR(1956, Fr.); GATES OF PARIS(1958, Fr./Ital.); GUINGUETTE(1959, Fr.); FANNY(1961); LOVE AT NIGHT(1961, Fr.); PEEK-A-BOO(1961, Fr.); WONDERS OF ALADDIN, THE(1961, Fr./Ital.); THREE FABLES OF LOVE(1963, Fr./Ital./Span.); PARIS WHEN IT SIZZLES(1964); UP FROM THE BEACH(1965); COUNTERFEIT CONSTABLE, THE(1966, Fr.); GIRL GAME(1968, Braz./Fr./Ital.); JONAH–WHO WILL BE 25 IN THE YEAR 2000(1976, Switz.)
Esther Bussler
SIDELONG GLANCES OF A PIGEON KICKER, THE(1970)
Raffaello Rossi Bussola
MARRIAGE–ITALIAN STYLE(1964, Fr./Ital.)
Ettore Bussoli
WHITE SISTER(1973, Ital./Span./Fr.)
Mark Busson
RETURN OF COUNT YORGA, THE(1971), makeup
Roger Bussonet
BARBER OF SEVILLE(1949, Fr.)
Bussy
LITTLE ARK, THE(1972)
Videt Bussy
GAS(1981, Can.)
Corinne Bustad
MEAL, THE(1975)
Maria Bustamante
YANCO(1964, Mex.)
Judith Bustany
ZERO TO SIXTY(1978), w
Budd Buster [George Selk]
BATTLE OF GREED(1934); CIRCLE OF DEATH(1935); CYCLONE RANGER(1935); LAWLESS BORDER(1935); WESTERN FRONTIER(1935); WILD MUSTANG(1935); DESERT GUNS(1936); DESERT JUSTICE(1936); RIDING AVENGER, THE(1936); SONG OF THE GRINGO(1936); TOLL OF THE DESERT(1936); ARIZONA DAYS(1937); BAR Z BAD MEN(1937); DOOMED AT SUNDOWN(1937); DRUMS OF DESTINY(1937); FIGHTING TEXAN(1937); GALLOPING DYNAMITE(1937); GUN LORDS OF STIRRUP BASIN(1937); GUN RANGER, THE(1937); GUNS IN THE DARK(1937); HEADIN' FOR THE RIO GRANDE(1937); HIT THE SADDLE(1937); LAWMAN IS BORN, A(1937); LEFT-HANDED LAW(1937); RAW TIMBER(1937); ROARING SIX GUNS(1937); SING, COWBOY, SING(1937); SINGING OUTLAW(1937); TRAIL OF VENGEANCE(1937); TRUSTED OUTLAW, THE(1937); UNDER STRANGE FLAGS(1937); WILD HORSE ROUND-UP(1937); COLORADO KID(1938); DESERT PATROL(1938); DURANGO VALLEY RAIDERS(1938); FEUD MAKER(1938); LAW COMMANDS, THE(1938); OLD LOUISIANA(1938); PAROLED–TO DIE(1938); ROLL ALONG, COWBOY(1938); SONGS AND BULLETS(1938); STRANGER FROM ARIZONA, THE(1938); THUNDER IN THE DESERT(1938); WHERE THE WEST BEGINS(1938); WHIRLWIND HORSEMAN(1938); COLORADO SUNSET(1939); DAUGHTER OF THE TONG(1939); FEUD OF THE RANGE(1939); FIGHTING RENEGADE(1939); FRONTIER SCOUT(1939); KNIGHT OF THE PLAINS(1939); LAW COMES TO TEXAS, THE(1939); LONE STAR PIONEERS(1939); WYOMING OUTLAW(1939); COURAGEOUS DR. CHRISTIAN, THE(1940); COVERED WAGON TRAILS(1940); DARK COMMAND, THE(1940); I TAKE THIS OATH(1940); MURDER ON THE YUKON(1940); PINTO CANYON(1940); ROCKY MOUNTAIN RANGERS(1940); STRAIGHT SHOOTER(1940); WEST OF PINTO BASIN(1940); BILLY THE KID WANTED(1941); BILLY THE KID'S FIGHTING PALS(1941); GANGS OF SONORA(1941); JESSE JAMES AT BAY(1941); LONE RIDER IN GHOST TOWN, THE(1941); SECRET EVIDENCE(1941); SIERRA SUE(1941); TEXAS MARSHAL, THE(1941); THUNDER OVER THE PRAIRIE(1941); TONTO BASIN OUTLAWS(1941); WEST OF CIMARRON(1941); BILLY THE KID TRAPPED(1942); DEEP IN THE HEART OF TEXAS(1942); DOWN RIO GRANDE WAY(1942); HEART OF THE RIO GRANDE(1942); LAW AND ORDER(1942); LONE STAR VIGILANTES, THE(1942); OVERLAND STAGECOACH(1942); ROCK RIVER RENEGADES(1942); SUNSET SERENADE(1942); TEXAS TO BATAAN(1942); THUNDER RIVER FEUD(1942); VALLEY OF HUNTED MEN(1942); WEST OF TOMBSTONE(1942); WESTWARD HO(1942); CATTLE STAMPEDE(1943); CHEYENNE ROUNDUP(1943); COWBOY COMMANDOS(1943); HAIL TO THE RANGERS(1943); HAUNTED RANCH, THE(1943); HITLER'S MADMAN(1943); OLD CHISHOLM TRAIL(1943); RAIDERS OF SAN JOAQUIN(1943); RAIDERS OF SUNSET PASS(1943); SANTA FE SCOUTS(1943);

THUNDERING TRAILS(1943); WOLVES OF THE RANGE(1943); BRAND OF THE DEVIL(1944); DEAD OR ALIVE(1944); FIREBRANDS OF ARIZONA(1944); FRONTIER OUTLAWS(1944); HIDDEN VALLEY OUTLAWS(1944); PINTO BANDIT, THE(1944); PRIDE OF THE PLAINS(1944); RIDERS OF THE SANTA FE(1944); THUNDERING GUN SLINGERS(1944); TRAIL OF TERROR(1944); TRIGGER TRAIL(1944); VALLEY OF VENGEANCE(1944); WILD HORSE PHANTOM(1944); APOLOGY FOR MURDER(1945); BORDER BADMEN(1945); CODE OF THE LAWLESS(1945); FIGHTING BILL CARSON(1945); FRONTIER FUGITIVES(1945); LONE TEXAS RANGER(1945); SALOME, WHERE SHE DANCED(1945); AMBUSH TRAIL(1946); FLYING SERPENT, THE(1946); GENTLEMEN WITH GUNS(1946); HOME ON THE RANGE(1946); HOODLUM SAINT, THE(1946); NAVAJO KID, THE(1946); OUTLAW OF THE PLAINS(1946); RUSTLER'S ROUNDUP(1946); SHERIFF OF REDWOOD VALLEY(1946); SIX GUN MAN(1946); SONG OF THE SIERRAS(1946); TERRORS ON HORSEBACK(1946); WEST OF THE ALAMO(1946); CHEYENNE TAKES OVER(1947); RAINBOW OVER THE ROCKIES(1947); SHADOW VALLEY(1947); VIGILANTES OF BOOMTOWN(1947); WILD FRONTIER, THE(1947); CHECK YOUR GUNS(1948); LOADED PISTOLS(1948); SIX-GUN LAW(1948); WESTWARD TRAIL, THE(1948); QUICK ON THE TRIGGER(1949); RIDING SHOTGUN(1954)
Misc. Talkies
SIX GUN JUSTICE(1935); TEXAS JACK(1935); TEXAS RAMBLER, THE(1935); VANISHING RIDERS(1935); WESTERN RACKETEERS(1935); BLAZING JUSTICE(1936); GUN GRIT(1936); BULLETS AND SADDLES(1943)
Budd L. Buster
MARKED MEN(1940)
John L. "Budd" Buster
PRAIRIE BADMEN(1946)
Buster Fite and His Six Saddle Tramps
ROLL ALONG, COWBOY(1938)
Buster The Dog
LUCKY DOG(1933); IT'S A GIFT(1934); NOW AND FOREVER(1934)
Buster the Horse
Silents
TUMBLING RIVER(1927)
Juan Bustillo Oro
MADCAP OF THE HOUSE(1950, Mex.), d, w
Antonio Bustos
TOAST TO LOVE(1951, Mex.), ed
Jorge Bustos
BRUTE, THE(1952, Mex.), ed; IMPORTANT MAN, THE(1961, Mex.), ed; CRIMINAL LIFE OF ARCHIBALDO DE LA CRUZ, THE(1962, Mex.), ed; DOCTOR OF DOOM(1962, Mex.), ed; EMPTY STAR, THE(1962, Mex.), ed; SHAME OF THE SABINE WOMEN, THE(1962, Mex.), ed; CURSE OF THE AZTEC MUMMY, THE(1965, Mex.), ed; ROBOT VS. THE AZTEC MUMMY, THE(1965, Mex.), ed; SPIRITISM(1965, Mex.), ed; TOM THUMB(1967, Mex.), ed; NIGHT OF THE BLOODY APES(1968, Mex.), ed
Jose Bustos
LAST REBEL, THE(1961, Mex.), ed; LITTLE RED RIDING HOOD(1963, Mex.), ed; QUEEN'S SWORDSMEN, THE(1963, Mex.), ed; LITTLE RED RIDING HOOD AND HER FRIENDS(1964, Mex.), ed; PUSS 'N' BOOTS(1964, Mex.), ed; LITTLE RED RIDING HOOD AND THE MONSTERS(1965, Mex.), ed; VAMPIRE, THE(1968, Mex.), ed
Jose W. Bustos
WHITE ORCHID, THE(1954), ed
Marujita Bustos
SOFT SKIN ON BLACK SILK(1964, Fr./Span.)
Butch & Buddy
LITTLE BIT OF HEAVEN, A(1940)
Butch and Buddy
SANDY IS A LADY(1940); SPRING PARADE(1940); JOHNNY DOUGHBOY(1943); LADY TAKES A CHANCE, A(1943)
Butch the Dog
MEET ME AT THE FAIR(1952)
Anne Butchart
AFFAIRS OF ADELAIDE(1949, U. S./Brit); BRAVE DON'T CRY, THE(1952, Brit.)
Ada Ruth Butcher
OUR HEARTS WERE GROWING UP(1946)
Arthur Butcher
COLDITZ STORY, THE(1955, Brit.)
Cyril Butcher
NIGHT BIRDS(1931, Brit.)
Dwight Butcher
RIDING HIGH(1943)
Edward Butcher
LAST OF THE DUANES(1930), p; BAD BOY(1935), p; IN OLD KENTUCKY(1935), p; IT'S A SMALL WORLD(1935), p; OUR LITTLE GIRL(1935), p
Edward W. Butcher
COUNTY CHAIRMAN, THE(1935), p
Ernest Butcher
KEY TO HARMONY(1935, Brit.); LIEUTENANT DARING, RN(1935, Brit.); SMALL MAN, THE(1935, Brit.); SONG OF THE ROAD(1937, Brit.); TALKING FEET(1937, Brit.); STEPPING TOES(1938, Brit.); ME AND MY PAL(1939, Brit.); OLD MOTHER RILEY IN BUSINESS(1940, Brit.); PACK UP YOUR TROUBLES(1940, Brit.); PIMPERNEL SMITH(1942, Brit.); IT'S IN THE BAG(1943, Brit.); WHEN WE ARE MARRIED(1943, Brit.); CANDLES AT NINE(1944, Brit.); IT HAPPENED ONE SUNDAY(1944, Brit.); DEAR MURDERER(1947, Brit.); TAWNY PIPIT(1947, Brit.); WHILE I LIVE(1947, Brit.); YEARS BETWEEN, THE(1947, Brit.); DIAMOND CITY(1949, Brit.); MEET SIMON CHERRY(1949, Brit.); MY BROTHER JONATHAN(1949, Brit.); HIGHLY DANGEROUS(1950, Brit.); MR. LORD SAYS NO(1952, Brit.); TERROR ON A TRAIN(1953); DESPERATE MAN, THE(1959, Brit.)
Joseph Butcher
HOLLYWOOD HIGH(1977)
Kim Butcher
FRIGHTMARE(1974, Brit.); CONFESSIONAL, THE(1977, Brit.)
Ambrosi Butchma
TARAS FAMILY, THE(1946, USSR)
Mary Ellen Bute
FINNEGANS WAKE(1965), p&d, w, ed

Walter "Doc" Butell
Silents
ONCE A PLUMBER(1920)
Lyudmila Butenina
DAY THE WAR ENDED, THE(1961, USSR)
Vladimir Butenko
WATERLOO(1970, Ital./USSR)
Claudia Butenuth
LAST VALLEY, THE(1971, Brit.); AMERICAN SUCCESS COMPANY, THE(1980)
Lou Butera
BALTIMORE BULLET, THE(1980)
1984
RACING WITH THE MOON(1984)
Sam Butera
RAT RACE, THE(1960); RAFFERTY AND THE GOLD DUST TWINS(1975)
Chief Buthelezi
ZULU(1964, Brit.)
Paul Butkevic
WATERLOO(1970, Ital./USSR)
Y. Butkova
Misc. Silents
DAYS OF OUR LIFE(1914, USSR)
Dick Butkus
GUS(1976); MOTHER, JUGS & SPEED(1976); SMORGASBORD(1983)
1984
JOHNNY DANGEROUSLY(1984)
Aaron C. Butler
1984
BLACK ROOM, THE(1984), p
Alexander Butler
MOUNTAINS O'MOURNE(1938, Brit.)
Silents
IN THE HANDS OF THE LONDON CROOKS(1913, Brit.), d; GIRL WHO LOVES A SOLDIER, THE(1916, Brit.), d; JUST A GIRL(1916, Brit.), d; JO THE CROSSING SWEEPER(1918, Brit.), d; ON LEAVE(1918, Brit.), d; ODDS AGAINST HER, THE(1919, Brit.), d; DAVID AND JONATHAN(1920, Brit.), d; HER STORY(1920, Brit.), d; KNOCKOUT, THE(1923, Brit.), d
Misc. Silents
FAIR IMPOSTER, A(1916, Brit.), d; PAIR OF SPECTACLES, A(1916, Brit.), d; VALLEY OF FEAR, THE(1916, Brit.), d; IN ANOTHER GIRL'S SHOES(1917, Brit.), d; LITTLE WOMEN(1917, Brit.), d; MY LADY'S DRESS(1917, Brit.), d; SORROWS OF SATAN, THE(1917, Brit.), d; BEETLE, THE(1919, Brit.), d; DAMAGED GOODS(1919, Brit.), d; DISAPPEARANCE OF THE JUDGE, THE(1919, Brit.), d; LAMP OF DESTINY(1919, Brit.), d; LIFE OF A LONDON ACTRESS, THE(1919, Brit.), d; THUNDERCLOUD, THE(1919, Brit.), d; LOVE IN THE WILDERNESS(1920, Brit.), d; NIGHT RIDERS, THE(1920, Brit.), d; UGLY DUCKLING, THE(1920, Brit.), d; FOR HER FATHER'S SAKE(1921, Brit.), d; MAISIE'S MARRIAGE(1923, Brit.), d; ROYAL DIVORCE, A(1923, Brit.), d; SHOULD A DOCTOR TELL?(1923, Brit.), d; NAPOLEON AND JOSEPHINE(1924, Brit.), d
Archie Butler
WYOMING(1940)
Artie Butler
LOVE MACHINE, THE,(1971), m; WHAT'S UP, DOC?(1972), m, md; HARRAD EXPERIMENT, THE(1973), m; AT LONG LAST LOVE(1975), md; RAFFERTY AND THE GOLD DUST TWINS(1975), m; FOR PETE'S SAKE(1977), m; RESCUERS, THE(1977), m; SEXTETTE(1978), m; O'HARA'S WIFE(1983), m
Assistant Butler
NINTH GUEST, THE(1934)
Barbara Butler
Silents
AMERICAN WAY, THE(1919); FLAPPER, THE(1920)
Barry Butler
STONE(1974, Aus.)
Betty Butler
FIGHTING COWBOY(1933); LIGHTNING RANGE(1934)
Bill Butler
FEARLESS FRANK(1967), ph; ONE MORE TIME(1970, Brit.), ed; CLOCKWORK ORANGE, A(1971, Brit.), ed; DRIVE, HE SAID(1971), ph; RETURN OF COUNT YORGA, THE(1971), ph; TOUCH OF CLASS, A(1973, Brit.), ph; CONVERSATION, THE(1974), ph; GREAT EXPECTATIONS(1975, Brit.), ed; JAWS(1975), ph; KILLER FORCE(1975, Switz./Ireland), ed; OLD DRACULA(1975, Brit.), ed; ONE FLEW OVER THE CUCKOO'S NEST(1975), ph; ALEX AND THE GYPSY(1976), ph; BINGO LONG TRAVELING ALL-STARS AND MOTOR KINGS, THE(1976), ph; BITTERSWEET LOVE(1976), ed; LIPSTICK(1976), ph; DEMON SEED(1977), ph; JOYRIDE(1977), ed; CAPRICORN ONE(1978), ph; DAMIEN—OMEN II(1978), ph; GREASE(1978), ph; ICE CASTLES(1978), ph; OUR WINNING SEASON(1978), ed; UNCLE JOE SHANNON(1978), ph; LOST AND FOUND(1979), ed; ROCKY II(1979), ph; CAN'T STOP THE MUSIC(1980), ph; GORP(1980), ed; HOW TO BEAT THE HIGH COST OF LIVING(1980), ed; IT'S MY TURN(1980), ph; NIGHT THE LIGHTS WENT OUT IN GEORGIA, THE(1981), ph; ON THE RIGHT TRACK(1981), ed; STRIPES(1981), ph; LITTLE SEX, A(1982), ed; ROCKY III(1982), ph; STING II, THE(1983), ph
1984
UP THE CREEK(1984), ed
Blake Butler
HELP!(1965, Brit.); LOVE IS A WOMAN(1967, Brit.); LOCK UP YOUR DAUGHTERS(1969, Brit.)
Bobby Butler
1984
BEAR, THE(1984)
Buddy Butler
PUTNEY SWOPE(1969); HI, MOM!(1970); SIDELONG GLANCES OF A PIGEON KICKER, THE(1970); WHERE'S POPPA?(1970)
Calvin Butler
CHICAGO 70(1970); CURTAINS(1983, Can.)
Carl Butler
SECOND FIDDLE TO A STEEL GUITAR(1965)
Carolyn Butler
DREAM GIRL(1947); VARIETY GIRL(1947)

Charles Butler
Silents
ARE YOU A MASON?(1915)
Charlie Butler
Silents
JOHN GLAYDE'S HONOR(1915)
Cindy Butler
GRAYEAGLE(1977); TOWN THAT DREADED SUNDOWN, THE(1977)
Claudia Butler
TELEFON(1977)
Crilly Butler
THAT'S MY BOY(1932)
Dave Butler
HOUSE OF WHIPCORD(1974, Brit.)
David Butler
FOX MOVIETONE FOLLIES(1929), d, w; SALUTE(1929), a, d; SUNNY SIDE UP(1929), d, w; HIGH SOCIETY BLUES(1930), d; JUST IMAGINE(1930), d, w; CONNECTICUT YANKEE, A(1931), d; BUSINESS AND PLEASURE(1932), d; DOWN TO EARTH(1932), d; HANDLE WITH CARE(1932), d, w; HOLD ME TIGHT(1933), d; MY WEAKNESS(1933), d, w; BOTTOMS UP(1934), d, w; BRIGHT EYES(1934), d, w; HANDY ANDY(1934), d; CAPTAIN JANUARY(1935), d; DOUBTING THOMAS(1935), d; LITTLE COLONEL, THE(1935), d; LITTLEST REBEL, THE(1935), d; PIGSKIN PARADE(1936), d; WHITE FANG(1936), d; ALI BABA GOES TO TOWN(1937), d; YOU'RE A SWEETHEART(1937), d; KENTUCKY(1938), d; KENTUCKY MOONSHINE(1938), d; STRAIGHT, PLACE AND SHOW(1938), d; EAST SIDE OF HEAVEN(1939), d, w; THAT'S RIGHT—YOU'RE WRONG(1939), p&d; IF I HAD MY WAY(1940), p&d, w; YOU'LL FIND OUT(1940), p&d; CAUGHT IN THE DRAFT(1941), d; PLAYMATES(1941), d, w; ROAD TO MOROCCO(1942), d; THANK YOUR LUCKY STARS(1943), a, d; THEY GOT ME COVERED(1943), d; PRINCESS AND THE PIRATE, THE(1944), d; SHINE ON, HARVEST MOON(1944), d; SAN ANTONIO(1945), d; TIME, THE PLACE AND THE GIRL, THE(1946), d; MY WILD IRISH ROSE(1947), d; TWO GUYS FROM TEXAS(1948), d; IT'S A GREAT FEELING(1949), a, d; JOHN LOVES MARY(1949), d; LOOK FOR THE SILVER LINING(1949), d; STORY OF SEABISCUIT, THE(1949), d; DAUGHTER OF ROSIE O'GRADY, THE(1950), d; TEA FOR TWO(1950), d; LULLABY OF BROADWAY, THE(1951), d; PAINTING THE CLOUDS WITH SUNSHINE(1951), d; WHERE'S CHARLEY?(1952, Brit.), d; APRIL IN PARIS(1953), d; BY THE LIGHT OF THE SILVERY MOON(1953), d; CALAMITY JANE(1953), d; COMMAND, THE(1954), d; KING RICHARD AND THE CRUSADERS(1954), d; GLORY(1955), p&d; JUMP INTO HELL(1955), d; GIRL HE LEFT BEHIND, THE(1956), d; RIGHT APPROACH, THE(1961), d; C'MON, LET'S LIVE A LITTLE(1967), d; CHRISTIAN LICORICE STORE, THE(1971), d; CRUCIBLE OF HORROR(1971, Brit.), d; SIMON, KING OF THE WITCHES(1971), ph; VOYAGE OF THE DAMNED(1976, Brit.), w; BEAR ISLAND(1980, Brit.-Can.), w; DANCE OF THE DWARFS(1983, U.S., Phil.), ph
Misc. Talkies
CHASING THROUGH EUROPE(1929), d
Silents
GREATEST THING IN LIFE, THE(1918); GIRL WHO STAYED AT HOME, THE(1919); NUGGET NELL(1919); PETAL ON THE CURRENT, THE(1919); FICKLE WOMEN(1920); GIRLS DON'T GAMBLE(1921); MAKING THE GRADE(1921); SKY PILOT, THE(1921); ACCORDING TO HOYLE(1922); FOG, THE(1923); HERO, THE(1923); NOISE IN NEWBORO, A(1923); POOR MEN'S WIVES(1923); ARIZONA EXPRESS, THE(1924); IN HOLLYWOOD WITH POTASH AND PERLMUTTER(1924); NARROW STREET, THE(1924); MAN ON THE BOX, THE(1925); PLASTIC AGE, THE(1925); WAGES FOR WIVES(1925); QUARTERBACK, THE(1926); WOMANPOWER(1926); NOBODY'S WIDOW(1927); RUSH HOUR, THE(1927); SEVENTH HEAVEN(1927); NEWS PARADE, THE(1928), d, w; PREP AND PEP(1928), d; MASKED EMOTIONS(1929), d
Misc. Silents
BETTER TIMES(1919); BONNIE, BONNIE LASSIE(1919); OTHER HALF, THE(1919); UNPAINTED WOMAN, THE(1919); UPSTAIRS AND DOWN(1919); COUNTY FAIR, THE(1920); TRIFLERS, THE(1920); SMILING ALL THE WAY(1921); BING BANG BOOM(1922); CONQUERING THE WOMAN(1922); MILKY WAY, THE(1922); WISE KID, THE(1922); CAUSE FOR DIVORCE(1923); DESIRE(1923); HOODMAN BLIND(1923); GOLD HUNTERS, THE(1925); HIS MAJESTY BUNKER BEAN(1925); PEOPLE VS. NANCY PRESTON, THE(1925); PHANTOM EXPRESS, THE(1925); PRIVATE AFFAIRS(1925); TRACKED IN THE SNOW COUNTRY(1925); OH, BABY!(1926); SAP, THE(1926); GIRL IN THE RAIN(1927); HIGH SCHOOL HERO(1927), d; WIN THAT GIRL(1928), d
David L. Butler
FRASIER, THE SENSUOUS LION(1973), ph
David W. Butler
Misc. Silents
DEATHLOCK, THE(1915)
Davis Butler
DELICIOUS(1931), d
Daws Butler
1001 ARABIAN NIGHTS(1959); HEY THERE, IT'S YOGI BEAR(1964); PHANTOM TOLLBOOTH, THE(1970)
Dick Butler
STUNTS(1977); HIGH COUNTRY, THE(1981, Can.)
Duke Butler
BUCK ROGERS IN THE 25TH CENTURY(1979)
Earlie J. Butler III
WANDERERS, THE(1979)
Eddie Butler
MY LITTLE CHICKADEE(1940)
Edith Butler
ODYSSEY OF THE PACIFIC(1983, Can./Fr.), m
Ellis Parker Butler
Silents
JACK KNIFE MAN, THE(1920), w
Eric Butler
THUMB TRIPPING(1972); H.O.T.S.(1979), art d
Ernest Butler
GAMBLER, THE(1974)
Eugene Butler
DIFFERENT STORY, A(1978); FORCE OF ONE, A(1979); I OUGHT TO BE IN PICTURES(1982)

F.R. Butler
Silents
SHEIK, THE(1921); BEYOND THE ROCKS(1922); MY AMERICAN WIFE(1923)
Misc. Silents
GREAT MOMENT, THE(1921)

Forrest T. Butler
OUT OF TOWNERS, THE(1970), cos

Frank Butler
UNTAMED(1929), w; MONTANA MOON(1930), w; NEW MOON(1930), w; STRICTLY UNCONVENTIONAL(1930), w; THOSE THREE FRENCH GIRLS(1930), w; THIS MODERN AGE(1931), w; FELLER NEEDS A FRIEND(1932), w; PROSPERITY(1932), w; COLLEGE HUMOR(1933), w; GIRL WITHOUT A ROOM(1933), w; WAY TO LOVE, THE(1933), w; WHITE WOMAN(1933), w; BABES IN TOYLAND(1934), w; LADIES SHOULD LISTEN(1934), w; SEARCH FOR BEAUTY(1934), w; BONNIE SCOTLAND(1935), w; CORONADO(1935), w; VAGABOND LADY(1935), w; MILKY WAY, THE(1936), w; PRINCESS COMES ACROSS, THE(1936), w; STRIKE ME PINK(1936), w; CHAMPAGNE WALTZ(1937), w; WAIKIKI WEDDING(1937), w; GIVE ME A SAILOR(1938), w; TROPIC HOLIDAY(1938), w; ISLAND OF LOST MEN(1939), w; NEVER SAY DIE(1939), w; PARIS HONEYMOON(1939), w; STAR MAKER, THE(1939), w; I WANT A DIVORCE(1940), w; RANGERS OF FORTUNE(1940), w; ROAD TO SINGAPORE(1940), w; UNTAMED(1940), w; ALOMA OF THE SOUTH SEAS(1941), w; ROAD TO ZANZIBAR(1941), w; BEYOND THE BLUE HORIZON(1942), w; MY FAVORITE BLONDE(1942), w; ROAD TO MOROCCO(1942), w; WAKE ISLAND(1942), w; CHINA(1943), w; HOSTAGES(1943), w; GOING MY WAY(1944), w; INCENDIARY BLONDE(1945), w; MEDAL FOR BENNY, A(1945), w; CALIFORNIA(1946), w; KID FROM BOOKLYN, THE(1946), w; GOLDEN EARRINGS(1947), w; PERILS OF PAULINE, THE(1947), w; VARIETY GIRL(1947); WELCOME STRANGER(1947), w; WHISPERING SMITH(1948), w; ROAD TO BALI(1952), w; STRANGE LADY IN TOWN(1955), w; MIRACLE, THE(1959), w
Silents
TAILOR MADE MAN, A(1922); CALL OF THE WILD, THE(1923); TIGER'S CLAW, THE(1923); KING OF THE WILD HORSES, THE(1924); COMPROMISE(1925); NO MAN'S LAW(1927), w; JUST MARRIED(1928), w
Misc. Silents
FIGHTING BUCKAROO, THE(1926); 30 BELOW ZERO(1926)

Fred Butler
Silents
DICTATOR, THE(1922); BLUFF(1924)
Misc. Silents
RED BLOOD AND BLUE(1925)

Fred J. Butler
Silents
FLYING TORPEDO, THE(1916); FICKLE WOMEN(1920), d; GIRLS DON'T GAMBLE(1921), d; MAKING THE GRADE(1921), d; ACCORDING TO HOYLE(1922); RACING HEARTS(1923); THREE WISE FOOLS(1923); WELCOME STRANGER(1924)
Misc. Silents
DEATHLOCK, THE(1915); LITTLE MEENA'S ROMANCE(1916); SUSAN ROCKS THE BOAT(1916); SMILING ALL THE WAY(1921), d; BING BANG BOOM(1922), d; BATTLING FOOL, THE(1924)

George Butler
CLOUDS OVER EUROPE(1939, Brit.)
Misc. Silents
WHEN IT WAS DARK(1919, Brit.)

Gerald Butler
FATAL NIGHT, THE(1948, Brit.), w; KISS THE BLOOD OFF MY HANDS(1948), w; THIRD TIME LUCKY(1950, Brit.), w; ON DANGEROUS GROUND(1951), w

Harold Butler
CHILDREN OF BABYLON(1980, Jamaica), m

Hugh Butler
OMAHA TRAIL, THE(1942), w; FIRST TIME, THE(1952), w

Hugo Butler
BIG CITY(1937), w; CHRISTMAS CAROL, A(1938), w; HUCKLEBERRY FINN(1939), w; SOCIETY LAWYER(1939), w; EDISON, THE MAN(1940), w; WYOMING(1940), w; YOUNG TOM EDISON(1940), w; BARNACLE BILL(1941), w; YANK ON THE BURMA ROAD, A(1942), w; LASSIE, COME HOME(1943), w; MISS SUSIE SLAGLE'S(1945), w; SOUTHERNER, THE(1945), w; FROM THIS DAY FORWARD(1946), w; ROUGHSHOD(1949), w; EYE WITNESS(1950, Brit.), w; WOMAN OF DISTINCTION, A(1950), w; HE RAN ALL THE WAY(1951), w; PROWLER, THE(1951), w; WORLD FOR RANSOM(1954), w; EVA(1962, Fr./Ital.), w; SODOM AND GOMORRAH(1962, U.S./Fr./Ital.), w; FACE IN THE RAIN, A(1963), w; LEGEND OF LYLAH CLARE, THE(1968), w

Jack Butler
PENNY POOL, THE(1937, Brit.); CALLING ALL CROOKS(1938, Brit.)

James Butler
NAVAL ACADEMY(1941)

Janet Butler
BROKEN HORSESHOE, THE(1953, Brit.); THERE WAS A YOUNG LADY(1953, Brit.)

Jay Butler
CARWASH(1976)

Jennifer Butler
1984
FIRESTARTER(1984), cos

Jerry Butler
MELINDA(1972), m; THING WITH TWO HEADS, THE(1972)
Misc. Talkies
IN LOVE(1983)

Jimmie Butler
AWAKENING OF JIM BURKE(1935)

Jimmy Butler
BATTLE OF GREED(1934); I'LL FIX IT(1934); MANHATTAN MELODRAMA(1934); MRS. WIGGS OF THE CABBAGE PATCH(1934); NO GREATER GLORY(1934); DARK ANGEL, THE(1935); DINKY(1935); LADDIE(1935); ROMANCE IN MANHATTAN(1935); WHEN A MAN'S A MAN(1935); EXCUSE MY GLOVE(1936, Brit.); COUNTY FAIR(1937); STELLA DALLAS(1937); WELLS FARGO(1937); BOYS TOWN(1938); SHOPWORN ANGEL(1938); CALL A MESSENGER(1939); ESCAPE, THE(1939); NURSE EDITH CAVELL(1939); WINTER CARNIVAL(1939); MILITARY ACADEMY(1940); TOUGH AS THEY COME(1942); GIRL CRAZY(1943); SOMEONE TO REMEMBER(1943); THIS IS THE ARMY(1943)

Jimmy Butler, Jr.
ONLY YESTERDAY(1933)

Joan Butler
OLD MOTHER RILEY AT HOME(1945, Brit.), w

John Butler
EXPENSIVE HUSBANDS(1937); SOME BLONDES ARE DANGEROUS(1937); ACCIDENTS WILL HAPPEN(1938); EXPOSED(1938); MARIE ANTOINETTE(1938); FRONTIER MARSHAL(1939); I STOLE A MILLION(1939); PRIDE OF THE BLUEGRASS(1939); TORCHY RUNS FOR MAYOR(1939); EARL OF CHICAGO, THE(1940); MAN FROM DAKOTA, THE(1940); THIRD FINGER, LEFT HAND(1940); WE WHO ARE YOUNG(1940); DESIGN FOR SCANDAL(1941); MOB TOWN(1941); EYES IN THE NIGHT(1942); FLY BY NIGHT(1942); DAISY KENYON(1947); DREAM GIRL(1947); FORCE OF EVIL(1948); SILENT CONFLICT(1948); SINISTER JOURNEY(1948); THAT WONDERFUL URGE(1948); IT HAPPENS EVERY SPRING(1949); RECKLESS MOMENTS, THE(1949); SET-UP, THE(1949); TOO LATE FOR TEARS(1949); UNDERCOVER MAN, THE(1949); CODE OF THE SILVER SAGE(1950); I'LL GET BY(1950); YELLOW CAB MAN, THE(1950); BRANDED(1951); PEOPLE AGAINST O'HARA, THE(1951); ROADBLOCK(1951); STRANGERS ON A TRAIN(1951); UNKNOWN MAN, THE(1951); PRIDE OF ST. LOUIS, THE(1952); FARMER TAKES A WIFE, THE(1953)
Silents
WET GOLD(1921); JOHN SMITH(1922)

John A. Butler
SENATOR WAS INDISCREET, THE(1947); SUN COMES UP, THE(1949); CONVICTED(1950); SIDE STREET(1950); SNIPER, THE(1952)

John E. Butler
PHANTOM SPEAKS, THE(1945), w

John K. Butler
BEYOND THE LAST FRONTIER(1943), w; RAIDERS OF SUNSET PASS(1943), w; SILVER SPURS(1943), w; GIRL WHO DARED, THE(1944), w; HIDDEN VALLEY OUTLAWS(1944), w; PRIDE OF THE PLAINS(1944), w; DON'T FENCE ME IN(1945), w; MAN FROM OKLAHOMA, THE(1945), w; SUNSET IN EL DORADO(1945), w; TELL IT TO A STAR(1945), w; UTAH(1945), w; VAMPIRE'S GHOST, THE(1945), w; AFFAIRS OF GERALDINE(1946), w; G.I. WAR BRIDES(1946), w; MY PAL TRIGGER(1946), w; ONE EXCITING WEEK(1946), w; MAIN STREET KID, THE(1947), w; ROBIN OF TEXAS(1947), w; CALIFORNIA FIREBRAND(1948), w; GALLANT LEGION, THE(1948), w; HEART OF VIRGINIA(1948), w; LIGHTNIN' IN THE FOREST(1948), w; OUT OF THE STORM(1948), w; SECRET SERVICE INVESTIGATOR(1948), w; DOWN DAKOTA WAY(1949), w; FLAMING FURY(1949), w; HIDEOUT(1949), w; POST OFFICE INVESTIGATOR(1949), w; RIM OF THE CANYON(1949), w; STREETS OF SAN FRANCISCO(1949), w; SUSANNA PASS(1949), w; BLONDE BANDIT, THE(1950), w; HARBOR OF MISSING MEN(1950), w; TARNISHED(1950), w; MISSING WOMEN(1951), w; PRIDE OF MARYLAND(1951), w; RODEO KING AND THE SENORITA(1951), w; SECRETS OF MONTE CARLO(1951), w; UTAH WAGON TRAIN(1951), w; TOUGHEST MAN IN ARIZONA(1952), w; DRUMS ACROSS THE RIVER(1954), w; OUTCAST, THE(1954), w; HEADLINE HUNTERS(1955), w; I COVER THE UNDERWORLD(1955), w; NO MAN'S WOMAN(1955), w; TERROR AT MIDNIGHT(1956), w; WHEN GANGLAND STRIKES(1956), w; AFFAIR IN RENO(1957), w; HELL'S CROSSROADS(1957), w; AMBUSH AT CIMARRON PASS(1958), w

Johnny Butler
MAKE WAY FOR A LADY(1936)

Kathleen Butler
FEATHERED SERPENT, THE(1934, Brit.), w; LITTLE BIT OF BLUFF, A(1935, Brit.), w; MARRY THE GIRL(1935, Brit.), w; OLD FAITHFUL(1935, Brit.), w; RIGHT AGE TO MARRY, THE(1935, Brit.), w; SHADOW OF MIKE EMERALD, THE(1935, Brit.), w; WIFE OR TWO, A(1935, Brit.), w; BUSMAN'S HOLIDAY(1936, Brit.), w; HAPPY FAMILY, THE(1936, Brit.), w; HEIRLOOM MYSTERY, THE(1936, Brit.), w; NOT SO DUSTY(1936, Brit.), w; NOTHING LIKE PUBLICITY(1936, Brit.), w; TO CATCH A THIEF(1936, Brit.), w; TOUCH OF THE MOON, A(1936, Brit.), w; TWICE BRANDED(1936, Brit.), w; FAREWELL TO CINDERELLA(1937, Brit.), w; FATHER STEPS OUT(1937, Brit.), w; STRANGE ADVENTURES OF MR. SMITH, THE(1937, Brit.), w; WHY PICK ON ME?(1937, Brit.), w; DARTS ARE TRUMPS(1938, Brit.), w; HIS LORDSHIP REGRETS(1938, Brit.), w; MIRACLES DO HAPPEN(1938, Brit.), w; WEDDINGS ARE WONDERFUL(1938, Brit.), w; HIS LORDSHIP GOES TO PRESS(1939, Brit.), w; GARRISON FOLLIES(1940, Brit.), w; FACING THE MUSIC(1941, Brit.), w; GERT AND DAISY'S WEEKEND(1941, Brit.), w; SHEEPDOG OF THE HILLS(1941, Brit.), w; FRONT LINE KIDS(1942, Brit.), w; GERT AND DAISY CLEAN UP(1942, Brit.), w; ROSE OF TRALEE(1942, Brit.), w; I'LL WALK BESIDE YOU(1943, Brit.), w; MY AIN FOLK(1944, Brit.), w; FOR YOU ALONE(1945, Brit.), w; VARIETY JUBILEE(1945, Brit.), w; I'LL TURN TO YOU(1946, Brit.), w; CALLING PAUL TEMPLE(1948, Brit.), w; TEMPTRESS, THE(1949, Brit.), w; NOT SO DUSTY(1956, Brit.), w

Kent Butler
WAVELENGTH(1983)

Larry Butler
DEVIL AT FOUR O'CLOCK, THE(1961), spec eff; PANIC IN YEAR ZERO!(1962), spec eff; MACKENNA'S GOLD(1969), spec eff; GOSPEL ROAD, THE(1973), m

Laurence Butler
ADVENTURES OF MARK TWAIN, THE(1944), ph

Lawerence Butler
SOUTH RIDING(1938, Brit.), spec eff

Lawrence Butler
THINGS TO COME(1936, Brit.), spec eff; DARK JOURNEY(1937, Brit.), spec eff; FIRE OVER ENGLAND(1937, Brit.), spec eff; MAN WHO COULD WORK MIRACLES, THE(1937, Brit.), spec eff; THIEF OF BAGHDAD, THE(1940, Brit.), spec eff; LYDIA(1941), spec eff; THAT HAMILTON WOMAN(1941), spec eff; CASABLANCA(1942), spec eff; JUNGLE BOOK(1942), spec eff; TO BE OR NOT TO BE(1942), spec eff; DESTINATION TOKYO(1944), spec eff; JANIE(1944), spec eff; HORN BLOWS AT MIDNIGHT, THE(1945), spec eff; SARATOGA TRUNK(1945), spec eff; LADY FROM SHANGHAI, THE(1948), spec eff

Lawrence W. Butler
THOUSAND AND ONE NIGHTS, A(1945), spec eff; TONIGHT AND EVERY NIGHT(1945), spec eff; ROBINSON CRUSOE ON MARS(1964), spec eff; IN HARM'S WAY(1965), spec eff; MAROONED(1969), spec eff

Lois Butler
MICKEY(1948); BOY FROM INDIANA(1950); HIGH LONESOME(1950)

Lori Butler
1984
MIKE'S MURDER(1984)
Lt. Col. Ewan Butler
DUNKIRK(1958, Brit.), w
Lynton Butler
1984
PALLET ON THE FLOOR(1984, New Zealand), d, w
M. Butler
PALM SPRINGS WEEKEND(1963), cos
Mary Ellen Butler
SAMURAI(1945)
Michael Butler
SEVEN SWEETHEARTS(1942); CHARLEY VARRICK(1973), ph; ELECTRA GLIDE IN BLUE(1973), a, w; HARRY AND TONTO(1974), a, ph; BRANNIGAN(1975, Brit.), w; MISSOURI BREAKS, THE(1976), ph; CAR, THE(1977), w; GAUNTLET, THE(1977), w; TELEFON(1977), ph; BUDDY HOLLY STORY, THE(1978), cos; JAWS II(1978), ph; HAIR(1979), p; WANDA NEVADA(1979), ph; SMALL CIRCLE OF FRIENDS, A(1980), ph; SMOKEY AND THE BANDIT II(1980), ph; BELLS(1981, Can.), w; CANNON-BALL RUN, THE(1981), ph; MEGAFORCE(1982), ph; DANCE OF THE DWARFS(1983, U.S., Phil.), ph
1984
FLASHPOINT(1984), w; PRODIGAL, THE(1984), cos
Michael C. Butler
92 IN THE SHADE(1975, U.S./Brit.), ph
Michael Philip Butler
DON IS DEAD, THE(1973), w
Mike Butler
UNDER THE RAINBOW(1981), cos
Patrick Butler
MARRYING KIND, THE(1952)
Paul Butler
SPOOK WHO SAT BY THE DOOR, THE(1973)
1984
OLD ENOUGH(1984)
Pearl Butler
SECOND FIDDLE TO A STEEL GUITAR(1965)
Philippe Butler
TELEFON(1977)
Richard Butler
HIDE AND SEEK(1964, Brit.); LOVE AND THE MIDNIGHT AUTO SUPPLY(1978), stunts
1984
SCRUBBERS(1984, Brit.)
Misc. Talkies
MAN WHO SAW TOMORROW, THE(1981)
Richard E. Butler
WHAT'S UP, DOC?(1972); PENNIES FROM HEAVEN(1981)
Robert Butler
GUNS IN THE HEATHER(1968, Brit.), d; COMPUTER WORE TENNIS SHOES, THE(1970), d; BAREFOOT EXECUTIVE, THE(1971), d; SCANDALOUS JOHN(1971), d; NOW YOU SEE HIM, NOW YOU DON'T(1972), d; ULTIMATE THRILL, THE(1974), d; HOT LEAD AND COLD FEET(1978), d; NIGHT OF THE JUGGLER(1980), d
1984
UP THE CREEK(1984), d
Misc. Talkies
UNDERGROUND ACES(1981), d
Rosita Butler
TO THE LAST MAN(1933); MAID OF SALEM(1937); TRUE CONFESSION(1937); HENRY ALDRICH FOR PRESIDENT(1941)
Roy Butler
RETURN OF DANIEL BOONE, THE(1941); SIERRA SUE(1941); HOME IN WYO-MIN'(1942); HOUSE OF ERRORS(1942); ICE-CAPADES REVUE(1942); FIGHTING BUCKAROO, THE(1943); FRONTIER LAW(1943); OLD CHISHOLM TRAIL(1943); WEST OF TEXAS(1943); RENEGADES OF THE RIO GRANDE(1945); HOODLUM SAINT, THE(1946); LAND OF THE LAWLESS(1947); TRAIL STREET(1947); FEUDIN', FUSSIN' AND A-FIGHTIN'(1948); GUN TALK(1948); DEPUTY MARSHAL(1949); SKY LINER(1949); STALLION CANYON(1949); BANDIT QUEEN(1950); FAST ON THE DRAW(1950); INDIAN TERRITORY(1950); KING OF THE BULLWHIP(1950); SUMMER STOCK(1950); FINGERPRINTS DON'T LIE(1951); GENE AUTRY AND THE MOUNTIES(1951); MY FAVORITE SPY(1951); SANTA FE(1951); SELLOUT, THE(1951); TEXANS NEVER CRY(1951); VENGEANCE VAL-LEY(1951); BLACK LASH, THE(1952); CARRIE(1952); FRONTIER PHANTOM, THE(1952); NIGHT RAIDERS(1952); GIRL WHO HAD EVERYTHING, THE(1953); MY DINNER WITH ANDRE(1981)
Roy E. Butler
ONE TOO MANY(1950)
Rudy Butler
DONDI(1961), set d
Sam Butler
PRIDE OF THE BLUEGRASS(1939)
Sarah Butler
YOUNG GIRLS OF ROCHEFORT, THE(1968, Fr.)
Shirley Butler
NEVER TAKE CANDY FROM A STRANGER(1961, Brit.)
Steve Butler
SUPER VAN(1977), ed
Ted Butler
WIZ, THE(1978); COOL WORLD, THE(1963); LOOKING UP(1977)
Tim Butler
TRACK OF THE MOONBEAST(1976)
Tracy Butler
WHAT A WAY TO GO(1964); CHANGES(1969), w
W.J. Butler
Misc. Silents
I ACCUSE(1916)
Walter Butler
Silents
ONE OF THE BEST(1927, Brit.); PASSION ISLAND(1927, Brit.)

Misc. Silents
WHITE HEAT(1926, Brit.); TOMMY ATKINS(1928, Brit.); TWO LITTLE DRUMMER BOYS(1928, Brit.); VICTORY(1928, Brit.)
Warde Q. Butler, Jr.
SIX PACK(1982)
Werner Butler
CONFESS DR. CORDA(1960, Ger.)
William Butler
BUONA SERA, MRS. CAMPBELL(1968, Ital.), ed; DUCHESS AND THE DIRTWA-TER FOX, THE(1976), ed
Silents
GOLD RUSH, THE(1925)
William J. Butler
Misc. Silents
GAMBLER OF THE WEST, THE(1915); SUSIE SNOWFLAKE(1916)
Wilmer Butler
RAIN PEOPLE, THE(1969), ph; HICKEY AND BOGGS(1972), ph; MANCHU EAGLE MURDER CAPER MYSTERY, THE(1975), ph
Wilmer C. Butler
ADAM'S WOMAN(1972, Austral.), ph; DEATHMASTER, THE(1972), ph; MELIN-DA(1972), ph
Butler-Glounder
LOST HORIZON(1973), spec eff
Butler-Glouner
PAJAMA PARTY(1964), spec eff; HEAD(1968), spec eff; COMIC, THE(1969), spec eff; IMPASSE(1969), spec eff; LIFE AND TIMES OF JUDGE ROY BEAN, THE(1972), spec eff
Butler-Glouner, Inc.
"X"-THE MAN WITH THE X-RAY EYES(1963), cos
Jan Butlin
ASSAULT(1971, Brit.)
Maryla Butorowicz
GUESTS ARE COMING(1965, Pol.)
Alfred Butow
RUMPELSTILTSKIN(1965, Ger.), art d; PUSS 'N' BOOTS(1967, Ger.), art d
Merritt Butrick
STAR TREK II: THE WRATH OF KHAN(1982); ZAPPED!(1982)
1984
STAR TREK III: THE SEARCH FOR SPOCK(1984)
Hillous Butrum
COUNTRY BOY(1966), a, md
Seweryn Butrym
KNIGHTS OF THE TEUTONIC ORDER, THE(1962, Pol.)
Johnny Butt
BLOCKADE(1928, Brit.); BLACKMAIL(1929, Brit.); CLUE OF THE NEW PIN, THE(1929, Brit.); INFORMER, THE(1929, Brit.); LAST POST, THE(1929, Brit.); SISTER TO ASSIST'ER, A(1930, Brit.)
Silents
FAR FROM THE MADDING CROWD(1915, Brit.); DIAMOND NECKLACE, THE(1921, Brit.); FOUR MEN IN A VAN(1921, Brit.); HEAD OF THE FAMILY, THE(1922, Brit.); SKIPPER'S WOOING, THE(1922, Brit.); MONKEY'S PAW, THE(1923, Brit.); PREHISTORIC MAN, THE(1924, Brit.); EVERY MOTHER'S SON(1926, Brit.); NELL GWYNNE(1926, Brit.); NELSON(1926, Brit.); PASSION ISLAND(1927, Brit.); PEEP BEHIND THE SCENES, A(1929, Brit.)
Misc. Silents
THREE MEN IN A BOAT(1920, Brit.); SAM'S BOY(1922, Brit.); WILL AND A WAY, A(1922, Brit.); CARRY ON!(1927, Brit.)
Lawson Butt
CITY OF PLAY(1929, Brit.); THOSE WHO LOVE(1929, Brit.)
Silents
STING OF THE LASH(1921); TEN COMMANDMENTS, THE(1923); DANTE'S IN-FERNO(1924); BELOVED ROGUE, THE(1927); FOREIGN DEVILS(1927); LADY OF THE LAKE, THE(1928, Brit.); RINGER, THE(1928, Brit.)
Misc. Silents
FLYING DUTCHMAN, THE(1923)
Lawsun Butt
Silents
ANY WOMAN(1925)
W. Lawson Butt
Silents
MALE AND FEMALE(1919); MIRACLE MAN, THE(1919); OUT OF THE STORM(1920); AFTERWARDS(1928, Brit.), d
Misc. Silents
DON CAESAR DE BAZAN(1915); DANGER TRAIL, THE(1917); GODDESS OF LOST LAKE, THE(1918); HER MAN(1918); ONE WOMAN, THE(1918); SHACKLED(1918); WOMAN ETERNAL, THE(1918); DESERT GOLD(1919); IT HAPPENED IN PA-RIS(1919); DANGEROUS DAYS(1920); LOVES OF LETTY, THE(1920); TIGER'S COAT, THE(1920); TONI(1928, Brit.)
Carl Buttenberger
GAMES(1967)
David Butter
HAVE A HEART(1934), d, w
Albert Butterfield
PENNY SERENADE(1941)
Everett Butterfield
Misc. Silents
MAGIC SKIN, THE(1915); SEVENTH NOON, THE(1915)
Herb Butterfield
BLUEPRINT FOR MURDER, A(1953)
Herbert Butterfield
NEVER FEAR(1950); HOUSE ON TELEGRAPH HILL(1951); SHIELD FOR MUR-DER(1954)
Maggie Butterfield
STRANGE BREW(1983)
Max Butterfield
HELL, HEAVEN OR HOBOKEN(1958, Brit.); GOOD COMPANIONS, THE(1957, Brit.); STOWAWAY GIRL(1957, Brit.); WOMEN IN A DRESSING GOWN(1957, Brit.); UP THE CREEK(1958, Brit.); AND WOMEN SHALL WEEP(1960, Brit.); TARNISHED HEROES(1961, Brit.)

Paul Butterfield
STEELYARD BLUES(1973), m
Roger Butterfield
PRIDE OF THE MARINES(1945), w
Roy Butterfield
LOVE BUG, THE(1968)
Ted Butterfield
DICK BARTON AT BAY(1950, Brit.)
Walton Butterfield
FAST COMPANY(1929), w
Orange [Opal] Butterfly
I AM A GROUPIE(1970, Brit.)
Charles Butterworth
LIFE OF THE PARTY, THE(1930); BARGAIN, THE(1931); ILLICIT(1931); MAD GENIUS, THE(1931); MANHATTAN PARADE(1931); SIDE SHOW(1931); BEAUTY AND THE BOSS(1932); LOVE ME TONIGHT(1932); MY WEAKNESS(1933); NUISANCE, THE(1933); PENTHOUSE(1933); BULLDOG DRUMMOND STRIKES BACK(1934); CAT AND THE FIDDLE(1934); HOLLYWOOD PARTY(1934); STUDENT TOUR(1934); BABY FACE HARRINGTON(1935); FORSAKING ALL OTHERS(1935); MAGNIFICENT OBSESSION(1935); NIGHT IS YOUNG, THE(1935); ORCHIDS TO YOU(1935); HALF ANGEL(1936); MOON'S OUR HOME, THE(1936); RAINBOW ON THE RIVER(1936); WE WENT TO COLLEGE(1936); SWING HIGH, SWING LOW(1937); EVERY DAY'S A HOLIDAY(1938); THANKS FOR THE MEMORY(1938); LET FREEDOM RING(1939); BOYS FROM SYRACUSE(1940); SECOND CHORUS(1940); BLONDE INSPIRATION(1941); ROAD SHOW(1941); SIS HOPKINS(1941); GIVE OUT, SISTERS(1942); NIGHT IN NEW ORLEANS, A(1942); WHAT'S COOKIN'?(1942); ALWAYS A BRIDESMAID(1943); SULTAN'S DAUGHTER, THE(1943); THIS IS THE ARMY(1943); BERMUDA MYSTERY(1944); FOLLOW THE BOYS(1944); DIXIE JAMBOREE(1945)
Donna Butterworth
FAMILY JEWELS, THE(1965); PARADISE, HAWAIIAN STYLE(1966)
Ed Butterworth
SCARFACE MOB, THE(1962), makeup; LOVE WITH THE PROPER STRANGER(1963), makeup; GOOD TIMES(1967), makeup; JUSTINE(1969), makeup; GREAT WHITE HOPE, THE(1970), makeup; MC CABE AND MRS. MILLER(1971), makeup; POSEIDON ADVENTURE, THE(1972), makeup; DEER HUNTER, THE(1978), makeup
Ernest Butterworth
OUT OF SINGAPORE(1932)
Silents
CRAB, THE(1917); ARIZONA(1918); GREATEST THING IN LIFE, THE(1918); MR. FIX-IT(1918), w; SAY! YOUNG FELLOW(1918); BROKEN BLOSSOMS(1919); KNICKERBOCKER BUCKAROO, THE(1919); SOUL OF YOUTH, THE(1920); WHAT'S YOUR HURRY?(1920); HER MAD BARGAIN(1921); NINETY AND NINE, THE(1922); NEVER THE TWAIN SHALL MEET(1925); DESERT'S PRICE, THE(1926)
Frank Butterworth
Silents
AMARILLY OF CLOTHESLINE ALLEY(1918)
Joe Butterworth
Silents
PENROD AND SAM(1923); GEARED TO GO(1924); NARROW STREET, THE(1924); NORTH OF NEVADA(1924); LITTLE ANNIE ROONEY(1925); ARIZONA BOUND(1927); THREE'S A CROWD(1927)
Misc. Silents
BLACK LIGHTING(1924); GOOD BAD BOY(1924)
Larry Butterworth
SERGEANT WAS A LADY, THE(1961), makeup
Mabel Butterworth
ISN'T IT ROMANTIC?(1948)
Peter Butterworth
WILLIAM COMES TO TOWN(1948, Brit.); ADVENTURES OF JANE, THE(1949, Brit.); BODY SAID NO!, THE(1950, Brit.); MISS PILGRIM'S PROGRESS(1950, Brit.); MYSTERY AT THE BURLESQUE(1950, Brit.); MR. DRAKE'S DUCK(1951, Brit.); OLD MOTHER RILEY'S JUNGLE TREASURE(1951, Brit.); PAUL TEMPLE'S TRIUMPH(1951, Brit.); ISLAND OF DESIRE(1952, Brit.); ISLAND RESCUE(1952, Brit.); PENNY PRINCESS(1953, Brit.); GAY DOG, THE(1954, Brit.); WILL ANY GENTLEMAN?(1955, Brit.); FUN AT ST. FANNY'S(1956, Brit.); BLOW YOUR OWN TRUMPET(1958, Brit.); TOM THUMB(1958, Brit./U.S.); ESCORT FOR HIRE(1960, Brit.); SPIDER'S WEB, THE(1960, Brit.); DAY THE EARTH CAUGHT FIRE, THE(1961, Brit.); MURDER SHE SAID(1961, Brit.); FATE TAKES A HAND(1962, Brit.); KILL OR CURE(1962, Brit.); LIVE NOW-PAY LATER(1962, Brit.); DOCTOR IN DISTRESS(1963, Brit.); MAID FOR MURDER(1963, Brit.); RESCUE SQUAD, THE(1963, Brit.); NEVER MENTION MURDER(1964, Brit.); AMOROUS ADVENTURES OF MOLL FLANDERS, THE(1965); CARRY ON COWBOY(1966, Brit.); CARRY ON SCREAMING(1966, Brit.); DON'T LOSE YOUR HEAD(1967, Brit.); FOLLOW THAT CAMEL(1967, Brit.); CARRY ON DOCTOR(1968, Brit.); CARRY ON, UP THE KHYBER(1968, Brit.); PRUDENCE AND THE PILL(1968, Brit.); CARRY ON CAMPING(1969, Brit.); CARRY ON HENRY VIII(1970, Brit.); CARRY ON ENGLAND(1976, Brit.); RITZ, THE(1976); ROBIN AND MARIAN(1976, Brit.); CARRY ON EMANUELLE(1978, Brit.); GREAT TRAIN ROBBERY, THE(1979, Brit.)
Shane Butterworth
EXORCIST II: THE HERETIC(1977)
Tyler Butterworth
DARLING(1965, Brit.); MAGNIFICENT TWO, THE(1967, Brit.)
Richard Buttery
Silents
PRIDE OF THE NORTH, THE(1920, Brit.)
Misc. Silents
I HEAR YOU CALLING ME(1919, Brit.); SILVER LINING, THE(1919, Brit.); SOUL'S CRUCIFIXION, A(1919, Brit.)
Douglas Buttleman
1984
RHINESTONE(1984)
Werner Buttler
THOUSAND EYES OF DR. MABUSE, THE(1960, Fr./Ital./Ger.); ONE, TWO, THREE(1961)
Cathy Buttner
PHANTOM OF THE PARADISE(1974)

Hansjoachim Buttner
PILLARS OF SOCIETY(1936, Ger.)
Michael Buttner
1984
CHINESE BOXES(1984, Ger./Brit.)
Wolfgang Buttner
LONGEST DAY, THE(1962); DEVIL IN SILK(1968, Ger.)
Jacques Buttnoir
GIRL FROM LORRAINE, A(1982, Fr./Switz.), art d
David Buttolph
NOW I'LL TELL(1934), m; WORLD MOVES ON, THE(1934), m; SHOW THEM NO MERCY(1935), m; EVERYBODY'S OLD MAN(1936), md; NAVY WIFE(1936), md; PIGSKIN PARADE(1936), md; DANGER–LOVE AT WORK(1937), md; FIFTY ROADS TO TOWN(1937), md; LOVE IS NEWS(1937), md; NANCY STEELE IS MISSING(1937), md; SECOND HONEYMOON(1937), md; YOU CAN'T HAVE EVERYTHING(1937), md; JOSETTE(1938), md; BARRICADE(1939), m; GORILLA, THE(1939), md; HOTEL FOR WOMEN(1939), md; STANLEY AND LIVINGSTONE(1939), m; THREE MUSKETEERS, THE(1939), md; WIFE, HUSBAND AND FRIEND(1939), md; CHAD HANNA(1940), m; FOUR SONS(1940), md; HE MARRIED HIS WIFE(1940), md; I WAS AN ADVENTURESS(1940), md; MAN I MARRIED, THE(1940), md; RETURN OF FRANK JAMES, THE(1940), m; STAR DUST(1940), md; LADY FOR A NIGHT(1941), m; SWAMP WATER(1941), m; TOBACCO ROAD(1941), m; WESTERN UNION(1941), m; IN OLD CALIFORNIA(1942), m; MOONTIDE(1942), md; MY FAVORITE BLONDE(1942), m; STREET OF CHANCE(1942), m; THIS GUN FOR HIRE(1942), m; THUNDER BIRDS(1942), m; WAKE ISLAND(1942), m; BOMBER'S MOON(1943), m; CORVETTE K-225(1943), m; CRASH DIVE(1943), m; GUADALCANAL DIARY(1943), m; IMMORTAL SERGEANT, THE(1943), m; BUFFALO BILL(1944), m; HITLER GANG, THE(1944), m; IN THE MEANTIME, DARLING(1944), m; 'TILL WE MEET AGAIN(1944), m; BULLFIGHTERS, THE(1945), m; CIRCUMSTANTIAL EVIDENCE(1945), m; HOUSE ON 92ND STREET, THE(1945), m; JUNIOR MISS(1945), m; NOB HILL(1945), m; SPIDER, THE(1945), m; WITHIN THESE WALLS(1945), m; HOME SWEET HOMICIDE(1946), m; IT SHOULDN'T HAPPEN TO A DOG(1946), m; JOHNNY COMES FLYING HOME(1946), m; MY DARLING CLEMENTINE(1946), m; SHOCK(1946), m; SOMEWHERE IN THE NIGHT(1946), m; STRANGE TRIANGLE(1946), m; 13 RUE MADELEINE(1946), md; BILL AND COO(1947), m; BOOMERANG(1947), m; BRASHER DOUBLOON, THE(1947), m; FOXES OF HARROW, THE(1947), m; KISS OF DEATH(1947), m; MOSS ROSE(1947), m; JUNE BRIDE(1948), m, md; ROPE(1948), m; SMART GIRLS DON'T TALK(1948), m; TO THE VICTOR(1948), m; COLORADO TERRITORY(1949), m; GIRL FROM JONES BEACH, THE(1949), m; JOHN LOVES MARY(1949), m; ONE LAST FLING(1949), m; ROSEANNA McCOY(1949), m; STORY OF SEABISCUIT, THE(1949), m, md; CHAIN LIGHTNING(1950), m; MONTANA(1950), m; PRETTY BABY(1950), m; REDHEAD AND THE COWBOY, THE(1950), m; RETURN OF THE FRONTIERSMAN(1950), m; THREE SECRETS(1950), m; ALONG THE GREAT DIVIDE(1951), m; ENFORCER, THE(1951), m; FIGHTING COAST GUARD(1951), m; FORT WORTH(1951), m; SELLOUT, THE(1951), m; SUBMARINE COMMAND(1951), m; CARSON CITY(1952), m; LONE STAR(1952), m; MAN BEHIND THE GUN, THE(1952), m; MY MAN AND I(1952), m; TALK ABOUT A STRANGER(1952), m; THIS WOMAN IS DANGEROUS(1952), m; WINNING TEAM, THE(1952), m; BEAST FROM 20,000 FATHOMS, THE(1953), m; HOUSE OF WAX(1953), m; SOUTH SEA WOMAN(1953), m; SYSTEM, THE(1953), m; THUNDER OVER THE PLAINS(1953), m; BOUNTY HUNTER, THE(1954), m; CRIME WAVE(1954), m; LONG JOHN SILVER(1954, Aus.), m; PHANTOM OF THE RUE MORGUE(1954), m; RIDING SHOTGUN(1954), m; SECRET OF THE INCAS(1954), m; I DIED A THOUSAND TIMES(1955), m; JUMP INTO HELL(1955), m, md; LONE RANGER, THE(1955), m, md; TARGET ZERO(1955), m; BURNING HILLS, THE(1956), m; CRY IN THE NIGHT, A(1956), m; SANTIAGO(1956), m; STEEL JUNGLE, THE(1956), m; BIG LAND, THE(1957), m; D.I., THE(1957), m; DEEP SIX, THE(1958), m; ONIONHEAD(1958), m; HORSE SOLDIERS, THE(1959), m; WESTBOUND(1959), m; GUNS OF THE TIMBERLAND(1960), m; PT 109(1963), m; MAN FROM GALVESTON, THE(1964), m
Charles Button
1984
OH GOD! YOU DEVIL(1984)
David Button
GROUND ZERO(1973)
Dick Button
YOUNG DOCTORS, THE(1961)
Peta Button
STRANGE AFFAIR, THE(1968, Brit.), set d; MAGIC CHRISTIAN, THE(1970, Brit.), set d
Ruth Button
1984
MUPPETS TAKE MANHATTAN, THE(1984)
Red Buttons
13 RUE MADELEINE(1946); SAYONARA(1957); IMITATION GENERAL(1958); BIG CIRCUS, THE(1959); ONE, TWO, THREE(1961); FIVE WEEKS IN A BALLOON(1962); GAY PURR-EE(1962); HATARI!(1962); LONGEST DAY, THE(1962); TICKLISH AFFAIR, A(1963); YOUR CHEATIN' HEART(1964); HARLOW(1965); UP FROM THE BEACH(1965); STAGECOACH(1966); THEY SHOOT HORSES, DON'T THEY?(1969); WHO KILLED MARY WHAT'SER NAME?(1971); POSEIDON ADVENTURE, THE(1972); GABLE AND LOMBARD(1976); PETE'S DRAGON(1977); VIVA KNIEVEL!(1977); MOVIE MOVIE(1978); C.H.O.M.P.S.(1979); WHEN TIME RAN OUT(1980)
Misc. Talkies
OFF YOUR ROCKER(1980)
Cpl. Red Buttons
WINGED VICTORY(1944)
Jack Buttram
RED RUNS THE RIVER(1963)
Pat Buttram
NATIONAL BARN DANCE(1944); STRAWBERRY ROAN, THE(1948); RIDERS IN THE SKY(1949); BEYOND THE PURPLE HILLS(1950); BLAZING SUN, THE(1950); INDIAN TERRITORY(1950); MULE TRAIN(1950); GENE AUTRY AND THE MOUNTIES(1951); HILLS OF UTAH(1951); SILVER CANYON(1951); TEXANS NEVER CRY(1951); VALLEY OF FIRE(1951); APACHE COUNTRY(1952); BARBED WIRE(1952); BLUE CANADIAN ROCKIES(1952); NIGHT STAGE TO GALVESTON(1952); OLD WEST, THE(1952); WAGON TEAM(1952); TWILIGHT OF HONOR(1963); ROUSTABOUT(1964); SERGEANT DEADHEAD(1965); SWEET RIDE, THE(1968); I SAILED TO TAHITI WITH AN ALL GIRL CREW(1969); ARISTOCATS, THE(1970); GATLING GUN, THE(1972); ROBIN HOOD(1973); RESCUERS, THE(1977); ANGELS BRIGADE(1980); FOX AND THE HOUND, THE(1981)

Graham Buttrose
OLIVER!(1968, Brit.)

Billy Butts
ALIAS JIMMY VALENTINE(1928); LONE STAR RANGER, THE(1930); MEDICINE MAN, THE(1930); ARE THESE OUR CHILDREN?(1931); YOUNG SINNERS(1931); LADY AND GENT(1932); NIGHT OF JUNE 13(1932); SCARLET RIVER(1933)
Silents
SPARROWS(1926); NONE BUT THE BRAVE(1928)
Misc. Silents
LONE HAND SAUNDERS(1926); BLACK ACE, THE(1928); TAKING A CHANCE(1928); WILD WEST ROMANCE(1928)

Dale Butts
DON'T FENCE ME IN(1945), m; GAY BLADES(1946), m; HELLDORADO(1946), m; HOME ON THE RANGE(1946), m; NIGHT TRAIN TO MEMPHIS(1946), m; ROLL ON TEXAS MOON(1946), md; SIOUX CITY SUE(1946), m; UNDER NEVADA SKIES(1946), md; INVISIBLE WALL, THE(1947), m; SECOND CHANCE(1947), m; DENVER KID, THE(1948), md; NIGHT TIME IN NEVADA(1948), m; PLUNDERERS, THE(1948), m; SON OF GOD'S COUNTRY(1948), m; DOWN DAKOTA WAY(1949), m; FAR FRONTIER, THE(1949), m; HELLFIRE(1949), m; LAST BANDIT, THE(1949), m; TOO LATE FOR TEARS(1949), m; SAVAGE HORDE, THE(1950), m; SOUTH OF CALIENTE(1951), md; CITY OF SHADOWS(1955), m; HELL'S OUTPOST(1955), md; LAY THAT RIFLE DOWN(1955), md

David Butts
PUTNEY SWOPE(1969)

Jimmy Butts
STRAIGHT FROM THE HEART(1935)

R. Dale Butts
HIT PARADE OF 1951(1950), m; ROCK ISLAND TRAIL(1950), m; SUNSET IN THE WEST(1950), m; TRIGGER, JR.(1950), md; WOMAN FROM HEADQUARTERS(1950), m; HEART OF THE ROCKIES(1951), m; IN OLD AMARILLO(1951), m; OH! SUSANNA(1951), m; SEA HORNET, THE(1951), m; SPOILERS OF THE PLAINS(1951), m; BAL TABARIN(1952), m; COLORADO SUNDOWN(1952), m; TOUGHEST MAN IN ARIZONA(1952), m; WAC FROM WALLA WALLA, THE(1952), m; WOMAN OF THE NORTH COUNTRY(1952), m; CHAMP FOR A DAY(1953), m; CITY THAT NEVER SLEEPS(1953), m; GERALDINE(1953), m; OLD OVERLAND TRAIL(1953), md; RED RIVER SHORE(1953), m; SAN ANTONE(1953), m; SEA OF LOST SHIPS(1953), m; SHADOWS OF TOMBSTONE(1953), m; HELL'S HALF ACRE(1954), m; OUTCAST, THE(1954), m; PHANTOM STALLION, THE(1954), m; SHANGHAI STORY, THE(1954), m; CAROLINA CANNONBALL(1955), m; DOUBLE JEOPARDY(1955), md; FIGHTING CHANCE, THE(1955), md; HEADLINE HUNTERS(1955), m; HELL'S OUTPOST(1955), m; I COVER THE UNDERWORLD(1955), m, md; LAY THAT RIFLE DOWN(1955), md; NO MAN'S WOMAN(1955), m, md; ROAD TO DENVER, THE(1955), m; SANTA FE PASSAGE(1955), m, md; VANISHING AMERICAN, THE(1955), m; ACCUSED OF MURDER(1956), m; DAKOTA INCIDENT(1956), m; MAN IS ARMED, THE(1956), m; STRANGE ADVENTURE, A(1956), md; STRANGER AT MY DOOR(1956), m; TERROR AT MIDNIGHT(1956), m; THUNDER OVER ARIZONA(1956), m, md; AFFAIR IN RENO(1957), m

Steve Butts
PACK, THE(1977); BLUE COLLAR(1978)

Tom Butts
RED RUNS THE RIVER(1963)

Tony Butula
DRAGSTRIP RIOT(1958)

Chief Butulezei
Misc. Talkies
TOKOLOSHE(1973)

N. Butuzov
GORDEYEV FAMILY, THE(1961, U.S.S.R.)

L. Butuzova
VIOLIN AND ROLLER(1962, USSR), ed

Ishaq Bux
NINE HOURS TO RAMA(1963, U.S./Brit.); INADMISSIBLE EVIDENCE(1968, Brit.); LEO THE LAST(1970, Brit.); HORSEMEN, THE(1971); VAULT OF HORROR, THE(1973, Brit.); RAIDERS OF THE LOST ARK(1981); MISSIONARY, THE(1982); PRIVATES ON PARADE(1982)
1984
PASSAGE TO INDIA, A(1984, Brit.); PRIVATES ON PARADE(1984, Brit.)

Kuda Bux
THEY CAME BY NIGHT(1940, Brit.)

Sarah Buxtom
1984
LOVELINES(1984)

Frank Buxton
WHAT'S UP, TIGER LILY?(1966), a, w

Henry J. Buxton
Silents
AMATEUR DEVIL, AN(1921), w

Judy Buxton
BAWDY ADVENTURES OF TOM JONES, THE(1976, Brit.); DEVIL WITHIN HER, THE(1976, Brit.)

Sheila Buxton
INBETWEEN AGE, THE(1958, Brit.); SHAKEDOWN, THE(1960, Brit.)

Susannah Buxton
RADIO ON(1980, Brit./Ger.), art d
1984
SCRUBBERS(1984, Brit.), cos

Vladimir Buyanovskiy
FORTY-NINE DAYS(1964, USSR)

Lillian Buyeff
ROGUE COP(1954); MARACAIBO(1958); SNOW QUEEN, THE(1959, USSR); LAD: A DOG(1962)

Sheep Buyer
PROUD REBEL, THE(1958)

Evelyn Buyers
LADY GODIVA RIDES AGAIN(1955, Brit.)

George Buza
1984
HIGHPOINT(1984, Can.)

Johannes Buzalaki
NOT RECONCILED, OR "ONLY VIOLENCE HELPS WHERE IT RULES"(1969, Ger.)

Johannes Buzalski
MARK OF THE DEVIL(1970, Ger./Brit.); MARK OF THE DEVIL II(1975, Ger./Brit.); OUR HITLER, A FILM FROM GERMANY(1980, Ger.)

Eddie Buzard
GENTLE JULIA(1936); HUMAN CARGO(1936)

Flo Buzby
SOMEONE TO REMEMBER(1943)

Zane Buzby
UP IN SMOKE(1978); OH, GOD!(1977); AMERICATHON(1979); NATIONAL LAMPOON'S CLASS REUNION(1982)
1984
THIS IS SPINAL TAP(1984)

Vasya Buzenkov
Misc. Silents
OLD AND NEW(1930, USSR)

Veronika Buzhinskava
Misc. Silents
CHILDREN OF STORM(1926, USSR)

Veronica Buzhinskaya
Misc. Silents
KATKA'S REINETTE APPLES(1926, USSR); PARISIAN COBBLER(1928, USSR)

Lando Buzzanca
DIVORCE, ITALIAN STYLE(1962, Ital.); SEDUCED AND ABANDONED(1964, Fr./Ital.); LITTLE NUNS, THE(1965, Ital.); AFTER THE FOX(1966, U.S./Brit./Ital.); LOVE AND MARRIAGE(1966, Ital.); SUCKER, THE(1966, Fr./Ital.); MADE IN ITALY(1967, Fr./Ital.); OPIATE '67(1967, Fr./Ital.); ROSE FOR EVERYONE, A(1967, Ital.); OPERATION ST. PETER'S(1968, Ital.); THOSE DARING YOUNG MEN IN THEIR JAUNTY JALOPIES(1969, Fr./Brit./Ital.); WHEN WOMEN HAD TAILS(1970, Ital.)

Eddie Buzzard
Misc. Talkies
BULLDOG COURAGE(1935)

Dino Buzzati
DESERT OF THE TARTARS, THE(1976 Fr./Ital./Iranian), w

Eddie Buzzell
LITTLE JOHNNY JONES(1930); HOLLYWOOD SPEAKS(1932), d; ANN CARVER'S PROFESSION(1933), d; CHILD OF MANHATTAN(1933), d; LOVE, HONOR, AND OH BABY!(1933), d, w; TRANSIENT LADY(1935), d, w; LUCKIEST GIRL IN THE WORLD, THE(1936), d; THREE MARRIED MEN(1936), d; AS GOOD AS MARRIED(1937), d; YOUNGEST PROFESSION, THE(1943); SONG OF THE THIN MAN(1947), d
Misc. Talkies
BIG TIMER(1932), d
Silents
MIDNIGHT LIFE(1928)

Edward Buzzell
LITTLE JOHNNY JONES(1930), w; VIRTUE(1932), d; CROSS COUNTRY CRUISE(1934), d; HUMAN SIDE, THE(1934), d; GIRL FRIEND, THE(1935), d; FAST COMPANY(1938), d; PARADISE FOR THREE(1938), d; AT THE CIRCUS(1939), d; HONOLULU(1939), d; GO WEST(1940), d; GET-AWAY, THE(1941), d; MARRIED BACHELOR(1941), d; OMAHA TRAIL, THE(1942), d; BEST FOOT FORWARD(1943), d; YOUNGEST PROFESSION, THE(1943), d; KEEP YOUR POWDER DRY(1945), d; EASY TO WED(1946), d; THREE WISE FOOLS(1946), d; NEPTUNE'S DAUGHTER(1949), d; EMERGENCY WEDDING(1950), d; WOMAN OF DISTINCTION, A(1950), d; CONFIDENTIAL CONNIE(1953), d; AIN'T MISBEHAVIN'(1955), d, w; MARY HAD A LITTLE(1961, Brit.), d

Edward N. Buzzell
SHIP AHOY(1942), d

Guido Buzzelli
INVESTIGATION OF A CITIZEN ABOVE SUSPICION(1970, Ital.)

Aldo Buzzi
WHITE LINE, THE(1952, Ital.), set d; VARIETY LIGHTS(1965, Ital.), art d, cos

Ruth Buzzi
FREAKY FRIDAY(1976); RECORD CITY(1978); APPLE DUMPLING GANG RIDES AGAIN, THE(1979); NORTH AVENUE IRREGULARS, THE(1979); SKATETOWN, U.S.A.(1979); VILLAIN, THE(1979); CHU CHU AND THE PHILLY FLASH(1981); BEING, THE(1983)
1984
SURF II(1984)

Signor Buzzi
Silents
ONE MORE AMERICAN(1918)

Tito Buzzo
LA DOLCE VITA(1961, Ital./Fr.)

Boris Byalik
GORDEYEV FAMILY, THE(1961, U.S.S.R.), w

Paul Byar
ALL FALL DOWN(1962)

Glenda Byars
1984
TIGHTROPE(1984)

Joe Byars
Misc. Talkies
DEATH RIDERS(1976)

Taylor Byars
TEENAGE MONSTER(1958), ph; CAT BURGLAR, THE(1961), ph; INTRUDER, THE(1962), ph; DESERT RAVEN, THE(1965), ph

Nigel Byass
DR. SIN FANG(1937, Brit.), w; AWAKENING, THE(1938, Brit.), w; CHINATOWN NIGHTS(1938, Brit.), w

Andrew Byatt
BIG CATCH, THE(1968, Brit.); THAT SUMMER(1979, Brit.); RADIO ON(1980, Brit./Ger.)
1984
SECRET PLACES(1984, Brit.)

Ariel Bybee
LA TRAVIATA(1982)

I. Bychkov
OPTIMISTIC TRAGEDY, THE(1964, USSR)
Glenn Bydwell
TERROR TRAIN(1980, Can.), prod d
Mary Bye
EXILE, THE(1947)
Victor Byelokurov
MILITARY SECRET(1945, USSR)
Anje Byer
1984
FOREVER YOUNG(1984, Brit.)
Charles Byer
TAXI 13(1928); DELIGHTFUL HOGUE(1929); MOLLY AND ME(1929); RED HOT SPEED ½(1929); SIDE STREET(1929)
Silents
NEW YORK(1927); ALEX THE GREAT(1928); BEAUTIFUL BUT DUMB(1928); DEAD MAN'S CURVE(1928)
Misc. Silents
SHANGHAI BOUND(1927); CLOTHES MAKE THE WOMAN(1928); HORSEMAN OF THE PLAINS, A(1928); RED RIDERS OF CANADA(1928)
Scotch Byerley
HARD COUNTRY(1981)
Orko Byerninen
OPTIMISTIC TRAGEDY, THE(1964, USSR)
Bill Byers
MOONCHILD(1972), m
Billy Byers
MAME(1974), md; WHITE LINE FEVER(1975, Can.), md
Bobbie Byers
WILD REBELS, THE(1967); SAVAGES FROM HELL(1968)
Brian Byers
YOU LIGHT UP MY LIFE(1977); HE KNOWS YOU'RE ALONE(1980)
Charles Byers
ROMANCE OF THE RIO GRANDE(1929)
Clara Byers
Misc. Silents
UNDER SOUTHERN SKIES(1915); HALF A ROGUE(1916); LITTLE MISS NOBO-DY(1917)
Lee Byers
Misc. Talkies
CURSE OF THE HEADLESS HORSEMAN(1972)
Patrick Byers
SCREAMS OF A WINTER NIGHT(1979)
Richard Byers
JIM, THE WORLD'S GREATEST(1976)
Wason Byers
JEDDA, THE UNCIVILIZED(1956, Aus.)
Ziggy Byfield
FINAL OPTION, THE(1983, Brit.)
1984
SLAYGROUND(1984, Brit.)
Jacqui Byford
LONG SHOT(1981, Brit.)
Joan Roy Byford
PHANTOM LIGHT, THE(1935, Brit.), w
June Byford
GOOD TIME GIRL(1950, Brit.)
Roy Byford
IMMORTAL GENTLEMAN(1935, Brit.); MUSEUM MYSTERY(1937, Brit.)
Silents
ON THE BANKS OF ALLAN WATER(1916, Brit.); MASTER OF CRAFT, A(1922, Brit.)
Pamela Bygrave
COME BACK PETER(1952, Brit.)
Anthony Bygraves
MAROC 7(1967, Brit.)
Max Bygraves
BLESS 'EM ALL(1949, Brit.); SKIMPY IN THE NAVY(1949, Brit.); TOM BROWN'S SCHOOLDAYS(1951, Brit.); CHARLEY MOON(1956, Brit.); BOBBIKINS(1959, Brit.); CRY FROM THE STREET, A(1959, Brit.); SPARE THE ROD(1961, Brit.)
Carsten Byhring
HUNGER(1968, Den./Norway/Swed.)
Spring Byington
LITTLE WOMEN(1933); AH, WILDERNESS!(1935); BROADWAY HOSTESS(1935); GREAT IMPERSONATION, THE(1935); LOVE ME FOREVER(1935); MUTINY ON THE BOUNTY(1935); ORCHIDS TO YOU(1935); WAY DOWN EAST(1935); WERE-WOLF OF LONDON, THE(1935); BACK TO NATURE(1936); CHARGE OF THE LIGHT BRIGADE, THE(1936); DODSWORTH(1936); EDUCATING FATHER(1936); EVERY SATURDAY NIGHT(1936); GIRL ON THE FRONT PAGE, THE(1936); PALM SPRINGS(1936); STAGE STRUCK(1936); THEODORA GOES WILD(1936); VOICE OF BUGLE ANN(1936); BIG BUSINESS(1937); BORROWING TROUBLE(1937); CLAR-ENCE(1937); FAMILY AFFAIR, A(1937); GREEN LIGHT(1937); HOT WATER(1937); HOTEL HAYWIRE(1937); IT'S LOVE I'M AFTER(1937); OFF TO THE RACES(1937); PENROD AND SAM(1937); ROAD BACK,THE(1937); BUCCANEER, THE(1938); DOWN ON THE FARM(1938); JEZEBEL(1938); LOVE ON A BUDGET(1938); PENROD AND HIS TWIN BROTHER(1938); SAFETY IN NUMBERS(1938); TRIP TO PARIS, A(1938); YOU CAN'T TAKE IT WITH YOU(1938); CHICKEN WAGON FAMILY(1939); EVERYBODY'S BABY(1939); JONES FAMILY IN HOLLYWOOD, THE(1939); QUICK MILLIONS(1939); STORY OF ALEXANDER GRAHAM BELL, THE(1939); TOO BUSY TO WORK(1939); BLUE BIRD, THE(1940); CHILD IS BORN, A(1940); LADDIE(1940); LUCKY PARTNERS(1940); MY LOVE CAME BACK(1940); ON THEIR OWN(1940); YOUNG AS YOU FEEL(1940); ARKANSAS JUDGE(1941); DEVIL AND MISS JONES, THE(1941); ELLERY QUEEN AND THE PERFECT CRIME(1941); MEET JOHN DOE(1941); VANISHING VIRGINIAN, THE(1941); WHEN LADIES MEET(1941); AFFAIRS OF MARTHA, THE(1942); RINGS ON HER FINGERS(1942); ROXIE HART(1942); WAR AGAINST MRS. HADLEY, THE(1942); HEAVENLY BODY, THE(1943); PRESENTING LILY MARS(1943); CAPTAIN EDDIE(1945); ENCHANTED COTTAGE, THE(1945); LETTER FOR EVIE, A(1945); SALTY O'ROURKE(1945); THRILL OF A ROMANCE(1945); DRAGONWYCH(1946); FAITHFUL IN MY FASH-ION(1946); LITTLE MISTER JIM(1946); MEET ME ON BROADWAY(1946); MY BROTHER TALKS TO HORSES(1946); CYNTHIA(1947); IT HAD TO BE YOU(1947);

LIVING IN A BIG WAY(1947); SINGAPORE(1947); B. F.'S DAUGHTER(1948); BIG WHEEL, THE(1949); IN THE GOOD OLD SUMMERTIME(1949); LOUISA(1950); PLEASE BELIEVE ME(1950); SKIPPER SURPRISED HIS WIFE, THE(1950); WALK SOFTLY, STRANGER(1950); ACCORDING TO MRS. HOYLE(1951); ANGELS IN THE OUTFIELD(1951); BANNERLINE(1951); BECAUSE YOU'RE MINE(1952); NO ROOM FOR THE GROOM(1952); ROCKET MAN, THE(1954); PLEASE DON'T EAT THE DAISIES(1960)
Vladimir Bykoff
GOIN' TO TOWN(1935); MAN WHO BROKE THE BANK AT MONTE CARLO, THE(1935); KLONDIKE ANNIE(1936)
Leonid Bykon
HOUSE ON THE FRONT LINE, THE(1963, USSR)
A. Bykov
KIEV COMEDY, A(1963, USSR)
I. Bykov
MARRIAGE OF BALZAMINOV, THE(1966, USSR)
Rolan Bykov
TIGER GIRL(1955, USSR); OVERCOAT, THE(1965, USSR); MARRIAGE OF BAL-ZAMINOV, THE(1966, USSR); MEET ME IN MOSCOW(1966, USSR); GIRL AND THE BUGLER, THE(1967, USSR)
Vera Bykova
RED AND THE WHITE, THE(1969, Hung./USSR)
Janusz Bylczynski
PASSENGER, THE(1970, Pol.)
Maggie Byle
EVERY LITTLE CROOK AND NANNY(1972)
Elvin Byler
HAPPY AS THE GRASS WAS GREEN(1973); HAZEL'S PEOPLE(1978)
Bobby Byles
WAR IS HELL(1964)
Glyn Byles
THIS, THAT AND THE OTHER(1970, Brit.), ed
Louis Byles
CROWNING EXPERIENCE, THE(1960)
Richard S. Bylin
YOUNG WARRIORS(1983), art d
Janet Bylund
BEYOND AND BACK(1978)
Jerome Bynder
1984
DELIVERY BOYS(1984)
John Byner
WHAT'S UP, DOC?(1972); GREAT SMOKEY ROADBLOCK, THE(1978); STROKER ACE(1983)
Misc. Talkies
PLEASURE DOING BUSINESS, A(1979)
Douglas Byng
HOTEL PARADISO(1966, U.S./Brit.)
Brenda Bynum
SHARKY'S MACHINE(1982)
Don Bynum
SOUNDER, PART 2(1976)
Inchib Byon
YONGKARI MONSTER FROM THE DEEP(1967 S.K.), ph
Arthur Byram
FANTASIA(1940), art d
Gene Byram
MRS. MINIVER(1942)
Ronald Byram
Silents
OUT OF THE SHADOW(1919)
Paul Byrar
ROSE BOWL STORY, THE(1952)
Beau Byrd
Misc. Silents
GIRL OF THE TIMBER CLAIMS, THE(1917)
Bob Byrd
Misc. Talkies
ASTROLOGER, THE(1979)
Bretton Byrd
SMILING ALONG(1938, Brit.), md; SAINT'S VACATION, THE(1941, Brit.), m, md; LOOK BEFORE YOU LOVE(1948, Brit.), m; MY SISTER AND I(1948, Brit.), m, md; TONY DRAWS A HORSE(1951, Brit.), m, md
Carl Byrd
FLAREUP(1969); TELEFON(1977)
1984
IRRECONCILABLE DIFFERENCES(1984)
Carolyn Byrd
AIRBORNE(1962)
Caruth C. Byrd
MURPH THE SURF(1974)
1984
HOLLYWOOD HIGH PART II(1984), d, w
Misc. Talkies
LONE STAR COUNTRY(1983), d
David Byrd
PIPE DREAMS(1976); ROLLERCOASTER(1977); TURNING POINT, THE(1977); SUNNYSIDE(1979); FORMULA, THE(1980); SOME KIND OF HERO(1982); MAN WITH TWO BRAINS, THE(1983)
1984
ALL OF ME(1984)
Donald Byrd
CORNBREAD, EARL AND ME(1975), m
Doyne Byrd
ACCEPTABLE LEVELS(1983, Brit.)
Evelyn Byrd
MANCHURIAN CANDIDATE, THE(1962)

George Byrd
MARRIAGE OF MARIA BRAUN, THE(1979, Ger.)
Jack Byrd
MAN BEHIND THE MASK, THE(1936, Brit.), w; ONE GOOD TURN(1936, Brit.), w; EVERYTHING IS RHYTHM(1940, Brit.), w
Joe Byrd
Misc. Talkies
DAUGHTER OF THE CONGO, A(1930)
John Byrd
RHYTHM RACKETEER(1937, Brit.), w; THREE SILENT MEN(1940, Brit.), w; FRONT LINE KIDS(1942, Brit.), w
Joseph Byrd
LIONS LOVE(1969), m; SKI BUM, THE(1971), m
Julian Byrd
DREAMER(1979)
Michael Byrd
WOMEN AND BLOODY TERROR(1970)
Miriam Byrd
1984
LIES(1984, Brit.)
Paul Byrd
SEVEN FACES OF DR. LAO(1964), spec eff; HAWAII(1966), spec eff
Ralph Byrd
BORDER CABALLERO(1936); HELL-SHIP MORGAN(1936); SWING TIME(1936); CRIMINALS OF THE AIR(1937); FIREFLY, THE(1937); MOTOR MADNESS(1937); PAID TO DANCE(1937); SAN QUENTIN(1937); TENDERFOOT GOES WEST, A(1937); TRIGGER TRIO, THE(1937); ARMY GIRL(1938); BORN TO BE WILD(1938); DOWN IN ARKANSAW(1938); FIGHTING THOROUGHBREDS(1939); MICKEY, THE KID(1939); S.O.S. TIDAL WAVE(1939); CAPTAIN IS A LADY, THE(1940); DARK STREETS OF CAIRO(1940); DRUMS OF THE DESERT(1940); GOLDEN FLEECING, THE(1940); HOWARDS OF VIRGINIA, THE(1940); MARK OF ZORRO, THE(1940); NORTHWEST MOUNTED POLICE(1940); PLAY GIRL(1940); SON OF MONTE CRISTO(1940); DESPERATE CARGO(1941); DR. KILDARE'S WEDDING DAY(1941); LIFE BEGINS FOR ANDY HARDY(1941); MISBEHAVING HUSBANDS(1941); NAVY BLUES(1941); PENALTY, THE(1941); YANK IN THE R.A.F., A(1941); BROADWAY BIG SHOT(1942); CAREFUL, SOFT SHOULDERS(1942); DUKE OF THE NAVY(1942); JUNGLE BOOK(1942); MANILA CALLING(1942); MOONTIDE(1942); TEN GENTLEMEN FROM WEST POINT(1942); TIME TO KILL(1942); GUADALCANAL DIARY(1943); MARGIN FOR ERROR(1943); THEY CAME TO BLOW UP AMERICA(1943); FOUR JILLS IN A JEEP(1944); TAMPICO(1944); DICK TRACY MEETS GRUESOME(1947); DICK TRACY'S DILEMMA(1947); STALLION ROAD(1947); ARGYLE SECRETS, THE(1948); CANON CITY(1948); JUNGLE GODDESS(1948); STAGE STRUCK(1948); THUNDER IN THE PINES(1949); RADAR SECRET SERVICE(1950); REDHEAD AND THE COWBOY, THE(1950); UNION STATION(1950); CLOSE TO MY HEART(1951); MY FAVORITE SPY(1951)
Misc. Talkies
S.O.S. COAST GUARD(1937)
Roxanne Byrd
TWO OF A KIND(1983)
Thomas Byrd
TWILIGHT ZONE–THE MOVIE(1983)
William Byrd
BETRAYAL, THE(1948)
Miriam Byrd-Nethery
BIG BUS, THE(1976)
Edye Byrde
BRONCO BILLY(1980)
1984
MOSCOW ON THE HUDSON(1984)
The Byrds
CANDY(1968, Ital./Fr.)
Stuart James Byre
DOOMSDAY MACHINE(1967), w
Robert Byrem
Misc. Silents
HIGHEST TRUMP, THE(1919)
Adrienne Byrne
MISCHIEF(1969, Brit.); MEMOIRS OF A SURVIVOR(1981, Brit.)
Alan Byrne
Silents
IMPOSSIBLE WOMAN, THE(1919, Brit.)
Andrew Byrne
Misc. Silents
EIGHT BELLS(1916)
Anne Byrne
END OF THE WORLD(in Our Usual Bed In a Night Full of Rain), THE*1/2 (1978, Ital.); MANHATTAN(1979)
Barbara Byrne
EXCALIBUR(1981)
Bob Byrne
MAIDSTONE(1970)
Bobby Byrne
THINGS ARE TOUGH ALL OVER(1982), ph; FIRST LOVE(1977), ph; SMOKEY AND THE BANDIT(1977), ph; BLUE COLLAR(1978), ph; END, THE(1978), ph; HOOPER(1978), ph; CALIFORNIA DREAMING(1979), ph; VILLAIN, THE(1979), ph; WALK PROUD(1979), ph; THOSE LIPS, THOSE EYES(1980), ph; PATERNITY(1981), ph; CHILLY SCENES OF WINTER(1982), ph; GOING BERSERK(1983), ph
1984
SIXTEEN CANDLES(1984), ph
Cecily Byrne
BROWN SUGAR(1931, Brit.); LOYALTIES(1934, Brit.); ALL AT SEA(1935, Brit.)
Charles Byrne
DEVIL'S AGENT, THE(1962, Brit.); QUACKSER FORTUNE HAS A COUSIN IN THE BRONX(1970)
Charlie Byrne
FREEDOM TO DIE(1962, Brit.)
David Byrne
TRUE STORY OF ESKIMO NELL, THE(1975, Aus.)

Dolly Byrne
Silents
ENTER MADAME(1922), w
Donn Byrne
HIS CAPTIVE WOMAN(1929), w; WINGS OF THE MORNING(1937, Brit.), w
Silents
ALL MAN(1918), w
Dorothea Donn Byrne
IRISH AND PROUD OF IT(1938, Ireland), w
Eddie Byrne
CAPTAIN BOYCOTT(1947, Brit.); ODD MAN OUT(1947, Brit.); SAINTS AND SINNERS(1949, Brit.); GENTLE GUNMAN, THE(1952, Brit.); ALBERT, R.N.(1953, Brit.); TIME GENTLEMEN PLEASE!(1953, Brit.); AUNT CLARA(1954, Brit.); BEAUTIFUL STRANGER(1954, Brit.); CHILDREN GALORE(1954, Brit.); TONIGHT'S THE NIGHT(1954, Brit.); TROUBLE IN THE GLEN(1954, Brit.); DIVIDED HEART, THE(1955, Brit.); LADY GODIVA RIDES AGAIN(1955, Brit.); ONE WAY OUT(1955, Brit.); SEA SHALL NOT HAVE THEM, THE(1955, Brit.); SQUARE RING, THE(1955, Brit.); STOLEN ASSIGNMENT(1955, Brit.); THREE CASES OF MURDER(1955, Brit.); EXTRA DAY, THE(1956, Brit.); IT'S GREAT TO BE YOUNG(1956, Brit.); KID FOR TWO FARTHINGS, A(1956, Brit.); ZARAK(1956, Brit.); ABANDON SHIP(1957, Brit.); ADMIRABLE CRICHTON, THE(1957, Brit.); DECISION AGAINST TIME(1957, Brit.); REACH FOR THE SKY(1957, Brit.); DANGEROUS YOUTH(1958, Brit.); DUNKIRK(1958, Brit.); FLOODS OF FEAR(1958, Brit.); MENACE IN THE NIGHT(1958, Brit.); ROONEY(1958, Brit.); WONDERFUL THINGS!(1958, Brit.); JACK THE RIPPER(1959, Brit.); MUMMY, THE(1959, Brit.); SCAPEGOAT, THE(1959, Brit.); BULLDOG BREED, THE(1960, Brit.); JACKPOT(1960, Brit.); SHAKEDOWN, THE(1960, Brit.); MARK, THE(1961, Brit.); BREAK, THE(1962, Brit.); LOCKER 69(1962, Brit.); MUTINY ON THE BOUNTY(1962); POT CARRIERS, THE(1962, Brit.); CRACKSMAN, THE(1963, Brit.); PUNCH AND JUDY MAN, THE(1963, Brit.); RUNNING MAN, THE(1963, Brit.); DEVILS OF DARKNESS, THE(1965, Brit.); JOHNNY NOBODY(1965, Brit.); ISLAND OF TERROR(1967, Brit.); GUNS IN THE HEATHER(1968, Brit.); VENGEANCE OF FU MANCHU, THE(1968, Brit./Ger./Hong Kong/Ireland); SINFUL DAVEY(1969, Brit.); WHERE'S JACK?(1969, Brit.); WEDDING NIGHT(1970, Ireland); STAR WARS(1977)
Edward Byrne
SAINTS AND SINNERS(1949, Brit.)
1984
CAL(1984, Ireland)
Francis Byrne
Silents
CONSPIRACY, THE(1914)
Gabriel Byrne
EXCALIBUR(1981); HANNAH K.(1983, Fr.); KEEP, THE(1983); WAGNER(1983, Brit./Hung./Aust.)
1984
REFLECTIONS(1984, Brit.)
Jacqueline Byrne
TRAIN OF EVENTS(1952, Brit.)
Jim Byrne
OUT OF THE BLUE(1982)
Joe Byrne
RECORD CITY(1978), p
John Byrne
GUERRILLA GIRL(1953), w; QUEEN OF THE PIRATES(1961, Ital./Ger.), w; RAGE OF THE BUCCANEERS(1963, Ital.), w; QUEEN OF THE NILE(1964, Ital.), w
John F. Byrne
Misc. Silents
EIGHT BELLS(1916), d
Katherine Byrne
FURTHER UP THE CREEK!(1958, Brit.)
Kiki Byrne
STOP THE WORLD–I WANT TO GET OFF(1966, Brit.), cos; PERFECT FRIDAY(1970, Brit.), cos
King Byrne
SILENT WITNESS, THE(1962)
Lennie Byrne
PIRATES OF PENZANCE, THE(1983)
Lou Byrne
AMERICANIZATION OF EMILY, THE(1964); SEND ME NO FLOWERS(1964); LORDS OF FLATBUSH, THE(1974)
Martha Byrne
EYES OF THE AMARYLLIS, THE(1982)
Mary Byrne
THEY GOT ME COVERED(1943)
Michael Byrne
CRIMSON BLADE, THE(1964, Brit.); HENRY VIII AND HIS SIX WIVES(1972, Brit.); BUTLEY(1974, Brit.); CONDUCT UNBECOMING(1975, Brit.); EAGLE HAS LANDED, THE(1976, Brit.); VAMPYRES, DAUGHTERS OF DRACULA(1977, Brit.); FORCE 10 FROM NAVARONE(1978, Brit.); MEDUSA TOUCH, THE(1978, Brit.)
1984
CHAMPIONS(1984)
Packie Byrne
BLACK JACK(1979, Brit.)
Patricia T. Byrne
NIGHT CALL NURSES(1974)
Patsy Byrne
RULING CLASS, THE(1972, Brit.); CLASS OF MISS MAC MICHAEL, THE(1978, Brit./U.S.); RETURN OF THE SOLDIER, THE(1983, Brit.)
Patti Tee Byrne
FUZZ(1972)
Paula Byrne
NARROWING CIRCLE, THE(1956, Brit.); WAY OUT, THE(1956, Brit.); KEY MAN, THE(1957, Brit.)
Peter Byrne
LARGE ROPE, THE(1953, Brit.); ROOMMATES(1962, Brit.); CARRY ON CABBIE(1963, Brit.); SWINGIN' MAIDEN, THE(1963, Brit.); FORCE BEYOND, THE(1978)
Roger Byrne
FORBIDDEN(1932)

Rosalind Byrne
Silents
CASEY AT THE BAT(1927)
Stafford Byrne
MADNESS OF THE HEART(1949, Brit.); HARASSED HERO, THE(1954, Brit.);
SANDS OF THE DESERT(1960, Brit.), w
Stuart J. Byrne
DESERTER, THE(1971 Ital./Yugo.), w
William Byrne
KNUTE ROCKNE–ALL AMERICAN(1940); RIO LOBO(1970)
Helena Byrne-Grant
DARK ANGEL, THE(1935)
Bara Byrnes
GIRL IN GOLD BOOTS(1968)
Misc. Talkies
EXTREME CLOSE-UP(1973)
Bobi Byrnes
GIRLS' TOWN(1959); NIGHT OF THE QUARTER MOON(1959)
Burke Byrnes
NEW CENTURIONS, THE(1972); SCORPIO(1973); TERMINAL MAN, THE(1974);
FUN WITH DICK AND JANE(1977); DIFFERENT STORY, A(1978); PROPHECY(1979);
10(1979); PRIVATE SCHOOL(1983)
Edd Byrnes
SECRET INVASION, THE(1964); BEACH BALL(1965); ANY GUN CAN PLAY(1968,
Ital./Span.); PAYMENT IN BLOOD(1968, Ital.); WICKED, WICKED(1973); STAR-
DUST(1974, Brit.); GREASE(1978)
Edward Byrnes
FEAR STRIKES OUT(1957); REFORM SCHOOL GIRL(1957); DARBY'S RAN-
GERS(1958)
Edward "Edd" Byrnes
JOHNNY TROUBLE(1957); LIFE BEGINS AT 17(1958); MARJORIE MORNING-
STAR(1958); UP PERISCOPE(1959); YELLOWSTONE KELLY(1959)
J. Byrnes
Silents
SONG OF THE WAGE SLAVE, THE(1915)
Ken Byrnes
SWEET CREEK COUNTY WAR, THE(1979), p
Maureen Byrnes
HURRY UP OR I'LL BE 30(1973); GOIN' SOUTH(1978)
Misc. Talkies
SUGAR COOKIES(1973)
Harold Byrns
GIRL ON THE BRIDGE, THE(1951), m; PICKUP(1951), m; SITUATION HOPELESS–
BUT NOT SERIOUS(1965), m
A.S. Byron
LADY AND GENT(1932); ONE SUNDAY AFTERNOON(1933); MADAME SPY(1934);
MENACE(1934); WHARF ANGEL(1934); WALKING ON AIR(1936); SECOND FID-
DLE(1939); RETURN OF FRANK JAMES, THE(1940)
A.S. "Pop" Byron
TWO FOR TONIGHT(1935); BRIDE COMES HOME(1936); STAR MAKER, THE(1939);
LILLIAN RUSSELL(1940)
Allan Byron
DANGER! WOMEN AT WORK(1943); GIRLS IN CHAINS(1943)
Arthur Byron
FAST LIFE(1932); MUMMY, THE(1932); COLLEGE COACH(1933); GABRIEL OVER
THE WHITE HOUSE(1933); MAYOR OF HELL, THE(1933); PRIVATE DETECTIVE
62(1933); SILK EXPRESS, THE(1933); TONIGHT IS OURS(1933); 20,000 YEARS IN
SING SING(1933); FOG OVER FRISCO(1934); HOUSE OF ROTHSCHILD, THE(1934);
MAN WITH TWO FACES, THE(1934); MARIE GALANTE(1934); NOTORIOUS SO-
PHIE LANG, THE(1934); PRESIDENT VANISHES, THE(1934); STAND UP AND
CHEER(1934 80m FOX bw); THAT'S GRATITUDE(1934); TWO ALONE(1934); CASINO
MURDER CASE, THE(1935); MURDER IN THE FLEET(1935); OIL FOR THE LAMPS
OF CHINA(1935); SECRET BRIDE, THE(1935); SHADOW OF A DOUBT(1935); WHOLE
TOWN'S TALKING, THE(1935); PRISONER OF SHARK ISLAND, THE(1936)
Arthur "Pop" Byron
MERRY WIDOW, THE(1934); WHOM THE GODS DESTROY(1934); MEN WITHOUT
NAMES(1935); SWEETHEARTS(1938)
Arthur S. Byron
YOU SAID A MOUTHFUL(1932); SHE MARRIED HER BOSS(1935); WINGS IN THE
DARK(1935)
Arthur S. "Pop" Byron
MILKY WAY, THE(1936); RETURN OF SOPHIE LANG, THE(1936)
Brook Byron
AUNTIE MAME(1958)
Carol Byron
PRIZE, THE(1963); DIMENSION 5(1966)
Carrol Byron
ASK ANY GIRL(1959)
Delma Byron
DIMPLES(1936); EVERYBODY'S OLD MAN(1936); LAUGHING AT TROUBLE(1937)
George Byron
DECEIVER, THE(1931); GOLD DUST GERTIE(1931); HUSH MONEY(1931); SOB
SISTER(1931); THEY NEVER COME BACK(1932); ICE-CAPADES REVUE(1942);
CHATTERBOX(1943); HOOSIER HOLIDAY(1943); THUMBS UP(1943); JAM-
BOREE(1944)
George Gordon [Lord] Byron
Silents
DON JUAN(1926), w
Jack Byron
SANTA FE TRAIL, THE(1930); SOCIAL LION, THE(1930); CLEARING THE RAN-
GE(1931); HARD HOMBRE(1931); TEN CENTS A DANCE(1931); GOLD(1932); ENTER
MADAME(1935); RIFF-RAFF(1936); LOVE IS NEWS(1937); MAYOR OF 44TH
STREET, THE(1942); 711 OCEAN DRIVE(1950), makeup; OUTCASTS OF POKER
FLAT, THE(1952); MURDER IS MY BEAT(1955), makeup; THIS ISLAND
EARTH(1955)
Silents
APRIL SHOWERS(1923); FIGHTING AMERICAN, THE(1924); AIR MAIL,
THE(1925); RUGGED WATER(1925); FOUR WALLS(1928)

Misc. Silents
FIGHT FOR HONOR, A(1924)
Jack [John] Byron
YOURS FOR THE ASKING(1936)
Jean Byron
VOODOO TIGER(1952); MAGNETIC MONSTER, THE(1953); SERPENT OF THE
NILE(1953); JUNGLE MOON MEN(1955); JOHNNY CONCHO(1956); THERE'S AL-
WAYS TOMORROW(1956); INVISIBLE INVADERS(1959); WALL OF NOISE(1963);
FLAREUP(1969)
Jeanne Byron
WHERE DOES IT HURT?(1972)
Jeffrey Byron
NICKELODEON(1976); INTERNATIONAL VELVET(1978, Brit.); SENIORS,
THE(1978); METALSTORM: THE DESTRUCTION OF JARED-SYN(1983)
Misc. Talkies
SENIORS, THE(1978)
John Byron
LORD BYRON OF BROADWAY(1930); MADAME SATAN(1930); WOMAN RACKET,
THE(1930); POPE JOAN(1972, Brit.)
Silents
SPITE MARRIAGE(1929)
Misc. Silents
FIGHTING JACK(1926)
Katherine Byron
MUMMY, THE(1932)
Kathleen Byron
YOUNG MR. PITT, THE(1942, Brit.); SILVER FLEET, THE(1945, Brit.); STAIRWAY
TO HEAVEN(1946, Brit.); BLACK NARCISSUS(1947, Brit.); HOUR OF GLORY(1949,
Brit.); MADNESS OF THE HEART(1949, Brit.); PRELUDE TO FAME(1950, Brit.);
FOUR DAYS(1951, Brit.); HELL IS SOLD OUT(1951, Brit.); I'LL NEVER FORGET
YOU(1951); LIFE IN HER HANDS(1951, Brit.); RELUCTANT WIDOW, THE(1951,
Brit.); SCARLET THREAD(1951, Brit.); TOM BROWN'S SCHOOLDAYS(1951, Brit.);
GAMBLER AND THE LADY, THE(1952, Brit.); MY DEATH IS A MOCKERY(1952,
Brit.); YOUNG BESS(1953); NIGHT OF THE FULL MOON, THE(1954, Brit.); PROFI-
LE(1954, Brit.); STAR OF MY NIGHT(1954, Brit.); HANDCUFFS, LONDON(1955, Brit.);
SECRET VENTURE(1955, Brit.); HAND IN HAND(1960, Brit.); BURN WITCH
BURN(1962); HAMMERHEAD(1968); ABDICATION, THE(1974, Brit.); CRAZE(1974,
Brit.); NOTHING BUT THE NIGHT(1975, Brit.); ELEPHANT MAN, THE(1980, Brit.)
Keith Byron
CHICAGO CONFIDENTIAL(1957); UNDER FIRE(1957); SPEED CRAZY(1959)
Marion Byron
BROADWAY BABIES(1929); FORWARD PASS, THE(1929); HIS CAPTIVE WO-
MAN(1929); SO LONG LETTY(1929); BAD MAN, THE(1930); GOLDEN DAWN(1930);
MATRIMONIAL BED, THE(1930); PLAYING AROUND(1930); SONG OF THE
WEST(1930); CHILDREN OF DREAMS(1931); GIRLS DEMAND EXCITEMENT(1931);
HEART OF NEW YORK(1932); BREED OF THE BORDER(1933); GIFT OF GAB(1934);
SWELL-HEAD(1935); FIVE OF A KIND(1938)
Silents
STEAMBOAT BILL, JR.(1928)
Marion "Peanuts" Byron
LOVE ME TONIGHT(1932); TENDERFOOT, THE(1932)
Melinda Byron
TEENAGE THUNDER(1957); 10 NORTH FREDERICK(1958)
Michael Byron
SHE BEAST, THE(1966, Brit./Ital./Yugo.), w; RIOT(1969)
Nicholas Byron
THING, THE(1951)
Nina Byron
Silents
TRUTHFUL TULLIVER(1917); JOHNNY GET YOUR GUN(1919)
Misc. Silents
HEIR OF THE AGES, THE(1917); TRUTHFUL TULLIVER(1917); BOOMERANG,
THE(1919); DUB, THE(1919)
Paul Byron
Silents
SECOND IN COMMAND, THE(1915)
Misc. Silents
BLACK SHEEP OF THE FAMILY, THE(1916); CHILD OF MYSTERY, A(1916);
SEEKERS, THE(1916); HEART STRINGS(1917)
Pop Byron
HIDEAWAY GIRL(1937); LOVE AND HISSES(1937); LOVE IS NEWS(1937); TIME
OUT FOR ROMANCE(1937); ALEXANDER'S RAGTIME BAND(1938); DISBAR-
RED(1939)
Richard Byron
ARE THESE OUR PARENTS?(1944); FACES IN THE FOG(1944); KID SISTER,
THE(1945)
Roy Byron
UNMASKED(1929)
Royal Byron
Silents
SINS OF SOCIETY(1915); QUEST OF LIFE, THE(1916)
Misc. Silents
LADY OF THE PHOTOGRAPH, THE(1917)
Walter Byron
SACRED FLAME, THE(1929); DANCERS, THE(1930); NOT DAMAGED(1930); LAST
FLIGHT, THE(1931); LEFTOVER LADIES(1931); LION AND THE LAMB(1931);
RECKLESS HOUR, THE(1931); YELLOW TICKET, THE(1931); CRUSADER,
THE(1932); MENACE, THE(1932); SAVAGE GIRL, THE(1932); SHOP ANGEL(1932);
SINNERS IN THE SUN(1932); SOCIETY GIRL(1932); THIS SPORTING AGE(1932);
THREE WISE GIRLS(1932); VANITY FAIR(1932); WEEK-ENDS ONLY(1932); CHARL-
IE CHAN'S GREATEST CASE(1933); EAST OF FIFTH AVE.(1933); GRAND
SLAM(1933); SLIGHTLY MARRIED(1933); ALL MEN ARE ENEMIES(1934); BIG
TIME OR BUST(1934); BRITISH AGENT(1934); MAN OF TWO WORLDS(1934); ONCE
TO EVERY WOMAN(1934); DON'T BET ON BLONDES(1935); FOLIES DER-
GERE(1935); MARY OF SCOTLAND(1936); AS GOOD AS MARRIED(1937); BACK IN
CIRCULATION(1937); MR. BOGGS STEPS OUT(1938); TRADE WINDS(1938); CRASH-
ING THRU(1939); DEATH GOES NORTH(1939); FRONTIER SCOUT(1939); ONE
NIGHT IN LISBON(1941); MRS. MINIVER(1942); NAZI AGENT(1942); ONCE UPON
A HONEYMOON(1942)

Misc. Talkies
EXPOSURE(1932)
Silents
AWAKENING, THE(1928); QUEEN KELLY(1929)
William Byron
SPIDER, THE(1940, Brit.)
Byron & Bean
Misc. Talkies
SUN TAN RANCH(1948)
The Byron Lee Band
DR. NU(1962)
R. Byron-Webber
Silents
MISSING THE TIDE(1918, Brit.), w; KEEPER OF THE DOOR(1919, Brit.), w; UNREST(1920, Brit.), w
Irena Byrska
CONTRACT, THE(1982, Pol.)
Irene Byrska
MAN OF IRON(1981, Pol.)
John Byrum
HAVE A NICE WEEKEND(1975), w; MAHOGANY(1975), w; HARRY AND WALTER GO TO NEW YORK(1976), w; HEART BEAT(1979), d&w; SPHINX(1981), w
1984
RAZOR'S EDGE, THE(1984), d, w; SCANDALOUS(1984), w
Lyle Byrum
1984
CHATTANOOGA CHOO CHOO(1984)
Jim Bysel
TERROR AT BLACK FALLS(1962)
Jim Bysol
COOL AND THE CRAZY, THE(1958)

Ellina Bystritskaya
AND QUIET FLOWS THE DON(1960 USSR)
Ashley Bystrom
1984
PRODIGAL, THE(1984)
Margareta Bystrom
TOUCH, THE(1971, U.S./Swed.)
Henning Bystron
TERROR IN THE JUNGLE(1968)
Doc Bytell
Silents
QUESTION OF HONOR, A(1922)
Walter Bytell
Silents
WILD AND WOOLLY(1917)
Reggie Rock Bythewood
1984
BROTHER FROM ANOTHER PLANET, THE(1984); EXTERMINATOR 2(1984)
Reginald Bythewood
FIGHT FOR YOUR LIFE(1977)
Hayong Byun
MONSTER WANGMAGWI(1967, S. K.), w
Soojai Byun
MONSTER WANGMAGWI(1967, S. K.), spec eff
Clement Bywood
LEGEND OF FRENCHIE KING, THE(1971, Fr./Ital./Span./Brit.), w
Pusante Byzantium
FOREIGNER, THE(1978)

C

C.J. the Orangutan
TARZAN, THE APE MAN(1981)

Alberto Ca'zorzi
TORPEDO BAY(1964, Ital./Fr.), w

James Caan
LADY IN A CAGE(1964); GLORY GUYS, THE(1965); RED LINE 7000(1965); EL DORADO(1967); GAMES(1967); COUNTDOWN(1968); JOURNEY TO SHILOH(1968); RAIN PEOPLE, THE(1969); SUMARINE X-1(1969, Brit.); RABBIT, RUN(1970); T.R. BASKIN(1971); GODFATHER, THE(1972); CINDERELLA LIBERTY(1973); SLITHER(1973); FREEBIE AND THE BEAN(1974); GAMBLER, THE(1974); GODFATHER, THE, PART II(1974); FUNNY LADY(1975); KILLER ELITE, THE(1975); ROLLERBALL(1975); HARRY AND WALTER GO TO NEW YORK(1976); SILENT MOVIE(1976); ANOTHER MAN, ANOTHER CHANCE(1977 Fr/US); BRIDGE TOO FAR, A(1977, Brit.); COMES A HORSEMAN(1978); CHAPTER TWO(1979); HIDE IN PLAIN SIGHT(1980), a, d; THIEF(1981); BOLERO(1982, Fr.); KISS ME GOODBYE(1982)
Misc. Talkies
GONE WITH THE WEST(1976)

Richard Caan
WAR OF THE WIZARDS(1983, Taiwan), d

Ronnie Caan
THIEF(1981), p

Cab Calloway
SENSATIONS OF 1945(1944)

Cab Calloway and Band
STORMY WEATHER(1943)

Cab Calloway and His Band
SINGING KID, THE(1936)

Cab Calloway and his Orchestra
INTERNATIONAL HOUSE(1933)

Cab Calloway Orchestra
HI-DE-HO(1947)

Emilio Gutierrez Caba
HUNT, THE(1967, Span.)

Robert Cabal
RIDE THE PINK HORSE(1947); SAXON CHARM, THE(1948); CRISIS(1950); FORBIDDEN JUNGLE(1950); MAN BEHIND THE GUN, THE(1952); MARA MARU(1952); ESCAPE TO BURMA(1955); HELL'S ISLAND(1955); WOMEN OF PITCAIRN ISLAND, THE(1957)

Oscar Caballero
TERRACE, THE(1964, Arg.)

Pilar Caballero
SAVAGE GUNS, THE(1962, U.S./Span.)

Los Caballeros de Villa de Leyva
PROUD AND THE DAMNED, THE(1972)

Bill Cabanne
SONG OF SCHEHERAZADE(1947); FIGHTER SQUADRON(1948); KING OF THE BANDITS(1948); KID MONK BARONI(1952)

Christine Cabanne
FLYING DEUCES, THE(1939)

Christy Cabanne
CONSPIRACY(1930), d; CONVICTED(1931), d; DAWN TRAIL, THE(1931), d; GRAFT(1931), d; SKY RAIDERS(1931), d; HEARTS OF HUMANITY(1932), d; HOTEL CONTINENTAL(1932), d; MIDNIGHT PATROL, THE(1932), d; RED-HAIRED ALIBI, THE(1932), d; UNWRITTEN LAW, THE(1932), d; WESTERN LIMITED(1932), d; DARING DAUGHTERS(1933), d; MIDSHIPMAN JACK(1933), d; WORLD GONE MAD, THE(1933), d; GIRL OF THE LIMBERLOST(1934), d; MONEY MEANS NOTHING(1934), d; ANOTHER FACE(1935), d; BEHIND GREEN LIGHTS(1935), d; JANE EYRE(1935), d; KEEPER OF THE BEES(1935), d; ONE FRIGHTENED NIGHT(1935), d; RENDEZVOUS AT MIDNIGHT(1935), d; STORM OVER THE ANDES(1935), d; LAST OUTLAW, THE(1936), d; ANNAPOLIS SALUTE(1937), d, w; CRIMINAL LAWYER(1937), d; DON'T TELL THE WIFE(1937), d; OUTCASTS OF POKER FLAT, THE(1937), d; WE WHO ARE ABOUT TO DIE(1937), d; WESTLAND CASE, THE(1937), d; YOU CAN'T BEAT LOVE(1937), d; EVERYBODY'S DOING IT(1938), d; NIGHT SPOT(1938), d; THIS MARRIAGE BUSINESS(1938), d; LEGION OF LOST FLYERS(1939), d; MUTINY ON THE BLACKHAWK(1939), d; SMASHING THE SPY RING(1939), d; TROPIC FURY(1939), d; ALIAS THE DEACON(1940), d; BLACK DIAMONDS(1940), d; DANGER ON WHEELS(1940), d; DEVIL'S PIPELINE, THE(1940), d; HOT STEEL(1940), d; MAN FROM MONTREAL, THE(1940), d; MUMMY'S HAND, THE(1940), d; SCATTERGOOD BAINES(1941), d; SCATTERGOOD MEETS BROADWAY(1941), d; SCATTERGOOD PULLS THE STRINGS(1941), d, w; CINDERELLA SWINGS IT(1942), d; DRUMS OF THE CONGO(1942), d; SCATTERGOOD RIDES HIGH(1942), d; SCATTERGOOD SURVIVES A MURDER(1942), d; TIMBER(1942), d; TOP SERGEANT(1942), d; KEEP 'EM SLUGGING(1943), d; DIXIE JAMBOREE(1945), d; MAN WHO WALKED ALONE, THE(1945), d&w; SENSATION HUNTERS(1945), d; SCARED TO DEATH(1947), d; BACK TRAIL(1948), d; KING OF THE BANDITS(1948), d, w; SILVER TRAILS(1948), d
Misc. Talkies
BROKEN HEARTS(1933), d; STORM OVER THE ANDES(1935), d; ROBIN HOOD OF MONTEREY(1947), d
Silents
DISHONORED MEDAL, THE(1914), d&w; ABSENTEE-NRA, THE(1915), d; DAPHNE AND THE PIRATE(1916), d; FLIRTING WITH FATE(1916), d&w; AT THE STAGE DOOR(1921), d&w; ALTARS OF DESIRE(1927), d; ANNAPOLIS(1928), d; NAMELESS MEN(1928), d
Misc. Silents
FAILURE, THE(1915), d; REGULAR FELLOW, A(1919), d; BURNT WINGS(1920), d; MASKED BRIDE, THE(1925), d; MIDSHIPMAN, THE(1925), d; MONTE CARLO(1926), d; DRIFTWOOD(1928), d; RESTLESS YOUTH(1928), d

Emilie Cabanne
PRISONER OF ZENDA, THE(1952)

Emily Cabanne
NINOTCHKA(1939)

W. Christy Cabanne
Silents
GANGSTERS OF NEW YORK, THE(1914), d; GREAT LEAP, THE(1914), d; LAMB, THE(1915), d, w; MARTYRS OF THE ALAMO, THE(1915), d, w; FLYING TORPEDO, THE(1916), d; PEST, THE(1919), d
Misc. Silents
DOUBLE TROUBLE(1915), d; ENOCH ARDEN(1915), d; LOST HOUSE, THE(1915), d; DIANA OF THE FOLLIES(1916), d; CYCLONE HIGGINS, D.D.(1918), d; MAYOR OF FILBERT, THE(1919), d; LIFE'S TWIST(1920), d

William Cabanne
FOREST RANGERS, THE(1942); MY FAVORITE BLONDE(1942); SWEATER GIRL(1942); THIS GUN FOR HIRE(1942); YOUNG AND WILLING(1943); JIGGS AND MAGGIE IN SOCIETY(1948); ROYAL WEDDING(1951); GENTLEMEN PREFER BLONDES(1953)
Silents
AVERAGE WOMAN, THE(1924), d

William Christy Cabanne
WHEN STRANGERS MEET(1934), d
Silents
REGGIE MIXES IN(1916), d; ONE OF MANY(1917), d&w; GOD'S OUTLAW(1919), d&w; NOTORIOUS MRS. SANDS, THE(1920), d; WHAT'S A WIFE WORTH?(1921), d&w; IS LOVE EVERYTHING?(1924), d, w; LEND ME YOUR HUSBAND(1924), d; SPITFIRE, THE(1924), d; YOUTH FOR SALE(1924), d
Misc. Silents
SOLD FOR MARRIAGE(1916), d; DRAFT 258(1917), d; MISS ROBINSON CRUSOE(1917), d; SLACKER, THE(1917), d; BELOVED CHEATER, THE(1920), d; STEALERS, THE(1920), d; TRIFLERS, THE(1920), d; BARRICADE, THE(1921), d; LIVE AND LET LIVE(1921), d; BEYOND THE RAINBOW(1922), d; TILL WE MEET AGAIN(1922), d; SIXTH COMMANDMENT, THE(1924), d

Naji Cabbay
KING OF THE KHYBER RIFLES(1953)

Virginia Cabell
PRINCESS COMES ACROSS, THE(1936)

Enrico Cabiati
TIME AND THE TOUCH, THE(1962), m

Renaldo Cabieri
PLACE FOR LOVERS, A(1969, Ital./Fr.), w

The Cabin Kids
MISSISSIPPI(1935); GIT ALONG, LITTLE DOGIES(1937); ROUNDUP TIME IN TEXAS(1937)

Giulietta Masina Cabiria
NIGHTS OF CABIRIA(1957, Ital.)

Cable
Misc. Talkies
BIJOU(1972)

Bill Cable
Misc. Talkies
LAST TANGO IN ACAPULCO, THE(1975)

Boyd Cable
Silents
SOMME, THE(1927, Brit.), w

Edward Cable
OCEAN'S ELEVEN(1960)

Richard Cable
SERENADE(1956)

Roy Cable
WEST OF ZANZIBAR(1954, Brit.)

Sue Cable
THUMBELINA(1970)

Tony Cabooch
LAUGH IT OFF(1939)

Michael Caborne
MY BROTHER JONATHAN(1949, Brit.)

Annette Cabot
HEIGHTS OF DANGER(1962, Brit.)

Bruce Cabot
LADY WITH A PAST(1932); ROADHOUSE MURDER, THE(1932); ANN VICKERS(1933); DISGRACED(1933); FLYING DEVILS(1933); GREAT JASPER, THE(1933); KING KONG(1933); LUCKY DEVILS(1933); MIDSHIPMAN JACK(1933); SCARLET RIVER(1933); FINISHING SCHOOL(1934); HIS GREATEST GAMBLE(1934); MEN OF THE NIGHT(1934); MURDER ON THE BLACKBOARD(1934); RED HEAD(1934); SHADOWS OF SING SING(1934); THEIR BIG MOMENT(1934); LET 'EM HAVE IT(1935); NIGHT ALARM(1935); SHOW THEM NO MERCY(1935); BIG GAME, THE(1936); DON'T GAMBLE WITH LOVE(1936); DON'T TURN'EM LOOSE(1936); FURY(1936); LAST OF THE MOHICANS, THE(1936); LEGION OF TERROR(1936); PENTHOUSE PARTY(1936); ROBIN HOOD OF EL DORADO(1936); SINNER TAKE ALL(1936); THREE WISE GUYS, THE(1936); BAD GUY(1937); LOVE TAKES FLIGHT(1937); BAD MAN OF BRIMSTONE(1938); SINNERS IN PARADISE(1938); SMASHING THE RACKETS(1938); TENTH AVENUE KID(1938); DODGE CITY(1939); HOMICIDE BUREAU(1939); MICKEY, THE KID(1939); MYSTERY OF THE WHITE ROOM(1939); CAPTAIN CAUTION(1940); GIRLS UNDER TWENTY-ONE(1940); MY SON IS GUILTY(1940); SUSAN AND GOD(1940); TORSO MURDER MYSTERY, THE(1940, Brit.); FLAME OF NEW ORLEANS, THE(1941); SUNDOWN(1941); PIERRE OF THE PLAINS(1942); SILVER QUEEN(1942); WILD BILL HICKOK RIDES(1942); DESERT SONG, THE(1943); DIVORCE(1945); FALLEN ANGEL(1945); SALTY O'ROURKE(1945); AVALANCHE(1946); SMOKY(1946); ANGEL AND THE BADMAN(1947); GUNFIGHTERS, THE(1947); GALLANT LEGION, THE(1948); SORROWFUL JONES(1949); FANCY PANTS(1950); ROCK ISLAND TRAIL(1950); BEST OF THE BADMEN(1951); KID MONK BARONI(1952); LOST IN ALASKA(1952); QUIET AMERICAN, THE(1958); SHERIFF OF FRACTURED JAW, THE(1958, Brit.); JOHN PAUL JONES(1959); LOVE SPECIALIST, THE(1959, Ital.); GOLIATH AND THE BARBARIANS(1960, Ital.); COMANCHEROS, THE(1961); RED CLOAK, THE(1961, Ital./Fr.); HATARI!(1962); ROMMEL'S TREASURE(1962, Ital.); LAW OF THE LAWLESS(1964); BLACK SPURS(1965); CAT BALLOU(1965); IN HARM'S WAY(1965); TOWN TAMER(1965); CHASE, THE(1966); WAR WAGON, THE(1967); GREEN BERETS, THE(1968); HELLFIGHTERS(1968); UNDEFEATED, THE(1969); CHISUM(1970); WUSA(1970); BIG JAKE(1971); DIAMONDS ARE FOREVER(1971, Brit.)

Ceil Cabot
RELUCTANT ASTRONAUT, THE(1967); SWEET CHARITY(1969); FREAKY FRIDAY(1976); NORTH AVENUE IRREGULARS, THE(1979); HERBIE GOES BANANAS(1980); NUDE BOMB, THE(1980)

Christopher Cabot
HEIGHTS OF DANGER(1962, Brit.); OH! WHAT A LOVELY WAR(1969, Brit.); MAN FRIDAY(1975, Brit.)

John Cabot
TWO-HEADED SPY, THE(1959, Brit.)

Judith Ogden Cabot
FRIENDS OF EDDIE COYLE, THE(1973)

Sebastian Cabot
DUAL ALIBI(1947, Brit.); ADVENTURES OF JANE, THE(1949, Brit.); DICK BARTON STRIKES BACK(1949, Brit.); THIRD TIME LUCKY(1950, Brit.); MIDNIGHT EPISODE(1951, Brit.); OLD MOTHER RILEY'S JUNGLE TREASURE(1951, Brit.); WONDER BOY(1951, Brit./Aust.); BABES IN BAGDAD(1952); IVANHOE(1952, Brit.); OLD MOTHER RILEY(1952, Brit.); SPIDER AND THE FLY, THE(1952, Br.); CAPTAIN'S PARADISE, THE(1953, Brit.); ALWAYS A BRIDE(1954, Brit.); LOVE LOTTERY, THE(1954, Brit.); ROMEO AND JULIET(1954, Brit.); KISMET(1955); WESTWARD HO THE WAGONS!(1956); BLACK PATCH(1957); DRAGON WELLS MASSACRE(1957); JOHNNY TREMAIN(1957); OMAR KHAYYAM(1957); IN LOVE AND WAR(1958); TERROR IN A TEXAS TOWN(1958); ANGRY HILLS, THE(1959, Brit.); SAY ONE FOR ME(1959); SEVEN THIEVES(1960); TIME MACHINE, THE(1960, Brit./U.S.); HEIGHTS OF DANGER(1962, Brit.); SWORD IN THE STONE, THE(1963); TWICE TOLD TALES(1963); FAMILY JEWELS, THE(1965); REDEEMER, THE(1965, Span.); JUNGLE BOOK, THE(1967)

Susan Cabot
ON THE ISLE OF SAMOA(1950); ENFORCER, THE(1951); FLAME OF ARABY(1951); PRINCE WHO WAS A THIEF, THE(1951); TOMAHAWK(1951); BATTLE AT APACHE PASS, THE(1952); DUEL AT SILVER CREEK, THE(1952); SON OF ALI BABA(1952); GUNSMOKE(1953); RIDE CLEAR OF DIABLO(1954); CARNIVAL ROCK(1957); SAGA OF THE VIKING WOMEN AND THEIR VOYAGE TO THE WATERS OF THE GREAT SEA SERPENT, THE(1957); SORORITY GIRL(1957); FORT MASSACRE(1958); MACHINE GUN KELLY(1958); WAR OF THE SATELLITES(1958); SURRENDER–HELL!(1959); WASP WOMAN, THE(1959)

Takis Cabouras
SERENITY(1962)

America Cabral
STRANGE WORLD(1952)

Sadi Cabral
VIOLENT AND THE DAMNED, THE(1962, Braz.)

Baby Cabrales
DYNAMITE JOHNSON(1978, Phil.), ph

Rudy Cabrales
STRYKER(1983, Phil.), ed

Arturo Cabre
COLOSSUS OF RHODES, THE(1961, Ital., Fr., Span.)

Mario Cabre
PANDORA AND THE FLYING DUTCHMAN(1951, Brit.)

John Cabrera
CAPTAIN APACHE(1971, Brit.), ph; CALL OF THE WILD(1972, Ger./ Span./Ital./ Fr.), ph; MAN CALLED NOON, THE(1973, Brit.), ph; CARAVAN TO VACCARES(1974, Brit./Fr), ph; PAPER TIGER(1975, Brit.), ph; WIDOWS' NEST(1977, U.S./Span.), ph; JAGUAR LIVES!(1979), ph; ZOMBIE CREEPING FLESH(1981, Ital./Span.), ph; CONAN THE BARBARIAN(1982), ph; NIGHT OF THE ZOMBIES(1983, Span./Ital.), ph; TRIUMPHS OF A MAN CALLED HORSE(1983, US/Mex.), ph
1984
HUNDRA(1984, Ital.), ph; YELLOW HAIR AND THE FORTRESS OF GOLD(1984), ph

Rafael Cabrera
WANDERERS, THE(1979)

Raul Cabrera
1984
CAGED WOMEN(1984, Ital./Fr.)

Susana Cabrera
RAGE(1966, U.S./Mex.)

Joe Cabrillas
MY FAVORITE WIFE(1940)

Carlo Cabrini
FIANCES, THE(1964, Ital.)

R. Cabutti
CHILDREN OF PARADISE(1945, Fr.), art d

John Cacavas
BLADE(1973), m; AIRPORT 1975(1974), m; AIRPORT '77(1977), m; COUNT DRACULA AND HIS VAMPIRE BRIDE(1978, Brit.), m; HANGAR 18(1980), m; SEPARATE WAYS(1981), m; MORTUARY(1983), m
1984
THEY'RE PLAYING WITH FIRE(1984), m

Roland Caccavo
HOME FREE ALL(1983)
1984
HOME FREE ALL(1984)

Robert Caccia
PEEK-A-BOO(1961, Fr.); TALL BLOND MAN WITH ONE BLACK SHOE, THE(1973, Fr.)

Tony Cacciotti
LONGEST YARD, THE(1974); HERO AT LARGE(1980)

Ernie Caceres
SUN VALLEY SERENADE(1941)

Richard Caceres
HAIR(1979)

Sally Caclough
PREHISTORIC WOMEN(1967, Brit.)

Michael Cacoyannis
CAESAR AND CLEOPATRA(1946, Brit.); ELECTRA(1962, Gr.), p,d&w; WASTREL, THE(1963, Ital.), d, w; ZORBA THE GREEK(1964, U.S./Gr.), p&d, w, ed; DAY THE FISH CAME OUT, THE(1967. Brit./Gr.), p,d&w; TROJAN WOMEN, THE(1971), p, d&w, ed; IPHIGENIA(1977, Gr.), d&w, ed

Cactus Mack
TIMBER STAMPEDE(1939); TWO-GUN TROUBADOR(1939); PRAIRIE PIONEERS(1941); SUNSET ON THE DESERT(1942); STAGECOACH TO MONTEREY(1944)

Libby Caculus
DRACULA(THE DIRTY OLD MAN) (1969)

Bertrand Cadart
MAD MAX(1979, Aus.)

Brian Cadd
ALVIN RIDES AGAIN(1974, Aus.), m

M. Brian Cadd
ALVIN PURPLE(1974, Aus.), ph

Raymond Caddell
THUNDER IN CAROLINA(1960)

Edward Caddick
VULTURE, THE(1967, U.S./Brit./Can.)

Jack Caddon
WANDA NEVADA(1979); WHERE THE BUFFALO ROAM(1980)

Alan Caddy
GREAT GUNDOWN, THE(1977), m

James F. Cade
DOUBLE LIFE, A(1947)

Rose Cade
Silents
SALVAGE(1921)

Paul Cadeac
FANTOMAS STRIKES BACK(1965, Fr./Ital.), p; FANTOMAS(1966, Fr./Ital.), p; OSS 117–MISSION FOR A KILLER(1966, Fr./Ital.), p; SHADOW OF EVIL(1967, Fr./Ital.), p; TWO OF US, THE(1968, Fr.), p

Lally Cadeau
THRESHOLD(1983, Can.); VIDEODROME(1983, Can.)

Ava Cadell
SPACED OUT(1981, Brit.); SMOKEY AND THE BANDIT–PART 3(1983)
1984
JUNGLE WARRIORS(1984, U.S./Ger./Mex.)

David Cadell
WOLFMAN(1979), art d

Don Cadell
SABOTEUR(1942); 'TILL WE MEET AGAIN(1944); CROSSFIRE(1947)

Jean Cadell
ESCAPE(1930, Brit.); LOVES OF ROBERT BURNS, THE(1930, Brit.); FIRES OF FATE(1932, Brit.); TIMBUCTOO(1933, Brit.); WIVES BEWARE(1933, Brit.); LITTLE FRIEND(1934, Brit.); LUCK OF A SAILOR, THE(1934, Brit.); DAVID COPPERFIELD(1935); LOVE FROM A STRANGER(1937, Brit.); PYGMALION(1938, Brit.); SOUTH RIDING(1938, Brit.); CONFIDENTIAL LADY(1939, Brit.); MOZART(1940, Brit.); QUIET WEDDING(1941, Brit.); YOUNG MR. PITT, THE(1942, Brit.); SOLDIER, SAILOR(1944, Brit.); RANDOLPH FAMILY, THE(1945, Brit.); I KNOW WHERE I'M GOING(1947, Brit.); JASSY(1948, Brit.); MARRY ME!(1949, Brit.); TIGHT LITTLE ISLAND(1949, Brit.); IF THIS BE SIN(1950, Brit.); MADELEINE(1950, Brit.); NO PLACE FOR JENNIFER(1950, Brit.); OBSESSED(1951, Brit.); RELUCTANT WIDOW, THE(1951, Brit.); I'M A STRANGER(1952, Brit.); MEET MR. LUCIFER(1953, Brit.); KEEP IT CLEAN(1956, Brit.); LET'S BE HAPPY(1957, Brit.); LITTLE HUT, THE(1957); SURGEON'S KNIFE, THE(1957, Brit.); MAD LITTLE ISLAND(1958, Brit.); TASTE OF MONEY, A(1960, Brit.); UPSTAIRS AND DOWNSTAIRS(1961, Brit.); IMMORAL CHARGE(1962, Brit.)
Silents
ALF'S BUTTON(1920, Brit.); ANNA THE ADVENTURESS(1920, Brit.)

Johnny Cadell
ROBBERY UNDER ARMS(1958, Brit.)

Simon Cadell
WATERSHIP DOWN(1978, Brit.)

Pierre Caden
YOUNG GIRLS OF ROCHEFORT, THE(1968, Fr.)

Richard Cadenas
SOME OF MY BEST FRIENDS ARE...(1971), ed

Garry Cadenat
1984
SUGAR CANE ALLEY(1984, Fr.)

Roberto Cadendo
SANTO CONTRA LA HIJA DE FRANKENSTEIN(1971, Mex.)

Kate Cadenhead
1984
SONGWRITER(1984)

Giuseppe Cadeo
ORGANIZER, THE(1964, Fr./Ital./Yugo.)

Rivers Cadet
OPEN ROAD, THE(1940, Fr.)

The Cadets of St. Basile-le-Grand Cadet Corps 2831
APPRENTICESHIP OF DUDDY KRAVITZ, THE(1974, Can.)

Donald Cadette
1984
OH GOD! YOU DEVIL(1984)

Dave Cadiente
PROFESSIONALS, THE(1966)
1984
STAR TREK III: THE SEARCH FOR SPOCK(1984)

David Cadiente
RAMPAGE(1963); RIDE THE WILD SURF(1964); BUCK ROGERS IN THE 25TH CENTURY(1979)

Vince Cadiente
PROFESSIONALS, THE(1966)

Vincent Cadiente
GREEN BERETS, THE(1968)

Pauline Cadieux
CORDELIA(1980, Fr., Can.), w

Rita Cadillac
ANY NUMBER CAN WIN(1963 Fr.); UNSATISFIED, THE(1964, Span.); PROSTITUTION(1965, Fr.); DAS BOOT(1982)

The Cadillacs
GO, JOHNNY, GO!(1959)
Pierre Cadiou
PICNIC ON THE GRASS(1960, Fr.), set d; MALPERTIUS(1972, Bel./Fr.), art d
1984
ERENDIRA(1984, Mex./Fr./Ger.), art d
Dusty Cadis
SANDPIPER, THE(1965)
Marinette Cadix
LIFE BEGINS TOMORROW(1952, Fr.), ed; LOVERS OF TERUEL, THE(1962, Fr.), ed
Marcel Cadiz
IT HAPPENED IN PARIS(1953, Fr.), ed
Emil Cadkin
BIG FIX, THE(1947), m, m; THREE ON A TICKET(1947), m; GUNSMOKE IN TUCSON(1958), md; KILLER SHREWS, THE(1959), m; DEVIL'S BEDROOM, THE(1964), m; NAVAJO RUN(1966), m
Ben Cadlett
SCAVENGERS, THE(1969); TRADER HORNEE(1970)
Charles Wakefield Cadman
SKY HAWK(1929), m/l
Josh Cadman
1984
ANGEL(1984)
Joshua Cadman
PENNIES FROM HEAVEN(1981)
Misc. Talkies
GOIN' ALL THE WAY(1982)
Michael Cadman
IF ...(1968, Brit.); TWISTED NERVE(1969, Brit.)
Lanell Cado
NIGHT TRAIN TO MUNDO FINE(1966)
Alice Cadogan
1984
BEVERLY HILLS COP(1984)
Therese Cadorette
ISABEL(1968, Can.)
Juliette Cadsow
WICKER MAN, THE(1974, Brit.)
Charles Cadwallader
CLANCY IN WALL STREET(1930), art d
Silents
PEACOCK ALLEY(1922), set d; SHERLOCK HOLMES(1922), art d; MAN BAIT(1926), art d; PRINCE OF PILSEN, THE(1926), art d; WHISPERING SMITH(1926), art d; JEWELS OF DESIRE(1927), art d; JIM THE CONQUEROR(1927), art d; NO CONTROL(1927), art d; RUSH HOUR, THE(1927), art d; NIGHT FLYER, THE(1928), art d; ON TO RENO(1928), art d; RED MARK, THE(1928), art d
Charles L. Cadwallader
Silents
MARRIED FLIRTS(1924), set d
A.A. Cadwell
Silents
ROYAL FAMILY, A(1915), ph
Arthur A. Cadwell
Silents
FINE FEATHERS(1921), ph; INNER MAN, THE(1922), ph
Arthur Cadwell
Silents
MADONNAS AND MEN(1920), ph
Daniel B. Cady
SWEET JESUS, PREACHER MAN(1973), p; BLACK SAMSON(1974), p, w; KISS OF THE TARANTULA(1975), p, w
Daniel Cady
KINFOLK(1970), p; SWEET TRASH(1970), p; GARDEN OF THE DEAD(1972), p; GRAVE OF THE VAMPIRE(1972), p
Frank Cady
SARGE GOES TO COLLEGE(1947); VIOLENCE(1947); BUNGALOW 13(1948); HE WALKED BY NIGHT(1948); CITY ACROSS THE RIVER(1949); LADY TAKES A SAILOR, THE(1949); PREJUDICE(1949); SKY DRAGON(1949); TAKE ONE FALSE STEP(1949); CONVICTED(1950); EMERGENCY WEDDING(1950); EXPERIMENT ALCATRAZ(1950); FATHER OF THE BRIDE(1950); GREAT RUPERT, THE(1950); PERFECT STRANGERS(1950); THREE HUSBANDS(1950); YOUNG MAN WITH A HORN(1950); BIG CARNIVAL, THE(1951); DEAR BRAT(1951); LET'S MAKE IT LEGAL(1951); SELLOUT, THE(1951); WHEN WORLDS COLLIDE(1951); ATOMIC CITY, THE(1952); HALF A HERO(1953); MARRY ME AGAIN(1953); REAR WINDOW(1954); INDIAN FIGHTER, THE(1955); TRIAL(1955); BAD SEED, THE(1956); GIRL MOST LIKELY, THE(1957); TIN STAR, THE(1957); MISSOURI TRAVELER, THE(1958); MAN WHO UNDERSTOOD WOMEN, THE(1959); SEVEN FACES OF DR. LAO(1964); GNOME-MOBILE, THE(1967); $1,000,000 DUCK(1971); ZANDY'S BRIDE(1974); HEARTS OF THE WEST(1975)
Fred Cady
WAY OUT WEST(1937)
Jeff Cady
GUESS WHAT HAPPENED TO COUNT DRACULA(1970)
Jerome Cady
LAURA(1944), w; PURPLE HEART, THE(1944), w; WING AND A PRAYER(1944), w; FOREVER AMBER(1947), w; CALL NORTHSIDE 777(1948), w; SAND(1949), w; CRY DANGER(1951), w
Jerry Cady
CHARLIE CHAN AT MONTE CARLO(1937), w; CHARLIE CHAN ON BROADWAY(1937), w; GREAT HOSPITAL MYSTERY, THE(1937), w; ARIZONA WILDCAT(1938), w; ISLAND IN THE SKY(1938), w; MR. MOTO'S GAMBLE(1938), w; ONE WILD NIGHT(1938), w; TIME OUT FOR MURDER(1938), w; FIVE CAME BACK(1939), w; FULL CONFESSION(1939), w; INSIDE STORY(1939), w; TWO THOROUGHBREDS(1939), w; WINNER TAKE ALL(1939), w; ANNE OF WINDY POPLARS(1940), w; CROSS COUNTRY ROMANCE(1940), w; LADDIE(1940), w; MARINES FLY HIGH, THE(1940), w; PLAY GIRL(1940), w; SUED FOR LIBEL(1940), w; YOU CAN'T FOOL YOUR WIFE(1940), w; MEXICAN SPITFIRE'S BABY(1941), w; OBLIGING YOUNG LADY(1941), w; REPENT AT LEISURE(1941), w; SAINT IN PALM SPRINGS, THE(1941), w; THEY MET IN ARGENTINA(1941), w; MEXICAN SPITFIRE AT SEA(1942), w; WHAT'S COOKIN'?(1942), w; GUADALCANAL DIA-

RY(1943), w; SILVER SKATES(1943), w; ROGER TOUHY, GANGSTER!(1944), w; MAN ALIVE(1945), w
Rice and Cady
IN OLD CHICAGO(1938)
Jordan Cael
CARNY(1980); ONE-TRICK PONY(1980)
Herb Caen
NORA PRENTISS(1947)
Massimo Caen
HOTEL SAHARA(1951, Brit.)
Giovanni Caenazzo
NEST OF VIPERS(1979, Ital.)
Ingrid Caern
FOX AND HIS FRIENDS(1976, Ger.)
"Caesar"
LAND OF NO RETURN, THE(1981)
Adolph Caesar
CHE!(1969); FIST OF FEAR, TOUCH OF DEATH(1980)
1984
SOLDIER'S STORY, A(1984)
Misc. Talkies
HITTER, THE(1979)
Art Caesar
STAR MAKER, THE(1939), w
Arthur Caesar
AVIATOR, THE(1929), w; SO LONG LETTY(1929), w; LIFE OF THE PARTY, THE(1930), w; SHE COULDN'T SAY NO(1930), w; THIS MAD WORLD(1930), w; THREE FACES EAST(1930), w; WIDE OPEN(1930), w; DIVORCE AMONG FRIENDS(1931), w; GOLD DUST GERTIE(1931), w; HER MAJESTY LOVE(1931), w; SIDE SHOW(1931), w; SOLDIER'S PLAYTHING, A(1931), w; FIREMAN, SAVE MY CHILD(1932), w; HEART OF NEW YORK(1932), w; TENDERFOOT, THE(1932), w; CHIEF, THE(1933), w; NO MARRIAGE TIES(1933), w; OBEY THE LAW(1933), w; MANHATTAN MELODRAMA(1934), w; THEIR BIG MOMENT(1934), w; ALIAS MARY DOW(1935), w; MC FADDEN'S FLATS(1935), w; TRANSIENT LADY(1935), w; ALONG CAME LOVE(1937), w; LITTLE MEN(1940), w; ADVENTURE IN WASHINGTON(1941), w; LOVES OF EDGAR ALLAN POE, THE(1942), w; NORTHWEST RANGERS(1942), w; ATLANTIC CITY(1944), w; I ACCUSE MY PARENTS(1945), w; ARSON, INC.(1949), w; ANNE OF THE INDIES(1951), w
Silents
HIS DARKER SELF(1924), w
Dina Caesar
FRONTIER UPRISING(1961)
Gaius Julius Caesar
CAESAR THE CONQUEROR(1963, Ital.), w
Harry Caesar
EMPEROR OF THE NORTH POLE(1973); LONGEST YARD, THE(1974); FAREWELL, MY LOVELY(1975); CASEY'S SHADOW(1978); END, THE(1978); SMALL CIRCLE OF FRIENDS, A(1980); BARBAROSA(1982); ESCAPE ARTIST, THE(1982)
1984
BREAKIN' 2: ELECTRIC BOOGALOO(1984); CITY HEAT(1984)
Irving Caesar
STRAIGHT, PLACE AND SHOW(1938), w
Julia Caesar
COUNT OF THE MONK'S BRIDGE, THE(1934, Swed.); ILLICIT INTERLUDE(1954, Swed.)
Sid Caesar
TARS AND SPARS(1946); GUILT OF JANET AMES, THE(1947); IT'S A MAD, MAD, MAD, MAD WORLD(1963); BUSYBODY, THE(1967); GUIDE FOR THE MARRIED MAN, A(1967); SPIRIT IS WILLING, THE(1967); AIRPORT 1975(1974); SILENT MOVIE(1976); FIRE SALE(1977); CHEAP DETECTIVE, THE(1978); GREASE(1978); FIENDISH PLOT OF DR. FU MANCHU, THE(1980); HISTORY OF THE WORLD, PART 1(1981); GREASE 2(1982)
1984
CANNONBALL RUN II(1984); OVER THE BROOKLYN BRIDGE(1984)
Vic Caesar
BARE KNUCKLES(1978), m
1984
HARDBODIES(1984), md
Caesar the Wolf Dog
TRAILING THE KILLER(1932)
Dante Caesari
WILD AND WONDERFUL(1964)
Julia Caeser
SWEDISH WEDDING NIGHT(1965, Swed.)
Jacques Caetelot
PRISONER OF THE VOLGA(1960, Fr./Ital.)
Jose Maria Cafarel
PASSENGER, THE(1975, Ital.)
Jose Maria Cafarell
SAVAGE PAMPAS(1967, Span./Arg.)
Jean Caffarel
EVE(1968, Brit./Span.)
Joe Caffarel
BANG BANG KID, THE(1968 U.S./Span./Ital.)
Jose Caffarel
DOCTOR ZHIVAGO(1965); TOUCH ME NOT(1974, Brit.)
Jose Maria Caffarel
HYPNOSIS(1966, Ger./Sp./Ital.); LIGHTNING BOLT(1967, Ital./Sp.); MADIGAN'S MILLIONS(1970, Span./Ital); TRISTANA(1970, Span./Ital./Fr.); LEONOR(1977, Fr./Span./Ital.)
Maurizio Caffarelli
HERCULES AND THE CAPTIVE WOMEN(1963, Fr./Ital.)
Cheri Caffaro
SAVAGE SISTERS(1974); H.O.T.S.(1979), w
Misc. Talkies
ABDUCTORS, THE(1972); GINGER(1972); GIRLS ARE FOR LOVING(1973); TOO HOT TO HANDLE(1976)

Jack Caffee
SHE WORE A YELLOW RIBBON(1949), spec eff; WAGONMASTER(1950), spec eff
John Cafferty
EDDIE AND THE CRUISERS(1983), m
Brando Caffey
VAN NUYS BLVD.(1979)
Frank Caffey
CARPETBAGGERS, THE(1964), prod d; PATTON(1970), p
Kreag Caffey
TWO-LANE BLACKTOP(1971)
Richard Caffey
BUCK ROGERS IN THE 25TH CENTURY(1979), p
Robert Caffey
FIVE BOLD WOMEN(1960)
Jenni Caffin
1984
SQUIZZY TAYLOR(1984, Aus.)
Yvonne Caffin
THEY WERE SISTERS(1945, Brit.), cos; DEAR MURDERER(1947, Brit.), cos; WHEN THE BOUGH BREAKS(1947, Brit.), cos; MIRANDA(1949, Brit.), cos; DAY TO REMEMBER, A(1953, Brit.), cos; DOCTOR IN THE HOUSE(1954, Brit.), cos; TO PARIS WITH LOVE(1955, Brit.), cos; TROUBLE IN STORE(1955, Brit.), cos; IRON PETTICOAT, THE(1956, Brit.), cos; DOCTOR AT LARGE(1957, Brit.), cos; MAD LITTLE ISLAND(1958, Brit.), cos; NIGHT TO REMEMBER, A(1958, Brit.), cos; CARRY ON CONSTABLE(1960, Brit.), cos; CONSPIRACY OF HEARTS(1960, Brit.), cos; DOCTOR IN LOVE(1960, Brit.), cos; FLAME OVER INDIA(1960, Brit.), cos; THIRTY NINE STEPS, THE(1960, Brit.), cos; NO LOVE FOR JOHNNIE(1961, Brit.), cos; SINGER NOT THE SONG, THE(1961, Brit.), cos; TIARA TAHITI(1962, Brit.), cos; DOCTOR IN DISTRESS(1963, Brit.), cos; NO, MY DARLING DAUGHTER(1964, Brit.), cos; YOUNG AND WILLING(1964, Brit.), cos; GYPSY GIRL(1966, Brit.), cos; MC GUIRE, GO HOME!(1966, Brit.), cos; CARRY ON CAMPING(1969, Brit.), cos; SOME GIRLS DO(1969, Brit.), cos; SOUTHERN STAR, THE(1969, Fr./Brit.), cos; EXECUTIONER, THE(1970, Brit.), cos
Frank Caffray
Misc. Silents
HATE TRAIL, THE(1922)
James Caffrey
SIEGE OF SIDNEY STREET, THE(1960, Brit.); ISLAND OF TERROR(1967, Brit.)
Peter Caffrey
CRIMINAL CONVERSATION(1980, Ireland); ANGEL(1982, Irish)
Sean Caffrey
RUN WITH THE WIND(1966, Brit.); TIME LOST AND TIME REMEMBERED(1966, Brit.); VIKING QUEEN, THE(1967, Brit.); WHEN DINOSAURS RULED THE EARTH(1971, Brit.); HUMAN FACTOR, THE(1979, Brit.); MOON OVER THE ALLEY(1980, Brit.)
Salvatore Cafiero
LOVE AND LARCENY(1963, Fr./Ital.)
Andrea Cagan
CAPTAIN MILKSHAKE(1970); HOT BOX, THE(1972, U.S./Phil.)
Misc. Talkies
TEENAGER(1975)
Carl-Henry Cagarp
MAGICIAN, THE(1959, Swed.), p
John Cage
DREAMS THAT MONEY CAN BUY(1948), m
Nicholas Cage
RUMBLE FISH(1983); VALLEY GIRL(1983)
Nicolas Cage
1984
BIRDY(1984); COTTON CLUB, THE(1984); RACING WITH THE MOON(1984)
Patricia Cage
WHEN TOMORROW DIES(1966, Can.)
Steven Cagen
CAT AND THE CANARY, THE(1979, Brit.), m
John Cagle
BEAST OF YUCCA FLATS, THE(1961), ph
Wade Cagle
FEAR STRIKES OUT(1957); YOUNG LIONS, THE(1958)
George Cagleton
BEHIND CITY LIGHTS(1945)
Anthony E. Caglia
LONE WOLF McQUADE(1983)
John Caglione
BASKET CASE(1982), spec eff; ZELIG(1983), makeup
John Caglione, Jr.
AMITYVILLE II: THE POSSESSION(1982), makeup
1984
C.H.U.D.(1984), makeup
Bill Cagney
ACE OF ACES(1933)
James Cagney
TIME OF YOUR LIFE, THE(1948); DOORWAY TO HELL(1930); SINNER'S HOLIDAY(1930); BLONDE CRAZY(1931); MILLIONAIRE, THE(1931); OTHER MEN'S WOMEN(1931); PUBLIC ENEMY, THE(1931); SMART MONEY(1931); CROWD ROARS, THE(1932); TAXI!(1932); WINNER TAKE ALL(1932); FOOTLIGHT PARADE(1933); HARD TO HANDLE(1933); LADY KILLER(1933); MAYOR OF HELL, THE(1933); PICTURE SNATCHER(1933); HE WAS HER MAN(1934); HERE COMES THE NAVY(1934); JIMMY THE GENT(1934); ST. LOUIS KID, THE(1934); CEILNG ZERO(1935); DEVIL DOGS OF THE AIR(1935); FRISCO KID(1935); G-MEN(1935); IRISH IN US, THE(1935); MIDSUMMER'S NIGHT'S DREAM, A(1935); MUTINY ON THE BOUNTY(1935); GREAT GUY(1936); SOMETHING TO SING ABOUT(1937); ANGELS WITH DIRTY FACES(1938); BOY MEETS GIRL(1938); EACH DAWN I DIE(1939); OKLAHOMA KID(1939); ROARING TWENTIES, THE(1939); FIGHTING 69TH, THE(1940); TORRID ZONE(1940); BRIDE CAME C.O.D., THE(1941); CITY FOR CONQUEST(1941); STRAWBERRY BLONDE, THE(1941); CAPTAINS OF THE CLOUDS(1942); YANKEE DOODLE DANDY(1942); JOHNNY COME LATELY(1943); BLOOD ON THE SUN(1945); 13 RUE MADELEINE(1946); WHITE HEAT(1949); KISS TOMORROW GOODBYE(1950); WEST POINT STORY, THE(1950); COME FILL THE CUP(1951); STARLIFT(1951); WHAT PRICE GLORY?(1952); LION IS IN THE STREETS, A(1953); LOVE ME OR LEAVE ME(1955); MISTER ROBERTS(1955); RUN

FOR COVER(1955); SEVEN LITTLE FOYS, THE(1955); THESE WILDER YEARS(1956); TRIBUTE TO A BADMAN(1956); MAN OF A THOUSAND FACES(1957); SHORT CUT TO HELL(1957), d; NEVER STEAL ANYTHING SMALL(1959); SHAKE HANDS WITH THE DEVIL(1959, Ireland); GALLANT HOURS, THE(1960); ONE, TWO, THREE(1961); RAGTIME(1981)
James Cagney, Jr.
GALLANT HOURS, THE(1960)
Jean Cagney
ALL WOMEN HAVE SECRETS(1939); GOLDEN GLOVES(1940); RHYTHM ON THE RIVER(1940)
Jeanne Cagney
TIME OF YOUR LIFE, THE(1948); QUEEN OF THE MOB(1940); YANKEE DOODLE DANDY(1942); QUICKSAND(1950); DON'T BOTHER TO KNOCK(1952); LION IS IN THE STREETS, A(1953); KENTUCKY RIFLE(1956); MAN OF A THOUSAND FACES(1957); TOWN TAMER(1965)
Tim Cagney
GOOD MORNING, MISS DOVE(1955)
William Cagney
TIME OF YOUR LIFE, THE(1948), p; PALOOKA(1934); FLIRTING WITH DANGER(1935); LOST IN THE STRATOSPHERE(1935); STOLEN HARMONY(1935); BRIDE CAME C.O.D., THE(1941), p; JOHNNY COME LATELY(1943), p; BLOOD ON THE SUN(1945), p; KISS TOMORROW GOODBYE(1950), a, p; ONLY THE VALIANT(1951), p; BUGLES IN THE AFTERNOON(1952), p; LION IS IN THE STREETS, A(1953), p
Mario Cagnion
TERROR IN THE JUNGLE(1968)
Edith Cagnon
DISPUTED PASSAGE(1939)
J. Leo Cagnon
THIRTEENTH LETTER, THE(1951)
Abraham Cahan
HESTER STREET(1975), w, d&w
Boyd Caheen
GENTLEMEN MARRY BRUNETTES(1955)
Bernard Cahier
GRAND PRIX(1966)
Barry Cahill
WHEN YOU COMIN' BACK, RED RYDER?(1979); THEN THERE WERE THREE(1961); SWEET BIRD OF YOUTH(1962); VALLEY OF THE DOLLS(1967); HANG'EM HIGH(1968); DADDY'S GONE A-HUNTING(1969); HAPPY ENDING, THE(1969); ...TICK...TICK...TICK...(1970); GROUNDSTAR CONSPIRACY, THE(1972, Can.); COFFY(1973); GRAND THEFT AUTO(1977); STRAIGHT TIME(1978); WRONG IS RIGHT(1982)
Cathy Cahill
SMOKEY AND THE BANDIT–PART 3(1983)
1984
HARRY AND SON(1984)
David Cahill
YOU CAN'T SEE 'ROUND CORNERS(1969, Aus.), d
Drew Cahill
SAILOR BEWARE(1951); MONEY FROM HOME(1953); SAD SACK, THE(1957)
G. M. Cahill
SURVIVAL RUN(1980), w
James Cahill
SANTA CLAUS CONQUERS THE MARTIANS(1964); EASY MONEY(1983)
Joe Cahill
FLIGHT OF THE DOVES(1971); SITTING TARGET(1972, Brit.); GREAT TRAIN ROBBERY, THE(1979, Brit.)
Kathy Cahill
DON'T ANSWER THE PHONE(1980), art d
Kathy Curtis Cahill
SCHIZOID(1980), art d
Lily Cahill
MY SIN(1931)
Lynette Cahill
SHADOW OF THE HAWK(1976, Can.), w
Marie Cahill
Silents
JUDY FORGOT(1915)
Hy Cahl
TEENAGE GANG DEBS(1966), w
Dan Cahn
HEAVEN WITH A GUN(1969), ed
Dann Cahn
FOREVER DARLING(1956), ed; PHYNX, THE(1970), ed; OCTAGON, THE(1980), ed; TOUGH ENOUGH(1983), ed
Edward Cahn
BROADWAY(1929), ed; LAST PERFORMANCE, THE(1929), ed; RADIO PATROL(1932), d; EMERGENCY CALL(1933), d; BAD GUY(1937), d; REDHEAD(1941), d; MAIN STREET AFTER DARK(1944), d; GAS HOUSE KIDS IN HOLLYWOOD(1947), d
Silents
MAN WHO LAUGHS, THE(1927), ed; JAZZ MAD(1928), ed; LOVE ME AND THE WORLD IS MINE(1928), ed
Edward L. Cahn
AFRAID TO TALK(1932), d; LAW AND ORDER(1932), d; LAUGHTER IN HELL(1933), d; CONFIDENTIAL(1935), d; DEATH DRIVES THROUGH(1935, Brit.), d; DANGEROUS PARTNERS(1945), d; BORN TO SPEED(1947), d; BUNGALOW 13(1948), d; CHECKERED COAT, THE(1948), d; I CHEATED THE LAW(1949), d; PREJUDICE(1949), d; DESTINATION MURDER(1950), p, d; EXPERIMENT ALCATRAZ(1950), p&d; GREAT PLANE ROBBERY(1950), d; TWO DOLLAR BETTOR(1951), p&d; BETRAYED WOMEN(1955), d; CREATURE WITH THE ATOM BRAIN(1955), d; GIRLS IN PRISON(1956), d; SHE-CREATURE, THE(1956), d; DRAGSTRIP GIRL(1957), d; FLESH AND THE SPUR(1957), d; INVASION OF THE SAUCER MEN(1957), d; MOTORCYCLE GANG(1957), d; RUNAWAY DAUGHTERS(1957), d; SHAKE, RATTLE, AND ROCK!(1957), d; VOODOO WOMAN(1957), d; ZOMBIES OF MORA TAU(1957), d; CURSE OF THE FACELESS MAN(1958), d; GUNS, GIRLS AND GANGSTERS(1958), d; HONG KONG CONFIDENTIAL(1958), d; IT! THE TERROR FROM BEYOND SPACE(1958), d; JET ATTACK(1958), d; SUICIDE BATTALION(1958), d; FOUR SKULLS OF JONATHAN DRAKE, THE(1959), d; INSIDE THE

MAFIA(1959), d; INVISIBLE INVADERS(1959), d; PIER 5, HAVANA(1959), d; RIOT IN JUVENILE PRISON(1959), d; VICE RAID(1959), d; CAGE OF EVIL(1960), d; DOG'S BEST FRIEND, A(1960), d; GUNFIGHTERS OF ABILENE(1960), d; MUSIC BOX KID, THE(1960), d; NOOSE FOR A GUNMAN(1960), d; OKLAHOMA TERRITORY(1960), d; THREE CAME TO KILL(1960), d; TWELVE HOURS TO KILL(1960), d; WALKING TARGET, THE(1960), d; BOY WHO CAUGHT A CROOK(1961), d; CLOWN AND THE KID, THE(1961), d; FIVE GUNS TO TOMBSTONE(1961), d; FRONTIER UPRISING(1961), d; GAMBLER WORE A GUN, THE(1961), d; GUN FIGHT(1961), d; OPERATION BOTTLENECK(1961), d; POLICE DOG STORY, THE(1961), d; SECRET OF DEEP HARBOR(1961), d; WHEN THE CLOCK STRIKES(1961), d; YOU HAVE TO RUN FAST(1961), d; GUN STREET(1962), d; INCIDENT IN AN ALLEY(1962), d; BEAUTY AND THE BEAST(1963), d

Julie Cahn
BORN LOSERS(1967)

Leo Cahn
LIFT, THE(1983, Neth.), spec eff

Phil Cahn
CLANCY IN WALL STREET(1930), ed; FLAMING GUNS(1933), ed; KING FOR A NIGHT(1933), ed; IMITATION OF LIFE(1934), ed; AFFAIR OF SUSAN(1935), ed; GREAT IMPERSONATION, THE(1935), ed; MANHATTAN MOON(1935), ed; PAROLE(1936), ed; POSTAL INSPECTOR(1936), ed; BEHIND THE MIKE(1937), ed; WESTBOUND LIMITED(1937), ed; RIO(1939), ed; MUMMY'S HAND, THE(1940), ed; WHERE DID YOU GET THAT GIRL?(1941), ed; WE'VE NEVER BEEN LICKED(1943), ed; PREJUDICE(1949), ed; FBI GIRL(1951), ed; LOST CONTINENT(1951), ed; BELA LUGOSI MEETS A BROOKLYN GORILLA(1952), ed

Philip Cahn
CROSS COUNTRY CRUISE(1934), ed; I'VE BEEN AROUND(1935), d; GIRL ON THE FRONT PAGE, THE(1936), ed; AS GOOD AS MARRIED(1937), ed; GIRL OVERBOARD(1937), ed; GIRL WITH IDEAS, A(1937), ed; MIGHTY TREVE, THE(1937), ed; DEVIL'S PARTY, THE(1938), ed; LITTLE TOUGH GUY(1938), ed; MAD ABOUT MUSIC(1938), ed; YOUTH TAKES A FLING(1938), ed; NEWSBOY'S HOME(1939), ed; SOCIETY SMUGGLERS(1939), ed; PRIVATE AFFAIRS(1940), ed; BUCK PRIVATES(1941), ed; HOLD THAT GHOST(1941), ed; IN THE NAVY(1941), ed; KEEP 'EM FLYING(1941), ed; ARABIAN NIGHTS(1942), ed; EAGLE SQUADRON(1942), ed; ALLERGIC TO LOVE(1943), ed; HOUSE OF FRANKENSTEIN(1944), ed; IN SOCIETY(1944), ed; LADIES COURAGEOUS(1944), ed; BAD MEN OF THE BORDER(1945), ed; I'LL REMEMBER APRIL(1945), ed; ON STAGE EVERYBODY(1945), ed; SENORITA FROM THE WEST(1945), p; BRUTE MAN, THE(1946), ed; HOUSE OF HORRORS(1946), ed; STRANGE CONQUEST(1946), ed; COPACABANA(1947), ed; NORTHWEST STAMPEDE(1948), ed; EXPERIMENT ALCATRAZ(1950), ed; STEEL HELMET, THE(1951), ed; BATTLES OF CHIEF PONTIAC(1952), ed; VERBOTEN!(1959), ed; MODERN MARRIAGE, A(1962), ed

Phillip Cahn
HIS EXCITING NIGHT(1938), ed; JURY'S SECRET, THE(1938), ed; BIG TOWN CZAR(1939), ed; THEY ASKED FOR IT(1939), ed; TWO BRIGHT BOYS(1939), ed; BLACK FRIDAY(1940), ed; SANDY GETS HER MAN(1940), ed; SANDY IS A LADY(1940), ed; RIDE 'EM COWBOY(1942), ed; TIME OF THEIR LIVES, THE(1946), ed; DESTINATION MURDER(1950), ed; I WAS AN AMERICAN SPY(1951), ed; PARK ROW(1952), ed

Sammy Cahn
ROOKIES ON PARADE(1941), w; LADIES' MAN(1947), m; TWO TICKETS TO BROADWAY(1951), w; THREE SAILORS AND A GIRL(1953), p; PETE KELLY'S BLUES(1955), m; OSCAR, THE(1966), m/l Ralph Rainger

William L. Cahn
LADY SURRENDERS, A(1930), ed

Richard Cahoon
PAINTED FACES(1929), ed; SHAKEDOWN, THE(1929), ed; BORDER ROMANCE(1930), ed; SWELLHEAD, THE(1930), w, ed; MAD PARADE, THE(1931), ed; MEN IN HER LIFE(1931), ed; WASHINGTON MERRY-GO-ROUND(1932), ed; CIRCUS QUEEN MURDER, THE(1933), ed; EAST OF FIFTH AVE.(1933), ed; WRECKER, THE(1933), ed; FOG(1934), ed; I'LL FIX IT(1934), ed; ONCE TO EVERY WOMAN(1934), ed; WHIRLPOOL(1934), ed; AIR HAWKS(1935), ed; BEHIND THE EVIDENCE(1935), ed; BLACK ROOM, THE(1935), ed; I'LL LOVE YOU ALWAYS(1935), ed; SHE MARRIED HER BOSS(1935), ed; COUNTERFEIT(1936), ed; MYSTERIOUS AVENGER, THE(1936), ed; PRESCOTT KID(1936), ed; PRIDE OF THE MARINES(1936), ed; CINDERELLA SWINGS IT(1942), ed; SCATTERGOOD SURVIVES A MURDER(1942), ed; MASSACRE RIVER(1949), ed; INDIAN FIGHTER, THE(1955), ed; MAGNIFICENT MATADOR, THE(1955), ed; NAVY WIFE(1956), ed; THREE FOR JAMIE DAWN(1956), ed

Richard H. Cahoon
CARNIVAL(1935), ed

Wyn Cahoon
AWFUL TRUTH, THE(1937); MURDER IN GREENWICH VILLAGE(1937); WHO KILLED GAIL PRESTON?(1938); WOMEN IN PRISON(1938)

Amin Cahudri
BLACK RODEO(1972), ph

Georges Cahuzac
Silents
NAPOLEON(1927, Fr.)

Carlo Caiano
NIGHTS OF LUCRETIA BORGIA, THE(1960, Ital.), p; NIGHTMARE CASTLE(1966, Ital.), p, w

Mario Caiano
NIGHTS OF LUCRETIA BORGIA, THE(1960, Ital.), w; PIRATE OF THE BLACK HAWK, THE(1961, Fr./Ital.), w; SULEIMAN THE CONQUEROR(1963, Ital.), w; TO KILL OR TO DIE(1973, Ital.), d, w

Alfred Caiazza
MAN IN THE GREY FLANNEL SUIT, THE(1956)

Jose Manuel Caicoya
HARBOR LIGHTS(1963)

Martin Caidin
MAROONED(1969), w

M. Caillard
Silents
NAPOLEON(1927, Fr.)

Gerard Caillaud
1984
UNTIL SEPTEMBER(1984)

Michele Caillaud
GERVAISE(1956, Fr.)

Raymond Caillava
DIARY OF A BAD GIRL(1958, Fr.), w; NIGHTS OF SHAME(1961, Fr.), w; VICE DOLLS(1961, Fr.), w

G.A. Caillavet
ROYAL AFFAIR, A(1950), w

Dollie Caillet
CALL NORTHSIDE 777(1948)

Lucien Caillet
WINNER'S CIRCLE, THE(1948), m&md; SPECIAL AGENT(1949), m; VANQUISHED, THE(1953), m; FUN ON A WEEKEND(1979), m

Lucien Cailliet
STATE DEPARTMENT–FILE 649(1949), m; THUNDER IN THE PINES(1949), m; TROUBLE PREFERRED(1949), m; CROSSWINDS(1951), m; HONG KONG(1951), m; BLAZING FOREST, THE(1952), m; CARIBBEAN(1952), m; JAMAICA RUN(1953), m; SANGAREE(1953), m; TROPIC ZONE(1953), m; NIGHT HOLDS TERROR, THE(1955), m, md; SECRET OF MY SUCCESS, THE(1965, Brit.), m

Haydee Caillot
AVIATOR'S WIFE, THE(1981, Fr.)

Alan Caillou
JOURNEY TO THE CENTER OF THE EARTH(1959); FIERCEST HEART, THE(1961); PIRATES OF TORTUGA(1961); FIVE WEEKS IN A BALLOON(1962); IT HAPPENED IN ATHENS(1962); LIST OF ADRIAN MESSENGER, THE(1963); RAMPAGE(1963), w; CLARENCE, THE CROSS-EYED LION(1965), a, w; STRANGE BEDFELLOWS(1965); VILLAGE OF THE GIANTS(1965); RARE BREED, THE(1966); HELLFIGHTERS(1968); LOSERS, THE(1970), a, w; EVEL KNIEVEL(1971), w; EVERYTHING YOU ALWAYS WANTED TO KNOW ABOUT SEX, BUT WE'RE AFRAID TO ASK(1972); ASSAULT ON AGATHON(1976, Brit./Gr.), w; HERBIE GOES TO MONTE CARLO(1977); KINGDOM OF THE SPIDERS(1977), w; SWORD AND THE SORCERER, THE(1982)
1984
ICE PIRATES, THE(1984)

Cailloux
LES MISERABLES(1936, Fr.)

Andre Cailloux
KAMOURASKA(1973, Can./Fr.)

Michael Caime
WRONG ARM OF THE LAW, THE(1963, Brit.)

Lamberto Caimi
SOUND OF TRUMPETS, THE(1963, Ital.), ph; FIANCES, THE(1964, Ital.), ph; MAN WHO CAME FOR COFFEE, THE(1970, Ital.), ph

Paul Caimi
1984
SILENT NIGHT, DEADLY NIGHT(1984), w

Ace Cain
DANGER TRAILS(1935); TOLL OF THE DESERT(1936)
Misc. Talkies
IRISH GRINGO, THE(1935); SIX GUN JUSTICE(1935)

Arthur Cain
FOOLS' PARADE(1971)

Chris Cain
1984
STONE BOY, THE(1984), d

Christopher Cain
SIXTH AND MAIN(1977), p,d&w
Misc. Talkies
ELMER(1977), d; GRAND JURY(1977), d

David Cain
Misc. Talkies
ATOR, THE INVINCIBLE(1984)

Dean Cain
1984
STONE BOY, THE(1984)

Frances Cain
GIRL TROUBLE(1942)

G. Cain
WONDERWALL(1969, Brit.), w

Georgia Cain
CHRISTMAS IN JULY(1940)

Guillermo Cain
VANISHING POINT(1971), w

James Cain
WHEN TOMORROW COMES(1939), w

James M. Cain
SHE MADE HER BED(1934), w; ALGIERS(1938), w; STAND UP AND FIGHT(1939), w; WIFE, HUSBAND AND FRIEND(1939), w; MONEY AND THE WOMAN(1940), w; DOUBLE INDEMNITY(1944), w; GYPSY WILDCAT(1944), w; MILDRED PIERCE(1945), w; POSTMAN ALWAYS RINGS TWICE, THE(1946), w; OUT OF THE PAST(1947), w; EVERYBODY DOES IT(1949), w; SERENADE(1956), w; SLIGHTLY SCARLET(1956), w; INTERLUDE(1957), w; OSSESSIONE(1959, Ital.), w; POSTMAN ALWAYS RINGS TWICE, THE(1981), w; BUTTERFLY(1982), w

Jane Cain
VANITY(1935)

Jess Cain
PINOCCHIO IN OUTER SPACE(1965, U.S./Bel.)

Jonathan Cain
WHALE OF A TALE, A(1977), m

Lisa Cain
SOLDIER, THE(1982)

Maurice Cain
LION OF THE DESERT(1981, Libya/Brit.), art d; SEA WOLVES, THE(1981, Brit.), art d; NATE AND HAYES(1983, U.S./New Zealand), prod d

Mo Cain
FINAL OPTION, THE(1983, Brit.), art d

Paula Cain
THANK GOD IT'S FRIDAY(1978), cos

Robert Cain
Silents
DAWN OF A TOMORROW, THE(1915); RUNNING FIGHT, THE(1915); ETERNAL GRIND, THE(1916); INNOCENT LIE, THE(1916); MY LADY INCOG(1916); ENVY(1917); KIDNAPPED(1917); MALE AND FEMALE(1919); WITCHING HOUR, THE(1921); BURNING SANDS(1922); IMPOSSIBLE MRS. BELLEW, THE(1922); REPORTED MISSING(1922); RACING HEARTS(1923); TIGER'S CLAW, THE(1923); ROSE OF PARIS, THE(1924); EVERY MAN'S WIFE(1925); WILDERNESS WOMAN, THE(1926); HUSBAND HUNTERS(1927)
Misc. Silents
LYDIA GILMORE(1916); CO-RESPONDENT, THE(1917); HUNGRY HEART, THE(1917); HER FINAL RECKONING(1918); WOMAN OF IMPULSE, A(1918); WOMAN'S EXPERIENCE, A(1918); IN MIZZOURA(1919); PAID IN FULL(1919); SHOD WITH FIRE(1920); CHILDREN OF JAZZ(1923); DRUMS OF FATE(1923); EVERLASTING WHISPER, THE(1925); WHEN THE DOOR OPENED(1925); DANCER OF PARIS, THE(1926); TOO MUCH MONEY(1926); RICH MEN'S SONS(1927)

Roger Cain
1984
INDIANA JONES AND THE TEMPLE OF DOOM(1984), art d

Shirley Cain
HONOURABLE MURDER, AN(1959, Brit.); VILLAIN(1971, Brit.)

Sid Cain
SHOUT AT THE DEVIL(1976, Brit.), prod d

Sidney Cain
FEAR IS THE KEY(1973), art d

Simon Cain
CHAIRMAN, THE(1969)

Syd Cain
FIRE DOWN BELOW(1957, U.S./Brit.), art d; DR. NO(1962, Brit.), art d; CALL ME BWANA(1963, Brit.), art d; FROM RUSSIA WITH LOVE(1963, Brit.), art d; SUMMER HOLIDAY(1963, Brit.), art d; AMOROUS ADVENTURES OF MOLL FLANDERS, THE(1965), art d; MISTER MOSES(1965), art d; FAHRENHEIT 451(1966, Brit.), art d; MC GUIRE, GO HOME!(1966, Brit.), art d; ON HER MAJESTY'S SECRET SERVICE(1969, Brit.), prod d; FRENZY(1972, Brit.), prod d; LIVE AND LET DIE(1973, Brit.), prod d, art d; GOLD(1974, Brit.), prod d; WILD GEESE, THE(1978, Brit.), prod d; LION OF THE DESERT(1981, Libya/Brit.), prod d; LOOPHOLE(1981, Brit.), prod d; SEA WOLVES, THE(1981, Brit.), prod d; FINAL OPTION, THE(1983, Brit.), prod d

Sydney Cain
ROAD TO HONG KONG, THE(1962, U.S./Brit.), art d

Ted Cain
WHEN JOHNNY COMES MARCHING HOME(1943), m

Viola Cain
Misc. Silents
ONE TOUCH OF NATURE(1917)

Virgil Cain
GAY SISTERS, THE(1942)

William B. Cain
DOGS OF WAR, THE(1980, Brit.)

William Cain
1984
ULTIMATE SOLUTION OF GRACE QUIGLEY, THE(1984)
Misc. Silents
WINNING OAR, THE(1927)

Derwent Hall Caine
Silents
CRIME AND PUNISHMENT(1917)
Misc. Silents
CHRISTIAN, THE(1915, Brit.); DEEMSTER, THE(1917); HUNS WIHIN OUR GATES(1918); DARBY AND JOAN(1919, Brit.)

Georgia Caine
GOOD INTENTIONS(1930); NIGHT WORK(1930); CRADLE SONG(1933); CALL IT LUCK(1934); COUNT OF MONTE CRISTO, THE(1934); EVELYN PRENTICE(1934); I AM SUZANNE(1934); LOVE TIME(1934); CRUSADES, THE(1935); HOORAY FOR LOVE(1935); SHE MARRIED HER BOSS(1935); NAVY BORN(1936); ONE RAINY AFTERNOON(1936); SING ME A LOVE SONG(1936); WHITE ANGEL, THE(1936); AFFAIRS OF CAPPY RICKS(1937); BILL CRACKS DOWN(1937); IT'S LOVE I'M AFTER(1937); TIME OUT FOR ROMANCE(1937); HIS EXCITING NIGHT(1938); JEZEBEL(1938); WOMEN ARE LIKE THAT(1938); BOY TROUBLE(1939); HONEYMOON IN BALI(1939); JUAREZ(1939); NO PLACE TO GO(1939); TOWER OF LONDON(1939); ALL THIS AND HEAVEN TOO(1940); BABIES FOR SALE(1940); CHILD IS BORN, A(1940); LONE WOLF MEETS A LADY, THE(1940); NOBODY'S CHILDREN(1940); REMEMBER THE NIGHT(1940); SANTA FE TRAIL(1940); GREAT LIE, THE(1941); HURRY, CHARLIE, HURRY(1941); MANPOWER(1941); NURSE'S SECRET, THE(1941); RIDIN' ON A RAINBOW(1941); YOU BELONG TO ME(1941); GENTLEMAN JIM(1942); HELLO ANNAPOLIS(1942); WIFE TAKES A FLYER, THE(1942); SKY'S THE LIMIT, THE(1943); HAIL THE CONQUERING HERO(1944); MIRACLE OF MORGAN'S CREEK, THE(1944); MR. SKEFFINGTON(1944); DOUBLE LIFE, A(1947); HIGH WALL, THE(1947); NORA PRENTISS(1947); GIVE MY REGARDS TO BROADWAY(1948); UNFAITHFULLY YOURS(1948); BEAUTIFUL BLONDE FROM BASHFUL BEND, THE(1949); KISS TOMORROW GOODBYE(1950); MAD WEDNESDAY(1950)

Hall Caine
Silents
CHRISTIAN, THE(1914), w; ETERNAL CITY, THE(1915), w; PRODIGAL SON, THE(1923, Brit.), w; BARBED WIRE(1927), w

Henry Caine
TEMPORARY WIDOW, THE(1930, Ger./Brit.); DREYFUS CASE, THE(1931, Brit.); NUMBER SEVENTEEN(1932, Brit.); SHADOW BETWEEN, THE(1932, Brit.); FIRE RAISERS, THE(1933, Brit.); GHOST TRAIN, THE(1933, Brit.); HER LAST AFFAIRE(1935, Brit.); BROWN WALLET, THE(1936, Brit.); HAIL AND FAREWELL(1936, Brit.); MAN BEHIND THE MASK, THE(1936, Brit.); STRANGE EXPERIMENT(1937, Brit.); SHOW GOES ON, THE(1938, Brit.); TOO DANGEROUS TO LIVE(1939, Brit.); HOUR OF GLORY(1949, Brit.); IF THIS BE SIN(1950, Brit.); PRIVATE INFORMATION(1952, Brit.); CHILDREN GALORE(1954, Brit.); GREEN SCARF, THE(1954, Brit.); SECRET, THE(1955, Brit.); CURSE OF FRANKENSTEIN, THE(1957, Brit.)

Howard Caine
FROM THE TERRACE(1960); PAY OR DIE(1960); JUDGMENT AT NUREMBERG(1961); BRUSHFIRE(1962); PRESSURE POINT(1962); MAN FROM THE DINERS' CLUB, THE(1963); ALVAREZ KELLY(1966); WATERMELON MAN(1970); 1776(1972); FORCED VENGEANCE(1982)

Irene Caine
WITNESS TO MURDER(1954), cos

Judy Caine
FLY NOW, PAY LATER(1969)

Michael Caine
HELL IN KOREA(1956, Brit.); HOW TO MURDER A RICH UNCLE(1957, Brit.); CARVE HER NAME WITH PRIDE(1958, Brit.); ROOM 43(1959, Brit.); TWO-HEADED SPY, THE(1959, Brit.); FOXHOLE IN CAIRO(1960, Brit.); ZULU(1964, Brit.); IPCRESS FILE, THE(1965, Brit.); ALFIE(1966, Brit.); FUNERAL IN BERLIN(1966, Brit.); GAMBIT(1966); SOLO FOR SPARROW(1966, Brit.); WRONG BOX, THE(1966, Brit.); BILLION DOLLAR BRAIN(1967, Brit.); HURRY SUNDOWN(1967); WOMAN TIMES SEVEN(1967, U.S./Fr./Ital.); DEADFALL(1968, Brit.); MAGUS, THE(1968, Brit.); BATTLE OF BRITAIN, THE(1969, Brit.); ITALIAN JOB, THE(1969, Brit.); PLAY DIRTY(1969, Brit.); TOO LATE THE HERO(1970); GET CARTER(1971, Brit.); KIDNAPPED(1971, Brit.); LAST VALLEY, THE(1971, Brit.); PULP(1972, Brit.); SLEUTH(1972, Brit.); X Y & ZEE(1972, Brit.); BLACK WINDMILL, THE(1974, Brit.); DESTRUCTORS, THE(1974, Brit.); MAN WHO WOULD BE KING, THE(1975, Brit.); PEEPER(1975); ROMANTIC ENGLISHWOMAN, THE(1975, Brit./Fr.); WILBY CONSPIRACY, THE(1975, Brit.); EAGLE HAS LANDED, THE(1976, Brit.); HARRY AND WALTER GO TO NEW YORK(1976); BRIDGE TOO FAR, A(1977, Brit.); CALIFORNIA SUITE(1978); SILVER BEARS(1978); SWARM, THE(1978); ASHANTI(1979); BEYOND THE POSEIDON ADVENTURE(1979); DRESSED TO KILL(1980); ISLAND, THE(1980); HAND, THE(1981); VICTORY(1981); DEATHTRAP(1982); BEYOND THE LIMIT(1983); EDUCATING RITA(1983)
1984
BLAME IT ON RIO(1984); JIGSAW MAN, THE(1984, Brit.)

Richard Caine
BORN AGAIN(1978)

Shakira Caine
MAN WHO WOULD BE KING, THE(1975, Brit.)

Shirley Caine
RETURN OF THE SOLDIER, THE(1983, Brit.)

Sir Hall Caine
Silents
MANXMAN, THE(1929, Brit.), w

Stanley Caine
ITALIAN JOB, THE(1969, Brit.)

Syd. Caine
ACES HIGH(1977, Brit.), set d

Sylvia Caine
Misc. Silents
FAIR MAID OF PERTH, THE(1923, Brit.)

Henry Cains
PRICE OF A SONG, THE(1935, Brit.)

Ruth Cains
MACHETE(1958)

Audrey Caire
THEY SAVED HITLER'S BRAIN(1964); JOE(1970)

Nicholas Cairis
NIGHT SCHOOL(1981); TERROR EYES(1981)

Andy Cairn
WALL STREET(1929)

James Cairncross
LONELINESS OF THE LONG DISTANCE RUNNER, THE(1962, Brit.); RING OF TERROR(1962), m; TOM JONES(1963, Brit.)

John Cairney
LUCKY JIM(1957, Brit.); MIRACLE IN SOHO(1957, Brit.); NIGHT AMBUSH(1958, Brit.); NIGHT TO REMEMBER, A(1958, Brit.); WINDOM'S WAY(1958, Brit.); SHAKE HANDS WITH THE DEVIL(1959, Ireland); MANIA(1961, Brit.); VICTIM(1961, Brit.); CLEOPATRA(1963); JASON AND THE ARGONAUTS(1963, Brit.); OPERATION BULLSHINE(1963, Brit.); DEVIL-SHIP PIRATES, THE(1964, Brit.); SPACEFLIGHT IC-1(1965, Brit.); STUDY IN TERROR, A(1966, Brit./Ger.); MARRIAGE OF CONVENIENCE(1970, Brit.)

Adrian Cairns
LINKS OF JUSTICE(1958); INNOCENT MEETING(1959, Brit.)

Cally Cairns
FATHER TAKES A WIFE(1941)

Dallas Cairns
Silents
PRINCESS OF HAPPY CHANCE, THE(1916, Brit.); UNREST(1920, Brit.), a, p&d; ROYAL OAK, THE(1923, Brit.); PEARL OF THE SOUTH SEAS(1927, Brit.)
Misc. Silents
COMRADESHIP(1919, Brit.); SILVER BRIDGE, THE(1920, Brit.), a, d; FOR VALOUR(1928, Brit.)

Dorothy Cairns
SIN TAKES A HOLIDAY(1930), w

Jessica Cairns
SOLUTION BY PHONE(1954, Brit.); STOLEN ASSIGNMENT(1955, Brit.); TIME OF HIS LIFE, THE(1955, Brit.); HIDEOUT, THE(1956, Brit.); ALIVE ON SATURDAY(1957, Brit.); NO TIME FOR TEARS(1957, Brit.); SCOTLAND YARD DRAGNET(1957, Brit.); MY WIFE'S FAMILY(1962, Brit.)

Jessie Cairns
HAUNTED STRANGLER, THE(1958, Brit.)

Joyce Cairns
GUNMAN HAS ESCAPED, A(1948, Brit.), w

Sally Cairns
COVERED WAGON TRAILS(1940); LOOK WHO'S LAUGHING(1941); PLAYMATES(1941); JOAN OF OZARK(1942); KING OF THE STALLIONS(1942); PARACHUTE NURSE(1942); CHANCE OF A LIFETIME, THE(1943); GIRL CRAZY(1943); COVER GIRL(1944)

The Cairoli Brothers
HAPPIDROME(1943, Brit.)

Joe Caites
SLIGHT CASE OF MURDER, A(1938); BROTHER ORCHID(1940)

Wilfred Caithness
LAD, THE(1935, Brit.); IMPROPER DUCHESS, THE(1936, Brit.); MAN BEHIND THE MASK, THE(1936, Brit.); MOUNTAINS O'MOURNE(1938, Brit.); SPY OF NAPOLEON(1939, Brit.); TWO FOR DANGER(1940, Brit.); MAN ABOUT THE HOUSE, A(1947, Brit.); SILVER DARLINGS, THE(1947, Brit.); MY SISTER AND I(1948, Brit.); NOTHING VENTURE(1948, Brit.); ONCE UPON A DREAM(1949, Brit.); WHILE THE

SUN SHINES(1950, Brit.); WINSLOW BOY, THE(1950); BRANDY FOR THE PARSON(1952, Brit.); TREASURE HUNT(1952, Brit.)

Wilfrid Caithness
CHECKMATE(1935, Brit,); TRIUMPH OF SHERLOCK HOLMES, THE(1935, Brit.); HEAD OFFICE(1936, Brit.); PERFECT CRIME, THE(1937, Brit.)

Elise Caitlin
HARD COUNTRY(1981)

Joe Caits
AFTER THE THIN MAN(1936); HOLLYWOOD COWBOY(1937); LIVE, LOVE AND LEARN(1937); MARRIED BEFORE BREAKFAST(1937); YOUTH ON PAROLE(1937); REFORMATORY(1938); INVITATION TO HAPPINESS(1939); GRANDPA GOES TO TOWN(1940)

Joseph Caits
AND SO THEY WERE MARRIED(1936); LADY AND THE MOB, THE(1939)

Aldo Caiva
THIS WINE OF LOVE(1948, Ital.), w

Joseph Caivelli
SPY WITH MY FACE, THE(1966), w

Gianni Cajafi
SEVEN SEAS TO CALAIS(1963, Ital.)

Levent Cakir
YOR, THE HUNTER FROM THE FUTURE(1983, Ital.)

Cal Shrum and His Rhythm Rangers
RANGERS TAKE OVER, THE(1942); LOST TRAIL, THE(1945)

Cal [Carl] Shrum and His Rhythm Rangers
THUNDER OVER THE PRAIRIE(1941)

Cal Shrum's Gang
SCATTERBRAIN(1940)

Cal Shrum's Rhythm Rangers
ROLLIN' HOME TO TEXAS(1941)

Cal Strumm's Rhythm Rangers
BAD MEN OF THUNDER GAP(1943)

Joseph Cala
1984
ANGEL(1984), a, w

Angelo Calabrese
WANDERING JEW, THE(1948, Ital.); RETURN OF THE BLACK EAGLE(1949, Ital.)

Francesca Calabrese
DEAF SMITH AND JOHNNY EARS(1973, Ital.), art d

Francesco Calabrese
FEW BULLETS MORE, A(1968, Ital./Span.), art d

Samuel Ray Calabrese
THEY RAN FOR THEIR LIVES(1968), p

Paul Calabria
1984
BODY DOUBLE(1984)

Thomas Calabro
1984
EXTERMINATOR 2(1984)

Gene Calahan
BUTTERFIELD 8(1960), set d

Helen Calahan
LORDS OF FLATBUSH, THE(1974)

Margarita Calahorra
MALOU(1983)

Clara Calamai
OSSESSIONE(1959, Ital.); WHITE NIGHTS(1961, Ital./Fr.); DEEP RED(1976, Ital.)

Calaman
GENERALS WITHOUT BUTTONS(1938, Fr.)

Aldo Calamara
EYE OF THE NEEDLE, THE(1965, Ital./Fr.), p; STAR PILOT(1977, Ital.), p

Nancy Calamatta
TRENCHCOAT(1983)

Stefano Calanchi
MASOCH(1980, Ital.)

Giuliana Calandra
DEEP RED(1976, Ital.)

Giulina Calandra
NEST OF VIPERS(1979, Ital.)

Giuseppe Calandra
SALVATORE GIULIANO(1966, Ital.)

Guiliana Calandra
ALL SCREWED UP(1976, Ital.)

Reno Calarco
Misc. Talkies
ROAD REBELS(1963), d

Shegundo Calarza
COUNTRY DOCTOR, THE(1963, Portuguese), m

Gian Pietro Calasso
STRANDED(1965)

Roman Calatayud
ADIOS GRINGO(1967, Ital./Fr./Span.), art d; VILLA RIDES(1968), set d

Van Calbert
RAINBOW RANCH(1933)

David Calcagni
Silents
AUCTION BLOCK, THE(1917), ph; OH, JOHNNY(1919), ph

Frank Calcagnini
LAST PORNO FLICK, THE(1974)

Hector Calcano
GAMES MEN PLAY, THE(1968, Arg.)

Sharon Calcraft
WINTER OF OUR DREAMS(1982, Aus.), m

Christine Calcutt
LONELY HEARTS(1983, Aus.)

Stephen Calcutt
FLASH GORDON(1980)

Orme Caldara
Silents
SPREADING DAWN, THE(1917)

M. R. Caldas
MAN COULD GET KILLED, A(1966)

Diana Caldenvood
CURTAIN UP(1952, Brit.)

A. A. Calder
Silents
PARTNERS OF THE NIGHT(1920), ph

Alexander Calder
DREAMS THAT MONEY CAN BUY(1948), w

Caleen Calder
HALF-BREED, THE(1952); SHE'S BACK ON BROADWAY(1953)

David Calder
SLEEPING DOGS(1977, New Zealand), m; SUPERMAN(1978); MOONLIGHTING(1982, Brit.)

Joseph Calder
Silents
FOUR HORSEMEN OF THE APOCALYPSE, THE(1921), art d; INFAMOUS MISS REVELL, THE(1921), art d; GOLDEN GIFT, THE(1922), art d; KISSES(1922), art d
Misc. Silents
HATE(1922), d

Judith Calder
KRAMER VS. KRAMER(1979)

King Calder
RAINS OF RANCHIPUR, THE(1955); ON THE THRESHOLD OF SPACE(1956); TIMETABLE(1956); HONG KONG CONFIDENTIAL(1958); MARDI GRAS(1958); THREE CAME TO KILL(1960); EVERYTHING'S DUCKY(1961); READY FOR THE PEOPLE(1964)

Anna Calder-Marshall
PUSSYCAT, PUSSYCAT, I LOVE YOU(1970); WUTHERING HEIGHTS(1970, Brit.); ZULU DAWN(1980, Brit.)
Misc. Talkies
TWO FACES OF EVIL, THE(1981, Brit.)

David Calderisi
1984
HIGHPOINT(1984, Can.)

Carlos Calderon
1984
ERENDIRA(1984, Mex./Fr./Ger.)

Fee Calderon
JOHNNY BANCO(1969, Fr./Ital./Ger.)

Guillermo Calderon
AZTEC MUMMY, THE(1957, Mex.), p, s; INVISIBLE MAN, THE(1958, Mex.), p; FRANKENSTEIN, THE VAMPIRE AND CO.(1961, Mex.), p; SPIRITISM(1965, Mex.), p, w; SANTO CONTRA LA HIJA DE FRANKENSTEIN(1971, Mex.), p

Jose Luis Calderon
SHARK(1970, U.S./Mex.), p

Juan Carlos Calderon
DAY THAT SHOOK THE WORLD, THE(1977, Yugo./Czech.), m

Norma Calderon
NAKED JUNGLE, THE(1953); MAN WITH THE GUN(1955)

Ruben A. Calderon
YOUNG AND EVIL(1962, Mex.), p

Sergio Calderon
IN-LAWS, THE(1979); HIGH RISK(1981)
1984
ERENDIRA(1984, Mex./Fr./Ger.); UNDER THE VOLCANO(1984)

William Calderon
SANTA CLAUS(1960, Mex.), p

Rita Calderoni
LADY OF MONZA, THE(1970, Ital.); QUIET PLACE IN THE COUNTRY, A(1970, Ital./Fr.); YEAR ONE(1974, Ital.); END OF THE GAME(1976, Ger./Ital.)

Diana Calderwood
REMARKABLE MR. KIPPS(1942, Brit.); SPRINGTIME(1948, Brit.); SOMETHING IN THE CITY(1950, Brit.); WALLET, THE(1952, Brit.); GLAD TIDINGS(1953, Brit.)

Anthony Caldeway
VIGILANTES OF DODGE CITY(1944), w

Richard Caldicot
ONE GOOD TURN(1955, Brit.); ROOM AT THE TOP(1959, Brit.); GET ON WITH IT(1963, Brit.); V.I.P.s, THE(1963, Brit.); SPY WHO CAME IN FROM THE COLD, THE(1965, Brit.); FIREPOWER(1979, Brit.)

Marjorie Caldicott
TWILIGHT HOUR(1944, Brit.)

Richard Caldicott
MAN WITH A MILLION(1954, Brit.); HORSE'S MOUTH, THE(1958, Brit.); COURT MARTIAL OF MAJOR KELLER, THE(1961, Brit.); BATTLEAXE, THE(1962, Brit.); DURANT AFFAIR, THE(1962, Brit.); YOU MUST BE JOKING!(1965, Brit.); CLUE OF THE TWISTED CANDLE(1968, Brit.); WEEKEND MURDERS, THE(1972, Ital.)

Sonny Caldinez
RAIDERS OF THE LOST ARK(1981)

Federico Caldara
MAGIC WORLD OF TOPO GIGIO, THE(1961, Ital.), d&w

A. A. Caldwell
Silents
WOMAN'S BUSINESS, A(1920), ph

Anne Caldwell
DIXIANA(1930), d&w; HALF SHOT AT SUNRISE(1930), w; FLYING DOWN TO RIO(1933), w

Arthur Caldwell, Jr.
Silents
INNER MAN, THE(1922)

Betty Caldwell
JINX MONEY(1948); ON OUR MERRY WAY(1948)
Misc. Silents
FANGS OF DESTINY(1927); PRINCE OF THE PLAINS(1927); WANDERER OF THE WEST(1927); DRIFTING KID, THE(1928); GREASED LIGHTING(1928)

Betty Ruth Caldwell
PRINCESS AND THE PIRATE, THE(1944)
Bill Caldwell
HER JUNGLE LOVE(1938)
Bobbie Caldwell
WEST POINT OF THE AIR(1935)
Bobby Caldwell
CIRCUS CLOWN(1934); STAND UP AND CHEER(1934 80m FOX bw); TEXAS
RANGERS, THE(1936); WINTERSET(1936); TEST PILOT(1938)
Cleatus Caldwell
SUSIE STEPS OUT(1946)
Dale Caldwell
HOLLYWOOD HIGH(1977)
Dan Caldwell
NIGHTMARE IN BLOOD(1978)
David Caldwell
KID FROM CANADA, THE(1957, Brit.)
Don Caldwell
LOOKIN' TO GET OUT(1982)
Dwight Caldwell
DEFENDERS OF THE LAW(1931), ed; SEA DEVILS(1931), ed; CHEATING
BLONDES(1933), ed; MOTIVE FOR REVENGE(1935), ed; NIGHT ALARM(1935), ed;
PERFECT CLUE, THE(1935), ed; RECKLESS ROADS(1935), ed; WESTERN COUR-
AGE(1935), ed; WESTERN FRONTIER(1935), ed; FUGITIVE SHERIFF, THE(1936),
ed; HEIR TO TROUBLE(1936), ed; HEROES OF THE RANGE(1936), ed; LAWLESS
RIDERS(1936), ed; UNKNOWN RANGER, THE(1936), ed; LAW OF THE RAN-
GER(1937), ed; NORTH OF NOME(1937), ed; OUTLAWS OF THE ORIENT(1937), ed;
RANGER COURAGE(1937), ed; RANGERS STEP IN, THE(1937), ed; RECKLESS
RANGER(1937), ed; RIO GRANDE RANGER(1937), ed; ROARING TIMBER(1937), ed;
SHADOWS OF THE ORIENT(1937), ed; TRAPPED BY G-MEN(1937), ed; TROUBLE
IN MOROCCO(1937), ed; UNDER SUSPICION(1937), ed; FLIGHT INTO NO-
WHERE(1938), ed; IN EARLY ARIZONA(1938), ed; MAKING THE HEAD-
LINES(1938), ed; PHANTOM GOLD(1938), ed; PIONEER TRAIL(1938), ed;
REFORMATORY(1938), ed; ROLLING CARAVANS(1938), ed; STAGECOACH
DAYS(1938), ed; FRONTIERS OF '49(1939), ed; FUGITIVE AT LARGE(1939), ed;
HIDDEN POWER(1939), ed; LAW COMES TO TEXAS, THE(1939), ed; LONE STAR
PIONEERS(1939), ed; STRANGE CASE OF DR. MEADE(1939), ed; TRAPPED IN THE
SKY(1939), ed; ELLERY QUEEN. MASTER DETECTIVE(1940), ed; FUGITIVE FROM
A PRISON CAMP(1940), ed; GREAT PLANE ROBBERY, THE(1940), ed; OUTSIDE
THE 3-MILE LIMIT(1940), ed; PASSPORT TO ALCATRAZ(1940), ed; ELLERY
QUEEN AND THE MURDER RING(1941), ed; ELLERY QUEEN AND THE PERFECT
CRIME(1941), ed; ELLERY QUEEN'S PENTHOUSE MYSTERY(1941), ed; GREAT
SWINDLE, THE(1941), ed; CLOSE CALL FOR ELLERY QUEEN, A(1942), ed; DES-
PERATE CHANCE FOR ELLERY QUEEN, A(1942), ed; ENEMY AGENTS MEET
ELLERY QUEEN(1942), ed; CRIME DOCTOR(1943), ed; CRIME DOCTOR'S STRANG-
EST CASE(1943), ed; NO PLACE FOR A LADY(1943), ed; SHADOWS IN THE
NIGHT(1944), ed; CRIME DOCTOR'S COURAGE, THE(1945), ed; CRIME DOCTOR'S
WARNING(1945), ed; VOICE OF THE WHISTLER(1945), ed; CRIME DOCTOR'S MAN
HUNT(1946), ed; JUST BEFORE DAWN(1946), ed; MYSTERIOUS INTRUDER(1946),
ed; SECRET OF THE WHISTLER(1946), ed; CRIME DOCTOR'S GAMBLE(1947), ed;
KEY WITNESS(1947), ed; MILLERSON CASE, THE(1947), ed; 13TH HOUR,
THE(1947), ed; RETURN OF THE WHISTLER, THE(1948), ed; TRAPPED BY BOS-
TON BLACKIE(1948), ed; TOP GUN(1955), ed; WILD YOUTH(1961), ed
Edgar Caldwell
STORY OF DR. WASSELL, THE(1944); DEADLINE AT DAWN(1946); NIGHT AND
DAY(1946); ROAD HOUSE(1948)
Erskine Caldwell
TOBACCO ROAD(1941), w; VOLCANO(1953, Ital.), w; GOD'S LITTLE ACRE(1958),
w; CLAUDELLE INGLISH(1961), w
Forbes Caldwell
CARNIVAL OF SOULS(1962)
Fred Caldwell
Silents
NIGHT LIFE IN HOLLYWOOD(1922), d&w; HURRICANE, THE(1926), d; NIGHT
WATCH, THE(1926), a, d
Misc. Silents
LONE HORSEMAN, THE(1923), d; WESTERN JUSTICE(1923), d
George Caldwell
RAT PFINK AND BOO BOO(1966); TO BE OR NOT TO BE(1983)
1984
DREAMSCAPE(1984)
Gisela Caldwell
TOGETHER FOR DAYS(1972)
Gwen Caldwell
TARZAN AND THE SLAVE GIRL(1950); TEN TALL MEN(1951); TWO TICKETS TO
BROADWAY(1951); SON OF SINBAD(1955)
H.H. Caldwell
CHRISTINA(1929), ed, w; LUCKY STAR(1929), ed; CITY GIRL(1930), ed
Silents
ALASKAN, THE(1924), t; WELCOME STRANGER(1924), t; BEN-HUR(1925), t;
PRAIRIE WIFE, THE(1925), t, ed; TORRENT, THE(1926), t; SEVENTH HEA-
VEN(1927), t, ed; SUNRISE–A SONG OF TWO HUMANS(1927), t, ed; AWAKENING,
THE(1928), t, ed; FOUR SONS(1928), t; GATEWAY OF THE MOON, THE(1928), t; NO
OTHER WOMAN(1928), t; ETERNAL LOVE(1929), t; EXALTED FLAPPER,
THE(1929), t, ed; FAR CALL, THE(1929), t, ed; RESCUE, THE(1929), t, ed
John C. Caldwell
THE BOSTON STRANGLER, THE(1968), spec eff
L. Scott Caldwell
WITHOUT A TRACE(1983)
1984
EXTERMINATOR 2(1984)
Louise Caldwell
AMAZING TRANSPARENT MAN, THE(1960), set d; MY DOG, BUDDY(1960), set d
Matilda Caldwell
JOHNNY ALLEGRO(1949)
Michael Caldwell
UP IN SMOKE(1978)

Orville Caldwell
HIS FAMILY TREE(1936); JUST AROUND THE CORNER(1938); LAST WARNING,
THE(1938)
Silents
FRENCH DOLL, THE(1923); LONELY ROAD, THE(1923); SCARLET LILY,
THE(1923); JUDGMENT OF THE HILLS(1927)
Misc. Silents
SIX-FIFTY, THE(1923); DAUGHTERS OF THE NIGHT(1924); SACKCLOTH AND
SCARLET(1925); FLAME OF THE ARGENTINE(1926); WIVES OF THE PROPHET,
THE(1926); HARVESTER, THE(1927); LITTLE YELLOW HOUSE, THE(1928); PATSY,
THE(1928)
Peter Caldwell
MANPOWER(1941); ONE FOOT IN HEAVEN(1941); TO BE OR NOT TO BE(1942)
Russ Caldwell
LOVE BUG, THE(1968)
Ruth Caldwell
PARTNERS IN TIME(1946)
Sarah Caldwell
MRS. BROWN, YOU'VE GOT A LOVELY DAUGHTER(1968, Brit.)
Thomas Caldwell
CASEY'S SHADOW(1978)
Virginia Caldwell
Silents
WHAT'S A WIFE WORTH?(1921)
Misc. Silents
RIGHT OF WAY, THE(1920)
Wehman Caldwell
1984
CHATTANOOGA CHOO CHOO(1984)
William Caldwell
UNDERGROUND AGENT(1942); HERE COME THE TIGERS(1978)
Cindy Cale
RENEGADE GIRLS(1974)
J.J. Cale
1984
MY BEST FRIEND'S GIRL(1984, Fr.), m
John Cale
RENEGADE GIRLS(1974), m
Katha Cale
LILITH(1964)
Noel Calef
STRANGER ON THE PROWL(1953, Ital.), a, p, w; TIGER BAY(1959, Brit.), w;
FRANTIC(1961, Fr.), w
Charles Calello
LONELY LADY, THE(1983), m
Charlie Calello
WHO KILLED TEDDY BEAR?(1965), m
Antonio Calenda
Misc. Talkies
ONE RUSSIAN SUMMER(1973), d
Francois Calepides
CIRCUS WORLD(1964)
John Caler
WRONG MAN, THE(1956); HUNTERS, THE(1958)
Johnny Caler
REVOLT OF MAMIE STOVER, THE(1956)
Anthony Calf
1984
OXFORD BLUES(1984)
Don Calfa
NO MORE EXCUSES(1968); CINDERELLA LIBERTY(1973); RAINBOW BOYS,
THE(1973, Can.); BANK SHOT(1974); RHINOCEROS(1974); PEEPER(1975); NICK-
ELODEON(1976); NEW YORK, NEW YORK(1977); FOUL PLAY(1978); ROSE,
THE(1979); 10(1979); 1941(1979); POSTMAN ALWAYS RINGS TWICE, THE(1981);
STAR CHAMBER, THE(1983)
Donald Calfa
GREASER'S PALACE(1972)
Nicole Calfan
BORSALINO(1970, Fr.); BURGLARS, THE(1972, Fr./Ital.); THREE MUSKETEERS,
THE(1974, Panama); FOUR MUSKETEERS, THE(1975); PERMISSION TO KILL(1975,
U.S./Aust.)
Andre Calgary
DOUBLE OR NOTHING(1937)
Steve Calgary
DOUBLE OR NOTHING(1937)
Louis Calgern
FIFTH AVENUE GIRL(1939)
Matilda Calhan
MADAME X(1966)
Louis Calhern
BLONDE CRAZY(1931); ROAD TO SINGAPORE(1931); STOLEN HEAVEN(1931);
AFRAID TO TALK(1932); NIGHT AFTER NIGHT(1932); OKAY AMERICA(1932);
THEY CALL IT SIN(1932); DIPLOMANIACS(1933); DUCK SOUP(1933); FRISCO
JENNY(1933); STRICTLY PERSONAL(1933); WOMAN ACCUSED(1933); WORLD
GONE MAD, THE(1933); 20,000 YEARS IN SING SING(1933); AFFAIRS OF CELLINI,
THE(1934); COUNT OF MONTE CRISTO, THE(1934); MAN WITH TWO FACES,
THE(1934); ARIZONIAN, THE(1935); LAST DAYS OF POMPEII, THE(1935); SWEET
ADELINE(1935); WOMAN WANTED(1935); GORGEOUS HUSSY, THE(1936); HER
HUSBAND LIES(1937); LIFE OF EMILE ZOLA, THE(1937); FAST COMPANY(1938);
CHARLIE MC CARTHY, DETECTIVE(1939); JUAREZ(1939); DR. EHRLICH'S MAGIC
BULLET(1940); I TAKE THIS WOMAN(1940); HEAVEN CAN WAIT(1943); NOBODY'S
DARLING(1943); BRIDGE OF SAN LUIS REY, THE(1944); UP IN ARMS(1944);
NOTORIOUS(1946); ARCH OF TRIUMPH(1948); RED DANUBE, THE(1949); RED
PONY, THE(1949); ANNIE GET YOUR GUN(1950); ASPHALT JUNGLE, THE(1950);
DEVIL'S DOORWAY(1950); LIFE OF HER OWN, A(1950); MAGNIFICENT YANKEE,
THE(1950); NANCY GOES TO RIO(1950); TWO WEEKS WITH LOVE(1950); MAN
WITH A CLOAK, THE(1951); BAD AND THE BEAUTIFUL, THE(1952); INVITA-
TION(1952); PRISONER OF ZENDA, THE(1952); WASHINGTON STORY(1952);
WE'RE NOT MARRIED(1952); CONFIDENTIAL CONNIE(1953); JULIUS CA-
ESAR(1953); LATIN LOVERS(1953); MAIN STREET TO BROADWAY(1953); RE-

MAINS TO BE SEEN(1953); ATHENA(1954); BETRAYED(1954); EXECUTIVE SUITE(1954); MEN OF THE FIGHTING LADY(1954); RHAPSODY(1954); STUDENT PRINCE, THE(1954); BLACKBOARD JUNGLE, THE(1955); PRODIGAL, THE(1955); FOREVER DARLING(1956); HIGH SOCIETY(1956)
Silents
BLOT, THE(1921)
Misc. Silents
TOO WISE WIVES(1921); WHAT'S WORTH WHILE?(1921); WOMAN, WAKE UP!(1922); LAST MOMENT, THE(1923)
Richard Calhoon
CRIME AND PUNISHMENT(1935), ed
Alice Calhoun
BRIDE OF THE DESERT(1929)
Silents
RAINBOW(1921); ANGEL OF CROOKED STREET, THE(1922); LITTLE WILD-CAT(1922); ONE STOLEN NIGHT(1923); FLOWING GOLD(1924); MAN ON THE BOX, THE(1925); KENTUCKY HANDICAP(1926); POWER OF THE WEAK, THE(1926); DOWN GRADE, THE(1927); ISLE OF FORGOTTEN WOMEN(1927)
Misc. Silents
THIRTEENTH CHAIR, THE(1919); CAPTAIN SWIFT(1920); DEADLINE AT ELEVEN(1920); SEA RIDER, THE(1920); CHARMING DECEIVER, THE(1921); CLOSED DOORS(1921); MATRIMONIAL WEB, THE(1921); PEGGY PUTS IT OVER(1921); PRINCESS JONES(1921); BLUE BLOOD(1922); GIRL IN HIS ROOM, THE(1922); GIRL'S DESIRE, A(1922); LITTLE MINISTER, THE(1922); MAN FROM BRODNEY'S, THE(1923); MAN NEXT DOOR, THE(1923); MASTERS OF MEN(1923); MIDNIGHT ALARM, THE(1923); PIONEER TRAILS(1923); BETWEEN FRIENDS(1924); CODE OF THE WILDERNESS(1924); EVERLASTING WHISPER, THE(1925); HAPPY WARRIOR, THE(1925); OTHER WOMAN'S STORY, THE(1925); PAMPERED YOUTH(1925); PART TIME WIFE(1925); FLYING HIGH(1926); HERO OF THE BIG SNOWS, A(1926); TENTACLES OF THE NORTH(1926); HIDDEN ACES(1927); IN THE FIRST DEGREE(1927); SAVAGE PASSIONS(1927); TRUNK MYSTERY, THE(1927)
Catherine Calhoun
Silents
DAUGHTER OF THE SEA, A(1915)
Cathleen Calhoun
Silents
UNDER FIRE(1926); WHAT HAPPENED TO FATHER(1927)
Misc. Silents
CALIBRE 45(1924); DON DARE DEVIL(1925)
Charles Calhoun
THEY WERE EXPENDABLE(1945)
D. D. Calhoun
Silents
ONE STOLEN NIGHT(1923), w
Grant Calhoun
GIRLS' SCHOOL(1950)
Jean Calhoun
GANGSTER, THE(1947); CAGED(1950)
Silents
ALIAS MIKE MORAN(1919); CUB REPORTER, THE(1922)
Misc. Silents
HIGH TIDE(1918); THIEVES(1919); HIS OWN LAW(1920); OFFICER 666(1920); THREE SEVENS(1921)
Jeanne Calhoun
Silents
SPLENDID SIN, THE(1919)
Joan Calhoun
ANGEL, ANGEL, DOWN WE GO(1969)
Julia Calhoun
Silents
JUST LIKE A WOMAN(1923)
Misc. Silents
MATCH-BREAKER, THE(1921)
Katherine Calhoun
Misc. Silents
DRAGON, THE(1916)
Kathleen Calhoun
Silents
MAN ON THE BOX, THE(1925)
Misc. Silents
WESTERN FEUDS(1924)
Pat Calhoun
Misc. Silents
MY UNMARRIED WIFE(1918)
Patrick Calhoun
Silents
ON TRIAL(1917)
Misc. Silents
LITTLE SHOES(1917); TRUANT SOUL, THE(1917); BLINDFOLDED(1918)
Richard Calhoun
THINGS ARE TOUGH ALL OVER(1982); PRIVATE SCANDAL, A(1932), ed
Rory Calhoun
GREAT JOHN L. THE(1945); NOB HILL(1945); ADVENTURE ISLAND(1947); RED HOUSE, THE(1947); THAT HAGEN GIRL(1947); MIRACULOUS JOURNEY(1948); MASSACRE RIVER(1949); SAND(1949); COUNTY FAIR(1950); RETURN OF THE FRONTIERSMAN(1950); TICKET TO TOMAHAWK(1950); I'D CLIMB THE HIGHEST MOUNTAIN(1951); MEET ME AFTER THE SHOW(1951); ROGUE RIVER(1951); WAY OF A GAUCHO(1952); WITH A SONG IN MY HEART(1952); HOW TO MARRY A MILLIONAIRE(1953); POWDER RIVER(1953); SILVER WHIP, THE(1953); BULLET IS WAITING, A(1954); DAWN AT SOCORRO(1954); FOUR GUNS TO THE BORDER(1954); RIVER OF NO RETURN(1954); YELLOW TOMAHAWK, THE(1954); AIN'T MISBEHAVIN'(1955); LOOTERS, THE(1955); SHOTGUN(1955), w; SPOILERS, THE(1955); TREASURE OF PANCHO VILLA, THE(1955); FLIGHT TO HONG KONG(1956); RAW EDGE(1956); RED SUNDOWN(1956); BIG CAPER, THE(1957); DOMINO KID(1957), a, p, w; HIRED GUN, THE(1957), a, p; RIDE OUT FOR REVENGE(1957); UTAH BLAINE(1957); APACHE TERRITORY(1958), a, p; SAGA OF HEMP BROWN, THE(1958); THUNDER IN CAROLINA(1960); COLOSSUS OF RHODES, THE(1961, Ital., Fr., Span.); SECRET OF MONTE CRISTO, THE(1961, Brit.); MARCO POLO(1962, Fr./Ital.); REQUIEM FOR A HEAVYWEIGHT(1962); FACE IN THE RAIN, A(1963); GUN HAWK, THE(1963); YOUNG AND THE BRAVE, THE(1963);

BLACK SPURS(1965); FINGER ON THE TRIGGER(1965, US/Span.); YOUNG FURY(1965); APACHE UPRISING(1966); OPERATION DELILAH(1966, U.S./Span.); DAYTON'S DEVILS(1968); OPERATION CROSS EAGLES(1969, U.S./Yugo.); NIGHT OF THE LEPUS(1972); WON TON TON, THE DOG WHO SAVED HOLLYWOOD(1976); LOVE AND THE MIDNIGHT AUTO SUPPLY(1978); MAIN EVENT, THE(1979); MOTEL HELL(1980)
1984
ANGEL(1984)
Misc. Talkies
GIRL OF THE NILE, THE(1967, US/ Ger.); OUR MEN IN BAGHDAD(1967, Ital.); WEST IS STILL WILD, THE(1977)
William Calhoun
Misc. Silents
COURAGE OF THE COMMONPLACE(1917); LADY OF THE PHOTOGRAPH, THE(1917); PRINCESS' NECKLACE, THE(1917); LITTLE MISS NO-ACCOUNT(1918); YOUTHFUL CHEATERS(1923); RED LOVE(1925)
Giulio Cali
UNFAITHFULS, THE(1960, Ital.); VARIETY LIGHTS(1965, Ital.)
Joseph Cali
VOICES(1979); COMPETITION, THE(1980); LONELY LADY, THE(1983)
Hank Calia
1984
CITY HEAT(1984)
Steve Calicchio
ENDLESS LOVE(1981)
Jeff Caliendo
PSYCHOTRONIC MAN, THE(1980)
Alberto Califano
PIRATES OF CAPRI, THE(1949)
John Califano
WANDERERS, THE(1979)
California Collegians
COLLEGE HOLIDAY(1936)
The California "Hessians"
HELL'S BLOODY DEVILS(1970)
California Opera Company
Misc. Talkies
H.M.S. PINAFORE(1951)
The Californian Collegians
TOP OF THE TOWN(1937)
Caligary Brothers
BELOVED IMPOSTER(1936, Brit.)
Caligola
MAN WHO WAGGED HIS TAIL, THE(1961, Ital./Span.)
William A. Calihan
MAGNIFICENT SEVEN RIDE, THE(1972), p
William Calihan, Jr.
FIGHTER ATTACK(1953), p
Ernesto Calindri
TIGER OF THE SEVEN SEAS(1964, Fr./Ital.); EYE OF THE NEEDLE, THE(1965, Ital./Fr.)
Ernesto Calindrini
LITTLE MARTYR, THE(1947, Ital.)
Toni Calio
TWO WOMEN(1961, Ital./Fr.)
Janet Calionzes
PASSPORT TO SUEZ(1943)
Clifford Calis
Misc. Silents
CHARITY CASTLE(1917)
Ugo Calise
SWEET SMELL OF LOVE(1966, Ital./Ger.), m
C. Calisti
MAN COULD GET KILLED, A(1966)
Calisto Calisti
SWORD OF THE CONQUEROR(1962, Ital.); OMICRON(1963, Ital.); BIG GUNDOWN, THE(1968, Ital.); BIGGEST BUNDLE OF THEM ALL, THE(1968)
Calisto
GOLDEN ARROW, THE(1964, Ital.)
Joan Calistri
RUN ACROSS THE RIVER(1961)
Darrel Calker
SINISTER JOURNEY(1948), md; FEDERAL MAN(1950), m
Darrell Calker
RENEGADE GIRL(1946), m; ADVENTURE ISLAND(1947), m; BACKLASH(1947), m; BIG TOWN(1947), m; I COVER BIG TOWN(1947), m; JEWELS OF BRANDENBURG(1947), m; SHOOT TO KILL(1947), m; ALBUQUERQUE(1948), m; BIG TOWN SCANDAL(1948), m; FIGHTING BACK(1948), m; HALF PAST MIDNIGHT(1948), m; TUCSON(1949), m; FIGHTING REDHEAD, THE(1950), m; FLYING SAUCER, THE(1950), m; FORBIDDEN JUNGLE(1950), m; CATTLE QUEEN(1951), m; FBI GIRL(1951), m; HOODLUM, THE(1951), m; JOE PALOOKA IN TRIPLE CROSS(1951), m; SAVAGE DRUMS(1951), m; SLAUGHTER TRAIL(1951), m; MARSHAL'S DAUGHTER, THE(1953), m; OUTLAW TREASURE(1955), m; FROM HELL IT CAME(1957), m; VOODOO WOMAN(1957), m; MY WORLD DIES SCREAMING(1958), m; AMAZING TRANSPARENT MAN, THE(1960), m; BEYOND THE TIME BARRIER(1960), m
Darril Calker
BORROWED TROUBLE(1948), md
Darryl Calker
MANHANDLED(1949), m; CHARTROOSE CABOOSE(1960), m
David Calkins
RESURRECTION(1980)
John Calkins
DIVORCE(1945); ROUGHLY SPEAKING(1945); BOY WITH THE GREEN HAIR, THE(1949)
Johnny Calkins
SULLIVANS, THE(1944); NIGHT EDITOR(1946); SONG OF ARIZONA(1946); GINGER(1947); LIFE WITH FATHER(1947); MOONRISE(1948); IT HAPPENS EVERY SPRING(1949)

Richard Calkins
1984
RACING WITH THE MOON(1984), a, stunts
Anthony Call
PEOPLE NEXT DOOR, THE(1970)
Anthony D. Call
GOING IN STYLE(1979)
Ed Call
ADAM AT 6 A.M.(1970); DIAMONDS ARE FOREVER(1971, Brit.); WALKING TALL(1973); KLANSMAN, THE(1974); CARBON COPY(1981)
Edward Call
I WANNA HOLD YOUR HAND(1978); MEAN DOG BLUES(1978)
1984
CRACKERS(1984); MICKI AND MAUDE(1984); NIGHTMARE ON ELM STREET, A(1984); WILD LIFE, THE(1984)
Inez Call
GALLANT LADY(1942)
John Call
INDIAN UPRISING(1951); BOOTS MALONE(1952); FEARLESS FAGAN(1952); HANGMAN'S KNOT(1952); YOUNG MAN WITH IDEAS(1952); KID FROM LEFT FIELD, THE(1953); LONG, LONG TRAILER, THE(1954); SANTA CLAUS CONQUERS THE MARTIANS(1964); ANDERSON TAPES, THE(1971)
John W. Call
SOAK THE RICH(1936)
Johnny Call
IRON MAN, THE(1951)
Joseph Call
SATURDAY NIGHT FEVER(1977)
Ken Call
CATTLE ANNIE AND LITTLE BRITCHES(1981); LOVELESS, THE(1982)
Kenny Call
1984
STARMAN(1984)
Maurice Call
BARONESS AND THE BUTLER, THE(1938)
Mildred Call
Silents
POLLY OF THE CIRCUS(1917)
Peggie Call
WHEN A GIRL'S BEAUTIFUL(1947)
Peggy Call
MR. BELVEDERE GOES TO COLLEGE(1949)
R. D. Call
48 HOURS(1982)
Zella Call
Misc. Silents
CORNER IN COTTON, A(1916)
Tessy Callado
1984
BLAME IT ON RIO(1984)
Andrew "Duke" Callaghan
JEREMIAH JOHNSON(1972), ph
Barry Callaghan
1984
LISTEN TO THE CITY(1984, Can.)
Duke Callaghan
SCALPHUNTERS, THE(1968), ph; TAKE, THE(1974), ph; YAKUZA, THE(1975, U.S./Jap.), ph; LAST HARD MEN, THE(1976), ph; CONAN THE BARBARIAN(1982), ph
1984
LOVELINES(1984), ph
Edna Callaghan
42ND STREET(1933)
George Callaghan
GENERAL JOHN REGAN(1933, Brit.); LONG SHOT, THE(1939), w
George H. Callaghan
ROMANCE RIDES THE RANGE(1936), p; MOONLIGHT ON THE RANGE(1937), p; SINGING BUCKAROO, THE(1937), p
John Callaghan
REFLECTIONS IN A GOLDEN EYE(1967)
Kymbra Callaghan
WITHOUT A TRACE(1983)
Larry D. Callaghan
WHOSE LIFE IS IT ANYWAY?(1981)
Mac Callaghan
TALK OF THE DEVIL(1937, Brit.)
Morley Callaghan
NOW THAT APRIL'S HERE(1958, Can.), w
Ray Callaghan
MELODY OF THE PLAINS(1937), p; INTERNECINE PROJECT, THE(1974, Brit.)
Vince Callaghan
THEY MIGHT BE GIANTS(1971), makeup
Vincent Callaghan
HOSPITAL, THE(1971), makeup; SHAMUS(1973), makeup
Andrew J. Callahan
Silents
BILLY JIM(1922), p
Bob Callahan
BATTLE OF GREED(1934); MILKY WAY, THE(1936); DRIFTIN' RIVER(1946)
Bobby Callahan
OUTLAW, THE(1943)
Cordelia Callahan
Silents
DOUBLING FOR ROMEO(1921); WATCH YOUR STEP(1922); ABRAHAM LINCOLN(1924)
Danna Callahan
REG'LAR FELLERS(1941)
Edna Callahan
PALMY DAYS(1931)

Foxy Callahan
BLACK MARKET RUSTLERS(1943)
G. Callahan
CAPTAIN TUGBOAT ANNIE(1945), w
Gene Callahan
HUSTLER, THE(1961), set d; MAD DOG COLL(1961), set d; SPLENDOR IN THE GRASS(1961), set d; CONNECTION, THE(1962), set d; DAVID AND LISA(1962), set d; LILITH(1964), set d; HARVEY MIDDLEMAN, FIREMAN(1965), prod d; GROUP, THE(1966), prod d; HURRY SUNDOWN(1967), prod d; FUNNY GIRL(1968), prod d; TRUMAN CAPOTE'S TRILOGY(1969), prod d; MAGIC GARDEN OF STANLEY SWEETHART, THE(1970), prod d; DEALING: OR THE BERKELEY-TO-BOSTON FORTY-BRICK LOST-BAG BLUES(1971), prod d; DOC(1971), prod d; EFFECT OF GAMMA RAYS ON MAN-IN-THE-MOON MARIGOLDS, THE(1972), prod d; FRIENDS OF EDDIE COYLE, THE(1973), prod d, art d; HAPPY HOOKER, THE(1975), prod d; STEPFORD WIVES, THE(1975), prod d; LAST TYCOON, THE(1976), prod d; NEXT MAN, THE(1976), prod d; FOR PETE'S SAKE(1977), art d; JULIA(1977), prod d; BLOODBROTHERS(1978), prod d; EYES OF LAURA MARS(1978), prod d; KING OF THE GYPSIES(1978), prod d; SEEMS LIKE OLD TIMES(1980), prod d; WHOSE LIFE IS IT ANYWAY?(1981), prod d; GREASE 2(1982), prod d; SURVIVORS, THE(1983), prod d
1984
PLACES IN THE HEART(1984), prod d
George Callahan
ADVENTURES OF KITTY O'DAY(1944), w; CALL OF THE JUNGLE(1944), w; CHARLIE CHAN IN BLACK MAGIC(1944), w; CHINESE CAT, THE(1944), w; JADE MASK, THE(1945), w; SCARLET CLUE, THE(1945), w; SHANGHAI COBRA, THE(1945), w; BEHIND THE MASK(1946), w; DARK ALIBI(1946), w; MISSING LADY, THE(1946), w; RED DRAGON, THE(1946), w; SHADOW RETURNS, THE(1946), w; STEP BY STEP(1946), w; BABE RUTH STORY, THE(1948), w; RED LIGHT(1949), w; BUNCO SQUAD(1950), w; PRISONERS IN PETTICOATS(1950), w; LUCKY NICK CAIN(1951), w
Harold Callahan
Silents
ANNE OF LITTLE SMOKY(1921)
Homer Bill Callahan
SONG OF THE DRIFTER(1948)
Jack Callahan
FURY, THE(1978)
James Callahan
CHARLIE CHAN IN THE SECRET SERVICE(1944), w; WALKING TARGET, THE(1960); EXPERIMENT IN TERROR(1962); MAN CALLED GANNON, A(1969); LADY SINGS THE BLUES(1972); OUTLAW BLUES(1977); INCHON(1981)
Jerry Callahan
Misc. Talkies
GUNNERS AND GUNS(1935), d
Margaret Callahan
HOT TIP(1935); SEVEN KEYS TO BALDPATE(1935); HIS FAMILY TREE(1936); LAST OUTLAW, THE(1936); MUSS 'EM UP(1936); SPECIAL INVESTIGATOR(1936)
Marion Callahan
MURDER AT THE VANITIES(1934)
Marlene Callahan
MAGIC SWORD, THE(1962)
Michael Callahan
TRUE CONFESSIONS(1981)
Mushy Callahan
MADISON SQUARE GARDEN(1932); PERSONALITY KID, THE(1934); IRISH IN US, THE(1935); HOUSE OF STRANGERS(1949); IRON MAN, THE(1951); STOP, YOU'RE KILLING ME(1952); FROM HERE TO ETERNITY(1953), tech adv; NUTTY PROFESSOR, THE(1963)
Pepe Callahan
SULLIVAN'S EMPIRE(1967); PINK JUNGLE, THE(1968); MACKENNA'S GOLD(1969); JOE KIDD(1972); LONG GOODBYE, THE(1973); APPLE DUMPLING GANG, THE(1975)
Robert Callahan
WIFE WANTED(1946), w
Robert E. Callahan
DAUGHTER OF THE WEST(1949), w
Tim Callahan
PRETTY POISON(1968)
Viola Callahan
LUCKIEST GIRL IN THE WORLD, THE(1936)
William Callahan
CHICKEN EVERY SUNDAY(1948)
Regan Callais
THEY LIVE BY NIGHT(1949)
Alex Callam
CHASING TROUBLE(1940); INVISIBLE KILLER, THE(1940); THUNDERING FRONTIER(1940); PAPER BULLETS(1941); CYCLONE KID, THE(1942); MIRACLE KID(1942); PHANTOM PLAINSMEN, THE(1942); RUBBER RACKETEERS(1942); WE WERE DANCING(1942); DARK MOUNTAIN(1944); THAT'S MY BABY(1944); ANCHORS AWEIGH(1945)
Callamand
MARIUS(1933, Fr.)
Lucien Callamand
PASSION FOR LIFE(1951, Fr.); UTOPIA(1952, Fr./Ital.)
D. Callan
Silents
LITTLE LORD FAUNTLEROY(1914, Brit.)
K. Callan
JOE(1970); LADY LIBERTY(1972, Ital./Fr.); HAIL(1973); TOUCH OF CLASS, A(1973, Brit.); FAST BREAK(1979); ONION FIELD, THE(1979); AMERICAN GIGOLO(1980); CHANGE OF SEASONS, A(1980)
Michael Callan
FLYING FONTAINES, THE(1959); THEY CAME TO CORDURA(1959); BECAUSE THEY'RE YOUNG(1960); PEPE(1960); GIDGET GOES HAWAIIAN(1961); MYSTERIOUS ISLAND(1961, U.S./Brit.); BON VOYAGE(1962); INTERNS, THE(1962); THIRTEEN WEST STREET(1962); VICTORS, THE(1963); NEW INTERNS, THE(1964); CAT BALLOU(1965); YOU MUST BE JOKING!(1965, Brit.); MAGNIFICENT SEVEN RIDE, THE(1972); FRASIER, THE SENSUOUS LION(1973); LEPKE(1975, U.S./Israel); RECORD CITY(1978); CAT AND THE CANARY, THE(1979, Brit.); DOUBLE EX-

POSURE(1982); CHAINED HEAT(1983 U.S./Ger.)

Shane Callan
FIRE AND ICE(1983)

Kay Callard
THEY WHO DARE(1954, Brit.); UNHOLY FOUR, THE(1954, Brit.); FINAL COLUMN, THE(1955, Brit.); JOE MACBETH(1955); STOLEN ASSIGNMENT(1955, Brit.); FIND THE LADY(1956, Brit.); WAY OUT, THE(1956, Brit.); CAT GIRL(1957); FIGHTING WILDCATS, THE(1957, Brit.); MAILBAG ROBBERY(1957, Brit.); SCOTLAND YARD DRAGNET(1957, Brit.); TWO GROOMS FOR A BRIDE(1957); UNDERCOVER GIRL(1957, Brit.); VIOLENT STRANGER(1957, Brit.); INTENT TO KILL(1958, Brit.); LINKS OF JUSTICE(1958); WOMAN POSSESSED, A(1958, Brit.); TOP FLOOR GIRL(1959, Brit.); ELECTRONIC MONSTER. THE(1960, Brit.); FREEDOM TO DIE(1962, Brit.); GREAT VAN ROBBERY, THE(1963, Brit.)
Misc. Talkies
ASSIGNMENT ABROAD(1955)

Charlie Callas
BIG MOUTH, THE(1967); SILENT MOVIE(1976); HIGH ANXIETY(1977); PETE'S DRAGON(1977); HISTORY OF THE WORLD, PART 1(1981); HYSTERICAL(1983)

Maria Callas
MEDEA(1971, Ital./Fr./Ger.)

Bill Callaway
GREAT NORTHFIELD, MINNESOTA RAID, THE(1972)

Cheryl Callaway
CRY VENGEANCE(1954); GOOD MORNING, MISS DOVE(1955); NIGHT OF THE HUNTER, THE(1955); KETTLES IN THE OZARKS, THE(1956); LEATHER SAINT, THE(1956); LINEUP, THE(1958)

James Callaway
JAWS OF SATAN(1980), w

Kirk Callaway
SUMMERTREE(1971)

William Callaway
ANNIE HALL(1977); FUN WITH DICK AND JANE(1977)

Stella Calle
MONSTER(1979)

C.P. Callegari
STROMBOLI(1950, Ital.), w

Gian Paolo Callegari
WARRIOR AND THE SLAVE GIRL, THE(1959, Ital.), w; HEAD OF A TYRANT(1960, Fr./Ital.), w; MINOTAUR, THE(1961, Ital.), w; 300 SPARTANS, THE(1962), w; GLADIATOR OF ROME(1963, Ital.), w; PONTIUS PILATE(1967, Fr./Ital.), d, w

Jean Paul Callegari
MYSTERY OF THE BLACK JUNGLE(1955), w

Joe Spurin Calleia
HIS WOMAN(1931)

Joseph Calleia
PUBLIC HERO NO. 1(1935); AFTER THE THIN MAN(1936); EXCLUSIVE STORY(1936); HIS BROTHER'S WIFE(1936); RIFF-RAFF(1936); ROBIN HOOD OF EL DORADO(1936), w; SINNER TAKE ALL(1936); SWORN ENEMY(1936); TOUGH GUY(1936); MAN OF THE PEOPLE(1937); ALGIERS(1938); BAD MAN OF BRIMSTONE(1938); MARIE ANTOINETTE(1938); FIVE CAME BACK(1939); FULL CONFESSION(1939); GOLDEN BOY(1939); JUAREZ(1939); MY LITTLE CHICKADEE(1940); WYOMING(1940); MONSTER AND THE GIRL, THE(1941); SUNDOWN(1941); GLASS KEY, THE(1942); JUNGLE BOOK(1942); CROSS OF LORRAINE, THE(1943); FOR WHOM THE BELL TOLLS(1943); CONSPIRATORS, THE(1944); DEADLINE AT DAWN(1946); GILDA(1946); BEGINNING OR THE END, THE(1947); LURED(1947); FOUR FACES WEST(1948); NOOSE HANGS HIGH, THE(1948); CAPTAIN CAREY, U.S.A(1950); PALOMINO, THE(1950); SILK NOOSE, THE(1950, Brit.); VENDETTA(1950); BRANDED(1951); LIGHT TOUCH, THE(1951); VALENTINO(1951); IRON MISTRESS, THE(1952); WHEN IN ROME(1952); YANKEE BUCCANEER(1952); CADDY, THE(1953); LITTLEST OUTLAW, THE(1955); TREASURE OF PANCHO VILLA, THE(1955); UNDERWATER!(1955); HOT BLOOD(1956); SERENADE(1956); WILD IS THE WIND(1957); LIGHT IN THE FOREST, THE(1958); TOUCH OF EVIL(1958); CRY TOUGH(1959); ALAMO, THE(1960); JOHNNY COOL(1963)

Cecelia Callejo
SALOME, WHERE SHE DANCED(1945); HOLIDAY IN HAVANA(1949)

Cecilia C. Callejo
DRAMATIC SCHOOL(1938)

Cecilia Callejo
OUTLAW EXPRESS(1938); RENEGADE RANGER(1938); IT'S A WONDERFUL WORLD(1939); ONLY ANGELS HAVE WINGS(1939); FALCON IN MEXICO, THE(1944); MARRIAGE IS A PRIVATE AFFAIR(1944); CISCO KID RETURNS, THE(1945)

Cecilla Callejo
PASSPORT TO ALCATRAZ(1940)

Mannela Callejo
FOR YOU I DIE(1947)

George "Red" Callender
ST. LOUIS BLUES(1958)

Joseph Callela
GORILLA, THE(1939)

Lucien Callemand
PARDON MY FRENCH(1951, U.S./Fr.)

John Callen
PICTURES(1982, New Zealand)

Red Callendar
NEW ORLEANS(1947)

Romaine Callendar
PEPPER(1936); 45 FATHERS(1937); MADEMOISELLE FIFI(1944)

Romain Callender
WUTHERING HEIGHTS(1939)

Romaine Callender
ALIBI FOR MURDER(1936); AND SO THEY WERE MARRIED(1936); HIGH TENSION(1936); THIRTY SIX HOURS TO KILL(1936); WHEN YOU'RE IN LOVE(1937); ONE WILD NIGHT(1938); SHARPSHOOTERS(1938); CAPTAIN CAUTION(1940); IT'S A DATE(1940); SUSAN AND GOD(1940); BODY DISAPPEARS, THE(1941); HONOLULU LU(1941); KISSES FOR BREAKFAST(1941); LADY IS WILLING, THE(1942); LUCKY LEGS(1942); WIFE TAKES A FLYER, THE(1942); YOU'RE TELLING ME(1942); TWO SENORITAS FROM CHICAGO(1943); YANKS AHOY(1943); ROAD TO UTOPIA(1945)

Guillermo Calleo
TREASURE OF THE SIERRA MADRE, THE(1948)

David Calles
I SELL ANYTHING(1934)

Gmo. Calles
SHE-DEVIL ISLAND(1936, Mex.)

Guilderma Calles
MY BROTHER, THE OUTLAW(1951)

Guillermo Calles
SEVEN CITIES OF GOLD(1955)

William Calles
LAST FRONTIER, THE(1955)

Willie Calles
CAPTAIN FROM CASTILE(1947)

Cecilia Calleto
BLOOD AND SAND(1941)

John Calley
FACE IN THE RAIN, A(1963), p; LOVED ONE, THE(1965), p; DON'T MAKE WAVES(1967), p; EYE OF THE DEVIL(1967, Brit.), p; ICE STATION ZEBRA(1968), p; CASTLE KEEP(1969), p; CATCH-22(1970), p

Dayton Callie
1984
PREPPIES(1984)

Lucien Callient
RED STALLION IN THE ROCKIES(1949), m

Lucien Calliet
LAST OUTPOST, THE(1951), m; CONFIDENCE GIRL(1952), m

George Calliga
ARTISTS AND MODELS ABROAD(1938); REUNION IN FRANCE(1942); ONE DANGEROUS NIGHT(1943); LADY IN THE DARK(1944); EASY TO WED(1946); TWO SMART PEOPLE(1946); SUN COMES UP, THE(1949); FOUR GIRLS IN TOWN(1956); ISTANBUL(1957)
Silents
KING OF KINGS, THE(1927)

Gianfranco Calligarich
FAMILY, THE(1974, Fr./Ital.), w

George Calligas
TWO-FACED WOMAN(1941)

William R. Callihan
OPERATION PETTICOAT(1959)

Michael Callin
THINGS HAPPEN AT NIGHT(1948, Brit.)

Dick Callinan
BANANAS(1971); LINCOLN CONSPIRACY, THE(1977)

Richard Callinan
PERSECUTION AND ASSASSINATION OF JEAN-PAUL MARAT AS PERFORMED BY THE INMATES OF THE ASYLUM OF CHARENTON UNDER THE DIRECTION OF THE MARQUIS DE SADE, THE(1967, Brit.); LIMBO(1972)

David Callis
WHAT'S YOUR RACKET?(1934)
Misc. Talkies
SISTER TO JUDAS(1933)
Silents
SIN SISTER, THE(1929)

Genevieve Callix
MOULIN ROUGE(1944, Fr.)

Marian Callopy
1984
MELVIN, SON OF ALVIN(1984, Aus.)

Helene Callot
JE T'AIME, JE T'AIME(1972, Fr./Swed.)

Simon Callow
1984
AMADEUS(1984)

Cab Calloway
MANHATTAN MERRY-GO-ROUND(1937); HI-DE-HO(1947); ST. LOUIS BLUES(1958); CINCINNATI KID, THE(1965); BLUES BROTHERS, THE(1980)

Cheryl Calloway
VIEW FROM POMPEY'S HEAD, THE(1955)

Cheryl Lynn Calloway
BRIDGES AT TOKO-RI, THE(1954)

Christopher L. Calloway
LANDLORD, THE(1970)

David Calloway
1984
HIGHWAY TO HELL(1984), p; RUNNING HOT(1984), p

Kirk Calloway
CINDERELLA LIBERTY(1973); SOUL OF NIGGER CHARLEY, THE(1973); MONKEY HUSTLE, THE(1976)
1984
WEEKEND PASS(1984)

Northern Calloway
TOGETHER FOR DAYS(1972)

William Calloway
Misc. Talkies
FLUSH(1981, Brit.)

Archie Callum
ROOM TO LET(1949, Brit.)

Marquita Callwood
Misc. Talkies
ANGELS(1976)

Alfred Callymore
COOL WORLD, THE(1963)

Calma
JOURNEY TO THE SEVENTH PLANET(1962, U.S./Swed.), makeup

Louise Calmenti
Silents
SIGN OF THE ROSE, THE(1922)

Bruce Calnan
OUTRAGEOUS!(1977, Can.), set d; HAPPY BIRTHDAY, GEMINI(1980), p

Matilda Calnan
GIDGET GOES TO ROME(1963); 8 ½(1963, Ital.); WAR OF THE ZOMBIES, THE(1965 Ital.); MADE IN PARIS(1966); STAR!(1968); DADDY'S GONE A-HUNTING(1969); TERROR IN THE WAX MUSEUM(1973); NICKELODEON(1976); SILVER STREAK(1976); OTHER SIDE OF MIDNIGHT, THE(1977); HUNTER, THE(1980)

Roy Calnek
Silents
ABIE'S IMPORTED BRIDE(1925), d&w
Misc. Silents
HEARTS OF THE WOODS(1921), d; PRINCE OF HIS RACE, THE(1926), d

Carla Calo
LAST OF THE VIKINGS, THE(1962, Fr./Ital.); CAESAR THE CONQUEROR(1963, Ital.); FURY OF THE PAGANS(1963, Ital.); BEBO'S GIRL(1964, Ital.); FISTFUL OF DOLLARS, A(1964, Ital./Ger./Span.); REVOLT OF THE MERCENARIES(1964, Ital./Span.); DOUBLE BED, THE(1965, Fr./Ital.); EYE OF THE NEEDLE, THE(1965, Ital./Fr.); 00-2 MOST SECRET AGENTS(1965, Ital.); TRAMPLERS, THE(1966, Ital.); HOW TO SEDUCE A PLAYBOY(1968, Aust./Fr./Ital.); BETTER A WIDOW(1969, Ital.)

Romano Calo
LAST CHANCE, THE(1945, Switz.)

Gloria Calomee
UNDER THE YUM-YUM TREE(1963); MADIGAN(1968); REIVERS, THE(1969); TOGETHER BROTHERS(1974); ROLLERCOASTER(1977)

Eugene T. Calongne
WACKY WORLD OF DR. MORGUS, THE(1962), p

Steve Calou
ONE FROM THE HEART(1982)

Orestes Calpini
GULLIVER'S TRAVELS(1939), anim d

Sam Calprice
JOAN OF ARC(1948)

Alfio Caltabiano
SEVEN SLAVES AGAINST THE WORLD(1965, Ital.), a, ch

Alfio Caltaviano
COLOSSUS OF RHODES, THE(1961, Ital., Fr., Span.)

Donald Calthorp
LOVE STORM, THE(1931, Brit.)

Dion Clayton Calthrop
SOUTHERN MAID, A(1933, Brit.), w
Silents
OLD COUNTRY, THE(1921, Brit.), w; OUT TO WIN(1923, Brit.), w

Donald Calthrop
ATLANTIC(1929 Brit.); BLACKMAIL(1929, Brit.); CLUE OF THE NEW PIN, THE(1929, Brit.); ALMOST A HONEYMOON(1930, Brit.); JUNO AND THE PAYCOCK(1930, Brit.); LOOSE ENDS(1930, Brit.); MURDER(1930, Brit.); SONG OF SOHO(1930, Brit.); SPANISH EYES(1930, Brit.); TWO WORLD(1930, Brit.); BELLS, THE(1931, Brit.); HER STRANGE DESIRE(1931, Brit.); MANY WATERS(1931, Brit.); UNEASY VIRTUE(1931, Brit.); FIRES OF FATE(1932, Brit.); MONEY FOR NOTHING(1932, Brit.); NUMBER SEVENTEEN(1932, Brit.); EARLY TO BED(1933, Brit./Ger.); F.P. 1(1933, Brit.); GHOST TRAIN, THE(1933, Brit.); ROME EXPRESS(1933, Brit.); THIS ACTING BUSINESS(1933, Brit.); FRIDAY THE 13TH(1934, Brit.); I WAS A SPY(1934, Brit.); IT'S A COP(1934, Brit.); NINE FORTY-FIVE(1934, Brit.); ORDERS IS ORDERS(1934, Brit.); SORRELL AND SON(1934, Brit.); STRIKE!(1934, Brit.); CLAIRVOYANT, THE(1935, Brit.); DIVINE SPARK, THE(1935, Brit./Ital.); MAN OF THE MOMENT(1935, Brit.); PHANTOM LIGHT, THE(1935, Brit.); SCROOGE(1935, Brit.); BROKEN BLOSSOMS(1936, Brit.); MAN BEHIND THE MASK, THE(1936, Brit.); MAN WHO LIVED AGAIN, THE(1936, Brit.); CAFE COLETTE(1937, Brit.); DREAMING LIPS(1937, Brit.); FIRE OVER ENGLAND(1937, Brit.); LOVE FROM A STRANGER(1937, Brit.); BAND WAGGON(1940, Brit.); LET GEORGE DO IT(1940, Brit.); MAJOR BARBARA(1941, Brit.)
Silents
ALTAR CHAINS(1916, Brit.); GAY LORD QUEX, THE(1917, Brit.); NELSON(1918, Brit.)
Misc. Silents
WANTED - A WIDOW(1916, Brit.); GOODBYE(1918, Brit.); SHOOTING STARS(1928); CLUE OF THE NEW PIN, THE(1929, Brit.); FLYING SQUAD, THE(1929)

David Caltrider
1984
TEACHERS(1984)

Joven Calub
LOST BATTALION(1961, U.S./Phil.), ed; KIDNAPPERS, THE(1964, U.S./Phil.), ed; MORO WITCH DOCTOR(1964, U.S./Phil.), ed; RAVAGERS, THE(1965, U.S./Phil.), ed

Jean Caludio
CROSSROADS(1938, Fr.)

Bong Calumpang
PASSIONATE STRANGERS, THE(1968, Phil.)

Dorothy Calve
SHADOWED EYES(1939, Brit.)

Jean Francois Calve
RED CLOAK, THE(1961, Ital./Fr.)

Jean-Francois Calve
BRIDE IS MUCH TOO BEAUTIFUL, THE(1958, Fr.); GIRL IN THE BIKINI, THE(1958, Fr.); ADORABLE LIAR(1962, Fr.); SHOCK TREATMENT(1973, Fr.)

Joseph Calvelli
MY SIX LOVES(1963), w; DEATH OF A GUNFIGHTER(1969), w

Adams R. Calvert
MOTEL HELL(1980), spec eff

Alice Calvert
CAESAR AND CLEOPATRA(1946, Brit.)

Bill Calvert
SHADOWED(1946), set d; OPERATION MAD BALL(1957), set d; FACE OF A FUGITIVE(1959), set d; MOUNTAIN ROAD, THE(1960), set d; GRAVY TRAIN, THE(1974), set d; ULTIMATE WARRIOR, THE(1975), set d; SIX WEEKS(1982)

C.C. Calvert
Silents
WALLS OF PREJUDICE(1920, Brit.), d; IN HIS GRIP(1921, Brit.), d; SILENT EVIDENCE(1922, Brit.), d

Misc. Silents
BRANDED(1920, Brit.), d; EDGE OF YOUTH, THE(1920, Brit.), d; ROSE IN THE DUST(1921, Brit.), d; WAY OF A MAN, THE(1921, Brit.), d; PRINCE OF LOVERS, A(1922, Brit.), d; BONNIE PRINCE CHARLIE(1923, Brit.), d; CITY OF YOUTH, THE(1928, Brit.), d

Camille Calvert
VALLEY GIRL(1983)

Capt. E. H. Calvert
MIGHTY BARNUM, THE(1934); MURDER AT GLEN ATHOL(1936)
Silents
SALLY(1925)

Captain E. H. Calvert
WESTERN COURAGE(1935)

Catherine Calvert
Silents
HEART OF MARYLAND, THE(1921); MORAL FIBRE(1921); GREEN CARAVAN, THE(1922, Brit.); INDIAN LOVE LYRICS, THE(1923, Brit.); OUT TO WIN(1923, Brit.)
Misc. Silents
BEHIND THE MASK(1917); OUTCAST(1917); PEDDLER, THE(1917); THINK IT OVER(1917); OUT OF THE NIGHT(1918); ROMANCE OF THE UNDERWORLD, A(1918); CAREER OF KATHERINE BUSH, THE(1919); MARRIAGE FOR CONVENIENCE(1919); DEAD MEN TELL NO TALES(1920); YOU FIND IT EVERYWHERE(1921); THAT WOMAN(1922)

Cecil Calvert
PATRICIA GETS HER MAN(1937, Brit.); CAESAR AND CLEOPATRA(1946, Brit.)
Silents
MANCHESTER MAN, THE(1920, Brit.)
Misc. Silents
SAVED FROM THE SEA(1920, Brit.)

Charles Calvert
SHADOW OF THE THIN MAN(1941); TROCADERO(1944); FEAR(1946); LOVE NEST(1951); CLOWN, THE(1953); SPRING AFFAIR(1960)
Silents
ACE OF HEARTS, THE(1916, Brit.), d
Misc. Silents
AVIATOR SPY, THE(1914, Brit.), d; FIENDS OF HELL(1914, Brit.), d; WRECKER OF LIVES, THE(1914, Brit.), d; AVENGING HAND, THE(1915, Brit.), d; SECRET SEVEN, THE(1915, Brit.), d; DISRAELI(1916, Brit.), d

Dave Calvert
KID COURAGEOUS(1935)

E.H. Calvert
CANARY MURDER CASE, THE(1929); DARK STREETS(1929); DARKENED ROOMS(1929); FAST COMPANY(1929); GREENE MURDER CASE, THE(1929); KIBITZER, THE(1929); LOVE PARADE, THE(1929); MIGHTY, THE(1929); STUDIO MURDER MYSTERY, THE(1929); THUNDERBOLT(1929); VIRGINIAN, THE(1929); WELCOME DANGER(1929); BEHIND THE MAKEUP(1930); BENSON MURDER CASE, THE(1930); BORDER LEGION, THE(1930); HALF SHOT AT SUNRISE(1930); LADIES LOVE BRUTES(1930); LET'S GO NATIVE(1930); MAN FROM WYOMING, A(1930); MEN ARE LIKE THAT(1930); ONLY THE BRAVE(1930); PEACOCK ALLEY(1930); SOCIAL LION, THE(1930); WIDOW FROM CHICAGO, THE(1930); WILD HORSE MESA(1932); MYSTERIOUS RIDER, THE(1933); HERE COMES THE GROOM(1934); RUMBA(1935); OREGON TRAIL, THE(1936); GLORY TRAIL, THE(1937)
Silents
SLIM PRINCESS, THE(1915), d; ACCORDING TO THE CODE(1916), a, d; SILENT PARTNER, THE(1923); BLUFF(1924); INEZ FROM HOLLYWOOD(1924); ONLY WOMAN, THE(1924); EAST OF SUEZ(1925); ELLA CINDERS(1926); LET 'ER GO GALLEGHER(1928); PREP AND PEP(1928)
Misc. Silents
ONE WONDERFUL NIGHT(1914), a, d; CRIMSON WING, THE(1915), a, d; DAUGHTER OF THE CITY, A(1915), a, d; MAN TRAIL, THE(1915), d; VULTURES OF SOCIETY(1916), a, d; WIZARD, THE(1927)

Eddie Calvert
BEYOND MOMBASA(1957)

Henry Calvert
WINDFLOWERS(1968); PHANTOM OF THE PARADISE(1974); ALL THE PRESIDENT'S MEN(1976)

James Dan Calvert
NASHVILLE(1975)

John Calvert
MARK OF THE WHISTLER, THE(1944); TEN CENTS A DANCE(1945); YOUTH ON TRIAL(1945); LAWLESS EMPIRE(1946); APPOINTMENT WITH MURDER(1948); DEVIL'S CARGO, THE(1948); SEARCH FOR DANGER(1949); GOLD FEVER(1952), a, p, w; DARK VENTURE(1956), d&w
Misc. Talkies
RETURN OF THE DURANGO KID(1945)

Keith Calvert
SMILEY GETS A GUN(1959, Brit.)

Louis Calvert
Misc. Silents
DAVID GARRICK(1913, Brit.)

Phyllis Calvert
CHARLEY'S(BIG-HEARTED) AUNT*1/2 (1940); SCHOOL FOR STARS(1935, Brit.); LET GEORGE DO IT(1940, Brit.); THEY CAME BY NIGHT(1940, Brit.); MAIL TRAIN(1941, Brit.); NEUTRAL PORT(1941, Brit.); REMARKABLE MR. KIPPS(1942, Brit.); YOUNG MR. PITT, THE(1942, Brit.); MAN IN GREY, THE(1943, Brit.); UNCENSORED(1944, Brit.); 2,000 WOMEN(1944, Brit.); MADONNA OF THE SEVEN MOONS(1945, Brit.); THEY WERE SISTERS(1945, Brit.); MAGIC BOW, THE(1947, Brit.); ROOT OF ALL EVIL(1947, Brit.); TIME OUT OF MIND(1947); BROKEN JOURNEY(1948, Brit.); MAN OF EVIL(1948, Brit.); MY OWN TRUE LOVE(1948); GOLDEN MADONNA, THE(1949, Brit.); APPOINTMENT WITH DANGER(1951); HER PANELLED DOOR(1951, Brit.); CRASH OF SILENCE(1952, Brit.); KISENGA, MAN OF AFRICA(1952, Brit.); MR. DENNING DRIVES NORTH(1953, Brit.); PROJECT M7(1953, Brit.); CHILD IN THE HOUSE(1956, Brit.); INDISCREET(1958); IT'S NEVER TOO LATE(1958, Brit.); LADY MISLAID(1958, Brit.); YOUNG AND THE GUILTY, THE(1958, Brit.); OSCAR WILDE(1960, Brit.); BATTLE OF THE VILLA FIORITA, THE(1965, Brit.); OH! WHAT A LOVELY WAR(1969, Brit.); TWISTED NERVE(1969, Brit.); WALKING STICK, THE(1970, Brit.)

Robert Calvert
DUTCHMAN(1966, Brit.)
Rod Calvert
UP FROM THE BEACH(1965)
Rosalee Calvert
TWO TICKETS TO BROADWAY(1951); LOUISIANA HUSSY(1960); IF A MAN
ANSWERS(1962)
Steve Calvert
BOWERY BOYS MEET THE MONSTERS, THE(1954); BRIDE AND THE BEAST,
THE(1958)
Toni Calvert
BLOOD FEAST(1963); SCUM OF THE EARTH(1963)
Vane Calvert
WESTERN JUSTICE(1935); $1,000,000 RACKET(1937); FEUD OF THE TRAIL(1938)
W. Calvert
Silents
IVANHOE(1913)
William Calvert
UNDERWORLD U.S.A.(1961), set d; TARAS BULBA(1962), set d; THREE STOOGES
MEET HERCULES, THE(1962), set d; MAIL ORDER BRIDE(1964), set d; RESTLESS
ONES, THE(1965), set d; RIDE BEYOND VENGEANCE(1966), set d
Corinne Calvet
ROPE OF SAND(1949); MY FRIEND IRMA GOES WEST(1950); WHEN WILLIE
COMES MARCHING HOME(1950); ON THE RIVERA(1951); PEKING EXPRESS(1951);
QUEBEC(1951); SAILOR BEWARE(1951); WHAT PRICE GLORY?(1952); FLIGHT TO
TANGIER(1953); POWDER RIVER(1953); THUNDER IN THE EAST(1953); SO THIS IS
PARIS(1954); FAR COUNTRY, THE(1955); PLUNDERERS OF PAINTED FLATS(1959);
BLUEBEARD'S TEN HONEYMOONS(1960, Brit.); ADVENTURES OF A YOUNG
MAN(1962); APACHE UPRISING(1966); DR. HECKYL AND MR. HYPE(1980); SWORD
AND THE SORCERER, THE(1982)
Misc. Talkies
TOO HOT TO HANDLE(1976)
Gerard Calvi
BIG CHIEF, THE(1960, Fr.), m; DEAD RUN(1961, Fr./Ital./Ger.), m; LA BELLE
AMERICAINE(1961, Fr.), m; PEEK-A-BOO(1961, Fr.), a, m; COUNTERFEIT CON-
STABLE, THE(1966, Fr.), m
Pino Calvi
REVENGERS, THE(1972, U.S./Mex.), m
Henry Calvin
BROKEN STAR, THE(1956); CRIME AGAINST JOE(1956); SIGN OF ZORRO,
THE(1960); TOBY TYLER(1960); BABES IN TOYLAND(1961); SHIP OF FOOLS(1965)
John Calvin
BABY BLUE MARINE(1976); CHEAP DETECTIVE, THE(1978); CALIFORNIA
DREAMING(1979); NORMA RAE(1979); FOOLIN' AROUND(1980); MAKING LO-
VE(1982)
1984
SWORDKILL(1984)
May Calvin
YELLOW STOCKINGS(1930, Brit.)
Patti "Moo-Moo" Calvin
KANSAS CITY BOMBER(1972)
Peggy Calvin
VOGUES OF 1938(1937)
Tony Calvin
DR. JEKYLL AND SISTER HYDE(1971, Brit.); FOURTEEN, THE(1973, Brit.);
THEATRE OF BLOOD(1973, Brit.)
Calvin College Theater Group
JONAH-WHO WILL BE 25 IN THE YEAR 2000(1976, Switz.)
Daniela Calvino
LA DOLCE VITA(1961, Ital./Fr.); EMPTY CANVAS, THE(1964, Fr./Ital.)
Italo Calvino
OF WAYWARD LOVE(1964, Ital./Ger.), w; TIKO AND THE SHARK(1966, U.S./Ital./
Fr.), w
Armando Calvo
ORLAK, THE HELL OF FRANKENSTEIN(1960, Mex.); WITCH'S MIRROR,
THE(1960, Mex.)
Eduardo Calvo
1984
IT'S NEVER TOO LATE(1984, Span.)
Eva Calvo
LIFE IN THE BALANCE, A(1955); CRIMINAL LIFE OF ARCHIBALDO DE LA
CRUZ, THE(1962, Mex.)
Jose Calvo
MAIN STREET(1956, Span.); TEACHER AND THE MIRACLE, THE(1961, Ital./
Span.); VIRIDIANA(1962, Mex./Span.); RUNNING MAN, THE(1963, Brit.); TRIS-
TANA(1970, Span./Ital./Fr.); MURDERS IN THE RUE MORGUE(1971)
Mauricia Calvo
NEST, THE(1982, Span.)
Oswaldo Calvo
DARKER THAN AMBER(1970); ABSENCE OF MALICE(1981)
Pablito Calvo
MAN WHO WAGGED HIS TAIL, THE(1961, Ital./Span.)
Pepe Calvo
FISTFUL OF DOLLARS, A(1964, Ital./Ger./Span.); SIX DAYS A WEEK(1966,
Fr./Ital./Span.); WEB OF VIOLENCE(1966, Ital./Span.); WEEKEND, ITALIAN
STYLE(1967, Fr./Ital./Span.); DAY OF ANGER(1970, Ital./Ger.)
Misc. Talkies
WHY KILL AGAIN?(1965)
Rafael Calvo
WARRIOR AND THE SLAVE GIRL, THE(1959, Ital.); LEGIONS OF THE NILE(1960,
Ital.)
Rafael Luis Calvo
KING OF KINGS(1961); COMMANDO(1962, Ital., Span., Bel., Ger.); MIGHTY UR-
SUS(1962, Ital./Span.); FALL OF THE ROMAN EMPIRE, THE(1964); UNINHIBITED,
THE(1968, Fr./Ital./Span.)
Rudy Calvo
UNHOLY ROLLERS(1972)

Fernando Calzado
COLOSSUS OF RHODES, THE(1961, Ital., Fr., Span.)
Flavio Calzavara
CARMELA(1949, Ital.), d, w
Phillippe Calzergues
LEFT-HANDED WOMAN, THE(1980, Ger.)
Cam
PIECES(1983, Span./Puerto Rico), m
Charles W. Camac
CHAMP, THE(1979)
Ahui Camacho
UNDER FIRE(1983)
Alejandro Camacho
HIGH RISK(1981)
Alex Camacho
MISSING(1982)
Cecelia Camacho
EAGLE'S WING(1979, Brit.)
Gloria Camacho
IF A MAN ANSWERS(1962)
Leu Camacho
SLAUGHTER'S BIG RIP-OFF(1973)
Margarita Camacho
REVOLT OF MAMIE STOVER, THE(1956)
Miguel Camacho
YOUNG LAND, THE(1959)
Sabu Camacho
AMERICAN GUERRILLA IN THE PHILIPPINES, AN(1950)
Jean-Paul Camail
1984
A NOS AMOURS(1984, Fr.), art d
Omar Camar
1984
MISSING IN ACTION(1984)
Carlos Camara
SURVIVE!(1977, Mex.)
Ousmane Camara
CEDDO(1978, Nigeria)
Beatrice Camaraut
1984
AMERICAN DREAMER(1984)
Aldo Camarda
DOG EAT DOG(1963, U.S./Ger./Ital.)
Robert Camardiel
UP THE MACGREGORS(1967, Ital./Span.); BIG GUNDOWN, THE(1968, Ital.)
Roberto Camardiel
MIGHTY URSUS(1962, Ital./Span.); SON OF CAPTAIN BLOOD, THE(1964, U.S./
Ital./Span.); ARIZONA COLT(1965, It./Fr./Span.); BACKFIRE(1965, Fr.); MURIE-
TA(1965, Span.); ADIOS GRINGO(1967, Ital./Fr./Span.); DJANGO KILL(1967, Ital./
Span.); FOR A FEW DOLLARS MORE(1967, Ital./Ger./Span.); THAT MAN GEOR-
GE!(1967, Fr./Ital./Span.); MR. SUPERINVISIBLE(1974, Ital./Span./Ger.)
Ana Camargo
LAWLESS LAND(1937); DESERT FURY(1947)
Anita Camargo
DESPERATE TRAILS(1939); GREEN HELL(1940)
Anna Camargo
TWILIGHT ON THE RIO GRANDE(1947)
Henry Camargo
ULZANA'S RAID(1972)
R. Camargo
POCKET MONEY(1972)
Ralph Camargo
WILD HARVEST(1962)
Dolores Camarillo
PEARL OF TLAYUCAN, THE(1964, Mex.)
George Camarinos III
GIRL FEVER(1961)
Claudio Camaso
10,000 DOLLARS BLOOD MONEY(1966, Ital.); WAKE UP AND DIE(1967, Fr./Ital.);
VENGEANCE(1968, Ital./Ger.)
Valentine Camax
ADVENTURES OF CAPTAIN FABIAN(1951); MR. HULOT'S HOLIDAY(1954, Fr.);
FOREIGN INTRIGUE(1956)
Kim Camba
PLAYMATES(1969, Fr./Ital.); MICHELLE(1970, Fr.)
George Cambanellis
CANNON AND THE NIGHTINGALE, THE(1969, Gr.)
Jacqueline Cambas
FALLING IN LOVE AGAIN(1980), ed; ZOOT SUIT(1981), ed; CAT PEOPLE(1982),
ed; PERSONAL BEST(1982), ed
1984
CITY HEAT(1984), ed; RACING WITH THE MOON(1984), ed; SURF II(1984), ed
Robert Cambel
ROCKY(1976), cos
Argyll Cambell
Silents
EARLY BIRD, THE(1925), w
Beatrice Cambell
HANGMAN WAITS, THE(1947, Brit.)
Jo Ann Cambell
GO, JOHNNY, GO!(1959)
Nell Cambell
1984
KILLING FIELDS, THE(1984, Brit.)
Patrick Cambell
CAPTAIN BOYCOTT(1947, Brit.), w
Webster Cambell
Misc. Silents
BRIGHT LIGHTS OF BROADWAY(1923), d

George Cambenellis
CANNON AND THE NIGHTINGALE, THE(1969, Gr.), p,d&w

Jacovos Cambenellis
CANNON AND THE NIGHTINGALE, THE(1969, Gr.), p,d&w

Don Cambern
ALEX AND THE GYPSY(1976), ed

Donn Cambern
EASY RIDER(1969), ed; 2000 YEARS LATER(1969), ed; DRIVE, HE SAID(1971), ed; LAST PICTURE SHOW, THE(1971), ed; BLUME IN LOVE(1973), ed; CINDERELLA LIBERTY(1973), ed; STEELYARD BLUES(1973), ed; HINDENBURG, THE(1975), ed; OTHER SIDE OF MIDNIGHT, THE(1977), ed; END, THE(1978), ed; HOOPER(1978), ed; TIME AFTER TIME(1979, Brit.), ed; SMOKEY AND THE BANDIT II(1980), ed; WILLIE AND PHIL(1980), ed; CANNONBALL RUN, THE(1981), ed; PATERNITY(1981), ed; TEMPEST(1982), ed; GOING BERSERK(1983), ed
1984
ROMANCING THE STONE(1984), ed

Louise Cambert
FRAGMENT OF FEAR(1971, Brit.)

Flora Cambi
MIRACLE IN MILAN(1951, Ital.)

Linda Cambi
TEENAGE GANG DEBS(1966)

Paul Cambo
DEVIL IS AN EMPRESS, THE(1939, Fr.)

Cambodian Art Preservation Group
1984
MICKI AND MAUDE(1984)

Robert Cambourakis
STOLEN KISSES(1969, Fr.); WILD CHILD, THE(1970, Fr.)

Bill Cambra
KILL SQUAD(1982)

Del Cambre
GLASS KEY, THE(1935); TUNDRA(1936); ARCTIC FURY(1949)

Adele Cambria
TEOREMA(1969, Ital.)

Ed Cambridge
LIMIT, THE(1972)

Edmund Cambridge
FINAL COMEDOWN, THE(1972); HIT MAN(1972); MELINDA(1972); TROUBLE MAN(1972)

Godfrey Cambridge
LAST ANGRY MAN, THE(1959); GONE ARE THE DAYS(1963); TROUBLEMAKER, THE(1964); BUSYBODY, THE(1967); PRESIDENT'S ANALYST, THE(1967); BIGGEST BUNDLE OF THEM ALL, THE(1968); BYE BYE BRAVERMAN(1968); COTTON COMES TO HARLEM(1970); WATERMELON MAN(1970); BEWARE! THE BLOB(1972); BISCUIT EATER, THE(1972); COME BACK CIHARLESTON BLUE(1972); FIVE ON THE BLACK HAND SIDE(1973); FRIDAY FOSTER(1975); WHIFFS(1975); SCOTT JOPLIN(1977)

Danone Camden
HARD COUNTRY(1981); TEXAS LIGHTNING(1981)

Dorothea Camden
Silents
SEVEN SISTERS, THE(1915)

Joan Camden
CAPTIVE CITY(1952); STOLEN IDENTITY(1953); STRANGE LADY IN TOWN(1955); CATERED AFFAIR, THE(1956); GUNFIGHT AT THE O.K. CORRAL(1957); TOWER OF LONDON(1962)

Tom Camden
ARIZONA TRAILS(1935), w

Joe Camel
PRISONER OF THE IRON MASK(1962, Fr./Ital.); SWORD OF THE CONQUEROR(1962, Ital.); MERCENARY, THE(1970, Ital./Span.)

Toni Camel
INCREDIBLY STRANGE CREATURES WHO STOPPED LIVING AND BECAME CRAZY MIXED-UP ZOMBIES, THE(1965)

Tony Camel
DEVIL'S SISTERS, THE(1966)

Camelia
CAIRO ROAD(1950, Brit.)

Camella
FLASH GORDON(1980)

Joey Camen
KING OF THE MOUNTAIN(1981)

Paul Camen
ON A CLEAR DAY YOU CAN SEE FOREVER(1970); STUDENT NURSES, THE(1970); METEOR(1979)

Cameo
Silents
PENROD AND SAM(1923); LEGEND OF HOLLYWOOD, THE(1924)

Cameo the Dog
Silents
HERO, THE(1923); HAM AND EGGS AT THE FRONT(1927)

Dolores Camerillo
MYSTERY IN MEXICO(1948)

Augusto Camerini
MILLER'S WIFE, THE(1957, Ital.), w

Mario Camerini
HONEYMOON DEFERRED(1951, Brit.), d; ULYSSES(1955, Ital.), d, w; WAR AND PEACE(1956, Ital./U.S.), w; MILLER'S WIFE, THE(1957, Ital.), d, w; AWAKENING, THE(1958, Ital.), d, w; RUN WITH THE DEVIL(1963, Fr./Ital.), d, w; AND SUDDENLY IT'S MURDER!(1964, Ital.), d

Hector Camerlynck
ONE NIGHT... A TRAIN(1968, Fr./Bel.)

Manuel Camero
Misc. Silents
TIGER LOVE(1924)

Cameron
NIGHT TIDE(1963)

1984
JIGSAW MAN, THE(1984, Brit.), prod d

Allan Cameron
FRENCH LIEUTENANT'S WOMAN, THE(1981), art d
1984
1984(1984, Brit.), prod d

Ann Cameron
TIME OF YOUR LIFE, THE(1948); FINISHING SCHOOL(1934); SINBAD THE SAILOR(1947); PRODIGAL, THE(1955)

Anne Cameron
MR. SKITCH(1933), w; MC CABE AND MRS. MILLER(1971); TICKET TO HEAVEN(1981), w

Art Cameron
SON OF PALEFACE(1952)

Audrey Cameron
CRIMSON CANDLE, THE(1934, Brit.); CRUCIFIX, THE(1934, Brit.)

Averil Cameron
MAKE WAY FOR TOMORROW(1937)

Avril Cameron
REMEMBER THE NIGHT(1940)

Basil Cameron
MAGIC BOW, THE(1947, Brit.), md

Ben Cameron
ROADBLOCK(1951); TURNING POINT, THE(1952)

Bill Cameron
JAZZ BABIES(1932), ed; BLUE SUNSHINE(1978)

Bob Cameron
CAESAR AND CLEOPATRA(1946, Brit.)

Brenda Cameron
WHILE I LIVE(1947, Brit.); NAUGHTY ARLETTE(1951, Brit.)

Bruce Cameron
HITLER'S CHILDREN(1942); RIDING HIGH(1943); KNICKERBOCKER HOLIDAY(1944); BERLIN EXPRESS(1948); SEALED CARGO(1951); GREATEST SHOW ON EARTH, THE(1952); SNIPER, THE(1952); SALOME(1953)

Carol Cameron
WOMAN IN THE WINDOW, THE(1945)

Cecile Cameron
VAGABOND KING, THE(1930)
Silents
GOLD RUSH, THE(1925); FANGS OF JUSTICE(1926)

Charles Cameron
END OF THE LINE, THE(1959, Brit.)

Cisse Cameron
PRIZE FIGHTER, THE(1979); HARD COUNTRY(1981); PORKY'S II: THE NEXT DAY(1983)

Cissie Cameron
BALTIMORE BULLET, THE(1980)

Colonel Cameron
BUCKET OF BLOOD(1934, Brit.)

Dave Cameron
1941(1979)

David Cameron
HIGH AND DRY(1954, Brit.); LOVING YOU(1957); SUDDENLY, LAST SUMMER(1959, Brit.); THOUSAND EYES OF DR. MABUSE, THE(1960, Fr./Ital./Ger.); DAWN(1979, Aus.); MAD MAX(1979, Aus.)

Dean Cameron
NORA PRENTISS(1947)

Don Cameron
Silents
LIGHTS OF NEW YORK, THE(1916)
Misc. Silents
KITTY MACKAY(1917); SALLY IN A HURRY(1917)

Donald Cameron
STALAG 17(1953)
Silents
EDUCATION OF ELIZABETH, THE(1921)
Misc. Silents
MUTE APPEAL, A(1917)

Douglas Cameron
INFORMATION RECEIVED(1962, Brit.)

Earl Cameron
POOL OF LONDON(1951, Brit.); HUNDRED HOUR HUNT(1953, Brit.); GREAT HOPE, THE(1954, Ital.); HEART OF THE MATTER, THE(1954, Brit.); SIMBA(1955, Brit.); WOMAN FOR JOE, THE(1955, Brit.); ODONGO(1956, Brit.); SAFARI(1956, Brit.); HEART WITHIN, THE(1957, Brit.); MARK OF THE HAWK, THE(1958); SAPPHIRE(1959, Brit.); KILLERS OF KILIMANJARO(1960, Brit.); TARZAN THE MAGNIFICENT(1960, Brit.); FLAME IN THE STREETS(1961, Brit.); TERM OF TRIAL(1962, Brit.); TARZAN'S THREE CHALLENGES(1963); GUNS AT BATASI(1964, Brit.); THUNDERBALL(1965, Brit.); SANDWICH MAN, THE(1966, Brit.); BATTLE BENEATH THE EARTH(1968, Brit.); TWO A PENNY(1968, Brit.); TWO GENTLEMEN SHARING(1969, Brit.); REVOLUTIONARY, THE(1970, Brit.); WARM DECEMBER, A(1973, Brit.); MOHAMMAD, MESSENGER OF GOD(1976, Lebanon/Brit.); CUBA(1979)

Elaine Ives Cameron
NIGHT DIGGER, THE(1971, Brit.); MOHAMMAD, MESSENGER OF GOD(1976, Lebanon/Brit.)

Elspet Cameron
1984
COMFORT AND JOY(1984, Brit.)

Gay Cameron
INTERLUDE(1968, Brit.)

Gene Cameron
Silents
SIGN OF THE ROSE, THE(1922); GAY RETREAT, THE(1927)

Herbert Cameron
DANNY BOY(1934, Brit.); ROLLING HOME(1935, Brit.); HAPPY DAYS ARE HERE AGAIN(1936, Brit.); LIVING DEAD, THE(1936, Brit.); AGAINST THE TIDE(1937, Brit.); CONCERNING MR. MARTIN(1937, Brit.); PHANTOM SHIP(1937, Brit.); 13 MEN AND A GUN(1938, Brit.); SPITFIRE(1943, Brit.); MY AIN FOLK(1944, Brit.); SAN DEMETRIO, LONDON(1947, Brit.); HIGH AND DRY(1954, Brit.)

Hope Cameron
CHAPMAN REPORT, THE(1962); TALES OF ORDINARY MADNESS(1983, Ital.)

Hugh Cameron
ONE HEAVENLY NIGHT(1931); BACK DOOR TO HEAVEN(1939); ONE THIRD OF A NATION(1939); TRACK THE MAN DOWN(1956, Brit.)
Silents
CAPPY RICKS(1921)
Misc. Silents
WEB OF DECEIT, THE(1920)

Ian Cameron
ISLAND AT THE TOP OF THE WORLD, THE(1974), w

Isla Cameron
ROOM AT THE TOP(1959, Brit.); INNOCENTS, THE(1961, U.S./Brit.); NIGHTMARE(1963, Brit.); PRIME OF MISS JEAN BRODIE, THE(1969, Brit.)

Jack Cameron
APPLAUSE(1929)

James Cameron
TELL ME LIES(1968, Brit.); STIR(1980, Aus.)
1984
TERMINATOR, THE(1984), d, w

Jean Cameron [Julia Thayer]
Misc. Talkies
IN OLD MONTANA(1939)

James Cameron [Ovidio Assonitis]
PIRANHA II: THE SPAWNING(1981, Neth.), d

Jim Cameron
EAGLE ROCK(1964, Brit.); BATTLE BEYOND THE STARS(1980), art d

Joanna Cameron
HOW TO COMMIT MARRIAGE(1969); I LOVE MY WIFE(1970); B.S. I LOVE YOU(1971); PRETTY MAIDS ALL IN A ROW(1971)

John Cameron
GRANDAD RUDD(1935, Aus.); GREAT GILBERT AND SULLIVAN, THE(1953, Brit.); POOR COW(1968, Brit.), md; KES(1970, Brit.), m, md; RISE AND RISE OF MICHAEL RIMMER, THE(1970, Brit.), m; THINK DIRTY(1970, Brit.), m; BLACK BEAUTY(1971, Brit./Ger./Span.), m; MADE(1972, Brit.), m, md; RULING CLASS, THE(1972, Brit.), m, md; STRANGE VENEGEANCE OF ROSALIE, THE(1972, Brit.), m, md; CHARLEY-ONE-EYE(1973, Brit.), m; NIGHT WATCH(1973, Brit.), m; SCALAWAG(1973, Yugo.), m; TOUCH OF CLASS, A(1973, Brit.), m; MOMENTS(1974, Brit.), m; OUT OF SEASON(1975, Brit.), m; WHIFFS(1975), m; WHO?(1975, Brit./Ger.), m; GREAT SCOUT AND CATHOUSE THURSDAY, THE(1976), m; I WILL...I WILL...FOR NOW(1976), m; NASTY HABITS(1976, Brit.), m; LOST AND FOUND(1979), m; SUNBURN(1979), m; MIRROR CRACK'D, THE(1980, Brit.), m; JIMMY THE KID(1982), m; SILVER DREAM RACER(1982, Brit.), md; WE OF THE NEVER NEVER(1983, Aus.)
1984
JIGSAW MAN, THE(1984, Brit.), m

Ken Cameron
MONKEY GRIP(1983, Aus.), d, w

Kimberly Cameron
H.O.T.S.(1979)

Kristine Cameron
MAHOGANY(1975)

Lady Mary Cameron
MANY HAPPY RETURNS(1934), w

Madge Cameron
SOL MADRID(1968)

Marjorie Cameron
HIGH, WIDE AND HANDSOME(1937)

Marlene Cameron
HAPPY TIME, THE(1952)

Michael Cameron
SOUL OF NIGGER CHARLEY, THE(1973)

Nomi Cameron
OEDIPUS REX(1957, Can.)

Oween Cameron
SPRING AFFAIR(1960)

Owen Cameron
NIGHT RUNNER, THE(1957), w

Patricia Cameron
KITTY(1945); DRESSED TO KILL(1946)

Pearl Cameron
CURSE OF THE WRAYDONS, THE(1946, Brit.); MYSTERY JUNCTION(1951, Brit.)

Ray Cameron
1984
BLOODBATH AT THE HOUSE OF DEATH(1984, Brit.), a, p,d&w

Rocky Cameron
WHITE STALLION(1947); ENCHANTED VALLEY, THE(1948); CALLAWAY WENT THATAWAY(1951)

Rod Cameron
OLD MAID, THE(1939); CHRISTMAS IN JULY(1940); NORTHWEST MOUNTED POLICE(1940); QUARTERBACK, THE(1940); RANGERS OF FORTUNE(1940); THOSE WERE THE DAYS(1940); BUY ME THAT TOWN(1941); HENRY ALDRICH FOR PRESIDENT(1941); I WANTED WINGS(1941); LIFE WITH HENRY(1941); MIDNIGHT ANGEL(1941); MONSTER AND THE GIRL, THE(1941); NIGHT OF JANUARY 16TH(1941); NO HANDS ON THE CLOCK(1941); NOTHING BUT THE TRUTH(1941); PARSON OF PANAMINT, THE(1941); COMMANDOS STRIKE AT DAWN, THE(1942); FLEET'S IN, THE(1942); FOREST RANGERS, THE(1942); PRIORITIES ON PARADE(1942); REMARKABLE ANDREW, THE(1942); STAR SPANGLED RHYTHM(1942); TRUE TO THE ARMY(1942); WAKE ISLAND(1942); GOOD FELLOWS, THE(1943); GUNG HO!(1943); HONEYMOON LODGE(1943); KANSAN, THE(1943); NO TIME FOR LOVE(1943); RIDING HIGH(1943); MRS. PARKINGTON(1944); OLD TEXAS TRAIL, THE(1944); RIDERS OF THE SANTA FE(1944); TRIGGER TRAIL(1944); BEYOND THE PECOS(1945); FRONTIER GAL(1945); RENEGADES OF THE RIO GRANDE(1945); SALOME, WHERE SHE DANCED(1945); SWING OUT, SISTER(1945); RUNAROUND, THE(1946); BELLE STARR'S DAUGHTER(1947); PIRATES OF MONTEREY(1947); PANHANDLE(1948); PLUNDERERS, THE(1948); RIVER LADY(1948); STRIKE IT RICH(1948); BRIMSTONE(1949); STAMPEDE(1949); DAKOTA LIL(1950); SHORT GRASS(1950); STAGE TO TUCSON(1950); CAVALRY SCOUT(1951); OH! SUSANNA(1951); SEA HORNET, THE(1951); FORT OSAGE(1952); JUNGLE, THE(1952); RIDE THE MAN DOWN(1952); WAGONS WEST(1952); WOMAN OF THE NORTH COUNTRY(1952); SAN ANTONE(1953); STEEL LADY, THE(1953); SOUTH-

WEST PASSAGE(1954); DOUBLE JEOPARDY(1955); FIGHTING CHANCE, THE(1955); HEADLINE HUNTERS(1955); HELL'S OUTPOST(1955); SANTA FE PASSAGE(1955); PASSPORT TO TREASON(1956, Brit.); YAQUI DRUMS(1956); SPOILERS OF THE FOREST(1957); MAN WHO DIED TWICE, THE(1958); GUN HAWK, THE(1963); BOUNTY KILLER, THE(1965); REQUIEM FOR A GUNFIGHTER(1965); THUNDER AT THE BORDER(1966, Ger./Yugo.); EVEL KNIEVEL(1971); LAST MOVIE, THE(1971); PSYCHIC KILLER(1975); JESSIE'S GIRLS(1976); LOVE AND THE MIDNIGHT AUTO SUPPLY(1978)
Misc. Talkies
BOSS OF BOOMTOWN(1944)

Ron Cameron
ELECTRONIC MONSTER. THE(1960, Brit.)

Rudolph Cameron
SONG OF THE WEST(1930); THREE HEARTS FOR JULIA(1943); VICIOUS CIRCLE, THE(1948)
Misc. Silents
CLOVER'S REBELLION(1917); MESSAGE OF THE MOUSE, THE(1917); MORE EXCELLENT WAY, THE(1917); ROSE O' THE SEA(1922); SHATTERED FAITH(1923); CONEY ISLAND(1928)

Rudy Cameron
QUEEN HIGH(1930); GILDED LILY, THE(1935); MAN WHO RECLAIMED HIS HEAD, THE(1935); PAGE MISS GLORY(1935); DOWN TO EARTH(1947)

Ruth Cameron
NIGHT THE LIGHTS WENT OUT IN GEORGIA, THE(1981)

Sean Cameron
LIMIT, THE(1972), w

Shirley Cameron
GUTTER GIRLS(1964, Brit.); SATURDAY NIGHT OUT(1964, Brit.); CADDIE(1976, Aus.); THIRST(1979, Aus.); ON THE RUN(1983, Aus.)
Misc. Talkies
DO YOU KNOW THIS VOICE?(1964)

Susan Cameron
E.T. THE EXTRA-TERRESTRIAL(1982)

Suzan Cameron
ANTI-CLOCK(1980)

Thomas Cameron
Misc. Silents
FORBIDDEN LOVE(1921)

Tina Leigh Cameron
SCARFACE(1983)

Tom Cameron
Silents
OTHER MAN'S WIFE, THE(1919)
Misc. Silents
CHILD OF THE WILD, A(1917); HEADIN' HOME(1920)

William Cameron
Silents
DESIRED WOMAN, THE(1918)

The Cameron Girls
Misc. Silents
MIDNIGHT AT MAXIM'S(1915)

Jo Cameron-Brown
PIRATES OF PENZANCE, THE(1983)

Charles Cameron
MAKE MINE A DOUBLE(1962, Brit.)

Bill Camfield
OUTLAWS IS COMING, THE(1965)

Terry Camilieri
BLUE FIN(1978, Aus.)

Valerie Camille
LA VIE DE CHATEAU(1967, Fr.); PLAYTIME(1973, Fr.)

George Camiller
MOHAMMAD, MESSENGER OF GOD(1976, Lebanon/Brit.); HUNGER, THE(1983)

Charles Camilleri
HOUSE OF 1,000 DOLLS(1967, Ger./Span./Brit.), m

Freda Camilleri
TRENCHCOAT(1983)

Terry Camilleri
CARS THAT ATE PARIS, THE(1974, Aus,); MONEY MOVERS(1978, Aus.); NIGHT OF THE PROWLER, THE(1979, Aus.); SUPERMAN III(1983)

Tony Camillo
HANGUP(1974), m; GETTING TOGETHER(1976), m; TENDER FLESH(1976), m

Gregory Camillucci
TOOTSIE(1982)

Poupee Camin
FASTEST GUITAR ALIVE, THE(1967)

Augusto Caminito
GRAND SLAM(1968, Ital., Span., Ger.), w; RUTHLESS FOUR, THE(1969, Ital./Ger.), w

Francisco Camiras
EVERY DAY IS A HOLIDAY(1966, Span.)

Sten-Goran Camitz
GEORGIA, GEORGIA(1972), ed

Peter Camlin
ARTISTS AND MODELS ABROAD(1938); HOUSE ACROSS THE BAY, THE(1940); PASSAGE TO MARSEILLE(1944); NIGHT AND DAY(1946); VOICE OF THE TURTLE, THE(1947); GIRL FROM JONES BEACH, THE(1949); ON THE RIVERA(1951); GENTLEMEN PREFER BLONDES(1953); MAN WHO KNEW TOO MUCH, THE(1956); FUNNY FACE(1957); PERFECT FURLOUGH, THE(1958); GOOD NEIGHBOR SAM(1964); MONKEYS, GO HOME!(1967)

Ursula Camm
NO SAFETY AHEAD(1959, Brit.); RUNNERS(1983, Brit.)

Pietro Cammarata
SALVATORE GIULIANO(1966, Ital.)

Donald Cammell
DUFFY(1968, Brit.), w; LA COLLECTIONNEUSE(1971, Fr.); DEMON SEED(1977), d; TILT(1979), w

Cora Camoin
BEAR, THE(1963, Fr.)
Rene Camoin
WOULD-BE GENTLEMAN, THE(1960, Fr.)
Francisco Camoiras
SAVAGE GUNS, THE(1962, U.S./Span.)
Quique Camoiras
SUPERSONIC MAN(1979, Span.)
Marc Camoletti
BOEING BOEING(1965), w
J. R. Camomile
SILVER BANDIT, THE(1950), p
James Camomile
NATIONAL LAMPOON'S CLASS REUNION(1982), spec eff
Adele Camondini
Silents
JOY GIRL, THE(1927), w
A.L. Camp
GETAWAY, THE(1972); SUGARLAND EXPRESS, THE(1974); HONEYSUCKLE ROSE(1980)
Aurore Camp
MYSTERIOUS ISLAND OF CAPTAIN NEMO, THE(1973, Fr./Ital. 87m Span./Cameroon), ed
Austen Camp
Misc. Silents
SOUL FOR SALE, A(1915, Brit.)
Austin Camp
Misc. Silents
CHANCE OF A LIFETIME, THE(1916, Brit.)
Charles Camp
KNOCK ON ANY DOOR(1949)
Colleen Camp
SMILE(1975); DEATH GAME(1977); LOVE AND THE MIDNIGHT AUTO SUPPLY(1978); APOCALYPSE NOW(1979); GAME OF DEATH, THE(1979); CLOUD DANCER(1980); THEY ALL LAUGHED(1981); SEDUCTION, THE(1982); SMOKEY AND THE BANDIT-PART 3(1983); VALLEY GIRL(1983)
1984
CITY GIRL, THE(1984); JOY OF SEX(1984); ROSEBUD BEACH HOTEL(1984)
Misc. Talkies
SWINGING CHEERLEADERS, THE(1974); EBONY, IVORY AND JADE(1977)
Gerard Camp
1984
LES COMPERES(1984, Fr.)
Halim Camp
UNDER FIRE(1983)
Hamilton Camp
PERILS OF PAULINE, THE(1967); COCKEYED COWBOYS OF CALICO COUNTY, THE(1970); NICKELODEON(1976); HEAVEN CAN WAIT(1978); STARCRASH(1979); ROADIE(1980); ALL NIGHT LONG(1981); S.O.B.(1981); EATING RAOUL(1982); EVILSPEAK(1982); SAFARI 3000(1982); TWICE UPON A TIME(1983); UNDER FIRE(1983)
1984
CITY HEAT(1984); MEATBALLS PART II(1984); NO SMALL AFFAIR(1984); ROSEBUD BEACH HOTEL(1984)
Helen Page Camp
COLD TURKEY(1971); GET TO KNOW YOUR RABBIT(1972); TELEFON(1977); ESCAPE ARTIST, THE(1982); FAST-WALKING(1982)
Hy Camp
HOLLYWOOD HIGH(1977)
Joe Camp
BENJI(1974), p&d&w; HAWMPS!(1976), p&d, w; FOR THE LOVE OF BENJI(1977), d&w; THE DOUBLE McGUFFIN(1979), p&d, w; OH, HEAVENLY DOG!(1980), a, p&d, w
Joey Camp
HAWMPS!(1976)
Judson Camp
1984
HARD CHOICES(1984)
Lubelle Camp
HONEYSUCKLE ROSE(1980); RAGGEDY MAN(1981)
Nancy S. Camp
TOUCH OF FLESH, THE(1960), w
Robin Camp
MRS. MIKE(1949); DARK CITY(1950); OUTRAGE(1950); SON OF DR. JEKYLL, THE(1951); WHEN I GROW UP(1951); MY COUSIN RACHEL(1952); TITANIC(1953); BLACK SHIELD OF FALWORTH, THE(1954); EXECUTIVE SUITE(1954)
Shep Camp
GREENE MURDER CASE, THE(1929); PLAYING AROUND(1930); SONG OF THE FLAME(1930)
Steve Camp
BUDDY HOLLY STORY, THE(1978)
Wadsworth Camp
LAST WARNING, THE(1929), w; HOUSE OF FEAR, THE(1939), w
Silents
SIGNAL TOWER, THE(1924), w
William Camp
IDOL ON PARADE(1959, Brit.), w
Wilson Camp
1984
NIGHT OF THE COMET(1984)
Jose Luis Campa
VIVA MARIA(1965, Fr./Ital.)
Miranda Campa
GIANT OF MARATHON, THE(1960, Ital.); NIGHT THEY KILLED RASPUTIN, THE(1962, Fr./Ital.); GLADIATOR OF ROME(1963, Ital.); PRIEST'S WIFE, THE(1971, Ital./Fr.)
Pio Campa
ISLAND OF PROCIDA, THE(1952, Ital.)

Roberto Campa
VIVA MARIA(1965, Fr./Ital.)
Rita Campagna
RED HEAD(1934)
Zanie Campan
ADVENTURES OF CAPTAIN FABIAN(1951)
Nina Campana
MELODY LINGERS ON, THE(1935); PETRIFIED FOREST, THE(1936); SUNSET OF POWER(1936); WHITE LEGION, THE(1936); IT COULD HAPPEN TO YOU(1937); IT HAPPENED OUT WEST(1937); ROOTIN' TOOTIN' RHYTHM(1937); CALL OF THE YUKON(1938); ARIZONA(1940); SOUTH OF PAGO PAGO(1940); ALOMA OF THE SOUTH SEAS(1941); HONOLULU LU(1941); TORTILLA FLAT(1942); HOMESTRETCH, THE(1947); STALLION ROAD(1947); TWILIGHT ON THE RIO GRANDE(1947); LOVES OF CARMEN, THE(1948)
Frank Campanella
SOMEBODY UP THERE LIKES ME(1956); FOUR BOYS AND A GUN(1957); STAGE STRUCK(1958); PARRISH(1961); VIEW FROM THE BRIDGE, A(1962, Fr./Ital.); WHO KILLED TEDDY BEAR?(1965); SECONDS(1966); PRODUCERS, THE(1967); WHAT'S SO BAD ABOUT FEELING GOOD?(1968); GANG THAT COULDN'T SHOOT STRAIGHT, THE(1971); STONE KILLER, THE(1973); CAPONE(1975); CHESTY ANDERSON, U.S. NAVY(1976); HEAVEN CAN WAIT(1978); NORTH AVENUE IRREGULARS, THE(1979); DEATH WISH II(1982)
1984
FLAMINGO KID, THE(1984)
Joe Campanella
Misc. Talkies
KINO, THE PADRE ON HORSEBACK(1977)
Joseph Campanella
MURDER, INC.(1960); YOUNG LOVERS, THE(1964); ST. VALENTINE'S DAY MASSACRE, THE(1967); BEN(1972); CHILD UNDER A LEAF(1975, Can.); METEOR(1979); HANGAR 18(1980); EARTHBOUND(1981)
Roy Campanella
ROOGIE'S BUMP(1954)
Vittorio Campanella
FINE PAIR, A(1969, Ital.)
Paddy Campanero
PHOBIA(1980, Can.)
P. F. Campanile
YOUNG HUSBANDS(1958, Ital./Fr.), w
Pasquale Festa Campanile
ASSASSIN, THE(1961, Ital./Fr.), w; ROCCO AND HIS BROTHERS(1961, Fr./Ital.), w; LA VIACCIA(1962, Fr./Ital.), w; CONJUGAL BED, THE(1963, Ital.), w; FOUR DAYS OF NAPLES, THE(1963, US/Ital.), w; LEOPARD, THE(1963, Ital.), w; WHITE VOICES(1965, Fr./Ital.), d, w; GIRL AND THE GENERAL, THE(1967, Fr./Ital.), d, w; MAIDEN FOR A PRINCE, A(1967, Fr./Ital.), d, w; CHASTITY BELT, THE(1968, Ital.), d; DROP DEAD, MY LOVE(1968, Italy), d; WHEN WOMEN HAD TAILS(1970, Ital.), d, w; BINGO BONGO(1983, Ital.), d; GIRL FROM TRIESTE, THE(1983, Ital.), d, w
Guerrino Campanili
IL GRIDO(1962, U.S./Ital.)
Carlo Campanini
ANYTHING FOR A SONG(1947, Ital.); SCHOOLGIRL DIARY(1947, Ital.); LADY IS FICKLE, THE(1948, Ital.); BANDIT, THE(1949, Ital.); BULLET FOR STEFANO(1950, Ital.); CENTO ANNI D'AMORE(1954, Ital.); RIFF RAFF GIRLS(1962, Fr./Ital.)
Pippo Campanini
LUNA(1979, Ital.)
I. Campanino
LA DOLCE VITA(1961, Ital./Fr.)
Al Campanis
BIG LEAGUER(1953)
Maria Campano
1984
BIZET'S CARMEN(1984, Fr./Ital.)
Nina Campano
OUTLAW EXPRESS(1938)
Adelino Campardo
SEDUCED AND ABANDONED(1964, Fr./Ital.)
Campas Indians
FITZCARRALDO(1982)
Francois Campaux
BLUE VEIL, THE(1947, Fr.), w; BLUE VEIL, THE(1951), w
Campbel
PONY EXPRESS RIDER(1976), cos
Campbell
FLAT TWO(1962, Brit.)
Adrienne Campbell
CLOSE ENCOUNTERS OF THE THIRD KIND(1977)
Alan Campbell
LADY BE CAREFUL(1936), w; MOON'S OUR HOME, THE(1936), w; SUZY(1936), w; THREE MARRIED MEN(1936), w; STAR IS BORN, A(1937), w; SWEETHEARTS(1938), w; TRADE WINDS(1938), w; LITTLE FOXES, THE(1941), w; WEEKEND FOR THREE(1941), w; TALES OF MANHATTAN(1942), w; FOREVER AND A DAY(1943), w; WOMAN ON THE RUN(1950), w; STAR IS BORN, A(1954), w; FUNNY MONEY(1983, Brit.)
Alec Campbell
MISSION TO MOSCOW(1943)
Alex Campbell
MAN IN THE GREY FLANNEL SUIT, THE(1956)
Alexander Campbell
KISS OF DEATH(1947); NAKED CITY, THE(1948); JIGSAW(1949); LOST BOUNDARIES(1949); DOWN THREE DARK STREETS(1954); MAGNIFICENT OBSESSION(1954); RAILS INTO LARAMIE(1954); THEM!(1954); MAN CALLED PETER, THE(1955); TEXAS LADY(1955); TO HELL AND BACK(1955); OUTSIDE THE LAW(1956); STORM CENTER(1956); NIGHT RUNNER, THE(1957); KATHY O'(1958); THIS HAPPY FEELING(1958); ANATOMY OF A MURDER(1959); SAY ONE FOR ME(1959)
Alice Campbell
JUGGERNAUT(1937, Brit.), w; TEMPTRESS, THE(1949, Brit.), w

Alistair Campbell
1984
COMFORT AND JOY(1984, Brit.)

Allan Campbell
Silents
FLORIDA ENCHANTMENT, A(1914)

Andrew Campbell
EYES OF ANNIE JONES, THE(1963, Brit.), set d; VILLAIN(1971, Brit.), set d; 10 RILLINGTON PLACE(1971, Brit.), set d

Ann Campbell
WELL DONE, HENRY(1936, Brit.)

Archie Campbell
NASHVILLE REBEL(1966)

Argyle Campbell
JEALOUSY(1934), w

Audrey Campbell
OLGA'S GIRLS(1964)

Bartley Campbell
Silents
SIBERIA(1926), w

Beatrice Campbell
WANTED FOR MURDER(1946, Brit.); MEET ME AT DAWN(1947, Brit.); THINGS HAPPEN AT NIGHT(1948, Brit.); MY BROTHER JONATHAN(1949, Brit.); NOW BARABBAS WAS A ROBBER(1949, Brit.); SILENT DUST(1949, Brit.); LAST HOLIDAY(1950, Brit.); LAUGHING LADY, THE(1950, Brit.); MUDLARK, THE(1950, Brit.); NO PLACE FOR JENNIFER(1950, Brit.); I'LL NEVER FORGET YOU(1951); LAUGHTER IN PARADISE(1951, Brit.); MASTER OF BALLANTRAE, THE(1953, U.S./Brit.); COCKLESHELL HEROES, THE(1955); WICKED WIFE(1955, Brit.)

Bettina Campbell
Misc. Silents
WHY MEN FORGET(1921, Brit.)

Beverly Campbell
D.O.A.(1950)

Bill Campbell
BREAKTHROUGH(1950)

Bob Campbell
FIVE GUNS WEST(1955)

Brigadier Hector Campbell
DRUMS(1938, Brit.), tech adv

Bruce Campbell
MR. DRAKE'S DUCK(1951, Brit.), m; MAN IN THE ROAD, THE(1957, Brit.), m; MARY HAD A LITTLE(1961, Brit.), m; JOHNNY GOT HIS GUN(1971), p; EVIL DEAD, THE(1983)

Caly Campbell
MISS SADIE THOMPSON(1953), makeup

Carole Ann Campbell
I'LL CRY TOMORROW(1955)

Cathy Campbell
WOMEN AND BLOODY TERROR(1970)

Catina Campbell
Misc. Silents
HOUND OF THE BASKERVILLES, THE(1921, Brit.)

Charles Campbell
13 RUE MADELEINE(1946); CAMPUS SLEUTH(1948); TURNING POINT, THE(1952)

Charles D. Campbell
DETECTIVE STORY(1951); MY FAVORITE SPY(1951)

Cherry Campbell
GILDED LILY, THE(1935)

Cheryl Campbell
HAWK THE SLAYER(1980, Brit.); CHARRIOTS OF FIRE(1981, Brit.); MC VICAR(1982, Brit.)
1984
GREYSTOKE: THE LEGEND OF TARZAN, LORD OF THE APES(1984)

Choker Campbell
SHAKE, RATTLE, AND ROCK!(1957)

Chris Campbell
1984
PHILADELPHIA EXPERIMENT, THE(1984), art d

Claribel Campbell
Silents
FLAMING BARRIERS(1924)
Misc. Silents
GIRL IN THE RAIN(1927)

Clay Campbell
YOU'LL NEVER GET RICH(1941), makeup; WHAT'S BUZZIN COUSIN?(1943), makeup; RETURN OF THE VAMPIRE, THE(1944), makeup; SONG TO REMEMBER, A(1945), makeup; TONIGHT AND EVERY NIGHT(1945), makeup; GILDA(1946), makeup; JOLSON STORY, THE(1946), makeup; DEAD RECKONING(1947), makeup; DOWN TO EARTH(1947), makeup; IT HAD TO BE YOU(1947), makeup; LADY FROM SHANGHAI, THE(1948), makeup; LOVES OF CARMEN, THE(1948), makeup; RETURN OF OCTOBER, THE(1948), makeup; KNOCK ON ANY DOOR(1949), makeup; LUST FOR GOLD(1949), makeup; MISS GRANT TAKES RICHMOND(1949), makeup; SHOCKPROOF(1949), makeup; TOKYO JOE(1949), makeup; IN A LONELY PLACE(1950), makeup; MOB, THE(1951), makeup; SIROCCO(1951), makeup; DEATH OF A SALESMAN(1952), makeup; MARRYING KIND, THE(1952), makeup; SCANDAL SHEET(1952), makeup; FROM HERE TO ETERNITY(1953), makeup; SALOME(1953), makeup; IT SHOULD HAPPEN TO YOU(1954), makeup; PUSHOVER(1954), makeup; MAN FROM LARAMIE, THE(1955), makeup; PICNIC(1955), makeup; HARDER THEY FALL, THE(1956), makeup; JUBAL(1956), makeup; NIGHTFALL(1956), makeup; SOLID GOLD CADILLAC, THE(1956), makeup; STORM CENTER(1956), makeup; GARMENT JUNGLE, THE(1957), makeup; LAST ANGRY MAN, THE(1959), makeup; THEY CAME TO CORDURA(1959), makeup

Colin Campbell
DECEIVER, THE(1931); GAY DIPLOMAT, THE(1931); ROAD TO SINGAPORE(1931); EIGHT GIRLS IN A BOAT(1934); SHOCK(1934); DARK ANGEL, THE(1935); SYLVIA SCARLETT(1936); WALLABY JIM OF THE ISLANDS(1937); SAN FRANCISCO DOCKS(1941); LIFE BEGINS AT 8:30(1942); MRS. MINIVER(1942); THIS ABOVE ALL(1942); JANE EYRE(1944); LODGER, THE(1944); NATIONAL VELVET(1944); FATAL WITNESS, THE(1945); SALOME, WHERE SHE DANCED(1945); SCOTLAND YARD INVESTIGATOR(1945, Brit.); NIGHT IN PARADISE, A(1946); WIFE OF MONTE CRISTO, THE(1946); EXILE, THE(1947); EXPOSED(1947); IVY(1947); LOVE FROM A STRANGER(1947); MOSS ROSE(1947); TWO MRS. CARROLLS, THE(1947); TEXAS, BROOKLYN AND HEAVEN(1948); ADVENTURES OF ICHABOD AND MR. TOAD(1949); FAN, THE(1949); MR. BELVEDERE GOES TO COLLEGE(1949); SABRINA(1954); LOST WORLD, THE(1960); TWO FOR THE SEESAW(1962); THREE STOOGES GO AROUND THE WORLD IN A DAZE, THE(1963); MY FAIR LADY(1964); SATURDAY NIGHT OUT(1964, Brit.); LEATHER BOYS, THE(1965, Brit.); MC GUIRE, GO HOME!(1966, Brit.)
Silents
SPOILERS, THE(1914), d, w; CARPET FROM BAGDAD, THE(1915), d; TILLIE'S TOMATO SURPRISE(1915); NE'ER-DO-WELL, THE(1916), d; CITY OF PURPLE DREAMS, THE(1918), d; MOON MADNESS(1920), d; NOTHING BUT THE TRUTH(1920), d; SWAMP, THE(1921), d; WHERE LIGHTS ARE LOW(1921), d; CARDIGAN(1922)
Misc. Silents
MONTE CRISTO(1912), d; CHIP OF THE FLYING U(1914), d; IN THE DAYS OF THE THUNDERING HERD(1914), d; STORY OF THE BLOOD RED ROSE, THE(1914), d; ROSARY, THE(1915), d; SWEET ALYSSUM(1915), d; GARDEN OF ALLAH, THE(1916), d; THOU SHALT NOT COVET(1916), d; UNTO THOSE WHO SIN(1916), d; BEWARE OF STRANGERS(1918), d; HOOSIER ROMANCE, A(1918), d; SEA FLOWER, THE(1918), d; WHO SHALL TAKE MY LIFE?(1918), d; YELLOW DOG, THE(1918), d; FRUITS OF PASSION(1919); LITTLE ORPHANT ANNIE(1919), d; RAILROADER, THE(1919), d; THUNDERBOLT, THE(1919), d; TONGUES OF FLAME(1919), d; BEAUTY MARKET, THE(1920), d; BIG HAPPINESS(1920), d; CORSICAN BROTHERS, THE(1920), d; WHEN DAWN CAME(1920), d; BLACK ROSES(1921), d; FIRST BORN, THE(1921), d; LURE OF JADE, THE(1921), d; MAN OF STONE, THE(1921), d; TWO KINDS OF WOMEN(1922), d; WORLD'S A STAGE, THE(1922), d; BUCKING THE BARRIER(1923), d; BUSTER, THE(1923), d; GRAIL, THE(1923), d; THREE WHO PAID(1923), d; BOWERY BISHOP, THE(1924), d; PAGAN PASSIONS(1924), d

Cordelia Campbell
HIT THE ICE(1943); LATE GEORGE APLEY, THE(1947)

Daisy Campbell
HIGH SEAS(1929, Brit.); INFORMER, THE(1929, Brit.); TESHA(1929, Brit.)
Silents
INDIAN LOVE LYRICS, THE(1923, Brit.); OUT TO WIN(1923, Brit.); FORBIDDEN CARGOES(1925, Brit.); IRISH DESTINY(1925, Brit.); LONDON(1926, Brit.); DAUGHTER IN REVOLT, A(1927, Brit.); POPPIES OF FLANDERS(1927, Brit.); AFTER THE VERDICT(1929, Brit.)

Daphne Campbell
OVERLANDERS, THE(1946, Brit./Aus.)

David Campbell
LIVING IDOL, THE(1957), ch; ALL THE RIGHT MOVES(1983), m
1984
NIGHT OF THE COMET(1984), m

Dean Campbell
TOP BANANA(1954)

Dennis Campbell
INJUN FENDER(1973)

Derek Campbell
RUNNING BRAVE(1983, Can.)

Diana Campbell
NO RESTING PLACE(1952, Brit.); TREASURE HUNT(1952, Brit.)

Diane Campbell
1984
HADLEY'S REBELLION(1984), prod d; PHILADELPHIA EXPERIMENT, THE(1984), set d

Don Campbell
MARS NEEDS WOMEN(1966); DEMONSTRATOR(1971, Aus.), w

Donalda Campbell
Misc. Silents
WHERE AMBITION LEADS(1919, Brit.)

Douglas Campbell
OEDIPUS REX(1957, Can.); WHEN TOMORROW DIES(1966, Can.); LOST AND FOUND(1979); IF YOU COULD SEE WHAT I HEAR(1982); STRANGE BREW(1983)

Dwight Campbell
AVENGING WATERS(1936), ed; WHISPERING ENEMIES(1939), ed

E. Murray Campbell
LAST OUTLAW, THE(1936), w

Edith Campbell
Misc. Silents
SPORTING DUCHESS, THE(1920)

Elaine Campbell
MOONLIGHT IN VERMONT(1943)

Elizabeth Campbell
BRIDAL PATH, THE(1959, Brit.); DOCTOR OF DOOM(1962, Mex.); PROFESSIONALS, THE(1966); DEMONSTRATOR(1971, Aus.), w

Emma Campbell
Silents
OUT OF THE SHADOW(1919); ROMANCE OF THE AIR, A(1919)
Misc. Silents
HIDDEN TRUTH, THE(1919)

Erma Campbell
ZELIG(1983)

Evelyn Campbell
WESTERN LIMITED(1932), w
Silents
BREAD(1918), w; NOBODY'S BRIDE(1923), w; EARLY TO WED(1926), w; GILDED BUTTERFLY, THE(1926), w; IRRESISTIBLE LOVER, THE(1927), w; MASKED ANGEL(1928), w

Flo Campbell
FIVE LITTLE PEPPERS AND HOW THEY GREW(1939)

Flora Campbell
GROUP, THE(1966)

Frances Rose Campbell
SUCH IS THE LAW(1930, Brit.)

Frances Ross Campbell
FOOTSTEPS IN THE NIGHT(1932, Brit.)

Gar Campbell
GLASS HOUSES(1972); DREAM ON(1981)
Gary Campbell
SOME OF MY BEST FRIENDS ARE...(1971)
Geordie Campbell
LADY LIBERTY(1972, Ital./Fr.)
George Campbell
VOICE IN THE NIGHT, A(1941, Brit.), w; CRY FOR HAPPY(1961), w
Silents
LIFE OF ROBERT BURNS, THE(1926, Brit.)
Glen Campbell
COOL ONES, THE(1967); TRUE GRIT(1969); NORWOOD(1970); ANY WHICH WAY YOU CAN(1980)
Graeme Campbell
MC CABE AND MRS. MILLER(1971)
H. R. Campbell
WEST POINT OF THE AIR(1935), art d
Harry Campbell
SKY GIANT(1938); VIVACIOUS LADY(1938)
Helen Campbell
Silents
LOVE'S WILDERNESS(1924), w
Howard Campbell
SOCIETY DOCTOR(1935), art d; SOCIETY LAWYER(1939), art d; SKY MURDER(1940), art d; TRIAL OF MARY DUGAN, THE(1941), art d; PILOT NO. 5(1943), art d; THREE HEARTS FOR JULIA(1943), art d; MAISIE GOES TO RENO(1944), art d; RATIONING(1944), art d; THIS MAN'S NAVY(1945), art d; WESTBOUND(1959), art d; BEACH BLANKET BINGO(1965), art d; HOW TO STUFF A WILD BIKINI(1965), art d; SERGEANT DEADHEAD(1965), art d; SKI PARTY(1965), art d
Huntley Campbell
SIMBA(1955, Brit.)
Ian Campbell
WICKER MAN, THE(1974, Brit.)
Isobel Campbell
GORBALS STORY, THE(1950, Brit.)
Ivar Campbell
REUNION(1932, Brit.), d; WATCH BEVERLY(1932, Brit.), p; COUNTY FAIR(1933, Brit.), p; DOSS HOUSE(1933, Brit.), p; EYES OF FATE(1933, Brit.), d; GOLDEN CAGE, THE(1933, Brit.), d; PARIS PLANE(1933, Brit.), p; SHE WAS ONLY A VILLAGE MAIDEN(1933, Brit.), p; WISHBONE, THE(1933, Brit.), p; BYPASS TO HAPPINESS(1934, Brit.), d; DESIGNING WOMEN(1934, Brit.), d; DIPLOMATIC LOVER, THE(1934, Brit.), w; WHITE ENSIGN(1934, Brit.), p; EXPERT'S OPINION(1935, Brit.), w; MAD HATTERS, THE(1935, Brit.), d; RADIO PIRATES(1935, Brit.), d; BELLES OF ST. CLEMENTS, THE(1936, Brit.), d, w; GRAND FINALE(1936, Brit.), d; CAPTAIN'S ORDERS(1937, Brit.), d; FEATHER YOUR NEST(1937, Brit.), w; TOO MANY HUSBANDS(1938, Brit.), p,d&w
J. A. Campbell
Silents
QUEEN MOTHER, THE(1916, Brit.), w
J. L. Campbell
Silents
FRENCH DRESSING(1927), w; ONE WOMAN TO ANOTHER(1927), w
J.F. Campbell
HERO(1982, Brit.), w, p,d&w
Jack Campbell
SNOW WHITE AND THE SEVEN DWARFS(1937), anim; FANTASIA(1940), anim; PINOCCHIO(1940), anim; DUMBO(1941), anim; RELUCTANT DRAGON, THE(1941), anim; MAKE MINE MUSIC(1946), anim; SONG OF THE SOUTH(1946), anim; FUN AND FANCY FREE(1947), anim; LADY AND THE TRAMP(1955), anim; 1001 ARABIAN NIGHTS(1959), anim
James Campbell
DEADLY DECOYS, THE(1962, Fr.); PLEASE, NOT NOW!(1963, Fr./Ital.), m; PLAYTIME(1973, Fr.), m; PASSENGER, THE(1975, Ital.)
Jan Campbell
HOMER(1970); CLASS OF '44(1973); SILENT PARTNER, THE(1979, Can.)
Jane Campbell
LOCAL COLOR(1978)
Jean Campbell
MAIDSTONE(1970); RECKONING, THE(1971, Brit.); LONELY HEARTS(1983, Aus.)
Jenni Campbell
DEATHCHEATERS(1976, Aus.), cos
Jerry Campbell
NIGHT THE LIGHTS WENT OUT IN GEORGIA, THE(1981); SIX PACK(1982)
Jim Campbell
SAGEBRUSH POLITICS(1930)
Jim Jack Campbell
ONE FROM THE HEART(1982)
Jo-Ann Campbell
HEY, LET'S TWIST!(1961)
Joan Campbell
FINNEGANS WAKE(1965)
Joe Campbell
Silents
BEAU REVEL(1921)
John Campbell
SULLIVANS, THE(1944); SWEET AND LOWDOWN(1944); MR. PERRIN AND MR. TRAILL(1948, Brit.); TOM BROWN'S SCHOOLDAYS(1951, Brit.)
John W. Campbell, Jr.
THING, THE(1982), w
John Wood Campbell, Jr.
THING, THE(1951), w
Joy Campbell
PUFNSTUF(1970)
Judy Campbell
CONVOY(1940); SALOON BAR(1940, Brit.); STRANGLER, THE(1941, Brit.); ADVENTURE IN BLACKMAIL(1943, Brit.); WORLD OWES ME A LIVING, THE(1944, Brit.); GREEN FOR DANGER(1946, Brit.); BONNIE PRINCE CHARLIE(1948, Brit.); THERE'S A GIRL IN MY SOUP(1970, Brit.); CRY OF THE PENGUINS(1972, Brit.)

Kane Campbell
ENCHANTED APRIL(1935), w
Kate Campbell
GHOST CITY(1932); GHOST VALLEY(1932); COME ON TARZAN(1933); GAMBLING SHIP(1933); MONTE CARLO NIGHTS(1934)
Katherine Campbell
Silents
MEASURE OF A MAN, THE(1916)
Keith Campbell
SNOWBOUND(1949, Brit.), w; STRONGROOM(1962, Brit.)
Ken Campbell
BIG RED ONE, THE(1980); BREAKING GLASS(1980, Brit.)
Kippy Campbell
WRONG MAN, THE(1956)
Larry Campbell
THEY ALL LAUGHED(1981)
Laura Campbell
1984
IRRECONCILABLE DIFFERENCES(1984)
Lindsay Campbell
IT!(1967, Brit.); CLOCKWORK ORANGE, A(1971, Brit.); SCHIZO(1977, Brit.); FFOLKES(1980, Brit.)
Lois Jane Campbell
CIMARRON(1931)
Louise Campbell
BULLDOG DRUMMOND COMES BACK(1937); BULLDOG DRUMMOND'S REVENGE(1937); NIGHT CLUB SCANDAL(1937); WILD MONEY(1937); BUCCANEER, THE(1938); BULLDOG DRUMMOND'S PERIL(1938); MEN WITH WINGS(1938); SCANDAL STREET(1938); STAR MAKER, THE(1939); ANNE OF WINDY POPLARS(1940); BOWERY BOY(1940); EMERGENCY SQUAD(1940); DEVIL SHIP(1947)
Maj. Gen. Douglas Campbell
OH! WHAT A LOVELY WAR(1969, Brit.), tech adv
Malcolm Campbell
AMERICAN WEREWOLF IN LONDON, AN(1981), ed; TRADING PLACES(1983), ed; TWILIGHT ZONE–THE MOVIE(1983), ed
Marcus Campbell
MERRY CHRISTMAS MR. LAWRENCE(1983, Jap./Brit.)
Margaret Campbell
ONE HYSTERICAL NIGHT(1930); TAKE THE HEIR(1930); GUNSLINGER(1956)
Silents
NOTORIOUS MISS LISLE, THE(1920); LYING LIPS(1921); CLEAN UP, THE(1923); LEGALLY DEAD(1923); LADY FROM HELL, THE(1926); CHILDREN OF DIVORCE(1927)
Misc. Silents
PLEASE GET MARRIED(1919); THEIR MUTUAL CHILD(1920); BECAUSE(1921, Brit.); HIS MYSTERY'S GIRL(1923); BETTER MAN, THE(1926)
Marguerite Campbell
HELLO, EVERYBODY(1933); JAM SESSION(1944); OUT OF THIS WORLD(1945); NIGHT IN PARADISE, A(1946); TOMORROW IS FOREVER(1946)
Mark Campbell
PENNIES FROM HEAVEN(1981)
Maurice Campbell
Silents
OH, LADY, LADY(1920), d; AMATEUR DEVIL, AN(1921), d; DUCKS AND DRAKES(1921), d; ONE WILD WEEK(1921), d; SPEED GIRL, THE(1921), d; EXCITERS, THE(1923), d
Misc. Silents
BURGLAR-PROOF(1920), d; FIRST LOVE(1921), d; MARCH HARE, THE(1921), d; TWO WEEKS WITH PAY(1921), d; MIDNIGHT(1922), d; THROUGH A GLASS WINDOW(1922), d; GIRLS MEN FORGET(1924), d; WANDERING FIRES(1925), d; BURNT FINGERS(1927), d
Michael Campbell
PERSECUTION(1974, Brit.), ed
Mick Campbell
MY CHILDHOOD(1972, Brit.), ph
Mike Campbell
CHARLEY-ONE-EYE(1973, Brit.), ed; RIDE A WILD PONY(1976, U.S./Aus.), ed; DEATH SHIP(1980, Can.), ed
Muriel Campbell
SHE MARRIED A COP(1939)
Murray Campbell
INBETWEEN AGE, THE(1958, Brit.)
Ned Campbell
NATIVE SON(1951, U.S., Arg.)
Neil Campbell
SUMMER OF SECRETS(1976, Aus.); SHOCK TREATMENT(1981)
Nell Campbell
LISZTOMANIA(1975, Brit.); ROCKY HORROR PICTURE SHOW, THE(1975, Brit.); JOURNEY AMONG WOMEN(1977, Aus.); PINK FLOYD–THE WALL(1982, Brit.)
Newton Campbell
Silents
DARING CHANCES(1924)
Nicholas Campbell
OMEN, THE(1976); BRIDGE TOO FAR, A(1977, Brit.); SPY WHO LOVED ME, THE(1977, Brit.); BROOD, THE(1979, Can.); SHAPE OF THINGS TO COME, THE(1979, Can.); YESTERDAY(1980, Can.); AMATEUR, THE(1982); DEAD ZONE, THE(1983)
Misc. Talkies
FAST COMPANY(1979); TRAPPED(1982)
Nick Campbell
DIRTY TRICKS(1981, Can.)
Norma Arden Campbell
BACHELOR PARTY, THE(1957)
Patrick Campbell
HELTER SKELTER(1949, Brit.), w; MISS ROBIN HOOD(1952, Brit.), w; HORSE'S MOUTH, THE(1953, Brit.), w; JACQUELINE(1956, Brit.), w; LUCKY JIM(1957, Brit.), w; LAW AND DISORDER(1958, Brit.), w; GO TO BLAZES(1962, Brit.), w; MODEL MURDER CASE, THE(1964, Brit.), w; ENTER LAUGHING(1967); CULPEPPER CATTLE COMPANY, THE(1972); SILENT MOVIE(1976); SATURDAY THE 14TH(1981); SMOKEY BITES THE DUST(1981)

Mrs. Patrick Campbell
DANCERS, THE(1930); ONE MORE RIVER(1934); OUTCAST LADY(1934); RIP TIDE(1934); CRIME AND PUNISHMENT(1935)
Paul Campbell
IT HAD TO BE YOU(1947); LAST DAYS OF BOOT HILL(1947); MILLIE'S DAUGHTER(1947); SPORT OF KINGS(1947); BUCKAROO FROM POWDER RIVER(1948); GALLANT BLADE, THE(1948); SIX-GUN LAW(1948); DESERT VIGILANTE(1949); ACROSS THE BADLANDS(1950); FRONTIER OUTPOST(1950); GREAT PLANE ROBBERY(1950); VIGILANTE HIDEOUT(1950); PECOS RIVER(1951); PRAIRIE ROUNDUP(1951); SMUGGLER'S GOLD(1951); SKY FULL OF MOON(1952), m/1; EGYPT BY THREE(1953); GOLDEN COACH, THE(1953, Fr./Ital.); DEADLY MANTIS, THE(1957)
Misc. Talkies
SMOKY RIVER SERENADE(1947); STRANGER FROM PONCA CITY, THE(1947); BLAZING ACROSS THE PECOS(1948)
Pauline Campbell
HICKEY AND BOGGS(1972), cos
Peggy Campbell
GLAMOUR(1934); WHEN A MAN SEES RED(1934); STONE OF SILVER CREEK(1935)
Misc. Talkies
BIG CALIBRE(1935)
R. Campbell
Silents
GOLD RUSH, THE(1925)
R. Wright Campbell
FIVE GUNS WEST(1955), w; GUN FOR A COWARD(1957), w; QUANTEZ(1957), w; MACHINE GUN KELLY(1958), w; TEENAGE CAVEMAN(1958), w; DEMENTIA 13(1963), p; YOUNG RACERS, THE(1963), w; MASQUE OF THE RED DEATH, THE(1964, U.S./Brit.), w; SECRET INVASION, THE(1964), w; HELL'S ANGELS ON WHEELS(1967), w; CAPTAIN NEMO AND THE UNDERWATER CITY(1969, Brit.), w
Ralph Campbell
SUPERCHICK(1973)
Raymond Campbell
PAISAN(1948, Ital.)
Reginald Campbell
GIRL FROM MANDALAY(1936), w; TUSK(1980, Fr.), w
Rheba Campbell
OUR RELATIONS(1936)
Robert Campbell
CELL 2455, DEATH ROW(1955); YOUNG RACERS, THE(1963)
Robert Wright Campbell
NIGHT FIGHTERS, THE(1960), w
Ron Campbell
9/30/55(1977)
Ross Campbell
FLASH THE SHEEPDOG(1967, Brit.); HUNCH, THE(1967, Brit.); WICKER MAN, THE(1974, Brit.)
Sally Campbell
JOURNEY AMONG WOMEN(1977, Aus.), set d; STARSTRUCK(1982, Aus.), set d
1984
PHAR LAP(1984, Aus.), set d
Scott Campbell
CAT ATE THE PARAKEET, THE(1972); SPLIT IMAGE(1982)
1984
BEAR, THE(1984)
Sean Campbell
SIDELONG GLANCES OF A PIGEON KICKER, THE(1970)
Shawn Campbell
RACHEL, RACHEL(1968); MAN ON A SWING(1974)
Sheena Campbell
RUN WITH THE WIND(1966, Brit.)
Sheila Campbell
EXPERT'S OPINION(1935, Brit.), w; BELLES OF ST. CLEMENTS, THE(1936, Brit.), w; FEATHER YOUR NEST(1937, Brit.), w
Sir Malcolm Campbell
BURN 'EM UP O'CONNER(1939), w
Stanley Campbell
DONDI(1961), makeup; LAST TIME I SAW ARCHIE, THE(1961), makeup; RAGE TO LIVE, A(1965), makeup
Stella Mervyn Campbell
Misc. Silents
SPINNER O' DREAMS(1918, Brit.)
Sterling Campbell
HANDS ACROSS THE TABLE(1935); LOVE IS NEWS(1937)
Misc. Talkies
BUSH PILOT(1947), d
Stewart Campbell
RETURN OF A MAN CALLED HORSE, THE(1976), prod d; URBAN COWBOY(1980), art d; INDEPENDENCE DAY(1983), prod d
Stu Campbell
SHAMPOO(1975), art d; JAWS II(1978), art d; SHOOT THE MOON(1982), art d
1984
BIRDY(1984), art d
Susan Campbell
LONG HAUL, THE(1957, Brit.)
Sussanah Campbell
WICKED DIE SLOW, THE(1968)
Thurston Campbell
CHILDREN OF BABYLON(1980, Jamaica)
Tim Campbell
GEORGE WASHINGTON CARVER(1940)
Tom Campbell
GALAXY OF TERROR(1981), spec eff; SPACE RAIDERS(1983), spec eff
Torquil Campbell
GOLDEN SEAL, THE(1983)
Vera Campbell
YELLOW CANARY, THE(1944, Brit.), ed; SO EVIL MY LOVE(1948, Brit.), ed; WOMAN HATER(1949, Brit.), ed; THEY WERE NOT DIVIDED(1951, Brit.), ed; FRIGHTENED BRIDE, THE(1952, Brit.), ed

Vicki Campbell
SHERLOCK HOLMES AND THE SECRET WEAPON(1942)
Violet Campbell
Silents
PHANTOM PICTURE, THE(1916, Brit.)
Virginia Campbell
UNCONQUERED(1947); THAT LADY IN ERMINE(1948); HOME TOWN STORY(1951)
Virita Campbell
THIS GUN FOR HIRE(1942)
Vivita Campbell
SHEPHERD OF THE HILLS, THE(1941)
W. Stewart Campbell
CHINATOWN(1974), art d; FORTUNE, THE(1975), art d; TRUE CONFESSIONS(1981), art d; RIGHT STUFF, THE(1983), art d
Wallace Campbell
CHARRIOTS OF FIRE(1981, Brit.)
Wardell Campbell
1984
KILLPOINT(1984)
Webster Campbell
LOVE RACKET, THE(1929); IN THE NEXT ROOM(1930)
Silents
BAB'S CANDIDATE(1920); MORAL FIBRE(1921), d; SINGLE TRACK, THE(1921), d; PACE THAT THRILLS, THE(1925), d
Misc. Silents
THROUGH THE WALL(1916); EVIL EYE, THE(1917); FETTERED WOMAN, THE(1917); LOVE DOCTOR, THE(1917); RENAISSANCE AT CHARLEROI, THE(1917); SATAN'S PRIVATE DOOR(1917); TRANSGRESSION(1917); GIRL OF TODAY, THE(1918); DEADLINE AT ELEVEN(1920); HUMAN COLLATERAL(1920); PLEASURE SEEKERS(1920); SEA RIDER, THE(1920); TOWER OF JEWELS, THE(1920); IT ISN'T BEING DONE THIS SEASON(1921); WHAT'S YOUR REPUTATION WORTH?(1921), d; DIVORCE COUPONS(1922), d; ISLAND WIVES(1922), d; VIRGIN'S SACRIFICE, A(1922), d
William Campbell
INGAGI(1931), d; HI-DE-HO(1947); BREAKING POINT, THE(1950); INSIDE THE WALLS OF FOLSOM PRISON(1951); PEOPLE AGAINST O'HARA, THE(1951); HOLIDAY FOR SINNERS(1952); BATTLE CIRCUS(1953); BIG LEAGUER(1953); CODE TWO(1953); ESCAPE FROM FORT BRAVO(1953); SMALL TOWN GIRL(1953); HIGH AND THE MIGHTY, THE(1954); BATTLE FLAME(1955); CELL 2455, DEATH ROW(1955); MAN WITHOUT A STAR(1955); RUNNING WILD(1955); BACKLASH(1956); LOVE ME TENDER(1956); MAN IN THE VAULT(1956); EIGHTEEN AND ANXIOUS(1957); DARBY'S RANGERS(1958), art d; MONEY, WOMEN AND GUNS(1958); NAKED AND THE DEAD, THE(1958); SHERIFF OF FRACTURED JAW, THE(1958, Brit.); NATCHEZ TRACE(1960); NIGHT OF EVIL(1962); DEMENTIA 13(1963); YOUNG RACERS, THE(1963); DISTANT TRUMPET, A(1964), art d; FBI CODE 98(1964), art d; HUSH... HUSH, SWEET CHARLOTTE(1964); SECRET INVASION, THE(1964); PORTRAIT IN TERROR(1965); BLOOD BATH(1966); MONEY TRAP, THE(1966); NIGHT OF THE GRIZZLY, THE(1966), art d; PRETTY MAIDS ALL IN A ROW(1971); STEAGLE, THE(1971), art d; BLACK GUNN(1972); DIRTY MARY, CRAZY LARRY(1974); OTHER SIDE OF THE MOUNTAIN–PART 2, THE(1978), art d
William [Bill] Campbell
OPERATION PACIFIC(1951)
William L. Campbell
WALK PROUD(1979), art d
Bonnie Campbell-Britton
1984
ICE PIRATES, THE(1984)
Ian Campbell-Gray
DANCE PRETTY LADY(1932, Brit.), art d; SOME DAY(1935, Brit.), art d
Anna Campbell-Jones
1984
SECRETS(1984, Brit.)
Hilda Campbell-Russell
2,000 WOMEN(1944, Brit.)
Frank Campeau
GAMBLERS, THE(1929); IN OLD ARIZONA(1929); IN THE HEADLINES(1929); SEA FURY(1929); ABRAHAM LINCOLN(1930); LAST OF THE DUANES(1930); LIGHTNIN'(1930); CAPTAIN THUNDER(1931); FIGHTING CARAVANS(1931); LASCA OF THE RIO GRANDE(1931); SOLDIER'S PLAYTHING, A(1931); GIRL OF THE RIO(1932); WHITE EAGLE(1932); SMOKY(1933); HOPALONG CASSIDY(1935); EVERYMAN'S LAW(1936); EMPTY SADDLES(1937); FIREFLY, THE(1937); BORDER WOLVES(1938); KING OF THE SIERRAS(1938); MARIE ANTOINETTE(1938); PAINTED TRAIL, THE(1938)
Silents
JORDAN IS A HARD ROAD(1915); MAN FROM PAINTED POST, THE(1917); MODERN MUSKETEER, A(1917); REACHING FOR THE MOON(1917); ARIZONA(1918); HEADIN' SOUTH(1918); MR. FIX-IT(1918); SAY! YOUNG FELLOW(1918); HIS MAJESTY THE AMERICAN(1919); KNICKERBOCKER BUCKAROO, THE(1919); WHEN THE CLOUDS ROLL BY(1920); KID, THE(1921); KILLER, THE(1921); SIN OF MARTHA QUEED, THE(1921); CRIMSON CHALLENGE, THE(1922); JUST TONY(1922); TRAP, THE(1922); ISLE OF LOST SHIPS, THE(1923); NORTH OF HUDSON BAY(1923); SPIDER AND THE ROSE, THE(1923); TO THE LAST MAN(1923); ALASKAN, THE(1924); NO MAN'S GOLD(1926); SEA HORSES(1926); LET IT RAIN(1927); POINTS WEST(1929)
Misc. Silents
WOOD NYMPH, THE(1916); HEART OF TEXAS RYAN, THE(1917); YOSEMITE TRAIL, THE(1922); HOODMAN BLIND(1923); MODERN MATRIMONY(1923); THREE WHO PAID(1923); NOT A DRUM WAS HEARD(1924); BATTLING BUNYON(1925); HEIR-LOONS(1925); MAN FROM RED GULCH, THE(1925); MANHATTAN MADNESS(1925); FRONTIER TRAIL, THE(1926); GOLDEN COCOON, THE(1926); HEART OF THE YUKON, THE(1927); CANDY KID, THE(1928)
George Campeau
TUGBOAT ANNIE SAILS AGAIN(1940); GREAT MR. NOBODY, THE(1941); MILLION DOLLAR BABY(1941); NURSE'S SECRET, THE(1941); STRAWBERRY BLONDE, THE(1941); NORA PRENTISS(1947)
Lauretta Campeau
CITIZEN SAINT(1947)

Laurette Campeau
SARUMBA(1950)
Ivar Campell
EXPERT'S OPINION(1935, Brit.), d
Paul Campellani
Silents
BABBLING TONGUES(1917)
Tony Campenero
OUR RELATIONS(1936)
El Teatro Campesino
WHICH WAY IS UP?(1977)
Elisabetta Campeti
LUNA(1979, Ital.)
Craig Campfield
TOGETHER BROTHERS(1974)
Frank Camphill
Silents
LONE EAGLE, THE(1927)
Edrioni G. Campi
MONGOLS, THE(1966, Fr./Ital.), md
Maria Campi
SHOE SHINE(1947, Ital.)
Anita Campillo
MAN FROM UTAH, THE(1934)
Lily Campillos
IMPASSE(1969)
Campion
PARISIAN, THE(1931, Fr.)
Anne Campion
DAMNED, THE(1948, Fr.)
Cyril Campion
WATCH BEVERLY(1932, Brit.), w; ASK BECCLES(1933, Brit.), w; ADMIRAL'S SECRET, THE(1934, Brit.), w; ADVENTURE LIMITED(1934, Brit.), w; CHANNEL CROSSING(1934, Brit.), w; FOUR MASKED MEN(1934, Brit.), w; LASH, THE(1934, Brit.), w; DEBT OF HONOR(1936, Brit.), w; IT'S YOU I WANT(1936, Brit.), w; TOUCH OF THE MOON, A(1936, Brit.), w; JUGGERNAUT(1937, Brit.), w; CONVICT 99(1938, Brit.), w; DISCOVERIES(1939, Brit.), w
Gerald Campion
MIRANDA(1949, Brit.); PICKWICK PAPERS, THE(1952, Brit.); TOP OF THE FORM(1953, Brit.); UP TO HIS NECK(1954, Brit.); LOVERS, HAPPY LOVERS!(1955, Brit.); FUN AT ST. FANNY'S(1956, Brit.); KEEP IT CLEAN(1956, Brit.); CARRY ON SERGEANT(1959, Brit.); INN FOR TROUBLE(1960, Brit.); SCHOOL FOR SCOUN-DRELS(1960, Brit.); DOUBLE BUNK(1961, Brit.); COMEDY MAN, THE(1964); JIG SAW(1965, Brit.); THOSE MAGNIFICENT MEN IN THEIR FLYING MACHINES; OR HOW I FLEWFROM LONDON TO PARIS IN 25 HOURS AND 11 MINUTES(1965, Brit.); HALF A SIXPENCE(1967, Brit.); SORCERERS, THE(1967, Brit.); CHITTY CHITTY BANG BANG(1968, Brit.)
Joyce Campion
QUIET DAY IN BELFAST, A(1974, Can.)
Leo Campion
FRENCH CANCAN(1956, Fr.)
Matthew Campion
BACK ROADS(1981); MOMMIE DEAREST(1981)
Nardi Reeder Campion
LONG GRAY LINE, THE(1955), w
Campion the horse
BLUE CANADIAN ROCKIES(1952)
Gaetano Campisi
LEAP INTO THE VOID(1982, Ital.)
Frank Campitelli
TOMB OF TORTURE(1966, Ital.), p, ph
Helen Campitelli
SQUEEZE PLAY(1981)
David Camplin
STUD, THE(1979, Brit.), ed
David Campling
MADE(1972, Brit.), ed; GOLDEN LADY, THE(1979, Brit.), ed
Del Campo
DEVIL ON HORSEBACK, THE(1936)
Pupi Campo
HOLE IN THE HEAD, A(1959)
Wally Campo
HELL SQUAD(1958); MACHINE GUN KELLY(1958); TANK COMMANDOS(1959); WARLOCK(1959); BEAST FROM THE HAUNTED CAVE(1960); SKI TROOP AT-TACK(1960); MASTER OF THE WORLD(1961); TALES OF TERROR(1962); SHOCK CORRIDOR(1963); STRANGLER, THE(1964); WAR IS HELL(1964); DEVIL'S AN-GELS(1967)
Wallace J. Campodanio
Misc. Talkies
MARK OF THE GUN(1969)
Carlo Campogalliani
GOLIATH AND THE BARBARIANS(1960, Ital.), d, w; MIGHTY URSUS(1962, Ital./Span.), d; SON OF SAMSON(1962, Fr./Ital./Yugo.), d; SWORD OF THE CON-QUEROR(1962, Ital.), d, w
Alfredo Campoli
STEPPING TOES(1938, Brit.); OLD MOTHER RILEY, DETECTIVE(1943, Brit.); DREAMING(1944, Brit.)
Merv Campone
TRAP, THE(1967, Can./Brit.)
Batista Campos
TROPICS(1969, Ital.)
Chela Campos
PASSION ISLAND(1943, Mex.)
Graciele Campos
TROPICS(1969, Ital.)
Jose Campos
Misc. Talkies
TERROR IN THE CRYPT(1963, Span./Ital.)

Jose Campos, Jr.
UNDER FIRE(1983)
Lidia Campos
WAY OF A GAUCHO(1952)
Magaly Campos
PASSION(1983, Fr./Switz.)
Marco Antonio Campos
LOS ASTRONAUTAS(1960, Mex.); LOS INVISIBLES(1961, Mex.)
Miguel Angel Perez Campos
1984
MIDSUMMER NIGHT'S DREAM, A(1984, Brit./Span.), p
Rafael Campos
BLACKBOARD JUNGLE, THE(1955); TRIAL(1955); SHARKFIGHTERS, THE(1956); DINO(1957); THIS COULD BE THE NIGHT(1957); LIGHT IN THE FOREST, THE(1958); TONKA(1958); SAVAGE SAM(1963); LADY IN A CAGE(1964); AGENT FOR H.A.R.M.(1966); APPALOOSA, THE(1966); MISTER BUDDWING(1966); GIRL IN GOLD BOOTS(1968); ASTRO-ZOMBIES, THE(1969); DOLL SQUAD, THE(1973); OK-LAHOMA CRUDE(1973); HANGUP(1974); SLUMBER PARTY '57(1977); WHERE THE BUFFALO ROAM(1980); HEARTBREAKER(1983)
Rose Marie Campos
NIGHTMARES(1983)
Vic Campos
Misc. Talkies
ADVERSARY, THE(1970)
Victor Campos
NEWMAN'S LAW(1974); MASTER GUNFIGHTER, THE(1975); BLACK SUN-DAY(1977); FIVE DAYS FROM HOME(1978); SCARFACE(1983)
Rafael Sanchez Campoy
GLASS SPHINX, THE(1968, Egypt/Ital./Span.), w
Jacques Campreaux
MYSTERIOUS ISLAND OF CAPTAIN NEMO, THE(1973, Fr./Ital. 87m Span./Cameroon), w
Michael Campus
Z.P.G.(1972), d; MACK, THE(1973), d; EDUCATION OF SONNY CARSON, THE(1974), d; PASSOVER PLOT, THE(1976, Israel), d
Michael I. Campus
SURVIVAL(1976), p&d
Roger Camras
ODE TO BILLY JOE(1976), p; HOMETOWN U.S.A.(1979), p
Rocky Camron
ARIZONA ROUNDUP(1942); OUTLAW TRAIL(1944); SONORA STAGE-COACH(1944); SONG OF OLD WYOMING(1945); WILDFIRE(1945); ROMANCE OF THE WEST(1946); FIGHTING STALLION, THE(1950)
Ken Camroux
BREAKING POINT(1976); IMPROPER CHANNELS(1981, Can.)
Beatrice Camurat
1984
HEAT OF DESIRE(1984, Fr.)
Albert Camus
STRANGER, THE(1967, Algeria/Fr./Ital.), w
Marcel Camus
BLACK ORPHEUS(1959 Fr./Ital./Braz.), d, w; DRAGON SKY(1964, Fr.), d, w
Mario Camus
1984
HOLY INNOCENTS, THE(1984, Span.), d, w
Vince Camuto
BANG THE DRUM SLOWLY(1973)
Carlos Alberto Camuyrano
1984
MEMOIRS OF PRISON(1984, Braz.), ed
Chester Can
GET-AWAY, THE(1941)
Marian Can
CELL 2455, DEATH ROW(1955)
Paul Can
CAPTAIN NEWMAN, M.D.(1963)
The Can Can Dancers
VARIETY(1935, Brit.)
Zoila Cana
HER BODYGUARD(1933)
Lena Canada
TOUCHED BY LOVE(1980), w
Ray Canada
I KILLED WILD BILL HICKOK(1956)
Roy Canada
GOLD RAIDERS, THE(1952); SON OF THE RENEGADE(1953); LAWLESS RIDER, THE(1954)
Canadian Army Orchestra
THIS MAN IS MINE(1946 Brit.)
John Canady
YANKS AHOY(1943)
Larry Canaga
STRAWBERRY STATEMENT, THE(1970)
Robert Canaga
HOW TO BEAT THE HIGH COST OF LIVING(1980)
Toni Canal
EVERY DAY IS A HOLIDAY(1966, Span.)
Giana Maria Canale
ALERT IN THE SOUTH(1954, Fr.)
Gianna Canale
GO FOR BROKE(1951)
Gianna Maria Canale
DEAD WOMAN'S KISS, A(1951, Ital.); MAN FROM CAIRO, THE(1953); MADAME DU BARRY(1954 Fr./Ital.); WHOLE TRUTH, THE(1958, Brit.); HERCULES(1959); SILENT ENEMY, THE(1959, Brit.); WARRIOR AND THE SLAVE GIRL, THE(1959, Ital.); MIGHTY CRUSADERS, THE(1961, Ital.); QUEEN OF THE PIRATES(1961, Ital./Ger.); SECRET OF MONTE CRISTO, THE(1961, Brit.); CENTURION, THE(1962, Fr./Ital.); NIGHT THEY KILLED RASPUTIN, THE(1962, Fr./Ital.); SLAVE, THE(1963, Ital.); ADVENTURES OF SCARAMOUCHE, THE(1964, Fr.); GOLIATH AND THE VAMPIRES(1964, Ital.); TIGER OF THE SEVEN SEAS(1964, Fr./Ital.); LION OF ST.

MARK(1967, Ital.)

Gianna Marie Canale
DEVIL'S COMMANDMENT, THE(1956, Ital.)
Misc. Talkies
COLOSSUS AND THE AMAZONS(1960)

Gianna-Maria Canale
NAPOLEON(1955, Fr.)

Joe Canalejas
MAN CALLED NOON, THE(1973, Brit.)

Jose Canalejas
HELLBENDERS, THE(1967, U.S./Ital./Span.); FEW BULLETS MORE, A(1968, Ital./Span.); GOD FORGIVES–I DON'T!(1969, Ital./Span.); MERCENARY, THE(1970, Ital./Span.)

Pedro Canalejas
MINUTE TO PRAY, A SECOND TO DIE, A(1968, Ital.)

Ricardo Canales
DOLORES(1949, Span.); INVINCIBLE GLADIATOR, THE(1963, c.u. Ital./Span.); UGLY ONES, THE(1968, Ital./Span.)

Susana Canales
JOHN PAUL JONES(1959); REVOLT OF THE MERCENARIES(1964, Ital./Span.)

Anna Maria Canali
RIGOLETTO(1949)

Lee Canalito
PARADISE ALLEY(1978)

Luca Canardi
NIGHT OF THE SHOOTING STARS, THE(1982, Ital.)

David Canary
HOMBRE(1967); ST. VALENTINE'S DAY MASSACRE, THE(1967); POSSE(1975); SHARK'S TREASURE(1975)
Misc. Talkies
JOHNNY FIRECLOUD(1975)

Gonzalo Canas
ADVENTURES OF SCARAMOUCHE, THE(1964, Fr.)

Bobby Canavarro
CLEOPATRA JONES AND THE CASINO OF GOLD(1975 U. S. Hong Kong)

Bill Canaway
IPCRESS FILE, THE(1965, Brit.), w

W. H. Canaway
BOY TEN FEET TALL, A(1965, Brit.), w

Linda Canby
NO WAY TO TREAT A LADY(1968)

Jacques Cancellier
1984
CHEECH AND CHONG'S THE CORSICAN BROTHERS(1984)

Alba Cancellieri
JULIET OF THE SPIRITS(1965, Fr./Ital./W.Ger.)

Antonella Cancellieri
LA NUIT DE VARENNES(1983, Fr./Ital.)

Antonia Cancellieri
NEST OF VIPERS(1979, Ital.)

Franco Cancellieri
IL GRIDO(1962, U.S./Ital.), p; GIRL GAME(1968, Braz./Fr./Ital.), p

Vladislav Cancura
CAPRICIOUS SUMMER(1968, Czech.), w

Ozualdo R. Candeias
MARGIN, THE,(1969, Braz.), p, d&w

Tom Candela
NIGHT SHIFT(1982)

Stelio Candelli
NIGHTS OF LUCRETIA BORGIA, THE(1960, Ital.); PLANET OF THE VAMPIRES(1965, U.S./Ital./Span.); LA CAGE AUX FOLLES II(1981, Ital./Fr.)

Stellio Candelli
HERCULES(1983)

Daniel Candib
ONE FROM THE HEART(1982)

Catherine Candida
FIRST TASTE OF LOVE(1962, Fr.)

Candy Candido
SOMETHING TO SING ABOUT(1937); COWBOY FROM BROOKLYN(1938); ONLY ANGELS HAVE WINGS(1939); CAMPUS RHYTHM(1943); RHYTHM PARADE(1943); SARGE GOES TO COLLEGE(1947); SMART POLITICS(1948); PETER PAN(1953); PLUNDERERS OF PAINTED FLATS(1959); SLEEPING BEAUTY(1959); PHANTOM TOLLBOOTH, THE(1970); HEY, GOOD LOOKIN'(1982)

Cindy Candido
GREAT RUPERT, THE(1950)

Johnny "Candy" Candido
ROBERTA(1935)

N. Candido
HUD(1963)

Nino Candido
PEACE KILLERS, THE(1971)

Joseph Candiotti
CINDERELLA LIBERTY(1973)

Doffy Candler
THIS STUFF'LL KILL YA!(1971)

Pete Candoli
KINGS GO FORTH(1958)

John Candy
IT SEEMED LIKE A GOOD IDEA AT THE TIME(1975, Can.); CLOWN MURDERS, THE(1976, Can.); LOST AND FOUND(1979); SILENT PARTNER, THE(1979, Can.); 1941(1979); BLUES BROTHERS, THE(1980); HEAVY METAL(1981, Can.); STRIPES(1981); GOING BERSERK(1983); NATIONAL LAMPOON'S VACATION(1983)
1984
SPLASH(1984)

Reuben Candy
MAD DOCTOR OF BLOOD ISLAND, THE(1969, Phil./U.S.), w

Candy & Coco
SADIE MCKEE(1934)

Candy and Coco
GIFT OF GAB(1934)

Charles Cane
TRUE TO LIFE(1943); MAYOR OF HELL, THE(1933); UNHOLY PARTNERS(1941); ALL THROUGH THE NIGHT(1942); BELLS OF CAPISTRANO(1942); BEYOND THE BLUE HORIZON(1942); LADY IN A JAM(1942); LUCKY JORDAN(1942); MAN IN THE TRUNK, THE(1942); MY FAVORITE BLONDE(1942); QUIET PLEASE, MURDER(1942); ALWAYS A BRIDESMAID(1943); DIXIE(1943); GILDERSLEEVE'S BAD DAY(1943); HELLO, FRISCO, HELLO(1943); HENRY ALDRICH HAUNTS A HOUSE(1943); HAIRY APE, THE(1944); LADY AND THE MONSTER, THE(1944); MRS. PARKINGTON(1944); SEVEN DAYS ASHORE(1944); DON JUAN QUILLIGAN(1945); DUFFY'S TAVERN(1945); LADY ON A TRAIN(1945); NOB HILL(1945); DARK CORNER, THE(1946); IT SHOULDN'T HAPPEN TO A DOG(1946); KID FROM BOOKLYN, THE(1946); VALLEY OF THE ZOMBIES(1946); DEAD RECKONING(1947); FRAMED(1947); GUILT OF JANET AMES, THE(1947); DARK PAST, THE(1948); FIGHTING MAD(1948); TENTH AVENUE ANGEL(1948); CALAMITY JANE AND SAM BASS(1949); FIGHTING KENTUCKIAN, THE(1949); GAL WHO TOOK THE WEST, THE(1949); PRISON WARDEN(1949); STREETS OF SAN FRANCISCO(1949); BLONDE BANDIT, THE(1950); CONVICTED(1950); IN A LONELY PLACE(1950); SOUTHSIDE 1-1000(1950); WOMAN ON PIER 13, THE(1950); BELLE LE GRAND(1951); BORN YESTERDAY(1951); NATIVE SON(1951, U.S., Arg.); SOLDIERS THREE(1951); KANSAS CITY CONFIDENTIAL(1952); LONE STAR(1952); MODELS, INC.(1952); RUBY GENTRY(1952); SCANDAL SHEET(1952); BIG HEAT, THE(1953); NO ESCAPE(1953); PERILOUS JOURNEY, A(1953); CRIME WAVE(1954); DANGEROUS MISSION(1954); LUCKY ME(1954); SHE COULDN'T SAY NO(1954); PRINCE OF PLAYERS(1955); REVENGE OF THE CREATURE(1955); DAY OF FURY, A(1956); STEEL JUNGLE, THE(1956); GUN BATTLE AT MONTEREY(1957); GAMBLER WORE A GUN, THE(1961)

Elliot W. Cane
1984
GREYSTOKE: THE LEGEND OF TARZAN, LORD OF THE APES(1984)

James Cane
HAROLD AND MAUDE(1971), set d

Jimmy Cane
JONIKO AND THE KUSH TA KA(1969)

Sid Cane
CASE OF PATTY SMITH, THE(1962)

Violet Cane
Silents
UNHOLY THREE, THE(1925)

Roberto Canedo
TREASURE OF THE SIERRA MADRE, THE(1948); DOCTOR OF DOOM(1962, Mex.)

Evadney Canegata
COOL WORLD, THE(1963)

Pheta Canegata
COOL WORLD, THE(1963)

William Canegata
COOL WORLD, THE(1963)

Antonio Canelli
REVOLT OF THE MERCENARIES(1964, Ital./Span.), p

John Canemaker
WORLD ACCORDING TO GARP, The(1982), anim

Alberto Canepa
1984
NOSTALGHIA(1984, USSR/Ital.)

Mario Canerini
SPIRIT AND THE FLESH, THE(1948, Ital.), p, w

George Canes
RIDER IN THE NIGHT, THE(1968, South Africa), art d

Francisco Canet
SAVAGE GUNS, THE(1962, U.S./Span.), art d; VIRIDIANA(1962, Mex./Span.), art d; GUNFIGHTERS OF CASA GRANDE(1965, U.S./Span.), art d; SCHEHERAZADE(1965, Fr./Ital./Span.), art d; MINNESOTA CLAY(1966, Ital./Fr./Span.), set d; SIX DAYS A WEEK(1966, Fr./Ital./Span.), set d; ISLAND OF THE DOOMED(1968, Span./Ger.), art d; UGLY ONES, THE(1968, Ital./Span.), art d

Maria Canete
MAD QUEEN, THE(1950, Span.)

Sergio Canevari
FACE IN THE RAIN, A(1963), art d; 00-2 MOST SECRET AGENTS(1965, Ital.), spec eff; SALVATORE GIULIANO(1966, Ital.), art d; WE STILL KILL THE OLD WAY(1967, Ital.), art d; BRUTE AND THE BEAST, THE(1968, Ital.), art d; DAY OF THE OWL, THE(1968, Ital./Fr.), art d; SARDINIA: RANSOM(1968, Ital.), art d; MAFIA(1969, Fr./Ital.), art d; BURN(1970), art d; QUIET PLACE IN THE COUNTRY, A(1970, Ital./Fr.), art d

Sergio Canevasi
PLUCKED(1969, Fr./Ital.), art d

Elsa Canevazzi
FACTS OF MURDER, THE(1965, Ital.)

Gianni Canfarelli
MOSES AND AARON(1975, Ger./Fr./Ital.), ph

Alyce Canfield
MODELS, INC.(1952), w; DEATH OVER MY SHOULDER(1958, Brit.), w

Bill Canfield
MADE FOR EACH OTHER(1971), set d

Don Canfield
Misc. Talkies
BEWARE THE BLACK WIDOW(1968)

Doris Canfield
CROSBY CASE, THE(1934); BIG BROWN EYES(1936)

Dorothy Canfield
TWO HEADS ON A PILLOW(1934), w

Kid Canfield
Silents
KID CANFIELD THE REFORM GAMBLER(1922), a, w&d

Mark Canfield [Darryl F. Zanuck]
MY MAN(1928), w; MADONNA OF AVENUE A(1929), w; MAYBE IT'S LOVE(1930), w; BABY FACE(1933), w; CRACK IN THE MIRROR(1960), w

Mary Grace Canfield
POLLYANNA(1960); DON'T MAKE WAVES(1967); ST. VALENTINE'S DAY MASSACRE, THE(1967); SOMETHING WICKED THIS WAY COMES(1983)
Misc. Talkies
HALF A HOUSE(1979)

William Canfield
Silents
KNIGHT OF THE RANGE, A(1916)
Misc. Silents
GLORIANA(1916)

Bruno Canfora
IT HAPPENED IN BROAD DAYLIGHT(1960, Ger./Switz.), m; MAN WHO WAGGED HIS TAIL, THE(1961, Ital./Span.), m; HUNS, THE(1962, Fr./Ital.), m

Hans Caninberg
HAMLET(1962, Ger.)

Hans Caninenberg
ODESSA FILE, THE(1974, Brit./Ger.)

James Canino
YOUNG AND DANGEROUS(1957); OCEAN'S ELEVEN(1960); INCIDENT IN AN ALLEY(1962); PARADISE ALLEY(1962)

Jim Canino
PLUNDER ROAD(1957)

Anna Canitano
FLESH AND BLOOD(1951, Brit.)

Angel Canizares
SAVAGE PAMPAS(1967, Span./Arg.), art d

Jose Canizares
STRANGE WORLD(1952), ed

Alex Cann
KANGAROO(1952)

Alexander Cann
NED KELLY(1970, Brit.); DEMONSTRATOR(1971, Aus.)

Bert Cann
Silents
JAILBIRD, THE(1920), ph; CHICKENS(1921), ph; ONE A MINUTE(1921), ph; ROOKIE'S RETURN, THE(1921), ph; SECOND HAND ROSE(1922), ph

David Cann
1984
1984(1984, Brit.)

Gary Cann
HOVERBUG(1970, Brit.)

Sally Cann
TO SIR, WITH LOVE(1967, Brit.)

Richard Cannaday
BEYOND AND BACK(1978)

Enzo Cannalvale
WHITE SISTER(1973, Ital./Span./Fr.)

Denis Cannan
ALIVE AND KICKING(1962, Brit.), w; TAMAHINE(1964, Brit.), w; WHY BOTHER TO KNOCK(1964, Brit.), w; AMOROUS ADVENTURES OF MOLL FLANDERS, THE(1965), w; BOY TEN FEET TALL, A(1965, Brit.), w; HIGH WIND IN JAMAICA, A(1965), w; MAYERLING(1968, Brit./Fr.), w; TELL ME LIES(1968, Brit.), w

Dennis Cannan
BEGGAR'S OPERA, THE(1953), a, w

Orio Cannarozzo
WE STILL KILL THE OLD WAY(1967, Ital.)

Enrica R. Cannataro
THIEF(1981)

Helena Canneli
JOY(1983, Fr./Can.)

Robert Hammer Cannerday
SCARFACE(1983)

Heather Canning
PERSECUTION AND ASSASSINATION OF JEAN-PAUL MARAT AS PERFORMED BY THE INMATES OF THE ASYLUM OF CHARENTON UNDER THE DIRECTION OF THE MARQUIS DE SADE, THE(1967, Brit.)

James Canning
BOYS IN COMPANY C, THE(1978, U.S./Hong Kong)

Jim Canning
FOG, THE(1980)

Thomas Canning
Silents
GENERAL POST(1920, Brit.); MONTY WORKS THE WIRES(1921, Brit.)

Victor Canning
GOLDEN SALAMANDER(1950, Brit.), w; SPY HUNT(1950), w; ASSASSIN, THE(1953, Brit.), w; HOUSE OF THE SEVEN HAWKS, THE(1959), w; MASQUERADE(1965, Brit.), w; LIMBO LINE, THE(1969, Brit.), w; SHARK(1970, U.S./Mex.), w; FAMILY PLOT(1976), w

Mitchell Cannold
GO TELL THE SPARTANS(1978), p

Greg Cannom
SWORD AND THE SORCERER, THE(1982), makeup

Bob Cannon
MELODY TIME(1948), animators

Carol Cannon
RACE WITH THE DEVIL(1975)

Chris Cannon
TALES FROM THE CRYPT(1972, Brit.)

Christopher Cannon
MISTER BROWN(1972)

David Cannon
Misc. Talkies
SEVERED ARM(1973)

Debbie Cannon
OPERATION EICHMANN(1961)

Diane [Dyan] Cannon
THIS REBEL BREED(1960)

Doc Pomeroy Cannon
Misc. Silents
PIDGIN ISLAND(1916)

"Doc" Pomeroy Cannon
Silents
PARSON OF PANAMINT, THE(1916)

Doran William Cannon
SKIDOO(1968), w; BREWSTER McCLOUD(1970), w; HEX(1973), w

Dyan Cannon
RISE AND FALL OF LEGS DIAMOND, THE(1960); BOB AND CAROL AND TED AND ALICE(1969); ANDERSON TAPES, THE(1971); DOCTORS' WIVES(1971); LOVE MACHINE, THE,(1971); SUCH GOOD FRIENDS(1971); BURGLARS, THE(1972, Fr./Ital.); LAST OF SHEILA, THE(1973); SHAMUS(1973); CHILD UNDER A LEAF(1975, Can.); HEAVEN CAN WAIT(1978); REVENGE OF THE PINK PANTHER(1978); COAST TO COAST(1980); HONEYSUCKLE ROSE(1980); AUTHOR! AUTHOR!(1982); DEATHTRAP(1982)

Edward Cannon
GOING IN STYLE(1979), w

Esma Cannon
FIVE POUND MAN, THE(1937, Brit.); LAST ADVENTURERS, THE(1937, Brit); I SEE ICE(1938); I MET A MURDERER(1939, Brit.); TROUBLE BREWING(1939, Brit.); U-BOAT 29(1939, Brit.); IT'S IN THE AIR(1940, Brit.); POISON PEN(1941, Brit.); QUIET WEDDING(1941, Brit.); YOUNG MR. PITT, THE(1942, Brit.); IT'S IN THE BAG(1943, Brit.); DON'T TAKE IT TO HEART(1944, Brit.); WAY AHEAD, THE(1945, Brit.); HOLIDAY CAMP(1947, Brit.); YEARS BETWEEN, THE(1947, Brit.); JASSY(1948, Brit.); FOOLS RUSH IN(1949, Brit.); HER MAN GILBEY(1949, Brit.); HUGGETTS ABROAD, THE(1949, Brit.); MARRY ME!(1949, Brit.); LAST HOLIDAY(1950, Brit.); CROW HOLLOW(1952, Brit.); DOUBLE CONFESSION(1953, Brit.); NOOSE FOR A LADY(1953, Brit.); STEEL KEY, THE(1953, Brit.); SLEEPING TIGER, THE(1954, Brit.); TOUCH OF THE SUN, A(1956, Brit.); OUT OF THE CLOUDS(1957, Brit.); PANIC IN THE PARLOUR(1957, Brit.); FURTHER UP THE CREEK!(1958, Brit.); THREE MEN IN A BOAT(1958, Brit.); EXPRESSO BONGO(1959, Brit.); I'M ALL RIGHT, JACK(1959, Brit.); JACK THE RIPPER(1959, Brit.); DOCTOR IN LOVE(1960, Brit.); INN FOR TROUBLE(1960, Brit.); BEWARE OF CHILDREN(1961, Brit.); CARRY ON REGARDLESS(1961, Brit.); MANIA(1961, Brit.); OVER THE ODDS(1961, Brit.); CARRY ON CRUISING(1962, Brit.); ON THE BEAT(1962, Brit.); ROOMMATES(1962, Brit.); WE JOINED THE NAVY(1962, Brit.); WHAT A CARVE UP!(1962, Brit.); CARRY ON CABBIE(1963, Brit.); FAST LADY, THE(1963, Brit.); HIDE AND SEEK(1964, Brit.); IN THE DOGHOUSE(1964, Brit.); NURSE ON WHEELS(1964, Brit.)

Esme Cannon
GUILT IS MY SHADOW(1950, Brit.)

Freddy Cannon
JUST FOR FUN(1963, Brit.); VILLAGE OF THE GIANTS(1965); JUNKMAN, THE(1982)

Glenn Cannon
COP HATER(1958); MAD DOG COLL(1961)

J.D. Cannon
AMERICAN DREAM, AN(1966); COOL HAND LUKE(1967); HEAVEN WITH A GUN(1969); KRAKATOA, EAST OF JAVA(1969); 1,000 PLANE RAID, THE(1969); COTTON COMES TO HARLEM(1970); LAWMAN(1971); SCORPIO(1973); RAISE THE TITANIC(1980, Brit.); DEATH WISH II(1982)
Misc. Talkies
ASYLUM FOR A SPY(1967)

Jack Cannon
ZELIG(1983)

Jimmy Cannon
POCKETFUL OF MIRACLES(1961), w

Joyce Cannon
MELODY AND ROMANCE(1937, Brit.); DOWN OUR ALLEY(1939, Brit.)

Kathy Cannon
FOOLS' PARADE(1971); PRIVATE DUTY NURSES(1972)

Kerry Cannon
PUNISHMENT PARK(1971)

Mary Cannon
SEED OF INNOCENCE(1980)
Misc. Talkies
TRUCKIN' MAN(1975)

Maureen Cannon
GALS, INCORPORATED(1943); GET GOING(1943)

Maurice Cannon
ROOTS OF HEAVEN, THE(1958)
Silents
ALASKAN, THE(1924); LOVE'S WILDERNESS(1924); SIDESHOW OF LIFE, THE(1924)

Michael Cannon
1984
TORCHLIGHT(1984), m

Norman Cannon
DISRAELI(1929); ANNIE, LEAVE THE ROOM(1935, Brit.), w

Orin Cannon
BURNT OFFERINGS(1976)

P. J. Cannon
Silents
HONOR SYSTEM, THE(1917)

Peter Cannon
RIDE IN THE WHIRLWIND(1966)

Pierre Cannon
TARGET: HARRY(1980)

Pomeroy Cannon
Silents
FOUR HORSEMEN OF THE APOCALYPSE, THE(1921)
Misc. Silents
MICROSCOPE MYSTERY, THE(1916); TRIFLING WOMEN(1922)

Pomeroy Doc Cannon
Silents
GOOD BAD MAN, THE(1916)

Pomeroy "Doc" Cannon
Misc. Silents
STAR ROVER, THE(1920)

Poppy Cannon
1984
EVIL THAT MEN DO, THE(1984), cos
Ray Cannon
OUTER GATE, THE(1937), d
Raymond Cannon
WHY LEAVE HOME?(1929), d; LADIES MUST PLAY(1930), p&d; HOTEL VARIE-TY(1933), d; SWING IT SAILOR(1937), d; SAMURAI(1945), d&w
Misc. Talkies
SWANEE RIVER(1931), d; BEHIND PRISON BARS(1937), d
Silents
NUGGET NELL(1919); OUT OF LUCK(1919); TRUE HEART SUSIE(1919); CHICK-ENS(1921); WATCH YOUR STEP(1922); NEVER SAY DIE(1924), w; GO WEST(1925), w; INTRODUCE ME(1925), w; CARNIVAL GIRL, THE(1926), w, t; TAXI! TAXI!(1927), w; RED WINE(1928), d, w; JOY STREET(1929), d, w
Misc. Silents
TURNING THE TABLES(1919); PENNY OF TOP HILL TRAIL(1921)
Robert J. Cannon
TOUCH OF FLESH, THE(1960)
Sherrill Cannon
GREAT MUPPET CAPER, THE(1981)
Thomas D. Cannon II
STUDENT BODIES(1981)
Tony Cannon
POST OFFICE INVESTIGATOR(1949)
Vince Cannon
BLADE(1973); TRACKDOWN(1976); YOUNGBLOOD(1978)
Misc. Talkies
MANHANDLERS, THE(1975)
William Cannon
SQUARE ROOT OF ZERO, THE(1964), p, d, w; SKIDOO(1968)
The Cannonball Adderley Quintet
PLAY MISTY FOR ME(1971)
Julie Cannons
DIAMOND STUD(1970)
Eddie Cano
FUN IN ACAPULCO(1963)
Lt. Col. Luis Cano
PRIDE AND THE PASSION, THE(1957), tech adv
Jean Canolle
THREE FACES OF SIN(1963, Fr./Ital.), w
David Canon
ADVENTURERS, THE(1970)
Jack Canon
Misc. Talkies
AXE(1977); LISA(1977)
Peter Canon
NEW KIND OF LOVE, A(1963); HINDENBURG, THE(1975); TOM HORN(1980)
Milena Canonero
CLOCKWORK ORANGE, A(1971, Brit.), cos; MIDNIGHT EXPRESS(1978, Brit.), cos; SHINING, THE(1980), cos; CHARRIOTS OF FIRE(1981, Brit.), cos; HUNGER, THE(1983), cos
1984
COTTON CLUB, THE(1984), cos; GIVE MY REGARDS TO BROAD STREET(1984, Brit.), cos
Juan Canos
UP THE SANDBOX(1972)
Anne Canova
IN CALIENTE(1935); ARTISTS AND MODELS(1937); THRILL OF A LIFETI-ME(1937)
Diana Canova
FIRST NUDIE MUSICAL, THE(1976)
Judy Canova
GOING HIGHBROW(1935); IN CALIENTE(1935); ARTISTS AND MODELS(1937); THRILL OF A LIFETIME(1937); SCATTERBRAIN(1940); PUDDIN' HEAD(1941); SIS HOPKINS(1941); JOAN OF OZARK(1942); SLEEPYTIME GAL(1942); TRUE TO THE ARMY(1942); CHATTERBOX(1943); SLEEPY LAGOON(1943); LOUISIANA HAY-RIDE(1944); HIT THE HAY(1945); SINGIN' IN THE CORN(1946); HONEY-CHILE(1951); OKLAHOMA ANNIE(1952); WAC FROM WALLA WALLA, THE(1952); UNTAMED HEIRESS(1954); CAROLINA CANNONBALL(1955); LAY THAT RIFLE DOWN(1955); ADVENTURES OF HUCKLEBERRY FINN, THE(1960); CANNON-BALL(1976, U.S./Hong Kong)
Pete Canova
IN CALIENTE(1935)
Tweeny Canova
UNTAMED HEIRESS(1954); LAY THAT RIFLE DOWN(1955)
Zeke Canova
IN CALIENTE(1935); ARTISTS AND MODELS(1937); THRILL OF A LIFETI-ME(1937)
The Canova Family
BROADWAY GONDOLIER(1935)
Antonio Canovas
ISLAND OF THE DOOMED(1968, Span./Ger.), ed
Reuben Canoy
PASSIONATE STRANGERS, THE(1968, Phil.), d&w
George Cansdale
SIMON AND LAURA(1956, Brit.)
Jacques Canselier
1984
UNTIL SEPTEMBER(1984)
Carmela Cansino
DOWN MEXICO WAY(1941); MASKED RIDER, THE(1941); TOO MANY BLON-DES(1941); RIDE 'EM COWBOY(1942)
Carmella Cansino
ALOMA OF THE SOUTH SEAS(1941)
Del Cansino
CITIZEN SAINT(1947)

Eduardo Cansino
CALL OF THE FLESH(1930), ch; GOLDEN DAWN(1930), ch; DANTE'S INFER-NO(1935), ch; LOVES OF CARMEN, THE(1948), ch; SALOME(1953); SOM-BRERO(1953)
Eduardo Cansino, Jr.
MISS SADIE THOMPSON(1953); MISSISSIPPI GAMBLER, THE(1953)
Enrique Cansino
MY BROTHER, THE OUTLAW(1951)
Jose Cansino
TOO MANY BLONDES(1941); LOVES OF CARMEN, THE(1948)
Vernon Cansino
SONG OF MY HEART(1947); LADY FROM SHANGHAI, THE(1948); LOVES OF CARMEN, THE(1948); MADONNA OF THE DESERT(1948)
Rita Cansino [Rita Hayworth]
CHARLIE CHAN IN EGYPT(1935); DANTE'S INFERNO(1935); PADDY O'DAY(1935); UNDER THE PAMPAS MOON(1935); HUMAN CARGO(1936); MEET NERO WOLFE(1936); HIT THE SADDLE(1937); TROUBLE IN TEXAS(1937); OLD LOUISIANA(1938); REBELLION(1938)
Misc. Talkies
REBELLION(1936)
Larry Cansler
SMOKEY AND THE BANDIT–PART 3(1983), m
1984
SONGWRITER(1984), m
Antonio Cantafora
DIRTY OUTLAWS, THE(1971, Ital.); BARON BLOOD(1972, Ital.)
1984
GABRIELA(1984, Braz.)
Gene Cantamessa
SEXTETTE(1978), m
Francesco Cantania
FORCE OF ARMS(1951)
Gil Cantanzaro, Jr.
ON THE RIGHT TRACK(1981)
Gil Cantanzaro, Sr.
ON THE RIGHT TRACK(1981)
Dario Cantarelli
NIGHT OF THE SHOOTING STARS, THE(1982, Ital.)
Nicola Cantatore
SEVEN SEAS TO CALAIS(1963, Ital.), art d
Kieran Canter
LONELY LADY, THE(1983)
1984
BURIED ALIVE(1984, Ital.)
Stanley Canter
ST. IVES(1976), p
Stanley S. Canter
HORNET'S NEST(1970), p; W. W. AND THE DIXIE DANCEKINGS(1975), p
1984
GREYSTOKE: THE LEGEND OF TARZAN, LORD OF THE APES(1984), p
Rosa Canterbet [Rosalino Caterbetti]
HEAT(1970, Arg.), ed
Jo Canterbury
TEEN-AGE STRANGLER(1967)
George Cantero
MORE AMERICAN GRAFFITI(1979); ESCAPE ARTIST, THE(1982)
1984
COTTON CLUB, THE(1984)
Cantinflas
AROUND THE WORLD IN 80 DAYS(1956); PEPE(1960); POR MIS PISTOLAS(1969, Mex.)
Guido Cantini
ETERNAL MELODIES(1948, Ital.), w
Charles Cantley
LIEUTENANT DARING, RN(1935, Brit.)
Shorty Cantlon
CROWD ROARS, THE(1932)
Wanda Cantlon
REPENT AT LEISURE(1941); HER HUSBAND'S AFFAIRS(1947); FOLLOW ME QUIETLY(1949); KID FROM GOWER GULCH, THE(1949); MISS GRANT TAKES RICHMOND(1949); RED ROCK OUTLAW(1950)
Charles Canton
DUFFY'S TAVERN(1945)
Mark Canton
DIE LAUGHING(1980), p
Neil Canton
1984
ADVENTURES OF BUCKAROO BANZAI: ACROSS THE 8TH DIMENSION, THE(1984), p
Howard Cantonwine
MERRY-GO-ROUND OF 1938(1937); YOU CAN'T HAVE EVERYTHING(1937)
Al Cantor
BREAKDOWN(1953); PRINCE OF PIRATES(1953)
Charles Cantor
STOP, YOU'RE KILLING ME(1952)
Eddie Cantor
CAUGHT SHORT(1930), w; GLORIFYING THE AMERICAN GIRL(1930); WHOOPEE(1930); MR. LEMON OF ORANGE(1931), w; PALMY DAYS(1931), a, w; KID FROM SPAIN, THE(1932); ROMAN SCANDALS(1933); KID MILLIONS(1934); STRIKE ME PINK(1936); ALI BABA GOES TO TOWN(1937); FORTY LITTLE MOTHERS(1940); THANK YOUR LUCKY STARS(1943); HOLLYWOOD CAN-TEEN(1944), a, p; SHOW BUSINESS(1944), a, p; ZIEGFELD FOLLIES(1945), w; IF YOU KNEW SUSIE(1948), a, p; STORY OF WILL ROGERS, THE(1952)
Silents
KID BOOTS(1926); SPECIAL DELIVERY(1927), a, w
Gerald Aleck Cantor
HIDE IN PLAIN SIGHT(1980)

Gerald Cantor
SOLDIER, THE(1982)

Herman Cantor
I WOULDN'T BE IN YOUR SHOES(1948); MUSIC MAN(1948); MYSTERY OF THE GOLDEN EYE, THE(1948); TROUBLE MAKERS(1948); TWO TICKETS TO BROADWAY(1951); YOU'RE IN THE NAVY NOW(1951); ROAD TO BALI(1952)

Julius Cantor
DEMOBBED(1944, Brit.), w

Lisa Cantor
STEAGLE, THE(1971)

Russell Cantor
TONIGHT WE SING(1953)

Sam Cantor
GOING WILD(1931)

Early Cantrell
ONE MYSTERIOUS NIGHT(1944); KEEP YOUR POWDER DRY(1945); WEST OF THE ALAMO(1946)

Ray Cantrell
HELLCATS, THE(1968)

Tom Cantrell
Misc. Talkies
ZOMBIE ISLAND MASSACRE(1984)

William Cantrell
SAME TIME, NEXT YEAR(1978)

Dolores Cantu
FORCE: FIVE(1981)

Maxie Cantway
KID FROM SPAIN, THE(1932)

Maxine Cantway
GOLD DIGGERS OF 1933(1933); LITTLE GIANT, THE(1933); 42ND STREET(1933); TWO IN A CROWD(1936)

Colin J. Cantwell
2001: A SPACE ODYSSEY(1968, U.S./Brit.), spec eff

Marietta Canty
LADY IS WILLING, THE(1942); MAGNIFICENT DOPE, THE(1942); SILVER QUEEN(1942); SPOILERS, THE(1942); HEAVENLY BODY, THE(1943); MEXICAN SPITFIRE'S BLESSED EVENT(1943); THREE HEARTS FOR JULIA(1943); GOIN' TO TOWN(1944); IRISH EYES ARE SMILING(1944); LADY IN THE DARK(1944); LAKE PLACID SERENADE(1944); SUNDAY DINNER FOR A SOLDIER(1944); HOME SWEET HOMICIDE(1946); JOHNNY COMES FLYING HOME(1946); SEARCHING WIND, THE(1946); CRIMSON KEY, THE(1947); DEAR RUTH(1947); SEA OF GRASS, THE(1947); BEST MAN WINS(1948); CHICAGO DEADLINE(1949); DEAR WIFE(1949); MOTHER IS A FRESHMAN(1949); MY FOOLISH HEART(1949); BRIGHT LEAF(1950); FATHER OF THE BRIDE(1950); TOAST OF NEW ORLEANS, THE(1950); BELLE LE GRAND(1951); FATHER'S LITTLE DIVIDEND(1951); STREETCAR NAMED DESIRE, A(1951); VALENTINO(1951); BAD AND THE BEAUTIFUL, THE(1952); DREAMBOAT(1952); I DON'T CARE GIRL, THE(1952); MAN CALLED PETER, THE(1955); REBEL WITHOUT A CAUSE(1955)

Cindy Canuelas
FAME(1980)

Bobby C. Canup
I'D CLIMB THE HIGHEST MOUNTAIN(1951)

Vic Canupe
LIMIT, THE(1972)

Pat Canuso
UNCLE SCAM(1981)

Edward "Tap" Canutt
IN LOVE AND WAR(1958); STATE FAIR(1962)

Joe Canutt
FAR HORIZONS, THE(1955); BEN HUR(1959); SPARTACUS(1960); PATTON(1970), stunts; SKYJACKED(1972); WHEN THE LEGENDS DIE(1972), stunts; SOYLENT GREEN(1973), stunts; DROWNING POOL, THE(1975); LAST HARD MEN, THE(1976), stunts; MAC ARTHUR(1977), stunts; MOTHER LODE(1982), d

Takima Canutt
Misc. Silents
TWO-FISTED SHERIFF, A(1925)

Tap Canutt
STRANGER WORE A GUN, THE(1953); LAWLESS RIDER, THE(1954); SPARTACUS(1960); COWBOYS, THE(1972)

Yakima Canutt
BAR L RANCH(1930); CANYON HAWKS(1930); CHEYENNE KID, THE(1930), a, w; FIREBRAND JORDAN(1930); LONESOME TRAIL, THE(1930); RIDIN' LAW(1930); HURRICANE HORSEMAN(1931); TWO-FISTED JUSTICE(1931); WESTWARD BOUND(1931); BATTLING BUCKAROO(1932); CHEYENNE CYCLONE, THE(1932); LAW AND LAWLESS(1932); RIDERS OF THE GOLDEN GULCH(1932), a, w; FIGHTING TEXANS(1933); RIDERS OF DESTINY(1933), a, stunts; SCARLET RIVER(1933); TELEGRAPH TRAIL, THE(1933); VIA PONY EXPRESS(1933); BLUE STEEL(1934); LUCKY TEXAN, THE(1934); MAN FROM HELL, THE(1934); MAN FROM UTAH, THE(1934); 'NEATH THE ARIZONA SKIES(1934); RANDY RIDES ALONE(1934); SAGEBRUSH TRAIL(1934); STAR PACKER, THE(1934); TEXAS TORNADO(1934); WEST OF THE DIVIDE(1934); CIRCLE OF DEATH(1935); CYCLONE OF THE SADDLE(1935); DANTE'S INFERNO(1935); DAWN RIDER(1935); LAWLESS FRONTIER, THE(1935); LAWLESS RANGE(1935); PALS OF THE RANGE(1935); PARADISE CANYON(1935); ROUGH RIDING RANGER(1935); TEXAS TERROR(1935); CHARGE OF THE LIGHT BRIGADE, THE(1936); KING OF THE PECOS(1936); LONELY TRAIL, THE(1936); OREGON TRAIL, THE(1936); WESTWARD HO(1936); WILDCAT TROOPER(1936); WINDS OF THE WASTELAND(1936); COME ON, COWBOYS(1937); GHOST TOWN GOLD(1937); GUNSMOKE RANCH(1937); HEART OF THE ROCKIES(1937); HIT THE SADDLE(1937); PRAIRIE THUNDER(1937); RANGE DEFENDERS(1937); RIDERS OF THE DAWN(1937); RIDERS OF THE ROCKIES(1937); RIDERS OF THE WHISTLING SKULL(1937); ROARIN' LEAD(1937); TROUBLE IN TEXAS(1937); OVERLAND STAGE RAIDERS(1938); SANTA FE STAMPEDE(1938); TEN LAPS TO GO(1938); COWBOYS FROM TEXAS(1939); FRONTIER VENGEANCE(1939); GONE WITH THE WIND(1939); KANSAS TERRORS, THE(1939); LIGHT THAT FAILED, THE(1939), stunts; NIGHT RIDERS, THE(1939); STAGECOACH(1939); WYOMING OUTLAW(1939); CARSON CITY KID(1940); DARK COMMAND, THE(1940); GHOST VALLEY RAIDERS(1940); OKLAHOMA RENEGADES(1940); ONE MILLION B.C.(1940), stunts; PIONEERS OF THE WEST(1940); RANGER AND THE LADY, THE(1940); UNDER TEXAS SKIES(1940); GAUCHOS OF EL DORADO(1941); GREAT TRAIN ROBBERY, THE(1941); KANSAS CYCLONE(1941); NEVADA CITY(1941);

PRAIRIE PIONEERS(1941); SHADOWS ON THE SAGE(1942); CALLING WILD BILL ELLIOTT(1943); FOR WHOM THE BELL TOLLS(1943); KING OF THE COWBOYS(1943); SANTA FE SCOUTS(1943); SONG OF TEXAS(1943); HIDDEN VALLEY OUTLAWS(1944); PRIDE OF THE PLAINS(1944); SHERIFF OF CIMARRON(1945), d; CARSON CITY RAIDERS(1948), d; OKLAHOMA BADLANDS(1948), d; SONS OF ADVENTURE(1948), d; ROCKY MOUNTAIN(1950); SHOWDOWN, THE(1950); LAWLESS RIDER, THE(1954), d; EL CID(1961, U.S./Ital.), stunts; WHERE EAGLES DARE(1968, Brit.), stunts
Misc. Talkies
TEXAN'S HONOR, A(1929); PUEBLO TERROR(1931); GUNS FOR HIRE(1932); TEXAN, THE(1932); WYOMING WHIRLWIND(1932); FIGHTING THROUGH(1934); OUTLAW RULE(1935)
Silents
GIRL WHO DARED, THE(1920); BRANDED A BANDIT(1924); RIDIN' MAD(1924)
Misc. Silents
FORBIDDEN RANGE, THE(1923); CACTUS CURE, THE(1925); HUMAN TORNADO, THE(1925); RIDIN' COMET(1925); ROMANCE AND RUSTLERS(1925); SCAR HANAN(1925); STRANGE RIDER(1925); WHITE THUNDER(1925); WOLVES OF THE ROAD(1925); DESERT GREED(1926); DEVIL HORSE, THE(1926); FIGHTING STALLION, THE(1926); BAD MEN'S MONEY(1929); CAPTAIN COWBOY(1929); RIDERS OF THE STORM(1929); THREE OUTCASTS, THE(1929)

Frank Canzano
1984
DELIVERY BOYS(1984)

Goffredo Canzano
SERAFINO(1970, Fr./Ital.)

Anna Canzi
FIANCES, THE(1964, Ital.)

Stefano Canzio
OPERATION KID BROTHER(1967, Ital.), w

Gabriel Canzona
FOREVER AND A DAY(1943); GANG'S ALL HERE, THE(1943); SWEET ROSIE O'GRADY(1943)

Tony Canzoneri
RINGSIDE(1949)

Gabriel Canzono
TWO SMART PEOPLE(1946)

Franz Cap
GREH(1962, Ger./Yugo.), d&w

Josef Cap
MATTER OF DAYS, A(1969, Fr./Czech.); SIGN OF THE VIRGIN(1969, Czech.)

Robert Capa
TEMPTATION(1946)

Frank Capacchione
LONGEST YARD, THE(1974), ed

Aldo Capacci
ANGELO IN THE CROWD(1952, Ital.)

Peter Capaldi
LOCAL HERO(1983, Brit.)

Otello Capanna
BEN HUR(1959)

Pietro Capanna
AVENGER, THE(1962, Fr./Ital.); SANDOKAN THE GREAT(1964, Fr./Ital./Span.); SECRET SEVEN, THE(1966, Ital./Span.)

Carlo Capannelle
SECRET OF SANTA VITTORIA, THE(1969)

Ernesto Caparros
MIRACLE WORKER, THE(1962), ph; WHAT'S SO BAD ABOUT FEELING GOOD?(1968), ph

P. Capdevielle
JUST A BIG, SIMPLE GIRL(1949, Fr.), m

Emil Cape
Misc. Talkies
SWEET SOUND OF DEATH(1965, U.S./Span.)

Giorgio Capecchi
SHIP OF CONDEMNED WOMEN, THE(1963, ITAL.)

Robert Capece
PARADES(1972); LINE, THE(1982)

Barney Capehart
KING KONG(1933)

Jimmy Capehorn
GO KART GO(1964, Brit.)

Karel Capek
LOSS OF FEELING(1935, USSR), w; SKELETON ON HORSEBACK(1940, Czech.), w; KRAKATIT(1948, Czech.), w

Fred Capel
JULES AND JIM(1962, Fr.), cos

Maxilyn Capel
BEYOND AND BACK(1978)

Jodie Capelan
SURF PARTY(1964), ed

Auguste Capelier
RIFIFI(1956, Fr.), art d; GIGOT(1962), art d; HORROR CHAMBER OF DR. FAUSTUS, THE(1962, Fr./Ital.), art d; BEHOLD A PALE HORSE(1964), art d; LADY L(1965, Fr./Ital.), art d; NIGHT OF THE GENERALS, THE(1967, Brit./Fr.), art d; FLEA IN HER EAR, A(1968, Fr.), art d; HELLO–GOODBYE(1970), art d; ONLY GAME IN TOWN, THE(1970), art d

Jad Capelja
PUBERTY BLUES(1983, Aus.)

Aina Capell
5 SINNERS(1961, Ger.); $100 A NIGHT(1968, Ger.)

Barbara Capell [Kapell]
WEREWOLF VS. THE VAMPIRE WOMAN, THE(1970, Span./Ger.)

Peter Capell
WALK EAST ON BEACON(1952); BURGLAR, THE(1956); PATHS OF GLORY(1957); FOR THE FIRST TIME(1959, U.S./Ger./Ital.); BETWEEN TIME AND ETERNITY(1960, Ger.); I AIM AT THE STARS(1960); ARMORED COMMAND(1961); BIG SHOW, THE(1961); ONE, TWO, THREE(1961); COUNTERFEIT TRAITOR, THE(1962); I DEAL IN DANGER(1966); ASSIGNMENT K(1968, Brit.); WILLY WONKA AND THE CHOCOLATE FACTORY(1971); ESCAPE TO THE SUN(1972, Fr./Ger./Israel); SOR-

CERER(1977); AMERICAN SUCCESS COMPANY, THE(1980)
1984
LITTLE DRUMMER GIRL, THE(1984)
Capella & Patricia
MOON OVER LAS VEGAS(1944)
Albert Capellaini
Silents
DAMSEL IN DISTRESS, A(1919), sup
Albert Capellani
Silents
COMMON LAW, THE(1916), d; AMERICAN MAID(1917), d; EYE FOR EYE(1918), d, w; OH, BOY!(1919), d&w; WILD GOOSE, THE(1921), d; SISTERS(1922), d
Misc. Silents
CAMILLE(1916), d; DARK SILENCE, THE(1916), d; LA VIE DE BOHEME(1916), d; EASIEST WAY, THE(1917), d; FOOLISH VIRGIN, THE(1917), d; DAYBREAK(1918), d; HOUSE OF MIRTH, THE(1918), d; RICHEST GIRL, THE(1918), d; SOCIAL HYPO-CRITES(1918), d; OUT OF THE FOG(1919), d; RED LANTERN, THE(1919), d; VIRTU-OUS MODEL, THE(1919), d; FORTUNE TELLER, THE(1920), d; YOUNG DIANA, THE(1922), d
Paul Capellani
Silents
COMMON LAW, THE(1916); ONE LAW FOR BOTH(1917)
Misc. Silents
CAMILLE(1916); DARK SILENCE, THE(1916); FEAST OF LIFE, THE(1916); RICH-EST GIRL, THE(1918); LE CARNIVAL DES VERITES(1920, Fr.); POSSESSION(1922, Brit.)
Frannye Capelle
ODE TO BILLY JOE(1976)
Jack Capelle
ODE TO BILLY JOE(1976)
Vittorio Capelli
TREE OF WOODEN CLOGS, THE(1979, Ital.)
Chris Capen
SWARM, THE(1978)
Boris Caper
GETTING OVER(1981), set d
John Caper
EQUINOX(1970), m
John Caper, Jr.
TRACK OF THUNDER(1967), md; POINT OF TERROR(1971), m; TRACK-DOWN(1976), md; JOYSTICKS(1983), m
Hedges Capers
WHO FEARS THE DEVIL(1972)
Virginia Capers
HOUSE OF WOMEN(1962); RIDE TO HANGMAN'S TREE, THE(1967); LOST MAN, THE(1969); GREAT WHITE HOPE, THE(1970); NORWOOD(1970); BIG JAKE(1971); LATE LIZ, THE(1971); SUPPORT YOUR LOCAL GUNFIGHTER(1971); LADY SINGS THE BLUES(1972); TROUBLE MAN(1972); FIVE ON THE BLACK HAND SIDE(1973); WORLD'S GREATEST ATHLETE, THE(1973); NORTH AVENUE IRREGULARS, THE(1979); TOY, THE(1982)
1984
TEACHERS(1984)
Renault Capes
DUAL ALIBI(1947, Brit.), w
Gwen Capetanos
SIXTH AND MAIN(1977), cos; MUPPET MOVIE, THE(1979), cos
L. Capetanos
Misc. Talkies
SUMMER RUN(1974), d
Leon Capetanos
SUMMER RUN(1974), a, d&w; GUMBALL RALLY, THE(1976), w; GREASED LIGHTNING(1977), w; TEMPEST(1982), w
1984
MOSCOW ON THE HUDSON(1984), w
Linda Capetta
ONLY WAY HOME, THE(1972)
David Capey
SECRET DOOR, THE(1964), ed
Lito Capina
CASTAWAY COWBOY, THE(1974)
Giorgio Capitani
VALIANT, THE(1962, Brit./Ital.), d, w; RUTHLESS FOUR, THE(1969, Ital./Ger.), d; I HATE BLONDES(1981, Ital.), d
Remo Capitani
ACE HIGH(1969, Ital.); GOD FORGIVES–I DON'T!(1969, Ital./Span.); THEY CALL ME TRINITY(1971, Ital.)
Roberto Capitani
LAST OF THE VIKINGS, THE(1962, Fr./Ital.), p; CAESAR THE CONQUEROR(1963, Ital.), p; FIVE GIANTS FROM TEXAS(1966, Ital./Span.), p
Don Capite
1984
HARRY AND SON(1984), w
Loretta Capitoli
NIGHTS OF CABIRIA(1957, Ital.); FACTS OF MURDER, THE(1965, Ital.)
Bill Capizzi
THEY CALL ME BRUCE(1982)
Benny Caplan
EXCUSE MY GLOVE(1936, Brit.)
Harry Caplan
CHARRO(1969), p
Jodie Caplan
GUILTY, THE(1947), ed; KILROY WAS HERE(1947), ed
Joseph B. Caplan
YANKEE FAKIR(1947), ed
Neil Caplan
1984
MIDSUMMER NIGHT'S DREAM, A(1984, Brit./Span.)

Phil Caplan
SOLOMON KING(1974), ph
Ronald I. Caplan
1984
WILD LIFE, THE(1984), cos
Rupert Caplan
FORBIDDEN JOURNEY(1950, Can.)
Twink Caplan
PENNIES FROM HEAVEN(1981)
Valerie Caplan
CHU CHU AND THE PHILLY FLASH(1981)
William B. Caplan
FINAL COMEDOWN, THE(1972), ph
Moran Caplat
ROYAL DIVORCE, A(1938, Brit.)
Norman Caplat
CHALLENGE, THE(1939, Brit.)
Scott Caple
RAIDERS OF THE LOST ARK(1981), anim
Carole Caplin
ACCIDENT(1967, Brit.)
Sidney Capo
DISTANT DRUMS(1951)
Anna Capodaglio
CARMELA(1949, Ital.)
John Capodice
Q(1982)
Tony Capodilupo
SIDELONG GLANCES OF A PIGEON KICKER, THE(1970); BELIEVE IN ME(1971); THEY MIGHT BE GIANTS(1971)
Renato Capogna
ACCATTONE!(1961, Ital.); HAWKS AND THE SPARROWS, THE(1967, Ital.)
Sergio Capogna
DIARY OF AN ITALIAN(1972, Ital.), d&w
Al Capogrossi
Misc. Talkies
BRANCHES(1971)
Pino Capogrosso
MIDAS RUN(1969), makeup
Enrico Capoleoni
STRANGER IN TOWN, A(1968, U.S./Ital.)
Lino Capolicchio
TAMING OF THE SHREW, THE(1967, U.S./Ital.); LAST DAYS OF MUSSOLINI(1974, Ital.); GARDEN OF THE FINZI-CONTINIS, THE(1976, Ital./Ger.); LION OF THE DESERT(1981, Libya/Brit.)
Edoardo Capolino
ALONE IN THE STREETS(1956, Ital.), p; EAST OF KILIMANJARO(1962, Brit./Ital.), p, d
Eduardo Capolino
FOUR WAYS OUT(1954, Ital.), p
Christopher Capon
SILVER DARLINGS, THE(1947, Brit.)
Paul Capon
RADIO LOVER(1936, Brit.), d; HIDDEN HOMICIDE(1959, Brit.), w
Clifford Capone
WINDOWS(1980), cos; TOUGH ENOUGH(1983), cos
Gino Capone
1984
CONQUEST(1984, Ital./Span./Mex.), w
Leonard Capone
WRONG MAN, THE(1956)
Aristide Caporale
AMARCORD(1974, Ital.)
Roberto Caporali
LA CAGE AUX FOLLES II(1981, Ital./Fr.)
Raffaele Caporilli
UNDER THE SUN OF ROME(1949, Ital.)
Truman Capote
BEAT THE DEVIL(1953), w; INDISCRETION OF AN AMERICAN WIFE(1954), w; BREAKFAST AT TIFFANY'S(1961), w; INNOCENTS, THE(1961, U.S./Brit.), w; TRU-MAN CAPOTE'S TRILOGY(1969), a, w; MURDER BY DEATH(1976)
Francesco Capotorto
THREE BROTHERS(1982, Ital.)
Maria Antonia Capotorto
THREE BROTHERS(1982, Ital.)
Jean Stanislas Capoul
1984
PERILS OF GWENDOLINE, THE(1984, Fr.)
Al Capp
LI'L ABNER(1940), w; THAT CERTAIN FEELING(1956); LI'L ABNER(1959), w
McClure Capp
ADVENTURES OF HUCKLEBERRY FINN, THE(1960), art d
Ernesto Capparos
ANDY(1965), ph
Joe Cappatta
1984
NO SMALL AFFAIR(1984)
Barbara Cappell
Misc. Talkies
WOMEN FOR SALE(1975)
Cappella and Patricia
COWBOY AND THE SENORITA(1944)
Albert Cappellani
Misc. Silents
INSIDE OF THE CUP, THE(1921), d
Paul Cappellani
Misc. Silents
LA VIE DE BOHEME(1916)

Claudio Cappelli
CONFORMIST, THE(1971, Ital., Fr)

Gian Carlo Cappelli
VOLCANO(1953, Ital.), ed

Giancarlo Cappelli
ANGELA(1955, Ital.), ed; DARK PURPOSE(1964), ed; TORPEDO BAY(1964, Ital./Fr.), ed; SWEET SMELL OF LOVE(1966, Ital./Ger.), ed; CANDY(1968, Ital./Fr.), ed

Graziana Cappellini
PRIEST OF LOVE(1981, Brit.)

Louis Cappetto
WILLIE AND PHIL(1980)

Joolia Cappleman
BLEAK MOMENTS(1972, Brit.)

Joe Cappo
ANGEL COMES TO BROOKLYN, AN(1945)

Joey Cappo
SUSPENSE(1946)

P.P. Capponi
SUBVERSIVES, THE(1967, Ital.)

Pier Paolo Capponi
KING OF HEARTS(1967, Fr./Ital.); SEATED AT HIS RIGHT(1968, Ital.); LADY OF MONZA, THE(1970, Ital.); CAT O'NINE TAILS(1971, Ital./Ger./Fr.); DIARY OF AN ITALIAN(1972, Ital.)

Vittorio Capprioli
MAGNIFICENT ONE, THE(1974, Fr./Ital.)

Al Capps
TRIBES(1970), m; WINDSPLITTER, THE(1971), m; CANNONBALL RUN, THE(1981), m; SHARKY'S MACHINE(1982), m; STROKER ACE(1983), m
1984
CANNONBALL RUN II(1984), m; HIGHWAY TO HELL(1984), m; RUNNING HOT(1984), m

H. McClure Capps
HARUM SCARUM(1965), art d

Henry Capps
PROUD AND THE DAMNED, THE(1972); DEATH WISH II(1982)

McClure Capps
PRIDE OF THE YANKEES, THE(1942), art d; NORTH STAR, THE(1943), art d; UP IN ARMS(1944), art d; WONDER MAN(1945), art d; RED HOUSE, THE(1947), art d; TARZAN AND THE HUNTRESS(1947), art d; TARZAN AND THE MERMAIDS(1948), art d; TARZAN'S MAGIC FOUNTAIN(1949), art d; TALES OF ROBIN HOOD(1951), art d; JACK AND THE BEANSTALK(1952), art d; CARELESS YEARS, THE(1957), art d; RIDE OUT FOR REVENGE(1957), art d; PROUD REBEL, THE(1958), art d; GO, JOHNNY, GO!(1959), art d

McLure Capps
MARAUDERS, THE(1947), ed

George Cappy
NEWS HOUNDS(1947), w

Cappy Barra Boys
RADIO STARS ON PARADE(1945)

The Cappy Barra Boys
ROCKIN' IN THE ROCKIES(1945)

Cappy Barra Harmonica Boys
SMART POLITICS(1948)

Cappy Barra's Harmonica Band
MAD ABOUT MUSIC(1938)

Frank Capra
DONOVAN AFFAIR, THE(1929), d; FLIGHT(1929), d, w; YOUNGER GENERATION(1929), d; LADIES OF LEISURE(1930), d; RAIN OR SHINE(1930), d; DIRIGIBLE(1931), d; MIRACLE WOMAN, THE(1931), d; PLATINUM BLONDE(1931), d; AMERICAN MADNESS(1932), d; FORBIDDEN(1932), d, w; BITTER TEA OF GENERAL YEN, THE(1933), d; LADY FOR A DAY(1933), d; BROADWAY BILL(1934), d; IT HAPPENED ONE NIGHT(1934), d; MR. DEEDS GOES TO TOWN(1936), p&d; LOST HORIZON(1937), p&d; YOU CAN'T TAKE IT WITH YOU(1938), p&d; MR. SMITH GOES TO WASHINGTON(1939), p&d; MEET JOHN DOE(1941), p&d; ARSENIC AND OLD LACE(1944), p&d; IT'S A WONDERFUL LIFE(1946), p&d, w; STATE OF THE UNION(1948), p&d; RIDING HIGH(1950), p&d; HERE COMES THE GROOM(1951), p&d; WESTWARD THE WOMEN(1951), w; HOLE IN THE HEAD, A(1959), p&d; POCKETFUL OF MIRACLES(1961), p&d
Silents
STRONG MAN, THE(1926), d, w; TRAMP, TRAMP, TRAMP(1926), w; LONG PANTS(1927), d; MATINEE IDOL, THE(1928), d; POWER OF THE PRESS, THE(1928), d; SO THIS IS LOVE(1928), d; WAY OF THE STRONG, THE(1928), d
Misc. Silents
FOR THE LOVE OF MIKE(1927), d; SAY IT WITH SABLES(1928), d; SUBMARINE(1928), d; THAT CERTAIN THING(1928), d

Frank Capra, Jr.
BILLY JACK GOES TO WASHINGTON(1977), p; BORN AGAIN(1978), p; BLACK MARBLE, THE(1980), p; EYE FOR AN EYE, AN(1981), p
1984
FIRESTARTER(1984), p

Jean Capra
TWO FOR DANGER(1940, Brit.); GIVE US THE MOON(1944, Brit.)

Sal A. Capra
SUPER VAN(1977), p

Tony Capra
SUMMERDOG(1977); LOVE IN A TAXI(1980)

Hugo Caprera
HAND IN THE TRAP, THE(1963, Arg./Span.)

Agnes Capri
MILKY WAY, THE(1969, Fr./Ital.)

Ahna Capri
COMPANY OF KILLERS(1970); DARKER THAN AMBER(1970); ENTER THE DRAGON(1973); SPECIALIST, THE(1975)
Misc. Talkies
PIRANHA, PIRANHA(1972); SPECIALIST, THE(1975)

Alaina Capri
GOOD MORNING... AND GOODBYE(1967)

Ann Capri
GIRLS ON THE BEACH(1965)

Anna Capri
KISSES FOR MY PRESIDENT(1964); ONE OF OUR SPIES IS MISSING(1966); BROTHERHOOD OF SATAN, THE(1971); PAYDAY(1972); BINGO LONG TRAVELING ALL-STARS AND MOTOR KINGS, THE(1976)

Juan Capri
UNSATISFIED, THE(1964, Span.)

Marcya Capri
Misc. Silents
MONEY MANIAC, THE(1921)

Tito Capri
PAYMENT IN BLOOD(1968, Ital.), w

Massimiliano Capriccioli
VIOLENT SUMMER(1961, Fr./Ital.), set d; CONJUGAL BED, THE(1963, Ital.), art d; RUN WITH THE DEVIL(1963, Fr./Ital.), art d; HE WHO SHOOTS FIRST(1966, Ital.), w; MINUTE TO PRAY, A SECOND TO DIE, A(1968, Ital.), art d

June Caprice
Silents
CAPRICE OF THE MOUNTAINS(1916); MISCHIEF MAKER, THE(1916); MODERN CINDERELLA, A(1917); DAMSEL IN DISTRESS, A(1919); OH, BOY!(1919); IN WALKED MARY(1920)
Misc. Silents
LITTLE MISS HAPPINESS(1916); RAGGED PRINCESS, THE(1916); CHILD OF THE WILD, A(1917); EVERY GIRL'S DREAM(1917); MISS U.S.A.(1917); PATSY(1917); SMALL TOWN GIRL, A(1917); UNKNOWN 274(1917); BLUE-EYED MARY(1918); CAMOUFLAGE KISS, A(1918); HEART OF ROMANCE, THE(1918); MISS INNOCENCE(1918); LOVE CHEAT, THE(1919); ROGUES AND ROMANCE(1920)

Anne Caprille
ANATOMY OF A MARRIAGE(MY DAYS WITH JEAN-MARC AND MY NIGHTS WITH FRANCOISE)**1/2 (1964 Fr.)

Rosa Caprino
SINGING BUCKAROO, THE(1937)

Carlo Caprioli
LISTEN, LET'S MAKE LOVE(1969, Fr./Ital.); SECRET OF SANTA VITTORIA, THE(1969)

Vittorio Caprioli
GENERALE DELLA ROVERE(1960, Ital./Fr.); NEOPOLITAN CAROUSEL(1961, Ital.); ZAZIE(1961, Fr.); ADIEU PHILLIPINE(1962, Fr./Ital.); MYTH, THE(1965, Ital.); VARIETY LIGHTS(1965, Ital.); WHITE VOICES(1965, Fr./Ital.); MAIDEN FOR A PRINCE, A(1967, Fr./Ital.); LISTEN, LET'S MAKE LOVE(1969, Fr./Ital.), d, w; TOUT VA BIEN(1973, Fr.); CATHERINE & CO.(1976, Fr.); CAFE EXPRESS(1980, Ital.); TRAGEDY OF A RIDICULOUS MAN, THE(1982, Ital.)

Vittorio Capriolli
WHERE THE HOT WIND BLOWS(1960, Fr., Ital.)

Mario Capriotti
TWO WOMEN(1961, Ital./Fr.), ph; GOLDEN ARROW, THE(1964, Ital.), ph; GUNMEN OF THE RIO GRANDE(1965, Fr./Ital./Span.), ph; JOHNNY YUMA(1967, Ital.), ph

Chantal Capron
1984
LE BAL(1984, Fr./Ital./Algeria)

Kate Capshaw
LITTLE SEX, A(1982)
1984
BEST DEFENSE(1984); DREAMSCAPE(1984); INDIANA JONES AND THE TEMPLE OF DOOM(1984); WINDY CITY(1984)

Capt. Bob Farnon
THIS MAN IS MINE(1946 Brit.)

Capt. John
SPECIAL AGENT K-7(1937)

"Captain" King of the Dogs
TIMBER TERRORS(1935)

Hal Captain
SUPPOSE THEY GAVE A WAR AND NOBODY CAME?(1970), w

Captain Boots
SILVER STALLION(1941)

John Capter, Jr.
HANG'EM HIGH(1968), md

Luigi Capuano
STORMBOUND(1951, Ital.), d; RED SHEIK, THE(1963, Ital.), w; TIGER OF THE SEVEN SEAS(1964, Fr./Ital.), d, w; MYSTERY OF THUG ISLAND, THE(1966, Ital./Ger.), d; LION OF ST. MARK(1967, Ital.), d, w
Misc. Talkies
FLYING SQUADRON(1952), d

Sam Capuano
PAY OR DIE(1960); HOODLUM PRIEST, THE(1961); CROSS AND THE SWITCHBLADE, THE(1970)

Fabrizio Capucci
GOLIATH AND THE BARBARIANS(1960, Ital.); DAVID AND GOLIATH(1961, Ital.); CRAZY DESIRE(1964, Ital.); EIGHTEEN IN THE SUN(1964, Ital.); RED LIPS(1964, Fr./Ital.); LOVE IN 4 DIMENSIONS(1965 Fr./Ital.); THEY CAME TO ROB LAS VEGAS(1969, Fr./Ital./Span./Ger.); TO COMMIT A MURDER(1970, Fr./Ital./Ger.)

Franco Capucci
WHITE SLAVE SHIP(1962, Fr./Ital.)

Roberto Capucci
TEOREMA(1969, Ital.), cos

Capucine
NORTH TO ALASKA(1960); SONG WITHOUT END(1960); LION, THE(1962, Brit.); WALK ON THE WILD SIDE(1962); PINK PANTHER, THE(1964); SEVENTH DAWN, THE(1964); WHAT'S NEW, PUSSYCAT?(1965, U.S./Fr.); HONEY POT, THE(1967, Brit.); QUEENS, THE(1968, Ital./Fr.); FELLINI SATYRICON(1969, Fr./Ital.); FRAULEIN DOKTOR(1969, Ital./Yugo.); RED SUN(1972, Fr./Ital./Span.); ARABIAN ADVENTURE(1979, Brit.); FROM HELL TO VICTORY(1979, Fr./Ital./Span.); JAGUAR LIVES(1979); NEST OF VIPERS(1979, Ital.); INCORRIGIBLE(1980, Fr.); CON ARTISTS, THE(1981, Ital.); TRAIL OF THE PINK PANTHER, THE(1982); CURSE OF THE PINK PANTHER(1983)

Bernard F. Caputo
DRIVE-IN(1976), ed; TOWING(1978), ed
Russell Car
OTHER PEOPLE'S SINS(1931, Brit.)
Car Hyson Dancers
STREET SINGER, THE(1937, Brit.)
The Car-Bert Dancers
IN OLD NEW MEXICO(1945)
Irene Cara
AARON LOVES ANGELA(1975); SPARKLE(1976); FAME(1980); D.C. CAB(1983)
1984
CITY HEAT(1984)
Gregorio Caraballo
W.I.A.(WOUNDED IN ACTION)*1/2 (1966), ed
James Carabatsos
HEROES(1977), w
Jim Carabatsos
BEYOND THE REEF(1981), w
Steve Carabatsos
TENTACLES(1977, Ital.), w
Steven Carabatsos
EL CONDOR(1970), w
Steven W. Carabatsos
REVENGERS, THE(1972, U.S./Mex.), w; LAST FLIGHT OF NOAH'S ARK, THE(1980), w
Mark Carabel
FIEND OF DOPE ISLAND(1961), w
Ezio Carabella
WHITE DEVIL, THE(1948, Ital.), m; DISHONORED(1950, Ital.), m; ISLAND OF PROCIDA, THE(1952, Ital.), m
Flora Carabella
END OF THE WORLD(in Our Usual Bed In a Night Full of Rain), THE*1/2 (1978, Ital.)
Fabrizio Caracciolo
SALAMANDER, THE(1983, U.S./Ital./Brit.), cos
Francesco Caracciolo
OPIATE '67(1967, Fr./Ital.)
Sacha Carafa
KREMLIN LETTER, THE(1970)
Christi Carafano
1984
SONGWRITER(1984)
Paul Carafotes
HEADIN' FOR BROADWAY(1980); ALL THE RIGHT MOVES(1983)
Misc. Talkies
CHOICES(1981)
Claudio Caramaschi
DEATH OF MARIO RICCI, THE(1983, Ital.)
Gian Carlo Caramello
CRAZY JOE(1974), m
Bob Caramico
BOSS NIGGER(1974), ph; MEAN JOHNNY BARROWS(1976), ph
Robert Caramico
ORGY OF THE DEAD(1965), ph; MOVIE STAR, AMERICAN STYLE, OR, LSD I HATE YOU!(1966), p, ph; ON HER BED OF ROSES(1966), p, ph; JOURNEY TO THE CENTER OF TIME(1967), ph; THAT TENDER TOUCH(1969), ph; GUESS WHAT HAPPENED TO COUNT DRACULA(1970), ph; WILD SCENE, THE(1970), ph; OCTA-MAN(1971), ph; DOBERMAN GANG, THE(1972), ph; HAPPY HOOKER GOES TO WASHINGTON, THE(1977), ph; SLUMBER PARTY '57(1977), ph; SLITHIS(1978), ph
Robert Caraminco
BLACK KLANSMAN, THE(1966), ph
Anna Caramini
8 ½(1963, Ital.)
Allen Caran
FUGITIVE LADY(1934)
Aida Carange
ZAZIE(1961, Fr.), makeup; JOY HOUSE(1964, Fr.), makeup; IS PARIS BUR-NING?(1966, U.S./Fr.), makeup; YOUNG GIRLS OF ROCHEFORT, THE(1968, Fr.), makeup; LES GAULOISES BLEUES(1969, Fr.), makeup
Hans Carate
INHERITANCE IN PRETORIA(1936, Ger.), m
Vincent Carato
HELL IN THE HEAVENS(1934)
Fred Carault
MY BABY IS BLACK!(1965, Fr.)
A. Caravaggi
GREEN TREE, THE(1965, Ital.)
Tony Caravajal
TEN DAYS TO TULARA(1958)
Carolyn Caraven
HI, MOM!(1970)
Dacosta Carayan
Misc. Talkies
RAPE KILLER, THE(1976), d
Costa Carayiannis
LAND OF THE MINOTAUR(1976, Gr.), d
Catherine Carayon
L'IMMORTELLE(1969, Fr./Ital./Turkey)
Jean-Marie Carayon
SMALL CHANGE(1976, Fr.)
Katy Carayon
SMALL CHANGE(1976, Fr.)
Janine Carazo
MALATESTA'S CARNIVAL(1973)
David Carb
CHATTERBOX(1936), w
Antonio Carbajal
LIFE IN THE BALANCE, A(1955)

Charles Carbajal
CAPTAIN SCARLETT(1953), ph
J. Carlos Carbajal
LITTLEST OUTLAW, THE(1955), ph; GALLANT ONE, THE(1964, U.S./Peru), ph
Lonny Carbajal
CHARLIE CHAN AND THE CURSE OF THE DRAGON QUEEN(1981)
Tony Carbajal
WOMAN'S DEVOTION, A(1956); LAST REBEL, THE(1961, Mex.); OF LOVE AND DESIRE(1963)
Emilio Carballido
MACARIO(1961, Mex.), w; TIME AND THE TOUCH, THE(1962), w
Dick Carballo
SLOW DANCING IN THE BIG CITY(1978); NIGHT OF THE ZOMBIES(1981)
Richard Carballo
GUESS WHAT WE LEARNED IN SCHOOL TODAY?(1970); STOOLIE, THE(1972)
Victoria Carbe
GUN RUNNER(1969); DIAMOND STUD(1970)
Misc. Talkies
DIAMOND STUD(1970)
B. D. Carber
Silents
NANCY COMES HOME(1918), w
Joe Carberry
SHORT EYES(1977)
Joseph Carberry
GOODBYE GIRL, THE(1977); NIGHT OF THE JUGGLER(1980); SURVIVORS, THE(1983); VIGILANTE(1983)
1984
MISSING IN ACTION(1984)
Emilio Carbillido
MUSHROOM EATER, THE(1976, Mex.), w
Barry Carbin
BEST LITTLE WHOREHOUSE IN TEXAS, THE(1982)
Christopher Carbis
PSYCHOTRONIC MAN, THE(1980)
Cesare Carboli
TEOREMA(1969, Ital.)
Gerald Carbonara
GERONIMO(1939), m
Gerard Carbonara
DR. CYCLOPS(1940), m; AMONG THE LIVING(1941), m; SHEPHERD OF THE HILLS, THE(1941), m; HENRY ALDRICH HAUNTS A HOUSE(1943), m
Carolina Carbonare
TWO WOMEN(1961, Ital./Fr.)
Virgilio Carbonari
LA BOHEME(1965, Ital.)
Gerard Carbonarn
AMERICAN EMPIRE(1942), m
Carbonaro
PIRANHA II: THE SPAWNING(1981, Neth.), spec eff
Anthony Carbone
BUCKET OF BLOOD, A(1959); INSIDE THE MAFIA(1959); LAST WOMAN ON EARTH, THE(1960); PIT AND THE PENDULUM, THE(1961); SPLIT, THE(1968); LAST PORNO FLICK, THE(1974); NEWMAN'S LAW(1974); SKATEBOARD(1978)
Antony Carbone
ARSON FOR HIRE(1959); CREATURE FROM THE HAUNTED SEA(1961); VIGI-LANTE FORCE(1976)
Gilberto Carbone
SWORD OF THE CONQUEROR(1962, Ital.), p
Ugo Carbone
WHITE VOICES(1965, Fr./Ital.); STRANGER IN TOWN, A(1968, U.S./Ital.)
Carmen Carbonell
DESPERATE ONES, THE(1968 U.S./Span.)
Emanuela Pala Carboni
RED DESERT(1965, Fr./Ital.)
Rino Carboni
FELLINI SATYRICON(1969, Fr./Ital.), makeup; ROMA(1972, Ital./Fr.), makeup
Norbert Carbonnaux
CANDIDE(1962, Fr.), d, w
Mario Carbuglia
VALACHI PAPERS, THE(1972, Ital./Fr.), art d
Fanny Carby
TEARS FOR SIMON(1957, Brit.); KITCHEN, THE(1961, Brit.); SPARROWS CAN'T SING(1963, Brit.); TRAITORS, THE(1963, Brit.); WHAT A CRAZY WORLD(1963, Brit.); SOME PEOPLE(1964, Brit.); FAMILY WAY, THE(1966, Brit.); IDOL, THE(1966, Brit.); SHARE OUT, THE(1966, Brit.); HOW I WON THE WAR(1967, Brit.); OH! WHAT A LOVELY WAR(1969, Brit.); JUNKET 89(1970, Brit.); ONE BRIEF SUMMER(1971, Brit.); DAY IN THE DEATH OF JOE EGG, A(1972, Brit.); ELEPHANT MAN, THE(1980, Brit.)
1984
LASSITER(1984)
Alvaro Carcano
IN-LAWS, THE(1979); HIGH RISK(1981); YELLOWBEARD(1983)
Emilio Carcano
ROMEO AND JULIET(1968, Brit./Ital.), art d
Gianfilipo Carcano
AMARCORD(1974, Ital.)
Laelita Carcano
DEVIL PROBABLY, THE(1977, FR.)
Alfons Carcasina
HYPNOSIS(1966, Ger./Sp./Ital.), p
Jose Maria Carcasona
BOLDEST JOB IN THE WEST, THE(1971, Ital.), p
Evie Carcroft
SOMEWHERE IN CAMP(1942, Brit.)
Aaron Card
Misc. Talkies
CRY TO THE WIND(1979)

Bob Card
RIDING THE CHEROKEE TRAIL(1941); STICK TO YOUR GUNS(1941)
Misc. Talkies
RIDERS OF RIO(1931)
Bonnie Card
Misc. Talkies
CRY TO THE WIND(1979)
Jack Card
HEROES DIE YOUNG(1960)
Kathryn Card
KISS AND TELL(1945); IT SHOULDN'T HAPPEN TO A DOG(1946); UNDERCURRENT(1946); BORN TO KILL(1947); HUCKSTERS, THE(1947); THAT HAGEN GIRL(1947); DARK PAST, THE(1948); SAINTED SISTERS, THE(1948); THREE DARING DAUGHTERS(1948); KISS FOR CORLISS, A(1949); MOTHER IS A FRESHMAN(1949); RECKLESS MOMENTS, THE(1949); HARRIET CRAIG(1950); SKIPPER SURPRISED HIS WIFE, THE(1950); MODEL AND THE MARRIAGE BROKER, THE(1951); NEVER TRUST A GAMBLER(1951); GIRL IN WHITE, THE(1952); PAULA(1952); SCANDAL SHEET(1952); YOU FOR ME(1952); IT HAPPENS EVERY THURSDAY(1953); REMAINS TO BE SEEN(1953); STAR IS BORN, A(1954); WOMAN'S WORLD(1954); DADDY LONG LEGS(1955); HOLLYWOOD OR BUST(1956); GOOD DAY FOR A HANGING(1958); HOME BEFORE DARK(1958); BECAUSE THEY'RE YOUNG(1960); PLEASE DON'T EAT THE DAISIES(1960); WALK ON THE WILD SIDE(1962); UNSINKABLE MOLLY BROWN, THE(1964); BIRDS AND THE BEES, THE(1965)
Ken Card
GUN LAW(1938); PAINTED DESERT, THE(1938); RENEGADE RANGER(1938); TROUBLE IN SUNDOWN(1939)
Lamar Card
CLONES, THE(1973), d; SAVAGE HARVEST(1981), p
Misc. Talkies
DISCO FEVER(1978), d
Robert Card
ACROSS THE PLAINS(1939)
Carlos Cardan
1984
ERENDIRA(1984, Mex./Fr./Ger.)
Romano Cardarelli
INVESTIGATION OF A CITIZEN ABOVE SUSPICION(1970, Ital.), prod d; SWEPT AWAY...BY AN UNUSUAL DESTINY IN THE BLUE SEA OF AUGUST(1975, Ital.), p; ALL SCREWED UP(1976, Ital.), p
Johnny Cardas
REBEL ROUSERS(1970)
Ugo Cardea
NIGHT PORTER, THE(1974, Ital./U.S.)
Richard Cardella
CRATER LAKE MONSTER, THE(1977), a, w
George Carden
SHERIFF OF FRACTURED JAW, THE(1958, Brit.), ch
Colby Cardenas
ISLAND CLAWS(1981), w
Elsa Cardenas
BRAVE ONE, THE(1956); GIANT(1956); FOR THE LOVE OF MIKE(1960); FUN IN ACAPULCO(1963); OF LOVE AND DESIRE(1963); TAGGART(1964); MADAME DEATH(1968, Mex.); WILD BUNCH, THE(1969)
Misc. Talkies
TEENAGE TEASE(1983)
Elsie Cardenas
DALTON THAT GOT AWAY(1960)
Hernan Cardenas
ISLAND CLAWS(1981), d, w
Leon Cardenas
FUN IN ACAPULCO(1963)
Mark Cardenas
1984
PURPLE RAIN(1984)
Martin Cardenas
1984
UNDER THE VOLCANO(1984), set d
Pilar Cardenas
BLOOD WEDDING(1981, Sp.)
Vicente Cardenas
BRAVE BULLS, THE(1951)
Elizabeth Carder
NIGHT SHIFT(1982)
Jane Cardew
SUBURBAN WIVES(1973, Brit.)
Phil Cardew
LADY OF VENGEANCE(1957, Brit), m; HIGH HELL(1958), m, md
Ronald Cardew
LUCKY JIM(1957, Brit.); FLAME OVER INDIA(1960, Brit.); MAN WITH THE GREEN CARNATION, THE(1960, Brit.)
Valerie Cardew
WOMAN'S VENGEANCE, A(1947); KISS THE BLOOD OFF MY HANDS(1948); THUNDER ON THE HILL(1951)
Denise Cardi
DAUGHTER OF THE SANDS(1952, Fr.)
Pat Cardi
BRAINSTORM(1965); AND NOW MIGUEL(1966); LET'S KILL UNCLE(1966); BATTLE FOR THE PLANET OF THE APES(1973); HORROR HIGH(1974)
Ray Cardi
SWEET CREEK COUNTY WAR, THE(1979)
Albert Cardiff
Misc. Talkies
KILLER'S CARNIVAL(1965), d
Jack Cardiff
GREAT, MEADOW, THE(1931), ph; AS YOU LIKE IT(1936, Brit.), ph; KNIGHT WITHOUT ARMOR(1937, Brit.), ph; WINGS OF THE MORNING(1937, Brit.), ph; FOUR FEATHERS, THE(1939, Brit.), ph; GREAT MR. HANDEL(1942, Brit.), ph; COLONEL BLIMP(1945, Brit.), ph; CAESAR AND CLEOPATRA(1946, Brit.), ph; STAIRWAY TO HEAVEN(1946, Brit.), ph; BLACK NARCISSUS(1947, Brit.), ph; RED

SHOES, THE(1948, Brit.), ph; SCOTT OF THE ANTARCTIC(1949, Brit.), ph; UNDER CAPRICORN(1949), ph; BLACK ROSE, THE(1950), ph; AFRICAN QUEEN, THE(1951, U.S./Brit.), ph; PANDORA AND THE FLYING DUTCHMAN(1951, Brit.), ph; IT STARTED IN PARADISE(1952, Brit.), ph; MAGIC BOX, THE(1952, Brit.), ph; MASTER OF BALLANTRAE, THE(1953, U.S./Brit.), ph; BAREFOOT CONTESSA, THE(1954), ph; CROSSED SWORDS(1954), ph; BRAVE ONE, THE(1956), ph; WAR AND PEACE(1956, Ital./U.S.), ph; LEGEND OF THE LOST(1957, U.S./Panama/Ital.), ph; PRINCE AND THE SHOWGIRL, THE(1957, Brit.), ph; INTENT TO KILL(1958, Brit.), d; VIKINGS, THE(1958), ph; BEYOND THIS PLACE(1959, Brit.), d; DIARY OF ANNE FRANK, THE(1959), ph; SONS AND LOVERS(1960, Brit.), d; FANNY(1961), ph; BIG MONEY, THE(1962, Brit.), ph; LION, THE(1962, Brit.), d; MY GEISHA(1962), d; LONG SHIPS, THE(1964, Brit./Yugo.), d; YOUNG CASSIDY(1965, U.S./Brit.), d; LIQUIDATOR, THE(1966, Brit.), d; DARK OF THE SUN(1968, Brit.), d; GIRL ON A MOTORCYCLE, THE(1968, Fr./Brit.), d, ph; SCALAWAG(1973, Yugo.), ph; MUTATIONS, THE(1974, Brit.), d; RIDE A WILD PONY(1976, U.S./Aus.), ph; BEHIND THE IRON MASK(1977), d; CROSSED SWORDS(1978), ph; DEATH ON THE NILE(1978, Brit.), ph; AVALANCHE EXPRESS(1979), ph; MAN, A WOMAN, AND A BANK, A(1979, Can.), ph; AWAKENING, THE(1980), ph; DOGS OF WAR, THE(1980, Brit.), ph; GHOST STORY(1981), ph; WICKED LADY, THE(1983, Brit.), ph
1984
CONAN THE DESTROYER(1984), ph; SCANDALOUS(1984), ph
Rodney Cardiff
DOCTOR IN DISTRESS(1963, Brit.)
Angela Cardile
DIVORCE, ITALIAN STYLE(1962, Ital.)
Cardillo
ANYTHING FOR A SONG(1947, Ital.), m
Pierre Cardin
EVA(1962, Fr./Ital.), cos; NEW KIND OF LOVE, A(1963), cos; V.I.P.s, THE(1963, Brit.), cos; MATA HARI(1965, Fr./Ital.), cos; YELLOW ROLLS-ROYCE, THE(1965, Brit.), cos; DANDY IN ASPIC, A(1968, Brit.), cos; IMMORTAL STORY, THE(1969, Fr.), cos; YOU ONLY LIVE ONCE(1969, Fr.), cos; HAPPY MOTHER'S DAY... LOVE, GEORGE(1973), cos
Marie Cardinal
MOUCHETTE(1970, Fr.)
Claudia Cardinale
AUSTERLITZ(1960, Fr./Ital./Yugo.); BIG DEAL ON MADONNA STREET, THE(1960); GIRL WITH A SUITCASE(1961, Fr./Ital.); ROCCO AND HIS BROTHERS(1961, Fr./Ital.); UPSTAIRS AND DOWNSTAIRS(1961, Brit.); BELL' ANTONIO(1962, Ital.); CARTOUCHE(1962, Fr./Ital.); LA VIACCIA(1962, Ital.); FIASCO IN MILAN(1963, Fr./Ital.); LEOPARD, THE(1963, Ital.); 8 ½(1963, Ital.); BEBO'S GIRL(1964, Ital.); CIRCUS WORLD(1964); PINK PANTHER, THE(1964); FACTS OF MURDER, THE(1965, Ital.); MAGNIFICENT CUCKOLD, THE(1965, Fr./Ital.); TIME OF INDIFFERENCE(1965, Fr./Ital.); BLINDFOLD(1966); LOST COMMAND, THE(1966); PROFESSIONALS, THE(1966); SANDRA(1966, Ital.); DON'T MAKE WAVES(1967); ROSE FOR EVERYONE, A(1967, Ital.); DAY OF THE OWL, THE(1968, Ital./Fr.); HELL WITH HEROES, THE(1968); FINE PAIR, A(1969, Ital.); MAFIA(1969, Fr./Ital.); ONCE UPON A TIME IN THE WEST(1969, U.S./Ital.); ADVENTURES OF GERARD, THE(1970, Brit.); CERTAIN, VERY CERTAIN, AS A MATTER OF FACT... PROBABLE(1970, Ital.); LEGEND OF FRENCHIE KING, THE(1971, Fr./Ital./Span./Brit.); POPSY POP(1971, Fr.); RED TENT, THE(1971, Ital./USSR); MIDNIGHT PLEASURES(1975, Ital.); CONVERSATION PIECE(1976, Ital., Fr.); GUN, THE(1978, Ital.); ESCAPE TO ATHENA(1979, Brit.); IMMORTAL BACHELOR, THE(1980, Ital.); FITZCARRALDO(1982); GIFT, THE(1983, Fr./Ital.); SALAMANDER, THE(1983, U.S./Ital./Brit.)
Misc. Talkies
ONE RUSSIAN SUMMER(1973)
Frank Cardinale
YOURS, MINE AND OURS(1968), cos
Mazzeno Cardinale
1984
HOUSE BY THE CEMETERY, THE(1984, Ital.), stunts
F. Cardinali
FURY OF HERCULES, THE(1961, Ital.), spec eff
Nazzareno Cardinali
1984
AFTER THE FALL OF NEW YORK(1984, Ital./Fr.), stunts; BLACK CAT, THE(1984, Ital./Brit.), stunts
Alice Cardinall
Silents
IN THE DAYS OF SAINT PATRICK(1920, Brit.)
Ana Cardini
1984
BURIED ALIVE(1984, Ital.)
George Cardini
THEY ALL LAUGHED(1981)
Beatrice Cardon
Misc. Talkies
SEAWOLF(1974)
John Cardona
1984
ALLEY CAT(1984)
Rene Cardona
RANCHO GRANDE(1938, Mex.); SANTA CLAUS(1960, Mex.), d, w; DOCTOR OF DOOM(1962, Mex.), d; TOM THUMB(1967, Mex.), d, w; NIGHT OF THE BLOODY APES(1968, Mex.), d, w
Rene Cardona, Jr.
SPIRITISM(1965, Mex.); NIGHT OF THE BLOODY APES(1968, Mex.), w; NIGHT OF A THOUSAND CATS(1974, Mex.), d; SURVIVE!(1977, Mex.), p&d, w; TINTORERA...-BLOODY WATERS(1977, Brit./Mex.), d; GUYANA, CULT OF THE DAMNED zero(1980, Mex./Span./Panama), p&d
Misc. Talkies
ROBINSON CRUSOE AND THE TIGER(1972), d; TREASURE OF THE AMAZON(1983), d
J.S. Cardone
SLAYER, THE(1982), d, w

Topper Carew
D.C. CAB(1983), p, d&w

Alexandria Carewe
Silents
IRON RING, THE(1917)

Arthur Carewe
Silents
MAD MARRIAGE, THE(1921); SHAM(1921); DADDY(1923)
Misc. Silents
GHOST BREAKER, THE(1922)

Arthur Edmund Carewe
PHANTOM OF THE OPERA, THE(1929); LIFE OF THE PARTY, THE(1930); MA-
TRIMONIAL BED, THE(1930); SWEET KITTY BELLAIRS(1930); CAPTAIN AP-
PLEJACK(1931); GOD'S GIFT TO WOMEN(1931); DOCTOR X(1932); MYSTERY OF
THE WAX MUSEUM, THE(1933)
Misc. Talkies
AFRICAN INCIDENT(1934)
Silents
PHANTOM OF THE OPERA, THE(1925); SILENT LOVER, THE(1926); CAT AND
THE CANARY, THE(1927)
Misc. Silents
CLAW, THE(1927)

Edward Carewe
Misc. Silents
TIME LOCK NO. 776(1915)

Edwin Carewe
EVANGELINE(1929), p&d; SPOILERS, THE(1930), p&d; RESURRECTION(1931),
p&d; ARE WE CIVILIZED?(1934), p, d
Silents
GOD'S HALF ACRE(1916), d; HER FIGHTING CHANCE(1917), d; TRAIL OF THE
SHADOW, THE(1917), d; EASY TO MAKE MONEY(1919), d; FALSE EVIDEN-
CE(1919), d; RIGHT TO LIE, THE(1919), d; ISOBEL(1920), d&w; HER MAD BAR-
GAIN(1921), d; INVISIBLE FEAR, THE(1921), d; PLAYTHINGS OF
DESTINY(1921), d; QUESTION OF HONOR, A(1922), d; SILVER WINGS(1922), d;
GIRL OF THE GOLDEN WEST, THE(1923), d; JOANNA(1925), d; MY SON(1925), d;
RAMONA(1928), d; EVANGELINE(1929), d
Misc. Silents
ACROSS THE PACIFIC(1914), d; CORA(1915), d; FINAL JUDGEMENT, THE(1915),
d; HOUSE OF TEARS, THE(1915), d; MARSE COVINGTON(1915), d; SOUL OF A
WOMAN, THE(1915), d; THREE OF US, THE(1915); DAWN OF LOVE, THE(1916), d;
HER GREAT PRICE(1916), d; SNOWBIRD, THE(1916), a, d; SUNBEAM, THE(1916),
d; UPSTART, THE(1916), d; BARRICADE, THE(1917), d; GREATEST POWER,
THE(1917), d; THEIR COMPACT(1917), d; VOICE OF CONSCIENCE, THE(1917), d;
HOUSE OF GOLD, THE(1918), d; SPLENDID SINNER, THE(1918), d; TRAIL TO
YESTERDAY, THE(1918), d; IT'S EASY TO MAKE MONEY(1919), d; SHADOWS OF
SUSPICION(1919), d; WAY OF THE STRONG, THE(1919), d; RIO GRANDE(1920), d;
WEB OF DECEIT, THE(1920), d; HABIT(1921), d; MY LADY'S LATCHKEY(1921), d;
I AM THE LAW(1922), d; BAD MAN, THE(1923), d; MIGHTY LAK' A ROSE(1923), d;
MADONNA OF THE STREETS(1924), d; SON OF THE SAHARA, A(1924), d; LADY
WHO LIED, THE(1925), d; WHY WOMEN LOVE(1925), d; HIGH STEPPERS(1926), d;
RESURRECTION(1927), d; REVENGE(1928), d

James Carewe
Misc. Silents
JUSTICE(1917, Brit.)

Mary Carewe
LADY TUBBS(1935)

Rita Carewe
Silents
JOANNA(1925); RAMONA(1928)
Misc. Silents
HIGH STEPPERS(1926); STRONGER WILL, THE(1928)

Anita Carey
1984
ORDEAL BY INNOCENCE(1984, Brit.)

Bill Carey
SWEETHEART OF SIGMA CHI(1933); SARATOGA(1937); SOMETHING TO SING
ABOUT(1937)

Bob Carey
FOR LOVE OF IVY(1968)

David Carey
BOY NAMED CHARLIE BROWN, A(1969); SNOOPY, COME HOME(1972)

Denis Carey
CHILDREN OF CHANCE(1949, Brit.); DAY OF THE JACKAL, THE(1973, Brit./Fr.)

Doris Carey
WORLD'S GREATEST SINNER, THE(1962)

Ed Carey
ARIZONA TRAILS(1935); LIGHTNIN' CRANDALL(1937)

Edward F. Carey
BADGE 373(1973)

Ernestine Gilbreth Carey
CHEAPER BY THE DOZEN(1950), w; BELLES ON THEIR TOES(1952), w

Gabrielle Carey
PUBERTY BLUES(1983, Aus.), w

Geoffrey Carey
EXPOSED(1983); STATE OF THINGS, THE(1983)

George Carey
SEX AND THE SINGLE GIRL(1964); CHROME AND HOT LEATHER(1971)
Misc. Talkies
AMAZING LOVE SECRET(1975)

George E. Carey
RIOT ON SUNSET STRIP(1967); WEEKEND WITH THE BABYSITTER(1970), a, p,
w; TOUCH OF SATAN, THE(1971), p; THING WITH TWO HEADS, THE(1972)
Misc. Talkies
BABYSITTER, THE(1969)

George F. Carey
WORLD'S GREATEST SINNER, THE(1962)

Hal Carey
EL DIABLO RIDES(1939)

Harry Carey
CAVALIER OF THE WEST(1931); TRADER HORN(1931); BORDER DEVILS(1932);
LAW AND ORDER(1932); NIGHT RIDER, THE(1932); WITHOUT HONORS(1932);
MAN OF THE FOREST(1933); THUNDERING HERD, THE(1934); BARBARY
COAST(1935); LAST OF THE CLINTONS, THE(1935); POWDERSMOKE RAN-
GE(1935); RUSTLER'S PARADISE(1935); WAGON TRAIL(1935); WILD MUS-
TANG(1935); ACCUSING FINGER, THE(1936); LAST OUTLAW, THE(1936); LITTLE
MISS NOBODY(1936); PRISONER OF SHARK ISLAND, THE(1936); SUTTER'S
GOLD(1936); VALIANT IS THE WORD FOR CARRIE(1936); ACES WILD(1937);
ANNAPOLIS SALUTE(1937); BORDER CAFE(1937); BORN RECKLESS(1937); DAN-
GER PATROL(1937); GHOST TOWN(1937); KID GALAHAD(1937); RACING LA-
DY(1937); SOULS AT SEA(1937); GATEWAY(1938); KING OF ALCATRAZ(1938); LAW
WEST OF TOMBSTONE, THE(1938); PORT OF MISSING GIRLS(1938); SKY
GIANT(1938); YOU AND ME(1938); BURN 'EM UP O'CONNER(1939); CODE OF THE
STREETS(1939); INSIDE INFORMATION(1939); MR. SMITH GOES TO WASHING-
TON(1939); STREET OF MISSING MEN(1939); BEYOND TOMORROW(1940); MY SON
IS GUILTY(1940); OUTSIDE THE 3-MILE LIMIT(1940); THEY KNEW WHAT THEY
WANTED(1940); AMONG THE LIVING(1941); PARACHUTE BATTALION(1941); SHE-
PHERD OF THE HILLS, THE(1941); SUNDOWN(1941); AIR FORCE(1943); HAPPY
LAND(1943); GREAT MOMENT, THE(1944); CHINA'S LITTLE DEVILS(1945); DUEL
IN THE SUN(1946); ANGEL AND THE BADMAN(1947); SEA OF GRASS, THE(1947);
SO DEAR TO MY HEART(1949); BALLAD OF JOSIE(1968); BANDOLERO!(1968)
Misc. Talkies
PORT OF MISSING GIRLS(1938)
Silents
JUDITH OF BETHULIA(1914); MASTER CRACKSMAN, THE(1914), a, d&w;
JUDGE NOT OR THE WOMAN OF MONA DIGGINGS(1915); JUST JIM(1915);
KNIGHT OF THE RANGE, A(1916); SECRET LOVE(1916); OUTCASTS OF POKER
FLAT, THE(1919); RIDERS OF VENGEANCE(1919), a, w; HUMAN STUFF(1920), a,
w; OVERLAND RED(1920); IF ONLY JIM(1921); WALLOP, THE(1921); KICK BACK,
THE(1922), a, w; MAN TO MAN(1922); CRASHIN' THRU(1923); ROARING
RAILS(1924); LITTLE JOURNEY, A(1927); SLIDE, KELLY, SLIDE(1927); TRAIL OF
'98, THE(1929)
Misc. Silents
BEHIND THE LINES(1916); LOVE'S LARIAT(1916), a, d; THREE GODFATHERS,
THE(1916); FIGHTING GRINGO, THE(1917); MARKED MAN, A(1917); SECRET MAN,
THE(1917); STRAIGHT SHOOTING(1917); BUCKING BROADWAY(1918); HELL
BENT(1918); PHANTOM RIDERS, THE(1918); SCARLET DROP, THE(1918);
THIEVES' GOLD(1918); THREE MOUNTED MEN(1918); WILD WOMEN(1918); WOM-
AN'S FOOL, A(1918); ACE OF THE SADDLE(1919); BARE FISTS(1919); FIGHT FOR
LOVE, A(1919); GUN-FIGHTIN' GENTLEMAN, A(1919); RIDER OF THE LAW(1919);
ROPED(1919); BLUE STREAK MCCOY(1920); BULLET-PROOF(1920); HEARTS
UP!(1920); MARKED MEN(1920); SUNDOWN SLIM(1920); DESPERATE
TRAILS(1921); FOX, THE(1921); FREEZE OUT, THE(1921); GOOD MEN AND
TRUE(1922); CANYON OF THE FOOLS(1923); DESERT DRIVEN(1923); MIRACLE
BABY, THE(1923); FLAMING FORTIES, THE(1924); LIGHTING RIDER, THE(1924);
NIGHT HAWK, THE(1924); TIGER THOMPSON(1924); BAD LANDS, THE(1925);
BEYOND THE BORDER(1925); MAN FROM RED GULCH, THE(1925); PRAIRIE
PIRATE, THE(1925); SILENT SANDERSON(1925); SOFT SHOES(1925); TEXAS
TRAIL, THE(1925); DRIFTIN' THRU(1926); FRONTIER TRAIL, THE(1926); SATAN
TOWN(1926); SEVENTH BANDIT, THE(1926); BORDER PATROL, THE(1928); BURN-
ING BRIDGES(1928)

Harry Carey, Jr.
SUNSET PASS(1933); PURSUED(1947); MOONRISE(1948); RED RIVER(1948);
THREE GODFATHERS, THE(1948); SHE WORE A YELLOW RIBBON(1949); COPPER
CANYON(1950); RIO GRANDE(1950); WAGONMASTER(1950); WARPATH(1951);
MONKEY BUSINESS(1952); WILD BLUE YONDER, THE(1952); BENEATH THE
12-MILE REEF(1953); GENTLEMEN PREFER BLONDES(1953); ISLAND IN THE
SKY(1953); NIAGARA(1953); SAN ANTONE(1953); SWEETHEARTS ON PARA-
DE(1953); OUTCAST, THE(1954); SILVER LODE(1954); HOUSE OF BAMBOO(1955);
LONG GRAY LINE, THE(1955); MISTER ROBERTS(1955); GREAT LOCOMOTIVE
CHASE, THE(1956); SEARCHERS, THE(1956); SEVENTH CAVALRY(1956); GUN THE
MAN DOWN(1957); KISS THEM FOR ME(1957); RIVER'S EDGE, THE(1957); FROM
HELL TO TEXAS(1958); ESCORT WEST(1959); RIO BRAVO(1959); GREAT IMPOS-
TOR, THE(1960); NOOSE FOR A GUNMAN(1960); TWO RODE TOGETHER(1961);
PUBLIC AFFAIR, A(1962); CHEYENNE AUTUMN(1964); RAIDERS, THE(1964);
TAGGART(1964); SHENANDOAH(1965); ALVAREZ KELLY(1966); BILLY THE KID
VS. DRACULA(1966); CYBORG 2087(1966); RARE BREED, THE(1966); WAY WEST,
THE(1967); DEVIL'S BRIGADE, THE(1968); DEATH OF A GUNFIGHTER(1969);
UNDEFEATED, THE(1969); DIRTY DINGUS MAGEE(1970); MOONSHINE WAR,
THE(1970); BIG JAKE(1971); ONE MORE TRAIN TO ROB(1971); SOMETHING
BIG(1971); TRINITY IS STILL MY NAME(1971, Ital.); CAHILL, UNITED STATES
MARSHAL(1973); MAN FROM THE EAST, A(1974, Ital./Fr.); TAKE A HARD RI-
DE(1975, U.S./Ital.); NICKELODEON(1976); LONG RIDERS, THE(1980); ENDAN-
GERED SPECIES(1982)
1984
GREMLINS(1984)

Harry Carey, Sr.
BAD COMPANY(1931); SPOILERS, THE(1942); RED RIVER(1948)

Harry D. Carey
Silents
KNIGHT OF THE RANGE, A(1916), w

James Carey
Misc. Silents
RIDING DOUBLE(1924)

Jeffrey Carey
LITTLE ROMANCE, A(1979, U.S./Fr.)

Joyce Carey
IN WHICH WE SERVE(1942, Brit.); BLITHE SPIRIT(1945, Brit.); BRIEF ENCOUN-
TER(1945, Brit.); JOHNNY IN THE CLOUDS(1945, Brit.); DULCIMER STREET(1948,
Brit.); OCTOBER MAN, THE(1948, Brit.); AMAZING MR. BEECHAM, THE(1949, Brit.);
ASTONISHED HEART, THE(1950, Brit.); IT'S HARD TO BE GOOD(1950, Brit.);
HAPPY GO LOVELY(1951, Brit.); CRY, THE BELOVED COUNTRY(1952, Brit.);
SECRET PEOPLE(1952, Brit.), w; BOTH SIDES OF THE LAW(1953, Brit.); END OF
THE AFFAIR, THE(1955, Brit.); STOLEN ASSIGNMENT(1955, Brit.); LOSER TAKES
ALL(1956, Brit.); HORSE'S MOUTH, THE(1958, Brit.), w; LIBEL(1959, Brit.); LET'S
GET MARRIED(1960, Brit.); GREYFRIARS BOBBY(1961, Brit.); NAKED EDGE,
THE(1961); PORTRAIT OF A SINNER(1961, Brit.); ALIVE AND KICKING(1962, Brit.);
NEARLY A NASTY ACCIDENT(1962, Brit.); EYES OF ANNIE JONES, THE(1963,
Brit.); V.I.P.s, THE(1963, Brit.); JOLLY BAD FELLOW, A(1964, Brit.); NICE GIRL LIKE

ME, A(1969, Brit.); LADY CAROLINE LAMB(1972, Brit./Ital.)
Silents
GOD AND THE MAN(1918, Brit.)
Misc. Silents
COLONEL NEWCOME THE PERFECT GENTLEMAN(1920, Brit.)
Kenneth Carey
WAGNER(1983, Brit./Hung./Aust.), prod d
Leonard Carey
LAUGHTER(1930); HONOR AMONG LOVERS(1931); MERRILY WE GO TO
HELL(1932); NICE WOMAN(1932); SHANGHAI EXPRESS(1932); THIS RECKLESS
AGE(1932); BOMBSHELL(1933); INFERNAL MACHINE(1933); LITTLE GIANT,
THE(1933); WORST WOMAN IN PARIS(1933); AGE OF INNOCENCE(1934); DOUBLE
DOOR(1934); GAMBLING LADY(1934); HIS GREATEST GAMBLE(1934); I SELL
ANYTHING(1934); LITTLE MINISTER, THE(1934); SMARTY(1934); GINGER(1935);
HOLD'EM YALE(1935); LADIES LOVE DANGER(1935); MAN WHO BROKE THE
BANK AT MONTE CARLO, THE(1935); OUR LITTLE GIRL(1935); TWO FOR TO-
NIGHT(1935); MILKY WAY, THE(1936); ROSE MARIE(1936); SMALL TOWN
GIRL(1936); TROUBLE FOR TWO(1936); UNGUARDED HOUR, THE(1936); WIFE
VERSUS SECRETARY(1936); ANGEL(1937); AWFUL TRUTH, THE(1937); EM-
PEROR'S CANDLESTICKS, THE(1937); HITTING A NEW HIGH(1937); LAST OF
MRS. CHEYNEY, THE(1937); NIGHT OF MYSTERY(1937); BULLDOG DRUMMOND
IN AFRICA(1938); FIVE LITTLE PEPPERS AND HOW THEY GREW(1939); LONE
WOLF SPY HUNT, THE(1939); STRONGER THAN DESIRE(1939); ZERO HOUR,
THE(1939); HIRED WIFE(1940); IN OLD MISSOURI(1940); PRIVATE AFFAIRS(1940);
REBECCA(1940); SING, DANCE, PLENTY HOT(1940); ACCENT ON LOVE(1941);
CONFIRM OR DENY(1941); MOON OVER HER SHOULDER(1941); MOUNTAIN
MOONLIGHT(1941); PRIVATE NURSE(1941); RAGE IN HEAVEN(1941); SUSPI-
CION(1941); THAT HAMILTON WOMAN(1941); TUXEDO JUNCTION(1941); WEST
POINT WIDOW(1941); GIVE OUT, SISTERS(1942); I MARRIED AN ANGEL(1942);
MRS. MINIVER(1942); SON OF FURY(1942); THIS ABOVE ALL(1942); HEAVEN CAN
WAIT(1943); YOUNGEST PROFESSION, THE(1943); GASLIGHT(1944); NATIONAL
VELVET(1944); ONCE UPON A TIME(1944); SECRETS OF SCOTLAND YARD(1944);
MINISTRY OF FEAR(1945); EXILE, THE(1947); FOREVER AMBER(1947); MOSS
ROSE(1947); SLIGHTLY FRENCH(1949); THAT FORSYTE WOMAN(1949); KIND
LADY(1951); STRANGERS ON A TRAIN(1951); LES MISERABLES(1952); SNOWS OF
KILIMANJARO, THE(1952); THUNDER IN THE EAST(1953)
Lucian Carey
Silents
DUKE STEPS OUT, THE(1929), w
Lynn Carey
LORD LOVE A DUCK(1966)
Macdonald Carey
DR. BROADWAY(1942); STAR SPANGLED RHYTHM(1942); TAKE A LETTER,
DARLING(1942); WAKE ISLAND(1942); SALUTE FOR THREE(1943); SHADOW OF A
DOUBT(1943); DREAM GIRL(1947); SUDDENLY IT'S SPRING(1947); VARIETY
GIRL(1947); HAZARD(1948); BRIDE OF VENGEANCE(1949); GREAT GATSBY,
THE(1949); SONG OF SURRENDER(1949); STREETS OF LAREDO(1949); COMMAN-
CHE TERRITORY(1950); COPPER CANYON(1950); GREAT MISSOURI RAID,
THE(1950); LAWLESS, THE(1950); MYSTERY SUBMARINE(1950); SOUTH SEA
SINNER(1950); CAVE OF OUTLAWS(1951); EXCUSE MY DUST(1951); LET'S MAKE
IT LEGAL(1951); MEET ME AFTER THE SHOW(1951); MY WIFE'S BEST
FRIEND(1952); COUNT THE HOURS(1953); HANNAH LEE(1953); FIRE OVER
AFRICA(1954, Brit.); ODONGO(1956, Brit.); STRANGER AT MY DOOR(1956); MAN OR
GUN(1958); BLUE DENIM(1959); JOHN PAUL JONES(1959); DEVIL'S AGENT,
THE(1962, Brit.); STRANGLEHOLD(1962, Brit.); TAMMY AND THE DOCTOR(1963);
THESE ARE THE DAMNED(1965, Brit.); END OF THE WORLD(1977); FOES(1977);
AMERICAN GIGOLO(1980)
Misc. Talkies
DEADLY AUGUST(1966); ACCESS CODE(1984)
Mary Jane Carey
KID MILLIONS(1934); FLYING DEUCES, THE(1939); LUSTY MEN, THE(1952);
FRENCH LINE, THE(1954)
Misc. Talkies
BORDER VENGEANCE(1935)
Michele Carey
SPY WITH MY FACE, THE(1966); EL DORADO(1967); LIVE A LITTLE, LOVE A
LITTLE(1968); SWEET RIDE, THE(1968); CHANGES(1969); DIRTY DINGUS MA-
GEE(1970); ANIMALS, THE(1971); SCANDALOUS JOHN(1971); CHOIRBOYS,
THE(1977)
Mike Carey
OLD CHISHOLM TRAIL(1943)
Olive Carey
TRADER HORN(1931); NAUGHTY MARIETTA(1935); ON DANGEROUS
GROUND(1951); WHIP HAND, THE(1951); FACE TO FACE(1952); MONKEY BUSI-
NESS(1952); AFFAIR WITH A STRANGER(1953); ROGUE COP(1954); COBWEB,
THE(1955); I DIED A THOUSAND TIMES(1955); PILLARS OF THE SKY(1956);
SEARCHERS, THE(1956); GUNFIGHT AT THE O.K. CORRAL(1957); NIGHT PAS-
SAGE(1957); RUN OF THE ARROW(1957); WINGS OF EAGLES, THE(1957); ALAMO,
THE(1960); TWO RODE TOGETHER(1961); BILLY THE KID VS. DRACULA(1966)
Paddy Carey
MEN OF IRELAND(1938, Ireland); KID FROM CANADA, THE(1957, Brit.), ph
Phil Carey
GUN FURY(1953); NEBRASKAN, THE(1953); MASSACRE CANYON(1954); OUT-
LAW STALLION, THE(1954); PUSHOVER(1954); THEY RODE WEST(1954); COUNT
THREE AND PRAY(1955); LONG GRAY LINE, THE(1955); THREE STRIPES IN THE
SUN(1955); WYOMING RENEGADES(1955); PORT AFRIQUE(1956, Brit.); PORTRAIT
IN SMOKE(1957, Brit.); SHADOW ON THE WINDOW, THE(1957); RETURN TO
WARBOW(1958); SCREAMING MIMI(1958)
Philip Carey
I WAS A COMMUNIST FOR THE F.B.I.(1951); INSIDE THE WALLS OF FOLSOM
PRISON(1951); OPERATION PACIFIC(1951); TANKS ARE COMING, THE(1951);
CATTLE TOWN(1952); MAN BEHIND THE GUN, THE(1952); SPRINGFIELD RI-
FLE(1952); THIS WOMAN IS DANGEROUS(1952); CALAMITY JANE(1953); TON-
KA(1958); TRUNK, THE(1961, Brit.); BLACK GOLD(1963); DEAD RINGER(1964);
TIME TRAVELERS, THE(1964); GREAT SIOUX MASSACRE, THE(1965); TOWN
TAMER(1965); THREE GUNS FOR TEXAS(1968); BACKTRACK(1969); ONCE YOU
KISS A STRANGER(1969); REBEL ROUSERS(1970); SEVEN MINUTES, THE(1971);
FIGHTING MAD(1976)

Misc. Talkies
CRACKLE OF DEATH(1974)
Phillip Carey
FORCE OF ARMS(1951); FBI CODE 98(1964)
Richard Carey
DRIVER, THE(1978)
Richenda Carey
1984
KIPPERBANG(1984, Brit.)
Roland Carey
SWORD OF EL CID, THE(1965, Span./Ital.)
Ron Carey
OUT OF TOWNERS, THE(1970); MADE FOR EACH OTHER(1971); WHO KILLED
MARY WHAT'SER NAME?(1971); SILENT MOVIE(1976); HIGH ANXIETY(1977);
FATSO(1980); HISTORY OF THE WORLD, PART 1(1981)
1984
JOHNNY DANGEROUSLY(1984)
Roy Carey
NO LADY(1931, Brit.)
Slim Carey
SINGING BUCKAROO, THE(1937)
Tim Carey
I'LL CRY TOMORROW(1955); KILLING, THE(1956); BAYOU(1957)
Timothy Carey
BLOODHOUNDS OF BROADWAY(1952); HELLGATE(1952); WHITE WITCH DOC-
TOR(1953); WILD ONE, THE(1953); ALASKA SEAS(1954); CRIME WAVE(1954); EAST
OF EDEN(1955); FINGER MAN(1955); FLIGHT TO HONG KONG(1956); FRANCIS IN
THE HAUNTED HOUSE(1956); LAST WAGON, THE(1956); NAKED GUN, THE(1956);
RUMBLE ON THE DOCKS(1956); CHAIN OF EVIDENCE(1957); PATHS OF GLO-
RY(1957); REVOLT IN THE BIG HOUSE(1958); UNWED MOTHER(1958); BOY AND
THE PIRATES, THE(1960); ONE-EYED JACKS(1961); SECOND TIME AROUND,
THE(1961); CONVICTS FOUR(1962); MERMAIDS OF TIBURON, THE(1962);
WORLD'S GREATEST SINNER, THE(1962, a, p,d&w; BIKINI BEACH(1964); RIO
CONCHOS(1964); SHOCK TREATMENT(1964); BEACH BLANKET BINGO(1965);
TIME FOR KILLING, A(1967); WATERHOLE NO. 3(1967); HEAD(1968); WHAT'S THE
MATTER WITH HELEN?(1971); GET TO KNOW YOUR RABBIT(1972); OUTFIT,
THE(1973); SPEEDTRAP(1978)
Timothy Agoglia Carey
PEEPER(1975); CHESTY ANDERSON, U.S. NAVY(1976); KILLING OF A CHINESE
BOOKIE, THE(1976); FAST-WALKING(1982)
Tom Carey
MINNIE AND MOSKOWITZ(1971); PLAZA SUITE(1971)
Tommy Carey
Silents
PAIR OF SIXES, A(1918)
Tristam Carey
SHE DIDN'T SAY NO!(1962, Brit.), m
Tristram Carey
SILENT PLAYGROUND, THE(1964, Brit.), m; TWIST OF SAND, A(1968, Brit.), m,
md
William Carey
OLD MAN RHYTHM(1935); ROBERTA(1935)
Edward C. Carfagno
MELINDA(1972), art d; SKYJACKED(1972), art d; MAN WHO LOVED CAT DANC-
ING, THE(1973), art d; SOYLENT GREEN(1973), art d; DEMON SEED(1977), prod d;
TIME AFTER TIME(1979, Brit.), prod d; LITTLE MISS MARKER(1980), prod d;
STING II, THE(1983), prod d
Edward Carfagno
TROUBLE WITH GIRLS(AND HOW TO GET INTO IT), THE*1/2 (1969), art d;
YOUNGEST PROFESSION, THE(1943), art d; BETWEEN TWO WOMEN(1944), art d;
THIN MAN GOES HOME, THE(1944), art d; OUR VINES HAVE TENDER GRA-
PES(1945), art d; SAILOR TAKES A WIFE, THE(1946), art d; SECRET HEART,
THE(1946), art d; GOOD NEWS(1947), art d; ON AN ISLAND WITH YOU(1948), art
d; BARKLEYS OF BROADWAY, THE(1949), art d; NEPTUNE'S DAUGHTER(1949),
art d; LADY WITHOUT PASSPORT, A(1950), art d; BAD AND THE BEAUTIFUL,
THE(1952), art d; WHEN IN ROME(1952), art d; GREAT DIAMOND ROBBERY(1953),
art d; JULIUS CAESAR(1953), art d; STORY OF THREE LOVES, THE(1953), art d;
DEEP IN MY HEART(1954), art d; EXECUTIVE SUITE(1954), art d; LONG, LONG
TRAILER, THE(1954), art d; TEA AND SYMPATHY(1956), art d; SOMETHING OF
VALUE(1957), art d; BEN HUR(1959), art d; ADA(1961), art d; GO NAKED IN THE
WORLD(1961), art d; PERIOD OF ADJUSTMENT(1962), art d; SUNDAY IN NEW
YORK(1963), art d; TICKLISH AFFAIR, A(1963), art d; SIGNPOST TO MUR-
DER(1964), art d; VIVA LAS VEGAS(1964), art d; 36 HOURS(1965), art d; GLASS
BOTTOM BOAT, THE(1966), art d; SPINOUT(1966), art d; DON'T MAKE WA-
VES(1967), art d; SHOES OF THE FISHERMAN, THE(1968), art d; EXTRAORDI-
NARY SEAMAN, THE(1969), art d; MALTESE BIPPY, THE(1969), art d;
MOONSHINE WAR, THE(1970), art d; TRAVELING EXECUTIONER, THE(1970), art
d; HINDENBURG, THE(1975), prod d; LAST HARD MEN, THE(1976), art d; LOOK-
ING FOR MR. GOODBAR(1977), art d; ONE AND ONLY, THE(1978), prod d; METE-
OR(1979), prod d; HONKYTONK MAN(1982), prod d; WRONG IS RIGHT(1982), prod
d; SUDDEN IMPACT(1983), prod d
1984
ALL OF ME(1984), prod d; CITY HEAT(1984), prod d; TIGHTROPE(1984), prod d
Edward Carfango
CINCINNATI KID, THE(1965), art d
Emilio Cargher
SECRET OF STAMBOUL, THE(1936, Brit.); MISSING, BELIEVED MARRIED(1937,
Brit.)
David Cargill
UPSTAIRS AND DOWNSTAIRS(1961, Brit.); INFORMATION RECEIVED(1962,
Brit.)
Henry Cargill
Silents
PURSUING VENGEANCE, THE(1916)
Patrick Cargill
SWORD AND THE ROSE, THE(1953); EXTRA DAY, THE(1956, Brit.); UP THE
CREEK(1958, Brit.); CARRY ON NURSE(1959, Brit.), w; CLUE OF THE SILVER KEY,
THE(1961, Brit.); TWICE AROUND THE DAFFODILS(1962, Brit.), w; CARRY ON
JACK(1963, Brit.); HI-JACKERS, THE(1963, Brit.); THIS IS MY STREET(1964, Brit.);
HELP!(1965, Brit.); COUNTESS FROM HONG KONG, A(1967, Brit.); STITCH IN TIME,

A(1967, Brit.); HAMMERHEAD(1968); INSPECTOR CLOUSEAU(1968, Brit.); MAGIC CHRISTIAN, THE(1970, Brit.); THINK DIRTY(1970, Brit.); UP POMPEII(1971, Brit.); PICTURE SHOW MAN, THE(1980, Aus.)

William Cargill
FIGHT FOR YOUR LIFE(1977)

Council Cargle
DETROIT 9000(1973)

David Cargo
GOOD GUYS AND THE BAD GUYS, THE(1969); UP IN THE CELLAR(1970); BUNNY O'HARE(1971)

Jean-Pierre Cargol
WILD CHILD, THE(1970, Fr.)

Tounet Cargol
WILD CHILD, THE(1970, Fr.)

Betty Cargyle
KID FROM BOOKLYN, THE(1946)

Glen Cargyle
WHITE CHRISTMAS(1954)

James Carhardt
CRY MURDER(1936), w

Arthur H. Carhart
RIDING ON(1937), w

Timothy Carhart
1984
GHOSTBUSTERS(1984)

Davina Carid
STOLEN LIFE(1939, Brit.)

Frank Carideo
SPIRIT OF NOTRE DAME, THE(1931)

Carmine Caridi
ANDERSON TAPES, THE(1971); GANG THAT COULDN'T SHOOT STRAIGHT, THE(1971); I COULD NEVER HAVE SEX WITH ANY MAN WHO HAS SO LITTLE REGARD FOR MY HUSBAND(1973); CRAZY JOE(1974); GAMBLER, THE(1974); GODFATHER, THE, PART II(1974); CARWASH(1976); CHEAP DETECTIVE, THE(1978); IN-LAWS, THE(1979); PRINCE OF THE CITY(1981)

Michael Caridia
GAMMA PEOPLE, THE(1956); TWO GROOMS FOR A BRIDE(1957); UP IN THE WORLD(1957, Brit.)

Lynn Caridine
COOLEY HIGH(1975); MONKEY HUSTLE, THE(1976)

Jean Carignan
FAR SHORE, THE(1976, Can.)

A. Carillo
CRISIS(1950)

Andy Carillo
SET-UP, THE(1949)

Leo Carillo
VIVA VILLA!(1934); IT HAD TO HAPPEN(1936); CHICKEN WAGON FAMILY(1939)

Mario Carillo
Silents
SLIM SHOULDERS(1922); PRISONER, THE(1923); ROSITA(1923); SONG OF LOVE, THE(1923); HIS HOUR(1924); EAGLE, THE(1925); EVE'S SECRET(1925); LURE OF THE WILD, THE(1925); BARRIER, THE(1926); TORRENT, THE(1926); TIME TO LOVE(1927); HOT NEWS(1928); JUST MARRIED(1928)
Misc. Silents
STAGE ROMANCE, A(1922); REMITTANCE WOMAN, THE(1923); HOW TO HANDLE WOMEN(1928)

Mary Carillo
LEGIONS OF THE NILE(1960, Ital.)
1984
HOLY INNOCENTS, THE(1984, Span.)

Tosh Carillo
Misc. Talkies
HORSE(1965)

Victor Carin
FLASH THE SHEEPDOG(1967, Brit.)

Larry Caringi
VICTORS, THE(1963)

Rudolph Caringi
WARM IN THE BUD(1970), p,d&w, ed

Luigi Carini
LOYALTY OF LOVE(1937, Ital.)

Carioca Boys
ROAD TO RIO(1947)

Marty Cariosa
RESTLESS BREED, THE(1957)

Joe Carioth
1984
FLASH OF GREEN, A(1984)

Len Cariou
LITTLE NIGHT MUSIC, A(1977, Aust./U.S./Ger.); ONE MAN(1979, Can.); FOUR SEASONS, THE(1981)
1984
LOUISIANE(1984, Fr./Can.)

Mara Carisi
OMICRON(1963, Ital.)

Georges Caristan
CEDDO(1978, Nigeria), ph

Carita
VIKING QUEEN, THE(1967, Brit.)

Adam Carl
1984
BUDDY SYSTEM, THE(1984)

Gilles Carl
FANTASTICA(1980, Can./Fr.), d&w

Joe Carl
TEL AVIV TAXI(1957, Israel), a, art d

Joseph Carl
HILL 24 DOESN'T ANSWER(1955, Israel), art d; SALLAH(1965, Israel), art d; IMPOSSIBLE ON SATURDAY(1966, Fr./Israel), set d

Kathryn Carl
PRIDE OF ST. LOUIS, THE(1952)

Kitty Carl
YOUR THREE MINUTES ARE UP(1973)
Misc. Talkies
KITTY CAN'T HELP IT(1975); CARHOPS(1980)

Raymond Carl
MR. HULOT'S HOLIDAY(1954, Fr.)

Renee Carl
PEPE LE MOKO(1937, Fr.)
Misc. Silents
LES MISERABLES(1927, Fr.)

Richard Carl
FOOLS' PARADE(1971)

Roger Carl
Misc. Silents
JADE CASKET, THE(1929, Fr.)

Rudolf Carl
DIE FLEDERMAUS(1964, Aust.)

Carl Hoff and Band
HIT PARADE, THE(1937)

Carla
WORM EATERS, THE(1981)

Olga Carlatos
THANOS AND DESPINA(1970, Fr./Gr.)

David Carlberg
E.T. THE EXTRA-TERRESTRIAL(1982)

Hildur Carlberg
Misc. Silents
PARSON'S WIDOW, THE(1920, Den.)

Lars-Owe Carlberg
WINTER LIGHT, THE(1963, Swed.); PASSION OF ANNA, THE(1970, Swed.), a, p; FANNY AND ALEXANDER(1983, Swed./Fr./Ger.)

Carole Carle
DOWNHILL RACER(1969)

Frankie Carle
MY DREAM IS YOURS(1949)

Gilles Carle
RED(1970, Can.), d, w

Philip Carle
Misc. Silents
IN A MOMENT OF TEMPTATION(1927), d

Richard Carle
THAT UNCERTAIN FEELING(1941); HIS GLORIOUS NIGHT(1929); IT CAN BE DONE(1929); MADAME X(1929); GRAND PARADE, THE(1930); LADY TO LOVE, A(1930); SIN TAKES A HOLIDAY(1930); FIREMAN, SAVE MY CHILD(1932); HAT CHECK GIRL(1932); NIGHT OF JUNE 13(1932); ONE HOUR WITH YOU(1932); ROCKABYE(1932); TENDERFOOT, THE(1932), w; DIPLOMANIACS(1933); GOLDEN HARVEST(1933); MAN HUNT(1933); MORNING GLORY(1933); PRIVATE JONES(1933); AFFAIRS OF A GENTLEMAN(1934); BELOVED(1934); CARAVAN(1934); GEORGE WHITE'S SCANDALS(1934); HAROLD TEEN(1934); HOLLYWOOD PARTY(1934); LAST ROUND-UP, THE(1934); MERRY WIDOW, THE(1934); OLD-FASHIONED WAY, THE(1934); SING AND LIKE IT(1934); SUCH WOMEN ARE DANGEROUS(1934); WAKE UP AND DREAM(1934); WITCHING HOUR, THE(1934); BABY FACE HARRINGTON(1935); GAY DECEPTION, THE(1935); GHOST WALKS, THE(1935); HOME ON THE RANGE(1935); I DREAM TOO MUCH(1935); LOVE IN BLOOM(1935); NIGHT LIFE OF THE GODS(1935); TOGETHER WE LIVE(1935); ANYTHING GOES(1936); ARIZONA MAHONEY(1936); ARIZONA RAIDERS, THE(1936); BRIDE COMES HOME(1936); CASE AGAINST MRS. AMES, THE(1936); COLLEGE HOLIDAY(1936); DANGEROUS(1936); DRIFT FENCE(1936); EASY TO TAKE(1936); LET'S SING AGAIN(1936); LITTLE RED SCHOOLHOUSE(1936); LOVE BEFORE BREAKFAST(1936); MAN I MARRY, THE(1936); MOONLIGHT ON THE PRAIRIE(1936); NEVADA(1936); ONE RAINY AFTERNOON(1936); SAN FRANCISCO(1936); SMALL TOWN GIRL(1936); SPENDTHRIFT(1936); TEXAS RANGERS, THE(1936); THREE OF A KIND(1936); TRAIL OF THE LONESOME PINE, THE(1936); I'LL TAKE ROMANCE(1937); IT'S ALL YOURS(1937); LOVE IN A BUNGALOW(1937); MAN IN BLUE, THE(1937); MARRIED BEFORE BREAKFAST(1937); MERRY-GO-ROUND OF 1938(1937); OUTCAST(1937); RACKETEERS IN EXILE(1937); RHYTHM IN THE CLOUDS(1937); SHE ASKED FOR IT(1937); SHE'S DANGEROUS(1937); THAT GIRL FROM PARIS(1937); TOP OF THE TOWN(1937); TRUE CONFESSION(1937); 45 FATHERS(1937); IT'S A WONDERFUL WORLD(1939); LIFE RETURNS(1939); MAISIE(1939); NINOTCHKA(1939); PERSONS IN HIDING(1939); REMEMBER?(1939); UNDERCOVER DOCTOR(1939); COMIN' ROUND THE MOUNTAIN(1940); GOLDEN FLEECING, THE(1940); GREAT McGINTY, THE(1940); LILLIAN RUSSELL(1940); MA, HE'S MAKING EYES AT ME(1940); ONE NIGHT IN THE TROPICS(1940); PAROLE FIXER(1940); SEVEN SINNERS(1940); BUY ME THAT TOWN(1941); DANGEROUS GAME, A(1941); DEVIL AND MISS JONES, THE(1941); MILLION DOLLAR BABY(1941); MOONLIGHT IN HAWAII(1941); MY LIFE WITH CAROLINE(1941); NEW WINE(1941)
Silents
COMING OF AMOS, THE(1925); ZANDER THE GREAT(1925); SOFT CUSHIONS(1927); WHILE THE CITY SLEEPS(1928)
Misc. Silents
MARY'S LAMB(1915); MAD MARRIAGE, THE(1925); BROTHERS(1929)

John Carlen
HOUSE OF DARK SHADOWS(1970)

Doug Carleson
BATTLE BEYOND THE STARS(1980)

Bob Carleton
BRINGING UP FATHER(1946); FALL GUY(1947)

Catherine Carleton [Boyle]
OLD MOTHER RILEY, HEADMISTRESS(1950, Brit.)

Claire Carleton
TIME OF YOUR LIFE, THE(1948); CROOKED ROAD, THE(1940); GRAND OLE OPRY(1940); MELODY AND MOONLIGHT(1940); SING, DANCE, PLENTY HOT(1940); GREAT TRAIN ROBBERY, THE(1941); PETTICOAT POLITICS(1941); GILDERSLEEVE ON BROADWAY(1943); LADY OF BURLESQUE(1943); ROOKIES

Paola Carlini
LUCIANO(1963, Ital.)

Paolo Carlini
ROMAN HOLIDAY(1953); IT STARTED IN NAPLES(1960); CHRONICLE OF ANNA MAGDALENA BACH(1968, Ital., Ger.)

Antonio Carlino
SHOE SHINE(1947, Ital.)

Bruno Carlino
LA TRAVIATA(1982), set d

Lewis John Carlino
SECONDS(1966), w; FOX, THE(1967), w; BROTHERHOOD, THE(1968), w; ME-CHANIC, THE(1972), p, w; REFLECTION OF FEAR, A(1973), w; CRAZY JOE(1974), w; SAILOR WHO FELL FROM GRACE WITH THE SEA, THE(1976, Brit.), d, w; I NEVER PROMISED YOU A ROSE GARDEN(1977), w; GREAT SANTINI, THE(1979), d, w; RESURRECTION(1980), w; CLASS(1983), d

Mary Carlise
DOWN TO EARTH(1932)

Olimpia Carlisi
CASANOVA(1976, Ital.); TRAGEDY OF A RIDICULOUS MAN, THE(1982, Ital.)

Olympia Carlisi
CATCH-22(1970)

Aileen Carlisle
MURDER AT MIDNIGHT(1931); TOO YOUNG TO MARRY(1931)

Alexandra Carlisle
Silents
TIDES OF FATE(1917)

Alexandria Carlisle
HALF A SINNER(1934)

Anne Carlisle
LIQUID SKY(1982), a, w
1984
PERFECT STRANGERS(1984)

Belinda Carlisle
1984
SWING SHIFT(1984)

Bill Carlisle
GOLD GUITAR, THE(1966)

Billie Carlisle
SHE SHALL HAVE MUSIC(1935, Brit.); SING AS YOU SWING(1937, Brit.)

Bruce Carlisle
FAST AND THE FURIOUS, THE(1954); FEMALE JUNGLE, THE(1955)

Carl Carlisle
MELODY IN THE DARK(1948, Brit.)

Chester Carlisle
GANGWAY FOR TOMORROW(1943); GOVERNMENT GIRL(1943); HEAVENLY DAYS(1944); MUSIC IN MANHATTAN(1944)

David Carlisle
APACHE WARRIOR(1957); UNDER FIRE(1957)

Eileen Carlisle
PLAY GIRL(1932)

Grace Carlisle
Misc. Silents
INTERNATIONAL MARRIAGE, AN(1916)

H.A. Carlisle
RECKLESS ROADS(1935), w

Harry Carlisle
REDS(1981)

Helen Grace Carlisle
MOTHERS CRY(1930), w; LIVE, LOVE AND LEARN(1937), w

Henry Carlisle
JEALOUSY(1931, Brit.); IF I WERE RICH(1936); SPORTING LOVE(1936, Brit.)

Isabel Carlisle
MARY BURNS, FUGITIVE(1935)

Jack Carlisle
MASQUERADE(1929); LAST MAN(1932); MASON OF THE MOUNTED(1932)
Silents
DIAMONDS ADRIFT(1921); IT CAN BE DONE(1921); DANGEROUS HOUR(1923)

Jame Carlisle
OBLIGING YOUNG LADY(1941)

James Carlisle
GOVERNMENT GIRL(1943); SOMEONE TO REMEMBER(1943); HEAVENLY DAYS(1944); SINCE YOU WENT AWAY(1944); THEY WERE EXPENDABLE(1945); WOMAN IN THE WINDOW, THE(1945); GIRL ON THE SPOT(1946); KID FROM BOOKLYN, THE(1946); NOCTURNE(1946); UNDERCURRENT(1946); SADDLE PALS(1947); EMERGENCY WEDDING(1950)

John Carlisle
WHO IS KILLING THE GREAT CHEFS OF EUROPE?(1978, US/Ger.)

Kenneth Carlisle
WATER GYPSIES, THE(1932, Brit.)

Kitty Carlisle
HERE IS MY HEART(1934); MURDER AT THE VANITIES(1934); SHE LOVES ME NOT(1934); NIGHT AT THE OPERA, A(1935); LARCENY WITH MUSIC(1943); HOLLY-WOOD CANTEEN(1944)

Mary Carlisle
MADAME SATAN(1930); GRAND HOTEL(1932); HER MAD NIGHT(1932); HOTEL CONTINENTAL(1932); NIGHT COURT(1932); THIS RECKLESS AGE(1932); COL-LEGE HUMOR(1933); EAST OF FIFTH AVE.(1933); LADIES MUST LOVE(1933); MEN MUST FIGHT(1933); SATURDAY'S MILLIONS(1933); SHOULD LADIES BEHA-VE?(1933); SWEETHEART OF SIGMA CHI(1933); HANDY ANDY(1934); MILLION DOLLAR RANSOM(1934); MURDER IN THE PRIVATE CAR(1934); ONCE TO EVERY WOMAN(1934); PALOOKA(1934); THAT'S GRATITUDE(1934); THIS SIDE OF HEAV-EN(1934); CHAMPAGNE FOR BREAKFAST(1935); GIRL O' MY DREAMS(1935); GRAND OLD GIRL(1935); GREAT HOTEL MURDER(1935); IT'S IN THE AIR(1935); KENTUCKY KERNELS(1935); KIND LADY(1935); OLD HOMESTEAD, THE(1935); ONE FRIGHTENED NIGHT(1935); SUPERSPEED(1935); LADY BE CAREFUL(1936); LOVE IN EXILE(1936, Brit.); DOUBLE OR NOTHING(1937); HOLD'EM NAVY!(1937); HOTEL HAYWIRE(1937); DR. RHYTHM(1938); HUNTED MEN(1938); ILLEGAL TRAFFIC(1938); SAY IT IN FRENCH(1938); TIP-OFF GIRLS(1938); TOUCHDOWN, ARMY(1938); BEWARE SPOOKS(1939); CALL A MESSENGER(1939); FIGHTING THOROUGHBREDS(1939); HAWAIIAN NIGHTS(1939); INSIDE INFORMA-TION(1939); ROVIN' TUMBLEWEEDS(1939); DANCE, GIRL, DANCE(1940); RAGS TO RICHES(1941); BABY FACE MORGAN(1942); TORPEDO BOAT(1942); DEAD MEN WALK(1943)

Norman Carlisle
JUNGLE BOOK, THE(1967), ed

Pat Carlisle
Misc. Talkies
DEVIL'S CANYON(1935)

Peggy Carlisle
HER MAN GILBEY(1949, Brit.)
Silents
MAN AND THE MOMENT, THE(1918, Brit.); KEEPER OF THE DOOR(1919, Brit.)
Misc. Silents
ROCKS OF VALPRE, THE(1919, Brit.); GOD'S GOOD MAN(1921, Brit.)

Peter Carlisle
AFTER THE BALL(1957, Brit.); NEVER TAKE CANDY FROM A STRANGER(1961, Brit.); CHARLIE BUBBLES(1968, Brit.); SECRETS OF SEX(1970, Brit.)

Richard Carlisle
PUBLIC OPINION(1935); WHEN A MAN'S A MAN(1935)

Rita Carlisle
WATERLOO BRIDGE(1931); VAMPIRE BAT, THE(1933)

Robert Carlisle
BROADWAY(1929), ed; LAST PERFORMANCE, THE(1929), ed; LAST WARNING, THE(1929), ed; SPIRIT OF NOTRE DAME, THE(1931), ed; NICE WOMAN(1932), ed; DON'T BET ON LOVE(1933), ed; LADIES MUST LOVE(1933), ed; SATURDAY'S MILLIONS(1933), ed; CROSBY CASE, THE(1934), ed; MOST PRECIOUS THING IN LIFE(1934), ed; POOR RICH, THE(1934), ed; BOY WHO CAUGHT A CROOK(1961), ed; GUN FIGHT(1961), ed; YOU HAVE TO RUN FAST(1961), ed; INCIDENT IN AN ALLEY(1962), ed; SAINTLY SINNERS(1962), ed; BEAUTY AND THE BEAST(1963), ed; SOFI(1967), p&d
Silents
COHENS AND THE KELLYS IN PARIS, THE(1928), ed

Robert Carlisle, Jr.
ULYSSES(1967, U.S./Brit.); UNDERGROUND(1970, Brit.)

Rodney Carlisle
LET'S LIVE AGAIN(1948), w

Sara Carlisle
LIQUID SKY(1982)

Spencer Carlisle
DEVIL'S PARTNER, THE(1958)

The Carlisles
JUMBO(1962)

Carlita
MONEY TRAP, THE(1966)

East Carlo
DEFIANCE(1980)

Idelma Carlo
PSYCHOUT FOR MURDER(1971, Arg./Ital.)

Joal Carlo
ADVENTURERS, THE(1970)

Johann Carlo
1984
NADIA(1984, U.S./Yugo.)

Jon Carlo
YOUNG SAVAGES, THE(1961)

Joseph Carlo
SATAN'S CHEERLEADERS(1977)

Val Carlo
ADVENTURES OF DON COYOTE(1947)

Frances Carlon
WHITE PARADE, THE(1934)

Alberto Carloni
WHITE NIGHTS(1961, Ital./Fr.)

Pietro Carloni
MORE THAN A MIRACLE(1967, Ital./Fr.); LOVE FACTORY(1969, Ital.)

Alexander Carlos
STRANGE WORLD(1952)

Christopher Carlos
TARZAN THE MAGNIFICENT(1960, Brit.); FURY AT SMUGGLERS BAY(1963, Brit.); NINE HOURS TO RAMA(1963, U.S./Brit.); TARZAN'S THREE CHALLEN-GES(1963); DR. TERROR'S HOUSE OF HORRORS(1965, Brit.)

Dan Carlos
SUNSHINE AHEAD(1936, Brit.)

Dolores Carlos
TASTE OF BLOOD, A(1967); MAFIA GIRLS, THE(1969)
Misc. Talkies
HIDEOUT IN THE SUN(1960)

Don Carlos
ROSE OF THE RANCHO(1936); GUN FURY(1953); LAWLESS STREET, A(1955); WYOMING RENEGADES(1955); FERRY TO HONG KONG(1959, Brit.); PROFESSION-ALS, THE(1966)

Eugenio Carlos
LOVE SLAVES OF THE AMAZONS(1957); MARIZINIA(1962, U.S./Braz.)

Flory Carlos
TERROR IS A MAN(1959, U.S./Phil.)

Franzi Carlos
Silents
OLD BILL THROUGH THE AGES(1924, Brit.)

Juan Carlos
SUMMERSKIN(1962, Arg.)

Michael Carlos
STORM BOY(1976, Aus.), m; BLUE FIN(1978, Aus.), m; LONG WEEKEND(1978, Aus.), m; ODD ANGRY SHOT, THE(1979, Aus.), m

Walter Carlos
CLOCKWORK ORANGE, A(1971, Brit.), m

Wendy Carlos
SHINING, THE(1980), m; TRON(1982), m

Carlos and Jeanette
Silents
WOMAN WHO SINNED, A(1925)
Carlos Molina and Orchestra
BELLE OF OLD MEXICO(1950)
Carlos Molina Orchestra
CLUB HAVANA(1946); ONE TOO MANY(1950)
Margit Carlquist
SMILES OF A SUMMER NIGHT(1957, Swed.)
Margit Carlqvist
LOVING COUPLES(1966, Swed.); LOVE MATES(1967, Swed.)
Carlsen
HUNGER(1968, Den./Norway/Swed.), w
Henning Carlsen
EPILOGUE(1967, Den.), d; HUNGER(1968, Den./Norway/Swed.), d; PEOPLE MEET AND SWEET MUSIC FILLS THE HEART(1969, Den./Swed.), p, d, w, ed
Traute Carlsen
HEIDI AND PETER(1955, Switz.)
Bob Carlson
BON VOYAGE, CHARLIE BROWN(AND DON'T COME BACK)*** (1980), anim; THREE CABALLEROS, THE(1944), anim; ALICE IN WONDERLAND(1951), anim; PETER PAN(1953), anim; 1001 ARABIAN NIGHTS(1959), anim; SIMON, KING OF THE WITCHES(1971); RACE FOR YOUR LIFE, CHARLIE BROWN(1977), anim; HEY, GOOD LOOKIN'(1982), anim
Casey Carlson
BON VOYAGE, CHARLIE BROWN(AND DON'T COME BACK)*** (1980)
Christine Carlson
VALENTINO(1977, Brit.)
Curtis Carlson
FEMALE RESPONSE, THE(1972)
Deborah Carlson
WITHOUT A TRACE(1983)
Erica Carlson
CAVEMAN(1981)
Erika Carlson
DEVIL'S RAIN, THE(1975, U.S./Mex.); GREAT SCOUT AND CATHOUSE THURSDAY, THE(1976); DEMONOID(1981)
Gene Carlson
PSYCHOPATH, THE(1973)
Misc. Talkies
EYE FOR AN EYE, AN(1975)
Glenn Carlson
TIME AFTER TIME(1979, Brit.)
Herbert Carlson
WACKIEST SHIP IN THE ARMY, THE(1961), w
Herren Carlson
BARBERINA(1932, Ger.), w
Jeff Carlson
SLAP SHOT(1977)
Jim Carlson
MISSION GALACTICA: THE CYLON ATTACK(1979), w
Jody Carlson
AMERICAN GRAFFITI(1973)
Johnny Carlson
THUNDER IN DIXIE(1965)
June Carlson
BACK TO NATURE(1936); EDUCATING FATHER(1936); EVERY SATURDAY NIGHT(1936); BORROWING TROUBLE(1937); CHECKERS(1937); HOT WATER(1937); OFF TO THE RACES(1937); DOWN ON THE FARM(1938); LOVE ON A BUDGET(1938); SAFETY IN NUMBERS(1938); TRIP TO PARIS, A(1938); EVERYBODY'S BABY(1939); JONES FAMILY IN HOLLYWOOD, THE(1939); QUICK MILLIONS(1939); TOO BUSY TO WORK(1939); ON THEIR OWN(1940); QUEEN OF THE YUKON(1940); YOUNG AS YOU FEEL(1940); VERY YOUNG LADY, A(1941); DELINQUENT DAUGHTERS(1944); COME OUT FIGHTING(1945); HAWK OF POWDER RIVER, THE(1948); MOM AND DAD(1948)
Karen Carlson
SHAME, SHAME, EVERYBODY KNOWS HER NAME(1969); STUDENT NURSES, THE(1970); CANDIDATE, THE(1972); BLACK OAK CONSPIRACY(1977); MATILDA(1978); OCTAGON, THE(1980)
1984
FLESHBURN(1984)
Les Carlson
HARD PART BEGINS, THE(1973, Can.); SHOOT(1976, Can.); LOVE AT FIRST SIGHT(1977, Can.); MR. PATMAN(1980, Can.); IMPROPER CHANNELS(1981, Can.); CHRISTMAS STORY, A(1983); DEAD ZONE, THE(1983); VIDEODROME(1983, Can.)
Misc. Talkies
RAKU FIRE(
Leslie Carlson
NEPTUNE FACTOR, THE(1973, Can.); DERANGED(1974, Can.); LOST AND FOUND(1979)
Lisa Carlson
ONE-TRICK PONY(1980)
Mats Carlson
PAISAN(1948, Ital.)
May Carlson
INTERNES CAN'T TAKE MONEY(1937)
Ora May Carlson
ONE MILLION B.C.(1940)
Philip Carlson
WHO'S THAT KNOCKING AT MY DOOR?(1968)
Ralph Carlson
REACHING OUT(1983)
Richard Carlson
DUKE OF WEST POINT, THE(1938); YOUNG IN HEART, THE(1938); DANCING CO-ED(1939); LITTLE ACCIDENT(1939); THESE GLAMOUR GIRLS(1939); WINTER CARNIVAL(1939); BEYOND TOMORROW(1940); GHOST BREAKERS, THE(1940); HOWARDS OF VIRGINIA, THE(1940); NO, NO NANETTE(1940); TOO MANY GIRLS(1940); BACK STREET(1941); HOLD THAT GHOST(1941); LITTLE FOXES, THE(1941); WEST POINT WIDOW(1941); AFFAIRS OF MARTHA, THE(1942); FLY BY NIGHT(1942); HIGHWAYS BY NIGHT(1942); MY HEART BELONGS TO DAD-

DY(1942); WHITE CARGO(1942); MAN FROM DOWN UNDER, THE(1943); PRESENTING LILY MARS(1943); STRANGER IN TOWN, A(1943); YOUNG IDEAS(1943); SO WELL REMEMBERED(1947, Brit.); BEHIND LOCKED DOORS(1948); SPIRITUALIST, THE(1948); KING SOLOMON'S MINES(1950); SOUND OF FURY, THE(1950); BLUE VEIL, THE(1951); MILLIONAIRE FOR CHRISTY, A(1951); VALENTINO(1951); FLAT TOP(1952); WHISPERING SMITH VERSUS SCOTLAND YARD(1952, Brit.); ALL I DESIRE(1953); IT CAME FROM OUTER SPACE(1953); MAGNETIC MONSTER, THE(1953); MAZE, THE(1953); SEMINOLE(1953); CREATURE FROM THE BLACK LAGOON(1954); RIDERS TO THE STARS(1954), a, d; BENGAZI(1955); LAST COMMAND, THE(1955); THREE FOR JAMIE DAWN(1956); APPOINTMENT WITH A SHADOW(1958), d; JOHNNY ROCCO(1958), w; SAGA OF HEMP BROWN, THE(1958), d; HELEN MORGAN STORY, THE(1959); TORMENTED(1960); KID RODELO(1966, U.S./Span.), a, d; POWER, THE(1968); CHANGE OF HABIT(1969); VALLEY OF GWANGI, THE(1969)
Misc. Talkies
HUMAN GORILLA(1948); APPOINTMENT WITH A SHADOW(1957), d
Robert Carlson
ICE STATION ZEBRA(1968)
Robert W. Carlson, Jr.
FANTASIA(1940), anim
Steve Carlson
DEADLIER THAN THE MALE(1967, Brit.); YOUNG WARRIORS, THE(1967); NOBODY'S PERFECT(1968); RASCAL(1969); CAREY TREATMENT, THE(1972); BROTHERS O'TOOLE, THE(1973); SLAP SHOT(1977)
Terry Lee Carlson
FREDDIE STEPS OUT(1946)
Verne Carlson
FLIGHT(1960), ph
Veronica Carlson
SMASHING TIME(1967 Brit.); DRACULA HAS RISEN FROM HIS GRAVE(1968, Brit.); HAMMERHEAD(1968); CROSSPLOT(1969, Brit.); FRANKENSTEIN MUST BE DESTROYED!(1969, Brit.); HORROR OF FRANKENSTEIN, THE(1970, Brit.); PUSSYCAT, PUSSYCAT, I LOVE YOU(1970); GHOUL, THE(1975, Brit.); OLD DRACULA(1975, Brit.)
Vicki Carlson
VIOLATED(1953)
Walter Carlson
BADLANDS OF DAKOTA(1941)
Wamp Carlson
DOUGHBOYS IN IRELAND(1943)
Wes Carlson
FALLGUY(1962)
The Carlsons
CULT OF THE COBRA(1955)
Carl Carlsson
PRIZE, THE(1963)
Erika Carlsson
GUYANA, CULT OF THE DAMNED(1980, Mex./Span./Panama)
Karin Carlsson
WALPURGIS NIGHT(1941, Swed.)
Lilian Carlsson
SHAME(1968, Swed.)
Karin Carlsson-Kavil
WOMAN'S FACE, A(1939, Swed.)
W. C. Carlston
Silents
FINAL CURTAIN, THE(1916)
W. T. Carlston
Silents
DANGER MARK, THE(1918)
Bess Carlton
LILITH(1964)
Catherine Carlton
I'LL NEVER FORGET YOU(1951)
Claire Carlton
GIRL FROM HAVANA(1940); GUN TOWN(1946); LINDA BE GOOD(1947); BUSTER KEATON STORY, THE(1957)
David B. Carlton
1984
SWING SHIFT(1984)
Eve Carlton
MILLION DOLLAR LEGS(1939); SING FOR YOUR SUPPER(1941)
George Carlton
AND NOW TOMORROW(1944); VAMPIRE'S GHOST, THE(1945); TIME OF THEIR LIVES, THE(1946)
Gina Carlton
LAST WALTZ, THE(1936, Brit.), p
Irvin Carlton
LET'S SCARE JESSICA TO DEATH(1971), makeup; STIGMA(1972), makeup
Jack Carlton
TELL NO TALES(1939)
Ken Carlton
THY NEIGHBOR'S WIFE(1953); MARAUDERS, THE(1955); TENDER HEARTS(1955); EDGE OF HELL(1956)
Larry Carlton
1984
AGAINST ALL ODDS(1984), m
Lewis Carlton
Misc. Silents
MYSTERY OF THE DIAMOND BELT(1914, Brit.)
Mark Carlton
JACKSON COUNTY JAIL(1976); GO TELL THE SPARTANS(1978); 1941(1979)
Neil Carlton
AGAINST THE TIDE(1937, Brit.)
Pamela Carlton
GREEN ICE(1981, Brit.), art d
Rena Carlton
Misc. Silents
TORCH BEARER, THE(1916)

Rex Carlton
GUILTY BYSTANDER(1950), p; BRAIN THAT WOULDN'T DIE, THE(1959), p, w; DEVIL'S HAND, THE(1961), p, w; UNEARTHLY STRANGER, THE(1964, Brit.), w; BLOOD OF DRACULA'S CASTLE(1967), p, w; NIGHTMARE IN WAX(1969), w

Robert Carlton
DARK ANGEL, THE(1935)

Sue Carlton
WHIRLPOOL(1949); JOE PALOOKA IN THE SQUARED CIRCLE(1950); MODELS, INC.(1952); SOMETHING TO LIVE FOR(1952); SON OF PALEFACE(1952); PHFFFT!(1954); SUSAN SLEPT HERE(1954)

Timothy Carlton
BABY LOVE(1969, Brit.); THAT LUCKY TOUCH(1975, Brit.); HIGH ROAD TO CHINA(1983)

Tommy Carlton
TARZAN'S SAVAGE FURY(1952)

Valerie Carlton
TRAPPED BY THE TERROR(1949, Brit.)

Vivienne Carlton
CRIMSON CULT, THE(1970, Brit.)

William Carlton
Misc. Silents
TEMPERED STEEL(1918)

William Carlton, Jr.
Misc. Silents
SPARK DIVINE, THE(1919)

William P. Carlton
TWO SINNERS(1935); RETURN OF JIMMY VALENTINE, THE(1936)
Misc. Silents
SOCIETY EXILE, A(1919)

Dr. Gus Carlucci
LONGEST YARD, THE(1974)

Aileen Carlyle
DUDE WRANGLER, THE(1930); MIRACLE WOMAN, THE(1931); STRANGER'S RETURN(1933); PEOPLE WILL TALK(1935); COUNTRY DOCTOR, THE(1936); ROSE MARIE(1936); HOLIDAY(1938); MIDNIGHT INTRUDER(1938); MARGIE(1940); MRS. MINIVER(1942); MEXICAN SPITFIRE'S BLESSED EVENT(1943); NOTORIOUS(1946); FATHER OF THE BRIDE(1950); HARVEY(1950); RETURN OF THE TEXAN(1952); STARS AND STRIPES FOREVER(1952); THREE FOR THE SHOW(1955)

Ailene Carlyle
THIS SIDE OF HEAVEN(1934)

Anthony Carlyle
Silents
GAMBLE WITH HEARTS, A(1923, Brit.), w; ALLEY CAT, THE(1929, Brit.), w

Betty Carlyle
SECRET LIFE OF WALTER MITTY, THE(1947)

Billie Carlyle
SUCH IS LIFE(1936, Brit.)

Chester Carlyle
LADIES COURAGEOUS(1944)

David Carlyle [Robert Paige]
CAIN AND MABEL(1936); CHEROKEE STRIP(1937); KID COMES BACK, THE(1937); MEET THE BOY FRIEND(1937); ONCE A DOCTOR(1937); RHYTHM IN THE CLOUDS(1937); SMART BLONDE(1937); TALENT SCOUT(1937)

Grace Carlyle
Silents
HELD TO ANSWER(1923); NOTORIOUS LADY, THE(1927)
Misc. Silents
EAGLE'S WINGS, THE(1916); SHE'S MY BABY(1927)

Helen Carlyle
FORGOTTEN COMMANDMENTS(1932)

Hugh Carlyle
Silents
ARIZONA(1918), ph

Jack Carlyle
CARNIVAL BOAT(1932); FORGOTTEN WOMEN(1932); GHOST CITY(1932); LAW OF THE NORTH(1932); LOST JUNGLE, THE(1934); MISSISSIPPI(1935)
Silents
GIRL WHO DARED, THE(1920); NORTH OF THE RIO GRANDE(1922); STORM-SWEPT(1923)

James Carlyle
TOAST OF NEW YORK, THE(1937)

John Carlyle
DANGEROUS PARTNERS(1945); THEY WERE EXPENDABLE(1945); WHAT NEXT, CORPORAL HARGROVE?(1945); DANGEROUS MISSION(1954); UNTAMED(1955)

Kathy Carlyle
WHEN HELL BROKE LOOSE(1958); PUSHER, THE(1960)

Milton Carlyle
VICE GIRLS, LTD.(1964)

Montgomery Carlyle
Silents
PENALTY, THE(1920); TWIN BEDS(1920)

Pat Carlyle
Misc. Talkies
IRISH GRINGO, THE(1935)

Richard Carlyle
GIRL IN THE SHOW, THE(1929); IN OLD CALIFORNIA(1929); IT CAN BE DONE(1929); VALIANT, THE(1929); GIRL OF THE GOLDEN WEST(1930); GUILTY?(1930); HIDE-OUT, THE(1930); KISMET(1930); MOUNTAIN JUSTICE(1930); PLAYING AROUND(1930); TOL'ABLE DAVID(1930); WEST OF BROADWAY(1931); SADDLE BUSTER, THE(1932); UNHOLY LOVE(1932); HAPPINESS C.O.D.(1935); SONS OF STEEL(1935); TARGET UNKNOWN(1951); IRON MISTRESS, THE(1952); TORPEDO RUN(1958); GALLANT HOURS, THE(1960); HARPER(1966); IN SEARCH OF HISTORIC JESUS(1980)
Misc. Talkies
BROTHERLY LOVE(1928); QUICK TRIGGER LEE(1931); LION MAN, THE(1936)
Silents
BACK HOME AND BROKE(1922); HALDANE OF THE SECRET SERVICE(1923); SHOOTIN' IRONS(1927); LINGERIE(1928)

Misc. Silents
BRIDGE OF SIGHS, THE(1915); TAKING A CHANCE(1928); CHILDREN OF THE RITZ(1929)

Rita Carlyle
BROTHERS(1930); MIDNIGHT CLUB(1933); LIMEHOUSE BLUES(1934); MENACE(1934); GILDED LILY, THE(1935); I FOUND STELLA PARISH(1935); LLOYDS OF LONDON(1936); HOUSE OF SECRETS, THE(1937); WE ARE NOT ALONE(1939)

Thomas Carlyle
Silents
ORPHANS OF THE STORM(1922), w

Carlyle Cousins
RADIO FOLLIES(1935, Brit.)

The Carlyle Cousins
FOR THE LOVE OF MIKE(1933, Brit.)

Richard Carlysle
HEARTS IN DIXIE(1929)

Sydney Carlysle
Misc. Talkies
WEEKEND LOVER(1969)

Michael Carman
MOUTH TO MOUTH(1978, Aus.)

Roberto Carmardiel
COLOSSUS OF RHODES, THE(1961, Ital., Fr., Span.)

Maria Grazia Carmassi
CLIMAX, THE(1967, Fr., Ital.)

Pamela Carme
SUCH IS THE LAW(1930, Brit.); LAZYBONES(1935, Brit.); YOUNG AND INNOCENT(1938, Brit.)

Eddie Carmel
50,000 B.C.(BEFORE CLOTHING)* (1963); BRAIN THAT WOULDN'T DIE, THE(1959)

Roger Carmel
GOODBYE CHARLIE(1964)

Roger C. Carmel
SILENCERS, THE(; STAGE STRUCK(1958); HOUSE IS NOT A HOME, A(1964); ART OF LOVE, THE(1965); ALVAREZ KELLY(1966); GAMBIT(1966); VENETIAN AFFAIR, THE(1967); SKULLDUGGERY(1970); BREEZY(1973); THUNDER AND LIGHTNING(1977); HARDLY WORKING(1981)

Carmen
LAST OF THE SECRET AGENTS?, THE(1966); HICKEY AND BOGGS(1972); NEST, THE(1982, Span.)

Jean Carmen
KISS AND MAKE UP(1934); YOUNG AND BEAUTIFUL(1934); ARIZONA GUNFIGHTER(1937); PAROLED FROM THE BIG HOUSE(1938); CRASHING THRU(1939); SMOKY TRAILS(1939)
Misc. Talkies
BORN TO BATTLE(1935)

Jean Carmen [Julia Thayer]
IN OLD MONTANA(1939)

Jeanne Carmen
WOLVES OF THE SEA(1938); THREE OUTLAWS, THE(1956); PORTLAND EXPOSE(1957); UNTAMED YOUTH(1957); WAR DRUMS(1957); MONSTER OF PIEDRAS BLANCAS, THE(1959)

Jeannie Carmen
DEVIL'S HAND, THE(1961)

Jewel Carmen
Silents
AMERICAN ARISTOCRACY(1916); FLIRTING WITH FATE(1916); MANHATTAN MADNESS(1916); AMERICAN METHODS(1917); TALE OF TWO CITIES, A(1917); BRIDE OF FEAR, THE(1918); KINGDOM OF LOVE, THE(1918); LES MISERABLES(1918); NOBODY(1921); SILVER LINING, THE(1921); BAT, THE(1926)
Misc. Silents
CHILDREN IN THE HOUSE, THE(1916); HALF BREED, THE(1916); SUNSHINE DAD(1916); CONQUEROR, THE(1917); TO HONOR AND OBEY(1917); WHEN A MAN SEES RED(1917); CONFESSION(1918); FALLEN ANGEL, THE(1918); GIRL WITH THE CHAMPAGNE EYES, THE(1918); LAWLESS LOVE(1918)

Julie Carmen
GLORIA(1980); NIGHT OF THE JUGGLER(1980)
Misc. Talkies
LAST PLANE OUT(1983)

Michael Carmen
RAW DEAL(1977, Aus.); 20TH CENTURY OZ(1977, Aus.)

Carmen Amaya and Her Company
FOLLOW THE BOYS(1944)

Carmen Amaya Dancers
PANAMA HATTIE(1942)

The Carmen Amaya Troupe
KNICKERBOCKER HOLIDAY(1944)

Carmen Cavallaro and his Orchestra
HOLLYWOOD CANTEEN(1944)

Carmen Cavallaro Orchestra
TIME, THE PLACE AND THE GIRL, THE(1946)

Julius Carmer
13 RUE MADELEINE(1946)

Jean Carmet
CONFESSIONS OF A ROGUE(1948, Fr.); MONSIEUR VINCENT(1949, Fr.); KNOCK(1955, Fr.); LA BELLE AMERICAINE(1961, Fr.); DEVIL AND THE TEN COMMANDMENTS, THE(1962, Fr.); ANY NUMBER CAN WIN(1963 Fr.); ELUSIVE CORPORAL, THE(1963, Fr.); COUNTERFEIT CONSTABLE, THE(1966, Fr.); VERY HAPPY ALEXANDER(1969, Fr.); AND SOON THE DARKNESS(1970, Brit.); TALL BLOND MAN WITH ONE BLACK SHOE, THE(1973, Fr.); DON'T CRY WITH YOUR MOUTH FULL(1974, Fr.); LE PETIT THEATRE DE JEAN RENOIR(1974, Fr.); JUST BEFORE NIGHTFALL(1975, Fr./Ital.); BLACK AND WHITE IN COLOR(1976, Fr.); ALICE, OR THE LAST ESCAPADE(1977, Fr.); VIOLETTE(1978, Fr.); CIRCLE OF DECEIT(1982, Fr./Ger.); LES MISERABLES(1982, Fr.)
1984
DOG DAY(1984, Fr.)

M. Carmet
THINGS OF LIFE, THE(1970, Fr./Ital./Switz.)

Maria Carmi
Misc. Silents
LOST IN THE DARK(1914, Ital.)
Mariz Carmi
Misc. Silents
TERESA RAQUIN(1915, Ital.)
Vera Carmi
ANYTHING FOR A SONG(1947, Ital.); ISLAND OF PROCIDA, THE(1952, Ital.); JOURNEY TO LOVE(1953, Ital.); FRIENDS FOR LIFE(1964, Ital.)
Evangeline Carmichael
WIRETAPPERS(1956)
H. Kenn Carmichael
MARK OF THE HAWK, THE(1958), w
Hoagy Carmichael
TOPPER(1937); TO HAVE AND HAVE NOT(1944); JOHNNY ANGEL(1945); BEST YEARS OF OUR LIVES, THE(1946); CANYON PASSAGE(1946), a, m/l; NIGHT SONG(1947); JOHNNY HOLIDAY(1949); YOUNG MAN WITH A HORN(1950); BELLES ON THEIR TOES(1952); LAS VEGAS STORY, THE(1952); TIMBERJACK(1955)
Ian Carmichael
DEAR MR. PROHACK(1949, Brit.); GAY LADY, THE(1949, Brit.); GHOST SHIP(1953, Brit.); MEET MR. LUCIFER(1953, Brit.); TIME GENTLEMEN PLEASE!(1953, Brit.); BETRAYED(1954); COLDITZ STORY, THE(1955, Brit.); STORM OVER THE NILE(1955, Brit.); PRIVATE'S PROGRESS(1956, Brit.); SIMON AND LAURA(1956, Brit.); BROTHERS IN LAW(1957, Brit.); LUCKY JIM(1957, Brit.); HAPPY IS THE BRIDE(1958, Brit.); I'M ALL RIGHT, JACK(1959, Brit.); LEFT, RIGHT AND CENTRE(1959); LIGHT UP THE SKY(1960, Brit.); SCHOOL FOR SCOUNDRELS(1960, Brit.); DOUBLE BUNK(1961, Brit.); BIG MONEY, THE(1962, Brit.); HEAVENS ABOVE!(1963, Brit.); CASE OF THE 44'S, THE(1964 Brit./Den.); HIDE AND SEEK(1964, Brit.); AMOROUS MR. PRAWN, THE(1965, Brit.); SMASHING TIME(1967 Brit.); MAGNIFICENT SEVEN DEADLY SINS, THE(1971, Brit.); FROM BEYOND THE GRAVE(1974, Brit.); LADY VANISHES, THE(1980, Brit.)
Judy Carmichael
SNAKE PEOPLE, THE(1968, Mex./U.S.)
Patricia Carmichael
DEAR, DEAD DELILAH(1972)
Patsy Carmichael
HEROES OF THE SADDLE(1940)
Ralph Carmichael
WIRETAPPERS(1956), m; PERSUADER, THE(1957), m, md; 4D MAN(1959), m, md; RESTLESS ONES, THE(1965), m; THREE WEEKS OF LOVE(1965), m; FOR PETE'S SAKE!(1966), m; CROSS AND THE SWITCHBLADE, THE(1970), m; LATE LIZ, THE(1971), m, md; JONI(1980), m
Stokeley Carmichael
TELL ME LIES(1968, Brit.)
Tullio Carminati
GALLANT LADY(1934); MOULIN ROUGE(1934); ONE NIGHT OF LOVE(1934); LET'S LIVE TONIGHT(1935); PARIS IN SPRING(1935); GIRLS IN THE STREET(1937, Brit.); SHOW GOES ON, THE(1938, Brit.); SAFARI(1940); SUICIDE LEGION(1940, Brit.); GOLDEN MADONNA, THE(1949, Brit.); BEAUTY AND THE DEVIL(1952, Fr./Ital.); ROMAN HOLIDAY(1953); JOAN AT THE STAKE(1954, Ital./Fr.); WAR AND PEACE(1956, Ital./U.S.); BREATH OF SCANDAL, A(1960); EL CID(1961, U.S./Ital.); ADVENTURES OF A YOUNG MAN(1962); SWORDSMAN OF SIENA, THE(1962, Fr./Ital.); CARDINAL, THE(1963)
Silents
BAT, THE(1926); STAGE MADNESS(1927)
Misc. Silents
DUCHESS OF BUFFALO, THE(1926); HONEYMOON HATE(1927)
Tullo Carminati
Silents
THREE SINNERS(1928)
Twilio Carminati
GIRL IN THE STREET(1938, Brit.)
Giuliano Carmineo
MIGHTY URSUS(1962, Ital./Span.), w
Chris Carmody
GLASS HOUSES(1972)
Don Carmody
TULIPS(1981, Can), p; PORKY'S(1982), p; PORKY'S II: THE NEXT DAY(1983), p; SPACEHUNTER: ADVENTURES IN THE FORBIDDEN ZONE(1983), p
1984
SURROGATE, THE(1984, Can.), p, d, w
John Carmody
BOOMERANG(1947); WARM IN THE BUD(1970); FARMER, THE(1977), w
Peter Carmody
FIRM MAN, THE(1975, Aus.); TRESPASSERS, THE(1976, Aus.)
Gabriel Carmona
PANDORA AND THE FLYING DUTCHMAN(1951, Brit.)
Gonzalo Carmona
TOM THUMB(1967, Mex.)
Guillermo Carmona
COMMANDO(1962, Ital., Span., Bel., Ger.)
Jerado Carmona
BOULEVARD NIGHTS(1979)
Louise Carmona
SUMMER CAMP(1979)
Luz Carmona
SHE-DEVIL ISLAND(1936, Mex.)
Mario Carmona
DAUGHTERS OF SATAN(1972), set d; SUPERBEAST(1972), set d
Nick Carmona
SWORD IN THE DESERT(1949), spec eff
Teodi Carmona
NO PLACE TO HIDE(1956), art d
Stella Carnacina
TORMENTED, THE(1978, Ital.)
Gianni Carnago
FINE PAIR, A(1969, Ital.)

Suzan Carnahan [Susan Peters]
SANTA FE TRAIL(1940)
Thomas Carnahan
Silents
CHRIS AND THE WONDERFUL LAMP(1917)
John Carnavale
SHADOW STRIKES, THE(1937)
Judy Carne
PAIR OF BRIEFS, A(1963, Brit.); AMERICANIZATION OF EMILY, THE(1964); ALL THE RIGHT NOISES(1973, Brit.)
Marcel Carne
PORT OF SHADOWS(1938, Fr.), d; BIZARRE BIZARRE(1939, Fr.), d; DAYBREAK(1940, Fr.), d; CHILDREN OF PARADISE(1945, Fr.), d; DEVIL'S ENVOYS, THE(1947, Fr.), d; GATES OF THE NIGHT(1950, Fr.), p&d; LA MARIE DU PORT(1951, Fr.), d, w; ADULTERESS, THE(1959, Fr.), d, w; CHEATERS, THE(1961, Fr.), d, w
Sturges Carne
GARDEN OF ALLAH, THE(1936), art d; LITTLE LORD FAUNTLEROY(1936), art d; SYLVIA SCARLETT(1936), art d; IT'S GREAT TO BE YOUNG(1946), art d; SINGIN' IN THE CORN(1946), art d; GALLANT BLADE, THE(1948), art d; LADY FROM SHANGHAI, THE(1948), art d; LONE WOLF AND HIS LADY, THE(1949), art d; RUSTY SAVES A LIFE(1949), art d; SONG OF INDIA(1949), art d
Sturges D. Carne
TANGIER(1946), art d
Andre Carnege
ORPHEUS(1950, Fr.)
Misc. Silents
REWARD OF FAITH(1929)
Dale Carnegie
JIGGS AND MAGGIE IN SOCIETY(1948)
Eddie Carnegie
OUR HEARTS WERE GROWING UP(1946); TROUBLE WITH WOMEN, THE(1947)
Hattie Carnegie
OUR BETTERS(1933), cos
Margaret Carnegie
MAD DOG MORGAN(1976,Aus.), w
Robert Carnegie
MOTHER'S DAY(1980)
Milton Carneiro
LOLLIPOP(1966, Braz.)
Cliff Carnell
SHADOWS(1960); TOO LATE BLUES(1962); MAN FROM THE DINERS' CLUB, THE(1963); UNDER THE YUM-YUM TREE(1963); LOLLIPOP COVER, THE(1965); PRIVATE DUTY NURSES(1972); WOMAN UNDER THE INFLUENCE, A(1974); WHITE BUFFALO, THE(1977)
Suzi Carnell
STUDS LONIGAN(1960); EXPLOSIVE GENERATION, THE(1961); RUNAWAY GIRL(1966)
Francesco Carnellitti
PRIEST OF LOVE(1981, Brit.)
Francesco Carnelutti
1984
BASILEUS QUARTET(1984, Ital.)
Antonio Carnera
EARTH ENTRANCED(1970, Braz.)
Primo Carnera
PRIZEFIGHTER AND THE LADY, THE(1933); MIGHTY JOE YOUNG(1949); CASANOVA'S BIG NIGHT(1954); PRINCE VALIANT(1954); KID FOR TWO FARTHINGS, A(1956, Brit.); HERCULES UNCHAINED(1960, Ital./Fr.)
Carnero
SOFT SKIN, THE(1964, Fr.)
Kim Carnes
C'MON, LET'S LIVE A LITTLE(1967)
Terrance Mario Carnes
GHOST STORY(1981)
Giuliana Carnescecchi
END OF THE WORLD(in Our Usual Bed In a Night Full of Rain), THE*1/2 (1978, Ital.)
Jack Carnevale
HIS NIGHT OUT(1935)
Ida Carnevali
1984
BIG MEAT EATER(1984, Can.)
Alan Carney
ADVENTURES OF A ROOKIE(1943); AROUND THE WORLD(1943); GANGWAY FOR TOMORROW(1943); GILDERSLEEVE'S BAD DAY(1943); MEXICAN SPITFIRE'S BLESSED EVENT(1943); MR. LUCKY(1943); ROOKIES IN BURMA(1943); GIRL RUSH(1944); SEVEN DAYS ASHORE(1944); STEP LIVELY(1944); RADIO STARS ON PARADE(1945); ZOMBIES ON BROADWAY(1945); GENIUS AT WORK(1946); VACATION IN RENO(1946); PRETENDER, THE(1947); HIDEOUT(1949); LI'L ABNER(1959); NORTH TO ALASKA(1960); ABSENT-MINDED PROFESSOR, THE(1961); SWINGIN' ALONG(1962); IT'S A MAD, MAD, MAD, MAD WORLD(1963); SON OF FLUBBER(1963); SYLVIA(1965); ADVENTURES OF BULLWHIP GRIFFIN, THE(1967); MONKEYS, GO HOME!(1967); WILD ROVERS(1971)
Art Carney
YELLOW ROLLS-ROYCE, THE(1965, Brit.); GUIDE FOR THE MARRIED MAN, A(1967); HARRY AND TONTO(1974); W. W. AND THE DIXIE DANCEKINGS(1975); WON TON TON, THE DOG WHO SAVED HOLLYWOOD(1976); LATE SHOW, THE(1977); SCOTT JOPLIN(1977); HOUSE CALLS(1978); MOVIE MOVIE(1978); GOING IN STYLE(1979); RAVAGERS, THE(1979); SUNBURN(1979); DEFIANCE(1980); ROADIE(1980); STEEL(1980); ST. HELENS(1981); TAKE THIS JOB AND SHOVE IT(1981); BETTER LATE THAN NEVER(1983)
1984
FIRESTARTER(1984); MUPPETS TAKE MANHATTAN, THE(1984); NAKED FACE, THE(1984)
Augustus Carney
Silents
MARTYRS OF THE ALAMO, THE(1915)
Bob Carney
KENTUCKY JUBILEE(1951); IT GROWS ON TREES(1952); PERILOUS JOURNEY, A(1953); ACCUSED OF MURDER(1956)

Brian Carney
HANKY-PANKY(1982)
Daniel Carney
NIGHT OF THE ASKARI(1978, Ger./South African), w; WILD GEESE, THE(1978, Brit.), w
Silents
AMERICA(1924)
Fred Carney
METEOR(1979); LOVING COUPLES(1980); BUSTIN' LOOSE(1981)
George Carney
COMMISSIONAIRE(1933, Brit.); EASY MONEY(1934, Brit.); GLIMPSE OF PARA-
DISE, A(1934, Brit.); LEST WE FORGET(1934, Brit.); MUSIC HALL(1934, Brit.); NIGHT
CLUB QUEEN(1934, Brit.); SAY IT WITH FLOWERS(1934, Brit.); CITY OF BEAUTI-
FUL NONSENSE, THE(1935, Brit.); COCK O' THE NORTH(1935, Brit.); FLOOD
TIDE(1935, Brit.); REAL BLOKE, A(1935, Brit.); SMALL MAN, THE(1935, Brit.);
VARIETY(1935, Brit.); WINDFALL(1935, Brit.); FORBIDDEN MUSIC(1936, Brit.); IT'S
IN THE BAG(1936, Brit.); TOMORROW WE LIVE(1936, Brit.); BEAUTY AND THE
BARGE(1937, Brit.); DREAMING LIPS(1937, Brit.); FATHER STEPS OUT(1937, Brit.);
LANCASHIRE LUCK(1937, Brit.); LITTLE MISS SOMEBODY(1937, Brit.); EASY
RICHES(1938, Brit.); MIRACLES DO HAPPEN(1938, Brit.); PAID IN ERROR(1938,
Brit.); WEDDINGS ARE WONDERFUL(1938, Brit.); COME ON GEORGE(1939, Brit.);
BRIGGS FAMILY, THE(1940, Brit.); CONVOY(1940, Brit.); STARS LOOK DOWN, THE(1940,
Brit.); COMMON TOUCH, THE(1941, Brit.); HARD STEEL(1941, Brit.); IN WHICH WE
SERVE(1942, Brit.); LADY IN DISTRESS(1942, Brit.); PLAYBOY, THE(1942, Brit.);
REMARKABLE MR. KIPPS(1942, Brit.); ROSE OF TRALEE(1942, Brit.); UNPUB-
LISHED STORY(1942, Brit.); NIGHT INVADER, THE(1943, Brit.); SCHWEIK'S NEW
ADVENTURES(1943, Brit.); WHEN WE ARE MARRIED(1943, Brit.); YOUNG MAN'S
FANCY(1943, Brit.); SOLDIER, SAILOR(1944, Brit.); THUNDER ROCK(1944, Brit.);
WELCOME, MR. WASHINGTON(1944, Brit.); LOVE ON THE DOLE(1945, Brit.);
WANTED FOR MURDER(1946, Brit.); WOMAN TO WOMAN(1946, Brit.); BRIGHTON
ROCK(1947, Brit.); FORTUNE LANE(1947, Brit.); I KNOW WHERE I'M GOING(1947,
Brit.); ROOT OF ALL EVIL, THE(1947, Brit.); TAWNY PIPIT(1947, Brit.); AGITATOR,
THE(1949, Brit.); WATERLOO ROAD(1949, Brit.); GOOD TIME GIRL(1950, Brit.); LITTLE
BALLERINA, THE(1951, Brit.)
Misc. Silents
SOME WAITER!(1916, Brit.), a, d
Grace Carney
OWL AND THE PUSSYCAT, THE(1970)
James Carney
REMBRANDT(1936, Brit.); ALF'S BUTTON AFLOAT(1938, Brit.); SEZ O'REILLY TO
MACNAB(1938, Brit.); DR. O'DOWD(1940, Brit.); HOUR OF GLORY(1949, Brit.);
PRINCE OF FOXES(1949); DANCE HALL(1950, Brit.); RELUCTANT WIDOW,
THE(1951, Brit.); GLORY AT SEA(1952, Brit.); LANDFALL(1953, Brit.); IMPUL-
SE(1955, Brit.)
John Carney
HAMLET(1969, Brit.)
1984
TOP SECRET!(1984)
John J. Carney
CLOCKWORK ORANGE, A(1971, Brit.)
1984
SWORD OF THE VALIANT(1984, Brit.)
Lucile Carney
Silents
DARK MIRROR, THE(1920)
Marion Carney
DRIFTIN' RIVER(1946); DAUGHTER OF THE WEST(1949)
Mary Carney
LAW FOR TOMBSTONE(1937)
Matt Carney
FAR FROM DALLAS(1972, Fr.); ONCE IN PARIS(1978)
Terry Carney
SCOTLAND YARD INSPECTOR(1952, Brit.); WOMAN IN HIDING(1953, Brit.)
Thom Carney
CELL 2455, DEATH ROW(1955); IT! THE TERROR FROM BEYOND SPACE(1958);
WHO'S MINDING THE MINT?(1967)
Will Carney
SUMMER SCHOOL TEACHERS(1977)
Suzanne Carnhan
MEET JOHN DOE(1941)
John Carnochan
INDEPENDENCE DAY(1976), ed; BOSS'S SON, THE(1978), ed
1984
HEARTBREAKERS(1984), ed
Angela Carnon
GUESS WHAT HAPPENED TO COUNT DRACULA(1970)
Misc. Talkies
YOUNG AND WILD(1975)
Morris Carnovsky
LIFE OF EMILE ZOLA, THE(1937); TOVARICH(1937); EDGE OF DARKNESS(1943);
ADDRESS UNKNOWN(1944); MASTER RACE, THE(1944); CORNERED(1945); MISS
SUSIE SLAGLE'S(1945); OUR VINES HAVE TENDER GRAPES(1945); RHAPSODY
IN BLUE(1945); DEAD RECKONING(1947); DISHONORED LADY(1947); MAN-EAT-
ER OF KUMAON(1948); SAIGON(1948); SIREN OF ATLANTIS(1948); GUN CRA-
ZY(1949); THIEVES' HIGHWAY(1949); CYRANO DE BERGERAC(1950); WESTERN
PACIFIC AGENT(1950); SECOND WOMAN, THE(1951); VIEW FROM THE BRIDGE,
A(1962, Fr./Ital.); GAMBLER, THE(1974)
Misc. Talkies
JOE PALOOKA IN THE KNOCKOUT(1947)
Alicia Caro
DAUGHTER OF DECEIT(1977, Mex.)
Cathia Caro
VIOLENT SUMMER(1961, Fr./Ital.)
Julia Delgado Caro
AGE OF INFIDELITY(1958, Span.)
Leticia Caro
1984
REVOLT OF JOB, THE(1984, Hung./Ger.)

Nidia Caro
HEROINA(1965)
Norman Caro
GIRO CITY(1982, Brit.)
Massimo Carocci
ADIOS SABATA(1971, Ital./Span.)
Philippe Caroit
AVIATOR'S WIFE, THE(1981, Fr.)
Ann Carol
GHOST RIDER, THE(1935)
Cindy Carol
GIDGET GOES TO ROME(1963); DEAR BRIGETTE(1965)
Jack Carol
KISS THE BLOOD OFF MY HANDS(1948); LINEUP, THE(1958); CRIMSON KIMO-
NO, THE(1959)
Joan Carol
LANCER SPY(1937); ONE MILE FROM HEAVEN(1937); WALKING DOWN BROAD-
WAY(1938); MR. MOTO'S LAST WARNING(1939); CHAMPAGNE CHARLIE(1944,
Brit.); UNEASY TERMS(1948, Brit.); JACK OF DIAMONDS, THE(1949, Brit.); DARK
LIGHT, THE(1951, Brit.); GHOST SHIP(1953, Brit.); GENTLE TOUCH, THE(1956,
Brit.); JOHNNY, YOU'RE WANTED(1956, Brit.); ROGUE'S YARN(1956, Brit.)
John Carol
PERFECT CRIME, THE(1937, Brit.); WINDMILL, THE(1937, Brit.); YOU LIVE AND
LEARN(1937, Brit.); DARK STAIRWAY, THE(1938, Brit.); THANK EVANS(1938, Brit.);
DUMMY TALKS, THE(1943, Brit.); SILVER FLEET, THE(1945, Brit.); IT ALWAYS
RAINS ON SUNDAY(1949, Brit.); PINK STRING AND SEALING WAX(1950, Brit.);
SPIDER AND THE FLY, THE(1952, Brit.)
Joseph Carol
LADIES OF THE CHORUS(1948), w
Judith Carol
DEAR MURDERER(1947, Brit.)
Lesley Carol
EMBEZZLER, THE(1954, Brit.)
Leslie Carol
GOOD COMPANIONS, THE(1957, Brit.)
Linda Carol
ANGEL IN MY POCKET(1969)
Lynn Carol
SAN FERRY ANN(1965, Brit.)
Lynne Carol
YANKS(1979)
Martine Carol
NOUS IRONS A PARIS(1949, Fr.); CAROLINE CHERIE(1951, Fr.); LOVERS OF
VERONA, THE(1951, Fr.); LES BELLES-DE-NUIT(1952, Fr.); LUCRECE BORGIA(1953,
Ital./Fr.); DAUGHTERS OF DESTINY(1954, Fr./Ital.); MADAME DU BARRY(1954
Fr./Ital.); SECRETS D'ALCOVE(1954, Fr./Ital.); LOLA MONTES(1955, Fr./Ger.);
ADORABLE CREATURES(1956, Fr.); AROUND THE WORLD IN 80 DAYS(1956);
DEFEND MY LOVE(1956, Ital.); FRENCH, THEY ARE A FUNNY RACE, THE(1956,
Fr.); ACTION OF THE TIGER(1957); NANA(1957, Fr./Ital.); NATHALIE(1958, Fr.);
TEN SECONDS TO HELL(1959); AUSTERLITZ(1960, Fr./Ital./Yugo.); NATHALIE,
AGENT SECRET(1960, Fr.); LOVE AND THE FRENCHWOMAN(1961, Fr.); COUN-
TERFEITERS OF PARIS, THE(1962, Fr., Ital.); HELL IS EMPTY(1967, Brit./Ital)
Misc. Talkies
ATOMIC AGENT(1959, Fr.)
Roger Carol
OPHELIA(1964, Fr.)
Sheila Carol
BEAST FROM THE HAUNTED CAVE(1960); SKI TROOP ATTACK(1960)
Sonia Carol
ROYAL DIVORCE, A(1938, Brit.)
Sue Carol
AIR CIRCUS, THE(1928); IT CAN BE DONE(1929); WHY LEAVE HOME?(1929);
AMOS 'N' ANDY(1930); BIG PARTY, THE(1930); DANCING SWEETIES(1930); GOLD-
EN CALF, THE(1930); LONE STAR RANGER, THE(1930); SHE'S MY WEAK-
NESS(1930); GRAFT(1931); IN THE LINE OF DUTY(1931); SECRET SINNERS(1933);
STRAIGHTAWAY(1934); DOCTOR'S DIARY, A(1937)
Misc. Talkies
CHASING THROUGH EUROPE(1929)
Silents
SLAVES OF BEAUTY(1927); SOFT CUSHIONS(1927); COHENS AND THE KELLYS
IN PARIS, THE(1928); WALKING BACK(1928); EXALTED FLAPPER, THE(1929);
GIRLS GONE WILD(1929)
Misc. Silents
BEAU BROADWAY(1928); CAPTAIN SWAGGER(1928); SKYSCRAPER(1928); WIN
THAT GIRL(1928)
Linda Carola
1984
MRS. SOFFEL(1984)
Joseph Carole
BABIES FOR SALE(1940), w; CONVICTED WOMAN(1940), w; MEN WITHOUT
SOULS(1940), w; MY SON IS GUILTY(1940), w; SCANDAL SHEET(1940), w; I'M
FROM ARKANSAS(1944), w; HOW DO YOU DO?(1946), w; RACING LUCK(1948), w;
TRIPLE THREAT(1948), w; MUTINEERS, THE(1949), w
The Carole Lombard Singers
FIREBALL 590(1966)
Nello Carolenuto
Silents
NERO(1922, U.S./Ital.)
Maria Grazia Caroli
TREE OF WOODEN CLOGS, THE(1979, Ital.)
Juan Carolilla
STOWAWAY GIRL(1957, Brit.)
Nancy Caroline
MACHISMO-40 GRAVES FOR 40 GUNS(1970)
Jimmy Caroll
GOOD COMPANIONS, THE(1957, Brit.)
John Caroll
MANTIS IN LACE(1968)

Linda Caroll
GEORGE(1973, U.S./Switz.)
Virginia Caroll
LOAN SHARK(1952)
Sal Carollo
SERPICO(1973)
1984
MOSCOW ON THE HUDSON(1984); SPLITZ(1984)
Barbara Caron
HAREM BUNCH; OR WAR AND PIECE, THE(1969); WILD, FREE AND HUNGRY(1970)
Misc. Talkies
CLASS OF '74(1972); BLUE MONEY(1975)
Danny Caron
PASSION FOR LIFE(1951, Fr.)
Doria Caron
BALL OF FIRE(1941); SHINE ON, HARVEST MOON(1944); CONFLICT(1945); MILDRED PIERCE(1945); I RING DOORBELLS(1946); ONE SUNDAY AFTERNOON(1948)
Elise Caron
COCKTAIL MOLOTOV(1980, Fr.)
Francois Caron
FIVE DAYS ONE SUMMER(1982)
Glen Caron
CONDORMAN(1981), w
Jacques Caron
QUEST FOR FIRE(1982, Fr./Can.)
Jeffery Caron
CAT ATE THE PARAKEET, THE(1972)
Leonard Caron
THOMAS CROWN AFFAIR, THE(1968)
Leslie Caron
AMERICAN IN PARIS, AN(1951); MAN WITH A CLOAK, THE(1951); GLORY ALLEY(1952); LILI(1953); STORY OF THREE LOVES, THE(1953); DADDY LONG LEGS(1955); GLASS SLIPPER, THE(1955); GABY(1956); DOCTOR'S DILEMMA, THE(1958, Brit.); GIGI(1958); MAN WHO UNDERSTOOD WOMEN, THE(1959); SUBTERRANEANS, THE(1960); FANNY(1961); GUNS OF DARKNESS(1962, Brit.); THREE FABLES OF LOVE(1963, Fr./Ital./Span.); FATHER GOOSE(1964); VERY SPECIAL FAVOR, A(1965); IS PARIS BURNING?(1966, U.S./Fr.); PROMISE HER ANYTHING(1966, Brit.); HEAD OF THE FAMILY(1967, Ital./Fr.); MADRON(1970, U.S./Israel); CHANDLER(1971); MAN WHO LOVED WOMEN, THE(1977, Fr.); VALENTINO(1977, Brit.); GOLDENGIRL(1979); CONTRACT, THE(1982, Pol.)
Misc. Talkies
NICOLE(1972)
Michel Caron
JOY(1983, Fr./Can.)
Pat Caron
SINGING COWBOY, THE(1936)
Patricia Caron
HOME TOWNERS, THE(1928); OH, YEAH!(1929); GIRLS ABOUT TOWN(1931); DANTE'S INFERNO(1935); SYLVIA SCARLETT(1936)
Silents
HONEYMOON FLATS(1928); JAZZ MAD(1928); IDAHO RED(1929)
Pauline Caron
BECKY SHARP(1935); COLLEEN(1936)
Pierre Caron
CINDERELLA(1937, Fr.), d
Richard Caron
SHADOW OF EVIL(1967, Fr./Ital.), w
Sandra Caron
SEA WIFE(1957, Brit.); LEATHER BOYS, THE(1965, Brit.); DON'T RAISE THE BRIDGE, LOWER THE RIVER(1968, Brit.); CARRY ON CAMPING(1969, Brit.); DIGBY, THE BIGGEST DOG IN THE WORLD(1974, Brit.)
Jack Carone
INDEPENDENCE DAY(1976)
Viti Caronia
HORNET'S NEST(1970)
Vittorio Caronia
NEXT!(1971, Ital./Span.), w
Bruno Carotenuto
WHERE THE HOT WIND BLOWS(1960, Fr., Ital.); VIOLENT SUMMER(1961, Fr./Ital.)
Mario Carotenuto
SCANDAL IN SORRENTO(1957, Ital./Fr.); IT HAPPENED IN ROME(1959, Ital.); LOVE AND LARCENY(1963, Fr./Ital.); HEAD OF THE FAMILY(1967, Ital./Fr.); IF IT'S TUESDAY, THIS MUST BE BELGIUM(1969); SCIENTIFIC CARDPLAYER, THE(1972, Ital.)
Memmo Carotenuto
BREAD, LOVE AND DREAMS(1953, Ital.); TOO BAD SHE'S BAD(1954, Ital.); LUCKY TO BE A WOMAN(1955, Ital.); FAREWELL TO ARMS, A(1957); BIG DEAL ON MADONNA STREET, THE(1960); WORLD IN MY POCKET, THE(1962, Fr./Ital./Ger.); LAZARILLO(1963, Span.); MALE COMPANION(1965, Fr./Ital.); MY WIFE'S ENEMY(1967, Ital.)
Memo Carotenuto
UMBERTO D(1955, Ital.)
A.J. Carothers
MIRACLE OF THE WHITE STALLIONS(1963), w; EMIL AND THE DETECTIVES(1964), w; HAPPIEST MILLIONAIRE, THE(1967), w; NEVER A DULL MOMENT(1968), w; HERO AT LARGE(1980), a, w
Homero Carpena
GAMES MEN PLAY, THE(1968, Arg.)
Betty Carpenter
Silents
KAISER, BEAST OF BERLIN, THE(1918); BURN 'EM UP BARNES(1921); DAWN OF THE EAST(1921); SUCH A LITTLE QUEEN(1921); CARDIGAN(1922)
Bill Carpenter
SAVAGE(1962)

Bonnie Carpenter
SHOOT THE MOON(1982)
Carleton Carpenter
LOST BOUNDARIES(1949); FATHER OF THE BRIDE(1950); SUMMER STOCK(1950); THREE LITTLE WORDS(1950); TWO WEEKS WITH LOVE(1950); VENGEANCE VALLEY(1951); WHISTLE AT EATON FALLS(1951); FEARLESS FAGAN(1952); SKY FULL OF MOON(1952); TAKE THE HIGH GROUND(1953); UP PERISCOPE(1959); SOME OF MY BEST FRIENDS ARE...(1971)
Carlton Carpenter
PROWLER, THE(1981)
Claude Carpenter
GHOST SHIP, THE(1943), set d; HIGHER AND HIGHER(1943), set d; MR. LUCKY(1943), set d; SKY'S THE LIMIT, THE(1943), set d; EXPERIMENT PERILOUS(1944), set d; STEP LIVELY(1944), set d; HAVING WONDERFUL CRIME(1945), set d; SPANISH MAIN, THE(1945), set d; NOTORIOUS(1946), set d; SINBAD THE SAILOR(1947), set d; PORTRAIT OF JENNIE(1949), set d; O. HENRY'S FULL HOUSE(1952), set d; STARS AND STRIPES FOREVER(1952), set d; WE'RE NOT MARRIED(1952), set d; GENTLEMEN PREFER BLONDES(1953), set d; VICKI(1953), set d; HATARI!(1962), set d; RED LINE 7000(1965), set d; TOWN TAMER(1965), set d; HARPER(1966), set d
Claude E. Carpenter
ONCE UPON A HONEYMOON(1942), set d
Constance Carpenter
JUST FOR A SONG(1930, Brit.); TWO WORLD(1930, Brit.); BROWN SUGAR(1931, Brit.)
Dale Carpenter
Misc. Talkies
FIRST TIME ROUND(1972)
David Carpenter
Misc. Talkies
TO LOVE, PERHAPS TO DIE(1975)
Don Carpenter
PAYDAY(1972), p, w
Ed Carpenter
NEW LAND, THE(1973, Swed.)
Edward Childs Carpenter
BACHELOR FATHER(1931), w; WHISTLING IN THE DARK(1933), w; ONE NEW YORK NIGHT(1935), w; PERFECT GENTLEMAN, THE(1935), w; WHISTLING IN THE DARK(1941), w; MAJOR AND THE MINOR, THE(1942), w; YOU'RE NEVER TOO YOUNG(1955), w
Silents
CAPTAIN COURTESY(1915), w; TONGUES OF MEN, THE(1916), w; LEOPARD LADY, THE(1928), w
Elliot Carpenter
STRIKE UP THE BAND(1940)
Elliott Carpenter
YES SIR, MR. BONES(1951)
Finele Carpenter
CANNONBALL RUN, THE(1981)
Florence Carpenter
Silents
PAIR OF SILK STOCKINGS, A(1918); TESTING BLOCK, THE(1920); SEA LION, THE(1921)
Misc. Silents
FACE VALUE(1918); UNCLE TOM'S CABIN(1918); JINX(1919); BELLE OF ALASKA(1922)
Francis Carpenter
Silents
COMMANDING OFFICER, THE(1915); GRETCHEN, THE GREENHORN(1916); LITTLE SCHOOL MA'AM, THE(1916); MARTHA'S VINDICATION(1916); PATRIOT, THE(1916); JACK AND THE BEANSTALK(1917); INFAMOUS MISS REVELL, THE(1921); RIP VAN WINKLE(1921)
Misc. Silents
GOING STRAIGHT(1916); ALADDIN AND THE WONDERFUL LAMP(1917); BABES IN THE WOODS(1917); TREASURE ISLAND(1917); FAN FAN(1918); TRUE BLUE(1918)
Frank "Red" Carpenter
LAWLESS RIDER, THE(1954); OUTLAW TREASURE(1955); I KILLED WILD BILL HICKOK(1956)
Freddie Carpenter
LADIES' DAY(1943); CARNIVAL(1946, Brit.), ch; EASY MONEY(1948, Brit.); SHOWTIME(1948, Brit.), d
Georges Carpenter
Misc. Silents
GIPSY CAVALIER, A(1922, Brit.)
Gloria Mitzi Carpenter
THIRTY SIX HOURS TO KILL(1936)
Grant Carpenter
Silents
SHE LOVES AND LIES(1920), w; LESSONS IN LOVE(1921), w; PRIDE OF PALOMAR, THE(1922), w; GOLD DIGGERS, THE(1923), w; SIXTY CENTS AN HOUR(1923), w
H.B. Carpenter
Silents
JULES OF THE STRONG HEART(1918); ONE MORE AMERICAN(1918); LAST CHANCE, THE(1926), d; RIDERS OF THE RIO GRANDE(1929)
Misc. Silents
SAGEBRUSH LADY, THE(1925), d; LOVIN' FOOL, THE(1926), d; LUCKY SPURS(1926), d; WESTERN TRAILS(1926), d
Hank Carpenter
ROLLIN' PLAINS(1938)
Harry Carpenter
MAGIC CHRISTIAN, THE(1970, Brit.)
Horace B. Carpenter
WEST OF THE ROCKIES(1929), a, d; SOUTH OF SONORA(1930); PARTNERS OF THE TRAIL(1931); WILD WEST WHOOPEE(1931); OUT OF SINGAPORE(1932); RIDERS OF THE DESERT(1932); SIGN OF THE CROSS, THE(1932); DUDE BANDIT, THE(1933); GUN LAW(1933); KING OF THE ARENA(1933); LONE AVENGER, THE(1933); GUN JUSTICE(1934); SMOKING GUNS(1934); WEST OF THE DIVIDE(1934); DESERT MESA(1935); IN OLD SANTA FE(1935); SMOKEY SMITH(1935);

WESTERN FRONTIER(1935); FUGITIVE SHERIFF, THE(1936); LAWLESS NINE-TIES, THE(1936); LAWLESS RIDERS(1936); LONELY TRAIL, THE(1936); MAN FROM GUN TOWN, THE(1936); BAR Z BAD MEN(1937); GIT ALONG, LITTLE DO-GIES(1937); GUN LORDS OF STIRRUP BASIN(1937); GUN RANGER, THE(1937); RANGE DEFENDERS(1937); ROGUE OF THE RANGE(1937); RUSTLER'S VAL-LEY(1937); TRAILING TROUBLE(1937); WHERE TRAILS DIVIDE(1937); COLORADO KID(1938); LAW COMMANDS, THE(1938); PAROLED–TO DIE(1938); PHANTOM RANGER(1938); PRIDE OF THE WEST(1938); STARLIGHT OVER TEXAS(1938); STRANGER FROM ARIZONA, THE(1938); SUNSET TRAIL(1938); COME ON RANG-ERS(1939); ROVIN' TUMBLEWEEDS(1939); SAGA OF DEATH VALLEY(1939); SPOIL-ERS OF THE RANGE(1939); ONE MAN'S LAW(1940); THUNDER OVER THE PRAIRIE(1941); WRANGLER'S ROOST(1941); BILLY THE KID TRAPPED(1942); HEART OF THE GOLDEN WEST(1942); IN OLD CALIFORNIA(1942); JOAN OF OZARK(1942); OUTLAWS OF PINE RIDGE(1942); ROLLING DOWN THE GREAT DIVIDE(1942); SHADOWS ON THE SAGE(1942); WESTWARD HO(1942); SILVER CITY RAIDERS(1943); CHEYENNE WILDCAT(1944); CODE OF THE PRAIRIE(1944); MARSHAL OF RENO(1944); RANGE LAW(1944); SHERIFF OF SUNDOWN(1944); SILVER CITY KID(1944); SONORA STAGECOACH(1944); VIGILANTES OF DODGE CITY(1944); COLORADO PIONEERS(1945); CORPUS CHRISTI BANDITS(1945); LONE TEXAS RANGER(1945)
Misc. Talkies
TRAILS OF THE GOLDEN WEST(1931); GALLOPING KID, THE(1932); PECOS DANDY, THE(1934), d
Silents
CALL OF THE NORTH, THE(1914); MAN FROM HOME, THE(1914); VIRGINIAN, THE(1914); ARAB, THE(1915); ARMSTRONG'S WIFE(1915); CARMEN(1915); GOLD-EN CHANCE, THE(1915); GOOSE GIRL, THE(1915); WOMAN, THE(1915); ANTON THE TERRIBLE(1916); JOAN THE WOMAN(1916); PLOW GIRL, THE(1916); RACE, THE(1916); NAN OF MUSIC MOUNTAIN(1917); WILD AND WOOLLY(1917), w; ARIZONA KID, THE(1929), a, d&w; FALSE FATHERS(1929), a, d
Misc. Silents
FOR THE DEFENCE(1916); HEIR TO THE HOORAH, THE(1916); WINNING OF SALLY TEMPLE, THE(1917); RIDING FOOL(1924), d; DESPERATE ODDS(1925), d; FANGS OF FATE(1925), d; JUST TRAVELIN'(1927), d

Horace Carpenter
BRIDE OF THE DESERT(1929); MANIAC(1934); DOOMED AT SUNDOWN(1937); GUNSMOKE RANCH(1937); KING OF THE NEWSBOYS(1938); RETURN OF THE APE MAN(1944); GREAT STAGECOACH ROBBERY(1945)
Silents
PUPPET CROWN, THE(1915); KING'S CREEK LAW(1923)
Misc. Silents
HEADIN' THROUGH(1924)

James Carpenter
DOUGHBOYS IN IRELAND(1943); TWO GIRLS AND A SAILOR(1944)
Misc. Silents
GENTLEMAN OF QUALITY, A(1919)

Jean Carpenter
WEEKEND AT THE WALDORF(1945)
Silents
HELEN'S BABIES(1924)
Misc. Silents
STAMPEDE, THE(1921)

Jeanne Carpenter
GLAMOROUS NIGHT(1937, Brit.)
Silents
WHAT NO MAN KNOWS(1921); SIGN OF THE ROSE, THE(1922); ASHES OF VENGEANCE(1923)

Jill Carpenter
CAESAR AND CLEOPATRA(1946, Brit.); SIEGE OF SIDNEY STREET, THE(1960, Brit.), makeup; INFORMATION RECEIVED(1962, Brit.), makeup; PHAEDRA(1962, U.S./Gr./Fr.), makeup; HELLFIRE CLUB, THE(1963, Brit.), makeup; SKULL, THE(1965, Brit.), makeup; PSYCHOPATH, THE(1966, Brit.), makeup; TRAITOR'S GATE(1966, Brit./Ger.), makeup; PRIVILEGE(1967, Brit.), makeup; TO SIR, WITH LOVE(1967, Brit.), makeup; TORTURE GARDEN(1968, Brit.), makeup; WHERE'S JACK?(1969, Brit.), makeup; HELL BOATS(1970, Brit.), makeup; MIND OF MR. SOAMES, THE(1970, Brit.), makeup; DRACULA A.D. 1972(1972, Brit.), makeup; LIV-ING FREE(1972, Brit.), makeup
1984
PASSAGE TO INDIA, A(1984, Brit.), makeup

Jimmy Carpenter
FOLLOW THE BOYS(1944); THEY LIVE IN FEAR(1944); TOGETHER AGAIN(1944)

John Carpenter
DANTE'S INFERNO(1935); NAVAJO TRAIL, THE(1945); SONG OF OLD WYO-MING(1945); TRAIL OF KIT CARSON(1945); EL PASO KID, THE(1946); SONG OF THE WASTELAND(1947); LARCENY(1948); RELENTLESS(1948); RED CANYON(1949); BORDER OUTLAWS(1950); FIGHTING STALLION, THE(1950); CATTLE QUEEN(1951); IRON MAN, THE(1951); LAW AND ORDER(1953); SON OF THE RENEGADE(1953), a, p, w; LAWLESS RIDER, THE(1954), p, w; OUTLAW TREAS-URE(1955), p, w; I KILLED WILD BILL HICKOK(1956), p, w; RED SUN-DOWN(1956); NO PLACE TO LAND(1958); TOMBOY AND THE CHAMP(1961); 7TH COMMANDMENT, THE(1961); DARK STAR(1975), p&d, w, m; ASSAULT ON PRE-CINCT 13(1976), d&w, m; NETWORK(1976); EYES OF LAURA MARS(1978), w; HAL-LOWEEN(1978), d&m, w; FOG, THE(1980), d, w, m; ESCAPE FROM NEW YORK(1981), d, w, m; HALLOWEEN II(1981), p&w, m; HALLOWEEN III: SEASON OF THE WITCH(1982), p, m; THING, THE(1982), d; TOOTSIE(1982); CHRIS-TINE(1983), d, m
1984
STARMAN(1984), d

Johnny Carpenter
BADMAN'S GOLD(1951); LAWLESS RIDER, THE(1954)

Joseph Carpenter
SHARK RIVER(1953), w

Josh [John] Carpenter
NORTHWEST TRAIL(1945)

Josh "John" Carpenter
SANTA FE SADDLEMATES(1945)

Ken Carpenter
TRUE TO LIFE(1943); RHYTHM ON THE RIVER(1940); NEW YORK TOWN(1941); ROAD TO ZANZIBAR(1941); SPIRIT OF STANFORD, THE(1942); MYSTERY BROAD-CAST(1943); WHAT A WOMAN!(1943); PHANTOM OF THE PARADISE(1974)

Kenneth Carpenter
MR. SMITH GOES TO WASHINGTON(1939)

Linda Carpenter
DIFFERENT STORY, A(1978); APOCALYPSE NOW(1979)

Lisa Carpenter
PICTURE OF DORIAN GRAY, THE(1945)

Marcel Carpenter
LOVE IN A FOUR LETTER WORLD(1970, Can.), cos; FORTUNE AND MEN'S EYES(1971, U.S./Can.), cos

Margert Carpenter
EXPERIMENT PERILOUS(1944), w

Merta Carpenter
Silents
ONLY SON, THE(1914); WHERE THE TRAIL DIVIDES(1914)

Paul Carpenter
SCHOOL FOR SECRETS(1946, Brit.); THIS MAN IS MINE(1946 Brit.); UNEASY TERMS(1948, Brit.); ALBERT, R.N.(1953, Brit.); LANDFALL(1953, Brit.); BLACK GLOVE(1954, Brit.); CHANCE MEETING(1954, Brit.); DIPLOMATIC PASSPORT(1954, Brit.); DUEL IN THE JUNGLE(1954, Brit.); HEATWAVE(1954, Brit.); JOHNNY ON THE SPOT(1954, Brit.); LAST MOMENT, THE(1954, Brit.); NIGHT PEOPLE(1954); PAID TO KILL(1954, Brit.); RED DRESS, THE(1954, Brit.); UNHOLY FOUR, THE(1954, Brit.); WEAK AND THE WICKED, THE(1954, Brit.); DOCTOR AT SEA(1955, Brit.); HORNET'S NEST, THE(1955, Brit.); ONE JUMP AHEAD(1955, Brit.); SEA SHALL NOT HAVE THEM, THE(1955, Brit.); SHADOW OF A MAN(1955, Brit.); STOCK CAR(1955, Brit.); BEHIND THE HEADLINES(1956, Brit.); FIRE MAIDENS FROM OUTER SPACE(1956, Brit.); IRON PETTICOAT, THE(1956, Brit.); NARROWING CIRCLE, THE(1956, Brit.); BLACK ICE(1957, Brit.); NO ROAD BACK(1957, Brit.); SCOTLAND YARD DRAGNET(1957, Brit.); UNDERCOVER GIRL(1957, Brit.); IN-TENT TO KILL(1958, Brit.); MURDER REPORTED(1958, Brit.); ACTION STA-TIONS(1959, Brit.); DATE AT MIDNIGHT(1960, Brit.); JET STORM(1961, Brit.); CALL ME BWANA(1963, Brit.); FIRST MEN IN THE MOON(1964, Brit.); PANIC(1966, Brit.)

Penny Carpenter
HARDER THEY FALL, THE(1956)

Pete Carpenter
VANISHING POINT(1971), m

Peter Carpenter
BLOOD MANIA(1971), a, p; POINT OF TERROR(1971), a, p; RABBIT TEST(1978), m

Ralph Carpenter
MAN WITH BOGART'S FACE, THE(1980)

Randall Carpenter
CANNIBAL GIRLS(1973)

Richard Carpenter
TARNISHED HEROES(1961, Brit.); DAMN THE DEFIANT!(1962, Brit.); PASSWORD IS COURAGE, THE(1962, Brit.); MYSTERY SUBMARINE(1963, Brit.); WINGS OF MYSTERY(1963, Brit.); ESCAPE BY NIGHT(1965, Brit.); TERRORNAUTS, THE(1967, Brit.)

Roy Carpenter
Silents
FLOWING GOLD(1924), ph; AS MAN DESIRES(1925), ph; KNOCKOUT, THE(1925), ph; UNGUARDED HOUR(1925), ph

Russ Carpenter
1984
SOLE SURVIVOR(1984), ph

Stephen Carpenter
DORM THAT DRIPPED BLOOD, THE(1983), d, w, ph
1984
POWER, THE(1984), d&w Jeffery Obrow, w, ph, ed
Misc. Talkies
PRANKS(1982), d

Sue Ann Carpenter
SIDEWINDER ONE(1977)

Teresa Carpenter
STAR 80(1983), d&w

Thelma Carpenter
WIZ, THE(1978)
1984
COTTON CLUB, THE(1984)

Virginia Carpenter
PHANTOM OF CHINATOWN(1940); OUTLAWS OF THE RIO GRANDE(1941); ROLLIN' HOME TO TEXAS(1941); GHOST TOWN LAW(1942); LONE STAR VIGI-LANTES, THE(1942)

Willie Carpenter
WIZ, THE(1978)

Carpenter Corps de Ballet
CARNIVAL(1946, Brit.)

Don Carpentier
1984
BOSTONIANS, THE(1984), art d

Francois Yves Carpentier
GREAT BIG THING, A(1968, U.S./Can.)

Georges Carpentier
HOLD EVERYTHING(1930)
Misc. Silents
WONDER MAN, THE(1920)

Louis-Michel Carpentier
GULLIVER'S TRAVELS(1977, Brit., Bel.), anim

Marcel Carpentier
LE DENIER MILLIARDAIRE(1934, Fr.); CARNIVAL IN FLANDERS(1936, Fr.); CAFE DE PARIS(1938, Fr.)

Luigi Carpentieri
DEVIL'S COMMANDMENT, THE(1956, Ital.), p; IT HAPPENED IN ROME(1959, Ital.), p; MARCO POLO(1962, Fr./Ital.), p, w; SON OF SAMSON(1962, Fr./Ital./Yugo.), p; STORY OF JOSEPH AND HIS BRETHREN THE(1962, Ital.), p; ATLAS AGAINST THE CYCLOPS(1963, Ital.), p; SAMSON AND THE SEVEN MIRACLES OF THE WORLD(1963, Fr./Ital.), p; SON OF THE RED CORSAIR(1963, Ital.), p; WITCH'S CURSE, THE(1963, Ital.), p; LOVE AND MARRIAGE(1966, Ital.), p; HILLS RUN RED, THE(1967, Ital.), p; MATCHLESS(1967, Ital.), p; NAVAJO JOE(1967, Ital./Span.), p; DAY OF THE OWL, THE(1968, Ital./Fr.), p; MAFIA(1969, Fr./Ital.), p

Larry Carper
DISTANT DRUMS(1951)
H.B. Carpernter
Misc. Silents
FLASHING STEEDS(1925), d
Horace Carpernter
Misc. Silents
BORDER RAIDERS, THE(1918)
Fabio Carpi
OF WAYWARD LOVE(1964, Ital./Ger.), w; WILD EYE, THE(1968, Ital.), w; WITCHES, THE(1969, Fr./Ital.), w; DIARY OF A SCHIZOPHRENIC GIRL(1970, Ital.), w
1984
BASILEUS QUARTET(1984, Ital.), d&w
Fiorenzo Carpi
ZAZIE(1961, Fr.), m; VERY PRIVATE AFFAIR, A(1962, Fr./Ital.), m; ITALIAN SECRET SERVICE(1968, Ital.), m; TILL MARRIAGE DO US PART(1979, Ital.), m
Florenzo Carpi
HE WHO SHOOTS FIRST(1966, Ital.), w; VACATION, THE(1971, Ital.), m
Pier Carpi
CAGLIOSTRO(1975, Ital.), w
Tito Carpi
KILL THEM ALL AND COME BACK ALONE(1970, Ital./Span.), w; JOHNNY HAMLET(1972, Ital.), w; CON MEN, THE(1973, Ital.,Span.), w; LOVES AND TIMES OF SCARAMOUCHE, THE(1976, Ital.), w; TENTACLES(1977, Ital.), w; NEW BARBARIANS, THE(1983, Ital.), w
1984
HUNTERS OF THE GOLDEN COBRA, THE(1984, Ital.), w; RUSH(1984, Ital.), w; WARRIORS OF THE WASTELAND(1984, Ital.), w
Carpio
DR. COPPELIUS(1968, U.S./Span.), cos
Roberto Carpio
SAVAGE PAMPAS(1967, Span./Arg.), set d; DR. COPPELIUS(1968, U.S./Span.), set d
Rustica Carpio
1984
BONA(1984, Phil.)
Carmen Carpoldi
NICE GIRL LIKE ME, A(1969, Brit.)
A.E. Carr
FROU-FROU(1955, Fr.), w
A.H.Z. Carr
LET'S GET MARRIED(1937), w
Adrian Carr
MAN FROM SNOWY RIVER, THE(1983, Aus.), ed; NOW AND FOREVER(1983, Aus.), d
Alan Carr
FIRST TIME, THE(1969), p
Albert Z. Carr
WOMEN ARE LIKE THAT(1938), w; JOHNNY NOBODY(1965, Brit.), w
Alexander Carr
NO GREATER LOVE(1932); UPTOWN NEW YORK(1932); DEATH KISS, THE(1933); HER SPLENDID FOLLY(1933); HYPNOTIZED(1933); OUT ALL NIGHT(1933); CHRISTMAS IN JULY(1940)
Misc. Talkies
I HATE WOMEN(1934)
Silents
IN HOLLYWOOD WITH POTASH AND PERLMUTTER(1924); APRIL FOOL(1926), a, w; BEAUTIFUL CHEAT, THE(1926); PARTNERS AGAIN(1926)
Misc. Silents
POTASH AND PERLMUTTER(1923)
Allan Carr
C. C. AND COMPANY(1971), p; GREASE(1978), p, w; CAN'T STOP THE MUSIC(1980), p, w; GREASE 2(1982), p
1984
CLOAK AND DAGGER(1984), p; WHERE THE BOYS ARE '84(1984), p
Anthony Carr
Misc. Talkies
RAPE KILLER, THE(1976)
Arnold Carr
TWO-MINUTE WARNING(1976)
Barney Carr
PICK A STAR(1937)
Bernard Carr
VIRGINIA JUDGE, THE(1935); WHO KILLED "DOC" ROBBIN?(1948), d
Betty Ann Carr
HANGAR 18(1980)
Betty Carr
SEVEN BRIDES FOR SEVEN BROTHERS(1954); CANCEL MY RESERVATION(1972)
Bob Carr
MODERN MARRIAGE, A(1962)
Bridget Carr
THAT MIDNIGHT KISS(1949); CRISIS(1950); LIFE OF HER OWN, A(1950); PLEASE BELIEVE ME(1950); SUMMER STOCK(1950); MARK OF THE RENEGADE(1951)
Bruce Carr
WITHOUT A TRACE(1983)
Cameron Carr
WAY OF LOST SOULS, THE(1929, Brit.); WOMAN HE SCORNED, THE(1930, Brit.); "W" PLAN, THE(1931, Brit.); DEADLOCK(1931, Brit.); ON THIN ICE(1933, Brit.); SCOOP, THE(1934, Brit.)
Silents
UNDER SUSPICION(1919, Brit.); DEAD CERTAINTY, A(1920, Brit.); PENNILESS MILLIONAIRE, THE(1921, Brit.); FOX FARM(1922, Brit.); OUT TO WIN(1923, Brit.); UNINVITED GUEST, THE(1923, Brit.); GAY CORINTHIAN, THE(1924); NETS OF DESTINY(1924, Brit.); NOTORIOUS MRS. CARRICK, THE(1924, Brit.); QUALIFIED ADVENTURER, THE(1925, Brit.); MR. NOBODY(1927, Brit.); POPPIES OF FLANDERS(1927, Brit.)
Misc. Silents
MEG O' THE WOODS(1918, Brit.); NATURE'S GENTLEMAN(1918, Brit.); RUGGED PATH, THE(1918, Brit.); TURF CONSPIRACY, A(1918, Brit.); DAUGHTER OF EVE,

A(1919, Brit.); GREAT COUP, A(1919, Brit.); HEARTS AND SADDLES(1919, Brit.); IN THE GLOAMING(1919, Brit.); SOUL'S CRUCIFIXION, A(1919, Brit.); HER SON(1920, Brit.); IMPERFECT LOVER, THE(1921, Brit.); LOUDWATER MYSTERY, THE(1921, Brit.); VI OF SMITH'S ALLEY(1921, Brit.); SCARLET LADY, THE(1922, Brit.); SON OF KISSING CUP(1922, Brit.); STIRRUP CUP SENSATION, THE(1924, Brit.); WARE CASE, THE(1928, Brit.)
Camilla Carr
BULLET FOR PRETTY BOY, A(1970); DON'T LOOK IN THE BASEMENT(1973); LOGAN'S RUN(1976); SCUM OF THE EARTH(1976); KEEP MY GRAVE OPEN(1980); MAKING LOVE(1982)
Carole Carr
DOWN AMONG THE Z MEN(1952, Brit.); LEFT, RIGHT AND CENTRE(1959)
Catherine Carr
Silents
ATOM, THE(1918), w; I LOVE YOU(1918), w; NOBODY'S KID(1921), w
Charles P. Carr
WESTMINSTER PASSION PLAY–BEHOLD THE MAN, THE(1951, Brit), a, w
Charmian Carr
SOUND OF MUSIC, THE(1965)
Claudia Carr
BLONDE BLACKMAILER(1955, Brit.)
Cynthia Carr
LAST HOUSE ON THE LEFT(1972)
Dan Carr
CHEYENNE AUTUMN(1964)
Darleen Carr
JUNGLE BOOK, THE(1967); MONKEYS, GO HOME!(1967); IMPOSSIBLE YEARS, THE(1968); DEATH OF A GUNFIGHTER(1969); BEGUILED, THE(1971)
David Carr
NEARLY A NASTY ACCIDENT(1962, Brit.), w
Dixie Carr
Silents
FALSE COLORS(1914); SECRET LOVE(1916)
Eddie Carr
LADIES OF THE CHORUS(1948)
Estelle Carr
PASSAGE WEST(1951)
Fatty Carr
LOVE IN THE DESERT(1929)
George Carr
MIDDLE WATCH, THE(1930, Brit.); CHINESE PUZZLE, THE(1932, Brit.); LIEUTENANT DARING, RN(1935, Brit.); VULTURE, THE(1937, Brit.)
Georgia Carr
WILL SUCCESS SPOIL ROCK HUNTER?(1957); HANDLE WITH CARE(1964)
1984
PHAR LAP(1984, Aus.)
Geraldine Carr
SNIPER, THE(1952); LONG, LONG TRAILER, THE(1954)
Gertrude Carr
GEORGE WASHINGTON SLEPT HERE(1942); DECEPTION(1946); ONE MORE TOMORROW(1946); NORA PRENTISS(1947)
Harry Carr
LAST COUPON, THE(1932, Brit.); RIDIN' DOWN THE TRAIL(1947); RUSTLERS OF DEVIL'S CANYON(1947)
Silents
I'LL GET HIM YET(1919), w; LITTLE MISS REBELLION(1920), w; OLD IRONSIDES(1926), w; WEDDING MARCH, THE(1927), w
Helen Carr
Silents
BEAUTIFUL CHEAT, THE(1926)
Henry Carr
ELEPHANT WALK(1954)
Silents
FLYING PAT(1920), w
Hope Carr
GUNMAN HAS ESCAPED, A(1948, Brit.)
Jack Carr
SHE DONE HIM WRONG(1933); LADIES IN DISTRESS(1938); LITTLE TOUGH GUY(1938); PERSONAL SECRETARY(1938); ONE HOUR TO LIVE(1939); WAY DOWN SOUTH(1939); ANGELS OVER BROADWAY(1940); BOWERY BOY(1940); EAST OF THE RIVER(1940); SAFARI(1940); FOUR JACKS AND A JILL(1941); PLAYMATES(1941); SPOOKS RUN WILD(1941); HILLBILLY BLITZKRIEG(1942); JOHNNY EAGER(1942); LUCKY LEGS(1942); TAKE MY LIFE(1942); TALK OF THE TOWN(1942); TORTILLA FLAT(1942); FALLEN SPARROW, THE(1943); FLIGHT FOR FREEDOM(1943); MORE THE MERRIER, THE(1943); SKY'S THE LIMIT, THE(1943); THEY GOT ME COVERED(1943); EVER SINCE VENUS(1944); I'LL BE SEEING YOU(1944); PRINCESS AND THE PIRATE, THE(1944); MURDER, MY SWEET(1945); MY SIX CONVICTS(1952); CHICAGO CONFIDENTIAL(1957); BULLWHIP(1958); SEVEN GUNS TO MESA(1958); TOUGHEST GUN IN TOMBSTONE(1958); PLATINUM HIGH SCHOOL(1960); PURPLE HILLS, THE(1961); RETURN TO PEYTON PLACE(1961); STATE FAIR(1962); 10 RILLINGTON PLACE(1971, Brit.)
Jack P. Carr
I CAN GET IT FOR YOU WHOLESALE(1951)
Jackie Carr
E.T. THE EXTRA-TERRESTRIAL(1982), set
1984
GREMLINS(1984), set d
Jane Carr
LET ME EXPLAIN, DEAR(1932); DICK TURPIN(1933, Brit.); CHURCH MOUSE, THE(1934, Brit.); KEEP IT QUIET(1934, Brit.); LORD EDGEWARE DIES(1934, Brit.); MURDER AT THE INN(1934, Brit.); NIGHT CLUB QUEEN(1934, Brit.); OH NO DOCTOR!(1934, Brit.); ON THE AIR(1934, Brit.); ORDERS IS ORDERS(1934, Brit.); OUTCAST, THE(1934, Brit.); THOSE WERE THE DAYS(1934, Brit.); YOUTHFUL FOLLY(1934, Brit.); ACE OF SPADES, THE(1935, Brit.); ANNIE, LEAVE THE ROOM(1935, Brit.); GET OFF MY FOOT(1935, Brit.); HELLO SWEETHEART(1935, Brit.); LAD, THE(1935, Brit.); NIGHT MAIL(1935, Brit.); TRIUMPH OF SHERLOCK HOLMES, THE(1935, Brit.); INTERRUPTED HONEYMOON, THE(1936, Brit.); IT'S YOU I WANT(1936, Brit.); MILLIONS(1936, Brit.); CAPTAIN'S ORDERS(1937, Brit.); LITTLE MISS SOMEBODY(1937, Brit.); MELODY AND ROMANCE(1937, Brit.); LILAC DOMINO, THE(1940, Brit.); SEVENTH SURVIVOR, THE(1941, Brit.); LADY

FROM LISBON(1942, Brit.); SABOTAGE AT SEA(1942, Brit.); ALIBI, THE(1943, Brit.); IT'S NOT CRICKET(1949, Brit.); TERROR STREET(1953); SAINT'S GIRL FRIDAY, THE(1954, Brit.); PRIME OF MISS JEAN BRODIE, THE(1969, Brit.)

Joan Carr
DEVOTION(1931); STOLEN HEAVEN(1931)

Joe E. Carr
IT ALWAYS RAINS ON SUNDAY(1949, Brit.)

Joey Carr
PASSPORT TO PIMLICO(1949, Brit.); HUE AND CRY(1950, Brit.)

John Carr
TALISMAN, THE(1966), p,d&w
Silents
POLLY OF THE CIRCUS(1917); KENTUCKIANS, THE(1921)

John Dickson Carr
MAN IN BLACK, THE(1950, Brit.), w; MAN WITH A CLOAK, THE(1951), w; DANGEROUS CROSSING(1953), w; CITY AFTER MIDNIGHT(1957, Brit.), w

John "Jack" Carr
HONKY TONK(1941)

June Carr
SON OF BILLY THE KID(1949); FRONTIER PHANTOM, THE(1952), w

Karen Carr
LIFE AND TIMES OF JUDGE ROY BEAN, THE(1972)

Larry Carr
PEGGY(1950); UNKNOWN MAN, THE(1951); HAS ANYBODY SEEN MY GAL?(1952); MAGNIFICENT ROUGHNECKS(1956); I WAS A TEENAGE FRANKENSTEIN(1958)

Laurence Carr
10(1979)

Lee-Ann Carr
1984
MUPPETS TAKE MANHATTAN, THE(1984)

Leland Carr
Silents
GOLD RUSH, THE(1925); DEVIL'S CHAPLAIN(1929)

Lena Carr
NIGHTWING(1979)

Louella Carr
Silents
OVER THE HILL TO THE POORHOUSE(1920)
Misc. Silents
HOME-KEEPING HEARTS(1921)

Marian Carr
SAN QUENTIN(1946); DEVIL THUMBS A RIDE, THE(1947); RING OF FEAR(1954); WORLD FOR RANSOM(1954); KISS ME DEADLY(1955); SEVEN LITTLE FOYS, THE(1955); GHOST TOWN(1956); INDESTRUCTIBLE MAN, THE(1956); NIGHTMARE(1956); WHEN GANGLAND STRIKES(1956)

Marion Carr
IT'S A WONDERFUL LIFE(1946); NORTHERN PATROL(1953); HARDER THEY FALL, THE(1956)

Mary Carr
LIGHTS OF NEW YORK(1928); SAILORS' HOLIDAY(1929); HOT CURVES(1930); JUST IMAGINE(1930); LADIES IN LOVE(1930); SECOND WIFE(1930); UTAH KID, THE(1930); BEYOND VICTORY(1931); HONEYMOON LANE(1931); KEPT HUSBANDS(1931); LAW OF THE TONG(1931); MIDNIGHT SPECIAL(1931); FIGHTING FOOL, THE(1932); FIGHTING MARSHAL, THE(1932); PACK UP YOUR TROUBLES(1932); GUN LAW(1933); POLICE CALL(1933); CHANGE OF HEART(1934); GAY BRIDE, THE(1934); LOUDSPEAKER, THE(1934); LOVE PAST THIRTY(1934); WHOM THE GODS DESTROY(1934); WORLD ACCUSES, THE(1935); FORBIDDEN TRAIL(1936); MUSIC FOR MADAME(1937); WEST OF RAINBOW'S END(1938); EAST SIDE OF HEAVEN(1939); MANHATTAN HEARTBEAT(1940); SHOP AROUND THE CORNER, THE(1940); MODEL WIFE(1941); EAGLE SQUADRON(1942); OREGON TRAIL(1945); FRIENDLY PERSUASION(1956)
Misc. Talkies
FIGHTING LADY(1935)
Silents
OVER THE HILL TO THE POORHOUSE(1920); SILVER WINGS(1922); LOYAL LIVES(1923); ON THE BANKS OF THE WABASH(1923); EAST OF BROADWAY(1924); ON THE STROKE OF THREE(1924); PAINTED PEOPLE(1924); ROULETTE(1924); BIG PAL(1925); EASY MONEY(1925); FIGHTING CUB, THE(1925); FLAMING WATERS(1925); HIS MASTER'S VOICE(1925); NIGHT SHIP, THE(1925); RED KIMONO(1925); WIZARD OF OZ, THE(1925); ATTA BOY!(1926); DAME CHANCE(1926); KING OF THE TURF, THE(1926); MIDNIGHT MESSAGE, THE(1926); NIGHT PATROL, THE(1926); NIGHT WATCH, THE(1926); PLEASURES OF THE RICH(1926); JESSE JAMES(1927); SHOW GIRL, THE(1927); SPECIAL DELIVERY(1927); SWELLHEAD, THE(1927); MILLION FOR LOVE, A(1928)
Misc. Silents
MRS. WIGGS OF THE CABBAGE PATCH(1919); THUNDERCLAP(1921); BROADWAY BROKE(1923); CUSTARD CUP, THE(1923); DARING YEARS, THE(1923); THREE O'CLOCK IN THE MORNING(1923); YOU ARE GUILTY(1923); DAMAGED HEARTS(1924); FOR SALE(1924); SPIRIT OF THE U.S.A., THE(1924); WHY MEN LEAVE HOME(1924); DRUSILLA WITH A MILLION(1925); GO STRAIGHT(1925); GOLD HUNTERS, THE(1925); PARASITE, THE(1925); RE-CREATION OF BRIAN KENT, THE(1925); SLAVE OF FASHION, A(1925); FALSE ALARM, THE(1926); FRENZIED FLAMES(1926); HER OWN STORY(1926); HIDDEN WAY, THE(1926); SOMEBODY'S MOTHER(1926); STOP, LOOK AND LISTEN(1926); WHOM SHALL I MARRY(1926); BETTER DAYS(1927); BLONDE OR BRUNETTE(1927); FALSE MORALS(1927); GOD'S GREAT WILDERNESS(1927); SOME MOTHER'S BOY(1929)

Mary Jane Carr
WESTWARD HO THE WAGONS!(1956), w

Mary Kennevan Carr
Silents
LIGHT AT DUSK, THE(1916)

May Beth Carr
Silents
OVER THE HILL TO THE POORHOUSE(1920)

Maybeth Carr
Silents
SILVER WINGS(1922)

Michael Carr
SLIPPY MCGEE(1948); TRAIN TO ALCATRAZ(1948); FLAME OF YOUTH(1949); HILLS OF OKLAHOMA(1950); PRISONERS IN PETTICOATS(1950); FRONT PAGE STORY(1954, Brit.), m; APACHE WARRIOR(1957); HE RIDES TALL(1964); CONVICT STAGE(1965); FORT COURAGEOUS(1965); WAR PARTY(1965); BEAU GESTE(1966)

Mrs. Carr
Silents
LOVE'S TOLL(1916)

Nat Carr
JAZZ SINGER, THE(1927); TALK OF HOLLYWOOD, THE(1929), a, w; FIFTY MILLION FRENCHMEN(1931); RAINBOW OVER BROADWAY(1933); BIG TIME OR BUST(1934); I CAN'T ESCAPE(1934); MARRYING WIDOWS(1934); RED BLOOD OF COURAGE(1935); NEXT TIME WE LOVE(1936); PORTIA ON TRIAL(1937); COMET OVER BROADWAY(1938); GIRLS ON PROBATION(1938); TORCHY GETS HER MAN(1938); ANGELS WASH THEIR FACES(1939); DARK VICTORY(1939); DODGE CITY(1939); EACH DAWN I DIE(1939); EVERYBODY'S HOBBY(1939); KID FROM KOKOMO, THE(1939); KID NIGHTINGALE(1939); KING OF THE UNDERWORLD(1939); ON TRIAL(1939); SECRET SERVICE OF THE AIR(1939); SMASHING THE MONEY RING(1939); THEY MADE ME A CRIMINAL(1939); TORCHY PLAYS WITH DYNAMITE(1939); WOMEN IN THE WIND(1939); CASTLE ON THE HUDSON(1940); FIGHTING 69TH, THE(1940); GRANNY GET YOUR GUN(1940); KING OF THE LUMBERJACKS(1940); 'TIL WE MEET AGAIN(1940); AFFECTIONATELY YOURS(1941); MANPOWER(1941); MILLION DOLLAR BABY(1941)
Misc. Talkies
MAN FROM ARIZONA, THE(1932)
Silents
APRIL FOOL(1926); COHENS AND KELLYS, THE(1926); PRIVATE IZZY MURPHY(1926); WATCH YOUR WIFE(1926)
Misc. Silents
MILLIONAIRES(1926)

Noreen Carr
VOGUES OF 1938(1937)

Pat Carr
THIN RED LINE, THE(1964), spec eff

Patricia Carr
MURDER CLINIC, THE(1967, Ital./Fr.)
Misc. Talkies
FALLS, THE(1980, Brit.)

Patti Carr
AMERICAN GIGOLO(1980)

Paul Carr
WRONG MAN, THE(1956); JAMBOREE(1957); YOUNG DON'T CRY, THE(1957); POSSE FROM HELL(1961); BEN(1972); DIRT GANG, THE(1972); EXECUTIVE ACTION(1973); BAT PEOPLE, THE(1974); TRUCK STOP WOMEN(1974); RAISE THE TITANIC(1980, Brit.)
Misc. Talkies
BRUTE CORPS(1972); MAN FOR HANGING, A(1972); CRAWLING ARM, THE(1973); SEVERED ARM(1973); SISTERS OF DEATH(1976)

Pauline Carr
Silents
BOWERY CINDERELLA(1927)

Percy Carr
Silents
ONE EXCITING NIGHT(1922); RAGGED EDGE, THE(1923)

R.S. Carr
RAMPANT AGE, THE(1930), w

Richard Carr
MAN FROM DEL RIO(1956), w; HELL IS FOR HEROES(1962), w; TOO LATE BLUES(1962), w; MALPAS MYSTERY, THE(1967, Brit.), m; HEAVEN WITH A GUN(1969), w; MACHO CALLAHAN(1970), w; AMERICANA(1981), w

Robert S. Carr
HOT STUFF(1929), w; WHY LEAVE HOME?(1929), w

Roger S. Carr
DEAD MAN'S FLOAT(1980), w

Ronald Carr
GONG SHOW MOVIE, THE(1980)

Rosemary Carr
Silents
OVER THE HILL TO THE POORHOUSE(1920)

Roy Carr
PASSPORT TO PIMLICO(1949, Brit.); GALLOPING MAJOR, THE(1951, Brit.)

Russell T. Carr
DOGS OF WAR, THE(1980, Brit.)

Sharon Carr
SMELL OF HONEY, A SWALLOW OF BRINE! A(1966)

Sonia Carr
KISMET(1944)

Stephen Carr
HELL'S ANGELS(1930); COLORADO RANGER(1950); CROOKED RIVER(1950); FAST ON THE DRAW(1950); HOSTILE COUNTRY(1950); MARSHAL OF HELDORADO(1950); WEST OF THE BRAZOS(1950); SUPERMAN AND THE MOLE MEN(1951)
Silents
POLLY OF THE CIRCUS(1917); OVER THE HILL TO THE POORHOUSE(1920); JANE EYRE(1921); NORTH OF 36(1924)
Misc. Silents
MATING, THE(1918); STREET OF SEVEN STARS, THE(1918); LITTLE OLD NEW YORK(1923); LIFE OF RILEY, THE(1927)

Steve Carr
OUTLAWS OF TEXAS(1950)

Terry Carr
ALMOST PERFECT AFFAIR, AN(1979), p

Thomas Carr
RANGE DEFENDERS(1937); YOUNG FUGITIVES(1938); BANDITS OF THE BADLANDS(1945), d; CHEROKEE FLASH, THE(1945), d; OREGON TRAIL(1945), d; ROUGH RIDERS OF CHEYENNE(1945), d; SANTA FE SADDLEMATES(1945), p&d; SHERIFF OF CIMARRON(1945), p; ALIAS BILLY THE KID(1946), d; DAYS OF BUFFALO BILL(1946), d; EL PASO KID, THE(1946), d; RED RIVER RENEGADES(1946), d; RIO GRANDE RAIDERS(1946), d; UNDERCOVER WOMAN, THE(1946), d; CODE OF THE SADDLE(1947), d; SONG OF THE WASTELAND(1947),

d; COLORADO RANGER(1950), d; CROOKED RIVER(1950), d; DALTON'S WOMEN, THE(1950), d; FAST ON THE DRAW(1950), d; HOSTILE COUNTRY(1950), d; MARSHAL OF HELDORADO(1950), d; OUTLAWS OF TEXAS(1950), d; WEST OF THE BRAZOS(1950), d; MAN FROM BLACK HILLS, THE(1952), d; MAVERICK, THE(1952), d; CAPTAIN SCARLETT(1953), d; FIGHTING LAWMAN, THE(1953), d; REBEL CITY(1953), d; STAR OF TEXAS(1953), d; TOPEKA(1953), d; BITTER CREEK(1954), d; DESPERADO, THE(1954), d; FORTYNINERS, THE(1954), d; BOBBY WARE IS MISSING(1955), d; THREE FOR JAMIE DAWN(1956), d; DINO(1957), d; TALL STRANGER, THE(1957), d; GUNSMOKE IN TUCSON(1958), d; CAST A LONG SHADOW(1959), d; SULLIVAN'S EMPIRE(1967), d

Misc. Talkies

WANTED DEAD OR ALIVE(1951), d; BEHIND SOUTHERN LINES(1952), d; HIRED GUN(1952), d; MAN FROM THE BLACK HILLS(1952), d; TRAIL OF THE ARROW(1952), d; WYOMING ROUNDUP(1952), d

Silents

IDOL DANCER, THE(1920)

Misc. Silents

HEART TO LET, A(1921); POLLY OF THE FOLLIES(1922)

Tom Carr

MEN WITHOUT LAW(1930); ONE MINUTE TO ZERO(1952)

Misc. Silents

WILD BULL'S LAIR, THE(1925)

Tommy Carr

Silents

WINGS(1927)

Trem Carr

BRIDE OF THE DESERT(1929), p; HEADIN' NORTH(1930), p; LAND OF MISSING MEN, THE(1930), p; NEAR THE RAINBOW'S END(1930), p; OKLAHOMA CYCLONE(1930), p; RAMPANT AGE, THE(1930), p; WORLDLY GOODS(1930), p; AT THE RIDGE(1931), p; DUGAN OF THE BAD LANDS(1931), p; MONTANA KID, THE(1931), p; MOTHER AND SON(1931), p; OKLAHOMA JIM(1931), p; SHIPS OF HATE(1931), p; SUNRISE TRAIL(1931), p; TWO-FISTED JUSTICE(1931), p; BROADWAY TO CHEYENNE(1932), p; GALLOPING THRU(1932), p; HIDDEN VALLEY(1932), p; HONOR OF THE MOUNTED(1932), p; LAND OF WANTED MEN(1932), p; LAW OF THE NORTH(1932), p; MAN FROM HELL'S EDGES(1932), p; MAN FROM NEW MEXICO, THE(1932), p; MASON OF THE MOUNTED(1932), p; RIDERS OF THE DESERT(1932), p; SINGLE-HANDED SANDERS(1932), p; SON OF OKLAHOMA(1932), p; SOUTH OF SANTA FE(1932), p; STRANGE ADVENTURE(1932), p; TEXAS BUDDIES(1932), p; TEXAS PIONEERS(1932), p; YOUNG BLOOD(1932), p; DIAMOND TRAIL(1933), p; FIGHTING CHAMP(1933), p; FIGHTING TEXANS(1933), p; FUGITIVE(1933), p; GALLANT FOOL, THE(1933), p; GALLOPING ROMEO(1933), p; LUCKY LARRIGAN(1933), p; MY MOTHER(1933), p; RAINBOW RANCH(1933), p; RANGER'S CODE, THE(1933), p; RETURN OF CASEY JONES(1933), p; SPHINX, THE(1933), p; WEST OF SINGAPORE(1933), p; KING KELLY OF THE U.S.A(1934), p; MANHATTAN LOVE SONG(1934), p; CAPPY RICKS RETURNS(1935), p; FRISCO WATERFRONT(1935), p; GREAT GOD GOLD(1935), p; HOOSIER SCHOOLMASTER(1935), p; KEEPER OF THE BEES(1935), p; MAKE A MILLION(1935), p; MYSTERY MAN, THE(1935), p; NUT FARM, THE(1935), p; TWO SINNERS(1935), p; CHEERS OF THE CROWD(1936), p; FORBIDDEN HEAVEN(1936), p; SEA SPOILERS, THE(1936), p; ADVENTURE'S END(1937), p; CALIFORNIA STRAIGHT AHEAD(1937), p; CONFLICT(1937), p; I COVER THE WAR(1937), p; IDOL OF THE CROWDS(1937), p; AIR DEVILS(1938), p; BLACK BANDIT(1938), p; GHOST TOWN RIDERS(1938), p; LAST STAND, THE(1938), p; MIDNIGHT INTRUDER(1938), p; OUTLAW EXPRESS(1938), p; PRISON BREAK(1938), p; SPY RING, THE(1938), p; STATE POLICE(1938), p; HONOR OF THE WEST(1939), p

Silents

MIDNIGHT WATCH, THE(1927), w; SHOW GIRL, THE(1927), p

Virginia Carr

NEW KIND OF LOVE, A(1963)

Walter Carr

WICKER MAN, THE(1974, Brit.)

William "Tex" Carr

JEANNE EAGELS(1957)

Phillipe Carr-Foster

BOOGEYMAN II(1983), ph

Neva Carr-Glyn

GIRLS PLEASE!(1934, Brit.); AGE OF CONSENT(1969, Austral.)

Rodney Carr-Smith

BARTLEBY(1970, Brit.), p&w; LOLLY-MADONNA XXX(1973), p, w

Doro Carra

RUTHLESS FOUR, THE(1969, Ital./Ger.)

Enzo Carra

LOVE AND MARRIAGE(1966, Ital.)

Mario Carra

DEAF SMITH AND JOHNNY EARS(1973, Ital.)

Raffaela Carra

VON RYAN'S EXPRESS(1965)

Raffaella Carra

CAESAR THE CONQUEROR(1963, Ital.); ORGANIZER, THE(1964, Fr./Ital./Yugo.); PONTIUS PILATE(1967, Fr./Ital.)

Saturno Carra

NARCO MEN, THE(1969, Span./Ital.)

Tino Carraco

ZIG-ZAG(1975, Fr/Ital.)

Bruce Carradine

Q(1982)

Buck Carradine

Misc. Talkies

DON'T GO INTO THE WOODS(1980)

Carolyn Carradine

STING II, THE(1983)

David Carradine

TAGGART(1964); BUS RILEY'S BACK IN TOWN(1965); VIOLENT ONES, THE(1967); TOO MANY THIEVES(1968); GOOD GUYS AND THE BAD GUYS, THE(1969); HEAVEN WITH A GUN(1969); YOUNG BILLY YOUNG(1969); MACHO CALLAHAN(1970); MC MASTERS, THE(1970); BOXCAR BERTHA(1972); MEAN STREETS(1973); DEATH RACE 2000(1975); BOUND FOR GLORY(1976); CANNONBALL(1976, U.S./Hong Kong); SERPENT'S EGG, THE(1977, Ger./U.S.); THUNDER AND LIGHTNING(1977); DEATHSPORT(1978); GRAY LADY DOWN(1978); CIRCLE

OF IRON(1979, Brit.); FAST CHARLIE... THE MOONBEAM RIDER(1979); CLOUD DANCER(1980); LONG RIDERS, THE(1980); AMERICANA(1981), a, p, d, m; Q(1982); SAFARI 3000(1982); TRICK OR TREATS(1982); LONE WOLF McQUADE(1983)

1984

ON THE LINE(1984, Span.); WARRIOR AND THE SORCERESS, THE(1984)

Misc. Talkies

YOU AND ME(1975), d; TRICK OR TREATS(1983)

John Carradine

UNDER TWO FLAGS(1936); TROUBLE WITH GIRLS(AND HOW TO GET INTO IT), THE*1/2 (1969); SIGN OF THE CROSS, THE(1932); INVISIBLE MAN, THE(1933); STORY OF TEMPLE DRAKE, THE(1933); CLIVE OF INDIA(1935); LES MISERABLES(1935); SHE GETS HER MAN(1935); DANIEL BOONE(1936); DIMPLES(1936); GARDEN OF ALLAH, THE(1936); MARY OF SCOTLAND(1936); MESSAGE TO GARCIA, A(1936); PRISONER OF SHARK ISLAND, THE(1936); RAMONA(1936); WHITE FANG(1936); WINTERSET(1936); ALI BABA GOES TO TOWN(1936); CAPTAINS COURAGEOUS(1937); DANGER–LOVE AT WORK(1937); HURRICANE, THE(1937); LAST GANGSTER, THE(1937); LAUGHING AT TROUBLE(1937); LOVE UNDER FIRE(1937); NANCY STEELE IS MISSING(1937); THANK YOU, MR. MOTO(1937); THIS IS MY AFFAIR(1937); ALEXANDER'S RAGTIME BAND(1938); FOUR MEN AND A PRAYER(1938); GATEWAY(1938); I'LL GIVE A MILLION(1938); INTERNATIONAL SETTLEMENT(1938); KENTUCKY MOONSHINE(1938); KIDNAPPED(1938); OF HUMAN HEARTS(1938); SUBMARINE PATROL(1938); CAPTAIN FURY(1939); DRUMS ALONG THE MOHAWK(1939); FIVE CAME BACK(1939); FRONTIER MARSHAL(1939); HOUND OF THE BASKERVILLES, THE(1939); JESSE JAMES(1939); MR. MOTO'S LAST WARNING(1939); STAGECOACH(1939); THREE MUSKETEERS, THE(1939); BRIGHAM YOUNG–FRONTIERSMAN(1940); CHAD HANNA(1940); GRAPES OF WRATH(1940); RETURN OF FRANK JAMES, THE(1940); BLOOD AND SAND(1941); MAN HUNT(1941); SWAMP WATER(1941); WESTERN UNION(1941); NORTHWEST RANGERS(1942); REUNION IN FRANCE(1942); SON OF FURY(1942); WHISPERING GHOSTS(1942); CAPTIVE WILD WOMAN(1943); GANGWAY FOR TOMORROW(1943); HITLER'S MADMAN(1943); I ESCAPED FROM THE GESTAPO(1943); ISLE OF FORGOTTEN SINS(1943); REVENGE OF THE ZOMBIES(1943); SILVER SPURS(1943); ADVENTURES OF MARK TWAIN, THE(1944); ALASKA(1944); BARBARY COAST GENT(1944); BLACK PARACHUTE, THE(1944); BLUEBEARD(1944); HOUSE OF FRANKENSTEIN(1944); INVISIBLE MAN'S REVENGE(1944); JUNGLE WOMAN(1944); MUMMY'S GHOST, THE(1944); RETURN OF THE APE MAN(1944); VOODOO MAN(1944); WATERFRONT(1944); CAPTAIN KIDD(1945); FALLEN ANGEL(1945); HOUSE OF DRACULA(1945); IT'S IN THE BAG(1945); DOWN MISSOURI WAY(1946); FACE OF MARBLE, THE(1946); PRIVATE AFFAIRS OF BEL AMI, THE(1947); C-MAN(1949); CASANOVA'S BIG NIGHT(1954); EGYPTIAN, THE(1954); JOHNNY GUITAR(1954); THUNDER PASS(1954); DESERT SANDS(1955); FEMALE JUNGLE, THE(1955); HALF HUMAN(1955, Jap.); KENTUCKIAN, THE(1955); STRANGER ON HORSEBACK(1955); AROUND THE WORLD IN 80 DAYS(1956); BLACK SLEEP, THE(1956); COURT JESTER, THE(1956); DARK VENTURE(1956); HIDDEN GUNS(1956); TEN COMMANDMENTS, THE(1956); HELL SHIP MUTINY(1957); STORY OF MANKIND, THE(1957); TRUE STORY OF JESSE JAMES, THE(1957); UNEARTHLY, THE(1957); LAST HURRAH, THE(1958); PROUD REBEL, THE(1958); SHOWDOWN AT BOOT HILL(1958); COSMIC MAN, THE(1959); INCREDIBLE PETRIFIED WORLD, THE(1959); INVISIBLE INVADERS(1959); OREGON TRAIL, THE(1959); ADVENTURES OF HUCKLEBERRY FINN, THE(1960); SEX KITTENS GO TO COLLEGE(1960); TARZAN THE MAGNIFICENT(1960, Brit.); INVASION OF THE ANIMAL PEOPLE(1962, U.S./Swed.); MAN WHO SHOT LIBERTY VALANCE, THE(1962); CHEYENNE AUTUMN(1964); PATSY, THE(1964); WIZARD OF MARS(1964); CURSE OF THE STONE HAND(1965, Mex/Chile); HOUSE OF THE BLACK DEATH(1965); PSYCHO A GO-GO!(1965); BILLY THE KID VS. DRACULA(1966); HOSTAGE, THE(1966); MUNSTER, GO HOME!(1966); NIGHT TRAIN TO MUNDO FINE(1966); BLOOD OF DRACULA'S CASTLE(1967); DR. TERROR'S GALLERY OF HORRORS(1967); HILLBILLYS IN A HAUNTED HOUSE(1967); HELICOPTER SPIES, THE(1968); MADAME DEATH(1968, Mex.); THEY RAN FOR THEIR LIVES(1968); ASTRO-ZOMBIES, THE(1969); CAIN'S WAY(1969); GOOD GUYS AND THE BAD GUYS, THE(1969); GUN RIDERS, THE(1969); VAMPIRES, THE(1969, Mex.); HELL'S BLOODY DEVILS(1970); HORROR OF THE BLOOD MONSTERS(1970, U.S./Phil.); IS THIS TRIP REALLY NECESSARY?(1970); MC MASTERS, THE(1970); SEVEN MINUTES, THE(1971); SHINBONE ALLEY(1971); BOXCAR BERTHA(1972); EVERYTHING YOU ALWAYS WANTED TO KNOW ABOUT SEX, BUT WE'RE AFRAID TO ASK(1972); GATLING GUN, THE(1972); MOONCHILD(1972); RICHARD(1972); BAD CHARLESTON CHARLIE(1973); BIG FOOT(1973); HEX(1973); LEGACY OF BLOOD(1973); SUPERCHICK(1973); TERROR IN THE WAX MUSEUM(1973); HOUSE OF SEVEN CORPSES, THE(1974); SILENT NIGHT, BLOODY NIGHT(1974); MARY, MARY, BLOODY MARY(1975, U.S./Mex.); KILLER INSIDE ME, THE(1976); LAST TYCOON, THE(1976); SHOOTIST, THE(1976); WON TON TON, THE DOG WHO SAVED HOLLYWOOD(1976); CRASH(1977); GOLDEN RENDEZVOUS(1977); SATAN'S CHEERLEADERS(1977); SENTINEL, THE(1977); SHOCK WAVES(1977); WHITE BUFFALO, THE(1977); BEES, THE(1978); SUNSET COVE(1978); MONSTER(1979); NOCTURNA(1979); VAMPIRE HOOKERS, THE(1979, Phil.); BOOGEY MAN, THE(1980); HOWLING, THE(1981); MONSTER CLUB, THE(1981, Brit.); NESTING, THE(1981); SATAN'S MISTRESS(1982); SCARECROW, THE(1982, New Zealand); SECRET OF NIMH, THE(1982); BOOGEYMAN II(1983); HOUSE OF LONG SHADOWS, THE(1983, Brit.)

1984

ICE PIRATES, THE(1984)

Misc. Talkies

BLOOD OF THE IRON MAIDEN(1969); RED ZONE CUBA(1972); DARK EYES(1980); MONSTROID(1980); FRANKENSTEIN'S ISLAND(1982); EVILS OF THE NIGHT(1983)

Keith Carradine

GUNFIGHT, A(1971); MC CABE AND MRS. MILLER(1971); EMPEROR OF THE NORTH POLE(1973); HEX(1973); THIEVES LIKE US(1974); IDAHO TRANSFER(1975); NASHVILLE(1975); LUMIERE(1976, Fr.); WELCOME TO L.A.(1976); DUELLISTS, THE(1977, Brit.); PRETTY BABY(1978); SGT. PEPPER'S LONELY HEARTS CLUB BAND(1978); ALMOST PERFECT AFFAIR, AN(1979); OLD BOYFRIENDS(1979); LONG RIDERS, THE(1980); SOUTHERN COMFORT(1981)

1984

CHOOSE ME(1984)

Misc. Talkies

RUN, RUN, JOE!(1974)

Robert Carradine

COWBOYS, THE(1972); MEAN STREETS(1973); ALOHA, BOBBY AND ROSE(1975); CANNONBALL(1976, U.S./Hong Kong); JACKSON COUNTY JAIL(1976); MASSACRE AT CENTRAL HIGH(1976); POM POM GIRLS, THE(1976); JOYRIDE(1977); ORCA(1977); BLACKOUT(1978, Fr./Can.); COMING HOME(1978); BIG RED ONE,

THE(1980); LONG RIDERS, THE(1980); HEARTACHES(1981, Can.); T.A.G.: THE ASSASSINATION GAME(1982); WAVELENGTH(1983)
1984
JUST THE WAY YOU ARE(1984); REVENGE OF THE NERDS(1984)

Bob Carraher
EXPERIMENT IN TERROR(1962)

Robert Carraher
GIRL NEXT DOOR, THE(1953); DANGEROUS MISSION(1954); BIG TIP OFF, THE(1955)

Bob Carrano
SKYDIVERS, THE(1963)

Ektor Carranza
WILD GYPSIES(1969), art d

J.P. Carranza
POCKET MONEY(1972)

Amalia Carrara
SHE AND HE(1969, Ital.)

Don Carrara
SHEILA LEVINE IS DEAD AND LIVING IN NEW YORK(1975)
1984
SWING SHIFT(1984)
Misc. Talkies
CURSE OF THE HEADLESS HORSEMAN(1972)

Fulvio Carrara
HERCULES, SAMSON & ULYSSES(1964, Ital.)

Nicola Carraro
RATATAPLAN(1979, Ital.), p; CAFE EXPRESS(1980, Ital.), p; EBOLI(1980, Ital.), p

Tina Carraro
CONSTANTINE AND THE CROSS(1962, Ital.)

Tino Carraro
HELL RAIDERS OF THE DEEP(1954, Ital.); LADY OF MONZA, THE(1970, Ital.); CAT O'NINE TAILS(1971, Ital./Ger./Fr.)

Anthony Carras
BLOOD AND STEEL(1959), ed; BUCKET OF BLOOD, A(1959), ed; BEAST FROM THE HAUNTED CAVE(1960), ph; HOUSE OF USHER(1960), ed; LAST WOMAN ON EARTH, THE(1960), ed; SKI TROOP ATTACK(1960), ed; MASTER OF THE WORLD(1961), ed; PIT AND THE PENDULUM, THE(1961), ed; PANIC IN YEAR ZERO!(1962), ed; TALES OF TERROR(1962), ed; "X"-THE MAN WITH THE X-RAY EYES(1963), ed; OPERATION BIKINI(1963), d, ed; COMEDY OF TERRORS, THE(1964), p, ed; TARZAN AND THE GREAT RIVER(1967, U.S./Switz.), ed

Costa Carras
IPHIGENIA(1977, Gr.)

Dora Carras
SEVEN DARING GIRLS(1962, Ger.); TURKISH CUCUMBER, THE(1963, Ger.)

Nicholas Carras
DRAGSTRIP RIOT(1958), m; FRANKENSTEIN'S DAUGHTER(1958), m; HELL'S FIVE HOURS(1958), m, md; MISSILE TO THE MOON(1959), m; WILLY(1963, U.S./Ger.), m; GIRL IN GOLD BOOTS(1968), m; DO NOT THROW CUSHIONS INTO THE RING(1970), m; 10 VIOLENT WOMEN(1982), m

Nicolas Carras
SHE DEMONS(1958), m

Robert Carras
DR. HECKYL AND MR. HYPE(1980), ph

Carrasco
SUMMERSKIN(1962, Arg.)

Ada Carrasco
BRAVADOS, THE(1958); NAZARIN(1968, Mex.); TWO MULES FOR SISTER SARA(1970)

Ernesto Carrasco
MACHO CALLAHAN(1970), set d; CHOSEN SURVIVORS(1974 U.S.-Mex.), set d; RETURN OF A MAN CALLED HORSE, THE(1976), set d

Herminio Carrasco
PRIEST OF LOVE(1981, Brit.)

James Carrasco
Silents
APACHE, THE(1925, Brit.)

Rene Carrasco
SCARFACE(1983)

Bob Carraway
GAMERA THE INVINCIBLE(1966, Jap.); SOLDIER BLUE(1970)

Tom Carray
NATCHEZ TRACE(1960), p

Robert Carrcart
DIME WITH A HALO(1963)

Bart Carre
BATTLING BUCKAROO(1932); FIGHTING COWBOY(1933); LIGHTNING RANGE(1934); TEXAS TORNADO(1934); CHEYENNE TORNADO(1935); WESTERN COURAGE(1935)
Misc. Talkies
RAWHIDE ROMANCE(1934)

Bartlett Carre
GUN SMOKE(1936), d
Misc. Talkies
OUTLAWS' HIGHWAY(1934); GUNSMOKE ON THE GUADALUPE(1935), d

Bartlett A. Carre
Misc. Silents
FLYING HOOFS(1925)

Ben Carre
PHANTOM OF THE OPERA, THE(1929), prod d; HOT FOR PARIS(1930), set d; NIGHT AT THE OPERA, A(1935), art d; GREAT GUY(1936), art d; MINE WITH THE IRON DOOR, THE(1936), art d
Silents
WISHING RING, THE(1914), art d; PRUNELLA(1918), art d; BOB HAMPTON OF PLACER(1921), art d; LIGHT IN THE DARK, THE(1922), ph; WHAT FOOLS MEN ARE(1922), art d; IN HOLLYWOOD WITH POTASH AND PERLMUTTER(1924), art d; STELLA DALLAS(1925), art d; DON JUAN(1926), art d; MARE NOSTRUM(1926), art d; SOFT CUSHIONS(1927), set d

Jeanine Carre
VACATION FROM MARRIAGE(1945, Brit.)

Jeanne Carre
LA NUIT DE VARENNES(1983, Fr./Ital.)

Leon Carre
DIARY OF A COUNTRY PRIEST(1954, Fr.), p

Lucien Carre
LE DENIER MILLIARDAIRE(1934, Fr.), art d; SIMPLE CASE OF MONEY, A(1952, Fr.), set d

Michel Carre
BRAT, THE(1930, Brit.), w; TARGET: HARRY(1980)

Carre and Cartingny
WITH A SMILE(1939, Fr.), art d&set d

Jaime Carreire
BLUE COLLAR(1978)

Dany Carrel
GATES OF PARIS(1958, Fr./Ital.); ENEMY GENERAL, THE(1960); MAIDEN, THE(1961, Fr.); WOMAN OF SIN(1961, Fr.); DIE GANS VON SEDAN(1962, Fr/Ger.); MILL OF THE STONE WOMEN(1963, Fr./Ital.); HANDS OF ORLAC, THE(1964, Brit./Fr.); LOVE ON THE RIVIERA(1964, Fr./Ital.); LA PRISONNIERE(1969, Fr./Ital.)

Jacqueline Carrel
LOVE AT NIGHT(1961, Fr.)

Lyne Carrel
PARIS DOES STRANGE THINGS(1957, Fr./Ital.)

Anita Carell
FLAME OF YOUTH(1949)

Lianella Carell
GOLD OF NAPLES(1957, Ital.)

Rudy Carrella
SHIP OF FOOLS(1965)

Gustavo Cesar Carreon
FOOL KILLER, THE(1965), m; VAMPIRES, THE(1969, Mex.), m

Tony Carreon
STRYKER(1983, Phil.)

Emile Carrer
BEN HUR(1959)

Emilio Carrer
DOCTOR ZHIVAGO(1965); LOST COMMAND, THE(1966)

Barbara Carrera
PUZZLE OF A DOWNFALL CHILD(1970); MASTER GUNFIGHTER, THE(1975); EMBRYO(1976); ISLAND OF DR. MOREAU, THE(1977); WHEN TIME RAN OUT(1980); CONDORMAN(1981); I, THE JURY(1982); LONE WOLF McQUADE(1983); NEVER SAY NEVER AGAIN(1983)

Dorothea Carrera
MARK OF THE DEVIL(1970, Ger./Brit.)

Enrique Carreras
MASTER OF HORROR(1965, Arg.), d

James Carreras
WHO KILLED VAN LOON?(1984, Brit.), p

Mercedes Carreras
MASTER OF HORROR(1965, Arg.)

Michael Carreras
YESTERDAY'S ENEMY(1959, Brit.), p; DARK LIGHT, THE(1951, Brit.), p; NEVER LOOK BACK(1952, Brit.), p; BLOOD ORANGE(1953, Brit.), p; FOUR SIDED TRIANGLE(1953), p; SPACEWAYS(1953, Brit.), p; WOMAN IN HIDING(1953, Brit.), p; BLACK GLOVE(1954, Brit.), p; BLACKOUT(1954, Brit.), p; UNHOLY FOUR, THE(1954, Brit.), p, w; RACE FOR LIFE, A(1955, Brit.), p; MEN OF SHERWOOD FOREST(1957, Brit.), p; SNORKEL, THE(1958, Brit.), p; STEEL BAYONET, THE(1958, Brit.), p&d; MAN WHO COULD CHEAT DEATH, THE(1959, Brit.), p; MUMMY, THE(1959, Brit.), p; TEN SECONDS TO HELL(1959), p; HELL IS A CITY(1960, Brit.), p; CURSE OF THE WEREWOLF, THE(1961), p; HOUSE OF FRIGHT(1961), p; PASSPORT TO CHINA(1961, Brit.), p&d; CASH ON DEMAND(1962, Brit.), p; SAVAGE GUNS, THE(1962, U.S./Span.), d; MANIAC(1963, Brit.), p; WHAT A CRAZY WORLD(1963, Brit.), p&d, w; CURSE OF THE MUMMY'S TOMB, THE(1965, Brit.), p&d; SHE(1965, Brit.), p; ONE MILLION YEARS B.C.(1967, Brit./U.S.), p, w; PREHISTORIC WOMEN(1967, Brit.), p&d; LOST CONTINENT, THE(1968, Brit.), p&d; MOON ZERO TWO(1970, Brit.), p, w; CREATURES THE WORLD FORGOT(1971, Brit.), p&w; CRESCENDO(1972, Brit.), p; CALL HIM MR. SHATTER(1976, Hong Kong), p, d

Nicolas Carreras
MASTER OF HORROR(1965, Arg.), p

Anne Carrere
GUTS IN THE SUN(1959, Fr.); CHECKERBOARD(1969, Fr.)

Christine Carrere
CADET-ROUSSELLE(1954, Fr.); LOVE IN A HOT CLIMATE(1958, Fr./Span.)

Ed Carrere
MY WILD IRISH ROSE(1947), art d

Edward Carrere
TWO GUYS FROM TEXAS(1948), art d; WINTER MEETING(1948), art d; FOUNTAINHEAD, THE(1949), art d; LADY TAKES A SAILOR, THE(1949), art d; WHITE HEAT(1949), art d; BREAKING POINT, THE(1950), art d; FLAME AND THE ARROW, THE(1950), art d; YOUNG MAN WITH A HORN(1950), art d; FORCE OF ARMS(1951), art d; JIM THORPE-ALL AMERICAN(1951), art d; PAINTING THE CLOUDS WITH SUNSHINE(1951), art d; RATON PASS(1951), art d; MIRACLE OF OUR LADY OF FATIMA, THE(1952), art d; STORY OF WILL ROGERS, THE(1952), art d; SHE'S BACK ON BROADWAY(1953), art d; SO THIS IS LOVE(1953), art d; SOUTH SEA WOMAN(1953), art d; DIAL M FOR MURDER(1954), art d; RIDING SHOTGUN(1954), art d; I DIED A THOUSAND TIMES(1955), art d; SINCERELY YOURS(1955), art d; HELEN OF TROY(1956, Ital), art d; SANTIAGO(1956), art d; SERENADE(1956), art d; SWEET SMELL OF SUCCESS(1957), art d; OLD MAN AND THE SEA, THE(1958), art d; RUN SILENT, RUN DEEP(1958), art d; SEPARATE TABLES(1958), art d; DEVIL'S DISCIPLE, THE(1959), art d; RABBIT TRAP, THE(1959), art d; TAKE A GIANT STEP(1959), art d; SUNRISE AT CAMPOBELLO(1960), art d; FRANCIS OF ASSISI(1961), art d; TARAS BULBA(1962), art d; CRITIC'S CHOICE(1963), art d; ISLAND OF LOVE(1963), art d; PLEASURE SEEKERS, THE(1964), art d; NEVER TOO LATE(1965), art d; THIRD DAY, THE(1965), art d; NOT WITH MY WIFE, YOU DON'T(1966), prod d; CAMELOT(1967), art d; WILD BUNCH, THE(1969), art d; THERE WAS A CROOKED MAN(1970), art d

Emilio Carrere
NO TIME FOR ECSTASY(1963, Fr.); CRACK IN THE WORLD(1965)

Fernando Carrere
NEW YORK CONFIDENTIAL(1955), prod d; PRIDE AND THE PASSION, THE(1957), art d; DEFIANT ONES, THE(1958), art d; KINGS GO FORTH(1958), art d; WINK OF AN EYE(1958), p; ON THE BEACH(1959), art d; PAY OR DIE(1960), prod d; CHILDREN'S HOUR, THE(1961), art d; JACK THE GIANT KILLER(1962), art d; GREAT ESCAPE, THE(1963), art d; PINK PANTHER, THE(1964), art d; YOUNG LOVERS, THE(1964), prod d; WHAT DID YOU DO IN THE WAR, DADDY?(1966), prod d; GUNN(1967), prod d&art d; WATERHOLE NO. 3(1967), art d; PARTY, THE(1968), prod d; DARLING LILI(1970), prod d; ZEPPELIN(1971, Brit.), prod d; SHEILA LEVINE IS DEAD AND LIVING IN NEW YORK(1975), prod d; WHIFFS(1975), art d; I WILL ...I WILL ...FOR NOW(1976), prod d; CONVOY(1978), prod d; FINAL COUNTDOWN, THE(1980), prod d; FOOLIN' AROUND(1980), prod d

Jacques Carrere
LUCRECE BORGIA(1953, Ital./Fr.), ed

Marlena Carrere
DAY THE FISH CAME OUT, THE(1967. Brit./Gr.)

Tonia Carrero
ALIAS BIG SHOT(1962, Argen.); VIOLENT AND THE DAMNED, THE(1962, Braz.)

Fernando Carrerre
GREAT RACE, THE(1965), prod d; CHARLEY VARRICK(1973), art d

Grant Carrett
BAD BASCOMB(1946), w

Franco Carretti
DUCK, YOU SUCKER!(1972, Ital.), cos

Jim Carrey
1984
FINDERS KEEPERS(1984)

Florence Carrez
TRIAL OF JOAN OF ARC(1965, Fr.)

Jean Carriaga
BLOOD ROSE, THE(1970, Fr.), w

Fablo Carriba
AUGUSTINE OF HIPPO(1973, Ital.)

Robert Carricart
JET ATTACK(1958); BLUEPRINT FOR ROBBERY(1961); RUN ACROSS THE RIVER(1961); FOLLOW THAT DREAM(1962); FUN IN ACAPULCO(1963); BLOOD ON THE ARROW(1964); GUNS OF DIABLO(1964); ROBIN AND THE SEVEN HOODS(1964); APACHE UPRISING(1966); WHAT DID YOU DO IN THE WAR, DADDY?(1966); PINK JUNGLE, THE(1968); VILLA RIDES(1968); WICKED DREAMS OF PAULA SCHULTZ, THE(1968); LAND RAIDERS(1969); DON IS DEAD, THE(1973); HERO AT LARGE(1980)

Robert Carricart, Jr.
R.P.M.(1970)

Allyn B. Carrick
Misc. Silents
HER STORY(1922), d

Anthony Carrick
JABBERWOCKY(1977, Brit.)
1984
CHAMPIONS(1984)

Antony Carrick
JULIA(1977); HOPSCOTCH(1980)

Edward Carrick
LOYALTIES(1934, Brit.), art d; WHEN THIEF MEETS THIEF(1937, Brit.), art d; CAPTAIN BOYCOTT(1947, Brit.), art d; MEN OF THE SEA(1951, Brit.), art d; SPIDER AND THE FLY, THE(1952, Brit.), art d; DIVIDED HEART, THE(1955, Brit.), art d; LIGHT TOUCH, THE(1955, Brit.), art d; GENTLE TOUCH, THE(1956, Brit.), art d; THIRD KEY, THE(1957, Brit.), art d; ONE THAT GOT AWAY, THE(1958, Brit.), art d; TIGER BAY(1959, Brit.), art d; CHANCE MEETING(1960, Brit.), art d; MACBETH(1963), art d; MANIAC(1963, Brit.), art d; HYSTERIA(1965, Brit.), prod d; NANNY, THE(1965, Brit.), prod d; SEASIDE SWINGERS(1965, Brit.), art d

Gene Carrick
GUN TOWN(1946); APPOINTMENT WITH MURDER(1948)

Herbert Carrick
MAGIC NIGHT(1932, Brit.)

J. B. Carrickford
Silents
IN THE DAYS OF SAINT PATRICK(1920, Brit.)

Richard Carrickford
I'LL NEVER FORGET YOU(1951)

Robert Carrickford
QUACKSER FORTUNE HAS A COUSIN IN THE BRONX(1970)

Monica Carrico
1984
HIGHWAY TO HELL(1984); RUNNING HOT(1984)

Michael Carridia
ODONGO(1956, Brit.)

John Carridine
CLEOPATRA(1934)

Carlos Carrido
MANILA CALLING(1942)

John Carrie
FAR FROM THE MADDING CROWD(1967, Brit.)

Steve Carrie
Misc. Silents
GOOD MEN AND BAD(1923)

Albert Carrier
TWO WEEKS IN ANOTHER TOWN(1962); THOROUGHLY MODERN MILLIE(1967); DESERT SANDS(1955); MAN WHO KNEW TOO MUCH, THE(1956); ISTANBUL(1957); PANAMA SAL(1957); DESERT HELL(1958); PERFECT FURLOUGH, THE(1958); WRECK OF THE MARY DEAR, THE(1959); SPRING AFFAIR(1960); TENDER IS THE NIGHT(1961); NEW KIND OF LOVE, A(1963); PRIZE, THE(1963); DO NOT DISTURB(1965); MAJOR DUNDEE(1965); MOMENT TO MOMENT(1966); FITZWILLY(1967); SECRET LIFE OF AN AMERICAN WIFE, THE(1968); SCARFACE(1983)

Eva Carrier
RED RUNS THE RIVER(1963), a, w

Gigi Carrier
HOT STUFF(1979)

Julie Carrier
CHILDREN, THE(1980)

Mathieu Carrier
YOUNG TORLESS(1968, Fr./Ger.)

Rick Carrier
STRANGERS IN THE CITY(1962), p,d&w, ph

Ronald Carrier
KNIGHTRIDERS(1981)

Suzy Carrier
CLANDESTINE(1948, Fr.)

Albert Carriere
CHANGE OF SEASONS, A(1980)

Anne Carriere
ROYAL AFFAIRS IN VERSAILLES(1957, Fr.)

Anne Marie Carriere
MY WIFE'S HUSBAND(1965, Fr./Ital.)

Augusta Carriere
MILKY WAY, THE(1969, Fr./Ital.)

Auguste Carriere
THAT OBSCURE OBJECT OF DESIRE(1977, Fr./Span.)

Henri Carriere
PAPILLON(1973), w

Jean-Claude Carriere
SUITOR, THE(1963, Fr.), w; DIARY OF A CHAMBERMAID(1964, Fr./Ital.), a, w; VIVA MARIA(1965, Fr./Ital.), w; DIABOLICAL DR. Z, THE(1966 Span./Fr.), w; HOTEL PARADISO(1966, U.S./Brit.), w; ATTACK OF THE ROBOTS(1967, Fr./Span.), w; THIEF OF PARIS, THE(1967, Fr./Ital.), w; YO YO(1967, Fr.), w; BELLE DE JOUR(1968, Fr.), w; MILKY WAY, THE(1969, Fr./Ital.), a, w; BORSALINO(1970, Fr.), w; TAKING OFF(1971), w; DISCREET CHARM OF THE BOURGEOISIE, THE(1972, Fr.), w; OUTSIDE MAN, THE(1973, U.S./FR.), w; PHANTOM OF LIBERTY, THE(1974, Fr.), w; LIZA(1976, Fr./Ital.), w; LEONOR(1977, Fr./Span./Ital.), w; THAT OBSCURE OBJECT OF DESIRE(1977, Fr./Span.), w; BUTTERFLY ON THE SHOULDER, A(1978, Fr.), w; ANGRY MAN, THE(1979 Fr./Can.), w; TIN DRUM, THE(1979, Ger./Fr./Yugo./Pol.), w; EVERY MAN FOR HIMSELF(1980, Fr.), w; ASSOCIATE, THE(1982 Fr./Ger.), w; CIRCLE OF DECEIT(1982, Fr./Ger.), w; DANTON(1983), w; RETURN OF MARTIN GUERRE, THE(1983, Fr.), w
1984
SWANN IN LOVE(1984, Fr.Ger.), w

Mathieu Carriere
TONIO KROGER(1968, Fr./Ger.); BLUEBEARD(1972); MALPERTIUS(1972, Bel./Fr.); MAN WITH THE TRANSPLANTED BRAIN, THE(1972, Fr./Ital./Ger.); GIORDANO BRUNO(1973, Ital.); POLICE PYTHON 357(1976, Fr.); CASE AGAINST FERRO, THE(1980, Fr.); AVIATOR'S WIFE, THE(1981, Fr.); EGON SCHIELE—EXCESS AND PUNISHMENT(1981, Ger.); ASSOCIATE, THE(1982 Fr./Ger.); BENVENUTA(1983, Fr.); LA PASSANTE(1983, Fr./Ger.)
1984
BAY BOY(1984, Can.); WOMAN IN FLAMES, A(1984, Ger.)

Matthieu Carriere
GATES TO PARADISE(1968, Brit./Ger.); COUP DE GRACE(1978, Ger./Fr.)

Nicole Carriere
MURMUR OF THE HEART(1971, Fr./Ital./Ger.)

Marieke Carrierre
SECOND WIND, A(1978, Fr.)

Louise Carrigan
1984
BOUNTY, THE(1984), set d

Thomas Carrigan
Silents
CROOKED ALLEY(1923)
Misc. Silents
LOVELY MARY(1916); TIGER'S CUB(1920); CROOKED ALLEY(1923)

Thomas J. Carrigan
Silents
DIMPLES(1916); DUST OF DESIRE(1919)
Misc. Silents
ROSE OF THE ALLEY(1916); CHECKERS(1919); LOVE'S FLAME(1920)

Tom Carrigan
BIG BROADCAST, THE(1932)
Silents
TRUTH, THE(1920); SALOMY JANE(1923)
Misc. Silents
ROOM AND BOARD(1921)

Lupe Carriles
BEAST OF HOLLOW MOUNTAIN, THE(1956); LA CUCARACHA(1961, Mex.)

Cely Carrillo
RAMPAGE(1963)

Daniel Carrillo
1984
WHERE IS PARSIFAL?(1984, Brit.), p

Elpidia Carrillo
BORDER, THE(1982); BEYOND THE LIMIT(1983); UNDER FIRE(1983)

Leo Carrillo
MISTER ANTONIO(1929); GUILTY GENERATION, THE(1931); HELL BOUND(1931); HOMICIDE SQUAD(1931); LASCA OF THE RIO GRANDE(1931); BROKEN WING, THE(1932); GIRL OF THE RIO(1932); BEFORE MORNING(1933); DECEPTION(1933); MEN ARE SUCH FOOLS(1933); MOONLIGHT AND PRETZELS(1933); OBEY THE LAW(1933); PARACHUTE JUMPER(1933); RACETRACK(1933); BAND PLAYS ON, THE(1934); FOUR FRIGHTENED PEOPLE(1934); GAY BRIDE, THE(1934); MANHATTAN MELODRAMA(1934); IN CALIENTE(1935); LOVE ME FOREVER(1935); WINNING TICKET, THE(1935); GAY DESPERADO, THE(1936); IF YOU COULD ONLY COOK(1936); MOONLIGHT MURDER(1936); BARRIER, THE(1937); HISTORY IS MADE AT NIGHT(1937); HOTEL HAYWIRE(1937); I PROMISE TO PAY(1937); MANHATTAN MERRY-GO-ROUND(1937); 52ND STREET(1937); ARIZONA WILDCAT(1938); BLOCKADE(1938); CITY STREETS(1938); FLIRTING WITH FATE(1938); GIRL OF THE GOLDEN WEST, THE(1938); LITTLE MISS ROUGHNECK(1938); TOO HOT TO HANDLE(1938); FISHERMAN'S WHARF(1939); GIRL AND THE GAMBLER, THE(1939); RIO(1939); SOCIETY LAWYER(1939); CAPTAIN CAUTION(1940); LILLIAN RUSSELL(1940); ONE NIGHT IN

THE TROPICS(1940); TWENTY MULE TEAM(1940); WYOMING(1940); BARNACLE BILL(1941); HONOLULU LU(1941); HORROR ISLAND(1941); KID FROM KANSAS, THE(1941); ROAD AGENT(1941); TIGHT SHOES(1941); AMERICAN EMPIRE(1942); DANGER IN THE PACIFIC(1942); ESCAPE FROM HONG KONG(1942); MEN OF TEXAS(1942); SIN TOWN(1942); TIMBER(1942); TOP SERGEANT(1942); UNSEEN ENEMY(1942); WHAT'S COOKIN'?(1942); CRAZY HOUSE(1943); FOLLOW THE BAND(1943); FRONTIER BADMEN(1943); LARCENY WITH MUSIC(1943); PHANTOM OF THE OPERA(1943); BOWERY TO BROADWAY(1944); GHOST CATCHERS(1944); GYPSY WILDCAT(1944); MOONLIGHT AND CACTUS(1944); CRIME, INC.(1945); MEXICANA(1945); UNDER WESTERN SKIES(1945); FUGITIVE, THE(1947); VALIANT HOMBRE, THE(1948); DARING CABALLERO, THE(1949); GAY AMIGO, THE(1949); SATAN'S CRADLE(1949); GIRL FROM SAN LORENZO, THE(1950); PANCHO VILLA RETURNS(1950, Mex.)

Ximenez Carrillo
TRISTANA(1970, Span./Ital./Fr.)

C. B. Carrington
KENTUCKY BLUE STREAK(1935), w

Carol Carrington
CHICAGO 70(1970)

Daisy Carrington
EXPOSED(1983)

Debbie Carrington
RETURN OF THE JEDI(1983)

Desmond Carrington
CALAMITY THE COW(1967, Brit.)

Elaine Sterne Carrington
ALIBI(1929), w

Evelyn C. Carrington
Silents
IN SEARCH OF A SINNER(1920); SALVATION NELL(1921)

Evelyn Carrington
PORT OF LOST DREAMS(1935); LIVING ON LOVE(1937)

Evelyn Carter Carrington
AFTER TONIGHT(1933)

Frank Carrington
Silents
$5,000,000 COUNTERFEITING PLOT, THE(1914)

Gail Carrington
FIRST TIME, THE(1969)

Hal Carrington
PASSION HOLIDAY(1963), ph

Helen Carrington
HEADS UP(1930); QUEEN HIGH(1930)

Jack Carrington
LADIES' DAY(1943); YOUTH RUNS WILD(1944); CRIME DOCTOR'S COURAGE, THE(1945); THEY WERE EXPENDABLE(1945); 13TH HOUR, THE(1947)

James Carrington
NOMADIC LIVES(1977)
1984
MIKE'S MURDER(1984)

Jane-Howard Carrington
KALEIDOSCOPE(1966, Brit.), w; WAIT UNTIL DARK(1967), w

Jim Carrington
1984
CITY GIRL, THE(1984)

Murray Carrington
Misc. Silents
IN SEARCH OF A HUSBAND(1915, Brit.)

Reginald Carrington
Silents
LIFE'S WHIRLPOOL(1917)
Misc. Silents
TO HIM THAT HATH(1918)

Robert Carrington
KALEIDOSCOPE(1966, Brit.), w; WAIT UNTIL DARK(1967), w; FEAR IS THE KEY(1973), w; VENOM(1982, Brit.), w

Thomas Carrington
Silents
IN WALKED MARY(1920)

Virginia Carrington
KILLING OF A CHINESE BOOKIE, THE(1976)

Gustavo Cesar Carrion
VAMPIRE'S COFFIN, THE(1958, Mex.), m; WITCH'S MIRROR, THE(1960, Mex.), m; EMPTY STAR, THE(1962, Mex.), m; SHAME OF THE SABINE WOMEN, THE(1962, Mex.), m; YANCO(1964, Mex.), m; LIVING COFFIN, THE(1965, Mex.), m; MAN AND THE MONSTER, THE(1965, Mex.), m; RAGE(1966, U.S./Mex.), m, md; VAMPIRE, THE(1968, Mex.), m; CURSE OF THE CRYING WOMAN, THE(1969, Mex.), m; LIVING HEAD, THE(1969, Mex.), m

Hector Carrion
LOVE HUNGER(1965, Arg.)

J. Antonio Carrion
Misc. Talkies
MUTHERS, THE(1976)

Pierre Carrive
1984
LE DERNIER COMBAT(1984, Fr.)

Marty Carrizosa
WALK THE PROUD LAND(1956)

Billy Carro
GUN MAN FROM BODIE, THE(1941)

Angela Carrol
CURTAINS(1983, Can.)

Leo G. Carrol
WUTHERING HEIGHTS(1939)

Liza Carrol
POOR COW(1968, Brit.)

Lucia Carrol
SANTA FE TRAIL(1940)

Marilyn Carrol
YOUNG AND DANGEROUS(1957)

Paul Carrol
MAIDSTONE(1970)

Regina Carrol
FEMALE BUNCH, THE(1969); SATAN'S SADISTS(1969); BLOOD OF FRANKENSTEIN(1970); JESSIE'S GIRLS(1976)
Misc. Talkies
NIGHTMARE BLOOD BATH(1971); ANGELS' WILD WOMEN(1972); BLACK HEAT(1976)

Vance Carrol
INSIDE INFORMATION(1934)

Victoria Carrol
HUSTLE(1975)

Vinnette Carrol
COTTON COMES TO HARLEM(1970)

Carrol Gibbons and his Savoy Orpheans
CALL ME MAME(1933, Brit.)

Carrol-Lewis
UNDERCOVER MAN(1942), ed

Carroll
ANGEL COMES TO BROOKLYN, AN(1945), m/l

Agatha Carroll
ROGUE'S YARN(1956, Brit.)

Ajax Carroll
Silents
PEG OF THE PIRATES(1918)

Alene Carroll
AIR MAIL(1932); DON'T GET PERSONAL(1936)

Alma Carroll
PARACHUTE NURSE(1942); PARDON MY GUN(1942); THEY ALL KISSED THE BRIDE(1942); SHE HAS WHAT IT TAKES(1943); SILVER CITY RAIDERS(1943); PRINCESS AND THE PIRATE, THE(1944); UP IN ARMS(1944); WONDER MAN(1945); TILL THE CLOUDS ROLL BY(1946); REDHEAD FROM MANHATTAN(1954)
Misc. Talkies
TORNADO IN THE SADDLE, A(1942); WYOMING HURRICANE(1944)

Ann Carroll
GARMENT JUNGLE, THE(1957); FEAR NO MORE(1961); WOMAN HUNT(1962); MARLOWE(1969)

Anna Lee Carroll
HEART IS A LONELY HUNTER, THE(1968)

Anne Carroll
ROAD TO DENVER, THE(1955); SON OF SINBAD(1955); NOT OF THIS EARTH(1957)

Annette Carroll
DARLING(1965, Brit.)

Arlene Carroll
NIGHT LIFE OF THE GODS(1935)

Barbara Carroll
I DON'T CARE GIRL, THE(1952); LAST DAYS OF POMPEII, THE(1960, Ital.); GOLIATH AGAINST THE GIANTS(1963, Ital./Span.)

Beeson Carroll
MISTER BUDDWING(1966); BANANAS(1971); LADY LIBERTY(1972, Ital./Fr.); SHAMUS(1973); WEREWOLF OF WASHINGTON(1973); SOMEBODY KILLED HER HUSBAND(1978); SPACEHUNTER: ADVENTURES IN THE FORBIDDEN ZONE(1983)

Belinda Carroll
NO LONGER ALONE(1978)

Bill Carroll
BEYOND AND BACK(1978)

Bob Carroll
1984
HIGHWAY TO HELL(1984); RUNNING HOT(1984)

Bob Carroll, Jr.
YOURS, MINE AND OURS(1968), w

Brandon Carroll
HELL SQUAD(1958); RIDE IN THE WHIRLWIND(1966)

Christopher Carroll
1984
MASS APPEAL(1984)

Christy Carroll
STOP THE WORLD–I WANT TO GET OFF(1966, Brit.)

Cliff Carroll
HARD PART BEGINS, THE(1973, Can.)

Curt Carroll
SAN ANTONE(1953), w

David Carroll
ABDUCTION(1975)

David-James Carroll
HERO AT LARGE(1980)

Dee Carroll
SWING OUT, SISTER(1945); MA AND PA KETTLE GO TO TOWN(1950); I WANT YOU(1951); THIS WOMAN IS DANGEROUS(1952); WAR ARROW(1953); TARANTULA(1955); DAY OF FURY, A(1956); SHOOT-OUT AT MEDICINE BEND(1957); FIVE BOLD WOMEN(1960); GNOME-MOBILE, THE(1967); GUIDE FOR THE MARRIED MAN, A(1967); HOTEL(1967); SPLIT, THE(1968); MARLOWE(1969); SWEET CHARITY(1969); CHRISTINE JORGENSEN STORY, THE(1970); KOTCH(1971); TERMINAL MAN, THE(1974); STUNT MAN, THE(1980)

Diahann Carroll
PORGY AND BESS(1959); GOODBYE AGAIN(1961); PARIS BLUES(1961); HURRY SUNDOWN(1967); SPLIT, THE(1968); CLAUDINE(1974)

Diane Carroll
CUBAN PETE(1946)

Earl Carroll
SO LONG LETTY(1929), w; MURDER AT THE VANITIES(1934), w; LOVE IS NEWS(1937), p; NIGHT AT EARL CARROLL'S, A(1940), p
Silents
12-10(1919, Brit.), w

Ed E. Carroll
HANGAR 18(1980)
Eddie Carroll
LAST OF THE SECRET AGENTS?, THE(1966)
Edwina Carroll
YESTERDAY'S ENEMY(1959, Brit.); GENGHIS KHAN(U.S./Brit./Ger./Yugo); TOWN LIKE ALICE, A(1958, Brit.); DEVIL'S DAFFODIL, THE(1961, Brit./Ger.); ROAD TO HONG KONG, THE(1962, U.S./Brit.); SOME MAY LIVE(1967, Brit.); 2001: A SPACE ODYSSEY(1968, U.S./Brit.); CARRY ON UP THE JUNGLE(1970, Brit.)
F.J. Carroll
Misc. Silents
FOR THE FREEDOM OF THE WORLD(1917), d
Fay Carroll
RADIO FOLLIES(1935, Brit.)
Gene Carroll
Silents
ADVENTUROUS SOUL, THE(1927), d; AIR MAIL PILOT, THE(1928), d
Georgia Carroll
PLAY GIRL(1940); MR. AND MRS. SMITH(1941); NAVY BLUES(1941); YOU'RE IN THE ARMY NOW(1941); ZIEGFELD GIRL(1941); MAN WHO CAME TO DINNER, THE(1942); YANKEE DOODLE DANDY(1942); AROUND THE WORLD(1943); DU BARRY WAS A LADY(1943); GIRL CRAZY(1943); CAROLINA BLUES(1944)
Gladys Hasty Carroll
AS THE EARTH TURNS(1934), w
Gordon Carroll
COOL HAND LUKE(1967), p; APRIL FOOLS, THE(1969), p; PAT GARRETT AND BILLY THE KID(1973), p; ALIEN(1979), p; BLUE THUNDER(1983), p
Heather Carroll
GUIDE FOR THE MARRIED MAN, A(1967)
Helen Carroll
LOVE THY NEIGHBOR(1940)
Helena Carroll
FRIENDS OF EDDIE COYLE, THE(1973); JERK, THE(1979); LOVING COUPLES(1980); GHOST STORY(1981)
J. Larry Carroll
TOURIST TRAP, THE(1979), p, w; DAY TIME ENDED, THE(1980, Span.), w
1984
SWORDKILL(1984), d
J. Scott Carroll
AND NOW MIGUEL(1966)
J. Winston Carroll
STRANGE BREW(1983)
1984
POLICE ACADEMY(1984)
Jack Carroll
JUNGLE GODDESS(1948); DARK CITY(1950)
Jack "Jidge" Carroll
FORTY GUNS(1957)
James Carroll
MELODY OF MY HEART(1936, Brit.); HE KNOWS YOU'RE ALONE(1980)
1984
GIRLS NIGHT OUT(1984)
Misc. Silents
SKINNER'S BABY(1917)
James C. Carroll
Silents
SKINNER'S DRESS SUIT(1917)
Misc. Silents
SKINNER'S BUBBLE(1917)
Janet Carroll
RISKY BUSINESS(1983)
Janice Carroll
SHANE(1953); STALAG 17(1953); HOW TO BE VERY, VERY, POPULAR(1955); LIEUTENANT WORE SKIRTS, THE(1956); APRIL FOOLS, THE(1969); HOW TO SEDUCE A WOMAN(1974); THREE THE HARD WAY(1974); HOW TO SUCCEED IN BUSINESS WITHOUT REALLY TRYING(1976); END, THE(1978); HARDCORE(1979); SECOND THOUGHTS(1983)
Jax Carroll
WILD RIDERS(1971)
Jean Carroll
MERMAIDS OF TIBURON, THE(1962); LEGEND OF LYLAH CLARE, THE(1968)
Jeanne Carroll
SING A JINGLE(1943)
Jill Carroll
HEART LIKE A WHEEL(1983); MAN WHO LOVED WOMEN, THE(1983); PSYCHO II(1983); SOMETHING WICKED THIS WAY COMES(1983)
Jim Carroll
1984
LISTEN TO THE CITY(1984, Can.)
Joan Carroll
TWO SISTERS(1938); BARRICADE(1939); ANNE OF WINDY POPLARS(1940); LADDIE(1940); PRIMROSE PATH(1940); OBLIGING YOUNG LADY(1941); PETTICOAT LARCENY(1943); MEET ME IN ST. LOUIS(1944); TOMORROW THE WORLD(1944); BELLS OF ST. MARY'S, THE(1945)
John Carroll
MONTE CARLO(1930); HI GAUCHO!(1936); MURDER ON A BRIDLE PATH(1936); MUSS 'EM UP(1936); DEATH IN THE SKY(1937); WE WHO ARE ABOUT TO DIE(1937); ROSE OF THE RIO GRANDE(1938); I AM A CRIMINAL(1939); ONLY ANGELS HAVE WINGS(1939); WOLF CALL(1939); CONGO MAISIE(1940); GO WEST(1940); HIRED WIFE(1940); SUSAN AND GOD(1940); LADY BE GOOD(1941); SUNNY(1941); THIS WOMAN IS MINE(1941); FLYING TIGERS(1942); PIERRE OF THE PLAINS(1942); RIO RITA(1942); HIT PARADE OF 1943(1943); YOUNGEST PROFESSION, THE(1943); BEDSIDE MANNER(1945); LETTER FOR EVIE, A(1945); FABULOUS TEXAN, THE(1947); FIESTA(1947); WYOMING(1947); ANGEL IN EXILE(1948); FLAME(1948); I, JANE DOE(1948); OLD LOS ANGELES(1948); AVENGERS, THE(1950); HIT PARADE OF 1951(1950); SURRENDER(1950); BELLE LE GRAND(1951); FARMER TAKES A WIFE, THE(1953); GERALDINE(1953); LIGHT TOUCH, THE(1955, Brit.); DECISION AT SUNDOWN(1957); SILKEN AFFAIR, THE(1957, Brit.); TWO GROOMS FOR A BRIDE(1957); PLUNDERERS OF PAINTED FLATS(1959); TIM(1981, Aus.), art d; SPLIT IMAGE(1982)

1984
CAREFUL, HE MIGHT HEAR YOU(1984, Aus.), art d
Misc. Talkies
DEATH IN THE AIR(1937); IN OLD LOS ANGELES(1948)
John Carroll, Jr.
PHANTOM RAIDERS(1940)
John W. Carroll
1984
MRS. SOFFEL(1984)
Johnny Carroll
ROCK BABY, ROCK IT(1957)
Joseph Carroll
Misc. Silents
LOVE THAT LIVES, THE(1917)
June Carroll
ANGEL COMES TO BROOKLYN, AN(1945), a, w; NEW FACES(1954)
Kent E. Carroll
ABDUCTION(1975), p, w
Lane Carroll
THE CRAZIES(1973)
Larry Carroll
TEXAS CHAIN SAW MASSACRE, THE(1974), ed; ROCKY(1976); ONE DARK NIGHT(1983)
1984
2010(1984)
Laura Carroll
SON OF SINBAD(1955)
Laurie Carroll
RUMBLE ON THE DOCKS(1956)
Leo Carroll
BARRETTS OF WIMPOLE STREET, THE(1934); SADIE MCKEE(1934); BULLDOG DRUMMOND'S SECRET POLICE(1939)
Leo G. Carroll
OUTCAST LADY(1934); CASINO MURDER CASE, THE(1935); CLIVE OF INDIA(1935); MURDER ON A HONEYMOON(1935); RIGHT TO LIVE, THE(1935); CAPTAINS COURAGEOUS(1937); LONDON BY NIGHT(1937); CHRISTMAS CAROL, A(1938); CHARLIE CHAN IN THE CITY OF DARKNESS(1939); PRIVATE LIVES OF ELIZABETH AND ESSEX, THE(1939); TOWER OF LONDON(1939); CHARLIE CHAN'S MURDER CRUISE(1940); REBECCA(1940); WATERLOO BRIDGE(1940); BAHAMA PASSAGE(1941); SCOTLAND YARD(1941); SUSPICION(1941); THIS WOMAN IS MINE(1941); HOUSE ON 92ND STREET, THE(1945); SPELLBOUND(1945); FOREVER AMBER(1947); PARADINE CASE, THE(1947); SONG OF LOVE(1947); TIME OUT OF MIND(1947); ENCHANTMENT(1948); SO EVIL MY LOVE(1948, Brit.); FATHER OF THE BRIDE(1950); HAPPY YEARS, THE(1950); DESERT FOX, THE(1951); FIRST LEGION, THE(1951); STRANGERS ON A TRAIN(1951); BAD AND THE BEAUTIFUL, THE(1952); ROGUE'S MARCH(1952); SNOWS OF KILIMANJARO, THE(1952); TREASURE OF THE GOLDEN CONDOR(1953); YOUNG BESS(1953); TARANTULA(1955); WE'RE NO ANGELS(1955); SWAN, THE(1956); NORTH BY NORTHWEST(1959); ONE PLUS ONE(1961, Can.); PARENT TRAP, THE(1961); PRIZE, THE(1963); THAT FUNNY FEELING(1965); ONE OF OUR SPIES IS MISSING(1966); ONE SPY TOO MANY(1966); SPY IN THE GREEN HAT, THE(1966); SPY WITH MY FACE, THE(1966); KARATE KILLERS, THE(1967); HELICOPTER SPIES, THE(1968); FROM NASHVILLE WITH MUSIC(1969)
Lewis Carroll
ALICE IN WONDERLAND(1933), w; ALICE IN WONDERLAND(1951), w, w; CHICAGO 70(1970), p&d; ALICE'S ADVENTURES IN WONDERLAND(1972, Brit.), d&w; JABBERWOCKY(1977, Brit.), w
Lisa Carroll
NATURAL ENEMIES(1979)
Lisa Hart Carroll
TERMS OF ENDEARMENT(1983)
Lucia Carroll
SERGEANT YORK(; ALWAYS A BRIDE(1940); TUGBOAT ANNIE SAILS AGAIN(1940); CITY, FOR CONQUEST(1941); HERE COMES HAPPINESS(1941); HIGH SIERRA(1941); KISSES FOR BREAKFAST(1941); MANPOWER(1941); MEET JOHN DOE(1941); NAVY BLUES(1941); NURSE'S SECRET, THE(1941); SHOT IN THE DARK, THE(1941); STRAWBERRY BLONDE, THE(1941); CAPTAINS OF THE CLOUDS(1942); WILD BILL HICKOK RIDES(1942); DANGER STREET(1947); NEVER WAVE AT A WAC(1952)
Lucie Carroll
MEET JOHN DOE(1941)
Mabel Z. Carroll
CONVICT'S CODE(1930), a, w
Madeleine Carroll
AMERICAN PRISONER, THE(1929 Brit.); ATLANTIC(1929 Brit.); CROOKED BILLET, THE(1930, Brit.); ESCAPE(1930, Brit.); KISSING CUP'S RACE(1930, Brit.); SCHOOL FOR SCANDAL, THE(1930, Brit.); YOUNG WOODLEY(1930, Brit.); "W" PLAN, THE(1931, Brit.); FASCINATION(1931, Brit.); FRENCH LEAVE(1931, Brit.); MADAME GUILLOTINE(1931, Brit.); WRITTEN LAW, THE(1931, Brit.); SLEEPING CAR(1933, Brit.); I WAS A SPY(1934, Brit.); WORLD MOVES ON, THE(1934); DICTATOR, THE(1935, Brit./Ger.); 39 STEPS, THE(1935, Brit.); CASE AGAINST MRS. AMES, THE(1936); GENERAL DIED AT DAWN, THE(1936); LLOYDS OF LONDON(1936); SECRET AGENT, THE(1936, Brit.); IT'S ALL YOURS(1937); ON THE AVENUE(1937); PRISONER OF ZENDA, THE(1937); BLOCKADE(1938); CAFE SOCIETY(1939); HONEYMOON IN BALI(1939); MY SON, MY SON!(1940); NORTHWEST MOUNTED POLICE(1940); SAFARI(1940); ONE NIGHT IN LISBON(1941); VIRGINIA(1941); MY FAVORITE BLONDE(1942); HIGH FURY(1947, Brit.); DON'T TRUST YOUR HUSBAND(1948); FAN, THE(1949)
Misc. Silents
FIRST BORN, THE(1928, Brit.); GUNS OF LOOS, THE(1928, Brit.)
Madeline Carroll
BAHAMA PASSAGE(1941)
Marcelle Carroll
Silents
NOTHING BUT THE TRUTH(1920)
Misc. Silents
MARBLE HEART, THE(1916)

Marilyn Carroll
DRAGSTRIP RIOT(1958)
Martha Carroll
DAKOTA(1945)
Martin Carroll
PRIVATE LIFE OF SHERLOCK HOLMES, THE(1970, Brit.); TERROR FROM UNDER THE HOUSE(1971, Brit.); TIME BANDITS(1981, Brit.)
Mary Carroll
KLONDIKE KATE(1944), ch; DESERT FOX, THE(1951); SECRET OF CONVICT LAKE, THE(1951); PRISONER OF ZENDA, THE(1952); BIG TIP OFF, THE(1955); FOXFIRE(1955); GOOD MORNING, MISS DOVE(1955); NO DOWN PAYMENT(1957); 10 NORTH FREDERICK(1958); WOMAN OBSESSED(1959)
Matt Carroll
STORM BOY(1976, Aus.), p; MONEY MOVERS(1978, Aus.), p; WEEKEND OF SHADOWS(1978, Aus.), p; BREAKER MORANT(1980, Aus.), p; CLUB, THE(1980, Aus.), p; PLUMBER, THE(1980, Aus.), p
Maxine Carroll
RACING FEVER(1964)
Merrie Carroll
HOME AND AWAY(1956, Brit.)
Mildred Carroll
TWO TICKETS TO BROADWAY(1951)
Moon Carroll
LAST OF MRS. CHEYNEY, THE(1929); LADY OF SCANDAL, THE(1930); LIGHT-NIN'(1930); THIRTEENTH CHAIR, THE(1930); DRACULA(1931)
Nancy Carroll
ABIE'S IRISH ROSE(1928); MANHATTAN COCKTAIL(1928); SHOPWORN ANGEL, THE(1928); CLOSE HARMONY(1929); DANCE OF LIFE, THE(1929); ILLUSION(1929); SWEETIE(1929); WOLF OF WALL STREET, THE(1929); DANGEROUS PARADIS-E(1930); DEVIL'S HOLIDAY, THE(1930); FOLLOW THRU(1930); HONEY(1930); LAUGHTER(1930); NIGHT ANGEL, THE(1931); PERSONAL MAID(1931); STOLEN HEAVEN(1931); BROKEN LULLABY(1932); HOT SATURDAY(1932); SCARLET DAWN(1932); UNDER-COVER MAN(1932); WAYWARD(1932); CHILD OF MANHAT-TAN(1933); I LOVE THAT MAN(1933); KISS BEFORE THE MIRROR, THE(1933); WOMAN ACCUSED(1933); JEALOUSY(1934); SPRINGTIME FOR HENRY(1934); TRANSATLANTIC MERRY-GO-ROUND(1934); AFTER THE DANCE(1935); ATLAN-TIC ADVENTURE(1935); I'LL LOVE YOU ALWAYS(1935); THAT CERTAIN AGE(1938); THERE GOES MY HEART(1938)
Silents
LADIES MUST DRESS(1927); EASY COME, EASY GO(1928); SIN SISTER, THE(1929)
Misc. Silents
CHICKEN A LA KING(1928); MANHATTAN COCKTAIL(1928); WATER HOLE, THE(1928)
Nilli Carroll
DESPERATE WOMEN, THE(?)
Pamela Carroll
MY HEART GOES CRAZY(1953, Brit.)
Pat Carroll
WITH SIX YOU GET EGGROLL(1968); BROTHERS O'TOOLE, THE(1973)
Paul Vincent Carroll
IT HAPPENED ONE SUNDAY(1944, Brit.), w; CAPTAIN BOYCOTT(1947, Brit.), w; BROTHERS, THE(1948, Brit.), w; SAINTS AND SINNERS(1949, Brit.), w; MIDNIGHT EPISODE(1951, Brit.), w; DEATH OF MICHAEL TURBIN, THE(1954, Brit.), w; DESTI-NATION MILAN(1954, Brit.), w; LAST MOMENT, THE(1954, Brit.), w; MARCH HARE, THE(1956, Brit.), w
Peggy Carroll
LADY TAKES A CHANCE, A(1943); MORE THE MERRIER, THE(1943); STRANGE LADY IN TOWN(1955), ch
Peter Carroll
LAST WAVE, THE(1978, Aus.); CHANT OF JIMMIE BLACKSMITH, THE(1980, Aus.); FATTY FINN(1980, Aus.)
Misc. Talkies
CASS(1977)
Regina Carroll
BRAIN OF BLOOD(1971, Phil.)
Misc. Talkies
BLAZING STEWARDESSES(1975)
Richard Carroll
LOVE TIME(1934), w; I CONQUER THE SEA(1936), w; FIVE CAME BACK(1939), w; APE, THE(1940), w; YOU CAN'T FOOL YOUR WIFE(1940), w; THREE GIRLS ABOUT TOWN(1941), w; FLIGHT LIEUTENANT(1942), w; TWO YANKS IN TRINI-DAD(1942), w; BACK FROM ETERNITY(1956), w
Richard A. Carroll
SUNBONNET SUE(1945), w
Robert Carroll
WALK EAST ON BEACON(1952); JAWS(1975)
Roberta Lee Carroll
I WANNA HOLD YOUR HAND(1978)
Ron Carroll
HAIL(1973)
Ronn Carroll
FRIDAY THE 13TH(1980); SPRING BREAK(1983)
1984
FRIDAY THE 13TH–THE FINAL CHAPTER(1984)
Ronnie Carroll
MAN IN THE DARK(1963, Brit.)
Sidney Carroll
THREE CASES OF MURDER(1955, Brit.), w; HUSTLER, THE(1961), w; BIG HAND FOR THE LITTLE LADY, A(1966), w; GAMBIT(1966), w; COUNT OF MONTE CRIS-TO(1976, Brit.), w
Susan Carroll
STANLEY(1973)
Susette Carroll
HISTORY OF THE WORLD, PART 1(1981)
Misc. Talkies
DISCO FEVER(1978)
Taylor Carroll
Silents
FIGHTING AMERICAN, THE(1924); SAWDUST TRAIL(1924)

Ted Carroll
DRACULA(1979); FLASH GORDON(1980)
Terry Carroll
LOVE KISS, THE(1930); CITY STREETS(1931); PERSONAL MAID(1931); BEFORE MORNING(1933)
Therese Carroll
WOMAN TO WOMAN(1946, Brit.)
Thomas C. Carroll
SUGAR HILL(1974)
Toni Carroll
ACTORS AND SIN(1952); FRENCH LINE, THE(1954)
Tony Carroll
HERCULES IN NEW YORK(1970)
Vana Carroll
MAN CALLED DAGGER, A(1967), cos
Vance Carroll
MAGNIFICENT OBSESSION(1935); YELLOW CARGO(1936); SWEETHEART OF THE NAVY(1937); SPEED LIMITED(1940)
Victoria Carroll
ART OF LOVE, THE(1965); HOW TO STUFF A WILD BIKINI(1965); LAST OF THE SECRET AGENTS?, THE(1966); FASTEST GUITAR ALIVE, THE(1967); ROAD HUS-TLERS, THE(1968); NIGHTMARE IN WAX(1969); BILLION DOLLAR HOBO, THE(1977); PANDEMONIUM(1982)
Vinette Carroll
ONE POTATO, TWO POTATO(1964); UP THE DOWN STAIRCASE(1967)
Vinnette Carroll
ALICE'S RESTAURANT(1969); REIVERS, THE(1969)
Virginia Carroll
ROBERTA(1935); TENDERFOOT GOES WEST, A(1937); TOAST OF NEW YORK, THE(1937); WOMEN OF GLAMOUR(1937); OKLAHOMA TERROR(1939); WATERLOO BRIDGE(1940); MASKED RIDER, THE(1941); MODEL WIFE(1941); PHANTOM COW-BOY, THE(1941); RAIDERS OF THE WEST(1942); LAKE PLACID SERENADE(1944); MAN FROM FRISCO(1944); G.I. WAR BRIDES(1946); MURDER IN THE MUSIC HALL(1946); LAST ROUND-UP, THE(1947); SMASH-UP, THE STORY OF A WO-MAN(1947); FRONTIER AGENT(1948); BAD MEN OF TOMBSTONE(1949); CRASH-ING THRU(1949); RIDERS OF THE WHISTLING PINES(1949); WAC FROM WALLA WALLA, THE(1952); PICKUP ON SOUTH STREET(1953); BIG TIP OFF, THE(1955); GOOD MORNING, MISS DOVE(1955); HEADLINE HUNTERS(1955); VIOLENT SATURDAY(1955); BIGGER THAN LIFE(1956); SPOILERS OF THE FOREST(1957); STORY ON PAGE ONE, THE(1959)
Misc. Talkies
PRAIRIE GUNSMOKE(1942); OVERLAND TRAILS(1948); TRIGGERMAN(1948)
W.A. Carroll
Silents
MOLLY ENTANGLED(1917); FIGHTING EDGE(1926); JOSSELYN'S WIFE(1926)
William Carroll
Silents
FIFTY CANDLES(1921); CHAIN LIGHTNING(1922); NORTH OF 36(1924)
Misc. Silents
EMBERS(1916); LORD LOVELAND DISCOVERS AMERICA(1916); REVELA-TIONS(1916); TWINKLER, THE(1916); DANGER WITHIN(1918); BILL HENRY(1919)
William A. Carroll
Silents
ALIMONY(1924); K–THE UNKNOWN(1924); ANCIENT HIGHWAY, THE(1925); COLLEGE DAYS(1926)
Misc. Silents
PURITY(1916); CONFIDENCE(1922)
Zelma Carroll
PENITENTE MURDER CASE, THE(1936), w
The Carroll Brothers
DON'T KNOCK THE TWIST(1962)
Carroll Gibbons and His Orchestra
SIDEWALKS OF LONDON(1940, Brit.); YANK IN LONDON, A(1946, Brit.)
Carroll Gibbons and His Savoy Orpheans
ROMANCE IN RHYTHM(1934, Brit.)
Carroll Gibbons and the Savoy Orpheans
I ADORE YOU(1933, Brit.)
Carroll Levis' Discoveries
LUCKY MASCOT, THE(1951, Brit.)
Carroll-MacDonald
WAY OUT WEST(1937), m
Vivian Carrols
Misc. Silents
MODERN CAIN, A(1925)
Carol Carrolton
LADY OF BURLESQUE(1943)
Sergio Carrone
NO ROOM TO DIE(1969, Ital.), d&w
Ric Carrott
MARATHON MAN(1976)
Misc. Talkies
SWINGING CHEERLEADERS, THE(1974)
Rick Carrott
MOTHER, JUGS & SPEED(1976)
Carrotte
WARRIORS, THE(1979)
Marie Carrozza
SONG OF BERNADETTE, THE(1943)
Burr Carruth
STRANDED(1935); GHOST TOWN GOLD(1937); LOVE IN A BUNGALOW(1937)
Carl Carruth
SONG OF KENTUCKY(1929), ed
Clyde Carruth
FOX MOVIETONE FOLLIES OF 1930(1930), ed; HAPPY DAYS(1930), ed; SOUP TO NUTS(1930), ed; TEMPLE TOWER(1930), ed; WILD COMPANY(1930), ed; THREE ROGUES(1931), ed
Misc. Silents
COWBOY KID, THE(1928), d

Dick Carruth
RETURN OF THE LASH(1947), md; THREE ON A TICKET(1947), md
Evelyn Carruth
MAN WITH THE GUN(1955), cos; KISS BEFORE DYING, A(1956), cos
Milton Carruth
PAD, THE(AND HOW TO USE IT)* (1966, Brit.), ed; SHANGHAI LADY(1929), ed; ALL QUIET ON THE WESTERN FRONT(1930), ed; NIGHT RIDE(1930), ed; OUTSIDE THE LAW(1930), ed; DRACULA(1931), ed; HEAVEN ON EARTH(1931), ed; IRON MAN, THE(1931), ed; LAW AND ORDER(1932), ed; MUMMY, THE(1932), ed; MURDERS IN THE RUE MORGUE(1932), ed; DESTINATION UNKNOWN(1933), ed; ONLY YESTERDAY(1933), ed; I LIKE IT THAT WAY(1934), ed; LITTLE MAN, WHAT NOW?(1934), ed; MAGNIFICENT OBSESSION(1935), ed; DRACULA'S DAUGHTER(1936), ed; LOVE LETTERS OF A STAR(1936), d&w; TWO IN A CROWD(1936), ed; BREEZING HOME(1937), d; LADY FIGHTS BACK(1937), d; MAN IN BLUE, THE(1937), d; REPORTED MISSING(1937), d; SHE'S DANGEROUS(1937), d; SOME BLONDES ARE DANGEROUS(1937), d; DESTRY RIDES AGAIN(1939), ed; LAUGH IT OFF(1939), ed; WHEN TOMORROW COMES(1939), ed; ALIAS THE DEACON(1940), ed; BOYS FROM SYRACUSE(1940), ed; ONE NIGHT IN THE TROPICS(1940), ed; ZANZIBAR(1940), ed; CRACKED NUTS(1941), ed; HELLZAPOPPIN'(1941), ed; MAN WHO LOST HIMSELF, THE(1941), ed; MEET THE CHUMP(1941), ed; MEN OF THE TIMBERLAND(1941), ed; SAN ANTONIO ROSE(1941), ed; BUTCH MINDS THE BABY(1942), ed; MUMMY'S TOMB, THE(1942), ed; MYSTERY OF MARIE ROGET, THE(1942), ed; NIGHT MONSTER(1942), ed; PRIVATE BUCKAROO(1942), ed; TOP SERGEANT(1942), ed; CAPTIVE WILD WOMAN(1943), ed; FOLLOW THE BAND(1943), ed; GUNG HO!(1943), ed; MAD GHOUL, THE(1943), ed; SHADOW OF A DOUBT(1943), ed; STRANGE DEATH OF ADOLF HITLER, THE(1943), ed; TWO TICKETS TO LONDON(1943), ed; DEAD MAN'S EYES(1944), ed; MOON OVER LAS VEGAS(1944), ed; TRIGGER TRAIL(1944), ed; WEIRD WOMAN(1944), ed; SUDAN(1945), ed; CANYON PASSAGE(1946), ed; NIGHT IN PARADISE, A(1946), ed; LOST MOMENT, THE(1947), ed; SMASH-UP, THE STORY OF A WOMAN(1947), ed; ANOTHER PART OF THE FOREST(1948), ed; FAMILY HONEYMOON(1948), ed; KISS THE BLOOD OFF MY HANDS(1948), ed; FRANCIS(1949), ed; GAL WHO TOOK THE WEST, THE(1949), ed; LADY GAMBLES, THE(1949), ed; LIFE OF RILEY, THE(1949), ed; WOMAN IN HIDING(1949), ed; KANSAS RAIDERS(1950), ed; LOUISA(1950), ed; ONE WAY STREET(1950), ed; SHAKEDOWN(1950), ed; APACHE DRUMS(1951), ed; FINDERS KEEPERS(1951), ed; FRANCIS GOES TO THE RACES(1951), ed; UP FRONT(1951), ed; FRANCIS GOES TO WEST POINT(1952), ed; IT GROWS ON TREES(1952), ed; TREASURE OF LOST CANYON, THE(1952), ed; ALL I DESIRE(1953), ed; BACK TO GOD'S COUNTRY(1953), ed; COLUMN SOUTH(1953), ed; FRANCIS COVERS THE BIG TOWN(1953), ed; REDHEAD FROM WYOMING, THE(1953), ed; TAKE ME TO TOWN(1953), ed; MAGNIFICENT OBSESSION(1954), ed; SIGN OF THE PAGAN(1954), ed; TAZA, SON OF COCHISE(1954), ed; CULT OF THE COBRA(1955), ed; FRANCIS IN THE NAVY(1955), ed; MAN FROM BITTER RIDGE, THE(1955), ed; ONE DESIRE(1955), ed; SMOKE SIGNAL(1955), ed; FRANCIS IN THE HAUNTED HOUSE(1956), ed; I'VE LIVED BEFORE(1956), ed; PILLARS OF THE SKY(1956), ed; TOY TIGER(1956), ed; WORLD IN MY CORNER(1956), ed; JOE BUTTERFLY(1957), ed; MY MAN GODFREY(1957), ed; FEMALE ANIMAL, THE(1958), ed; ONCE UPON A HORSE(1958), ed; PERFECT FURLOUGH, THE(1958), ed; THIS HAPPY FEELING(1958), ed; IMITATION OF LIFE(1959), ed; PILLOW TALK(1959), ed; HELL BENT FOR LEATHER(1960), ed; LEECH WOMAN, THE(1960), ed; PORTRAIT IN BLACK(1960), ed; BACK STREET(1961), ed; FLOWER DRUM SONG(1961), ed; IF A MAN ANSWERS(1962), ed; TAMMY AND THE DOCTOR(1963), ed; THRILL OF IT ALL, THE(1963), ed; BEDTIME STORY(1964), ed; I'D RATHER BE RICH(1964), ed; ART OF LOVE, THE(1965), ed; MADAME X(1966), ed
Nathan Carruth
LET'S BE RITZY(1934), ed
William Carruth
NICKELODEON(1976), ed; SAINT JACK(1979), ed; CADDY SHACK(1980), ed
1984
STRANGERS KISS(1984), ed
Bruce Carruther
BOMBA AND THE JUNGLE GIRL(1952)
Ben Carruthers
SHADOWS(1960); GUNS OF THE TREES(1964); LILITH(1964); DIRTY DOZEN, THE(1967, Brit.); FEARLESS FRANK(1967); UNKNOWN MAN OF SHANDIGOR, THE(1967, Switz.); RIOT(1969); MAN IN THE WILDERNESS(1971, U.S./Span.)
Benito Carruthers
GOLDSTEIN(1964); HIGH WIND IN JAMAICA, A(1965); LOST CONTINENT, THE(1968, Brit.); UNIVERSAL SOLDIER(1971, Brit.)
Bruce Carruthers
HEART OF THE NORTH(1938); MINISTRY OF FEAR(1945); THEY WERE EXPENDABLE(1945); CALCUTTA(1947); GENE AUTRY AND THE MOUNTIES(1951); CARRIE(1952)
James Carruthers
TOOTSIE(1982)
Leto Carruthers
EYE WITNESS(1950, Brit.), ed
Lito Carruthers
DAUGHTER OF DARKNESS(1948, Brit.), ed; HIDDEN ROOM, THE(1949, Brit.), ed; SILENT DUST(1949, Brit.), ed; TEMPTATION HARBOR(1949, Brit.), ed; VALLEY OF EAGLES(1952, Brit.), ed; FUSS OVER FEATHERS(1954, Brit.), ed; TURN THE KEY SOFTLY(1954, Brit.), ed; FIRE MAIDENS FROM OUTER SPACE(1956, Brit.), ed; LIFE IN EMERGENCY WARD 10(1959, Brit.), ed; MISSILE FROM HELL(1960, Brit.), ed; TOO HOT TO HANDLE(1961, Brit.), ed
Steve Carruthers
HOLLOW TRIUMPH(1948); PROWLER, THE(1951); DREAMBOAT(1952); CLOWN, THE(1953); DREAM WIFE(1953); PEPE(1960); HOUSE IS NOT A HOME, A(1964)
Steven Carruthers
ANGELA(1955, Ital.), w
Jack Carry
HAWK OF WILD RIVER, THE(1952); GUN BELT(1953); MAN FROM LARAMIE, THE(1955)
Jean Carry
THIS WOMAN IS DANGEROUS(1952)
Julius J. Carry III
FISH THAT SAVED PITTSBURGH, THE(1979)

Steven Wayne Carry
Misc. Talkies
EVIDENCE OF POWER(1979)
Betty Carse
THREE ON A MATCH(1932)
Wally Carsell
GUILTY, THE(1947)
Gastone Carsetti
WARRIORS FIVE(1962), art d; PRIMITIVE LOVE(1966, Ital.), art d; ACE HIGH(1969, Ital.), art d; GOD FORGIVES–I DON'T!(1969, Ital./Span.), art d; LONG RIDE FROM HELL, A(1970, Ital.), set d; STREET PEOPLE(1976, U.S./Ital.), art d
Gastoni Carsetti
BLINDMAN(1972, Ital.), art d
Barbara Carson
MADE FOR EACH OTHER(1971)
Bartlett Carson
MACHISMO–40 GRAVES FOR 40 GUNS(1970)
Bill Carson
GOODBYE PORK PIE(1981, New Zealand)
Bob Carson
AMBUSH TRAIL(1946); MY DREAM IS YOURS(1949); COUNTY FAIR(1950); RADAR SECRET SERVICE(1950); TWO LOST WORLDS(1950); ACTORS AND SIN(1952); GREATEST SHOW ON EARTH, THE(1952); MAN OF CONFLICT(1953); MURDER WITHOUT TEARS(1953); THREE SAILORS AND A GIRL(1953); DEEP IN MY HEART(1954); EXECUTIVE SUITE(1954); GANG BUSTERS(1955); LADY AND THE TRAMP(1955), anim; SLEEPING BEAUTY(1959), anim; PATSY, THE(1964)
Carrol Davis Carson
PRIVATE BENJAMIN(1980)
Chad Carson
FAREWELL PERFORMANCE(1963, Brit.)
Charles Carson
VICTORIA THE GREAT(1937, Brit.); DREYFUS CASE, THE(1931, Brit.); MANY WATERS(1931, Brit.); CHINESE PUZZLE, THE(1932, Brit.); LEAP YEAR(1932, Brit.); MARRY ME(1932, Brit.); THERE GOES THE BRIDE(1933, Brit.); BLIND JUSTICE(1934, Brit.); BROKEN MELODY, THE(1934, Brit.); FATHER AND SON(1934, Brit.); NO ESCAPE(1934, Brit.); PERFECT FLAW, THE(1934, Brit.); WHISPERING TONGUES(1934, Brit.); INVITATION TO THE WALTZ(1935, Brit.); MEN OF TOMORROW(1935, Brit.); SANDERS OF THE RIVER(1935, Brit.); SCROOGE(1935, Brit.); BELOVED VAGABOND, THE(1936, Brit.); HEAD OFFICE(1936, Brit.); I STAND CONDEMNED(1936, Brit.); SECRET AGENT, THE(1936, Brit.); THINGS TO COME(1936, Brit.); APRIL BLOSSOMS(1937, Brit.); DARK JOURNEY(1937, Brit.); DREAMING LIPS(1937, Brit.); FIRE OVER ENGLAND(1937, Brit.); FOREVER YOURS(1937, Brit.); GLAMOROUS NIGHT(1937, Brit.); OLD MOTHER RILEY(1937, Brit.); SATURDAY NIGHT REVUE(1937, Brit.); TALK OF THE DEVIL(1937, Brit.); WEEKEND MILLIONAIRE(1937, Brit.); WHO KILLED FEN MARKHAM?(1937, Brit.); I MARRIED A SPY(1938); NO PARKING(1938, Brit.); OH BOY!(1938, Brit.); RETURN OF THE FROG, THE(1938, Brit.); SIXTY GLORIOUS YEARS(1938, Brit.); WE'RE GOING TO BE RICH(1938, Brit.); SAINT IN LONDON, THE(1939, Brit.); CAPTAIN MOONLIGHT(1940, Brit.); LION HAS WINGS, THE(1940, Brit.); SPARE A COPPER(1940, Brit.); COMMON TOUCH, THE(1941, Brit.); COURAGEOUS MR. PENN, THE(1941, Brit.); QUIET WEDDING(1941, Brit.); WINGS AND THE WOMAN(1942, Brit.); AMAZING MR. FORREST, THE(1943, Brit.); BATTLE FOR MUSIC(1943, Brit.); DUMMY TALKS, THE(1943, Brit.); PINK STRING AND SEALING WAX(1950, Brit.); LADY WITH A LAMP, THE(1951, Brit.); CRY, THE BELOVED COUNTRY(1952, Brit.); MOULIN ROUGE(1952); MASTER OF BALLANTRAE, THE(1953, U.S./Brit.); BEAU BRUMMELL(1954); DUEL IN THE JUNGLE(1954, Brit.); DAM BUSTERS, THE(1955, Brit.); LET'S BE HAPPY(1957, Brit.); REACH FOR THE SKY(1957, Brit.); SILKEN AFFAIR, THE(1957, Brit.); BOBBIKINS(1959, Brit.); SANDS OF THE DESERT(1960, Brit.); STORY OF DAVID, A(1960, Brit.); MACBETH(1963); THREE LIVES OF THOMASINA, THE(1963, U.S./Brit.); CURSE OF THE FLY(1965, Brit.); LADY CAROLINE LAMB(1972, Brit./Ital.)
Cindy Carson
Misc. Talkies
FRONTIER WOMAN(1956)
Dale Carson
BATTLING MARSHAL(1950)
Darwyn Carson
TRUE CONFESSIONS(1981); SIX WEEKS(1982); UNCOMMON VALOR(1983)
1984
BEVERLY HILLS COP(1984)
David Carson
FUNHOUSE, THE(1981)
Doris Carson
MOONLIGHT AND PRETZELS(1933)
Frances Carson
JAVA HEAD(1935, Brit.); FOREIGN CORRESPONDENT(1940); LIFE WITH HENRY(1941); SMILIN' THROUGH(1941); TWO-FACED WOMAN(1941); PACIFIC RENDEZVOUS(1942); SABOTEUR(1942); SCATTERGOOD RIDES HIGH(1942); SHADOW OF A DOUBT(1943)
Frank G. Carson
THIRTY FOOT BRIDE OF CANDY ROCK, THE(1959), ph
Fred Carson
CHARGE AT FEATHER RIVER, THE(1953); WALL OF NOISE(1963); REQUIEM FOR A GUNFIGHTER(1965)
Freddie Carson
SON OF THE RENEGADE(1953)
Ganahl Carson
DEVIL'S PLAYGROUND(1937), spec eff; LOST HORIZON(1937), spec eff; START CHEERING(1938), spec eff
Hunter Carson
1984
PARIS, TEXAS(1984, Ger./Fr.)
Jack Carson
CIRCLE OF DEATH(1935); CRASHING HOLLYWOOD(1937); HIGH FLYERS(1937); MUSIC FOR MADAME(1937); REPORTED MISSING(1937); STAGE DOOR(1937); STAND-IN(1937); TOAST OF NEW YORK, THE(1937); TOO MANY WIVES(1937); YOU ONLY LIVE ONCE(1937); BRINGING UP BABY(1938); CAREFREE(1938); GO CHASE YOURSELF(1938); HAVING WONDERFUL TIME(1938); LAW OF THE UNDERWORLD(1938); MAID'S NIGHT OUT(1938); MR. DOODLE KICKS OFF(1938); NIGHT SPOT(1938); QUICK MONEY(1938); SAINT IN NEW YORK, THE(1938); SHE'S GOT

EVERYTHING(1938); THIS MARRIAGE BUSINESS(1938); VIVACIOUS LADY(1938); DESTRY RIDES AGAIN(1939); ESCAPE, THE(1939); FIFTH AVENUE GIRL(1939); HONEYMOON'S OVER, THE(1939); KID FROM TEXAS, THE(1939); LEGION OF LOST FLYERS(1939); MR. SMITH GOES TO WASHINGTON(1939); ALIAS THE DEACON(1940); ENEMY AGENT(1940); GIRL IN 313(1940); I TAKE THIS WOMAN(1940); LOVE THY NEIGHBOR(1940); LUCKY PARTNERS(1940); PAROLE FIXER(1940); QUEEN OF THE MOB(1940); SANDY GETS HER MAN(1940); SHOOTING HIGH(1940); TYPHOON(1940); YOUNG AS YOU FEEL(1940); BLUES IN THE NIGHT(1941); BRIDE CAME C.O.D., THE(1941); LOVE CRAZY(1941); MR. AND MRS. SMITH(1941); NAVY BLUES(1941); STRAWBERRY BLONDE, THE(1941); GENTLEMAN JIM(1942); HARD WAY, THE(1942); LARCENY, INC.(1942); MALE ANIMAL, THE(1942); WINGS FOR THE EAGLE(1942); PRINCESS O'ROURKE(1943); THANK YOUR LUCKY STARS(1943); ARSENIC AND OLD LACE(1944); DOUGHGIRLS, THE(1944); HOLLYWOOD CANTEEN(1944); MAKE YOUR OWN BED(1944); SHINE ON, HARVEST MOON(1944); MILDRED PIERCE(1945); ROUGHLY SPEAKING(1945); ONE MORE TOMORROW(1946); TIME, THE PLACE AND THE, THE(1946); LOVE AND LEARN(1947); APRIL SHOWERS(1948); ROMANCE ON THE HIGH SEAS(1948); TWO GUYS FROM TEXAS(1948); IT'S A GREAT FEELING(1949); JOHN LOVES MARY(1949); MY DREAM IS YOURS(1949); BRIGHT LEAF(1950); GOOD HUMOR MAN, THE(1950); GROOM WORE SPURS, THE(1951); MR. UNIVERSE(1951); DANGEROUS WHEN WET(1953); PHFFFT!(1954); RED GARTERS(1954); STAR IS BORN, A(1954); AIN'T MISBEHAVIN'(1955); BOTTOM OF THE BOTTLE, THE(1956); MAGNIFICENT ROUGHNECKS(1956); TARNISHED ANGELS, THE(1957); TATTERED DRESS, THE(1957); CAT ON A HOT TIN ROOF(1958); RALLY 'ROUND THE FLAG, BOYS!(1958); BRAMBLE BUSH, THE(1960); CIRCUS OF HORRORS(1960, Brit.); KING OF THE ROARING TWENTIES–THE STORY OF ARNOLD ROTHSTEIN(1961); BLOOD BEAST FROM OUTER SPACE(1965, Brit.)

James Carson
MOONLIGHT AND PRETZELS(1933); SWISS MISS(1938); ONE OF OUR AIRCRAFT IS MISSING(1942, Brit.); MAN IN GREY, THE(1943, Brit.); UNCENSORED(1944, Brit.); MARK OF CAIN, THE(1948, Brit.)

James B. Carson
HARMONY LANE(1935); LOVE ON THE RUN(1936); FIREFLY, THE(1937); MURDER GOES TO COLLEGE(1937); CRIME SCHOOL(1938); FAST COMPANY(1938); GIRL DOWNSTAIRS, THE(1938); SECRETS OF AN ACTRESS(1938); THREE LOVES HAS NANCY(1938); DISPUTED PASSAGE(1939); LADY IN QUESTION, THE(1940); ROAD TO ZANZIBAR(1941); I MARRIED AN ANGEL(1942)

Jean Carson
DATE WITH A DREAM, A(1948, Brit.); LOVE IN PAWN(1953, Brit.); PHENIX CITY STORY, THE(1955); ALLIGATOR NAMED DAISY, AN(1957, Brit.); AS LONG AS THEY'RE HAPPY(1957, Brit.); I MARRIED A MONSTER FROM OUTER SPACE(1958); HERE COME THE JETS(1959); SANCTUARY(1961); ONE MAN'S WAY(1964); GUNN(1967); WARNING SHOT(1967); PARTY, THE(1968); FUN WITH DICK AND JANE(1977)

Jean-Philippe Carson
GLASS CAGE, THE(1964), ph; SERPENTS OF THE PIRATE MOON, THE(1973)

Jean-Phillippe Carson
GOLDSTEIN(1964), ph

Jeanne Carson
MY FAIR LADY(1964)

Jeannie Carson
MAD LITTLE ISLAND(1958, Brit.); SEVEN KEYS(1962, Brit.)

Jerome Carson
MINSTREL MAN(1944)

Jill Carson
UGLY DUCKLING, THE(1959, Brit.); VILLAGE OF DAUGHTERS(1962, Brit.); PRIZE, THE(1963); V.I.P.s, THE(1963, Brit.); INCREDIBLY STRANGE CREATURES WHO STOPPED LIVING AND BECAME CRAZY MIXED-UP ZOMBIES, THE(1965)

John Carson
BLACK LASH, THE(1952); THUNDER OVER THE PLAINS(1953); QUENTIN DURWARD(1955); RAMSBOTTOM RIDES AGAIN(1956, Brit.); INTENT TO KILL(1958, Brit.); LADY IS A SQUARE, THE(1959, Brit.); GUNS OF DARKNESS(1962, Brit.); LOCKER 69(1962, Brit.); SEVEN KEYS(1962, Brit.); ACCIDENTAL DEATH(1963, Brit.); SET-UP, THE(1963, Brit.); MASTER SPY(1964, Brit.); SMOKESCREEN(1964, Brit.); ACT OF MURDER(1965, Brit.); PLAGUE OF THE ZOMBIES, THE(1966, Brit.); THUNDERBIRD 6(1968, Brit.); MAN WHO HAUNTED HIMSELF, THE(1970, Brit.); TASTE THE BLOOD OF DRACULA(1970, Brit.); CAPTAIN KRONOS: VAMPIRE HUNTER(1974, Brit.)
Misc. Talkies
MAN IN A LOOKING GLASS, A(1965, Brit.)

John David Carson
PRETTY MAIDS ALL IN A ROW(1971); DAY OF THE DOLPHIN, THE(1973); SAVAGE IS LOOSE, THE(1974); CREATURE FROM BLACK LAKE, THE(1976); STAY HUNGRY(1976); EMPIRE OF THE ANTS(1977); CHARGE OF THE MODEL-T'S(1979); FIFTH FLOOR, THE(1980)

Johnny Carson
LOOKING FOR LOVE(1964)

Kay Carson
WINTER A GO-GO(1965), ch

Ken Carson
IN OLD MONTEREY(1939); SO DEAR TO MY HEART(1949)

Kit Carson
LADY IN THE DARK(1944); OBJECTIVE, BURMA!(1945); OUTCASTS OF POKER FLAT, THE(1952); CITY OF BAD MEN(1953); FANGS OF THE ARCTIC(1953); SHADOW ON THE WINDOW, THE(1957), ph
Silents
PONY EXPRESS RIDER(1926)
Misc. Silents
COWBOY COURAGE(1925); HIS GREATEST BATTLE(1925); RIDIN' WILD(1925); TWIN SIX O'BRIEN(1926); WALLOPING KID(1926); FORBIDDEN TRAILS(1928)

L.M. Kit Carson
DAVID HOLZMAN'S DIARY(1968); LAST WORD, THE(1979), w; BREATHLESS(1983), w
1984
CHINESE BOXES(1984, Ger./Brit.), a, w; PARIS, TEXAS(1984, Ger./Fr.), w

Lucky Carson
CHUKA(1967)

May Carson
Misc. Silents
FIGHTING RANGER, THE(1922); GUILTY(1922)

Neke Carson
LIQUID SKY(1982)

Nina Carson
Misc. Talkies
CHERRY HILL HIGH(1977)

Peggy Carson
GORILLA MAN(1942); ADVENTURES IN IRAQ(1943); SHINE ON, HARVEST MOON(1944)

Percy Carson
RENEGADES OF THE RIO GRANDE(1945)

Renee Carson
GHOST AND THE GUEST(1943); PHANTOM OF THE OPERA(1943); FOUR JILLS IN A JEEP(1944); DON JUAN QUILLIGAN(1945); HOUSE ON 92ND STREET, THE(1945); ROYAL SCANDAL, A(1945); DEADLINE FOR MURDER(1946); RAZOR'S EDGE, THE(1946); SHOCK(1946)

Renie Carson
PICTURE OF DORIAN GRAY, THE(1945)

Robert Carson
LAST GANGSTER, THE(1937), w; STAR IS BORN, A(1937), w; MEN WITH WINGS(1938), w; BEAU GESTE(1939), w; LIGHT THAT FAILED, THE(1939), w; FIVE LITTLE PEPPERS IN TROUBLE(1940); JUNGLE MAN(1941); SAINT IN PALM SPRINGS, THE(1941); WESTERN UNION(1941), w; ACROSS THE PACIFIC(1942), w; PHANTOM KILLER(1942); TUTTLES OF TAHITI(1942), w; DESPERADOES, THE(1943), w; BEDSIDE MANNER(1945), w; PERILOUS HOLIDAY(1946), w; YOU GOTTA STAY HAPPY(1948), w; ONCE MORE, MY DARLING(1949), w; FIGHTING STALLION, THE(1950); INDIAN TERRITORY(1950); MULE TRAIN(1950); REFORMER AND THE REDHEAD, THE(1950), p,d&w; GROOM WORE SPURS, THE(1951), w; SAILOR BEWARE(1951); FOR MEN ONLY(1952); JUST FOR YOU(1952), w; RED SNOW(1952); NO ESCAPE(1953); PUSHOVER(1954); STAR IS BORN, A(1954), w; AIN'T MISBEHAVIN'(1955), w; YOU'RE NEVER TOO YOUNG(1955); BUNDLE OF JOY(1956), w; ACTION OF THE TIGER(1957), w; ADVANCE TO THE REAR(1964); STAR IS BORN, A(1976), w

Robert B. Carson
LOVE ME OR LEAVE ME(1955)

Robert M. Carson
WE SHALL RETURN(1963), p

Robert S. Carson
TOO MUCH, TOO SOON(1958); GREAT RACE, THE(1965); GNOME-MOBILE, THE(1967)

Shawn Carson
FUNHOUSE, THE(1981); SOMETHING WICKED THIS WAY COMES(1983)

Sonny Carson [Iwina Lmiri Abubadika]
EDUCATION OF SONNY CARSON, THE(1974), w

Sue Carson
BEST OF EVERYTHING, THE(1959)

Sunset Carson
CODE OF THE PRAIRIE(1944); FIREBRANDS OF ARIZONA(1944); BANDITS OF THE BADLANDS(1945); BELLS OF ROSARITA(1945); CHEROKEE FLASH, THE(1945); OREGON TRAIL(1945); ROUGH RIDERS OF CHEYENNE(1945); SANTA FE SADDLEMATES(1945); SHERIFF OF CIMARRON(1945); ALIAS BILLY THE KID(1946); DAYS OF BUFFALO BILL(1946); EL PASO KID, THE(1946); RED RIVER RENEGADES(1946); RIO GRANDE RAIDERS(1946); DEADLINE(1948); BATTLING MARSHAL(1950); SEABO(1978)
Misc. Talkies
BORDERTOWN TRAIL(1944); CALL OF THE ROCKIES(1944); FIGHTING MUSTANG(1948); SUNSET CARSON RIDES AGAIN(1948); RIO GRANDE(1949)

Sunset Carson [Michael Harrison]
JANIE(1944)

Tony Carson
MADAME CURIE(1943); THEY WERE EXPENDABLE(1945); DESIRE ME(1947)

Willie May Carson
Silents
LEOPARD LADY, THE(1928)
Misc. Silents
BIG STAKES(1922); HELLHOUNDS OF THE WEST(1922)

Carson Robinson and His Pioneers
VARIETY HOUR(1937, Brit.)

The Carsons
OLD MOTHER RILEY'S CIRCUS(1941, Brit.)

Bruce Carstairs
SPY WITH A COLD NOSE, THE(1966, Brit.)

John Paddy Carstairs
FOOTSTEPS IN THE NIGHT(1932, Brit.), w; LOVE ON THE SPOT(1932, Brit.), w; NINE TILL SIX(1932), w; WATER GYPSIES, THE(1932, Brit.), w; WOMAN IN CHAINS(1932, Brit.), w; PARIS PLANE(1933, Brit.), d; BOOMERANG(1934, Brit.), w; IT'S A BOY(1934, Brit.), w; IT'S A COP(1934, Brit.), w; LOST IN THE LEGION(1934, Brit.), w; HOPE OF HIS SIDE(1935, Brit.), w; WHILE PARENTS SLEEP(1935, Brit.), w; CAPTAIN'S TABLE, THE(1936, Brit.), w; GAY BRIDE(1936, Brit.), w; TROUBLE AHEAD(1936, Brit.), w; DOUBLE EXPOSURES(1937, Brit.), d; HOLIDAY'S END(1937, Brit.), d; INCIDENT IN SHANGHAI(1937, Brit.), d&w; MISSING, BELIEVED MARRIED(1937, Brit.), d; NIGHT RIDE(1937, Brit.), d; LASSIE FROM LANCASHIRE(1938, Brit.), d; YANK AT OXFORD, A(1938), w; SAINT IN LONDON, THE(1939, Brit.), d; TWO'S COMPANY(1939, Brit.), w; LAMBETH WALK, THE(1940, Brit.), d; SECOND MR. BUSH, THE(1940, Brit.), d; SPARE A COPPER(1940, Brit.), d; HE FOUND A STAR(1941, Brit.), d; MAXWELL ARCHER, DETECTIVE(1942, Brit.), d; DANCING WITH CRIME(1947, Brit.), d; AMAZING MR. BEECHAM, THE(1949, Brit.), d; FOOLS RUSH IN(1949, Brit.), d; SLEEPING CAR TO TRIESTE(1949, Brit.), d; TONY DRAWS A HORSE(1951, Brit.), d; LITTLE BIG SHOT(1952, Brit.), w; MADE IN HEAVEN(1952, Brit.), d; TREASURE HUNT(1952, Brit.), d; YOU CAN'T BEAT THE IRISH(1952, Brit.), d; TOP OF THE FORM(1953, Brit.), d; CROWDED DAY, THE(1954, Brit.), d; UP TO HIS NECK(1954, Brit.), d, w; MAN OF THE MOMENT(1955, Brit.), d, w; ONE GOOD TURN(1955, Brit.), d, w; TROUBLE IN STORE(1955, Brit.), d, w; YANK IN ERMINE, A(1955, Brit.), d; JUMPING FOR JOY(1956, Brit.), d; JUST MY LUCK(1957, Brit.), d; UP IN THE WORLD(1957, Brit.), d; SQUARE PEG, THE(1958, Brit.), d; AND THE SAME TO YOU(1960, Brit.), w; SANDS OF THE DESERT(1960, Brit.), d, w; TOMMY THE TOREADOR(1960, Brit.), d; WEEKEND WITH LULU, A(1961, Brit.), d; BIG MONEY, THE(1962, Brit.), d; DEVIL'S AGENT, THE(1962, Brit.), d

Peter Carsten
DEVIL STRIKES AT NIGHT, THE(1959, Ger.); UNDER TEN FLAGS(1960, U.S./Ital.); COMMANDO(1962, Ital., Span., Bel., Ger.); GREH(1962, Ger./Yugo.); GIRL FROM HONG KONG(1966, Ger.); MY NAME IS PECOS(1966, Ital.); QUILLER MEMORANDUM, THE(1966, Brit.); STUDY IN TERROR, A(1966, Brit./Ger.); TENDER SCOUNDREL(1967, Fr./Ital.); U-47 LT. COMMANDER PRIEN(1967, Ger.); DARK OF THE SUN(1968, Brit.); VENGEANCE OF FU MANCHU, THE(1968, Brit./Ger./Hong Kong/Ireland); ZEPPELIN(1971, Brit.); MR. SUPERINVISIBLE(1974, Ital./Span./Ger.), a, p; SQUEEZE, THE(1980, Ital.); TWILIGHT TIME(1983, U.S./Yugo.)

Lina Carstens
GIRL FROM THE MARSH CROFT, THE(1935, Ger.); AFFAIRS OF DR. HOLL(1954, Ger.); MAN WHO WALKED THROUGH THE WALL, THE(1964, Ger.); TWO IN A SLEEPING BAG(1964, Ger.)

Niels Carstens
LURE OF THE JUNGLE, THE(1970, Den.), ph

Margit Carstensen
BITTER TEARS OF PETRA VON KANT, THE(1972, Ger.); MOTHER KUSTERS GOES TO HEAVEN(1976, Ger.); CHINESE ROULETTE(1977, Ger.); POSSESSION(1981, Fr./Ger.)

Rolf Carston
NOW THAT APRIL'S HERE(1958, Can.); STEEL BAYONET, THE(1958, Brit.)

Greg Carswell
LIVING LEGEND(1980)

Maria Carta
GODFATHER, THE, PART II(1974)

Edward Cartagmo
WONDERFUL WORLD OF THE BROTHERS ERIMM, THE(1962), art d

Anna Cartaret
DATELINE DIAMONDS(1966, Brit.)

Eric Carte
BEAST MUST DIE, THE(1974, Brit.)

Carmen Cartellieri
Misc. Silents
PAREMA, CRERATURE FROM THE STARWORLD(1922, Aust.); HANDS OF ORLAC, THE(1925, Aust.)

Kenneth Carten
IN WHICH WE SERVE(1942, Brit.)

Marilu Carteny
BANDITS OF ORGOSOLO(1964, Ital.), cos; SALVATORE GIULIANO(1966, Ital.), cos; BULLET FOR THE GENERAL, A(1967, Ital.), cos; MAFIA(1969, Fr./Ital.), cos; ONCE UPON A TIME IN THE WEST(1969, U.S./Ital.)

Alan Carter
MAN WHO LOVED REDHEADS, THE(1955, Brit.), ch

Allan Carter
DRAGSTRIP RIOT(1958)

Angel Carter
HOT SPUR(1968)

Ann Carter
LAST OF THE DUANES(1941); COMMANDOS STRIKE AT DAWN, THE(1942); I MARRIED A WITCH(1942); NORTH STAR, THE(1943); CURSE OF THE CAT PEOPLE, THE(1944); INCENDIARY BLONDE(1945); CHILD OF DIVORCE(1946); SEARCHING WIND, THE(1946); FABULOUS DORSEYS, THE(1947); SONG OF LOVE(1947); TWO MRS. CARROLLS, THE(1947); CONNECTICUT YANKEE IN KING ARTHUR'S COURT, A(1949); MEMBER OF THE WEDDING, THE(1952)

Anne Carter
RUTHLESS(1948)

Arthur Carter
OPERATION MAD BALL(1957), w

Audrey Carter
NOTORIOUS AFFAIR, A(1930), w

Ben Carter
ADVENTURE'S END(1937); HAVING WONDERFUL TIME(1938); TELL NO TALES(1939); CHAD HANNA(1940); EARL OF PUDDLESTONE(1940); LITTLE OLD NEW YORK(1940); MARYLAND(1940); SAFARI(1940); SOUTH TO KARANGA(1940); TIN PAN ALLEY(1940); DRESSED TO KILL(1941); RIDE ON VAQUERO(1941); SLEEPERS WEST(1941); REAP THE WILD WIND(1942); YOUNG AMERICA(1942); CRASH DIVE(1943); HAPPY GO LUCKY(1943); BOWERY TO BROADWAY(1944); DIXIE JAMBOREE(1945); LADY ON A TRAIN(1945); SCARLET CLUE, THE(1945); DARK ALIBI(1946); HARVEY GIRLS, THE(1946); NIGHT WITHOUT SLEEP(1952); REDHEAD FROM MANHATTAN(1954)

Benny Carter
MAN CALLED ADAM, A(1966), m; BUCK AND THE PREACHER(1972), m

Betty Carter
INSIDE THE LINES(1930); MONTE CARLO STORY, THE(1957, Ital.)
Silents
AFTER THE VERDICT(1929, Brit.)
Misc. Silents
WINE OF LIFE, THE(1924, Brit.); DOLORES(1928, Brit.); WARE CASE, THE(1928, Brit.)

Bill Carter
MY KINGDOM FOR A COOK(1943); BATTLE OF THE WORLDS(1961, Ital.)

Blanche Carter
MELODY LANE(1929)

Boake Carter
DEAD MARCH, THE(1937)

Calvert Carter
Silents
WILD AND WOOLLY(1917); LYING LIPS(1921); SLAVE OF DESIRE(1923); ABRAHAM LINCOLN(1924)
Misc. Silents
BROADWAY FEVER(1929)

Catherine Carter
Silents
GREYHOUND, THE(1914)

Cathy Carter
IT HAPPENED ON 5TH AVENUE(1947); HUNTED, THE(1948); KING OF THE BANDITS(1948)

Charles Carter
Misc. Silents
WORLD, THE FLESH AND THE DEVIL, THE(1914, Brit.)

Charlotte Carter
HUNGRY WIVES(1973)

Cheryl Carter
MISTER BROWN(1972); HARD COUNTRY(1981); NIGHT SHIFT(1982); DOCTOR DETROIT(1983); OSTERMAN WEEKEND, THE(1983)
1984
2010(1984)

Chet Carter
MORE AMERICAN GRAFFITI(1979)

Chris Carter
Misc. Talkies
MARK OF THE GUN(1969)

Cicily Carter
GLENN MILLER STORY, THE(1953)

Claire Carter
BLOW OUT(1981)

Conlan Carter
QUICK, BEFORE IT MELTS(1964); WHITE LIGHTNING(1973)

Daniel D. Carter [Daniel Cohen]
Silents
MASTER MIND, THE(1914), w; MASTER MIND, THE(1920), w

Dave Carter
STRANGE AFFAIR, THE(1968, Brit.)

Desmond Carter
JUST FOR A SONG(1930, Brit.), w; OUT OF THE BLUE(1931, Brit.), w

Diane Carter
1984
BEST DEFENSE(1984)

Dick Carter
WEST OF CARSON CITY(1940)
Misc. Silents
LET HIM BUCK(1924); RECKLESS RIDING BILL(1924); RANGER BILL(1925); BATTLIN' BILL(1927); GOLDEN TRAIL, THE(1927); PIONEERS OF THE WEST(1927)

Dixie Carter
GOING BERSERK(1983)

Don Carter
SUPERDAD(1974); CAT MURKIL AND THE SILKS(1976); FREAKY FRIDAY(1976)

Donald Carter
CLUE OF THE MISSING APE, THE(1953, Brit.), w

Donnie Carter
TWO LITTLE BEARS, THE(1961); FOLLOW ME, BOYS!(1966)

Doug Carter
EASY TO LOOK AT(1945); DANGER WOMAN(1946); LETTER FROM AN UNKNOWN WOMAN(1948); WINTER MEETING(1948); MILKMAN, THE(1950); SHAKEDOWN(1950); TEXAS CARNIVAL(1951); MA AND PA KETTLE AT THE FAIR(1952); GIRL WHO HAD EVERYTHING, THE(1953)

Douglas Carter
FRONTIER GAL(1945); SENORITA FROM THE WEST(1945); BLUE DAHLIA, THE(1946); FORCE OF EVIL(1948); STATE OF THE UNION(1948); WALLS OF JERICHO(1948); CHICAGO DEADLINE(1949); RED, HOT AND BLUE(1949); SORROWFUL JONES(1949); SUN COMES UP, THE(1949); MYSTERY STREET(1950); WABASH AVENUE(1950); CARRIE(1952)
Silents
LOVE IS AN AWFUL THING(1922)

Duane Carter
LIVELY SET, THE(1964)

Ellis Carter
INDIAN UPRISING(1951), ph; CAPTAIN JOHN SMITH AND POCAHONTAS(1953), ph; ROYAL AFRICAN RIFLES, THE(1953), ph; HUMAN JUNGLE, THE(1954), ph; MOLE PEOPLE, THE(1956), ph; DEADLY MANTIS, THE(1957), ph; OREGON PASSAGE(1958), ph; NIGHT OF THE QUARTER MOON(1959), ph; LEECH WOMAN, THE(1960), ph; PURPLE GANG, THE(1960), ph; SEVEN WAYS FROM SUNDOWN(1960), ph

Ellis W. Carter
BIG TOWN AFTER DARK(1947), ph; BIG TOWN SCANDAL(1948), ph; CAGED FURY(1948), ph; DISASTER(1948), ph; DYNAMITE(1948), ph; MR. RECKLESS(1948), ph; SHAGGY(1948), ph; SPEED TO SPARE(1948), ph; WATERFRONT AT MIDNIGHT(1948), ph; EL PASO(1949), ph; RANGER OF CHEROKEE STRIP(1949), ph; SPECIAL AGENT(1949), ph; BLONDE BANDIT, THE(1950), ph; GUNMEN OF ABILENE(1950), ph; HILLS OF OKLAHOMA(1950), ph; LONELY HEARTS BANDITS(1950), ph; OLD FRONTIER, THE(1950), ph; PRISONERS IN PETTICOATS(1950), ph; UNMASKED(1950), ph; VANISHING WESTERNER, THE(1950), ph; BAREFOOT MAILMAN, THE(1951), ph; HAVANA ROSE(1951), ph; MAGIC CARPET, THE(1951), ph; SUNNY SIDE OF THE STREET(1951), ph; TEXAS RANGERS, THE(1951), ph; CALIFORNIA CONQUEST(1952), ph; OUTLAW WOMEN(1952), ph; RAINBOW 'ROUND MY SHOULDER(1952), ph; SOUND OFF(1952), ph; THIEF OF DAMASCUS(1952), ph; ARROW IN THE DUST(1954), ph; BLACK DAKOTAS, THE(1954), ph; RUNNING WILD(1955), ph; DAY OF FURY, A(1956), ph; FLIGHT TO HONG KONG(1956), ph; RIVER CHANGES, THE(1956), ph; INCREDIBLE SHRINKING MAN, THE(1957), ph; LAND UNKNOWN, THE(1957), ph; MONOLITH MONSTERS, THE(1957), ph; SLIM CARTER(1957), ph; DAMN CITIZEN(1958), ph; CURSE OF THE UNDEAD(1959), ph; WIZARD OF BAGHDAD, THE(1960), ph; FIERCEST HEART, THE(1961), ph; PIRATES OF TORTUGA(1961), ph; SECOND TIME AROUND, THE(1961), ph; DIARY OF A MADMAN(1963), ph; HOOTENANNY HOOT(1963), ph; SHOWDOWN(1963), ph; TWICE TOLD TALES(1963), ph; HE RIDES TALL(1964), ph; KISSIN' COUSINS(1964), ph; YOUR CHEATIN' HEART(1964), ph

Eric Carter
IT!(1967, Brit.), makeup

Everett Carter
LAW OF THE RANGE(1941), m; MASKED RIDER, THE(1941), ph; FIGHTING BILL FARGO(1942), m

Fleurette Carter
NAKED ZOO, THE(1970)

Logan Carter
1984
LOVE STREAMS(1984); REPO MAN(1984)

Louise Carter
BLONDIE OF THE FOLLIES(1932); BROKEN LULLABY(1932); HELL'S HIGH-WAY(1932); I AM A FUGITIVE FROM A CHAIN GANG(1932); LAST MILE, THE(1932); MADAME BUTTERFLY(1932); TESS OF THE STORM COUNTRY(1932); TWO AGAINST THE WORLD(1932); WEEK-END MARRIAGE(1932); BEAUTY FOR SALE(1933); EAST OF FIFTH AVE.(1933); JENNIE GERHARDT(1933); MONKEY'S PAW, THE(1933); PILGRIMAGE(1933); RIGHT TO ROMANCE(1933); THIS DAY AND AGE(1933); BELOVED(1934); READY FOR LOVE(1934); YOU'RE TELLING ME(1934); MYSTERY OF EDWIN DROOD, THE(1935); PADDY O'DAY(1935); RECKLESS ROADS(1935); STRAIGHT FROM THE HEART(1935); ROSE OF THE RANCHO(1936); ANGEL(1937); LAST TRAIN FROM MADRID, THE(1937); INSIDE STORY(1939); NANCY DREW AND THE HIDDEN STAIRCASE(1939)
Silents
IN BORROWED PLUMES(1926); STRIVING FOR FORTUNE(1926)
Misc. Silents
SUBSTITUTE WIFE, THE(1925)

Lucy Carter
Misc. Silents
MADAME SHERRY(1917)

Lynda Carter
BOBBIE JO AND THE OUTLAW(1976)

Lynn Carter
PORT OF NEW YORK(1949); MAN FROM O.R.G.Y., THE(1970)

Lynne Carter
EXPERIMENT ALCATRAZ(1950)

Malik Carter
BLACK BELT JONES(1974); EMMA MAE(1976); PENITENTIARY II(1982)

Margaret Carter
EMIL(1938, Brit.), w

Marya Carter
PHANTOM PLANET, THE(1961)

Maurice Carter
GENGHIS KHAN(U.S./Brit./Ger./Yugo), art d; LADY VANISHES, THE(1938, Brit.), set d; ROOT OF ALL EVIL, THE(1947, Brit.), art d; SNOWBOUND(1949, Brit.), art d; GOOD TIME GIRL(1950, Brit.), art d; MR. DRAKE'S DUCK(1951, Brit.), art d; WHITE CORRIDORS(1952, Brit.), art d; DAY TO REMEMBER, A(1953, Brit.), art d; DESPERATE MOMENT(1953, Brit.), art d; I BELIEVE IN YOU(1953, Brit.), art d; PENNY PRINCESS(1953, Brit.), art d; LAND OF FURY(1955 Brit.), art d; TO PARIS WITH LOVE(1955, Brit.), art d; DOCTOR AT LARGE(1957, Brit.), art d; SPANISH GARDENER, THE(1957, Span.), prod d; WIND CANNOT READ, THE(1958, Brit.), art d; FOLLOW A STAR(1959, Brit.), art d; BOY WHO STOLE A STAR, THE(1960, Brit.), art d; DOCTOR IN LOVE(1960, Brit.), art d; DOUBLE BUNK(1961, Brit.), art d; FRIGHTENED CITY, THE(1961, Brit.), art d; NO LOVE FOR JOHN-NIE(1961, Brit.), art d; RING-A-DING RHYTHM(1962, Brit. 73m Amicus/COL bw (G.B: IT'S TRAD, DAD!), art d; PAIR OF BRIEFS, A(1963, Brit.), art d; SWORD OF LANCELOT(1963, Brit.), art d; BECKET(1964, Brit.), art d; GUNS AT BATASI(1964, Brit.), art d; IN THE DOGHOUSE(1964, Brit.), art d; NO, MY DARLING DAUGHT-ER(1964, Brit.), art d; YOU MUST BE JOKING!(1965, Brit.), art d; FIGHTING PRINCE OF DONEGAL, THE(1966, Brit.), art d; KALEIDOSCOPE(1966, Brit.), art d; QUILLER MEMORANDUM, THE(1966, Brit.), art d; FATHOM(1967), art d; ANNE OF THE THOUSAND DAYS(1969, Brit.), prod d; BATTLE OF BRITAIN, THE(1969, Brit.), art d; VILLAIN(1971, Brit.), art d; 10 RILLINGTON PLACE(1971, Brit.), art d; FEAR IS THE KEY(1973), art d; INNOCENT BYSTANDERS(1973, Brit.), art d; FROM BEYOND THE GRAVE(1974, Brit.), art d; LAND THAT TIME FORGOT, THE(1975, Brit.), set d; PEOPLE THAT TIME FORGOT, THE(1977, Brit.), prod d; GREAT TRAIN ROBBERY, THE(1979, Brit.), prod d

Mel Carter
CAT FROM OUTER SPACE, THE(1978)
1984
ANGEL(1984)

Michael Carter
JANIE(1944); KEEP, THE(1983); RETURN OF THE JEDI(1983)

Midge Carter
ZULU DAWN(1980, Brit.)

Mike Carter
DRAUGHTSMAN'S CONTRACT, THE(1983, Brit.)

Miki Carter
TARZAN AND THE LOST SAFARI(1957, Brit.), ph; TARZAN'S FIGHT FOR LI-FE(1958), ph

Mitch Carter
HARD COUNTRY(1981)
1984
SAVAGE STREETS(1984)

Monte Carter
MELODY LANE(1929); VICE SQUAD, THE(1931); NO LIVING WITNESS(1932); RED HEAD(1934); MAKE A MILLION(1935); WHAT PRICE CRIME?(1935); $1,000,000 RACKET(1937); SUNSET MURDER CASE(1941)
Silents
MIDNIGHT LIFE(1928)

Monti Carter
STREET SCENE(1931)

Mrs. Leslie Carter
ROCKY MOUNTAIN MYSTERY(1935)
Silents
SCALES OF JUSTICE, THE(1914)

Nan Carter
Silents
SERPENT, THE(1916)

Nat Carter
THERE'S ALWAYS VANILLA(1972)

Neil Carter
OBJECTIVE, BURMA!(1945)

Nell Carter
HAIR(1979); BACK ROADS(1981); MODERN PROBLEMS(1981)

Nick Carter
REDEEMER, THE(1978)

Paul Carter [Paolo Magalotti]
UP THE MACGREGORS(1967, Ital./Span.); SEVEN GUNS FOR THE MACGRE-GORS(1968, Ital./Span.)

Paulina Carter
MY GAL LOVES MUSIC(1944)

Peter Carter
ROWDYMAN, THE(1973, Can.), d; HIGH-BALLIN'(1978), d; CREEPER, THE(1980, Can.), a, d; KLONDIKE FEVER(1980), d
1984
HIGHPOINT(1984, Can.), d

Phil Carter
DIRTYMOUTH(1970)

Phyllis Carter
SINS OF THE FATHERS(1948, Can.)

R. Carter
ALIBI, THE(1943, Brit.), w

Reggie Carter
DR. NO(1962, Brit.)

Reginald Carter
YOICKS!(1932, Brit.)
Silents
WHITE FLOWER, THE(1923)

Richard Carter
SLAUGHTER ON TENTH AVENUE(1957), w; KOTCH(1971), p; SECOND-HAND HEARTS(1981), art d
1984
ADVENTURES OF BUCKAROO BANZAI: ACROSS THE 8TH DIMENSION, THE(1984), art d
Silents
TONY RUNS WILD(1926)

Robert Peyton Carter
Silents
SACRED SILENCE(1919), w

Rod Carter
48 HOURS TO ACAPULCO(1968, Ger.)

Roger Carter
1984
REVENGE OF THE NERDS(1984)

Ron Carter
DESPERATE CHARACTERS(1971), m

Ronald Carter
TRICK BABY(1973)

Rosanna Carter
NIGHT OF THE JUGGLER(1980)
1984
BROTHER FROM ANOTHER PLANET, THE(1984)

Roy Carter
SHADOWED EYES(1939, Brit.), w

Ruth Carter
1984
ADERYN PAPUR(1984, Brit.), w

Sally Carter
DO NOT THROW CUSHIONS INTO THE RING(1970)

T.K. Carter
SEED OF INNOCENCE(1980); SEEMS LIKE OLD TIMES(1980); SOUTHERN COM-FORT(1981); THING, THE(1982); DOCTOR DETROIT(1983)

Ted Carter
LONG RIDE FROM HELL, A(1970, Ital.)

Terry Carter
PARRISH(1961); COMPANY OF KILLERS(1970); ABBY(1974); BENJI(1974); FOXY DROWN(1974); BATTLESTAR GALACTICA(1979)
Misc. Talkies
BOOTS TURNER(1973); BROTHER ON THE RUN(1973)

Thomas Carter
INDEPENDENCE DAY(1976); MONKEY HUSTLE, THE(1976); ALMOST SUM-MER(1978); WHOSE LIFE IS IT ANYWAY?(1981)

Tina Carter
GAMES, THE(1970)

Tom Carter
RETURN OF DANIEL BOONE, THE(1941); GENTLEMAN FROM TEXAS(1946)

Virginia Carter
NIGHT OF EVIL(1962)

Walter Carter
PATRICK THE GREAT(1945)

Waverly Carter
NOTORIOUS AFFAIR, A(1930), w

Wes Carter
WHY RUSSIANS ARE REVOLTING(1970)

Wilfred Carter
HOT MILLIONS(1968, Brit.)

William Carter
WHERE DO WE GO FROM HERE?(1945); DRAGONWYCH(1946); I'VE ALWAYS LOVED YOU(1946)

Winifred Carter
MRS. FITZHERBERT(1950, Brit.), w

Wylie Carter
CAPTURE THAT CAPSULE(1961)

The Carter Family
Misc. Talkies
ROAD TO NASHVILLE(1967)

Douglas Carther
SCENE OF THE CRIME(1949)

Margaret Carthew
GOLD DIGGERS OF 1933(1933); STRAWBERRY BLONDE, THE(1941)

Caroline Cartier
LUMIERE(1976, Fr.)

Francois Cartier
MODERN PROBLEMS(1981)
Gerard Cartier
MATHIAS SANDORF(1963, Fr.), w
Jean-Pierre Cartier
RED(1970, Can.)
Joyzelle Jacques Cartier
WHOOPEE(1930)
Max Cartier
ASSASSIN, THE(1961, Ital./Fr.); ROCCO AND HIS BROTHERS(1961, Fr./Ital.); SALVATORE GIULIANO(1966, Ital.)
Rudolph Cartier
MAN FROM MOROCCO, THE(1946, Brit.), w; CORRIDOR OF MIRRORS(1948, Brit.), p, w; PASSIONATE SUMMER(1959, Brit.), d
Walter Cartier
SOMEBODY UP THERE LIKES ME(1956); FIDDLER ON THE ROOF(1971)
Henri Cartier-Bresson
RULES OF THE GAME, THE(1939, Fr.)
Bob Cartland
1984
PLOUGHMAN'S LUNCH, THE(1984, Brit.)
Robert Cartland
GUNMAN HAS ESCAPED, A(1948, Brit.)
Bill Cartledge
NEWSBOY'S HOME(1939); PLAYMATES(1941); FOREVER AND A DAY(1943); HARRIGAN'S KID(1943); RED STALLION, THE(1947); RACING LUCK(1948); FIGHTING FOOLS(1949); LADY GAMBLES, THE(1949); KEY TO THE CITY(1950); CRAZY OVER HORSES(1951); SHANE(1953)
Billy Cartledge
UNFAITHFULLY YOURS(1948); ESCAPE TO BURMA(1955); SEARCHERS, THE(1956)
William Cartledge
SPLENDOR(1935); LADY'S FROM KENTUCKY, THE(1939); I TAKE THIS WOMAN(1940); UNDERCURRENT(1946); DEAR WIFE(1949); COURT JESTER, THE(1956)
William J. Cartledge
STORY OF SEABISCUIT, THE(1949); DARK CITY(1950)
Katrin Cartlidge
1984
SACRED HEARTS(1984, Brit.)
Audrey Carton
GAY LOVE(1936, Brit.), w
Brian Carton
TASTE OF EXCITEMENT(1969, Brit.), w
Leone Carton
Misc. Silents
SHIFTING SANDS(1918)
Pauline Carton
BLOOD OF A POET, THE(1930, Fr.); PARISIAN, THE(1931, Fr.); AMERICAN LOVE(1932, Fr.); FROM TOP TO BOTTOM(1933, Fr.); BONNE CHANCE(1935, Fr.); STORY OF A CHEAT, THE(1938, Fr.); AFFAIR LAFONT, THE(1939, Fr.); CONFLICT(1939, Fr.); CONFESSIONS OF A NEWLYWED(1941, Fr.); PRIZE, THE(1952, Fr.); CARNIVAL(1953, Fr.); NAPOLEON(1955, Fr.); ROYAL AFFAIRS IN VERSAILLES(1957, Fr.)
R.C. Carton
ROLLING IN MONEY(1934, Brit.), w
Valerie Carton
LAST MOMENT, THE(1954, Brit.)
Waveney Carton
GAY LOVE(1936, Brit.), w
Angela Cartwright
SOMEBODY UP THERE LIKES ME(1956); LAD: A DOG(1962); SOUND OF MUSIC, THE(1965); BEYOND THE POSEIDON ADVENTURE(1979)
Bill Cartwright
DREAM MAKER, THE(1963, Brit.); SWINGIN' MAIDEN, THE(1963, Brit.); HIDE AND SEEK(1964, Brit.)
Bob Cartwright
HEROES OF TELEMARK, THE(1965, Brit.), set d; COUNTESS FROM HONG KONG, A(1967, Brit.), art d; SCROOGE(1970, Brit.), art d; ELEPHANT MAN, THE(1980, Brit.), art d
1984
BOUNTY, THE(1984), set d; SECRET PLACES(1984, Brit.), art d
Cecil Cartwright
CRY, THE BELOVED COUNTRY(1952, Brit.)
Christine Cartwright
1984
LASSITER(1984)
Ed Cartwright
RIDERS OF THE CACTUS(1931)
Gary Cartwright
J.W. COOP(1971), w
Geoff Cartwright
AGE OF CONSENT(1969, Austral.)
Jean Cartwright
MAGIC SPECTACLES(1961)
John Cartwright
OFFICER AND A GENTLEMAN, AN(1982), art d
John V. Cartwright
FIRST MONDAY IN OCTOBER(1981), art d; KISS ME GOODBYE(1982), art d
Jorja Cartwright
HEAVEN ONLY KNOWS(1947)
Lynn Cartwright
BLACK PATCH(1957); CRY BABY KILLER, THE(1958); QUEEN OF OUTER SPACE(1958); GIRLS ON THE BEACH(1965); SENIORS, THE(1978)
1984
LOVELINES(1984)
Malou Cartwright
Misc. Talkies
GROOVE ROOM, THE(1974, Brit.)

Nancy Cartwright
TWILIGHT ZONE–THE MOVIE(1983)
Peggy Cartwright
MAGIC NIGHT(1932, Brit.)
Silents
AFRAID TO FIGHT(1922); PENROD(1922); IRON HORSE, THE(1924)
Misc. Silents
LOVE(1920); ROBIN HOOD, JR.(1923); LADY OF QUALITY, A(1924)
Percy Cartwright
ROOM 43(1959, Brit.); HOUSE OF FRIGHT(1961)
Randy Cartwright
FOX AND THE HOUND, THE(1981), anim
Robert Cartwright
ONLY TWO CAN PLAY(1962, Brit.), set d; MARY, QUEEN OF SCOTS(1971, Brit.), art d; PUBLIC EYE, THE(1972, Brit.), art d; DAY OF THE JACKAL, THE(1973, Brit./Fr.), set d; OPTIMISTS, THE(1973, Brit.), art d; HANOVER STREET(1979, Brit.), art d; PRAYING MANTIS(1982, Brit.), prod d
Veronica Cartwright
IN LOVE AND WAR(1958); CHILDREN'S HOUR, THE(1961); BIRDS, THE(1963); SPENCER'S MOUNTAIN(1963); ONE MAN'S WAY(1964); GOIN' SOUTH(1978); INVASION OF THE BODY SNATCHERS(1978); ALIEN(1979); NIGHTMARES(1983); RIGHT STUFF, THE(1983)
William Cartwright
DEVIL'S BRIGADE, THE(1968), ed; BRIDGE AT REMAGEN, THE(1969), ed
Janet Jane Carty
ADVISE AND CONSENT(1962)
Sheila Carty
TREASURE HUNT(1952, Brit.)
Todd Carty
KRULL(1983)
Tommy Carty
SUNRISE AT CAMPOBELLO(1960)
Calogero Caruana
MAN OF LA MANCHA(1972)
Louis Caruana
PULP(1972, Brit.)
Mary Caruana
PULP(1972, Brit.)
Carmen Carulla
ALEXANDER THE GREAT(1956)
Carlo Carunchio
'TIS A PITY SHE'S A WHORE(1973, Ital.), w
Al Caruso
LOVES OF CARMEN, THE(1948)
Anthony Caruso
THEY WON'T BELIEVE ME(1947); BRIDE WORE CRUTCHES, THE(1940); JOHNNY APOLLO(1940); NORTHWEST MOUNTED POLICE(1940); TALL, DARK AND HANDSOME(1941); ACROSS THE PACIFIC(1942); ALWAYS IN MY HEART(1942); SUNDAY PUNCH(1942); GHOST AND THE GUEST(1943); GIRL FROM MONTEREY, THE(1943); WATCH ON THE RHINE(1943); WHISTLING IN BROOKLYN(1943); AND NOW TOMORROW(1944); RACKET MAN, THE(1944); STORY OF DR. WASSELL, THE(1944); CRIME DOCTOR'S COURAGE, THE(1945); DON JUAN QUILLIGAN(1945); OBJECTIVE, BURMA!(1945); PRIDE OF THE MARINES(1945); STORK CLUB, THE(1945); BLUE DAHLIA, THE(1946); LAST CROOKED MILE, THE(1946); MONSIEUR BEAUCAIRE(1946); NIGHT EDITOR(1946); TARZAN AND THE LEOPARD WOMAN(1946); THE CATMAN OF PARIS(1946); DEVIL SHIP(1947); ESCAPE ME NEVER(1947); NEWS HOUNDS(1947); WILD HARVEST(1947); INCIDENT(1948); TO THE VICTOR(1948); ANNA LUCASTA(1949); BRIDE OF VENGEANCE(1949); ILLEGAL ENTRY(1949); SCENE OF THE CRIME(1949); SONG OF INDIA(1949); THREAT, THE(1949); UNDERCOVER MAN, THE(1949); ASPHALT JUNGLE, THE(1950); PRISONERS IN PETTICOATS(1950); TARZAN AND THE SLAVE GIRL(1950); ACCORDING TO MRS. HOYLE(1951); HIS KIND OF WOMAN(1951); BLACKBEARD THE PIRATE(1952); BOOTS MALONE(1952); DESERT PURSUIT(1952); PALS OF THE GOLDEN WEST(1952); DESERT LEGION(1953); FIGHTER ATTACK(1953); FORT ALGIERS(1953); RAIDERS OF THE SEVEN SEAS(1953); STEEL LADY, THE(1953); BOY FROM OKLAHOMA, THE(1954); CATTLE QUEEN OF MONTANA(1954); DRUM BEAT(1954); PASSION(1954); PHANTOM OF THE RUE MORGUE(1954); SASKATCHEWAN(1954); CITY OF SHADOWS(1955); JAIL BUSTERS(1955); MAGNIFICENT MATADOR, THE(1955); SANTA FE PASSAGE(1955); TENNESSEE'S PARTNER(1955); TOUGHEST MAN ALIVE(1955); CRY IN THE NIGHT, A(1956); HELL ON FRISCO BAY(1956); WALK THE PROUD LAND(1956); WHEN GANGLAND STRIKES(1956); BIG LAND, THE(1957); JOE DAKOTA(1957); LAWLESS EIGHTIES, THE(1957); OKLAHOMAN, THE(1957); BADLANDERS, THE(1958); FORT MASSACRE(1958); LEGION OF THE DOOMED(1958); NEVER STEAL ANYTHING SMALL(1959); WONDERFUL COUNTRY, THE(1959); MOST DANGEROUS MAN ALIVE, THE(1961); ESCAPE FROM ZAHRAIN(1962); WHERE LOVE HAS GONE(1964); SYLVIA(1965); YOUNG DILLINGER(1965); NEVER A DULL MOMENT(1968); FLAP(1970); MEAN JOHNNY BARROWS(1976)
Misc. Talkies
LEGEND OF EARL DURAND, THE(1974); CLAWS(1977)
Anthony L. Caruso
LUCKY JORDAN(1942)
Bruno Caruso
MAFIOSO(1962, Ital.), w
David Caruso
WITHOUT WARNING(1980); FIRST BLOOD(1982); OFFICER AND A GENTLEMAN, AN(1982)
1984
THIEF OF HEARTS(1984)
Dee Caruso
WHICH WAY TO THE FRONT?(1970), w; WORLD'S GREATEST ATHLETE, THE(1973), w
Dorothy Caruso
GREAT CARUSO, THE(1951), w
E. Caruso
LOVE FACTORY(1969, Ital.)
Elmo Caruso
EMBALMER, THE(1966, Ital.)

Enrico Caruso
Silents
MY COUSIN(1918)
Misc. Silents
SPLENDID ROMANCE, THE(1918)
Fred Caruso
HAPPY HOOKER, THE(1975), p; WINTER KILLS(1979), p
Jeanine Caruso
MADAME BOVARY(1949)
Joe Caruso
SOMEONE(1968); DRIFTER(1975)
Josie Caruso
DAWN OF THE DEAD(1979), cos
Margherita Caruso
GOSPEL ACCORDING TO ST. MATTHEW, THE(1966, Fr., Ital.)
Mickey Caruso
ULTIMATE WARRIOR, THE(1975); SEMI-TOUGH(1977)
Nicholas Caruso
IN GAY MADRID(1930)
Silents
JAZZLAND(1928)
Pino Caruso
MALICIOUS(1974, Ital.)
Richard Caruso
1984
BLAME IT ON THE NIGHT(1984)
Robert Caruso
STUNT MAN, THE(1980)
Tony Caruso
DON'T GAMBLE WITH STRANGERS(1946); IRON MISTRESS, THE(1952); MAN BEHIND THE GUN, THE(1952); BABY FACE NELSON(1957)
Tony [Anthony] Caruso
THAT NIGHT WITH YOU(1945); MY FAVORITE BRUNETTE(1947)
Burr Caruth
DOUBLE DOOR(1934); PURSUIT OF HAPPINESS, THE(1934); READY FOR LOVE(1934); COWBOY AND THE KID,THE(1936); HARVESTER, THE(1936); GUNSMOKE RANCH(1937); TOUGH TO HANDLE(1937); RED RIVER RANGE(1938); UNDER WESTERN STARS(1938); COME ON RANGERS(1939); INVITATION TO HAPPINESS(1939); KONGA, THE WILD STALLION(1939); NEW FRONTIER(1939); ROCKY MOUNTAIN RANGERS(1940); PHANTOM COWBOY, THE(1941); RIDIN' ON A RAINBOW(1941); CALLING WILD BILL ELLIOTT(1943); ADVENTURES OF MARK TWAIN, THE(1944)
Lilo Caruthers
IS YOUR HONEYMOON REALLY NECESSARY?(1953, Brit.), ed
Carl Carvahal
MOST DANGEROUS MAN ALIVE, THE(1961), ph
Alfonso Carvajal
MAD DOCTOR OF BLOOD ISLAND, THE(1969, Phil./U.S.); BEAST OF BLOOD(1970, U.S./Phil.); BLACK MAMA, WHITE MAMA(1973)
Alfonzo Carvajal
NO PLACE TO HIDE(1956)
Florence Carvajal
Misc. Talkies
PAY OR DIE(1982)
Tony Carvajal
TREASURE OF PANCHO VILLA, THE(1955)
Betty Carvalho
BOULEVARD NIGHTS(1979)
Claire Carvalho
RACETRACK(1933), w
Jose Carvalho
IN THE WHITE CITY(1983, Switz./Portugal)
Mlle. Carvalho
Silents
NAPOLEON(1927, Fr.)
Hugo Carvana
ANTONIO DAS MORTES(1970, Braz.); EARTH ENTRANCED(1970, Braz.); ALL NUDITY SHALL BE PUNISHED(1974, Brazil)
Paolo Carvara
BLACK BELLY OF THE TARANTULA, THE(1972, Ital.), d
Rex Carvel
MYSTERY OF ROOM 13(1941, Brit.)
Carven
EDWARD AND CAROLINE(1952, Fr.), cos
Michael Carven
MEGAFORCE(1982)
Mircha Carven
STATUE, THE(1971, Brit.)
Brent Carver
CROSS COUNTRY(1983, Can.)
Briana Carver
OPENING NIGHT(1977)
Cathy Carver
DO NOT THROW CUSHIONS INTO THE RING(1970)
Cynthia May Carver
SECOND GREATEST SEX, THE(1955)
Danelle Carver
Misc. Talkies
AFFAIRS OF ROBIN HOOD, THE(1981)
Frances Carver
CROSS MY HEART(1937, Brit.), ph
Francis Carver
CROSS CURRENTS(1935, Brit.), ph; LUCKY DAYS(1935, Brit.), ph; MAD HATTERS, THE(1935, Brit.), ph; CHICK(1936, Brit.), ph; HOUSE BROKEN(1936, Brit.), ph; LOVE AT SEA(1936, Brit.), ph; MAN BEHIND THE MASK, THE(1936, Brit.), ph; TICKET OF LEAVE(1936, Brit.), ph; CAVALIER OF THE STREETS, THE(1937, Brit.), ph; INCIDENT IN SHANGHAI(1937, Brit.), ph; LANCASHIRE LUCK(1937, Brit.), ph; MISSING, BELIEVED MARRIED(1937, Brit.), ph; MR. SMITH CARRIES ON(1937, Brit.), ph; MUSEUM MYSTERY(1937, Brit.), ph; NIGHT RIDE(1937, Brit.), ph; TALK OF THE DEVIL(1937, Brit.), ph; LIGHTNING CONDUCTOR(1938, Brit.), ph; NO

PARKING(1938, Brit.), ph; SPOT OF BOTHER, A(1938, Brit.), ph; LAMBETH WALK, THE(1940, Brit.), ph; PLAYBOY, THE(1942, Brit.), ph; SILVER DARLINGS, THE(1947, Brit.), ph
Dr. George Washington Carver
GEORGE WASHINGTON CARVER(1940)
H.P. Carver
SILENT ENEMY, THE(1930), d
Jann Carver
ARENA, THE(1973), ed
Jim Carver
MARK OF THE WITCH(1970), set d
Kathryn Carver
NO DEFENSE(1929)
Silents
OUTCAST(1928)
Misc. Silents
SERENADE(1927); SERVICE FOR LADIES(1927); HIS PRIVATE LIFE(1928); NO DEFENSE(1929)
Lilian Carver
HARDER THEY FALL, THE(1956)
Louis Carver
Silents
SCARAMOUCHE(1923)
Louise Carver
SAP, THE(1929); TONIGHT AT TWELVE(1929); BACK PAY(1930); BIG TRAIL, THE(1930); MAN FROM BLANKLEY'S, THE(1930); SIDE SHOW(1931); RIDERS OF THE DESERT(1932); DEVIL'S BROTHER, THE(1933); HALLELUJAH, I'M A BUM(1933); ROMAN SCANDALS(1933); KID MILLIONS(1934); EVERY NIGHT AT EIGHT(1935)
Silents
EXTRA GIRL, THE(1923); BACKSTAGE(1927); FORTUNE HUNTER, THE(1927)
Misc. Silents
BREED OF THE BORDER, THE(1924)
Lynn Carver
HUCKLEBERRY FINN(1939)
Lynne Carver
KID MILLIONS(1934); BRIDE WORE RED, THE(1937); MADAME X(1937); MAYTIME(1937); CHRISTMAS CAROL, A(1938); EVERYBODY SING(1938); YOUNG DR. KILDARE(1938); CALLING DR. KILDARE(1939); WITHIN THE LAW(1939); BITTER SWEET(1940); BROADWAY MELODY OF 1940(1940); DULCY(1940); SPORTING BLOOD(1940); IN OLD CALIFORNIA(1942); MAN FROM CHEYENNE(1942); SUNSET ON THE DESERT(1942); YOKEL BOY(1942); BATAAN(1943); HUMAN COMEDY, THE(1943); LAW OF THE VALLEY(1944); FLAME OF THE WEST(1945); DRIFTING ALONG(1946); CARTER CASE, THE(1947); CROSSED TRAILS(1948)
Marjorie L. Carver
MEXICAN HAYRIDE(1948)
Mary Carver
GOODBYE, MY FANCY(1951); FROM HERE TO ETERNITY(1953); BIGGER THAN LIFE(1956); EMERGENCY HOSPITAL(1956); KATHY O'(1958); PAY OR DIE(1960); GLASS HOUSES(1972); I NEVER PROMISED YOU A ROSE GARDEN(1977)
1984
PROTOCOL(1984)
Peter Carver
HIDDEN HOMICIDE(1959, Brit.); IN THE WAKE OF A STRANGER(1960, Brit.); SUNDOWNERS, THE(1960); WALKABOUT(1971, Aus./U.S.)
R. P. Carver
VIKING, THE(1931), ed
Randall Carver
Misc. Talkies
TIME TO RUN(1974)
Richard Carver
SILENT ENEMY, THE(1930), w
Robert D. Carver
HONKYTONK MAN(1982)
Steve Carver
ARENA, THE(1973), d; BIG BAD MAMA(1974), d; CAPONE(1975), d; DRUM(1976), d; FAST CHARLIE... THE MOONBEAM RIDER(1979), d; EYE FOR AN EYE, AN(1981), d; LONE WOLF McQUADE(1983), p, d
Steven Carver
STEEL(1980), d
Tina Carver
INSIDE DETROIT(1955); CRY IN THE NIGHT, A(1956); HARDER THEY FALL, THE(1956); HELL ON FRISCO BAY(1956); URANIUM BOOM(1956); CHAIN OF EVIDENCE(1957); FROM HELL IT CAME(1957); MAN WHO TURNED TO STONE, THE(1957)
William Carver
ON THE YARD(1978)
Gordon Carveth
LIFE BEGINS AT 40(1935); WILD HARVEST(1947); CHICAGO DEADLINE(1949); MILKMAN, THE(1950); SON OF PALEFACE(1952)
Dana Carvey
1984
RACING WITH THE MOON(1984)
Dane Carvey
1984
THIS IS SPINAL TAP(1984)
H. J. Carvill
Silents
BRANDED WOMAN, THE(1920)
Henry Carvill
DISRAELI(1929)
Silents
SHACKLES OF GOLD(1922)
Henry J. Carville
Silents
GUILTY OF LOVE(1920)
William E. Carville
POCO...LITTLE DOG LOST(1977), w

Darlene Carviotto
HUMAN EXPERIMENTS(1980)
Richard Carwardine
DOCTOR FAUSTUS(1967, Brit.)
Arthur Carwew
Misc. Silents
HIS WIFE'S HUSBAND(1922)
Doreen Carwithen
THREE CASES OF MURDER(1955, Brit.), m; HEIGHTS OF DANGER(1962, Brit.), m
Carol Cary
WEDNESDAY CHILDREN, THE(1973)
Christopher Cary
MARLOWE(1969); RAID ON ROMMEL(1971); WHITE BUFFALO, THE(1977); SWORD AND THE SORCERER, THE(1982)
Claibane Cary
SPORTING CLUB, THE(1971)
Falkland Cary
SCOTLAND YARD DRAGNET(1957, Brit.), w; WATCH IT, SAILOR!(1961, Brit.), w
Falkland D. Cary
NO ROAD BACK(1957, Brit.), w
Falkland L. Cary
PANIC IN THE PARLOUR(1957, Brit.), w
Geoffrey Cary
JOY(1983, Fr./Can.)
Jill Cary
ASSAULT(1971, Brit.)
Joyce Cary
KISENGA, MAN OF AFRICA(1952, Brit.), w
Lucian Cary
SATURDAY'S MILLIONS(1933), w; STRAIGHT FROM THE SHOULDER(1936), w; DUKE COMES BACK, THE(1937), w; DUKE OF CHICAGO(1949), w
Silents
WHITE FLANNELS(1927), w
Ned Cary
MINX, THE(1969)
Tristan Cary
FLESH IS WEAK, THE(1957, Brit.), m; TREAD SOFTLY STRANGER(1959, Brit.), m; BLOOD FROM THE MUMMY'S TOMB(1972, Brit.), m
Tristram Cary
LADYKILLERS, THE(1956, Brit.), m; TIME WITHOUT PITY(1957, Brit.), m; TOWN ON TRIAL(1957, Brit.), m; BOY WHO STOLE A MILLION, THE(1960, Brit.), m; BOY TEN FEET TALL, A(1965, Brit.), m; FIVE MILLION YEARS TO EARTH(1968, Brit.), m
Ronnie Caryl
OPERATION THIRD FORM(1966, Brit.)
Zoe Caryl
1984
SECRET PLACES(1984, Brit.)
Billy Caryll
MARRY ME(1932, Brit.); REGAL CAVALCADE(1935, Brit.); BITER BIT, THE(1937, Brit.); LASSIE FROM LANCASHIRE(1938, Brit.); I DIDN'T DO IT(1945, Brit.)

Antonio Casa
YOUNG REBEL, THE(1969, Fr./Ital./Span.)
R. Casa
COUNSEL FOR ROMANCE(1938, Fr.)
Roberto Della Casa
I HATE BLONDES(1981, Ital.)
Casa d'Arte Firenze
MYSTERY OF THUG ISLAND, THE(1966, Ital./Ger.), cos
Antonio Casa Monica
ORGANIZER, THE(1964, Fr./Ital./Yugo.)
Casa Nuova Girls
ONE PRECIOUS YEAR(1933, Brit.)
Casablanca Records and Filmworks
FIFTH FLOOR, THE(1980), m
Enrico Casadei
DEAF SMITH AND JOHNNY EARS(1973, Ital.)
Yvonne Casadei
8 ½(1963, Ital.); JULIET OF THE SPIRITS(1965, Fr./Ital./W.Ger.)
Casadessus
ROTHSCHILD(1938, Fr.)
Gisele Casadessus
VERDICT(1975, Fr./Ital.)
Gisele Casadesus
ETERNAL HUSBAND, THE(1946, Fr.)
Mathilde Casadesus
LE PLAISIR(1954, Fr.); GERVAISE(1956, Fr.); LOVE IS MY PROFESSION(1959, Fr.); CANDIDE(1962, Fr.); FIVE MILES TO MIDNIGHT(1963, U.S./Fr./Ital.); MURDER AT 45 R.P.M.(1965, Fr.)
Eduardo Casado
MYSTERY IN MEXICO(1948)
J.J. Martinez Casado
SHE-DEVIL ISLAND(1936, Mex.)
Juan Martinez Casado
SANTA(1932, Mex.)
Mario Casado
LOVE HUNGER(1965, Arg.); HEAT(1970, Arg.)
Eloy Casados
1984
CLOAK AND DAGGER(1984)
Eloy Phil Casados
PIECES OF DREAMS(1970); WALK PROUD(1979); UNDER FIRE(1983)
1984
SACRED GROUND(1984)
Alessandro Casagrande
MATA HARI'S DAUGHTER(1954, Fr./Ital), m

Antonio Casagrande
ARABELLA(1969, U.S./Ital.)
Wilma Casagrande
DEATH TOOK PLACE LAST NIGHT(1970, Ital./Ger.)
Maria Casajuana
Silents
GIRL IN EVERY PORT, A(1928)
Antonio Casale
GOOD, THE BAD, AND THE UGLY, THE(1967, Ital./Span.)
Nino Casale
DUCK, YOU SUCKER!(1972, Ital.)
Marta Casanas
HEROINA(1965)
Jeannette Casanave
RABID(1976, Can.)
Santos Casani
LOST IN THE LEGION(1934, Brit.); SPIES OF THE AIR(1940, Brit.)
Delia Casanova
ALSINO AND THE CONDOR(1983, Nicaragua)
1984
ERENDIRA(1984, Mex./Fr./Ger.)
Ermando Casanova
TEN DAYS' WONDER(1972, Fr.)
Fernando Casanova
EL(1955, Mex.); SANTO CONTRA EL CEREBRO DIABOLICO zero(1962, Mex.)
Jorge Casanova
LOS ASTRONAUTAS(1960, Mex.); SANTO CONTRA LA HIJA DE FRANKEN-STEIN(1971, Mex.)
Carlos Casaravilla
PRIDE AND THE PASSION, THE(1957); AGE OF INFIDELITY(1958, Span.); MAN WHO WAGGED HIS TAIL, THE(1961, Ital./Span.); COMMANDO(1962, Ital., Span., Bel., Ger.); LAZARILLO(1963, Span.); 55 DAYS AT PEKING(1963); FACE OF TER-ROR(1964, Span.); PYRO(1964, U.S./Span.); SON OF CAPTAIN BLOOD, THE(1964, U.S./Ital./Span.); REDEEMER, THE(1965, Span.); PLACE CALLED GLORY, A(1966, Span./Ger.); RETURN OF THE SEVEN(1966, Span.); FEW BULLETS MORE, A(1968, Ital./Span.); SAUL AND DAVID(1968, Ital./Span.); HORSEMEN, THE(1971)
Ann Casares
UP THE MACGREGORS(1967, Ital./Span.)
Maria Casares
CHILDREN OF PARADISE(1945, Fr.); ORPHEUS(1950, Fr.); TESTAMENT OF ORPHEUS, THE(1962, Fr.); LADIES OF THE PARK(1964, Fr.)
Guy Casaril
LEGEND OF FRENCHIE KING, THE(1971, Fr./Ital./Span./Brit.), d, w; PIAF–THE EARLY YEARS(1982, U.S./Fr.), d, w
Gabrielle Casartelli
LYONS MAIL, THE(1931, Brit.)
Carlos Casarvilla
CEREMONY, THE(1963, U.S./Span.); WEB OF FEAR(1966, Fr./Span.)
Antonio Casas
COLOSSUS OF RHODES, THE(1961, Ital., Fr., Span.); REVOLT OF THE SLAVES, THE(1961, Ital./Span./Ger.); REDEEMER, THE(1965, Span.); HYPNOSIS(1966, Ger./Sp./Ital.); MINNESOTA CLAY(1966, Ital./Fr./Span.); PISTOL FOR RINGO, A(1966, Ital./Span.); RETURN OF RINGO, THE(1966, Ital./Span.); SON OF A GUNFIGHT-ER(1966, U.S./Span.); SOUND OF HORROR(1966, Span.); TEXICAN, THE(1966, U.S./Span.); GOOD, THE BAD, AND THE UGLY, THE(1967, Ital./Span.); BIG GUNDOWN, THE(1968, Ital.); TRISTANA(1970, Span./Ital./Fr.)
Alberto Casati
LA FUGA(1966, Ital.), p
Georges Casati
DON'T PLAY WITH MARTIANS(1967, Fr.), p; DEADLY TRAP, THE(1972, Fr./Ital.), p; GODSON, THE(1972, Ital./Fr.)
Franco Casavola
DIFFICULT YEARS(1950, Ital.), m
Larry Casazza
FACE IN THE CROWD, A(1957)
Frederik Casby
1984
ELEMENT OF CRIME, THE(1984, Den.)
The Cascades
CATALINA CAPER, THE(1967)
Jacinto Cascales
SUMMERSKIN(1962, Arg.), ed; HAND IN THE TRAP, THE(1963, Arg./Span.), ed; TERRACE, THE(1964, Arg.), ed; THE EAVESDROPPER(1966, U.S./Arg.), ed; CURI-OUS DR. HUMPP(1967, Arg.), ed
Jose Antonio Cascales
GLASS SPHINX, THE(1968, Egypt/Ital./Span.), w
Michael Casconi
NIGHT OF THE ZOMBIES(1981)
Penny Casdagli
PUPPET ON A CHAIN(1971, Brit.)
Anna Case
Misc. Silents
HIDDEN TRUTH, THE(1919)
Bonnie Carol Case
WEDDING IN WHITE(1972, Can.)
Brad Case
MAKE MINE MUSIC(1946), anim; SHINBONE ALLEY(1971), anim; MOUSE AND HIS CHILD, THE(1977), anim
Brandy Case
MY BODY HUNGERS(1967)
Carol Case
Misc. Talkies
STREET GIRLS(1975)
Carroll Case
BILLY THE KID VS. DRACULA(1966), p; EYE FOR AN EYE, AN(1966), p; JESSE JAMES MEETS FRANKENSTEIN'S DAUGHTER(1966), p; TWO MULES FOR SIS-TER SARA(1970), p

Charles Case
BODYGUARD(1948)
Dale Case
WAR BETWEEN MEN AND WOMEN, THE(1972), anim
Geoffrey Case
TROG(1970, Brit.)
Gerald Case
MUSEUM MYSTERY(1937, Brit.); LION HAS WINGS, THE(1940, Brit.); IN WHICH WE SERVE(1942, Brit.); ADVENTURESS, THE(1946, Brit.); CAESAR AND CLEOPATRA(1946, Brit.); HENRY V(1946, Brit.); NIGHT BOAT TO DUBLIN(1946, Brit.); WHEN THE BOUGH BREAKS(1947, Brit.); MAN ON THE RUN(1949, Brit.); MEET SIMON CHERRY(1949, Brit.); NOW BARABBAS WAS A ROBBER(1949, Brit.); DANCING YEARS, THE(1950, Brit.); ASSASSIN FOR HIRE(1951, Brit.); CLOUDBURST(1952, Brit.); STRANGER IN BETWEEN, THE(1952, Brit.); FAKE, THE(1953, Brit.); LANDFALL(1953, Brit.); MURDER ON MONDAY(1953, Brit.); LADY OF VENGEANCE(1957, Brit); MAILBAG ROBBERY(1957, Brit.); SAFECRACKER, THE(1958, Brit.); LADY IS A SQUARE, THE(1959, Brit.); INVASION QUARTET(1961, Brit.); ACCIDENTAL DEATH(1963, Brit.); THIRD SECRET, THE(1964, Brit.); ELEPHANT MAN, THE(1980, Brit.)
Henry Case
NO SMOKING(1955, Brit.), d
John Case
MONTY PYTHON'S LIFE OF BRIAN(1979, Brit.)
Justin Case
SUPERMAN III(1983)
Kathleen Case
JUNCTION CITY(1952); LAST OF THE PONY RIDERS(1953); HUMAN DESIRE(1954); RUNNING WILD(1955); SECOND GREATEST SEX, THE(1955); CALLING HOMICIDE(1956)
Kathy Case
TWO TICKETS TO BROADWAY(1951)
Lee Case
DINER(1982)
Marianna Case
FATE IS THE HUNTER(1964); DIMENSION 5(1966); GNOME-MOBILE, THE(1967); WINNING(1969)
Martin Case
IF THIS BE SIN(1950, Brit.)
Mary Case
JOE(1970)
Rena Case
TIME OF YOUR LIFE, THE(1948)
Robert Case
WIND AND THE LION, THE(1975); CONFESSIONS OF AMANS, THE(1977)
Robert Ormond Case
GIRL FROM ALASKA(1942), w
Thomas Case
1984
PROTOCOL(1984), makeup
Tom Case
JENNY(1969), makeup; SHAMPOO(1975), makeup; THIEVES(1977), makeup
Willard Case
Silents
RANSOM, THE(1916)
Colette Casel
TALL BLOND MAN WITH ONE BLACK SHOE, THE(1973, Fr.)
Marissa Casel
1984
HUNDRA(1984, Ital.)
William Casel
SILENT ENEMY, THE(1930), ph
Gordon Casell
OPERATION PETTICOAT(1959); WILD HARVEST(1962)
Alberto Casella
DEATH TAKES A HOLIDAY(1934), w
Martin Casella
POLTERGEIST(1982); SIX WEEKS(1982); HEART LIKE A WHEEL(1983)
Ernest Caselli
Silents
MERCHANT OF VENICE, THE(1916, Brit.)
Richard Caselnova
SCARFACE(1983)
Adriana Caselotti
SNOW WHITE AND THE SEVEN DWARFS(1937)
Tom Casement
DEVIL'S ROCK(1938, Brit.)
Jeannette Casenave
OH, HEAVENLY DOG!(1980)
Clem Caserta
1984
FALLING IN LOVE(1984); ONCE UPON A TIME IN AMERICA(1984); POPE OF GREENWICH VILLAGE, THE(1984)
Frankie Caserta
1984
ONCE UPON A TIME IN AMERICA(1984)
Fernando Izcaino Cases
BATTLE OF THE AMAZONS(1973, Ital./Span.), w
Tiziana Casetti
MINOTAUR, THE(1961, Ital.); PRISONER OF THE IRON MASK(1962, Fr./Ital.)
Bernie Casey
GUNS OF THE MAGNIFICENT SEVEN(1969); ...TICK...TICK...TICK...(1970); BLACK GUNN(1972); BOXCAR BERTHA(1972); HIT MAN(1972); CLEOPATRA JONES(1973); MAURIE(1973); CORNBREAD, EARL AND ME(1975); DR. BLACK AND MR. HYDE(1976); MAN WHO FELL TO EARTH, THE(1976, Brit.); BROTHERS(1977); SHARKY'S MACHINE(1982); NEVER SAY NEVER AGAIN(1983)
1984
REVENGE OF THE NERDS(1984)
Misc. Talkies
BLACK CHARIOT(1971); MAURIE(1973)

Chick Casey
PARADISE ALLEY(1978)
Claude Casey
SQUARE DANCE JUBILEE(1949); KENTUCKY JUBILEE(1951); MOONSHINE MOUNTAIN(1964); FORTY ACRE FEUD(1965)
Colleen Casey
FRATERNITY ROW(1977)
Corey Casey
STRYKER(1983, Phil.)
David Casey
SWEENEY 2(1978, Brit.)
Dolores Casey
ROMAN SCANDALS(1933); BIG BROWN EYES(1936); ARTISTS AND MODELS ABROAD(1938); DR. RHYTHM(1938); ILLEGAL TRAFFIC(1938); MEN WITH WINGS(1938); SAY IT IN FRENCH(1938); TROPIC HOLIDAY(1938); CAFE SOCIETY(1939)
Emmett Casey
DU BARRY WAS A LADY(1943); SALOME, WHERE SHE DANCED(1945)
Frank Casey
HERO AT LARGE(1980)
Gertrude Casey
WESTWARD HO THE WAGONS!(1956), cos; JOHNNY TREMAIN(1957), cos; OLD YELLER(1957), cos; LIGHT IN THE FOREST, THE(1958), cos; TONKA(1958), cos; DARBY O'GILL AND THE LITTLE PEOPLE(1959), cos; SHAGGY DOG, THE(1959), cos; POLLYANNA(1960), cos; TOBY TYLER(1960), cos; BON VOYAGE(1962), cos; MOON PILOT(1962), cos; SAVAGE SAM(1963), cos; MISADVENTURES OF MERLIN JONES, THE(1964), cos; TIGER WALKS, A(1964), cos; MONKEY'S UNCLE, THE(1965), cos; UGLY DACHSHUND, THE(1966), cos
Jack Casey
GHOST PATROL(1936); RENEGADES OF THE RIO GRANDE(1945)
James Casey
MEXICAN SPITFIRE'S BABY(1941), w
John Casey
LURE OF THE ISLANDS(1942)
1984
CLOAK AND DAGGER(1984), cos
Kenneth Casey
Misc. Silents
ADVENTURER, THE(1920)
Kevin Casey
SKYDIVERS, THE(1963)
Larry Casey
GAY DECEIVERS, THE(1969)
Lawrence Casey
STUDENT NURSES, THE(1970); GREAT WALDO PEPPER, THE(1975); ACAPULCO GOLD(1978); BORDERLINE(1980)
Leonard Casey
UNTAMED(1955)
Lesley Casey
Silents
OTHER MAN'S WIFE, THE(1919)
Leslie Casey
Silents
WORLD'S CHAMPION, THE(1922); ONE MILLION IN JEWELS(1923); STORMY SEAS(1923)
Lucille Casey
MEET THE PEOPLE(1944); ZIEGFELD FOLLIES(1945); HARVEY GIRLS, THE(1946); HOODLUM SAINT, THE(1946); NOCTURNE(1946); TILL THE CLOUDS ROLL BY(1946); DOWN TO EARTH(1947); MEXICAN HAYRIDE(1948)
Marie-Pierre Casey
THINGS OF LIFE, THE(1970, Fr./Ital./Switz.)
1984
ONE DEADLY SUMMER(1984, Fr.)
Melinda Ann Casey
WRONG IS RIGHT(1982)
Patricia Casey
Misc. Talkies
FADE-IN(1968)
Rosemary Casey
FOOLS FOR SCANDAL(1938), w
Sally Casey
MARS NEEDS WOMEN(1966)
Sean Casey
1984
LAST HORROR FILM, THE(1984)
Sharon Casey
ROLLOVER(1981)
Shaun Casey
ANNIE HALL(1977)
Shawn Casey
THEY ALL LAUGHED(1981)
Stuart Casey
CAPTAIN BLOOD(1935)
Sue Casey
SECRET LIFE OF WALTER MITTY, THE(1947); GREAT SINNER, THE(1949); IT'S A GREAT FEELING(1949); NEPTUNE'S DAUGHTER(1949); FOR HEAVEN'S SAKE(1950); MY FAVORITE SPY(1951); SCARF, THE(1951); SECRETS OF MONTE CARLO(1951); LAS VEGAS STORY, THE(1952); ROAD TO BALI(1952); FRENCH LINE, THE(1954); OTHER WOMAN, THE(1954); THREE RING CIRCUS(1954); SON OF SINBAD(1955); ERRAND BOY, THE(1961); JUMBO(1962); NEW KIND OF LOVE, A(1963); BEACH GIRLS AND THE MONSTER(1965); SWAMP COUNTRY(1966); CAMELOT(1967); CATALINA CAPER, THE(1967); PAINT YOUR WAGON(1969); MAIN EVENT, THE(1979); HYSTERICAL(1983)
Taggart Casey
DELICATE DELINQUENT, THE(1957); JUVENILE JUNGLE(1958); NORTH BY NORTHWEST(1959); SEX AND THE SINGLE GIRL(1964)
Taggart Casey
LONELY MAN, THE(1957); HELLER IN PINK TIGHTS(1960)

Terence Casey
KENTUCKY MINSTRELS(1934, Brit.)
Thomas Casey
DEATH CURSE OF TARTU(1967), set d; FLESH FEAST(1970), w, ph
Tony Casey
GUNMAN HAS ESCAPED, A(1948, Brit.)
Van Casey
THUNDER IN CAROLINA(1960)
Warren Casey
GREASE(1978), w
Aubrey Cash
DANGER BY MY SIDE(1962, Brit.), w; NIGHT WITHOUT PITY(1962, Brit.), w; TOUCH OF DEATH(1962, Brit.), w
Bubbles Cash
MARS NEEDS WOMEN(1966)
Don Cash
LURED(1947), makeup; PRETENDER, THE(1947), makeup; STRIKE IT RICH(1948), makeup; FIGHTING KENTUCKIAN, THE(1949), makeup; NIGHT OF THE HUNTER, THE(1955), makeup; DEFIANT ONES, THE(1958), makeup; DINOSAURUS(1960), makeup; YOUR CHEATIN' HEART(1964), makeup; HARUM SCARUM(1965), makeup; WHAT'S UP, DOC?(1972), makeup
Don L. Cash
DEMON SEED(1977), makeup
Donald Cash, Jr.
WAY WE WERE, THE(1973), makeup
Ellis Lamar Cash
CONRACK(1974)
Fred Cash
THREE THE HARD WAY(1974)
Jerry Cash
STRAWBERRY STATEMENT, THE(1970), makeup
Jim S. Cash
POSTMAN ALWAYS RINGS TWICE, THE(1981)
Jimmy Cash
HAT CHECK HONEY(1944)
Johnny Cash
FIVE MINUTES TO LIVE(1961); HOOTENANNY HOOT(1963); GUNFIGHT, A(1971); GOSPEL ROAD, THE(1973), p, w
June Cash
GOSPEL ROAD, THE(1973), p
June Carter Cash
GOSPEL ROAD, THE(1973)
Rosalind Cash
KLUTE(1971); OMEGA MAN, THE(1971); HICKEY AND BOGGS(1972); MELINDA(1972); NEW CENTURIONS, THE(1972); ALL-AMERICAN BOY, THE(1973); AMAZING GRACE(1974); UPTOWN SATURDAY NIGHT(1974); CORNBREAD, EARL AND ME(1975); DR. BLACK AND MR. HYDE(1976); MONKEY HUSTLE, THE(1976); CLASS OF MISS MAC MICHAEL, THE(1978, Brit./U.S.); WRONG IS RIGHT(1982)
1984
ADVENTURES OF BUCKAROO BANZAI: ACROSS THE 8TH DIMENSION, THE(1984); GO TELL IT ON THE MOUNTAIN(1984)
Misc. Talkies
KEEPING ON(1981)
Shirley Cash
HELL'S CHOSEN FEW(1968)
Georgann Cashen
GIANT(1956)
Mary Ann Cashen
GIANT(1956)
Katy Cashfield
NAKED FURY(1959, Brit.)
Bank Cashier
NOW BARABBAS WAS A ROBBER(1949, Brit.)
Isidor Cashier
Silents
BROKEN HEARTS(1926)
Isidore Cashier
CANTOR'S SON, THE(1937); GREEN FIELDS(1937)
Misc. Talkies
HIS WIFE'S LOVER(1931); DOBBIN, THE(1939); JEWISH MELODY, THE(1940)
Bonnie Cashin
IN THE MEANTIME, DARLING(1944), cos; LAURA(1944), cos; FALLEN ANGEL(1945), cos; HOUSE ON 92ND STREET, THE(1945), cos; TREE GROWS IN BROOKLYN, A(1945), cos; THREE LITTLE GIRLS IN BLUE(1946), cos; NIGHTMARE ALLEY(1947), cos; CRY OF THE CITY(1948), cos; IRON CURTAIN, THE(1948), cos; LUCK OF THE IRISH(1948), cos; SCUDDA-HOO! SCUDDA-HAY!(1948), cos; SNAKE PIT, THE(1948), cos; UNFAITHFULLY YOURS(1948), cos; IT HAPPENS EVERY SPRING(1949), cos; MR. BELVEDERE GOES TO COLLEGE(1949), cos; YOU'RE MY EVERYTHING(1949), cos
Michael Cashman
I'VE GOTTA HORSE(1965, Brit.); UNMAN, WITTERING AND ZIGO(1971, Brit.); MADE(1972, Brit.); X Y & ZEE(1972, Brit.)
Genevieve Casile
SEVEN CAPITAL SINS(1962, Fr./Ital.); SEA PIRATE, THE(1967, Fr./Span./Ital.)
Maria Pia Casilio
BREAD, LOVE AND DREAMS(1953, Ital.); UMBERTO D(1955, Ital.); ANGELS OF DARKNESS(1956, Ital.); NEOPOLITAN CAROUSEL(1961, Ital.)
Maria Pia Casillo-Ciro
INDISCRETION OF AN AMERICAN WIFE(1954, U.S./Ital.)
Golda Casimir
MAIN ATTRACTION, THE(1962, Brit.); THREE SPARE WIVES(1962, Brit.); VILLAGE OF DAUGHTERS(1962, Brit.); HELP!(1965, Brit.); BERSERK(1967); HALF A SIXPENCE(1967, Brit.); SMASHING TIME(1967 Brit.); TROG(1970, Brit.)
Charles M. Casinelli
LOST, LONELY AND VICIOUS(1958), p; LOUISIANA HUSSY(1960), p
Claudio Casinelli
TEMPTER, THE(1974, Ital./Brit.)

Anna Casini
LUXURY GIRLS(1953, Ital.)
Enzo Casini
ORGANIZER, THE(1964, Fr./Ital./Yugo.)
Stefanio Casini
SUSPIRIA(1977, Ital.)
Tatiana Casini
DEVIL, THE(1963), ed; DEVIL IN LOVE, THE(1968, Ital.), ed; JOHNNY HAMLET(1972, Ital.), ed; ARABIAN NIGHTS(1980, Ital./Fr.), ed
Tatiana Morigi Casini
KILL THEM ALL AND COME BACK ALONE(1970, Ital./Span.), ed
James Casino
ROCKY II(1979)
James J. Casino
MOVIE MOVIE(1978); PARADISE ALLEY(1978)
Jimmy Casino
FOXFIRE(1955); I'VE LIVED BEFORE(1956); ISLAND, THE(1980)
Johnny Casino
TREASURE OF MONTE CRISTO(1949)
George Casir
HOUSE IS NOT A HOME, A(1964)
Karl Casitzky
TERROR OF TINY TOWN, THE(1938)
Ted Caskey
RACING LUCK(1935)
Christopher Casler
Misc. Talkies
TEENAGE GRAFFITI(1977), d
Lucky Casner
GREEN HELMET, THE(1961, Brit.)
Philip Casnoff
MESSAGE FROM SPACE(1978, Jap.); GORP(1980)
Maria Caso
1984
HOT MOVES(1984), set d
Maria Rebman Caso
1984
BEAR, THE(1984), set d; TERMINATOR, THE(1984), set d
Egidio Casolari
RUN FOR YOUR WIFE(1966, Fr./Ital.); TIGER AND THE PUSSYCAT, THE(1967, U.S., Ital.)
Barbara Cason
HONEYMOON KILLERS, THE(1969); HOUSE OF DARK SHADOWS(1970); COLD TURKEY(1971); EXORCIST II: THE HERETIC(1977)
Bob Cason
GHOST GUNS(1944); LAND OF THE OUTLAWS(1944); WILD HORSE PHANTOM(1944); FIGHTING BILL CARSON(1945); HIS BROTHER'S GHOST(1945); SHADOWS OF DEATH(1945); STAGECOACH OUTLAWS(1945); HER HUSBAND'S AFFAIRS(1947); LAST ROUND-UP, THE(1947); LONE HAND TEXAN, THE(1947); RELENTLESS(1948); SIX-GUN LAW(1948); BIG SOMBRERO, THE(1949); LARAMIE(1949); JUBAL(1956)
Misc. Talkies
SUNSET CARSON RIDES AGAIN(1948)
Chuck [Bob] Cason
SON OF A BADMAN(1949)
John Cason
RIDERS OF THE BADLANDS(1941); DOWN RIO GRANDE WAY(1942); RAIDERS OF THE RANGE(1942); RAIDERS OF THE WEST(1942); SHADOWS ON THE SAGE(1942); SONORA STAGECOACH(1944); SPOOK TOWN(1944); MARK OF THE LASH(1948); BLAZING TRAIL, THE(1949); CHALLENGE OF THE RANGE(1949); RED DESERT(1949); RIMFIRE(1949); RINGSIDE(1949); TOUGH ASSIGNMENT(1949); COLORADO RANGER(1950); CROOKED RIVER(1950); FAST ON THE DRAW(1950); HOSTILE COUNTRY(1950); MARSHAL OF HELDORADO(1950); REDWOOD FOREST TRAIL(1950); RUSTLERS ON HORSEBACK(1950); STREETS OF GHOST TOWN(1950); TRAVELING SALESWOMAN(1950); WEST OF THE BRAZOS(1950); FORT SAVAGE RAIDERS(1951); PRAIRIE ROUNDUP(1951); THUNDERING TRAIL, THE(1951); BLACK HILLS AMBUSH(1952); HAWK OF WILD RIVER, THE(1952); KID FROM BROKEN GUN, THE(1952); VOODOO TIGER(1952); WAGON TEAM(1952); FROM HERE TO ETERNITY(1953); GUN FURY(1953); RED RIVER SHORE(1953); SAVAGE FRONTIER(1953); CATTLE QUEEN OF MONTANA(1954); SASKATCHEWAN(1954); COUNT THREE AND PRAY(1955); HE LAUGHED LAST(1956); JUBAL(1956); OVER-EXPOSED(1956); STORM RIDER, THE(1957); SNOWFIRE(1958); CIMARRON(1960)
John [Bob] Cason
DEAD MAN'S GOLD(1948); WYOMING RENEGADES(1955)
John L. "Bob" Cason
DEATH VALLEY OUTLAWS(1941); GHOST OF HIDDEN VALLEY(1946); OUTLAW OF THE PLAINS(1946); OVERLAND RIDERS(1946)
John L. Cason
WESTWARD HO(1942); PRAIRIE BADMEN(1946); RANGE LAND(1949)
Vickey Cason
WALK, DON'T RUN(1966)
Eric P. Caspar
DEAD PIGEON ON BEETHOVEN STREET(1972, Ger.)
George Caspar
FOR LOVE AND MONEY(1967)
Horst Caspar
KOLBERG(1945, Ger.)
Bibi Caspari
QUEST FOR FIRE(1982, Fr./Can.)
Ragnvald Caspari
EDVARD MUNCH(1976, Norway/Swed.)
Vera Caspary
WORKING GIRLS(1931), w; NIGHT OF JUNE 13(1932), w; PRIVATE SCANDAL(1934), w; SUCH WOMEN ARE DANGEROUS(1934), w; I'LL LOVE YOU ALWAYS(1935), w; PARTY WIRE(1935), w; EASY LIVING(1937), w; SCANDAL STREET(1938), w; SERVICE DE LUXE(1938), w; SING, DANCE, PLENTY HOT(1940), w; LADY FROM LOUISIANA(1941), w; LADY BODYGUARD(1942), w; LAURA(1944), w; BEDELIA(1946, Brit.), w; OUT OF THE BLUE(1947), w; LETTER TO THREE WIVES, A(1948), w; THREE HUSBANDS(1950), w; I CAN GET IT FOR YOU

WHOLESALE(1951), w; BLUE GARDENIA, THE(1953), w; GIVE A GIRL A BREAK(1953), w; LES GIRLS(1957), w; BACHELOR IN PARADISE(1961), w

Julie Caspell
1984
UP THE CREEK(1984)

Bill Casper
SLUMBER PARTY '57(1977), ed

Billy Casper
NOW YOU SEE HIM, NOW YOU DON'T(1972)

Mike Casper
PURSUIT OF D.B. COOPER, THE(1981)

Robert Casper
STUDS LONIGAN(1960); RIGHT APPROACH, THE(1961)

Debbie Casperson
STROKER ACE(1983)

Michael Caspi
MOUSE ON THE MOON, THE(1963, Brit.)

Joe Caspolich
THUNDER IN CAROLINA(1960)

Charles Cass
SCREAMERS(1978, Ital.)

Dave Cass
SHENANDOAH(1965); BOY WHO CRIED WEREWOLF, THE(1973); GOODBYE GIRL, THE(1977); MR. BILLION(1977); HOT LEAD AND COLD FEET(1978); TRON(1982); SMOKEY AND THE BANDIT–PART 3(1983)
Misc. Talkies
DISCIPLES OF DEATH(1975); ENTER THE DEVIL(1975)

David Cass
DIRTY DINGUS MAGEE(1970); SUPPOSE THEY GAVE A WAR AND NOBODY CAME?(1970); TWO-MINUTE WARNING(1976); ISLAND OF DR. MOREAU, THE(1977); SMOKEY AND THE BANDIT–PART 3(1983), stunts

Henry Cass
LANCASHIRE LUCK(1937, Brit.), d; FACTS OF LOVE(1949, Brit.), d; GLASS MOUNTAIN, THE(1950, Brit), d, w; LAST HOLIDAY(1950, Brit.), d; NO PLACE FOR JENNIFER(1950, Brit.), d; CASTLE IN THE AIR(1952, Brit.), d; FATHER'S DOING FINE(1952, Brit.), d; YOUNG WIVES' TALE(1954, Brit.), d; WINDFALL(1955 Brit.), d; BOND OF FEAR(1956, Brit.), d; BREAKAWAY(1956, Brit.), d; BOOBY TRAP(1957, Brit.), d; CROOKED SKY, THE(1957, Brit.), d; HIGH TERRACE(1957, Brit.), d; PROFESSOR TIM(1957, Ireland), d; TWO GROOMS FOR A BRIDE(1957), d; BLOOD OF THE VAMPIRE(1958, Brit.), d; BOYD'S SHOP(1960, Brit.), d; HAND, THE(1960, Brit.), d; MAN WHO COULDN'T WALK, THE(1964, Brit.), d; MR. BROWN COMES DOWN THE HILL(1966, Brit.), p&d, w; GIVE A DOG A BONE(1967, Brit.), p,d, w; HAPPY DEATHDAY(1969, Brit.), d&w

Lou Cass
YOU BELONG TO ME(1934); FAKE'S PROGRESS(1950, Brit.)

Mama Cass
PUFNSTUF(1970)

Martin Cass
MAN WHO COULDN'T WALK, THE(1964, Brit.)

Mary Cass
Misc. Talkies
BROAD COALITION, THE(1972); WHAT DO I TELL THE BOYS AT THE STATION(1972)

Maurice Cass
MAN WHO BROKE THE BANK AT MONTE CARLO, THE(1935); TWO FOR TONIGHT(1935); WHISPERING SMITH SPEAKS(1935); CHARLIE CHAN AT THE OPERA(1936); EVERYBODY'S OLD MAN(1936); KING OF BURLESQUE(1936); PEPPER(1936); PIGSKIN PARADE(1936); PROFESSIONAL SOLDIER(1936); WIFE VERSUS SECRETARY(1936); ALI BABA GOES TO TOWN(1937); BIG TOWN GIRL(1937); CHAMPAGNE WALTZ(1937); DANGER–LOVE AT WORK(1937); EXILED TO SHANGHAI(1937); FIREFLY, THE(1937); LADY ESCAPES, THE(1937); LAST TRAIN FROM MADRID, THE(1937); LIFE BEGINS IN COLLEGE(1937); MAYTIME(1937); SHE HAD TO EAT(1937); THIN ICE(1937); WIFE, DOCTOR AND NURSE(1937); WOMEN OF GLAMOUR(1937); BREAKING THE ICE(1938); DESPERATE ADVENTURE, A(1938); DRAMATIC SCHOOL(1938); EXPOSED(1938); GANGS OF NEW YORK(1938); GOLD DIGGERS IN PARIS(1938); JOSETTE(1938); LONE WOLF IN PARIS, THE(1938); MAKING THE HEADLINES(1938); PARADISE FOR THREE(1938); SUNSET TRAIL(1938); WALKING DOWN BROADWAY(1938); WHEN WERE YOU BORN?(1938); ROSE OF WASHINGTON SQUARE(1939); SECOND FIDDLE(1939); LADY WITH RED HAIR(1940); NO, NO NANETTE(1940); SON OF MONTE CRISTO(1940); BLOOD AND SAND(1941); CHARLEY'S AUNT(1941); COUNTRY FAIR(1941); WEEKEND IN HAVANA(1941); MY HEART BELONGS TO DADDY(1942); TOO MANY WOMEN(1942); GOOD FELLOWS, THE(1943); YOUTH ON PARADE(1943); IRISH EYES ARE SMILING(1944); MRS. PARKINGTON(1944); UP IN ARMS(1944); EASY TO LOOK AT(1944); HER LUCKY NIGHT(1945); HIT THE HAY(1945); SHE GETS HER MAN(1945); WONDER MAN(1945); IDEA GIRL(1946); NOTORIOUS LONE WOLF, THE(1946); SPOOK BUSTERS(1946); THE CATMAN OF PARIS(1946); HIGH CONQUEST(1947); SADDLE PALS(1947); SONG OF MY HEART(1947); SPOILERS OF THE NORTH(1947); GIRL FROM MANHATTAN(1948); STATE OF THE UNION(1948); FOLLOW ME QUIETLY(1949); ONCE MORE, MY DARLING(1949); SORROWFUL JONES(1949); KID MONK BARONI(1952); SOMETHING TO LIVE FOR(1952); WE'RE NOT MARRIED(1952)
Misc. Talkies
BEYOND THE MOON(1964)

Monty Cass
RED RIVER VALLEY(1936)

Peggy Cass
MARRYING KIND, THE(1952); AUNTIE MAME(1958); GIDGET GOES HAWAIIAN(1961); IF IT'S TUESDAY, THIS MUST BE BELGIUM(1969); PADDY(1970, Irish)

Ronald Cass
GO TO BLAZES(1962, Brit.), w; WONDERFUL TO BE YOUNG!(1962, Brit.), w; SUMMER HOLIDAY(1963, Brit.), w; FRENCH DRESSING(1964, Brit.), w; SWINGER'S PARADISE(1965, Brit.), w

Terrell Cass
YEAR OF THE YAHOO(1971)

The Cass Country Boys
SADDLE PALS(1947); TWILIGHT ON THE RIO GRANDE(1947); BUCKAROO FROM POWDER RIVER(1948)

The Cass County Boys
SIOUX CITY SUE(1946); LAST DAYS OF BOOT HILL(1947); ROBIN OF TEXAS(1947); TRAIL TO SAN ANTONE(1947); HOLIDAY RHYTHM(1950); KID FROM AMARILLO, THE(1951); BLUE CANADIAN ROCKIES(1952); ON TOP OF OLD SMOKY(1953)

Cass County Trio
TUCSON(1949)

Bill Cassady
PEGGY(1950); AMAZING COLOSSAL MAN, THE(1957)

Carolyn Cassady
HEART BEAT(1979), w

John Cassady
SUPERMAN(1978); MOUSE AND THE WOMAN, THE(1981, Brit.); TRAIL OF THE PINK PANTHER, THE(1982); VICTOR/VICTORIA(1982)
Misc. Talkies
VOICE OVER(1983)

Leon J. Cassady
ON THE YARD(1978)

Michel Cassagne
EVERY MAN FOR HIMSELF(1980, Fr.); DEATH OF MARIO RICCI, THE(1983, Ital.)

Marguerite Cassan
SYLVIA AND THE PHANTOM(1950, Fr.); PICNIC ON THE GRASS(1960, Fr.); LE PETIT THEATRE DE JEAN RENOIR(1974, Fr.)

Gino Cassani
LE MANS(1971)

Aurino Cassanio
BLACK ORPHEUS(1959 Fr./Ital./Braz.)

Gianbatista Cassarino
HIDEOUS SUN DEMON, THE(1959), d

Alexandra Cassavetes
HUSBANDS(1970)
1984
LOVE STREAMS(1984)

John Cassavetes
TAXI(1953); NIGHT HOLDS TERROR, THE(1955); CRIME IN THE STREETS(1956); AFFAIR IN HAVANA(1957); EDGE OF THE CITY(1957); SADDLE THE WIND(1958); SHADOWS(1960), d; VIRGIN ISLAND(1960, Brit.); TOO LATE BLUES(1962), p&d, w; CHILD IS WAITING, A(1963), d; KILLERS, THE(1964); DEVIL'S ANGELS(1967); DIRTY DOZEN, THE(1967, Brit.); FACES(1968), d&w, ed; ROSEMARY'S BABY(1968); IF IT'S TUESDAY, THIS MUST BE BELGIUM(1969); HUSBANDS(1970), a, d&w; MACHINE GUN McCAIN(1970, Ital.); MINNIE AND MOSKOWITZ(1971), a, d&w; WOMAN UNDER THE INFLUENCE, A(1974), d&w; CAPONE(1975); KILLING OF A CHINESE BOOKIE, THE(1976), d&w; MIKEY AND NICKY(1976); TWO-MINUTE WARNING(1976); OPENING NIGHT(1977), a, d&w; BRASS TARGET(1978); FURY, THE(1978); GLORIA(1980), p,d&w; WHOSE LIFE IS IT ANYWAY?(1981); INCUBUS, THE(1982, Can.); TEMPEST(1982); MARVIN AND TIGE(1983)
1984
LOVE STREAMS(1984), a, d, w
Misc. Talkies
BANDITS IN ROME(1967, Ital.)

Jon Cassavetes
WEBSTER BOY, THE(1962, Brit.)

Katherine Cassavetes
MINNIE AND MOSKOWITZ(1971); WOMAN UNDER THE INFLUENCE, A(1974); OPENING NIGHT(1977)

Nick Cassavetes
HUSBANDS(1970); WOMAN UNDER THE INFLUENCE, A(1974)

Zan Cassavetes
WOMAN UNDER THE INFLUENCE, A(1974)

Janine Casse
PHAEDRA(1962, U.S./Gr./Fr.), makeup

Ted Cassedy
HARRAD EXPERIMENT, THE(1973), w

Cindy Cassel
EMIL AND THE DETECTIVES(1964)

Jean Pierre Cassel
ANYONE CAN PLAY(1968, Ital.); FROM HELL TO VICTORY(1979, Fr./Ital./Span.)

Jean-Pierre Cassel
JOKER, THE(1961, Fr.); CANDIDE(1962, Fr.); ELUSIVE CORPORAL, THE(1963, Fr.); HIGH INFIDELITY(1965, Fr./Ital.); MALE COMPANION(1965, Fr./Ital.); THOSE MAGNIFICENT MEN IN THEIR FLYING MACHINES; OR HOW I FLEWFROM LONDON TO PARIS IN 25 HOURS AND 11 MINUTES(1965, Brit.); IS PARIS BURNING?(1966, U.S./Fr.); BEAUTIFUL SWINDLERS, THE(1967, Fr./Ital./Jap./Neth.); KILLING GAME, THE(1968, Fr.); L'ARMEE DES OMBRES(1969, Fr./Ital.); OH! WHAT A LOVELY WAR(1969, Brit.); DISCREET CHARM OF THE BOURGEOISIE, THE(1972, Fr.); MALPERTIUS(1972, Bel./Fr.); BAXTER(1973, Brit.); MURDER ON THE ORIENT EXPRESS(1974, Brit.); THREE MUSKETEERS, THE(1974, Panama); FOUR MUSKETEERS, THE(1975); FRENCH WAY, THE(1975, Fr.); THAT LUCKY TOUCH(1975, Brit.); TWIST, THE(1976, Fr.); NO TIME FOR BREAKFAST(1978, Fr.); WHO IS KILLING THE GREAT CHEFS OF EUROPE?(1978, US/Ger.); LA VIE CONTINUE(1982, Fr.); TROUT, THE(1982, Fr.)

Louis Cassel
MY NAME IS PECOS(1966, Ital.)

Matthew Cassel
WOMAN UNDER THE INFLUENCE, A(1974)

Sandra Cassel
LAST HOUSE ON THE LEFT(1972)

Seymour Cassel
JUKE BOX RACKET(1960); TOO LATE BLUES(1962); WEBSTER BOY, THE(1962, Brit.); KILLERS, THE(1964); COOGAN'S BLUFF(1968); FACES(1968); SWEET RIDE, THE(1968); REVOLUTIONARY, THE(1970, Brit.); MINNIE AND MOSKOWITZ(1971); KILLING OF A CHINESE BOOKIE, THE(1976); BLACK OAK CONSPIRACY(1977); DEATH GAME(1977); SCOTT JOPLIN(1977); VALENTINO(1977, Brit.); CONVOY(1978); CALIFORNIA DREAMING(1979); RAVAGERS, THE(1979); SUNBURN(1979); MOUNTAIN MEN, THE(1980); KING OF THE MOUNTAIN(1981); DOUBLE EXPOSURE(1982)
1984
LOVE STREAMS(1984)

W. Cassel
Silents
UNDER FIRE(1926)
Alan Cassell
MONEY MOVERS(1978, Aus.); CATHY'S CHILD(1979, Aus.); BREAKER MORANT(1980, Aus.); CLUB, THE(1980, Aus.); FIRE IN THE STONE, THE(1983, Aus.); PUBERTY BLUES(1983, Aus.)
1984
SQUIZZY TAYLOR(1984, Aus.)
Jean-Pierre Cassell
SEVEN CAPITAL SINS(1962, Fr./Ital.)
Malcolm Cassell
ROOM FOR ONE MORE(1952); KID FROM LEFT FIELD, THE(1953); OPERATION PETTICOAT(1959); PIRATES OF TORTUGA(1961)
Seymour Cassell
MURDER, INC.(1960); LAST TYCOON, THE(1976)
Wally Cassell
UNTIL THEY SAIL(1957); HUMAN COMEDY, THE(1943); THOUSANDS CHEER(1943); NATIONAL VELVET(1944); THIN MAN GOES HOME, THE(1944); THIRTY SECONDS OVER TOKYO(1944); ANCHORS AWEIGH(1945); DANGEROUS PARTNERS(1945); STORY OF G.I. JOE, THE(1945); GALLANT BESS(1946); POSTMAN ALWAYS RINGS TWICE, THE(1946); RAMROD(1947); HOMECOMING(1948); JOAN OF ARC(1948); LOVES OF CARMEN, THE(1948); SAIGON(1948); SUMMER HOLIDAY(1948); ARCTIC MANHUNT(1949); SANDS OF IWO JIMA(1949); STREETS OF SAN FRANCISCO(1949); WE WERE STRANGERS(1949); WHITE HEAT(1949); HIGHWAY 301(1950); QUICKSAND(1950); LITTLE BIG HORN(1951); OH! SUSANNA(1951); ONE MINUTE TO ZERO(1952); SOUND OFF(1952); THUNDERBIRDS(1952); WILD BLUE YONDER, THE(1952); BREAKDOWN(1953); CITY THAT NEVER SLEEPS(1953); ISLAND IN THE SKY(1953); LAW AND ORDER(1953); PRINCESS OF THE NILE(1954); FRESH FROM PARIS(1955); PARIS FOLLIES OF 1956(1955); TIMBERJACK(1955); ACCUSED OF MURDER(1956); I, MOBSTER(1959); SCARFACE MOB, THE(1962)
Walter Cassell
WINE, WOMEN AND HORSES(1937); COME ON, THE(1956)
Adrianna Cassellotti
BRIDE WORE RED, THE(1937)
Bernard Casselman
LAST MOVIE, THE(1971)
Kevin Casselman
FANTASIES(1981), p
Lavinia Cassels
TRUMAN CAPOTE'S TRILOGY(1969)
Andrew Cassese
1984
REVENGE OF THE NERDS(1984)
J.S. Casshyap
NINE HOURS TO RAMA(1963, U.S./Brit.)
Alan Cassidy
GREAT BRAIN, THE(1978), w
Arthur Cassidy
MAN BEAST(1956), w
Asa Cassidy
Misc. Silents
WONDERS OF THE SEA(1922)
Bill Cassidy
SPOOK CHASERS(1957); MAN IN THE NET, THE(1959); ROCKY(1976), prod d
Daniel Cassidy, Jr.
Misc. Talkies
HORSE(1965)
Diane Cassidy
EVERYTHING I HAVE IS YOURS(1952); INVITATION(1952); LOVELY TO LOOK AT(1952)
Ed Cassidy
NO MAN'S RANGE(1935); MEN OF THE PLAINS(1936); MILLIONAIRE KID(1936); RIO GRANDE ROMANCE(1936); ROGUES' TAVERN, THE(1936); WINDS OF THE WASTELAND(1936); ACES WILD(1937); BOOTHILL BRIGADE(1937); BOOTS OF DESTINY(1937); CHEYENNE RIDES AGAIN(1937); FIGHTING TEXAN(1937); MOONLIGHT ON THE RANGE(1937); RED ROPE, THE(1937); ROARING SIX GUNS(1937); SILVER TRAIL, THE(1937); SUNDOWN SAUNDERS(1937); BORDER WOLVES(1938); FRONTIER TOWN(1938); IN EARLY ARIZONA(1938); MEXICALI KID, THE(1938); OUTLAW EXPRESS(1938); PAINTED TRAIL, THE(1938); RAWHIDE(1938); WHERE THE BUFFALO ROAM(1938); COLORADO SUNSET(1939); DESPERATE TRAILS(1939); FRONTIERS OF '49(1939); MOUNTAIN RHYTHM(1939); TRIGGER SMITH(1939); WILD HORSE CANYON(1939); RAGTIME COWBOY JOE(1940); BURY ME NOT ON THE LONE PRAIRIE(1941); GANG'S ALL HERE(1941); RAWHIDE RANGERS(1941); RIDIN' ON A RAINBOW(1941); RIDING THE CHEROKEE TRAIL(1941); ROBBERS OF THE RANGE(1941); SAN FRANCISCO DOCKS(1941); WIDE OPEN TOWN(1941); HOUSE OF ERRORS(1942); SILVER QUEEN(1942); CATTLE STAMPEDE(1943); MAN FROM THUNDER RIVER, THE(1943); SAGEBRUSH LAW(1943); SANTA FE SCOUTS(1943); THUNDERING TRAILS(1943); WOLVES OF THE RANGE(1943); BRAND OF THE DEVIL(1944); DEVIL RIDERS(1944); GREAT MIKE, THE(1944); RAIDERS OF RED GAP(1944); RUSTLER'S HIDEOUT(1944); DALTONS RIDE AGAIN, THE(1945); STAGECOACH OUTLAWS(1945); SUNSET IN EL DORADO(1945); DEVIL BAT'S DAUGHTER, THE(1946); PRAIRIE BADMEN(1946); BORDER FEUD(1947); FABULOUS TEXAN, THE(1947); TAKE ME OUT TO THE BALL GAME(1949); FENCE RIDERS(1950); TRAIN TO TOMBSTONE(1950); NIGHT RAIDERS(1952)
Edward Cassidy
COURAGEOUS AVENGER, THE(1935); CROOKED TRAIL, THE(1936); FACE IN THE FOG, A(1936); FEUD OF THE WEST(1936); ROARIN' GUNS(1936); SONG OF THE GRINGO(1936); SPEED REPORTER(1936); TOLL OF THE DESERT(1936); UNDERCOVER MAN(1936); VALLEY OF THE LAWLESS(1936); COME ON, COWBOYS(1937); GHOST TOWN(1937); HIT THE SADDLE(1937); HITTIN' THE TRAIL(1937); IDAHO KID, THE(1937); LAW AND LEAD(1937); LAWLESS LAND(1937); RIO GRANDE RANGER(1937); SANTA FE BOUND(1937); TEX RIDES WITH THE BOY SCOUTS(1937); TRAILING TROUBLE(1937); CASSIDY OF BAR 20(1938); MAN FROM MUSIC MOUNTAIN(1938); PURPLE VIGILANTES, THE(1938); RED RIVER RANGE(1938); ROLLIN' PLAINS(1938); STARLIGHT OVER TEXAS(1938); UTAH TRAIL(1938); COWBOYS FROM TEXAS(1939); ROVIN' TUMBLEWEEDS(1939); SILVER ON THE SAGE(1939); SON OF FRANKENSTEIN(1939); GAUCHO SERENA-

DE(1940); KNIGHTS OF THE RANGE(1940); RIDERS OF PASCO BASIN(1940); HONKY TONK(1941); WYOMING WILDCAT(1941); ARIZONA ROUNDUP(1942); MAD MONSTER, THE(1942); PHANTOM PLAINSMEN, THE(1942); PIRATES OF THE PRAIRIE(1942); SOMBRERO KID, THE(1942); STARDUST ON THE SAGE(1942); SUNSET ON THE DESERT(1942); AVENGING RIDER, THE(1943); COWBOY IN THE CLOUDS(1943); BOSS OF THE RAWHIDE(1943); FRONTIER OUTLAWS(1944); FUZZY SETTLES DOWN(1944); HIDDEN VALLEY OUTLAWS(1944); PINTO BANDIT, THE(1944); SPOOK TOWN(1944); TUCSON RAIDERS(1944); VALLEY OF VENGEANCE(1944); WHISPERING SKULL, THE(1944); ALONG THE NAVAJO TRAIL(1945); ARSON SQUAD(1945); COLORADO PIONEERS(1945); CORPUS CHRISTI BANDITS(1945); ENEMY OF THE LAW(1945); MARKED FOR MURDER(1945); NAVAJO TRAIL, THE(1945); SHERIFF OF CIMARRON(1945); THREE IN THE SADDLE(1945); UTAH(1945); YOUTH AFLAME(1945); ALIAS BILLY THE KID(1946); AMBUSH TRAIL(1946); DAYS OF BUFFALO BILL(1946); EL PASO KID, THE(1946); NAVAJO KID, THE(1946); ROLL ON TEXAS MOON(1946); STAGECOACH TO DENVER(1946); SUN VALLEY CYCLONE(1946); BUFFALO BILL RIDES AGAIN(1947); HOMESTEADERS OF PARADISE VALLEY(1947); OREGON TRAIL SCOUTS(1947); BOLD FRONTIERSMAN, THE(1948); DESPERADOES OF DODGE CITY(1948); ROUGHSHOD(1949); SAVAGE HORDE, THE(1950); TRAIL OF ROBIN HOOD(1950); BUCKAROO SHERIFF OF TEXAS(1951); MILLION DOLLAR PURSUIT(1951); OKLAHOMA JUSTICE(1951); BLACK HILLS AMBUSH(1952); DESPERADOES OUTPOST(1952); TALK ABOUT A STRANGER(1952); WACO(1952); DREAM WIFE(1953); FIRST TRAVELING SALESLADY, THE(1956)
Misc. Talkies
PECOS KID, THE(1935); RECKLESS BUCKAROO, THE(1935); VENGEANCE OF RANNAH(1936); TRIGGER LAW(1944); ROARING RANGERS(1946); VALLEY OF FEAR(1947)
Ellen Cassidy
Misc. Silents
MILADY O' THE BEAN STALK(1918); LOVE, HONOR AND ?(1919); POOR, DEAR MARGARET KIRBY(1921); DARK SECRETS(1923)
J. M. Cassidy
Silents
GOOSE GIRL, THE(1915)
Jack Cassidy
LOOK IN ANY WINDOW(1961); CHAPMAN REPORT, THE(1962); FBI CODE 98(1964); COCKEYED COWBOYS OF CALICO COUNTY, THE(1970); MR. MAGOO'S HOLIDAY FESTIVAL(1970); BUNNY O'HARE(1971); EIGER SANCTION, THE(1975); W.C. FIELDS AND ME(1976); PRIVATE FILES OF J. EDGAR HOOVER, THE(1978)
James F. Cassidy
SANTA FE STAMPEDE(1938)
Jay Lash Cassidy
END OF AUGUST, THE(1982), ed; WALTZ ACROSS TEXAS(1982), ed
1984
ROADHOUSE 66(1984), ed
Joanna Cassidy
LAUGHING POLICEMAN, THE(1973); OUTFIT, THE(1973); BANK SHOT(1974); NIGHT CHILD(1975, Brit./Ital.); STEPFORD WIVES, THE(1975); STAY HUNGRY(1976); LATE SHOW, THE(1977); STUNTS(1977); OUR WINNING SEASON(1978); GLOVE, THE(1980); NIGHT GAMES(1980); BLADE RUNNER(1982); UNDER FIRE(1983)
Misc. Talkies
GLOVE, THE(1979)
John Cassidy
YANKS(1979)
John "Doc" Cassidy
CARNY(1980)
Katherine Cassidy
FRENCH LINE, THE(1954); SON OF SINBAD(1955)
Martin Cassidy
WHY WOULD I LIE(1980); HALLOWEEN III: SEASON OF THE WITCH(1982)
Mary Cassidy
WHEN THE DALTONS RODE(1940)
Maureen Cassidy
CARELESS YEARS, THE(1957); RUNAWAY DAUGHTERS(1957)
Michael Cassidy
1984
CITY HEAT(1984)
Mike Cassidy
METALSTORM: THE DESTRUCTION OF JARED-SYN(1983)
1984
ROMANCING THE STONE(1984)
Morley F. Cassidy
ON SUCH A NIGHT(1937), w
Patrick Cassidy
OFF THE WALL(1983)
1984
JUST THE WAY YOU ARE(1984)
Regina Cassidy
UNDER AGE(1964)
Richard Cassidy
NOW AND FOREVER(1983, Aus.), w
Robert Cassidy
HIT AND RUN(1957)
Susan Cassidy
TORTURE DUNGEON(1970)
Ted Cassidy
BUTCH CASSIDY AND THE SUNDANCE KID(1969); MACKENNA'S GOLD(1969); LIMIT, THE(1972); SLAMS, THE(1973); HARRY AND WALTER GO TO NEW YORK(1976); LAST REMAKE OF BEAU GESTE, THE(1977); GOIN' COCONUTS(1978)
Misc. Talkies
POOR PRETTY EDDIE(1975); HEARTBREAK MOTEL(1978); SUNSHINE RUN(1979)
William Cassidy
NIGHT IN HEAVEN, A(1983), prod d
William J. Cassidy
ROCKY III(1982), prod d; RISKY BUSINESS(1983), prod d
1984
KARATE KID, THE(1984), prod d

Alan Cassie
FATHOM(1967), set d; WATCHER IN THE WOODS, THE(1980, Brit.), art d; DRAGONSLAYER(1981), art d; LORDS OF DISCIPLINE, THE(1983), art d; PIRATES OF PENZANCE, THE(1983), art d

Allan Cassie
1984
INDIANA JONES AND THE TEMPLE OF DOOM(1984), art d

Iain Cassie
XTRO(1983, Brit.), w

Richard Cassilly
FIDELIO(1970, Ger.)

Barry Cassin
ULYSSES(1967, U.S./Brit.); MC KENZIE BREAK, THE(1970)

Antonio Cassinelli
AIDA(1954, Ital.)

Claudio Cassinelli
CHINA IS NEAR(1968, Ital.); DEVIL IS A WOMAN, THE(1975, Brit./Ital.); SCREAMERS(1978, Ital.); SLAVE OF THE CANNIBAL GOD(1979, Ital.); HERCULES(1983)
Misc. Talkies
LOVE UNDER THE ELMS(1973)

Dolores Cassinelli
Silents
RIGHT TO LIE, THE(1919); ANNE OF LITTLE SMOKY(1921); SECRETS OF PARIS, THE(1922); JAMESTOWN(1923); LEND ME YOUR HUSBAND(1924); UNGUARDED HOUR, THE(1925)
Misc. Silents
LAFAYETTE, WE COME!(1918); UNKNOWN LOVE, THE(1919); VIRTUOUS MODEL, THE(1919); HIDDEN LIGHT(1920); TARNISHED REPUTATIONS(1920); WEB OF DECEIT, THE(1920); CHALLENGE, THE(1922); DANGEROUS MONEY(1924); MIDNIGHT GIRL, THE(1925)

Madeline Cassinelli
Misc. Silents
WITH WINGS OUTSPREAD(1922)

Joe Cassini
WILD GYPSIES(1969), ch

Leonard Cassini
SOLDIER'S TALE, THE(1964, Brit.), p

Nadia Cassini
PULP(1972, Brit.); STARCRASH(1979)

Oleg Cassini
SHANGHAI GESTURE, THE(1941), cos; GHOST AND MRS. MUIR, THE(1942), cos; TALES OF MANHATTAN(1942), cos; RAZOR'S EDGE, THE(1946), cos; THAT WONDERFUL URGE(1948), cos; WHIRLPOOL(1949), cos; NIGHT AND THE CITY(1950, Brit.), cos; WHERE THE SIDEWALK ENDS(1950), a, cos; MATING SEASON, THE(1951), cos; RAMPAGE(1963), cos

Stefania Cassini
COCKTAIL MOLOTOV(1980, Fr.)

John Cassisi
BUGSY MALONE(1976, Brit.)

Ellen Cassity
Silents
OTHER MAN'S WIFE, THE(1919); SHACKLES OF GOLD(1922)
Misc. Silents
VOICE OF DESTINY, THE(1918); CHECKERS(1919); THROUGH THE TOILS(1919); BROADWAY AND HOME(1920); PASSERS-BY(1920); VICE OF FOOLS, THE(1920); HIGHEST BIDDER, THE(1921); MIRACLE OF MANHATTAN, THE(1921)

James C. Cassity
MAN OR GUN(1958), w

David Cassling
UNCLE SCAM(1981)

Judy Cassmore
FOXY DROWN(1974)

Sergio Cassner
MARK OF THE DEVIL(1970, Ger./Brit.), w

Carla Cassola
DEATH RIDES A HORSE(1969, Ital.)

Carlo Cassola
BEBO'S GIRL(1964, Ital.), w; LA VISITA(1966, Ital./Fr.), w

Ann Casson
ESCAPE(1930, Brit.); BACHELOR'S BABY(1932, Brit.); DANCE PRETTY LADY(1932, Brit.); MARRIAGE BOND, THE(1932, Brit.); NUMBER SEVENTEEN(1932, Brit.); SHADOW BETWEEN, THE(1932, Brit.); GEORGE AND MARGARET(1940, Brit.)

Christopher Casson
ZARDOZ(; CAPTAIN LIGHTFOOT(1955); SIEGE OF SIDNEY STREET, THE(1960, Brit.); DEVIL'S AGENT, THE(1962, Brit.); JOHNNY NOBODY(1965, Brit.); EDUCATING RITA(1983)

John Casson
ON THE BEACH(1959)

Lewis Casson
VICTORIA THE GREAT(1937, Brit.); ESCAPE(1930, Brit.); CRIME ON THE HILL(1933, Brit.); LITTLE FRIEND(1934, Brit.); NIGHT CLUB QUEEN(1934, Brit.); CALLING THE TUNE(1936, Brit.); RHODES(1936, Brit.); SIXTY GLORIOUS YEARS(1938, Brit.); SOUTH RIDING(1938, Brit.); WINSLOW BOY, THE(1950); MEN OF THE SEA(1951, Brit.); SHAKE HANDS WITH THE DEVIL(1959, Ireland); UNCLE VANYA(1977, Brit.)

Maxine Casson
LOVE IS A SPLENDID ILLUSION(1970, Brit.); BAWDY ADVENTURES OF TOM JONES, THE(1976, Brit.)

Marc Cassot
DEMONIAQUE(1958, Fr.); GAME OF TRUTH, THE(1961, Fr.); PASSION OF SLOW FIRE, THE(1962, Fr.); OTHER ONE, THE(1967,Fr.)

Renato Casstellani
DREAMS IN A DRAWER(1957, Fr./Ital.), d&w

Emanuele Cassuto
LA NOTTE(1961, Fr./Ital.), p

Joseph Cassuto
HORNET'S NEST(1970)

Edward Cast
DEADLY RECORD(1959, Brit.); TIGER BAY(1959, Brit.); LINDA(1960, Brit.); PROFESSIONALS, THE(1960, Brit.); PAYROLL(1962, Brit.); DREAM MAKER, THE(1963, Brit.); SEVENTY DEADLY PILLS(1964, Brit.); MALPAS MYSTERY, THE(1967, Brit.); CHAIRMAN, THE(1969); 10 RILLINGTON PLACE(1971, Brit.)

Ted Cast
DR. CRIPPEN(1963, Brit.)

Edward Castagna
JOHNNY TROUBLE(1957)

Joe Castagna
THAT TENDER TOUCH(1969)

Bianca Castagnetta
DIVORCE, ITALIAN STYLE(1962, Ital.)

Robert B. Castaine
ATLANTIC CITY(1944)

Robert Castaine
WHERE DO WE GO FROM HERE?(1945)

Claude Castaing
CASQUE D'OR(1956, Fr.)

Dany Castaing
CONFIDENTIALLY YOURS(1983, Fr.)

Jean-Pierre Castaldi
FRENCH CONNECTION 11(1975); MOONRAKER(1979, Brit.)

Anne Castaldini
LONG SHADOW, THE(1961, Brit.)

Paul Castaldini
BOTTOMS UP(1960, Brit.)

Ernest Castaldo
HOUSEHOLDER, THE(1963, US/India)

Bruno Castan
WANDERER, THE(1969, Fr.)

Pulchier Castan
1984
LES COMPERES(1984, Fr.)

Luis Aceves Castaneda
AZTEC MUMMY, THE(1957, Mex.); GINA(1961, Fr./Mex.); SANTO CONTRA EL CEREBRO DIABOLICO zero(1962, Mex.); CURSE OF THE AZTEC MUMMY, THE(1965, Mex.); ROBOT VS. THE AZTEC MUMMY, THE(1965, Mex.); NAZARIN(1968, Mex.); DEATH IN THE GARDEN(1977, Fr./Mex.)

Movita Castaneda
FLYING DOWN TO RIO(1933); MUTINY ON THE BOUNTY(1935); MYSTERIOUS DESPERADO, THE(1949); FEDERAL MAN(1950); PETTY GIRL, THE(1950); SADDLE LEGION(1951)

Jean-Michel Castanie
1984
LE DERNIER COMBAT(1984, Fr.)

Jean Castanier
CRIME OF MONSIEUR LANGE, THE(1936, Fr.), w, set d; PARIS DOES STRANGE THINGS(1957, Fr./Ital.); BOUDU SAVED FROM DROWNING(1967, Fr.), set d

Xavier Castano
GIRL FROM LORRAINE, A(1982, Fr./Switz.), ed

The Castaways
IT'S A BIKINI WORLD(1967)

Ron Casteel
GROUND ZERO(1973)

Mario Castegnaro
ARCH OF TRIUMPH(1948), ed

Colette Castel
TRUTH, THE(1961, Fr./Ital.); DAY AND THE HOUR, THE(1963, Fr./ Ital.); TASTE FOR WOMEN, A(1966, Fr./Ital.)

Jany Castel
ROYAL AFFAIRS IN VERSAILLES(1957, Fr.)

Lillian Castel
STRAIGHT FROM THE HEART(1935)

Lou Castel
BULLET FOR THE GENERAL, A(1967, Ital.); FIST IN HIS POCKET(1968, Ital.); GALILEO(1968, Ital./Bul.); THANK YOU, AUNT(1969, Ital.); NADA GANG, THE(1974, Fr./Ital.); AMERICAN FRIEND, THE(1977, Ger.); EYES, THE MOUTH, THE(1982, Ital./Fr.)

Norma Castel
OPEN SEASON(1974, U.S./Span.)

Robert Castel
TALL BLOND MAN WITH ONE BLACK SHOE, THE(1973, Fr.)

William Castelet
Misc. Silents
BUNCH OF KEYS, A(1915)

Lou Castell
CASSANDRA CROSSING, THE(1977)

Charles Castella
DON'T BE A DUMMY(1932, Brit.); WOMANHOOD(1934, Brit.); ROLLING HOME(1935, Brit.); BITER BIT, THE(1937, Brit.); OLD MOTHER RILEY IN PARIS(1938, Brit.); WE'RE GOING TO BE RICH(1938, Brit.); THAT'S THE TICKET(1940, Brit.)

Donato Castellaneta
LA DOLCE VITA(1961, Ital./Fr.); MANDRAGOLA(1966 Fr./Ital.)

Bruto Castellani
Silents
QUO VADIS?(1913, Ital.)

Franco Castellani
ANGEL WORE RED, THE(1960); OPIATE '67(1967, Fr./Ital.)

Giuseppe Castellani
DIRTY OUTLAWS, THE(1971, Ital.)

Renato Castellani
CUCKOO CLOCK, THE(1938, Ital.), w; UNDER THE SUN OF ROME(1949, Ital.), d, w; ROMEO AND JULIET(1954, Brit.), d&w; AND THE WILD, WILD WOMEN(1961, Ital.), d; MARRIAGE–ITALIAN STYLE(1964, Fr./Ital.), w; MY WIFE'S ENEMY(1967, Ital.), w; KISS THE OTHER SHEIK(1968, Ital./Fr.), w; GHOSTS, ITALIAN STYLE(1969, Ital./Fr.), d, w

Vanni Castellani
SHE AND HE(1969, Ital.), a, set d&cos; THAT SPLENDID NOVEMBER(1971, Ital./Fr.), a, art d

Franco Castellano
TWELVE-HANDED MEN OF MARS, THE(1964, Ital./Span.), d&w; FASCIST, THE(1965, Ital.), w; HOURS OF LOVE, THE(1965, Ital.), w; LITTLE NUNS, THE(1965, Ital.), w; WAR ITALIAN STYLE(1967, Ital.), w; THREE NIGHTS OF LOVE(1969, Ital.), w

Giuseppe Castellano
DEATH RIDES A HORSE(1969, Ital.)

Jason Castellano
1984
BUDDY SYSTEM, THE(1984)

Joe Castellano
1984
NATURAL, THE(1984)

John Castellano
LAST DETAIL, THE(1973)

Richard Castellano
FINE MADNESS, A(1966); LOVERS AND OTHER STRANGERS(1970); GODFATHER, THE(1972); NIGHT OF THE JUGGLER(1980)

Anzo G. Castellari
Misc. Talkies
ANONYMOUS AVENGER, THE(1976, Ital.), d

Enzo G. Castellari [Enzo Girolami]
JOHNNY HAMLET(1972, Ital.), d; NEW BARBARIANS, THE(1983, Ital.), d&w

Enzo Girolami Castellari
1984
WARRIORS OF THE WASTELAND(1984, Ital.), d, w

Bertrand Castelli
THUNDER IN THE SUN(1959); RICHARD(1972), p, w

Delores Castelli
Misc. Talkies
TRAIL TO MEXICO(1946)

Ernst Castelli
CHRONICLE OF ANNA MAGDALENA BACH(1968, Ital., Ger.)

Philippe Castelli
ELUSIVE CORPORAL, THE(1963, Fr.); GALIA(1966, Fr./Ital.)
1984
PAR OU T'ES RENTRE? ON T'A PAS VUE SORTIR(1984, Fr./Tunisia)

R. Castelli
THIS WINE OF LOVE(1948, Ital.), w; MAN COULD GET KILLED, A(1966)

Don Castello
NEW ADVENTURES OF TARZAN(1935); TARZAN AND THE GREEN GODDESS(1938)

Florencio Castello
SOMBRERO(1953); EXTERMINATING ANGEL, THE(1967, Mex.)

William Castello
MAN ON A TIGHTROPE(1953)

Willy Castello
GREAT IMPERSONATION, THE(1935); MELODY TRAIL(1935); SPECIAL AGENT K-7(1937); FOREIGN CORRESPONDENT(1940); MAD YOUTH(1940); WE WERE DANCING(1942)

Peter Castellotti
1984
BROADWAY DANNY ROSE(1984)

Nino Castelnuevo
ANGEL WORE RED, THE(1960); BRUTE AND THE BEAST, THE(1968, Ital.)

Nino Castelnuovo
EVERYBODY GO HOME!(1962, Fr./Ital.); HUNCHBACK OF ROME, THE(1963, Ital.); UMBRELLAS OF CHERBOURG, THE(1964, Fr./Ger.); CAVERN, THE(1965, Ital./Ger.); EYE OF THE NEEDLE, THE(1965, Ital./Fr.); FACTS OF MURDER, THE(1965, Ital.); REWARD, THE(1965); YOUNG WORLD, A(1966, Fr./Ital.); CHASTITY BELT, THE(1968, Ital.); CAMILLE 2000(1969); LES CREATURES(1969, Fr./Swed.); CERTAIN, VERY CERTAIN, AS A MATTER OF FACT... PROBABLE(1970, Ital,); FIVE MAN ARMY, THE(1970, Ital.); PSYCHOUT FOR MURDER(1971, Arg./Ital.)

Mario Castelnuovo-Tedesco
DOWN TO EARTH(1947), m; TIME OUT OF MIND(1947), m; LOVES OF CARMEN, THE(1948), m; EVERYBODY DOES IT(1949), m; MASK OF THE AVENGER(1951), m; BRIGAND, THE(1952), m

Jacques Castelot
CHILDREN OF PARADISE(1945, Fr.); LES MAINS SALES(1954, Fr.); OBSESSION(1954, Fr./Ital.); COUNT OF MONTE-CRISTO(1955, Fr., Ital.); NANA(1957, Fr./Ital.); FOLIES BERGERE(1958, Fr.); FORBIDDEN FRUIT(1959, Fr.); MARIE OF THE ISLES(1960, Fr.); LAFAYETTE(1963, Fr.)

Araceli Ladewuen Castelun
1984
UNDER THE VOLCANO(1984)

Movita Castenada
HURRICANE, THE(1937); FORT APACHE(1948); RED LIGHT(1949); KIM(1950); WAGONMASTER(1950); SOLDIERS THREE(1951)

Movita Castenda
RIDE, VAQUERO!(1953)

Movita Casteneda
FURIES, THE(1950)

Castel Casti
CONFIDENTIALLY YOURS(1983, Fr.)

Countess Iphigeni Castiglioni
LIFE OF EMILE ZOLA, THE(1937)

Iphigenie Castiglioni
STORY OF LOUIS PASTEUR, THE(1936); MAYTIME(1937); SEPTEMBER AFFAIR(1950); REAR WINDOW(1954); THREE COINS IN THE FOUNTAIN(1954); FUNNY FACE(1957); WILD IS THE WIND(1957); COMANCHEROS, THE(1961); ROME ADVENTURE(1962)

Lynn Castile
MARSHAL OF AMARILLO(1948)

Patricio Castilla
SELF-PORTRAIT(1973, U.S./Chile)

G. Castilli
AIDA(1954, Ital.), w

Chuy Castillion
PAN-AMERICANA(1945)

Jesus Castillion
PAN-AMERICANA(1945)

Castillo
YELLOW ROLLS-ROYCE, THE(1965, Brit.), cos

Alex Castillo
HEAT(1970, Arg.)

Antonio Castillo
NICHOLAS AND ALEXANDRA(1971, Brit.), cos

Aurora Castillo
TWO FLAGS WEST(1950)

Braulio Castillo
HARBOR LIGHTS(1963)

Candy Castillo
MODERN ROMANCE(1981)

Carmen Castillo
Silents
WOMAN WISE(1928)

Enrique Castillo
BORDERLINE(1980); LOSIN' IT(1983)
1984
EL NORTE(1984)

Fernando Castillo
WARRIORS, THE(1979)

Gerald Castillo
HERO AT LARGE(1980)

Gloria Castillo
NIGHT OF THE HUNTER, THE(1955); VANISHING AMERICAN, THE(1955); INVASION OF THE SAUCER MEN(1957); REFORM SCHOOL GIRL(1957); RUNAWAY DAUGHTERS(1957); TEENAGE MONSTER(1958); YOU'VE GOT TO BE SMART(1967)

Jessica Castillo
GLORIA(1980)

Leo Castillo
THREE VIOLENT PEOPLE(1956)

M. du P. Castillo
BRAVE BULLS, THE(1951)

Mary Lou Castillo
SALT OF THE EARTH(1954)

Michael [Miguel del] Castillo
ONE STEP TO HELL(1969, U.S./Ital./Span.)

Toto Castillo
1984
MISSING IN ACTION(1984), art d

Viki Castillo
EMBALMER, THE(1966, Ital.)

Jesus Castillon
TROPIC HOLIDAY(1938)

Mario Castillon
FOXTROT(1977, Mex./Swiss)

Iphigenie Castinglioni
VALERIE(1957)

Castle
STORY OF VERNON AND IRENE CASTLE, THE(1939), cos

Agnes Castle
SWEET KITTY BELLAIRS(1930), w
Silents
SECRET ORCHARD(1915), w; ROSE OF THE WORLD(1918), w

Anita Castle
WEST OF SONORA(1948); JUNCTION CITY(1952)

Ann Castle
V.I.P.s, THE(1963, Brit.); GUTTER GIRLS(1964, Brit.)

Connie Castle
LAS VEGAS STORY, THE(1952)

David Castle
WHERE THE BUFFALO ROAM(1980)

Dennis Castle
ROSSITER CASE, THE(1950, Brit.); SING ALONG WITH ME(1952, Brit.); KEY MAN, THE(1957, Brit.); SCHOOL FOR SEX(1969, Brit.)

Dick Castle
FOR SINGLES ONLY(1968)

Dolores Castle
GANGSTER, THE(1947); WEST TO GLORY(1947); CRY OF THE CITY(1948); JUNGLE GODDESS(1948); CRISS CROSS(1949); GIRL FROM JONES BEACH, THE(1949); RED PONY, THE(1949); PAINTING THE CLOUDS WITH SUNSHINE(1951); STARLIFT(1951); STRIP, THE(1951)

Don Castle
LOVE FINDS ANDY HARDY(1938); OUT WEST WITH THE HARDYS(1938); RICH MAN, POOR GIRL(1938); YOUNG DR. KILDARE(1938); HARDYS RIDE HIGH, THE(1939); NICK CARTER, MASTER DETECTIVE(1939); THESE GLAMOUR GIRLS(1939); THUNDER AFLOAT(1939); I TAKE THIS WOMAN(1940); NORTHWEST PASSAGE(1940); STRIKE UP THE BAND(1940); SUSAN AND GOD(1940); WE WHO ARE YOUNG(1940); POWER DIVE(1941); WORLD PREMIERE(1941); YOU'RE THE ONE(1941); STAR SPANGLED RHYTHM(1942); TOMBSTONE, THE TOWN TOO TOUGH TO DIE(1942); WAKE ISLAND(1942); SEARCHING WIND, THE(1946); BORN TO SPEED(1947); GUILTY, THE(1947); HIGH TIDE(1947); INVISIBLE WALL, THE(1947); LIGHTHOUSE(1947); ROSES ARE RED(1947); SEVEN WERE SAVED(1947); I WOULDN'T BE IN YOUR SHOES(1948); MADONNA OF THE DESERT(1948); PERILOUS WATERS(1948); STRIKE IT RICH(1948); WHO KILLED "DOC" ROBBIN?(1948); STAMPEDE(1949); MOTOR PATROL(1950); BIG LAND, THE(1957); GUNFIGHT AT THE O.K. CORRAL(1957)
Misc. Talkies
IN SELF DEFENSE(1947)

Donald Castle
Silents
AUTUMN OF PRIDE, THE(1921, Brit.)

Edmond Castle
LA MARSEILLAISE(1938, Fr.)
Egerton Castle
SWEET KITTY BELLAIRS(1930), w
Silents
SECRET ORCHARD(1915), w; ROSE OF THE WORLD(1918), w
Gabe Castle
SNIPER'S RIDGE(1961)
Gene Castle
GOODBYE GIRL, THE(1977); NEW YORK, NEW YORK(1977); KISS ME GOOD-
BYE(1982), a, ch; HYSTERICAL(1983)
Hubert Castle
SENSATIONS OF 1945(1944)
Irene Castle
STORY OF VERNON AND IRENE CASTLE, THE(1939), w
Silents
AMATEUR WIFE, THE(1920); NO TRESPASSING(1922); SLIM SHOULDERS(1922);
BROADWAY AFTER DARK(1924)
Misc. Silents
WHIRL OF LIFE, THE(1915); MARK OF CAIN, THE(1917); STRANDED IN AR-
CADY(1917); CONVICT 993(1918); FIRST LAW, THE(1918); GIRL FROM BOHEMIA,
THE(1918); HILLCREST MYSTERY, THE(1918); MYSTERIOUS CLIENT, THE(1918);
VENGEANCE IS MINE(1918); FIRING LINE, THE(1919); INVISIBLE BOND,
THE(1920); FRENCH HEELS(1922)
Jack Castle
Silents
TERROR OF BAR X, THE(1927)
James W. Castle
Misc. Silents
HER VOCATION(1915), d; TEST, THE(1915), d
Jay Castle
DISTANCE(1975), w
Joan Castle
HUSH MONEY(1931); MR. LEMON OF ORANGE(1931); YOUNG SINNERS(1931);
SING A JINGLE(1943)
John Castle
CRIMSON CIRCLE, THE(1930, Brit.); PASSWORD IS COURAGE, THE(1962, Brit.),
d&w; BLOW-UP(1966, Brit.); STING OF DEATH(1966); LION IN WINTER, THE(1968,
Brit.); PROMISE, THE(1969, Brit.); MADE(1972, Brit.); MAN OF LA MANCHA(1972);
ANTONY AND CLEOPATRA(1973, Brit.); ELIZA FRASER(1976, Aus.); INCREDIBLE
SARAH, THE(1976, Brit.); EAGLE'S WING(1979, Brit.); NEVER NEVER LAND(1982)
Lillian Castle
CHAMPAGNE WALTZ(1937); THEY GOT ME COVERED(1943); EXILE, THE(1947);
SET-UP, THE(1949)
Linda Castle
SHAKEDOWN, THE(1960, Brit.); SHE KNOWS Y'KNOW(1962, Brit.); YOUNG,
WILLING AND EAGER(1962, Brit.); FRIENDS AND NEIGHBORS(1963, Brit.)
Mary Castle
TOUGHER THEY COME, THE(1950); CRIMINAL LAWYER(1951); PRAIRIE
ROUNDUP(1951); TEXANS NEVER CRY(1951); WHEN THE REDSKINS RODE(1951);
EIGHT IRON MEN(1952); LAWLESS BREED, THE(1952); GUNSMOKE(1953); WHITE
FIRE(1953, Brit.); CRASHING LAS VEGAS(1956); YAQUI DRUMS(1956); LAST
STAGECOACH WEST, THE(1957); JAILBREAKERS, THE(1960); THREAT, THE(1960)
Maxine Castle
MONKEY BUSINESS(1931)
Michael Castle
VAN NUYS BLVD.(1979); DON'T ANSWER THE PHONE(1980), w
Michael D. Castle
BEACH GIRLS(1982), p
1984
WEEKEND PASS(1984), p
Mike Castle
CURIOUS FEMALE, THE(1969); GAS-S-S-S!(1970)
Nicholas Castle
HOLD THAT CO-ED(1938), ch; STRAIGHT, PLACE AND SHOW(1938), ch; UP THE
RIVER(1938), ch; WHILE NEW YORK SLEEPS(1938), ch; YOUNG PEOPLE(1940), ch;
YOUTH WILL BE SERVED(1940), ch
Nick Castle
LIFE BEGINS IN COLLEGE(1937), ch; LOVE AND HISSES(1937), ch; JOSET-
TE(1938), ch; LITTLE MISS BROADWAY(1938), ch; RASCALS(1938), ch; SALLY,
IRENE AND MARY(1938), ch; EVERYTHING HAPPENS AT NIGHT(1939), staging;
SWANEE RIVER(1939), ch; DOWN ARGENTINE WAY(1940), ch; BUCK PRIVA-
TES(1941), ch; HELLZAPOPPIN'(1941), ch; IN THE NAVY(1941), ch; ROOKIES ON
PARADE(1941), ch; SAN ANTONIO ROSE(1941), ch; JOAN OF OZARK(1942), ch;
MAYOR OF 44TH STREET, THE(1942), ch; MISS ANNIE ROONEY(1942), ch; MOON-
LIGHT MASQUERADE(1942), ch; RIDE 'EM COWBOY(1942), ch; AROUND THE
WORLD(1943), ch; HIT PARADE OF 1943(1943), ch; JOHNNY DOUGHBOY(1943), ch;
NOBODY'S DARLING(1943), ch; TWO SENORITAS FROM CHICAGO(1943), ch;
WHAT'S BUZZIN COUSIN?(1943), ch; SHOW BUSINESS(1944), ch; SOMETHING
FOR THE BOYS(1944), ch; MEXICANA(1945), ch; NOB HILL(1945), ch; EARL CAR-
ROLL SKETCHBOOK(1946), ch; SUSPENSE(1946), ch; THRILL OF BRAZIL,
THE(1946), ch; LUXURY LINER(1948), ch; SAXON CHARM, THE(1948), ch; SHAM-
ROCK HILL(1949), ch; YOU'RE MY EVERYTHING(1949), ch; SUMMER
STOCK(1950), ch; RICH, YOUNG AND PRETTY(1951), ch; ROYAL WEDDING(1951),
ch; STRIP, THE(1951), ch; EVERYTHING I HAVE IS YOURS(1952), ch; SKIRTS
AHOY!(1952), ch; STARS AND STRIPES FOREVER(1952), ch; HERE COME THE
GIRLS(1953), ch; SWEETHEARTS ON PARADE(1953), ch; LIVING IT UP(1954), ch;
RED GARTERS(1954), ch; THREE RING CIRCUS(1954), ch; ARTISTS AND MO-
DELS(1955); SEVEN LITTLE FOYS, THE(1955), ch; ANYTHING GOES(1956), ch;
BUNDLE OF JOY(1956), ch; PARDNERS(1956), ch; THAT CERTAIN FEELING(1956),
ch; DELICATE DELINQUENT, THE(1957), ch; ROCK-A-BYE BABY(1958), ch; SING,
BOY, SING(1958), ch; BELLBOY, THE(1960), ch; CINDERFELLA(1960), ch; ERRAND
BOY, THE(1961), ch; POCKETFUL OF MIRACLES(1961), ch; STATE FAIR(1962), ch;
BIRDS AND THE BEES, THE(1965), ch; HALLOWEEN(1978), ch; SKATETOWN, U.S-
.A.(1979), w; ESCAPE FROM NEW YORK(1981), w; T.A.G.: THE ASSASSINATION
GAME(1982), d&w
1984
LAST STARFIGHTER, THE(1984), d

Peggie Castle
AIR CADET(1951); GOLDEN HORDE, THE(1951); PAYMENT ON DEMAND(1951);
PRINCE WHO WAS A THIEF, THE(1951); HAREM GIRL(1952); INVASION U.S-
.A.(1952); WAGONS WEST(1952); COW COUNTRY(1953); I, THE JURY(1953); SON OF
BELLE STARR(1953); 99 RIVER STREET(1953); JESSE JAMES' WOMEN(1954);
LONG WAIT, THE(1954); OVERLAND PACIFIC(1954); WHITE ORCHID, THE(1954);
YELLOW TOMAHAWK, THE(1954); FINGER MAN(1955); TALL MAN RIDING(1955);
TARGET ZERO(1955); MIRACLE IN THE RAIN(1956); OKLAHOMA WOMAN,
THE(1956); QUINCANNON, FRONTIER SCOUT(1956); TWO-GUN LADY(1956); BACK
FROM THE DEAD(1957); COUNTERFEIT PLAN, THE(1957, Brit.); HELL'S CROSS-
ROADS(1957); SEVEN HILLS OF ROME, THE(1958)
Peggy Castle
WOMAN IN HIDING(1949); BUCCANEER'S GIRL(1950); I WAS A SHOPLIF-
TER(1950); BEGINNING OF THE END(1957)
Richard Castle
RUNNING WILD(1955); SIX BRIDGES TO CROSS(1955); TO HELL AND BACK(1955)
Robert Castle
Silents
SINGLE STANDARD, THE(1929)
Roy Castle
HELLO LONDON(1958, Brit.); DR. TERROR'S HOUSE OF HORRORS(1965, Brit.);
DR. WHO AND THE DALEKS(1965, Brit.); PLANK, THE(1967, Brit.); CARRY ON, UP
THE KHYBER(1968, Brit.)
Ruth Castle
HARPOON(1948)
Toni [Mary] Castle
MEXICAN HAYRIDE(1948)
Vernon Castle
Misc. Silents
WHIRL OF LIFE, THE(1915)
Walter H. Castle
BEAT GENERATION, THE(1959), ph; BIG OPERATOR, THE(1959), ph
Wayne Castle
IDOL OF THE CROWDS(1937)
William C. Castle
DAY OF THE LOCUST, THE(1975)
William Castle
MAN WHO CRIED WOLF, THE(1937); HE STAYED FOR BREAKFAST(1940); LADY
IN QUESTION, THE(1940); NORTH TO THE KLONDIKE(1942), w; CHANCE OF A
LIFETIME, THE(1943), d; KLONDIKE KATE(1944), d; MARK OF THE WHISTLER,
THE(1944), d; SHE'S A SOLDIER TOO(1944), d; WHEN STRANGERS MARRY(1944),
d; WHISTLER, THE(1944), d; CRIME DOCTOR'S WARNING(1945), d; VOICE OF THE
WHISTLER(1945), d, w; CRIME DOCTOR'S MAN HUNT(1946), d; JUST BEFORE
DAWN(1946), d; MYSTERIOUS INTRUDER(1946), d; CRIME DOCTOR'S GAM-
BLE(1947), d; GENTLEMAN FROM NOWHERE, THE(1948), d; TEXAS, BROOKLYN
AND HEAVEN(1948), d; JOHNNY STOOL PIGEON(1949), d; UNDERTOW(1949), d;
IT'S A SMALL WORLD(1950), d, w; CAVE OF OUTLAWS(1951), d; FAT MAN,
THE(1951), d; HOLLYWOOD STORY(1951), d; CHARGE OF THE LANCERS(1953), d;
CONQUEST OF COCHISE(1953), d; SERPENT OF THE NILE(1953),
d; SLAVES OF BABYLON(1953), d; BATTLE OF ROGUE RIVER(1954), d; DRUMS
OF TAHITI(1954), d; IRON GLOVE, THE(1954), d; JESSE JAMES VERSUS THE
DALTONS(1954), d; LAW VS. BILLY THE KID, THE(1954), d; MASTERSON OF
KANSAS(1954), d; SARACEN BLADE, THE(1954), d; AMERICANO, THE(1955), d;
DUEL ON THE MISSISSIPPI(1955), d; GUN THAT WON THE WEST, THE(1955), d;
NEW ORLEANS UNCENSORED(1955), d; HOUSTON STORY, THE(1956), d; URANI-
UM BOOM(1956), d; HOUSE ON HAUNTED HILL(1958), p&d; MACABRE(1958),
p&d; TINGLER, THE(1959), p&d; THIRTEEN GHOSTS(1960), p&d; HOMICI-
DAL(1961), a, p&d; MR. SARDONICUS(1961), a, p&d; ZOTZ!(1962), p&d; OLD DARK
HOUSE, THE(1963, Brit.), p, d; THIRTEEN FRIGHTENED GIRLS(1963), p&d;
NIGHT WALKER, THE(1964), p&d; STRAIT-JACKET(1964), p&d; I SAW WHAT YOU
DID(1965), p&d; BUSYBODY, THE(1967), p&d; SPIRIT IS WILLING, THE(1967),
p&d; PROJECT X(1968), p, d; ROSEMARY'S BABY(1968), a, p; RIOT(1969), p;
SHANKS(1974), a, d; BUG(1975), p, w; SHAMPOO(1975)
Misc. Talkies
RETURN OF RUSTY, THE(1946), d
Sherle Castle [Mrs. Edgar G. Ulmer]
THUNDER OVER TEXAS(1934), w
Robert Castleberry
HARD TIMES(1975)
Mary Castleman
Silents
ROMANCE OF HAPPY VALLEY, A(1919), w
William Allen Castleman
TRADER HORNEE(1970), p; WRESTLER, THE(1974), m
Misc. Talkies
BUMMER(1973), d; JOHNNY FIRECLOUD(1975), d
William Castleman
BIG BIRD CAGE, THE(1972), m
Ross Allen Castlen
WOMAN IN RED, THE(1935)
Mario Castlenuovo-Tedesco
LONG WAIT, THE(1954), m
Lord Castlerosse
WINGS AND THE WOMAN(1942, Brit.), w
Viscount Castlerosse
BLAME THE WOMAN(1932, Brit.), w; REMARKABLE MR. KIPPS(1942, Brit.);
YOUNG MR. PITT, THE(1942, Brit.), w
Neil Castles
THUNDER IN CAROLINA(1960)
Barbara Castleton
Silents
ON TRIAL(1917); JUST SYLVIA(1918); MAN WHO TURNED WHITE, THE(1919);
BRANDING IRON, THE(1920); OUT OF THE STORM(1920); SHAMS OF SOCIE-
TY(1921); STREETS OF NEW YORK, THE(1922); NET, THE(1923)
Misc. Silents
FOR THE FREEDOM OF THE WORLD(1917); EMPTY POCKETS(1918); HEART OF
A GIRL(1918); HEREDITY(1918); PARENTAGE(1918); VENGEANCE(1918); ROUGH-
NECK, THE(1919); SILVER KING, THE(1919); WHAT LOVE FORGIVES(1919); DAN-
GEROUS DAYS(1920); DANGEROUS HOURS(1920); CHILD THOU GAVEST ME,
THE(1921); FALSE FRONTS(1922)

Paul A. Castleton
BANDIT OF SHERWOOD FOREST, THE(1946), w
Ralph Jarvis Caston
STALAG 17(1953)
Ana Castor
DIABOLICAL DR. Z, THE(1966 Span./Fr.); WEEKEND, ITALIAN STYLE(1967, Fr./Ital./Span.); NARCO MEN, THE(1969, Span./Ital.)
Chris Castor
NO PLACE FOR JENNIFER(1950, Brit.)
Amedeo Castracane
HORNET'S NEST(1970)
John Castranova
DIRTY MARY, CRAZY LARRY(1974)
Thomas Castranova
BALTIMORE BULLET, THE(1980)
Jose G. Castrillo
THAT HOUSE IN THE OUTSKIRTS(1980, Span.), w
Giselda Castrini
AVANTI!(1972)
Arturo Bigoton Castro
CHIQUTTO PERO PICOSO(1967, Mex.)
Bob Castro
LEATHER GLOVES(1948); HOUSE OF STRANGERS(1949); JEOPARDY(1953); SECOND CHANCE(1953)
Carlos Castro
GLORIA(1980)
Emmanuelle Castro
1984
GABRIELA(1984, Braz.), ed
Fidel Castro
HOLIDAY IN MEXICO(1946)
Isabelita Castro
MEDAL FOR BENNY, A(1945)
Israel Castro
GLORIA(1980)
Luis Castro
WITCH WITHOUT A BROOM, A(1967, U.S./Span.), spec eff; DESPERATE ONES, THE(1968 U.S./Span.)
Raul Castro
LIGHT AT THE EDGE OF THE WORLD, THE(1971, U.S./Span./Lichtenstein); VALDEZ IS COMING(1971); CHATO'S LAND(1972)
Raul Medoza Castro
EL CONDOR(1970)
Alicia Castro-Leal
UP THE SANDBOX(1972)
To Castronova
LEPKE(1975, U.S./Israel)
Tom Castronova
MAD DOG COLL(1961)
Nancy Caswell
SCAREHEADS(1931)
Silents
KINGDOM OF LOVE, THE(1918)
Misc. Silents
UNDER CRIMSON SKIES(1920)
Ozzie Caswell
BOMBA AND THE HIDDEN CITY(1950), md; COUNTY FAIR(1950), m; LOST VOLCANO, THE(1950), m, md; MOTOR PATROL(1950), md; BLUE BLOOD(1951), m
Jacqueline Cat
WHEREVER SHE GOES(1953, Aus.)
Cat Stevens and the Can
DEEP END(1970 Ger./U.S.), m
Francisco Catala
1984
DEMONS IN THE GARDEN(1984, Span.)
Muriel Catala
VERDICT(1975, Fr./Ital.)
Joe Catalanatto
TOWN THAT DREADED SUNDOWN, THE(1977), a, spec eff
Catalano
PEARLS OF THE CROWN(1938, Fr.)
Clare Catalano
MERCHANT OF SLAVES(1949, Ital.), titles; PEDDLIN' IN SOCIETY(1949, Ital.), titles; BITTER RICE(1950, Ital.), titles; NEOPOLITAN CAROUSEL(1961, Ital.), titles
Elisabeta Catalano
8 ½(1963, Ital.)
Rolando Catalano
VILLAGE, THE(1953, Brit./Switz.)
Rudy Cataldi
SHINBONE ALLEY(1971), anim
Gaspare Cataldo
DUEL WITHOUT HONOR(1953, Ital.), w
Clare Cataleno
WHITE LINE, THE(1952, Ital.), w
Ennio Catalfamo
SUPERFLY T.N.T.(1973)
Catalina
NEST, THE(1982, Span.)
The Catalinas
MOONSHINE MOUNTAIN(1964)
Ettore Catallucci
MAGIC WORLD OF TOPO GIGIO, THE(1961, Ital.), spec eff; GOSPEL ACCORDING TO ST. MATTHEW, THE(1966, Fr., Ital.), spec eff
Bruco Cataneo
AUGUSTINE OF HIPPO(1973, Ital.)
Antonio Catania
WHITE LINE, THE(1952, Ital.)

Brigitte Catapano
THEY ALL LAUGHED(1981)
Johnnie Catcher
CURE FOR LOVE, THE(1950, Brit.)
Johnny Catcher
MURDER IN REVERSE(1946, Brit.); MR. POTTS GOES TO MOSCOW(1953, Brit.)
Bill Catching
NORTH BY NORTHWEST(1959); OPERATION CIA(1965); RIDE BEYOND VENGEANCE(1966); HEAVEN WITH A GUN(1969); RUN, ANGEL, RUN(1969), stunts; MAN WITH BOGART'S FACE, THE(1980)
Dorothy Catching
METEOR(1979)
Dottie Catching
DEAD AND BURIED(1981)
William Catching
MAN FROM LARAMIE, THE(1955)
Frank Catchlove
KANGAROO(1952)
Eve Catchpole
MURDER IN REVERSE(1946, Brit.), ed
Gertrudien Cate
LAST CHANCE, THE(1945, Switz.)
Jacques Catelain
ENTENTE CORDIALE(1939, Fr.); THIS LOVE OF OURS(1945)
Jaque Catelain
LA MARSEILLAISE(1938, Fr.); FRENCH CANCAN(1956, Fr.); PARIS DOES STRANGE THINGS(1957, Fr./Ital.)
Misc. Silents
LE TORRENT(1918, Fr.); ROSE FRANCE(1919, Fr.); LE CARNIVAL DES VERITES(1920, Fr.); L'HOMME DU LARGE(1920, Fr.); ELDORADO(1921, Fr.); DON JUAN ET FAUST(1923, Fr.); KOENIGSMARK(1923, Fr.); LA MARCHAND DE PLAISIR(1923, Fr.), a, d; L'INHUMAINE(1923, Fr.); LA GALERIE DES MONSTRES(1924, Fr.), d; LE PRINCE CHARMANT(1925, Fr.); LE DIABLE AU COEUR(1928, Fr.); L'OCCIDENT(1928, Fr.)
Sergio Catellani
BLACK SPIDER, THE(1983, Swit.)
Ralph Catellanos
Misc. Talkies
WEAPONS OF DEATH(1982)
Phil Catelli
Misc. Talkies
CUTTING LOOSE(1980)
Victor A. Catena
FISTFUL OF DOLLARS, A(1964, Ital./Ger./Span.), w; SANDOKAN THE GREAT(1964, Fr./Ital./Span.), w
Luciano Catenacci
KILL BABY KILL(1966, Ital.), p; BIG AND THE BAD, THE(1971, Ital./Fr./Span.); TWO SUPER COPS(1978, Ital.); LION OF THE DESERT(1981, Libya/Brit.)
John Cater
DECLINE AND FALL... OF A BIRD WATCHER(1969, Brit.); ABOMINABLE DR. PHIBES, THE(1971, Brit.); LOOT(1971, Brit.); DOCTOR PHIBES RISES AGAIN(1972, Brit.); CAPTAIN KRONOS: VAMPIRE HUNTER(1974, Brit.); RISING DAMP(1980, Brit.)
Carmelina Caterina
DAWN(1979, Aus.)
Lina Caterini
LA STRADA(1956, Ital.), ed
Albert Cates
MISSING(1982)
Darren Cates
TEX(1982)
G. Lewis Cates
LAST MARRIED COUPLE IN AMERICA, THE(1980)
Gilbert Cates
I NEVER SANG FOR MY FATHER(1970), p&d; SUMMER WISHES, WINTER DREAMS(1973), d; ONE SUMMER LOVE(1976), p&d; PROMISE, THE(1979), d; LAST MARRIED COUPLE IN AMERICA, THE(1980), d; OH GOD! BOOK II(1980), p&d
Jim Cates
Misc. Talkies
DEATH RIDERS(1976)
Joe Cates
EDDIE AND THE CRUISERS(1983)
Joseph Cates
GIRL OF THE NIGHT(1960), d; WHO KILLED TEDDY BEAR?(1965), d; FAT SPY(1966), d
Madelyn Cates
DEVIL AND MAX DEVLIN, THE(1981); JEKYLL AND HYDE...TOGETHER AGAIN(1982)
Madlyn Cates
PRODUCERS, THE(1967)
Marie Louise Cates
MADAME CURIE(1943)
Phoebe Cates
FAST TIMES AT RIDGEMONT HIGH(1982); PARADISE(1982); PRIVATE SCHOOL(1983)
1984
GREMLINS(1984)
Countess Vera Cathcart
Silents
WOMAN TEMPTED, THE(1928, Brit.), w
Daniel Cathcart
LAST GANGSTER, THE(1937), art d; CASS TIMBERLANE(1947), art d; LAW AND THE LADY, THE(1951), art d
Daniel B. Cathcart
LET FREEDOM RING(1939), art d; 6000 ENEMIES(1939), art d; I LOVE YOU AGAIN(1940), art d; DR. JEKYLL AND MR. HYDE(1941), art d; TWO-FACED WOMAN(1941), art d, set d; ZIEGFELD GIRL(1941), art d; WHITE CARGO(1942), art d; THOUSANDS CHEER(1943), art d; KISMET(1944), art d; LOST IN A HAREM(1944), art d; WEEKEND AT THE WALDORF(1945), art d; TILL THE CLOUDS ROLL BY(1946), art d; TWO SISTERS FROM BOSTON(1946), art d; UNFINISHED DANCE,-

THE(1947), art d; B. F.'S DAUGHTER(1948), art d; JULIA MISBEHAVES(1948), art d; TAKE ME OUT TO THE BALL GAME(1949), art d; THAT FORSYTE WOMAN(1949), art d; HAPPY YEARS, THE(1950), art d; MRS. O'MALLEY AND MR. MALONE(1950), art d; PLEASE BELIEVE ME(1950), art d; SIDE STREET(1950), art d; TOAST OF NEW ORLEANS, THE(1950), art d; INSIDE STRAIGHT(1951), art d; WESTWARD THE WOMEN(1951), art d; SKIRTS AHOY!(1952), art d; WASHINGTON STORY(1952), art d; DREAM WIFE(1953), art d; GLASS SLIPPER, THE(1955), art d; INTERRUPTED MELODY(1955), art d; GABY(1956), art d; OPPOSITE SEX, THE(1956), art d; SEVENTH SIN, THE(1957), art d; LAW AND JAKE WADE, THE(1958), art d; HANGING TREE, THE(1959), art d

Daniel R. Cathcart
SOMBRERO(1953), art d

Darrell Cathcart
SEABO(1978), ph; WOLFMAN(1979), ph; LIVING LEGEND(1980), ph; FINAL EXAM(1981), ph

Darryl Cathcart
LADY GREY(1980), ph
1984
RARE BREED(1984), ph

Dick Cathcart
DRAGNET(1954); PETE KELLY'S BLUES(1955); BATTLE STATIONS(1956); LAST TIME I SAW ARCHIE, THE(1961)

S. L. Cathcart-Jones
CAPTAINS OF THE CLOUDS(1942)

Margaret Cathell
Misc. Talkies
BLUE SEXTET(1972)

Willa Cather
LOST LADY, A(1934), w
Silents
LOST LADY, A(1924), w

Web Catherfield
REINCARNATE, THE(1971, Can.), cos

George Cathery
RUN ACROSS THE RIVER(1961)

Dalton Cathey
1984
BREAKIN'(1984)

John Cathey
AVALANCHE(1978)

Ralph Cathey
WHAT A MAN!(1944)

Dermot Cathie
THEY CAME FROM BEYOND SPACE(1967, Brit.)

George Cathrey
ETERNALLY YOURS(1939); RAFFLES(1939); FOREIGN CORRESPONDENT(1940); PARIS CALLING(1941)

Iphigenie Catiglioni
CONQUEST OF SPACE(1955)

Patrice Catineau
GERVAISE(1956, Fr.)

Patrice Catineaud
GERVAISE(1956, Fr,)

Clare Catlano
WITHOUT PITY(1949, Ital.), titles

Lloyd Catlett
TRON(1982)

Lorenzo Catlett
MURDER A LA MOD(1968)

Loyd Catlett
LAST PICTURE SHOW, THE(1971); WINTER KILLS(1979); AMERICAN SUCCESS COMPANY, THE(1980); HALLOWEEN III: SEASON OF THE WITCH(1982); 48 HOURS(1982)

Mary Jo Catlett
SEMI-TOUGH(1977); CHAMP, THE(1979); BEACH GIRLS(1982); BEST LITTLE WHOREHOUSE IN TEXAS, THE(1982); O'HARA'S WIFE(1983)

Walter Catlett
MARRIED IN HOLLYWOOD(1929); WHY LEAVE HOME?(1929), a, w; BIG PARTY, THE(1930); FLORODORA GIRL, THE(1930); GOLDEN CALF, THE(1930); HAPPY DAYS(1930); LET'S GO PLACES(1930); FRONT PAGE, THE(1931); MAKER OF MEN(1931); PALMY DAYS(1931); PLATINUM BLONDE(1931); BIG CITY BLUES(1932); COCK OF THE AIR(1932); EXPERT, THE(1932); IT'S TOUGH TO BE FAMOUS(1932); OKAY AMERICA(1932); RAIN(1932); ROCKABYE(1932); SPORT PARADE, THE(1932); ARIZONA TO BROADWAY(1933); MAMA LOVES PAPA(1933); ONLY YESTERDAY(1933); PRIVATE JONES(1933); CAPTAIN HATES THE SEA, THE(1934); OLSEN'S BIG MOMENT(1934); UNKNOWN BLONDE(1934); AFFAIR OF SUSAN(1935); EVERY NIGHT AT EIGHT(1935); LIGHTNING STRIKES TWICE(1935); TALE OF TWO CITIES, A(1935); BANJO ON MY KNEE(1936); CAIN AND MABEL(1936); FOLLOW YOUR HEART(1936); FOUR DAYS WONDER(1936); MR. DEEDS GOES TO TOWN(1936); SING ME A LOVE SONG(1936); WE WENT TO COLLEGE(1936); DANGER–LOVE AT WORK(1937); LOVE IS NEWS(1937); LOVE UNDER FIRE(1937); ON THE AVENUE(1937); VARSITY SHOW(1937); WAKE UP AND LIVE(1937); BRINGING UP BABY(1938); EVERY DAY'S A HOLIDAY(1938); EXILE EXPRESS(1939); GOING PLACES(1939); KID NIGHTINGALE(1939); ZAZA(1939); COMIN' ROUND THE MOUNTAIN(1940); HALF A SINNER(1940); LI'L ABNER(1940); PINOCCHIO(1940); POP ALWAYS PAYS(1940); QUARTERBACK, THE(1940); SPRING PARADE(1940); BAD MEN OF MISSOURI(1941); HELLO SUCKER(1941); HONEYMOON FOR THREE(1941); HORROR ISLAND(1941); IT STARTED WITH EVE(1941); MANPOWER(1941); MILLION DOLLAR BABY(1941); REMEDY FOR RICHES(1941); SING ANOTHER CHORUS(1941); STEEL AGAINST THE SKY(1941); UNFINISHED BUSINESS(1941); WILD MAN OF BORNEO, THE(1941); YOU'RE THE ONE(1941); BETWEEN US GIRLS(1942); GIVE OUT, SISTERS(1942); HEART OF THE GOLDEN WEST(1942); MAISIE GETS HER MAN(1942); MY GAL SAL(1942); STAR SPANGLED RHYTHM(1942); WILD BILL HICKOK RIDES(1942); YANKEE DOODLE DANDY(1942); COWBOY IN MANHATTAN(1943); FIRED WIFE(1943); GET GOING(1943); HIS BUTLER'S SISTER(1943); HIT PARADE OF 1943(1943); HOW'S ABOUT IT?(1943); THEY GOT ME COVERED(1943); WEST SIDE KID(1943); GHOST CATCHERS(1944); HI BEAUTIFUL(1944); HAT CHECK HONEY(1944); HER PRIMITIVE MAN(1944); LADY, LET'S DANCE(1944); LAKE PLACID SERENADE(1944); MY GAL LOVES MUSIC(1944); PARDON MY RHYTHM(1944); UP IN ARMS(1944); 3 IS A

FAMILY(1944); I LOVE A BANDLEADER(1945); MAN WHO WALKED ALONE, THE(1945); RIVERBOAT RHYTHM(1946); SLIGHTLY SCANDALOUS(1946); I'LL BE YOURS(1947); ARE YOU WITH IT?(1948); MR. RECKLESS(1948); BOY WITH THE GREEN HAIR, THE(1949); DANCING IN THE DARK(1949); HENRY, THE RAINMAKER(1949); INSPECTOR GENERAL, THE(1949); LEAVE IT TO HENRY(1949); LOOK FOR THE SILVER LINING(1949); FATHER MAKES GOOD(1950); FATHER'S WILD GAME(1950); FATHER TAKES THE AIR(1951); HERE COMES THE GROOM(1951); HONEYCHILE(1951); DAVY CROCKETT AND THE RIVER PIRATES(1956); FRIENDLY PERSUASION(1956); BEAU JAMES(1957)
Silents
SECOND YOUTH(1924); SUMMER BACHELORS(1926)

Gwen Catley
WE'LL SMILE AGAIN(1942, Brit.); THEATRE ROYAL(1943, Brit.)

Darrell Catling
FLYING EYE, THE(1955, Brit.), w; CAT GANG, THE(1959, Brit.), d

Frederick Catling
Misc. Silents
UNTO EACH OTHER(1929, Brit.)

Jane Catling
1984
BEDROOM EYES(1984, Can.)

David Cato
CAPTAIN FROM CASTILE(1947)

Jo Levitt Cato
JUD(1971)

Minto Cato
END OF THE RIVER, THE(1947, Brit.)

Pier Luigi Catocci
BEBO'S GIRL(1964, Ital.)

Lauderic Caton
WALKING ON AIR(1946, Brit.)

Michael Caton
LAST OF THE KNUCKLEMEN, THE(1981, Aus.); MONKEY GRIP(1983, Aus.)

Patti Caton
JOE(1970)

Phil Caton
SILVER BEARS(1978)

Presley Caton
GAMBLER, THE(1974); ABDUCTION(1975)

Douglas Cator
Silents
LIVINGSTONE(1925, Brit.)

Leo Catozzo
NIGHTS OF CABIRIA(1957, Ital.), ed; ATTILA(1958, Ital.), ed; THIS ANGRY AGE(1958, Ital./Fr.), ed; LA DOLCE VITA(1961, Ital./Fr.), ed; RITA(1963, Fr./Ital.), ed; STEPPE, THE(1963, Fr./Ital.), ed; 8 ½(1963, Ital.), ed

Jack Catron
HOSTILE GUNS(1967)

Jerry Catron
POINT BLANK(1967); WUSA(1970)

Catron and Pop
SONG OF THE OPEN ROAD(1944)

Tom Catronova
1984
NINJA III–THE DOMINATION(1984)

Edith Catry
PLAYMATES(1969, Fr./Ital.)

The Cats and the Fiddle
DUKE IS THE TOPS, THE(1938)

Dorothy Catt
FALL OF THE HOUSE OF USHER, THE(1952, Brit.), w

Rene Salvatore Catta
MY UNCLE ANTOINE(1971, Can.)

Bruno Cattanco
MYTH, THE(1965, Ital.)

Amelia Cattaneo
Silents
QUO VADIS?(1913, Ital.)

Bruno Cattaneo
BEST OF ENEMIES, THE(1962); DON'T LOOK NOW(1973, Brit./Ital.)

Princess Alma Cattaneo
ROMAN HOLIDAY(1953)

Henry Rico Cattani
TOBRUK(1966); WHAT DID YOU DO IN THE WAR, DADDY?(1966)

Rice Cattani
OUTSIDE MAN, THE(1973, U.S./FR.)

Rico Cattani
POINT BLANK(1967); ST. VALENTINE'S DAY MASSACRE, THE(1967); BAMBOO SAUCER, THE(1968); HOW SWEET IT IS(1968)

Christine Cattell
1984
BEDROOM EYES(1984, Can.)

Irene Cattell
ANOTHER LANGUAGE(1933)

James Catti
JIM, THE WORLD'S GREATEST(1976), art d

Honorine Catto
IMPROPER DUCHESS, THE(1936, Brit.)

Max Catto
DAUGHTER OF DARKNESS(1948, Brit.), w; TAKE ME TO PARIS(1951, Brit.), w; BAD BLONDE(1953, Brit.), w; WEST OF ZANZIBAR(1954, Brit.), w; PRIZE OF GOLD, A(1955), w; HELL IN KOREA(1956, Brit.), w; TRAPEZE(1956), w; FIRE DOWN BELOW(1957, U.S./Brit.), w; SEVEN THIEVES(1960), w; DEVIL AT FOUR O'CLOCK, THE(1961), w; MISTER MOSES(1965), w; MURPHY'S WAR(1971, Brit.), w

Sandy Catton
PHANTOM OF THE PARADISE(1974)

Leo Cattozo
LA STRADA(1956, Ital.), ed

Leo Cattozzo
WOMAN OF THE RIVER(1954, Fr./Ital.), ed; ULYSSES(1955, Ital.), ed; WAR AND PEACE(1956, Ital./U.S.), ed

Kim Cattrall
TRIBUTE(1980, Can.); ROSEBUD(1975); TICKET TO HEAVEN(1981); PORKY'S(1982)
1984
POLICE ACADEMY(1984)
Misc. Talkies
DEADLY HARVEST(1972)

Gary Catus
KLANSMAN, THE(1974)

James Catusi
PARADES(1972); DEATH PLAY(1976); LINE, THE(1982)

Jean Cau
GAME IS OVER, THE(1967, Fr.), w; BORSALINO(1970, Fr.), w

Manuel Cauchi
HANNAH K.(1983, Fr.)

Daniel Cauchy
COUNT OF MONTE-CRISTO(1955, Fr., Ital.); LOVE AT NIGHT(1961, Fr.); I SPIT ON YOUR GRAVE(1962, Fr.); GENDARME OF ST. TROPEZ, THE(1966, Fr./Ital.)

M. Caudani
BANDIT, THE(1949, Ital.), w

Al Caudebec
RIDE THE MAN DOWN(1952)

Lane Caudell
SATAN'S CHEERLEADERS(1977); GOODBYE FRANKLIN HIGH(1978)

Ruby Caudill
COAL MINER'S DAUGHTER(1980)

Bert Caudle, Jr.
GENTLE RAIN, THE(1966, Braz.), a, p

Pete Caudreaux
VIOLATED(1953)

Cary Caughlin
1984
ON THE LINE(1984, Span.), ed

Alan Cauldwell
GOD TOLD ME TO(1976)

Brenda Cauldwell
FLIGHT OF THE DOVES(1971)

Brendan Cauldwell
PLAYBOY OF THE WESTERN WORLD, THE(1963, Ireland); ULYSSES(1967, U.S./Brit.)

Claudia Cauldwell
CAGED(1950)

Bernard Cauley
TOP O' THE MORNING(1949)

Betty Caulfield
GIRL IN THE RED VELVET SWING, THE(1955); GOOD MORNING, MISS DOVE(1955); MAN CALLED PETER, THE(1955); BIGGER THAN LIFE(1956)

Dan Caulfield
JOANNA(1968, Brit.); TALES FROM THE CRYPT(1972, Brit.)

Joan Caulfield
DUFFY'S TAVERN(1945); MISS SUSIE SLAGLE'S(1945); BLUE SKIES(1946); MONSIEUR BEAUCAIRE(1946); DEAR RUTH(1947); UNSUSPECTED, THE(1947); VARIETY GIRL(1947); WELCOME STRANGER(1947); LARCENY(1948); SAINTED SISTERS, THE(1948); DEAR WIFE(1949); PETTY GIRL, THE(1950); LADY SAYS NO, THE(1951); RAINS OF RANCHIPUR, THE(1955); CATTLE KING(1963); RED TOMAHAWK(1967); BUCKSKIN(1968); DARING DOBERMANS, THE(1973); PONY EXPRESS RIDER(1976)

Mason Caulfield
CREMATORS, THE(1972)

Maxwell Caulfield
GREASE 2(1982)
1984
ELECTRIC DREAMS(1984)

Michael Caulfield
STORM BOY(1976, Aus.); TIM(1981, Aus.); FIGHTING BACK(1983, Brit.), d

Ward Caulfield
Misc. Silents
IRISH EYES(1918)

Daryl Caulker
SON OF THE RENEGADE(1953), m

Zella Caull
Misc. Silents
DOCTOR AND THE WOMAN, THE(1918)

Julian Caunter
NO HAUNT FOR A GENTLEMAN(1952, Brit.), w

Tony Caunter
HILL, THE(1965, Brit.); IPCRESS FILE, THE(1965, Brit.); TWIST OF SAND, A(1968, Brit.); ADDING MACHINE, THE(1969); MIND OF MR. SOAMES, THE(1970, Brit.); ASPHYX, THE(1972, Brit.); MR. QUILP(1975, Brit.)

Chief Caupolican
WHOOPEE(1930)

Robert Caus
FAT ANGELS(1980, U.S./Span.)

Buddy Causey, Jr.
EASY RIDER(1969)

J. P Caussade
CLOPORTES(1966, Fr., Ital.)

Jean Roger Caussimon
FANTOMAS(1966, Fr./Ital.); TIGHT SKIRTS, LOOSE PLEASURES(1966, Fr.)

Jean-Roger Caussimon
RED, INN, THE(1954, Fr.); FRENCH CANCAN(1956, Fr.); RETURN OF DR. MABUSE, THE(1961, Ger./Fr./Ital.); LAFAYETTE(1963, Fr.); JUDGE AND THE ASSASSIN, THE(1979, Fr.)

David Caute
WINSTANLEY(1979, Brit.), w

Robert Cauterio
FAREWELL TO ARMS, A(1932)
Silents
LADY ROBINHOOD(1925)

Robert Cautier
Silents
HEADS UP(1925)

Robert Cautiero
BRIDE FOR SALE(1949)

Charles Cautley
Misc. Silents
RINGING THE CHANGES(1929, Brit.)

Pattrick Cauvin
LITTLE ROMANCE, A(1979, U.S./Fr.), w

Gregory La Cava
Misc. Silents
TELL IT TO SWEENEY(1927), d

Allan Cavaen
SPECIAL AGENT(1935)

Cesare Cavagna
MORGAN THE PIRATE(1961, Fr./Ital.), ed

Gary Cavagnaro
DRIVE-IN(1976)

Gary Lee Cavagnaro
BAD NEWS BEARS, THE(1976)

Cavalcanti
FOR THEM THAT TRESPASS(1949, Brit.), d

Alberto Cavalcanti
TURNED OUT NICE AGAIN(1941, Brit.), art d; BIG BLOCKADE, THE(1942, Brit.), p; SOMEWHERE IN FRANCE(1943, Brit.), p; CHAMPAGNE CHARLIE(1944, Brit.), d; 48 HOURS(1944, Brit.), d; DEAD OF NIGHT(1946, Brit.), d; I BECAME A CRIMINAL(1947), d; NICHOLAS NICKLEBY(1947, Brit.), d; AFFAIRS OF A ROGUE, THE(1949, Brit.), d; MONSTER OF HIGHGATE PONDS, THE(1961, Brit.), d
Misc. Silents
EN RADE(1927, Fr.), d; LE TRAIN SANS YEUX(1928, Fr.), d; YVETTE(1928, Fr.), d; LA JALOUSIE DU BARBOUILLE(1929, Fr.), d; LE CAPITAINE FRACASSE(1929, Fr.), d

Emanoel Cavalcanti
BYE-BYE BRASIL(1980, Braz.)

Emanuel Cavalcanti
EARTH ENTRANCED(1970, Braz.)

Raymond Cavaleri
R.P.M.(1970); LEPKE(1975, U.S./Israel)

Sylvia Cavalho
Silents
SANCTUARY(1916, Brit.)

Alain Cavalier
CROSS OF THE LIVING(1963), w; LA VIE DE CHATEAU(1967, Fr.), w

Joe Cavalier
TWIST ALL NIGHT(1961)

M. Cavalier
TRUTH, THE(1961, Fr./Ital.)

Marjorie Cavalier
EIGHT GIRLS IN A BOAT(1934)

Nita Cavalier
CROSS-EXAMINATION(1932)
Misc. Silents
DEAD LINE, THE(1926); TWIN TRIGGERS(1926)

Sebastian Cavalier
FINGER ON THE TRIGGER(1965, US/Span.)

Gianni Cavalieri
WHITE LINE, THE(1952, Ital.); TWO NIGHTS WITH CLEOPATRA(1953, Ital.)

Gino Cavalieri
TO LIVE IN PEACE(1947, Ital.); WHITE LINE, THE(1952, Ital.); PRIEST'S WIFE, THE(1971, Ital./Fr.)

Lina Cavalieri
Silents
MANON LESCAUT(1914); ETERNAL TEMPTRESS, THE(1917)
Misc. Silents
LOVE'S CONQUEST(1918); WOMAN OF IMPULSE, A(1918); TWO BRIDES, THE(1919)

Luciano Cavalieri
PRISONER OF THE IRON MASK(1962, Fr./Ital.), ed

Jean Cavall
ADULTEROUS AFFAIR(1966)

Julie Cavall
NAKED FURY(1959, Brit.)

Carmen Cavallaro
DIAMOND HORSESHOE(1945); OUT OF THIS WORLD(1945)

Gaylord Cavallaro
COMPANIONS IN CRIME(1954, Brit.); HARASSED HERO, THE(1954, Brit.); HORNET'S NEST, THE(1955, Brit.); PICKUP ALLEY(1957, Brit.); MURDER REPORTED(1958, Brit.); SUBWAY IN THE SKY(1959, Brit.); BEYOND THE CURTAIN(1960, Brit.); BOY WHO STOLE A MILLION, THE(1960, Brit.); NEVER TAKE CANDY FROM A STRANGER(1961, Brit.); HOT MONEY GIRL(1962, Brit./Ger.)

Giacomo Cavalleri
TREE OF WOODEN CLOGS, THE(1979, Ital.)

Vincent Cavalleri
HIDE IN PLAIN SIGHT(1980)

Gaylord Cavallero
UPSTAIRS AND DOWNSTAIRS(1961, Brit.)

Olimpia Cavalli
LA VIACCIA(1962, Fr./Ital.); LEOPARD, THE(1963, Ital.); 8 ½(1963, Ital.)

Robert Cavallo
1984
PURPLE RAIN(1984), p

Secondino Cavallo
WONDERS OF ALADDIN, THE(1961, Fr./Ital.), ch

Victor Cavallo
TRAGEDY OF A RIDICULOUS MAN, THE(1982, Ital.); MOON IN THE GUTTER, THE(1983, Fr./Ital.)

Alan Cavan
OFFICER 13(1933); NEW FRONTIER, THE(1935); RED SALUTE(1935); NATION AFLAME(1937)

Allan Cavan
MILLION DOLLAR COLLAR, THE(1929); TRESPASSER, THE(1929); SHADOW OF THE LAW(1930); CITY STREETS(1931); NO LIMIT(1931); THIRTEENTH GUEST, THE(1932); MADAME DU BARRY(1934); IT'S A GREAT LIFE(1936); HIT THE SADDLE(1937); SUBMARINE D-1(1937); TOAST OF NEW YORK, THE(1937); ACCIDENTS WILL HAPPEN(1938); KING OF THE NEWSBOYS(1938); OLD LOUISIANA(1938); REBELLION(1938); COME ON RANGERS(1939); IN OLD MONTANA(1939); MR. SMITH GOES TO WASHINGTON(1939); NIGHT AT EARL CARROLL'S, A(1940)
Silents
WHEN ODDS ARE EVEN(1923)

Allen Cavan
INTRUDER, THE(1932); MAYTIME(1937); I AM A CRIMINAL(1939)

Barbara Cavan
HIS EXCELLENCY(1952, Brit.); GOOD BEGINNING, THE(1953, Brit.); LARGE ROPE, THE(1953, Brit.); ROOM IN THE HOUSE(1955, Brit.); YOU CAN'T ESCAPE(1955, Brit.); HELEN OF TROY(1956, Ital); IT'S NEVER TOO LATE(1958, Brit.); NEXT TO NO TIME(1960, Brit.); HIDE AND SEEK(1964, Brit.); TAMAHINE(1964, Brit.)

James Cavan
PARASITE(1982)
1984
WOMAN IN RED, THE(1984)

Jess Cavan
IN EARLY ARIZONA(1938); SAGA OF DEATH VALLEY(1939); SHERIFF OF TOMBSTONE(1941); FIREBRANDS OF ARIZONA(1944); MOJAVE FIREBRAND(1944); TOPEKA TERROR, THE(1945); DAYS OF BUFFALO BILL(1946)

Jesse Cavan
FRONTIERSMAN, THE(1938)

Taylor Cavan
MEET THE MISSUS(1940), w; PETTICOAT POLITICS(1941), w; MARSHAL OF RENO(1944), w

Ann Cavanagh
LANDSLIDE(1937, Brit.)

James Cavanagh
FAMILY SECRET, THE(1951), w

James P. Cavanagh
MURDER AT THE GALLOP(1963, Brit.), w

John Cavanagh
SECRET OF MY SUCCESS, THE(1965, Brit.), cos

Lynne Cavanagh
THREE CARD MONTE(1978, Can.)

Paul Cavanagh
TESHA(1929, Brit.); DEVIL TO PAY, THE(1930); GRUMPY(1930); STORM, THE(1930); STRICTLY UNCONVENTIONAL(1930); VIRTUOUS SIN(1930); ALWAYS GOODBYE(1931); BORN TO LOVE(1931); HEARTBREAK(1931); SQUAW MAN, THE(1931); TRANSGRESSION(1931); UNFAITHFUL(1931); BILL OF DIVORCEMENT, A(1932); DEVIL'S LOTTERY(1932); THE CRASH(1932); KENNEL MURDER CASE, THE(1933); SIN OF NORA MORAN(1933); MENACE(1934); NOTORIOUS SOPHIE LANG, THE(1934); SHOOT THE WORKS(1934); TARZAN AND HIS MATE(1934); UNCERTAIN LADY(1934); GOIN' TO TOWN(1935); ONE EXCITING ADVENTURE(1935); SPLENDOR(1935); THUNDER IN THE NIGHT(1935); WITHOUT REGRET(1935); CHAMPAGNE CHARLIE(1936); CRIME OVER LONDON(1936, Brit.); CAFE COLETTE(1937, Brit.); RENO(1939); UNDER-PUP, THE(1939); WITHIN THE LAW(1939); I TAKE THIS WOMAN(1940); LOST ON THE WESTERN FRONT(1940, Brit.); CASE OF THE BLACK PARROT, THE(1941); MAISIE WAS A LADY(1941); PASSAGE FROM HONG KONG(1941); SHADOWS ON THE STAIRS(1941); CAPTAINS OF THE CLOUDS(1942); EAGLE SQUADRON(1942); GORILLA MAN(1942); HARD WAY, THE(1942); PACIFIC RENDEZVOUS(1942); STRANGE CASE OF DR. RX, THE(1942); ADVENTURES IN IRAQ(1943); MAISIE GOES TO RENO(1944); MAN IN HALF-MOON STREET, THE(1944); MARRIAGE IS A PRIVATE AFFAIR(1944); SCARLET CLAW, THE(1944); HOUSE OF FEAR, THE(1945); THIS MAN'S NAVY(1945); WOMAN IN GREEN, THE(1945); CLUB HAVANA(1946); HUMORESQUE(1946); NIGHT AND DAY(1946); NIGHT IN PARADISE, A(1946); VERDICT, THE(1946); WIFE WANTED(1946); DISHONORED LADY(1947); IVY(1947); BABE RUTH STORY, THE(1948); BLACK ARROW(1948); SECRET BEYOND THE DOOR, THE(1948); YOU GOTTA STAY HAPPY(1948); MADAME BOVARY(1949); HIJACKED(1950); HIT PARADE OF 1951(1950); IROQUOIS TRAIL, THE(1950); ROGUES OF SHERWOOD FOREST(1950); BRIDE OF THE GORILLA(1951); DESERT FOX, THE(1951); HOLLYWOOD STORY(1951); SON OF DR. JEKYLL(1951); STRANGE DOOR, THE(1951); TALES OF ROBIN HOOD(1951); GOLDEN HAWK, THE(1952); PLYMOUTH ADVENTURE(1952); ALL-AMERICAN, THE(1953); BANDITS OF CORSICA, THE(1953); BLADES OF THE MUSKETEERS(1953); CHARADE(1953); FLAME OF CALCUTTA(1953); HOUSE OF WAX(1953); MISSISSIPPI GAMBLER, THE(1953); PORT SINISTER(1953); CASANOVA'S BIG NIGHT(1954); IRON GLOVE, THE(1954); KHYBER PATROL(1954); LAW VS. BILLY THE KID, THE(1954); MAGNIFICENT OBSESSION(1954); RAID, THE(1954); DIANE(1955); KING'S THIEF, THE(1955); PRODIGAL, THE(1955); PURPLE MASK, THE(1955); SCARLET COAT, THE(1955); BLONDE BAIT(1956, U.S./Brit.); FRANCIS IN THE HAUNTED HOUSE(1956); MAN WHO TURNED TO STONE, THE(1957); SHE DEVIL(1957); IN THE MONEY(1958); FOUR SKULLS OF JONATHAN DRAKE, THE(1959)
Misc. Silents
TWO LITTLE DRUMMER BOYS(1928, Brit.); RUNAWAY PRINCESS, THE(1929, Brit.)

Seamus Cavanagh
GENTLE GUNMAN, THE(1952, Brit.)

Stan Cavanagh
STRANDED(1935)

Arthur Cavanaugh
DEADLY TRAP, THE(1972, Fr./Ital.), w

Florence Cavanaugh
IRON MAJOR, THE(1943), w

Hobart Cavanaugh
BROADWAY THROUGH A KEYHOLE(1933); CONVENTION CITY(1933); DEVIL'S MATE(1933); FOOTLIGHT PARADE(1933); FROM HEADQUARTERS(1933); GOLD DIGGERS OF 1933(1933); GOODBYE AGAIN(1933); HAVANA WIDOWS(1933); HEADLINE SHOOTER(1933); I COVER THE WATERFRONT(1933); LILLY TURNER(1933); MARY STEVENS, M.D.(1933); MAYOR OF HELL, THE(1933); MY WOMAN(1933); NO MARRIAGE TIES(1933); PICTURE SNATCHER(1933); PRIVATE DETECTIVE 62(1933); STATE FAIR(1933); STUDY IN SCARLET, A(1933); DARK HAZARD(1934); EASY TO LOVE(1934); FASHIONS OF 1934(1934); FIREBIRD, THE(1934); HAROLD TEEN(1934); HI, NELLIE!(1934); HOUSEWIFE(1934); I SELL ANYTHING(1934); I'VE GOT YOUR NUMBER(1934); JIMMY THE GENT(1934); KANSAS CITY PRINCESS(1934); KEY, THE(1934); LOST LADY, A(1934); MADAME DU BARRY(1934); MANDALAY(1934); MERRY WIVES OF RENO, THE(1934); MODERN HERO, A(1934); MOULIN ROUGE(1934); NOW I'LL TELL(1934); ST. LOUIS KID, THE(1934); VERY HONORABLE GUY, A(1934); WONDER BAR(1934); BORDERTOWN(1935); BROADWAY GONDOLIER(1935); CAPTAIN BLOOD(1935); DON'T BET ON BLONDES(1935); DR. SOCRATES(1935); I AM A THIEF(1935); I LIVE FOR LOVE(1935); MIDSUMMER'S NIGHT'S DREAM, A(1935); PAGE MISS GLORY(1935); STEAMBOAT ROUND THE BEND(1935); WE'RE IN THE MONEY(1935); WHILE THE PATIENT SLEPT(1935); WINGS IN THE DARK(1935); CAIN AND MABEL(1936); COLLEEN(1936); HEARTS DIVIDED(1936); HERE COMES CARTER(1936); LADY CONSENTS, THE(1936); LOVE BEGINS AT TWENTY(1936); LOVE LETTERS OF A STAR(1936); SING ME A LOVE SONG(1936); STAGE STRUCK(1936); TWO AGAINST THE WORLD(1936); WIFE VERSUS SECRETARY(1936); CARNIVAL QUEEN(1937); GIRL OVERBOARD(1937); GREAT O'MALLEY, THE(1937); LOVE IN A BUNGALOW(1937); MIGHTY TREVE, THE(1937); MYSTERIOUS CROSSING(1937); NIGHT KEY(1937); REPORTED MISSING(1937); THAT'S MY STORY(1937); THREE SMART GIRLS(1937); COWBOY FROM BROOKLYN(1938); STRANGE FACES(1938); CAREER(1939); CHICKEN WAGON FAMILY(1939); COVERED TRAILER, THE(1939); HONEYMOON'S OVER, THE(1939); I STOLE A MILLION(1939); IDIOT'S DELIGHT(1939); NAUGHTY BUT NICE(1939); NEVER SAY DIE(1939); ORPHANS OF THE STREET(1939); RENO(1939); ROSE OF WASHINGTON SQUARE(1939); TELL NO TALES(1939); THAT'S RIGHT–YOU'RE WRONG(1939); ZENOBIA(1939); ANGEL FROM TEXAS, AN(1940); CHARTER PILOT(1940); CHILD IS BORN, A(1940); GHOST COMES HOME, THE(1940); GREAT PLANE ROBBERY, THE(1940); HIRED WIFE(1940); LOVE, HONOR AND OH, BABY!(1940); PUBLIC DEB NO. 1(1940); SANTA FE TRAIL(1940); SHOOTING HIGH(1940); STAGE TO CHINO(1940); STREET OF MEMORIES(1940); YOU CAN'T FOOL YOUR WIFE(1940); DOWN IN SAN DIEGO(1941); HORROR ISLAND(1941); I WANTED WINGS(1941); LAND OF THE OPEN RANGE(1941); MEET THE CHUMP(1941); PLAYMATES(1941); REACHING FOR THE SUN(1941); SKYLARK(1941); THERE'S MAGIC IN MUSIC(1941); THIEVES FALL OUT(1941); JACKASS MAIL(1942); LADY IN A JAM(1942); MAGNIFICENT DOPE, THE(1942); MY FAVORITE SPY(1942); PITTSBURGH(1942); STAND BY FOR ACTION(1942); TRAGEDY AT MIDNIGHT, A(1942); WHISTLING IN DIXIE(1942); DANGEROUS BLONDES(1943); GILDERSLEEVE ON BROADWAY(1943); JACK LONDON(1943); KANSAN, THE(1943); MAN FROM DOWN UNDER, THE(1943); PILOT NO. 5(1943); SCREAM IN THE DARK, A(1943); SWEET ROSIE O'GRADY(1943); WHAT A WOMAN!(1943); KISMET(1944); LOUISIANA HAYRIDE(1944); SAN DIEGO, I LOVE YOU(1944); TOGETHER AGAIN(1944); DON JUAN QUILLIGAN(1945); I'LL REMEMBER APRIL(1945); LADY ON A TRAIN(1945); ROUGHLY SPEAKING(1945); BLACK ANGEL(1946); CINDERELLA JONES(1946); FAITHFUL IN MY FASHION(1946); LITTLE IODINE(1946); MARGIE(1946); NIGHT AND DAY(1946); SPIDER WOMAN STRIKES BACK, THE(1946); DRIFTWOOD(1947); EASY COME, EASY GO(1947); BEST MAN WINS(1948); INSIDE STORY, THE(1948); LETTER TO THREE WIVES, A(1948); UP IN CENTRAL PARK(1948); STELLA(1950)

James Cavanaugh
VENGEANCE(1964)

James J. Cavanaugh
JOKER IS WILD, THE(1957)

Jimmy Cavanaugh
PEPE(1960)

Larry Cavanaugh
DOGS OF WAR, THE(1980, Brit.), spec eff; SMALL CIRCLE OF FRIENDS, A(1980), spec eff

Marie Cavanaugh
GIRL IN TROUBLE(1963)

Michael Cavanaugh
GAUNTLET, THE(1977); HEROES(1977); OVER-UNDER, SIDEWAYS-DOWN(1977); ANY WHICH WAY YOU CAN(1980); FORCED VENGEANCE(1982); HEART LIKE A WHEEL(1983)

Paul Cavanaugh
TONIGHT IS OURS(1933); CURTAIN AT EIGHT(1934); GOD IS MY PARTNER(1957)

Richard Cavanaugh
RANCHO DELUXE(1975)

W.H. Cavanaugh
Misc. Silents
EVANGELINE(1914, Can.), d

William Cavanaugh
Silents
TRAFFIC IN SOULS(1913); $5,000,000 COUNTERFEITING PLOT, THE(1914); DOWN TO THE SEA IN SHIPS(1923)
Misc. Silents
MORGAN'S RAIDERS(1918)

Glen Cavander
TUGBOAT ANNIE SAILS AGAIN(1940)

Kenneth Cavander
GIRL ON APPROVAL(1962, Brit.), w

Liliana Cavani
CANNIBALS, THE(1970, Ital.), d, w; NIGHT PORTER, THE(1974, Ital./U.S.), d, w
1984
BEYOND GOOD AND EVIL(1984, Ital./Fr./Ger.), d, w

Martin Cavani
1984
AMADEUS(1984)

J. Cortes Cavanillas
ROMAN HOLIDAY(1953)

Elisa Cavanna
Silents
IT'S THE OLD ARMY GAME(1926)

Elise Cavanna
INFERNAL MACHINE(1933); YOU'RE TELLING ME(1934); I DREAM TOO MUCH(1935); HAVING WONDERFUL TIME(1938); THREE LOVES HAS NANCY(1938); NAUGHTY BUT NICE(1939)

Wendy Cavanough
Misc. Talkies
BEACH BUNNIES(1977)

Paolo Cavara
WILD EYE, THE(1968, Ital.), d, w; DEAF SMITH AND JOHNNY EARS(1973, Ital.), d, w

Jimmy Cavaretta
Misc. Talkies
NOT MY DAUGHTER(1975)

Arnold Cavasos
1984
LAST NIGHT AT THE ALAMO(1984)

James Cavasos
GUNFIGHT, A(1971)

Walter Cavazzuti
ALLEGRO NON TROPPO(1977, Ital.), anim

Claude Cave
COOL WORLD, THE(1963)

Daphne Cave
TEENAGE BAD GIRL(1959, Brit.)

Des Cave
Misc. Talkies
PHILADELPHIA HERE I COME(1975)

Desmond Cave
OUTSIDER, THE(1980)

Grace Cave
FAMILY LIFE(1971, Brit.)

Rita Cave
ROMANY LOVE(1931, Brit.); VARIETY(1935, Brit.)

L. Cave-Chinn
MANIACS ON WHEELS(1951, Brit.), ph

Rene Caveau
BLUE VEIL, THE(1947, Fr.), ph

The Cavegirls
50,000 B.C.(BEFORE CLOTHING)* (1963)

Dallas Cavell
LONELINESS OF THE LONG DISTANCE RUNNER, THE(1962, Brit.)

Marc Cavell
DIANE(1955); BIG NIGHT, THE(1960); PURPLE GANG, THE(1960); ADVENTURES OF A YOUNG MAN(1962); CAPTAIN NEWMAN, M.D.(1963); OPERATION BIKINI(1963); BUS RILEY'S BACK IN TOWN(1965); GREATEST STORY EVER TOLD, THE(1965); YOUNG FURY(1965); WILD ANGELS, THE(1966); COOL HAND LUKE(1967); DEVIL'S ANGELS(1967); LOVE-INS, THE(1967); CALIFORNIA SPLIT(1974)

Mark Cavell
MAN FROM THE ALAMO, THE(1953); THUNDER IN THE EAST(1953)

Maurice Cavell
CITIZEN SAINT(1947); UP FRONT(1951)

Daniel Cavelli
DAYDREAMER, THE(1966), ph

Allan Caven
CODE OF THE RANGE(1937)

Allen Caven
IN OLD KENTUCKY(1935)

Donann Caven
MELANIE(1982, Can.)

Ingrid Caven
AMERICAN SOLDIER, THE(1970 Ger.); MOTHER KUSTERS GOES TO HEAVEN(1976, Ger.); WHY DOES HERR R. RUN AMOK?(1977, Ger.); DESPAIR(1978, Ger.); IN A YEAR OF THIRTEEN MOONS(1980, Ger.); MALOU(1983)

Taylor Caven
CHINA PASSAGE(1937), w; SHOULD HUSBANDS WORK?(1939), w; MONEY TO BURN(1940), w; GAY VAGABOND, THE(1941), w; ARIZONA TERRORS(1942), w; JESSE JAMES, JR.(1942), w; JAMBOREE(1944), w; SILVER CITY KID(1944), w; DANNY BOY(1946), w; UNTAMED FURY(1947), w

Glen Cavendar
TORCHY PLAYS WITH DYNAMITE(1939)
Misc. Talkies
NEVADA BUCKAROO, THE(1931)

Ben Cavender
DANGEROUSLY THEY LIVE(1942)

Glen Cavender
G-MEN(1935); GOOSE AND THE GANDER, THE(1935); STRANDED(1935); STAGE STRUCK(1936); SAN QUENTIN(1937); GIRLS ON PROBATION(1938); PATIENT IN ROOM 18, THE(1938); CODE OF THE SECRET SERVICE(1939); EVERYTHING HAPPENS AT NIGHT(1939); KING OF THE UNDERWORLD(1939); SECRET SERVICE OF THE AIR(1939); MAN I MARRIED, THE(1940); MAN WHO TALKED TOO MUCH, THE(1940); MEET JOHN DOE(1941); SHE COULDN'T SAY NO(1941); UNDERGROUND(1941); MALE ANIMAL, THE(1942); NORTHERN PURSUIT(1943); WATCH ON THE RHINE(1943)
Silents
SUBMARINE PIRATE, A(1915); KEEP SMILING(1925); GENERAL, THE(1927)
Misc. Silents
WHAT LOVE WILL DO(1921)

Glenn Cavender
GEORGE WASHINGTON SLEPT HERE(1942); TRUCK BUSTERS(1943)

Kenneth Cavender
IMPERSONATOR, THE(1962, Brit.), w

Reg W. Cavender
HEIGHTS OF DANGER(1962, Brit.), ph

Cecilia Cavendish
FLAW, THE(1955, Brit.)

Constance Cavendish
THAT FORSYTE WOMAN(1949); LADY POSSESSED(1952); BUSTER KEATON STORY, THE(1957); MR. SARDONICUS(1961); LIST OF ADRIAN MESSENGER, THE(1963)

David Cavendish
DOUBLE TROUBLE(1941); RANDOM HARVEST(1942); UNDERCURRENT(1946); EXILE, THE(1947); IVY(1947); LADY IN THE LAKE(1947); LIFE WITH FATHER(1947); LOVE FROM A STRANGER(1947); MADAME BOVARY(1949); YOUNG BESS(1953)

Kay Cavendish
POET'S PUB(1949, Brit.)

Robert W. Cavendish
ACROSS THE BADLANDS(1950)

Alice Cavenna
I MET MY LOVE AGAIN(1938)

Al Cavens
CLASH BY NIGHT(1952); FRENCH LINE, THE(1954); FIRST TRAVELING SALESLADY, THE(1956); BOY AND THE PIRATES, THE(1960)

Albert Cavens
CYRANO DE BERGERAC(1950)

Allen Cavens
EVER SINCE EVE(1937)

Fred Cavens
BREED OF THE BORDER(1933); LOVE ON THE RUN(1936); CAFE METROPOLE(1937); ARTISTS AND MODELS ABROAD(1938); MAN IN THE IRON MASK, THE(1939); EXILE, THE(1947); LYDIA BAILEY(1952)
Silents
KING OF KINGS, THE(1927)

Don Caverhill
SECOND COMING OF SUZANNE, THE(1974), m

Jim Caverhill
THREE CARD MONTE(1978, Can.), m

Alice Cavers
SPECTER OF THE ROSE(1946)

Clinton Cavers
PINK FLOYD–THE WALL(1982, Brit.), art d; QUEST FOR FIRE(1982, Fr./Can.), art d; HUNGER, THE(1983), art d
1984
ANOTHER COUNTRY(1984, Brit.), art d

Frank Cavestani
EVENTS(1970); CHINA SYNDROME, THE(1979)
1984
MIKE'S MURDER(1984)
Misc. Talkies
BRAND X(1970)

Dick Cavett
ANNIE HALL(1977); POWER PLAY(1978, Brit./Can.); HEALTH(1980); SIMON(1980)

Frank Cavett
VANITY STREET(1932), w; RULERS OF THE SEA(1939), w; SECOND CHORUS(1940), Hunter; TOM BROWN'S SCHOOL DAYS(1940), w; SYNCOPATION(1942), w; GOING MY WAY(1944), w; CORN IS GREEN, THE(1945), w; SMASH-UP, THE STORY OF A WOMAN(1947), w; ACROSS THE WIDE MISSOURI(1951), w; GREATEST SHOW ON EARTH, THE(1952), w

Frank Morgan Cavett
FORSAKING ALL OTHERS(1935), w

Des Cavez
PADDY(1970, Irish)

Liliana Caviani
GALILEO(1968, Ital./Bul.), d, w

Sylvio Cavicchia
Silents
NAPOLEON(1927, Fr.)

Maria E. Cavieres
SELF-PORTRAIT(1973, U.S./Chile)

Joy Cavill
NICKEL QUEEN, THE(1971, Aus.), w; DAWN(1979, Aus.), p, w

Alin Cavin
ARE WE CIVILIZED?(1934)

Donann Cavin
CIRCLE OF TWO(1980, Can.)

Gerard Cavin
SHERLOCK HOLMES AND THE SECRET WEAPON(1942)

Jess Cavin
OUTLAWS OF PINE RIDGE(1942); FIGHTING VALLEY(1943); COLORADO PIONEERS(1945); HIGH BARBAREE(1947)
Silents
RAMONA(1928); DESERT RIDER, THE(1929)

R. A. Cavin
Silents
KINKAID, GAMBLER(1916)

Cathryn Caviness
Misc. Talkies
BLOOD OF JESUS(1941)

Jessie Cavitt
QUEEN FOR A DAY(1951)

Robert Cawdron
DOWN AMONG THE Z MEN(1952, Brit.); SHADOW MAN(1953, Brit.); FEET OF CLAY(1960, Brit.); OCTOBER MOTH(1960, Brit.); FRIGHTENED CITY, THE(1961, Brit.); SATURDAY NIGHT AND SUNDAY MORNING(1961, Brit.); CROSSTRAP(1962, Brit.); FIGHTING PRINCE OF DONEGAL, THE(1966, Brit.); SHUTTERED ROOM, THE(1968, Brit.); PRIVATE LIFE OF SHERLOCK HOLMES, THE(1970, Brit.); S(1974)

Bob Cawley
Misc. Talkies
TREASURE OF TAYOPA(1974), d

Dell Cawley
Misc. Silents
TOILERS OF THE SEA(1923 US/Ital.)

Olive Cawley
VOGUES OF 1938(1937)

Pat Cawley
ANDY HARDY COMES HOME(1958); PARTY GIRL(1958)

Constance Cawlfield
ROSE, THE(1979)

Joe Cawthon
SNIPER'S RIDGE(1961)

James Cawthorn
LAND THAT TIME FORGOT, THE(1975, Brit.), w

Joe Cawthorn
GOLD DIGGERS OF 1935(1935); BRIDES ARE LIKE THAT(1936); FRESHMAN LOVE(1936)

Joseph Cawthorn
DANCE HALL(1929); JAZZ HEAVEN(1929); SPEAKEASY(1929); STREET GIRL(1929); TAMING OF THE SHREW, THE(1929); DIXIANA(1930); PRINCESS AND THE PLUMBER, THE(1930); KIKI(1931); PEACH O' RENO(1931); TAILOR MADE MAN, A(1931); LOVE ME TONIGHT(1932); WHITE ZOMBIE(1932); BEST OF ENEMIES(1933); BLONDIE JOHNSON(1933); BROKEN DREAMS(1933); MADE ON BROADWAY(1933); MEN ARE SUCH FOOLS(1933); WHISTLING IN THE DARK(1933); CAT AND THE FIDDLE(1934); GLAMOUR(1934); HOUSEWIFE(1934); HUMAN SIDE, THE(1934); LAST GENTLEMAN, THE(1934); LAZY RIVER(1934); MUSIC IN THE AIR(1934); BRIGHT LIGHTS(1935); GO INTO YOUR DANCE(1935); HARMONY LANE(1935); MAYBE IT'S LOVE(1935); NAUGHTY MARIETTA(1935); PAGE MISS GLORY(1935); SMART GIRL(1935); SWEET ADELINE(1935); SWEET MUSIC(1935); CRIME OVER LONDON(1936, Brit.); HOT MONEY(1936); ONE RAINY AFTERNOON(1936); LILLIAN RUSSELL(1940); SCATTERBRAIN(1940); SO ENDS OUR NIGHT(1941); POSTMAN DIDN'T RING, THE(1942)
Silents
SILK LEGS(1927); HOLD 'EM YALE!(1928)
Misc. Silents
VERY CONFIDENTIAL(1927)

Joseph M. Cawthorn
YOUNG AND BEAUTIFUL(1934)

Alec Cawthorne
SLEUTH(1972, Brit.)

Ann Cawthorne
HITCHHIKERS, THE(1972), p,d&w

Joe Cawthorne
VERY HONORABLE GUY, A(1934)

Joseph Cawthorne
RUNAROUND, THE(1931); THEY CALL IT SIN(1932); GRAND SLAM(1933); TWENTY MILLION SWEETHEARTS(1934)

Peter Cawthorne
ONE HYSTERICAL NIGHT(1930)

Joyce Cay
HIGH(1968, Can.)

Andre Cayatte
STORMY WATERS(1946, Fr.), w; LOVERS OF VERONA, THE(1951, Fr.), d, w; WE ARE ALL MURDERERS(1957), d, w; MIRROR HAS TWO FACES, THE(1959, Fr.), d, w; TOMORROW IS MY TURN(1962, Fr./Ital./Ger.), d, w; TWO ARE GUILTY(1964, Fr.), d, w; VERDICT(1975, Fr./Ital.), d, w

Nicole Cayatte
HEAT OF MIDNIGHT(1966, Fr.), ed

Paul Cayatte
WE ARE ALL MURDERERS(1957), ed; MIRROR HAS TWO FACES, THE(1959, Fr.), ed; DANIELLA BY NIGHT(1962, Fr/Ger.), ed; DEVIL AND THE TEN COMMANDMENTS, THE(1962, Fr.), ed; SWEET ECSTASY(1962, Fr.), ed; CROSS OF THE LIVING(1963, Fr.), ed; FIRE IN THE FLESH(1964, Fr.), ed; TWO ARE GUILTY(1964, Fr.), ed; SYMPHONY FOR A MASSACRE(1965, Fr./Ital.), ed; YOUNG WORLD, A(1966, Fr./Ital.), ed; THAT MAN GEORGE!(1967, Fr./Ital./Span.), ed; DIABOLICALLY YOURS(1968, Fr.), ed; BORSALINO(1970, Fr.), ed; MYSTERIOUS ISLAND OF CAPTAIN NEMO, THE(1973, Fr./Ital. 87m Span./Cameroon), ed; VERDICT(1975, Fr./Ital.), ed

Juan Caycho
DAUGHTER OF THE SUN GOD(1962)

Howard Caye
CRIMSON CIRCLE, THE(1930, Brit.), w

Kim Cayer
SCREWBALLS(1983)

Catana Cayetano
UNCLE TOM'S CABIN(1969, Fr./Ital./Ger./Yugo.)

Andre Cayette
ANATOMY OF A MARRIAGE(MY DAYS WITH JEAN-MARC AND MY NIGHTS WITH FRANCOISE)**1/2 (1964 Fr.), p&d, w

Adrien Cayla-Legrand
DAY OF THE JACKAL, THE(1973, Brit./Fr.)

Rose Caylor
SPRING TONIC(1935), w; FINGERS AT THE WINDOW(1942), w

Dorival Caymmi
WILD PACK, THE(1972)

Jean Cayrol
MURIEL(1963, Fr./Ital.), w

Cayton
JOURNEY TO THE BEGINNING OF TIME(1966, Czech), w

William Cayton
JOURNEY TO THE BEGINNING OF TIME(1966, Czech), p

Ben J. Caza
SUDDEN FURY(1975, Can.), p

John Cazabon
MASSACRE HILL(1949, Brit.); CRASH OF SILENCE(1952, Brit.); CURTAIN UP(1952, Brit.); BACKFIRE!(1961, Brit.); MARY HAD A LITTLE(1961, Brit.); SNAKE WOMAN, THE(1961, Brit.)

Joelle Cazal
PARIS IN THE MONTH OF AUGUST(1968, Fr.)

D.J. Cazale
WILD WOMEN OF WONGO, THE(1959), ed

John Cazale
GODFATHER, THE(1972); CONVERSATION, THE(1974); GODFATHER, THE, PART II(1974); DOG DAY AFTERNOON(1975); DEER HUNTER, THE(1978)

Juan Cazalilla
MURIETA(1965, Span.); PISTOL FOR RINGO, A(1966, Ital./Span.); MERCENARY, THE(1970, Ital./Span.); LIGHT AT THE EDGE OF THE WORLD, THE(1971, U.S./Span./Lichtenstein); WIND AND THE LION, THE(1975)

Pam Cazano
SLUMBER PARTY MASSACRE, THE(1982)

Bernard Cazassus
SMUGGLERS, THE(1969, Fr.); EVERY MAN FOR HIMSELF(1980, Fr.); ENTRE NOUS(1983, Fr.)

Alex Caze [Rene Plaissetty]
MISSION TO MOSCOW(1943)

Isolde Cazelet
HAUNTING OF M, THE(1979)

Huynh Cazenas
HOA-BINH(1971, Fr.)

Paul Cazeneuve
Silents
BIG TOWN IDEAS(1921); QUEEN OF SHEBA, THE(1921); FRENCH DOLL, THE(1923); SIX DAYS(1923)
Misc. Silents
ADVENTURER, THE(1920); HEART STRINGS(1920); HER HONOR THE MAYOR(1920), d; SPIRIT OF GOOD, THE(1920), d; SUNSET SPRAGUE(1920), d

Christopher Cazenove
JULIUS CAESAR(1929, Brit.); THERE'S A GIRL IN MY SOUP(1970, Brit.); ROYAL FLASH(1975, Brit.); EAST OF ELEPHANT ROCK(1976, Brit.); ZULU DAWN(1980, Brit.); EYE OF THE NEEDLE(1981); HEAT AND DUST(1983, Brit.)
1984
UNTIL SEPTEMBER(1984)

Clive Cazes
THAT RIVIERA TOUCH(1968, Brit.)

Jean Jacques Caziot
QUARTET(1981, Brit./Fr.), art d

Jean-Jacques Caziot
MURMUR OF THE HEART(1971, Fr./Ital./Ger.), art d; LA PASSANTE(1983, Fr./Ger.), ph

Otello Cazzola
QUIET PLACE IN THE COUNTRY, A(1970, Ital./Fr.)

The CBS-KMBC Texas Rangers
COLORADO SUNSET(1939)

Bruna Cealti
TWO WOMEN(1961, Ital./Fr.)

Arthur Ceasar
PISTOL PACKIN' MAMA(1943), w

Rafael Ceballos
LIVING IDOL, THE(1957), ed

Larry Ceballos
GOLD DIGGERS OF BROADWAY(1929), ch; HONKY TONK(1929), ch; IS EVERYBODY HAPPY?(1929), ch; ON WITH THE SHOW(1929), ch; PARIS(1929), ch; SALLY(1929), ch; SMILING IRISH EYES(1929), ch; GOLDEN DAWN(1930), md; HOLD EVERYTHING(1930), ch; NO, NO NANETTE(1930), ch; TOP SPEED(1930), ch; BRIGHT LIGHTS(1931), ch; DIPLOMANIACS(1933), ch; GIRL WITHOUT A ROOM(1933), ch; SITTING PRETTY(1933), ch; CAT'S PAW, THE(1934), ch; TRANSATLANTIC MERRY-GO-ROUND(1934), ch; REDHEADS ON PARADE(1935), ch; FOLLOW YOUR HEART(1936), ch; MUSIC GOES ROUND, THE(1936), ch; MAKE A WISH(1937), ch; HE LOVED AN ACTRESS(1938, Brit.), ch; ONE NIGHT IN THE TROPICS(1940), ch; SING, DANCE, PLENTY HOT(1940), ch; SPRING PARADE(1940), ch; POT O' GOLD(1941), ch; SING ANOTHER CHORUS(1941), ch; COWBOY AND THE SENORITA(1944), ch; LIGHTS OF OLD SANTA FE(1944), ch; SAN FERNANDO VALLEY(1944), ch; SONG OF NEVADA(1944), ch; YELLOW ROSE OF TEXAS, THE(1944), ch; DAKOTA(1945), ch; DON'T FENCE ME IN(1945), ch; FLAME OF THE BARBARY COAST(1945), ch; SONG FOR MISS JULIE, A(1945), ch; SUNSET IN EL DORADO(1945), ch; UTAH(1945), ch; MEET THE NAVY(1946, Brit.), m; QUEEN OF BURLESQUE(1946), ch; COPACABANA(1947), ch; I'LL GET BY(1950), ch

Rene Ceballos
FAN, THE(1981)

Rossi Ceballos
VAMPIRES, THE(1969, Mex.)

Maria Cebotari
DREAM OF BUTTERFLY, THE(1941, Ital.)

Fernando Cebrian
SWORD OF EL CID, THE(1965, Span./Ital.); TRISTANA(1970, Span./Ital./Fr.)

M. Cebulski
JOVITA(1970, Pol.)

Daniel Ceccaldi
LIGHT ACROSSS THE STREET, THE(1957, Fr.); NANA(1957, Fr./Ital.); SOFT SKIN, THE(1964, Fr.); THAT MAN FROM RIO(1964, Fr./Ital.); FRIEND OF THE FAMILY(1965, Fr./Ital.); HOW NOT TO ROB A DEPARTMENT STORE(1965, Fr./Ital.); CLOPORTES(1966, Fr., Ital.); UPPER HAND, THE(1967, Fr./Ital./Ger.); POSTMAN GOES TO WAR, THE(1968, Fr.); STOLEN KISSES(1969, Fr.); BED AND BOARD(1971, Fr.); CHLOE IN THE AFTERNOON(1972, Fr.); DON'T CRY WITH YOUR MOUTH FULL(1974, Fr.); INCORRIGIBLE(1980, Fr.); CHARLES AND LUCIE(1982, Fr.)

Franco Ceccarelli
OPERATION KID BROTHER(1967, Ital.); WATERLOO(1970, Ital./USSR)

Lanfranco Ceccarelli
WHITE NIGHTS(1961, Ital./Fr.); BIG GUNDOWN, THE(1968, Ital.)

Luigi Ceccarelli
1984
CAGED WOMEN(1984, Ital./Fr.), m

Marcello Ceccarelli
GOSPEL ACCORDING TO ST. MATTHEW, THE(1966, Fr., Ital.), makeup; LONG RIDE FROM HELL, A(1970, Ital.), makeup

Mathilde Ceccarelli
TEN DAYS' WONDER(1972, Fr.)

Pietro Ceccarelli
TARTARS, THE(1962, Ital./Yugo.); REBEL GLADIATORS, THE(1963, Ital.); SEVEN SLAVES AGAINST THE WORLD(1965, Ital.)

Andrea Cecchi
BLACK SUNDAY(1961, Ital.); LADY WITHOUT CAMELLIAS, THE(1981, Ital.)

Carlo Cecchi
LE MANS(1971)

Dario Cecchi
NAKED MAJA, THE(1959, Ital./U.S.), cos; SAVAGE INNOCENTS, THE(1960, Brit.), art d; VIOLENT SUMMER(1961, Fr./Ital.), set d; BEST OF ENEMIES, THE(1962), cos; SWINDLE, THE(1962, Fr./Ital.), set d; RUN WITH THE DEVIL(1963, Fr./Ital.), art d

Emilio Cecchi
UNDER THE SUN OF ROME(1949, Ital.), w
Maria Barony Cecchi
SEVEN HILLS OF ROME, THE(1958), cos
Mario Cecchi
DUCH IN ORANGE SAUCE(1976, Ital.), p
Subo Cecchi
BEST OF ENEMIES, THE(1962), w
Cesare Ceccia
COLOSSUS OF RHODES, THE(1961, Ital., Fr., Span.), prod d
Bart Ceccon
MY WAY(1974, South Africa)
Aldo Cecconi
TRAMPLERS, THE(1966, Ital.); WATERLOO(1970, Ital./USSR)
Anthony Cecere
THING, THE(1982)
Dominic A. Cecere
WORLD ACCORDING TO GARP, The(1982)
Tony Cecere
DEAD AND BURIED(1981); SOLDIER, THE(1982); METALSTORM: THE DESTRUC-
TION OF JARED-SYN(1983)
Ed Cecil
GUILTY?(1930); FEROCIOUS PAL(1934); HIS FIGHTING BLOOD(1935); HOLLY-
WOOD BOULEVARD(1936); JUVENILE COURT(1938); SAY IT IN FRENCH(1938);
MAN FROM TUMBLEWEEDS, THE(1940); THIRD FINGER, LEFT HAND(1940)
Edward Cecil
PHANTOM OF THE OPERA, THE(1929); LOTUS LADY(1930); RESURREC-
TION(1931); SECRET MENACE(1931); CATTLE THIEF, THE(1936); PORT OF HA-
TE(1939); RIDERS OF THE FRONTIER(1939)
Silents
CAPTAIN OF THE GRAY HORSE TROOP, THE(1917); BREAD(1918); RISKY ROAD,
THE(1918); OFF-SHORE PIRATE, THE(1921); LOVE GAMBLER, THE(1922); SCAR-
LET CAR, THE(1923); SWORD OF VALOR, THE(1924); PHANTOM OF THE OPERA,
THE(1925); TOP OF NEW YORK, THE(1925); WHAT HAPPENED TO JONES(1926);
CHEATERS(1927); JAZZLAND(1928); SKY RIDER, THE(1928)
Misc. Silents
AFTER THE WAR(1918); COVE OF MISSING MEN(1918); DANGER ZONE,
THE(1918); GIRL FROM BOHEMIA, THE(1918); MAN WHO WOULDN'T TELL,
THE(1918); WILD CAT OF PARIS, THE(1919); BLACKMAIL(1920); CINDERELLA'S
TWIN(1920); GREATER CLAIM, THE(1921); PARTED CURTAINS(1921); THERE ARE
NO VILLAINS(1921); HIDDEN LOOT(1925); SMOKE EATERS, THE(1926); DESERT
OF THE LOST, THE(1927); HOOF MARKS(1927)
Edwin Cecil
Misc. Silents
LOVE THIEF, THE(1916)
Evelyn Cecil
Misc. Silents
ANGEL OF THE WARD, THE(1915, Brit.)
Henry Cecil
BROTHERS IN LAW(1957, Brit.), w
Jane Cecil
BRUBAKER(1980); PATERNITY(1981); TAPS(1981); WITHOUT A TRACE(1983)
Jonathan Cecil
OTLEY(1969, Brit.); RISE AND RISE OF MICHAEL RIMMER, THE(1970, Brit.);
CATCH ME A SPY(1971, Brit./Fr.); BARRY LYNDON(1975, Brit.); HISTORY OF THE
WORLD, PART 1(1981); AND THE SHIP SAILS ON(1983, Ital./Fr.)
Mary Cecil
WOMEN, THE(1939)
Nora Cecil
CAVALIER, THE(1928); SEVEN FOOTPRINTS TO SATAN(1929); LITTLE ACCI-
DENT(1930); ONLY SAPS WORK(1930); SEVEN DAYS LEAVE(1930); RULING
VOICE, THE(1931); STREET SCENE(1931); HOT SATURDAY(1932); PACK UP YOUR
TROUBLES(1932); BITTER TEA OF GENERAL YEN, THE(1933); DESIGN FOR
LIVING(1933); DR. BULL(1933); HOLD YOUR MAN(1933); LITTLE GIANT,
THE(1933); PEG O' MY HEART(1933); CHAINED(1934); HOLLYWOOD PARTY(1934);
LITTLE MISS MARKER(1934); MERRY WIDOW, THE(1934); OLD-FASHIONED
WAY, THE(1934); ONCE TO EVERY WOMAN(1934); SEARCH FOR BEAUTY(1934);
TWENTY MILLION SWEETHEARTS(1934); UPPER WORLD(1934); YOU'RE TELL-
ING ME(1934); CAR 99(1935); WAY DOWN EAST(1935); COLLEGE HOLIDAY(1936);
DANCING PIRATE(1936); FURY(1936); GIRL OF THE OZARKS(1936); POPPY(1936);
UNDER YOUR SPELL(1936); CHAMPAGNE WALTZ(1937); EASY LIVING(1937);
NIGHT OF MYSTERY(1937); NOTHING SACRED(1937); PARTNERS IN CRI-
ME(1937); INTERNATIONAL SETTLEMENT(1938); KING OF ALCATRAZ(1938); MR.
BOGGS STEPS OUT(1938); ST. LOUIS BLUES(1939); STAGECOACH(1939); UNION
PACIFIC(1939); WHAT A LIFE(1939); LUCKY PARTNERS(1940); GIRL, A GUY AND
A GOB, A(1941); OBLIGING YOUNG LADY(1941); I MARRIED A WITCH(1942);
TISH(1942); WIFE TAKES A FLYER, THE(1942); UNKNOWN GUEST, THE(1943);
MIRACLE OF MORGAN'S CREEK, THE(1944); THIN MAN GOES HOME, THE(1944);
TOGETHER AGAIN(1944); LADY ON A TRAIN(1945); MISSING LADY, THE(1946);
MOURNING BECOMES ELECTRA(1947); SEA OF GRASS, THE(1947)
Silents
ARRIVAL OF PERPETUA, THE(1915); AMERICAN BUDS(1918); APPEARANCE OF
EVIL(1918); PRUNELLA(1918); MISS CRUSOE(1919); FORTUNE HUNTER,
THE(1927); SENSATION SEEKERS(1927)
Misc. Silents
ROYAL ROMANCE(1917); RED FOAM(1920); CHIP OF THE FLYING U(1926);
CAVALIER, THE(1928)
Sylvia Cecil
MAIL TRAIN(1941, Brit.)
Walter Cecil
Silents
MANON LESCAUT(1914)
Cecil Stewart and His Royal Rogues
ALWAYS LEAVE THEM LAUGHING(1949)
Cecile
JONAH–WHO WILL BE 25 IN THE YEAR 2000(1976, Switz.)
Riva Spier Cecile
RABID(1976, Can.)

Ernando Cecilia
Silents
NERO(1922, U.S./Ital.)
Jon Cecka
PORKY'S(1982)
Elayne Cedar
PONY EXPRESS RIDER(1976), art d; GET CRAZY(1983), art d
Jon Cedar
CONCORDE, THE–AIRPORT '79(; QUICK AND THE DEAD, THE(1963); LITTLE
CIGARS(1973); SWASHBUCKLER(1976); DAY OF THE ANIMALS(1977); MANITOU,
THE(1978), a, w; DEATH HUNT(1981); SECOND THOUGHTS(1983)
Larry Cedar
TWILIGHT ZONE–THE MOVIE(1983)
1984
DREAMSCAPE(1984); EL NORTE(1984)
Ralph Cedar
SHE HAD TO CHOOSE(1934), d; PERFECT CLUE, THE(1935), w; MEET THE
MAYOR(1938), d; WEST OF ABILENE(1940), d
Silents
WIFE SAVERS(1928), d
Jon Ceddar
Misc. Talkies
KISS DADDY GOODBYE(1981)
Elayne Barbara Ceder
AMERICAN HOT WAX(1978), art d; WHEN A STRANGER CALLS(1979), prod d
Elayne Ceder
SECOND COMING OF SUZANNE, THE(1974), art d; SMALL TOWN IN TEXAS,
A(1976), art d; EVERY WHICH WAY BUT LOOSE(1978), art d; FIREFOX(1982), art d
Evelyn Ceder
WOMAN ON PIER 13, THE(1950)
Ralph Ceder
CAPTAIN BILL(1935, Brit.), d; STRICTLY ILLEGAL(1935, Brit.), d
Artur Cederborg
COUNT OF THE MONK'S BRIDGE, THE(1934, Swed.)
Ingrid Cedergren
SCORCHY(1976)
Gosta Cederlund
DOLLAR(1938, Swed.); WOMAN'S FACE, A(1939, Swed.); TORMENT(1947, Swed.);
VALLEY OF EAGLES(1952, Brit.); MATTER OF MORALS, A(1961, U.S./Swed.)
Leslie Cederquist
Misc. Talkies
GIRLS NEXT DOOR, THE(1979)
Sven Cederstrand
LAUGHING IN THE SUNSHINE(1953, Brit./Swed.), w
Ron Cedillos
BREAKER! BREAKER!(1977)
Cy Ceeder
FOUND ALIVE(1934)
Aat Ceelen
LIFT, THE(1983, Neth.)
Leonard Ceeley
MOONLIGHT MURDER(1936); DAY AT THE RACES, A(1937)
Irene Cefaro
SWINDLE, THE(1962, Fr./Ital.)
Ceffie
SERGEANTS 3(1962)
Elisa Cegani
FABIOLA(1951, Ital.); LUXURY GIRLS(1953, Ital.); TIMES GONE BY(1953, Ital.);
NANA(1957, Fr./Ital.); ANATOMY OF LOVE(1959, Ital.); CONSTANTINE AND THE
CROSS(1962, Ital.); RELUCTANT SAINT, THE(1962, U.S./Ital.); DOLL THAT TOOK
THE TOWN, THE(1965, Ital.); VERY HANDY MAN, A(1966, Fr./Ital.); SAUL AND
DAVID(1968, Ital./Span.); SICILIAN CLAN, THE(1970, Fr.)
1984
BEYOND GOOD AND EVIL(1984, Ital./Fr./Ger.)
Edward Cehman
LITTLE TOUGH GUY(1938)
Pina Cei
LOVE AND ANARCHY(1974, Ital.); LA TRAVIATA(1982)
1984
JOKE OF DESTINY LYING IN WAIT AROUND THE CORNER LIKE A STREET-
BANDIT, A(1984, Ital.)
Antoinette Ceillier
HOUSE OF MYSTERY(1941, Brit.)
Setoki Ceinaturoga
DOVE, THE(1974, Brit.)
Turk Cekovsky
DELIRIUM(1979)
Paloma Cela
TOWN CALLED HELL, A(1971, Span./Brit.)
Violeta Cela
1984
CONQUEST(1984, Ital./Span./Mex.)
Guidio Celano
THIS ANGRY AGE(1958, Ital./Fr.)
Guido Celano
FEDORA(1946, Ital.); DEPORTED(1950); NEVER TAKE NO FOR AN ANSWER(1952,
Brit./Ital.); THIEF OF VENICE, THE(1952); MAN FROM CAIRO, THE(1953); LOVES
OF THREE QUEENS, THE(1954, Ital./Fr.); WAR AND PEACE(1956, Ital./U.S.);
ATTILA(1958, Ital.); SEVEN HILLS OF ROME, THE(1958); TEMPEST(1958, Ital./
Yugo./Fr.); FIVE BRANDED WOMEN(1960); JOURNEY TO THE LOST CITY(1960,
Ger./Fr./Ital.); GREAT WAR, THE(1961, Fr., Ital.); PHAROAH'S WOMAN, THE(1961,
Ital.); BARABBAS(1962, Ital.); SWORD OF THE CONQUEROR(1962, Ital.); FLYING
SAUCER, THE(1964, Ital.); SEVEN DWARFS TO THE RESCUE(1965, Ital.);
HYPNOSIS(1966, Ger./Sp./Ital.); HILLS RUN RED, THE(1967, Ital.); L'IMMORTEL-
LE(1969, Fr./Ital./Turkey)
Alva Celauro
SWIMMER, THE(1968)

Willard Cele
PENNYWHISTLE BLUES, THE(1952, South Africa)

Yasemin Celenk
YOR, THE HUNTER FROM THE FUTURE(1983, Ital.)

Adriano Celentano
LA DOLCE VITA(1961, Ital./Fr.); SERAFINO(1970, Fr./Ital.); WHITE SISTER(1973, Ital./Span./Fr.); CON ARTISTS, THE(1981, Ital.); BINGO BONGO(1983, Ital.)

John Celentano
JEANNE EAGELS(1957)

Celeste
FLASH GORDON(1980)

Olga Celeste
CLEOPATRA(1934)

Celestin
RULES OF THE GAME, THE(1939, Fr.)

Jack Celestin
GABLES MYSTERY, THE(1931, Brit.), w; SILENT WITNESS, THE(1932), w; CRIME ON THE HILL(1933, Brit.), w; LINE ENGAGED(1935, Brit.), w; LOVE TEST, THE(1935, Brit.), w; WINDFALL(1935, Brit.), w; CRIMES OF STEPHEN HAWKE, THE(1936, Brit.), w; JURY'S EVIDENCE(1936, Brit.), w; GABLES MYSTERY, THE(1938, Brit.), w

Pierre Celeyron
1984
SWANN IN LOVE(1984, Fr.Ger.)

Adolfo Celi
AGONY AND THE ECSTASY, THE(1965); MALE COMPANION(1965, Fr./Ital.); THUNDERBALL(1965, Brit.); VON RYAN'S EXPRESS(1965); EL GRECO(1966, Ital., Fr.); GRAND PRIX(1966); BOBO, THE(1967, Brit.); DEATH SENTENCE(1967, Ital.); HEAD OF THE FAMILY(1967, Ital./Fr.); HONEY POT, THE(1967, Brit.); KING OF HEARTS(1967, Fr./Ital.); OPERATION KID BROTHER(1967, Ital.); AND THERE CAME A MAN(1968, Ital.); DANGER: DIABOLIK(1968, Ital./Fr.); GRAND SLAM(1968, Ital., Span., Ger.); MIDAS RUN(1969); DETECTIVE BELLI(1970, Ital.); IN SEARCH OF GREGORY(1970, Brit./Ital.); DIRTY HEROES(1971, Ital./Fr./Ger.); FRAGMENT OF FEAR(1971, Brit.); MURDERS IN THE RUE MORGUE(1971); BROTHER SUN, SISTER MOON(1973, Brit./Ital.); ITALIAN CONNECTION, THE(1973, U.S./Ital./Ger.); PHANTOM OF LIBERTY, THE(1974, Fr.); TEMPTER, THE(1974, Ital./Brit.); DEVIL IS A WOMAN, THE(1975, Brit./Ital.); TEN LITTLE INDIANS(1975, Ital./Fr./Span./Ger.); NEXT MAN, THE(1976); GOODNIGHT, LADIES AND GENTLEMEN(1977, Ital.); CAFE EXPRESS(1980, Ital.); MONSIGNOR(1982)
Misc. Talkies
SEVEN TIMES SEVEN(1973, Ital.)

Adolph Celi
HITLER: THE LAST TEN DAYS(1973, Brit./Ital.)

Adolpho Celi
THAT MAN FROM RIO(1964, Fr./Ital.)

Celia
JUST BEFORE NIGHTFALL(1975, Fr./Ital.); BODY AND SOUL(1981), cos

Hikmet Celik
YOL(1982, Turkey)

Nikolai Celikhovsky
MISSION TO MOSCOW(1943)

Stanislawa Celinska
YOUNG GIRLS OF WILKO, THE(1979, Pol./Fr.)

Mary Celio
1984
IMPULSE(1984)

Jose Luis Celis
LA CUCARACHA(1961, Mex.), w; LITTLE ANGEL(1961, Mex.), p, w

Debbie Celiz
AMERICAN GRAFFITI(1973)

Cell Block Seven
ROCK BABY, ROCK IT(1957)

Ettore Cella
PORTRAIT OF A WOMAN(1946, Fr.); IT HAPPENED IN BROAD DAYLIGHT(1960, Ger./Switz.); UNWILLING AGENT(1968, Ger.)

Gianfranco Cella
FIST IN HIS POCKET(1968, Ital.)

Maria Cellario
SIDELONG GLANCES OF A PIGEON KICKER, THE(1970); WITHOUT A TRA-CE(1983)

Liliana Celli
COME SEPTEMBER(1961)

Paolo Celli
1984
RUSH(1984, Ital.)

Teresa Celli
BORDER INCIDENT(1949); ASPHALT JUNGLE, THE(1950); BLACK HAND, THE(1950); CRISIS(1950); RIGHT CROSS(1950); GREAT CARUSO, THE(1951)

Andre Cellier
RIFF RAFF GIRLS(1962, Fr./Ital.); CONFESSION, THE(1970, Fr.)

Antoinette Cellier
LATE EXTRA(1935, Brit.); MUSIC HATH CHARMS(1935, Brit.); REGAL CAVALCADE(1935, Brit.); DEATH CROONS THE BLUES(1937, Brit.); RIVER OF UNREST(1937, Brit.); SILENT BARRIERS(1937, Brit.); TENTH MAN, THE(1937, Brit.); GABLES MYSTERY, THE(1938, Brit.); LUCKY TO ME(1939, Brit.); HEADLINE(1943, Brit.); BEES IN PARADISE(1944, Brit.); RANDOLPH FAMILY, THE(1945, Brit.); END OF THE RIVER, THE(1947, Brit.)

Antoinettee Cellier
WHO IS GUILTY?(1940, Brit.)

Caroline Cellier
LIFE LOVE DEATH(1969, Fr./Ital.); THIS MAN MUST DIE(1970, Fr./Ital.)

Frank Cellier
HER REPUTATION(1931, Brit.); TIN GODS(1932, Brit.); DOSS HOUSE(1933, Brit.); FIRE RAISERS, THE(1933, Brit.); GOLDEN CAGE, THE(1933, Brit.); COLONEL BLOOD(1934, Brit.); POWER(1934, Brit.); WOMAN IN COMMAND, THE(1934 Brit.); DICTATOR, THE(1935, Brit./Ger.); LORNA DOONE(1935, Brit.); 39 STEPS, THE(1935, Brit.); LADY JANE GREY(1936, Brit.); MAN WHO LIVED AGAIN, THE(1936, Brit.); MISTER HOBO(1936, Brit.); PASSING OF THE THIRD FLOOR BACK, THE(1936, Brit.); RHODES(1936, Brit.); ACTION FOR SLANDER(1937, Brit.); NON-STOP NEW YORK(1937, Brit.); TAKE MY TIP(1937, Brit.); YOU'RE IN THE ARMY NOW(1937,

Brit.); KATE PLUS TEN(1938, Brit.); ROYAL DIVORCE, A(1938, Brit.); SIXTY GLORIOUS YEARS(1938, Brit.); WARE CASE, THE(1939, Brit.); MIDAS TOUCH, THE(1940, Brit.); SPIDER, THE(1940, Brit.); BLACK SHEEP OF WHITEHALL, THE(1941 Brit.); BOMBSIGHT STOLEN(1941, Brit.); GIRL IN DISTRESS(1941, Brit.); QUIET WEDDING(1941, Brit.); BIG BLOCKADE, THE(1942, Brit.); SHIPS WITH WINGS(1942, Brit.); GIVE US THE MOON(1944, Brit.); LOVE ON THE DOLE(1945, Brit.); MAGIC BOW, THE(1947, Brit.); BLIND GODDESS, THE(1948, Brit.); EASY MONEY(1948, Brit.); QUIET WEEKEND(1948, Brit.)

Peter Cellier
OTHELLO(1965, Brit.); MORGAN!(1966, Brit.); YOUNG WINSTON(1972, Brit.); LUTHER(1974); BARRY LYNDON(1975, Brit.); MAN FRIDAY(1975, Brit.); JABBER-WOCKY(1977, Brit.); CHARIOTS OF FIRE(1981, Brit.); AND THE SHIP SAILS ON(1983, Ital./Fr.)

Joseph Cellini
MOTOR PSYCHO(1965)

Nikki Cellini
TOP BANANA(1954)

Celina Cely
MADAME(1963, Fr./Ital./Span.)

Susan Cembrowska
PHANTOM PLANET, THE(1961)

Iga Cembrzynska
SALTO(1966, Pol.); JOVITA(1970, Pol.); SARAGOSSA MANUSCRIPT, THE(1972, Pol.)

Beatrice Cenci
SKY ABOVE HEAVEN(1964, Fr./Ital.)

Blaise Cendrars
SUTTER'S GOLD(1936), w

Michel Cenet
MOTHER AND THE WHORE, THE(1973, Fr.), ph; CELINE AND JULIE GO BOATING(1974, Fr.), ph

Olivia Cenizal
KIDNAPPERS, THE(1964, U.S./Phil.)

Marino Cenna
PADRE PADRONE(1977, Ital.); LEAP INTO THE VOID(1982, Ital.)

Pasquale Cennamo
GOLD OF NAPLES(1957, Ital.); YESTERDAY, TODAY, AND TOMORROW(1964, Ital./Fr.)

Centa
WAGES OF FEAR, THE(1955, Fr./Ital.)

Antonio Centa
BALL AT THE CASTLE(1939, Ital.); GLASS MOUNTAIN, THE(1950, Brit)

Tony Centa
FUGITIVE LADY(1951)

Andres Centenera
TWILIGHT PEOPLE(1972, Phil.)

Lia Centeno
WAY OF A GAUCHO(1952)

Centre De Danse Classique Dancers
YELLOW HAT, THE(1966, Brit.)

Toni Ceo
SIGN OF AQUARIUS(1970)

Gerardo Cepeda
SANTO Y BLUE DEMON CONTRA LOS MONSTRUOS(1968, Mex.); HIGH RISK(1981)

Francois Ceppi
NO TIME FOR BREAKFAST(1978, Fr.), ed

Mario Cequi
ISLAND OF PROCIDA, THE(1952, Ital.), d

Tommy Cerafice
YOU'VE GOT TO WALK IT LIKE YOU TALK IT OR YOU'LL LOSE THAT BEAT(1971)

C.W. Ceram
VALLEY OF THE KINGS(1954), w

Armand Cerami
CALIFORNIA SUITE(1978)

Matteo Cerami
BLOW TO THE HEART(1983, Ital.)

Vincenzo Cerami
DIRTY OUTLAWS, THE(1971, Ital.), w; BLINDMAN(1972, Ital.), w; EYES, THE MOUTH, THE(1982, Ital./Fr.), w; LEAP INTO THE VOID(1982, Ital.), w; BLOW TO THE HEART(1983, Ital.), w

Armand Cerani
BLUES BROTHERS, THE(1980)

Clorindo Cerato
SENSUALITA(1954, Ital.)

Frederique Cerbonnet
LOULOU(1980, Fr.)

Fernando Cerchio
HEAD OF A TYRANT(1960, Fr./Ital.), d, w; HEROD THE GREAT(1960, Ital.), w; DESERT WARRIOR(1961 Ital./Span.), d; CLEOPATRA'S DAUGHTER(1963, Fr., Ital.), d, w; RED SHEIK, THE(1963, Ital.), d; QUEEN OF THE NILE(1964, Ital.), d, w; INVASION 1700(1965, Fr./Ital./Yugo.), d; LIPSTICK(1965, Fr./Ital.), ed; WEB OF VIOLENCE(1966, Ital./Span.), w

Marcel Cerdan, Jr.
1984
EDITH AND MARCEL(1984, Fr.)

Giancarlo Cereda
ALLEGRO NON TROPPO(1977, Ital.), anim

Huw Ceredig
MOUSE AND THE WOMAN, THE(1981, Brit.); GIRO CITY(1982, Brit.)

Mario Cereli
DRIVER'S SEAT, THE(1975, Ital.), art d

Virginia Cerenio
CHAN IS MISSING(1982)

Michele Cerf
BEAU PERE(1981, Fr.), cos; WOMAN NEXT DOOR, THE(1981, Fr.), cos
1984
MY BEST FRIEND'S GIRL(1984, Fr.), cos

Jaques Cey
HOUSE OF THE ARROW, THE(1953, Brit.)
Ron Cey
Q(1982)
Hasan Ceylan
FROM RUSSIA WITH LOVE(1963, Brit.)
George Cezar
CROOKED WEB, THE(1955)
Paul Cezeneuve
Misc. Silents
IRON HEART, THE(1920), d; SQUARE SHOOTER, THE(1920), d
Connie Cezon
FEMALE JUNGLE, THE(1955); ERRAND BOY, THE(1961)
Lord Cezon
RUGGLES OF RED GAP(1935)
T'ang Juo Ch'ing
OUT OF THE TIGER'S MOUTH(1962)
Stanley Cha
HOLD BACK THE NIGHT(1956)
Cha-bing
SINGAPORE(1947)
Habib Chaari
1984
MISUNDERSTOOD(1984)
J. J. Chaback
FRANCES(1982)
Lydia Chaban
QUEST FOR FIRE(1982, Fr./Can.)
Jacques Chabannes
PALACE OF NUDES(1961, Fr./Ital.), w
Jacques Chabassol
WOMEN AND WAR(1965, Fr.)
Ray Chabeau
SWEET CHARITY(1969)
M. E. Chaber
MAN INSIDE, THE(1958, Brit.), w
Chabing
CHINESE RING, THE(1947); SHANGHAI CHEST, THE(1948); I WAS AN AMERI-
CAN SPY(1951)
Amedee Chabot
SILENCERS, THE(; FOR THOSE WHO THINK YOUNG(1964); HOUSE IS NOT A
HOME, A(1964); MUSCLE BEACH PARTY(1964); MURDERERS' ROW(1966); GNOME-
MOBILE, THE(1967)
Irene Chabrier
JOKER, THE(1961, Fr.); ZAZIE(1961, Fr.); MALE COMPANION(1965, Fr./Ital.)
Claude Chabrol
BREATHLESS(1959, Fr.), art d; COUSINS, THE(1959, Fr.), p&d, w; LE BEAU
SERGE(1959, Fr.), d&w; WEB OF PASSION(1961, Fr.), d; PARIS BELONGS TO
US(1962, Fr.); SEVEN CAPITAL SINS(1962, Fr./Ital.), d; LANDRU(1963, Fr./Ital), a,
d; THIRD LOVER, THE(1963, Fr./Ital.), d; OPHELIA(1964, Fr.), d, w; BEAUTIFUL
SWINDLERS, THE(1967, Fr./Ital./Jap./Neth.), d; CHAMPAGNE MURDERS,
THE(1968, Fr.), d; LES BICHES(1968, Fr.), a, d, w; SIX IN PARIS(1968, Fr.), a, d, w;
LA FEMME INFIDELE(1969, Fr./Ital.), d&w; THIS MAN MUST DIE(1970, Fr./Ital.),
d, w; WHO'S GOT THE BLACK BOX?(1970, Fr./Gr./Ital.), a, d; LE BOUCHER(1971,
Fr./Ital.), d&w; DOCTEUR POPAUL(1972, Fr.), d; TEN DAYS' WONDER(1972, Fr.), d;
NADA GANG, THE(1974, Fr./Ital.), d, w; JUST BEFORE NIGHTFALL(1975, Fr./Ital.),
d&w; DIRTY HANDS(1976, Fr/Ital./Ger.), d, w; TWIST, THE(1976, Fr.), d, w; AL-
ICE, OR THE LAST ESCAPADE(1977, Fr.), d, w; BLOOD RELATIVES(1978, Fr./Can.),
d, w; VIOLETTE(1978, Fr.), d; HORSE OF PRIDE(1980, Fr.), d, w; HATTER'S
GHOST, THE(1982, Fr.), d&w
Jean-Pierre Chabrol
SHOCK TROOPS(1968, Ital./Fr.), d&w
Mathieu Chabrol
HATTER'S GHOST, THE(1982, Fr.), m
Thomas Chabrol
ALICE, OR THE LAST ESCAPADE(1977, Fr.)
A. Chabrov
Misc. Silents
SATAN TRIUMPHANT(1917, USSR)
Raymonde Chabrun
MOUCHETTE(1970, Fr.)
Dorothy Chace
PARADES(1972)
H. Haile Chace
HOT CARS(1956), w
Haile Chace
MONSTER OF PIEDRAS BLANCAS, THE(1959), w; V.D.(1961), d&w
Chachita
1984
ROMANCING THE STONE(1984)
Juan Chacon
SALT OF THE EARTH(1954)
Miguel Chacour
ECHOES OF SILENCE(1966)
Tom Chadbon
BEAST MUST DIE, THE(1974, Brit.); TESS(1980, Fr./Brit.)
Arthur Chadbourne
Misc. Talkies
ASTROLOGER, THE(1975)
Richard Chadbourne II
Misc. Talkies
YOU AND ME(1975)
Karla Chadimova
DEVIL'S TRAP, THE(1964, Czech.); SWEET LIGHT IN A DARK ROOM(1966, Czech.);
MARKETA LAZAROVA(1968, Czech.); SEVENTH CONTINENT, THE(1968, Czech./
Yugo.); SKI FEVER(1969, U.S./Aust./Czech.)
Chris Chadman
1984
MUPPETS TAKE MANHATTAN, THE(1984), ch

Christopher Chadman
1984
FLAMINGO KID, THE(1984)
Wallace Chadweel
ADAM HAD FOUR SONS(1941)
Wallace Chadwell
BRINGING UP FATHER(1946)
Cyril Chadwick
BLACK WATCH, THE(1929); LAST OF MRS. CHEYNEY, THE(1929); LADY OF
SCANDAL, THE(1930); ONCE A GENTLEMAN(1930); TEMPLE TOWER(1930); THIR-
TEENTH CHAIR, THE(1930); BIG BLUFF, THE(1933); SENSATION HUNTERS(1934);
HATE IN PARADISE(1938, Brit.)
Silents
MRS. BLACK IS BACK(1914); ON THE QUIET(1918); OUT YONDER(1920); STRAN-
GER'S BANQUET(1922); THIRTY DAYS(1922); DON'T MARRY FOR MONEY(1923);
LITTLE CHURCH AROUND THE CORNER(1923); SLANDER THE WOMAN(1923);
SOCIAL CODE, THE(1923); IRON HORSE, THE(1924); PETER PAN(1924); STORM
DAUGHTER, THE(1924); FORTY WINKS(1925); FOREIGN DEVILS(1927); IS ZAT
SO?(1927); ACTRESS, THE(1928); EXCESS BAGGAGE(1928)
Misc. Silents
SMUGGLERS, THE(1916); MISLEADING LADY, THE(1920); RUSTLE OF SILK,
THE(1923); HAPPINESS(1924); HEART BUSTER, THE(1924); MAN WHO CAME
BACK, THE(1924); BEST BAD MAN, THE(1925); HUNTED WOMAN, THE(1925);
SPORTING LIFE(1925); GIGOLO(1926); HOLD THAT LION(1926)
Helen Chadwick
Misc. Silents
VENGEANCE IS MINE(1918); CALEB PIPER'S GIRL(1919)
Helene Chadwick
FATHER AND SON(1929); MEN ARE LIKE THAT(1930); HELL BOUND(1931);
FRISCO KID(1935); MISSISSIPPI(1935); SCHOOL FOR GIRLS(1935); SAN FRANCIS-
CO(1936); STAR IS BORN, A(1937)
Silents
NAULAHKA, THE(1918); ADVENTURE IN HEARTS, AN(1919); FROM THE
GROUND UP(1921); MADE IN HEAVEN(1921); DUST FLOWER, THE(1922); GIM-
MIE(1923); RENO(1923); HER OWN FREE WILL(1924); PLEASURES OF THE
RICH(1926); BACHELOR'S BABY, THE(1927); STAGE KISSES(1927); STOLEN
PLEASURES(1927)
Misc. Silents
T.N.T(THE NAKED TRUTH) (1924); CHALLENGE, THE(1916); ANGEL FACTORY,
THE(1917); IRON HEART, THE(1917); GIRLS(1919); GO GET 'EM GARRINGER(1919);
HEARTSEASE(1919); LONG ARM OF MANNISTER, THE(1919); SOLITARY SIN,
THE(1919); VERY GOOD YOUNG MAN, A(1919); CUP OF FURY, THE(1920); CUPID,
THE COWPUNCHER(1920); SCRATCH MY BACK(1920); DANGEROUS CURVE
AHEAD(1921); GODLESS MEN(1921); BROTHERS UNDER THE SKIN(1922); GLORI-
OUS FOOL, THE(1922); SIN FLOOD, THE(1922); YELLOW MEN AND GOLD(1922);
QUICKSANDS(1923); BORDER LEGION, THE(1924); DARK SWAN, THE(1924); LOVE
OF WOMEN(1924); MASKED DANCER, THE(1924); TROUPING WITH ELLEN(1924);
WHY MEN LEAVE HOME(1924); RE-CREATION OF BRIAN KENT, THE(1925);
DANCING DAYS(1926); GOLDEN COCOON, THE(1926); HARD BOILED(1926); STILL
ALARM, THE(1926); ROSE OF KILDARE, THE(1927); CONFESSIONS OF A WI-
FE(1928); MODERN MOTHERS(1928); SAY IT WITH SABLES(1928); WOMEN WHO
DARE(1928)
I. E. Chadwick
COUNTY FAIR, THE(1932), p; FAME STREET(1932), p; OLIVER TWIST(1933), p
Silents
MASKED ANGEL(1928), p
I.E. Chadwick
FLAMES(1932), w; LEGION OF MISSING MEN(1937), p; OUTER GATE, THE(1937),
p; HER FIRST ROMANCE(1940), p; REDHEAD(1941), p
Ida May Chadwick
PARDON MY GUN(1930)
Joseph Chadwick
RIM OF THE CANYON(1949), w
June Chadwick
GOLDEN LADY, THE(1979, Brit.); FORBIDDEN WORLD(1982)
1984
LAST HORROR FILM, THE(1984); THIS IS SPINAL TAP(1984)
Lee Chadwick
STRANGE ADVENTURE(1932), w
Les Chadwick
FERRY ACROSS THE MERSEY(1964, Brit.)
Lisa Chadwick
1984
SWING SHIFT(1984)
Nancy Chadwick
FIRST NUDIE MUSICAL, THE(1976); YOU LIGHT UP MY LIFE(1977), a, cos
Robin Chadwick
HAMLET(1969, Brit.); JULIUS CAESAR(1970, Brit.)
Rose Chadwick
Misc. Silents
TRACY THE OUTLAW(1928)
Warren Chadwick
SCARED TO DEATH(1981), ed
1984
HOLLYWOOD HIGH PART II(1984), ed; JUNGLE WARRIORS(1984, U.S./Ger./
Mex.), ed
Sam Chadwyck
TIMERIDER(1983)
Afred Chafe
TRAUMA(1962)
Verena Chaffe
WAY WE LIVE, THE(1946, Brit.)
Joan Chaffee
UP IN ARMS(1944)
Suzy Chaffee
BENJAMIN(1973, Ger.)
Edward Chaffers
MALTA STORY(1954, Brit.)

Don Chaffey
CROOKED ROAD, THE(, d, w; SKID KIDS(1953, Brit.), d; GIRL IN THE PICTURE, THE(1956, Brit.), d; SECRET TENT, THE(1956, Brit.), d; FLESH IS WEAK, THE(1957, Brit.), d; TIME IS MY ENEMY(1957, Brit.), d; MAN UPSTAIRS, THE(1959, Brit.), d, w; QUESTION OF ADULTERY, A(1959, Brit.), d; BREAKOUT(1960, Brit.), d; DENTIST IN THE CHAIR(1960, Brit.), d; LIES MY FATHER TOLD ME(1960, Brit.), p, d; GREYFRIARS BOBBY(1961, Brit.), d; MATTER OF WHO, A(1962, Brit.), d; NEARLY A NASTY ACCIDENT(1962, Brit.), d; STOLEN PLANS, THE(1962, Brit.), art d; WEBSTER BOY, THE(1962, Brit.), d; JASON AND THE ARGONAUTS(1963, Brit.), d; THREE LIVES OF THOMASINA, THE(1963, U.S./Brit.), d; JOLLY BAD FELLOW, A(1964, Brit.), d; ONE MILLION YEARS B.C.(1967, Brit./U.S.), d; VIKING QUEEN, THE(1967, Brit.), d; TWIST OF SAND, A(1968, Brit.), d; CREATURES THE WORLD FORGOT(1971, Brit.), d; CHARLEY-ONE-EYE(1973, Brit.), d; PERSECUTION(1974, Brit.), d; RIDE A WILD PONY(1976, U.S./Aus.), d; PETE'S DRAGON(1977), d; MAGIC OF LASSIE, THE(1978), d; C.H.O.M.P.S.(1979), d

John Chaffey
OPTIMISTS, THE(1973, Brit.)

Robina Chaffey
MAD MAX(1979, Aus.)

Donald Chaffin
TITANIC(1953); TATTERED DRESS, THE(1957)

1984
FLETCH(1984)

John Chaffin
JUST FOR THE HELL OF IT(1968); SHE-DEVILS ON WHEELS(1968)

Susan Chafitz
TAKING OFF(1971)

Chaflan
GUADALAJARA(1943, Mex.); PASSION ISLAND(1943, Mex.)

Walmor Chagas
XICA(1982, Braz.)

Charles Chagnon
HARRY'S WAR(1981)

Francis Chagril
DEEP BLUE SEA, THE(1955, Brit.), m/1

Francis Chagrin
CONTINENTAL EXPRESS(1939, Brit.), m; LAST HOLIDAY(1950, Brit.), m; CASTLE IN THE AIR(1952, Brit.), m; INSPECTOR CALLS, AN(1954, Brit.), m; COLDITZ STORY, THE(1955, Brit.), m; INTRUDER, THE(1955, Brit.), m; SIMBA(1955, Brit.), m; THE BEACHCOMBER(1955, Brit.), m; CHARLEY MOON(1956, Brit.), m; NO TIME FOR TEARS(1957, Brit.), m; SNORKEL, THE(1958, Brit.), m; STRANGE AFFECTION(1959, Brit.), m; GREYFRIARS BOBBY(1961, Brit.), m; MONSTER OF HIGHGATE PONDS, THE(1961, Brit.), m; IN THE COOL OF THE DAY(1963), m; CLUE OF THE TWISTED CANDLE(1968, Brit.), m; MARRIAGE OF CONVENIENCE(1970, Brit.), m

Julian Chagrin
DANGER ROUTE(1968, Brit.); ALFRED THE GREAT(1969, Brit.); GREAT MCGONAGALL, THE(1975, Brit.)

Nicholas Chagrin
PIRATES OF PENZANCE, THE(1983)

Abdallah Chahed
L'ETOILE DU NORD(1983, Fr.)

James Chai
NIGHTBEAST(1982), makeup

Po Chai
JUNGLE OF CHANG(1951)

Enrique Chaico
WAY OF A GAUCHO(1952)

Y. Chaika
Misc. Silents
ISLE OF OBLIVION(1917, USSR); INFINITE SORROW(1922, USSR)

Janice Chaikelson
CITY ON FIRE(1979 Can.)

Steven Chaikelson
CITY ON FIRE(1979 Can.)

Joseph Chaikin
ME AND MY BROTHER(1969)

Judy Howard Chaikin
JOHNNY GOT HIS GUN(1971)

Jacques Chailieux
GOING PLACES(1974, Fr.)

F.T. Chaillee
Silents
ANNE OF GREEN GABLES(1919)

Gerard Chaillou
DIVA(1982, Fr.)

Luciano Chailly
LUCIANO(1963, Ital.), m

Barbara Chain
MR. MAGOO'S HOLIDAY FESTIVAL(1970), w

Mike Chain
DARK AT THE TOP OF THE STAIRS, THE(1960)

Des Roberts Chainer
BLACK ANGELS, THE(1970)

Roy Chaio
GAME OF DEATH, THE(1979)

Chaiporn
OPERATION CIA(1965)

Norman C. Chaitin
SMALL HOURS, THE(1962), p,d&w, ed

Acho Chakatouny
Silents
NAPOLEON(1927, Fr.)

F. Chakhava
DRAGONFLY, THE(1955 USSR)

Maury Chakin
NOTHING PERSONAL(1980, Can.)

George Chakiris
WHITE CHRISTMAS(1954); GIRL RUSH, THE(1955); UNDER FIRE(1957); WEST SIDE STORY(1961); DIAMOND HEAD(1962); TWO AND TWO MAKE SIX(1962, Brit.); KINGS OF THE SUN(1963); BEBO'S GIRL(1964, Ital.); FLIGHT FROM ASHIYA(1964, U.S./Jap.); SQUADRON 633(1964, U.S./Brit.); 633 SQUADRON(1964); IS PARIS BURNING?(1966, U.S./Fr.); MC GUIRE, GO HOME!(1966, Brit.); DAY THE HOTLINE GOT HOT, THE(1968, Fr.); YOUNG GIRLS OF ROCHEFORT, THE(1968, Fr.); BIG CUBE, THE(1969); JEKYLL AND HYDE...TOGETHER AGAIN(1982)

M.R.B. Chakrabandhu
BRIDGE ON THE RIVER KWAI, THE(1957)

Tulshi Chakraborty
PATHER PANCHALI(1958, India)

Khagesh Chakravarty
GODDESS, THE(1962, India)

Mihir Rakhal Chakravarty
TWO DAUGHTERS(1963, India)

S. Alke Chakravarty
WORLD OF APU, THE(1960, India)

Dennis Chaldecott
DARK ANGEL, THE(1935)

Fay Chaldecott
DARK ANGEL, THE(1935); DAVID COPPERFIELD(1935); TALE OF TWO CITIES, A(1935); LLOYDS OF LONDON(1936)

Rich Chalet
IMPOSSIBLE YEARS, THE(1968)

Frank Chalfant
O.S.S.(1946)

Feodor Chaliapin
DON QUIXOTE(1935, Fr.); LAW OF THE JUNGLE(1942); FOR WHOM THE BELL TOLLS(1943); MISSION TO MOSCOW(1943); SEVENTH VICTIM, THE(1943); THREE RUSSIAN GIRLS(1943); ROYAL SCANDAL, A(1945); ZIEGFELD FOLLIES(1945); PRISONER OF THE VOLGA(1960, Fr./Ital.); FRANCIS OF ASSISI(1961); NIGHT THEY KILLED RASPUTIN, THE(1962, Fr./Ital.); SODOM AND GOMORRAH(1962, U.S./Fr./Ital.)

Feodor Chaliapin, Jr.
LANCER SPY(1937); EXILE EXPRESS(1939)

Al Chalk
AMERICAN HOT WAX(1978)

Gary Chalk
GREY FOX, THE(1983, Can.)

Harvey Chalk
CURUCU, BEAST OF THE AMAZON(1956); LOVE SLAVES OF THE AMAZONS(1957)

William Challee
WITHOUT RESERVATIONS(1946); DAYS OF GLORY(1944); DESTINATION TOKYO(1944); NONE BUT THE LONELY HEART(1944); SEVENTH CROSS, THE(1944); GOD IS MY CO-PILOT(1945); MISS SUSIE SLAGLE'S(1945); SONG TO REMEMBER, A(1945); TOKYO ROSE(1945); DEADLINE AT DAWN(1946); NOCTURNE(1946); BOOMERANG(1947); DESPERATE(1947); GUILT OF JANET AMES, THE(1947); SEA OF GRASS, THE(1947); FORCE OF EVIL(1948); TAP ROOTS(1948); BLACK BOOK, THE(1949); PORT OF NEW YORK(1949); OUTRAGE(1950); ON DANGEROUS GROUND(1951); WHIP HAND, THE(1951); THIS WOMAN IS DANGEROUS(1952); GLENN MILLER STORY, THE(1953); CHICAGO SYNDICATE(1955); MAN WITHOUT A STAR(1955); DESPERADOES ARE IN TOWN, THE(1956); CALYPSO HEAT WAVE(1957); RAINTREE COUNTY(1957); TWILIGHT FOR THE GODS(1958); STORY ON PAGE ONE, THE(1959); NOOSE FOR A GUNMAN(1960); PLUNDERERS, THE(1960); NIGHTMARE IN THE SUN(1964); CINCINNATI KID, THE(1965); BILLY THE KID VS. DRACULA(1966); FIVE EASY PIECES(1970); ZACHARIAH(1971); GREAT NORTHFIELD, MINNESOTA RAID, THE(1972); MOONCHILD(1972); IRISH WHISKEY REBELLION(1973)

Paul Challen
LAST VALLEY, THE(1971, Brit.)

Percy Challenger
SKY HAWK(1929)

Silents
ASHES OF HOPE(1917); FLAMES OF CHANCE, THE(1918); FLY GOD, THE(1918); NANCY COMES HOME(1918); BLIND HUSBANDS(1919); HER MAD BARGAIN(1921); NOBODY'S FOOL(1921); STING OF THE LASH(1921); GALLOPING KID, THE(1922); KISSED(1922); TAKING CHANCES(1922); TRACKED TO EARTH(1922); WILD HONEY(1922); SWORD OF VALOR, THE(1924); WHEEL OF DESTINY, THE(1927)
Misc. Silents
MEDICINE MAN, THE(1917); LONELY WOMAN, THE(1918); HEART OF TWENTY, THE(1920); MAGNIFICENT BRUTE, THE(1921); WOLVES OF THE NORTH(1921); SMILING JIM(1922); SINGLE HANDED(1923)

Rudy Challenger
CHANGE OF MIND(1969); COOL BREEZE(1972); HIT MAN(1972); DETROIT 9000(1973); SHEBA BABY(1975)

Leading Aircraftsman Bromley Challenor
JOURNEY TOGETHER(1946, Brit.)

Pauline Challenor
GO KART GO(1964, Brit.); HOUSE THAT SCREAMED, THE(1970, Span.)

Barbara Challis
FAMILY HONEYMOON(1948); LARCENY(1948); SAXON CHARM, THE(1948)

Chris Challis
SHOT IN THE DARK, A(1964), ph; RETURN FROM THE ASHES(1965, U.S./Brit.), ph; FORCE 10 FROM NAVARONE(1978, Brit.), ph

Christopher Challis
DRUMS(1938, Brit.), ph; HOUR OF GLORY(1949, Brit.), ph; FIGHTING PIMPERNEL, THE(1950, Brit.), ph; TALES OF HOFFMANN, THE(1951, Brit.), ph; WILD HEART, THE(1952, Brit.), ph; GENEVIEVE(1953, Brit.), ph; GREAT GILBERT AND SULLIVAN, THE(1953, Brit.), ph; SAADIA(1953), ph; TWICE UPON A TIME(1953, Brit.), ph; ANGELS ONE FIVE(1954, Brit.), ph; FIRE OVER AFRICA(1954, Brit.), ph; FLAME AND THE FLESH(1954), ph; FOOTSTEPS IN THE FOG(1955, Brit.), ph; QUENTIN DURWARD(1955), ph; OH ROSALINDA(1956, Brit.), ph; MIRACLE IN SOHO(1957, Brit.), ph; PURSUIT OF THE GRAF SPEE(1957, Brit.), ph; RAISING A RIOT(1957, Brit.), ph; SPANISH GARDENER, THE(1957, Span.), ph; FLOODS OF FEAR(1958, Brit.), ph; NIGHT AMBUSH(1958, Brit.), ph; ROONEY(1958, Brit.), ph; WINDOM'S WAY(1958, Brit.), ph; CAPTAIN'S TABLE, THE(1960, Brit.), ph; CHANCE MEETING(1960, Brit.), ph; GRASS IS GREENER, THE(1960), ph; NEVER LET

GO(1960, Brit.), ph; SINK THE BISMARCK!(1960, Brit.), ph; SURPRISE PACKAGE(1960), ph; FIVE GOLDEN HOURS(1961, Brit.), ph; FLAME IN THE STREETS(1961, Brit.), ph; DAMN THE DEFIANT!(1962, Brit.), ph; VICTORS, THE(1963, Brit.), ph; LONG SHIPS, THE(1964, Brit./Yugo.), ph; THOSE MAGNIFICENT MEN IN THEIR FLYING MACHINES; OR HOW I FLEWFROM LONDON TO PARIS IN 25 HOURS AND 11 MINUTES(1965, Brit.), ph; ARABESQUE(1966), ph; KALEIDOSCOPE(1966, Brit.), ph; TWO FOR THE ROAD(1967, Brit.), ph; CHITTY CHITTY BANG BANG(1968, Brit.), ph; DANDY IN ASPIC, A(1968, Brit.), ph; STAIRCASE(1969 U.S./Brit./Fr.), ph; PRIVATE LIFE OF SHERLOCK HOLMES, THE(1970, Brit.), ph; CATCH ME A SPY(1971, Brit./Fr.), ph; MARY, QUEEN OF SCOTS(1971, Brit.), ph; VILLAIN(1971, Brit.), ph; BOY WHO TURNED YELLOW, THE(1972, Brit.), ph; PUBLIC EYE, THE(1972, Brit.), ph; LITTLE PRINCE, THE(1974, Brit.), ph; MR. QUILP(1975, Brit.), ph; INCREDIBLE SARAH, THE(1976, Brit.), ph; DEEP, THE(1977), ph; MIRROR CRACK'D, THE(1980, Brit.), ph; EVIL UNDER THE SUN(1982, Brit.), ph

1984

RIDDLE OF THE SANDS, THE(1984, Brit.), ph; SECRETS(1984, Brit.), ph; TOP SECRET!(1984), ph

Christopher G. Challis
END OF THE RIVER, THE(1947, Brit.), ph

Drummond Challis
1984
RIDDLE OF THE SANDS, THE(1984, Brit.), p

John Challis
YELLOW SUBMARINE(1958, Brit.), animation; WHERE HAS POOR MICKEY GONE?(1964, Brit.)

Carla Challomer
NO TIME FOR TEARS(1957, Brit.)

Carla Challoner
CLUE OF THE MISSING APE, THE(1953, Brit.); HEART OF A CHILD(1958, Brit.); SOAPBOX DERBY(1958, Brit.); CIRCUS OF HORRORS(1960, Brit.); TO SIR, WITH LOVE(1967, Brit.); WHERE'S JACK?(1969, Brit.)

Pauline Challoner
GATES TO PARADISE(1968, Brit./Ger.); HERE WE GO ROUND THE MULBERRY BUSH(1968, Brit.); ONE BRIEF SUMMER(1971, Brit.)

Ed Chalmers
TERROR EYES(1981)

Edward Chalmers, Jr.
JAWS(1975)

Kendal Chalmers
HOT ICE(1952, Brit.)

Rosemary Chalmers
MURDER CAN BE DEADLY(1963, Brit.)

Steven Chalmers
Silents
LOOKING FOR TROUBLE(1926), w

Terry Chalmers
POWERFORCE(1983), w

Thomas Chalmers
ROMANOFF AND JULIET(1961); ALL THE WAY HOME(1963); OUTRAGE, THE(1964)

Tom Chalmers
Silents
BLIND ALLEYS(1927)

W.G. Chalmers
THUNDER OVER TANGIER(1957, Brit.), p; YOU PAY YOUR MONEY(1957, Brit.), p; INBETWEEN AGE, THE(1958, Brit.), p; MARK OF THE PHOENIX(1958, Brit.), p

William G. Chalmers
MILLION DOLLAR MANHUNT(1962, Brit.), p

Caria Chaloner
SAY HELLO TO YESTERDAY(1971, Brit.)

Jan Chaloupek
90 DEGREES IN THE SHADE(1966, Czech./Brit.), ed

Hugh Chaloupka
SIGN OF ZORRO, THE(1960), ed

Josef Chaloupka
DIVINE EMMA, THE(1983, Czech,), md

Syd Chalton
SPOTLIGHT SCANDALS(1943)

Jacques Chalvet
COW AND I, THE(1961, Fr., Ital., Ger.), art d; THERESE(1963, Fr.), art d

Leo Chalzel
COME ON, MARINES(1934); MEN IN WHITE(1934)

Sydney Chama
WILD GEESE, THE(1978, Brit.)

Tom T. Chamales
NEVER SO FEW(1959), w

Chamarat
CARNIVAL OF SINNERS(1947, Fr.)

George Chamarat
FRENCH TOUCH, THE(1954, Fr.); WOULD-BE GENTLEMAN, THE(1960, Fr.)

Georges Chamarat
LES MAINS SALES(1954, Fr.); DIABOLIQUE(1955, Fr.); ADORABLE CREATURES(1956, Fr.); FERNANDEL THE DRESSMAKER(1957, Fr.); JULIETTA(1957, Fr.); ROYAL AFFAIRS IN VERSAILLES(1957, Fr.); BIG CHIEF, THE(1960, Fr.); LOVE AND THE FRENCHWOMAN(1961, Fr.); LOVE AT NIGHT(1961, Fr.); THIEF OF BAGHDAD, THE(1961, Ital./Fr.); WOMAN OF SIN(1961, Fr.); TOMORROW IS MY TURN(1962, Fr./Ital./Ger.); WHERE THE TRUTH LIES(1962, Fr.); MARRIAGE OF FIGARO, THE(1963, Fr.); UP FROM THE BEACH(1965); CLOPORTES(1966, Fr., Ital.)

Christina Chamaret
DON'T CRY WITH YOUR MOUTH FULL(1974, Fr.)

George Chamaret
GIVE ME MY CHANCE(1958, Fr.); MIRROR HAS TWO FACES, THE(1959, Fr.)

Omar Chambati
BORN FREE(1966)

Cathy Chamberlain
HAPPY BIRTHDAY, GEMINI(1980), m

Cyril Chamberlain
JAILBIRDS(1939, Brit.); STOLEN LIFE(1939, Brit.); THIS MAN IN PARIS(1939, Brit.); WHAT WOULD YOU DO, CHUMS?(1939, Brit.); OLD MOTHER RILEY IN BUSINESS(1940, Brit.); OLD MOTHER RILEY IN SOCIETY(1940, Brit.); POISON PEN(1941, Brit.); DANCING WITH CRIME(1947, Brit.); UPTURNED GLASS, THE(1947, Brit.); DARK ROAD, THE(1948, Brit.); DULCIMER STREET(1948, Brit.); GIRL IN THE PAINTING, THE(1948, Brit.); BOYS IN BROWN(1949, Brit.); DON'T EVER LEAVE ME(1949, Brit.); IT'S NOT CRICKET(1949, Brit.); MARRY ME!(1949, Brit.); MY BROTHER'S KEEPER(1949, Brit.); QUARTET(1949, Brit.); STOP PRESS GIRL(1949, Brit.); STAGE FRIGHT(1950, Brit.); ADVENTURERS, THE(1951, Brit.); BLACKMAILED(1951, Brit.); LAVENDER HILL MOB, THE(1951, Brit.); MANIACS ON WHEELS(1951, Brit.); OLD MOTHER RILEY'S JUNGLE TREASURE(1951, Brit.); SCARLET THREAD(1951, Brit.); SING ALONG WITH ME(1952, Brit.); FOLLY TO BE WISE(1953); PROJECT M7(1953, Brit.); COMPANIONS IN CRIME(1954, Brit.); DIAMOND WIZARD, THE(1954, Brit.); DOCTOR IN THE HOUSE(1954, Brit.); EMBEZZLER, THE(1954, Brit.); HELL BELOW ZERO(1954, Brit.); YOU KNOW WHAT SAILORS ARE(1954, Brit.); DOCTOR AT SEA(1955, Brit.); IMPULSE(1955, Brit.); LADY GODIVA RIDES AGAIN(1955, Brit.); MAN OF THE MOMENT(1955, Brit.); TROUBLE IN STORE(1955, Brit.); WINDFALL(1955 Brit.); GAMMA PEOPLE, THE(1956); SIMON AND LAURA(1956, Brit.); WAY OUT, THE(1956, Brit.); DOCTOR AT LARGE(1957, Brit.); GREEN MAN, THE(1957, Brit.); NO TIME FOR TEARS(1957, Brit.); RAISING A RIOT(1957, Brit.); ROCK AROUND THE WORLD(1957, Brit.); TEARS FOR SIMON(1957, Brit.); UP IN THE WORLD(1957, Brit.); BLUE MURDER AT ST. TRINIAN'S(1958, Brit.); CHAIN OF EVENTS(1958, Brit.); CROSS-UP(1958); DUKE WORE JEANS, THE(1958, Brit.); MAN WHO WOULDN'T TALK, THE(1958, Brit.); MAN WITH A GUN(1958, Brit.); NIGHT TO REMEMBER, A(1958, Brit.); WONDERFUL THINGS!(1958, Brit.); CARRY ON NURSE(1959, Brit.); CARRY ON SERGEANT(1959, Brit.); UGLY DUCKLING, THE(1959, Brit.); CARRY ON CONSTABLE(1960, Brit.); PLEASE TURN OVER(1960, Brit.); FLAME IN THE STREETS(1961, Brit.); PURE HELL OF ST. TRINIAN'S, THE(1961, Brit.); TWO-WAY STRETCH(1961, Brit.); UPSTAIRS AND DOWNSTAIRS(1961, Brit.); CARRY ON CRUISING(1962, Brit.); CARRY ON TEACHER(1962, Brit.); NEARLY A NASTY ACCIDENT(1962, Brit.); ON THE BEAT(1962, Brit.); ROOMMATES(1962, Brit.); CARRY ON CABBIE(1963, Brit.); GET ON WITH IT(1963, Brit.); OPERATION BULLSHINE(1963, Brit.); SWINGIN' MAIDEN, THE(1963, Brit.); RING OF SPIES(1964, Brit.); TWO LEFT FEET(1965, Brit.); GREAT ST. TRINIAN'S TRAIN ROBBERY, THE(1966, Brit.); GYPSY GIRL(1966, Brit.)

Diane Chamberlain
GALLIPOLI(1981, Aus.)

George Agnew Chamberlain
RED HOUSE, THE(1947, Brit.), d&w; SCUDDA-HOO! SCUDDA-HAY!(1948), w; APRIL LOVE(1957), w

Holland Chamberlain
THIEVES' HIGHWAY(1949)

Howland Chamberlain
SONG IS BORN, A(1948); EDGE OF DOOM(1950); SURRENDER(1950); KRAMER VS. KRAMER(1979)

J.R. Chamberlain
Silents
BAR SINISTER, THE(1917)

Jan Chamberlain
HAPPY MOTHER'S DAY... LOVE, GEORGE(1973)

Kenneth Chamberlain
REDS(1981)

Lee Chamberlain
ALL AT SEA(1970, Brit.)

Lois Chamberlain
SPRING BREAK(1983)

Maggie Chamberlain
ETERNAL SUMMER(1961)

Margaret Chamberlain
Misc. Talkies
TUCK EVERLASTING(1981)

Paul G. Chamberlain
CYNTHIA(1947), set d; GOOD NEWS(1947), set d

Peggy Chamberlain
MA, HE'S MAKING EYES AT ME(1940)

Richard Chamberlain
SECRET OF THE PURPLE REEF, THE(1960); THUNDER OF DRUMS, A(1961); TWILIGHT OF HONOR(1963); JOY IN THE MORNING(1965); PETULIA(1968, U.S./Brit.); MADWOMAN OF CHAILLOT, THE(1969); JULIUS CAESAR(1970, Brit.); MUSIC LOVERS, THE(1971, Brit.); LADY CAROLINE LAMB(1972, Brit./Ital.); THREE MUSKETEERS, THE(1974, Panama); TOWERING INFERNO, THE(1974); FOUR MUSKETEERS, THE(1975); COUNT OF MONTE CRISTO(1976, Brit.); SLIPPER AND THE ROSE, THE(1976, Brit.); LAST WAVE, THE(1978, Aus.); SWARM, THE(1978); BELLS(1981, Can.)

Riley Chamberlain
Misc. Silents
NAIDRA, THE DREAM WOMAN(1914, Ger.)

Roy Chamberlain
MELODY LANE(1941), m

William Chamberlain
IMITATION GENERAL(1958), w

William N. Chamberlain
SMALL CIRCLE OF FRIENDS, A(1980)

Wilt Chamberlain
1984
CONAN THE DESTROYER(1984)

Win Chamberlain
Misc. Talkies
BRAND X(1970), d

Winthrop Chamberlain
Misc. Silents
MARRYING MONEY(1915)

Cyril Chamberlin
BULLDOG BREED, THE(1960, Brit.)

George Andrew Chamberlin
HOME IN INDIANA(1944), w

Howland Chamberlin
BEST YEARS OF OUR LIVES, THE(1946); BRUTE FORCE(1947); DRIFT-
WOOD(1947); WEB, THE(1947); ANGEL IN EXILE(1948); FEUDIN', FUSSIN' AND
A-FIGHTIN'(1948); FORCE OF EVIL(1948); AND BABY MAKES THREE(1949); FRAN-
CIS(1949); HOUSE BY THE RIVER(1950); MISTER 880(1950); BIG NIGHT, THE(1951);
NO QUESTIONS ASKED(1951); PICKUP(1951); RACKET, THE(1951); HIGH
NOON(1952); BARBAROSA(1982)
1984
ELECTRIC DREAMS(1984)
Lee Chamberlin
UP THE SANDBOX(1972); UPTOWN SATURDAY NIGHT(1974); LET'S DO IT
AGAIN(1975)
1984
BEAT STREET(1984)
Mark Chamberlin
GHOST STORY(1981)
Riley Chamberlin
Misc. Silents
PRUDENCE THE PIRATE(1916); HER NEW YORK(1917)
Andrews Chambers
END OF AUGUST, THE(1982)
Anne Chambers
SLEEPING CAR TO TRIESTE(1949, Brit.)
Barbars Chambers
Silents
NEW YORK(1927), w
Barry Chambers
LONELY HEARTS(1983, Aus.)
Bonita Chambers
PREMONITION, THE(1976)
Cullen G. Chambers
STUDENT BODIES(1981)
Don Chambers
HELL SQUAD(1958)
Dudley Chambers
FINGERPRINTS DON'T LIE(1951), m; MASK OF THE DRAGON(1951), m
Everett Chambers
RUN ACROSS THE RIVER(1961), p, d; TESS OF THE STORM COUNTRY(1961), p;
TOO LATE BLUES(1962); LOLLIPOP COVER, THE(1965), p&d, w
Frank Chambers
TAPS(1981)
Haddon Chambers
Silents
CAPTAIN SWIFT(1914), w; IMPOSSIBLE WOMAN, THE(1919, Brit.), w
Harley Chambers
WYOMING(1940)
Hennen Chambers
FADE TO BLACK(1980)
James Cox Chambers
1984
ALPHABET CITY(1984)
Jerry Chambers
FISH THAT SAVED PITTSBURGH, THE(1979); NEW YEAR'S EVIL(1980)
John Chambers
HUMAN DUPLICATORS, THE(1965), makeup; PLANET OF THE APES(1968),
makeup; ESCAPE FROM THE PLANET OF THE APES(1971), makeup; SLAUGHTER-
HOUSE-FIVE(1972), makeup; SUPERBEAST(1972), makeup; SCHLOCK(1973);
SSSSSSSS(1973), makeup; ISLAND OF DR. MOREAU, THE(1977), makeup; NATION-
AL LAMPOON'S CLASS REUNION(1982), makeup
Misc. Talkies
69 MINUTES(1977)
Julia Chambers
MOONLIGHTING(1982, Brit.)
Karl Chambers
TOOMORROW(1970, Brit.)
Kathleen Chambers
Silents
ABRAHAM LINCOLN(1924); KING OF KINGS, THE(1927)
Kellett Chambers
Silents
AMERICAN WIDOW, AN(1917), w
Lester Chambers
Silents
FINE FEATHERS(1915); JUNGLE TRAIL, THE(1919)
Misc. Silents
SPAN OF LIFE, THE(1914); AT BAY(1915); DIVORCED(1915); BIG JIM GAR-
RITY(1916); WAGER, THE(1916); BRINGING UP BETTY(1919); FALLEN IDOL,
A(1919); SHOULD A HUSBAND FORGIVE?(1919)
Lowell Chambers
1984
RED DAWN(1984), set d
Lucinda Chambers
ISADORA(1968, Brit.)
Margaret Chambers
WOMAN TO WOMAN(1929)
Marie Chambers
Silents
"THAT ROYLE GIRL"(1925)
Misc. Silents
FIFTY-FIFTY(1916); WOMAN IN THE CASE, A(1916); MATERNITY(1917)
Marilyn Chambers
RABID(1976, Can.); PROTECTORS, BOOK 1, THE(1981)
Misc. Talkies
ANGEL OF H.E.A.T.(1982)
Mary Chambers
Misc. Silents
GAY OLD DOG, THE(1919)

Michael "Boogaloo Shrimp" Chambers
1984
BREAKIN'(1984); BREAKIN' 2: ELECTRIC BOOGALOO(1984)
Nancy Chambers
SCREWBALLS(1983)
Phil Chambers
BIG HEAT, THE(1953); TUMBLEWEED(1953); BOUNTY HUNTER, THE(1954);
EXECUTIVE SUITE(1954); OVERLAND PACIFIC(1954); PUSHOVER(1954); ROGUE
COP(1954); FOXFIRE(1955); RAGE AT DAWN(1955); RUN FOR COVER(1955); BACK-
LASH(1956); DAY OF FURY, A(1956); MOLE PEOPLE, THE(1956); DRANGO(1957);
RAINTREE COUNTY(1957); WILL SUCCESS SPOIL ROCK HUNTER?(1957); GOOD
DAY FOR A HANGING(1958); SUMMER PLACE, A(1959); SIX BLACK HORSES(1962);
FOR LOVE OR MONEY(1963)
Phillip Chambers
RICOCHET ROMANCE(1954)
Ralph Chambers
PAJAMA GAME, THE(1957)
Ralph W. Chambers
Silents
ANOTHER SCANDAL(1924)
Richard Chambers
TOO LATE BLUES(1962)
Robert Chambers
JAWS(1975)
Silents
COMMON LAW, THE(1923), w
Robert W. Chambers
COMMON LAW, THE(1931), w; OPERATOR 13(1934), w
Silents
COMMON LAW, THE(1916), w; DANGER MARK, THE(1918), w; AMAZING LOV-
ERS(1921), w; CARDIGAN(1922), w; AMERICA(1924), w, t
Shirley Chambers
HALF-NAKED TRUTH, THE(1932); KID FROM SPAIN, THE(1932); MELODY
CRUISE(1933); MERRY WIDOW, THE(1934); VIVA VILLA!(1934); CALM YOUR-
SELF(1935); LAST GANGSTER, THE(1937); NOTHING SACRED(1937)
Sid Chambers
KANGAROO(1952)
Stan Chambers
WAR OF THE COLOSSAL BEAST(1958)
Steve Chambers
LONG RIDERS, THE(1980); URBAN COWBOY(1980)
Steve D. Chambers
MOUNTAIN MEN, THE(1980)
Stevins Chambers
DEVIL'S PLOT, THE(1948, Brit.)
Syd Chambers
WHEREVER SHE GOES(1953, Aus.); LONG JOHN SILVER(1954, Aus.)
Terry Chambers
BREAKER! BREAKER!(1977), w; REVENGE OF THE SHOGUN WOMEN(1982,
Taiwan), w
Wheaton Chambers
ROSE BOWL(1936); STORY OF LOUIS PASTEUR, THE(1936); DISBARRED(1939);
INVITATION TO HAPPINESS(1939); FOREIGN CORRESPONDENT(1940); SLIGHT-
LY HONORABLE(1940); PRAIRIE PIONEERS(1941); LIFE BEGINS AT 8:30(1942);
OUTLAWS OF PINE RIDGE(1942); THEY ALL KISSED THE BRIDE(1942); WIFE
TAKES A FLYER, THE(1942); BEYOND THE LAST FRONTIER(1943); DRUMS OF FU
MANCHU(1943); GANGWAY FOR TOMORROW(1943); HEAVENLY BODY,
THE(1943); IRON MAJOR, THE(1943); PHANTOM OF THE OPERA(1943); SEVENTH
VICTIM, THE(1943); THIS LAND IS MINE(1943); FALCON IN HOLLYWOOD,
THE(1944); FALCON OUT WEST, THE(1944); GIRL RUSH(1944); NEVADA(1944);
TALL IN THE SADDLE(1944); APOLOGY FOR MURDER(1945); MARSHAL OF
LAREDO(1945); MILDRED PIERCE(1945); PEOPLE ARE FUNNY(1945); STATE
FAIR(1945); EL PASO KID, THE(1946); FLYING SERPENT, THE(1946); MURDER IN
THE MUSIC HALL(1946); SO GOES MY LOVE(1946); STAGECOACH TO DEN-
VER(1946); TANGIER(1946); TIME OF THEIR LIVES, THE(1946); UNDERCUR-
RENT(1946); CRIME DOCTOR'S GAMBLE(1947); LADY IN THE LAKE(1947); MAGIC
TOWN(1947); MONSIEUR VERDOUX(1947); ON THE OLD SPANISH TRAIL(1947);
POSSESSED(1947); SEA OF GRASS, THE(1947); WILD FRONTIER, THE(1947); GUN
TALK(1948); HOMECOMING(1948); SONG OF THE DRIFTER(1948); THREE DARING
DAUGHTERS(1948); DEPUTY MARSHAL(1949); EAST SIDE, WEST SIDE(1949);
GREAT SINNER, THE(1949); MISSISSIPPI RHYTHM(1949); NOT WANTED(1949);
UNDERCOVER MAN, THE(1949); BARON OF ARIZONA, THE(1950); BETWEEN
MIDNIGHT AND DAWN(1950); MAGNIFICENT YANKEE, THE(1950); PEGGY(1950);
SECRET FURY, THE(1950); WEST POINT STORY, THE(1950); DAY THE EARTH
STOOD STILL, THE(1951); LORNA DOONE(1951); NIGHT INTO MORNING(1951);
PROWLER, THE(1951); SON OF DR. JEKYLL, THE(1951); UNKNOWN MAN,
THE(1951); WELL, THE(1951); LAWLESS BREED, THE(1952); MA AND PA KETTLE
AT THE FAIR(1952); WAGONS WEST(1952); SLAVES OF BABYLON(1953); BIG
CHASE, THE(1954); PEACEMAKER, THE(1956); OKLAHOMAN, THE(1957)
Whitman Chambers
MURDER ON THE CAMPUS(1934), w; SENSATION HUNTERS(1934), w; SINNER
TAKE ALL(1936), w; TOKYO ROSE(1945), w; SHADOW OF A WOMAN(1946), w; BIG
TOWN AFTER DARK(1947), w; I COVER BIG TOWN(1947), w; JUNGLE
FLIGHT(1947), w; BLONDE ICE(1949), w; MANHANDLED(1949), w; SPECIAL
AGENT(1949), w; COME ON, THE(1956), w
Robert Chamblee
KILLER INSIDE ME, THE(1976), w
Carlos Chambliss
CONRACK(1974)
John L. Chambliss
FINAL EXAM(1981), p
Woodrow Chambliss
WILD SEED(1965); WILD COUNTRY, THE(1971); COUNT YOUR BULLETS(1972);
DEVIL'S RAIN, THE(1975, U.S./Mex.); SGT. PEPPER'S LONELY HEARTS CLUB
BAND(1978); SECOND-HAND HEARTS(1981)
Misc. Talkies
GLEN AND RANDA(1971)

Woody Chambliss
GREASER'S PALACE(1972)
Johnny Chambot
GYPSY FURY(1950, Fr.)
Gerard Chambre
ENTRE NOUS(1983, Fr.)
Maurice Chambreuil
IDIOT, THE(1948, Fr.)
Krzysztof Chamiec
WALKOVER(1969, Pol.)
Pierre Chaminade
HOUSE OF THE ARROW, THE(1953, Brit.); GOLDEN MASK, THE(1954, Brit.); MARK OF THE PHOENIX(1958, Brit.)
Alain Chammas
1984
BUDDY SYSTEM, THE(1984), p
Jocelyne Chamonin
PARSIFAL(1983, Fr.)
Champ Jr. the Horse
OLD WEST, THE(1952)
Champagne
Misc. Silents
CATHERINE(1924, Fr.)
Adrine Champagne
THUNDER BAY(1953)
Andree Champagne
DECOY FOR TERROR(1970, Can.)
Clarence Champagne
PSYCHO(1960), spec eff
Jacques Champagne
QUEBEC(1951)
Jean Champagne
FRENCH POSTCARDS(1979)
Lyne Champagne
MY UNCLE ANTOINE(1971, Can.)
Mons. Champagne
NOUS IRONS A PARIS(1949, Fr.)
Pierre Champagne
Misc. Silents
LA FILLE DE L'EAU(1924, Fr.)
Helen Champan
LAST ANGRY MAN, THE(1959)
Patricia Champane
ENTRE NOUS(1983, Fr.)
Georges Champavert
Misc. Silents
L'OEIL DE SAINT-YVES(1919, Fr.), d; MEA CULPA(1919, Fr.), d; LE REMOUS(1920, Fr.), d; L'ETE DE LA SAINT MARTIN(1920, Fr.), d; LA HURLE(1921, Fr.), d; LE PORION(1921, Fr.), d; L'EVASION(1922, Fr.), d; LA NEUVAINE DE COLETTE(1925, Fr.), d
Albert Champeaux
JOHNNY THE GIANT KILLER(1953, Fr.), anim
Andree Champeaux
DIVA(1982, Fr.)
Marcel Champel
NIGHT OF LUST(1965, Fr.); RETURN OF MARTIN GUERRE, THE(1983, Fr.)
Jim Champin
DAFFY DUCK'S MOVIE: FANTASTIC ISLAND(1983), ed
Champion
COMIN' ROUND THE MOUNTAIN(1936); BIG SHOW, THE(1937); HILLS OF UTAH(1951); TEXICAN, THE(1966, U.S./Span.), w
Misc. Silents
SILENT SENTINEL(1929)
Bob Champion
1984
CHAMPIONS(1984), w
Claude Champion
EVERY MAN FOR HIMSELF(1980, Fr.)
Gower Champion
TILL THE CLOUDS ROLL BY(1946); MR. MUSIC(1950), a, ch; SHOW BOAT(1951); EVERYTHING I HAVE IS YOURS(1952), a, ch; LOVELY TO LOOK AT(1952); GIVE A GIRL A BREAK(1953), a, ch; JUPITER'S DARLING(1955); THREE FOR THE SHOW(1955); GIRL MOST LIKELY, THE(1957), ch; MY SIX LOVES(1963), d; BANK SHOT(1974), d
Harry Champion
ON THE AIR(1934, Brit.)
Jean Champion
MURIEL(1963, Fr./Ital.); UMBRELLAS OF CHERBOURG, THE(1964, Fr./Ger.); THIEF OF PARIS, THE(1967, Fr./Ital.); DAY FOR NIGHT(1973, Fr.); INVITATION, THE(1975, Fr./Switz.); MARCH OR DIE(1977, Brit.); COUP DE TORCHON(1981, Fr.)
John C. Champion
PANHANDLE(1948), p, w; STAMPEDE(1949), p, w; HELLGATE(1952), p, w; TEXICAN, THE(1966, U.S./Span.), p; ATTACK ON THE IRON COAST(1968, U.S./Brit.), p, w; SUMARINE X-1(1969, Brit.), p, w; LAST ESCAPE, THE(1970, Brit.), w
John Champion
DRAGONFLY SQUADRON(1953), p, w; SHOTGUN(1955), p, w; ZERO HOUR!(1957), p, w; MUSTANG COUNTRY(1976), p,d&w
Marc Champion
SLIPSTREAM(1974, Can.), ph; SUNDAY IN THE COUNTRY(1975, Can.), ph; BREAKING POINT(1976), ph; PARTNERS(1976, Can.), ph; ANGELA(1977, Can.), ph; WHY SHOOT THE TEACHER(1977, Can.), ph; I, MAUREEN(1978, Can.), ph; OUT OF THE BLUE(1982), ph
Michael Champion
WHEN A STRANGER CALLS(1979); WHOLLY MOSES(1980); HISTORY OF THE WORLD, PART 1(1981); WOMAN INSIDE, THE(1981)
1984
BEVERLY HILLS COP(1984)

Pokey Champion
FOLIES DERGERE(1935)
Champion Egmund of Send
HOUND OF THE BASKERVILLES(1932, Brit.)
Champion the Dog
Silents
SKY RIDER, THE(1928)
Champion the Horse
MELODY TRAIL(1935); SAGEBRUSH TROUBADOR(1935); SINGING VAGABOND, THE(1935); TUMBLING TUMBLEWEEDS(1935); RED RIVER VALLEY(1936); RIDE, RANGER, RIDE(1936); SINGING COWBOY, THE(1936); GIT ALONG, LITTLE DO-GIES(1937); OH, SUSANNA(1937); OLD CORRAL, THE(1937); PUBLIC COWBOY NO. 1(1937); ROOTIN' TOOTIN' RHYTHM(1937); ROUNDUP TIME IN TEXAS(1937); SPRINGTIME IN THE ROCKIES(1937); YODELIN' KID FROM PINE RIDGE(1937); GOLD MINE IN THE SKY(1938); MAN FROM MUSIC MOUNTAIN(1938); OLD BARN DANCE, THE(1938); RHYTHM OF THE SADDLE(1938); IN OLD MONTEREY(1939); MEXICALI ROSE(1939); MOUNTAIN RHYTHM(1939); ROVIN' TUM-BLEWEEDS(1939); SOUTH OF THE BORDER(1939); GAUCHO SERENADE(1940); MELODY RANCH(1940); RANCHO GRANDE(1940); RIDE, TENDERFOOT, RI-DE(1940); SHOOTING HIGH(1940); RIDIN' ON A RAINBOW(1941); SIERRA SUE(1941); SINGING HILL, THE(1941); SUNSET IN WYOMING(1941); UNDER FIESTA STARS(1941); STARDUST ON THE SAGE(1942); SIOUX CITY SUE(1946); TRAIL TO SAN ANTONE(1947); STRAWBERRY ROAN, THE(1948); BIG SOMBRERO, THE(1949); RIDERS OF THE WHISTLING PINES(1949); TEXANS NEVER CRY(1951); OLD WEST, THE(1952); GOLDTOWN GHOST RIDERS(1953); LAST OF THE PONY RIDERS(1953); PACK TRAIN(1953)
Champion Jr. the Horse
LAST ROUND-UP, THE(1947); ROBIN OF TEXAS(1947); SADDLE PALS(1947); TWILIGHT ON THE RIO GRANDE(1947); LOADED PISTOLS(1948); RIDERS IN THE SKY(1949); RIM OF THE CANYON(1949); SONS OF NEW MEXICO(1949); COW TOWN(1950); INDIAN TERRITORY(1950); MULE TRAIN(1950); GENE AUTRY AND THE MOUNTIES(1951); SILVER CANYON(1951); VALLEY OF FIRE(1951); WHIRL-WIND(1951); NIGHT STAGE TO GALVESTON(1952); WAGON TEAM(1952); ON TOP OF OLD SMOKY(1953); WINNING OF THE WEST(1953)
Alice Champlin
1984
POWER, THE(1984)
Irene Champlin
GUERRILLA GIRL(1953)
Jean Champommier
LITTLE BOY LOST(1953)
Michel Champommier
LITTLE BOY LOST(1953)
Jacques Champreux
MY BABY IS BLACK!(1965, Fr.); JUDEX(1966, Fr./Ital.), w; SHADOWMAN(1974, Fr./Ital.), a, w
Champy the Bull
TOMBOY AND THE CHAMP(1961)
Charles Chan
LOVERS AND LUGGERS(1938, Aus.)
Charlie Chan
VENGEANCE OF THE DEEP(1940, Aus.)
Doris Chan
LADY FROM SHANGHAI, THE(1948)
Duke Chan
THEY MET IN BOMBAY(1941)
Elizabeth Chan
PORTRAIT IN BLACK(1960)
Frances Chan
PASSPORT TO SUEZ(1943); CHARLIE CHAN IN BLACK MAGIC(1944); GOD IS MY CO-PILOT(1945); SAMURAI(1945)
George Chan
DANTE'S INFERNO(1935); GENERAL DIED AT DAWN, THE(1936); LOST HORI-ZON(1937); SONG OF THE THIN MAN(1947); HE WALKED BY NIGHT(1948); SAIGON(1948); SORROWFUL JONES(1949); MACAO(1952); BLOOD ALLEY(1955); JUMP INTO HELL(1955); LEFT HAND OF GOD, THE(1955); SOLDIER OF FOR-TUNE(1955); TARGET ZERO(1955); PAL JOEY(1957); KILLERS, THE(1964), art d; GAILY, GAILY(1969), art d; HAWAIIANS, THE(1970), art d
George B. Chan
ORGANIZATION, THE(1971), art d; FORCED VENGEANCE(1982), prod d
Grace Chan
INCHON(1981)
Helen Chan
STUDENT TOUR(1934)
Henry Chan
GLADIATORS, THE(1970, Swed.)
Jackie Chan
BIG BRAWL, THE(1980); CANNONBALL RUN, THE(1981)
1984
CANNONBALL RUN II(1984)
Jacqueline Chan
WORLD OF SUZIE WONG, THE(1960)
Jacqui Chan
CLEOPATRA(1963); KRAKATOA, EAST OF JAVA(1969)
Janet Chan
1984
REPO MAN(1984)
Joyce Chan
SECRET, THE(1979, Hong Kong), w
Kim Chan
OWL AND THE PUSSYCAT, THE(1970); SOUP FOR ONE(1982); KING OF COMEDY, THE(1983)
1984
COTTON CLUB, THE(1984); MOSCOW ON THE HUDSON(1984); OVER THE BROOKLYN BRIDGE(1984)
Look Chan
NOW AND FOREVER(1934)

Luke Chan
SECRETS OF WU SIN(1932); STUDENT TOUR(1934); MYSTERIOUS MR. WONG(1935); WITHOUT REGRET(1935); WEST OF SHANGHAI(1937); REAL GLORY, THE(1939); SOMEWHERE I'LL FIND YOU(1942); BEHIND THE RISING SUN(1943); MISSION TO MOSCOW(1943); PURPLE HEART, THE(1944); STORY OF DR. WASSELL, THE(1944); SAMURAI(1945); WELL-GROOMED BRIDE, THE(1946); SINGAPORE(1947); SAIGON(1948)

Lum Chan
BRIDE OF THE DESERT(1929)

Mary Chan
SAIGON(1948)

Maureen Chan
Misc. Talkies
CRYPT OF DARK SECRETS(1976)

Michael Paul Chan
THIEF(1981)
1984
RUNAWAY(1984)

Mike Chan
CARDIAC ARREST(1980)

Neil Chan
AVIATOR'S WIFE, THE(1981, Fr.)

Oie Chan
KEYS OF THE KINGDOM, THE(1944); STORY OF DR. WASSELL, THE(1944); SAIGON(1948)

Ole Chan
DAUGHTER OF THE DRAGON(1931)

Oy Chan
BLOOD ON THE SUN(1945)

Robert Chan
CROCODILE(1979, Thai./Hong Kong), p

Roy Chan
CHAN IS MISSING(1982)

Silan Chan
MALAYA(1950)

Spencer Chan
GENERAL DIED AT DAWN, THE(1936); SWING HIGH, SWING LOW(1937); ACROSS THE PACIFIC(1942); PURPLE HEART, THE(1944); FIRST YANK INTO TOKYO(1945); CHINESE RING, THE(1947); TREASURE OF THE SIERRA MADRE, THE(1948); STATE DEPARTMENT-FILE 649(1949); WE WERE STRANGERS(1949); MALAYA(1950); TIMBER FURY(1950); LAW AND THE LADY, THE(1951); FORBIDDEN(1953); THIS ISLAND EARTH(1955); FLOWER DRUM SONG(1961)

Thomas Chan
GENERAL DIED AT DAWN, THE(1936)

Unicorn Chan
BRUCE LEE-TRUE STORY(1976, Chi.)

Victoria Chan
OUT OF THE TIGER'S MOUTH(1962)

Kao Chan-Fei
FIGHT TO THE LAST(1938, Chi.)

Shalom Chanach
SEED OF INNOCENCE(1980), m

Andre Chanal
SEVEN CAPITAL SINS(1962, Fr./Ital.)

Anna Chance
SECOND CHOICE(1930)

Diana Chance
MAN WHO HAD POWER OVER WOMEN, THE(1970, Brit.)

John Newton Chance
FLYING EYE, THE(1955, Brit.), w; CROSSTRAP(1962, Brit.), w

John T. Chance
ASSAULT ON PRECINCT 13(1976), ed

Kim Chance
HIGH SCHOOL CONFIDENTIAL(1958)

Larry Chance
BATTLES OF CHIEF PONTIAC(1952); ROAD TO BALI(1952); KING RICHARD AND THE CRUSADERS(1954); RIVER OF NO RETURN(1954); ROSE TATTOO, THE(1955); GIRL IN BLACK STOCKINGS(1957); WAR DRUMS(1957); FORT BOWIE(1958); FORT MASSACRE(1958); TIMBUKTU(1959); HARUM SCARUM(1965)

Lightnin' Chance
THAT TENNESSEE BEAT(1966)

Naomi Chance
DEAD ON COURSE(1952, Brit.); GAMBLER AND THE LADY, THE(1952, Brit.); IT STARTED IN PARADISE(1952, Brit.); BLOOD ORANGE(1953, Brit.); END OF THE ROAD, THE(1954, Brit.); SAINT'S GIRL FRIDAY, THE(1954, Brit.); TERROR SHIP(1954, Brit.); TOUCH OF THE SUN, A(1956, Brit.); SUSPENDED ALIBI(1957, Brit.); MAN INSIDE, THE(1958, Brit.); MAN WITH THE GREEN CARNATION, THE(1960, Brit.); OPERATION BULLSHINE(1963, Brit.); HE WHO RIDES A TIGER(1966, Brit.)

Jules Chancel
LOVE PARADE, THE(1929), w

John Chancellor
OPEN ALL NIGHT(1934, Brit.), w; KING OF THE DAMNED(1936, Brit.), w; PAID IN ERROR(1938, Brit.), w

Joyce Chancellor
NORAH O'NEALE(1934, Brit.)

Norman Chancer
VALENTINO(1977, Brit.); EMPIRE STRIKES BACK, THE(1980); OUTLAND(1981); RAGTIME(1981); REDS(1981); VICTOR/VICTORIA(1982); LOCAL HERO(1983, Brit.); LORDS OF DISCIPLINE, THE(1983)

Robert Chandeau
PICNIC ON THE GRASS(1960, Fr.); VICE DOLLS(1961, Fr.)

Michel Chanderli
MORE(1969, Luxembourg)

Dick Chandlee
HENRY ALDRICH GETS GLAMOUR(1942); MAJOR AND THE MINOR, THE(1942); YANKEE DOODLE DANDY(1942); CLANCY STREET BOYS(1943); KEEP 'EM SLUGGING(1943); WE'VE NEVER BEEN LICKED(1943)

Harry Chandlee
WHAT A MAN(1930), ed; RAINBOW ON THE RIVER(1936), w; OUR TOWN(1940), w; ADVENTURES OF MARK TWAIN, THE(1944), w; 3 IS A FAMILY(1944), w; JOLSON STORY, THE(1946), w; TARZAN'S MAGIC FOUNTAIN(1949), w
Silents
NATION'S PERIL, THE(1915), w; FALSE BRANDS(1922), w; ONE LAW FOR THE WOMAN(1924), w; ANYTHING ONCE(1925), w; BOWERY CINDERELLA(1927), t; NO BABIES WANTED(1928), t, ed

Harry E. Chandlee
RENO(1930), w; PLATINUM BLONDE(1931), w

Allen Chandler
TEENAGE ZOMBIES(1960), ph

Anna Chandler
BIG BROADCAST, THE(1932); MADAME RACKETEER(1932); REDHEAD(1941); MASTER MINDS(1949)

Betty Chandler
DON'T LOOK IN THE BASEMENT(1973)

Bill Chandler
LET'S GO NAVY(1951); JUBILEE TRAIL(1954)

Bob Chandler
Silents
LAST STRAW, THE(1920)

Chic Chandler
HAROLD TEEN(1934)
Misc. Talkies
IN PARIS, A.W.O.L.(1936)

Chick Chandler
BLOOD MONEY(1933); MELODY CRUISE(1933); SWEEPINGS(1933); PARTY'S OVER, THE(1934); ALIAS MARY DOW(1935); CIRCUMSTANTIAL EVIDENCE(1935); LIGHTNING STRIKES TWICE(1935); MURDER ON A HONEYMOON(1935); STAR FOR A NIGHT(1936); STRAIGHT FROM THE SHOULDER(1936); TANGO(1936); THREE OF A KIND(1936); BORN RECKLESS(1937); LADY FIGHTS BACK(1937); LOVE AND HISSES(1937); OFF TO THE RACES(1937); ONE MILE FROM HEAVEN(1937); PORTIA ON TRIAL(1937); SING AND BE HAPPY(1937); TIME OUT FOR ROMANCE(1937); WOMAN-WISE(1937); CITY GIRL(1938); KENTUCKY(1938); MR. MOTO TAKES A CHANCE(1938); SPEED TO BURN(1938); TIME OUT FOR MURDER(1938); WHILE NEW YORK SLEEPS(1938); HOLLYWOOD CAVALCADE(1939); HOTEL FOR WOMEN(1939); INSIDE STORY(1939); MISSING EVIDENCE(1939); MYSTERIOUS MISS X, THE(1939); ROSE OF WASHINGTON SQUARE(1939); SWANEE RIVER(1939); TOO BUSY TO WORK(1939); CHARTER PILOT(1940); FREE, BLONDE AND 21(1940); HONEYMOON DEFERRED(1940); ON THEIR OWN(1940); PIER 13(1940); BLONDIE IN SOCIETY(1941); BRIDE CAME C.O.D., THE(1941); CADET GIRL(1941); PEOPLE VS. DR. KILDARE, THE(1941); PUDDIN' HEAD(1941); REMEMBER THE DAY(1941); RIDE, KELLY, RIDE(1941); SAILORS ON LEAVE(1941); TWO IN A TAXI(1941); BABY FACE MORGAN(1942); BIG SHOT, THE(1942); GENTLEMAN AT HEART, A(1942); HOME IN WYOMIN'(1942); I WAKE UP SCREAMING(1942); SPRINGTIME IN THE ROCKIES(1942); ACTION IN THE NORTH ATLANTIC(1943); HE HIRED THE BOSS(1943); HI DIDDLE DIDDLE(1943); MINESWEEPER(1943); RHYTHM PARADE(1943); SPY TRAIN(1943); WEST SIDE KID(1943); YOUTH ON PARADE(1943); IRISH EYES ARE SMILING(1944); JOHNNY DOESN'T LIVE HERE ANY MORE(1944); MAISIE GOES TO RENO(1944); SEVEN DOORS TO DEATH(1944); CAPTAIN EDDIE(1945); CHICAGO KID, THE(1945); LEAVE IT TO BLONDIE(1945); NOB HILL(1945); DO YOU LOVE ME?(1946); MOTHER WORE TIGHTS(1947); BLONDIE'S REWARD(1948); EVERY GIRL SHOULD BE MARRIED(1948); FAMILY HONEYMOON(1948); MUSIC MAN(1948); HOLIDAY AFFAIR(1949); CURTAIN CALL AT CACTUS CREEK(1950); GREAT RUPERT, THE(1950); LOST CONTINENT(1951); MR. IMPERIUM(1951); SHOW BOAT(1951); AARON SLICK FROM PUNKIN CRICK(1952); STEEL TOWN(1952); PRIVATE EYES(1953); IT SHOULD HAPPEN TO YOU(1954); STAR IS BORN, A(1954); THERE'S NO BUSINESS LIKE SHOW BUSINESS(1954); THREE RING CIRCUS(1954); UNTAMED HEIRESS(1954); BATTLE FLAME(1955); NAKED GUN, THE(1956); DANGEROUS CHARTER(1962); IT'S A MAD, MAD, MAD, MAD WORLD(1963); NIGHTMARE IN THE SUN(1964); GIRL WHO KNEW TOO MUCH, THE(1969)

Chris Chandler
HELLFIGHTERS(1968)

Collin Chandler
LOVE ON THE DOLE(1945, Brit.)

Dan Chandler
FLIPPER'S NEW ADVENTURE(1964)
Misc. Talkies
KING FRAT(1979)

David Chandler
WINTER WONDERLAND(1947), w; APACHE DRUMS(1951), w; YOU NEVER CAN TELL(1951), w; JACK MCCALL, DESPERADO(1953), w; CALYPSO HEAT WAVE(1957), w; TOMAHAWK TRAIL(1957), w; BEYOND AND BACK(1978)

David Roy Chandler
WHITE BUFFALO, THE(1977)

Diana Chandler
SLEEPING CAR TO TRIESTE(1949, Brit.); WOMAN HATER(1949, Brit.)

Dick Chandler
TOM BROWN'S SCHOOL DAYS(1940); NOTHING BUT THE TRUTH(1941)

Don Chandler
ISLAND CLAWS(1981), spec eff

Ed Chandler
HIGH SPEED(1932); HERE COMES CARTER(1936); ROAD GANG(1936); GONE WITH THE WIND(1939); RETURN OF DR. X, THE(1939); RETURN OF THE APE MAN(1944); NIGHT EDITOR(1946); NORA PRENTISS(1947)

Eddie Chandler
BORROWED WIVES(1930); CARNIVAL BOAT(1932); STATE TROOPER(1933); NAME THE WOMAN(1934); HIS NIGHT OUT(1935); MAN ON THE FLYING TRAPEZE, THE(1935); UNKNOWN WOMAN(1935); WILD BRIAN KENT(1936); CASE OF THE STUTTERING BISHOP, THE(1937); KID GALAHAD(1937); OVER THE GOAL(1937); SHE LOVED A FIREMAN(1937); OVER THE WALL(1938); PENROD AND HIS TWIN BROTHER(1938); YOU CAN'T CHEAT AN HONEST MAN(1939); DANGER ON WHEELS(1940); SLIGHTLY HONORABLE(1940); DESTROYER(1943); SHE HAS WHAT IT TAKES(1943); CHARLIE CHAN IN THE SECRET SERVICE(1944); LOUISIANA HAYRIDE(1944); CAPTAIN TUGBOAT ANNIE(1945)
Silents
YOUNG WHIRLWIND(1928)

Misc. Silents
FLASHING FANGS(1926)
Eddy Chandler
WELCOME DANGER(1929); BORN TO LOVE(1931); PLATINUM BLONDE(1931); STRANGE ADVENTURE(1932); DEATH KISS, THE(1933); DAMES(1934); GIRL IN DANGER(1934); IT HAPPENED ONE NIGHT(1934); MADAME SPY(1934); TWENTIETH CENTURY(1934); ALIBI IKE(1935); CAR 99(1935); DESERT TRAIL(1935); GOOSE AND THE GANDER, THE(1935); LIVING ON VELVET(1935); MAGNIFICENT OBSESSION(1935); MISS PACIFIC FLEET(1935); RED SALUTE(1935); SPECIAL AGENT(1935); GREAT GUY(1936); LONE WOLF RETURNS, THE(1936); POLO JOE(1936); SHOW BOAT(1936); STAGE STRUCK(1936); TWO IN A CROWD(1936); LOVE IS NEWS(1937); PERFECT SPECIMEN, THE(1937); PUBLIC WEDDING(1937); COWBOY FROM BROOKLYN(1938); GOLD IS WHERE YOU FIND IT(1938); MAD MISS MANTON, THE(1938); PROFESSOR BEWARE(1938); SHOPWORN ANGEL(1938); STRANGE FACES(1938); TORCHY BLANE IN CHINATOWN(1938); YOU CANT TAKE IT WITH YOU(1938); YOUNG FUGITIVES(1938); ANGELS WASH THEIR FACES(1939); EACH DAWN I DIE(1939); FOR LOVE OR MONEY(1939); GOING PLACES(1939); I STOLE A MILLION(1939); MR. SMITH GOES TO WASHINGTON(1939); ONE HOUR TO LIVE(1939); PIRATES OF THE SKIES(1939); ROARING TWENTIES, THE(1939); SECRET SERVICE OF THE AIR(1939); THEY MADE ME A CRIMINAL(1939); TORCHY PLAYS WITH DYNAMITE(1939); YOU CANT GET AWAY WITH MURDER(1939); DOUBLE ALIBI(1940); FRAMED(1940); FUGITIVE FROM JUSTICE, A(1940); INVISIBLE STRIPES(1940); KNUTE ROCKNE–ALL AMERICAN(1940); LOVE, HONOR AND OH, BABY(1940); SANTA FE TRAIL(1940); THEY DRIVE BY NIGHT(1940); BALL OF FIRE(1941); BRIDE CAME C.O.D., THE(1941); HIGH SIERRA(1941); MANPOWER(1941); NINE LIVES ARE NOT ENOUGH(1941); STRAWBERRY BLONDE, THE(1941); I MARRIED A WITCH(1942); LADY IN A JAM(1942); LARCENY, INC.(1942); MAN WHO CAME TO DINNER, THE(1942); STRANGE CASE OF DR. RX, THE(1942); SWEATER GIRL(1942); THIS GUN FOR HIRE(1942); YOU'RE TELLING ME(1942); GHOST AND THE GUEST(1943); MORE THE MERRIER, THE(1943); REVEILLE WITH BEVERLY(1943); SECRETS OF THE UNDERGROUND(1943); SLEEPY LAGOON(1943); JUNGLE CAPTIVE(1945); MEDAL FOR BENNY, A(1945); WOMAN IN THE WINDOW, THE(1945); BEAUTIFUL CHEAT, THE(1946); DEADLINE AT DAWN(1946); BRUTE FORCE(1947)
Edward Chandler
SHE GOES TO WAR(1929); DIXIANA(1930); HERE COMES THE NAVY(1934); CALL OF THE JUNGLE(1944)
Edward S. Chandler
TRUE TO LIFE(1943)
Edwin Chandler
YOU CANT RUN AWAY FROM IT(1956); WHERE THERE'S LIFE(1947); IT SHOULD HAPPEN TO YOU(1954); LAWLESS STREET, A(1955)
Fletcher Chandler
HIDEOUT(1949)
Gene Chandler
DON'T KNOCK THE TWIST(1962)
Geoffrey Chandler
DREAM MAKER, THE(1963, Brit.)
George Chandler
VIRGINIAN, THE(1929); FLORODORA GIRL, THE(1930); IN GAY MADRID(1930); LAST DANCE, THE(1930); LIGHT OF WESTERN STARS, THE(1930); MANSLAUGHTER(1930); ONLY SAPS WORK(1930); DOCTORS' WIVES(1931); MAN OF THE WORLD(1931); TOO MANY COOKS(1931); BEAST OF THE CITY, THE(1932); BLESSED EVENT(1932); ME AND MY GAL(1932); TENDERFOOT, THE(1932); FOOTLIGHT PARADE(1933); KENNEL MURDER CASE, THE(1933); KEYHOLE, THE(1933); LADY KILLER(1933); PICTURE SNATCHER(1933); FOG OVER FRISCO(1934); HE WAS HER MAN(1934); HI, NELLIE!(1934); MUSIC IN THE AIR(1934); TWENTY MILLION SWEETHEARTS(1934); BROADWAY GONDOLIER(1935); MARY BURNS, FUGITIVE(1935); MURDER MAN(1935); STAR OF MIDNIGHT(1935); STARS OVER BROADWAY(1935); WOMAN IN RED, THE(1935); COUNTRY DOCTOR, THE(1936); FURY(1936); HERE COMES TROUBLE(1936); LIBELED LADY(1936); OLD HUTCH(1936); PRINCESS COMES ACROSS, THE(1936); REUNION(1936); SPEED(1936); SWORN ENEMY(1936); THREE MEN ON A HORSE(1936); CHARLIE CHAN AT THE OLYMPICS(1937); DANGER–LOVE AT WORK(1937); GO-GETTER, THE(1937); GOD'S COUNTRY AND THE WOMAN(1937); MANNEQUIN(1937); NOTHING SACRED(1937); SARATOGA(1937); SMALL TOWN BOY(1937); STAR IS BORN, A(1937); THEY GAVE HIM A GUN(1937); TIME OUT FOR ROMANCE(1937); WAKE UP AND LIVE(1937); WOMAN CHASES MAN(1937); JOY OF LIVING(1938); MEN WITH WINGS(1938); MR. MOTO TAKES A VACATION(1938); SECRETS OF A NURSE(1938); SHINING HOUR, THE(1938); SHOPWORN ANGEL(1938); THREE COMRADES(1938); THREE LOVES HAS NANCY(1938); VIVACIOUS LADY(1938); BEAU GESTE(1939); CALLING ALL MARINES(1939); I STOLE A MILLION(1939); JESSE JAMES(1939); KING OF THE TURF(1939); LIGHT THAT FAILED, THE(1939); MR. SMITH GOES TO WASHINGTON(1939); SECOND FIDDLE(1939); THOU SHALT NOT KILL(1939); YOUNG MR. LINCOLN(1939); ARIZONA(1940); MELODY RANCH(1940); RETURN OF FRANK JAMES, THE(1940); SHOOTING HIGH(1940); DOUBLE DATE(1941); GIRL, A GUY AND A GOB, A(1941); HELLZAPOPPIN'(1941); MAD DOCTOR, THE(1941); MODEL WIFE(1941); MOUNTAIN MOONLIGHT(1941); OBLIGING YOUNG LADY(1941); PRIVATE NURSE(1941); REACHING FOR THE SUN(1941); REMEMBER THE DAY(1941); REPENT AT LEISURE(1941); TOBACCO ROAD(1941); WESTERN UNION(1941); CASTLE IN THE DESERT(1942); FOREST RANGERS, THE(1942); GREAT MAN'S LADY, THE(1942); ISLE OF MISSING MEN(1942); NIGHT IN NEW ORLEANS, A(1942); NIGHT TO REMEMBER, A(1942); PARDON MY SARONG(1942); POWERS GIRL, THE(1942); ROXIE HART(1942); SCATTERGOOD SURVIVES A MURDER(1942); ALLERGIC TO LOVE(1943); HERS TO HOLD(1943); HI, BUDDY(1943); LADY OF BURLESQUE(1943); NEVER A DULL MOMENT(1943); OX-BOW INCIDENT, THE(1943); SECRETS OF THE UNDERGROUND(1943); SWEET ROSIE O'GRADY(1943); THEY GOT ME COVERED(1943); BUFFALO BILL(1944); CHINESE CAT, THE(1944); GOIN' TO TOWN(1944); IRISH EYES ARE SMILING(1944); IT HAPPENED TOMORROW(1944); JOHNNY DOESN'T LIVE HERE ANY MORE(1944); SINCE YOU WENT AWAY(1944); STEP LIVELY(1944); TALL IN THE SADDLE(1944); THREE MEN IN WHITE(1944); CAPTAIN EDDIE(1945); COLONEL EFFINGHAM'S RAID(1945); LADY ON A TRAIN(1945); MAN FROM OKLAHOMA, THE(1945); PARDON MY PAST(1945); PATRICK THE GREAT(1945); SHANGHAI COBRA, THE(1945); STRANGE CONFESSION(1945); TELL IT TO A STAR(1945); THIS MAN'S NAVY(1945); WITHOUT LOVE(1945); BEHIND THE MASK(1946); GLASS ALIBI, THE(1946); GUY COULD CHANGE, A(1946); KID FROM BROOKLYN, THE(1946); LITTLE GIANT(1946); LOVER COME BACK(1946); MISSING LADY, THE(1946); STRANGE IMPERSONATION(1946); SUSPENSE(1946); DEAD RECKONING(1947); IT HAD TO BE YOU(1947); MAGIC

TOWN(1947); MICHIGAN KID, THE(1947); NIGHT SONG(1947); NIGHTMARE ALLEY(1947); ROAD TO RIO(1947); SADDLE PALS(1947); SECRET LIFE OF WALTER MITTY, THE(1947); SINBAD THE SAILOR(1947); VIGILANTES RETURN, THE(1947); GIRL FROM MANHATTAN(1948); HOLLOW TRIUMPH(1948); IF YOU KNEW SUSIE(1948); LIGHTNIN' IN THE FOREST(1948); MIRACLE OF THE BELLS, THE(1948); PALEFACE, THE(1948); RACE STREET(1948); SONS OF ADVENTURE(1948); KNOCK ON ANY DOOR(1949); ONCE MORE, MY DARLING(1949); HAPPY YEARS, THE(1950); KANSAS RAIDERS(1950); NEXT VOICE YOU HEAR, THE(1950); PERFECT STRANGERS(1950); PRETTY BABY(1950); SINGING GUNS(1950); TRIPLE TROUBLE(1950); ACROSS THE WIDE MISSOURI(1951); DOUBLE DYNAMITE(1951); WESTWARD THE WOMEN(1951); HANS CHRISTIAN ANDERSEN(1952); MEET ME AT THE FAIR(1952); MY MAN AND I(1952); SOMEBODY LOVES ME(1952); THIS WOMAN IS DANGEROUS(1952); WAC FROM WALLA WALLA, THE(1952); ISLAND IN THE SKY(1953); HIGH AND THE MIGHTY, THE(1954); RAILS INTO LARAMIE(1954); STEEL CAGE, THE(1954); APACHE AMBUSH(1955); GIRL RUSH, THE(1955); GUNSIGHT RIDGE(1957); SPRING REUNION(1957); DEAD RINGER(1964); LAW OF THE LAWLESS(1964); APACHE UPRISING(1966); GHOST AND MR. CHICKEN, THE(1966); BUCKSKIN(1968); ONE MORE TRAIN TO ROB(1971); PICKUP ON 101(1972); CAPONE(1975); ESCAPE TO WITCH MOUNTAIN(1975); APPLE DUMPLING GANG RIDES AGAIN, THE(1979)
Silents
KID'S CLEVER, THE(1929)
Misc. Silents
BLACK HILLS(1929)
Harry Chandler
IT HAPPENED OUT WEST(1937), w
Helen Chandler
MOTHER'S BOY(1929); SALUTE(1929); SKY HAWK(1929); MOTHERS CRY(1930); OUTWARD BOUND(1930); ROUGH ROMANCE(1930); DAYBREAK(1931); DRACULA(1931); FANNY FOLEY HERSELF(1931); LAST FLIGHT, THE(1931); SALVATION NELL(1931); HOUSE DIVIDED, A(1932); VANITY STREET(1932); ALIMONY MADNESS(1933); BEHIND JURY DOORS(1933, Brit.); CHRISTOPHER STRONG(1933); DANCE MALL HOSTESS(1933); GOODBYE AGAIN(1933); WORST WOMAN IN PARIS(1933); LONG LOST FATHER(1934); MIDNIGHT ALIBI(1934); IT'S A BET(1935, Brit.); RADIO FOLLIES(1935, Brit.); MR. BOGGS STEPS OUT(1938); UNFINISHED SYMPHONY, THE(1953, Aust./Brit.)
Silents
JOY GIRL, THE(1927)
Jack Chandler
SOUP FOR ONE(1982)
James Chandler
YOUNG CAPTIVES, THE(1959); DON'T KNOCK THE TWIST(1962); JUMBO(1962); SWEET BIRD OF YOUTH(1962); HEAVEN WITH A GUN(1969)
Jane Chandler
MEN ON HER MIND(1944)
Janet Chandler
GOLDEN WEST, THE(1932); COWBOY HOLIDAY(1934); HOUSE OF DANGER(1934); CYCLONE OF THE SADDLE(1935); ROUGH RIDING RANGER(1935)
Misc. Talkies
MILLION DOLLAR HAUL(1935); NOW OR NEVER(1935)
Jeff Chandler
INVISIBLE WALL, THE(1947); JOHNNY O'CLOCK(1947); ROSES ARE RED(1947); ABANDONED(1949); MR. BELVEDERE GOES TO COLLEGE(1949); SWORD IN THE DESERT(1949); BROKEN ARROW(1950); DEPORTED(1950); DOUBLE CROSSBONES(1950); TWO FLAGS WEST(1950); BIRD OF PARADISE(1951); FLAME OF ARABY(1951); IRON MAN, THE(1951); SMUGGLER'S ISLAND(1951); BATTLE AT APACHE PASS, THE(1952); BECAUSE OF YOU(1952); RED BALL EXPRESS(1952); YANKEE BUCCANEER(1952); EAST OF SUMATRA(1953); GREAT SIOUX UPRISING, THE(1953); WAR ARROW(1953); SIGN OF THE PAGAN(1954); TAZA, SON OF COCHISE(1954); YANKEE PASHA(1954); FEMALE ON THE BEACH(1955); FOXFIRE(1955); SPOILERS, THE(1955); AWAY ALL BOATS(1956); PILLARS OF THE SKY(1956); TOY TIGER(1956); DRANGO(1957); JEANNE EAGELS(1957); MAN IN THE SHADOW(1957); TATTERED DRESS, THE(1957); LADY TAKES A FLYER, THE(1958); RAW WIND IN EDEN(1958); JAYHAWKERS, THE(1959); STRANGER IN MY ARMS(1959); TEN SECONDS TO HELL(1959); THUNDER IN THE SUN(1959); PLUNDERERS, THE(1960); STORY OF DAVID, A(1960, Brit.); RETURN TO PEYTON PLACE(1961); MERRILL'S MARAUDERS(1962)
Jeffrey Chandler
HIGH WIND IN JAMAICA, A(1965); HALF A SIXPENCE(1967, Brit.); HEADLINE HUNTERS(1968, Brit.); OLIVER!(1968, Brit.); DAVID COPPERFIELD(1970, Brit.)
Jene Chandler
STRANGE SHADOWS IN AN EMPTY ROOM(1977, Can./Ital.)
Jeremy Chandler
DOCTOR FAUSTUS(1967, Brit.)
Joan Chandler
HUMORESQUE(1946); ROPE(1948); DRAGSTRIP RIOT(1958); HOW TO MAKE A MONSTER(1958)
John Chandler
PACIFIC ADVENTURE(1947, Aus.), w; MAD DOG COLL(1961); SHOOT OUT(1971); PAT GARRETT AND BILLY THE KID(1973); WISHBONE CUTTER(1978); LITTLE DRAGONS, THE(1980)
John D. Chandler
CAPONE(1975)
John David Chandler
SCORCHY(1976)
John Davis Chandler
YOUNG SAVAGES, THE(1961); RIDE THE HIGH COUNTRY(1962); THOSE CALLOWAYS(1964); MAJOR DUNDEE(1965); ONCE A THIEF(1965); GOOD GUYS AND THE BAD GUYS, THE(1969); HOOKED GENERATION, THE(1969); BARQUERO(1970); ULTIMATE THRILL, THE(1974); WALKING TALL, PART II(1975); MAKO: THE JAWS OF DEATH(1976); SWORD AND THE SORCERER, THE(1982); TRIUMPHS OF A MAN CALLED HORSE(1983, US/Mex.)
Karen Chandler
MODERN ROMANCE(1981)
Kerry Chandler
BIONIC BOY, THE(1977, Hong Kong/Phil.)
Lane Chandler
CORPSE CAME C.O.D., THE(; SERGEANT YORK(; FORWARD PASS, THE(1929); STUDIO MURDER MYSTERY, THE(1929); FIREBRAND JORDAN(1930); ROUGH WATERS(1930); HURRICANE HORSEMAN(1931); UNDER TEXAS SKIES(1931);

BATTLING BUCKAROO(1932); CHEYENNE CYCLONE, THE(1932); SIGN OF THE CROSS, THE(1932); CORRUPTION(1933); DELUGE(1933); DEVIL'S BROTHER, THE(1933); EAGLE AND THE HAWK, THE(1933); ROMAN SCANDALS(1933); VIA PONY EXPRESS(1933); WAR OF THE RANGE(1933); BEYOND THE LAW(1934); GIRL FROM MISSOURI, THE(1934); MERRY WIDOW, THE(1934); NOW I'LL TELL(1934); SAGEBRUSH TRAIL(1934); TEXAS TORNADO(1934); FLASH GORDON(1936); HEARTS IN BONDAGE(1936); LAWLESS NINETIES, THE(1936); RETURN OF JIMMY VALENTINE, THE(1936); STORMY TRAILS(1936); WINDS OF THE WASTELAND(1936); CONFESSION(1937); FIREFLY, THE(1937); GO-GETTER, THE(1937); IDAHO KID, THE(1937); KID GALAHAD(1937); LAW AND LEAD(1937); LAW OF THE RANGER(1937); PLAINSMAN, THE(1937); RECKLESS RANGER(1937); ROSALIE(1937); SAN QUENTIN(1937); SEA RACKETEERS(1937); SHE LOVED A FIREMAN(1937); SINGING MARINE, THE(1937); THREE SMART GIRLS(1937); ANGELS WITH DIRTY FACES(1938); CAMPUS CONFESSIONS(1938); FIRST 100 YEARS, THE(1938); HEART OF ARIZONA(1938); HEROES OF THE ALAMO(1938); I AM THE LAW(1938); LAND OF FIGHTING MEN(1938); MARIE ANTOINETTE(1938); TOO HOT TO HANDLE(1938); TWO-GUN JUSTICE(1938); COME ON RANGERS(1939); LAW COMES TO TEXAS, THE(1939); MADE FOR EACH OTHER(1939); MAN IN THE IRON MASK, THE(1939); MAN OF CONQUEST(1939); NORTH OF THE YUKON(1939); OKLAHOMA FRONTIER(1939); OUTPOST OF THE MOUNTIES(1939); SAGA OF DEATH VALLEY(1939); SECRET SERVICE OF THE AIR(1939); SOUTHWARD HO!(1939); ST. LOUIS BLUES(1939); TAMING OF THE WEST, THE(1939); UNION PACIFIC(1939); YOU CAN'T GET AWAY WITH MURDER(1939); CHARLIE CHAN IN PANAMA(1940); GREAT PLANE ROBBERY, THE(1940); HI-YO SILVER(1940); HOWARDS OF VIRGINIA, THE(1940); INVISIBLE STRIPES(1940); MAN FROM MONTREAL, THE(1940); MURDER IN THE AIR(1940); MY LITTLE CHICKADEE(1940); NORTHWEST MOUNTED POLICE(1940); PIONEERS OF THE WEST(1940); PONY POST(1940); SANTA FE TRAIL(1940); VIRGINIA CITY(1940); I WANTED WINGS(1941); LAST OF THE DUANES(1941); ROAD SHOW(1941); ROUNDUP, THE(1941); SIX GUN GOLD(1941); INVISIBLE AGENT(1942); MOONLIGHT IN HAVANA(1942); PRIDE OF THE YANKEES, THE(1942); REAP THE WILD WIND(1942); SECRET ENEMIES(1942); SUNDOWN JIM(1942); THEY DIED WITH THEIR BOOTS ON(1942); BEHIND PRISON WALLS(1943); FLESH AND FANTASY(1943); IN OLD OKLAHOMA(1943); NORTH STAR, THE(1943); PHANTOM OF THE OPERA(1943); RIDING HIGH(1943); TENTING TONIGHT ON THE OLD CAMP GROUND(1943); THEY CAME TO BLOW UP AMERICA(1943); THEY GOT ME COVERED(1943); WILD HORSE RUSTLERS(1943); CASANOVA BROWN(1944); DESTINATION TOKYO(1944); DESTINY(1944); FOLLOW THE BOYS(1944); GREAT MIKE, THE(1944); HEAVENLY DAYS(1944); JANIE(1944); LADY AND THE MONSTER, THE(1944); LAURA(1944); LAW OF THE SADDLE(1944); LOUISIANA HAYRIDE(1944); OKLAHOMA RAIDERS(1944); ONCE UPON A TIME(1944); RIDERS OF THE SANTA FE(1944); RUSTLER'S HIDEOUT(1944); SILVER CITY KID(1944); STORY OF DR. WASSELL, THE(1944); TRIGGER TRAIL(1944); ALONG CAME JONES(1945); SAN ANTONIO(1945); SARATOGA TRUNK(1945); SENORITA FROM THE WEST(1945); SPIDER, THE(1945); BANDIT OF SHERWOOD FOREST, THE(1946); CALIFORNIA(1946); DARK HORSE, THE(1946); DARK MIRROR, THE(1946); DUEL IN THE SUN(1946); IDEA GIRL(1946); IT'S A WONDERFUL LIFE(1946); LITTLE GIANT(1946); LOVER COME BACK(1946); MONSIEUR BEAUCAIRE(1946); TOMORROW IS FOREVER(1946); PURSUED(1947); SONG OF MY HEART(1947); UNCONQUERED(1947); VIGILANTES RETURN, THE(1947); BIG CLOCK, THE(1948); CAMPUS SLEUTH(1948); MONEY MADNESS(1948); NORTHWEST STAMPEDE(1948); PALEFACE, THE(1948); RED RIVER(1948); RETURN OF THE BADMEN(1948); SONG IS BORN, A(1948); SOUTHERN YANKEE, A(1948); LONE WOLF AND HIS LADY, THE(1949); RIDERS OF THE WHISTLING PINES(1949); SAMSON AND DELILAH(1949); TULSA(1949); MONTANA(1950); OUTCAST OF BLACK MESA(1950); CATTLE QUEEN(1951); MILLIONAIRE FOR CHRISTY, A(1951); PRAIRIE ROUNDUP(1951); SANTA FE(1951); WELL, THE(1951); GREATEST SHOW ON EARTH, THE(1952); HAWK OF WILD RIVER, THE(1952); LION AND THE HORSE, THE(1952); LUSTY MEN, THE(1952); RANCHO NOTORIOUS(1952); SAN FRANCISCO STORY, THE(1952); CHARGE AT FEATHER RIVER, THE(1953); TAKE ME TO TOWN(1953); THUNDER OVER THE PLAINS(1953); BORDER RIVER(1954); RETURN TO TREASURE ISLAND(1954); SILVER LODE(1954); INDIAN FIGHTER, THE(1955); LONE RANGER, THE(1955); PRINCE OF PLAYERS(1955); SHOTGUN(1955); TALL MAN RIDING(1955); FIRST TRAVELING SALESLADY, THE(1956); STORM RIDER, THE(1957); QUANTRILL'S RAIDERS(1958); SPACE MASTER X-7(1958); NOOSE FOR A GUNMAN(1960); LITTLE SHEPHERD OF KINGDOM COME(1961); REQUIEM FOR A GUNFIGHTER(1965)

Misc. Talkies

BEYOND THE LAW(1930); RIDERS OF RIO(1931); GUNS FOR HIRE(1932); LAWLESS VALLEY(1932); RECKLESS RIDER, THE(1932); WYOMING WHIRLWIND(1932); TROUBLE BUSTERS(1933); LONE BANDIT, THE(1934); OUTLAW TAMER, THE(1934); NORTH OF ARIZONA(1935); TERROR TRAIL(1946); TWO-FISTED STRANGER(1946)

Silents

LOVE AND LEARN(1928); RED HAIR(1928); SINGLE STANDARD, THE(1929)

Misc. Silents

OPEN RANGE(1927); FIRST KISS, THE(1928); LEGION OF THE CONDEMNED(1928)

Lane R. Chandler

CREATURE WITH THE ATOM BRAIN(1955)

Lee Chandler

CYCLE SAVAGES(1969)

Mack Chandler

SCENE OF THE CRIME(1949); MYSTERY STREET(1950); MILLION DOLLAR MERMAID(1952); FROM HERE TO ETERNITY(1953); CRIME WAVE(1954); UNDERSEA GIRL(1957)

Mandy Chandler

Misc. Talkies

SWINGING COEDS, THE(1976)

Michael Chandler

NEVER CRY WOLF(1983), ed

1984

AMADEUS(1984), ed

Mimi Chandler

HENRY ALDRICH SWINGS IT(1943); AND THE ANGELS SING(1944)

Patti Chandler

PAJAMA PARTY(1964); BEACH BLANKET BINGO(1965); DR. GOLDFOOT AND THE BIKINI MACHINE(1965); HOW TO STUFF A WILD BIKINI(1965); SERGEANT DEADHEAD(1965); FIREBALL 590(1966); GHOST IN THE INVISIBLE BIKINI(1966); MILLION EYES OF SU-MURU, THE(1967, Brit.)

Paul Chandler

Misc. Talkies

VOICE OVER(1983)

Perdita Chandler

GLASS MENAGERIE, THE(1950); GREAT JEWEL ROBBER, THE(1950); PEOPLE AGAINST O'HARA, THE(1951); PHONE CALL FROM A STRANGER(1952); SCANDAL AT SCOURIE(1953); JET PILOT(1957)

Pierre Chandler

FRENCH LINE, THE(1954)

Raymond Chandler

FALCON TAKES OVER, THE(1942), w; TIME TO KILL(1942), w; AND NOW TOMORROW(1944), w; DOUBLE INDEMNITY(1944), w; MURDER, MY SWEET(1945), w; UNSEEN, THE(1945), w; BIG SLEEP, THE(1946), w; BLUE DAHLIA, THE(1946), w; BRASHER DOUBLOON, THE(1947), w; LADY IN THE LAKE(1947), w; STRANGERS ON A TRAIN(1951), w; MARLOWE(1969), w; LONG GOODBYE, THE(1973), w; FAREWELL, MY LOVELY(1975), w

Richard Chandler

SHE HAS WHAT IT TAKES(1943)

Robert Chandler

Silents

AVENGING TRAIL, THE(1918); GO WEST, YOUNG MAN(1919); HOME STUFF(1921)

Misc. Silents

QUICK TRIGGERS(1928); HAWK OF THE HILLS(1929)

Robert B. Chandler

1984

CANNONBALL RUN II(1984)

Shirley Chandler

GYPSY(1962)

Simon Chandler

VICTOR/VICTORIA(1982)

1984

BOUNTY, THE(1984)

Tanis Chandler

JANIE(1944); CORNERED(1945); DICK TRACY(1945); AFFAIRS OF GERALDINE(1946); BIG SLEEP, THE(1946); SHADOWS OVER CHINATOWN(1946); SPOOK BUSTERS(1946); THE CATMAN OF PARIS(1946); LURED(1947); SPIRIT OF WEST POINT, THE(1947); TRAP, THE(1947); SIXTEEN FATHOMS DEEP(1948); ACCORDING TO MRS. HOYLE(1951)

Vern Chandler

MISSOURI BREAKS, THE(1976)

Vivenne Chandler

CLOCKWORK ORANGE, A(1971, Brit.)

Vivienne Chandler

LUST FOR A VAMPIRE(1971, Brit.); VICTOR/VICTORIA(1982); DRAUGHTSMAN'S CONTRACT, THE(1983, Brit.)

1984

PLOUGHMAN'S LUNCH, THE(1984, Brit.)

Warren Chandler

Silents

ADVENTURE SHOP, THE(1918); MAN AND HIS WOMAN(1920)

Misc. Silents

GRAY TOWERS MYSTERY, THE(1919); MY HUSBAND'S OTHER WIFE(1919)

Winnie Chandler

SUMMER AND SMOKE(1961)

John Chandos

INVADERS, THE,(1941); NEXT OF KIN(1942, Brit.); SPITFIRE(1943, Brit.); NICHOLAS NICKLEBY(1947, Brit.); FOUR AGAINST FATE(1952, Brit.); SECRET PEOPLE(1952, Brit.); LONG MEMORY, THE(1953, Brit.); TERROR STREET(1953); COURT MARTIAL(1954, Brit.); LOVE LOTTERY, THE(1954, Brit.); ONE WAY OUT(1955, Brit.); SIMBA(1955, Brit.); SHIP THAT DIED OF SHAME, THE(1956, Brit.); DOCTOR AT LARGE(1957, Brit.); GREEN MAN, THE(1957, Brit.); PURSUIT OF THE GRAF SPEE(1957, Brit.); TIME WITHOUT PITY(1957, Brit.); I ACCUSE(1958, Brit.); WITNESS, THE(1959, Brit.); JUNGLE STREET GIRLS(1963, Brit.); LITTLE ONES, THE(1965, Brit.); TWO GENTLEMEN SHARING(1969, Brit.)

Ram Chandra

RAINS OF RANCHIPUR, THE(1955)

Chandra Kaly and His Dancers

TIME, THE PLACE AND THE GIRL, THE(1946)

Chandra Kaly Dancers

CRAZY HOUSE(1943)

The Chandra-Kaly and Hi Dancers

ABBOTT AND COSTELLO MEET THE MUMMY(1955)

B. Chandragupta

APARAJITO(1959, India), art d

Bansi Chandragupta

RIVER, THE(1951), set d; GODDESS, THE(1962, India), art d; MUSIC ROOM, THE(1963, India), art d; TWO DAUGHTERS(1963, India), art d; KANCHENJUNGHA(1966, India), art d; GURU, THE(1969, U.S./India), art d; HULLABALOO OVER GEORGIE AND BONNIE'S PICTURES(1979, Brit.), artd

B. Chandrasherkhra

TUSK(1980, Fr.)

Haile Chane

ROADRACERS, THE(1959)

Chanel

PALMY DAYS(1931), cos; TONIGHT OR NEVER(1931), cos; GREEKS HAD A WORD FOR THEM(1932), cos; LAST YEAR AT MARIENBAD(1962, Fr./Ital.), cos; DAY OF THE JACKAL, THE(1973, Brit./Fr.), cos

Coco Chanel

RULES OF THE GAME, THE(1939, Fr.), cos

Granier Chanel

LA MARSEILLAISE(1938, Fr.), cos

Helen Chanel

TERROR OF THE BLACK MASK(1967, Fr./Ital.)

Helene Chanel

PRICE OF FLESH, THE(1962, Fr.); SAMSON AND THE SEVEN MIRACLES OF THE WORLD(1963, Fr./Ital.); WITCH'S CURSE, THE(1963, Ital.); HEAT(1970, Arg.)

Lorraine Chanel
MAGNIFICENT MATADOR, THE(1955); REVENGERS, THE(1972, U.S./Mex.)
Barbara Chaney
SOUNDER, PART 2(1976)
Bill Chaney
BLOCK BUSTERS(1944); ONCE UPON A TIME(1944); LAWLESS RIDER, THE(1954); I KILLED WILD BILL HICKOK(1956)
Billy Chaney
PLAYMATES(1941); LOVE THAT BRUTE(1950)
Bob Chaney
Misc. Talkies
INSTRUCTOR, THE(1983)
Creighton Chaney
CHEYENNE RIDES AGAIN(1937)
Misc. Talkies
MARRIAGE BARGAIN, THE(1935)
Creighton Chaney [Lon Chaney, Jr.]
BIRD OF PARADISE(1932); LUCKY DEVILS(1933); SCARLET RIVER(1933); SON OF THE BORDER(1933); LIFE OF VERGIE WINTERS, THE(1934); SIXTEEN FATHOMS DEEP(1934); ACCENT ON YOUTH(1935); ROSE BOWL(1936); SINGING COWBOY, THE(1936); ANGEL'S HOLIDAY(1937); CHARLIE CHAN ON BROADWAY(1937); LIFE BEGINS IN COLLEGE(1937); LOVE AND HISSES(1937); MIDNIGHT TAXI(1937); OLD CORRAL, THE(1937); SECOND HONEYMOON(1937); SLAVE SHIP(1937); THIN ICE(1937); WIFE, DOCTOR AND NURSE(1937); WILD AND WOOLLY(1937); CITY GIRL(1938); HAPPY LANDING(1938); JOSETTE(1938); MR. MOTO'S GAMBLE(1938); PASSPORT HUSBAND(1938); ROAD DEMON(1938); CHARLIE CHAN IN THE CITY OF DARKNESS(1939); FRONTIER MARSHAL(1939); JESSE JAMES(1939); OF MICE AND MEN(1939); UNION PACIFIC(1939); NORTHWEST MOUNTED POLICE(1940); ONE MILLION B.C.(1940); BADLANDS OF DAKOTA(1941); BILLY THE KID(1941); MAN MADE MONSTER(1941); SAN ANTONIO ROSE(1941); TOO MANY BLONDES(1941); WOLF MAN, THE(1941); GHOST OF FRANKENSTEIN, THE(1942); MUMMY'S TOMB, THE(1942); NORTH TO THE KLONDIKE(1942); SHERLOCK HOLMES AND THE VOICE OF TERROR(1942); CALLING DR. DEATH(1943); CRAZY HOUSE(1943); EYES OF THE UNDERWORLD(1943); FRANKENSTEIN MEETS THE WOLF MAN(1943); FRONTIER BADMEN(1943); SCREAM IN THE NIGHT(1943); SON OF DRACULA(1943); COBRA WOMAN(1944); FOLLOW THE BOYS(1944); HOUSE OF FRANKENSTEIN(1944); MUMMY'S CURSE, THE(1944); MUMMY'S GHOST, THE(1944); WEIRD WOMAN(1944); DALTONS RIDE AGAIN, THE(1945); FROZEN GHOST, THE(1945); HERE COME THE CO-EDS(1945); PILLOW OF DEATH(1945); STRANGE CONFESSION(1945); MY FAVORITE BRUNETTE(1947); ABBOTT AND COSTELLO MEET FRANKENSTEIN(1948); SIXTEEN FATHOMS DEEP(1948); CAPTAIN CHINA(1949); THERE'S A GIRL IN MY HEART(1949); ONCE A THIEF(1950); BRIDE OF THE GORILLA(1951); FLAME OF ARABY(1951); INSIDE STRAIGHT(1951); ONLY THE VALIANT(1951); BATTLES OF CHIEF PONTIAC(1952); BLACK CASTLE, THE(1952); BUSHWHACKERS, THE(1952); HIGH NOON(1952); SPRINGFIELD RIFLE(1952); THIEF OF DAMASCUS(1952); LION IS IN THE STREETS, A(1953); RAIDERS OF THE SEVEN SEAS(1953); BIG CHASE, THE(1954); CASANOVA'S BIG NIGHT(1954); JIVARO(1954); PASSION(1954); BIG HOUSE, U.S.A.(1955); I DIED A THOUSAND TIMES(1955); NOT AS A STRANGER(1955); SILVER STAR, THE(1955); BLACK SLEEP, THE(1956); MANFISH(1956); PARDNERS(1956); CYCLOPS(1957); DANIEL BOONE, TRAIL BLAZER(1957); MONEY, WOMEN AND GUNS(1958); ALLIGATOR PEOPLE, THE(1959); FACE OF THE SCREAMING WEREWOLF(1959, Mex.); NIGHT OF THE GHOULS(1959); CHIVATO(1961); REBELLION IN CUBA(1961); DEVIL'S MESSENGER, THE(1962 U.S./Swed.); HAUNTED PALACE, THE(1963); LAW OF THE LAWLESS(1964); STAGE TO THUNDER ROCK(1964); WITCHCRAFT(1964, Brit.); BLACK SPURS(1965); HOUSE OF THE BLACK DEATH(1965); TOWN TAMER(1965); YOUNG FURY(1965); JOHNNY RENO(1966); DR. TERROR'S GALLERY OF HORRORS(1967); HILLBILLYS IN A HAUNTED HOUSE(1967); WELCOME TO HARD TIMES(1967); BUCKSKIN(1968); FIREBALL JUNGLE(1968); SPIDER BABY(1968); FEMALE BUNCH, THE(1969); BLOOD OF FRANKENSTEIN(1970)
Misc. Talkies
BRIDE OF THE GORILLA(1951)
Debi Chaney
DELIRIUM(1979)
Dick Chaney
BOLD AND THE BRAVE, THE(1956), cos
Frances Chaney
WHIPPED, THE(1950); SEVEN UPS, THE(1973)
Hank Edds Faye Chaney
HOW TO SAVE A MARRIAGE–AND RUIN YOUR LIFE(1968), make up
J. Benton Chaney
MAN FROM MUSIC MOUNTAIN(1943), w; LARAMIE TRAIL, THE(1944), w
Jan Chaney
MY GUN IS QUICK(1957)
Lon Chaney
PHANTOM OF THE OPERA, THE(1929); UNHOLY THREE, THE(1930); GIRL O' MY DREAMS(1935); DEAD MAN'S EYES(1944); GHOST CATCHERS(1944); HOUSE OF DRACULA(1945); ALBUQUERQUE(1948); COUNTERFEITERS, THE(1948); BEHAVE YOURSELF(1951); BLACK PIRATES, THE(1954, Mex.); BOY FROM OKLAHOMA, THE(1954); INDIAN FIGHTER, THE(1955); INDESTRUCTIBLE MAN, THE(1956); DEFIANT ONES, THE(1958); APACHE UPRISING(1966)
Silents
GILDED SPIDER, THE(1916); ANTHING ONCE(1917); FLASHLIGHT, THE(1917); RESCUE, THE(1917); BROADWAY SCANDAL(1918); KAISER, BEAST OF BERLIN, THE(1918); FALSE FACES(1919); MIRACLE MAN, THE(1919); NOMADS OF THE NORTH(1920); PENALTY, THE(1920); TREASURE ISLAND(1920); ACE OF HEARTS, THE(1921); OUTSIDE THE LAW(1921); BLIND BARGAIN, A(1922); LIGHT IN THE DARK, THE(1922); OLIVER TWIST(1922); SHADOWS(1922); TRAP, THE(1922); ALL THE BROTHERS WERE VALIANT(1923); HUNCHBACK OF NOTRE DAME, THE(1923); SHOCK(1923); HE WHO GETS SLAPPED(1924); MONSTER, THE(1925); PHANTOM OF THE OPERA, THE(1925); TOWER OF LIES(1925); UNHOLY THREE, THE(1925); BLACK BIRD, THE(1926); ROAD TO MANDALAY, THE(1926); TELL IT TO THE MARINES(1926); LONDON AFTER MIDNIGHT(1927); MOCKERY(1927); MR. WU(1927); UNKNOWN, THE(1927); BIG CITY, THE(1928); LAUGH, CLOWN, LAUGH(1928); WEST OF ZANZIBAR(1928); WHILE THE CITY SLEEPS(1928); THUNDER(1929); WHERE EAST IS EAST(1929)
Misc. Silents
FORBIDDEN ROOM, THE(1914); RICHIELIEU(1914); BOBBIE OF THE BALLET(1916); GRASP OF GREED, THE(1916); GRIP OF JEALOUSY, THE(1916); IF MY

COUNTRY SHOULD CALL(1916); MARK OF CAIN, THE(1916); PLACE BEYOND THE WINDS, THE(1916); PRICE OF SILENCE, THE(1916); DOLL'S HOUSE, A(1917); FIRES OF REBELLION(1917); GIRL IN THE CHECKERED COAT, THE(1917); HELL MORGAN'S GIRL(1917); PAY ME(1917); PIPER'S PRICE, THE(1917); TRIUMPH(1917); BROADWAY LOVE(1918); GRAND PASSION, THE(1918); RIDDLE GAWNE(1918); SCARLET CAR, THE(1918); TALK OF THE TOWN(1918); THAT DEVIL, BATEESE(1918); MAN'S COUNTRY, A(1919); PAID IN ADVANCE(1919); VICTORY(1919); WHEN BEARCAT WENT DRY(1919); WICKED DARLING, THE(1919); BITS OF LIFE(1921); NIGHT ROSE, THE(1921); FLESH AND BLOOD(1922); QUINCY ADAMS SAWYER(1922); WHILE PARIS SLEEPS(1923); NEXT CORNER, THE(1924)
Richard Chaney
DRANGO(1957), cos
Stewart Chaney
UP IN ARMS(1944), art d; KID FROM BOOKLYN, THE(1946), art d
Will Chaney
HONKY(1971), p, w
William Chaney
PRIDE OF THE YANKEES, THE(1942)
Anna Chang
HATCHET MAN, THE(1932)
Bobby Chang
HOLIDAY RHYTHM(1950)
Chang Yao Chang
RETURN OF THE DRAGON(1974, Chin.), ed
Danny Chang
HONG KONG(1951); BATTLE CIRCUS(1953); SOUTH SEA WOMAN(1953); SOLDIER OF FORTUNE(1955); CHINA DOLL(1958)
David Chang
DRACULA AND THE SEVEN GOLDEN VAMPIRES(1978, Brit./Chi.)
George Chang
WEST OF RAINBOW'S END(1938)
Grace Chang
NEXT TO NO TIME(1960, Brit.)
Harry Chang
GHOST OF THE CHINA SEA(1958); RAGGEDY ANN AND ANDY(1977), ed
Dr. Hugh Ho Chang
SO PROUDLY WE HAIL(1943)
Jane Chang
OPERATION BOTTLENECK(1961); SEVEN WOMEN(1966)
Jeffrey Chang
HAWAIIANS, THE(1970)
Jenifer Chang
LIQUID SKY(1982)
John W. T. Chang
LOVE IS A MANY-SPLENDORED THING(1955)
Kathryn Chang
LOVE ISLAND(1952)
Key Chang
PURPLE HEART, THE(1944); PRISON SHIP(1945)
Keye Chang
FIRST YANK INTO TOKYO(1945)
King Ho Chang
PICCADILLY(1932, Brit.)
King Hoo Chang
SON OF THE GODS(1930)
Li Chang
FEMALE PRINCE, THE(1966, Hong Kong)
Mei Chung Chang
REVENGE OF THE SHOGUN WOMEN(1982, Taiwan), d
Melie Chang
LITTLE TOKYO, U.S.A.(1942)
Paul Chang
MILLION EYES OF SU-MURU, THE(1967, Brit.)
Peter Chang
YANK IN INDO-CHINA, A(1952)
Roger Chang
1984
NIGHTSONGS(1984)
Sheilah Chang
OPEN THE DOOR AND SEE ALL THE PEOPLE(1964)
Tanya Chang
HAWAIIANS, THE(1970)
Tisa Chang
AMBUSH BAY(1966)
Tong-hui Chang
MARINE BATTLEGROUND(1966, U.S/S.K.)
Vincent Chang
MANFISH(1956)
W. T. Chang
MACAO(1952); BLOOD ALLEY(1955)
Wah Chang
DINOSAURUS(1960), spec eff; TIME MACHINE, THE(1960; Brit./U.S.), spec eff; MASTER OF THE WORLD(1961), spec eff; WONDERFUL WORLD OF THE BROTHERS ERIMM, THE(1962), spec eff; SEVEN FACES OF DR. LAO(1964), spec eff; POWER, THE(1968), spec eff
Yankee Chang
GIDGET GOES HAWAIIAN(1961); SEVEN WOMEN FROM HELL(1961); DIAMOND HEAD(1962)
Yanqui Chang
RIDE THE WILD SURF(1964)
Yun Kui Chang
JUNGLE HEAT(1957)
Zon Su Chang
REVENGE OF THE SHOGUN WOMEN(1982, Taiwan), ph
Chang the Elephant
JUNGLE OF CHANG(1951)
Chang-Fu
SHARK WOMAN, THE(1941)

Ken Chapin
SOMETHING WILD(1961); UNMARRIED WOMAN, AN(1978); STARDUST MEMORIES(1980); WINDOWS(1980); ZELIG(1983)

Martha Chapin
VICE RACKET(1937); LIGHTNING STRIKES WEST(1940), w
Misc. Talkies
GAMBLING WITH SOULS(1936)

Michael Chapin
NIGHT EDITOR(1946); SONG OF ARIZONA(1946); CALL NORTHSIDE 777(1948); UNDER CALIFORNIA STARS(1948); STRANGE BARGAIN(1949); SUMMER STOCK(1950); ARIZONA MANHUNT(1951); BUCKAROO SHERIFF OF TEXAS(1951); DAKOTA KID, THE(1951); WELLS FARGO GUNMASTER(1951); SPRINGFIELD RIFLE(1952); WAGONS WEST(1952); WILD HORSE AMBUSH(1952); PRIDE OF THE BLUE GRASS(1954)

Miles Chapin
LADYBUG, LADYBUG(1963); BLESS THE BEASTS AND CHILDREN(1971); TO FIND A MAN(1972); FRENCH POSTCARDS(1979); HAIR(1979); BUDDY BUDDY(1981); FUNHOUSE, THE(1981); FUNNY FARM, THE(1982, Can.); PANDEMONIUM(1982); GET CRAZY(1983)

Mrs. Chapin
Silents
OTHER MAN, THE(1918)

Robert Chapin
BORROWING TROUBLE(1937), w; CHECKERS(1937), w; HOT WATER(1937), w; ALWAYS IN TROUBLE(1938), w; PASSPORT HUSBAND(1938), w; SAFETY IN NUMBERS(1938), w; WALKING DOWN BROADWAY(1938), w; BLONDIE BRINGS UP BABY(1939), w; BLONDIE TAKES A VACATION(1939), w; EVERYBODY'S BABY(1939), w; BABIES FOR SALE(1940), w; BOWERY BOY(1940), w; LITTLE ORVIE(1940), w; ISLE OF MISSING MEN(1942), w; PRISONER OF JAPAN(1942), w; G.I. HONEYMOON(1945), w

Sandy Chapin
FIRST MONDAY IN OCTOBER(1981)

Steve Chapin
LAST HOUSE ON THE LEFT(1972), m

Theodore Chapin
Silents
PENROD(1922)

Tom Chapin
LORD OF THE FLIES(1963, Brit.)

Dominique Chapius
1984
SUGAR CANE ALLEY(1984, Fr.), ph

Arnold Chapkis
I START COUNTING(1970, Brit.), art d; RUNNERS(1983, Brit.), prod d

Jack Chaplain
GIT!(1965)

Claudie Chapland
ROYAL AFFAIRS IN VERSAILLES(1957, Fr.)

S. Chaplesky
Misc. Silents
ON THE WARSAW HIGHROAD(1916, USSR)

N. Chapligin
VOW, THE(1947, USSR.); ADMIRAL NAKHIMOV(1948, USSR)

Ann Chaplin
KID FOR TWO FARTHINGS, A(1956, Brit.)

Anne Morrison Chaplin
BIG CITY(1948), w

Charles Chaplin
MODERN TIMES(1936), a, p,d&w, m; GREAT DICTATOR, THE(1940), a, p,d&w; MONSIEUR VERDOUX(1947), a, p,d&w, m; LIMELIGHT(1952), a, p,d&w, m, ch; KING IN NEW YORK, A(1957, Brit.), a, p,d&w, m; COUNTESS FROM HONG KONG, A(1967, Brit.), a, p, d,w&m; SMILE(1975), m
Silents
TILLIE'S PUNCTURED ROMANCE(1914); KID, THE(1921), a, p,d&w; NUT, THE(1921); PILGRIM, THE(1923), a, d&w; SOULS FOR SALE(1923); WOMAN OF PARIS, A(1923), a, p,d&w; GOLD RUSH, THE(1925), a, p,d&w; CIRCUS, THE(1928), a, p,d&w, m&ed; SHOW PEOPLE(1928); CITY LIGHTS(1931), a, p,d&w, m
Misc. Silents
CARMEN(1916), a, d; SHOULDER ARMS(1917), a, d

Charles Chaplin, Jr.
LIMELIGHT(1952); FANGS OF THE WILD(1954); COURT-MARTIAL OF BILLY MITCHELL, THE(1955); HIGH SCHOOL CONFIDENTIAL(1958); BEAT GENERATION, THE(1959); BIG OPERATOR, THE(1959); GIRLS' TOWN(1959); NIGHT OF THE QUARTER MOON(1959); SEX KITTENS GO TO COLLEGE(1960)

Charles F. Chaplin
TROCADERO(1944), w

Charlie Chaplin
Misc. Silents
ESSANAY-CHAPLIN REVUE OF 1916, THE(1916), a, d

Christopher Chaplin
1984
WHERE IS PARSIFAL?(1984, Brit.)

Esme V. Chaplin
MURDER(1930, Brit.)

Geraldine Chaplin
LIMELIGHT(1952); DOCTOR ZHIVAGO(1965); COP-OUT(1967, Brit.); COUNTESS FROM HONG KONG, A(1967, Brit.); HAWAIIANS, THE(1970); Z.P.G.(1972); INNOCENT BYSTANDERS(1973, Brit.); THREE MUSKETEERS, THE(1974, Panama); FOUR MUSKETEERS, THE(1975); NASHVILLE(1975); BUFFALO BILL AND THE INDIANS, OR SITTING BULL'S HISTORY LESSON(1976); WELCOME TO L.A.(1976); ROSELAND(1977); ADOPTION, THE(1978, Fr.); REMEMBER MY NAME(1978); WEDDING, A(1978); MAIS OU ET DONC ORNICAR(1979, Fr.); MIRROR CRACK'D, THE(1980, Brit.); BOLERO(1982, Fr.)
1984
LIFE IS A BED OF ROSES(1984, Fr.); LOVE ON THE GROUND(1984,Fr.)

Jennifer Chaplin
ZAPPED!(1982)

Josephine Chaplin
LIMELIGHT(1952); COUNTESS FROM HONG KONG, A(1967, Brit.); ESCAPE TO THE SUN(1972, Fr./Ger./Israel); SHADOWMAN(1974, Fr./Ital.); NO TIME FOR BREAKFAST(1978, Fr.)
1984
BAY BOY(1984, Can.)

Lita Grey Chaplin
DEVIL'S SLEEP, THE(1951)

Michael Chaplin
LIMELIGHT(1952); KING IN NEW YORK, A(1957, Brit.); PROMISE HER ANYTHING(1966, Brit.); SANDWICH MAN, THE(1966, Brit.)

Mildred Harris Chaplin
Silents
INFERIOR SEX, THE(1920); POLLY OF THE STORM COUNTRY(1920)
Misc. Silents
OLD DAD(1920); WOMAN IN HIS HOUSE, THE(1920)

Nancy Chaplin
EBB TIDE(1937)

Oona Chaplin
BROKEN ENGLISH(1981)

Prescott Chaplin
LAUGHING AT LIFE(1933), w; PRIVATE JONES(1933), w; NEVER GIVE A SUCKER AN EVEN BREAK(1941), w; SLEEPY LAGOON(1943), w; MY BUDDY(1944), w; FLAME OF THE BARBARY COAST(1945), w; WOMAN OF THE NORTH COUNTRY(1952), w; ISLAND OF LOST WOMEN(1959), w

Saul Chaplin
ROOKIES ON PARADE(1941), w; TWO YANKS IN TRINIDAD(1942), m/l; IT'S GREAT TO BE YOUNG(1946), md; ON THE TOWN(1949), m; SUMMER STOCK(1950), md; AMERICAN IN PARIS, AN(1951), md; LOVELY TO LOOK AT(1952), md; GIVE A GIRL A BREAK(1953), md; KISS ME KATE(1953), md; SEVEN BRIDES FOR SEVEN BROTHERS(1954), md; INTERRUPTED MELODY(1955), md; JUPITER'S DARLING(1955), md; HIGH SOCIETY(1956), m; TEAHOUSE OF THE AUGUST MOON, THE(1956), m, md; MERRY ANDREW(1958), m; WEST SIDE STORY(1961), md; STAR!(1968), p

Sidney Chaplin
HO(1968, Fr.)

Syd Chaplin
Silents
BETTER 'OLE, THE(1926)
Misc. Silents
MISSING LINK, THE(1927)

Sydney Chaplin
LIMELIGHT(1952); LAND OF THE PHARAOHS(1955); ABDULLAH'S HAREM(1956, Brit./Egypt.); DEADLIEST SIN, THE(1956, Brit.); FOUR GIRLS IN TOWN(1956); PILLARS OF THE SKY(1956); QUANTEZ(1957); FOLLOW THAT MAN(1961, Brit.); COUNTESS FROM HONG KONG, A(1967, Brit.); ADDING MACHINE, THE(1969); SICILIAN CLAN, THE(1970, Fr.); SATAN'S CHEERLEADERS(1977)
Misc. Talkies
PSYCHO SISTERS(1972)
Silents
SUBMARINE PIRATE, A(1915), a, d; KING, QUEEN, JOKER(1921), a, d&w; PILGRIM, THE(1923); RENDEZVOUS, THE(1923); MAN ON THE BOX, THE(1925); OH, WHAT A NURSE!(1926); FORTUNE HUNTER, THE(1927)
Misc. Silents
SHOULDER ARMS(1917); HER TEMPORARY HUSBAND(1923); GALLOPING FISH(1924); PERFECT FLAPPER, THE(1924); CHARLEY'S AUNT(1925); SKIRTS(1928, Brit.)

Victoria Chaplin
COUNTESS FROM HONG KONG, A(1967, Brit.)

Adele Chapman
GOODBYE PORK PIE(1981, New Zealand)

Alan Chapman
1984
DARK ENEMY(1984, Brit.)

Ann Chapman
YOUNG GIRLS OF ROCHEFORT, THE(1968, Fr.)

Anne Chapman
FINDERS KEEPERS, LOVERS WEEPERS(1968)

Antony Chapman
OUT(1982), prod d

Audrey Chapman
Silents
GARRISON'S FINISH(1923)
Misc. Silents
MONEY CHANGERS, THE(1920); FALSE WOMEN(1921); GOD'S GOLD(1921)

Audry Chapman
Silents
DADDY LONG LEGS(1919)

Ben Chapman
DEVIL'S PIPELINE, THE(1940), w; LEATHER-PUSHERS, THE(1940), w; DANGEROUS GAME, A(1941), w; SIX LESSONS FROM MADAME LA ZONGA(1941), w; TIMBER(1942), w; TOP SERGEANT(1942), w; CREATURE FROM THE BLACK LAGOON(1954); RHINO(1964), p

Blanche Chapman
Misc. Silents
MRS. WIGGS OF THE CABBAGE PATCH(1914)

Bob Chapman
FOR MEN ONLY(1952)

Ceil Chapman
PROMISES, PROMISES(1963), cos

Christopher Chapman
Misc. Talkies
KELLY(1981, Can.), d

Constance Chapman
LONG AGO, TOMORROW(1971, Brit.); SAY HELLO TO YESTERDAY(1971, Brit.); DAY IN THE DEATH OF JOE EGG, A(1972, Brit.); O LUCKY MAN!(1973, Brit.); HEDDA(1975, Brit.); IN CELEBRATION(1975, Brit.)

Consuela Chapman
MUSIC LOVERS, THE(1971, Brit.)
Craig Chapman
PRIME CUT(1972)
David Chapman
SOMEBODY KILLED HER HUSBAND(1978), art d; SEDUCTION OF JOE TYNAN, THE(1979), art d; FOUR FRIENDS(1981), prod d; WOLFEN(1981), art d
1984
COTTON CLUB, THE(1984), art d
Dian Finn Chapman
GREAT BANK HOAX, THE(1977), cos
Dianne Finn Chapman
SQUIRM(1976), cos; ROSELAND(1977), cos
Don Chapman
BORDER LAW(1931); STATE TROOPER(1933)
Eddie Chapman
JOEY BOY(1965, Brit.), w; TRIPLE CROSS(1967, Fr./Brit.), w
Edith Chapman
Silents
PRETTY SISTER OF JOSE(1915)
Edward Chapman
CASTE(1930, Brit.); JUNO AND THE PAYCOCK(1930, Brit.); MURDER(1930, Brit.); LEAP OF FAITH(1931, Brit.); SKIN GAME, THE(1931, Brit.); TILLY OF BLOOMSBURY(1931, Brit.); FLYING SQUAD, THE(1932, Brit.); HAPPY EVER AFTER(1932, Ger./Brit.); CHURCH MOUSE, THE(1934, Brit.); GIRLS WILL BE BOYS(1934, Brit.); GUEST OF HONOR(1934, Brit.); MISTER CINDERS(1934, Brit.); DIVINE SPARK, THE(1935, Brit./Ital.); REGAL CAVALCADE(1935, Brit.); RUNAWAY QUEEN, THE(1935, Brit.); REMBRANDT(1936, Brit.); SOMEONE AT THE DOOR(1936, Brit.); THINGS TO COME(1936, Brit.); APRIL BLOSSOMS(1937, Brit.); MAN WHO COULD WORK MIRACLES, THE(1937, Brit.); WHO KILLED JOHN SAVAGE?(1937, Brit.); CITADEL, THE(1938); I'VE GOT A HORSE(1938, Brit.); MARIGOLD(1938, Brit.); INSPECTOR HORNLEIGH ON HOLIDAY(1939, Brit.); NURSEMAID WHO DISAPPEARED, THE(1939, Brit.); THERE AIN'T NO JUSTICE(1939, Brit.); BRIGGS FAMILY, THE(1940, Brit.); CONVOY(1940); LAW AND DISORDER(1940, Brit.); ONE NIGHT IN PARIS(1940, Brit.); SECRET FOUR, THE(1940, Brit.); GIRL IN DISTRESS(1941, Brit.); MAIL TRAIN(1941, Brit.); POISON PEN(1941, Brit.); PROUD VALLEY, THE(1941, Brit.); TURNED OUT NICE AGAIN(1941, Brit.); SHIPS WITH WINGS(1942, Brit.); WINGS AND THE WOMAN(1942, Brit.); MR. PERRIN AND MR. TRAILL(1948, Brit.); OCTOBER MAN, THE(1948, Brit.); HISTORY OF MR. POLLY, THE(1949, Brit.); IT ALWAYS RAINS ON SUNDAY(1949, Brit.); MAN ON THE RUN(1949, Brit.); MADELEINE(1950, Brit.); NIGHT AND THE CITY(1950, Brit.); CRASH OF SILENCE(1952, Brit.); HIS EXCELLENCY(1952, Brit.); MAGIC BOX, THE(1952, Brit.); PROMOTER, THE(1952, Brit.); SPIDER AND THE FLY, THE(1952, Brit.); WILD HEART, THE(1952, Brit.); DAY TO REMEMBER, A(1953, Brit.); FOLLY TO BE WISE(1953); CROWDED DAY, THE(1954, Brit.); END OF THE ROAD, THE(1954, Brit.); INTRUDER, THE(1955, Brit.); LOVE MATCH, THE(1955, Brit.); YANK IN ERMINE, A(1955, Brit.); BHOWANI JUNCTION(1956); LISBON(1956); DOCTOR AT LARGE(1957, Brit.); JUST MY LUCK(1957, Brit.); X THE UNKNOWN(1957, Brit.); INNOCENT SINNERS(1958, Brit.); SQUARE PEG, THE(1958, Brit.); YOUNG AND THE GUILTY, THE(1958, Brit.); BULLDOG BREED, THE(1960, Brit.); OSCAR WILDE(1960, Brit.); SCHOOL FOR SCOUNDRELS(1960, Brit.); PORTRAIT OF A SINNER(1961, Brit.); HIDE AND SEEK(1964, Brit.); EARLY BIRD, THE(1965, Brit.); JOEY BOY(1965, Brit.); STITCH IN TIME, A(1967, Brit.); MAN WHO HAUNTED HIMSELF, THE(1970, Brit.)
Edyth Chapman
NAVY BLUES(1930)
Silents
NORTH OF THE RIO GRANDE(1922)
Misc. Silents
TAKE THE HEIR(1930)
Edythe Chapman
IDLE RICH, THE(1929); TWIN BEDS(1929); DOUBLE CROSS ROADS(1930); MAN TROUBLE(1930); TAKE THE HEIR(1930); UP THE RIVER(1930)
Silents
GOLDEN CHANCE, THE(1915); ANTON THE TERRIBLE(1916); PLOW GIRL, THE(1916); HUCK AND TOM(1918); SAY! YOUNG FELLOW(1918); ALIAS MIKE MORAN(1919); KNICKERBOCKER BUCKAROO, THE(1919); HUCKLEBERRY FINN(1920); OUT OF THE STORM(1920); BUNTY PULLS THE STRINGS(1921); JUST OUT OF COLLEGE(1921); ONE WILD WEEK(1921); TALE OF TWO WORLDS, A(1921); WIFE'S AWAKENING, A(1921); BEYOND THE ROCKS(1922); SATURDAY NIGHT(1922); SLEEPWALKER, THE(1922); TAILOR MADE MAN, A(1922); YOUTH TO YOUTH(1922); DIVORCE(1923); MIRACLE MAKERS, THE(1923); MY AMERICAN WIFE(1923); TEN COMMANDMENTS, THE(1923); BREAKING POINT, THE(1924); IN THE NAME OF LOVE(1925); LAZYBONES(1925); LEARNING TO LOVE(1925); PRIDE OF THE FORCE, THE(1925); SOUL MATES(1925); ONE MINUTE TO PLAY(1926); RUNAWAY, THE(1926); AMERICAN BEAUTY(1927); CRYSTAL CUP, THE(1927); MAN CRAZY(1927)
Misc. Silents
HEIR TO THE HOORAH, THE(1916); PUBLIC OPINION(1916); COUNTESS CHARMING, THE(1917); MORMON MAID, A(1917); TOM SAWYER(1917); BOUND IN MOROCCO(1918); ONLY ROAD, THE(1918); SANDY(1918); SPIRIT OF '17, THE(1918); WHISPERING CHORUS, THE(1918); FAITH(1919); FLAME OF THE DESERT(1919); INNOCENT ADVENTURESS, AN(1919); SECRET SERVICE(1919); COUNTY FAIR, THE(1920); DOUBLE-DYED DECIEVER, A(1920); LADYFINGERS(1921); GIRL I LOVED, THE(1923); DAUGHTERS OF PLEASURE(1924); WISE VIRGIN, THE(1924); WORLDLY GOODS(1924); FAITHFUL WIVES(1926); COUNT OF TEN, THE(1928); HAPPINESS AHEAD(1928); LOVE HUNGRY(1928); SYNTHETIC SIN(1929)
Eileen Chapman
2,000 WEEKS(1970, Aus.); FIRM MAN, THE(1975, Aus.); BREAK OF DAY(1977, Aus.)
Emogene Chapman
STAKEOUT!(1962), art d
Eric Chapman
FINGER ON THE TRIGGER(1965, US/Span.); CHRISTMAS KID, THE(1968, U.S., Span.); NICHOLAS AND ALEXANDRA(1971, Brit.)
Eve Chapman
MUSIC HALL(1934, Brit.)
Frank Chapman
Misc. Silents
DEFEAT OF THE CITY, THE(1917)

Fred Chapman
NOBODY'S CHILDREN(1940); WOMAN IN THE WINDOW, THE(1945); WE WERE STRANGERS(1949)
Freddie Chapman
SHERIFF OF LAS VEGAS(1944); COLORADO PIONEERS(1945); CORPUS CHRISTI BANDITS(1945); GREAT STAGECOACH ROBBERY(1945); TRAIL OF KIT CARSON(1945)
George Chapman
Silents
CATCH AS CATCH CAN(1927)
Misc. Silents
SPEED LIMIT, THE(1926)
Georgie Chapman
Misc. Silents
CROSSED SIGNALS(1926)
Graham Chapman
DOCTOR IN TROUBLE(1970, Brit.); MAGIC CHRISTIAN, THE(1970, Brit.), a, w; RISE AND RISE OF MICHAEL RIMMER, THE(1970, Brit.), a, w; MAGNIFICENT SEVEN DEADLY SINS, THE(1971, Brit.), w; STATUE, THE(1971, Brit.); AND NOW FOR SOMETHING COMPLETELY DIFFERENT(1972, Brit.), a, w; RENTADICK(1972, Brit.), w; MONTY PYTHON AND THE HOLY GRAIL(1975, Brit.), a, w; ODD JOB, THE(1978, Brit.), a, p, w; MONTY PYTHON'S LIFE OF BRIAN(1979, Brit.), a, w; MONTY PYTHON'S THE MEANING OF LIFE(1983, Brit.), a, w; YELLOWBEARD(1983), a, w
Helen Chapman
O.S.S.(1946); SMOOTH AS SILK(1946); THRILL OF BRAZIL, THE(1946); BORROWED TROUBLE(1946); NIGHT HAS A THOUSAND EYES(1948); CHICAGO DEADLINE(1949); MY FAVORITE SPY(1951); CONFIDENCE GIRL(1952); FRENCH LINE, THE(1954); SON OF SINBAD(1955)
Misc. Talkies
OUTLAW ROUNDUP(1944)
Hugh Chapman
MY SON IS GUILTY(1940); WOMAN ON THE BEACH, THE(1947)
Irene Chapman
NEW KIND OF LOVE, A(1963)
Janet Chapman
BROADWAY MUSKETEERS(1938); HEART OF THE NORTH(1938); LITTLE MISS THOROUGHBRED(1938); ON TRIAL(1939); NOBODY'S CHILDREN(1940); PRIDE OF THE YANKEES, THE(1942); PRESENTING LILY MARS(1943)
Joan Chapman
FIRST BLOOD(1982), ed
John Chapman
DRY ROT(1956, Brit.), w; NOT WANTED ON VOYAGE(1957, Brit.); NOTHING BARRED(1961, Brit.), w; MAKE MINE A DOUBLE(1962, Brit.), a, w; NOT NOW DARLING(1975, Brit.), w; THERE GOES THE BRIDE(1980, Brit.), w
John T. Chapman
SATAN IN HIGH HEELS(1962), w
Judith Chapman
SCALPEL(1976)
Judy Chapman
FRANKIE AND JOHNNY(1966)
Lee Chapman
HOW COME NOBODY'S ON OUR SIDE?(1975), w
Leigh Chapman
LAW OF THE LAWLESS(1964); SWINGIN' SUMMER, A(1965), w; PROFESSIONALS, THE(1966); DIRTY MARY, CRAZY LARRY(1974), w; TRUCK TURNER(1974), w; BOARDWALK(1979), w; OCTAGON, THE(1980), w; STEEL(1980), w
Lonnie Chapman
NORMA RAE(1979)
Lonny Chapman
EAST OF EDEN(1955); YOUNG AT HEART(1955); BABY DOLL(1956); COVENANT WITH DEATH, A(1966); HOUR OF THE GUN(1967); REIVERS, THE(1969); STALKING MOON, THE(1969); TAKE THE MONEY AND RUN(1969); I WALK THE LINE(1970); COWBOYS, THE(1972); WELCOME HOME, SOLDIER BOYS(1972); WHERE THE RED FERN GROWS(1974); MOVING VIOLATION(1976); BAD NEWS BEARS GO TO JAPAN, THE(1978); WHEN TIME RAN OUT(1980); AMY(1981); BORDER, THE(1982)
Misc. Talkies
WITCH WHO CAME FROM THE SEA, THE(1976)
Marcia Chapman
GIRL FROM HAVANA, THE(1929)
Margaret Chapman
NO BLADE OF GRASS(1970, Brit.)
Margot Chapman
MADELEINE IS(1971, Can.)
Marguerite Chapman
CHARLIE CHAN AT THE WAX MUSEUM(1940); ON THEIR OWN(1940); BODY DISAPPEARS, THE(1941); GIRL, A GUY AND A GOB, A(1941); NAVY BLUES(1941); YOU'RE IN THE ARMY NOW(1941); DARING YOUNG MAN, THE(1942); MAN'S WORLD, A(1942); MEET THE STEWARTS(1942); PARACHUTE NURSE(1942); SPIRIT OF STANFORD, THE(1942); SUBMARINE RAIDER(1942); APPOINTMENT IN BERLIN(1943); DESTROYER(1943); MURDER IN TIMES SQUARE(1943); MY KINGDOM FOR A COOK(1943); ONE DANGEROUS NIGHT(1943); STRANGE AFFAIR(1944); COUNTER-ATTACK(1945); PARDON MY PAST(1945); MR. DISTRICT ATTORNEY(1946); ONE WAY TO LOVE(1946); WALLS CAME TUMBLING DOWN, THE(1946); CORONER CREEK(1948); GALLANT BLADE, THE(1948); RELENTLESS(1948); GREEN PROMISE, THE(1949); KANSAS RAIDERS(1950); FLIGHT TO MARS(1951); BLOODHOUNDS OF BROADWAY(1952); MAN BAIT(1952, Brit.); SEA TIGER(1952); SEVEN YEAR ITCH, THE(1955); AMAZING TRANSPARENT MAN, THE(1960)
Marian Chapman
LITTLE BALLERINA, THE(1951, Brit.)
Matthew Chapman
1984
STRANGERS KISS(1984), d, w
Misc. Talkies
HUSSY(1979), d

Michael Chapman
LAST DETAIL, THE(1973), a, ph; WHITE DAWN, THE(1974), ph; FRONT, THE(1976), ph; NEXT MAN, THE(1976), ph; TAXI DRIVER(1976), ph; INVASION OF THE BODY SNATCHERS(1978), ph; HARDCORE(1979), ph; WANDERERS, THE(1979), ph; RAGING BULL(1980), ph; DEAD MEN DON'T WEAR PLAID(1982), ph; PERSONAL BEST(1982), ph; ALL THE RIGHT MOVES(1983), d; MAN WITH TWO BRAINS, THE(1983), ph

Mike Chapman
FINGERS(1978), ph

Nolia Chapman
SATAN IN HIGH HEELS(1962)

Patricia Chapman
Misc. Talkies
MAN'S BEST FRIEND(1935)

Pattee Chapman
MR. BELVEDERE GOES TO COLLEGE(1949); TAKE CARE OF MY LITTLE GIRL(1951); PRIDE OF ST. LOUIS, THE(1952); WAC FROM WALLA WALLA, THE(1952); TEENAGE REBEL(1956); SUMMER AND SMOKE(1961); MODERN MARRIAGE, A(1962)

Paul S. Chapman
IPCRESS FILE, THE(1965, Brit.)

Priscilla Chapman
FAN, THE(1981), w

Reed Chapman
Misc. Silents
FOREST KING, THE(1922)

Richard Chapman
AMAZING DOBERMANS, THE(1976), w

Robert Chapman
WHEN WORLDS COLLIDE(1951); DELAVINE AFFAIR, THE(1954, Brit.), w; ONE JUMP AHEAD(1955, Brit.), w; BEHIND THE HEADLINES(1956, Brit.), w; MURDER REPORTED(1958, Brit.), w

Robin Chapman
TOO HOT TO HANDLE(1961, Brit.); THOSE MAGNIFICENT MEN IN THEIR FLYING MACHINES; OR HOW I FLEWFROM LONDON TO PARIS IN 25 HOURS AND 11 MINUTES(1965, Brit.); TRIPLE ECHO, THE(1973, Brit.), w; FORCE 10 FROM NAVARONE(1978, Brit.), w

Sean Chapman
PARTY PARTY(1983, Brit.)

Sue Chapman
LONELY HEARTS(1983, Aus.)

Ted Chapman
MAGIC GARDEN OF STANLEY SWEETHART, THE(1970), ed; BANANAS(1971); DON'T ANSWER THE PHONE(1980)

Tedwell Chapman
FABULOUS SUZANNE, THE(1946), w; RUNAWAY BUS, THE(1954, Brit.)

Tom Chapman
HANGAR 18(1980), w

Vern Chapman
LUCK OF GINGER COFFEY, THE(1964, U.S./Can.)

Virginia Chapman
MOB, THE(1951)

William Chapman
TORTURE SHIP(1939); THERE'S MAGIC IN MUSIC(1941)

Xavier Chapman
REVENGE OF THE CHEERLEADERS(1976), ch

Benjamin F. Chapman, Jr.
JUNGLE MOON MEN(1955)

Ted Chapman, Jr.
PRETTY BOY FLOYD(1960)

Jean Chapot
SKY ABOVE HEAVEN(1964, Fr./Ital.), w; CHARLES AND LUCIE(1982, Fr.), w, ed

Shantel R. Chappel
1984
TEACHERS(1984)

Tina Chappel
1984
HEARTBREAKERS(1984)

Bertram Chappell
SECOND BEST SECRET AGENT IN THE WHOLE WIDE WORLD, THE(1965, Brit.), m

Connery Chappell
BELOVED IMPOSTER(1936, Brit.), w; DANGEROUS MEDICINE(1938, Brit.), w; NURSEMAID WHO DISAPPEARED, THE(1939, Brit.), w; TOO DANGEROUS TO LIVE(1939, Brit.), w

Dorothy Chappell
Misc. Silents
HANDCUFFS OR KISSES(1921)

Edward Chappell
MADRON(1970, U.S./Israel), w

Eric Chappell
RISING DAMP(1980, Brit.), w

Janet Chappell
VIRGIN AND THE GYPSY, THE(1970, Brit.)

John Chappell
STRONGROOM(1962, Brit.); MYSTERY SUBMARINE(1963, Brit.); NICKELODEON(1976); OTHER SIDE OF MIDNIGHT, THE(1977); FAST BREAK(1979); 10(1979); BRUBAKER(1980); HARD COUNTRY(1981)

Norman Chappell
CARRY ON CABBIE(1963, Brit.); 80,000 SUSPECTS(1963, Brit.); JIG SAW(1965, Brit.); HOW I WON THE WAR(1967, Brit.); CARRY ON HENRY VIII(1970, Brit.)

William Chappell
WINSLOW BOY, THE(1950), cos; FLESH AND BLOOD(1951, Brit.); PRINCE AND THE SHOWGIRL, THE(1957, Brit.), ch; TRIAL, THE(1963, Fr./Ital./Ger.)

Yvonne Chappelle
Silents
AS A WOMAN SOWS(1916)

Walter Chappen
Misc. Silents
NAN O' THE BACKWOODS(1915)

Jean-Francois Chappey
SIX IN PARIS(1968, Fr.)

Dawn Chapple
LADY GODIVA RIDES AGAIN(1955, Brit.)

Alain-Patrick Chappuis
Misc. Talkies
BLUE MONEY(1975), a, d

Anne Chappuis
BENVENUTA(1983, Fr.)

Dominique Chapuis
COUNTRYMAN(1982, Jamaica), ph

Emeric Chapuis
1984
HERE COMES SANTA CLAUS(1984)

Pierre-Alain Chapuis
1984
FIRST NAME: CARMEN(1984, Fr.)

Carol Chaput
LOVE CHILD(1982)

Winston Char
HAWAIIANS, THE(1970)

Ross Charap
ME, NATALIE(1969)

Henri Charbakshi
LAST AFFAIR, THE(1976), p,d&w, ed

Philip Charbert
THIS WOMAN IS MINE(1941)

Jeanne Charblay
LOVE IN THE AFTERNOON(1957)

Odette Charblay
LOVE IN THE AFTERNOON(1957)

Joseph Charboneau
1984
NATURAL, THE(1984)

Charbonnier
CRIME OF MONSIEUR LANGE, THE(1936, Fr.)

Pierre Charbonnier
MAN ESCAPED, A(1957, Fr.), art d; NAKED AUTUMN(1963, Fr.), art d; PICKPOCKET(1963, Fr.), art d; TRIAL OF JOAN OF ARC(1965, Fr.), art d; AU HASARD, BALTHAZAR(1970, Fr.), art d; GENTLE CREATURE, A(1971, Fr.), art d; LANCELOT OF THE LAKE(1975, Fr.), prod d

Marcel Charbrie
Misc. Silents
REWARD OF FAITH(1929)

Jerry Charburn
WORLD IS JUST A 'B' MOVIE, THE(1971)

Jacques Charby
RISE OF LOUIS XIV, THE(1970, Fr.)

Marjorie Chard
INSIDE THE ROOM(1935, Brit.); CHEER UP!(1936, Brit.); MINSTREL BOY, THE(1937, Brit.)
Silents
VEILED WOMAN, THE(1917, Brit.)

Denise Chardein
GINA(1961, Fr./Mex.), ed

Jon Chardiet
1984
BEAT STREET(1984)

Lyne Chardonnet
MAYERLING(1968, Brit./Fr.); CHANEL SOLITAIRE(1981)

Pyotr Chardynin
Misc. Silents
CHRYSANTHEMUMS(1914, USSR), d; WOMAN OF TOMORROW(1914, USSR), d; FLOOD(1915, USSR), d; LOVE OF A STATE COUNCILLOR(1915, USSR), d; STORY OF SEVEN WHO WERE HANGED(1920, USSR), d

Pytor Chardynin
Misc. Silents
VOLGA AND SIBERIA(1914, USSR); NATASHA ROSTOVA(1915, USSR), d

M. Chardynini
YOLANTA(1964, USSR), ed

Gina Chare
FIRE DOWN BELOW(1957, U.S./Brit.)

Eric Charell
CONGRESS DANCES(1932, Ger.), d

Erick Charell
ZIEGFELD FOLLIES(1945), w

Erik Charell
CARAVAN(1934), p&d; WHAT A WOMAN!(1943), w; CASBAH(1948), w; WHITE HORSE INN, THE(1959, Ger.), p, w

Stefano Charelli
TOWN CALLED HELL, A(1971, Span./Brit.)

O.B. Charence
EYES OF FATE(1933, Brit.)

Francois Charet
FRIEND OF THE FAMILY(1965, Fr./Ital.)

Alexander Chargonin
Misc. Silents
IN THE WHIRLWIND OF REVOLUTION(1922, USSR), d

Zharira Charifai
JUDITH(1965)

Andre Chariot
MISSISSIPPI GAMBLER, THE(1953)

The Charioteers
ROAD SHOW(1941)

Andre Charise
UNDER MY SKIN(1950); CIRCLE OF DECEPTON(1961, Brit.); RETURN FROM THE ASHES(1965, U.S./Brit.); THERE'S A GIRL IN MY SOUP(1970, Brit.); UNDERGROUND(1970, Brit.)

Andre Charisse
MADAME BOVARY(1949); LIGHT TOUCH, THE(1951); ROYAL WEDDING(1951); IDOL ON PARADE(1959, Brit.); RISK, THE(1961, Brit.); S(1974)

Cyd Charisse
SILENCERS, THE(; TWO WEEKS IN ANOTHER TOWN(1962); MISSION TO MOSCOW(1943); SOMETHING TO SHOUT ABOUT(1943); ZIEGFELD FOLLIES(1945); HARVEY GIRLS, THE(1946); THREE WISE FOOLS(1946); TILL THE CLOUDS ROLL BY(1946); FIESTA(1947); UNFINISHED DANCE,THE(1947); KISSING BANDIT, THE(1948); ON AN ISLAND WITH YOU(1948); EAST SIDE, WEST SIDE(1949); TENSION(1949); MARK OF THE RENEGADE(1951); SINGIN' IN THE RAIN(1952); WILD NORTH, THE(1952); BAND WAGON, THE(1953); SOMBRERO(1953); BRIGADOON(1954); DEEP IN MY HEART(1954); IT'S ALWAYS FAIR WEATHER(1955); MEET ME IN LAS VEGAS(1956); SILK STOCKINGS(1957); PARTY GIRL(1958); TWILIGHT FOR THE GODS(1958); FIVE GOLDEN HOURS(1961, Brit.); BLACK TIGHTS(1962, Fr.); MAROC 7(1967, Brit.); WON TON TON, THE DOG WHO SAVED HOLLYWOOD(1976); WARLORDS OF ATLANTIS(1978, Brit.)

Nico Charisse
SULTAN'S DAUGHTER, THE(1943), ch

Charita
SONS OF THE DESERT(1933)

C.C. Charity
GREAT SCOUT AND CATHOUSE THURSDAY, THE(1976)

David Charkham
2001: A SPACE ODYSSEY(1968, U.S./Brit.)

Bernard Charlan
VERY HAPPY ALEXANDER(1969, Fr.)

Charlatan Prods
BIG CUBE, THE(1969), spec eff

Gerald Charlebois
SHOOT-OUT AT MEDICINE BEND(1957)

Robert Charlebois
MAN ON A TIGHTROPE(1953); GENIUS, THE(1976, Ital./Fr./Ger.)

Jaime Charlemagne
PIE IN THE SKY(1964)

Annette Charles
GREASE(1978); IN SEARCH OF HISTORIC JESUS(1980)

Arlene Charles
DR. GOLDFOOT AND THE BIKINI MACHINE(1965); WINTER A GO-GO(1965); CLAMBAKE(1967); I SAILED TO TAHITI WITH AN ALL GIRL CREW(1969)

Bob Charles
PLEASURE PLANTATION(1970)

Bryan Charles
DEMENTED(1980)

Captain Charles
Silents
CABARET, THE(1918); OLDEST LAW, THE(1918)

Charles Charles
Misc. Silents
SHALL WE FORGIVE HER?(1917)

Charles W. Charles
Misc. Silents
PAWN OF FATE, THE(1916)

Charlie Charles
HEAVEN CAN WAIT(1978)

Colin Charles
1984
GREYSTOKE: THE LEGEND OF TARZAN, LORD OF THE APES(1984)

David Charles
MEATBALLS(1979, Can.), art d

Ernest Charles
POINT OF TERROR(1971)

Ernest A. Charles
POINT OF TERROR(1971), w

Frances Charles
BEYOND THE FOREST(1949); PERFECT STRANGERS(1950); WOMAN FROM HEADQUARTERS(1950); YUKON GOLD(1952)

Francis Charles
DOWN AMONG THE Z MEN(1952, Brit.), w

Francisco Charles
1984
SUGAR CANE ALLEY(1984, Fr.)

Frank Charles
DANGER TOMORROW(1960, Brit.), w

Fred Charles
WILD ONES ON WHEELS(1967), p

Glenn Charles
COVER GIRL(1944)

Gloria Charles
FRIDAY THE 13TH PART III(1982)

Grahame Charles
TO SIR, WITH LOVE(1967, Brit.)

Henry Charles
GOING APE!(1981)

Hugh Charles
I WOULDN'T BE IN YOUR SHOES(1948); JOE PALOOKA IN WINNER TAKE ALL(1948); WINTER MEETING(1948); YOUNG MAN WITH A HORN(1950)

Irene Charles
1,000 SHAPES OF A FEMALE(1963)

Iris Charles
IT'S A GRAND OLD WORLD(1937, Brit.)

Irwin Charles
YOUR NUMBER'S UP(1931)

Jacqueline Charles
LIFE IN HER HANDS(1951, Brit.)

Joan Charles
UNASHAMED(1938)

John Charles
SPOOK WHO SAT BY THE DOOR, THE(1973); GOODBYE PORK PIE(1981, New Zealand), m
1984
UTU(1984, New Zealand), m

Silents
BURIED TREASURE(1921)

Misc. Silents
TOLL OF LOVE, THE(1914); HOUSE OF A THOUSAND CANDLES, THE(1915); MILLIONAIRE BABY, THE(1915); TEXAS STEER, A(1915); JEALOUSY(1916); VICTIM, THE(1916); VEILED MARRIAGE, THE(1920); LAW OF COMPENSATION(1927)

Lady Mount Charles
CAPTAIN LIGHTFOOT(1955)

Leon Charles
DILLINGER(1945), w; FLAME OF ARABY(1951); FOXFIRE(1955); MIDNIGHT LACE(1960); CAPER OF THE GOLDEN BULLS, THE(1967); NIGHT OF THE WITCHES(1970); SCOTT JOPLIN(1977)
1984
HOUSE WHERE DEATH LIVES, THE(1984)

Leslie Charles
SINBAD THE SAILOR(1947); ROAD TO BALI(1952)

Lewis Charles
THEY LIVE BY NIGHT(1949); PANIC IN THE STREETS(1950); FINGER MAN(1955); ROSE TATTOO, THE(1955); TO CATCH A THIEF(1955); BIGGER THAN LIFE(1956); MONKEY ON MY BACK(1957); SWEET SMELL OF SUCCESS(1957); UNDERSEA GIRL(1957); PARTY GIRL(1958); AL CAPONE(1959); 48 HOURS TO LIVE(1960, Brit./Swed.); THREE STOOGES MEET HERCULES, THE(1962); WHO'S GOT THE ACTION?(1962); ISLAND OF LOVE(1963); SOLDIER IN THE RAIN(1963); HOUSE IS NOT A HOME, A(1964); TOPAZ(1969, Brit.); HUMAN FACTOR, THE(1975)

Lord Mount Charles
CAPTAIN LIGHTFOOT(1955)

Lucille Charles
LOVES OF CARMEN, THE(1948)

Marco Charles
Misc. Silents
CUPID'S KNOCKOUT(1926)

Maria Charles
GUNMAN HAS ESCAPED, A(1948, Brit.); DEADLY AFFAIR, THE(1967, Brit.); GREAT EXPECTATIONS(1975, Brit.); VICTOR/VICTORIA(1982)

Marion Charles
SOYLENT GREEN(1973)

Martha Charles
INDEPENDENCE DAY(1976)

Martin Charles
TWISTED NERVE(1969, Brit.), ed; SOPHIE'S PLACE(1970), ed; THERE'S A GIRL IN MY SOUP(1970, Brit.), ed; LOOT(1971, Brit.), ed; UNDERCOVERS HERO(1975, Brit.), ed

Mary Charles
COUNSEL'S OPINION(1933, Brit.); MONEY TALKS(1933, Brit.)

Moie Charles
GENTLE SEX, THE(1943, Brit.), w; MASTER OF BANKDAM, THE(1947, Brit.), w; WHEN THE BOUGH BREAKS(1947, Brit.), w; DARK SECRET(1949, Brit.), w; HELL IS SOLD OUT(1951, Brit.), w; SCARLET THREAD(1951, Brit.), w; CROWDED DAY, THE(1954, Brit.), w

Mona Charles
1984
WEEKEND PASS(1984)

Noel Charles
GENIE, THE(1953, Brit.), w

R.K. Charles
GIRL ON A CHAIN GANG(1966)

Ray Charles
SWINGIN' ALONG(1962); BLUES FOR LOVERS(1966, Brit.); BLUES BROTHERS, THE(1980); OCTOPUSSY(1983, Brit.)

Rene Charles
ROYAL AFFAIRS IN VERSAILLES(1957, Fr.)

Richard Charles
HAPPY BIRTHDAY, DAVY(1970), ed

Robert Charles
RETURN OF THE APE MAN(1944), w; VOODOO MAN(1944), w

Rosaline Charles
LOVE PARADE, THE(1929)

Rudolph Charles
TARZAN'S DEADLY SILENCE(1970)

Sonny Charles
Misc. Talkies
BLACK CONNECTION, THE(1974)

Spencer Charles
GAMBLING SHIP(1933)

Theresa Charles
HER PANELLED DOOR(1951, Brit.), w

Tom T. Charles
GO NAKED IN THE WORLD(1961), w

Tommy Charles
SHAKE, RATTLE, AND ROCK!(1957)

Tony Charles
RECKONING, THE(1971, Brit.)

Vernon Charles
FALL OF THE HOUSE OF USHER, THE(1952, Brit.)

Victor Charles
PASSION HOLIDAY(1963)

Woody Charles
SUMMER STORM(1944)

Zachary Charles
MA AND PA KETTLE AT THE FAIR(1952)

Zachary A. Charles
FLYING MISSILE(1950); GAMBLING HOUSE(1950)
The Charles Austin Group
SCREAM, BABY, SCREAM(1969), m
Charles B. Cochran's Young Ladies
IT'S IN THE BAG(1936, Brit.)
Charles Barnet and His Orchestra
JUKE BOX JENNY(1942)
Charles McDevitt's Skiffle Group
ROCK AROUND THE WORLD(1957, Brit.)
Charles Weidman Dancers
FOLLIES GIRL(1943)
B. Charles-Deane
VOICE WITHIN, THE(1945, Brit.), w
Liz Charles-Williams
DEADLIER THAN THE MALE(1967, Brit.), w; SOME GIRLS DO(1969, Brit.), w; OPEN SEASON(1974, U.S./Span.), w

Ian Charleson
JUBILEE(1978, Brit.); CHARRIOTS OF FIRE(1981, Brit.); GANDHI(1982); ASCEND-ANCY(1983, Brit.)
1984
GREYSTOKE: THE LEGEND OF TARZAN, LORD OF THE APES(1984); LOUI-SIANE(1984, Fr./Can.)
Kate Charleson
1984
DREAMSCAPE(1984)
Leslie Charleson
LOVELY WAY TO DIE, A(1968); DAY OF THE DOLPHIN, THE(1973)
Mary Charleson
Silents
MR. BARNES OF NEW YORK(1914); SYLVIA GRAY(1914); SEALED LIPS(1915); HUMAN STUFF(1920)
Misc. Silents
WHAT HAPPENED TO JONES(1915); COUNTRY THAT GOD FORGOT, THE(1916); PASSERS-BY(1916); PRINCE CHAP, THE(1916); LITTLE SHOES(1917); SAINT'S ADVENTURE, THE(1917); SATAN'S PRIVATE DOOR(1917); TRUANT SOUL, THE(1917); HUMDRUM BROWN(1918); LONG LANE'S TURNING, THE(1919); UP-STAIRS AND DOWN(1919)
Ray Charleson
HOPSCOTCH(1980); SHOCK TREATMENT(1981)
Anne Charleston
2,000 WEEKS(1970, Aus.)
Kate Charleston
TERMS OF ENDEARMENT(1983)
Mary Charleston
Silents
WITHOUT HOPE(1914); HIS ROBE OF HONOR(1918)
Milton Charleston
SHE WROTE THE BOOK(1946)
Ray Charleston
HAWK THE SLAYER(1980, Brit.)
David Charlesworth
DOUBLE, THE(1963, Brit); DEVIL DOLL(1964, Brit.)
John Charlesworth
CHRISTMAS CAROL, A(1951, Brit.); TOM BROWN'S SCHOOLDAYS(1951, Brit.); MAGIC BOX, THE(1952, Brit.); HORSE'S MOUTH, THE(1953, Brit.); BATTLE HELL(1956, Brit.); ADVENTURES OF HAL 5, THE(1958, Brit.); MAN UPSTAIRS, THE(1959, Brit.); NAVY HEROES(1959, Brit.); NO SAFETY AHEAD(1959, Brit.); QUESTION OF ADULTERY, A(1959, Brit.); DATE AT MIDNIGHT(1960, Brit.); DEAD LUCKY(1960, Brit.); SO EVIL SO YOUNG(1961, Brit.); JOHN OF THE FAIR(1962, Brit.)
Peter Charlesworth
MAN AT THE TOP(1973, Brit.), p
Tom Charlesworth
PROBLEM GIRLS(1953)
Sylvaine Charlet
CHLOE IN THE AFTERNOON(1972, Fr.)
Sylviane Charlet
ONCE IN PARIS(1978)
George Charleton
LADY GAMBLES, THE(1949)
G. Charlia
Misc. Silents
SOUL OF FRANCE(1929, Fr.)
Geores Charlia
Misc. Silents
EN RADE(1927, Fr.)
Charlie
NAKED KISS, THE(1964); PLEASE STAND BY(1972)
Charlie Barnet and his Orchestra
IDEA GIRL(1946)
Charlie Barnet and Orchestra
SONG IS BORN, A(1948)
Charlie Barnet Orchestra
JAM SESSION(1944); MUSIC IN MANHATTAN(1944)
Charlie Cairoli & Paul
SECRET PEOPLE(1952, Brit.)
The Charlie Daniels Band
URBAN COWBOY(1980)
Charlie Naughton & Jimmy Gold
FROZEN LIMITS, THE(1939, Brit.)
Charlie Spivak and His Orchestra
FOLLOW THE BOYS(1944)
Charlie Spivak and Orchestra
PIN UP GIRL(1944)

Charlie the Cougar
CHARLIE, THE LONESOME COUGAR(1967)
June Charlier
NAUGHTY ARLETTE(1951, Brit.); PROFILE(1954, Brit.); LADY GODIVA RIDES AGAIN(1955, Brit.)
Margot Charlier
THIEF(1981)
Geo Charliot
Misc. Silents
LA BELLE NIVERNAISE(1923, Fr.)
Charlita
BRIMSTONE(1949); BRAVE BULLS, THE(1951); COME FILL THE CUP(1951); LET'S GO NAVY(1951); SOUTH OF CALIENTE(1951); TEN TALL MEN(1951); BELA LUGOSI MEETS A BROOKLYN GORILLA(1952); RANCHO NOTORIOUS(1952); TOUGHEST MAN IN ARIZONA(1952); RIDE, VAQUERO!(1953); MASSACRE CANYON(1954); GREEN FIRE(1955); NAKED DAWN, THE(1955); WOMEN OF PITCAIRN ISLAND, THE(1957); BILLY THE KID VS. DRACULA(1966); EL DORADO(1967)
The Charlivels
TWO TICKETS TO BROADWAY(1951)
Andre Charlot
ARABIAN NIGHTS(1942); FALCON'S BROTHER, THE(1942); ABOVE SUSPI-CION(1943); CONSTANT NYMPH, THE(1943); FALCON STRIKES BACK, THE(1943); FALLEN SPARROW, THE(1943); HEAVENLY BODY, THE(1943); MAN FROM DOWN UNDER, THE(1943); MELODY PARADE(1943); SONG OF BERNADETTE, THE(1943); THEY CAME TO BLOW UP AMERICA(1943); THUMBS UP(1943); ACTION IN ARABIA(1944); SUMMER STORM(1944); DELIGHTFULLY DANGEROUS(1945); DOLLY SISTERS, THE(1945); LADY ON A TRAIN(1945); PARIS UNDER-GROUND(1945); THIS LOVE OF OURS(1945); YOLANDA AND THE THIEF(1945); DEADLINE FOR MURDER(1946); O.S.S.(1946); RAZOR'S EDGE, THE(1946); TEMPTA-TION(1946); FOXES OF HARROW, THE(1947); SONG OF LOVE(1947); JULIA MIS-BEHAVES(1948); SAIGON(1948); GREAT SINNER, THE(1949); I WAS A MALE WAR BRIDE(1949); THAT FORSYTE WOMAN(1949); ANNIE GET YOUR GUN(1950); FLAME OF ARABY(1951); LAW AND THE LADY, THE(1951); INTERRUPTED MELODY(1955)
Berenoff and Charlot
FACE AT THE WINDOW, THE(1932, Brit.)
Georges Charlot
SEASON FOR LOVE, THE(1963, Fr.), prod d; NIGHT WATCH, THE(1964, Fr./Ital.), p
Jean Charlot
MEMENTO MEI(1963)
Martin Charlot
MEMENTO MEI(1963), p,d,ph&ed
Misc. Talkies
APOCALYPSE 3:16(1964), d
Philip Charlot
MAN WHO COULD WORK MIRACLES, THE(1937, Brit.), ed; MOONLIGHT SONA-TA(1938, Brit.), ed; RETURN OF THE SCARLET PIMPERNEL(1938, Brit.), ed; CONTI-NENTAL EXPRESS(1939, Brit.), ed; LADY IN DISTRESS(1942, Brit.), ed
Charlotte
QUICK, LET'S GET MARRIED(1965)
Misc. Silents
CHARLOTTE(1917); FROZEN WARNING, THE(1918)
Charlotte the Elephant
SMOKEY AND THE BANDIT II(1980)
Mary Charlson
Misc. Silents
BURNING THE CANDLE(1917)
Bill Charlton
NED KELLY(1970, Brit.); MONKEY GRIP(1983, Aus.)
Bob Charlton
DETROIT 9000(1973)
Bobby Charlton
HARDER THEY COME, THE(1973, Jamaica)
Elizabeth Charlton
SPACE RAIDERS(1983)
Fluff Charlton
FRESH FROM PARIS(1955); PARIS FOLLIES OF 1956(1955)
Howard Charlton
WHAT THE BUTLER SAW(1950, Brit.)
John Charlton
SCHOOL FOR SCANDAL, THE(1930, Brit.)
Maureen Charlton
RETURN OF THE JEDI(1983)
Michael Charlton
WATERFRONT WOMEN(1952, Brit.), ed
Warwick Charlton
EYES THAT KILL(1947, Brit.), d&w
A. J. Charlwood
Silents
IVANHOE(1913)
Charly Baumann's Tiger Group
HIPPODROME(1961, Aust./Ger.)
Harry Charman
NIGHT INVADER, THE(1943, Brit)
The Charmers
SOUTH OF DIXIE(1944)
Tony Charmoli
WHAT'S THE MATTER WITH HELEN?(1971), ch
Jacques Charmont
KILL! KILL! KILL!(1972, Fr./Ger./Ital./Span.), m
Charmy
Silents
NAPOLEON(1927, Fr.), cos
Jean-Claude Charnay
RISE OF LOUIS XIV, THE(1970, Fr.)
Claude Charney
EROTIQUE(1969, Fr.)

Eva Charney
FIRST TIME, THE(1983)
Jack Charney
PLUNDER ROAD(1957), w
Jean Charney
DOWN AMONG THE SHELTERING PALMS(1953); WEREWOLF, THE(1956); THREE STOOGES IN ORBIT, THE(1962)
Jordan Charney
HOSPITAL, THE(1971); NETWORK(1976); THOSE LIPS, THOSE EYES(1980); FIRST MONDAY IN OCTOBER(1981); SEPARATE WAYS(1981); FRANCES(1982)
1984
GHOSTBUSTERS(1984)
Kim Charney
SUDDENLY(1954); AT GUNPOINT(1955); BOBBY WARE IS MISSING(1955); BOTTOM OF THE BOTTLE, THE(1956); WEREWOLF, THE(1956); GUNS OF FORT PETTICOAT, THE(1957); CRASH LANDING(1958); GIRL IN THE WOODS(1958); MAN FROM GOD'S COUNTRY(1958); QUANTRILL'S RAIDERS(1958); HEY BOY! HEY GIRL!(1959); HOW THE WEST WAS WON(1962)
Libby Charney
SINGING BLACKSMITH(1938)
Susan Charney
TOMB OF THE UNDEAD(1972)
Martin Charnin
ANNIE(1982), w
Michael Charnley
SET, THE(1970, Aus.)
Stu Charno
FRIDAY THE 13TH PART II(1981)
1984
HARD TO HOLD(1984)
Stuart Charno
CHRISTINE(1983)
Anthony Charnota
SAM'S SONG(1971); DON IS DEAD, THE(1973); TRICK BABY(1973); SHOOT IT: BLACK, SHOOT IT: BLUE(1974); SURVIVAL RUN(1980); LOOKER(1981); LUNCH WAGON(1981)
1984
CITY HEAT(1984)
Anthony R. Charnota
SOME KIND OF HERO(1982)
Carole Charnow
1984
SUPERGIRL(1984)
Suzanne Charny
SWEET CHARITY(1969); STEAGLE, THE(1971)
Charo
TIGER BY THE TAIL(1970); CONCORDE, THE–AIRPORT '79(1979)
Frank Charolla
HARD RIDE, THE(1971); WILD RIDERS(1971), a, stunts
Andre Charon
SO BIG(1932)
Jacques Charon
COLONEL CHABERT(1947, Fr.); WOULD-BE GENTLEMAN, THE(1960, Fr.); CARTOUCHE(1962, Fr./Ital.); IN THE FRENCH STYLE(1963, U.S./Fr.); DOUBLE BED, THE(1965, Fr./Ital.); FLEA IN HER EAR, A(1968, Fr.), d
Irwin Charone
CACTUS FLOWER(1969)
Jacquimine Charott-Lodwidge
EMILY(1976, Brit.), art d
V. Charova
Misc. Silents
CURSED MILLIONS(1917, USSR)
Gustave Charpentier
LOUISE(1940, Fr.), w
Jean Charpentier
TRIAL, THE(1963, Fr./Ital./Ger.), set d
Petra Charpentier
GREAT GAY ROAD, THE(1931, Brit.)
Suzanne Charpentier [Annabella]
Silents
NAPOLEON(1927, Fr.)
Charpin
THEY WERE FIVE(1938, Fr.); BAKER'S WIFE, THE(1940, Fr.); THEY MET ON SKIS(1940, Fr.); WELL-DIGGER'S DAUGHTER, THE(1946, Fr.); WHIRLWIND OF PARIS(1946, Fr.); BLUE VEIL, THE(1947, Fr.)
Fernand Charpin
MARIUS(1933, Fr.); CESAR(1936, Fr.); PEPE LE MOKO(1937, Fr.)
Fernand Charpin
FANNY(1948, Fr.)
Pierre Charras
CHARLES AND LUCIE(1982, Fr.)
Janine Charrat
SCHEHERAZADE(1965, Fr./Ital./Span.), ch
Gertrude Charre
TRAVELING SALESWOMAN(1950)
Michel Charrel
DEAD RUN(1961, Fr./Ital./Ger.); BELLE DE JOUR(1968, Fr.); LA FEMME INFIDELE(1969, Fr./Ital.); THIS MAN MUST DIE(1970, Fr./Ital.); MURMUR OF THE HEART(1971, Fr./Ital./Ger.)
Henri Charret
DEVIL'S DAUGHTER(1949, Fr.)
Henri Charrett
CONFESSIONS OF A ROGUE(1948, Fr.)
Henry Charrett
ROYAL AFFAIR, A(1950)
Georges Charrier
THIS MAN MUST DIE(1970, Fr./Ital.)

Jacques Charrier
ANATOMY OF A MARRIAGE(MY DAYS WITH JEAN-MARC AND MY NIGHTS WITH FRANCOISE)**1/2 (1964 Fr.); BABETTE GOES TO WAR(1960, Fr.); CHEATERS, THE(1961, Fr.); LA BELLE AMERICAINE(1961, Fr.); THIRD LOVER, THE(1963, Fr./Ital.); OLDEST PROFESSION, THE(1968, Fr./Ital./Ger.); LES CREATURES(1969, Fr./Swed.); WINTER WIND(1970, Fr./Hung.), a, p; EGLANTINE(1972, Fr.), p
Christian Charriere
JOY(1983, Fr./Can.), w
Henri Charriere
POPSY POP(1971, Fr.), a, w
Jean-Jacques Charriere
ONCE IN PARIS(1978)
Arthur Charrington
Misc. Silents
GRIP OF IRON, THE(1913, Brit.), d
Victor Charrington
CANDIDATE FOR MURDER(1966, Brit.)
Jacques Charron
RED, INN, THE(1954, Fr.)
Pierre Charron
DOULOS–THE FINGER MAN(1964, Fr./Ital.), set d; GREED IN THE SUN(1965, Fr./Ital.), set d; WEEKEND AT DUNKIRK(1966, Fr./Ital.), set d; FLEA IN HER EAR, A(1968, Fr.), set d; HELLO–GOODBYE(1970), set d; DAY OF THE JACKAL, THE(1973, Brit./Fr.), set d; JULIA(1977), set d
Ruth Charron
COUNTRY BOY(1966)
Sonie Charsaky
RAINS CAME, THE(1939)
Boris Charsky
Silents
CAPTAIN LASH(1929)
Misc. Silents
RED DANCE, THE(1928)
Ron Charter
OUT OF THE BLUE(1982)
Leslie Charteris
MIDNIGHT CLUB(1933), w; SAINT IN NEW YORK, THE(1938), w; SAINT IN LONDON, THE(1939, Brit.), w; SAINT STRIKES BACK, THE(1939), w; SAINT TAKES OVER, THE(1940), w; SAINT'S DOUBLE TROUBLE, THE(1940), w; SAINT IN PALM SPRINGS, THE(1941), w; SAINT'S VACATION, THE(1941, Brit.), w; SAINT MEETS THE TIGER, THE(1943, Brit.), w; LADY ON A TRAIN(1945), w; RIVER GANG(1945), w; TWO SMART PEOPLE(1946), w; SAINT'S GIRL FRIDAY, THE(1954, Brit.), w
Christopher Charters
1984
ULTIMATE SOLUTION OF GRACE QUIGLEY, THE(1984)
Michael Charters
1984
ULTIMATE SOLUTION OF GRACE QUIGLEY, THE(1984)
Spencer Charters
BAT WHISPERS, THE(1930); WHOOPEE(1930); EX-BAD BOY(1931); FRONT PAGE, THE(1931); LONELY WIVES(1931); PALMY DAYS(1931); TRAVELING HUSBANDS(1931); CENTRAL PARK(1932); CROOKED CIRCLE(1932); FAMOUS FERGUSON CASE, THE(1932); HOLD'EM JAIL(1932); JEWEL ROBBERY(1932); MATCH KING, THE(1932); MOVIE CRAZY(1932); TENDERFOOT, THE(1932); THREE ON A MATCH(1932); BROADWAY BAD(1933); FEMALE(1933); KENNEL MURDER CASE, THE(1933); LADY KILLER(1933); SO THIS IS AFRICA(1933); 20,000 YEARS IN SING SING(1933); BLIND DATE(1934); CIRCUS CLOWN(1934); FASHIONS OF 1934(1934); FIREBIRD, THE(1934); HALF A SINNER(1934); HIPS, HIPS, HOORAY(1934); IT'S A GIFT(1934); LOUDSPEAKER, THE(1934); MILLION DOLLAR RANSOM(1934); PURSUIT OF HAPPINESS, THE(1934); ST. LOUIS KID, THE(1934); SUCCESS AT ANY PRICE(1934); WAKE UP AND DREAM(1934); WONDER BAR(1934); ALIBI IKE(1935); DON'T BET ON BLONDES(1935); GHOST WALKS, THE(1935); GOOSE AND THE GANDER, THE(1935); IN PERSON(1935); MURDER ON A HONEYMOON(1935); NUT FARM, THE(1935); RAVEN, THE(1935); SECRET BRIDE, THE(1935); STAR OF MIDNIGHT(1935); STRANDED(1935); WELCOME HOME(1935); WHISPERING SMITH SPEAKS(1935); $1,000 A MINUTE(1935); ALL-AMERICAN CHUMP(1936); BANJO ON MY KNEE(1936); CAREER WOMAN(1936); COLLEEN(1936); DON'T GET PERSONAL(1936); EX-MRS. BRADFORD, THE(1936); F MAN(1936); FARMER IN THE DELL, THE(1936); FOUR DAYS WONDER(1936); HARVESTER, THE(1936); LADY FROM NOWHERE(1936); LIBELED LADY(1936); LOVE ON A BET(1936); MINE WITH THE IRON DOOR, THE(1936); MOON'S OUR HOME, THE(1936); MR. DEEDS GOES TO TOWN(1936); MURDER ON A BRIDLE PATH(1936); POSTAL INSPECTOR(1936); SPENDTHRIFT(1936); TILL WE MEET AGAIN(1936); BACK IN CIRCULATION(1937); BEHIND THE MIKE(1937); BIG TOWN GIRL(1937); CHECKERS(1937); DANGER-LOVE AT WORK(1937); DANGEROUS NUMBER(1937); EMPEROR'S CANDLESTICKS, THE(1937); EVER SINCE EVE(1937); FIFTY ROADS TO TOWN(1937); FUGITIVE IN THE SKY(1937); GIRL LOVES BOY(1937); HURRICANE, THE(1937); LADY BEHAVE(1937); MARRIED BEFORE BREAKFAST(1937); MIGHTY TREVE, THE(1937); MOUNTAIN MUSIC(1937); PERFECT SPECIMEN, THE(1937); PICK A STAR(1937); PRISONER OF ZENDA, THE(1937); VENUS MAKES TROUBLE(1937); WAIKIKI WEDDING(1937); WELLS FARGO(1937); WIFE, DOCTOR AND NURSE(1937); BREAKING THE ICE(1938); CRIME SCHOOL(1938); FIVE OF A KIND(1938); FORBIDDEN VALLEY(1938); FOUR'S A CROWD(1938); IN OLD CHICAGO(1938); JOY OF LIVING(1938); MR. BOGGS STEPS OUT(1938); MR. CHUMP(1938); ONE WILD NIGHT(1938); PROFESSOR BEWARE(1938); ROAD TO RENO, THE(1938); STABLEMATES(1938); STRANGE FACES(1938); TEXANS, THE(1938); THREE BLIND MICE(1938); THREE COMRADES(1938); VIVACIOUS LADY(1938); BOY TROUBLE(1939); COVERED TRAILER, THE(1939); DODGE CITY(1939); DRUMS ALONG THE MOHAWK(1939); EXILE EXPRESS(1939); FLYING IRISHMAN, THE(1939); HOTEL IMPERIAL(1939); HUNCHBACK OF NOTRE DAME, THE(1939); I'M FROM MISSOURI(1939); IN NAME ONLY(1939); INSIDE STORY(1939); JESSE JAMES(1939); OKLAHOMA KID(1939); SECOND FIDDLE(1939); ST. LOUIS BLUES(1939); THEY ASKED FOR IT(1939); THEY MADE HER A SPY(1939); TOPPER TAKES A TRIP(1939); TWO THOROUGHBREDS(1939); UNDER-PUP, THE(1939); UNEXPECTED FATHER(1939); WOMAN DOCTOR(1939); WOMEN IN THE WIND(1939); YES, MY DARLING DAUGHTER(1939); YOUNG MR. LINCOLN(1939); ALIAS THE DEACON(1940); BLONDIE PLAYS CUPID(1940); DOCTOR TAKES A WIFE(1940); FIVE LITTLE PEPPERS AT HOME(1940); FRIENDLY NEIGHBORS(1940); GIRL FROM GOD'S COUNTRY(1940); GOLDEN FLEECING, THE(1940); HE MARRIED HIS WIFE(1940); KITTY FOYLE(1940); LUCKY CISCO KID(1940);

MARYLAND(1940); MEET THE MISSUS(1940); OUR TOWN(1940); REMEMBER THE NIGHT(1940); SANTA FE TRAIL(1940); THREE FACES WEST(1940); VIRGINIA CITY(1940); HIGH SIERRA(1941); LADY FROM CHEYENNE(1941); LOOK WHO'S LAUGHING(1941); MAN AT LARGE(1941); MIDNIGHT ANGEL(1941); MOON OVER MIAMI(1941); PETTICOAT POLITICS(1941); SHE COULDN'T SAY NO(1941); SINGING HILL, THE(1941); SO ENDS OUR NIGHT(1941); TOBACCO ROAD(1941); JUKE GIRL(1942); NIGHT BEFORE THE DIVORCE, THE(1942); PACIFIC BLACKOUT(1942); POSTMAN DIDN'T RING, THE(1942); PRIDE OF THE YANKEES, THE(1942); REMARKABLE ANDREW, THE(1942); RIGHT TO THE HEART(1942); SCATTERGOOD SURVIVES A MURDER(1942); SILVER QUEEN(1942); THEY DIED WITH THEIR BOOTS ON(1942); YANKEE DOODLE DANDY(1942); SLIGHTLY DANGEROUS(1943); ARSENIC AND OLD LACE(1944); CARTER CASE, THE(1947)

Silents
NUMBER 17(1920); JANICE MEREDITH(1924)

Eric Chartier
TOUT VA BIEN(1973, Fr.)

Samuel M. Chartock
TOYS ARE NOT FOR CHILDREN(1972), p

Robert Chartoff
POINT BLANK(1967), p; SPLIT, THE(1968), p; THEY SHOOT HORSES, DON'T THEY?(1969), p; LEO THE LAST(1970, Brit.), p; STRAWBERRY STATEMENT, THE(1970), p; BELIEVE IN ME(1971), p; GANG THAT COULDN'T SHOOT STRAIGHT, THE(1971), p; MECHANIC, THE(1972), p; NEW CENTURIONS, THE(1972), p; THUMB TRIPPING(1972), p; UP THE SANDBOX(1972), p; BUSTING(1974), p; GAMBLER, THE(1974), p; S(1974), p; BREAKOUT(1975), p; PEEPER(1975), p; NICKELODEON(1976), p; ROCKY(1976), p; NEW YORK, NEW YORK(1977), p; VALENTINO(1977, Brit.), p; UNCLE JOE SHANNON(1978), p; ROCKY II(1979), p; RAGING BULL(1980), p; TRUE CONFESSIONS(1981), p; ROCKY III(1982), p; RIGHT STUFF, THE(1983), p

Marcel Charton
MY LIFE TO LIVE(1963, Fr.)

Lois Chartrand
GREAT MISSOURI RAID, THE(1950); PLACE IN THE SUN, A(1951)

Annie Charvein
EXPOSED(1983), ed

Denise Charvein
TWO OF US, THE(1968, Fr.), ed

Jean Charvein
SINGAPORE, SINGAPORE(1969, Fr./Ital.), ph; GODSON, THE(1972, Ital./Fr.), ph; BUTTERFLY ON THE SHOULDER, A(1978, Fr.), ph

Marcel Charvey
DESPERATE DECISION(1954, Fr.); COUNTERFEITERS OF PARIS, THE(1962, Fr., Ital.); CLOPORTES(1966, Fr., Ital.); PARIS IN THE MONTH OF AUGUST(1968, Fr.)

Paul Charvonneau
MY BODYGUARD(1980)

Tex Charwate
Silents
PECK'S BAD GIRL(1918), w

Chas
CRIME OF HELEN STANLEY(1934), w

Adam Chase
SUZANNE(1980, Can.)

Adelaide M. Chase
Misc. Silents
MOTHERHOOD; LIFE'S GREATEST MIRACLE(1928)

Alden Chase
CHANCE AT HEAVEN(1933); CAROLINA(1934); GREEN EYES(1934); MAN'S GAME, A(1934); COWBOY MILLIONAIRE(1935); FIGHTING YOUTH(1935); LITTLE COLONEL, THE(1935); PRESCOTT KID, THE(1936); FORTY NAUGHTY GIRLS(1937); ROGUE OF THE RANGE(1937); UNDER WESTERN STARS(1938); BURIED ALIVE(1939); CODE OF THE CACTUS(1939); EAST SIDE KIDS(1940); GUN CODE(1940); BILLY THE KID'S RANGE WAR(1941); LONE RIDER CROSSES THE RIO, THE(1941); LONE RIDER IN GHOST TOWN, THE(1941); PAPER BULLETS(1941)
Misc. Talkies
SIX-GUN TRAIL(1938)

Alden [Stephen] Chase
MILLIONS IN THE AIR(1935); DESIRE(1936); FRESHMAN YEAR(1938); NEW MOON(1940)

Alden "Stephen" Chase
RIGHT TO ROMANCE(1933); FLYING WILD(1941)

[Stephen] Alden Chase
HEART OF ARIZONA(1938)

Annazette Chase
MACK, THE(1973); TRUCK TURNER(1974); SOUNDER, PART 2(1976); GREATEST, THE(1977, U.S./Brit.); TOY, THE(1982)
Misc. Talkies
BLACK STREETFIGHTER(1976); BLACK FIST(1977)

Barbara Chase
NINE TO FIVE(1980)
Misc. Talkies
GHOSTS OF HANLEY HOUSE, THE(1974)

Barrie Chase
WHITE CHRISTMAS(1954); OPPOSITE SEX, THE(1956); MARDI GRAS(1958); PARTY GIRL(1958); GEORGE RAFT STORY, THE(1961); CAPE FEAR(1962); IT'S A MAD, MAD, MAD, MAD WORLD(1963); FLIGHT OF THE PHOENIX, THE(1965)

Barry Chase
SWORD AND THE SORCERER, THE(1982)

Betty Barrie Chase
SILK STOCKINGS(1957)

Borden Chase
UNDER PRESSURE(1935), w; MIDNIGHT TAXI(1937), w; DEVIL'S PARTY, THE(1938), w; BLUE, WHITE, AND PERFECT(1941), w; DR. BROADWAY(1942), w; NAVY COMES THROUGH, THE(1942), w; DESTROYER(1943), w; HARRIGAN'S KID(1943), w; FIGHTING SEABEES, THE(1944), w; FLAME OF THE BARBARY COAST(1945), w; THIS MAN'S NAVY(1945), w; I'VE ALWAYS LOVED YOU(1946), w; TYCOON(1947), w; MAN FROM COLORADO, THE(1948), w; RED RIVER(1948), w; GREAT JEWEL ROBBER, THE(1950), w; MONTANA(1950), w; WINCHESTER '73(1950), w; IRON MAN, THE(1951), w; BEND OF THE RIVER(1952), w; LONE STAR(1952), w; WORLD IN HIS ARMS, THE(1952), w; HIS MAJESTY O'KEEFE(1953), w; VERA CRUZ(1954), w; FAR COUNTRY, THE(1955), w; BACK-LASH(1956), w; NIGHT PASSAGE(1957), w; RIDE A CROOKED TRAIL(1958), w; MUTINY ON THE BOUNTY(1962), w; GUNFIGHTERS OF CASA GRANDE(1965, U.S./Span.), w; BACKTRACK(1969), w; MAN CALLED GANNON, A(1969), w

Bordon Chase
SEA DEVILS(1953), w; MAN WITHOUT A STAR(1955), w

Brandon Chase
FOUR FOR THE MORGUE(1962), p; ALLIGATOR(1980), p; SWORD AND THE SORCERER, THE(1982), p

Brian Chase
SMASH PALACE(1982, New Zealand)

Charles Chase
Silents
TILLIE'S PUNCTURED ROMANCE(1914)

Charley Chase
MODERN LOVE(1929); SONS OF THE DESERT(1933); KELLY THE SECOND(1936)
Misc. Talkies
NEIGHBORHOOD HOUSE(1936)

Chaz Chase
MAN ON THE EIFFEL TOWER, THE(1949)

Chaz. Chase
START CHEERING(1938)

Chevy Chase
GROOVE TUBE, THE(1974); TUNNELVISION(1976); FOUL PLAY(1978); CADDY SHACK(1980); OH, HEAVENLY DOG!(1980); SEEMS LIKE OLD TIMES(1980); MODERN PROBLEMS(1981); UNDER THE RAINBOW(1981); DEAL OF THE CENTURY(1983); NATIONAL LAMPOON'S VACATION(1983)
1984
FLETCH(1984)

Chris Chase
ALL THAT JAZZ(1979)

Clarence Chase
MAN FROM COLORADO, THE(1948)

Colin Chase
GODLESS GIRL, THE(1929); LONE STAR RANGER, THE(1930); RENEGADES(1930); CYCLONE RANGER(1935); FEUD OF THE TRAIL(1938)
Silents
PARSON OF PANAMINT, THE(1916); IRON HORSE, THE(1924); KING OF KINGS, THE(1927); AIR LEGION, THE(1929)
Misc. Silents
RIGHT DIRECTION, THE(1916); ROAD TO LOVE, THE(1916); BRANDED SOUL, A(1917); HER OWN PEOPLE(1917); SPIRIT OF ROMANCE, THE(1917); STRANGE TRANSGRESSOR, A(1917); MORAL LAW, THE(1918); WIVES AND OTHER WIVES(1919); BUCKING THE BARRIER(1923); SNOWDRIFT(1923); SILVER FINGERS(1926)

Colin "Bud" Chase
Misc. Silents
FATHER AND THE BOYS(1915)

David Chase
GRAVE OF THE VAMPIRE(1972), w; SILHOUETTES(1982)

Dorrit Chase
THERE'S ALWAYS VANILLA(1972)

Duane Chase
SOUND OF MUSIC, THE(1965); FOLLOW ME, BOYS!(1966)

Florence Chase
Misc. Silents
WOMAN ABOVE REPROACH, THE(1920)

Francis S. Chase, Jr.
BUCKSKIN LADY, THE(1957), w

Frank Chase
WINCHESTER '73(1950); BEND OF THE RIVER(1952); HORIZONS WEST(1952); RED BALL EXPRESS(1952); WORLD IN HIS ARMS, THE(1952); SEMINOLE(1953); THUNDER BAY(1953); SASKATCHEWAN(1954); MAN WITHOUT A STAR(1955); BACKLASH(1956); CREATURE WALKS AMONG US, THE(1956); FOUR GIRLS IN TOWN(1956); WALK THE PROUD LAND(1956); BEGINNING OF THE END(1957); JOE BUTTERFLY(1957); NIGHT PASSAGE(1957); ATTACK OF THE 50 FOOT WOMAN(1958); RAWHIDE TRAIL, THE(1958); RIDE A CROOKED TRAIL(1958); SULLIVAN'S EMPIRE(1967), w
Misc. Talkies
RAWHIDE TRAIL, THE(1950)

Gary Chase
1984
BLAME IT ON THE NIGHT(1984)

George Chase
Silents
EVIDENCE(1918)
Misc. Silents
GUN WOMAN, THE(1918)

Gertrude Chase
Silents
ENCHANTED COTTAGE, THE(1924), t

Gregory Chase
WITHOUT A TRACE(1983)

Guy [Alden] Chase
FRONTIER SCOUT(1939)

Haile Chase
OPERATION PETTICOAT(1959)

Howard Chase
SHE MARRIED HER BOSS(1935); MAN FROM MUSIC MOUNTAIN(1938); MEET JOHN DOE(1941)

Ilka Chase
CARELESS AGE(1929); PARIS BOUND(1929); RICH PEOPLE(1929); SOUTH SEA ROSE(1929); WHY LEAVE HOME?(1929); FAST AND LOOSE(1930); FLORODORA GIRL, THE(1930); FREE LOVE(1930); GOLDEN CALF, THE(1930); LET'S GO PLACES(1930); ON YOUR BACK(1930); RED HOT RHYTHM(1930); GAY DIPLOMAT, THE(1931); ONCE A SINNER(1931); ANIMAL KINGDOM, THE(1932); LADY CONSENTS, THE(1936); SOAK THE RICH(1936); STRONGER THAN DESIRE(1939); NOW, VOYAGER(1942); NO TIME FOR LOVE(1943); MISS TATLOCK'S MILLIONS(1948); IT SHOULD HAPPEN TO YOU(1954); JOHNNY DARK(1954); BIG KNIFE, THE(1955); OCEAN'S ELEVEN(1960)

Soumitra Chatterjee
WORLD OF APU, THE(1960, India); GODDESS, THE(1962, India); TWO DAUGH-TERS(1963, India)
1984
HOME AND THE WORLD, THE(1984, India)
Swatilekha Chatterjee
1984
HOME AND THE WORLD, THE(1984, India)
Vivienne Chatteron
ANNIE LAURIE(1936, Brit.)
Ann Chatterton
ROCK 'N' ROLL HIGH SCHOOL(1979)
Robert Wade Chatterton
KID FROM BOOKLYN, THE(1946)
Ruth Chatterton
SINS OF THE FATHERS(1928); CHARMING SINNERS(1929); DOCTOR'S SE-CRET(1929); DUMMY, THE(1929); MADAME X(1929); ANYBODY'S WOMAN(1930); LADY OF SCANDAL, THE(1930); LAUGHING LADY, THE(1930); SARAH AND SON(1930); MAGNIFICENT LIE(1931); ONCE A LADY(1931); RIGHT TO LOVE, THE(1931); UNFAITHFUL(1931); RICH ARE ALWAYS WITH US, THE(1932); THE CRASH(1932); TOMORROW AND TOMORROW(1932); FEMALE(1933); FRISCO JEN-NY(1933); LILLY TURNER(1933); JOURNAL OF A CRIME(1934); DOD-SWORTH(1936); GIRLS' DORMITORY(1936); LADY OF SECRETS(1936); RAT, THE(1938, Brit.); ROYAL DIVORCE, A(1938, Brit.)
Misc. Silents
SINS OF THE FATHER(1928)
Thomas Chatterton
FIGHT TO THE FINISH, A(1937); VENUS MAKES TROUBLE(1937)
Silents
GILDED DREAM, THE(1920)
Misc. Silents
BLUFF(1916); BELOVED ROGUES(1917)
Tom Chatterton
WITHOUT RESERVATIONS(1946); BOSS RIDER OF GUN CREEK(1936); SAND-FLOW(1937); TOAST OF NEW YORK, THE(1937); SUDDEN BILL DORN(1938); UNDER WESTERN STARS(1938); ARIZONA LEGION(1939); LAUGH IT OFF(1939); OKLAHOMA KID, THE(1939); ROVIN' TUMBLEWEEDS(1939); COVERED WAGON DAYS(1940); PONY POST(1940); SON OF ROARING DAN(1940); TRAIL BLAZERS, THE(1940); DESERT BANDIT(1941); HONKY TONK(1941); OUTLAWS OF THE CHEROKEE TRAIL(1941); RAIDERS OF THE RANGE(1942); DRUMS OF FU MAN-CHU(1943); SANTA FE SCOUTS(1943); CHEYENNE WILDCAT(1944); CODE OF THE PRAIRIE(1944); MAN FROM FRISCO(1944); MARSHAL OF RENO(1944); TUCSON RAIDERS(1944); COLORADO PIONEERS(1945); LONE TEXAS RANGER(1945); MAR-SHAL OF LAREDO(1945); ALIAS BILLY THE KID(1946); CONQUEST OF CHEYENNE(1946); HOME ON THE RANGE(1946); LAWLESS EMPIRE(1946); LOCK-ET, THE(1946); SHERIFF OF REDWOOD VALLEY(1946); STAGECOACH TO DEN-VER(1946); SMASH-UP, THE STORY OF A WOMAN(1947); CARSON CITY RAIDERS(1948); FAMILY HONEYMOON(1948); HEART OF VIRGINIA(1948); HIGH-WAY 13(1948); MARSHAL OF AMARILLO(1948); OUTLAW BRAND(1948); SECRET BEYOND THE DOOR, THE(1948); GUN LAW JUSTICE(1949); WAGON WHEELS WESTWARD(1956)
Silents
PRICE OF SILENCE, THE(1920, Brit.)
Misc. Silents
SOUL ENSLAVED, A(1916); WHITHER THOU GOEST(1917); HER HUSBAND'S FRIEND(1920); WOULD YOU FORGIVE?(1920)
Vivienne Chatterton
LOVE UP THE POLE(1936, Brit.); DINNER AT THE RITZ(1937, Brit.); FATHER STEPS OUT(1937, Brit.); LITTLE MISS SOMEBODY(1937, Brit.); MAYFAIR MELO-DY(1937, Brit.); MOUNTAINS O'MOURNE(1938, Brit.); DOWN OUR ALLEY(1939, Brit.)
Daniel Chatto
PRIEST OF LOVE(1981, Brit.); QUARTET(1981, Brit./Fr.)
1984
RAZOR'S EDGE, THE(1984)
Tom Chatto
GIRL IN THE PICTURE, THE(1956, Brit.); ENEMY FROM SPACE(1957, Brit.); OSCAR WILDE(1960, Brit.); FROZEN DEAD, THE(1967, Brit.); IT!(1967, Brit.); BATTLE OF BRITAIN(1969, Brit.); MY LOVER, MY SON(1970, Brit.); ASSAULT(1971, Brit.); WHEN EIGHT BELLS TOLL(1971, Brit.); ROMANTIC ENGLISHWOMAN, THE(1975, Brit./Fr.); HUMAN FACTOR, THE(1979, Brit.)
Sid Chatton
TOO YOUNG TO KNOW(1945); TOP SECRET AFFAIR(1957)
Sydney Chatton
LOVING YOU(1957); PAL JOEY(1957); ONCE UPON A HORSE(1958)
Hariendernath Chattopadaya
HOUSEHOLDER, THE(1963, US/India)
Joy Chatwin
ILLEGAL(1932, Brit.)
Lily Mo Chau
MAGNIFICENT CONCUBINE, THE(1964, Hong Kong)
Nam Chau
YANK IN VIET-NAM, A(1964)
Tom Do-Trong Chau
Misc. Talkies
SOLDIER'S STORY, THE(1981)
Vo Doan Chau
QUIET AMERICAN, THE(1958)
L.W. Chaudet
Misc. Silents
EDGE OF THE LAW(1917), d; FOLLOW THE GIRL(1917), d; LONG LANE'S TURN-ING, THE(1919), d
Louis Chaudet
Silents
FOOLS OF FORTUNE(1922), d; KINGFISHER'S ROOST, THE(1922), d&w; MAN OF NERVE, A(1925), d; CAPTAIN'S COURAGE, A(1926), d; EYES RIGHT(1926), d
Misc. Silents
BLUE BONNET, THE(1920), d; DEFYING DESTINY(1923), d; FIGHTING JACK(1926), d; LIGHTING BILL(1926), d; SPEEDING HOOFS(1927), d; OUTCAST SOULS(1928), d

Louis W. Chaudet
Misc. Silents
HOOP-LA(1919), d
Louis William Chaudet
Misc. Silents
GIRL OF MY DREAMS, THE(1918), d; LOVE CALL, THE(1919), d; COMMON SENSE(1920), d
Louis Wm. Chaudet
Misc. Silents
SOCIETY'S DRIFTWOOD(1917), d
Amin Chaudhri
VICE GIRLS, LTD.(1964), p, d, ph&ed; WICKED DIE SLOW, THE(1968), ph
Jacques-Rene Chauffard
BLOOD AND ROSES(1961, Fr./Ital.)
R.J. Chauffard
FRENCH CANCAN(1956, Fr.); LA GUERRE EST FINIE(1967, Fr./Swed.); SOLO(1970, Fr.)
Andre Chaumeau
RETURN OF MARTIN GUERRE, THE(1983, Fr.)
1984
CHEECH AND CHONG'S THE CORSICAN BROTHERS(1984)
Francois Chaumette
NIGHT AFFAIR(1961, Fr.); GALIA(1966, Fr./Ital.); BEAUTIFUL PRISONER, THE(1983, Fr.)
Monique Chaumette
CONFESSION, THE(1970, Fr.); DON'T TOUCH WHITE WOMEN!(1974, Fr.); LACE-MAKER, THE(1977, Fr.); JUDGE AND THE ASSASSIN, THE(1979, Fr.); HATTER'S GHOST, THE(1982, Fr.)
1984
SUNDAY IN THE COUNTRY, A(1984, Fr.)
Yen Chaun
EMPRESS WU(1965, Hong Kong)
Norman Chauncer
GREAT GATSBY, THE(1974)
Chaussettes Noires, Les
TALES OF PARIS(1962)
Emil Chautard
CAUGHT IN THE FOG(1928); MARIANNE(1929); TIMES SQUARE(1929); JUST LIKE HEAVEN(1930); TIGER ROSE(1930); ROAD TO RENO(1931); MAN FROM YESTERDAY, THE(1932); DEVIL'S IN LOVE, THE(1933); MAN OF TWO WORLDS(1934)
Silents
ADORATION(1928)
Misc. Silents
WHISPERING SHADOWS(1922), d; HIS TIGER LADY(1928)
Emile Chautard
SOUTH SEA ROSE(1929); L'ENIGMATIQUE MONSIEUR PARKES(1930); MAN FROM WYOMING, A(1930); MOROCCO(1930); COCK OF THE AIR(1932); SHANGHAI EXPRESS(1932); RIP TIDE(1934); VIVA VILLA!(1934); WONDER BAR(1934)
Silents
ARRIVAL OF PERPETUA, THE(1915), d; ALL MAN(1916), d; FRIDAY THE 13TH(1916), d; ETERNAL TEMPTRESS, THE(1917), d; MAN WHO FORGOT, THE(1917), d&w; MARRIAGE PRICE(1919), d; OUT OF THE SHADOW(1919), d; YOUTH TO YOUTH(1922), p&d; BROKEN HEARTS OF HOLLYWOOD(1926); NOW WE'RE IN THE AIR(1927); SEVENTH HEAVEN(1927); LILAC TIME(1928); NOOSE, THE(1928); OLYMPIC HERO, THE(1928)
Misc. Silents
BOSS, THE(1915), d; HEART OF A HERO, THE(1916), d; HUMAN DRIFT-WOOD(1916), d; LOVE'S CRUCIBLE(1916), d; SUDDEN RICHES(1916), d; FAMILY HONOR, THE(1917), d; FIRES OF YOUTH(1917), d; FORGET-ME-NOTS(1917), d; HEART OF EZRA GREER, THE(1917), d; HUNGRY HEART, A(1917), d; MAG-DA(1917), d; UNDER FALSE COLORS(1917), d; WEB OF DESIRE, THE(1917), d; DAUGHTER OF THE OLD SOUTH, A(1918), d; HER FINAL RECKONING(1918), d; HOUSE OF GLASS, THE(1918), d; MARIONETTES, THE(1918), d; ORDEAL OF ROSETTA, THE(1918), d; UNDER THE GREENWOOD TREE(1918), d; EYES OF THE SOUL(1919), d; HIS PARISIAN WIFE(1919), d; MYSTERY OF THE YELLOW ROOM, THE(1919), d; PAID IN FULL(1919), d; BLACK PANTHER'S CUB, THE(1921), d; FORSAKING ALL OTHERS(1922), d; GLORY OF CLEMENTINA, THE(1922), d; LIVING LIES(1922), d; DAYTIME WIVES(1923), d; UNTAMED YOUTH(1924), d; WHISPERING SAGE(1927); OUT OF THE RUINS(1928)
Andre Chautin
MAMBA(1930), art d
Cesar Chauveau
SICILIAN CLAN, THE(1970, Fr.)
Jacqueline Chauveau
MURMUR OF THE HEART(1971, Fr./Ital./Ger.)
Laetitia Chauveau
ADOLESCENT, THE(1978, Fr./W.Ger.)
Zoe Chauveau
Misc. Talkies
LONGSHOT(1982)
Charles Chauvel
IN THE WAKE OF THE BOUNTY(1933, Aus.), p,d&w; HERITAGE(1935, Aus.), d&w; UNCIVILISED(1937, Aus.), d&w; FORTY THOUSAND HORSEMEN(1941, Aus.), p&d; RUGGED O'RIORDANS, THE(1949, Aus.), p&d, w; RATS OF TOBRUK(1951, Aus.), p, d; JEDDA, THE UNCIVILIZED(1956, Aus.), p&d, w
Elsa Chauvel
RUGGED O'RIORDANS, THE(1949, Aus.), w; JEDDA, THE UNCIVILIZED(1956, Aus.), w
Jean-Francois Chauvel
1984
LE CRABE TAMBOUR(1984, Fr.), w
Mrs. Chauvel
FORTY THOUSAND HORSEMEN(1941, Aus.), w; RATS OF TOBRUK(1951, Aus.), w
Virginia Chauvernet
JEALOUSY(1929)
Elisabeth Chauvet
RATTLERS(1976)

Elizabeth Chauvet
TRACKDOWN(1976)
Misc. Talkies
RATTLERS(1976)
Elizabeth G. Chauvet
Misc. Talkies
BRIDGE IN THE JUNGLE, THE(1971)
Ilizabeth Chauvin
TOUT VA BIEN(1973, Fr.)
Lilyan Chauvin
TWO WEEKS IN ANOTHER TOWN(1962); LES GIRLS(1957); LOST, LONELY AND VICIOUS(1958); PERFECT FURLOUGH, THE(1958); BLOODLUST(1959); WRECK OF THE MARY DEAR, THE(1959); NORTH TO ALASKA(1960); WALK LIKE A DRAGON(1960); BACK STREET(1961); TICKLE ME(1965); MACHISMO–40 GRAVES FOR 40 GUNS(1970); MEPHISTO WALTZ, THE(1971); OTHER SIDE OF MIDNIGHT, THE(1977); PRIVATE BENJAMIN(1980)
1984
SILENT NIGHT, DEADLY NIGHT(1984)
Martine Chauvin
1984
LE BAL(1984, Fr./Ital./Algeria)
Yvette Chauvire
NEOPOLITAN CAROUSEL(1961, Ital.)
Sylvia Chavalho
Silents
SANCTUARY(1916, Brit.), w
Joe Chavalier
MR. BILLION(1977), set d
Louis Chavance
L'ATALANTE(1947, Fr.), ed; RAVEN, THE(1948, Fr.), w; LA MARIE DU PORT(1951, Fr.), w; THIRTEENTH LETTER, THE(1951), w; LIGHT ACROSSS THE STREET, THE(1957, Fr.), w
Francois Chavane
BACK TO THE WALL(1959, Fr.), p, w; PASSION OF SLOW FIRE, THE(1962, Fr.), p
Philip Chavannes
1984
MAJDHAR(1984, Brit.), ph
Melinda Chavaria
MOLLY AND LAWLESS JOHN(1972)
D. Chavchavadze
Misc. Silents
CONQUEST OF THE CAUCASUS(1913, USSR)
Eka Chavchavadze
Misc. Silents
SABA(1929, USSR)
Kotti Chave
DOLLAR(1938, Swed.); JUST ONCE MORE(1963, Swed.)
Zoe Chaveau
VIOLETTE(1978, Fr.)
Rudolph Chavers
WINGS OVER HONOLULU(1937); GAMBLING SHIP(1939)
Eduardo Chaves
STARLIGHT OVER TEXAS(1938)
Jose Chaves
TARZAN'S DEADLY SILENCE(1970)
Luiz Chaves
MARGIN, THE,(1969, Braz.), m
Anna Chavez
1984
DREAMSCAPE(1984)
Ben Chavez
MEXICAN HAYRIDE(1948); MARA MARU(1952)
Carlos Chavez
JAILBREAKERS, THE(1960); TWO MULES FOR SISTER SARA(1970), cos; REVENGERS, THE(1972, U.S./Mex.), cos
David Chavez
HISTORY OF THE WORLD, PART 1(1981)
Ernie Chavez
RING, THE(1952)
Gloria Chavez
SURVIVE!(1977, Mex.)
Jose Chavez
ADVENTURES OF ROBINSON CRUSOE, THE(1954); BEAST OF HOLLOW MOUNTAIN, THE(1956); IMPORTANT MAN, THE(1961, Mex.); PEARL OF TLAYUCAN, THE(1964, Mex.); MAN AND THE MONSTER, THE(1965, Mex.); MIGHTY JUNGLE, THE(1965, U.S./Mex.); PROFESSIONALS, THE(1966); VAMPIRE, THE(1968, Mex.); TWO MULES FOR SISTER SARA(1970); CULPEPPER CATTLE COMPANY, THE(1972)
1984
ROMANCING THE STONE(1984)
Julio Chavez
STANLEY(1973), ed
Julio C. Chavez
RACING FEVER(1964), ph; DEVIL'S SISTERS, THE(1966), ph, ed; STING OF DEATH(1966), ph, ed; DEATH CURSE OF TARTU(1967), ph&ed; WILD REBELS, THE(1967), ed; HOOKED GENERATION, THE(1969), ed; SCREAM, BABY, SCREAM(1969), ph
Ramon Chavez
PURSUIT OF D.B. COOPER, THE(1981)
Nora Chavooshian
1984
BROTHER FROM ANOTHER PLANET, THE(1984), prod d
Nora Chavoosian
1984
ALMOST YOU(1984), art d; RECKLESS(1984), set d
Betty Chay
SON OF FRANKENSTEIN(1939); ILLEGAL ENTRY(1949)

Lillian Chay
WHEN A MAN RIDES ALONE(1933)
Paddy Chayefsky
DOUBLE LIFE, A(1947); AS YOUNG AS YOU FEEL(1951), w; MARTY(1955), w; CATERED AFFAIR, THE(1956), w; BACHELOR PARTY, THE(1957), w; MIDDLE OF THE NIGHT(1959), w; AMERICANIZATION OF EMILY, THE(1964), w; PAINT YOUR WAGON(1969), w; HOSPITAL, THE(1971), w; NETWORK(1976), w
Anita Chayes
Misc. Talkies
BAR MITSVE(1935)
Sunny Chayes
1984
DUBEAT-E-O(1984), cos
V. Chayeva
RESURRECTION(1963, USSR)
Paddy Chayevsky
GODDESS, THE(1958), w
Maury Chaykin
KIDNAPPING OF THE PRESIDENT, THE(1980, Can.); DEATH HUNT(1981); SOUP FOR ONE(1982); CURTAINS(1983, Can.); OF UNKNOWN ORIGIN(1983, Can.); WARGAMES(1983)
1984
HARRY AND SON(1984); HIGHPOINT(1984, Can.); MRS. SOFFEL(1984)
Boris Chaykovskiy
SUMMER TO REMEMBER, A(1961, USSR), m; MARRIAGE OF BALZAMINOV, THE(1966, USSR), m
Kubi Chaza
LIVE AND LET DIE(1973, Brit.)
Robert Chazal
GAME OF TRUTH, THE(1961, Fr.), w
Marie-Anne Chazelk
FRENCH POSTCARDS(1979)
Bachar Chbib
1984
MEMOIRS(1984, Can.), p&d, w, ed
Michael Cheal
NOTORIOUS CLEOPATRA, THE(1970)
Loia Cheaney
SUBMARINE D-1(1937); THAT CERTAIN WOMAN(1937); AMAZING DR. CLITTERHOUSE, THE(1938); MYSTERY HOUSE(1938); SISTERS, THE(1938); SLIGHT CASE OF MURDER, A(1938); WOMEN ARE LIKE THAT(1938); KID FROM KOKOMO, THE(1939)
Lois Cheaney
FOOTLOOSE HEIRESS, THE(1937); TORCHY PLAYS WITH DYNAMITE(1939)
Lola Cheaney
BELOVED BRAT(1938); TORCHY GETS HER MAN(1938); ON TRIAL(1939)
Hally Cheater
CALL A MESSENGER(1939)
Jack Cheatham
SHANGHAIED LOVE(1931); HOLD YOUR MAN(1933); JEALOUSY(1934); ST. LOUIS KID, THE(1934); UPPER WORLD(1934); WHARF ANGEL(1934); ALIBI IKE(1935); CAR 99(1935); HIS FIGHTING BLOOD(1935); MURDER MAN(1935); RED SALUTE(1935); NEXT TIME WE LOVE(1936); PETRIFIED FOREST, THE(1936); WEDDING PRESENT(1936); PAID TO DANCE(1937); TEST PILOT(1938); STRANGER ON THE THIRD FLOOR(1940); MEET JOHN DOE(1941); TWO LATINS FROM MANHATTAN(1941); BROADWAY BIG SHOT(1942); MEN OF SAN QUENTIN(1942); QUIET PLEASE, MURDER(1942); SABOTEUR(1942); FLIGHT FOR FREEDOM(1943); CRIME BY NIGHT(1944); THEY WERE EXPENDABLE(1945); CRACK-UP(1946); DARK MIRROR, THE(1946); DEADLINE AT DAWN(1946); GIRL ON THE SPOT(1946); HOODLUM SAINT, THE(1946); IN FAST COMPANY(1946); KID FROM BROOKLYN, THE(1946); KILLERS, THE(1946); HARD BOILED MAHONEY(1947); KILLER AT LARGE(1947); SECRET LIFE OF WALTER MITTY, THE(1947); UNSUSPECTED, THE(1947); ON OUR MERRY WAY(1948); FLAXY MARTIN(1949)
The Cheatin' Hearts
SECOND FIDDLE TO A STEEL GUITAR(1965)
Leon Cheatom
SMOKEY AND THE BANDIT–PART 3(1983)
Ed Cheatwood
Misc. Talkies
BLACK LOLITA(1975)
Martha Cheavens
PENNY SERENADE(1941), w; SUNDAY DINNER FOR A SOLDIER(1944), w
M. Chebotarenko
SHE-WOLF, THE(1963, USSR)
Boris Chebotaryov
SUN SHINES FOR ALL, THE(1961, USSR), art d; RED AND THE WHITE, THE(1969, Hung./USSR), art d
Andrea Checchi
SCHOOLGIRL DIARY(1947, Ital.); WALLS OF MALAPAGA, THE(1950, Fr./Ital.); STORMBOUND(1951, Ital.); TIMES GONE BY(1953, Ital.); GOLIATH AND THE BARBARIANS(1960, Ital.); THOUSAND EYES OF DR. MABUSE, THE(1960, Fr./Ital./Ger.); ASSASSIN, THE(1961, Ital./Fr.); TWO WOMEN(1961, Ital./Fr.); LAST OF THE VIKINGS, THE(1962, Fr./Ital.); ROMMEL'S TREASURE(1962, Ital.); ERIK THE CONQUEROR(1963, Fr./Ital.); VERONA TRIAL, THE(1963, Ital.); TORPEDO BAY(1964, Ital./Fr.); ITALIANO BRAVA GENTE(1965, Ital./USSR); BULLET FOR THE GENERAL, A(1967, Ital.); MADE IN ITALY(1967, Fr./Ital.); MY WIFE'S ENEMY(1967, Ital.); WATERLOO(1970, Ital./USSR)
Giovanni Checchi
TENTH VICTIM, THE(1965, Fr./Ital.), set d
Robert Checchi
DON'T CRY, IT'S ONLY THUNDER(1982), prod d
1984
BUDDY SYSTEM, THE(1984), set d; MASS APPEAL(1984), set d
Andrea Checcki
EARTH CRIES OUT, THE(1949, Ital.)
Al Checco
HOTEL(1967); BULLITT(1968); PARTY, THE(1968); I LOVE MY WIFE(1970); SKIN GAME(1971); GLASS HOUSES(1972); WORLD'S GREATEST ATHLETE, THE(1973); PETE'S DRAGON(1977); HOW TO BEAT THE HIGH COST OF LIVING(1980)

Misc. Talkies
EXTREME CLOSE-UP(1973)
Augusta Checcotti
CASANOVA '70(1965, Ital.)
Chechik-Efrati
Misc. Silents
MABUL(1927, USSR)
Natasha Chechyotkina
SUMMER TO REMEMBER, A(1961, USSR)
P. Chechyotkina
SUMMER TO REMEMBER, A(1961, USSR), ed; DUEL, THE(1964, USSR), ed
Sylwester Checinski
YELLOW SLIPPERS, THE(1965, Pol.), d
Chubby Checker
TEENAGE MILLIONAIRE(1961); TWIST AROUND THE CLOCK(1961); DON'T KNOCK THE TWIST(1962); RING-A-DING RHYTHM(1962, Brit. 73m Amicus/COL bw (G.B: IT'S TRAD, DAD!)
The Checkerboard Band
SOUTH OF THE BORDER(1939)
The Checkmates, Ltd.
Misc. Talkies
BLACK CONNECTION, THE(1974)
Alexis Checnakov
SPYLARKS(1965, Brit.)
Al Checo
ANGEL IN MY POCKET(1969)
C.C Cheddon
HOUSE OF DANGER(1934), w
America Chedister
Silents
DAWN OF THE EAST(1921); ATTA BOY!(1926)
Alan Chee
WALK, DON'T RUN(1966)
Chang Chee
BRUCE LEE–TRUE STORY(1976, Chi.), ph
Leung Pui Chee
CHAN IS MISSING(1982)
Douglas Cheek
1984
C.H.U.D.(1984), d
Cheeka
SILENT ENEMY, THE(1930)
Tyrus Cheeney
RICHARD(1972)
Beryl Cheers
TOUCH AND GO(1955); SQUEEZE A FLOWER(1970, Aus.)
Ted Cheesman
KING KONG(1933), ed; SON OF KONG(1933), ed; RED MORNING(1935), ed; TO BEAT THE BAND(1935), ed; WANTED: JANE TURNER(1936), ed; ANNAPOLIS SALUTE(1937), ed; DANGER PATROL(1937), ed; WE'RE ON THE JURY(1937), ed; YOU CAN'T BEAT LOVE(1937), ed; I'M FROM THE CITY(1938), ed; LAW OF THE UNDERWORLD(1938), ed; MAID'S NIGHT OUT(1938), ed; MR. DOODLE KICKS OFF(1938), ed; MIGHTY JOE YOUNG(1949), ed
Cheeta
MOON PILOT(1962)
Jack Cheetham
PENAL CODE, THE(1933)
Robert Cheetham
BORN FREE(1966)
John Cheever
SWIMMER, THE(1968), w
Harold Cheevers
SYLVIA SCARLETT(1936)
Jack Chefe
MY MAN GODFREY(1936); ESPIONAGE(1937); WE HAVE OUR MOMENTS(1937); KING OF THE NEWSBOYS(1938); FLYING DEUCES, THE(1939); I TAKE THIS WOMAN(1940); PERFECT SNOB, THE(1941); CROSSROADS(1942); MAD MARTINDALES, THE(1942); TALES OF MANHATTAN(1942); ABOVE SUSPICION(1943); DIXIE DUGAN(1943); THAT'S MY BABY(1944); TO HAVE AND HAVE NOT(1944); DICK TRACY(1945); IT'S A PLEASURE(1945); NAUGHTY NINETIES, THE(1945); SUDAN(1945); GILDA(1946); LIVE WIRES(1946); NOBODY LIVES FOREVER(1946); POSTMAN ALWAYS RINGS TWICE, THE(1946); SUSPENSE(1946); TANGIER(1946); HIGH WALL, THE(1947); MY FAVORITE BRUNETTE(1947); APPOINTMENT WITH MURDER(1948); LARCENY(1948); SAIGON(1948); ABBOTT AND COSTELLO MEET THE KILLER, BORIS KARLOFF(1949); EVERYBODY DOES IT(1949); ILLEGAL ENTRY(1949); THAT FORSYTE WOMAN(1949); SHAKEDOWN(1950); SPY HUNT(1950); DOUBLE DYNAMITE(1951); FAT MAN, THE(1951); MY FAVORITE SPY(1951); ON THE RIVERA(1951); DREAM WIFE(1953); GENTLEMEN PREFER BLONDES(1953); DANGEROUS MISSION(1954); FRENCH LINE, THE(1954); CRASHING LAS VEGAS(1956); FUNNY FACE(1957); PERFECT FURLOUGH, THE(1958)
Andre Cheff
RED, INN, THE(1954, Fr.)
Philip Chege
HUMAN FACTOR, THE(1979, Brit.); SAVAGE HARVEST(1981)
Ann Chegwidden
ROCK AROUND THE WORLD(1957, Brit.), ed; PETTICOAT PIRATES(1961, Brit.), ed; TRIAL AND ERROR(1962, Brit.), ed; CROOKS IN CLOISTERS(1964, Brit.), ed; MASQUE OF THE RED DEATH, THE(1964, U.S./Brit.), ed; DALEKS–INVASION EARTH 2155 A.D.(1966, Brit.), ed; THOSE FANTASTIC FLYING FOOLS(1967, Brit.), ed; TWO A PENNY(1968, Brit.), ed; AND SOON THE DARKNESS(1970, Brit.), ed; LAST GRENADE, THE(1970, Brit.), ed; WUTHERING HEIGHTS(1970, Brit.), ed; HIDING PLACE, THE(1975), ed
Jeffrey Chegwin
EGGHEAD'S ROBOT(1970, Brit.)
Keith Chegwin
EGGHEAD'S ROBOT(1970, Brit.); MACBETH(1971, Brit.); TROUBLESOME DOUBLE, THE(1971, Brit.)

Cheng Cheh
TRIPLE IRONS(1973, Hong Kong), d
Gueye Cheick
END OF A PRIEST(1970, Czech.)
Chang Chein
MERMAID, THE(1966, Hong Kong), w
Jacques Chein-Lit
FLY NOW, PAY LATER(1969), ed
Jeanne Cheiral
Misc. Silents
CRAINQUEBILLE(1922, Fr.)
Micheline Cheirel
CARNIVAL IN FLANDERS(1936, Fr.); THEY WERE FIVE(1938, Fr.); HOLD BACK THE DAWN(1941); I MARRIED AN ANGEL(1942); CORNERED(1945); DEVOTION(1946); FLIGHT TO NOWHERE(1946); SO DARK THE NIGHT(1946); CRIME DOCTOR'S GAMBLE(1947); JEWELS OF BRANDENBURG(1947)
Jadwige Chejnacka
FIRST START(1953, Pol.)
Chang Chek
FEMALE PRINCE, THE(1966, Hong Kong), w
Mark Cheka
GEORG(1964)
S. Chekan
DEVOTION(1955, USSR)
Stanislav Chekan
WAR AND PEACE(1968, USSR)
V. Chekan
MUMU(1961, USSR), ed
A. Chekayevskiy
HAMLET(1966, USSR)
R. Chekhikvadze
DRAGONFLY, THE(1955 USSR)
Anton Chekhov
SUMMER STORM(1944), w; ANNA CROSS, THE(1954, USSR), w; SIGN OF VENUS, THE(1955, Ital.), w; UNCLE VANYA(1958), w; STEPPE, THE(1963, Fr./Ital.), w; HOUSE WITH AN ATTIC, THE(1964, USSR), w; SEA GULL, THE(1968), w; EVENT, AN(1970, Yugo.), w; UNCLE VANYA(1972, USSR), w; THREE SISTERS(1974, Brit.), w; THREE SISTERS, THE(1977), w; UNCLE VANYA(1977, Brit.), w
Anton Pavlovich Chekhov
THREE TALES OF CHEKHOV(1961, USSR), w; LADY WITH THE DOG, THE(1962, USSR), w; DUEL, THE(1964, USSR), w; THREE SISTERS, THE(1969, USSR), d&w
Michael Chekhov
SONG OF RUSSIA(1943); IN OUR TIME(1944); SPELLBOUND(1945); ABIE'S IRISH ROSE(1946); CROSS MY HEART(1946); SPECTER OF THE ROSE(1946); TEXAS, BROOKLYN AND HEAVEN(1948); HOLIDAY FOR SINNERS(1952); INVITATION(1952); RHAPSODY(1954)
Mikhail Chekhov
Misc. Silents
TERCENTENARY OF THE ROMANOV DYNASTY'S ACCESSION TO THE THRONE(1913, USSR); WHEN THE STRINGS OF THE HEART SOUND(1914, USSR)
P. Chekin
TSAR'S BRIDE, THE(1966, USSR)
V. Chekoerski
HAMLET(1966, USSR)
Anton Chekov
BLACK SABBATH(1963, Ital.), w
Olga Chekova
Misc. Silents
CITY OF TEMPTATION(1929, Brit.); PAWNS OF PASSION(1929, Fr./USSR)
A. Chekulaeva
LOSS OF FEELING(1935, USSR)
Y. Chekulayev
NIGHT BEFORE CHRISTMAS, A(1963, USSR)
Yu. Chekulayev
JACK FROST(1966, USSR); WAR AND PEACE(1968, USSR)
A. Chekulayeva
Misc. Silents
YOUR ACQUAINTANCE(1927, USSR)
Z. Chekulayeva
NIGHT BEFORE CHRISTMAS, A(1963, USSR); LAST GAME, THE(1964, USSR); NINE DAYS OF ONE YEAR(1964, USSR); GARNET BRACELET, THE(1966, USSR)
Chela & Dorvay
SUCH IS LIFE(1936, Brit.)
Chela and Doray
TROPICAL TROUBLE(1936, Brit.)
A. Chelenov
ROMEO AND JULIET(1955, USSR), ph
Arman Chelieu
TOAST TO LOVE(1951, Mex.), d, w
Kathy Chelimsky
TWO FOR THE ROAD(1967, Brit.)
Thomas Chelimsky
CHARADE(1963)
B. M. Chelintsev
MYSTERIOUS ISLAND(1941, USSR), d, w
Chelito and Gabriel
WITH LOVE AND KISSES(1937)
Frank Chelland
TO CATCH A THIEF(1955)
Alida Chelli
SUCKER, THE(1966, Fr./Ital.); THEY'RE A WEIRD MOB(1966, Aus.)
Luigi Chellini
Silents
CABIRIA(1914, Ital.)
Chelsea
JUBILEE(1978, Brit.), m
Peter Chelsom
AMERICAN SUCCESS COMPANY, THE(1980)

Cher Chelton
FRATERNITY ROW(1977)
Tsila Chelton
PEPPERMINT SODA(1979, Fr.)
Tsilla Chelton
LES GAULOISES BLEUES(1969, Fr.); VERY HAPPY ALEXANDER(1969, Fr.); TEN DAYS' WONDER(1972, Fr.); SHANKS(1974)
Carlos Chemenal
CEREMONY, THE(1963, U.S./Span.)
Henri Chemin
MAN AND A WOMAN, A(1966, Fr.)
Mic Cheminal
FIRST TIME, THE(1978, Fr.), cos
A. Chemodurov
DREAM OF A COSSACK(1982, USSR)
Anatoliy Chemodurov
DESTINY OF A MAN(1961, USSR)
China Chen
FRIDAY THE 13TH PART II(1981)
Christopher Chen
INN OF THE SIXTH HAPPINESS, THE(1958)
K.S. Chen
AMSTERDAM KILL, THE(1978, Hong Kong), art d
Leo Chen
MOUNTAIN ROAD, THE(1960)
Li Chen
GOLIATHON(1979, Hong Kong), w
Lin Chen
INN OF THE SIXTH HAPPINESS, THE(1958); SATAN NEVER SLEEPS(1962)
Lo Chen
SHEPHERD GIRL, THE(1965, Hong Kong), d&w; VERMILION DOOR(1969, Hong Kong), d
Robert Chen
DEVIL WOMAN(1976, Phil.)
Sherry Chen
HOT POTATO(1976), cos
Si Lan Chen
PEKING EXPRESS(1951)
Si-Lan Chen
ANNA AND THE KING OF SIAM(1946); SLAVE GIRL(1947), ch
Si-Len Chen
KEYS OF THE KINGDOM, THE(1944)
Silan Chen
SOUTH SEA SINNER(1950)
Tina Chen
ALICE'S RESTAURANT(1969); HAWAIIANS, THE(1970); THREE DAYS OF THE CONDOR(1975)
Patrick Chenais
SNOW(1983, Fr.)
Pierre Chenal
CRIME AND PUNISHMENT(1935, Fr.), d, w; ALIBI, THE(1939, Fr.), d; NATIVE SON(1951,U.S., Arg.), d, w; NIGHT THEY KILLED RASPUTIN, THE(1962, Fr./Ital.), d, w
Yvonne Chenal
LOOK WHO'S LAUGHING(1941)
Lawrence Chenault
Misc. Talkies
TEN MINUTES TO LIVE(1932); VEILED ARISTOCRATS(1932)
Misc. Silents
BURDEN OF RACE, THE(1921); CRIMSON SKULL, THE(1921); GUNSAULUS MYSTERY, THE(1921); SECRET SORROW(1921); SYMBOL OF THE UNCONQUERED(1921); BIRTHRIGHT(1924); BRUTE, THE(1925); DEVIL'S DISCIPLE, THE(1926); PRINCE OF HIS RACE, THE(1926); TEN NIGHTS IN A BARROOM(1926); HOUSE BEHIND THE CEDARS, THE(1927); CHILDREN OF FATE(1928)
Reed Chenault
GRAND THEFT AUTO(1977)
Ivan Chendey
SHADOWS OF FORGOTTEN ANCESTORS(1967, USSR), w
Ronald Chenery
MOHAMMAD, MESSENGER OF GOD(1976, Lebanon/Brit.); FUNNY MONEY(1983, Brit.)
Victor Chenet
HIGH TIDE AT NOON(1957, Brit.)
Guillaume Cheneviere
JONAH-WHO WILL BE 25 IN THE YEAR 2000(1976, Switz.)
Frances Cheney
WHEN I GROW UP(1951)
J. Benton Cheney
GAME THAT KILLS, THE(1937), w; OLD WYOMING TRAIL, THE(1937), w; MARINES ARE HERE, THE(1938), w; ROCKY MOUNTAIN RANGERS(1940), w; BORDER VIGILANTES(1941), w; DOOMED CARAVAN(1941), w; IN OLD COLORADO(1941), w; OUTLAWS OF THE DESERT(1941), w; PIRATES ON HORSEBACK(1941), w; RIDERS OF THE TIMBERLINE(1941), w; STICK TO YOUR GUNS(1941), w; TWILIGHT ON THE TRAIL(1941), w; WIDE OPEN TOWN(1941), w; LONE PRAIRIE, THE(1942), w; PIRATES OF THE PRAIRIE(1942), w; ROMANCE ON THE RANGE(1942), w; SHADOWS ON THE SAGE(1942), w; UNDERCOVER MAN(1942), w; FIGHTING FRONTIER(1943), w; HANDS ACROSS THE BORDER(1943), w; KING OF THE COWBOYS(1943), w; MAN FROM THUNDER RIVER, THE(1943), w; SILVER SPURS(1943), w; MYSTERY MAN(1944), w; OUTLAWS OF THE ROCKIES(1945), w; ROCKIN' IN THE ROCKIES(1945), w; COWBOY BLUES(1946), w; GENTLEMAN FROM TEXAS(1946), w; UNDER ARIZONA SKIES(1946), w; UNDER NEVADA SKIES(1946), w; HOPPY'S HOLIDAY(1947), w; LAND OF THE LAWLESS(1947), w; PRAIRIE EXPRESS(1947), w; RAIDERS OF THE SOUTH(1947), w; SONG OF THE WASTELAND(1947), w; BACK TRAIL(1948), w; CALIFORNIA FIREBRAND(1948), w; COWBOY CAVALIER(1948), w; FRONTIER AGENT(1948), w; GUN TALK(1948), w; GUNNING FOR JUSTICE(1948), w; LIGHTNIN' IN THE FOREST(1948), w; OUTLAW BRAND(1948), w; PARTNERS OF THE SUNSET(1948), w; PHANTOM VALLEY(1948), w; SILVER TRAILS(1948), w; GUN RUNNER(1949), w; HIDDEN DANGER(1949), w; LAW OF THE WEST(1949), w; TRAIL'S END(1949), w; OVER THE BORDER(1950), w

Matthew Cheney
RAT FINK(1965), d&w
Cecil Cheng
COUNTESS FROM HONG KONG, A(1967, Brit.); CHAIRMAN, THE(1969)
John Cheng
CLEOPATRA JONES AND THE CASINO OF GOLD(1975 U. S. Hong Kong)
Louis Cheng
GLADIATORS, THE(1970, Swed.)
Mary Cheng
MILLION EYES OF SU-MURU, THE(1967, Brit.)
Shih Cheng
DRAGON INN(1968, Chi.)
Stephen Cheng
WEREWOLF OF WASHINGTON(1973)
Tony Cheng
SEVENTH DAWN, THE(1964)
Y.C. Cheng
FIGHT TO THE LAST(1938, Chi.), d
Yung Cheng
FLYING GUILLOTINE, THE(1975, Chi.)
Chel Chenier
SMITHEREENS(1982)
Katia Chenko
PLAYMATES(1969, Fr./Ital.); FIENDISH PLOT OF DR. FU MANCHU, THE(1980)
Lois Chenney
ESPIONAGE AGENT(1939)
Debbie Chenoweth
VAN NUYS BLVD.(1979)
Deborah Chenoweth
SKATETOWN, U.S.A.(1979)
Bernard Chentrier
RED(1970, Can.), ph
A. Chepurko
TRAIN GOES TO KIEV, THE(1961, USSR), cos
A. Chepurnon
NO GREATER LOVE(1944, USSR)
Cher
CHASTITY(1969); COME BACK TO THE 5 & DIME, JIMMY DEAN, JIMMY DEAN(1982); SILKWOOD(1983)
Piero Cherardi
WAR AND PEACE(1956, Ital./U.S.), set d; UNDER TEN FLAGS(1960, U.S./Ital.), cos
Patrice Chereau
DANTON(1983)
Gwen Cherell
WALKING STICK, THE(1970, Brit.)
Omar Cheriff
GOHA(1958, Tunisia)
Saada Cheritel
STRANGER, THE(1967, Algeria/Fr./Ital.)
V. Cheriyak
SKY CALLS, THE(1959, USSR)
Mera Cheriyan
DREAM ON(1981), set d
Nikolai Cherkasov
IN THE NAME OF LIFE(1947, USSR)
N.P. Cherkasov-Sergeyev
GENERAL SUVOROV(1941, USSR)
Nikolai Cherkassov
IVAN THE TERRIBLE(Part I, 1947, USSR); BALTIC DEPUTY(1937, USSR); ALEXANDER NEVSKY(1939); CAPTAIN GRANT'S CHILDREN(1939, USSR); SPRING(1948, USSR); DON QUIXOTE(1961, USSR)
Eddie Cherkose
SIERRA SUE(1941); MELODY PARADE(1943), m; BOWERY CHAMPS(1944)
Edward Cherkose
CAMPUS RHYTHM(1943), m
Cy Chermak
4D MAN(1959), w
George Chermanoff
PASSPORT TO SUEZ(1943)
Dick Cherney
CEILNG ZERO(1935)
Linda Cherney
SCREAMING MIMI(1958)
Rudy Cherney
TEMPEST(1982)
Joseph Cherniavsky
GIVE AND TARE(1929), m; HIS LUCKY DAY(1929), m; LAST WARNING, THE(1929), m; SHOW BOAT(1929), m
Cayle Chernin
GOIN' DOWN THE ROAD(1970, Can.)
Kayle Chernin
LOVE IN A FOUR LETTER WORLD(1970, Can.)
Jay Chernis
TROCADERO(1944), m; IDENTITY UNKNOWN(1945), md
N. Chernobayeva
Misc. Silents
BLOODY EAST, THE(1915, USSR)
Joel Chernoff
LOOSE SHOES(1980), p
Steven Chernoff
GOSPEL ROAD, THE(1973)
B. Chernova
Misc. Silents
KATKA'S REINETTE APPLES(1926, USSR)
N. Chernova
Misc. Silents
DOUBLE, THE(1916, USSR)

Lyubov Chernoval
LULLABY(1961, USSR)
Sonia Chernus
OUTLAW JOSEY WALES, THE(1976), w
Sonja Chernus
BIG FIX, THE(1947), w
Ye. Chernyayaev
PEACE TO HIM WHO ENTERS(1963, USSR), art d
Ye. Chernyayev
MY NAME IS IVAN(1963, USSR), art d
Frank Rosbert Cheroka
Misc. Silents
WHEEL OF DEATH, THE(1916, Brit.)
Cherokee
LONE HAND, THE(1953); I AM A GROUPIE(1970, Brit.)
Eddie Cherokose
GOLD MINE IN THE SKY(1938)
Andre Cheron
FOUR DEVILS(1929); LOVE PARADE, THE(1929); THEY HAD TO SEE PARIS(1929);
VEILED WOMAN, THE(1929); L'ENIGMATIQUE MONSIEUR PARKES(1930); OH,
FOR A MAN!(1930); SEA LEGS(1930); HUSH MONEY(1931); I LIKE YOUR NER-
VE(1931); MAN OF THE WORLD(1931); EMMA(1932); INTERNATIONAL
HOUSE(1933); BLACK CAT, THE(1934); CAROLINA(1934); KANSAS CITY PRIN-
CESS(1934); NOW AND FOREVER(1934); RIP TIDE(1934); VIVA VILLA!(1934); CAP-
TAIN BLOOD(1935); DRESSED TO THRILL(1935); GIRL FROM TENTH AVENUE,
THE(1935); WHITE COCKATOO(1935); COLLEEN(1936); PRINCESS COMES ACROSS,
THE(1936); WIDOW FROM MONTE CARLO, THE(1936); WIFE VERSUS SECRE-
TARY(1936); CAFE METROPOLE(1937); ESPIONAGE(1937); GOD'S COUNTRY AND
THE WOMAN(1937); THAT CERTAIN WOMAN(1937); ARTISTS AND MODELS
ABROAD(1938); NAVY SECRETS(1939); OUT WEST WITH THE PEPPERS(1940);
TWO-FACED WOMAN(1941)
Silents
MARRIAGE CLAUSE, THE(1926); EVENING CLOTHES(1927); KING OF KINGS,
THE(1927)
Peter Lawrence Cherone
VOICES(1979)
George Cherques
KILLER FISH(1979, Ital./Braz.)
Jorge Cherques
1984
MEMOIRS OF PRISON(1984, Braz.)
Gwen Cherrell
TRAIN OF EVENTS(1952, Brit.); DON'T TALK TO STRANGE MEN(1962, Brit.), w
Gwen Cherrill
ONE WILD OAT(1951, Brit.); FABIAN OF THE YARD(1954, Brit.)
Roger Cherrill
JUST MY LUCK(1957, Brit.), ed; SQUARE PEG, THE(1958, Brit.), ed; FOLLOW A
STAR(1959, Brit.), ed; MAKE MINE MINK(1960, Brit.), ed; FLAME IN THE
STREETS(1961, Brit.), ed; SINGER NOT THE SONG, THE(1961, Brit.), ed; KIND OF
LOVING, A(1962, Brit.), ed; LIVE NOW-PAY LATER(1962, Brit.), ed; BILLY
LIAR(1963, Brit.), ed; IN THE DOGHOUSE(1964, Brit.), ed; THIS IS MY STREET(1964,
Brit.), ed; NAKED PREY, THE(1966, U.S./South Africa), ed
Virginia Cherrill
BRAT, THE(1931); DELICIOUS(1931); GIRLS DEMAND EXCITEMENT(1931);
CHARLIE CHAN'S GREATEST CASE(1933); FAST WORKERS(1933); LADIES MUST
LOVE(1933); NUISANCE, THE(1933); HE COULDN'T TAKE IT(1934); MONEY
MAD(1934, Brit.); WHITE HEAT(1934); LATE EXTRA(1935, Brit.); WHAT PRICE
CRIME?(1935); TROUBLED WATERS(1936, Brit.)
Silents
CITY LIGHTS(1931)
Paki Cherrington
GOODBYE PORK PIE(1981, New Zealand)
Ruth Cherrington
UNCLE HARRY(1945); CAUGHT IN THE FOG(1928); LONE WOLF'S DAUGHTER,
THE(1929); SHE MARRIED HER BOSS(1935); EMPTY SADDLES(1937); I WANT A
DIVORCE(1940); OBLIGING YOUNG LADY(1941); GIRL TROUBLE(1942); FALCON
AND THE CO-EDS, THE(1943); MADAME CURIE(1943); MARGIN FOR ERROR(1943);
YOUNGEST PROFESSION, THE(1943); SEVEN DAYS ASHORE(1944); TWO GIRLS
AND A SAILOR(1944); BEHIND THE MASK(1946); DRAGONWYCH(1946); STOLEN
LIFE, A(1946); SEA OF GRASS, THE(1947)
Silents
MY HOME TOWN(1928)
Alan Cherry
HARRY'S WAR(1981)
Carl Cherry
1984
REVENGE OF THE NERDS(1984)
Charles Cherry
Misc. Silents
MUMMY AND THE HUMMINGBIRD, THE(1915); PASSERS-BY(1916)
Don Cherry
HOLY MOUNTAIN, THE(1973, U.S./Mex.), m
Donald Cherry
ZERO IN THE UNIVERSE(1966), m
Eugene Cherry
1984
BLESS THEIR LITTLE HEARTS(1984)
Helen Cherry
COURTNEY AFFAIR, THE(1947, Brit.); MARK OF CAIN, THE(1948, Brit.); FOR
THEM THAT TRESPASS(1949, Brit.); ADAM AND EVELYNE(1950, Brit.); LAST
HOLIDAY(1950, Brit.); HER PANELLED DOOR(1951, Brit.); OPERATION DISAS-
TER(1951, Brit.); THEY WERE NOT DIVIDED(1951, Brit.); CASTLE IN THE AIR(1952,
Brit.); HIS EXCELLENCY(1952, Brit.); YOUNG WIVES' TALE(1954, Brit.); THREE
CASES OF MURDER(1955, Brit.); HIGH FLIGHT(1957, Brit.); NAKED EDGE,
THE(1961); DEVIL'S AGENT, THE(1962, Brit.); FLIPPER'S NEW ADVENTURE(1964);
TOMORROW AT TEN(1964, Brit.); CHARGE OF THE LIGHT BRIGADE, THE(1968,
Brit.); HARD CONTRACT(1969); 11 HARROWHOUSE(1974, Brit.); CONDUCT UNBE-
COMING(1975, Brit.); NO LONGER ALONE(1978)

Jack Cherry
HOUSE ON 92ND STREET, THE(1945)
Joretta Cherry
UNDER AGE(1964)
Kate Cherry
Silents
RECKLESS YOUTH(1922)
Kathy Cherry
HYSTERICAL(1983)
Malcolm Cherry
Silents
FAR FROM THE MADDING CROWD(1915, Brit.); WELSH SINGER, A(1915, Brit.);
PLACE IN THE SUN, A(1916, Brit.); CALL OF YOUTH, THE(1920, Brit.)
Misc. Silents
GRIM JUSTICE(1916, Brit.); MY LADY'S DRESS(1917, Brit.); LINKED BY FA-
TE(1919, Brit.); MEMBER OF THE TATTERSALL'S, A(1919, Brit.); SWEET-
HEARTS(1919, Brit.); CALL OF YOUTH, THE(1921, Brit.)
Ray Cherry
INDEPENDENCE DAY(1976)
Robert Cherry
GOOD GIRLS GO TO PARIS(1939); JOAN OF OZARK(1942); SWEATER GIRL(1942);
REVENGE OF THE ZOMBIES(1943); YOU'RE A LUCKY FELLOW, MR. SMITH(1943);
SINCE YOU WENT AWAY(1944); CORN IS GREEN, THE(1945); EGG AND I,
THE(1947); MANHATTAN ANGEL(1948); ROAD HOUSE(1948); VICIOUS CIRCLE,
THE(1948); TRAVELING SALESWOMAN(1950); RED BADGE OF COURAGE,
THE(1951); O. HENRY'S FULL HOUSE(1952); NIGHTFALL(1956); TOY, THE(1982)
Stanley Z. Cherry
BUNNY O'HARE(1971), w
William T. Cherry III
SCREAMS OF A WINTER NIGHT(1979), spec eff
Rex Cherryman
Silents
IN FOR THIRTY DAYS(1919); SUNSHINE TRAIL, THE(1923)
Jack Chertok
THEY ALL COME OUT(1939), p; PENALTY, THE(1941), p; EYES IN THE
NIGHT(1942), p; JOE SMITH, AMERICAN(1942), p; KID GLOVE KILLER(1942), p;
OMAHA TRAIL, THE(1942), p; NORTHERN PURSUIT(1943), p; CONSPIRATORS,
THE(1944), p; CORN IS GREEN, THE(1945), p; STRANGE WOMAN, THE(1946), p;
DISHONORED LADY(1947), p
Gennadiy Chertov
SONS AND MOTHERS(1967, USSR)
Evgeni Cherviakov
Misc. Silents
CITIES AND YEARS(1931, USSR), d
Mikhail Abramovich Chervinskiy
SONG OVER MOSCOW(1964, USSR), w
Richard Cherwin
FACES IN THE FOG(1944), md; BANDITS OF THE BADLANDS(1945), md; BEHIND
CITY LIGHTS(1945), m; CHEROKEE FLASH, THE(1945), md; CORPUS CHRISTI
BANDITS(1945), md; GANGS OF THE WATERFRONT(1945), m; GREAT STAGE-
COACH ROBBERY(1945), md; LONE TEXAS RANGER(1945), md; MARSHAL OF
LAREDO(1945), md; OREGON TRAIL(1945), md; PHANTOM OF THE PLAINS(1945),
md; PHANTOM SPEAKS, THE(1945), md; ROAD TO ALCATRAZ(1945), md; ROUGH
RIDERS OF CHEYENNE(1945), md; SANTA FE SADDLEMATES(1945), md; SCOT-
LAND YARD INVESTIGATOR(1945, Brit.), md; SHERIFF OF CIMARRON(1945), md;
SONG OF MEXICO(1945), md; SPORTING CHANCE, A(1945), md; THREE'S A
CROWD(1945), md; TIGER WOMAN, THE(1945), md; TOPEKA TERROR, THE(1945),
md; TRAIL OF KIT CARSON(1945), md; VAMPIRE'S GHOST, THE(1945), md; CON-
QUEST OF CHEYENNE(1946), md; DAYS OF BUFFALO BILL(1946), md; GUY
COULD CHANGE, A(1946), md; PASSKEY TO DANGER(1946), m; SHERIFF OF
REDWOOD VALLEY(1946), md; SUN VALLEY CYCLONE(1946), md; UNDERCOV-
ER WOMAN, THE(1946), md; VALLEY OF THE ZOMBIES(1946), md; PILGRIM
LADY, THE(1947), md; WAGON WHEELS WESTWARD(1956), md
Tom Cherwin
SMITHEREENS(1982)
Karen Cheryl
1984
HERE COMES SANTA CLAUS(1984)
George Chesbro
RIDERS OF BLACK MOUNTAIN(1941); SAVAGE HORDE, THE(1950); MAN WHO
WOULD NOT DIE, THE(1975), w
Chris Chescoe
1984
DARK ENEMY(1984, Brit.)
George Chesebro
HANDCUFFED(1929); SHOULD A GIRL MARRY?(1929); SHOW BOAT(1929); AIR
POLICE(1931); FIRST AID(1931); KID FROM ARIZONA, THE(1931); SKY SPIDER,
THE(1931); WILD WEST WHOOPEE(1931); BEHIND STONE WALLS(1932); GORILLA
SHIP, THE(1932); TEX TAKES A HOLIDAY(1932); TOMBSTONE CANYON(1932);
FIGHTING CHAMP(1933); LUCKY LARRIGAN(1933); FIGHTING HERO(1934); COW-
BOY AND THE BANDIT, THE(1935); COYOTE TRAILS(1935); CYCLONE OF THE
SADDLE(1935); DANGER AHEAD(1935); DANGER TRAILS(1935); FIGHTING
CABALLERO(1935); FIGHTING TROOPER, THE(1935); GALLANT DEFEND-
ER(1935); IN OLD SANTA FE(1935); PALS OF THE RANGE(1935); ROUGH RIDING
RANGER(1935); TUMBLING TUMBLEWEEDS(1935); WILD MUSTANG(1935); CA-
RYL OF THE MOUNTAINS(1936); LAWLESS NINETIES, THE(1936); LUCKY TER-
ROR(1936); MAN FROM GUN TOWN, THE(1936); MYSTERIOUS AVENGER,
THE(1936); RED RIVER VALLEY(1936); RETURN OF JIMMY VALENTINE,
THE(1936); SPEED REPORTER(1936); TOLL OF THE DESERT(1936); TRAIL
DUST(1936); BORDERLAND(1937); DEVIL'S SADDLE LEGION, THE(1937); DODGE
CITY TRAIL(1937); EMPTY HOLSTERS(1937); GAME THAT KILLS, THE(1937);
HILLS OF OLD WYOMING(1937); OLD WYOMING TRAIL, THE(1937); PINTO
RUSTLERS(1937); PRAIRIE THUNDER(1937); ROAMING COWBOY, THE(1937);
ROARIN' LEAD(1937); SPRINGTIME IN THE ROCKIES(1937); TWO-FISTED SHE-
RIFF(1937); TWO GUN LAW(1937); WESTBOUND MAIL(1937); CALL OF THE
ROCKIES(1938); CATTLE RAIDERS(1938); JUVENILE COURT(1938); LAW OF THE
PLAINS(1938); LAWLESS VALLEY(1938); MEXICALI KID, THE(1938); OUTLAWS OF
SONORA(1938); OUTLAWS OF THE PRAIRIE(1938); PURPLE VIGILANTES,
THE(1938); SANTA FE STAMPEDE(1938); STARLIGHT OVER TEXAS(1938); LET US
LIVE(1939); MAN FROM SUNDOWN, THE(1939); NEW FRONTIER(1939); OK-

LAHOMA FRONTIER(1939); RANGE WAR(1939); RIDERS OF BLACK RIVER(1939); RIO GRANDE(1939); ROUGH RIDERS' ROUNDUP(1939); SMASHING THE MONEY RING(1939); SMOKY TRAILS(1939); SONG OF THE BUCKAROO(1939); SOUTHWARD HO!(1939); WALL STREET COWBOY(1939); CHEYENNE KID, THE(1940); FRONTIER CRUSADER(1940); GUN CODE(1940); KID FROM SANTA FE, THE(1940); LAND OF THE SIX GUNS(1940); LIGHTNING STRIKES WEST(1940); MELODY RANCH(1940); PINTO CANYON(1940); PIONEER DAYS(1940); PIONEERS OF THE FRONTIER(1940); PIONEERS OF THE WEST(1940); RIDERS FROM NOWHERE(1940); STRANGER FROM TEXAS, THE(1940); TEXAS STAGECOACH(1940); WEST OF PINTO BASIN(1940); WILD HORSE VALLEY(1940); YOUNG BUFFALO BILL(1940); BILLY THE KID'S FIGHTING PALS(1941); KING OF DODGE CITY(1941); LONE RIDER AMBUSHED, THE(1941); LONE RIDER IN GHOST TOWN, THE(1941); MEDICO OF PAINTED SPRINGS, THE(1941); OUTLAWS OF THE RIO GRANDE(1941); PALS OF THE PECOS(1941); PIONEERS, THE(1941); SADDLE MOUNTAIN ROUNDUP(1941); TRAIL OF THE SILVER SPURS(1941); WILDCAT OF TUCSON(1941); WRANGLER'S ROOST(1941); BILLY THE KID TRAPPED(1942); JESSE JAMES, JR.(1942); LONE RIDER IN CHEYENNE, THE(1942); LONE STAR VIGILANTES, THE(1942); ROLLING DOWN THE GREAT DIVIDE(1942); THUNDER RIVER FEUD(1942); BLACK MARKET RUSTLERS(1943); TWO FISTED JUSTICE(1943); ARIZONA WHIRLWIND(1944); BLAZING FRONTIER(1944); BOSS OF THE RAWHIDE(1944); DEATH RIDES THE PLAINS(1944); DEATH VALLEY RANGERS(1944); DEVIL RIDERS(1944); DRIFTER, THE(1944); MARSHAL OF GUNSMOKE(1944); RAIDERS OF RED GAP(1944); THUNDERING GUN SLINGERS(1944); COLORADO PIONEERS(1945); MARSHAL OF LAREDO(1945); OUTLAWS OF THE ROCKIES(1945); SALOME, WHERE SHE DANCED(1945); SANTA FE SADDLEMATES(1945); SHERIFF OF CIMARRON(1945); STAGECOACH OUTLAWS(1945); TRAIL OF KIT CARSON(1945); CARAVAN TRAIL, THE(1946); DAYS OF BUFFALO BILL(1946); GENTLEMEN WITH GUNS(1946); LANDRUSH(1946); LAWLESS EMPIRE(1946); OVERLAND RIDERS(1946); RAINBOW OVER TEXAS(1946); SINGIN' IN THE CORN(1946); STAGECOACH TO DENVER(1946); SUN VALLEY CYCLONE(1946); TERRORS ON HORSEBACK(1946); CHEYENNE TAKES OVER(1947); FIGHTING VIGILANTES, THE(1947); HOMESTEADERS OF PARADISE VALLEY(1947); LONE HAND TEXAN, THE(1947); RETURN OF THE LASH(1947); SHADOW VALLEY(1947); SONG OF THE WASTELAND(1947); STAGE TO MESA CITY(1947); VIGILANTES OF BOOMTOWN(1947); WYOMING(1947); BLACK HILLS(1948); CHECK YOUR GUNS(1948); FRONTIER REVENGE(1948); FURY AT FURNACE CREEK(1948); GALLANT LEGION, THE(1948); SIX-GUN LAW(1948); TORNADO RANGE(1948); WEST OF SONORA(1948); CHALLENGE OF THE RANGE(1949); DEATH VALLEY GUNFIGHTER(1949); DESERT VIGILANTE(1949); LAST BANDIT, THE(1949); LUST FOR GOLD(1949); RENEGADES OF THE SAGE(1949); ROLL, THUNDER, ROLL(1949); TRAIL'S END(1949); COLORADO RANGER(1950); CROOKED RIVER(1950); FAST ON THE DRAW(1950); FRISCO TORNADO(1950); GUNMEN OF ABILENE(1950); GUNSLINGERS(1950); HORSEMEN OF THE SIERRAS(1950); HOSTILE COUNTRY(1950); LIGHTNING GUNS(1950); MARSHAL OF HELDORADO(1950); SALT LAKE RAIDERS(1950); STREETS OF GHOST TOWN(1950); TEXAS DYNAMO(1950); TRAIL OF ROBIN HOOD(1950); TRAVELING SALESWOMAN(1950); WEST OF THE BRAZOS(1950); CYCLONE FURY(1951); KENTUCKY JUBILEE(1951); KID FROM AMARILLO, THE(1951); NIGHT RIDERS OF MONTANA(1951); SNAKE RIVER DESPERADOES(1951); THUNDERING TRAIL, THE(1951); FRONTIER PHANTOM, THE(1952); JUNCTION CITY(1952); LAST OF THE COMANCHES(1952); MONTANA BELLE(1952); MONTANA TERRITORY(1952); SNIPER, THE(1952); WINNING OF THE WEST(1953); WAGON WHEELS WESTWARD(1956)

Misc. Talkies
LARIATS AND SIXSHOOTERS(1931); SHERIFF'S SECRET, THE(1931); FORTYFIVE CALIBRE ECHO(1932); BORDER GUNS(1934); BORDER MENACE, THE(1934); RAWHIDE MAIL(1934); DEFYING THE LAW(1935); LARAMIE KID, THE(1935); PHANTOM COWBOY, THE(1935); WESTERN RACKETEERS(1935); WOLF RIDERS(1935); ROAMIN' WILD(1936); LAW OF THE WILD(1941); FIGHTING FRONTIERSMAN, THE(1946); GUNNING FOR VENGEANCE(1946)

Silents
RISKY ROAD, THE(1918); RUSTLER'S RANCH(1926)

Misc. Silents
BECAUSE OF THE WOMAN(1917); BROADWAY ARIZONA(1917); INDISCREET CORINNE(1917); MR. OPP(1917); SHOW-DOWN, THE(1917); MODERN LOVE(1918); RIDERS OF THE NIGHT(1918); RECOIL, THE(1921); BLIND CIRCUMSTANCES(1922); DIAMOND CARLISLE(1922); FOR LOVE OF SERVICE(1922); HATE TRAIL, THE(1922); MENACING PAST, THE(1922); SAFE GUARDED(1924); WOLF BLOOD(1925), a, d; BLOCK SIGNAL, THE(1926); SILENT AVENGER, THE(1927)

George N. Chesebro
Misc. Silents
HUMANIZING MR. WINSBY(1916); LAND JUST OVER YONDER, THE(1916)

George Chesebrough
COUNTY FAIR, THE(1932)

Anna Cheselka
RACERS, THE(1955); MIDNIGHT LACE(1960)

Ted Cheseman
OUTCASTS OF POKER FLAT, THE(1937), ed

Grahame Chesewright
SCARAB MURDER CASE, THE(1936, Brit.)

Elizabeth Cheshire
LOOKING FOR MR. GOODBAR(1977); MELVIN AND HOWARD(1980); DEAD KIDS(1981 Aus./New Zealand)

Geoffrey Cheshire
SKULL, THE(1965, Brit.); DALEKS–INVASION EARTH 2155 A.D.(1966, Brit.); ON HER MAJESTY'S SECRET SERVICE(1969, Brit.)

Harry Cheshire
CHILD OF DIVORCE(1946); DICK TRACY VS. CUEBALL(1946); IF I'M LUCKY(1946); IT'S A WONDERFUL LIFE(1946); SIOUX CITY SUE(1946); SMOOTH AS SILK(1946); HER HUSBAND'S AFFAIRS(1947); HOMESTRETCH, THE(1947); I WONDER WHO'S KISSING HER NOW(1947); INVISIBLE WALL, THE(1947); MOTHER WORE TIGHTS(1947); NIGHTMARE ALLEY(1947); SHOOT TO KILL(1947); SPORT OF KINGS(1947); BLACK EAGLE(1948); FOR THE LOVE OF MARY(1948); INCIDENT(1948); RACING LUCK(1948); SIXTEEN FATHOMS DEEP(1948); BRIDE FOR SALE(1949); CHICAGO DEADLINE(1949); FIGHTING MAN OF THE PLAINS(1949); IMPACT(1949); IT HAPPENS EVERY SPRING(1949); LADY TAKES A SAILOR, THE(1949); MA AND PA KETTLE(1949); MISS GRANT TAKES RICHMOND(1949); RIDERS OF THE WHISTLING PINES(1949); SAND(1949); CHAIN GANG(1950); COUNTY FAIR(1950); GIRLS' SCHOOL(1950); LONELY HEARTS BANDITS(1950); LUCKY LOSERS(1950); NO SAD SONGS FOR ME(1950); PAID IN FULL(1950);

SEPTEMBER AFFAIR(1950); SQUARE DANCE KATY(1950); WOMAN OF DISTINCTION, A(1950); WOMAN ON PIER 13, THE(1950); BLUE BLOOD(1951); RHUBARB(1951); THUNDER IN GOD'S COUNTRY(1951); CARBINE WILLIAMS(1952); DREAMBOAT(1952); FLESH AND FURY(1952); HERE COME THE NELSONS(1952); MA AND PA KETTLE AT THE FAIR(1952); PHONE CALL FROM A STRANGER(1952); SNIPER, THE(1952); ESCAPE FROM FORT BRAVO(1953); DANGEROUS MISSION(1954); FIREMAN SAVE MY CHILD(1954); PHFFFT!(1954); PRIDE OF THE BLUE GRASS(1954); SEVEN LITTLE FOYS, THE(1955); BOSS, THE(1956); FIRST TRAVELING SALESLADY, THE(1956); LOVING YOU(1957); MY MAN GODFREY(1957); RESTLESS BREED, THE(1957); LET'S MAKE LOVE(1960); ERRAND BOY, THE(1961)

Harry "Pappy" Cheshire
BARNYARD FOLLIES(1940); HI, NEIGHBOR(1942); O, MY DARLING CLEMENTINE(1943); SWING YOUR PARTNER(1943); SING, NEIGHBOR, SING(1944)

Harry V. Cheshire
ADVENTURES OF GALLANT BESS(1948); LUCKY JORDAN(1942); AFFAIRS OF GERALDINE(1946); TRAFFIC IN CRIME(1946); FABULOUS TEXAN, THE(1947); HUCKSTERS, THE(1947); PILGRIM LADY, THE(1947); SPRINGTIME IN THE SIERRAS(1947); TENDER YEARS, THE(1947); FLAME, THE(1948); MOONRISE(1948); SLIPPY MCGEE(1948); BRIMSTONE(1949); ARIZONA COWBOY, THE(1950); PATSY, THE(1964)

Harry V. "Pappy" Cheshire
SMOKY MOUNTAIN MELODY(1949)

Robin Chesler
LEPKE(1975, U.S./Israel)

Bob Cheslock
JACK OF DIAMONDS(1967, U.S./Ger.)

Bernard Chesnais
FIRST TASTE OF LOVE(1962, Fr.), w

Patrick Chesnai?
COCKTAIL MOLOTOV(1980, Fr.)

Alexis Chesnakoff
ADVENTURE FOR TWO(1945, Brit.)

Alexis Chesnakov
THIRD MAN, THE(1950, Brit.); NEVER LET ME GO(1953, U.S./Brit.); OPERATION DIPLOMAT(1953, Brit.); TAKE A POWDER(1953, Brit.); LOVE LOTTERY, THE(1954, Brit.)

Patrick Chesnals
GIRL FROM LORRAINE, A(1982, Fr./Switz.)

Al Chesney
1984
SPLASH(1984)

Arthur Chesney
FRENCH LEAVE(1931, Brit.); FIRES OF FATE(1932, Brit.); INDISCRETIONS OF EVE(1932, Brit.); LORD BABS(1932, Brit.); SHADOW BETWEEN, THE(1932, Brit.); CHELSEA LIFE(1933, Brit.); FORTUNATE FOOL, THE(1933, Brit.); NIGHT OF THE GARTER(1933, Brit.); COLONEL BLOOD(1934, Brit.); SORRELL AND SON(1934, Brit.); YOUTHFUL FOLLY(1934, Brit.); RUNAWAY QUEEN, THE(1935, Brit.); CHICK(1936, Brit.); SENSATION(1936, Brit.); GIRLS IN THE STREET(1937, Brit.); PLEASE TEACHER(1937, Brit.); SONG OF THE FORGE(1937, Brit.); YOU'RE IN THE ARMY NOW(1937, Brit.); GIRL IN THE STREET(1938, Brit.); I KNOW WHERE I'M GOING(1947, Brit.); FLAMINGO AFFAIR, THE(1948, Brit.)

Silents
LODGER, THE(1926, Brit.)

Misc. Silents
LIGHTS O' LONDON, THE(1914, Brit.)

Diana Chesney
LOVE IN WAITING(1948, Brit.); ROCK YOU SINNERS(1957, Brit.); SON OF A STRANGER(1957, Brit.); WOMAN OF MYSTERY, A(1957, Brit.); LINKS OF JUSTICE(1958); GIDEON OF SCOTLAND YARD(1959, Brit.); HONOURABLE MURDER, AN(1959, Brit.); MAN ACCUSED(1959); TOP FLOOR GIRL(1959, Brit.); WEB OF SUSPICION(1959, Brit.); SHAKEDOWN, THE(1960, Brit.); STRONGROOM(1962, Brit.); MUNSTER, GO HOME(1966); KING'S PIRATE(1967); SWASHBUCKLER(1976)

Nancy Chesney
1984
MRS. SOFFEL(1984)

Ronald Chesney
FACING THE MUSIC(1941, Brit.); THEY MET IN THE DARK(1945, Brit.); VALUE FOR MONEY(1957, Brit.); I'VE GOTTA HORSE(1965, Brit.), w; ON THE BUSES(1972, Brit.), p

Tyrus Chesney
SHAME, SHAME, EVERYBODY KNOWS HER NAME(1969)

Bruce Chesse
THX 1138(1971)

Dion Chesse
MORE AMERICAN GRAFFITI(1979)

Dion M. Chesse
THX 1138(1971)

Ralph Chesse
THX 1138(1971); MR. BILLION(1977); CHU CHU AND THE PHILLY FLASH(1981)

Chris Chesser
1984
NIGHT OF THE COMET(1984)

Gordon E. "Chet" Chessher
1984
BEAR, THE(1984)

Jennifer Chessman
WILD PARTY, THE(1975)

Ted Chessman
EVERYBODY'S DOING IT(1938), ed

Tod Chessman
Silents
ONE MAN DOG, THE(1929), ed

Treasure Chest
POPDOWN(1968, Brit.)

Chester
CRASHOUT(1955), w

Chester the Chimp
FIVE WEEKS IN A BALLOON(1962)
Alfred Chester
MIRACLE IN HARLEM(1948)
Alfred "Slick" Chester
TEMPTATION(1936); UNDERWORLD(1937)
Misc. Talkies
HARLEM AFTER MIDNIGHT(1934)
Alma Chester
BELOVED BACHELOR, THE(1931); SUNDOWN TRAIL(1931); WHEN A MAN RIDES ALONE(1933); COWBOY HOLIDAY(1934); DUDE RANGER, THE(1934); DEVIL'S PLAYGROUND(1937); OLD WYOMING TRAIL, THE(1937)
Angelyn Chester
THREE THE HARD WAY(1974)
Basil Chester
BIG CARNIVAL, THE(1951)
Beatrice Chester
Silents
ELEVENTH HOUR, THE(1922, Brit.)
Betty Chester
BE MINE TONIGHT(1933, Brit.)
Cheerful Charlie Chester
HOLIDAY CAMP(1947, Brit.)
Colby Chester
CHARLEY VARRICK(1973); EXECUTIVE ACTION(1973); DOVE, THE(1974, Brit.); HINDENBURG, THE(1975); LAST MARRIED COUPLE IN AMERICA, THE(1980)
Dot Chester
GET HEP TO LOVE(1942)
George Chester
EGYPTIAN. THE(1954)
George Randolph Chester
NEW ADVENTURES OF GET-RICH-QUICK WALLINGFORD, THE(1931), w
Silents
LAVENDER BATH LADY, THE(1922), w; SCARLET CAR, THE(1923), w; SOFT CUSHIONS(1927), w; HEAD OF THE FAMILY, THE(1928), w
Misc. Silents
SON OF WALLINGFORD, THE(1921), d
Hal Chester
BEAST FROM 20,000 FATHOMS, THE(1953), p
Hal E. Chester
JOE PALOOKA, CHAMP(1946), p, w; FIGHTING MAD(1948), p; JOE PALOOKA IN WINNER TAKE ALL(1948), p; SMART WOMAN(1948), p; JOE PALOOKA IN THE BIG FIGHT(1949), p; JOE PALOOKA IN THE COUNTERPUNCH(1949), p; HUMPHREY TAKES A CHANCE(1950), p; JOE PALOOKA IN THE SQUARED CIRCLE(1950), p; JOE PALOOKA MEETS HUMPHREY(1950), p; WHIPPED, THE(1950), p; HIGHWAYMAN, THE(1951), p; JOE PALOOKA IN TRIPLE CROSS(1951), p; MODELS, INC.(1952), p; CRASHOUT(1955), p; BOLD AND THE BRAVE, THE(1956), p; WEAPON, THE(1957, Brit.), p, w; CURSE OF THE DEMON(1958), p, w; TWO-HEADED SPY, THE(1959, Brit.), p; SCHOOL FOR SCOUNDRELS(1960, Brit.), p, w; HIS AND HERS(1961, Brit.), p, w; HIDE AND SEEK(1964, Brit.), p; DOUBLE MAN, THE(1967), p; SECRET WAR OF HARRY FRIGG, THE(1968), p; TAKE A GIRL LIKE YOU(1970, Brit,), p
Hally Chester
CRIME SCHOOL(1938); JUVENILE COURT(1938); LITTLE TOUGH GUY(1938); LITTLE TOUGH GUYS IN SOCIETY(1938); CODE OF THE STREETS(1939); NEWSBOY'S HOME(1939); WHEN TOMORROW COMES(1939); EAST SIDE KIDS(1940); YOU'RE NOT SO TOUGH(1940); HIT THE ROAD(1941); MOB TOWN(1941)
Holly Chester
BOYS OF THE CITY(1940)
Lila Chester
Misc. Silents
CARDINAL RICHELIEU'S WARD(1914)
Lila Hayward Chester
Silents
SINS OF SOCIETY(1915)
Misc. Silents
UNPARDONABLE SIN, THE(1916)
Lillian Chester
Silents
BLACK BEAUTY(1921), w
Lloyd Chester
WOLF DOG(1958, Can.)
Louise Chester
ONLY WAY HOME, THE(1972)
Noel Chester
LORD JIM(1965, Brit.)
Peggy Chester
CAVALIER OF THE STREETS, THE(1937, Brit.)
Robert Chester
Misc. Silents
SOME WAITER!(1916, Brit.)
Virginia Chester
Silents
OUTCASTS OF POKER FLAT, THE(1919)
Misc. Silents
DEMON, THE(1918)
William Chester
Silents
GIRL WHO WOULDN'T QUIT, THE(1918)
Chester Hale Girls
LOVE AT FIRST SIGHT(1930)
Chester's Performing Dogs
MUSIC HALL(1934, Brit.)
G.K. Chesterton
DETECTIVE, THE(1954, Qit.), w
Gilbert K. Chesterton
FATHER BROWN, DETECTIVE(1935), w

Robert Chestnut
1984
WILD LIFE, THE(1984)
Wayne Everett Chestnut
BURY ME AN ANGEL(1972)
Graham Cheswright
FIRE OVER ENGLAND(1937, Brit.)
Cheta the Chimp
TARZAN, THE APE MAN(1932); TARZAN ESCAPES(1936); TARZAN'S SECRET TREASURE(1941); TARZAN TRIUMPHS(1943); TARZAN'S DESERT MYSTERY(1943); TARZAN AND THE LEOPARD WOMAN(1946); TARZAN'S MAGIC FOUNTAIN(1949); TARZAN AND THE SLAVE GIRL(1950); TARZAN'S PERIL(1951); TARZAN AND THE SHE-DEVIL(1953); TARZAN'S HIDDEN JUNGLE(1955); TARZAN AND THE LOST SAFARI(1957, Brit.); TARZAN'S FIGHT FOR LIFE(1958); TARZAN'S JUNGLE REBELLION(1970)
Cheta the Chimpanzee
TARZAN'S NEW YORK ADVENTURE(1942)
Cheta the Monkey
TARZAN AND THE HUNTRESS(1947)
Jack Chete
HOLIDAY AFFAIR(1949)
Warren Chetham-Strode
ODETTE(1951, Brit.), w
Alfredo Chetta
BOBO, THE(1967, Brit.)
Nicholas Chetta
FOUR FOR THE MORGUE(1962)
Viktor Chetverikov
LULLABY(1961, USSR); SANDU FOLLOWS THE SUN(1965, USSR)
Ann Chetwidden
KILL ME TOMORROW(1958, Brit.), ed
Gloria Carlin Chetwynd
SHOOT(1976, Can.)
Lionel Chetwynd
APPRENTICESHIP OF DUDDY KRAVITZ, THE(1974, Can.), w; TWO SOLITUDES(1978, Can.), d&w; QUINTET(1979), w
R. Chetwynd-Hayes
FROM BEYOND THE GRAVE(1974, Brit.), w
Ronald Chetwynd-Hayes
MONSTER CLUB, THE(1981, Brit.), w
Michael Cheuk
GLADIATORS, THE(1970, Swed.)
George Cheung
AMSTERDAM KILL, THE(1978, Hong Kong); GOING BERSERK(1983)
George Kee Cheung
KILLER ELITE, THE(1975); BEACH GIRLS(1982)
Louie Cheung
Silents
BRANDING IRON, THE(1920); TALE OF TWO WORLDS, A(1921)
Margaret Cheung
MILLION EYES OF SU-MURU, THE(1967, Brit.)
Susan Cheung
1984
STREETS OF FIRE(1984)
Lita Cheuret
WORDS AND MUSIC(1929)
Annie Chevaldonne
SMALL CHANGE(1976, Fr.)
Albert Chevalier
MY OLD DUTCH(1934, Brit.), w; EVERYTHING IS THUNDER(1936, Brit.); NONSTOP NEW YORK(1937, Brit.); SABOTAGE(1937, Brit.); STRANGE BOARDERS(1938, Brit.); YOUNG AND INNOCENT(1938, Brit.); MILLIONS LIKE US(1943, Brit.); FIVE ANGLES ON MURDER(1950, Brit.); TROUBLE IN THE GLEN(1954, Brit.)
Silents
MY OLD DUTCH(1915, Brit.), a, w
Misc. Silents
BOTTLE, THE(1915, Brit.); MIDDLEMAN, THE(1915, Brit.); FALLEN STAR, A(1916, Brit.)
Anna Chevalier
Silents
TABU(1931)
Bliss Chevalier
Silents
ON RECORD(1917); KID, THE(1921)
Misc. Silents
BETTY TAKES A HAND(1918); BIGGEST SHOW ON EARTH, THE(1918)
Christian Chevalier
EGLANTINE(1972, Fr.), m
Gigi Chevalier
HARVEY MIDDLEMAN, FIREMAN(1965)
Giuseppe Chevalier
MAN COULD GET KILLED, A(1966), set d
Jacques Chevalier
ONE, TWO, THREE(1961); MADEMOISELLE(1966, Fr./Brit.)
Joe Chevalier
REFLECTIONS IN A GOLDEN EYE(1967), set d; GIRL FROM PETROVKA, THE(1974), set d; PRISONER OF ZENDA, THE(1979), set d; MONSIGNOR(1982), set d
Louise Chevalier
UP FROM THE BEACH(1965); HOW TO STEAL A MILLION(1966); LA FEMME INFIDELE(1969, Fr./Ital.); THIS MAN MUST DIE(1970, Fr./Ital.); DEADLY TRAP, THE(1972, Fr./Ital.)
Marian Chevalier
RASPUTIN(1932, Ger.)
Maurice Chevalier
INNOCENTS OF PARIS(1929); LOVE PARADE, THE(1929); BIG POND, THE(1930); PLAYBOY OF PARIS(1930); SMILING LIEUTENANT, THE(1931); LOVE ME TONIGHT(1932); MAKE ME A STAR(1932); ONE HOUR WITH YOU(1932); BEDTIME STORY, A(1933); WAY TO LOVE, THE(1933); MERRY WIDOW, THE(1934); FOLIES DERGERE(1935); BELOVED VAGABOND, THE(1936, Brit.); BREAK THE

NEWS(1938, Brit.); PERSONAL COLUMN(1939, Fr.); WITH A SMILE(1939, Fr.); MAN OF THE HOUR, THE(1940, Fr.), a, w; MAN ABOUT TOWN(1947, Fr.); JUST ME(1950, Fr.); ROYAL AFFAIR, A(1950); SCHLAGER-PARADE(1953); CENTO ANNI D'AMORE(1954, Ital.); MY SEVEN LITTLE SINS(1956, Fr./Ital.); LOVE IN THE AFTERNOON(1957); GIGI(1958); COUNT YOUR BLESSINGS(1959); BREATH OF SCANDAL, A(1960); CAN-CAN(1960); PEPE(1960); FANNY(1961); BLACK TIGHTS(1962, Fr.); IN SEARCH OF THE CASTAWAYS(1962, Brit.); JESSICA(1962, U.S./Ital./Fr.); NEW KIND OF LOVE, A(1963); I'D RATHER BE RICH(1964); PANIC BUTTON(1964); MONKEYS, GO HOME!(1967); ARISTOCATS, THE(1970)

Olivia Chevalier
LOVE IN THE AFTERNOON(1957)

Paul Chevalier
MORE DEADLY THAN THE MALE(1961, Brit.), w

Yvonne Chevalier
Misc. Silents
FORTUNES OF FIFI, THE(1917)

L. Chevallier
MADEMOISELLE(1966, Fr./Brit.)

Robert Chevassu
TWO OR THREE THINGS I KNOW ABOUT HER(1970, Fr.)

Maxine Chevelier
SINGAPORE(1947)

Roy P. Cheverton
LOVE IS A CAROUSEL(1970), p, d, ph

Edmond Chevie
ROCK, PRETTY BABY(1956), p; EIGHTEEN AND ANXIOUS(1957), p

Hector Chevigny
YOU CAN'T ESCAPE FOREVER(1942), w

Dick Chevillat
SHE GETS HER MAN(1945), w; NEPTUNE'S DAUGHTER(1949), w

Francis Chevillon
RETURN OF MARTIN GUERRE, THE(1983, Fr.)

Maurice Chevit
TWO ARE GUILTY(1964, Fr.); SLEEPING CAR MURDER THE(1966, Fr.)

Cecile Chevreau
DEADLOCK(1943, Brit.); CANDLELIGHT IN ALGERIA(1944, Brit.); MELBA(1953, Brit.); SPACEWAYS(1953, Brit.); PAID TO KILL(1954, Brit.); PRIVATE POOLEY(1962, Brit./E. Ger.)

Lita Chevret
LOCKED DOOR, THE(1929); WORDS AND MUSIC(1929); PAY OFF, THE(1930); EVERYTHING'S ROSIE(1931); KEPT HUSBANDS(1931); LAUGH AND GET RICH(1931); ROYAL BED, THE(1931); GIRL CRAZY(1932); LADIES OF THE JURY(1932); ROCKABYE(1932); SYMPHONY OF SIX MILLION(1932); DARING DAUGHTERS(1933); GOLDIE GETS ALONG(1933); MAN WHO DARED, THE(1933); GLAMOUR(1934); DANTE'S INFERNO(1935); ESCAPADE(1935); FOLLOW THE FLEET(1936); ROMEO AND JULIET(1936); ESPIONAGE(1937); SANDFLOW(1937); REBELLIOUS DAUGHTERS(1938); WOMEN, THE(1939); FATAL HOUR, THE(1940); MIDNIGHT LIMITED(1940); MY LITTLE CHICKADEE(1940); PHILADELPHIA STORY, THE(1940)

Jean Chevrier
MESSALINE(1952, Fr./Ital.); AFFAIRS OF MESSALINA, THE(1954, Ital.); NAPOLEON(1955, Fr.); DOCTORS, THE(1956, Fr.); TONIGHT THE SKIRTS FLY(1956, Fr.); ROYAL AFFAIRS IN VERSAILLES(1957, Fr.)

Alex Chevron
FOLIES DERGERE(1935)

John Chevron
GOLIATH AND THE SINS OF BABYLON(1964, Ital.)

Jon Chevron
HATARI!(1962); SHAFT IN AFRICA(1973)

Caroline Chew
GOOD EARTH, THE(1937)

Frank Chew
GANG WAR(1928); CHINATOWN NIGHTS(1929)
Silents
FOREIGN DEVILS(1927); FAR CALL, THE(1929)

Gloria Ann Chew
CHINA'S LITTLE DEVILS(1945)

Laureen Chew
CHAN IS MISSING(1982)

Richard Chew
WHEN YOU COMIN' BACK, RED RYDER?(1979), ed; CONVERSATION, THE(1974), ed; ONE FLEW OVER THE CUCKOO'S NEST(1975), ed; STAR WARS(1977), ed; GOIN' SOUTH(1978), ed; MY FAVORITE YEAR(1982), ed; RISKY BUSINESS(1983), ed

Sam Chew
SKIN GAME(1971); THIS IS A HIJACK(1973); RATTLERS(1976); LOVE AND BULLETS(1979, Brit.); TIME WALKER(1982); 10 TO MIDNIGHT(1983)
Misc. Talkies
RATTLERS(1976)

Sam Chew, Jr.
SWEET RIDE, THE(1968); CHANGES(1969); FORTY CARATS(1973); SERIAL(1980)

Virgilia Chew
FUGITIVE KIND, THE(1960)

Chewikar
CAIRO(1963)

Wallace Chewing
MONSIEUR VERDOUX(1947), ph

Edward Entero Chey
1984
KILLING FIELDS, THE(1984, Brit.)

Katherine Krapum Chey
1984
KILLING FIELDS, THE(1984, Brit.)

Pemylot Cheydon
NIGHT CREATURE(1979), ph

Georges Cheyko
DON'T TEMPT THE DEVIL(1964, Fr./Ital.), p; LIARS, THE(1964, Fr.), p

Norman Cheyne
Silents
GIRL WHO LOVES A SOLDIER, THE(1916, Brit.)

Peter Cheyney
WIFE OF GENERAL LING, THE(1938, Brit.), w; UNEASY TERMS(1948, Brit.), w; DIPLOMATIC COURIER(1952), w; MEET MR. CALLAGHAN(1954, Brit.), w; YOUR TURN, DARLING(1963, Fr.), w

The Chez Paree Adorables
SOMEBODY LOVES ME(1952)

Chao Li Chi
OPEN THE DOOR AND SEE ALL THE PEOPLE(1964)

Chao-Li Chi
BIG BRAWL, THE(1980); EYEWITNESS(1981)

Chiu Ah Chi
SECRET, THE(1979, Hong Kong)

Dr. Hsin Kung Chuan Chi
THIRTY SECONDS OVER TOKYO(1944)

Greta Chi
FIVE GATES TO HELL(1959); LISETTE(1961); FATHOM(1967)

Huang Pei Chi
CALL HIM MR. SHATTER(1976, Hong Kong)

Lin Chen Chi
CLEOPATRA JONES AND THE CASINO OF GOLD(1975 U. S. Hong Kong)

Liu Chi
SHEPHERD GIRL, THE(1965, Hong Kong), ph; VERMILION DOOR(1969, Hong Kong), ph

Lo Chi
EMPRESS WU(1965, Hong Kong)

Mar Chi
WHITE ROSE OF HONG KONG(1965, Jap.)

Pham Phuoc Chi
YANK IN VIET-NAM, A(1964)

Yang Chi-ching
LOVE ETERNE, THE(1964, Hong Kong); LADY GENERAL, THE(1965, Hong Kong); SHEPHERD GIRL, THE(1965, Hong Kong); VERMILION DOOR(1969, Hong Kong)

Cheng Chi-hung
1984
AH YING(1984, Hong Kong)

Chan Chi-jui
ENCHANTING SHADOW, THE(1965, Hong Kong), ed

Chen Chi-jui
LAST WOMAN OF SHANG, THE(1964, Hong Kong), art d; LOVE ETERNE, THE(1964, Hong Kong), art d; GRAND SUBSTITUTION, THE(1965, Hong Kong), art d; MERMAID, THE(1966, Hong Kong), art d

Yu Chi-kung
DRAGON INN(1968, Chi.)

Kuo Chia
SACRED KNIVES OF VENGEANCE, THE(1974, Hong Kong), w

Jean Cesar Chiabaut
FIRST TIME, THE(1978, Fr.), ph

Minoru Chiaki
SEVEN SAMURAI, THE(1956, Jap.); GIGANTIS(1959, Jap./U.S.); HIDDEN FORTRESS, THE(1959, Jap.); IKIRU(1960, Jap.); THRONE OF BLOOD(1961, Jap.); LOWER DEPTHS, THE(1962, Jap.); IDIOT, THE(1963, Jap.); YOUTH AND HIS AMULET, THE(1963, Jap.); INHERITANCE, THE(1964, Jap.); FACE OF ANOTHER, THE(1967, Jap.); I LIVE IN FEAR(1967, Jap.)

Jeanine Chialvo
PUBERTY BLUES(1983, Aus.), ed

Milvia Chianelli
VITELLONI(1956, Ital./Fr.)

Dominic Chianese
FUZZ(1972); GODFATHER, THE, PART II(1974); DOG DAY AFTERNOON(1975); ALL THE PRESIDENT'S MEN(1976); ON THE YARD(1978); ...AND JUSTICE FOR ALL(1979); FIREPOWER(1979, Brit.); FORT APACHE, THE BRONX(1981)

Dominick Chianese
FINGERS(1978)

Francesco Saverio Chianese
LA CAGE AUX FOLLES II(1981, Ital./Fr.), art d; KRULL(1983), art d; AMADEUS(1984), art d & set d

David Chiang
TRIPLE IRONS(1973, Hong Kong)

George Chiang
MAME(1974); CHARLIE CHAN AND THE CURSE OF THE DRAGON QUEEN(1981)

Ma Chi Chiang
EXIT THE DRAGON, ENTER THE TIGER(1977, Hong Kong)

Sylvia Chiang
SECRET, THE(1979, Hong Kong)

Renata Chiantioni
CROSSED SWORDS(1954)

Ernato Chiantoni
ROMANOFF AND JULIET(1961)

Renato Chiantoni
BAREFOOT CONTESSA, THE(1954); MAN WHO WAGGED HIS TAIL, THE(1961, Ital./Span.); ARIZONA COLT(1965, It./Fr./Span.); WEB OF VIOLENCE(1966, Ital./Span.); SECRET OF SANTA VITTORIA, THE(1969)

Roy Chiao
GOLDEN NEEDLES(1974)
1984
INDIANA JONES AND THE TEMPLE OF DOOM(1984)

Cristofaro Chiapparino
THREE BROTHERS(1982, Ital.)

Maurizio Chiara
ANGEL WORE RED, THE(1960), cos

Piero Chiara
MAN WHO CAME FOR COFFEE, THE(1970, Ital.), w

Tommaso Chiaretti
HUNCHBACK OF ROME, THE(1963, Ital.), w

Margherita Chiari
TRAGEDY OF A RIDICULOUS MAN, THE(1982, Ital.)
Mario Chiari
MIRACLE IN MILAN(1951, Ital.), w; BELLISSIMA(1952, Ital.); LOVES OF THREE QUEENS, THE(1954, Ital./Fr.), art d; TOO BAD SHE'S BAD(1954, Ital.), art d; VITELLONI(1956, Ital./Fr.), art d; WAR AND PEACE(1956, Ital./U.S.), art d; TEMPEST(1958, Ital./Yugo./Fr.), art d; THIS ANGRY AGE(1958, Ital./Fr.), art d; NEOPOLITAN CAROUSEL(1961, Ital.), art d; WHITE NIGHTS(1961, Ital./Fr.), art d; RELUCTANT SAINT, THE(1962, U.S./Ital.), art d; HUNCHBACK OF ROME, THE(1963, Ital.), art d; SON OF THE RED CORSAIR(1963, Ital.), art d; CONQUERED CITY(1966, Ital.), art d; DOCTOR DOLITTLE(1967), prod d; WEEKEND, ITALIAN STYLE(1967, Fr./Ital./Span.), art d; QUEENS, THE(1968, Ital./Fr.), art d; FRAULEIN DOKTOR(1969, Ital./Yugo.), prod d; DESERTER, THE(1971 Ital./Yugo.), prod d; LUDWIG(1973, Ital./Ger./Fr.), art d; KING KONG(1976), prod d; WOMANLIGHT(1979, Fr./Ger./Ital.), art d; CLAIR DE FEMME(1980,Fr.), art d
Maurizio Chiari
MAGNIFICENT CUCKOLD, THE(1965, Fr./Ital.), art d, cos; RUN FOR YOUR WIFE(1966, Fr./Ital.), art d; DEVIL IN LOVE, THE(1968, Ital.), cos; TREASURE OF SAN GENNARO(1968, Fr./Ital./Ger.), cos
Ugo Chiari
GLADIATORS, THE(1970, Swed.)
Vito Chiari
PEDDLIN' IN SOCIETY(1949, Ital.); HEART AND SOUL(1950, Ital.)
Walter Chiari
BELLISSIMA(1952, Ital.); DONATELLA(1956, Ital.); LITTLE HUT, THE(1957); NANA(1957, Fr./Ital.); BONJOUR TRISTESSE(1958); LET'S TALK ABOUT WOMEN(1964, Fr./Ital.); LOVE, THE ITALIAN WAY(1964, Ital.); DAY IN COURT, A(1965, Ital.); SUCKER, THE(1966, Fr./Ital.); THEY'RE A WEIRD MOB(1966, Aus.); CHIMES AT MIDNIGHT(1967, Span.,Switz.); MADE IN ITALY(1967, Fr./Ital.); GIRL GAME(1968, Braz./Fr./Ital.); THOSE DARING YOUNG MEN IN THEIR JAUNTY JALOPIES(1969, Fr./Brit./ Ital.); SQUEEZE A FLOWER(1970, Aus.); VALACHI PAPERS, THE(1972, Ital./Fr.); ZIG-ZAG(1975, Fr/Ital.)
Deborah Chiariamonte
OSTERMAN WEEKEND, THE(1983)
Luigi Chiarini
INDISCRETION OF AN AMERICAN WIFE(1954, U.S./Ital.), w
Violetta Chiarini
IN SEARCH OF GREGORY(1970, Brit./Ital.)
Jerry Chiat
FUNNY FACE(1957)
S. Chiatsintova
VOW, THE(1947, USSR.)
M. Chiaureli
THEY WANTED PEACE(1940, USSR), d&w
Mikhail Chiaureli
VOW, THE(1947, USSR.), d, w
Misc. Silents
MURDER OF GENERAL GRYAZNOV, THE(1921, USSR); SABA(1929, USSR), d
Hisa Chiba
JAPANESE WAR BRIDE(1952)
Ichiro Chiba
SEVEN SAMURAI, THE(1956, Jap.); IKIRU(1960, Jap.)
Nobuo Chiba
MY GEISHA(1962)
Shigeki Chiba
NO GREATER LOVE THAN THIS(1969, Jap.), w
Shinichi "Sonny" Chiba
TERROR BENEATH THE SEA(1966, Jap.)
Sonny Chiba
VIRUS(1980, Jap.); TIME SLIP(1981, Jap.), a, ch; BUSHIDO BLADE, THE(1982 Brit./U.S.)
Misc. Talkies
BODYGUARD, THE(1976)
Sonny [Shinichi] Chiba
MESSAGE FROM SPACE(1978, Jap.)
Toshio Chiba
BUDDHA(1965, Jap.)
Yasuke Chiba
DAPHNE, THE(1967), d
Yasuki Chiba
NIGHT IN HONG KONG, A(1961, Jap.), d; DIFFERENT SONS(1962, Jap.), d; STAR OF HONG KONG(1962, Jap.), d; HONOLULU-TOKYO-HONG KONG(1963, Hong Kong/Jap.), d; NIGHT IN BANGKOK(1966, Jap.), d
Marissa Chibas
1984
COLD FEET(1984)
Nikolai Chibbius
ROAD HOME, THE(1947, USSR)
Chicago Cubs
DEATH ON THE DIAMOND(1934)
Ben Nye Chicago Historical Society
ST. VALENTINE'S DAY MASSACRE, THE(1967), makeup
Chicago Vice Commission
Silents
IS YOUR DAUGHTER SAFE?(1927)
Lokelani S. Chicarell
HAWAII(1966)
Emily Chicester
Misc. Silents
BURGLAR-PROOF(1920)
Chichay [Amparo Custodio]
NO MAN IS AN ISLAND(1962)
Pierre Chicherio
PRICE OF FLESH, THE(1962, Fr.), w
Dan Chichester
1984
RED DAWN(1984), cos

Emily Chichester
Silents
GOD'S OUTLAW(1919); NUGGET NELL(1919); OUT OF LUCK(1919); MISS HOBBS(1920)
Misc. Silents
PEPPY POLLY(1919); ONCE TO EVERY WOMAN(1920); RIDER OF THE KING LOG, THE(1921); WEDDING BELLS(1921)
D. Chichinadze
DRAGONFLY, THE(1955 USSR)
Chichuahua
LAST SUNSET, THE(1961)
Chick
JAIL BAIT(1954)
Chick Farr and Farland
MURDER AT THE CABARET(1936, Brit.)
Chickie and Buck
COWBOY CANTEEN(1944)
The Chico Hamilton Quintet
SWEET SMELL OF SUCCESS(1957)
Chico the Horse
FRONTIER DAYS(1934)
Michele Chicoine
EXPLOSION(1969, Can.)
Michelle Chicoine
Misc. Talkies
TOMORROW MAN, THE(1979)
Etienne Chicot
LIKE A TURTLE ON ITS BACK(1981, Fr.)
Rita Joelson Chidester
CINDERELLA LIBERTY(1973)
Denmore Chief
LONG SHOT, THE(1939)
Chief Akawanush
SILENT ENEMY, THE(1930)
Chief American Horse
TOMAHAWK(1951)
Chief Bad Bear
TOMAHAWK(1951)
Chief Big Tree
FIGHTING CARAVANS(1931); RED FORK RANGE(1931); GOLDEN WEST, THE(1932); KING OF THE ARENA(1933); CAT'S PAW, THE(1934); WHEELS OF DESTINY(1934); SINGING VAGABOND, THE(1935); HILLS OF OLD WYOMING(1937); LOST HORIZON(1937); MAID OF SALEM(1937); GIRL OF THE GOLDEN WEST, THE(1938); STAGECOACH(1939); SUSANNAH OF THE MOUNTIES(1939); BRIGHAM YOUNG-FRONTIERSMAN(1940); HUDSON'S BAY(1940); WESTERN UNION(1941)
Silents
HUNTRESS, THE(1923); IRON HORSE, THE(1924); DESERT'S TOLL, THE(1926); RANSON'S FOLLY(1926); PAINTED PONIES(1927); OVERLAND TELEGRAPH, THE(1929); SIOUX BLOOD(1929)
Misc. Silents
SPOILERS OF THE WEST(1927)
Chief Blue Eagle
GUNMAN'S WALK(1958)
Chief Bright Fire
PONY SOLDIER(1952)
Chief Dan George
SMITH(1969); LITTLE BIG MAN(1970); CANCEL MY RESERVATION(1972); BEARS AND I, THE(1974); HARRY AND TONTO(1974); COLD JOURNEY(1975, Can.); OUTLAW JOSEY WALES, THE(1976); SHADOW OF THE HAWK(1976, Can.); SPIRIT OF THE WIND(1979)
Chief Dark Hawk
RIDERS OF THE DAWN(1937)
Chief David Perez Espinosa
FITZCARRALDO(1982)
Chief Eagle Wing
Silents
RANSON'S FOLLY(1926)
Chief Joe Buffalo
SHERIFF OF FRACTURED JAW, THE(1958, Brit.)
Chief John Big Tree
DESTRY RIDES AGAIN(1939); TOO MANY GIRLS(1940); SHE WORE A YELLOW RIBBON(1949); DEVIL'S DOORWAY(1950)
Chief Jonas Applegarth
SHERIFF OF FRACTURED JAW, THE(1958, Brit.)
Chief Little Wolf
WE'RE IN THE MONEY(1935)
Chief Lomoiro
VISIT TO A CHIEF'S SON(1974)
Chief Long Lance
SILENT ENEMY, THE(1930)
Chief Many Treaties
OUTLAW EXPRESS(1938); PIONEERS, THE(1941); KING OF THE STALLIONS(1942); LAW RIDES AGAIN, THE(1943); BUFFALO BILL(1944); LAST OF THE REDMEN(1947); BLACK BART(1948); SUNDOWN RIDERS(1948)
Chief Miguel
FITZCARRALDO(1982)
Chief Nicolas
FITZCARRALDO(1982)
Chief Nipo T. Strongheart
PONY SOLDIER(1952), tech adv
Chief Pascal
FITZCARRALDO(1982)
Chief Sky Eagle
SHE WORE A YELLOW RIBBON(1949)
Chief Soldani
PIONEERS, THE(1941)

Chief Standing Bear
SANTA FE TRAIL, THE(1930); CONQUERING HORDE, THE(1931); TEXAS PION-EERS(1932); CYCLONE OF THE SADDLE(1935); FIGHTING PIONEERS(1935)
Silents
WHITE OAK(1921)
Chief Thunder Cloud
99 WOUNDS(1931); CYCLONE OF THE SADDLE(1935); FIGHTING PIONEERS(1935); RUSTLER'S PARADISE(1935); SINGING VAGABOND, THE(1935); RIDERS OF THE WHISTLING SKULL(1937); MURDER ON THE YUKON(1940); LAW RIDES AGAIN, THE(1943); SONORA STAGECOACH(1944); RENEGADE GIRL(1946); I KILLED GERONIMO(1950); INDIAN TERRITORY(1950)
Misc. Talkies
BLAZING ACROSS THE PECOS(1948); CALL OF THE FOREST(1949)
Chief Thunder-Cloud
HI-YO SILVER(1940); SHUT MY BIG MOUTH(1942)
Chief Thunderbird
LAUGHING BOY(1934); FOR THE SERVICE(1936); SILLY BILLIES(1936); NORTH-WEST MOUNTED POLICE(1940); FALCON OUT WEST, THE(1944)
Chief Thundercloud
RAMONA(1936); RENFREW OF THE ROYAL MOUNTED(1937); CAT AND THE CANARY, THE(1939); FIGHTING MAD(1939); UNION PACIFIC(1939); HUDSON'S BAY(1940); NORTHWEST MOUNTED POLICE(1940); TYPHOON(1940); WYO-MING(1940); YOUNG BUFFALO BILL(1940); WESTERN UNION(1941); KING OF THE STALLIONS(1942); LADY IN A JAM(1942); MY GAL SAL(1942); BUFFALO BILL(1944); OUTLAW TRAIL(1944); NOB HILL(1945); BADMAN'S TERRITORY(1946); ROMANCE OF THE WEST(1946); SENATOR WAS INDISCREET, THE(1947); PRAI-RIE, THE(1948); COLT .45(1950); DAVY CROCKETT, INDIAN SCOUT(1950); TICKET TO TOMAHAWK(1950); TRAVELING SALESWOMAN(1950); SANTA FE(1951)
Chief Thundersky
INDIAN TERRITORY(1950)
Chief Tug Smith
WHITE BUFFALO, THE(1977); SUPERMAN(1978); WINDWALKER(1980)
Chief White Horse
STAGECOACH(1939)
Chief White Spear
Silents
IRON HORSE, THE(1924); PAINTED PONIES(1927)
Chief Whitehorse
Silents
WAR PAINT(1926)
Chief Yellow Robe
SILENT ENEMY, THE(1930)
Chief Yowlache
Silents
ELLA CINDERS(1926); WAR PAINT(1926)
Chief Yowlachi
CANYON PASSAGE(1946); BOWERY BUCKAROOS(1947)
Chief Yowlachie
SANTA FE TRAIL, THE(1930); NORTHWEST MOUNTED POLICE(1940); OUTLAWS OF THE CHEROKEE TRAIL(1941); KING OF THE STALLIONS(1942); RIDE 'EM COWBOY(1942); OREGON TRAIL SCOUTS(1947); SENATOR WAS INDISCREET, THE(1947); PALEFACE, THE(1948); PRAIRIE, THE(1948); MA AND PA KETT-LE(1949); MY FRIEND IRMA(1949); CHEROKEE UPRISING(1950); INDIAN TERRI-TORY(1950); MY FRIEND IRMA GOES WEST(1950); TICKET TO TOMAHAWK(1950); TRAVELING SALESWOMAN(1950); PAINTED HILLS, THE(1951); WARPATH(1951); LONE STAR(1952); PATHFINDER, THE(1952); SPIRIT OF ST. LOUIS, THE(1957); HELLER IN PINK TIGHTS(1960)
Michael Chieffo
LAST AMERICAN VIRGIN, THE(1982)
The Chieftans
GREY FOX, THE(1983, Can.), m
Chen Ying Chieh
GRAND SUBSTITUTION, THE(1965, Hong Kong)
Han Ying Chieh
FISTS OF FURY(1973, Chi.)
Jen Chieh
LOVE ETERNE, THE(1964, Hong Kong)
Li Chieh
DRAGON INN(1968, Chi.)
Tsao Chien
DRAGON INN(1968, Chi.)
Stefano Chierchie
CLIMAX, THE(1967, Fr., Ital.)
Yvan Chiffre
ANATOMY OF A MARRIAGE(MY DAYS WITH JEAN-MARC AND MY NIGHTS WITH FRANCOISE)**1/2 (1964 Fr.)
1984
CHEECH AND CHONG'S THE CORSICAN BROTHERS(1984)
Chignone
THIEF OF BAGHDAD, THE(1961, Ital./Fr.)
Ch'eng Pin Chih
RETURN OF THE DRAGON(1974, Chin.)
Huang Jen Chih
RETURN OF THE DRAGON(1974, Chin.)
Yeh Ling Chih
BLOOD MONEY(1974, U.S./Hong Kong/Ital./Span.)
Yang Chih-ching
MAGNIFICENT CONCUBINE, THE(1964, Hong Kong); ENCHANTING SHADOW, THE(1965, Hong Kong)
Ku Chih-hui
FISTS OF FURY(1973, Chi.), m
Wang Chih-po
MAGNIFICENT CONCUBINE, THE(1964, Hong Kong), w
Paul Chihara
DEATH RACE 2000(1975), m; DANDY, THE ALL AMERICAN GIRL(1976), m; I NEVER PROMISED YOU A ROSE GARDEN(1977), m; BAD NEWS BEARS GO TO JAPAN, THE(1978), m; PRINCE OF THE CITY(1981), m; SURVIVORS, THE(1983), m
1984
CRACKERS(1984), m; IMPULSE(1984), m

Akiko Chihaya
Misc. Silents
CROSSWAYS(1928, Jap.)
Yang Chihching
LAST WOMAN OF SHANG, THE(1964, Hong Kong)
Monzaemon Chikamatsu
PRODIGAL SON, THE(1964, Jap.), w; DOUBLE SUICIDE(1970, Jap.), w
Inoue Chikaya
TORA! TORA! TORA!(1970, U.S./Jap.), ed
M. Chikhladze
THEY WANTED PEACE(1940, USSR)
Mikhail Chikiryov
DUEL, THE(1964, USSR), makeup; WAR AND PEACE(1968, USSR), makeup
Hayde Chikly
Misc. Silents
GIRL FROM CARTHAGE, THE(1924, Tunisia)
Scemana Chikly
Misc. Silents
GIRL FROM CARTHAGE, THE(1924, Tunisia), d
Mikhail Chikovani
WAR AND PEACE(1968, USSR), cos
Nani Chikvinidze
STEPCHILDREN(1962, USSR)
John E. Chilberg II
BATTLESTAR GALACTICA(1979), art d
1984
STAR TREK III: THE SEARCH FOR SPOCK(1984), art d
Barbara Chilcott
STOP ME BEFORE I KILL!(1961, Brit.); TRAP, THE(1967, Can./Brit.); LIES MY FATHER TOLD ME(1975, Can.)
Beth Child
1984
CAREFUL, HE MIGHT HEAR YOU(1984, Aus.); RAZORBACK(1984, Aus.)
Cyd Child
PINK PANTHER STRIKES AGAIN, THE(1976, Brit.); STICK UP, THE(1978, Brit.)
Jennifer Child
1984
THIS IS SPINAL TAP(1984)
Jeremy Child
PRIVILEGE(1967, Brit.); DECLINE AND FALL... OF A BIRD WATCHER(1969, Brit.); OH! WHAT A LOVELY WAR(1969, Brit.); PLAY DIRTY(1969, Brit.); GLADIATORS, THE(1970, Swed.); YOUNG WINSTON(1972, Brit.); EMILY(1976, Brit.); STUD, THE(1979, Brit.); SIR HENRY AT RAWLINSON END(1980, Brit.); CHANEL SOLI-TAIRE(1981); HIGH ROAD TO CHINA(1983)
1984
GIVE MY REGARDS TO BROAD STREET(1984, Brit.)
Kirsty Child
PICNIC AT HANGING ROCK(1975, Aus.)
Marilyn Child
MAN WHO LOVED WOMEN, THE(1983)
Matthew Child
SUDDEN IMPACT(1983)
O. Child
Silents
GANGSTERS OF NEW YORK, THE(1914)
Richard Washburn Child
FORGOTTEN FACES(1936), w; GENTLEMAN AFTER DARK, A(1942), w
Erskine Childers
1984
RIDDLE OF THE SANDS, THE(1984, Brit.), w
Ethel Childers
Misc. Silents
FLASHING STEEDS(1925)
Naomi Childers
MIGHTY BARNUM, THE(1934); WHITE HEAT(1934); SAN FRANCISCO(1936); LOST ANGEL(1944); MRS. PARKINGTON(1944); WEEKEND AT THE WAL-DORF(1945); ZIEGFELD FOLLIES(1945); COCKEYED MIRACLE, THE(1946); SEA OF GRASS, THE(1947)
Silents
MR. BARNES OF NEW YORK(1914); TANGLE, THE(1914); ISLAND OF REGENER-ATION, THE(1915); COURAGE(1921); SUCCESS(1923)
Misc. Silents
TURN OF THE ROAD, THE(1915); DEVIL'S PRIZE, THE(1916); FATHERS OF MEN(1916); FOOTLIGHTS OF FATE, THE(1916); PRICE OF FAME, THE(1916); WRITING ON THE WALL, THE(1916); AUCTION OF VIRTUE, THE(1917); AFTER HIS OWN HEART(1919); BLIND MAN'S EYES(1919); DIVORCEE, THE(1919); HU-MAN DESIRE, THE(1919); LORD AND LADY ALGY(1919); SHADOWS OF SUSPI-CION(1919); DUDS(1920); EARTHBOUND(1920); GAY LORD QUEX, THE(1920); STREET CALLED STRAIGHT, THE(1920); HOLD YOUR HORSES(1921); MR. BARNES OF NEW YORK(1922)
Charles Childerstone
BETRAYAL(1932, Brit.); I'LL STICK TO YOU(1933, Brit.); THIRTEENTH CANDLE, THE(1933, Brit.); LITTLE FRIEND(1934, Brit.); MURDER IN THE FAMILY(1938, Brit.)
Ernest Childerstone
GREAT STUFF(1933, Brit.)
Dancing Children
SANTA'S CHRISTMAS CIRCUS(1966)
Children of the Corona Academy
OLD MAC(1961, Brit.)
The Children's Film Unit
1984
DARK ENEMY(1984, Brit.), w
Alice Childress
UPTIGHT(1968); HERO AIN'T NOTHIN' BUT A SANDWICH, A(1977), w
Alvin Childress
ANNA LUCASTA(1958); MAN IN THE NET, THE(1959); THUNDERBOLT AND LIGHTFOOT(1974); DARKTOWN STRUTTERS(1975); DAY OF THE LOCUST, THE(1975); BINGO LONG TRAVELING ALL-STARS AND MOTOR KINGS, THE(1976); MAIN EVENT, THE(1979)

Misc. Talkies
KEEP PUNCHING(1939)
Lee Childress
TERROR IN THE JUNGLE(1968)
Scott Childress
TOGETHER FOR DAYS(1972)
Deborah Childs
MELODY(1971, Brit.)
Herbert Childs
WAY OF A GAUCHO(1952), w
1984
FLASH OF GREEN, A(1984)
Peter Childs
O LUCKY MAN!(1973, Brit.); DIRTY KNIGHT'S WORK(1976, Brit.)
Ray Childs
Misc. Silents
LURE OF THE WEST(1925); BEYOND ALL ODDS(1926); BORN TO BATTLE(1926)
Maj. Richard W.N. Childs, USAR
TOKYO FILE 212(1951)
Sally Childs
DOUBLE EXPOSURE(1982), makeup
Stephen Childs
ALL AT SEA(1970, Brit.)
Sylvia Childs
JUST MY LUCK(1957, Brit.)
Ted Childs
SWEENEY(1977, Brit.), p; SWEENEY 2(1978, Brit.), p; QUATERMASS CONCLU-SION(1980, Brit.), p
Tracy Childs
RICHARD'S THINGS(1981, Brit.)
Linden Chiles
SANCTUARY(1961); RAGE TO LIVE, A(1965); INCIDENT AT PHANTOM HILL(1966); TEXAS ACROSS THE RIVER(1966); COUNTERPOINT(1967); SULLIVAN'S EMPIRE(1967); EYE OF THE CAT(1969); WHERE THE BUFFALO ROAM(1980); FORBIDDEN WORLD(1982)
1984
CLOAK AND DAGGER(1984)
Lois Chiles
WAY WE WERE, THE(1973); TOGETHER FOR DAYS(1972); GREAT GATSBY, THE(1974); COMA(1978); DEATH ON THE NILE(1978, Brit.); MOONRAKER(1979, Brit.)
1984
RAW COURAGE(1984)
Misc. Talkies
TOGETHER FOR DAYS(1972)
Chill Wills and his Avalon Boys
BAR 20 RIDES AGAIN(1936)
Chill Wills and the Avalon Boys
IT'S A GIFT(1934); CALL OF THE PRAIRIE(1936); HIDEAWAY GIRL(1937)
Doris Chillcot
WOLFPEN PRINCIPLE, THE(1974, Can.)
Maj. Alexander Chilton
Silents
DRESS PARADE(1927), w
Charles Chilton
OH! WHAT A LOVELY WAR(1969, Brit.), w
Chilton & Thomas
LOVE AND HISSES(1937); SING AS YOU SWING(1937, Brit.)
Colin Chilvers
SUPERMAN(1978), spec eff; SATURN 3(1980), spec eff; SUPERMAN II(1980), spec eff; CONDORMAN(1981), spec eff; INCUBUS, THE(1982, Can.), spec eff; SUPERMAN III(1983), spec eff
Simon Chilvers
HIGH ROLLING(1977, Aus.); BUDDIES(1983, Aus.)
Gregori Chimara
Misc. Silents
CROWN OF THORNS(1934, Ger.)
Alberto Chimens
HERCULES VS THE GIANT WARRIORS(1965 Fr./Ital.), p
Melissa Chimenti
CHINO(1976, Ital., Span., Fr.)
Robert Chimento
1984
FLESHBURN(1984)
Alberto Chimenz
PLANETS AGAINST US, THE(1961, Ital./Fr.), p
Chin
COUNTRYMAN(1982, Jamaica)
Anthony Chin
ABOMINABLE SNOWMAN OF THE HIMALAYAS, THE(1957, Brit.); SAVAGE INNOCENTS, THE(1960, Brit.); COUNTESS FROM HONG KONG, A(1967, Brit.); MATTER OF INNOCENCE, A(1968, Brit.)
Clint Chin
UNMARRIED WOMAN, AN(1978); TEMPEST(1982)
Glen Chin
JEKYLL AND HYDE...TOGETHER AGAIN(1982)
Gum Chin
LADY TO LOVE, A(1930)
John Chin
MAKE A FACE(1971)
Lu Chin
DRAGON INN(1968, Chi.)
Mary Ann Chin
DON'T GO IN THE HOUSE(1980)
Michael Chin
CHAN IS MISSING(1982), ph
Mona Chin
HEROSTRATUS(1968, Brit.)

Mr. Chin
LEGACY OF BLOOD(1973)
Sophie Chin
LEFT HAND OF GOD, THE(1955)
Tsai Chin
INN OF THE SIXTH HAPPINESS, THE(1958); VIOLENT PLAYGROUND(1958, Brit.); HOT MONEY GIRL(1962, Brit./Ger.); COOL MIKADO, THE(1963, Brit.); FACE OF FU MANCHU, THE(1965, Brit.); INVASION(1965, Brit.); BLOW-UP(1966, Brit.); BRIDES OF FU MANCHU, THE(1966, Brit.); YOU ONLY LIVE TWICE(1967, Brit.); BLOOD OF FU MANCHU, THE(1968, Brit.); CASTLE OF FU MANCHU, THE(1968, Ger./Span./Ital./Brit.); VENGEANCE OF FU MANCHU, THE(1968, Brit./Ger./Hong Kong/Ireland); VIRGIN SOLDIERS, THE(1970, Brit.)
Hu Chin-chuan
SONS OF GOOD EARTH(1967, Hong Kong), d&w; DRAGON INN(1968, Chi.), d
Wang Chin-Feng
FIVE FINGERS OF DEATH(1973, Hong Kong)
Chen Chin-shen
LAST WOMAN OF SHANG, THE(1964, Hong Kong), art d; GRAND SUBSTITUTION, THE(1965, Hong Kong), art d
Trovadores Chinacos
GAY DESPERADO, THE(1936)
Chinchilla
TREASURE ISLAND(1972, Brit./Span./Fr./Ger.)
J.L. Chinchilla
HORSEMEN, THE(1971)
People of ChincoteaqueËVirginia
MISTY(1961)
the Chinese Baby
AMAZING MRS. HOLLIDAY(1943)
1000 Chinese Laborers
Silents
IRON HORSE, THE(1924)
Anthony Ching
DEAD PIGEON ON BEETHOVEN STREET(1972, Ger.)
Bill [William] Ching
TALL MAN RIDING(1955)
Bo Ching
PETTICOAT FEVER(1936); FIRST YANK INTO TOKYO(1945)
Chen Chang Ching
1984
PERILS OF GWENDOLINE, THE(1984, Fr.)
Hoo Ching
Misc. Silents
WAR OF THE TONGS, THE(1917)
Li Ching
MERMAID, THE(1966, Hong Kong); TRIPLE IRONS(1973, Hong Kong)
Lin Ching
MAGNIFICENT CONCUBINE, THE(1964, Hong Kong)
Nellie Gee Ching
PAL JOEY(1957)
William Brooks Ching
MAGNIFICENT MATADOR, THE(1955)
William Ching
BUCK PRIVATES COME HOME(1947); MICHIGAN KID, THE(1947); SOMETHING IN THE WIND(1947); SONG OF SCHEHERAZADE(1947); WISTFUL WIDOW OF WAGON GAP, THE(1947); D.O.A.(1950); IN A LONELY PLACE(1950); SHOWDOWN, THE(1950); SURRENDER(1950); BELLE LE GRAND(1951); OH! SUSANNA(1951); SEA HORNET, THE(1951); BAL TABARIN(1952); NEVER WAVE AT A WAC(1952); PAT AND MIKE(1952); WILD BLUE YONDER, THE(1952); GIVE A GIRL A BREAK(1953); MOONLIGHTER, THE(1953); SCARED STIFF(1953); MY WORLD DIES SCREAMING(1958); ESCORT WEST(1959)
Yang Che Ching
SACRED KNIVES OF VENGEANCE, THE(1974, Hong Kong)
Yeh Ching
MERMAID, THE(1966, Hong Kong)
Chang Ching-chu
FISTS OF FURY(1973, Chi.), ed
Chen Ching-chu
FISTS OF FURY(1973, Chi.), ph
Hung Ching-yun
LOVERS' ROCK(1966, Taiwan), ph
Kieu Chinh
YANK IN VIET-NAM, A(1964); OPERATION CIA(1965)
Lieu Chinh
ANGELS BRIGADE(1980)
L. Chinidzhanei
DREAM COME TRUE, A(1963, USSR)
Garry Chiniquy
HEY THERE, IT'S YOGI BEAR(1964), anim
Gerry Chiniquy
INCREDIBLE MR. LIMPET, THE(1964), spec eff; RAGGEDY ANN AND ANDY(1977), anim
Roland Chiniquy
PUFNSTUF(1970), spec eff
Chinita
HIT PARADE OF 1943(1943); MY GAL LOVES MUSIC(1944)
Chinita Guadalajara Trio
ALLERGIC TO LOVE(1943)
Allan Chinn
CHINA SYNDROME, THE(1979)
Anthony Chinn
NEXT TO NO TIME(1960, Brit.); SATAN NEVER SLEEPS(1962); TARZAN'S THREE CHALLENGES(1963); CHAIRMAN, THE(1969); KREMLIN LETTER, THE(1970); REVENGE OF THE PINK PANTHER(1978); RAIDERS OF THE LOST ARK(1981); HIGH ROAD TO CHINA(1983)
B. Cave Chinn
Misc. Silents
WHERE THE RAINBOW ENDS(1921, Brit.)

Bob Chinn
FIRST YANK INTO TOKYO(1945)
Lori Tan Chinn
AUTHOR! AUTHOR!(1982)
Robert C. Chinn
Misc. Talkies
PANAMA RED(1976), d
Tony Chinn
GAMBLERS, THE(1969)
Dennis Chinnery
WHITE FIRE(1953, Brit.); DELAYED ACTION(1954, Brit.); EMBEZZLER, THE(1954, Brit.); PLAGUE OF THE ZOMBIES, THE(1966, Brit.)
Giuseppe Chinnici
MONSTER OF THE ISLAND(1953, Ital.)
Kakuko Chino
SNOW COUNTRY(1969, Jap.)
Chinook
WOLF HUNTERS, THE(1949); CALL OF THE KLONDIKE(1950); NORTHWEST TERRITORY(1952)
Chinook the Dog
YUKON MANHUNT(1951); YUKON GOLD(1952); FANGS OF THE ARCTIC(1953); NORTHERN PATROL(1953)
Chinook the Wonder Dog
TRAIL OF THE YUKON(1949); SNOW DOG(1950)
Paul Chinpae
SAND PEBBLES, THE(1966)
Anna Maria Chio
MEDEA(1971, Ital./Fr./Ger.)
Annamaria Chio
LAST REBEL, THE(1971)
Sam Chiodi
WHAT'S UP FRONT(1964)
Fred Chiodo
GET OUTTA TOWN(1960)
Sam Chiodo
GET OUTTA TOWN(1960)
Carlo Chionetti
RED DESERT(1965, Fr./Ital.)
Becky Chipman
ISLAND WOMEN(1958)
"Chippie" Chipman
ISLAND WOMEN(1958)
Eve Chipman
SONG AT EVENTIDE(1934, Brit.); BIRDS OF A FEATHER(1935, Brit.); IT HAPPENED IN PARIS(1935, Brit.); SAILING ALONG(1938, Brit.); OLD MOTHER RILEY, DETECTIVE(1943, Brit.)
Eveline Chipman
Misc. Silents
SACRIFICE(1929, Brit.)
Michele Chiponski
MIDDLE AGE CRAZY(1980, Can.)
Elinor Chipp
Silents
AMAZING WIFE, THE(1919), w
Jimmy Chipperfield
THREE LIVES OF THOMASINA, THE(1963, U.S./Brit.), animal
Ray Chippeway
PHYNX, THE(1970)
Jan Chippman
ILLIAC PASSION, THE(1968)
Chiquita
HANDS ACROSS THE BORDER(1943); JAGUAR(1956)
Chiquita Hernandez Orchestra
LAWLESS LAND(1937)
Chiquito
TNT JACKSON(1975)
Misc. Talkies
BAMBOO GODS AND IRON MEN(1974)
Harry Chira
Silents
IDOL OF THE STAGE, THE(1916)
Mario Chirai
MAN CALLED SLEDGE, A(1971, Ital.), prod d
Armand Chirard
SYMPHONIE FANTASTIQUE(1947, Fr.), ph
George Chirello
MACBETH(1948)
George Shorty Chirello
FOLLOW THE BOYS(1944)
George "Shorty" Chirello
LADY FROM SHANGHAI, THE(1948); JUST ACROSS THE STREET(1952); GOLDEN BLADE, THE(1953)
Paul Chirelstein
BUGSY MALONE(1976, Brit.)
G. H. Chirgwin
Silents
BLIND BOY, THE(1917, Brit.)
George H. Chirgwin
Silents
BLIND BOY, THE(1917, Brit.), w
Michael Chirgwin
ROAD WARRIOR, THE(1982, Aus.), ed
Afte Chiriaeff
1984
HEY BABE!(1984, Can.), ed
Lee Chirillo
YAKUZA, THE(1975, U.S./Jap.)

B. Chirkov
1812(1944, USSR)
Boris Chirkov
GREAT CITIZEN, THE(1939, USSR); NEW HORIZONS(1939, USSR); NEW TEACHER, THE(1941, USSR); DREAM OF A COSSACK(1982, USSR)
B. Chirskov
WINGS OF VICTORY(1941, USSR), w
Alex Chirva
MISSION TO MOSCOW(1943)
Gianluigi Chirzzi
MALICIOUS(1974, Ital.)
Kid Chisel
DILLINGER(1945)
Arthur Chishlom
Misc. Silents
BLADYS OF THE STEWPONY(1919, Brit.)
Robert Chishold
FATHER O'FLYNN(1938, Irish)
Anthony Chisholm
PUTNEY SWOPE(1969)
Arthur Chisholm
Misc. Silents
ANGEL OF THE WARD, THE(1915, Brit.)
D. Scatty Chisholm
FOLLOW THE SUN(1951)
Floyd Chisholm
ROSELAND(1977)
George Chisholm
MOUSE ON THE MOON, THE(1963, Brit.); KNACK ... AND HOW TO GET IT, THE(1965, Brit.); SUPERMAN III(1983)
Jack Chisholm
NORTHERN FRONTIER(1935)
Jim Chisholm
LOVE MERCHANT, THE(1966)
Robert Chisholm
LOTTERY BRIDE, THE(1930); COCK O' THE NORTH(1935, Brit.)
Ronald Chisholm
ROSIE!(1967)
Fiona Chislett
NEXT TO NO TIME(1960, Brit.)
Frank Chisnell
IT HAPPENED IN SOHO(1948, Brit.), p&d
H. C. Chisolm
Silents
GOLD RUSH, THE(1925)
Kid Chissell
EX-CHAMP(1939); KNOCKOUT(1941); MY BUDDY(1944); SONG OF ARIZONA(1946); LIKELY STORY, A(1947); GRAND CANYON(1949); SORROWFUL JONES(1949)
Noble "Kid" Chissell
HOME IN INDIANA(1944); JEALOUSY(1945); SET-UP, THE(1949); HELLCATS, THE(1968); THEY SHOOT HORSES, DON'T THEY?(1969); MACHISMO–40 GRAVES FOR 40 GUNS(1970)
Misc. Talkies
WEST IS STILL WILD, THE(1977)
Sandra Chistolini
LEOPARD, THE(1963, Ital.)
A. Chistyakov
DESERTER(1934, USSR); NEW HORIZONS(1939, USSR)
Misc. Silents
MOTHER(1926, USSR)
A.P. Chistyakov
Misc. Silents
END OF ST. PETERSBURG, THE(1927, USSR)
Alexander Chistyakov
THIRTEEN, THE(1937, USSR)
Christopher Chitell
WEEKEND MURDERS, THE(1972, Ital.)
Leela Chitnis
GUIDE, THE(1965, U.S./India)
Chitorin
Misc. Silents
STORY OF SEVEN WHO WERE HANGED(1920, USSR)
Ashay Chitre
Misc. Talkies
GREAT MONKEY RIP-OFF, THE(1979)
Luciano Chittarini
COLOSSUS OF RHODES, THE(1961, Ital., Fr., Span.), w
Chris Chittel
WILD GEESE, THE(1978, Brit.)
Chris Chittell
LAST VALLEY, THE(1971, Brit.); ZULU DAWN(1980, Brit.)
Christopher Chittell
TO SIR, WITH LOVE(1967, Brit.); CHARGE OF THE LIGHT BRIGADE, THE(1968, Brit.); BEAST IN THE CELLAR, THE(1971, Brit.); LONG AGO, TOMORROW(1971, Brit.)
Al Chittenden
NEW ORLEANS UNCENSORED(1955)
Frank Chittenden
STRANGER IN TOWN(1957, Brit.), w
Gano Chittenden
GIRL WHO DARED, THE(1944), art d; MARSHAL OF RENO(1944), art d; MY BEST GAL(1944), art d; SAN ANTONIO KID, THE(1944), art d; SECRETS OF SCOTLAND YARD(1944), art d; SING, NEIGHBOR, SING(1944), art d; STAGECOACH TO MONTEREY(1944), art d; STORM OVER LISBON(1944), art d; STRANGERS IN THE NIGHT(1944), art d; THREE LITTLE SISTERS(1944), art d; TUCSON RAIDERS(1944), art d; DAKOTA(1945), art d; FLAME OF THE BARBARY COAST(1945), art d; GIRLS OF THE BIG HOUSE(1945), art d; GRISSLY'S MILLIONS(1945), art d; OREGON TRAIL(1945), art d; STEPPIN' IN SOCIETY(1945), art d; SWINGIN' ON A RAINBOW(1945), art d; UTAH(1945), art d; GAY BLADES(1946), art d; HELL-

DORADO(1946), art d; MY PAL TRIGGER(1946), art d; PLAINSMAN AND THE LADY(1946), art d; RIO GRANDE RAIDERS(1946), art d; SIOUX CITY SUE(1946), art d; TRAFFIC IN CRIME(1946), art d; TRAIL TO SAN ANTONE(1947), art d; WEB OF DANGER, THE(1947), art d; FLAME, THE(1948), art d; STRIKE IT RICH(1948), art d

Ugo Chitti
BEBO'S GIRL(1964, Ital.)

Bob Chitty
GLENROWAN AFFAIR, THE(1951, Aus.)

Eric Chitty
EYE WITNESS(1950, Brit.); FIRST MEN IN THE MOON(1964, Brit.); DOCTOR ZHIVAGO(1965); LOLA(1971, Brit./Ital.); PLEASE SIR(1971, Brit.); STATUE, THE(1971, Brit.); GREAT EXPECTATIONS(1975, Brit.)

Erick Chitty
HORROR OF IT ALL, THE(1964, Brit.)

Erik Chitty
FORBIDDEN(1949, Brit.); JOHN WESLEY(1954, Brit.); WINDFALL(1955 Brit.); RAISING A RIOT(1957, Brit.); TIME IS MY ENEMY(1957, Brit.); ZOO BABY(1957, Brit.); DEVIL'S DISCIPLE, THE(1959); LEFT, RIGHT AND CENTRE(1959); DAY THEY ROBBED THE BANK OF ENGLAND, THE(1960, Brit.); ROOMMATES(1962, Brit.); NICE GIRL LIKE ME, A(1969, Brit.); SONG OF NORWAY(1970); LUST FOR A VAMPIRE(1971, Brit.); RAILWAY CHILDREN, THE(1971, Brit.); VAULT OF HORROR, THE(1973, Brit.); FLYING SORCERER, THE(1974, Brit.); SEVEN-PER-CENT SOLUTION, THE(1977, Brit.)

Susan Richards Chitty
SONG OF NORWAY(1970)

Joie Chitwood
FIREBALL JUNGLE(1968); LIVE AND LET DIE(1973, Brit.), a, stunts; STUNTS(1977)

Tim Chitwood
HOT STUFF(1979)

Joie Chitwood, Jr.
THUNDER AND LIGHTNING(1977), stunts

Gaetano Chiurazzi
UNDER THE SUN OF ROME(1949, Ital.)

Isabella Chiurco
WARRIORS FIVE(1962)

Natale Chiusano
Silents
CABIRIA(1914, Ital.), ph

S. Chiusi
THEY CALL ME TRINITY(1971, Ital.), spec eff

Naiyana Chivanand
1 2 3 MONSTER EXPRESS(1977, Thai.)

David Chivers
HIDDEN HOMICIDE(1959, Brit.)

Nigel Chivers
Misc. Talkies
MR. HORATIO KNIBBLES(1971)

Chiyaki
THREE STRIPES IN THE SUN(1955)

Yuko Chiyo
WEIRD LOVE MAKERS, THE(1963, Jap.)

A. Chizova
DIMKA(1964, USSR)

N. Chkeidze
THEY WANTED PEACE(1940, USSR)

Revas Chkheidze
FATHER OF A SOLDIER(1966, USSR), d, w

G. Chmara
CASE VAN GELDERN(1932, Ger.)

Gregor Chmara
Misc. Silents
CRIME AND PUNISHMENT(1929, Ger.); RASPUTIN(1929, USSR); STRANGE CASE OF DISTRICT ATTORNEY M.(1930)

Gregori Chmara
PARIS DOES STRANGE THINGS(1957, Fr./Ital.)

Raduz Chmelik
MATTER OF DAYS, A(1969, Fr./Czech.)

N.P. Chmelioff
HOUSE OF DEATH(1932, USSR)

Tadeusz Chmielewski
EVE WANTS TO SLEEP(1961, Pol.), d, w

Feliks Chmurkowski
SARAGOSSA MANUSCRIPT, THE(1972, Pol.)

Emily Cho
LITTLE BIG MAN(1970)

Hyon Cho
STILL OF THE NIGHT(1982)

Keiko Cho
YOUNG GUY GRADUATES(1969, Jap.)

Lim Cho-Cho
Misc. Silents
SONG OF CHINA(1936, Chi.)

Wu Cho-hua
SACRED KNIVES OF VENGEANCE, THE(1974, Hong Kong), ph

Bennett Choate
SWAMP THING(1982), cos

Tim Choate
EUROPEANS, THE(1979, Brit.); JANE AUSTEN IN MANHATTAN(1980); TIMES SQUARE(1980); FIRST TIME, THE(1983)

Tom Choate
GHOST STORY(1981)

Frantisek Chocholaty
FIFTH HORSEMAN IS FEAR, THE(1968, Czech.)

The Chocolate Watch Band
RIOT ON SUNSET STRIP(1967)

Daniel Chodes
FRANCES(1982)

Edward Chodorev
WORLD CHANGES, THE(1933), w

Edward Chodorov
YELLOW JACK(1938), w; CAPTURED(1933), w; MAYOR OF HELL, THE(1933), w; DESIRABLE(1934), p; MADAME DU BARRY(1934), w; ALIBI IKE(1935), p; KIND LADY(1935), w; LIVING ON VELVET(1935), p; SWEET ADELINE(1935), p; CRAIG'S WIFE(1936), p; RICH MAN, POOR GIRL(1938), p; SPRING MADNESS(1938), p, w; WOMAN AGAINST WOMAN(1938), p, w; TELL NO TALES(1939), p; MAN FROM DAKOTA, THE(1940), p; THOSE ENDEARING YOUNG CHARMS(1945), w; UNDER-CURRENT(1946), w; HUCKSTERS, THE(1947), w; ROAD HOUSE(1948), p, w; KIND LADY(1951), w; OH, MEN! OH, WOMEN!(1957), w

Jerome Chodorov
CASE OF THE LUCKY LEGS, THE(1935), w; ALL OVER TOWN(1937), w; DEVIL'S PLAYGROUND(1937), w; REPORTED MISSING(1937), w; CONSPIRACY(1939), w; DULCY(1940), w; MAD EMPRESS, THE(1940), w; TWO GIRLS ON BROADWAY(1940), w; LOUISIANA PURCHASE(1941), w; MURDER IN THE BIG HOUSE(1942), w; MY SISTER EILEEN(1942), w; JUNIOR MISS(1945), w; THOSE ENDEARING YOUNG CHARMS(1945), w; MAN FROM TEXAS, THE(1948), w; MY SISTER EILEEN(1955), w; HAPPY ANNIVERSARY(1959), w

Jerry Chodorov
DANCING FEET(1936), w; GENTLEMAN FROM LOUISIANA(1936), w

Al Choi
MISSION OVER KOREA(1953)

Joseph H. Choi
TRUE CONFESSIONS(1981)

Elizabeth Choice
1984
SECRETS(1984, Brit.)

Choir Of The Welsh Guards
I'LL TURN TO YOU(1946, Brit.)

Wieslawa Chojkowska
PASSENGER, THE(1970, Pol.), cos

Gyuli Chokhonelidze
THERE WAS AN OLD COUPLE(1967, USSR); WAR AND PEACE(1968, USSR)

Reina Chokoyeva
MORNING STAR(1962, USSR)

Nicole Chollet
LOVE AND THE FRENCHWOMAN(1961, Fr.); NAKED AUTUMN(1963, Fr.); UP FROM THE BEACH(1965); THIEF OF PARIS, THE(1967, Fr./Ital.)

John Chollot
DRAGONWYCH(1946)

Mary Cholmondeley
Silents
RED POTTAGE(1918, Brit.), w

Henri Chomette
Misc. Silents
LE CHAUFFEUR DE MADEMOISELLE(1928, Fr.), d

Marvin Chomsky
BUBBLE, THE(1967), art d; EVEL KNIEVEL(1971), d; MURPH THE SURF(1974), d

Marvin J. Chomsky
MACKINTOSH & T.J.(1975), d; GOOD LUCK, MISS WYCKOFF(1979), d
1984
TANK(1984), d

Billy Chong
Misc. Talkies
HARD WAY TO DIE, A(1980)

Lin Chong
STAR OF HONG KONG(1962, Jap.)

Michael Chong
DEATH MACHINES(1976)

Mona Chong
SECOND BEST SECRET AGENT IN THE WHOLE WIDE WORLD, THE(1965, Brit.); VENGEANCE OF FU MANCHU, THE(1968, Brit./Ger./Hong Kong/Ireland); ON HER MAJESTY'S SECRET SERVICE(1969, Brit.); PEOPLE MEET AND SWEET MUSIC FILLS THE HEART(1969, Den./Swed.)

Peter Chong
AROUND THE WORLD(1943); PURPLE HEART, THE(1944); UP IN ARMS(1944); FIRST YANK INTO TOKYO(1945); INTRIGUE(1947); EASTER PARADE(1948); TO THE ENDS OF THE EARTH(1948); PEKING EXPRESS(1951); MISS SADIE THOMPSON(1953); REMAINS TO BE SEEN(1953); SOUTH SEA WOMAN(1953); TORCH SONG(1953); LEFT HAND OF GOD, THE(1955); TRIBUTE TO A BADMAN(1956); INN OF THE SIXTH HAPPINESS, THE(1958); THIS EARTH IS MINE(1959); MOUNTAIN ROAD, THE(1960)

Peter Goo Chong
MISSION TO MOSCOW(1943)

Phil Chong
1984
STAR TREK III: THE SEARCH FOR SPOCK(1984)

Rae Dawn Chong
STONY ISLAND(1978); QUEST FOR FIRE(1982, Fr./Can.)
1984
BEAT STREET(1984); CHEECH AND CHONG'S THE CORSICAN BROTHERS(1984); CHOOSE ME(1984); FEAR CITY(1984)

Robbi Chong
1984
CHEECH AND CHONG'S THE CORSICAN BROTHERS(1984)

Sheila Chong
ISLAND OF DESIRE(1952, Brit.)

Thomas Chong
THINGS ARE TOUGH ALL OVER(1982), w; CHEECH AND CHONG'S NEXT MOVIE(1980), a, d, w; CHEECH AND CHONG'S NICE DREAMS(1981), a, d, w; STILL SMOKIN'(1983), d, w
1984
CHEECH AND CHONG'S THE CORSICAN BROTHERS(1984), a, d, w

Tommy Chong
UP IN SMOKE(1978), a, w; THINGS ARE TOUGH ALL OVER(1982); STILL SMOKIN'(1983); YELLOWBEARD(1983)

Wong Chong
KING OF CHINATOWN(1939)

Wong Show Chong
LADY FROM SHANGHAI, THE(1948)

Leo Chooluck
PLUNDER ROAD(1957), p

Leon Chooluck
HELL ON DEVIL'S ISLAND(1957), p; MURDER BY CONTRACT(1958), p; CITY OF FEAR(1959), p; THREE BLONDES IN HIS LIFE(1961), d; TAKE A HARD RIDE(1975, U.S./Ital.), p

Farid Chopel
1984
MY BEST FRIEND'S GIRL(1984, Fr.)

Georgie Choper
FATHER TAKES A WIFE(1941)

Chopin
RULES OF THE GAME, THE(1939, Fr.), m; DREAM OF BUTTERFLY, THE(1941, Ital.), m; FIVE EASY PIECES(1970), m

Frederic Chopin
I'VE ALWAYS LOVED YOU(1946), m; CRIES AND WHISPERS(1972, Swed.), m

Frederic Francois Chopin
RISK, THE(1961, Brit.), m; ISADORA(1968, Brit.), m

Frederick Chopin
HAUNTING OF M, THE(1979), m

Kate Chopin
END OF AUGUST, THE(1982), w

The Choppers Gang
BLACK ANGELS, THE(1970)

Ram Chopra
DOCTOR FAUSTUS(1967, Brit.)

Sudha Chopra
HEAT AND DUST(1983, Brit.)

Vinod Chopra
TIGER AND THE FLAME, THE(1955, India), ch

Michael Choquet
DON'T CRY WITH YOUR MOUTH FULL(1974, Fr.), m

Michel Choquet
JE T'AIME, JE T'AIME(1972, Fr./Swed.)

Elie Choraqui
AND NOW MY LOVE(1975, Fr.)

Ray Chordes
IT'S A BIG COUNTRY(1951), w

The Chords
STARS ON PARADE(1944)

Sonny Choree
HER JUNGLE LOVE(1938); RED CANYON(1949)

Marie Chorie
WHITE FANG(1936)

Danny Chorlton
INTERRUPTED JOURNEY, THE(1949, Brit.), ed

Michael C. Chorlton
HIGH TREASON(1937, Brit.), ed; AVENGERS, THE(1942, Brit.), ed; SQUADRON LEADER X(1943, Brit.), ed; SILVER FLEET, THE(1945, Brit.), ed

Michael Chorlton
JUGGERNAUT(1937, Brit.), ed; LOVE ON THE DOLE(1945, Brit.), ed; RANDOLPH FAMILY, THE(1945, Brit.), ed

Jo-Ann Chorney
1984
BLAME IT ON THE NIGHT(1984), set d

Alexander Chorny
1984
JAZZMAN(1984, USSR)

L. Chorny
Misc. Silents
CONQUEST OF THE CAUCASUS(1913, USSR), d

J. Chorodov
TIKI TIKI(1971, Can.), w

Gertrude Chorre
FROZEN JUSTICE(1929); SEA OF GRASS, THE(1947); WE WERE STRANGERS(1949)

Sonny Chorre
EBB TIDE(1937); UNION PACIFIC(1939)

Suni Chorre
JOE PALOOKA IN THE COUNTERPUNCH(1949)

Sunny Chorre
RIDE, RANGER, RIDE(1936)

Chorus and Orchestra of the Rome Opera
LA TRAVIATA(1968, Ital.)

Chorus of United Nations
THOUSANDS CHEER(1943)

Irena Chorynska
1984
SHIVERS(1984, Pol.), ed

Cyril Chosack
MAN WITHOUT A FACE, THE(1935, Brit.)

Al Chosis
NIGHT IN PARADISE, A(1946)

Neil Chotem
U-TURN(1973, Can.), m

Andre E. Chotin
CLANDESTINE(1948, Fr.), d

Claude Choublier
LOVE ON A PILLOW(1963, Fr./Ital.), w; NUTTY, NAUGHTY CHATEAU(1964, Fr./Ital.), w; VICE AND VIRTUE(1965, Fr./Ital.), w

Choudens
BATTLE, THE(1934, Fr.), ed

Arpen Choudhury
GODDESS, THE(1962, India)

Mohammed Chouly
CIRCLE OF DECEIT(1982, Fr./Ger.)

Elie Chouraqui
MY FIRST LOVE(1978, Fr.), p,d&w

Etchika Choureau
DARBY'S RANGERS(1958); LAFAYETTE ESCADRILLE(1958); PROSTITUTION(1965, Fr.); PARIS IN THE MONTH OF AUGUST(1968, Fr.)

Rene-Pierre Chouteau
WAR OF THE BUTTONS(1963 Fr.), md

Elizabeth Chouvalidze
ONE MAN(1979, Can.)

Aen Ling Chow
FORBIDDEN(1953); LOVE IS A MANY-SPLENDORED THING(1955)

Aen-Ling Chow
BACK AT THE FRONT(1952)

Chin Kuang Chow
CHINA SKY(1945)

David Chow
SAMURAI(1945); DRAGON'S GOLD(1954); DIMENSION 5(1966); WRECKING CREW, THE(1968); SKI BUM, THE(1971); CONQUEST OF THE PLANET OF THE APES(1972); THREE THE HARD WAY(1974); BRUCE LEE–TRUE STORY(1976, Chi.); CHARLIE CHAN AND THE CURSE OF THE DRAGON QUEEN(1981)

Hinsing Chow
PROSTITUTION(1965, Fr.)

Marilyn Chow
CALCUTTA(1947)

Michael Chow
VIOLENT PLAYGROUND(1958, Brit.); SAVAGE INNOCENTS, THE(1960, Brit.); MARCO POLO(1962, Fr./Ital.); 55 DAYS AT PEKING(1963); MODESTY BLAISE(1966, Brit.); YOU ONLY LIVE TWICE(1967, Brit.); JOANNA(1968, Brit.); WHO IS KILLING THE GREAT CHEFS OF EUROPE?(1978, US/Ger.); HAMMETT(1982)

Noel Chow
SEVENTH DAWN, THE(1964)

Raymond Chow
DEEP THRUST–THE HAND OF DEATH(1973, Hong Kong), p; FISTS OF FURY(1973, Chi.), p; RETURN OF THE DRAGON(1974, Chin.), p; MAN FROM HONG KONG(1975), p; GAME OF DEATH, THE(1979), p

S.T. Chow
HONG KONG AFFAIR(1958), ph

Wayne Chow
HAWAIIANS, THE(1970)

S.S. Chowdhary
FLAME OVER INDIA(1960, Brit.)

Nilima Roy Chowdhury
KANCHENJUNGHA(1966, India)

Ah Chong Choy
THE BEACHCOMBER(1955, Brit.)

Diana Choy
1984
ELECTRIC DREAMS(1984)

Eugene Choy
1984
SLAPSTICK OF ANOTHER KIND(1984)

Eugene G. Choy
CHU CHU AND THE PHILLY FLASH(1981)

Hew Thian Choy
SEVENTH DAWN, THE(1964)

Steve Choy
HAWAIIANS, THE(1970)

Abdelhaq Chraibi
MAN WHO KNEW TOO MUCH, THE(1956)

Vlasta Chramostova
CREMATOR, THE(1973, Czech.)

Georges Chretelain
TESTAMENT OF ORPHEUS, THE(1962, Fr.)

Diane Chretien
CHRONOPOLIS(1982, Fr.), anim

Don Crichton
GIRL RUSH, THE(1955)

Kyle Chrichton
HAPPIEST MILLIONAIRE, THE(1967), w

Chris
WEDDINGS AND BABIES(1960)

Marilyn Chris
LOVE WITH THE PROPER STRANGER(1963); HONEYMOON KILLERS, THE(1969); JOHN AND MARY(1969); PEOPLE NEXT DOOR, THE(1970); RHINOCEROS(1974); LOOKING UP(1977); BLACK MARBLE, THE(1980); LOVING COUPLES(1980)

Chris Barber and His Jazz Band
LOOK BACK IN ANGER(1959)

Chris Barber's Jazz Band
RING-A-DING RHYTHM(1962, Brit. 73m Amicus/COL bw (G.B: IT'S TRAD, DAD!)

Chris O'Brien's Caribbeans
ROCK AROUND THE WORLD(1957, Brit.)

Nils Olaf Chrisander
Misc. Silents
FIGHTING LOVE(1927), d; HEART THIEF, THE(1927), d

Pat Chrisman
Silents
SKY HIGH(1922); ROMANCE LAND(1923); OH, YOU TONY!(1924)
Misc. Silents
ROUGH RIDING ROMANCE(1919); TEXAN, THE(1920); RIDIN' ROMEO, A(1921)

Fred Chriss
MALIBU BEACH(1978), art d

Kid Chrissell
SUSPENSE(1946)

Harry P. Christ [Harry Fraser]
CAVALIER OF THE WEST(1931), w; BORDER DEVILS(1932), w; NIGHT RIDER, THE(1932), w; WITHOUT HONORS(1932), w

The Christa Ballet
LITTLE MISS DEVIL(1951, Egypt)
Ivo G. Christante
1984
BREAKIN'(1984), prod d
Marina Christelis
KILLER FORCE(1975, Switz./Ireland)
Marya Christen
STAY AWAY, JOE(1968); DIRTY DINGUS MAGEE(1970)
Chris Christenberry
LITTLE CIGARS(1973), d
Benjamin Christensen
HOUSE OF HORROR(1929), d; MYSTERIOUS ISLAND(1929), d; SEVEN FOOT-PRINTS TO SATAN(1929), d
Silents
MOCKERY(1927), d, w
Misc. Silents
WITCHCRAFT THROUGH THE AGES(1921, Swed.), a, d; MICHAEL(1924, Ger.); DEVIL'S CIRCUS, THE(1926), d; CHAINED(1927, Ger.); HAUNTED HOUSE, THE(1928), d; HAWK'S NEST, THE(1928), d; SEVEN FOOTPRINTS TO SATAN(1929), d
Bent Christensen
CASE OF THE 44'S, THE(1964 Brit./Den.), a, p; WEEKEND(1964, Den.), p; EPI-LOGUE(1967, Den.), p; HAGBARD AND SIGNE(1968, Den./Iceland/Swed.), p; PEO-PLE MEET AND SWEET MUSIC FILLS THE HEART(1969, Den./Swed.), p; ONLY WAY, THE(1970, Panama/Den./U.S.), d, w; Z.P.G.(1972)
Bo Christensen
OPERATION LOVEBIRDS(1968, Den.), p
Carlos Hugo Christensen
VIOLENT AND THE DAMNED, THE(1962, Braz.), d, w; CURSE OF THE STONE HAND(1965, Mex/Chile), d
Carol Christensen
FRECKLES(1960); BIG SHOW, THE(1961); SWINGIN' ALONG(1962); THREE STOOGES IN ORBIT, THE(1962)
Caroline Christensen
APOLLO GOES ON HOLIDAY(1968, Ger./Swed.)
Charles Christensen
HIS NIGHT OUT(1935), w
Chris Christensen
IT TAKES ALL KINDS(1969, U.S./Aus.)
Don Christensen
MIGHTY MOUSE IN THE GREAT SPACE CHASE(1983), p
Emil Hass Christensen
ORDET(1957, Den.)
Greta Christensen
PAN-AMERICANA(1945)
Harley Christensen
1984
RED DAWN(1984)
Hass Christensen
ERIC SOYA'S "17"(1967, Den.)
J.E. Christensen
GET YOURSELF A COLLEGE GIRL(1964), spec eff
John Christensen
HAPPY DAYS(1930)
Margaret Christensen
SMILEY(1957, Brit.); SMILEY GETS A GUN(1959, Brit.)
Michael Christensen
POPEYE(1980)
Nils Reinhardt Christensen
PASSIONATE DEMONS, THE(1962, Norway), d
Per Christensen
PASSIONATE DEMONS, THE(1962, Norway)
Robert Christensen
J.W. COOP(1971)
Rolf Christensen
PASSIONATE DEMONS, THE(1962, Norway)
Shirley Ann Christensen
TORCH SINGER(1933)
Wes C. Christensen
STAMPEDE(1949)
Wes Christensen
DOMINO KID(1957)
Benjamin Christenson
HAUNTED HOUSE, THE(1928), d
Irma Christensson
DEVIL'S WANTON, THE(1962, Swed.)
Frank Christi
STEAGLE, THE(1971); DON IS DEAD, THE(1973); HIT(1973); TERMINAL IS-LAND(1973)
Sal Christi
CROSS AND THE SWITCHBLADE, THE(1970)
Beulah Christian
NOTORIOUS(1946); MISS TATLOCK'S MILLIONS(1948); MATING SEASON, THE(1951)
Carl Christian
TORPEDO ALLEY(1953); WRITTEN ON THE WIND(1956); SOMETHING OF VAL-UE(1957)
Chad Christian
1984
POWER, THE(1984)
Chris Christian
CIRCUS OF HORRORS(1960, Brit.)
Curt Christian
BOY WHO STOLE A MILLION, THE(1960, Brit.)
Diana Christian
TOUGHEST MAN IN ARIZONA(1952)

Elsa Christian
PARADISE FOR THREE(1938)
Gina Christian
DEATH VALLEY(1982)
Gloria Christian
PARIS MODEL(1953)
H. R. Christian
ACT OF VENGEANCE(1974), w; KING OF THE MOUNTAIN(1981), w
H.R. Christian
BLACK MAMA, WHITE MAMA(1973), w
Hans Christian
ALMOST ANGELS(1962)
Helen Christian
BACK DOOR TO HEAVEN(1939)
Ian Christian
POOR COW(1968, Brit.)
John Christian
DELINQUENT DAUGHTERS(1944); MILDRED PIERCE(1945); GUERRILLA GIRL(1953), p,d,ed; PROWLER, THE(1981)
Kurt Christian
NINE HOURS TO RAMA(1963, U.S./Brit.); LONG DUEL, THE(1967, Brit.); FRAG-MENT OF FEAR(1971, Brit.); LAST VALLEY, THE(1971, Brit.); POPE JOAN(1972, Brit.); GOLDEN VOYAGE OF SINBAD, THE(1974, Brit.); PAPER TIGER(1975, Brit.); SINBAD AND THE EYE OF THE TIGER(1977, U.S./Brit.)
Lee Christian
DOLL SQUAD, THE(1973)
Leigh Christian
BEYOND ATLANTIS(1973, Phil.); WORLD'S GREATEST ATHLETE, THE(1973); BUTTERFLY(1982)
Linda Christian
UP IN ARMS(1944); HOLIDAY IN MEXICO(1946); GREEN DOLPHIN STREET(1947); TARZAN AND THE MERMAIDS(1948); BATTLE ZONE(1952); HAPPY TIME, THE(1952); SLAVES OF BABYLON(1953); ATHENA(1954); THUNDERSTORM(1956); HOUSE OF THE SEVEN HAWKS, THE(1959); DEVIL'S HAND, THE(1961); V.I.P.s, THE(1963, Brit.); MOMENT OF TRUTH, THE(1965, Ital./Span.); HOW TO SEDUCE A PLAYBOY(1968, Aust./Fr./Ital.)
Lisa Christian
Misc. Talkies
LEGACY OF SATAN(1973)
Madonna Christian
STROKER ACE(1983)
Mary Christian
Silents
KISS FOR CINDERELLA, A(1926)
Melissa Christian
1984
BODY DOUBLE(1984)
Michael Christian
WHERE ANGELS GO...TROUBLE FOLLOWS(1968); 2000 YEARS LATER(1969); GREAT GUNDOWN, THE(1977)
Misc. Talkies
TO HELL YOU PREACH(1972); POOR PRETTY EDDIE(1975); HEARTBREAK MOTEL(1978); HOLLYWOOD KNIGHT(1979)
Nilo Christian
KITCHEN, THE(1961, Brit.)
Paul Christian
BAGDAD(1949); NO TIME FOR FLOWERS(1952); THIEF OF VENICE, THE(1952); BEAST FROM 20,000 FATHOMS, THE(1953); JOURNEY TO THE LOST CITY(1960, Ger./Fr./Ital.); ROMMEL'S TREASURE(1962, Ital.)
Ray Christian
"IMP"PROBABLE MR. WEE GEE, THE(1966)
Rob Christian
PATSY, THE(1964)
Robert Christian
AIRBORNE(1962); SOME OF MY BEST FRIENDS ARE...(1971); ...AND JUSTICE FOR ALL(1979); SEDUCTION OF JOE TYNAN, THE(1979); BUSTIN' LOOSE(1981); PRINCE OF THE CITY(1981)
Roger Christian
MUSCLE BEACH PARTY(1964); RIDE THE WILD SURF(1964), m/l "Ride the Wild Surf," Jan Berry; RETURN TO MACON COUNTY(1975), m; LAST REMAKE OF BEAU GESTE, THE(1977), set d; STAR WARS(1977), set d; MONTY PYTHON'S LIFE OF BRIAN(1979, Brit.), art d; SENDER, THE(1982, Brit.), d
Scott Christian
GUMSHOE(1972, Brit.)
Susanne Christian
PATHS OF GLORY(1957)
Tawn Christian
NIGHTHAWKS(1981)
Tina Chad Christian
BABY LOVE(1969, Brit.), w
Tony Christian
TARGET UNKNOWN(1951)
Christian-Jacque
ANGEL AND SINNER(1947, Fr.), d; LUCRECE BORGIA(1953, Ital./Fr.), d&w; THE DIRTY GAME(1966, Fr./Ital./Ger.), d, w
Christian-Jaque
SYMPHONIE FANTASTIQUE(1947, Fr.), d; GYPSY FURY(1950, Fr.), d, w; FAN-FAN THE TULIP(1952, Fr.), p&d, w; MADAME DU BARRY(1954 Fr./Ital.), d, w; ADORABLE CREATURES(1956, Fr.), d, w; NANA(1957, Fr./Ital.), d, w; NA-THALIE(1958, Fr.), p&d; LAW IS THE LAW, THE(1959, Fr.), d; DEAD RUN(1961, Fr./Ital./Ger.), d, w; MADAME(1963, Fr./Ital./Span.), d, w; DON'T TEMPT THE DEVIL(1964, Fr./Ital.), d, w; MAN FROM COCODY(1966, Fr/Ital.), d, w; MARCO THE MAGNIFICENT(1966, Ital./Fr./Yugo./Egypt/Afghanistan), d; LADY HAMIL-TON(1969, Ger./Ital./Fr.), d, w; LEGEND OF FRENCHIE KING, THE(1971, Fr./Ital./Span./Brit.), d
Rita Christiana
ROAD TO MOROCCO(1942)

Rita Christiani
TALES OF MANHATTAN(1942); HAPPY GO LUCKY(1943); THANK YOUR LUCKY STARS(1943)
The Christianis
SENSATIONS OF 1945(1944)
Bill Christians
SO FINE(1981), cos
Broeken Christians
Misc. Silents
DEEP WATERS(1920)
Mady Christians
BECAUSE I LOVED YOU(1930, Ger.); EMPRESS AND I, THE(1933, Ger.); HEART SONG(1933, Brit.); MANULESCU(1933, Ger.); WICKED WOMAN, A(1934); ESCAPADE(1935); SHIP CAFE(1935); COME AND GET IT(1936); HEIDI(1937); SEVENTH HEAVEN(1937); WOMAN I LOVE, THE(1937); TENDER COMRADE(1943); ADDRESS UNKNOWN(1944); ALL MY SONS(1948); LETTER FROM AN UNKNOWN WOMAN(1948)
Misc. Silents
RUNAWAY PRINCESS, THE(1929, Brit.)
Margarete Christians
Silents
AUDREY(1916)
Rudolph Christians
Silents
FOOLISH WIVES(1920); HER FIVE-FOOT HIGHNESS(1920); HUMAN STUFF(1920)
Misc. Silents
BURNT WINGS(1920); SECRET GIFT, THE(1920)
Arthur Christiansen
DAY THE EARTH CAUGHT FIRE, THE(1961, Brit.); 80,000 SUSPECTS(1963, Brit.); LURE OF THE JUNGLE, THE(1970, Den.), ph
Cay Christiansen
GOLDEN MOUNTAINS(1958, Den.)
Cheryl Christiansen
SWEET CHARITY(1969); LAUGHING POLICEMAN, THE(1973)
Ellen Christiansen
1984
FIRST TURN-ON!, THE(1984), art d
Elsa Christiansen
AS GOOD AS MARRIED(1937)
Greta Christiansen
FALCON IN HOLLYWOOD, THE(1944)
Harvey Christiansen
HONEYSUCKLE ROSE(1980); RESURRECTION(1980)
Henning Christiansen
CASE OF THE 44'S, THE(1964 Brit./Den.), ph
Per Christiansen
SUICIDE MISSION(1956, Brit.)
Robert Christiansen
ADAM AT 6 A.M.(1970), p; HIDE IN PLAIN SIGHT(1980), p
Sigurd Wesley Christiansen
TWO LIVING, ONE DEAD(1964, Brit./Swed.), w
Todd Christiansen
GOIN' HOME(1976)
Al Christianson
HORRIBLE DR. HICHCOCK, THE(1964, Ital.)
Dean Christianson
MOONSHINE COUNTY EXPRESS(1977)
Lila Christianson
LOOKER(1981)
Lorna Christianson
LOOKER(1981)
Shawn Christianson
SMILE(1975)
Jacques Christiany
Misc. Silents
L'AUBERGE ROUGE(1923, Fr.)
Robert Christides
RELUCTANT DEBUTANTE, THE(1958), set d; VISIT, THE(1964, Ger./Fr./Ital./U.S.), set d; HOTEL PARADISO(1966, U.S./Brit.), set d; KING OF HEARTS(1967, Fr./Ital.), set d; MAGNIFICENT ONE, THE(1974, Fr./Ital.), set d
A.E. Christie
BIRTH OF A BABY(1938), d
Agatha Christie
ALIBI(1931, Brit.), w; BLACK COFFEE(1931, Brit.), w; LORD EDGEWARE DIES(1934, Brit.), w; LOVE FROM A STRANGER(1937, Brit.), w; AND THEN THERE WERE NONE(1945), w; LOVE FROM A STRANGER(1947), w; WITNESS FOR THE PROSECUTION(1957), w; SPIDER'S WEB, THE(1960, Brit.), w; MURDER SHE SAID(1961, Brit.), w; MURDER AHOY(1964, Brit.), w; MURDER MOST FOUL(1964, Brit.), w; TEN LITTLE INDIANS(1965, U.S.), w; ALPHABET MURDERS, THE(1966), w; ENDLESS NIGHT(1971, Brit.), d&w; MURDER ON THE ORIENT EXPRESS(1974, Brit.), w; TEN LITTLE INDIANS(1975, Ital./Fr./Span./Ger.), w; DEATH ON THE NILE(1978, Brit.), w; MIRROR CRACK'D, THE(1980, Brit.), w; EVIL UNDER THE SUN(1982, Brit.), w
1984
ORDEAL BY INNOCENCE(1984, Brit.), w
Silents
PASSING OF MR. QUIN, THE(1928, Brit.), w
Al Christie
CARNATION KID(1929), p; CHARLEY'S AUNT(1930), p&d; SWEETHEARTS ON PARADE(1930), p; HALF A SINNER(1940), p&d
Misc. Silents
MRS. PLUM'S PUDDING(1915), d; SO LONG LETTY(1920), d; SEE MY LAWYER(1921), d
Audrey Christie
KEEPER OF THE FLAME(1942); DEADLINE–U.S.A.(1952); CAROUSEL(1956); SPLENDOR IN THE GRASS(1961); UNSINKABLE MOLLY BROWN, THE(1964); HARLOW(1965); FRANKIE AND JOHNNY(1966); BALLAD OF JOSIE(1968); MAME(1974); HARPER VALLEY, P.T.A.(1978)

Barbara Christie
ROGUE'S YARN(1956, Brit.)
C. Christie
WINDJAMMER, THE(1931, Brit.)
Campbell Christie
SOMEONE AT THE DOOR(1936, Brit.), w; JASSY(1948, Brit.), w; SOMEONE AT THE DOOR(1950, Brit.), w; HIS EXCELLENCY(1952, Brit.), w; COURT MARTIAL(1954, Brit.), w; WICKED WIFE(1955, Brit.), w; THIRD KEY, THE(1957, Brit.), w
Dick Christie
ANY WHICH WAY YOU CAN(1980); HONKY TONK FREEWAY(1981); LOOKER(1981)
Donna Christie [Ornella Micheli]
HORRIBLE DR. HICHCOCK, THE(1964, Ital.), ed; GHOST, THE(1965, Ital.), ed
Dorothy Christie
GOLD DUST GERTIE(1931); SOMEONE AT THE DOOR(1936, Brit.), w; THEY SHALL HAVE MUSIC(1939); JASSY(1948, Brit.), w; SOMEONE AT THE DOOR(1950, Brit.), w; HIS EXCELLENCY(1952, Brit.), w; COURT MARTIAL(1954, Brit.), w; WICKED WIFE(1955, Brit.), w; THIRD KEY, THE(1957, Brit.), w
George Stuart Christie
Misc. Silents
DUCHESS OF DOUBT, THE(1917); SOWERS AND REAPERS(1917)
Gordon Christie
LITTLEST HORSE THIEVES, THE(1977)
Helen Christie
UP FOR THE CUP(1950, Brit.); FLESH AND BLOOD(1951, Brit.); CASTLE IN THE AIR(1952, Brit.); WIDE BOY(1952, Brit.); DECLINE AND FALL... OF A BIRD WATCHER(1969, Brit.); LUST FOR A VAMPIRE(1971, Brit.)
Howard Christie
STRIKE ME PINK(1936); ABBOTT AND COSTELLO MEET THE INVISIBLE MAN(1951), p; COMIN' ROUND THE MOUNTAIN(1951), p; GOLDEN HORDE, THE(1951), p; AGAINST ALL FLAGS(1952), p; LOST IN ALASKA(1952), p; YANKEE BUCCANEER(1952), p; ABBOTT AND COSTELLO GO TO MARS(1953), p, w; BACK TO GOD'S COUNTRY(1953), p; LONE HAND, THE(1953), p; SEMINOLE(1953), p; ABBOTT AND COSTELLO MEET DR. JEKYLL AND MR. HYDE(1954), p; FIREMAN SAVE MY CHILD(1954), p; YANKEE PASHA(1954), p; ABBOTT AND COSTELLO MEET THE KEYSTONE KOPS(1955), p; ABBOTT AND COSTELLO MEET THE MUMMY(1955), p; LOOTERS, THE(1955), p; PURPLE MASK, THE(1955), p; SMOKE SIGNAL(1955), p; AWAY ALL BOATS(1956), p; CONGO CROSSING(1956), p; EVERYTHING BUT THE TRUTH(1956), p; I'VE LIVED BEFORE(1956), p; PRICE OF FEAR, THE(1956), p; SHOWDOWN AT ABILENE(1956), p; TOY TIGER(1956), p; JOE DAKOTA(1957), p; KETTLES ON OLD MACDONALD'S FARM, THE(1957), p; MONOLITH MONSTERS, THE(1957), p; LAST OF THE FAST GUNS, THE(1958), p; NO NAME ON THE BULLET(1959), p; RAIDERS, THE(1964), p; SWORD OF ALI BABA, THE(1965), p; GUNFIGHT IN ABILENE(1967), p; RIDE TO HANGMAN'S TREE, THE(1967), p; JOURNEY TO SHILOH(1968), p; NOBODY'S PERFECT(1968), p; MAN CALLED GANNON, A(1969), p
Howard "Red" Christie
LOVE BEFORE BREAKFAST(1936); NEWSBOY'S HOME(1939)
Ivan Christie
SON OF THE GODS(1930)
Silents
RAINBOW(1921)
Jimmy Christie
OPENING NIGHT(1977)
Julie Christie
BILLY LIAR(1963, Brit.); CROOKS ANONYMOUS(1963, Brit.); FAST LADY, THE(1963, Brit.); DOCTOR ZHIVAGO(1965); YOUNG CASSIDY(1965, U.S./Brit.); FAHRENHEIT 451(1966, Brit.); FAR FROM THE MADDING CROWD(1967, Brit.); PETULIA(1968, U.S./Brit.); IN SEARCH OF GREGORY(1970, Brit./Ital.); GO-BETWEEN, THE(1971, Brit.); MC CABE AND MRS. MILLER(1971); DON'T LOOK NOW(1973, Brit./Ital.); NASHVILLE(1975); SHAMPOO(1975); DEMON SEED(1977); HEAVEN CAN WAIT(1978); MEMOIRS OF A SURVIVOR(1981, Brit.); HEAT AND DUST(1983, Brit.); RETURN OF THE SOLDIER, THE(1983, Brit.)
Misc. Talkies
GOLD DIGGERS, THE(1984, Brit.)
Keith Christie
ALL NIGHT LONG(1961, Brit.)
Madeleine Christie
BACKFIRE!(1961, Brit.); ONE PLUS ONE(1961, Can.); BROTHERLY LOVE(1970, Brit.)
1984
ELECTRIC DREAMS(1984); IT'S NEVER TOO LATE(1984, Span.)
Margot Christie
ONE PLUS ONE(1961, Can.)
Paul Christie
1984
GIRLS NIGHT OUT(1984)
Pearl Christie
MONKEY GRIP(1983, Aus.)
Robert Christie
BLOODY BROOD, THE(1959, Can.); ONE PLUS ONE(1961, Can.); INCREDIBLE JOURNEY, THE(1963); NOTHING PERSONAL(1980, Can.)
Shannon Christie
BIG BAD MAMA(1974)
Stuart Christie
SKY RAIDERS, THE(1938, Brit.)
Van Christie
MARCO(1973)
Katia Christina
SPIRITS OF THE DEAD(1969, Fr./Ital.); ADVENTURERS, THE(1970); PUSSYCAT, PUSSYCAT, I LOVE YOU(1970)
Teresa Christina [Delores Taylor]
BILLY JACK(1971), w; BILLY JACK GOES TO WASHINGTON(1977), w
Christine
CROSS OF THE LIVING(1963, Fr.), p, w; TAKE HER BY SURPRISE(1967, Can.), cos
Eva Christine
Misc. Talkies
IDEAL MARRIAGE, THE(1970)

Lilian Christine
Silents
HUNTINGTOWER(1927, Brit.)
Lillian Christine
PAID IN ERROR(1938, Brit.)
Marilyn Christine
KEEP YOUR POWDER DRY(1945)
Virgina Christine
MISSION TO MOSCOW(1943)
Virginia Christine
EDGE OF DARKNESS(1943); TRUCK BUSTERS(1943); MUMMY'S CURSE, THE(1944); OLD TEXAS TRAIL, THE(1944); GIRLS OF THE BIG HOUSE(1945); PHANTOM OF THE PLAINS(1945); HOUSE OF HORRORS(1946); IDEA GIRL(1946); INNER CIRCLE, THE(1946); KILLERS, THE(1946); MURDER IS MY BUSINESS(1946); MYSTERIOUS MR. VALENTINE, THE(1946); GANGSTER, THE(1947); INVISIBLE WALL, THE(1947); NIGHT WIND(1948); WOMEN IN THE NIGHT(1948); COVER-UP(1949); SPECIAL AGENT(1949); CYRANO DE BERGERAC(1950); HIGH NOON(1952); NEVER WAVE AT A WAC(1952); WOMAN THEY ALMOST LYNCHED, THE(1953); DRAGNET(1954); COBWEB, THE(1955); GOOD MORNING, MISS DOVE(1955); NOT AS A STRANGER(1955); INVASION OF THE BODY SNATCHERS(1956); KILLER IS LOOSE, THE(1956); NIGHTMARE(1956); CARELESS YEARS, THE(1957); JOHNNY TREMAIN(1957); SPIRIT OF ST. LOUIS, THE(1957); THREE BRAVE MEN(1957); FLAMING STAR(1960); JUDGMENT AT NUREMBERG(1961); INCIDENT IN AN ALLEY(1962); CATTLE KING(1963); FOUR FOR TEXAS(1963); PRIZE, THE(1963); KILLERS, THE(1964); ONE MAN'S WAY(1964); RAGE TO LIVE, A(1965); BILLY THE KID VS. DRACULA(1966); GUESS WHO'S COMING TO DINNER(1967); IN ENEMY COUNTRY(1968); HAIL, HERO!(1969)
Paul Christman
TRIPLE THREAT(1948)
Bill Christmas
THIN RED LINE, THE(1964); KID RODELO(1966, U.S./Span.)
Eric Christmas
MONTE WALSH(1970); HAROLD AND MAUDE(1971); JOHNNY GOT HIS GUN(1971); LAST TYCOON, THE(1976); ATTACK OF THE KILLER TOMATOES(1978); ENEMY OF THE PEOPLE, AN(1978); CHANGELING, THE(1980, Can.); MIDDLE AGE CRAZY(1980, Can.); PORKY'S(1982); PORKY'S II: THE NEXT DAY(1983)
1984
ALL OF ME(1984); PHILADELPHIA EXPERIMENT, THE(1984)
Leonard Christmas
HARLEM RIDES THE RANGE(1939)
Gil Christner
MORE AMERICAN GRAFFITI(1979)
1984
SUBURBIA(1984)
Raymond Christodoulou
FROM BEYOND THE GRAVE(1974, Brit.), w; NUTCRACKER(1982, Brit.), a, w
Pericles Christofarides
FORTUNE TELLER, THE(1961, Gr.)
Scott Christoffel
JAWS 3-D(1983)
Debbie Christoffersen
1984
WEEKEND PASS(1984)
Phillip Christon
1984
SWING SHIFT(1984)
Francoise Christophe
WALK INTO HELL(1957, Aus.); TESTAMENT OF ORPHEUS, THE(1962, Fr.); ERIK THE CONQUEROR(1963, Fr./Ital.); FANTOMAS(1966, Fr./Ital.); KING OF HEARTS(1967, Fr./Ital.); CAROLINE CHERIE(1968, Fr.); BORSALINO(1970, Fr.)
Jean Christophe
ONE-EYED SOLDIERS(1967, U.S./Brit./Yugo.), d&w
Pascale Christophe
ACES HIGH(1977, Brit.); PIAF–THE EARLY YEARS(1982, U.S./Fr.)
Bill Christopher
FORTUNE COOKIE, THE(1966)
Bob Christopher
BUDDY HOLLY STORY, THE(1978)
David Christopher
1984
HOT MOVES(1984)
Dennis Christopher
BLOOD AND LACE(1971); YOUNG GRADUATES, THE(1971); 9/30/55(1977); WEDDING, A(1978); BREAKING AWAY(1979); CALIFORNIA DREAMING(1979); LAST WORD, THE(1979); FADE TO BLACK(1980); CHARRIOTS OF FIRE(1981, Brit.); DON'T CRY, IT'S ONLY THUNDER(1982)
Misc. Talkies
DIDN'T YOU HEAR(1983)
Eunice Christopher
AUDREY ROSE(1977); OTHER SIDE OF MIDNIGHT, THE(1977)
Eve Christopher
KLANSMAN, THE(1974)
Faith Christopher
TERROR IN THE JUNGLE(1968); POM POM GIRLS, THE(1976)
Guy Christopher
LEPKE(1975, U.S./Israel)
Inge Christopher
"RENT-A-GIRL"(1965)
James Christopher
WORLD IS JUST A 'B' MOVIE, THE(1971)
Jean Christopher
ADULTEROUS AFFAIR(1966); DECOY FOR TERROR(1970, Can.)
John Christopher
NO BLADE OF GRASS(1970, Brit.), w
Jordan Christopher
FAT SPY(1966); RETURN OF THE SEVEN(1966, Span.); ANGEL, ANGEL, DOWN WE GO(1969); TREE, THE(1969); SIDELONG GLANCES OF A PIGEON KICKER, THE(1970); STAR 80(1983)

Kathie Christopher
Misc. Talkies
TEENAGE HITCHHIKERS(1975)
Kathy Christopher
DUCHESS AND THE DIRTWATER FOX, THE(1976)
Misc. Talkies
BEASTS(1983)
Kay Christopher
LOCKET, THE(1946); DESPERATE(1947); DICK TRACY'S DILEMMA(1947); WOMAN ON THE BEACH, THE(1947); PREJUDICE(1949); SOUTH OF RIO(1949); CODE OF THE SILVER SAGE(1950); CORKY OF GASOLINE ALLEY(1951); GASOLINE ALLEY(1951); ONE MINUTE TO ZERO(1952)
Marcelle Christopher
LADY EVE, THE(1941); LAS VEGAS NIGHTS(1941)
Milbourne Christopher
Misc. Talkies
MODERN DAY HOUDINI(1983)
Robert Christopher
BAREFOOT CONTESSA, THE(1954); BEDEVILLED(1955); THREE OUTLAWS, THE(1956); BUSTER KEATON STORY, THE(1957); DEATH IN SMALL DOSES(1957); DISEMBODIED, THE(1957); SPOOK CHASERS(1957); DECKS RAN RED, THE(1958); HELL'S FIVE HOURS(1958); WALKING TARGET, THE(1960); OPERATION EICHMANN(1961); CONVICTS FOUR(1962); AGENT FOR H.A.R.M.(1966)
Robin Christopher
EQUINOX(1970)
Russell Christopher
LA TRAVIATA(1982)
Sam Christopher
SQUARES(1972)
Thom Christopher
VOICES(1979); SPACE RAIDERS(1983)
Tony Christopher
SOMETHING WICKED THIS WAY COMES(1983)
William Christopher
PRIVATE NAVY OF SGT. O'FARRELL, THE(1968); WITH SIX YOU GET EGGROLL(1968)
Stefanianna Christopherson
GRASSHOPPER, THE(1970)
Paul Christopoulos
LOOKING UP(1977)
Tani Christou
OEDIPUS THE KING(1968, Brit.), m
Al Christy
IN COLD BLOOD(1967)
Ann Christy
FOURTH ALARM, THE(1930); BEHIND STONE WALLS(1932)
Silents
KID SISTER, THE(1927); SPEEDY(1928); JUST OFF BROADWAY(1929); LARIAT KID, THE(1929)
Beryl Christy
NAKED WORLD OF HARRISON MARKS, THE(1967, Brit.)
Bill Christy
SONG OF THE OPEN ROAD(1944); BEHIND THE MASK(1946); LIVE WIRES(1946)
Dorothy Christy
BIG MONEY(1930); EXTRAVAGANCE(1930); GOT WHAT SHE WANTED(1930); SHE GOT WHAT SHE WANTED(1930); SO THIS IS LONDON(1930); BIG BUSINESS GIRL(1931); CAUGHT CHEATING(1931); CONVICTED(1931); GRIEF STREET(1931); NIGHT LIFE IN RENO(1931); PARLOR, BEDROOM AND BATH(1931); ARM OF THE LAW(1932); COHENS, AND KELLYS IN HOLLYWOOD, THE(1932); DEVIL AND THE DEEP(1932); DEVIL PAYS, THE(1932); FORBIDDEN COMPANY(1932); SHOP ANGEL(1932); UNEXPECTED FATHER(1932); UNION DEPOT(1932); LAWYER MAN(1933); ONLY YESTERDAY(1933); SECOND HAND WIFE(1933); SLIGHTLY MARRIED(1933); SONS OF THE DESERT(1933); BRIGHT EYES(1934); KISS AND MAKE UP(1934); LOVE BIRDS(1934); SERVANTS' ENTRANCE(1934); SIX-DAY BIKE RIDER(1934); DARING YOUNG MAN, THE(1935); I'VE BEEN AROUND(1935); ONE EXCITING ADVENTURE(1935); LOVE IS NEWS(1937); SLAVE SHIP(1937); YOU CAN'T HAVE EVERYTHING(1937); MARIE ANTOINETTE(1938); SWEETHEARTS(1938); WOMAN AGAINST WOMAN(1938); EAST SIDE OF HEAVEN(1939); ROUGH RIDERS' ROUNDUP(1939); SIERRA SUE(1941); FALCON AND THE CO-EDS, THE(1943); YOUNGEST PROFESSION, THE(1943); ARMY WIVES(1944); COWBOY AND THE SENORITA(1944); LAURA(1944); DAKOTA(1945); FASHION MODEL(1945); GEORGE WHITE'S SCANDALS(1945); JUNIOR MISS(1945); WEEKEND AT THE WALDORF(1945); LITTLE GIANT(1946); LITTLE MISS BIG(1946); LOVER COME BACK(1946); MAGNIFICENT ROGUE, THE(1946); UNDERCURRENT(1946); DREAM GIRL(1947); PILGRIM LADY, THE(1947); SECRET LIFE OF WALTER MITTY, THE(1947); SMASH-UP, THE STORY OF A WOMAN(1947); UNFAITHFUL, THE(1947); FIGHTING BACK(1948); HOMECOMING(1948); SILVER RIVER(1948); FOUNTAINHEAD, THE(1949); SO BIG(1953)
Eileen Christy
I DREAM OF JEANIE(1952); THUNDERBIRDS(1952); PERILOUS JOURNEY, A(1953); SWEETHEARTS ON PARADE(1953)
Floyd Christy
TURN OFF THE MOON(1937)
Grace Christy
ROMANCE OF THE WEST(1946)
Gus Christy
MICKEY ONE(1965)
Harold Christy
Silents
ATTA BOY!(1926), t
Howard Christy
SING SINNER, SING(1933), d
Ivan Christy
SEVEN FOOTPRINTS TO SATAN(1929); LONE WOLF RETURNS, THE(1936)
Silents
NEVADA(1927)
Misc. Silents
ISLAND WIVES(1922)

James Christy
GAILY, GAILY(1969)
James V. Christy
RIGHT HAND OF THE DEVIL, THE(1963); ROOMMATES, THE(1973); RAGING BULL(1980)
Jan Christy
HOPPY SERVES A WRIT(1943)
Jimmy Christy
LAUGHING POLICEMAN, THE(1973)
Ken Christy
FOREIGN CORRESPONDENT(1940); THIRD FINGER, LEFT HAND(1940); BALL OF FIRE(1941); BURMA CONVOY(1941); DOWN IN SAN DIEGO(1941); HARMON OF MICHIGAN(1941); HERE COMES MR. JORDAN(1941); LOVE CRAZY(1941); SAN FRANCISCO DOCKS(1941); SHADOW OF THE THIN MAN(1941); SIX LESSONS FROM MADAME LA ZONGA(1941); WHISTLING IN THE DARK(1941); ARABIAN NIGHTS(1942); BIG SHOT, THE(1942); LADY GANGSTER(1942); MANILA CAL-LING(1942); MAYOR OF 44TH STREET, THE(1942); THIS TIME FOR KEEPS(1942); GILDERSLEEVE'S BAD DAY(1943); HE HIRED THE BOSS(1943); HELLO, FRISCO, HELLO(1943); HIT THE ICE(1943); LAUGH YOUR BLUES AWAY(1943); NORTHERN PURSUIT(1943); SECRETS OF THE UNDERGROUND(1943); BIG NOISE, THE(1944); WILSON(1944); COLONEL EFFINGHAM'S RAID(1945); CRY OF THE CITY(1948); SCUDDA-HOO! SCUDDA-HAY!(1948); SITTING PRETTY(1948); DEVIL'S HENCH-MEN, THE(1949); TRAPPED(1949); CHEAPER BY THE DOZEN(1950); JACKPOT, THE(1950); NO WAY OUT(1950); SUNSET BOULEVARD(1950); BIG CARNIVAL, THE(1951); CALL ME MISTER(1951); MODEL AND THE MARRIAGE BROKER, THE(1951); PLACE IN THE SUN, A(1951); BOOTS MALONE(1952); GREATEST SHOW ON EARTH, THE(1952); ABBOTT AND COSTELLO GO TO MARS(1953); KID FROM LEFT FIELD, THE(1953); INSIDE DETROIT(1955); MY SISTER EILEEN(1955); BLACKJACK KETCHUM, DESPERADO(1956); WEREWOLF, THE(1956); ESCAPE FROM SAN QUENTIN(1957); FURY AT SHOWDOWN(1957); OUTLAW'S SON(1957); UTAH BLAINE(1957)
Kenneth Christy
LUCKY JORDAN(1942); NO TIME FOR LOVE(1943)
Laclede Christy
STORM OVER THE ANDES(1935), w
Michael Christy
EYE FOR AN EYE, AN(1981)
Nan Christy
Silents
LOVE LIAR, THE(1916); ON THE QUIET(1918)
Misc. Silents
QUEST, THE(1915); LEOPARD'S BRIDE, THE(1916)
Ted Christy
NO HOLDS BARRED(1952)
Vic Christy
PRINCESS AND THE PIRATE, THE(1944); CHALLENGE TO BE FREE(1976)
Whitey Christy
SPRINGTIME IN THE SIERRAS(1947)
Maja Chrolowska
MAN OF IRON(1981, Pol.), art d
Chris Chronopolis
DELIRIUM(1979)
Gene Chronopoulos
HUSTLE(1975)
Mary Chronopoulou
NAKED BRIGADE, THE(1965, U.S./Gr.); RED LANTERNS(1965, Gr.); FEAR, THE(1967, Gr.)
Enrico Chroscicki
BEYOND THE LAW(1967, Ital.), p; DEATH RIDES A HORSE(1969, Ital.), p; DAY OF ANGER(1970, Ital./Ger.), p; BIG AND THE BAD, THE(1971, Ital./Fr./Span.), p
Henry Chroscicki
RUN FOR YOUR WIFE(1966, Fr./Ital.), p
Henryk Chroscicki
CONJUGAL BED, THE(1963, Ital.), p; MAGNIFICENT CUCKOLD, THE(1965, Fr./Ital.), p
Douglas W. Chruchill
PLATINUM BLONDE(1931), w
Allen Chrysler
FLAMING FRONTIER(1958, Can.)
Charles Chrysler
ESCAPADE(1935)
Kenneth Chryst
GLASS KEY, THE(1942); STREET OF CHANCE(1942)
Kenny Chryst
BABY FACE MORGAN(1942)
Belle Chrystal
WARM CORNER, A(1930, Brit.); HINDLE WAKES(1931, Brit.); HOBSON'S CHOI-CE(1931, Brit.); FRIDAY THE 13TH(1934, Brit.); GIRL IN THE FLAT, THE(1934, Brit.); YOUTHFUL FOLLY(1934, Brit.); KEY TO HARMONY(1935, Brit.); LIVING DEAD, THE(1936, Brit.); BREAKERS AHEAD(1938, Brit.); YELLOW SANDS(1938, Brit.); POISON PEN(1941, Brit.)
Belle Chrystall
CRIMINAL AT LARGE(1932, Brit.); EDGE OF THE WORLD, THE(1937, Brit.); FOLLOW YOUR STAR(1938, Brit.); CASTLE OF CRIMES(1940, Brit.)
Eric Lin Moon Chu
HAWAIIANS, THE(1970)
Kaisen Chu
IN GOD WE TRUST(1980)
Leemei Chu
DRAGON'S GOLD(1954)
Leemoi Chu
FORBIDDEN(1953)
Paul Chu
OPEN THE DOOR AND SEE ALL THE PEOPLE(1964)
Chu-Lai-Chit
SAMSON AND THE SEVEN MIRACLES OF THE WORLD(1963, Fr./Ital.)
Andrew Chua
SAINT JACK(1979)

Chu Shao Chuan
THIS ANGRY AGE(1958, Ital./Fr.)
King Chuan
SONS OF GOOD EARTH(1967, Hong Kong)
Margaret Tu Chuan
MADAME WHITE SNAKE(1963, Hong Kong)
Yen Chuan
MAGNIFICENT CONCUBINE, THE(1964, Hong Kong)
Chiao Chuang
LOVERS' ROCK(1966, Taiwan)
Tsao Chuang-Sheng
TRIPLE IRONS(1973, Hong Kong), art d
L. Chubarov
SUN SHINES FOR ALL, THE(1961, USSR)
Paul Chubb
KITTY AND THE BAGMAN(1983, Aus.)
Kenneth Chuck
CHINESE RING, THE(1947); INTRIGUE(1947)
Mama Chuck
Misc. Talkies
FRIDAY ON MY MIND(1970)
Chuck Banks' Big Band
WEDDING, A(1978)
Chuck Faulkner Band
SONG OF THE OPEN ROAD(1944)
The Chuckles
GIRL CAN'T HELP IT, THE(1956)
Byron Chudnow
DOBERMAN GANG, THE(1972), d; AMAZING DOBERMANS, THE(1976), d
Byron Ross Chudnow
DARING DOBERMANS, THE(1973), d
Dave Chudnow
BEASTS OF BERLIN(1939), m; BURIED ALIVE(1939), md; BILLY THE KID'S FIGHTING PALS(1941), md; PERILOUS WATERS(1948), md
David Chudnow
PRISON TRAIN(1938), md; PANAMA PATROL(1939), md; TORTURE SHIP(1939), m; I TAKE THIS OATH(1940), md; INSIDE THE LAW(1942), md; MAD MONSTER, THE(1942), m; QUEEN OF BROADWAY(1942), md; RUBBER RACKETEERS(1942), md; THEY RAID BY NIGHT(1942), m; BEHIND PRISON WALLS(1943), md; COR-REGIDOR(1943), md; HARVEST MELODY(1943), md; UNKNOWN GUEST, THE(1943), md; MACHINE GUN MAMA(1944), m, md; MONSTER MAKER, THE(1944), md; NABONGA(1944), m; SWEETHEARTS OF THE U.S.A.(1944), md; SWING HOSTESS(1944), md; BIG SHOW-OFF, THE(1945), md; GREAT FLAMA-RION, THE(1945), md; IN OLD NEW MEXICO(1945), m; KID SISTER, THE(1945), md; PEOPLE ARE FUNNY(1945), md; SONG FOR MISS JULIE, A(1945), md; BLACK BEAUTY(1946), md; DEVIL'S PLAYGROUND, THE(1946), md; FOOL'S GOLD(1946), m; MR. ACE(1946), md; RENEGADE GIRL(1946), md; SCANDAL IN PARIS(1946), md; UNEXPECTED GUEST(1946), m; CHRISTMAS EVE(1947), md; DANGEROUS VENTURE(1947), m; GUILTY, THE(1947), md; HEAVEN ONLY KNOWS(1947), md; HOPPY'S HOLIDAY(1947), m; JEWELS OF BRANDENBURG(1947), md; LU-RED(1947), md; MARAUDERS, THE(1947), m; SHOOT TO KILL(1947), md; STORK BITES MAN(1947), md; BIG TOWN SCANDAL(1948), md; ENCHANTED VALLEY, THE(1948), m; FIGHTING BACK(1948), md; GAY INTRUDERS, THE(1948), md; GIRL FROM MANHATTAN(1948), md; HALF PAST MIDNIGHT(1948), md; HIGH-WAY 13(1948), m; LET'S LIVE AGAIN(1948), md; ON OUR MERRY WAY(1948), md; STRIKE IT RICH(1948), md; WATERFRONT AT MIDNIGHT(1948), md; EL PA-SO(1949), md; GREAT DAN PATCH, THE(1949), md; LUCKY STIFF, THE(1949), md; MANHANDLED(1949), md; MISS MINK OF 1949(1949), md; THUNDER IN THE PINES(1949), md; TROUBLE PREFERRED(1949), m; EAGLE AND THE HAWK, THE(1950), md; FIGHTING REDHEAD, THE(1950), m; JACKIE ROBINSON STORY, THE(1950), m; LAWLESS, THE(1950), md; TRIPOLI(1950), m; VALENTINO(1951), m; RED PLANET MARS(1952), m; RUBY GENTRY(1952), md; DOBERMAN GANG, THE(1972), p; DARING DOBERMANS, THE(1973), p; AMAZING DOBERMANS, THE(1976), p
Davis Chudnow
TOWN WENT WILD, THE(1945), md
Dick Chudnow
HYSTERICAL(1983); OFF THE WALL(1983), a, w
Craig Chudy
OTHER SIDE OF THE MOUNTAIN-PART 2, THE(1978); TRON(1982)
Craig W. Chudy
BILLIE(1965)
K.I. Chugonov
Misc. Silents
RIVALS(1933, USSR)
Chugunov
ON HIS OWN(1939, USSR)
Grigori Chukhrai
BALLAD OF A SOLDIER(1960, USSR), d, w
Grigoriy Chukhray
CLEAR SKIES(1963, USSR), d; THERE WAS AN OLD COUPLE(1967, USSR), d
Dru-Ann Chukron
NEIGHBORS(1981)
Fred A. Chulack
LITTLE ARK, THE(1972), ed; MITCHELL(1975), ed
1984
LOVELINES(1984), ed
Fred Chulack
SPARTACUS(1960), ed; DARKER THAN AMBER(1970), ed; OUT OF TOWNERS, THE(1970), ed; C. C. AND COMPANY(1971), ed; LAST HARD MEN, THE(1976), ed; HERO AIN'T NOTHIN' BUT A SANDWICH, A(1977), ed; DREAMER(1979), ed; TOUCHED BY LOVE(1980), ed; PRIVATE LESSONS(1981), ed; PRIVATE SCHOOL(1983), ed; TIME TO DIE, A(1983), ed
William Chulack
PIECES OF DREAMS(1970), ed
William K. Chulack
OUTSIDE MAN, THE(1973, U.S./FR.), ed

Fred A. Chulak
BALLAD OF JOSIE(1968), ed
Fred Chulak
JORY(1972), ed
Cornell Chulay
CHEAP DETECTIVE, THE(1978)
Babs Chulla
1984
RUNAWAY(1984)
R. Chumak
WAR AND PEACE(1968, USSR)
V. Chumak
DAY THE WAR ENDED, THE(1961, USSR)
Howard Chuman
THREE CAME HOME(1950); HALLS OF MONTEZUMA(1951); I WAS AN AMERI-CAN SPY(1951); SECRETS OF MONTE CARLO(1951); MARA MARU(1952); FAIR WIND TO JAVA(1953); FORBIDDEN(1953)
Chumey Chumez
FAT ANGELS(1980, U.S./Span.), w
A. Chumina
JACK FROST(1966, USSR)
Kam Fong Chun
GHOST OF THE CHINA SEA(1958); SEVEN WOMEN FROM HELL(1961); DIA-MOND HEAD(1962)
William Chun
STEEL HELMET, THE(1951); MISSION OVER KOREA(1953)
Yen Chun
GRAND SUBSTITUTION, THE(1965, Hong Kong), a, d
Betty Chung
ENTER THE DRAGON(1973)
C.M. Chung
SECRET, THE(1979, Hong Kong), ph
David Chung
1984
NINJA III-THE DOMINATION(1984); REPO MAN(1984)
Doris Chung
LEFT HAND OF GOD, THE(1955)
Dorothy Chung
ANNA AND THE KING OF SIAM(1946)
Dr. E.Y. Chung
DISPUTED PASSAGE(1939)
Emma Chung
1984
HOTEL NEW HAMPSHIRE, THE(1984)
Esmond Chung
WHEN TIME RAN OUT(1980)
Frances Chung
SAIGON(1948); WOMEN IN THE NIGHT(1948)
George Chung
FIRST YANK INTO TOKYO(1945)
Gum Chung
GAMBLING SHIP(1933)
Ida F. O. Chung
1984
NIGHTSONGS(1984)
Jane Chung
PAL JOEY(1957)
Jennifer Chung
1984
KILLPOINT(1984), set d
Kei Chung
LOVE IS A MANY-SPLENDORED THING(1955); WAR IS HELL(1964)
Kei Thing Chung
ROGUES' REGIMENT(1948); HOUSE ON TELEGRAPH HILL(1951); I WAS AN AMERICAN SPY(1951)
Liu Chung
Misc. Silents
MYSTIC FACES(1918)
Paul Chang Chung
EMPRESS WU(1965, Hong Kong)
Walter Chung
Silents
DINTY(1920)
Wang Chung
TRIPLE IRONS(1973, Hong Kong)
Wong Chung
BARBARY COAST(1935); FORBIDDEN TRAIL(1936)
Young Sup Chung
1984
HOTEL NEW HAMPSHIRE, THE(1984)
Wan Chung-shan
DRAGON INN(1968, Chi.)
Chang Chung-wen
EMPRESS WU(1965, Hong Kong)
N. Churakovska
COSSACKS OF THE DON(1932, USSR)
Church
MARATHON MAN(1976)
Allen Church
BOY FROM INDIANA(1950)
Blanch Church
MILLIONAIRE KID(1936), w
Bob Church
VIDEODROME(1983, Can.)
Clair Church
$1,000 A MINUTE(1935), w
Claire Church
HEADLINE WOMAN, THE(1935), w; NAVY BORN(1936), w

Elaine Church
JUSTINE(1969)
Esme Church
AUTUMN CROCUS(1934, Brit.); LOVE, LIFE AND LAUGHTER(1934, Brit.); MISTER CINDERS(1934, Brit.); OLD ROSES(1935, Brit.); MEN OF THE SEA(1951, Brit.)
Fred Church
SOUTH OF SONORA(1930); RIDERS OF THE CACTUS(1931); WILD WEST WHOOPEE(1931)
Misc. Talkies
DEVIL'S CANYON(1935)
Silents
CLEVER MRS. CARFAX, THE(1917); ANGEL CHILD(1918)
Misc. Silents
LONG CHANCE, THE(1915); ROMANCE OF BILLY GOAT HILL, A(1916); SECRET OF THE SWAMP, THE(1916); BLINDNESS OF DIVORCE, THE(1918); MADAME DUBARRY(1918); MAN FROM NEW YORK, THE(1923); PRINCE OF THE SAD-DLE(1926); SIGNAL FIRES(1926); STACKED CARDS(1926); TWO FISTED BUCK-AROO(1926); LONE RIDER, THE(1927); UNKNOWN RIDER, THE(1929); WESTERN METHODS(1929)
Gilbert Church
CURSE OF THE WRAYDONS, THE(1946, Brit.), p; BLACK MEMORY(1947, Brit.), p; MYSTERIOUS MR. NICHOLSON, THE(1947, Brit.), p; GREED OF WILLIAM HART, THE(1948, Brit.), p; TEMPTRESS, THE(1949, Brit.), p; KING OF THE UNDER-WORLD(1952, Brit.), p; SKID KIDS(1953, Brit.), p; TIM DRISCOLL'S DONKEY(1955, Brit.), p; ADVENTURES OF HAL 5, THE(1958, Brit.), p
John Church
SQUADRON 633(1964, U.S./Brit.); 633 SQUADRON(1964)
Judy Church
TAKING TIGER MOUNTAIN(1983, U.S./Welsh)
Madeline Church
BLOODY KIDS(1983, Brit.)
Norris Church
JETLAG(1981, U.S./Span.)
Pat Church
INTERNES CAN'T TAKE MONEY(1937)
Peter Church
STAR!(1968); KILLER FORCE(1975, Switz./Ireland), art d
Sandra Church
MUGGER, THE(1958); UGLY AMERICAN, THE(1963)
Stanley Church
GREAT JEWEL ROBBER, THE(1950); FRIDAY THE 13TH... THE ORPHAN(1979)
Suzanne Church
GREAT MUPPET CAPER, THE(1981)
Misc. Talkies
CHILD'S PLAY(1984, Brit.)
Thornton Church
Silents
BRAZEN BEAUTY(1918)
Misc. Silents
DECIDING KISS, THE(1918)
Tony Church
WORK IS A FOUR LETTER WORD(1968, Brit.); TESS(1980, Fr./Brit.); KRULL(1983)
1984
PLAGUE DOGS, THE(1984, U.S./Brit.)
Melinda Churcher
CROMWELL(1970, Brit.); LUST FOR A VAMPIRE(1971, Brit.)
Misc. Talkies
LOVE PILL, THE(1971)
Anne Churchill
1984
THIS IS SPINAL TAP(1984)
Berton Churchill
NOTHING BUT THE TRUTH(1929); SECRETS OF A SECRETARY(1931); AFRAID TO TALK(1932); AIR EAGLES(1932); AMERICAN MADNESS(1932); BIG STAMPEDE, THE(1932); BILLION DOLLAR SCANDAL(1932); CABIN IN THE COTTON(1932); CROOKED CIRCLE(1932); DARK HORSE, THE(1932); FALSE FACES(1932); I AM A FUGITIVE FROM A CHAIN GANG(1932); IF I HAD A MILLION(1932); IMPATIENT MAIDEN(1932); MADAME BUTTERFLY(1932); OKAY AMERICA(1932); RICH ARE ALWAYS WITH US, THE(1932); SCANDAL FOR SALE(1932); TAXI!(1932); TWO SECONDS(1932); WEEK-ENDS ONLY(1932); AVENGER, THE(1933); BIG BRAIN, THE(1933); DR. BULL(1933); ELMER THE GREAT(1933); EMPLOYEE'S ENTRAN-CE(1933); FROM HELL TO HEAVEN(1933); HARD TO HANDLE(1933); HER FIRST MATE(1933); HEROES FOR SALE(1933); LADIES MUST LOVE(1933); LAUGHTER IN HELL(1933); LITTLE GIANT, THE(1933); MASTER OF MEN(1933); MYSTERIOUS RIDER, THE(1933); ONLY YESTERDAY(1933); PRIVATE JONES(1933); SO THIS IS AFRICA(1933); BABBITT(1934); BACHELOR BAIT(1934); DAMES(1934); FRIENDS OF MR. SWEENEY(1934); FRONTIER MARSHAL(1934); HALF A SINNER(1934); HI, NELLIE!(1934); JUDGE PRIEST(1934); KID MILLIONS(1934); LET'S BE RITZY(1934); MENACE(1934); MURDER IN THE PRIVATE CAR(1934); RED HEAD(1934); STRICT-LY DYNAMITE(1934); TAKE THE STAND(1934); BACHELOR OF ARTS(1935); CORONADO(1935); COUNTY CHAIRMAN, THE(1935); I LIVE FOR LOVE(1935); NIGHT AT THE RITZ, A(1935); PAGE MISS GLORY(1935); RAINMAKERS, THE(1935); SING SING NIGHTS(1935); SPANISH CAPE MYSTERY(1935); STEAM-BOAT ROUND THE BEND(1935); VAGABOND LADY(1935); $10 RAISE(1935); BUNK-ER BEAN(1936); COLLEEN(1936); DARK HOUR, THE(1936); DIMPLES(1936); DIZZY DAMES(1936); PAROLE(1936); THREE OF A KIND(1936); UNDER YOUR SPELL(1936); YOU MAY BE NEXT(1936); PARNELL(1937); PUBLIC WEDDING(1937); RACING LADY(1937); SING AND BE HAPPY(1937); SINGING MARINE, THE(1937); WILD AND WOOLLY(1937); YOU CAN'T BEAT LOVE(1937); COWBOY AND THE LADY, THE(1938); DANGER ON THE AIR(1938); DOWN IN ARKANSAW(1938); FOUR MEN AND A PRAYER(1938); HE COULDN'T SAY NO(1938); IN OLD CHICA-GO(1938); KENTUCKY MOONSHINE(1938); LADIES IN DISTRESS(1938); MEET THE MAYOR(1938); QUICK MONEY(1938); SWEETHEARTS(1938); WIDE OPEN FA-CES(1938); ANGELS WASH THEIR FACES(1939); DAUGHTERS COURA-GEOUS(1939); HERO FOR A DAY(1939); ON YOUR TOES(1939); SHOULD HUSBANDS WORK?(1939); STAGECOACH(1939); BROTHER RAT AND A BA-BY(1940); CROSS COUNTRY ROMANCE(1940); I'M NOBODY'S SWEETHEART NOW(1940); PUBLIC DEB NO. 1(1940); SATURDAY'S CHILDREN(1940); SO THIS IS LONDON(1940, Brit.); TURNABOUT(1940); TWENTY MULE TEAM(1940); WAY OF ALL FLESH, THE(1940)

Misc. Silents
ROAD CALLED STRAIGHT, THE(1919); TONGUES OF FLAME(1924)
Bonnie Jean Churchill
GIVE ME A SAILOR(1938)
Burton Churchill
HUSBAND'S HOLIDAY(1931); WASHINGTON MASQUERADE(1932); GOLDEN HARVEST(1933)
Diana Churchill
SALLY BISHOP(1932, Brit.); FOREIGN AFFAIRES(1935, Brit.); DISHONOR BRIGHT(1936, Brit.); POT LUCK(1936, Brit.); SENSATION(1936, Brit.); DOMINANT SEX, THE(1937, Brit.); HOUSEMASTER(1938, Brit.); JANE STEPS OUT(1938, Brit.); YES, MADAM?(1938, Brit.); SCHOOL FOR HUSBANDS(1939, Brit.); CASTLE OF CRIMES(1940, Brit.); LAW AND DISORDER(1940, Brit.); SPIDER, THE(1940, Brit.); HISTORY OF MR. POLLY, THE(1949, Brit.); SCOTT OF THE ANTARCTIC(1949, Brit.); WINTER'S TALE, THE(1968, Brit.)
Donald Churchill
YESTERDAY'S ENEMY(1959, Brit.); VICTIM(1961, Brit.); SPACEFLIGHT IC-1(1965, Brit.); WILD AFFAIR, THE(1966, Brit.); ZEPPELIN(1971, Brit.), w; GREAT TRAIN ROBBERY, THE(1979, Brit.); HOUND OF THE BASKERVILLES, THE(1983, Brit.)
Douglas Churchill
RENO(1930), w
Edward Churchill
ROCKY RHODES(1934), w; EXCLUSIVE(1937); FORCED LANDING(1941), w; POWER DIVE(1941), w
Frank Churchill
SNOW WHITE AND THE SEVEN DWARFS(1937), m; BAMBI(1942), m
Joan Churchill
PUNISHMENT PARK(1971), ph
Marguerite Churchill
PLEASURE CRAZED(1929); SEVEN FACES(1929); THEY HAD TO SEE PARIS(1929); VALIANT, THE(1929); BIG TRAIL, THE(1930); BORN RECKLESS(1930); GOOD INTENTIONS(1930); HARMONY AT HOME(1930); AMBASSADOR BILL(1931); CHARLIE CHAN CARRIES ON(1931); GIRLS DEMAND EXCITEMENT(1931); QUICK MILLIONS(1931); RIDERS OF THE PURPLE SAGE(1931); FORGOTTEN COMMANDMENTS(1932); GIRL WITHOUT A ROOM(1933); SPEED DEVILS(1935); ALIBI FOR MURDER(1936); FINAL HOUR, THE(1936); LEGION OF TERROR(1936); MAN HUNT(1936); MURDER BY AN ARISTOCRAT(1936); WALKING DEAD, THE(1936); BUNCO SQUAD(1950)
Marquerite Churchill
DRACULA'S DAUGHTER(1936); PENTHOUSE PARTY(1936)
Maude Churchill
ODETTE(1951, Brit.), cos; WEEKEND WITH LULU, A(1961, Brit.), cos; HAUNTING, THE(1963), cos; MURDER AT THE GALLOP(1963, Brit.), cos
Odette Sansom Churchill
ODETTE(1951, Brit.), tech adv
Randolph Churchill
PARNELL(1937)
Robert B. Churchill
BORN TO SPEED(1947), w; WEST TO GLORY(1947), w
Robert Churchill
FIGHTING VIGILANTES, THE(1947), w; LIGHTHOUSE(1947), w
Sarah Churchill
WHO'S YOUR LADY FRIEND?(1937, Brit.); HE FOUND A STAR(1941, Brit.); SPRING MEETING(1941, Brit.); ALL OVER THE TOWN(1949, Brit.); ROYAL WEDDING(1951); FABIAN OF THE YARD(1954, Brit.); IMMORAL CHARGE(1962, Brit.)
Savannah Churchill
MIRACLE IN HARLEM(1948)
Misc. Talkies
SOULS OF SIN(1949)
Spencer Churchill
RECKONING, THE(1971, Brit.)
Winston Churchill
EXTRAORDINARY SEAMAN, THE(1969)
Sir Winston Churchill
YOUNG WINSTON(1972, Brit.), w
Inna Churikova
JACK FROST(1966, USSR)
V. Churkin
SONS AND MOTHERS(1967, USSR)
Blanche Churms
Silents
JOYOUS ADVENTURES OF ARISTIDE PUJOL, THE(1920, Brit.)
Rudy Churney
JOE(1970)
Lea Chursina
HOUSE ON THE FRONT LINE, THE(1963, USSR); WHEN THE TREES WERE TALL(1965, USSR)
B. Churskov
DREAM OF A COSSACK(1982, USSR), w
Gilles Chusseau
SIX IN PARIS(1968, Fr.)
Chute the Kangaroo
WILD INNOCENCE(1937, Aus.)
George Chuvalo
STONE COLD DEAD(1980, Can.)
I. Chuvelef
CAPTAIN GRANT'S CHILDREN(1939, USSR)
I. Chuvelev
SKI BATTALION(1938, USSR); ON HIS OWN(1939, USSR)
Yu. Chuveleva
WAR AND PEACE(1968, USSR)
Ivan Chuvelov
Misc. Silents
END OF ST. PETERSBURG, THE(1927, USSR)
V. Chuvelov
Misc. Silents
END OF ST. PETERSBURG, THE(1927, USSR)

Don Chuy
EVERYTHING YOU ALWAYS WANTED TO KNOW ABOUT SEX, BUT WE'RE AFRAID TO ASK(1972)
Chuy Reyes and his Mambo Orchestra
HOLIDAY RHYTHM(1950)
Chuy Reyes and Orchestra
EVERYBODY'S DANCIN'(1950)
Chuy Reyes' Orchestra
PAN-AMERICANA(1945)
Ivan Chuyelyov
Misc. Silents
WHITE EAGLE, THE(1928, USSR)
Maria Chwalibog
JOAN OF THE ANGELS(1962, Pol.)
Jan Chwiej
ON THE YARD(1978)
Herbert Chwoika
POSSESSION(1981, Fr./Ger.)
Eugeniusz Chylek
JOHNNY ON THE RUN(1953, Brit.)
V. Chyornyy
LAST GAME, THE(1964, USSR)
Vera Chytilova
DAISIES(1967, Czech.), d, w
CI-PA-ROMA
THIS MAN CAN'T DIE(1970, Ital.), spec eff
Bill Ciaccia
SPRING FEVER(1983, Can.)
Marissa Ciampaglia
VAMPIRE AND THE BALLERINA, THE(1962, Ital.), ch
Elgin Ciampi
STRANGERS IN THE CITY(1962), w; ZEBRA IN THE KITCHEN(1965), w
Paola Ciampi
LEAP INTO THE VOID(1982, Ital.)
Yves Ciampi
PERFECTIONIST, THE(1952, Fr.), d, w; TIME BOMB(1961, Fr./Ital.), d, w; SKY ABOVE HEAVEN(1964, Fr./Ital.), d, w; MATTER OF DAYS, A(1969, Fr./Czech.), p&d, w
Antonio Cianci
CONDEMNED OF ALTONA, THE(1963); SAMSON AND THE SEVEN MIRACLES OF THE WORLD(1963, Fr./Ital.); WITCH'S CURSE, THE(1963, Ital.)
Andy Cianella
GOODBYE COLUMBUS(1969), makeup
Edward Cianelli [Eduardo Ciannelli]
VOLCANO(1953, Ital.)
Lewis Cianelli
TERESA(1951)
Cianfanelli
MOST WANTED MAN, THE(1962, Fr./Ital.)
E. Cianfelli
MAN COULD GET KILLED, A(1966)
Giovanni Cianfriglia
SANDOKAN THE GREAT(1964, Fr./Ital./Span.); FIVE GIANTS FROM TEXAS(1966, Ital./Span.); TRAMPLERS, THE(1966, Ital.)
John Cianfrone
NIGHTHAWKS(1981)
Valeria Ciangotini
EXTERMINATORS, THE(1965 Fr.)
Valeria Ciangottini
FROM A ROMAN BALCONY(1961, Fr./Ital.); LA DOLCE VITA(1961, Ital./Fr.); VICE AND VIRTUE(1965, Fr./Ital.); TIGHT SKIRTS, LOOSE PLEASURES(1966, Fr.)
Valerie Ciangottini
FAMILY DIARY(1963 Ital.)
Leo Ciani
NUNZIO(1978); WARRIORS, THE(1979)
Suzanne Ciani
INCREDIBLE SHRINKING WOMAN, THE(1981), m
Andrew Ciannella
STRANGER IS WATCHING, A(1982), makeup
Eduardo Ciannelli
REUNION IN VIENNA(1933); SCOUNDREL, THE(1935); WINTERSET(1936); CRIMINAL LAWYER(1937); GIRL FROM SCOTLAND YARD, THE(1937); HITTING A NEW HIGH(1937); LEAGUE OF FRIGHTENED MEN(1937); MARKED WOMAN(1937); ON SUCH A NIGHT(1937); SUPER SLEUTH(1937); BLIND ALIBI(1938); LAW OF THE UNDERWORLD(1938); ANGELS WASH THEIR FACES(1939); BULLDOG DRUMMOND'S BRIDE(1939); GUNGA DIN(1939); RISKY BUSINESS(1939); SOCIETY LAWYER(1939); FOREIGN CORRESPONDENT(1940); FORGOTTEN GIRLS(1940); KITTY FOYLE(1940); MUMMY'S HAND, THE(1940); OUTSIDE THE 3-MILE LIMIT(1940); STRANGE CARGO(1940); ZANZIBAR(1940); ELLERY QUEEN'S PENTHOUSE MYSTERY(1941); PARIS CALLING(1941); THEY MET IN BOMBAY(1941); CAIRO(1942); DR. BROADWAY(1942); CONSTANT NYMPH, THE(1943); FLIGHT FOR FREEDOM(1943); THEY GOT ME COVERED(1943); CONSPIRATORS, THE(1944); MASK OF DIMITRIOS, THE(1944); PASSAGE TO MARSEILLE(1944); STORM OVER LISBON(1944); BELL FOR ADANO, A(1945); CRIME DOCTOR'S WARNING(1945); DILLINGER(1945); INCENDIARY BLONDE(1945); CALIFORNIA(1946); GILDA(1946); HEARTBEAT(1946); JOE PALOOKA, CHAMP(1946); PERILOUS HOLIDAY(1946); WIFE OF MONTE CRISTO, THE(1946); CRIME DOCTOR'S GAMBLE(1947); I LOVE TROUBLE(1947); LOST MOMENT, THE(1947); SEVEN KEYS TO BALDPATE(1947); CREEPER, THE(1948); ON OUR MERRY WAY(1948); TO THE VICTOR(1948); PRINCE OF FOXES(1949); RAPTURE(1950, Ital.); FUGITIVE LADY(1951); PEOPLE AGAINST O'HARA, THE(1951); MAMBO(1955); STRANGER'S HAND, THE(1955, Brit.); HELEN OF TROY(1956, Ital); LOVE SLAVES OF THE AMAZONS(1957); ATTILA(1958, Ital.); HOUSEBOAT(1958); MONSTER FROM THE GREEN HELL(1958); SHIP OF CONDEMNED WOMEN, THE(1963, Ital.); VISIT, THE(1964, Ger./Fr./Ital./U.S.); CHASE, THE(1966); SPY IN THE GREEN HAT, THE(1966); BROTHERHOOD, THE(1968); BOOT HILL(1969, Ital.); MACKENNA'S GOLD(1969); SECRET OF SANTA VITTORIA, THE(1969); STILETTO(1969)
Misc. Talkies
ROSE OF SANTA ROSA(1947); MASSACRE AT GRAND CANYON(1965)

Edward Ciannelli
  YOU CAN'T ESCAPE FOREVER(1942)
Edward [Eduardo] Ciannelli
  I WAS A PRISONER ON DEVIL'S ISLAND(1941)
Lewis Ciannelli
  SACCO AND VANZETTI(1971, Ital./Fr.)
Lewis E. Ciannelli
  MURDER CLINIC, THE(1967, Ital./Fr.), p&d
Eloisa Cianni
  PIRATE OF THE BLACK HAWK, THE(1961, Fr./Ital.)
A. Ciaognini
  RING AROUND THE CLOCK(1953, Ital.), m
Roberta Ciappi
  BRUCE LEE-TRUE STORY(1976, Chi.)
Carl Ciarfalio
  1984
  AGAINST ALL ODDS(1984)
Francesco Ciarletta
  SUCKER, THE(1966, Fr./Ital.), art d
Giovanni Ciarlo
  CRIME AT PORTA ROMANA(1980, Ital.), ph
Joe Ciasulli
  1984
  CHATTANOOGA CHOO CHOO(1984)
Romeo Ciatti
  NIGHT EVELYN CAME OUT OF THE GRAVE, THE(1973, Ital.), ed
Luigi Ciavarro
  ONCE UPON A TIME IN THE WEST(1969, U.S./Ital.)
Colley Cibber
  RICHARD III(1956, Brit.), w
Nada Cibic
  ROMANCE OF A HORSE THIEF(1971)
Caroline Cibot
  1984
  A NOS AMOURS(1984, Fr.)
Jose Cibrian
  MAN AND THE BEAST, THE(1951, Arg.); GAMES MEN PLAY, THE(1968, Arg.)
Chick Cicarelli
  DRUMS OF TABU, THE(1967, Ital./Span.)
Luigi Ciccarese
  1984
  CAGED WOMEN(1984, Ital./Fr.), ph
Janet Cicchese
  1984
  BOSTONIANS, THE(1984)
Anthony Ciccolini
  POPI(1969), ed
Chic Ciccolini
  WHERE'S POPPA?(1970), ed
Roy Ciccolini
  HUNCHBACK OF ROME, THE(1963, Ital.)
Michael Ciccone
  DR. HECKYL AND MR. HYPE(1980)
Steve Ciccone
  DR. HECKYL AND MR. HYPE(1980)
Leo Ciceri
  JOSEPHINE AND MEN(1955, Brit.)
Fernando Cicero
  STEPPE, THE(1963, Fr./Ital.); SALVATORE GIULIANO(1966, Ital.)
Mike Cichette
  FORT APACHE, THE BRONX(1981)
Martin Cichy
  COVERED WAGON TRAILS(1930); DOWN TO THEIR LAST YACHT(1934); HOUSE ACROSS THE BAY, THE(1940); AIR RAID WARDENS(1943); CORNERED(1945); FOLLOW ME QUIETLY(1949); GAL WHO TOOK THE WEST, THE(1949); GOLDEN BLADE, THE(1953); FOXFIRE(1955)
Silents
  RIDERS OF THE RIO GRANDE(1929)
Misc. Silents
  CODE OF THE WEST(1929); O'MALLEY RIDES ALONE(1930)
Bino Cicogna
  REVENGE AT EL PASO(1968, Ital.), p; MACHINE GUN McCAIN(1970, Ital.), p
Marina Cicogna
  MEDEA(1971, Ital./Fr./Ger.), p; MASTER TOUCH, THE(1974, Ital./Ger.), p
Alessandro Cicognini
  SHOE SHINE(1947, Ital.), m; MIRACLE IN MILAN(1951, Ital.), m; STORMBOUND(1951, Ital.), m; THIEF OF VENICE, THE(1952), m; LITTLE WORLD OF DON CAMILLO, THE(1953, Fr./Ital.), m; TIMES GONE BY(1953, Ital.), m; HELLO, ELEPHANT(1954, Ital.), m; INDISCRETION OF AN AMERICAN WIFE(1954, U.S./Ital.), m; FRISKY(1955, Ital.), m; LUCKY TO BE A WOMAN(1955, Ital.), m; SUMMERTIME(1955, Ital.), m; ULYSSES(1955, Ital.), m; LOSER TAKES ALL(1956, Brit.), m; GOLD OF NAPLES(1957, Ital.), m; ANNA OF BROOKLYN(1958, Ital.), m; BLACK ORCHID(1959), m; BREATH OF SCANDAL, A(1960), m; IT STARTED IN NAPLES(1960), m; PIGEON THAT TOOK ROME, THE(1962), m
Allessandro Cicognini
  BREAD, LOVE AND DREAMS(1953, Ital.), m; TOO BAD SHE'S BAD(1954, Ital.), m
Alsandro Cicognini
  FAST AND SEXY(1960, Fr./Ital.), m
Pierangelo Cicoletti
  SUSPIRIA(1977, Ital.), cos
Piero Cicoletti
  LION OF THE DESERT(1981, Libya/Brit.), cos
Jean Paul Ciebert
  BLOCKHOUSE, THE(1974, Brit.), w
Jan Ciecierski
  ASHES AND DIAMONDS(1961, Pol.); CONDUCTOR, THE(1981, Pol.)
Anna Ciepiela
  JOVITA(1970, Pol.)

Anna Ciepielewska
  JOAN OF THE ANGELS(1962, Pol.); PASSENGER, THE(1970, Pol.)
Maria Ciesielska
  PASSENGER, THE(1970, Pol.)
Piotr Cieslak
  MAN OF MARBLE(1979, Pol.)
Leslie Cifarelli
  RENT CONTROL(1981)
Antonio Cifariello
  SCANDAL IN SORRENTO(1957, Ital./Fr.); AWAKENING, THE(1958, Ital.); IT HAPPENED IN ROME(1959, Ital.); NEOPOLITAN CAROUSEL(1961, Ital.); IN SEARCH OF THE CASTAWAYS(1962, Brit.); JESSICA(1962, U.S./Ital./Fr.); DOLL THAT TOOK THE TOWN, THE(1965, Ital.)
Antonio Ciffariello
  YOUNG HUSBANDS(1958, Ital./Fr.)
Alessandro Cigognini
  UMBERTO D(1955, Ital.), m
Allesandro Cigognini
  BICYCLE THIEF, THE(1949, Ital.), m
Laci Cigoj
  CAVE OF THE LIVING DEAD(1966, Yugo./Ger.)
Cigolani
  PAISAN(1948, Ital.)
Emilio Cigoli
  LITTLE MARTYR, THE(1947, Ital.); RITA(1963, Fr./Ital.)
Giovanna Cigoli
  LITTLE MARTYR, THE(1947, Ital.)
Emilio Cigoll
  SHOE SHINE(1947, Ital.)
Barbara Cihlar
  DEVONSVILLE TERROR, THE(1983)
Karl Cik
  SONS OF SATAN(1969, Ital./Fr./Ger.)
Cilea
  ANYTHING FOR A SONG(1947, Ital.), m
Diana Cilento
  DUET FOR FOUR(1982, Aus.)
Diane Cilento
  DEAD ON COURSE(1952, Brit.); MOULIN ROUGE(1952); MEET MR. LUCIFER(1953, Brit.); PASSING STRANGER, THE(1954, Brit.); PASSAGE HOME(1955, Brit.); WOMAN FOR JOE, THE(1955, Brit.); ANGEL WHO PAWNED HER HARP, THE(1956, Brit.); ADMIRABLE CRICHTON, THE(1957, Brit.); TRUTH ABOUT WOMEN, THE(1958, Brit.); JET STORM(1961, Brit.); NAKED EDGE, THE(1961, Brit.); STOP ME BEFORE I KILL!(1961, Brit.); I THANK A FOOL(1962, Brit.); TOM JONES(1963, Brit.); RATTLE OF A SIMPLE MAN(1964, Brit.); THIRD SECRET, THE(1964, Brit.); AGONY AND THE ECSTASY, THE(1965); HOMBRE(1967); YOU ONLY LIVE TWICE(1967, Brit.); NEGATIVES(1968, Brit.); Z.P.G.(1972); HITLER: THE LAST TEN DAYS(1973, Brit./Ital.); WICKER MAN, THE(1974, Brit.)
Misc. Talkies
  ALL HALLOWE'EN(1952)
Wayne Cilento
  ANNIE(1982)
Miles Ciletti
  KILLING OF A CHINESE BOOKIE, THE(1976)
Luis Cilia
  VOYAGE OF SILENCE(1968, Fr.), m
Jana Cilliers
  GAME FOR VULTURES, A(1980, Brit.)
Norbert Cills
Misc. Silents
  KEITH OF THE BORDER(1918); LAW'S OUTLAW, THE(1918)
Natalie Cilona
  HERO AT LARGE(1980)
Ricky Cilona
  SQUEEZE A FLOWER(1970, Aus.)
Luigi Cimara
  LOYALTY OF LOVE(1937, Ital.); ANYTHING FOR A SONG(1947, Ital.); CENTO ANNI D'AMORE(1954, Ital.)
Luigi Cimari
  DESTINY(1938)
Gaetano Cimarosa
  DAY OF THE OWL, THE(1968, Ital./Fr.); MAFIA(1969, Fr./Ital.)
Michele Cimarosa
  BROTHERHOOD, THE(1968)
Matt Cimber
  BLACK SIX, THE(1974), p&d; BUTTERFLY(1982), p&d, w; TIME TO DIE, A(1983), d, w
  1984
  HUNDRA(1984, Ital.), d, w; YELLOW HAIR AND THE FORTRESS OF GOLD(1984), d, w
Misc. Talkies
  CALLIOPE(1971), d; CANDY TANGERINE MAN, THE(1975), d; LADY COCOA(1975), d; WITCH WHO CAME FROM THE SEA, THE(1976), d; FAKE-OUT(1982), d
Dr. Pietro Cimini
  ONE NIGHT OF LOVE(1934), md
Cimino
  SUPERARGO VERSUS DIABOLICUS(1966, Ital./Span.), set d
Franco Cimino
  L'AVVENTURA(1960, Ital.)
Leonard Cimino
  MONSIGNOR(1982)
Leonardo Cimino
  MAD DOG COLL(1961); QUICK, LET'S GET MARRIED(1965); STILETTO(1969); COTTON COMES TO HARLEM(1970); COME BACK CIHARLESTON BLUE(1972); JEREMY(1973); HIDE IN PLAIN SIGHT(1980); STARDUST MEMORIES(1980); AMITYVILLE II: THE POSSESSION(1982)
  1984
  DUNE(1984)

Mario Cimino
EXPERIMENT IN TERROR(1962); WHAT DID YOU DO IN THE WAR, DAD-DY?(1966)

Michael Cimino
SILENT RUNNING(1972), w; MAGNUM FORCE(1973), w; THUNDERBOLT AND LIGHTFOOT(1974), d&w; DEER HUNTER, THE(1978), p, d; HEAVEN'S GATE(1980), d&w

Michael Ciminod
ROSE, THE(1979), w

Frank J. Cimorelli
DEATH VALLEY(1982)

Teresa Cimpera
LEGEND OF FRENCHIE KING, THE(1971, Fr./Ital./Span./Brit.)

Shirley Cina
SOLDIER, THE(1982)

Nick Cinardo
1984
SPLASH(1984)

Martin Cinchy
TAMPICO(1944)

Cincinnati Reds
DEATH OF THE DIAMOND(1934)

Billy Cinders
Silents
LAW OF THE SNOW COUNTRY, THE(1926)

Cinedepth
CAPTAIN MILKSHAKE(1970), spec eff

Cinema Research Corp
TWO LITTLE BEARS, THE(1961), spec eff

Cingalee
CAN YOU HEAR ME MOTHER?(1935, Brit.)

Al Cingolani
SCARECROW(1973); HARDCORE(1979)

Elisabetta Cini
8 ½(1963, Ital.)

Isabella Cini
SHE AND HE(1969, Ital.)

Ruggero Cini
OPEN SEASON(1974, U.S./Span.), m

Cosimo Cinieri
TRAGEDY OF A RIDICULOUS MAN, THE(1982, Ital.)

Claudio Cinini
CRIME AT PORTA ROMANA(1980, Ital.), art d

R. Cinquini
HANNIBAL(1960, Ital.), ed

Renato Cinquini
MIGHTY CRUSADERS, THE(1961, Ital.), ed; QUEEN OF THE PIRATES(1961, Ital./Ger.), ed; FALL OF ROME, THE(1963, Ital.), ed; RAGE OF THE BUC-CANEERS(1963, Ital.), ed; SECRET MARK OF D'ARTAGNAN, THE(1963, Fr./Ital.), ed; QUEEN OF THE NILE(1964, Ital.), ed; SON OF CAPTAIN BLOOD, THE(1964, U.S./Ital./Span.), ed; TIGER OF THE SEVEN SEAS(1964, Fr./Ital.), ed; CAVERN, THE(1965, Ital./Ger.), ed; NIGHTMARE CASTLE(1966, Ital.), ed; SPY IN YOUR EYE(1966, Ital.), ed; JOURNEY BENEATH THE DESERT(1967, Fr./Ital.), ed; MIS-SION STARDUST(1968, Ital./Span./Ger.), ed; RUTHLESS FOUR, THE(1969, Ital./Ger.), ed; THREE NIGHTS OF LOVE(1969, Ital.), ed

Robert Cinquini
PRISONER OF THE VOLGA(1960, Fr./Ital.), ed

Roberta Cinquini
YOUNG HUSBANDS(1958, Ital./Fr.), ed

Roberto Cinquini
HERCULES' PILLS(1960, Ital.), ed; DIVORCE, ITALIAN STYLE(1962, Ital.), ed; SON OF SAMSON(1962, Fr./Ital./Yugo.), ed; LADY DOCTOR, THE(1963, Fr./Ital./Span.), ed; SQUARE OF VIOLENCE(1963, U.S./Yugo.), ed; CRAZY DESIRE(1964, Ital.), ed; FISTFUL OF DOLLARS, A(1964, Ital./Ger./Span.), ed; KAPO(1964, Ital./Fr./Yugo.), ed; SEDUCED AND ABANDONED(1964, Fr./Ital.), ed; FACTS OF MURDER, THE(1965, Ital.), ed; HOURS OF LOVE, THE(1965, Ital.), ed; LITTLE NUNS, THE(1965, Ital.), ed; SALLAH(1965, Israel), ed; PLACE CALLED GLORY, A(1966, Span./Ger.), ed; SPY IN YOUR EYE(1966, Ital.), ed; SEVEN GOLDEN MEN(1969, Fr./Ital./Span.), ed

Antonio Cintado
UGLY ONES, THE(1968, Ital./Span.); TRISTANA(1970, Span./Ital./Fr.)

Frederick Cintron
MAN, WOMAN AND CHILD(1983)

Sharon Cintron
HOW SWEET IT IS(1968)

Charles Cioffi
KLUTE(1971); SHAFT(1971); DON IS DEAD, THE(1973); CRAZY JOE(1974); RE: LUCKY LUCIANO(1974, Fr./Ital.); NEXT MAN, THE(1976); OTHER SIDE OF MID-NIGHT, THE(1977); GRAY LADY DOWN(1978); TIME AFTER TIME(1979, Brit.); MISSING(1982); ALL THE RIGHT MOVES(1983)

Mario Cioffi
NEOPOLITAN CAROUSEL(1961, Ital.)

Augusta Ciolli
MARTY(1955); FAST AND SEXY(1960, Fr./Ital.); LOVE WITH THE PROPER STRANGER(1963)

Franco Ciolli
ORGANIZER, THE(1964, Fr./Ital./Yugo.)

Marcello Ciorciolini
HUNS, THE(1962, Fr./Ital.), w

Richard Ciotti
WARRIORS, THE(1979)

Cipa
LADY FRANKENSTEIN(1971, Ital.), spec eff

Berenica Cipcus
MONDO TRASHO(1970)

Tubby Cipen
ALONG CAME SALLY(1934, Brit.)

Eddie Cipot
1984
NATURAL, THE(1984)

Jerry Cipperley
LOVE IS A FUNNY THING(1970, Fr./Ital.)

Leone Ciprelli
DISHONORED(1950, Ital.), w

Angela Cipriani
FRANKENSTEIN-ITALIAN STYLE(1977, Ital.), ed

Carla Cipriani
VACATION, THE(1971, Ital.), art d

Mario Cipriani
ACCATTONE!(1961, Ital.); WITCHES, THE(1969, Fr./Ital.)

S.W. Cipriani
TENTACLES(1977, Ital.), m

Stelvio Cipriani
STRANGER RETURNS, THE(1968, U.S./Ital./Ger./Span.), m; UGLY ONES, THE(1968, Ital./Span.), m; ANONYMOUS VENETIAN, THE(1971), m; COME-TOGETHER(1971), m; NIGHT HAIR CHILD(1971, Brit.), m; BLINDMAN(1972, Ital.), m; FRANKENSTEIN-ITALIAN STYLE(1977, Ital.), m; TAKE ALL OF ME(1978, Ital.), m

Mme. Felco Cipriano
TRAPEZE(1956)

Karen Ciral
UNDERTAKER AND HIS PALS, THE(1966); GOOD MORNING... AND GOOD-BYE(1967); CYCLE SAVAGES(1969); FM(1978)

The Circle Jerks
1984
REPO MAN(1984)

Chapman's Circus
MAKE-UP(1937, Brit.)

Clyde Beatty Circus
RING OF FEAR(1954)

B.J. Cirell
TATTOO(1981)

Charles Cirillo
NIGHT SONG(1947)

Charlie Cirillo
SQUARE DANCE JUBILEE(1949)

Claudio Cirillo
THIS MAN CAN'T DIE(1970, Ital.), ph; MOST WONDERFUL EVENING OF MY LIFE, THE(1972, Ital./Fr.), ph; ROCCO PAPALEO(1974, Ital./Fr.), ph; SCENT OF A WOMAN(1976, Ital.), ph; TWO SUPER COPS(1978, Ital.), ph; DESIRE, THE INTERI-OR LIFE(1980, Ital,/Ger.), ph

Joe Cirillo
TWO OF A KIND(1983)
1984
GHOSTBUSTERS(1984); SPLASH(1984)

Michael Cirillo
JOAN OF ARC(1948)

Michael A. Cirillo
SORROWFUL JONES(1949); MY FAVORITE SPY(1951); SON OF PALEFACE(1952)

Tony Cirillo
STORY OF DR. WASSELL, THE(1944); SORROWFUL JONES(1949)

Albert Cirimele
ONE DARK NIGHT(1983)

Natale Cirino
APPOINTMENT FOR MURDER(1954, Ital.)

Nick Cirino
Misc. Talkies
BURNOUT(1979)

Cirino and The Bowties
ROCK, ROCK, ROCK!(1956)

Jacques Ciron
INNOCENTS IN PARIS(1955, Brit.); FRENCH CANCAN(1956, Fr.); LADY L(1965, Fr./Ital.); BRAIN, THE(1969, Fr./US)

Sam Cirone
THIEF(1981)

George Cisar
CALL NORTHSIDE 777(1948); JOHNNY HOLIDAY(1949); TEEN-AGE CRIME WAVE(1955); DON'T KNOCK THE ROCK(1956); EMERGENCY HOSPITAL(1956); NIGHTFALL(1956); SCANDAL INCORPORATED(1956); WEREWOLF, THE(1956); ABDUCTORS, THE(1957); BROTHERS RICO, THE(1957); BUCKSKIN LADY, THE(1957); CHICAGO CONFIDENTIAL(1957); JAILHOUSE ROCK(1957); JET AT-TACK(1958); EDGE OF ETERNITY(1959); SOME CAME RUNNING(1959); VICE RAID(1959); MARRIED TOO YOUNG(1962); VIVA LAS VEGAS(1964); BILLY THE KID VS. DRACULA(1966); SPLIT, THE(1968); ...TICK...TICK...TICK...(1970)

Patricia Cisarano
1984
SKYLINE(1984, Spain)

Karel Cisarovsky
ROCKET TO NOWHERE(1962, Czech.), spec eff; VOYAGE TO THE END OF THE UNIVERSE(1963, Czech.), spec eff

Jean-Paul Cisife
CONFESSION, THE(1970, Fr.)

Mario Cisneros
HERBIE GOES BANANAS(1980)

Max Cisneros
THOMASINE AND BUSHROD(1974)

Marcella Cisney
UNDERCOVER MAN, THE(1949); HARD, FAST, AND BEAUTIFUL(1951)

Michael Cisney
CRISS CROSS(1949); JOLSON SINGS AGAIN(1949); MISS GRANT TAKES RICH-MOND(1949); ONCE MORE, MY DARLING(1949); UNDERCOVER MAN, THE(1949); PEGGY(1950)

Mamadou Cisoko
MANDABI(1970, Fr./Senegal)

Marina Cisternas
FRENCH LINE, THE(1954)
Raymond Cistheri
MELINDA(1972), w
Kasey Ciszk
YOU LIGHT UP MY LIFE(1977)
Phyliss Citas
GRAND THEFT AUTO(1977)
Sam Citen
EAST SIDE SADIE(1929), ed
Rosalie Citera
UP THE ACADEMY(1980)
Tom Citera
UP THE ACADEMY(1980)
Tommy Citera
FORTY DEUCE(1982)
Sonia Citicica
KILLER FISH(1979, Ital./Braz.)
Serge Citon
LAST OF SHEILA, THE(1973)
Michelle Citron
1984
WHAT YOU TAKE FOR GRANTED(1984), p,d&w, ed
Milton Citron
GALLANT ONE, THE(1964, U.S./Peru), ed
Sam Citron
BIRTH OF A BABY(1938), ed; TEVYA(1939), ed
Franco Citti
ACCATTONE!(1961, Ital.); MAMMA ROMA(1962, Ital.); SEATED AT HIS RIGHT(1968, Ital.); KILL THEM ALL AND COME BACK ALONE(1970, Ital./Span.); GODFATHER, THE(1972); LUNA(1979, Ital.); ARABIAN NIGHTS(1980, Ital./Fr.)
Misc. Talkies
BLACK JESUS(1971, Ital.)
Giulio Citti
LA DOLCE VITA(1961, Ital./Fr.)
Stepanka Cittova
FIFTH HORSEMAN IS FEAR, THE(1968, Czech.)
Jim City
DREAMS COME TRUE(1936, Brit.); TOWN THAT DREADED SUNDOWN, THE(1977)
M. Ciudad
WIND AND THE LION, THE(1975)
Sabatino Ciuffini
GOLD FOR THE CAESARS(1964), w; SEVEN REVENGES, THE(1967, Ital.), w; SONNY AND JED(1974, Ital.), w; SUPER FUZZ(1981), w
Sabatino Ciuffino
GIANT OF METROPOLIS, THE(1963, Ital.), w
Sabatino Ciuffni
TARTARS, THE(1962, Ital./Yugo.), w
Mara Ciukleva
MERCHANT OF SLAVES(1949, Ital.); CITY OF WOMEN(1980, Ital./Fr.)
Tommy Ciulla
PURSUIT OF D.B. COOPER, THE(1981)
Richard Ciupka
YESTERDAY(1980, Can.), ph; ATLANTIC CITY(1981, U.S./Can.), ph; DIRTY TRICKS(1981, Can.), ph; MELANIE(1982, Can.), ph; JOY(1983, Fr./Can.), ph
Carlo Civallero
HIS LAST TWELVE HOURS(1953, Ital.), p; LUXURY GIRLS(1953, Ital.), p; TIMES GONE BY(1953, Ital.), p; FRIENDS FOR LIFE(1964, Ital.), p
Pierangelo Civera
ASSASSINATION OF TROTSKY, THE(1972 Fr./Ital.)
Osvaldo Civirani
FABIOLA(1951, Ital.), ph; HERCULES AGAINST THE SONS OF THE SUN(1964, Span./Ital.), p,d&w
Misc. Talkies
DEVIL HAS SEVEN FACES, THE(1977), d
Diane Civita
1984
EL NORTE(1984)
Loudde Claar
SINCE YOU WENT AWAY(1944)
Loudie Claar
NORTH STAR, THE(1943)
Plinio Clabassi
JOAN AT THE STAKE(1954, Ital./Fr.)
Herbert Clache
Silents
SONG OF THE WAGE SLAVE, THE(1915), d
Ake Claesson
NIGHT IS MY FUTURE(1962, Swed.); LOVE MATES(1967, Swed.)
Don Clafa
SHANKS(1974)
George Claff
MEET ME AT DAWN(1947, Brit.), makeup; HORROR HOTEL(1960, Brit.), makeup; ROMEO AND JULIET(1966, Brit.), makeup; STOP THE WORLD–I WANT TO GET OFF(1966, Brit.), makeup
Renee Claff
MINI-AFFAIR, THE(1968, Brit.), makeup
Charles Clague
NEW ADVENTURES OF TARZAN(1935), art d; IDOL OF THE CROWDS(1937), art d; DEADLY GAME, THE(1941), art d; KING OF THE ZOMBIES(1941), art d; LET'S GO COLLEGIATE(1941), art d; SWING IN THE SADDLE(1944), art d; LET'S GO STEADY(1945), art d; OUTLAWS OF THE ROCKIES(1945), art d; BOSTON BLACKIE AND THE LAW(1946), art d; COWBOY BLUES(1946), art d; DESERT HORSEMAN, THE(1946), art d; LANDRUSH(1946), art d; LAWLESS EMPIRE(1946), art d; LAST DAYS OF BOOT HILL(1947), art d; LONE WOLF IN MEXICO, THE(1947), art d; MILLIE'S DAUGHTER(1947), art d; SPORT OF KINGS(1947), art d; PHANTOM VALLEY(1948), art d; SONG OF IDAHO(1948), art d; WEST OF SONORA(1948), art d; WHIRLWIND RAIDERS(1948), art d; DESERT VIGILANTE(1949), art d; LARAMIE(1949), art d; QUICK ON THE TRIGGER(1949), art d; RENEGADES OF THE SAGE(1949), art d; SOUTH OF DEATH VALLEY(1949), art d; FRONTIER OUTPOST(1950), art d; HORSEMEN OF THE SIERRAS(1950), art d; INDIAN TERRITORY(1950), art d; LIGHTNING GUNS(1950), art d; MULE TRAIN(1950), art d; OUTCAST OF BLACK MESA(1950), art d; RAIDERS OF TOMAHAWK CREEK(1950), art d; STREETS OF GHOST TOWN(1950), art d; TEXAS DYNAMO(1950), art d; FORT SAVAGE RAIDERS(1951), art d; GENE AUTRY AND THE MOUNTIES(1951), art d; HILLS OF UTAH(1951), art d; KID FROM AMARILLO, THE(1951), art d; PECOS RIVER(1951), art d; PRAIRIE ROUNDUP(1951), art d; RIDIN' THE OUTLAW TRAIL(1951), art d; SNAKE RIVER DESPERADOES(1951), art d; VALLEY OF FIRE(1951), art d; WHIRLWIND(1951), art d; HAWK OF WILD RIVER, THE(1952), art d; JUNCTION CITY(1952), art d; KID FROM BROKEN GUN, THE(1952), art d; LARAMIE MOUNTAINS(1952), art d; MONTANA TERRITORY(1952), art d; NIGHT STAGE TO GALVESTON(1952), art d; OLD WEST, THE(1952), art d; SMOKY CANYON(1952), art d; WAGON TEAM(1952), art d
A. C. T. Clair
FIRE MAIDENS FROM OUTER SPACE(1956, Brit.), ed
Bernice Clair
MOONLIGHT AND PRETZELS(1933)
Blanche Le Clair
JEALOUSY(1929)
Cyrielle Clair
TUSK(1980, Fr.)
Edith Clair
GET OUTTA TOWN(1960)
Ethlyne Clair
SECOND CHOICE(1930)
Silents
PAINTED PONIES(1927); HEY RUBE!(1928); GUN LAW(1929); WILD BLOOD(1929)
Misc. Silents
HERO ON HORSEBACK, A(1927); THREE MILES UP(1927); GUARDIANS OF THE WILD(1928); RIDING FOR FAME(1928)
George Clair
Silents
OLIVER TWIST, JR.(1921); SECRET OF THE HILLS, THE(1921)
Imogen Clair
MUSIC LOVERS, THE(1971, Brit.)
Jany Clair
LEGIONS OF THE NILE(1960, Ital.); PLANETS AGAINST US, THE(1961, Ital./Fr.); NIGHT THEY KILLED RASPUTIN, THE(1962, Fr./Ital.); PRISONER OF THE IRON MASK(1962, Fr./Ital.); CONQUEST OF MYCENE(1965, Ital., Fr.); EXTERMINATORS, THE(1965 Fr.); HERCULES AGAINST THE MOON MEN(1965, Fr./Ital.); ROAD TO FORT ALAMO, THE(1966, Fr./Ital.)
Malcolm St. Clair
Misc. Silents
FLEET'S IN, THE(1928), d
Mavis Clair
PRICE OF A SONG, THE(1935, Brit.); TENTH MAN, THE(1937, Brit.); SO THIS IS LONDON(1940, Brit.); MISSING TEN DAYS(1941, Brit.); ADVENTURE FOR TWO(1945, Brit.)
Mildred Clair
Misc. Silents
TREASON(1918)
Nadege Clair
1984
THREE CROWNS OF THE SAILOR(1984, Fr.)
Philippe Clair
UPPER HAND, THE(1967, Fr./Ital./Ger.)
1984
PAR OU T'ES RENTRE? ON T'A PAS VUE SORTIR(1984, Fr./Tunisia), a, d, w
Rene Clair
UNDER THE ROOFS OF PARIS(1930, Fr.), d&w; A NOUS LA LIBERTE(1931, Fr.), d&w, ed; MILLION, THE(1931, Fr.), d, w; LE DENIER MILLIARDAIRE(1934, Fr.), d&w; GHOST GOES WEST, THE(1936), d, w; BREAK THE NEWS(1938, Brit.), p&d; FLAME OF NEW ORLEANS, THE(1941), d; I MARRIED A WITCH(1942), d; FOREVER AND A DAY(1943), p&d; IT HAPPENED TOMORROW(1944), d, w; AND THEN THERE WERE NONE(1945), d; MAN ABOUT TOWN(1947, Fr.), p&d, w; BEAUTY AND THE DEVIL(1952, Fr./Ital.), d, w; LES BELLES-DE-NUIT(1952, Fr.), d&w; GRAND MANEUVER, THE(1956, Fr.), p&d, w; GATES OF PARIS(1958, Fr./Ital.), d, w; LOVE AND THE FRENCHWOMAN(1961, Fr.), w; THREE FABLES OF LOVE(1963, Fr./Ital./Span.), d, w
Silents
ITALIAN STRAW HAT, AN(1927, Fr.), d&w
Misc. Silents
PARIS QUI DORT(1924, Fr.), d; LE FANTOME DU MOULIN ROUGE(1925, Fr.), d; LE VOYAGE IMAGINAIRE(1926, Fr.), d; LA PROIE DU VENT(1927, Fr.), d; LES DEUX TIMIDES(1929, Fr.), d
Richard Clair
MOVIE STAR, AMERICAN STYLE, OR, LSD I HATE YOU!(1966); ON HER BED OF ROSES(1966); BEWARE! THE BLOB(1972), w
Suzanne Clair
SPITFIRE(1943, Brit.)
Adele Claire
PATSY, THE(1964); ONE WAY WAHINI(1965); DESTRUCTORS, THE(1968); WICKED DREAMS OF PAULA SCHULTZ, THE(1968); GOODBYE, NORMA JEAN(1976)
Alden Claire
RIDERS OF BLACK MOUNTAIN(1941)
Arleen Claire
SPECTER OF THE ROSE(1946)
Bernice Claire
NO, NO NANETTE(1930); NUMBERED MEN(1930); SONG OF THE FLAME(1930); SPRING IS HERE(1930); TOP SPEED(1930); KISS ME AGAIN(1931); TWO HEARTS IN HARMONY(1935, Brit.)
Clariet Claire
Silents
RIP VAN WINKLE(1914)
Cyrielle Claire
1984
SWORD OF THE VALIANT(1984, Brit.)

Dina Claire
GYPSY(1962)
Dorothy Claire
CAT BALLOU(1965); DIRTYMOUTH(1970)
Edith Claire
PEYTON PLACE(1957); THREE BRAVE MEN(1957)
Ethlyn Claire
GOD'S GIFT TO WOMEN(1931)
Ethlyne Claire
FROM HEADQUARTERS(1929)
George Claire, Jr.
Misc. Silents
SOUL'S CYCLE, THE(1916)
Gertrude Claire
Silents
ARYAN, THE(1916); JUNGLE CHILD, THE(1916); LIEUT. DANNY, U.S.A.(1916);
MARKET OF VAIN DESIRE, THE(1916); PEGGY(1916); CRAB, THE(1917); FEMALE
OF THE SPECIES(1917); WOODEN SHOES(1917); NINE O'CLOCK TOWN, A(1918);
WHEN DO WE EAT?(1918); LITTLE COMRADE(1919); PETAL ON THE CURRENT,
THE(1919); ROMANCE AND ARABELLA(1919); PARIS GREEN(1920); INVISIBLE
POWER, THE(1921); SIN OF MARTHA QUEED, THE(1921); ENVIRONMENT(1922);
OLIVER TWIST(1922); RIDIN' WILD(1922); SUPER-SEX, THE(1922); DAUGHTERS
OF TODAY(1924); LADIES TO BOARD(1924); ROMANCE ROAD(1925); TUM-
BLEWEEDS(1925); WEDDING SONG, THE(1925); LITTLE IRISH GIRL, THE(1926);
OUT OF THE WEST(1926); MARRIED ALIVE(1927); WE'RE ALL GAMBLERS(1927)
Misc. Silents
COWARD, THE(1915); BLUE BLAZES RAWDEN(1918); HARD BOILED(1919);
JINX(1919); STEPPING OUT(1919); CRADLE OF COURAGE, THE(1920); GREATER
THAN LOVE(1920); HAIL THE WOMAN(1921); SOCIETY SECRETS(1921); THINGS
MEN DO(1921); CRUSADER, THE(1922); HUMAN HEARTS(1922); HEART BANDIT,
THE(1924)
Imogen Claire
HENRY VIII AND HIS SIX WIVES(1972, Brit.); SAVAGE MESSIAH(1972, Brit.);
LISZTOMANIA(1975, Brit.); TOMMY(1975, Brit.); FLASH GORDON(1980); SHOCK
TREATMENT(1981)
Ina Claire
AWFUL TRUTH, THE(1929); ROYAL FAMILY OF BROADWAY, THE(1930); RE-
BOUND(1931); GREEKS HAD A WORD FOR THEM(1932); NINOTCHKA(1939);
CLAUDIA(1943); STAGE DOOR CANTEEN(1943); FIDDLER ON THE ROOF(1971)
Silents
PUPPET CROWN, THE(1915); WILD GOOSE CHASE, THE(1915)
Misc. Silents
POLLY WITH A PAST(1920)
Jan Claire
MADMAN(1982)
Laurene Claire
MY BODY HUNGERS(1967)
Linda Claire
GEORGE WHITE'S SCANDALS(1945)
Loraine Claire
LOVE MERCHANT, THE(1966)
Marie Claire
PUTNEY SWOPE(1969)
Marion Claire
MAKE A WISH(1937)
Mary Claire
CONSTANT NYMPH, THE(1933, Brit.)
Mavis Claire
CASE OF THE FRIGHTENED LADY, THE(1940. Brit.)
Ray Claire
SADDLE MOUNTAIN ROUNDUP(1941), ed; COWBOY COMMANDOS(1943), ed
Roy Claire
CIRCLE OF DEATH(1935), w; GUN SMOKE(1936), ed; ARIZONA GUNFIGHT-
ER(1937), ed; BORDER PHANTOM(1937), ed; GUN RANGER, THE(1937), ed; LAW-
MAN IS BORN, A(1937), ed; RED ROPE, THE(1937), ed; ROGUE OF THE
RANGE(1937), ed; DESERT PATROL(1938), ed; DURANGO VALLEY RAID-
ERS(1938), ed; FEUD MAKER(1938), ed; PAROLED–TO DIE(1938), ed; RANGE
BUSTERS, THE(1940), ed; TRAILING DOUBLE TROUBLE(1940), ed; WEST OF
PINTO BASIN(1940), ed; FUGITIVE VALLEY(1941), ed; KID'S LAST RIDE,
THE(1941), ed; TONTO BASIN OUTLAWS(1941), ed; TRAIL OF THE SILVER
SPURS(1941), ed; TUMBLEDOWN RANCH IN ARIZONA(1941), ed; UNDER-
GROUND RUSTLERS(1941), ed; WRANGLER'S ROOST(1941), ed; PRIDE OF THE
ARMY(1942), ed; ROCK RIVER RENEGADES(1942), ed; TEXAS TO BATAAN(1942),
ed; THUNDER RIVER FEUD(1942), ed; TRAIL RIDERS(1942), ed; WAR DOGS(1942),
ed; BLACK MARKET RUSTLERS(1943), ed; TWO FISTED JUSTICE(1943), ed
Shirley Claire
MUSIC MAN, THE(1962)
Sidney Claire
LOVE COMES ALONG(1930), m; CRIME OF DR. FORBES(1936), m
Susan Claire
SONG OF NORWAY(1970)
Willis Claire
FUGITIVE FROM JUSTICE, A(1940); IN OLD MISSOURI(1940); NIGHT AND
DAY(1946)
Zola Claire
Silents
GILDED DREAM, THE(1920)
Claire and Arene
FOLLIES GIRL(1943)
Aime Clairiond
MONSIEUR VINCENT(1949, Fr.)
Denny Clairmont
WORLD IS JUST A 'B' MOVIE, THE(1971), ph
Aime Clairond
LA MARSEILLAISE(1938, Fr.)
Jacques Clairoux
CITY ON FIRE(1979 Can.), ed

Laurence Clairval
MARRIED WOMAN, THE(1965, Fr.), cos
Georges Claisse
IS PARIS BURNING?(1966, U.S./Fr.); CHARLES AND LUCIE(1982, Fr.); FIVE DAYS
ONE SUMMER(1982)
Gayle Claitman
TIKI TIKI(1971, Can.)
Frank Clake
I ACCUSE(1958, Brit.), ed
Leopold Clam
YOUNG LORD, THE(1970, Ger.)
Renee Clama
DEVIL'S MAZE, THE(1929, Brit.); TAXI FOR TWO(1929, Brit.); GREAT GAME,
THE(1930); LATIN LOVE(1930, Brit.); SYMPHONY IN TWO FLATS(1930, Brit.);
NEVER TROUBLE TROUBLE(1931, Brit.); NO LADY(1931, Brit.); SPORT OF KINGS,
THE(1931, Brit.); STRONGER SEX, THE(1931, Brit.); MAN THEY COULDN'T AR-
REST, THE(1933, Brit.)
Silents
ADVENTUROUS YOUTH(1928, Brit.)
Clara Clamai
WITCHES, THE(1969, Fr./Ital.)
Dolores Claman
CAPTAIN APACHE(1971, Brit.), m
Elizabeth Claman
PLAY IT AS IT LAYS(1972)
Mel Claman
LONG SHOT(1981, Brit.)
A. Pismo Clamm
FLY NOW, PAY LATER(1969), a, m
Bob Clampett
BUGS BUNNY, SUPERSTAR(1975)
Clampham & Dwyer
SING AS YOU SWING(1937, Brit.)
Georgia Clancey
SEPTEMBER AFFAIR(1950)
Margaret Clancey
YOUNG AMERICA(1932), ed; SPLENDOR(1935), ed; GAY DESPERADO, THE(1936),
ed
Margaret V. Clancey
THEY HAD TO SEE PARIS(1929), ed; LILIOM(1930), ed; YOUNG AS YOU
FEEL(1931), ed
Silents
SLAVES OF BEAUTY(1927), ed
Vernon Clancey
FRENCH LEAVE(1937, Brit.), w; SATURDAY NIGHT REVUE(1937, Brit.), w; DEAD
MEN ARE DANGEROUS(1939, Brit.), w; FLYING FIFTY-FIVE(1939, Brit.), w; WANT-
ED BY SCOTLAND YARD(1939, Brit.), w
Vernon J. Clancey
SAVE A LITTLE SUNSHINE(1938, Brit.), w
Bill Clancy
NICE GIRL LIKE ME, A(1969, Brit.)
Carl Stearns Clancy
Silents
ADVENTUROUS SEX, THE(1925), w
Deidre Clancy
GIRL FROM PETROVKA, THE(1974), cos
Deirdre Clancy
VIRGIN AND THE GYPSY, THE(1970, Brit.), cos; LIGHT AT THE EDGE OF THE
WORLD, THE(1971, U.S./Span./Lichtenstein), cos
Ellen Clancy
SHE MARRIED HER BOSS(1935); PRAIRIE THUNDER(1937); SERGEANT MUR-
PHY(1938)
Ellen Clancy [Janet Shaw]
IT'S LOVE I'M AFTER(1937)
Georgia Clancy
FURIES, THE(1950); TWO TICKETS TO BROADWAY(1951)
Jacques Clancy
FRIEND WILL COME TONIGHT, A(1948, Fr.); LOVE IS MY PROFESSION(1959, Fr.);
LOVE AT NIGHT(1961, Fr.)
Jim Clancy
TOY, THE(1982)
Kitty Clancy
MIDNIGHT MADONNA(1937)
Louise B. Clancy
Silents
HIGH HEELS(1921), w
Margaret Clancy
ANNABELLE'S AFFAIRS(1931), ed; BAD GIRL(1931), ed; EAST LYNNE(1931), ed;
HEARTBREAK(1931), ed; AFTER TOMORROW(1932), ed; DANCE TEAM(1932), ed;
SOCIETY GIRL(1932), ed; BEST OF ENEMIES(1933), ed; CAVALCADE(1933), ed;
SHANGHAI MADNESS(1933), ed; STAND UP AND CHEER(1934 80m FOX bw), ed;
ONE RAINY AFTERNOON(1936), ed; HISTORY IS MADE AT NIGHT(1937), ed;
ADVENTURES OF TOM SAWYER, THE(1938), ed
Margaret V. Clancy
MOTHER KNOWS BEST(1928), ed; PRINCESS AND THE PLUMBER, THE(1930),
ed; SONG O' MY HEART(1930), ed
Silents
FOUR SONS(1928), ed
Melinda Clancy
TALES FROM THE CRYPT(1972, Brit.); CONFESSIONAL, THE(1977, Brit.)
Nora Clancy
Silents
KNOCKNAGOW(1918, Ireland)
Tom Clancy
KILLER ELITE, THE(1975); SWASHBUCKLER(1976)
Vernon Clancy
NIGHT ALONE(1938, Brit.), w

Frances Clanton
Misc. Silents
HIS MAJESTY BUNKER BEAN(1918)
Jimmy Clanton
GO, JOHNNY, GO!(1959); TEENAGE MILLIONAIRE(1961)
Ralph Clanton
CYRANO DE BERGERAC(1950); THEY WERE NOT DIVIDED(1951, Brit.); HOT CARS(1956); VAGABOND KING, THE(1956); JOHNNY TREMAIN(1957); NO TIME TO BE YOUNG(1957); PHARAOH'S CURSE(1957); UNDERSEA GIRL(1957); 27TH DAY, THE(1957); THEY MIGHT BE GIANTS(1971); TRADING PLACES(1983)
Ronnie Clanton
FORT APACHE, THE BRONX(1981)
Rony Clanton
EDUCATION OF SONNY CARSON, THE(1974); NIGHT OF THE JUGGLER(1980)
1984
COTTON CLUB, THE(1984)
Yves Claoue
MURDER AT 45 R.P.M.(1965, Fr.), m
Charles Clapham
MATTER OF MURDER, A(1949, Brit.)
Charlie Clapham
MY WIFE'S FAMILY(1941, Brit.)
Leonard Clapham
Silents
HER FIVE-FOOT HIGHNESS(1920); LONG CHANCE, THE(1922); OUR HOSPITALITY(1923); TO THE LAST MAN(1923); AIR HAWK, THE(1924)
Misc. Silents
UNDER NORTHERN LIGHTS(1920); GHOST CITY(1921); SHELL SHOCKED SAMMY(1923); WITH NAKED FISTS(1923); RIDING DOUBLE(1924)
Peter Clapham
SAILOR WHO FELL FROM GRACE WITH THE SEA, THE(1976, Brit.)
Clapham & Dwyer
RADIO FOLLIES(1935, Brit.)
Clapham and Dwyer
ON THE AIR(1934, Brit.)
Leonard Claphman
Misc. Silents
PERFECT ALIBI, THE(1924)
Leonard Clapman
Misc. Silents
SHIELD OF SILENCE, THE(1925)
Cecil B. Clapp
Silents
SABLE LORCHA, THE(1915), w
Gordon Clapp
RUNNING(1979, Can.); RETURN OF THE SECAUCUS SEVEN(1980)
Dick Clappin
MONKEY GRIP(1983, Aus.)
Eric Clapton
SLIPSTREAM(1974, Can.), m; TOMMY(1975, Brit.)
Patricia Clapton
KITCHEN, THE(1961, Brit.)
Charles Claque
SILVER CANYON(1951), art d
Fanny Clar
L'ATALANTE(1947, Fr.)
Sonia Clara
EARTH ENTRANCED(1970, Braz.)
Alan Clare
SEVEN KEYS(1962, Brit.), m
Caroline Clare
OFF THE RECORD(1939)
Colleen Clare
LAST OF MRS. CHEYNEY, THE(1937); WE'RE ON THE JURY(1937)
Diane Clare
DESERT ATTACK(1958, Brit.); INDISCREET(1958); RELUCTANT DEBUTANTE, THE(1958); LET'S GET MARRIED(1960, Brit.); GREEN HELMET, THE(1961, Brit.); NAKED EDGE, THE(1961); WHISTLE DOWN THE WIND(1961, Brit.); L-SHAPED ROOM, THE(1962, Brit.); DOUBLE, THE(1963, Brit); HAUNTING, THE(1963); MURDER ON THE CAMPUS(1963, Brit.); WITCHCRAFT(1964, Brit.); PLAGUE OF THE ZOMBIES, THE(1966, Brit.); WRONG BOX, THE(1966, Brit.); VULTURE, THE(1967, U.S./Brit./Can.); HAND OF NIGHT, THE(1968, Brit.); TRYGON FACTOR, THE(1969, Brit.)
Fernand Clare
HEAT OF THE SUMMER(1961, Fr.), m
Frances Clare
WILD HEART, THE(1952, Brit.)
Jack Clare
Silents
BLIND BOY, THE(1917, Brit.), a, d
Madeline [Madelyn] Clare
Misc. Silents
MISLEADING WIDOW, THE(1919); DISCARDED WOMAN, THE(1920)
Madelyn Clare
Silents
IF WOMEN ONLY KNEW(1921)
Misc. Silents
YOUNG AMERICA(1918); FALSE FRONTS(1922); MARK OF THE BEAST(1923)
Malcolm Clare
FRIGHTENED CITY, THE(1961, Brit.); FINDERS KEEPERS(1966, Brit.), ch
Marvis Clare
Misc. Silents
ROGUES OF THE TURF(1923, Brit.)
Mary Clare
FEATHER, THE(1929, Brit.); BILL'S LEGACY(1931, Brit.); CARMEN(1931, Brit.); HINDLE WAKES(1931, Brit.); KEEPERS OF YOUTH(1931, Brit.); MANY WATERS(1931, Brit.); SHADOWS(1931, Brit.); OUTSIDER, THE(1933, Brit.); NIGHT CLUB QUEEN(1934, Brit.); POWER(1934, Brit.); SAY IT WITH FLOWERS(1934, Brit.); CLAIRVOYANT, THE(1935, Brit.); LINE ENGAGED(1935, Brit.); LORNA DOONE(1935, Brit.); REAL BLOKE, A(1935, Brit.); MISTER HOBO(1936, Brit.); PASSING

OF THE THIRD FLOOR BACK, THE(1936, Brit.); CITADEL, THE(1938); CLIMBING HIGH(1938, Brit.); LADY VANISHES, THE(1938, Brit.); RAT, THE(1938, Brit.); YOUNG AND INNOCENT(1938, Brit.); CHALLENGE, THE(1939, Brit.); MILL ON THE FLOSS(1939, Brit.); MRS. PYM OF SCOTLAND YARD(1939, Brit.); THERE AIN'T NO JUSTICE(1939, Brit.); BRIGGS FAMILY, THE(1940, Brit.); FUGITIVE, THE(1940, Brit.); OLD BILL AND SON(1940, Brit.); GIRL MUST LIVE, A(1941, Brit.); NEXT OF KIN(1942, Brit.); TERROR HOUSE(1942, Brit.); HUNDRED POUND WINDOW, THE(1943, Brit.); FIDDLERS THREE(1944, Brit.); YOU CAN'T DO WITHOUT LOVE(1946, Brit.); PATIENT VANISHES, THE(1947, Brit.); ESTHER WATERS(1948, Brit.); THREE WEIRD SISTERS, THE(1948, Brit.); CARDBOARD CAVALIER, THE(1949, Brit.); MY BROTHER JONATHAN(1949, Brit.); BLACK ROSE, THE(1950); MRS. FITZHERBERT(1950, Brit.); OLIVER TWIST(1951, Brit.); PORTRAIT OF CLARE(1951, Brit.); HOLIDAY WEEK(1952, Brit.); MOULIN ROUGE(1952); BEGGAR'S OPERA, THE(1953); MY HEART GOES CRAZY(1953, Brit.); PENNY PRINCESS(1953, Brit.); MAMBO(1955, Ital.); PRICE OF SILENCE, THE(1960, Brit.)
Misc. Silents
SKIN GAME, THE(1920, Brit.); FOOLISH MONTE CARLO(1922); GIPSY CAVALIER, A(1922, Brit.); PRINCE OF LOVERS, A(1922, Brit.); BECKET(1923, Brit.); CONSTANT NYMPH, THE(1928, Brit.)
Mavis Clare
DOUBLE EXPOSURES(1937, Brit.)
Misc. Silents
LOWLAND CINDERELLA, A(1921, Brit.)
Mildred Clare
Misc. Talkies
SKYBOUND(1935)
Myrtle Clare
IN COLD BLOOD(1967)
Norman R. Clare
WORLD OF APU, THE(1960, India), titles
Pat Clare
MAYTIME IN MAYFAIR(1952, Brit.)
Paul Clare
Misc. Talkies
HER UNBORN CHILD(1933)
Phyllis Clare
ROADHOUSE MURDER, THE(1932); FLAW, THE(1933, Brit.); JUST MY LUCK(1933, Brit.); ALONG CAME SALLY(1934, Brit.); ROMANCE IN RHYTHM(1934, Brit.); CLIVE OF INDIA(1935); STOKER, THE(1935, Brit.); HIS BROTHER'S WIFE(1936); HOT NEWS(1936, Brit.); CONVICTED(1938); MANHATTAN SHAKEDOWN(1939)
Misc. Talkies
ALONG CAME SALLY(1933)
Sidney Clare
DELIGHTFUL HOGUE(1929), m/l Oscar Levant; JAZZ HEAVEN(1929), m; CAN THIS BE DIXIE?(1936), m
Suzanne Clare
PIMPERNEL SMITH(1942, Brit.)
Willis Clare
STORY OF VERNON AND IRENE CASTLE, THE(1939)
Wyn Clare
WONDERFUL STORY, THE(1932, Brit.)
O.B. Clarece
TURNED OUT NICE AGAIN(1941, Brit.)
Arthur Claremont
Silents
LOVE AT THE WHEEL(1921, Brit.)
Leonard Claremont
WINGS OF CHANCE(1961, Can.), ph
G. C. Claren
ELISABETH OF AUSTRIA(1931, Ger.), w
Clarence
CLARENCE, THE CROSS-EYED LION(1965)
Silents
CIRCUS ACE, THE(1927)
Monique Clarence
LOVE AT NIGHT(1961, Fr.)
O. B. Clarence
KEEPERS OF YOUTH(1931, Brit.); MAN FROM CHICAGO, THE(1931, Brit.); MAGIC NIGHT(1932, Brit.); PERFECT UNDERSTANDING(1933, Brit.); FRIDAY THE 13TH(1934, Brit.); KING OF PARIS, THE(1934, Brit.); WOMAN IN COMMAND, THE(1934 Brit.); BARNACLE BILL(1935, Brit.); CAPTAIN BILL(1935, Brit.); DOMMED CARGO(1936, Brit.); OLD IRON(1938, Brit.); JAMAICA INN(1939, Brit.); ME AND MY PAL(1939, Brit.); MILL ON THE FLOSS(1939, Brit.); IT'S IN THE AIR(1940, Brit.); MISSING PEOPLE, THE(1940, Brit.); OLD MOTHER RILEY IN BUSINESS(1940, Brit.); SALOON BAR(1940, Brit.); COURAGEOUS MR. PENN, THE(1941, Brit.); MAIL TRAIN(1941, Brit.); OLD MOTHER RILEY'S CIRCUS(1941, Brit.); ON APPROVAL(1944, Brit.); GREAT DAY(1945, Brit.); JOHNNY IN THE CLOUDS(1945, Brit.); PLACE OF ONE'S OWN, A(1945, Brit.); MEET ME AT DAWN(1947, Brit.); NO ROOM AT THE INN(1950, Brit.); INHERITANCE, THE(1951, Brit.)
Silents
LONDON PRIDE(1920, Brit.)
O.B. Clarence
BELLS, THE(1931, Brit.); BARTON MYSTERY, THE(1932, Brit.); FLAG LIEUTENANT, THE(1932, Brit.); WHERE IS THIS LADY?(1932, Brit.); DISCORD(1933, Brit.); EXCESS BAGGAGE(1933, Brit.); FALLING FOR YOU(1933, Brit.); HEART SONG(1933, Brit.); HIS GRACE GIVES NOTICE(1933, Brit.); I ADORE YOU(1933, Brit.); SHOT IN THE DARK, A(1933, Brit.); DOUBLE EVENT, THE(1934, Brit.); FATHER AND SON(1934, Brit.); FEATHERED SERPENT, THE(1934, Brit.); GREAT DEFENDER, THE(1934, Brit.); LADY IN DANGER(1934, Brit.); SILVER SPOON, THE(1934, Brit.); SONG AT EVENTIDE(1934, Brit.); NO MONKEY BUSINESS(1935, Brit.); PRIVATE SECRETARY, THE(1935, Brit.); SCARLET PIMPERNEL, THE(1935, Brit.); SQUIBS(1935, Brit.); ALL IN(1936, Brit.); CARDINAL, THE(1936, Brit.); EAST MEETS WEST(1936, Brit.); KING OF HEARTS(1936, Brit.); DINNER AT THE RITZ(1937, Brit.); PYGMALION(1938, Brit.); RETURN OF THE SCARLET PIMPERNEL(1938, Brit.); SPY FOR A DAY(1939, Brit.); STOLEN LIFE(1939, Brit.); RETURN TO YESTERDAY(1940, Brit.); QUIET WEDDING(1941, Brit.); FRONT LINE KIDS(1942, Brit.); GREAT EXPECTATIONS(1946, Brit.); SCHOOL FOR SECRETS(1946, Brit.); MAGIC BOW, THE(1947, Brit.); WHILE THE SUN SHINES(1950, Brit.)

Misc. Silents
LIBERTY HALL(1914, Brit.); LITTLE HOUR OF PETER WELLS, THE(1920, Brit.)
Clarence Muse Singers
GENTLEMAN FROM DIXIE(1941)
Hal Clarendon
Silents
CONSPIRACY, THE(1914); DAY OF DAYS, THE(1914); HIS LAST DOLLAR(1914);
LITTLE GRAY LADY, THE(1914); ONE OF OUR GIRLS(1914); PRIDE OF JENNICO,
THE(1914); SCALES OF JUSTICE, THE(1914); DAVID HARUM(1915); ONE
DAY(1916), a, d
Misc. Silents
LADY OF QUALITY, A(1913); LEAH KLESCHNA(1913); MARTA OF THE LOW-
LANDS(1914); WOMAN'S TRIUMPH, A(1914); ALMA, WHERE DO YOU LIVE?(1917),
d; PHANTOM HONEYMOON, THE(1919)
Jean Clarendon
MISSISSIPPI(1935); MOURNING BECOMES ELECTRA(1947)
Paula Clarendon
CLASS(1983)
Carlos Clarens
LIONS LOVE(1969)
G. Claret
RULES OF THE GAME, THE(1939, Fr.), m
Needham Clarge
HATE IN PARADISE(1938, Brit.)
Norman Claridge
DANCE PRETTY LADY(1932, Brit.); HIDEOUT(1948, Brit.); DARK MAN, THE(1951,
Brit.); WOMAN EATER, THE(1959, Brit.); THEY CAME FROM BEYOND SPACE(1967,
Brit.); TORTURE GARDEN(1968, Brit.); CLEGG(1969, Brit.); CRY OF THE PEN-
GUINS(1972, Brit.); BROTHERS AND SISTERS(1980, Brit.)
Clarie Wear's Embassy Orchestra
ALIBI, THE(1943, Brit.)
Clarieux
BATTLE OF THE RAILS(1949, Fr.)
Jean Clarieux
CASQUE D'OR(1956, Fr.); BERNADETTE OF LOURDES(1962, Fr.); MILKY WAY,
THE(1969, Fr./Ital.)
Hans Clarin
SPESSART INN, THE(1961, Ger.); 24 HOURS TO KILL(1966, Brit.)
Irene Clarin
FRIENDS AND HUSBANDS(1983, Ger.)
Aime Clariond
LUCREZIA BORGIA(1937, Fr.); ENTENTE CORDIALE(1939, Fr.); ETERNAL HUS-
BAND, THE(1946, Fr.); COLONEL CHABERT(1947, Fr.); DEADLIER THAN THE
MALE(1957, Fr.); ROYAL AFFAIRS IN VERSAILLES(1957, Fr.); NATHALIE(1958,
Fr.); MISTRESS FOR THE SUMMER, A(1964, Fr./Ital.)
Alme Clariond
CRIME AND PUNISHMENT(1935, Fr.)
Simone Claris
PEEK-A-BOO(1961, Fr.)
Clark
SUSPICION(1941), art d; TOM(1973), w
Misc. Talkies
BAD BUNCH, THE(1976), d
A. J. Clark
1984
NUMBER ONE(1984, Brit.)
Al Clark
YOU CAN'T RUN AWAY FROM IT(1956), ed; 3:10 TO YUMA(1957), ed; IMPORTANT
WITNESS, THE(1933), ed; MEN OF THE NIGHT(1934), ed; CASE OF THE MISSING
MAN, THE(1935), ed; GUARD THAT GIRL(1935), ed; REVENGE RIDER, THE(1935),
ed; DANGEROUS INTRIGUE(1936), ed; END OF THE TRAIL(1936), ed; LEGION OF
TERROR(1936), ed; MORE THAN A SECRETARY(1936), ed; AWFUL TRUTH,
THE(1937), ed; DEVIL IS DRIVING, THE(1937), ed; IT HAPPENED IN HOLLY-
WOOD(1937), ed; LET'S GET MARRIED(1937), ed; HOLIDAY(1938), ed; LADY OB-
JECTS, THE(1938), ed; LITTLE ADVENTURESS, THE(1938), ed; MAIN EVENT,
THE(1938), ed; SQUADRON OF HONOR(1938), ed; WHEN G-MEN STEP IN(1938), ed;
GOOD GIRLS GO TO PARIS(1939), ed; LET US LIVE(1939), ed; MR. SMITH GOES TO
WASHINGTON(1939), ed; NORTH OF SHANGHAI(1939), ed; CAFE HOSTESS(1940),
ed; ESCAPE TO GLORY(1940), ed; LADY IN QUESTION, THE(1940), ed; LONE WOLF
MEETS A LADY, THE(1940), ed; LONE WOLF STRIKES, THE(1940), ed; MAN WITH
NINE LIVES, THE(1940), ed; PRAIRIE SCHOONERS(1940), ed; DEVIL COMMANDS,
THE(1941), ed; LADIES IN RETIREMENT(1941), ed; RICHEST MAN IN TOWN(1941),
ed; THEY DARE NOT LOVE(1941), ed; ADVENTURES OF MARTIN EDEN,
THE(1942), ed; BLONDIE FOR VICTORY(1942), ed; MEET THE STEWARTS(1942),
ed; APPOINTMENT IN BERLIN(1943), ed; IT'S A GREAT LIFE(1943), ed; SHE HAS
WHAT IT TAKES(1943), ed; WHAT A WOMAN!(1943), ed; ADDRESS UN-
KNOWN(1944), ed; ONE MYSTERIOUS NIGHT(1944), ed; SHE'S A SWEET-
HEART(1944), ed; COUNTER-ATTACK(1945), ed; GAY SENORITA, THE(1945), ed;
GIRL OF THE LIMBERLOST, THE(1945), ed; LEAVE IT TO BLONDIE(1945), ed;
GALLANT JOURNEY(1946), ed; PHANTOM THIEF, THE(1946), ed; TARS AND
SPARS(1946), ed; BLONDIE'S ANNIVERSARY(1947), ed; HER HUSBAND'S AF-
FAIRS(1947), ed; I LOVE TROUBLE(1947), ed; JOHNNY O'CLOCK(1947), ed;
SWORDSMAN, THE(1947), ed; BLONDIE'S REWARD(1948), ed; BLONDIE'S SE-
CRET(1948), ed; FULLER BRUSH MAN(1948), ed; ALL THE KING'S MEN(1949), ed;
SLIGHTLY FRENCH(1949), ed; UNDERCOVER MAN, THE(1949), ed; WE WERE
STRANGERS(1949), ed; CONVICTED(1950), ed; EMERGENCY WEDDING(1950), ed;
PETTY GIRL, THE(1950), ed; FAMILY SECRET, THE(1951), ed; LORNA DOO-
NE(1951), ed; NEVER TRUST A GAMBLER(1951), ed; SMUGGLER'S GOLD(1951),
ed; TEXAS RANGERS, THE(1951), ed; BOOTS MALONE(1952), ed; LAST OF THE
COMANCHES(1952), ed; CONQUEST OF COCHISE(1953), ed; NEBRASKAN,
THE(1953), ed; WILD ONE, THE(1953), ed; 5,000 FINGERS OF DR. T. THE(1953), ed;
BAD FOR EACH OTHER(1954), ed; NAKED ALIBI(1954), ed; SIGN OF THE PA-
GAN(1954), ed; TANGANYIKA(1954), ed; BRING YOUR SMILE ALONG(1955), ed;
CHIEF CRAZY HORSE(1955), ed; GUN THAT WON THE WEST, THE(1955), ed; LAST
FRONTIER, THE(1955), ed; NEW ORLEANS UNCENSORED(1955), ed; JUBAL(1956),
ed; MIAMI EXPOSE(1956), ed; DECISION AT SUNDOWN(1957), ed; GUNS OF FORT
PETTICOAT(1957), ed; TALL T, THE(1957), ed; APACHE TERRITORY(1958),
ed; BUCHANAN RIDES ALONE(1958), ed; COWBOY(1958), ed; LINEUP, THE(1958),
ed; SENIOR PROM(1958), ed; GUNMEN FROM LAREDO(1959), ed; HEY BOY! HEY
GIRL!(1959), ed; THIRTY FOOT BRIDE OF CANDY ROCK, THE(1959), ed; ALL THE

YOUNG MEN(1960), ed; MAN ON A STRING(1960), ed; PEPE(1960), ed; INTERNS,
THE(1962), ed; THIRTEEN WEST STREET(1962), ed; UNDERWATER CITY,
THE(1962), ed; HOOTENANNY HOOT(1963), ed; CHARRO(1969), ed
Alan Clark
LOCAL HERO(1983, Brit.)
Alan R. Clark
HIGH WALL, THE(1947), w
Albert Clark
JUSTICE OF THE RANGE(1935), ed
Albert C. Clark
TICKET TO PARADISE(1936), ed
Alex Clark
HALLS OF ANGER(1970)
Alexander Clark
DOUBLE LIFE, A(1947); GOD TOLD ME TO(1976)
Andy Clark
BEGGARS OF LIFE(1928); HIT THE DECK(1930)
Misc. Silents
KNIGHTS OF THE SQUARE TABLE(1917)
Angela Clark
MIRACLE OF OUR LADY OF FATIMA, THE(1952); HOUDINI(1953)
Anice Clark
LOOK OUT SISTER(1948)
Arlette Clark
TENDER IS THE NIGHT(1961)
Arthur Clark
HUSBANDS(1970)
Asa Clark
ANGEL ON MY SHOULDER(1946), ed; BADGE OF MARSHAL BRENNAN,
THE(1957), ed; NO PLACE TO LAND(1958), ed; WHEN HELL BROKE LOOSE(1958),
ed; PLUNDERERS OF PAINTED FLATS(1959), ed; TANK COMMANDOS(1959), ed
Asa Boyd Clark
PRETENDER, THE(1947), ed; APPOINTMENT WITH MURDER(1948), ed; DEVIL'S
CARGO, THE(1948), ed; SEARCH FOR DANGER(1949), ed; ONCE A THIEF(1950), ed
B.D. Clark
GALAXY OF TERROR(1981), d, w
Barbara Clark
JOAN OF OZARK(1942); MAYOR OF 44TH STREET, THE(1942)
Barry Clark
FLOWER THIEF, THE(1962)
Benjamin Clark
CHILDREN SHOULDN'T PLAY WITH DEAD THINGS(1972), w; DEATH-
DREAM(1972, Can.), p&d
Bernadette Clark
Misc. Talkies
LOST CITY, THE(1982)
Betty Ross Clark
THREE MARRIED MEN(1936); BRIDE FOR HENRY, A(1937)
Silents
BREWSTER'S MILLIONS(1921)
Misc. Silents
IF I WERE KING(1920); FOX, THE(1921); MOTHER O' MINE(1921); TRAVELING
SALESMAN, THE(1921); AT THE SIGN OF THE JACK O'LANTERN(1922)
Bill Clark
YOUNG FURY(1965)
Billy Clark
MA AND PA KETTLE AT THE FAIR(1952); MA AND PA KETTLE ON VACA-
TION(1953); MA AND PA KETTLE AT WAIKIKI(1955)
Bob Clark
TRIBUTE(1980, Can.), d; THUNDER TRAIL(1937); FRENCHMAN'S CREEK(1944);
FEAR(1946), spec eff; YOUNG WIVES' TALE(1954, Brit.), makeup; WHY BOTHER TO
KNOCK(1964, Brit.), makeup; SHE MAN, THE(1967), d, w; DEATHDREAM(1972,
Can.), p&d, makeup; BLACK CHRISTMAS(1974, Can.), p&d; BREAKING
POINT(1976), p, d; MEAT CLEAVER MASSACRE(1977); MURDER BY DE-
CREE(1979, Brit.), p, d, w; PORKY'S(1982), p, d&w; CHRISTMAS STORY, A(1983),
p, d, w; PORKY'S II: THE NEXT DAY(1983), p, d, w
1984
RHINESTONE(1984), d, m/1
Bobby Clark
GOLDWYN FOLLIES, THE(1938); SAGEBRUSH FAMILY TRAILS WEST,
THE(1940); RIM OF THE CANYON(1949); SONS OF NEW MEXICO(1949); KEN-
TUCKY JUBILEE(1951); SILVER CANYON(1951); OLD WEST, THE(1952); BRING
YOUR SMILE ALONG(1955); INVASION OF THE BODY SNATCHERS(1956); RAN-
SOM(1956); REBEL IN TOWN(1956); DESTINATION 60,000(1957); GUN DUEL IN
DURANGO(1957); HAPPY ROAD, THE(1957); FEMALE BUNCH, THE(1969); SA-
TAN'S SADISTS(1969); WILD WHEELS(1969), a, stunts; RED, WHITE AND BLACK,
THE(1970); LIMIT, THE(1972)
Misc. Talkies
RIO GRANDE(1949)
Brett Clark
NIGHT SHIFT(1982)
Brian Clark
SERENITY(1962); WHOSE LIFE IS IT ANYWAY?(1981), w
Brian Patrick Clark
BLOOD AND GUTS(1978, Can.)
Bridgetta Clark
Silents
CONQUERING POWER, THE(1921); FOUR HORSEMEN OF THE APOCALYPSE,
THE(1921); MORALS(1921); GOLDEN GIFT, THE(1922)
Bruce Clark
NAKED ANGELS(1969), d&w; SKI BUM, THE(1971), a, d, w, ed; HAMMER(1972),
d
Bryan Clark
TRADING PLACES(1983)
Bryan E. Clark
ALL THE PRESIDENT'S MEN(1976)
Buddy Clark
SEVEN DAYS LEAVE(1942); MELODY TIME(1948); SUBTERRANEANS,
THE(1960); YOUNG FURY(1965), cos

Camilla Clark
Silents
GOLDEN GIFT, THE(1922); SECOND HAND ROSE(1922)
Misc. Silents
FALSE KISSES(1921)

Candy Clark
WHEN YOU COMIN' BACK, RED RYDER?(1979); FAT CITY(1972); AMERICAN GRAFFITI(1973); I WILL ...I WILL ...FOR NOW(1976); MAN WHO FELL TO EARTH, THE(1976, Brit.); CITIZENS BAND(1977); BIG SLEEP, THE½(1978, Brit.); MORE AMERICAN GRAFFITI(1979); Q(1982); AMITYVILLE 3-D(1983); BLUE THUNDER(1983)
1984
HAMBONE AND HILLIE(1984)

Caroll Clark
NEVER A DULL MOMENT(1968), art d

Carrol Clark
FRENCH LINE, THE(1954), art d; BON VOYAGE(1962), art d

Carroll Clark
BIG MONEY(1930), art d; HELL'S ANGELS(1930), art d; HOLIDAY(1930), art d; SIN TAKES A HOLIDAY(1930), art d; SWING HIGH(1930), art d; SUICIDE FLEET(1931), art d; TIP-OFF, THE(1931), art d; BILL OF DIVORCEMENT, A(1932), art d; BIRD OF PARADISE(1932), art d; CARNIVAL BOAT(1932), art d; CONQUERORS, THE(1932), art d; FREIGHTERS OF DESTINY(1932), art d; HELL'S HIGHWAY(1932), art d; HOLD'EM JAIL(1932), art d; PHANTOM OF CRESTWOOD, THE(1932), ph, art d; ROCKABYE(1932), art d; SADDLE BUSTER, THE(1932), art d; SECRETS OF THE FRENCH POLICE(1932), art d; STATE'S ATTORNEY(1932), art d; SYMPHONY OF SIX MILLION(1932), art d; WESTWARD PASSAGE(1932), art d; WHAT PRICE HOLLYWOOD?(1932), art d; WOMAN COMMANDS, A(1932), art d; FLYING DOWN TO RIO(1933), art d; KING KONG(1933), art d; MELODY CRUISE(1933), art d; MONKEY'S PAW, THE(1933), art d; PROFESSIONAL SWEETHEART(1933), art d; GAY DIVORCEE, THE(1934), art d; LITTLE MINISTER, THE(1934), art d; OF HUMAN BONDAGE(1934), art d; SPITFIRE(1934), art d; THIS MAN IS MINE(1934), art d; IN PERSON(1935), art d; ROBERTA(1935), art d; TOP HAT(1935), art d; VILLAGE TALE(1935), art d; MARY OF SCOTLAND(1936), art d; PLOUGH AND THE STARS, THE(1936), art d; SWING TIME(1936), art d; STAGE DOOR(1937), art d; CAREFREE(1938), art d; JOY OF LIVING(1938), art d; MAD MISS MANTON, THE(1938), art d; VIVACIOUS LADY(1938), art d; LUCKY PARTNERS(1940), art d; PRIMROSE PATH(1940), art d; HIGHWAYS BY NIGHT(1942), art d; HITLER'S CHILDREN(1942), art d; JOAN OF PARIS(1942), art d; MEXICAN SPITFIRE SEES A GHOST(1942), art d; MY FAVORITE SPY(1942), art d; NAVY COMES THROUGH, THE(1942), art d; SEVEN DAYS LEAVE(1942), art d; FLIGHT FOR FREEDOM(1943), art d; GILDERSLEEVE'S BAD DAY(1943), art d; IRON MAJOR, THE(1943), art d; SKY'S THE LIMIT, THE(1943), art d; TENDER COMRADE(1943), art d; GILDERSLEEVE'S GHOST(1944), art d; MY PAL, WOLF(1944), art d; STEP LIVELY(1944), art d; YOUTH RUNS WILD(1944), art d; CORNERED(1945), art d; ENCHANTED COTTAGE, THE(1945), art d; MURDER, MY SWEET(1945), art d; SPANISH MAIN, THE(1945), art d; NOTORIOUS(1946), art d; BACHELOR AND THE BOBBY-SOXER, THE(1947), art d; SINBAD THE SAILOR(1947), art d; TYCOON(1947), art d; EVERY GIRL SHOULD BE MARRIED(1948), art d; I REMEMBER MAMA(1948), art d; MR. BLANDINGS BUILDS HIS DREAM HOUSE(1948), art d; BRIDE FOR SALE(1949), art d; HOLIDAY AFFAIR(1949), art d; STRANGE BARGAIN(1949), art d; WOMAN'S SECRET, A(1949), art d; SECRET FURY, THE(1950), art d; PAYMENT ON DEMAND(1951), art d; TWO TICKETS TO BROADWAY(1951), art d; CLASH BY NIGHT(1952), art d; TRAIL GUIDE(1952), art d; ANGEL FACE(1953), art d; SECOND CHANCE(1953), art d; TARZAN AND THE SHE-DEVIL(1953), art d; VICE SQUAD(1953), art d; SHE COULDN'T SAY NO(1954), art d; DOUBLE JEOPARDY(1955), art d; HEADLINE HUNTERS(1955), art d; LAY THAT RIFLE DOWN(1955), art d; ONE DESIRE(1955), art d; GREAT LOCOMOTIVE CHASE, THE(1956), art d; WHILE THE CITY SLEEPS(1956), art d; JOHNNY TREMAIN(1957), art d; OLD YELLER(1957), art d; LIGHT IN THE FOREST, THE(1958), art d; DARBY O'GILL AND THE LITTLE PEOPLE(1959), art d; SHAGGY DOG, THE(1959), art d; POLLYANNA(1960), art d; TEN WHO DARED(1960), art d; TOBY TYLER(1960), art d; ABSENT-MINDED PROFESSOR, THE(1961), art d; PARENT TRAP, THE(1961), art d; MOON PILOT(1962), art d; INCREDIBLE JOURNEY, THE(1963), art d; SAVAGE SAM(1963), art d; SON OF FLUBBER(1963), art d; SUMMER MAGIC(1963), art d; MARY POPPINS(1964), art d; MISADVENTURES OF MERLIN JONES, THE(1964), art d; THOSE CALLOWAYS(1964), art d; TIGER WALKS, A(1964), art d; MONKEY'S UNCLE, THE(1965), art d; THAT DARN CAT(1965), art d; FOLLOW ME, BOYS!(1966), art d; LT. ROBIN CRUSOE, U.S.N.(1966), art d; UGLY DACHSHUND, THE(1966), art d; GNOME-MOBILE, THE(1967), art d; HAPPIEST MILLIONAIRE, THE(1967), art d; MONKEYS, GO HOME(1967), art d; HORSE IN THE GRAY FLANNEL SUIT, THE(1968), art d; LOVE BUG, THE(1968), art d; ONE AND ONLY GENUINE ORIGINAL FAMILY BAND, THE(1968), art d

Charles Clark
CHARLIE CHAN IN HONOLULU(1938), ph; CADET GIRL(1941), ph; COWBOY AND THE BLONDE, THE(1941), ph

Charles C. Clark
IRON CURTAIN, THE(1948), ph

Charles Dow Clark
BAT WHISPERS, THE(1930); HALF-NAKED TRUTH, THE(1932); LADIES OF THE JURY(1932)
Silents
PROHIBITION(1915); OLD HOME WEEK(1925)
Misc. Silents
CONFIDENCE MAN, THE(1924)

Charles G. Clark
BIG LIFT, THE(1950), ph; OH, MEN! OH, WOMEN!(1957), ph

Chris Clark
LADY SINGS THE BLUES(1972), w

Christopher Clark
UNCONQUERED(1947)

Christy Clark
SEVEN ALONE(1975)

Cliff Clark
CORPSE CAME C.O.D., THE(; ADVENTURES OF GALLANT BESS(1948); MOUNTAIN MUSIC(1937); COCOANUT GROVE(1938); DAREDEVIL DRIVERS(1938); HE COULDN'T SAY NO(1938); KENTUCKY(1938); MR. MOTO'S GAMBLE(1938); PATIENT IN ROOM 18, THE(1938); TIME OUT FOR MURDER(1938); WHILE NEW YORK SLEEPS(1938); FAST AND FURIOUS(1939); HONOLULU(1939); INSIDE STORY(1939); IT'S A WONDERFUL WORLD(1939); JOE AND ETHEL TURP CALL ON

THE PRESIDENT(1939); MIRACLES FOR SALE(1939); MISSING EVIDENCE(1939); THEY MADE ME A CRIMINAL(1939); TORCHY PLAYS WITH DYNAMITE(1939); WITHIN THE LAW(1939); YOUNG MR. LINCOLN(1939); BLACK DIAMONDS(1940); CHARLIE CHAN'S MURDER CRUISE(1940); CROSS COUNTRY ROMANCE(1940); DOUBLE ALIBI(1940); DR. EHRLICH'S MAGIC BULLET(1940); GRAPES OF WRATH(1940); HONEYMOON DEFERRED(1940); INVISIBLE STRIPES(1940); KNUTE ROCKNE–ALL AMERICAN(1940); MARYLAND(1940); MURDER IN THE AIR(1940); SANTA FE TRAIL(1940); SLIGHTLY HONORABLE(1940); STRANGER ON THE THIRD FLOOR(1940); THREE CHEERS FOR THE IRISH(1940); WAGON TRAIN(1940); YOU'RE NOT SO TOUGH(1940); BABES ON BROADWAY(1941); BLUE, WHITE, AND PERFECT(1941); FOR BEAUTY'S SAKE(1941); GOLDEN HOOFS(1941); LAW OF THE TROPICS(1941); MANPOWER(1941); MOB TOWN(1941); NINE LIVES ARE NOT ENOUGH(1941); SEA WOLF, THE(1941); STRANGE ALIBI(1941); THIEVES FALL OUT(1941); TRIAL OF MARY DUGAN, THE(1941); WAGONS ROLL AT NIGHT, THE(1941); WASHINGTON MELODRAMA(1941); WESTERN UNION(1941); DANGEROUSLY THEY LIVE(1942); FALCON'S BROTHER, THE(1942); FINGERS AT THE WINDOW(1942); HENRY ALDRICH, EDITOR(1942); HIGHWAYS BY NIGHT(1942); JAIL HOUSE BLUES(1942); KID GLOVE KILLER(1942); MADAME SPY(1942); MOKEY(1942); MUMMY'S TOMB, THE(1942); SECRET ENEMIES(1942); STREET OF CHANCE(1942); WHO IS HOPE SCHUYLER?(1942); WILD BILL HICKOK RIDES(1942); FALCON AND THE CO-EDS, THE(1943); FALCON IN DANGER, THE(1943); FALCON STRIKES BACK, THE(1943); KEEP 'EM SLUGGING(1943); LADIES' DAY(1943); PETTICOAT LARCENY(1943); SLIGHTLY DANGEROUS(1943); BARBARY COAST GENT(1944); DESTINATION TOKYO(1944); FALCON OUT WEST, THE(1944); IN THE MEANTIME, DARLING(1944); MISSING JUROR, THE(1944); ONCE UPON A TIME(1944); BURY ME DEAD(1947); CASS TIMBERLANE(1947); HER HUSBAND'S AFFAIRS(1947); IT HAD TO BE YOU(1947); PHILO VANCE'S GAMBLE(1947); 13TH HOUR, THE(1947); DEEP WATERS(1948); FALSE PARADISE(1948); FORCE OF EVIL(1948); FORT APACHE(1948); HOLLOW TRIUMPH(1948); I, JANE DOE(1948); MR. BLANDINGS BUILDS HIS DREAM HOUSE(1948); RAW DEAL(1948); SMART WOMAN(1948); SORRY, WRONG NUMBER(1948); SOUTHERN YANKEE, A(1948); TROUBLE MAKERS(1948); CRIME DOCTOR'S DIARY, THE(1949); FIGHTING MAN OF THE PLAINS(1949); FLAMING FURY(1949); HOME OF THE BRAVE(1949); HOMICIDE(1949); MISS GRANT TAKES RICHMOND(1949); POST OFFICE INVESTIGATOR(1949); POWDER RIVER RUSTLERS(1949); ROSEANNA McCOY(1949); SHOCKPROOF(1949); STRATTON STORY, THE(1949); CARIBOO TRAIL, THE(1950); FULLER BRUSH GIRL, THE(1950); GUNFIGHTER, THE(1950); MEN, THE(1950); ROOKIE FIREMAN(1950); SOUND OF FURY, THE(1950); VIGILANTE HIDEOUT(1950); CAVALRY SCOUT(1951); DESERT OF LOST MEN(1951); JOE PALOOKA IN TRIPLE CROSS(1951); MR. IMPERIUM(1951); MY FORBIDDEN PAST(1951); OPERATION PACIFIC(1951); OVERLAND TELEGRAPH(1951); SADDLE LEGION(1951); SECOND WOMAN, THE(1951); SELLOUT, THE(1951); SILVER CITY(1951); SUGARFOOT(1951); WARPATH(1951); CARRIE(1952); CRIPPLE CREEK(1952); FRANCIS GOES TO WEST POINT(1952); HIGH NOON(1952); HURRICANE SMITH(1952); IT GROWS ON TREES(1952); PRIDE OF ST. LOUIS, THE(1952); SCANDAL SHEET(1952); SNIPER, THE(1952); HOUDINI(1953); SOUTH SEA WOMAN(1953); WAR OF THE WORLDS, THE(1953)

Colbert Clark
LOST JUNGLE, THE(1934), w; YOUNG AND BEAUTIFUL(1934), w; BEHIND GREEN LIGHTS(1935), w; IN OLD SANTA FE(1935), w; MARINES ARE COMING, THE(1935), w; DANCING FEET(1936), p; LAUGHING IRISH EYES(1936), p; MEET THE BOY FRIEND(1937), p; WRONG ROAD, THE(1937), p; BOOGIE MAN WILL GET YOU, THE(1942), p; CANAL ZONE(1942), p; JUNIOR ARMY(1943), p; MURDER IN TIMES SQUARE(1943), p; SHE HAS WHAT IT TAKES(1943), p; OUTLAWS OF THE ROCKIES(1945), p; ROCKIN' IN THE ROCKIES(1945), p; COWBOY BLUES(1946), p; DESERT HORSEMAN, THE(1946), p; LANDRUSH(1946), p; LAWLESS EMPIRE(1946), p; LAST DAYS OF BOOT HILL(1947), p; LONE HAND TEXAN, THE(1947), p; BUCKAROO FROM POWDER RIVER(1948), p; PHANTOM VALLEY(1948), p; SIX-GUN LAW(1948), p; SONG OF IDAHO(1948), p; WEST OF SONORA(1948), p; WHIRLWIND RAIDERS(1948), p; BLAZING TRAIL, THE(1949), p; CHALLENGE OF THE RANGE(1949), p; DESERT VIGILANTE(1949), p; EL DORADO PASS(1949), p; LARAMIE(1949), p; QUICK ON THE TRIGGER(1949), p; RENEGADES OF THE SAGE(1949), p; SMOKY MOUNTAIN MELODY(1949), p; SOUTH OF DEATH VALLEY(1949), p; ACROSS THE BADLANDS(1950), p; FRONTIER OUTPOST(1950), p; HOEDOWN(1950), p; HORSEMEN OF THE SIERRAS(1950), p; LIGHTNING GUNS(1950), p; OUTCAST OF BLACK MESA(1950), p; RAIDERS OF TOMAHAWK CREEK(1950), p; STREETS OF GHOST TOWN(1950), p; TEXAS DYNAMO(1950), p; BANDITS OF EL DORADO(1951), p; BONANZA TOWN(1951), p; CYCLONE FURY(1951), p; FORT SAVAGE RAIDERS(1951), p; KID FROM AMARILLO, THE(1951), p; PECOS RIVER(1951), p; PRAIRIE ROUNDUP(1951), p; RIDIN' THE OUTLAW TRAIL(1951), p; SNAKE RIVER DESPERADOES(1951), p; HAWK OF WILD RIVER, THE(1952), p; JUNCTION CITY(1952), p; KID FROM BROKEN GUN, THE(1952), p; LARAMIE MOUNTAINS(1952), p; MONTANA TERRITORY(1952), p; ROUGH, TOUGH WEST, THE(1952), p; SMOKY CANYON(1952), p

Collbert Clark
ATLANTIC CONVOY(1942), p

Cordy Clark
WALK ON THE WILD SIDE(1962); WHO'S MINDING THE MINT?(1967); FOR LOVE OF IVY(1968); HILLS HAVE EYES, THE(1978)

Curtis Clark
GIRO CITY(1982, Brit.), ph; DRAUGHTSMAN'S CONTRACT, THE(1983, Brit.), ph; NELLY'S VERSION(1983, Brit.), ph

Dan Clark
AIR CIRCUS, THE(1928), ph; HARMONY AT HOME(1930), ph; MY PAL, THE KING(1932), ph; RIDER OF DEATH VALLEY(1932), ph; TEXAS BAD MAN(1932), ph; FOURTH HORSEMAN, THE(1933), ph; HIDDEN GOLD(1933), ph; RUSTLERS' ROUNDUP(1933), ph; STRAIGHTAWAY(1934), ph; SONG OF THE SADDLE(1936), ph
Silents
DO AND DARE(1922), ph; JUST TONY(1922), ph; ROMANCE LAND(1923), ph; STEPPING FAST(1923), ph; DICK TURPIN(1925), ph; LUCKY HORSESHOE, THE(1925), ph; RIDERS OF THE PURPLE SAGE(1925), ph; GREAT K & A TRAIN ROBBERY, THE(1926), ph; NO MAN'S GOLD(1926), ph; ARIZONA WILDCAT(1927), ph; BRONCHO TWISTER(1927), ph; CIRCUS ACE, THE(1927), ph; LAST TRAIL, THE(1927), ph; OUTLAWS OF RED RIVER(1927), ph; SILVER VALLEY(1927), ph; TUMBLING RIVER(1927), ph; DAREDEVIL'S REWARD(1928), ph

Dane Clark
MONEY AND THE WOMAN(1940); GLASS KEY, THE(1942); PRIDE OF THE YANKEES, THE(1942); SUNDAY PUNCH(1942); TENNESSEE JOHNSON(1942); WAKE ISLAND(1942); ACTION IN THE NORTH ATLANTIC(1943); DESTINATION

TOKYO(1944); HOLLYWOOD CANTEEN(1944); VERY THOUGHT OF YOU, THE(1944); GOD IS MY CO-PILOT(1945); PRIDE OF THE MARINES(1945); HER KIND OF MAN(1946); STOLEN LIFE, A(1946); DEEP VALLEY(1947); THAT WAY WITH WOMEN(1947); EMBRACEABLE YOU(1948); MOONRISE(1948); WHIPLASH(1948); WITHOUT HONOR(1949); BACKFIRE(1950); BARRICADE(1950); HIGHLY DANGEROUS(1950, Brit.); FORT DEFIANCE(1951); NEVER TRUST A GAMBLER(1951); GAMBLER AND THE LADY, THE(1952, Brit.); BLACKOUT(1954, Brit.); GO, MAN, GO!(1954); PAID TO KILL(1954, Brit.); THUNDER PASS(1954); PORT OF HELL(1955); TOUGHEST MAN ALIVE(1955); MAN IS ARMED, THE(1956); MASSACRE(1956); OUTLAW'S SON(1957); MC MASTERS, THE(1970); WOMAN INSIDE, THE(1981)
Misc. Talkies
TIME RUNNING OUT(1950); BLOOD SONG(1982)

Daniel B. Clark
LAST OF THE DUANES(1930), ph; ROUGH ROMANCE(1930), ph; DESTRY RIDES AGAIN(1932), ph; SMOKY(1933), ph; CHARLIE CHAN IN EGYPT(1935), ph; LADIES LOVE DANGER(1935), ph; BACK TO NATURE(1936), ph; COUNTRY DOCTOR, THE(1936), ph; EDUCATING FATHER(1936), ph; HUMAN CARGO(1936), ph; PEPPER(1936), ph; REUNION(1936), ph; ANGEL'S HOLIDAY(1937), ph; BORN RECKLESS(1937), ph; HOLY TERROR, THE(1937), ph; SING AND BE HAPPY(1937), ph; STEP LIVELY, JEEVES(1937), ph; CHANGE OF HEART(1938), ph; FIVE OF A KIND(1938), ph

Daniel C. Clark
CHARLIE CHAN AT THE CIRCUS(1936), ph; CHARLIE CHAN AT MONTE CARLO(1937), ph; CHARLIE CHAN AT THE OLYMPICS(1937), ph

Daniel Clark
WHY LEAVE HOME?(1929), ph; LONE STAR RANGER, THE(1930), ph; THREE ROGUES(1931), ph; RAINBOW TRAIL(1932), ph; SILK HAT KID(1935), ph; THIS IS THE LIFE(1935), ph; CHAMPAGNE CHARLIE(1936), ph
Silents
LADIES TO BOARD(1924), ph; OH, YOU TONY!(1924), ph; RAINBOW TRAIL, THE(1925), ph; TONY RUNS WILD(1926), ph; YANKEE SENOR, THE(1926), ph; RED WINE(1928), ph

Daniel R. Clark
CHECKERS(1937), ph

Dave Clark
HAVING A WILD WEEKEND(1965, Brit.), a, md

David Clark
MOONLIGHT IN HAVANA(1942); HOMECOMING(1948); MAN FROM COLORADO, THE(1948); MY FRIEND IRMA GOES WEST(1950); SING AND SWING(1964, Brit.)

David Scott Clark
TRIAL OF BILLY JACK, THE(1974)

Davidson Clark
OLD-FASHIONED WAY, THE(1934); COWBOY IN THE CLOUDS(1943); WILSON(1944); COME OUT FIGHTING(1945); DUFFY'S TAVERN(1945); GREATEST SHOW ON EARTH, THE(1952)

Davison Clark
DISHONORED(1931); VICE SQUAD, THE(1931); BLONDE VENUS(1932); THIS IS THE NIGHT(1932); LADIES THEY TALK ABOUT(1933); TORCH SINGER(1933); MIGHTY BARNUM, THE(1934); SCARLET EMPRESS, THE(1934); WE LIVE AGAIN(1934); GOOSE AND THE GANDER, THE(1935); LES MISERABLES(1935); SECRET BRIDE, THE(1935); VIRGINIA JUDGE, THE(1935); BANJO ON MY KNEE(1936); MESSAGE TO GARCIA, A(1936); MURDER WITH PICTURES(1936); EMPEROR'S CANDLESTICKS, THE(1937); LOVE IS NEWS(1937); PLAINSMAN, THE(1937); SLIM(1937); SOULS AT SEA(1937); THIS IS MY AFFAIR(1937); BORN TO BE WILD(1938); JEZEBEL(1938); WESTERN JAMBOREE(1938); HOTEL IMPERIAL(1939); OKLAHOMA TERROR(1939); SECRET SERVICE OF THE AIR(1939); NORTHWEST MOUNTED POLICE(1940); RETURN OF FRANK JAMES, THE(1940); THREE MEN FROM TEXAS(1940); PRAIRIE PIONEERS(1941); SIX GUN GOLD(1941); COME ON DANGER(1942); DOWN RIO GRANDE WAY(1942); REAP THE WILD WIND(1942); DEATH VALLEY MANHUNT(1943); FIGHTING FRONTIER(1943); HAIL TO THE RANGERS(1943); JACK LONDON(1943); LAW OF THE NORTHWEST(1943); SONG OF BERNADETTE, THE(1943); ADVENTURES OF MARK TWAIN, THE(1944); STORY OF DR. WASSELL, THE(1944); TRIGGER TRAIL(1944); GANGS OF THE WATERFRONT(1945); HONEYMOON AHEAD(1945); OUT OF THIS WORLD(1945); ROGUES GALLERY(1945); SEA OF GRASS, THE(1947); UNCONQUERED(1947); B. F.'S DAUGHTER(1948); CRY OF THE CITY(1948); FOUR FACES WEST(1948); STATE OF THE UNION(1948); SAMSON AND DELILAH(1949); SAND(1949); CAGED(1950); LONE STAR(1952)
Misc. Talkies
RIDING THROUGH NEVADA(1942)

Dawn Clark
STRIPES(1981)

Dean Clark
ARISTOCATS, THE(1970)

Dennis Clark
AMERICAN GRAFFITI(1973), art d

Dennis Lynton Clark
MAN CALLED HORSE, A(1970), prod d; MAN IN THE WILDERNESS(1971, U.S./Span.), prod d, cos; NEPTUNE FACTOR, THE(1973, Can.), prod d; COMES A HORSEMAN(1978), w

Dick Clark
JAMBOREE(1957); BECAUSE THEY'RE YOUNG(1960); YOUNG DOCTORS, THE(1961); KILLERS THREE(1968), a, p, w; PSYCH-OUT(1968), p; SAVAGE SEVEN, THE(1968), p; WILD IN THE STREETS(1968); PHYNX, THE(1970); DARK, THE(1979), p

Dolores Clark
LIFE AND TIMES OF JUDGE ROY BEAN, THE(1972)

Don Clark
KETTLES ON OLD MACDONALD'S FARM, THE(1957)
Silents
NORTH OF HUDSON BAY(1923), ph
Misc. Silents
FIGHTING GUIDE, THE(1922), d

Donald Clark
FATHER'S LITTLE DIVIDEND(1951)

Donald Henderson Clark
FEMALE(1933), w

Doran Clark
WARRIORS, THE(1979)

Doreena Clark
WHISTLE DOWN THE WIND(1961, Brit.)

Doris Clark
LEO THE LAST(1970, Brit.)

Dorothy Clark
Misc. Silents
LOVE NEVER DIES(1916); YAQUI, THE(1916)

Dorothy Love Clark
Misc. Silents
HUMDRUM BROWN(1918)

Dort Clark
KISS OF DEATH(1947); SLEEPING CITY, THE(1950); ST. BENNY THE DIP(1951); ER LOVE A STRANGER(1958); BELLS ARE RINGING(1960); FATE IS THE HUNTER(1964); I'D RATHER BE RICH(1964); IN HARM'S WAY(1965); LOVED ONE, THE(1965); FOOLS' PARADE(1971); SKIN GAME(1971); EVERYTHING YOU ALWAYS WANTED TO KNOW ABOUT SEX, BUT WE'RE AFRAID TO ASK(1972)

Downing Clark
Silents
AMERICA(1924)

Dudley Clark
THERE WAS A YOUNG MAN(1937, Brit.), w

E. Holman Clark
Silents
MESSAGE FROM MARS, A(1913, Brit.); RED POTTAGE(1918, Brit.); HER HERITAGE(1919, Brit.); FALSE EVIDENCE(1922, Brit.)

Ed Clark
BEDTIME FOR BONZO(1951); LITTLE EGYPT(1951); HERE COME THE NELSONS(1952)
Silents
KAISER, BEAST OF BERLIN, THE(1918)

Eddie Clark
FALCON OUT WEST, THE(1944); HEAVENLY DAYS(1944)

Edward Clark
UNMASKED(1929), w; ONE HOUR LATE(1935); BALL OF FIRE(1941); SWAMP WATER(1941); ROXIE HART(1942); PHANTOM OF THE OPERA(1943); SONG OF BERNADETTE, THE(1943); EXPERIMENT PERILOUS(1944); WHERE DO WE GO FROM HERE?(1945); FALCON'S ALIBI, THE(1946); NOCTURNE(1946); O.S.S.(1946); FABULOUS DORSEYS, THE(1947); MY WILD IRISH ROSE(1947); NIGHTMARE ALLEY(1947); SENATOR WAS INDISCREET, THE(1947); WELCOME STRANGER(1947); WALLS OF JERICHO(1948); WHEN MY BABY SMILES AT ME(1948); DANCING IN THE DARK(1949); OH, YOU BEAUTIFUL DOLL(1949); MA AND PA KETTLE GO TO TOWN(1950); MILKMAN, THE(1950); PETTY GIRL, THE(1950); TICKET TO TOMAHAWK(1950); BRANDED(1951); CATTLE QUEEN(1951); DANGER ZONE(1951); MILLION DOLLAR PURSUIT(1951); MR. BELVEDERE RINGS THE BELL(1951); SAVAGE DRUMS(1951); STRANGERS ON A TRAIN(1951); CARRIE(1952); MILLION DOLLAR MERMAID(1952); THUNDERING CARAVANS(1952); EASY TO LOVE(1953); EL PASO STAMPEDE(1953); FLAME OF CALCUTTA(1953); HOUDINI(1953); IT HAPPENS EVERY THURSDAY(1953); MONEY FROM HOME(1953); TOPEKA(1953); CRASHOUT(1955); HELL'S OUTPOST(1955)
Silents
ETERNAL LOVE(1917); BROKEN HEARTS OF HOLLYWOOD(1926), w; PRIVATE IZZY MURPHY(1926), w; GAY OLD BIRD, THE(1927), w; HILLS OF KENTUCKY(1927), w; SALLY IN OUR ALLEY(1927), w; SILKS AND SADDLES(1929), w

Elia Clark
STREET OF SINNERS(1957)

Ellen Clark
CHRISTINE JORGENSEN STORY, THE(1970)

Ellery H. Clark
CARIBBEAN(1952), w

Elsie Clark
ACCENT ON YOUTH(1935)

Ernest Clark
CIRCUS CLOWN(1934); PRIVATE ANGELO(1949, Brit.); MUDLARK, THE(1950, Brit.); BEAU BRUMMELL(1954); DETECTIVE, THE(1954, Qit.); DOCTOR IN THE HOUSE(1954, Brit.); DAM BUSTERS, THE(1955, Brit.); STARS IN YOUR EYES(1956, Brit.); 1984(1956, Brit.); BABY AND THE BATTLESHIP, THE(1957, Brit.); BIRTHDAY PRESENT, THE(1957, Brit.); DECISION AGAINST TIME(1957, Brit.); TIME WITHOUT PITY(1957, Brit.); WOMAN OF MYSTERY, A(1957, Brit.); BLIND SPOT(1958, Brit.); I ACCUSE(1958, Brit.); SAFECRACKER, THE(1958, Brit.); TALE OF TWO CITIES, A(1958, Brit.); SINK THE BISMARCK!(1960, Brit.); THREE ON A SPREE(1961, Brit.); TIME TO REMEMBER(1962, Brit.); BILLY LIAR(1963, Brit.); DEVIL-SHIP PIRATES, THE(1964, Brit.); MASTER SPY(1964, Brit.); NOTHING BUT THE BEST(1964, Brit.); TOMORROW AT TEN(1964, Brit.); YOUNG AND WILLING(1964, Brit.); CUCKOO PATROL(1965, Brit.); MASQUERADE(1965, Brit.); SECRET OF MY SUCCESS, THE(1965, Brit.); ARABESQUE(1966); FINDERS KEEPERS(1966, Brit.); IT!(1967, Brit.); STITCH IN TIME, A(1967, Brit.); ATTACK ON THE IRON COAST(1968, U.S./Brit.); SALT & PEPPER(1968, Brit.); CASTLE KEEP(1969); EXECUTIONER, THE(1970, Brit.); SONG OF NORWAY(1970); GANDHI(1982)

Estelle Clark
Silents
HIS SECRETARY(1925); MERRY WIDOW, THE(1925); TILLIE THE TOILER(1927); CROWD, THE(1928)

Ethel Clark
HEADLEYS AT HOME, THE(1939)

Eugene Clark
IMPROPER CHANNELS(1981, Can.)

F. Clark
Silents
NOBODY'S WIFE(1918), w

Frank Clark
ROARING RANCH(1930); SPURS(1930); CROSS-EXAMINATION(1932); LOST SQUADRON, THE(1932); MEN WITH WINGS(1938); SUNDOWN(1941); CALL ME MISTER(1951); BHOWANI JUNCTION(1956), ed; BARRETTS OF WIMPOLE STREET, THE(1957), ed; STRANGE SHADOWS IN AN EMPTY ROOM(1977, Can./Ital.), w
Misc. Talkies
BORDER MENACE, THE(1934); WHIRLWIND RIDER, THE(1935)

Frank C. Clark-

Silents

SPOILERS, THE(1914); CARPET FROM BAGDAD, THE(1915); NE'ER-DO-WELL, THE(1916); MAN FROM PAINTED POST, THE(1917); CITY OF PURPLE DREAMS, THE(1918); LIVE WIRES(1921); MAID OF THE WEST(1921); ROOKIE'S RETURN, THE(1921); BLUE BLOOD(1925), w; AIR PATROL, THE(1928); MY HOME TOWN(1928)

Misc. Silents

CHIP OF THE FLYING U(1914); CYCLE OF FATE, THE(1916); PRICE OF SILENCE, THE(1917); WESTERN BLOOD(1918); TRIXIE FROM BROADWAY(1919); WILDERNESS TRAIL, THE(1919); LITTLE MISS HAWKSHAW(1921), d; WANDERER OF THE WEST(1927)

Frank C. Clark

BEYOND THE REEF(1981), d

Frank H. Clark

LONE RIDER, THE(1930), w

Frank Howard Clark

SHADOW RANCH(1930), w; UTAH KID, THE(1930), w; FIGHTING FOOL, THE(1932), w; FIGHTING MARSHAL, THE(1932), w; HEART PUNCH(1932), w; WILD HORSE MESA(1932), w; RUSTLERS' ROUNDUP(1933), w; TRAVELING SALESLADY, THE(1935), w; O'MALLEY OF THE MOUNTED(1936), w; TWO IN REVOLT(1936), w

Silents

AMAZING IMPOSTER, THE(1919), w; BILLY JIM(1922), w; AMERICAN MANNERS(1924), w; IN HIGH GEAR(1924), w; LAUGHING AT DANGER(1924), w; JIMMIE'S MILLIONS(1925), w; HAUNTED RANGE, THE(1926), w; NIGHT PATROL, THE(1926), w; UNDER FIRE(1926), w; BANDIT'S SON, THE(1927), w; BOY RIDER, THE(1927), w; SPLITTING THE BREEZE(1927), w; AVENGING RIDER, THE(1928), w; BANTAM COWBOY, THE(1928), w; CAPTAIN CARELESS(1928), w; DESERT PIRATE, THE(1928), w; DOG LAW(1928); MAN IN THE ROUGH(1928); PHANTOM OF THE RANGE(1928), w; AMAZING VAGABOND(1929), w; FRECKLED RASCAL, THE(1929), w; IDAHO RED(1929), w; LITTLE SAVAGE, THE(1929), w; ONE MAN DOG, THE(1929), w; PALS OF THE PRAIRIE(1929), w

Misc. Silents

WIZARD OF THE SADDLE(1928), d

Frank M. Clark

Silents

OUTLAWED(1929)

Franklyn Clark

SATAN'S BED(1965)

Fred Clark

RIDE THE PINK HORSE(1947); UNSUSPECTED, THE(1947); CRY OF THE CITY(1948); FURY AT FURNACE CREEK(1948); HAZARD(1948); MR. PEABODY AND THE MERMAID(1948); TWO GUYS FROM TEXAS(1948); ALIAS NICK BEAL(1949); FLAMINGO ROAD(1949); LADY TAKES A SAILOR, THE(1949); WHITE HEAT(1949); YOUNGER BROTHERS, THE(1949); EAGLE AND THE HAWK, THE(1950); JACKPOT, THE(1950); MRS. O'MALLEY AND MR. MALONE(1950); RETURN OF THE FRONTIERSMAN(1950); SUNSET BOULEVARD(1950); TREASURE ISLAND(1950, Brit.); HOLLYWOOD STORY(1951); LEMON DROP KID, THE(1951); MEET ME AFTER THE SHOW(1951); PLACE IN THE SUN, A(1951); DREAMBOAT(1952); THREE FOR BEDROOM C(1952); CADDY, THE(1953); HERE COME THE GIRLS(1953); HOW TO MARRY A MILLIONAIRE(1953); STARS ARE SINGING, THE(1953); LIVING IT UP(1954); ABBOTT AND COSTELLO MEET THE KEYSTONE KOPS(1955); COURT-MARTIAL OF BILLY MITCHELL, THE(1955); DADDY LONG LEGS(1955); HOW TO BE VERY, VERY, POPULAR(1955); BACK FROM ETERNITY(1956); MIRACLE IN THE RAIN(1956); SOLID GOLD CADILLAC, THE(1956); FUZZY PINK NIGHTGOWN, THE(1957); JOE BUTTERFLY(1957); AUNTIE MAME(1958); MARDI GRAS(1958); IT STARTED WITH A KISS(1959); MATING GAME, THE(1959); BELLS ARE RINGING(1960); VISIT TO A SMALL PLANET(1960); ADVENTURES OF A YOUNG MAN(1962); BOYS' NIGHT OUT(1962); ZOTZ!(1962); MOVE OVER, DARLING(1963); PASSIONATE THIEF, THE(1963, Ital.); JOHN GOLDFARB, PLEASE COME HOME(1964); BIRDS AND THE BEES, THE(1965); CURSE OF THE MUMMY'S TOMB, THE(1965, Brit.); DR. GOLDFOOT AND THE BIKINI MACHINE(1965); SERGEANT DEADHEAD(1965); WHEN THE BOYS MEET THE GIRLS(1965); WAR ITALIAN STYLE(1967, Ital.); EVE(1968, Brit./Span.); HORSE IN THE GRAY FLANNEL SUIT, THE(1968); SKIDOO(1968); I SAILED TO TAHITI WITH AN ALL GIRL CREW(1969); DON'T GO NEAR THE WATER(1975)

Freddy Clark

HELL, HEAVEN OR HOBOKEN(1958, Brit.); WRONG BOX, THE(1966, Brit.)

Frederick Clark

EVER SINCE EVE(1937); FIRST 100 YEARS, THE(1938); KID FROM KOKOMO, THE(1939); SUNDOWN(1941)

Frederick R. Clark

THEN THERE WERE THREE(1961)

1984

TANK(1984)

G. Davidson Clark

Misc. Silents

FORTUNATE YOUTH, THE(1916)

G. Davison Clark

GREAT POWER, THE(1929)

Gage Clark

INVISIBLE BOY, THE(1957); I WANT TO LIVE!(1958); RETURN OF DRACULA, THE(1958); POLLYANNA(1960)

Gary Clark

BACKTRACK(1969)

Geoffrey Clark

LIEUTENANT DARING, RN(1935, Brit.); CAFE MASCOT(1936, Brit.); FULL SPEED AHEAD(1936, Brit.); MUSEUM MYSTERY(1937, Brit.); KATE PLUS TEN(1938, Brit.)

George Clark

FOOLS RUSH IN(1949, Brit.), ed; GUILT IS MY SHADOW(1950, Brit.), ed; TENDER IS THE NIGHT(1961)

Silents

DOUBLE LIFE OF MR. ALFRED BURTON, THE(1919, Brit.), p; FANCY DRESS(1919, Brit.), p

Misc. Silents

I WILL(1919, Brit.), d

George Dow Clark

OKAY AMERICA(1932)

Gerry Clark

THAT SINKING FEELING(1979, Brit.)

Gilbert Clark

BELLAMY TRIAL, THE(1929), cos; IRON MASK, THE(1929), cos

Silents

ENEMY, THE(1927), cos; FAIR CO-ED, THE(1927), cos; IN OLD KENTUCKY(1927), cos; WHILE THE CITY SLEEPS(1928), cos

Glen Clark

1984

SONGWRITER(1984)

Gloria Clark

PERILOUS JOURNEY, A(1953); DIARY OF A MADMAN(1963); DEAR BRIGITTE(1965)

Gordon Clark

ONCE UPON A HONEYMOON(1942); FIRST COMES COURAGE(1943); IMMORTAL SERGEANT, THE(1943); IRON MAJOR, THE(1943); OLD ACQUAINTANCE(1943); THIS LAND IS MINE(1943); QUEEN OF BURLESQUE(1946); BELLS OF SAN FERNANDO(1947); EXILE, THE(1947); INTRIGUE(1947); SINBAD THE SAILOR(1947); SONG OF MY HEART(1947); ROGUES' REGIMENT(1948); UNDER MY SKIN(1950); WHERE DANGER LIVES(1950); WINNING TEAM, THE(1952); PARIS PLAYBOYS(1954); WRONG MAN, THE(1956); LAST GUNFIGHTER, THE(1961, Can.)

Graham Clark

WILD GEESE, THE(1978, Brit.)

Graydon Clark

BLACK SHAMPOO(1976), d, w

Greydon Clark

SATAN'S SADISTS(1969); HELL'S BLOODY DEVILS(1970); TOM(1973), a, d; PSYCHIC KILLER(1975), a, w; SATAN'S CHEERLEADERS(1977), d, w; HI-RIDERS(1978), d&w; ANGELS BRIGADE(1980), p&d, w; RETURN, THE(1980), p&d; WITHOUT WARNING(1980), p&d; JOYSTICKS(1983), p&d; WACKO(1983), p&d

Misc. Talkies

BAD BUNCH, THE(1976)

Gwen Clark

YEARS BETWEEN, THE(1947, Brit.)

Gwen Clark [Jane Hylton]

GIRL IN A MILLION, A(1946, Brit.)

Harry Clark

ABSOLUTE QUIET(1936), w; CRY MURDER(1936); NEW FACES OF 1937(1937), w; AND ONE WAS BEAUTIFUL(1940), w; DOWN IN SAN DIEGO(1941), w; ICE-CAPADES(1941); MIGHTY MCGURK, THE(1946), w; PROJECT X(1949); PAINTING THE CLOUDS WITH SUNSHINE(1951), w; TAXI(1953)

Harvey Clark

ANYBODY'S WOMAN(1930); MAN TROUBLE(1930); SEVEN KEYS TO BALDPATE(1930); UP THE RIVER(1930); WHAT A MAN(1930); CRACKED NUTS(1931); DANCING DYNAMITE(1931); DECEIVER, THE(1931); GOING WILD(1931); MILLIE(1931); DOWN TO EARTH(1932); HAT CHECK GIRL(1932); RED HEADED WOMAN(1932); THOSE WE LOVE(1932); I LOVE THAT MAN(1933); MAN'S CASTLE, A(1933); SHRIEK IN THE NIGHT, A(1933); SITTING PRETTY(1933); STRICTLY PERSONAL(1933); WEST OF SINGAPORE(1933); CHARLIE CHAN'S COURAGE(1934); PECK'S BAD BOY(1934); PICTURE BRIDES(1934); PADDY O'DAY(1935); BOSS RIDER OF GUN CREEK(1936); FURY(1936); SINGING COWBOY, THE(1936); SITTING ON THE MOON(1936); THREE GODFATHERS(1936); BLONDE TROUBLE(1937); BOSS OF LONELY VALLEY(1937); DANCE, CHARLIE, DANCE(1937); DANGEROUS HOLIDAY(1937); EMPEROR'S CANDLESTICKS, THE(1937); EMPTY SADDLES(1937); INTERNES CAN'T TAKE MONEY(1937); IT'S LOVE I'M AFTER(1937); LAW FOR TOMBSTONE(1937); SOULS AT SEA(1937); TOAST OF NEW YORK, THE(1937); WOMEN OF GLAMOUR(1937); ARSENE LUPIN RETURNS(1938); DANGEROUS TO KNOW(1938); I AM THE LAW(1938); MOTHER CAREY'S CHICKENS(1938); PARTNERS OF THE PLAINS(1938); SPAWN OF THE NORTH(1938); THREE COMRADES(1938)

Silents

FRAME UP, THE(1917); IN BAD(1918); THIS HERO STUFF(1919); ARABIAN KNIGHT, AN(1920); ALIAS JULIUS CAESAR(1922); SHATTERED IDOLS(1922); THELMA(1922); SECOND HAND LOVE(1923); ROUGHNECK, THE(1924); ARIZONA ROMEO, THE(1925); BLUE BLOOD(1925); CAMILLE(1927); IN OLD KENTUCKY(1927); BEAUTIFUL BUT DUMB(1928); FLOATING COLLEGE, THE(1928); HEAD MAN, THE(1928); OLYMPIC HERO, THE(1928); TOILERS, THE(1928)

Misc. Silents

LAND O' LIZARDS(1916); LONESOME TOWN(1916); VOICE OF LOVE, THE(1916); ENVIRONMENT(1917); GENTLE INTRUDER, THE(1917); NEW YORK LUCK(1917); SNAP JUDGEMENT(1917); GOLDEN FLEECE, THE(1918); HIGH STAKES(1918); POWERS THAT PREY(1918); SHIFTING SANDS(1918); PRUDENCE ON BROADWAY(1919); RESTLESS SOULS(1919); SIX FEET FOUR(1919); WHOM THE GODS WOULD DESTROY(1919); DANGEROUS TALENT, THE(1920); MILESTONES(1920); THEIR MUTUAL CHILD(1920); VALLEY OF TOMORROW, THE(1920); MONEY TO BURN(1922); SECRETS(1924); COWBOY AND THE COUNTESS, THE(1926); PALACE OF PLEASURE, THE(1926); NIGHT BIRD, THE(1928); WOMAN AGAINST THE WORLD, A(1928)

Herbert Clark

BIG NEWS(1929); BRIDE OF THE REGIMENT(1930); IN GAY MADRID(1930)

Holman Clark

Misc. Silents

BRASS BOTTLE, THE(1914, Brit.)

Hope Clark

BOOK OF NUMBERS(1973)

Ida May Clark

Silents

AMAZING WIFE, THE(1919), d&w

J. Nesbit Clark

FAN, THE(1981)

J.D. Clark

WANDA NEVADA(1979)

J.J. Clark

VERDICT, THE(1982)

J.L. Clark

TEXAS LIGHTNING(1981); TRICK OR TREATS(1982)

J.R. Clark

GRAVEYARD OF HORROR(1971, Span.); SSSSSSSS(1973); HANGAR 18(1980)

Jack Clark
THREE-CORNERED MOON(1933); HOME ON THE RANGE(1935); MURDER WITH PICTURES(1936); EBB TIDE(1937); HOTEL HAYWIRE(1937); WELLS FARGO(1937)
Silents
FROM THE MANGER TO THE CROSS(1913); AUDREY(1916); INNOCENT LIE, THE(1916)
Misc. Silents
LAST OF THE MAFFIA, THE(1915)

Jack J. Clark
Misc. Talkies
HOWDY BROADWAY(1929)
Silents
LOVE AND LEARN(1928)

Jacki Clark
D.C. CAB(1983)

Jacqueline Clark
BLITHE SPIRIT(1945, Brit.); QUEEN OF SPADES(1948, Brit.); NIGHT AFTER NIGHT AFTER NIGHT(1970, Brit.)

James Clark
UNDER THE RED ROBE(1937, Brit.), ed; WINGS OF THE MORNING(1937, Brit.), ed; ONE WISH TOO MANY(1956, Brit.), ed; GRASS IS GREENER, THE(1960), ed; SURPRISE PACKAGE(1960), ed; INNOCENTS, THE(1961, U.S./Brit.), ed; TERM OF TRIAL(1962, Brit.), ed; CHARADE(1963), ed; PUMPKIN EATER, THE(1964, Brit.), ed; DARLING(1965, Brit.), ed; CHRISTMAS TREE, THE(1966, Brit.), d, w; VAMPYRES, DAUGHTERS OF DRACULA(1977, Brit.), m

James B. Clark
DINNER AT THE RITZ(1937, Brit.), ed; SMILING ALONG(1938, Brit.), ed; INSPECTOR HORNLEIGH(1939, Brit.), ed; RETURN OF THE CISCO KID(1939), ed; CHARLIE CHAN AT THE WAX MUSEUM(1940), ed; HE MARRIED HIS WIFE(1940), ed; SO THIS IS LONDON(1940, Brit.), ed; HOW GREEN WAS MY VALLEY(1941), ed; SUN VALLEY SERENADE(1941), ed; VERY YOUNG LADY, A(1941), ed; CHINA GIRL(1942), ed; ICELAND(1942), ed; ROXIE HART(1942), ed; TEN GENTLEMEN FROM WEST POINT(1942), ed; HOLY MATRIMONY(1943), ed; IMMORTAL SERGEANT, THE(1943), ed; STORMY WEATHER(1943), ed; BUFFALO BILL(1944), ed; KEYS OF THE KINGDOM, THE(1944), ed; CAPTAIN EDDIE(1945), ed; LEAVE HER TO HEAVEN(1946), ed; SOMEWHERE IN THE NIGHT(1946), ed; FOXES OF HARROW, THE(1947), ed; LATE GEORGE APLEY, THE(1947), ed; MOSS ROSE(1947), ed; ROAD HOUSE(1948), ed; WALLS OF JERICHO(1948), ed; I WAS A MALE WAR BRIDE(1949), ed; MY BLUE HEAVEN(1950), ed; WHEN WILLIE COMES MARCHING HOME(1950), ed; BIRD OF PARADISE(1951), ed; DESERT FOX, THE(1951), ed; SECRET OF CONVICT LAKE, THE(1951), ed; YOU'RE IN THE NAVY NOW(1951), ed; DIPLOMATIC COURIER(1952), ed; DREAMBOAT(1952), ed; FIVE FINGERS(1952), ed; STARS AND STRIPES FOREVER(1952), ed; WHITE WITCH DOCTOR(1953), ed; GARDEN OF EVIL(1954), ed; HELL AND HIGH WATER(1954), ed; HOUSE OF BAMBOO(1955), ed; RACERS, THE(1955), ed; BETWEEN HEAVEN AND HELL(1956), ed; GIRL CAN'T HELP IT, THE(1956), ed; LIEUTENANT WORE SKIRTS, THE(1956), ed; 23 PACES TO BAKER STREET(1956), ed; AFFAIR TO REMEMBER, AN(1957), ed; UNDER FIRE(1957), d; SIERRA BARON(1958), d; VILLA!(1958), d; DOG OF FLANDERS, A(1959), d; SAD HORSE, THE(1959), d; ONE FOOT IN HELL(1960), d; BIG SHOW, THE(1961), p, d; MISTY(1961), d; DRUMS OF AFRICA(1963), d; FLIPPER(1963), d; ISLAND OF THE BLUE DOLPHINS(1964), d; AND NOW MIGUEL(1966), d; MY SIDE OF THE MOUNTAIN(1969), d; LITTLE ARK, THE(1972), d

James H. Clark
YOUNG PEOPLE(1940), ed

James R. Clark
GOLDEN HOOFS(1941), ed

Jameson Clark
TIGHT LITTLE ISLAND(1949, Brit.); BRAVE DON'T CRY, THE(1952, Brit.); HIGH AND DRY(1954, Brit.); LITTLE KIDNAPPERS, THE(1954, Brit.); SCOTCH ON THE ROCKS(1954, Brit.); BOND OF FEAR(1956, Brit.); HIGH TERRACE(1957, Brit.); LET'S BE HAPPY(1957, Brit.); LONG HAUL, THE(1957, Brit.); THIRD KEY, THE(1957, Brit.); X THE UNKNOWN(1957, Brit.); KEY, THE(1958, Brit.); MAD LITTLE ISLAND(1958, Brit.); BEYOND THIS PLACE(1959, Brit.); BRIDAL PATH, THE(1959, Brit.); BATTLE OF THE SEXES, THE(1960, Brit.); THIRTY NINE STEPS, THE(1960, Brit.); GREYFRIARS BOBBY(1961); PAIR OF BRIEFS, A(1963, Brit.); RING OF BRIGHT WATER(1969, Brit.)

Janet Clark
EXPERIMENT PERILOUS(1944); NO ROOM FOR THE GROOM(1952); MOVIE STUNTMEN(1953), w; GREAT BANK ROBBERY, THE(1969)

Janet E. Clark
I LOVE YOU, ALICE B. TOKLAS!(1968); SUPPOSE THEY GAVE A WAR AND NOBODY CAME?(1970)

Janet Elsie Clark
ROMANCE IN THE DARK(1938)

Jason Clark
ELECTRA GLIDE IN BLUE(1973); MIXED COMPANY(1974); TRIAL OF BILLY JACK, THE(1974); PURSUIT(1975); WANDA NEVADA(1979)

Jean Clark
SKY LINER(1949); HARD ROAD, THE(1970)

Jerry Clark
1984
FLASH OF GREEN, A(1984)

Jerry L. Clark
1984
INITIATION, THE(1984)

Jesse Clark
HELL'S PLAYGROUND(1967), d

Jill Clark
WHERE THE RED FERN GROWS(1974); TEX(1982)

Jim Clark
THINK DIRTY(1970, Brit.), d; RENTADICK(1972, Brit.), d; X Y & ZEE(1972, Brit.), ed; MADHOUSE(1974, Brit.), d; ADVENTURES OF SHERLOCK HOLMES' SMARTER BROTHER, THE(1975, Brit.), ed; DAY OF THE LOCUST, THE(1975), ed; MARATHON MAN(1976), ed; LAST REMAKE OF BEAU GESTE, THE(1977), ed; AGATHA(1979, Brit.), ed; YANKS(1979), ed; HONKY TONK FREEWAY(1981), ed; PRIVATES ON PARADE(1982), ed
1984
HOT DOG...THE MOVIE(1984), ed; KILLING FIELDS, THE(1984, Brit.), ed; PRIVATES ON PARADE(1984, Brit.), ed, ed

Jimmy Clark
EVE OF ST. MARK, THE(1944); THEY LIVE IN FEAR(1944); GIRL OF THE LIMBERLOST, THE(1945); ON STAGE EVERYBODY(1945); STRANGE ILLUSION(1945); SENATOR WAS INDISCREET, THE(1947); VIOLENCE(1947); MOM AND DAD(1948)

Joe Clark
DULCIMER STREET(1948, Brit.); CONSTANT HUSBAND, THE(1955, Brit.)

John Clark
KANGAROO(1952); OUTCASTS OF THE CITY(1958); SECRET CEREMONY(1968, Brit.), art d; LAND RAIDERS(1969); EL CONDOR(1970); LIGHT AT THE EDGE OF THE WORLD, THE(1971, U.S./Span./Lichtenstein); RAILWAY CHILDREN, THE(1971, Brit.), art d; SEVERED HEAD, A(1971, Brit.), art d; TOWN CALLED HELL, A(1971, Span./Brit.); ZEPPELIN(1971, Brit.); JESUS CHRIST, SUPERSTAR(1973), art d; OFFENSE, THE(1973, Brit.), art d; TOMMY(1975, Brit.), art d

John G. Clark
HOUSE ON SORORITY ROW, THE(1983), p

John J. Clark
Silents
PAJAMAS(1927)

Johnny Clark
JIVE JUNCTION(1944); LOCKET, THE(1946)

Joseph Clark
MEDUSA TOUCH, THE(1978, Brit.); BIG RED ONE, THE(1980); SIX WEEKS(1982)

Judy Clark
UNCLE HARRY(1945); SOUTH OF SANTA FE(1942); SWING YOUR PARTNER(1943); BEAUTIFUL BUT BROKE(1944); MINSTREL MAN(1944); NIGHT CLUB GIRL(1944); RECKLESS AGE(1944); KID SISTER, THE(1945); PENTHOUSE RHYTHM(1945); IN FAST COMPANY(1946); JUNIOR PROM(1946); THAT'S MY GAL(1947); TWO BLONDES AND A REDHEAD(1947); GIRL ON THE BRIDGE, THE(1951); CROOKED WEB, THE(1955)

Kathie Clark
METALSTORM: THE DESTRUCTION OF JARED-SYN(1983), cos

Ken Clark
BETWEEN HEAVEN AND HELL(1956); LAST WAGON, THE(1956); LOVE ME TENDER(1956); ON THE THRESHOLD OF SPACE(1956); PROUD ONES, THE(1956); SOUTH PACIFIC(1958); ATTACK OF THE GIANT LEECHES(1959); TWELVE TO THE MOON(1960); ROAD TO FORT ALAMO, THE(1966, Fr./Ital.); MISSION BLOODY MARY(1967, Fr./Ital./Span.); MAN CALLED SLEDGE, A(1971, Ital.); TARZANA, THE WILD GIRL(1973)
Misc. Talkies
FURY ON THE BOSPHOROUS(1965, Brit.); FULLER REPORT, THE(1966); TIFFANY MEMORANDUM(1966)

Kendall Clark
SHRIKE, THE(1955); SIX BRIDGES TO CROSS(1955); DAMN CITIZEN(1958)

Kory Clark
Misc. Talkies
STRAIGHT JACKET(1980)

L.C. Clark
SYMPHONY OF LIVING(1935), ed

L.V. Clark
WARRIORS, THE(1955), makeup; LONG AND THE SHORT AND THE TALL, THE(1961, Brit.), makeup

Larry Clark
PASSING THROUGH(1977), d, w, ed

Laurence Clark
ALL THE KING'S HORSES(1935), w

Laurence Mery Clark
RETURN OF THE SOLDIER, THE(1983, Brit.), ed

Lee Clark
YOU WERE MEANT FOR ME(1948), ch; WHEN WILLIE COMES MARCHING HOME(1950)

Leroy Clark, Jr.
SHEBA BABY(1975)

Les Clark
SNOW WHITE AND THE SEVEN DWARFS(1937), anim; FANTASIA(1940), anim, anim; PINOCCHIO(1940), anim; DUMBO(1941), anim; THREE CABALLEROS, THE(1944), anim; DO YOU LOVE ME?(1946), anim; MAKE MINE MUSIC(1946), anim; SONG OF THE SOUTH(1946), anim; FUN AND FANCY FREE(1947), anim d; WALLS OF JERICHO(1948); WHEN MY BABY SMILES AT ME(1948); YOU WERE MEANT FOR ME(1948); SO DEAR TO MY HEART(1949), anim; ALICE IN WONDERLAND(1951), anim d; SOMEBODY LOVES ME(1952); PETER PAN(1953), anim; COUNTRY GIRL, THE(1954); LADY AND THE TRAMP(1955), anim d; DEVIL'S HAIRPIN, THE(1957); SLEEPING BEAUTY(1959), d; ONE HUNDRED AND ONE DALMATIANS(1961), anim

Lester Clark
WHITE CHRISTMAS(1954)

Lex Clark
MANGANINNIE(1982, Aus.)

Liddy Clark
TOUCH AND GO(1955); SIDECAR RACERS(1975, Aus.); BLUE FIN(1978, Aus.); KITTY AND THE BAGMAN(1983, Aus.)

Lili Clark
SHOCK TREATMENT(1964)

Linda Clark
1984
HOTEL NEW HAMPSHIRE, THE(1984)

Logan Clark
CHECKERED FLAG OR CRASH(1978)

Lon Clark
GENTLE RAIN, THE(1966, Braz.)

Lorraine Clark
GEORGE WHITE'S SCANDALS(1945); HAVING WONDERFUL CRIME(1945)

Lou Clark
SLENDER THREAD, THE(1965)

Louise Clark
TO HAVE AND HAVE NOT(1944); CATAMOUNT KILLING, THE(1975, Ger.)
Misc. Silents
IN THE HOLLOW OF HER HAND(1918)

Lyle Clark
MAGNIFICENT YANKEE, THE(1950); STARLIFT(1951)
M. Clark
POCKET MONEY(1972)
Mack Clark
UP THE RIVER(1930)
Mae Clark
HITCH HIKE LADY(1936); BREACH OF PROMISE(1942, Brit.); DAREDEVILS OF THE CLOUDS(1948); WICHITA(1955)
Mamo Clark
MUTINY ON THE BOUNTY(1935); HURRICANE, THE(1937); WALLABY JIM OF THE ISLANDS(1937); AIR DEVILS(1938); BOOLOO(1938); HAWAII CALLS(1938); MUTINY ON THE BLACKHAWK(1939); GIRL FROM GOD'S COUNTRY(1940); ONE MILLION B.C.(1940)
Margaret Clark
SHOOT THE MOON(1982)
Marguerite Clark
Silents
PRETTY SISTER OF JOSE(1915); PRINCE AND THE PAUPER, THE(1915); SEVEN SISTERS, THE(1915); STILL WATERS(1915); MICE AND MEN(1916); OUT OF THE DRIFTS(1916); AMAZONS, THE(1917); BAB'S BURGLAR(1917); BAB'S DIARY(1917); LITTLE MISS HOOVER(1918); OUT OF A CLEAR SKY(1918); PRUNELLA(1918); EASY TO GET(1920)
Misc. Silents
(; CRUCIBLE, THE(1914); WILDFLOWER(1914); GRETNA GREEN(1915); HELENE OF THE NORTH(1915); LITTLE LADY EILEEN(1916); MISS GEORGE WASHINGTON(1916); MOLLY MAKE-BELIEVE(1916); SILKS AND SATINS(1916); BAB'S MATINEE IDOL(1917); FORTUNES OF FIFI, THE(1917); SNOW WHITE(1917); VALENTINE GIRL, THE(1917); RICH MAN, POOR MAN(1918); SEVEN SWANS, THE(1918); UNCLE TOM'S CABIN(1918); GIRLS(1919); LUCK IN PAWN(1919); MRS. WIGGS OF THE CABBAGE PATCH(1919); THREE MEN AND A GIRL(1919); WIDOW BY PROXY(1919); ALL OF A SUDDEN PEGGY(1920); GIRL NAMED MARY, A(1920); SCRAMBLED WIVES(1921)
Marguertie Clark
Misc. Silents
LET'S ELOPE(1919)
Marie Clark
STONE COLD DEAD(1980, Can.)
Marilyn Clark
SHADOWS(1960); TOO LATE BLUES(1962); HORROR OF PARTY BEACH, THE(1964); SLAVES(1969)
Marlene Clark
FOR LOVE OF IVY(1968); LANDLORD, THE(1970); CLAY PIGEON(1971); SLAUGHTER(1972); GANJA AND HESS(1973); BEAST MUST DIE, THE(1974, Brit.); NEWMAN'S LAW(1974); NIGHT OF THE COBRA WOMAN(1974, U.S./Phil.); LORD SHANGO(1975); SWITCHBLADE SISTERS(1975)
Misc. Talkies
BLOOD COUPLE(1974)
Mary Higgins Clark
STRANGER IS WATCHING, A(1982), w
Mary Kai Clark
9/30/55(1977)
Mathew Clark
SOME KIND OF HERO(1982)
Matt Clark
IN THE HEAT OF THE NIGHT(1967); WILL PENNY(1968); BRIDGE AT REMAGEN, THE(1969); HOMER(1970), w; MACHO CALLAHAN(1970); MONTE WALSH(1970); GRISSOM GANG, THE(1971); HONKY(1971); COWBOYS, THE(1972); CULPEPPER CATTLE COMPANY, THE(1972); GREAT NORTHFIELD, MINNESOTA RAID, THE(1972); JEREMIAH JOHNSON(1972); LIFE AND TIMES OF JUDGE ROY BEAN, THE(1972); EMPEROR OF THE NORTH POLE(1973); LAUGHING POLICEMAN, THE(1973); PAT GARRETT AND BILLY THE KID(1973); WHITE LIGHTNING(1973); TERMINAL MAN, THE(1974); HEARTS OF THE WEST(1975); KID VENGEANCE(1977); OUTLAW BLUES(1977); DRIVER, THE(1978); DREAMER(1979); BRUBAKER(1980); EYE FOR AN EYE, AN(1981); LEGEND OF THE LONE RANGER, THE(1981); RUCKUS(1981); HONKYTONK MAN(1982); SOME KIND OF HERO(1982); LOVE LETTERS(1983)
1984
ADVENTURES OF BUCKAROO BANZAI: ACROSS THE 8TH DIMENSION, THE(1984); COUNTRY(1984)
Maurice Clark
THREE RUSSIAN GIRLS(1943), w; THREE LITTLE SISTERS(1944), w; BOY, A GIRL, AND A DOG, A(1946), w
Michael Clark
KELLY'S HEROES(1970, U.S./Yugo.)
Milas Clark
GOOD MORNING, MISS DOVE(1955)
Milas Clark, Jr.
BWANA DEVIL(1953); BAND OF ANGELS(1957)
Nerida Clark
PUBERTY BLUES(1983, Aus.)
Neville Clark
BARRETTS OF WIMPOLE STREET, THE(1934); LOST PATROL, THE(1934); STUDENT TOUR(1934); CLIVE OF INDIA(1935); WELL DONE, HENRY(1936, Brit.), p
Norma Clark
WARNING SHOT(1967)
Old Joe Clark
SECOND FIDDLE TO A STEEL GUITAR(1965)
Olga Printzlau Clark
Silents
SCARLET SIN, THE(1915), w
Oliver Clark
LANDLORD, THE(1970); THEY MIGHT BE GIANTS(1971); GREAT GATSBY, THE(1974); STAR IS BORN, A(1976); ANOTHER MAN, ANOTHER CHANCE(1977 Fr/US); FIRE SALE(1977); LAST MARRIED COUPLE IN AMERICA, THE(1980); DEADHEAD MILES(1982); DOCTOR DETROIT(1983)
Ossie Clark
TOWN CALLED HELL, A(1971, Span./Brit.), cos

1984
BIGGER SPLASH, A(1984)
P.G. Clark
LURE, THE(1933, Brit.); BORROWED CLOTHES(1934, Brit.)
Pat Clark
TOO YOUNG TO KNOW(1945)
Patricia Clark
NIGHT AND DAY(1946)
Pauelle Clark
NIGHT WALKER, THE(1964)
Paul Clark
BOY MEETS GIRL(1938)
Paule Clark
PICTURE MOMMY DEAD(1966)
Paulle Clark
MY FAIR LADY(1964); HARLOW(1965); WHAT'S THE MATTER WITH HELEN?(1971)
1984
COVERGIRL(1984, Can.)
Peggy Clark
1984
RACING WITH THE MOON(1984)
Penny Clark
MEMOIRS OF A SURVIVOR(1981, Brit.), p; ASCENDANCY(1983, Brit.), p; NELLY'S VERSION(1983, Brit.), p
Peter Clark
SCOBIE MALONE(1975, Aus.), m; BLOODY KIDS(1983, Brit.)
Petula Clark
QUERY(1945, Brit.); STRAWBERRY ROAN(1945, Brit.); GAY INTRUDERS, THE(1946, Brit.); MURDER IN REVERSE(1946, Brit.); I KNOW WHERE I'M GOING(1947, Brit.); EASY MONEY(1948, Brit.); HERE COME THE HUGGETTS(1948, Brit.); VICE VERSA(1948, Brit.); VOTE FOR HUGGETT(1948, Brit.); DON'T EVER LEAVE ME(1949, Brit.); HUGGETTS ABROAD, THE(1949, Brit.); DANCE HALL(1950, Brit.); MADAME LOUISE(1951, Brit.); NAUGHTY ARLETTE(1951, Brit.); MADE IN HEAVEN(1952, Brit.); PROMOTER, THE(1952, Brit.); WHITE CORRIDORS(1952, Brit.); MY HEART GOES CRAZY(1953, Brit.); GAY DOG, THE(1954, Brit.); HAPPINESS OF THREE WOMEN, THE(1954, Brit.); RUNAWAY BUS, THE(1954, Brit.); TRACK THE MAN DOWN(1956, Brit.); CITY AFTER MIDNIGHT(1957, Brit.); 6.5 SPECIAL(1958, Brit.); FINIAN'S RAINBOW(1968); GOODBYE MR. CHIPS(1969, U.S./Brit.); NEVER NEVER LAND(1982)
Phil Clark
DIRTY HARRY(1971)
Phillip Clark
ALONE IN THE DARK(1982)
Polly Clark
MAN UPSTAIRS, THE(1959, Brit.)
R. Clark
TEMPTATION HARBOR(1949, Brit.), makeup
Ralph O. Clark
SNIPER, THE(1952)
Randy Clark
SKATEBOARD(1978)
Redfield Clark
Misc. Silents
SPITFIRE, THE(1914)
Richard Clark
CORNERED(1945); NOTORIOUS(1946)
Richard Dale Clark
TATTERED DRESS, THE(1957)
Robert Clark
DILLINGER(1945), spec eff; SILVER DARLINGS, THE(1947, Brit.), makeup; DAM BUSTERS, THE(1955, Brit.), p; HIDEOUS SUN DEMON, THE(1959)
Robert B. Clark
MOONRUNNERS(1975), p
Robin Clark
PRIZE FIGHTER, THE(1979)
Robin Sanders Clark
NONE BUT THE LONELY HEART(1944); TITANIC(1953)
Roger Clark
HONOLULU LU(1941); SECRETS OF THE LONE WOLF(1941); YOU BELONG TO ME(1941); LADY IS WILLING, THE(1942); MAN WHO RETURNED TO LIFE, THE(1942); MEET THE STEWARTS(1942); SUBMARINE RAIDER(1942); THEY ALL KISSED THE BRIDE(1942); TWO YANKS IN TRINIDAD(1942); WIFE TAKES A FLYER, THE(1942); DESTROYER(1943); GIRLS IN CHAINS(1943); LAUGH YOUR BLUES AWAY(1943); ONE DANGEROUS NIGHT(1943); SO THIS IS WASHINGTON(1943); SWING YOUR PARTNER(1943); EVE OF ST. MARK, THE(1944); FACES IN THE FOG(1944); IN THE MEANTIME, DARLING(1944); PIN UP GIRL(1944); SOMETHING FOR THE BOYS(1944); SWEET AND LOWDOWN(1944); DETOUR(1945); SONG FOR MISS JULIE, A(1945); LOST LAGOON(1958); ANGEL BABY(1961); MONSTER(1979)
Ron Clark
NORMAN...IS THAT YOU?(1976), w; SILENT MOVIE(1976), w; HIGH ANXIETY(1977), a, w; REVENGE OF THE PINK PANTHER(1978), w; HISTORY OF THE WORLD, PART 1(1981); FUNNY FARM, THE(1982, Can.), d&w
Ronald Clark
THUNDER OVER TANGIER(1957, Brit.); TERROR FROM UNDER THE HOUSE(1971, Brit.); MACKINTOSH MAN, THE(1973, Brit.); EAT MY DUST!(1976), stunts
Ronnie Clark
MONKEY BUSINESS(1952)
Roy Clark
DREAMING LIPS(1937, Brit.), ph; GIRL IN THE TAXI(1937, Brit.), ph; SKY'S THE LIMIT, THE(1937, Brit.), ph; LARCENY STREET(1941, Brit.), ph; MATILDA(1978)
Silents
AVALANCHE(1928), ph; SUNSET PASS(1929), ph
Royce Clark
COAL MINER'S DAUGHTER(1980); NIGHT THE LIGHTS WENT OUT IN GEORGIA, THE(1981)

Royden Clark
COLT .45(1950); THEM!(1954); GREAT BANK ROBBERY, THE(1969)
Roydon Clark
RIDE THE MAN DOWN(1952); BADLANDS OF MONTANA(1957); ESCAPE FROM RED ROCK(1958)
Rudd Clark
LOST IN THE STRATOSPHERE(1935)
Russ Clark
SINNERS IN THE SUN(1932); SHE LEARNED ABOUT SAILORS(1934); MAN WHO RECLAIMED HIS HEAD, THE(1935); MEN WITHOUT NAMES(1935); PADDY O'-DAY(1935); SHE GETS HER MAN(1935); CRIME PATROL, THE(1936); LIVE, LOVE AND LEARN(1937); MAN WHO CRIED WOLF, THE(1937); SLAVE SHIP(1937); INTERNATIONAL SETTLEMENT(1938); MR. MOTO'S GAMBLE(1938); INVITATION TO HAPPINESS(1939); LONE WOLF SPY HUNT, THE(1939); MADE FOR EACH OTHER(1939); MILLION DOLLAR LEGS(1939); PHILADELPHIA STORY, THE(1940); DANCE HALL(1941); DATE WITH THE FALCON, A(1941); I WANTED WINGS(1941); LAST OF THE DUANES(1941); FOOTLIGHT SERENADE(1942); I WAKE UP SCREAMING(1942); SING YOUR WORRIES AWAY(1942); IRON MAJOR, THE(1943); LADIES' DAY(1943); SHOW BUSINESS(1944); STORY OF DR. WASSELL, THE(1944); WILSON(1944); CALIFORNIA(1946); VALLEY OF THE ZOMBIES(1946); MOSS ROSE(1947); PURSUED(1947); COME TO THE STABLE(1949); WHEN WILLIE COMES MARCHING HOME(1950); MONKEY BUSINESS(1952); PAT AND MIKE(1952); WINNING TEAM, THE(1952)
Russell Clark
1984
BODY ROCK(1984)
Sanders Clark
GOD IS MY CO-PILOT(1945); JOAN OF ARC(1948); LES MISERABLES(1952); DIAL M FOR MURDER(1954)
Sandra Clark
1984
SCREAM FOR HELP(1984)
Sanford Clark
1984
C.H.U.D.(1984)
Sheila Clark
SHOW BOAT(1951)
Sis Clark
ATLANTIC CITY(1981, U.S./Can.)
Stephen Clark
MAD MAX(1979, Aus.)
Misc. Talkies
LAW OF THE WILD(1941)
Steve Clark
MAN TRAILER, THE(1934); ALIAS JOHN LAW(1935); DANGER TRAILS(1935); NO MAN'S RANGE(1935); CARYL OF THE MOUNTAINS(1936); CAVALCADE OF THE WEST(1936); LAST OF THE WARRENS, THE(1936); LAWLESS NINETIES, THE(1936); PRESCOTT KID, THE(1936); TOO MUCH BEEF(1936); VALLEY OF THE LAWLESS(1936); WEST OF NEVADA(1936); ARIZONA GUNFIGHTER(1937); BOOTHILL BRIGADE(1937); GAMBLING TERROR, THE(1937); GUN LORDS OF STIRRUP BASIN(1937); GUNS IN THE DARK(1937); LAWMAN IS BORN, A(1937); ONE MAN JUSTICE(1937); RIDERS OF THE DAWN(1937); RIDIN' THE LONE TRAIL(1937); SILVER TRAIL, THE(1937); TRAIL OF VENGEANCE(1937); TWO-FISTED SHERIFF(1937); WESTERN GOLD(1937); WHERE TRAILS DIVIDE(1937); CATTLE RAIDERS(1938); DESERT PATROL(1938); DURANGO VALLEY RAIDERS(1938); FEUD MAKER(1938); HEROES OF THE ALAMO(1938); JUVENILE COURT(1938); OUTLAWS OF THE PRAIRIE(1938); PAROLED–TO DIE(1938); RANGER'S ROUNDUP, THE(1938); ROMANCE OF THE ROCKIES(1938); SOUTH OF ARIZONA(1938); THUNDER IN THE DESERT(1938); KNIGHT OF THE PLAINS(1939); ROLL, WAGONS, ROLL(1939); THUNDERING WEST, THE(1939); WESTERN CARAVANS(1939); DURANGO KID, THE(1940); KID FROM SANTA FE, THE(1940); LAND OF THE SIX GUNS(1940); PINTO CANYON(1940); WESTBOUND STAGE(1940); BILLY THE KID IN SANTA FE(1941); DRIFTIN' KID, THE(1941); KING OF DODGE CITY(1941); LONE RIDER AMBUSHED, THE(1941); LONE RIDER CROSSES THE RIO, THE(1941); LONE RIDER IN GHOST TOWN, THE(1941); MEDICO OF PAINTED SPRINGS, THE(1941); NORTH FROM LONE STAR(1941); OUTLAWS OF THE PANHANDLE(1941); PINTO KID, THE(1941); RETURN OF DANIEL BOONE, THE(1941); SADDLE MOUNTAIN ROUNDUP(1941); SON OF DAVY CROCKETT, THE(1941); TRAIL OF THE SILVER SPURS(1941); TUMBLEDOWN RANCH IN ARIZONA(1941); UNDERGROUND RUSTLERS(1941); ARIZONA ROUNDUP(1942); ARIZONA STAGECOACH(1942); DAWN ON THE GREAT DIVIDE(1942); DEVIL'S TRAIL, THE(1942); DOWN RIO GRANDE WAY(1942); LONE STAR VIGILANTES, THE(1942); ROCK RIVER RENEGADES(1942); TEXAS TO BATAAN(1942); THUNDER RIVER FEUD(1942); TRAIL RIDERS(1942); BLACK MARKET RUSTLERS(1943); CATTLE STAMPEDE(1943); COWBOY COMMANDOS(1943); HAUNTED RANCH, THE(1943); LAND OF HUNTED MEN(1943); MAN OF COURAGE(1943); STRANGER FROM PECOS, THE(1943); CHEYENNE WILDCAT(1944); COWBOY FROM LONESOME RIVER(1944); DEATH VALLEY RANGERS(1944); GHOST GUNS(1944); LAND OF THE OUTLAWS(1944); LAW MEN(1944); LAW OF THE VALLEY(1944); MARKED TRAILS(1944); PARTNERS OF THE TRAIL(1944); RANGE LAW(1944); RIDING WEST(1944); VALLEY OF VENGEANCE(1944); FLAME OF THE WEST(1945); FRONTIER FEUD(1945); LOST TRAIL, THE(1945); OUTLAWS OF THE ROCKIES(1945); SONG OF OLD WYOMING(1945); STAGECOACH OUTLAWS(1945); BORDER BANDITS(1946); DRIFTING ALONG(1946); GENTLEMAN FROM TEXAS(1946); PRAIRIE BADMEN(1946); RUSTLER'S ROUNDUP(1946); SIX GUN MAN(1946); TERRORS ON HORSEBACK(1946); THUNDER TOWN(1946); UNDER ARIZONA SKIES(1946); CHEYENNE TAKES OVER(1947); FIGHTING VIGILANTES, THE(1947); FLASHING GUNS(1947); GHOST TOWN RENEGADES(1947); LAND OF THE LAWLESS(1947); LAST ROUND-UP, THE(1947); PRAIRIE EXPRESS(1947); RANGE BEYOND THE BLUE(1947); SIX GUN SERENADE(1947); STAGE TO MESA CITY(1947); COURTIN' TROUBLE(1948); COWBOY CAVALIER(1948); CROSSED TRAILS(1948); FIGHTING RANGER, THE(1948); HAWK OF POWDER RIVER, THE(1948); OKLAHOMA BLUES(1948); RANGE RENEGADES(1948); RANGERS RIDE, THE(1948); SONG OF THE DRIFTER(1948); SUNDOWN RIDERS(1948); TORNADO RANGE(1948); UNDER CALIFORNIA STARS(1948); BANDIT KING OF TEXAS(1949); GUN RUNNER(1949); HIDDEN DANGER(1949); LAST BANDIT, THE(1949); LAW OF THE WEST(1949); LAWLESS CODE(1949); NAVAJO TRAIL RAIDERS(1949); RANGE LAND(1949); RIDE, RYDER, RIDE!(1949); STAMPEDE(1949); TWELVE O'CLOCK HIGH(1949); WESTERN RENEGADES(1949); GUNMEN OF ABILENE(1950); GUNSLINGERS(1950); OUTLAW GOLD(1950); WEST OF WYOMING(1950); ABILENE

TRAIL(1951); LONGHORN, THE(1951); MONTANA DESPERADO(1951); SILVER CANYON(1951); STAGE TO BLUE RIVER(1951); NIGHT RAIDERS(1952); NIGHT STAGE TO GALVESTON(1952); COW COUNTRY(1953); GHOST OF ZORRO(1959); INCREDIBLY STRANGE CREATURES WHO STOPPED LIVING AND BECAME CRAZY MIXED-UP ZOMBIES, THE(1965)
Misc. Talkies
TRIGGER FINGERS(1946); SIX GUN MESA(1950)
Steven Clark
PHANTOM RANCHER(1940); CALL ME MISTER(1951); SATURDAY'S HERO(1951); FOR MEN ONLY(1952); SECURITY RISK(1954)
Stuart Clark
GOSPEL ROAD, THE(1973)
Susan Clark
BANNING(1967); COOGAN'S BLUFF(1968); MADIGAN(1968); COLOSSUS: THE FORBIN PROJECT(1969); TELL THEM WILLIE BOY IS HERE(1969); SKULLDUGGERY(1970); SKIN GAME(1971); VALDEZ IS COMING(1971); SHOWDOWN(1973); AIRPORT 1975(1974); MIDNIGHT MAN, THE(1974); APPLE DUMPLING GANG, THE(1975); NIGHT MOVES(1975); CITY ON FIRE(1979 Can.); NORTH AVENUE IRREGULARS, THE(1979); PROMISES IN THE DARK(1979); REAL LIFE(1979); DOUBLE NEGATIVE(1980, Can.); NOBODY'S PERFEKT(1981); PORKY'S(1982)
Misc. Talkies
BODY BENEATH, THE(1970)
Sylvia Clark
MELODY CLUB(1949, Brit.)
T.E.B. Clark
ALL AT SEA(1958, Brit.), w
Tammy Clark
GIRL IN TROUBLE(1963)
Thomas "Knobby" Clark
MC KENZIE BREAK, THE(1970), spec eff; UNDERGROUND(1970, Brit.), spec eff
Tiffany Clark
SURVIVORS, THE(1983)
Tim T. Clark
SOMETHING WICKED THIS WAY COMES(1983)
Tom Clark
BLACK OAK CONSPIRACY(1977), p
Trilby Clark
DEVIL'S MAZE, THE(1929, Brit.); COMPULSORY HUSBAND, THE(1930, Brit.); HARMONY HEAVEN(1930, Brit.); SQUEAKER, THE(1930, Brit.); 99 WOUNDS(1931)
Silents
JUST OFF BROADWAY(1924); PASSING OF MR. QUIN, THE(1928, Brit.)
Misc. Silents
BIG DAN(1923); PRAIRIE PIRATE, THE(1925); SILENT SANDERSON(1925); TRIPLE ACTION(1925); SATAN TOWN(1926); CARRY ON!(1927, Brit.); IN THE FIRST DEGREE(1927); CHICK(1928, Brit.); GOD'S CLAY(1928, Brit.); MARIA MARTEN(1928, Brit.)
Valeria Rae Clark
DEATHSPORT(1978)
Valerie Clark
SKATEBOARD(1978)
Vera Clark
Silents
BACHELOR'S PARADISE(1928), w
Violet Clark
Silents
MADONNAS AND MEN(1920), w; RED LANE, THE(1920), w; SLANDER THE WOMAN(1923), w; NOT SO LONG AGO(1925), w
Violet T. Clark
Silents
WOMAN'S BUSINESS, A(1920), w
Wallace Clark
ATTORNEY FOR THE DEFENSE(1932); EVER IN MY HEART(1933)
Silents
20,000 LEAGUES UNDER THE SEA(1916)
Wallis Clark
ALIAS THE DOCTOR(1932); FINAL EDITION(1932); HELL'S HOUSE(1932); I AM A FUGITIVE FROM A CHAIN GANG(1932); IF I HAD A MILLION(1932); MADAME BUTTERFLY(1932); MY PAL, THE KING(1932); NIGHT MAYOR, THE(1932); NIGHT OF JUNE 13(1932); SHOPWORN(1932); BUREAU OF MISSING PERSONS(1933); DOUBLE HARNESS(1933); KISS BEFORE THE MIRROR, THE(1933); LADY FOR A DAY(1933); LUXURY LINER(1933); NO MAN OF HER OWN(1933); POLICE CAR 17(1933); PRIVATE JONES(1933); THEY JUST HAD TO GET MARRIED(1933); WORKING MAN, THE(1933); WORLD CHANGES, THE(1933); WORLD GONE MAD, THE(1933); 42ND STREET(1933); CHEATING CHEATERS(1934); CRIME DOCTOR, THE(1934); I'LL FIX IT(1934); IT HAPPENED ONE NIGHT(1934); I'VE GOT YOUR NUMBER(1934); LIFE OF VERGIE WINTERS, THE(1934); MASSACRE(1934); MEANEST GAL IN TOWN, THE(1934); NAME THE WOMAN(1934); SHE HAD TO CHOOSE(1934); STAND UP AND CHEER(1934 80m FOX bw); BORDERTOWN(1935); CHAMPAGNE FOR BREAKFAST(1935); CHINATOWN SQUAD(1935); ENTER MADAME(1935); IT HAPPENED IN NEW YORK(1935); MUTINY ON THE BOUNTY(1935); SECRET BRIDE, THE(1935); COME CLOSER, FOLKS(1936); EASY MONEY(1936); FORBIDDEN TRAIL(1936); GREAT GUY(1936); GREAT ZIEGFELD, THE(1936); IT HAD TO HAPPEN(1936); PAROLE(1936); POSTAL INSPECTOR(1936); ROMEO AND JULIET(1936); UNGUARDED HOUR, THE(1936); WHIPSAW(1936); BIG BUSINESS(1937); ESCAPE BY NIGHT(1937); I PROMISE TO PAY(1937); LAST OF MRS. CHEYNEY, THE(1937); ROSALIE(1937); SHE HAD TO EAT(1937); TRAPPED BY G-MEN(1937); WILDCATTER, THE(1937); WOMAN IN DISTRESS(1937); HIGGINS FAMILY, THE(1938); HUNTED MEN(1938); YOU CAN'T TAKE IT WITH YOU(1938); ALLEGHENY UPRISING(1939); GONE WITH THE WIND(1939); I STOLE A MILLION(1939); MAIN STREET LAWYER(1939); SMUGGLED CARGO(1939); STAR REPORTER(1939); MURDER BY INVITATION(1941); PENNY SERENADE(1941); GENTLEMAN JIM(1942); REMARKABLE ANDREW, THE(1942); TOMBSTONE, THE TOWN TOO TOUGH TO DIE(1942); YANKEE DOODLE DANDY(1942); DESERT SONG, THE(1943); HUMAN COMEDY, THE(1943); JACK LONDON(1943); MISSION TO MOSCOW(1943); NORTHERN PURSUIT(1943); YOU'RE A LUCKY FELLOW, MR. SMITH(1943); FOLLOW THE BOYS(1944); LADY AND THE MONSTER, THE(1944); MRS. PARKINGTON(1944); SINCE YOU WENT AWAY(1944); UNCERTAIN GLORY(1944); CONFLICT(1945); FIRST YANK INTO TOKYO(1945); MILDRED PIERCE(1945); SAN ANTONIO(1945); WITHOUT LOVE(1945); FREE FOR ALL(1949); THAT FORSYTE WOMAN(1949); TOAST OF NEW ORLEANS, THE(1950); CRIMINAL

LAWYER(1951); LAS VEGAS STORY, THE(1952); SHE COULDN'T SAY NO(1954)

Walter Van Tilburg Clark
OX-BOW INCIDENT, THE(1943), w

Westcott Clark
TREASURE ISLAND(1934)

William Clark
MIDNIGHT MAN, THE(1974)
1984
BIRDY(1984)

William G. Clark
FIRST MONDAY IN OCTOBER(1981)

Clark & McCullough
Silents
TWO FLAMING YOUTHS(1927)

Clark and Dexter
HOLY TERROR, THE(1937)

Clark Sisters
1001 ARABIAN NIGHTS(1959)

D.A. Clark-Smith
HIGH FINANCE(1933, Brit.)

Alan Clarke
SCUM(1979, Brit.), d

Alex Clarke
LEARNING TREE, THE(1969)

Alexander Clarke
COMPUTER WORE TENNIS SHOES, THE(1970)

Angela Clarke
DOUBLE LIFE, A(1947); NIGHT SONG(1947); MR. SOFT TOUCH(1949); MRS. MIKE(1949); UNDERCOVER MAN, THE(1949); CAPTAIN CAREY, U.S.A(1950); GUN-FIGHTER, THE(1950); KILLER THAT STALKED NEW YORK, THE(1950); OUT-RAGE(1950); UNDERCOVER GIRL(1950); DARLING, HOW COULD YOU!(1951); GREAT CARUSO, THE(1951); HARLEM GLOBETROTTERS, THE(1951); IT'S A BIG COUNTRY(1951); MY FAVORITE SPY(1951); WHEN IN ROME(1952); BENEATH THE 12-MILE REEF(1953); HOUSE OF WAX(1953); SAVAGE, THE(1953); EGYPTIAN, THE(1954); SEVEN LITTLE FOYS, THE(1955); INTERNS, THE(1962); BLIND-FOLD(1966); HARRAD SUMMER, THE(1974)

Anthony Clarke
PAUL AND MICHELLE(1974, Fr./Brit.)

Arthur C. Clarke
2001: A SPACE ODYSSEY(1968, U.S./Brit.), w
1984
2010(1984), a, w

Barbara Clarke
PUTNEY SWOPE(1969)

Basil Clarke
HENRY VIII AND HIS SIX WIVES(1972, Brit.); MOON OVER THE ALLEY(1980, Brit.)
1984
TAIL OF THE TIGER(1984, Aus.)

Bellenden Clarke
MAD HATTERS, THE(1935, Brit.)

Betsy Ross Clarke
AGE FOR LOVE, THE(1931); JUDGE HARDY'S CHILDREN(1938)

Betty Ross Clarke
MURDERS IN THE RUE MORGUE(1932); LOVE FINDS ANDY HARDY(1938); SWEETHEARTS(1938); TOO HOT TO HANDLE(1938); WOMAN AGAINST WO-MAN(1938); UNTAMED(1940)
Misc. Silents
ROMANCE(1920); VERY IDEA, THE(1920); HER SOCIAL VALUE(1921); LUCKY CARSON(1921); MAN FROM DOWNING STREET, THE(1922); COST OF BEAUTY, THE(1924, Brit.); STRAWS IN THE WIND(1924, Brit.)

Bobby Clarke
Misc. Silents
MARRIED PEOPLE(1922)

Burke Clarke
WAYWARD(1932)

Caitlin Clarke
DRAGONSLAYER(1981)

Cam Clarke
BAKER'S HAWK(1976)

Caprice Clarke
GOODBYE GIRL, THE(1977)

Carroll Clarke
GHOST VALLEY(1932), art d

Charles Clarke
MASQUERADE(1929), ph; NOT QUITE DECENT(1929), ph; VEILED WOMAN, THE(1929), ph; WORDS AND MUSIC(1929), ph; OH, FOR A MAN!(1930), ph; ANNABELLE'S AFFAIRS(1931), ph; GIRLS DEMAND EXCITEMENT(1931), ph; GOOD SPORT(1931), ph; MEN ON CALL(1931), ph; HOT PEPPER(1933), ph; SECOND HAND WIFE(1933), ph; CAT AND THE FIDDLE(1934), ph; TARZAN AND HIS MATE(1934), ph; CASINO MURDER CASE, THE(1935), ph; PERFECT GENTLEMAN, THE(1935), ph; PURSUIT(1935), ph; SHADOW OF A DOUBT(1935), ph; WINNING TICKET, THE(1935), ph; WOMAN WANTED(1935), ph; ALL-AMERICAN CHUMP(1936), ph; GARDEN MURDER CASE, THE(1936), ph; MOONLIGHT MUR-DER(1936), ph; TROUBLE FOR TWO(1936), ph; MAN OF THE PEOPLE(1937), ph; STAND-IN(1937), ph; THIRTEENTH CHAIR, THE(1937), ph; UNDER COVER OF NIGHT(1937), ph; MR. MOTO TAKES A VACATION(1938), ph; SAFETY IN NUM-BERS(1938), ph; PARDON OUR NERVE(1939), ph; RETURN OF THE CISCO KID(1939), ph; BRIDE WORE CRUTCHES, THE(1940), ph; STREET OF MEMO-RIES(1940), ph; VIVA CISCO KID(1940), ph; YESTERDAY'S HEROES(1940), ph; YOUNG AS YOU FEEL(1940), ph; ACCENT ON LOVE(1941), ph; DEAD MEN TELL(1941), ph; FOR BEAUTY'S SAKE(1941), ph; LAST OF THE DUANES(1941), ph; MARRY THE BOSS' DAUGHTER(1941), ph; MURDER AMONG FRIENDS(1941), ph; PERFECT SNOB, THE(1941), ph; ROMANCE OF THE RIO GRANDE(1941), ph; CAREFUL, SOFT SHOULDERS(1942), ph; GENTLEMAN AT HEART, A(1942), ph; IT HAPPENED IN FLATBUSH(1942), ph; MOONTIDE(1942), ph; THRU DIFFERENT EYES(1942), ph; TIME TO KILL(1942), ph; GUADALCANAL DIARY(1943), ph; HEL-LO, FRISCO, HELLO(1943), ph; LADIES OF WASHINGTON(1944), ph; TAM-PICO(1944), ph; JUNIOR MISS(1945), ph; MOLLY AND ME(1945), ph; THUNDERHEAD-SON OF FLICKA(1945), ph; MARGIE(1946), ph; SMOKY(1946), ph;

CAPTAIN FROM CASTILE(1947), ph; MIRACLE ON 34TH STREET, THE(1947), ph; GREEN GRASS OF WYOMING(1948), ph; YOUNGER BROTHERS, THE(1949), art d; THREE SECRETS(1950), art d; SUDDENLY(1954), ph; TRICK BABY(1973)
Silents
ONE MINUTE TO PLAY(1926), ph; HAM AND EGGS AT THE FRONT(1927), ph; SINGED(1927), ph; RILEY THE COP(1928), ph; SHARP SHOOTERS(1928), ph; EX-ALTED FLAPPER, THE(1929), ph; SIN SISTER, THE(1929), ph

Charles C. Clarke
THAT WONDERFUL URGE(1948), ph

Charles G. Clarke
NIX ON DAMES(1929), ph; SONG OF KENTUCKY(1929), ph; SO THIS IS LON-DON(1930), ph; TEMPLE TOWER(1930), ph; TOO BUSY TO WORK(1932), ph; EVE-LYN PRENTICE(1934), ph; FRONTIER MARSHAL(1939), ph; SAND(1949), ph; SLATTERY'S HURRICANE(1949), ph; I'LL GET BY(1950), ph; GOLDEN GIRL(1951), ph; KANGAROO(1952), ph; RED SKIES OF MONTANA(1952), ph; STARS AND STRIPES FOREVER(1952), ph; CITY OF BAD MEN(1953), ph; DESTINATION GO-BI(1953), ph; BLACK WIDOW(1954), ph; BRIDGES AT TOKO-RI, THE(1954), ph; NIGHT PEOPLE(1954), ph; PRINCE OF PLAYERS(1955), ph; VIOLENT SATUR-DAY(1955), ph; VIRGIN QUEEN, THE(1955), ph; CAROUSEL(1956), ph; MAN IN THE GREY FLANNEL SUIT, THE(1956), ph; STOPOVER TOKYO(1957), ph; THREE BRAVE MEN(1957), ph; WAYWARD BUS, THE(1957), ph; BARBARIAN AND THE GEISHA, THE(1958), ph; HUNTERS, THE(1958), ph; HOLIDAY FOR LOVERS(1959), ph; HOUND-DOG MAN(1959), ph; PRIVATE'S AFFAIR, A(1959), ph; SOUND AND THE FURY, THE(1959), ph; THESE THOUSAND HILLS(1959), ph; FLAMING STAR(1960), ph; RETURN TO PEYTON PLACE(1961), ph; MADISON AVENUE(1962), ph
Silents
FLAMING BARRIERS(1924), ph; WHISPERING SMITH(1926), ph; RACING ROMEO(1927), ph; FOUR SONS(1928), ph

Charles H. Clarke
ROAD TO RENO, THE(1938), art d; DARK PASSAGE(1947), art d; BIG PUNCH, THE(1948), art d; BIG TOWN SCANDAL(1948), art d; WHIPLASH(1948), art d; CAGED(1950), art d; MONTANA(1950), art d; PRETTY BABY(1950), art d; WEST POINT STORY, THE(1950), art d; ENFORCER, THE(1951), art d; STARLIFT(1951), art d; TOMORROW IS ANOTHER DAY(1951), art d; SHE'S WORKING HER WAY THROUGH COLLEGE(1952), art d; STOP, YOU'RE KILLING ME(1952), art d; EDDIE CANTOR STORY, THE(1953), art d

Charles M. Clarke
RETURN OF THE FRONTIERSMAN(1950), art d

Cheryll Clarke
PRINCESS OF THE NILE(1954); OH, MEN! OH, WOMEN!(1957)

Cliff Clarke
GOOD SAM(1948)

Col. George E. Clarke
BACK TO BATAAN(1945), tech adv

Dallas Clarke
BATTLE BEYOND THE STARS(1980)

Dan Clarke
TERROR TRAIL(1933), ph

Darby Clarke
LOST HORIZON(1937)

David Clarke
DEADLY GAME, THE(1941); KNOCKOUT(1941); MILLION DOLLAR BABY(1941); FOREIGN AGENT(1942); GENTLEMAN AFTER DARK, A(1942); SWELL GUY(1944); KILLER McCOY(1947); LONG NIGHT, THE(1947); BERLIN EXPRESS(1948); STATE OF THE UNION(1948); ABANDONED(1949); ADAM'S RIB(1949); BOY WITH THE GREEN HAIR, THE(1949); ILLEGAL ENTRY(1949); INTRUDER IN THE DUST(1949); RED CANYON(1949); SANDS OF IWO JIMA(1949); SET-UP, THE(1949); THIEVES' HIGHWAY(1949); TOO LATE FOR TEARS(1949); WAKE OF THE RED WITCH(1949); BLONDE BANDIT, THE(1950); GUNFIGHTER, THE(1950); WABASH AVENUE(1950); HOUSE ON TELEGRAPH HILL(1951); EDGE OF THE CITY(1957); GREAT ST. LOUIS BANK ROBBERY, THE(1959); FRONT, THE(1976)

Davidson Clarke
REAP THE WILD WIND(1942)

Davison Clarke
HERE COMES CARTER(1936); AVENGING RIDER, THE(1943)

Don Clarke
SUSPENSE(1946)

Donald Henderson Clarke
BORN RECKLESS(1930), w; MILLIE(1931), w; IMPATIENT MAIDEN(1932), w; WOMEN MEN MARRY, THE(1937), w; HOUSEKEEPER'S DAUGHTER(1939), w; GHOST SHIP, THE(1943), w; MILLIE'S DAUGHTER(1947), w

Dorothy Clarke
KID FROM BROOKLYN, THE(1946)

Downing Clarke
Silents
KNOW YOUR MEN(1921); WHEN KNIGHTHOOD WAS IN FLOWER(1922); MON-SIEUR BEAUCAIRE(1924)
Misc. Silents
REMODELING HER HUSBAND(1920); WONDER MAN, THE(1920); GHOST IN THE GARRET, THE(1921)

E. Holman Clarke
Silents
ONCE ABOARD THE LUGGER(1920, Brit.)

Edward Clarke
Misc. Silents
CAPTAIN SWIFT(1920)

Ernest Clarke
1984
MEMED MY HAWK(1984, Brit.)

F. Clarke
SPRING IN PARK LANE(1949, Brit.), ed

Frank Clarke
HANDCUFFED(1929); HELL'S ANGELS(1930); FLYING DEUCES, THE(1939), a, tech adv; CONSPIRATOR(1949, Brit.), ed; MINIVER STORY, THE(1950, Brit./U.S.), ed; CALLING BULLDOG DRUMMOND(1951, Brit.), ed; IVANHOE(1952, Brit.), ed; KNIGHTS OF THE ROUND TABLE(1953), ed; MOGAMBO(1953), ed; NEVER LET ME GO(1953, U.S./Brit.), ed; TERROR ON A TRAIN(1953), ed; BEAU BRUM-MELL(1954), ed; BEDEVILLED(1955), ed; ACTION OF THE TIGER(1957), ed; TOM THUMB(1958, Brit./U.S.), ed; LIBEL(1959, Brit.), ed; DAY THEY ROBBED THE

BANK OF ENGLAND, THE(1960, Brit.), ed; GREEN HELMET, THE(1961, Brit.), ed;
I THANK A FOOL(1962, Brit.), ed; LIGHT IN THE PIAZZA(1962), ed; MATTER OF
WHO, A(1962, Brit.), ed; COME FLY WITH ME(1963), ed; V.I.P.s, THE(1963, Brit.), ed;
YELLOW ROLLS-ROYCE, THE(1965, Brit.), ed; BLOW-UP(1966, Brit.), ed; MATTER
OF INNOCENCE, A(1968, Brit.), ed; LOCK UP YOUR DAUGHTERS(1969, Brit.), ed;
NO BLADE OF GRASS(1970, Brit.), ed

Frank I. Clarke
STATE OF THE UNION(1948)

Frederick Clarke
BLOSSOMS ON BROADWAY(1937); HAPPY GO LUCKY(1943)

Gage Clarke
BAD SEED, THE(1956); NIGHTMARE(1956); FURY AT SHOWDOWN(1957); VALER-
IE(1957); BROTHERS KARAMAZOV, THE(1958); MIDNIGHT LACE(1960); ABSENT-
MINDED PROFESSOR, THE(1961); MONKEY'S UNCLE, THE(1965)

Gary Clarke
DRAGSTRIP RIOT(1958); HOW TO MAKE A MONSTER(1958); MISSILE TO THE
MOON(1959); DATE BAIT(1960); PASSION STREET, U.S.A.(1964); WILD, WILD
WINTER(1966)
Misc. Talkies
STRIKE ME DEADLY(1963); CONFESSIONS OF TOM HARRIS(1972)

Gayle Clarke
WILD GYPSIES(1969)

Geoffrey Clarke
HOT NEWS(1936, Brit.); STRANGE CARGO(1936, Brit.)

George Clarke
HERE'S GEORGE(1932, Brit.)
Silents
TIGER WOMAN, THE(1917)
Misc. Silents
MAN'S MAKING, THE(1915); RIGHTS OF MAN, THE(1915); FLAMES OF JOHAN-
NIS, THE(1916); MARRIAGES ARE MADE(1918)

Gordon B. Clarke
FROM THE TERRACE(1960); HUSTLER, THE(1961)

Grant Clarke
Silents
SECOND HAND ROSE(1922), w; CASEY AT THE BAT(1927), t

Harvey Clarke
HIS LUCKY DAY(1929)
Silents
ELOPE IF YOU MUST(1922); MIXED FACES(1922); HE WHO GETS SLAPPED(1924);
TRAGEDY OF YOUTH, THE(1928)
Misc. Silents
SIGN OF THE SPADE, THE(1916); INNOCENCE OF LIZETTE, THE(1917); DON'T
SHOOT(1922); MEN OF ZANSIBAR, THE(1922); RAINBOW, THE(1929)

Hope Clarke
CHANGE OF MIND(1969); GOING HOME(1971); PIECE OF THE ACTION, A(1977);
BODY AND SOUL(1981), ch
1984
BEAT STREET(1984)

J. I. C. Clarke
Silents
GILDED CAGE, THE(1916), w

J. Vyne Clarke
MOUNTAIN, THE(1935, Brit.)

Jack Clarke
FLYING DOCTOR, THE(1936, Aus.); MAN IN THE WATER, THE(1963)

Jacqueline Clarke
GREAT DAY(1945, Brit.); JOHNNY IN THE CLOUDS(1945, Brit.); ESCAPE(1948,
Brit.)

James Clarke
WE'RE GOING TO BE RICH(1938, Brit.), ed; MUMMY, THE(1959, Brit.)

James Kenelm Clarke
GOT IT MADE(1974, Brit.), p&d, w, m; WILDCATS OF ST. TRINIAN'S, THE(1980,
Brit.), m; FUNNY MONEY(1983, Brit.), d&w

Jameson Clarke
WEE GEORDIE(1956, Brit.)

Jason Clarke
CHASTITY(1969)

Jean Clarke
GOODBYE AGAIN(1961); THERE WAS A CROOKED MAN(1962, Brit.)

Joe Clarke
GALLOPING MAJOR, THE(1951, Brit.); LAVENDER HILL MOB, THE(1951, Brit.);
MC CABE AND MRS. MILLER(1971); BASKET CASE(1982)

John Clarke
OPERATION BOTTLENECK(1961); YOU HAVE TO RUN FAST(1961); GUN
STREET(1962); THIN RED LINE, THE(1964); FINGER ON THE TRIGGER(1965,
US/Span.); SATAN BUG, THE(1965); TALL WOMEN, THE(1967, Aust./Ital./Span.);
WITCH WITHOUT A BROOM, A(1967, U.S./Span.); SHALAKO(1968, Brit.); DE-
SPERADOS, THE(1969); LAST DAY OF THE WAR, THE(1969, U.S./Ital./Span.);
CANNON FOR CORDOBA(1970); LONELY HEARTS(1983, Aus.), w

June Clarke
ZOO BABY(1957, Brit.)

Keith Clarke
WILD ONE, THE(1953)

Kendell Clarke
JOHNNY GOT HIS GUN(1971)

Kenelm Clarke
MUSIC MACHINE, THE(1979, Brit.), w

Kenneth B. Clarke
ROUGH ROMANCE(1930), w
Silents
IMMEDIATE LEE(1916), w; PRISONER OF THE PINES(1918), w; KINGDOM
WITHIN, THE(1922), w; IF I MARRY AGAIN(1925), w; WAGES FOR WIVES(1925),
w; EARLY TO WED(1926), w; WOMANPOWER(1926), w

Kenny Clarke
TWO ARE GUILTY(1964, Fr.)

Leslie Clarke
CHAMPAGNE CHARLIE(1944, Brit.); FOR THOSE IN PERIL(1944, Brit.)

Lillian Clarke
Silents
HUN WITHIN, THE(1918)

Logan Clarke
BOYS IN COMPANY C, THE(1978, U.S./Hong Kong); SWEET SIXTEEN(1983)

Loretta Clarke
WHERE'S JACK?(1969, Brit.)

Lydia Clarke
ATOMIC CITY, THE(1952); GREATEST SHOW ON EARTH, THE(1952); BAD FOR
EACH OTHER(1954); WILL PENNY(1968)

Madison Clarke
INCREDIBLY STRANGE CREATURES WHO STOPPED LIVING AND BECAME
CRAZY MIXED-UP ZOMBIES, THE(1965)

Mae Clarke
WATERLOO BRIDGE(1931); THOROUGHLY MODERN MILLIE(1967); BIG TI-
ME(1929); NIX ON DAMES(1929); DANCERS, THE(1930); FALL GUY, THE(1930);
FRANKENSTEIN(1931); FRONT PAGE, THE(1931); GOOD BAD GIRL, THE(1931);
MEN ON CALL(1931); PUBLIC ENEMY, THE(1931); RECKLESS LIVING(1931);
FINAL EDITION(1932); IMPATIENT MAIDEN(1932); NIGHT WORLD(1932); PEN-
GUIN POOL MURDER, THE(1932); THREE WISE GIRLS(1932); AS THE DEVIL
COMMANDS(1933); FAST WORKERS(1933); LADY KILLER(1933); PAROLE
GIRL(1933); PENTHOUSE(1933); TURN BACK THE CLOCK(1933); FLAMING
GOLD(1934); LET'S TALK IT OVER(1934); MAN WITH TWO FACES, THE(1934);
NANA(1934); THIS SIDE OF HEAVEN(1934); DARING YOUNG MAN, THE(1935);
SILK HAT KID(1935); GREAT GUY(1936); HEARTS IN BONDAGE(1936); HOUSE OF
A THOUSAND CANDLES, THE(1936); WILD BRIAN KENT(1936); HATS OFF(1937);
OUTLAWS OF THE ORIENT(1937); TROUBLE IN MOROCCO(1937); WOMEN IN
WAR(1940); SAILORS ON LEAVE(1941); FLYING TIGERS(1942); LADY FROM
CHUNGKING(1943); HERE COME THE WAVES(1944); KITTY(1945); GUN RUN-
NER(1949); STREETS OF SAN FRANCISCO(1949); DUCHESS OF IDAHO(1950);
MRS. O'MALLEY AND MR. MALONE(1950); CALLAWAY WENT THATAWAY(1951);
GREAT CARUSO, THE(1951); MR. IMPERIUM(1951); PEOPLE AGAINST O'HARA,
THE(1951); ROYAL WEDDING(1951); THREE GUYS NAMED MIKE(1951); BECAUSE
OF YOU(1952); HORIZONS WEST(1952); LOVE IS BETTER THAN EVER(1952); PAT
AND MIKE(1952); SINGIN' IN THE RAIN(1952); SKIRTS AHOY!(1952); THUNDER-
BIRDS(1952); MAGNIFICENT OBSESSION(1954); I DIED A THOUSAND TI-
MES(1955); NOT AS A STRANGER(1955); WOMEN'S PRISON(1955); CATERED
AFFAIR, THE(1956); COME NEXT SPRING(1956); DESPERADOES ARE IN TOWN,
THE(1956); MOHAWK(1956); RIDE THE HIGH IRON(1956); VOICE IN THE MIR-
ROR(1958); ASK ANY GIRL(1959); BIG HAND FOR THE LITTLE LADY, A(1966)

Margaret Clarke
FRENZY(1946, Brit.)

Marguerite Clarke
Silents
GOOSE GIRL, THE(1915)

Mary Clarke
STRANGER IN HOLLYWOOD(1968)

Matt Clarke
OUTLAW JOSEY WALES, THE(1976)

Mavis Clarke
BATTLE FOR MUSIC(1943, Brit.)

Melita Clarke
LUST FOR A VAMPIRE(1971, Brit.)

Michael Clarke
CARNIVAL(1946, Brit.); GIRL ON APPROVAL(1962, Brit.)

Neville Clarke
HATE IN PARADISE(1938, Brit.), p

Nigel Clarke
SAN DEMETRIO, LONDON(1947, Brit.); TIME GENTLEMEN PLEASE!(1953, Brit.)

Nobby Clarke
1984
SWORD OF THE VALIANT(1984, Brit.), spec eff

Oz Clarke
SUPERMAN(1978)

P.L. Clarke
Misc. Talkies
MAN WHO SAW TOMORROW, THE(1981)

Paul Clarke
CRY TOUGH(1959)

Phil Clarke
CASE OF PATTY SMITH, THE(1962)

Philip Clarke
LURE, THE(1933, Brit.)

Richard Clarke
CHARLIE CHAN IN THE CITY OF DARKNESS(1939); SWANEE RIVER(1939); MAN
WHO WOULDN'T TALK, THE(1940); DESPERATE CARGO(1941); RIOT
SQUAD(1941); CITY OF SILENT MEN(1942); GALLANT LADY(1942); PRISON
GIRL(1942); GIRLS IN CHAINS(1943); WORLD OWES ME A LIVING, THE(1944, Brit.);
DANGEROUS EXILE(1958, Brit.); NIGHT TO REMEMBER, A(1958, Brit.); FIVE TO
ONE(1963, Brit.); SIEGE OF THE SAXONS(1963, Brit.); TO HAVE AND TO HOLD(1963,
Brit.); JOHN AND MARY(1969); MIDNIGHT COWBOY(1969); SIDELONG GLANCES
OF A PIGEON KICKER, THE(1970)
Silents
IRON RING, THE(1917)
Misc. Silents
MAID OF BELGIUM, THE(1917); SOUL WITHOUT WINDOWS, A(1918)

Robert Clarke
FALCON IN HOLLYWOOD, THE(1944); ENCHANTED COTTAGE, THE(1945);
FIRST YANK INTO TOKYO(1945); GAME OF DEATH, A(1945); MAN ALIVE(1945);
RADIO STARS ON PARADE(1945); THOSE ENDEARING YOUNG CHARMS(1945);
WANDERER OF THE WASTELAND(1945); CRIMINAL COURT(1946); GENIUS AT
WORK(1946); LADY LUCK(1946); SAN QUENTIN(1946); SUNSET PASS(1946); CODE
OF THE WEST(1947); DESPERATE(1947); FARMER'S DAUGHTER, THE(1947);
THUNDER MOUNTAIN(1947); UNDER THE TONTO RIM(1947); FIGHTING FATHER
DUNNE(1948); IF YOU KNEW SUSIE(1948); LADIES OF THE CHORUS(1948);
RETURN OF THE BADMEN(1948); RIDERS OF THE RANGE(1949); OUTRAGE(1950);
CASA MANANA(1951); HARD, FAST, AND BEAUTIFUL(1951); MAN FROM PLANET
X, THE(1951); PISTOL HARVEST(1951); STREET BANDITS(1951); TALES OF ROBIN
HOOD(1951); CAPTIVE WOMEN(1952); FABULOUS SENORITA, THE(1952); BLADES
OF THE MUSKETEERS(1953); CAPTAIN JOHN SMITH AND POCAHONTAS(1953);

SWORD OF VENUS(1953); BLACK PIRATES, THE(1954, Mex.); MY MAN GOD-FREY(1957); ASTOUNDING SHE-MONSTER, THE(1958); DEEP SIX, THE(1958); DATE WITH DEATH, A(1959); HIDEOUS SUN DEMON, THE(1959), p, d, w; INCREDIBLE PETRIFIED WORLD, THE(1959); TIMBUKTU(1959); BEYOND THE TIME BARRIER(1960), a, p; CASH McCALL(1960); LAST TIME I SAW ARCHIE, THE(1961); MODERN MARRIAGE, A(1962); SECRET FILE: HOLLYWOOD(1962); TERROR OF THE BLOODHUNTERS(1962); CLAY(1964 Aus.); RESTLESS ONES, THE(1965); ZEBRA IN THE KITCHEN(1965)

Misc. Talkies
OUTLAW QUEEN(1957); FRANKENSTEIN'S ISLAND(1982)

Robin Brent Clarke
VALENTINO(1977, Brit.)

Robin Clarke
DEATH SENTENCE(1967, Ital.); FROM BEYOND THE GRAVE(1974, Brit.), w; GREEK TYCOON, THE(1978); LOVE AND BULLETS(1979, Brit.); SUNBURN(1979); FORMULA, THE(1980); BOXOFFICE(1982); HORROR PLANET(1982, Brit.)

Misc. Talkies
INSEMINOID(1980)

Ron Clarke
INADMISSIBLE EVIDENCE(1968, Brit.)

Ronald Clarke
HELL DRIVERS(1958, Brit.); UP THE JUNCTION(1968, Brit.)

Roy Clarke
DOOMED AT SUNDOWN(1937), ed; LILAC DOMINO, THE(1940, Brit.), ph

Russ Clarke
WINTER MEETING(1948)

Sheila Clarke
ROUND TRIP(1967)

Shirley Clarke
CONNECTION, THE(1962), p, d, ed; COOL WORLD, THE(1963), d, w, ed; LIONS LOVE(1969); MARCH ON PARIS 1914–OF GENERALOBERST ALEXANDER VON KLUCK–AND HIS MEMORY OF JESSIE HOLLADAY(1977), ed

Misc. Talkies
PORTRAIT OF JASON(1967), d

Sylvia Clarke
GREAT GILBERT AND SULLIVAN, THE(1953, Brit.)

T.E.B. Clarke
FOR THOSE IN PERIL(1944, Brit.), w; DEAD OF NIGHT(1946, Brit.), w; JOHNNY FRENCHMAN(1946, Brit.), w; AGAINST THE WIND(1948, Brit.), w; PASSPORT TO PIMLICO(1949, Brit.), w; BLUE LAMP, THE(1950, Brit.), w; HUE AND CRY(1950, Brit.), w; MAGNET, THE(1950, Brit.), w; ENCORE(1951, Brit.), w; LAVENDER HILL MOB, THE(1951, Brit.), w; TRAIN OF EVENTS(1952, Brit.), w; TITFIELD THUNDERBOLT, THE(1953, Brit.), w; RAINBOW JACKET, THE(1954, Brit.), w; WHO DONE IT?(1956, Brit.), w; LAW AND DISORDER(1958, Brit.), w; TALE OF TWO CITIES, A(1958, Brit.), w; GIDEON OF SCOTLAND YARD(1959, Brit.), w; SONS AND LOVERS(1960, Brit.), w; MAN COULD GET KILLED, A(1966, Brit.), w; HITCH IN TIME, A(1978, Brit.), w

Thomas Clarke
DU BARRY WAS A LADY(1943); LORDS OF FLATBUSH, THE(1974)

Tom Clarke
CRIME WAVE(1954)

Trevor Clarke
1984
CHAMPIONS(1984)

Vanessa Clarke
PRIVILEGE(1967, Brit.), cos

W. B. Clarke
Silents
NORTH OF THE RIO GRANDE(1922); BREAKING POINT, THE(1924)

Wallace Clarke
Silents
ELUSIVE ISABEL(1916)

Walter Clarke
Silents
CLIMBERS, THE(1915)

Walter D. Clarke, Jr.
GREAT GUY(1936)

Warren Clarke
CLOCKWORK ORANGE, A(1971, Brit.); ANTONY AND CLEOPATRA(1973, Brit.); O LUCKY MAN!(1973, Brit.); HAWK THE SLAYER(1980, Brit.); FIREFOX(1982); ENIGMA(1983)
1984
LASSITER(1984); REAL LIFE(1984, Brit.); TOP SECRET!(1984)

Misc. Talkies
GREAT RIVIERA BANK ROBBERY, THE(1979)

Westcott B. Clarke
TRIAL OF MARY DUGAN, THE(1929)
Silents
SAFETY LAST(1923); ABRAHAM LINCOLN(1924); FINNEGAN'S BALL(1927)

Willis Clarke
HIDDEN GOLD(1933)

Zelah Clarke
RICHARD'S THINGS(1981, Brit.)

S. Clarke-Hook
Silents
JACK, SAM AND PETE(1919, Brit.), w

Michael Clarke-Lawrence
FOREPLAY(1975)

D.A. Clarke-Smith
ATLANTIC(1929 Brit.); BRACELETS(1931, Brit.); SHADOWS(1931, Brit.); CRIMINAL AT LARGE(1932, Brit.); HELP YOURSELF(1932, Brit.); ILLEGAL(1932, Brit.); MICHAEL AND MARY(1932, Brit.); OLD MAN, THE(1932, Brit.); GOOD COMPANIONS(1933, Brit.); HEAD OF THE FAMILY(1933, Brit.); I'M AN EXPLOSIVE(1933, Brit.); MAYFAIR GIRL(1933, Brit.); SMITHY(1933, Brit.); THIRTEENTH CANDLE, THE(1933, Brit.); TURKEY TIME(1933, Brit.); WALTZ TIME(1933, Brit.); WHITE FACE(1933, Brit.); CUP OF KINDNESS, A(1934, Brit.); DESIGNING WOMEN(1934, Brit.); FEATHERED SERPENT, THE(1934, Brit.); FRIDAY THE 13TH(1934, Brit.); GHOUL, THE(1934, Brit.); KEEP IT QUIET(1934, Brit.); MONEY MAD(1934, Brit.); PASSING SHADOWS(1934, Brit.); PERFECT FLAW, THE(1934, Brit.); WARN LONDON!(1934, Brit.); WHEN LONDON SLEEPS(1934, Brit.); KEY TO HARMONY(1935, Brit.); LORNA

DOONE(1935, Brit.); REGAL CAVALCADE(1935, Brit.); HAPPY FAMILY, THE(1936, Brit.); MURDER BY ROPE(1936, Brit.); SOUTHERN ROSES(1936, Brit.); LITTLE MISS SOMEBODY(1937, Brit.); SPLINTERS IN THE AIR(1937, Brit.); I'VE GOT A HORSE(1938, Brit.); FLYING FIFTY-FIVE(1939, Brit.); WANTED BY SCOTLAND YARD(1939, Brit.); FRIEDA(1947, Brit.); PICKWICK PAPERS, THE(1952, Brit.); SOMETHING MONEY CAN'T BUY(1952, Brit.); SWORD AND THE ROSE, THE(1953); MAN WHO NEVER WAS, THE(1956, Brit.); BABY AND THE BATTLESHIP, THE(1957, Brit.)

Zoe Clarke-Williams
NUNZIO(1978)

Frank Clarks
GOLDEN HEAD, THE(1965, Hung., U.S.), ed

Channing Clarkson
COACH(1978); BEACH GIRLS(1982)

John Clarkson
RAGTIME(1981)

Lana Clarkson
FAST TIMES AT RIDGEMONT HIGH(1982); DEATHSTALKER(1983, Arg./U.S.)
1984
BLIND DATE(1984); DEATHSTALKER, THE(1984)

Stephen Clarkson
CHILDREN OF THE FOG(1935, Brit.), w; MR. SMITH CARRIES ON(1937, Brit.), w; CLIMBING HIGH(1938, Brit.), w; SPOT OF BOTHER, A(1938, Brit.), w; DUAL ALIBI(1947, Brit.), w; DEATM GOES TO SCHOOL(1953, Brit.), d, w

Alme Clarlond
BLUE VEIL, THE(1947, Fr.)

Tamara Clarrett
DOCTOR DETROIT(1983)

Clary
CROSSROADS(1938, Fr.)

Charles Clary
SAILORS' HOLIDAY(1929); KISMET(1930); NIGHT WORK(1930)
Silents
CARPET FROM BAGDAD, THE(1915); PENITENTES, THE(1915); EACH PEARL A TEAR(1916); JOAN THE WOMAN(1916); TENNESSEE'S PARDNER(1916); HONOR SYSTEM, THE(1917); INNOCENT SINNER, THE(1917); TALE OF TWO CITIES, A(1917); EXTRAVAGANCE(1919); SPLENDID SIN, THE(1919); PENALTY, THE(1920); CONNECTICUT YANKEE AT KING ARTHUR'S COURT, A(1921); SEA LION, THE(1921); RICH MEN'S WIVES(1922); MONEY! MONEY!(1923); NOBODY'S MONEY(1923); SIX DAYS(1923); EMPTY HANDS(1924); IN FAST COMPANY(1924); ON TIME(1924); ENEMY OF MEN, AN(1925); JIMMIE'S MILLIONS(1925); KISS BARRIER, THE(1925); AUCTION BLOCK, THE(1926); BEVERLY OF GRAUSTARK(1926); BLIND GODDESS, THE(1926); BLUE STREAK, THE(1926); RED DICE(1926); KING OF KINGS, THE(1927); PRETTY CLOTHES(1927); SMILE, BROTHER, SMILE(1927); JAZZ MAD(1928); NAMELESS MEN(1928); POWER OF THE PRESS, THE(1928); EXALTED FLAPPER, THE(1929); EYES OF THE UNDERWORLD(1929)

Misc. Silents
FIFTH MAN, THE(1914); STORY OF THE BLOOD RED ROSE, THE(1914); ROSARY, THE(1915); STRATHMORE(1915); BLACKLIST(1916); CONQUEROR, THE(1917); HIGH FINANCE(1917); PRICE OF SILENCE, THE(1917); ROSE OF BLOOD, THE(1917); SILENT LIE, THE(1917); SOUL OF SATAN, THE(1917); SPY, THE(1917); TO HONOR AND OBEY(1917); BLINDNESS OF DIVORCE, THE(1918); FALLEN ANGEL, THE(1918); FOR LIBERTY(1918); MADAME DUBARRY(1918); SCARLET ROAD, THE(1918); STRANGE WOMAN, THE(1918); TRUE BLUE(1918); CALL OF THE SOUL, THE(1919); DAY SHE PAID, THE(1919); GIRL WITH NO REGRETS, THE(1919); LONE STAR RANGER, THE(1919); MAN HUNTER, THE(1919); WOLVES OF THE NIGHT(1919); LIGHT WOMAN, A(1920); STREET CALLED STRAIGHT, THE(1920); WOMAN IN ROOM 13, THE(1920); DON'T NEGLECT YOUR WIFE(1921); HOLE IN THE WALL, THE(1921); SUNSET JONES(1921); FLAMING HOUR, THE(1922); HATE(1922); HEROES AND HUSBANDS(1922); SKIN DEEP(1922); TWO KINDS OF WOMEN(1922); VERY TRULY YOURS(1922); CAUSE FOR DIVORCE(1923); MICHAEL O'HALLORAN(1923); BEHIND THE CURTAIN(1924); WHISPERED NAME, THE(1924); SUPER SPEED(1925); MODERN YOUTH(1926); SATAN TOWN(1926); THRILLING YOUTH(1926); WHISPERING WIRES(1926); HIS FOREIGN WIFE(1927); LAND OF THE LAWLESS(1927); WHAT PRICE LOVE(1927)

Danielle Clary
GIRL FEVER(1961)

Leo Clary
LOVE NEST(1951)

Michael Clary
ANDERSON TAPES, THE(1971)

Robert Clary
TEN TALL MEN(1951); THIEF OF DAMASCUS(1952); NEW FACES(1954); NEW KIND OF LOVE, A(1963); HINDENBURG, THE(1975)

Tom Clasen
1984
LAST HORROR FILM, THE(1984), w

The Clash
RUDE BOY(1980, Brit.)

Charlotte Clasis
LA BETE HUMAINE(1938, Fr.)

Buck Class
IN LOVE AND WAR(1958); THUNDERING JETS(1958); 10 NORTH FREDERICK(1958); BELOVED INFIDEL(1959); BLUE DENIM(1959); HOLIDAY FOR LOVERS(1959)

Dave Class
APPLE DUMPLING GANG RIDES AGAIN, THE(1979)

Robert Clathworthy
IT HAPPENS EVERY THURSDAY(1953), art d

Bert Clatworthy
ONCE MORE, MY DARLING(1949), art d

George R. Clatworthy
HOW TO SAVE A MARRIAGE–AND RUIN YOUR LIFE(1968), prod d

Robert C. Clatworthy
LADY ON A TRAIN(1945), art d

Robert Clatworthy
CHRISTMAS HOLIDAY(1944), art d; PHANTOM LADY(1944), art d; EASY TO LOOK AT(1945), art d; FRISCO SAL(1945), art d; JUNGLE CAPTIVE(1945), art d; SHE GETS HER MAN(1945), art d; THIS LOVE OF OURS(1945), art d; RUNAROUND,

THE(1946), art d; SMOOTH AS SILK(1946), art d; VARIETY GIRL(1947), art d; HAZARD(1948), art d; ISN'T IT ROMANTIC?(1948), art d; WOMAN IN HIDING(1949), art d; SHAKEDOWN(1950), art d; KATIE DID IT(1951), art d; LITTLE EGYPT(1951), art d; HORIZONS WEST(1952), art d; SAN FRANCISCO STORY, THE(1952), art d; SCARLET ANGEL(1952), art d; STEEL TOWN(1952), art d; DESERT LEGION(1953), art d; LAW AND ORDER(1953), art d; WINGS OF THE HAWK(1953), art d; FEMALE ON THE BEACH(1955), art d; FOXFIRE(1955), art d; SECOND GREATEST SEX, THE(1955), art d; SIX BRIDGES TO CROSS(1955), art d; TO HELL AND BACK(1955), art d; PRICE OF FEAR, THE(1956), art d; WRITTEN ON THE WIND(1956), art d; DEADLY MANTIS, THE(1957), art d; INCREDIBLE SHRINKING MAN, THE(1957), art d; NIGHT PASSAGE(1957), art d; FEMALE ANIMAL, THE(1958), art d; ONCE UPON A HORSE(1958), art d; TOUCH OF EVIL(1958), art d; CURSE OF THE UNDEAD(1959), art d; NEVER STEAL ANYTHING SMALL(1959), art d; WILD AND THE INNOCENT, THE(1959), art d; LEECH WOMAN, THE(1960), art d; MIDNIGHT LACE(1960), art d; POLLYANNA(1960), art d; PSYCHO(1960), prod d; LOVER COME BACK(1961), art d; PARENT TRAP, THE(1961), art d; FORTY POUNDS OF TROUBLE(1962), art d; THAT TOUCH OF MINK(1962), art d; SUMMER MAGIC(1963), art d; BEDTIME STORY(1964), art d; INVITATION TO A GUNFIGHTER(1964), art d; SEND ME NO FLOWERS(1964), art d; INSIDE DAISY CLOVER(1965), prod d; SHIP OF FOOLS(1965), prod d; GUESS WHO'S COMING TO DINNER(1967), prod d; CACTUS FLOWER(1969), set d; SECRET OF SANTA VITTORIA, THE(1969), prod d; R.P.M.(1970), prod d; SCANDALOUS JOHN(1971), prod d; WILD COUNTRY, THE(1971), prod d; BUTTERFLIES ARE FREE(1972), prod d; FORTY CARATS(1973), prod d; CASTAWAY COWBOY, THE(1974), set d; REPORT TO THE COMMISSIONER(1975), prod d; CARWASH(1976), art d; FROM NOON TO THREE(1976), prod d; TREASURE OF MATECUMBE(1976), prod d; ANOTHER MAN, ANOTHER CHANCE(1977 Fr/US), art d

Rosemary Clatworthy
FORTY POUNDS OF TROUBLE(1962), cos

Felix Claude
DEVIL'S DAUGHTER(1949, Fr.)

Jean Claude
NIGHT OF LUST(1965, Fr.)

Pierre Claude
WITHOUT PITY(1949, Ital.)

Toby Claude
Silents
NO CONTROL(1927)
Misc. Silents
CLINGING VINE, THE(1926)

Claude-Antoine
ANTONIO DAS MORTES(1970, Braz.), p

Paul Claudel
JOAN AT THE STAKE(1954, Ital./Fr.), w

Claudia
DEAD AND BURIED(1981), set d; ESCAPE FROM NEW YORK(1981), set d

Yvonne Claudie
GERVAISE(1956, Fr.); FOUR HUNDRED BLOWS, THE(1959)

Annette Claudier
HANGING TREE, THE(1959); MARATHON MAN(1976); TWILIGHT ZONE–THE MOVIE(1983)

Claudio
RASPUTIN(1939, Fr.)

Andrea Claudio
FM(1978); WINTER KILLS(1979)

Jean Claudio
MOULIN ROUGE(1952); PARIS DOES STRANGE THINGS(1957, Fr./Ital.); DANGEROUS EXILE(1958, Brit.); PICNIC ON THE GRASS(1960, Fr.); DARLING(1965, Brit.); MAGNIFICENT CUCKOLD, THE(1965, Fr./Ital.); BEAUTY JUNGLE, THE(1966, Brit.); HEAT OF MIDNIGHT(1966, Fr.); TRIPLE CROSS(1967, Fr./Brit.); WITNESS OUT OF HELL(1967, Ger./Yugo.); SABRA(1970, Fr./Ital./Israel)

Lou Claudio
GUESS WHAT HAPPENED TO COUNT DRACULA(1970), ch

Marieluise Claudius
MAN WHO WAS SHERLOCK HOLMES, THE(1937, Ger.)

Paul Claudon
SUITOR, THE(1963, Fr.), p; YO YO(1967, Fr.), p; GOING PLACES(1974, Fr.), p; GET OUT YOUR HANDKERCHIEFS(1978, Fr.), p

Peter Claughton
POOR COW(1968, Brit.)

Erich Claunick
JUDGE AND THE SINNER, THE(1964, Ger.), ph

Erich Claunigk
ROSES FOR THE PROSECUTOR(1961, Ger.), ph

Elly Claus
SOLDIER OF ORANGE(1979, Dutch), cos
1984
FOURTH MAN, THE(1984, Neth.), cos

Jack Claus
ROAD TO BALI(1952)

Bo Clausen
SOMEWHERE IN TIME(1980)

Carl Clausen
KILLER AT LARGE(1936), w
Silents
PERFECT CRIME, A(1921), w

Claus Clausen
DEVIL MAKES THREE, THE(1952)

Frimann Falck Clausen
HUNGER(1968, Den./Norway/Swed.); ONE DAY IN THE LIFE OF IVAN DENISOVICH(1971, U.S./Brit./Norway)

Richard Clausen
Misc. Talkies
REFLECTIONS FROM A BRASS BED(1976), d

Nils Clausnitzer
SNOW WHITE(1965, Ger.); SNOW WHITE AND ROSE RED(1966, Ger.)

Bill Clauson
WISTFUL WIDOW OF WAGON GAP, THE(1947); CANON CITY(1948); MIRACLE OF THE BELLS, THE(1948); YOU GOTTA STAY HAPPY(1948); LOUISA(1950)

Billy Clauson
MAJOR AND THE MINOR, THE(1942)

Elliott Clauson
Silents
ANOTHER MAN'S WIFE(1924), w

Ernest Clauson
JAZZ SINGER, THE(1927)

Henry Clauss
Silents
SAPHEAD, THE(1921)

Joy Claussen
DIARY OF A BACHELOR(1964); TROUBLEMAKER, THE(1964)

Kleber Claux
KANGAROO(1952)

Moria Claux
ROAD WARRIOR, THE(1982, Aus.)

Antoni Clave
HANS CHRISTIAN ANDERSEN(1952), art d, cos

Andre Claveau
FRENCH CANCAN(1956, Fr.); LACOMBE, LUCIEN(1974), m

Clavel
ANGEL AND SINNER(1947, Fr.), art d

Aurora Clavel
GUNS FOR SAN SEBASTIAN(1968, U.S./Fr./Mex./Ital.); WILD BUNCH, THE(1969); SOLDIER BLUE(1970); WRATH OF GOD, THE(1972); PAT GARRETT AND BILLY THE KID(1973)

Maurice Clavel
CROSS OF THE LIVING(1963. Fr.), w; MISTRESS FOR THE SUMMER, A(1964, Fr./Ital.), w

Robert Clavel
MAXIME(1962, Fr.), art d; MONKEY IN WINTER, A(1962, Fr.), set d; PASSION OF SLOW FIRE, THE(1962, Fr.), art d; TOMORROW IS MY TURN(1962, Fr./Ital./Ger.), art d; MARRIAGE OF FIGARO, THE(1963, Fr.), art d; PLEASE, NOT NOW!(1963, Fr./Ital.), art d; LADIES OF THE PARK(1964, Fr.), art d; GREED IN THE SUN(1965, Fr./ Ital.), art d; RAVISHING IDIOT, A(1966, Ital./Fr.), art d; WEEKEND AT DUNKIRK(1966, Fr./Ital.), art d; UPPER HAND, THE(1967, Fr./Ital./Ger.), art d; 25TH HOUR, THE(1967, Fr./Ital./Yugo.), prod d; BELLE DE JOUR(1968, Fr.), art d; GUNS FOR SAN SEBASTIAN(1968, U.S./Fr./Mex./Ital.), art d; TO COMMIT A MURDER(1970, Fr./Ital./Ger.), art d; VERDICT(1975, Fr./Ital.), art d

Aurora Clavell
MAJOR DUNDEE(1965)

James Clavell
FLY, THE(1958), w; FIVE GATES TO HELL(1959), p,d&w; WATUSI(1959), w; WALK LIKE A DRAGON(1960), p&d, w; GREAT ESCAPE, THE(1963), w; SQUADRON 633(1964, U.S./Brit.), w; 633 SQUADRON(1964), w; KING RAT(1965), w; SATAN BUG, THE(1965), w; TO SIR, WITH LOVE(1967, Brit.), p,d&w; WHERE'S JACK?(1969, Brit.), d; LAST VALLEY, THE(1971, Brit.), p,d&w

Michaela Clavell
OCTOPUSSY(1983, Brit.)

Bob Claver
JAWS OF SATAN(1980), d

Eric Clavering
MR. SATAN(1938, Brit.); FROZEN LIMITS, THE(1939, Brit.); WHERE'S THAT FIRE?(1939, Brit.); GASBAGS(1940, Brit.); THREE COCKEYED SAILORS(1940, Brit.); FACING THE MUSIC(1941, Brit.); INVADERS, THE,(1941); NEUTRAL PORT(1941, Brit.); SOUTH AMERICAN GEORGE(1941, Brit.); FRONT LINE KIDS(1942, Brit.); MUCH TOO SHY(1942, Brit.); TOWER OF TERROR, THE(1942, Brit.); SAINT MEETS THE TIGER, THE(1943, Brit.); SUSPECTED PERSON(1943, Brit.); PATIENT VANISHES, THE(1947, Brit.); INCREDIBLE JOURNEY, THE(1963); ISABEL(1968, Can.); TO KILL A CLOWN(1972); SUDDEN FURY(1975, Can.); SUNDAY IN THE COUNTRY(1975, Can.); IMPROPER CHANNELS(1981, Can.)
Misc. Talkies
UNDERCOVER MEN(1935)

Capt. E. H. Clavert
DEATH FROM A DISTANCE(1936)

Queti Clavijo
SOFT SKIN ON BLACK SILK(1964, Fr./Span.)

Antonio Espino Clavillazo
CASTLE OF THE MONSTERS(1958, Mex.)

Pat Clavin
PORTRAIT IN SMOKE(1957, Brit.); ELECTRONIC MONSTER. THE(1960, Brit.); MAN WHO COULDN'T WALK, THE(1964, Brit.)

Jim Clawin
LAUGHING POLICEMAN, THE(1973)

Mary Ellen Clawsen
INCREDIBLE TWO-HEADED TRANSPLANT, THE(1971)

Dal Clawson
SYNCOPATION(1929), ph; LOVE AT FIRST SIGHT(1930), ph; LOVE KISS, THE(1930), ph
Silents
HYPOCRITES(1914), ph; CIVILIZATION(1916), ph; DUMB GIRL OF PORTICI(1916), ph; RED, RED HEART, THE(1918), ph; MIDNIGHT ROMANCE, A(1919), ph; WHAT DO MEN WANT?(1921), ph; ANOTHER SCANDAL(1924), ph

Elliot Clawson
SAL OF SINGAPORE(1929), w; THIRTEENTH CHAIR, THE(1930), w

Elliot J. Clawson
Silents
CODE OF MARCIA GRAY(1916), w; KENTUCKY CINDERELLA, A(1917), w

Elliott Clawson
FLYING FOOL(1929), w; HIGH VOLTAGE(1929), w; LEATHERNECK, THE(1929), w
Silents
KAISER, BEAST OF BERLIN, THE(1918), w; ROAD TO MANDALAY, THE(1926), w; LET 'ER GO GALLEGHER(1928), w; WEST OF ZANZIBAR(1928), w

Elliott J. Clawson
PHANTOM OF THE OPERA, THE(1929), w
Silents
TRUTH WAGON, THE(1914), w; PHANTOM OF THE OPERA, THE(1925), w; WHISPERING SMITH(1926), w

Stewart Kirk Clawson
BIG CARNIVAL, THE(1951)
Tim Clawson
THEY CALL ME BRUCE(1982), w
Oliver Claxton
LUCKY NIGHT(1939), w
William Claxton
KIT CARSON(1940), ed; CHEERS FOR MISS BISHOP(1941), ed; CORSICAN BROTHERS, THE(1941), ed; INTERNATIONAL LADY(1941), ed; FRIENDLY ENEMIES(1942), ed; FIGHTING BUCKAROO, THE(1943), ed; HAIL TO THE RANGERS(1943), ed; DANGEROUS YEARS(1947), ed; INVISIBLE WALL, THE(1947), ed; JEWELS OF BRANDENBURG(1947), ed; MISS MINK OF 1949(1949), ed; TUCSON(1949), d; HOME TOWN STORY(1951), ed; FANGS OF THE WILD(1954), d, w; STAGECOACH TO FURY(1956), d; QUIET GUN, THE(1957), d
William F. Claxton
DANGEROUS MILLIONS(1946), ed; DEADLINE FOR MURDER(1946), ed; RENDEZVOUS 24(1946), ed; STRANGE JOURNEY(1946), ed; BACKLASH(1947), ed; FIGHTING BACK(1948), ed; HALF PAST MIDNIGHT(1948), d; NIGHT WIND(1948), ed; GOLDEN GLOVES STORY, THE(1950), ed; ROCKABILLY BABY(1957), p&d; YOUNG AND DANGEROUS(1957), p&d; I'LL GIVE MY LIFE(1959), d; DESIRE IN THE DUST(1960), p&d; YOUNG JESSE JAMES(1960), d; LAW OF THE LAWLESS(1964), d; STAGE TO THUNDER ROCK(1964), d; NIGHT OF THE LEPUS(1972), d
Misc. Talkies
ALL THAT I HAVE(1951), d
Willian F. Claxton
GOD IS MY PARTNER(1957), d
Andrew Clay
WACKO(1983)
1984
MAKING THE GRADE(1984)
Bertha M. Clay
Silents
THORNS AND ORANGE BLOSSOMS(1922), w
Cassius Clay [Muhammad Ali]
REQUIEM FOR A HEAVYWEIGHT(1962)
Charles Clay
IT'S A WONDERFUL WORLD(1956, Brit.); HIGH FLIGHT(1957, Brit.); TRUE AS A TURTLE(1957, Brit.); END OF THE LINE, THE(1959, Brit.); MAN WHO LIKED FUNERALS, THE(1959, Brit.); MOUSE THAT ROARED, THE(1959, Brit.); OPERATION CUPID(1960, Brit.)
Ford Clay
TERMINAL ISLAND(1973)
Harry Clay
GHOST SHIP, THE(1943); GOVERNMENT GIRL(1943); FALCON OUT WEST, THE(1944); MARINE RAIDERS(1944); MUSIC IN MANHATTAN(1944); YOUTH RUNS WILD(1944); HAVING WONDERFUL CRIME(1945)
Henry Clay
FEAR(1946)
Jennifer Clay
1984
SUBURBIA(1984)
Jim Clay [Aldo Cecconi]
SECRET AGENT FIREBALL(1965, Fr./Ital.)
John Clay
VARIETY(1935, Brit.)
Juanin Clay
LEGEND OF THE LONE RANGER, THE(1981); WARGAMES(1983)
Lang Clay
MAIDSTONE(1970)
Melvin Clay
SPOOK WHO SAT BY THE DOOR, THE(1973), w
Mitchell Clay
ROOMMATES, THE(1973), makeup
Monica Clay
LADY WITHOUT CAMELLIAS, THE(1981, Ital.)
Nicholas Clay
THESE ARE THE DAMNED(1965, Brit.); NIGHT DIGGER, THE(1971, Brit.); DARWIN ADVENTURE, THE(1972, Brit.); VICTOR FRANKENSTEIN(1975, Swed./Ireland); ZULU DAWN(1980, Brit.); EXCALIBUR(1981); LADY CHATTERLEY'S LOVER(1981, Fr./Brit.); EVIL UNDER THE SUN(1982, Brit.); HOUND OF THE BASKERVILLES, THE(1983, Brit.)
Misc. Talkies
CHILD'S PLAY(1984, Brit.)
Noland Clay
STALKING MOON, THE(1969)
Peter Clay
HENRY VIII AND HIS SIX WIVES(1972, Brit.)
Philippe Clay
FRENCH CANCAN(1956, Fr.); HUNCHBACK OF NOTRE DAME, THE(1957, Fr.); NATHALIE(1958, Fr.); ROAD TO SHAME, THE(1962, Fr.); MAN FROM COCODY(1966, Fr./Ital.); SHANKS(1974)
Phillipe Clay
BELL, BOOK AND CANDLE(1958)
Rachel Clay
MONSTER OF HIGHGATE PONDS, THE(1961, Brit.); THESE ARE THE DAMNED(1965, Brit.)
Stanley Clay
MAN FRIDAY(1975, Brit.); CANNONBALL(1976, U.S./Hong Kong)
Virginia Clay
GOOD BEGINNING, THE(1953, Brit.); TOWN LIKE ALICE, A(1958, Brit.); MY WIFE'S FAMILY(1962, Brit.); MAN WHO HAD POWER OVER WOMEN, THE(1970, Brit.)
Whit Clay
FAST CHARLIE... THE MOONBEAM RIDER(1979)
Doug Claybourne
ESCAPE ARTIST, THE(1982), p; BLACK STALLION RETURNS, THE(1983), p; RUMBLE FISH(1983), p

Jill Clayburgh
WEDDING PARTY, THE(1969); PORTNOY'S COMPLAINT(1972); THIEF WHO CAME TO DINNER, THE(1973); TERMINAL MAN, THE(1974); GABLE AND LOMBARD(1976); SILVER STREAK(1976); SEMI-TOUGH(1977); UNMARRIED WOMAN, AN(1978); LUNA(1979, Ital.); STARTING OVER(1979); IT'S MY TURN(1980); FIRST MONDAY IN OCTOBER(1981); I'M DANCING AS FAST AS I CAN(1982); HANNAH K.(1983, Fr.)
Misc. Talkies
TELEPHONE BOOK, THE(1971)
George Claydon
BERSERK(1967); DEVIL WITHIN HER, THE(1976, Brit.)
Lillian Clayes
SOMETHING TO LIVE FOR(1952)
Larry Clayman
J.W. COOP(1971)
Ocean Claypool
ROSALIE(1937); DRAMATIC SCHOOL(1938)
Ocean Claypoole
MARIE ANTOINETTE(1938)
Berenice Clayre
LADY ICE(1973)
Allie Clayton
SECOND FIDDLE TO A STEEL GUITAR(1965), makeup
Arthur Clayton
THREE LIVE GHOSTS(1929); GIRL OF THE PORT(1930); ROAD TO SINGAPORE(1931); CRIMSON ROMANCE(1934); GREEN EYES(1934); MENACE(1934); WHITE HEAT(1934); DEPUTY DRUMMER, THE(1935, Brit.); ONE GOOD TURN(1936, Brit.)
Silents
IN FOLLY'S TRAIL(1920); MISTRESS OF SHENSTONE, THE(1921); BETTER 'OLE, THE(1926); OUTLAWS OF RED RIVER(1927)
Misc. Silents
CONFESSIONS OF A WIFE(1928)
Barbara Clayton
Silents
NAUGHTY NANETTE(1927)
Bob Clayton
DISC JOCKEY(1951); BELLBOY, THE(1960)
Cecil Clayton
DOSS HOUSE(1933, Brit.)
Curtiss Clayton
1984
ON THE LINE(1984, Span.), ed
Don Clayton
MISSION TO MOSCOW(1943)
Eddie Clayton
DANCING SWEETIES(1930); GUILTY?(1930); WAY OF ALL MEN, THE(1930); PICK-UP(1933)
Silents
LADY BE GOOD(1928); ROAD HOUSE(1928); WHY BE GOOD?(1929)
Edward Clayton
COLLEGE COQUETTE, THE(1929); PICK A STAR(1937)
Ethel Clayton
TRUE TO LIFE(1943); CALL OF THE CIRCUS(1930); HIT THE DECK(1930); ALL-AMERICAN, THE(1932); HOTEL CONTINENTAL(1932); THRILL OF YOUTH(1932); PRIVATE JONES(1933); SECRETS(1933); EASY LIVING(1937); EXCLUSIVE(1937); HOLD'EM NAVY!(1937); KING OF GAMBLERS(1937); MAKE WAY FOR TOMORROW(1937); SOULS AT SEA(1937); ARTISTS AND MODELS ABROAD(1938); COCOANUT GROVE(1938); IF I WERE KING(1938); MEN WITH WINGS(1938); SAY IT IN FRENCH(1938); YOU AND ME(1938); CAFE SOCIETY(1939); WEST POINT WIDOW(1941); LADY BODYGUARD(1942); LUCKY JORDAN(1942); MAJOR AND THE MINOR, THE(1942); PERILS OF PAULINE, THE(1947)
Silents
DAUGHTERS OF MEN(1914); FORTUNE HUNTER, THE(1914); HOUSE NEXT DOOR, THE(1914); BROKEN CHAINS(1916); HIDDEN SCAR, THE(1916); JOURNEY'S END(1918); MAN HUNT, THE(1918); CROOKED STREETS(1920); LADY IN LOVE, A(1920); SINS OF ROZANNE(1920); BEYOND(1921); EXIT THE VAMP(1921); SHAM(1921); WEALTH(1921); CRADLE, THE(1922); IF I WERE QUEEN(1922); PRINCESS FROM HOBOKEN, THE(1927)
Misc. Silents
GAMBLERS, THE(1914); LION AND THE MOUSE, THE(1914); WOLF, THE(1914); COLLEGE WIDOW, THE(1915); DARKNESS BEFORE DAWN, THE(1915); SPORTING DUCHESS, THE(1915); DOLLARS AND THE WOMAN(1916); GREAT DIVIDE, THE(1916); HIS BROTHER'S WIFE(1916); HUSBAND AND WIFE(1916); MADNESS OF HELEN, THE(1916); WOMAN'S WAY, A(1916); BONDAGE OF FEAR, THE(1917); DORMANT POWER, THE(1917); EASY MONEY(1917); MAN'S WOMAN(1917); SOULS ADRIFT(1917); STOLEN PARADISE, THE(1917); WEB OF DESIRE, THE(1917); WOMAN BENEATH, THE(1917); YANKEE PLUCK(1917); GIRL WHO CAME BACK, THE(1918); MYSTERY OF A GIRL, THE(1918); SOUL WITHOUT WINDOWS, A(1918); STOLEN HOURS(1918); WHIMS OF SOCIETY, THE(1918); WITCH WOMAN, THE(1918); WOMAN'S WEAPONS(1918); MAGGIE PEPPER(1919), a, d; MEN, WOMEN AND MONEY(1919); MORE DEADLY THAN THE MALE(1919); PETTIGREW'S GIRL(1919); SPORTING CHANCE, A(1919); VICKY VAN(1919); CITY SPARROW, THE(1920); LADDER OF LIES, THE(1920); YOUNG MRS. WINTHROP(1920); 13TH COMMANDMENT, THE(1920); PRICE OF POSSESSION, THE(1921); FOR THE DEFENSE(1922); HER OWN MONEY(1922); CAN A WOMAN LOVE TWICE?(1923); REMITTANCE WOMAN, THE(1923); MANSION OF ACHING HEARTS, THE(1925); WINGS OF YOUTH(1925); BAR-C MYSTERY, THE(1926); HIS NEW YORK WIFE(1926); RISKY BUSINESS(1926)
Gilbert Clayton
LOCKED DOOR, THE(1929); ARM OF THE LAW(1932); STAND UP AND CHEER(1934 80m FOX bw); WE LIVE AGAIN(1934)
Silents
MARK OF ZORRO(1920); BLOOD AND SAND(1922); BELOW THE LINE(1925); PARTNERS AGAIN(1926)
Gregory Clayton
PERSONAL BEST(1982)

Hampton Clayton
COOL WORLD, THE(1963)
Helena Clayton
Misc. Talkies
RED ROSES OF PASSION(1967)
Hyde Clayton
BEYOND AND BACK(1978); TAKE DOWN(1979)
Jack Clayton
DARK RED ROSES(1930, Brit.); GOOD DIE YOUNG, THE(1954, Brit.), p; I AM A
CAMERA(1955, Brit.), p; DRY ROT(1956, Brit.), p; PANIC IN THE PARLOUR(1957,
Brit.), p; STORY OF ESTHER COSTELLO, THE(1957, Brit.), p; THREE MEN IN A
BOAT(1958, Brit.), p; WHOLE TRUTH, THE(1958, Brit.), p; ROOM AT THE TOP(1959,
Brit.), d; INNOCENTS, THE(1961, U.S./Brit.), p&d; PUMPKIN EATER, THE(1964,
Brit.), d; OUR MOTHER'S HOUSE(1967, Brit.), p&d; SOMETHING WICKED THIS
WAY COMES(1983), d
James Clayton
Misc. Talkies
FRONTIER WOMAN(1956)
James F. Clayton
SEXTETTE(1978), art d
Jan Clayton
FATHER IS A PRINCE(1940); FLIGHT ANGELS(1940); SHOWDOWN, THE(1940);
SIX GUN GOLD(1941); LOVES OF EDGAR ALLAN POE, THE(1942); THIS MAN'S
NAVY(1945); SNAKE PIT, THE(1948); WOLF HUNTERS, THE(1949)
Jane Clayton
IN OLD MEXICO(1938); SUNSET TRAIL(1938); LLANO KID, THE(1940)
Jill Clayton
DARK RED ROSES(1930, Brit.)
John Clayton
SIDECAR RACERS(1975, Aus.); HIGH ROLLING(1977, Aus.); SUMMERDOG(1977),
p&d; DAWN(1979, Aus.); NEWSFRONT(1979, Aus.); PALM BEACH(1979, Aus.)
Misc. Talkies
REDNECK MILLER(1977), d
Kathryn Clayton
DEMENTED(1980)
Keeva Clayton
RUMBLE FISH(1983)
Ken Clayton
LOST, LONELY AND VICIOUS(1958)
Kenneth Clayton
PIED PIPER, THE(1972, Brit.), md
Kenny Clayton
FOURTEEN, THE(1973, Brit.), m; RAGMAN'S DAUGHTER, THE(1974, Brit.), m
Link Clayton
MY FRIEND IRMA GOES WEST(1950)
Lou Clayton
ROADHOUSE NIGHTS(1930)
Marguerite Clayton
Silents
ACCORDING TO THE CODE(1916); NIGHT WORKERS, THE(1917); INSIDE THE
LINES(1918); BULLIN' THE BULLSHEVIKI(1919); NEW MOON, THE(1919); CURSE
OF DRINK, THE(1922); BARRIERS OF THE LAW(1925); POWER OF THE WEAK,
THE(1926)
Misc. Silents
DAUGHTER OF THE CITY, A(1915); PRINCE OF GRAUSTARK, THE(1916); VUL-
TURES OF SOCIETY(1916); DREAM DOLL, THE(1917); TWO-BITS SEATS(1917);
HIT-THE-TRAIL HOLLIDAY(1918); MAN OF BRONZE, THE(1918); DANGEROUS
TOYS(1921); FORBIDDEN LOVE(1921); CANYON OF THE FOOLS(1923); MEN IN
THE RAW(1923); WHAT LOVE WILL DO(1923); FLASHING SPURS(1924); STREET
OF TEARS, THE(1924); TIGER THOMPSON(1924); STRAIGHT THROUGH(1925);
WOLF BLOOD(1925); PALM BEACH GIRL, THE(1926); SKY HIGH CORRAL(1926);
TWIN FLAPPERS(1927); INSPIRATION(1928)
Marion Clayton
ALL QUIET ON THE WESTERN FRONT(1930); BARRETTS OF WIMPOLE STREET,
THE(1934); LADIES LOVE DANGER(1935); MAGNIFICENT OBSESSION(1935);
MUTINY ON THE BOUNTY(1935)
Merry Clayton
1984
BLAME IT ON THE NIGHT(1984)
Paul Clayton
ARABIAN NIGHTS(1942)
Powell Clayton
TRAIL OF THE LONESOME PINE, THE(1936)
Richard Clayton
OUR NEIGHBORS–THE CARTERS(1939); BROTHER RAT AND A BABY(1940);
FATHER IS A PRINCE(1940); FIGHTING 69TH, THE(1940); INVISIBLE STRI-
PES(1940); KNUTE ROCKNE–ALL AMERICAN(1940); MURDER IN THE AIR(1940);
MY LOVE CAME BACK(1940); THEY DRIVE BY NIGHT(1940); GREAT LIE,
THE(1941); HIGH SIERRA(1941); STRAWBERRY BLONDE, THE(1941); VERY
YOUNG LADY, A(1941); MOTHER IS A FRESHMAN(1949)
Robert Clayton
Misc. Talkies
CAPTAIN CELLULOID VS THE FILM PIRATES(1974)
Rosy Clayton
CHARRIOTS OF FIRE(1981, Brit.)
Toni Clayton
WINNING(1969); CHRISTIAN LICORICE STORE, THE(1971); SKYJACKED(1972)
William A. Clayton
Misc. Talkies
TEN MINUTES TO LIVE(1932)
William A. Clayton, Jr.
Misc. Silents
PRINCE OF HIS RACE, THE(1926)
Xernona Clayton
HOUSE ON SKULL MOUNTAIN, THE(1974)
James Claytor
PANDEMONIUM(1982), art d

June Clayworth
GOOD FAIRY, THE(1935); LADY TUBBS(1935); STRANGE WIVES(1935); TRAN-
SIENT LADY(1935); TWO-FISTED GENTLEMAN(1936); BETWEEN TWO WO-
MEN(1937); LIVE, LOVE AND LEARN(1937); MARRIED BEFORE
BREAKFAST(1937); ALMOST A GENTLEMAN(1939); CRIMINAL COURT(1946);
TRUTH ABOUT MURDER, THE(1946); BEAT THE BAND(1947); DICK TRACY
MEETS GRUESOME(1947); BODYGUARD(1948); WHITE TOWER, THE(1950); AT
SWORD'S POINT(1951); DREAM WIFE(1953); ROCKET MAN, THE(1954); THERE'S
ALWAYS TOMORROW(1956); MARRIAGE-GO-ROUND(1960)
Peter Cleall
CONFESSIONS OF A POP PERFORMER(1975, Brit.)
Charles Cleary
Silents
MAN'S PREROGATIVE, A(1915)
Dawn Cleary
CHRISTIAN LICORICE STORE, THE(1971); NIGHT GOD SCREAMED, THE(1975)
Jimmy Cleary
GIRL, A GUY AND A GOB, A(1941)
John Cleary
FOUR DESPERATE MEN(1960, Brit.), w
Jon Cleary
SUNDOWNERS, THE(1960), w; GREEN HELMET, THE(1961, Brit.), w; HIGH COM-
MISSIONER, THE(1968, U.S./Brit.), w; YOU CAN'T SEE 'ROUND CORNERS(1969,
Aus.), w; SCOBIE MALONE(1975, Aus.), w; SIDECAR RACERS(1975, Aus.), w; HIGH
ROAD TO CHINA(1983), w
Leo Cleary
DANCE, GIRL, DANCE(1940); YOU CAN'T FOOL YOUR WIFE(1940); JOHNNY
HOLIDAY(1949); RED MENACE, THE(1949); WHITE HEAT(1949); BELLS OF
CORONADO(1950); STORM WARNING(1950); DESERT OF LOST MEN(1951); CONFI-
DENCE GIRL(1952); DREAMBOAT(1952); KID FROM LEFT FIELD, THE(1953);
HUMAN JUNGLE, THE(1954)
Leo T. Cleary
STATE PENITENTIARY(1950); PRIDE OF ST. LOUIS, THE(1952)
Sgt. Cleary
NIGHT PEOPLE(1954)
Val Cleary
Misc. Silents
WHISPERING PALMS(1923)
Redmond Cleason
STEEL(1980)
Arthur Cleave
Silents
ADVENTURES OF MR. PICKWICK, THE(1921, Brit.); BACHELORS' CLUB,
THE(1921, Brit.); MASTER OF CRAFT, A(1922, Brit.); OLD BILL THROUGH THE
AGES(1924, Brit.)
Van Cleave
SAINTED SISTERS, THE(1948), m; GOLDBERGS, THE(1950), m; MR. MUSIC(1950),
md; QUEBEC(1951), m; RHUBARB(1951), m; OFF LIMITS(1953), m; CONQUEST OF
SPACE(1955), m; LUCY GALLANT(1955), m, md; LONELY MAN, THE(1957), m;
COLOSSUS OF NEW YORK, THE(1958), m; SPACE CHILDREN, THE(1958), m; THAT
KIND OF WOMAN(1959), md; BLUEPRINT FOR ROBBERY(1961), m
Bill Cleaver
WHERE THE LILIES BLOOM(1974), w
Brian Cleaver
INADMISSIBLE EVIDENCE(1968, Brit.)
Kathleen Cleaver
ZABRISKIE POINT(1970)
Vera Cleaver
WHERE THE LILIES BLOOM(1974), w
Zelda Cleaver
BAND OF ANGELS(1957); CAT ON A HOT TIN ROOF(1958)
Claudie Cleaves
ROTHSCHILD(1938, Fr.)
Robert Cleaves
YOUNG SAVAGES, THE(1961); THIRTEEN WEST STREET(1962); NOT WITH MY
WIFE, YOU DON'T!(1966); BORN LOSERS(1967); PROJECT X(1968); TARGETS(1968);
FLAP(1970); THREE THE HARD WAY(1974)
Sally Cleaves
SPIRAL ROAD, THE(1962)
Yvonne Clech
WOMAN OF SIN(1961, Fr.); ZAZIE(1961, Fr.); FIRE WITHIN, THE(1964, Fr./Ital.);
LIFE UPSIDE DOWN(1965, Fr.)
Hervey M. Cleckley, M.D.
THREE FACES OF EVE, THE(1957), p,d&w
Sara Clee
THAT'LL BE THE DAY(1974, Brit.); FLAME(1975, Brit.); SWEET WILLIAM(1980,
Brit.)
John Cleese
INTERLUDE(1968, Brit.); MAGIC CHRISTIAN, THE(1970, Brit.); RISE AND RISE OF
MICHAEL RIMMER, THE(1970, Brit.), w; STATUE, THE(1971, Brit.); AND NOW
FOR SOMETHING COMPLETELY DIFFERENT(1972, Brit.), a, w; REN-
TADICK(1972, Brit.), w; MONTY PYTHON AND THE HOLY GRAIL(1975, Brit.), a, w;
MONTY PYTHON'S LIFE OF BRIAN(1979, Brit.), a, w; GREAT MUPPET CAPER,
THE(1981); TIME BANDITS(1981, Brit.); PRIVATES ON PARADE(1982); MONTY
PYTHON'S THE MEANING OF LIFE(1983, Brit.), a, w; YELLOWBEARD(1983)
1984
PRIVATES ON PARADE(1984, Brit.)
Jon Cleese
MAGIC CHRISTIAN, THE(1970, Brit.), w
Barbara Clegg
DREAM MAKER, THE(1963, Brit.)
Brendan Clegg
HILLS OF DONEGAL, THE(1947, Brit.); MR. PERRIN AND MR. TRAILL(1948, Brit.)
Cy Clegg
TIGER ROSE(1930); PAINTED DESERT, THE(1931)
Georgina Clegg
WORLD IS JUST A 'B' MOVIE, THE(1971)

Tom Clegg
MOBY DICK(1956, Brit.); MARK OF THE PHOENIX(1958, Brit.); MISSILE FROM HELL(1960, Brit.); JOHN OF THE FAIR(1962, Brit.); ROOMMATES(1962, Brit.); THIS SPORTING LIFE(1963, Brit.); CARRY ON CLEO(1964, Brit.); CARRY ON SPYING(1964, Brit.); CARRY ON SCREAMING(1966, Brit.); GREAT CATHERINE(1968, Brit.); DECLINE AND FALL... OF A BIRD WATCHER(1969, Brit.); CARRY ON LOVING(1970, Brit.), d; LOVE IS A SPLENDID ILLUSION(1970, Brit.), d; SWEENEY 2(1978, Brit.), d; MC VICAR(1982, Brit.), d

Tommy Clegg
FAKE, THE(1953, Brit.); EXTRA DAY, THE(1956, Brit.); HIDEOUT, THE(1956, Brit.)

V.V. Clegg
Misc. Silents
LUCKY SPURS(1926), d

Gregory Cleghorne
WARRIORS, THE(1979)

John Clein
HEARTS OF HUMANITY(1932), p; TWO HEARTS IN HARMONY(1935, Brit.), p; MILL ON THE FLOSS(1939, Brit.), p; ROOM 43(1959, Brit.), p; INFORMATION RECEIVED(1962, Brit.), p; DR. CRIPPEN(1963, Brit.), p
Misc. Talkies
KEEP PUNCHING(1939), d

John Cleland
FANNY HILL: MEMOIRS OF A WOMAN OF PLEASURE zero(1965), w

Jim Clem
BOOTLEGGERS(1974)

Jimmy Clem
WINTERHAWK(1976); GRAYEAGLE(1977); TOWN THAT DREADED SUNDOWN, THE(1977); NORSEMAN, THE(1978); EVICTORS, THE(1979)

Majel Cleman
GIRL IN THE GLASS CAGE, THE(1929)

Dora Clemant
STAND UP AND CHEER(1934 80m FOX bw); STUDENT TOUR(1934); MY AMERICAN WIFE(1936); MR. SMITH GOES TO WASHINGTON(1939); WOMEN, THE(1939); YOU CAN'T CHEAT AN HONEST MAN(1939); THOSE WERE THE DAYS(1940)

Doris Clemence
WICKHAM MYSTERY, THE(1931, Brit.)

Brian Clemens
DEPRAVED, THE(1957, Brit.), w; OPERATION MURDER(1957, Brit.), w; THREE SUNDAYS TO LIVE(1957, Brit.), w; WOMAN OF MYSTERY, A(1957, Brit.), w; BETRAYAL, THE(1958, Brit.), w; LINKS OF JUSTICE(1958), w; MOMENT OF INDISCRETION(1958, Brit.), w; ON THE RUN(1958, Brit.), w; THREE CROOKED MEN(1958, Brit.), w; WOMAN POSSESSED, A(1958, Brit.), w; CHILD AND THE KILLER, THE(1959, Brit.), w; CRASH DRIVE(1959, Brit.), w; HIGH JUMP(1959, Brit.), w; HONOURABLE MURDER, AN(1959, Brit.), w; INNOCENT MEETING(1959, Brit.), w; TOP FLOOR GIRL(1959, Brit.), w; WEB OF SUSPICION(1959, Brit.), w; IDENTITY UNKNOWN(1960, Brit.), w; COURT MARTIAL OF MAJOR KELLER, THE(1961, Brit.), w; HIGHWAY TO BATTLE(1961, Brit.), w; MIDDLE COURSE, THE(1961, Brit.), w; PURSUERS, THE(1961, Brit.), w; TARNISHED HEROES(1961, Brit.), w; TRANSATLANTIC(1961, Brit.), w; TWO WIVES AT ONE WEDDING(1961, Brit.), w; FATE TAKES A HAND(1962, Brit.), w; RETURN OF A STRANGER(1962, Brit.), w; SILENT INVASION, THE(1962, Brit.), w; SPANISH SWORD, THE(1962, Brit.), w; TELL-TALE HEART, THE(1962, Brit.), w; GREAT VAN ROBBERY, THE(1963, Brit.), w; STATION SIX-SAHARA(1964, Brit./Ger.), w; CORRUPT ONES, THE(1967, Ger.), w; AND SOON THE DARKNESS(1970, Brit.), p, w; DR. JEKYLL AND SISTER HYDE(1971, Brit.), w; SEE NO EVIL(1971, Brit.), w; CAPTAIN KRONOS: VAMPIRE HUNTER(1974, Brit.), p, d&w; GOLDEN VOYAGE OF SINBAD, THE(1974, Brit.), w; WATCHER IN THE WOODS, THE(1980, Brit.), w

George Clemens
ARIZONA MAHONEY(1936), ph; BIG BROWN EYES(1936), ph; DESERT GOLD(1936), ph; HOLLYWOOD BOULEVARD(1936), ph; KLONDIKE ANNIE(1936), ph; RETURN OF SOPHIE LANG, THE(1936), ph; WIVES NEVER KNOW(1936), ph; CLARENCE(1937), ph; HIDEAWAY GIRL(1937), ph

Gertrude Clemens
WAR IS A RACKET(1934)

Gregory Clemens
FOES(1977)

Gunther Clemens
MARK OF THE DEVIL(1970, Ger./Brit.); FIVE DAYS ONE SUMMER(1982)

Harold Clemens
LADY ICE(1973), w

William Clemens
GHOST VALLEY(1932), ed; HAUNTED GOLD(1932), ed; RIDE HIM, COWBOY(1932), ed; FROM HEADQUARTERS(1933), ed; MAN FROM MONTEREY, THE(1933), ed; SOMEWHERE IN SONORA(1933), ed; TELEGRAPH TRAIL, THE(1933), ed; DOCTOR MONICA(1934), ed; EASY TO LOVE(1934), ed; HAPPINESS AHEAD(1934), ed; JOURNAL OF A CRIME(1934), ed; KEY, THE(1934), ed; DEVIL DOGS OF THE AIR(1935), ed; I FOUND STELLA PARISH(1935), ed; OIL FOR THE LAMPS OF CHINA(1935), ed; PAGE MISS GLORY(1935), ed; CASE OF THE VELVET CLAWS, THE(1936), d; DOWN THE STRETCH(1936), d; HERE COMES CARTER(1936), d; LAW IN HER HANDS, THE(1936), d; MAN HUNT(1936), d; MURDER OF DR. HARRIGAN, THE(1936), ed; CASE OF THE STUTTERING BISHOP, THE(1937), d; FOOTLOOSE HEIRESS, THE(1937), d; MISSING WITNESSES(1937), d; ONCE A DOCTOR(1937), d; TALENT SCOUT(1937), d; ACCIDENTS WILL HAPPEN(1938), d; MR. CHUMP(1938), d; NANCY DREW-DETECTIVE(1938), d; TORCHY BLANE IN PANAMA(1938), d; DEAD END KIDS ON DRESS PARADE(1939), d; NANCY DREW-REPORTER(1939), d; NANCY DREW AND THE HIDDEN STAIRCASE(1939), d; NANCY DREW, TROUBLE SHOOTER(1939), d; CALLING PHILO VANCE(1940), d; DEVIL'S ISLAND(1940), d; KING OF THE LUMBERJACKS(1940), p&d; KNOCKOUT(1941), d; NIGHT OF JANUARY 16TH(1941), d; SHE COULDN'T SAY NO(1941), d; LADY BODYGUARD(1942), d; NIGHT IN NEW ORLEANS, A(1942), d; SWEATER GIRL(1942), d; FALCON AND THE CO-EDS, THE(1943), d; FALCON IN DANGER, THE(1943), d; CRIME BY NIGHT(1944), d; 13TH HOUR, THE(1947), d

Leroy Clemens
LOVE, LIVE AND LAUGH(1929), w; HALF A SINNER(1934), w; ALIAS THE DEACON(1940), w
Silents
ALOMA OF THE SOUTH SEAS(1926), w

Paul Clemens
PASSAGE, THE(1979, Brit.); PROMISES IN THE DARK(1979); BEAST WITHIN, THE(1982)
1984
THEY'RE PLAYING WITH FIRE(1984)

Pilar Clemens
SAUL AND DAVID(1968, Ital./Span.)

Walter Clemens
YOUNG GO WILD, THE(1962, Ger.)

William B. Clemens
KANSAS CITY PRINCESS(1934), ed

Zeke Clemens
CODE OF THE RANGERS(1938)

Jimmie Clemens, Jr.
HELLO, FRISCO, HELLO(1943)

Clement
Misc. Silents
LA ZOME DE LA MORT(1917, Fr.)

Andre Clement
SYMPHONIE PASTORALE(1948, Fr.); DAUGHTERS OF DESTINY(1954, Fr./Ital.)

Andree Clement
DEVIL'S DAUGHTER(1949, Fr.); JUST A BIG, SIMPLE GIRL(1949, Fr.); BACK STREETS OF PARIS(1962, Fr.)

Aurore Clement
LACOMBE, LUCIEN(1974); LOVERS AND LIARS(1981, Ital.); HATTER'S GHOST, THE(1982, Fr.)
1984
LE CRABE TAMBOUR(1984, Fr.); PARIS, TEXAS(1984, Ger./Fr.)

C. Clement
VOW, THE(1947, USSR.), titles

Carolie Clement
AVIATOR'S WIFE, THE(1981, Fr.)

Charles Clement
IVAN THE TERRIBLE(Part I, 1947, USSR), titles; LAD FROM OUR TOWN(1941, USSR), English titles; HEROES ARE MADE(1944, USSR), titles; RAINBOW, THE(1944, USSR), titles; THREE HOURS(1944, Fr.), titles; LAST HILL, THE(1945, USSR), titles; MILITARY SECRET(1945, USSR), titles; DARK IS THE NIGHT(1946, USSR), titles; SIX P.M.(1946, USSR), titles; TARAS FAMILY, THE(1946, USSR), titles; WELL-DIGGER'S DAUGHTER, THE(1946, Fr.), ed; CARNIVAL OF SINNERS(1947, Fr.), titles; IN THE NAME OF LIFE(1947, USSR), titles; JENNY LAMOUR(1948, Fr.), ed; MARRIAGE IN THE SHADOWS(1948, Ger.), titles; MONTE CASSINO(1948, Ital.), titles; PORTRAIT OF INNOCENCE(1948, Fr.), titles; GERMANY, YEAR ZERO(1949, Ger.), titles; CHILDREN OF CHAOS(1950, Fr.), ed; HEART AND SOUL(1950, Ital.), titles; OUR DAILY BREAD(1950, Ger.), titles; JAIL BAIT(1954), ed; WOZZECK(1962, E. Ger.), titles

Clay Clement
EVENINGS FOR SALE(1932); MANHATTAN TOWER(1932); WASHINGTON MERRY-GO-ROUND(1932); BUREAU OF MISSING PERSONS(1933); DON'T BET ON LOVE(1933); HOLD ME TIGHT(1933); PAST OF MARY HOLMES, THE(1933); SECOND HAND WIFE(1933); SON OF A SAILOR(1933); TONIGHT IS OURS(1933); WORKING MAN, THE(1933); WORLD CHANGES, THE(1933); HOUSE OF MYSTERY(1934); I SELL ANYTHING(1934); I'VE GOT YOUR NUMBER(1934); JOURNAL OF A CRIME(1934); LET'S BE RITZY(1934); MURDER IN THE CLOUDS(1934); PERSONALITY KID, THE(1934); SIDE STREETS(1934); ST. LOUIS KID(1934); THIN MAN, THE(1934); UPPER WORLD(1934); WONDER BAR(1934); CHINATOWN SQUAD(1935); DINKY(1935); DON'T BET ON BLONDES(1935); STREAMLINE EXPRESS(1935); SWEET MUSIC(1935); GREAT ZIEGFELD, THE(1936); HEARTS IN BONDAGE(1936); HITCH HIKE LADY(1936); LEATHERNECKS HAVE LANDED, THE(1936); LEAVENWORTH CASE, THE(1936); LET'S SING AGAIN(1936); NOBODY'S FOOL(1936); THREE WISE GUYS, THE(1936); TWO AGAINST THE WORLD(1936); WHIPSAW(1936); WIFE VERSUS SECRETARY(1936); BAD GUY(1937); ROSALIE(1937); ARSON GANG BUSTERS(1938); KING OF ALCATRAZ(1938); TRIP TO PARIS, A(1938); DISBARRED(1939); EACH DAWN I DIE(1939); GIRL FROM RIO, THE(1939); OFF THE RECORD(1939); ROARING TWENTIES, THE(1939); SOCIETY SMUGGLERS(1939); STAR REPORTER(1939); GRANNY GET YOUR GUN(1940); I'M STILL ALIVE(1940); PASSPORT TO ALCATRAZ(1940); BOOMERANG(1947)
Misc. Talkies
NUMBERED WOMAN(1938)
Misc. Silents
STOLEN HONOR(1918)

Clay Clement, Jr.
Silents
APPEARANCE OF EVIL(1918)

Coralie Clement
PEPPERMINT SODA(1979, Fr.)

David Clement
STRANGE BREW(1983)
1984
POLICE ACADEMY(1984)

Dick Clement
JOKERS, THE(1967, Brit.), w; HANNIBAL BROOKS(1969, Brit.), w; OTLEY(1969, Brit.), d, w; CATCH ME A SPY(1971, Brit./Fr.), d, w; SEVERED HEAD, A(1971, Brit.), d; VILLAIN(1971, Brit.), w; LIKELY LADS, THE(1976, Brit.), w; DOING TIME(1979, Brit.), d, w; PRISONER OF ZENDA, THE(1979), w; BULLSHOT(1983), d

Dora Clement
IN OLD KENTUCKY(1935); MAN WHO BROKE THE BANK AT MONTE CARLO, THE(1935); PRIVATE WORLDS(1935); SHE MARRIED HER BOSS(1935); FORGOTTEN FACES(1936); I MARRIED A DOCTOR(1936); KING OF HOCKEY(1936); EASY LIVING(1937); NOBODY'S BABY(1937); HAWAII CALLS(1938); HOLD THAT CO-ED(1938); MY LUCKY STAR(1938); UNDER WESTERN STARS(1938); FOR LOVE OR MONEY(1939); GOLDEN BOY(1939); GOOD GIRLS GO TO PARIS(1939); MA, HE'S MAKING EYES AT ME(1940); NO, NO NANETTE(1940); SPORTING BLOOD(1940); BUCK PRIVATES(1941); LADY EVE, THE(1941); LUCKY DEVILS(1941); OBLIGING YOUNG LADY(1941); SUN VALLEY SERENADE(1941); UNFINISHED BUSINESS(1941); WHISTLING IN THE DARK(1941); TOO MANY WOMEN(1942)

Eloise Clement
Silents
JUST SYLVIA(1918); OLDEST LAW, THE(1918)

Misc. Silents
BURDEN OF PROOF, THE(1918)
Greta Clement
PRETENDER, THE(1947)
Jack Clement
DEAR, DEAD DELILAH(1972), p
Johnny Clement
TRIPLE THREAT(1948)
Joseph Clement
Silents
ON THE BANKS OF THE WABASH(1923), art d
Kay Clement
Silents
AIN'T LOVE FUNNY?(1927), w
Keith Clement
WHISTLE DOWN THE WIND(1961, Brit.)
Leroy Clement
Silents
ALIAS THE DEACON(1928), w
Lyle Clement
MARKED MEN(1940); CRACKED NUTS(1941)
Marc Clement
1984
NIGHT SHADOWS(1984)
Michel Clement
REACH FOR THE SKY(1957, Brit.)
Myra Clement
CATHY'S CURSE(1977, Can.), w
Rene Clement
BEAUTY AND THE BEAST(1947, Fr.), tech adv; DAMNED, THE(1948, Fr.), d, w; MR. ORCHID(1948, Fr.), d; BATTLE OF THE RAILS(1949, Fr.), p&d; WALLS OF MALAPAGA, THE(1950, Fr./Ital.), d; FORBIDDEN GAMES(1953, Fr.), d, w; LOVERS, HAPPY LOVERS!(1955, Brit.), d, w; GERVAISE(1956, Fr.), d; THIS ANGRY AGE(1958, Ital./Fr.), d, w; PURPLE NOON(1961, Fr./Ital.), d, w; DAY AND THE HOUR, THE(1963, Fr./ Ital.), d, w; JOY HOUSE(1964, Fr.), d, w; IS PARIS BURNING?(1966, U.S./Fr.), d; RIDER ON THE RAIN(1970, Fr./Ital.), d; AND HOPE TO DIE(1972 Fr/US), d; DEADLY TRAP, THE(1972, Fr./Ital.), d
Sam Clement
YOUNG NURSES, THE(1973), ph
Travers Clement
LAZARILLO(1963, Span.), titles
Clement-Thierry
LOVE AND DEATH(1975)
Ralph Clemente
CAYMAN TRIANGLE, THE(1977), w
Roberto Clemente
ODD COUPLE, THE(1968)
Steve Clemente
KING OF THE ARENA(1933); FIGHTING RANGER, THE(1934); MURDER IN THE MUSEUM(1934); HILLS OF OLD WYOMING(1937); IT HAPPENED OUT WEST(1937); STAGECOACH(1939); VALLEY OF THE SUN(1942)
Anna Maria Clementelli
I HATE BLONDES(1981, Ital.), p
Silvio Clementelli
DEFEND MY LOVE(1956, Ital.), p; PASSIONATE THIEF, THE(1963, Ital.), p; DROP DEAD, MY LOVE(1968, Italy), p; SARDINIA: RANSOM(1968, Ital.), p; THREE NIGHTS OF LOVE(1969, Ital.), p; CERTAIN, VERY CERTAIN, AS A MATTER OF FACT... PROBABLE(1970, Ital.), p; LADY OF MONZA, THE(1970, Ital.), p; WHEN WOMEN HAD TAILS(1970, Ital.), p; 'TIS A PITY SHE'S A WHORE(1973, Ital.), p; MALICIOUS(1974, Ital.), p; I HATE BLONDES(1981, Ital.), p
Margareth Clementi
MEDEA(1971, Ital./Fr./Ger.); ARABIAN NIGHTS(1980, Ital./Fr.)
Pierre Clementi
LEOPARD, THE(1963, Ital.); HOW NOT TO ROB A DEPARTMENT STORE(1965, Fr./Ital.); BELLE DE JOUR(1968, Fr.); BENJAMIN(1968, Fr.); SHOCK TROOPS(1968, Ital./Fr.); LISTEN, LET'S MAKE LOVE(1969, Fr./Ital.); MILKY WAY, THE(1969, Fr./Ital.); CANNIBALS, THE(1970, Ital.); WHEEL OF ASHES(1970, Fr.); CONFORMIST, THE(1971, Ital., Fr); STEPPENWOLF(1974); QUARTET(1981, Brit./Fr.); EXPOSED(1983)
1984
DOG DAY(1984, Fr.)
Steve Clementi
Silents
ARIZONA CATCLAW, THE(1919)
Steve Clemento
MOST DANGEROUS GAME, THE(1932); KING KONG(1933); SON OF KONG(1933); KID MILLIONS(1934); VIVA VILLA!(1934)
Silents
TEMPTRESS, THE(1926)
Misc. Silents
DOUBLE O, THE(1921)
Albert Clements
ISLAND OF ALLAH(1956)
Brian Clements
WOMAN'S TEMPTATION, A(1959, Brit.), w
Calvin Clements
FIRECREEK(1968), w; KANSAS CITY BOMBER(1972), w
Calvin Clements, Jr.
WILD COUNTRY, THE(1971), w
Candice Clements
MANIAC(1980)
Charles Clements
THEY ARE NOT ANGELS(1948, Fr.), titles; SIN YOU SINNERS(1963)
Colin Clements
SWEETHEARTS ON PARADE(1930), w; NOTORIOUS GENTLEMAN, A(1935), w; HER FIRST BEAU(1941), w; SMOOTH AS SILK(1946), w
Silents
OH, WHAT A NIGHT!(1926), w

Dudley Clements
BIG SHOT, THE(1937); HIDEAWAY(1937); NEW FACES OF 1937(1937); NIGHT CLUB SCANDAL(1937); OUTCASTS OF POKER FLAT, THE(1937); TOAST OF NEW YORK, THE(1937); TOO MANY WIVES(1937); TRUE CONFESSION(1937); YOU CAN'T BUY LUCK(1937); TEST PILOT(1938)
Hal Clements
SEVENTEEN(1940)
Silents
MAN WHO COULD NOT LOSE, THE(1914); ARMSTRONG'S WIFE(1915)
Misc. Silents
SECRETARY OF FRIVOLOUS AFFAIRS, THE(1915); UNKNOWN, THE(1915); MISS JACKIE OF THE ARMY(1917); MOLLY, GO GET 'EM(1918)
Hale Clements
Silents
AMERICAN LIVE WIRE, AN(1918)
Harold Clements
COUNTERFEIT KILLER, THE(1968), w
John Clements
DIVINE SPARK, THE(1935, Brit./Ital.); REMBRANDT(1936, Brit.); THINGS TO COME(1936, Brit.); TICKET OF LEAVE(1936, Brit.); KNIGHT WITHOUT ARMOR(1937, Brit.); SOUTH RIDING(1938, Brit.); FOUR FEATHERS, THE(1939, Brit.); CONVOY(1940); HIDDEN MENACE, THE(1940, Brit.); THIS ENGLAND(1941, Brit.); SHIPS WITH WINGS(1942, Brit.); AT DAWN WE DIE(1943, Brit.); THEY CAME TO A CITY(1944, Brit.); UNDERGROUND GUERRILLAS(1944, Brit.); CALL OF THE BLOOD(1948, Brit.), a, d, w; TRAIN OF EVENTS(1952, Brit.); SILENT ENEMY, THE(1959, Brit.); MIND BENDERS, THE(1963, Brit.); OH! WHAT A LOVELY WAR(1969, Brit.); GANDHI(1982)
Marjorie Clements
DEAD OR ALIVE(1944); OLD TEXAS TRAIL, THE(1944)
Mary Frye Clements
Misc. Silents
JANE EYRE(1914)
Richard Clements
PEEPER(1975), m
Ron Clements
FOX AND THE HOUND, THE(1981), anim
Roy Clements
Silents
KING SPRUCE(1920), d; NOBODY'S FOOL(1921), w; MARSHAL OF MONEYMINT, THE(1922), d&w; NINE AND THREE-FIFTHS SECONDS(1925), w; WANTED–A COWARD(1927), p&d
Misc. Silents
CROWN JEWELS(1918), d; WHEN A WOMAN STRIKES(1919), d; TIGER'S COAT, THE(1920), d; DOUBLE O, THE(1921), d; MOTION TO ADJOURN, A(1921), d; SPARKS OF FLINT(1921), d; DESERT BRIDEGROOM, A(1922), d; DESERT'S CRUCIBLE, THE(1922), d; TWO-FISTED JEFFERSON(1922), d; TONGUES OF SCANDAL(1927), d
Sir John Clements
ONCE IN A NEW MOON(1935, Brit.)
Stanley Clements
AIR STRIKE(1955); ACCENT ON LOVE(1941); DOWN IN SAN DIEGO(1941); TALL, DARK AND HANDSOME(1941); I WAKE UP SCREAMING(1942); 'NEATH BROOKLYN BRIDGE(1942); ON THE SUNNY SIDE(1942); RIGHT TO THE HEART(1942); SMART ALECKS(1942); GHOSTS ON THE LOOSE(1943); MORE THE MERRIER, THE(1943); SWEET ROSIE O'GRADY(1943); THANK YOUR LUCKY STARS(1943); THEY GOT ME COVERED(1943); YOU'RE A LUCKY FELLOW, MR. SMITH(1943); GIRL IN THE CASE(1944); GOING MY WAY(1944); SEE MY LAWYER(1945); VARIETY GIRL(1947); BABE RUTH STORY, THE(1948); BIG TOWN SCANDAL(1948); CANON CITY(1948); HAZARD(1948); JOE PALOOKA IN WINNER TAKE ALL(1948); RACING LUCK(1948); BAD BOY(1949); JOHNNY HOLIDAY(1949); MR. SOFT TOUCH(1949); DESTINATION MURDER(1950); MILITARY ACADEMY WITH THAT TENTH AVENUE GANG(1950); PRIDE OF MARYLAND(1951); ARMY BOUND(1952); BOOTS MALONE(1952); JET JOB(1952); HOT NEWS(1953); OFF LIMITS(1953); WHITE LIGHTNING(1953); ROCKET MAN, THE(1954); MAD AT THE WORLD(1955); ROBBER'S ROOST(1955); FIGHTING TROUBLE(1956); HOT SHOTS(1956); LAST OF THE DESPERADOES(1956); WIRETAPPERS(1956); HOLD THAT HYPNOTIST(1957); LOOKING FOR DANGER(1957); SPOOK CHASERS(1957); UP IN SMOKE(1957); DEVIL'S PARTNER, THE(1958), w; IN THE MONEY(1958); NICE LITTLE BANK THAT SHOULD BE ROBBED, A(1958); SNIPER'S RIDGE(1961); SAINTLY SINNERS(1962); IT'S A MAD, MAD, MAD, MAD WORLD(1963); TAMMY AND THE DOCTOR(1963); PANIC IN THE CITY(1968); HOT LEAD AND COLD FEET(1978)
Stanley "Stash" Clements
SALTY O'ROURKE(1945)
Steve Clements
Silents
GIRL WHO DARED, THE(1920); RAINBOW TRAIL, THE(1925)
Misc. Silents
CRASHIN' THROUGH(1924); RIDING ROMANCE(1926)
Ted Clements
SERVANT, THE(1964, Brit.), art d; HEROES OF TELEMARK, THE(1965, Brit.), set d
Vassar Clements
NASHVILLE(1975)
Veola Clements
CONRACK(1974)
Warren Clements
1984
SOLDIER'S STORY, A(1984)
William Clements
SADDLE BUSTER, THE(1932), ed
Zeke Clements
Misc. Talkies
VALLEY OF BLOOD(1973)
Larry Clementson
NEW LAND, THE(1973, Swed.)
Trudy Clemes
STARTING OVER(1979)

FROM FRISCO(1944); MY BEST GAL(1944); MY PAL, WOLF(1944); WHEN THE LIGHTS GO ON AGAIN(1944); YELLOW ROSE OF TEXAS, THE(1944); DAKOTA(1945); GOD IS MY CO-PILOT(1945); HER HIGHNESS AND THE BELLBOY(1945); IT'S IN THE BAG(1945); SENORITA FROM THE WEST(1945); SHE WOULDN'T SAY YES(1945); SONG OF THE SARONG(1945); SUNBONNET SUE(1945); ANGEL ON MY SHOULDER(1946); BLUE SIERRA(1946); COURAGE OF LASSIE(1946); LITTLE GIANT(1946); RUNAROUND, THE(1946); SHOW-OFF, THE(1946); STEP BY STEP(1946); WAKE UP AND DREAM(1946); WILD BEAUTY(1946); EASY COME, EASY GO(1947); I WONDER WHO'S KISSING HER NOW(1947); MOTHER WORE TIGHTS(1947); MY WILD IRISH ROSE(1947); WISTFUL WIDOW OF WAGON GAP, THE(1947); ALBUQUERQUE(1948); DATE WITH JUDY, A(1948); FURY AT FURNACE CREEK(1948); MIRACULOUS JOURNEY(1948); PLUNDERERS, THE(1948); KAZAN(1949); MISS GRANT TAKES RICHMOND(1949); RIMFIRE(1949); BOY FROM INDIANA(1950); PLEASE BELIEVE ME(1950); TRIGGER, JR.(1950); FLAMING FEATHER(1951); FORT DEFIANCE(1951); CARSON CITY(1952); CRIPPLE CREEK(1952); WAC FROM WALLA WALLA, THE(1952); AFFAIR WITH A STRANGER(1953); SAN ANTONE(1953); WALKING MY BABY BACK HOME(1953); FIREMAN SAVE MY CHILD(1954); OUTLAW'S DAUGHTER, THE(1954); RACING BLOOD(1954); RAILS INTO LARAMIE(1954); UNTAMED HEIRESS(1954)
Misc. Talkies
HOME IN SAN ANTONE(1949)
Georgine Cleveland
MY SIX LOVES(1963); I'D RATHER BE RICH(1964)
John Cleveland
MAYOR OF 44TH STREET, THE(1942), w; NEW FACES(1954), w
Kenneth Cleveland
LILLI MARLENE(1951, Brit.)
Madge Cleveland
SING, BOY, SING(1958); WALKING TARGET, THE(1960)
Odessa Cleveland
HUCKLEBERRY FINN(1974)
Patience Cleveland
FITZWILLY(1967)
1984
LIES(1984, Brit.)
Val Cleveland
Silents
BEAUTY AND BULLETS(1928), t; EYES OF THE UNDERWORLD(1929), t; GRIT WINS(1929), t; SKY SKIDDER, THE(1929), w; SLIM FINGERS(1929), t
Helen Cleveley
PANDORA AND THE FLYING DUTCHMAN(1951, Brit.)
Hugh Clevely
MAXWELL ARCHER, DETECTIVE(1942, Brit.), w
Beatrice Clevener
Silents
DAN(1914)
Philippe Clevenot
CELINE AND JULIE GO BOATING(1974, Fr.)
Edith Clever
ADOLESCENT, THE(1978, Fr./W.Ger.); LEFT-HANDED WOMAN, THE(1980, Ger.); PARSIFAL(1983, Fr.)
Helen Cleverley
INSPECTOR CALLS, AN(1954, Brit.)
Lynne Clevers
CARNIVAL IN FLANDERS(1936, Fr.)
The Cleves
THREE TO GO(1971, Aus.), m
Howard Clewes
GREEN GROW THE RUSHES(1951, Brit.), w; LONG MEMORY, THE(1953, Brit.), w; ONE THAT GOT AWAY, THE(1958, Brit.), w; STEEL BAYONET(1958, Brit.), w; DAY THEY ROBBED THE BANK OF ENGLAND, THE(1960, Brit.), w; UP FROM THE BEACH(1965), w
Lorraine Clewes
JAILBIRDS(1939, Brit.); PRISON WITHOUT BARS(1939, Brit.); CURSE OF THE WRAYDONS, THE(1946, Brit.); DESTINATION MILAN(1954, Brit.); MAN WHO WOULDN'T TALK, THE(1958, Brit.); IT TAKES A THIEF(1960, Brit.); SENTENCED FOR LIFE(1960, Brit.); PIRATES OF BLOOD RIVER, THE(1962, Brit.)
Lorreaine Clewes
OPEN SEASON(1974, U.S./Span.)
Carl Clewing
Silents
ONE ARABIAN NIGHT(1921, Ger.)
Eric Cleworth
PETER PAN(1953), anim; SLEEPING BEAUTY(1959), anim; ONE HUNDRED AND ONE DALMATIANS(1961), anim; ARISTOCATS, THE(1970), w, anim
Erik Cleworth
LADY AND THE TRAMP(1955), anim
Hetty Clews
VISITOR, THE(1973, Can.)
Angela Clianto
Misc. Talkies
RAPE KILLER, THE(1976)
Martin Clichy
SCARLET ANGEL(1952)
James Clifden
SO GOES MY LOVE(1946), w
Jeannette Cliff
HIDING PLACE, THE(1975)
Jimmy Cliff
HARDER THEY COME, THE(1973, Jamaica), a, m
John Cliff
BEYOND THE PURPLE HILLS(1950); LAW OF THE BADLANDS(1950); MILKMAN, THE(1950); BEST OF THE BADMEN(1951); BACK TO GOD'S COUNTRY(1953); DEVIL'S CANYON(1953); SECOND CHANCE(1953); DEMETRIUS AND THE GLADIATORS(1954); FIREMAN SAVE MY CHILD(1954); JESSE JAMES VERSUS THE DALTONS(1954); LAW VS. BILLY THE KID(1954); RIVER OF NO RETURN(1954); SIEGE AT RED RIVER, THE(1954); BULLET FOR JOEY, A(1955); FINGER MAN(1955); ILLEGAL(1955); MAN FROM BITTER RIDGE, THE(1955); DANCE WITH ME, HENRY(1956); MIDNIGHT STORY, THE(1957); GUNSMOKE IN TUCSON(1958); I WAS A TEENAGE FRANKENSTEIN(1958); LEGEND OF TOM

DOOLEY, THE(1959); OKLAHOMA TERRITORY(1960); THREE STOOGES MEET HERCULES, THE(1962); GNOME-MOBILE, THE(1967); GOOD TIMES(1967); MONEY JUNGLE, THE(1968); NEVER A DULL MOMENT(1968)
Laddie Cliff
SLEEPING CAR(1933, Brit.); HAPPY(1934, Brit.); SPORTING LOVE(1936, Brit.); OVER SHE GOES(1937, Brit.)
Misc. Silents
CARD, THE(1922, Brit.)
Oliver Cliff
EDDY DUCHIN STORY, THE(1956); SOLID GOLD CADILLAC, THE(1956)
H. Cooper Cliffe
Silents
ARMS AND THE WOMAN(1916); ARGYLE CASE, THE(1917); LOVE'S REDEMPTION(1921); WOMAN GOD CHANGED(1921); MISSING MILLIONS(1922); MONSIEUR BEAUCAIRE(1924)
Misc. Silents
ENEMY TO SOCIETY, AN(1915); FINAL JUDGEMENT, THE(1915); TABLES TURNED(1915); EXTRAVAGANCE(1916); KISS OF HATE, THE(1916); PARISIAN ROMANCE, A(1916); RAFFLES, THE AMATEUR CRACKSMAN(1917)
Henry Cooper Cliffe
Misc. Silents
GOLD AND THE WOMAN(1916); DEVIL'S GARDEN, THE(1920)
Ruth Cliffoer
Silents
DON MIKE(1927)
Cal Clifford
WEDNESDAY CHILDREN, THE(1973), p
Carmen Clifford
BLUE DAHLIA, THE(1946); MAN WITH A CLOAK, THE(1951); STRIP, THE(1951)
Carmes Clifford
ROYAL WEDDING(1951)
Charles L. Clifford
ARMY GIRL(1938), w; REAL GLORY, THE(1939), w; THEY SHALL HAVE MUSIC(1939), w
Colleen Clifford
1984
CAREFUL, HE MIGHT HEAR YOU(1984, Aus.)
Cynthia Clifford
ROYAL DEMAND, A(1933, Brit.)
Dr. Hubert Clifford
MINE OWN EXECUTIONER(1948, Brit.), md; NIGHT BEAT(1948, Brit.), md; FALLEN IDOL, THE(1949, Brit.), md; SAINTS AND SINNERS(1949, Brit.), md; SEVEN DAYS TO NOON(1950, Brit.), md; WINSLOW BOY, THE(1950), md; OPERATION X(1951, Brit.), md; PANDORA AND THE FLYING DUTCHMAN(1951, Brit.), md; WONDER BOY(1951, Brit./Aust.), md; CRY, THE BELOVED COUNTRY(1952, Brit.), md
Frances Clifford
TOMBSTONE, THE TOWN TOO TOUGH TO DIE(1942)
Francis Clifford
GUNS OF DARKNESS(1962, Brit.), w; NAKED RUNNER, THE(1967, Brit.), w
Gary Clifford
SUBTERFUGE(1969, US/Brit.)
Gordon Clifford
PARADISE CANYON(1935); SUBMARINE D-1(1937)
Misc. Silents
OIL AND ROMANCE(1925); QUEEN OF SPADES(1925); WEST OF THE MOJAVE(1925); FIGHTING GOB, THE(1926); SHEEP TRAIL(1926); WILDCAT, THE(1926)
Graeme Clifford
IMAGES(1972, Ireland), ed; DON'T LOOK NOW(1973, Brit./Ital.), ed; ROCKY HORROR PICTURE SHOW, THE(1975, Brit.), ed; MAN WHO FELL TO EARTH, THE(1976, Brit.), ed; CONVOY(1978), ed; F.I.S.T.(1978), ed; POSTMAN ALWAYS RINGS TWICE, THE(1981), ed; FRANCES(1982), d
Harry Clifford
KNIGHTS FOR A DAY(1937, Brit.)
Misc. Silents
MASTER OF GRAY, THE(1918, Brit.)
Herbert Clifford
TRIPLE DECEPTION(1957, Brit.), m
Hubert Clifford
IDEAL HUSBAND, AN(1948, Brit.), md; IF THIS BE SIN(1950, Brit.), md; STRANGER IN BETWEEN, THE(1952, Brit.), m; RIVER BEAT(1954), m; BACHELOR OF HEARTS(1958, Brit.), m; HELL DRIVERS(1958, Brit.), m; ONE THAT GOT AWAY, THE(1958, Brit.), m
Jack Clifford
CAUGHT(1931); SKIPPY(1931); SUNRISE TRAIL(1931); FAITHLESS(1932); GOLD(1932); LAW OF THE SEA(1932); LOCAL BAD MAN(1932); SOUTH OF SANTA FE(1932); TOMBSTONE CANYON(1932); ONE SUNDAY AFTERNOON(1933); POOR RICH, THE(1934); GALLANT DEFENDER(1935); ONE-WAY TICKET(1935); REVENGE RIDER, THE(1935); DIMPLES(1936); KING OF THE PECOS(1936); LONE WOLF RETURNS, THE(1936); MAN FROM GUN TOWN, THE(1936); MILKY WAY, THE(1936); SPEED(1936); TIMOTHY'S QUEST(1936); HIGH, WIDE AND HANDSOME(1937); MIDNIGHT MADONNA(1937); ONE MAN JUSTICE(1937); RACKETEERS IN EXILE(1937); COLORADO TRAIL(1938); IRISH AND PROUD OF IT(1938, Ireland); ANGELS WASH THEIR FACES(1939); YOU CAN'T CHEAT AN HONEST MAN(1939); MURDER ON THE YUKON(1940); RAGTIME COWBOY JOE(1940); SKY BANDITS, THE(1940); WHEN THE DALTONS RODE(1940); YUKON FLIGHT(1940); BANDIT TRAIL, THE(1941); CONFESSIONS OF BOSTON BLACKIE(1941); SIX LESSONS FROM MADAME LA ZONGA(1941); MY FAVORITE BLONDE(1942); DUMMY TALKS, THE(1943, Brit.), w; OLD TEXAS TRAIL, THE(1944); PRACTICALLY YOURS(1944); TRAIL TO GUNSIGHT(1944); HONEYMOON AHEAD(1945); ROCKIN' IN THE ROCKIES(1945); SALOME, WHERE SHE DANCED(1945); SENORITA FROM THE WEST(1945); BLUE DAHLIA, THE(1946); CANYON PASSAGE(1946); TO EACH HIS OWN(1946); MY FAVORITE BRUNETTE(1947); WHERE THERE'S LIFE(1947); I, JANE DOE(1948)
Silents
SWEET ADELINE(1926)
Jake Clifford
GENTLE ANNIE(1944)

Jefferson Clifford
DEADLIEST SIN, THE(1956, Brit.); BRIDAL PATH, THE(1959, Brit.)

Jeffrey Clifford
ROAD WARRIOR, THE(1982, Aus.), spec eff

Jill Clifford
I'LL NEVER FORGET YOU(1951); NO HIGHWAY IN THE SKY(1951, Brit.); SING ALONG WITH ME(1952, Brit.); KNIGHTS OF THE ROUND TABLE(1953); JUST MY LUCK(1957, Brit.)

John Clifford
GOOD COMPANIONS(1933, Brit.); FRIDAY THE 13TH(1934, Brit.); ROOM TO LET(1949, Brit.); LAUGHING LADY, THE(1950, Brit.); DIAMOND SAFARI(1958); CARNIVAL OF SOULS(1962), w; SUBTERFUGE(1969, US/Brit.)

Johns Clifford
IDEAL HUSBAND, AN(1948, Brit.)

Kathleen Clifford
Silents
ANGEL CHILD(1918); WHEN THE CLOUDS ROLL BY(1920); KICK IN(1922); NO MORE WOMEN(1924); EXCESS BAGGAGE(1928)
Misc. Silents
LAW THAT DIVIDES, THE(1919); RICHARD, THE LION-HEARTED(1923); LOVE GAMBLE, THE(1925)

Kim Clifford
CHARIOTS OF FIRE(1981, Brit.)

Larry Clifford
JOHNNY EAGER(1942)

Marjorie Clifford
Misc. Silents
WINDING TRAIL, THE(1921)

Michael A. Clifford
THING, THE(1982), spec eff

Mike Clifford
VILLAGE OF THE GIANTS(1965); SHEBA BABY(1975)

Mikel Clifford
Misc. Talkies
JACKPOT(1982)

Molly Clifford
LEAVE IT TO BLANCHE(1934, Brit.)

Molly Hamley Clifford
JOY RIDE(1935, Brit.); PAY BOX ADVENTURE(1936, Brit.); THERE WAS A YOUNG MAN(1937, Brit.); UNDER SECRET ORDERS(1943, Brit.); SHADOW MAN(1953, Brit.); GENTLE TOUCH, THE(1956, Brit.)

Mrs. W. K. Clifford
Silents
LIKENESS OF THE NIGHT, THE(1921, Brit.), w

Neil Clifford
CLASS OF 1984(1982, Can.)

Peggy Ann Clifford
FORBIDDEN(1949, Brit.); KIND HEARTS AND CORONETS(1949, Brit.); JOSEPHINE AND MEN(1955, Brit.); HAPPY IS THE BRIDE(1958, Brit.); HAUNTED STRANGLER, THE(1958, Brit.); ON THE BEAT(1962, Brit.); SPARROWS CAN'T SING(1963, Brit.); CUCKOO PATROL(1965, Brit.); TWO LEFT FEET(1965, Brit.); VOICES(1973, Brit.)

Peggyann Clifford
MAN OF THE MOMENT(1955, Brit.); TIME OF HIS LIFE, THE(1955, Brit.); IT'S A GREAT DAY(1956, Brit.); DOCTOR AT LARGE(1957, Brit.); TEARS FOR SIMON(1957, Brit.); MY WIFE'S FAMILY(1962, Brit.); UNDER MILK WOOD(1973, Brit.)

Ruth Clifford
ONLY YESTERDAY(1933); ELMER AND ELSIE(1934); STAND UP AND CHEER(1934 80m FOX bw); DANTE'S INFERNO(1935); HOLD'EM YALE(1935); PADDY O'DAY(1935); SHE MARRIED HER BOSS(1935); STOLEN HARMONY(1935); HOLLYWOOD BOULEVARD(1936); TO MARY–WITH LOVE(1936); FOUR MEN AND A PRAYER(1938); SAILOR'S LADY(1940); ALONG THE RIO GRANDE(1941); MR. CELEBRITY(1942); IN THE MEANTIME, DARLING(1944); KEYS OF THE KINGDOM, THE(1944); CRY OF THE CITY(1948); LUCK OF THE IRISH(1948); UNFAITHFULLY YOURS(1948); EVERYBODY DOES IT(1949); FATHER WAS A FULLBACK(1949); NOT WANTED(1949); PREJUDICE(1949); SLATTERY'S HURRICANE(1949); YOU'RE MY EVERYTHING(1949); SUNSET BOULEVARD(1950); WAGONMASTER(1950); COBWEB, THE(1955); MAN CALLED PETER, THE(1955); PRINCE OF PLAYERS(1955); MAN IN THE GREY FLANNEL SUIT, THE(1956); SEARCHERS, THE(1956); LAST HURRAH, THE(1958); TWO RODE TOGETHER(1961); I'D RATHER BE RICH(1964)
Silents
ETERNAL LOVE(1917); KENTUCKY CINDERELLA, A(1917); KAISER, BEAST OF BERLIN, THE(1918); RED, RED HEART, THE(1918); CABARET GIRL, THE(1919); DANGEROUS AGE, THE(1922); MY DAD(1922); APRIL SHOWERS(1923); MOTHERS-IN-LAW(1923); ABRAHAM LINCOLN(1924); AS MAN DESIRES(1925); DEVIL'S APPLE TREE(1929); ETERNAL WOMAN, THE(1929)
Misc. Silents
BEHIND THE LINES(1916); DESIRE OF THE MOTH, THE(1917); DOOR BETWEEN, THE(1917); MOTHER O'MINE(1917); MYSTERIOUS MR. TILLER, THE(1917); POLLY PUT THE KETTLE ON(1917); SAVAGE, THE(1917); FIRES OF YOUTH(1918); GUILT OF SILENCE, THE(1918); HANDS DOWN(1918); HUNGRY EYES(1918); LURE OF LUXURY, THE(1918); MIDNIGHT MADNESS(1918); BLACK GATE, THE(1919); GAME'S UP, THE(1919); MILLIONAIRE PIRATE, THE(1919); TROPICAL LOVE(1921); DAUGHTERS OF THE RICH(1923); FACE ON THE BARROOM FLOOR, THE(1923); TRUXTON KING(1923); BUTTERFLY(1924); TORNADO, THE(1924); WHISPERED NAME, THE(1924); HER HUSBAND'S SECRET(1925); LOVE HOUR, THE(1925); STORM BREAKER, THE(1925); BROODING EYES(1926); LEW TYLER'S WIVES(1926); TYPHOON LOVE(1926); THRILL SEEKERS, THE(1927)

Ruth E. Clifford
LODGER, THE(1944)

Sid Clifford
ANGEL BABY(1961), set d

Sidney Clifford
SHADOWS IN THE NIGHT(1944), set d; WHISTLER, THE(1944), set d; POWER OF THE WHISTLER, THE(1945), set d; FRAMED(1947), set d; SWORDSMAN, THE(1947), set d; JUNGLE JIM(1948), set d; MAN FROM COLORADO, THE(1948), set d; SECRET OF ST. IVES, THE(1949), set d; GOLDEN HAWK, THE(1952), set d; LAST TRAIN FROM BOMBAY(1952), set d; PATHFINDER, THE(1952), set d; VOODOO TIGER(1952), set d; JESSE JAMES VERSUS THE DALTONS(1954), set d; MOUN-

TAIN ROAD, THE(1960), set d; DON'T KNOCK THE TWIST(1962), set d; WILD WESTERNERS, THE(1962), set d; MAD ROOM, THE(1969), set d

Tom Clifford
PART TIME WIFE(1930)

Tommy Clifford
SONG O' MY HEART(1930)

Veronica Clifford
I'LL NEVER FORGET WHAT'S 'IS NAME(1967, Brit.); SEBASTIAN(1968, Brit.) 1984 SECRET PLACES(1984, Brit.)

W. C. Clifford
Silents
CHEATERS(1927), w

W. K. Clifford
Silents
EVE'S LOVER(1925), w

W.H. Clifford
Misc. Silents
DENNY FROM IRELAND(1918), d

William Clifford
Silents
SECOND IN COMMAND, THE(1915); SILENT VOICE, THE(1915); MY LADY INCOG(1916), w; PARADISE GARDEN(1917); TALE OF TWO CITIES, A(1917); AVENGING TRAIL, THE(1918); GAMBLING IN SOULS(1919); NOTORIOUS MISS LISLE, THE(1920); MASK, THE(1921); ASHES OF VENGEANCE(1923); OUT OF THE PAST(1927)
Misc. Silents
ROSEMARY(1915); BAIT, THE(1916); HEART OF TARA, THE(1916); HIDDEN LAW, THE(1916); LEOPARD'S BRIDE, THE(1916); SINS OF HER PARENT(1916); OUT OF THE WRECK(1917); SQUARE DECEIVER, THE(1917); UNDER HANDICAP(1917); YOUNG MOTHER HUBBARD(1917); LANDLOPER, THE(1918); MAN OF HONOR, A(1919); CONFESSION, THE(1920); THREE MILES UP(1927)

William H. Clifford
Silents
WRATH OF THE GODS, THE or THE DESTRUCTION OF SAKURA JIMA(1914), w; ETERNAL GRIND, THE(1916), w; NEARLY A KING(1916), w; OUT OF THE DRIFTS(1916), w; SPIDER, THE(1916), w; RIDERS OF THE DAWN(1920), w
Misc. Silents
LONG ARM OF MANNISTER, THE(1919); MAN ALONE, THE(1923), d; SOULS IN BONDAGE(1923), d; MISSING DAUGHTERS(1924), d

Vala Clifton
EVERY DAY IS A HOLIDAY(1966, Span.)

Brooke Clift
TOGETHER FOR DAYS(1972)

Brooks Clift
VICE GIRLS, LTD.(1964)

Denison Clift
CITY OF PLAY(1929, Brit.), d, w; HIGH SEAS(1929, Brit.), d, w; TAXI FOR TWO(1929, Brit.), d; SCOTLAND YARD(1930), w; MAN ABOUT TOWN(1932), w; WARN LONDON!(1934, Brit.), w; ALL THAT GLITTERS(1936, Brit.), w; LAST ADVENTURERS, THE(1937, Brit.), w; PHANTOM SHIP(1937, Brit.), d; SCOTLAND YARD(1941), w; END OF THE ROAD(1944), w; SECRETS OF SCOTLAND YARD(1944), w
Silents
DIVORCE TRAP, THE(1919), w; DIAMOND NECKLACE, THE(1921, Brit.), d&w; OLD WIVES' TALE, THE(1921, Brit.), d&w; OUT TO WIN(1923, Brit.), d&w; PORTS OF CALL(1925), d; YANKEE CLIPPER, THE(1927), w; PARADISE(1928, Brit.), d; POWER OVER MEN(1929, Brit.)
Misc. Silents
SONIA(1921, Brit.), d; WHY MEN FORGET(1921, Brit.), d; WOMAN OF NO IMPORTANCE, A(1921, Brit.), d; BENTLEY'S CONSCIENCE(1922, Brit.), d; BILL FOR DIVORCEMENT, A(1922), d; DIANA OF THE CROSSWAYS(1922, Brit.), d; LOVES OF MARY, QUEEN OF SCOTS, THE(1923), d; THIS FREEDOM(1923, Brit.), d; FLAMES OF DESIRE(1924), d; GREAT DIAMOND MYSTERY, THE(1924), d; HONOR AMONG MEN(1924), d

Dennison Clift
Silents
AND A STILL, SMALL VOICE(1918), w; MIDNIGHT PATROL, THE(1918), w; GAMBLING IN SOULS(1919), w; SPLENDID SIN, THE(1919), w; LAST STRAW, THE(1920), d&w
Misc. Silents
IRON HEART, THE(1920), d; WHAT WOULD YOU DO?(1920), d; THERE'S MILLIONS IN IT(1924), d

Faith Clift
CAPTAIN APACHE(1971, Brit.)

Lawrence Clift
NIGHTMARE CASTLE(1966, Ital.)

Montgomery Clift
RED RIVER(1948); SEARCH, THE(1948); HEIRESS, THE(1949); BIG LIFT, THE(1950); PLACE IN THE SUN, A(1951); FROM HERE TO ETERNITY(1953); I CONFESS(1953); INDISCRETION OF AN AMERICAN WIFE(1954, U.S./Ital.); RAINTREE COUNTY(1957); LONELYHEARTS(1958); YOUNG LIONS, THE(1958); SUDDENLY, LAST SUMMER(1959, Brit.); WILD RIVER(1960); JUDGMENT AT NUREMBERG(1961); MISFITS, THE(1961); FREUD(1962); DEFECTOR, THE(1966, Ger./Fr.)

Sten Clift
$100 A NIGHT(1968, Ger.), m

Adele Clifton
Silents
ATTA BOY'S LAST RACE(1916); NINA, THE FLOWER GIRL(1917)

Barry Clifton
GIRL IN THE CROWD, THE(1934, Brit.); WIDOW'S MIGHT(1934, Brit.); FLAME IN THE HEATHER(1935, Brit.); HONEYMOON FOR THREE(1935, Brit.)

Bernard Clifton
MERRY COMES TO STAY(1937, Brit.); UNDER A CLOUD(1937, Brit.)

Charles Clifton
STOOLIE, THE(1972), ph

Dorinda Clifton
GIRL OF THE LIMBERLOST, THE(1945); MARAUDERS, THE(1947); GOLDEN BLADE, THE(1953)

Elmer Clifton
MAID TO ORDER(1932), d; CYCLONE OF THE SADDLE(1935), d, w; FIGHTING CABALLERO(1935), d, w; PALS OF THE RANGE(1935), d, w; RIP ROARING RILEY(1935), d; ROUGH RIDING RANGER(1935), d, w; WILDCAT TROOPER(1936), d; CRIME AFLOAT(1937), d; CRUSADE AGAINST RACKETS(1937), d; DEATH IN THE SKY(1937), d; MILE A MINUTE LOVE(1937), d; CALIFORNIA FRONTIER(1938), d; LAW OF THE TEXAN(1938), d; PAROLED FROM THE BIG HOUSE(1938), d; SKULL AND CROWN(1938), d; STRANGER FROM ARIZONA, THE(1938), d; TEN LAPS TO GO(1938), d; WOLVES OF THE SEA(1938), d&w; CRASHING THRU(1939), d; ISLE OF DESTINY(1940), d; WEST OF PINTO BASIN(1940), w; CITY OF MISSING GIRLS(1941), d; I'LL SELL MY LIFE(1941), d, w; SWAMP WOMAN(1941), d; TRAIL OF THE SILVER SPURS(1941), w; DEEP IN THE HEART OF TEXAS(1942), d; RANGERS TAKE OVER, THE(1942), w; SUNDOWN KID, THE(1942), d; BAD MEN OF THUNDER GAP(1943), w; CHEYENNE ROUNDUP(1943), w; DAYS OF OLD CHEYENNE(1943), d; FRONTIER LAW(1943), d&w; OLD CHISHOLM TRAIL(1943), d&w; RAIDERS OF SAN JOAQUIN(1943), d&w; RETURN OF THE RANGERS, THE(1943), d&w; BOSS OF THE RAWHIDE(1944), d&w; BRAND OF THE DEVIL(1944), w; GANGSTERS OF THE FRONTIER(1944), d&w; GUNS OF THE LAW(1944), d&w; GUNSMOKE MESA(1944), w; PINTO BANDIT, THE(1944), d&w; SEVEN DOORS TO DEATH(1944), d&w; SPOOK TOWN(1944), d&w; WHISPERING SKULL, THE(1944), d; FRONTIER FUGITIVES(1945), w; LIGHTNING RAIDERS(1945), w; THREE IN THE SADDLE(1945), d, w; YOUTH AFLAME(1945), d, w; AMBUSH TRAIL(1946), w; OUTLAW OF THE PLAINS(1946), w; SONG OF THE SIERRAS(1946), w; RAINBOW OVER THE ROCKIES(1947), w; WEST TO GLORY(1947), w; JUDGE, THE(1949), d, w; NOT WANTED(1949), d; QUICK ON THE TRIGGER(1949), w; OUTCAST OF BLACK MESA(1950), w; SILVER BANDIT, THE(1950), d
Misc. Talkies
DARK ENDEAVOUR(1933), d; CAPTURED IN CHINATOWN(1935), d; GAMBLING WITH SOULS(1936), d; ASSASSIN OF YOUTH(1937), d; DEATH IN THE AIR(1937), d; BLOCKED TRAIL, THE(1943), d; SWING, COWBOY, SWING(1944), d
Silents
JOHN BARLEYCORN(1914); BIRTH OF A NATION, THE(1915); LILY AND THE ROSE, THE(1915); ACQUITTED(1916); INTOLERANCE(1916); LITTLE SCHOOL MA'AM, THE(1916); OLD FOLKS AT HOME, THE(1916); HIGH SPEED(1917), d; NINA, THE FLOWER GIRL(1917); EAGLE, THE(1918), d; I'LL GET HIM YET(1919), d; NUGGET NELL(1919), d; OUT OF LUCK(1919), d; DOWN TO THE SEA IN SHIPS(1923), d; WARRENS OF VIRGINIA, THE(1924), d; BEAUTIFUL BUT DUMB(1928), d; LET 'ER GO GALLEGHER(1928), d; DEVIL'S APPLE TREE(1929), d
Misc. Silents
FOX WOMAN, THE(1915); STRATHMORE(1915); MISSING LINKS, THE(1916); FLAME OF YOUTH, THE(1917), d; FLIRTING WITH DEATH(1917), d; HER OFFICAL FATHERS(1917), d; HIGH SIGN, THE(1917), d; MAN TRAP, THE(1917), d; MIDNIGHT MAN(1917), d; STORMY KNIGHT, A(1917), d; BATTLING JANE(1918), d; BRACE UP(1918), d; FLASH OF FATE, THE(1918), d; GUILT OF SILENCE, THE(1918), d; HOPE CHEST, THE(1918), d; KISS OR KILL(1918), d; SMASHING THROUGH(1918), d; TWO-SOUL WOMAN, THE(1918), d; WINNER TAKES ALL(1918), d; BOOTS(1919), d; I'LL GET HIM YET(1919), d; PEPPY POLLY(1919), d; TURNING THE TABLES(1919), d; MARY ELLEN COMES TO TOWN(1920), d; SIX CYLINDER LOVE(1923), d; DAUGHTERS OF THE NIGHT(1924), d; TRUTH ABOUT MEN(1926), d; WIVES AT AUCTION(1926), d; WRECK OF THE HESPERUS, THE(1927), d; TROPICAL NIGHTS(1928), d; VIRGIN LIPS(1928), d

Elmer P. Clifton
DEAD OR ALIVE(1944), d

Emma Bell Clifton
Silents
CONQUERED HEARTS(1918), w

Ethel Clifton
MAN WHO LOST HIMSELF, THE(1941)
Misc. Silents
SECRET ROOM, THE(1915)

F. G. Clifton
Silents
ON THE BANKS OF ALLAN WATER(1916, Brit.)

Frank M. Clifton
Silents
RIDIN' THE WIND(1925), w; HANDS ACROSS THE BORDER(1926), w; DON MIKE(1927), w; JESSE JAMES(1927), w; SILVER COMES THROUGH(1927), w; KIT CARSON(1928), w; PIONEER SCOUT, THE(1928), w; SUNSET LEGION, THE(1928), w

Gerard Clifton
MEN OF STEEL(1932, Brit.)

Harry Clifton
BUCKET OF BLOOD(1934, Brit.), p; NORAH O'NEALE(1934, Brit.), p
Misc. Silents
MAN AND BEAST(1917)

Herbert Clifton
FALSE PRETENSES(1935); HIGH FLYERS(1937); SHE'S GOT EVERYTHING(1938); RAFFLES(1939); RIDE, TENDERFOOT, RIDE(1940); CONFESSIONS OF BOSTON BLACKIE(1941); MRS. MINIVER(1942); THIS ABOVE ALL(1942); LADY AND THE MONSTER, THE(1944); LODGER, THE(1944); IVY(1947)

Hugh Clifton
Silents
MR. JUSTICE RAFFLES(1921, Brit.); NARROW VALLEY, THE(1921, Brit.); PIPES OF PAN, THE(1923, Brit.)
Misc. Silents
JOHN FORREST FINDS HIMSELF(1920, Brit.); DOLLARS IN SURREY(1921, Brit.); TANSY(1921, Brit.); SIMPLE SIMON(1922, Brit.)

Jane Clifton
CLINIC, THE(1983, Aus.)

Lotta Clifton
Silents
INTOLERANCE(1916)

Mike Clifton
UNCLE HARRY(1945)

Patti Clifton
MASTER GUNFIGHTER, THE(1975)

Wallace C. Clifton
Silents
AMERICAN WAY, THE(1919), w; LOVE IN A HURRY(1919), w

Wallace Clifton
Silents
CHEATED HEARTS(1921), w; HIGH HEELS(1921), w; MILLIONAIRE, THE(1921), w; TORRENT, THE(1921), w; OUT OF THE SILENT NORTH(1922), w; TRACKED TO EARTH(1922), w

M. E. Clifton-James
BLANCHE FURY(1948, Brit.)

Joel Climenhaga
ONE WAY TICKET TO HELL(1955)

Amparo Climent
1984
DEMONS IN THE GARDEN(1984, Span.)

Jose Climent
DRACULA VERSUS FRANKENSTEIN(1972, Span.), ph

Pilar Climent
SONNY AND JED(1974, Ital.)

Jim Climer
DELTA FACTOR, THE(1970), stunts

David Climie
DESERT MICE(1960, Brit.), w

Capt. William J. Clinch
I WANTED WINGS(1941), m/1

Al Cline
NOOSE FOR A GUNMAN(1960), ph

Benjamin Cline
GIRL IN DANGER(1934), ph; REVENGE RIDER, THE(1935), ph

Bill Cline
Silents
ARIZONA CYCLONE(1928), ph

Bob Cline
HOUSE OF ERRORS(1942), ph; WHITE GORILLA(1947), ph

Cynthia Cline
UFO: TARGET EARTH(1974)

Eddie Cline
HIS LUCKY DAY(1929), p; IN THE NEXT ROOM(1930), d; LEATHERNECKING(1930), d; PAROLE GIRL(1933), d; SO THIS IS AFRICA(1933), d; YOU CAN'T CHEAT AN HONEST MAN(1939), d; NIGHT CLUB GIRL(1944), d; PENTHOUSE RHYTHM(1945), d; BRINGING UP FATHER(1946), d, m; JIGGS AND MAGGIE IN SOCIETY(1948), d, w; JIGGS AND MAGGIE OUT WEST(1950), w
Silents
THREE AGES, THE(1923), d; RAG MAN, THE(1925), d; LET IT RAIN(1927), d; HEAD MAN, THE(1928), d; VAMPING VENUS(1928), d
Misc. Silents
GOOD BAD BOY(1924), d; CRASH, THE(1928), d

Edward Cline
FORWARD PASS, THE(1929), d; HOOK, LINE AND SINKER(1930), d; SWEET MAMA(1930), d; WIDOW FROM CHICAGO, THE(1930), d; GIRL HABIT(1931), d; NAUGHTY FLIRT, THE(1931), d; MILLION DOLLAR LEGS(1932), d; FORTY NAUGHTY GIRLS(1937), d; HIGH FLYERS(1937), d; ON AGAIN-OFF AGAIN(1937), d; BANK DICK, THE(1940), d; MY LITTLE CHICKADEE(1940), d; HELLO SUCKER(1941), d; NEVER GIVE A SUCKER AN EVEN BREAK(1941), d; SEE MY LAWYER(1945), d
Silents
ALONG CAME RUTH(1924), d; OLD CLOTHES(1925), d
Misc. Silents
LITTLE ROBINSON CRUSOE(1924), d; LADIES' NIGHT IN A TURKISH BATH(1928), d; BROADWAY FEVER(1929), d

Edward E. Cline
CRACKED NUTS(1941), d

Edward F Cline
COWBOY MILLIONAIRE(1935), d

Edward F. Cline
CRACKED NUTS(1931), d; DUDE RANGER, THE(1934), d; PECK'S BAD BOY(1934), d; WHEN A MAN'S A MAN(1935), d; F MAN(1936), d; IT'S A GREAT LIFE(1936), d; BREAKING THE ICE(1938), d; GO CHASE YOURSELF(1938), d; HAWAII CALLS(1938), d; PECK'S BAD BOY WITH THE CIRCUS(1938), d; VILLAIN STILL PURSUED HER, THE(1940), d; MEET THE CHUMP(1941), d; BEHIND THE EIGHT BALL(1942), d; GIVE OUT, SISTERS(1942), d; PRIVATE BUCKAROO(1942), d; SNUFFY SMITH, YARD BIRD(1942), d; WHAT'S COOKIN'?(1942), d; HE'S MY GUY(1943), d; GHOST CATCHERS(1944), d, w; HAT CHECK HONEY(1944), d; MOONLIGHT AND CACTUS(1944), d; SLIGHTLY TERRIFIC(1944), d; SWINGTIME JOHNNY(1944), d
Misc. Talkies
FIGHTING TO LIVE(1934), d
Silents
CIRCUS DAYS(1923), d, w; CAPTAIN JANUARY(1924), d; SOFT CUSHIONS(1927), d
Misc. Silents
MEANEST MAN IN THE WORLD, THE(1923), d; WHEN A MAN'S A MAN(1924), d

George Cline
Silents
JANICE MEREDITH(1924)

Hall Cline
Silents
OLD AGE HANDICAP(1928); GIRLS WHO DARE(1929)

Harry Cline
WALK IN THE SUN, A(1945)

Kathy Cline
RING OF FEAR(1954)

Robert C. Cline
SPOOK TOWN(1944), ph

Robert Cline
CORRUPTION(1933), ph; FIGHTING PIONEERS(1935), ph; LAST OF THE CLINTONS, THE(1935), ph; LAWLESS BORDER(1935), ph; RUSTLER'S PARADISE(1935), ph; WAGON TRAIL(1935), ph; WILD MUSTANG(1935), ph; MEN OF THE

PLAINS(1936), ph; ROMANCE RIDES THE RANGE(1936), ph; TOLL OF THE DESERT(1936), ph; ACES WILD(1937), ph; ARIZONA GUNFIGHTER(1937), ph; GHOST TOWN(1937), ph; IDAHO KID, THE(1937), ph; MOONLIGHT ON THE RANGE(1937), ph; RIDIN' THE LONE TRAIL(1937), ph; COLORADO KID(1938), ph; DESERT PATROL(1938), ph; DUKE IS THE TOPS, THE(1938), ph; DURANGO VALLEY RAIDERS(1938), ph; FEUD MAKER(1938), ph; HEROES OF THE ALAMO(1938), ph; LAND OF FIGHTING MEN(1938), ph; PAROLED—TO DIE(1938), ph; THUNDER IN THE DESERT(1938), ph; AM I GUILTY?(1940), ph; BOYS OF THE CITY(1940), ph; THAT GANG OF MINE(1940), ph; FUGITIVE VALLEY(1941), ph; KID'S LAST RIDE, THE(1941), ph; PRIDE OF THE BOWERY(1941), ph; SADDLE MOUNTAIN ROUND-UP(1941), ph; TONTO BASIN OUTLAWS(1941), ph; TRAIL OF THE SILVER SPURS(1941), ph; TUMBLEDOWN RANCH IN ARIZONA(1941), ph; UNDERGROUND RUSTLERS(1941), ph; WRANGLER'S ROOST(1941), ph; BOMBS OVER BURMA(1942), ph; LONE STAR LAW MEN(1942), ph; RANGERS TAKE OVER, THE(1942), ph; ROCK RIVER RENEGADES(1942), ph; SECRETS OF A CO-ED(1942), ph; TEXAS TO BATAAN(1942), ph; THUNDER RIVER FEUD(1942), ph; TRAIL RIDERS(1942), ph; WAR DOGS(1942), ph; BAD MEN OF THUNDER GAP(1943), ph; BLACK RAVEN, THE(1943), ph; CATTLE STAMPEDE(1943), ph; GHOST AND THE GUEST(1943), ph; MY SON, THE HERO(1943), ph; RETURN OF THE RANGERS, THE(1943), ph; TWO FISTED JUSTICE(1943), ph; UNDERDOG, THE(1943), ph; WESTERN CYCLONE(1943), ph; WILD HORSE RUSTLERS(1943), ph; WOLVES OF THE RANGE(1943), ph; BLAZING FRONTIER(1944), ph; BOSS OF THE RAWHIDE(1944), ph; CONTENDER, THE(1944), ph; DEAD OR ALIVE(1944), ph; DEATH RIDES THE PLAINS(1944), ph; DEVIL RIDERS(1944), ph; DRIFTER, THE(1944), ph; FRONTIER OUTLAWS(1944), ph; GANGSTERS OF THE FRONTIER(1944), ph; LAW OF THE SADDLE(1944), ph; MEN ON HER MIND(1944), ph; MONSTER MAKER, THE(1944), ph; NABONGA(1944), ph; RAIDERS OF RED GAP(1944), ph; SEVEN DOORS TO DEATH(1944), ph; SHAKE HANDS WITH MURDER(1944), ph; THUNDERING GUN SLINGERS(1944), ph; WATERFRONT(1944), ph; FLAMING BULLETS(1945), ph; FRONTIER FUGITIVES(1945), ph; I ACCUSE MY PARENTS(1945), ph; THREE IN THE SADDLE(1945), ph; PRAIRIE BADMEN(1946), ph; SECRETS OF A SORORITY GIRL(1946), ph; THUNDER TOWN(1946), ph; BUFFALO BILL RIDES AGAIN(1947), ph; LAW OF THE LASH(1947), ph; RANGE BEYOND THE BLUE(1947), ph; WILD COUNTRY(1947), ph

Robert E. Cline
Silents
DEVIL DOGS(1928), ph; OBEY YOUR HUSBAND(1928), ph

Rocky Cline
SIREN OF ATLANTIS(1948), spec eff

Rosco Cline
QUIET AMERICAN, THE(1958), spec eff

Roscoe Cline
LION IS IN THE STREETS, A(1953), spec eff; KINGS OF THE SUN(1963), spec eff; DUEL AT DIABLO(1966), spec eff; MARCO THE MAGNIFICENT(1966, Ital./Fr./Yugo./Egypt/Afghanistan), spec eff

Roscoe S. Cline
PARK ROW(1952), spec eff; JOHN PAUL JONES(1959), spec eff

Rusty Cline
ROLLIN' HOME TO TEXAS(1941)

Walter Cline
TOOTSIE(1982)

Wilfred Cline
PAINTING THE CLOUDS WITH SUNSHINE(1951), ph; GIANT GILA MONSTER, THE(1959), ph; KILLER SHREWS, THE(1959), ph

Wilfred M. Cline
CAPTAINS OF THE CLOUDS(1942), ph; FIGHTER SQUADRON(1948), ph; ONE SUNDAY AFTERNOON(1948), ph; ROMANCE ON THE HIGH SEAS(1948), spec eff; MY DREAM IS YOURS(1949), ph; TEA FOR TWO(1950), ph; LULLABY OF BROADWAY, THE(1951), ph; RATON PASS(1951), ph; SHE'S WORKING HER WAY THROUGH COLLEGE(1952), ph; APRIL IN PARIS(1953), ph; HIDDEN FEAR(1957), ph; MARDI GRAS(1958), ph

Wilfrid Cline
MAN FROM HELL'S EDGES(1932), ph; ADVENTURES OF TOM SAWYER, THE(1938), ph; HAPPY GO LUCKY(1943), ph; FIRST TEXAN, THE(1956), ph; LAST WAGON, THE(1956), ph; NAVY WIFE(1956), ph; APRIL LOVE(1957), ph; DINO(1957), ph; TALL STRANGER, THE(1957), ph; BATTLE OF THE CORAL SEA(1959), ph; BECAUSE THEY'RE YOUNG(1960), ph

Wilfrid M. Cline
HEART OF THE NORTH(1938), ph; FIESTA(1947), ph; IT'S A GREAT FEELING(1949), ph; STORY OF SEABISCUIT, THE(1949), ph; TASK FORCE(1949), ph; COLT .45(1950), ph; DAUGHTER OF ROSIE O'GRADY, THE(1950), ph; SUGARFOOT(1951), ph; BUGLES IN THE AFTERNOON(1952), ph; STORY OF WILL ROGERS, THE(1952), ph; BY THE LIGHT OF THE SILVERY MOON(1953), ph; CALAMITY JANE(1953), ph; COMMAND, THE(1954), ph; LUCKY ME(1954), ph; AIN'T MISBEHAVIN'(1955), ph; GLORY(1955), ph; INDIAN FIGHTER, THE(1955), ph; SECOND GREATEST SEX, THE(1955), ph; TALL MAN RIDING(1955), ph; TEN WANTED MEN(1955), ph; FROM HELL TO TEXAS(1958), ph; FACE OF A FUGITIVE(1959), ph; TINGLER, THE(1959), ph

Will Cline
LAW OF THE NORTH(1932), ph

Debra Clinger
MIDNIGHT MADNESS(1980)

Edith Clinton
EXILE, THE(1947)

Edward Clinton
HONKY TONK FREEWAY(1981), w

Geoffrey Clinton
Silents
GLORIOUS ADVENTURE, THE(1922, U.S./Brit.)

George S. Clinton
APPLE, THE(1980 U.S./Ger.); STILL SMOKIN'(1983), m

Gordon Clinton
GREAT GILBERT AND SULLIVAN, THE(1953, Brit.)

Jack R. Clinton
NEW YORK, NEW YORK(1977)
1984
NO SMALL AFFAIR(1984)

Lois Clinton
EASY LIVING(1937)

Mildred Clinton
NEW LEAF, A(1971); SERPICO(1973); ALICE, SWEET ALICE(1978)

Stanley Clinton
WALKING ON AIR(1946, Brit.), ph; DARK ROAD, THE(1948, Brit.), ph; DICK BARTON–SPECIAL AGENT(1948, Brit.), ph; MY HANDS ARE CLAY(1948, Irish), ph; IT'S A WONDERFUL DAY(1949, Brit.), ph; DICK BARTON AT BAY(1950, Brit.), ph; GORBALS STORY, THE(1950, Brit.), ph

Steve Clinton
WHO'S BEEN SLEEPING IN MY BED?(1963)

Terry Clinton
OF HUMAN BONDAGE(1964, Brit.)

Vivien Clinton
CRY, THE BELOVED COUNTRY(1952, Brit.)

Walter Clinton
HEADLINE CRASHER(1937); FOR LOVE OR MONEY(1939); GYPSY WILDCAT(1944); DANCING IN THE DARK(1949); BLONDE BANDIT, THE(1950); IT GROWS ON TREES(1952); LET'S DO IT AGAIN(1953); MARJORIE MORNINGSTAR(1958)

V.C. Clinton-Baddeley
HIS LORDSHIP(1932, Brit.); BORN THAT WAY(1937, Brit.), w

The Clippers
ENTERTAINER, THE(1960, Brit.)

Edward Clisbee
Misc. Silents
PITFALL, THE(1915)

Jack Clisby
STANLEY AND LIVINGSTONE(1939); LOOK OUT SISTER(1948); KNOCK ON ANY DOOR(1949); BOMBA AND THE JUNGLE GIRL(1952)

Neal Clisby
FRENCHMAN'S CREEK(1944)

Jimmy Clitheroe
MUCH TOO SHY(1942, Brit.); RHYTHM SERENADE(1943, Brit.); SCHOOL FOR RANDLE(1949, Brit.); SOMEWHERE IN POLITICS(1949, Brit.); STARS IN YOUR EYES(1956, Brit.); THOSE FANTASTIC FLYING FOOLS(1967, Brit)

Colin Clive
JOURNEY'S END(1930); FRANKENSTEIN(1931); STRONGER SEX, THE(1931, Brit.); LILY CHRISTINE(1932, Brit.); CHRISTOPHER STRONG(1933); LOOKING FORWARD(1933); KEY, THE(1934); ONE MORE RIVER(1934); CLIVE OF INDIA(1935); GIRL FROM TENTH AVENUE, THE(1935); JANE EYRE(1935); MAD LOVE(1935); MAN WHO BROKE THE BANK AT MONTE CARLO, THE(1935); RIGHT TO LIVE, THE(1935); WIDOW FROM MONTE CARLO, THE(1936); HISTORY IS MADE AT NIGHT(1937); WOMAN I LOVE, THE(1937)

Donald Clive
WILLIAM COMES TO TOWN(1948, Brit.); MYSTERY AT THE BURLESQUE(1950, Brit.)

E.E. Clive
INVISIBLE MAN, THE(1933); BULLDOG DRUMMOND STRIKES BACK(1934); CHARLIE CHAN IN LONDON(1934); GAY DIVORCEE, THE(1934); LONG LOST FATHER(1934); ONE MORE RIVER(1934); POOR RICH, THE(1934); RIP TIDE(1934); ATLANTIC ADVENTURE(1935); CAPTAIN BLOOD(1935); FATHER BROWN, DETECTIVE(1935); FEATHER IN HER HAT, A(1935); MAN WHO BROKE THE BANK AT MONTE CARLO, THE(1935); MYSTERY OF EDWIN DROOD(1935); PAGE MISS GLORY(1935); REMEMBER LAST NIGHT(1935); STARS OVER BROADWAY(1935); TALE OF TWO CITIES, A(1935); WE'RE IN THE MONEY(1935); ALL-AMERICAN CHUMP(1936); CAIN AND MABEL(1936); CHARGE OF THE LIGHT BRIGADE, THE(1936); DARK HOUR, THE(1936); DRACULA'S DAUGHTER(1936); GOLDEN ARROW, THE(1936); ISLE OF FURY(1936); LIBELED LADY(1936); LITTLE LORD FAUNTLEROY(1936); LLOYDS OF LONDON(1936); LOVE BEFORE BREAKFAST(1936); PALM SPRINGS(1936); PICCADILLY JIM(1936); SHOW BOAT(1936); SYLVIA SCARLETT(1936); TARZAN ESCAPES(1936); TICKET TO PARADISE(1936); TROUBLE FOR TWO(1936); UNGUARDED HOUR, THE(1936); WIDOW FROM MONTE CARLO, THE(1936); BEG, BORROW OR STEAL(1937); BULLDOG DRUMMOND COMES BACK(1937); BULLDOG DRUMMOND ESCAPES(1937); CAMILLE(1937); EMPEROR'S CANDLESTICKS, THE(1937); GREAT GARRICK, THE(1937); IT'S LOVE I'M AFTER(1937); LIVE, LOVE AND LEARN(1937); LOVE UNDER FIRE(1937); MAID OF SALEM(1937); NIGHT MUST FALL(1937); ON THE AVENUE(1937); PERSONAL PROPERTY(1937); READY, WILLING AND ABLE(1937); ROAD BACK, THE(1937); THEY WANTED TO MARRY(1937); ARSENE LUPIN RETURNS(1938); BULLDOG DRUMMOND IN AFRICA(1938); BULLDOG DRUMMOND'S PERIL(1938); FIRST 100 YEARS, THE(1938); GATEWAY(1938); KIDNAPPED(1938); LAST WARNING, THE(1938); SUBMARINE PATROL(1938); ADVENTURES OF SHERLOCK HOLMES, THE(1939); ARREST BULLDOG DRUMMOND(1939, Brit.); BACHELOR MOTHER(1939); BULLDOG DRUMMOND'S BRIDE(1939); BULLDOG DRUMMOND'S SECRET POLICE(1939); HONEYMOON'S OVER, THE(1939); HOUND OF THE BASKERVILLES, THE(1939); I'M FROM MISSOURI(1939); LITTLE PRINCESS, THE(1939); MAN ABOUT TOWN(1939); MR. MOTO'S LAST WARNING(1939); RAFFLES(1939); ROSE OF WASHINGTON SQUARE(1939); WE ARE NOT ALONE(1939); ADVENTURE IN DIAMONDS(1940); CONGO MAISIE(1940); EARL OF CHICAGO, THE(1940); FOREIGN CORRESPONDENT(1940); PRIDE AND PREJUDICE(1940)

Henry Clive
OBEY THE LAW(1933)
Silents
FIGHTING ODDS(1917); I WANT TO FORGET(1918)
Misc. Silents
HER SILENT SACRIFICE(1917); ON THE JUMP(1918); OATH, THE(1921)

Iris Clive
RENEGADES OF THE RIO GRANDE(1945); CAT CREEPS, THE(1946); SONG OF THE SIERRAS(1946); WEST OF THE ALAMO(1946)
Misc. Talkies
LONESOME TRAIL(1945)

Iris Clive [Eden]
SOUTH OF DIXIE(1944)

Joe Clive
SHE COULDN'T TAKE IT(1935)

John Clive
YELLOW SUBMARINE(1958, Brit.); SMASHING TIME(1967 Brit.); MINI-AFFAIR, THE(1968, Brit.); ITALIAN JOB, THE(1969, Brit.); NICE GIRL LIKE ME, A(1969, Brit.); CLOCKWORK ORANGE, A(1971, Brit.); NO LONGER ALONE(1978); REVENGE OF THE PINK PANTHER(1978)

Madeline Clive
MADIGAN(1968)

Robert Clive
WEST OF SINGAPORE(1933, ph; HE SNOOPS TO CONQUER(1944, Brit.)

Vincent Clive
WATCH BEVERLY(1932, Brit.)

Al Cliver
ZOMBIE(1980, Ital.)
1984
BLACK CAT, THE(1984, Ital./Brit.)
Misc. Talkies
MISTER SCARFACE(1977); ENDGAME(1984)

Theodore Cloak
JULIUS CAESAR(1952)

Maurice Cloche
DOCTEUR LAENNEC(1949, Fr.), p&d; MONSIEUR VINCENT(1949, Fr.), d, w; NEVER TAKE NO FOR AN ANSWER(1952, Brit./Ital.), d, w; SELLERS OF GIRLS(1967, Fr.), d&w; VISCOUNT, THE(1967, Fr./Span./Ital./Ger.), d

Rene Cloerea
ENOUGH ROPE(1966, Fr./Ital./Ger.), m

Paul Cloerec
CAGE OF NIGHTINGALES, A(1947, Fr.), m; RED AND THE BLACK, THE(1954, Fr./Ital.), m

Rene Cloerec
DEVIL IN THE FLESH, THE(1949, Fr.), m; LOVE STORY(1949, Fr.), m; SYLVIA AND THE PHANTOM(1950, Fr.), m; ADVENTURES OF CAPTAIN FABIAN(1951), m; DISOBEDIENT(1953, Brit.), m; JOHNNY THE GIANT KILLER(1953, Fr.), m; RED, INN, THE(1954, Fr.), m; LOVE IS MY PROFESSION(1959, Fr.), m; STORY OF THE COUNT OF MONTE CRISTO, THE(1962, Fr./Ital.), m

Rene Cloeree
MR. ORCHID(1948, Fr.), w; GAME OF LOVE, THE(1954, Fr.), m

Anna Cloete
HELLIONS, THE(1962, Brit.)

Stuart Cloete
FIERCEST HEART, THE(1961), w

Charles Cloffi
THIEF WHO CAME TO DINNER, THE(1973)

Butler Clonebaugh [Gustau_von Seyffertiz]
Misc. Silents
'TILL I COME BACK TO YOU(1918)

G. Butler Clonebaugh
Misc. Silents
SECRET GARDEN, THE(1919), d

Ralph Cloninger
Misc. Silents
MAN WHO WON, THE(1923); WINDS OF THE PAMPAS(1927)

Rosemary Clooney
HERE COME THE GIRLS(1953); STARS ARE SINGING, THE(1953); DEEP IN MY HEART(1954); RED GARTERS(1954); WHITE CHRISTMAS(1954)

Hans Peter Cloos
GERMANY IN AUTUMN(1978, Ger.), a, d

Ghislain Cloquest
FOUR FRIENDS(1981), ph

Ghislain Cloquet
LA BELLE AMERICAINE(1961, Fr.), ph; NUDE IN HIS POCKET(1962, Fr.), ph; FIRE WITHIN, THE(1964, Fr./Ital.), ph; NIGHT WATCH, THE(1964, Fr./Ital.), ph; MICKEY ONE(1965), ph; BENJAMIN(1968, Fr.), ph; ONE NIGHT... A TRAIN(1968, Fr./Bel.), ph; YOUNG GIRLS OF ROCHEFORT, THE(1968, Fr.), ph; MARRY ME! MARRY ME!(1969, Fr.), ph; AU HASARD, BALTHAZAR(1970, Fr.), ph; MOUCHETTE(1970, Fr.), ph; GENTLE CREATURE, A(1971, Fr.), ph; NATHALIE GRANGER(1972, Fr.), ph; DONKEY SKIN(1975, Fr.), ph; LOVE AND DEATH(1975), ph; TESS(1980, Fr./Brit.), ph; FOUR FRIENDS(1981), ph; I SENT A LETTER TO MY LOVE(1981, Fr.), ph

Leon Clore
PASSING STRANGER, THE(1954, Brit.), p; VIRGIN ISLAND(1960, Brit.), p; MORGAN!(1966, Brit.), p; ALL NEAT IN BLACK STOCKINGS(1969, Brit.), p; FRENCH LIEUTENANT'S WOMAN, THE(1981), p

Rene Clorec
FOUR BAGS FULL(1957, Fr./Ital.), m; GREEN MARE, THE(1961, Fr./Ital.), m

Enrico Clori
DISILLUSION(1949, Ital.)

Harry Clork
DIAMOND JIM(1935), w; HIS NIGHT OUT(1935), w; KING SOLOMON OF BROADWAY(1935), w; MR. DYNAMITE(1935), w; PRINCESS O'HARA(1935), w; REMEMBER LAST NIGHT(1935), w; FLYING HOSTESS(1936), w; MAN I MARRY, THE(1936), w; MILKY WAY, THE(1936), w; OH DOCTOR(1937), w; WHEN'S YOUR BIRTHDAY?(1937), w; FLIRTING WITH FATE(1938), w; LAUGH IT OFF(1939), w; CAPTAIN IS A LADY, THE(1940), w; LA CONGA NIGHTS(1940), w; MOON OVER BURMA(1940), w; LAS VEGAS NIGHTS(1941), w; WHISTLING IN THE DARK(1941), w; BORN TO SING(1942), w; SHIP AHOY(1942), w; BROADWAY RHYTHM(1944), w; SEE MY LAWYER(1945), w; KID FROM BOOKLYN, THE(1946), w; THRILL OF BRAZIL, THE(1946), w; SAINTED SISTERS, THE(1948), w; TEA FOR TWO(1950), w; MA AND PA KETTLE AT WAIKIKI(1955), w

Alberto Closas
AGE OF INFIDELITY(1958, Span.); GIRL FROM VALLADOLIO(1958, Span.)

Enrique Closas
CEREMONY, THE(1963, U.S./Span.)

Del Close
AMERICAN GRAFFITI(1973); LAST AFFAIR, THE(1976); THIEF(1981)

Glenn Close
WORLD ACCORDING TO GARP, The(1982); BIG CHILL, THE(1983)
1984
NATURAL, THE(1984); STONE BOY, THE(1984)

Ivy Close
Silents
LURE OF LONDON, THE(1914, Brit.); DARKEST LONDON(1915, Brit.); WARE CASE, THE(1917, Brit.); ADAM BEDE(1918, Brit.); MISSING THE TIDE(1918, Brit.); NELSON(1918, Brit.); PEEP BEHIND THE SCENES, A(1918, Brit.); FLAG LIEUTENANT, THE(1919, Brit.); WORLDLINGS, THE(1920, Brit.)
Misc. Silents
HOUSE OPPOSITE, THE(1917, Brit.); DARBY AND JOAN(1919, Brit.); HER CROSS(1919, Brit.); IRRESISTIBLE FLAPPER, THE(1919, Brit.); EXPIATION(1922, Brit.); WAS SHE JUSTIFIED?(1922, Brit.); LA ROUE(1923, Fr.)

James Close
DEVIL'S ROCK(1938, Brit.)

John Close
WHERE THE SIDEWALK ENDS(1950); GUY WHO CAME BACK, THE(1951); LET'S GO NAVY(1951); PAT AND MIKE(1952); RED SKIES OF MONTANA(1952); YOU FOR ME(1952); ABOVE AND BEYOND(1953); FANGS OF THE ARCTIC(1953); FARMER TAKES A WIFE, THE(1953); GENTLEMEN PREFER BLONDES(1953); TORPEDO ALLEY(1953); DRIVE A CROOKED ROAD(1954); THEM!(1954); FINGER MAN(1955); SUDDEN DANGER(1955); BEGINNING OF THE END(1957); CHAIN OF EVIDENCE(1957); STORM RIDER, THE(1957); THREE BRAVE MEN(1957); NO TIME FOR SERGEANTS(1958); OUTCASTS OF THE CITY(1958); STREET OF DARKNESS(1958); PURPLE GANG, THE(1960); CONVICTS FOUR(1962); SLIME PEOPLE, THE(1963)
Misc. Talkies
STREET OF DARKNESS(1958)

John V. Close
KOREA PATROL(1951); SAILOR BEWARE(1951); SUBMARINE COMMAND(1951)

Johnny Close
GIRL ON THE BRIDGE, THE(1951)

Juanita Close
ON THE THRESHOLD OF SPACE(1956); PROUD ONES, THE(1956); THREE BRAVE MEN(1957)

Julian Close
UP IN THE AIR(1969, Brit.); REVOLUTIONARY, THE(1970, Brit.)

Pat Close
SUNRISE AT CAMPOBELLO(1960)

William Close
VOICE OF THE HURRICANE(1964)

Ron Closky
MOONSHINE MOUNTAIN(1964), ed

Richie Closs
WHITE RAT(1972)

Emmanuel Clot
LOVE ON THE RUN(1980, Fr.)

Carmen Clothier
CONFIDENCE GIRL(1952)

Gary L. Clothier
ACE ELI AND RODGER OF THE SKIES(1973)

Robert Clothier
SILENCE OF THE NORTH(1981, Can.)
1984
FINDERS KEEPERS(1984)

William Clothier
FOR YOU I DIE(1947), ph; SOFIA(1948), ph; CONFIDENCE GIRL(1952), ph; PHANTOM FROM SPACE(1953), ph; SEA CHASE, THE(1955), ph; TOP OF THE WORLD(1955), ph; BOMBERS B-52(1957), ph; DRAGON WELLS MASSACRE(1957), ph; GUN THE MAN DOWN(1957), ph; CHINA DOLL(1958), ph; DARBY'S RANGERS(1958), ph; FORT DOBBS(1958), ph; LAFAYETTE ESCADRILLE(1958), ph; ESCORT WEST(1959), ph; HORSE SOLDIERS, THE(1959), ph; DEADLY COMPANIONS, THE(1961), ph; MERRILL'S MARAUDERS(1962), ph; DONOVAN'S REEF(1963), ph; CHEYENNE AUTUMN(1964), ph; DISTANT TRUMPET, A(1964), ph; FIRECREEK(1968), ph; UNDEFEATED, THE(1969), ph; CHEYENNE SOCIAL CLUB, THE(1970), ph; RIO LOBO(1970), ph; BIG JAKE(1971), ph

William H. Clothier
ONCE A THIEF(1950), ph; ISLAND IN THE SKY(1953), ph; HIGH AND THE MIGHTY, THE(1954), ph; KILLERS FROM SPACE(1954), ph; TRACK OF THE CAT(1954), ph; BLOOD ALLEY(1955), ph; GANG BUSTERS(1955), p, ph; SINCERELY YOURS(1955), ph; GOODBYE, MY LADY(1956), ph; MAN IN THE VAULT(1956), ph; SEVEN MEN FROM NOW(1956), ph; ALAMO, THE(1960), ph; COMANCHEROS, THE(1961), ph; RING OF FIRE(1961), ph; TOMBOY AND THE CHAMP(1961), ph; MAN WHO SHOT LIBERTY VALANCE, THE(1962), ph; MC LINTOCK!(1963), ph; SHENANDOAH(1965), ph; RARE BREED, THE(1966), ph; STAGECOACH(1966), ph; WAY...WAY OUT(1966), ph; WAR WAGON, THE(1967), ph; WAY WEST, THE(1967), ph; BANDOLERO!(1968), ph; DEVIL'S BRIGADE, THE(1968), ph; HELLFIGHTERS(1968), ph; CHISUM(1970), ph; TRAIN ROBBERS, THE(1973), ph

Clotilde
PATERNITY(1981)

Belinda Cloud
1984
WHAT YOU TAKE FOR GRANTED(1984)

Chief Dark Cloud
Misc. Silents
WHAT AM I BID?(1919)

Dark Cloud
Silents
DISHONORED MEDAL, THE(1914); PENITENTES, THE(1915)
Misc. Silents
WOMAN UNTAMED, THE(1920)

Margaret Cloud
Misc. Silents
HE WHO LAUGHS LAST(1925); BROADWAY MADNESS(1927)

Mrs. Dark Cloud
Silents
CRIMSON CHALLENGE, THE(1922)

Paul Cloud
1941(1979)

Red Cloud
HOW THE WEST WAS WON(1962)

Tom Cloud
LADY GODIVA(1955)
Elizabeth Cloud-Miller
LUCY GALLANT(1955)
Cloudia
THOSE LIPS, THOSE EYES(1980), set d
1984
BODY DOUBLE(1984), set d
Inez Clough
Misc. Silents
SIMP, THE(1921); TIES OF BLOOD(1921); EASY MONEY(1922)
Ann Philip Clouse
DREAMS OF GLASS(1969), art d
Jim Clouse
PURSUIT OF D.B. COOPER, THE(1981)
Robert Clouse
DREAMS OF GLASS(1969), p,d&w; DARKER THAN AMBER(1970), d; ENTER THE DRAGON(1973), d; HAPPY MOTHER'S DAY... LOVE, GEORGE(1973), w; BLACK BELT JONES(1974), d; GOLDEN NEEDLES(1974), d; ULTIMATE WARRIOR, THE(1975), d&w; PACK, THE(1977), d&w; AMSTERDAM KILL, THE(1978, Hong Kong), d, w; GAME OF DEATH, THE(1979), d; BIG BRAWL, THE(1980), d&w; FORCE: FIVE(1981), d&w; DEADLY EYES(1982), d
Misc. Talkies
BLACK BELT JONES(1974), d
J. Storer Clouston
U-BOAT 29(1939, Brit.), w
Raymond Cloutier
RED(1970, Can.); TWO SOLITUDES(1978, Can.); CORDELIA(1980, Fr., Can.)
Misc. Talkies
RIEL(1979)
Suzanne Cloutier
TEMPTATION(1946); FOUR AGAINST FATE(1952, Brit.); DOCTOR IN THE HOUSE(1954, Brit.); OTHELLO(1955, U.S./Fr./Ital.); ROMANOFF AND JULIET(1961)
Henri G. Clouzot
WAGES OF FEAR, THE(1955, Fr./Ital.), p&d, w
Henri-Georges Clouzot
LE MONDE TREMBLERA(1939, Fr.), w; MURDERER LIVES AT NUMBER 21, THE(1947, Fr.), d, w; JENNY LAMOUR(1948, Fr.), d, w; RAVEN, THE(1948, Fr.), d, w; STRANGERS IN THE HOUSE(1949, Fr.), w; MANON(1950, Fr.), d, w; DIABOLIQUE(1955, Fr.), p&d, w; TRUTH, THE(1961, Fr./Ital.), d, w; LA PRISONNIERE(1969, Fr./Ital.), d, w
Jean Clouzot
DANIELLA BY NIGHT(1962, Fr/Ger.), w
Vera Clouzot
DIABOLIQUE(1955, Fr.); WAGES OF FEAR, THE(1955, Fr./Ital.); TRUTH, THE(1961, Fr./Ital.), w
Robert Clovel
NATHALIE, AGENT SECRET(1960, Fr.), set d
Cecil Clovelly
SO YOUNG, SO BAD(1950); TWO GALS AND A GUY(1951)
Silents
DR. JEKYLL AND MR. HYDE(1920)
David Clover
MALIBU BEACH(1978); WARGAMES(1983)
Ed Clover
1984
DUBEAT-E-O(1984), ph
Mary Cloverdale
Silents
OUT YONDER(1920)
George Clow
STARK FEAR(1963); RUN FOR YOUR WIFE(1966, Fr./Ital.); ONLY WAY HOME, THE(1972)
Alan Clowes
REINCARNATE, THE(1971, Can.)
John L. Clowes
GRAND PRIX(1934, Brit.), d&w
St. John L. Clowes
GRAND PRIX(1934, Brit.), p; BATTLE FOR MUSIC(1943, Brit.), w; SOLDIER, SAILOR(1944, Brit.), w
Misc. Silents
FROZEN FATE(1929, Brit.), d
St. John Legh Clowes
DEAR MURDERER(1947, Brit.), w; NO ORCHIDS FOR MISS BLANDISH(1948, Brit.), d&w; THINGS HAPPEN AT NIGHT(1948, Brit.), w
May Cloy
KNICKERBOCKER HOLIDAY(1944)
Misc. Silents
BLUFF(1916); MILLION FOR MARY, A(1916); PECK O' PICKLES(1916); THREE PALS(1916); BELOVED ROGUES(1917); BROTH FOR SUPPER(1919)
David Clrake
NARROW MARGIN, THE(1952)
Malay Clu
LAST OUTPOST, THE(1935)
Daniel Clucas
HIGH ROAD TO CHINA(1983)
E.B. Clucher [Enzo Barboni]
UNHOLY FOUR, THE(1969, Ital.), d; THEY CALL ME TRINITY(1971, Ital.), d&w; TRINITY IS STILL MY NAME(1971, Ital.), d&w; MAN FROM THE EAST, A(1974, Ital./Fr.), d&w
Penny Cluer
WICKER MAN, THE(1974, Brit.)
Jack Cluett
WHAT! NO BEER?(1933), w
Jennifer Cluff
FINAL CUT, THE(1980, Aus.)
1984
BROTHERS(1984, Aus.)

Misc. Talkies
DEATHGAMES(1981)
Franco Cluffi
LUCIANO(1963, Ital.)
Kirk Clugeston
OLIVER!(1968, Brit.)
H. M. Clugston
Silents
NAVIGATOR, THE(1924)
H. N. Clugston
BULLDOG DRUMMOND STRIKES BACK(1934)
Katherine Clugston
FINISHING SCHOOL(1934), w; LAST GENTLEMAN, THE(1934), w
Robert Clugston
Silents
KICK IN(1917)
Misc. Silents
ISLE OF LOVE, THE(1916); HUNTING OF THE HAWK, THE(1917); SIREN, THE(1917)
Woodworth Clum
WALK THE PROUD LAND(1956), w
Peter Clume
BLAST OF SILENCE(1961)
Raymond Clumy
SECOND BUREAU(1936, Fr.), ph
Anne Clune
HANDS OF ORLAC, THE(1964, Brit./Fr.); OBLONG BOX, THE(1969, Brit.); HANDS OF THE RIPPER(1971, Brit.)
Peter Clune
JUKE BOX RACKET(1960); DIRTYMOUTH(1970)
Misc. Talkies
BLUE SEXTET(1972)
Peter H. Clune
STIGMA(1972)
William Clune
MOLLY MAGUIRES, THE(1970)
Alec Clunes
SALOON BAR(1940, Brit.); THREE COCKEYED SAILORS(1940, Brit.); ONE OF OUR AIRCRAFT IS MISSING(1942, Brit.); NOW BARABBAS WAS A ROBBER(1949, Brit.); MELBA(1953, Brit.); QUENTIN DURWARD(1955); RICHARD III(1956, Brit.); TIGER IN THE SMOKE(1956, Brit.); TOMORROW AT TEN(1964, Brit.)
Genevieve Cluny
COUSINS, THE(1959, Fr.); JOKER, THE(1961, Fr.); HOUSE OF CARDS(1969)
Harold Clurman
DEADLINE AT DAWN(1946), d
May Cluskey
OF HUMAN BONDAGE(1964, Brit.); YOUNG CASSIDY(1965, U.S./Brit.); ULYSSES(1967, U.S./Brit.); RYAN'S DAUGHTER(1970, Brit.)
Chester Clute
DANCE, CHARLIE, DANCE(1937); EXCLUSIVE(1937); GREAT GARRICK, THE(1937); LIVE, LOVE AND LEARN(1937); LIVING ON LOVE(1937); NAVY BLUES(1937); THERE GOES MY GIRL(1937); TRUE CONFESSION(1937); WRONG ROAD, THE(1937); ANNABEL TAKES A TOUR(1938); ARSENE LUPIN RETURNS(1938); ARTISTS AND MODELS ABROAD(1938); COMET OVER BROADWAY(1938); GO CHASE YOURSELF(1938); HE COULDN'T SAY NO(1938); LETTER OF INTRODUCTION(1938); MR. CHUMP(1938); RASCALS(1938); RECKLESS LIVING(1938); SERVICE DE LUXE(1938); YOU CAN'T TAKE IT WITH YOU(1938); DANCING CO-ED(1939); DODGE CITY(1939); EAST SIDE OF HEAVEN(1939); HONEYMOON'S OVER, THE(1939); I WAS A CONVICT(1939); LAUGH IT OFF(1939); MIRACLES FOR SALE(1939); PARDON OUR NERVE(1939); SPELLBINDER, THE(1939); TELEVISION SPY(1939); TELL NO TALES(1939); BLONDIE ON A BUDGET(1940); DANCE, GIRL, DANCE(1940); DOCTOR TAKES A WIFE(1940); HIRED WIFE(1940); INVISIBLE STRIPES(1940); LITTLE BIT OF HEAVEN, A(1940); LOVE THY NEIGHBOR(1940); MILLIONAIRES IN PRISON(1940); MY FAVORITE WIFE(1940); PUBLIC DEB NO. 1(1940); REMEMBER THE NIGHT(1940); TOO MANY GIRLS(1940); TWO GIRLS ON BROADWAY(1940); FOOTLIGHT FEVER(1941); HOLD BACK THE DAWN(1941); MANPOWER(1941); NEW YORK TOWN(1941); PERFECT SNOB, THE(1941); SCATTERGOOD MEETS BROADWAY(1941); SHE COULDN'T SAY NO(1941); SHE KNEW ALL THE ANSWERS(1941); SUN VALLEY SERENADE(1941); THEY MET IN ARGENTINA(1941); THREE GIRLS ABOUT TOWN(1941); UNFINISHED BUSINESS(1941); FLEET'S IN, THE(1942); FOREST RANGERS, THE(1942); GEORGE WASHINGTON SLEPT HERE(1942); GET HEP TO LOVE(1942); JOAN OF OZARK(1942); JUST OFF BROADWAY(1942); LADY IS WILLING, THE(1942); LARCENY, INC.(1942); MAN WHO CAME TO DINNER, THE(1942); MEET THE STEWARTS(1942); MY FAVORITE SPY(1942); PARDON MY SARONG(1942); SPOILERS, THE(1942); STAR SPANGLED RHYTHM(1942); THIS GUN FOR HIRE(1942); VALLEY OF THE SUN(1942); WIFE TAKES A FLYER, THE(1942); YANKEE DOODLE DANDY(1942); CHATTERBOX(1943); CRAZY HOUSE(1943); DESPERADOES, THE(1943); DU BARRY WAS A LADY(1943); FALSE FACES(1943); GOOD FELLOWS, THE(1943); HERE COMES ELMER(1943); MORE THE MERRIER, THE(1943); NO PLACE FOR A LADY(1943); SING A JINGLE(1943); SOMEONE TO REMEMBER(1943); SO'S YOUR UNCLE(1943); WEST SIDE KID(1943); ARSENIC AND OLD LACE(1944); EVER SINCE VENUS(1944); FALCON IN HOLLYWOOD, THE(1944); HAT CHECK HONEY(1944); JOHNNY DOESN'T LIVE HERE ANY MORE(1944); LAKE PLACID SERENADE(1944); MY GAL LOVES MUSIC(1944); NOTHING BUT TROUBLE(1944); RATIONING(1944); RECKLESS AGE(1944); SAN DIEGO, I LOVE YOU(1944); THIN MAN GOES HOME, THE(1944); ABBOTT AND COSTELLO IN HOLLYWOOD(1945); ANCHORS AWEIGH(1945); ARSON SQUAD(1945); BLONDE RANSOM(1945); CLOCK, THE(1945); DANGEROUS PARTNERS(1945); EARL CARROLL'S VANITIES(1945); GUEST WIFE(1945); LADY ON A TRAIN(1945); MAN WHO WALKED ALONE, THE(1945); MILDRED PIERCE(1945); ON STAGE EVERYBODY(1945); ROUGHLY SPEAKING(1945); SARATOGA TRUNK(1945); SHE GETS HER MAN(1945); SHE WENT TO THE RACES(1945); SWING OUT, SISTER(1945); TWO O'CLOCK COURAGE(1945); WONDER MAN(1945); ANGEL ON MY SHOULDER(1946); CINDERELLA JONES(1946); DOWN MISSOURI WAY(1946); GENTLEMAN MISBEHAVES, THE(1946); NIGHT AND DAY(1946); ONE EXCITING WEEK(1946); SECRET HEART, THE(1946); SPOOK BUSTERS(1946); TO EACH HIS OWN(1946); TWO SISTERS FROM BOSTON(1946); CRIMSON KEY, THE(1947); DEAD RECKONING(1947); EASY COME, EASY GO(1947); HIT PARADE OF 1947(1947); IT HAPPENED ON 5TH AVENUE(1947); LIKELY STORY, A(1947);

PERILS OF PAULINE, THE(1947); SOMETHING IN THE WIND(1947); SUDDENLY IT'S SPRING(1947); WEB OF DANGER, THE(1947); BLONDIE'S REWARD(1948); JOE PALOOKA IN WINNER TAKE ALL(1948); MARY LOU(1948); ON AN ISLAND WITH YOU(1948); ON OUR MERRY WAY(1948); STRANGE MRS. CRANE, THE(1948); TRAIN TO ALCATRAZ(1948); BLONDIE'S BIG DEAL(1949); GIRL FROM JONES BEACH, THE(1949); MARY RYAN, DETECTIVE(1949); MASTER MINDS(1949); MY DREAM IS YOURS(1949); RINGSIDE(1949); SQUARE DANCE JUBILEE(1949); HUMPHREY TAKES A CHANCE(1950); LUCKY LOSERS(1950); KENTUCKY JUBILEE(1951); STOP THAT CAB(1951); COLORADO SUNDOWN(1952)

John Clute
WINTER KEPT US WARM(1968, Can.), w

Sid Clute
BIG HEAT, THE(1953); CRIME AND PUNISHMENT, U.S.A.(1959); INSIDE THE MAFIA(1959); FIVE BRANDED WOMEN(1960)

Sidney Clute
THEN THERE WERE THREE(1961); CRY OF BATTLE(1963); I LOVE YOU, ALICE B. TOKLAS!(1968); SAM WHISKEY(1969); WHO FEARS THE DEVIL(1972); EXECUTIVE ACTION(1973); WALKING TALL(1973); BREAKOUT(1975); MITCHELL(1975); VIVA KNIEVEL!(1977); BIG FIX, THE(1978); STING II, THE(1983)

George Clutesi
NIGHTWING(1979); PROPHECY(1979); SPIRIT OF THE WIND(1979); RUNNING BRAVE(1983, Can.)
1984
ISAAC LITTLEFEATHERS(1984, Can.)
Misc. Talkies
KELLY(1981, Can.)

G.H. Clutsam
MIMI(1935, Brit.), m; BIG FELLA(1937, Brit.), m; HEART'S DESIRE(1937, Brit.), md

Francois Cluzet
COCKTAIL MOLOTOV(1980, Fr.); HORSE OF PRIDE(1980, Fr.); ENTRE NOUS(1983, Fr.)
1984
ONE DEADLY SUMMER(1984, Fr.)

Clyde
EVERY WHICH WAY BUT LOOSE(1978)

Andy Clyde
MIDNIGHT DADDIES(1929); SHOULD A GIRL MARRY?(1929); MILLION DOLLAR LEGS(1932); LITTLE MINISTER, THE(1934); ANNIE OAKLEY(1935); MC FADDEN'S FLATS(1935); ROMANCE IN MANHATTAN(1935); VILLAGE TALE(1935); STRAIGHT FROM THE SHOULDER(1936); TWO IN A CROWD(1936); YELLOW DUST(1936); BARRIER, THE(1937); RED LIGHTS AHEAD(1937); BAD LANDS(1939); IT'S A WONDERFUL WORLD(1939); ABE LINCOLN IN ILLINOIS(1940); CHEROKEE STRIP(1940); THREE MEN FROM TEXAS(1940); BORDER VIGILANTES(1941); DOOMED CARAVAN(1941); IN OLD COLORADO(1941); OUTLAWS OF THE DESERT(1941); PIRATES ON HORSEBACK(1941); RIDERS OF THE TIMBERLINE(1941); SECRETS OF THE WASTELANDS(1941); STICK TO YOUR GUNS(1941); TWILIGHT ON THE TRAIL(1941); WIDE OPEN TOWN(1941); THIS ABOVE ALL(1942); UNDERCOVER MAN(1942); BAR 20(1943); BORDER PATROL(1943); COLT COMRADES(1943); FALSE COLORS(1943); HOPPY SERVES A WRIT(1943); LEATHER BURNERS, THE(1943); LOST CANYON(1943); RIDERS OF THE DEADLINE(1943); FORTY THIEVES(1944); LUMBERJACK(1944); MYSTERY MAN(1944); TEXAS MASQUERADE(1944); ROUGHLY SPEAKING(1945); DEVIL'S PLAYGROUND, THE(1946); FOOL'S GOLD(1946); GREEN YEARS, THE(1946); PLAINSMAN AND THE LADY(1946); UNEXPECTED GUEST(1946); DANGEROUS VENTURE(1947); HOPPY'S HOLIDAY(1947); MARAUDERS, THE(1947); BORROWED TROUBLE(1948); DEAD DON'T DREAM, THE(1948); FALSE PARADISE(1948); SILENT CONFLICT(1948); SINISTER JOURNEY(1948); STRANGE GAMBLE(1948); SUNDOWN RIDERS(1948); CRASHING THRU(1949); RANGE LAND(1949); RIDERS OF THE DUSK(1949); SHADOWS OF THE WEST(1949); ARIZONA TERRITORY(1950); CHEROKEE UPRISING(1950); FENCE RIDERS(1950); GUNSLINGERS(1950); OUTLAWS OF TEXAS(1950); SILVER RAIDERS(1950); ABILENE TRAIL(1951); CAROLINA CANNONBALL(1955); ROAD TO DENVER, THE(1955)
Misc. Talkies
SONG OF THE PRAIRIE(1945); THAT TEXAS JAMBOREE(1946); THROW A SADDLE ON A STAR(1946); HAUNTED TRAILS(1949)
Silents
GOOD-BYE KISS, THE(1928)
Misc. Silents
SHIPS OF THE NIGHT(1928)

Craig Clyde
HANGAR 18(1980)

Dave Clyde
TONIGHT AND EVERY NIGHT(1945)

David Clyde
HARD ROCK HARRIGAN(1935); MAN ON THE FLYING TRAPEZE, THE(1935); GIRL FROM MANDALAY(1936); MESSAGE TO GARCIA, A(1936); PRINCESS COMES ACROSS, THE(1936); ROSE MARIE(1936); SUZY(1936); ANOTHER DAWN(1937); BULLDOG DRUMMOND ESCAPES(1937); FURY AND THE WOMAN(1937); LANCER SPY(1937); LOST HORIZON(1937); LOVE UNDER FIRE(1937); BULLDOG DRUMMOND'S PERIL(1938); KIDNAPPED(1938); ARREST BULLDOG DRUMMOND(1939, Brit.); DEATH OF A CHAMPION(1939); RULERS OF THE SEA(1939); WE ARE NOT ALONE(1939); ADVENTURE IN DIAMONDS(1940); EARL OF CHICAGO, THE(1940); I TAKE THIS WOMAN(1940); MY SON, MY SON!(1940); PHILADELPHIA STORY, THE(1940); WATERLOO BRIDGE(1940); FEMININE TOUCH, THE(1941); H.M. PULHAM, ESQ.(1941); ONE NIGHT IN LISBON(1941); RAGE IN HEAVEN(1941); SMILIN' THROUGH(1941); THEY MET IN BOMBAY(1941); GAY SISTERS, THE(1942); GREAT MAN'S LADY, THE(1942); MRS. MINIVER(1942); NIGHTMARE(1942); NOW, VOYAGER(1942); MYSTERIOUS DOCTOR, THE(1943); PRINCESS O'ROURKE(1943); FRENCHMAN'S CREEK(1944); HOUR BEFORE THE DAWN, THE(1944); JANE EYRE(1944); LODGER, THE(1944); NONE BUT THE LONELY HEART(1944); SCARLET CLAW, THE(1944); UNINVITED, THE(1944); HOUSE OF FEAR, THE(1945); LOST WEEKEND, THE(1945); LOVE LETTERS(1945); MINISTRY OF FEAR(1945); MOLLY AND ME(1945); SALTY O'ROURKE(1945); DEVOTION(1946); TWO YEARS BEFORE THE MAST(1946)

Jean Clyde
MARIGOLD(1938, Brit.); POISON PEN(1941, Brit.)

Jeremy Clyde
GREAT ST. TRINIAN'S TRAIN ROBBERY, THE(1966, Brit.); SILVER BEARS(1978); FFOLKES(1980, Brit.)

Jonathan Clyde
FOLLOW THAT HORSE!(1960, Brit.)

June Clyde
TANNED LEGS(1929); CUCKOOS, THE(1930); HIT THE DECK(1930); MIDNIGHT MYSTERY(1930); BRANDED MEN(1931); MAD PARADE, THE(1931); MEN ARE LIKE THAT(1931); MORALS FOR WOMEN(1931); SECRET WITNESS, THE(1931); ALL-AMERICAN, THE(1932); COHENS, AND KELLYS IN HOLLYWOOD, THE(1932); FILE 113(1932); RACING YOUTH(1932); RADIO PATROL(1932); STEADY COMPANY(1932); STRANGE ADVENTURE(1932); TESS OF THE STORM COUNTRY(1932); THRILL OF YOUTH(1932); FORGOTTEN(1933); HER RESALE VALUE(1933); HOLD ME TIGHT(1933); ONLY YESTERDAY(1933); STUDY IN SCARLET, A(1933); HOLLYWOOD MYSTERY(1934); HOLLYWOOD PARTY(1934); CHARING CROSS ROAD(1935, Brit.); DANCE BAND(1935, Brit.); NO MONKEY BUSINESS(1935, Brit.); SHE SHALL HAVE MUSIC(1935, Brit.); FORBIDDEN MUSIC(1936, Brit.); KING OF THE CASTLE(1936, Brit.); AREN'T MEN BEASTS?(1937, Brit.); INTIMATE RELATIONS(1937, Brit.); LET'S MAKE A NIGHT OF IT(1937, Brit.); MAKE-UP(1937, Brit.); SAM SMALL LEAVES TOWN(1937, Brit.); WEDDINGS ARE WONDERFUL(1938, Brit.); HIS LORDSHIP GOES TO PRESS(1939, Brit.); SCHOOL FOR HUSBANDS(1939, Brit.); COUNTRY FAIR(1941); SEALED LIPS(1941); UNFINISHED BUSINESS(1941); HI'YA, CHUM(1943); SEVEN DOORS TO DEATH(1944); HOLLYWOOD AND VINE(1945); BEHIND THE MASK(1946); TREASURE HUNT(1952, Brit.); AFFAIR IN MONTE CARLO(1953, Brit.); NIGHT WITHOUT STARS(1953, Brit.); LOVE LOTTERY, THE(1954, Brit.); AFTER THE BALL(1957, Brit.); STORY OF ESTHER COSTELLO, THE(1957, Brit.)
Misc. Talkies
I HATE WOMEN(1934)

Thomas Clyde
HOSTAGE, THE(1956, Brit.), p; CHASE A CROOKED SHADOW(1958, Brit.), p; FOLLOW THAT HORSE!(1960, Brit.), p; GUNS OF DARKNESS(1962, Brit.), p; MALAGA(1962, Brit.), p; WORK IS A FOUR LETTER WORD(1968, Brit.), p

Walter Clyde
GOING HIGHBROW(1935); STRANDED(1935); STAGE STRUCK(1936); SUBMARINE D-1(1937)

The Clyde Valley Stompers
DREAM MAKER, THE(1963, Brit.)

Gail Clymer
EMBASSY(1972, Brit.)

John B. Clymer
COLLEGE LOVE(1929), w; GIRL OVERBOARD(1929), w; HIS LUCKY DAY(1929), w; LOVE TRAP, THE(1929), w; WHAT MEN WANT(1930), w; HOUSE DIVIDED, A(1932), w; EMERGENCY CALL(1933), w; THANKS FOR LISTENING(1937), w; GENTLEMAN MISBEHAVES, THE(1946), w
Silents
DRIFTER, THE(1916), w; ON RECORD(1917), w; RIDDLE: WOMAN, THE(1920), w; ACCORDING TO HOYLE(1922), w; HILLS OF MISSING MEN(1922), w; PHYLLIS OF THE FOLLIES(1928), w

John Clymer
Silents
LONE EAGLE, THE(1927), w

Warren Clymer
WHERE'S POPPA?(1970), art d; NEW LEAF, A(1971), art d; GODFATHER, THE(1972), art d; RIVALS(1972), prod d, art d

Robert Clymire
CURSE OF BIGFOOT, THE(1972)

Fiona Clyne
HIGH AND DRY(1954, Brit.); BRIDAL PATH, THE(1959, Brit.)

Paula Clyne
SILVER DARLINGS, THE(1947, Brit.)

Phema Clyne
SILVER DARLINGS, THE(1947, Brit.)

Terrell Tanen CMI Ltd.
BOOGEYMAN II(1983), ed

Jan Cmiral
90 DEGREES IN THE SHADE(1966, Czech./Brit.)

Joyce Coad
DEVOTION(1931); X MARKS THE SPOT(1931); CAPTURED(1933)
Silents
SCARLET LETTER, THE(1926); CHILDREN OF DIVORCE(1927); ONE WOMAN TO ANOTHER(1927)
Misc. Silents
MAGIC GARDEN, THE(1927); MOTHER(1927)

Simon Coady
MOUSE AND THE WOMAN, THE(1981, Brit.); GIRO CITY(1982, Brit.)

Terrance P. Coady
VISITING HOURS(1982, Can.)

Dena Coaker
ALOMA OF THE SOUTH SEAS(1941)

Marion Coakley
Silents
ENCHANTED COTTAGE, THE(1924)
Misc. Silents
LOST BATALLION, THE(1919)

Pattie Coakley
Silents
KISS FOR CINDERELLA, A(1926)

Fraser Coalter
Silents
SOCIETY SCANDAL, A(1924)

Lorenza Coalville
DEVIL DOLL(1964, Brit.)

Ray Selfe Coast to Coast Ltd.
1984
DON'T OPEN TILL CHRISTMAS(1984, Brit.), ed

Martha Coastworth
RACING FEVER(1964)

Albert Coates
SONG OF RUSSIA(1943), md; TWO GIRLS AND A SAILOR(1944)

Anne Coates
BECKET(1964, Brit.), ed; ACES HIGH(1977, Brit.), ed

Anne V. Coates
PICKWICK PAPERS, THE(1952, Brit.), ed; FORBIDDEN CARGO(1954, Brit.), ed; TO PARIS WITH LOVE(1955, Brit.), ed; WICKED WIFE(1955, Brit.), ed; TEARS FOR SIMON(1957, Brit.), ed; HORSE'S MOUTH, THE(1958, Brit.), ed; TRUTH ABOUT WOMEN, THE(1958, Brit.), ed; TUNES OF GLORY(1960, Brit.), ed; LAWRENCE OF ARABIA(1962, Brit.), ed; WHY BOTHER TO KNOCK(1964, Brit.), ed; THOSE MAGNIFICENT MEN IN THEIR FLYING MACHINES; OR HOW I FLEWFROM LONDON TO PARIS IN 25 HOURS AND 11 MINUTES(1965, Brit.), ed; YOUNG CASSIDY(1965, U.S./Brit.), ed; HOTEL PARADISO(1966, U.S./Brit.), ed; GREAT CATHERINE(1968, Brit.), ed; ADVENTURERS, THE(1970), ed; FRIENDS(1971, Brit.), ed; PUBLIC EYE, THE(1972, Brit.), ed; NELSON AFFAIR, THE(1973, Brit.), ed; MURDER ON THE ORIENT EXPRESS(1974, Brit.), ed; 11 HARROWHOUSE(1974, Brit.), ed; MAN FRIDAY(1975, Brit.), ed; EAGLE HAS LANDED, THE(1976, Brit.), ed; MEDUSA TOUCH, THE(1978, Brit.), p, ed; LEGACY(1979, Brit.), ed; ELEPHANT MAN, THE(1980, Brit.), ed; RAGTIME(1981), ed; PIRATES OF PENZANCE, THE(1983), ed
1984
GREYSTOKE: THE LEGEND OF TARZAN, LORD OF THE APES(1984), ed

Athol Coates
EAGLE IN A CAGE(1971, U.S./Yugo.)

Carolyn Coates
HUSTLER, THE(1961); EFFECT OF GAMMA RAYS ON MAN-IN-THE-MOON MARIGOLDS, THE(1972); MOMMIE DEAREST(1981); POSTMAN ALWAYS RINGS TWICE, THE(1981)
1984
BUDDY SYSTEM, THE(1984)

Eric Coates
OLD CURIOSITY SHOP, THE(1935, Brit.), m; DAM BUSTERS, THE(1955, Brit.), m

Francis Coates
XTRO(1983, Brit.), spec eff

Franklin B. Coates
Silents
ROMANCE OF THE AIR, A(1919), a, w; JESSE JAMES AS THE OUTLAW(1921), d&w; JESSE JAMES UNDER THE BLACK FLAG(1921), a, d&w

John Coates
TRUE AS A TURTLE(1957, Brit.), w

Kevin Coates
BUCK ROGERS IN THE 25TH CENTURY(1979)

Leonard Coates
NAKED ANGELS(1969)

Lewis Coates
STARCRASH(1979), d, w; ALIEN CONTAMINATION(1982, Ital.), d&w; HERCULES(1983), d&w

Paul Coates
TIJUANA STORY, THE(1957)

Phyllis Coates
SMART GIRLS DON'T TALK(1948); KISS IN THE DARK, A(1949); MY FOOLISH HEART(1949); BLUES BUSTERS(1950); MY BLUE HEAVEN(1950); OUTLAWS OF TEXAS(1950); CANYON RAIDERS(1951); LONGHORN, THE(1951); NEVADA BADMEN(1951); OKLAHOMA JUSTICE(1951); STAGE TO BLUE RIVER(1951); SUPERMAN AND THE MOLE MEN(1951); CANYON AMBUSH(1952); FARGO(1952); FLAT TOP(1952); INVASION U.S.A.(1952); MAVERICK, THE(1952); EL PASO STAMPEDE(1953); HERE COME THE GIRLS(1953); MARSHAL OF CEDAR ROCK(1953); SHE'S BACK ON BROADWAY(1953); TOPEKA(1953); GIRLS IN PRISON(1956); CHICAGO CONFIDENTIAL(1957); BLOOD ARROW(1958); CATTLE EMPIRE(1958); I WAS A TEENAGE FRANKENSTEIN(1958); INCREDIBLE PETRIFIED WORLD, THE(1959); BABY MAKER, THE(1970)
Misc. Talkies
MAN FROM SONORA(1951); GUNS ALONG THE BORDER(1952); HIRED GUN(1952); WYOMING ROUNDUP(1952)

Phyllis Coates
Misc. Talkies
CLAW MONSTERS, THE(1966)

Robert M. Coates
EDGE OF FURY(1958), w

Shirley Coates
GRAPES OF WRATH(1940); INTERNATIONAL SQUADRON(1941); HENRY AND DIZZY(1942); YOUNGEST PROFESSION, THE(1943); HENRY ALDRICH PLAYS CUPID(1944)

Tommy Coates
UNDER THE PAMPAS MOON(1935); ALONG CAME JONES(1945); DESERT HORSEMAN, THE(1946)

Claude Coats
SNOW WHITE AND THE SEVEN DWARFS(1937), anim; THREE CABALLEROS, THE(1944), art d; FUN AND FANCY FREE(1947), art d; LADY AND THE TRAMP(1955), art d

Don Coats
ROCK BABY, ROCK IT(1957)

Edith Coats
BEGGAR'S OPERA, THE(1953)

John Coats
FOES(1977), a, d&w, spec eff

Mike Coats
TEX(1982)

Richard Coats
FOES(1977), p

Tommy Coats
TUMBLING TUMBLEWEEDS(1935); THUNDER TRAIL(1937); OVERLAND STAGE RAIDERS(1938); WYOMING OUTLAW(1939); JESSE JAMES, JR.(1942); FUGITIVE FROM SONORA(1943); SIOUX CITY SUE(1946); FEUDIN', FUSSIN' AND A-FIGHTIN'(1948); GRAND CANYON TRAIL(1948); SAN ANTONE AMBUSH(1949)

Fred Cob
JUMBO(1962)

Necmettin Cobanoglu
YOL(1982, Turkey)

Menggie Cobarrubias
JAGUAR(1980, Phil.)

Anthony Cobb
MOTHER DIDN'T TELL ME(1950)

Cpl. Lee J. Cobb
WINGED VICTORY(1944)

David Cobb
DR. FRANKENSTEIN ON CAMPUS(1970, Can.), w
1984
RHINESTONE(1984)

Dita Cobb
HOW TO SEDUCE A WOMAN(1974)

Ed Cobb
TRAITOR, THE(1936); CALIFORNIA MAIL, THE(1937); CHEROKEE STRIP(1937); TALES OF TERROR(1962)

Eddie Cobb
STORMY(1935); SMOKE TREE RANGE(1937); CATTLE RAIDERS(1938); OUTLAWS OF THE PRAIRIE(1938); LONE WOLF SPY HUNT, THE(1939); LONE WOLF STRIKES, THE(1940); PONY POST(1940); MEET JOHN DOE(1941); SALOME, WHERE SHE DANCED(1945)

Edmond Cobb
FUGITIVE SHERIFF, THE(1936); SANTA FE TRAIL(1940); PRAIRIE STRANGER(1941); JACK LONDON(1943); STRANGER FROM PECOS, THE(1943); BELLS OF CORONADO(1950)

Edmun Cobb
AVENGING WATERS(1936)

Edmund Cobb
BEYOND THE RIO GRANDE(1930); WHOOPEE(1930); LAW OF THE RIO GRANDE(1931); WILD HORSE(1931); DARING DANGER(1932); DYNAMITE RANCH(1932); HUMAN TARGETS(1932); LONE TRAIL, THE(1932); MC KENNA OF THE MOUNTED(1932); RIDER OF DEATH VALLEY(1932); RIDERS OF THE GOLDEN GULCH(1932); COME ON TARZAN(1933); DEADWOOD PASS(1933); FOURTH HORSEMAN, THE(1933); GUN LAW(1933); RUSTY RIDES ALONE(1933); SMOKING GUNS(1934); ARIZONA BADMAN(1935); CHEYENNE TORNADO(1935); DANGER TRAILS(1935); GALLANT DEFENDER(1935); NAUGHTY MARIETTA(1935); RUSTLER'S PARADISE(1935); SINGING VAGABOND, THE(1935); DARKEST AFRICA(1936); LIGHTNING BILL CARSON(1936); MYSTERIOUS AVENGER, THE(1936); PRESCOTT KID, THE(1936); RIDE 'EM COWBOY(1936); SHOW BOAT(1936); WESTERNER, THE(1936); CODE OF THE RANGE(1937); EMPTY HOLSTERS(1937); GAME THAT KILLS, THE(1937); LAND BEYOND THE LAW(1937); MIGHTY TREVE, THE(1937); ONE MAN JUSTICE(1937); SPRINGTIME IN THE ROCKIES(1937); SUNDOWN SAUNDERS(1937); TWO-FISTED SHERIFF(1937); CALL OF THE ROCKIES(1938); COLORADO TRAIL(1938); GOLD IS WHERE YOU FIND IT(1938); I'M FROM THE CITY(1938); JUVENILE COURT(1938); LAW OF THE PLAINS(1938); SERGEANT MURPHY(1938); SOUTH OF ARIZONA(1938); WEST OF CHEYENNE(1938); WEST OF SANTA FE(1938); WILD HORSE RODEO(1938); BLUE MONTANA SKIES(1939); LAW COMES TO TEXAS, THE(1939); LET US LIVE(1939); MAN FROM SUNDOWN, THE(1939); MR. SMITH GOES TO WASHINGTON(1939); NORTH OF THE YUKON(1939); OUTPOST OF THE MOUNTIES(1939); RIDERS OF BLACK RIVER(1939); SPOILERS OF THE RANGE(1939); TEXAS STAMPEDE(1939); THUNDERING WEST, THE(1939); WESTERN CARAVANS(1939); BLAZING SIX SHOOTERS(1940); DARK COMMAND, THE(1940); HIS GIRL FRIDAY(1940); MELODY RANCH(1940); MY SON IS GUILTY(1940); ONE MAN'S LAW(1940); PIONEERS OF THE FRONTIER(1940); PRAIRIE SCHOONERS(1940); STRANGER FROM TEXAS, THE(1940); TEXAS TERRORS(1940); WEST OF CARSON CITY(1940); ACROSS THE SIERRAS(1941); BACK IN THE SADDLE(1941); I WAS A PRISONER ON DEVIL'S ISLAND(1941); KING OF DODGE CITY(1941); MAN FROM MONTANA(1941); MEDICO OF PAINTED SPRINGS, THE(1941); NORTH FROM LONE STAR(1941); RETURN OF DANIEL BOONE, THE(1941); RIDERS OF THE BADLANDS(1941); SON OF DAVY CROCKETT, THE(1941); TEXAS(1941); TONTO BASIN OUTLAWS(1941); WILDCAT OF TUCSON(1941); WYOMING WILDCAT(1941); ALIAS BOSTON BLACKIE(1942); DEEP IN THE HEART OF TEXAS(1942); DEVIL'S TRAIL, THE(1942); DOWN RIO GRANDE WAY(1942); GLASS KEY, THE(1942); HEART OF THE RIO GRANDE(1942); LONE PRAIRIE, THE(1942); LONE STAR VIGILANTES, THE(1942); MY FAVORITE BLONDE(1942); SABOTAGE SQUAD(1942); SHUT MY BIG MOUTH(1942); STARDUST ON THE SAGE(1942); WESTWARD HO(1942); DESTROYER(1943); HAIL TO THE RANGERS(1943); MAN FROM THUNDER RIVER, THE(1943); MISSION TO MOSCOW(1943); NORTH STAR, THE(1943); OLD CHISHOLM TRAIL(1943); OUTLAWS OF STAMPEDE PASS(1943); SAGEBRUSH LAW(1943); SILVER CITY RAIDERS(1943); SIX GUN GOSPEL(1943); CALIFORNIA JOE(1944); CYCLONE PRAIRIE RANGERS(1944); DOUBLE INDEMNITY(1944); LAW MEN(1944); LAW OF THE VALLEY(1944); MARSHAL OF RENO(1944); MISSING JUROR, THE(1944); OLD TEXAS TRAIL, THE(1944); OUTLAWS OF SANTA FE(1944); RAIDERS OF THE BORDER(1944); SWEETHEARTS OF THE U.S.A.(1944); TEXAS KID, THE(1944); BAD MEN OF THE BORDER(1945); CHEROKEE FLASH, THE(1945); CODE OF THE LAWLESS(1945); FALCON IN SAN FRANCISCO, THE(1945); FRONTIER FEUD(1945); MAN FROM OKLAHOMA, THE(1945); NAVAJO TRAIL, THE(1945); RENEGADES OF THE RIO GRANDE(1945); SANTA FE SADDLEMATES(1945); SUNSET IN EL DORADO(1945); DAYS OF BUFFALO BILL(1946); EL PASO KID, THE(1946); FALCON'S ALIBI, THE(1946); PHANTOM THIEF, THE(1946); RED RIVER RENEGADES(1946); RENEGADE GIRL(1946); RIO GRANDE RAIDERS(1946); RUSTLER'S ROUNDUP(1946); SANTA FE UPRISING(1946); SONG OF ARIZONA(1946); STAGECOACH TO DENVER(1946); SUN VALLEY CYCLONE(1946); BRUTE FORCE(1947); BUFFALO BILL RIDES AGAIN(1947); FLASHING GUNS(1947); HOMESTRETCH, THE(1947); LAND OF THE LAWLESS(1947); LAST FRONTIER UPRISING(1947); MICHIGAN KID, THE(1947); OREGON TRAIL SCOUTS(1947); ROBIN OF TEXAS(1947); WISTFUL WIDOW OF WAGON GAP, THE(1947); BOLD FRONTIERSMAN, THE(1948); CARSON CITY RAIDERS(1948); FAMILY HONEYMOON(1948); FEUDIN', FUSSIN' AND A-FIGHTIN'(1948); FURY AT FURNACE CREEK(1948); HEART OF VIRGINIA(1948); LETTER FROM AN UNKNOWN WOMAN(1948); MYSTERY OF THE GOLDEN EYE, THE(1948); RIVER LADY(1948); STREET WITH NO NAME, THE(1948); DARING CABALLERO, THE(1949); FAR FRONTIER, THE(1949); GUN LAW JUSTICE(1949); HIDDEN DANGER(1949); LUST FOR GOLD(1949); RED CANYON(1949); SAN ANTONE AMBUSH(1949); SHERIFF OF WICHITA(1949); TAKE ONE FALSE STEP(1949); WYOMING BANDIT, THE(1949); ARIZONA COWBOY, THE(1950); COMMANCHE TERRITORY(1950); FRISCO TORNADO(1950); GIRL FROM SAN LORENZO, THE(1950); HILLS OF OKLAHOMA(1950); MA AND PA KETTLE GO TO TOWN(1950); VANISHING WESTERNER, THE(1950); WINCHESTER '73(1950); MONTANA DESPERADO(1951); CONFIDENCE GIRL(1952); MA AND PA KETTLE AT THE FAIR(1952); SOMETHING FOR THE BIRDS(1952); REDHEAD FROM WYOMING, THE(1953); BROKEN LANCE(1954); EGYPTIAN, THE(1954); MA AND PA KETTLE AT HOME(1954); RIVER OF NO RETURN(1954);

GIRL IN THE RED VELVET SWING, THE(1955); LAY THAT RIFLE DOWN(1955); LUCY GALLANT(1955); ONE DESIRE(1955); VIOLENT MEN, THE(1955); HIDDEN GUNS(1956); OKLAHOMA WOMAN, THE(1956); AMAZING COLOSSAL MAN, THE(1957); DRAGSTRIP GIRL(1957); MOTORCYCLE GANG(1957); RUNAWAY DAUGHTERS(1957); LAST HURRAH, THE(1958); UNDERWATER CITY, THE(1962); BOUNTY KILLER, THE(1965); REQUIEM FOR A GUNFIGHTER(1965); JOHNNY RENO(1966)
Misc. Talkies
TANGLED FORTUNES(1932); RACKETEER ROUND-UP(1934); RAWHIDE TER-ROR, THE(1934); GUNNERS AND GUNS(1935); LIGHTNING TRIGGERS(1935); TRACY RIDES(1935); GALLOPING THUNDER(1946)
Silents
AT DEVIL'S GORGE(1923); PLAYING IT WILD(1923); STING OF THE SCORPION, THE(1923); LOOKING FOR TROUBLE(1926); LITTLE BIG HORN(1927); YOUNG WHIRLWIND(1928)
Misc. Silents
SOCIAL BRIARS(1918); FINDERS KEEPERS(1921); OUT OF THE DEPTHS(1921), a, d; BATTLING BATES(1923); LAW RUSTLERS, THE(1923); RIDERS OF THE RAN-GE(1923); BLASTED HOPES(1924); CALIFORNIA IN '49(1924); CUPID'S RUST-LER(1924); MIDNIGHT SHADOWS(1924); RANGE BLOOD(1924); RODEO MIXUP, A(1924); WESTERN FEUDS(1924); WESTERN YESTERDAYS(1924); GALLOPING COWBOY, THE(1926); GENERAL CUSTER AT LITTLE BIG HORN(1926); FANGS OF DESTINY(1927); WOLF'S TRAIL(1927); CALL OF THE HEART(1928); FOUR-FOOTED RANGER, THE(1928); HOUND OF THE SILVER CREEK, THE(1928)
Edmund F. Cobb
DETECTIVE STORY(1951)
Misc. Silents
CAPTAIN JINKS OF THE HORSE MARINES(1916); DESERT SCORPION, THE(1920); WOLVES OF THE STREET(1920)
Elisabeth Cobb
SHE WAS A LADY(1934), w
Humphrey Cobb
SAN QUENTIN(1937), w; PATHS OF GLORY(1957), w
Hutton Cobb
1984
UNTIL SEPTEMBER(1984)
Irvin S. Cobb
WOMAN ACCUSED(1933), w; STEAMBOAT ROUND THE BEND(1935); EVERY-BODY'S OLD MAN(1936); PEPPER(1936); ARKANSAS TRAVELER, THE(1938); HA-WAII CALLS(1938); YOUNG IN HEART, THE(1938); OUR LEADING CITIZEN(1939), w; SUN SHINES BRIGHT, THE(1953), w
Silents
ARAB, THE(1915); FIGHTING ODDS(1917), w; PECK'S BAD BOY(1921), t
Jack Cobb
TOYS ARE NOT FOR CHILDREN(1972)
Jane Cobb
NIGHT TRAIN(1940, Brit.)
Joe Cobb
WHERE DID YOU GET THAT GIRL?(1941)
John Cobb
Misc. Silents
LURE OF A WOMAN, THE(1921)
Kacey Cobb
CRATER LAKE MONSTER, THE(1977)
Lee Cobb
SONG OF BERNADETTE, THE(1943)
Lee J. Cobb
NORTH OF THE RIO GRANDE(1937); RUSTLER'S VALLEY(1937); DANGER ON THE AIR(1938); GOLDEN BOY(1939); THIS THING CALLED LOVE(1940); MEN OF BOYS TOWN(1941); PARIS CALLING(1941); BUCKSKIN FRONTIER(1943); MOON IS DOWN, THE(1943); TONIGHT WE RAID CALAIS(1943); ANNA AND THE KING OF SIAM(1946); BOOMERANG(1947); CAPTAIN FROM CASTILE(1947); JOHNNY O'-CLOCK(1947); CALL NORTHSIDE 777(1948); DARK PAST, THE(1948); LUCK OF THE IRISH(1948); MIRACLE OF THE BELLS, THE(1948); THIEVES' HIGHWAY(1949); FAMILY SECRET, THE(1951); MAN WHO CHEATED HIMSELF, THE(1951); SIROC-CO(1951); FIGHTER, THE(1952); TALL TEXAN, THE(1953); DAY OF TRIUMPH(1954); GORILLA AT LARGE(1954); ON THE WATERFRONT(1954); YANKEE PASHA(1954); LEFT HAND OF GOD, THE(1955); RACERS, THE(1955); ROAD TO DENVER, THE(1955); MAN IN THE GREY FLANNEL SUIT, THE(1956); MIAMI EXPOSE(1956); GARMENT JUNGLE, THE(1957); THREE FACES OF EVE, THE(1957); 12 ANGRY MEN(1957); BROTHERS KARAMAZOV, THE(1958); MAN OF THE WEST(1958); PARTY GIRL(1958); BUT NOT FOR ME(1959); GREEN MANSIONS(1959); TRAP, THE(1959); EXODUS(1960); FOUR HORSEMEN OF THE APOCALYPSE, THE(1962); HOW THE WEST WAS WON(1962); COME BLOW YOUR HORN(1963); OUR MAN FLINT(1966); IN LIKE FLINT(1967); COOGAN'S BLUFF(1968); DAY OF THE OWL, THE(1968, Ital./Fr.); MACKENNA'S GOLD(1969); MAFIA(1969, Fr./Ital.); THEY CAME TO ROB LAS VEGAS(1969, Fr./Ital./Span./Ger.); LIBERATION OF L.B. JONES, THE(1970); MACHO CALLAHAN(1970); LAWMAN(1971); EXORCIST, THE(1973); MAN WHO LOVED CAT DANCING, THE(1973); BLOOD, SWEAT AND FEAR(1975, Ital.); THAT LUCKY TOUCH(1975, Brit.)
Marcel Cobb
Misc. Talkies
REDNECK MILLER(1977)
Randall Cobb
CHAMP, THE(1979)
Randall "Tex" Cobb
UNCOMMON VALOR(1983)
Ron Cobb
1984
LAST STARFIGHTER, THE(1984), prod d
Ronn Cobb
CONAN THE BARBARIAN(1982), prod d
Tracy Cobb
MOTHER DIDN'T TELL ME(1950)
Ty Cobb
Misc. Silents
SOMEWHERE IN GEORGIA(1916)

Clifford Cobbe
THREADS(1932, Brit.); BOB'S YOUR UNCLE(1941, Brit.); KING ARTHUR WAS A GENTLEMAN(1942, Brit.); MILLIONS LIKE US(1943, Brit.); UNCENSORED(1944, Brit.); GALLOPING MAJOR, THE(1951, Brit.)
Silents
FLAMES(1917, Brit.)
Misc. Silents
RUSSIA - LAND OF TOMORROW(1919, Brit.)
Gordon Cobbledock
KID FROM CLEVELAND, THE(1949)
Jonathan Cobbler
LINCOLN CONSPIRACY, THE(1977), w
Bill Cobbs
GREASED LIGHTNING(1977); HERO AIN'T NOTHIN' BUT A SANDWICH, A(1977); SILKWOOD(1983); TRADING PLACES(1983)
1984
BROTHER FROM ANOTHER PLANET, THE(1984); COTTON CLUB, THE(1984)
Misc. Talkies
HITTER, THE(1979)
Joe Cobbs
MEET ME IN ST. LOUIS(1944)
Rebecca Cobbs
CONRACK(1974)
Brian Cobby
BREAKING POINT, THE(1961, Brit.); TELL-TALE HEART, THE(1962, Brit.); GREAT ARMORED CAR SWINDLE, THE(1964)
Misc. Talkies
FOR MEMBERS ONLY(1960)
Sandy Cobe
TERROR ON TOUR(1980), p; TO ALL A GOODNIGHT(1980), p
Giancarlo Cobelli
WHITE, RED, YELLOW, PINK(1966, Ital.); TAMING OF THE SHREW, THE(1967, U.S./Ital.); LOVE FACTORY(1969, Ital.)
Shimon Coben
TWO KOUNEY LEMELS(1966, Israel), md
Robert Cobert
LADYBUG, LADYBUG(1963), md; HOUSE OF DARK SHADOWS(1970), m, md; NIGHT OF DARK SHADOWS(1971), m, md; BURNT OFFERINGS(1976), m; SCAL-PEL(1976), m
Sir Alan Cobham
KING'S CUP, THE(1933, Brit.), d, w
Misc. Silents
FLIGHT COMMANDER, THE(1927)
Franco Cobianchi
THIEF OF BAGHDAD, THE(1961, Ital./Fr.)
Hester Coblentz
YELLOW SUBMARINE(1958, Brit.), animation
James Coblentz
STILL SMOKIN'(1983), ed
1984
STREETS OF FIRE(1984), ed
Jim Coblentz
FOXES(1980), ed
James Coblenz
IT'S MY TURN(1980), ed
Martin Coblenz
STRANGE INVADERS(1983), spec eff
Walter Coblenz
CANDIDATE, THE(1972), p; ALL THE PRESIDENT'S MEN(1976), p; ONION FIELD, THE(1979), p; LEGEND OF THE LONE RANGER, THE(1981), p; STRANGE INVADERS(1983), p
Jan Cobler
Misc. Talkies
ON THE LAM(1972)
Jan Rita Cobler
OUTLAW BLUES(1977)
John Cobley
ELIZA FRASER(1976, Aus.)
Roberto Cobo
LOS OLVIDADOS(1950, Mex.)
Charles Coborn
VARIETY JUBILEE(1945, Brit.)
Dick Cobos
RIO LOBO(1970), makeup; POCKET MONEY(1972), makeup
Gerald Cobos
DEVIL MADE A WOMAN, THE(1962, Span.)
German Cobos
CASTILIAN, THE(1963, Span./U.S.); LADY DOCTOR, THE(1963, Fr./Ital./Span.); TAXI FOR TOBRUK(1965, Fr./Span./Ger.)
Juan Cobos
WEB OF VIOLENCE(1966, Ital./Span.), w; BANDIDOS(1967, Ital.), w
Richard Cobos
WINGS OF CHANCE(1961, Can.), makeup; WILD SEED(1965), makeup; HAIL, HERO!(1969), makeup; MAN CALLED HORSE, A(1970), makeup; KANSAS CITY BOMBER(1972), makeup
Art Coburn
DOUBLES(1978), ed
Arthur Coburn
1984
BEVERLY HILLS COP(1984), ed
Brian Coburn
RETURN OF MR. MOTO, THE(1965, Brit.); FIDDLER ON THE ROOF(1971); MARY, QUEEN OF SCOTS(1971, Brit.); LOVE AND DEATH(1975); DIRTY KNIGHT'S WORK(1976, Brit.); OCTOPUSSY(1983, Brit.); TRENCHCOAT(1983)
1984
LASSITER(1984); SWORD OF THE VALIANT(1984, Brit.)
Buck Coburn
GUN SMOKE(1936)

Misc. Talkies
GUNSMOKE ON THE GUADALUPE(1935)

Charles Coburn
YELLOW JACK(1938); SAY IT WITH FLOWERS(1934, Brit.); PEOPLE'S ENEMY, THE(1935); LORD JEFF(1938); OF HUMAN HEARTS(1938); VIVACIOUS LADY(1938); BACHELOR MOTHER(1939); IDIOT'S DELIGHT(1939); IN NAME ONLY(1939); MADE FOR EACH OTHER(1939); STANLEY AND LIVINGSTONE(1939); STORY OF ALEXANDER GRAHAM BELL, THE(1939); CAPTAIN IS A LADY, THE(1940); EDISON, THE MAN(1940); FLORIAN(1940); ROAD TO SINGAPORE(1940); THREE FACES WEST(1940); DEVIL AND MISS JONES, THE(1941); H.M. PULHAM, ESQ.(1941); LADY EVE, THE(1941); OUR WIFE(1941); UNEXPECTED UNCLE(1941); GEORGE WASHINGTON SLEPT HERE(1942); IN THIS OUR LIFE(1942); KING'S ROW(1942); CONSTANT NYMPH, THE(1943); FOREVER AND A DAY(1943); HEAVEN CAN WAIT(1943); MORE THE MERRIER, THE(1943); MY KINGDOM FOR A COOK(1943); PRINCESS O'ROURKE(1943); IMPATIENT YEARS, THE(1944); KNICKERBOCKER HOLIDAY(1944); TOGETHER AGAIN(1944); WILSON(1944); COLONEL EFFINGHAM'S RAID(1945); OVER 21(1945); RHAPSODY IN BLUE(1945); ROYAL SCANDAL, A(1945); SHADY LADY(1945); GREEN YEARS, THE(1946); LURED(1947); PARADINE CASE, THE(1947); B. F.'S DAUGHTER(1948); GREEN GRASS OF WYOMING(1948); DOCTOR AND THE GIRL, THE(1949); EVERYBODY DOES IT(1949); GAL WHO TOOK THE WEST, THE(1949); IMPACT(1949); YES SIR, THAT'S MY BABY(1949); LOUISA(1950); MR. MUSIC(1950); PEGGY(1950); HIGHWAYMAN, THE(1951); HAS ANYBODY SEEN MY GAL?(1952); MONKEY BUSINESS(1952); GENTLEMEN PREFER BLONDES(1953); TROUBLE ALONG THE WAY(1953); LONG WAIT, THE(1954); ROCKET MAN, THE(1954); HOW TO BE VERY, VERY, POPULAR(1955); AROUND THE WORLD IN 80 DAYS(1956); POWER AND THE PRIZE, THE(1956); HOW TO MURDER A RICH UNCLE(1957, Brit.); STORY OF MANKIND, THE(1957); TOWN ON TRIAL(1957, Brit.); JOHN PAUL JONES(1959); REMARKABLE MR. PENNYPACKER, THE(1959); STRANGER IN MY ARMS(1959); PEPE(1960)

Frank Coburn
OPERATION DISASTER(1951, Brit.)

Gladys Coburn
Silents
BATTLE OF LIFE, THE(1916)
Misc. Silents
PRIMITIVE CALL, THE(1917); HEART STRINGS(1920); OUT OF THE SHOWS(1920); EAST LYNNE(1921); GOD'S CRUCIBLE(1921)

Helen Coburn
SKYSCRAPER SOULS(1932)

James Coburn
FACE OF A FUGITIVE(1959); RIDE LONESOME(1959); MAGNIFICENT SEVEN, THE(1960); HELL IS FOR HEROES(1962); CHARADE(1963); GREAT ESCAPE, THE(1963); AMERICANIZATION OF EMILY, THE(1964); MAN FROM GALVESTON, THE(1964); HIGH WIND IN JAMAICA, A(1965); LOVED ONE, THE(1965); MAJOR DUNDEE(1965); DEAD HEAT ON A MERRY-GO-ROUND(1966); OUR MAN FLINT(1966); WHAT DID YOU DO IN THE WAR, DADDY?(1966); IN LIKE FLINT(1967); PRESIDENT'S ANALYST, THE(1967); WATERHOLE NO. 3(1967); CANDY(1968, Ital./Fr.); DUFFY(1968, Brit.); HARD CONTRACT(1969); CAREY TREATMENT, THE(1972); DUCK, YOU SUCKER!(1972, Ital.); HONKERS, THE(1972); HARRY IN YOUR POCKET(1973); LAST OF SHEILA(1973); PAT GARRETT AND BILLY THE KID(1973); INTERNECINE PROJECT, THE(1974, Brit.); REASON TO LIVE, A REASON TO DIE, A(1974, Ital./Fr./Ger./Span.); BITE THE BULLET(1975); HARD TIMES(1975); LAST HARD MEN, THE(1976); MIDWAY(1976); SKY RIDERS(1976, U.S./Gr.); CROSS OF IRON(1977, Brit., Ger.); CIRCLE OF IRON(1979, Brit.), w; FIREPOWER(1979, Brit.); GOLDENGIRL(1979); MUPPET MOVIE, THE(1979); BALTIMORE BULLET, THE(1980); LOVING COUPLES(1980); MR. PATMAN(1980, Can.); HIGH RISK(1981); LOOKER(1981)

Jim Coburn
SCREWBALLS(1983)

Norman Coburn
CIRCLE OF DECEPTON(1961, Brit.); OPERATION SNAFU(1965, Brit.)

W. Coburn
Silents
KAISER, BEAST OF BERLIN, THE(1918)

Wallace D. Coburn
Misc. Silents
GOLDEN GODDESS, THE(1916)

Walt Coburn
RUSTY RIDES ALONE(1933), w; WESTERNER, THE(1936), w; RETURN OF WILD BILL, THE(1940), w; SHOOT OUT AT BIG SAG(1962), w

Walter J. Coburn
Silents
BACK TRAIL, THE(1924), w

Fred Coby
WITHOUT RESERVATIONS(1946); COUNTERFEITERS, THE(1948); JUNGLE GODDESS(1948); MAN FROM COLORADO, THE(1948); PRAIRIE, THE(1948); THREE MUSKETEERS, THE(1948); STATE DEPARTMENT–FILE 649(1949); WHITE HEAT(1949); HALLS OF MONTEZUMA(1951); MOB, THE(1951); HORIZONS WEST(1952); PAT AND MIKE(1952); SCARLET ANGEL(1952); DEVIL'S CANYON(1953); ILLEGAL(1955); FURY AT GUNSIGHT PASS(1956); TEN COMMANDMENTS, THE(1956); JAILHOUSE ROCK(1957); MY MAN GODFREY(1957); NIGHT THE WORLD EXPLODED, THE(1957); NO TIME FOR SERGEANTS(1958); EXPERIMENT IN TERROR(1962)

Michael Coby
SUPERSONIC MAN(1979, Span.)
Misc. Talkies
BITCH, THE(1979)

Ron Coby
JAMBOREE(1957)

Shailar Coby
TOURIST TRAP, THE(1979)

Imogene Coca
PROMISES, PROMISES(1963); UNDER THE YUM-YUM TREE(1963); RABBIT TEST(1978); NATIONAL LAMPOON'S VACATION(1983)
1984
NOTHING LASTS FOREVER(1984)

Otello Cocchi
EYE OF THE NEEDLE, THE(1965, Ital./Fr.), p

Aurelio Coccia
Silents
ARGENTINE LOVE(1924); ALOMA OF THE SOUTH SEAS(1926)

Phil Coccioletti
LOVE LETTERS(1983)

Alice Cocea
SWEET SKIN(1965, Fr./Ital.)

Ed Coch, Jr.
PATHFINDER, THE(1952)

Eduardo Coch
KANSAS CITY CONFIDENTIAL(1952)

Edward Coch
FRENCH LINE, THE(1954); SARACEN BLADE, THE(1954); CREATURE WITH THE ATOM BRAIN(1955); SEMINOLE UPRISING(1955); HELL ON DEVIL'S ISLAND(1957)

Edward Coch, Jr.
HORIZONS WEST(1952); RIDING SHOTGUN(1954)

Charles Cochberg
SEQUOIA(1934), ed

Barbara Cochran
END OF THE LINE, THE(1959, Brit.)

Dorcas Cochran
SWING IT SOLDIER(1941), w; FIGHTING BILL FARGO(1942), w; FRISCO LILL(1942), w; JUKE BOX JENNY(1942), w; SWING OUT THE BLUES(1943), w; GIRL IN THE CASE(1944), w; GIRL ON THE SPOT(1946), w; WIFE OF MONTE CRISTO, THE(1946), w

Eddie Cochran
GIRL CAN'T HELP IT, THE(1956); UNTAMED YOUTH(1957); GO, JOHNNY, GO!(1959); RADIO ON(1980, Brit./Ger.), m

Frances Cochran
Silents
KID, THE(1921)

Frank Cochran
TICKET OF LEAVE MAN, THE(1937, Brit.)

Gifford Cochran
EMPEROR JONES, THE(1933), p

Hank Cochran
HONEYSUCKLE ROSE(1980)

Ian Cochran
1984
BOLERO(1984)

Jeane Cochran
HALF-BREED, THE(1952)

John Cochran
EXTRAORDINARY SEAMAN, THE(1969)

John J. Cochran
NIGHTMARE IN BLOOD(1978)

Kevin Cochran
GLENN MILLER STORY, THE(1953)

Linda Cochran
TWO THOUSAND MANIACS!(1964)

Mickey Cochran
SLEEPING CITY, THE(1950)

Paul R. Cochran
PICNIC(1955)

Philip G. Cochran
JET PILOT(1957), ph

R.H. Cochran
Silents
ARRIVAL OF PERPETUA, THE(1915), w

Rice E. Cochran
MR. SCOUTMASTER(1953), w

Robert Cochran
GLIMPSE OF PARADISE, A(1934, Brit.); THIRD CLUE, THE(1934, Brit.); SANDERS OF THE RIVER(1935, Brit.); SCROOGE(1935, Brit.); I STAND CONDEMNED(1936, Brit.); LIMPING MAN, THE(1936, Brit.); NO ESCAPE(1936, Brit.); MAN WHO COULD WORK MIRACLES, THE(1937, Brit.); OH BOY!(1938, Brit.); MYSTERY OF ROOM 13(1941, Brit.)

Steve Cochran
BOSTON BLACKIE BOOKED ON SUSPICION(1945); BOSTON BLACKIE'S RENDEZVOUS(1945); GAY SENORITA, THE(1945); WONDER MAN(1945); BEST YEARS OF OUR LIVES, THE(1946); CHASE, THE(1946); KID FROM BOOKLYN, THE(1946); COPACABANA(1947); SONG IS BORN, A(1948); WHITE HEAT(1949); DALLAS(1950); DAMNED DON'T CRY, THE(1950); HIGHWAY 301(1950); STORM WARNING(1950); INSIDE THE WALLS OF FOLSOM PRISON(1951); JIM THORPE–ALL AMERICAN(1951); RATON PASS(1951); TANKS ARE COMING, THE(1951); TOMORROW IS ANOTHER DAY(1951); LION AND THE HORSE, THE(1952); OPERATION SECRET(1952); BACK TO GOD'S COUNTRY(1953); DESERT SONG, THE(1953); SHARK RIVER(1953); SHE'S BACK ON BROADWAY(1953); CARNIVAL STORY(1954); PRIVATE HELL 36(1954); COME NEXT SPRING(1956); SLANDER(1956); WEAPON, THE(1957, Brit.); QUANTRILL'S RAIDERS(1958); BEAT GENERATION, THE(1959); BIG OPERATOR, THE(1959); I, MOBSTER(1959); DEADLY COMPANIONS, THE(1961); IL GRIDO(1962, U.S./Ital.); OF LOVE AND DESIRE(1963); TELL ME IN THE SUNLIGHT(1967), a, p&d, w

Steven Cochran
MOZAMBIQUE(1966, Brit.)

Elaine Cochrane
MY MAN GODFREY(1936)

Frank Cochrane
YELLOW MASK, THE(1930, Brit.); CHU CHIN CHOW(1934, Brit.); HELL'S CARGO(1935, Brit.); BULLDOG DRUMMOND AT BAY(1937, Brit.); TENTH MAN, THE(1937, Brit.); WHAT A MAN!(1937, Brit.); DARK SANDS(1938, Brit.); PIRATES OF THE SEVEN SEAS(1941, Brit.); WARNING TO WANTONS, A(1949, Brit.)

George Cochrane
Silents
SPINDLE OF LIFE, THE(1917), d

Lucy Cochrane
GEORGE WHITE'S SCANDALS(1945)

Michael Cochrane
VICTORY(1981); RETURN OF THE SOLDIER, THE(1983, Brit.)
1984
REAL LIFE(1984, Brit.)
Nan Cochrane
IT CAN BE DONE(1929), w
Nick Cochran
PRIORITIES ON PARADE(1942); HERE COMES ELMER(1943)
Peggy Cochrane
RADIO FOLLIES(1935, Brit.)
Robert Cochrane
TROOPSHIP(1938, Brit.)
Talie Cochrane
Misc. Talkies
SWEET SAVIOR(1971); FUGITIVE GIRLS(1975)
Tallie Cochrane
DAN'S MOTEL(1982)
Jack Cock
GREAT GAME, THE(1930)
Silents
WINNING GOAL, THE(1929, Brit.)
Bruce Cockburn
GOIN' DOWN THE ROAD(1970, Can.), m
Daisy Cockburn
1984
SECRETS(1984, Brit.)
Inez Cocke
INTERLUDE(1957), w
William Cocklin
TERROR IN THE JUNGLE(1968)
Harley Cockliss
GLITTERBALL, THE(1977, Brit.), d
Helga Cockova
TRANSPORT FROM PARADISE(1967, Czech.)
Joan Cockram
Misc. Silents
HOBSON'S CHOICE(1920, Brit.)
Robert Cockran
AGAINST THE TIDE(1937, Brit.)
Alston Cockrell
HOLD'EM NAVY!(1937)
Eustace Cockrell
FAST COMPANY(1953), w; TENNESSEE CHAMP(1954), w
Francis Cockrell
AGE OF CONSENT(1932), w; SPORT PARADE, THE(1932), w; FAMILY SECRET, THE(1951), w; RHUBARB(1951), w; INFERNO(1953), w; RAID, THE(1954), w; ON THE THRESHOLD OF SPACE(1956), w
Francis M. Cockrell
WALKING ON AIR(1936), w; PROFESSOR BEWARE(1938), w; PROFESSIONALS, THE(1966), w
Frank Cockrell
LADY IN A JAM(1942), w; DARK WATERS(1944), w
Gary Cockrell
TARZAN THE MAGNIFICENT(1960, Brit.); CROSSTRAP(1962, Brit.); LOLITA(1962); TIARA TAHITI(1962, Brit.); TWO AND TWO MAKE SIX(1962, Brit.); WAR LOVER, THE(1962, U.S./Brit.); BLAZE OF GLORY(1963, Brit.); AMERICANIZATION OF EMILY, THE(1964); MAN IN THE MIDDLE(1964, U.S./Brit.); WHY BOTHER TO KNOCK(1964, Brit.); BEDFORD INCIDENT, THE(1965, Brit.); OPERATION SNAFU(1965, Brit.); MAN OUTSIDE, THE(1968, Brit.); TWILIGHT'S LAST GLEAMING(1977, U.S./Ger.)
Marian Cockrell
DARK WATERS(1944), w
Marion B. Cockrell
PROFESSOR BEWARE(1938), w; PROFESSIONALS, THE(1966), w
Sue Cockrell
SHARKY'S MACHINE(1982)
John Mills Cockwell
HUMONGOUS(1982, Can.), m
Cocky Two Bull
SAFARI 3000(1982)
Coco
SLEEPING CAR TO TRIESTE(1949, Brit.); HURRICANE(1979), cos
James Coco
ENSIGN PULVER(1964); GENERATION(1969); STRAWBERRY STATEMENT, THE(1970); TELL ME THAT YOU LOVE ME, JUNIE MOON(1970); NEW LEAF, A(1971); SUCH GOOD FRIENDS(1971); MAN OF LA MANCHA(1972); WILD PARTY, THE(1975); MURDER BY DEATH(1976); BYE BYE MONKEY(1978, Ital/Fr.); CHARLESTON(1978, Ital.); CHEAP DETECTIVE, THE(1978); SCAVENGER HUNT(1979); WHOLLY MOSES(1980); ONLY WHEN I LAUGH(1981)
1984
MUPPETS TAKE MANHATTAN, THE(1984)
Sasha Coco
CIRCUS OF HORRORS(1960, Brit.)
The Community Players of Cocoanut Grove
Silents
ONCE UPON A TIME(1922)
George Cocos
LOVE IN THE AFTERNOON(1957)
Jean Cocteau
BLOOD OF A POET, THE(1930, Fr.), d&w; ETERNAL RETURN, THE(1943, Fr.), w; BEAUTY AND THE BEAST(1947, Fr.), d&w; EAGLE WITH TWO HEADS(1948, Fr.), d&w; RUY BLAS(1948, Fr.), w; LES PARENTS TERRIBLES(1950, Fr.), a, d&w; ORPHEUS(1950, Fr.), a, d&w; DAUGHTER OF THE SANDS(1952, Fr.), w; LES ENFANTS TERRIBLES(1952, Fr.), a, w; DISOBEDIENT(1953, Brit.), d&w; TESTAMENT OF ORPHEUS, THE(1962, Fr.), a, d&w; LADIES OF THE PARK(1964, Fr.), w
Frank Coda
NO SAFETY AHEAD(1959, Brit.); PRIZE OF ARMS, A(1962, Brit.); TOUCH OF DEATH(1962, Brit.); OH! WHAT A LOVELY WAR(1969, Brit.); GET CHARLIE TULLY(1976, Brit.); FINAL CONFLICT, THE(1981)

Elsie Codd
Silents
KID, THE(1921)
Nick Coddington
1984
MICKI AND MAUDE(1984)
Grant Code
MIRACLE WORKER, THE(1962); SUMMER WISHES, WINTER DREAMS(1973)
Ann Codee
UNDER THE PAMPAS MOON(1935); BRILLIANT MARRIAGE(1936); HI GAUCHO!(1936); EXPENSIVE HUSBANDS(1937); JEZEBEL(1938); CHARLIE CHAN IN THE CITY OF DARKNESS(1939); ARISE, MY LOVE(1940); CAPTAIN CAUTION(1940); DRUMS OF THE DESERT(1940); CHARLIE CHAN IN RIO(1941); COME LIVE WITH ME(1941); ARMY SURGEON(1942); REUNION IN FRANCE(1942); OLD ACQUAINTANCE(1943); PARIS AFTER DARK(1943); TONIGHT WE RAID CALAIS(1943); YOUNGEST PROFESSION, THE(1943); BATHING BEAUTY(1944); MARRIAGE IS A PRIVATE AFFAIR(1944); MR. SKEFFINGTON(1944); MRS. PARKINGTON(1944); MUMMY'S CURSE, THE(1944); HANGOVER SQUARE(1945); HER HIGHNESS AND THE BELLBOY(1945); JOHNNY ANGEL(1945); KITTY(1945); THIS LOVE OF OURS(1945); TONIGHT AND EVERY NIGHT(1945); HOLIDAY IN MEXICO(1946); IT'S GREAT TO BE YOUNG(1946); SO DARK THE NIGHT(1946); TILL THE CLOUDS ROLL BY(1946); OTHER LOVE, THE(1947); UNFINISHED DANCE,- THE(1947); THAT MIDNIGHT KISS(1949); UNDER MY SKIN(1950); WHEN WILLIE COMES MARCHING HOME(1950); AMERICAN IN PARIS, AN(1951); DETECTIVE STORY(1951); LADY PAYS OFF, THE(1951); MR. IMPERIUM(1951); ON THE RIVERA(1951); WHAT PRICE GLORY?(1952); DANGEROUS WHEN WET(1953); KISS ME KATE(1953); WAR OF THE WORLDS, THE(1953); LAST TIME I SAW PARIS, THE(1954); SO THIS IS PARIS(1954); DADDY LONG LEGS(1955); INTERRUPTED MELODY(1955); KINGS GO FORTH(1958); YOUNG LIONS, THE(1958)
Ralph Coder
PAPER MOON(1973)
Corinne Coderey
INVITATION, THE(1975, Fr./Switz.)
Claude Codgen
Misc. Talkies
FOLLOW ME(1969)
Teresa Codling
KADOYNG(1974, Brit.); ELEPHANT MAN, THE(1980, Brit.); PIRATES OF PENZANCE, THE(1983); WICKED LADY, THE(1983, Brit.)
Betty Codreano
TRAPEZE(1956)
The Codreanos
TRAPEZE(1956)
Bruce Bushman Tom Codrick
FANTASIA(1940), art d
Tom Codrick
SNOW WHITE AND THE SEVEN DWARFS(1937), art d
Ann Codrington
LUCKY DAYS(1935, Brit.); PRICE OF WISDOM, THE(1935, Brit.); SILENT PASSENGER, THE(1935, Brit.); I'LL TURN TO YOU(1946, Brit.); POET'S PUB(1949, Brit.); NO PLACE FOR JENNIFER(1950, Brit.); ROSSITER CASE, THE(1950, Brit.); LADY WITH A LAMP, THE(1951, Brit.); PORTRAIT OF CLARE(1951, Brit.)
Albert Cody
Silents
JOYOUS LIAR, THE(1919)
Bill Cody
DUGAN OF THE BAD LANDS(1931); MONTANA KID, THE(1931); OKLAHOMA JIM(1931); UNDER TEXAS SKIES(1931); LAND OF WANTED MEN(1932); LAW OF THE NORTH(1932); MASON OF THE MOUNTED(1932); TEXAS PIONEERS(1932); FRONTIER DAYS(1934); CYCLONE RANGER(1935); LAWLESS BORDER(1935); FIGHTING GRINGO, THE(1939); STAGECOACH(1939); JOAN OF ARC(1948)
Misc. Talkies
BORDER GUNS(1934); BORDER MENACE, THE(1934); RECKLESS BUCKAROO, THE(1935); SIX GUN JUSTICE(1935); TEXAS RAMBLER, THE(1935); VANISHING RIDERS(1935); WESTERN RACKETEERS(1935); BLAZING JUSTICE(1936); OUTLAWS OF THE RANGE(1936)
Silents
FIGHTING SMILE, THE(1925); RIDERS OF MYSTERY(1925); KING OF THE SADDLE(1926); LADDIE BE GOOD(1928), a, p, w; EYES OF THE UNDERWORLD(1929); SLIM FINGERS(1929)
Misc. Silents
BORDER JUSTICE(1925); COLD NERVE(1925); DANGEROUS ODDS(1925); FIGHTING SHERIFF, THE(1925); LOVE ON THE RIO GRANDE(1925); MOCCASINS(1925); GALLOPING COWBOY, THE(1926); ARIZONA WHIRLWIND, THE(1927); BORN TO BATTLE(1927); GOLD FROM WEEPAH(1927); PRICE OF FEAR, THE(1928); TIP-OFF, THE(1929); WOLVES OF THE CITY(1929)
Bill Cody, Jr.
FRONTIER DAYS(1934); ROMANCE OF THE ROCKIES(1938); DESPERATE TRAILS(1939); DESTRY RIDES AGAIN(1939); BAD MAN FROM RED BUTTE(1940); TWO-FISTED RANGERS(1940); RAIDERS OF THE WEST(1942)
Misc. Talkies
BORDER GUNS(1934); RECKLESS BUCKAROO, THE(1935); VANISHING RIDERS(1935); OUTLAWS OF THE RANGE(1936)
Billy Cody, Jr.
GIRL OF THE GOLDEN WEST, THE(1938)
Deborah Cody
1984
IRRECONCILABLE DIFFERENCES(1984)
Emma Cody
PLASTIC DOME OF NORMA JEAN, THE(1966)
Eric Cody
FORT UTAH(1967); HOSTILE GUNS(1967); ARIZONA BUSHWHACKERS(1968)
Francis R. Cody
BUNNY O'HARE(1971)
Harry Cody
MISSISSIPPI(1935); SLIGHT CASE OF MURDER, A(1938); MARK OF THE LASH(1948); ADAM'S RIB(1949); PEOPLE AGAINST O'HARA, THE(1951); UNKNOWN MAN, THE(1951); VANQUISHED, THE(1953); LAST TIME I SAW PARIS, THE(1954)

Iron Eyes Cody
FIGHTING CARAVANS(1931); OKLAHOMA JIM(1931); 99 WOUNDS(1931); RIDER OF DEATH VALLEY(1932); TEXAS PIONEERS(1932); WHISTLIN' DAN(1932); WILD GIRL(1932); KING OF THE ARENA(1933); FARMER TAKES A WIFE, THE(1935); RIDE, RANGER, RIDE(1936); TOLL OF THE DESERT (1936); TREACHERY RIDES THE RANGE(1936); PRAIRIE THUNDER(1937); RIDERS OF THE WHISTLING SKULL(1937); OLD LOUISIANA(1938); CRASHING THRU(1939); UNION PACIFIC(1939); GREEN HELL(1940); KIT CARSON(1940); PONY POST(1940); TOO MANY GIRLS(1940); YOUNG BILL HICKOK(1940); YOUNG BUFFALO BILL(1940); OUTLAWS OF THE CHEROKEE TRAIL(1941); SADDLEMATES(1941); KING OF THE STALLIONS(1942); SPRINGTIME IN THE ROCKIES(1942); VALLEY OF THE SUN(1942); PLAINSMAN AND THE LADY(1946); UNDER NEVADA SKIES(1946); BOWERY BUCKAROOS(1947); LAST ROUND-UP, THE(1947); SENATOR WAS INDISCREET, THE(1947); UNCONQUERED(1947); GALLANT LEGION, THE(1948); INDIAN AGENT(1948); PALEFACE, THE(1948); TRAIN TO ALCATRAZ(1948); MASSACRE RIVER(1949); SAND(1949); TULSA(1949); BROKEN ARROW(1950); CALIFORNIA PASSAGE(1950); CHEROKEE UPRISING(1950); NORTH OF THE GREAT DIVIDE(1950); BIG CARNIVAL, THE(1951); FORT DEFIANCE(1951); RED MOUNTAIN(1951); FORT OSAGE(1952); LOST IN ALASKA(1952); MEET ME AT THE FAIR(1952); MONTANA BELLE(1952); NIGHT RAIDERS(1952); SON OF PALEFACE(1952); FAST COMPANY(1953); SITTING BULL(1954); WHITE FEATHER(1955); WESTWARD HO THE WAGONS(1956); WILD DAKOTAS, THE(1956); GUN FOR A COWARD(1957); GUN FEVER(1958); HELLER IN PINK TIGHTS(1960); BLACK GOLD(1963); GREAT SIOUX MASSACRE, THE(1965); FASTEST GUITAR ALIVE, THE(1967); COCKEYED COWBOYS OF CALICO COUNTY, THE(1970); EL CONDOR(1970); MAN CALLED HORSE, A(1970); GRAYEAGLE(1977)

J. W. Cody
WAGON TRACKS WEST(1943); LAST ROUND-UP, THE(1947); BULLWHIP(1958)

Kathleen Cody
SNOWBALL EXPRESS(1972); CHARLEY AND THE ANGEL(1973); HOT SUMMER WEEK(1973, Can.); SUPERDAD(1974)

Lara Cody
I'M DANCING AS FAST AS I CAN(1982)
1984
THIS IS SPINAL TAP(1984)

Laura Cody
BATTLE BEYOND THE STARS(1980)

Lew Cody
WHAT A WIDOW(1930); BEYOND VICTORY(1931); COMMON LAW, THE(1931); DISHONORED(1931); DIVORCE AMONG FRIENDS(1931); MEET THE WIFE(1931); SPORTING BLOOD(1931); SWEEPSTAKES(1931); THREE GIRLS LOST(1931); THREE ROGUES(1931); WOMAN OF EXPERIENCE, A(1931); X MARKS THE SPOT(1931); CRUSADER, THE(1932); FILE 113(1932); MADISON SQUARE GARDEN(1932); PARISIAN ROMANCE, A(1932); TENDERFOOT, THE(1932); UNDER-COVER MAN(1932); UNWRITTEN LAW, THE(1932); 70,000 WITNESSES(1932); BY APPOINTMENT ONLY(1933); I LOVE THAT MAN(1933); SITTING PRETTY(1933); PRIVATE SCANDAL(1934); SHOOT THE WORKS(1934); WINE, WOMEN, AND SONG(1934)
Silents
ARE YOU LEGALLY MARRIED?(1919); MICKEY(1919); OCCASIONALLY YOURS(1920); SECRETS OF PARIS, THE(1922); VALLEY OF SILENT MEN, THE(1922); JACQUELINE, OR BLAZING BARRIERS(1923); LAWFUL LARCENY(1923); RENO(1923); RUPERT OF HENTZAU(1923); SOULS FOR SALE(1923); NELLIE, THE BEAUTIFUL CLOAK MODEL(1924); REVELATION(1924); HIS SECRETARY(1925); MAN AND MAID(1925); ADAM AND EVIL(1927); ON ZE BOULEVARD(1927); TEA FOR THREE(1927); SINGLE MAN, A(1929)
Misc. Silents
TREASURE OF THE SEA(1918); BROKEN BUTTERFLY, THE(1919); DON'T CHANGE YOUR HUSBAND(1919); LIFE LINE, THE(1919); MEN, WOMEN AND MONEY(1919); BELOVED CHEATER, THE(1920); SIGN ON THE DOOR, THE(1921); DANGEROUS PASTIME(1922); WITHIN THE LAW(1923); DEFYING THE LAW(1924); SHOOTING OF DAN MCGREW, THE(1924); SO THIS IS MARRIAGE(1924); THREE WOMEN(1924); WOMAN ON THE JURY, THE(1924); EXCHANGE OF WIVES(1925); SLAVE OF FASHION, A(1925); SPORTING VENUS, THE(1925); TIME, THE COMEDIAN(1925); GAY DECEIVER, THE(1926); MONTE CARLO(1926); DEMI-BRIDE, THE(1927); BABY CYCLONE, THE(1928); BEAU BROADWAY(1928); WICKEDNESS PREFERRED(1928)

Lewis J. Cody
Silents
BRIDE'S SILENCE, THE(1917); BRIDE'S AWAKENING, THE(1918); AS THE SUN WENT DOWN(1919)
Misc. Silents
BRANDED SOUL, A(1917); GAME OF WITS, A(1917); BORROWED CLOTHES(1918); DADDY'S GIRL(1918); FOR HUSBANDS ONLY(1918); OUR BETTER SELVES(1919)

Mike Cody
GYPSY(1962)

Robert Cody
FOLIES DERGERE(1935)

Barry Coe
HOUSE OF BAMBOO(1955); LOVE ME TENDER(1956); ON THE THRESHOLD OF SPACE(1956); PEYTON PLACE(1957); BRAVADOS, THE(1958); THUNDERING JETS(1958); BUT NOT FOR ME(1959); PRIVATE'S AFFAIR, A(1959); ONE FOOT IN HELL(1960); WIZARD OF BAGHDAD, THE(1960); 300 SPARTANS, THE(1962); CAT, THE(1966); FANTASTIC VOYAGE(1966); SEVEN MINUTES, THE(1971); DOCTOR DEATH: SEEKER OF SOULS(1973); MAC ARTHUR(1977); JAWS II(1978)

Charles Francis Coe
GAY BRIDE, THE(1934), w; NANCY STEELE IS MISSING(1937), w

David Allan Coe
SEABO(1978); TAKE THIS JOB AND SHOVE IT(1981)

David Allen Coe
SEABO(1978), m; LADY GREY(1980); TAKE THIS JOB AND SHOVE IT(1981), w

Fred Coe
LEFT-HANDED GUN, THE(1958), p; MIRACLE WORKER, THE(1962), p; THOUSAND CLOWNS, A(1965), p&d; THIS PROPERTY IS CONDEMNED(1966), w; ME, NATALIE(1969), d

George Coe
DISTANCE(1975), p; STEPFORD WIVES, THE(1975); FRENCH POSTCARDS(1979); KRAMER VS. KRAMER(1979); FIRST DEADLY SIN, THE(1980); BUSTIN' LOOSE(1981); AMATEUR, THE(1982); ENTITY, THE(1982)

1984
FLASH OF GREEN, A(1984); HOUSE OF GOD, THE(1984); MICKI AND MAUDE(1984)

John Coe
SEDUCERS, THE(1962); COOGAN'S BLUFF(1968); ME AND MY BROTHER(1969)

Kelvin Coe
DON QUIXOTE(1973, Aus.)

Kenton Coe
BIRDS COME TO DIE IN PERU(1968, Fr.), m

Peter Coe
GUNG HO!(1943); FOLLOW THE BOYS(1944); GYPSY WILDCAT(1944); HOUSE OF FRANKENSTEIN(1944); MUMMY'S CURSE, THE(1944); MY OWN TRUE LOVE(1948); SANDS OF IWO JIMA(1949); SWORD IN THE DESERT(1949); ROCKY MOUNTAIN(1950); DIPLOMATIC COURIER(1952); HELLGATE(1952); ROAD TO BALI(1952); WILD BLUE YONDER, THE(1952); ARROWHEAD(1953); DESERT LEGION(1953); FLIGHT TO TANGIER(1953); HINDU, THE(1953, Brit.); ALASKA SEAS(1954); PASSION(1954); ESCAPE TO BURMA(1955); SHOTGUN(1955); SMOKE SIGNAL(1955); TEN COMMANDMENTS, THE(1956); HELL SHIP MUTINY(1957); LOUISIANA HUSSY(1960); OKEFENOKEE(1960); PRIZE, THE(1963); SECRET INVASION, THE(1964); TOBRUK(1966); LOCK UP YOUR DAUGHTERS(1969, Brit.), d; VIGILANTE FORCE(1976)

Phyllis Coe
ROCK, ROCK, ROCK!(1956), w

Richard Coe
SMASHING TIME(1967 Brit.)

Rose Coe
MELODY LANE(1929)

Vivien Coe
YANKEE DOODLE DANDY(1942)

Vivian Coe [Austin]
GOLDWYN FOLLIES, THE(1938)

Coedel
PORTRAIT OF INNOCENCE(1948, Fr.)

Lucien Coedel
CARMEN(1946, Ital.); BELLMAN, THE(1947, Fr.); IDIOT, THE(1948, Fr.); STRANGERS IN THE HOUSE(1949, Fr.)

Susie Coelho
NORSEMAN, THE(1978)

Ethan Coen
1984
BLOOD SIMPLE(1984), p, w

Franklin Coen
LIVING ON LOVE(1937), w; WE'RE ON THE JURY(1937), w; EXPOSED(1938), w; QUICK MONEY(1938), w; FORGED PASSPORT(1939), w; GLORY BRIGADE, THE(1953), w; FOUR GUNS TO THE BORDER(1954), w; JOHNNY DARK(1954), w; CHIEF CRAZY HORSE(1955), w; KISS OF FIRE(1955), w; THIS ISLAND EARTH(1955), w; INTERLUDE(1957), w; NIGHT OF THE QUARTER MOON(1959), w; TRAIN, THE(1965, Fr./Ital./U.S.), w; ALVAREZ KELLY(1966), w; BLACK GUNN(1972), w; TAKE, THE(1974), w

Franklyn Coen
FIGHTING THOROUGHBREDS(1939), w

Guido Coen
SHE SHALL HAVE MURDER(1950, Brit.), p; GOLDEN LINK, THE(1954, Brit.), p; MEET MR. CALLAGHAN(1954, Brit.), p; HORNET'S NEST, THE(1955, Brit.), p; ONE JUMP AHEAD(1955, Brit.), p; BEHIND THE HEADLINES(1956, Brit.), p; DATE WITH DISASTER(1957, Brit.), p; MAN WITHOUT A BODY, THE(1957, Brit.), p; THERE'S ALWAYS A THURSDAY(1957, Brit.), p; KILL HER GENTLY(1958, Brit.), p; MURDER REPORTED(1958, Brit.), p; END OF THE LINE, THE(1959, Brit.), p; NAKED FURY(1959, Brit.), p&w; STRICTLY CONFIDENTIAL(1959, Brit.), p; WOMAN EATER, THE(1959, Brit.), p; GENTLE TRAP, THE(1960, Brit.), p; OPERATION CUPID(1960, Brit.), p; DANGEROUS AFTERNOON(1961, Brit.), p; STRONGROOM(1962, Brit.), p; JUNGLE STREET GIRLS(1963, Brit.), p, w; PLEASURE LOVERS, THE(1964, Brit.), p, w; PANIC(1966, Brit.), p, d&w; BABY LOVE(1969, Brit.), p, w; ONE BRIEF SUMMER(1971, Brit.), p, w

Joel Coen
1984
BLOOD SIMPLE(1984), d, w

Massino Coen
SNOWBOUND(1949, Brit.)

Joseph Coencas
VERY NATURAL THING, A(1974), w

Carlotta Coer
Misc. Silents
CAUGHT IN THE ACT(1918)

Carlotta Coerr
JEALOUSY(1929)

Josef Coesfeld
ONE, TWO, THREE(1961), Makeup; JUDGE AND THE SINNER, THE(1964, Ger.), makeup; ONE-TRICK PONY(1980), makeup

Morne Coetzer, Jr.
SEVEN AGAINST THE SUN(1968, South Africa)

Damon Cofer
BAD COMPANY(1972)

Marina Coffa
LAST REBEL, THE(1971)

Jean-Pierre Coffe
VIOLETTE(1978, Fr.)

Pierre Coffe
1984
SWANN IN LOVE(1984, Fr.Ger.)

Lenore Coffee
POSSESSED(1931), w; SQUAW MAN, THE(1931), w; ARSENE LUPIN(1932), w; DOWNSTAIRS(1932), w; NIGHT COURT(1932), w; TORCH SINGER(1933), w; ALL MEN ARE ENEMIES(1934), w; EVELYN PRENTICE(1934), w; SUCH WOMEN ARE DANGEROUS(1934), w; AGE OF INDISCRETION(1935), w; VANESSA, HER LOVE STORY(1935), w; SUZY(1936), w; FOUR DAUGHTERS(1938), w; WHITE BANNERS(1938), w; GOOD GIRLS GO TO PARIS(1939), w; MY SON, MY SON!(1940), w; WAY OF ALL FLESH, THE(1940), w; GREAT LIE, THE(1941), w; GAY SISTERS, THE(1942), w; OLD ACQUAINTANCE(1943), w; MARRIAGE IS A PRIVATE AFFAIR(1944), w; 'TILL WE MEET AGAIN(1944), w; TOMORROW IS FOREVER(1946),

w; GUILT OF JANET AMES, THE(1947), w; BEYOND THE FOREST(1949), w; LIGHTNING STRIKES TWICE(1951), w; SUDDEN FEAR(1952), w; END OF THE AFFAIR, THE(1955, Brit.), w; YOUNG AT HEART(1955), w; ANOTHER TIME, ANOTHER PLACE(1958), w; CASH McCALL(1960), w
Silents
RIGHT THAT FAILED, THE(1922), w; TEMPTATION(1923), w
Lenore J. Coffee
BISHOP MURDER CASE, THE(1930), w; MOTHERS CRY(1930), w; FOUR FRIGHTENED PEOPLE(1934), w
Silents
FORBIDDEN WOMAN, THE(1920), w; SHERLOCK BROWN(1921), w; ROSE OF PARIS, THE(1924), w; VOLGA BOATMAN, THE(1926), w; NIGHT OF LOVE, THE(1927), w; CHICAGO(1928), w
Leonore Coffee
FOOTSTEPS IN THE FOG(1955, Brit.), w
Leonore J. Coffee
STREET OF CHANCE(1930), w
Stuart Coffee
SHAME, SHAME, EVERYBODY KNOWS HER NAME(1969)
Ciquita Coffelli
HUNS, THE(1962, Fr./Ital.)
Jack Coffer
WAY WEST, THE(1967)
Coffey
FEMALE TROUBLE(1975)
Bob Coffey
1984
ELECTRIC DREAMS(1984)
Cameron Coffey
GODLESS GIRL, THE(1929)
Silents
POLLY OF THE STORM COUNTRY(1920); LITTLE CLOWN, THE(1921)
Misc. Silents
PASSING THRU(1921)
Christopher Coffey
CHANGE OF SEASONS, A(1980)
Clark Coffey
Misc. Silents
CUPID'S RUSTLER(1924)
Denise Coffey
WALTZ OF THE TOREADORS(1962, Brit.); YOUNG AND WILLING(1964, Brit.); GEORGY GIRL(1966, Brit.); FAR FROM THE MADDING CROWD(1967, Brit.); START THE REVOLUTION WITHOUT ME(1970); PERCY(1971, Brit.); SIR HENRY AT RAWLINSON END(1980, Brit.); ANOTHER TIME, ANOTHER PLACE(1983, Brit.)
1984
ANOTHER TIME, ANOTHER PLACE(1984, Brit.)
Dennis Coffey
MARDI GRAS MASSACRE(1978), m
Frank Coffey
GONE TO THE DOGS(1939, Aus.), w; RANGLE RIVER(1939, Aus.), ed; THAT CERTAIN SOMETHING(1941, Aus.), ph
Jack Coffey
MOONLIGHT IN VERMONT(1943)
Joe Coffey
PRODUCERS, THE(1967), ph; HELLCATS, THE(1968)
Joseph Coffey
UP THE DOWN STAIRCASE(1967), ph; FOR LOVE OF IVY(1968), ph
Lt. Col. Edward H. Coffey
STORY OF G.I. JOE, THE(1945), tech adv
Robert Coffey
EXPERIMENT IN TERROR(1962)
Tom Coffey
TYCOON(1947); UNDERCOVER MAN, THE(1949)
Peter Coffield
TIMES SQUARE(1980); ONLY WHEN I LAUGH(1981)
Adeline Hayden Coffin
Silents
AFTER MANY DAYS(1919, Brit.); KNAVE OF HEARTS, THE(1919, Brit.); POWER OF RIGHT, THE(1919, Brit.); KISSING CUP'S RACE(1920, Brit.); DON QUIXOTE(1923, Brit.); IN THE BLOOD(1923, Brit.); PRODIGAL SON, THE(1923, Brit.); ALLEY OF GOLDEN HEARTS, THE(1924, Brit.); FLYING FIFTY-FIVE, THE(1924, Brit.); AFRAID OF LOVE(1925, Brit.); WOMAN TEMPTED, THE(1928, Brit.)
Estelle Coffin
Silents
FLOOR ABOVE, THE(1914)
Eugene Coffin
HAPPENING, THE(1967), cos
Fred Coffin
KING OF THE GYPSIES(1978); WITHOUT A TRACE(1983)
Fredrick Coffin
ONE SUMMER LOVE(1976)
Gene Coffin
LOLITA(1962), cos; YELLOW ROLLS-ROYCE, THE(1965, Brit.), cos; PRODUCERS, THE(1967), cos; DON'T DRINK THE WATER(1969), cos; GOODBYE COLUMBUS(1969), cos; BANANAS(1971), cos; EDUCATION OF SONNY CARSON, THE(1974), cos; LOVIN' MOLLY(1974), prod d
Hayden Coffin
SCHOOL FOR SCANDAL, THE(1930, Brit.)
Silents
QUEEN OF MY HEART(1917, Brit.)
Misc. Silents
BIGAMIST, THE(1916)
Ida Coffin
AM I GUILTY?(1940)
Mrs. Hayden Coffin
OTHER PEOPLE'S SINS(1931, Brit.)
Tris [Tristram] Coffin
OKLAHOMA TERROR(1939); OVERLAND MAIL(1939); ARIZONA FRONTIER(1940); CHASING TROUBLE(1940); QUEEN OF THE YUKON(1940); RHYTHM OF THE RIO GRANDE(1940); UP IN THE AIR(1940); WEST OF PINTO BASIN(1940);

ARIZONA BOUND(1941); FORBIDDEN TRAILS(1941); KING OF DODGE CITY(1941); LET'S GO COLLEGIATE(1941); MAN BETRAYED, A(1941); NO GREATER SIN(1941); TONTO BASIN OUTLAWS(1941); YOU'RE OUT OF LUCK(1941); BELLS OF CAPISTRANO(1942); CORPSE VANISHES, THE(1942); COWBOY SERENADE(1942); DAWN ON THE GREAT DIVIDE(1942); DEVIL'S TRAIL, THE(1942); MEET THE MOB(1942); POLICE BULLETS(1942); DESTROYER(1943); LADY IN THE DARK(1944); DANGEROUS MONEY(1946); GENTLEMAN FROM TEXAS(1946); INVISIBLE INFORMER(1946); MYSTERIOUS MR. VALENTINE, THE(1946); RIO GRANDE RAIDERS(1946); SIOUX CITY SUE(1946); UNDER ARIZONA SKIES(1946); UNDER NEVADA SKIES(1946); BLACKMAIL(1947); FABULOUS TEXAN, THE(1947); LAND OF THE LAWLESS(1947); LOUISIANA(1947); POSSESSED(1947); TRAIL TO SAN ANTONE(1947); VOICE OF THE TURTLE, THE(1947); CALIFORNIA FIREBRAND(1948); DESPERADOES OF DODGE CITY(1948); HUNTED, THE(1948); ROMANCE ON THE HIGH SEAS(1948); SHANGHAI CHEST, THE(1948); ANGELS IN DISGUISE(1949); CRASHING THRU(1949); DESERT VIGILANTE(1949); FLAMINGO ROAD(1949); FOUNTAINHEAD, THE(1949); LAWLESS CODE(1949); MY DREAM IS YOURS(1949); RANGE JUSTICE(1949); RIDERS OF THE DUSK(1949); BARON OF ARIZONA, THE(1950); DAMNED DON'T CRY, THE(1950); OLD FRONTIER, THE(1950); OUTRAGE(1950); PYGMY ISLAND(1950); RADAR SECRET SERVICE(1950); SHORT GRASS(1950); SQUARE DANCE KATY(1950); UNDERCOVER GIRL(1950); ACCORDING TO MRS. HOYLE(1951); BUCKAROO SHERIFF OF TEXAS(1951); FAT MAN, THE(1951); LADY PAYS OFF, THE(1951); MASK OF THE AVENGER(1951); ON THE LOOSE(1951); PAINTING THE CLOUDS WITH SUNSHINE(1951); QUEEN FOR A DAY(1951); RHUBARB(1951); RODEO KING AND THE SENORITA(1951); KID FROM BROKEN GUN, THE(1952); NORTHWEST TERRITORY(1952); SMOKY CANYON(1952); COMBAT SQUAD(1953); HANNAH LEE(1953); LATIN LOVERS(1953); LAW AND ORDER(1953); SALOME(1953); FIREMAN SAVE MY CHILD(1954); STAR IS BORN, A(1954); CREATURE WITH THE ATOM BRAIN(1955); SCARLET COAT, THE(1955); FIRST TRAVELING SALESLADY, THE(1956); MAN IN THE GREY FLANNEL SUIT, THE(1956); MAVERICK QUEEN, THE(1956); LAST STAGECOACH WEST, THE(1957); NIGHT THE WORLD EXPLODED, THE(1957); MA BARKER'S KILLER BROOD(1960); SILENT WITNESS, THE(1962); CRAWLING HAND, THE(1963); GOOD NEIGHBOR SAM(1964); ZEBRA IN THE KITCHEN(1965); BAREFOOT EXECUTIVE, THE(1971)
Misc. Talkies
NORTH OF THE ROCKIES(1942); PRAIRIE GUNSMOKE(1942); TORNADO IN THE SADDLE, A(1942); COSMO JONES, CRIME SMASHER(1943); VIGILANTES RIDE, THE(1944); VALLEY OF FEAR(1947); MARSHALS IN DISGUISE(1954); ALIENS FROM ANOTHER PLANET(1967)
Anne Marie Coffinet
ANY NUMBER CAN WIN(1963 Fr.)
Anne-Marie Coffinet
MONKEY IN WINTER, A(1962, Fr.); SUNDAYS AND CYBELE(1962, Fr.); NO TIME FOR ECSTASY(1963, Fr.); LIARS, THE(1964, Fr.); TIGHT SKIRTS, LOOSE PLEASURES(1966, Fr.); MOON IN THE GUTTER, THE(1983, Fr./Ital.)
Christian Coffinet
WOMAN OF SIN(1961, Fr.), w
Noel Coffman
1984
FULL MOON IN PARIS(1984, Fr.)
Tony Coffman
HOT STUFF(1979)
Dennis Coffy
BLACK BELT JONES(1974), m
Frank Coffyn
Silents
RANSON'S FOLLY(1926)
Misc. Silents
DEADWOOD COACH, THE(1924)
Pauline Coffyn
Misc. Silents
PASSERS-BY(1920)
Adolfo Cofino
UP THE MACGREGORS(1967, Ital./Span.), art d; SPIRIT OF THE BEEHIVE, THE(1976, Span.), art d; JAGUAR LIVES(1979), art d
Alma Cogan
FOR BETTER FOR WORSE(1954, Brit.)
Dick Cogan
DANCING IN THE DARK(1949); JOLSON SINGS AGAIN(1949); WILD WEED(1949); EXPERIMENT ALCATRAZ(1950); JACKPOT, THE(1950); MAGNIFICENT YANKEE, THE(1950); YOUNG MAN WITH A HORN(1950); STREET BANDITS(1951); UNKNOWN WORLD(1951); DON'T BOTHER TO KNOCK(1952); IRON MISTRESS, THE(1952); MY SIX CONVICTS(1952)
Fanny Cogan
Misc. Silents
SHELL GAME, THE(1918)
Henri Cogan
THAT MAN IN ISTANBUL(1966, Fr./Ital./Span.); MADWOMAN OF CHAILLOT, THE(1969); HIT(1973)
Henry Cogan
YOUR TURN, DARLING(1963, Fr.); LIQUIDATOR, THE(1966, Brit.)
James Cogan
Silents
RISE OF JENNIE CUSHING, THE(1917)
Lick Cogan
MEET ME AFTER THE SHOW(1951)
Nathan Cogan
TEL AVIV TAXI(1957, Israel)
Rhodie Cogan
WATERMELON MAN(1970); YOUR THREE MINUTES ARE UP(1973)
Shaye Cogan
COMIN' ROUND THE MOUNTAIN(1951); JACK AND THE BEANSTALK(1952); MISTER ROCK AND ROLL(1957)
David J. Cogen
RUN ACROSS THE RIVER(1961), p
Carol Coggin
FIRST MONDAY IN OCTOBER(1981)

Thomas C. Coggin
TOMORROW(1972)

Roger Coggio
SELLERS OF GIRLS(1967, Fr.); LES CARABINIERS(1968, Fr./Ital.); IMMORTAL STORY, THE(1969, Fr.); TIME OF THE WOLVES(1970, Fr.)

Ambrose Coghill
DOCTOR FAUSTUS(1967, Brit.); CHARGE OF THE LIGHT BRIGADE, THE(1968, Brit.); OH! WHAT A LOVELY WAR(1969, Brit.)

Bridget Coghill
DOCTOR FAUSTUS(1967, Brit.)

Gordon Coghill
Misc. Silents
WAY OF THE WORLD, THE(1920, Brit.)

Joy Coghill
JACOB TWO-TWO MEETS THE HOODED FANG(1979, Can.)

Nevill Coghill
DOCTOR FAUSTUS(1967, Brit.), a, d, w

Charles Coghlan
Silents
JIM THE PENMAN(1921)
Misc. Silents
THOU SHALT NOT KILL(1915)

Eileen Coghlan
THOUSANDS CHEER(1943); DARK WATERS(1944); TWO TICKETS TO BROAD-WAY(1951); FRENCH LINE, THE(1954)

Frank Coghlan, Jr.
PUBLIC ENEMY, THE(1931); MAKE WAY FOR A LADY(1936); BLAZING BARRI-ERS(1937); SATURDAY'S HEROES(1937); ANGELS WITH DIRTY FACES(1938); HIS EXCITING NIGHT(1938); SERVICE DE LUXE(1938); BOY'S REFORMATORY(1939); DAY-TIME WIFE(1939); EAST SIDE OF HEAVEN(1939); LUCKY NIGHT(1939); MEET DR. CHRISTIAN(1939); OFF THE RECORD(1939); SECOND FIDDLE(1939); FIGHT-ING 69TH, THE(1940); FREE, BLONDE AND 21(1940); GOLDEN GLOVES(1940); KNUTE ROCKNE–ALL AMERICAN(1940); MURDER OVER NEW YORK(1940); STAR DUST(1940); THOSE WERE THE DAYS(1940); HENRY ALDRICH FOR PRESI-DENT(1941); OUT OF THE FOG(1941); UNFINISHED BUSINESS(1941); ANDY HARDY'S DOUBLE LIFE(1942); COURTSHIP OF ANDY HARDY, THE(1942); FOOT-LIGHT SERENADE(1942); GIRL TROUBLE(1942); MAN WHO CAME TO DINNER, THE(1942); RINGS ON HER FINGERS(1942); TO THE SHORES OF TRIPOLI(1942); FOLLOW THE BAND(1943); THIS IS THE ARMY(1943); YOUTH ON PARADE(1943); ONE MORE TOMORROW(1946)

Frank "Junior" Coghlan, Jr.
HAPPINESS C.O.D.(1935); LITTLE RED SCHOOLHOUSE(1936)

Junior Coghlan
SQUARE SHOULDERS(1929); GIRL SAID NO, THE(1930); IT PAYS TO ADVER-TISE(1931); PENROD AND SAM(1931); HELL'S HOUSE(1932); DRUM TAPS(1933); RACETRACK(1933); IN THE MONEY(1934); KENTUCKY BLUE STREAK(1935); STRANDED(1935); CHARLIE CHAN AT THE RACE TRACK(1936); GONE WITH THE WIND(1939)
Silents
RUBBER TIRES(1927); SLIDE, KELLY, SLIDE(1927); YANKEE CLIPPER, THE(1927); LET 'ER GO GALLEGHER(1928); MARKED MONEY(1928)
Misc. Silents
LAST FRONTIER, THE(1926); COUNTRY DOCTOR, THE(1927); HARP IN HOCK, A(1927)

Junior Coghlan [Frank Coghlan, Jr.]
RIVER'S END(1931); UNION DEPOT(1932)

Phillis Coghlan
DARK ANGEL, THE(1935); CHARGE OF THE LIGHT BRIGADE, THE(1936)

Phyllis Coghlan
I FOUND STELLA PARISH(1935); RIGHT TO LIVE, THE(1935); TOP HAT(1935); ANGEL(1937); PARNELL(1937); SCARLET COAT, THE(1955)

Rose Coghlan
JENNIE GERHARDT(1933); FINISHING SCHOOL(1934)
Silents
SECRETS OF PARIS, THE(1922); UNDER THE RED ROBE(1923)
Misc. Silents
THOU SHALT NOT KILL(1915); FADED FLOWER, THE(1916)

Rose Coghlan II
HOT SATURDAY(1932)

Eileen Coghlin
FORCE OF EVIL(1948); NO MINOR VICES(1948)

Laura Cogin
YOUNG WARRIORS(1983), cos

Nick Cogley
ABIE'S IRISH ROSE(1928); COHENS AND KELLYS IN AFRICA, THE(1930); CROSSFIRE(1933)
Silents
INSIDE THE LINES(1918); BEATING THE GAME(1921); GUILE OF WOMEN(1921); ONE CLEAR CALL(1922); CRINOLINE AND ROMANCE(1923); ABRAHAM LIN-COLN(1924); HEY! HEY! COWBOY(1927); IN OLD KENTUCKY(1927)
Misc. Silents
OLD NEST, THE(1921)

Julia Coglin
RED AND THE WHITE, THE(1969, Hung./USSR)

Monsieur Cognac
WILD AND WONDERFUL(1964)

George M. Cohan
HOME TOWNERS, THE(1928), w; FAST COMPANY(1929), w; LITTLE JOHNNY JONES(1930), w; SEVEN KEYS TO BALDPATE(1930), w; SO THIS IS LONDON(1930), w; MIRACLE MAN, THE(1932), w; PHANTOM PRESIDENT, THE(1932); ELMER THE GREAT(1933), w; GAMBLING(1934), a, w; SEVEN KEYS TO BALDPATE(1935), w; SONG AND DANCE MAN, THE(1936), w; TIMES SQUARE PLAYBOY(1936), w; COWBOY QUARTERBACK(1939), w; LADIES MUST LIVE(1940), w; LITTLE NEL-LIE KELLY(1940), w; SO THIS IS LONDON(1940, Brit.), w; MEANEST MAN IN THE WORLD, THE(1943), w
Silents
MIRACLE MAN, THE(1919), w; PRINCE THERE WAS, A(1921), w
Misc. Silents
BROADWAY JONES(1917); SEVEN KEYS TO BALDPATE(1917); HIT-THE-TRAIL HOLLIDAY(1918)

Helen Cohan
LIGHTNIN'(1930); PENAL CODE, THE(1933)

Helene Cohan
KISS AND MAKE UP(1934)

Millard Cohan
PASSOVER PLOT, THE(1976, Israel), w

Morrie Cohan
IRON MAN, THE(1931); I'M NO ANGEL(1933); BELLE OF THE NINETIES(1934); MILKY WAY, THE(1936)

Morry Cohan
STEADY COMPANY(1932)

Tony Cohan
MAKE A FACE(1971), m

Patti Cohane
TOOTSIE(1982)

Edward Cohem
FIRE OVER ENGLAND(1937, Brit.), spec eff

Alain Cohen
TWO OF US, THE(1968, Fr.)

Alaine Cohen
FIRST TIME, THE(1978, Fr.)

Albert Cohen
TIMES SQUARE LADY(1935), w

Albert J. Cohen
I SELL ANYTHING(1934), w; KING SOLOMON OF BROADWAY(1935), w; NIGHT AT THE RITZ, A(1935), w; MOONLIGHT MURDER(1936), w; INVISIBLE ENE-MY(1938), w; WHO KILLED AUNT MAGGIE?(1940), p; ANGELS WITH BROKEN WINGS(1941), p; DEVIL PAYS OFF, THE(1941), p; DOCTORS DON'T TELL(1941), p; LADY FOR A NIGHT(1941), p; PUDDIN' HEAD(1941), p; ROOKIES ON PARA-DE(1941), p; SAILORS ON LEAVE(1941), p; PARDON MY STRIPES(1942), p; REMEMBER PEARL HARBOR(1942), p; SLEEPYTIME GAL(1942), p; CHATTER-BOX(1943), p; HIT PARADE OF 1943(1943), p; SLEEPY LAGOON(1943), p; THUMBS UP(1943), p; YOUTH ON PARADE(1943), p; ATLANTIC CITY(1944), p; CASANOVA IN BURLESQUE(1944), p; FIGHTING SEABEES, THE(1944), p; EARL CARROLL'S VANITIES(1945), p; WALLS CAME TUMBLING DOWN, THE(1946), p; LET'S LIVE A LITTLE(1948), w; PREHISTORIC WOMEN(1950), p; LADY PAYS OFF, THE(1951), p, w; BECAUSE OF YOU(1952), p; HORIZONS WEST(1952), p; MEET ME AT THE FAIR(1952), p; CITY BENEATH THE SEA(1953), p; EAST OF SUMATRA(1953), p; GIRLS IN THE NIGHT(1953), p; GLASS WEB, THE(1953), p; GREAT SIOUX UPRIS-ING, THE(1953), p; VEILS OF BAGDAD, THE(1953), p; BORDER RIVER(1954), p; PLAYGIRL(1954), p; SIGN OF THE PAGAN(1954), p; SO THIS IS PARIS(1954), p; TANGANYIKA(1954), p; SECOND GREATEST SEX, THE(1955), p; NEVER SAY GOODBYE(1956), p; OUTSIDE THE LAW(1956), p; ISTANBUL(1957), p; NIGHT RUNNER, THE(1957), p; ISLAND OF LOST WOMEN(1959), p; NAKED BRIGADE, THE(1965, U.S./Gr.), p, w

Albert Jay Cohen
UNKNOWN ISLAND(1948), p

Alejandro Cohen
STATE OF SIEGE(1973, Fr./U.S./Ital./Ger.)

Alison Cohen
FIRST NUDIE MUSICAL, THE(1976)

Barney Cohen
STUNTS(1977), w; FRENCH QUARTER(1978), w
1984
FRIDAY THE 13TH–THE FINAL CHAPTER(1984), w

Barry Cohen
Misc. Talkies
JOE AND MAXI(1980)

Bella Cohen
FOR THE LOVE O'LIL(1930), w

Bella Cohen [Spewack]
NUISANCE, THE(1933), w

Ben Cohen
BORDER PATROLMAN, THE(1936), w; SIX GUN SERENADE(1947), w

Ben S. Cohen
NEW ADVENTURES OF TARZAN(1935), p; TARZAN AND THE GREEN GOD-DESS(1938), p

Bennet Cohen
IN OLD CHEYENNE(1931), w
Silents
MIND OVER MOTOR(1923), t

Bennett Cohen
SENOR AMERICANO(1929), w; FIGHTING LEGION, THE(1930), w; MOUNTAIN JUSTICE(1930), w; PARADE OF THE WEST(1930), w; SONS OF THE SADDLE(1930), w; UNDER MONTANA SKIES(1930), w; LAW OF THE RIO GRANDE(1931), d, w; WEST OF CHEYENNE(1931), w; COME ON DANGER!(1932), w; LONE TRAIL, THE(1932), w; SUNSET TRAIL(1932), w; TEXAS GUN FIGHTER(1932), w; WILDER-NESS MAIL(1935), w; AMBUSH VALLEY(1936), w; SWIFTY(1936), w; FIGHTING DEPUTY, THE(1937), w; MELODY OF THE PLAINS(1937), w; RAW TIMBER(1937), w; LAW COMMANDS, THE(1938), w; RENEGADE RANGER(1938), w; SKULL AND CROWN(1938), w; SOUTH OF ARIZONA(1938), w; FRONTIER VENGEANCE(1939), w; RIDERS OF BLACK RIVER(1939), w; GHOST VALLEY RAIDERS(1940), w; ONE MAN'S LAW(1940), w; PIONEER DAYS(1940), w; DESERT BANDIT(1941), w; MAN FROM MONTANA(1941), w; TWO GUN SHERIFF(1941), w; WYOMING WILD-CAT(1941), w; COME ON DANGER(1942), w; FALSE COLORS(1943), w; RIDERS OF THE DEADLINE(1943), w; SAGEBRUSH LAW(1943), w; GHOST GUNS(1944), w; SILVER CITY KID(1944), w; TRAIL TO GUNSIGHT(1944), w; BEYOND THE PE-COS(1945), w; CHEROKEE FLASH, THE(1945), p, w; OREGON TRAIL(1945), p; ROUGH RIDERS OF CHEYENNE(1945), p; SANTA FE SADDLEMATES(1945), w; SHERIFF OF CIMARRON(1945), w; ALIAS BILLY THE KID(1946), p; EL PASO KID, THE(1946), p; LAWLESS EMPIRE(1946), w; RED RIVER RENEGADES(1946), p; RIO GRANDE RAIDERS(1946), p; HOPPY'S HOLIDAY(1947), w; RIDIN' DOWN THE TRAIL(1947), p, w; OKLAHOMA BLUES(1948), w
Silents
BRIDE OF FEAR, THE(1918), w; CROSS BREED(1927), w; AVENGING SHADOW, THE(1928), w

Bennett R. Cohen
BAR L RANCH(1930), w; SONG OF THE CABELLERO(1930), w; WALLABY JIM OF THE ISLANDS(1937), w; FEMALE FUGITIVE(1938), w; WEST OF SANTA FE(1938), w; NORTH OF THE YUKON(1939), w; THUNDERING WEST, THE(1939), w; WEST-

ERN CARAVANS(1939), w; BANDIT RANGER(1942), w; RED RIVER ROBIN HOOD(1943), w; BANDITS OF THE BADLANDS(1945), p; KING OF THE BANDITS(1948), w; DEVIL'S CANYON(1953), w

Bennett Ray Cohen
Silents
FAME AND FORTUNE(1918), w

Charles Cohen
Misc. Silents
PERILS OF PORK PIE, THE(1916, Brit.)

Claude Cohen
MAMMA DRACULA(1980, Bel./Fr.), ed

Dael Cohen
DANIEL(1983)

Danny Cohen
HITCHHIKERS, THE(1972), m
Misc. Talkies
JOE AND MAXI(1980)

Darren Cohen
NORMAN LOVES ROSE(1982, Aus.)

David Hayyad Cohen
EXTERMINATING ANGEL, THE(1967, Mex.)

Dean Cohen
COOL WORLD, THE(1963)

Dick Cohen
SCARECROW IN A GARDEN OF CUCUMBERS(1972), ed

Donald J. Cohen
FIVE GOLDEN DRAGONS(1967, Brit.), ed

Edward Cohen
THINGS TO COME(1936, Brit.), spec eff; DARK JOURNEY(1937, Brit.), spec eff; MAN WHO COULD WORK MIRACLES, THE(1937, Brit.), spec eff; STORM IN A TEACUP(1937, Brit.), spec eff; SOUTH RIDING(1938, Brit.), spec eff; GENTLEMAN FROM ARIZONA, THE(1940), ph

Eli Cohen
JESUS(1979)

Ellis Cohen
DEFIANCE(1980), cos; SAVAGE HARVEST(1981), cos

Emanual Cohen
LOVE ON TOAST(1937), p

Emanuel Cohen
GIRL FROM SCOTLAND YARD, THE(1937), p; MIDNIGHT MADONNA(1937), p; MIND YOUR OWN BUSINESS(1937), p; ON SUCH A NIGHT(1937), p; OUTCAST(1937), p; DR. RHYTHM(1938), p; EVERY DAY'S A HOLIDAY(1938), p

Emanuel R. Cohen
GO WEST, YOUNG MAN(1936), p

Emma Cohen
LEGEND OF FRENCHIE KING, THE(1971, Fr./Ital./Span./Brit.)
Misc. Talkies
APARTMENT ON THE THIRTEENTH FLOOR(1973)

Emmanuel Cohen
DEVIL AND THE DEEP(1932), p; PENNIES FROM HEAVEN(1936), p

Ernest Cohen
BEDTIME STORY, A(1933), p

Esther Cohen
HOT TOMORROWS(1978)

Fred Cohen
1984
SPLATTER UNIVERSITY(1984), ph

Gabe Cohen
NOTHING PERSONAL(1980, Can.)
1984
POWER, THE(1984)

Gerard Bernard Cohen
ECHOES(1983), m

Germaine Cohen
LE GAI SAVOIR(1968, Fr.), ed

Gilda Cohen
ELEPHANT MAN, THE(1980, Brit.)

Harold D. Cohen
HAIL, HERO!(1969), p; I WALK THE LINE(1970), p

Harriet Cohen
LADY SURRENDERS, A(1947, Brit.)

Harry Cohen
I'M AN EXPLOSIVE(1933, Brit.), p

Henry Cohen
RECOMMENDATION FOR MERCY(1975, Can.)

Herb Cohen
TWO HUNDRED MOTELS(1971, Brit.), p

Herman Cohen
RIVER BEAT(1954), p; TARGET EARTH(1954), p; BRASS LEGEND, THE(1956), p; MAGNIFICENT ROUGHNECKS(1956), p; BLOOD OF DRACULA(1957), p; CRIME OF PASSION(1957), p; I WAS A TEENAGE WEREWOLF(1957), p; HOW TO MAKE A MONSTER(1958), w; I WAS A TEENAGE FRANKENSTEIN(1958), p; HEADLESS GHOST, THE(1959, Brit.), p, w; HORRORS OF THE BLACK MUSEUM(1959, U.S./Brit.), p, w; 1001 ARABIAN NIGHTS(1959), anim; KONGA(1961, Brit.), p, w; BLACK ZOO(1963), p, w; BERSERK(1967), p, w; SOPHIE'S PLACE(1970), a, p; TROG(1970, Brit.), p; CRAZE(1974, Brit.), p, w; STRANGER'S GUNDOWN, THE(1974, Ital.), p

Howard Cohen
VAMPIRE HOOKERS, THE(1979, Phil.), w; DEATHSTALKER(1983, Arg./U.S.), w
1984
DEATHSTALKER, THE(1984), w

Howard R. Cohen
UNHOLY ROLLERS(1972), w; YOUNG NURSES, THE(1973), w; SATURDAY THE 14TH(1981), d&w; SPACE RAIDERS(1983), d&w; STRYKER(1983, Phil.), w

Ian Cohen
WARRIORS, THE(1979)

Irving Cohen
GOLDEN BOY(1939); TRACKS(1977), p

Jack Cohen
JERUSALEM FILE, THE(1972, U.S./Israel)

Jacky Cohen
TENANT, THE(1976, Fr.)

Jacques Cohen
HANNAH K.(1983, Fr.)

Jeffrey Cohen
CLASS OF '44(1973)
1984
HOTEL NEW HAMPSHIRE, THE(1984)

Jerry Cohen
STUDENT BODY, THE(1976), ed; NEW GIRL IN TOWN(1977), ed

Joe Cohen
Misc. Talkies
JOE AND MAXI(1980)

Joel Cohen
STRANGE INVADERS(1983)

Jonathan Cohen
1984
MARIGOLDS IN AUGUST(1984, S. Africa), p

Judith Cohen
SO FINE(1981)

Julie Cohen
1984
ONCE UPON A TIME IN AMERICA(1984)

Ken Cohen
LOOKIN' TO GET OUT(1982)

Larry Cohen
I DEAL IN DANGER(1966), w; RETURN OF THE SEVEN(1966, Span.), w; DADDY'S GONE A-HUNTING(1969), w; EL CONDOR(1970), w; BLACK CAESAR(1973), p,d&w; HELL UP IN HARLEM(1973), p,d&w; IT'S ALIVE(1974), p,d&w; GOD TOLD ME TO(1976), p,d&w; IT LIVES AGAIN(1978), p,d&w; PRIVATE FILES OF J. EDGAR HOOVER, THE(1978), p,d&w; AMERICAN SUCCESS COMPANY, THE(1980), w; FULL MOON HIGH(1982), p,d&w; I, THE JURY(1982), w; Q(1982), p,d&w
1984
PERFECT STRANGERS(1984), d&w; SCANDALOUS(1984), w; SPECIAL EFFECTS(1984), d&w
Misc. Talkies
BONE(1972), d

Laurence Cohen
CHARLIE CHAN AND THE CURSE OF THE DRAGON QUEEN(1981)

Laurence J. Cohen
S(1974), w

Laurence Robert Cohen
SCREAM, BABY, SCREAM(1969), w

Lawrence D. Cohen
CARRIE(1976), w; GHOST STORY(1981), w

Lawrence J. Cohen
START THE REVOLUTION WITHOUT ME(1970), w; BIG BUS, THE(1976), p&w

Leonard Cohen
MC CABE AND MRS. MILLER(1971), m

Lester Cohen
DANGEROUS CURVES(1929), w; NAGANA(1933), w; ONE MAN'S JOURNEY(1933), w; SWEEPINGS(1933), w; OF HUMAN BONDAGE(1934), w; BREAK OF HEARTS(1935), w; THREE SONS(1939), w

Lynn Cohen
WITHOUT A TRACE(1983)

M. Charles Cohen
DRYLANDERS(1963, Can.), w

Martin B. Cohen
NIGHTMARE IN WAX(1969), p; REBEL ROUSERS(1970), p&d; w; HUMANOIDS FROM THE DEEP(1980), p, w; HOUSE WHERE EVIL DWELLS, THE(1982), p

Martin C. Cohen
I KILLED THAT MAN(1942), ed

Martin Cohen
CATSKILL HONEYMOON(1950), p

Martin G. Cohen
ANYTHING FOR A THRILL(1937), p; UNKNOWN GUEST, THE(1943), ed; CAPTAIN TUGBOAT ANNIE(1945), ed

Marty Cohen
CALL OF THE JUNGLE(1944), ed; CISCO KID RETURNS, THE(1945), ed

Marvin Cohen
FORT APACHE, THE BRONX(1981); JETLAG(1981, U.S./Span.)

Maury Cohen
IN LOVE WITH LIFE(1934), p; SOCIETY FEVER(1935), p; LIVING ON LOVE(1937), p; DOUBLE DANGER(1938), p

Maury M. Cohen
ESCAPADE(1932), p; FIFTEEN WIVES(1934), p; CONDEMNED TO LIVE(1935), p; GHOST WALKS, THE(1935), p; ONE IN A MILLION(1935), p; PORT OF LOST DREAMS(1935), p; PUBLIC OPINION(1935), p; SYMPHONY OF LIVING(1935), p; BRIDGE OF SIGHS(1936), p; BRILLIANT MARRIAGE(1936), p; DEATH FROM A DISTANCE(1936), p; EASY MONEY(1936), p; HITCH HIKE TO HEAVEN(1936), p; IT COULDN'T HAVE HAPPENED–BUT IT DID(1936), p; MURDER AT GLEN ATHOL(1936), p; TANGO(1936), p; THREE OF A KIND(1936), p

Maxi Cohen
Misc. Talkies
JOE AND MAXI(1980), a, d

Michael Cohen
MY FATHER'S HOUSE(1947, Palestine); BOYS IN COMPANY C, THE(1978, U.S./Hong Kong)

Mike Cohen
Misc. Talkies
ONE ARMED EXECUTIONER(1980)

Mrs. Cohen
Silents
LOVE GAMBLER, THE(1922)

Nancy Cohen
CITY NEWS(1983)

Nat Cohen
MISS PILGRIM'S PROGRESS(1950, Brit.), p; MYSTERY AT THE BURLES-QUE(1950, Brit.), p; DUKE WORE JEANS, THE(1958, Brit.), p; CARRY ON SER-GEANT(1959, Brit.), p

Nathan Cohen
SONG AND THE SILENCE, THE(1969), p,d,w,ph&m

Noa Cohen
1984
QUESTION OF SILENCE(1984, Neth.)

Noam Cohen
JESUS CHRIST, SUPERSTAR(1973)

Nole R. Cohen
1984
FIRSTBORN(1984)

Norman Cohen
BREATH OF LIFE(1962, Brit.), p; RUNAWAY, THE(1964, Brit.), ed; ALF 'N' FAMI-LY(1968, Brit.), d; DAD'S ARMY(1971, Brit.), d; ADOLF HITLER–MY PART IN HIS DOWNFALL(1973, Brit.), d; CONFESSIONS OF A POP PERFORMER(1975, Brit.), d; CONFESSIONS FROM A HOLIDAY CAMP(1977, Brit.), d; STAND UP VIRGIN SOLDIERS(1977, Brit.), d

Norman I. Cohen
DEATH PLAY(1976), p

Octavus Roy Cohen
WHY BRING THAT UP?(1929), w; OTHER TOMORROW, THE(1930), w; SOCIAL LION, THE(1930), w; BIG GAMBLE, THE(1931), w; CURTAIN AT EIGHT(1934), w; TRANSIENT LADY(1935), w; VIRGINIA JUDGE, THE(1935), w; THEY MET IN A TAXI(1936), w; JIM HANVEY, DETECTIVE(1937), w; I LOVE YOU AGAIN(1940), w; PITTSBURGH KID, THE(1941), w; GALLANT LADY(1942), w; PRISON GIRL(1942), w
Silents
MATRIMANIAC, THE(1916), w; KAISER'S SHADOW, THE(1918), w; DOLLARS AND SENSE(1920), w; RED DICE(1926), w

Olivier Cohen
ENTRE NOUS(1983, Fr.), d&w

R. P. Cohen
KING OF THE MOUNTAIN(1981)

Ralph Cohen
CRIME DOCTOR(1943), p

Rob Cohen
WIZ, THE(1978), p; MAHOGANY(1975), p; BINGO LONG TRAVELING ALL-STARS AND MOTOR KINGS, THE(1976), p; ALMOST SUMMER(1978), p; THANK GOD IT'S FRIDAY(1978), p; SMALL CIRCLE OF FRIENDS, A(1980), d
1984
SCANDALOUS(1984), d, w

Robert Carl Cohen
Misc. Talkies
JENNIE, WIFE/CHILD(1968), d

Ronald Cohen
RUNNING(1979, Can.), p; MIDDLE AGE CRAZY(1980, Can.), p

Ronald I. Cohen
HARRY TRACY–DESPERADO(1982, Can.), p

Ronald M. Cohen
BLUE(1968), w; GOOD GUYS AND THE BAD GUYS, THE(1969), p, w; TWILIGHT'S LAST GLEAMING(1977, U.S./Ger.), w

Ronnie Cohen
MY FATHER'S HOUSE(1947, Palestine)

Sammy Cohen
ARIZONA TO BROADWAY(1933); SAILOR'S LUCK(1933); TOO MUCH HAR-MONY(1933); SWELL-HEAD(1935); HERE COMES TROUBLE(1936); RIP ROARIN' BUCKAROO(1936); TWO MINUTES TO PLAY(1937); 45 FATHERS(1937); BATTLE OF BROADWAY(1938); PHANTOM OF THE RANGE, THE(1938); FIGHTING 69TH, THE(1940); DUKE OF THE NAVY(1942); MR. HEX(1946)
Silents
RETURN OF PETER GRIMM, THE(1926); SKYROCKET, THE(1926); WHAT PRICE GLORY(1926); AUCTIONEER, THE(1927); GAY RETREAT, THE(1927); HOME-SICK(1928)
Misc. Silents
PLASTERED IN PARIS(1928); WHY SAILORS GO WRONG(1928)

Samuel H. Cohen
TWO SISTERS(1938), w

Sandy Cohen
SUPER VAN(1977), p

Sanford Cohen
EDGE, THE(1968)

Sarah Cohen
FIDDLER ON THE ROOF(1971)

Shachar Cohen
1984
SAHARA(1984)

Shura Cohen
LEGACY, THE(1979, Brit.), cos

Sol Cohen
Silents
SCARS OF JEALOUSY(1923), m

Thomas A. Cohen
1984
MASSIVE RETALIATION(1984), p&d

William Cohen
MALIBU HIGH(1979)

Zvulun Cohen
JESUS CHRIST, SUPERSTAR(1973)

Sarah Cohen-Sali
PASSION(1983, Fr./Switz.)

Robert Cohert
LADYBUG, LADYBUG(1963), m

William A. Cohill
Silents
LIFE WITHOUT SOUL(1916)

William Cohill
Silents
HER FIGHTING CHANCE(1917); EYE FOR EYE(1918)
Misc. Silents
LOVE OF WOMEN, THE(1915); RATED AT $10.000.000(1915); VOICES FROM THE PAST(1915); CRUCIAL TEST, THE(1916); FORTUNATE YOUTH, THE(1916)

Al Cohn
NUMBERED MEN(1930), w; SWEETHEARTS ON PARADE(1930), w; MYSTERY RANCH(1932), w; SON OF A SAILOR(1933), w; HAROLD TEEN(1934), w
Silents
ON TIME(1924), w

Albert J. Cohn
MAN FROM FRISCO(1944), p

Alfred A. Cohn
JAZZ SINGER, THE(1927), w; CARNATION KID(1929), w; LAST WARNING, THE(1929), w; FEET FIRST(1930), w; HOLY TERROR, A(1931), w
Silents
FRENCH DOLL, THE(1923), t; JAZZMANIA(1923), t; IN FAST COMPANY(1924), w; LEGEND OF HOLLYWOOD, THE(1924), w, t; COHENS AND KELLYS, THE(1926), w; CAT AND THE CANARY, THE(1927), w; COHENS AND THE KELLYS IN PARIS, THE(1928), w

Art Cohn
ILLEGAL ENTRY(1949), w; SET-UP, THE(1949), w; STROMBOLI(1950, Ital.), w; TALL TARGET, THE(1951), w; TOMORROW IS ANOTHER DAY(1951), w; CARBINE WILLIAMS(1952), w; GLORY ALLEY(1952), w; RED SKIES OF MONTANA(1952), w; FATAL DESIRE(1953), w; GIRL WHO HAD EVERYTHING, THE(1953), w; MEN OF THE FIGHTING LADY(1954), w; TENNESSEE CHAMP(1954), w; JOKER IS WILD, THE(1957), w; TEN THOUSAND BEDROOMS(1957), w; SEVEN HILLS OF ROME, THE(1958), w

Arthur Cohn
WOMAN TIMES SEVEN(1967, U.S./Fr./Ital.), p; PLACE FOR LOVERS, A(1969, Ital./Fr.), p; SUNFLOWER(1970, Fr./Ital.), p; BLACK AND WHITE IN COLOR(1976, Fr.), p; GARDEN OF THE FINZI-CONTINIS, THE(1976, Ital./Ger.), p; ADOPTION, THE(1978, Fr.), p

Ben Cohn
Silents
CODE OF THE RANGE(1927), d

Bennett Cohn
AIR POLICE(1931), w, ed; ARIZONA NIGHTS(1934), w
Silents
GREY DEVIL, THE(1926), d; WEST OF THE RAINBOW'S END(1926), d; LAFFIN' FOOL, THE(1927), d; LADDIE BE GOOD(1928), d; LAWLESS LEGION, THE(1929), w
Misc. Silents
FIGHTIN' ODDS(1925), d; DANGEROUS TRAFFIC(1926), d; HI-JACKING RUS-TLERS(1926), d; MIDNIGHT FACES(1926), d; RIDIN' GENT, A(1926), d; ROARING BILL ATWOOD(1926), d; WHERE THE NORTH HOLDS SWAY(1927), d

Bruce Cohn
DOGS(1976), p; ACAPULCO GOLD(1978), p; GOOD GUYS WEAR BLACK(1978), w

Gordon Cohn
MUSCLE BEACH PARTY(1964)

Harry Cohn
ACQUITTED(1929), p; BROADWAY HOOFER, THE(1929), p; BROADWAY SCAN-DALS(1929), p; MEXICALI ROSE(1929), p; SONG OF LOVE, THE(1929), p; BROTH-ERS(1930), p; FOR THE LOVE O'LIL(1930), p; HELL'S ISLAND(1930), p; LADIES OF LEISURE(1930), p; MADONNA OF THE STREETS(1930), p; SHADOW RANCH(1930), p; SISTERS(1930), p; SOLDIERS AND WOMEN(1930), p; SQUEALER, THE(1930), p; VENGEANCE(1930), p; CRIMINAL CODE(1931), p; DAWN TRAIL, THE(1931), p; DIRIGIBLE(1931), p; GUILTY GENERATION, THE(1931), p; MIRACLE WOMAN, THE(1931), p; PLATINUM BLONDE(1931), p; TEN CENTS A DANCE(1931), p; BE-HIND THE MASK(1932), p; FORBIDDEN(1932), p; SHOPWORN(1932), p; BROAD-WAY BILL(1934), p; IT HAPPENED ONE NIGHT(1934), p; ONE NIGHT OF LOVE(1934), p; BROADWAY MELODY OF 1936(1935), w; LAST GANGSTER, THE(1937), p; MARIGOLD MAN(1970); TAXI DRIVER(1976); ESCAPE ARTIST, THE(1982)
Silents
ONLY A SHOP GIRL(1922), p; INNOCENCE(1923), p; LURE OF THE WILD, THE(1925), p; WHEN THE WIFE'S AWAY(1926), sup; ALIAS THE LONE WOLF(1927), p; BACHELOR'S BABY, THE(1927), sup; CLOWN, THE(1927), p; ISLE OF FORGOTTEN WOMEN(1927), p; KID SISTER, THE(1927), p; SALLY IN OUR ALLEY(1927), p; STAGE KISSES(1927), p; STOLEN PLEASURES(1927), sup; SWELL-HEAD, THE(1927), p; WANDERING GIRLS(1927), p; WARNING, THE(1927), p; AFTER THE STORM(1928), p; MATINEE IDOL, THE(1928), p; NAME THE WO-MAN(1928), p; RANSOM(1928), p; RUNAWAY GIRLS(1928), p; SCARLET LADY, THE(1928), p; SINNER'S PARADE(1928), p; SO THIS IS LOVE(1928), p; WAY OF THE STRONG, THE(1928), p; ETERNAL WOMAN, THE(1929), p

J.J. Cohn
THIRTEENTH CHAIR, THE(1937), p; OUT WEST WITH THE HARDYS(1938), p

Jack Cohn
YOUNGER GENERATION(1929), p; LAST PARADE, THE(1931), p
Silents
APACHE, THE(1928), p; NOTHING TO WEAR(1928), p; POWER OF THE PRESS, THE(1928), p; OBJECT–ALIMONY(1929), p

Joseph Cohn
MY BODYGUARD(1980)

Martin C. Cohn
HEADLINE CRASHER(1937), ed

Martin Cohn
LEFTOVER LADIES(1931), ed; TOUGH TO HANDLE(1937), ed; DANGER AHEAD(1940), ed; LADY AT MIDNIGHT(1948), ed; STRANGE MRS. CRANE, THE(1948), ed; GAY AMIGO, THE(1949), ed

Martin G. Cohn
UNMASKED(1929), ed; LOST ZEPPELIN(1930), ed; ALIAS THE BAD MAN(1931), ed; MORALS FOR WOMEN(1931), ed; LAST MILE, THE(1932), ed; LENA RI-VERS(1932), ed; MAN CALLED BACK, THE(1932), ed; STRANGERS OF THE EVEN-ING(1932), ed; DEATH KISS, THE(1933), ed; DELUGE(1933), ed; LAST OF THE PAGANS(1936), ed; GALLOPING DYNAMITE(1937), ed; SING WHILE YOU'RE ABLE(1937), ed; SWING IT, PROFESSOR(1937), ed; THANKS FOR LIS-TENING(1937), ed; WITH LOVE AND KISSES(1937), ed; YOUNG DYNAMITE(1937), ed; RACING BLOOD(1938), ed; TERROR OF TINY TOWN, THE(1938), ed; YUKON FLIGHT(1940), ed; BORROWED HERO(1941), ed; DEADLY GAME, THE(1941), ed;

MURDER BY INVITATION(1941), ed; SUNSET MURDER CASE(1941), ed; GIRLS' TOWN(1942), ed; MAN WITH TWO LIVES, THE(1942), ed; ONE THRILLING NIGHT(1942), ed; GENTLE GANGSTER, A(1943), ed; SPY TRAIN(1943), ed; SULTAN'S DAUGHTER, THE(1943), ed; CHARLIE CHAN IN THE SECRET SERVICE(1944), ed; JOHNNY DOESN'T LIVE HERE ANY MORE(1944), ed; WHEN STRANGERS MARRY(1944), ed; VALIANT HOMBRE, THE(1948), ed; ZAMBA(1949), ed; TOKYO FILE 212(1951), ed

Silents
EVERY WOMAN'S PROBLEM(1921), ed; NAMELESS MEN(1928), ed; SCARLET DOVE, THE(1928), ed; STORMY WATERS(1928), ed

Martin J. Cohn
TAKE MY LIFE(1942), ed

Marty Cohn
HEADING FOR HEAVEN(1947), ed; KILLER DILL(1947), ed; DARING CABALLERO, THE(1949), ed; SATAN'S CRADLE(1949), ed; GIRL FROM SAN LORENZO, THE(1950), ed

Mary Cohn
DEADLINE(1948), ed

Maurice Cohn
RED BLOOD OF COURAGE(1935), p

Nik Cohn
SATURDAY NIGHT FEVER(1977), w; STAYING ALIVE(1983), w

Paul Cohn
LILIOM(1935, Fr.), art d

Phil Cohn
ALIAS MARY DOW(1935), ed

Philip Cohn
SECRET OF THE BLUE ROOM(1933), ed

Ralph Cohn
FIGHT TO THE FINISH, A(1937), p; FIND THE WITNESS(1937), p; GIRLS CAN PLAY(1937), p; PAID TO DANCE(1937), p; JUVENILE COURT(1938), p; MAIN EVENT, THE(1938), p; WHO KILLED GAIL PRESTON?(1938), p; CONVICTED WOMAN(1940), p; GIRLS UNDER TWENTY-ONE(1940), p; LONE WOLF KEEPS A DATE, THE(1940), p; LONE WOLF MEETS A LADY, THE(1940), p; LONE WOLF TAKES A CHANCE, THE(1941), p; MEET BOSTON BLACKIE(1941), p; PHANTOM SUBMARINE, THE(1941), p; UNDER AGE(1941), p; NO PLACE FOR A LADY(1943), p; LITTLE IODINE(1946), p; SUSIE STEPS OUT(1946), p; ADVENTURES OF DON COYOTE(1947), p; STORK BITES MAN(1947), p; SLEEP, MY LOVE(1948), p

Robert Cohn
ADVENTURES IN SILVERADO(1948), p; RUSTY LEADS THE WAY(1948), p; KAZAN(1949), p; KILLER THAT STALKED NEW YORK, THE(1950), p; PALOMINO, THE(1950), p; BAREFOOT MAILMAN, THE(1951), p; MISSION OVER KOREA(1953), p; INTERNS, THE(1962), p; NEW INTERNS, THE(1964), p

Robin Cohn
BLACK EAGLE(1948), p

Stephen Cohn
ONE FROM THE HEART(1982)

Stewart Cohn
RUNAWAY GIRL(1966), w

Tracey Cohn
WORLD'S GREATEST LOVER, THE(1977); HERO AT LARGE(1980)

Daniel Cohn-Bendit
MISTER FREEDOM(1970, Fr.); WIND FROM THE EAST(1970, Fr./Ital./Ger.), d, w

Gilbert Cohn-Seat
LADY CHATTERLEY'S LOVER(1959, Fr.), p

Roy J. Cohoe
WINDWALKER(1980)

Terence Coholey
Misc. Talkies
BEGGING THE RING(1979, Brit.)

Ronald Cohoon
INCREDIBLE JOURNEY, THE(1963)

Frank B. Coigne
Misc. Silents
BATTLE OF BALLOTS, THE(1915), d

Marvin Coil
CHINA SKY(1945), ed; MAN ALIVE(1945), ed; FALCON'S ADVENTURE, THE(1946), ed; GENIUS AT WORK(1946), ed; RIVERBOAT RHYTHM(1946), ed; SAN QUENTIN(1946), ed; MY SON, JOHN(1952), ed; ALIAS JESSE JAMES(1959), ed; YOUNG FURY(1965), ed

Marvin J. Coil
AVENGERS, THE(1950), ed

Paul Coilet
DAUGHTERS OF DARKNESS(1971, Bel./ Fr./ Ger./ Ital.), p

Carlos Coimbra
GIVEN WORD, THE(1964, Braz.), ed

The Four Coins
JAMBOREE(1957)

Stephen Coit
COUNTDOWN(1968)

Steve Coit
FEAR AND DESIRE(1953); LONG GOODBYE, THE(1973)

Joe Coits
BURIED ALIVE(1939)

Ed Coke
PERFECT STRANGERS(1950)

Eddie Coke
LITTLE ACCIDENT(1939); YOU'LL NEVER GET RICH(1941); HITLER–DEAD OR ALIVE(1942); MADAME SPY(1942); MOONLIGHT IN HAVANA(1942); GOOD MORNING, JUDGE(1943); GUY NAMED JOE, A(1943); HE'S MY GUY(1943); SALUTE FOR THREE(1943); IT HAPPENED TOMORROW(1944); SENATOR WAS INDISCREET, THE(1947); SUDDENLY IT'S SPRING(1947); ABBOTT AND COSTELLO MEET THE KILLER, BORIS KARLOFF(1949)

Edward Coke
TALK OF THE TOWN(1942); LADY FROM SHANGHAI, THE(1948); SHANGHAI CHEST, THE(1948)

Peter Coke
MISSING, BELIEVED MARRIED(1937, Brit.); RETURN OF CAROL DEANE, THE(1938, Brit.); SMILING ALONG(1938, Brit.); CHEER BOYS CHEER(1939, Brit.); GENTLEMAN'S GENTLEMAN, A(1939, Brit.); I MET A MURDERER(1939, Brit.);

NURSEMAID WHO DISAPPEARED, THE(1939, Brit.); BROKEN HORSESHOE, THE(1953, Brit.); EXTRA DAY, THE(1956, Brit.); CARRY ON ADMIRAL(1957, Brit.); JOHN AND JULIE(1957, Brit.); UP THE CREEK(1958, Brit.); MAKE MINE MINK(1960, Brit.), w

Rene Coke
SATELLITE IN THE SKY(1956), cos; ACCURSED, THE(1958, Brit.), cos; GIRL HUNTERS, THE(1963, Brit.), cos

Richard Coke
INQUEST(1939, Brit.)

John Coker
REACH FOR GLORY(1963, Brit.)

Salami Coker
SINBAD AND THE EYE OF THE TIGER(1977, U.S./Brit.)

Bud Cokes
SMART GIRLS DON'T TALK(1948); SALOME(1953); LITTLE BIG MAN(1970)

Curtis Cokes
FAT CITY(1972)

Husein Cokic
APACHE GOLD(1965, Ger.); KAYA, I'LL KILL YOU(1969, Yugo./Fr.)

Robert Cokjlat
MY BOYS ARE GOOD BOYS(1978)

Harley Cokliss
THAT SUMMER(1979, Brit.), d; BATTLETRUCK(1982), d, w
Misc. Talkies
BATTLE OF BILLY'S POND(1976), d

Col. Stoopnagle and Budd
INTERNATIONAL HOUSE(1933)

Corrado Colabucci
1984
BASILEUS QUARTET(1984, Ital.), cos

Dick Colacino
SWEET CHARITY(1969)

Robert Colan
THOSE DIRTY DOGS(1974, U.S./Ital./Span.), ed

Victor Colane
BUT NOT IN VAIN(1948, Brit.)

Otello Colangeli
DAY THE SKY EXPLODED, THE(1958, Fr./Ital.), ed; TEMPEST(1958, Ital./Yugo./Fr.), ed; NUDE ODYSSEY(1962, Fr./Ital.), ed; FRIENDS FOR LIFE(1964, Ital.), ed; HERCULES VS THE GIANT WARRIORS(1965 Fr./Ital.), ed; SNOW DEVILS, THE(1965, Ital.), ed; MONGOLS, THE(1966, Fr./Ital.), ed; PRIMITIVE LOVE(1966, Ital.), ed; SECRET SEVEN, THE(1966, Ital./Span.), ed; LIGHTNING BOLT(1967, Ital./Sp.), ed; MAIDEN FOR A PRINCE, A(1967, Fr./Ital.), ed; OPERATION KID BROTHER(1967, Ital.), ed; YOUNG, THE EVIL AND THE SAVAGE, THE(1968, Ital.), ed; DIRTY HEROES(1971, Ital./Fr./Ger.), ed

Otello Colangelli
THIS WINE OF LOVE(1948, Ital.), ed; GLADIATORS 7(1964, Span./Ital.), ed

Antonio Colantuoni
00-2 MOST SECRET AGENTS(1965, Ital.), p

Colette Colas
FIRST TASTE OF LOVE(1962, Fr.)

Daniel Colas
1984
MY BEST FRIEND'S GIRL(1984, Fr.)

Rene Colas
CRIME AND PUNISHMENT(1935, Fr.), ph; PEEK-A-BOO(1961, Fr.), ph

Rens Colas
MAN STOLEN(1934, Fr.), ph

Manfredo Colasanti
BRASIL ANNO 2,000(1968, Braz.)

Veniero Colasanti
FABIOLA(1951, Ital.), set d; 55 DAYS AT PEKING(1963), prod d, set d, cos; ROVER, THE(1967, Ital.), cos; MATTER OF TIME, A(1976, Ital./U.S.), prod d

Nicholas Colasanto
COUNTERFEIT KILLER, THE(1968); FAT CITY(1972); FAMILY PLOT(1976); RAGING BULL(1980)

Nick Colasanto
MANCHU EAGLE MURDER CAPER MYSTERY, THE(1975)

Colasson
PERSONAL COLUMN(1939, Fr.), art d&set d

Maurice Colasson
LONG ABSENCE, THE(1962, Fr./Ital.), art d; LAFAYETTE(1963, Fr.), art d, set d; POPPY IS ALSO A FLOWER, THE(1966), art d; MAYERLING(1968, Brit./Fr.), art d; SHOCK TROOPS(1968, Ital./Fr.), art d

Quito Colayco
1984
ALLEY CAT(1984), m

Janet Colazzo
THIEVES(1977)

Bob Colbeit
HAVE ROCRET, WILL TRAVEL(1959)

Angel Colbert
Misc. Talkies
FIVE ANGRY WOMEN(1975)

Claudette Colbert
UNDER TWO FLAGS(1936); WITHOUT RESERVATIONS(1946); HOLE IN THE WALL(1929); LADY LIES, THE(1929); BIG POND, THE(1930); L'ENIGMATIQUE MONSIEUR PARKES(1930); MANSLAUGHTER(1930); YOUNG MAN OF MANHATTAN(1930); HIS WOMAN(1931); HONOR AMONG LOVERS(1931); SECRETS OF A SECRETARY(1931); SMILING LIEUTENANT, THE(1931); MAKE ME A STAR(1932); MAN FROM YESTERDAY, THE(1932); MISLEADING LADY, THE(1932); PHANTOM PRESIDENT, THE(1932); SIGN OF THE CROSS, THE(1932); WISER SEX, THE(1932); I COVER THE WATERFRONT(1933); THREE-CORNERED MOON(1933); TONIGHT IS OURS(1933); TORCH SINGER(1933); CLEOPATRA(1934); FOUR FRIGHTENED PEOPLE(1934); IMITATION OF LIFE(1934); IT HAPPENED ONE NIGHT(1934); GILDED LILY, THE(1935); PRIVATE WORLDS(1935); SHE MARRIED HER BOSS(1935); BRIDE COMES HOME(1935); I MET HIM IN PARIS(1937); MAID OF SALEM(1937); TOVARICH(1937); BLUEBEARD'S EIGHTH WIFE(1938); DRUMS ALONG THE MOHAWK(1939); IT'S A WONDERFUL WORLD(1939); MIDNIGHT(1939); ZAZA(1939); ARISE, MY LOVE(1940); BOOM TOWN(1940); REMEMBER THE DAY(1941); SKY-

LARK(1941); PALM BEACH STORY, THE(1942); NO TIME FOR LOVE(1943); SO PROUDLY WE HAIL(1943); PRACTICALLY YOURS(1944); SINCE YOU WENT AWAY(1944); GUEST WIFE(1945); SECRET HEART, THE(1946); TOMORROW IS FOREVER(1946); EGG AND I, THE(1947); FAMILY HONEYMOON(1948); SLEEP, MY LOVE(1948); BRIDE FOR SALE(1949); SECRET FURY, THE(1950); THREE CAME HOME(1950); LET'S MAKE IT LEGAL(1951); THUNDER ON THE HILL(1951); OUTPOST IN MALAYA(1952, Brit.); DAUGHTERS OF DESTINY(1954, Fr./Ital.); TEXAS LADY(1955); ROYAL AFFAIRS IN VERSAILLES(1957, Fr.); PARRISH(1961)
Misc. Silents
FOR THE LOVE OF MIKE(1927)
Curt Colbert
PSYCHOTRONIC MAN, THE(1980)
Dorothy Colbert
FUNNY FACE(1957)
Keith Colbert
1984
FIRESTARTER(1984)
Nicholas Colbert
BATTLE BEYOND THE SUN(1963), w
Norma Colbert
CITY OF CHANCE(1940), ed
Norman Colbert
CITY GIRL(1938), ed; MR. MOTO TAKES A VACATION(1938), ed; MYSTERIOUS MR. MOTO(1938), ed; TRIP TO PARIS, A(1938), ed; WALKING DOWN BROAD-WAY(1938), ed; WHILE NEW YORK SLEEPS(1938), ed; BOY FRIEND(1939), ed; CHARLIE CHAN AT TREASURE ISLAND(1939), ed; CHASING DANGER(1939), ed; EVERYBODY'S BABY(1939), ed; HEAVEN WITH A BARBED WIRE FENCE(1939), ed; INSIDE STORY(1939), ed; MR. MOTO'S LAST WARNING(1939), ed; FREE, BLONDE AND 21(1940), ed; VIVA CISCO KID(1940), ed; DANCING MASTERS, THE(1943), ed; JITTERBUGS(1943), ed; BERMUDA MYSTERY(1944), ed; BIG NOISE, THE(1944), ed; CIRCUMSTANTIAL EVIDENCE(1945), ed; DOLL FACE(1945), ed; DON JUAN QUILLIGAN(1945), ed; SPIDER, THE(1945), ed; IF I'M LUCKY(1946), ed; STRANGE TRIANGLE(1946), ed; BIG FIX, THE(1947), ed, d; IT'S A JOKE, SON!(1947), ed; LOST HONEYMOON(1947), ed; OUT OF THE BLUE(1947), ed; BEHIND LOCKED DOORS(1948), ed; IN THIS CORNER(1948), ed; MAN FROM TEXAS, THE(1948), ed; MICKEY(1948), ed; SPIRITUALIST, THE(1948), ed; PORT OF NEW YORK(1949), ed; RED STALLION IN THE ROCKIES(1949), ed
Pam Colbert
SURF PARTY(1964); COME SPY WITH ME(1967)
Pat Colbert
HYSTERICAL(1983)
Patrick Colbert
SHIPMATES O' MINE(1936, Brit.)
Peter Colbert
GENTLE GIANT(1967), ed; GET TO KNOW YOUR RABBIT(1972), ed
Ray Colbert
FIRST MONDAY IN OCTOBER(1981)
Misc. Talkies
R.S.V.P.(1984)
Robert Colbert
UNDER FIRE(1957); JOY RIDE(1958); CLAUDELLE INGLISH(1961); FEVER IN THE BLOOD, A(1961); LAWYER, THE(1969)
Misc. Talkies
ALIENS FROM ANOTHER PLANET(1967)
Stanley Colbert
PRIVATE PROPERTY(1960), p; EXPLOSIVE GENERATION, THE(1961), p; HOR-NET'S NEST(1970), w
Marie Colbin
MALOU(1983)
Marion Colbin
Silents
CRITICAL AGE, THE(1923)
Red Colbin
FRANCES(1982)
Rod Colbin
CHANGE OF SEASONS, A(1980); YES, GIORGIO(1982)
William Colbin
Silents
CRITICAL AGE, THE(1923)
June Colbourne
SIN YOU SINNERS(1963)
Maurice Colbourne
ARMS AND THE MAN(1932, Brit.); BROTHER ALFRED(1932, Brit.); MAGIC BOX, THE(1952, Brit.); KING OF THE KHYBER RIFLES(1953); I'M ALL RIGHT, JACK(1959, Brit.); WALK IN THE SHADOW(1966, Brit.); CRY OF THE BAN-SHEE(1970, Brit.); DUELLISTS, THE(1977, Brit.); LITTLEST HORSE THIEVES, THE(1977); VENOM(1982, Brit.)
Marcel Colbrant
GULLIVER'S TRAVELS(1977, Brit., Bel.), anim
1984
SMURFS AND THE MAGIC FLUTE, THE(1984, Fr./Belg.), anim
Ed Colbrook
GANG BUSTERS(1955)
Albert Colby
Silents
ALL OF A SUDDEN NORMA(1919)
Anita Colby
BRIDE WALKS OUT, THE(1936); MARY OF SCOTLAND(1936); WALKING ON AIR(1936); COVER GIRL(1944); BRUTE FORCE(1947); WIND AND THE LION, THE(1975)
Barbara Colby
PETULIA(1968, U.S./Brit.); CALIFORNIA SPLIT(1974); MEMORY OF US(1974)
Charles Colby
Silents
ACE OF ACTION(1926)
Misc. Silents
THUNDERING THROUGH(1925)

Fred Colby
DON RICARDO RETURNS(1946); SWEETHEART OF SIGMA CHI(1946)
James Colby
Misc. Talkies
KILLING GROUND, THE(1972)
Marian Colby
ISLE OF FORGOTTEN SINS(1943)
Marion Colby
MOTHER IS A FRESHMAN(1949); SON OF BILLY THE KID(1949)
Pat Colby
UNTIL THEY SAIL(1957)
Phil Colby
PIRANHA II: THE SPAWNING(1981, Neth.)
Ralph Colby
UTAH(1945)
Robert Colby
Misc. Talkies
CHOPPER SQUAD(1971)
Ronald Colby
YOU'RE A BIG BOY NOW(1966); FINIAN'S RAINBOW(1968); RAIN PEOPLE, THE(1969), p; HAMMETT(1982), p; ONE FROM THE HEART(1982)
1984
STARMAN(1984)
William Colby
IN THE MEANTIME, DARLING(1944); SWEET AND LOWDOWN(1944)
Thomas Colchart
BATTLE BEYOND THE SUN(1963), p, d
Mabel Colcord
LITTLE WOMEN(1933); DAVID COPPERFIELD(1935); IRISH IN US, THE(1935); NO MORE LADIES(1935); LAW IN HER HANDS, THE(1936); STORY OF LOUIS PAS-TEUR, THE(1936); THREE MARRIED MEN(1936); FIREFLY, THE(1937); GREAT O'MALLEY, THE(1937); STELLA DALLAS(1937); COWBOY AND THE LADY, THE(1938); MYSTERIOUS RIDER, THE(1938); SHOP AROUND THE CORNER, THE(1940); INVISIBLE AGENT(1942)
Ray Colcord
DEVONSVILLE TERROR, THE(1983), m
Alfredo Alvarez Colderon
ABSENCE OF MALICE(1981)
Anthony Coldeway
NOAH'S ARK(1928), w; WOMEN THEY TALK ABOUT(1928), w; FROZEN RI-VER(1929), w; GREYHOUND LIMITED, THE(1929), w; CROSS STREETS(1934), w; IN SPITE OF DANGER(1935), w; MEN OF THE HOUR(1935), w; TRAILIN' WEST(1936), w; BLAZING SIXES(1937), w; DRAEGERMAN COURAGE(1937), w; GUNS OF THE PECOS(1937), w; OVER THE GOAL(1937), w; WHITE BON-DAGE(1937), w; ACCIDENTS WILL HAPPEN(1938), w; TORCHY BLANE IN PANA-MA(1938), w; WHEN WERE YOU BORN?(1938), w; PACIFIC LINER(1939), w; SMASHING THE MONEY RING(1939), w; DEVIL'S ISLAND(1940), w; TEXAS TER-RORS(1940), w; TULSA KID, THE(1940), W; UNDER TEXAS SKIES(1940), w; NURSE'S SECRET, THE(1941), w; SHADOWS ON THE STAIRS(1941), w; WYOMING WILDCAT(1941), w; GORILLA MAN(1942), w; HIDDEN HAND, THE(1942), w; LADY GANGSTER(1942), w; CALLING WILD BILL ELLIOTT(1943), w; DEATH VALLEY MANHUNT(1943), w; SCREAM IN THE DARK, A(1943), w; WEST SIDE KID(1943), w; CODE OF THE PRAIRIE(1944), w; MARSHAL OF RENO(1944), w; TUCSON RAIDERS(1944), w; PRAIRIE EXPRESS(1947), w
Silents
WHEN EAST COMES WEST(1922), w; GENTLEMAN OF LEISURE, A(1923), w; RUGGLES OF RED GAP(1923), w; BEGGAR ON HORSEBACK(1925), w; CO-BRA(1925), w; ALMOST A LADY(1926), w; CRIMSON CITY, THE(1928), w
Anthony Coldewey
TWIN HUSBANDS(1934), w; BUSSES ROAR(1942), w
Silents
PRINCE OF PILSEN, THE(1926), w; GINSBERG THE GREAT(1927), w; JEWELS OF DESIRE(1927), w; OLD SAN FRANCISCO(1927), w; SILVER SLAVE, THE(1927), w; RECKLESS CHANCES(5 reels), d&w
Louise Coldren
DELIVERANCE(1972)
John Coldrosen
BUDDY HOLLY STORY, THE(1978), w
Golda Coldwell
Misc. Silents
YAQUI, THE(1916)
Al Cole
HARD RIDE, THE(1971)
Albert Cole
FEMALE BUNCH, THE(1969); INCREDIBLE TWO-HEADED TRANSPLANT, THE(1971); SWEET SUGAR(1972); TERMINAL ISLAND(1973); LEPKE(1975, U.S./Israel)
Alexandra Cole
DR. BUTCHER, M.D.(1982, Ital.)
Roger Cole
LADY IN THE LAKE(1947)
Annie Cole
DON'T CRY WITH YOUR MOUTH FULL(1974, Fr.)
Betty Cole
FROM NOON TO THREE(1976); NEW YORK, NEW YORK(1977); POSTMAN ALWAYS RINGS TWICE, THE(1981); WHOSE LIFE IS IT ANYWAY?(1981)
Buddy Cole
JOHNNY HOLIDAY(1949)
Carol Cole
TAKING OF PELHAM ONE, TWO, THREE, THE(1974); MAD ROOM, THE(1969); MODEL SHOP, THE(1969); PROMISE AT DAWN(1970, U.S./Fr.)
Carole Cole
SILENCERS, THE(
Carolea Cole
SON OF SINBAD(1955)
Cece Cole
1984
PROTOCOL(1984)

Clay Cole
TWIST AROUND THE CLOCK(1961)
Corinne Cole
MURDERERS' ROW(1966); SWINGER, THE(1966); WHO'S MINDING THE MINT?(1967); PARTY, THE(1968); LIMIT, THE(1972)
Cornelius Cole
SHINBONE ALLEY(1971), prod d
Cornelius "Corny" Cole
RAGGEDY ANN AND ANDY(1977), prod d
Corny Cole
MR. MAGOO'S HOLIDAY FESTIVAL(1970), prod d
"Corny" Cole
GAY PURR-EE(1962), prod d
Dallas Cole
1984
CITY HEAT(1984)
David Cole
CHRISTOPHER COLUMBUS(1949, Brit.); QUARTET(1949, Brit.); SON OF DR. JEKYLL, THE(1951); VOICE OF THE HURRICANE(1964); FOUL PLAY(1978)
Debra Cole
TOY, THE(1982)
Delana Renay Cole
TOY, THE(1982)
Dona Cole
LONG GRAY LINE, THE(1955); BEAST WITH A MILLION EYES, THE(1956)
Doris Cole
SURRENDER(1950)
Douglas Cole
PARALLELS(1980, Can.), ph
Elizabeth Cole
PEER GYNT(1965), cos; HAWAII(1966)
Enid Cole
WOMAN AGAINST THE WORLD(1938)
Frederick Cole
Misc. Silents
DARING DAYS(1925)
Gene Cole
HAPPY GO LUCKY(1943)
George Cole
BOMBSIGHT STOLEN(1941, Brit.); THOSE KIDS FROM TOWN(1942, Brit.); HENRY V(1946, Brit.); JOURNEY TOGETHER(1946, Brit.); MY BROTHER'S KEEPER(1949, Brit.); QUARTET(1949, Brit.); CHRISTMAS CAROL, A(1951, Brit.); FLESH AND BLOOD(1951, Brit.); LAUGHTER IN PARADISE(1951, Brit.); OPERATION DISASTER(1951, Brit.); MR. LORD SAYS NO(1952, Brit.); PASSIONATE SENTRY, THE(1952, Brit.); SPIDER AND THE FLY, THE(1952, Brit.); WILD HEART, THE(1952, Brit.); CLUE OF THE MISSING APE, THE(1953, Brit.); FOLLY TO BE WISE(1953); MR. POTTS GOES TO MOSCOW(1953, Brit.); BELLES OF ST. TRINIAN'S, THE(1954, Brit.); TONIGHT'S THE NIGHT(1954, Brit.); ADVENTURES OF SADIE, THE(1955, Brit.); CONSTANT HUSBAND, THE(1955, Brit.); INTRUDER, THE(1955, Brit.); LADY GODIVA RIDES AGAIN(1955, Brit.); PRIZE OF GOLD, A(1955); QUENTIN DURWARD(1955); WHERE THERE'S A WILL(1955, Brit.); WILL ANY GENTLEMAN?(1955, Brit.); IT'S A WONDERFUL WORLD(1956, Brit.); GREEN MAN, THE(1957, Brit.); WEAPON, THE(1957, Brit.); BLUE MURDER AT ST. TRINIAN'S(1958, Brit.); BRIDAL PATH, THE(1959, Brit.); DON'T PANIC CHAPS!(1959, Brit.); TOO MANY CROOKS(1959, Brit.); ANATOMIST, THE(1961, Brit.); PURE HELL OF ST. TRINIAN'S, THE(1961, Brit.); CLEOPATRA(1963); ONE WAY PENDULUM(1965, Brit.); GREAT ST. TRINIAN'S TRAIN ROBBERY, THE(1966, Brit.); VAMPIRE LOVERS, THE(1970, Brit.); FRIGHT(1971, Brit.); TAKE ME HIGH(1973, Brit.); GONE IN 60 SECONDS(1974); DR. SYN, ALIAS THE SCARECROW(1975); BLUE BIRD, THE(1976); DOUBLE NICKELS(1977)
Grover Cole
MISSION MARS(1968), cos
Inez Cole
PRISON GIRL(1942)
Jack Cole
EADIE WAS A LADY(1945), a, ch; TONIGHT AND EVERY NIGHT(1945), md, ch; GILDA(1946), ch; JOLSON STORY, THE(1946), ch; TARS AND SPARS(1946), ch; THRILL OF BRAZIL, THE(1946), ch; DOWN TO EARTH(1947), ch; DAVID AND BATHSHEBA(1951), ch; MEET ME AFTER THE SHOW(1951), ch; ON THE RIVERA(1951), ch; I DON'T CARE GIRL, THE(1952), ch; MERRY WIDOW, THE(1952), ch; FARMER TAKES A WIFE, THE(1953), ch; GENTLEMEN PREFER BLONDES(1953), ch; RIVER OF NO RETURN(1954), ch; GENTLEMEN MARRY BRUNETTES(1955), ch; KISMET(1955), ch; THREE FOR THE SHOW(1955), ch; DESIGNING WOMAN(1957), a, ch; LES GIRLS(1957), ch; LET'S MAKE LOVE(1960), ch
Jacquelin Cole
SATAN'S CHEERLEADERS(1977)
Jacqueline Cole
Misc. Talkies
BAD BUNCH, THE(1976)
Jacquin Cole
TOM(1973)
Jacqulin Cole
ANGELS BRIGADE(1980); JOYSTICKS(1983)
Janine Cole
PHOBIA(1980, Can.)
Joe Cole
WILD GEESE, THE(1978, Brit.)
Joel Cole
SCUM OF THE EARTH(1976)
Jonathan Cole
TILL DEATH(1978)
Jude Cole
1984
WHERE THE BOYS ARE '84(1984)
Julie Dawn Cole
WILLY WONKA AND THE CHOCOLATE FACTORY(1971); THAT LUCKY TOUCH(1975, Brit.)

June Cole
THIS IS MY AFFAIR(1937)
Karen Margret Cole
NIGHT IN HEAVEN, A(1983)
Kay Cole
HELLO DOWN THERE(1969); COMA(1978)
King Cole
DAYS OF HEAVEN(1978)
Lee Cole
CREATURE WASN'T NICE,THE(1981), prod d, art d
Leslie Cole
THREADS(1932, Brit.); INCREDIBLE TWO-HEADED TRANSPLANT, THE(1971)
Lester Cole
PAINTED FACES(1929); LOVE AT FIRST SIGHT(1930); IF I HAD A MILLION(1932), w; CHARLIE CHAN'S GREATEST CASE(1933), w; WALLS OF GOLD(1933), w; PURSUED(1934), w; SLEEPERS EAST(1934), w; WILD GOLD(1934), w; TOO TOUGH TO KILL(1935), w; UNDER PRESSURE(1935), w; FOLLOW YOUR HEART(1936), w; HITCH HIKE LADY(1936), w; PRESIDENT'S MYSTERY, THE(1936), w; AFFAIRS OF CAPPY RICKS(1937), w; MAN IN BLUE, THE(1937), w; SOME BLONDES ARE DANGEROUS(1937), w; CRIME OF DR. HALLET(1938), w; JURY'S SECRET, THE(1938), w; MIDNIGHT INTRUDER(1938), w; SINNERS IN PARADISE(1938), w; BIG GUY, THE(1939), w; I STOLE A MILLION(1939), w; PIRATES OF THE SKIES(1939), w; WINTER CARNIVAL(1939), w; HOUSE OF THE SEVEN GABLES, THE(1940), w; INVISIBLE MAN RETURNS, THE(1940), w; WHEN THE DALTONS RODE(1940), w; AMONG THE LIVING(1941), w; FOOTSTEPS IN THE DARK(1941), w; MIDNIGHT ANGEL(1941), w; NIGHT PLANE FROM CHUNGKING(1942), w; PACIFIC BLACKOUT(1942), w; HOSTAGES(1943), w; NONE SHALL ESCAPE(1944), w; BLOOD ON THE SUN(1945), w; MEN IN HER DIARY(1945), w; OBJECTIVE, BURMA!(1945), w; STRANGE CONQUEST(1946), w; FIESTA(1947), w; HIGH WALL, THE(1947), w; ROMANCE OF ROSY RIDGE, THE(1947), w
Linda Cole
UP THE JUNCTION(1968, Brit.)
Lyn Cole
GREEN HELMET, THE(1961, Brit.)
Lynne Cole
JUST MY LUCK(1957, Brit.)
Major Cole
PUTNEY SWOPE(1969)
Martin Cole
BLACK BEAUTY(1946), ed
Martin G. Cole
PAPER BULLETS(1941), ed
Mary Cole
CLOTHES AND THE WOMAN(1937, Brit.); HE LOVED AN ACTRESS(1938, Brit.); MR. SATAN(1938, Brit.)
Max Cole
TEN GENTLEMEN FROM WEST POINT(1942)
Michael Cole
BUBBLE, THE(1967); CHUKA(1967); WICKER MAN, THE(1974, Brit.); DOUBLE NICKELS(1977)
Misc. Talkies
FORBID THEM NOT(1961)
Mildred Cole
MARSHAL OF AMARILLO(1948)
Nat King Cole
NIGHT OF THE QUARTER MOON(1959)
Nat "King" Cole
BLUE GARDENIA, THE(1953); SMALL TOWN GIRL(1953); SCARLET HOUR, THE(1956); CHINA GATE(1957); ISTANBUL(1957); ST. LOUIS BLUES(1958); CAT BALLOU(1965)
Misc. Talkies
KILLER DILLER(1948)
Nikki Cole
WHEN TOMORROW DIES(1966, Can.)
Norman Cole
NEW INTERNS, THE(1964); WANDERLOVE(1970)
Olivia Cole
HEROES(1977); COMING HOME(1978); SOME KIND OF HERO(1982)
1984
GO TELL IT ON THE MOUNTAIN(1984)
Paul Cole
HORROR OF DRACULA, THE(1958, Brit.); NEXT TO NO TIME(1960, Brit.); PLEASE TURN OVER(1960, Brit.); CARRY ON TEACHER(1962, Brit.); MOUSE ON THE MOON, THE(1963, Brit.)
Phyllis Cole
MOTORCYCLE GANG(1957); THE HYPNOTIC EYE(1960)
Ralph Cole, Jr.
1984
DELIVERY BOYS(1984)
Ray Cole
INCIDENT, THE(1967)
Robert Cole
THIS LOVE OF OURS(1945); MY SIX LOVES(1963); JOHNNY GOT HIS GUN(1971)
Roger Cole
THEY WERE EXPENDABLE(1945); GIRL ON THE SPOT(1946); HOODLUM SAINT, THE(1946); WHITE TIE AND TAILS(1946); FORCE OF EVIL(1948); IT'S A BIG COUNTRY(1951)
Ronnie Cole
EDUCATION OF SONNY CARSON, THE(1974)
Rosalie Cole
CHILD, THE(1977)
Royal Cole
GHOST OF ZORRO(1959), w
Royal K. Cole
VALLEY OF THE ZOMBIES(1946), w; BLACKMAIL(1947), w; EXPOSED(1947), w; CALIFORNIA FIREBRAND(1948), w; ALIMONY(1949), w; PAROLE, INC.(1949), w
Russel Cole
BANK DICK, THE(1940)

S. Cole
DANCE BAND(1935, Brit.), ed
Sandy Cole
DOC(1971), cos; DEMON SEED(1977), cos
Selette Cole
GIRL IN LOVER'S LANE, THE(1960); WHY MUST I DIE?(1960); STRANGLER, THE(1964)
Sidney Cole
FREEDOM OF THE SEAS(1934, Brit.), ed; HIGH COMMAND(1938, Brit.), ed; ADVENTURE IN BLACKMAIL(1943, Brit.), ed; FOR THOSE IN PERIL(1944, Brit.), ed; THEY CAME TO A CITY(1944, Brit.), w; UNDERGROUND GUERRILLAS(1944, Brit.), ed; SAN DEMETRIO, LONDON(1947, Brit.), ed; AGAINST THE WIND(1948, Brit.), p; MEN OF THE SEA(1951, Brit.), p; SECRET PEOPLE(1952, Brit.), p; TRAIN OF EVENTS(1952, Brit.), d; ANGEL WHO PAWNED HER HARP, THE(1956, Brit.), p, w; SUICIDE MISSION(1956, Brit.), w; KITCHEN, THE(1961, Brit.), p&w; SWORD OF SHERWOOD FOREST(1961, Brit.), p
Slim Cole
TEXAS BAD MAN(1932)
Silents
PROWLERS OF THE NIGHT(1926)
Sophie Cole
Silents
MONEY ISN'T EVERYTHING(1925, Brit.), w
Stan Cole
NEPTUNE FACTOR, THE(1973, Can.), ed; BLACK CHRISTMAS(1974, Can.), ed; BREAKING POINT(1976), ed; JACOB TWO-TWO MEETS THE HOODED FANG(1979, Can.), ed; MURDER BY DECREE(1979, Brit.), ed; KLONDIKE FEVER(1980), ed; PHOBIA(1980, Can.), ed; PORKY'S(1982), ed; CHRISTMAS STORY, A(1983), ed; PORKY'S II: THE NEXT DAY(1983), ed
1984
RHINESTONE(1984), ed
Stephanie Cole
THAT SUMMER(1979, Brit.)
Steve Cole
THEY ALL LAUGHED(1981)
Sue Cole
THIS, THAT AND THE OTHER(1970, Brit.)
Sydney Cole
GASLIGHT(1940), ed
Tina Cole
PALM SPRINGS WEEKEND(1963)
Tommy Cole
WESTWARD HO THE WAGONS!(1956)
Tony Cole
TAKE ME HIGH(1973, Brit.), m
Valerie Cole
THIS ABOVE ALL(1942)
Vincent Cole
APPRENTICESHIP OF DUDDY KRAVITZ, THE(1974, Can.)
Walter P. Cole
Silents
UNHOLY THREE, THE(1925)
Trevor Cole-Rees
SHALAKO(1968, Brit.), makeup
Charles Colean
KNOCK ON ANY DOOR(1949); SCANDAL SHEET(1952)
Chuck Colean
JEALOUSY(1934); I WAS A COMMUNIST FOR THE F.B.I.(1951)
Forrest Colebank
HUCKLEBERRY FINN(1974)
Eddie Colebrook
HE STAYED FOR BREAKFAST(1940)
Edward Colebrook
IT COULD HAPPEN TO YOU(1937); TOM, DICK AND HARRY(1941); DESTINATION UNKNOWN(1942)
Catherine Coleburn
Silents
SOCIETY SCANDAL, A(1924)
A. E. Coleby
Silents
KENT, THE FIGHTING MAN(1916, Brit.), d; HOLY ORDERS(1917, Brit.), a, d; JUST DECEPTION, A(1917, Brit.), d; GREAT GAME, THE(1918, Brit.), a, d&w; PRIDE OF THE NORTH, THE(1920, Brit.), d&w; LONG ODDS(1922, Brit.), a, d&w; PRODIGAL SON, THE(1923, Brit.), d&w; REST CURE, THE(1923, Brit.), d&w; FLYING FIFTY-FIVE, THE(1924, Brit.), d&w; PREHISTORIC MAN, THE(1924, Brit.), d; OVER THE STICKS(1929, Brit.), d
Misc. Silents
BLACKMAILERS, THE(1915, Brit.), d; FIGHTING COBBLER, THE(1915, Brit.), a, d; MYSTERIES OF LONDON, THE(1915, Brit.), d; CHAINS OF BONDAGE(1916, Brit.), d; KENT THE FIGHTING MAN(1916, Brit.), a, d; TREASURE OF HEAVEN, THE(1916, Brit.), a, d; WHEEL OF DEATH, THE(1916, Brit.), d; FOR ALL ETERNITY(1917, Brit.), a, d; PIT-BOY'S ROMANCE, A(1917, Brit.), a, d; STRONG MAN'S WEAKNESS, A(1917, Brit.), a, d; MATT(1918, Brit.), a, d; SECRET WOMAN, THE(1918, Brit.), a, d; THELMA(1918, Brit.), d; I HEAR YOU CALLING ME(1919, Brit.), d; SILVER LINING, THE(1919, Brit.), d; CALL OF THE ROAD, THE(1920, Brit.), d; HOUR OF THE TRIAL, THE(1920, Brit.), d; WAY OF THE WORLD, THE(1920, Brit.), a, d; CHILDREN OF COURAGE(1921, Brit.), d; FIFTH FORM AT ST. DOMINIC'S, THE(1921, Brit.), d; RIGHT TO LIVE, THE(1921, Brit.), d; PEACEMAKER, THE(1922, Brit.), d; GREAT PRINCE SHAN, THE(1924, Brit.), d; SEN YAN'S DEVOTION(1924, Brit.), d; UNTO EACH OTHER(1929, Brit.), d
Robert Coleby
LAST RUN, THE(1971); PLUMBER, THE(1980, Aus.); NOW AND FOREVER(1983, Aus.)
Forrest R. Colee
COLT .45(1950)
Kim Colefax
1984
GIMME AN 'F'(1984), prod d

Larry Colelay
ULZANA'S RAID(1972)
Ann Coleman
DAY OF THE LOCUST, THE(1975); HONKY TONK FREEWAY(1981)
Barbara Coleman
AROUND THE WORLD(1943); FALCON AND THE CO-EDS, THE(1943); GOVERNMENT GIRL(1943); SHOW BUSINESS(1944)
Beatrice Coleman
MURDER WITH PICTURES(1936)
Ben Coleman
CHASTITY(1969), ph
Betty Coleman
SWEET JESUS, PREACHER MAN(1973)
Bill Coleman
SECRET AGENT SUPER DRAGON(1966, Fr./Ital./Ger./Monaco), w
Bob Coleman
WHERE DANGER LIVES(1950)
Booth Coleman
FLIGHT TO HONG KONG(1956); MY GUN IS QUICK(1957)
Boothe Coleman
GLOBAL AFFAIR, A(1964)
Brian Coleman
SWORD OF HONOUR(1938, Brit.); LADY IN DISTRESS(1942, Brit.); BIG FRAME, THE(1953, Brit.)
Bruce Coleman
IN GAY MADRID(1930); CONFESSIONS OF A CO-ED(1931)
Bryan Coleman
JASSY(1948, Brit.); OUTPOST IN MALAYA(1952, Brit.); TRAIN OF EVENTS(1952, Brit.); LANDFALL(1953, Brit.); SWORD AND THE ROSE, THE(1953); YOU KNOW WHAT SAILORS ARE(1954, Brit.); LOSER TAKES ALL(1956, Brit.); ROCK AROUND THE WORLD(1957, Brit.); SUSPENDED ALIBI(1957, Brit.); HAND, THE(1960, Brit.); CROOKS ANONYMOUS(1963, Brit.); LIFE IN DANGER(1964, Brit.); MR. BROWN COMES DOWN THE HILL(1966, Brit.); GIVE A DOG A BONE(1967, Brit.); HAPPY DEATHDAY(1969, Brit.); ZEPPELIN(1971, Brit.)
Brysis Coleman
Silents
ARIZONA DAYS(1928), w; WEST OF SANTA FE(1928), w
C. C. Coleman
LEGION OF TERROR(1936), d; CODE OF THE RANGE(1937), d
C. C. Coleman, Jr.
CRIMINALS OF THE AIR(1937), d; DODGE CITY TRAIL(1937), d; FIGHT TO THE FINISH, A(1937), d; PAROLE RACKET(1937), d; FLIGHT TO FAME(1938), d; HIGHWAY PATROL(1938), d; SQUADRON OF HONOR(1938), d; WHEN G-MEN STEP IN(1938), d; HOMICIDE BUREAU(1939), d; MISSING DAUGHTERS(1939), d; MY SON IS A CRIMINAL(1939), d; OUTPOST OF THE MOUNTIES(1939), d; SPOILERS OF THE RANGE(1939), d
Caryl Coleman
DON'T GAMBLE WITH STRANGERS(1946), w; WIFE WANTED(1946), w; BLACK GOLD(1947), w; MAIN STREET KID, THE(1947), w
Charles Coleman
LAWFUL LARCENY(1930); ONCE A GENTLEMAN(1930); WHAT A MAN(1930); BACHELOR APARTMENT(1931); HIGH STAKES(1931); HEART OF NEW YORK(1932); JEWEL ROBBERY(1932); MERRILY WE GO TO HELL(1932); ONE HOUR WITH YOU(1932); PLAY GIRL(1932); SILVER DOLLAR(1932); WINNER TAKE ALL(1932); AS THE DEVIL COMMANDS(1933); DIPLOMANIACS(1933); LITTLE GIANT, THE(1933); MIDNIGHT CLUB(1933); SAILOR BE GOOD(1933); SITTING PRETTY(1933); BORN TO BE BAD(1934); DOWN TO THEIR LAST YACHT(1934); GALLANT LADY(1934); GAY DIVORCEE, THE(1934); HOUSEWIFE(1934); LADY BY CHOICE(1934); MERRY FRINKS, THE(1934); MILLION DOLLAR RANSOM(1934); SHOCK(1934); BECKY SHARP(1935); GOOSE AND THE GANDER, THE(1935); MAGNIFICENT OBSESSION(1935); MAN WHO BROKE THE BANK AT MONTE CARLO, THE(1935); NO MORE LADIES(1935); RENDEZVOUS(1935); COLLEEN(1936); DON'T GET PERSONAL(1936); EVERYBODY'S OLD MAN(1936); FURY(1936); GREAT ZIEGFELD, THE(1936); HER MASTER'S VOICE(1936); HIS FAMILY TREE(1936); LLOYDS OF LONDON(1936); MUMMY'S BOYS(1936); POOR LITTLE RICH GIRL(1936); RETURN OF SOPHIE LANG, THE(1936); WALKING ON AIR(1936); WHIPSAW(1936); WIDOW FROM MONTE CARLO, THE(1936); CAPTAINS COURAGEOUS(1937); DANGER-LOVE AT WORK(1937); DOUBLE WEDDING(1937); FIGHT FOR YOUR LADY(1937); GO-GETTER, THE(1937); LAST GANGSTER, THE(1937); LOVE IS NEWS(1937); MERRY-GO-ROUND OF 1938(1937); SHALL WE DANCE(1937); THERE GOES MY GIRL(1937); THREE SMART GIRLS(1937); TOO MANY WIVES(1937); 100 MEN AND A GIRL(1937); ALEXANDER'S RAGTIME BAND(1938); BLOND CHEAT(1938); CHRISTMAS CAROL, A(1938); GATEWAY(1938); LITTLE MISS BROADWAY(1938); RAGE OF PARIS, THE(1938); THAT CERTAIN AGE(1938); FIRST LOVE(1939); IN NAME ONLY(1939); MEXICAN SPITFIRE(1939); THEY SHALL HAVE MUSIC(1939); YOU CAN'T CHEAT AN HONEST MAN(1939); EARL OF CHICAGO, THE(1940); MEXICAN SPITFIRE OUT WEST(1940); MICHAEL SHAYNE, PRIVATE DETECTIVE(1940); WESTERNER, THE(1940); BUCK PRIVATES(1941); DESIGN FOR SCANDAL(1941); FREE AND EASY(1941); IT STARTED WITH EVE(1941); MELODY LANE(1941); MOONLIGHT IN HAWAII(1941); REPENT AT LEISURE(1941); SIS HOPKINS(1941); WEST POINT WIDOW(1941); ALMOST MARRIED(1942); ARABIAN NIGHTS(1942); GREAT IMPERSONATION, THE(1942); LADY IN A JAM(1942); MISS ANNIE ROONEY(1942); PITTSBURGH(1942); THEY ALL KISSED THE BRIDE(1942); TWIN BEDS(1942); AIR RAID WARDENS(1943); DU BARRY WAS A LADY(1943); GIRL CRAZY(1943); HE HIRED THE BOSS(1943); HI' YA, SAILOR(1943); IT AIN'T HAY(1943); IT COMES UP LOVE(1943); MEXICAN SPITFIRE'S BLESSED EVENT(1943); PETTICOAT LARCENY(1943); SHE'S FOR ME(1943); FRENCHMAN'S CREEK(1944); IN SOCIETY(1944); JANE EYRE(1944); LADY IN THE DARK(1944); MARRIAGE IS A PRIVATE AFFAIR(1944); ONCE UPON A TIME(1944); WHISTLER, THE(1944); WHITE CLIFFS OF DOVER, THE(1944); ANCHORS AWEIGH(1945); KITTY(1945); MISSING CORPSE, THE(1945); PICTURE OF DORIAN GRAY, THE(1945); STORK CLUB, THE(1945); ZIEGFELD FOLLIES(1945); CLUNY BROWN(1946); IN FAST COMPANY(1946); MAGNIFICENT ROGUE, THE(1946); MONSIEUR BEAUCAIRE(1946); NEVER SAY GOODBYE(1946); RUNAROUND, THE(1946); IMPERFECT LADY, THE(1947); LOVE FROM A STRANGER(1947); PILGRIM LADY, THE(1947); VARIETY GIRL(1947); GRAND CANYON TRAIL(1948); STATE OF THE UNION(1948); THREE DARING DAUGHTERS(1948); TROUBLE MAKERS(1948); MY FRIEND IRMA(1949); DOUBLE DYNAMITE(1951); SALT OF THE EARTH(1954)

Silents
SECOND HAND LOVE(1923); SANDY(1926)
Misc. Silents
THAT FRENCH LADY(1924); VAGABOND TRAIL, THE(1924)
Charles C. Coleman
VOICE IN THE NIGHT(1934), d; SHINING HOUR, THE(1938)
Charles C. Coleman, Jr.
PAID TO DANCE(1937), d; SHADOW, THE(1937), d
Charles E. Coleman
EMBARRASSING MOMENTS(1934)
Cherrie Coleman
Silents
CRIME AND PUNISHMENT(1917)
Clarke Coleman
JEKYLL AND HYDE...TOGETHER AGAIN(1982)
Claudia Coleman
I COVER THE WATERFRONT(1933); SON OF THE BORDER(1933); WARRIOR'S HUSBAND, THE(1933); BIG HEARTED HERBERT(1934); MERRY WIDOW, THE(1934); OPERATOR 13(1934); FRISCO KID(1935); LET'S LIVE TONIGHT(1935); PAGE MISS GLORY(1935); RECKLESS(1935); STRANDED(1935); COUNTRY BEYOND, THE(1936); HUMAN CARGO(1936); KING OF BURLESQUE(1936); LADY FROM NOWHERE(1936); LITTLE MISS NOBODY(1936); NAVY BORN(1936); REUNION(1936); UNDER YOUR SPELL(1936); YOU CAN'T HAVE EVERYTHING(1937); KEEP SMILING(1938); PENROD AND HIS TWIN BROTHER(1938); TEST PILOT(1938)
Cy Coleman
FATHER GOOSE(1964), m; TROUBLEMAKER, THE(1964), m; ART OF LOVE, THE(1965), m; SWEET CHARITY(1969), w, m
1984
GARBO TALKS(1984), m
Dabney Coleman
TROUBLE WITH GIRLS(AND HOW TO GET INTO IT), THE*1/2 (1969); SLENDER THREAD, THE(1965); THIS PROPERTY IS CONDEMNED(1966); SCALPHUNTERS, THE(1968); DOWNHILL RACER(1969); I LOVE MY WIFE(1970); CINDERELLA LIBERTY(1973); DOVE, THE(1974, Brit.); TOWERING INFERNO, THE(1974); BITE THE BULLET(1975); OTHER SIDE OF THE MOUNTAIN, THE(1975); MIDWAY(1976); ROLLING THUNDER(1977); VIVA KNIEVEL(1977); NORTH DALLAS FORTY(1979); HOW TO BEAT THE HIGH COST OF LIVING(1980); MELVIN AND HOWARD(1980); NOTHING PERSONAL(1980, Can.); MODERN PROBLEMS(1981); ON GOLDEN POND(1981); TOOTSIE(1982); YOUNG DOCTORS IN LOVE(1982); WARGAMES(1983)
1984
CLOAK AND DAGGER(1984); MUPPETS TAKE MANHATTAN, THE(1984)
Misc. Talkies
BLACK FIST(1977)
Dabney Coleman, Jr.
NINE TO FIVE(1980)
Deanna Dae Coleman
STUNT MAN, THE(1980)
Deanne Coleman
STUNTS(1977)
Don Coleman
Silents
APACHE RAIDER, THE(1928)
Misc. Silents
DEVIL'S TWIN, THE(1927); BLACK ACE, THE(1928); BOSS OF RUSTLER'S ROOST, THE(1928); BRONC STOMPER, THE(1928); .45 CALIBRE WAR(1929)
E. Bradley Coleman
ADAM'S RIB(1949)
Edward Coleman
SHAGGY DOG, THE(1959), ph; AMBUSHERS, THE(1967), ph; GNOME-MOBILE, THE(1967), ph
Elizabeth Coleman
DRUMS OF JEOPARDY(1931), cos; MURDER AT MIDNIGHT(1931), cos; STRANGERS OF THE EVENING(1932), cos; TOMBSTONE CANYON(1932), cos; PICTURE BRIDES(1934), cos
Emil Coleman
NOB HILL(1945)
Frank Coleman
TRUE TO LIFE(1943); SIN TOWN(1942); VALLEY OF THE SUN(1942)
Gary Coleman
ON THE RIGHT TRACK(1981); JIMMY THE KID(1982)
Harry Coleman
Silents
GOLD RUSH, THE(1925)
Herbert Coleman
BATTLE AT BLOODY BEACH(1961), d; POSSE FROM HELL(1961), d
Irene Coleman
JEALOUSY(1934); GOLD DIGGERS OF 1937(1936); STAGE STRUCK(1936); HERO FOR A DAY(1939)
Jack Coleman
Misc. Silents
TOM BROWN'S SCHOOLDAYS(1916, Brit.)
Jacqueline Coleman
STAR 80(1983)
James Coleman
DAUGHTER OF THE TONG(1939)
Jean Coleman
G.I. JANE(1951)
Jim Coleman
SHOW BOAT(1929)
Joey Coleman
MAX DUGAN RETURNS(1983)
1984
BAD MANNERS(1984)
Juan Coleman
TOY, THE(1982)
King Coleman
UP THE ACADEMY(1980)

Layne Coleman
HUMONGOUS(1982, Can.)
Leo Coleman
MEDIUM, THE(1951); WOMAN OF THE RIVER(1954, Fr./Ital.), ch; LA DOLCE VITA(1961, Ital./Fr.); ERIK THE CONQUEROR(1963, Fr./Ital.), ch
Leroy Coleman
RIDE THE HIGH COUNTRY(1962), art d; VENETIAN AFFAIR, THE(1967), art d; FOR SINGLES ONLY(1968), art d; SPEEDWAY(1968), art d; TIME TO SING, A(1968), art d; SUPPORT YOUR LOCAL SHERIFF(1969), art d; BALLAD OF CABLE HOGUE, THE(1970), art d
Lisa Coleman
1984
PURPLE RAIN(1984)
Lonnie Coleman
HOT SPELL(1958), w
Lynn Wood Coleman
MA AND PA KETTLE GO TO TOWN(1950)
Madelyn Coleman
LIANNA(1983)
Majel Coleman
Silents
CORPORAL KATE(1926); KING OF KINGS, THE(1927)
Misc. Silents
WEST OF BROADWAY(1926); ALMOST HUMAN(1927)
Major Coleman
ROMANCE OF THE RIO GRANDE(1929)
Marilyn Coleman
UP THE SANDBOX(1972); WILLIE DYNAMITE(1973); LOOKING FOR MR. GOODBAR(1977); WHICH WAY IS UP?(1977); REMEMBER MY NAME(1978); VICE SQUAD(1982)
Michael Coleman
PETER RABBIT AND TALES OF BEATRIX POTTER(1971, Brit.)
Nancy Coleman
DANGEROUSLY THEY LIVE(1942); DESPERATE JOURNEY(1942); GAY SISTERS, THE(1942); KING'S ROW(1942); EDGE OF DARKNESS(1943); IN OUR TIME(1944); DEVOTION(1946); HER SISTER'S SECRET(1946); MOURNING BECOMES ELECTRA(1947); VIOLENCE(1947); THAT MAN FROM TANGIER(1953); SLAVES(1969)
Ornette Coleman
CHAPPAQUA(1967); BOXOFFICE(1982), m
Pat Coleman
HELLGATE(1952)
Patricia Coleman
ABOVE SUSPICION(1943), w; BLONDE FEVER(1944), w
Peter Coleman
INQUEST(1931, Brit.); COLLISION(1932, Brit.)
Silents
HANDY ANDY(1921, Brit.)
Retta Coleman
NAKED CITY, THE(1948)
Rev. Carlton Coleman
CLAUDINE(1974)
Richard Coleman
ROTTEN TO THE CORE(1956, Brit.); GIRLS AT SEA(1958, Brit.); BEN HUR(1959); NAVY LARK, THE(1959, Brit.); EXORCISM AT MIDNIGHT(1966, Brit. revised 1973, U.S.); COUNTDOWN TO DANGER(1967, Brit.); 10 RILLINGTON PLACE(1971, Brit.); FINAL OPTION, THE(1983, Brit.)
Robert Coleman
MOONLIGHT IN VERMONT(1943); PATRICK THE GREAT(1945); FABULOUS TEXAN, THE(1947)
Robin Coleman
HALLOWEEN 11(1981)
1984
AMERICAN DREAMER(1984)
Ronald Coleman
Misc. Silents
HER NIGHT OF ROMANCE(1924)
Rosemary Coleman
FOUR JACKS AND A JILL(1941); MAYOR OF 44TH STREET, THE(1942); POWERS GIRL, THE(1942)
Ruth Coleman
CRIME NOBOBY SAW, THE(1937); DOCTOR'S DIARY, A(1937); HEADIN' EAST(1937); NIGHT OF MYSTERY(1937); WALLABY JIM OF THE ISLANDS(1937); WILD MONEY(1937); OUTSIDE OF PARADISE(1938); KILLERS OF THE WILD(1940)
Misc. Talkies
TOPA TOPA(1938)
Ted Coleman
PRIVILEGED(1982, Brit.)
Theo Coleman
PARACHUTE NURSE(1942)
Thomas A. Coleman
STANLEY AND LIVINGSTONE(1939)
Tom Coleman
TOAST OF NEW YORK, THE(1937); HOODLUM SAINT, THE(1946); LOCKET, THE(1946); MAGNIFICENT DOLL(1946); SPOOK BUSTERS(1946); SENATOR WAS INDISCREET, THE(1947); WHERE THERE'S LIFE(1947); WOMAN'S SECRET, A(1949)
Verena Coleman
DARWIN ADVENTURE, THE(1972, Brit.), cos; PHASE IV(1974), cos; GET CHARLIE TULLY(1976, Brit.), cos
Vincent Coleman
Silents
PRODIGAL WIFE, THE(1918); PARTNERS OF THE NIGHT(1920); SUCH A LITTLE QUEEN(1921); HAS THE WORLD GONE MAD!(1923)
Misc. Silents
LAW OF NATURE, THE(1919); SCARLET TRAIL, THE(1919); SHOULD A HUSBAND FORGIVE?(1919); FOR THE FREEDOM OF IRELAND(1920); GOOD REFERENCES(1920); MAGIC CUP, THE(1921); PRINCESS JONES(1921); PURPLE HIGHWAY, THE(1923); SALOME(1923)

William Coleman
HIS ROYAL HIGHNESS(1932, Aus.), set d

Wilson Coleman
DOSS HOUSE(1933, Brit.); BORROW A MILLION(1934, Brit.); GRAND PRIX(1934, Brit.); KENTUCKY MINSTRELS(1934, Brit.); LEST WE FORGET(1934, Brit.); MUSIC HALL(1934, Brit.); SAY IT WITH FLOWERS(1934, Brit.); BLUE SMOKE(1935, Brit.); FLOOD TIDE(1935, Brit.); REAL BLOKE, A(1935, Brit.); SEXTON BLAKE AND THE MADEMOISELLE(1935, Brit.); BLIND MAN'S BLUFF(1936, Brit.); DON'T RUSH ME(1936, Brit.); TOILERS OF THE SEA(1936, Brit.); WEDNESDAY'S LUCK(1936, Brit.); BLACK TULIP, THE(1937, Brit.); DOCTOR SYN(1937, Brit.); STEPPING TO-ES(1938, Brit.); GIRL MUST LIVE, A(1941, Brit.)

Edward Colemans
MAN BEHIND THE GUN, THE(1952)

Louise Colembet
COME TO THE STABLE(1949)

Beatrice Colen
AMERICAN POP(1981)

Alison Coleridge
SHINING, THE(1980)

Barbara Coleridge
ONE PLUS ONE(1969, Brit.)

Ethel Coleridge
ONE EMBARRASSING NIGHT(1930, Brit.); PLUNDER(1931, Brit.); KEEP YOUR SEATS PLEASE(1936, Brit.); LABURNUM GROVE(1936, Brit.); FEATHER YOUR NEST(1937, Brit.); SCOTLAND YARD COMMANDS(1937, Brit.); SECOND BEST BED(1937, Brit.); PENNY PARADISE(1938, Brit.); WOMEN AREN'T ANGELS(1942, Brit.); WHEN WE ARE MARRIED(1943, Brit.); QUERY(1945, Brit.); MURDER IN REVERSE(1946, Brit.); LOVES OF JOANNA GODDEN, THE(1947, Brit.); CLOUDED CRYSTAL, THE(1948, Brit.); COLONEL BOGEY(1948, Brit.); SONG FOR TOMORROW, A(1948, Brit.); VENGEANCE IS MINE(1948, Brit.); FALLEN IDOL, THE(1949, Brit.)

Samuel Taylor Coleridge
Silents
ANCIENT MARINER, THE(1925), w

Sylvia Coleridge
CROSS MY HEART(1937, Brit.); I MET A MURDERER(1939, Brit.); JAILBIRDS(1939, Brit.); LONG AGO, TOMORROW(1971, Brit.); HUMAN FACTOR, THE(1979, Brit.); TESS(1980, Fr./Brit.);
1984
SECRET PLACES(1984, Brit.)

Andrea Coles
EASY MONEY(1983)

Betty Coles
SLAMS, THE(1973)

Celeste Coles
EXILE, THE(1931)

Charles Coles
ROCKY II(1979)

Charles "Honi" Coles
1984
COTTON CLUB, THE(1984)

John Coles
DIRTY LITTLE BILLY(1972), spec eff; SLITHER(1973), spec eff

Marshall Coles, Sr.
ZELIG(1983)

Michael Coles
MAN DETAINED(1961, Brit.); DAMN THE DEFIANT!(1962, Brit.); PRIVATE POT-TER(1963, Brit.); NEVER MENTION MURDER(1964, Brit.); DR. WHO AND THE DALEKS(1965, Brit.); UNDERWORLD INFORMERS(1965, Brit.); SOLO FOR SPAR-ROW(1966, Brit.); THANK YOU ALL VERY MUCH(1969, Brit.); DRACULA A.D. 1972(1972, Brit.); I WANT WHAT I WANT(1972, Brit.); FLAME(1975, Brit.); SWEE-NEY(1977, Brit.); COUNT DRACULA AND HIS VAMPIRE BRIDE(1978, Brit.)

Mildred Coles
FIFTH AVENUE GIRL(1939); LADIES MUST LIVE(1940); MONEY AND THE WOMAN(1940); PLAY GIRL(1940); SANTA FE TRAIL(1940); HERE COMES HAPPI-NESS(1941); HURRY, CHARLIE, HURRY(1941); LADY SCARFACE(1941); MEET JOHN DOE(1941); SCATTERGOOD MEETS BROADWAY(1941); SLEEPYTIME GAL(1942); SO THIS IS WASHINGTON(1943); BACK TRAIL(1948); BUNGALOW 13(1948); DESPERADOES OF DODGE CITY(1948); OKLAHOMA BADLANDS(1948); SONG OF THE DRIFTER(1948); BLONDE ICE(1949)

Sandra Coles
ONCE UPON A TIME(1944)

Stanley Coles
SGT. PEPPER'S LONELY HEARTS CLUB BAND(1978)

Veniero Colesanti
EL CID(1961, U.S./Ital.), art d&cos

Robert F. Colesberry
1984
RECKLESS(1984)

Alan Coleshill
SOAPBOX DERBY(1958, Brit.); UGLY DUCKLING, THE(1959, Brit.); CIRCUS FRIENDS(1962, Brit.)

Jan Colet
HALF A SIXPENCE(1967, Brit.)

Lino Coletta
AVANTI!(1972)

Colette
SEVEN DEADLY SINS, THE(1953, Fr./Ital.), w

Ann Colette
WHO'S THAT KNOCKING AT MY DOOR?(1968)

Anne Colette
SEASON FOR LOVE, THE(1963, Fr.)

Grace Colette
MICKEY ONE(1965)

Marie Colette
Misc. Silents
SAHARA LOVE(1926, Brit.)

Verne Colette
ST. BENNY THE DIP(1951)

Duilio Coletti
MERCHANT OF SLAVES(1949, Ital.), d; BULLET FOR STEFANO(1950, Ital.), d; HEART AND SOUL(1950, Ital.), d; GREAT HOPE, THE(1954, Ital.), d, w; HELL RAIDERS OF THE DEEP(1954, Ital.), d, w; HOUSE OF INTRIGUE, THE(1959, Ital.), p,d&w; UNDER TEN FLAGS(1960, U.S./Ital.), d; OPERATION CROSS-BOW(1965, U.S./Ital.), w; FRAULEIN DOKTOR(1969, Ital./Yugo.), w; CHINO(1976, Ital., Span., Fr.), p

Duillo Coletti
UNDER TEN FLAGS(1960, U.S./Ital.), w

Dullio Coletti
EARTH CRIES OUT, THE(1949, Ital.), d

Frank Coletti
INVISIBLE KILLER, THE(1940)

Jean-Michel Coletti
1984
L'ARGENT(1984, Fr./Switz.)

Sonio Coletti
RING AROUND THE CLOCK(1953, Ital.), p

Thomas Coley
DR. CYCLOPS(1940)

Eileen Colgan
QUACKSER FORTUNE HAS A COUSIN IN THE BRONX(1970)

Joe Colgan
HARD ROAD, THE(1970)

Michael Colgan
DONOVAN'S BRAIN(1953); FORTY-NINTH MAN, THE(1953); TOPEKA(1953); VIGI-LANTE TERROR(1953); BATTLE TAXI(1955)

Valerie Colgan
LORDS OF DISCIPLINE, THE(1983)

Russell W. Colgin
YOUNG WARRIORS(1983), w

Michael Colicchio
QUICK, LET'S GET MARRIED(1965), m; ROAD HUSTLERS, THE(1968), m&md

Victor Colicchio
1984
DELIVERY BOYS(1984)

John Colicos
FORBIDDEN JOURNEY(1950, Can.); BOND OF FEAR(1956, Brit.); MURDER ON APPROVAL(1956, Brit.); PASSPORT TO TREASON(1956, Brit.); WAR DRUMS(1957); ANNE OF THE THOUSAND DAYS(1969, Brit.); DOCTORS' WIVES(1971); RAID ON ROMMEL(1971); RED SKY AT MORNING(1971); WRATH OF GOD, THE(1972); SCORPIO(1973); BREAKING POINT(1976); DRUM(1976); KING SOLOMON'S TREAS-URE(1978, Can.); BATTLESTAR GALACTICA(1979); CHANGELING, THE(1980, Can.); CONQUEST OF THE EARTH(1980); PHOBIA(1980, Can.); POSTMAN ALWAYS RINGS TWICE, THE(1981)

Hadley Coliman
THEY SHOOT HORSES, DON'T THEY?(1969)

Amy Colin
NIGHT AFFAIR(1961, Fr.)

David Colin, Jr.
BEYOND THE DOOR(1975, Ital./U.S.); BEYOND THE DOOR II(1979, Ital.)

Fernando Alvarez Carces Colin
SANTO CONTRA EL CEREBRO DIABOLICO zero(1962, Mex.), ph

Fernando Alvarez Garces Colin
LOS AUTOMATAS DE LA MUERTE(1960, Mex.), ph; ORLAK, THE HELL OF FRANKENSTEIN(1960, Mex.), ph; NEUTRON CONTRA EL DR. CARONTE(1962, Mex.), ph; NEUTRON EL ENMASCARADO NEGRO(1962, Mex.), ph

Georges Colin
END OF THE WORLD, THE(1930, Fr.); OPEN ROAD, THE(1940, Fr.)

Ian Colin
BLUE SMOKE(1935, Brit.); CROSS CURRENTS(1935, Brit.); LATE EXTRA(1935, Brit.); SMALL MAN, THE(1935, Brit.); BLIND MAN'S BLUFF(1936, Brit.); MEN OF YESTERDAY(1936, Brit.); TOILERS OF THE SEA(1936, Brit.); BORN THAT WAY(1937, Brit.); IT'S NEVER TOO LATE TO MEND(1937, Brit.); DARTS ARE TRUMPS(1938, Brit.); OUTSIDER, THE(1940, Brit.); LAST LOAD, THE(1948, Brit.); QUEEN OF SPADES(1948, Brit.); ADVENTURES OF JANE, THE(1949, Brit.); TRAPPED BY THE TERROR(1949, Brit.); WINSLOW BOY, THE(1950); BIG CHANCE, THE(1957, Brit.); TWO-HEADED SPY, THE(1959, Brit.); WHITE TRAP, THE(1959, Brit.); WITNESS IN THE DARK(1959, Brit.); DANGEROUS AFTERNOON(1961, Brit.); STRONGROOM(1962, Brit.)

Jean Colin
HATE SHIP, THE(1930, Brit.); COMPROMISED!(1931, Brit.); LORD BABS(1932, Brit.); CHARING CROSS ROAD(1935, Brit.); SUCH IS LIFE(1936, Brit.); HE LOVED AN ACTRESS(1938, Brit.); MIKADO, THE(1939, Brit.); LAUGH IT OFF(1940, Brit.); BOB'S YOUR UNCLE(1941, Brit.); LAST HOLIDAY(1950, Brit.); SCOTCH ON THE ROCKS(1954, Brit.)

Joel Colin
BONNIE PARKER STORY, THE(1958)

Lotte Colin
PLAY DIRTY(1969, Brit.), w

Sid Colin
GAY ADVENTURE, THE(1953, Brit.), w; ONE GOOD TURN(1955, Brit.), w; I ONLY ASKED!(1958, Brit.), w; NAVY LARK, THE(1959, Brit.), w; UGLY DUCKLING, THE(1959, Brit.), w; TOMMY THE TOREADOR(1960, Brit.), w; UP POMPEII(1971, Brit.), w; UP THE CHASTITY BELT(1971, Brit.), w; UP THE FRONT(1972, Brit.), w; IT'S NOT THE SIZE THAT COUNTS(1979, Brit.), w

Stephanie Colin
MR. BILLION(1977), cos

Peter Colingwood
GREEN HELMET, THE(1961, Brit.)

Charlie Colins
CONFIDENCE GIRL(1952)

Gaetano Colisano
HORNET'S NEST(1970)

Rick Colitti
PIE IN THE SKY(1964)

Rik Colitti
VOICES(1979); FORT APACHE, THE BRONX(1981)

1984
POPE OF GREENWICH VILLAGE, THE(1984)

Giuseppe Colizzi
RED LIPS(1964, Fr./Ital.); REVENGE AT EL PASO(1968, Ital.), p, d&w; GOD FORGIVES-I DON'T!(1969, Ital./Span.), d, w; ALL THE WAY, BOYS(1973, Ital.), d&w

Gouseppe Colizzi
BOOT HILL(1969, Ital.), d

Guiseppe Colizzi
ACE HIGH(1969, Ital.), d

Ronald Colizzo
DUCHESS AND THE DIRTWATER FOX, THE(1976)

Christopher Coll
WALK A CROOKED PATH(1969, Brit.)

Jose Luis Coll
NOT ON YOUR LIFE(1965, Ital./Span.)

Julio Coll
PYRO(1964, U.S./Span.), d; NARCO MEN, THE(1969, Span./Ital.), d, w

Marvin Coll
DICK TRACY'S DILEMMA(1947), ed

Ramon Coll
SWEET SUGAR(1972)

Richard Coll
WHO'S THAT KNOCKING AT MY DOOR?(1968), ph

Tom Coll
FUNHOUSE, THE(1981), set d; HARDLY WORKING(1981), set d; SPRING BREAK(1983), set d

Yvonne Coll
GODFATHER, THE, PART II(1974)

Elizabeth Colla
ZIGZAG(1970)

Richard A. Colla
YOUNG SINNER, THE(1965); ZIGZAG(1970), d; FUZZ(1972), d; OLLY, OLLY, OXEN FREE(1978), p&d, w; BATTLESTAR GALACTICA(1979), d

Franco Collace
DUCK, YOU SUCKER!(1972, Ital.)

Dominique Colladant
NOSFERATU, THE VAMPIRE(1979, Fr./Ger.), makeup

Maria Jose Collado
GUNFIGHTERS OF CASA GRANDE(1965, U.S./Span.); SON OF A GUNFIGHT-ER(1966, U.S./Span.)

Tony Collado
GETTING TOGETHER(1976)

Misc. Talkies
FEELIN' UP(1983)

Jerome Collamore
FOR LOVE OF IVY(1968); KLUTE(1971); ARTHUR(1981); ANNIE(1982)

Dominique Collandant
1984
PERILS OF GWENDOLINE, THE(1984, Fr.), makeup

Russell Collar
SINISTER HANDS(1932)

Cyril Collard
1984
A NOS AMOURS(1984, Fr.)

Jack Collard
VERDICT, THE(1982)

Viera Collaro
CRY DR. CHICAGO(1971)

Yanou Collart
1984
AMERICAN DREAMER(1984)

Dora Collazo-Levy
OLIVER'S STORY(1978)

Bonar Colleano
STAIRWAY TO HEAVEN(1946, Brit.); WANTED FOR MURDER(1946, Brit.); ONE NIGHT WITH YOU(1948, Brit); SALT TO THE DEVIL(1949, Brit.); SLEEPING CAR TO TRIESTE(1949, Brit.); DANCE HALL(1950, Brit.); GOOD TIME GIRL(1950, Brit.); MANIACS ON WHEELS(1951, Brit.); POOL OF LONDON(1951, Brit.); TALE OF FIVE WOMEN, A(1951, Brit.); EIGHT IRON MEN(1952); IS YOUR HONEYMOON REALLY NECESSARY?(1953, Brit.); ESCAPE BY NIGHT(1954, Brit.); FLAME AND THE FLESH(1954); JOE MACBETH(1955); SEA SHALL NOT HAVE THEM, THE(1955, Brit.); STARS IN YOUR EYES(1956, Brit.); ZARAK(1956, Brit.); FIRE DOWN BE-LOW(1957, U.S./Brit.); PICKUP ALLEY(1957, Brit.); TIME IS MY ENEMY(1957, Brit.); DEATH OVER MY SHOULDER(1958, Brit.); MAN INSIDE, THE(1958, Brit.); TANK FORCE(1958, Brit.); THEM NICE AMERICANS(1958, Brit.)

Con Colleano
FLESH AND FANTASY(1943)

Garry Colleano
FOLLOW THAT MAN(1961, Brit.)

Gary Colleano
CARRY ON COWBOY(1966, Brit.)

Mark Colleano
BOYS OF PAUL STREET, THE(1969, Hung./US); UP IN THE AIR(1969, Brit.); HORNET'S NEST(1970); HORSEMEN, THE(1971); LADY CHATTERLEY'S LO-VER(1981, Fr./Brit.); LION OF THE DESERT(1981, Libya/Brit.)

Bonar Colleano, Jr.
JOHNNY IN THE CLOUDS(1945, Brit.); MERRY-GO-ROUND(1948, Brit.)

Bonar Colleano [Jr.]
WHILE THE SUN SHINES(1950, Brit.)

Brian Colleary
WANDERERS, THE(1979)

Collective "Rote Ruebe"
GERMANY IN AUTUMN(1978, Ger.)

Robert Collector
1984
JUNGLE WARRIORS(1984, U.S./Ger./Mex.), w

The Collectors
DON'T LET THE ANGELS FALL(1969, Can.), m

Doris Colleen
CIGARETTE GIRL(1947); GUILT OF JANET AMES, THE(1947); HER HUSBAND'S AFFAIRS(1947); LITTLE MISS BROADWAY(1947)

G. Collegare
RING AROUND THE CLOCK(1953, Ital.), w

Gina Collens
TELL ME THAT YOU LOVE ME, JUNIE MOON(1970)

Barbara Collentine
EXPERIMENT IN TERROR(1962); THAT TOUCH OF MINK(1962); DIFFERENT STORY, A(1978)
1984
SAM'S SON(1984)

Robin Coller
GROUNDSTAR CONSPIRACY, THE(1972, Can.)

Russ Coller
THERE'S MAGIC IN MUSIC(1941)

Bill Colleran
HAMLET(1964), d&ph

Jean Colleran
COVER GIRL(1944)

Christopher Collet
SLEEPAWAY CAMP(1983)
1984
FIRSTBORN(1984)

Joris Collet
DAUGHTERS OF DARKNESS(1971, Bel./ Fr./ Ger./ Ital.)

Pierre Collet
TIME BOMB(1961, Fr./Ital.); ROAD TO SHAME, THE(1962, Fr.); DIARY OF A CHAMBERMAID(1964, Fr./Ital.); FANTOMAS(1966, Fr./Ital.); MADEMOI-SELLE(1966, Fr./Brit.); LIFE LOVE DEATH(1969, Fr./Ital.); HIT(1973); FRENCH CONNECTION 11(1975); INVITATION, THE(1975, Fr./Switz.)

Rae Collet
CAPTAIN'S ORDERS(1937, Brit.)

Marie Collett
1984
GIVE MY REGARDS TO BROAD STREET(1984, Brit.)

Rae Collett
COMMAND PERFORMANCE(1937, Brit.)

Rex Collett
IT HAPPENED HERE(1966, Brit.)

Buddy Collette
TRAUMA(1962), m, md

Chea Collette
SIX WEEKS(1982)

Thomas Collette
WHOSE LIFE IS IT ANYWAY?(1981)

Ricky Colletti
MURDER, INC.(1960)

Don Pedro Colley
BENEATH THE PLANET OF THE APES(1970); THX 1138(1971); LEGEND OF NIGGER CHARLEY, THE(1972); BLACK CAESAR(1973); THIS IS A HIJACK(1973); WORLD'S GREATEST ATHLETE, THE(1973); SUGAR HILL(1974)

Isabel Colley
MARLOWE(1969)

Ken Colley
MAHLER(1974, Brit.); MONTY PYTHON'S LIFE OF BRIAN(1979, Brit.)

Kenneth Colley
HOW I WON THE WAR(1967, Brit.); JOKERS, THE(1967, Brit.); MUSIC LOVERS, THE(1971, Brit.); HITLER: THE LAST TEN DAYS(1973, Brit./Ital.); JUGGER-NAUT(1974, Brit.); EMPIRE STRIKES BACK, THE(1980); FIREFOX(1982); GIRO CITY(1982, Brit.); RETURN OF THE JEDI(1983)

Martin Colley
GETAWAY, THE(1972)

Ernesto Colli
SPIRITS OF THE DEAD(1969, Fr./Ital.); CLARETTA AND BEN(1983, Ital., Fr.)

Franco Delli Colli
SWEET SMELL OF LOVE(1966, Ital./Ger.), ph; DJANGO KILL(1967, Ital./Span.), ph

Ombretta Colli
GLADIATOR OF ROME(1963, Ital.); SLAVE, THE(1963, Ital.); SNOW DEVILS, THE(1965, Ital.)

Tonino Delli Colli
FUGITIVE LADY(1951), ph; ISLAND OF PROCIDA, THE(1952, Ital.), ph; DONA-TELLA(1956, Ital.), ph; ACCATTONE!(1961, Ital.), ph; THIEF OF BAGHDAD, THE(1961, Ital./Fr.), ph; MANDRAGOLA(1966 Fr./Ital.), ph; VERY HANDY MAN, A(1966, Fr./Ital.), ph; BEAUTIFUL SWINDLERS, THE(1967, Fr./Ital./Jap./Neth.), ph; DAY OF THE OWL, THE(1968, Ital./Fr.), ph; PILGRIMAGE(1972), ph; DEAF SMITH AND JOHNNY EARS(1973, Ital.), ph; LACOMBE, LUCIEN(1974), ph; SEVEN BEAU-TIES(1976, Ital.), ph; VIVA ITALIA(1978, Ital.), ph; TALES OF ORDINARY MAD-NESS(1983, Ital.), ph; TRENCHCOAT(1983), ph

Tonio Delli Colli
1984
ONCE UPON A TIME IN AMERICA(1984), ph

Erland Colliander
DOLLAR(1938, Swed.)

Cyril Collick
OPERATION CIA(1965)

J. Craig Collicut
NORTHVILLE CEMETERY MASSACRE, THE(1976)

Biff Collie
SING, BOY, SING(1958)

James Collie
SHEPHERD OF THE HILLS, THE(1964)

Alys Collier
Misc. Silents
VICAR OF WAKEFIELD, THE(1913, Brit.)

Armalie Collier
LOVESICK(1983)

Buster Collier
Misc. Talkies
HER SECRET(1933)
Buster Collier, Jr.
REDUCING(1931); SPORTING CHANCE(1931)
Claude Collier
TO PARIS WITH LOVE(1955, Brit.)
Constance Collier
RETURN OF THE RAT, THE(1929, Brit.), w; PETER IBBETSON(1935), w; SHADOW OF A DOUBT(1935); GIRLS' DORMITORY(1936); LITTLE LORD FAUNTLEROY(1936); PROFESSIONAL SOLDIER(1936); CLOTHES AND THE WOMAN(1937, Brit.); DAMSEL IN DISTRESS, A(1937); STAGE DOOR(1937); THUNDER IN THE CITY(1937, Brit.); WEE WILLIE WINKIE(1937); RAT, THE(1938, Brit.), w; ZAZA(1939); HALF A SINNER(1940); SUSAN AND GOD(1940); KITTY(1945); DARK CORNER, THE(1946); MONSIEUR BEAUCAIRE(1946); PERILS OF PAULINE, THE(1947); GIRL FROM MANHATTAN(1948); IDEAL HUSBAND, AN(1948, Brit.); ROPE(1948); WHIRLPOOL(1949)
Silents
CODE OF MARCIA GRAY(1916); TONGUES OF MEN, THE(1916); IMPOSSIBLE WOMAN, THE(1919, Brit.); RAT, THE(1925, Brit.), w; WHEN BOYS LEAVE HOME(1928, Brit.), w
Misc. Silents
MACBETH(1916); BLEAK HOUSE(1920, Brit.)
Don Collier
SEVEN WAYS FROM SUNDOWN(1960); TWELVE HOURS TO KILL(1960); SAFE AT HOME(1962); INCIDENT AT PHANTOM HILL(1966); PARADISE, HAWAIIAN STYLE(1966); EL DORADO(1967); WAR WAGON, THE(1967); FIVE CARD STUD(1968); UNDEFEATED, THE(1969); FLAP(1970)
Ed Collier
GROUNDSTAR CONSPIRACY, THE(1972, Can.)
Edwin Collier
MC CABE AND MRS. MILLER(1971)
Gail Collier
SKATETOWN, U.S.A.(1979)
Harry Collier
Silents
THOU SHALT NOT(1914)
Ian Collier
HAMLET(1969, Brit.); NEXT MAN, THE(1976)
James Collier
ESCAPE FROM ALCATRAZ(1979)
James F. Collier
RESTLESS ONES, THE(1965), w; FOR PETE'S SAKE!(1966), d&w; TWO A PENNY(1968, Brit.), d; HIDING PLACE, THE(1975), d; JONI(1980), d&w
1984
PRODIGAL, THE(1984), d&w
Jim Collier
FRANKENSTEIN MUST BE DESTROYED!(1969, Brit.)
John Collier
SYLVIA SCARLETT(1936), w; ELEPHANT BOY(1937, Brit.), w; HER CARDBOARD LOVER(1942), w; DECEPTION(1946), w; ROSEANNA McCOY(1949), w; STORY OF THREE LOVES, THE(1953), w; I AM A CAMERA(1955, Brit.), w; WAR LORD, THE(1965), w; SOME CALL IT LOVING(1973), p,d&w
Kathryn Collier
BILL OF DIVORCEMENT(1940); WATERLOO BRIDGE(1940)
Lesley Collier
PETER RABBIT AND TALES OF BEATRIX POTTER(1971, Brit.); STORIES FROM A FLYING TRUNK(1979, Brit.)
Lois Collier
DESPERATE ADVENTURE, A(1938); GAUCHOS OF EL DORADO(1941); OUTLAWS OF THE CHEROKEE TRAIL(1941); WEST OF CIMARRON(1941); PHANTOM PLAINSMEN, THE(1942); RAIDERS OF THE RANGE(1942); WESTWARD HO(1942); YOKEL BOY(1942); GET GOING(1943); MY SON, THE HERO(1943); SANTA FE SCOUTS(1943); SHE'S FOR ME(1943); COBRA WOMAN(1944); FOLLOW THE BOYS(1944); JUNGLE WOMAN(1944); LADIES COURAGEOUS(1944); WEIRD WOMAN(1944); CRIMSON CANARY(1945); NAUGHTY NINETIES, THE(1945); PENTHOUSE RHYTHM(1945); CAT CREEPS, THE(1946); NIGHT IN CASABLANCA, A(1946); WILD BEAUTY(1946); SLAVE GIRL(1947); ARTHUR TAKES OVER(1948); OUT OF THE STORM(1948); MISS MINK OF 1949(1949); HUMPHREY TAKES A CHANCE(1950); RHYTHM INN(1951)
Lols Collier
GIRL ON THE SPOT(1946)
Marian Collier
ROADRACERS, THE(1959); PAY OR DIE(1960); LAST CHALLENGE, THE(1967); NOBODY'S PERFECT(1968); COMPANY OF KILLERS(1970); THREE THE HARD WAY(1974); HUNTING PARTY, THE(1977, Brit.)
Marion Collier
YOUNG AND DANGEROUS(1957)
Patience Collier
THIRD SECRET, THE(1964, Brit.); WILD AFFAIR, THE(1966, Brit.); BABY LOVE(1969, Brit.); DECLINE AND FALL... OF A BIRD WATCHER(1969, Brit.); HOUSE OF CARDS(1969); PERFECT FRIDAY(1970, Brit.); THINK DIRTY(1970, Brit.); FIDDLER ON THE ROOF(1971); COUNTESS DRACULA(1972, Brit.); NATIONAL HEALTH, OR NURSE NORTON'S AFFAIR, THE(1973, Brit.); FRENCH LIEUTENANT'S WOMAN, THE(1981)
Richard Collier
SUDDENLY(1954); BIGGER THAN LIFE(1956); REVOLT OF MAMIE STOVER, THE(1956); SCARLET HOUR, THE(1956); TEENAGE REBEL(1956); THIS COULD BE THE NIGHT(1957); RALLY 'ROUND THE FLAG, BOYS!(1958); SAY ONE FOR ME(1959); NORTH TO ALASKA(1960); PLEASE DON'T EAT THE DAISIES(1960); MR. HOBBS TAKES A VACATION(1962); CHASE, THE(1966); GOOD TIMES(1967); HELLO, DOLLY!(1969); CHEYENNE SOCIAL CLUB, THE(1970); BLAZING SADDLES(1974)
Ron Collier
FAN'S NOTES, A(1972, Can.), m; PAPERBACK HERO(1973, Can.), m
Ryan Collier
NEW YEAR'S EVIL(1980)

Sherlee Collier
RETURN OF THE VAMPIRE, THE(1944); VALLEY OF DECISION, THE(1945); ENCHANTMENT(1948); KIND LADY(1951)
Shirley Collier
TWO TICKETS TO LONDON(1943)
Sue Collier
KISS THEM FOR ME(1957)
Terence Collier
Silents
LOST PATROL, THE(1929, Brit.)
Valerie Collier
INADMISSIBLE EVIDENCE(1968, Brit.)
Wayne Collier
DIARY OF A MADMAN(1963)
William Collier
HOTTENTOT, THE(1929), w; STREET SCENE(1931); GLAMOUR GIRL(1938, Brit.), p; MR. SATAN(1938, Brit.), p; GOING PLACES(1939), w; PAPER ORCHID(1949, Brit.), p
Silents
NEVER SAY DIE(1924), w
Misc. Silents
NO-GOOD GUY, THE(1916); SERVANT QUESTION, THE(1920)
William Collier, Jr.
LION AND THE MOUSE, THE(1928); WOMEN THEY TALK ABOUT(1928); BACHELOR GIRL, THE(1929); COLLEGE COQUETTE, THE(1929); DONOVAN AFFAIR, THE(1929); HARDBOILED ROSE(1929); NEW ORLEANS(1929); ONE STOLEN NIGHT(1929); TWO MEN AND A MAID(1929); FOX MOVIETONE FOLLIES OF 1930(1930); LUMMOX(1930); MELODY MAN(1930); RAIN OR SHINE(1930); ROYAL ROMANCE, A(1930); BIG GAMBLE, THE(1931); BROADMINDED(1931); CIMARRON(1931); LITTLE CAESAR(1931); SECRET WITNESS, THE(1931); SOUL OF THE SLUMS(1931); COUNTY FAIR, THE(1932); DANCERS IN THE DARK(1932); EXPOSED(1932); FIGHTING GENTLEMAN, THE(1932); FILE 113(1932); PHANTOM EXPRESS, THE(1932); BEHIND JURY DOORS(1933, Brit.); FORGOTTEN(1933); MARK IT PAID(1933); STORY OF TEMPLE DRAKE, THE(1933); ALL OF ME(1934); PEOPLE'S ENEMY, THE(1935); PUBLIC STENOGRAPHER(1935)
Misc. Talkies
BEWARE OF BACHELORS(1928); SPEED DEMON(1933)
Silents
EVERYBODY'S SWEETHEART(1920); SOUL OF YOUTH, THE(1920); AT THE STAGE DOOR(1921); HEART OF MARYLAND, THE(1921); CARDIGAN(1922); ENEMIES OF WOMEN, THE(1923); LOYAL LIVES(1923); PLEASURE MAD(1923); LIGHTHOUSE BY THE SEA, THE(1924); DEVIL'S CARGO, THE(1925); EVE'S SECRET(1925); RECKLESS SEX, THE(1925); RAINMAKER, THE(1926); BACKSTAGE(1927); CONVOY(1927); STRANDED(1927); SUNSET DERBY, THE(1927); FLOATING COLLEGE, THE(1928); NIGHT OF MYSTERY, A(1928); SO THIS IS LOVE(1928); TRAGEDY OF YOUTH, THE(1928)
Misc. Silents
BUGLE CALL, THE(1916); AGE OF DESIRE, THE(1923); FOOLS' HIGHWAY(1924); LEAVE IT TO GERRY(1924); VERDICT, THE(1925); GOD GAVE ME TWENTY CENTS(1926); LADY OF THE HAREM, THE(1926); LUCKY LADY, THE(1926); WANDERER, THE(1926); BROKEN GATE, THE(1927); COLLEGE WIDOW, THE(1927); DEARIE(1927); DESIRED WOMAN, THE(1927); RED SWORD, THE(1929); TIDE OF EMPIRE(1929)
William "Buster" Collier, Jr.
Silents
SECRETS OF PARIS, THE(1922)
Misc. Silents
GIRL FROM PORCUPINE, THE(1921)
William Collier, Sr.
NOTHING BUT THE TRUTH(1929), w; FREE AND EASY(1930); HAPPY DAYS(1930); HARMONY AT HOME(1930), a, w; HIGH SOCIETY BLUES(1930); SHE'S MY WEAKNESS(1930); UP THE RIVER(1930), a, w; ANNABELLE'S AFFAIRS(1931); BRAT, THE(1931); MR. LEMON OF ORANGE(1931); SEAS BENEATH, THE(1931); SIX CYLINDER LOVE(1931); AFTER TOMORROW(1932); HOT SATURDAY(1932); MADISON SQUARE GARDEN(1932); STEPPING SISTERS(1932), a, w; WASHINGTON MASQUERADE(1932); CHEATERS(1934); CROSBY CASE, THE(1934); SUCCESSFUL FAILURE, A(1934); ANNAPOLIS FAREWELL(1935); MURDER MAN(1935); BRIDE COMES HOME(1936); CAIN AND MABEL(1936); GIVE US THIS NIGHT(1936); LOVE ON A BET(1936); VALIANT IS THE WORD FOR CARRIE(1936); JOSETTE(1938); SAY IT IN FRENCH(1938); THANKS FOR THE MEMORY(1938); DISPUTED PASSAGE(1939); I'M FROM MISSOURI(1939); INVITATION TO HAPPINESS(1939); PERSONS IN HIDING(1939); TELEVISION SPY(1939); MIRACLE ON MAIN STREET, A(1940); THERE'S MAGIC IN MUSIC(1941); YANKEE DOODLE DANDY(1942), tech adv
Collier Sisters
WORDS AND MUSIC(1929)
Joe Colligan
Misc. Talkies
GOIN' ALL THE WAY(1982)
Richard Colligan
PROWLER, THE(1981)
Rosemary Colligan
RUN FOR THE HILLS(1953); FRENCH LINE, THE(1954)
Yves Collignon
LA NUIT DE VARENNES(1983, Fr./Ital.)
A. E. Collin
SPY IN THE SKY(1958)
Fabien Collin
PLAYTIME(1963, Fr.), d
Francoise Collin
MARRIED WOMAN, THE(1965, Fr.), ed; BAND OF OUTSIDERS(1966, Fr.), ed; PIERROT LE FOU(1968, Fr./Ital.), ed; CANNABIS(1970, Fr.), ed; TWO OR THREE THINGS I KNOW ABOUT HER(1970, Fr.), ed
Ian Collin
WINGS OVER AFRICA(1939)
Ivor Collin
SWORD OF SHERWOOD FOREST(1961, Brit.), tech adv

Jack Collin
GOIN' COCONUTS(1978)
Joel Collin
WOMEN OF PITCAIRN ISLAND, THE(1957)
John Collin
PIRATES OF BLOOD RIVER, THE(1962, Brit.); DEAD MAN'S CHEST(1965, Brit.); DEVIL'S OWN, THE(1967, Brit.); STAR!(1968); BEFORE WINTER COMES(1969, Brit.); LAST ESCAPE, THE(1970, Brit.); INNOCENT BYSTANDERS(1973, Brit.); MAN AT THE TOP(1973, Brit.); ALL CREATURES GREAT AND SMALL(1975, Brit.); TESS(1980, Fr./Brit.)
Paul Colline
ROYAL AFFAIRS IN VERSAILLES(1957, Fr.)
Joe Colling
BEAU GESTE(1939)
Patricia Collinge
LITTLE FOXES, THE(1941); SHADOW OF A DOUBT(1943); TENDER COMRADE(1943); CASANOVA BROWN(1944); TERESA(1951); WASHINGTON STORY(1952); NUN'S STORY, THE(1959)
Andy Collings
CORPSE GRINDERS, THE(1972)
Anne Collings
NOW THAT APRIL'S HERE(1958, Can.); MASK, THE(1961, Can.); SEVEN ALONE(1975)
Misc. Talkies
ESCAPE FROM ANGOLA(1976)
Benita Collings
SUNSTRUCK(1973, Aus.)
C. F. Collings
Silents
GIRL WHO TOOK THE WRONG TURNING, THE(1915, Brit.)
Cliff Collings
LINE, THE(1982)
David Collings
JOANNA(1968, Brit.); SCROOGE(1970, Brit.); MAHLER(1974, Brit.); HENNESSY(1975, Brit.); THIRTY NINE STEPS, THE(1978, Brit.)
Jeannie Collings
CONFESSIONS OF A WINDOW CLEANER(1974, Brit.); CARRY ON ENGLAND(1976, Brit.); EMILY(1976, Brit.)
Joe Collings
LIGHT THAT FAILED, THE(1939)
Lisa Collings
LOVE IS A SPLENDID ILLUSION(1970, Brit.); MUTATIONS, THE(1974, Brit.)
Monte Collings
HOUSE OF ERRORS(1942)
Pierre Collings
HOLE IN THE WALL(1929), w; DANGEROUS NAN McGREW(1930), w
Silents
ALIMONY(1924), ph; GOOD AND NAUGHTY(1926), w; GRAND DUCHESS AND THE WAITER, THE(1926), w; SOCIAL CELEBRITY, A(1926), w; KNOCKOUT REILLY(1927), w; TIME TO LOVE(1927), w
Russell Collings
STOLEN LIFE, A(1946), spec eff
Charles Collingwood
SHARKFIGHTERS, THE(1956); DARK CRYSTAL, THE(1982, Brit.)
Lyn Collingwood
PALM BEACH(1979, Aus.)
Monica Collingwood
BISHOP'S WIFE, THE(1947), ed; FANGS OF THE WILD(1954), ed; LASSIE'S GREAT ADVENTURE(1963), ed
Peter Collingwood
PANIC IN THE PARLOUR(1957, Brit.); UP THE CREEK(1958, Brit.); FOLLOW THAT HORSE!(1960, Brit.); MORGAN!(1966, Brit.); ADAM'S WOMAN(1972, Austral.); DEATHCHEATERS(1976, Aus.); CROSSTALK(1982, Aus.)
Alan Collins
DEAD RUN(1961, Fr./Ital./Ger.); WEREWOLF IN A GIRL'S DORMITORY(1961, Ital./Aust.); DEVIL'S MAN, THE(1967, Ital.); YOUNG, THE EVIL AND THE SAVAGE, THE(1968, Ital.); HATCHET FOR A HONEYMOON(1969, Span./Ital.); VON RICHTHOFEN AND BROWN(1970), ed; BARON BLOOD(1972, Ital.); MERRY WIVES OF TOBIAS ROUKE, THE(1972, Can.), ed; PRIVATE DUTY NURSES(1972), ed; I ESCAPED FROM DEVIL'S ISLAND(1973), ed; WHAT'S NEXT?(1975, Brit.); LOVE AT FIRST SIGHT(1977, Can.), ed; DIRTY TRICKS(1981, Can.), ed; YOR, THE HUNTER FROM THE FUTURE(1983, Ital.)
1984
HUNTERS OF THE GOLDEN COBRA, THE(1984, Ital.); LAST HUNTER, THE(1984, Ital.)
Alan Collins [Luciano Pigozzi]
SECRET AGENT FIREBALL(1965, Fr./Ital.); WHAT!(1965, Fr./Brit./Ital.); TERROR CREATURES FROM THE GRAVE(1967, U.S./Ital.); ONE STEP TO HELL(1969, U.S./Ital./Span.); SABATA(1969, Ital.)
Alana Collins
EVEL KNIEVEL(1971); NIGHT CALL NURSES(1974)
Allan Collins
BROOD, THE(1979, Can.), ed; TULIPS(1981, Can), ed
Amber Collins [Ombretta Colli]
WAR BETWEEN THE PLANETS(1971, Ital.)
Ann Collins
DRIFTER(1975)
Anne Collins
BLOODY BROOD, THE(1959, Can.)
Anthony Collins
VICTORIA THE GREAT(1937, Brit.), m; NURSE EDITH CAVELL(1939), md; IRENE(1940), md; NO, NO NANETTE(1940), md; TOM BROWN'S SCHOOL DAYS(1940), m; SUNNY(1941), md; UNEXPECTED UNCLE(1941), m; DESTROYER(1943), m; FOREVER AND A DAY(1943), md; YANK IN LONDON, A(1946, Brit.), m; FABULOUS TEXAN, THE(1947), m; LADY WITH A LAMP, THE(1951, Brit.), m; ODETTE(1951, Brit.), m; MACAO(1952), m; TRENT'S LAST CASE(1953, Brit.), m; ADVENTURES OF ROBINSON CRUSOE, THE(1954), m; LAUGHING ANNE(1954, Brit./U.S.), m

Arthur Greville Collins
FROM HEADQUARTERS(1933), w; MODERN HERO, A(1934), d; DON'T BET ON BLONDES(1935), w; PERSONAL MAID'S SECRET(1935), d; NOBODY'S FOOL(1936), d; THANK YOU, JEEVES(1936), d; WIDOW FROM MONTE CARLO, THE(1936), d; PARADISE ISLE(1937), d; SALESLADY(1938), d; LITTLE AUSTRALIANS(1940, Aus.), d
Barry Collins
TIME OF THE HEATHEN(1962); FIENDISH PLOT OF DR. FU MANCHU, THE(1980), ch
Bill Collins
RED, WHITE AND BLACK, THE(1970); INCREDIBLE TWO-HEADED TRANSPLANT, THE(1971); JUD(1971); WILD RIDERS(1971)
Bill Hugh Collins
PROWLER, THE(1981)
Bob Collins
SCHLOCK(1973), ph
1984
POLICE ACADEMY(1984)
Bobby Collins
MOTHER'S DAY(1980)
Boon Collins
BUTCHER BAKER(NIGHTMARE MAKER)* (1982), w; SALLY FIELDGOOD & CO.(1975, Can.), d, w
Brent Collins
VORTEX(1982)
Burton Collins
PRINCE OF THE CITY(1981); DANIEL(1983)
1984
BEST DEFENSE(1984)
C. E. Collins
Silents
KISMET(1920)
C. Pat Collins
SAN FRANCISCO(1936); SCUDDA-HOO! SCUDDA-HAY!(1948)
Candace Collins
CLASS(1983); SMOKEY AND THE BANDIT–PART 3(1983)
Cathy Collins
COLOR ME BLOOD RED(1965)
Charles Collins
DANCING PIRATE(1936); SWING HOSTESS(1944); BLUEPRINT FOR MURDER, A(1953)
Charlie Collins
STEEL TRAP, THE(1952)
Chic Collins
MY MAN GODFREY(1936)
Chick Collins
MILLION DOLLAR LEGS(1932); KISS AND MAKE UP(1934); SOMETHING TO SING ABOUT(1937); CITY GIRL(1938); I AM THE LAW(1938); LITTLE OLD NEW YORK(1940); SAINT IN PALM SPRINGS, THE(1941); SULLIVAN'S TRAVELS(1941); QUIET PLEASE, MURDER(1942); DANCING MASTERS, THE(1943); FALLEN ANGEL(1945); FULLER BRUSH MAN(1948); GOOD HUMOR MAN, THE(1950); MILKMAN, THE(1950)
Choo Choo Collins
BUSYBODY, THE(1967)
Choo-Choo Collins
GIRL FEVER(1961)
Chris Collins
GLADIATORS, THE(1970, Swed.), cos
Claude Collins
SHOW BOAT(1929)
Colleen Collins
I, MAUREEN(1978, Can.)
Connie Collins
ATLANTIC CITY(1981, U.S./Can.)
Cora Sue Collins
CASE OF CLARA DEANE, THE(1932); SMILIN' THROUGH(1932); STRANGE CASE OF CLARA DEANE, THE(1932); UNEXPECTED FATHER(1932); JENNIE GERHARDT(1933); MYSTERIOUS RIDER, THE(1933); PICTURE SNATCHER(1933); QUEEN CHRISTINA(1933); SIN OF NORA MORAN(1933); THEY JUST HAD TO GET MARRIED(1933); TORCH SINGER(1933); BLACK MOON(1934); EVELYN PRENTICE(1934); RIP TIDE(1934); SCARLET LETTER, THE(1934); TREASURE ISLAND(1934); ANNA KARENINA(1935); DARK ANGEL, THE(1935); ELINOR NORTON(1935); HARMONY LANE(1935); LITTLE MEN(1935); MAD LOVE(1935); MAGNIFICENT OBSESSION(1935); MARY BURNS, FUGITIVE(1935); NAUGHTY MARIETTA(1935); PUBLIC HERO NO. 1(1935); TWO SINNERS(1935); WORLD ACCUSES, THE(1935); DEVIL'S SQUADRON(1936); HARVESTER, THE(1936); PENTHOUSE PARTY(1936); THREE MARRIED MEN(1936); ADVENTURES OF TOM SAWYER, THE(1938); BAD LITTLE ANGEL(1939); STOP, LOOK, AND LOVE(1939); BLOOD AND SAND(1941); GET HEP TO LOVE(1942); JOHNNY DOUGHBOY(1943); ROUGHLY SPEAKING(1945); WEEKEND AT THE WALDORF(1945); YOUTH ON TRIAL(1945)
Corny Collins
YOUNG GO WILD, THE(1962, Ger.); PRIEST OF ST. PAULI, THE(1970, Ger.)
Courtney Collins
Silents
IN THE STRETCH(1914)
Dale Collins
SAL OF SINGAPORE(1929), w; SHIP FROM SHANGHAI, THE(1930), w; HIS WOMAN(1931), w; RICH AND STRANGE(1932, Brit.), w
David Collins
1984
PIGS(1984, Ireland), p
Dean Collins
SING A JINGLE(1943); JUNIOR PROM(1946), ch
Denver John Collins
DOC(1971); WATCHED(1974)
Dick Collins
Silents
LOVE IN A HURRY(1919)

Dimity Collins

NEGATIVES(1968, Brit.), set d; MUMSY, NANNY, SONNY, AND GIRLY(1970, Brit.), set d; DAY IN THE DEATH OF JOE EGG, A(1972, Brit.), set d

Eddie Collins

ALEXANDER'S RAGTIME BAND(1938); ALWAYS IN TROUBLE(1938); CHARLIE CHAN IN HONOLULU(1938); DOWN ON THE FARM(1938); IN OLD CHICAGO(1938); JOSETTE(1938); KENTUCKY MOONSHINE(1938); LITTLE MISS BROADWAY(1938); PENROD AND HIS TWIN BROTHER(1938); SALLY, IRENE AND MARY(1938); UP THE RIVER(1938); CHARLIE CHAN IN RENO(1939); DRUMS ALONG THE MOHAWK(1939); HEAVEN WITH A BARBED WIRE FENCE(1939); HOLLYWOOD CAVALCADE(1939); NEWS IS MADE AT NIGHT(1939); QUICK MILLIONS(1939); STOP, LOOK, AND LOVE(1939); YOUNG MR. LINCOLN(1939); BLUE BIRD, THE(1940); RETURN OF FRANK JAMES, THE(1940)

Edward Collins

Misc. Talkies

GOD BLESS DR. SHAGETZ(1977), d

Edwin J. Collins

Silents

EUGENE ARAM(1914, Brit.), d&w; BLIND BOY, THE(1917, Brit.), d; GOD AND THE MAN(1918, Brit.), d; STARTING POINT, THE(1919, Brit.), d; GOD IN THE GARDEN, THE(1921, Brit.), d&w; GREEN CARAVAN, THE(1922, Brit.), d&w; GAMBLE WITH HEARTS, A(1923, Brit.), d

Misc. Silents

TOM JONES(1917, Brit.), d; IN THE GLOAMING(1919, Brit.), d; HARD CASH(1921, Brit.), d; MISS CHARITY(1921, Brit.), d; SINGLE LIFE(1921, Brit.), d; STELLA(1921), d

Elaine Collins

1984

GREYSTOKE: THE LEGEND OF TARZAN, LORD OF THE APES(1984)

Ernie Collins

Silents

KENT, THE FIGHTING MAN(1916, Brit.)

Misc. Silents

GREEN ORCHARD, THE(1916, Brit.); WHEN PARIS SLEEPS(1917, Brit.); WHERE AMBITION LEADS(1919, Brit.)

Frank J. Collins

MOUTHPIECE, THE(1932), w; MAN WHO TALKED TOO MUCH, THE(1940), w; ILLEGAL(1955), w

G. Pat Collins

HALF-MARRIAGE(1929); BE YOURSELF(1930); MANSLAUGHTER(1930); ONLY SAPS WORK(1930); NO LIMIT(1931); VICE SQUAD, THE(1931); HOLD YOUR MAN(1933); BIG SHAKEDOWN, THE(1934); CRIME DOCTOR, THE(1934); FOG(1934); KEEP 'EM ROLLING(1934); MANHATTAN MELODRAMA(1934); ALIBI IKE(1935); BABY FACE HARRINGTON(1935); MR. DYNAMITE(1935); WEST OF THE PECOS(1935); WEST POINT OF THE AIR(1935); IT HAD TO HAPPEN(1936); CARNIVAL QUEEN(1937); DOUBLE WEDDING(1937); WITH LOVE AND KISSES(1937); INVISIBLE STRIPES(1940); KING OF THE LUMBERJACKS(1940); THEY DIED WITH THEIR BOOTS ON(1942); JUNGLE PATROL(1948); NAKED CITY, THE(1948); UP IN CENTRAL PARK(1948); FLAMING FURY(1949); FOUNTAINHEAD, THE(1949); SCENE OF THE CRIME(1949); WHITE HEAT(1949); WOMAN ON PIER 13, THE(1950); WILD NORTH, THE(1952); ABOVE AND BEYOND(1953); CLOWN, THE(1953); BETRAYED WOMEN(1955); BIG TIP OFF, THE(1955); NAKED STREET, THE(1955); NIGHT FREIGHT(1955); YAQUI DRUMS(1956)

Silents

RACKET, THE(1928)

Gary Collins

PIGEON THAT TOOK ROME, THE(1962); STRANDED(1965); ANGEL IN MY POCKET(1969); AIRPORT(1970); KILLER FISH(1979, Ital./Braz.); HANGAR 18(1980)

Misc. Talkies

STREETS OF HONG KONG(1979)

Gene Collins

MARGIE(1940); PRIDE OF THE YANKEES, THE(1942); GANGSTER, THE(1947); GINGER(1947); FIGHTING FATHER DUNNE(1948); WALLS OF JERICHO(1948); I SHOT JESSE JAMES(1949); MILITARY ACADEMY WITH THAT TENTH AVENUE GANG(1950); WHEN WILLIE COMES MARCHING HOME(1950); WHEN WORLDS COLLIDE(1951); HAPPY TIME, THE(1952); MIRACLE OF THE HILLS, THE(1959); DESPERATE ONES, THE(1968 U.S./Span.), ch; KELLY'S HEROES(1970, U.S./Yugo.); DOC(1971)

George Collins

CENTRAL PARK(1932)

George Pat Collins

I AM A FUGITIVE FROM A CHAIN GANG(1932); GIRL MISSING(1933); HARD TO HANDLE(1933); HEROES FOR SALE(1933); MAYOR OF HELL, THE(1933); PARACHUTE JUMPER(1933); PICTURE SNATCHER(1933); SILK EXPRESS, THE(1933); 20,000 YEARS IN SING SING(1933); PERSONALITY KID, THE(1934); VERY HONORABLE GUY, A(1934); BLACK FURY(1935)

Georgie Collins

VISITOR, THE(1973, Can.)

Gerry Collins

UNDERCOVER GIRL(1957, Brit.)

Gunther Collins

SWINGIN' AFFAIR, A(1963), p, w; JUD(1971), d&w

Hal Collins

FREDDIE STEPS OUT(1946), w; HIGH SCHOOL HERO(1946), w; JUNIOR PROM(1946), w; SARGE GOES TO COLLEGE(1947), w; VACATION DAYS(1947), w; CAMPUS SLEUTH(1948), w; SMART POLITICS(1948), w, m/l; LOVE-INS, THE(1967), w; FOR SINGLES ONLY(1968), w

Harriet Collins

LOOPHOLE(1981, Brit.)

Harry Collins

FASHIONS OF 1934(1934), w

Helen Collins

FLYING DOWN TO RIO(1933); DOWN TO THEIR LAST YACHT(1934)

Ivy Collins

MYSTERIOUS MR. NICHOLSON, THE(1947, Brit.); DULCIMER STREET(1948, Brit.)

Jack Collins

FEAR IN THE NIGHT(1947); ROCK, ROCK, ROCK!(1956); FRANKENSTEIN 1970(1958), art d; ISLAND OF LOST WOMEN(1959), art d; GET TO KNOW YOUR RABBIT(1972); OTHER, THE(1972); STING, THE(1973); TOWERING INFERNO, THE(1974); EXORCIST II: THE HERETIC(1977), art d; PETE'S DRAGON(1977); LAST

WORD, THE(1979), prod d; JEKYLL AND HYDE...TOGETHER AGAIN(1982); PSYCHO FROM TEXAS(1982)

Silents

IS THAT NICE?(1926), w; AIN'T LOVE FUNNY?(1927), t

Jack T. Collins

GIRL IN BLACK STOCKINGS(1957), prod d; JERK, THE(1979), prod d

Jackie Collins

ROCK YOU SINNERS(1957, Brit.); UNDERCOVER GIRL(1957, Brit.); ALL AT SEA(1958, Brit.); INTENT TO KILL(1958, Brit.); SAFECRACKER, THE(1958, Brit.); ROOM 43(1959, Brit.); DURING ONE NIGHT(1962, Brit.); STUD, THE(1979, Brit.), w; YESTERDAY'S HERO(1979, Brit.), w; WORLD IS FULL OF MARRIED MEN, THE(1980, Brit.), w

Jane Collins

ALL CREATURES GREAT AND SMALL(1975, Brit.)

Jayne Collins

Misc. Talkies

LAST KIDS ON EARTH, THE(1983)

Jeff Collins

YELLOW SUBMARINE(1958, Brit.), animation

Jill Collins

JOURNEY INTO DARKNESS(1968, Brit.)

Jo Collins

HOW TO STUFF A WILD BIKINI(1965); SERGEANT DEADHEAD(1965); SKI PARTY(1965); FIREBALL 590(1966); LORD LOVE A DUCK(1966)

Joab Collins

ELEPHANT CALLED SLOWLY, AN(1970, Brit.)

Joan Collins

JUDGMENT DEFERRED(1952, Brit.); DECAMERON NIGHTS(1953, Brit.); I BELIEVE IN YOU(1953, Brit.); SLASHER, THE(1953, Brit.); GOOD DIE YOUNG, THE(1954, Brit.); TURN THE KEY SOFTLY(1954, Brit.); WOMAN'S ANGLE, THE(1954, Brit.); ADVENTURES OF SADIE, THE(1955, Brit.); GIRL IN THE RED VELVET SWING, THE(1955); LADY GODIVA RIDES AGAIN(1955, Brit.); LAND OF THE PHARAOHS(1955); SQUARE RING, THE(1955, Brit.); VIRGIN QUEEN, THE(1955); OPPOSITE SEX, THE(1956); ISLAND IN THE SUN(1957); SEA WIFE(1957, Brit.); STOPOVER TOKYO(1957); WAYWARD BUS, THE(1957); BRAVADOS, THE(1958); RALLY 'ROUND THE FLAG, BOYS!(1958); ESTHER AND THE KING(1960, U.S./Ital.); SEVEN THIEVES(1960); ROAD TO HONG KONG, THE(1962, U.S./Brit.); ONE MILLION DOLLARS(1965, Ital.); WARNING SHOT(1967); IF IT'S TUESDAY, THIS MUST BE BELGIUM(1969); SUBTERFUGE(1969, US/Brit.); EXECUTIONER, THE(1970, Brit.); UP IN THE CELLAR(1970); QUEST FOR LOVE(1971, Brit.); TERROR FROM UNDER THE HOUSE(1971, Brit.); FEAR IN THE NIGHT(1972, Brit.); TALES FROM THE CRYPT(1972, Brit.); TALES THAT WITNESS MADNESS(1973, Brit.); DARK PLACES(1974, Brit.); ALFIE DARLING(1975, Brit.); BAWDY ADVENTURES OF TOM JONES, THE(1976, Brit.); DEVIL WITHIN HER, THE(1976, Brit.); GREAT ADVENTURE, THE(1976, Span./Ital.); EMPIRE OF THE ANTS(1977); BIG SLEEP, THE½(1978, Brit.); ZERO TO SIXTY(1978); STUD, THE(1979, Brit.); SUNBURN(1979); GAME FOR VULTURES, A(1980, Brit.); HOMEWORK(1982); NUTCRACKER(1982, Brit.)

Misc. Talkies

CAN HIERONYMUS MERKIN EVER FORGET MERCY HUMPPE AND FIND TRUE HAPPINESS?(1969); AQUARIAN, THE(1972); BITCH, THE(1979); NUTCRACKER(1984)

Joe Collins

THIN RED LINE, THE(1964)

Joel Collins

DINO(1957); MOVE OVER, DARLING(1963)

John Collins

Misc. Silents

ON DANGEROUS PATHS(1915), d

John D. Collins

DRACULA HAS RISEN FROM HIS GRAVE(1968, Brit.)

John H. Collins

Silents

GLADIOLA(1915), d; INNOCENCE OF RUTH, THE(1916), d; ALADDIN'S OTHER LAMP(1917), d; GIRL WITHOUT A SOUL, THE(1917), d&w

Misc. Silents

COHEN'S LUCK(1915), d; GREATER THAN ART(1915), d; PLOUGHSHARE, THE(1915), d; SLAVEY STUDENT, THE(1915), d; COSSACK WHIP, THE(1916), d; FLOWER OF NO MAN'S LAND, THE(1916), d; GATES OF EDEN, THE(1916), d; HIS SISTER'S CHAMPION(1916), d; LIGHT OF HAPPINESS, THE(1916), d; BLUE JEANS(1917), d; GOD'S LAW AND MAN'S(1917), d; LADY BARNACLE(1917), d; MORTAL SIN, THE(1917), d; FLOWER OF THE DUSK(1918), d; OPPORTUNITY(1918), d; RIDERS OF THE NIGHT(1918), d; WEAVER OF DREAMS(1918), d; WINDING TRAIL, THE(1918), d; GOLD CURE, THE(1919), d

Jolina Collins

1984

LONELY GUY, THE(1984)

Jonathan Collins

DECLINE AND FALL... OF A BIRD WATCHER(1969, Brit.)

Johnnie Collins III

BREEZY(1973); GREAT SMOKEY ROADBLOCK, THE(1978)

Jose Collins

FACING THE MUSIC(1933, Brit.)

Silents

NOBODY'S CHILD(1919, Brit.)

Misc. Silents

LIGHT THAT FAILED, THE(1916); WOMAN'S HONOR, A(1916); SWORD OF DAMOCLES, THE(1920, Brit.)

Julie Collins

TROUBLESOME DOUBLE, THE(1971, Brit.)

June Collins

SHIRLEY THOMPSON VERSUS THE ALIENS(1968, Aus.)

Kathleen Collins

BORDER DEVILS(1932)

Misc. Talkies

CRUZ BROTHERS AND MISS MALLOY, THE(1979), d; LOSING GROUND(1982), d

Silents

BLACK CYCLONE(1925); UNKNOWN CAVALIER, THE(1926); SOMEWHERE IN SONORA(1927); GRIT WINS(1929)

Richard Collins
RULERS OF THE SEA(1939), w; ONE CROWDED NIGHT(1940), w; LADY SCAR-FACE(1941), w; SONG OF RUSSIA(1943), w; THOUSANDS CHEER(1943), w; LITTLE GIANT(1946), w; CHINA VENTURE(1953), w; ADVENTURES OF HAJJI BA-BA(1954), w; BOB MATHIAS STORY, THE(1954), w; RIOT IN CELL BLOCK 11(1954), w; CULT OF THE COBRA(1955), w; KISS OF FIRE(1955), w; MY GUN IS QUICK(1957), w; BADLANDERS, THE(1958), w; SPANISH AFFAIR(1958, Span.), w; EDGE OF ETERNITY(1959), w; PAY OR DIE(1960), w

Robert Collins
WALK PROUD(1979), d; SAVAGE HARVEST(1981), d, w

Roberta Collins
BIG DOLL HOUSE, THE(1971); UNHOLY ROLLERS(1972); AROUSERS, THE(1973); ROOMMATES, THE(1973); WONDER WOMEN(1973, Phil.); RENEGADE GIRLS(1974); THREE THE HARD WAY(1974); DEATH RACE 2000(1975); TRAIN RIDE TO HOLLY-WOOD(1975); MATILDA(1978); SATURDAY THE 14TH(1981); DEATH WISH II(1982)
1984
HARDBODIES(1984)
Misc. Talkies
BIG DOLL HOUSE, THE(1971); WOMEN IN CAGES(1972); DEADLY AND THE BEAUTIFUL(1974); WHISKEY MOUNTAIN(1977)

Rosie Collins
TERROR(1979, Brit.)

Roy Collins
ROSE MARIE(1954)

Rufus Collins
SUMMER OF SECRETS(1976, Aus.); SHOCK TREATMENT(1981); BRITTANIA HOSPITAL(1982, Brit.); HUNGER, THE(1983)

Russell Collins
SEEDS OF FREEDOM(1943, USSR); CLOSE-UP(1948); SHOCKPROOF(1949); WALK-ING HILLS, THE(1949); SLEEPING CITY, THE(1950); DESTINATION GOBI(1953); MISS SADIE THOMPSON(1953); MONTE CARLO BABY(1953, Fr.); NIAGARA(1953); BAD DAY AT BLACK ROCK(1955); CANYON CROSSROADS(1955); LAST FRON-TIER, THE(1955); SOLDIER OF FORTUNE(1955); ENEMY BELOW, THE(1957); RAINTREE COUNTY(1957); MATCHMAKER, THE(1958); RABBIT TRAP, THE(1959); FAIL SAFE(1964); THOSE CALLOWAYS(1964); WHEN THE BOYS MEET THE GIRLS(1965); DEAD KIDS(1981 Aus./New Zealand), art d; PICTURES(1982, New Zealand), art d

Sewell Collins
DEVIL'S MAZE, THE(1929, Brit.), w; BRACELETS(1931, Brit.), d&w; GENTLEMAN OF PARIS, A(1931), w; ANNE ONE HUNDRED(1933, Brit.), w; LASH, THE(1934, Brit.), w; NINE FORTY-FIVE(1934, Brit.), w

Shannon Collins
PIRANHA(1978)

Sheldon Collins
PRESIDENT'S ANALYST, THE(1967)

Sid Collins
CARRY ON SPYING(1964, Brit.), w

Spelman B. Collins
SO DEAR TO MY HEART(1949)

Stephen Collins
ALL THE PRESIDENT'S MEN(1976); BETWEEN THE LINES(1977); FEDORA(1978, Ger./Fr.); PROMISE, THE(1979); STAR TREK: THE MOTION PICTURE(1979); LOV-ING COUPLES(1980)

Steven Collins
FROZEN ALIVE(1966, Brit./Ger.), ed; SUNSCORCHED(1966, Span./Ger.), ed

Sunny Collins
Misc. Talkies
FOX AFFAIR, THE(1978)

Suzanne Collins
1984
NINJA III–THE DOMINATION(1984)

Suzette Collins
EUREKA(1983, Brit.)

Ted Collins
HELLO, EVERYBODY(1933); OUT OF THE PAST(1947)

Terri Collins
TALES OF A SALESMAN(1965)

Tom Collins
NORAH O'NEALE(1934, Brit.); BURN 'EM UP O'CONNER(1939); FAST AND LOOSE(1939); TELL NO TALES(1939); THESE GLAMOUR GIRLS(1939); DANCING ON A DIME(1940); DR. KILDARE GOES HOME(1940); DR. KILDARE'S STRANGE CASE(1940); I TAKE THIS WOMAN(1940)
Misc. Silents
BROMLEY CASE, THE(1920), d; CIRCUMSTANTIAL EVIDENCE(1920), d; SCRAP OF PAPER, THE(1920), d; TRAIL OF THE CIGARETTE, THE(1920), d; WALL STREET MYSTERY, THE(1920), d

Tracey Collins
ON THE RUN(1969, Brit.)

Tracy Collins
TROUBLESOME DOUBLE, THE(1971, Brit.)

Wilkie Collins
MOONSTONE, THE(1934), w; CRIMES AT THE DARK HOUSE(1940, Brit.), w; WOMAN IN WHITE, THE(1948), w
Silents
SHE LOVES AND LIES(1920), w

William Collins
SEXTON BLAKE AND THE MADEMOISELLE(1935, Brit.); MURDER BY RO-PE(1936, Brit.)

William E. Collins
Silents
KISS IN TIME, A(1921), ph; LOVE CHARM, THE(1921), ph

Winnie Collins
YELLOW MASK, THE(1930, Brit.)

Madeleine Collinson
COME BACK PETER(1971, Brit.); LOVE MACHINE, THE,(1971); TWINS OF EVIL(1971, Brit.)

Mary Collinson
COME BACK PETER(1971, Brit.); LOVE MACHINE, THE,(1971); TWINS OF EVIL(1971, Brit.)

Peter Collinson
PENTHOUSE, THE(1967, Brit.), d&w; LONG DAY'S DYING, THE(1968, Brit.), p, d; UP THE JUNCTION(1968, Brit.), d; ITALIAN JOB, THE(1969, Brit.), d; YOU CAN'T WIN 'EM ALL(1970, Brit.), d; FRIGHT(1971, Brit.), d; INNOCENT BYSTAN-DERS(1973, Brit.), d; MAN CALLED NOON, THE(1973, Brit.), d; OPEN SEASON(1974, U.S./Span.), d; STRAIGHT ON TILL MORNING(1974, Brit.), p&d; SPIRAL STAIR-CASE, THE(1975, Brit.), d; TEN LITTLE INDIANS(1975, Ital./Fr./Span./Ger.), d; SELL OUT, THE(1976), d; TOMORROW NEVER COMES(1978, Brit./Can.), d; EARTHLING, THE(1980), d

Tara Collinson
FRIGHT(1971, Brit.)

Wilson Collinson
MAISIE(1939), w; MAISIE WAS A LADY(1941), w; MAISIE GETS HER MAN(1942), w; MAISIE GOES TO RENO(1944), w

Collinson & Dean
ON VELVET(1938, Brit.)

Anthony Collis
PICCADILLY INCIDENT(1948, Brit.), md

Jack Collis
VIOLENT ROAD(1958), art d; I DEAL IN DANGER(1966), art d; HELLO DOWN THERE(1969), art d; DARKER THAN AMBER(1970), art d; DELTA FACTOR, THE(1970), art d; MAGNUM FORCE(1973), art d; SAVE THE TIGER(1973), art d; LAST TYCOON, THE(1976), art d; FOUR SEASONS, THE(1981), prod d; PATER-NITY(1981), prod d; NIGHT SHIFT(1982), prod d; NATIONAL LAMPOON'S VACA-TION(1983), prod d

Jack T. Collis
HELL BOUND(1957), prod d; BORN RECKLESS(1959), art d; GIRLS' TOWN(1959), art d; UP PERISCOPE(1959), art d; NORTH AVENUE IRREGULARS, THE(1979), art d; LONG RIDERS, THE(1980), prod d; TEX(1982), prod d
1984
IMPULSE(1984), a, prod d; SPLASH(1984), prod d

Wilson Collison
EXPENSIVE WOMEN(1931), w; CRUSADER, THE(1932), w; RED DUST(1932), w; RED-HAIRED ALIBI, THE(1932), w; THREE WISE GIRLS(1932), w; NIGHT OF THE GARTER(1933, Brit.), w; SING SINNER, SING(1933), w; SMART GIRL(1935), w; WOMAN WANTED(1935), w; MAD MISS MANTON, THE(1938), w; THERE'S AL-WAYS A WOMAN(1938), w; THERE'S THAT WOMAN AGAIN(1938), w; CONGO MAISIE(1940), w; GOLD RUSH MAISIE(1940), w; MOON OVER BURMA(1940), w; SWING SHIFT MAISIE(1943), w; UP IN MABEL'S ROOM(1944), w; GETTING GER-TIE'S GARTER(1945), w; UP GOES MAISIE(1946), w; MOGAMBO(1953), w

Peter Collister
SUMMER LOVERS(1982), ph

Rick Colliti
LOVE AND BULLETS(1979, Brit.)

Luigi Collo
CAT O'NINE TAILS(1971, Ital./Ger./Fr.), w

Daureen Collodel
1984
WEEKEND PASS(1984)

Collodi [Carlo Lorenzini]
PINOCCHIO(1940), w

Carlo Collodi
PINOCCHIO IN OUTER SPACE(1965, U.S./Bel.), w; PINOCCHIO(1969, E. Ger.), w

Roy Collodi
GIRL, THE BODY, AND THE PILL, THE(1967), a, ph; JUST FOR THE HELL OF IT(1968), ph; SHE-DEVILS ON WHEELS(1968), a, ph

Jean Collomb
MY BABY IS BLACK!(1965, Fr.), ph; LIVE FOR LIFE(1967, Fr./Ital.); TO BE A CROOK(1967, Fr.), ph; LIFE LOVE DEATH(1969, Fr./Ital.), a, ph; CROOK, THE(1971, Fr.), ph; AND NOW MY LOVE(1975, Fr.), ph; CAT AND MOUSE(1978, Fr.), ph

John Collum
KID MILLIONS(1934); TOM BROWN'S SCHOOL DAYS(1940); FORCE OF EVIL(1948); LOUISA(1950)

Eve Collyer
THE BOSTON STRANGLER, THE(1968)

June Collyer
ILLUSION(1929); LOVE DOCTOR, THE(1929); NOT QUITE DECENT(1929); RIVER OF ROMANCE(1929); CHARLEY'S AUNT(1930); EXTRAVAGANCE(1930); MAN FROM WYOMING, A(1930); SWEET KITTY BELLAIRS(1930); THREE SISTERS, THE(1930); ALEXANDER HAMILTON(1931); BRAT, THE(1931); DAMAGED LO-VE(1931); DRUMS OF JEOPARDY(1931); DUDE RANCH(1931); HONEYMOON LANE(1931); KISS ME AGAIN(1931); REVENGE AT MONTE CARLO(1933); BEFORE MIDNIGHT(1934); CHEATERS(1934); GHOST WALKS, THE(1935); LOST IN THE STRATOSPHERE(1935); MURDER BY TELEVISION(1935); FACE IN THE FOG, A(1936)
Silents
FOUR SONS(1928); RED WINE(1928); WOMAN WISE(1928)
Misc. Silents
HANGMAN'S HOUSE(1928); ME, GANGSTER(1928)

Ben Colman
BATTLESTAR GALACTICA(1979), ph; CONQUEST OF THE EARTH(1980), ph

Booth Colman
BIG SKY, THE(1952); LIVING IT UP(1954); SECRET OF THE INCAS(1954); THEM!(1954); MOONFLEET(1955); WORLD WITHOUT END(1956); BEAST OF BUDA-PEST, THE(1958); CASE AGAINST BROOKLYN, THE(1958); ERRAND BOY, THE(1961); ROMANOFF AND JULIET(1961); RAIDERS FROM BENEATH THE SEA(1964); WILD ON THE BEACH(1965); RUNAWAY GIRL(1966); MARYJANE(1968); LAWYER, THE(1969); SCANDALOUS JOHN(1971); NORMA RAE(1979)

Bryan Colman
BLOOD OF THE VAMPIRE(1958, Brit.)

Chubby Colman
SCARLET WEEKEND, A(1932)

Colleen Colman
COLLEEN(1936)

Edward Colman
DRAGNET(1954), ph; BLACK PATCH(1957), ph; D.I., THE(1957), ph; –30–(1959), ph; ABSENT-MINDED PROFESSOR, THE(1961), ph; BABES IN TOYLAND(1961), ph; BIG RED(1962), ph; SAVAGE SAM(1963), ph; SON OF FLUBBER(1963), ph; MARY POPPINS(1964), ph; MISADVENTURES OF MERLIN JONES, THE(1964), ph; THOSE CALLOWAYS(1964), ph; MONKEY'S UNCLE, THE(1965), ph; THAT DARN

CAT(1965), ph; UGLY DACHSHUND, THE(1966), ph; ADVENTURES OF BULLWHIP GRIFFIN, THE(1967), ph; HAPPIEST MILLIONAIRE, THE(1967), ph; BLACK-BEARD'S GHOST(1968), ph; LOVE BUG, THE(1968), ph

Edward Colman [Cohen]
DRUMS(1938, Brit.), spec eff

Eric Colman
SPLENDID FELLOWS(1934, Aus.); FLYING DOCTOR, THE(1936, Aus.)

Irene Colman
FUGITIVE LADY(1934); THREE MEN ON A HORSE(1936); MAN WHO LOST HIMSELF, THE(1941); MODEL WIFE(1941); NEVER GIVE A SUCKER AN EVEN BREAK(1941)

Julian Colman
ZORRO, THE GAY BLADE(1981)

Katya Colman
WAITRESS(1982)

Ronald Colman
UNDER TWO FLAGS(1936); BULLDOG DRUMMOND(1929); CONDEMNED(1929); DEVIL TO PAY, THE(1930); RAFFLES(1930); ARROWSMITH(1931); UNHOLY GARDEN, THE(1931); CYNARA(1932); MASQUERADER, THE(1933); BULLDOG DRUMMOND STRIKES BACK(1934); CLIVE OF INDIA(1935); MAN WHO BROKE THE BANK AT MONTE CARLO, THE(1935); TALE OF TWO CITIES, A(1935); LOST HORIZON(1937); PRISONER OF ZENDA, THE(1937); IF I WERE KING(1938); LIGHT THAT FAILED, THE(1939); LUCKY PARTNERS(1940); MY LIFE WITH CAROLINE(1941); RANDOM HARVEST(1942); TALK OF THE TOWN(1942); KISMET(1944); DOUBLE LIFE, A(1947); LATE GEORGE APLEY, THE(1947); CHAMPAGNE FOR CAESAR(1950); AROUND THE WORLD IN 80 DAYS(1956); STORY OF MANKIND, THE(1957)
Silents
ANNA THE ADVENTURESS(1920, Brit.); WHITE SISTER, THE(1923); DARK ANGEL, THE(1925); LADY WINDERMERE'S FAN(1925); ROMOLA(1925); STELLA DALLAS(1925); BEAU GESTE(1926); KIKI(1926); WINNING OF BARBARA WORTH, THE(1926); NIGHT OF LOVE, THE(1927); TWO LOVERS(1928); RESCUE, THE(1929)
Misc. Silents
TOILERS, THE(1919, Brit.); BLACK SPIDER, THE(1920, Brit.); SON OF DAVID, A(1920, Brit.); TARNISH(1924); DARK ANGEL, THE(1925); HER SISTER FROM PARIS(1925); HIS SUPREME MOMENT(1925); SPORTING VENUS, THE(1925); THIEF IN PARADISE, A(1925); MAGIC FLAME, THE(1927)

Edward Colmans
MY DREAM IS YOURS(1949); SIROCCO(1951); CALIFORNIA CONQUEST(1952); IRON MISTRESS, THE(1952); SNOWS OF KILIMANJARO, THE(1952); THIEF OF DAMASCUS(1952); CONQUEST OF COCHISE(1953); PRINCE OF PIRATES(1953); WAR OF THE WORLDS, THE(1953); JUBILEE TRAIL(1954); SECRET OF THE INCAS(1954); HEADLINE HUNTERS(1955); LOVE IS A MANY-SPLENDORED THING(1955); SANTIAGO(1956); HELL ON DEVIL'S ISLAND(1957); ISTANBUL(1957); GUN RUNNERS, THE(1958); THIRD VOICE, THE(1960); DIARY OF A MADMAN(1963); HELLFIGHTERS(1968)

Eric Colmar
CAPTIVE WOMEN(1952); CAPTAIN JOHN SMITH AND POCAHONTAS(1953); PORT SINISTER(1953); PROBLEM GIRLS(1953); SWORD OF VENUS(1953)

Eric Colmer
DRAGON'S GOLD(1954)

Walter Colmes
HARVEST MELODY(1943), p; THAT'S MY BABY(1944), p; TROCADERO(1944), p; IDENTITY UNKNOWN(1945), p, d; WOMAN WHO CAME BACK(1945), p&d; ACCOMPLICE(1946), d; FRENCH KEY, THE(1946), p&d; BURNING CROSS, THE(1947), p&d; ROAD TO THE BIG HOUSE(1947), p, d; WINTER WONDERLAND(1947), p; KID FROM CLEVELAND, THE(1949), p

Ignazio Colnaghi
MAGIC WORLD OF TOPO GIGIO, THE(1961, Ital.)

Giancarlo Colobaioni
HORNET'S NEST(1970)

Valerio Colobaioni
HORNET'S NEST(1970)

Joel Colodner
KIRLIAN WITNESS, THE(1978)

Bernadette Cologne
ZOOT SUIT(1981)

Ayberk Colok
1984
HORSE, THE(1984, Turk.)

Ronald Colomaioni
HORNET'S NEST(1970)

Marc Colombani
PIRATE MOVIE, THE(1982, Aus.)

Marisa Colomber
8 ½(1963, Ital.)

Louise Colombet
O.S.S.(1946); RAZOR'S EDGE, THE(1946); HOMECOMING(1948); SUMMER HOLIDAY(1948); LIGHT TOUCH, THE(1951); LAST OF THE SECRET AGENTS?, THE(1966)

Mme. Louise Colombet
GOLDEN EARRINGS(1947)

Christopher Colombi, Jr.
DEER HUNTER, THE(1978)

Myriam Colombi
BURGLARS, THE(1972, Fr./Ital.)

Jacques Colombier
EDWARD AND CAROLINE(1952, Fr.), set d; WE ARE ALL MURDERERS(1957), art d; COUNTERFEITERS OF PARIS, THE(1962, Fr., Ital.), set d; MAGNIFICENT TRAMP, THE(1962, Fr./Ital.), art d

Michael Colombier
STEEL(1980), m

Michel Colombier
YOUNG WORLD, A(1966, Fr./Ital.), m; EVERY BASTARD A KING(1968, Israel), m; PAUL AND MICHELLE(1974, Fr./Brit.), m
1984
AGAINST ALL ODDS(1984), m; PURPLE RAIN(1984), m

Pierre Colombier
FOLIES BERGERE(1958, Fr.), set d

Misc. Silents
LE NOEL DU PERE LATHUILE(1922, Fr.), d; LE TAXI 313 x 7(1922, Fr.), d; MONSIEUR LEBIDOIS PROPRIETAIRE(1922, Fr.), d; SOIREE DE REVEILLON(1922, Fr.), d; PAR DESSUS LE MUR(1923, Fr.), d; PETIT HOTEL A LOUER(1923, Fr.), d; LE MARIAGE DE ROSINE(1925, Fr.), d; JIM LA HOULETTE, ROI DES VOLEURS(1926, Fr.), d; L'AME DU MOTEUR: LE CARBURATEUR(1926, Fr.), d; PARIS EN CINQ JOURS(1926, Fr.), d; LES TRANSATLANTIQUES(1928, Fr.), d; PETITE FILLE(1928, Fr.), d; DOLLY(1929, Fr.), d

Willy Colombini
HERCULES, SAMSON & ULYSSES(1964, Ital.)

Al Colombo
JALNA(1935), m; ROMANCE IN MANHATTAN(1935), md; VILLAGE TALE(1935), m; SUNDOWNERS, THE(1950), m

Albert Colombo
UNDER WESTERN STARS(1938), md; FEDERAL FUGITIVES(1941), m; BLACK HAND, THE(1950), m

Alberto Colombo
HOORAY FOR LOVE(1935), md; POWDERSMOKE RANGE(1935), md; HIS FAMILY TREE(1936), md; TWO IN REVOLT(1936), md; DANGEROUS HOLIDAY(1937), m; ESCAPE BY NIGHT(1937), md; HIT PARADE, THE(1937), md; HIT THE SADDLE(1937), m; IT COULD HAPPEN TO YOU(1937), m; LADY BEHAVE(1937), md; MANHATTAN MERRY-GO-ROUND(1937), md; PORTIA ON TRIAL(1937), md; SEA RACKETEERS(1937), md; SHEIK STEPS OUT, THE(1937), md; WRONG ROAD, THE(1937), md; GOLD MINE IN THE SKY(1938), m; MAMA RUNS WILD(1938), md; ROMANCE ON THE RUN(1938), md; GO FOR BROKE(1951), m; IT'S A BIG COUNTRY(1951), m; HOLIDAY FOR SINNERS(1952), md; ROGUE'S MARCH(1952), m; YOU FOR ME(1952), md; BIG LEAGUER(1953), m; CODE TWO(1953), m; FAST COMPANY(1953), md

Alice Colombo
END OF THE WORLD(in Our Usual Bed In a Night Full of Rain), THE*1/2 (1978, Ital.)

Arrigo Colombo
FISTFUL OF DOLLARS, A(1964, Ital./Ger./Span.), p; FAMILY, THE(1974, Fr./Ital.), p; SEVEN BEAUTIES(1976, Ital.), p

Arrigo [Harry] Colombo
SACCO AND VANZETTI(1971, Ital./Fr.), p

Carla Colombo
SOUND OF TRUMPETS, THE(1963, Ital.), ed; FIANCES, THE(1964, Ital.), ed

Fernando Colombo
1984
SKYLINE(1984, Spain), d&w

Harry Colombo
GRAND SLAM(1968, Ital., Span., Ger.), p

Hary Colombo
END OF THE WORLD(in Our Usual Bed In a Night Full of Rain), THE*1/2 (1978, Ital.), p

Paolo Colombo
AGOSTINO(1962, Ital.)

Pia Colombo
OH! WHAT A LOVELY WAR(1969, Brit.)

Harry Colomby
1984
JOHNNY DANGEROUSLY(1984), w

Scott Colomby
CADDY SHACK(1980); PORKY'S(1982); PORKY'S II: THE NEXT DAY(1983)

Alex Colon
TAKING OF PELHAM ONE, TWO, THREE, THE(1974); WHEN YOU COMIN' BACK, RED RYDER?(1979); CROSS AND THE SWITCHBLADE, THE(1970); HOSPITAL, THE(1971); SUPER COPS, THE(1974); ULTIMATE WARRIOR, THE(1975); SPECIAL DELIVERY(1976); BACK ROADS(1981); DEAL OF THE CENTURY(1983)

Louis Colon
WAY OUT(1966)

Miriam Colon
CROWDED PARADISE(1956); BATTLE AT BLOODY BEACH(1961); ONE-EYED JACKS(1961); OUTSIDER, THE(1962); HARBOR LIGHTS(1963); THUNDER ISLAND(1963); APPALOOSA, THE(1966); POSSESSION OF JOEL DELANEY, THE(1972); BACK ROADS(1981); SCARFACE(1983)

Richard Colon
FLASHDANCE(1983)

Willie Colon
LAST FIGHT, THE(1983); VIGILANTE(1983)
Misc. Talkies
LAST FIGHT, THE(1983)

Bob Colona
LIKE FATHER LIKE SON(1961)

Bob Colonna
YOUNG SINNER, THE(1965)

G.A. Colonna
PIRATES OF CAPRI, THE(1949), w

Golfiero Colonna
CALYPSO(1959, Fr./It.), d; NUDE ODYSSEY(1962, Fr./Ital.), p, w

Jerry Colonna
ROSALIE(1937); 52ND STREET(1937); COLLEGE SWING(1938); GARDEN OF THE MOON(1938); LITTLE MISS BROADWAY(1938); PORT OF SEVEN SEAS(1938); VALLEY OF THE GIANTS(1938); NAUGHTY BUT NICE(1939); SWEEPSTAKES WINNER(1939); COMIN' ROUND THE MOUNTAIN(1940); MELODY AND MOONLIGHT(1940); ROAD TO SINGAPORE(1940); ICE-CAPADES(1941); SIS HOPKINS(1941); YOU'RE THE ONE(1941); ICE-CAPADES REVUE(1942); PRIORITIES ON PARADE(1942); STAR SPANGLED RHYTHM(1942); TRUE TO THE ARMY(1942); ATLANTIC CITY(1944); IT'S IN THE BAG(1945); MAKE MINE MUSIC(1946); ROAD TO RIO(1947); ALICE IN WONDERLAND(1951); KENTUCKY JUBILEE(1951); MEET ME IN LAS VEGAS(1956); ANDY HARDY COMES HOME(1958); ROAD TO HONG KONG, THE(1962, U.S./Brit.)

Hortensia Colorado
1984
IRRECONCILABLE DIFFERENCES(1984)

Tita Colorado
EASY RIDER(1969)

Colosantis and Benda
HUNCHBACK OF NOTRE DAME, THE(1957, Fr.), cos
Clara Colosimo
SERAFINO(1970, Fr./Ital.); ALFREDO, ALFREDO(1973, Ital.)
Max Colpet
ONCE A THIEF(1950), w
Louisa Colpeyn
BAND OF OUTSIDERS(1966, Fr.); MARRY ME! MARRY ME!(1969, Fr.)
Luisa Colpeyn
PASSION OF SLOW FIRE, THE(1962, Fr.)
Henri Colpi
HIROSHIMA, MON AMOUR(1959, Fr./Jap.), ed; LAST YEAR AT MARIEN-BAD(1962, Fr./Ital.), ed; LONG ABSENCE, THE(1962, Fr./Ital.), d; DESTROY, SHE SAID(1969, Fr.), ed; MYSTERIOUS ISLAND OF CAPTAIN NEMO, THE(1973, Fr./Ital. 87m Span./Cameroon), d
Cissie Colpitts
BILLY JACK(1971)
Frank Colson
MONTE CARLO STORY, THE(1957, Ital.)
Headley Colson
SKIN GAME, THE(1965, Brit.)
Kevin Colson
NIGHT WATCH(1973, Brit.)
Janice Colson-Dodge
FARMER, THE(1977), w
Rolf Colstan
BLOODY BROOD, THE(1959, Can.)
Robert Colston
KING OF COMEDY, THE(1983)
Alvin Colt
STILETTO(1969), cos
Bobby Colt
CATSKILL HONEYMOON(1950)
John Drew Colt
DOUBLE LIFE, A(1947)
Marshall Colt
NORTH DALLAS FORTY(1979); THOSE LIPS, THOSE EYES(1980)
Peter Colt
SHOTGUN WEDDING, THE(1963)
Samuel Barrymore Colt
STAR IS BORN, A(1954)
Samuel Colt
MATING SEASON, THE(1951); JOHNNY TROUBLE(1957); THREE BRAVE MEN(1957)
Giulio Coltellacci
ULYSSES(1955, Ital.), cos; CASANOVA '70(1965, Ital.), cos; TENTH VICTIM, THE(1965, Fr./Ital.), cos; MORE THAN A MIRACLE(1967, Ital./Fr.), cos; QUIET PLACE IN THE COUNTRY, A(1970, Ital./Fr.), cos
Guido Coltellacci
MAMBO(1955, Ital.), cos
Guilio Coltellacci
HERCULES(1959, Ital.), cos
Luciana Coltellesi
TWO WOMEN(1961, Ital./Fr.)
Eli Colter
UNTAMED BREED, THE(1948), w
Tony Colti
ON A CLEAR DAY YOU CAN SEE FOREVER(1970)
Chevi Colton
1984
FALLING IN LOVE(1984)
Jacque Lynn Colton
FEMALE RESPONSE, THE(1972); DR. HECKYL AND MR. HYPE(1980); MR. MOM(1983)
John Colton
SHANGHAI LADY(1929), w; CALL OF THE FLESH(1930), w; ROGUE SONG, THE(1930), w; CUBAN LOVE SONG,THE(1931), w; RAIN(1932), w; LAUGHING BOY(1934), w; WEREWOLF OF LONDON, THE(1935), w; THE INVISIBLE RAY(1936), w; SHANGHAI GESTURE, THE(1941), w; UNDER CAPRICORN(1949), w; STRAIGHT TIME(1978); TIME AFTER TIME(1979, Brit.)
Silents
ALL DOLLED UP(1921), w; WOMAN WHO WALKED ALONE, THE(1922), w; EXCITERS, THE(1923), w; CAPTAIN SALVATION(1927), t; ENEMY, THE(1927), t; DIVINE WOMAN, THE(1928), t; SADIE THOMPSON(1928), w; TELLING THE WORLD(1928), ed; TWO LOVERS(1928), t; WILD ORCHIDS(1929), w
Joseph Colton
GAY DOG, THE(1954, Brit.), w
Nikola Colton
. NIGHT THE LIGHTS WENT OUT IN GEORGIA, THE(1981)
Richard Colton
HAIR(1979)
Rita Colton
PROJECT X(1949)
Scott Colton
ALL-AMERICAN SWEETHEART(1937); AWFUL TRUTH, THE(1937); MURDER IN GREENWICH VILLAGE(1937); WILDCATTER, THE(1937); EXTORTION(1938); I AM THE LAW(1938); LITTLE MISS ROUGHNECK(1938); WOMEN IN PRISON(1938)
Trax Colton
MARRIAGE-GO-ROUND, THE(1960); IT HAPPENED IN ATHENS(1962)
John Coltrane
CAT IN THE SACK, THE(1967, Can.), m
Rexx Coltrane
BEING, THE(1983)
Robbie Coltrane
FLASH GORDON(1980); SUBWAY RIDERS(1981); KRULL(1983)
1984
CHINESE BOXES(1984, Ger./Brit.); GHOST DANCE(1984, Brit.); LOOSE CONNECTIONS(1984, Brit.); SCRUBBERS(1984, Brit.)

Suzanne Coltrin
WHERE THE BUFFALO ROAM(1980)
Guido Colucci
Misc. Silents
MYSTERY OF ROOM 13, THE(1915); TELLTALE STEP, THE(1917)
Mario Colucci
Misc. Talkies
SOMETHING CREEPING IN THE DARK(1972, Ital.), d
Coluche
1984
MY BEST FRIEND'S GIRL(1984, Fr.)
Michel Coluche
BANZAI(1983, Fr.)
Padraic Colum
HANSEL AND GRETEL(1954), w
Anthony Columbia
HARRY AND WALTER GO TO NEW YORK(1976)
The Columbia Choir
ON VELVET(1938, Brit.)
Michel Columbier
COLOSSUS: THE FORBIN PROJECT(1969), m
Al Columbo
MESSENGER OF PEACE(1950), md
Albert Columbo
MURDER ON A HONEYMOON(1935), md
Alberti Columbo
M'LISS(1936), md
Alberto Columbo
ANNIE OAKLEY(1935), md; CHASING YESTERDAY(1935), md; ANY MAN'S WIFE(1936), m; YELLOW DUST(1936), md; ARMY GIRL(1938), m; BORN TO BE WILD(1938), md; GANGS OF NEW YORK(1938), m; KING OF THE NEWS-BOYS(1938), m; LADIES IN DISTRESS(1938), md; OLD BARN DANCE, THE(1938), md; PRISON NURSE(1938), md; PURPLE VIGILANTES, THE(1938), md; HI-YO SILVER(1940), md; SOUTH OF PANAMA(1941), md
Franco Columbo
CONAN THE BARBARIAN(1982)
Russ Columbo
BROADWAY THROUGH A KEYHOLE(1933); WAKE UP AND DREAM(1934)
Russell Columbo
HELLO SISTER(1930), m
Russell "Russ" Columbo
WOLF SONG(1929); TEXAN, THE(1930)
Franco Columbu
1984
TERMINATOR, THE(1984)
Chris Columbus
1984
GREMLINS(1984), w; RECKLESS(1984), w
Effi Columbus
DREAM OF KINGS, A(1969)
Veniero Colusanti
FALL OF THE ROMAN EMPIRE, THE(1964), prod d, set d
F. Romana Coluzzi
CON MEN, THE(1973, Ital.,Span.)
Francesca Romana Coluzzi
MAN WHO CAME FOR COFFEE, THE(1970, Ital.); SERAFINO(1970, Fr./Ital.); ITALIAN CONNECTION, THE(1973, U.S./Ital./Ger.)
Jane Colvard
COUNTRY BOY(1966)
Alice Ross Colver
Silents
ON THIN ICE(1925), w
Helen Colvig
PSYCHO(1960), cos; KILLERS, THE(1964), cos; MC HALE'S NAVY(1964), cos; NIGHT WALKER, THE(1964), cos; SWORD OF ALI BABA, THE(1965), cos; AP-PALOOSA, THE(1966), cos; INCIDENT AT PHANTOM HILL(1966), cos; OUT OF SIGHT(1966), cos; PLAINSMAN, THE(1966), cos; TEXAS ACROSS THE RIVER(1966), cos; TROUBLE WITH ANGELS, THE(1966), cos; GUNFIGHT IN ABILENE(1967), cos; ROUGH NIGHT IN JERICHO(1967), cos; COOGAN'S BLUFF(1968), cos; CHANGE OF HABIT(1969), cos; DEATH OF A GUNFIGHTER(1969), cos; LOVE GOD?, THE(1969), cos; MAN CALLED GANNON, A(1969), cos; SAM WHISKEY(1969), cos; COCKEYED COWBOYS OF CALICO COUNTY, THE(1970), cos; I LOVE MY WI-FE(1970), cos; TWO MULES FOR SISTER SARA(1970), cos; BEGUILED, THE(1971), cos; HOW TO FRAME A FIGG(1971), cos; MINNIE AND MOSKOWITZ(1971), cos; PLAY MISTY FOR ME(1971), cos; GREAT NORTHFIELD, MINNESOTA RAID, THE(1972), cos; CHARLEY VARRICK(1973), cos
Pinto Colvig
SNOW WHITE AND THE SEVEN DWARFS(1937); RELUCTANT DRAGON, THE(1941); VARIETY GIRL(1947); MAN FROM BUTTON WILLOW, THE(1965)
Billy Colvill
BLOODY KIDS(1983, Brit.)
John Colville
ONE BRIEF SUMMER(1971, Brit.), ed
Lorenza Colville
PORT AFRIQUE(1956, Brit.)
Peter Colville
THREE TO GO(1971, Aus.)
Billy Colvin
NIX ON DAMES(1929); WALL STREET(1929)
Jack Colvin
HOW SWEET IT IS(1968); VIVA MAX!(1969); MONTE WALSH(1970); HICKEY AND BOGGS(1972); JEREMIAH JOHNSON(1972); LIFE AND TIMES OF JUDGE ROY BEAN, THE(1972); SCORPIO(1973); STONE KILLER, THE(1973); CRAZY WORLD OF JULIUS VROODER, THE(1974); TERMINAL MAN, THE(1974); ROOSTER COG-BURN(1975); EMBRYO(1976)
Marion Colvin
Silents
BRANDING IRON, THE(1920)

Norm Colvin
SILKWOOD(1983)
William Colvin
COHENS AND KELLYS IN SCOTLAND, THE(1930); SOLDIERS AND WO-
MEN(1930)
William P. Colvin
GIRL WITHOUT A ROOM(1933)
Chuck Colwell
SOLOMON KING(1974), ph, ed
Gary Colwell
1984
POLICE ACADEMY(1984)
James Colwell
Silents
AFTER THE BALL(1924), w
Misc. Silents
GREAT ALONE, THE(1922), d
Robert T. Colwell
STRICTLY DYNAMITE(1934), w
Angel Coly [Otello Colangeli]
HORROR CASTLE(1965, Ital.), ed; WILD, WILD PLANET, THE(1967, Ital.), ed
Gus Coma
COME BACK PETER(1971, Brit.), ph
Corinne Comacho
MARLOWE(1969)
M. Avilla Comacho
MISSING(1982)
Joe Comadore
TANGANYIKA(1954); SHRIKE, THE(1955)
Cornel Coman
FANTASTIC COMEDY, A(1975, Rum.)
Adele Comandini
HELL BOUND(1931), w; GIRL OF THE LIMBERLOST(1934), w; JANE EYRE(1935),
w; THREE SMART GIRLS(1937), w; BEYOND TOMORROW(1940), w; HER FIRST
ROMANCE(1940), w; ALWAYS IN MY HEART(1942), w; MATING OF MILLIE,
THE(1948), w; FLAME OF THE ISLANDS(1955), w
Jeffrey Comanor
PHANTOM OF THE PARADISE(1974)
Edward Comans
TWO WEEKS IN ANOTHER TOWN(1962)
Richard Comar
ONE MAN(1979, Can.); VISITING HOURS(1982, Can.)
Clarence Comas
RED, WHITE AND BLACK, THE(1970)
Mario Comaschi
WHITE SISTER(1973, Ital./Span./Fr.)
A.B. Comathiere
EXILE, THE(1931)
Misc. Talkies
TEN MINUTES TO LIVE(1932); THIRTY YEARS LATER(1938)
A.G. Comathieri
DRUMS O' VOODOO(1934)
Jean Combal
MONTE CARLO STORY, THE(1957, Ital.)
Jesus Combarro
TRISTANA(1970, Span./Ital./Fr.)
Boyce Combe
Silents
RENO(1923)
Muriel Combe
WOMAN NEXT DOOR, THE(1981, Fr.)
Pat Combe
HOLLYWOOD BARN DANCE(1947)
Vivian Combe
DEATH GOES NORTH(1939)
Bobbie Comber
BROTHER ALFRED(1932, Brit.); FORTUNATE FOOL, THE(1933, Brit.); LILIES OF
THE FIELD(1934, Brit.); ACE OF SPADES, THE(1935, Brit.); LAZYBONES(1935, Brit.);
SCANDALS OF PARIS(1935, Brit.); SINGING THROUGH(1935, Brit.); DON'T RUSH
ME(1936, Brit.); EXCUSE MY GLOVE(1936, Brit.); SPORTING LOVE(1936, Brit.);
SINGING COP, THE(1938, Brit.); LOST ON THE WESTERN FRONT(1940, Brit.)
Misc. Talkies
BE CAREFUL, MR. SMITH(1935)
Christian Comber
GREAT PONY RAID, THE(1968, Brit.)
Jeanette Comber
PANCHO VILLA RETURNS(1950, Mex.)
Tully Comber
FLAG LIEUTENANT, THE(1932, Brit.); SONG AT EVENTIDE(1934, Brit.); BARNA-
CLE BILL(1935, Brit.); OFF THE DOLE(1935, Brit.); END OF THE ROAD, THE(1936,
Brit.); CROSS MY HEART(1937, Brit.); HONEYMOON MERRY-GO-ROUND(1939,
Brit.)
Edward Combermere
Silents
DAWN(1917, Brit.); GREATEST WISH IN THE WORLD, THE(1918, Brit.)
Misc. Silents
BETTA THE GYPSY(1918, Brit.)
Maria Comberti
STATUE, THE(1971, Brit.)
Carol Joyce Combes
GAY SISTERS, THE(1942)
Marcel Combes
HEAT OF THE SUMMER(1961, Fr.), ph; MARTIAN IN PARIS, A(1961, Fr.), ph; SIN
ON THE BEACH(1964, Fr.), ph
Norman Combes
KILL OR BE KILLED(1980)
Michael Smith Combination
NO PLACE TO HIDE(1975), m

Clyde Combo
OVERLANDERS, THE(1946, Brit./Aus.); BUSH CHRISTMAS(1947, Brit.); KAN-
GAROO(1952)
Kako y Su Combo
HEROINA(1965)
George Combret
MARIE OF THE ISLES(1960, Fr.), w
Georges Combret
RASPOUTINE(1954, Fr.), d, w; MARIE OF THE ISLES(1960, Fr.), d; FRUSTRA-
TIONS(1967, Fr./Ital.), p&d, w
Barbara Combs
FORCE OF EVIL(1948)
Frederick Combs
BOYS IN THE BAND, THE(1970)
Gary Combs
WHAT'S THE MATTER WITH HELEN?(1971); LIFE AND TIMES OF JUDGE ROY
BEAN, THE(1972); PEEPER(1975); TWO-MINUTE WARNING(1976); MOONSHINE
COUNTY EXPRESS(1977), stunts; VILLAIN, THE(1979), stunts; HERO AT LAR-
GE(1980); LOOKER(1981); HANKY-PANKY(1982); UNDER FIRE(1983), stunts
Gilbert B. Combs
STAR 80(1983)
Gary M. Combs
MITCHELL(1975)
Gilbert Combs
NATIONAL LAMPOON'S ANIMAL HOUSE(1978); UNDER FIRE(1983)
Jean Combs
HUCKLEBERRY FINN(1974)
Jeffrey Combs
HONKY TONK FREEWAY(1981); WHOSE LIFE IS IT ANYWAY?(1981); FRIGHT-
MARE(1983); MAN WITH TWO BRAINS, THE(1983)
Mike Combs
HEX(1973)
Pat Combs
IT HAPPENS EVERY SPRING(1949); MOTHER IS A FRESHMAN(1949); MILK-
MAN, THE(1950); PLACE IN THE SUN, A(1951)
Misc. Talkies
SECOND CHANCE(1950)
Betty Comden
GOOD NEWS(1947), w; BARKLEYS OF BROADWAY, THE(1949), w; ON THE
TOWN(1949), w; SINGIN' IN THE RAIN(1952), w; BAND WAGON, THE(1953), w; IT'S
ALWAYS FAIR WEATHER(1955), w; AUNTIE MAME(1958), w; BELLS ARE RING-
ING(1960), w, m; WHAT A WAY TO GO(1964), w
1984
GARBO TALKS(1984)
Barbara Comeau
ATLAS(1960), cos
Jerry Comeaux
LIVE AND LET DIE(1973, Brit.), stunts
Members of the Comedie Francaise
Silents
QUEEN ELIZABETH(1912, Fr.)
Members and Students of the Comedie-Francaise
MARRIAGE OF FIGARO, THE(1963, Fr.)
John Comeford
RISING OF THE MOON, THE(1957, Ireland)
Kathleen Comegys
BIRTH OF A BABY(1938); MR. BELVEDERE RINGS THE BELL(1951); FIRST TIME,
THE(1952); MIRACLE WORKER, THE(1962)
Joceline Comellas
QUARTET(1981, Brit./Fr.)
Josine Comellas
TESS(1980, Fr./Brit.)
1984
CHEECH AND CHONG'S THE CORSICAN BROTHERS(1984)
Alberto Comenar
VALDEZ IS COMING(1971), makeup
Luigi Comencini
BEHIND CLOSED SHUTTERS(1952, Ital.), d; BREAD, LOVE AND DREAMS(1953,
Ital.), d&w; HEIDI(1954, Switz.), d; FRISKY(1955, Ital.), d, w; SIGN OF VENUS,
THE(1955, Ital.), w; EVERYBODY GO HOME!(1962, Fr./Ital.), d, w; BEBO'S
GIRL(1964, Ital.), d, w; BAMBOLE!(1965, Ital.), d; SIX DAYS A WEEK(1966, Fr./Ital./
Span.), d, w; ITALIAN SECRET SERVICE(1968, Ital.), d, w; THREE NIGHTS OF
LOVE(1969, Ital.), d; SCIENTIFIC CARDPLAYER, THE(1972, Ital.), d; GOODNIGHT,
LADIES AND GENTLEMEN(1977, Ital.), d&w; TILL MARRIAGE DO US PART(1979,
Ital.), d, w
Anjanette Comer
QUICK, BEFORE IT MELTS(1964); LOVED ONE, THE(1965); APPALOOSA,
THE(1966); BANNING(1967); GUNS FOR SAN SEBASTIAN(1968, U.S./Fr./Mex./Ital.);
IN ENEMY COUNTRY(1968); FIRECHASERS, THE(1970, Brit.); RABBIT, RUN(1970);
BABY, THE(1973); NIGHT OF A THOUSAND CATS(1974, Mex.); LEPKE(1975,
U.S./Israel); MANCHU EAGLE MURDER CAPER MYSTERY, THE(1975); FIRE
SALE(1977)
John Comer
I'M ALL RIGHT, JACK(1959, Brit.); HEAVENS ABOVE!(1963, Brit.); FAMILY WAY,
THE(1966, Brit.); HAPPY DEATHDAY(1969, Brit.); THERE'S A GIRL IN MY
SOUP(1970, Brit.); WUTHERING HEIGHTS(1970, Brit.); CRY OF THE PEN-
GUINS(1972, Brit.); LOVERS, THE(1972, Brit.)
Mark Comer
GROUND ZERO(1973), m
Phil Comer
GROUND ZERO(1973), m
Sam Comer
NO TIME FOR LOVE(1943), set d; FRENCHMAN'S CREEK(1944), set d; BLUE
DAHLIA, THE(1946), set d; BRIDE WORE BOOTS, THE(1946), set d; CALIFOR-
NIA(1946), set d; O.S.S.(1946), set d; OUR HEARTS WERE GROWING UP(1946), set d;
PERFECT MARRIAGE, THE(1946), set d; SEARCHING WIND, THE(1946), set d;
STRANGE LOVE OF MARTHA IVERS, THE(1946), set d; TO EACH HIS OWN(1946),
set d; CALCUTTA(1947), set d; DEAR RUTH(1947), set d; DESERT FURY(1947), set d;
GOLDEN EARRINGS(1947), set d; IMPERFECT LADY, THE(1947), set d; SUDDEN-
LY IT'S SPRING(1947), set d; TROUBLE WITH WOMEN, THE(1947), set d; UNCON-

QUERED(1947), set d; VARIETY GIRL(1947), set d; WELCOME STRANGER(1947), set d; WHERE THERE'S LIFE(1947), set d; BIG CLOCK, THE(1948), set d; EMPEROR WALTZ, THE(1948), set d; FOREIGN AFFAIR, A(1948), set d; I WALK ALONE(1948), set d; MISS TATLOCK'S MILLIONS(1948), set d; MY OWN TRUE LOVE(1948), set d; NIGHT HAS A THOUSAND EYES(1948), set d; PALEFACE, THE(1948), set d; SEALED VERDICT(1948), set d; SORRY, WRONG NUMBER(1948), set d; ACCUSED, THE(1949), set d; ALIAS NICK BEAL(1949), set d; CHICAGO DEADLINE(1949), set d; CONNECTICUT YANKEE IN KING ARTHUR'S COURT, A(1949), set d; RED, HOT AND BLUE(1949), set d; ROPE OF SAND(1949), set d; SAMSON AND DELI-LAH(1949), set d; SORROWFUL JONES(1949), set d; STREETS OF LAREDO(1949), set d; TOP O' THE MORNING(1949), set d; DARK CITY(1950), set d; FILE ON THELMA JORDAN, THE(1950), set d; FURIES, THE(1950), set d; NO MAN OF HER OWN(1950), set d; SUNSET BOULEVARD(1950), set d; UNION STATION(1950), set d; BIG CARNIVAL, THE(1951), set d; WHEN WORLDS COLLIDE(1951), set d; GREAT-EST SHOW ON EARTH, THE(1952), set d; HURRICANE SMITH(1952), set d; JUST FOR YOU(1952), set d; ROAD TO BALI(1952), set d; SOMEBODY LOVES ME(1952), set d; STOOGE, THE(1952), set d; TURNING POINT, THE(1952), set d; FOREVER FEMALE(1953), set d; HOUDINI(1953), set d; LITTLE BOY LOST(1953), set d; SAV-AGE, THE(1953), set d; STALAG 17(1953), set d; WAR OF THE WORLDS, THE(1953), set d; COUNTRY GIRL, THE(1954), set d; ELEPHANT WALK(1954), set d; REAR WINDOW(1954), set d; RED GARTERS(1954), set d; SABRINA(1954), set d; WHITE CHRISTMAS(1954), set d; DESPERATE HOURS, THE(1955), set d; RUN FOR CO-VER(1955), set d; TO CATCH A THIEF(1955), set d; WE'RE NO ANGELS(1955), set d; MAN WHO KNEW TOO MUCH, THE(1956), set d; MOUNTAIN, THE(1956), set d; PROUD AND THE PROFANE, THE(1956), set d; RAINMAKER, THE(1956), set d; TEN COMMANDMENTS, THE(1956), set d; DEVIL'S HAIRPIN, THE(1957), set d; FUNNY FACE(1957), set d; JOKER IS WILD, THE(1957), set d; SHORT CUT TO HELL(1957), set d; GEISHA BOY, THE(1958), set d; MARACAIBO(1958), set d; ROCK-A-BYE BABY(1958), set d; SPACE CHILDREN, THE(1958), set d; TEACHER'S PET(1958), set d; VERTIGO(1958), set d; ALIAS JESSE JAMES(1959), set d; CA-REER(1959), set d; RAT RACE, THE(1960), set d; VISIT TO A SMALL PLANET(1960), set d; ERRAND BOY, THE(1961), set d; LADIES MAN, THE(1961), set d; LOVE IN A GOLDFISH BOWL(1961), set d; ON THE DOUBLE(1961), set d; ONE-EYED JACKS(1961), set d; PLEASURE OF HIS COMPANY, THE(1961), set d; POCKETFUL OF MIRACLES(1961), set d; SUMMER AND SMOKE(1961), set d; GIRL NAMED TAMIRO, A(1962), set d; GIRLS! GIRLS! GIRLS!(1962), set d; HATARI!(1962), set d; HELL IS FOR HEROES(1962), set d; MAN WHO SHOT LIBERTY VALANCE, THE(1962), set d; PIGEON THAT TOOK ROME, THE(1962), set d; COME BLOW YOUR HORN(1963), set d; FUN IN ACAPULCO(1963), set d; HUD(1963), set d; LOVE WITH THE PROPER STRANGER(1963), set d; MC LINTOCK!(1963), set d; MY SIX LOVES(1963), set d; NEW KIND OF LOVE, A(1963), set d; NUTTY PROFESSOR, THE(1963), set d; PAPA'S DELICATE CONDITION(1963), set d; WHO'S BEEN SLEEP-ING IN MY BED?(1963), set d; WIVES AND LOVERS(1963), set d; DISORDERLY ORDERLY, THE(1964), set d; HOUSE IS NOT A HOME, A(1964), set d; LADY IN A CAGE(1964), set d; LAW OF THE LAWLESS(1964), set d; PATSY, THE(1964), set d; ROUSTABOUT(1964), set d; STAGE TO THUNDER ROCK(1964), set d; STRANGLER, THE(1964), set d; WHERE LOVE HAS GONE(1964), set d; FAMILY JEWELS, THE(1965), set d; RED LINE 7000(1965), set d; SONS OF KATIE ELDER, THE(1965), set d; SYLVIA(1965), set d; YOUNG FURY(1965), set d; PARADISE, HAWAIIAN STYLE(1966), set d

Tony Comer
I'M ALL RIGHT, JACK(1959, Brit.)

Sheridan Comerate
3:10 TO YUMA(1957); JEANNE EAGELS(1957); OPERATION MAD BALL(1957); CRASH LANDING(1958); LIVE FAST, DIE YOUNG(1958); STORY ON PAGE ONE, THE(1959); ICE PALACE(1960)

Janet Comerford
SON OF SINBAD(1955)

Lorraine Comerford
KNOCK ON ANY DOOR(1949)

Jeff Comeron
Misc. Talkies
TIME OF FURY(1968)

Luis Comeron
THAT MAN IN ISTANBUL(1966, Fr./Ital./Span.), w; THEY CAME TO ROB LAS VEGAS(1969, Fr./Ital./Span./Ger.), w

A. B. Comethiere
BLACK KING(1932)

Alex Comfort
1984
JOY OF SEX(1984), w

Brian Comfort
ASPHYX, THE(1972, Brit.), w

Charles Comfort
ON THE NICKEL(1980)

David Comfort
LAST MARRIED COUPLE IN AMERICA, THE(1980)

John Comfort
CODE 7, VICTIM 5(1964, Brit.), prod d

Lance Comfort
COURAGEOUS MR. PENN, THE(1941, Brit.), d; THOSE KIDS FROM TOWN(1942, Brit.), d; ESCAPE TO DANGER(1943, Brit.), d; OLD MOTHER RILEY, DETEC-TIVE(1943, Brit.), d; SQUADRON LEADER X(1943, Brit.), d; WHEN WE ARE MAR-RIED(1943, Brit.), d; GREAT DAY(1945, Brit.), d; BEDELIA(1946, Brit.), d; HOTEL RESERVE(1946, Brit.), d; DAUGHTER OF DARKNESS(1948, Brit.), d; HATTER'S CASTLE(1948, Brit.), d; SILENT DUST(1949, Brit.), d; TEMPTATION HARBOR(1949, Brit.), d; HOME TO DANGER(1951, Brit.), p; PORTRAIT OF CLARE(1951, Brit.), d; GENIE, THE(1953, Brit.), d; GIRL ON THE PIER, THE(1953, Brit.), p, d; BANG! YOU'RE DEAD(1954, Brit.), p&d; EIGHT O'CLOCK WALK(1954, Brit.), d; LAST MOMENT, THE(1954, Brit.), d; PORT OF ESCAPE(1955, Brit.), p; AT THE STROKE OF NINE(1957, Brit.), d; MAN IN THE ROAD, THE(1957, Brit.), d; THUNDER OVER TANGIER(1957, Brit.), d; MENACE IN THE NIGHT(1958, Brit.), d; UGLY DUCK-LING, THE(1959, Brit.), d; BREAKING POINT, THE(1961, Brit.), d; PIT OF DARK-NESS(1961, Brit.), p,d&w; BREAK, THE(1962, Brit.), d; TOUCH OF DEATH(1962, Brit.), d; YOUNG, WILLING AND EAGER(1962, Brit.), d; MAN IN THE DARK(1963, Brit.), d; MURDER CAN BE DEADLY(1963, Brit.), d; SWITCH, THE(1963, Brit.), p; GREAT ARMORED CAR SWINDLE, THE(1964, Brit.), d; SING AND SWING(1964, Brit.), p&d; TOMORROW AT TEN(1964, Brit.), d; BE MY GUEST(1965, Brit.), p&d; DEVILS OF DARKNESS, THE(1965, Brit.), d; MAKE MINE A MILLION(1965, Brit.), d

Madi Comfort
KISS ME DEADLY(1955)

Will Levington Comfort
SOMEWHERE IN SONORA(1933), w
Silents
SOMEWHERE IN SONORA(1927), w

The Comfortable Chair
HOW TO COMMIT MARRIAGE(1969)

Paul Comi
IN LOVE AND WAR(1958); YOUNG LIONS, THE(1958); PORK CHOP HILL(1959); WARLOCK(1959); DARK AT THE TOP OF THE STAIRS, THE(1960); CAPE FEAR(1962); FORTY POUNDS OF TROUBLE(1962); OUTSIDER, THE(1962); FBI CODE 98(1964); BLINDFOLD(1966); CONQUEST OF THE PLANET OF THE APES(1972); TOWERING INFERNO, THE(1974); DEATH WISH II(1982)
1984
BEST DEFENSE(1984)

Lou Comici
VISITOR, THE(1980, Ital./U.S.), w

Dorothy Comingore
COMET OVER BROADWAY(1938); TRADE WINDS(1938); GOOD GIRLS GO TO PARIS(1939); CITIZEN KANE(1941); HAIRY APE, THE(1944); ANY NUMBER CAN PLAY(1949); BIG NIGHT, THE(1951)

Joe Cominguez
TORRID ZONE(1940)

Pat Comiskey
HARDER THEY FALL, THE(1956); GUN BATTLE AT MONTEREY(1957)

C. Comisky
BATTLE BEYOND THE STARS(1980), spec eff

Chuck Comisky
WILD PARTY, THE(1975); STRANGE INVADERS(1983), spec eff

Rex Commack
HUCKLEBERRY FINN(1974)

Thomas Commack
DEVIL'S BEDROOM, THE(1964)

Police Commandant
PASSPORT TO HELL(1932)

Commander Cody and the Lost Planet Airmen
HOLLYWOOD BOULEVARD(1976)

Sgt. Eugene C. Commander, USMC
BACK TO BATAAN(1945)

Adele Commandini
GIRL FROM WOOLWORTH'S, THE(1929), w; LOVE RACKET, THE(1929), w; PLAY-ING AROUND(1930), w; COUNTRY BEYOND, THE(1936), w; ROAD TO RENO, THE(1938), w; GOOD LUCK, MR. YATES(1943), w; NIGHT CLUB GIRL(1944), w; CHRISTMAS IN CONNECTICUT(1945), w; DANGER SIGNAL(1945), w; STRANGE ILLUSION(1945), w

Thomas Commerford
Misc. Silents
GRAUSTARK(1915); WHITE SISTER, THE(1915)

Land Commissioner
WILD BILL HICKOK RIDES(1942)

The Committee
PETULIA(1968, U.S./Brit.); WHERE IT'S AT(1969)

The Committee
STEELYARD BLUES(1973)

Franco Committeri
WEEKEND MURDERS, THE(1972, Ital.), p; GOODNIGHT, LADIES AND GENTLE-MEN(1977, Ital.), p; PASSION OF LOVE(1982, Ital./Fr.), a, p

Jim Commock
DEAD MAN'S EVIDENCE(1962, Brit.), ed

The Commodores
SCOTT JOPLIN(1977); THANK GOD IT'S FRIDAY(1978)

David Commons
PARIS MODEL(1953), spec eff; ROBOT MONSTER(1953), spec eff; ANGRY BREED, THE(1969), p&d

Sam Comner
HOUSEBOAT(1958), set d

Don Como
Misc. Talkies
UNKNOWN POWERS(1979), d

Josell Como
FIVE WILD GIRLS(1966, Fr.)

Perry Como
SOMETHING FOR THE BOYS(1944); DOLL FACE(1945); IF I'M LUCKY(1946)

Rosella Como
TALL WOMEN, THE(1967, Aust./Ital./Span.)

Rossella Como
SEVEN HILLS OF ROME, THE(1958); 8 ½(1963, Ital.)

Michel Comobier
DIRTY MONEY(1977, Fr.), m

Michel Comobler
COP, A(1973, Fr.), m

Jean-Louis Comolli
ALPHAVILLE, A STRANGE CASE OF LEMMY CAUTION(1965, Fr.); LES CARABINIERS(1968, Fr./Ital.)

Mathilda Comont
CUBAN LOVE SONG,THE(1931); ESCAPADE(1935); WATERFRONT LADY(1935)

Mathilde Comont
CALL OF THE FLESH(1930); JUST LIKE HEAVEN(1930); LASH, THE(1930); ROMANCE(1930); SEA BAT, THE(1930); ALONG CAME YOUTH(1931); HARD HOM-BRE(1931); LADY WHO DARED, THE(1931); DESIGN FOR LIVING(1933); LAUGH-ING AT LIFE(1933); ALL MEN ARE ENEMIES(1934); CEILNG ZERO(1935); ANTHONY ADVERSE(1936); POOR LITTLE RICH GIRL(1936); GO-GETTER, THE(1937); GOD'S COUNTRY AND THE WOMAN(1937)
Silents
ROSITA(1923); HIS HOUR(1924); THIEF OF BAGDAD, THE(1924); ENCHANTED HILL, THE(1926); FAR CRY, THE(1926); GILDED HIGHWAY, THE(1926); PUP-PETS(1926); SEA BEAST, THE(1926); VOLCANO(1926); WHAT PRICE GLORY(1926); RAMONA(1928)

Misc. Silents
WOMAN'S WAY, A(1928)

Matilda Comont
Silents
KISMET(1920)

Soni Compagna
RUN FOR YOUR WIFE(1966, Fr./Ital.)

Achille Compagnoni
GREAT WAR, THE(1961, Fr., Ital.)

J. Companeez
LOWER DEPTHS, THE(1937, Fr.), w; ALIBI, THE(1939, Fr.), w; ALIBI, THE(1943, Brit.), w

Jacques Companeez
PERSONAL COLUMN(1939, Fr.), w; I WAS AN ADVENTURESS(1940), w; IT HAPPENED IN GIBRALTAR(1943, Fr.), w; LURED(1947), w; DAMNED, THE(1948, Fr.), w; FRIEND WILL COME TONIGHT, A(1948, Fr.), w; CROSSROADS OF PASSION(1951, Fr.), d; TALE OF FIVE WOMEN, A(1951, Brit.), w; SHADOW OF THE EAGLE(1955, Brit.), w; THEY WERE SO YOUNG(1955), w; ADORABLE CREATURES(1956, Fr.), w; CASQUE D'OR(1956, Fr.), w; FOLIES BERGERE(1958, Fr.), w; FORBIDDEN FRUIT(1959, Fr.), w; MAIDEN, THE(1961, Fr.), w; VIENNA WALTZES(1961, Aust.), w

Joseph Companeez
LOVER'S NET(1957, Fr.), w

Nina Companeez
ADORABLE LIAR(1962, Fr.), w, ed; BENJAMIN(1968, Fr.), w; BYE BYE BARBARA(1969, Fr.), w, ed

Companeez and Jacoby
BETRAYAL(1939, Fr.), w

Jacques Companez
THREE HOURS(1944, Fr.), w

Carroll and Company
MARRIAGE ON THE ROCKS(1965), cos

Compinsky
SNOW CREATURE, THE,(1954), md

Alec Compinsky
NO PLACE TO LAND(1958), md; FOUR FAST GUNS(1959), md; PLUNDERERS OF PAINTED FLATS(1959), md

Manuel Compinsky
KILLERS FROM SPACE(1954), m; SNOW CREATURE, THE,(1954), m; BIG BLUFF, THE(1955), m

Vera Complojer
SPESSART INN, THE(1961, Ger.)

Brian Comport
MUMSY, NANNY, SONNY, AND GIRLY(1970, Brit.), w

Bruce Comport
MAN OF VIOLENCE(1970, Brit.), w

Betty Compson
BARKER, THE(1928); GREAT GABBO, THE(1929); ON WITH THE SHOW!(1929); SKIN DEEP(1929); STREET GIRL(1929); TIME, THE PLACE AND THE GIRL, THE(1929); WEARY RIVER(1929); WOMAN TO WOMAN(1929); BLAZE O' GLORY(1930); BOUDOIR DIPLOMAT(1930); CASE OF SERGEANT GRISCHA, THE(1930); CZAR OF BRODWAY, THE(1930); GOT WHAT SHE WANTED(1930); INSIDE THE LINES(1930); ISLE OF ESCAPE(1930); MIDNIGHT MYSTERY(1930); SHE GOT WHAT SHE WANTED(1930); SPOILERS, THE(1930); THOSE WHO DANCE(1930); GAY DIPLOMAT, THE(1931); LADY REFUSES, THE(1931); THREE WHO LOVED(1931); VIRTUOUS HUSBAND(1931); SILVER LINING(1932); DESTINATION UNKNOWN(1933); WEST OF SINGAPORE(1933); NOTORIOUS BUT NICE(1934); FALSE PRETENSES(1935); AUGUST WEEK-END(1936, Brit.); BULLDOG EDITION(1936); HOLLYWOOD BOULEVARD(1936); KILLER AT LARGE(1936); LAUGHING IRISH EYES(1936); MILLIONAIRE KID(1936); CIRCUS GIRL(1937); FEDERAL BULLETS(1937); GOD'S COUNTRY AND THE MAN(1937); TWO MINUTES TO PLAY(1937); BLONDES AT WORK(1938); PORT OF MISSING GIRLS(1938); SLIGHT CASE OF MURDER, A(1938); TORCHY BLANE IN PANAMA(1938); TWO-GUN JUSTICE(1938); UNDER THE BIG TOP(1938); COWBOYS FROM TEXAS(1939); HOTEL IMPERIAL(1939); MYSTIC CIRCLE MURDER(1939); NEWS IS MADE AT NIGHT(1939); LAUGHING AT DANGER(1940); MAD YOUTH(1940); STRANGE CARGO(1940); INVISIBLE GHOST, THE(1941); MR. AND MRS. SMITH(1941); ROAR OF THE PRESS(1941); DANGER! WOMEN AT WORK(1943); HER ADVENTUROUS NIGHT(1946); HARD BOILED MAHONEY(1947); SECOND CHANCE(1947); HERE COMES TROUBLE(1948)
Misc. Talkies
WOMAN PURSUED(1931); GUILTY OR NOT GUILTY(1932); MANHATTAN BUTTERFLY(1935); DRAGNET, THE(1936); PORT OF MISSING GIRLS(1938)
Silents
DEVIL'S TRAIL, THE(1919); LIGHT OF VICTORY(1919); MIRACLE MAN, THE(1919); PRISONERS OF LOVE(1921); ALWAYS THE WOMAN(1922); KICK IN(1922); OVER THE BORDER(1922); TO HAVE AND TO HOLD(1922); ROYAL OAK, THE(1923, Brit.); WHITE FLOWER, THE(1923); ENEMY SEX, THE(1924); RAMSHACKLE HOUSE(1924); STRANGER, THE(1924); BEGGAR ON HORSEBACK(1925); EVE'S SECRET(1925); NEW LIVES FOR OLD(1925); PATHS TO PARADISE(1925); PONY EXPRESS, THE(1925); CHEATING CHEATERS(1927); LADYBIRD, THE(1927); BIG CITY, THE(1928); LOVE ME AND THE WORLD IS MINE(1928); MASKED ANGEL(1928); SCARLET SEAS(1929)
Misc. Silents
BORDER RAIDERS, THE(1918); PRODIGAL LIAR, THE(1919); AT THE END OF THE WORLD(1921); FOR THOSE WE LOVE(1921); LADIES MUST LIVE(1921); LITTLE MINISTER, THE(1921); BONDED WOMAN, THE(1922); GREEN TEMPTATION, THE(1922); LAW AND THE WOMAN, THE(1922); RUSTLE OF SILK, THE(1923); WOMAN TO WOMAN(1923, Brit.); WOMAN WITH FOUR FACES, THE(1923); FAST SET, THE(1924); FEMALE, THE(1924); GARDEN OF WEEDS, THE(1924); MIAMI(1924); WHITE SHADOWS(1924, Brit.); COUNSEL FOR THE DEFENSE(1925); LOCKED DOORS(1925); BELLE OF BROADWAY, THE(1926); PALACE OF PLEASURE, THE(1926); WISE GUY, THE(1926); SAY IT WITH DIAMONDS(1927); TEMPTATIONS OF A SHOP GIRL(1927); COURT-MARTIAL(1928); DESERT BRIDE, THE(1928); DOCKS OF NEW YORK, THE(1928); LIFE'S MOCKERY(1928)

Athol Compton
GAMES, THE(1970); LAST WAVE, THE(1978, Aus.)

Betty Compton
TOO MANY MILLIONS(1934, Brit.)

Charles Compton
FLEMISH FARM, THE(1943, Brit.)
Misc. Silents
SPHINX, THE(1916)

David Compton
DEATHWATCH(1980, Fr./Ger.), w

Denis Compton
FINAL TEST, THE(1953, Brit.); SMALL TOWN STORY(1953, Brit.)

Dixey Compton
Misc. Silents
MAN O' WARS MAN, THE(1914)

Dixie Compton
Silents
SENATOR, THE(1915)

Fay Compton
FASHIONS IN LOVE(1929); BATTLE OF GALLIPOLI(1931, Brit.); LOVE STORM, THE(1931, Brit.); UNEASY VIRTUE(1931, Brit.); AUTUMN CROCUS(1934, Brit.); SONG AT EVENTIDE(1934, Brit.); STRAUSS' GREAT WALTZ(1934, Brit.); WRATH OF JEALOUSY(1936, Brit.); MILL ON THE FLOSS(1939, Brit.); SO THIS IS LONDON(1940, Brit.); PRIME MINISTER, THE(1941, Brit.); NICHOLAS NICKLEBY(1947, Brit.); ODD MAN OUT(1947, Brit.); DULCIMER STREET(1948, Brit.); ESTHER WATERS(1948, Brit.); AFFAIRS OF ADELAIDE(1949, U. S./Brit); BLACKMAILED(1951, Brit.); LAUGHTER IN PARADISE(1951, Brit.); LADY POSSESSED(1952); AUNT CLARA(1954, Brit.); OTHELLO(1955, U.S./Fr./Ital.); DOUBLE CROSS(1956, Brit.); STORY OF ESTHER COSTELLO, THE(1957, Brit.); TOWN ON TRIAL(1957, Brit.); HAUNTING, THE(1963); I START COUNTING(1970, Brit.); VIRGIN AND THE GYPSY, THE(1970, Brit.); UNCLE VANYA(1977, Brit.)
Silents
LABOUR LEADER, THE(1917, Brit.); ONE SUMMER'S DAY(1917, Brit.); JUDGE NOT(1920, Brit.); OLD WIVES' TALE, THE(1921, Brit.); ELEVENTH COMMANDMENT, THE(1924, Brit.); ROBINSON CRUSOE(1927, Brit.); SOMEHOW GOOD(1927, Brit.); ZERO(1928, Brit.)
Misc. Silents
WOMAN OF NO IMPORTANCE, A(1921, Brit.); BILL FOR DIVORCEMENT, A(1922); DIANA OF THE CROSSWAYS(1922, Brit.); HOUSE OF PERIL, THE(1922, Brit.); LOVES OF MARY, QUEEN OF SCOTS, THE(1923); THIS FREEDOM(1923, Brit.); CLAUDE DUVAL(1924, Brit.); HAPPY ENDING, THE(1925, Brit.); SETTLED OUT OF COURT(1925, Brit.)

Forrest Compton
OUTSIDER, THE(1962)

Francis Compton
SOAK THE RICH(1936); MR. AND MRS. SMITH(1941); RAGE IN HEAVEN(1941); SHE KNEW ALL THE ANSWERS(1941); WITNESS FOR THE PROSECUTION(1957)

Gary Compton
1984
RHINESTONE(1984)

John Compton
MILDRED PIERCE(1945); PRIDE OF THE MARINES(1945); SAN ANTONIO(1945); TOO YOUNG TO KNOW(1945); NIGHT AND DAY(1946); CHEYENNE(1947); NORA PRENTISS(1947); GLASS MENAGERIE, THE(1950); NAVY BOUND(1951); OH! SUSANNA(1951); FRIENDLY PERSUASION(1956); THUNDER OVER ARIZONA(1956); SPOILERS OF THE FOREST(1957)

Joyce Compton
WILD PARTY, THE(1929); DANGEROUS CURVES(1929); SALUTE(1929); SKY HAWK(1929); HIGH SOCIETY BLUES(1930); LIGHTNIN'(1930); THREE SISTERS, THE(1930); WILD COMPANY(1930); ANNABELLE'S AFFAIRS(1931); GOOD SPORT(1931); THREE GIRLS LOST(1931); THREE ROGUES(1931); UP POPS THE DEVIL(1931); WOMEN OF ALL NATIONS(1931); AFRAID TO TALK(1932); BEAUTY PARLOR(1932); FALSE FACES(1932); HAT CHECK GIRL(1932); IF I HAD A MILLION(1932); LADY AND GENT(1932); LENA RIVERS(1932); PARISIAN ROMANCE, A(1932); UNDER EIGHTEEN(1932); UNHOLY LOVE(1932); WESTWARD PASSAGE(1932); ONLY YESTERDAY(1933); SING SINNER, SING(1933); AFFAIRS OF A GENTLEMAN(1934); IMITATION OF LIFE(1934); KING KELLY OF THE U.S.A(1934); TRUMPET BLOWS, THE(1934); WHITE PARADE, THE(1934); COLLEGE SCANDAL(1935); GO INTO YOUR DANCE(1935); LET 'EM HAVE IT(1935); MAGNIFICENT OBSESSION(1935); HARVESTER, THE(1936); LOVE BEFORE BREAKFAST(1936); MURDER WITH PICTURES(1936); SITTING ON THE MOON(1936); STAR FOR A NIGHT(1936); TRAPPED BY TELEVISION(1936); UNDER YOUR SPELL(1936); VALLEY OF THE LAWLESS(1936); AWFUL TRUTH, THE(1937); CHINA PASSAGE(1937); COUNTRY GENTLEMEN(1937); KID GALAHAD(1937); PICK A STAR(1937); RHYTHM IN THE CLOUDS(1937); SEA RACKETEERS(1937); SMALL TOWN BOY(1937); TOAST OF NEW YORK, THE(1937); TOP OF THE TOWN(1937); WE HAVE OUR MOMENTS(1937); WINGS OVER HONOLULU(1937); ARTISTS AND MODELS ABROAD(1938); LAST WARNING, THE(1938); LOVE ON A BUDGET(1938); MANPROOF(1938); SPRING MADNESS(1938); TRADE WINDS(1938); WOMEN ARE LIKE THAT(1938); YOU AND ME(1938); BALALAIKA(1939); ESCAPE TO PARADISE(1939); FLYING IRISHMAN, THE(1939); GOING PLACES(1939); HOTEL FOR WOMEN(1939); RENO(1939); ROSE OF WASHINGTON SQUARE(1939); HONEYMOON DEFERRED(1940); I TAKE THIS OATH(1940); LET'S MAKE MUSIC(1940); SKY MURDER(1940); THEY DRIVE BY NIGHT(1940); TURNABOUT(1940); VILLAIN STILL PURSUED HER, THE(1940); WHO KILLED AUNT MAGGIE?(1940); CITY, FOR CONQUEST(1941); MANPOWER(1941); MOON OVER HER SHOULDER(1941); SCATTERGOOD MEETS BROADWAY(1941); ZIEGFELD GIRL(1941); BEDTIME STORY(1942); THUNDER BIRDS(1942); TOO MANY WOMEN(1942); GENTLE GANGSTER, A(1943); LET'S FACE IT(1943); SILVER SKATES(1943); SILVER SPURS(1943); SWING OUT THE BLUES(1943); CHRISTMAS IN CONNECTICUT(1945); DANGER SIGNAL(1945); HITCHHIKE TO HAPPINESS(1945); MILDRED PIERCE(1945); PILLOW TO POST(1945); ROUGHLY SPEAKING(1945); BEHIND THE MASK(1946); DARK ALIBI(1946); NIGHT AND DAY(1946); EXPOSED(1947); LINDA BE GOOD(1947); SCARED TO DEATH(1947); INCIDENT(1948); SORRY, WRONG NUMBER(1948); SOUTHERN YANKEE, A(1948); GRAND CANYON(1949); JET PILOT(1957); PERSUADER, THE(1957); GIRL IN THE WOODS(1958)
Misc. Talkies
FIGHTING FOR JUSTICE(1932)
Silents
WHAT FOOLS MEN(1925); SYNCOPATING SUE(1926); ANKLES PREFERRED(1927)

Misc. Silents
BROADWAY LADY(1925); SOFT LIVING(1928)
Juleen Compton
STRANDED(1965), a, p,d&w; PLASTIC DOME OF NORMA JEAN, THE(1966), p, d&w
Julie Compton
BEHOLD MY WIFE(1935)
Juliette Compton
WOMAN TO WOMAN(1929); ANYBODY'S WOMAN(1930); LADIES OF LEISURE(1930); MOROCCO(1930); COMPROMISED(1931); HUSBAND'S HOLIDAY(1931); KICK IN(1931); RICH MAN'S FOLLY(1931); UNFAITHFUL(1931); WOMEN LOVE ONCE(1931); DEVIL AND THE DEEP(1932); MAN CALLED BACK, THE(1932); MATCH KING, THE(1932); NO ONE MAN(1932); STRANGERS IN LOVE(1932); WESTWARD PASSAGE(1932); BERKELEY SQUARE(1933); MASQUERADER, THE(1933); PEG O' MY HEART(1933); COUNT OF MONTE CRISTO, THE(1934); GRAND CANARY(1934); IRENE(1940); THAT HAMILTON WOMAN(1941)
Silents
HUMAN DESIRES(1924, Brit.); AFRAID OF LOVE(1925, Brit.); CHINESE BUNGALOW, THE(1926, Brit.); NELL GWYNNE(1926, Brit.); FAKE, THE(1927, Brit.); WOMAN TEMPTED, THE(1928, Brit.)
Misc. Silents
GAYEST OF THE GAY, THE(1924, Brit.); WINE OF LIFE, THE(1924, Brit.); TRAINER AND THE TEMPTRESS(1925, Brit.); CHINESE BUNGALOW, THE(1926, Brit.); WHITE HEAT(1926, Brit.); SCARLET DAREDEVIL, THE(1928, Brit.)
Lt. Cdr. Phillip Compton
DESTINATION TOKYO(1944), tech adv
Lynn Compton
FORBIDDEN(1932)
Madge Compton
RANDOLPH FAMILY, THE(1945, Brit.)
Philip Compton
GIRO CITY(1982, Brit.)
Richard Compton
GUN RUNNER(1969), d&w; RUN, ANGEL, RUN(1969), w; ANGELS DIE HARD(1970), a, d&w; DIAMOND STUD(1970); MACON COUNTY LINE(1974), d, w; RETURN TO MACON COUNTY(1975), d&w; MANIAC!(1977), d; RAVAGERS, THE(1979), d
S. Compton
COCAINE COWBOYS(1979), w
Sharon Compton
QUEEN OF BLOOD(1966), cos; CALIFORNIA SPLIT(1974); AVALANCHE(1978), prod d; DEATHSPORT(1978), art d; DR. HECKYL AND MR. HYPE(1980); TARGET: HARRY(1980), prod d; BARBAROSA(1982)
Spencer Compton
Misc. Talkies
ANGELS(1976), d
Todd Compton
Misc. Talkies
POSSE FROM HEAVEN(1975)
Tony Compton
1984
RHINESTONE(1984)
Viola Compton
THE BLACK HAND GANG(1930, Brit.); COMPROMISED!(1931, Brit.); THIRD TIME LUCKY(1931, Brit.); LOOKING ON THE BRIGHT SIDE(1932, Brit.); EXCESS BAGGAGE(1933, Brit.); GOOD COMPANIONS(1933, Brit.); MEDICINE MAN, THE(1933, Brit.); SMITHY(1933, Brit.); DARK WORLD(1935, Brit.); BIG NOISE, THE(1936, Brit.); FIND THE LADY(1936, Brit.); HAPPY DAYS ARE HERE AGAIN(1936, Brit.); LAST JOURNEY, THE(1936, Brit.); MAN IN THE MIRROR, THE(1936, Brit.); SHADOW, THE(1936, Brit.); UNDER PROOF(1936, Brit.); WHO GOES NEXT?(1938, Brit.)
Silents
POLLY OF THE CIRCUS(1917)
Clark Comstock
Silents
SHOCKING NIGHT, A(1921); SINGING RIVER(1921); RIDE FOR YOUR LIFE(1924); LOOKING FOR TROUBLE(1926); HEY! HEY! COWBOY(1927); SILVER VALLEY(1927); SINGED(1927); AVENGING SHADOW, THE(1928); HUNTED MEN(1930); OKLAHOMA SHERIFF, THE(1930)
Misc. Silents
EAGLE'S NEST(1915); RANGER AND THE LAW, THE(1921); BLAZING ARROWS(1922); CALGARY STAMPEDE, THE(1925); MAN IN THE SADDLE, THE(1926); MAN FROM NOWHERE, THE(1930)
Frank Comstock
LAST TIME I SAW ARCHIE, THE(1961), m, md
Howard W. Comstock
DOCTOR X(1932), w
Howard Warren Comstock
STEPPING SISTERS(1932), w
Sal Comstock
WILD RIDERS(1971), w
William Comstock
HERE COMES ELMER(1943)
Michele Comte
TESTAMENT OF ORPHEUS, THE(1962, Fr.)
Francois Comtet
ENIGMA(1983), art d
Guy Comtois
TERROR TRAIN(1980, Can.), art d; QUEST FOR FIRE(1982, Fr./Can.), prod d
1984
BODY ROCK(1984), prod d
David Comville
PRIZE OF ARMS, A(1962, Brit.)
Sally Conabere
PICTURE SHOW MAN, THE(1980, Aus.)
Misc. Talkies
LITTLE FELLER, THE(1979)
Sidney Conabere
MAN OF VIOLENCE(1970, Brit.)

Syd Conabere
PETERSEN(1974, Aus.); TRESPASSERS, THE(1976, Aus.)
Bill Conant
Silents
ARIZONA KID, THE(1929)
Oliver Conant
SUMMER OF '42(1971); CLASS OF '44(1973)
James Conaty
POSSESSED(1947); EMERGENCY WEDDING(1950); GIRL IN THE RED VELVET SWING, THE(1955)
Charles Conaway
SUGARLAND EXPRESS, THE(1974)
Jan Conaway
GIDGET GOES HAWAIIAN(1961)
Jeff Conaway
JENNIFER ON MY MIND(1971); EAGLE HAS LANDED, THE(1976, Brit.); I NEVER PROMISED YOU A ROSE GARDEN(1977); GREASE(1978)
1984
COVERGIRL(1984, Can.)
Cari Conboy
CARNIVAL OF SOULS(1962)
Giuseppe Conca
MADAME BUTTERFLY(1955 Ital./Jap.), md
Kiko Concalves
STATUE, THE(1971, Brit.)
Jack Concannon
M(1970)
Mike Concannon
TEENAGE ZOMBIES(1960)
Baby Conceicao
XICA(1982, Braz.)
Maria Conceicao
GIVEN WORD, THE(1964, Braz.)
Antoinette Concello
GREATEST SHOW ON EARTH, THE(1952)
M. Concepcion
STORM OVER TIBET(1952)
Maria Conchita
1984
FEAR CITY(1984)
Georges Conchon
STRANGER, THE(1967, Algeria/Fr./Ital.), w; BLACK AND WHITE IN COLOR(1976, Fr.), w
Emillio Concini
ALWAYS VICTORIOUS(1960, Ital.), w
Alice Concord
Silents
MORAL FIBRE(1921)
Lillian Concord
Misc. Silents
HERITAGE OF HATE, THE(1916); GIRL FROM RECTOR'S, THE(1917); TROUBLEMAKERS(1917)
Mabel Concord
SMOKE TREE RANGE(1937)
Anton Conde
REBELLION OF THE HANGED, THE(1954, Mex.), ed
Antonio Conde
NIGHT OF THE BLOODY APES(1968, Mex.), m
Antonio D. Conde
PLUNDER OF THE SUN(1953), m
Antonio Diaz Conde
PEARL, THE(1948, U.S./Mex.), m; TORCH, THE(1950), m; STRONGHOLD(1952, Mex.), md; CURSE OF THE AZTEC MUMMY, THE(1965, Mex.), m; ROBOT VS. THE AZTEC MUMMY, THE(1965, Mex.), m; CURSE OF THE DOLL PEOPLE, THE(1968, Mex.), m
Carlos Conde
CALLAWAY WENT THATAWAY(1951); MY FAVORITE SPY(1951); RATON PASS(1951); MY MAN AND I(1952); JEOPARDY(1953)
Diaz Conde
TORCH, THE(1950), md
Eduardo Conde
1984
BLAME IT ON RIO(1984)
Fred Conde
TASTE OF HELL, A(1973), ph
Freddie Conde
BIG DOLL HOUSE, THE(1971), ph
Gene Conde
HUMAN TORNADO, THE(1976), ph
Rita Conde
RIDE THE PINK HORSE(1947); CRISIS(1950); BRAVE BULLS, THE(1951); TEN TALL MEN(1951); SOMBRERO(1953); BARQUERO(1970); WORLD'S GREATEST LOVER, THE(1977); TIME AFTER TIME(1979, Brit.)
Tony Conde
KID FROM BOOKLYN, THE(1946)
Zedra Conde
FALCON OUT WEST, THE(1944); KISMET(1944)
Conden and Bohland
MURDER IN THE MUSIC HALL(1946)
Candi Conder
COLOR ME BLOOD RED(1965)
Jay Conder
STACY'S KNIGHTS(1983)
George Condert
Silents
ALL FOR A GIRL(1915), ph
Carlos Condi
CRISIS(1950)

David Condi
LOVE SLAVES OF THE AMAZONS(1957), ch
Fernanda Condi
LOVE SLAVES OF THE AMAZONS(1957), ch
Win Condict
SLITHIS(1978)
Steve Condit
TO KILL A MOCKINGBIRD(1962); ROUSTABOUT(1964); YOUNG FURY(1965)
Laura Duke Condominas
LANCELOT OF THE LAKE(1975, Fr.)
Bob Condon
TRUE AND THE FALSE, THE(1955, Swed.), w
Charles Condon
CAUGHT IN THE FOG(1928), w; LAND OF THE SILVER FOX(1928), w; MARK IT PAID(1933), w; SOLDIERS OF THE STORM(1933), w; THREE MESQUITEERS, THE(1936), w; GALLOPING DYNAMITE(1937), w; SING WHILE YOU'RE ABLE(1937), w; MYSTIC CIRCLE MURDER(1939), w; OKLAHOMA RENEGADES(1940), w
Silents
RED WINE(1928), w; JOY STREET(1929), w
Charles R. Condon
BROTHERS(1930), w; GET THAT GIRL(1932), d; SPEED MADNESS(1932), w; DEATH IN THE SKY(1937), w; DAREDEVIL DRIVERS(1938), w; TEN LAPS TO GO(1938), w
Silents
DOG OF THE REGIMENT(1927), w; JAWS OF STEEL(1927), w; ONE-ROUND HOGAN(1927), w; WHAT HAPPENED TO FATHER(1927), w
David Condon
NO HOLDS BARRED(1952); CLIPPED WINGS(1953); JALOPY(1953); PRIVATE EYES(1953); JUNGLE GENTS(1954); HIGH SOCIETY(1955); JAIL BUSTERS(1955); CRASHING LAS VEGAS(1956); DIG THAT URANIUM(1956); SPY CHASERS(1956); HOLD THAT HYPNOTIST(1957); LOOKING FOR DANGER(1957)
Eva Condon
KISS OF DEATH(1947); WALK EAST ON BEACON(1952)
Frank Condon
Silents
SEALED LIPS(1915), w; CITY OF SILENT MEN(1921), w; CRAZY TO MARRY(1921), w; MAN WHO SAW TOMORROW, THE(1922), w; SIXTY CENTS AN HOUR(1923), w; LEGEND OF HOLLYWOOD, THE(1924), w; NO CONTROL(1927), w; RUBBER TIRES(1927), w
David Condon [David Gorcey]
PARIS PLAYBOYS(1954)
Geraldine Condon
Silents
INFAMOUS MISS REVELL, THE(1921)
Hobart Condon
HOME IN INDIANA(1944)
Jack Condon
Silents
PENROD(1922)
Jackie Condon
Silents
DOCTOR JACK(1922)
James Condon
SCOBIE MALONE(1975, Aus.); TIM(1981, Aus.)
R. Condon
CRIME OF HELEN STANLEY(1934), w
Richard Condon
HAPPY THIEVES, THE(1962), w; MANCHURIAN CANDIDATE, THE(1962), w; WINTER KILLS(1979), w
Robert Condon
HOME IN INDIANA(1944); WING AND A PRAYER(1944)
William Condon
DEAD KIDS(1981 Aus./New Zealand), w; STRANGE INVADERS(1983), w
Bobby Condor
STACY'S KNIGHTS(1983)
George A. Condor
NAVY SPY(1937), p
Jennifer Condos
THINGS ARE TOUGH ALL OVER(1982)
Nick Condos
DANCING FEET(1936)
Steve Condos
MEET ME AFTER THE SHOW(1951)
William Condos
QUEEN OF BLOOD(1966), makeup
Condos & Brandow
SHE'S BACK ON BROADWAY(1953)
Condos Bros
HAPPY LANDING(1938)
Condos Brothers
MIDSHIPMAID GOB(1932, Brit.); MOON OVER MIAMI(1941); HEY, ROOKIE(1944); PIN UP GIRL(1944); TIME, THE PLACE AND THE GIRL, THE(1946)
The Condos Brothers
WAKE UP AND LIVE(1937); SONG OF THE OPEN ROAD(1944)
Tim Condron
PLAGUE OF THE ZOMBIES, THE(1966, Brit.)
Valerie Condroyer
1984
A NOS AMOURS(1984, Fr.), ed
Wolfgang Condrus
GIRL AND THE LEGEND, THE(1966, Ger.)
Arthur Condy
Silents
ONLY A MILL GIRL(1919, Brit.)
Paul Condylis
NEVER A DULL MOMENT(1968); SWEET RIDE, THE(1968); TARGETS(1968); WHAT'S UP, DOC?(1972)

Bill Cone
PHANTASM(1979)
C. Edward Cone
Misc. Silents
GIRL ALASKA, THE(1919)
Nancy Cone
1984
MISSING IN ACTION(1984), cos; NINJA III–THE DOMINATION(1984), cos
Cone School Girls
STEPPING TOES(1938, Brit.)
David Conell
HI, MOM!(1970)
E.S. Conerly
SALT OF THE EARTH(1954)
Tristam Cones
VILLAGE OF DAUGHTERS(1962, Brit.), ed; PLAY IT COOL(1963, Brit.), ed; WRONG ARM OF THE LAW, THE(1963, Brit.), ed; SEASIDE SWINGERS(1965, Brit.), ed; THREE HATS FOR LISA(1965, Brit.), ed; FINDERS KEEPERS(1966, Brit.), ed; MALPAS MYSTERY, THE(1967, Brit.), ed; TRAP, THE(1967, Can./Brit.), ed; MRS. BROWN, YOU'VE GOT A LOVELY DAUGHTER(1968, Brit.), ed; SOUTHERN STAR, THE(1969, Fr./Brit.), ed; MUMSY, NANNY, SONNY, AND GIRLY(1970, Brit.), ed; ABOMINABLE DR. PHIBES, THE(1971, Brit.), ed; WHAT CHANGED CHARLEY FARTHING?(1976, Brit.), p
Tristam V. Cones
WHO SLEW AUNTIE ROO?(1971, U.S./Brit.), ed
Tristan Cones
COOL IT, CAROL!(1970, Brit.), ed; DOCTOR PHIBES RISES AGAIN(1972, Brit.), ed
Tristram Cones
PAYROLL(1962, Brit.), ed; BAY OF SAINT MICHEL, THE(1963, Brit.), ed
Myrtis Coney
Misc. Silents
DUPLICITY OF HARGRAVES, THE(1917)
The Coney Island Kids
ROCK, ROCK, ROCK!(1956)
Klary Confalonieri
EMBASSY(1972, Brit.), set d
Claude Confortes
WAR OF THE BUTTONS(1963 Fr.); BEHOLD A PALE HORSE(1964); THINGS OF LIFE, THE(1970, Fr./Ital./Switz.)
Donna Conforti
SANTA CLAUS CONQUERS THE MARTIANS(1964)
Gene Conforti
HAWMPS!(1976)
Gino Conforti
HOW SWEET IT IS(1968); VIVA MAX!(1969); FUZZ(1972); MAN OF LA MANCHA(1972)
Leo Conforti
CLOWN AND THE KIDS, THE(1968, U.S./Bulgaria)
Harold Congdon
YOU'LL LIKE MY MOTHER(1972)
James Congdon
LEFT-HANDED GUN, THE(1958); 4D MAN(1959); GROUP, THE(1966); 300 YEAR WEEKEND(1971); SUMMERDOG(1977); REFUGE(1981); SEEDS OF EVIL(1981)
Jim Congdon
PEGGY(1950); WHEN WORLDS COLLIDE(1951)
John C. Conger
TERMS OF ENDEARMENT(1983)
Logan Conger
LOUISIANA(1947)
Mairead Ni Conghaile
POITIN(1979, Irish)
Vittorio Congia
CAT O'NINE TAILS(1971, Ital./Ger./Fr.)
The Congoroos
RIDE 'EM COWBOY(1942)
Jules Conjager
DRAGNET PATROL(1932), ph
William Conkiln
Misc. Silents
YELLOW PAWN, THE(1916)
Tony Conkle
MARLOWE(1969)
Betty Conklin
ACT OF VENGEANCE(1974), w
Bill Conklin
GRAND THEFT AUTO(1977)
1984
THEY'RE PLAYING WITH FIRE(1984)
Charles Conklin
Silents
FIGHTING EDGE(1926)
Misc. Silents
GEORGE(; SEVEN SINNERS(1925); FIGHTING EDGE, THE(1926); HARD BOILED(1926)
Charles [Heinie] Conklin
Silents
BELOW THE LINE(1925)
Chester Conklin
HAUNTED HOUSE, THE(1928); TAXI 13(1928); VARSITY(1928); FAST COMPANY(1929); HOUSE OF HORROR(1929); PHANTOM OF THE OPERA, THE(1929); STUDIO MURDER MYSTERY, THE(1929); VIRGINIAN, THE(1929); LOVE TRADER(1930); SWING HIGH(1930); HER MAJESTY LOVE(1931); HALLELUJAH, I'M A BUM(1933); CALL OF THE PRAIRIE(1936); MODERN TIMES(1936); PREVIEW MURDER MYSTERY(1936); FORLORN RIVER(1937); HOTEL HAYWIRE(1937); SING, COWBOY, SING(1937); EVERY DAY'S A HOLIDAY(1938); HOLLYWOOD CAVALCADE(1939); ZENOBIA(1939); CHIP OF THE FLYING U(1940); GREAT DICTATOR, THE(1940); LI'L ABNER(1940); HARMON OF MICHIGAN(1941); HERE COMES MR. JORDAN(1941); HONOLULU LU(1941); SULLIVAN'S TRAVELS(1941); I MARRIED A WITCH(1942); IN OLD CALIFORNIA(1942); PALM BEACH STORY, THE(1942); SONS OF THE PIONEERS(1942); VALLEY OF THE SUN(1942); AROUND

THE WORLD(1943); ADVENTURES OF MARK TWAIN, THE(1944); GOODNIGHT SWEETHEART(1944); HAIL THE CONQUERING HERO(1944); KNICKERBOCKER HOLIDAY(1944); MAN FROM FRISCO(1944); MIRACLE OF MORGAN'S CREEK, THE(1944); SUNDAY DINNER FOR A SOLDIER(1944); FEAR(1946); HOODLUM SAINT, THE(1946); LITTLE GIANT(1946); SHE WROTE THE BOOK(1946); SINGIN' IN THE CORN(1946); SMOOTH AS SILK(1946); PERILS OF PAULINE, THE(1947); SONG OF SCHEHERAZADE(1947); SONG OF THE WASTELAND(1947); SPRINGTIME IN THE SIERRAS(1947); TROUBLE WITH WOMEN, THE(1947); ISN'T IT ROMANTIC?(1948); BEAUTIFUL BLONDE FROM BASHFUL BEND, THE(1949); GOLDEN STALLION, THE(1949); KNOCK ON ANY DOOR(1949); FANCY PANTS(1950); HUMPHREY TAKES A CHANCE(1950); LET'S DANCE(1950); MILKMAN, THE(1950); NEVER A DULL MOMENT(1950); SHAKEDOWN(1950); MY FAVORITE SPY(1951); SON OF PALEFACE(1952); APACHE WOMAN(1955); BEAST WITH A MILLION EYES, THE(1956); ROCK-A-BYE BABY(1958); PARADISE ALLEY(1962); BIG HAND FOR THE LITTLE LADY, A(1966)
Silents
TILLIE'S PUNCTURED ROMANCE(1914); ANNA CHRISTIE(1923); SOULS FOR SALE(1923); ANOTHER MAN'S WIFE(1924); NORTH OF NEVADA(1924); GREAT LOVE, THE(1925); GREED(1925); ONE YEAR TO LIVE(1925); PHANTOM OF THE OPERA, THE(1925); WINDING STAIR, THE(1925); BEHIND THE FRONT(1926); NERVOUS WRECK, THE(1926); SOCIAL CELEBRITY, A(1926); WILDERNESS WOMAN, THE(1926); TWO FLAMING YOUTHS(1927); GENTLEMEN PREFER BLONDES(1928); TILLIE'S PUNCTURED ROMANCE(1928); STAIRS OF SAND(1929); SUNSET PASS(1929)
Misc. Silents
SKIRTS(1921); GALLOPING FISH(1924); MIDNIGHT LOVERS(1926); SAY IT AGAIN(1926); WE'RE IN THE NAVY NOW(1926); CABARET(1927); KISS IN A TAXI, A(1927); MCFADDEN FLATS(1927); RUBBER HEELS(1927); TELL IT TO SWEENEY(1927); BIG NOISE, THE(1928); FOOLS FOR LUCK(1928); MARQUIS PREFERRED(1929)
Frank Conklin
FEDERAL MAN-HUNT(1939); REMEMBER THE NIGHT(1940)
Frank R. Conklin
MAD PARADE, THE(1931), w
Hal Conklin
SPIELER, THE(1929), w; SILVER LINING(1932), w; SIX BRIDGES TO CROSS(1955)
Silents
JUST LIKE A WOMAN(1923), w
Han Conklin
Silents
TRAMP, TRAMP, TRAMP(1926), w
Heimie Conklin
NIGHT PARADE(1929, Brit.)
Heinie Conklin
AIR CIRCUS, THE(1928); SIDE STREET(1929); ALL QUIET ON THE WESTERN FRONT(1930); TIGER ROSE(1930); LAW OF THE NORTH(1932); ME AND MY GAL(1932); MILLION DOLLAR LEGS(1932); ONE WAY PASSAGE(1932); TRAILING THE KILLER(1932); WHAT PRICE HOLLYWOOD?(1932); BOWERY, THE(1933); KEYHOLE, THE(1933); PRIVATE DETECTIVE 62(1933); RIDERS OF DESTINY(1933); SHE DONE HIM WRONG(1933); DEATH OF THE DIAMOND(1934); PERSONALITY KID, THE(1934); GIRL FROM TENTH AVENUE, THE(1935); MAN ON THE FLYING TRAPEZE, THE(1935); MURDER MAN(1935); RUGGLES OF RED GAP(1935); STEAMBOAT ROUND THE BEND(1935); AFTER THE THIN MAN(1936); RHYTHM ON THE RANGE(1936); WEDDING PRESENT(1936); GIRL WITH IDEAS, A(1937); LIVE, LOVE AND LEARN(1937); MOUNTAIN JUSTICE(1937); OH DOCTOR(1937); CITY GIRL(1938); LITTLE MISS BROADWAY(1938); PROFESSOR BEWARE(1938); STRANGE FACES(1938); FRONTIER MARSHAL(1939); HOLLYWOOD CAVALCADE(1939); INVITATION TO HAPPINESS(1939); LET FREEDOM RING(1939); NEWSBOY'S HOME(1939); OUR LEADING CITIZEN(1939); TELL NO TALES(1939); COURAGEOUS DR. CHRISTIAN, THE(1940); DR. CHRISTIAN MEETS THE WOMEN(1940); MARGIE(1940); WESTERNER, THE(1940); YOU'RE NOT SO TOUGH(1940); CAUGHT IN THE DRAFT(1941); DOUBLE CROSS(1941); HONKY TONK(1941); TRAMP, TRAMP, TRAMP(1942); YOU'RE TELLING ME(1942); LOST IN A HAREM(1944); HOODLUM SAINT, THE(1946); PERILS OF PAULINE, THE(1947); FAMILY HONEYMOON(1948); LOADED PISTOLS(1948); ROAD HOUSE(1948); NEPTUNE'S DAUGHTER(1949); SMOKY MOUNTAIN MELODY(1949); COUNTY FAIR(1950); TRAVELING SALESWOMAN(1950); MONKEY BUSINESS(1952); VICKI(1953); ABBOTT AND COSTELLO MEET THE KEYSTONE KOPS(1955)
Silents
SUBMARINE PIRATE, A(1915); GOLD RUSH, THE(1925); NIGHT CRY, THE(1926); CHEATERS(1927); HAM AND EGGS AT THE FRONT(1927)
Misc. Silents
CLASH OF THE WOLVES(1925); SAP, THE(1926); HORSEMAN OF THE PLAINS, A(1928); TRICK OF HEARTS, A(1928)
Patricia Conklin
COAST TO COAST(1980)
Peggy Conklin
PRESIDENT VANISHES, THE(1934); ONE-WAY TICKET(1935); DEVIL IS A SISSY, THE(1936); HER MASTER'S VOICE(1936)
Rus Conklin
UNCONQUERED(1947); HURRICANE ISLAND(1951); GREATEST SHOW ON EARTH, THE(1952); SON OF PALEFACE(1952)
Russ Conklin
SIREN OF ATLANTIS(1948); HAREM GIRL(1952); PATHFINDER, THE(1952); WILD NORTH, THE(1952); SEMINOLE UPRISING(1955)
Shirley Conklin
TROG(1970, Brit.)
William Conklin
Misc. Talkies
DIVINE LADY, THE(1929)
Silents
DAN(1914); PIERRE OF THE PLAINS(1914); JOAN THE WOMAN(1916); LAW OF THE LAND, THE(1917); PRICE MARK, THE(1917); SOLD AT AUCTION(1917); HAIRPINS(1920); RED HOT DOLLARS(1920); SEX(1920); BEAU REVEL(1921); BLIND HEARTS(1921); LURE OF YOUTH, THE(1921); LONELY ROAD, THE(1923); GOLDFISH, THE(1924); NEVER SAY DIE(1924); PORTS OF CALL(1925); RAG MAN, THE(1925); OLD IRONSIDES(1926); OUTLAWS OF RED RIVER(1927); TUMBLING RIVER(1927)

Misc. Silents
RAGGED EARL, THE(1914); INHERITED PASSIONS(1916); SHRINE OF HAPPINESS, THE(1916); SPELLBOUND(1916); SULTANA, THE(1916); DEVIL'S BAIT, THE(1917); GOLDEN RULE KATE(1917); LOVE LETTERS(1917); MASKED HEART, THE(1917); NORTH OF FIFTY-THREE(1917); OUT OF THE WRECK(1917); PRISON WITHOUT WALLS, THE(1917); SERPENT'S TOOTH, THE(1917); STOLEN PLAY, THE(1917); FLARE-UP SAL(1918); LOVE ME(1918); MATING OF MARCELLA, THE(1918); TYRANT FEAR(1918); COME AGAIN SMITH(1919); DRIFTERS, THE(1919); HAY FOOT, STRAW FOOT(1919); WHAT EVERY WOMAN LEARNS(1919); WHEN FATE DECIDES(1919); BRUTE MASTER, THE(1920); LOVE MADNESS(1920); WOMAN IN THE SUITCASE, THE(1920); OTHER WOMAN, THE(1921); IRON TO GOLD(1922); UNFOLDMENT, THE(1922); WHEN HUSBANDS DECEIVE(1922); WOMAN HE MARRIED, THE(1922); DAYTIME WIVES(1923); MAN ALONE, THE(1923); FIFTH AVENUE MODELS(1925); GENTLEMAN ROUGHNECK, A(1925); SWEET ROSIE O'GRADY(1926); LIFE'S CROSSROADS(1928); SHANGHAI ROSE(1929)
Chris Conkling
LORD OF THE RINGS, THE(1978), w
Donna Conkling
HIDEOUS SUN DEMON, THE(1959)
Xaudra Conkling
HIDEOUS SUN DEMON, THE(1959)
Heinie Conklon
MODERN TIMES(1936)
Bud Conlan
THOMASINE AND BUSHROD(1974)
Francis X. Conlan
Silents
BRAVE AND BOLD(1918)
Misc. Silents
FATAL HOUR, THE(1920)
Frank Conlan
SCOUNDREL, THE(1935); ANGELS OVER BROADWAY(1940); CHAD HANNA(1940); BILLY THE KID(1941); DEVIL AND DANIEL WEBSTER, THE(1941); CRYSTAL BALL, THE(1943); STRANGLER OF THE SWAMP(1945); MY DARLING CLEMENTINE(1946); NO MINOR VICES(1948); RACHEL AND THE STRANGER(1948); BLACK BOOK, THE(1949); PERFECT STRANGERS(1950); WINCHESTER '73(1950)
Misc. Silents
BOUGHT AND PAID FOR(1916)
James Conlan
BELLE OF THE NINETIES(1934)
Joe Conlan
CONCRETE JUNGLE, THE(1982), m
Joseph Conlan
KILL SQUAD(1982), m
Amelia Conley
SPELL OF THE HYPNOTIST(1956)
Barbara Conley
Misc. Silents
GIRL WHO WON OUT, THE(1917)
Bing Conley
MY LITTLE CHICKADEE(1940); NIGHT UNTO NIGHT(1949)
Corrine Conley
RETURN OF COUNT YORGA, THE(1971)
Dan Conley
1984
MRS. SOFFEL(1984), set d
Darlene Conley
FACES(1968); CAPTAIN MILKSHAKE(1970); PLAY IT AS IT LAYS(1972)
Effie Conley
Misc. Silents
WALK-OFFS, THE(1920)
Gator Conley
URBAN COWBOY(1980)
Harry Conley
OLD HOMESTEAD, THE(1935)
Joe Conley
SCARLET HOUR, THE(1956); BLUEPRINT FOR ROBBERY(1961); CASE OF PATTY SMITH, THE(1962); 80 STEPS TO JONAH(1969)
John Conley
CRIME OF PASSION(1957); HEAVEN'S GATE(1980)
Onest Conley
GRAND OLD GIRL(1935); RACING LUCK(1935); GOLDEN BOY(1939); SHE KNEW ALL THE ANSWERS(1941); JUNGLE GODDESS(1948)
Onset [Tom-Tom] Conley
THRILL OF BRAZIL, THE(1946)
Rene Conley
GREAT SCOUT AND CATHOUSE THURSDAY, THE(1976), cos
Renie Conley
CARAVANS(1978, U.S./Iranian), cos; BODY HEAT(1981), cos
Tommy Conley
QUEEN OF THE MOB(1940)
Truman Conley
RED RUNS THE RIVER(1963)
William "Bing" Conley
TWO YANKS IN TRINIDAD(1942)
James Conlin
FREE SOUL, A(1931); BOWERY, THE(1933); SHE LEARNED ABOUT SAILORS(1934); 365 NIGHTS IN HOLLYWOOD(1934); ROSE BOWL(1936); ROSE MARIE(1936); CRASHING HOLLYWOOD(1937); FIND THE WITNESS(1937); OLD ACQUAINTANCE(1943); THIS IS THE ARMY(1943)
James "Jimmy" Conlin
MAN WHO FOUND HIMSELF, THE(1937)
Jim Conlin
SHINING HOUR, THE(1938); IDIOT'S DELIGHT(1939)
Jimmy Conlin
FOOTLIGHT PARADE(1933); AND SUDDEN DEATH(1936); CAPTAINS COURAGEOUS(1937); MANNEQUIN(1937); MOUNTAIN MUSIC(1937); COCOANUT GROVE(1938); COMET OVER BROADWAY(1938); HARD TO GET(1938); PRISON

FARM(1938); SWEETHEARTS(1938); NAUGHTY BUT NICE(1939); $1,000 A TOUCH-DOWN(1939); ANGELS OVER BROADWAY(1940); CHARLIE CHAN AT THE WAX MUSEUM(1940); CHRISTMAS IN JULY(1940); GREAT McGINTY, THE(1940); HONEYMOON DEFERRED(1940); THIRD FINGER, LEFT HAND(1940); TWO GIRLS ON BROADWAY(1940); GAY FALCON, THE(1941); LADY EVE, THE(1941); OBLIGING YOUNG LADY(1941); RIDIN' ON A RAINBOW(1941); SULLIVAN'S TRAVELS(1941); BROADWAY(1942); FOREST RANGERS, THE(1942); ICE-CAPADES REVUE(1942); LADY IS WILLING, THE(1942); MADAME SPY(1942); PALM BEACH STORY, THE(1942); REMARKABLE ANDREW, THE(1942); WOMAN OF THE YEAR(1942); DIXIE(1943); PETTICOAT LARCENY(1943); ALI BABA AND THE FORTY THIEVES(1944); AND THE ANGELS SING(1944); ARMY WIVES(1944); HAIL THE CONQUERING HERO(1944); MAN FROM FRISCO(1944); MIRACLE OF MORGAN'S CREEK, THE(1944); SUMMER STORM(1944); ANGEL COMES TO BROOKLYN, AN(1945); DON JUAN QUILLIGAN(1945); FALLEN ANGEL(1945); HONEYMOON AHEAD(1945); IT'S A PLEASURE(1945); PICTURE OF DORIAN GRAY, THE(1945); TOWN WENT WILD, THE(1945); CROSS MY HEART(1946); TWO SISTERS FROM BOSTON(1946); DICK TRACY'S DILEMMA(1947); HUCKSTERS, THE(1947); IT'S A JOKE, SON!(1947); MOURNING BECOMES ELECTRA(1947); SEVEN KEYS TO BALDPATE(1947); TROUBLE WITH WOMEN, THE(1947); HAZARD(1948); SMART WOMAN(1948); KNOCK ON ANY DOOR(1949); PREJUDICE(1949); TULSA(1949); GREAT RUPERT, THE(1950); MAD WEDNESDAY(1950); OPERATION HAYLIFT(1950); SIDESHOW(1950); ON DANGEROUS GROUND(1951); IT HAPPENS EVERY THURSDAY(1953); SEVEN LITTLE FOYS, THE(1955); ANATOMY OF A MURDER(1959); THIRTY FOOT BRIDE OF CANDY ROCK, THE(1959)

Joe Conlin
THIEF, THE(1952)
Richard Conlin
ANGELS IN THE OUTFIELD(1951), w
Terence Conlin
LABURNUM GROVE(1936, Brit.); FLYING FIFTY-FIVE(1939, Brit.)
Terry Conlin
IRISH FOR LUCK(1936, Brit.); FALSE EVIDENCE(1937, Brit.); KATHLEEN(1938, Ireland); IT'S IN THE BAG(1943, Brit.); SUSPECTED PERSON(1943, Brit.); LOVE ON THE DOLE(1945, Brit.); PATIENT VANISHES, THE(1947, Brit.)
Thomas Conlin
CAUGHT SHORT(1930)
Casey Conlon
GUARDIAN OF THE WILDERNESS(1977), w
Danny Conlon
PUNISHMENT PARK(1971)
Dolores Conlon
DOUGHGIRLS, THE(1944)
Frank Conlon
LYDIA(1941); SIDE STREET(1950)
James Conlon
BRIDE COMES HOME(1936); ADVENTUROUS BLONDE(1937); BROADWAY MUSKETEERS(1938); TORCHY BLANE IN PANAMA(1938); NO PLACE TO GO(1939); CALLING PHILO VANCE(1940); MY LITTLE CHICKADEE(1940)
Jeff Conlon
MY LITTLE CHICKADEE(1940)
Jimmy Conlon
SECOND CHORUS(1940); UNEXPECTED UNCLE(1941); HITLER'S MADMAN(1943)
Joseph Conlon
CHAINED HEAT(1983 U.S./Ger.), m
Noel Conlon
POLTERGEIST(1982)
1984
RAW COURAGE(1984)
Paul Conlon
SCATTERBRAIN(1940), w
Tom Conlon
OVER THE HILL(1931); LAUGHTER IN HELL(1933); ONLY YESTERDAY(1933)
Tommy Conlon
REBECCA OF SUNNYBROOK FARM(1932); SIGN OF THE CROSS, THE(1932); THOSE WE LOVE(1932); YOUNG AMERICA(1932); NO MAN OF HER OWN(1933)
Misc. Talkies
CONSTANT WOMAN, THE(1933)
William Conlon
Misc. Silents
IN MIZZOURA(1914)
Onest A. Conly
VENGEANCE(1930)
Onest Conly
THOROUGHBRED, THE(1930); THIS DAY AND AGE(1933)
Marie Conmee
AMBUSH IN LEOPARD STREET(1962, Brit.); STORK TALK(1964, Brit.); EDUCATING RITA(1983)
Billy Conn
PITTSBURGH KID, THE(1941)
Capt. Jacob Conn
FOUND ALIVE(1934), w
Didi Conn
RAGGEDY ANN AND ANDY(1977); YOU LIGHT UP MY LIFE(1977); ALMOST SUMMER(1978); GREASE(1978); GREASE 2(1982)
Frank Conn
YOU LIGHT UP MY LIFE(1977); CALIFORNIA SUITE(1978)
Harry W. Conn
TRANSATLANTIC MERRY-GO-ROUND(1934), w
Martin G. Conn
WILD HORSE ROUND-UP(1937), p; COUNTERFEITERS, THE(1948), ed
Maurice A. Conn
RACING BLOOD(1938), p
Maurice Conn
CODE OF THE MOUNTED(1935), p; FIGHTING TROOPER, THE(1935), p; NORTHERN FRONTIER(1935), p; TRAILS OF THE WILD(1935), p; WILDERNESS MAIL(1935), p; PHANTOM PATROL(1936), p; SONG OF THE TRAIL(1936), p; TIMBER WAR(1936), p; WILDCAT TROOPER(1936), p; FIGHTING TEXAN(1937), p; GALLOPING DYNAMITE(1937), p; HEADLINE CRASHER(1937), p; ROARING SIX GUNS(1937), p; ROUGH RIDIN' RHYTHM(1937), p; SING WHILE YOU'RE ABLE(1937), p; SWING IT, PROFESSOR(1937), p; THANKS FOR LISTENING(1937),

p; TOUGH TO HANDLE(1937), p; WHISTLING BULLETS(1937), p; WITH LOVE AND KISSES(1937), p; GUNSMOKE TRAIL(1938), p; LAND OF FIGHTING MEN(1938), p; PHANTOM RANGER(1938), p; TWO-GUN JUSTICE(1938), p; WEST OF RAINBOW'S END(1938), p; WHERE THE WEST BEGINS(1938), p; FRONTIER SCOUT(1939), p
Maurice D. Conn
DRAGNET(1974), p, w
Maurice H. Conn
HIS FIGHTING BLOOD(1935), p; COUNTERFEITERS, THE(1948), p, w; ZAMBA(1949), p, w
Tom D. Connachie
DEATH OF MICHAEL TURBIN, THE(1954, Brit.), p
Lit Connah
NIGHT THE LIGHTS WENT OUT IN GEORGIA, THE(1981)
Bob Connally
TAKE A CHANCE(1933), ch
Merrill Connally
CLOSE ENCOUNTERS OF THE THIRD KIND(1977)
Merrill L. Connally
SUGARLAND EXPRESS, THE(1974)
Jean-Paul Connart
LA BALANCE(1983, Fr.)
Richard Connaught
CLOCKWORK ORANGE, A(1971, Brit.); TALES THAT WITNESS MADNESS(1973, Brit.)
Shane Connaughton
1984
EVERY PICTURE TELLS A STORY(1984, Brit.), w; FOUR DAYS IN JULY(1984)
The Connecticut Yankees
VAGABOND LOVER(1929)
Barbara Connell
MAKE A FACE(1971), ed
Betty Connell
SHE-DEVILS ON WHEELS(1968)
Bill Connell
GREASED LIGHTNING(1977); STROKER ACE(1983)
Cayce Connell
SPRING FEVER(1983, Can.)
Charles Connell
RIDERS OF THE CACTUS(1931), p, w
David Connell
CROSS AND THE SWITCHBLADE, THE(1970); GORDON'S WAR(1973); WOLFEN(1981)
Del Connell
THREE CABALLEROS, THE(1944), w; ALICE IN WONDERLAND(1951), w
Diana Connell
DOUBLE CONFESSION(1953, Brit.)
Edward Connell
EQUINOX(1970)
Eric Connell
PORT AFRIQUE(1956, Brit.)
Gordon Connell
ROSEMARY'S BABY(1968)
Howard Connell
GORBALS STORY, THE(1950, Brit.); FABIAN OF THE YARD(1954, Brit.); FUSS OVER FEATHERS(1954, Brit.); LITTLE KIDNAPPERS, THE(1954, Brit.); MYSTERY ON BIRD ISLAND(1954, Brit.); SCOTCH ON THE ROCKS(1954, Brit.)
Jack Connell
GOODBYE GEMINI(1970, Brit.)
James Connell
WIZARDS(1977)
James R. Connell
UNTAMED WOMEN(1952), set d; GOLDEN MISTRESS, THE(1954), art d
Jane Connell
LADYBUG, LADYBUG(1963); TRUMAN CAPOTE'S TRILOGY(1969); KOTCH(1971); MAME(1974); WON TON TON, THE DOG WHO SAVED HOLLYWOOD(1976); HOUSE CALLS(1978); RABBIT TEST(1978)
Jim Connell
WILD ONE, THE(1953)
John Connell
FAIL SAFE(1964); THREE DAYS OF THE CONDOR(1975)
Laura Connell
OCEAN'S ELEVEN(1960)
Linda Connell
CAPE CANAVERAL MONSTERS(1960)
Maureen Connell
HELL, HEAVEN OR HOBOKEN(1958, Brit.); MURDER ON APPROVAL(1956, Brit.); PORT AFRIQUE(1956, Brit.); ABOMINABLE SNOWMAN OF THE HIMALAYAS, THE(1957, Brit.); LUCKY JIM(1957, Brit.); TOWN ON TRIAL(1957, Brit.); WHITE HUNTRESS(1957, Brit.); KILL HER GENTLY(1958, Brit.); STORMY CROSSING(1958, Brit.); CROWNING TOUCH, THE(1959, Brit.); MAN UPSTAIRS, THE(1959, Brit.); NEXT TO NO TIME(1960, Brit.); ECHO OF BARBARA(1961, Brit.); DANGER BY MY SIDE(1962, Brit.); SKYJACKED(1972)
Misc. Talkies
BLACK TIDE(1958)
Merle Connell
DEVIL'S SLEEP, THE(1951), d; UNEARTHLY, THE(1957), ph; CAPE CANAVERAL MONSTERS(1960), ph
Miranda Connell
ADMIRABLE CRICHTON, THE(1957, Brit.)
Paul Connell
YOU CAN'T BEAT THE IRISH(1952, Brit.); HELL BELOW ZERO(1954, Brit.); CONSTANT HUSBAND, THE(1955, Brit.); LADY GODIVA RIDES AGAIN(1955, Brit.); ONE DAY IN THE LIFE OF IVAN DENISOVICH(1971, U.S./Brit./Norway)
Richard Connell
DARK STREETS(1929), w; SEVEN FACES(1929), w; NOT DAMAGED(1930), w; MOST DANGEROUS GAME, THE(1932), w; F MAN(1936), w; MILKY WAY, THE(1936), w; OUR RELATIONS(1936), w; LOVE ON TOAST(1937), w; DR. RHYTHM(1938), w; BROTHER ORCHID(1940), w; HIRED WIFE(1940), w; MEET JOHN DOE(1941), w; NICE GIRL?(1941), w; RIO RITA(1942), w; PRESENTING LILY MARS(1943), w; TWO GIRLS AND A SAILOR(1944), w; GAME OF DEATH, A(1945),

w; HER HIGHNESS AND THE BELLBOY(1945), w; THRILL OF A ROMANCE(1945), w; KID FROM BOOKLYN, THE(1946), w; LUXURY LINER(1948), w; RUN FOR THE SUN(1956), w
Silents
PAINTED PEOPLE(1924), w; BRIGHT LIGHTS(1925), w; NEW YEAR'S EVE(1929), w

Thelma Connell
FOLLY TO BE WISE(1953), ed; BELLES OF ST. TRINIAN'S, THE(1954, Brit.), ed; TALE OF THREE WOMEN, A(1954, Brit.), d; LADY GODIVA RIDES AGAIN(1955, Brit.), ed; WEE GEORDIE(1956, Brit.), ed; NIGHT WE GOT THE BIRD, THE(1961, Brit.), ed; PURE HELL OF ST. TRINIAN'S, THE(1961, Brit.), ed; ONLY TWO CAN PLAY(1962, Brit.), ed; BARBER OF STAMFORD HILL, THE(1963, Brit.), ed; HIDE AND SEEK(1964, Brit.), ed; RING OF SPIES(1964, Brit.), ed; AMOROUS MR. PRAWN, THE(1965, Brit.), ed; DR. TERROR'S HOUSE OF HORRORS(1965, Brit.), ed; HILL, THE(1965, Brit.), ed; ALFIE(1966, Brit.), ed; DEADLY AFFAIR, THE(1967, Brit.), ed; ISLAND OF TERROR(1967, Brit.), ed; DANDY IN ASPIC, A(1968, Brit.), ed; APPOINT-MENT, THE(1969), ed; VIRGIN SOLDIERS, THE(1970, Brit.), ed; BUTTERCUP CHAIN, THE(1971, Brit.), ed; ONE DAY IN THE LIFE OF IVAN DENISOVICH(1971, U.S./Brit./Norway), ed; SEE NO EVIL(1971, Brit.), ed; PAUL AND MICHELLE(1974, Fr./Brit.), ed; TERRORISTS, THE(1975, Brit.), ed; OPERATION DAYBREAK(1976, U.S./Brit./Czech.), ed

Tracy Connell
RETURN OF MR. MOTO, THE(1965, Brit.)

W. Merle Connell
UNTAMED WOMEN(1952), d; FLESH MERCHANT, THE(1956), p&d

W.M. Connell
Misc. Talkies
TROUBLE AT MELODY MESA(1949), d

Barbara Connell,
MAKE A FACE(1971), w

Thelma Connelli
STRANGER ON THE PROWL(1953, Ital.), ed

Bobby Connelly
READY, WILLING AND ABLE(1937), ch; HONOLULU(1939), ch
Silents
ISLAND OF REGENERATION, THE(1915); PRINCE IN A PAWNSHOP, A(1916); OUT OF A CLEAR SKY(1918); CHILD FOR SALE, A(1920); SIN THAT WAS HIS, THE(1920); WIDE-OPEN TOWN, A(1922)
Misc. Silents
TURN OF THE ROAD, THE(1915); BRITTON OF THE SEVENTH(1916); FATHERS OF MEN(1916); LAW DECIDES, THE(1916); SUSPECT, THE(1916); HER RIGHT TO LIVE(1917); INTRIGUE(1917); BEYOND THE LAW(1918); WHAT LOVE FORGIVES(1919); OLD OAKEN BUCKET, THE(1921)

Chris Connelly
WHAT A WAY TO GO(1964); NORSEMAN, THE(1978)

Christopher Connelly
MOVE OVER, DARLING(1963); CORKY(1972); THEY ONLY KILL THEIR MASTERS(1972); BENJI(1974); HAWMPS!(1976); EARTHBOUND(1981); LIAR'S MOON(1982)
Misc. Talkies
RAIDERS OF ATLANTIS(1983)

Darlene Connelly
DIRTY HARRY(1971)

E.J. Connelly
Misc. Silents
SHORE ACRES(1914)

Ed Connelly
SKYJACKED(1972)
Silents
CONFLICT, THE(1921)

Edward Connelly
Misc. Talkies
BROTHERLY LOVE(1928)
Silents
EASY TO MAKE MONEY(1919); DANGEROUS TO MEN(1920); CONQUERING POWER, THE(1921); FOUR HORSEMEN OF THE APOCALYPSE, THE(1921); SAP-HEAD, THE(1921); KISSES(1922); PRISONER OF ZENDA, THE(1922); RED HOT ROMANCE(1922); SEEING'S BELIEVING(1922); HER FATAL MILLIONS(1923); SCARAMOUCHE(1923); SLAVE OF DESIRE(1923); GOLDFISH, THE(1924); REVELATION(1924); MERRY WIDOW, THE(1925); UNHOLY THREE, THE(1925); BROWN OF HARVARD(1926); TORRENT, THE(1926); ACROSS THE SINGAPORE(1928); MYSTERIOUS LADY, THE(1928); DESERT RIDER, THE(1929)
Misc. Silents
MARSE COVINGTON(1915); JEANNE OF THE GUTTER(1919); LION'S DEN, THE(1919); PARISIAN TIGRESS, THE(1919); CINDERELLA'S TWIN(1920); SHORE ACRES(1920); SOMEONE IN THE HOUSE(1920); WILLOW TREE, THE(1920); TRIFLING WOMEN(1922); WHERE THE PAVEMENT ENDS(1923); ONLY THING, THE(1925); LOVERS?(1927); SHOW, THE(1927); WINNERS OF THE WILDERNESS(1927); FORBIDDEN HOURS(1928)

Edward J. Connelly
Silents
FALSE EVIDENCE(1919); JOHNNY-ON-THE-SPOT(1919)
Misc. Silents
RED LANTERN, THE(1919)

Erwin Connelly
FAIR WARNING(1931); UNDER SUSPICION(1931)
Silents
MAN FROM BEYOND, THE(1922); BEGGAR ON HORSEBACK(1925); SEVEN CHANCES(1925); BLIND GODDESS, THE(1926); KIKI(1926); SON OF THE SHEIK(1926); WINNING OF BARBARA WORTH, THE(1926); CHEATING CHEATERS(1927); RUBBER TIRES(1927)

Glenn Connelly
WHERE WERE YOU WHEN THE LIGHTS WENT OUT?(1968), cos; WITH SIX YOU GET EGGROLL(1968), cos

Helen Connelly
Misc. Silents
HER RIGHT TO LIVE(1917)

Jack Connelly
Silents
OLD MAID'S BABY, THE(1919)
Misc. Silents
EGG CRATE WALLOP, THE(1919); ONE-WAY TRAIL, THE(1920)

Jane Connelly
Silents
MAN FROM BEYOND, THE(1922); SHERLOCK, JR.(1924)

Joe Connelly
PRIVATE WAR OF MAJOR BENSON, THE(1955), w; MUNSTER, GO HOME(1966), p, w; CHANGE OF HABIT(1969), p

John Connelly
WHY RUSSIANS ARE REVOLTING(1970)

Lex Connelly
J.W. COOP(1971)

Marc C. Connelly
Silents
WHISPERS(1920), w

Marc Connelly
NOT SO DUMB(1930), w; MAKE ME A STAR(1932), w; CRADLE SONG(1933), w; ELMER AND ELSIE(1934), w; GREEN PASTURES(1936), d, w; CAPTAINS COURAGEOUS(1937), w; DULCY(1940), w; WILD MAN OF BORNEO, THE(1941), w; I MARRIED A WITCH(1942), w; REUNION IN FRANCE(1942), w; IMPOSTER, THE(1944), w; MERTON OF THE MOVIES(1947), w; FABIOLA(1951, Ital.), w; CROWDED PARADISE(1956), w; SPIRIT OF ST. LOUIS, THE(1957); TALL STORY(1960)
Silents
DULCY(1923), w; MERTON OF THE MOVIES(1924), w; BEGGAR ON HORSEBACK(1925), w; EXIT SMILING(1926), w

Paul Connelly
TOP O' THE MORNING(1949)

Peggy Connelly
GIRL IN THE RED VELVET SWING, THE(1955); HOUSEBOAT(1958)

Randolph Connelly
SECRETS(1933)

Regina Connelly
Misc. Silents
HOODMAN BLIND(1923)

Walter Connelly
Misc. Silents
MARKED WOMAN, THE(1914)

Allen Conner
WOMEN WITHOUT NAMES(1940)

David Conner
CROSS COUNTRY(1983, Can.)

Edric Conner
FIRE DOWN BELOW(1957, U.S./Brit.)

Francis Conner
MISTER ROBERTS(1955)

Gilbert Conner
PILLARS OF THE SKY(1956)

Jeremy Conner
CARRY ON ENGLAND(1976, Brit.)

Kenneth Conner
CARRY ON CABBIE(1963, Brit.)

Kevin Conner
LAND THAT TIME FORGOT, THE(1975, Brit.), d

Paige Conner
VISITOR, THE(1980, Ital./U.S.)

Robert Conner
LAUGHING LADY, THE(1950, Brit.)

Tami Conner
SING, BOY, SING(1958)

W.A. Conner
Misc. Talkies
COCAINE FIENDS(1937), d

Whitfield Conner
SARACEN BLADE, THE(1954)

Alice Conners
EACH DAWN I DIE(1939)

B. Richard Conners
SCAVENGERS, THE(1969), ed

Barry Conners
BLACK CAMEL, THE(1931), w; SPIDER, THE(1931), w; BACHELOR'S AFFAIRS(1932), w; CHANDU THE MAGICIAN(1932), w; TOO BUSY TO WORK(1932), w; TRIAL OF VIVIENNE WARE, THE(1932), w; HOT PEPPER(1933), w; ALWAYS A BRIDE(1940), w; PIER 13(1940), w

Buck Conners
TRAILS OF DANGER(1930)
Misc. Silents
OUTLAWED(1921); BIFF BANG BUDDY(1924)

Harry Conners
BRIDES ARE LIKE THAT(1936), w

Julie Conners
CURIOUS FEMALE, THE(1969); COUNT YORGA, VAMPIRE(1970)

Ralph Conners
RAW WEEKEND(1964)

Ray Conners
WRONG IS RIGHT(1982)

William Conners
SWEET TRASH(1970)

Jason Connery
LORDS OF DISCIPLINE, THE(1983)
1984
DREAM ONE(1984, Brit./Fr.)

Neil Connery
OPERATION KID BROTHER(1967, Ital.); BODY STEALERS, THE(1969)
Misc. Talkies
OUT OF THIN AIR(1969)

Sean Connery
ZARDOZ(; LET'S MAKE UP(1955, Brit.); ACTION OF THE TIGER(1957); NO ROAD BACK(1957, Brit.); ANOTHER TIME, ANOTHER PLACE(1958); HELL DRIVERS(1958, Brit.); NIGHT TO REMEMBER, A(1958, Brit.); DARBY O'GILL AND THE LITTLE PEOPLE(1959); TARZAN'S GREATEST ADVENTURE(1959, Brit.); TIME LOCK(1959, Brit.); FRIGHTENED CITY, THE(1961, Brit.); DR. NO(1962, Brit.); LONGEST DAY, THE(1962); FROM RUSSIA WITH LOVE(1963, Brit.); GOLDFINGER(1964, Brit.); MARNIE(1964); WOMAN OF STRAW(1964, Brit.); HILL, THE(1965, Brit.); OPERATION SNAFU(1965, Brit.); THUNDERBALL(1965, Brit.); FINE MADNESS, A(1966); YOU ONLY LIVE TWICE(1967, Brit.); SHALAKO(1968, Brit.); MOLLY MAGUIRES, THE(1970); ANDERSON TAPES, THE(1971); DIAMONDS ARE FOREVER(1971, Brit.); RED TENT, THE(1971, Ital./USSR); MURDER ON THE ORIENT EXPRESS(1974, Brit.); MAN WHO WOULD BE KING, THE(1975, Brit.); TERRORISTS, THE(1975, Brit.); WIND AND THE LION, THE(1975); NEXT MAN, THE(1976); ROBIN AND MARIAN(1976, Brit.); BRIDGE TOO FAR, A(1977, Brit.); CUBA(1979); GREAT TRAIN ROBBERY, THE(1979, Brit.); METEOR(1979); OUTLAND(1981); TIME BANDITS(1981, Brit.); FIVE DAYS ONE SUMMER(1982); WRONG IS RIGHT(1982); NEVER SAY NEVER AGAIN(1983)
1984
SWORD OF THE VALIANT(1984, Brit.)
Robert Conness
Silents
GLADIOLA(1915); HOUSE OF THE LOST CORD, THE(1915); JUNE FRIDAY(1915); PAIR OF SIXES, A(1918)
Misc. Silents
CHILDREN OF EVE, THE(1915); ON DANGEROUS PATHS(1915); PLOUGHSHARE, THE(1915); TRAGEDIES OF THE CRYSTAL GLOBE, THE(1915); TRUTH ABOUT HELEN, THE(1915); MARTYRDOM OF PHILLIP STRONG, THE(1916); MESSAGE TO GARCIA, A(1916); WITCHING HOUR, THE(1916); GHOST OF OLD MORRO, THE(1917); MASTER PASSION, THE(1917); RAINBOW, THE(1917); SONG OF SIXPENCE, A(1917)
Cecil Conney
MADNESS OF THE HEART(1949, Brit.), ph
Tom D. Connochie
LAST MOMENT, THE(1954, Brit.), p
James Connock
NO ROAD BACK(1957, Brit.), ed
Jim Connock
MASTER PLAN, THE(1955, Brit.), ed; SHADOW OF FEAR(1956, Brit.), ed; MAN IN THE ROAD, THE(1957, Brit.), ed; HOT MONEY GIRL(1962, Brit./Ger.), ed; NAKED WORLD OF HARRISON MARKS, THE(1967, Brit.), ed; HANNIE CALDER(1971, Brit.), ed; WELCOME TO THE CLUB(1971), ed; DIGBY, THE BIGGEST DOG IN THE WORLD(1974, Brit.), ed
Roger Connock
CHRISTINE KEELER AFFAIR, THE(1964, Brit.), m
Ginger Connolley
SUBWAY EXPRESS(1931)
Barbara Connolly
Misc. Silents
LITTLE RED DECIDES(1918)
Billy Connolly
ABSOLUTION(1981, Brit.)
Bob Connolly
I DOOD IT(1943), ch
Bobby Connolly
MOONLIGHT AND PRETZELS(1933), ch; FLIRTATION WALK(1934), ch; BROADWAY HOSTESS(1935), ch; G-MEN(1935), ch; SHIPMATES FOREVER(1935), ch; STARS OVER BROADWAY(1935), ch; SWEET ADELINE(1935), ch; SWEET MUSIC(1935), ch; CAIN AND MABEL(1936), ch; COLLEEN(1936), ch; SING ME A LOVE SONG(1936), ch; SINGING KID, THE(1936), ch; SONS O' GUNS(1936), ch; DEVIL'S SADDLE LEGION, THE(1937), d; EXPENSIVE HUSBANDS(1937), p&d; KING AND THE CHORUS GIRL, THE(1937), ch; MELODY FOR TWO(1937), ch; FOOLS FOR SCANDAL(1938), d; PATIENT IN ROOM 18, THE(1938), d; SWING YOUR LADY(1938), ch; AT THE CIRCUS(1939), ch; WIZARD OF OZ, THE(1939), ch; BROADWAY MELODY OF 1940(1940), ch; TWO GIRLS ON BROADWAY(1940), ch; FOR ME AND MY GAL(1942), ch; SHIP AHOY(1942), ch
Christopher Connolly
1990: THE BRONX WARRIORS(1983, Ital.)
Edward Connolly
Silents
IN OLD KENTUCKY(1920)
Erwin Connolly
Silents
SHERLOCK, JR.(1924)
Ginger Connolly
TOAST OF NEW YORK, THE(1937)
Jack Connolly
Silents
LITTLE PATRIOT, A(1917); DOLLY'S VACATION(1918); WOLVERINE, THE(1921); WOMAN'S PLACE(1921); NIGHT LIFE IN HOLLYWOOD(1922); MYSTERIOUS WITNESS, THE(1923)
Misc. Silents
BLUEBEARD, JR.(; GATES OF DOOM, THE(1917); JEWEL IN PAWN, A(1917); MATE OF THE SALLY ANN, THE(1917); MILADY O' THE BEAN STALK(1918); VOICE OF DESTINY, THE(1918); LITTLE DIPLOMAT, THE(1919); SAWDUST DOLL, THE(1919); BUBBLES(1920); LINCOLN HIGHWAYMAN, THE(1920); TOO MUCH MARRIED(1921); BROADWAY MADONNA, THE(1922)
James Connolly
DAY THE FISH CAME OUT(1967. Brit./Gr.)
John M. Connolly, Capt. USN
ICE STATION ZEBRA(1968), tech adv
John Connolly
1984
HARD CHOICES(1984)
Michael Connolly
1984
MUPPETS TAKE MANHATTAN, THE(1984)

Mike Connolly
I'LL CRY TOMORROW(1955), w
Molly Connolly
PRIMROSE PATH, THE(1934, Brit.)
Myles Connolly
VERY IDEA, THE(1929), p; HE KNEW WOMEN(1930), p; HOOK, LINE AND SINKER(1930), p; CONSOLATION MARRIAGE(1931), m; SIN SHIP(1931), p; FACE IN THE SKY(1933), w; RIGHT TO ROMANCE(1933), w; HIS GREATEST GAMBLE(1934), p; LET'S TRY AGAIN(1934), p; PALM SPRINGS(1936), w; I PROMISE TO PAY(1937), p; IT HAPPENED IN HOLLYWOOD(1937), w; WIVES UNDER SUSPICION(1938), w; YOUTH TAKES A FLING(1938), w; HOUSE ACROSS THE BAY, THE(1940), w; MAISIE WAS A LADY(1941), w; TARZAN'S SECRET TREASURE(1941), w; BETWEEN US GIRLS(1942), w; TARZAN'S NEW YORK ADVENTURE(1942), w; MUSIC FOR MILLIONS(1944), w; STRANGE MR. GREGORY, THE(1945), w; TILL THE CLOUDS ROLL BY(1946), w; TWO SISTERS FROM BOSTON(1946), w; UNFINISHED DANCE,THE(1947), w; STATE OF THE UNION(1948), w; HERE COMES THE GROOM(1951), w; HANS CHRISTIAN ANDERSEN(1952), w; MY SON, JOHN(1952), w
Nora Connolly
1984
RAZOR'S EDGE, THE(1984)
Norma Connolly
WRONG MAN, THE(1956); THIRD OF A MAN(1962); OTHER, THE(1972); THEY ONLY KILL THEIR MASTERS(1972)
Patricia Connolly
COLOR ME DEAD(1969, Aus.)
Peggy Connolly
1984
BLOOD SIMPLE(1984), ed
Randolph Connolly
DARK ANGEL, THE(1935)
Ray Connolly
STARDUST(1974, Brit.), w; THAT'LL BE THE DAY(1974, Brit.), w
1984
FOREVER YOUNG(1984, Brit.), w
Rita Connolly
Silents
AUDREY(1916)
Sybil Connolly
TROUBLE WITH ANGELS, THE(1966), cos
Tame Connolly
LOVE CHILD(1982)
Walter Connolly
MAN AGAINST WOMAN(1932); WASHINGTON MERRY-GO-ROUND(1932); BITTER TEA OF GENERAL YEN, THE(1933); EAST OF FIFTH AVE.(1933); LADY FOR A DAY(1933); MAN'S CASTLE, A(1933); MASTER OF MEN(1933); NO MORE ORCHIDS(1933); PADDY, THE NEXT BEST THING(1933); BROADWAY BILL(1934); CAPTAIN HATES THE SEA, THE(1934); EIGHT GIRLS IN A BOAT(1934); IT HAPPENED ONE NIGHT(1934); LADY BY CHOICE(1934); ONCE TO EVERY WOMAN(1934); SERVANTS' ENTRANCE(1934); TWENTIETH CENTURY(1934); WHOM THE GODS DESTROY(1934); FATHER BROWN, DETECTIVE(1935); ONE-WAY TICKET(1935); SHE COULDN'T TAKE IT(1935); SO RED THE ROSE(1935); WHITE LIES(1935); KING STEPS OUT, THE(1936); LIBELED LADY(1936); MUSIC GOES ROUND, THE(1936); SOAK THE RICH(1936); FIRST LADY(1937); GOOD EARTH, THE(1937); LEAGUE OF FRIGHTENED MEN(1937); LET'S GET MARRIED(1937); NANCY STEELE IS MISSING(1937); NOTHING SACRED(1937); FOUR'S A CROWD(1938); GIRL DOWNSTAIRS, THE(1938); PENITENTIARY(1938); START CHEERING(1938); TOO HOT TO HANDLE(1938); BRIDAL SUITE(1939); COAST GUARD(1939); FIFTH AVENUE GIRL(1939); GOOD GIRLS GO TO PARIS(1939); GREAT VICTOR HERBERT, THE(1939); HUCKLEBERRY FINN(1939); THOSE HIGH GREY WALLS(1939)
Bobby Connolly
GO INTO YOUR DANCE(1935), ch
Barry Connons
GAY CABALLERO, THE(1932), w
Alan Connor
DUKE OF WEST POINT, THE(1938)
Alice Connor
COMET OVER BROADWAY(1938)
Allan Connor
Silents
LINDA(1929)
Allen Connor
KISS BEFORE THE MIRROR, THE(1933); MAGNIFICENT OBSESSION(1935); THREE MESQUITEERS, THE(1936); GUNSMOKE RANCH(1937)
Silents
ISLE OF LOST MEN(1928)
Bob Connor
VENGEANCE IS MINE(1948, Brit.)
Buck Connor
WESTERNER, THE(1940)
Della Connor
Silents
DANGER SIGNAL, THE(1915); SENTIMENTAL LADY, THE(1915); SCARLET ROAD, THE(1916)
Misc. Silents
COMMUTORS, THE(1915); GREEN CLOAK, THE(1915); WHO'S WHO IN SOCIETY(1915); WOMAN NEXT DOOR, THE(1915)
Edgar Connor
KID FROM SPAIN, THE(1932); HALLELUJAH, I'M A BUM(1933)
Edric Connor
CRY, THE BELOVED COUNTRY(1952, Brit.); HEART OF THE MATTER, THE(1954, Brit.), m; WEST OF ZANZIBAR(1954, Brit.); MOBY DICK(1956, Brit.); ROOTS OF HEAVEN, THE(1958); VIKINGS, THE(1958); BEASTS OF MARSEILLES, THE(1959, Brit.); VIRGIN ISLAND(1960, Brit.); KING OF KINGS(1961); FOUR FOR TEXAS(1963); ONLY WHEN I LARF(1968, Brit.)
Edward Connor
Silents
ANNE OF LITTLE SMOKY(1921), d, w

Elisa Connor
EASY LIVING(1937)
Frank Connor
LET'S DO IT AGAIN(1953); BATTLE STATIONS(1956); THESE WILDER YEARS(1956); BEGINNING OF THE END(1957)
Gene Connor
FANDANGO(1970)
Joe Connor
SOUTH SEA WOMAN(1953)
Kenneth Connor
POISON PEN(1941, Brit.); DON'T SAY DIE(1950, Brit.); MARILYN(1953, Brit.); THERE WAS A YOUNG LADY(1953, Brit.); BLACK RIDER, THE(1954, Brit.); LADYKILLERS, THE(1956, Brit.); DAVY(1958, Brit.); CARRY ON NURSE(1959, Brit.); CARRY ON SERGEANT(1959, Brit.); CARRY ON CONSTABLE(1960, Brit.); DENTIST IN THE CHAIR(1960, Brit.); CARRY ON REGARDLESS(1961, Brit.); HIS AND HERS(1961, Brit.); WATCH YOUR STERN(1961, Brit.); WEEKEND WITH LULU, A(1961, Brit.); CARRY ON CRUISING(1962, Brit.); CARRY ON TEACHER(1962, Brit.); NEARLY A NASTY ACCIDENT(1962, Brit.); WHAT A CARVE UP!(1962, Brit.); GET ON WITH IT(1963, Brit.); CARRY ON CLEO(1964, Brit.); CUCKOO PATROL(1965, Brit.); GONKS GO BEAT(1965, Brit.); MAKE MINE A MILLION(1965, Brit.); CAPTAIN NEMO AND THE UNDERWATER CITY(1969, Brit.); CARRY ON HENRY VIII(1970, Brit.); CARRY ON UP THE JUNGLE(1970, Brit.); CARRY ON ENGLAND(1976, Brit.); CARRY ON EMANUELLE(1978, Brit.)
Misc. Talkies
CARRY ON GIRLS(1974, Brit.)
Kevin Connor
OH! WHAT A LOVELY WAR(1969, Brit.), ed; MAGIC CHRISTIAN, THE(1970, Brit.), ed; ROMANCE OF A HORSE THIEF(1971), ed; YOUNG WINSTON(1972, Brit.), ed; HITLER: THE LAST TEN DAYS(1973, Brit./Ital.), ed; FROM BEYOND THE GRAVE(1974, Brit.), d; AT THE EARTH'S CORE(1976, Brit.), d; DIRTY KNIGHT'S WORK(1976, Brit.), d; PEOPLE THAT TIME FORGOT, THE(1977, Brit.), d; WARLORDS OF ATLANTIS(1978, Brit.), d; ARABIAN ADVENTURE(1979, Brit.), d; MOTEL HELL(1980, d; HOUSE WHERE EVIL DWELLS, THE(1982), d
Michael Connor
THIRD MAN, THE(1950, Brit.)
Paige Connor
NIGHT THEY ROBBED BIG BERTHA'S, THE(1975); LITTLE DARLINGS(1980)
Patrick Connor
HELL, HEAVEN OR HOBOKEN(1958, Brit.); KILL HER GENTLY(1958, Brit.); HEADLESS GHOST, THE(1959, Brit.); QUEEN'S GUARDS, THE(1963, Brit.); STRANGE AFFAIR, THE(1968, Brit.); FLAME(1975, Brit.); EYE OF THE NEEDLE(1981)
Philip Connor
WESTERNER, THE(1940)
Ralph Connor
Silents
SKY PILOT, THE(1921), w; CRITICAL AGE, THE(1923), w
Reardon Connor
SHAKE HANDS WITH THE DEVIL(1959, Ireland), w
Tami Connor
PEYTON PLACE(1957)
Tim Connor
MASTER MINDS(1949); SHE KNOWS Y'KNOW(1962, Brit.)
Trudy Connor
SINGAPORE, SINGAPORE(1969, Fr./Ital.)
Una O. Connor
CLUNY BROWN(1946)
Velma Connor
Misc. Silents
SCRAPPIN' KID, THE(1926); TERROR, THE(1926)
Whitfield Connor
TAP ROOTS(1948); SCARLET ANGEL(1952); CITY OF BAD MEN(1953); PRESIDENT'S LADY, THE(1953); PRINCE OF PIRATES(1953); BUTTERFIELD 8(1960)
Willis Connor
QUICK, LET'S GET MARRIED(1965), art d
Alice Connors
ESPIONAGE AGENT(1939); OFF THE RECORD(1939); WOMEN IN THE WIND(1939)
Barry Connors
CHARLIE CHAN CARRIES ON(1931), w; RIDERS OF THE PURPLE SAGE(1931), w; WOMEN OF ALL NATIONS(1931), w; CHARLIE CHAN'S CHANCE(1932), w; HAT CHECK GIRL(1932), w; ME AND MY GAL(1932), w; RAINBOW TRAIL(1932), w; PILGRIMAGE(1933), w
Barry L. Connors
MIAMI EXPOSE(1956)
Buck Connors
HELL'S HEROES(1930); DAWN TRAIL, THE(1931); DESERT VENGEANCE(1931); LAST ROUND-UP, THE(1934); THUNDERING HERD, THE(1934); ALIAS JOHN LAW(1935); NO MAN'S RANGE(1935); LAW RIDES, THE(1936); WEST OF SANTA FE(1938)
Silents
TRACKED TO EARTH(1922); BACK TRAIL, THE(1924); YELLOW BACK, THE(1926); GRIT WINS(1929)
Misc. Silents
PHANTOM RIDERS, THE(1918); ACTION(1921); MOJAVE KID, THE(1927); SHOOTING STRAIGHT(1927); SLINGSHOT KID, THE(1927); CRIMSON CANYON, THE(1928); PHANTOM FLYER, THE(1928)
Bull Connors
COMMON LAW WIFE(1963)
Carol Connors
RED LINE 7000(1965); CATALINA CAPER, THE(1967); CHEAPER TO KEEP HER(1980), m/l
Misc. Talkies
ROAD OF DEATH(1977)
Chuck Connors
PAT AND MIKE(1952); DRAGONFLY SQUADRON(1953); SOUTH SEA WOMAN(1953); TROUBLE ALONG THE WAY(1953); HUMAN JUNGLE, THE(1954); NAKED ALIBI(1954); GOOD MORNING, MISS DOVE(1955); TARGET ZERO(1955); THREE STRIPES IN THE SUN(1955); HOLD BACK THE NIGHT(1956); HOT ROD GIRL(1956); WALK THE DARK STREET(1956); DEATH IN SMALL DOSES(1957);

DESIGNING WOMAN(1957); HIRED GUN, THE(1957); OLD YELLER(1957); TOMAHAWK TRAIL(1957); BIG COUNTRY, THE(1958); LADY TAKES A FLYER, THE(1958); GERONIMO(1962); FLIPPER(1963); MOVE OVER, DARLING(1963); SYNANON(1965); CAPTAIN NEMO AND THE UNDERWATER CITY(1969, Brit.); KILL THEM ALL AND COME BACK ALONE(1970, Ital./Span.); DESERTER, THE(1971 Ital./Yugo.); SUPPORT YOUR LOCAL GUNFIGHTER(1971); EMBASSY(1972, Brit.); PROUD AND THE DAMNED, THE(1972); MAD BOMBER, THE(1973); SOYLENT GREEN(1973); 99 AND 44/100% DEAD(1974); PANCHO VILLA(1975, Span.); WOLF LARSEN(1978, Ital.); TOURIST TRAP, THE(1979); VIRUS(1980, Jap.); AIRPLANE II: THE SEQUEL(1982);
Misc. Talkies
UNDER THE SIGN OF CAPRICORN(1971); TARGET EAGLE(1982)
Floraine Connors
UNSTRAP ME(1968)
George Connors
Silents
JAWS OF STEEL(1927)
Misc. Silents
BRONCHO BUSTER, THE(1927); HANDS OFF(1927)
Jim Connors
STAR SPANGLED GIRL(1971); CANNONBALL(1976, U.S./Hong Kong)
Joan Connors
DIARY OF A HIGH SCHOOL BRIDE(1959); TANK COMMANDOS(1959); DIME WITH A HALO(1963); GUN HAWK, THE(1963); SANDPIPER, THE(1965)
John Connors
FIRST TRAVELING SALESLADY, THE(1956)
Julie Connors
Misc. Talkies
SINNER'S BLOOD(1970)
Kasey Connors
I'M DANCING AS FAST AS I CAN(1982)
Katherine Connors
CARIBBEAN MYSTERY, THE(1945)
Kathleen Connors
13 MEN AND A GUN(1938, Brit.), w; FATAL NIGHT, THE(1948, Brit.), w; TONIGHT'S THE NIGHT(1954, Brit.), ed
Misc. Silents
HELL ROARIN' REFORM(1919)
Kay Connors
LAURA(1944); DO YOU LOVE ME?(1946); IF I'M LUCKY(1946); RENDEZVOUS 24(1946)
Michael Connors
LIVE FAST, DIE YOUNG(1958); SUICIDE BATTALION(1958); DALTON THAT GOT AWAY(1960); GOOD NEIGHBOR SAM(1964); PANIC BUTTON(1964); WHERE LOVE HAS GONE(1964); HARLOW(1965); SITUATION HOPELESS–BUT NOT SERIOUS(1965); STAGECOACH(1966); KISS THE GIRLS AND MAKE THEM DIE(1967, U.S./Ital.)
Michael "Touch" Connors
DAY OF TRIUMPH(1954); FIVE GUNS WEST(1955); DAY THE WORLD ENDED, THE(1956)
Mike Connors
AVALANCHE EXPRESS(1979)
Susan Connors
1984
HIGHPOINT(1984, Can.)
Tom Connors
NATIVE LAND(1942)
Touch [Michael] Connors
SUDDEN FEAR(1952); FORTY-NINTH MAN, THE(1953); ISLAND IN THE SKY(1953); SKY COMMANDO(1953); TWINKLE IN GOD'S EYE, THE(1955); OKLAHOMA WOMAN, THE(1956); SWAMP WOMEN(1956); TEN COMMANDMENTS, THE(1956); FLESH AND THE SPUR(1957); SHAKE, RATTLE, AND ROCK!(1957); VOODOO WOMAN(1957)
Debbie Connoyer
JAWS 3-D(1983)
Alberto Conocchia
8 ½(1963, Ital.)
Mario Conocchia
LA DOLCE VITA(1961, Ital./Fr.); 8 ½(1963, Ital.); JULIET OF THE SPIRITS(1965, Fr./Ital./W.Ger.)
Dennis Conoley
ON THE RUN(1969, Brit.)
Billy Conolly
BULLSHOT(1983)
Dickie Conon
GOLDEN GLOVES STORY, THE(1950)
Brucie Conover
FROM THE MIXED-UP FILES OF MRS. BASIL E. FRANKWEILER(1973)
Holly Conover
SEABO(1978)
Teresa Conover
TWO WISE MAIDS(1937)
Theresa Conover
SILVER DOLLAR(1932)
Theresa Maxwell Conover
QUEEN HIGH(1930); KID FROM SPAIN, THE(1932); BRIEF MOMENT(1933); MEN OF AMERICA(1933); CHAINED(1934); HALF A SINNER(1934); MISSISSIPPI(1935); NIGHT LIFE OF THE GODS(1935); PETER IBBETSON(1935); RAINBOW ON THE RIVER(1936); FREE AND EASY(1941)
Silents
JUST SYLVIA(1918); DAUGHTER PAYS, THE(1920); LIGHT IN THE DARK, THE(1922); WHEN KNIGHTHOOD WAS IN FLOWER(1922)
Theresa Maxwell Conovor
MIGHTY BARNUM, THE(1934)
Conrad
Misc. Talkies
COUNTRY BLUE(1975), d

Alan Conrad
BARRETTS OF WIMPOLE STREET, THE(1934); SURVIVAL RUN(1980)
1984
EVIL THAT MEN DO, THE(1984)
Arthur Conrad
Silents
NIGHT PATROL, THE(1926)
Barbara Conrad
Silents
LOST CHORD, THE(1917, Brit.)
Misc. Silents
IN SEARCH OF A HUSBAND(1915, Brit.); VERDICT OF THE HEART, THE(1915, Brit.); LITTLE DAMOZEL, THE(1916, Brit.)
Barnaby Conrad
FLIGHT(1960)
Barraby Conrad
FLIGHT(1960), w
Bart Conrad
FIVE FINGER EXERCISE(1962); MISTER BUDDWING(1966)
Charles Conrad
STORM WARNING(1950); GUY WHO CAME BACK, THE(1951); I'VE LIVED BEFORE(1956); PLUNDER ROAD(1957)
Charles J. Conrad
PEGGY(1950); TATTERED DRESS, THE(1957); HELL'S FIVE HOURS(1958)
Christopher Conrad
BORN AGAIN(1978)
Con Conrad
SONG OF KENTUCKY(1929), w; THEY HAD TO SEE PARIS(1929), m; FOX MOVIE-TONE FOLLIES OF 1930(1930), m
Connie Conrad
KNICKERBOCKER HOLIDAY(1944); DEADLINE AT DAWN(1946); KNOCK ON ANY DOOR(1949)
Ed Conrad
HOT MONEY(1936); SHE KNEW ALL THE ANSWERS(1941)
Eddie Conrad
BLAZE O' GLORY(1930); MELODY LINGERS ON, THE(1935); STARS OVER BROADWAY(1935); BIG BROWN EYES(1936); HAPPY LANDING(1938); I'LL GIVE A MILLION(1938); JUST AROUND THE CORNER(1938); ADVENTURES OF JANE ARDEN(1939); IN OLD MONTEREY(1939); I WAS AN ADVENTURESS(1940); SAPS AT SEA(1940); BEHIND THE NEWS(1941); HURRY, CHARLIE, HURRY(1941); INVISIBLE WOMAN, THE(1941); MURDER AMONG FRIENDS(1941); YOU'RE THE ONE(1941)
Eddy Conrad
EVERY NIGHT AT EIGHT(1935); I LIVE FOR LOVE(1935); BOY MEETS GIRL(1938); GATEWAY(1938); MY LUCKY STAR(1938); ROMANCE IN THE DARK(1938); ICE FOLLIES OF 1939(1939); MIDNIGHT(1939); TOPPER TAKES A TRIP(1939); FOREIGN CORRESPONDENT(1940); MAN FROM MONTREAL, THE(1940); INTERNATIONAL SQUADRON(1941); LADY SCARFACE(1941); ROAD TO ZANZIBAR(1941); THAT NIGHT IN RIO(1941); WEST POINT WIDOW(1941)
Edith Conrad
LADY BY CHOICE(1934); UNEXPECTED UNCLE(1941); SEVENTH VICTIM, THE(1943)
Edward Conrad
CHAD HANNA(1940); DOWN ARGENTINE WAY(1940); LUCKY PARTNERS(1940); GREAT AMERICAN BROADCAST, THE(1941)
Eugene Conrad
ABOUT FACE(1942), w; MOONLIGHT IN VERMONT(1943), w; SING A JINGLE(1943), w; YANKS AHOY(1943), w; BABES ON SWING STREET(1944), w; CHIP OFF THE OLD BLOCK(1944), w; HI, GOOD-LOOKIN'(1944), w; MOONLIGHT AND CACTUS(1944), w; MY GAL LOVES MUSIC(1944), w; PARDON MY RHYTHM(1944), w; SINGING SHERIFF, THE(1944), w; SWING OUT, SISTER(1944), w; GAS HOUSE KIDS GO WEST(1947), w; LOVE AND LEARN(1947), w; PHILO VANCE'S GAMBLE(1947), w; COBRA STRIKES, THE(1948), w
Frank Conrad
ON THE YARD(1978)
Gabriel Conrad
BUSHWHACKERS, THE(1952)
George Conrad
JACKPOT, THE(1950); FIXED BAYONETS(1951); HALLS OF MONTEZUMA(1951); IT'S A BIG COUNTRY(1951); BIG BLUFF, THE(1955)
Harold Conrad
SUNNY SIDE OF THE STREET(1951), w; BEYOND THE LAW(1968); WILD 90(1968); MAIDSTONE(1970); GREATEST, THE(1977, U.S./Brit.)
Hildegard Conrad
NAKED AMONG THE WOLVES(1967, Ger.), ed
Jack Conrad
SURRENDER(1931); GLASS ALIBI, THE(1946); BRASHER DOUBLOON, THE(1947); ROAD TO THE BIG HOUSE(1947); MONKEY HUSTLE, THE(1976), m; HOWLING, THE(1981), p
Misc. Talkies
COUNTRY BLUE(1975)
Jack H. Conrad
MOONCHILD(1972), ed
Jan Conrad
HARRY BLACK AND THE TIGER(1958, Brit.); MAN WHO WOULDN'T TALK, THE(1958, Brit.); MISSILE FROM HELL(1960, Brit.); SILENT INVASION, THE(1962, Brit.); MOUSE ON THE MOON, THE(1963, Brit.); HEROES OF TELEMARK, THE(1965, Brit.); ISADORA(1968, Brit.)
Jean Conrad
FURTHER UP THE CREEK!(1958, Brit.)
Jess Conrad
UGLY DUCKLING, THE(1959, Brit.); TOO YOUNG TO LOVE(1960, Brit.); KONGA(1961, Brit.); BOYS, THE(1962, Brit.); YOUNG, WILLING AND EAGER(1962, Brit.); FRIENDS AND NEIGHBORS(1963, Brit.); QUEEN'S GUARDS, THE(1963, Brit.); GOLDEN HEAD, THE(1965, Hung., U.S.); SKIN GAME, THE(1965, Brit.); HELL IS EMPTY(1967, Brit./Ital); ASSASSINATION BUREAU, THE(1969, Brit.); COOL IT, CAROL!(1970, Brit.)
Misc. Talkies
ALIKI-MY LOVE(1963, U.S./Gr.); DIRTIEST GIRL I EVER MET, THE(1973)

Jim Conrad
CURE FOR LOVE, THE(1950, Brit.)
Johnny Conrad
ONCE UPON A COFFEE HOUSE(1965), ch
Joseph Conrad
DANGEROUS PARADISE(1930), w; SABOTAGE(1937, Brit.), w; VICTORY(1940), w; FACE TO FACE(1952), w; OUTCAST OF THE ISLANDS(1952, Brit.), w; LAUGHING ANNE(1954, Brit./U.S.), w; LORD JIM(1965, Brit.), w; ROVER, THE(1967, Ital.), w; DUELLISTS, THE(1977, Brit.), w
Silents
LORD JIM(1925), w; RESCUE, THE(1929), w
Karen Conrad
SHOCK CORRIDOR(1963); NAKED KISS, THE(1964)
Les Conrad
1984
CHAMPIONS(1984)
Linda Conrad
DEMON LOVER, THE(1977)
Mabel Conrad
INVISIBLE AGENT(1942)
Marion Conrad
WHAT'S NEW, PUSSYCAT?(1965, U.S./Fr.)
Mark Conrad
STACY'S KNIGHTS(1983)
Maxine Conrad
$1,000 A TOUCHDOWN(1939); TWO GIRLS ON BROADWAY(1940)
Michael Conrad
REQUIEM FOR A HEAVYWEIGHT(1962); WAR LORD, THE(1965); BLACKBEARD'S GHOST(1968); SOL MADRID(1968); THREE GUNS FOR TEXAS(1968); CASTLE KEEP(1969); THEY SHOOT HORSES, DON'T THEY?(1969); MONTE WALSH(1970); HEAD ON(1971); TODD KILLINGS, THE(1971); COP, A(1973, Fr.); SCREAM BLACULA SCREAM(1973); LONGEST YARD, THE(1974); W(1974); BABY BLUE MARINE(1976); HARRY AND WALTER GO TO NEW YORK(1976); CATTLE ANNIE AND LITTLE BRITCHES(1981)
Mike Conrad
GANGSTER, THE(1947); BANDIT QUEEN(1950); THUMB TRIPPING(1972)
Mikel Conrad
BORDER FEUD(1947); UNTAMED FURY(1947); CHECK YOUR GUNS(1948); MAN FROM COLORADO, THE(1948); PHANTOM VALLEY(1948); ABBOTT AND COSTELLO MEET THE KILLER, BORIS KARLOFF(1949); ARCTIC MANHUNT(1949); FRANCIS(1949); MR. SOFT TOUCH(1949); SAND(1949); TAKE ONE FALSE STEP(1949); FLYING SAUCER, THE(1950), a, p&d, w; MILLION DOLLAR PURSUIT(1951); HOODLUM EMPIRE(1952); UNTAMED WOMEN(1952)
Nancy Conrad
MURPH THE SURF(1974)
Misc. Talkies
SUDDEN DEATH(1977)
Paul Conrad
EVER SINCE VENUS(1944); U-BOAT PRISONER(1944); DOCKS OF NEW ORLEANS(1948)
Pete Conrad
HOT STUFF(1979); PORKY'S(1982); PORKY'S II: THE NEXT DAY(1983)
Peter Conrad
FUNHOUSE, THE(1981); SMOKEY AND THE BANDIT-PART 3(1983)
Randall Conrad
EDGE, THE(1968); DOZENS, THE(1981), p&d, w, ed
Robert Conrad
THUNDERING JETS(1958); PALM SPRINGS WEEKEND(1963); YOUNG DILLINGER(1965); MURPH THE SURF(1974); LADY IN RED, THE(1979); WRONG IS RIGHT(1982)
Misc. Talkies
SUDDEN DEATH(1977)
Scott Conrad
DEAD PEOPLE(1974), ed; BOY AND HIS DOG, A(1975), ed; ROCKY(1976), ed; OUTLAW BLUES(1977), ed; WANDA NEVADA(1979), ed; CHEECH AND CHONG'S NEXT MOVIE(1980), ed; HOLLYWOOD KNIGHTS, THE(1980), ed; CHEECH AND CHONG'S NICE DREAMS(1981), ed; SPACEHUNTER: ADVENTURES IN THE FORBIDDEN ZONE(1983), ed
1984
HEY BABE!(1984, Can.), ed
Sid Conrad
KING KONG(1976); DIFFERENT STORY, A(1978)
Thomas Conrad
GRASS EATER, THE(1961), ed; SHELL SHOCK(1964), ed; EXILES, THE(1966), ed
Tom Conrad
GREEN SLIME, THE(1969)
Walter Conrad
FULL OF LIFE(1956); JEANNE EAGELS(1957)
William Conrad
KILLERS, THE(1946); BODY AND SOUL(1947); ARCH OF TRIUMPH(1948); FOUR FACES WEST(1948); JOAN OF ARC(1948); SORRY, WRONG NUMBER(1948); TO THE VICTOR(1948); ANY NUMBER CAN PLAY(1949); EAST SIDE, WEST SIDE(1949); TENSION(1949); DIAL 1119(1950); MILKMAN, THE(1950); ONE WAY STREET(1950); CRY DANGER(1951); RACKET, THE(1951); SWORD OF MONTE CRISTO, THE(1951); LONE STAR(1952); CRY OF THE HUNTED(1953); DESERT SONG, THE(1953); NAKED JUNGLE, THE(1953); FIVE AGAINST THE HOUSE(1955); CONQUEROR, THE(1956); JOHNNY CONCHO(1956); RIDE BACK, THE(1957), a, p; -30-(1959); MAN FROM GALVESTON, THE(1964), d; BATTLE OF THE BULGE(1965); BRAINSTORM(1965), p&d; MY BLOOD RUNS COLD(1965), p&d; TWO ON A GUILLOTINE(1965), p&d; AMERICAN DREAM, AN(1966), p; COVENANT WITH DEATH, A(1966), p; COOL ONES THE(1967), p; FIRST TO FIGHT(1967), p; CHUBASCO(1968), p; COUNTDOWN(1968), p; MOONSHINE COUNTY EXPRESS(1977)
Misc. Silents
LAST OF THE MAFFIA, THE(1915)
Hans Conradi
TRUNKS OF MR. O.F., THE(1932, Ger.), p
Kurt Conradi
GREAT BRITISH TRAIN ROBBERY, THE(1967, Ger.)

Marion Conradi
BECAUSE I LOVED YOU(1930, Ger.)

Joan Conrath
GIRLS ON THE BEACH(1965)

Don Conreaux
PAD, THE(AND HOW TO USE IT)* (1966, Brit.)

Hans Conried
DRAMATIC SCHOOL(1938); IT'S A WONDERFUL WORLD(1939); DULCY(1940); DATE WITH THE FALCON, A(1941); GAY FALCON, THE(1941); MAISIE WAS A LADY(1941); UNDERGROUND(1941); UNEXPECTED UNCLE(1941); WEEKEND FOR THREE(1941); BIG STREET, THE(1942); BLONDIE'S BLESSED EVENT(1942); FALCON TAKES OVER, THE(1942); HITLER'S CHILDREN(1942); JOURNEY INTO FEAR(1942); NIGHTMARE(1942); ONCE UPON A HONEYMOON(1942); PACIFIC RENDEZVOUS(1942); SABOTEUR(1942); UNDERGROUND AGENT(1942); WIFE TAKES A FLYER, THE(1942); CRAZY HOUSE(1943); HIS BUTLER'S SISTER(1943); HOSTAGES(1943); LADY TAKES A CHANCE, A(1943); MRS. PARKINGTON(1944); PASSAGE TO MARSEILLE(1944); SENATOR WAS INDISCREET, THE(1947); BARKLEYS OF BROADWAY, THE(1949); BRIDE FOR SALE(1949); MY FRIEND IRMA(1949); ON THE TOWN(1949); NANCY GOES TO RIO(1950); SUMMER STOCK(1950); BEHAVE YOURSELF(1951); LIGHT TOUCH, THE(1951); NEW MEXICO(1951); RICH, YOUNG AND PRETTY(1951); TEXAS CARNIVAL(1951); TOO YOUNG TO KISS(1951); BIG JIM McLAIN(1952); THREE FOR BEDROOM C(1952); WORLD IN HIS ARMS, THE(1952); AFFAIRS OF DOBIE GILLIS, THE(1953); PETER PAN(1953); SIREN OF BAGDAD(1953); TWONKY, THE(1953); 5,000 FINGERS OF DR. T. THE(1953); DAVY CROCKETT, KING OF THE WILD FRONTIER(1955); YOU'RE NEVER TOO YOUNG(1955); BUS STOP(1956); JET PILOT(1957); MONSTER THAT CHALLENGED THE WORLD, THE(1957); BIG BEAT, THE(1958); ROCK-A-BYE BABY(1958); JUKE BOX RHYTHM(1959); 1001 ARABIAN NIGHTS(1959); MAGIC FOUNTAIN, THE(1961); MY SIX LOVES(1963); PATSY, THE(1964); ROBIN AND THE SEVEN HOODS(1964); BIRDS AND THE BEES, THE(1965); PHANTOM TOLLBOOTH, THE(1970); BROTHERS O'TOOLE, THE(1973); SHAGGY D.A., THE(1976); CAT FROM OUTER SPACE, THE(1978); OH GOD! BOOK II(1980)
Misc. Talkies
CRICKET OF THE HEARTH, THE(1968); MAGIC PONY(1979)

Trilby Conried
TWONKY, THE(1953)

Allen Conroy
NEW FACES(1954)

Bert Conroy
REVENGE OF THE CHEERLEADERS(1976)

Brendan Conroy
1984
BOUNTY, THE(1984)

Burt Conroy
LAST OF THE RED HOT LOVERS(1972); FUTUREWORLD(1976)

Cindy Conroy
COME SEPTEMBER(1961)

Frances Conroy
MANHATTAN(1979)
1984
FALLING IN LOVE(1984)

Frank Conroy
ROYAL FAMILY OF BROADWAY, THE(1930); BAD COMPANY(1931); MANHATTAN PARADE(1931); POSSESSED(1931); WEST OF BROADWAY(1931); DISORDERLY CONDUCT(1932); GRAND HOTEL(1932); HELL DIVERS(1932); ACE OF ACES(1933); ANN CARVER'S PROFESSION(1933); KENNEL MURDER CASE, THE(1933); MIDNIGHT MARY(1933); NIGHT FLIGHT(1933); STORM AT DAYBREAK(1933); CAT AND THE FIDDLE(1934); CRIME DOCTOR, THE(1934); EVELYN PRENTICE(1934); FRONTIER MARSHAL(1934); I'LL FIX IT(1934); KEEP 'EM ROLLING(1934); LITTLE MINISTER, THE(1934); LITTLE MISS MARKER(1934); MANHATTAN MELODRAMA(1934); RETURN OF THE TERROR(1934); SUCH WOMEN ARE DANGEROUS(1934); UPPER WORLD(1934); WEDNESDAY'S CHILD(1934); WHITE PARADE, THE(1934); CALL OF THE WILD(1935); CHARLIE CHAN IN EGYPT(1935); DANTE'S INFERNO(1935); I LIVE MY LIFE(1935); LAST DAYS OF POMPEII, THE(1935); SHE COULDN'T TAKE IT(1935); SHOW THEM NO MERCY(1935); WEST POINT OF THE AIR(1935); CHARLIE CHAN AT THE OPERA(1936); GORGEOUS HUSSY, THE(1936); MEET NERO WOLFE(1936); NOBODY'S FOOL(1936); WHITE ANGEL, THE(1936); BIG BUSINESS(1937); EMPEROR'S CANDLESTICKS, THE(1937); LAST GANGSTER, THE(1937); LOVE IS NEWS(1937); MUSIC FOR MADAME(1937); NANCY STEELE IS MISSING(1937); STOLEN HOLIDAY(1937); THAT I MAY LIVE(1937); THIS IS MY AFFAIR(1937); WELLS FARGO(1937); THIS WOMAN IS MINE(1941); ADVENTURES OF MARTIN EDEN, THE(1942); CROSSROADS(1942); LOVES OF EDGAR ALLAN POE, THE(1942); CRASH DIVE(1943); LADY OF BURLESQUE(1943); OX-BOW INCIDENT, THE(1943); THAT HAGEN GIRL(1947); ALL MY SONS(1948); FOR THE LOVE OF MARY(1948); NAKED CITY, THE(1948); ROGUES' REGIMENT(1948); SEALED VERDICT(1948); SNAKE PIT, THE(1948); THREAT, THE(1949); DAY THE EARTH STOOD STILL, THE(1951); LIGHTNING STRIKES TWICE(1951); LAST MILE, THE(1959); YOUNG PHILADELPHIANS, THE(1959); BRAMBLE BUSH, THE(1960); BEYOND THE LAW(1968), m

Grant Conroy
CHANGES(1969)

J. Clayton Conroy
THOSE LIPS, THOSE EYES(1980)

James Conroy
STRANGE BREW(1983)

Jarlath Conroy
HEAVEN'S GATE(1980)

Laurence Conroy
NOTORIOUS LANDLADY, THE(1962); CLARENCE, THE CROSS-EYED LION(1965); KING RAT(1965); ASSAULT ON A QUEEN(1966)

Michael Conroy
FIRST OFFENDERS(1939); NEWSBOY'S HOME(1939); CASTLE ON THE HUDSON(1940); FUGITIVE FROM JUSTICE, A(1940)

Pat Conroy
CONRACK(1974), w; GREAT SANTINI, THE(1979), w; LORDS OF DISCIPLINE, THE(1983), w

Rebecca Conroy
Silents
GOLD RUSH, THE(1925)

Sue Conroy
GIRL HABIT(1931)

Susan Conroy
UNMASKED(1929)
Misc. Talkies
UNMASKED(1929)
Misc. Silents
UNMASKED(1929)

Thom Conroy
MAN WITH THE GUN(1955); YOUNG SAVAGES, THE(1961); ROBIN AND THE SEVEN HOODS(1964); SECONDS(1966)

Tom Conroy
TEN TALL MEN(1951)

Francesco Consalvo
LA DOLCE VITA(1961, Ital./Fr.)

Gennaro Consalvo
ATLANTIC CITY(1981, U.S./Can.)

Lamberto Consani
LEAP INTO THE VOID(1982, Ital.)

Bill Conselman, Jr.
MILLION DOLLAR LEGS(1939)

William Conselman
LOVE AMONG THE MILLIONAIRES(1930), w; WHOOPEE(1930), w; CONNECTICUT YANKEE, A(1931), w; HEARTBREAK(1931), w; SIX CYLINDER LOVE(1931), w; THREE ROGUES(1931), w; YOUNG SINNERS(1931), w; BUSINESS AND PLEASURE(1932), w; STEPPING SISTERS(1932), w; YOUNG AMERICA(1932), w; ARIZONA TO BROADWAY(1933), w; JIMMY AND SALLY(1933), w; MAD GAME, THE(1933), w; BRIGHT EYES(1934), w; FRONTIER MARSHAL(1934), w; LOVE TIME(1934), w; ORIENT EXPRESS(1934), w; 365 NIGHTS IN HOLLYWOOD(1934), w; DOUBTING THOMAS(1935), w; LITTLE COLONEL, THE(1935), w; PIGSKIN PARADE(1936), w; PRIVATE NUMBER(1936), w; STOWAWAY(1936), w; FIFTY ROADS TO TOWN(1937), w; GREAT HOSPITAL MYSTERY, THE(1937), w; ON THE AVENUE(1937), w; THAT I MAY LIVE(1937), w; SMILING ALONG(1938, Brit.), w; EAST SIDE OF HEAVEN(1939), w; THAT'S RIGHT–YOU'RE WRONG(1939), w; IF I HAD MY WAY(1940), w
Silents
BRIGHT LIGHTS(1925), t; ELLA CINDERS(1926), w; GAY RETREAT, THE(1927), w; PAJAMAS(1927), w; SILK LEGS(1927), sup; WAY OF THE STRONG, THE(1928), w

William Conselman, Jr.
SAILOR'S LADY(1940); LAST OF THE DUANES(1941), w; RIDE, KELLY, RIDE(1941), w; LONE STAR RANGER(1942), w

William M. Conselman
LIFE BEGINS AT 40(1935), w
Silents
SLAVES OF BEAUTY(1927), w; NEWS PARADE, THE(1928), w

Louis Consentino
BADGE 373(1973)

Isobel Conser
MY HANDS ARE CLAY(1948, Irish)

Bob Considine
BABE RUTH STORY, THE(1948), w; HOODLUM EMPIRE(1952), w

Charlotte Considine
DOCTOR, YOU'VE GOT TO BE KIDDING(1967); SPEEDWAY(1968)

John Considine
GREATEST STORY EVER TOLD, THE(1965); TARZAN'S DEADLY SILENCE(1970), w; DOCTOR DEATH: SEEKER OF SOULS(1973); CALIFORNIA SPLIT(1974); THIRSTY DEAD, THE(1975); BUFFALO BILL AND THE INDIANS, OR SITTING BULL'S HISTORY LESSON(1976); WELCOME TO L.A.(1976); LATE SHOW, THE(1977); WEDDING, A(1978), a, w; WHEN TIME RAN OUT(1980); ENDANGERED SPECIES(1982)
1984
CHOOSE ME(1984)
Misc. Talkies
BRAINWASH(1982, Brit.); CIRCLE OF POWER(1984)

John Considine, Jr.
ABRAHAM LINCOLN(1930), ed; SHE WANTED A MILLIONAIRE(1932), p; GAY BRIDE, THE(1934), p; HAVE A HEART(1934), p; THIS SIDE OF HEAVEN(1934), p; BLACKMAIL(1939), p; SOCIETY LAWYER(1939), p; MEN OF BOYS TOWN(1941), p; REUNION IN FRANCE(1942)

John W. Considine
ARSENE LUPIN RETURNS(1938), p
Silents
TEMPEST(1928), p

John W. Considine, Jr.
BAD ONE, THE(1930), p; PUTTIN' ON THE RITZ(1930), p, w; DISORDERLY CONDUCT(1932), d; EVELYN PRENTICE(1934), p; SEQUOIA(1934), p; BROADWAY MELODY OF 1936(1935), p; MAD LOVE(1935), p; THREE LIVE GHOSTS(1935), p; ABSOLUTE QUIET(1936), p; ROBIN HOOD OF EL DORADO(1936), p; VOICE OF BUGLE ANN(1936), p; EMPEROR'S CANDLESTICKS, THE(1937), p; PERSONAL PROPERTY(1937), p; BOYS TOWN(1938), p; HOLD THAT KISS(1938), p; OF HUMAN HEARTS(1938), p; STRONGER THAN DESIRE(1939), p; EDISON, THE MAN(1940), p; THIRD FINGER, LEFT HAND(1940), p; YOUNG TOM EDISON(1940), p; DESIGN FOR SCANDAL(1941), p; MARRIED BACHELOR(1941), p; JACKASS MAIL(1942), p; JOHNNY EAGER(1942), p; YANK AT ETON, A(1942), p; SALUTE TO THE MARINES(1943), p; THREE HEARTS FOR JULIA(1943), p
Silents
SON OF THE SHEIK(1926), p

Mildred Considine
Silents
ALL WRONG(1919), w; REAL ADVENTURE, THE(1922), w

Robert Considine
LADIES' DAY(1943), w; THIRTY SECONDS OVER TOKYO(1944), w

Tim Considine
CLOWN, THE(1953); EXECUTIVE SUITE(1954); HER TWELVE MEN(1954); PRIVATE WAR OF MAJOR BENSON, THE(1955); UNCHAINED(1955); SHAGGY DOG, THE(1959); SUNRISE AT CAMPOBELLO(1960); PATTON(1970); TARZAN'S DEADLY SILENCE(1970), w; DARING DOBERMANS, THE(1973)

Alberto Consiglio
OPEN CITY(1946, Ital.), w

Ignazio Consiglio
VOLCANO(1953, Ital.)
Ermanno Consolazione
MACHINE GUN McCAIN(1970, Ital.)
Michael Consoldane
MOMENT BY MOMENT(1978)
Enzo Consoli
OPERATION KID BROTHER(1967, Ital.); VIOLENT FOUR, THE(1968, Ital.)
Consolidated Film Industries
KID FROM CLEVELAND, THE(1949), spec eff
Bill Constable
MAN WITH THE GREEN CARNATION, THE(1960, Brit.), art d; SIEGE OF THE SAXONS(1963, Brit.), art d; DR. WHO AND THE DALEKS(1965, Brit.), art d; SKULL, THE(1965, Brit.), art d; PSYCHOPATH, THE(1966, Brit.), art d; DEADLY BEES,- THE(1967, Brit.), art d; TERRORNAUTS, THE(1967, Brit.), prod d; THEY CAME FROM BEYOND SPACE(1967, Brit.), prod d; DANGER ROUTE(1968, Brit.), prod d; SALT & PEPPER(1968, Brit.), prod d; TORTURE GARDEN(1968, Brit.), prod d; MIND OF MR. SOAMES, THE(1970, Brit.), prod d; SCREAM AND SCREAM AGAIN(1970, Brit.), prod d
David A. Constable
KING KONG(1976), art d
David Constable
METEOR(1979), art d
June Constable
DUCHESS AND THE DIRTWATER FOX, THE(1976)
Trevor Constable
DESERT RATS, THE(1953)
William Constable
HELLIONS, THE(1962, Brit.), art d; JUST FOR FUN(1963, Brit.), art d; LONG SHIPS, THE(1964, Brit./Yugo.), art d; DR. TERROR'S HOUSE OF HORRORS(1965, Brit.), art d
Ira Constad
ISLAND OF ALLAH(1956)
Constance
KING OF HEARTS(1936, Brit.); SUDDENLY, A WOMAN!(1967, Den.)
Al Constance
FOLIES DERGERE(1935)
Marian Constance
Silents
REDEEMING SIN, THE(1925), w; BRIDE OF THE STORM(1926), w; GILDED HIGHWAY, THE(1926), w
Denis Constanduros
HOLIDAY CAMP(1947, Brit.), w; HERE COME THE HUGGETTS(1948, Brit.), w; VOTE FOR HUGGETT(1948, Brit.), w; FACTS OF LOVE(1949, Brit.), w; HUGGETTS ABROAD, THE(1949, Brit.), w
Mabel Constanduros
HOPE OF HIS SIDE(1935, Brit.); ROSE OF TRALEE(1942, Brit.); SALUTE JOHN CITIZEN(1942, Brit.); I'LL WALK BESIDE YOU(1943, Brit.), w; MY AIN FOLK(1944, Brit.); VARIETY JUBILEE(1945, Brit.), w; CARAVAN(1946, Brit.); GAY INTRUDERS, THE(1946, Brit.); THIS MAN IS MINE(1946 Brit.), w; BAD SISTER(1947, Brit.); HOLIDAY CAMP(1947, Brit.), w; EASY MONEY(1948, Brit.); HERE COME THE HUGGETTS(1948, Brit.), w; VOTE FOR HUGGETT(1948, Brit.), w; FACTS OF LO-VE(1949, Brit.), w; HUGGETTS ABROAD, THE(1949, Brit.), w
Marita Constaniou
ANGRY HILLS, THE(1959, Brit.)
Aina Constant
BELLS OF ST. MARY'S, THE(1945); JOHNNY ANGEL(1945); THOSE ENDEARING YOUNG CHARMS(1945); ZIEGFELD FOLLIES(1945)
Claudia Constant
RACKET, THE(1951)
Gilbert Constant
LOVE IN THE AFTERNOON(1957)
Jacques Constant
PEPE LE MOKO(1937, Fr.), w
Lee Constant
VIOLENT YEARS, THE(1956)
Madeleine Constant
FIVE WILD GIRLS(1966, Fr.)
Yvonne Constant
GIGOT(1962); MAXIME(1962, Fr.); MONKEYS, GO HOME!(1967)
Lambros Constantaras
ANNA OF RHODES(1950, Gr.)
Peter Constanti
SUMMER PLACE, A(1959)
Ernst Constantin
QUESTION 7(1961, U.S./Ger.)
Jean Constantin
FOUR HUNDRED BLOWS, THE(1959), m; LOVE AND THE FRENCHWOMAN(1961, Fr.), m; CANDIDE(1962, Fr.); WISE GUYS(1969, Fr./Ital.)
Michael Constantin
COLD SWEAT(1974, Ital., Fr.)
Michel Constantin
NIGHT WATCH, THE(1964, Fr./Ital.); SOUTHERN STAR, THE(1969, Fr./Brit.); VERY CURIOUS GIRL, A(1970, Fr.); OUTSIDE MAN, THE(1973, U.S./FR.); FAMILY, THE(1974, Fr./Ital.); BEYOND FEAR(1977, Fr.); COUNTERFEIT COMMANDOS(1981, Ital.)
Nitza Constantin
PRISONER OF THE VOLGA(1960, Fr./Ital.)
Constantine
SPECTER OF THE ROSE(1946)
Andreas Constantine
KITCHEN, THE(1961, Brit.)
Eddie Constantine
EGYPT BY THREE(1953); FOLIES BERGERE(1958, Fr.); ROOM 43(1959, Brit.); S.O.S. PACIFIC(1960, Brit.); CLEO FROM 5 TO 7(1961, Fr.); HOT MONEY GIRL(1962, Brit./Ger.); RIFF RAFF GIRLS(1962, Fr./Ital.); EMPIRE OF NIGHT, THE(1963, Fr.); YOUR TURN, DARLING(1963, Fr.); ALPHAVILLE, A STRANGE CASE OF LEMMY CAUTION(1965, Fr.); HAIL MAFIA(1965, Fr./Ital.); ATTACK OF THE ROBOTS(1967, Fr./Span.); LIONS LOVE(1969); IT LIVES AGAIN(1978); BOXOFFICE(1982); LONG GOOD FRIDAY, THE(1982, Brit.)

1984
FLIGHT TO BERLIN(1984, Ger./Brit.)
Frixos Constantine
LAND OF THE MINOTAUR(1976, Gr.), p
Mathew Constantine
MAD MAX(1979, Aus.)
Michael Constantine
LAST MILE, THE(1959); HUSTLER, THE(1961); ISLAND OF LOVE(1963); LON-NIE(1963); QUICK, BEFORE IT MELTS(1964); BEAU GESTE(1966); HAWAII(1966); IN ENEMY COUNTRY(1968); SKIDOO(1968); DON'T DRINK THE WATER(1969); IF IT'S TUESDAY, THIS MUST BE BELGIUM(1969); JUSTINE(1969); REIVERS, THE(1969); DIRTY HEROES(1971, Ital./Fr./Ger.); PEEPER(1975); VOYAGE OF THE DAM-NED(1976, Brit.); NORTH AVENUE IRREGULARS, THE(1979)
Tony Constantine
HAIR(1979)
Paul Constantineau
FREEWHEELIN'(1976)
Rene Constantineau
QUEBEC(1951); DON'T DRINK THE WATER(1969)
Beatrice Constantini
MILKY WAY, THE(1969, Fr./Ital.)
Enzo Constantini
300 SPARTANS, THE(1962), set d
Giorgio Constantini
STRANGER'S HAND, THE(1955, Brit.); WAR AND PEACE(1956, Ital./U.S.)
Nino Constantini
Misc. Silents
MAUPRAT(1926, Fr.); 6 ½ X 11(1927, Fr.)
Richard Constantini
ATTENTION, THE KIDS ARE WATCHING(1978, Fr.)
Alexandro Constantino
BLACK ORPHEUS(1959 Fr./Ital./Braz.)
Stack Constantino
MAGUS, THE(1968, Brit.)
Consuelo
Misc. Silents
FOLLY OF VANITY, THE(1924)
British Consul
NEUTRAL PORT(1941, Brit.)
Andre Contant
GOLDEN MISTRESS, THE(1954)
Livia Contardi
MIGHTY CRUSADERS, THE(1961, Ital.); ERIK THE CONQUEROR(1963, Fr./Ital.); WAR OF THE ZOMBIES, THE(1965 Ital.)
John Contardo
SCARFACE(1983)
D. Constantine Conte
DEATH VENGEANCE(1982), p
1984
HARD TO HOLD(1984), p
Fred Conte
HARLOW(1965)
John Conte
CROWD ROARS, THE(1932); EACH DAWN I DIE(1939); INDIANAPOLIS SPEED-WAY(1939); OUR NEIGHBORS–THE CARTERS(1939); THOUSANDS CHEER(1943); LOST IN A HAREM(1944); MAN WITH THE GOLDEN ARM, THE(1955); TRAU-MA(1962); CARPETBAGGERS, THE(1964)
Maria-Pia Conte
LOVE IS A FUNNY THING(1970, Fr./Ital.)
Nicholas Conte
HEAVEN WITH A BARBED WIRE FENCE(1939)
Paolo Conte
1984
JOKE OF DESTINY LYING IN WAIT AROUND THE CORNER LIKE A STREET-BANDIT, A(1984, Ital.), m
Richard Conte
GUADALCANAL DIARY(1943); PURPLE HEART, THE(1944); BELL FOR ADANO, A(1945); CAPTAIN EDDIE(1945); SPIDER, THE(1945); WALK IN THE SUN, A(1945); SOMEWHERE IN THE NIGHT(1946); 13 RUE MADELEINE(1946); OTHER LOVE, THE(1947); CALL NORTHSIDE 777(1948); CRY OF THE CITY(1948); BIG JACK(1949); HOUSE OF STRANGERS(1949); THIEVES' HIGHWAY(1949); WHIRLPOOL(1949); SLEEPING CITY, THE(1950); HOLLYWOOD STORY(1951); RAGING TIDE, THE(1951); UNDER THE GUN(1951); FIGHTER, THE(1952); RAIDERS, THE(1952); BLUE GARDENIA, THE(1953); DESERT LEGION(1953); SLAVES OF BABY-LON(1953); HIGHWAY DRAGNET(1954); BENGAZI(1955); BIG COMBO, THE(1955); BIG TIP OFF, THE(1955); CASE OF THE RED MONKEY(1955, Brit.); I'LL CRY TOMORROW(1955); NEW YORK CONFIDENTIAL(1955); RACE FOR LIFE, A(1955, Brit.); TARGET ZERO(1955); FULL OF LIFE(1956); BROTHERS RICO, THE(1957); THIS ANGRY AGE(1958, Ital./Fr.); THEY CAME TO CORDURA(1959); OCEAN'S ELEVEN(1960); PEPE(1960); EYES OF ANNIE JONES, THE(1963, Brit.); WHO'S BEEN SLEEPING IN MY BED?(1963); CIRCUS WORLD(1964); GREATEST STORY EVER TOLD, THE(1965); SYNANON(1965); ASSAULT ON A QUEEN(1966); DEATH SENTENCE(1967, Ital.); HOTEL(1967); TONY ROME(1967); LADY IN CEMENT(1968); EXPLOSION(1969, Can.); OPERATION CROSS EAGLES(1969, U.S./Yugo.), a, d; GOD-FATHER, THE(1972); NO WAY OUT(1975, Ital./Fr.)
Misc. Talkies
1931, ONCE UPON A TIME IN NEW YORK(1972); SHOOT FIRST, DIE LATER(1973)
Robert Conte
THRILL OF BRAZIL, THE(1946); APPOINTMENT WITH MURDER(1948); LIGHT TOUCH, THE(1951); THIEF OF DAMASCUS(1952)
Ruth Conte
RICH AND FAMOUS(1981)
Steve Conte
CATTLE QUEEN(1951); GOLDTOWN GHOST RIDERS(1953); WIRETAPPERS(1956); TEENAGE ZOMBIES(1960); DANGEROUS CHARTER(1962); TERROR OF THE BLOODHUNTERS(1962); ATTACK OF THE MAYAN MUMMY(1963, U.S./Mex.); FLAREUP(1969); OTHER SIDE OF THE MOUNTAIN–PART 2, THE(1978); FAST BREAK(1979); ONION FIELD, THE(1979)

John Conteh
MAN AT THE TOP(1973, Brit.)
Sandro Contenenza
FEMALE BUTCHER, THE(1972, Ital./Span.), w
J. Burgi Conter
DRUMS O' VOODOO(1934, ph; MUGGER, THE(1958), ph
Norma Conterno
Misc. Silents
CYCLONE BUDDY(1924)
Roberto Contero
EMBALMER, THE(1966, Ital.)
John G. Contes
300 SPARTANS, THE(1962)
Albert Conti
JAZZ HEAVEN(1929); LADY OF THE PAVEMENTS(1929); SATURDAY'S CHIL-
DREN(1929); BLUSHING BRIDES(1930); MADAME SATAN(1930); MELODY
MAN(1930); MONTE CARLO(1930); MOROCCO(1930); OH, FOR A MAN!(1930); ONE
ROMANTIC NIGHT(1930); OUR BLUSHING BRIDES(1930); SEA LEGS(1930); SUCH
MEN ARE DANGEROUS(1930); GANG BUSTER, THE(1931); JUST A GIGOLO(1931);
STRANGERS MAY KISS(1931); THIS MODERN AGE(1931); AS YOU DESIRE
ME(1932); DOOMED BATTALION, THE(1932); FREAKS(1932); LADY WITH A
PAST(1932); NIGHT CLUB LADY(1932); SHOPWORN(1932); GIGOLETTES OF PA-
RIS(1933); LOVE IS LIKE THAT(1933); MEN ARE SUCH FOOLS(1933); SHANGHAI
MADNESS(1933); TOPAZE(1933); TORCH SINGER(1933); BELOVED(1934); BLACK
CAT, THE(1934); ELMER AND ELSIE(1934); GAMBLING LADY(1934); LOVE TI-
ME(1934); NANA(1934); CRUSADES, THE(1935); DIAMOND JIM(1935); GOIN' TO
TOWN(1935); HANDS ACROSS THE TABLE(1935); HERE'S TO ROMANCE(1935);
MILLS OF THE GODS(1935); SYMPHONY OF LIVING(1935); CASE AGAINST MRS.
AMES, THE(1936); COLLEGIATE(1936); FATAL LADY(1936); HOLLYWOOD BOULE-
VARD(1936); NEXT TIME WE LOVE(1936); ONE IN A MILLION(1936); DANGEROUS-
LY YOURS(1937); I'LL TAKE ROMANCE(1937); THREE SMART GIRLS(1937);
ALWAYS GOODBYE(1938); GATEWAY(1938); SUEZ(1938); EVERYTHING HAPPENS
AT NIGHT(1939); MY GAL SAL(1942)
Silents
MERRY-GO-ROUND(1923); EAGLE, THE(1925); MERRY WIDOW, THE(1925); OLD
LOVES AND NEW(1926); WATCH YOUR WIFE(1926); CAMILLE(1927); WEDDING
MARCH, THE(1927); ALEX THE GREAT(1928); LOVE ME AND THE WORLD IS
MINE(1928); MAGNIFICENT FLIRT, THE(1928); SHOW PEOPLE(1928); STOCKS
AND BLONDES(1928); TEMPEST(1928); CAPTAIN LASH(1929); EXALTED FLAP-
PER, THE(1929)
Alberti Conti
NIGHT IS YOUNG, THE(1935)
Aldo Conti
WILD, WILD PLANET, THE(1967, Ital.)
Audrey Conti
INVASION OF THE SAUCER MEN(1957); SPOOK CHASERS(1957)
Beppe Conti
RED DESERT(1965, Fr./Ital.)
Bill Conti
HARRY AND TONTO(1974), m; NEXT STOP, GREENWICH VILLAGE(1976), m;
ROCKY(1976), m; CITIZENS BAND(1977), m; BIG FIX, THE(1978), m; F.I.S.T.(1978),
m; FIVE DAYS FROM HOME(1978), m; PARADISE ALLEY(1978), m; SLOW DANC-
ING IN THE BIG CITY(1978), m; UNCLE JOE SHANNON(1978), m; UNMARRIED
WOMAN, AN(1978), m; DREAMER(1979), m; GOLDENGIRL(1979), m; MAN, A
WOMAN, AND A BANK, A(1979, Can.), m; ROCKY II(1979), m; SEDUCTION OF JOE
TYNAN, THE(1979), m; FORMULA, THE(1980), m; GLORIA(1980), m; PRIVATE
BENJAMIN(1980), m; CARBON COPY(1981), m; FOR YOUR EYES ONLY(1981), m;
NEIGHBORS(1981), m; VICTORY(1981), m; I, THE JURY(1982), m; ROCKY III(1982),
m; SPLIT IMAGE(1982), m; THAT CHAMPIONSHIP SEASON(1982), m; BAD
BOYS(1983), m; RIGHT STUFF, THE(1983), m
1984
BEAR, THE(1984), m; KARATE KID, THE(1984), m; MASS APPEAL(1984), m;
UNFAITHFULLY YOURS(1984), m
C. Conti
JULIE THE REDHEAD(1963, Fr.)
Capt. Albert Conti
HEARTBREAK(1931)
Carla Conti
LA FUGA(1966, Ital.), w
Carlos Conti
EXPOSED(1983), set d
Diana Conti
TEENAGE GANG DEBS(1966)
Dino Conti
1984
LAST HUNTER, THE(1984, Ital.)
Gabriella Conti
MAFIOSO(1962, Ital.)
Gerard Conti
MY BODY HUNGERS(1967), p
Gino Conti
STREET ANGEL(1928); MAKING THE GRADE(1929)
Joe Conti
EAST OF THE RIVER(1940); BIG BOSS, THE(1941); HERE COMES MR. JOR-
DAN(1941)
Juan-Carlos Conti
1984
AMERICAN DREAMER(1984), set d
Louise Conti
Silents
PRODIGAL SON, THE(1923, Brit.)
Marie-Catherine Conti
1984
UNTIL SEPTEMBER(1984)
Mario Conti
PAISAN(1948, Ital.), p; SEVEN BEAUTIES(1976, Ital.)
Peter Conti
1984
POPE OF GREENWICH VILLAGE, THE(1984)

Pino Conti
Silents
MR. JUSTICE RAFFLES(1921, Brit.); OLD CURIOSITY SHOP, THE(1921, Brit.);
INDIAN LOVE LYRICS, THE(1923, Brit.)
Steve Conti
GUNFIRE(1950)
Tom Conti
FLAME(1975, Brit.); GALILEO(1975, Brit.); DUELLISTS, THE(1977, Brit.); FULL
CIRCLE(1977, Brit./Can.); HAUNTING OF JULIA, THE(1981, Brit./Can.); MERRY
CHRISTMAS MR. LAWRENCE(1983, Jap./Brit.); REUBEN, REUBEN(1983)
1984
AMERICAN DREAMER(1984)
Continenza
DONATELLA(1956, Ital.), w; LOVES OF HERCULES, THE(1960), w
Alessandro Continenza
TOO BAD SHE'S BAD(1954, Ital.), w; LUCKY TO BE A WOMAN(1955, Ital.), w;
MILLER'S WIFE, THE(1957, Ital.), w; TOTO IN THE MOON(1957, Ital.), w;
DAY THE SKY EXPLODED, THE(1958, Fr./Ital.), w; TRAPPED IN TANGIERS(1960,
Ital./Span.), w; HERCULES AND THE CAPTIVE WOMEN(1963, Fr./Ital.), w; HER-
CULES IN THE HAUNTED WORLD(1964, Ital.), w; OF WAYWARD LOVE(1964,
Ital./Ger.), w; DAY IN COURT, A(1965, Ital.), w
Allesandro Continenza
HANNIBAL(1960, Ital.), w
Sandro Continenza
APPOINTMENT FOR MURDER(1954, Ital.), w; MINOTAUR, THE(1961, Ital.), w;
SWORDSMAN OF SIENA, THE(1962, Fr./Ital.), w; LOVE AND LARCENY(1963,
Fr./Ital.), w; GLADIATORS 7(1964, Span./Ital.), w; HE WHO SHOOTS FIRST(1966,
Ital.), w; SECRET SEVEN, THE(1966, Ital./Span.), w; MISSION BLOODY MARY(1967,
Fr./Ital./Span.), w; DON'T OPEN THE WINDOW(1974, Ital.), w
Sandro Contineza
WHITE SLAVE SHIP(1962, Fr./Ital.), w
Aldo Contini
BINGO BONGO(1983, Ital.), ph
Alfio Contini
HUNS, THE(1962, Fr./Ital.), ph; EASY LIFE, THE(1963, Ital.), ph; MY SON, THE
HERO(1963, Ital./Fr.), ph; TWELVE-HANDED MEN OF MARS, THE(1964, Ital./
Span.), ph; LOVE AND MARRIAGE(1966, Ital.), ph; OPIATE '67(1967, Fr./Ital.), ph;
ROSE FOR EVERYONE, A(1967, Ital.), ph; GALILEO(1968, Ital./Bul.), ph; FINE PAIR,
A(1969, Ital.), ph; GOD FORGIVES—I DON'T!(1969, Ital./Span.), ph; ZABRISKIE
POINT(1970), ph; PRIEST'S WIFE, THE(1971, Ital./Fr.), ph; TROJAN WOMEN,
THE(1971), ph; LADY LIBERTY(1972, Ital./Fr.), ph; WHITE SISTER(1973, Ital./
Span./Fr.), ph; NIGHT PORTER, THE(1974, Ital./U.S.), ph; STORY WITHOUT
WORDS(1981, Ital.), ph; GIRL FROM TRIESTE, THE(1983, Ital.), ph
Dick Contino
BEAT GENERATION, THE(1959); DADDY-O(1959); GIRLS' TOWN(1959); BIG
NIGHT, THE(1960)
Alfio Contiui
CERTAIN, VERY CERTAIN, AS A MATTER OF FACT... PROBABLE(1970, Ital,), ph
Nacho Contla
CHIQUTTO PERO PICOSO(1967, Mex.)
Bergi Contner
WANDERING JEW, THE(1933), ph
Burdi Contner
COP HATER(1958), ph
Burgi Contner
GREEN FIELDS(1937), ph
Durgi J. Contner
ROOGIE'S BUMP(1954), ph
J. Burgi Contner
MARINES COME THROUGH, THE(1943), ph; FOUR BOYS AND A GUN(1957), ph;
STREET OF SINNERS(1957), ph; LIGHT FANTASTIC(1964), ph; KILLERS
THREE(1968), ph; THREE IN THE ATTIC(1968), ph
James A. Contner
TIMES SQUARE(1980), ph; NIGHTHAWKS(1981), ph; SO FINE(1981), ph; EDDIE
MACON'S RUN(1983), ph; JAWS 3-D(1983), ph; TOUGH ENOUGH(1983), ph
1984
FLAMINGO KID, THE(1984), ph; WHERE THE BOYS ARE '84(1984), ph
James Contner
CRUISING(1980), ph
Chantal Contouri
TOUCH AND GO(1955); ALVIN RIDES AGAIN(1974, Aus.); THIRST(1979, Aus.); DAY
AFTER HALLOWEEN, THE(1981, Aus.)
Nacho Contra
DAUGHTER OF DECEIT(1977, Mex.)
Didi Contractor
GURU, THE(1969, U.S./India), art d
Doris Contreras
SIERRA BARON(1958)
Enrique Contreras
EL DORADO(1967)
James Contreras
LAST MOVIE, THE(1971)
Luis Contreras
HEART BEAT(1979); 1941(1979); LONG RIDERS, THE(1980); BARBAROSA(1982); 48
HOURS(1982)
Martha Contreras
STATE OF SIEGE(1973, Fr./U.S./Ital./Ger.)
Mickey Contreras
CRISIS(1950)
Miguel Contreras
SOMBRERO(1953); SECRET OF THE INCAS(1954)
Robert Contreras
PROFESSIONALS, THE(1966)
Roberto Contreras
BEAST OF HOLLOW MOUNTAIN, THE(1956); RIDE A VIOLENT MILE(1957);
FLAME BARRIER, THE(1958); GOLD OF THE SEVEN SAINTS(1961); CALIFOR-
NIA(1963); MARA OF THE WILDERNESS(1966); TOPAZ(1969, Brit.); DARK,
THE(1979); BARBAROSA(1982); SCARFACE(1983)

Nora Controne
FAME(1980)
Tom Conventry
Misc. Silents
CIGARETTE MAKER'S ROMANCE, A(1920, Brit.)
Anita Converse
FADE TO BLACK(1980)
Cleo Converse
LADY FRANKENSTEIN(1971, Ital.), ed
Frank Converse
HOUR OF THE GUN(1967); HURRY SUNDOWN(1967); ROWDYMAN, THE(1973, Can.); PILOT, THE(1979); BUSHIDO BLADE, THE(1982 Brit./U.S.); SPRING FEVER(1983, Can.)
Patsy Converse
CHILD OF DIVORCE(1946)
Peggy Converse
GIRL OF THE LIMBERLOST, THE(1945); JUST BEFORE DAWN(1946); RAILROADED(1947); RUSTY LEADS THE WAY(1948); DEVIL'S HENCHMEN, THE(1949); FATHER IS A BACHELOR(1950); FAMILY SECRET, THE(1951); MISS SADIE THOMPSON(1953); DRUM BEAT(1954); THEY RODE WEST(1954); DAY OF THE BAD MAN(1958); THING THAT COULDN'T DIE, THE(1958); VOICE IN THE MIRROR(1958)
Roger Converse
YELLOW JACK(1938); MY DEAR MISS ALDRICH(1937); NAVY BLUE AND GOLD(1937); FAST COMPANY(1938); FIRST 100 YEARS, THE(1938); MARIE ANTOINETTE(1938); SHINING HOUR, THE(1938); SHOPWORN ANGEL(1938); SWEETHEARTS(1938); TEST PILOT(1938); THREE COMRADES(1938); YOUNG DR. KILDARE(1938)
Sue Ann Converse
WEDDING PARTY, THE(1969)
Thelma Converse
Silents
SOCIETY SCANDAL, A(1924)
Tony Converse
WEDDING PARTY, THE(1969)
Cleofe Conversi
KILL OR BE KILLED(1967, Ital.), ed
Francesco Conversi
SACCO AND VANZETTI(1971, Ital./Fr.)
Luciano Conversi
BIBLE...IN THE BEGINNING, THE(1966)
Spartaco Conversi
BULLET FOR THE GENERAL, A(1967, Ital.); BIG GUNDOWN, THE(1968, Ital.); ONCE UPON A TIME IN THE WEST(1969, U.S./Ital.); LONG RIDE FROM HELL, A(1970, Ital.)
Con Convert
TENDER IS THE NIGHT(1961)
Spanny Convery [Spartaco Conversi]
SABATA(1969, Ital.)
David Conville
DIPLOMATIC PASSPORT(1954, Brit.); CURSE OF THE WEREWOLF, THE(1961); EVIL OF FRANKENSTEIN, THE(1964, Brit.)
Robert Conville
Silents
STILL WATERS(1915); MICE AND MEN(1916); NANETTE OF THE WILDS(1916); OUT OF THE DRIFTS(1916); SIN THAT WAS HIS, THE(1920); SOUTH SEA LOVE(1923)
Misc. Silents
COTTON AND CATTLE(1921); COWBOY ACE, A(1921); FLOWING GOLD(1921); OUT OF THE CLOUDS(1921); RANGE PIRATE, THE(1921); RUSTLERS OF THE NIGHT(1921); TRAIL TO RED DOG, THE(1921)
Bert Convy
GUNMAN'S WALK(1958); BUCKET OF BLOOD, A(1959); SUSAN SLADE(1961); ACT ONE(1964); GIVE HER THE MOON(1970, Fr./Ital.); SEMI-TOUGH(1977); JENNIFER(1978); RACQUET(1979); HERO AT LARGE(1980); CANNONBALL RUN, THE(1981)
Alban Conway
DANCE PRETTY LADY(1932, Brit.); MURDER BY ROPE(1936, Brit.)
Alvin Conway
SATURDAY NIGHT REVUE(1937, Brit.)
Becky Conway
URBAN COWBOY(1980)
Bert Conway
NATIVE LAND(1942); MAN FROM TEXAS, THE(1948); OPEN SECRET(1948); YOU GOTTA STAY HAPPY(1948); CITY ACROSS THE RIVER(1949); FIGHTING FOOLS(1949); JOE PALOOKA IN THE BIG FIGHT(1949); ONCE MORE, MY DARLING(1949); PINKY(1949); TRAPPED(1949); JOE PALOOKA MEETS HUMPHREY(1950); PRISONERS IN PETTICOATS(1950); WOMAN FROM HEADQUARTERS(1950); ROCK, ROCK, ROCK!(1956); LITTLE BIG MAN(1970); CAT ATE THE PARAKEET, THE(1972); DRAGNET(1974); SPIKES GANG, THE(1974); RANCHO DELUXE(1975); ON THE NICKEL(1980)
Bob Conway
CHARLEY'S AUNT(1941)
Booth Conway
Silents
MARRIED TO A MORMAN(1922, Brit.); NELL GWYNNE(1926, Brit.)
Misc. Silents
LOVE TRAIL, THE(1916, Brit.); PAIR OF SPECTACLES, A(1916, Brit.); VALLEY OF FEAR, THE(1916, Brit.); CALL OF THE SEA, THE(1919); WESTWARD HO!(1919, Brit.); LITTLE WELSH GIRL, THE(1920, Brit.)
Blade Stanhope Conway [Bob Cummings]
SONS OF THE DESERT(1933)
Carl Conway
SAFECRACKER, THE(1958, Brit.); IDOL ON PARADE(1959, Brit.); WOMAN'S TEMPTATION, A(1959, Brit.); GREAT VAN ROBBERY, THE(1963, Brit.)

Christine Conway
WE OF THE NEVER NEVER(1983, Aus.)
Curt Conway
DOUBLE LIFE, A(1947); GENTLEMAN'S AGREEMENT(1947); SINGAPORE(1947); T-MEN(1947); CASBAH(1948); NAKED CITY, THE(1948); RAW DEAL(1948); SAXON CHARM, THE(1948); ILLEGAL ENTRY(1949); KNOCK ON ANY DOOR(1949); LADY GAMBLES, THE(1949); THEY LIVE BY NIGHT(1949); WOMAN'S SECRET, A(1949); GODDESS, THE(1958); WIND ACROSS THE EVERGLADES(1958); RUN ACROSS THE RIVER(1961); HUD(1963); INVITATION TO A GUNFIGHTER(1964); MACHO CALLAHAN(1970); MAURIE(1973)
Cyril Conway
INSPECTOR HORNLEIGH ON HOLIDAY(1939, Brit.); OPERATION DIAMOND(1948, Brit.); ROOM TO LET(1949, Brit.); SPRING IN PARK LANE(1949, Brit.); HIGH TREASON(1951, Brit.); HOME TO DANGER(1951, Brit.); FOUR AGAINST FATE(1952, Brit.); GLORY AT SEA(1952, Brit.); LITTLE BIG SHOT(1952, Brit.); BEGGAR'S OPERA, THE(1953, Brit.); TWILIGHT WOMEN(1953, Brit.); RUNAWAY BUS, THE(1954, Brit.); EVIL UNDER THE SUN(1982, Brit.); VENOM(1982, Brit.); WICKED LADY, THE(1983, Brit.)
Misc. Talkies
UNDEFEATED, THE(1951, Brit.)
Dan Conway
Misc. Talkies
BLAST-OFF GIRLS(1967)
Edith Conway
Misc. Silents
SUBMARINE EYE, THE(1917)
Frank Conway
1984
PIGS(1984, Ireland), art d
Gary Conway
SAGA OF THE VIKING WOMEN AND THEIR VOYAGE TO THE WATERS OF THE GREAT SEA SERPENT, THE(1957); HOW TO MAKE A MONSTER(1958); I WAS A TEENAGE FRANKENSTEIN(1958); YOUNG GUNS OF TEXAS(1963); BLACK GUNN(1972); FARMER, THE(1977), a, p; FIRE IN THE STONE, THE(1983, Aus.), d
Gerry Conway
FIRE AND ICE(1983), w
1984
CONAN THE DESTROYER(1984), w
Gordon Conway
ROME EXPRESS(1933, Brit.), cos
Harold Conway
BATTLE IN OUTER SPACE(1960)
Harold S. Conway
MYSTERIANS, THE(1959, Jap.)
Helen Conway
THREE HEARTS FOR JULIA(1943), set d; YOUNGEST PROFESSION, THE(1943), set d; LOST ANGEL(1944), set d; MAISIE GOES TO RENO(1944), set d
Hugh Conway
Silents
AUNT RACHEL(1920, Brit.), w; LAST ROSE OF SUMMER, THE(1920, Brit.), w
J. W. Conway
Silents
MILLION DOLLAR ROBBERY, THE(1914)
Jack Conway
ALIAS JIMMY VALENTINE(1928), d; OUR MODERN MAIDENS(1929), d; UNTAMED(1929), d; NEW MOON(1930), d; THEY LEARNED ABOUT WOMEN(1930), d; UNHOLY THREE, THE(1930), d; EASIEST WAY, THE(1931), d; JUST A GIGOLO(1931), p&d; ARSENE LUPIN(1932), d; BUT THE FLESH IS WEAK(1932), d; RED HEADED WOMAN(1932), d; HELL BELOW(1933), d; NUISANCE, THE(1933), d; SOLITAIRE MAN, THE(1933), d; GAY BRIDE, THE(1934), d; GIRL FROM MISSOURI, THE(1934), d; TARZAN AND HIS MATE(1934), d; VIVA VILLA!(1934), d; ONE NEW YORK NIGHT(1935), d; TALE OF TWO CITIES, A(1935), d; LIBELED LADY(1936), d; SARATOGA(1937), d; TOO HOT TO HANDLE(1938), d; YANK AT OXFORD, A(1938), d; LADY OF THE TROPICS(1939), d; LET FREEDOM RING(1939), d; BOOM TOWN(1940), d; NORTHWEST PASSAGE(1940), d; HONKY TONK(1941), d; LOVE CRAZY(1941), d; CROSSROADS(1942), d; ASSIGNMENT IN BRITTANY(1943), d; DRAGON SEED(1944), d; HIGH BARBAREE(1947), d; HUCKSTERS, THE(1947), d; JULIA MISBEHAVES(1948), d
Silents
PENITENTES, THE(1915), d; MEASURE OF A MAN, THE(1916), d; RIDERS OF THE DAWN(1920), d; KILLER, THE(1921), d; MILLIONAIRE, THE(1921), d; RAGE OF PARIS, THE(1921), d; ACROSS THE DEAD-LINE(1922), d; LONG CHANCE, THE(1922), d; STEP ON IT!(1922), d; PRISONER, THE(1923), d; SAWDUST(1923), d; WHAT WIVES WANT(1923), d; ROUGHNECK, THE(1924), d; SOUL MATES(1925), d; BROWN OF HARVARD(1926), d; KICK-OFF, THE(1926), t; NEVADA(1927), t; TWELVE MILES OUT(1927), d; TWO FLAMING YOUTHS(1927), t; WE'RE ALL GAMBLERS(1927), t; FLYING ROMEOS(1928), t; SALLY OF THE SCANDALS(1928), t; SMART SET, THE(1928), d; STOCKS AND BLONDES(1928), t; WHILE THE CITY SLEEPS(1928), d; OUR MODERN MAIDENS(1929), d
Misc. Silents
VALLEY OF THE MOON, THE(1914); CAPTAIN MACKLIN(1915), a, d; BECKONING TRAIL, THE(1916), d; MAINSPRING, THE(1916), d; SILENT BATTLE, THE(1916), d; SOCIAL BUCCANEER, THE(1916), d; BECAUSE OF THE WOMAN(1917), d; BOND OF FEAR, THE(1917), d; CHARMER, THE(1917), d; COME THROUGH(1917), d; HER SOUL'S INSPIRATION(1917), d; JEWEL IN PAWN, A(1917), d; LITTLE ORPHAN, THE(1917), a, d; POLLY REDHEAD(1917), d; DESERT LAW(1918), d; DIPLOMATIC MISSION, A(1918), d; HER DECISION(1918), d; LITTLE RED DECIDES(1918), d; YOU CAN'T BELIEVE EVERYTHING(1918), d; LOMBARDI, LTD.(1919), d; RESTLESS SOULS(1919); ROYAL DEMOCRAT, A(1919); DWELLING PLACE OF LIGHT, THE(1920), d; MONEY CHANGERS, THE(1920), d; DAUGHTER OF THE LAW, A(1921), d; KISS, THE(1921), d; SPENDERS, THE(1921), d; ANOTHER MAN'S SHOES(1922), d; DON'T SHOOT(1922), d; LUCRETIA LOMBARD(1923), d; QUICKSANDS(1923), d; TRIMMED IN SCARLET(1923), d; HEART BUSTER, THE(1924), d; TROUBLE SHOOTER, THE(1924), d; HUNTED WOMAN, THE(1925), d; ONLY THING, THE(1925), d; UNDERSTANDING HEART, THE(1927), d; BRINGING UP FATHER(1928), d
Jack [Hugh Ryan] Conway
Misc. Silents
SERVANT IN THE HOUSE, THE(1920), d

Jack W. Conway
Silents
KNOCKOUT REILLY(1927), t
James Conway
EARTHBOUND(1981), d
James L. Conway
LINCOLN CONSPIRACY, THE(1977), d; BEYOND AND BACK(1978), d; FALL OF THE HOUSE OF USHER, THE(1980), d; HANGAR 18(1980), d, w; IN SEARCH OF HISTORIC JESUS(1980), p; BOOGENS, THE(1982), d
Jeff Conway
PETE'S DRAGON(1977)
Joseph Conway
RING OF TERROR(1962)
Julie Conway
AROUND THE WORLD(1943); SWING FEVER(1943)
Karla Conway
FIREBALL 590(1966)
Kevin Conway
BELIEVE IN ME(1971); PORTNOY'S COMPLAINT(1972); SLAUGHTERHOUSE-FIVE(1972); SHAMUS(1973); F.I.S.T.(1978); PARADISE ALLEY(1978); FUNHOUSE, THE(1981)
1984
FLASHPOINT(1984)
Lita Conway
TRAILING DOUBLE TROUBLE(1940); SADDLE MOUNTAIN ROUNDUP(1941)
Melba Conway
Misc. Talkies
LAST MOMENT, THE(1976)
Melora Conway
THAT TOUCH OF MINK(1962); VENGEANCE(1964); LAST MOMENT, THE(1966)
Michele Conway
1984
LOVE STREAMS(1984)
Mike Conway
LAST GUNFIGHTER, THE(1961, Can.)
Mila Conway
NIGHT OF THE JUGGLER(1980)
Morgan Conway
HAPPY LANDING(1934); LOOKING FOR TROUBLE(1934); CRIME RING(1938); ILLEGAL TRAFFIC(1938); NURSE FROM BROOKLYN(1938); SINNERS IN PARADISE(1938); BLACKWELL'S ISLAND(1939); CHARLIE CHAN IN RENO(1939); GRAND JURY SECRETS(1939); KID FROM KOKOMO, THE(1939); NORTH OF SHANGHAI(1939); OFF THE RECORD(1939); PRIVATE DETECTIVE(1939); SECRET SERVICE OF THE AIR(1939); SPELLBINDER, THE(1939); TELEVISION SPY(1939); WINGS OF THE NAVY(1939); BROTHER ORCHID(1940); FLORIAN(1940); FUGITIVE FROM JUSTICE, A(1940); MILLIONAIRES IN PRISON(1940); SAINT TAKES OVER, THE(1940); SUED FOR LIBEL(1940); THREE CHEERS FOR THE IRISH(1940); BELLS OF CAPISTRANO(1942); DESPERATE CHANCE FOR ELLERY QUEEN, A(1942); SING YOUR WORRIES AWAY(1942); CANYON CITY(1943); JACK LONDON(1943); TORNADO(1943); DICK TRACY(1945); BADMAN'S TERRITORY(1946); DICK TRACY VS. CUEBALL(1946); TRUTH ABOUT MURDER, THE(1946); VACATION IN RENO(1946)
Pamela Conway
STRONGROOM(1962, Brit.); HEROES OF TELEMARK, THE(1965, Brit.); STITCH IN TIME, A(1967, Brit.)
Pat Conway
AMOS 'N' ANDY(1930); ANNAPOLIS STORY, AN(1955); FLIGHT TO HONG KONG(1956); SCREAMING EAGLES(1956); DEADLY MANTIS, THE(1957); DESTINATION 60,000(1957); UNDERSEA GIRL(1957); GERONIMO(1962); BRIGHTY OF THE GRAND CANYON(1967)
Patricia Ann Conway
ROSEMARY'S BABY(1968)
Patrick Conway
INVITATION(1952); ABOVE AND BEYOND(1953)
Philip Conway
FURY AND THE WOMAN(1937), w
Richard Conway
FLASH GORDON(1980), spec eff
Richard S. Conway
YANKEE FAKIR(1947), w; ONCE A THIEF(1950), w
Robert Conway
DOWN ARGENTINE WAY(1940); FOUR SONS(1940); YOUTH WILL BE SERVED(1940); COWBOY AND THE BLONDE, THE(1941); MOON OVER MIAMI(1941); OLD HOMESTEAD, THE(1942); TO THE SHORES OF TRIPOLI(1942); CHATTERBOX(1943); FIGHTING MAD(1948); JOE PALOOKA IN THE COUNTERPUNCH(1949)
Russ Conway
DOUBLE LIFE, A(1947); LARCENY(1948); NAKED CITY, THE(1948); ONE TOUCH OF VENUS(1948); WINNER'S CIRCLE, THE(1948); HEIRESS, THE(1949); I WAS A MALE WAR BRIDE(1949); LADY TAKES A SAILOR, THE(1949); TRAPPED(1949); TWELVE O'CLOCK HIGH(1949); LAWLESS, THE(1950); MILITARY ACADEMY WITH THAT TENTH AVENUE GANG(1950); PRISONERS IN PETTICOATS(1950); WHEN WILLIE COMES MARCHING HOME(1950); CALL ME MISTER(1951); I WAS A COMMUNIST FOR THE F.B.I.(1951); LET'S GO NAVY(1951); DIPLOMATIC COURIER(1952); FORT OSAGE(1952); JET JOB(1952); MY SIX CONVICTS(1952); OUTCASTS OF POKER FLAT, THE(1952); ABBOTT AND COSTELLO GO TO MARS(1953); JENNIFER(1953); ONE GIRL'S CONFESSION(1953); SAFARI DRUMS(1953); VICKI(1953); KILLER LEOPARD(1954); LOOTERS, THE(1955); TALL MAN RIDING(1955); LOVE ME TENDER(1956); SOMEBODY UP THERE LIKES ME(1956); BERNARDINE(1957); MIDNIGHT STORY, THE(1957); PORTLAND EXPOSE(1957); FLOOD TIDE(1958); FORT DOBBS(1958); JOHNNY ROCCO(1958); SCREAMING SKULL, THE(1958); BRAMBLE BUSH, THE(1960); TWELVE HOURS TO KILL(1960); WEEKEND WITH LULU, A(1961, Brit.); WHATEVER HAPPENED TO BABY JANE?(1962); DREAM MAKER, THE(1963, Brit.); GUNS OF DIABLO(1964); LIVELY SET, THE(1964); OUR MAN FLINT(1966); C'MON, LET'S LIVE A LITTLE(1967); INTERVAL(1973, Mex./U.S.); WORLD'S GREATEST ATHLETE, THE(1973)
Russell Conway
WEB, THE(1947); TOMAHAWK(1951); TURNING POINT, THE(1952); WAR OF THE WORLDS, THE(1953); TOP OF THE WORLD(1955)

Shirl Conway
HELTER SKELTER(1949, Brit.); YOU CAN'T FOOL AN IRISHMAN(1950, Ireland)
Steve Conway
GIRL ON THE PIER, THE(1953, Brit.)
Stewart Conway
MUSIC BOX KID, THE(1960); TWELVE HOURS TO KILL(1960)
Tanya Conway
PASSION STREET, U.S.A.(1964)
Teresa Conway
SORCERESS(1983)
Tim Conway
MC HALE'S NAVY(1964); MC HALE'S NAVY JOINS THE AIR FORCE(1965); WORLD'S GREATEST ATHLETE, THE(1973); APPLE DUMPLING GANG, THE(1975); GUS(1976); SHAGGY D.A., THE(1976); BILLION DOLLAR HOBO, THE(1977), a, w; THEY WENT THAT-A-WAY AND THAT-A-WAY(1978), a, w; APPLE DUMPLING GANG RIDES AGAIN, THE(1979); PRIZE FIGHTER, THE(1979), a, w; PRIVATE EYES, THE(1980), a, w
1984
CANNONBALL RUN II(1984)
Tom Conway
SKY MURDER(1940); BAD MAN, THE(1941); FREE AND EASY(1941); LADY BE GOOD(1941); MR. AND MRS. NORTH(1941); PEOPLE VS. DR. KILDARE, THE(1941); TARZAN'S SECRET TREASURE(1941); TRIAL OF MARY DUGAN, THE(1941); WILD MAN OF BORNEO, THE(1941); CAT PEOPLE(1942); FALCON'S BROTHER, THE(1942); GRAND CENTRAL MURDER(1942); MRS. MINIVER(1942); RIO RITA(1942); FALCON AND THE CO-EDS, THE(1943); FALCON IN DANGER, THE(1943); FALCON STRIKES BACK, THE(1943); I WALKED WITH A ZOMBIE(1943); SEVENTH VICTIM, THE(1943); FALCON IN HOLLYWOOD, THE(1944); FALCON IN MEXICO, THE(1944); FALCON OUT WEST, THE(1944); NIGHT OF ADVENTURE, A(1944); FALCON IN SAN FRANCISCO, THE(1945); TWO O'CLOCK COURAGE(1945); CRIMINAL COURT(1946); FALCON'S ADVENTURE, THE(1946); FALCON'S ALIBI, THE(1946); WHISTLE STOP(1946); LOST HONEYMOON(1947); REPEAT PERFORMANCE(1947); BUNGALOW 13(1948); CHALLENGE, THE(1948); CHECKERED COAT, THE(1948); ONE TOUCH OF VENUS(1948); THIRTEEN LEAD SOLDIERS(1948); I CHEATED THE LAW(1949); GREAT PLANE ROBBERY(1950); BRIDE OF THE GORILLA(1951); PAINTING THE CLOUDS WITH SUNSHINE(1951); CONFIDENCE GIRL(1952); BLOOD ORANGE(1953, Brit.); NORMAN CONQUEST(1953, Brit.); PARIS MODEL(1953); PETER PAN(1953); TARZAN AND THE SHE-DEVIL(1953); PRINCE VALIANT(1954); BREAKAWAY(1956, Brit.); DEATH OF A SCOUNDREL(1956); LAST MAN TO HANG, THE(1956, Brit.); MURDER ON APPROVAL(1956, Brit.); SHE-CREATURE, THE(1956); OPERATION MURDER(1957, Brit.); VOODOO WOMAN(1957); ATOMIC SUBMARINE, THE(1960); TWELVE TO THE MOON(1960); ONE HUNDRED AND ONE DALMATIANS(1961); WHAT A WAY TO GO(1964); FUN ON A WEEKEND(1979)
Misc. Talkies
BRIDE OF THE GORILLA(1951)
William E. Conway
GHOST STORY(1981)
Carolyn Conwell
TORN CURTAIN(1966); THE BOSTON STRANGLER, THE(1968); ADAM AT 6 A.M.(1970); MAGNIFICENT SEVEN RIDE, THE(1972)
Mary Conwell
UNTAMED FURY(1947)
Nula Conwell
ELEPHANT MAN, THE(1980, Brit.); BLOODY KIDS(1983, Brit.)
Russell H. Conwell
Silents
JOHNNY RING AND THE CAPTAIN'S SWORD(1921), w
D'Arcy Conyers
GIRDLE OF GOLD(1952, Brit.), p; GAY ADVENTURE, THE(1953, Brit.); NOTHING BARRED(1961, Brit.), p, d
Darcy Conyers
JACK OF DIAMONDS, THE(1949, Brit.); HA' PENNY BREEZE(1950, Brit.), a, p; DEAD ON COURSE(1952, Brit.); SECRET OF THE FOREST, THE(1955, Brit.), d, w; TIME OF HIS LIFE, THE(1955, Brit.); DEVIL'S PASS, THE(1957, Brit.), d&w; SOAP BOX DERBY(1958, Brit.), d, w; NIGHT WE GOT THE BIRD, THE(1961, Brit.), p, d, w; MAKE MINE A DOUBLE(1962, Brit.), d; IN THE DOGHOUSE(1964, Brit.), d
Joseph Conyers
Silents
OH, BOY!(1919)
Fred Conyngham
INDISCRETIONS OF EVE(1932, Brit.); KEY TO HARMONY(1935, Brit.); RADIO FOLLIES(1935, Brit.); SCHOOL FOR STARS(1935, Brit.); BALL AT SAVOY(1936, Brit.); BELOVED IMPOSTER(1936, Brit.); CHICK(1936, Brit.); CROUCHING BEAST, THE(1936, U. S./Brit.); SHE KNEW WHAT SHE WANTED(1936, Brit.); MINSTREL BOY, THE(1937, Brit.); SAM SMALL LEAVES TOWN(1937, Brit.); WAKE UP FAMOUS(1937, Brit.); ROSE OF TRALEE(1938, Ireland); WHEN YOU COME HOME(1947, Brit.), a, ch
Koo Coo
FREAKS(1932)
Ry Cooder
BLUE COLLAR(1978), m; LONG RIDERS, THE(1980), m; SOUTHERN COMFORT(1981), m; BORDER, THE(1982), m
1984
PARIS, TEXAS(1984, Ger./Fr.), m; STREETS OF FIRE(1984), m
Ted Coodley
VOODOO ISLAND(1957), makeup; EXPLOSIVE GENERATION, THE(1961), makeup; HOODLUM PRIEST, THE(1961), makeup; PANIC IN YEAR ZERO!(1962), makeup; "X"—THE MAN WITH THE X-RAY EYES(1963), makeup; HAUNTED PALACE, THE(1963), makeup; OPERATION BIKINI(1963), makeup; RAVEN, THE(1963), makeup; YOUNG AND THE BRAVE, THE(1963), makeup; MUSCLE BEACH PARTY(1964), makeup; SURF PARTY(1964), makeup; DR. GOLDFOOT AND THE BIKINI MACHINE(1965), makeup; MUTINY IN OUTER SPACE(1965), makeup; SKI PARTY(1965), makeup; JESSE JAMES MEETS FRANKENSTEIN'S DAUGHTER(1966), makeup; TRIP, THE(1967), makeup; 40 GUNS TO APACHE PASS(1967), makeup; KILLERS THREE(1968), makeup; THREE IN THE ATTIC(1968), makeup; LAST MOVIE, THE(1971), makeup

Millard Coody
LAWTON STORY, THE(1949); PRINCE OF PEACE, THE(1951)
Gene Coogan
GIRL OF THE GOLDEN WEST, THE(1938); STRANGE CARGO(1940); B. F.'S DAUGHTER(1948); STATE OF THE UNION(1948); FATHER OF THE BRIDE(1950); PLYMOUTH ADVENTURE(1952); ISLAND IN THE SKY(1953); LAST TIME I SAW PARIS, THE(1954); ROGUE COP(1954); GUN GLORY(1957); GUN FIGHT(1961)
George Coogan
ESCAPE FROM TERROR(1960), d
Jack Coogan, Sr.
Silents
KID, THE(1921); MY BOY(1922), sup; OLIVER TWIST(1922), sup; TROUBLE(1922), p; CIRCUS DAYS(1923), sup; JOHNNY GET YOUR HAIR CUT(1927), sup
Jackie Coogan
FREE AND EASY(1930); TOM SAWYER(1930); HUCKLEBERRY FINN(1931); HOME ON THE RANGE(1935); COLLEGE SWING(1938); MILLION DOLLAR LEGS(1939); SKY PATROL(1939); KILROY WAS HERE(1947); FRENCH LEAVE(1948); SKIPA-LONG ROSENBLOOM(1951); OUTLAW WOMEN(1952); MESA OF LOST WOMEN, THE(1956); PROUD ONES, THE(1956); BUSTER KEATON STORY, THE(1957); EIGHT-EEN AND ANXIOUS(1957); JOKER IS WILD, THE(1957); HIGH SCHOOL CONFI-DENTIAL(1958); LONELYHEARTS(1958); NO PLACE TO LAND(1958); SPACE CHILDREN, THE(1958); BEAT GENERATION, THE(1959); BIG OPERATOR, THE(1959); NIGHT OF THE QUARTER MOON(1959); ESCAPE FROM TERROR(1960), a, d; SEX KITTENS GO TO COLLEGE(1960); WHEN THE GIRLS TAKE OVER(1962); JOHN GOLDFARB, PLEASE COME HOME(1964); GIRL HAPPY(1965); FINE MAD-NESS, A(1966); SHAKIEST GUN IN THE WEST, THE(1968); MARLOWE(1969); CAHILL, UNITED STATES MARSHAL(1973); MANCHU EAGLE MURDER CAPER MYSTERY, THE(1975); WON TON TON, THE DOG WHO SAVED HOL-LYWOOD(1976); DR. HECKYL AND MR. HYPE(1980); HUMAN EX-PERIMENTS(1980); ESCAPE ARTIST, THE(1982)
1984
PREY, THE(1984)
Silents
KID, THE(1921); PECK'S BAD BOY(1921); MY BOY(1922); OLIVER TWIST(1922); TROUBLE(1922); CIRCUS DAYS(1923); DADDY(1923); LONG LIVE THE KING(1923); OLD CLOTHES(1925); RAG MAN, THE(1925); JOHNNY GET YOUR HAIR CUT(1927)
Misc. Silents
BOY OF FLANDERS, A(1924); LITTLE ROBINSON CRUSOE(1924); BUGLE CALL, THE(1927); BUTTONS(1927)
Jackie Coogan, Sr.
Silents
RAG MAN, THE(1925), sup
Peter Coogan
1984
SWORD OF THE VALIANT(1984, Brit.)
Richard Coogan
THREE HOURS TO KILL(1954); VICE RAID(1959); GIRL ON THE RUN(1961)
Robert Coogan
SKIPPY(1931); SOOKY(1931); MIRACLE MAN, THE(1932); SKY BRIDE(1932); JOHNNY DOUGHBOY(1943); KILROY WAS HERE(1947); FRENCH LEAVE(1948); MASTER MINDS(1949); HUMPHREY TAKES A CHANCE(1950); JOE PALOOKA IN THE SQUARED CIRCLE(1950); JOE PALOOKA MEETS HUMPHREY(1950); GHOST CHASERS(1951); THIRD OF A MAN(1962)
Ad Cook
Misc. Silents
WESTERN GRIT(1924), d
Alan Cook
THANK YOUR LUCKY STARS(1943)
Alice Cook
BABES IN TOYLAND(1934); PAINTED VEIL, THE(1934)
Ancel Cook
RATTLERS(1976); GRAND THEFT AUTO(1977)
Ancil Cook
Misc. Talkies
STARBIRD AND SWEET WILLIAM(1975)
Baldy Cook
LUCKY NIGHT(1939)
Barbara Cook
SPRING FEVER(1983, Can.)
Bernie Cook
GAL YOUNG UN(1979)
Beryl Cook
NICE GIRL LIKE ME, A(1969, Brit.)
Billy Cook
MEN WITH WINGS(1938); SONS OF THE LEGION(1938); BEAU GESTE(1939); DISPUTED PASSAGE(1939); INVITATION TO HAPPINESS(1939); TOM SAWYER, DETECTIVE(1939); NAVAL ACADEMY(1941); MAJOR AND THE MINOR, THE(1942)
Brian Cook
HARPER VALLEY, P.T.A.(1978)
Bruce Cook
1984
CENSUS TAKER, THE(1984), d, w, ed
Carlo Cook
PAGAN LOVE SONG(1950)
Carole Cook
PALM SPRINGS WEEKEND(1963); INCREDIBLE MR. LIMPET, THE(1964); GAUNTLET, THE(1977); AMERICAN GIGOLO(1980); SUMMER LOVERS(1982)
1984
GRANDVIEW, U.S.A.(1984); SIXTEEN CANDLES(1984)
Caroline Cook
SON OF FRANKENSTEIN(1939)
Charles E. Cook
Silents
LIVE WIRES(1921), w
Chris Cook
TWO GENTLEMEN SHARING(1969, Brit.), set d
Christopher Cook
MAN CALLED PETER, THE(1955); PRINCE OF PLAYERS(1955); SWAN, THE(1956); PERCY(1971, Brit.), set d

Clyde Cook
DANGEROUS WOMAN(1929); IN THE HEADLINES(1929); JAZZ HEAVEN(1929); MASQUERADE(1929); SPIELER, THE(1929); TAMING OF THE SHREW, THE(1929); DAWN PATROL, THE(1930); DUDE WRANGLER, THE(1930); OFFICER O'BRIEN(1930); SUNNY(1930); WINGS OF ADVENTURE(1930); WOMEN EVERY-WHERE(1930); DAYBREAK(1931); GOD IS MY WITNESS(1931); NEVER THE TWAIN SHALL MEET(1931); SECRET WITNESS, THE(1931); DICK TURPIN(1933, Brit.), p; OLIVER TWIST(1933); WEST OF SINGAPORE(1933); SHOCK(1934); BARBARY COAST(1935); CALM YOURSELF(1935); INFORMER, THE(1935); WHITE ANGEL, THE(1936); ANOTHER DAWN(1937); BULLDOG DRUMMOND ESCAPES(1937); LANCER SPY(1937); LOVE UNDER FIRE(1937); SOULS AT SEA(1937); WEE WILLIE WINKIE(1937); BULLDOG DRUMMOND'S PERIL(1938); KIDNAPPED(1938); STORM OVER BENGAL(1938); ARREST BULLDOG DRUMMOND(1939, Brit.); LIGHT THAT FAILED, THE(1939); LITTLE PRINCESS, THE(1939); DANCE, GIRL, DANCE(1940); SEA HAWK, THE(1940); LADIES IN RETIREMENT(1941); SUSPICION(1941); KLON-DIKE FURY(1942); WHITE CARGO(1942); FOREVER AND A DAY(1943); MAN FROM DOWN UNDER, THE(1943); MYSTERIOUS DOCTOR, THE(1943); FOLLOW THE BOYS(1944); WHITE CLIFFS OF DOVER, THE(1944); TO EACH HIS OWN(1946); VERDICT, THE(1946); PRIDE OF MARYLAND(1951); LOOSE IN LONDON(1953); MAZE, THE(1953); ABBOTT AND COSTELLO MEET DR. JEKYLL AND MR. HYDE(1954)
Misc. Talkies
BEWARE OF BACHELORS(1928); TUGBOAT PRINCESS(1936)
Silents
GREATER LAW, THE(1917), ph; ALL WRONG(1919), ph; HE WHO GETS SLAPPED(1924); MISS NOBODY(1926); WINNING OF BARBARA WORTH, THE(1926); BARBED WIRE(1927); BRUTE, THE(1927); SAILOR'S SWEETHEART, A(1927); WHITE GOLD(1927); CAPTAIN LASH(1929); STRONG BOY(1929)
Misc. Silents
SKIRTS(1921); SO THIS IS MARRIAGE(1924); BUSH LEAGUER, THE(1927); CLIMB-ERS, THE(1927); GOOD TIME CHARLEY(1927); SIMPLE SIS(1927); BEWARE OF MARRIED MEN(1928); CELEBRITY(1928); DOCKS OF NEW YORK, THE(1928); DOMESTIC TROUBLES(1928); FIVE AND TEN CENT ANNIE(1928); PAY AS YOU ENTER(1928); THROUGH THE BREAKERS(1928)
David Cook
KIND OF LOVING, A(1962, Brit.); KING AND COUNTRY(1964, Brit.); WHO IS KILLING THE GREAT CHEFS OF EUROPE?(1978, US/Ger.)
Dempsey Cook
OLIVER!(1968, Brit.)
Diana Cook
ONE IN A MILLION(1936); MERMAIDS OF TIBURON, THE(1962)
Diane Cook
ROBERTA(1935); THIN ICE(1937)
Donald Cook
MAD GENIUS, THE(1931); PARTY HUSBAND(1931); PUBLIC ENEMY, THE(1931); SAFE IN HELL(1931); SIDE SHOW(1931); UNFAITHFUL(1931); CONQUERORS, THE(1932); HEART OF NEW YORK(1932); MAN WHO PLAYED GOD, THE(1932); TAXI!(1932); TRIAL OF VIVIENNE WARE, THE(1932); BABY FACE(1933); BRIEF MOMENT(1933); CIRCUS QUEEN MURDER, THE(1933); FRISCO JENNY(1933); JENNIE GERHARDT(1933); KISS BEFORE THE MIRROR, THE(1933); PRIVATE JONES(1933); WOMAN I STOLE, THE(1933); WORLD CHANGES, THE(1933); FOG(1934); FUGITIVE LADY(1934); FURY OF THE JUNGLE(1934); JEALOU-SY(1934); LONG LOST FATHER(1934); MOST PRECIOUS THING IN LIFE(1934); NINTH GUEST, THE(1934); VIVA VILLA!(1934); WHIRLPOOL(1934); BEHIND THE EVIDENCE(1935); CASINO MURDER CASE, THE(1935); CONFIDENTIAL(1935); GIGOLETTE(1935); HERE COMES THE BAND(1935); LADIES LOVE DANGER(1935); MOTIVE FOR REVENGE(1935); MURDER IN THE FLEET(1935); NIGHT IS YOUNG, THE(1935); SPANISH CAPE MYSTERY(1935); CAN THIS BE DIXIE?(1936); DAN MATTHEWS(1936); GIRL FROM MANDALAY(1936); LEAVENWORTH CASE, THE(1936); RING AROUND THE MOON(1936); SHOW BOAT(1936); BEWARE OF LADIES(1937); CIRCUS GIRL(1937); TWO WISE MAIDS(1937); BOWERY TO BROAD-WAY(1944); MURDER IN THE BLUE ROOM(1944); BLONDE RANSOM(1945); HERE COME THE CO-EDS(1945); OUR VERY OWN(1950); VENGEANCE(1964)
Misc. Talkies
CALLING OF DAN MATTHEWS, THE(1936); ELLIS ISLAND(1936)
Donald Cook, Sr.
PATRICK THE GREAT(1945)
Doria Cook
HEX(1973); MAME(1974); PARALLAX VIEW, THE(1974); SWARM, THE(1978); FAST BREAK(1979)
Ed Cook
LET'S GET MARRIED(1937); LIKE FATHER LIKE SON(1961); VENGEANCE(1964); YOUNG SINNER, THE(1965); GLORY STOMPERS, THE(1967); IF HE HOLLERS, LET HIM GO(1968)
Edwin Cook
BORN LOSERS(1967); YOUNG RUNAWAYS, THE(1968)
Elisha Cook
INDIAN FIGHTER, THE(1955); VOODOO ISLAND(1957); HOUSE ON HAUNTED HILL(1958); DAY OF THE OUTLAW(1959); COLLEGE CONFIDENTIAL(1960); HAUNTED PALACE, THE(1963); SPY IN THE GREEN HAT, THE(1966); WELCOME TO HARD TIMES(1967); ELECTRA GLIDE IN BLUE(1973); EMPEROR OF THE NORTH POLE(1973); ST. IVES(1976); CHAMP, THE(1979); 1941(1979); CARNY(1980); TOM HORN(1980); HARRY'S WAR(1981); HAMMETT(1982)
Elisha Cook, Jr.
SERGEANT YORK(; PIGSKIN PARADE(1936); TWO IN A CROWD(1936); BREEZ-ING HOME(1937); DANGER–LOVE AT WORK(1937); DEVIL IS DRIVING, THE(1937); LIFE BEGINS IN COLLEGE(1937); LOVE IS NEWS(1937); THEY WON'T FOR-GET(1937); WIFE, DOCTOR AND NURSE(1937); MY LUCKY STAR(1938); SUBMA-RINE PATROL(1938); THREE BLIND MICE(1938); GRAND JURY SECRETS(1939); NEWSBOY'S HOME(1939); PUBLIC DEB NO. 1(1940); STRANGER ON THE THIRD FLOOR(1940); TIN PAN ALLEY(1940); BALL OF FIRE(1941); HELLZAPOPPIN'(1941); LOVE CRAZY(1941); MALTESE FALCON, THE(1941); MAN AT LARGE(1941); A-HAUNTING WE WILL GO(1942); GENTLEMAN AT HEART, A(1942); I WAKE UP SCREAMING(1942); IN THIS OUR LIFE(1942); MANILA CALLING(1942); SLEEPY-TIME GAL(1942); WILDCAT(1942); DARK MOUNTAIN(1944); DARK WATERS(1944); PHANTOM LADY(1944); UP IN ARMS(1944); DILLINGER(1945); WHY GIRLS LEAVE HOME(1945); BIG SLEEP, THE(1946); BLONDE ALIBI(1946); CINDERELLA JO-NES(1946); FALCON'S ALIBI, THE(1946); JOE PALOOKA, CHAMP(1946); TWO SMART PEOPLE(1946); BORN TO KILL(1947); FALL GUY(1947); GANGSTER, THE(1947); LONG NIGHT, THE(1947); FLAXY MARTIN(1949); GREAT GATSBY,

THE(1949); BEHAVE YOURSELF(1951); DON'T BOTHER TO KNOCK(1952); I, THE JURY(1953); SHANE(1953); THUNDER OVER THE PLAINS(1953); DRUM BEAT(1954); OUTLAW'S DAUGHTER(1954); TIMBERJACK(1955); TRIAL(1955); ACCUSED OF MURDER(1956); KILLING, THE(1956); BABY FACE NELSON(1957); CHICAGO CONFIDENTIAL(1957); LONELY MAN, THE(1957); PLUNDER ROAD(1957); PLATINUM HIGH SCHOOL(1960); ONE-EYED JACKS(1961); BLACK ZOO(1963); JOHNNY COOL(1963); PAPA'S DELICATE CONDITION(1963); BLOOD ON THE ARROW(1964); GLASS CAGE, THE(1964); ROSEMARY'S BABY(1968); GREAT BANK ROBBERY, THE(1969); EL CONDOR(1970); BLACULA(1972); GREAT NORTHFIELD, MINNESOTA RAID, THE(1972); OUTFIT, THE(1973); PAT GARRETT AND BILLY THE KID(1973); DEAD PEOPLE(1974); BLACK BIRD, THE(1975); WINTERHAWK(1976)
Misc. Talkies
HER UNBORN CHILD(1933)

Ella May Cook
RIDING SPEED(1934), w

Estelle Cook
Silents
KID, THE(1921)

Evelyn Cook
WEST OF THE LAW(1942)

Fielder Cook
PATTERNS(1956), d; BIG HAND FOR THE LITTLE LADY, A(1966), p&d; HOW TO SAVE A MARRIAGE-AND RUIN YOUR LIFE(1968), d; PRUDENCE AND THE PILL(1968, Brit.), d; EAGLE IN A CAGE(1971, U.S./Yugo.), d; FROM THE MIXED-UP FILES OF MRS. BASIL E. FRANKWEILER(1973), d

Frank Cook
VILLAGE BARN DANCE(1940); BUCK PRIVATES(1941)

Fred Cook
HOT ROCK, THE(1972)

Frederic Cook
JACKSON COUNTY JAIL(1976); TRUE CONFESSIONS(1981)

Fredric Cook
SCHIZOID(1980)

Genadee Cook
Misc. Talkies
CLOSET CASANOVA, THE(1979)

George Cook
MIKADO, THE(1967, Brit.)

Glen Cook
Misc. Silents
SADDLE KING, THE(1929)

J. Fielder Cook
HOME IS THE HERO(1959, Ireland), d

James Cook
BLADE(1973)

Jim Cook
THIRD OF A MAN(1962)

Jimmie Cook
DRUMS O' VOODOO(1934)

Jo Cook
MOON ZERO TWO(1970, Brit.), ch

Joe Cook
RAIN OR SHINE(1930); ARIZONA MAHONEY(1936); LEGACY OF BLOOD(1978), set d

Joe Cook, Jr.
THIS IS THE ARMY(1943); YOU GOTTA STAY HAPPY(1948)

John C. Cook
SHARK WOMAN, THE(1941), ph

John Cook
SAFARI(1956); ADDING MACHINE, THE(1969)
Silents
ROMANCE OF TARZAN, THE(1918); EYES OF THE HEART(1920)
Misc. Silents
RIGHT TO BE HAPPY, THE(1917); THIEVES' GOLD(1918)

Johnnie Cook
Misc. Silents
LIKE WILDFIRE(1917); POINTING FINGER, THE(1919)

Joseph Cook
WHERE HAS POOR MICKEY GONE?(1964, Brit.)

Judy Cook
MAN FROM FRISCO(1944); PRIVATE AFFAIRS OF BEL AMI, THE(1947)

Kenneth Cook
OUTBACK(1971, Aus.), w

Larry Cook
LANDLORD, THE(1970); TROUBLE MAN(1972)

Lawrence Cook
MAN, THE(1972); SPOOK WHO SAT BY THE DOOR, THE(1973); LORD SHANGO(1975)

Lee Cook
MAIDSTONE(1970)

Lem Cook
1984
NINJA III-THE DOMINATION(1984)

Lillian Cook
Silents
MOTHER(1914); COTTON KING, THE(1915); AS IN A LOOKING GLASS(1916); COMMON LAW, THE(1916); DEVIL'S PLAYGROUND, THE(1918)
Misc. Silents
(; CAMILLE(1916); BETSY ROSS(1917)

Linda Cook
Misc. Talkies
ALL THE YOUNG WIVES(1975); NAKED RIVER(1977)

Louise Cook
EXILE, THE(1931)

Lt. Egbert Cook
Silents
LONE EAGLE, THE(1927)

Luci Ann Cook
MURDERERS' ROW(1966)

Lucius Cook
GOODBYE, MY FANCY(1951); LONE STAR(1952)

Malcolm Cook
LUTHER(1974), ed

Mara Cook
SWARM, THE(1978)

Marianne Cook
FOUR GIRLS IN TOWN(1956); INTERLUDE(1957)

Mary Lou Cook
NIGHT AT EARL CARROLL'S, A(1940); MELODY LANE(1941); MOONLIGHT IN HAWAII(1941); SAN ANTONIO ROSE(1941); RIDE 'EM COWBOY(1942); DESTRUCTORS, THE(1968)

Maxine Cook
STRIKE UP THE BAND(1940)

Michelle Cook
MRS. BROWN, YOU'VE GOT A LOVELY DAUGHTER(1968, Brit.)

Myron Cook
SILENCERS, THE(; AMAZING COLOSSAL MAN, THE(1957); CHICAGO CONFIDENTIAL(1957)

Nathan Cook
ABBY(1974); LAST WORD, THE(1979); NATIONAL LAMPOON'S VACATION(1983)

Patrick Cook
1984
MAN OF FLOWERS(1984, Aus.)

Paul Cook
DAMIEN-OMEN II(1978); LADIES AND GENTLEMEN, THE FABULOUS STAINS(1982)

Paul M. Cook
SOMEWHERE IN TIME(1980)

Perry Cook
MARYJANE(1968); UNHOLY ROLLERS(1972)

Peter Cook
WRONG BOX, THE(1966, Brit.); BEDAZZLED(1967, Brit.), a, w; DANDY IN ASPIC, A(1968, Brit.); BED SITTING ROOM, THE(1969, Brit.); THOSE DARING YOUNG MEN IN THEIR JAUNTY JALOPIES(1969, Fr./Brit./ Ital.); RISE AND RISE OF MICHAEL RIMMER, THE(1970, Brit.), a, w; ADVENTURES OF BARRY McKENZIE(1972, Austral.); HOUND OF THE BASKERVILLES, THE(1980, Brit.), a, w; YELLOWBEARD(1983), a, w
1984
SUPERGIRL(1984)
Misc. Talkies
RISE AND RISE OF MICHAEL RIMMER, THE(1970, Brit.)

Phyllis Cook
THREE HEARTS FOR JULIA(1943)

Ralph Cook
FLYING LEATHERNECKS(1951)

Randy Cook
DAY TIME ENDED, THE(1980, Span.), David Allen; Q(1982), spec eff

Ray Cook
GOODBYE AGAIN(1933)
1984
CAREFUL, HE MIGHT HEAR YOU(1984, Aus.), m

Robert Cook
1984
RHINESTONE(1984)

Robin Cook
COMA(1978), w; SPHINX(1981), w

Roderick Cook
IDOL ON PARADE(1959, Brit.); OUR TIME(1974); GREAT WALDO PEPPER, THE(1975); GIRLFRIENDS(1978)
1984
AMADEUS(1984); GARBO TALKS(1984); SILENT MADNESS(1984)

Ron Cook
1984
NUMBER ONE(1984, Brit.); SCANDALOUS(1984)

Rowena Cook
KIT CARSON(1940)

T. S. Cook
CHINA SYNDROME, THE(1979), w

Tommy Cook
GOOD LUCK, MR. YATES(1943); HI, BUDDY(1943); MR. WINKLE GOES TO WAR(1944); GAY SENORITA, THE(1945); STRANGE HOLIDAY(1945); WANDERER OF THE WASTELAND(1945); GALLANT JOURNEY(1946); HUMORESQUE(1946); SONG OF ARIZONA(1946); TARZAN AND THE LEOPARD WOMAN(1946); HOMESTRETCH, THE(1947); CRY OF THE CITY(1948); MICHAEL O'HALLORAN(1948); BAD BOY(1949); DAUGHTER OF THE WEST(1949); KID FROM CLEVELAND, THE(1949); AMERICAN GUERRILLA IN THE PHILIPPINES, AN(1950); PANIC IN THE STREETS(1950); VICIOUS YEARS, THE(1950); BATTLE AT APACHE PASS, THE(1952); STALAG 17(1953); THUNDER PASS(1954); BATTLE FLAME(1955); CANYON CROSSROADS(1955); TEEN-AGE CRIME WAVE(1955); MOHAWK(1956); NIGHT PASSAGE(1957); ALASKA PASSAGE(1959); MISSILE TO THE MOON(1959); WHEN THE GIRLS TAKE OVER(1962); SEND ME NO FLOWERS(1964); THING WITH TWO HEADS, THE(1972); ROLLERCOASTER(1977), w

Vera Cook
WINSLOW BOY, THE(1950); BRIDES OF DRACULA, THE(1960, Brit.); NEVER TAKE CANDY FROM A STRANGER(1961, Brit.); SHADOW OF THE CAT, THE(1961, Brit.); CASH ON DEMAND(1962, Brit.); KISS OF EVIL(1963, Brit.); HELP!(1965, Brit.)

Virginia Cook
SHED NO TEARS(1948), w

W. Cook
Misc. Silents
UNKNOWN LOVE, THE(1919)

Walter Cook
JOAN OF ARC(1948); NIGHT HAS A THOUSAND EYES(1948)

Warren Cook
Silents
INFIDELITY(1917); PRIDE OF THE CLAN, THE(1917); AVENGING TRAIL, THE(1918); CHALLENGE ACCEPTED, THE(1918); DOLL'S HOUSE, A(1918); RIGHT

TO LIE, THE(1919); FLAPPER, THE(1920); WHISPERS(1920); FIGHTER, THE(1921); JOHN SMITH(1922); SLIM SHOULDERS(1922); SILENT COMMAND, THE(1923); HIS DARKER SELF(1924); SHORE LEAVE(1925)
Misc. Silents
SHINE GIRL, THE(1916); SNOWBIRD, THE(1916); EXILE(1917); HER FINAL RECKONING(1918); INTERLOPER, THE(1918); SUSPICION(1918); WOMAN(1919); BROADWAY AND HOME(1920); HIS WIFE'S FRIEND(1920); MANHATTAN KNIGHT, A(1920); POINT OF VIEW, THE(1920); WOMAN GOD SENT, THE(1920); BROKEN VIOLIN, THE(1923); LUNATIC AT LARGE, THE(1927)

Whitfeld Cook
SAILOR TAKES A WIFE, THE(1946), w

Whitfield Cook
SECRET HEART, THE(1946), w; HIGH BARBAREE(1947), w; BIG CITY(1948), w; STAGE FRIGHT(1950, Brit.), w; STRANGERS ON A TRAIN(1951), w

Will Cook
TWO RODE TOGETHER(1961), w; TRAMPLERS, THE(1966, Ital.), w

William Cook
Silents
PATCHWORK GIRL OF OZ, THE(1914)

William Wallace Cook
Silents
SUNSHINE TRAIL, THE(1923), w

William Walllace Cook
Silents
SONORA KID, THE(1927), w

Willis Cook
NEW YORK CONFIDENTIAL(1955), spec eff; PRIDE AND THE PASSION, THE(1957), spec eff; DEVIL AT FOUR O'CLOCK, THE(1961), spec eff; PROFESSIONALS, THE(1966), spec eff; HAPPENING, THE(1967), spec eff; HURRY SUNDOWN(1967), spec eff; MACKENNA'S GOLD(1969), spec eff; MOLLY MAGUIRES, THE(1970), spec eff

Windy Cook
COURAGE OF LASSIE(1946); SWING PARADE OF 1946(1946)

Al Cooke
DEFENDERS OF THE LAW(1931); MYSTERY TRAIN(1931)
Silents
SMALL TOWN IDOL, A(1921); ONE MINUTE TO PLAY(1926)
Misc. Silents
HER FATHER SAID NO(1927); LEGIONNAIRES IN PARIS(1927)

Alan Cooke
FOLLOW THE BOYS(1944); FLAT TWO(1962, Brit.), d; MIND OF MR. SOAMES, THE(1970, Brit.), d
1984
NADIA(1984, U.S./Yugo.), d

Alice Cooke
OUR RELATIONS(1936)

Alistair Cooke
THREE FACES OF EVE, THE(1957)

Allan Cooke
SPECTER OF THE ROSE(1946)

Allen Cooke
GEORGE WHITE'S SCANDALS(1945)

Baldwin Cooke
PARDON US(1931); PACK UP YOUR TROUBLES(1932); SONS OF THE DESERT(1933); HOLLYWOOD PARTY(1934); OUR RELATIONS(1936); SWISS MISS(1938)

Baldwin G. Cooke
Silents
HIS LAST DOLLAR(1914), w

Baldy Cooke
OF MICE AND MEN(1939); NAZI AGENT(1942)

Beach Cooke
Silents
CLASSMATES(1924); NECESSARY EVIL, THE(1925)

Beryl Cooke
FUSS OVER FEATHERS(1954, Brit.); LOVERS, HAPPY LOVERS!(1955, Brit.); MONSTER OF HIGHGATE PONDS, THE(1961, Brit.)

Brian Cooke
NO SEX PLEASE–WE'RE BRITISH(1979, Brit.), w

C.J. Cooke
NIGHTMARE(1981)

Caroline Cooke
HOUSE OF THE SEVEN GABLES, THE(1940); WOLF MAN, THE(1941); MYSTERY OF MARIE ROGET, THE(1942); STRICTLY IN THE GROOVE(1942); KEEP 'EM SLUGGING(1943)

Christopher Cooke
VIOLENT PLAYGROUND(1958, Brit.); WOMAN'S TEMPTATION, A(1959, Brit.)

Donna Cooke
SENTIMENTAL JOURNEY(1946)

Doria Cooke
RANCHO DELUXE(1975)

Ethyle Cooke
Misc. Silents
FUGITIVE, THE(1916); PILLORY, THE(1916); SAINT, DEVIL AND WOMAN(1916); HER LIFE AND HIS(1917); SMALL TOWN GIRL, A(1917)

Evelyn Cooke
LITTLE JOE, THE WRANGLER(1942); MUG TOWN(1943)

Frank Cooke
Silents
MILLION DOLLAR ROBBERY, THE(1914)
Misc. Silents
THREE MUST-GET-THERES, THE(1922)

Gerry Cooke
PAPERBACK HERO(1973, Can.)

Gregory Cooke
1984
NADIA(1984, U.S./Yugo.)

Hal Cooke
MAN WHO CRIED WOLF, THE(1937); SWEETHEARTS(1938); MR. SMITH GOES TO WASHINGTON(1939); I LOVE YOU AGAIN(1940); TRIAL OF MARY DUGAN, THE(1941); NAZI AGENT(1942); PACIFIC RENDEZVOUS(1942); THEY ALL KISSED THE BRIDE(1942)

Harry Cooke
KISS OF DEATH(1947)

Jennifer C. Cooke
1984
GIMME AN 'F'(1984)

Jill Cooke
PETER RABBIT AND TALES OF BEATRIX POTTER(1971, Brit.)

John B. Cooke
Silents
MISSING MILLIONS(1922)

John Cooke
Misc. Silents
HOOP-LA(1919)

Johnnie Cooke
Misc. Silents
COMMON PROPERTY(1919); WEAKER VESSEL, THE(1919); ALIAS MISS DODD(1920)

Johnny Cooke
Silents
PRINCE OF AVENUE A., THE(1920)

Juliet Cooke
ALL THINGS BRIGHT AND BEAUTIFUL(1979, Brit.)

Lucius Cooke
IMPACT(1949)

Malcolm Cooke
FAR FROM THE MADDING CROWD(1967, Brit.), ed; CASTLE KEEP(1969), ed; FRAGMENT OF FEAR(1971, Brit.), ed; ENGLANO MADE ME(1973, Brit.), ed; THEATRE OF BLOOD(1973, Brit.), ed; BUTLEY(1974, Brit.), ed; BRANNIGAN(1975, Brit.), ed; SKY RIDERS(1976, U.S./Gr.), ed; DEATH ON THE NILE(1978, Brit.), ed; FLASH GORDON(1980), ed; ZULU DAWN(1980, Brit.), ed; HOUND OF THE BASKERVILLES, THE(1983, Brit.), ed
1984
SUPERGIRL(1984), ed

Marjorie Benton Cooke
Silents
LITTLE 'FRAID LADY, THE(1920), w; MAD MARRIAGE, THE(1921), w

Maurice Cooke
SKATETOWN, U.S.A.(1979)

Michele Cooke
JOANNA(1968, Brit.)

Peter Cooke
TARZAN GOES TO INDIA(1962, U.S./Brit./Switz.)

Ray Cooke
MAMMY(1930); SWEETHEARTS ON PARADE(1930); TRUE TO THE NAVY(1930); BLONDE CRAZY(1931); GIRLS DEMAND EXCITEMENT(1931); MIDNIGHT PATROL, THE(1932); TAXI!(1932); FLYING DOWN TO RIO(1933); I'M NO ANGEL(1933); LADY KILLER(1933); HOLLYWOOD PARTY(1934); JEALOUSY(1934); MAN WITH TWO FACES, THE(1934); NOW I'LL TELL(1934); 365 NIGHTS IN HOLLYWOOD(1934); OUR RELATIONS(1936); PICK A STAR(1937); ROARING TWENTIES, THE(1939); INVISIBLE STRIPES(1940); PRIMROSE PATH(1940); STRANGER ON THE THIRD FLOOR(1940); THIRD FINGER, LEFT HAND(1940); MODEL WIFE(1941); NAVY BLUES(1941); PLAYMATES(1941); WEST POINT WIDOW(1941)

Stanley Cooke
ROAD TO FORTUNE, THE(1930, Brit.)

Terry Cooke
ONE WISH TOO MANY(1956, Brit.); AFTER THE BALL(1957, Brit.)

Victor Ray Cooke
KING OF THE NEWSBOYS(1938)

Virginia M. Cooke
TOMBOY AND THE CHAMP(1961), w

Jack Cookerly
INVASION OF THE STAR CREATURES(1962), m; SHOOT OUT AT BIG SAG(1962), m

Shirley Cooklin
ADDING MACHINE, THE(1969)

Jim Cookman
RENT CONTROL(1981), ed

Curtis Cooksey
MISLEADING LADY, THE(1932); BECAUSE YOU'RE MINE(1952); GIRL IN WHITE, THE(1952); SCARAMOUCHE(1952); YOUNG MAN WITH IDEAS(1952); TAXI(1953); DEATH OF A SCOUNDREL(1956); STORM CENTER(1956)
Misc. Silents
FAITH AND FORTUNE(1915); SELF MADE WIDOW(1917); WOMAN BENEATH, THE(1917); DIAMONDS AND PEARLS(1918); TRAP, THE(1918); SILVER HORDE, THE(1920); VIRGIN'S SACRIFICE, A(1922)

Darryl Cooksey
1984
NEVERENDING STORY, THE(1984, Ger.)

Alma Cookson
GOOD BEGINNING, THE(1953, Brit.)

Barrie Cookson
CLOCKWORK ORANGE, A(1971, Brit.)

Catherine Cookson
JACQUELINE(1956, Brit.), w; ROONEY(1958, Brit.), w

Georgina Cookson
I DIDN'T DO IT(1945, Brit.); WOMAN HATER(1949, Brit.); SOLUTION BY PHONE(1954, Brit.); YOUR PAST IS SHOWING(1958, Brit.); QUESTION OF ADULTERY, A(1959, Brit.); SHAKEDOWN, THE(1960, Brit.); FIVE GOLDEN HOURS(1961, Brit.); HOT MONEY GIRL(1962, Brit./Ger.); LIVE NOW-PAY LATER(1962, Brit.); NEVER PUT IT IN WRITING(1964); WOMAN OF STRAW(1964, Brit.); DARLING(1965, Brit.); WOMAN WHO WOULDN'T DIE, THE(1965, Brit.); YOUR MONEY OR YOUR WIFE(1965, Brit.); COUNTERFEIT CONSTABLE, THE(1966, Fr.); WALK A CROOKED PATH(1969, Brit.)

Peter Cookson
GUY NAMED JOE, A(1943); ADVENTURES OF KITTY O'DAY(1944); DETECTIVE KITTY O'DAY(1944); GIRL WHO DARED, THE(1944); IMPOSTER, THE(1944); SHADOW OF SUSPICION(1944); SWINGTIME JOHNNY(1944); BEHIND CITY LIGHTS(1945); G.I. HONEYMOON(1945); DON'T GAMBLE WITH STRANGERS(1946); FEAR(1946); STRANGE CONQUEST(1946)

S. A. Cookson
MANY WATERS(1931, Brit.)
Silents
HAMLET(1913, Brit.)

S.A. Cookson
WHAT HAPPENED TO HARKNESS(1934, Brit.)

Gomer Cool
LAW OF THE RANGE(1941), m

Harold N. Cooledge, Jr.
MIDNIGHT MAN, THE(1974)

Kees Coolen
1984
QUESTION OF SILENCE(1984, Neth.)

John Cooler
LINCOLN CONSPIRACY, THE(1977)

Bill Cooley
PLOUGH AND THE STARS, THE(1936), makeup

Bobby Cooley
SHEBA BABY(1975)

Charles Cooley
WHERE THERE'S LIFE(1947); PALEFACE, THE(1948); FANCY PANTS(1950); LEMON DROP KID, THE(1951); MY FAVORITE SPY(1951)

Charley Cooley
MY FAVORITE BRUNETTE(1947); CHICAGO DEADLINE(1949); SORROWFUL JONES(1949); SON OF PALEFACE(1952)

Ernest Cooley
SHEBA BABY(1975)

Frank Cooley
Silents
FIRST YEAR, THE(1926); WANTED–A COWARD(1927)

Hal Cooley
Silents
OLD FASHIONED BOY, AN(1920); TEN DOLLAR RAISE, THE(1921); PAINTED FLAPPER, THE(1924)
Misc. Silents
COURTESAN, THE(1916); DAUGHTER OF THE DON, THE(1917); DECIDING KISS, THE(1918); LEAVE IT TO ME(1920); TOMBOY, THE(1921); HER NIGHT OF NIGHTS(1922); WHITE SIN, THE(1924)

Hal [Hallam] Cooley
Misc. Silents
GIRL DODGER, THE(1919)

Hallam Cooley
LITTLE WILDCAT, THE(1928); BLACK WATERS(1929); FANCY BAGGAGE(1929); IN THE HEADLINES(1929); PARIS BOUND(1929); SO LONG LETTY(1929); STOLEN KISSES(1929); TONIGHT AT TWELVE(1929); BACK PAY(1930); HOLIDAY(1930); SOUP TO NUTS(1930); WEDDING RINGS(1930); WHAT MEN WANT(1930); SPORTING BLOOD(1931); TOO MANY COOKS(1931); FRISCO JENNY(1933); DANCING MASTERS, THE(1943)
Silents
WHAT DO MEN WANT?(1921); KINGDOM WITHIN, THE(1922); ONE WEEK OF LOVE(1922); ARE YOU A FAILURE?(1923); DOLLAR DEVILS(1923); NEVER SAY DIE(1924); MONSTER, THE(1925); FOREVER AFTER(1926); LADIES AT PLAY(1926); LADIES MUST DRESS(1927); WEDDING BILL$(1927)
Misc. Silents
HAPPY THOUGH MARRIED(1919); MORE DEADLY THAN THE MALE(1919); UPSTAIRS(1919); BEWARE OF THE BRIDE(1920); LIGHT WOMAN, A(1920); TRUMPET ISLAND(1920); FOOLISH AGE, THE(1921); MAN WITH TWO MOTHERS, THE(1922); MONEY TO BURN(1922); UP AND AT 'EM(1922); WISE KID, THE(1922); GOING UP(1923); SPORTING YOUTH(1924); STOP FLIRTING(1925); THOROUGHBRED, THE(1925); HER WILD OAT(1927)

Hallem Cooley
Misc. Silents
NO PLACE TO GO(1927)

Isabel Cooley
SUICIDE BATTALION(1958); YOUNGBLOOD(1978); CHAPTER TWO(1979); ESCAPE ARTIST, THE(1982)

Isabelle Cooley
RAINTREE COUNTY(1957); ANNA LUCASTA(1958); I PASSED FOR WHITE(1960); CLEOPATRA(1963); UPTIGHT(1968)

Jack Cooley
WIND AND THE LION, THE(1975)

James Cooley
NO LIVING WITNESS(1932); WIND AND THE LION, THE(1975)
Silents
LITTLE GRAY LADY, THE(1914); ETERNAL SAPHO, THE(1916); ASHES OF VENGEANCE(1923); SONG OF LOVE, THE(1923)
Misc. Silents
WILDFLOWER(1914); CONCEALED TRUTH, THE(1915); COQUETTE, THE(1915); FORBIDDEN FRUIT(1916); IMMORTAL FLAME, THE(1916); TALE OF TWO NATIONS, A(1917); DISCARDED WOMAN, THE(1920)

Jim Cooley
JOAN OF ARC(1948)

Lee Cooley
SWING HIGH, SWING LOW(1937)

Marjorie Cooley
GIRLS OF THE ROAD(1940); WEST OF ABILENE(1940); GREAT COMMANDMENT, THE(1941); TRAITOR WITHIN, THE(1942)

Ron Cooley
LIFE BEGINS IN COLLEGE(1937)

Spade Cooley
HOME IN WYOMIN'(1942); CHATTERBOX(1943); OUTLAWS OF THE ROCKIES(1945); ROCKIN' IN THE ROCKIES(1945); VACATION DAYS(1947); KID FROM GOWER GULCH, THE(1949); SQUARE DANCE JUBILEE(1949); BORDER OUTLAWS(1950); EVERYBODY'S DANCIN'(1950), a, w; SILVER BANDIT, THE(1950);

CASA MANANA(1951)

Ted Cooley
FIREBALL 590(1966), makeup

Willard Cooley
Silents
RUGGED WATER(1925); ENCHANTED HILL, THE(1926)
Misc. Silents
MADNESS OF LOVE, THE(1922)

William Cooley
FLIPPER'S NEW ADVENTURE(1964)

Carl Coolidge
MURDER BY TELEVISION(1935), w

Edwina Coolidge
I MARRIED AN ANGEL(1942)

Karl Coolidge
Silents
SPINDLE OF LIFE, THE(1917), w

Martha Coolidge
VALLEY GIRL(1983), d
1984
CITY GIRL, THE(1984), p&d, w; JOY OF SEX(1984), d

Philip Coolidge
BOOMERANG(1947); SHARKFIGHTERS, THE(1956); SLANDER(1956); I WANT TO LIVE!(1958); IT HAPPENED TO JANE(1959); MATING GAME, THE(1959); NORTH BY NORTHWEST(1959); TINGLER, THE(1959); BECAUSE THEY'RE YOUNG(1960); BRAMBLE BUSH, THE(1960); INHERIT THE WIND(1960); HAMLET(1964); GREATEST STORY EVER TOLD, THE(1965); RUSSIANS ARE COMING, THE RUSSIANS ARE COMING, THE(1966); NEVER A DULL MOMENT(1968)

Rita Coolidge
VANISHING POINT(1971); PAT GARRETT AND BILLY THE KID(1973)

Maud Cooling
Misc. Silents
BOY GIRL, THE(1917); SUSAN'S GENTLEMAN(1917)

Maude Cooling
Silents
ETERNAL MAGDALENE, THE(1919)

Joan Cooly
2,000 WEEKS(1970, Aus.), makeup

Carol Coombe
HELP YOURSELF(1932, Brit.); GHOST TRAIN, THE(1933, Brit.); MY LUCKY STAR(1933, Brit.); MAN WHO RECLAIMED HIS HEAD, THE(1935); MAN WITHOUT A FACE, THE(1935, Brit.); STRAIGHT FROM THE HEART(1935)

Carole Coombe
WOMAN TO WOMAN(1946, Brit.)

Guy Coombes
Silents
BAB'S DIARY(1917); WHEN KNIGHTHOOD WAS IN FLOWER(1922)

Norman Coombes
GOLD(1974, Brit.); MY WAY(1974, South Africa)

Pat Coombes
ALF 'N' FAMILY(1968, Brit.)

Boyce Coombs
Misc. Silents
ROYAL ROMANCE(1917)

Carol Coombs
MAN WHO RETURNED TO LIFE, THE(1942); PERFECT MARRIAGE, THE(1946); SENTIMENTAL JOURNEY(1946); KNOCK ON ANY DOOR(1949); MATING SEASON, THE(1951)

Carol Joyce Coombs
ADVENTURES OF MARK TWAIN, THE(1944)

Guy Coombs
Silents
CELEBRATED CASE, A(1914); BAB'S BURGLAR(1917)
Misc. Silents
SCHOOL FOR SCANDAL, THE(1914); BARBARA FRIETCHIE(1915); CALL OF THE DANCE, THE(1915); MY MADONNA(1916); TWO MEN AND A WOMAN(1917); FLOWER OF THE DUSK(1918); LOADED DICE(1918); WRONG WOMAN, THE(1920)

Jackie Coombs
Silents
OH, WHAT A NIGHT!(1926); CALLAHANS AND THE MURPHYS, THE(1927); WAY OF ALL FLESH, THE(1927); RANSOM(1928)

Murray Coombs
NATIONAL VELVET(1944)

Pat Coombs
CRY WOLF(1968, Brit.); ADOLF HITLER–MY PART IN HIS DOWNFALL(1973, Brit.); GET CHARLIE TULLY(1976, Brit.)

Vivian Coombs
SPECIAL INSPECTOR(1939)

Jan Coomer
GIDGET GOES TO ROME(1963)

Carol Coomes
IT'S A WONDERFUL LIFE(1946)

Caroline Coon
RUDE BOY(1980, Brit.)

Carolyn Coon
HOUSE OF 1,000 DOLLS(1967, Ger./Span./Brit.)

Gene L. Coon
GIRL IN THE KREMLIN, THE(1957), w; MAN IN THE SHADOW(1957), w; NO NAME ON THE BULLET(1959), w; KILLERS, THE(1964), w; RAIDERS, THE(1964), w; FIRST TO FIGHT(1967), w; JOURNEY TO SHILOH(1968), w

Dorothy Coonan
GOLD DIGGERS OF 1933(1933); WILD BOYS OF THE ROAD(1933); 42ND STREET(1933); STORY OF G.I. JOE, THE(1945)

Dorothy Rae Coonan
KID FROM SPAIN, THE(1932)

Gerry Coonan
LADY OF BURLESQUE(1943)

Sheila Coonan
THIRTEENTH LETTER, THE(1951); ECHOES(1983)
Sheila M. Coonan
WITHOUT A TRACE(1983)
Cecil Cooney
SILVER FLEET, THE(1945, Brit.), ph; PASSPORT TO PIMLICO(1949, Brit.), ph; SHADOW OF THE EAGLE(1955, Brit.), ph
Cecil R. Cooney
BEACH RED(1967), ph
Dennis Cooney
FITZWILLY(1967)
Kevin Cooney
DEADLY BLESSING(1981)
Ray Cooney
HAND, THE(1960, Brit.), a, w; NIGHT WE GOT THE BIRD, THE(1961, Brit.), w; MAKE MINE A DOUBLE(1962, Brit.); WHAT A CARVE UP!(1962, Brit.), w; NOT NOW DARLING(1975, Brit.), a, d; THERE GOES THE BRIDE(1980, Brit.), p, w
Raymond Cooney
MY BROTHER JONATHAN(1949, Brit.)
Thomas D. Cooney
WIN, PLACE, OR STEAL(1975), p
Val Cooney
SMILEY GETS A GUN(1959, Brit.)
Mrs. Coonleu
Silents
STELLA MARIS(1918)
C.C. Coons
RIOT SQUAD(1941), w
Johnny Coons
TELL THEM WILLIE BOY IS HERE(1969)
Bill Coontz
LAWLESS RIDER, THE(1954); HIDDEN GUNS(1956); RAIDERS OF OLD CALIFORNIA(1957); FRANKENSTEIN'S DAUGHTER(1958); LITTLEST HOBO, THE(1958); NO PLACE TO LAND(1958); SHE DEMONS(1958); LONE TEXAN(1959)
Eddie Coonz
STARLIFT(1951)
Chuck Coop
KING OF COMEDY, THE(1983)
Denys Coop
HANGMAN WAITS, THE(1947, Brit.), ph; AFFAIRS OF ADELAIDE(1949, U. S./Brit.), ph; KIND OF LOVING, A(1962, Brit.), ph; BILLY LIAR(1963, Brit.), ph; MIND BENDERS, THE(1963, Brit.), ph; THIS SPORTING LIFE(1963, Brit.), ph; KING AND COUNTRY(1964, Brit.), ph; BUNNY LAKE IS MISSING(1965), ph; ONE WAY PENDULUM(1965, Brit.), ph; ARRIVEDERCI, BABY!(1966, Brit.), ph; TRAITOR'S GATE(1966, Brit./Ger.), ph; DOUBLE MAN, THE(1967), ph; BIRTHDAY PARTY, THE(1968, Brit.), ph; MY SIDE OF THE MOUNTAIN(1969), ph; EXECUTIONER, THE(1970, Brit.), ph; 10 RILLINGTON PLACE(1971, Brit.), ph; ASYLUM(1972, Brit.), ph; DARWIN ADVENTURE, THE(1972, Brit.), ph; LITTLE ARK, THE(1972), ph; AND NOW THE SCREAMING STARTS(1973, Brit.), ph; VAULT OF HORROR, THE(1973, Brit.), ph; ROSEBUD(1975), ph; SUPERMAN(1978), spec eff; VENOM(1982, Brit.), ph
Franco Coop
DEFEAT OF HANNIBAL, THE(1937, Ital.); GOLDEN MADONNA, THE(1949, Brit.); NEOPOLITAN CAROUSEL(1961, Ital.)
Richard Coopan
REVOLT OF MAMIE STOVER, THE(1956)
Alice Cooper
SEXTETTE(1978); SGT. PEPPER'S LONELY HEARTS CLUB BAND(1978); ROADIE(1980)
Andrew "Buzz" Cooper
GETTING OVER(1981)
Anita Cooper
SOMETHING WILD(1961)
Ann Cooper
BLUE SUNSHINE(1978)
Anthony Kemble Cooper
ADVENTURES OF SHERLOCK HOLMES, THE(1939); I WAS AN ADVENTURESS(1940)
Arissa Cooper
MOULIN ROUGE(1952)
Arthur Cooper
NOTHING LIKE PUBLICITY(1936, Brit.), w
Arthur S. Cooper
CONNECTING ROOMS(1971, Brit.), p
Ashley Cooper
BEGGAR STUDENT, THE(1931,Brit.)
Silents
PARTNERS OF THE TIDE(1921); SHADOWS OF CONSCIENCE(1921); GAY AND DEVILISH(1922); SON OF THE WOLF, THE(1922); TILLIE(1922); PARADISE(1926)
Misc. Silents
ROBIN HOOD, JR.(1923)
B.C Cooper
1984
SONGWRITER(1984)
Barbara Cooper
TONIGHT FOR SURE(1962), set d
Barry Cooper
FEAR NO EVIL(1981)
Ben Cooper
SIDE STREET(1950); THUNDERBIRDS(1952); FLIGHT NURSE(1953); PERILOUS JOURNEY, A(1953); SEA OF LOST SHIPS(1953); WOMAN THEY ALMOST LYNCHED, THE(1953); JOHNNY GUITAR(1954); OUTCAST, THE(1954); ETERNAL SEA, THE(1955); FIGHTING CHANCE, THE(1955); HEADLINE HUNTERS(1955); HELL'S OUTPOST(1955); LAST COMMAND, THE(1955); ROSE TATTOO, THE(1955); REBEL IN TOWN(1956); STRANGE ADVENTURE, A(1956); DUEL AT APACHE WELLS(1957); OUTLAW'S SON(1957); CHARTROOSE CABOOSE(1960); GUNFIGHT AT COMANCHE CREEK(1964); RAIDERS, THE(1964); ARIZONA RAIDERS(1965); WACO(1966); FASTEST GUITAR ALIVE, THE(1967); RED TOMAHAWK(1967); ONE MORE TRAIN TO ROB(1971); SUPPORT YOUR LOCAL GUNFIGHTER(1971)

Bernie Cooper
1984
REAL LIFE(1984, Brit.), w
Betty Cooper
HIDDEN ROOM, THE(1949, Brit.); STOP PRESS GIRL(1949, Brit.); DARK MAN, THE(1951, Brit.); LADY WITH A LAMP, THE(1951, Brit.); MANIACS ON WHEELS(1951, Brit.); ISLAND RESCUE(1952, Brit.); SCOTLAND YARD INSPECTOR(1952, Brit.); MEN ARE CHILDREN TWICE(1953, Brit.); ACROSS THE BRIDGE(1957, Brit.); HEART WITHIN, THE(1957, Brit.); TEENAGE BAD GIRL(1959, Brit.); BEDAZZLED(1967, Brit.)
Betty Jane Cooper
COLLEGIATE(1936)
Bigelow Cooper
Silents
EUGENE ARAM(1915); EXCITERS, THE(1923); ANOTHER SCANDAL(1924)
Misc. Silents
MAGIC SKIN, THE(1915); SHADOWS FROM THE PAST(1915); TRAGEDIES OF THE CRYSTAL GLOBE, THE(1915); HEART OF THE HILLS, THE(1916); MARTYRDOM OF PHILLIP STRONG, THE(1916); WHEN LOVE IS KING(1916); GHOST OF OLD MORRO, THE(1917); GOD OF LITTLE CHILDREN(1917); GREAT BRADLEY MYSTERY, THE(1917); PASSION(1917); WHERE LOVE IS(1917); WOOING OF PRINCESS PAT, THE(1918); COUNTRY COUSIN, THE(1919); PERILOUS VALLEY(1920); PROPHET'S PARADISE, THE(1922); BAD COMPANY(1925); WHITE MICE(1926); BROADWAY DRIFTER, THE(1927)
Bob Cooper
LONNIE(1963), m
Misc. Talkies
I WAS A TEENAGE ALIEN(1980), d
Bobbie Cooper
LITTLE MEN(1940)
Bobby Cooper
H.M. PULHAM, ESQ.(1941); MAGNIFICENT AMBERSONS, THE(1942); SECRETS OF SCOTLAND YARD(1944); STRANGE VOYAGE(1945); GALLANT JOURNEY(1946); MY REPUTATION(1946)
Bonnie Cooper
FANDANGO(1970)
Brigid Cooper
LADY IN DISTRESS(1942, Brit.), w
Bunny Cooper
DIANE(1955)
Carolyn Cooper
SPIDER BABY(1968)
Cary Cooper
HANGING TREE, THE(1959)
Silents
HALF A BRIDE(1928)
Cathey Cooper
HANDLE WITH CARE(1964)
Charles Cooper
MR. H. C. ANDERSEN(1950, Brit.); WRONG MAN, THE(1956); DOG'S BEST FRIEND, A(1960); GUN FIGHT(1961); FBI CODE 98(1964); BIG BOUNCE, THE(1969)
Chris Cooper
STEP DOWN TO TERROR(1958), w
Christine Cooper
PAID IN FULL(1950)
Clancey Cooper
WEST OF TOMBSTONE(1942); NORA PRENTISS(1947)
Clancy Cooper
FLIGHT LIEUTENANT(1942); JUKE GIRL(1942); MAN WHO RETURNED TO LIFE, THE(1942); MAN'S WORLD, A(1942); NATIVE LAND(1942); STREET OF CHANCE(1942); UNSEEN ENEMY(1942); DEAD MAN'S GULCH(1943); DEERSLAYER(1943); GIRLS IN CHAINS(1943); CYCLONE PRAIRIE RANGERS(1944); RIDING WEST(1944); SUNDOWN VALLEY(1944); THIN MAN GOES HOME, THE(1944); TIMBER QUEEN(1944); WHISTLER, THE(1944); DANGER SIGNAL(1945); DANGEROUS PARTNERS(1945); ENCHANTED FOREST, THE(1945); MILDRED PIERCE(1945); WITHOUT LOVE(1945); BELOW THE DEADLINE(1946); BLUE SIERRA(1946); COURAGE OF LASSIE(1946); DRAGONWYCH(1946); IT SHOULDN'T HAPPEN TO A DOG(1946); SOMEWHERE IN THE NIGHT(1946); WIFE OF MONTE CRISTO, THE(1946); DARK PASSAGE(1947); DEEP VALLEY(1947); GANGSTER, THE(1947); HER HUSBAND'S AFFAIRS(1947); NIGHTMARE ALLEY(1947); RAILROADED(1947); JOAN OF ARC(1948); LULU BELLE(1948); MAN FROM TEXAS, THE(1948); ROAD HOUSE(1948); SAINTED SISTERS, THE(1948); MARY RYAN, DETECTIVE(1949); MR. BELVEDERE GOES TO COLLEGE(1949); PRISON WARDEN(1949); SONG OF SURRENDER(1949); WHIRLPOOL(1949); CONVICTED(1950); DAKOTA LIL(1950); FILE ON THELMA JORDAN, THE(1950); GREAT RUPERT, THE(1950); WHERE THE SIDEWALK ENDS(1950); DISTANT DRUMS(1951); HE RAN ALL THE WAY(1951); DEADLINE-U.S.A.(1952); LYDIA BAILEY(1952); MAN BEHIND THE GUN, THE(1952); WILD NORTH, THE(1952); ALL THE BROTHERS WERE VALIANT(1953); PICKUP ON SOUTH STREET(1953); SILVER WHIP, THE(1953); LIVING IT UP(1954); REDHEAD FROM MANHATTAN(1954); SQUARE JUNGLE, THE(1955); SOMEBODY UP THERE LIKES ME(1956); OH, MEN! OH, WOMEN!(1957); TRUE STORY OF JESSE JAMES, THE(1957); SHERIFF OF FRACTURED JAW, THE(1958, Brit.); TIME TO LOVE AND A TIME TO DIE, A(1958); WILD YOUTH(1961); INCIDENT IN AN ALLEY(1962); SAINTLY SINNERS(1962)
Misc. Talkies
RIDING THROUGH NEVADA(1942)
Clara Cooper
Silents
HARD TIMES(1915, Brit.)
Claude Cooper
STRUGGLE, THE(1931)
Courtney Riley Cooper
PLAINSMAN, THE(1937), w; DESPERATE TRAILS(1939), w
Courtney Ryley Cooper
WEARY RIVER(1929), w
Silents
STEP ON IT!(1922), w; SAWDUST(1923), w

Cynthia Cooper
TOUCH AND GO(1955)

D. P. Cooper
INQUEST(1939, Brit.), ph

D.P. Cooper
LAST POST, THE(1929, Brit.), ph; TOILERS OF THE SEA(1936, Brit.), ph; GREED OF WILLIAM HART, THE(1948, Brit.), ph

Dave Cooper
FUNNY MONEY(1983, Brit.)
1984
SHEENA(1984)

David Cooper
TATTOOED STRANGER, THE(1950), ed; THAT NIGHT(1957), ed; VIOLATORS, THE(1957), ed; SOLDIER, THE(1982)

Dee Cooper
CHEYENNE TAKES OVER(1947); GHOST TOWN RENEGADES(1947); PIONEER JUSTICE(1947); RAIDERS OF THE SOUTH(1947); RETURN OF THE LASH(1947); STAGE TO MESA CITY(1947); CHECK YOUR GUNS(1948); GUNNING FOR JUSTICE(1948); BRAND OF FEAR(1949); CRASHING THRU(1949); OUTLAW COUNTRY(1949); RANGE LAND(1949); RIDERS OF THE DUSK(1949); SHADOWS OF THE WEST(1949); WESTERN RENEGADES(1949)

Dennis Cooper
SENSATION HUNTERS(1945), w; WOMAN WHO CAME BACK(1945), w; FEAR(1946), w; CITY ACROSS THE RIVER(1949), w

Dennis J. Cooper
WHEN STRANGERS MARRY(1944), w

Deryn Cooper
SKIN DEEP(1978, New Zealand)

Donny Cooper
RUNNING(1979, Can.)

Dorothy Cooper
DATE WITH JUDY, A(1948), w; ON AN ISLAND WITH YOU(1948), w; DUCHESS OF IDAHO, THE(1950), w; RICH, YOUNG AND PRETTY(1951), w; SMALL TOWN GIRL(1953), w; LET'S BE HAPPY(1957, Brit.), w; FLOOD TIDE(1958), w

Douglas Cooper
JANIE(1944); INJUN FENDER(1973), p; DRAGONSLAYER(1981)

Dulcie Cooper
FACE ON THE BARROOM FLOOR, THE(1932)
Silents
CHARGE IT(1921); DESERT BLOSSOMS(1921); WHAT NO MAN KNOWS(1921); DO AND DARE(1922)
Misc. Silents
LIVE AND LET LIVE(1921)

Ed Cooper
ENTER ARSENE LUPIN(1944)

Edmund Cooper
INVISIBLE BOY, THE(1957), w

Edna Mae Cooper
Silents
OLD WIVES FOR NEW(1918); MALE AND FEMALE(1919); PUTTING IT OVER(1919); KING OF KINGS, THE(1927)

Edna May Cooper
TEN COMMANDMENTS, THE(1956)

Edward Ashley Cooper
MEN OF STEEL(1932, Brit.); TIMBUCTOO(1933, Brit.); OLD FAITHFUL(1935, Brit.)

Edward Cooper
DIPLOMANIACS(1933); FEMALE(1933); OFFICER 13(1933); WORKING MAN, THE(1933); KEY, THE(1934); CLIVE OF INDIA(1935); DARK ANGEL, THE(1935); I FOUND STELLA PARISH(1935); PAGE MISS GLORY(1935); PERFECT GENTLEMAN, THE(1935); SHE MARRIED HER BOSS(1935); HUMAN CARGO(1936); SYLVIA SCARLETT(1936); TO MARY–WITH LOVE(1936); UNDER YOUR SPELL(1936); HEAD OVER HEELS IN LOVE(1937, Brit.); LOVE IS NEWS(1937); ON THE AVENUE(1937); SING AND BE HAPPY(1937); HOLIDAY(1938); RASCALS(1938); SAILING ALONG(1938, Brit.); WIFE, HUSBAND AND FRIEND(1939); FREE, BLONDE AND 21(1940); MARRY THE BOSS' DAUGHTER(1941); MRS. MINIVER(1942); DU BARRY WAS A LADY(1943); FRENCHMAN'S CREEK(1944); MAN IN HALF-MOON STREET, THE(1944); COLONEL BLIMP(1945, Brit.); KITTY(1945); TONIGHT AND EVERY NIGHT(1945); 13 RUE MADELEINE(1946)

Edwin Cooper
BLONDIE KNOWS BEST(1946); SING WHILE YOU DANCE(1946); GUILT OF JANET AMES, THE(1947); HUCKSTERS, THE(1947); B. F.'S DAUGHTER(1948); HOMECOMING(1948); STATE OF THE UNION(1948); LOST BOUNDARIES(1949); RAGTIME(1981)

Elliott Cooper
ACES HIGH(1977, Brit.)

Everett Cooper
MAC ARTHUR(1977)

Ferderick Cooper
GREAT MR. HANDEL, THE(1942, Brit.)

Florice Cooper
Silents
ONE SPLENDID HOUR(1929)

Frederick Cooper
DARK SANDS(1938, Brit.); UNPUBLISHED STORY(1942, Brit.); ESCAPE TO DANGER(1943, Brit.); WARN THAT MAN(1943, Brit.); THUNDER ROCK(1944, Brit.); THEY KNEW MR. KNIGHT(1945, Brit.); HENRY V(1946, Brit.)
Silents
EVERY MOTHER'S SON(1926, Brit.); ONLY WAY, THE(1926, Brit.)

Garry Cooper
QUADROPHENIA(1979, Brit.)
1984
KIPPERBANG(1984, Brit.); 1984(1984, Brit.)

Gary Cooper
SERGEANT YORK(; SHOPWORN ANGEL, THE(1928); VIRGINIAN, THE(1929); WOLF SONG(1929); MAN FROM WYOMING, A(1930); MOROCCO(1930); ONLY THE BRAVE(1930); SEVEN DAYS LEAVE(1930); SPOILERS, THE(1930); TEXAN, THE(1930); CITY STREETS(1931); FIGHTING CARAVANS(1931); HIS WOMAN(1931); I TAKE THIS WOMAN(1931); DEVIL AND THE DEEP(1932); FAREWELL TO ARMS, A(1932); IF I HAD A MILLION(1932); MAKE ME A STAR(1932); ALICE IN WONDERLAND(1933); DESIGN FOR LIVING(1933); ONE SUNDAY AFTERNOON(1933); TO-

DAY WE LIVE(1933); NOW AND FOREVER(1934); OPERATOR 13(1934); LIVES OF A BENGAL LANCER(1935); PETER IBBETSON(1935); WEDDING NIGHT, THE(1935); DESIRE(1936); GENERAL DIED AT DAWN, THE(1936); HOLLYWOOD BOULEVARD(1936); MR. DEEDS GOES TO TOWN(1936); PLAINSMAN, THE(1937); SOULS AT SEA(1937); ADVENTURES OF MARCO POLO, THE(1938); BLUEBEARD'S EIGHTH WIFE(1938); COWBOY AND THE LADY, THE(1938); BEAU GESTE(1939); REAL GLORY, THE(1939); NORTHWEST MOUNTED POLICE(1940); WESTERNER, THE(1940); BALL OF FIRE(1941); MEET JOHN DOE(1941); PRIDE OF THE YANKEES, THE(1942); FOR WHOM THE BELL TOLLS(1943); CASANOVA BROWN(1944); STORY OF DR. WASSELL, THE(1944); ALONG CAME JONES(1945), a, p; SARATOGA TRUNK(1945); CLOAK AND DAGGER(1946); UNCONQUERED(1947); VARIETY GIRL(1947); GOOD SAM(1948); FOUNTAINHEAD, THE(1949); IT'S A GREAT FEELING(1949); TASK FORCE(1949); BRIGHT LEAF(1950); DALLAS(1950); DISTANT DRUMS(1951); IT'S A BIG COUNTRY(1951); STARLIFT(1951); YOU'RE IN THE NAVY NOW(1951); HIGH NOON(1952); SPRINGFIELD RIFLE(1952); BLOWING WILD(1953); RETURN TO PARADISE(1953); GARDEN OF EVIL(1954); VERA CRUZ(1954); COURT-MARTIAL OF BILLY MITCHELL, THE(1955); FRIENDLY PERSUASION(1956); LOVE IN THE AFTERNOON(1957); MAN OF THE WEST(1958); 10 NORTH FREDERICK(1958); ALIAS JESSE JAMES(1959); THEY CAME TO CORDURA(1959); WRECK OF THE MARY DEAR, THE(1959); NAKED EDGE, THE(1961)
Silents
WINNING OF BARBARA WORTH, THE(1926); ARIZONA BOUND(1927); CHILDREN OF DIVORCE(1927); IT(1927); NEVADA(1927); WINGS(1927); BEAU SABREUR(1928); LILAC TIME(1928)
Misc. Silents
LAST OUTLAW, THE(1927); DOOMSDAY(1928); FIRST KISS, THE(1928); LEGION OF THE CONDEMNED(1928); BETRAYAL(1929)

George A. Cooper
WORLD, THE FLESH, AND THE DEVIL, THE(1932, Brit.), d; HIS GRACE GIVES NOTICE(1933, Brit.), d; HOME, SWEET HOME(1933, Brit.), d; MAN OUTSIDE, THE(1933, Brit.), d; MANNEQUIN(1933, Brit.), d; ROOF, THE(1933, Brit.), d; BLACK ABBOT, THE(1934, Brit.), d; CASE FOR THE CROWN, THE(1934, Brit.), p&d; TANGLED EVIDENCE(1934, Brit.), d; ANYTHING MIGHT HAPPEN(1935, Brit.), d; SEXTON BLAKE AND THE BEARDED DOCTOR(1935, Brit.), p&d; WOLVES OF THE UNDERWORLD(1935, Brit.), d; ROYAL EAGLE(1936, Brit.), d; SHADOW, THE(1936, Brit.), d; DOWN OUR ALLEY(1939, Brit.), d; MEN WITHOUT HONOUR(1939, Brit.), w; OLD MOTHER RILEY AT HOME(1945, Brit.), w; WHAT DO WE DO NOW?(1945, Brit.), w; LOYAL HEART(1946, Brit.), w; SECRET PLACE, THE(1958, Brit.); VIOLENT PLAYGROUND(1958, Brit.); FOLLOW THAT HORSE!(1960, Brit.); HELL IS A CITY(1960, Brit.); CRACKSMAN, THE(1963, Brit.); NIGHTMARE(1963, Brit.); TOM JONES(1963, Brit.); BARGEE, THE(1964, Brit.); FERRY ACROSS THE MERSEY(1964, Brit.); YOUNG AND WILLING(1964, Brit.); BRAIN, THE(1965, Ger./Brit.); LIFE AT THE TOP(1965, Brit.); SMASHING TIME(1967 Brit.); DRACULA HAS RISEN FROM HIS GRAVE(1968, Brit.); STRANGE AFFAIR, THE(1968, Brit.); ON HER MAJESTY'S SECRET SERVICE(1969, Brit.); RISE AND RISE OF MICHAEL RIMMER, THE(1970, Brit.); START THE REVOLUTION WITHOUT ME(1970); WHAT BECAME OF JACK AND JILL?(1972, Brit.)
Silents
ELEVENTH COMMANDMENT, THE(1924, Brit.), d; IF YOUTH BUT KNEW(1926, Brit.), d; FAKE, THE(1927, Brit.), w; FURTHER ADVENTURES OF THE FLAG LIEUTENANT(1927, Brit.), w
Misc. Silents
HIS WIFE'S HUSBAND(1922, Brit.), d; CLAUDE DUVAL(1924, Brit.), d; HAPPY ENDING, THE(1925, Brit.), d; SETTLED OUT OF COURT(1925, Brit.), d; SOMEBODY'S DARLING(1925, Brit.), d; MASTER AND MAN(1929, Brit.), d

George Cooper
BARKER, THE(1928); SAILORS' HOLIDAY(1929); UNHOLY NIGHT, THE(1929); GIRL OF THE GOLDEN WEST(1930); NUMBERED MEN(1930); PAID(1930); RENEGADES(1930); SHOOTING STRAIGHT(1930); UNDER A TEXAS MOON(1930); GENTLEMAN'S FATE(1931); LAUGHING SINNERS(1931); FLAMES(1932); I AM A FUGITIVE FROM A CHAIN GANG(1932); SKY DEVILS(1932); UPTOWN NEW YORK(1932); EVER IN MY HEART(1933); GRAND SLAM(1933); HAVANA WIDOWS(1933); MARY STEVENS, M.D.(1933); SOLDIERS OF THE STORM(1933); MURDER IN THE CLOUDS(1934); PERSONALITY KID, THE(1934); RETURN OF THE TERROR(1934); DOUBTING THOMAS(1935); WEST OF THE PECOS(1935); ADVENTURE IN MANHATTAN(1936); FEDERAL AGENT(1936); FORBIDDEN TRAIL(1936); MISSING GIRLS(1936); MR. DEEDS GOES TO TOWN(1936); RIDE 'EM COWBOY(1936); SITTING ON THE MOON(1936); DODGE CITY TRAIL(1937), ph; DUKE COMES BACK, THE(1937); LIVE, LOVE AND LEARN(1937); PORTIA ON TRIAL(1937); RIDERS OF THE DAWN(1937); STEP LIVELY, JEEVES(1937); THAT I MAY LIVE(1937); THINK FAST, MR. MOTO(1937); WE'RE ON THE JURY(1937); WHEN YOU'RE IN LOVE(1937); MISSING GUEST, THE(1938); SAY IT IN FRENCH(1938); SWEETHEARTS(1938); LUCKY NIGHT(1939); WESTERN CARAVANS(1939), ph; CROSSFIRE(1947); NIGHT SONG(1947); BLOOD ON THE MOON(1948); FLAMING FURY(1949); ROUGHSHOD(1949); ZAMBA(1949); MYSTERY STREET(1950); EIGHT IRON MEN(1952); KISENGA, MAN OF AFRICA(1952); OKINAWA(1952); MEN OF THE FIGHTING LADY(1954); PASSING STRANGER, THE(1954, Brit.); STEEL CAGE, THE(1954); MIRACLE IN SOHO(1957, Brit.); DIAMONDS ARE FOREVER(1971, Brit.); BLACK WINDMILL, THE(1974, Brit.); GREATEST, THE(1977, U.S./Brit.); STAR CHAMBER, THE(1983)
1984
LASSITER(1984)
Silents
WHEELS OF JUSTICE(1915); NIGHT OUT, A(1916); AUCTION BLOCK, THE(1917); SUZANNA(1922); ETERNAL THREE, THE(1923); LITTLE CHURCH AROUND THE CORNER(1923); LOVE LETTER, THE(1923); NTH COMMANDMENT, THE(1923); NEVER SAY DIE(1924); NO MORE WOMEN(1924); TORMENT(1924); DEVIL'S CARGO, THE(1925); GOOSE WOMAN, THE(1925); JUST A WOMAN(1925); LAWFUL CHEATERS(1925); NEW COMMANDMENT, THE(1925); BARRIER, THE(1926); RED DICE(1926); LOVELORN, THE(1927); LILAC TIME(1928); DEVIL'S APPLE TREE(1929); TRAIL OF '98, THE(1929)
Misc. Silents
PAWNS OF MARS(1915); THOU ART THE MAN(1915); HUNTED WOMAN, THE(1916); THOU ART THE MAN(1916); VITAL QUESTION, THE(1916); FIELDS OF HONOR(1918); WOMAN ETERNAL, THE(1918); BIRTH OF A SOUL(1920); TURN TO THE RIGHT(1922); SHRIEK OF ARABY, THE(1923); RIDERS UP(1924); PALS FIRST(1926); TIN HATS(1926); BARKER, THE(1928)

George Lane Cooper
HISTORY OF THE WORLD, PART 1(1981)
Georgia Cooper
DESIRABLE(1934); STRANDED(1935); THEODORA GOES WILD(1936); WHEN YOU'RE IN LOVE(1937); HOMICIDE BUREAU(1939); JOHNNY EAGER(1942); MAN FROM THUNDER RIVER, THE(1943); MUSIC IN MANHATTAN(1944)
Georgie Cooper
SHOW THEM NO MERCY(1935); MOON'S OUR HOME, THE(1936); IT'S LOVE I'M AFTER(1937); PAID TO DANCE(1937); SISTERS, THE(1938); LADY EVE, THE(1941)
Gerald Cooper
MEN OF TOMORROW(1935, Brit.); YOUNG MR. PITT, THE(1942, Brit.)
Giles Cooper
UNMAN, WITTERING AND ZIGO(1971, Brit.), w
Ginny Cooper
DEATH WISH II(1982)
Gladys Cooper
IRON DUKE, THE(1935, Brit.); KITTY FOYLE(1940); REBECCA(1940); BLACK CAT, THE(1941); GAY FALCON, THE(1941); THAT HAMILTON WOMAN(1941); YANK IN THE R.A.F., A(1941); EAGLE SQUADRON(1942); NOW, VOYAGER(1942); THIS ABOVE ALL(1942); FOREVER AND A DAY(1943); MR. LUCKY(1943); PRINCESS O'ROURKE(1943); SONG OF BERNADETTE, THE(1943); MRS. PARKINGTON(1944); WHITE CLIFFS OF DOVER, THE(1944); LOVE LETTERS(1945); VALLEY OF DECISION, THE(1945); BEWARE OF PITY(1946, Brit.); COCKEYED MIRACLE, THE(1946); GREEN YEARS, THE(1946); BISHOP'S WIFE, THE(1947); GREEN DOLPHIN STREET(1947); HOMECOMING(1948); PIRATE, THE(1948); MADAME BOVARY(1949); SECRET GARDEN, THE(1949); AT SWORD'S POINT(1951); THUNDER ON THE HILL(1951); MAN WHO LOVED REDHEADS, THE(1955, Brit.); SEPARATE TABLES(1958); LIST OF ADRIAN MESSENGER, THE(1963); MY FAIR LADY(1964); HAPPIEST MILLIONAIRE, THE(1967); NICE GIRL LIKE ME, A(1969, Brit.)
Misc. Silents
MY LADY'S DRESS(1917, Brit.); SORROWS OF SATAN, THE(1917); HEADIN' NORTH(1921); BOHEMIAN GIRL, THE(1922, Brit.); BONNIE PRINCE CHARLIE(1923, Brit.)
Glancy Cooper
CENTENNIAL SUMMER(1946)
Goerge Cooper
WEST OF RAINBOW'S END(1938)
Harrison Cooper
CAVALIER, THE(1928), ph
Harry Cooper
THOMAS CROWN AFFAIR, THE(1968)
Silents
AVENGING SHADOW, THE(1928), ph; HEROIC LOVER, THE(1929), ph
Harry E. Cooper
CADDY, THE(1953)
Henry Cooper
ROYAL FLASH(1975, Brit.)
Horace Cooper
RIP TIDE(1934); WHERE'S CHARLEY?(1952, Brit.)
Inez Cooper
MARRIED BACHELOR(1941); MR. AND MRS. NORTH(1941); SHADOW OF THE THIN MAN(1941); WHISTLING IN THE DARK(1941); AFFAIRS OF MARTHA, THE(1942); I MARRIED AN ANGEL(1942); RIO RITA(1942); STAND BY FOR ACTION(1942); DU BARRY WAS A LADY(1943); GIRL CRAZY(1943); WINGS OVER THE PACIFIC(1943); FLIGHT TO NOWHERE(1946); LADY CHASER(1946); BARKLEYS OF BROADWAY, THE(1949); BORDER TREASURE(1950)
Misc. Talkies
RIDING THE CALIFORNIA TRAIL(1947)
Irene K. Cooper
THUNDERBOLT AND LIGHTFOOT(1974)
Irissa Cooper
GAMBLER AND THE LADY, THE(1952, Brit.); LIMPING MAN, THE(1953, Brit.)
Irving H. Cooper
JET OVER THE ATLANTIC(1960), w
Isabel Chabing Cooper
UNCONQUERED(1947)
Isabel Cooper
SO PROUDLY WE HAIL(1943); STORY OF DR. WASSELL, THE(1944)
J. Cooper
Misc. Silents
WHEN LONDON BURNED(1915, Brit.)
J. Gordon Cooper
Misc. Silents
SIN TOWN(1929), d
Jack Cooper
MIDNIGHT DADDIES(1929); THREE LIVE GHOSTS(1929); OUR RELATIONS(1936); CRIMINALS OF THE AIR(1937), w; RODEO RHYTHM(1941); LAUGHING ANNE(1954, Brit./U.S.); SWORD OF SHERWOOD FOREST(1961, Brit.), a, tech adv; MACKINTOSH MAN, THE(1973, Brit.)
Silents
CARNIVAL GIRL, THE(1926); WOLF'S CLOTHING(1927)
Misc. Silents
SKIRTS(1921)
Jackie Cooper
SUNNY SIDE UP(1929); CHAMP, THE(1931); SKIPPY(1931); SOOKY(1931); YOUNG DONOVAN'S KID(1931); DIVORCE IN THE FAMILY(1932); FELLER NEEDS A FRIEND(1932); BOWERY, THE(1933); BROADWAY TO HOLLYWOOD(1933); LONE COWBOY(1934); PECK'S BAD BOY(1934); TREASURE ISLAND(1934); DINKY(1935); O'SHAUGHNESSY'S BOY(1935); DEVIL IS A SISSY, THE(1936); TOUGH GUY(1936); BOY OF THE STREETS(1937); GANGSTER'S BOY(1938); THAT CERTAIN AGE(1938); WHITE BANNERS(1938); BIG GUY, THE(1939); NEWSBOY'S HOME(1939); SPIRIT OF CULVER, THE(1939); STREETS OF NEW YORK(1939); TWO BRIGHT BOYS(1939); WHAT A LIFE(1939); GALLANT SONS(1940); RETURN OF FRANK JAMES, THE(1940); SEVENTEEN(1940); GLAMOUR BOY(1941); HER FIRST BEAU(1941); LIFE WITH HENRY(1941); ZIEGFELD GIRL(1941); MEN OF TEXAS(1942); NAVY COMES THROUGH, THE(1942); SYNCOPATION(1942); WHERE ARE YOUR CHILDREN?(1943); KILROY WAS HERE(1947); STORK BITES MAN(1947); FRENCH LEAVE(1948); EVERYTHING'S DUCKY(1961); LOVE MACHINE, THE(1971); STAND UP AND BE COUNTED(1972), d; CHOSEN SURVIVORS(1974 U.S.-Mex.); PINK PANTHER STRIKES AGAIN, THE(1976, Brit.); SUPERMAN(1978); SUPERMAN

II(1980); SUPERMAN III(1983)
James A. Cooper
Silents
CAPTAIN'S CAPTAIN, THE(1919), w
James Fenimore Cooper
LAST OF THE MOHICANS, THE(1936), w; PIONEERS, THE(1941), w; DEERSLAYER(1943), w; LAST OF THE REDMEN(1947), w; PRAIRIE, THE(1948), w; IROQUOIS TRAIL, THE(1950), w; PATHFINDER, THE(1952), w; DEERSLAYER, THE(1957), w
Silents
LAST OF THE MOHICANS, THE(1920), w
Jamie Cooper
DARK SIDE OF TOMORROW, THE(1970)
Jason Cooper
PRIVILEGED(1982, Brit.), prod d
Jeanne Cooper
MAN FROM THE ALAMO, THE(1953); REDHEAD FROM WYOMING, THE(1953); SHADOWS OF TOMBSTONE(1953); NAKED STREET, THE(1955); CALLING HOMICIDE(1956); HOUSTON STORY, THE(1956); OVER-EXPOSED(1956); FIVE STEPS TO DANGER(1957); PLUNDER ROAD(1957); UNWED MOTHER(1958); LET NO MAN WRITE MY EPITAPH(1960); HOUSE OF WOMEN(1962); INTRUDER, THE(1962); THIRTEEN WEST STREET(1962); BLACK ZOO(1963); GLORY GUYS, THE(1965); TONY ROME(1967); THE BOSTON STRANGLER, THE(1968); THERE WAS A CROOKED MAN(1970); KANSAS CITY BOMBER(1972); ALL-AMERICAN BOY, THE(1973)
Jed Cooper
1984
VAMPING(1984)
Jeff Cooper
DUEL AT DIABLO(1966); BORN LOSERS(1967); IMPOSSIBLE YEARS, THE(1968); CIRCLE OF IRON(1979, Brit.)
Misc. Talkies
KNIFE FOR THE LADIES, A(1973)
Jerry Cooper
DEAD END(1937); HOLLYWOOD HOTEL(1937); MELODY PARADE(1943); HOT RHYTHM(1944)
Joan Cooper
RULING CLASS, THE(1972, Brit.); BAWDY ADVENTURES OF TOM JONES, THE(1976, Brit.); SWEET WILLIAM(1980, Brit.)
John C. Cooper
HAUNTED STRANGLER, THE(1958, Brit.), w; FIRST MAN INTO SPACE(1959, Brit.), w; PROJECTED MAN(1967, Brit.), w
John Cooper
LIVING ON VELVET(1935); RACE FOR LIFE, A(1955, Brit.)
1984
MY KIND OF TOWN(1984, Can.)
Ken Cooper
COMIN' ROUND THE MOUNTAIN(1936); GUNS AND GUITARS(1936); RED RIVER VALLEY(1936); SINGING COWBOY, THE(1936); RIDERS OF THE WHISTLING SKULL(1937); ROUNDUP TIME IN TEXAS(1937); COWBOY SERENADE(1942); HOME IN WYOMIN'(1942); JESSE JAMES, JR.(1942); SONS OF THE PIONEERS(1942); COW TOWN(1950)
Kenny Cooper
STORMY(1935)
Kevin Cooper
PETULIA(1968, U.S./Brit.)
Kia Cooper
BUSTIN' LOOSE(1981)
Kip Cooper
Silents
RIDERS OF THE RIO GRANDE(1929)
Larry Cooper
HOMETOWN U.S.A.(1979)
Lester Cooper
MEET THE NAVY(1946, Brit.), w
Lillian Cooper
THREE LIVE GHOSTS(1935)
Lillian Kemble Cooper
PERSONAL MAID'S SECRET(1935); READY, WILLING AND ABLE(1937); GONE WITH THE WIND(1939); KING'S THIEF, THE(1955); MOONFLEET(1955)
Lily Kemble Cooper
SO BIG(1953)
Linda Cooper
MARYJANE(1968)
Louise Cooper
BLACK JACK(1979, Brit.)
M. Lisa Cooper
1984
HOT DOG...THE MOVIE(1984)
Maggie Cooper
EYE FOR AN EYE, AN(1981)
1984
LAST STARFIGHTER, THE(1984)
Marc Cooper
SHARK(1970, U.S./Mex.), p
Marie Cooper
WORDS AND MUSIC(1929)
Marilyn Cooper
SURVIVORS, THE(1983)
Mark Cooper
SKI FEVER(1969, U.S./Aust./Czech.), p
Marty Cooper
TRIBES(1970), m
Mary Cooper
BRIGHT VICTORY(1951)
Mary Louise Cooper
THESE THREE(1936)
Maury Cooper
COMA(1978)

Maxine Cooper
KISS ME DEADLY(1955); AUTUMN LEAVES(1956); ZERO HOUR!(1957); WHATEVER HAPPENED TO BABY JANE?(1962)

Melville Cooper
BISHOP MISBEHAVES, THE(1933); LEAVE IT TO ME(1933, Brit.); WIVES BEWARE(1933, Brit.); PRIVATE LIFE OF DON JUAN, THE(1934, Brit.); SCARLET PIMPERNEL, THE(1935, Brit.); GORGEOUS HUSSY, THE(1936); GREAT GARRICK, THE(1937); LAST OF MRS. CHEYNEY, THE(1937); THIN ICE(1937); TOVARICH(1937); ADVENTURES OF ROBIN HOOD, THE(1938); COMET OVER BROADWAY(1938); DAWN PATROL, THE(1938); DRAMATIC SCHOOL(1938); FOUR'S A CROWD(1938); GARDEN OF THE MOON(1938); GOLD DIGGERS IN PARIS(1938); HARD TO GET(1938); WOMEN ARE LIKE THAT(1938); BLIND ALLEY(1939); I'M FROM MISSOURI(1939); SUN NEVER SETS, THE(1939); TWO BRIGHT BOYS(1939); ESCAPE TO GLORY(1940); MURDER OVER NEW YORK(1940); PRIDE AND PREJUDICE(1940); REBECCA(1940); TOO MANY HUSBANDS(1940); FLAME OF NEW ORLEANS, THE(1941); LADY EVE, THE(1941); SCOTLAND YARD(1941); YOU BELONG TO ME(1941); AFFAIRS OF MARTHA, THE(1942); LIFE BEGINS AT 8:30(1942); RANDOM HARVEST(1942); THIS ABOVE ALL(1942); HIT PARADE OF 1943(1943); HOLY MATRIMONY(1943); IMMORTAL SERGEANT, THE(1943); MY KINGDOM FOR A COOK(1943); HEARTBEAT(1946); 13 RUE MADELEINE(1946); IMPERFECT LADY, THE(1947); ENCHANTMENT(1948); AND BABY MAKES THREE(1949); LOVE HAPPY(1949); RED DANUBE, THE(1949); FATHER OF THE BRIDE(1950); LET'S DANCE(1950); PETTY GIRL, THE(1950); WHIPPED, THE(1950); IT SHOULD HAPPEN TO YOU(1954); DIANE(1955); KING'S THIEF, THE(1955); MOONFLEET(1955); AROUND THE WORLD IN 80 DAYS(1956); BUNDLE OF JOY(1956); STORY OF MANKIND, THE(1957); FROM THE EARTH TO THE MOON(1958)
Misc. Talkies
RETURN OF GILBERT AND SULLIVAN(1952)

Merian C. Cooper
MOST DANGEROUS GAME, THE(1932), p; ROAR OF THE DRAGON(1932), w; AFTER TONIGHT(1933), p; BED OF ROSES(1933), p; DOUBLE HARNESS(1933), p; IF I WERE FREE(1933), p; KING KONG(1933), a, p&d; w; MELODY CRUISE(1933), p; MONKEY'S PAW, THE(1933), p; RIGHT TO ROMANCE(1933), p; FINISHING SCHOOL(1934), p; FLAMING GOLD(1934), p; LAST DAYS OF POMPEII, THE(1935), p; SHE(1935), p; TOY WIFE, THE(1938), p; FUGITIVE, THE(1947), p; FORT APACHE(1948), p; THREE GODFATHERS, THE(1948), p; MIGHTY JOE YOUNG(1949), p, w; SHE WORE A YELLOW RIBBON(1949), p; RIO GRANDE(1950), p; WAGONMASTER(1950), p; QUIET MAN, THE(1952), p; SUN SHINES BRIGHT, THE(1953), p; SEARCHERS, THE(1956), p
Silents
CHANG(1927), p,d&w; FOUR FEATHERS(1929), d, ph

Miriam Cooper
Silents
DISHONORED MEDAL, THE(1914); HOME SWEET HOME(1914); BIRTH OF A NATION, THE(1915); INTOLERANCE(1916); HONOR SYSTEM, THE(1917); INNOCENT SINNER, THE(1917); KINDRED OF THE DUST(1922); IS MONEY EVERYTHING?(1923); AFTER THE BALL(1924)
Misc. Silents
BETRAYED(1917); SILENT LIE, THE(1917); PRUSSIAN CUR, THE(1918); WOMAN AND THE LAW(1918); EVANGELINE(1919); SHOULD A HUSBAND FORGIVE?(1919); DEEP PURPLE, THE(1920); OATH, THE(1921); SERENADE(1921); BROKEN WING, THE(1923); DAUGHTERS OF THE RICH(1923); GIRL WHO CAME BACK, THE(1923); HER ACCIDENTAL HUSBAND(1923)

Mr. Jack Cooper
Silents
DADDY(1923), w

Mrs. Jack Cooper
Silents
DADDY(1923), w

Muriel Cooper
WORM EATERS, THE(1981)

Neil Cooper
GETTING TOGETHER(1976), cos

Olive Cooper
CONFIDENTIAL(1935), w; HOT TIP(1935), w; STREAMLINE EXPRESS(1935), w; DANCING FEET(1936), w; FOLLOW YOUR HEART(1936), w; HEARTS IN BONDAGE(1936), w; LAUGHING IRISH EYES(1936), w; NAVY BORN(1936), w; RETURN OF JIMMY VALENTINE, THE(1936), w; HAPPY-GO-LUCKY(1937), w; JIM HANVEY, DETECTIVE(1937), w; JOIN THE MARINES(1937), w; LADY BEHAVE(1937), w; RHYTHM IN THE CLOUDS(1937), w; ANNABEL TAKES A TOUR(1938), w; ORPHANS OF THE STREET(1939), w; SHE MARRIED A COP(1939), w; BORDER LEGION, THE(1940), w; YOUNG BILL HICKOK(1940), w; DOWN MEXICO WAY(1941), w; GREAT TRAIN ROBBERY, THE(1941), w; ICE-CAPADES(1941), w; IN OLD CHEYENNE(1941), w; ROBIN HOOD OF THE PECOS(1941), w; SHERIFF OF TOMBSTONE(1941), w; SINGING HILL, THE(1941), w; CALL OF THE CANYON(1942), w; COWBOY SERENADE(1942), w; IDAHO(1943), w; KING OF THE COWBOYS(1943), w; NOBODY'S DARLING(1943), w; SHANTYTOWN(1943), w; MY BEST GAL(1944), w; SONG OF NEVADA(1944), w; THREE LITTLE SISTERS(1944), w; SWINGIN' ON A RAINBOW(1945), w; BAMBOO BLONDE, THE(1946), w; SIOUX CITY SUE(1946), w; BANDIT KING OF TEXAS(1949), w; BIG SOMBRERO, THE(1949), w; OUTCASTS OF THE TRAIL(1949), w; HILLS OF OKLAHOMA(1950), w

Oliver Cooper
COCOANUT GROVE(1938), w

Pat Cooper
UNCLE SCAM(1981); DEATH VENGEANCE(1982)

Paul Cooper
SPIRITS OF THE DEAD(1969, Fr./Ital.)

Peggy Cooper
STUDENT BODIES(1981)

Pete Cooper
DYNAMITE JOHNSON(1978, Phil.); FIRECRACKER(1981); STRYKER(1983, Phil.)
Misc. Talkies
ONE ARMED EXECUTIONER(1980)

Peter Cooper
HANNIE CALDER(1971, Brit.), w

Philip Cooper
FARMER TAKES A WIFE, THE(1935); UNDER THE PAMPAS MOON(1935)

Philip Friend John Cooper
WARN THAT MAN(1943, Brit.)

Phillip Cooper
CUBAN LOVE SONG,THE(1931); VIVA VILLA!(1934); COME AND GET IT(1936)

Ralph Cooper
LLOYDS OF LONDON(1936); POOR LITTLE RICH GIRL(1936), ch; WHITE HUNTER(1936); DARK MANHATTAN(1937), a, p; DUKE IS THE TOPS, THE(1938); AM I GUILTY?(1940); GANG WAR(1940)
Misc. Talkies
BARGAIN WITH BULLETS(1937)

Ray Cooper
LIVES OF A BENGAL LANCER(1935); MILKY WAY, THE(1936); SPANISH MAIN, THE(1945); POPEYE(1980)
1984
SCRUBBERS(1984, Brit.), m

Richard Cooper
BED AND BREAKFAST(1930, Brit.); HOUSE OF THE ARROW, THE(1930, Brit.); KISSING CUP'S RACE(1930, Brit.); LAST HOUR, THE(1930, Brit.); LORD RICHARD IN THE PANTRY(1930, Brit.); MYSTERY AT THE VILLA ROSE(1930, Brit.); BLACK COFFEE(1931, Brit.); OFFICER'S MESS, THE(1931, Brit.); FIRST MRS. FRASER, THE(1932, Brit.); HOME, SWEET HOME(1933, Brit.); MANNEQUIN(1933, Brit.); BLACK ABBOT, THE(1934, Brit.); FOUR MASKED MEN(1934, Brit.); LORD EDGEWARE DIES(1934, Brit.); ACE OF SPADES, THE(1935, Brit.); ANNIE, LEAVE THE ROOM(1935, Brit.); THAT'S MY UNCLE(1935, Brit.); THREE WITNESSES(1935, Brit.); WHO KILLED FEN MARKHAM?(1937, Brit.); STEPPING TOES(1938, Brit.); SHIPYARD SALLY(1940, Brit.); MAIL TRAIN(1941, Brit.)

Rick Cooper
UNDERTAKER AND HIS PALS, THE(1966); THAT TENDER TOUCH(1969); TORA! TORA! TORA!(1970, U.S./Jap.)

Ricky Cooper
HAIL MAFIA(1965, Fr./Ital.)

Robert Cooper
PEER GYNT(1965), a, ph; RUNNING(1979, Can.), p; MIDDLE AGE CRAZY(1980, Can.), p; BELLS(1981, Can.), p; UTILITIES(1983, Can.), p

Rosemary Cooper
Silents
MAILMAN, THE(1923); WHITE FLANNELS(1927)
Misc. Silents
RETURN OF BOSTON BLACKIE, THE(1927)

Rowena Cooper
MEMOIRS OF A SURVIVOR(1981, Brit.)
1984
LITTLE DRUMMER GIRL, THE(1984)

Roy Cooper
300 YEAR WEEKEND(1971); SIMON(1980)

Sally Cooper
JOAN OF ARC(1948); KIND LADY(1951)

Sammy Cooper
Silents
OUR MRS. McCHESNEY(1918)

Scott Cooper
1984
BREAKIN'(1984)

Sheryl Cooper
ROADIE(1980)

Stan Cooper
Misc. Talkies
SOMETHING CREEPING IN THE DARK(1972, Ital.)

Stanley Cooper
Misc. Talkies
HANGING WOMAN, THE(1976)

Stuart Cooper
DIRTY DOZEN, THE(1967, Brit.); I'LL NEVER FORGET WHAT'S 'IS NAME(1967, Brit.); SUBTERFUGE(1969, US/Brit.); LITTLE MALCOLM(1974, Brit.), d; OVERLORD(1975, Brit.), d, w

Susan Cooper
FRANCHETTE; LES INTRIGUES(1969)

Tabi Cooper
HEY, GOOD LOOKIN'(1982)
Misc. Talkies
HEROWORK(1977)

Tamar Cooper
NOT OF THIS EARTH(1957); NICKELODEON(1976); RUBY(1977)

Ted Cooper
ARIZONA MANHUNT(1951); THING, THE(1951); WILD HORSE AMBUSH(1952); PHANTOM FROM SPACE(1953); WILD ONE, THE(1953); 20,000 LEAGUES UNDER THE SEA(1954)

Terence Cooper
NO SAFETY AHEAD(1959, Brit.); TOP FLOOR GIRL(1959, Brit.); MAN IN THE MIDDLE(1964, U.S./Brit.); WALK A TIGHTROPE(1964, U.S./Brit.); CASINO ROYALE(1967, Brit.); BEYOND REASONABLE DOUBT(1980, New Zeal.)
1984
HEART OF THE STAG(1984, New Zealand); PALLET ON THE FLOOR(1984, New Zealand)

Terrence Cooper
CALCULATED RISK(1963, Brit.)

Tex Cooper
OUTLAW DEPUTY, THE(1935); FUGITIVE SHERIFF, THE(1936); OLD WYOMING TRAIL, THE(1937); RECKLESS RANGER(1937); RIDERS OF THE DAWN(1937); TWO-FISTED SHERIFF(1937); TWO GUN LAW(1937); HEROES OF THE ALAMO(1938); UNDER WESTERN STARS(1938); WEST OF CHEYENNE(1938); MAN FROM SUNDOWN, THE(1939); OKLAHOMA KID, THE(1939); DARK COMMAND, THE(1940); MELODY RANCH(1940); WAGONS WESTWARD(1940); ACROSS THE SIERRAS(1941); KING OF DODGE CITY(1941); NORTH FROM LONE STAR(1941); RETURN OF DANIEL BOONE, THE(1941); TUMBLEDOWN RANCH IN ARIZONA(1941); UNDERGROUND RUSTLERS(1941); WRANGLER'S ROOST(1941); OVERLAND STAGECOACH(1942); BLACK MARKET RUSTLERS(1943); CATTLE STAMPEDE(1943); FRONTIER LAW(1943); OUTLAWS OF STAMPEDE PASS(1943); OX-BOW INCIDENT, THE(1943); PRAIRIE RUSTLERS(1945); SUNSET IN EL DORADO(1945); GUN TOWN(1946); ROMANCE OF THE WEST(1946); QUICK ON THE

TRIGGER(1949); KING OF THE BULLWHIP(1950)

"Tex" Cooper
Silents
MAN WORTH WHILE, THE(1921)

Thomas Cooper
DAWN OVER IRELAND(1938, Irish), p&d, w

Tom Cooper
TROUBLE IN TEXAS(1937); DAWN OVER IRELAND(1938, Irish)
Misc. Talkies
UNCLE NICK(1938), d

Tommy Cooper
AND THE SAME TO YOU(1960, Brit.); COOL MIKADO, THE(1963, Brit.); PLANK, THE(1967, Brit.)

Trevor Cooper
MOONLIGHTING(1982, Brit.)

Trudi Cooper
Misc. Talkies
SPITTIN' IMAGE(1983)

Velma Cooper
J.W. COOP(1971)

Vic Cooper
TOOMORROW(1970, Brit.)

Violet Kemble Cooper
FOUNTAIN, THE(1934); THE INVISIBLE RAY(1936)

Walter Cooper
GANG WAR(1940), w; THIEVES LIKE US(1974)
Silents
ANGEL OF CROOKED STREET, THE(1922)

Wilkie Cooper
CONQUEST OF THE AIR(1940), ph; DESIGN FOR MURDER(1940, Brit.), ph; BIG BLOCKADE, THE(1942, Brit.), ph; SHIPS WITH WINGS(1942, Brit.), ph; MY LEARNED FRIEND(1943, Brit.), ph; SOMEWHERE IN FRANCE(1943, Brit.), ph; CHAMPAGNE CHARLIE(1944, Brit.), ph; FIDDLERS THREE(1944, Brit.), ph; UNDERGROUND GUERRILLAS(1944, Brit.), ph; 48 HOURS(1944, Brit.), ph; HALF-WAY HOUSE, THE(1945, Brit.), ph; NOTORIOUS GENTLEMAN(1945, Brit.), ph; ADVENTURESS, THE(1946, Brit.), ph; GREEN FOR DANGER(1946, Brit.), ph; CAPTAIN BOYCOTT(1947, Brit.), ph; CALL OF THE BLOOD(1948, Brit.), ph; DULCIMER STREET(1948, Brit.), ph; MINE OWN EXECUTIONER(1948, Brit.), ph; HASTY HEART, THE(1949), ph; MAN ON THE RUN(1949, Brit.), ph; SILENT DUST(1949, Brit.), ph; STAGE FRIGHT(1950, Brit.), ph; LONG DARK HALL, THE(1951, Brit.), ph; MADAME LOUISE(1951, Brit.), ph; PICKWICK PAPERS, THE(1952, Brit.), ph; DISOBEDIENT(1953, Brit.), ph; HUNDRED HOUR HUNT(1953, Brit.), ph; LANDFALL(1953, Brit.), ph; SEA DEVILS(1953), ph; TIME GENTLEMEN PLEASE!(1953, Brit.), ph; DANCE LITTLE LADY(1954, Brit.), ph; THEY WHO DARE(1954, Brit.), ph; WHAT EVERY WOMAN WANTS(1954, Brit.), ph; ADVENTURES OF SADIE, THE(1955, Brit.), ph; END OF THE AFFAIR, THE(1955, Brit.), ph; LADY GODIVA RIDES AGAIN(1955, Brit.), ph; SVENGALI(1955, Brit.), ph; IT'S A WONDERFUL WORLD(1956, Brit.), ph; PORT AFRIQUE(1956, Brit.), ph; POSTMARK FOR DANGER(1956, Brit.), ph; WEE GEORDIE(1956, Brit.), ph; ABANDON SHIP!(1957, Brit.), ph; ADMIRABLE CRICHTON, THE(1957, Brit.), ph; SEVENTH VOYAGE OF SINBAD, THE(1958), ph; BEASTS OF MARSEILLES, THE(1959, Brit.), ph; BEYOND THIS PLACE(1959, Brit.), ph; SUBWAY IN THE SKY(1959, Brit.), ph; I AIM AT THE STARS(1960), ph; S.O.S. PACIFIC(1960, Brit.), ph; THREE WORLDS OF GULLIVER, THE(1960, Brit.), ph; MYSTERIOUS ISLAND(1961, U.S./Brit.), ph; DESERT PATROL(1962, Brit.), ph; HOT MONEY GIRL(1962, Brit./Ger.), ph; VALIANT, THE(1962, Brit./Ital.), ph; JASON AND THE ARGONAUTS(1963, Brit.), ph; MANIAC(1963, Brit.), ph; MOUSE ON THE MOON, THE(1963, Brit.), ph; SIEGE OF THE SAXONS(1963, Brit.), ph; EAST OF SUDAN(1964, Brit.), ph; FIRST MEN IN THE MOON(1964, Brit.), ph; MAN IN THE MIDDLE(1964, U.S./Brit.), ph; AMOROUS MR. PRAWN, THE(1965, Brit.), ph; TWO LEFT FEET(1965, Brit.), ph; ONE MILLION YEARS B.C.(1967, Brit./U.S.), ph; HAMMERHEAD(1968), ph; LAND RAIDERS(1969), ph; RUN WILD, RUN FREE(1969, Brit.), ph; PLEASE SIR(1971, Brit.), ph

William Cooper
Silents
CRIMSON DOVE, THE(1917), ph

Willis Cooper
THANK YOU, MR. MOTO(1937), w; MR. MOTO TAKES A CHANCE(1938), w; SON OF FRANKENSTEIN(1939), w

Wilmuth Cooper
PREMONITION, THE(1976)

Winifred Cooper
RICH AND STRANGE(1932, Brit.), ed; OUTSIDER, THE(1933, Brit.), ed; TWO WHO DARED(1937, Brit.), ed; TORPEDOED!(1939), ed; CANDLELIGHT IN ALGERIA(1944, Brit.), ed

Wyatt Cooper
SANCTUARY(1961); CHAPMAN REPORT, THE(1962), w

H. Cooper-Willis
Misc. Silents
PRIMROSE PATH, THE(1915)

Chad Cooperman
ROCKY III(1982)

J.M. Coopersmith
TAKE THE HEIR(1930), m

Helen Cooperstein
MOURNING SUIT, THE(1975, Can.)

Bernard Coote
VIOLENT MOMENT(1966, Brit.), p

Bert Coote
SUCH IS THE LAW(1930, Brit.); BRACELETS(1931, Brit.); TWO HEARTS IN WALTZ TIME(1934, Brit.)

Berte Coote
LATIN LOVE(1930, Brit.)

David Coote
JOHNNY ON THE RUN(1953, Brit.); SECRET CAVE, THE(1953, Brit.); LOVERS, HAPPY LOVERS!(1955, Brit.); TIM DRISCOLL'S DONKEY(1955, Brit.); MURDER REPORTED(1958, Brit.); INNOCENT MEETING(1959, Brit.)

Lissa Coote
F.J. HOLDEN, THE(1977, Aus.), art d; STARSTRUCK(1982, Aus.), set d

Robert Coote
LOYALTIES(1934, Brit.); SHEIK STEPS OUT, THE(1937); THIRTEENTH CHAIR, THE(1937); BLOND CHEAT(1938); GIRL DOWNSTAIRS, THE(1938); YANK AT OXFORD, A(1938); BAD LANDS(1939); GUNGA DIN(1939); MR. MOTO'S LAST WARNING(1939); NURSE EDITH CAVELL(1939); RANGLE RIVER(1939, Aus.); VIGIL IN THE NIGHT(1940); YOU CAN'T FOOL YOUR WIFE(1940); COMMANDOS STRIKE AT DAWN, THE(1942); GHOST AND MRS. MUIR, THE(1942); FOREVER AND A DAY(1943); CLOAK AND DAGGER(1946); STAIRWAY TO HEAVEN(1946, Brit.); EXILE, THE(1947); FOREVER AMBER(1947); LURED(1947); BERLIN EXPRESS(1948); THREE MUSKETEERS, THE(1948); RED DANUBE(1949); FIGHTING PIMPERNEL, THE(1950, Brit.); DESERT FOX, THE(1951); SOLDIERS THREE(1951); MERRY WIDOW, THE(1952); PRISONER OF ZENDA, THE(1952); SCARAMOUCHE(1952); CONSTANT HUSBAND, THE(1955, Brit.); OTHELLO(1955, U.S./Fr./Ital.); SWAN, THE(1956); HELLO LONDON(1958, Brit.); HORSE'S MOUTH, THE(1958, Brit.); MERRY ANDREW(1958); LEAGUE OF GENTLEMEN, THE(1961, Brit.); V.I.P.s, THE(1963, Brit.); GOLDEN HEAD, THE(1965, Hung., U.S.); MAN COULD GET KILLED, A(1966); SWINGER, THE(1966); COOL ONES THE(1967); PRUDENCE AND THE PILL(1968, Brit.); KENNER(1969); UP THE FRONT(1972, Brit.); THEATRE OF BLOOD(1973, Brit.)

Robert "Bobby" Coote
HOUSE OF FEAR, THE(1939)

John Copage
KILLERS, THE(1964); WITH SIX YOU GET EGGROLL(1968); SIMON, KING OF THE WITCHES(1971)

David Cope
OUT(1982), m

James R. Cope
1984
MISUNDERSTOOD(1984)

John Cope
GOING MY WAY(1944), set d

Kennedy Cope
FATHER CAME TOO(1964, Brit.)

Kenneth Cope
GENGHIS KHAN(U.S./Brit./Ger./Yugo); BATTLE HELL(1956, Brit.); X THE UNKNOWN(1957, Brit.); DANGEROUS YOUTH(1958, Brit.); DUNKIRK(1958, Brit.); TANK FORCE(1958, Brit.); LADY IS A SQUARE, THE(1959, Brit.); NAKED FURY(1959, Brit.); UNSTOPPABLE MAN, THE(1961, Brit.); CONCRETE JUNGLE, THE(1962, Brit.); DEATH TRAP(1962, Brit.); JUNGLE STREET GIRLS(1963, Brit.); PLEASURE LOVERS, THE(1964, Brit.); TOMORROW AT TEN(1964, Brit.); CHANGE PARTNERS(1965, Brit.); THESE ARE THE DAMNED(1965, Brit.); DATELINE DIAMONDS(1966, Brit.); TWIST OF SAND, A(1968, Brit.); DESPERADOS, THE(1969); TOUCH OF THE OTHER, A(1970, Brit.); ISLAND OF THE BURNING DAMNED(1971, Brit.); GEORGE AND MILDRED(1980, Brit.)
Misc. Talkies
SHE'LL FOLLOW YOU ANYWHERE(1971)

Nigel Cope
Misc. Silents
NAUGHTY HUSBANDS(1930, Brit.)

Jacques Copeau
COURIER OF LYONS(1938, Fr.); AFFAIR LAFONT, THE(1939, Fr.); CONFLICT(1939, Fr.)

James Copedge
THANK YOUR LUCKY STARS(1943)

Jodie Copelan
SNOW CREATURE, THE,(1954), ed; BATTLE TAXI(1955), ed; APACHE WARRIOR(1957), ed; DEERSLAYER, THE(1957), ed; KRONOS(1957), ed; UNDER FIRE(1957), ed; MACHETE(1958), ed; NIGHT OF THE BLOOD BEAST(1958), ed; BATTLE AT BLOODY BEACH(1961), ed; LITTLE SHEPHERD OF KINGDOM COME(1961), ed; PURPLE HILLS, THE(1961), ed; SEVEN WOMEN FROM HELL(1961), ed; FIREBRAND, THE(1962), ed; IT HAPPENED IN ATHENS(1962), ed; WOMAN HUNT(1962), ed; DAY MARS INVADED EARTH, THE(1963), ed; HARBOR LIGHTS(1963), ed; HOUSE OF THE DAMNED(1963), ed; NIGHT TIDE(1963), ed; THUNDER ISLAND(1963), ed; YELLOW CANARY, THE(1963), ed; YOUNG GUNS OF TEXAS(1963), ed; YOUNG SWINGERS, THE(1963), ed; STAGE TO THUNDER ROCK(1964), ed; WILD ON THE BEACH(1965), ed; 1,000 PLANE RAID, THE(1969), ed; SMALL TOWN IN TEXAS, A(1976), ed

Sheila Copelan
VIOLATORS, THE(1957)

Bill Copeland
DEAD ZONE, THE(1983)

Carl Copeland
HEARTLAND(1980), art d

J. David Copeland
MIDSUMMER NIGHT'S SEX COMEDY, A(1982)

Jack L. Copeland
HELL'S FIVE HOURS(1958), p,d&w

James Copeland
SAILOR OF THE KING(1953, Brit.); HIGH AND DRY(1954, Brit.); SCOTCH ON THE ROCKS(1954, Brit.); INNOCENTS IN PARIS(1955, Brit.); LAND OF FURY(1955, Brit.); YOU LUCKY PEOPLE(1955, Brit.); MAD LITTLE ISLAND(1958, Brit.); FAREWELL PERFORMANCE(1963, Brit.); BIG CATCH, THE(1968, Brit.); TORTURE GARDEN(1968, Brit.); PRIVATE LIFE OF SHERLOCK HOLMES, THE(1970, Brit.)

Jimmy Copeland
RACE FOR LIFE, A(1955, Brit.)

Joan Copeland
GODDESS, THE(1958); MIDDLE OF THE NIGHT(1959); ROSELAND(1977); IT'S MY TURN(1980); LITTLE SEX, A(1982)

Jodie Copeland
AMBUSH AT CIMARRON PASS(1958), d; LASERBLAST(1978), ed

Lisa Copeland
JACKSON COUNTY JAIL(1976)

Maurice Copeland
NEXT MAN, THE(1976); SEDUCTION OF JOE TYNAN, THE(1979); ARTHUR(1981); BLOW OUT(1981)

Maurice D. Copeland
TRADING PLACES(1983)
Morey Copeland
NIGHT OF EVIL(1962)
Nicholas Copeland
LEGION OF TERROR(1936)
Nick Copeland
FEET FIRST(1930); DECEIVER, THE(1931); HELL CAT, THE(1934); HERE COMES THE NAVY(1934); MAN'S GAME, A(1934); MURDER IN THE CLOUDS(1934); STUDENT TOUR(1934); THIN MAN, THE(1934); TWENTIETH CENTURY(1934); CASE OF THE CURIOUS BRIDE, THE(1935); GOOSE AND THE GANDER, THE(1935); I LIVE FOR LOVE(1935); MISS PACIFIC FLEET(1935); O'SHAUGHNESSY'S BOY(1935); SWEET ADELINE(1935); COWBOY STAR, THE(1936); MAN HUNT(1936); MORE THAN A SECRETARY(1936); TREACHERY RIDES THE RANGE(1936); MIDNIGHT MADONNA(1937); SARATOGA(1937); TRUE CONFESSION(1937); JUVENILE COURT(1938); MAIN EVENT, THE(1938); MEET THE MAYOR(1938); SWISS MISS(1938); TEST PILOT(1938); WHO KILLED GAIL PRESTON?(1938); YOU CAN'T TAKE IT WITH YOU(1938); MR. SMITH GOES TO WASHINGTON(1939); TELL NO TALES(1939); ENEMY AGENT(1940); NEW MOON(1940)
Rene Copeland
REUBEN, REUBEN(1983)
Roger Copeland
1984
RIVER RAT, THE(1984)
Stewart Copeland
RUMBLE FISH(1983), m
William Copeland
PRINCE OF PIRATES(1953), w; LONNIE(1963), w; SECRET OF THE SACRED FOREST, THE(1970), p, w
Campbell Copelin
TWO MINUTES' SILENCE(1934, Brit.); IT ISN'T DONE(1937, Aus.); TALL TIMBERS(1937, Aus.); LOVERS AND LUGGERS(1938, Aus.); TYPHOON TREASURE(1939, Brit.); VENGEANCE OF THE DEEP(1940, Aus.); KISS THE BLOOD OFF MY HANDS(1948); SWORD IN THE DESERT(1949); TWELVE O'CLOCK HIGH(1949); ROGUES OF SHERWOOD FOREST(1950); THREE CAME HOME(1950); MIDNIGHT EPISODE(1951, Brit.); PORTRAIT OF CLARE(1951, Brit.)
Mike Copeman
1984
AMERICAN NIGHTMARE(1984)
David Coplan
JUST WILLIAM'S LUCK(1948, Brit.), p; WILLIAM COMES TO TOWN(1948, Brit.), p; LUCKY MASCOT, THE(1951, Brit.), p
Fred Coplan
ONE STEP TO HELL(1969, U.S./Ital./Span.)
Jodie Coplan
AIR PATROL(1962), ed
Aaron Copland
OF MICE AND MEN(1939), m; OUR TOWN(1940), m; NORTH STAR, THE(1943), m; HEIRESS, THE(1949), m; RED PONY, THE(1949), m; SOMETHING WILD(1961), m; LOVE AND MONEY(1982), m, md
Nick Copland
OUR RELATIONS(1936)
Ronda Copland
YOUR THREE MINUTES ARE UP(1973); RANCHO DELUXE(1975)
John Coplans
BORN IN FLAMES(1983)
Elbert Coplen, Jr.
BACHELOR MOTHER(1939)
Yorke Coplen
Misc. Talkies
URUBU(1948)
Geoffrey Copleston
SUPERARGO VERSUS DIABOLICUS(1966, Ital./Span.); HILLS RUN RED, THE(1967, Ital.); NIGHT PORTER, THE(1974, Ital./U.S.)
1984
BLACK CAT, THE(1984, Ital./Brit.)
Billy Copley
MAIDSTONE(1970)
Gerald L.C. Copley
BORN FREE(1966), w
Lewis Copley
OPERATION EICHMANN(1961), w
Marjorie Copley
SONG OF BERNADETTE, THE(1943)
Paul Copley
ALFIE DARLING(1975, Brit.); ZULU DAWN(1980, Brit.)
Misc. Talkies
DOLL'S EYE(1982)
Peter Copley
FIGHTING PIMPERNEL, THE(1950, Brit.); GOLDEN SALAMANDER(1950, Brit.); HOUR OF THIRTEEN, THE(1952, Brit.); PROMOTER, THE(1952, Brit.); CLUE OF THE MISSING APE, THE(1953, Brit.); SAADIA(1953); SWORD AND THE ROSE, THE(1953); FOREIGN INTRIGUE(1956); PERIL FOR THE GUY(1956, Brit.); JUST MY LUCK(1957, Brit.); MAN WITHOUT A BODY, THE(1957, Brit.); TIME WITHOUT PITY(1957, Brit.); FOLLOW THAT HORSE!(1960, Brit.); VICTIM(1961, Brit.); KING AND COUNTRY(1964, Brit.); THIRD SECRET, THE(1964, Brit.); KNACK ... AND HOW TO GET IT, THE(1965, Brit.); FIVE MILLION YEARS TO EARTH(1968, Brit.); SHOES OF THE FISHERMAN, THE(1968); FRANKENSTEIN MUST BE DESTROYED!(1969, Brit.); WALK A CROOKED PATH(1969, Brit.); ALL AT SEA(1970, Brit.); MOSQUITO SQUADRON(1970, Brit.); JANE EYRE(1971, Brit.); WHAT BECAME OF JACK AND JILL?(1972, Brit.); GAWAIN AND THE GREEN KNIGHT(1973, Brit.); SHOUT AT THE DEVIL(1976, Brit.)
Teri Copley
NEW YEAR'S EVIL(1980)
Campbell Copling
Misc. Talkies
TIMBERLAND TERROR(1940, Aus.)

Copoeira Dancers of Cangiquinha
GIVEN WORD, THE(1964, Braz.)
Tony Coppala
THRILL OF A ROMANCE(1945)
James Coppedge
ONE MILLION B.C.(1940)
Alec Coppel
JUST LIKE A WOMAN(1939, Brit.), w; OVER THE MOON(1940, Brit.), w; WHO IS GUILTY?(1940, Brit.), w; SMITHY(1946, Aus.), w; PACIFIC ADVENTURE(1947, Aus.), w; HIDDEN ROOM, THE(1949, Brit.), w; WOMAN HATER(1949, Brit.), w; LUCKY MASCOT, THE(1951, Brit.), w; NO HIGHWAY IN THE SKY(1951, Brit.), w; SMART ALEC(1951, Brit.), w; SCHOOL FOR BRIDES(1952, Brit.), w; CAPTAIN'S PARADISE, THE(1953, Brit.), w; MR. DENNING DRIVES NORTH(1953, Brit.), w; BLACK KNIGHT, THE(1954), w; HELL BELOW ZERO(1954, Brit.), w; APPOINTMENT WITH A SHADOW(1958), w; GAZEBO, THE(1959), w; SWORDSMAN OF SIENA, THE(1962, Fr./Ital.), w; MOMENT TO MOMENT(1966), w; BLISS OF MRS. BLOSSOM, THE(1968, Brit.), w; STATUE, THE(1971, Brit.), w
Alex Coppel
VERTIGO(1958), w
Hazel Coppen
TWO LEFT FEET(1965, Brit.)
William Coppen
RETURN OF THE JEDI(1983)
Isabelle Coppens
Misc. Talkies
THAT GIRL IS A TRAMP(1974)
Myra Copper
GAZEBO, THE(1959), w
Olive Copper
MYSTERIOUS MISS X, THE(1939), w
Stuart Copper
DISAPPEARANCE, THE(1981, Brit./Can.), d
Copper the Horse
TORNADO RANGE(1948); WESTWARD TRAIL, THE(1948)
David Copperfield
TERROR TRAIN(1980, Can.)
Doug Coppin
BUCKAROO FROM POWDER RIVER(1948)
Douglas D. Coppin
HER HUSBAND'S AFFAIRS(1947); IT HAD TO BE YOU(1947)
Grace Coppin
NAKED CITY, THE(1948); LOST BOUNDARIES(1949); SO YOUNG, SO BAD(1950)
Hazel Coppin
PRESS FOR TIME(1966, Brit.)
Tyler Coppin
ROAD WARRIOR, THE(1982, Aus.)
David Copping
NED KELLY(1970, Brit.); PICNIC AT HANGING ROCK(1975, Aus.), art d; STORM BOY(1976, Aus.), prod d; LET THE BALLOON GO(1977, Aus.), art d; MONEY MOVERS(1978, Aus.), art d; CLUB, THE(1980, Aus.), art d; PICTURE SHOW MAN, THE(1980, Aus.), art d; PUBERTY BLUES(1983, Aus.), prod d; RETURN OF CAPTAIN INVINCIBLE, THE(1983, Aus./U.S.), prod d
1984
SECOND TIME LUCKY(1984, Aus./New Zealand), prod d
Misc. Talkies
OUTBREAK OF HOSTILITIES(1979), d
Robin Copping
2,000 WEEKS(1970, Aus.), ph; STORK(1971, Aus.), ph; LIBIDO(1973, Aus.), ph; ALVIN RIDES AGAIN(1974, Aus.), d, ph; PETERSEN(1974, Aus.), ph; END PLAY(1975, Aus.), ph; ELIZA FRASER(1976, Aus.), ph; PIRATE MOVIE, THE(1982, Aus.), ph
Joe Coppini
TRENCHCOAT(1983)
Rusty Coppleman
WONDERWALL(1969, Brit.), ed
Geoffrey Coppleston
MATTER OF TIME, A(1976, Ital./U.S.)
Geoffrey Copplestone
WAR AND PEACE(1956, Ital./U.S.); BREAD AND CHOCOLATE(1978, Ital.)
Jeffrey Copplestone
GIRL WHO COULDN'T SAY NO, THE(1969, Ital.)
Ed Coppo
MURDER MAN(1935)
Edward Coppo
BEAST OF THE CITY, THE(1932)
Andrea Coppola
1984
WARRIORS OF THE WASTELAND(1984, Ital.)
Carmen Coppola
TONIGHT FOR SURE(1962), m&md
Carmine Coppola
GODFATHER, THE, PART II(1974), m, md; HARRY AND WALTER GO TO NEW YORK(1976); APOCALYPSE NOW(1979), m; BLACK STALLION, THE(1979), m; ONE FROM THE HEART(1982); OUTSIDERS, THE(1983), m
Silents
NAPOLEON(1927, Fr.), m
Francesco Coppola
MORE THAN A MIRACLE(1967, Ital./Fr.)
Francis Coppola
TONIGHT FOR SURE(1962), p,d&w; TERROR, THE(1963), p&d; ONE FROM THE HEART(1982), d, w
1984
COTTON CLUB, THE(1984), d, w
Francis Ford Coppola
MAGIC VOYAGE OF SINBAD, THE(1962, USSR), w; PLAYGIRLS AND THE BELLBOY, THE(1962,Ger.), d, w; DEMENTIA 13(1963), d&w; IS PARIS BURNING?(1966, U.S./Fr.), w; THIS PROPERTY IS CONDEMNED(1966), w; YOU'RE A BIG BOY NOW(1966), d&w; FINIAN'S RAINBOW(1968), d; RAIN PEOPLE, THE(1969), d&w; PATTON(1970), w; GODFATHER, THE(1972), d, w; AMERICAN GRAFFITI(1973), p; CONVERSATION, THE(1974), p,d&w; GODFATHER, THE, PART II(1974), p, d, w; APOCALYPSE NOW(1979), p&d, w, m; OUTSIDERS, THE(1983), d;

RUMBLE FISH(1983), d, w
Frank Coppola
1984
BUDDY SYSTEM, THE(1984)
Giovanna Coppola
WHAT DID YOU DO IN THE WAR, DADDY?(1966)
Giuseppe Coppola
HORNET'S NEST(1970)
Italia Coppola
ONE FROM THE HEART(1982)
Marc Coppola
1984
COTTON CLUB, THE(1984)
Nicholas Coppola
FAST TIMES AT RIDGEMONT HIGH(1982)
Sam Coppola
NO WAY TO TREAT A LADY(1968); ANDERSON TAPES, THE(1971); CRAZY JOE(1974); KING OF THE GYPSIES(1978)
Misc. Talkies
INTERPLAY(1970)
Sam J. Coppola
GANG THAT COULDN'T SHOOT STRAIGHT, THE(1971); SATURDAY NIGHT FEVER(1977); WITHOUT A TRACE(1983)
Talia Coppola [Shire]
WILD RACERS, THE(1968); DUNWICH HORROR, THE(1970); GAS-S-S-S!(1970)
Vincent Coppola
GODFATHER, THE, PART II(1974)
Kathryn Copponex
NEW ORLEANS AFTER DARK(1958)
Stelvio Copriani
TWITCH OF THE DEATH NERVE(1973, Ital.), m
Harold Cops
RIO LOBO(1970)
Douglas Copsey
BRONCO BILLY(1980)
the Coptic Priests of the Church of Abu Sefen
EGYPT BY THREE(1953)
J. Coquelin
CAFE DE PARIS(1938, Fr.)
Jean Coquelin
DAVID GOLDER(1932, Fr.); END OF A DAY, THE(1939, Fr.); CARNIVAL OF SINNERS(1947, Fr.)
Jean-Paul Coquelin
NIGHT WATCH, THE(1964, Fr./Ital.)
Fernand Coquet
MADE IN U.S.A.(1966, Fr.)
John Coquillion
THIRTY NINE STEPS, THE(1978, Brit.), ph
John Coquillon
TOTO AND THE POACHERS(1958, Brit.), w, ph; IMPERSONATOR, THE(1962, Brit.), ph; CONQUEROR WORM, THE(1968, Brit.), ph; OBLONG BOX, THE(1969, Brit.), ph; CRY OF THE BANSHEE(1970, Brit.), ph; SCREAM AND SCREAM AGAIN(1970, Brit.), ph; WUTHERING HEIGHTS(1970, Brit.), ph; STRAW DOGS(1971, Brit.), ph; RENTADICK(1972, Brit.), ph; NATIONAL HEALTH, OR NURSE NORTON'S AFFAIR, THE(1973, Brit.), ph; PAT GARRETT AND BILLY THE KID(1973), ph; TRIPLE ECHO, THE(1973, Brit.), ph; INSIDE OUT(1975, Brit.), ph; WILBY CONSPIRACY, THE(1975, Brit.), ph; ECHOES OF A SUMMER(1976), ph; CROSS OF IRON(1977, Brit., Ger.), ph; CHANGELING, THE(1980, Can.), ph; FINAL ASSIGNMENT(1980, Can.), ph; MR. PATMAN(1980, Can.), ph; ABSOLUTION(1981, Brit.), ph; AMATEUR, THE(1982), ph; PRAYING MANTIS(1982, Brit.), ph; OSTERMAN WEEKEND, THE(1983), ph
Johnnie Coquillon
LAST RHINO, THE(1961, Brit.), p
Johnny Coquillon
CRIMSON CULT, THE(1970, Brit.), ph; EGGHEAD'S ROBOT(1970, Brit.), ph
Gloria Coral
POR MIS PISTOLAS(1969, Mex.)
Tito Coral
MARIE GALANTE(1934); GOIN' TO TOWN(1935)
Coralie
JONAH–WHO WILL BE 25 IN THE YEAR 2000(1976, Switz.)
Jean Coralli
TURNING POINT, THE(1977), ch
Vera Coralli
Misc. Silents
CHRYSANTHEMUMS(1914, USSR); LOVE OF A STATE COUNCILLOR(1915, USSR); NATASHA ROSTOVA(1915, USSR); SINGED WINGS(1915, USSR); GRIFFON OF AN OLD WARRIOR(1916, USSR); ALARM, THE(1917, USSR)
Allan Coran
WIDOW FROM CHICAGO, THE(1930)
Marusa [Maria Esther] Coran
HEAT(1970, Arg.)
Greg Corarito
HARD TRAIL(1969), a, d&w; DIAMOND STUD(1970), d; HARD ROAD, THE(1970)
Misc. Talkies
DIAMOND STUD(1970), d
Gregory Corarito
Misc. Talkies
CARNAL MADNESS(1975), d
Bruno Corazzari
LONG RIDE FROM HELL, A(1970, Ital.); MERCENARY, THE(1970, Ital./Span.); MAN CALLED SLEDGE, A(1971, Ital.); HANNAH K.(1983, Fr.)
Mike Corb
WILD ANGELS, THE(1966), m
Kate Corbaley
Silents
REAL FOLKS(1918), w; DESERT BLOSSOMS(1921), w

Laura Corbay
ROAD TO RIO(1947); PALEFACE, THE(1948)
Eduardo Corbe
HOT STUFF(1979)
1984
WHERE THE BOYS ARE '84(1984)
Roger Corbeau
SYMPHONIE PASTORALE(1948, Fr.), ph
Yves Corbeil
TROUBLE-FETE(1964, Can.)
Jean-Claude Corbel
1984
LIFE IS A BED OF ROSES(1984, Fr.)
Vincenzo Corbella
LA NOTTE(1961, Fr./Ital.)
A. G. Corbelle
Silents
MY COUSIN(1918)
Vanni Corbellini
BLOW TO THE HEART(1983, Ital.)
Richard Corben
HEAVY METAL(1981, Can.), w, anim
Ben Corbett
BAR L RANCH(1930); LONESOME TRAIL, THE(1930); MEN WITHOUT LAW(1930); PHANTOM OF THE DESERT(1930); RIDIN' LAW(1930); SHADOW RANCH(1930); CAVALIER OF THE WEST(1931); KID FROM ARIZONA, THE(1931); WEST OF CHEYENNE(1931); WESTWARD BOUND(1931); WILD WEST WHOOPEE(1931); HELL FIRE AUSTIN(1932); PARTNERS(1932); SADDLE BUSTER, THE(1932); SHOTGUN PASS(1932); TEX TAKES A HOLIDAY(1932); COME ON TARZAN(1933); GUN LAW(1933); STRAWBERRY ROAN(1933); ARIZONA NIGHTS(1934); GUN JUSTICE(1934); HONOR OF THE RANGE(1934); LAST ROUND-UP, THE(1934); SMOKING GUNS(1934); TEXAS TORNADO(1934); TRAIL DRIVE, THE(1934); ARIZONA BADMAN(1935); COWBOY AND THE BANDIT, THE(1935); COYOTE TRAILS(1935); IVORY-HANDLED GUN(1935); PALS OF THE RANGE(1935); FOR THE SERVICE(1936); MOONLIGHT ON THE PRAIRIE(1936); SUNSET OF POWER(1936); EMPTY HOLSTERS(1937); EMPTY SADDLES(1937); HOPALONG RIDES AGAIN(1937); LAW FOR TOMBSTONE(1937); SANDFLOW(1937); TEXAS TRAIL(1937); GOLD MINE IN THE SKY(1938); HEROES OF THE ALAMO(1938); LAWLESS VALLEY(1938); OVERLAND EXPRESS, THE(1938); SIX SHOOTIN' SHERIFF(1938); CODE OF THE CACTUS(1939); COME ON RANGERS(1939); FIGHTING GRINGO, THE(1939); FIGHTING RENEGADE(1939); LAW COMES TO TEXAS, THE(1939); RACKETEERS OF THE RANGE(1939); TEXAS WILDCATS(1939); TIMBER STAMPEDE(1939); TRIGGER FINGERS ½(1939); ARIZONA GANGBUSTERS(1940); STRAIGHT SHOOTER(1940); IN OLD CHEYENNE(1941); GHOST TOWN LAW(1942); PIRATES OF THE PRAIRIE(1942); HOPPY SERVES A WRIT(1943); SAGEBRUSH LAW(1943); WAGON TRACKS WEST(1943); LAND OF THE OUTLAWS(1944); LAW MEN(1944); PARTNERS OF THE TRAIL(1944); RANGE LAW(1944); ENEMY OF THE LAW(1945); FOOL'S GOLD(1946); MAN FROM COLORADO, THE(1948); SILVER RIVER(1948); COLT .45(1950); MONTANA DESPERADO(1951); SPRINGFIELD RIFLE(1952), a, tech adv; CHARGE AT FEATHER RIVER, THE(1953); DRUM BEAT(1954), tech adv
Misc. Talkies
FORTY-FIVE CALIBRE ECHO(1932); GIRL TROUBLE(1933); TROUBLE BUSTERS(1933); BORDER MENACE, THE(1934); FIGHTING THROUGH(1934); LONE BANDIT, THE(1934); OUTLAW TAMER, THE(1934); POTLUCK PARDS(1934); WEST ON PARADE(1934); BORDER VENGEANCE(1935); WESTERN RACKETEERS(1935); LIGHTNING CARSON RIDES AGAIN(1938); SIX-GUN TRAIL(1938)
Silents
KINGFISHER'S ROOST, THE(1922); LURE OF GOLD(1922); SOUTH OF NORTHERN LIGHTS(1922); MAN FROM WYOMING, THE(1924); OUTLAW'S DAUGHTER, THE(1925); LAW OF THE SNOW COUNTRY, THE(1926); MAN FROM HARDPAN, THE(1927); SOMEWHERE IN SONORA(1927)
Misc. Silents
RANGELAND(1922); SHADOWS OF CHINATOWN(1926); BOSS OF RUSTLER'S ROOST, THE(1928); BRONC STOMPER, THE(1928); FEARLESS RIDER, THE(1928); .45 CALIBRE WAR(1929)
Benny Corbett
RIO RITA(1929); GUN SMOKE(1936); OUTLAW'S PARADISE(1939); MARKED TRAILS(1944); COUNTY FAIR(1950); DALLAS(1950)
Silents
ONE GLORIOUS SCRAP(1927); ARIZONA CYCLONE(1928); ROYAL RIDER, THE(1929)
Bernie Corbett
Misc. Silents
SAGEBRUSH LADY, THE(1925)
Carol Corbett
THOMAS CROWN AFFAIR, THE(1968)
Ed Corbett
1984
CRACKERS(1984)
Glenn Corbett
FIREBALL, THE(1950); VIOLENT YEARS, THE(1956); CRIMSON KIMONO, THE(1959); ALL THE YOUNG MEN(1960); MAN ON A STRING(1960); MOUNTAIN ROAD, THE(1960); HOMICIDAL(1961); PIRATES OF BLOOD RIVER, THE(1962, Brit.); SHENANDOAH(1965); GUNS IN THE HEATHER(1968, Brit.); THIS SAVAGE LAND(1969); CHISUM(1970); BIG JAKE(1971); DEAD PIGEON ON BEETHOVEN STREET(1972, Ger.); RIDE IN A PINK CAR(1974, Can.); MIDWAY(1976); NEW GIRL IN TOWN(1977)
Gretchen Corbett
OUT OF IT(1969); LET'S SCARE JESSICA TO DEATH(1971); OTHER SIDE OF THE MOUNTAIN–PART 2, THE(1978); JAWS OF SATAN(1980)
Misc. Talkies
PSI FACTOR(1980, Brit.)
Harry Corbett
NOWHERE TO GO(1959, Brit.); IT'S NOT THE SIZE THAT COUNTS(1979, Brit.), w
Harry H. Corbett
PASSING STRANGER, THE(1954, Brit.); FLOODS OF FEAR(1958, Brit.); SHAKE HANDS WITH THE DEVIL(1959, Ireland); BIG DAY, THE(1960, Brit.); COVER GIRL KILLER(1960, Brit.); IN THE WAKE OF A STRANGER(1960, Brit.); SHAKEDOWN, THE(1960, Brit.); UNSTOPPABLE MAN, THE(1961, Brit.); TIME TO REMEM-

J. Corbett—
BER(1962, Brit.); SPARROWS CAN'T SING(1963, Brit.); WHAT A CRAZY WORLD(1963, Brit.); BARGEE, THE(1964, Brit.); LADIES WHO DO(1964, Brit.); RATTLE OF A SIMPLE MAN(1964, Brit.); SOME PEOPLE(1964, Brit.); BOY TEN FEET TALL, A(1965, Brit.); JOEY BOY(1965, Brit.); CARRY ON SCREAMING(1966, Brit.); SANDWICH MAN, THE(1966, Brit.); MARRIAGE OF CONVENIENCE(1970, Brit.); SOPHIE'S PLACE(1970); MAGNIFICENT SEVEN DEADLY SINS, THE(1971, Brit.); STEPTOE AND SON(1972, Brit.); JABBERWOCKY(1977, Brit.); IT'S NOT THE SIZE THAT COUNTS(1979, Brit.); SILVER DREAM RACER(1982, Brit.)

J. Corbett
RIVER OF UNREST(1937, Brit.), ed

James Corbett
CHINESE BUNGALOW, THE(1930, Brit.), w; DEAD MEN TELL NO TALES(1939, Brit.), ed; CHINESE DEN, THE(1940, Brit.), w; MEET THE DUKE(1949, Brit.), d
Silents
CHINESE BUNGALOW, THE(1926, Brit.), w

James "Gentleman Jim" Corbett
Misc. Silents
LADY AND THE BURGLAR, THE(1915)

James J. Corbett
HAPPY DAYS(1930); GENTLEMAN JIM(1942), w
Silents
BROADWAY AFTER DARK(1924)
Misc. Silents
BURGLAR AND THE LADY, THE(1914); OTHER GIRL, THE(1916); BEAUTY SHOP, THE(1922)

James J. "Gentleman Jim" Corbett
Silents
PRINCE OF AVENUE A., THE(1920)

Jean Corbett
TWO TICKETS TO BROADWAY(1951); DREAMBOAT(1952); LAS VEGAS STORY, THE(1952); ROAD TO BALI(1952); ROBE, THE(1953); PAL JOEY(1957); YOUNG STRANGER, THE(1957)

Jim Corbett
MAN-EATER OF KUMAON(1948), w

Joan Corbett
ROBE, THE(1953)

Kaye Corbett
RUNNING BRAVE(1983, Can.)

Leonora Corbett
LOVE ON WHEELS(1932, Brit.); CONSTANT NYMPH, THE(1933, Brit.); FRIDAY THE 13TH(1934, Brit.); LADY IN DANGER(1934, Brit.); WARN LONDON!(1934, Brit.); WILD BOY(1934, Brit.); REGAL CAVALCADE(1935, Brit.); HAPPY FAMILY, THE(1936, Brit.); LIVING DANGEROUSLY(1936, Brit.); HEART'S DESIRE(1937, Brit.); PRICE OF FOLLY, THE(1937, Brit.); NIGHT ALONE(1938, Brit.); TROOPSHIP(1938, Brit.); FINGERS(1940, Brit.); UNDER YOUR HAT(1940, Brit.)

Louis J. Corbett
TIOGA KID, THE(1948)

Marjorie Corbett
THARK(1932, Brit.); TURKEY TIME(1933, Brit.); BROKEN ROSARY, THE(1934, Brit.); GIRL IN THE CROWD, THE(1934, Brit.); CHILDREN OF THE FOG(1935, Brit.); PRICE OF A SONG, THE(1935, Brit.); WINDFALL(1935, Brit.); PAY BOX ADVENTURE(1936, Brit.); REVERSE BE MY LOT, THE(1938, Brit.)

Pamela Corbett
TOM(1973)
Misc. Talkies
BAD BUNCH, THE(1976)

Ronald Corbett
FUN AT ST. FANNY'S(1956, Brit.); MAD LITTLE ISLAND(1958, Brit.)

Ronnie Corbett
TOP OF THE FORM(1953, Brit.); CASINO ROYALE(1967, Brit.); RISE AND RISE OF MICHAEL RIMMER, THE(1970, Brit.); SOME WILL, SOME WON'T(1970, Brit.); NO SEX PLEASE–WE'RE BRITISH(1979, Brit.)

Roy Corbett
CADDIE(1976, Aus.)

Scott Corbett
LOVE NEST(1951), w

Tom Corbett
SEPARATION(1968, Brit.)

Will Corbett
Misc. Silents
SOMEWHERE IN GEORGIA(1916)

William Corbett
UNMASKED(1929)
Misc. Talkies
UNMASKED(1929)
Misc. Silents
SOULS IN BONDAGE(1916)

Barry Corbin
ANY WHICH WAY YOU CAN(1980); STIR CRAZY(1980); URBAN COWBOY(1980); DEAD AND BURIED(1981); NIGHT THE LIGHTS WENT OUT IN GEORGIA, THE(1981); HONKYTONK MAN(1982); SIX PACK(1982); BALLAD OF GREGORIO CORTEZ, THE(1983); MAN WHO LOVED WOMEN, THE(1983); WARGAMES(1983)

Virginia Lee Corbin
FOOTLIGHTS AND FOOLS(1929); MORALS FOR WOMEN(1931); X MARKS THE SPOT(1931); FORGOTTEN WOMEN(1932); SHOTGUN PASS(1932)
Silents
JACK AND THE BEANSTALK(1917); ENEMIES OF CHILDREN(1923); HANDSOME BRUTE, THE(1925); HANDS UP(1926); LADIES AT PLAY(1926); DRIVEN FROM HOME(1927); PLAY SAFE(1927); HEAD OF THE FAMILY, THE(1928); JAZZLAND(1928)
Misc. Silents
ALADDIN AND THE WONDERFUL LAMP(1917); BABES IN THE WOODS(1917); TREASURE ISLAND(1917); FAN FAN(1918); CHORUS LADY, THE(1924); CITY THAT NEVER SLEEPS, THE(1924); CLOUD RIDER, THE(1925); HEADLINES(1925); LILLIES OF THE STREETS(1925); NORTH STAR(1925); THREE KEYS(1925); WHOLE TOWN'S TALKING, THE(1926); PERFECT SAP, THE(1927); BARE KNEES(1928); LITTLE SNOB, THE(1928)

Robert Corbins
Misc. Silents
FOOLISH MONTE CARLO(1922)

Bruno Corbucci
SLAVE, THE(1963, Ital.), w; GLADIATORS 7(1964, Span./Ital.), w; DJANGO(1966 Ital./Span.), w; HATE FOR HATE(1967, Ital.), w; BATTLE OF THE AMAZONS(1973, Ital./Span.), w; CRIME AT PORTA ROMANA(1980, Ital.), d, w

Enzo Corbucci
EVIL EYE(1964 Ital.), w

Serge Corbucci
CON ARTISTS, THE(1981, Ital.), d

Sergio Corbucci
LAST DAYS OF POMPEII, THE(1960, Ital.), w; DUEL OF THE TITANS(1963, Ital.), d, w; SLAVE, THE(1963, Ital.), d; TWO COLONELS, THE(1963, Ital.), w; GOLIATH AND THE VAMPIRES(1964, Ital.), d, w; DJANGO(1966 Ital./Span.), d, w; MAN WHO LAUGHS, THE(1966, Ital.), d, w; MINNESOTA CLAY(1966, Ital./Fr./Span.), d, w; RINGO AND HIS GOLDEN PISTOL(1966, Ital.), d; HELLBENDERS, THE(1967, U.S./Ital./Span.), d; NAVAJO JOE(1967, Ital./Span.), d; DROP THEM OR I'LL SHOOT(1969, Fr./Ger./Span.), p&d, w; COMPANEROS(1970 Ital./Span./Ger.), d, w; MERCENARY, THE(1970, Ital./Span.), d; JOHNNY HAMLET(1972, Ital.), w; SONNY AND JED(1974, Ital.), d, w; SUPER FUZZ(1981), d, w

Bob Corby
ESCAPE TO BURMA(1955)

Ellen Corby
THEY WON'T BELIEVE ME(1947); TWILIGHT ON THE TRAIL(1941), w; CORNERED(1945); CRACK-UP(1946); DARK CORNER, THE(1946); FROM THIS DAY FORWARD(1946); IN OLD SACRAMENTO(1946); IT'S A WONDERFUL LIFE(1946); LOCKET, THE(1946); LOVER COME BACK(1946); SISTER KENNY(1946); SPIRAL STAIRCASE, THE(1946); TILL THE END OF TIME(1946); FOREVER AMBER(1947); HOPPY'S HOLIDAY(1947), w; DARK PAST, THE(1948); FIGHTING FATHER DUNNE(1948); I REMEMBER MAMA(1948); IF YOU KNEW SUSIE(1948); NOOSE HANGS HIGH, THE(1948); STRIKE IT RICH(1948); CAPTAIN CHINA(1949); LITTLE WOMEN(1949); MADAME BOVARY(1949); MIGHTY JOE YOUNG(1949); RUSTY SAVES A LIFE(1949); WOMAN'S SECRET, A(1949); CAGED(1950); EDGE OF DOOM(1950); GUNFIGHTER, THE(1950); HARRIET CRAIG(1950); MA AND PA KETTLE GO TO TOWN(1950); PEGGY(1950); ANGELS IN THE OUTFIELD(1951); BAREFOOT MAILMAN, THE(1951); GOODBYE, MY FANCY(1951); HERE COMES THE GROOM(1951); MATING SEASON, THE(1951); ON MOONLIGHT BAY(1951); SEA HORNET, THE(1951); BIG TREES, THE(1952); FEARLESS FAGAN(1952); LION IS IN THE STREETS, A(1953); MONSOON(1953); SHANE(1953); VANQUISHED, THE(1953); WOMAN THEY ALMOST LYNCHED, THE(1953); ABOUT MRS. LESLIE(1954); BOWERY BOYS MEET THE MONSTERS, THE(1954); SABRINA(1954); SUSAN SLEPT HERE(1954); UNTAMED HEIRESS(1954); ILLEGAL(1955); SLIGHTLY SCARLET(1956); STAGECOACH TO FURY(1956); ALL MINE TO GIVE(1957); GOD IS MY PARTNER(1957); NIGHT PASSAGE(1957); ROCKABILLY BABY(1957); SEVENTH SIN, THE(1957); AS YOUNG AS WE ARE(1958); MACABRE(1958); VERTIGO(1958); VISIT TO A SMALL PLANET(1960); POCKETFUL OF MIRACLES(1961); SAINTLY SINNERS(1962); CARETAKERS, THE(1963); FOUR FOR TEXAS(1963); HUSH... HUSH, SWEET CHARLOTTE(1964); STRANGLER, THE(1964); FAMILY JEWELS, THE(1965); GHOST AND MR. CHICKEN, THE(1966); GLASS BOTTOM BOAT, THE(1966); NIGHT OF THE GRIZZLY, THE(1966); GNOME-MOBILE, THE(1967); LEGEND OF LYLAH CLARE, THE(1968); ANGEL IN MY POCKET(1969); FINE PAIR, A(1969, Ital.); SUPPORT YOUR LOCAL GUNFIGHTER(1971); NAPOLEON AND SAMANTHA(1972)

Francis Corby
BABES IN TOYLAND(1934), ph; BOHEMIAN GIRL, THE(1936), ph; ROLLIN' PLAINS(1938), ph; STARLIGHT OVER TEXAS(1938), ph; WHERE THE BUFFALO ROAM(1938), ph; LURE OF THE WASTELAND(1939), ph; SONG OF THE BUCKAROO(1939), ph

Michael Corby
1984
SCREAM FOR HELP(1984)

Travers Corby
Misc. Silents
HERE HE COMES(1926), d

Ann Corcoran
ESCAPE FROM CRIME(1942); IN THE MEANTIME, DARLING(1944); TAKE IT OR LEAVE IT(1944); DANCING IN THE DARK(1949)

Billy Corcoran
WHAT A WAY TO GO(1964)

Brian Corcoran
UNTAMED(1955); CAT ON A HOT TIN ROOF(1958); IN LOVE AND WAR(1958); LONG, HOT SUMMER, THE(1958); BABES IN TOYLAND(1961)

Donna Corcoran
ANGELS IN THE OUTFIELD(1951); DON'T BOTHER TO KNOCK(1952); MILLION DOLLAR MERMAID(1952); YOUNG MAN WITH IDEAS(1952); DANGEROUS WHEN WET(1953); SCANDAL AT SCOURIE(1953); GYPSY COLT(1954); MOONFLEET(1955); VIOLENT SATURDAY(1955)

E. Corcoran
Silents
KAISER, BEAST OF BERLIN, THE(1918)

Ethel Corcoran
Silents
PRICE FOR FOLLY, A(1915); NIGHT OUT, A(1916)

Frances G. Corcoran
Silents
ARRIVAL OF PERPETUA, THE(1915), w

George Corcoran
NOT DAMAGED(1930); MEN ON CALL(1931)

George "Red" Corcoran
PART TIME WIFE(1930)

Hugh Corcoran
HALF A HERO(1953); NO PLACE TO HIDE(1956); SEARCH FOR BRIDEY MURPHY, THE(1956); CAT ON A HOT TIN ROOF(1958); MANITOU, THE(1978)

Jane Corcoran
FURY(1936)

John Corcoran
SOMEBODY KILLED HER HUSBAND(1978)

Kathryn Cordes
SILHOUETTES(1982)
Helene Cordet
LIMPING MAN, THE(1953, Brit.); THREE STEPS IN THE DARK(1953, Brit.); TALE OF THREE WOMEN, A(1954, Brit.)
Louise Cordet
JUST FOR FUN(1963, Brit.)
Regis Cordic
WILD PARTY, THE(1975); MOUSE AND HIS CHILD, THE(1977)
Regis J. Cordic
SEVEN MINUTES, THE(1971); NEWMAN'S LAW(1974); TELEFON(1977)
Pierre Cordier
DEAD RUN(1961, Fr./Ital./Ger.)
Robert Cordier
INJUN FENDER(1973), p, d&w
Margaret Cordin
MERRY-G0-ROUND(1948, Brit.), p
Joe Zammit Cordina
PULP(1972, Brit.)
Harry Cording
PATRIOT, THE(1928); SINS OF THE FATHERS(1928); CHRISTINA(1929); ISLE OF LOST SHIPS(1929); SQUALL, THE(1929); BRIDE OF THE REGIMENT(1930); CAPTAIN OF THE GUARD(1930); ROUGH ROMANCE(1930); CONQUERING HORDE, THE(1931); HONOR OF THE FAMILY(1931); MATA HARI(1931); FILE 113(1932); FORGOTTEN COMMANDMENTS(1932); INTRUDER, THE(1932); NIGHT BEAT(1932); TEXAS CYCLONE(1932); WORLD AND THE FLESH, THE(1932); CAPTURED(1933); ROMAN SCANDALS(1933); TO THE LAST MAN(1933); BLACK CAT, THE(1934); GREAT EXPECTATIONS(1934); TREASURE ISLAND(1934); VIVA VILLA!(1934); WE LIVE AGAIN(1934); CAPTAIN BLOOD(1935); CHARLIE CHAN IN PARIS(1935); CRUSADES, THE(1935); MAN WHO RECLAIMED HIS HEAD, THE(1935); MUTINY ON THE BOUNTY(1935); NAUGHTY MARIETTA(1935); STRANGE WIVES(1935); DANIEL BOONE(1936); ROAD GANG(1936); SUTTER'S GOLD(1936); SUZY(1936); WHITE ANGEL, THE(1936); PRINCE AND THE PAUPER, THE(1937); ADVENTURES OF MARCO POLO, THE(1938); ADVENTURES OF ROBIN HOOD, THE(1938); CRIME SCHOOL(1938); PAINTED DESERT, THE(1938); VALLEY OF THE GIANTS(1938); ARIZONA LEGION(1939); DESTRY RIDES AGAIN(1939); EACH DAWN I DIE(1939); LIGHT THAT FAILED, THE(1939); MARSHAL OF MESA CITY, THE(1939); NORTH OF THE YUKON(1939); RACKETEERS OF THE RANGE(1939); SON OF FRANKENSTEIN(1939); SUN NEVER SETS, THE(1939); TOWER OF LONDON(1939); WE ARE NOT ALONE(1939); DARK COMMAND, THE(1940); DEVIL'S ISLAND(1940); GRAPES OF WRATH(1940); GREAT PLANE ROBBERY, THE(1940); HOUSE OF THE SEVEN GABLES, THE(1940); INVISIBLE MAN RETURNS, THE(1940); LAW AND ORDER(1940); PASSPORT TO ALCATRAZ(1940); SANTA FE TRAIL(1940); SEA HAWK, THE(1940); STAGE TO CHINO(1940); STRANGE CARGO(1940); TEXAS STAGECOACH(1940); TRAIL OF THE VIGILANTES(1940); VIRGINIA CITY(1940); WHEN THE DALTONS RODE(1940); BURY ME NOT ON THE LONE PRAIRIE(1941); LADY FROM CHEYENNE(1941); MUTINY IN THE ARCTIC(1941); RAGE IN HEAVEN(1941); RAIDERS OF THE DESERT(1941); RAWHIDE RANGERS(1941); RIDERS OF THE BADLANDS(1941); SAN FRANCISCO DOCKS(1941); THEY MET IN BOMBAY(1941); WOLF MAN, THE(1941); ARABIAN NIGHTS(1942); GHOST OF FRANKENSTEIN, THE(1942); PITTSBURGH(1942); ROAD TO MOROCCO(1942); SHERLOCK HOLMES AND THE SECRET WEAPON(1942); SHERLOCK HOLMES AND THE VOICE OF TERROR(1942); SON OF FURY(1942); YANK AT ETON, A(1942); FOR WHOM THE BELL TOLLS(1943); FUGITIVE FROM SONORA(1943); MAN FROM THE RIO GRANDE, THE(1943); MISSION TO MOSCOW(1943); SONG OF BERNADETTE, THE(1943); ALI BABA AND THE FORTY THIEVES(1944); GYPSY WILDCAT(1944); HOUR BEFORE THE DAWN, THE(1944); KISMET(1944); LOST IN A HAREM(1944); MAN IN HALF-MOON STREET, THE(1944); MRS. PARKINGTON(1944); PASSAGE TO MARSEILLE(1944); PEARL OF DEATH, THE(1944); SHERLOCK HOLMES AND THE SPIDER WOMAN(1944); HOUSE OF FEAR, THE(1945); SAN ANTONIO(1945); SUDAN(1945); BANDIT OF SHERWOOD FOREST, THE(1946); DRESSED TO KILL(1946); FOOL'S GOLD(1946); HOT CARGO(1946); NIGHT IN PARADISE, A(1946); RENEGADE GIRL(1946); TERROR BY NIGHT(1946); CALCUTTA(1947); DANGEROUS VENTURE(1947); EXILE, THE(1947); MARAUDERS, THE(1947); SLAVE GIRL(1947); WOMAN'S VENGEANCE, A(1947); KISS THE BLOOD OFF MY HANDS(1948); SOUTHERN YANKEE, A(1948); TAP ROOTS(1948); THAT LADY IN ERMINE(1948); THIRTEEN LEAD SOLDIERS(1948); FIGHTING O'FLYNN, THE(1949); ROPE OF SAND(1949); SAMSON AND DELILAH(1949); SECRET OF ST. IVES, THE(1949); CONVICTED(1950); FORTUNES OF CAPTAIN BLOOD(1950); LAST OF THE BUCCANEERS(1950); TYRANT OF THE SEA(1950); AL JENNINGS OF OKLAHOMA(1951); MASK OF THE AVENGER(1951); SANTA FE(1951); AGAINST ALL FLAGS(1952); BIG TREES, THE(1952); BRAVE WARRIOR(1952); CRIPPLE CREEK(1952); MA AND PA KETTLE AT THE FAIR(1952); NIGHT STAGE TO GALVESTON(1952); ROAD TO BALI(1952); MAN IN THE ATTIC(1953); TITANIC(1953); TREASURE OF THE GOLDEN CONDOR(1953); ABBOTT AND COSTELLO MEET DR. JEKYLL AND MR. HYDE(1954); DEMETRIUS AND THE GLADIATORS(1954); JUNGLE GENTS(1954); KILLER LEOPARD(1954); KING RICHARD AND THE CRUSADERS(1954)
Silents
KNOCKOUT, THE(1925); DAREDEVIL'S REWARD(1928); RESCUE, THE(1929)
John Cording
ONE DAY IN THE LIFE OF IVAN DENISOVICH(1971, U.S./Brit./Norway); TERRORISTS, THE(1975, Brit.); SUPERMAN(1978)
Blaine Cordner
BEFORE MORNING(1933)
Pancho Cordoba
LONG GOODBYE, THE(1973)
Pedro de Cordoba
RANGE WAR(1939)
Misc. Silents
TEMPTATION(1916)
PedroDe Cordoba
ANTHONY ADVERSE(1936)
Amy Cordone
SONG OF THE ISLANDS(1942)
Michele Cordous
DESPERATE DECISION(1954, Fr.)

Caesar Cordova
SHARK'S TREASURE(1975); WHERE THE BUFFALO ROAM(1980); CUTTER AND BONE(1981); NIGHTHAWKS(1981); SCARFACE(1983)
Misc. Talkies
DEATH ON CREDIT(1976)
Fabian Gregory Cordova
ZANDY'S BRIDE(1974)
Francisco Cordova
PEARL OF TLAYUCAN, THE(1964, Mex.); BUTCH CASSIDY AND THE SUNDANCE KID(1969)
Fred Cordova
RIDE 'EM COWGIRL(1939); MASKED RIDER, THE(1941); NORTH TO THE KLONDIKE(1942); IT AIN'T HAY(1943); HOUSE OF DRACULA(1945); PIRATES OF MONTEREY(1947); MADAME BOVARY(1949)
Herma Cordova
WATCH ON THE RHINE(1943)
Lee Cordova
WHEN A MAN RIDES ALONE(1933)
Misc. Talkies
QUICK TRIGGER LEE(1931)
Linda Cordova
VIRGIN SACRIFICE(1959); LONG ROPE, THE(1961); HOMBRE(1967)
Margarita Cordova
ONE-EYED JACKS(1961)
Marguerita Cordova
GUNS OF DIABLO(1964)
Pancho Cordova
RAGE(1966, U.S./Mex.); EXTERMINATING ANGEL, THE(1967, Mex.); GUNS FOR SAN SEBASTIAN(1968, U.S./Fr./Mex./Ital.); TWO MULES FOR SISTER SARA(1970); WRATH OF GOD, THE(1972)
Victoria Cordova
THEY MET IN ARGENTINA(1941)
Dorothy Cordray
MUG TOWN(1943)
Allan Corduner
RETURN OF THE SOLDIER, THE(1983, Brit.); YENTL(1983)
Harry Cordwell
ISADORA(1968, Brit.), set d; PRIVATE LIFE OF SHERLOCK HOLMES, THE(1970, Brit.), set d; GUMSHOE(1972, Brit.), set d; O LUCKY MAN!(1973, Brit.), set d; S(1974), set d; NASTY HABITS(1976, Brit.), set d; VICTOR/VICTORIA(1982), set d
1984
SCANDALOUS(1984), set d
John Beresford Cordwell
SOUTHERN MAID, A(1933, Brit.)
Annie Cordy
RIDER ON THE RAIN(1970, Fr./Ital.); CAT, THE(1975, Fr.)
Anny Cordy
ROYAL AFFAIRS IN VERSAILLES(1957, Fr.)
Henry Cordy
HOUSE ON 92ND STREET, THE(1945)
Mita Cordy
HOUSE ON 92ND STREET, THE(1945)
Raymond Cordy
A NOUS LA LIBERTE(1931, Fr.); MILLION, THE(1931, Fr.); LE DENIER MILLIARDAIRE(1934, Fr.); RUNAWAY LADIES(1935, Brit.); SLIPPER EPISODE, THE(1938, Fr); THEY WERE FIVE(1938, Fr.); TESTAMENT OF DR. MABUSE, THE(1943, Ger.); MAN ABOUT TOWN(1947, Fr.); BEAUTY AND THE DEVIL(1952, Fr./Ital.); LES BELLES-DE-NUIT(1952, Fr.); GRAND MANEUVER, THE(1956, Fr.); GIRL IN THE BIKINI, THE(1958, Fr.)
Gina Core
MY GUN IS QUICK(1957)
Harold Core
THIN RED LINE, THE(1964)
Natalie Core
MUSIC MAN, THE(1962); MY FAIR LADY(1964); NOT WITH MY WIFE, YOU DON'T!(1966); WHY WOULD I LIE(1980); HYSTERICAL(1983)
1984
ICE PIRATES, THE(1984)
Traci Core
WIZ, THE(1978)
Genie Coree
UNDERWATER WARRIOR(1958)
Everett Coreill
HERE COME THE GIRLS(1953)
Belinda Corell
SANTO CONTRA LA INVASION DE LOS MARCIANOS(1966, Mex.)
Maria Jesus Corella
MURIETA(1965, Span.)
Arcangelo Corelli
GIRL WITH THE GOLDEN EYES, THE(1962, Fr.), m
Bruno Corelli
PIRATE AND THE SLAVE GIRL, THE(1961, Fr./Ital.)
Marie Corelli
Silents
SORROWS OF SATAN(1926), w
Lotus Corelli
DELINQUENTS, THE(1957)
Marie Corelli
Silents
HOLY ORDERS(1917, Brit.), w; INNOCENT(1921, Brit.), w; THELMA(1922), w
Nick Corello
HIDE IN PLAIN SIGHT(1980); LAST FIGHT, THE(1983)
Jordan Corenweth
CARBINE WILLIAMS(1952)
Carol Cores
MALE AND FEMALE SINCE ADAM AND EVE(1961, Arg.)
Ben Corett
WAY OUT WEST(1937)

Antonio Corevi
 HERCULES, SAMSON & ULYSSES(1964, Ital.); WAR OF THE ZOMBIES, THE(1965 Ital.); HONEY POT, THE(1967, Brit.)
Tony Corevi
 LAST MAN ON EARTH, THE(1964, U.S./Ital.)
Adele Corey
1984
 HEARTBREAKERS(1984)
Bob Corey
 EARL OF CHICAGO, THE(1940); LOVE FROM A STRANGER(1947)
Brigitte Corey
 FURY OF HERCULES, THE(1961, Ital.); SAMSON(1961, Ital.)
Don Corey
 WILL SUCCESS SPOIL ROCK HUNTER?(1957); ROOKIE, THE(1959)
Eugene Corey
Silents
 EVIDENCE(1918); FLAMES OF CHANCE, THE(1918); ORDEAL, THE(1922)
Misc. Silents
 LAW OF THE GREAT NORTHWEST, THE(1918); RESTITUTION(1918); VELVET HAND, THE(1918); SOUTH OF THE EQUATOR(1924)
George Corey
 MR. WINKLE GOES TO WAR(1944), w
Invin Corey
 COMEBACK TRAIL, THE(1982)
Irwin Corey
 HOW TO COMMIT MARRIAGE(1969); THIEVES(1977); STUCK ON YOU(1983)
1984
 CRACKERS(1984)
Misc. Talkies
 FAIRY TALES(1979)
Isabelle Corey
 AND GOD CREATED WOMAN(1957, Fr.); YOUNG HUSBANDS(1958, Ital./Fr.); IT HAPPENED IN ROME(1959, Ital.); HEAD OF A TYRANT(1960, Fr./Ital.); FROM A ROMAN BALCONY(1961, Fr./Ital.); LAST OF THE VIKINGS, THE(1962, Fr./Ital.); INVINCIBLE GLADIATOR, THE(1963, c.u. Ital./Span.)
James Corey
 MOUNTED STRANGER, THE(1930); PRAIRIE STRANGER(1941)
Misc. Silents
 BURNING TRAIL, THE(1925)
James "Jim" Corey
 WESTERNER, THE(1940)
Jeff Corey
 THIRD FINGER, LEFT HAND(1940); DEVIL AND DANIEL WEBSTER, THE(1941); PARIS CALLING(1941); PETTICOAT POLITICS(1941); RELUCTANT DRAGON, THE(1941); SMALL TOWN DEB(1941); YOU BELONG TO ME(1941); GIRL TROUBLE(1942); MAN WHO WOULDN'T DIE, THE(1942); NORTH TO THE KLONDIKE(1942); POSTMAN DIDN'T RING, THE(1942); ROXIE HART(1942); FRANKENSTEIN MEETS THE WOLF MAN(1943); MOON IS DOWN, THE(1943); MY FRIEND FLICKA(1943); CALIFORNIA(1946); IT SHOULDN'T HAPPEN TO A DOG(1946); KILLERS, THE(1946); SOMEWHERE IN THE NIGHT(1946); BRUTE FORCE(1947); GANGSTER, THE(1947); HOPPY'S HOLIDAY(1947); MIRACLE ON 34TH STREET, THE(1947); RAMROD(1947); UNCONQUERED(1947); ALIAS A GENTLEMAN(1948); CANON CITY(1948); FLAME, THE(1948); HOMECOMING(1948); I, JANE DOE(1948); JOAN OF ARC(1948); KIDNAPPED(1948); LET'S LIVE AGAIN(1948); SOUTHERN YANKEE, A(1948); BAGDAD(1949); CITY ACROSS THE RIVER(1949); FOLLOW ME QUIETLY(1949); HIDEOUT(1949); HOME OF THE BRAVE(1949); ROUGHSHOD(1949); WAKE OF THE RED WITCH(1949); BRIGHT LEAF(1950); NEVADAN, THE(1950); NEXT VOICE YOU HEAR, THE(1950); OUTRIDERS, THE(1950); ROCK ISLAND TRAIL(1950); SINGING GUNS(1950); FOURTEEN HOURS(1951); NEVER TRUST A GAMBLER(1951); NEW MEXICO(1951); ONLY THE VALIANT(1951); PRINCE WHO WAS A THIEF, THE(1951); RAWHIDE(1951); RED MOUNTAIN(1951); SUPERMAN AND THE MOLE MEN(1951); BALCONY, THE(1963); YELLOW CANARY, THE(1963); LADY IN A CAGE(1964); CINCINNATI KID, THE(1965); MICKEY ONE(1965); ONCE A THIEF(1965); SECONDS(1966); IN COLD BLOOD(1967); THE BOSTON STRANGLER, THE(1968); BUTCH CASSIDY AND THE SUNDANCE KID(1969); IMPASSE(1969); TRUE GRIT(1969); BENEATH THE PLANET OF THE APES(1970); COVER ME BABE(1970); GETTING STRAIGHT(1970); LITTLE BIG MAN(1970); THEY CALL ME MISTER TIBBS(1970); CATLOW(1971, Span.); CLAY PIGEON(1971); SHOOT OUT(1971); PAPER TIGER(1975, Brit.); LAST TYCOON, THE(1976); PREMONITION(1976); MOONSHINE COUNTY EXPRESS(1977); OH, GOD!(1977); JENNIFER(1978); WILD GEESE, THE(1978, Brit.); BUTCH AND SUNDANCE: THE EARLY DAYS(1979); BATTLE BEYOND THE STARS(1980); SWORD AND THE SORCERER, THE(1982)
1984
 CONAN THE DESTROYER(1984)
Misc. Talkies
 UP RIVER(1979)
Jill Corey
 SENIOR PROM(1958)
Jim Corey
 COURTIN' WILDCATS(1929); FIGHTING THRU(1931); RANGE FEUD, THE(1931); RED FORK RANGE(1931); TWO GUN MAN, THE(1931); CORNERED(1932); HAUNTED GOLD(1932); COME ON TARZAN(1933); FOURTH HORSEMAN, THE(1933); MAN FROM MONTEREY, THE(1933); SOMEWHERE IN SONORA(1933); TERROR TRAIL(1933); FIGHTING RANGER, THE(1934); LAST ROUND-UP, THE(1934); LOST JUNGLE, THE(1934); SMOKING GUNS(1934); IN OLD SANTA FE(1935); NO MAN'S RANGE(1935); OUTLAW DEPUTY, THE(1935); GUNS AND GUITARS(1936); HEIR TO TROUBLE(1936); TRAIL OF THE LONESOME PINE, THE(1936); COME ON, COWBOYS(1937); GUN LORDS OF STIRRUP BASIN(1937); GUNS IN THE DARK(1937); LAND BEYOND THE LAW(1937); LEFT-HANDED LAW(1937); MYSTERY RANGE(1937); PRAIRIE THUNDER(1937); RECKLESS RANGER(1937); RIDERS OF THE DAWN(1937); RIO GRANDE RANGER(1937); ROUNDUP TIME IN TEXAS(1937); SPRINGTIME IN THE ROCKIES(1937); TRAIL OF VENGEANCE(1937); YODELIN' KID FROM PINE RIDGE(1937); FEUD OF THE TRAIL(1938); FRONTIERSMAN, THE(1938); GOLD MINE IN THE SKY(1938); OUTLAWS OF SONORA(1938); OUTLAWS OF THE PRAIRIE(1938); ROMANCE OF THE ROCKIES(1938); SUNSET TRAIL(1938); IN OLD MONTEREY(1939); SILVER ON THE SAGE(1939); SOUTHWARD HO!(1939); TRIGGER SMITH(1939); GAUCHO SERENADE(1940); LAW AND ORDER(1940); ONE MAN'S LAW(1940); RETURN OF WILD BILL, THE(1940); THREE MEN FROM TEXAS(1940); BURY ME NOT ON THE LONE PRAIRIE(1941); DESERT

BANDIT(1941); IN OLD CHEYENNE(1941); LAW OF THE RANGE(1941); MEDICO OF PAINTED SPRINGS, THE(1941); ROBIN HOOD OF THE PECOS(1941); SHEPHERD OF THE HILLS, THE(1941); SIX GUN GOLD(1941); TONTO BASIN OUTLAWS(1941); WRANGLER'S ROOST(1941); DOWN RIO GRANDE WAY(1942); JESSE JAMES, JR.(1942); STAGECOACH BUCKAROO(1942); HAUNTED RANCH, THE(1943)
Silents
 WESTERN VENGEANCE(1924); HAIR TRIGGER BAXTER(1926); HEY! HEY! COWBOY(1927); LARIAT KID, THE(1929); POINTS WEST(1929)
Misc. Silents
 HEADIN' WEST(1922); PAYABLE ON DEMAND(1924); PERFECT ALIBI, THE(1924)
Jonathan Corey
 FILE ON THELMA JORDAN, THE(1950)
Joseph Corey
 ACCUSED OF MURDER(1956); GABY(1956); DELICATE DELINQUENT, THE(1957)
Mike Corey
 GOD TOLD ME TO(1976), ed
Milton Corey, Sr.
 RAWHIDE(1951)
Phil Corey
 GRIZZLY(1976), spec eff
Prof. Irwin Corey
 CARWASH(1976)
1984
 STUCK ON YOU(1984)
Robin Corey
 FILE ON THELMA JORDAN, THE(1950)
Victor Corey
 WORLD'S GREATEST SINNER, THE(1962)
Wendell Corey
 DESERT FURY(1947); I WALK ALONE(1948); MAN-EATER OF KUMAON(1948); SEARCH, THE(1948); SORRY, WRONG NUMBER(1948); ACCUSED, THE(1949); ANY NUMBER CAN PLAY(1949); HOLIDAY AFFAIR(1949); FILE ON THELMA JORDAN, THE(1950); FURIES, THE(1950); GREAT MISSOURI RAID, THE(1950); HARRIET CRAIG(1950); NO SAD SONGS FOR ME(1950); RICH, YOUNG AND PRETTY(1951); CARBINE WILLIAMS(1952); MY MAN AND I(1952); WILD BLUE YONDER, THE(1952); WILD NORTH, THE(1952); JAMAICA RUN(1953); HELL'S HALF ACRE(1954); LAUGHING ANNE(1954, Brit./U.S.); REAR WINDOW(1954); BIG KNIFE, THE(1955); BOLD AND THE BRAVE, THE(1956); KILLER IS LOOSE, THE(1956); RACK, THE(1956); RAINMAKER, THE(1956); LOVING YOU(1957); LIGHT IN THE FOREST, THE(1958); ALIAS JESSE JAMES(1959); BLOOD ON THE ARROW(1964); AGENT FOR H.A.R.M.(1966); CYBORG 2087(1966); PICTURE MOMMY DEAD(1966); WACO(1966); WOMEN OF THE PREHISTORIC PLANET(1966); RED TOMAHAWK(1967); BUCKSKIN(1968); ASTRO-ZOMBIES, THE(1969)
Robert Corff
 GAS-S-S-S!(1970)
John Corfield
 TURN OF THE TIDE(1935, Brit.), p; DEBT OF HONOR(1936, Brit.), p; LASSIE FROM LANCASHIRE(1938, Brit.), p; MEET MR. PENNY(1938, Brit.), p; NIGHT JOURNEY(1938, Brit.), p; DEAD MEN TELL NO TALES(1939, Brit.), p; OLD MOTHER RILEY JOINS UP(1939, Brit.), p; WHAT WOULD YOU DO, CHUMS?(1939, Brit.), p; AMONG HUMAN WOLVES(1940 Brit.), p; BLACKOUT(1940, Brit.), p; CROOKS TOUR(1940, Brit.), p; GASLIGHT(1940), p; LAUGH IT OFF(1940, Brit.), p; OLD MOTHER RILEY IN BUSINESS(1940, Brit.), p; OLD MOTHER RILEY IN SOCIETY(1940, Brit.), p; SECOND MR. BUSH, THE(1940, Brit.), p; SPIES OF THE AIR(1940, Brit.), p; HE FOUND A STAR(1941, Brit.), p; MYSTERY OF ROOM 13(1941, Brit.), p; THIS ENGLAND(1941, Brit.), p; HEADLINE(1943, Brit.), p; LOOK BEFORE YOU LOVE(1948, Brit.), p; MY SISTER AND I(1948, Brit.), p
Danielle Corgan
 CLASS OF MISS MAC MICHAEL, THE(1978, Brit./U.S.)
Will Cori
Silents
 AMATEUR GENTLEMAN, THE(1920, Brit.)
Aurora Coria
 HERBIE GOES BANANAS(1980)
Gia Corides
Misc. Talkies
 LOVELETTERS FROM TERALBA ROAD(1977)
John Corigliano
 ALTERED STATES(1980), m
Owen Corin
Silents
 AWAKENING, THE(1928)
Ann Corio
 SWAMP WOMAN(1941); JUNGLE SIREN(1942); SARONG GIRL(1943); SULTAN'S DAUGHTER, THE(1943); CALL OF THE JUNGLE(1944)
Rafael Corio
 LADIES SHOULD LISTEN(1934); RUMBA(1935); DOUGHNUTS AND SOCIETY(1936); FARMER IN THE DELL, THE(1936); SOPHIE LANG GOES WEST(1937); CODE OF THE SECRET SERVICE(1939); ONLY ANGELS HAVE WINGS(1939); OPENED BY MISTAKE(1940); TORRID ZONE(1940)
Ana Corita
Misc. Talkies
 FORTRESS OF THE DEAD(1965)
Charles Cork
 WHAT'S NEXT?(1975, Brit.); LONG GOOD FRIDAY, THE(1982, Brit.); MC VICAR(1982, Brit.); VENOM(1982, Brit.)
Charlie Cork
 MC VICAR(1982, Brit.)
Kevin Cork
1984
 FINDERS KEEPERS(1984)
Kevin Harrison Cork
 SUPERMAN III(1983)
Rafael Corkidi
 HOLY MOUNTAIN, THE(1973, U.S./Mex.), ph
Raphael Corkidi
 EL TOPO(1971, Mex.), ph

Daniel Bryan Corkill
WITHOUT A TRACE(1983)
Danny Corkill
1984
DUNE(1984); MRS. SOFFEL(1984)
Michael Corkran
TWILIGHT WOMEN(1953, Brit.)
Corky
LONDON BY NIGHT(1937); WHEN'S YOUR BIRTHDAY?(1937)
"Corky"
GARDEN OF ALLAH, THE(1936)
Corky the Dog
LITTLE RED SCHOOLHOUSE(1936)
Anthony Corlan
WALK WITH LOVE AND DEATH, A(1969); SOMETHING FOR EVERYONE(1970); TASTE THE BLOOD OF DRACULA(1970, Brit.); VAMPIRE CIRCUS(1972, Brit.)
Stephanie Corler
PARSIFAL(1983, Fr.)
Irene Corlett
FOUR GIRLS IN TOWN(1956)
Al Corley
HONKY TONK FREEWAY(1981)
1984
TORCHLIGHT(1984)
Alford Corley
SQUEEZE PLAY(1981)
Bob Corley
FORTY ACRE FEUD(1965); LEGEND OF BLOOD MOUNTAIN, THE(1965), w
Cynthia Corley
SENATOR WAS INDISCREET, THE(1947); MR. PEABODY AND THE MERMAID(1948); QUEEN FOR A DAY(1951)
Francis Corley
RENFREW OF THE ROYAL MOUNTED(1937), ph
Pat Corley
LAW AND DISORDER(1974); SUPER COPS, THE(1974); AUDREY ROSE(1977); BAD NEWS BEARS IN BREAKING TRAINING, THE(1977); NIGHTWING(1979); ONION FIELD, THE(1979); ROSE, THE(1979); BLACK MARBLE, THE(1980); LOVING COUPLES(1980); ON THE NICKEL(1980); HAND, THE(1981); TRUE CONFESSIONS(1981); HANKY-PANKY(1982); NIGHT SHIFT(1982); CURSE OF THE PINK PANTHER(1983)
1984
AGAINST ALL ODDS(1984)
Rex Corley
WHERE THE RED FERN GROWS(1974)
Adele Corliss
GILDED LILY, THE(1935)
Allene Corliss
I MET MY LOVE AGAIN(1938), w
Michael Corlton
LATE AT NIGHT(1946, Brit.), d
Bart Cormack
SIDEWALKS OF LONDON(1940, Brit.)
Bartlett Cormack
GENTLEMEN OF THE PRESS(1929), w; GREENE MURDER CASE, THE(1929), w; WOMAN TRAP(1929), w; BENSON MURDER CASE, THE(1930), w; LAUGHING LADY, THE(1930), w; SPOILERS, THE(1930), w; FRONT PAGE, THE(1931), w; KICK IN(1931), w; IS MY FACE RED?(1932), w; PHANTOM OF CRESTWOOD, THE(1932), w; THIRTEEN WOMEN(1932), w; PAST OF MARY HOLMES, THE(1933), p; THIS DAY AND AGE(1933), w; FOUR FRIGHTENED PEOPLE(1934), w; TRUMPET BLOWS, THE(1934), w; DOUBTING THOMAS(1935), w; ORCHIDS TO YOU(1935), w; FURY(1936), w; UNHOLY PARTNERS(1941), w; RACKET, THE(1951), w
Silents
RACKET, THE(1928), w
George Cormack
TROUBLE IN THE GLEN(1954, Brit.); SMALLEST SHOW ON EARTH, THE(1957, Brit.); ROBBERY UNDER ARMS(1958, Brit.); MATTER OF WHO, A(1962, Brit.); PIED PIPER, THE(1972, Brit.)
James Cormack
ELEPHANT MAN, THE(1980, Brit.)
Robert Cormack
FANTASIA(1940), art d, art d; MAKE MINE MUSIC(1946), d
Avery Corman
OH, GOD!(1977), w; KRAMER VS. KRAMER(1979), w
Chip Corman
DIRTY OUTLAWS, THE(1971, Ital.)
Chip Corman [Andrea Giordana]
JOHNNY HAMLET(1972, Ital.)
Corki Corman
NIGHT SHIFT(1982)
E. W. Corman
Silents
RANSON'S FOLLY(1926)
Evelyne Corman
NIGHTS OF SHAME(1961, Fr.)
Gene Corman
HOT CAR GIRL(1958), p; NIGHT OF THE BLOOD BEAST(1958), p, w; ATTACK OF THE GIANT LEECHES(1959), p; BLOOD AND STEEL(1959), p; I, MOBSTER(1959), p; BEAST FROM THE HAUNTED CAVE(1960), p; SECRET OF THE PURPLE REEF, THE(1960), p, w; VALLEY OF THE REDWOODS(1960), p, w; CAT BURGLAR, THE(1961), p; TOWER OF LONDON(1962), p; SECRET INVASION, THE(1964), p; SKI PARTY(1965), p; TOBRUK(1966), p; VON RICHTHOFEN AND BROWN(1970), p; YOU CAN'T WIN 'EM ALL(1970, Brit.), p; COOL BREEZE(1972), p; HIT MAN(1972), p; PRIVATE PARTS(1972), p; I ESCAPED FROM DEVIL'S ISLAND(1973), p; VIGILANTE FORCE(1976), p; BIG RED ONE, THE(1980), p; TARGET: HARRY(1980), p
Julie Corman
STUDENT TEACHERS, THE(1973), p; YOUNG NURSES, THE(1973), p; NIGHT CALL NURSES(1974), p; CRAZY MAMA(1975), p; MOVING VIOLATION(1976), p; SUMMER SCHOOL TEACHERS(1977), p; LADY IN RED, THE(1979), p; SATURDAY THE 14TH(1981), p

Lawrence Corman
Misc. Silents
BLACK GOLD(1928); FLYING ACE(1928)
Leonard Corman
TERROR EYES(1981)
Marvin Corman
MAHOGANY(1975)
Roger Corman
FAST AND THE FURIOUS, THE(1954), p, w; HIGHWAY DRAGNET(1954), w; MONSTER FROM THE OCEAN FLOOR, THE(1954), p; APACHE WOMAN(1955), p, d; FIVE GUNS WEST(1955), p&d; DAY THE WORLD ENDED, THE(1956), ptd; GUNSLINGER(1956), p&d; IT CONQUERED THE WORLD(1956), p&d; OKLAHOMA WOMAN, THE(1956), p&d; SWAMP WOMEN(1956), d; ATTACK OF THE CRAB MONSTERS(1957), p&d; CARNIVAL ROCK(1957), p, d; NAKED PARADISE(1957), p&d; NOT OF THIS EARTH(1957), p&d; ROCK ALL NIGHT(1957), p&d; SAGA OF THE VIKING WOMEN AND THEIR VOYAGE TO THE WATERS OF THE GREAT SEA SERPENT, THE(1957), p&d; SORORITY GIRL(1957), p&d; TEENAGE DOLL(1957), p&d; UNDEAD, THE(1957), p&d; MACHINE GUN KELLY(1958), p&d; SHE-GODS OF SHARK REEF(1958), d; TEENAGE CAVEMAN(1958), p&d; WAR OF THE SATELLITES(1958), p, d; BUCKET OF BLOOD, A(1959), p&d; I, MOBSTER(1959), p, d; T-BIRD GANG(1959), p; WASP WOMAN, THE(1959), p&d; ATLAS(1960), p&d; HOUSE OF USHER(1960), p&d; LAST WOMAN ON EARTH, THE(1960), p&d; SKI TROOP ATTACK(1960), p&d; CREATURE FROM THE HAUNTED SEA(1961), a, p&d; LITTLE SHOP OF HORRORS(1961), p&d; PIT AND THE PENDULUM, THE(1961), p&d; INTRUDER, THE(1962), p&d; PREMATURE BURIAL, THE(1962), p&d; TOWER OF LONDON(1962), d; "X"-THE MAN WITH THE X-RAY EYES(1963), p&d; DEMENTIA 13(1963), p; HAUNTED PALACE, THE(1963), p&d; RAVEN, THE(1963), p&d; TERROR, THE(1963), p&d; YOUNG RACERS, THE(1963), p&d; MASQUE OF THE RED DEATH, THE(1964, U.S./Brit.), p&d; SECRET INVASION, THE(1964), d; TOMB OF LIGEIA, THE(1965, Brit.), p&d; VOYAGE TO THE PLANET OF PREHISTORIC WOMEN(1966), p; WILD ANGELS, THE(1966), p&d; ST. VALENTINE'S DAY MASSACRE, THE(1967), p&d; TRIP, THE(1967), p&d; BLOODY MAMA(1970), p&d; GAS-S-S-S!(1970), p&d; VON RICHTHOFEN AND BROWN(1970), d; BOXCAR BERTHA(1972), p; I ESCAPED FROM DEVIL'S ISLAND(1973), p; BIG BAD MAMA(1974), p; GODFATHER, THE, PART II(1974); BORN TO KILL(1975), p; CAPONE(1975), p; DEATH RACE 2000(1975), p; CANNONBALL(1976, U.S./Hong Kong); EAT MY DUST!(1976), p; FIGHTING MAD(1976), p; THUNDER AND LIGHTNING(1977), p; AVALANCHE(1978), p; DEATHSPORT(1978), p; FAST CHARLIE... THE MOONBEAM RIDER(1979), p; SAINT JACK(1979), p; GALAXY OF TERROR(1981), p; HOWLING, THE(1981); SMOKEY BITES THE DUST(1981), p; FORBIDDEN WORLD(1982), p; LOVE LETTERS(1983), p; SPACE RAIDERS(1983), p; STATE OF THINGS, THE(1983)
1984
SWING SHIFT(1984)
Corki Corman-Grazer
1984
SPLASH(1984)
Evelyne Cormand
DON JUAN(1956, Aust.)
Al Cormier
BARN OF THE NAKED DEAD(1976)
Dean Cormier
CASEY'S SHADOW(1978)
Gerald Cormier
BARN OF THE NAKED DEAD Zero(1976), p&d
Jerald Cormier
TALISMAN, THE(1966)
Robert Cormier
I AM THE CHEESE(1983), a, w
Thelma Cormier
CASEY'S SHADOW(1978)
Eugene Cormon
Silents
CELEBRATED CASE, A(1914), w; ORPHANS OF THE STORM(1922), w
Danielle Corn
HELL'S ANGELS '69(1969)
Lester Corn
BEGINNING OF THE END(1957), w
Jack Cornall
BALLAD OF A GUNFIGHTER(1964), ed; CAT, THE(1966), ed
Leonora Cornall
STONE(1974, Aus.)
Peter Cornberg
LAST MOVIE, THE(1971), set d; MOONRUNNERS(1975), prod d; CANNONBALL(1976, U.S./Hong Kong)
Catherine Corne
1984
CHEECH AND CHONG'S THE CORSICAN BROTHERS(1984), cos
Leonce Corne
LE CIEL EST A VOUS(1957, Fr.); WE ARE ALL MURDERERS(1957); PARIS IN THE MONTH OF AUGUST(1968, Fr.); VERY HAPPY ALEXANDER(1969, Fr.)
Alain Corneau
POLICE PYTHON 357(1976, Fr.), d, w; CASE AGAINST FERRO, THE(1980, Fr.), d, w; CHOICE OF ARMS(1983, Fr.), d, w
Cornejo
CONFESSIONS OF AMANS, THE(1977), cos
Faustino Cornejo
AWFUL DR. ORLOFF, THE(1964, Span./Fr.)
Humberto Cornejo
LAZARILLO(1963, Span.), cos
The Cornel Trio
SCHLAGER-PARADE(1953)
Cornelia and Eddie
MOUNTAINS O'MOURNE(1938, Brit.)
Hans Cornelis
LUCKY STAR, THE(1980, Can.)
Michael Cornelison
WHERE THE BUFFALO ROAM(1980)

Bill Cornelius
LONG GOOD FRIDAY, THE(1982, Brit.)
Billy Cornelius
CARRY ON SCREAMING(1966, Brit.); CARRY ON HENRY VIII(1970, Brit.); MIND OF MR. SOAMES, THE(1970, Brit.); WHEN DINOSAURS RULED THE EARTH(1971, Brit.)
Don Cornelius
NO WAY BACK(1976); ROADIE(1980)
Eugene Cornelius
RUN, ANGEL, RUN(1969); LOSERS, THE(1970)
Henry Cornelius
GHOST GOES WEST, THE(1936), ed; FOREVER YOURS(1937, Brit.), ed; MEN ARE NOT GODS(1937, Brit.), ed; DRUMS(1938, Brit.), ed; FOUR FEATHERS, THE(1939, Brit.), ed; LION HAS WINGS, THE(1940, Brit.), ed; GIRL ON THE CANAL, THE(1947, Brit.), p; IT ALWAYS RAINS ON SUNDAY(1949, Brit.), p, w; PASSPORT TO PIMLICO(1949, Brit.), d; HUE AND CRY(1950, Brit.), p; GALLOPING MAJOR, THE(1951, Brit.), d, w; GENEVIEVE(1953, Brit.), p&d; I AM A CAMERA(1955, Brit.), d; NEXT TO NO TIME(1960, Brit.), d&w
Joe Cornelius
FILE OF THE GOLDEN GOOSE, THE(1969, Brit.); CARRY ON LOVING(1970, Brit.); TROG(1970, Brit.)
Marjorie Cornelius
ON HER MAJESTY'S SECRET SERVICE(1969, Brit.), cos
Verna Cornelius
1984
IRRECONCILABLE DIFFERENCES(1984)
Ann Cornell
GOLD FEVER(1952); DARK VENTURE(1956)
Anna Cornell
SEARCH FOR DANGER(1949)
Bob Cornell
CHARLEY'S AUNT(1941); I WAKE UP SCREAMING(1942)
Connie Cornell
UNFINISHED DANCE,THE(1947)
Dale Cornell
ADDRESS UNKNOWN(1944); MY REPUTATION(1946)
Dolores Cornell
NATIVE LAND(1942)
Elmer Cornell
STOLEN HEAVEN(1931)
Evans W. Cornell
REQUIEM FOR A GUNFIGHTER(1965), w
Harry Cornell
STRANGE WIVES(1935)
James A. Cornell
HURRICANE SMITH(1952); REAR WINDOW(1954)
James Cornell
STORY OF DR. WASSELL, THE(1944); EASY COME, EASY GO(1947); RED, HOT AND BLUE(1949); SORROWFUL JONES(1949); YOU'RE IN THE NAVY NOW(1951); CARRIE(1952)
Jane Cornell
BRITANNIA OF BILLINGSGATE(1933, Brit.); CONSTANT NYMPH, THE(1933, Brit.); GOOD COMPANIONS(1933, Brit.); WALTZ TIME(1933, Brit.); LADY IN DANGER(1934, Brit.); ORDERS IS ORDERS(1934, Brit.); POWER(1934, Brit.); SOME DAY(1935, Brit.)
Jonas Cornell
HUGS AND KISSES(1968, Swed.), d&w
Katharine Cornell
STAGE DOOR CANTEEN(1943)
Lillian Cornell
BUCK BENNY RIDES AGAIN(1940); DANCING ON A DIME(1940); NIGHT AT EARL CARROLL'S, A(1940); QUARTERBACK, THE(1940); RHYTHM ON THE RIVER(1940); LAS VEGAS NIGHTS(1941); YOU'RE THE ONE(1941); GALS, INCORPORATED(1943); GET GOING(1943); MAD GHOUL, THE(1943); MOON OVER LAS VEGAS(1944); SLIGHTLY TERRIFIC(1944); SWEETHEARTS OF THE U.S.A.(1944)
Lydia Cornell
BLOOD TIDE(1982)
Lyn Cornell
JUST FOR FUN(1963, Brit.)
Melva Cornell
FOX MOVIETONE FOLLIES(1929)
Oyer Cornell
SLIGHTLY TERRIFIC(1944)
Pamela Cornell
MILLIONAIRESS, THE(1960, Brit.), set d; I LIKE MONEY(1962, Brit.), set d; I THANK A FOOL(1962, Brit.), set d; MALAGA(1962, Brit.), art d; V.I.P.s, THE(1963, Brit.), set d; YELLOW ROLLS-ROYCE, THE(1965, Brit.), set d; KHARTOUM(1966, Brit.), set d; DEADLY AFFAIR, THE(1967, Brit.), set d; DON'T RAISE THE BRIDGE, LOWER THE RIVER(1968, Brit.), set d; GREAT CATHERINE(1968, Brit.), set d; PRIME OF MISS JEAN BRODIE, THE(1969, Brit.), set d; HELLO–GOODBYE(1970), set d; SCROOGE(1970, Brit.), set d; WALKING STICK, THE(1970, Brit.), set d; MARY, QUEEN OF SCOTS(1971, Brit.), set d
Paul Cornell
DEADLY SPAWN, THE(1983), m
Peter Cornell
HUGS AND KISSES(1968, Swed.)
Phyllis Cornell
SHADOW OF FEAR(1956, Brit.)
Richard Cornell
CHEER UP AND SMILE(1930), w
Robert Cornell
SMALL TOWN DEB(1941); YOUNG AMERICA(1942)
Sam Cornell
SHINBONE ALLEY(1971), prod d
Harry Cornelli
Misc. Silents
MARY OF THE MOVIES(1923)

Betty Corner
FORCE OF EVIL(1948); UNION STATION(1950)
Harry Corner
SAVAGE SISTERS(1974), w
James Corner
WHAT A LIFE(1939); WINTER CARNIVAL(1939); SCATTERGOOD PULLS THE STRINGS(1941)
Michael Corner
FRATERNITY ROW(1977), m
Sally Corner
LEATHER GLOVES(1948); ONCE MORE, MY DARLING(1949); TASK FORCE(1949); DARK CITY(1950); HARVEY(1950); TWO FLAGS WEST(1950); SCARLET ANGEL(1952); ROBE, THE(1953); MAN CALLED PETER, THE(1955)
Lola Cornero
Silents
AS GOD MADE HER(1920, Brit.)
Francisco Cornet
COMMANDO(1962, Ital., Span., Bel., Ger.)
Alan G. Cornett
1984
TANK(1984)
Stuart Cornfeld
ELEPHANT MAN, THE(1980, Brit.), p
Hubert Cornfield
SUDDEN DANGER(1955), d; LURE OF THE SWAMP(1957), d; PLUNDER ROAD(1957), d; THIRD VOICE, THE(1960), p, d&w; PRESSURE POINT(1962), d, w; NIGHT OF THE FOLLOWING DAY, THE(1969, Brit.), p&d, w
Stuart Cornfield
FATSO(1980), p; FAST TIMES AT RIDGEMONT HIGH(1982)
Bill Cornford
HANG YOUR HAT ON THE WIND(1969)
Phillip Cornford
KITTY AND THE BAGMAN(1983, Aus.), w
Robert Cornford
ALL NEAT IN BLACK STOCKINGS(1969, Brit.), m
William Cornford
LINCOLN CONSPIRACY, THE(1977), art d
Walter Cornick
Misc. Silents
MIDNIGHT ACE, THE(1928)
Edward Corniglion-Molinier
HATRED(1941, Fr.), p
Dr. Robert E. Cornish
LIFE RETURNS(1939)
John R. Cornish
Silents
NUGGET NELL(1919), w
Reginald Cornish
REVOLUTIONARY, THE(1970, Brit.)
Richard Cornish
OBLONG BOX, THE(1969, Brit.); CROMWELL(1970, Brit.); ABDICATION, THE(1974, Brit.); INTERNECINE PROJECT, THE(1974, Brit.)
Vera Cornish
Silents
WON BY A HEAD(1920, Brit.)
Misc. Silents
LONDON FLAT MYSTERY, A(1915, Brit.); QUICKSANDS(1917)
Harold Cornsweet
DESERT HAWK, THE(1950); WABASH AVENUE(1950); CALLAWAY WENT THATAWAY(1951); CLOUDS OVER ISRAEL(1966, Israel), p; RETURN TO CAMPUS(1975), p,d&w
Bob Cornthwaite
SOMETHING TO LIVE FOR(1952)
Robert Cornthwaite
HIS KIND OF WOMAN(1951); THING, THE(1951); MONKEY BUSINESS(1952); WAR OF THE WORLDS, THE(1953); KISS ME DEADLY(1955); PURPLE MASK, THE(1955); STRANGER ON HORSEBACK(1955); LEATHER SAINT, THE(1956); ON THE THRESHOLD OF SPACE(1956); HELL ON DEVIL'S ISLAND(1957); SPIRIT OF ST. LOUIS, THE(1957); DAY OF THE OUTLAW(1959); TEN SECONDS TO HELL(1959); WHATEVER HAPPENED TO BABY JANE?(1962); GHOST AND MR. CHICKEN, THE(1966); RIDE TO HANGMAN'S TREE, THE(1967); WATERHOLE NO. 3(1967); COLOSSUS: THE FORBIN PROJECT(1969); PEACE KILLERS, THE(1971); JOURNEY THROUGH ROSEBUD(1972); FUTUREWORLD(1976); DEAL OF THE CENTURY(1983); DOCTOR DETROIT(1983)
Robert R. Cornthwaite
UNION STATION(1950)
Roberto Cornthwaite
MARK OF THE RENEGADE(1951)
Aurora Cornu
CLAIRE'S KNEE(1971, Fr.); CHLOE IN THE AFTERNOON(1972, Fr.)
Richard Cornu
SECRET OF MAGIC ISLAND, THE(1964, Fr./Ital.), m
Ann Cornwall
THEY WON'T BELIEVE ME(1947); WIDOW FROM CHICAGO, THE(1930); YOU CAN'T TAKE IT WITH YOU(1938); KNOCK ON ANY DOOR(1949)
Silents
COLLEGE(1927)
Anne Cornwall
TRUE CONFESSION(1937); MR. SMITH GOES TO WASHINGTON(1939); UNTAMED(1955)
Silents
KNIFE, THE(1918); HER GILDED CAGE(1922); SEVENTH DAY, THE(1922); TO HAVE AND TO HOLD(1922); DULCY(1923); GOLD DIGGERS, THE(1923); ONLY 38(1923); ARIZONA EXPRESS, THE(1924); ROUGHNECK, THE(1924); INTRODUCE ME(1925); KEEP SMILING(1925); RAINBOW TRAIL, THE(1925)
Misc. Silents
GIRL IN THE RAIN, THE(1920); LA LA LUCILLE(1920); PATH SHE CHOSE, THE(1920); 40-HORSE HAWKINS(1924); WRONG DOERS(1925); FLAMING FRONTIER, THE(1926); RACING BLOOD(1926); SPLENDID CRIME, THE(1926); UNDER WESTERN SKIES(1926); EYES OF THE TOTEM(1927); HEART OF THE

YUKON, THE(1927)
Charlotte Cornwall
STARDUST(1974, Brit.)
Dan Cornwall
KING AND COUNTRY(1964, Brit.)
Jack Cornwall
KING DINOSAUR(1955), ed
Judy Cornwall
DR. TERROR'S HOUSE OF HORRORS(1965, Brit.)
Roy Cornwall
BURNING AN ILLUSION(1982, Brit.), ph
Bruce Cornwell
GAL YOUNG UN(1979)
David Cornwell
1984
LITTLE DRUMMER GIRL, THE(1984)
Judy Cornwell
THOSE FANTASTIC FLYING FOOLS(1967, Brit); TWO FOR THE ROAD(1967, Brit.); CRY WOLF(1968, Brit.); WILD RACERS, THE(1968); BROTHERLY LOVE(1970, Brit.); PADDY(1970, Irish); THINK DIRTY(1970, Brit.); WUTHERING HEIGHTS(1970, Brit.); WHO SLEW AUNTIE ROO?(1971, U.S./Brit.)
O'Kane Cornwell
Silents
SCARAMOUCHE(1923), cos
Roger Cornwell
ENEMY BELOW, THE(1957)
Tom Cornwell
WOMAN UNDER THE INFLUENCE, A(1974), ed; KILLING OF A CHINESE BOOKIE, THE(1976), ed; OPENING NIGHT(1977), ed
Stan Cornyn
PHYNX, THE(1970), w
Sal Corolio
LAST FIGHT, THE(1983)
Joe Corolla
HEAVEN CAN WAIT(1978)
Elvira Corona
DIARY OF A HIGH SCHOOL BRIDE(1959); SIGN OF ZORRO, THE(1960)
Fidel Corona
DRIVER, THE(1978)
Isabela Corona
PASSION ISLAND(1943, Mex.); WITCH'S MIRROR, THE(1960, Mex.)
John Corona
THINGS ARE TOUGH ALL OVER(1982)
Luis Corona
BRAVE BULLS, THE(1951)
Sergio Corona
TERRACE, THE(1964, Arg.)
The Corona Babes
TALKING FEET(1937, Brit.)
Corona Kids
VARIETY PARADE(1936, Brit.)
The Girls of the Corona Stage School
WEB OF SUSPICION(1959, Brit.)
Celestino Coronado
HAMLET(1976, Brit.), p&d, w, set d
1984
MIDSUMMER NIGHT'S DREAM, A(1984, Brit./Span.), d&w
Clet Coroner
BACKFIRE(1965, Fr.), w
Jacqueline Corot
RISE OF LOUIS XIV, THE(1970, Fr.)
Corps de Ballet
ESCAPE ME NEVER(1947)
Corps of Cadets of the Virginia Military Institute
MARDI GRAS(1958)
Eugene Corr
OVER-UNDER, SIDEWAYS-DOWN(1977, d, w, ed; NEVER CRY WOLF(1983), w
Bruna Corra
AGE OF INFIDELITY(1958, Span.)
Doro Corra
GUNS OF THE BLACK WITCH(1961, Fr./Ital.)
Teodoro Corra
STRANGER'S GUNDOWN, THE(1974, Ital.), p
Nelly Corradi
BARBER OF SEVILLE, THE(1947, Ital.); THIS WINE OF LOVE(1948, Ital.)
Rita Corradini
TALES OF ORDINARY MADNESS(1983, Ital.), cos
Geno Corrado
Silents
SLANDER THE WOMAN(1923); DESERT FLOWER, THE(1925)
Misc. Silents
MODERN YOUTH(1926)
Gino Corrado
IRON MASK, THE(1929); SENOR AMERICANO(1929); LORD BYRON OF BROADWAY(1930); NOTORIOUS AFFAIR, A(1930); OH! SAILOR, BEHAVE!(1930); SONG OF THE CABELLERO(1930); THOSE WHO DANCE(1930); LAST PARADE, THE(1931); MAN FROM DEATH VALLEY, THE(1931); LOVE IS A RACKET(1932); FLYING DOWN TO RIO(1933); KEYHOLE, THE(1933); OBEY THE LAW(1933); PICTURE SNATCHER(1933); WHITE SISTER, THE(1933); CHAINED(1934); HE WAS HER MAN(1934); LADY BY CHOICE(1934); MERRY WIDOW, THE(1934); NANA(1934); WONDER BAR(1934); ENTER MADAME(1935); FLIRTING WITH DANGER(1935); MAGNIFICENT OBSESSION(1935); MAN WHO BROKE THE BANK AT MONTE CARLO, THE(1935); NIGHT AT THE OPERA, A(1935); ON PROBATION(1935); PARADISE CANYON(1935); RENDEZVOUS(1935); TOP HAT(1935); WITHOUT REGRET(1935); DODSWORTH(1936); OREGON TRAIL, THE(1936); ANGEL(1937); CAFE METROPOLE(1937); DAUGHTER OF SHANGHAI(1937); ESPIONAGE(1937); FIGHT FOR YOUR LADY(1937); SWING HIGH, SWING LOW(1937); BORN TO FIGHT(1938); DANGEROUS TO KNOW(1938); DR. RHYTHM(1938); REBELLION(1938); ROSE OF THE RIO GRANDE(1938); CHARLIE CHAN IN THE CITY OF DARKNESS(1939); NEVER SAY DIE(1939); DANCE, GIRL, DANCE(1940); FOREIGN CORRESPOND-

ENT(1940); KITTY FOYLE(1940); MARK OF ZORRO, THE(1940); NEW MOON(1940); THAT NIGHT IN RIO(1941); CASABLANCA(1942); I MARRIED AN ANGEL(1942); SECRET AGENT OF JAPAN(1942); TALES OF MANHATTAN(1942); TALK OF THE TOWN(1942); WE WERE DANCING(1942); CLANCY STREET BOYS(1943); HELLO, FRISCO, HELLO(1943); MISSION TO MOSCOW(1943); MAN FROM FRISCO(1944); SHINE ON, HARVEST MOON(1944); STORM OVER LISBON(1944); BELL FOR ADANO, A(1945); SARATOGA TRUNK(1945); SUNSET IN EL DORADO(1945); TWO SISTERS FROM BOSTON(1946); DREAM GIRL(1947); MY WILD IRISH ROSE(1947); ROAD TO RIO(1947); WEB, THE(1947); I WALK ALONE(1948); HARVEY(1950); THREE COINS IN THE FOUNTAIN(1954)
Silents
ADAM'S RIB(1923); MY AMERICAN WIFE(1923); ROSE OF PARIS, THE(1924); OFF THE HIGHWAY(1925); AMATEUR GENTLEMAN, THE(1926); WHITE BLACK SHEEP, THE(1926); SUNRISE–A SONG OF TWO HUMANS(1927); COHENS AND THE KELLYS IN PARIS, THE(1928); GUN RUNNER, THE(1928)
Misc. Silents
RECKLESS SPEED(1924); HE WHO LAUGHS LAST(1925); NEVER TOO LATE(1925); UNEASY PAYMENTS(1927); DEVIL'S SKIPPER, THE(1928); HOUSE OF SCANDAL, THE(1928); PROWLERS OF THE SEA(1928)
Karen Corrado
Misc. Talkies
TEAM-MATES(1978)
Tony Corrado
OPERATION PETTICOAT(1959)
Malissa Corragio
EVENTS(1970)
Delores Corral
LOVES OF CARMEN, THE(1948)
Helen Corran
BUGSY MALONE(1976, Brit.)
Angelo Corrao
1984
FIRSTBORN(1984), ed
Sadie Corre
MR. QUILP(1975, Brit.)
Fernando Corredor
MONSTER(1979)
Adrian Correger
LOOT(1971, Brit.)
Marinho Correia
SEA GYPSIES, THE(1978), animal t
Charles Correll
MOVING VIOLATION(1976), ph; MANIAC!(1977), ph; NATIONAL LAMPOON'S ANIMAL HOUSE(1978), ph; FAST BREAK(1979), ph; IN GOD WE TRUST(1980), ph; CHEECH AND CHONG'S NICE DREAMS(1981), ph
1984
JOY OF SEX(1984), ph; STAR TREK III: THE SEARCH FOR SPOCK(1984), ph
Charles V. Correll
AMOS 'N' ANDY(1930)
Mady Correll
MIDNIGHT MADONNA(1937); INVISIBLE ENEMY(1938); GIRL, A GUY AND A GOB, A(1941); OLD CHISHOLM TRAIL(1943); TEXAS MASQUERADE(1944); MONSIEUR VERDOUX(1947)
Robert Scott Correll
STORY OF WILL ROGERS, THE(1952); THEM!(1954)
Socrates Corres
NAKED BRIGADE, THE(1965, U.S./Gr.)
Addrienne Corri
WOMAN TIMES SEVEN(1967, U.S./Fr./Ital.)
Adrienne Corri
NAUGHTY ARLETTE(1951, Brit.); RIVER, THE(1951); DEVIL GIRL FROM MARS(1954, Brit.); LEASE OF LIFE(1954, Brit.); LITTLE KIDNAPPERS, THE(1954, Brit.); MAKE ME AN OFFER(1954, Brit.); MEET MR. CALLAGHAN(1954, Brit.); BEHIND THE HEADLINES(1956, Brit.); GENTLE TOUCH, THE(1956, Brit.); SHIELD OF FAITH, THE(1956, Brit.); BIG CHANCE, THE(1957, Brit.); SECOND FIDDLE(1957, Brit.); SURGEON'S KNIFE, THE(1957, Brit.); THREE MEN IN A BOAT(1958, Brit.); DYNAMITE JACK(1961, Fr.); PORTRAIT OF A SINNER(1961, Brit.); CORRIDORS OF BLOOD(1962, Brit.); TELL-TALE HEART, THE(1962, Brit.); HELLFIRE CLUB, THE(1963, Brit.); SWORD OF LANCELOT(1963, Brit.); BUNNY LAKE IS MISSING(1965); DOCTOR ZHIVAGO(1965); STUDY IN TERROR, A(1966, Brit./Ger.); AFRICA–TEXAS STYLE!(1967 U.S./Brit.); VIKING QUEEN, THE(1967, Brit.); CRY WOLF(1968, Brit.); FILE OF THE GOLDEN GOOSE, THE(1969, Brit.); MOON ZERO TWO(1970, Brit.); CLOCKWORK ORANGE, A(1971, Brit.); VAMPIRE CIRCUS(1972, Brit.); MADHOUSE(1974, Brit.); ROSEBUD(1975); REVENGE OF THE PINK PANTHER(1978); HUMAN FACTOR, THE(1979, Brit.)
Nick Corri
1984
NIGHTMARE ON ELM STREET, A(1984)
Will Corri
Silents
GREATEST WISH IN THE WORLD, THE(1918, Brit.)
Franco Corridoni
INVESTIGATION OF A CITIZEN ABOVE SUSPICION(1970, Ital.), makeup
Giovanni Corridoni
MINUTE TO PRAY, A SECOND TO DIE, A(1968, Ital.), spec eff
Corridori
PIRANHA II: THE SPAWNING(1981, Neth.), spec eff
A. Corridori
GREAT WHITE, THE(1982, Ital.), spec eff
Antonio Corridori
1990: THE BRONX WARRIORS(1983, Ital.), spec eff
Delia Corrie
DOOMSDAY AT ELEVEN(1963 Brit.)
Eric Corrie
FIRE OVER AFRICA(1954, Brit.); HELL IN KOREA(1956, Brit.); JOHNNY, YOU'RE WANTED(1956, Brit.); ROGUE'S YARN(1956, Brit.); IDOL ON PARADE(1959, Brit.); NAKED FURY(1959, Brit.); WATCH YOUR STERN(1961, Brit.); SWINGIN' MAIDEN, THE(1963, Brit.); CRIMSON BLADE, THE(1964, Brit.); GREAT ARMORED CAR SWINDLE, THE(1964)

Maggie Corrie
  BLOOD AND LACE(1971)
Sadie Corrie
  DOWN OUR ALLEY(1939, Brit.); RETURN OF THE JEDI(1983)
Will Corrie
Silents
  HARD TIMES(1915, Brit.); ADAM BEDE(1918, Brit.); AS HE WAS BORN(1919, Brit.);
  FANCY DRESS(1919, Brit.); MARCH HARE, THE(1919, Brit.)
Misc. Silents
  TOM JONES(1917, Brit.)
Bob Corrigan
Misc. Talkies
  TREASURE OF TAYOPA(1974)
Brian Corrigan
  BEING THERE(1979)
D'Arcy Corrigan
  LAST WARNING, THE(1929); MAN FROM BLANKLEY'S, THE(1930); LAW AND
  ORDER(1932); MURDERS IN THE RUE MORGUE(1932); INFORMER, THE(1935);
  STEAMBOAT ROUND THE BEND(1935); KLONDIKE ANNIE(1936); LLOYDS OF
  LONDON(1936); MARY OF SCOTLAND(1936); PLOUGH AND THE STARS,
  THE(1936); ALL OVER TOWN(1937); PRISONER OF ZENDA, THE(1937); STAGE
  DOOR(1937); BRINGING UP BABY(1938); CHRISTMAS CAROL, A(1938); TOY WIFE,
  THE(1938); MAN IN THE IRON MASK, THE(1939); NIGHT OF NIGHTS, THE(1939);
  $1,000 A TOUCHDOWN(1939); GREAT COMMANDMENT, THE(1941)
Silents
  LADY ROBINHOOD(1925); MERRY WIDOW, THE(1925); ELLA CINDERS(1926);
  EXIT SMILING(1926)
Douglas Corrigan
  FLYING IRISHMAN, THE(1939)
Emmet Corrigan
  DIRIGIBLE(1931)
Emmett Corrigan
  LION AND THE MOUSE, THE(1928); SOLDIERS AND WOMEN(1930); AMERICAN
  TRAGEDY, AN(1931); CORSAIR(1931); BEAST OF THE CITY, THE(1932); GOLDEN
  WEST, THE(1932); MAN AGAINST WOMAN(1932); NIGHT MAYOR, THE(1932);
  SILVER DOLLAR(1932); WORLD AND THE FLESH, THE(1932); BITTER TEA OF
  GENERAL YEN, THE(1933)
Silents
  PARTNERS OF THE NIGHT(1920); RENDEZVOUS, THE(1923)
Misc. Silents
  GREATER LOVE HATH NO MAN(1915); TURMOIL, THE(1924)
James Corrigan
Silents
  JACK KNIFE MAN, THE(1920); BREWSTER'S MILLIONS(1921); LAVENDER AND
  OLD LACE(1921); PECK'S BAD BOY(1921); SKY PILOT, THE(1921); FRONT PAGE
  STORY, A(1922); APRIL SHOWERS(1923); DIVORCE(1923); LAW FORBIDS,
  THE(1924); MAN FROM WYOMING, THE(1924); AUCTION BLOCK, THE(1926);
  JOHNNY GET YOUR HAIR CUT(1927)
Misc. Silents
  HER REPUTATION(1923)
Lee Corrigan
1984
  PRODIGAL, THE(1984)
Lloyd Corrigan
  MYSTERIOUS DR. FU MANCHU, THE(1929), w; SATURDAY NIGHT KID,
  THE(1929), w; SWEETIE(1929), w; ANYBODY'S WAR(1930), w; FOLLOW
  THRU(1930), d&w; RETURN OF DR. FU MANCHU, THE(1930), w; ALONG CAME
  YOUTH(1931), d; BELOVED BACHELOR, THE(1931), d; DAUGHTER OF THE DRAG-
  ON(1931), d, w; DUDE RANCH(1931), w; LAWYER'S SECRET, THE(1931), w; BROK-
  EN WING, THE(1932), d; NO ONE MAN(1932), d; HE LEARNED ABOUT
  WOMEN(1933), d; BY YOUR LEAVE(1935), d; MURDER ON A HONEYMOON(1935),
  d; DANCING PIRATE(1936), d; HOLD'EM NAVY!(1937), w; LADY BEHAVE(1937), d;
  NIGHT KEY(1937), d; CAMPUS CONFESSIONS(1938), w; TOUCHDOWN, ARM-
  MY(1938), w; BOY TROUBLE(1939), w; NIGHT WORK(1939), w; CAPTAIN CAU-
  TION(1940); DARK STREETS OF CAIRO(1940); GHOST BREAKERS, THE(1940);
  HIGH SCHOOL(1940); LADY IN QUESTION, THE(1940); PUBLIC DEB NO. 1(1940);
  QUEEN OF THE MOB(1940); RETURN OF FRANK JAMES, THE(1940); SPORTING
  BLOOD(1940); TWO GIRLS ON BROADWAY(1940); YOUNG TOM EDISON(1940);
  CONFESSIONS OF BOSTON BLACKIE(1941); GIRL, A GUY AND A GOB, A(1941);
  GREAT COMMANDMENT, THE(1941); KATHLEEN(1941); MEN OF BOYS
  TOWN(1941); MEXICAN SPITFIRE'S BABY(1941); WHISTLING IN THE DARK(1941);
  ALIAS BOSTON BLACKIE(1942); BOMBAY CLIPPER(1942); BOSTON BLACKIE
  GOES HOLLYWOOD(1942); GREAT MAN'S LADY, THE(1942); HITLER'S CHIL-
  DREN(1942); LONDON BLACKOUT MURDERS(1942); LUCKY JORDAN(1942); MAI-
  SIE GETS HER MAN(1942); MYSTERY OF MARIE ROGET, THE(1942); NORTH TO
  THE KLONDIKE(1942); TENNESSEE JOHNSON(1942); TREAT 'EM ROUGH(1942);
  WIFE TAKES A FLYER, THE(1942); AFTER MIDNIGHT WITH BOSTON BLACK-
  IE(1943); CAPTIVE WILD WOMAN(1943); CHANCE OF A LIFETIME, THE(1943);
  EYES OF THE UNDERWORLD(1943); KING OF THE COWBOYS(1943); MANTRAP,
  THE(1943); NOBODY'S DARLING(1943); SECRETS OF THE UNDERGROUND(1943);
  STAGE DOOR CANTEEN(1943); TARZAN'S DESERT MYSTERY(1943); GAMBLER'S
  CHOICE(1944); GOODNIGHT SWEETHEART(1944); LAKE PLACID SERENA-
  DE(1944); LIGHTS OF OLD SANTA FE(1944); PASSPORT TO DESTINY(1944);
  RECKLESS AGE(1944); ROSIE THE RIVETER(1944); SINCE YOU WENT
  AWAY(1944); SONG OF NEVADA(1944); THIN MAN GOES HOME, THE(1944);
  BOSTON BLACKIE BOOKED ON SUSPICION(1945); BRING ON THE GIRLS(1945);
  CRIME DOCTOR'S COURAGE, THE(1945); FIGHTING GUARDSMAN, THE(1945);
  BANDIT OF SHERWOOD FOREST, THE(1946); CHASE, THE(1946); LADY
  LUCK(1946); SHADOWED(1946); SHE-WOLF OF LONDON(1946); TWO SMART PEO-
  PLE(1946); BLAZE OF NOON(1947); GHOST GOES WILD, THE(1947); STALLION
  ROAD(1947); ADVENTURES OF CASANOVA(1948); BIG CLOCK, THE(1948); BRIDE
  GOES WILD, THE(1948); DATE WITH JUDY, A(1948); HOMICIDE FOR THREE(1948);
  MR. RECKLESS(1948); RETURN OF OCTOBER, THE(1948); STRIKE IT RICH(1948);
  AND BABY MAKES THREE(1949); BLONDIE HITS THE JACKPOT(1949); DANCING
  IN THE DARK(1949); GIRL FROM JONES BEACH, THE(1949); CYRANO DE
  BERGERAC(1950); FATHER IS A BACHELOR(1950); MY FRIEND IRMA GOES
  WEST(1950); WHEN WILLIE COMES MARCHING HOME(1950); GHOST CHA-
  SERS(1951); HER FIRST ROMANCE(1951); LAST OUTPOST, THE(1951); NEW MEX-
  ICO(1951); SIERRA PASSAGE(1951); RAINBOW 'ROUND MY SHOULDER(1952);
  SON OF PALEFACE(1952); MARRY ME AGAIN(1953); STARS ARE SINGING,

THE(1953); BOWERY BOYS MEET THE MONSTERS, THE(1954); RETURN FROM
THE SEA(1954); FRESH FROM PARIS(1955); PARIS FOLLIES OF 1956(1955); HID-
DEN GUNS(1956); MANCHURIAN CANDIDATE, THE(1962); IT'S A MAD, MAD,
MAD, MAD WORLD(1963)
Misc. Talkies
  ALIAS MR. TWILIGHT(1946); HOME IN SAN ANTONE(1949)
Silents
  CAMPUS FLIRT, THE(1926), w; HANDS UP(1926), w; MISS BREWSTER'S MIL-
  LIONS(1926), w; WET PAINT(1926), w; IT(1927); SHE'S A SHEIK(1927), w; WED-
  DING BILL$(1927), w; FIFTY-FIFTY GIRL, THE(1928), w; HOT NEWS(1928), w; RED
  HAIR(1928), w; WHAT A NIGHT!(1928), w
Ray Corrigan
  DANTE'S INFERNO(1935); LEATHERNECKS HAVE LANDED, THE(1936); THREE
  MESQUITEERS, THE(1936); COME ON, COWBOYS(1937); COUNTRY GENT-
  LEMEN(1937); GHOST TOWN GOLD(1937); GUNSMOKE RANCH(1937); HEART OF
  THE ROCKIES(1937); HIT THE SADDLE(1937); JOIN THE MARINES(1937); RANGE
  DEFENDERS(1937); RIDERS OF THE WHISTLING SKULL(1937); ROARIN'
  LEAD(1937); TRIGGER TRIO, THE(1937); CALL THE MESQUITEERS(1938); HEROES
  OF THE HILLS(1938); OUTLAWS OF SONORA(1938); OVERLAND STAGE RAI-
  DERS(1938); PALS OF THE SADDLE(1938); PURPLE VIGILANTES, THE(1938); RED
  RIVER RANGE(1938); RIDERS OF THE BLACK HILLS(1938); SANTA FE STAM-
  PEDE(1938); WILD HORSE RODEO(1938); NEW FRONTIER(1939); NIGHT RIDERS,
  THE(1939); THREE TEXAS STEERS(1939); WYOMING OUTLAW(1939); RANGE
  BUSTERS, THE(1940); TRAILING DOUBLE TROUBLE(1940); WEST OF PINTO
  BASIN(1940); FUGITIVE VALLEY(1941); KID'S LAST RIDE, THE(1941); SADDLE
  MOUNTAIN ROUNDUP(1941); TRAIL OF THE SILVER SPURS(1941); TUMBLE-
  DOWN RANCH IN ARIZONA(1941); UNDERGROUND RUSTLERS(1941); WRAN-
  GLER'S ROOST(1941); ARIZONA STAGECOACH(1942); ROCK RIVER
  RENEGADES(1942); STRANGE CASE OF DR. RX, THE(1942); THUNDER RIVER
  FEUD(1942); BLACK MARKET RUSTLERS(1943); COWBOY COMMANDOS(1943);
  LAND OF HUNTED MEN(1943); RENEGADE GIRL(1946); ZAMBA(1949); KILLER
  APE(1953); DOMINO KID(1957)
Misc. Talkies
  BOOT HILL BANDITS(1942); TEXAS TROUBLE SHOOTERS(1942); BULLETS AND
  SADDLES(1943)
Ray "Crash" Corrigan
  TONTO BASIN OUTLAWS(1941); DR. RENAULT'S SECRET(1942); SHE'S FOR
  ME(1943); WHITE GORILLA(1947); TRAIL OF ROBIN HOOD(1950); APACHE AM-
  BUSH(1955); ZOMBIES OF MORA TAU(1957); IT! THE TERROR FROM BEYOND
  SPACE(1958)
Shirley Corrigan
  DR. JEKYLL AND THE WOLFMAN(1971, Span.)
Tom Corrigan
  AIR MAIL(1932)
Aaron Corrin
  MY BRILLIANT CAREER(1980, Aus.)
John Corrington
  VON RICHTHOFEN AND BROWN(1970), w; ARENA, THE(1973), w
John William Corrington
  OMEGA MAN, THE(1971), w; BOXCAR BERTHA(1972), w; BATTLE FOR THE
  PLANET OF THE APES(1973), w
Joyce Corrington
  VON RICHTHOFEN AND BROWN(1970), w; ARENA, THE(1973), w
Joyce H. Corrington
  OMEGA MAN, THE(1971), w; BOXCAR BERTHA(1972), w
Joyce Hooper Corrington
  BATTLE FOR THE PLANET OF THE APES(1973), w
Andre Corriveau
  FOND MEMORIES(1982, Can.), ed
Marguerite Corriveau
  OH, HEAVENLY DOG!(1980)
Ken Corrone
  FORBIDDEN ZONE(1980), set d
Graham Corry
  INN OF THE DAMNED(1974, Aus.); 27A(1974, Aus.)
Josephine Corry
  MADAME BUTTERFLY(1955 Ital./Jap.)
Mark E. Corry
1984
  BEVERLY HILLS COP(1984)
Will Corry
  WILD IN THE COUNTRY(1961); STRATEGY OF TERROR(1969); TWO-LANE
  BLACKTOP(1971), w
Bill Corsair
  VORTEX(1982)
Frank Corsara
  GOIN' TO TOWN(1935)
Franco Corsaro
  TWO WEEKS IN ANOTHER TOWN(1962); PRESCRIPTION FOR ROMANCE(1937);
  GREEN HELL(1940); MARK OF ZORRO, THE(1940); MY FAVORITE WIFE(1940);
  DOWN IN SAN DIEGO(1941); FOR WHOM THE BELL TOLLS(1943); HEAVENLY
  BODY, THE(1943); WE'VE NEVER BEEN LICKED(1943); MRS. PARKINGTON(1944);
  CRIME DOCTOR'S WARNING(1945); WITHOUT LOVE(1945); DANGEROUS MIL-
  LIONS(1946); DECOY(1946); ARCH OF TRIUMPH(1948); BLACK MAGIC(1949);
  PRINCE OF FOXES(1949); FOUR GIRLS IN TOWN(1956); ISTANBUL(1957); TOP
  SECRET AFFAIR(1957); PAY OR DIE(1960)
Frank Corsaro
  EMPEROR WALTZ, THE(1948); RACHEL, RACHEL(1968)
Franco Corsarro
  WESTERN TRAILS(1938)
Aneta Corsaut
  TOOLBOX MURDERS, THE(1978)
Anita Corseaut
  BLOB, THE(1958)
Frank Corsentino
  SIMON, KING OF THE WITCHES(1971); MOONCHILD(1972)
Misc. Talkies
  UP YOUR ALLEY(1975); MELON AFFAIR, THE(1979)

Antonio Corsi
Misc. Silents
FALSE WOMEN(1921)
J. Corsi
RING AROUND THE CLOCK(1953, Ital.), w
Jacopo Corsi
RED CLOAK, THE(1961, Ital./Fr.), w
Ron Corsi
ETERNAL SUMMER(1961)
Silvana Corsini
ACCATTONE!(1961, Ital.); MAMMA ROMA(1962, Ital.)
Salvatore Corsitto
GODFATHER, THE(1972)
Arturo Corso
STRANGER IN TOWN, A(1968, U.S./Ital.)
Bob Corso
DOC SAVAGE... THE MAN OF BRONZE(1975)
Chris Corso
FIRST NUDIE MUSICAL, THE(1976)
Gene Corso
SHEPHERD OF THE HILLS, THE(1964), spec eff
Gregory Corso
ME AND MY BROTHER(1969)
John Corso
COAL MINER'S DAUGHTER(1980), prod d
John W. Corso
PARADISE ALLEY(1978), prod d; XANADU(1980), prod d; HEARTBEEPS(1981), d;
PSYCHO II(1983), prod d
1984
SIXTEEN CANDLES(1984), prod d
Marge Corso
BEACH PARTY(1963), cos
Margo Corso
MACHINE GUN KELLY(1958), cos
Marjorie Corso
HIGH SCHOOL HELLCATS(1958), cos; TEENAGE CAVEMAN(1958), cos; I, MOB-
STER(1959), cos; MISSILE TO THE MOON(1959), cos; WHY MUST I DIE?(1960), cos;
PIT AND THE PENDULUM, THE(1961), cos; NUN AND THE SERGEANT, THE(1962),
cos; PANIC IN YEAR ZERO!(1962), cos; PREMATURE BURIAL, THE(1962), cos;
DIARY OF A MADMAN(1963), cos; HAUNTED PALACE, THE(1963), cos; RAVEN,
THE(1963), cos; TERROR, THE(1963), cos; TWICE TOLD TALES(1963), cos; COMEDY
OF TERRORS, THE(1964), cos; MUSCLE BEACH PARTY(1964), cos; PAJAMA
PARTY(1964), cos; WICKED DREAMS OF PAULA SCHULTZ, THE(1968), cos
Marjorie D. Corso
BULLWHIP(1958), cos
Robert Corso
STRANGERS IN THE CITY(1962); PIPE DREAMS(1976)
Sam Corso
DRUMS O' VOODOO(1934), art d; WINDOW, THE(1949), art d; TATTOOED STRAN-
GER, THE(1950), art d
Silents
SUMMER BACHELORS(1926), art d
Steve Corso
OLD LOUISIANA(1938), makeup; REBELLION(1938), makeup
Bill Corson
HAVING WONDERFUL TIME(1938); MR. DOODLE KICKS OFF(1938)
Corrine Corson
JOY(1983, Fr./Can.)
Stanley Corson
RIO LOBO(1970)
William Corson
HIDEAWAY(1937); MUSIC FOR MADAME(1937); NEW FACES OF 1937(1937);
STAGE DOOR(1937); SUPER SLEUTH(1937); THERE GOES MY GIRL(1937); DOUBLE
DANGER(1938); GO CHASE YOURSELF(1938); SKY GIANT(1938)
Michael Corston
DON'T PANIC CHAPS!(1959, Brit.), w
Alexander Cort
JOHN AND MARY(1969)
Bill Cort
BANNING(1967); WACKIEST WAGON TRAIN IN THE WEST, THE(1976)
Bud Cort
BREWSTER McCLOUD(1970); GAS-S-S-S!(1970); M(1970); STRAWBERRY STATE-
MENT, THE(1970); TRAVELING EXECUTIONER, THE(1970); HAROLD AND
MAUDE(1971); WHY SHOOT THE TEACHER(1977, Can.); DIE LAUGHING(1980);
SHE DANCES ALONE(1981, Aust./U.S.); HYSTERICAL(1983); LOVE LETTERS(1983)
1984
ELECTRIC DREAMS(1984); SECRET DIARY OF SIGMUND FREUD, THE(1984)
Harvey Cort
VIXENS, THE(1969), d, w
Hugh Cort
PORTRAIT OF CLARE(1951, Brit.)
Michael Cort
Misc. Talkies
ZETA ONE(1969), d
Van Cort
MAIL ORDER BRIDE(1964), d&w
William Cort
BIG HAND FOR THE LITTLE LADY, A(1966); GLASS HOUSES(1972)
1984
BREAKIN' 2: ELECTRIC BOOGALOO(1984)
John Cortay
CRY OF THE CITY(1948); GREAT SINNER, THE(1949); FILE ON THELMA JOR-
DAN, THE(1950); SUNSET BOULEVARD(1950); ROMAN HOLIDAY(1953)
Ernesto Cortazar
SHE-DEVIL ISLAND(1936, Mex.), w; GUADALAJARA(1943, Mex.), w
Julio Cortazar
BLOW-UP(1966, Brit.), w

Tony Corteggiani
LA BETE HUMAINE(1938, Fr.); RULES OF THE GAME, THE(1939, Fr.); CASQUE
D'OR(1956, Fr.)
Georg Corten
HOW TO SEDUCE A PLAYBOY(1968, Aust./Fr./Ital.)
Marilu Corteny
GOD FORGIVES-I DON'T!(1969, Ital./Span.), cos
Antonio Cortes
DIABOLICAL DR. Z, THE(1966 Span./Fr.), art d; VISCOUNT, THE(1967, Fr./Span./
Ital./Ger.), cos; DESPERATE ONES, THE(1968 U.S./Span.), art d; THEY CAME TO
ROB LAS VEGAS(1969, Fr./Ital./Span./Ger.), art d
Armand Cortes
CROSSROADS(1942)
Silents
HOW MOLLY MADE GOOD(1915)
Misc. Silents
BIG SISTER, THE(1916)
Carlos Cortes
JORY(1972)
Fernando Cortes
CREATURE OF THE WALKING DEAD(1960, Mex.), d, w
Hercules Cortes
WITCH WITHOUT A BROOM, A(1967, U.S./Span.); KILL THEM ALL AND COME
BACK ALONE(1970, Ital./Span.); PIZZA TRIANGLE, THE(1970, Ital./Span.)
Mapy Cortes
SEVEN DAYS LEAVE(1942)
Margarita Cortes
PORTRAIT OF MARIA(1946, Mex.)
Robert Cortes
1984
CRACKERS(1984), p; RIVER, THE(1984), p
Valentina Cortesa
BLACK MAGIC(1949); THIEVES' HIGHWAY(1949); HOUSE ON TELEGRAPH
HILL(1951); SECRET PEOPLE(1952, Brit.); BAREFOOT CONTESSA, THE(1954);
SHADOW OF THE EAGLE(1955, Brit.); ANGELS OF DARKNESS(1956, Ital.); MAGIC
FIRE(1956); WHEN TIME RAN OUT(1980)
Elvira Cortese
CONVERSATION PIECE(1976, Ital., Fr.)
Enrico Cortese
LEGEND OF NIGGER CHARLEY, THE(1972), makeup; NASTY HABITS(1976,
Brit.), makeup
Joe Cortese
JESSIE'S GIRLS(1976); MONSIGNOR(1982)
Joseph Cortese
DEATH COLLECTOR(1976); WINDOWS(1980); WORLDS APART(1980, U.S., Israel);
EVILSPEAK(1982)
Misc. Talkies
FAMILY ENFORCER(1978)
Leonardo Cortese
LOST HAPPINESS(1948, Ital.); VERGINITA(1953, Ital.); VALIANT, THE(1962, Brit./
Ital.)
Luigi Cortese
JUDEX(1966, Fr./Ital.)
Valentina Cortese
UNA SIGNORA DELL'OVEST(1942, Ital); WANDERING JEW, THE(1948, Ital.);
BULLET FOR STEFANO(1950, Ital.); MALAYA(1950); CROSSROADS OF PAS-
SION(1951, Fr.); CALABUCH(1956, Span./Ital.); BARABBAS(1962, Ital.); LE AMI-
CHE(1962, Ital.); SQUARE OF VIOLENCE(1963, U.S./Yugo.); EVIL EYE(1964 Ital.);
VISIT, THE(1964, Ger./Fr./Ital./U.S.); JULIET OF THE SPIRITS(1965, Fr./Ital./
W.Ger.); LEGEND OF LYLAH CLARE, THE(1968); LISTEN, LET'S MAKE LOVE(1969,
Fr./Ital.); SECRET OF SANTA VITTORIA, THE(1969); FIRST LOVE(1970, Ger./Switz.);
GIVE HER THE MOON(1970, Fr./Ital.); MADLY(1970, Fr.); ASSASSINATION OF
TROTSKY, THE(1972 Fr./Ital.); BROTHER SUN, SISTER MOON(1973, Brit./Ital.);
DAY FOR NIGHT(1973, Fr.); WIDOWS' NEST(1977, U.S./Span.)
Valentine Cortese
GLASS MOUNTAIN, THE(1950, Brit)
Giulio Cortesi
Silents
LOVES OF RICARDO, THE(1926)
Mrs. Giulio Cortesi
Silents
LOVES OF RICARDO, THE(1926)
Elena Cortesina
THE EAVESDROPPER(1966, U.S./Arg.)
Anita Cortez
Silents
OH, JOHNNY(1919)
Armand Cortez
STORY OF VERNON AND IRENE CASTLE, THE(1939); SONG OF BERNADETTE,
THE(1943)
Silents
SCARAB RING, THE(1921)
Misc. Silents
WOMAN'S HONOR, A(1916); ROAD BETWEEN, THE(1917); MATRIMONIAL WEB,
THE(1921)
Armando Cortez
KIDNAPPERS, THE(1964, U.S./Phil.)
Arthur Cortez
CONSTANT HUSBAND, THE(1955, Brit.); DIVIDED HEART, THE(1955, Brit.); SEE
HOW THEY RUN(1955, Brit.)
Bella Cortez
TARTARS, THE(1962, Ital./Yugo.); GIANT OF METROPOLIS, THE(1963, Ital.);
SEVEN TASKS OF ALI BABA, THE(1963, Ital.); SEVEN REVENGES, THE(1967, Ital.)
Misc. Talkies
TAUR THE MIGHTY(1960)
Carlos Cortez
CANDY MAN, THE(1969)

Celia Cortez
PALACE OF NUDES(1961, Fr./Ital.)
Diego Cortez
OFFENDERS, THE(1980)
Endrew Cortez
FLIGHT(1960)
Erlinda Cortez
AMERICAN GUERRILLA IN THE PHILIPPINES, AN(1950)
Espanita Cortez
GIRL IN THE BIKINI, THE(1958, Fr.); FEMALE, THE(1960, Fr.)
Ester Cortez
FLIGHT(1960)
Johnny Cortez
SAMAR(1962)
Juan Cortez
SEVEN GOLDEN MEN(1969, Fr./Ital./Span.)
Katherine Cortez
Misc. Talkies
ELECTRIC CHAIR, THE(1977)
Leon Cortez
STRIP TEASE MURDER(1961, Brit.); GANG WAR(1962, Brit.); I COULD GO ON SINGING(1963); SECRETS OF A WINDMILL GIRL(1966, Brit.)
Lita Cortez
THREE ON THE TRAIL(1936); REBELLION(1938); ARIZONA GANGBUSTERS(1940); LONG VOYAGE HOME, THE(1940)
Maria Cortez
RIDE THE PINK HORSE(1947)
Misc. Talkies
KAHUNA!(1981)
Maro Cortez
MOON OVER BURMA(1940)
Mary Cortez
BLACK PIT OF DOCTOR M(1958, Mex.)
Ricardo Cortez
MIDSTREAM(1929); NEW ORLEANS(1929); PHANTOM IN THE HOUSE, THE(1929); YOUNGER GENERATION(1929); HER MAN(1930); LOST ZEPPELIN(1930); MONTANA MOON(1930); BAD COMPANY(1931); BEHIND OFFICE DOORS(1931); BIG BUSINESS GIRL(1931); ILLICIT(1931); MALTESE FALCON, THE(1931); RECKLESS LIVING(1931); TEN CENTS A DANCE(1931); TRANSGRESSION(1931); WHITE SHOULDERS(1931); FLESH(1932); IS MY FACE RED?(1932); MEN OF CHANCE(1932); NO ONE MAN(1932); PHANTOM OF CRESTWOOD, THE(1932); SYMPHONY OF SIX MILLION(1932); THIRTEEN WOMEN(1932); BIG EXECUTIVE(1933); BROADWAY BAD(1933); HOUSE ON 56TH STREET(1933); MIDNIGHT MARY(1933); TORCH SINGER(1933); BIG SHAKEDOWN, THE(1934); FIREBIRD, THE(1934); HAT, COAT AND GLOVE(1934); LOST LADY, A(1934); MAN WITH TWO FACES, THE(1934); MANDALAY(1934); FRISCO KID(1935); I AM A THIEF(1935); MANHATTAN MOON(1935); SHADOW OF A DOUBT(1935); SPECIAL AGENT(1935); WHITE COCKATOO(1935); CASE OF THE BLACK CAT, THE(1936); MAN HUNT(1936); MURDER OF DR. HARRIGAN, THE(1936); POSTAL INSPECTOR(1936); WALKING DEAD, THE(1936); CALIFORNIAN, THE(1937); HER HUSBAND LIES(1937); TALK OF THE DEVIL(1937, Brit.); WEST OF SHANGHAI(1937); CITY GIRL(1938); CHARLIE CHAN IN RENO(1939), d; CHASING DANGER(1939), d; ESCAPE, THE(1939), d; HEAVEN WITH A BARBED WIRE FENCE(1939), d; INSIDE STORY(1939), d; CITY OF CHANCE(1940), d; FREE, BLONDE AND 21(1940), d; GIRL IN 313(1940), d; MURDER OVER NEW YORK(1940); ROMANCE OF THE RIO GRANDE(1941); SHOT IN THE DARK, THE(1941); WORLD PREMIERE(1941); I KILLED THAT MAN(1942); RUBBER RACKETEERS(1942); TOMORROW WE LIVE(1942); MAKE YOUR OWN BED(1944); INNER CIRCLE, THE(1946); LOCKET, THE(1946); BLACKMAIL(1947); MYSTERY IN MEXICO(1948); BUNCO SQUAD(1950); LAST HURRAH, THE(1958)
Silents
SIXTY CENTS AN HOUR(1923); ARGENTINE LOVE(1924); BEDROOM WINDOW, THE(1924); SOCIETY SCANDAL, A(1924); IN THE NAME OF LOVE(1925); NOT SO LONG AGO(1925); PONY EXPRESS, THE(1925); CAT'S PAJAMAS, THE(1926); SORROWS OF SATAN(1926); TORRENT, THE(1926); VOLCANO(1926); BY WHOSE HAND?(1927); MOCKERY(1927); NEW YORK(1927); EXCESS BAGGAGE(1928); GRAIN OF DUST, THE(1928)
Misc. Silents
CHILDREN OF JAZZ(1923); CITY THAT NEVER SLEEPS, THE(1924); NEXT CORNER, THE(1924); THIS WOMAN(1924); PRIVATE LIFE OF HELEN OF TROY, THE(1927); LADIES OF THE NIGHT CLUB(1928); LOST ZEPPELIN, THE(1929)
Ricards Cortez
WONDER BAR(1934)
Richard Cortez
MR. MOTO'S LAST WARNING(1939); WHO IS HOPE SCHUYLER?(1942)
Richardo Cortez
Silents
GUN RUNNER, THE(1928)
Misc. Silents
FEET OF CLAY(1924); SPANIARD, THE(1925); SWAN, THE(1925); EAGLE OF THE SEA, THE(1926); PROWLERS OF THE SEA(1928)
Rudolf Cortez
LEMONADE JOE(1966, Czech.); TRANSPORT FROM PARADISE(1967, Czech.)
Stanely Cortez
PERSONAL SECRETARY(1938), ph
Stanley Cortez
FOUR DAYS WONDER(1936), ph; ARMORED CAR(1937), ph; WILDCATTER, THE(1937), ph; DANGER ON THE AIR(1938), ph; EXPOSED(1938), ph; LADY IN THE MORGUE(1938), ph; LAST EXPRESS, THE(1938), ph; FOR LOVE OR MONEY(1939), ph; FORGOTTEN WOMAN, THE(1939), ph; HAWAIIAN NIGHTS(1939), ph; LAUGH IT OFF(1939), ph; RISKY BUSINESS(1939), ph; THEY ASKED FOR IT(1939), ph; ALIAS THE DEACON(1940), ph; LEATHER-PUSHERS, THE(1940), ph; LOVE, HONOR AND OH, BABY(1940), ph; MARGIE(1940), ph; MEET THE WILDCAT(1940), ph; BADLANDS OF DAKOTA(1941), ph; BLACK CAT, THE(1941), ph; DANGEROUS GAME, A(1941), ph; MOONLIGHT IN HAWAII(1941), ph; SAN ANTONIO ROSE(1941), ph; SEALED LIPS(1941), ph; BOMBAY CLIPPER(1942), ph; EAGLE SQUADRON(1942), ph; MAGNIFICENT AMBERSONS, THE(1942), ph; POWERS GIRL, THE(1942), ph; FLESH AND FANTASY(1943), ph; SINCE YOU WENT AWAY(1944), ph; SMASH-UP, THE STORY OF A WOMAN(1947), ph; SECRET BEYOND THE DOOR, THE(1948), ph; SMART WOMAN(1948), ph; MAN ON THE EIFFEL TOWER,

THE(1949), ph; ADMIRAL WAS A LADY, THE(1950), ph; WHIPPED, THE(1950), ph; BASKETBALL FIX, THE(1951), ph; FORT DEFIANCE(1951), ph; ABBOTT AND COSTELLO MEET CAPTAIN KIDD(1952), ph; MODELS, INC.(1952), ph; STRONGHOLD(1952, Mex.), ph; DIAMOND QUEEN, THE(1953), ph; SHARK RIVER(1953), ph; DRAGON'S GOLD(1954), ph; RIDERS TO THE STARS(1954), ph; BLACK TUESDAY(1955), ph; NIGHT OF THE HUNTER, THE(1955), ph; MAN FROM DEL RIO(1956), ph; THREE FACES OF EVE, THE(1957), ph; TOP SECRET AFFAIR(1957), ph; ANGRY RED PLANET, THE(1959), ph; THUNDER IN THE SUN(1959), ph; VICE RAID(1959), ph; DINOSAURUS(1960), ph; BACK STREET(1961), ph; SHOCK CORRIDOR(1963), ph; CANDIDATE, THE(1964), ph; NAKED KISS, THE(1964), ph; NIGHTMARE IN THE SUN(1964), ph; THEY SAVED HITLER'S BRAIN(1964), ph; YOUNG DILLINGER(1965), ph; GHOST IN THE INVISIBLE BIKINI(1966), ph; NAVY VS. THE NIGHT MONSTERS, THE(1966), ph; BLUE(1968), ph; BRIDGE AT REMAGEN, THE(1969), ph; ANOTHER MAN, ANOTHER CHANCE(1977 Fr/US), ph
Tony Cortez
DEVIL'S RAIN, THE(1975, U.S./Mex.)
Cortez and Galante
STRANGE WIVES(1935)
Sylvain Corthay
MICHELLE(1970, Fr.)
Herbert Corthell
ONLY YESTERDAY(1933); SATURDAY'S MILLIONS(1933); BOMBAY MAIL(1934); LET'S TALK IT OVER(1934); LONE COWBOY(1934); UNCERTAIN LADY(1934); FIRETRAP, THE(1935); CRIME PATROL, THE(1936); DANCING FEET(1936); STORY OF LOUIS PASTEUR, THE(1936); BLAZING BARRIERS(1937); ESPIONAGE(1937); MAN IN BLUE, THE(1937); RENFREW OF THE ROYAL MOUNTED(1937); SING YOU SINNERS(1938); ROLLIN' WESTWARD(1939); DANGER ON WHEELS(1940); PRIMROSE PATH(1940); DUKE OF THE NAVY(1942); SLEEPY LAGOON(1943); KNICKERBOCKER HOLIDAY(1944); LADY IN THE DARK(1944)
Silents
CLASSMATES(1924); SECOND YOUTH(1924)
Basilio Cortijo
TROJAN WOMEN, THE(1971), spec eff
Larry Cortinez
MR. MAJESTYK(1974)
Generoso Cortini
MARRIAGE–ITALIAN STYLE(1964, Fr./Ital.)
Tiziano Cortini
LA DOLCE VITA(1961, Ital./Fr.); MATCHLESS(1967, Ital.)
Anthony Cortino
EXPOSED(1983)
1984
MOSCOW ON THE HUDSON(1984)
Nicholas Cortland
FROGS(1972); DAY OF THE LOCUST, THE(1975); BEAR ISLAND(1980, Brit.-Can.)
1984
NEW YORK NIGHTS(1984)
Carol Cortne
BOXOFFICE(1982)
Sergio Cortona
KNIVES OF THE AVENGER(1967, Ital.); ZOMBIE CREEPING FLESH(1981, Ital./Span.), p
Jerry Cortwright
GIANT GILA MONSTER, THE(1959)
Clair Corvalho
SILVER LINING(1932), w
Dolores Corvall
DALLAS(1950)
Pietro Corvelatti
IL GRIDO(1962, U.S./Ital.)
John Corvello
MAX DUGAN RETURNS(1983)
Manola Corvera
IT SEEMED LIKE A GOOD IDEA AT THE TIME(1975, Can.), anim
Maria Corvin
SET-UP, THE(1963, Brit.)
Aleka Corwin
FINAL TERROR, THE(1983), art d
Alexia Corwin
BEING, THE(1983), art d
Arlene Corwin
JUKE BOX RACKET(1960); 1,000 SHAPES OF A FEMALE(1963), m
Norman Corwin
FOREVER AND A DAY(1943), w; ONCE UPON A TIME(1944), w; BLUE VEIL, THE(1951), w; SCANDAL AT SCOURIE(1953), w; LUST FOR LIFE(1956), w; NO PLACE TO HIDE(1956), w; NAKED MAJA, THE(1959, Ital./U.S.), w; STORY OF RUTH, THE(1960), w; MADISON AVENUE(1962), w
Alexandra Corwin-Hankin
OPENING NIGHT(1977), cos
Assemblyman Ken Cory
CANDIDATE, THE(1972)
Bob Cory
LOVE ON THE RUN(1936); LAST OF MRS. CHEYNEY, THE(1937)
Desmond Cory
MARK OF THE PHOENIX(1958, Brit.), w; DEADFALL(1968, Brit.), d&w; ENGLANO MADE ME(1973, Brit.), w
Henry Cory
HOT TIMES(1974)
Joel Cory
THREE TOUGH GUYS(1974, U.S./Ital.)
John Cory
RETURN OF MONTE CRISTO, THE(1946)
Ken Cory
WITHOUT A TRACE(1983)
Kenneth Cory
HERO AT LARGE(1980); ENDLESS LOVE(1981)

Phil Cory
DOMINO PRINCIPLE, THE(1977), spec eff; SCAVENGER HUNT(1979), spec eff
1984
PROTOCOL(1984), spec eff
Philip Cory
1984
CANNONBALL RUN II(1984), spec eff
Ray Cory
PERILOUS HOLIDAY(1946), spec eff; ASSIGNMENT–PARIS(1952), ph; LAST OF THE COMANCHES(1952), ph; FLAME OF CALCUTTA(1953), ph; HAVE ROCRET, WILL TRAVEL(1959), ph; HEY BOY! HEY GIRL!(1959), ph
Robert Cory
HUDSON'S BAY(1940); MAN IN HALF-MOON STREET, THE(1944); CORN IS GREEN, THE(1945); GOLDEN EARRINGS(1947)
Steve Cory
CLAMBAKE(1967); MARYJANE(1968); MECHANIC, THE(1972)
Betty Coryell
VELVET TRAP, THE(1966)
William Coryn
NO TIME FOR BREAKFAST(1978, Fr.)
Clayton Corzatte
CINDERELLA LIBERTY(1973)
1984
PRODIGAL, THE(1984)
C.P. Corzilius
DISORDER AND EARLY TORMENT(1977, Ger.)
Vickie Cos
GOOD NEIGHBOR SAM(1964); STRAIT-JACKET(1964)
Loren Cosand
TOYS IN THE ATTIC(1963), makeup; WHO'S GOT THE ACTION?(1962), makeup; KISS ME, STUPID(1964), makeup; MURDERERS' ROW(1966), makeup
John Cosar
Misc. Silents
LITTLE SHEPHERD OF BARGIAN ROW, THE(1916)
Bruce Dennis Cosbey
OTHER SIDE OF THE MOUNTAIN, THE(1975)
Jackie Cosbey
CAROLINA(1934)
Ronald Cosbey
EAST LYNNE(1931); MAN FROM YESTERDAY, THE(1932); BROADWAY BAD(1933); HOUSEWIFE(1934); SUTTER'S GOLD(1936)
Ronnie Cosbey
IRON MASTER, THE(1933); CAROLINA(1934); NOW AND FOREVER(1934); NOW I'LL TELL(1934); REGISTERED NURSE(1934); I LIVE MY LIFE(1935); STRAIGHT FROM THE HEART(1935); NEXT TIME WE LOVE(1936); MARINES ARE HERE, THE(1938); TELEPHONE OPERATOR(1938)
Ronnie Cosbey, Jr.
PERSONAL MAID'S SECRET(1935)
Bill Cosby
HICKEY AND BOGGS(1972); MAN AND BOY(1972); UPTOWN SATURDAY NIGHT(1974); LET'S DO IT AGAIN(1975); MOTHER, JUGS & SPEED(1976); PIECE OF THE ACTION, A(1977); CALIFORNIA SUITE(1978); DEVIL AND MAX DEVLIN, THE(1981)
Ed Cosby
BLACK SAMSON(1974), art d
Ronnie Cosby
KING OF THE JUNGLE(1933); CIRCUS CLOWN(1934); OIL FOR THE LAMPS OF CHINA(1935); WEST POINT OF THE AIR(1935); BOULDER DAM(1936); MOONLIGHT ON THE PRAIRIE(1936)
Vivian Cosby
MIND READER, THE(1933), w
Cyndie Coscarelli
JIM, THE WORLD'S GREATEST(1976); KENNY AND CO.(1976), cos
D.A. Coscarelli
JIM, THE WORLD'S GREATEST(1976)
Don A. Coscarelli
PHANTASM(1979), p, d,w,ph&ed
Don Coscarelli
JIM, THE WORLD'S GREATEST(1976), p, d&w, ph, ed; KENNY AND CO.(1976), p,d,w&ph, ed; BEASTMASTER, THE(1982), d, w
S.T. Coscarelli
KENNY AND CO.(1976), a, art d
Shirley Coscarelli
JIM, THE WORLD'S GREATEST(1976)
Marcello Coscia
DAY THE SKY EXPLODED, THE(1958, Fr./Ital.), w; WHITE SLAVE SHIP(1962, Fr./Ital.), w; FANTASTIC THREE, THE(1967, Ital./Ger./Fr./Yugo.), w; MISSION BLOODY MARY(1967, Fr./Ital./Span.), w; GRAND SLAM(1968, Ital., Span., Ger.), w; DORIAN GRAY(1970, Ital./Brit./Ger./Liechtenstein), w; DON'T OPEN THE WINDOW(1974, Ital.), w
Amanda Cosell
BLUE MURDER AT ST. TRINIAN'S(1958, Brit.)
Howard Cosell
BANANAS(1971); WORLD'S GREATEST ATHLETE, THE(1973); TWO-MINUTE WARNING(1976)
1984
BROADWAY DANNY ROSE(1984)
Nicholas Cosentino
WOMAN IN THE DARK(1952), w
Richard Cosentino
STINGRAY(1978); DREAMER(1979); STUCKEY'S LAST STAND(1980)
Jack Cosgrave
Silents
GIRLS DON'T GAMBLE(1921)
Luke Cosgrave
LIGHTNIN'(1930); SQUAW MAN, THE(1931); SINNERS IN THE SUN(1932); KEY, THE(1934); STEAMBOAT ROUND THE BEND(1935); MARRIED BEFORE BREAKFAST(1937); MAYTIME(1937); HOLIDAY(1938); MY GAL SAL(1942)

Silents
CODE OF THE SEA(1924); FLAMING BARRIERS(1924); MERTON OF THE MOVIES(1924); JEWELS OF DESIRE(1927); GENTLEMEN PREFER BLONDES(1928); RED MARK, THE(1928)
Misc. Silents
HOLLYWOOD(1923); WELCOME HOME(1925)
Robert Cosgrif
Silents
GOING THE LIMIT(1925)
Robert Cosgriff
CAUGHT IN THE ACT(1941), w
Robert James Cosgriff
ROARING TIMBER(1937), w; NAVAL ACADEMY(1941), w
Jack Cosgrose
BEYOND TOMORROW(1940), spec eff
Douglas Cosgrove
HUSH MONEY(1931); SCARLET WEEKEND, A(1932); SHE WANTED A MILLIONAIRE(1932); TOO BUSY TO WORK(1932); LADY KILLER(1933); MAN WHO DARED, THE(1933); AMONG THE MISSING(1934); DANCING MAN(1934); FOG OVER FRISCO(1934); I'VE GOT YOUR NUMBER(1934); MAN WITH TWO FACES, THE(1934); ST. LOUIS KID, THE(1934); UPPER WORLD(1934); WINDS OF THE WASTELAND(1936)
Jack Cosgrove
DEATH FROM A DISTANCE(1936), spec eff; NOTHING SACRED(1937), spec eff; PRISONER OF ZENDA, THE(1937), spec eff; STAR IS BORN, A(1937), spec eff; YOUNG IN HEART, THE(1938), spec eff; GONE WITH THE WIND(1939), spec eff; INTERMEZZO: A LOVE STORY(1939), spec eff; MADE FOR EACH OTHER(1939), spec eff; KIT CARSON(1940), spec eff; MEET JOHN DOE(1941), spec eff; SO ENDS OUR NIGHT(1941), spec eff; PRIDE OF THE YANKEES, THE(1942), spec eff; ACTION IN THE NORTH ATLANTIC(1943), spec eff; THIS IS THE ARMY(1943), spec eff; PASSAGE TO MARSEILLE(1944), spec eff; SINCE YOU WENT AWAY(1944), ph, spec eff; SPELLBOUND(1945), spec eff; DUEL IN THE SUN(1946), spec eff; JOAN OF ARC(1948), spec eff; SHE WORE A YELLOW RIBBON(1949), spec eff; FLIGHT TO MARS(1951), spec eff; INVADERS FROM MARS(1953), spec eff; SEPTEMBER STORM(1960), spec eff
Silents
DAPHNE AND THE PIRATE(1916); INTOLERANCE(1916); HEARTS OF THE WORLD(1918); MAKING THE GRADE(1921)
John Cosgrove
Silents
QUEEN OF SHEBA, THE(1921)
Misc. Silents
QUEEN O' TURF(1922)
Luke Cosgrove
Silents
DUKE STEPS OUT, THE(1929)
Ralph Coshan
1984
STARMAN(1984)
Gordana Cosic
FRONTIER HELLCAT(1966, Fr./Ital./Ger./Yugo.)
Marinko Cosic
RAMPAGE AT APACHE WELLS(1966, Ger./Yugo.)
Renee Cosima
ORPHEUS(1950, Fr.); LES ENFANTS TERRIBLES(1952, Fr.); SELLERS OF GIRLS(1967, Fr.)
Sam Coslow
LIMEHOUSE BLUES(1934), m; ALL THE KING'S HORSES(1935), m; RUGGLES OF RED GAP(1935), m; MOUNTAIN MUSIC(1937), m; DREAMING OUT LOUD(1940), p; SUNSET MURDER CASE(1941), m; SOUTH OF DIXIE(1944), w; OUT OF THIS WORLD(1945), p, w; COPACABANA(1947), p; AS LONG AS THEY'RE HAPPY(1957, Brit.), m/l
Edgar Cosma
UP FROM THE BEACH(1965), m, md
Valdimar Cosma
VERY HAPPY ALEXANDER(1969, Fr.), md
Valdimir Cosma
1984
LE BAL(1984, Fr./Ital./Algeria), md
Vladimar Cosma
VERY HAPPY ALEXANDER(1969, Fr.), m
Vladimir Cosma
NEITHER BY DAY NOR BY NIGHT(1972, U.S./Israel), m; DAYDREAMER, THE(1975, Fr.), m; CATHERINE & CO.(1976, Fr.), m; DRACULA AND SON(1976, Fr.), m; ACE OF ACES(1982, Fr./Ger.), m; DIVA(1982, Fr.), m; BANZAI(1983, Fr.), m; LA BOUM(1983, Fr.), m
1984
JUST THE WAY YOU ARE(1984), m; LE BAL(1984, Fr./Ital./Algeria), m; LES COMPERES(1984, Fr.), m; TO CATCH A COP(1984, Fr.), m
George P. Cosmatos
ESCAPE TO ATHENA(1979, Brit.), d, w
George Pan Cosmatos
MASSACRE IN ROME(1973, Ital.), d, w; CASSANDRA CROSSING, THE(1977), d; OF UNKNOWN ORIGIN(1983, Can.), d
Robert Kaiz Cosmatos
CASSANDRA CROSSING, THE(1977), w
Yorgo Pan Cosmatos
Misc. Talkies
BELOVED, THE(1972), d
Eusebia Cosme
PAWNBROKER, THE(1965)
Sergio Cosmei
TURKISH CUCUMBER, THE(1963, Ger.)
James Cosmo
BATTLE OF BRITAIN, THE(1969, Brit.); VIRGIN SOLDIERS, THE(1970, Brit.); ASSAULT(1971, Brit.); YOUNG WINSTON(1972, Brit.)
Michael Cosmo
BEN HUR(1959)

Nicholas Coster
CONCORDE, THE–AIRPORT '79(; ALL THE PRESIDENT'S MEN(1976); MAC ARTHUR(1977); BIG FIX, THE(1978); ELECTRIC HORSEMAN, THE(1979); GOLDEN-GIRL(1979)

Nick Coster
TITANIC(1953)

Nicolas Coster
OUTCAST, THE(1954); CITY OF SHADOWS(1955); LIGHT FANTASTIC(1964); MY BLOOD RUNS COLD(1965); SPORTING CLUB, THE(1971); SLOW DANCING IN THE BIG CITY(1978); JUST YOU AND ME, KID(1979); LITTLE DARLINGS(1980); STIR CRAZY(1980); WHY WOULD I LIE(1980); PURSUIT OF D.B. COOPER, THE(1981); REDS(1981)

Mary Costes
NIGHT IS OURS(1930, Fr.); ABDULLAH'S HAREM(1956, Brit./Egypt.)

Carmen Costi
NO DRUMS, NO BUGLES(1971)

Maria Costi
BAREFOOT BATTALION, THE(1954, Gr.); TO HELL AND BACK(1955)

Thomas Costich
BLOODY MAMA(1970), cos

George Costigan
SAILOR'S RETURN, THE(1978, Brit.); BLOODY KIDS(1983, Brit.)

Jim Costigan
GRAND THEFT AUTO(1977)

Andrew Costikyan
PRIME TIME, THE(1960), ph

Andrew M. Costikyan
BANANAS(1971), ph

Andy Costikyan
BEAST FROM THE HAUNTED CAVE(1960), ph; SKI TROOP ATTACK(1960), ph

Breck Costin
HUMANOIDS FROM THE DEEP(1980); LOVE AND MONEY(1982); MAN WITH TWO BRAINS, THE(1983); 10 TO MIDNIGHT(1983)

Robert Costley
TOY, THE(1982)

Kevin Costner
NIGHT SHIFT(1982); STACY'S KNIGHTS(1983); TABLE FOR FIVE(1983); TESTAMENT(1983)

Logan Costumes
NOTORIOUS CLEOPATRA, THE(1970), cos

Callisto Cosulich
PLANET OF THE VAMPIRES(1965, U.S./Ital./Span.), w

Guido Cosulich
BRASIL ANNO 2,000(1968, Braz.), ph

Harry Coswick
RETURN OF JESSE JAMES, THE(1950), ed; BUCKSKIN LADY, THE(1957), ed; GUN BATTLE AT MONTEREY(1957), ed; GUNS OF DIABLO(1964), ed; JOHNNY TIGER(1966), ed

David Cota
TAMPICO(1944); VOICE IN THE WIND(1944); ALONG THE NAVAJO TRAIL(1945); MILDRED PIERCE(1945); PAN-AMERICANA(1945); PERILOUS HOLIDAY(1946); TWO SMART PEOPLE(1946); SECRET BEYOND THE DOOR, THE(1948); THREE DARING DAUGHTERS(1948); CRISIS(1950); KING OF THE KHYBER RIFLES(1953)

Gaspare Cotaldo
WHITE DEVIL, THE(1948, Ital.), w

Tom Cote
LIQUID SKY(1982)

Celia Susan Cotelo
VAN, THE(1977), w; MALIBU BEACH(1978), w

Paul Coteret
FRUIT IS RIPE, THE(1961, Fr./Ital.), ph

Peter Cotes
FINGERS(1940, Brit.); PASTOR HALL(1940, Brit.); GENTLE SEX, THE(1943, Brit.); DON'T TAKE IT TO HEART(1944, Brit.); JOHNNY IN THE CLOUDS(1945, Brit.); BEWARE OF PITY(1946, Brit.); UPTURNED GLASS, THE(1947, Brit.); YOUNG AND THE GUILTY, THE(1958, Brit.), d

Enzo Coticchia
BAD BLONDE(1953, Brit.)

Giuli Cotignoli
RED DESERT(1965, Fr./Ital.)

Gordon Cotler
HORIZONTAL LIEUTENANT, THE(1962), w; ARABESQUE(1966), w; BLACK BIRD, THE(1975), w

Lanny Cotler
EARTHLING, THE(1980), w

Carl Cotner
MELODY RANCH(1940)

Douglas Cotner
STUDENT BODIES(1981)

Frank Cotner
Silents
WESTERN HEARTS(1921), ph; FIGHTING CUB, THE(1925), ph; HAUNTED RANGE, THE(1926), ph; WINGS(1927), ph; OLD CODE, THE(1928), ph; PHANTOM RIDER, THE(1929), ph

Mario Cotone
THREE(1969, Brit.); GODFATHER, THE, PART II(1974); TAKE ALL OF ME(1978, Ital.), p

Anne-Marie Cotret
LOLA(1961, Fr./Ital.), ed; BAY OF ANGELS(1964, Fr.), ed; UMBRELLAS OF CHERBOURG, THE(1964, Fr./Ger.), ed; MANON 70(1968, Fr.), ed; MISTER FREEDOM(1970, Fr.), ed

Marie Cotret
DONKEY SKIN(1975, Fr.), ed

Carlos Cotrim
VIOLENT AND THE DAMNED, THE(1962, Braz.)

Stephanie Cotsirilos
BEYOND THE LIMIT(1983)
1984
MOSCOW ON THE HUDSON(1984)

Staats Cotsworth
PEYTON PLACE(1957); THEY MIGHT BE GIANTS(1971)

Jonathan Cott
MAN WITH A CLOAK, THE(1951); NIGHT INTO MORNING(1951); PEOPLE AGAINST O'HARA, THE(1951); SELLOUT, THE(1951); SHADOW IN THE SKY(1951); STRIP, THE(1951); TOO YOUNG TO KISS(1951); BAD AND THE BEAUTIFUL, THE(1952); DESPERATE SEARCH(1952); EVERYTHING I HAVE IS YOURS(1952); FEARLESS FAGAN(1952); SCARAMOUCHE(1952); SKY FULL OF MOON(1952); ABOVE AND BEYOND(1953); ALL THE BROTHERS WERE VALIANT(1953); BATTLE CIRCUS(1953); CLOWN, THE(1953); CODE TWO(1953); CRY OF THE HUNTED(1953); DREAM WIFE(1953); FAST COMPANY(1953); GIRL WHO HAD EVERYTHING, THE(1953); SMALL TOWN GIRL(1953); EXECUTIVE SUITE(1954)

Jonathan E. Cott
LONE STAR(1952)

Jonathon Cott
GIRL IN WHITE, THE(1952)

Vittorio Cottafavi
WARRIOR AND THE SLAVE GIRL, THE(1959, Ital.), d; LEGIONS OF THE NILE(1960, Ital.), d, w; GOLIATH AND THE DRAGON(1961, Ital./Fr.), d; HERCULES AND THE CAPTIVE WOMEN(1963, Fr./Ital.), d, w

Richard Cottan
1984
PLOUGHMAN'S LUNCH, THE(1984, Brit.)

Carolina Cotten
SMOKY MOUNTAIN MELODY(1949)

Joseph Cotten
CITIZEN KANE(1941); LYDIA(1941); JOURNEY INTO FEAR(1942), a, w; MAGNIFICENT AMBERSONS, THE(1942); HERS TO HOLD(1943); SHADOW OF A DOUBT(1943); GASLIGHT(1944); I'LL BE SEEING YOU(1944); SINCE YOU WENT AWAY(1944); LOVE LETTERS(1945); DUEL IN THE SUN(1946); FARMER'S DAUGHTER, THE(1947); BEYOND THE FOREST(1949); PORTRAIT OF JENNIE(1949); UNDER CAPRICORN(1949); SEPTEMBER AFFAIR(1950); THIRD MAN, THE(1950, Brit.); TWO FLAGS WEST(1950); WALK SOFTLY, STRANGER(1950); HALF ANGEL(1951); MAN WITH A CLOAK, THE(1951); PEKING EXPRESS(1951); STEEL TRAP, THE(1952); UNTAMED FRONTIER(1952); WILD HEART, THE(1952, Brit.); BLUEPRINT FOR MURDER, A(1953); EGYPT BY THREE(1953); NIAGARA(1953); OTHELLO(1955, U.S./Fr./Ital.); SPECIAL DELIVERY(1955, Ger.); BOTTOM OF THE BOTTLE, THE(1956); KILLER IS LOOSE, THE(1956); HALLIDAY BRAND, THE(1957); FROM THE EARTH TO THE MOON(1958); TOUCH OF EVIL(1958); ANGEL WORE RED, THE(1960); LAST SUNSET, THE(1961); HUSH... HUSH, SWEET CHARLOTTE(1964); GREAT SIOUX MASSACRE, THE(1965); MONEY TRAP, THE(1966); OSCAR, THE(1966); TRAMPLERS, THE(1966, Ital.); BRIGHTY OF THE GRAND CANYON(1967); HELLBENDERS, THE(1967, U.S./Ital./Span.); JACK OF DIAMONDS(1967, U.S./Ger.); SOME MAY LIVE(1967, Brit.); PETULIA(1968, U.S./Brit.); LATITUDE ZERO(1969, U.S./Jap.); GRASSHOPPER, THE(1970); TORA! TORA! TORA!(1970, U.S./Jap.); ABOMINABLE DR. PHIBES, THE(1971, Brit.); LADY FRANKENSTEIN(1971, Ital.); BARON BLOOD(1972, Ital.); DOOMSDAY VOYAGE(1972); SCIENTIFIC CARDPLAYER, THE(1972, Ital.); DELICATE BALANCE, A(1973); SOYLENT GREEN(1973); AIRPORT '77(1977); TWILIGHT'S LAST GLEAMING(1977, U.S./Ger.); CARAVANS(1978, U.S./Iranian); SCREAMERS(1978, Ital.); GUYANA, CULT OF THE DAMNED(1980, Mex./Span./Panama); HEARSE, THE(1980); HEAVEN'S GATE(1980); SURVIVOR(1980, Aus.)
1984
HOUSE WHERE DEATH LIVES, THE(1984)
Misc. Talkies
PERFECT CRIME(; WHITE COMANCHE(1967); TIMBER TRAMPS(1975); HOUSE WHERE DEATH LIVES, THE(1982)

Peter Cotten
WOMAN HATER(1949, Brit.)

Fanny Cottencon
NORTH STAR, THE(1982, Fr.); PARADISE POUR TOUS(1982, Fr.); L'ETOILE DU NORD(1983, Fr.)

Margot Cottens
NUN AT THE CROSSROADS, A(1970, Ital./Span.)

Catherine Cotter
RESCUE SQUAD(1935); UNDER THE PAMPAS MOON(1935); PINTO RUSTLERS(1937); SUNDOWN SAUNDERS(1937)
Misc. Talkies
TEXAS RAMBLER, THE(1935); OUTLAWS OF THE RANGE(1936)

Ed Cotter
LEO AND LOREE(1980), ed

Jayne Cotter
UNDERCURRENT(1946)

John Cotter
MOUNTAIN FAMILY ROBINSON(1979), d

Richard Cotter
Silents
MY OLD DUTCH(1915, Brit.)

Dorothy Cotterell
ORPHAN OF THE WILDERNESS(1937, Aus.), w

Geoffrey Cotterell
TIARA TAHITI(1962, Brit.), w

Ralph Cotterell
JOURNEY AMONG WOMEN(1977, Aus.)

Paul Cotteret
CAGE OF NIGHTINGALES, A(1947, Fr.), ph

Chrissie Cotterill
1984
SCRUBBERS(1984, Brit.)

Helen Cotterill
DAVID COPPERFIELD(1970, Brit.); NO LONGER ALONE(1978)

Ralph Cotterill
DEATHCHEATERS(1976, Aus.); BLUE FIN(1978, Aus.); CHAIN REACTION(1980, Aus.); SURVIVOR(1980, Aus.)

Enzo Cottichia
GAMBLER AND THE LADY, THE(1952, Brit.)

LaDonna Cottier
DEADWOOD'76(1965)

Anne Cottingham
ROSE BOWL STORY, THE(1952)
Graham Cottle
TRIPLE ECHO, THE(1973, Brit.), p
Herman Cottman
PANIC IN THE STREETS(1950)
Max Cotto
HAPPY FAMILY, THE(1936, Brit.), w
Andre Cotton
POSTMAN GOES TO WAR, THE(1968, Fr.), p
Barry Cotton
SUMMER SOLDIERS(1972, Jap.)
Billie Cotton
Misc. Silents
EARTHBOUND(1920)
Carolina Cotton
I'M FROM ARKANSAS(1944); SING, NEIGHBOR, SING(1944); OUTLAWS OF THE ROCKIES(1945); COWBOY BLUES(1946); STALLION CANYON(1949); HOEDOWN(1950); APACHE COUNTRY(1952); BLUE CANADIAN ROCKIES(1952); ROUGH, TOUGH WEST, THE(1952)
Misc. Talkies
TEXAS PANHANDLE(1945)
Col. Robert C. Cotton
REMEMBER PEARL HARBOR(1942), tech adv
Diana Cotton
MAN FROM TORONTO, THE(1933, Brit.); WALTZ TIME(1933, Brit.); LITTLE FRIEND(1934, Brit.); POWER(1934, Brit.)
Donavan Cotton
FARMER'S OTHER DAUGHTER, THE(1965)
Evelyn Cotton
PROUD AND THE PROFANE, THE(1956)
George Cotton
CURSE OF THE LIVING CORPSE, THE(1964)
Harry Cotton
UP THE MACGREGORS(1967, Ital./Span.); SEVEN GUNS FOR THE MACGREGORS(1968, Ital./Span.)
James Cotton
PSYCH-OUT(1968), set d
Joan Cotton
RETURN OF THE FLY(1959)
Larry Cotton
POT O' GOLD(1941)
Lucy Cotton
Silents
LIFE WITHOUT SOUL(1916); PRODIGAL WIFE, THE(1918); SIN THAT WAS HIS, THE(1920); MAN WHO, THE(1921)
Misc. Silents
BLIND LOVE, THE(1920); BROKEN MELODY, THE(1920); MIRACLE OF LOVE, THE(1920); MISLEADING LADY, THE(1920); DEVIL, THE(1921); WHISPERING SHADOWS(1922)
Oliver Cotton
HERE WE GO ROUND THE MULBERRY BUSH(1968, Brit.); FIREFOX(1982)
Thomas J. Cotton
COURT JESTER, THE(1956)
Tommy Cotton
MY GAL SAL(1942)
The Cotton Club Orchestra
TAXI!(1932)
The Cotton Sisters
I'LL REMEMBER APRIL(1945)
Bill Cottrell
RELUCTANT DRAGON, THE(1941), w; MELODY TIME(1948), w; ALICE IN WONDERLAND(1951), w; CAPTAIN KIDD AND THE SLAVE GIRL(1954)
Cherry Cottrell
FIGHTING PIMPERNEL, THE(1950, Brit.)
Dorothy Cottrell
WILD INNOCENCE(1937, Aus.), w; SECRET OF THE PURPLE REEF, THE(1960), w
Mike Cottrell
FLASH GORDON(1980); HISTORY OF THE WORLD, PART 1(1981); RETURN OF THE JEDI(1983)
Pierre Cottrell
MY NIGHT AT MAUD'S(1970, Fr.), p; CLAIRE'S KNEE(1971, Fr.), p; CHLOE IN THE AFTERNOON(1972, Fr.), p; MOTHER AND THE WHORE, THE(1973, Fr.), p
William Cottrell
SNOW WHITE AND THE SEVEN DWARFS(1937), d; PINOCCHIO(1940), w; THREE CABALLEROS, THE(1944), w; VARIETY GIRL(1947), Puppeteer; NAKED CITY, THE(1948); MAN ON THE EIFFEL TOWER, THE(1949); STRANGE DOOR, THE(1951); LES MISERABLES(1952); MY PAL GUS(1952); CAPTAIN JOHN SMITH AND POCAHONTAS(1953); DONOVAN'S BRAIN(1953); JULIUS CAESAR(1953); LOOSE IN LONDON(1953); TITANIC(1953); RETURN TO TREASURE ISLAND(1954)
Campbell Cotts
IDOL OF PARIS(1948, Brit.); DEAR MR. PROHACK(1949, Brit.); GAY LADY, THE(1949, Brit.); STOP PRESS GIRL(1949, Brit.); WEAKER SEX, THE(1949, Brit.); ANGEL WITH THE TRUMPET(1950, Brit.); LAST HOLIDAY(1950, Brit.); ENCORE(1951, Brit.); HOUR OF THIRTEEN, THE(1952); MURDER ON APPROVAL(1956, Brit.); DOCTOR AT LARGE(1957, Brit.); GOOD COMPANIONS, THE(1957, Brit.); JUST MY LUCK(1957, Brit.); THREE MEN IN A BOAT(1958, Brit.)
Gerald Cotts
PUT UP OR SHUT UP(1968, Arg.), ph; PUTNEY SWOPE(1969), ph; DEATH PLAY(1976), ph
Anny Coty
Misc. Silents
CAFE ELECTRIC(1927, Aust.)
Chana Coubert
EVIL EYE(1964 Ital.)
Henri Coubet
RETURN OF DR. MABUSE, THE(1961, Ger./Fr./Ital.)

Bill Couch
SILENCERS, THE(; MA BARKER'S KILLER BROOD(1960); WALKING TARGET, THE(1960); KING'S PIRATE(1967); LOVE BUG, THE(1968); SPLIT, THE(1968); MAROONED(1969); RUSSIAN ROULETTE(1975), stunts; KING KONG(1976), stunts; LOGAN'S RUN(1976), stunts; MEAN DOG BLUES(1978), stunts; METEOR(1979); DEAD AND BURIED(1981)
1984
GHOSTBUSTERS(1984), stunts
Bill Couch, Jr.
DEAD AND BURIED(1981)
Charles Couch
JEANNE EAGELS(1957); DEAD AND BURIED(1981)
Chuck Couch
KING'S PIRATE(1967)
Desmond Couch
1984
RIVER, THE(1984)
Lionel Couch
SONS AND LOVERS(1960, Brit.), art d; CARRY ON REGARDLESS(1961, Brit.), art d; CARRY ON TEACHER(1962, Brit.), art d; PLAY IT COOL(1963, Brit.), art d; NIGHT MUST FALL(1964, Brit.), art d; NURSE ON WHEELS(1964, Brit.), art d; CASINO ROYALE(1967, Brit.), art d; VENGEANCE OF SHE, THE(1968, Brit.), art d; ANNE OF THE THOUSAND DAYS(1969, Brit.), art d; CARRY ON CAMPING(1969, Brit.), art d; CARRY ON HENRY VIII(1970, Brit.), art d; CARRY ON LOVING(1970, Brit.), art d; DOCTOR IN TROUBLE(1970, Brit.), art d; ASSAULT(1971, Brit.), art d; COUNT DRACULA AND HIS VAMPIRE BRIDE(1978, Brit.), art d; AWAKENING, THE(1980), art d
Robert Couch
HALLELUJAH(1929)
Wendy Lee Couch
MELVIN AND HOWARD(1980)
William Couch
JEANNE EAGELS(1957); FINAL COUNTDOWN, THE(1980)
William T. Couch
DIRTY HARRY(1971)
Cristel Couchane-Lehman
1984
CHEECH AND CHONG'S THE CORSICAN BROTHERS(1984)
Brian Coucher
O LUCKY MAN!(1973, Brit.)
Pierre Couderc
COLLEGE LOVE(1929), w; CAPTAIN THUNDER(1931), w
Silents
PATCHWORK GIRL OF OZ, THE(1914)
Peggy Coudray
Silents
KNIGHT OF THE RANGE, A(1916)
Robert Coudy
ONCE MORE, MY DARLING(1949)
Jerome Couelle
LOVE IN A FOUR LETTER WORLD(1970, Can.), art d
Jack C. Couffer
RUNNING TARGET(1956), p, w
Jack Couffer
EDGE OF FURY(1958), ph; SAVAGE EYE, THE(1960), ph; NIKKI, WILD DOG OF THE NORTH(1961, U.S./Can.), d, ph; LEGEND OF LOBO, THE(1962), ph; MEDIUM COOL(1969), w; RING OF BRIGHT WATER(1969, Brit.), d, w; DARWIN ADVENTURE, THE(1972, Brit.), d, w, ph; LIVING FREE(1972, Brit.), d, ph; JONATHAN LIVINGSTON SEAGULL(1973), ph; NEVER CRY WOLF(1983), p
Paul Coufos
BATTLESTAR GALACTICA(1979)
James Cougar
BLACKENSTEIN(1973)
Rosalie Coughenour
EVERY GIRL SHOULD BE MARRIED(1948)
William Coughey
Misc. Silents
BEWARE OF THE LAW(1922)
Charles Coughlan
ROYAL BOX, THE(1930), w
Frank Coughlan, Jr.
RED LIGHTS AHEAD(1937)
Ian Coughlan
Misc. Talkies
ALISON'S BIRTHDAY(1979, Aus.), d
Junior Coughlan
Silents
GREAT LOVE, THE(1925); MIKE(1926); SKYROCKET, THE(1926)
Phyllis Coughlan
CHARLIE CHAN IN LONDON(1934); COURT JESTER, THE(1956)
Rose Coughlan
Misc. Silents
SPORTING DUCHESS, THE(1915); HERE SURRENDER(1916)
Don Coughlin
MORE AMERICAN GRAFFITI(1979)
Ian Coughlin
Misc. Talkies
SPIRAL BUREAU, THE(1974), d
Frank Coughlin, Jr.
ANGELS WASH THEIR FACES(1939)
James Coughlin
MY SON IS GUILTY(1940)
Kevin Coughlin
STORM CENTER(1956); DEFIANT ONES, THE(1958); HAPPY ANNIVERSARY(1959); DUEL AT DIABLO(1966); MARYJANE(1968); WILD IN THE STREETS(1968); YOUNG RUNAWAYS, THE(1968); GAY DECEIVERS, THE(1969)
Phyllis Coughlin
THIRD OF A MAN(1962)

Helen Couglin
Misc. Silents
GREAT PHYSICIAN, THE(1913)
Jarvis Couillard
PREJUDICE(1949), w
Francois Cousineau
SUZANNE(1980, Can.), m
Harry Y. Coul
POLICE DOG STORY, THE(1961)
Jovy Couldry
POWERFORCE(1983)
Patricia Coulet
LOULOU(1980, Fr.)
Yvonne Coulette
SECRET PEOPLE(1952, Brit.)
Mamadou Coulibaly
BLACK AND WHITE IN COLOR(1976, Fr.)
Deborah Coulls
LADY, STAY DEAD(1982, Aus.)
George Coulouris
ASSASSINATION BUREAU, THE(1969, Brit.)
George Coulouris
CROOKED ROAD, THE(; CHRISTOPHER BEAN(1933); ALL THIS AND HEAVEN TOO(1940); LADY IN QUESTION, THE(1940); CITIZEN KANE(1941); ASSIGNMENT IN BRITTANY(1943); FOR WHOM THE BELL TOLLS(1943); THIS LAND IS MINE(1943); WATCH ON THE RHINE(1943); BETWEEN TWO WORLDS(1944); MASTER RACE, THE(1944); MR. SKEFFINGTON(1944); NONE BUT THE LONELY HEART(1944); CONFIDENTIAL AGENT(1945); HOTEL BERLIN(1945); LADY ON A TRAIN(1945); SONG TO REMEMBER, A(1945); CALIFORNIA(1946); MR. DISTRICT ATTORNEY(1946); NOBODY LIVES FOREVER(1946); VERDICT, THE(1946); WHERE THERE'S LIFE(1947); BEYOND GLORY(1948); JOAN OF ARC(1948); SLEEP, MY LOVE(1948); SOUTHERN YANKEE, A(1948); KILL OR BE KILLED(1950); ISLAND RESCUE(1952, Brit.); OUTCAST OF THE ISLANDS(1952, Brit.); ASSASSIN, THE(1953, Brit.); DAY TO REMEMBER, A(1953, Brit.); DOCTOR IN THE HOUSE(1954, Brit.); DUEL IN THE JUNGLE(1954, Brit.); HEART OF THE MATTER, THE(1954, Brit.); RUNAWAY BUS, THE(1954, Brit.); DOCTOR AT SEA(1955, Brit.); RACE FOR LIFE, A(1955, Brit.); TECKMAN MYSTERY, THE(1955, Brit.); PRIVATE'S PROGRESS(1956, Brit.); DOCTOR AT LARGE(1957, Brit.); MAN WITHOUT A BODY, THE(1957, Brit.); TARZAN AND THE LOST SAFARI(1957, Brit.); I ACCUSE(1958, Brit.); KILL ME TOMORROW(1958, Brit.); LAW AND DISORDER(1958, Brit.); SPY IN THE SKY(1958); TANK FORCE(1958, Brit.); BEASTS OF MARSEILLES, THE(1959, Brit.); SON OF ROBIN HOOD(1959, Brit.); WOMAN EATER, THE(1959, Brit.); BLUEBEARD'S TEN HONEYMOONS(1960, Brit.); BOY WHO STOLE A MILLION, THE(1960, Brit.); CONSPIRACY OF HEARTS(1960, Brit.); SURPRISE PACKAGE(1960); KING OF KINGS(1961); BIG MONEY, THE(1962, Brit.); DOG AND THE DIAMONDS, THE(1962, Brit.); FURY AT SMUGGLERS BAY(1963, Brit.); IN THE COOL OF THE DAY(1963); SKULL, THE(1965, Brit.); ARABESQUE(1966); TOO MANY THIEVES(1968); LAND RAIDERS(1969); NO BLADE OF GRASS(1970, Brit.); BLOOD FROM THE MUMMY'S TOMB(1972, Brit.); MAHLER(1974, Brit.); MURDER ON THE ORIENT EXPRESS(1974, Brit.); LAST DAYS OF MAN ON EARTH, THE(1975, Brit.); RITZ, THE(1976); SHOUT AT THE DEVIL(1976, Brit.); TEMPTER, THE(1978, Ital.); IT'S NOT THE SIZE THAT COUNTS(1979, Brit.); BEYOND THE FOG(1981, Brit.); LONG GOOD FRIDAY, THE(1982, Brit.)
Catherine Coulson
BREAKFAST IN BED(1978), p; TRICK OR TREATS(1982)
Frank Coulson
NEVER TAKE NO FOR AN ANSWER(1952, Brit./Ital.)
Peter Coulson
SWEET WILLIAM(1980, Brit.), ed; BLOODY KIDS(1983, Brit.), ed; RUNNERS(1983, Brit.), ed
Roy Coulson
Silents
ABABIAN KNIGHT, AN(1920); IF ONLY JIM(1921); ROBIN HOOD(1922); SCARAMOUCHE(1923); DON Q, SON OF ZORRO(1925); NEVER THE TWAIN SHALL MEET(1925); TEMPTRESS, THE(1926)
Clare Coulter
BY DESIGN(1982)
Craig Coulter
SATURDAY THE 14TH(1981)
Elizabeth Coulter
PICTURES(1982, New Zealand)
Frazer Coulter
Silents
LOVE'S REDEMPTION(1921); HEART RAIDER, THE(1923)
Misc. Silents
HIS BROTHER'S KEEPER(1921); GOVERNOR'S LADY, THE(1923)
Jean Ann Coulter
END, THE(1978)
Jean Coulter
JAWS II(1978)
Lucia Coulter
Silents
LONDON AFTER MIDNIGHT(1927), cos; UNKNOWN, THE(1927), cos; DESERT RIDER, THE(1929), cos; OVERLAND TELEGRAPH, THE(1929), cos
Luke Coulter
LOCAL HERO(1983, Brit.)
Martin Coulter
WAR OF THE WORLDS, THE(1953)
Michael Coulter
THAT SINKING FEELING(1979, Brit.), ph; GREGORY'S GIRL(1982, Brit.), ph
Stephen Coulter
EMBASSY(1972, Brit.), w
C.F. Counce
GIRL IN TROUBLE(1963)
Elizabeth Council
I PASSED FOR WHITE(1960)
Tom Cound
KING OF THE KHYBER RIFLES(1953); IT SHOULD HAPPEN TO YOU(1954); SCARLET COAT, THE(1955); INCIDENT IN AN ALLEY(1962); BEAUTY AND THE BEAST(1963); MY FAIR LADY(1964)

John Coundley
GREEN HELMET, THE(1961, Brit.)
Francine Counihan
COVER GIRL(1944)
Robert Counsel
GENTLE PEOPLE AND THE QUIET LAND, THE(1972)
Elizabeth Counsell
MIND BENDERS, THE(1963, Brit.); SPYLARKS(1965, Brit.); HOT MILLIONS(1968, Brit.)
John Counsell
VANITY(1935); PRISON BREAKER(1936, Brit.); RETURN OF THE SCARLET PIMPERNEL(1938, Brit.)
Mildred Counselman
Silents
ETERNAL TEMPTRESS, THE(1917)
Nikki Counselman
I NEVER SANG FOR MY FATHER(1970); HAVE A NICE WEEKEND(1975)
William Counselman
SOPHOMORE, THE(1929), p; RED HOT RHYTHM(1930), w; WEEK-ENDS ONLY(1932), w; HANDY ANDY(1934), w; I BELIEVED IN YOU(1934), w; SHE LEARNED ABOUT SAILORS(1934), w; SO THIS IS LONDON(1940, Brit.), w
William Counselman, Jr.
YESTERDAY'S HEROES(1940), w
William H. Counselman, Jr.
BOY FRIEND(1939)
Mary Count
ARENA, THE(1973)
Count Basie and His Band
STAGE DOOR CANTEEN(1943)
Count Basie and His Octet
MADE IN PARIS(1966)
Count Basie and His Orchestra
REVEILLE WITH BEVERLY(1943); TOP MAN(1943); SEX AND THE SINGLE GIRL(1964)
Count Basie and Orchestra
HIT PARADE OF 1943(1943)
Count Basie Orchestra
CRAZY HOUSE(1943); JAMBOREE(1957)
Margaret Countenay
ISADORA(1968, Brit.)
Susan Counter
FOR LOVE OR MONEY(1963)
Tom Counter
HAREM BUNCH; OR WAR AND PIECE, THE(1969)
Countess Liev de Maigret
ONE RAINY AFTERNOON(1936)
The Countess of Massarne
Silents
GREAT LOVE, THE(1918)
Catherine Countiss
Misc. Silents
AVALANCHE, THE(1915); MODERN MAGDALEN, A(1915)
Country Joe [McDonald] and The Fish
CAPTAIN MILKSHAKE(1970), m; GAS-S-S-S!(1970), m; ZACHARIAH(1971)
Countryman
COUNTRYMAN(1982, Jamaica)
Eleanor Counts
GOOD GIRLS GO TO PARIS(1939); MILLION DOLLAR LEGS(1939); LOOK WHO'S LAUGHING(1941); NOTHING BUT THE TRUTH(1941); UNEXPECTED UNCLE(1941); BORDER BUCKAROOS(1943); DESTROYER(1943); THANK YOUR LUCKY STARS(1943); FOLLOW THE BOYS(1944); NOCTURNE(1946); UNSUSPECTED, THE(1947)
Elinor Counts
HONOLULU LU(1941)
Gerald J. Counts
STRIPES(1981)
Kevin Coupe
CHILD'S PLAY(1972)
Barbara Couper
HEAVEN IS ROUND THE CORNER(1944, Brit.); STORY OF SHIRLEY YORKE, THE(1948, Brit.); DARK SECRET(1949, Brit.); LAST DAYS OF DOLWYN, THE(1949, Brit.); HAPPY GO LOVELY(1951, Brit.); LADY WITH A LAMP, THE(1951, Brit.); PAUL TEMPLE'S TRIUMPH(1951, Brit.); WEAK AND THE WICKED, THE(1954, Brit.); MENACE IN THE NIGHT(1958, Brit.); AMOROUS ADVENTURES OF MOLL FLANDERS, THE(1965); GREAT ST. TRINIAN'S TRAIN ROBBERY, THE(1966, Brit.); GOODBYE MR. CHIPS(1969, U.S./Brit.)
Max Couper
JOE(1970)
Francois Couperin
CAT IN THE SACK, THE(1967, Can.), m
Diana Coupland
MILLIONAIRESS, THE(1960, Brit.); FAMILY WAY, THE(1966, Brit.); CHARLIE BUBBLES(1968, Brit.); RISE AND RISE OF MICHAEL RIMMER, THE(1970, Brit.); SPRING AND PORT WINE(1970, Brit.); TWELVE CHAIRS, THE(1970); OPERATION DAYBREAK(1976, U.S./Brit./Czech.)
Misc. Talkies
BLESS THIS HOUSE(1972, Brit.)
Henri Coupon
VERDICT(1975, Fr./Ital.), w
Danielle Couprayen
HAIL MAFIA(1965, Fr./Ital.)
Alexander Courage
HOT ROD RUMBLE(1957), m; SHAKE, RATTLE, AND ROCK!(1957), m; SIERRA STRANGER(1957), m, md; SUN ALSO RISES, THE(1957), m; UNDERSEA GIRL(1957), m, md; HANDLE WITH CARE(1958), m; LEFT-HANDED GUN, THE(1958), m; TOKYO AFTER DARK(1959), m; FOLLOW THE BOYS(1963), m; DOCTOR DOLITTLE(1967), md

Carolyn Courage
TERROR(1979, Brit.)

C. Courant
ME AND MARLBOROUGH(1935, Brit.), ph

Curt Courant
RASPUTIN(1932, Ger.), ph; PERFECT UNDERSTANDING(1933, Brit.), ph; IRON DUKE, THE(1935, Brit.), ph; MAN WHO KNEW TOO MUCH, THE(1935, Brit.), ph; BROKEN BLOSSOMS(1936, Brit.), ph; MAN IN THE MIRROR, THE(1936, Brit.), ph; PASSING OF THE THIRD FLOOR BACK, THE(1936, Brit.), ph; SHE KNEW WHAT SHE WANTED(1936, Brit.), ph; HIDEOUT IN THE ALPS(1938, Brit.), ph; LA BETE HUMAINE(1938, Fr.), ph; BETRAYAL(1939, Fr.), ph; SPY OF NAPOLEON(1939, Brit.), ph; DAYBREAK(1940, Fr.), ph; MONSIEUR VERDOUX(1947), ph
Silents
WOMAN ON THE MOON, THE(1929, Ger.), ph

Curtis Courant
IT HAPPENED IN ATHENS(1962), ph

Madeleine Courau
YOUR SHADOW IS MINE(1963, Fr./Ital.), w

Pierre Courau
LAST YEAR AT MARIENBAD(1962, Fr./Ital.), p; YOUR SHADOW IS MINE(1963, Fr./Ital.), p

Robin Courbet
THIS, THAT AND THE OTHER(1970, Brit.)

Nicole Courcel
LA MARIE DU PORT(1951, Fr.); ROYAL AFFAIRS IN VERSAILLES(1957, Fr.); CASE OF DR. LAURENT(1958, Fr.); NIGHTS OF SHAME(1961, Fr.); VICE DOLLS(1961, Fr.); SUNDAYS AND CYBELE(1962, Fr.); TESTAMENT OF ORPHEUS, THE(1962, Fr.); TOMORROW IS MY TURN(1962, Fr./Ital./Ger.); MAN WHO WALKED THROUGH THE WALL, THE(1964, Ger.); STOP TRAIN 349(1964, Fr./Ital./Ger.); NIGHT OF THE GENERALS, THE(1967, Brit./Fr.)

Christiane Courcelles
JUDEX(1966, Fr./Ital.), cos

Francine Coureau
TRIAL, THE(1963, Fr./Ital./Ger.), set d

Carlos Couret
LAZARILLO(1963, Span.), p

Val Couret
HAREM BUNCH; OR WAR AND PIECE, THE(1969)

Devereaux Courier
REAP THE WILD WIND(1942)

John Courier
SIERRA BARON(1958)

Robert Courleigh
WINTER KILLS(1979)

Courme
LA CHIENNE(1975, Fr.)

Charles Courney
COW COUNTRY(1953)

Pat Courney
PICCADILLY NIGHTS(1930, Brit.)

Michel Cournot
WEEKEND(1968, Fr./Ital.); LES GAULOISES BLEUES(1969, Fr.), d&w

Serge Coursan
L'ETOILE DU NORD(1983, Fr.)

Jim Coursar
SIGN OF AQUARIUS(1970)

Dennis Court
MASSACRE AT CENTRAL HIGH(1976)

Edward Court
PICK A STAR(1937), ch

Emerton Court
THUNDER OVER TANGIER(1957, Brit.)

Gordon Court
LUCKY JADE(1937, Brit.)

Hazel Court
UNDERCOVER AGENT(1935, Brit.); CHAMPAGNE CHARLIE(1944, Brit.); DREAMING(1944, Brit.); CARNIVAL(1946, Brit.); DEAR MURDERER(1947, Brit.); HOLIDAY CAMP(1947, Brit.); MEET ME AT DAWN(1947, Brit.); ROOT OF ALL EVIL, THE(1947, Brit.); BOND STREET(1948, Brit.); MY SISTER AND I(1948, Brit.); SHOWTIME(1948, Brit.); FORBIDDEN(1949, Brit.); GHOST SHIP(1953, Brit.); DEVIL GIRL FROM MARS(1954, Brit.); SCARLET WEB, THE(1954, Brit.); TALE OF THREE WOMEN, A(1954, Brit.); BEHIND THE HEADLINES(1956, Brit.); NARROWING CIRCLE, THE(1956, Brit.); CURSE OF FRANKENSTEIN, THE(1957, Brit.); HOUR OF DECISION(1957, Brit.); WOMAN OF MYSTERY, A(1957, Brit.); MAN WHO COULD CHEAT DEATH, THE(1959, Brit.); MAN WHO WAS NOBODY, THE(1960, Brit.); MODEL FOR MURDER(1960, Brit.); SHAKEDOWN, THE(1960, Brit.); DR. BLOOD'S COFFIN(1961); MARY HAD A LITTLE(1961, Brit.); PREMATURE BURIAL, THE(1962, Brit.); RAVEN, THE(1963); MASQUE OF THE RED DEATH, THE(1964, U.S./Brit.); FINAL CONFLICT, THE(1981)
Misc. Talkies
BREAKOUT(1959)

Jason Court
1984
GRANDVIEW, U.S.A.(1984); UP THE CREEK(1984)

Joanne Court
CAIRO(1963), w

Marion Court
Silents
NEW CHAMPION(1925)

R. Brian Court
MR. HULOT'S HOLIDAY(1954, Fr.), art d

Cast of The Court of the Missing Heirs
SEVEN DAYS LEAVE(1942)

Suzanne Courtal
FORBIDDEN GAMES(1953, Fr.)

Gerald Courtemarch
SOMETHING TO LIVE FOR(1952)

Daphne Courtenay
HAPPY ENDING, THE(1931, Brit.); POLITICAL PARTY, A(1933, Brit.); CAPTAIN'S TABLE, THE(1936, Brit.)

David Courtenay
PRIZE OF ARMS, A(1962, Brit.)

Dick Courtenay
GALLOPING MAJOR, THE(1951, Brit.)

Dolores Courtenay
Silents
EDUCATION OF NICKY, THE(1921, Brit.)

George Courtenay
Silents
IVANHOE(1913)

Helen Courtenay
Misc. Silents
SHADOW, THE(1921)

Joan Courtenay
TWO WEEKS IN ANOTHER TOWN(1962)

Margaret Courtenay
HOT MILLIONS(1968, Brit.); UNDER MILK WOOD(1973, Brit.); GET CHARLIE TULLY(1976, Brit.); INCREDIBLE SARAH, THE(1976, Brit.); MIRROR CRACK'D, THE(1980, Brit.); OH, HEAVENLY DOG!(1980)

Syd Courtenay
KISS ME, SERGEANT(1930, Brit.), a, w; NOT SO QUIET ON THE WESTERN FRONT(1930, Brit.), a, w; WHY SAILORS LEAVE HOME(1930, Brit.), a, w; BILL'S LEGACY(1931, Brit.), a, w; OLD SOLDIERS NEVER DIE(1931, Brit.), w; POOR OLD BILL(1931, Brit.), a, w; WHAT A NIGHT!(1931, Brit.), a, w; LAST COUPON, THE(1932, Brit.), a, w; OLD SPANISH CUSTOMERS(1932, Brit.), a, w; TONIGHT'S THE NIGHT(1932, Brit.), a, w; HAWLEY'S OF HIGH STREET(1933, Brit.), a, w; POLITICAL PARTY, A(1933, Brit.), w; PRIDE OF THE FORCE, THE(1933, Brit.), a, w; LOST IN THE LEGION(1934, Brit.), a, w; OUTCAST, THE(1934, Brit.), w; CAPTAIN BILL(1935, Brit.), w; STOKER, THE(1935, Brit.), a, w; STRICTLY ILLEGAL(1935, Brit.), a, w; MAN BEHIND THE MASK, THE(1936, Brit.), w; ONE GOOD TURN(1936, Brit.), w; COTTON QUEEN(1937, Brit.), a, w; DARBY AND JOAN(1937, Brit.), d&w, d, w; SING AS YOU SWING(1937, Brit.), w; REVERSE BE MY LOT, THE(1938, Brit.), w; EVERYTHING IS RHYTHM(1940, Brit.), w

Tom Courtenay
LONELINESS OF THE LONG DISTANCE RUNNER, THE(1962, Brit.); BILLY LIAR(1963, Brit.); PRIVATE POTTER(1963, Brit.); KING AND COUNTRY(1964, Brit.); DOCTOR ZHIVAGO(1965); KING RAT(1965); OPERATION CROSSBOW(1965, U.S./Ital.); DAY THE FISH CAME OUT, THE(1967. Brit./Gr.); NIGHT OF THE GENERALS, THE(1967, Brit./Fr.); DANDY IN ASPIC, A(1968, Brit.); OTLEY(1969, Brit.); CATCH ME A SPY(1971, Brit./Fr.); ONE DAY IN THE LIFE OF IVAN DENISOVICH(1971, U.S./Brit./Norway); DRESSER, THE(1983)

William Courtenay
EVIDENCE(1929); SACRED FLAME, THE(1929); THREE FACES EAST(1930); WAY OF ALL MEN, THE(1930)
Silents
SEALED LIPS(1915); KICK IN(1917)
Misc. Silents
ISLAND OF SURPRISE, THE(1916); NINETY AND NINE, THE(1916); ROMANTIC JOURNEY, THE(1916); HUNTING OF THE HAWK, THE(1917); RECOIL, THE(1917)

Philip Courter
RED RUNS THE RIVER(1963)

Gene Courtier
BLOOD FEAST(1963)

Christi Courtland
LAST MAN ON EARTH, THE(1964, U.S./Ital.)

Jerome Courtland
TOGETHER AGAIN(1944); KISS AND TELL(1945); MAN FROM COLORADO, THE(1948); BATTLEGROUND(1949); MAKE BELIEVE BALLROOM(1949); TOKYO JOE(1949); WALKING HILLS, THE(1949); PALOMINO, THE(1950); WHEN YOU'RE SMILING(1950); WOMAN OF DISTINCTION, A(1950); BAREFOOT MAILMAN, THE(1951); SANTA FE(1951); SUNNY SIDE OF THE STREET(1951); TEXAS RANGERS, THE(1951); CRIPPLE CREEK(1952); TAKE THE HIGH GROUND(1953); BAMBOO PRISON, THE(1955); TONKA(1958); BLACK SPURS(1965); RESTLESS ONES, THE(1965); ESCAPE TO WITCH MOUNTAIN(1975), p; RIDE A WILD PONY(1976, U.S./Aus.), p; PETE'S DRAGON(1977), p; RETURN FROM WITCH MOUNTAIN(1978), p; AMY(1981), p; DEVIL AND MAX DEVLIN, THE(1981), p
Misc. Talkies
QUEEN OF THE SEAS(1960)

John Courtland
SPORTING CLUB, THE(1971), ph

Stephen Courtleigh
YELLOWNECK(1955); NORTH TO ALASKA(1960)

William Courtleigh
Silents
MOON MADNESS(1920); POLLYANNA(1920); HANDLE WITH CARE(1922)
Misc. Silents
BETTER MAN, THE(1914); HEART OF A LION, THE(1918); MADAME X(1920); ASHES(1922); MIDNIGHT(1922)

William Courtleigh, Jr.
Silents
NIGHTINGALE, THE(1914); OUT OF THE DRIFTS(1916); RAINBOW PRINCESS, THE(1916)
Misc. Silents
SUSIE SNOWFLAKE(1916); UNDER COVER(1916); MISS U.S.A.(1917); BY RIGHT OF PURCHASE(1918)

Bert Courtley
ALL NIGHT LONG(1961, Brit.)

Ann Courtneidge
SAFARI 3000(1982)

Charles Courtneidge
LOVE LIES(1931, Brit.)

Cicely Courtneidge
HAPPY EVER AFTER(1932, Ger./Brit.); FALLING FOR YOU(1933, Brit.); GHOST TRAIN, THE(1933, Brit.); NIGHT AND DAY(1933, Brit.); ALONG CAME SALLY(1934, Brit.); THINGS ARE LOOKING UP(1934, Brit.); WOMAN IN COMMAND, THE(1934 Brit.); ME AND MARLBOROUGH(1935, Brit.); PERFECT GENTLEMAN, THE(1935); EVERYBODY DANCE(1936, Brit.); TAKE MY TIP(1937, Brit.); UNDER YOUR

HAT(1940, Brit.); MISS TULIP STAYS THE NIGHT(1955, Brit.); SPIDER'S WEB, THE(1960, Brit.); L-SHAPED ROOM, THE(1962, Brit.); THOSE MAGNIFICENT MEN IN THEIR FLYING MACHINES; OR HOW I FLEWFROM LONDON TO PARIS IN 25 HOURS AND 11 MINUTES(1965, Brit.); WRONG BOX, THE(1966, Brit.); NOT NOW DARLING(1975, Brit.)
Misc. Talkies
ALONG CAME SALLY(1933)

Alan D. Courtney
NIGHT DIGGER, THE(1971, Brit.), p

Alex Courtney
ENTER THE NINJA(1982)

Alicia Courtney
Misc. Talkies
JUST THE TWO OF US(1975)

Alisa Courtney
DARK SIDE OF TOMORROW, THE(1970)

Bessie Courtney
HANGMAN WAITS, THE(1947, Brit.)

Bob Courtney
ROCK, PRETTY BABY(1956); SUMMER LOVE(1958); DINGAKA(1965, South Africa); AFTER YOU, COMRADE(1967, S. Afr.); CAPETOWN AFFAIR(1967, U.S./South Afr.); JACKALS, THE(1967, South Africa)

Carter Courtney
STIGMA(1972)

Catherine Courtney
GOOD GIRLS GO TO PARIS(1939); ANGELS OVER BROADWAY(1940); COURAGEOUS DR. CHRISTIAN, THE(1940); DOCTOR TAKES A WIFE(1940)

Charles Courtney
LOVE'S OLD SWEET SONG(1933, Brit.); LOUISA(1950); AT GUNPOINT(1955); FRIENDLY PERSUASION(1956); TEENAGE THUNDER(1957); TEENAGE MONSTER(1958); SANTEE(1973)

Chuck Courtney
IT GROWS ON TREES(1952); BORN TO THE SADDLE(1953); TWO GUNS AND A BADGE(1954); LONG GRAY LINE, THE(1955); LINEUP, THE(1958); SOME CAME RUNNING(1959); SPARTACUS(1960); MAN'S FAVORITE SPORT [?](1964); BILLY THE KID VS. DRACULA(1966); EL DORADO(1967); RIO LOBO(1970); COWBOYS, THE(1972); MURPH THE SURF(1974), p

Daphne Courtney
FATHER AND SON(1934, Brit.); OH DADDY!(1935, Brit.); BED AND BREAKFAST(1936, Brit.); MURDER BY ROPE(1936, Brit.); THEY ARE NOT ANGELS(1948, Fr.)

David Courtney
INFORMATION RECEIVED(1962, Brit.); TELL-TALE HEART, THE(1962, Brit.)

Del Courtney
IT CAME FROM BENEATH THE SEA(1955); HIDEOUS SUN DEMON, THE(1959)

Don Courtney
KENNER(1969), spec eff; MORE AMERICAN GRAFFITI(1979), spec eff

Donald Courtney
POCKET MONEY(1972), spec eff; HOMEBODIES(1974), spec eff

Elizabeth Courtney
NOTORIOUS LANDLADY, THE(1962), cos

Gavin Courtney
1984
SUBURBIA(1984)

Gene Courtney
WILD IS MY LOVE(1963)

George Courtney
INCIDENT IN SHANGHAI(1937, Brit.)

Inez Courtney
LOOSE ANKLES(1930); NOT DAMAGED(1930); SONG OF THE FLAME(1930); SPRING IS HERE(1930); SUNNY(1930); BRIGHT LIGHTS(1931); HOT HEIRESS(1931); BIG CITY BLUES(1932); CHEATING BLONDES(1933); HOLD YOUR MAN(1933); I LOVE THAT MAN(1933); WORLD GONE MAD, THE(1933); BROADWAY BILL(1934); JEALOUSY(1934); AFFAIR OF SUSAN(1935); ANOTHER FACE(1935); BREAK OF HEARTS(1935); GIRL FRIEND, THE(1935); MAGNIFICENT OBSESSION(1935); MILLIONS IN THE AIR(1935); RAVEN, THE(1935); SHIP CAFE(1935); SWEEPSTAKE ANNIE(1935); BRILLIANT MARRIAGE(1936); DIZZY DAMES(1936); IT COULDN'T HAVE HAPPENED–BUT IT DID(1936); LET'S SING AGAIN(1936); SUZY(1936); WEDDING PRESENT(1936); ARMORED CAR(1937); CLARENCE(1937); HIT PARADE, THE(1937); HURRICANE, THE(1937); PARTNERS IN CRIME(1937); THIRTEENTH MAN, THE(1937); TIME OUT FOR ROMANCE(1937); CRIME RING(1938); FIVE OF A KIND(1938); HAVING WONDERFUL TIME(1938); LETTER OF INTRODUCTION(1938); BEAUTY FOR THE ASKING(1939); BLONDIE MEETS THE BOSS(1939); MISSING EVIDENCE(1939); WHEN TOMORROW COMES(1939); FARMER'S DAUGHTER, THE(1940); SHOP AROUND THE CORNER, THE(1940); TURNABOUT(1940)

James Courtney
AIR STRIKE(1955); IRON MAJOR, THE(1943); STORY OF DR. WASSELL, THE(1944)

Jill Courtney
FORTUNE AND MEN'S EYES(1971, U.S./Can.), ch

Lynn Courtney
SHE FREAK(1967)

Margaret Courtney
LIGHT TOUCH, THE(1955, Brit.)

Mark Courtney
MORE AMERICAN GRAFFITI(1979); DEAD AND BURIED(1981)

Michael Courtney
MORE AMERICAN GRAFFITI(1979); DEAD AND BURIED(1981)

Nicholas Courtney
TAKE A GIRL LIKE YOU(1970, Brit,)

Pat Courtney
Silents
NELSON(1926, Brit.); AFTERWARDS(1928, Brit.); HIS HOUSE IN ORDER(1928, Brit.)

Scott Courtney
TAKE MY TIP(1937, Brit.), ch

Sheila Courtney
Silents
HIS HOUSE IN ORDER(1928, Brit.)

Stella Courtney
OH! WHAT A LOVELY WAR(1969, Brit.); FIDDLER ON THE ROOF(1971)

Syd Courtney
DOCTOR'S ORDERS(1934, Brit.), w

William B. Courtney
Silents
ARTIE, THE MILLIONAIRE KID(1916), w; BLACK BEAUTY(1921), w; HEART OF MARYLAND, THE(1921), w; MORAL FIBRE(1921), w

Colette Courtois
KAMOURASKA(1973, Can./Fr.)

Leon Courtois
Silents
NAPOLEON(1927, Fr.)

Nicole Courtois
WISE GUYS(1969, Fr./Ital.), ed

Reine Courtois
WISE GUYS(1969, Fr./Ital.)

Juliette Courtot
Silents
DOWN TO THE SEA IN SHIPS(1923)

Marguerite Courtot
Silents
CELEBRATED CASE, A(1914); KISS, THE(1916); CRIME AND PUNISHMENT(1917); PERFECT LOVER, THE(1919); CRADLE BUSTER, THE(1922); DOWN TO THE SEA IN SHIPS(1923); JACQUELINE, OR BLAZING BARRIERS(1923); OUTLAWS OF THE SEA(1923); STEADFAST HEART, THE(1923)
Misc. Silents
PRETENDERS, THE(1915); SECRET ROOM, THE(1915); VANDERHOFF AFFAIR, THE(1915); DEAD ALIVE, THE(1916); FEATHERTOP(1916); ROLLING STONES(1916); NATURAL LAW, THE(1917); UNBELIEVER, THE(1918); TEETH OF THE TIGER, THE(1919); UNDERCURRENT, THE(1919); ROGUES AND ROMANCE(1920); SILAS MARNER(1922); MEN, WOMEN AND MONEY(1924)

Billy Courtright
Misc. Silents
HARD BOILED(1919)

Clyde Courtright
NAZI AGENT(1942)

William Courtright
Silents
JAILBIRD, THE(1920); PARIS GREEN(1920); ROOKIE'S RETURN, THE(1921); SPEED GIRL, THE(1921); SUNSHINE TRAIL, THE(1923); GRAND DUCHESS AND THE WAITER, THE(1926); REGULAR SCOUT, A(1926); DON MIKE(1927); JESSE JAMES(1927); SILVER COMES THROUGH(1927); KIT CARSON(1928); PIONEER SCOUT, THE(1928); SUNSET LEGION, THE(1928)
Misc. Silents
LADY OF RED BUTTE, THE(1919); ALL AROUND FRYING PAN(1925); ARIZONA NIGHTS(1927)

Clyde Courtwright
SHE COULDN'T SAY NO(1954)

William Courtwright
Silents
LURE OF YOUTH, THE(1921); MILLIONAIRE, THE(1921); ARE PARENTS PEOPLE?(1925); ATTA BOY!(1926); HANDS ACROSS THE BORDER(1926); MY BEST GIRL(1927)
Misc. Silents
EXTRAVAGANCE(1921); MAN UNDER COVER, THE(1922); HEART BUSTER, THE(1924); TOUGH GUY, THE(1926)

Nathalie Courval
AND NOW MY LOVE(1975, Fr.); CATHERINE & CO.(1976, Fr.)

Albert de Courville
REBEL SON, THE ½(1939, Brit.), d

Isobel Couser
THIS OTHER EDEN(1959, Brit.)

Pascal Cousin
SPIRITS OF THE DEAD(1969, Fr./Ital.), w

Cousin Emmy
SWING IN THE SADDLE(1944)

Cousin Jody
FROM NASHVILLE WITH MUSIC(1969)

Andre Cousineau
ANGELA(1977, Can.)

Andree Cousineau
STONE COLD DEAD(1980, Can.)

Jean Cousineau
TAKE IT ALL(1966, Can.), m; MY UNCLE ANTOINE(1971, Can.), m; FOND MEMORIES(1982, Can.), m

Maggie Cousineau
RETURN OF THE SECAUCUS SEVEN(1980)

Frank Cousins
THUNDERBALL(1965, Brit.); O LUCKY MAN!(1973, Brit.)

John Cousins
WATCH BEVERLY(1932, Brit.), w; SHE WAS ONLY A VILLAGE MAIDEN(1933, Brit.), w; CHILDREN OF THE FOG(1935, Brit.), w; MR. SMITH CARRIES ON(1937, Brit.), w; SPOT OF BOTHER, A(1938, Brit.), w; GLASS MOUNTAIN, THE(1950, Brit), w; TARZAN'S PERIL(1951), w; RAW DEAL(1977, Aus.)

Julie Cousins
BLOB, THE(1958)

Kay Cousins
RESTLESS ONES, THE(1965)

Margaret Cousins
LUCY GALLANT(1955), w

A. Cousminer
FIGHTING CARAVANS(1931), m

Sophie Coussein
MADEMOISELLE(1966, Fr./Brit.), ed; SHAMELESS OLD LADY, THE(1966, Fr.), ed; TWO OF US, THE(1968, Fr.), ed; MARRY ME! MARRY ME!(1969, Fr.), ed; MAN WITH CONNECTIONS, THE(1970, Fr.), ed; MADAME ROSA(1977, Fr.), ed; LOULOU(1980, Fr.), ed

1984
A NOS AMOURS(1984, Fr.), ed

Maurice Coussoneau
ME(1970, Fr.)

Desiree Cousteau
RENEGADE GIRLS(1974)

J. Paul Coutan-Laboureur
FRUSTRATIONS(1967, Fr./Ital.), art d; CHECKERBOARD(1969, Fr.), art d

Kurt Coutant
LOUISE(1940, Fr.), ph

Raoul Coutard
BREATHLESS(1959, Fr.), ph; LOLA(1961, Fr./Ital.), ph; WOMAN IS A WOMAN, A(1961, Fr./Ital.), ph; DOLL, THE(1962, Fr.), ph; JULES AND JIM(1962, Fr.), ph; SHOOT THE PIANO PLAYER(1962, Fr.), ph; ARMY GAME, THE(1963, Fr.), ph; CONTEMPT(1963, Fr./Ital.), ph; LOVE AT TWENTY(1963, Fr./Ital./Jap./Pol./Ger.), ph; MY LIFE TO LIVE(1963, Fr.), ph; TIME OUT FOR LOVE(1963, Ital./Fr.), ph; SOFT SKIN, THE(1964, Fr.), ph; ALPHAVILLE, A STRANGE CASE OF LEMMY CAUTION(1965, Fr.), ph; HAIL MAFIA(1965, Fr./Ital.), ph; LE PETIT SOLDAT(1965, Fr.), ph; MALE COMPANION(1965, Fr./Ital.), ph; MARRIED WOMAN, THE(1965, Fr.), ph; BAND OF OUTSIDERS(1966, Fr.), ph; DEFECTOR, THE(1966, Ger./Fr.), ph; MADE IN U.S.A.(1966, Fr.), ph; LA CHINOISE(1967, Fr.), ph; SAILOR FROM GIBRALTAR, THE(1967, Brit.), ph; BRIDE WORE BLACK, THE(1968, Fr./Ital.), ph; LES CARABINIERS(1968, Fr./Ital.), ph; PIERROT LE FOU(1968, Fr./Ital.), ph; WEEKEND(1968, Fr./Ital.), ph; Z(1969, Fr./Algeria), ph; CONFESSION, THE(1970, Fr.), ph; TWO OR THREE THINGS I KNOW ABOUT HER(1970, Fr.), ph; HOA-BINH(1971, Fr.), d&w; EMBASSY(1972, Brit.), ph; JERUSALEM FILE, THE(1972, U.S./Israel), ph; PASSION(1983, Fr./Switz.), ph
1984
FIRST NAME: CARMEN(1984, Fr.), ph; LE CRABE TAMBOUR(1984, Fr.), ph

Andre Couteaux
MALE COMPANION(1965, Fr./Ital.), w

Coutelain
FANNY(1948, Fr.), ph

Eduardo Coutelen
CAULDRON OF BLOOD(1971, Span.)

Henry Coutet
LOVE AND DEATH(1975)

Bob Coutiere
BRIDE WORE RED, THE(1937)

George Coutoupis
1984
WHERE THE BOYS ARE '84(1984)

Earle Couttie
WATCH YOUR STERN(1961, Brit.), w

E. Compton Coutts
Misc. Silents
HOME(1915, Brit.)

Jean Coutu
NIKKI, WILD DOG OF THE NORTH(1961, U.S./Can.)

Bill Couturie
TWICE UPON A TIME(1983), p, w

Michele Couty
L'ETOILE DU NORD(1983, Fr.)

David Couwlier
THINGS ARE TOUGH ALL OVER(1982)

Gianfranco Couyoumdjian
1984
HUNTERS OF THE GOLDEN COBRA, THE(1984, Ital.), p, w; LAST HUNTER, THE(1984, Ital.), p

Lawrence Couzens
1984
NATURAL, THE(1984)

Paul Couzens
F.J. HOLDEN, THE(1977, Aus.)

Michael Couzzi
SALOME(1953)

Anna Maria Covacci
LISTEN, LET'S MAKE LOVE(1969, Fr./Ital.)

Alvaro Covacevich
NEW LOVE(1968, Chile), d&w, m

De Forest Covan
NEW YORK, NEW YORK(1977)

De Forrest Covan
REFORM SCHOOL(1939)

DeForest Covan
CARMEN JONES(1954); LIVING BETWEEN TWO WORLDS(1963); DAY OF THE LOCUST, THE(1975); ROCKY(1976); WHEN A STRANGER CALLS(1979); HONKYTONK MAN(1982)

DeForrest Covan
TAKE MY LIFE(1942)

Ellie Covan
SOUP FOR ONE(1982)

Roberto Covarrubias
BOULEVARD NIGHTS(1979)

Kenneth Cove
GAY ADVENTURE, THE(1953, Brit.); ROOMMATES(1962, Brit.); EVIL OF FRANKENSTEIN, THE(1964, Brit.)

Martin Cove
COPS AND ROBBERS(1973)

Michael Cove
DEATHCHEATERS(1976, Aus.), w; FIGHTING BACK(1983, Brit.), a, w

Richard Cove
LOVE MERCHANT, THE(1966), m, md

Gene Covelli
BREAKDOWN(1953)

Angela Covello
TORSO(1974, Ital.)

Edwina Coven
GREAT ST. TRINIAN'S TRAIN ROBBERY, THE(1966, Brit.)

Laurence Coven
SOMEWHERE IN TIME(1980)

Covent Garden Chorus
MELODY OF MY HEART(1936, Brit.)

Brian Coventry
BATTLE BEYOND THE STARS(1980)

Florence Coventry
Silents
FINAL CURTAIN, THE(1916)

Miss Coventry
Silents
DANGER SIGNAL, THE(1915)

Tom Coventry
UNDER THE GREENWOOD TREE(1930, Brit.)
Silents
KENT, THE FIGHTING MAN(1916, Brit.); NEW CLOWN, THE(1916, Brit.); AUTOCRAT, THE(1919, Brit.); FATHER O'FLYNN(1919, Brit.); BRENDA OF THE BARGE(1920, Brit.); GLORIOUS ADVENTURE, THE(1922, U.S./Brit.); MONKEY'S PAW, THE(1923, Brit.); PADDY, THE NEXT BEST THING(1923, Brit.); NELL GWYNNE(1926, Brit.); MUMSIE(1927, Brit.)
Misc. Silents
FIVE NIGHTS(1915, Brit.); DOUBLE EVENT, THE(1921, Brit.); SAM'S BOY(1922, Brit.); SPORTING INSTINCT, THE(1922, Brit.)

Franklin Cover
WHAT'S SO BAD ABOUT FEELING GOOD?(1968)

Franklin E. Cover
MIRAGE(1965)

Marie Coverdale
Silents
SILVER LINING, THE(1921)

Eric Coverly
MANFISH(1956); COME SPY WITH ME(1967)

Con Covert
FANTASM(1976, Aus.)
Misc. Talkies
FRIDAY ON MY MIND(1970); SCREAM IN THE STREETS, A(1972)

Grahame Covert
DESPERATE(1947)

Annabelle Covey
BELLES OF ST. TRINIAN'S, THE(1954, Brit.)

Lynn Covey
1984
PLACES IN THE HEART(1984)

Everett Covin
PRIVATE BENJAMIN(1980)

Ada Hall Covington
HURRY SUNDOWN(1967)

Alfred E. Covington
PRIZE FIGHTER, THE(1979)

Bruce Covington
PHANTOM OF THE OPERA, THE(1929); DIXIANA(1930); UNDER A TEXAS MOON(1930); FOLIES DERGERE(1935); MISSISSIPPI(1935)
Silents
FIGHTING COWARD, THE(1924); LOVE'S WILDERNESS(1924); PHANTOM OF THE OPERA, THE(1925)
Misc. Silents
TROUBLES OF A BRIDE(1924); FLYING HORSEMAN, THE(1926)

Danny Covington
HOPSCOTCH(1980)

Fred Covington
NORMA RAE(1979); NIGHT THE LIGHTS WENT OUT IN GEORGIA, THE(1981)
Misc. Talkies
BRASS RING, THE(1975)

Julie Covington
ADVENTURES OF BARRY McKENZIE(1972, Austral.); ASCENDANCY(1983, Brit.)

Suzanne Covington
HARRY AND WALTER GO TO NEW YORK(1976)

Toni Covington
PRIVATE LIVES OF ADAM AND EVE, THE(1961)

Z. Wall Covington
Silents
FAITH HEALER, THE(1921), w; KINGDOM WITHIN, THE(1922)

Nich Covvacevich
WEST SIDE STORY(1961)

Cowan
JOURNEY AMONG WOMEN(1977, Aus.), ph

Ashley Cowan
FLAME, THE(1948); SNAKE PIT, THE(1948); SORRY, WRONG NUMBER(1948); WHISPERING SMITH(1948); NO MAN OF HER OWN(1950); DEADLINE-U.S.A.(1952); TITANIC(1953); KING'S THIEF, THE(1955); LOVE IS A MANY-SPLENDORED THING(1955); MOONFLEET(1955); SCARLET COAT, THE(1955); TO HELL AND BACK(1955); VIRGIN QUEEN, THE(1955); D-DAY, THE SIXTH OF JUNE(1956); 23 PACES TO BAKER STREET(1956); IN THE MONEY(1958); YOUNG LIONS, THE(1958); WRECK OF THE MARY DEAR, THE(1959); MUTINY ON THE BOUNTY(1962); CRAWLING HAND, THE(1963)

Ashlye Cowan
DO YOU LOVE ME?(1946)

Barry Cowan
UNDERGROUND(1970, Brit.)

Bob Cowan
UNSTRAP ME(1968), m

Bunny Cowan
WILLIE McBEAN AND HIS MAGIC MACHINE(1965, U.S./Jap.)

Charlie Cowan
HEAVEN CAN WAIT(1978)

Claudia Cowan
1984
LOVELINES(1984)
David Cowan
1984
CHILDREN OF THE CORN(1984)
Doris Cowan
HIGH(1968, Can.)
Douglas Cowan
THIRTY SECONDS OVER TOKYO(1944); ANCHORS AWEIGH(1945); THRILL OF A ROMANCE(1945); COURAGE OF LASSIE(1946)
James R. Cowan
COCOANUTS, THE(1929), p
Jane Cowan
HENRY AND DIZZY(1942); YOU'RE TELLING ME(1942)
Jeanne Cowan
SEA WOLF, THE(1941)
Jerome Cowan
BELOVED ENEMY(1936); HURRICANE, THE(1937); NEW FACES OF 1937(1937); SHALL WE DANCE(1937); VOGUES OF 1938(1937); YOU ONLY LIVE ONCE(1937); GOLDWYN FOLLIES, THE(1938); THERE'S ALWAYS A WOMAN(1938); EAST SIDE OF HEAVEN(1939); EXILE EXPRESS(1939); GRACIE ALLEN MURDER CASE(1939); GREAT VICTOR HERBERT, THE(1939); OLD MAID, THE(1939); SAINT STRIKES BACK, THE(1939); SHE MARRIED A COP(1939); ST. LOUIS BLUES(1939); CASTLE ON THE HUDSON(1940); FRAMED(1940); MA, HE'S MAKING EYES AT ME(1940); MEET THE WILDCAT(1940); MELODY RANCH(1940); QUARTERBACK, THE(1940); STREET OF MEMORIES(1940); TORRID ZONE(1940); VICTORY(1940); WOLF OF NEW YORK(1940); AFFECTIONATELY YOURS(1941); BUGLE SOUNDS, THE(1941); CITY, FOR CONQUEST(1941); GREAT LIE, THE(1941); HIGH SIERRA(1941); KISS THE BOYS GOODBYE(1941); KISSES FOR BREAKFAST(1941); MALTESE FALCON, THE(1941); MR. AND MRS. NORTH(1941); ONE FOOT IN HEAVEN(1941); OUT OF THE FOG(1941); RAGS TO RICHES(1941); ROUNDUP, THE(1941); SINGAPORE WOMAN(1941); TOO MANY BLONDES(1941); FRISCO LILL(1942); GENTLEMAN AT HEART, A(1942); GIRL FROM ALASKA(1942); JOAN OF OZARK(1942); MOONTIDE(1942); STREET OF CHANCE(1942); THRU DIFFERENT EYES(1942); WHO DONE IT?(1942); CRIME DOCTOR'S STRANGEST CASE(1943); FIND THE BLACKMAILER(1943); HI' YA, SAILOR(1943); LADIES' DAY(1943); MISSION TO MOSCOW(1943); NO PLACE FOR A LADY(1943); SILVER SPURS(1943); SING A JINGLE(1943); SONG OF BERNADETTE, THE(1943); CRIME BY NIGHT(1944); GUEST IN THE HOUSE(1944); MR. SKEFFINGTON(1944); SOUTH OF DIXIE(1944); BEHIND CITY LIGHTS(1945); BLONDE RANSOM(1945); CRIME DOCTOR'S COURAGE, THE(1945); DIVORCE(1945); FOG ISLAND(1945); GETTING GERTIE'S GARTER(1945); G.I. HONEYMOON(1945); HITCHHIKE TO HAPPINESS(1945); JUNGLE CAPTIVE(1945); BLONDE KNOWS BEST(1946); CLAUDIA AND DAVID(1946); DEADLINE AT DAWN(1946); DEADLINE FOR MURDER(1946); FLIGHT TO NOWHERE(1946); KID FROM BOOKLYN, THE(1946); MR. ACE(1946); MURDER IN THE MUSIC HALL(1946); MY REPUTATION(1946); NIGHT IN PARADISE, A(1946); ONE EXCITING WEEK(1946); ONE WAY TO LOVE(1946); PERFECT MARRIAGE, THE(1946); BLONDIE IN THE DOUGH(1947); BLONDIE'S ANNIVERSARY(1947); BLONDIE'S BIG MOMENT(1947); BLONDIE'S HOLIDAY(1947); CRY WOLF(1947); DANGEROUS YEARS(1947); DRIFTWOOD(1947); MIRACLE ON 34TH STREET, THE(1947); RIFFRAFF(1947); UNFAITHFUL, THE(1947); ARTHUR TAKES OVER(1948); BLONDIE'S REWARD(1948); BLONDIE'S SECRET(1948); JUNE BRIDE(1948); NIGHT HAS A THOUSAND EYES(1948); SO THIS IS NEW YORK(1948); WALLFLOWER(1948); ALWAYS LEAVE THEM LAUGHING(1949); BLONDIE HITS THE JACKPOT(1949); BLONDIE'S BIG DEAL(1949); FOUNTAINHEAD, THE(1949); GIRL FROM JONES BEACH, THE(1949); SCENE OF THE CRIME(1949); DALLAS(1950); JOE PALOOKA MEETS HUMPHREY(1950); PEGGY(1950); WEST POINT STORY, THE(1950); WHEN YOU'RE SMILING(1950); YOUNG MAN WITH A HORN(1950); CRIMINAL LAWYER(1951); DISC JOCKEY(1951); FAT MAN, THE(1951); SYSTEM, THE(1953); HAVE ROCRET, WILL TRAVEL(1959); PRIVATE PROPERTY(1960); VISIT TO A SMALL PLANET(1960); ALL IN A NIGHT'S WORK(1961); POCKETFUL OF MIRACLES(1961); BLACK ZOO(1963); CRITIC'S CHOICE(1963); JOHN GOLDFARB, PLEASE COME HOME(1964); FRANKIE AND JOHNNY(1966); PENELOPE(1966); GNOME-MOBILE, THE(1967); COMIC, THE(1969)
Misc. Talkies
MAGNIFICENT ADVENTURE, THE(1952)
Jules Cowan
CROSSFIRE(1933); FIGHTING PARSON, THE(1933)
Karla Cowan
ARIZONA CYCLONE(1934)
Misc. Talkies
RIDERS OF RIO(1931); GALLOPING KID, THE(1932)
Kenneth Cowan
SIEGE OF THE SAXONS(1963, Brit.)
Larry Cowan
HEY THERE, IT'S YOGI BEAR(1964), ed; MAN CALLED FLINTSTONE, THE(1966), ed; CHARLOTTE'S WEB(1973), ed
Lester Cowan
WHOLE TOWN'S TALKING, THE(1935), p; YOU CAN'T CHEAT AN HONEST MAN(1939), p; MY LITTLE CHICKADEE(1940), p; LADIES IN RETIREMENT(1941), p; COMMANDOS STRIKE AT DAWN, THE(1942), p; TOMORROW THE WORLD(1944), p; STORY OF G.I. JOE, THE(1945), p; ONE TOUCH OF VENUS(1948), p; LOVE HAPPY(1949), p; MAIN STREET TO BROADWAY(1953), p
Lore Cowan
SPRINGTIME(1948, Brit.), w
Lynn Cowan
STUDENT TOUR(1934)
Silents
COMPROMISE(1925); SOCIAL HIGHWAYMAN, THE(1926)
Maurice Cowan
WANTED FOR MURDER(1946, Brit.), w; YANK IN LONDON, A(1946, Brit.), w; SPRINGTIME(1948, Brit.), p; FOUR AGAINST FATE(1952, Brit.), p; MURDER ON MONDAY(1953, Brit.), p; TURN THE KEY SOFTLY(1954, Brit.), p, w; UP TO HIS NECK(1954, Brit.), w; MAN OF THE MOMENT(1955, Brit.), w; ONE GOOD TURN(1955, Brit.), p, w; TROUBLE IN STORE(1955, Brit.), p, w; GYPSY AND THE GENTLEMAN, THE(1958, Brit.), p; OPERATION AMSTERDAM(1960, Brit.), p; WATCH IT, SAILOR!(1961, Brit.), p

Paul Cowan
GOLDEN LADY, THE(1979, Brit.), p
Robert Cowan
PITFALL(1948), makeup; VARAN THE UNBELIEVABLE(1962, U.S./Jap.), makeup
Robert A. Cowan
SPLIT IMAGE(1982)
Sada Cowan
WOMAN IN THE DARK(1934), w; FORBIDDEN HEAVEN(1936), w; STOP, LOOK, AND LOVE(1939), w
Silents
CHARGE IT(1921), w; COURAGE(1921), w; WHAT NO MAN KNOWS(1921), w; SILENT PARTNER, THE(1923), w; CHARMER, THE(1925), w; EAST OF SUEZ(1925), w; IN THE NAME OF LOVE(1925), w; NEW COMMANDMENT, THE(1925), w; RECKLESS LADY, THE(1926), w; STAND AND DELIVER(1928), w
Tom Cowan
OFFICE PICNIC, THE(1974, Aus.), p,d&w; PURE S(1976, Aus.), ph; JOURNEY AMONG WOMEN(1977, Aus.), d, w; MOUTH TO MOUTH(1978, Aus.), ph; DIMBOOLA(1979, Aus.), ph; WINTER OF OUR DREAMS(1982, Aus.), ph
Misc. Talkies
SWEET DREAMERS(1981), d
Will Cowan
ARIZONA CYCLONE(1941), p; LAW OF THE RANGE(1941), p; MAN FROM MONTANA(1941), p; MASKED RIDER, THE(1941), p; RAWHIDE RANGERS(1941), p; FIGHTING BILL FARGO(1942), p; STAGECOACH BUCKAROO(1942), p; GALS, INCORPORATED(1943), p; GET GOING(1943), p; HAT CHECK HONEY(1944), p; JUNGLE WOMAN(1944), p; HONEYMOON AHEAD(1945), p; BIG BEAT, THE(1958), p&d; THING THAT COULDN'T DIE, THE(1958), p&d
William Cowan
HE'S MY GUY(1943), p; FROZEN GHOST, THE(1945), p
Herbert "Cowboy" Coward
DELIVERANCE(1972)
Neville Coward
SMELL OF HONEY, A SWALLOW OF BRINE! A(1966)
Noel Coward
PRIVATE LIVES(1931), w; BITTER SWEET(1933, Brit.), w; CAVALCADE(1933), w; DESIGN FOR LIVING(1933), w; TONIGHT IS OURS(1933), w; SCOUNDREL, THE(1935); BITTER SWEET(1940), w, m; IN WHICH WE SERVE(1942, Brit.), a, p, d, w, m; WE WERE DANCING(1942), w; THIS HAPPY BREED(1944, Brit.), p, w, m; BLITHE SPIRIT(1945, Brit.), p&w, w; BRIEF ENCOUNTER(1945, Brit.), p, w; ASTONISHED HEART, THE(1950, Brit.), a, w, m; TONIGHT AT 8:30(1953, Brit.), w; AROUND THE WORLD IN 80 DAYS(1956); GRASS IS GREENER, THE(1960), m; OUR MAN IN HAVANA(1960, Brit.); SURPRISE PACKAGE(1960); PARIS WHEN IT SIZZLES(1964); BUNNY LAKE IS MISSING(1965); BOOM!(1968); MATTER OF INNOCENCE, A(1968, Brit.), w; ITALIAN JOB, THE(1969, Brit.)
Silents
HEARTS OF THE WORLD(1918); EASY VIRTUE(1927, Brit.), w; VORTEX, THE(1927, Brit.), w
Nargis Cowasji
GURU, THE(1969, U.S./India)
Cowboy Copas
SQUARE DANCE JUBILEE(1949)
The Cowboy Island Band
COCAINE COWBOYS(1979)
Deidre Cowden
DOCTOR DETROIT(1983)
Deirdre L. Cowden
FLASHDANCE(1983)
Jack Cowden
FLIPPER(1963), w; SALTY(1975), w; ISLAND CLAWS(1981), w
Jack Cowell
WESTERN JUSTICE(1935); WHAT PRICE CRIME?(1935); BARS OF HATE(1936); FACE IN THE FOG, A(1936); KELLY OF THE SECRET SERVICE(1936); MEN OF THE PLAINS(1936); PRISON SHADOWS(1936); TOO MUCH BEEF(1936)
Jo Ann Cowell
KLANSMAN, THE(1974)
John Cowell
RIP ROARING RILEY(1935); ROGUES' TAVERN, THE(1936)
Lorna Cowell
HELLIONS, THE(1962, Brit.)
Shirley Cowell
HOT STUFF(1979)
John Cowells
Misc. Talkies
BULLDOG COURAGE(1935)
Jules Cowels
Silents
BAR SINISTER, THE(1917)
Henry Cowen
GONE ARE THE DAYS(1963), m
Lawrence Cowen
WORLD, THE FLESH, AND THE DEVIL, THE(1932, Brit.), w
Misc. Silents
HIDDEN HAND, THE(1916, Brit.), d
Ron Cowen
SUMMERTREE(1971), w
Will Cowen
CUBAN PETE(1946), p
William Cowen
KONGO(1932), d; OLIVER TWIST(1933), d
William J. Cowen
HALF-MARRIAGE(1929), d; WOMAN UNAFRAID(1934), d
Silents
NED MCCOBB'S DAUGHTER(1929), d
William Joyce Cowen
THEY GAVE HIM A GUN(1937), w; GOOD GIRLS GO TO PARIS(1939), w
Brad Cowgill
PINK MOTEL(1983)
1984
HOLLYWOOD HIGH PART II(1984)

Richard Cowgill
1984
POWER, THE(1984)
Joan Cowick
SHIPYARD SALLY(1940, Brit.)
Laura Cowie
BLIND SPOT(1932, Brit.); SECRET OF STAMBOUL, THE(1936, Brit.)
Misc. Silents
UNDER SUSPICION(1916, Brit.); VICAR OF WAKEFIELD, THE(1916, Brit.)
Susanne Cowie
1984
HEART OF THE STAG(1984, New Zealand)
Darry Cowl
PLEASE! MR. BALZAC(1957, Fr.); SPUTNIK(1960, Fr.); LOVE AND THE FRENCH-WOMAN(1961, Fr.); MARTIAN IN PARIS, A(1961, Fr.); MAGNIFICENT TRAMP, THE(1962, Fr./Ital.); TALES OF PARIS(1962, Fr./Ital.); LADY DOCTOR, THE(1963, Fr./Ital./Span.); DOUBLE BED, THE(1965, Fr./Ital.), a, w; SWEET SKIN(1965, Fr./Ital.); UP TO HIS EARS(1966, Fr./Ital.); DON'T TOUCH WHITE WOMEN!(1974, Fr.)
George Cowl
JAZZ CINDERELLA(1930); RIP TIDE(1934); EASY LIVING(1937); GLASS KEY, THE(1942)
Misc. Talkies
SECRETS OF HOLLYWOOD(1933)
Silents
DAN(1914); IRON RING, THE(1917); TIDES OF FATE(1917), d; WOODEN SHOES(1917); GRIM GAME, THE(1919); LOVE, HONOR AND OBEY(1920); PRISONER, THE(1923); 'MARRIAGE LICENSE?'(1926); ADVENTURER, THE(1928)
Misc. Silents
(, d; BELOVED ADVENTURESS, THE(1917), d; BETSY ROSS(1917), d; HER HOUR(1917), d; YOUTH(1917); MYSTERY OF THE YELLOW ROOM, THE(1919); GLORY OF CLEMENTINA, THE(1922); FASHIONABLE FAKERS(1923); JADE CUP, THE(1926)
Henry Cowl
NIGHT OF THE LEPUS(1972), animal t
Jane Cowl
SMILIN' THROUGH(1932), w; SMILIN' THROUGH(1941), w; STAGE DOOR CANTEEN(1943); ONCE MORE, MY DARLING(1949); NO MAN OF HER OWN(1950); SECRET FURY, THE(1950); PAYMENT ON DEMAND(1951)
Silents
SPREADING DAWN, THE(1917); LILAC TIME(1928), w
Misc. Silents
GARDEN OF LIES, THE(1915)
Richard S. Cowl
THREAT, THE(1960); CHOPPERS, THE(1961); DEADWOOD'76(1965)
Albert Cowles
UNMASKED(1929), w
Denis Cowles
HOLIDAY'S END(1937, Brit.); YOU'RE IN THE ARMY NOW(1937, Brit.); GOLDFINGER(1964, Brit.); WRONG BOX, THE(1966, Brit.)
Silents
ONCE ABOARD THE LUGGER(1920, Brit.)
Misc. Silents
TOWN OF CROOKED WAYS, THE(1920, Brit.)
Dennis Cowles
DOUBLE EXPOSURES(1937, Brit.); TALK OF THE DEVIL(1937, Brit.); RETURN OF THE FROG, THE(1938, Brit.); HOME FROM HOME(1939, Brit.)
Misc. Silents
HIS OTHER WIFE(1921, Brit.)
Ed Cowles
Silents
SPOOK RANCH(1925)
J.D. Cowles
Silents
ROYAL FAMILY, A(1915)
James Cowles
GOIN' TO TOWN(1935)
Jules Cowles
HIS FIRST COMMAND(1929); LEATHERNECK, THE(1929); SAL OF SINGAPORE(1929); ONE HYSTERICAL NIGHT(1930); HEAVEN ON EARTH(1931); SEA DEVILS(1931); SECRET MENACE(1931); RENEGADES OF THE WEST(1932); LEMON DROP KID, THE(1934); PURSUIT OF HAPPINESS, THE(1934); SCARLET LETTER, THE(1934); BARBARY COAST(1935); LAW BEYOND THE RANGE(1935); MISSISSIPPI(1935); DOUBLE WEDDING(1937); RICH MAN, POOR GIRL(1938)
Silents
STORK'S NEST, THE(1915); PERSUASIVE PEGGY(1917); IDOL OF THE NORTH, THE(1921); LORD JIM(1925); LOST WORLD, THE(1925); SEVEN CHANCES(1925); SCARLET LETTER, THE(1926); LONDON AFTER MIDNIGHT(1927); DOG LAW(1928); ISLE OF LOST MEN(1928)
Misc. Silents
BOOTLEGGERS, THE(1922); LOVE BANDIT, THE(1924); MAN RUSTLIN'(1926); BRINGING UP FATHER(1928); TERROR(1928)
Julius D. Cowles
Misc. Silents
HIS GREAT TRIUMPH(1916)
Mathew Cowles
HAPPY HOOKER, THE(1975)
Matthew Cowles
ME, NATALIE(1969); PEOPLE NEXT DOOR, THE(1970); THEY MIGHT BE GIANTS(1971); FRIENDS OF EDDIE COYLE, THE(1973); SLAP SHOT(1977); WORLD ACCORDING TO GARP, The(1982); EDDIE MACON'S RUN(1983)
Peggy Cowles
ALL-AMERICAN BOY, THE(1973)
Sage Cowles
WARM IN THE BUD(1970)
Virginia Spencer Cowles
LADIES COURAGEOUS(1944), w
Anthony Cowley
1984
HIGHWAY TO HELL(1984), art d; RUNNING HOT(1984), art d

Eric Cowley
ESCAPE(1930, Brit.); JEWEL, THE(1933, Brit.); LUCKY DAYS(1935, Brit.); PRICE OF WISDOM, THE(1935, Brit.); DEBT OF HONOR(1936, Brit.); GRAND FINALE(1936, Brit.); BIG FELLA(1937, Brit.)
Graeme Cowley
SMASH PALACE(1982, New Zealand), ph
1984
UTU(1984, New Zealand), ph
Hilda Cowley
Misc. Silents
CARD, THE(1922, Brit.); PALAVER(1926, Brit.)
John Cowley
RISING OF THE MOON, THE(1957, Ireland); IDOL ON PARADE(1959, Brit.); LIES MY FATHER TOLD ME(1960, Brit.); POACHER'S DAUGHTER, THE(1960, Brit.); DEVIL'S AGENT, THE(1962, Brit.); UNDERWORLD INFORMERS(1965, Brit.); YOUNG CASSIDY(1965, U.S./Brit.)
Brenda Cowling
UP IN THE AIR(1969, Brit.); RAILWAY CHILDREN, THE(1971, Brit.); YOUNG WINSTON(1972, Brit.); BLACK WINDMILL, THE(1974, Brit.); JABBERWOCKY(1977, Brit.); OCTOPUSSY(1983, Brit.)
Bruce Cowling
TILL THE CLOUDS ROLL BY(1946); HIGH BARBAREE(1947); IT HAPPENED IN BROOKLYN(1947); SONG OF THE THIN MAN(1947); BATTLEGROUND(1949); STRATTON STORY, THE(1949); AMBUSH(1950); DEVIL'S DOORWAY(1950); LADY WITHOUT PASSPORT, A(1950); CAUSE FOR ALARM(1951); PAINTED HILLS, THE(1951); BATTLE AT APACHE PASS, THE(1952); GUN BELT(1953); CANNIBAL ATTACK(1954); MASTERSON OF KANSAS(1954); TO HELL AND BACK(1955)
Geraldine Cowper
WICKER MAN, THE(1974, Brit.)
Gerry Cowper
RETURN OF THE SOLDIER, THE(1983, Brit.)
Jacqueline Cowper
WHO SLEW AUNTIE ROO?(1971, U.S./Brit.)
Nichola Cowper
NICE GIRL LIKE ME, A(1969, Brit.)
Nicola Cowper
1984
WINTER FLIGHT(1984, Brit.)
Peter Cowper
MY BLOODY VALENTINE(1981, Can.)
William Cowper
Silents
STORK'S NEST, THE(1915); DIMPLES(1916)
A. Cox
WINDBAG THE SAILOR(1937, Brit.), art d
Alex Cox
1984
REPO MAN(1984), a, d&w
Alfred Cox
YESTERDAY'S ENEMY(1959, Brit.), ed; I ONLY ASKED!(1958, Brit.), ed; REVENGE OF FRANKENSTEIN, THE(1958, Brit.), ed; HOUND OF THE BASKERVILLES, THE(1959, Brit.), ed; MUMMY, THE(1959, Brit.), ed; BRIDES OF DRACULA, THE(1960, Brit.), ed; STRANGLERS OF BOMBAY, THE(1960, Brit.), ed; CURSE OF THE WEREWOLF, THE(1961), ed; NEVER TAKE CANDY FROM A STRANGER(1961, Brit.), ed; PASSPORT TO CHINA(1961, Brit.), ed; WATCH IT, SAILOR!(1961, Brit.), ed; PHANTOM OF THE OPERA, THE(1962, Brit.), ed; DIE, MONSTER, DIE(1965, Brit.), ed; TOMB OF LIGEIA, THE(1965, Brit.), ed
Arthur Cox
FAHRENHEIT 451(1966, Brit.)
Ashley Cox
DRIVE-IN(1976); KING OF THE MOUNTAIN(1981); LOOKER(1981); NIGHT SHIFT(1982)
Babs Cox
FRENCH LINE, THE(1954)
Barry Cox
ITALIAN JOB, THE(1969, Brit.)
Beau Cox
ON THE RUN(1983, Aus.)
Betsy Cox
HUSTLE(1975), cos; SPECIAL DELIVERY(1976), cos; BREAKING AWAY(1979), cos; PRIVATE BENJAMIN(1980), cos; SEEMS LIKE OLD TIMES(1980), cos; LOOKER(1981), cos; BEST FRIENDS(1982), cos; DOCTOR DETROIT(1983), cos
1984
LONELY GUY, THE(1984), cos; WINDY CITY(1984), cos
Bobby Cox
LITTLE MEN(1935)
Brian Cox
HAMMERHEAD(1968), cos; MAN WHO HAD POWER OVER WOMEN, THE(1970, Brit.), cos; LOOT(1971, Brit.), cos; NICHOLAS AND ALEXANDRA(1971, Brit.); IN CELEBRATION(1975, Brit.)
Buddy Cox
COURAGE OF THE WEST(1937); RECKLESS RANGER(1937); ROAMING COWBOY, THE(1937); STUNT PILOT(1939)
Carol Cox
SECOND-HAND HEARTS(1981)
Cathy Cox
HELLER IN PINK TIGHTS(1960)
Clifford Cox
PRIZE OF ARMS, A(1962, Brit.); TWISTED NERVE(1969, Brit.)
David Cox
ALIAS JIMMY VALENTINE(1928), cos; BROADWAY MELODY, THE(1929), cos; HIS GLORIOUS NIGHT(1929), cos; MADAME X(1929), cos; WONDER OF WOMEN(1929), cos; FREE AND EASY(1930), cos; LOVE IN THE ROUGH(1930), cos; NAVY BLUES(1930), cos; SINS OF THE CHILDREN(1930), cos; STRICTLY UNCONVENTIONAL(1930), cos; THEY LEARNED ABOUT WOMEN(1930), cos; UNHOLY THREE, THE(1930), cos; WAY OUT WEST(1930), cos; WISE GIRLS(1930), cos; WOMAN RACKET, THE(1930), cos; RACKETY RAX(1932), cos; SOCIETY GIRL(1932), cos; TESS OF THE STORM COUNTRY(1932), cos; TRIAL OF VIVIENNE WARE, THE(1932), cos; WOMAN IN ROOM 13, THE(1932), cos; FACE IN THE SKY(1933), cos; SECOND HAND WIFE(1933), cos

Silents
OUR DANCING DAUGHTERS(1928), cos; WHERE EAST IS EAST(1929), cos

Derek Cox
PERFECT FRIDAY(1970, Brit.); WALKING STICK, THE(1970, Brit.)

Don Cox
SEED(1931); NIGHT IN HEAVEN, A(1983)
1984
WHERE THE BOYS ARE '84(1984)

Douglas Cox
Silents
PICTURE OF DORIAN GRAY, THE(1916, Brit.)
Misc. Silents
COAL KING, THE(1915, Brit.)

Enrique Cox
MIRAGE(1972, Peru)

Ernest Cox
Misc. Silents
WILL OF HER OWN, A(1915, Brit.)

Frank Cox
UP JUMPED A SWAGMAN(1965, Brit.); FAHRENHEIT 451(1966, Brit.)

Fred Cox
UP JUMPED A SWAGMAN(1965, Brit.); FAHRENHEIT 451(1966, Brit.)

George L. Cox
Misc. Silents
HELLION, THE(1919), d; TIGER LILY, THE(1919), d; BLUE MOON, THE(1920), d; DANGEROUS TALENT, THE(1920), d; GAMESTERS, THE(1920), d; HOUSE OF TOYS, THE(1920), d; LIFE IN THE ORANGE GROVES(1920), d; LIGHT WOMAN, A(1920), d; THEIR MUTUAL CHILD(1920), d; THIRTIETH PIECE OF SILVER, THE(1920), d; WEEK-END, THE(1920), d; PARISIAN SCANDAL, A(1921), d; PAYMENT GUARANTEED(1921), d; SUNSET JONES(1921), d

Hal Wilson Cox
FROM THE EARTH TO THE MOON(1958), art d

Ian Cox
HELL BOATS(1970, Brit.), tech adv

J. J. Cox
ARMS AND THE MAN(1932, Brit.), ph; LETTING IN THE SUNSHINE(1933, Brit.), ph

Jack Cox
BLACKMAIL(1929, Brit.), ph; LADY FROM THE SEA, THE(1929, Brit.), ph; ALMOST A HONEYMOON(1930, Brit.), ph; JUNO AND THE PAYCOCK(1930, Brit.), ph; MURDER(1930, Brit.), ph; GLAMOUR(1931, Brit.), ph; LAST COUPON, THE(1932, Brit.), ph; NUMBER SEVENTEEN(1932, Brit.), ph; OVER THE GARDEN WALL(1934, Brit.), ph; MIMI(1935, Brit.), ph; MUSIC HATH CHARMS(1935, Brit.), ph; REGAL CAVALCADE(1935, Brit.), ph; MAN WHO LIVED AGAIN, THE(1936, Brit.), ph; RED WAGON(1936), ph; DOCTOR SYN(1937, Brit.), ph; OKAY FOR SOUND(1937, Brit.), ph; SECOND BEST BED(1937, Brit.), ph; TWO WHO DARED(1937, Brit.), ph; WINDBAG THE SAILOR(1937, Brit.), ph; GIRL THIEF, THE(1938), ph; LADY VANISHES, THE(1938, Brit.), ph; MAN WITH 100 FACES, THE(1938, Brit.), ph; SHOW GOES ON, THE(1938, Brit.), ph; STRANGE BOARDERS(1938, Brit.), ph; TO THE VICTOR(1938, Brit.), ph; THEY CAME BY NIGHT(1940, Brit.), ph; BOMBSIGHT STOLEN(1941, Brit.), ph; GIRL MUST LIVE, A(1941, Brit.), ph; HI, GANG!(1941, Brit.), ph; I THANK YOU(1941, Brit.), ph; MAIL TRAIN(1941, Brit.), ph; NEUTRAL PORT(1941, Brit.), ph; BACK ROOM BOY(1942, Brit.), ph; ADVENTURE IN BLACKMAIL(1943, Brit.), ph; MILLIONS LIKE US(1943, Brit.), ph; WE DIVE AT DAWN(1943, Brit.), ph; 2,000 WOMEN(1944, Brit.), ph; MADONNA OF THE SEVEN MOONS(1945, Brit.), ph; THEY WERE SISTERS(1945, Brit.), ph; WICKED LADY, THE(1946, Brit.), ph; HOLIDAY CAMP(1947, Brit.), ph; MAGIC BOW, THE(1947, Brit.), ph; IDOL OF PARIS(1948, Brit.), ph; ONCE UPON A DREAM(1949, Brit.), ph; CURE FOR LOVE, THE(1950, Brit.), ph; MR. DRAKE'S DUCK(1951, Brit.), ph; TRAVELLER'S JOY(1951, Brit.), ph; BABES IN BAGDAD(1952), ph; DEVIL GIRL FROM MARS(1954, Brit.), ph; STAR OF MY NIGHT(1954, Brit.), ph; TALE OF THREE WOMEN, A(1954, Brit.), ph; THREE CORNERED FATE(1954, Brit.), ph; MAN OF THE MOMENT(1955, Brit.), ph; ONE GOOD TURN(1955, Brit.), ph; JUMPING FOR JOY(1956, Brit.), ph; JUST MY LUCK(1957, Brit.), ph; UP IN THE WORLD(1957, Brit.), ph; SQUARE PEG, THE(1958, Brit.), ph
1984
RARE BREED(1984), p
Silents
FARMER'S WIFE, THE(1928, Brit.), ph; MANXMAN, THE(1929, Brit.), ph

Jack J. Cox
MIDDLE WATCH, THE(1930, Brit.), ph

Jacqueline Cox
SECRET OF THE FOREST, THE(1955, Brit.)

Jewell Cox
Misc. Silents
FOOLISH LIVES(1922)

Jim Cox
UNTIL THEY SAIL(1957)

Joe Anthony Cox
DR. HECKYL AND MR. HYPE(1980); PENITENTIARY II(1982)

Joel Cox
FAREWELL, MY LOVELY(1975), ed; ENFORCER, THE(1976), ed; GAUNTLET, THE(1977), ed; EVERY WHICH WAY BUT LOOSE(1978), ed; BRONCO BILLY(1980), ed; HONKYTONK MAN(1982), ed; SUDDEN IMPACT(1983), ed
1984
TIGHTROPE(1984), ed

Joel E. Cox
DEATH VALLEY(1982), ed

John C. Cox
HEART'S DESIRE(1937, Brit.), ph

John Cox
RICH AND STRANGE(1932, Brit.), ph; CAR 99(1935); FRIENDS AND NEIGHBORS(1963, Brit.), set d

John Cox, Jr.
FOUR HOURS TO KILL(1935)

John J. Cox
LOVE HABIT, THE(1931, Brit.), ph; LOVE STORM, THE(1931, Brit.), ph; SKIN GAME, THE(1931, Brit.), ph; LUCKY GIRL(1932, Brit.), ph; HAWLEY'S OF HIGH STREET(1933, Brit.), ph; SLEEPLESS NIGHTS(1933, Brit.), ph; GREAT DEFENDER, THE(1934, Brit.), ph; YOU MADE ME LOVE YOU(1934, Brit.), ph; 18 MINUTES(1935,

Brit.), ph; INSPECTOR HORNLEIGH ON HOLIDAY(1939, Brit.), ph; GHOST TRAIN, THE(1941, Brit.), ph; ADVENTURES OF TARTU(1943, Brit.), ph
Silents
RING, THE(1927, Brit.), ph; CHAMPAGNE(1928, Brit.), ph

Jonathan Cox
WHAT'S GOOD FOR THE GOOSE(1969, Brit.)

Lambert Cox
ROMEO AND JULIET(1966, Brit.)

Lamont Cox
UNDER FIRE(1983)

Lili Cox
CHARLES AND LUCIE(1982, Fr.)

Linda Cox
PHANTOM OF THE PARADISE(1974)

Marilyn Cox
COOL WORLD, THE(1963)

Mary Agen Cox
SCREAMS OF A WINTER NIGHT(1979)

Mary Cox
1984
RAW COURAGE(1984), w

Merle Cox
SNOW WHITE AND THE SEVEN DWARFS(1937), anim

Michael Cox
BLOODTHIRSTY BUTCHERS(1970)

Michael Graham Cox
WHERE THE BULLETS FLY(1966, Brit.); WOMEN IN LOVE(1969, Brit.); OPTIMISTS, THE(1973, Brit.)
1984
LITTLE DRUMMER GIRL, THE(1984)

Mitchell Cox
STRAIT-JACKET(1964)

Monty Cox
1984
ICE PIRATES, THE(1984)

Morgan Cox
BILL CRACKS DOWN(1937), w; DESPERATE CARGO(1941), w; ROAD AGENT(1941), w; RAIDERS OF SAN JOAQUIN(1943), w

Morgan B. Cox
DRUMS OF FU MANCHU(1943), w; FRONTIER BADMEN(1943), w; JUNGLE CAPTIVE(1945), p; DANGER WOMAN(1946), p

Myron Cox
WE'RE IN THE MONEY(1935)

Nigel Cox
HALLUCINATION GENERATION(1966), p

Patricia Cox
DON QUIXOTE(1973, Aus.)

Paul Cox
GIRL GRABBERS, THE(1968); ILLUMINATIONS(1976, Aus.), d&w; INSIDE LOOKING OUT(1977, Aus.), p&d, w, ph, ed; LONELY HEARTS(1983, Aus.), d, w
1984
MAN OF FLOWERS(1984, Aus.), p, d, w

Peter Cox
DEVIL'S PLAYGROUND, THE(1976, Aus.); MONKEY GRIP(1983, Aus.)
1984
POLICE ACADEMY(1984)

Phyllis Cox
I PASSED FOR WHITE(1960)

Rich Cox
YELLOW SUBMARINE(1958, Brit.), animation

Richard Cox
BETWEEN THE LINES(1977); CRUISING(1980); KING OF THE MOUNTAIN(1981)
1984
OASIS, THE(1984)

Roger Cox
SUNSTRUCK(1973, Aus.)

Ronnie Cox
HUGO THE HIPPO(1976, Hung./U.S.)

Ronny Cox
DELIVERANCE(1972); HAPPINESS CAGE, THE(1972); BOUND FOR GLORY(1976); CAR, THE(1977); GRAY LADY DOWN(1978); HARPER VALLEY, P.T.A.(1978); ONION FIELD, THE(1979); TAPS(1981); BEAST WITHIN, THE(1982); SOME KIND OF HERO(1982)
1984
BEVERLY HILLS COP(1984); RAW COURAGE(1984), a, p, w
Misc. Talkies
ONE LAST RIDE(1980)

Ruby Cox
Misc. Silents
GIRL OF LOST LAKE, THE(1916)

Rusty Cox
WIND AND THE LION, THE(1975)

Ruth Cox
ATTIC, THE(1979); SWAP MEET(1979)

Sandy Cox
PUNISHMENT PARK(1971)

Sheila Cox
OH! WHAT A LOVELY WAR(1969, Brit.)

Terence Cox
Misc. Talkies
TRUCKIN' BUDDY McCOY(1983)

Terry Cox
SEED(1931)

Tony Cox
JEKYLL AND HYDE...TOGETHER AGAIN(1982); RETURN OF THE JEDI(1983)

Valerie Cox
WIRE SERVICE(1942)

Victor Cox
RECKLESS RANGER(1937); SPRINGTIME IN THE ROCKIES(1937); IN OLD MONTEREY(1939); MEET ME IN ST. LOUIS(1944); LOST TRAIL, THE(1945); LAND OF THE LAWLESS(1947); BOY FROM INDIANA(1950); COW TOWN(1950)

Vincent Cox
WILD SEASON(1968, South Africa), ph; CREATURES THE WORLD FORGOT(1971, Brit.), ph; KILLER FORCE(1975, Switz./Ireland), ph; DEMON, THE(1981, S. Africa), ph

Vincent G. Cox
MY WAY(1974, South Africa), ph

Virginia Cox
BROTHERS IN THE SADDLE(1949)

Vivian A. Cox
TREAD SOFTLY(1952, Brit.), p; DETECTIVE, THE(1954, Qit.), p; PRISONER, THE(1955, Brit.), p; TEARS FOR SIMON(1957, Brit.), p; TRIPLE DECEPTION(1957, Brit.), p; BACHELOR OF HEARTS(1958, Brit.), p; DEADLY RECORD(1959, Brit.), p, w; WATCH YOUR STERN(1961, Brit.), w; SWINGIN' MAIDEN, THE(1963, Brit.), w

Vivian Cox
VERY EDGE, THE(1963, Brit.), w

Wally Cox
STATE FAIR(1962); SPENCER'S MOUNTAIN(1963); FATE IS THE HUNTER(1964); BEDFORD INCIDENT, THE(1965, Brit.); MORITURI(1965); YELLOW ROLLS-ROYCE, THE(1965, Brit.); GUIDE FOR THE MARRIED MAN, A(1967); ONE AND ONLY GENUINE ORIGINAL FAMILY BAND, THE(1968); BOATNIKS, THE(1970); COCK-EYED COWBOYS OF CALICO COUNTY, THE(1970); UP YOUR TEDDY BEAR(1970); BAREFOOT EXECUTIVE, THE(1971)

Wesley Cox
HELL ON WHEELS(1967), w

William R. Cox
VEILS OF BAGDAD, THE(1953), w; TANGANYIKA(1954), w; NATCHEZ TRACE(1960), w

Wilma Cox
SHE LEARNED ABOUT SAILORS(1934); PICK A STAR(1937)

Amanda Coxall
PERIL FOR THE GUY(1956, Brit.)

George Harmon Coxe
MURDER WITH PICTURES(1936), w; WOMEN ARE TROUBLE(1936), w; HERE'S FLASH CASEY(1937), w; ARSENE LUPIN RETURNS(1938), w; HIDDEN EYE, THE(1945), w

Amanda Coxell
SALVAGE GANG, THE(1958, Brit.)

Ed Coxen
KING OF THE ARENA(1933); GUN JUSTICE(1934); SMOKING GUNS(1934); WHEELS OF DESTINY(1934); GHOST RIDER, THE(1935); RIDERS OF THE DAWN(1937); CATTLE RAIDERS(1938); SOUTH OF ARIZONA(1938); DOWN THE WYOMING TRAIL(1939); TEXAS STAMPEDE(1939); ONE MILLION B.C.(1940); KING OF DODGE CITY(1941)
Silents
QUICKSANDS(1918)
Misc. Silents
MADAM WHO?(1917); MAN'S MAN, A(1917); WHO SHALL TAKE MY LIFE?(1918)

Edward Coxen
SPOILERS, THE(1930); TRAIL DRIVE, THE(1934); CODE OF THE RANGE(1937); THUNDER TRAIL(1937)
Silents
CARMEN OF THE KLONDIKE(1918); GO WEST, YOUNG MAN(1919); IN OLD KENTUCKY(1920); OUR HOSPITALITY(1923); SCARAMOUCHE(1923); TEMPORARY MARRIAGE(1923); SINGER JIM MCKEE(1924)
Misc. Silents
VOICE OF LOVE, THE(1916); WOMAN'S DARING, A(1916); BEWARE OF STRANGERS(1918); CRIME OF THE HOUR(1918); HONOR'S CROSS(1918); MOTHER, I NEED YOU(1918); WITHIN THE CUP(1918); MORE DEADLY THAN THE MALE(1919); HONOR BOUND(1920); MOUNTAIN MADNESS(1920); NINE POINTS OF THE LAW(1922); STRANGER OF THE HILLS, THE(1922); VEILED WOMAN, THE(1922); FLYING DUTCHMAN, THE(1923); FOOLISH MOTHERS(1923); FLASHING SPURS(1924)

Elizabeth Coxhead
CRY FROM THE STREET, A(1959, Brit.), w

Ed Coxon
WEST OF RAINBOW'S END(1938)

Charles Coy
GUN FIGHT(1961)

Johnnie Coy
BRING ON THE GIRLS(1945)

Johnny Coy
ON STAGE EVERYBODY(1945); THAT'S THE SPIRIT(1945); EARL CARROLL SKETCHBOOK(1946); LADIES' MAN(1947); VARIETY GIRL(1947); TOP BANANA(1954)

Walter Coy
LOVE LETTERS OF A STAR(1936); BARRICADE(1950); COLT .45(1950); SADDLE TRAMP(1950); UNDER MEXICALI STARS(1950); FBI GIRL(1951); FLAT TOP(1952); LUSTY MEN, THE(1952); SO BIG(1953); SIGN OF THE PAGAN(1954); THEM!(1954); CULT OF THE COBRA(1955); RUNNING WILD(1955); ON THE THRESHOLD OF SPACE(1956); PILLARS OF THE SKY(1956); SEARCHERS, THE(1956); YOUNG GUNS, THE(1956); JOHNNY TREMAIN(1957); JUVENILE JUNGLE(1958); GUNFIGHT AT DODGE CITY, THE(1959); GUNMEN FROM LAREDO(1959); NORTH BY NORTHWEST(1959); TRAP, THE(1959); WARLOCK(1959); CASH McCALL(1960); FIVE GUNS TO TOMBSTONE(1961); I EAT YOUR SKIN(1971)

Ellen Coyle
GHOST OF HIDDEN VALLEY(1946), w; OVERLAND RIDERS(1946), w

Jack Coyle
ONE FRIGHTENED NIGHT(1935), spec eff

James J. Coyle
HOUSE ON 92ND STREET, THE(1945)

John Coyle
HE SNOOPS TO CONQUER(1944, Brit.); GEORGE IN CIVVY STREET(1946, Brit.); THIS MAN IS MINE(1946 Brit.); SAN DEMETRIO, LONDON(1947, Brit.)

John T. Coyle
HIT PARADE, THE(1937), spec eff; DESPERATE CARGO(1941), p, w; GREAT COMMANDMENT, THE(1941), p; DUKE OF THE NAVY(1942), p; MIRACLE KID(1942), p, w; SMART GUY(1943), p; DAY OF TRIUMPH(1954), d

Richard Coyler
OUT OF IT(1969)

Bill Coyne
1984
SUBURBIA(1984)

Jeanne Coyne
SINGIN' IN THE RAIN(1952); KISS ME KATE(1953)

Kathleen Coyne
1984
SAM'S SON(1984)

Maureen Coyne
RIGHT STUFF, THE(1983)

Nancy Marlowe Coyne
CHEAP DETECTIVE, THE(1978)

Peter Coyote
DIE LAUGHING(1980); TELL ME A RIDDLE(1980); SOUTHERN COMFORT(1981); ENDANGERED SPECIES(1982); E.T. THE EXTRA-TERRESTRIAL(1982); OUT(1982); CROSS CREEK(1983); TIMERIDER(1983)
1984
HEARTBREAKERS(1984); SLAYGROUND(1984, Brit.); STRANGERS KISS(1984)

Percy Coyte
STRAWBERRY ROAN(1945, Brit.); GREEN FINGERS(1947)

James Cozart
WHY RUSSIANS ARE REVOLTING(1970), ph

Edmund Cozens
EYES OF FATE(1933, Brit.)

Peter Cozens
UNPUBLISHED STORY(1942, Brit.); UNCENSORED(1944, Brit.)

Bernie Cozier
CITY BENEATH THE SEA(1953)

Arthur Cozine
Silents
PRICE FOR FOLLY, A(1915); LIGHTS OF NEW YORK, THE(1916); NIGHT OUT, A(1916)

James Gould Cozzens
DR. BULL(1933), w; BY LOVE POSSESSED(1961), w

Mimi Cozzens
SPRING BREAK(1983)

Luigi Cozzi
FOUR FLIES ON GREY VELVET(1972, Ital.), w; TAKE ALL OF ME(1978, Ital.), d, w

William Cozzo
BRUTE FORCE(1947)

Michele Cozzoli
GUNS OF THE BLACK WITCH(1961, Fr./Ital.), m; PIRATE AND THE SLAVE GIRL, THE(1961, Fr./Ital.), m

Bill Crabb
1984
TANK(1984)

Brian Crabb
SPRING FEVER(1983, Can.)

Buster Crabbe
KING OF THE JUNGLE(1933); MAN OF THE FOREST(1933); SWEETHEART OF SIGMA CHI(1933); TARZAN THE FEARLESS(1933); TO THE LAST MAN(1933); BADGE OF HONOR(1934); BILLY THE KID WANTED(1934); BILLY THE KID'S ROUNDUP(1941); JUNGLE MAN(1941); BILLY THE KID TRAPPED(1942); JUNGLE SIREN(1942); LAW AND ORDER(1942); MYSTERIOUS RIDER, THE(1942); QUEEN OF BROADWAY(1942); SHERIFF OF SAGE VALLEY(1942); CATTLE STAMPEDE(1943); KID RIDES AGAIN, THE(1943); WESTERN CYCLONE(1943); BLAZING FRONTIER(1944); CONTENDER, THE(1944); DEVIL RIDERS(1944); DRIFTER, THE(1944); FRONTIER OUTLAWS(1944); FUZZY SETTLES DOWN(1944); NABONGA(1944); RUSTLER'S HIDEOUT(1944); THUNDERING GUN SLINGERS(1944); VALLEY OF VENGEANCE(1944); WILD HORSE PHANTOM(1944); BORDER BADMEN(1945); FIGHTING BILL CARSON(1945); HIS BROTHER'S GHOST(1945); LIGHTNING RAIDERS(1945); PRAIRIE RUSTLERS(1945); SHADOWS OF DEATH(1945); STAGECOACH OUTLAWS(1945); GENTLEMEN WITH GUNS(1946); GHOST OF HIDDEN VALLEY(1946); OUTLAW OF THE PLAINS(1946); OVERLAND RIDERS(1946); PRAIRIE BADMEN(1946); SWAMP FIRE(1946); TERRORS ON HORSEBACK(1946); LAST OF THE REDMEN(1947); CAGED FURY(1948); CAPTIVE GIRL(1950); GUN BROTHERS(1956); LAWLESS EIGHTIES, THE(1957); BADMAN'S COUNTRY(1958); ARIZONA RAIDERS(1965); BOUNTY KILLERS, THE(1965); IT FELL FROM THE SKY(1980); COMEBACK TRAIL, THE(1982)

Byron L. Crabbe
KING KONG(1933), spec eff; SON OF KONG(1933), spec eff

James Crabbe
JUST WILLIAM'S LUCK(1948, Brit.); WILLIAM COMES TO TOWN(1948, Brit.); GAY ADVENTURE, THE(1953, Brit.); PROPER TIME, THE(1959), ph

Kerry Crabbe
MEMOIRS OF A SURVIVOR(1981, Brit.), w

Larry ["Buster"] Crabbe
ISLAND OF LOST SOULS(1933); SEARCH FOR BEAUTY(1934); SHE HAD TO CHOOSE(1934); THUNDERING HERD, THE(1934); WE'RE RICH AGAIN(1934); YOU'RE TELLING ME(1934); WANDERER OF THE WASTELAND(1935); DESERT GOLD(1936); DRIFT FENCE(1936); FLASH GORDON(1936); LADY BE CAREFUL(1936); NEVADA(1936); ROSE BOWL(1936); FORLORN RIVER(1937); KING OF GAMBLERS(1937); MURDER GOES TO COLLEGE(1937); SOPHIE LANG GOES WEST(1937); THRILL OF A LIFETIME(1937); HUNTED MEN(1938); ILLEGAL TRAFFIC(1938); TIP-OFF GIRLS(1938); COLORADO SUNSET(1939); MILLION DOLLAR LEGS(1939); UNMARRIED(1939); SAILOR'S LADY(1940); WILDCAT(1942)

Larry Crabbe
HOLD'EM YALE(1935); ARIZONA MAHONEY(1936); ARIZONA RAIDERS, THE(1936); DAUGHTER OF SHANGHAI(1937); CALL A MESSENGER(1939)

James Crabe
LIKE FATHER LIKE SON(1961), ph; HONKERS, THE(1972), ph; W. W. AND THE DIXIE DANCEKINGS(1975), ph; ROCKY(1976), ph; SEXTETTE(1978), ph; THANK GOD IT'S FRIDAY(1978), ph; CHINA SYNDROME, THE(1979), ph; PLAYERS(1979), ph; FORMULA, THE(1980), ph; HOW TO BEAT THE HIGH COST OF LIVING(1980), ph; NIGHT SHIFT(1982), ph
1984
KARATE KID, THE(1984), ph

James A. Crabe
YOUNG SINNER, THE(1965), ph; ZIGZAG(1970), ph; BALTIMORE BULLET, THE(1980), ph

Jim Crabe
SAVE THE TIGER(1973), ph; RHINOCEROS(1974), ph; ENTERTAINER, THE(1975), ph

Arthur Crabtree
CHARLEY'S(BIG-HEARTED) AUNT*1/2 (1940), ph; OUT OF THE BLUE(1931, Brit.), ph; MAID OF THE MOUNTAINS, THE(1932, Brit.), ph; EVERYBODY DANCE(1936, Brit.), ph; FIRST OFFENCE(1936, Brit.), ph; POT LUCK(1936, Brit.), ph; OH, MR. PORTER!(1937, Brit.), ph; SILENT BARRIERS(1937, Brit.), ph; WHERE THERE'S A WILL(1937, Brit.), ph; ALF'S BUTTON AFLOAT(1938, Brit.), ph; BANK HOLIDAY(1938, Brit.), ph; CONVICT 99(1938, Brit.), ph; HEY! HEY! U.S.A.(1938, Brit.), ph; OLD BONES OF THE RIVER(1938, Brit.), ph; SEZ O'REILLY TO MACNAB(1938, Brit.), ph; FROZEN LIMITS, THE(1939, Brit.), ph; FOR FREEDOM(1940, Brit.), ph; GASBAGS(1940, Brit.), ph; I THANK YOU(1941, Brit.), ph; MAIL TRAIN(1941, Brit.), ph; NEUTRAL PORT(1941, Brit.), ph; ONCE A CROOK(1941, Brit.), ph; SOUTH AMERICAN GEORGE(1941, Brit.), ph; KING ARTHUR WAS A GENTLEMAN(1942, Brit.), ph; MUCH TOO SHY(1942, Brit.), ph; REMARKABLE MR. KIPPS(1942, Brit.), ph; MAN IN GREY, THE(1943, Brit.), ph; UNCENSORED(1944, Brit.), d; MADONNA OF THE SEVEN MOONS(1945, Brit.), ph; RANDOLPH FAMILY, THE(1945, Brit.), ph; THEY WERE SISTERS(1945, Brit.), d; CARAVAN(1946, Brit.), d; DEAR MURDERER(1947, Brit.), d; CALENDAR, THE(1948, Brit.), d; MAN OF EVIL(1948, Brit.), ph; DON'T EVER LEAVE ME(1949, Brit.), d; WATERLOO ROAD(1949, Brit.), ph; LILLI MARLENE(1951, Brit.), d; HOLIDAY WEEK(1952, Brit.), d; WEDDING OF LILLI MARLENE, THE(1953, Brit.), d; FIGHTING WILDCATS, THE(1957, Brit.), d; DEATH OVER MY SHOULDER(1958, Brit.), d; FIEND WITHOUT A FACE(1958), d; STRANGE CASE OF DR. MANNING, THE(1958, Brit.), d; HORRORS OF THE BLACK MUSEUM(1959, U.S./Brit.), d

Brian Crabtree
NO BLADE OF GRASS(1970, Brit.)

Buddy Crabtree
LEGEND OF BOGGY CREEK, THE(1973)

Donald Crabtree
HUSTLER, THE(1961); MAN CALLED ADAM, A(1966)

Jeff Crabtree
LEGEND OF BOGGY CREEK, THE(1973)

Michael Crabtree
TENDER MERCIES(1982)
1984
NIGHT PATROL(1984)

Paul Crabtree
COUNTRY BOY(1966), a, w; JOHNNY TIGER(1966), w; TRACK OF THUNDER(1967)

Toni Crabtree
GREATEST, THE(1977, U.S./Brit.); EYES OF A STRANGER(1980)

Leo Cracknell
RANGLE RIVER(1939, Aus.)

Leonard Cracknell
TERRORNAUTS, THE(1967, Brit.)

Ruth Cracknell
SMILEY GETS A GUN(1959, Brit.); SINGER AND THE DANCER, THE(1977, Aus.); NIGHT OF THE PROWLER, THE(1979, Aus.); CHANT OF JIMMIE BLACKSMITH, THE(1980, Aus.)

Andrew Craddock
JOHNNY RENO(1966), w; FORT UTAH(1967), w; RED TOMAHAWK(1967), w; ARIZONA BUSHWHACKERS(1968), w

John Craddock
GOSPEL ROAD, THE(1973), ed

Teresa Craddock
OCTOPUSSY(1983, Brit.)

Mark Crader
PUMPKIN EATER, THE(1964, Brit.)

Ian Crafford
BEYOND THE REEF(1981), ed; NEVER SAY NEVER AGAIN(1983), ed

Charles Craft
RICH PEOPLE(1929), ed; BIG SHOT, THE(1931), ed; TIP-OFF, THE(1931), ed; LADY WITH A PAST(1932), ed; PANAMA FLO(1932), ed; WESTWARD PASSAGE(1932), ed; DOWN TO THE SEA(1936), ed; GENTLEMAN FROM LOUISIANA(1936), ed; ADVENTURE'S END(1937), ed; CALIFORNIA STRAIGHT AHEAD(1937), ed; COURAGE OF THE WEST(1937), ed; I COVER THE WAR(1937), ed; IDOL OF THE CROWDS(1937), ed; SECRET VALLEY(1937), ed; SINGING OUTLAW(1937), ed; AIR DEVILS(1938), ed; LAST STAND, THE(1938), ed; OUTLAW EXPRESS(1938), ed; SPY RING, THE(1938), ed; STATE POLICE(1938), ed; WESTERN TRAILS(1938), ed; BARNYARD FOLLIES(1940), ed; FRIENDLY NEIGHBORS(1940), ed; BAD MAN OF DEADWOOD(1941), ed; GAUCHOS OF EL DORADO(1941), ed; IN OLD CHEYENNE(1941), ed; KANSAS CYCLONE(1941), ed; MAN BETRAYED, A(1941), ed; MOUNTAIN MOONLIGHT(1941), ed; ROBIN HOOD OF THE PECOS(1941), ed; ROOKIES ON PARADE(1941), ed; TUXEDO JUNCTION(1941), ed; JOAN OF OZARK(1942), ed; LONDON BLACKOUT MURDERS(1942), ed; REMEMBER PEARL HARBOR(1942), ed; SHEPHERD OF THE OZARKS(1942), ed; TRAITOR WITHIN, THE(1942), ed; BEYOND THE LAST FRONTIER(1943), ed; OVERLAND MAIL ROBBERY(1943), ed; PURPLE V, THE(1943), ed; RIDERS OF THE RIO GRANDE(1943), ed; SANTA FE SCOUTS(1943), ed; WAGON TRACKS WEST(1943), ed; BENEATH WESTERN SKIES(1944), ed; CHEYENNE WILDCAT(1944), ed; MARSHAL OF RENO(1944), ed; OUTLAWS OF SANTA FE(1944), ed; PRIDE OF THE PLAINS(1944), ed; SILVER CITY KID(1944), ed; VIGILANTES OF DODGE CITY(1944), ed; CHEROKEE FLASH, THE(1945), ed; CORPUS CHRISTI BANDITS(1945), ed; DON'T FENCE ME IN(1945), ed; GREAT STAGECOACH ROBBERY(1945), ed; LONE TEXAS RANGER(1945), ed;

MARSHAL OF LAREDO(1945), ed; PHANTOM OF THE PLAINS(1945), ed; TOPEKA TERROR, THE(1945), ed; ALIAS BILLY THE KID(1946), ed; CONQUEST OF CHEYENNE(1946), ed; HOME ON THE RANGE(1946), ed; OUT CALIFORNIA WAY(1946), ed; SUN VALLEY CYCLONE(1946), ed; HIGH CONQUEST(1947), ed; HOMESTEADERS OF PARADISE VALLEY(1947), ed; LAST FRONTIER UPRISING(1947), ed; TRAIL TO SAN ANTONE(1947), ed; SIXTEEN FATHOMS DEEP(1948), ed; ALASKA PATROL(1949), ed; YOUNG DANIEL BOONE(1950), ed; UNDERWATER WARRIOR(1958), ed; FLIPPER'S NEW ADVENTURE(1964), ed
Silents
GATE CRASHER, THE(1928), ed; KID'S CLEVER, THE(1929), ed

Gene Craft
DEVIL'S HAND, THE(1961)

Gere Craft
FEAR STRIKES OUT(1957)

Robert Craft
Misc. Silents
WHITE RIDER, THE(1920)

W. James Craft
Silents
CLOWN, THE(1927), d

William Craft
THEY ALL LAUGHED(1981)

William J. Craft
COHENS AND KELLYS IN ATLANTIC CITY, THE(1929), d; RUNAROUND, THE(1931), d
Silents
ANOTHER MAN'S BOOTS(1922), d; FALSE BRANDS(1922), d, w; WOLF PACK(1922), d&w; PRIDE OF SUNSHINE ALLEY(1924), d; KING OF THE SADDLE(1926), d; POWER OF THE WEAK, THE(1926), d
Misc. Silents
WHITE RIDER, THE(1920), d; HEADIN' WEST(1922), d; SAVED BY RADIO(1922), d; FLASH, THE(1923), d; POWER DIVINE, THE(1923), d; SMILIN' ON(1923), d; WAY OF THE TRANSGRESSOR, THE(1923), d; BIG TIMBER(1924), d; THAT MAN JACK!(1925), d; GALLOPING COWBOY, THE(1926), d; ARIZONA WHIRLWIND, THE(1927), d; WRECK, THE(1927), d; HOW TO HANDLE WOMEN(1928), d

William James Craft
SKINNER STEPS OUT(1929), d; COHENS AND KELLYS IN SCOTLAND, THE(1930), d; CZAR OF BRODWAY, THE(1930), d; DAMES AHOY(1930), d; EMBARRASSING MOMENTS(1930), d; LITTLE ACCIDENT(1930), d; ONE HYSTERICAL NIGHT(1930), d; SEE AMERICA THIRST(1930), d; HONEYMOON LANE(1931), d
Silents
PAINTING THE TOWN(1927), d; GATE CRASHER, THE(1928), d, w; KID'S CLEVER, THE(1929), d
Misc. Silents
LOVE'S BATTLE(1920), d; BATTLING MASON(1924), d; RECKLESS SPEED(1924), d; SOUTH OF THE EQUATOR(1924), d; BLOODHOUND, THE(1925), d; GALLOPING VENGENCE(1925), d; RANGE TERROR, THE(1925), d; BIRDS OF PREY(1927), d; HERO FOR A NIGHT, A(1927), d; POOR GIRLS(1927), d; HOT HEELS(1928), d

Richard Crafter
SATAN'S SLAVE(1976, Brit.), p; TERROR(1979, Brit.), p

Chuck Crafts
PSYCHO II(1983), makeup

Rita Crafts
HERO AT LARGE(1980)
Misc. Talkies
GHOSTS THAT STILL WALK(1977)

Bill Crago
ADVENTURES IN IRAQ(1943); AIR FORCE(1943); MURDER ON THE WATERFRONT(1943); TRUCK BUSTERS(1943)

Richard Cragun
TURNING POINT, THE(1977)

Joseph Crahan
JUDGMENT AT NUREMBERG(1961)

Alan Craig
GOLD(1974, Brit.)

Alec Craig
MUTINY ON THE BOUNTY(1935); MARY OF SCOTLAND(1936); WINTERSET(1936); CHINA PASSAGE(1937); CRASHING HOLLYWOOD(1937); HIDEAWAY(1937); MEET THE MISSUS(1937); SUPER SLEUTH(1937); THAT GIRL FROM PARIS(1937); THERE GOES MY GIRL(1937); WISE GIRL(1937); WOMAN I LOVE, THE(1937); DOUBLE DANGER(1938); SHE'S GOT EVERYTHING(1938); VIVACIOUS LADY(1938); CONFESSIONS OF A NAZI SPY(1939); LET US LIVE(1939); LONE WOLF SPY HUNT, THE(1939); THEY MADE HER A SPY(1939); ABE LINCOLN IN ILLINOIS(1940); EARL OF CHICAGO, THE(1940); GOLDEN GLOVES(1940); PHANTOM RAIDERS(1940); QUEEN OF THE MOB(1940); SEA HAWK, THE(1940); STRANGER ON THE THIRD FLOOR(1940); THREE CHEERS FOR THE IRISH(1940); TOM BROWN'S SCHOOL DAYS(1940); BARNACLE BILL(1941); DATE WITH THE FALCON, A(1941); DEVIL AND DANIEL WEBSTER, THE(1941); MR. AND MRS. SMITH(1941); SHINING VICTORY(1941); SUSPICION(1941); THAT HAMILTON WOMAN(1941); THREE GIRLS ABOUT TOWN(1941); LIFE BEGINS AT 8:30(1942); LOVES OF EDGAR ALLAN POE, THE(1942); MAD MARTINDALES, THE(1942); MRS. MINIVER(1942); NIGHT BEFORE THE DIVORCE, THE(1942); ORCHESTRA WIVES(1942); ROXIE HART(1942); TENNESSEE JOHNSON(1942); THIS ABOVE ALL(1942); TO BE OR NOT TO BE(1942); UNDYING MONSTER, THE(1942); WILDCAT(1942); WRECKING CREW(1942); ACTION IN THE NORTH ATLANTIC(1943); APPOINTMENT IN BERLIN(1943); CALLING DR. DEATH(1943); FOREVER AND A DAY(1943); HOLY MATRIMONY(1943); JOHNNY COME LATELY(1943); LASSIE, COME HOME(1943); NORTHERN PURSUIT(1943); CAREER GIRL(1944); DANGEROUS PASSAGE(1944); GASLIGHT(1944); JANE EYRE(1944); JUNGLE WOMAN(1944); NATIONAL VELVET(1944); SHERLOCK HOLMES AND THE SPIDER WOMAN(1944); WHITE CLIFFS OF DOVER, THE(1944); HOUSE OF FEAR, THE(1945); KITTY(1945); LOVE LETTERS(1945); TONIGHT AND EVERY NIGHT(1945); TREE GROWS IN BROOKLYN, A(1945); WOMAN IN THE WINDOW, THE(1945); GIRL ON THE SPOT(1946); THREE STRANGERS(1946)

Alex Craig
DISPATCH FROM REUTERS, A(1940); GHOST SHIP, THE(1943)

Alison Craig
STAGE DOOR(1937)

Anthony Scott Craig
FEMALE RESPONSE, THE(1972)
Bette Craig
JUMP(1971)
Bill Craig
WHAT AM I BID?(1967)
Blanche Craig
DARKENED ROOMS(1929); DYNAMITE(1930); I LIVE MY LIFE(1935); PETER IBBETSON(1935); DESIRE(1936)
Silents
DAWN OF A TOMORROW, THE(1915); RISE OF JENNIE CUSHING, THE(1917); I WANT TO FORGET(1918); LOYAL LIVES(1923); MODERN MARRIAGE(1923); POLICE PATROL, THE(1925)
Misc. Silents
MAGIC CUP, THE(1921); THEN CAME THE WOMAN(1926)
Bob Craig
1984
NINJA III-THE DOMINATION(1984)
Bradford Craig
DOBERMAN GANG, THE(1972), m
Carl Craig
TOM(1973)
Carolyn Craig
GIANT(1956); FURY AT SHOWDOWN(1957); GUNSIGHT RIDGE(1957); PORTLAND EXPOSE(1957); APACHE TERRITORY(1958); HOUSE ON HAUNTED HILL(1958); STUDS LONIGAN(1960)
Catherine Craig
DOOMED TO DIE(1940); LAS VEGAS NIGHTS(1941); LOUISIANA PURCHASE(1941); NOTHING BUT THE TRUTH(1941); ONE NIGHT IN LISBON(1941); WEST POINT WIDOW(1941); PARACHUTE NURSE(1942); YOU WERE NEVER LOVELIER(1942); SPY TRAIN(1943); HERE COME THE WAVES(1944); LADY IN THE DARK(1944); STORY OF DR. WASSELL, THE(1944); DUFFY'S TAVERN(1945); LOVE LETTERS(1945); MONSIEUR BEAUCAIRE(1946); O.S.S.(1946); PERFECT MARRIAGE, THE(1946); STRANGE LOVE OF MARTHA IVERS, THE(1946); PRETENDER, THE(1947); SEVEN WERE SAVED(1947); VARIETY GIRL(1947); ALBUQUERQUE(1948); APPOINTMENT WITH MURDER(1948); EL PASO(1949); NO MAN OF HER OWN(1950)
Misc. Silents
HELLHOUNDS OF THE WEST(1922)
Charles Craig
MELBA(1953, Brit.); NIGHT OF THE LIVING DEAD(1968)
Silents
COMMON LAW, THE(1916); SERPENT, THE(1916); POOR LITTLE RICH GIRL, A(1917); FLAPPER, THE(1920); NOTHING BUT THE TRUTH(1920); AT THE STAGE DOOR(1921); BRIDE FOR A NIGHT, A(1923); ONE MILLION IN JEWELS(1923); POLICE PATROL, THE(1925)
Misc. Silents
LAST DOOR, THE(1921); BLONDE VAMPIRE, THE(1922); MADNESS OF LOVE, THE(1922)
Colin Craig
JACK THE RIPPER(1959, Brit.), w
Silents
OLD CURIOSITY SHOP, THE(1921, Brit.)
Misc. Silents
MARY-FIND-THE-GOLD(1921, Brit.)
Dan Craig
1,000 SHAPES OF A FEMALE(1963)
Dave Craig
FARMER, THE(1977)
David Craig
LILITH(1964); SQUEEZE, THE(1977, Brit.), w
Davina Craig
I LIVED WITH YOU(1933, Brit.); ARE YOU A MASON?(1934, Brit.); TANGLED EVIDENCE(1934, Brit.); WIDOW'S MIGHT(1934, Brit.); ANNIE, LEAVE THE ROOM(1935, Brit.); PRIVATE SECRETARY, THE(1935, Brit.); CROWN VS STEVENS(1936); LOVE UP THE POLE(1936, Brit.); WHERE THERE'S A WILL(1936, Brit.); GIRLS IN THE STREET(1937, Brit.); GIRL IN THE STREET(1938, Brit.); HIDEOUT IN THE ALPS(1938, Brit.); SOUTH RIDING(1938, Brit.); DEMON BARBER OF FLEET STREET, THE(1939, Brit.); HOOTS MON!(1939, Brit.); SUICIDE LEGION(1940, Brit.); TORSO MURDER MYSTERY, THE(1940, Brit.); FARMER'S WIFE, THE(1941, Brit.); I'LL TURN TO YOU(1946, Brit.)
Dean Craig
HILLS RUN RED, THE(1967, Ital.), w
Dean Craig [Mario Pierotti]
MATCHLESS(1967, Ital.), w; NAVAJO JOE(1967, Ital./Span.), w
Diane Craig
NED KELLY(1970, Brit.); MANGO TREE, THE(1981, Aus.)
Misc. Talkies
NEWMAN SHAME, THE(1977); ROSES BLOOM TWICE(1977)
Don Craig
VICE GIRLS, LTD.(1964)
Donald Craig
FRANCES(1982)
E. Gordon Craig
WICKHAM MYSTERY, THE(1931, Brit.), p; COLLISION(1932, Brit.), p
Ed Craig
OPERATION DAMES(1959)
Edith Craig
HARMONY LANE(1935); THREE MEN ON A HORSE(1936); GO CHASE YOURSELF(1938); LETTER OF INTRODUCTION(1938); SMASHING THE RACKETS(1938)
Silents
GOD AND THE MAN(1918, Brit.); IMPOSSIBLE WOMAN, THE(1919, Brit.); GOD IN THE GARDEN, THE(1921, Brit.); FIRES OF FATE(1923, Brit.)
Misc. Silents
DESERT SHEIK, THE(1924)
Faye Craig
JUNGLE STREET GIRLS(1963, Brit.)

Garret Craig
HE WALKED BY NIGHT(1948)
Garrett Craig
AFFECTIONATELY YOURS(1941); DIVE BOMBER(1941); MILLION DOLLAR BABY(1941); SHOT IN THE DARK, THE(1941); WHITE HEAT(1949); HEAVEN CAN WAIT(1978)
George Craig
SHAME, SHAME, EVERYBODY KNOWS HER NAME(1969), m; LITTLE MOTHER(1973, U.S./Yugo./Ger.), m; WOMEN IN CELL BLOCK 7(1977, Ital./U.S.), m
Gordan Craig
Silents
SOMME, THE(1927, Brit.), p
Gordon Craig
BLOCKADE(1928, Brit.), p; INQUEST(1931, Brit.), p; JEALOUSY(1931, Brit.), p; OTHER WOMAN, THE(1931, Brit.), p; WINDJAMMER, THE(1931, Brit.), p; CALLBOX MYSTERY, THE(1932, Brit.), p; THREADS(1932, Brit.), p; CRUCIFIX, THE(1934, Brit.), p; HAMMER THE TOFF(1952, Brit.); TAKE A POWDER(1953, Brit.); TWILIGHT WOMEN(1953, Brit.); WORK IS A FOUR LETTER WORD(1968, Brit.)
Silents
DOUBLE LIFE OF MR. ALFRED BURTON, THE(1919, Brit.); MIRIAM ROZELLA(1924, Brit.)
Misc. Silents
ROSE IN THE DUST(1921, Brit.)
H.A.L. Craig
ADVENTURES OF GERARD, THE(1970, Brit.), w; WATERLOO(1970, Ital./USSR), w; MOHAMMAD, MESSENGER OF GOD(1976, Lebanon/Brit.), w; FOXTROT(1977, Mex./Swiss), w; LION OF THE DESERT(1981, Libya/Brit.), w
Hal Craig
YOU'RE TELLING ME(1934); TWO FOR TONIGHT(1935); GOD'S COUNTRY AND THE WOMAN(1937); PERFECT SPECIMEN, THE(1937); SINGING MARINE, THE(1937); TIME OUT FOR ROMANCE(1937); TOAST OF NEW YORK, THE(1937); WHO KILLED GAIL PRESTON?(1938); THEY MADE ME A CRIMINAL(1939); GOOD MORNING, JUDGE(1943); MIRACLE OF MORGAN'S CREEK, THE(1944); WOMAN IN THE WINDOW, THE(1945); LIKELY STORY, A(1947); UNSUSPECTED, THE(1947)
Silents
SCRAPPER, THE(1922); AFTER A MILLION(1924); LOVE AND LEARN(1928)
Harry A. L. Craig
ANZIO(1968, Ital.), w
Helen Craig
SNAKE PIT, THE(1948); THEY LIVE BY NIGHT(1949); SPORTING CLUB, THE(1971); RANCHO DELUXE(1975); HEROES(1977)
Hilton Craig
FABIAN OF THE YARD(1954, Brit.), ph; SOLUTION BY PHONE(1954, Brit.), ph
Ian Craig
UNDER CAPRICORN(1949), ph
Ivan Craig
JUST WILLIAM'S LUCK(1948, Brit.); WILLIAM COMES TO TOWN(1948, Brit.); HIGH JINKS IN SOCIETY(1949, Brit.); MATTER OF MURDER, A(1949, Brit.); SKIMPY IN THE NAVY(1949, Brit.); DANGEROUS ASSIGNMENT(1950, Brit.); MISS PILGRIM'S PROGRESS(1950, Brit.); MYSTERY AT THE BURLESQUE(1950, Brit.); YOU CAN'T FOOL AN IRISHMAN(1950, Ireland); SIX MEN, THE(1951, Brit.); STORY OF ROBIN HOOD, THE(1952, Brit.); DEVIL'S JEST, THE(1954, Brit.); HELL BELOW ZERO(1954, Brit.); PROFILE(1954, Brit.); FLYING EYE, THE(1955, Brit.); MAN OF THE MOMENT(1955, Brit.); PRIZE OF GOLD, A(1955); ROBBERY WITH VIOLENCE(1958, Brit.)
Jack Craig
KONGA(1961, Brit.), makeup
James Craig
BIG BROADCAST, THE(1932); JOSSER ON THE FARM(1934, Brit.); LOVE TEST, THE(1935, Brit.); BORN TO THE WEST(1937); THUNDER TRAIL(1937); PRIDE OF THE WEST(1938); BLONDIE MEETS THE BOSS(1939); GOOD GIRLS GO TO PARIS(1939); LONE WOLF SPY HUNT, THE(1939); MAN THEY COULD NOT HANG, THE(1939); NORTH OF SHANGHAI(1939); TAMING OF THE WEST, THE(1939); ENEMY AGENT(1940); HOUSE ACROSS THE BAY, THE(1940); I'M NOBODY'S SWEETHEART NOW(1940); KITTY FOYLE(1940); LAW AND ORDER(1940); SEVEN SINNERS(1940); SOUTH TO KARANGA(1940); TWO-FISTED RANGERS(1940); ZANZIBAR(1940); DEVIL AND DANIEL WEBSTER, THE(1941); UNEXPECTED UNCLE(1941); FRIENDLY ENEMIES(1942); NORTHWEST RANGERS(1942); OMAHA TRAIL, THE(1942); SEVEN MILES FROM ALCATRAZ(1942); VALLEY OF THE SUN(1942); HEAVENLY BODY, THE(1943); HUMAN COMEDY, THE(1943); SWING SHIFT MAISIE(1943); GENTLE ANNIE(1944); KISMET(1944); LOST ANGEL(1944); MARRIAGE IS A PRIVATE AFFAIR(1944); DANGEROUS PARTNERS(1945); OUR VINES HAVE TENDER GRAPES(1945); SHE WENT TO THE RACES(1945); BOYS' RANCH(1946); LITTLE MISTER JIM(1946); DARK DELUSION(1947); MAN FROM TEXAS, THE(1948); NORTHWEST STAMPEDE(1948); LADY WITHOUT PASSPORT, A(1950); SIDE STREET(1950); DRUMS IN THE DEEP SOUTH(1951); STRIP, THE(1951); HURRICANE SMITH(1952); CODE TWO(1953); FORT VENGEANCE(1953); LAST OF THE DESPERADOES(1956); MASSACRE(1956); WHILE THE CITY SLEEPS(1956); CYCLOPS(1957); GHOST DIVER(1957); NAKED IN THE SUN(1957); PERSUADER, THE(1957); SHOOT-OUT AT MEDICINE BEND(1957); WOMEN OF PITCAIRN ISLAND, THE(1957); MAN OR GUN(1958); FOUR FAST GUNS(1959); FORT UTAH(1967); HOSTILE GUNS(1967); ARIZONA BUSHWHACKERS(1968); DEVIL'S BRIGADE, THE(1968); IF HE HOLLERS, LET HIM GO(1968)
Janette Craig
SEASON OF PASSION(1961, Aus./Brit.)
John Craig
SILENCE(1931); GAMBLER WORE A GUN, THE(1961); SHOCK CORRIDOR(1963); DEVIL'S ANGELS(1967); ONE AND ONLY GENUINE ORIGINAL FAMILY BAND, THE(1968); SWEET CHARITY(1969); HOMEBODIES(1974); HOW TO SEDUCE A WOMAN(1974); PENNIES FROM HEAVEN(1981)
Johnny Craig
TALES FROM THE CRYPT(1972, Brit.), w
Kay Craig
GIRL WITH GREEN EYES(1964, Brit.)
Kenneth Craig
REEFER MADNESS(1936)
L. Michael Craig
TAPS(1981)

Larry Craig
SHE'S WORKING HER WAY THROUGH COLLEGE(1952)
Louis Craig
OF UNKNOWN ORIGIN(1983, Can.), spec eff
Lynn Craig
INNOCENTS IN PARIS(1955, Brit.)
Marla Craig
PHANTOM PLANET, THE(1961), cos; SAINTLY SINNERS(1962)
May Craig
QUIET MAN, THE(1952); RISING OF THE MOON, THE(1957, Ireland); BOYD'S SHOP(1960, Brit.); JOHNNY NOBODY(1965, Brit.); YOUNG CASSIDY(1965, U.S./Brit.)
Michael Craig
PASSPORT TO PIMLICO(1949, Brit.); EMBEZZLER, THE(1954, Brit.); LOVE LOTTERY, THE(1954, Brit.); MALTA STORY(1954, Brit.); HANDCUFFS, LONDON(1955, Brit.); PASSAGE HOME(1955, Brit.); SVENGALI(1955, Brit.); BLACK TENT, THE(1956, Brit.); BLONDE SINNER(1956, Brit.); EYEWITNESS(1956, Brit.); CAMPBELL'S KINGDOM(1957, Brit.); HIGH TIDE AT NOON(1957, Brit.); TRIPLE DECEPTION(1957, Brit.); ELEPHANT GUN(1959, Brit.); LIFE IN EMERGENCY WARD 10(1959, Brit.); SAPPHIRE(1959, Brit.); SILENT ENEMY, THE(1959, Brit.); ANGRY SILENCE, THE(1960, Brit.), a, w; DOCTOR IN LOVE(1960, Brit.); MYSTERIOUS ISLAND(1961, U.S./Brit.); TROUBLE IN THE SKY(1961, Brit.); UPSTAIRS AND DOWNSTAIRS(1961, Brit.); DESERT PATROL(1962, Brit.); PAYROLL(1962, Brit.); CAPTIVE CITY, THE(1963, Ital.); PAIR OF BRIEFS, A(1963, Brit.); STOLEN HOURS(1963); SWINGIN' MAIDEN, THE(1963, Brit.); NO, MY DARLING DAUGHTER(1964, Brit.); LIFE AT THE TOP(1965, Brit.); CONQUERED CITY(1966, Ital.); MODESTY BLAISE(1966, Brit.); SANDRA(1966, Ital.); WALK IN THE SHADOW(1966, Brit.); STAR!(1968); ROYAL HUNT OF THE SUN, THE(1969, Brit.); BROTHERLY LOVE(1970, Brit.); LOLA(1971, Brit./Ital.); TOWN CALLED HELL, A(1971, Span./Brit.); VAULT OF HORROR, THE(1973, Brit.); INN OF THE DAMNED(1974, Aus.); RIDE A WILD PONY(1976, U.S./Aus.); IRISHMAN, THE(1978, Aus.); ESCAPE 2000(1983, Aus.); KILLING OF ANGEL STREET, THE(1983, Aus.), w
Misc. Talkies
NIGHT OF THE ASSASSIN, THE(1972); ROSES BLOOM TWICE(1977)
Miss B. Craig
Silents
GANGSTERS OF NEW YORK, THE(1914)
Monica Craig
ROCKERS(1980)
Neil Craig
Silents
CRASHIN' THRU(1923)
Nell Craig
CIMARRON(1931); COME ON DANGER!(1932); CAT'S PAW, THE(1934); CHANGE OF HEART(1934); THIS SIDE OF HEAVEN(1934); GOIN' TO TOWN(1935); HANDS ACROSS THE TABLE(1935); MAN WHO RECLAIMED HIS HEAD, THE(1935); SHE GETS HER MAN(1935); KLONDIKE ANNIE(1936); PAID TO DANCE(1937); THERE'S THAT WOMAN AGAIN(1938); TOO HOT TO HANDLE(1938); WHO KILLED GAIL PRESTON?(1938); YOU CAN'T TAKE IT WITH YOU(1938); YOUNG DR. KILDARE(1938); CALLING DR. KILDARE(1939); HOMICIDE BUREAU(1939); LADY'S FROM KENTUCKY, THE(1939); OUR LEADING CITIZEN(1939); SECRET OF DR. KILDARE, THE(1939); SERGEANT MADDEN(1939); WOMEN, THE(1939); DR. KILDARE GOES HOME(1940); DR. KILDARE'S CRISIS(1940); DR. KILDARE'S STRANGE CASE(1940); EDISON, THE MAN(1940); I LOVE YOU AGAIN(1940); I TAKE THIS WOMAN(1940); NOBODY'S CHILDREN(1940); DR. KILDARE'S VICTORY(1941); DR. KILDARE'S WEDDING DAY(1941); PEOPLE VS. DR. KILDARE, THE(1941); WEST POINT WIDOW(1941); CALLING DR. GILLESPIE(1942); DR. GILLESPIE'S NEW ASSISTANT(1942); HENRY ALDRICH GETS GLAMOUR(1942); MY FAVORITE BLONDE(1942); TAKE A LETTER, DARLING(1942); DR. GILLESPIE'S CRIMINAL CASE(1943); THREE HEARTS FOR JULIA(1943); BETWEEN TWO WOMEN(1944); CASANOVA BROWN(1944); HENRY ALDRICH PLAYS CUPID(1944); OUR HEARTS WERE YOUNG AND GAY(1944); PRACTICALLY YOURS(1944); THREE MEN IN WHITE(1944); FASHION MODEL(1945); OUT OF THIS WORLD(1945); OUR HEARTS WERE GROWING UP(1946); DARK DELUSION(1947); POSSESSED(1947)
Silents
BREAKER, THE(1916); QUEEN OF SHEBA, THE(1921); FLIRT, THE(1922); ABYSMAL BRUTE, THE(1923); ABRAHAM LINCOLN(1924)
Misc. Silents
TRUFFLERS, THE(1917); COMMON PROPERTY(1919); DESPERATE HERO, THE(1920); HER FIRST ELOPEMENT(1920); PASSION'S PLAYGROUND(1920); POOR SIMP, THE(1920); BOY OF FLANDERS, A(1924)
Nobel Craig
SSSSSSSS(1973)
Noel Craig
RIVALS(1972)
Pauline Craig
ONE IN A MILLION(1936); THIN ICE(1937)
Phillip Craig
1984
MRS. SOFFEL(1984)
Robert Craig
Silents
NEW KLONDIKE, THE(1926); QUARTERBACK, THE(1926)
Sarah Craig
WE OF THE NEVER NEVER(1983, Aus.)
Simon Craig
DEAD ZONE, THE(1983)
Skip Craig
1001 ARABIAN NIGHTS(1959), ed
Stuart Craig
ELEPHANT MAN, THE(1980, Brit.), prod d; SATURN 3(1980), prod d; HISTORY OF THE WORLD, PART 1(1981), prod d; GANDHI(1982), prod d
1984
CAL(1984, Ireland), p, prod d; GREYSTOKE: THE LEGEND OF TARZAN, LORD OF THE APES(1984), prod d
Teddy Gordon Craig
Silents
TRUE TILDA(1920, Brit.)

Tony Craig
TOOTSIE(1982); REACHING OUT(1983)
Walter Craig
SIDE STREET(1950)
Wendy Craig
SECRET PLACE, THE(1958, Brit.); ROOM AT THE TOP(1959, Brit.); MIND BENDERS, THE(1963, Brit.); SERVANT, THE(1964, Brit.); NANNY, THE(1965, Brit.); I'LL NEVER FORGET WHAT'S 'IS NAME(1967, Brit.); JUST LIKE A WOMAN(1967, Brit.)
Windy Craig
ZELIG(1983)
Yvonne Craig
EIGHTEEN AND ANXIOUS(1957); GENE KRUPA STORY, THE(1959); GIDGET(1959); YOUNG LAND, THE(1959); HIGH TIME(1960); BY LOVE POSSESSED(1961); SEVEN WOMEN FROM HELL(1961); IT HAPPENED AT THE WORLD'S FAIR(1963); ADVANCE TO THE REAR(1964); KISSIN' COUSINS(1964); QUICK, BEFORE IT MELTS(1964); SKI PARTY(1965); MARS NEEDS WOMEN(1966); ONE OF OUR SPIES IS MISSING(1966); ONE SPY TOO MANY(1966); IN LIKE FLINT(1967); HOW TO FRAME A FIGG(1971)
Harry A.L. Craigh
FRAULEIN DOKTOR(1969, Ital./Yugo.), w
Robert Craighead
1984
BEAR, THE(1984)
Jill Craigie
MAKE-UP(1937, Brit.); WAY WE LIVE, THE(1946, Brit.), p,d&w; BLUE SCAR(1949, Brit.), d&w; MAN WITH A MILLION(1954, Brit.), w; WINDOM'S WAY(1958, Brit.), w
Elizabeth Craik
Silents
JOHN HALIFAX, GENTLEMAN(1915, Brit.), w
Kim Craik
DAVID COPPERFIELD(1970, Brit.)
Mrs. Craik
JOHN HALIFAX–GENTLEMAN(1938, Brit.), w
Marty Crail
STUDS LONIGAN(1960)
Rita Crailey
LAST DAYS OF DOLWYN, THE(1949, Brit.)
Bill Crain
Misc. Talkies
KID FROM NOT SO BIG, THE(1978), d
Earl Crain
CURTAIN AT EIGHT(1934), ed
Silents
JOYOUS TROUBLEMAKERS, THE(1920); BLUSHING BRIDE, THE(1921); QUEEN OF SHEBA, THE(1921); STEELHEART(1921); LAVENDER BATH LADY, THE(1922); PENROD(1922)
Misc. Silents
ORPHAN, THE(1920)
Earl Crain, Sr.
HOMICIDE FOR THREE(1948), ed
Earl N. Crain
BEHIND JURY DOORS(1933, Brit.), ph
Jeanne Crain
GANG'S ALL HERE, THE(1943); HOME IN INDIANA(1944); IN THE MEANTIME, DARLING(1944); WINGED VICTORY(1944); STATE FAIR(1945); CENTENNIAL SUMMER(1946); LEAVE HER TO HEAVEN(1946); MARGIE(1946); APARTMENT FOR PEGGY(1948); LETTER TO THREE WIVES, A(1948); YOU WERE MEANT FOR ME(1948); FAN, THE(1949); PINKY(1949); CHEAPER BY THE DOZEN(1950); I'LL GET BY(1950); MODEL AND THE MARRIAGE BROKER, THE(1951); PEOPLE WILL TALK(1951); TAKE CARE OF MY LITTLE GIRL(1951); BELLES ON THEIR TOES(1952); O. HENRY'S FULL HOUSE(1952); CITY OF BAD MEN(1953); DANGEROUS CROSSING(1953); VICKI(1953); DUEL IN THE JUNGLE(1954, Brit.); GENTLEMEN MARRY BRUNETTES(1955); MAN WITHOUT A STAR(1955); SECOND GREATEST SEX, THE(1955); FASTEST GUN ALIVE(1956); JOKER IS WILD, THE(1957); TATTERED DRESS, THE(1957); GUNS OF THE TIMBERLAND(1960); TWENTY PLUS TWO(1961); MADISON AVENUE(1962); QUEEN OF THE NILE(1964, Ital.); INVASION 1700(1965, Fr./Ital./Yugo.); HOT RODS TO HELL(1967); PONTIUS PILATE(1967, Fr./Ital.); SKYJACKED(1972); NIGHT GOD SCREAMED, THE(1975)
William Crain
BLACULA(1972), d; DR. BLACK AND MR. HYDE(1976), d
Larry Craine
DESIREE(1954)
Frank Cram
DARK SANDS(1938, Brit.)
Mildred Cram
BEHIND THE MAKEUP(1930), w; THIS MODERN AGE(1931), w; AMATEUR DADDY(1932), w; FAITHLESS(1932), w; SINNERS IN THE SUN(1932), w; NAVY BORN(1936), w; WINGS OVER HONOLULU(1937), w; LOVE AFFAIR(1939), w; BEYOND TOMORROW(1940), w; AFFAIR TO REMEMBER, AN(1957), w
Norman Cram
RIDE A VIOLENT MILE(1957)
Richard Cramen
SCREAM IN THE NIGHT(1943)
Angela Cramer
RANCHO DELUXE(1975)
Barry Cramer
MADELEINE IS(1971, Can.)
Bud Cramer
1984
HOT AND DEADLY(1984)
Dick Cramer
BIG NEWS(1929); TRESPASSER, THE(1929); BLONDE CRAZY(1931); LADIES' MAN(1931); PAINTED DESERT, THE(1931); PLATINUM BLONDE(1931); POCATELLO KID(1932); DANGER AHEAD(1935); O'MALLEY OF THE MOUNTED(1936); RIP ROARIN' BUCKAROO(1936); GUNS IN THE DARK(1937); LIGHTNIN' CRANDALL(1937); NIGHT CLUB SCANDAL(1937); RANGERS STEP IN, THE(1937); ROAMING COWBOY, THE(1937); TRAIL OF VENGEANCE(1937); TRUSTED OUTLAW, THE(1937); TWO-FISTED SHERIFF(1937); WHERE TRAILS DIVIDE(1937); WOMAN CHASES MAN(1937); PAINTED TRAIL, THE(1938); PHANTOM OF THE RANGE, THE(1938); PHANTOM RANGER(1938); SONGS AND BULLETS(1938); BAD

BOY(1939); IN OLD MONTANA(1939); ARIZONA FRONTIER(1940); SAPS AT SEA(1940); STRANGE CARGO(1940); TRAILING DOUBLE TROUBLE(1940); WEST OF PINTO BASIN(1940); UNDERGROUND RUSTLERS(1941); ARIZONA STAGE-COACH(1942); BILLY THE KID TRAPPED(1942); BROADWAY BIG SHOT(1942); PIRATES OF THE PRAIRIE(1942); ROCK RIVER RENEGADES(1942); THUNDER RIVER FEUD(1942); TRAIL RIDERS(1942); TWO FISTED JUSTICE(1943)

Misc. Talkies
DEFYING THE LAW(1935)

Dick [Richard] Cramer
SATURDAY'S MILLIONS(1933)

Duncan Cramer
NIX ON DAMES(1929), set d; ARE YOU THERE?(1930), art d; CRAZY THAT WAY(1930), art d; SCOTLAND YARD(1930), art d; UP THE RIVER(1930), set d; AMBASSADOR BILL(1931), art d; DISORDERLY CONDUCT(1932), art d; REBECCA OF SUNNYBROOK FARM(1932), art d; YOUNG AMERICA(1932), art d; LIFE IN THE RAW(1933), art d; STATE FAIR(1933), art d; SHE LEARNED ABOUT SAILORS(1934), set d; LIFE BEGINS AT 40(1935), art d; MUSIC IS MAGIC(1935), art d; HUMAN CARGO(1936), art d; RAMONA(1936), art d; STAR FOR A NIGHT(1936), art d; CRACK-UP, THE(1937), art d; DANGER–LOVE AT WORK(1937), art d; YOU CAN'T HAVE EVERYTHING(1937), art d; FIGHTING SEABEES, THE(1944), art d; DE-LIGHTFULLY DANGEROUS(1945), art d; WOMAN IN THE WINDOW, THE(1945), art d; DARK MIRROR, THE(1946), prod d; FOUR FACES WEST(1948), art d; LULU BELLE(1948), art d; ON OUR MERRY WAY(1948), art d; D.O.A.(1950), art d; FLAM-ING STAR(1960), art d; HIGH TIME(1960), art d; LOST WORLD, THE(1960), art d; MARRIAGE-GO-ROUND, THE(1960), art d; NORTH TO ALASKA(1960), art d; ONE FOOT IN HELL(1960), art d; WIZARD OF BAGHDAD, THE(1960), art d; FIERCEST HEART, THE(1961), art d; MISTY(1961), art d; RIGHT APPROACH, THE(1961), art d; SANCTUARY(1961), art d; SEVEN WOMEN FROM HELL(1961), art d; MADISON AVENUE(1962), art d; SWINGIN' ALONG(1962), art d; HARLOW(1965), art d

Frank Cramer [Gianfranco Paolini]
ADIOS SABATA(1971, Ital./Span.), w

Fred Cramer
SILVER STREAK(1976), spec eff; DEER HUNTER, THE(1978), spec eff; 10(1979), spec eff
1984
KILLING FIELDS, THE(1984, Brit.), spec eff

Gary Cramer
MIGHTY GORGA, THE(1969), ph

Grant Cramer
NEW YEAR'S EVIL(1980)
1984
HARDBODIES(1984)

Guillermo Cramer
LIVING HEAD, THE(1969, Mex.)

Jeffrey Cramer
1984
AMERICAN DREAMER(1984)

Joe Cramer
TRIAL OF BILLY JACK, THE(1974), p

Joey Cramer
1984
RUNAWAY(1984)

Kay Cramer
MAGIC SPECTACLES(1961)

Marc Cramer
BRIDE BY MISTAKE(1944); CANTERVILLE GHOST, THE(1944); MADEMOISELLE FIFI(1944); MY PAL, WOLF(1944); FIRST YANK INTO TOKYO(1945); ISLE OF THE DEAD(1945); JOHNNY ANGEL(1945); PAN-AMERICANA(1945); THOSE ENDEAR-ING YOUNG CHARMS(1945); GENIUS AT WORK(1946); LITTLE IODINE(1946); RIVERBOAT RHYTHM(1946); ADVENTURES OF DON COYOTE(1947)

Marguerite Cramer
WILD PARTY, THE(1929)

Massey Cramer
LEGEND OF BLOOD MOUNTAIN, THE(1965), d, w
Misc. Talkies
LEGEND OF BLOOD MOUNTAIN, THE(1965), d

Michael Cramer
PLAYGIRLS AND THE BELLBOY, THE(1962,Ger.); HYPNOSIS(1966, Ger./Sp./Ital.); U-47 LT. COMMANDER PRIEN(1967, Ger.)

Norma Jean Cramer
CARBINE WILLIAMS(1952)

Paul Cramer
WEST OF WYOMING(1950)

Richard Cramer
ILLUSION(1929); KID GLOVES(1929); CAPTAIN OF THE GUARD(1930); HELL'S ISLAND(1930); MURDER ON THE ROOF(1930); SWEET MAMA(1930); THOSE WHO DANCE(1930); AIR POLICE(1931); ANYBODY'S BLONDE(1931); DANCING DYNA-MITE(1931); IN THE LINE OF DUTY(1931); NECK AND NECK(1931); NIGHT BEAT(1932); STRANGE LOVE OF MOLLY LOUVAIN, THE(1932); TENDERFOOT, THE(1932); UNEXPECTED FATHER(1932); FOURTH HORSEMAN, THE(1933); PRI-VATE JONES(1933); CAT'S PAW, THE(1934); HOLLYWOOD PARTY(1934); SHE GETS HER MAN(1935); TRAIL OF TERROR(1935); FRONTIER JUSTICE(1936); SPEED REPORTER(1936); SUTTER'S GOLD(1936); COURAGE OF THE WEST(1937); CRU-SADE AGAINST RACKETS(1937); SANTA FE BOUND(1937); CLIPPED WINGS(1938); RANGER'S ROUNDUP, THE(1938); ROLLING CARAVANS(1938); THUNDER IN THE DESERT(1938); FEUD OF THE RANGE(1939); KNIGHT OF THE PLAINS(1939); LAND OF THE SIX GUNS(1940); LEGION OF THE LAWLESS(1940); NORTHWEST PASSAGE(1940); PIONEER DAYS(1940); DOUBLE TROUBLE(1941); SCARLET STREET(1945); SONG OF OLD WYOMING(1945); LAW OF THE LASH(1947); WILD COUNTRY(1947); SANTA FE(1951)
Misc. Talkies
LAWLESS VALLEY(1932); RAWHIDE MAIL(1934); JUDGMENT BOOK, THE(1935); PHANTOM COWBOY, THE(1935); RIDDLE RANCH(1936)

Rychard Cramer
FLYING DEUCES, THE(1939)

Rychard [Richard] Cramer
PACK UP YOUR TROUBLES(1932)

Sharon Cramer
FIREBALL JUNGLE(1968)

Susan Cramer
DEAR BRIGETTE(1965)

Susanne Cramer
INDECENT(1962, Ger.); BEDTIME STORY(1964); TWO IN A SLEEPING BAG(1964, Ger.)

Duncan Crammer
CAFE METROPOLE(1937), art d

Harold Cramp
SMOKY(1946), set d

Barbara Crampton
1984
BODY DOUBLE(1984)

Gerry Crampton
HEROES OF TELEMARK, THE(1965, Brit.), stunts; HIGH COMMISSIONER, THE(1968, U.S./Brit.); CROMWELL(1970, Brit.), stunts; DEATHLINE(1973, Brit.); HENNESSY(1975, Brit.), stunts; EAGLE HAS LANDED, THE(1976, Brit.), stunts; RAIDERS OF THE LOST ARK(1981)

Howard Crampton
Silents
TRAFFIC IN SOULS(1913); 20,000 LEAGUES UNDER THE SEA(1916); BRONZE BELL, THE(1921)
Misc. Silents
HUMDRUM BROWN(1918); WIFE HE BOUGHT, THE(1918); SOMEONE IN THE HOUSE(1920); MAN WHO MARRIED HIS OWN WIFE, THE(1922)

Phillip Crampton
STORM CENTER(1956)

Michael Crand
GAWAIN AND THE GREEN KNIGHT(1973, Brit.)

Brad Crandal
BEYOND AND BACK(1978)

Bill Crandall
BIG LEAGUER(1953)

Bob Crandall
SIX-GUN RHYTHM(1939), ed

Brad Crandall
LINCOLN CONSPIRACY, THE(1977); IN SEARCH OF HISTORIC JESUS(1980)

Eddie Crandall
HELL ON WHEELS(1967); FROM NASHVILLE WITH MUSIC(1969), p&d

Edward Crandall
GLORIFYING THE AMERICAN GIRL(1930); OVER THE HILL(1931); DANCE TEAM(1932)

Eric Crandall
NORSEMAN, THE(1978)

Patti Crandall
INCREDIBLY STRANGE CREATURES WHO STOPPED LIVING AND BECAME CRAZY MIXED-UP ZOMBIES, THE(1965)

Robert Crandall
EVIDENCE(1929), ed; DOORWAY TO HELL(1930), ed; OH! SAILOR, BEHA-VE!(1930), ed; SECOND CHOICE(1930), ed; FIFTY MILLION FRENCHMEN(1931), ed; THUNDER MOUNTAIN(1935), ed; WHISPERING SMITH SPEAKS(1935), ed; BORDER PATROLMAN, THE(1936), ed; LET'S SING AGAIN(1936), ed; RAINBOW ON THE RIVER(1936), ed; WILD BRIAN KENT(1936), ed; HEADIN' EAST(1937), ed; HOLLYWOOD COWBOY(1937), ed; PARK AVENUE LOGGER(1937), ed; WINDJAM-MER(1937), ed; GLADIATOR, THE(1938), ed; HOLLYWOOD ROUNDUP(1938), ed; RAWHIDE(1938), ed; BEASTS OF BERLIN(1939), ed; ISLE OF DESTINY(1940), ed; EMERGENCY LANDING(1941), ed; FLYING BLIND(1941), ed; FORCED LAND-ING(1941), ed; MISBEHAVING HUSBANDS(1941), ed; POWER DIVE(1941), ed; BROADWAY BIG SHOT(1942), ed; MR. CELEBRITY(1942), ed; SNUFFY SMITH, YARD BIRD(1942), ed; GIRL FROM MONTEREY, THE(1943), ed; CAREER GIRL(1944), ed.; DEVIL RIDERS(1944), ed; JIVE JUNCTION(1944), ed; TROCADE-RO(1944), ed; 3 IS A FAMILY(1944), ed; DIXIE JAMBOREE(1945), ed; LAND OF THE LAWLESS(1947), ed; UNTAMED FURY(1947), ed; FLYING SAUCER, THE(1950), ed; DARWIN ADVENTURE, THE(1972, Brit.), ph

Robert G. Crandall
DANGER! WOMEN AT WORK(1943), ed

Robert O. Crandall
FLIRTING WITH FATE(1938), ed; LADY IN THE DEATH HOUSE(1944), ed; MA-CHINE GUN MAMA(1944), ed; TARZAN AND THE AMAZONS(1945), ed; TARZAN AND THE LEOPARD WOMAN(1946), ed; HARPOON(1948), ed

Roland Crandall
GULLIVER'S TRAVELS(1939), anim d

Steve Crandall
EASY LIVING(1949); GAL WHO TOOK THE WEST, THE(1949)

Suzi Crandall
DECEPTION(1946); NIGHT SONG(1947); THAT WAY WITH WOMEN(1947); MARK OF THE LASH(1948); STATION WEST(1948); THEY LIVE BY NIGHT(1949)

Yusef Crandall
DESTINATION MILAN(1954, Brit.)

Robert Crandell
KING OF THE ROYAL MOUNTED(1936), ed; HOLLYWOOD BARN DANCE(1947), ed

Anita Crane
NEW YEAR'S EVIL(1980)

Barbara Crane
SORORITY GIRL(1957)

Barry Crane
CONQUEST OF THE EARTH(1980), d

Beverlee Crane
BLONDE DYNAMITE(1950)

Beverly Crane
EMERGENCY WEDDING(1950)

Bill Crane
BROTHER JOHN(1971)

Bob Crane
MAN-TRAP(1961); RETURN TO PEYTON PLACE(1961); WICKED DREAMS OF PAULA SCHULTZ, THE(1968); SUPERDAD(1974); GUS(1976)

Carl Crane
GAMERA VERSUS VIRAS(1968, Jap)
Carleton Crane
CASE OF PATTY SMITH, THE(1962)
Christian Crane
1984
IMPULSE(1984)
Colin Crane
ON THE BEACH(1959)
Colleen Crane
GIANT(1956)
Cornelius Crane
TAHITIAN, THE(1956), p
Cynthia Crane
NOBODY'S CHILDREN(1940)
Dagne Crane
DIARY OF A BACHELOR(1964); BANANAS(1971)
David Crane
MICKEY ONE(1965)
Derek Crane
MURDER IN MISSISSIPPI(1965)
Dick Crane
KEEP 'EM FLYING(1941); THIS IS THE ARMY(1943); HONEYMOON OF TER-
ROR(1961)
Doc Crane
Silents
POLLYANNA(1920)
Dorothy Crane
Silents
GOLD RUSH, THE(1925)
Doug Crane
RAGGEDY ANN AND ANDY(1977), anim
Frank Crane
SPEED REPORTER(1936)
Silents
MISS CRUSOE(1919), d; PRAISE AGENT, THE(1919), d; MASTER STROKE,
A(1920); LITTLE WILDCAT(1922); FAIR PLAY(1925), d
Misc. Silents
MAN WHO FOUND HIMSELF, THE(1915), d; MOONSTONE, THE(1915), d;
STRANDED IN ARCADY(1917), d; THAIS(1917), d; VENGEANCE IS MINE(1918),
d; HIS FATHER'S WIFE(1919), d; SCAR, THE(1919), d; UNVEILING HAND, THE(1919),
d; GIRL'S DESIRE, A(1922); TONS OF MONEY(1924, Brit.), d
Frank H. Crane
Silents
FAMILY CUPBOARD, THE(1915), d&w; STOLEN VOICE(1915), w; AS IN A LOOK-
ING GLASS(1916), d; NEIGHBORS(1918), d; WANTED FOR MURDER(1919), d; PUP-
PET MAN, THE(1921, Brit.), d; HUTCH STIRS 'EM UP(1923, Brit.), d
Misc. Silents
PAYING THE PRICE(1916), d; WHOSO TAKETH A WIFE(1916), d; LIFE MASK,
THE(1918), d; HER GAME(1919), d; DOOR THAT HAS NO KEY, THE(1921, Brit.), d;
GRASS ORPHAN, THE(1922, Brit.), d; PAUPER MILLIONAIRE, THE(1922, Brit.), d
Frank Hall Crane
MASON OF THE MOUNTED(1932); 'NEATH THE ARIZONA SKIES(1934); TOAST
OF NEW YORK, THE(1937)
Misc. Talkies
MYSTERY RANCH(1934)
Silents
AS YE SOW(1914), d
Misc. Silents
FATE'S BOOMERANG(1916), d; MAN WHO STOOD STILL, THE(1916), d; WORLD
AGAINST HIM, THE(1916), d; JADE CUP, THE(1926), d; TRUNK MYSTERY,
THE(1927), d
Fred Crane
GONE WITH THE WIND(1939); GAY AMIGO, THE(1949)
Freya Crane
Misc. Talkies
SCORING(1980)
George Crane
DOG OF FLANDERS, A(1935), ed; SECOND WIFE(1936), ed
Hamilton Crane
Misc. Silents
BULLDOGS OF THE TRAIL, THE(1915)
Harold Crane
KISS OF DEATH(1947); NAKED CITY, THE(1948)
Harry Crane
AIR RAID WARDENS(1943), w; LOST IN A HAREM(1944), w; ZIEGFELD FOL-
LIES(1945), w; HARVEY GIRLS, THE(1946), w; TWO SISTERS FROM BOSTON(1946),
w; SONG OF THE THIN MAN(1947), w; TAKE ME OUT TO THE BALL GAME(1949),
w
Helen Crane
HOLE IN THE WALL(1929)
Hilary Crane
WARM DECEMBER, A(1973, Brit.)
Irene Crane
I'LL TAKE ROMANCE(1937)
Irving Crane
BALTIMORE BULLET, THE(1980)
James Crane
DRAKE CASE, THE(1929); ONE NIGHT AT SUSIE'S(1930); DUDE RANCH(1931);
LADY AND GENT(1932); MUMMY, THE(1932); TWO KINDS OF WOMEN(1932);
GOOD DAME(1934); NOBODY'S CHILDREN(1940)
James L. Crane
Misc. Silents
HIS BRIDAL NIGHT(1919); MISLEADING WIDOW, THE(1919); WANTED - A
HUSBAND(1919); DARK LANTERN, A(1920); SADIE LOVE(1920); SINNERS(1920)
Jimmy Crane
BELLS OF ST. MARY'S, THE(1945); DICK TRACY VS. CUEBALL(1946); MAGIC
TOWN(1947); MOONRISE(1948); SUN COMES UP, THE(1949)

Joan Crane
ATTACK ON THE IRON COAST(1968, U.S./Brit.); SOPHIE'S PLACE(1970)
Judith Crane
MANTIS IN LACE(1968)
Kenneth B. Crane
MANSTER, THE(1962, Jap.), d
Kenneth Crane
DAVY CROCKETT, INDIAN SCOUT(1950), ed; IROQUOIS TRAIL, THE(1950), ed;
TIMETABLE(1956), ed; DESTINATION 60,000(1957), ed; MONSTER FROM THE
GREEN HELL(1958), d; FLIGHT THAT DISAPPEARED, THE(1961), ed; FRONTIER
UPRISING(1961), ed; GAMBLER WORE A GUN, THE(1961), ed; SECRET OF DEEP
HARBOR(1961), ed; DEADLY DUO(1962), ed; GUN STREET(1962), ed; MANSTER,
THE(1962, Jap.), ed; DEVIL'S ANGELS(1967), ed; THUNDER ALLEY(1967), ed;
WEDDING NIGHT(1970, Ireland), ed; HARD RIDE, THE(1971), ed
Kenneth G. Crane
HALF HUMAN(1955, Jap.), d; WHEN HELL BROKE LOOSE(1958), d
Kenny Crane
PLEASE MURDER ME(1956), ed
Larry Crane
CRISIS(1950)
Misc. Talkies
BEWARE THE BLACK WIDOW(1968), d
Les Crane
AMERICAN DREAM, AN(1966)
Lillian Crane
Silents
KID, THE(1921)
Lloyd Crane
GIRL FROM SCOTLAND YARD, THE(1937)
Lloyd Crane [Jon Hall]
MIND YOUR OWN BUSINESS(1937)
Lor Crane
HAUNTED(1976), m
Mack Crane
BOMBSHELL(1933), w
Madge Crane
BACHELOR'S DAUGHTERS, THE(1946); DECOY(1946); CONFIDENCE GIRL(1952)
Marlene Crane
GIANT(1956)
Michael Crane
AT THE EARTH'S CORE(1976, Brit.)
Mrs. Gardener Crane
GIRLS IN CHAINS(1943)
Mrs. Gardner Crane
HOLD THAT GHOST(1941)
Mrs. Gardner Crane
ALL THIS AND HEAVEN TOO(1940); MEET JOHN DOE(1941); RANDOM HAR-
VEST(1942); BEDSIDE MANNER(1945)
Norma Crane
TEA AND SYMPATHY(1956); ALL IN A NIGHT'S WORK(1961); PENELOPE(1966);
SWEET RIDE, THE(1968); THEY CALL ME MISTER TIBBS(1970); FIDDLER ON THE
ROOF(1971)
Odgen Crane
Silents
HER FIVE-FOOT HIGHNESS(1920)
Ogden Crane
Silents
END OF THE TRAIL, THE(1916); PARSON OF PANAMINT, THE(1916); WHEN A
WOMAN SINS(1918); INVISIBLE FEAR, THE(1921)
Misc. Silents
HORNET'S NEST, THE(1919); DWELLING PLACE OF LIGHT, THE(1920)
Peter Crane
WHITE HUNTRESS(1957, Brit.), p; ASSASSIN(1973, Brit.), d; MOMENTS(1974,
Brit.), p, d
Phillip Crane
POLLY OF THE CIRCUS(1932)
Phyllis Crane
FORWARD PASS, THE(1929); SO THIS IS COLLEGE(1929); STOLEN KISSES(1929);
COLLEGE LOVERS(1930); GIRL SAID NO, THE(1930); TEN CENTS A DANCE(1931);
MEN OF THE NIGHT(1934); EVERY NIGHT AT EIGHT(1935); SPLENDOR(1935); MY
MAN GODFREY(1936); TWO IN A CROWD(1936)
Richard Crane
WE WHO ARE YOUNG(1940); IN THE NAVY(1941); SAINT IN PALM SPRINGS,
THE(1941); EAGLE SQUADRON(1942); FLYING TIGERS(1942); PHANTOM PLAINS-
MEN, THE(1942); THIS TIME FOR KEEPS(1943); HAPPY LAND(1943); RIDERS OF
THE DEADLINE(1943); SO PROUDLY WE HAIL(1943); SOMEONE TO REMEM-
BER(1943); FOLLOW THE BOYS(1944); NONE SHALL ESCAPE(1944); WING AND A
PRAYER(1944); CAPTAIN EDDIE(1945); BEHIND GREEN LIGHTS(1946); JOHNNY
COMES FLYING HOME(1946); ANGEL ON THE AMAZON(1948); ARTHUR TAKES
OVER(1948); CAMPUS HONEYMOON(1948); DYNAMITE(1948); TRIPLE
THREAT(1948); WATERFRONT AT MIDNIGHT(1948); LADY WITHOUT PASSPORT,
A(1950); LAST OUTPOST, THE(1951); MAN IN THE SADDLE(1951); IRON MISTRESS,
THE(1952); LEADVILLE GUNSLINGER(1952); THUNDERING CARAVANS(1952);
NEANDERTHAL MAN, THE(1953); WINNING OF THE WEST(1953); WOMAN THEY
ALMOST LYNCHED(1953); ETERNAL SEA, THE(1955); NO MAN'S WO-
MAN(1955); EDDY DUCHIN STORY, THE(1956); BAILOUT AT 43,000(1957); DEEP
SIX, THE(1958); DEVIL'S PARTNER, THE(1958); ALLIGATOR PEOPLE, THE(1959);
BATTLE CRY(1959); THIRTEEN FIGHTING MEN(1960); HOUSE OF THE DAM-
NED(1963); SURF PARTY(1964)
Misc. Talkies
BEYOND THE MOON(1964)
Richard O. Crane
SUSAN AND GOD(1940)
Rita Crane
LOVE KISS, THE(1930)
Roy Crane
REMEMBER THE NIGHT(1940); FOUR JACKS AND A JILL(1941)

Sandra Crane
MEAT CLEAVER MASSACRE(1977)

Stephen Crane
CRY OF THE WEREWOLF(1944); CRIME DOCTOR'S COURAGE, THE(1945); TO-NIGHT AND EVERY NIGHT(1945); RED BADGE OF COURAGE, THE(1951), d&w; FACE TO FACE(1952), w; FACE OF FIRE(1959, U.S./Brit.), w

Ward Crane
PHANTOM OF THE OPERA, THE(1929)
Silents
BROADWAY ROSE(1922); DESTINY'S ISLE(1922); NO TRESPASSING(1922); ENE-MIES OF CHILDREN(1923); PLEASURE MAD(1923); EMPTY HANDS(1924); GAM-BLING WIVES(1924); SHERLOCK, JR.(1924); BORROWED FINERY(1925); CRIMSON RUNNER, THE(1925); PHANTOM OF THE OPERA, THE(1925); BLIND GODDESS, THE(1926); AUCTIONEER, THE(1927); DOWN THE STRETCH(1927); RUSH HOUR, THE(1927); HONEYMOON FLATS(1928)
Misc. Silents
FRISKY MRS. JOHNSON, THE(1920); HARRIET AND THE PIPER(1920); LUCK OF THE IRISH, THE(1920); SOMETHING DIFFERENT(1920); YELLOW TAIFUN, THE(1920); YELLOW TYPHOON, THE(1920); HEEDLESS MOTHS(1921); FRENCH HEELS(1922); CLASSIFIED(1925); HOW BAXTER BUTTED IN(1925); MILLION DOLLAR HANDICAP, THE(1925); PEACOCK FEATHERS(1925); BOY FRIEND, THE(1926); FLAMING FRONTIER, THE(1926); RISKY BUSINESS(1926); SPORTING LOVER, THE(1926); THAT MODEL FROM PARIS(1926); UNDER WESTERN SKIES(1926); BEAUTY SHOPPERS(1927); LADY IN ERMINE, THE(1927)

William Crane
WRONG MAN, THE(1956)

William H. Crane
Silents
DAVID HARUM(1915); SAPHEAD, THE(1921); SOULS FOR SALE(1923); THREE WISE FOOLS(1923)

Kenneth G. Cranel
PAWNEE(1957), ed

Sally Cranfield
1984
SUPERGIRL(1984)

Jean Cranford
FEUD OF THE RANGE(1939)

Robert Cranford
STRANGLER, THE(1964)

Kenneth Cranham
OLIVER!(1968, Brit.); OTLEY(1969, Brit.); ALL THE WAY UP(1970, Brit.); FRAG-MENT OF FEAR(1971, Brit.); BROTHER SUN, SISTER MOON(1973, Brit./Ital.); JOSEPH ANDREWS(1977, Brit.)

Kenneth Cranhan
ROBIN AND MARIAN(1976, Brit.)

John Cranko
TURNING POINT, THE(1977), ch

James Cranna
THX 1138(1971); AMERICAN GRAFFITI(1973); TIME AFTER TIME(1979, Brit.); DIE LAUGHING(1980); SHOOT THE MOON(1982); TWICE UPON A TIME(1983)

Jim Cranna
STEELYARD BLUES(1973); SUNSHINE BOYS, THE(1975)

Robert Cransac
RISE OF LOUIS XIV, THE(1970, Fr.)

Joseph Patrick Cranshaw
UNDER AGE(1964)

Pat Cranshaw
MARS NEEDS WOMEN(1966); THUNDER AND LIGHTNING(1977); SGT. PEPPER'S LONELY HEARTS CLUB BAND(1978); GONG SHOW MOVIE, THE(1980)

Patrick Cranshaw
AMAZING TRANSPARENT MAN, THE(1960); PRIVATE EYES, THE(1980)

Sen. Alan Cranston
CANDIDATE, THE(1972)

Claudia Cranston
IT'S A BIG COUNTRY(1951), w

Helga Cranston
DAYDREAK(1948, Brit.), ed; HAMLET(1948, Brit.), ed; MADNESS OF THE HEART(1949, Brit.), ed; IT'S HARD TO BE GOOD(1950, Brit.), ed; FINAL TEST, THE(1953, Brit.), ed; DIAMOND WIZARD, THE(1954, Brit.), ed; RICHARD III(1956, Brit.), ed; SAINT JOAN(1957), ed; BONJOUR TRISTESSE(1958), ed; THEY WERE TEN(1961, Israel), ed; REBELS AGAINST THE LIGHT(1964), ed; SANDS OF BEER-SHEBA(1966, U.S./Israel), ed; SIMCHON FAMILY, THE(1969, Israel), ed

Joe Cranston
GO, JOHNNY, GO!(1959)

Joseph Cranston
TRAUMA(1962), p

Joseph L. Cranston
CORPSE GRINDERS, THE(1972), w

Kyle Edward Cranston
10 TO MIDNIGHT(1983)

Peter Cranwell
SEMINOLE(1953); FIGHTING PRINCE OF DONEGAL, THE(1966, Brit.)

Joe Cranzano
LOVING(1970), makeup; OWL AND THE PUSSYCAT, THE(1970), makeup

Howard Marion Crasford
LONGEST DAY, THE(1962)

Antonio Crast
WANDERING JEW, THE(1948, Ital.); SON OF THE RED CORSAIR(1963, Ital.)

Mimmo Crau
YETI(1977, Ital.)

Paul Crauchet
WOMAN OF SIN(1961, Fr.); WAR OF THE BUTTONS(1963 Fr.); LA GUERRE EST FINIE(1967, Fr./Swed.); HO!(1968, Fr.); LAST ADVENTURE, THE(1968, Fr./Ital.); ZITA(1968, Fr.); L'ARMEE DES OMBRES(1969, Fr./Ital.); WITHOUT APPARENT MOTIVE(1972, Fr.); COP, A(1973, Fr.); BEYOND FEAR(1977, Fr.); DIRTY MO-NEY(1977, Fr.); BUTTERFLY ON THE SHOULDER, A(1978, Fr.)

Jan Cravan
SMASH-UP, THE STORY OF A WOMAN(1947)

Nick Cravat
MY FRIEND IRMA(1949); FILE ON THELMA JORDAN, THE(1950); FLAME AND THE ARROW, THE(1950); TEN TALL MEN(1951); CRIMSON PIRATE, THE(1952); VEILS OF BAGDAD, THE(1953); KING RICHARD AND THE CRUSADERS(1954); THREE RING CIRCUS(1954); DAVY CROCKETT, KING OF THE WILD FRON-TIER(1955); STORY OF MANKIND, THE(1957); RUN SILENT, RUN DEEP(1958); CAT BALLOU(1965); WAY WEST, THE(1967); SCALPHUNTERS, THE(1968); VALDEZ IS COMING(1971); ULZANA'S RAID(1972); MIDNIGHT MAN, THE(1974); ISLAND OF DR. MOREAU, THE(1977)

Noel Cravat
RIOT SQUAD(1941); SHADOW OF THE THIN MAN(1941); SECRET AGENT OF JAPAN(1942); MISSION TO MOSCOW(1943); ALI BABA AND THE FORTY THIE-VES(1944); WONDER MAN(1945); RAZOR'S EDGE, THE(1946); WALLS CAME TUM-BLING DOWN(1946); THREE ON A TICKET(1947); IRON CURTAIN, THE(1948); MUTINEERS, THE(1949); PAROLE, INC.(1949); FEDERAL MAN(1950); SOUTH SEA WOMAN(1953); 5,000 FINGERS OF DR. T. THE(1953); CAPTAIN KIDD AND THE SLAVE GIRL(1954); DRAGON'S GOLD(1954); FLIGHT TO HONG KONG(1956)

Jeff Cravath
LIFE BEGINS IN COLLEGE(1937)

Alan Craven
TWO-GUN JUSTICE(1938)

Eddie Craven
GILDED LILY, THE(1935); SPLENDOR(1935); INVISIBLE MENACE, THE(1938); DOWN MISSOURI WAY(1946); TILL THE END OF TIME(1946)

Edward Craven
ONE HOUR LATE(1935)

Elizabeth Craven
OH! WHAT A LOVELY WAR(1969, Brit.)

Elsie Craven
Misc. Silents
LES CLOCHES DE CORNEVILLE(1917, Brit.)

Frank Craven
VERY IDEA, THE(1929); TOO MANY COOKS(1931), w; FIRST YEAR, THE(1932), w; HANDLE WITH CARE(1932), w; HER FIRST MATE(1933), w; SONS OF THE DES-ERT(1933), w; STATE FAIR(1933); CITY LIMITS(1934); HE WAS HER MAN(1934); HUMAN SIDE, THE(1934), w; LET'S TALK IT OVER(1934); THAT'S GRATITU-DE(1934), a, d&w; ANNAPOLIS FAREWELL(1935), w; BARBARY COAST(1935); CAR 99(1935); VAGABOND LADY(1935); HARVESTER, THE(1936); SMALL TOWN GIRL(1936); BLOSSOMS ON BROADWAY(1937); PENROD AND SAM(1937); PENROD AND HIS TWIN BROTHER(1938); YOU'RE ONLY YOUNG ONCE(1938); MIRACLES FOR SALE(1939); OUR NEIGHBORS–THE CARTERS(1939); DREAMING OUT LOUD(1940); OUR TOWN(1940), a, w; CITY, FOR CONQUEST(1941); LADY FROM CHEYENNE(1941); RICHEST MAN IN TOWN(1941); GIRL TROUBLE(1942); IN THIS OUR LIFE(1942); KEEPER OF THE FLAME(1942); PITTSBURGH(1942); THRU DIFFERENT EYES(1942); DANGEROUS BLONDES(1943); HARRIGAN'S KID(1943); JACK LONDON(1943); SON OF DRACULA(1943); DESTINY(1944); MY BEST GAL(1944); WHEN THE LIGHTS GO ON AGAIN(1944), w; COLONEL EFFINGHAM'S RAID(1945); FOREVER YOURS(1945)
Silents
NEW BROOMS(1925), w; FIRST YEAR, THE(1926), w

Garth Craven
PAT GARRETT AND BILLY THE KID(1973), ed; BRING ME THE HEAD OF ALFREDO GARCIA(1974), ed; KILLER ELITE, THE(1975), ed; I NEVER PROMISED YOU A ROSE GARDEN(1977), ed; CONVOY(1978), ed; AVALANCHE EX-PRESS(1979), ed; I, THE JURY(1982), ed; EDUCATING RITA(1983), ed

Gemma Craven
SLIPPER AND THE ROSE, THE(1976, Brit.); WAGNER(1983, Brit./Hung./Aust.)

Hazel Craven
LORD BYRON OF BROADWAY(1930); KID FROM SPAIN, THE(1932)

Howard Craven
THAT CERTAIN SOMETHING(1941, Aus.)

Jackie Craven
EGYPT BY THREE(1953)

James Craven
CAVALIER OF THE STREETS, THE(1937, Brit.); SAM SMALL LEAVES TOWN(1937, Brit.); WINGS OVER AFRICA(1939); DOWN IN SAN DIEGO(1941); TUMBLEDOWN RANCH IN ARIZONA(1941); YANK IN THE R.A.F., A(1941); INVISIBLE AGENT(1942); LITTLE JOE, THE WRANGLER(1942); SHERLOCK HOLMES AND THE SECRET WEAPON(1942); SON OF FURY(1942); TODAY I HANG(1942); FLESH AND FANTASY(1943); IMMORTAL SERGEANT, THE(1943); DAYS OF BUFFALO BILL(1946); MURDER IN THE MUSIC HALL(1946); O.S.S.(1946); SHERIFF OF REDWOOD VALLEY(1946); 13 RUE MADELEINE(1946); EXILE, THE(1947); FOREV-ER AMBER(1947); MONSIEUR VERDOUX(1947); DESPERADOES OF DODGE CI-TY(1948); JOHNNY BELINDA(1948); MILLION DOLLAR WEEKEND(1948); STRANGE GAMBLE(1948); CLAY PIGEON, THE(1949); FIGHTING O'FLYNN, THE(1949); SAMSON AND DELILAH(1949); SWORD IN THE DESERT(1949); TRIAL WITHOUT JURY(1950); DAVID AND BATHSHEBA(1951); DAY THE EARTH STOOD STILL, THE(1951); WELLS FARGO GUNMASTER(1951); AGAINST ALL FLAGS(1952); LES MISERABLES(1952); OLD WEST, THE(1952); BLADES OF THE MUSKETEERS(1953); EAST OF SUMATRA(1953); PROJECT MOONBASE(1953); SHE COULDN'T SAY NO(1954); PURPLE HAZE(1982)

Jenny Craven
1984
ORDEAL BY INNOCENCE(1984, Brit.), p

John Craven
OVER THE GOAL(1937); DR. GILLESPIE'S CRIMINAL CASE(1943); HUMAN COMEDY, THE(1943); SOMEONE TO REMEMBER(1943); MEET THE PEOPLE(1944); PURPLE HEART, THE(1944); FLIGHT TO NOWHERE(1946); SWELL GUY(1946); COUNT THE HOURS(1953); SECURITY RISK(1954); BATTLE STATIONS(1956); FRIENDLY PERSUASION(1956); HOLD BACK THE NIGHT(1956); NAVY WI-FE(1956); LET'S MAKE LOVE(1960); OCEAN'S ELEVEN(1960); WILD SCENE, THE(1970)

Mary Craven
STRAIGHT TIME(1978)

Matt Craven
MEATBALLS(1979, Can.); HOG WILD(1980, Can.); HAPPY BIRTHDAY TO ME(1981)

Noreen Craven
GENTLE SEX, THE(1943, Brit.)

Paul Craven
ONLY THING YOU KNOW, THE(1971, Can.), m
Robin Craven
GAMERA THE INVINCIBLE(1966, Jap.)
Timothy Craven
TOUCH OF THE OTHER, A(1970, Brit.)
Walter Craven
Silents
KIDNAPPED(1917); GREAT ADVENTURE, THE(1918)
Misc. Silents
UNWELCOME MRS. HATCH, THE(1914); DESTROYING ANGEL, THE(1915)
Wes Craven
YOU'VE GOT TO WALK IT LIKE YOU TALK IT OR YOU'LL LOSE THAT BEAT(1971), ed; LAST HOUSE ON THE LEFT(1972), d,w&ed; HILLS HAVE EYES, THE(1978), d&w, ed; DEADLY BLESSING(1981), d, w; SWAMP THING(1982), d&w
1984
NIGHTMARE ON ELM STREET, A(1984), d&w
Fred Cravens
MISSISSIPPI GAMBLER, THE(1953)
Mozelle Cravens
RAIDERS OF SUNSET PASS(1943)
Mario Craveri
FATHER'S DILEMMA(1952, Ital.), ph
Paoli Craveri
ANGELINA(1948, Ital.), ph
Noel Cravet
ESCAPE IN THE FOG(1945); KILLERS, THE(1946)
Clara Cravey
DR. COPPELIUS(1968, U.S./Span.)
Darlene Craviotto
I NEVER PROMISED YOU A ROSE GARDEN(1977)
Alice Crawford
Silents
GLORIOUS ADVENTURE, THE(1922, U.S./Brit.)
Andrew Crawford
DEAR MURDERER(1947, Brit.); BROKEN JOURNEY(1948, Brit.); BROTHERS, THE(1948, Brit.); DULCIMER STREET(1948, Brit.); LOVE IN WAITING(1948, Brit.); SMUGGLERS, THE(1948, Brit.); BOYS IN BROWN(1949, Brit.); DIAMOND CITY(1949, Brit.); GAY LADY, THE(1949, Brit.); ONE WILD OAT(1951, Brit.); OPERATION DISASTER(1951, Brit.); BITTER VICTORY(1958, Fr.); SHADOW OF THE CAT, THE(1961, Brit.); QUEEN'S GUARDS, THE(1963, Brit.); 80,000 SUSPECTS(1963, Brit.); JULIUS CAESAR(1970, Brit.)
Anne Crawford
PRISON WITHOUT BARS(1939, Brit.); PETERVILLE DIAMOND, THE(1942, Brit.); WINGS AND THE WOMAN(1942, Brit.); DARK TOWER, THE(1943, Brit.); HEADLINE(1943, Brit.); HUNDRED POUND WINDOW, THE(1943, Brit.); MILLIONS LIKE US(1943, Brit.); NIGHT INVADER, THE(1943, Brit.); 2,000 WOMEN(1944, Brit.); THEY WERE SISTERS(1945, Brit.); BEDELIA(1946, Brit.); CARAVAN(1946, Brit.); MASTER OF BANKDAM, THE(1947, Brit.); BLIND GODDESS, THE(1948, Brit.); DAUGHTER OF DARKNESS(1948, Brit.); NIGHT BEAT(1948, Brit.); IT'S HARD TO BE GOOD(1950, Brit.); TRIO(1950, Brit.); THUNDER ON THE HILL(1951); TONY DRAWS A HORSE(1951, Brit.); BOTH SIDES OF THE LAW(1953, Brit.); KNIGHTS OF THE ROUND TABLE(1953); MAD ABOUT MEN(1954, Brit.)
Bobby Crawford
DUEL AT DIABLO(1966)
Boyd Crawford
JUDGE HARDY'S CHILDREN(1938)
Broderick Crawford
TIME OF YOUR LIFE, THE(1948); WOMAN CHASES MAN(1937); START CHEERING(1938); AMBUSH(1939); BEAU GESTE(1939); ETERNALLY YOURS(1939); ISLAND OF LOST MEN(1939); REAL GLORY, THE(1939); SUDDEN MONEY(1939); UNDERCOVER DOCTOR(1939); I CAN'T GIVE YOU ANYTHING BUT LOVE, BABY(1940); SEVEN SINNERS(1940); SLIGHTLY HONORABLE(1940); TEXAS RANGERS RIDE AGAIN(1940); TRAIL OF THE VIGILANTES(1940); WHEN THE DALTONS RODE(1940); BADLANDS OF DAKOTA(1941); BLACK CAT, THE(1941); SOUTH OF TAHITI(1941); TIGHT SHOES(1941); BROADWAY(1942); BUTCH MINDS THE BABY(1942); LARCENY, INC.(1942); MEN OF TEXAS(1942); NORTH TO THE KLONDIKE(1942); SIN TOWN(1942); BLACK ANGEL(1946); RUNAROUND, THE(1946); SLAVE GIRL(1947); FLAME, THE(1948); SEALED VERDICT(1948); ALL THE KING'S MEN(1949); ANNA LUCASTA(1949); BAD MEN OF TOMBSTONE(1949); KISS IN THE DARK, A(1949); NIGHT UNTO NIGHT(1949); CARGO TO CAPETOWN(1950); CONVICTED(1950); BORN YESTERDAY(1951); MOB, THE(1951); LAST OF THE COMANCHES(1952); LONE STAR(1952); SCANDAL SHEET(1952); STOP, YOU'RE KILLING ME(1952); LAST POSSE, THE(1953); DOWN THREE DARK STREETS(1954); HUMAN DESIRE(1954); NIGHT PEOPLE(1954); BIG HOUSE, U.S.A.(1955); NEW YORK CONFIDENTIAL(1955); NOT AS A STRANGER(1955); BETWEEN HEAVEN AND HELL(1956); FASTEST GUN ALIVE(1956); DECKS RAN RED, THE(1958); GOLIATH AND THE DRAGON(1961, Ital./Fr.); CONVICTS FOUR(1962); LAST OF THE VIKINGS, THE(1962, Fr./Ital.); SWINDLE, THE(1962, Fr./Ital.); CASTILIAN, THE(1963, Span./U.S.); SQUARE OF VIOLENCE(1963, U.S./Yugo.); HOUSE IS NOT A HOME, A(1964); UP FROM THE BEACH(1965); KID RODELO(1966, U.S./Span.); OSCAR, THE(1966); TEXICAN, THE(1966, U.S./Span.); RED TOMAHAWK(1967); VULTURE, THE(1967, U.S./Brit./Can.); HELL'S BLOODY DEVILS(1969); CANDIDATE, THE(1972); EMBASSY(1972, Brit.); TERROR IN THE WAX MUSEUM(1973); WON TON TON, THE DOG WHO SAVED HOLLYWOOD(1976); PRIVATE FILES OF J. EDGAR HOOVER, THE(1978); LITTLE ROMANCE, A(1979, U.S./Fr.); HARLEQUIN(1980, Aus.); THERE GOES THE BRIDE(1980, Brit.); LIAR'S MOON(1982)
Misc. Talkies
GREGORIO(1968); UPPERCRUST, THE(1982)
Caritz Crawford
GIRL SAID NO, THE(1937)
Carol Ann Crawford
1984
ANOTHER TIME, ANOTHER PLACE(1984, Brit.)
Christina Crawford
FORCE OF IMPULSE(1961); WILD IN THE COUNTRY(1961); MOMMIE DEAREST(1981), w

Clifton Crawford
Misc. Silents
GALLOPER, THE(1915)
Clyde Crawford
DRIVE, HE SAID(1971)
David Crawford
TO KILL A MOCKINGBIRD(1962); DAWN OF THE DEAD(1979)
Dennis Crawford
LAST HOUSE ON DEAD END STREET(1977)
Misc. Talkies
FUN HOUSE, THE(1977)
Don Crawford
C'MON, LET'S LIVE A LITTLE(1967); CHANGE OF MIND(1969)
Earl Crawford
ARIZONA(1940); NAVAJO TRAIL, THE(1945)
Ellen Crawford
1984
BEST DEFENSE(1984); TEACHERS(1984)
Ethel Marie Crawford
BOOK OF NUMBERS(1973)
F. Marion Crawford
SON OF INDIA(1931), w
Florence Crawford
Misc. Silents
PATH OF HAPPINESS, THE(1916)
Francis Marion Crawford
WHITE SISTER, THE(1933), w
Silents
WHITE SISTER, THE(1923), w
George Crawford
DICK BARTON STRIKES BACK(1949, Brit.); DICK BARTON AT BAY(1950, Brit.)
Gwen Crawford
FALCON IN HOLLYWOOD, THE(1944); HERE COME THE WAVES(1944); LADIES COURAGEOUS(1944); BELLS OF ST. MARY'S, THE(1945); FIRST YANK INTO TOKYO(1945)
Howard Crawford
HASTY HEART, THE(1949)
Howard Marion Crawford
BORN FOR GLORY(1935, Brit.); MUSIC HATH CHARMS(1935, Brit.); MISTER HOBO(1936, Brit.); NOTORIOUS GENTLEMAN(1945, Brit.); MAN ON THE RUN(1949, Brit.); HIS EXCELLENCY(1952, Brit.); MAN IN THE WHITE SUIT, THE(1952); WHERE'S CHARLEY?(1952, Brit.); KNIGHTS OF THE ROUND TABLE(1953); DON'T BLAME THE STORK(1954, Brit.); PAID TO KILL(1954, Brit.); RAINBOW JACKET, THE(1954, Brit.); WEST OF ZANZIBAR(1954, Brit.); BIRTHDAY PRESENT, THE(1957, Brit.); REACH FOR THE SKY(1957, Brit.); NOWHERE TO GO(1959, Brit.); SILENT ENEMY, THE(1959, Brit.); FOXHOLE IN CAIRO(1960, Brit.); VIRGIN ISLAND(1960, Brit.); LAWRENCE OF ARABIA(1962, Brit.); LIFE IN DANGER(1964, Brit.); MAN IN THE MIDDLE(1964, U.S./Brit.); TAMAHINE(1964, Brit.); BRIDES OF FU MANCHU, THE(1966, Brit.); SECRETS OF A WINDMILL GIRL(1966, Brit.); BLOOD OF FU MANCHU, THE(1968, Brit.); CASTLE OF FU MANCHU, THE(1968, Ger./Span./Ital./Brit.); VENGEANCE OF FU MANCHU, THE(1968, Brit./Ger./Hong Kong/Ireland)
J.A. Crawford
STRIPES(1981)
Jack Crawford
HARD TO HANDLE(1933)
Silents
BATTLE CRY OF PEACE, THE(1915)
Jim Crawford
HIS MAJESTY O'KEEFE(1953)
Jimmy Crawford
PLAY IT COOL(1963, Brit.)
Joan Crawford
OUR MODERN MAIDENS(1929); UNTAMED(1929); BLUSHING BRIDES(1930); MONTANA MOON(1930); OUR BLUSHING BRIDES(1930); PAID(1930); DANCE, FOOLS, DANCE(1931); LAUGHING SINNERS(1931); POSSESSED(1931); THIS MODERN AGE(1931); GRAND HOTEL(1932); LETTY LYNTON(1932); RAIN(1932); DANCING LADY(1933); TODAY WE LIVE(1933); CHAINED(1934); SADIE MCKEE(1934); FORSAKING ALL OTHERS(1935); I LIVE MY LIFE(1935); NO MORE LADIES(1935); GORGEOUS HUSSY, THE(1936); LOVE ON THE RUN(1936); BRIDE WORE RED, THE(1937); LAST OF MRS. CHEYNEY, THE(1937); MANNEQUIN(1937); SHINING HOUR, THE(1938); ICE FOLLIES OF 1939(1939); WOMEN, THE(1939); STRANGE CARGO(1940); SUSAN AND GOD(1940); WHEN LADIES MEET(1941); WOMAN'S FACE(1941); REUNION IN FRANCE(1942); THEY ALL KISSED THE BRIDE(1942); ABOVE SUSPICION(1943); HOLLYWOOD CANTEEN(1944); MILDRED PIERCE(1945); HUMORESQUE(1946); DAISY KENYON(1947); POSSESSED(1947); FLAMINGO ROAD(1949); IT'S A GREAT FEELING(1949); DAMNED DON'T CRY, THE(1950); HARRIET CRAIG(1950); GOODBYE, MY FANCY(1951); SUDDEN FEAR(1952); THIS WOMAN IS DANGEROUS(1952); TORCH SONG(1953); JOHNNY GUITAR(1954); FEMALE ON THE BEACH(1955); QUEEN BEE(1955); AUTUMN LEAVES(1956); STORY OF ESTHER COSTELLO(1957, Brit.); BEST OF EVERYTHING, THE(1959); WHATEVER HAPPENED TO BABY JANE?(1962); CARETAKERS, THE(1963); STRAIT-JACKET(1964); I SAW WHAT YOU DID(1965); BERSERK(1967); KARATE KILLERS, THE(1967); TROG(1970, Brit.)
Silents
OLD CLOTHES(1925); TRAMP, TRAMP, TRAMP(1926); TAXI DANCER, THE(1927); TWELVE MILES OUT(1927); UNKNOWN, THE(1927); ACROSS THE SINGAPORE(1928); FOUR WALLS(1928); LAW OF THE RANGE, THE(1928); OUR DANCING DAUGHTERS(1928); WEST POINT(1928); DUKE STEPS OUT, THE(1929); OUR MODERN MAIDENS(1929)
Misc. Silents
SALLY, IRENE AND MARY(1925); BOOB, THE(1926); PARIS(1926); SPRING FEVER(1927); UNDERSTANDING HEART, THE(1927); WINNERS OF THE WILDERNESS(1927); DREAM OF LOVE(1928); ROSE-MARIE(1928)
Joanna Crawford
DEAR HEART(1964); MY SIDE OF THE MOUNTAIN(1969), w; LITTLE ARK, THE(1972), w; BIRCH INTERVAL(1976), a, w
John Crawford
WITHOUT RESERVATIONS(1946); PHANTOM OF 42ND STREET, THE(1945); THOROUGHBREDS(1945); TIME OF THEIR LIVES, THE(1946); SONS OF ADVENTURE(1948); CYRANO DE BERGERAC(1950); LONELY HEARTS BANDITS(1950);

MYSTERY STREET(1950); UNION STATION(1950); HONEYCHILE(1951); I WAS A COMMUNIST FOR THE F.B.I.(1951); RATON PASS(1951); ACTORS AND SIN(1952); GREATEST SHOW ON EARTH, THE(1952); NORTHWEST TERRITORY(1952); OLD OKLAHOMA PLAINS(1952); SCARAMOUCHE(1952); STOP, YOU'RE KILLING ME(1952); BIG HEAT, THE(1953); CONQUEST OF COCHISE(1953); MAN CRAZY(1953); MARSHAL OF CEDAR ROCK(1953); REBEL CITY(1953); SALOME(1953); SERPENT OF THE NILE(1953); SLAVES OF BABYLON(1953); STAR OF TEXAS(1953); THREE SAILORS AND A GIRL(1953); BATTLE OF ROGUE RIVER(1954); CAPTAIN KIDD AND THE SLAVE GIRL(1954); MAN IN THE GREY FLANNEL SUIT, THE(1956); COURAGE OF BLACK BEAUTY(1957); FLOODS OF FEAR(1958, Brit.); INTENT TO KILL(1958, Brit.); KEY, THE(1958, Brit.); ORDERS TO KILL(1958, Brit.); SATAN'S SATELLITES(1958); SPACE CHILDREN, THE(1958); GHOST OF ZORRO(1959); JOHN PAUL JONES(1959); EXODUS(1960); HELL IS A CITY(1960, Brit.); MAN WHO WAS NOBODY, THE(1960, Brit.); PICCADILLY THIRD STOP(1960, Brit.); LONG SHADOW, THE(1961, Brit.); DEVIL'S MESSENGER, THE(1962 U.S./Swed.); IMPERSONATOR, THE(1962, Brit.); LONGEST DAY, THE(1962); 300 SPARTANS, THE(1962); CAPTAIN SINDBAD(1963); COME FLY WITH ME(1963); JASON AND THE ARGONAUTS(1963, Brit.); VICTORS, THE(1963); AMERICANIZATION OF EMILY, THE(1964); GREATEST STORY EVER TOLD, THE(1965); I SAW WHAT YOU DID(1965); DUEL AT DIABLO(1966); BALLAD OF CABLE HOGUE, THE(1970), w; MISS JESSICA IS PREGNANT(1970); J.W. COOP(1971); NAPOLEON AND SAMANTHA(1972); POSEIDON ADVENTURE, THE(1972); TROUBLE MAN(1972); TOWERING INFERNO, THE(1974); NIGHT MOVES(1975); ENFORCER, THE(1976); OUTLAW BLUES(1977); APPLE DUMPLING GANG RIDES AGAIN, THE(1979); DREAMER(1979); TILT(1979); BOOGENS, THE(1982)
Misc. Talkies
CRAWLING ARM, THE(1973); SEVERED ARM(1973); HOLLYWOOD KNIGHT(1979)
John Robert Crawford
RED LINE 7000(1965)
Johnny Crawford
INDIAN PAINT(1965); RESTLESS ONES, THE(1965); VILLAGE OF THE GIANTS(1965); EL DORADO(1967); NAKED APE, THE(1973); INBREAKER, THE(1974, Can.); GREAT TEXAS DYNAMITE CHASE, THE(1976)
Junia Crawford
GIRL IN THE PICTURE, THE(1956, Brit.); TONS OF TROUBLE(1956, Brit.); DOCTOR AT LARGE(1957, Brit.); MIRACLE IN SOHO(1957, Brit.); ALL AT SEA(1958, Brit.)
Katherine Crawford
CITY OF MISSING GIRLS(1941); WALK IN THE SPRING RAIN, A(1970)
Misc. Talkies
RIDING WITH DEATH(1976)
Kathryn Crawford
MODERN LOVE(1929); SENOR AMERICANO(1929); CLIMAX, THE(1930); CONCENTRATIN' KID, THE(1930); HIDE-OUT, THE(1930); MOUNTAIN JUSTICE(1930); RED HOT RHYTHM(1930); SAFETY IN NUMBERS(1930); FLYING HIGH(1931); EMMA(1932); NEW MORALS FOR OLD(1932); SKYWAY(1933)
Silents
KID'S CLEVER, THE(1929); KING OF THE RODEO(1929)
Kelton Crawford
PANIC IN YEAR ZERO!(1962)
Lana Crawford
MANCHURIAN CANDIDATE, THE(1962)
Les Crawford
INNOCENT BYSTANDERS(1973, Brit.), stunts; FLASH GORDON(1980)
Leslie Crawford
HIDE AND SEEK(1964, Brit.); ON HER MAJESTY'S SECRET SERVICE(1969, Brit.); TAMARIND SEED, THE(1974, Brit.)
Lester Crawford
FIFTY MILLION FRENCHMEN(1931); MY WOMAN(1933)
Lilybell Crawford
THOMASINE AND BUSHROD(1974); MAN WHO FELL TO EARTH, THE(1976, Brit.)
Loraine Crawford
MATCHMAKER, THE(1958)
Lorraine Crawford
MEXICAN HAYRIDE(1948); GIRL FROM JONES BEACH, THE(1949); GREAT SINNER, THE(1949); WHITE CHRISTMAS(1954); STRANGERS WHEN WE MEET(1960); PATSY, THE(1964)
Martha Crawford
UNSUSPECTED, THE(1947)
Melville Crawford
SEND FOR PAUL TEMPLE(1946, Brit.); WOMAN TO WOMAN(1946, Brit.); GUNMAN HAS ESCAPED, A(1948, Brit.); SCOTT OF THE ANTARCTIC(1949, Brit.)
Merritt Crawford
Silents
BATTLES OF THE CORONEL AND FALKLAND ISLANDS, THE(1928, Brit.), w
Michael Crawford
BLOW YOUR OWN TRUMPET(1958, Brit.); SOAPBOX DERBY(1958, Brit.); WAR LOVER, THE(1962, U.S./Brit.); TWO LIVING, ONE DEAD(1964, Brit./Swed.); KNACK ... AND HOW TO GET IT, THE(1965, Brit.); TWO LEFT FEET(1965, Brit.); FUNNY THING HAPPENED ON THE WAY TO THE FORUM, A(1966); HOW I WON THE WAR(1967, Brit.); JOKERS, THE(1967, Brit.); HELLO, DOLLY!(1969); GAMES, THE(1970); HELLO—GOODBYE(1970); ALICE'S ADVENTURES IN WONDERLAND(1972, Brit.); CONDORMAN(1981)
Misc. Talkies
PRELUDE TO TAURUS(1972)
Morris DeCamp Crawford
Silents
KNOCKOUT, THE(1925), w
Nancy Crawford
WITCHMAKER, THE(1969)
Nancy Voyles Crawford
SIDEWINDER ONE(1977), w; CARAVANS(1978, U.S./Iranian), w
Ned Crawford
KID FROM KOKOMO, THE(1939)
Ninette Crawford
PARACHUTE NURSE(1942)
Oliver Crawford
MAN FROM THE ALAMO, THE(1953), w; STEEL CAGE, THE(1954), w; GIRL IN THE WOODS(1958), w

Patrick M. Crawford
PRIVATE EYES, THE(1980), ed
Pauline Crawford
NUTCRACKER(1982, Brit.)
Peggy Crawford
MURDER AT THE CABARET(1936, Brit.)
Percy Crawford
Silents
MARCH HARE, THE(1919, Brit.)
Pete Crawford
WEST OF THE ROCKIES(1929)
Richard Crawford
CAPTAIN MILKSHAKE(1970), p&d, w
Silents
NIGHT BRIDE, THE(1927)
Robert Crawford
LAW OF THE RANGE(1941), m
Robert Crawford, Jr.
GREAT IMPOSTOR, THE(1960); WONDERFUL WORLD OF THE BROTHERS ERIMM, THE(1962); INDIAN PAINT(1965); HAWAII(1966)
Robert Crawford, Sr.
INDIAN PAINT(1965), a, ed
Robert L. Crawford
LITTLE ROMANCE, A(1979, U.S./Fr.), p; WORLD ACCORDING TO GARP, The(1982), p
1984
LITTLE DRUMMER GIRL, THE(1984), p
Sam Crawford
Silents
COLLEGE(1927)
Sarah Crawford
VALLEY OF EAGLES(1952, Brit.)
Stuart Crawford
DR. KILDARE'S VICTORY(1941); MR. AND MRS. NORTH(1941); NAZI AGENT(1942); SHIP AHOY(1942); YANK ON THE BURMA ROAD, A(1942); NEVER A DULL MOMENT(1943); CRIME BY NIGHT(1944)
Terrayne Crawford
SAM'S SONG(1971); SHARKY'S MACHINE(1982)
Terry Crawford
HOUSE OF DARK SHADOWS(1970); MAIDSTONE(1970)
W. Lane Crawford
WHEN THE DEVIL WAS WELL(1937, Brit.), w
Wayne Crawford
BARRACUDA(1978), p&w; VALLEY GIRL(1983), a, p, w
1984
NIGHT OF THE COMET(1984), p
Wayne David Crawford
BARRACUDA(1978)
William Crawford
SYNANON(1965)
Melville Crawfurd
I'LL TURN TO YOU(1946, Brit.)
Constance Crawley
Silents
THAIS(1914), a, d
Misc. Silents
FATAL NIGHT, THE(1915); EMBERS(1916); LORD LOVELAND DISCOVERS AMERICA(1916); POWDER(1916); REVELATIONS(1916)
Sandy Crawley
SILENT PARTNER, THE(1979, Can.)
Frank Crawshaw
KATHLEEN(1938, Ireland); THREE WEIRD SISTERS, THE(1948, Brit.); MR. H. C. ANDERSEN(1950, Brit.); HALF A SIXPENCE(1967, Brit.); MAN OUTSIDE, THE(1968, Brit.); OLIVER!(1968, Brit.)
Eliot Crawshay-Williams
FASCINATION(1931, Brit.), w; RESERVED FOR LADIES(1932, Brit.), w
Lew Crawson
DUKE IS THE TOPS, THE(1938), ch
Letty Craydon
KANGAROO(1952)
Misc. Talkies
LET GEORGE DO IT(1938, Aus.)
Jonathan Crayford
1984
PALLET ON THE FLOOR(1984, New Zealand), m
Dani Crayne
AIN'T MISBEHAVIN'(1955); DAY OF FURY, A(1956); UNGUARDED MOMENT, THE(1956); WORLD IN MY CORNER(1956); WRITTEN ON THE WIND(1956); SHOOT-OUT AT MEDICINE BEND(1957); STORY OF MANKIND, THE(1957)
Frank Hall Crayne
THERE'S THAT WOMAN AGAIN(1938)
Hessel Crayne
Silents
HANDY ANDY(1921, Brit.)
Michael Craze
TWO LEFT FEET(1965, Brit.); NEITHER THE SEA NOR THE SAND(1974, Brit.); TERROR(1979, Brit.)
Peter Craze
SECRET OF BLOOD ISLAND, THE(1965, Brit.); BEAST IN THE CELLAR, THE(1971, Brit.); TERROR(1979, Brit.)
Wanda Crazer
Silents
ABRAHAM LINCOLN(1924)
The Crazy World of Arthur Brown
COMMITTEE, THE(1968, Brit.)
Everett Creach
WAY WEST, THE(1967); LOVE BUG, THE(1968); GREAT BANK ROBBERY, THE(1969); TELL THEM WILLIE BOY IS HERE(1969); BIG JAKE(1971); EVEL KNIEVEL(1971), stunts; WRATH OF GOD, THE(1972), stunts; CAR, THE(1977), stunts; DRIVER, THE(1978), stunts; STRAIGHT TIME(1978), stunts; TIME AFTER

TIME(1979, Brit.), stunts; MAN WITH BOGART'S FACE, THE(1980); MOTEL HELL(1980)
1984
BEST DEFENSE(1984), stunts

Everett L. Creach
PROPHECY(1979)

Everett Louis Creach
DIRTY HARRY(1971)

Linda Creagan
HUNGRY WIVES(1973)

Joe Creaghe
UP IN SMOKE(1978)

June Creaghe
UP IN SMOKE(1978)

Robert Cream
GENTLE RAIN, THE(1966, Braz.), w

Rev. Francis B. Creamer, Jr.
DEATHTRAP(1982)

John Creamer
HARD TIMES(1975)

Massey Creamer
RAGE, THE(1963, U.S./Mex.), p

Stanley Creamer
MOONSHINE COUNTY EXPRESS(1977)

William Creamer
1984
BLOOD SIMPLE(1984)

Patrick Crean
MASTER OF BALLANTRAE, THE(1953, U.S./Brit.), ch; WAR AND PEACE(1956, Ital./U.S.); FAREWELL TO ARMS, A(1957); SEVEN HILLS OF ROME, THE(1958); NAKED MAJA, THE(1959, Ital./U.S.); TREAD SOFTLY STRANGER(1959, Brit.); SWORD OF SHERWOOD FOREST(1961, Brit.), a, tech adv

Charles Creasap
BLAST OF SILENCE(1961)

John Creasey
SALUTE THE TOFF(1952, Brit.), w

Bob Creassman
DESTINATION TOKYO(1944)

Pauline Creasman
CAGED(1950)

Sammy Creason
1984
SONGWRITER(1984)

Victor Creatore
PURPLE GANG, THE(1960); POINT BLANK(1967); THOMAS CROWN AFFAIR, THE(1968)

Gladys Crebbin
Silents
MONEY ISN'T EVERYTHING(1925, Brit.)

Bill Creber
DOMINO PRINCIPLE, THE(1977), prod d
1984
PRODIGAL, THE(1984), prod d

Lew Creber
LINDA BE GOOD(1947), art d

Lewis Creber
CRACK-UP, THE(1937), art d; THINK FAST, MR. MOTO(1937), art d; WILD AND WOOLLY(1937), art d; MYSTERIOUS MR. MOTO(1938), art d; STRAIGHT, PLACE AND SHOW(1938), art d; FRONTIER MARSHAL(1939), art d; GORILLA, THE(1939), art d; GIRL IN 313(1940), art d; PIER 13(1940), art d; SHOOTING HIGH(1940), art d; YESTERDAY'S HEROES(1940), art d; SUN VALLEY SERENADE(1941), art d; A-HAUNTING WE WILL GO(1942), art d; IT HAPPENED IN FLATBUSH(1942), art d; MAN WHO WOULDN'T DIE, THE(1942), art d; MANILA CALLING(1942), art d; POSTMAN DIDN'T RING, THE(1942), art d; UNDYING MONSTER, THE(1942), art d; WHISPERING GHOSTS(1942), art d; DIXIE DUGAN(1943), art d; MARGIN FOR ERROR(1943), art d; PURPLE HEART, THE(1944), art d; ROGER TOUHY, GANGSTER!(1944), art d; WING AND A PRAYER(1944), art d; WINGED VICTORY(1944), art d; HOUSE ON 92ND STREET, THE(1945), art d; STATE FAIR(1945), art d; IT HAPPENED ON 5TH AVENUE(1947), art d; MILLION DOLLAR WEEKEND(1948), art d; PERILOUS WATERS(1948), art d; PREJUDICE(1949), art d; DESTINATION GOBI(1953), art d; GLORY BRIGADE, THE(1953), art d; FLIM-FLAM MAN, THE(1947), art d

Lewis H. Creber
WALKING DOWN BROADWAY(1938), art d; HIGH TIDE(1947), art d; DISASTER(1948), art d; DYNAMITE(1948), art d; SPEED TO SPARE(1948), art d; STRIKE IT RICH(1948), art d; WATERFRONT AT MIDNIGHT(1948), art d; EL DASO(1949), art d; LUCKY STIFF, THE(1949), art d; MANHANDLED(1949), art d; SPECIAL AGENT(1949), art d; EAGLE AND THE HAWK, THE(1950), art d; LAWLESS, THE(1950), art d; TRIPOLI(1950), art d; HONG KONG(1951), art d; LAST OUTPOST, THE(1951), art d; D-DAY, THE SIXTH OF JUNE(1956), art d; LAST WAGON, THE(1956), art d; ON THE THRESHOLD OF SPACE(1956), art d

Lewis W. Creber
MR. RECKLESS(1948), art d

William Creber
RIO CONCHOS(1964), art d; GREATEST STORY EVER TOLD, THE(1965), art d; DETECTIVE, THE(1968), art d; PLANET OF THE APES(1968), art d; THREE IN THE ATTIC(1968), prod d; JUSTINE(1969), art d; BENEATH THE PLANET OF THE APES(1970), art d; ESCAPE FROM THE PLANET OF THE APES(1971), art d; POSEIDON ADVENTURE, THE(1972), prod d; TOWERING INFERNO, THE(1974), prod d; HOPSCOTCH(1980), prod d

William J. Creber
SUPERDAD(1974), art d; ANY WHICH WAY YOU CAN(1980), art d; SIX PACK(1982), prod d; YES, GIORGIO(1982), prod d

Joseph Crebun
I LOVE A MYSTERY(1945)

Mike Crecco
NAKED IN THE SUN(1957)

Lony Crechales
KILLING KIND, THE(1973), w

Tony Crechales
BLOOD MANIA(1971), w; POINT OF TERROR(1971), w; IMPULSE(1975), w; ATTIC, THE(1979), w

Curtis Credel
OTHER SIDE OF THE MOUNTAIN–PART 2, THE(1978); HARD COUNTRY(1981)
1984
FIRESTARTER(1984)

The Credibility Gap
CRACKING UP(1977)

Patricia Cree
RAISING A RIOT(1957, Brit.)

Celeste Creech
TRICK BABY(1973)

Jim Creech
HELL WITH HEROES, THE(1968); IN ENEMY COUNTRY(1968); JIGSAW(1968); NOBODY'S PERFECT(1968)

Creed
WHILE THE SUN SHINES(1950, Brit.), cos

Roger Creed
WITHOUT RESERVATIONS(1946); FIVE GRAVES TO CAIRO(1943); MIRACLE OF MORGAN'S CREEK, THE(1944); CRACK-UP(1946); DEADLINE AT DAWN(1946); NOCTURNE(1946); O.S.S.(1946); WELL-GROOMED BRIDE, THE(1946); JOAN OF ARC(1948); MIRACLE OF THE BELLS, THE(1948); MY FAVORITE SPY(1951); LAS VEGAS STORY, THE(1952); TALL MAN RIDING(1955); GUNFIGHT AT THE O.K. CORRAL(1957); KETTLES ON OLD MACDONALD'S FARM, THE(1957); RAIDERS FROM BENEATH THE SEA(1964); ROBIN AND THE SEVEN HOODS(1964); JESSE JAMES MEETS FRANKENSTEIN'S DAUGHTER(1966); DELTA FACTOR, THE(1970), stunts; MOLLY MAGUIRES, THE(1970), stunts; THERE WAS A CROOKED MAN(1970), stunts; PIRANHA(1978); NORTH AVENUE IRREGULARS, THE(1979); HOPSCOTCH(1980)

Roger V. Creed
ROUSTABOUT(1964)

Wendy Creed
1984
ALMOST YOU(1984)

Richard Creedon
SNOW WHITE AND THE SEVEN DWARFS(1937), w

Coleman Creel
SUMMERSPELL(1983)

Ken Creel
PUFNSTUF(1970)

James A. Creelman
MOST DANGEROUS GAME, THE(1932), w
Silents
ALOMA OF THE SOUTH SEAS(1926), w

James Ashman Creelman
HALF SHOT AT SUNRISE(1930), w

James Ashmore Creelman
CIRCUS KID, THE(1928), w; GANG WAR(1928), w; LAST PERFORMANCE, THE(1929), w; VAGABOND LOVER(1929), p, w; DANGER LIGHTS(1930), s; HONOR OF THE FAMILY(1931), w; DANCERS IN THE DARK(1932), w; SOCIAL REGISTER(1934), w; EAST OF JAVA(1935), w; LAST DAYS OF POMPEII, THE(1935), w
Silents
SECOND FIDDLE(1923), w; GRIT(1924), w; SINNERS IN HEAVEN(1924), w; COMING OF AMOS, THE(1925), w; FINE MANNERS(1926), w; UNTAMED LADY, THE(1926), w; AIR LEGION, THE(1929), w
Misc. Silents
HIGH HAT(1927), d

James Creelman
KING KONG(1933), w; THESE THIRTY YEARS(1934), w; KING KONG(1976), w

Jack Creenhalgh
CODE OF THE RANGERS(1938), ph

Erica Creer
CIRCLE OF IRON(1979, Brit.); DOGS OF WAR, THE(1980, Brit.); GREAT MUPPET CAPER, THE(1981)

Ray Creevey
GRASS EATER, THE(1961), set d

Eddie Cregar
EXILE, THE(1947)

Laird Cregar
HUDSON'S BAY(1940); OH JOHNNY, HOW YOU CAN LOVE!(1940); BLOOD AND SAND(1941); CHARLEY'S AUNT(1941); BLACK SWAN, THE(1942); I WAKE UP SCREAMING(1942); JOAN OF PARIS(1942); RINGS ON HER FINGERS(1942); TEN GENTLEMEN FROM WEST POINT(1942); THIS GUN FOR HIRE(1942); HEAVEN CAN WAIT(1943); HELLO, FRISCO, HELLO(1943); HOLY MATRIMONY(1943); LODGER, THE(1944); HANGOVER SQUARE(1945)

Lawrence Cregar
JOHNNY ONE-EYE(1950); UNDERCOVER GIRL(1950)

Lewis Creger
BUFFALO BILL(1944), art d

Dorothy Crehan
I WAS A TEENAGE WEREWOLF(1957); REFORM SCHOOL GIRL(1957)

Joe Crehan
BLACK FURY(1935); CRIME TAKES A HOLIDAY(1938); MIDNIGHT INTRUDER(1938); DODGE CITY(1939); RETURN OF DR. X, THE(1939); GIRL TROUBLE(1942); CHARLIE CHAN IN BLACK MAGIC(1944); CAPTAIN TUGBOAT ANNIE(1945); SILVER RIVER(1948); AMAZON QUEST(1949)

Joseph Crehan
SECRETS OF A SECRETARY(1931); STOLEN HEAVEN(1931); HOLD THE PRESS(1933); AGAINST THE LAW(1934); HELL CAT, THE(1934); HERE COMES THE NAVY(1934); IT HAPPENED ONE NIGHT(1934); JIMMY THE GENT(1934); LINEUP, THE(1934); LOST LADY, A(1934); MAN WITH TWO FACES, THE(1934); VOICE IN THE NIGHT(1934); ALIBI IKE(1935); BRIGHT LIGHTS(1935); CASE OF THE LUCKY LEGS, THE(1935); DEVIL DOGS OF THE AIR(1935); DINKY(1935); DON'T BET ON BLONDES(1935); FRISCO KID(1935); FRONT PAGE WOMAN(1935); GO INTO YOUR DANCE(1935); MAN OF IRON(1935); OIL FOR THE LAMPS OF CHINA(1935); PAGE MISS GLORY(1935); PAYOFF, THE(1935); SECRET BRIDE, THE(1935); SHIPMATES FOREVER(1935); SPECIAL AGENT(1935); STRANDED(1935); STRANGE WI-

VES(1935); TRAVELING SALESLADY, THE(1935); WE'RE IN THE MONEY(1935); ANTHONY ADVERSE(1936); BENGAL TIGER(1936); BOULDER DAM(1936); BULLETS OR BALLOTS(1936); CAIN AND MABEL(1936); CHINA CLIPPER(1936); DOWN THE STRETCH(1936); EARTHWORM TRACTORS(1936); GOLD DIGGERS OF 1937(1936); HERE COMES CARTER(1936); JAILBREAK(1936); KING OF HOCKEY(1936); LAW IN HER HANDS, THE(1936); MURDER BY AN ARISTOCRAT(1936); MURDER OF DR. HARRIGAN, THE(1936); ROAD GANG(1936); SINGING KID, THE(1936); TRAILIN' WEST(1936); BORN RECKLESS(1937); CASE OF THE STUTTERING BISHOP, THE(1937); CHEROKEE STRIP(1937); DRAEGERMAN COURAGE(1937); DUKE COMES BACK, THE(1937); GIRLS CAN PLAY(1937); GO-GETTER, THE(1937); GOD'S COUNTRY AND THE WOMAN(1937); GUNS OF THE PECOS(1937); HER HUSBAND'S SECRETARY(1937); HERE'S FLASH CASEY(1937); KID COMES BACK, THE(1937); KID GALAHAD(1937); MARRIED BEFORE BREAKFAST(1937); MIDNIGHT COURT(1937); MIDNIGHT MADONNA(1937); ONCE A DOCTOR(1937); OUTLAWS OF THE ORIENT(1937); SMART BLONDE(1937); TALENT SCOUT(1937); THERE GOES MY GIRL(1937); THIS IS MY AFFAIR(1937); WRONG ROAD, THE(1937); ALEXANDER'S RAGTIME BAND(1938); BILLY THE KID RETURNS(1938); FOUR'S A CROWD(1938); GIRLS ON PROBATION(1938); GOLDWYN FOLLIES, THE(1938); HAPPY LANDING(1938); ILLEGAL TRAFFIC(1938); MAMA RUNS WILD(1938); NIGHT SPOT(1938); WOMAN AGAINST WOMAN(1938); BABES IN ARMS(1939); BEHIND PRISON GATES(1939); BLACKMAIL(1939); GERONIMO(1939); MAISIE(1939); NAVY SECRETS(1939); NEWSBOY'S HOME(1939); PRIDE OF THE NAVY(1939); PRIVATE DETECTIVE(1939); ROARING TWENTIES, THE(1939); SOCIETY LAWYER(1939); ST. LOUIS BLUES(1939); STANLEY AND LIVINGSTONE(1939); STAR MAKER, THE(1939); STAR REPORTER(1939); TELL NO TALES(1939); UNION PACIFIC(1939); WE ARE NOT ALONE(1939); WHISPERING ENEMIES(1939); WINGS OF THE NAVY(1939); YOU CAN'T GET AWAY WITH MURDER(1939); BROTHER ORCHID(1940); EMERGENCY SQUAD(1940); FIGHTING 69TH, THE(1940); GAUCHO SERENADE(1940); HOUSE ACROSS THE BAY, THE(1940); INVISIBLE STRIPES(1940); MUSIC IN MY HEART(1940); PUBLIC DEB NO. 1(1940); SANTA FE TRAIL(1940); SECRET SEVEN, THE(1940); TEXAS RANGERS RIDE AGAIN(1940); CASE OF THE BLACK PARROT, THE(1941); CITY, FOR CONQUEST(1941); DOCTORS DON'T TELL(1941); HERE COMES HAPPINESS(1941); HERE COMES MR. JORDAN(1941); LIFE BEGINS FOR ANDY HARDY(1941); LOVE CRAZY(1941); MAN BETRAYED, A(1941); MANPOWER(1941); NEVADA CITY(1941); NINE LIVES ARE NOT ENOUGH(1941); SCATTERGOOD BAINES(1941); SEALED LIPS(1941); TEXAS(1941); WASHINGTON MELODRAMA(1941); GAY SISTERS, THE(1942); HELLO ANNAPOLIS(1942); LARCENY, INC.(1942); MEN OF TEXAS(1942); MURDER IN THE BIG HOUSE(1942); THEY DIED WITH THEIR BOOTS ON(1942); TO THE SHORES OF TRIPOLI(1942); TREAT 'EM' ROUGH(1942); TRUE TO THE ARMY(1942); WILD BILL HICKOK RIDES(1942); YOU CAN'T ESCAPE FOREVER(1942); EYES OF THE UNDERWORLD(1943); FALSE FACES(1943); FLESH AND FANTASY(1943); HANDS ACROSS THE BORDER(1943); HIT THE ICE(1943); HONEYMOON LODGE(1943); IRON MAJOR, THE(1943); JOHNNY COME LATELY(1943); JUNIOR ARMY(1943); KEEP 'EM SLUGGING(1943); MISSION TO MOSCOW(1943); MR. LUCKY(1943); MYSTERY BROADCAST(1943); OLD ACQUAINTANCE(1943); SHE HAS WHAT IT TAKES(1943); WOMAN OF THE TOWN, THE(1943); ADVENTURES OF MARK TWAIN, THE(1944); MISSING JUROR, THE(1944); NAVY WAY, THE(1944); ONE MYSTERIOUS NIGHT(1944); PHANTOM LADY(1944); ROGER TOUHY, GANGSTER!(1944); SHINE ON, HARVEST MOON(1944); WHEN THE LIGHTS GO ON AGAIN(1944); BREWSTER'S MILLIONS(1945); CHICAGO KID, THE(1945); DICK TRACY(1945); LADY ON A TRAIN(1945); MAN ALIVE(1945); YOUTH ON TRIAL(1945); ZIEGFELD FOLLIES(1945); BAD BASCOMB(1946); BEHIND THE MASK(1946); BIG SLEEP, THE(1946); DANGEROUS MONEY(1946); DEADLINE AT DAWN(1946); DICK TRACY VS. CUEBALL(1946); FALCON'S ADVENTURE, THE(1946); GIRL ON THE SPOT(1946); GUY COULD CHANGE, A(1946); MAGNIFICENT DOLL(1946); NIGHT TRAIN TO MEMPHIS(1946); O.S.S.(1946); PHANTOM THIEF, THE(1946); PLAINSMAN AND THE LADY(1946); SHADOW RETURNS, THE(1946); DEAD RECKONING(1947); DICK TRACY MEETS GRUESOME(1947); FOXES OF HARROW, THE(1947); LOUISIANA(1947); MONSIEUR VERDOUX(1947); PHILO VANCE'S GAMBLE(1947); SEA OF GRASS, THE(1947); TRESPASSER, THE(1947); TROUBLE WITH WOMEN, THE(1947); APRIL SHOWERS(1948); BECAUSE OF EVE(1948); BLONDIE'S SECRET(1948); COUNTESS OF MONTE CRISTO, THE(1948); ENCHANTED VALLEY, THE(1948); GALLANT LEGION, THE(1948); GOOD SAM(1948); HOMECOMING(1948); HOMICIDE FOR THREE(1948); HUNTED, THE(1948); NIGHT TIME IN NEVADA(1948); SONG IS BORN, A(1948); STREET CORNER(1948); SUNDOWN IN SANTA FE(1948); TRIPLE THREAT(1948); ALIAS THE CHAMP(1949); DANCING IN THE DARK(1949); DUKE OF CHICAGO(1949); LAST BANDIT, THE(1949); PREJUDICE(1949); RED DESERT(1949); RINGSIDE(1949); STATE DEPARTMENT–FILE 649(1949); TULSA(1949); ARIZONA COWBOY, THE(1950); MALAYA(1950); SQUARE DANCE KATY(1950); TOUGHER THEY COME, THE(1950); TRIPLE TROUBLE(1950); PRIDE OF MARYLAND(1951); ROADBLOCK(1951); DEADLINE–U.S.A.(1952); CRAZYLEGS, ALL AMERICAN(1953); HIGHWAY DRAGNET(1954)

Misc. Talkies
CADETS ON PARADE(1942)

Lewis Creher
KENTUCKY MOONSHINE(1938), art d

Norma Creiger
SINBAD THE SAILOR(1947)

Connie Creighton
HAPPIDROME(1943, Brit.)

Liza Creighton
SALLY FIELDGOOD & CO.(1975, Can.)

Patsy Creighton
MATING OF MILLIE, THE(1948); ADVENTURE IN BALTIMORE(1949)

Sally Creighton
THING, THE(1951); HAS ANYBODY SEEN MY GAL?(1952)

Walter Creighton
ONE FAMILY(1930, Brit.), d; BELOVED VAGABOND, THE(1936, Brit.), w

Jack Creley
CANADIANS, THE(1961, Brit.); DR. STRANGELOVE: OR HOW I LEARNED TO STOP WORRYING AND LOVE THE BOMB(1964); CHANGE OF MIND(1969); REINCARNATE, THE(1971, Can.); TULIPS(1981, Can); IF YOU COULD SEE WHAT I HEAR(1982); VIDEODROME(1983, Can.)

Joseph Creman
FULLER BRUSH GIRL, THE(1950)

Linda Cremeans
HARDCORE(1979)

Bruno Cremer
IS PARIS BURNING?(1966, U.S./Fr.); MARCO THE MAGNIFICENT(1966, Ital./Fr./Yugo./Egypt/Afghanistan); OBJECTIVE 500 MILLION(1966, Fr.); STRANGER, THE(1967, Algeria/Fr./Ital.); LE VIOL(1968, Fr./Swed.); SHOCK TROOPS(1968, Ital./Fr.); BYE BYE BARBARA(1969, Fr.); LES GAULOISES BLEUES(1969, Fr.); FRENCH CONSPIRACY, THE(1973, Fr.); SORCERER(1977)

Lance Cremer
MR. SYCAMORE(1975)

France Cremieux
CHAPPAQUA(1967)

Henri Cremieux
PERSONAL COLUMN(1939, Fr.); ORPHEUS(1950, Fr.); MR. PEEK-A-BOO(1951, Fr.); LE PLAISIR(1954, Fr.); HOLIDAY FOR HENRIETTA(1955, Fr.); WE ARE ALL MURDERERS(1957); LAW IS THE LAW, THE(1959, Fr.); NUDE IN A WHITE CAR(1960, Fr.); WOMAN OF SIN(1961, Fr.); LOVERS ON A TIGHTROPE(1962, Fr.); TESTAMENT OF ORPHEUS, THE(1962, Fr.); SEVENTH JUROR, THE(1964, Fr.); TWO ARE GUILTY(1964, Fr.); YOUNG GIRLS OF ROCHEFORT, THE(1968, Fr.); GIVE HER THE MOON(1970, Fr./Ital.)

Carlo Cremona
AUGUSTINE OF HIPPO(1973, Ital.), w

Italo Cremona
CARMELA(1949, Ital.), w

Joe Cremona
1984
SUPERGIRL(1984)

Paul Cremonesi
EAGLE AND THE HAWK, THE(1933); MAYTIME(1937); ARTISTS AND MODELS ABROAD(1938)

Richard Crenna
IT GROWS ON TREES(1952); PRIDE OF ST. LOUIS, THE(1952); RED SKIES OF MONTANA(1952); OUR MISS BROOKS(1956); OVER-EXPOSED(1956); JOHN GOLDFARB, PLEASE COME HOME(1964); MADE IN PARIS(1966); SAND PEBBLES, THE(1966); WAIT UNTIL DARK(1967); STAR!(1968); MAROONED(1969); MIDAS RUN(1969); CATLOW(1971, Span.); DESERTER, THE(1971 Ital./Yugo.); DOCTORS' WIVES(1971); RED SKY AT MORNING(1971); COP, A(1973, Fr.); JONATHAN LIVINGSTON SEAGULL(1973); MAN CALLED NOON, THE(1973, Brit.); BREAKHEART PASS(1976); DIRTY MONEY(1977, Fr.); EVIL, THE(1978); WILD HORSE HANK(1979, Can.); DEATH SHIP(1980, Can.); STONE COLD DEAD(1980, Can.); BODY HEAT(1981); FIRST BLOOD(1982); TABLE FOR FIVE(1983)
1984
FLAMINGO KID, THE(1984)

Hugh Crenshaw
FREE, WHITE AND 21(1963)

Aiden Crenwell
BOYD'S SHOP(1960, Brit.)

D. Creona
COSSACKS IN EXILE(1939, Ukrainian)

Dimitri Creona
GIRL FROM POLTAVA(1937)

Nini Crepon
SNOW(1983, Fr.)

Pamela Cresant
SMALL CIRCLE OF FRIENDS, A(1980)

Vince Cresceman
RETURN OF COUNT YORGA, THE(1971), art d

Antonio Crescenzi
NEXT!(1971, Ital./Span.), p

G. Luigi Crescenzi
DIRTY OUTLAWS, THE(1971, Ital.)

Gianluigi Crescenzi
SWEET SMELL OF LOVE(1966, Ital./Ger.); HILLS RUN RED, THE(1967, Ital.)

Isa Crescenzi
WARRIOR EMPRESS, THE(1961, Ital./Fr.); LOVE IN 4 DIMENSIONS(1965 Fr./Ital.)

Vince Cresciman
BITTERSWEET LOVE(1976), art d

Vincent Cresciman
STEELYARD BLUES(1973), art d; THIS IS A HIJACK(1973), art d; LEPKE(1975, U.S./Israel), set d
1984
RED DAWN(1984), art d

Vincent M. Cresciman
TRACKDOWN(1976), art d

Margery Cresley
REVENGE OF FRANKENSTEIN, THE(1958, Brit.)

Joan Crespi
SHAME OF THE SABINE WOMEN, THE(1962, Mex.)

Bill Crespinel
RADAR SECRET SERVICE(1950)

William T. Crespinel
Silents
GLORIOUS ADVENTURE, THE(1922, U.S./Brit.), ph

Israel Crespo
1984
DELIVERY BOYS(1984)

Jose Crespo
REVENGE AT MONTE CARLO(1933); HOLLYWOOD MYSTERY(1934); SENORA CASADA NECEISITA MARIDO(1935); STORM OVER THE ANDES(1935); RASCALS(1938)
Silents
JOY STREET(1929)

Mario Crespo, Jr.
RUN FOR THE ROSES(1978), p

Maud Cressall
Silents
MAN AND THE MOMENT, THE(1918, Brit.)
Misc. Silents
BARTON MYSTERY, THE(1920, Brit.); SCARLET KISS, THE(1920, Brit.); TINTED VENUS, THE(1921, Brit.)

Alex Cressan
TAMANGO(1959, Fr.)
Bob Cresse
SURFTIDE 77(1962)
R.W. Cresse
HOT SPUR(1968), p, w; HAREM BUNCH; OR WAR AND PIECE, THE(1969), p&w; SCAVENGERS, THE(1969), p, w
Dan Cressey
TECKMAN MYSTERY, THE(1955, Brit); WRONG BOX, THE(1966, Brit.)
John Cressey
SHADES OF SILK(1979, Can.)
Babe Cressman
Misc. Silents
DURAND OF THE BAD LANDS(1917)
James Cresson
GREENWICH VILLAGE STORY(1963); TRAVELS WITH MY AUNT(1972, Brit.), p; ABDICATION, THE(1974, Brit.), p; MAME(1974), p
Pierre Cressoy
CAROLINE CHERIE(1951, Fr.); WAR OF THE WORLDS, THE(1953); HELL RAIDERS OF THE DEEP(1954, Ital.); WALK INTO HELL(1957, Aus.); UNFAITHFULS, THE(1960, Ital.); DAVID AND GOLIATH(1961, Ital.); MARCO POLO(1962, Fr./Ital.); HERCULES VS THE GIANT WARRIORS(1965 Fr./Ital.); MONGOLS, THE(1966, Fr./Ital.); NAVAJO JOE(1967, Ital./Span.)
John Cresswell
FIVE ANGLES ON MURDER(1950, Brit.), w; SO LITTLE TIME(1953, Brit.), w; THREE'S COMPANY(1953, Brit.), w; ADVENTURE IN THE HOPFIELDS(1954, Brit.), w; BLONDE SINNER(1956, Brit.), w; CHARLEY MOON(1956, Brit.), w; PORT AFRIQUE(1956, Brit.), w; CAST A DARK SHADOW(1958, Brit.), w; BEYOND THE CURTAIN(1960, Brit.), w; SPARE THE ROD(1961, Brit.), w
Peter Cresswell
BELL-BOTTOM GEORGE(1943, Brit.), w; MEET ME AT DAWN(1947, Brit.), d; SHOWTIME(1948, Brit.), w; WHO KILLED VAN LOON?(1984, Brit.), w
Dan Cressy
MAN UPSTAIRS, THE(1959, Brit.)
John Cressy
SHADES OF SILK(1979, Can.), ph
Patricia Crest
BRAMBLE BUSH, THE(1960)
Rene Creste
Misc. Silents
VENDEMIAIRE(1919, Fr.)
Vasco Creti
BALL AT THE CASTLE(1939, Ital.)
Michel Creton
SHOCK TROOPS(1968, Ital./Fr.); MILKY WAY, THE(1969, Fr./Ital.); MISTER FREEDOM(1970, Fr.); BEYOND FEAR(1977, Fr.)
Alfredo B. Crevenna
INVISIBLE MAN, THE(1958, Mex.), d; YOUNG AND EVIL(1962, Mex.), d; GIGANTES PLANETARIOS(1965, Mex.), d; SANTO CONTRA LA INVASION DE LOS MARCIANOS(1966, Mex.), d
Alfredo Crevenna
REBELLION OF THE HANGED, THE(1954, Mex.), d
John Crewdson
FOLLOW THAT HORSE!(1960, Brit.); JET STORM(1961, Brit.); SQUADRON 633(1964, U.S./Brit.), stunts; ON HER MAJESTY'S SECRET SERVICE(1969, Brit.)
John M. Crewdson
PRIVATE FILES OF J. EDGAR HOOVER, THE(1978), tech adv
Robert Crewdson
ONE THAT GOT AWAY, THE(1958, Brit.); TWO-HEADED SPY, THE(1959, Brit.); BLOOD BEAST FROM OUTER SPACE(1965, Brit.); PSYCHOPATH, THE(1966, Brit.); TROG(1970, Brit.)
Bob Crewe
BARBARELLA(1968, Fr./Ital.), m
Robin Crewe
GYPSY GIRL(1966, Brit.)
Laurie Crewes
RAIN PEOPLE, THE(1969)
Jerry Crews
SUNRISE AT CAMPOBELLO(1960)
Laura Hope Crews
CHARMING SINNERS(1929); NEW MORALS FOR OLD(1932); BLIND ADVENTURE(1933); EVER IN MY HEART(1933); FEMALE(1933); I LOVED YOU WEDNESDAY(1933); IF I WERE FREE(1933); OUT ALL NIGHT(1933); SILVER CORD(1933); AGE OF INNOCENCE(1934); RAFTER ROMANCE(1934); BEHOLD MY WIFE(1935); ESCAPADE(1935); LIGHTNING STRIKES TWICE(1935); MELODY LINGERS ON, THE(1935); HER MASTER'S VOICE(1936); ANGEL(1937); CAMILLE(1937); CONFESSION(1937); ROAD BACK,THE(1937); DR. RHYTHM(1938); SISTERS, THE(1938); THANKS FOR THE MEMORY(1938); GONE WITH THE WIND(1939); IDIOT'S DELIGHT(1939); RAINS CAME, THE(1939); REMEMBER?(1939); RENO(1939); STAR MAKER, THE(1939); GIRL FROM AVENUE A(1940); I'M NOBODY'S SWEETHEART NOW(1940); LADY WITH RED HAIR(1940); FLAME OF NEW ORLEANS, THE(1941); ONE FOOT IN HEAVEN(1941); MAN WHO CAME TO DINNER, THE(1942)
Misc. Silents
FIGHTING HOPE, THE(1915)
Marlena Crews
FRATERNITY ROW(1977)
Mike Crews
1984
MAKING THE GRADE(1984)
Philip Crews
RETURN TO MACON COUNTY(1975)
Jacques Crey
DOUBLE BUNK(1961, Brit.)
Barry Creyton
THEY'RE A WEIRD MOB(1966, Aus.)
Jitka Crhova
DAISIES(1967, Czech.)

Cristobal Criado
OPEN SEASON(1974, U.S./Span.), makeup
Mik Cribben
NIGHTMARE(1981)
Bernard Cribbens
DANGEROUS DAVIES–THE LAST DETECTIVE(1981, Brit.)
Bernard Cribbins
DAVY(1958, Brit.); DUNKIRK(1958, Brit.); TOMMY THE TOREADOR(1960, Brit.); WORLD OF SUZIE WONG, THE(1960); NOTHING BARRED(1961, Brit.); PASSPORT TO CHINA(1961, Brit.); TWO-WAY STRETCH(1961, Brit.); BEST OF ENEMIES, THE(1962); GIRL ON THE BOAT, THE(1962, Brit.); CARRY ON JACK(1963, Brit.); MOUSE ON THE MOON, THE(1963, Brit.); WRONG ARM OF THE LAW, THE(1963, Brit.); CARRY ON SPYING(1964, Brit.); CROOKS IN CLOISTERS(1964, Brit.); CUP FEVER(1965, Brit.); MAKE MINE A MILLION(1965, Brit.); SHE(1965, Brit.); YOU MUST BE JOKING!(1965, Brit.); COUNTERFEIT CONSTABLE, THE(1966, Fr.); DALEKS–INVASION EARTH 2155 A.D.(1966, Brit.); SANDWICH MAN, THE(1966, Brit.); CASINO ROYALE(1967, Brit.); DON'T RAISE THE BRIDGE, LOWER THE RIVER(1968, Brit.); RAILWAY CHILDREN, THE(1971, Brit.); FRENZY(1972, Brit.); WATER BABIES, THE(1979, Brit.); ADVENTURES OF PICASSO, THE(1980, Swed.)
Misc. Talkies
GHOST OF A CHANCE, A(1968, Brit.)
Otis Criblecoblis [W.C. Fields]
NEVER GIVE A SUCKER AN EVEN BREAK(1941), w
Charles Crichton
SANDERS OF THE RIVER(1935, Brit.), ed; THINGS TO COME(1936, Brit.), ed; ELEPHANT BOY(1937, Brit.), ed; PRISON WITHOUT BARS(1939, Brit.), ed; OLD BILL AND SON(1940, Brit.), ed; THIEF OF BAGHDAD, THE(1940, Brit.), ed; TWENTY-ONE DAYS TOGETHER(1940, Brit.), ed; NINE MEN(1943, Brit.), p, ed; FOR THOSE IN PERIL(1944, Brit.), d; GIRL ON THE CANAL, THE(1947, Brit.), d; AGAINST THE WIND(1948, Brit.), d; ANOTHER SHORE(1948, Brit.), d; DANCE HALL(1950, Brit.), d; HUE AND CRY(1950, Brit.), d; LAVENDER HILL MOB, THE(1951, Brit.), d; STRANGER IN BETWEEN, THE(1952, Brit.), d; TRAIN OF EVENTS(1952, Brit.), d; TITFIELD THUNDERBOLT, THE(1953, Brit.), d; LOVE LOTTERY, THE(1954, Brit.), d; DIVIDED HEART, THE(1955, Brit.), d; DECISION AGAINST TIME(1957, Brit.), d; FLOODS OF FEAR(1958, Brit.), d, w; LAW AND DISORDER(1958, Brit.), d; BATTLE OF THE SEXES, THE(1960, Brit.), d; BOY WHO STOLE A MILLION, THE(1960, Brit.), d, w; THIRD SECRET, THE(1964, Brit.), d; HE WHO RIDES A TIGER(1966, Brit.), d
Don Crichton
STAR!(1968); CHU CHU AND THE PHILLY FLASH(1981), ch
Douglas Crichton
DEALING: OR THE BERKELEY-TO-BOSTON FORTY-BRICK LOST-BAG BLUES(1971), w
Knox Crichton
THINGS HAPPEN AT NIGHT(1948, Brit.)
Michael Crichton
ANDROMEDA STRAIN, THE(1971), w; DEALING: OR THE BERKELEY-TO-BOSTON FORTY-BRICK LOST-BAG BLUES(1971), w; WESTWORLD(1973), d&w; TERMINAL MAN, THE(1974), p,d&w; COMA(1978), d&w; GREAT TRAIN ROBBERY, THE(1979, Brit.), d&w; LOOKER(1981), d&w
1984
RUNAWAY(1984), d&w
Ollie Crichton
PACIFIC DESTINY(1956, Brit.)
Robert Crichton
GREAT IMPOSTOR, THE(1960), w; SECRET OF SANTA VITTORIA, THE(1969), w
William Crichton
HIGH AND DRY(1954, Brit.)
Ed Crick
RIVER NIGER, THE(1976)
Monte Crick
WHAT DO WE DO NOW?(1945, Brit.)
The Crickets
JUST FOR FUN(1963, Brit.)
David Crickett
HARD STEEL(1941, Brit.)
Mathieu Crico
1984
SUGAR CANE ALLEY(1984, Fr.)
Tom Criddle
MIDSUMMERS NIGHT'S DREAM, A(1961, Czech)
Dorothy Crider
GREATEST SHOW ON EARTH, THE(1952); GUNS OF FORT PETTICOAT, THE(1957); WILD AND WONDERFUL(1964), w
Gordon Crier
WHAT WOULD YOU DO, CHUMS?(1939, Brit.), w; BLACK GLOVE(1954, Brit.)
Jennifer Crier
MY FAIR LADY(1964)
Ann Crilley
CADDY SHACK(1980)
Andy Crim
Misc. Talkies
IN THE RAPTURE(1976)
W.W. Crimans
Misc. Silents
DAREDEVIL, THE(1918)
Marisa Crimi
GIANT OF MARATHON, THE(1960, Ital.), cos; NUN AT THE CROSSROADS, A(1970, Ital./Span.), cos
Ann Duncan Crimmins
PILGRIMAGE(1972), p
Dan Crimmins
SMILING IRISH EYES(1929); WHITE ZOMBIE(1932); MISSISSIPPI(1935); VAGABOND LADY(1935); JUNGLE PRINCESS, THE(1936)
Silents
JOHNNY GET YOUR GUN(1919); PINK TIGHTS(1920); MIDNIGHT EXPRESS, THE(1924); NOT SO LONG AGO(1925); PRETTY LADIES(1925)

Jeannine Crispin
FROM TOP TO BOTTOM(1933, Fr.)
Armando Crispini
Misc. Talkies
AUTOPSY(1980, Ital.), d
Armando Crispino
DEAD ARE ALIVE, THE(1972, Yugo./Ger./Ital.), d, w; FRANKENSTEIN-ITALIAN STYLE(1977, Ital.), d
Diana Crispo
PSYCHOUT FOR MURDER(1971, Arg./Ital.), w; STORY WITHOUT WORDS(1981, Ital.), w
Vittoria Crispo
BREAD, LOVE AND DREAMS(1953, Ital.); TREASURE OF SAN GENNARO(1968, Fr./Ital./Ger.)
Vittorio Crispo
PRIEST'S WIFE, THE(1971, Ital./Fr.)
Lamar Criss
CLASS OF '44(1973)
Sonny Criss
TWO ARE GUILTY(1964, Fr.)
Forrest Crissey
Silents
BAB'S CANDIDATE(1920), w
H. T. Crist
Silents
NO BABIES WANTED(1928), w
Harry P. Crist
Misc. Silents
CACTUS TRAILS(1927), d
Paul Crist
DARK, THE(1979)
Linda Cristal
COMANCHE(1956); FIEND WHO WALKED THE WEST, THE(1958); LAST OF THE FAST GUNS, THE(1958); PERFECT FURLOUGH, THE(1958); CRY TOUGH(1959); ALAMO, THE(1960); LEGIONS OF THE NILE(1960, Ital.); PHAROAH'S WOMAN, THE(1961, Ital.); TWO RODE TOGETHER(1961); PANIC IN THE CITY(1968); MR. MAJESTYK(1974); LOVE AND THE MIDNIGHT AUTO SUPPLY(1978)
Misc. Talkies
SLAVE GIRLS OF SHEBA(1960); HUGHES AND HARLOW: ANGELS IN HELL(1978)
Perla Cristal
AWFUL DR. ORLOFF, THE(1964, Span./Fr.); TALL WOMEN, THE(1967, Aust./Ital./Span.); WITCH WITHOUT A BROOM, A(1967, U.S./Span.); CHRISTMAS KID, THE(1968, U.S., Span.); SEVEN GUNS FOR THE MACGREGORS(1968, Ital./Span.)
Misc. Talkies
WHITE COMANCHE(1967); BEHIND THE SHUTTERS(1976, Span.)
Franco Cristaldi
BIG DEAL ON MADONNA STREET, THE(1960), p; ASSASSIN, THE(1961, Ital./Fr.), p; WHITE NIGHTS(1961, Ital./Fr.), p; DIVORCE, ITALIAN STYLE(1962, Ital.), p; FIASCO IN MILAN(1963, Fr./Ital.), p; OMICRON(1963, Ital.), p; BEBO'S GIRL(1964, Ital.), p; ORGANIZER, THE(1964, Fr./Ital./Yugo.), p; SEDUCED AND ABAN-DONED(1964, Fr./Ital.), p; TIME OF INDIFFERENCE(1965, Fr./Ital.), p; SAL-VATORE GIULIANO(1966, Ital.), p; SANDRA(1966, Ital.), p; ROSE FOR EVERYONE, A(1967, Ital.), p; CHINA IS NEAR(1968, Ital.), p; RED TENT, THE(1971, Ital./USSR), p; AMARCORD(1974, Ital.), p; RE: LUCKY LUCIANO(1974, Fr./Ital.), p; RATATA-PLAN(1979, Ital.), p; WIFEMISTRESS(1979, Ital.), p; CAFE EXPRESS(1980, Ital.), p; EBOLI(1980, Ital.), p; AND THE SHIP SAILS ON(1983, Ital./Fr.), p
Giorgio Cristallani
LEGIONS OF THE NILE(1960, Ital.), w
Dhia Cristani
OSSESSIONE(1959, Ital.)
Gabriella Cristani
TRAGEDY OF A RIDICULOUS MAN, THE(1982, Ital.), ed
Gabrielle Cristani
DEVIL'S MAN, THE(1967, Ital.), p
Ivo Cristante
PRIVATE SCHOOL(1983), prod d
Ivo G. Cristante
1984
WEEKEND PASS(1984), art d
Aldo Cristiani
MYSTERY OF THUG ISLAND, THE(1966, Ital./Ger.); WEB OF VIOLENCE(1966, Ital./Span.)
Antoinette Cristiani
ROPE OF FLESH(1965)
Belmonte Cristiani
THIS IS THE ARMY(1943)
Gabriella Cristiani
LUNA(1979, Ital.), ed
Tina Cristiani
BADGE 373(1973)
The Cristianis
CAROLINA BLUES(1944)
The Cristianos Troupe
SEE MY LAWYER(1945)
Corky Cristians
JUMBO(1962); UNSTRAP ME(1968)
Sebastian Cristillo
WAVE, A WAC AND A MARINE, A(1944), p; LITTLE GIANT(1946)
Olinto Cristina
LITTLE MARTYR, THE(1947, Ital.); CROSSROADS OF PASSION(1951, Fr.)
Mayra Cristine
DEATH CURSE OF TARTU(1967)
Raffaele Cristini
SEDUCED AND ABANDONED(1964, Fr./Ital.), makeup
Rita Cristinziano
Misc. Talkies
VALLEY OF BLOOD(1973)

Corinna Cristobal
TAKING OFF(1971)
Michael Cristofer
ENTERTAINER, THE(1975); ENEMY OF THE PEOPLE, AN(1978)
1984
FALLING IN LOVE(1984), w; LITTLE DRUMMER GIRL, THE(1984)
Michael Ivan Cristofer
CRAZY WORLD OF JULIUS VROODER, THE(1974)
Ciro Cristofoletti
DEATH IN VENICE(1971, Ital./Fr.)
Dorothy Cristy
PLAYBOY OF PARIS(1930)
Criswell
NIGHT OF THE GHOULS(1959); PLAN 9 FROM OUTER SPACE(1959); ORGY OF THE DEAD zero(1965)
Dude Criswell
JALOPY(1953)
Floyd Criswell
LIFE BEGINS AT 40(1935); MEET JOHN DOE(1941); SAN FRANCISCO DOCKS(1941); DELINQUENT DAUGHTERS(1944)
James Lee Crite
LEGEND OF THE LONE RANGER, THE(1981)
Ernie Crites
RAT FINK(1965)
Dianne Crittenden
SUNDAY LOVERS(1980, Ital./Fr.)
Dwight Crittenden
Silents
HOODLUM THE(1919); BOB HAMPTON OF PLACER(1921); HIGH HEELS(1921); TALE OF TWO WORLDS, A(1921)
Misc. Silents
STAR ROVER, THE(1920); OLD NEST, THE(1921); WOMAN'S SIDE, THE(1922)
Emily Crittenden
SUNDOWN RIDERS(1948)
James Crittenden
TURNING POINT, THE(1977)
1984
CRIMES OF PASSION(1984)
Jordon Crittenden
GET TO KNOW YOUR RABBIT(1972), w
Linda Crittenden
T.R. BASKIN(1971)
T. Dwight Crittenden
Silents
MIRACLE MAN, THE(1919)
T.C. Crittenden
Misc. Silents
MOTHER'S SECRET, A(1918)
T.D. Crittenden
Misc. Silents
ISLE OF LIFE, THE(1916)
Guerrino Crivello
BLACK BELLY OF THE TARANTULA, THE(1972, Ital.)
Tom Crizer
MY PAL, THE KING(1932), w
Silents
KID BROTHER, THE(1927), w; SPORTING GOODS(1928), w
Thomas J. Crizer
Silents
GRANDMA'S BOY(1922), w; WHY WORRY(1923), ed
Jana Crkalova
LOVES OF A BLONDE(1966, Czech.)
Zvonimir Crnko
RAMPAGE AT APACHE WELLS(1966, Ger./Yugo.)
Marija Crnobori
TEMPEST(1958, Ital./Yugo./Fr.)
Carlo Croccolo
GRAN VARIETA(1955, Ital.); JESSICA(1962, U.S./Ital./Fr.); RELUCTANT SAINT, THE(1962, U.S./Ital.); PANIC BUTTON(1964); TWELVE-HANDED MEN OF MARS, THE(1964, Ital./Span.); YESTERDAY, TODAY, AND TOMORROW(1964, Ital./Fr.); YELLOW ROLLS-ROYCE, THE(1965, Brit.); AFTER THE FOX(1966, U.S./Brit./Ital.); BIGGEST BUNDLE OF THEM ALL, THE(1968); DANGER: DIABOLIK(1968, Ital./Fr.)
Alfred Croce
CITY ACROSS THE RIVER(1949)
Edgar Croce
ONCE IN PARIS(1978)
Gerard Croce
ONCE IN PARIS(1978), a, p
Raimondo Crocianai
DESERT OF THE TARTARS, THE(1976 Fr./Ital./Iranian), ed
Raimondo Crociani
MOST WONDERFUL EVENING OF MY LIFE, THE(1972, Ital./Fr.), ed; SPECIAL DAY, A(1977, Ital./Can.), ed; PASSION OF LOVE(1982, Ital./Fr.), ed; LA NUIT DE VARENNES(1983, Fr./Ital.), ed
1984
LE BAL(1984, Fr./Ital./Algeria), ed
Vincenzo Crocitti
HUMAN FACTOR, THE(1975)
Barry Crocker
SQUEEZE A FLOWER(1970, Aus.); ADVENTURES OF BARRY McKENZIE(1972, Austral.); BARRY MC KENZIE HOLDS HIS OWN(1975, Aus.)
Emerson Crocker
TREASURE OF LOST CANYON, THE(1952), w
Frankie Crocker
FIVE ON THE BLACK HAND SIDE(1973); DARKTOWN STRUTTERS(1975); THAT'S THE WAY OF THE WORLD(1975)
1984
BREAKIN' 2: ELECTRIC BOOGALOO(1984)

George Crocker
Silents
PAYING THE LIMIT(1924), ph
Harry Crocker
H.M. PULHAM, ESQ.(1941); GENTLEMAN JIM(1942); NIGHT FOR CRIME, A(1942); GREAT JOHN L. THE(1945); SONG FOR MISS JULIE, A(1945); NIGHT AND DAY(1946); DANCING IN THE DARK(1949)
Silents
SALLY IN OUR ALLEY(1927); TILLIE THE TOILER(1927); CIRCUS, THE(1928)
Misc. Silents
BECKY(1927); SOUTH SEA LOVE(1927)
Henry Crocker
GOOD COMPANIONS(1933, Brit.); TWO OF US, THE(1938, Brit.)
John Crocker
MOONRAKER, THE(1958, Brit.); INVASION QUARTET(1961, Brit.)
Lou Crocker
HOLLYWOOD AND VINE(1945)
Mickey Crocker
RIGHT STUFF, THE(1983)
C. H. Crocker-King
Silents
ONE EXCITING NIGHT(1922)
Charles Crocker-King
CRIME OF DR. FORBES(1936)
Charles Crockett
ABRAHAM LINCOLN(1930); EX-FLAME(1931); GUILTY HANDS(1931)
Silents
ARIZONA BOUND(1927); PRINCESS FROM HOBOKEN, THE(1927)
Misc. Silents
MILLIONAIRE COWBOY, THE(1924); INTO HER KINGDOM(1926); GINGHAM GIRL, THE(1927)
Dick Crockett
WEEKEND AT THE WALDORF(1945); DARK HORSE, THE(1946); POSTMAN ALWAYS RINGS TWICE, THE(1946); PANHANDLE(1948); MILKMAN, THE(1950); WABASH AVENUE(1950); SEALED CARGO(1951); ALL ASHORE(1953); CRUISIN' DOWN THE RIVER(1953); JALOPY(1953); TOPEKA(1953); DRIVE A CROOKED ROAD(1954); PUSHOVER(1954); DAVY CROCKETT AND THE RIVER PIRATES(1956); OVER-EXPOSED(1956); BABY FACE NELSON(1957); GARMENT JUNGLE, THE(1957); MISTER CORY(1957); OPERATION MAD BALL(1957); ESCAPE FROM RED ROCK(1958); PERFECT FURLOUGH, THE(1958); IT HAPPENED TO JANE(1959); OPERATION PETTICOAT(1959); HIGH TIME(1960); SPARTACUS(1960); STRANGERS WHEN WE MEET(1960); DAYS OF WINE AND ROSES(1962); EXPERIMENT IN TERROR(1962); NOTORIOUS LANDLADY, THE(1962); BATMAN(1966); GUNN(1967); KARATE KILLERS, THE(1968); PARTY, THE(1968); MOONSHINE WAR, THE(1970); DIAMONDS ARE FOREVER(1971, Brit.); WILD ROVERS(1971); GETAWAY, THE(1972); PINK PANTHER STRIKES AGAIN, THE(1976, Brit.); REVENGE OF THE PINK PANTHER(1978), stunts; 10(1979), stunts
Eric Crockett
Silents
EXTRA GIRL, THE(1923), ph
Jan Crockett
DIARY OF A BACHELOR(1964)
Karlene Crockett
CHARLIE CHAN AND THE CURSE OF THE DRAGON QUEEN(1981)
1984
MASSIVE RETALIATION(1984)
Lucy Herndon Crockett
PROUD AND THE PROFANE, THE(1956), d&w
Lute Crockett
KEY LARGO(1948); LADY TAKES A SAILOR, THE(1949); COLT .45(1950); WEST POINT STORY, THE(1950)
Luther Crockett
WOLF HUNTERS, THE(1949); I KILLED GERONIMO(1950); KILL THE UMPIRE(1950); MALAYA(1950); ONE TOO MANY(1950); RIDER FROM TUCSON(1950); BONANZA TOWN(1951); CUBAN FIREBALL(1951); GOLDEN GIRL(1951); HALF ANGEL(1951); MR. BELVEDERE RINGS THE BELL(1951); DEADLINE-U.S.A.(1952); SCANDAL SHEET(1952); WOMAN IN THE DARK(1952)
Michael Crockett
OPERATION THIRD FORM(1966, Brit.)
Richard Crockett
THIS MAN'S NAVY(1945); STREET OF DARKNESS(1958); DIRTY HARRY(1971)
Fred Crodova
FEATHERED SERPENT, THE(1948)
Lia Croelli
BITTER RICE(1950, Ital.)
Francis Croese
DON QUIXOTE(1973, Aus.)
Colin Crofk
IT'S A WONDERFUL WORLD(1956, Brit.)
Leonard Crofoot
ECHOES(1983)
Leonard John Crofoot
REFLECTION OF FEAR, A(1973)
Al Croft
THERE'S ALWAYS VANILLA(1972)
Alvin C. Croft
THE CRAZIES(1973), p
Ann Croft
STOCK CAR(1955, Brit.)
Charles Croft
CODE OF THE OUTLAW(1942), ed
Colin Croft
TREAD SOFTLY(1952, Brit.); LADY OF VENGEANCE(1957, Brit); ROCK YOU SINNERS(1957, Brit.); ACCURSED, THE(1958, Brit.); HIGH HELL(1958); GREAT MACARTHY, THE(1975, Aus.); WILD DUCK, THE(1983, Aus.)
1984
CAREFUL, HE MIGHT HEAR YOU(1984, Aus.); FANTASY MAN(1984, Aus.)

David Croft
DAD'S ARMY(1971, Brit.), w; NOT NOW DARLING(1975, Brit.), d
Douglas Croft
REMEMBER THE DAY(1941); FLIGHT LIEUTENANT(1942); GEORGE WASHINGTON SLEPT HERE(1942); PRIDE OF THE YANKEES, THE(1942); YANKEE DOODLE DANDY(1942); HARRIGAN'S KID(1943); PRESENTING LILY MARS(1943); RIVER GANG(1945); KILLER McCOY(1947)
Misc. Talkies
NOT A LADIES MAN(1942)
Jon Croft
MIND OF MR. SOAMES, THE(1970, Brit.); WHEN EIGHT BELLS TOLL(1971, Brit.); REMEMBRANCE(1982, Brit.)
Misc. Talkies
BEGGING THE RING(1979, Brit.)
Julie Croft
INSPECTOR CLOUSEAU(1968, Brit.)
Leila Croft
LOVE IN THE AFTERNOON(1957); COMEDY MAN, THE(1964); STOP THE WORLD--I WANT TO GET OFF(1966, Brit.)
Mary Jane Croft
KATHY O'(1958)
Michael Croft
SPARE THE ROD(1961, Brit.), w
Paddy Croft
FINNEGANS WAKE(1965); JUST TELL ME WHAT YOU WANT(1980)
Paul Croft
ECHO MURDERS, THE(1945, Brit.); CAESAR AND CLEOPATRA(1946, Brit.)
Peter Croft
EAST MEETS WEST(1936, Brit.); KING OF THE DAMNED(1936, Brit.); LADY JANE GREY(1936, Brit.); YOU'RE IN THE ARMY NOW(1937, Brit.); YANK AT OXFORD, A(1938); MURDER WILL OUT(1939, Brit.); PHANTOM STRIKES, THE(1939, Brit.); BRIGGS FAMILY, THE(1940, Brit.); FLYING FORTRESS(1942, Brit.); GOOSE STEPS OUT, THE(1942, Brit.); DANCING WITH CRIME(1947, Brit.); ESCAPE(1948, Brit.); POET'S PUB(1949, Brit.)
Sylvia Croft
WHO SLEW AUNTIE ROO?(1971, U.S./Brit.), makeup; SUPERMAN(1978), makeup
Valerie Croft
LOVE IN THE AFTERNOON(1957); COMEDY MAN, THE(1964); STOP THE WORLD--I WANT TO GET OFF(1966, Brit.)
Wal Croft
Silents
LIFE OF ROBERT BURNS, THE(1926, Brit.)
Rupert Croft-Brooke
ESCAPE BY NIGHT(1965, Brit.), w
Rupert Croft-Cooke
FATAL WITNESS, THE(1945), w; BEASTS OF MARSEILLES, THE(1959, Brit.), w
Desmond Crofton
SORCERER(1977)
Betsy Crofts
PETTY GIRL, THE(1950)
Charles Crofts
GLEN OR GLENDA(1953)
Daniel Crohem
PARIS BELONGS TO US(1962, Fr.); DOULOS--THE FINGER MAN(1964, Fr./Ital.)
Hugh Croise
Silents
FOUR MEN IN A VAN(1921, Brit.), d&w
Misc. Silents
JUDGED BY APPEARANCES(1916, Brit.), d; BALL OF FORTUNE, THE(1926, Brit.), d
Hans Croiset
1984
QUESTION OF SILENCE(1984, Neth.)
Max Croiset
DOG OF FLANDERS, A(1959); LITTLE ARK, THE(1972)
Nicole Croisille
UNDERGROUND(1970, Brit.); BOLERO(1982, Fr.)
Betty Croissant
TERMS OF ENDEARMENT(1983)
Harry Croizet
BUT NOT IN VAIN(1948, Brit.)
Edward Croke
MEDIUM COOL(1969)
C. H. Croker-King
Silents
QUESTION OF TRUST, A(1920, Brit.); EXPERIMENT, THE(1922, Brit.)
Misc. Silents
FOUR JUST MEN, THE(1921, Brit.)
Charles Croker-King
LLOYDS OF LONDON(1936); WHITE ANGEL, THE(1936)
Dick Crokett
GOLD RAIDERS, THE(1952)
Trevor Crole-Rees
NEVER LET GO(1960, Brit.), makeup; PAYROLL(1962, Brit.), makeup; FAMILY WAY, THE(1966, Brit.), makeup; NAKED PREY, THE(1966, U.S./South Africa), makeup; BLISS OF MRS. BLOSSOM, THE(1968, Brit.), makeup; MATTER OF INNOCENCE, A(1968, Brit.), makeup; EXECUTIONER, THE(1970, Brit.), makeup; KELLY'S HEROES(1970, U.S./Yugo.), makeup; DOCTOR PHIBES RISES AGAIN(1972, Brit.), makeup; I WANT WHAT I WANT(1972, Brit.), makeup
Gladys Crolius
SHANNONS OF BROADWAY, THE(1929)
Louise Crolius
Silents
ALSTER CASE, THE(1915)
Henri Crolla
LA PARISIENNE(1958, Fr./Ital.), m; COME DANCE WITH ME(1960, Fr.), m; LOVE AND THE FRENCHWOMAN(1961, Fr.), m; TIME BOMB(1961, Fr./Ital.), m

Ann Croman
Misc. Silents
FLAME OF YOUTH, THE(1917)
Andee Cromarty
CONFESSIONS OF A WINDOW CLEANER(1974, Brit.); CONFESSIONS OF A POP PERFORMER(1975, Brit.); AT THE EARTH'S CORE(1976, Brit.)
Donald Crombie
CADDIE(1976, Aus.), d; IRISHMAN, THE(1978, Aus.), d, w; CATHY'S CHILD(1979, Aus.), d; KILLING OF ANGEL STREET, THE(1983, Aus.), d; KITTY AND THE BAGMAN(1983, Aus.), d
Lillian Crombie
JOURNEY AMONG WOMEN(1977, Aus.)
Maureen Crombie
GREAT ST. TRINIAN'S TRAIN ROBBERY, THE(1966, Brit.)
Michael Crombie
VANDERGILT DIAMOND MYSTERY, THE(1936), w
Tony Crombie
SPIDER'S WEB, THE(1960, Brit.), m; TELL-TALE HEART, THE(1962, Brit.), m
George Crome
ONE BIG AFFAIR(1952), ed
Bob Cromer
FOLLOW THE FLEET(1936)
Dean Cromer
HANNAH LEE(1953); FORTYNINERS, THE(1954); THEM!(1954); TIGHT SPOT(1955); MONOLITH MONSTERS, THE(1957)
John Cromer
MEMOIRS OF A SURVIVOR(1981, Brit.)
Tex Cromer
EVERYBODY'S DANCIN'(1950)
Jean Cromie
1984
THIS IS SPINAL TAP(1984)
Larry Cromlen
SINS OF THE FATHERS(1948, Can.), p
Alice Cromley
RED RUNS THE RIVER(1963), cos
Bernard Crommbe
POURQUOI PAS!(1979, Fr.)
Fernand Crommelynck
MAGNIFICENT CUCKOLD, THE(1965, Fr./Ital.), w
Richard Crommie
FLIGHT(1960)
Charles Crompton
Silents
DOLL'S HOUSE, A(1918)
Colin Crompton
CONFESSIONS FROM A HOLIDAY CAMP(1977, Brit.)
R. Crompton
Silents
MESSAGE FROM MARS, A(1913, Brit.)
Richmal Crompton
JUST WILLIAM(1939, Brit.), w; JUST WILLIAM'S LUCK(1948, Brit.), w; WILLIAM COMES TO TOWN(1948, Brit.), w
Gloria Cromwell
SOUP FOR ONE(1982)
Helen Cromwell
SILVER CORD(1933)
James Cromwell
MURDER BY DEATH(1976); CHEAP DETECTIVE, THE(1978); NOBODY'S PERFEKT(1981); MAN WITH TWO BRAINS, THE(1983)
1984
HOUSE OF GOD, THE(1984); OH GOD! YOU DEVIL(1984); REVENGE OF THE NERDS(1984); TANK(1984)
John Cromwell
CLOSE HARMONY(1929), d; DANCE OF LIFE, THE(1929), a, d; DUMMY, THE(1929); MIGHTY, THE(1929), a, d; FOR THE DEFENSE(1930), d; STREET OF CHANCE(1930), a, d; TEXAN, THE(1930), d; TOM SAWYER(1930), d; RICH MAN'S FOLLY(1931), d; SCANDAL SHEET(1931), d; UNFAITHFUL(1931), d; VICE SQUAD, THE(1931), d; WORLD AND THE FLESH, THE(1932), d; ANN VICKERS(1933), d; DOUBLE HARNESS(1933), d; SILVER CORD(1933), d; SWEEPINGS(1933), d; FOUNTAIN, THE(1934), d; OF HUMAN BONDAGE(1934), d; SPITFIRE(1934), p; THIS MAN IS MINE(1934), d; I DREAM TOO MUCH(1935), d; JALNA(1935), d; VILLAGE TALE(1935), d; BANJO ON MY KNEE(1936), d; LITTLE LORD FAUNTLEROY(1936), d; TO MARY-WITH LOVE(1936), d; PRISONER OF ZENDA, THE(1937), d; ALGIERS(1938), d; IN NAME ONLY(1939), d; MADE FOR EACH OTHER(1939), d; ABE LINCOLN IN ILLINOIS(1940), d; VICTORY(1940), d; SO ENDS OUR NIGHT(1941), d; SON OF FURY(1942), d; SINCE YOU WENT AWAY(1944), d; ENCHANTED COTTAGE, THE(1945), d; ANNA AND THE KING OF SIAM(1946), d; DEAD RECKONING(1947), d; NIGHT SONG(1947), d; CAGED(1950), d; COMPANY SHE KEEPS, THE(1950), d; RACKET, THE(1951), d; TOP SECRET AFFAIR(1957); GODDESS, THE(1958), d; SCAVENGERS, THE(1959, U.S./Phil.), d; MATTER OF MORALS, A(1961, U.S./Swed.), d; THREE WOMEN(1977); WEDDING, A(1978)
Josephine Cromwell
Misc. Silents
BAD BOYS(1917)
O'Kane Cromwell
Silents
WAY DOWN EAST(1920), cos
Richard Cromwell
TOL'ABLE DAVID(1930); FIFTY FATHOMS DEEP(1931); MAKER OF MEN(1931); SHANGHAIED LOVE(1931); AGE OF CONSENT(1932); EMMA(1932); STRANGE LOVE OF MOLLY LOUVAIN, THE(1932); THAT'S MY BOY(1932); TOM BROWN OF CULVER(1932); HOOPLA(1933); THIS DAY AND AGE(1933); ABOVE THE CLOUDS(1934); AMONG THE MISSING(1934); CAROLINA(1934); MOST PRECIOUS THING IN LIFE(1934); NAME THE WOMAN(1934); WHEN STRANGERS MEET(1934); ANNAPOLIS FAREWELL(1935); LIFE BEGINS AT 40(1935); LIVES OF A BENGAL LANCER(1935); MC FADDEN'S FLATS(1935); MEN OF THE HOUR(1935); UNKNOWN WOMAN(1935); POPPY(1936); ROAD BACK,THE(1937); WRONG ROAD, THE(1937); COME ON, LEATHERNECKS(1938); JEZEBEL(1938); STORM OVER BENGAL(1938); TORPEDOED!(1939); YOUNG MR. LINCOLN(1939); ENEMY

AGENT(1940); VILLAGE BARN DANCE(1940); VILLAIN STILL PURSUED HER, THE(1940); PARACHUTE BATTALION(1941); RIOT SQUAD(1941); BABY FACE MORGAN(1942); BUNGALOW 13(1948)
Misc. Talkies
COSMO JONES, CRIME SMASHER(1943)
Robert Cromwell
LADY LIBERTY(1972, Ital./Fr.)
Claudia Cron
DINER(1982); HIT AND RUN(1982); SOUP FOR ONE(1982); RUNNING BRAVE(1983, Can.)
Edward Cronajer
CONQUERORS, THE(1932), ph
George Crone
GET THAT GIRL(1932), d; SPEED MADNESS(1932), d; FLAMING GOLD(1934), ed; RICHEST GIRL IN THE WORLD, THE(1934), ed; SING AND LIKE IT(1934), ed; STRICTLY DYNAMITE(1934), ed; GRAND OLD GIRL(1935), ed; GRIDIRON FLASH(1935), ed; HOORAY FOR LOVE(1935), ed; OLD MAN RHYTHM(1935), ed; TO BEAT THE BAND(1935), ed; MAKE WAY FOR A LADY(1936), ed; TWO IN THE DARK(1936), ed; FIGHT FOR YOUR LADY(1937), ed; NEW FACES OF 1937(1937), ed; QUICK MONEY(1938), ed; ROOM SERVICE(1938), ed; ALLEGHENY UPRISING(1939), ed; BEAUTY FOR THE ASKING(1939), ed; SWISS FAMILY ROBINSON(1940), ed; WILDCAT BUS(1940), ed; GAY FALCON, THE(1941), ed; GIRL, A GUY AND A GOB, A(1941), ed; SEVEN MILES FROM ALCATRAZ(1942), ed; FALCON IN DANGER, THE(1943), ed; FALCON STRIKES BACK, THE(1943), ed; FOREVER AND A DAY(1943), ed; GANGWAY FOR TOMORROW(1943), ed; MY BROTHER, THE OUTLAW(1951), ed; LIFE IN THE BALANCE, A(1955), ed
George J. Crone
BLAZE O' GLORY(1930), d; WHAT A MAN(1930), d
Silents
NEVER SAY DIE(1924), d; INTRODUCE ME(1925), d; THAT'S MY BABY(1926), w; LET IT RAIN(1927), w; FLOATING COLLEGE, THE(1928), d
George W. Crone
RENO(1930), d
Kenneth Crone
SUGARLAND EXPRESS, THE(1974)
Lewis Crone
DELIVERANCE(1972)
Penny Crone
HERO AT LARGE(1980)
Robert Crone
I, MAUREEN(1978, Can.)
S.R. Crone
RAINBOW MAN(1929), ed
David Cronenberg
CRIMES OF THE FUTURE(1969, Can.), p,d,w&ph; STEREO(1969, Can.), p,d,w,ph&ed; RABID(1976, Can.), d&w; THEY CAME FROM WITHIN(1976, Can.), d&w; BROOD, THE(1979, Can.), d&w; SCANNERS(1981, Can.), d&w; DEAD ZONE, THE(1983), d; VIDEODROME(1983, Can.), d&w
Misc. Talkies
FAST COMPANY(1979), d
Philippe Cronenberver
LA CAGE AUX FOLLES II(1981, Ital./Fr.)
Jordan Cronenweth
COUNT YOUR BULLETS(1972), ph; NICKEL RIDE, THE(1974), ph; ZANDY'S BRIDE(1974), ph; CITIZENS BAND(1977), ph; CUTTER AND BONE(1981), ph; BLADE RUNNER(1982), ph
Jordan S. Cronenweth
FRONT PAGE, THE(1974), ph; GABLE AND LOMBARD(1976), ph
Jordon Cronenweth
TRUMAN CAPOTE'S TRILOGY(1969), ph
Jordan Croneweth
BREWSTER McCLOUD(1970), ph; PLAY IT AS IT LAYS(1972), ph; ALTERED STATES(1980), ph; BEST FRIENDS(1982), ph
Jordon Croneweth
ROLLING THUNDER(1977), ph
A.J. Cronin
GRAND CANARY(1934), w; ONCE TO EVERY WOMAN(1934), w; CITADEL, THE(1938), w; STARS LOOK DOWN, THE(1940, Brit.), w; VIGIL IN THE NIGHT(1940), w; SHINING VICTORY(1941), w; KEYS OF THE KINGDOM, THE(1944), w; GREEN YEARS, THE(1946), w; HATTER'S CASTLE(1948, Brit.), w; SPANISH GARDENER, THE(1957, Span.), w; BEYOND THIS PLACE(1959, Brit.), w
Alyce Cronin
SON OF SINBAD(1955)
Brian Cronin
WHAT A CRAZY WORLD(1963, Brit.)
Charles R. Cronin
1984
RECKLESS(1984)
Dorothy Cronin
PENNIES FROM HEAVEN(1981)
Isaac Cronin
CHAN IS MISSING(1982), w
Jackie Cronin
CROSS AND THE SWITCHBLADE, THE(1970)
Jean Cronin
KID FROM BOOKLYN, THE(1946)
Jim Cronin
DREAM WIFE(1953)
Joe Cronin
PLEASE DON'T EAT THE DAISIES(1960); BACK STREET(1961)
John Cronin
TWIST AROUND THE CLOCK(1961); THREE NUTS IN SEARCH OF A BOLT(1964)
Kevin Cronin
FM(1978)
Marion W. Cronin
YOUNG GIANTS(1983), ed
Michael Cronin
JOHNNY ON THE SPOT(1954, Brit.), w; YOU PAY YOUR MONEY(1957, Brit.), w; DEATHMASTER, THE(1972); HOPSCOTCH(1980)

Patrick Cronin
1984
SPLASH(1984)
Paul Cronin
CHILDREN SHOULDN'T PLAY WITH DEAD THINGS(1972)
Sherrie Lee Cronin
WORLD IS FULL OF MARRIED MEN, THE(1980, Brit.)
Tandy Cronin
1984
ONCE UPON A TIME IN AMERICA(1984)
Wally Cronin
1984
REPO MAN(1984)
Edward Cronjager
LOVE DOCTOR, THE(1929), ph; NOTHING BUT THE TRUTH(1929), ph; VIRGINIAN, THE(1929), ph; WHEEL OF LIFE(1929), ph; HE KNEW WOMEN(1930), ph; LOVIN' THE LADIES(1930), ph; SEVEN KEYS TO BALDPATE(1930), ph; SHOOTING STRAIGHT(1930), ph; CIMARRON(1931), ph; PUBLIC DEFENDER, THE(1931), ph; SECRET SERVICE(1931), ph; YOUNG DONOVAN'S KID(1931), ph; BIRD OF PARADISE(1932), ph; HELL'S HIGHWAY(1932), ph; LOST SQUADRON, THE(1932), ph; ROAR OF THE DRAGON(1932), ph; ANN VICKERS(1933), ph; DIPLOMANIACS(1933), ph; IF I WERE FREE(1933), ph; MONKEY'S PAW, THE(1933), ph; NO OTHER WOMAN(1933), ph; PROFESSIONAL SWEETHEART(1933), ph; DOWN TO THEIR LAST YACHT(1934), ph; SPITFIRE(1934), ph; STRICTLY DYNAMITE(1934), ph; ENCHANTED APRIL(1935), ph; IN PERSON(1935), ph; JALNA(1935), ph; KENTUCKY KERNELS(1935), ph; LIGHTNING STRIKES TWICE(1935), ph; NITWITS, THE(1935), ph; ROBERTA(1935), ph; ONE IN A MILLION(1936), ph; SPECIAL INVESTIGATOR(1936), ph; TEXAS RANGERS, THE(1936), ph; THREE MARRIED MEN(1936), ph; THIN ICE(1937), ph; WAKE UP AND LIVE(1937), ph; WIFE, DOCTOR AND NURSE(1937), ph; GATEWAY(1938), ph; ISLAND IN THE SKY(1938), ph; KEEP SMILING(1938), ph; RASCALS(1938), ph; CHICKEN WAGON FAMILY(1939), ph; ESCAPE, THE(1939), ph; EVERYTHING HAPPENS AT NIGHT(1939), ph; GORILLA, THE(1939), ph; HEAVEN WITH A BARBED WIRE FENCE(1939), ph; TOO BUSY TO WORK(1939), ph; WINNER TAKE ALL(1939), ph; GAY CABALLERO, THE(1940), ph; GIRL IN 313(1940), ph; I WAS AN ADVENTURESS(1940), ph; YOUNG PEOPLE(1940), ph; YOUTH WILL BE SERVED(1940), ph; RISE AND SHINE(1941), ph; SUN VALLEY SERENADE(1941), ph; VERY YOUNG LADY, A(1941), ph; WESTERN UNION(1941), ph; FRIENDLY ENEMIES(1942), ph; GIRL TROUBLE(1942), ph; I WAKE UP SCREAMING(1942), ph; LIFE BEGINS AT 8:30(1942), ph; PIED PIPER, THE(1942), ph; TO THE SHORES OF TRIPOLI(1942), ph; GANG'S ALL HERE, THE(1943), ph; HEAVEN CAN WAIT(1943), ph; MARGIN FOR ERROR(1943), ph; HOME IN INDIANA(1944), ph; COLONEL EFFINGHAM'S RAID(1945), ph; NOB HILL(1945), ph; CANYON PASSAGE(1946), ph; DO YOU LOVE ME?(1946), ph; DESERT FURY(1947), ph; HONEYMOON(1947), ph; COUNTESS OF MONTE CRISTO, THE(1948), ph; DON'T TRUST YOUR HUSBAND(1948), ph; ON OUR MERRY WAY(1948), ph; RELENTLESS(1948), ph; CAPTURE, THE(1950), ph; HOUSE BY THE RIVER(1950), ph; BEST OF THE BADMEN(1951), ph; I'D CLIMB THE HIGHEST MOUNTAIN(1951), ph; TWO TICKETS TO BROADWAY(1951), ph; BLOODHOUNDS OF BROADWAY(1952), ph; LURE OF THE WILDERNESS(1952), ph; BENEATH THE 12-MILE REEF(1953), ph; POWDER RIVER(1953), ph; TREASURE OF THE GOLDEN CONDOR(1953), ph; SIEGE AT RED RIVER, THE(1954), ph; DEVIL'S PARTNER, THE(1958), ph; THREAT, THE(1960), ph
Silents
WOMANHANDLED(1925), ph; LET'S GET MARRIED(1926), ph; QUARTERBACK, THE(1926), ph; KNOCKOUT REILLY(1927), ph; JUST MARRIED(1928), ph; SPORTING GOODS(1928), ph; WARMING UP(1928), ph; WHAT A NIGHT!(1928), ph
Edward J. Cronjager
SWEEPINGS(1933), ph
Henry Cronjager
PARTY GIRL(1930), ph; ACE OF ACES(1933), ph; GIGOLETTES OF PARIS(1933), ph; NO MARRIAGE TIES(1933), ph; RAYMIE(1960), ph; SQUAD CAR(1961), ph; HANDS OF A STRANGER(1962), ph
Silents
DADDY LONG LEGS(1919), ph; JUST AROUND THE CORNER(1921), ph; LOVE LIGHT, THE(1921), ph; TOL'ABLE DAVID(1921), ph; BACK HOME AND BROKE(1922), ph; SEVENTH DAY, THE(1922), ph; SONNY(1922), ph; SINNERS IN HEAVEN(1924), ph; CLOTHES MAKE THE PIRATE(1925), ph; CORPORAL KATE(1926), ph; OLD LOVES AND NEW(1926), ph; LINDA(1929), ph
Jules Cronjager
ANYBODY'S BLONDE(1931), ph; FIRST AID(1931), ph; HELL BENT FOR 'FRISCO(1931), ph; KID FROM ARIZONA, THE(1931), ph; NECK AND NECK(1931), ph; SKY SPIDER, THE(1931), ph; SOUL OF THE SLUMS(1931), ph; WILD WEST WHOOPEE(1931), ph; ALIAS MARY SMITH(1932), ph; BEHIND STONE WALLS(1932), ph; DOCKS OF SAN FRANCISCO(1932), ph; DYNAMITE DENNY(1932), ph; GORILLA SHIP, THE(1932), ph; HELL'S HEADQUARTERS(1932), ph; HER MAD NIGHT(1932), ph; MIDNIGHT MORALS(1932), ph; MIDNIGHT WARNING, THE(1932), ph; MONSTER WALKS, THE(1932), ph; NIGHT BEAT(1932), ph; NO LIVING WITNESS(1932), ph; SALLY OF THE SUBWAY(1932), ph; SIN'S PAYDAY(1932), ph; TANGLED DESTINIES(1932), ph; WIDOW IN SCARLET(1932), ph; DANCE MALL HOSTESS(1933), ph; EASY MILLIONS(1933), ph; HER SPLENDID FOLLY(1933), ph; JUSTICE TAKES A HOLIDAY(1933), ph; MALAY NIGHTS(1933), ph; UNDER SECRET ORDERS(1933), ph
Silents
FORTUNE'S CHILD(1919), ph; MISS DULCIE FROM DIXIE(1919), ph; GREATER THAN FAME(1920), ph; CLAY DOLLARS(1921), ph; JOHN SMITH(1922), ph; LOVE IS AN AWFUL THING(1922), ph; ONE WEEK OF LOVE(1922), ph; RECKLESS YOUTH(1922), ph; REPORTED MISSING(1922), ph; SHADOWS OF THE SEA(1922), ph; STORM DAUGHTER, THE(1924), ph; IS THAT NICE?(1926), ph; ISLE OF RETRIBUTION, THE(1926), ph; KING OF THE TURF, THE(1926), ph; COWARD, THE(1927), ph; HOME STRUCK(1927), ph; LITTLE WILD GIRL, THE(1928), ph; OLD AGE HANDICAP(1928), ph; GIRLS WHO DARE(1929), ph
William Cronjager
VIGILANTE FORCE(1976), ph
William H. Cronjager
HOW TO SEDUCE A WOMAN(1974), ph
Kathy Cronkite
TRIAL OF BILLY JACK, THE(1974); NETWORK(1976); WHICH WAY IS UP?(1977)

Ed Cronley
CRIME, INC.(1945)
Mark Cronogue
'84
COLD FEET(1984); PREPPIES(1984)
Anne Cronwall
Misc. Silents
EVERYTHING BUT THE TRUTH(1920)
Hume Cronyn
CROSS OF LORRAINE, THE(1943); PHANTOM OF THE OPERA(1943); SHADOW OF A DOUBT(1943); LIFEBOAT(1944); MAIN STREET AFTER DARK(1944); SEVENTH CROSS, THE(1944); LETTER FOR EVIE, A(1945); ZIEGFELD FOLLIES(1945); GREEN YEARS, THE(1946); POSTMAN ALWAYS RINGS TWICE, THE(1946); SAILOR TAKES A WIFE, THE(1946); SECRET HEART, THE(1946); BEGINNING OR THE END, THE(1947); BRUTE FORCE(1947); BRIDE GOES WILD(1948); ROPE(1948), w; TOP O' THE MORNING(1949); UNDER CAPRICORN(1949), w; PEOPLE WILL TALK(1951); CROWDED PARADISE(1956); SUNRISE AT CAMPOBELLO(1960); CLEOPATRA(1963); HAMLET(1964); ARRANGEMENT, THE(1969); GAILY, GAILY(1969); THERE WAS A CROOKED MAN(1970); CONRACK(1974); PARALLAX VIEW, THE(1974); HONKY TONK FREEWAY(1981); ROLLOVER(1981); WORLD ACCORDING TO GARP, The(1982)
1984
IMPULSE(1984)
Tandy Cronyn
PRAISE MARX AND PASS THE AMMUNITION(1970, Brit.)
Donald Crook
PENGUIN POOL MURDER, THE(1932)
Wade Crookham
FIRST NUDIE MUSICAL, THE(1976)
Henry Croom
BLUE DAHLIA, THE(1946)
James Croome
NEW HOTEL, THE(1932, Brit.)
Liane Croon
RUMPELSTILTSKIN(1965, Ger.)
Colin Crop
Silents
BROKEN ROMANCE, A(1929, Brit.)
Anna Cropper
ALL NEAT IN BLACK STOCKINGS(1969, Brit.); CROMWELL(1970, Brit.); PRAYING MANTIS(1982, Brit.)
Steve Cropper
BLUES BROTHERS, THE(1980)
Annette Crosbie
BRIDAL PATH, THE(1959, Brit.); GYPSY GIRL(1966, Brit.); PUBLIC EYE, THE(1972, Brit.); SLIPPER AND THE ROSE, THE(1976, Brit.); HAWK THE SLAYER(1980, Brit.)
1984
ORDEAL BY INNOCENCE(1984, Brit.)
Gladys Crosbie
BRITTANIA HOSPITAL(1982, Brit.)
Martin Crosbie
OF HUMAN BONDAGE(1964, Brit.); YOUNG CASSIDY(1965, U.S./Brit.); LOCK UP YOUR DAUGHTERS(1969, Brit.); QUACKSER FORTUNE HAS A COUSIN IN THE BRONX(1970); UNDERGROUND(1970, Brit.)
Bing Crosby
CONFESSIONS OF A CO-ED(1931); REACHING FOR THE MOON(1931); BIG BROADCAST, THE(1932); COLLEGE HUMOR(1933); GOING HOLLYWOOD(1933); TOO MUCH HARMONY(1933); HERE IS MY HEART(1934); SHE LOVES ME NOT(1934); WE'RE NOT DRESSING(1934); BIG BROADCAST OF 1936, THE(1935); MISSISSIPPI(1935); TWO FOR TONIGHT(1935); ANYTHING GOES(1936); PENNIES FROM HEAVEN(1936); RHYTHM ON THE RANGE(1936); DOUBLE OR NOTHING(1937); WAIKIKI WEDDING(1937); DR. RHYTHM(1938); SING YOU SINNERS(1938); EAST SIDE OF HEAVEN(1939); PARIS HONEYMOON(1939); STAR MAKER, THE(1939); IF I HAD MY WAY(1940); RHYTHM ON THE RIVER(1940); ROAD TO SINGAPORE(1940); BIRTH OF THE BLUES(1941); ROAD TO ZANZIBAR(1941); HOLIDAY INN(1942); MY FAVORITE BLONDE(1942); ROAD TO MOROCCO(1942); STAR SPANGLED RHYTHM(1942); DIXIE(1943); GOING MY WAY(1944); HERE COME THE WAVES(1944); PRINCESS AND THE PIRATE, THE(1944); BELLS OF ST. MARY'S, THE(1945); DUFFY'S TAVERN(1945); ROAD TO UTOPIA(1945); BLUE SKIES(1946); MY FAVORITE BRUNETTE(1947); ROAD TO RIO(1947); VARIETY GIRL(1947); WELCOME STRANGER(1947); EMPEROR WALTZ, THE(1948); ADVENTURES OF ICHABOD AND MR. TOAD(1949); CONNECTICUT YANKEE IN KING ARTHUR'S COURT, A(1949); DOWN MEMORY LANE(1949); TOP O' THE MORNING(1949); MR. MUSIC(1950); RIDING HIGH(1950); HERE COMES THE GROOM(1951); GREATEST SHOW ON EARTH, THE(1952); JUST FOR YOU(1952); ROAD TO BALI(1952); SON OF PALEFACE(1952); LITTLE BOY LOST(1953); SCARED STIFF(1953); COUNTRY GIRL, THE(1954); WHITE CHRISTMAS(1954); ANYTHING GOES(1956); HIGH SOCIETY(1956); MAN ON FIRE(1957); ALIAS JESSE JAMES(1959); SAY ONE FOR ME(1959); HIGH TIME(1960); LET'S MAKE LOVE(1960); PEPE(1960); ROAD TO HONG KONG, THE(1962, U.S./Brit.); ROBIN AND THE SEVEN HOODS(1964); STAGECOACH(1966)
Bob Crosby
TROUBLE IN TEXAS(1937); LET'S MAKE MUSIC(1940); ROOKIES ON PARADE(1941); SIS HOPKINS(1941); KANSAS CITY KITTY(1944); MEET MISS BOBBY SOCKS(1944); MY GAL LOVES MUSIC(1944); SEE HERE, PRIVATE HARGROVE(1944); SINGING SHERIFF, THE(1944); PILLOW TO POST(1945); JOAN OF ARC(1948); WHEN YOU'RE SMILING(1950); TWO TICKETS TO BROADWAY(1951); ROAD TO BALI(1952); SENIOR PROM(1958); FIVE PENNIES, THE(1959)
Cathy Crosby
BEAT GENERATION, THE(1959); GIRLS' TOWN(1959); NIGHT OF THE QUARTER MOON(1959); COLLEGE CONFIDENTIAL(1960)
Cathy Lee Crosby
LAUGHING POLICEMAN, THE(1973); TRACKDOWN(1976); COACH(1978); DARK, THE(1979)
Chris Crosby
HOOTENANNY HOOT(1963); YOUR CHEATIN' HEART(1964)
Denise Crosby
TRAIL OF THE PINK PANTHER, THE(1982); 48 HOURS(1982); CURSE OF THE PINK PANTHER(1983); MAN WHO LOVED WOMEN, THE(1983)

Dennis Crosby
DUFFY'S TAVERN(1945); OUT OF THIS WORLD(1945); SERGEANTS 3(1962)
Don Crosby
NEWSFRONT(1979, Aus.); CHANT OF JIMMIE BLACKSMITH, THE(1980, Aus.); HEATWAVE(1983, Aus.)
Elizabeth Crosby
SINGER AND THE DANCER, THE(1977, Aus.)
Eve Crosby
BLOOD(1974, Brit.)
Floyd Crosby
MY FATHER'S HOUSE(1947, Palestine), ph; BRAVE BULLS, THE(1951), ph; HIGH NOON(1952), ph; MAN CRAZY(1953), ph; MAN IN THE DARK(1953), ph; MYSTERY LAKE(1953), ph; STEEL LADY, THE(1953), ph; FAST AND THE FURIOUS, THE(1954), ph; MONSTER FROM THE OCEAN FLOOR, THE(1954), ph; APACHE WOMAN(1955), ph; FIVE GUNS WEST(1955), ph; HELL'S HORIZON(1955), ph; NAKED STREET, THE(1955), ph; SHACK OUT ON 101(1955), ph; ATTACK OF THE CRAB MONSTERS(1957), ph; CARNIVAL ROCK(1957), ph; HELL CANYON OUT-LAWS(1957), ph; NAKED PARADISE(1957), ph; REFORM SCHOOL GIRL(1957), ph; RIDE OUT FOR REVENGE(1957), ph; ROCK ALL NIGHT(1957), ph; TEENAGE DOLL(1957), ph; CRY BABY KILLER, THE(1958), ph; HOT ROD GANG(1958), ph; MACHINE GUN KELLY(1958), ph; OLD MAN AND THE SEA, THE(1958), ph; SHE-GODS OF SHARK REEF(1958), ph; SUICIDE BATTALION(1958), ph; TEENAGE CAVEMAN(1958), ph; WAR OF THE SATELLITES(1958), ph; WOLF LARSEN(1958), ph; CRIME AND PUNISHMENT, U.S.A.(1959), ph; I, MOBSTER(1959), ph; MIRACLE OF THE HILLS, THE(1959), ph; ROOKIE, THE(1959), ph; WONDERFUL COUNTRY, THE(1959), ph; FRECKLES(1960), ph; HIGH-POWERED RIFLE, THE(1960), ph; HOUSE OF USHER(1960), ph; TWELVE HOURS TO KILL(1960), ph; WALK TALL(1960), ph; COLD WIND IN AUGUST(1961), ph; EXPLOSIVE GENERATION, THE(1961), ph; GAMBLER WORE A GUN, THE(1961), ph; LITTLE SHEPHERD OF KINGDOM COME(1961), ph; PIT AND THE PENDULUM, THE(1961), ph; PURPLE HILLS, THE(1961), ph; SEVEN WOMEN FROM HELL(1961), ph; TWO LITTLE BEARS, THE(1961), ph; FIREBRAND, THE(1962), ph; HAND OF DEATH(1962), ph; PREMATURE BURIAL, THE(1962), ph; TALES OF TERROR(1962), ph; TERROR AT BLACK FALLS(1962), ph; WOMAN HUNT(1962), ph; "X"–THE MAN WITH THE X-RAY EYES(1963), ph; BLACK ZOO(1963), ph; HAUNTED PALACE, THE(1963), ph; RAVEN, THE(1963), ph; YELLOW CANARY, THE(1963), ph; YOUNG RACERS, THE(1963), ph; BIKINI BEACH(1964), ph; COMEDY OF TERRORS, THE(1964), ph; PAJAMA PARTY(1964), ph; RAIDERS FROM BENEATH THE SEA(1964), ph; BEACH BLANKET BINGO(1965), ph; HOW TO STUFF A WILD BIKINI(1965), ph; INDIAN PAINT(1965), ph; SALLAH(1965, Israel), ph; SERGEANT DEAD-HEAD(1965), ph; FIREBALL 590(1966), ph; AROUSERS, THE(1973), ph
Silents
TABU(1931), ph
Floyd D. Crosby
SNOW CREATURE, THE,(1954), ph; BLOOD AND STEEL(1959), ph; COOL ONES THE(1967), ph
Gary Crosby
STAR SPANGLED RHYTHM(1942); DUFFY'S TAVERN(1945); OUT OF THIS WORLD(1945); MARDI GRAS(1958); HOLIDAY FOR LOVERS(1959); PRIVATE'S AFFAIR, A(1959); BATTLE AT BLOODY BEACH(1961); RIGHT APPROACH, THE(1961); TWO TICKETS TO PARIS(1962); OPERATION BIKINI(1963); GIRL HAP-PY(1965); MORITURI(1965); WHICH WAY TO THE FRONT?(1970)
Gene Crosby
Silents
LONE WAGON, THE(1924)
Misc. Silents
WEST VS. EAST(1922); SMILIN' ON(1923); LET HIM BUCK(1924); NORTH OF ALASKA(1924); BATTLIN' BILL(1927)
Harry Crosby
FRIDAY THE 13TH(1980)
Irene Crosby
CLASH BY NIGHT(1952)
Jack Crosby
DR. RHYTHM(1938), ch; SOUTH OF PAGO PAGO(1940), ch; PLAYMATES(1941), ch; DARK WATERS(1944), ch; LAKE PLACID SERENADE(1944), ch; NATIONAL BARN DANCE(1944), ch; PEOPLE ARE FUNNY(1945), ch; WHISTLE STOP(1946), ch; UNCONQUERED(1947), ch
Silents
NORTH WIND'S MALICE, THE(1920)
Misc. Silents
(; SLOTH(1917); WRONG WOMAN, THE(1920); PROXIES(1921)
James A. Crosby
Silents
PATCHWORK GIRL OF OZ, THE(1914), ph
Joan Crosby
SHAGGY D.A., THE(1976); SUMMERSPELL(1983)
Juliette Crosby
CHARMING SINNERS(1929); PARIS BOUND(1929)
Kathy Crosby
Misc. Talkies
CALL ME BY MY RIGHTFUL NAME(1973)
Lindsay Crosby
DUFFY'S TAVERN(1945); OUT OF THIS WORLD(1945); SERGEANTS 3(1962); GIRLS FROM THUNDER STRIP, THE(1966); GLORY STOMPERS, THE(1967); FREE GRASS(1969); BIG FOOT(1973); SANTEE(1973); MURPH THE SURF(1974)
Lindsay H. Crosby
MECHANIC, THE(1972)
Lou Crosby
DAYS OF GLORY(1944); BEHIND THE MASK(1946)
Louis Crosby
LAST ROUND-UP, THE(1947)
Lucinda Crosby
WARGAMES(1983)
Marshall Crosby
DAD AND DAVE COME TO TOWN(1938, Aus.); THAT CERTAIN SOMETHING(1941, Aus.); OVERLANDERS, THE(1946, Brit./Aus.); SMITHY(1946, Aus.); PACIFIC AD-VENTURE(1947, Aus.); CHANT OF JIMMIE BLACKSMITH, THE(1980, Aus.)

Mary Crosby
1984
ICE PIRATES, THE(1984)
Misc. Talkies
LAST PLANE OUT(1983); CHILD'S PLAY(1984, Brit.)
Matthew Crosby
CHANT OF JIMMIE BLACKSMITH, THE(1980, Aus.)
Percy Crosby
SKIPPY(1931), w; SOOKY(1931), w
Phil Crosby
ROBIN AND THE SEVEN HOODS(1964)
Philip Crosby
DUFFY'S TAVERN(1945)
Phillip Crosby
OUT OF THIS WORLD(1945); SERGEANTS 3(1962); NONE BUT THE BRAVE(1965, U.S./Jap.)
Ronnie Crosby
EVER IN MY HEART(1933); LITTLE MEN(1935); PUBLIC OPINION(1935)
Vivian Crosby
TRICK FOR TRICK(1933), w
Wade Crosby
MARIE ANTOINETTE(1938); RIDE A CROOKED MILE(1938); ARIZONA(1940); WAGON TRAIN(1940); CITADEL OF CRIME(1941); SIGN OF THE WOLF(1941); GENTLEMAN JIM(1942); IN OLD CALIFORNIA(1942); SHEPHERD OF THE OZARKS(1942); THEY DIED WITH THEIR BOOTS ON(1942); HEADIN' FOR GOD'S COUNTRY(1943); WOMAN OF THE TOWN, THE(1943); GENTLE ANNIE(1944); BANDITS OF THE BADLANDS(1945); JOHNNY ANGEL(1945); ROUGH RIDERS OF CHEYENNE(1945); IN OLD SACRAMENTO(1946); NIGHT IN PARADISE, A(1946); TRAFFIC IN CRIME(1946); ALONG THE OREGON TRAIL(1947); SECRET LIFE OF WALTER MITTY, THE(1947); SINBAD THE SAILOR(1947); WISTFUL WIDOW OF WAGON GAP, THE(1947); PALEFACE, THE(1948); TIMBER TRAIL, THE(1948); UNDER CALIFORNIA STARS(1948); BLACK BOOK, THE(1949); ROSE OF THE YUKON(1949); STREETS OF LAREDO(1949); HIT PARADE OF 1951(1950); TALES OF ROBIN HOOD(1951); VALLEY OF FIRE(1951); INVASION U.S.A.(1952); HITCH-HIKER, THE(1953); LADY WANTS MINK, THE(1953); OLD OVERLAND TRAIL(1953); PRISONERS OF THE CASBAH(1953); J.W. COOP(1971); WEST-WORLD(1973)
Warren Crosby
TANK BATTALION(1958)
William G. Crosby
Silents
ENCHANTED ISLAND, THE(1927), d
Zelda Crosby
Silents
DOLL'S HOUSE, A(1918)
Paula Croset [Paula Corday]
EXILE, THE(1947)
Paul H. Crosfield
MANOLIS(1962, Brit.), p&d
Alan Crosland
JAZZ SINGER, THE(1927), d; GENERAL CRACK(1929), d; ON WITH THE SHOW(1929), d; BIG BOY(1930), d; FURIES, THE(1930), d; SONG OF THE FLA-ME(1930), d; VIENNESE NIGHTS(1930), d; CAPTAIN THUNDER(1931), d; CHIL-DREN OF DREAMS(1931), d; SILVER LINING(1932), d; WEEK-ENDS ONLY(1932), d; CASE OF THE HOWLING DOG, THE(1934), d; MASSACRE(1934), d; MIDNIGHT ALIBI(1934), d; PERSONALITY KID, THE(1934), d; GREAT IMPER-SONATION, THE(1935), d; IT HAPPENED IN NEW YORK(1935), d; KING SOLOMON OF BROADWAY(1935), d; LADY TUBBS(1935), d; MR. DYNAMITE(1935), d; WHITE COCKATOO(1935), d; BLOWING WILD(1953), ed; NATCHEZ TRACE(1960), d
Silents
CHRIS AND THE WONDERFUL LAMP(1917), d; FLAPPER, THE(1920), d; GREAT-ER THAN FAME(1920), d; SHADOWS OF THE SEA(1922), d; SLIM SHOUL-DERS(1922), d; ENEMIES OF WOMEN, THE(1923), d; UNDER THE RED ROBE(1923), d; SINNERS IN HEAVEN(1924), d; COMPROMISE(1925), d; DON JUAN(1926), d; OLD SAN FRANCISCO(1927), d; SCARLET LADY, THE(1928), d
Misc. Silents
APPLE-TREE GIRL, THE(1917), d; KNIGHTS OF THE SQUARE TABLE(1917), d; LIGHT IN DARKNESS(1917), d; LITTLE CHEVALIER, THE(1917), d; UNBELIEVER, THE(1918), d; WHIRLPOOL, THE(1918), d; COUNTRY COUSIN, THE(1919), d; BROADWAY AND HOME(1920), d; POINT OF VIEW, THE(1920), d; YOUTHFUL FOLLY(1920), d; IS LIFE WORTH LIVING?(1921), d; ROOM AND BOARD(1921), d; WORLDS APART(1921), d; FACE IN THE FOG, THE(1922), d; PROPHET'S PARA-DISE, THE(1922), d; SNITCHING HOUR, THE(1922), d; WHY ANNOUNCE YOUR MARRIAGE?(1922), d; MIAMI(1924), d; THREE WEEKS(1924), d; UNGUARDED WOMEN(1924), d; BOBBED HAIR(1925), d; CONTRABAND(1925), d; WHEN A MAN LOVES(1927), d
Alan Crosland, Jr.
VERY THOUGHT OF YOU, THE(1944), ed; PILLOW TO POST(1945), ed; DECEP-TION(1946), ed; UNFAITHFUL, THE(1947), ed; SILVER RIVER(1948), ed; ADVEN-TURES OF DON JUAN(1949), ed; TASK FORCE(1949), ed; BREAKING POINT, THE(1950), ed; FLAME AND THE ARROW, THE(1950), ed; YOUNG MAN WITH A HORN(1950), ed; COME FILL THE CUP(1951), ed; OPERATION PACIFIC(1951), ed; TOMORROW IS ANOTHER DAY(1951), ed; IRON MISTRESS, THE(1952), ed; ROOM FOR ONE MORE(1952), ed; WINNING TEAM, THE(1952), ed; JAZZ SINGER, THE(1953), ed; APACHE(1954), ed; VERA CRUZ(1954), ed; ALL MINE TO GI-VE(1957), ed; SWEET SMELL OF SUCCESS(1957), ed
Allan Crosland
Silents
KIDNAPPED(1917), d; BELOVED ROGUE, THE(1927), d
Juanita Crosland
MR. DEEDS GOES TO TOWN(1936)
Marjorie Crosland
LOUISA(1950)
Bill Crosley
JOHN LOVES MARY(1949), makeup
Elaine Crosley
CURTAINS(1983, Can.)

Frank Crosley
SCREAMING SKULL, THE(1958), ph
Hella Crosley
CLOAK AND DAGGER(1946)
Sid Crosley
CIRCUS KID, THE(1928)
Henrietta Crosman
ROYAL FAMILY OF BROADWAY, THE(1930); PILGRIMAGE(1933); AMONG THE MISSING(1934); CAROLINA(1934); MENACE(1934); SUCH WOMEN ARE DANGEROUS(1934); THREE ON A HONEYMOON(1934); DARK ANGEL, THE(1935); ELINOR NORTON(1935); RIGHT TO LIVE, THE(1935); CHARLIE CHAN'S SECRET(1936); FOLLOW YOUR HEART(1936); GIRL OF THE OZARKS(1936); HITCH HIKE TO HEAVEN(1936); MOON'S OUR HOME, THE(1936); PERSONAL PROPERTY(1937)
Silents
HOW MOLLY MADE GOOD(1915)
Misc. Silents
UNWELCOME MRS. HATCH, THE(1914); SUPREME TEST, THE(1915)
Maurice Crosnier
LAST OF SHEILA, THE(1973)
Al Cross
MURDER AT DAWN(1932)
Alexander Cross
BLACKMAILER(1936); CHINA CLIPPER(1936); FURY(1936); I MET HIM IN PARIS(1937); LAW FOR TOMBSTONE(1937); TEXAS TRAIL(1937)
Alfred Cross
SMART WOMAN(1931); SIN'S PAYDAY(1932); MYSTERY OF MR. X, THE(1934)
Ben Cross
CHARIOTS OF FIRE(1981, Brit.)
Beverley Cross
LONG SHIPS, THE(1964, Brit./Yugo.), w; HALF A SIXPENCE(1967, Brit.), w; SINBAD AND THE EYE OF THE TIGER(1977, U.S./Brit.), w; CLASH OF THE TITANS(1981), w
Beverly Cross
GENGHIS KHAN(U.S./Brit./Ger./Yugo), w; JASON AND THE ARGONAUTS(1963, Brit.), w
Bill Cross
BLACK OAK CONSPIRACY(1977); I OUGHT TO BE IN PICTURES(1982); PARTNERS(1982); 48 HOURS(1982)
Billy Cross
HEART BEAT(1979)
Brewster Cross
IT HAPPENED HERE(1966, Brit.)
Charles Cross
LAS VEGAS STORY, THE(1952)
Cyril Cross
HIDE AND SEEK(1964, Brit.); WORK IS A FOUR LETTER WORD(1968, Brit.); DULCIMA(1971, Brit.); OPERATION DAYBREAK(1976, U.S./Brit./Czech.)
David Cross
NIGHT HOLDS TERROR, THE(1955); CREATION OF THE HUMANOIDS(1962); MAGIC SWORD, THE(1962)
David R. Cross
DECKS RAN RED, THE(1958)
Dennis Cross
BRASS LEGEND, THE(1956); CRIME OF PASSION(1957); NAKED IN THE SUN(1957); HOW TO MAKE A MONSTER(1958); 80 STEPS TO JONAH(1969); MRS. POLLIFAX-SPY(1971)
Ed Cross
BLACK GESTAPO, THE(1975); PSYCHIC KILLER(1975)
Edward Cross
ST. IVES(1976)
Edwin Cross
FOUND ALIVE(1934)
Elizabeth Cross
MISSING(1982)
Eric Cross
LURE, THE(1933, Brit.), ph; MONEY FOR SPEED(1933, Brit.), ph; ON THIN ICE(1933, Brit.), ph; SPORTING LOVE(1936, Brit.), ph; MAKE-UP(1937, Brit.), ph; PHANTOM SHIP(1937, Brit.), ph; SPLINTERS IN THE AIR(1937, Brit.), ph; SONG OF FREEDOM(1938, Brit.), ph; SONS OF THE SEA(1939, Brit.), ph; BLACK SHEEP OF WHITEHALL, THE(1941 Brit.), ph; SHIPS WITH WINGS(1942, Brit.), ph; FLEMISH FARM, THE(1943, Brit.), ph; DON'T TAKE IT TO HEART(1944, Brit.), ph; TAWNY PIPIT(1947, Brit.), ph; QUIET WEEKEND(1948, Brit.), ph; CHANCE OF A LIFETIME(1950, Brit.), ph; DARK MAN, THE(1951, Brit.), ph; PRIVATE INFORMATION(1952, Brit.), ph; STRANGER IN BETWEEN, THE(1952, Brit.), ph; DEATM GOES TO SCHOOL(1953, Brit.), ph; GENIE, THE(1953, Brit.), ph; GLAD TIDINGS(1953, Brit.), ph; I'LL GET YOU(1953, Brit.), ph; NORMAN CONQUEST(1953, Brit.), ph; FOREVER MY HEART(1954, Brit.), ph; LITTLE KIDNAPPERS, THE(1954, Brit.), ph; ESCAPADE(1955, Brit.), ph; FUN AT ST. FANNY'S(1956, Brit.), ph; PRIVATE'S PROGRESS(1956, Brit.), ph; HIGH TERRACE(1957, Brit.), ph; HIGH TIDE AT NOON(1957, Brit.), ph; CROSS-UP(1958), ph; ONE THAT GOT AWAY, THE(1958, Brit.), ph; THREE MEN IN A BOAT(1958, Brit.), ph; DEADLY RECORD(1959, Brit.), ph; MAN WHO LIKED FUNERALS, THE(1959, Brit.), ph; TIGER BAY(1959, Brit.), ph; WHITE TRAP, THE(1959, Brit.), ph; BEYOND THE CURTAIN(1960, Brit.), ph; IN THE WAKE OF A STRANGER(1960, Brit.), ph; INN FOR TROUBLE(1960, Brit.), ph
George Cross
SQUATTER'S DAUGHTER(1933, Aus.); WE DIVE AT DAWN(1943, Brit.); NOTORIOUS GENTLEMAN(1945, Brit.); DULCIMER STREET(1948, Brit.); GREAT GILBERT AND SULLIVAN, THE(1953, Brit.); SMALLEST SHOW ON EARTH, THE(1957, Brit.)
Gerald Cross
MURDER SHE SAID(1961, Brit.); MURDER AHOY(1964, Brit.)
H. B. Cross
CHOSEN SURVIVORS(1974 U.S.-Mex.), w
H. B. Cross [Harry Spalding]
TEENAGE MILLIONAIRE(1961), w
Harley Cross
1984
MRS. SOFFEL(1984)

Henry Cross
AIR PATROL(1962), w; HARBOR LIGHTS(1963), w; EARTH DIES SCREAMING, THE(1964, Brit.), w
Henry Cross [Harry Spalding]
YOUNG GUNS OF TEXAS(1963), w; NIGHT TRAIN TO PARIS(1964, Brit.), w
Hugh Cross
MILLIONS LIKE US(1943, Brit.); JUST WILLIAM'S LUCK(1948, Brit.); WILLIAM COMES TO TOWN(1948, Brit.); WARNING TO WANTONS, A(1949, Brit.); SEVEN DAYS TO NOON(1950, Brit.); SVENGALI(1955, Brit.); COURT MARTIAL OF MAJOR KELLER, THE(1961, Brit.)
J. H. Martin Cross
Silents
WHEN SCOUTING WON(1930, Brit.), d&w
James Cross
SHIP AHOY(1942); SOMEBODY LOVES ME(1952); JOKER IS WILD, THE(1957); SQUAD CAR(1961)
Jennifer Cross
DOUBLE CONFESSION(1953, Brit.)
Jimmy Cross
BEHIND GREEN LIGHTS(1946); DO YOU LOVE ME?(1946); FRENCH LEAVE(1948); G.I. JANE(1951); LEAVE IT TO THE MARINES(1951); LET'S GO NAVY(1951); MR. IMPERIUM(1951); NO HOLDS BARRED(1952); LOVE ME OR LEAVE ME(1955); SQUARE JUNGLE, THE(1955); NORTH BY NORTHWEST(1959); EVERYTHING'S DUCKY(1961); THREE NUTS IN SEARCH OF A BOLT(1964); DAY OF THE NIGHTMARE(1965); GUIDE FOR THE MARRIED MAN, A(1967)
Larry Cross
GOOD COMPANIONS, THE(1957, Brit.); PORTRAIT IN SMOKE(1957, Brit.); TIME LOCK(1959, Brit.); ELECTRONIC MONSTER. THE(1960, Brit.); GIRL HUNTERS, THE(1963, Brit.); MOUSE ON THE MOON, THE(1963, Brit.); BATTLE BENEATH THE EARTH(1968, Brit.); MAN OUTSIDE, THE(1968, Brit.); EMBASSY(1972, Brit.); 11 HARROWHOUSE(1974, Brit.); WIND AND THE LION, THE(1975)
Lewin Cross
KEY, THE(1934)
Mary Cross
STONE KILLER, THE(1973)
Milton Cross
THIS WINE OF LOVE(1948, Ital.); GROUNDS FOR MARRIAGE(1950)
Murphy Cross
ANNIE(1982)
Oliver A. Cross
CARRIE(1952)
Oliver Cross
GUY NAMED JOE, A(1943); MISSION TO MOSCOW(1943); POSTMAN ALWAYS RINGS TWICE, THE(1946); UNDERCURRENT(1946); RACE STREET(1948); IN A LONELY PLACE(1950); GIRL IN THE RED VELVET SWING, THE(1955); PAL JOEY(1957)
Silents
DR. JIM(1921); SHARK MASTER, THE(1921)
Peter Cross
ADIOS GRINGO(1967, Ital./Fr./Span.)
Peter Cross [Pierre Cressoy]
SEVEN GUNS FOR THE MACGREGORS(1968, Ital./Span.)
Piero Cross
MISSING(1982)
Rhoda Cross
NOT DAMAGED(1930); UNDER SUSPICION(1931)
Robin White Cross
WAR AND PEACE(1956, Ital./U.S.)
Roland Cross
ANDROCLES AND THE LION(1952), ed
Ruth Cross
Silents
QUESTION OF HONOR, A(1922), w
Victoria Cross
Silents
PAULA(1915, Brit.), w
Walter Cross
MOULIN ROUGE(1952); SCHLAGER-PARADE(1953); INSPECTOR CALLS, AN(1954, Brit.)
Warren Cross
DESTINATION TOKYO(1944)
Wellington Cross
Misc. Silents
GREY PARASOL, THE(1918)
Marshall Crossby
HIS ROYAL HIGHNESS(1932, Aus.); HARMONY ROW(1933, Aus.)
Rupert Crosse
SHADOWS(1960); TOO LATE BLUES(1962); WILD SEED(1965); RIDE IN THE WHIRLWIND(1966); TO TRAP A SPY(1966); WATERHOLE NO. 3(1967); REIVERS, THE(1969)
Vaughn Crosskill
SMILE ORANGE(1976, Jamaican)
Alan Crossland
Silents
EVERYBODY'S SWEETHEART(1920), d
Jackie Crossland
MC CABE AND MRS. MILLER(1971)
Marjorie Crossland
CAGED(1950); COMPANY SHE KEEPS, THE(1950); BRIGHT VICTORY(1951); I WANT YOU(1951); TAKE CARE OF MY LITTLE GIRL(1951); CAPTIVE CITY(1952)
Stephen Crossland
KES(1970, Brit.)
Doyle Crossley
LOVE UP THE POLE(1936, Brit.)
Hella Crossley
MASK OF DIMITRIOS, THE(1944)
Peter Crossley
BLUE FIN(1978, Aus.)

Syd Crossley
ATLANTIC(1929 Brit.); YOUNGER GENERATION(1929); HATE SHIP, THE(1930, Brit.); JUST FOR A SONG(1930, Brit.); MIDDLE WATCH, THE(1930, Brit.); SUSPENSE(1930, Brit.); FLYING FOOL, THE(1931, Brit.); MAN FROM CHICAGO, THE(1931, Brit.); TRAPPED IN A SUBMARINE(1931, Brit.); HERE'S GEORGE(1932, Brit.); HIGH SOCIETY(1932, Brit.); LAST COUPON, THE(1932, Brit.); LUCKY LADIES(1932, Brit.); MAYOR'S NEST, THE(1932, Brit.); TONIGHT'S THE NIGHT(1932, Brit.); BERMONDSEY KID, THE(1933, Brit.); FOR THE LOVE OF MIKE(1933, Brit.); KING'S CUP, THE(1933, Brit.); LEAVE IT TO ME(1933, Brit.); LETTING IN THE SUNSHINE(1933, Brit.); MEDICINE MAN, THE(1933, Brit.); MEET MY SISTER(1933, Brit.); UMBRELLA, THE(1933, Brit.); MASTER AND MAN(1934, Brit.); NIGHT CLUB QUEEN(1934, Brit.); OVER THE GARDEN WALL(1934, Brit.); THOSE WERE THE DAYS(1934, Brit.); YOU MADE ME LOVE YOU(1934, Brit.); DANDY DICK(1935, Brit.); DEPUTY DRUMMER, THE(1935, Brit.); HONEYMOON FOR THREE(1935, Brit.); JIMMY BOY(1935, Brit.); CHEER UP!(1936, Brit.); FULL SPEED AHEAD(1936, Brit.); GIVE HER A RING(1936, Brit.); LIMPING MAN, THE(1936, Brit.); MAN BEHIND THE MASK, THE(1936, Brit.); PAY BOX ADVENTURE(1936, Brit.); QUEEN OF HEARTS(1936, Brit.); BOYS WILL BE GIRLS(1937, Brit.); FEATHER YOUR NEST(1937, Brit.); LUCKY JADE(1937, Brit.); MURDER ON DIAMOND ROW(1937, Brit.); OLD MOTHER RILEY(1937, Brit.); PEARLS BRING TEARS(1937, Brit.); SWEET DEVIL(1937, Brit.); THERE WAS A YOUNG MAN(1937, Brit.); LITTLE DOLLY DAYDREAM(1938, Brit.); PENNY PARADISE(1938, Brit.); WE'RE GOING TO BE RICH(1938, Brit.); YOUNG AND INNOCENT(1938, Brit.); COME ON GEORGE(1939, Brit.); TWO'S COMPANY(1939, Brit.); EVERYTHING IS RHYTHM(1940, Brit.); OLD MOTHER RILEY'S CIRCUS(1941, Brit.); MAXWELL ARCHER, DETECTIVE(1942, Brit.)
Silents
KEEP SMILING(1925); AIN'T LOVE FUNNY?(1927); JEWELS OF DESIRE(1927); PLAY SAFE(1927); FANGS OF THE WILD(1928); INTO NO MAN'S LAND(1928); PRIDE OF DONEGAL, THE(1929, Brit.)
Misc. Silents
ROMANTIC ROGUE(1927)

Melville Crossman
HARDBOILED ROSE(1929), w; DARK HORSE, THE(1932), w; THIS IS MY AFFAIR(1937), w; YANK IN THE R.A.F., A(1941), w; CHINA GIRL(1942), w
Silents
IRISH HEARTS(1927), w

Melville Crossman [Darryl F. Zanuck]
STATE STREET SADIE(1928), w; TENDERLOIN(1928), w; LIFE OF THE PARTY, THE(1930), w; THANKS A MILLION(1935), w; THUNDER BIRDS(1942), w; PURPLE HEART, THE(1944), w
Silents
SLIGHTLY USED(1927), w

Robert Crosson
WHITE CHRISTMAS(1954); I COVER THE UNDERWORLD(1955)
1984
MIKE'S MURDER(1984)

Tom Crossman
LITTLE ONES, THE(1965, Brit.)

E. B. Crosswhite
MURDER IN THE MUSEUM(1934), w

Julie Crosthwaite
MADHOUSE(1974, Brit.)

Benjamin "Scatman" Crothers
KING OF MARVIN GARDENS, THE(1972)

Rachel Crothers
LET US BE GAY(1930), w; WHEN LADIES MEET(1933), w; SPLENDOR(1935), w; CAPTAIN IS A LADY, THE(1940), w; SUSAN AND GOD(1940), w; WHEN LADIES MEET(1941), w
Silents
NICE PEOPLE(1922), w; LITTLE JOURNEY, A(1927), w

Sam Behrman Rachel Crothers
AS HUSBANDS GO(1934), w

Scat Man Crothers
PATSY, THE(1964)

Scatman Crothers
YES SIR, MR. BONES(1951); EAST OF SUMATRA(1953); WALKING MY BABY BACK HOME(1953); JOHNNY DARK(1954); BETWEEN HEAVEN AND HELL(1956); SINS OF RACHEL CADE, THE(1960); LADY IN A CAGE(1964); THREE ON A COUCH(1966); ARISTOCATS, THE(1970); BLOODY MAMA(1970); GREAT WHITE HOPE, THE(1970); CHANDLER(1971); LADY SINGS THE BLUES(1972); DETROIT 9000(1973); BLACK BELT JONES(1974); TRUCK TURNER(1974); COONSKIN(1975); FORTUNE, THE(1975); FRIDAY FOSTER(1975); CHESTY ANDERSON, U.S. NAVY(1976); SHOOTIST, THE(1976); SILVER STREAK(1976); STAY HUNGRY(1976); CHEAP DETECTIVE, THE(1978); MEAN DOG BLUES(1978); SCAVENGER HUNT(1979); BRONCO BILLY(1980); SHINING, THE(1980); DEADLY EYES(1982); ZAPPED!(1982); TWO OF A KIND(1983)
Misc. Talkies
RETURN OF GILBERT AND SULLIVAN(1952); BLACK BELT JONES(1974)

"Scatman" Crothers
MEET ME AT THE FAIR(1952)

Sherman "Scatman" Crothers
ONE FLEW OVER THE CUCKOO'S NEST(1975)

Sharon Crouch
MY BRILLIANT CAREER(1980, Aus.)

William Forest Crouch
Misc. Talkies
REET, PETITE AND GONE(1947), d

Brian Croucher
MADE(1972, Brit.)
1984
SCRUBBERS(1984, Brit.)

Roger Croucher
GENGHIS KHAN(U.S./Brit./Ger./Yugo); BLACK TORMENT, THE(1965, Brit.); FIGHTING PRINCE OF DONEGAL, THE(1966, Brit.)

Avery Crounse
1984
EYES OF FIRE(1984), d&w

Lindsay Crouse
BETWEEN THE LINES(1977); SLAP SHOT(1977); PRINCE OF THE CITY(1981); VERDICT, THE(1982); DANIEL(1983)
1984
ICEMAN(1984); PLACES IN THE HEART(1984)

Lindsay Ann Crouse
ALL THE PRESIDENT'S MEN(1976)

Peter Crouse
STRATTON STORY, THE(1949)

Russel Crouse
ANYTHING GOES(1936), w; BIG BROADCAST OF 1938, THE(1937), w; GREAT VICTOR HERBERT, THE(1939), w; LIFE WITH FATHER(1947), w; STATE OF THE UNION(1948), w; CALL ME MADAM(1953), w; REMAINS TO BE SEEN(1953), w; WOMAN'S WORLD(1954), w; TALL STORY(1960), w; SOUND OF MUSIC, THE(1965), w

Russell Crouse
MOUNTAIN MUSIC(1937), w; ARTISTS AND MODELS ABROAD(1938), w; YOKEL BOY(1942), w; HASTY HEART, THE(1949), p; ANYTHING GOES(1956), w

Laurence Croutz
Silents
MY SON(1925), ed

Henri Crouzat
TEMPTATION(1962, Fr.), w

Roger Crouzet
LETTERS FROM MY WINDMILL(1955, Fr.); FRUIT IS RIPE, THE(1961, Fr./Ital.); NIGHT ENCOUNTER(1963, Fr./Ital.); THIEF OF PARIS, THE(1967, Fr./Ital.); THINGS OF LIFE, THE(1970, Fr./Ital./Switz.); BLUE COUNTRY, THE(1977, Fr.)

Luciano Crovato
SILHOUETTES(1982); TRENCHCOAT(1983)

Junius Crovins
Silents
GRIT(1924), set d

Alvin Crow
ROADIE(1980); ENDANGERED SPECIES(1982)

Angela Crow
SHADOW OF THE CAT, THE(1961, Brit.)

Carl Crow
SHELL SHOCK(1964); MUTINY IN OUTER SPACE(1965)
Misc. Talkies
PREMONITION(1972)

Clarence Crow
OTHER, THE(1972)

James H. Crow
MOTHER LODE(1982), art d

Scott Crow
1984
BUDDY SYSTEM, THE(1984)

Slim Crow
ILLEGAL ENTRY(1949)

Ronnie Crowbey
DANCE MALL HOSTESS(1933)

Peter Crowcroft
ON A CLEAR DAY YOU CAN SEE FOREVER(1970)

Graham Crowden
DEAD MAN'S CHEST(1965, Brit.); ONE WAY PENDULUM(1965, Brit.); MORGAN!(1966, Brit.); IF ...(1968, Brit.); FILE OF THE GOLDEN GOOSE, THE(1969, Brit.); LEO THE LAST(1970, Brit.); RISE AND RISE OF MICHAEL RIMMER, THE(1970, Brit.); VIRGIN SOLDIERS, THE(1970, Brit.); NIGHT DIGGER, THE(1971, Brit.); PERCY(1971, Brit.); UP THE CHASTITY BELT(1971, Brit.); RULING CLASS, THE(1972, Brit.); SOMETHING TO HIDE(1972, Brit.); O LUCKY MAN!(1973, Brit.); ABDICATION, THE(1974, Brit.); LITTLE PRINCE, THE(1974, Brit.); LAST DAYS OF MAN ON EARTH, THE(1975, Brit.); JABBERWOCKY(1977, Brit.); FOR YOUR EYES ONLY(1981); BRITTANIA HOSPITAL(1982, Brit.); MISSIONARY, THE(1982)

Charles Crowder
SACCO AND VANZETTI(1971, Ital./Fr.)

Jack Crowder
OUT OF TOWNERS, THE(1970)

Michael Crowdson
PRELUDE TO FAME(1950, Brit.)

Francis Crowdy
MARK OF CAIN, THE(1948, Brit.), w; GIDEON OF SCOTLAND YARD(1959, Brit.)

Miriam Crowdy
DANGEROUS ASSIGNMENT(1950, Brit.), p

Ben Crowe
GLENROWAN AFFAIR, THE(1951, Aus.)

Bill Crowe
GLENROWAN AFFAIR, THE(1951, Aus.)

Cameron Crowe
FAST TIMES AT RIDGEMONT HIGH(1982), w
1984
WILD LIFE, THE(1984), p, w

Christopher Crowe
NIGHTMARES(1983), p, w

Deanna Crowe
1984
EXTERMINATOR 2(1984); MISSING IN ACTION(1984)

Dorothy Crowe
HOUSE ON SKULL MOUNTAIN, THE(1974), set d

Eileen Crowe
PLOUGH AND THE STARS, THE(1936); HUNGRY HILL(1947, Brit.); TOP O' THE MORNING(1949); QUIET MAN, THE(1952); STEEL TOWN(1952); RISING OF THE MOON, THE(1957, Ireland); HOME IS THE HERO(1959, Ireland); SHAKE HANDS WITH THE DEVIL(1959, Ireland); BOYD'S SHOP(1960, Brit.); NIGHT FIGHTERS, THE(1960); GIRL WITH GREEN EYES(1964, Brit.)

Eleanor Crowe
Silents
END OF THE TRAIL, THE(1916); FIRES OF CONSCIENCE(1916)

Lt. Col. H.P. Crowe, USMC
SANDS OF IWO JIMA(1949)
Ivan Crowe
BILL'S LEGACY(1931, Brit.)
James Crowe
CORPSE CAME C.O.D., THE(, set d; NIGHT EDITOR(1946), set d; PERSONALITY KID(1946), set d; TALK ABOUT A LADY(1946), set d; JOHNNY O'CLOCK(1947), set d; WHEN A GIRL'S BEAUTIFUL(1947), set d; WOMAN FROM TANGIER, THE(1948), set d; MISS GRANT TAKES RICHMOND(1949), set d; SLIGHTLY FRENCH(1949), set d; TOKYO JOE(1949), set d; WALKING HILLS, THE(1949), set d; CONVICTED(1950), set d; EIGHT IRON MEN(1952), set d; HAPPY TIME, THE(1952), set d; LARAMIE MOUNTAINS(1952), set d; RAINBOW 'ROUND MY SHOULDER(1952), set d; SNIPER, THE(1952), set d; TARGET HONG KONG(1952), set d; WAGON TEAM(1952), set d; GUN FURY(1953), art d; DRIVE A CROOKED ROAD(1954), set d; PUSHOVER(1954), set d; MAN FROM LARAMIE, THE(1955); YOUNG SAVAGES, THE(1961), set d
James A. Crowe
CRIMSON KIMONO, THE(1959), set d
James M. Crowe
THRILL OF BRAZIL, THE(1946), set d; COWBOY(1958), set d; MAN ON A STRING(1960), set d; WHO WAS THAT LADY?(1960), set d; MR. SARDONICUS(1961), set d; SAIL A CROOKED SHIP(1961), set d; TWO RODE TOGETHER(1961), set d; EXPERIMENT IN TERROR(1962), set d; SAFE AT HOME(1962), set d; ZOTZ!(1962), set d; THREE STOOGES GO AROUND THE WORLD IN A DAZE, THE(1963), set d; OUTLAWS IS COMING, THE(1965), set d
Jamie Crowe
WHITE DOG(1982)
Patti Crowe
TWO GALS AND A GUY(1951)
Bubbles Crowell
WORDS AND MUSIC(1929)
Hank Crowell
FLASHDANCE(1983)
Josephine Crowell
Silents
AVENGING CONSCIENCE, THE(1914); HOME SWEET HOME(1914); BIRTH OF A NATION, THE(1915); PENITENTES, THE(1915); INTOLERANCE(1916); LITTLE SCHOOL MA'AM, THE(1916); MARTHA'S VINDICATION(1916); OLD FOLKS AT HOME, THE(1916); REBECCA OF SUNNYBROOK FARM(1917); BRAVEST WAY, THE(1918); HEARTS OF THE WORLD(1918); STELLA MARIS(1918); CROOKED STREETS(1920); DANGEROUS TO MEN(1920); FLAMES OF THE FLESH(1920); GREATEST QUESTION, THE(1920); BUNTY PULLS THE STRINGS(1921); HOME STUFF(1921); HOMESPUN VAMP, A(1922); LIGHTS OF THE DESERT(1922); SEEING'S BELIEVING(1922); SHATTERED IDOLS(1922); ASHES OF VENGEANCE(1923); NOBODY'S MONEY(1923); RUPERT OF HENTZAU(1923); YESTERDAY'S WIFE(1923); FLOWING GOLD(1924); HOT WATER(1924); MERRY WIDOW, THE(1925); NEW BROOMS(1925); YELLOW FINGERS(1926); KING OF KINGS, THE(1927); MAN WHO LAUGHS, THE(1927); SPEEDY(1928)
Misc. Silents
BETSY'S BURGLAR(1917); DIANE OF THE GREEN VAN(1919); WHITE LIES(1920); MINNIE(1922); SPORTING VENUS, THE(1925)
W.B.F. Crowell
Misc. Silents
DUNGEON, THE(1922)
William Crowell
REVOLT OF THE ZOMBIES(1936); FIREFLY, THE(1937); GLORY TRAIL, THE(1937); ANGELS WITH DIRTY FACES(1938)
Misc. Silents
HOUSE BEHIND THE CEDARS, THE(1927)
Larry Crowhurst
GLENROWAN AFFAIR, THE(1951, Aus.); KANGAROO(1952)
Shelley Crowhurst
PSYCHE 59(1964, Brit.); GREAT PONY RAID, THE(1968, Brit.)
Joseph Crowingham
YOUR THREE MINUTES ARE UP(1973), art d
Dave Crowley
FUGITIVE, THE(1940, Brit.); SAINTS AND SINNERS(1949, Brit.); TEMPTATION HARBOR(1949, Brit.); WATERLOO ROAD(1949, Brit.); LAUGHING ANNE(1954, Brit./U.S.); LAST VALLEY, THE(1971, Brit.)
David Crowley
I'LL BE YOUR SWEETHEART(1945, Brit.); WAR AND PEACE(1956, Ital./U.S.); STEEL BAYONET, THE(1958, Brit.); FIRST BLOOD(1982); OUT OF THE BLUE(1982)
David L. Crowley
GREY FOX, THE(1983, Can.)
Dermot Crowley
GIRO CITY(1982, Brit.); OCTOPUSSY(1983, Brit.); RETURN OF THE JEDI(1983)
Ed Crowley
MADIGAN(1968); LOVING(1970); BANANAS(1971); WHO SAYS I CAN'T RIDE A RAINBOW!(1971); SERPICO(1973); THREE DAYS OF THE CONDOR(1975); NETWORK(1976); FAN, THE(1981)
1984
GARBO TALKS(1984)
Evin Crowley
RYAN'S DAUGHTER(1970, Brit.)
Ginger Crowley
SHE'S WORKING HER WAY THROUGH COLLEGE(1952)
Jack Crowley
FABIAN OF THE YARD(1954, Brit.)
Jan Crowley
1984
SILENT ONE, THE(1984, New Zealand), w
Jane Crowley
LONG VOYAGE HOME, THE(1940); THEY WERE EXPENDABLE(1945); CALL NORTHSIDE 777(1948); NIGHT HAS A THOUSAND EYES(1948); CAGED(1950); GOOD MORNING, MISS DOVE(1955)
Jeananne Crowley
EDUCATING RITA(1983)

Jim Crowley
SPIRIT OF NOTRE DAME, THE(1931)
Joy Crowley
NIGHT DIGGER, THE(1971, Brit.), w
Kathleen Crowley
FARMER TAKES A WIFE, THE(1953); SABRE JET(1953); SILVER WHIP, THE(1953); TARGET EARTH(1954); CITY OF SHADOWS(1955); FEMALE JUNGLE, THE(1955); SEVEN CITIES OF GOLD(1955); TEN WANTED MEN(1955); WESTWARD HO THE WAGONS!(1956); PHANTOM STAGECOACH, THE(1957); QUIET GUN, THE(1957); FLAME BARRIER, THE(1958); CURSE OF THE UNDEAD(1959); REBEL SET, THE(1959); SHOWDOWN(1963); FBI CODE 98(1964); DOWNHILL RACER(1969); LAWYER, THE(1969)
Mart Crowley
BOYS IN THE BAND, THE(1970), p, w; NIJINSKY(1980, Brit.)
Matt Crowley
MOB, THE(1951); SOMEBODY UP THERE LIKES ME(1956); APRIL LOVE(1957); YOUNG DOCTORS, THE(1961)
Michael Crowley
UNDER FIRE(1983)
Pat Crowley
FOREVER FEMALE(1953); MONEY FROM HOME(1953); RED GARTERS(1954); SQUARE JUNGLE, THE(1955); HOLLYWOOD OR BUST(1956); THERE'S ALWAYS TOMORROW(1956); WALK THE PROUD LAND(1956); WILD WOMEN OF WONGO, THE(1959); KEY WITNESS(1960); OFF THE WALL(1977)
Patricia Crowley
SCARFACE MOB, THE(1962); WHEELER DEALERS, THE(1963); TO TRAP A SPY(1966); BISCUIT EATER, THE(1972)
Paul Crowley
SECOND HAND WIFE(1933), art d
Stephen Ellsworth Crowley
FLIGHT THAT DISAPPEARED, THE(1961)
Suzan Crowley
DRAUGHTSMAN'S CONTRACT, THE(1983, Brit.)
1984
SUCCESS IS THE BEST REVENGE(1984, Brit.)
Tim Crowley
AMERICAN GRAFFITI(1973)
William Crowley
Silents
OTHER MAN'S WIFE, THE(1919), ph
William X. Crowley
MR. MUGGS STEPS OUT(1943), w; SPOTLIGHT SCANDALS(1943), w; FOLLOW THE LEADER(1944), w; WHAT A MAN!(1944), w; TRAIL OF THE YUKON(1949), d
Bruce Crowling
WESTWARD THE WOMEN(1951)
Alfred W. Crown
HAMLET(1964), p; LAST SUMMER(1969), p; TAKING OFF(1971), p
Claudia Crown
YOUNG DOCTORS IN LOVE(1982)
Elliot Crown
CITY NEWS(1983)
Patricia Crown
LOVE AND DEATH(1975)
Stanley Crown
HARMON OF MICHIGAN(1941)
Erica Crowne
THREE TO GO(1971, Aus.)
Erika Crowne
NED KELLY(1970, Brit.)
Diane Crowther
YELLOW SUBMARINE(1958, Brit.), animation
Duane Crowther
MOUSE AND HIS CHILD, THE(1977), anim
Graeme Crowther
FLASH GORDON(1980)
John Crowther
OSCAR, THE(1966); KILL AND KILL AGAIN(1981), w
1984
EVIL THAT MEN DO, THE(1984), w; MISSING IN ACTION(1984), w
Leslie Crowther
OVER THE ODDS(1961, Brit.)
Patsy Crowther
HOT MILLIONS(1968, Brit.)
Ernest Croxford
DOSS HOUSE(1933, Brit.)
L.O. Croxton
FALCON IN HOLLYWOOD, THE(1944), art d
Lucien Croxton
RENEGADE RANGER(1938), art d
Lucius Croxton
FALCON OUT WEST, THE(1944), art d; NEVADA(1944), art d; GAME OF DEATH, A(1945), art d; MAMA LOVES PAPA(1945), art d; ROAD TO ALCATRAZ(1945), art d; TELL IT TO A STAR(1945), md; WANDERER OF THE WASTELAND(1945), art d; WEST OF THE PECOS(1945), art d; WHAT A BLONDE(1945), art d; DING DONG WILLIAMS(1946), art d; FALCON'S ALIBI, THE(1946), art d; RIVERBOAT RHYTHM(1946), art d; SUNSET PASS(1946), art d; MASSACRE RIVER(1949), art d; FORT DEFIANCE(1951), art d; MUSCLE BEACH PARTY(1964), art d
Lucius O. Croxton
DICK TRACY VS. CUEBALL(1946), art d; SAN QUENTIN(1946), art d; DICK TRACY'S DILEMMA(1947), art d; SEVEN KEYS TO BALDPATE(1947), art d; WILD HORSE MESA(1947), art d; MICHAEL O'HALLORAN(1948), art d; WESTERN HERITAGE(1948), art d; ROUGHSHOD(1949), art d
Homer Croy
DOWN TO EARTH(1932), w; COHENS AND KELLYS IN TROUBLE, THE(1933), w; LADY TUBBS(1935), w; HARVESTER, THE(1936), w; DOWN ON THE FARM(1938), w; I'M FROM MISSOURI(1939), w; FAMILY HONEYMOON(1948), w; I SHOT JESSE JAMES(1949), d&w

John Croyden
WHITE CORRIDORS(1952, Brit.), p; HIGH WIND IN JAMAICA, A(1965), p

Joan Croydon
BAD SEED, THE(1956)

John Croydon
COLONEL BOGEY(1948, Brit.), p; BADGER'S GREEN(1949, Brit.), p; ONE WILD OAT(1951, Brit.), p; SING ALONG WITH ME(1952, Brit.), p; DELAVINE AFFAIR, THE(1954, Brit.), p; TARZAN AND THE LOST SAFARI(1957, Brit.), p; WHITE HUNTRESS(1957, Brit.), p; FIEND WITHOUT A FACE(1958), p; HAUNTED STRANGLER, THE(1958, Brit.), p; FIRST MAN INTO SPACE(1959, Brit.), p; CORRIDORS OF BLOOD(1962, Brit.), p; PROJECTED MAN, THE(1967, Brit.), p

Peter Croydon
FIRST TRAVELING SALESLADY, THE(1956)

Lou Croyton
SHACK OUT ON 101(1955), art d

Edmee Crozet
DEATH OF MARIO RICCI, THE(1983, Ital.)

Emmet Crozier
Silents
BLIND ALLEYS(1927), w

Helen Crozier
FOXES OF HARROW, THE(1947); TAKE ONE FALSE STEP(1949); THEY LIVE BY NIGHT(1949)

Judith Crozier
1984
CONSTANCE(1984, New Zealand), prod d

Reid Cruckshanks
ANDERSON TAPES, THE(1971)

Coleen Crudden
PHANTOM OF THE PARADISE(1974)

Aldo Crudo
THREE STOOGES VS. THE WONDER WOMEN(1975, Ital./Chi.), w

Carl Crudup
J.D.'S REVENGE(1976); MONKEY HUSTLE, THE(1976)

Carl W. Crudup
GAMBLER, THE(1974)

Will Cruft
SEE HOW THEY RUN(1955, Brit.)

Paul A. Cruger
Silents
EASY PICKINGS(1927), w

Aureio Crugnola
ADVENTURERS, THE(1970), art d

Aurelio Crugnola
IT HAPPENED IN ATHENS(1962), set d; MARCO POLO(1962, Fr./Ital.), art d; LITTLE NUNS, THE(1965, Ital.), set d; LOVE AND MARRIAGE(1966, Ital.), art d; HILLS RUN RED, THE(1967, Ital.), art d; NAVAJO JOE(1967, Ital./Span.), art d; HOUSE OF CARDS(1969), art d; STORY OF A WOMAN(1970, U.S./Ital.), art d; SACCO AND VANZETTI(1971, Ital./Fr.), art d; SNOW JOB(1972), art d; CHE?(1973, Ital./Fr./Ger.), art d; EIGER SANCTION, THE(1975), art d; MAHOGANY(1975), art d; CASSANDRA CROSSING, THE(1977), art d; ASHANTI(1979), prod d; BLACK STALLION RETURNS, THE(1983), art d

Aurelio Crugnolla
STARCRASH(1979), prod d

Andrew Cruickshank
AULD LANG SYNE(1937, Brit.); IDOL OF PARIS(1948, Brit.); MARK OF CAIN, THE(1948, Brit.); FORBIDDEN(1949, Brit.); PAPER ORCHID(1949, Brit.); EYE WITNESS(1950, Brit.); RELUCTANT WIDOW, THE(1951, Brit.); IVORY HUNTER(1952, Brit.); CRUEL SEA, THE(1953); JOHN WESLEY(1954, Brit.); RICHARD III(1956, Brit.); SECRET TENT, THE(1956, Brit.); JOHN AND JULIE(1957, Brit.); PURSUIT OF THE GRAF SPEE(1957, Brit.); STORY OF ESTHER COSTELLO, THE(1957, Brit.); INNOCENT SINNERS(1958, Brit.); QUESTION OF ADULTERY, A(1959, Brit.); KIDNAPPED(1960); STRANGLERS OF BOMBAY, THE(1960, Brit.); EL CID(1961, U.S./Ital.); GREYFRIARS BOBBY(1961, Brit.); LIVE NOW-PAY LATER(1962, Brit.); THERE WAS A CROOKED MAN(1962, Brit.); WE JOINED THE NAVY(1962, Brit.); COME FLY WITH ME(1963); MURDER MOST FOUL(1964, Brit.); WAGNER(1983, Brit./Hung./Aust.)

Art Cruickshank
DOCTOR DOLITTLE(1967), spec eff; FLIM-FLAM MAN, THE(1967), spec eff; GUIDE FOR THE MARRIED MAN, A(1967), spec eff; ST. VALENTINE'S DAY MASSACRE, THE(1967), spec eff; VALLEY OF THE DOLLS(1967), spec eff; DETECTIVE, THE(1968), spec eff; PLANET OF THE APES(1968), spec eff; SECRET LIFE OF AN AMERICAN WIFE, THE(1968), spec eff; STAR!(1968), spec eff; THE BOSTON STRANGLER, THE(1968), spec eff; BUTCH CASSIDY AND THE SUNDANCE KID(1969), spec eff; HARD CONTRACT(1969), spec eff; HELLO, DOLLY!(1969), spec eff; JOHN AND MARY(1969), spec eff; 100 RIFLES(1969), spec eff; M(1970), spec eff; MOVE(1970), spec eff; ONLY GAME IN TOWN, THE(1970), spec eff; PATTON(1970), spec eff; TORA! TORA! TORA!(1970, U.S./Jap.), spec eff; SNOWBALL EXPRESS(1972), spec eff; WORLD'S GREATEST ATHLETE, THE(1973), spec eff; HERBIE RIDES AGAIN(1974), spec eff; ESCAPE TO WITCH MOUNTAIN(1975), spec eff; FREAKY FRIDAY(1976), spec eff; GUS(1976), spec eff; HERBIE GOES TO MONTE CARLO(1977), spec eff; PETE'S DRAGON(1977), spec eff; CAT FROM OUTER SPACE, THE(1978), spec eff; RETURN FROM WITCH MOUNTAIN(1978), spec eff; NORTH AVENUE IRREGULARS, THE(1979), spec eff; HERBIE GOES BANANAS(1980), spec eff; LAST FLIGHT OF NOAH'S ARK, THE(1980), spec eff; WATCHER IN THE WOODS, THE(1980, Brit.), spec eff

Enid Cruickshank
GEORGE IN CIVVY STREET(1946, Brit.)

Gladys Cruickshank
KISS ME, SERGEANT(1930, Brit.); NOT SO QUIET ON THE WESTERN FRONT(1930, Brit.); WHY SAILORS LEAVE HOME(1930, Brit.)

Larry Cruickshank
GRAND THEFT AUTO(1977)

Rufus Cruickshank
LILLI MARLENE(1951, Brit.); THEY WERE NOT DIVIDED(1951, Brit.); NO HAUNT FOR A GENTLEMAN(1952, Brit.); NAKED HEART, THE(1955, Brit.); YOU LUCKY PEOPLE(1955, Brit.)

Reid Cruickshanks
SOMETHING WILD(1961); DIRTYMOUTH(1970); JOE(1970); HIGH PLAINS DRIFTER(1973); NIGHT SHIFT(1982); 48 HOURS(1982); JOYSTICKS(1983)
1984
FLETCH(1984)

Andrew Cruikshank
ANGEL WITH THE TRUMPET, THE(1950, Brit.); THIRTY NINE STEPS, THE(1960, Brit.)

Art Cruikshank
FANTASTIC VOYAGE(1966), spec eff; IN LIKE FLINT(1967), spec eff; LADY IN CEMENT(1968), spec eff; UNDEFEATED, THE(1969), spec eff; ISLAND AT THE TOP OF THE WORLD, THE(1974), spec eff; HOT LEAD AND COLD FEET(1978), spec eff

Reid Cruikshank
STOOLIE, THE(1972)

Rufus Cruikshank
WOMAN'S ANGLE, THE(1954, Brit.)

Sally Cruikshank
TWILIGHT ZONE-THE MOVIE(1983), anim

Reid Cruikshanks
HOSPITAL, THE(1971)
1984
SWING SHIFT(1984)

Christopher Cruise
HANSEL AND GRETEL(1965, Ger.), w

Tom Cruise
ENDLESS LOVE(1981); TAPS(1981); ALL THE RIGHT MOVES(1983); LOSIN' IT(1983); OUTSIDERS, THE(1983); RISKY BUSINESS(1983)

Christopher Cruize
STATUE, THE(1971, Brit.)

Bob Crumb
WILD GUITAR(1962)

Connie Crump
PASSION HOLIDAY(1963)

Freddie Crump
KING ARTHUR WAS A GENTLEMAN(1942, Brit.); WALKING ON AIR(1946, Brit.)

Owen Crump
SILVER RIVER(1948), p; NIGHT UNTO NIGHT(1949), p; RIVER CHANGES, THE(1956), p,d&w; MANHUNT IN THE JUNGLE(1958), w; COUCH, THE(1962), p&d, w; GUNN(1967), p; ZEPPELIN(1971, Brit.), p, w

Pete Crump
BRONCO BUSTER(1952)

Hugh Crumplin
Silents
POWER OVER MEN(1929, Brit.)

Charles Crumpton
Misc. Silents
GREEN-EYED MONSTER, THE(1916)

Jim Crumrine
1984
MISSING IN ACTION(1984)

Tony Crupi
HERO AT LARGE(1980); TWO OF A KIND(1983)

Craig Cruse
1984
RIVER RAT, THE(1984)

Gerald Cruse
BLOOD WATERS OF DOCTOR Z(1982)

William Cruse
DAMNATION ALLEY(1977), art d

Willian Cruse
AMITYVILLE HORROR, THE(1979), ph

Beegie Cruser
COUNTRY BOY(1966)

The Crusher
WRESTLER, THE(1974)

Arnold Crust
FIREPOWER(1970$c Brit.), ed; DEATH WISH II(1982), ed; WICKED LADY, THE(1983, Brit.), ed

Gary Crutcher
NAME OF THE GAME IS KILL, THE(1968), w; STANLEY(1973), a, w; SUPERCHICK(1973), a, w

Jack Crutcher
HERE COME THE MARINES(1952), w; NO HOLDS BARRED(1952), w; JALOPY(1953), w

Robert Riley Crutcher
GIRL TROUBLE(1942), w; KEY TO THE CITY(1950), w

Sgt. Norvell Crutcher
JOURNEY TOGETHER(1946, Brit.)

T. Renee Crutcher
1984
TANK(1984)

Jim Crutchfield
NASTY RABBIT, THE(1964), w

Les Crutchfield
LAST TRAIN FROM GUN HILL(1959), w; TARZAN'S GREATEST ADVENTURE(1959, Brit.), w

Geoffrey Crutchley
AND NOW THE SCREAMING STARTS(1973, Brit.)

Kate Crutchley
PROSTITUTE(1980, Brit.)

Leigh Crutchley
DYNAMITERS, THE(1956, Brit.); HOUSE IN THE WOODS, THE(1957, Brit.); HELLIONS, THE(1962, Brit.)

Roassalie Crutchley
BEYOND THIS PLACE(1959, Brit.)

Rosalee Crutchley
MAN OF LA MANCHA(1972)

Rosalie Crutchley
TAKE MY LIFE(1948, Brit.); SALT TO THE DEVIL(1949, Brit.); PRELUDE TO FAME(1950, Brit.); LADY WITH A LAMP, THE(1951, Brit.); QUO VADIS(1951); SWORD AND THE ROSE, THE(1953); FLAME AND THE FLESH(1954); MAKE ME AN OFFER(1954, Brit.); MALTA STORY(1954, Brit.); GAMMA PEOPLE, THE(1956); MIRACLE IN SOHO(1957, Brit.); NO TIME FOR TEARS(1957, Brit.); SPANISH GARDENER, THE(1957, Span.); TALE OF TWO CITIES, A(1958, Brit.); BEASTS OF MARSEILLES, THE(1959, Brit.); NUN'S STORY, THE(1959); SONS AND LO-VERS(1960, Brit.); GREYFRIARS BOBBY(1961, Brit.); NO LOVE FOR JOHNNIE(1961, Brit.); FREUD(1962); HAUNTING, THE(1963); BEHOLD A PALE HORSE(1964); MODEL MURDER CASE, THE(1964, Brit.); WUTHERING HEIGHTS(1970, Brit.); CREATURES THE WORLD FORGOT(1971, Brit.); WHO SLEW AUNTIE ROO?(1971, U.S./Brit.); BLOOD FROM THE MUMMY'S TOMB(1972, Brit.); MAHLER(1974, Brit.); MOHAMMAD, MESSENGER OF GOD(1976, Lebanon/Brit.); KEEP, THE(1983)
1984
MEMED MY HAWK(1984, Brit.)
Rosalie Crutchley
AND NOW THE SCREAMING STARTS(1973, Brit.)
Sally Crute
Silents
HOUSE OF THE LOST CORD, THE(1915); LIGHT AT DUSK, THE(1916); POWER OF DECISION, THE(1917); AVENGING TRAIL, THE(1918); EYE FOR EYE(1918); AMAZ-ING LOVERS(1921)
Misc. Silents
MATCH-MAKERS, THE(1916); BLUE JEANS(1917); POOR RICH MAN, THE(1918); TWILIGHT(1919); ATONEMENT(1920); BLIND WIVES(1920); EVEN AS EVE(1920); GARTER GIRL, THE(1920); IT ISN'T BEING DONE THIS SEASON(1921); PER-JURY(1921)
Abigail Cruttenden
1984
KIPPERBANG(1984, Brit.)
Mina Cruvi
TEL AVIV TAXI(1957, Israel)
Angel Crux
I WAS AN AMERICAN SPY(1951)
Alejandro Cruz
AZTEC MUMMY, THE(1957, Mex.); CURSE OF THE AZTEC MUMMY, THE(1965, Mex.); ROBOT VS. THE AZTEC MUMMY(1965, Mex.); CEREBROS DIABOLI-COS(1966, Mex.); BLUE DEMON VERSUS THE INFERNAL BRAINS(1967, Mex.); SANTO CONTRA BLUE DEMON EN LA ATLANTIDA(1968, Mex.)
Alejandro Cruz [Blue Demon]
SANTO Y BLUE DEMON CONTRA LOS MONSTRUOS(1968, Mex.)
Alfredo Santa Cruz
MAGNIFICENT BANDITS, THE(1969, Ital./Span.)
Angel Cruz
MANILA CALLING(1942); SOMEWHERE I'LL FIND YOU(1942); WAKE IS-LAND(1942); DESTINATION TOKYO(1944); PURPLE HEART, THE(1944); BACK TO BATAAN(1945); DIXIE JAMBOREE(1945); SAIGON(1948)
Angelo Cruz
TYPHOON(1940); LURE OF THE ISLANDS(1942)
Brandon Cruz
80 STEPS TO JONAH(1969); BAD NEWS BEARS, THE(1976); ONE AND ONLY, THE(1978)
Carmellio Cruz
GENTLE RAIN, THE(1966, Braz.), art d
Celia Cruz
AFFAIR IN HAVANA(1957)
Cesar A. Cruz
LOVE IS A CAROUSEL(1970), ed
Charles Cruz
Silents
WAS IT BIGAMY?(1925)
Misc. Silents
NIGHT MESSAGE, THE(1924); VIRTUE'S REVOLT(1924)
Chris Cruz
TNT JACKSON(1975)
Cintia Cruz
1984
ALPHABET CITY(1984)
Ediberto Cruz
ROLLER BOOGIE(1979), ed
Ernesto Gomez Cruz
1984
EL NORTE(1984); ERENDIRA(1984, Mex./Fr./Ger.); EVIL THAT MEN DO, THE(1984)
Francisco Cruz
CURSE OF THE VAMPIRES(1970, Phil., U.S.)
Gregory N. Cruz
SCARFACE(1983)
Irene Cruz
COUNTRY DOCTOR, THE(1963, Portuguese)
James Cruz
Misc. Silents
CARDINAL RICHELIEU'S WARD(1914); PATRIOT AND THE SPY, THE(1915)
Javier Ruvalcaba Cruz
1984
EVIL THAT MEN DO, THE(1984), ph
Jorge B. Cruz
LITTLE MISS MARKER(1980)
Mara Cruz
HYPNOSIS(1966, Ger./Sp./Ital.); TALL WOMEN, THE(1967, Aust./Ital./Span.); TREASURE OF MAKUBA, THE(1967, U.S./Span.); NUN AT THE CROSSROADS, A(1970, Ital./Span.)
Octaio Cruz
UNDER FIRE(1983)
Rafael Cruz
EASY MONEY(1983)

Rodell Cruz
RAW FORCE(1982), set d
Salvador Cruz
LUPE(1967)
Vera Cruz
WARRIOR AND THE SLAVE GIRL, THE(1959, Ital.)
James Cruze
GREAT GABBO, THE(1929), p&d; COCK O' THE WALK(1930), p; COSTELLO CASE, THE(1930), p; GOT WHAT SHE WANTED(1930), d; HELLO SISTER(1930), p; ONCE A GENTLEMAN(1930), p&d; SHE GOT WHAT SHE WANTED(1930), d; HELL BOUND(1931), p; SALVATION NELL(1931), d; WOMEN GO ON FOREVER(1931), p; IF I HAD A MILLION(1932), d; WASHINGTON MERRY-GO-ROUND(1932), d; I COVER THE WATERFRONT(1933), d; MR. SKITCH(1933), d; RACETRACK(1933), p&d; SAILOR BE GOOD(1933), d; DAVID HARUM(1934), d; THEIR BIG MO-MENT(1934), d; HELLDORADO(1935), d; TWO FISTED(1935), d; SUTTER'S GOLD(1936), d; WRONG ROAD, THE(1937), d; COME ON, LEATHERNECKS(1938), d; GANGS OF NEW YORK(1938), d; PRISON NURSE(1938), d
Silents
ARMSTRONG'S WIFE(1915); NAN OF MUSIC MOUNTAIN(1917); ADVENTURE IN HEARTS, AN(1919), d; ALIAS MIKE MORAN(1919), d; HAWTHORNE OF THE U.S.A.(1919), d; JOHNNY GET YOUR GUN(1919), d; ROARING ROAD, THE(1919), d; ALWAYS AUDACIOUS(1920), d; FOOD FOR SCANDAL(1920), d; CHARM SCHOOL, THE(1921), d; CRAZY TO MARRY(1921), d; GASOLINE GUS(1921), d; DICTATOR, THE(1922), d; THIRTY DAYS(1922), d; COVERED WAGON, THE(1923), p&d; RUG-GLES OF RED GAP(1923), d; ENEMY SEX, THE(1924), d; FIGHTING COWARD, THE(1924), d; MERTON OF THE MOVIES(1924), p&d; BEGGAR ON HORSEBACK(1925), d; PONY EXPRESS, THE(1925), d; OLD IRONSIDES(1926), d; CITY GONE WILD, THE(1927), d; WE'RE ALL GAMBLERS(1927), d; EXCESS BAG-GAGE(1928), d; NIGHT FLYER, THE(1928), p; ON TO RENO(1928), d; RED MARK, THE(1928), p; WIFE SAVERS(1928), p; DUKE STEPS OUT, THE(1929), d; MAN'S MAN, A(1929), d
Misc. Silents
ROBIN HOOD(1913); FROU FROU(1914); JOSEPH IN THE LAND OF EGYPT(1914); SNOWBIRD, THE(1916); HER TEMPTATION(1917); WEB OF LIFE, THE(1917); CITY OF DIM FACE, THE(1918); SOURCE, THE(1918); TOO MANY MILLIONS(1918), d; WILD YOUTH(1918); DUB, THE(1919), d; LOTTERY MAN, THE(1919), d; LOVE BURGLAR, THE(1919), d; VALLEY OF THE GIANTS, THE(1919), d; YOU'RE FI-RED(1919), d; FULL HOUSE, A(1920), d; MRS. TEMPLE'S TELEGRAM(1920), d; SINS OF ST. ANTHONY, THE(1920), d; TERROR ISLAND(1920), d; WHAT HAP-PENED TO JONES(1920), d; DOLLAR-A-YEAR MAN, THE(1921), d; IS MATRIMONY A FAILURE?(1922), d; OLD HOMESTEAD, THE(1922), d; ONE GLORIOUS DAY(1922), d; HOLLYWOOD(1923), d; TO THE LADIES(1923), d; CITY THAT NEV-ER SLEEPS, THE(1924), d; GARDEN OF WEEDS(1924), d; GOOSE HANGS HIGH, THE(1925), d; MARRY ME(1925), d; WAKING UP THE TOWN(1925), d; WELCOME HOME(1925), d; MANNEQUIN(1926), d; WE'RE ALL GAMBLERS(1927), d; MATING CALL, THE(1928), d
Jessie Cruzon
Misc. Silents
GALLOPING ON(1925)
Virginia Cruzon
ZIEGFELD GIRL(1941); UP IN ARMS(1944); GEORGE WHITE'S SCANDALS(1945); HAVING WONDERFUL CRIME(1945); EMERGENCY WEDDING(1950)
Barry Cryer
LITTLE OF WHAT YOU FANCY, A(1968, Brit.); MAGNIFICENT SEVEN DEADLY SINS, THE(1971, Brit.), w
1984
BLOODBATH AT THE HOUSE OF DEATH(1984, Brit.)
David Cryer
ESCAPE FROM ALCATRAZ(1979); AMERICAN GIGOLO(1980)
Jon Cryer
1984
NO SMALL AFFAIR(1984)
Sherwood Cryer
URBAN COWBOY(1980)
Anita Crystal
DEVIL'S SISTERS, THE(1966)
Billy Crystal
RABBIT TEST(1978)
1984
THIS IS SPINAL TAP(1984)
Danny Crystal
SOME KIND OF A NUT(1969)
Leon Crystal
TEVYA(1939), titles
Richard Crystal
FUN WITH DICK AND JANE(1977); BLUE SUNSHINE(1978)
Zsuzsa Csakany
CONFIDENCE(1980, Hung.), ed
Laszlo Csakanyi
DIALOGUE(1967, Hung.)
Karoly Csaki
CONFIDENCE(1980, Hung.)
A.S. Csaky
1984
PROTOCOL(1984)
Miklos Csanyi
WINTER WIND(1970, Fr./Hung.)
Eva Csapo
MOSES AND AARON(1975, Ger./Fr./Ital.)
Zsuzsa Csekany
MEPHISTO(1981, Ger.), ed
Nancy Cser
JOY(1983, Fr./Can.)
Gyorgy Cserhalmi
MEPHISTO(1981, Ger.)
Ervin Csomak
FATHER(1967, Hung.)

Larry Csonka
MIDWAY(1976)
Josef Csor
MEPHISTO(1981, Ger.)
Gyula Csortos
HIPPOLYT, THE LACKEY(1932, Hung.)
Laszlo Csurka
ROUND UP, THE(1969, Hung.)
Maria Jesus Cuadra
PRICE OF POWER, THE(1969, Ital./Span.)
Luis Cuadrado
HUNT, THE(1967, Span.), ph; SONNY AND JED(1974, Ital.), ph; SPIRIT OF THE BEEHIVE, THE(1976, Span.), ph
Maria Cuadros
PEARL, THE(1948, U.S./Mex.)
Jackie Cubat
COMANCHEROS, THE(1961)
Emilio Cubero
SUBWAY RIDERS(1981)
Jaime P. Cubero
NUN AT THE CROSSROADS, A(1970, Ital./Span.), art d
Jaime Perez Cubero
KID RODELO(1966, U.S./Span.), art d; HELLBENDERS, THE(1967, U.S./Ital./Span.), art d; MISSION STARDUST(1968, Ital./Span./Ger.), art d; SEVEN GUNS FOR THE MACGREGORS(1968, Ital./Span.), art d; ONE STEP TO HELL(1969, U.S./Ital./Span.), art d; SEVEN GOLDEN MEN(1969, Fr./Ital./Span.), prod d; KILL THEM ALL AND COME BACK ALONE!(1970, Ital./Span.), set d
James Perez Cubero
NEXT!(1971, Ital./Span.), art d
Raul Perez Cubero
HUNCHBACK OF THE MORGUE, THE(1972, Span.), ph; MUSHROOM EATER, THE(1976, Mex.), ph
Cubero y Galicia
MYSTERIOUS ISLAND OF CAPTAIN NEMO, THE(1973, Fr./Ital. 87m Span./Cameroon), prod d
Joseph Cuby
CONSPIRACY OF HEARTS(1960, Brit.); NINE HOURS TO RAMA(1963, U.S./Brit.); SWINGER'S PARADISE(1965, Brit.); TO SIR, WITH LOVE(1967, Brit.); TRYGON FACTOR, THE(1969, Brit.)
Franco Cucca
TODAY IT'S ME...TOMORROW YOU!(1968, Ital.), p
Antonio Cuccarre
CAMMINA CAMMINA(1983, Ital.)
Milo G. Cuccia
COUNT DRACULA(1971, Sp., Ital., Ger., Brit.), w
Cucciola
GREATEST SHOW ON EARTH, THE(1952)
Riccardo Cucciolla
ITALIANO BRAVA GENTE(1965, Ital./USSR); SIX DAYS A WEEK(1966, Fr./Ital./Span.); GRAND SLAM(1968, Ital., Span., Ger.); SACCO AND VANZETTI(1971, Ital./Fr.); COP, A(1973, Fr.); DIRTY MONEY(1977, Fr.)
Peppeddu Cuccu
BANDITS OF ORGOSOLO(1964, Ital.)
Mike Cuchar
MARCH ON PARIS 1914–OF GENERALOBERST ALEXANDER VON KLUCK–AND HIS MEMORY OF JESSIE HOLLADAY(1977), ph
Jose Cuchillo
RIO BRAVO(1959)
Enrico Cucinelli
HAPPY DAYS(1930)
Warren Cucurullo
LUNCH WAGON(1981)
Amilda Cuddy
WHERE DANGER LIVES(1950)
Bob Cudlip
NO HOLDS BARRED(1952)
Cliff Cudney
FRIDAY THE 13TH PART II(1981), a, stunts; NESTING, THE(1981); NIGHTHAWKS(1981); SLEEPAWAY CAMP(1983), stunts
1984
ONCE UPON A TIME IN AMERICA(1984)
Roger Cudney
SLAUGHTER(1972); CATTLE ANNIE AND LITTLE BRITCHES(1981); TRIUMPHS OF A MAN CALLED HORSE(1983, US/Mex.)
1984
EVIL THAT MEN DO, THE(1984)
Robert Cudney, Jr.
CATTLE ANNIE AND LITTLE BRITCHES(1981)
William Cuellar
SOUP FOR ONE(1982)
Pedro F Cuenca
CARMEN(1949, Span.)
Ernani Cuenco
1984
CAGED FURY(1984, Phil.), m
June Cuendet
HERE COME THE CO-EDS(1945)
James Cuenet
BEAUTY AND THE DEVIL(1952, Fr./Ital.), ed; DAUGHTERS OF DESTINY(1954, Fr./Ital.), ed; OBSESSION(1954, Fr./Ital.), ed; SECRETS D'ALCOVE(1954, Fr./Ital.), ed; COW AND I, THE(1961, Fr., Ital., Ger.), ed
Alma Cuervo
SO FINE(1981)
Gemma Cuervo
I HATE MY BODY(1975, Span./Switz.)
Conchita Cuetos
FACE OF TERROR(1964, Span.); OPEN SEASON(1974, U.S./Span.)

Antonio Cuevas
THAT HOUSE IN THE OUTSKIRTS(1980, Span.), w
Bob Cuff
VENGEANCE OF SHE, THE(1968, Brit.), spec eff; MACKENNA'S GOLD(1969), spec eff
Evelyne Cuffee
MELINDA(1972)
Xavier Cugat
WHITE ZOMBIE(1932, m; HOLIDAY IN MEXICO(1946); THIS TIME FOR KEEPS(1947); DATE WITH JUDY, A(1948); LUXURY LINER(1948); NEPTUNE'S DAUGHTER(1949); CHICAGO SYNDICATE(1955); DONATELLA(1956, Ital.), a, m; EDDY DUCHIN STORY, THE(1956); MONITORS, THE(1969); PHYNX, THE(1970)
Marcel Cugola
DEAD MAN'S FLOAT(1980, Aus.)
Steve Cuiffo
JACK AND THE BEANSTALK(1970), ed
Edward Cuitino
MALE AND FEMALE SINCE ADAM AND EVE(1961, Arg.)
Janez Cuk
SERGEANT JIM(1962, Yugo.)
Frances Cuka
OVER THE ODDS(1961, Brit.); SCROOGE(1970, Brit.); HENRY VIII AND HIS SIX WIVES(1972, Brit.); WATCHER IN THE WOODS, THE(1980, Brit.)
George Cukor
TARNISHED LADY(1931), d; GRUMPY(1930), d; ROYAL FAMILY OF BROADWAY, THE(1930), d; VIRTUOUS SIN, THE(1930), d; GIRLS ABOUT TOWN(1931), d; BILL OF DIVORCEMENT, A(1932), d; ONE HOUR WITH YOU(1932), d; ROCKABYE(1932), d; WHAT PRICE HOLLYWOOD?(1932), d; DINNER AT EIGHT(1933), d; LITTLE WOMEN(1933), d; OUR BETTERS(1933), d; DAVID COPPERFIELD(1935), d; NO MORE LADIES(1935), d; ROMEO AND JULIET(1936), d; SYLVIA SCARLETT(1936), d; CAMILLE(1937), d; PRISONER OF ZENDA, THE(1937), d; HOLIDAY(1938), d; I MET MY LOVE AGAIN(1938), d; GONE WITH THE WIND(1939), d; WOMEN, THE(1939), d; ZAZA(1939), d; PHILADELPHIA STORY, THE(1940), d; SUSAN AND GOD(1940), d; TWO-FACED WOMAN(1941), d; WOMAN'S FACE(1941), d; HER CARDBOARD LOVER(1942), d; KEEPER OF THE FLAME(1942), d; GASLIGHT(1944), d; WINGED VICTORY(1944), d; DESIRE ME(1947), d; DOUBLE LIFE, A(1947), d; ADAM'S RIB(1949), d; EDWARD, MY SON(1949, U.S./Brit.), d; LIFE OF HER OWN, A(1950), d; BORN YESTERDAY(1951), d; MODEL AND THE MARRIAGE BROKER, THE(1951), d; MARRYING KIND, THE(1952), d; PAT AND MIKE(1952), d; ACTRESS, THE(1953), d; IT SHOULD HAPPEN TO YOU(1954), d; STAR IS BORN, A(1954), d; BHOWANI JUNCTION(1956), d; LES GIRLS(1957), d; WILD IS THE WIND(1957), d; HELLER IN PINK TIGHTS(1960), d; LET'S MAKE LOVE(1960), d; SONG WITHOUT END(1960), d; CHAPMAN REPORT, THE(1962), d; MY FAIR LADY(1964), d; JUSTINE(1969), d; TRAVELS WITH MY AUNT(1972, Brit.), d; BLUE BIRD, THE(1976), d; RICH AND FAMOUS(1981), d
Angela Culbert
ROOM AT THE TOP(1959, Brit.)
Patricia Culbert
WILD RACERS, THE(1968)
Tim Culbertson
WALK PROUD(1979); WINTER KILLS(1979); EYE FOR AN EYE, AN(1981)
Melinda Culea
LITTLE SEX, A(1982)
Christopher Culhane
Misc. Talkies
YOUNG AND WILD(1975)
Clare Culhane
TO BE OR NOT TO BE(1983)
James Culhane
SNOW WHITE AND THE SEVEN DWARFS(1937), anim
Candace Culkin
UP THE DOWN STAIRCASE(1967)
Christopher Culkin
HAMLET(1964)
Frankie Cull
PIRATES OF PENZANCE, THE(1983)
Graham Cull
LORDS OF DISCIPLINE, THE(1983)
Peter Cullan
TIKI TIKI(1971, Can.)
Albert Cullaz
PARDON MY FRENCH(1951, U.S./Fr.)
Alan Cullen
SUPERMAN(1978)
Allen Cullen
O LUCKY MAN!(1973, Brit.)
Bill Cullen
IT HAPPENED TO JANE(1959)
Christine Cullen
GREAT MUPPET CAPER, THE(1981)
Cul Cullen
GREAT MACARTHY, THE(1975, Aus.); SCOBIE MALONE(1975, Aus.)
Fred Cullen
MAN FROM SNOWY RIVER, THE(1983, Aus.), w
1984
SQUIZZY TAYLOR(1984, Aus.)
Hedley Cullen
STORM BOY(1976, Aus.); LAST WAVE, THE(1978, Aus.)
James F. Cullen
Silents
SUMMER BACHELORS(1926)
Misc. Silents
CHAINS OF EVIDENCE(1920)
James V. Cullen
DEVIL'S RAIN, THE(1975, U.S./Mex.), p
John Cullen
Misc. Talkies
CAPTAIN CELLULOID VS THE FILM PIRATES(1974)

Kerrie Cullen
UNDER FIRE(1983)
Lorraine Cullen
DIARY OF A MAD HOUSEWIFE(1970); LOVING(1970)
Max Cullen
OFFICE PICNIC, THE(1974, Aus.); SUMMERFIELD(1977, Aus.); BLUE FIN(1978, Aus.); DIMBOOLA(1979, Aus.); ODD ANGRY SHOT, THE(1979, Aus.); HARD KNOCKS(1980, Aus.); MY BRILLIANT CAREER(1980, Aus.); HOODWINK(1981, Aus.); STARSTRUCK(1982, Aus.)
Nan Cullen
EARLY BIRD, THE(1936, Brit.); LUCK OF THE IRISH, THE(1937, Ireland)
Nancy Cullen
DEVIL'S ROCK(1938, Brit.)
Peter Cullen
PROLOGUE(1970, Can.); HEIDI'S SONG(1982)
Robert Cullen
IT'S A COP(1934, Brit.), w; AS YOU LIKE IT(1936, Brit.), w
Robert J. Cullen
KING'S CUP, THE(1933, Brit.), d; ESCAPE ME NEVER(1935, Brit.), w
Silents
EVERY MOTHER'S SON(1926, Brit.), d; DAWN(1928, Brit.), w
Robert Culler
HOUSE ON 92ND STREET, THE(1945)
Sid Culler
MELODY RANCH(1940), w
Christine Cullers
OCTOPUSSY(1983, Brit.)
Neil Culleton
LUNCH HOUR(1962, Brit.)
Cliff Culley
HANDS OF THE RIPPER(1971, Brit.), spec eff; JANE EYRE(1971, Brit.), spec eff; UNIDENTIFIED FLYING ODDBALL, THE(1979, Brit.), spec eff
1984
SWORD OF THE VALIANT(1984, Brit.), spec eff
Frederick Culley
MADAME GUILLOTINE(1931, Brit.); PRIVATE LIFE OF HENRY VIII, THE(1933); ONCE A THIEF(1935, Brit.); MEN OF YESTERDAY(1936, Brit.); ANNIE LAURIE(1936, Brit.); DINNER AT THE RITZ(1937, Brit.); KNIGHT WITHOUT ARMOR(1937, Brit.); MR. SMITH CARRIES ON(1937, Brit.); TALK OF THE DEVIL(1937, Brit.); DRUMS(1938, Brit.); RAT, THE(1938, Brit.); SPECIAL EDITION(1938, Brit.); SWORD OF HONOUR(1938, Brit.); FOUR FEATHERS, THE(1939, Brit.); REBEL SON, THE ½(1939, Brit.); TORPEDOED!(1939); CONQUEST OF THE AIR(1940); YOUNG MR. PITT, THE(1942, Brit.); BELLS GO DOWN, THE(1943, Brit.); UNCENSORED(1944, Brit.)
John C. Culley
Silents
PENNINGTON'S CHOICE(1915), w
John K. Culley
ATTACK OF THE KILLER TOMATOES(1978), ph
Niel Culley
1984
SWORD OF THE VALIANT(1984, Brit.), spec eff
Russell A. Culley
LONG NIGHT, THE(1947), spec eff
Wilf Culley
KING OF THE GRIZZLIES(1970), set d
Zara Culley
SUGAR HILL(1974)
James Culliford
ENTERTAINER, THE(1960, Brit.); FIVE MILLION YEARS TO EARTH(1968, Brit.); TRYGON FACTOR, THE(1969, Brit.); DEATHLINE(1973, Brit.)
Peyo Culliford
1984
SMURFS AND THE MAGIC FLUTE, THE(1984, Fr./Belg.), w
Alan Cullimore
VENGEANCE IS MINE(1948, Brit.), d&w; PENNY POINTS TO PARADISE(1951, Brit.), p
Alan J. Cullimore
CLOUDED CRYSTAL, THE(1948, Brit.), d&w
Arthur Cullin
Silents
FIRES OF FATE(1923, Brit.)
Misc. Silents
BONNIE MARY(1918, Brit.); NATURE'S GENTLEMAN(1918, Brit.); BLOOD MONEY(1921, Brit.); SIGN OF FOUR, THE(1923, Brit.)
Arthur M. Cullin
Silents
GREAT ADVENTURE, THE(1915, Brit.); ANSWER, THE(1916, Brit.); LOVE(1916, Brit.)
Charise Cullin
COWBOYS, THE(1972)
Thomas Cullinan
BEGUILED, THE(1971), w
David Cullinane
PLAY DEAD(1981)
Margaret Cullington
Silents
CAROLYN OF THE CORNERS(1919); MAD MARRIAGE, THE(1921); EXCITEMENT(1924)
Webster Cullinson
Silents
AIR HAWK, THE(1924)
Webster Cullison
Silents
IN FOR THIRTY DAYS(1919), d; LAST CHANCE, THE(1921), d
Misc. Silents
FIGHTING STRANGER, THE(1921), d; GOD'S GOLD(1921), d; BATTLING BATES(1923), d

Joseph Culliton
SOMEBODY KILLED HER HUSBAND(1978)
Patrick Culliton
TOWERING INFERNO, THE(1974); SWARM, THE(1978); BEYOND THE POSEIDON ADVENTURE(1979)
Desmond Cullon-Jones
GREAT ARMORED CAR SWINDLE, THE(1964)
Albert Culloz
AMAZING MONSIEUR FABRE, THE(1952, Fr.)
Catherine Culloz
AMAZING MONSIEUR FABRE, THE(1952, Fr.)
Charles Cullum
SELF-MADE LADY(1932, Brit.); PERFECT UNDERSTANDING(1933, Brit.); BORROW A MILLION(1934, Brit.); TO BE A LADY(1934, Brit.); CAPTAIN MOONLIGHT(1940, Brit.), w; BONNIE PRINCE CHARLIE(1948, Brit.); AMAZING MR. BEECHAM, THE(1949, Brit.); IT'S NOT CRICKET(1949, Brit.); RUN FOR YOUR MONEY, A(1950, Brit.); ISLAND RESCUE(1952, Brit.); MAN IN THE WHITE SUIT, THE(1952); ALL AT SEA(1958, Brit.); RELUCTANT DEBUTANTE, THE(1958); GAMES THAT LOVERS PLAY(1971, Brit.)
John Cullum
ALL THE WAY HOME(1963); HAMLET(1964); HAWAII(1966); 1776(1972)
1984
ACT, THE(1984); PRODIGAL, THE(1984)
Paul Cullum
TAKING TIGER MOUNTAIN(1983, U.S./Welsh), w
Ridgwell Cullum
Silents
TRAIL OF THE AXE, THE(1922), w
Desmond Cullum-Jones
BIG SWITCH, THE(1970, Brit.); MR. QUILP(1975, Brit.)
Cliff Cully
KIDNAPPED(1971, Brit.), spec eff
Russell Cully
MOURNING BECOMES ELECTRA(1947), spec eff; EVERY GIRL SHOULD BE MARRIED(1948), spec eff
Russell A. Cully
WITHOUT RESERVATIONS(1946), spec eff; THEY WON'T BELIEVE ME(1947), spec eff; CRIMINAL COURT(1946), spec eff; FALCON'S ADVENTURE, THE(1946), spec. eff; IT'S A WONDERFUL LIFE(1946), spec eff; LOCKET, THE(1946), spec eff; NOCTURNE(1946), spec eff; STEP BY STEP(1946), spec eff; VACATION IN RENO(1946), spec eff; BACHELOR AND THE BOBBY-SOXER, THE(1947), spec eff; CROSSFIRE(1947), spec eff; DESPERATE(1947), spec eff; DICK TRACY MEETS GRUESOME(1947), spec eff; LIKELY STORY, A(1947), spec eff; NIGHT SONG(1947), spec eff; OUT OF THE PAST(1947), spec eff; RIFFRAFF(1947), spec eff; TRAIL STREET(1947), spec eff; WOMAN ON THE BEACH, THE(1947), spec eff; GOOD SAM(1948), spec eff; I REMEMBER MAMA(1948), spec eff; MR. BLANDINGS BUILDS HIS DREAM HOUSE(1948), spec eff; RACE STREET(1948), spec eff; RACHEL AND THE STRANGER(1948), spec eff; RETURN OF THE BADMEN(1948), spec eff; STATION WEST(1948), spec eff; VELVET TOUCH, THE(1948), spec eff; WESTERN HERITAGE(1948), spec eff; THEY LIVE BY NIGHT(1949), spec eff; WINDOW, THE(1949), spec eff; WOMAN'S SECRET, A(1949), spec eff
Zara Cully
LIBERATION OF L.B. JONES, THE(1970); WUSA(1970); BROTHER JOHN(1971); DARKTOWN STRUTTERS(1975)
E.G. Culman
JIM, THE WORLD'S GREATEST(1976), art d
Nino Culotta
THEY'RE A WEIRD MOB(1966, Aus.), w
John Culow
Silents
ETERNAL CITY, THE(1915)
Jason Culp
HICKEY AND BOGGS(1972)
Nancy Culp
YOU'RE NEVER TOO YOUNG(1955)
Paul Culp
COOL AND THE CRAZY, THE(1958)
Robert Culp
PT 109(1963); SUNDAY IN NEW YORK(1963); RAIDERS, THE(1964); RHINO(1964); BOB AND CAROL AND TED AND ALICE(1969); NAME FOR EVIL, A(1970); HANNIE CALDER(1971, Brit.); HICKEY AND BOGGS(1972), a, d; CASTAWAY COWBOY, THE(1974); INSIDE OUT(1975, Brit.); BREAKING POINT(1976); GREAT SCOUT AND CATHOUSE THURSDAY, THE(1976); SKY RIDERS(1976, U.S./Gr.); GOLDENGIRL(1979)
Peter Culpan
PATRICK(1979, Aus.)
Stuart Culpepper
NORMA RAE(1979)
Fred Culpitt
KEEP YOUR SEATS PLEASE(1936, Brit.)
Eileen Culshaw
TOO MANY MILLIONS(1934, Brit.)
Eric Culton
PIRATES OF CAPRI, THE(1949)
K.E.B. Culvan
HEY, ROOKIE(1944), w
Calvin Culver
Misc. Talkies
FUN AND GAMES(1973); SCORE(1973)
Carol Culver
1941(1979)
Howard B. Culver
CATTLE EMPIRE(1958)
Howard Culver
BLACK WHIP, THE(1956); HOT CAR GIRL(1958); SWARM, THE(1978)
Lillian Culver
CARBINE WILLIAMS(1952); DREAM WIFE(1953); EASY TO LOVE(1953); NIGHTFALL(1956); GARMENT JUNGLE, THE(1957); JEANNE EAGELS(1957)

Michael Culver
BODY STEALERS, THE(1969); CROSSPLOT(1969, Brit.); GOODBYE MR. CHIPS(1969, U.S./Brit.); CONDUCT UNBECOMING(1975, Brit.); EMPIRE STRIKES BACK, THE(1980)
1984
PASSAGE TO INDIA, A(1984, Brit.)
Misc. Talkies
FAST KILL(1973)
Robin Culver
SUBURBAN WIVES(1973, Brit.)
Roland Culver
FASCINATION(1931, Brit.); 77 PARK LANE(1931, Brit.); C.O.D.(1932, Brit.); HER FIRST AFFAIRE(1932, Brit.); LOVE ON WHEELS(1932, Brit.); HEAD OF THE FAMILY(1933, Brit.); HER IMAGINARY LOVER(1933, Brit.); MAYFAIR GIRL(1933, Brit.); THERE GOES THE BRIDE(1933, Brit.); BORROW A MILLION(1934, Brit.); FATHER AND SON(1934, Brit.); LUCKY LOSER(1934, Brit.); SCOOP, THE(1934, Brit.); TWO HEARTS IN WALTZ TIME(1934, Brit.); OH, WHAT A NIGHT(1935); WOLVES OF THE UNDERWORLD(1935, Brit.); ACCUSED(1936, Brit.); GAIETY GIRLS, THE(1938, Brit.); BLIND FOLLY(1939, Brit.); FRENCH WITHOUT TEARS(1939, Brit.); FINGERS(1940, Brit.); NIGHT TRAIN(1940, Brit.); OLD BILL AND SON(1940, Brit.); QUIET WEDDING(1941, Brit.); THIS ENGLAND(1941, Brit.); AVENGERS, THE(1942, Brit.); ONE OF OUR AIRCRAFT IS MISSING(1942, Brit.); TALK ABOUT JACQUELINE(1942, Brit.); UNPUBLISHED STORY(1942, Brit.); SPITFIRE(1943, Brit.); GIVE US THE MOON(1944, Brit.); ON APPROVAL(1944, Brit.); SECRET MISSION(1944, Brit.); COLONEL BLIMP(1945, Brit.); RANDOLPH FAMILY, THE(1945, Brit.); VACATION FROM MARRIAGE(1945, Brit.); DEAD OF NIGHT(1946, Brit.); TO EACH HIS OWN(1946); WANTED FOR MURDER(1946, Brit.); DOWN TO EARTH(1947); SINGAPORE(1947); ISN'T IT ROMANTIC?(1948); GREAT LOVER, THE(1949); HER MAN GILBEY(1949, Brit.); TRIO(1950, Brit.); ENCORE(1951, Brit.); HOTEL SAHARA(1951, Brit.); OBSESSED(1951, Brit.); HOUR OF THIRTEEN, THE(1952); MAGIC BOX, THE(1952, Brit.); FOLLY TO BE WISE(1953); SHOOT FIRST(1953, Brit.); BETRAYED(1954); HOLLY AND THE IVY, THE(1954, Brit.); LIGHT TOUCH, THE(1955, Brit.); MAN WHO LOVED REDHEADS, THE(1955, Brit.); TECKMAN MYSTERY, THE(1955, Brit); SAFARI(1956); SHIP THAT DIED OF SHAME, THE(1956, Brit.); ALLIGATOR NAMED DAISY, AN(1957, Brit.); LIGHT FINGERS(1957, Brit.); SCOTLAND YARD DRAGNET(1957, Brit.); BONJOUR TRISTESSE(1958); MAD LITTLE ISLAND(1958, Brit.); TRUTH ABOUT WOMEN, THE(1958, Brit.); CIRCLE, THE(1959, Brit.); NEXT TO NO TIME(1960, Brit.); TERM OF TRIAL(1962, Brit.); PAIR OF BRIEFS, A(1963, Brit.); SWINGIN' MAIDEN, THE(1963, Brit.); THUNDERBALL(1965, Brit.); YELLOW ROLLS-ROYCE, THE(1965, Brit.); MAN COULD GET KILLED, A(1966); IN SEARCH OF GREGORY(1970, Brit./Ital.); RISE AND RISE OF MICHAEL RIMMER, THE(1970, Brit.); FRAGMENT OF FEAR(1971, Brit.); LEGEND OF HELL HOUSE, THE(1973, Brit.); MACKINTOSH MAN, THE(1973, Brit.); NELSON AFFAIR, THE(1973, Brit.); UNCANNY, THE(1977, Brit./Can.); GREEK TYCOON, THE(1978); NO LONGER ALONE(1978); ROUGH CUT(1980, Brit.); MISSIONARY, THE(1982); NEVER NEVER LAND(1982)
Sidney Culver
BELOVED IMPOSTER(1936, Brit.)
The Personnel of Culver Military Academy Units of Indiana
TOM BROWN OF CULVER(1932)
Peter Culverwell
ENIGMA(1983), ed
Necati Cumali
DRY SUMMER(1967, Turkey), w
John Cumberland
Silents
BABY MINE(1917)
Misc. Silents
GAY OLD DOG, THE(1919)
Marten Cumberland
INSIDE THE ROOM(1935, Brit.), w
Roscoe Cumberland
HARLEM GLOBETROTTERS, THE(1951)
Heshimu Cumbuka
SUNNYSIDE(1979)
Ji-Tu Cumbuka
UPTIGHT(1968); CHANGE OF HABIT(1969); TOP OF THE HEAP(1972); UP THE SANDBOX(1972); LOST IN THE STARS(1974); MANDINGO(1975); BOUND FOR GLORY(1976); DR. BLACK AND MR. HYDE(1976); FUN WITH DICK AND JANE(1977); WALK PROUD(1979)
Jitu Cumbuka
BLACULA(1972); MAURIE(1973)
Mwako Cumbuka
HIT(1973); TOGETHER BROTHERS(1974); ONE FLEW OVER THE CUCKOO'S NEST(1975)
William Cumby
GREEN PASTURES(1936)
Fred Cumings
SLAUGHTER IN SAN FRANCISCO(1981), ed
The Cummerford Dancers
NORAH O'NEALE(1934, Brit.)
Charles Cumming
Misc. Silents
CHALICE OF SORROW, THE(1916)
David Cumming
ROBBERY WITH VIOLENCE(1958, Brit.), w
Dorothy Cumming
WIND, THE(1928); APPLAUSE(1929); KITTY(1929, Brit.)
Silents
NOTORIOUS MISS LISLE, THE(1920); NOTORIOUS MRS. SANDS, THE(1920); DON'T TELL EVERYTHING(1921); NELLIE, THE BEAUTIFUL CLOAK MODEL(1924); NEW COMMANDMENT, THE(1925); DANCING MOTHERS(1926); KISS FOR CINDERELLA, A(1926); IN OLD KENTUCKY(1927); KING OF KINGS, THE(1927); LOVELORN, THE(1927); DIVINE WOMAN, THE(1928); OUR DANCING DAUGHTERS(1928)
Misc. Silents
IDOLS OF CLAY(1920); WOMAN AND THE PUPPET, THE(1920); WOMAN WHO UNDERSTOOD, A(1920); CHEAT, THE(1923); TWENTY-ONE(1923); COAST OF FOLLY, THE(1925); MANICURE GIRL, THE(1925); ONE WAY STREET(1925); BUTTERFLIES IN THE RAIN(1926); MADEMOISELLE MODISTE(1926); FORBIDDEN

HOURS(1928); KITTY(1929, Brit.)
Dorothy G. Cumming
Misc. Silents
SNOW WHITE(1917)
George W. Cumming
MR. BILLION(1977)
A.B. Cummings
TYPHOON TREASURE(1939, Brit.), ph
Alastair Cummings
DRAUGHTSMAN'S CONTRACT, THE(1983, Brit.)
Barbara Cummings
LILLI MARLENE(1951, Brit.)
Bert Cummings
Silents
JACK O'HEARTS(1926)
Bill Cummings
SECRET OF MONTE CRISTO, THE(1961, Brit.); CARRY ON SPYING(1964, Brit.); THUNDERBALL(1965, Brit.)
Billy Cummings
SULLIVANS, THE(1944); SUNDAY DINNER FOR A SOLDIER(1944); THREE MEN IN WHITE(1944); CIRCUMSTANTIAL EVIDENCE(1945); COLORADO PIONEERS(1945); OREGON TRAIL SCOUTS(1947); FIGHTING FATHER DUNNE(1948)
Bob Cummings
MY GEISHA(1962); BEACH PARTY(1963); CARPETBAGGERS, THE(1964); WHAT A WAY TO GO(1964); PROMISE HER ANYTHING(1966, Brit.); STAGECOACH(1966)
1984
STAR TREK III: THE SEARCH FOR SPOCK(1984)
Brian Cummings
CALIFORNIA SUITE(1978); WHERE THE BUFFALO ROAM(1980)
Burton Cummings
MELANIE(1982, Can.)
Chris Cummings
1984
MRS. SOFFEL(1984)
Constance Cummings
CRIMINAL CODE(1931); GUILTY GENERATION, THE(1931); LAST PARADE, THE(1931); LOVER COME BACK(1931); TRAVELING HUSBANDS(1931); AMERICAN MADNESS(1932); ATTORNEY FOR THE DEFENSE(1932); BEHIND THE MASK(1932); BILLION DOLLAR SCANDAL(1932); LAST MAN(1932); MOVIE CRAZY(1932); NIGHT AFTER NIGHT(1932); WASHINGTON MERRY-GO-ROUND(1932); BROADWAY THROUGH A KEYHOLE(1933); CHARMING DECEIVER, THE(1933, Brit.); MIND READER, THE(1933); CHANNEL CROSSING(1934, Brit.); GLAMOUR(1934); LOOKING FOR TROUBLE(1934); THIS MAN IS MINE(1934); REMEMBER LAST NIGHT(1935); DOMMED CARGO(1936, Brit.); STRANGERS ON A HONEYMOON(1937, Brit.); BUSMAN'S HONEYMOON(1940, Brit.); THIS ENGLAND(1941, Brit.); SOMEWHERE IN FRANCE(1943, Brit.); BLITHE SPIRIT(1945, Brit.); MAN IN THE DINGHY, THE(1951, Brit.); THREE'S COMPANY(1953, Brit.); FINGER OF GUILT(1956, Brit.); JOHN AND JULIE(1957, Brit.); BATTLE OF THE SEXES, THE(1960, Brit.); IN THE COOL OF THE DAY(1963); BOY TEN FEET TALL, A(1965, Brit.); JANE EYRE(1971, Brit.)
Misc. Talkies
BIG TIMER(1932)
Dale Cummings
ENEMY BELOW, THE(1957); OPERATION PETTICOAT(1959); BUONA SERA, MRS. CAMPBELL(1968, Ital.); ONE STEP TO HELL(1969, U.S./Ital./Span.)
Dick Cummings
Silents
WOLF LAW(1922)
Misc. Silents
ADORABLE SAVAGE, THE(1920)
Dorothy Cummings
Misc. Silents
FEMALE, THE(1924)
Dwight Cummings
RECKONING, THE(1932), d; SAGINAW TRAIL(1953), w
Eugene Cummings
CRIME PATROL, THE(1936), d
George Cummings
Silents
MAN'S LAW AND GOD'S(1922)
Howard Cummings
1984
GIRLS NIGHT OUT(1984), prod d
Hugh Cummings
PARDON MY GUN(1930), w; MEN ARE LIKE THAT(1931); BIG RACE, THE(1934), w; HOT TIP(1935), w; EARTHWORM TRACTORS(1936), w; POLO JOE(1936), w; PENROD AND SAM(1937), w; PENROD AND HIS TWIN BROTHER(1938), w; SWEEPSTAKES WINNER(1939), w
Irving Cummings
BEHIND THAT CURTAIN(1929), d; IN OLD ARIZONA(1929), d; NOT QUITE DECENT(1929), d; CAMEO KIRBY(1930), d; DEVIL WITH WOMEN, A(1930), d; ON THE LEVEL(1930), d; CISCO KID(1931), d; HOLY TERROR, A(1931), d; ATTORNEY FOR THE DEFENSE(1932), d; MAN AGAINST WOMAN(1932), d; NIGHT CLUB LADY(1932), d; MAD GAME, THE(1933), d; MAN HUNT(1933), d; WOMAN I STOLE, THE(1933), d; GRAND CANARY(1934), d; I BELIEVED IN YOU(1934), d; WHITE PARADE, THE(1934), d; CURLY TOP(1935), d; IT'S A SMALL WORLD(1935), d; GIRLS' DORMITORY(1936), d; POOR LITTLE RICH GIRL(1936), d; WHITE HUNTER(1936), d; MERRY-GO-ROUND OF 1938(1937), d; VOGUES OF 1938(1937), d; JUST AROUND THE CORNER(1938), d; LITTLE MISS BROADWAY(1938), d; EVERYTHING HAPPENS AT NIGHT(1939), d; HOLLYWOOD CAVALCADE(1939), d; STORY OF ALEXANDER GRAHAM BELL, THE(1939), d; DOWN ARGENTINE WAY(1940), d; LILLIAN RUSSELL(1940), d; BELLE STARR(1941), d; LOUISIANA PURCHASE(1941), d; THAT NIGHT IN RIO(1941), d; MY GAL SAL(1942), d; SPRINGTIME IN THE ROCKIES(1942), d; SWEET ROSIE O'GRADY(1943), d; WHAT A WOMAN!(1943), p&d; IMPATIENT YEARS, THE(1944), p&d; DOLLY SISTERS, THE(1945), d
Silents
LAST VOLUNTEER, THE(1914); UNCLE TOM'S CABIN(1914); GILDED CAGE, THE(1916); HIDDEN SCAR, THE(1916); AMERICAN WIDOW, AN(1917); ROUND UP,

THE(1920); SEX(1920); SAPHEAD, THE(1921); ENVIRONMENT(1922), d; JILT, THE(1922), d; PAID BACK(1922), d; DRUG TRAFFIC, THE(1923), d; EAST SIDE-WEST SIDE(1923), p&d; RUPERT OF HENTZAU(1923), d; IN EVERY WOMAN'S LIFE(1924), d; ROSE OF PARIS, THE(1924), d; AS MAN DESIRES(1925), a, d; DESERT FLOWER, THE(1925), d; JUST A WOMAN(1925), d; ONE YEAR TO LIVE(1925), d; JOHNSTOWN FLOOD, THE(1926), d; BERTHA, THE SEWING MACHINE GIRL(1927), d; BRUTE, THE(1927), d

Misc. Silents

LURE OF THE MASK, THE(1915); THREE OF US, THE(1915); FEUD GIRL, THE(1916); PAMELA'S PAST(1916); SALESLADY, THE(1916); WORLD'S GREAT SNARE, THE(1916); MAN'S LAW, A(1917); ROYAL ROMANCE(1917); SISTER AGAINST SISTER(1917); WHIP, THE(1917); WRATH OF LOVE(1917); DEBT OF HONOR, THE(1918); HEART OF A GIRL(1918); INTERLOPER, THE(1918); MERELY PLAYERS(1918); STRUGGLE EVERLASTING, THE(1918); TOYS OF FATE(1918); WOMAN WHO GAVE, THE(1918); BLUFFER, THE(1919); EVERYWOMAN(1919); GREATER SINNER, THE(1919); HER CODE OF HONOR(1919); MANDARIN'S GOLD(1919); SCAR, THE(1919); SOME BRIDE(1919); UNVEILING HAND, THE(1919); WHAT EVERY WOMAN LEARNS(1919); BEAUTIFULLY TRIMMED(1920); LADDER OF LIES, THE(1920); OLD DAD(1920); BROAD DAYLIGHT(1922), d; FLESH AND BLOOD(1922), d; MAN FROM HELL'S RIVER, THE(1922), a, d; BROKEN HEARTS OF BROADWAY, THE(1923); DANCING CHEAT, THE(1924), d; FOOLS' HIGHWAY(1924), d; RIDERS UP(1924), d; STOLEN SECRETS(1924), d; INFATUATION(1925), d; COUNTRY BEYOND, THE(1926), d; MIDNIGHT KISS, THE(1926), d; RUSTLING FOR CUPID(1926), d; DRESSED TO KILL(1928), d; PORT OF MISSING GIRLS, THE(1928), d; ROMANCE OF THE UNDERWORLD(1928), d

Irving Cummings, Jr.

YESTERDAY'S HEROES(1940), w; LAST OF THE DUANES(1941), w; RIDE, KELLY, RIDE(1941), w; LONE STAR RANGER(1942), w; HE HIRED THE BOSS(1943), w; DANGEROUS MILLIONS(1946), w; DEADLINE FOR MURDER(1946), w; JEWELS OF BRANDENBURG(1947), w; SIGN OF THE RAM, THE(1948), p; WHERE DANGER LIVES(1950), p; DOUBLE DYNAMITE(1951); GIRL IN EVERY PORT, A(1952), p

Irving Cummings, Sr.

DOUBLE DYNAMITE(1951), d

Jack Cummings

YELLOW JACK(1938), p; WINNING TICKET, THE(1935), p; BORN TO DANCE(1936), p; BROADWAY MELODY OF '38(1937), p; LISTEN, DARLING(1938), p; HONOLULU(1939), p; BROADWAY MELODY OF 1940(1940), p; GO WEST(1940), p; TWO GIRLS ON BROADWAY(1940), p; SHIP AHOY(1942), p; I DOOD IT(1943), p; BATHING BEAUTY(1944), p; BROADWAY RHYTHM(1944), p; EASY TO WED(1946), p; FIESTA(1947), p; IT HAPPENED IN BROOKLYN(1947), p; ROMANCE OF ROSY RIDGE, THE(1947), p; NEPTUNE'S DAUGHTER(1949), p; STRATTON STORY, THE(1949), p; THREE LITTLE WORDS(1950), p; TWO WEEKS WITH LOVE(1950), p; EXCUSE MY DUST(1951), p; TEXAS CARNIVAL(1951), p; LOVELY TO LOOK AT(1952), p; GIVE A GIRL A BREAK(1953), p; KISS ME KATE(1953), p; SOMBRERO(1953), p; LAST TIME I SAW PARIS, THE(1954), p; SEVEN BRIDES FOR SEVEN BROTHERS(1954), p; INTERRUPTED MELODY(1955), p; MANY RIVERS TO CROSS(1955), p; TEAHOUSE OF THE AUGUST MOON, THE(1956), p; BLUE ANGEL, THE(1959), p; CAN-CAN(1960), p; SECOND TIME AROUND, THE(1961), p; BACHELOR FLAT(1962), p; VIVA LAS VEGAS(1964), p

John Cummings

MARCO POLO JUNIOR(1973, Aus.), ph; RETURN OF THE JEDI(1983)

Kay Cummings

GOODBYE COLUMBUS(1969); WHY WOULD I LIE(1980)

Mrs. Irving Cummings

Misc. Silents

DANGEROUS PASTIME(1922)

Pat Cummings

WAY OF ALL MEN, THE(1930)

Patrick Cummings

PROMISES, PROMISES(1963), cos; CONVICT STAGE(1965), cos; FORT COURAGEOUS(1965), cos; DOC SAVAGE... THE MAN OF BRONZE(1975), cos

Patrick W. Cummings

GUN THE MAN DOWN(1957), cos

Peg Cummings

HOW TO BEAT THE HIGH COST OF LIVING(1980), set d; IN GOD WE TRUST(1980), set d

1984

MEATBALLS PART II(1984), art d; WOMAN IN RED, THE(1984), set d

Quinn Cummings

GOODBYE GIRL, THE(1977)

Richard Cummings

SOCIAL LION, THE(1930)

Silents

DAPHNE AND THE PIRATE(1916); REACHING FOR THE MOON(1917); BLIND HUSBANDS(1919); LITTLE COMRADE(1919); PRINCE OF AVENUE A., THE(1920); NO WOMAN KNOWS(1921)

Misc. Silents

DOUBLE TROUBLE(1915); WOLF-MAN, THE(1915); BAD BOYS(1917); MAN OF BRONZE, THE(1918); DELICIOUS LITTLE DEVIL, THE(1919); LITTLE WHITE SAVAGE, THE(1919); TOMBOY, THE(1921)

Robert Cummings

CONVICT'S CODE(1930); MILLIONS IN THE AIR(1935); SO RED THE ROSE(1935); VIRGINIA JUDGE, THE(1935); ACCUSING FINGER, THE(1936); ARIZONA MAHONEY(1936); BORDER FLIGHT(1936); DESERT GOLD(1936); FORGOTTEN FACES(1936); HOLLYWOOD BOULEVARD(1936); THREE CHEERS FOR LOVE(1936); HIDEAWAY GIRL(1937); LAST TRAIN FROM MADRID, THE(1937); SOPHIE LANG GOES WEST(1937); SOULS AT SEA(1937); WELLS FARGO(1937); COLLEGE SWING(1938); I STAND ACCUSED(1938); TEXANS, THE(1938); TOUCHDOWN, ARMY(1938); YOU AND ME(1938); CHARLIE MC CARTHY, DETECTIVE(1939); EVERYTHING HAPPENS AT NIGHT(1939); RIO(1939); THREE SMART GIRLS GROW UP(1939); UNDER-PUP, THE(1939); AND ONE WAS BEAUTIFUL(1940); ONE NIGHT IN THE TROPICS(1940); PRIVATE AFFAIRS(1940); SPRING PARADE(1940); DEVIL AND MISS JONES, THE(1941); FREE AND EASY(1941); IT STARTED WITH EVE(1941); MOON OVER MIAMI(1941); BETWEEN US GIRLS(1942); KING'S ROW(1942); SABOTEUR(1942); FLESH AND FANTASY(1943); FOREVER AND A DAY(1943); PRINCESS O'ROURKE(1943); YOU CAME ALONG(1945); BRIDE WORE BOOTS, THE(1946); CHASE, THE(1946); HEAVEN ONLY KNOWS(1947); LOST MOMENT, THE(1947); LET'S LIVE A LITTLE(1948), a, p; SLEEP, MY LOVE(1948); ACCUSED, THE(1949); BLACK BOOK, THE(1949); FREE FOR ALL(1949); TELL IT TO THE JUDGE(1949); FOR HEAVEN'S SAKE(1950); PAID IN FULL(1950); PETTY GIRL,

THE(1950); BAREFOOT MAILMAN, THE(1951); FIRST TIME, THE(1952); MARRY ME AGAIN(1953); DIAL M FOR MURDER(1954); LUCKY ME(1954); HOW TO BE VERY, VERY, POPULAR(1955); FIVE GOLDEN DRAGONS(1967, Brit.)

Silents

JUNGLE, THE(1914); LITTLE GRAY LADY, THE(1914); CUB, THE(1915); HEART OF THE BLUE RIDGE, THE(1915); IVORY SNUFF BOX, THE(1915); RUNNING FIGHT, THE(1915); BRAND OF COWARDICE, THE(1916); FRUITS OF DESIRE, THE(1916); CRIME AND PUNISHMENT(1917); DEVIL'S PLAYGROUND, THE(1918)

Misc. Silents

AWAKENING OF HELENA RICHIE, THE(1916); CAMILLE(1916); MILLION A MINUTE, A(1916); PAYING THE PRICE(1916); RICH MAN'S PLAYTHING, A(1917); TRAP, THE(1918); GOLDEN SHOWER, THE(1919); FACE AT YOUR WINDOW(1920)

Robert Cummings, Sr.

FIRST LADY(1937); LIFE OF EMILE ZOLA, THE(1937); THEY WON'T FORGET(1937); I AM THE LAW(1938); OKLAHOMA FRONTIER(1939)

Robert H. Cummings

HELL SHIP MUTINY(1957), ph

Robert W. Cummings

Misc. Silents

VIRTUOUS MEN(1919)

Ron Cummings

WHERE THE BUFFALO ROAM(1980)

Ross Cummings

ONLY WAY HOME, THE(1972)

Ruth Cummings

BRIDGE OF SAN LUIS REY, THE(1929), w; OUR MODERN MAIDENS(1929), titles; DAYBREAK(1931), w; NEVER THE TWAIN SHALL MEET(1931), w; BY CANDLE-LIGHT(1934), w

Silents

TOWER OF LIES, THE(1925), t; ALTARS OF DESIRE(1927), t; ANNIE LAURIE(1927), t; CALIFORNIA(1927), t; FOREIGN DEVILS(1927), t; IN OLD KENTUCKY(1927), t; LOVE(1927), t; QUALITY STREET(1927), t; ADVENTURER, THE(1928), t; MYSTERIOUS LADY, THE(1928), t; OUR DANCING DAUGHTERS(1928), t; WOMAN OF AFFAIRS, A(1928), t; OUR MODERN MAIDENS(1929), t; WILD ORCHIDS(1929), t

Samuel Cummings

WAR IS A RACKET(1934), p&d

Sanford Cummings

LONE WOLF IN MEXICO, THE(1947), p

Susan Cummings

SECRET OF TREASURE MOUNTAIN(1956); SWAMP WOMEN(1956); TOMAHAWK TRAIL(1957); UTAH BLAINE(1957); MAN FROM GOD'S COUNTRY(1958); VERBOTEN!(1959); STREET IS MY BEAT, THE(1966)

Misc. Talkies

NEW DAY AT SUNDOWN(1957)

Thomas Cummings

Silents

CARDIGAN(1922)

Vicki Cummings

I CAN GET IT FOR YOU WHOLESALE(1951)

Bill Cummins

PINK PANTHER STRIKES AGAIN, THE(1976, Brit.)

Danny Cummins

ULYSSES(1967, U.S./Brit.); WHERE'S JACK?(1969, Brit.); PADDY(1970, Irish); QUACKSER FORTUNE HAS A COUSIN IN THE BRONX(1970)

Diane Cummins

Misc. Talkies

NIGHT TO DISMEMBER, A(1983)

Don Cummins

SLITHIS(1978); ESCAPE FROM ALCATRAZ(1979)

Misc. Talkies

ELECTRIC CHAIR, THE(1977)

Dwight Cummins

RIVER, THE(1928), w; THUNDERHEAD-SON OF FLICKA(1945), w; SMOKY(1946), w; LOADED PISTOLS(1948), w; STRAWBERRY ROAN, THE(1948), w; COWBOY AND THE INDIANS, THE(1949), w; SMOKY(1966), w

Silents

FANGS OF THE WILD(1928), w; NONE BUT THE BRAVE(1928), w; NEW YEAR'S EVE(1929), w

Eli Cummins

TENDER MERCIES(1982); LONE WOLF McQUADE(1983); TOUGH ENOUGH(1983)

G. M. Cummins

LOOSE ENDS(1975), ed

Gerard Cummins

1984

REFLECTIONS(1984, Brit.)

Greg Cummins

PERSONALS, THE(1982), ph

Gregory M. Cummins

LOOSE ENDS(1975), ph

Jackie Cummins

THREE ON A SPREE(1961, Brit.), cos; GUTTER GIRLS(1964, Brit.), cos; BRAIN, THE(1965, Ger./Brit.), cos; SKULL, THE(1965, Brit.), cos

Janis Cummins

SMOKEY AND THE BANDIT-PART 3(1983)

Josephine Cummins

RAINTREE COUNTY(1957)

Juliette Cummins

1984

HIGHWAY TO HELL(1984); RUNNING HOT(1984)

Laura Cummins

PLAYGIRLS AND THE BELLBOY, THE(1962,Ger.)

Lt. Joe Cummins

FLIRTATION WALK(1934)

Marie Susanna Cummins

Silents

LAMPLIGHTER, THE(1921), w

Peggy Cummins
DR. O'DOWD(1940, Brit.); SALUTE JOHN CITIZEN(1942, Brit.); OLD MOTHER RILEY, DETECTIVE(1943, Brit.); WELCOME, MR. WASHINGTON(1944, Brit.); LATE GEORGE APLEY, THE(1947); MOSS ROSE(1947); ESCAPE(1948, Brit.); GREEN GRASS OF WYOMING(1948); GUN CRAZY(1949); HER MAN GILBEY(1949, Brit.); IF THIS BE SIN(1950, Brit.); OPERATION X(1951, Brit.); PASSIONATE SENTRY, THE(1952, Brit.); BOTH SIDES OF THE LAW(1953, Brit.); MEET MR. LUCIFER(1953, Brit.); ALWAYS A BRIDE(1954, Brit.); LOVE LOTTERY, THE(1954, Brit.); CASH ON DELIVERY(1956, Brit.); MARCH HARE, THE(1956, Brit.); CARRY ON ADMIRAL(1957, Brit.); CURSE OF THE DEMON(1958); HELL DRIVERS(1958, Brit.); CAPTAIN'S TABLE, THE(1960, Brit.); DENTIST IN THE CHAIR(1960, Brit.); IN THE DOGHOUSE(1964, Brit.); YOUR MONEY OR YOUR WIFE(1965, Brit.)

Peter Cummins
FIRM MAN, THE(1975, Aus.); GREAT MACARTHY, THE(1975, Aus.); REMOVALISTS, THE(1975, Aus.); SUNDAY TOO FAR AWAY(1975, Aus.); STORM BOY(1976, Aus.); HIGH ROLLING(1977, Aus.)

Ralph Cummins
Silents
WHERE MEN ARE MEN(1921), w; LOADED DOOR, THE(1922), w

Ron Cummins
HOT ROD HULLABALOO(1966); DOG DAY AFTERNOON(1975); WHICH WAY IS UP?(1977); STAR CHAMBER, THE(1983)

Vicki Cummins
TIME AND THE TOUCH, THE(1962)

Alan J. Cumner-Price
PRESSURE(1976, Brit.), ed

Basil Cunard
NIGHT ALONE(1938, Brit.); INQUEST(1939, Brit.); THREE SILENT MEN(1940, Brit.); DULCIMER STREET(1948, Brit.); MAN ON THE RUN(1949, Brit.); MY BROTHER JONATHAN(1949, Brit.); OUTSIDER, THE(1949, Brit.); NO ROOM AT THE INN(1950, Brit.); ISN'T LIFE WONDERFUL!(1953, Brit.); HELL BELOW ZERO(1954, Brit.)

Grace Cunard
UNTAMED(1929); LADY SURRENDERS, A(1930); RESURRECTION(1931); FOURTH HORSEMAN, THE(1933); LADIES THEY TALK ABOUT(1933); MAN WHO RECLAIMED HIS HEAD, THE(1935); SHOW BOAT(1936); WINGS OVER HONOLULU(1937); MUMMY'S TOMB, THE(1942); NORTH STAR, THE(1943); CASANOVA BROWN(1944); EASY TO LOOK AT(1945); GREAT STAGECOACH ROBBERY(1945); MAGNIFICENT DOLL(1946)
Silents
WASHINGTON AT VALLEY FORGE(1914), a, d&w; CAMPBELLS ARE COMING, THE(1915), a, w; KISS BARRIER, THE(1925); OUTWITTED(1925); MASKED ANGEL(1928)
Misc. Silents
IN TREASON'S GRASP(1917); SOCIETY'S DRIFTWOOD(1917); AFTER THE WAR(1918); HELL'S CRATER(1918); GIRL IN THE TAXI, THE(1921); HEART OF LINCOLN, THE(1922); EMBLEMS OF LOVE(1924); LAST MAN ON EARTH, THE(1924); PRICE OF FEAR, THE(1928)

Mina Cunard
Misc. Silents
SIGN OF THE POPPY, THE(1916); WHAT LOVE CAN DO(1916)

Myna Cunard
GOOD MORNING, MISS DOVE(1955); JEANNE EAGELS(1957)

Myra Cunard
UNTAMED(1955)

C. Thomas Cuncliffe
ON THE RIGHT TRACK(1981)

Christopher Cunday
FOG, THE(1980)

Pamela Cundell
HALF A SIXPENCE(1967, Brit.); MRS. BROWN, YOU'VE GOT A LOVELY DAUGHTER(1968, Brit.); EMILY(1976, Brit.); MEMOIRS OF A SURVIVOR(1981, Brit.); WICKED LADY, THE(1983, Brit.)

Dean Cundey
WHERE THE RED FERN GROWS(1974), ph; BARE KNUCKLES(1978), ph; HALLOWEEN(1978), ph; CHARGE OF THE MODEL-T'S(1979), ph; ROCK 'N' ROLL HIGH SCHOOL(1979), ph; ROLLER BOOGIE(1979), ph; FOG, THE(1980), ph; JAWS OF SATAN(1980), ph; ESCAPE FROM NEW YORK(1981), ph; HALLOWEEN 11(1981), ph; HALLOWEEN III: SEASON OF THE WITCH(1982), ph; THING, THE(1982), ph; D.C. CAB(1983), ph; PSYCHO II(1983), ph
1984
ROMANCING THE STONE(1984), ph

Michelle Cundey
1984
BAD MANNERS(1984)

Dean Cundy
SATAN'S CHEERLEADERS(1977), ph; ANGELS BRIGADE(1980), ph; GALAXINA(1980), ph; WITHOUT WARNING(1980), ph; SEPARATE WAYS(1981), ph

Lawrence J. Cuneo
HOUR OF THE GUN(1967), set d

Lester Cuneo
TERROR, THE(1928)
Silents
PENNINGTON'S CHOICE(1915); SECOND IN COMMAND, THE(1915); SILENT VOICE, THE(1915); BIG TREMAINE(1916); HAUNTED PAJAMAS(1917); PARADISE GARDEN(1917); ARE ALL MEN ALIKE?(1920); FOOD FOR SCANDAL(1920); MASKED AVENGER, THE(1922); EAGLE'S FEATHER, THE(1923)
Misc. Silents
MISTER 44(1916); PIDGIN ISLAND(1916); RIVER OF ROMANCE, THE(1916); HIDDEN SPRING, THE(1917); PROMISE, THE(1917); UNDER HANDICAP(1917); DESERT LOVE(1920); LONE HAND WILSON(1920); TERROR, THE(1920); RANGER AND THE LAW, THE(1921); BLAZING ARROWS(1922); BLUE BLAZES(1922); SILVER SPURS(1922); TRAPPED IN THE AIR(1922); FIGHTING JIM GRANT(1923); VENGEANCE OF PIERRE, THE(1923); LONE HAND TEXAS(1924); RIDIN' FOOL(1924); WESTERN GRIT(1924); HEARTS OF THE WEST(1925); RANGE VULTURES(1925); TWO FISTED THOMPSON(1925); WESTERN PROMISE(1925)

Jesse Cuneta
1984
MISSING IN ACTION(1984)

Sergio Cunevari
GIORDANO BRUNO(1973, Ital.), art d

Dick Cunha
FRANKENSTEIN'S DAUGHTER(1958), d

Richard Cunha
MISSILE TO THE MOON(1959), d; GIRL IN ROOM 13(1961, U.S./Braz.), d, w

Richard E. Cunha
GIANT FROM THE UNKNOWN(1958), d, ph; SHE DEMONS(1958), d, w; SILENT WITNESS, THE(1962), ph

Rick Cunha
BEST FRIENDS(1975), m

J. M. Cunilles
NIGHT OF THE ZOMBIES(1983, Span./Ital.), w

J.M. Cunilles
ZOMBIE CREEPING FLESH(1981, Ital./Span.), w

Ronald Cunliffe
HAVING A WILD WEEKEND(1965, Brit.)

Phil Cunneen
BREAKER MORANT(1980, Aus.), m

George Cunnigmfee
RECOMMENDATION FOR MERCY(1975, Can.)

Robert Cunnignham
I, THE JURY(1953)

Pat Cunning
RAMPANT AGE, THE(1930)

Patrick Cunning
HIS PRIVATE SECRETARY(1933)
Misc. Silents
VERY CONFIDENTIAL(1927)

Alvin Cunningham
1984
KILLPOINT(1984)

Anne Cunningham
SEQUOIA(1934), w; BITTER HARVEST(1963, Brit.); THIS SPORTING LIFE(1963, Brit.); CARNABY, M.D.(1967, Brit.); MAN AT THE TOP(1973, Brit.)

Beryl Cunningham
CURSE OF THE VOODOO(1965, Brit.); DEATH TOOK PLACE LAST NIGHT(1970, Ital./Ger.); DORIAN GRAY(1970, Ital./Brit./Ger./Liechtenstein); WEEKEND MURDERS, THE(1972, Ital.); TARZANA, THE WILD GIRL(1973); SCREAMERS(1978, Ital.)

Billy Cunningham
YOU'VE GOT TO WALK IT LIKE YOU TALK IT OR YOU'LL LOSE THAT BEAT(1971), a, m

Bob Cunningham
SUN ALSO RISES, THE(1957); JOHN PAUL JONES(1959); ANGEL WORE RED, THE(1960); FIVE BRANDED WOMEN(1960); RUNNING MAN, THE(1963, Brit.); PHONY AMERICAN, THE(1964, Ger.); POPPY IS ALSO A FLOWER, THE(1966); SHALAKO(1968, Brit.); GAMES, THE(1970); EARTHQUAKE(1974)

Cecil Cunningham
THEIR OWN DESIRE(1929); ANYBODY'S WOMAN(1930); PLAYBOY OF PARIS(1930); MATA HARI(1931); SAFE IN HELL(1931); SUSAN LENOX–HER FALL AND RISE(1931); BLONDE VENUS(1932); IF I HAD A MILLION(1932); IMPATIENT MAIDEN(1932); LOVE IS A RACKET(1932); LOVE ME TONIGHT(1932); RICH ARE ALWAYS WITH US, THE(1932); THOSE WE LOVE(1932); WET PARADE, THE(1932); FROM HELL TO HEAVEN(1933); LADIES THEY TALK ABOUT(1933); LIFE OF VERGIE WINTERS, THE(1934); MANHATTAN LOVE SONG(1934); RETURN OF THE TERROR(1934); WE LIVE AGAIN(1934); PEOPLE WILL TALK(1935); COME AND GET IT(1936); MR. DEEDS GOES TO TOWN(1936); ARTISTS AND MODELS(1937); AWFUL TRUTH, THE(1937); DAUGHTER OF SHANGHAI(1937); KING OF GAMBLERS(1937); NIGHT CLUB SCANDAL(1937); SWING HIGH, SWING LOW(1937); THIS WAY PLEASE(1937); BLOND CHEAT(1938); COLLEGE SWING(1938); FOUR MEN AND A PRAYER(1938); GIRLS' SCHOOL(1938); KENTUCKY MOONSHINE(1938); MARIE ANTOINETTE(1938); SCANDAL STREET(1938); WIVES UNDER SUSPICION(1938); YOU AND ME(1938); FAMILY NEXT DOOR, THE(1939); IT'S A WONDERFUL WORLD(1939); LADY OF THE TROPICS(1939); LAUGH IT OFF(1939); WINTER CARNIVAL(1939); CAPTAIN IS A LADY, THE(1940); GREAT PROFILE, THE(1940); KITTY FOYLE(1940); LILLIAN RUSSELL(1940); NEW MOON(1940); PLAY GIRL(1940); BACK STREET(1941); BLOSSOMS IN THE DUST(1941); HURRY, CHARLIE, HURRY(1941); REPENT AT LEISURE(1941); AFFAIRS OF MARTHA, THE(1942); ARE HUSBANDS NECESSARY?(1942); CAIRO(1942); COWBOY SERENADE(1942); HIDDEN HAND, THE(1942); I MARRIED AN ANGEL(1942); TWIN BEDS(1942); WIFE TAKES A FLYER, THE(1942); ABOVE SUSPICION(1943); DU BARRY WAS A LADY(1943); IN OLD OKLAHOMA(1943); WONDER MAN(1945); MY REPUTATION(1946)

Chris Cunningham
STORY OF G.I. JOE, THE(1945); CHARGE OF THE LIGHT BRIGADE, THE(1968, Brit.); DRACULA HAS RISEN FROM HIS GRAVE(1968, Brit.); GUMSHOE(1972, Brit.)

Christopher Cunningham
LUST FOR A VAMPIRE(1971, Brit.)

Colin Cunningham
MELODY OF MY HEART(1936, Brit.); ONE PLUS ONE(1969, Brit.)

Copper Cunningham
TAXI DRIVER(1976)
1984
BROTHER FROM ANOTHER PLANET, THE(1984)

Dan Cunningham
WOODEN HORSE, THE(1951); LAST MAN TO HANG, THE(1956, Brit.); RICHARD III(1956, Brit.)

David Cunningham
BABYLON(1980, Brit.)
1984
GHOST DANCE(1984, Brit.), m

Don Cunningham
DIAMOND WIZARD, THE(1954, Brit.)

Dorothy Cunningham
PIRANHA II: THE SPAWNING(1981, Neth.)

E.V. Cunningham
SYLVIA(1965), w

E.V. Cunningham [Evan Hunter]
PENELOPE(1966), w
Edward Cunningham
THAT CHAMPIONSHIP SEASON(1982)
Fairy Cunningham
FILE ON THELMA JORDAN, THE(1950)
Frank Cunningham
NATCHEZ TRACE(1960)
George Cunningham
OUR MODERN MAIDENS(1929), ch
Silents
OUR MODERN MAIDENS(1929), ch; THUNDER(1929), ch
J. Cunningham
WINDJAMMER, THE(1931, Brit.)
Jack Cunningham
WHITE SHADOWS IN THE SOUTH SEAS(1928), w; CLEARING THE RANGE(1931), w; DECEIVER, THE(1931), w; GUILTY GENERATION, THE(1931), w; SHANG-HAIED LOVE(1931), w; JAZZ BABIES(1932), w; RIDER OF DEATH VALLEY(1932), w; TEXAS BAD MAN(1932), w; FLAMING GUNS(1933), w; FOURTH HORSEMAN, THE(1933), w; MAN OF THE FOREST(1933), w; RUSTLERS' ROUNDUP(1933), w; SUNSET PASS(1933), w; TERROR TRAIL(1933), w; TO THE LAST MAN(1933), w; UNDER THE TONTO RIM(1933), w; DOUBLE DOOR(1934), w; IT'S A GIFT(1934), w; LAST ROUND-UP, THE(1934), w; OLD-FASHIONED WAY, THE(1934), w; PURSUIT OF HAPPINESS, THE(1934), w; THUNDERING HERD, THE(1934), w; WAGON WHEELS(1934), w; MAN ON THE FLYING TRAPEZE, THE(1935), w; MISSISSIP-PI(1935), w; EASY TO TAKE(1936), p; PENROD AND SAM(1937); ARKANSAS TRAV-ELER, THE(1938), w; PAINTED DESERT, THE(1938), w; PENROD AND HIS TWIN BROTHER(1938); PROFESSOR BEWARE(1938), w; UNION PACIFIC(1939), w; DIAL M FOR MURDER(1954), w; HIGH TERRACE(1957, Brit.); DUBLIN NIGHTMARE(1958, Brit.); TIME LOCK(1959, Brit.); SNAKE WOMAN, THE(1961, Brit.); QUARE FELLOW, THE(1962, Brit.); PROFESSIONALS, THE(1966), w
Silents
EVIDENCE(1918), w; NARROW PATH, THE(1918), w; REAL FOLKS(1918), w; ADELE(1919), w; ALL OF A SUDDEN NORMA(1919), w; ALL WRONG(1919), w; JOYOUS LIAR, THE(1919), w; DEVIL TO PAY, THE(1920), w; GREEN FLAME, THE(1920), w; WHERE LIGHTS ARE LOW(1921), w; WIFE'S AWAKENING, A(1921), w; BEYOND THE ROCKS(1922), w; COVERED WAGON, THE(1923), w; GENTLE-MAN OF LEISURE, A(1923), w; HEART RAIDER, THE(1923), w; TIGER'S CLAW, THE(1923), w; DON Q, SON OF ZORRO(1925), w; JUST A WOMAN(1925), w; BLACK PIRATE, THE(1926), w; CAPTAIN SALVATION(1927), w; ADVENTURER, THE(1928), w
James Cunningham
CONDEMNED TO DEATH(1932, Brit.)
Jenni Cunningham
WE OF THE NEVER NEVER(1983, Aus.)
Joe Cunningham
HOT MONEY(1936); SENSATION(1936, Brit.); COUNTRY GENTLEMEN(1937); FUGITIVE IN THE SKY(1937); KID GALAHAD(1937); PRESCRIPTION FOR RO-MANCE(1937); ANGELS WITH DIRTY FACES(1938); BLONDES AT WORK(1938); FOUR'S A CROWD(1938); KING OF THE NEWSBOYS(1938); THEY DRIVE BY NIGHT(1938, Brit.); TORCHY BLANE IN PANAMA(1938); TORCHY GETS HER MAN(1938); 13 MEN AND A GUN(1938, Brit.); BLACKWELL'S ISLAND(1939); DOWN OUR ALLEY(1939, Brit.); GOING PLACES(1939); INVITATION TO HAPPINESS(1939); SECRET SERVICE OF THE AIR(1939); TORCHY PLAYS WITH DYNAMITE(1939); TORCHY RUNS FOR MAYOR(1939); FUGITIVE, THE(1940, Brit.); IT'S IN THE AIR(1940, Brit.); TOM, DICK AND HARRY(1941); ABOUT FACE(1942); BROAD-WAY(1942); DUDES ARE PRETTY PEOPLE(1942); I LIVE ON DANGER(1942); NAVY COMES THROUGH, THE(1942); TALK OF THE TOWN(1942); TAKE A POWDER(1953, Brit.)
John Cunningham
FLOATING DUTCHMAN, THE(1953, Brit.); BIG FIX, THE(1978); LOST AND FOUND(1979)
John M. Cunningham
STRANGER WORE A GUN, THE(1953), w; DAY OF THE BAD MAN(1958), w
John W. Cunningham
HIGH NOON(1952), w
Joseph Cunningham
FLYING SQUAD, THE(1932, Brit.); LORD BABS(1932, Brit.); CALL IT LUCK(1934), w; CHINA CLIPPER(1936); SMART BLONDE(1937); NIGHT ALONE(1938, Brit.); REBEL SON, THE ½(1939, Brit.)
June Cunningham
SMALLEST SHOW ON EARTH, THE(1957, Brit.); HORRORS OF THE BLACK MUSEUM(1959, U.S./Brit.); STRANGE AFFECTION(1959, Brit.); PART-TIME WI-FE(1961, Brit.); THREE ON A SPREE(1961, Brit.); DESIGN FOR LOVING(1962, Brit.); SMALL WORLD OF SAMMY LEE, THE(1963, Brit.)
Kathy Cunningham
HUNTER, THE(1980)
Kitty Cunningham
GOLD DIGGERS OF 1933(1933)
Loretta Cunningham
THIS LOVE OF OURS(1945)
Margo Cunningham
TASTE OF HONEY, A(1962, Brit.); PRIME OF MISS JEAN BRODIE, THE(1969, Brit.); SAILOR WHO FELL FROM GRACE WITH THE SEA, THE(1976, Brit.)
Maureen Cunningham
WONDER MAN(1945)
Michael Cunningham
1984
SPLATTER UNIVERSITY(1984), w
Neil Cunningham
VICTOR/VICTORIA(1982); BLOODY KIDS(1983, Brit.); DRAUGHTSMAN'S CON-TRACT, THE(1983, Brit.)
Noel John Cunningham
HERE COME THE TIGERS(1978)
Owen Cunningham
VOODOO ISLAND(1957); WAKE ME WHEN IT'S OVER(1960)
Ralph Cunningham
TERROR IN THE WAX MUSEUM(1973)

Robert Cunningham
SHARK RIVER(1953); SPECIAL DELIVERY(1955, Ger.); WAR AND PEACE(1956, Ital./U.S.); BADLANDS OF MONTANA(1957); IT STARTED WITH A KISS(1959); NO SURVIVORS, PLEASE(1963, Ger.); CIRCUS WORLD(1964)
Misc. Silents
LUCK OF THE NAVY, THE(1927, Brit.)
Ron Cunningham
LILITH(1964)
Sarah Cunningham
NAKED CITY, THE(1948); COWBOYS, THE(1972); I NEVER PROMISED YOU A ROSE GARDEN(1977); FRANCES(1982)
Sean S. Cunningham
LAST HOUSE ON THE LEFT(1972), p; HERE COME THE TIGERS(1978), p, d; FRIDAY THE 13TH(1980), p&d; STRANGER IS WATCHING, A(1982), d; SPRING BREAK(1983), p&d
Steve Cunningham
VISITOR, THE(1980, Ital./U.S.)
Susan Cunningham
SPRING BREAK(1983), ed
Susan E. Cunningham
HERE COME THE TIGERS(1978), art d; FRIDAY THE 13TH PART II(1981), ed; STRANGER IS WATCHING, A(1982), ed
Vera Cunningham
Silents
LOVE IN A WOOD(1915, Brit.)
William Cunningham
CONSOLATION MARRIAGE(1931), w
Zamah Cunningham
DREAM GIRL(1947); KEY TO THE CITY(1950); HERE COME THE GIRLS(1953); BABY, THE RAIN MUST FALL(1965)
Tana Cunningham-Curtis
ATTIC, THE(1979), set d
James Oliver Cunvood
COUNTRY BEYOND, THE(1936), w
Alain Cuny
DEVIL'S ENVOYS, THE(1947, Fr.); STRANGE DECEPTION(1953, Ital.); ANITA GARIBALDI(1954, Ital.); HUNCHBACK OF NOTRE DAME, THE(1957, Fr.); LOVERS, THE(1959, Fr.); LA DOLCE VITA(1961, Ital./Fr.); CROSS OF THE LIVING(1963, Fr.); BANANA PEEL(1965, Fr.); FELLINI SATYRICON(1969, Fr./Ital.); MILKY WAY, THE(1969, Fr./Ital.); DON'T TOUCH WHITE WOMEN!(1974, Fr.); LADY WITHOUT CAMELLIAS, THE(1981, Ital.)
1984
BASILEUS QUARTET(1984, Ital.)
Sam Cupae
1984
MICKI AND MAUDE(1984)
Eduard Cupak
SIR, YOU ARE A WIDOWER(1971, Czech.)
Franca Cupane
GOSPEL ACCORDING TO ST. MATTHEW, THE(1966, Fr., Ital.)
Francesco Cupano
VOLCANO(1953, Ital.)
Cvetka Cupar
ENGLANO MADE ME(1973, Brit.)
Suzanne Cupito
GYPSY(1962); STAGE TO THUNDER ROCK(1964)
Suzanne Cupito [Morgan Brittany]
YOURS, MINE AND OURS(1968)
Francesco Cuppini
ITALIAN CONNECTION, THE(1973, U.S./Ital./Ger.), set d
Roland Cupram
ADMIRABLE CRICHTON, THE(1957, Brit.)
Carlo Cura
GENGHIS KHAN(U.S./Brit./Ger./Yugo)
Harcourt Curacao
LONG HAUL, THE(1957, Brit.); STOWAWAY GIRL(1957, Brit.); SECRET MAN, THE(1958, Brit.); TWO GENTLEMEN SHARING(1969, Brit.)
Michael Curb
BIG BOUNCE, THE(1969), m
Mike Curb
DEVIL'S ANGELS(1967), m; GLORY STOMPERS, THE(1967), m; IT'S A BIKINI WORLD(1967), m; KILLERS THREE(1968), m; MARYJANE(1968), m; SAVAGE SEV-EN, THE(1968), m; WILD RACERS, THE(1968), m; DEVIL'S 8, THE(1969), m; FIVE THE HARD WAY(1969), m; ...TICK...TICK...TICK...(1970), md
Bill Curbishley
QUADROPHENIA(1979, Brit.), p; MC VICAR(1982, Brit.), p
Elvira Curci
CASE AGAINST MRS. AMES, THE(1936); ALWAYS IN MY HEART(1942); MY SON, THE HERO(1943); PHANTOM OF THE OPERA(1943); SONG OF BERNADETTE, THE(1943); WATCH ON THE RHINE(1943); STANDING ROOM ONLY(1944); CLOAK AND DAGGER(1946); SHADOW OF A WOMAN(1946); SONG OF MY HEART(1947); RATON PASS(1951)
Gennaro Curci
MELODY LINGERS ON, THE(1935); AND SO THEY WERE MARRIED(1936); LONE WOLF RETURNS, THE(1936); LOVE ON THE RUN(1936); ESPIONAGE(1937); I MET HIM IN PARIS(1937); I'LL TAKE ROMANCE(1937); MANHATTAN MERRY-GO-ROUND(1937); ARTISTS AND MODELS ABROAD(1938); JUAREZ(1939); MID-NIGHT(1939)
Anthony Curcio
GROUND ZERO(1973)
Dino Curcio
RE: LUCKY LUCIANO(1974, Fr./Ital.)
Enzo Curcio
YOUNG REBEL, THE(1969, Fr./Ital./Span.)
Frank Curcio
GOODBYE, NORMA JEAN(1976)
Claude Curdle [Richard Haydn]
MR. MUSIC(1950)

Roger Curel
KILLING GAME, THE(1968, Fr.)
Cureli
YOUNG HUSBANDS(1958, Ital./Fr.), w
Silvia Curetti
WHITE LINE, THE(1952, Ital.)
A.J. Curi
TENTACLES(1977, Ital.), ed
Angelo Curi
BURNING YEARS, THE(1979, Ital.), ed
Raffaele Curi
GARDEN OF THE FINZI-CONTINIS, THE(1976, Ital./Ger.)
Robert Curi
VISITOR, THE(1980, Ital./U.S.), ed
Eve Curie
MADAME CURIE(1943), w
Sandra Curie
RIO LOBO(1970)
Alberto Hernandez Curiel
CASTLE OF THE MONSTERS(1958, Mex.), p
Federico Curiel
LOS AUTOMATAS DE LA MUERTE(1960, Mex.), d; LAST REBEL, THE(1961, Mex.); NEUTRON CONTRA EL DR. CARONTE(1962, Mex.), d; NEUTRON EL ENMAS-CARADO NEGRO(1962, Mex.), d; SANTO CONTRA EL CEREBRO DIABOLICO zero(1962, Mex.), d, w; CEREBROS DIABOLICOS(1966, Mex.), d&w; VAMPIRES, THE(1969, Mex.), d, w; VENGEANCE OF THE VAMPIRE WOMEN, THE(1969, Mex.), d
Frederick Curiel
LIVING HEAD, THE(1969, Mex.), w
Gonzalo Curiel
MASSACRE(1956), m, md
Herbert Curiel
SPY IN THE SKY(1958); BOY WHO STOLE A MILLION, THE(1960, Brit.); RUNNING MAN, THE(1963, Brit.)
Jan Curik
TRANSPORT FROM PARADISE(1967, Czech.), ph; DAY THAT SHOOK THE WORLD, THE(1977, Yugo./Czech.), ph
Raphael Curio
MARK OF ZORRO, THE(1940)
Federic Curiosi
DEFEAT OF HANNIBAL, THE(1937, Ital.), p
Curitan
RUY BLAS(1948, Fr.)
Leo Curlay
JOHNNY HOLIDAY(1949)
Helen Curley
ROMANCE RIDES THE RANGE(1936), ed
James Curley
Silents
INTOLERANCE(1916)
Leo Curley
SPEED DEVILS(1935); SCARLET ANGEL(1952); SOMETHING FOR THE BIRDS(1952); CITY OF BAD MEN(1953); HOUSE OF WAX(1953); PRESIDENT'S LADY, THE(1953); ROBE, THE(1953); IT SHOULD HAPPEN TO YOU(1954); OUR MISS BROOKS(1956)
Malcolm Curley
WHEN THE LEGENDS DIE(1972)
Pauline Curley
LOCKED DOOR, THE(1929)
Silents
LIFE WITHOUT SOUL(1916); CASSIDY(1917); JUDGE HER NOT(1921); PONY EXPRESS RIDER(1926); WEST OF THE RAINBOW'S END(1926); CODE OF THE RANGE(1927); DEVIL DOGS(1928)
Misc. Silents
CASE AT LAW, A(1917); SQUARE DECEIVER, THE(1917); BOUND IN MOROC-CO(1918); HER BOY(1918); LANDLOPER, THE(1918); LEND ME YOUR NAME(1918); MAN BENEATH, THE(1919); SOLITARY SIN, THE(1919); HANDS OFF(1921); PRAI-RIE MYSTERY, THE(1922); MIDNIGHT SECRETS(1924); SHACKLES OF FEAR(1924); TRAIL OF VENGEANCE, THE(1924); COWBOY COURAGE(1925); HIS GREATEST BATTLE(1925); RIDIN' WILD(1925); MILLIONAIRE ORPHAN, THE(1926); TWIN SIX O'BRIEN(1926); THUNDERBOLT'S TRACKS(1927)
Curly
FOR LOVE AND MONEY(1967)
Ralph Curly
NIGHT TO REMEMBER, A(1942)
Curly Clements and his Rodeo Rangers
SIX-GUN LAW(1948)
Tim Curnen
FORBIDDEN WORLD(1982), w
1984
SWORDKILL(1984), w
David Curnick
LIFE AND TIMES OF CHESTER-ANGUS RAMSGOOD, THE(1971, Can.), d,w&ph, ed; KEEPER, THE(1976, Can.), w
Richard Curnock
DUBLIN NIGHTMARE(1958, Brit.); PARADISE(1982)
Graham Curnow
THREE MEN IN A BOAT(1958, Brit.); HORRORS OF THE BLACK MUSEUM(1959, U.S./Brit.)
Roland Curram
GOOD BEGINNING, THE(1953, Brit.); TOP OF THE FORM(1953, Brit.); UP TO HIS NECK(1954, Brit.); SILENT PLAYGROUND, THE(1964, Brit.); DARLING(1965, Brit.); PANIC(1966, Brit.); DECLINE AND FALL... OF A BIRD WATCHER(1969, Brit.); THINK DIRTY(1970, Brit.)
Ronald Curram
DUNKIRK(1958, Brit.); GREEN HELMET, THE(1961, Brit.)
Adrian Curran
1984
ONCE UPON A TIME IN AMERICA(1984)

Bill Curran
GRAVEYARD OF HORROR(1971, Span.); SPIKES GANG, THE(1974)
Charles Curran
NO MARRIAGE TIES(1933), w; ADVENTURES OF JANE ARDEN(1939), w; HEROES IN BLUE(1939), w
Chris Curran
YOUNG CASSIDY(1965, U.S./Brit.); ULYSSES(1967, U.S./Brit.); WEDDING NIGHT(1970, Ireland); COLD RIVER(1982)
Dandy Curran
BLOOD ON THE ARROW(1964); BRIGHTY OF THE GRAND CANYON(1967)
Eileen Curran
MEN OF IRELAND(1938, Ireland)
Homer Curran
SONG OF NORWAY(1970), w
Joavan Curran
LILITH(1964)
Leigh Curran
I NEVER PROMISED YOU A ROSE GARDEN(1977); REDS(1981); LITTLE SEX, A(1982)
Lynette Curran
HEATWAVE(1983, Aus.)
Misc. Talkies
COUNTRY TOWN(1971)
Pamela Curran
THRILL OF IT ALL, THE(1963); UNDER THE YUM-YUM TREE(1963); GIRL HAPPY(1965); LOVED ONE, THE(1965); MUTINY IN OUTER SPACE(1965); CHASE, THE(1966)
Paul Curran
JOHN PAUL JONES(1959); NOTHING BUT THE BEST(1964, Brit.); WILD AFFAIR, THE(1966, Brit.); DECLINE AND FALL... OF A BIRD WATCHER(1969, Brit.); JAB-BERWOCKY(1977, Brit.); HUMAN FACTOR, THE(1979, Brit.)
Pearl Lenore Curran
Silents
WHAT HAPPENED TO ROSA?(1921), w
Peter Curran
WHEN DINOSAURS RULED THE EARTH(1971, Brit.), ed
Roland Curran
I'LL NEVER FORGET WHAT'S 'IS NAME(1967, Brit.); GET CHARLIE TULLY(1976, Brit.)
Thomas A. Curran
PHANTOM IN THE HOUSE, THE(1929); MILKY WAY, THE(1936); OUR LEADING CITIZEN(1939)
Silents
MODERN MONTE CRISTO, A(1917)
Misc. Silents
SILAS MARNER(1916); WORLD AND THE WOMAN, THE(1916); AMATEUR OR-PHAN, AN(1917)
Thomas Curran
KIBITZER, THE(1929); WORLDLY GOODS(1930); COWBOY MILLIONAIRE(1935); PAROLE(1936); POLO JOE(1936)
Silents
EARL OF PAWTUCKET, THE(1915); OBJECT-ALIMONY(1929)
Misc. Silents
GREATER LOVE HATH NO MAN(1915); WHEN LOVE WAS BLIND(1917)
Tom Curran
YOURS FOR THE ASKING(1936); CHAMPAGNE WALTZ(1937)
Silents
ANNE AGAINST THE WORLD(1929)
W. Hughes Curran
Silents
FRESHIE, THE(1922), d&w
Misc. Silents
BLAZE AWAY(1922), d; TRAIL OF HATE(1922), d
William Curran
Misc. Silents
TRIAL MARRIAGE(1928), d; UNGUARDED GIRLS(1929), d
William Hughes Curran
Silents
DANGEROUS HOUR(1923), d; KNOCK ON THE DOOR, THE(1923), d; PREPARED TO DIE(1923), d
Misc. Silents
SCARLET YOUTH(1928), d
Wolf Curran
IRISH AND PROUD OF IT(1938, Ireland)
Enzo Currelli
STEPPE, THE(1963, Fr./Ital.), w
Cal Currens
DESTRUCTORS, THE(1968); PANIC IN THE CITY(1968)
Lee Curreri
FAME(1980)
Bill Currie
EVERYTHING IS RHYTHM(1940, Brit.)
Cherie Currie
FOXES(1980); PARASITE(1982); TWILIGHT ZONE–THE MOVIE(1983); WAVE-LENGTH(1983)
1984
ROSEBUD BEACH HOTEL(1984)
Clive Currie
MAGIC NIGHT(1932, Brit.); MONEY MEANS NOTHING(1932, Brit.); LEAVE IT TO ME(1933, Brit.)
Silents
OLD BILL THROUGH THE AGES(1924, Brit.)
Finlay Currie
CRIMINAL AT LARGE(1932, Brit.); OLD MAN, THE(1932, Brit.); EXCESS BAG-GAGE(1933, Brit.); GOOD COMPANIONS(1933, Brit.); ROME EXPRESS(1933, Brit.); LITTLE FRIEND(1934, Brit.); MISTER CINDERS(1934, Brit.); MY OLD DUTCH(1934, Brit.); ORDERS IS ORDERS(1934, Brit.); BIG SPLASH, THE(1935, Brit.); PRINCESS CHARMING(1935, Brit.); GAY ADVENTURE, THE(1936, Brit.); GAY LOVE(1936, Brit.); IMPROPER DUCHESS, THE(1936, Brit.); CATCH AS CATCH CAN(1937, Brit.); COMMAND PERFORMANCE(1937, Brit.); EDGE OF THE WORLD, THE(1937, Brit.);

GLAMOROUS NIGHT(1937, Brit.); WANTED(1937, Brit.); AROUND THE TOWN(1938, Brit.); CLAYDON TREASURE MYSTERY, THE(1938, Brit.); FOLLOW YOUR STAR(1938, Brit.); GAIETY GIRLS, THE(1938, Brit.); INVADERS, THE,(1941); AVENGERS, THE(1942, Brit.); BELLS GO DOWN, THE(1943, Brit.); SHIPBUILDERS, THE(1943, Brit.); THEATRE ROYAL(1943, Brit.); WARN THAT MAN(1943, Brit.); THUNDER ROCK(1944, Brit.); UNDERGROUND GUERRILLAS(1944, Brit.); DON CHICAGO(1945, Brit.); THEY MET IN THE DARK(1945, Brit.); GREAT EXPECTATIONS(1946, Brit.); SCHOOL FOR SECRETS(1946, Brit.); TROJAN BROTHERS, THE(1946); WOMAN TO WOMAN(1946, Brit.); I KNOW WHERE I'M GOING(1947, Brit.); BONNIE PRINCE CHARLIE(1948, Brit.); BROTHERS, THE(1948, Brit.); MR. PERRIN AND MR. TRAILL(1948, Brit.); SO EVIL MY LOVE(1948, Brit.); SPRINGTIME(1948, Brit.); HISTORY OF MR. POLLY, THE(1949, Brit.); MY BROTHER JONATHAN(1949, Brit.); SLEEPING CAR TO TRIESTE(1949, Brit.); TIGHT LITTLE ISLAND(1949, Brit.); BLACK ROSE, THE(1950); MUDLARK, THE(1950, Brit.); TREASURE ISLAND(1950, Brit.); TRIO(1950, Brit.); PEOPLE WILL TALK(1951); QUO VADIS(1951); IVANHOE(1952, Brit.); KANGAROO(1952); STARS AND STRIPES FOREVER(1952); WALK EAST ON BEACON(1952); TREASURE OF THE GOLDEN CONDOR(1953); END OF THE ROAD, THE(1954, Brit.); ROB ROY, THE HIGHLAND ROGUE(1954, Brit.); CAPTAIN LIGHTFOOT(1955); DEADLY GAME, THE(1955, Brit.); FOOTSTEPS IN THE FOG(1955, Brit.); KING'S RHAPSODY(1955, Brit.); AROUND THE WORLD IN 80 DAYS(1956); ZARAK(1956, Brit.); ABANDON SHIP(1957, Brit.); CAMPBELL'S KINGDOM(1957, Brit.); LITTLE HUT, THE(1957); SAINT JOAN(1957); DANGEROUS EXILE(1958, Brit.); NAKED EARTH, THE(1958, Brit.); TEMPEST(1958, Ital./Fr.); 6.5 SPECIAL(1958, Brit.); BEN HUR(1959); ADVENTURES OF HUCKLEBERRY FINN, THE(1960); ANGEL WORE RED, THE(1960); HAND IN HAND(1960, Brit.); KIDNAPPED(1960); CLUE OF THE SILVER KEY, THE(1961, Brit.); FIVE GOLDEN HOURS(1961, Brit.); FRANCIS OF ASSISI(1961); GO TO BLAZES(1962, Brit.); LISA(1962, Brit.); STORY OF JOSEPH AND HIS BRETHREN THE(1962, Ital.); BILLY LIAR(1963, Brit.); CLEOPATRA(1963); CRACKSMAN, THE(1963, Brit.); MURDER AT THE GALLOP(1963, Brit.); THREE LIVES OF THOMASINA, THE(1963, U.S./Brit.); WEST 11(1963, Brit.); FALL OF THE ROMAN EMPIRE, THE(1964); WHO WAS MADDOX?(1964, Brit.); AMOROUS MR. PRAWN, THE(1965, Brit.); BATTLE OF THE VILLA FIORITA, THE(1965, Brit.); BUNNY LAKE IS MISSING(1965)

Finley Currie
OPERATION X(1951, Brit.); CORRIDORS OF BLOOD(1962, Brit.)

George Currie
Silents
IT'S THE OLD ARMY GAME(1926)

Iris Currie
1984
BAY BOY(1984, Can.)

Louise Currie
DUDE COWBOY(1941); LOOK WHO'S LAUGHING(1941); PINTO KID, THE(1941); BASHFUL BACHELOR, THE(1942); STARDUST ON THE SAGE(1942); APE MAN, THE(1943); AROUND THE WORLD(1943); FORTY THIEVES(1944); MILLION DOLLAR KID(1944); PRACTICALLY YOURS(1944); SENSATIONS OF 1945(1944); VOODOO MAN(1944); LOVE LETTERS(1945); GUN TOWN(1946); WILD WEST(1946); BACKLASH(1947); CHINESE RING, THE(1947); CRIMSON KEY, THE(1947); SECOND CHANCE(1947); THREE ON A TICKET(1947); PRAIRIE OUTLAWS(1948); AND BABY MAKES THREE(1949)
Misc. Talkies
BILLY THE KID OUTLAWED(1940); BILLY THE KID'S GUN JUSTICE(1940)

Michael Currie
TROUBLEMAKER, THE(1964); DEAD AND BURIED(1981); FIREFOX(1982); HALLOWEEN III: SEASON OF THE WITCH(1982); SUDDEN IMPACT(1983)
1984
PHILADELPHIA EXPERIMENT, THE(1984)

Sandee Currie
TERROR TRAIN(1980, Can.); GAS(1981, Can.)

Sandra Currie
Misc. Talkies
CLASS OF '74(1972)

Sheila Currie
CURTAINS(1983, Can.)

Sondra Currie
POLICEWOMAN(1974); JESSIE'S GIRLS(1976); LAST MARRIED COUPLE IN AMERICA, THE(1980); CONCRETE JUNGLE, THE(1982)

Arthur Currier
Misc. Silents
GIRL OF THE LIMBERLOST, A(1924)

Dick Currier
CAMPUS RYTHM(1943), ed; MELODY PARADE(1943), ed; MYSTERY OF THE 13TH GUEST, THE(1943), ed; NEARLY EIGHTEEN(1943), ed; LEAVE IT TO THE IRISH(1944), ed; CHINA'S LITTLE DEVILS(1945), ed; JADE MASK, THE(1945), ed; LAWTON STORY, THE(1949), ed; NIGHT OF THE BLOOD BEAST(1958), ed

Frank Currier
Silents
BRAT, THE(1919)

Frank Currier
Silents
JUGGERNAUT, THE(1915); CASSIDY(1917); HIS FATHER'S SON(1917); OUTWITTED(1917); TRAIL OF THE SHADOW, THE(1917); ALMOST MARRIED(1919); EASY TO MAKE MONEY(1919); SHOULD A WOMAN TELL?(1920); CLAY DOLLARS(1921); MAN WHO, THE(1921); ROOKIE'S RETURN, THE(1921); WITHOUT LIMIT(1921); RECKLESS YOUTH(1922); WOMAN WHO FOOLED HERSELF, THE(1922); FOG, THE(1923); STEPHEN STEPS OUT(1923); FAMILY SECRET, THE(1924); REVELATION(1924); ROSE OF PARIS, THE(1924); BEN-HUR(1925); GREAT LOVE, THE(1925); EXQUISITE SINNER, THE(1926); FIRST YEAR, THE(1926); TELL IT TO THE MARINES(1926); ANNIE LAURIE(1927); CALIFORNIA(1927); CALLAHANS AND THE MURPHYS, THE(1927); ENEMY, THE(1927); FOREIGN DEVILS(1927); ACROSS THE SINGAPORE(1928); EASY COME, EASY GO(1928); TELLING THE WORLD(1928)
Misc. Silents
GREEN STOCKINGS(1916); HIS WIFE'S GOOD NAME(1916); HUNTED WOMAN, THE(1916); NINETY AND NINE, THE(1916); DUCHESS OF DOUBT, THE(1917); END OF THE TOUR, THE(1917); GRAFTERS(1917); GREATEST POWER, THE(1917); HER FATHER'S KEEPER(1917); SOWERS AND REAPERS(1917); BRASS CHECK, THE(1918); HIS BONDED WIFE(1918); OPPORTUNITY(1918); REVELATION(1918); SOCIAL HYPOCRITES(1918); SYLVIA ON A SPREE(1918); TOYS OF FATE(1918); WINNING OF BEATRICE, THE(1918); WITH NEATNESS AND DISPATCH(1918);

BLIND MAN'S EYES(1919); GREAT ROMANCE, THE(1919); IT'S EASY TO MAKE MONEY(1919); PEGGY DOES HER DARNDEST(1919); RED LANTERN, THE(1919); CHEATER, THE(1920); MISLEADING LADY, THE(1920); PLEASURE SEEKERS(1920); MY OLD KENTUCKY HOME(1922); SNITCHING HOUR, THE(1922); WHY ANNOUNCE YOUR MARRIAGE?(1922); TENTS OF ALLAH, THE(1923); VICTOR, THE(1923); RED LILY, THE(1924); TROUBLE SHOOTER, THE(1924); LIGHTS OF OLD BROADWAY(1925); TOO MANY KISSES(1925); WHITE DESERT, THE(1925)

Lauren Currier
CUJO(1983), w

Mary Currier
THAT UNCERTAIN FEELING(1941); RACKET BUSTERS(1938); DARK VICTORY(1939); EVERYTHING'S ON ICE(1939); GREAT VICTOR HERBERT, THE(1939); BABIES FOR SALE(1940); BLONDIE ON A BUDGET(1940); FATHER IS A PRINCE(1940); FIVE LITTLE PEPPERS IN TROUBLE(1940); I LOVE YOU AGAIN(1940); KITTY FOYLE(1940); MA, HE'S MAKING EYES AT ME(1940); NO, NO NANETTE(1940); NOBODY'S CHILDREN(1940); ADVENTURE IN WASHINGTON(1941); FACE BEHIND THE MASK, THE(1941); HERE COMES MR. JORDAN(1941); LIFE WITH HENRY(1941); YOU'LL NEVER GET RICH(1941); GIRL TROUBLE(1942); JACKASS MAIL(1942); SHIP AHOY(1942); IRON MAJOR, THE(1943); FALCON IN MEXICO, THE(1944); MEET MISS BOBBY SOCKS(1944); ONCE UPON A TIME(1944); RETURN OF THE APE MAN(1944); STANDING ROOM ONLY(1944); STARS ON PARADE(1944); STORY OF DR. WASSELL, THE(1944); UNWRITTEN CODE, THE(1944); VOODOO MAN(1944); BEDSIDE MANNER(1945); DICK TRACY(1945); HOLD THAT BLONDE(1945); STORK CLUB, THE(1945); VALLEY OF DECISION, THE(1945); YOUTH ON TRIAL(1945); CRIME OF THE CENTURY(1946); SECRET OF THE WHISTLER(1946); SOMEWHERE IN THE NIGHT(1946); BODY AND SOUL(1947); DARK DELUSION(1947); MAGIC TOWN(1947); ANGEL IN EXILE(1948); JOAN OF ARC(1948); RUSTY LEADS THE WAY(1948); TRAPPED BY BOSTON BLACKIE(1948)

Richard C. Currier
DOCTOR'S DIARY, A(1937), ed; COSMIC MAN, THE(1959), ed

Richard Currier
PARDON US(1931), ed; PACK UP YOUR TROUBLES(1932), ed; MAMA LOVES PAPA(1933), ed; ELMER AND ELSIE(1934), ed; MANY HAPPY RETURNS(1934), ed; MELODY IN SPRING(1934), ed; MAN ON THE FLYING TRAPEZE(1935), ed; PEOPLE WILL TALK(1935), ed; VIRGINIA JUDGE, THE(1935), ed; TILL WE MEET AGAIN(1936), ed; WIVES NEVER KNOW(1936), ed; WOMAN TRAP(1936), ed; KING OF THE ZOMBIES(1941), ed; TANKS A MILLION(1941), ed; FLYING WITH MUSIC(1942), ed; HAY FOOT(1942), ed; REVENGE OF THE ZOMBIES(1943), ed; SILVER SKATES(1943), ed; WOMEN IN BONDAGE(1943), ed; YANKS AHOY(1943), ed; ALASKA(1944), ed; DETECTIVE KITTY O'DAY(1944), ed; HOT RHYTHM(1944), ed; LADY, LET'S DANCE(1944), ed; DIVORCE(1945), ed; SCARLET CLUE, THE(1945), ed; SUNBONNET SUE(1945), ed; THERE GOES KELLY(1945), ed; HIGH SCHOOL HERO(1946), ed; IN FAST COMPANY(1946), ed; MR. HEX(1946), ed; SPOOK BUSTERS(1946), ed; SWING PARADE OF 1946(1946), ed; THERE'S A GIRL IN MY HEART(1949), ed; CATTLE QUEEN(1951), ed; TALES OF ROBIN HOOD(1951), ed; UNEARTHLY, THE(1957), ed
Silents
DESERT'S TOLL, THE(1926), ed

Terrence Currier
HIDE IN PLAIN SIGHT(1980); BLOW OUT(1981)

Victor Currier
PERFECT CRIME, THE(1928), w

Richard Curriers
WIFE WANTED(1946), ed

Farid Currim
SEA WOLVES, THE(1981, Brit.)

Brenda C. Currin
IN COLD BLOOD(1967)

Brenda Currin
BELL JAR, THE(1979); REDS(1981); TAPS(1981); WORLD ACCORDING TO GARP, The(1982); GOING BERSERK(1983)
1984
C.H.U.D.(1984); THIEF OF HEARTS(1984)

Jay Currin
SERIAL(1980)

Lynette Currin
CADDIE(1976, Aus.)

Christopher Curry
PURSUIT OF D.B. COOPER, THE(1981)
1984
C.H.U.D.(1984)

Helen Curry
WINTER KILLS(1979)

Hugh Curry
HARD PART BEGINS, THE(1973, Can.)

Ian Curry
TRIAL AND ERROR(1962, Brit.)

John Curry
Silents
IN OLD KENTUCKY(1920); FAITH HEALER, THE(1921)

Judge Peter Michael Curry
SUGARLAND EXPRESS, THE(1974)

Julia Curry
LEGACY OF BLOOD(1978)

Julian Curry
SMASHING TIME(1967 Brit.); MINI-AFFAIR, THE(1968, Brit.); VICTORY(1981); MISSIONARY, THE(1982)

Kathryn Curry
AWFUL TRUTH, THE(1937)

Kristen Curry
Misc. Talkies
LEGEND OF THE WILD(1981)

Louis Curry
DOUBLE TROUBLE(1941)

Louise Curry
QUEEN FOR A DAY(1951)

Mark Curry
BUGSY MALONE(1976, Brit.)
Mason Curry
SNIPER'S RIDGE(1961)
Michael Curry
LOVING COUPLES(1980)
Nathan Curry
TARZAN AND HIS MATE(1934); HARLEM ON THE PRAIRIE(1938); CONGO MAISIE(1940); SOUTH OF SUEZ(1940)
Rahsaan Curry
HAIR(1979)
Shaun Curry
LOVE IS A WOMAN(1967, Brit.); UP THE JUNCTION(1968, Brit.); LAST SHOT YOU HEAR, THE(1969, Brit.); GUNS AND THE FURY, THE(1983)
Steve Curry
HOT TIMES(1974)
Steven Curry
Misc. Talkies
GLEN AND RANDA(1971)
Tim Curry
ROCKY HORROR PICTURE SHOW, THE(1975, Brit.); SHOUT, THE(1978, Brit.); TIMES SQUARE(1980); ANNIE(1982)
1984
PLOUGHMAN'S LUNCH, THE(1984, Brit.)
Anne Curson
KITTY(1945); MINISTRY OF FEAR(1945); IRON CURTAIN, THE(1948)
Dieter Curt
DEAD MEN DON'T WEAR PLAID(1982); TO BE OR NOT TO BE(1983)
Fred Curt
PUFNSTUF(1970)
Curt Barrett and The Trailsman
DRIFTING ALONG(1946); GENTLEMAN FROM TEXAS(1946); RAIDERS OF THE SOUTH(1947)
Curt Barrett's Trailsmen
MASK OF THE DRAGON(1951)
Hoyt Curtain
JONIKO AND THE KUSH TA KA(1969), m
Ian Curteis
PROJECTED MAN, THE(1967, Brit.), d
Sylvain Curtel
CHARLES AND LUCIE(1982, Fr.)
Hoyt S. Curten
HEIDI'S SONG(1982), m
Ermanno Curti
STAR PILOT(1977, Ital.), p, w
Ezio Curti
WHITE SISTER(1973, Ital./Span./Fr.)
Franio Curti
WHITE SISTER(1973, Ital./Span./Fr.)
Grazia Curti
MAGIC WORLD OF TOPO GIGIO, THE(1961, Ital.), anim
A.V. Curtice
TREASURE AT THE MILL(1957, Brit.), p
Emmanuel Curtil
LES MISERABLES(1982, Fr.)
Hoyt Curtin
C.H.O.M.P.S.(1979), m
Jane Curtin
HOW TO BEAT THE HIGH COST OF LIVING(1980)
Robert Curtin
1984
CLOAK AND DAGGER(1984)
Valerie Curtin
ALICE DOESN'T LIVE HERE ANYMORE(1975); ALL THE PRESIDENT'S MEN(1976); MOTHER, JUGS & SPEED(1976); SILENT MOVIE(1976); SILVER STREAK(1976); DIFFERENT STORY, A(1978); GREAT SMOKEY ROADBLOCK, THE(1978); ...AND JUSTICE FOR ALL(1979), w; INSIDE MOVES(1980), w; WHY WOULD I LIE(1980); BEST FRIENDS(1982), w
1984
UNFAITHFULLY YOURS(1984), w
Alan Curtis
YELLOW JACK(1938); SMARTEST GIRL IN TOWN(1936); WALKING ON AIR(1936); WINTERSET(1936); CHINA PASSAGE(1937); DON'T TELL THE WIFE(1937); FIREFLY, THE(1937); MANNEQUIN(1937); DUKE OF WEST POINT, THE(1938); SHOPWORN ANGEL(1938); BURN 'EM UP O'CONNER(1939); GOOD GIRLS GO TO PARIS(1939); HOLLYWOOD CAVALCADE(1939); SERGEANT MADDEN(1939); FOUR SONS(1940); BUCK PRIVATES(1941); HIGH SIERRA(1941); NEW WINE(1941); WE GO FAST(1941); REMEMBER PEARL HARBOR(1942); CRAZY HOUSE(1943); GUNG HO!(1943); HITLER'S MADMAN(1943); TWO TICKETS TO LONDON(1943); DESTINY(1944); FOLLOW THE BOYS(1944); INVISIBLE MAN'S REVENGE(1944); PHANTOM LADY(1944); DALTONS RIDE AGAIN, THE(1945); FRISCO SAL(1945); NAUGHTY NINETIES, THE(1945); SEE MY LAWYER(1945); SHADY LADY(1945); FLIGHT TO NOWHERE(1946); INSIDE JOB(1946); RENEGADE GIRL(1946); PHILO VANCE'S GAMBLE(1947); PHILO VANCE'S SECRET MISSION(1947); ENCHANTED VALLEY, THE(1948); APACHE CHIEF(1949); PIRATES OF CAPRI, THE(1949); CARRY ON HENRY VIII(1970, Brit.)
Misc. Talkies
THREE DIMENSIONS OF GRETA(1973)
Alfie Curtis
ELEPHANT MAN, THE(1980, Brit.)
Alice F. Curtis
MAN WHO FOUND HIMSELF, THE(1937), w
Ann Curtis
MIDSUMMER NIGHT'S DREAM, A(1969, Brit.), cos
Anthony [Tony] Curtis
FRANCIS(1949); JOHNNY STOOL PIGEON(1949); LADY GAMBLES, THE(1949); I WAS A SHOPLIFTER(1950); SIERRA(1950); WINCHESTER '73(1950)

Antone Curtis
TRIBES(1970)
Arlo Curtis
SAVAGE WILD, THE(1970)
Barry Curtis
3:10 TO YUMA(1957); MARRYING KIND, THE(1952); ONE DESIRE(1955); MISSOURI TRAVELER, THE(1958)
Beatrice Curtis
AND SO THEY WERE MARRIED(1936); MR. DEEDS GOES TO TOWN(1936); THEODORA GOES WILD(1936); DEVIL'S PLAYGROUND(1937); GIRLS CAN PLAY(1937); LOST HORIZON(1937); PAID TO DANCE(1937); SHADOW, THE(1937); VENUS MAKES TROUBLE(1937); YOU CAN'T TAKE IT WITH YOU(1938); GOOD GIRLS GO TO PARIS(1939); HOMICIDE BUREAU(1939); LET US LIVE(1939); LONE WOLF SPY HUNT, THE(1939)
Betty Joy Curtis
PAN-AMERICANA(1945)
Billy Curtis
TERROR OF TINY TOWN, THE(1938); THREE TEXAS STEERS(1939); HELLZAPOPPIN'(1941); MEET JOHN DOE(1941); LUCKY LEGS(1942); MY GAL SAL(1942); SABOTEUR(1942); TRAMP, TRAMP, TRAMP(1942); WINGS FOR THE EAGLE(1942); INCENDIARY BLONDE(1945); THREE WISE FOOLS(1946); APRIL SHOWERS(1948); HOMICIDE FOR THREE(1948); PYGMY ISLAND(1950); SUPERMAN AND THE MOLE MEN(1951); THING, THE(1951); TWO TICKETS TO BROADWAY(1951); PRINCESS OF THE NILE(1954); THREE RING CIRCUS(1954); JUNGLE MOON MEN(1955); CONQUEROR, THE(1956); COURT JESTER, THE(1956); INCREDIBLE SHRINKING MAN, THE(1957); OUT OF SIGHT(1966); NORWOOD(1970); DIRTY HARRY(1971); HIGH PLAINS DRIFTER(1973); LITTLE CIGARS(1973); HOW TO SEDUCE A WOMAN(1974); EATING RAOUL(1982)
Bob Curtis
DEADLINE(1948); BRAND OF FEAR(1949); GUN LAW JUSTICE(1949); LAWLESS CODE(1949); SKY DRAGON(1949)
Bruce Cohn Curtis
OTLEY(1969, Brit.), p; LONG AGO, TOMORROW(1971, Brit.), p; JOYRIDE(1977), p; ROLLER BOOGIE(1979), p; HELL NIGHT(1981), p; SEDUCTION, THE(1982), p
1984
DREAMSCAPE(1984), p; FEAR CITY(1984), p
Carolyn Curtis
MESQUITE BUCKAROO(1939)
Catherine Curtis
Misc. Silents
SHEPHERD OF THE HILLS, THE(1920)
Cathrine Curtis
Silents
SKY PILOT, THE(1921), p
Christy Curtis
PRIVATE SCHOOL(1983)
Clarene Curtis
KID FROM SANTA FE, THE(1940)
Clarissa Curtis
PALS OF THE SILVER SAGE(1940)
Clive Curtis
WILD GEESE, THE(1978, Brit.); OCTOPUSSY(1983, Brit.), stunts
1984
LASSITER(1984)
Craig Curtis
SUNRISE AT CAMPOBELLO(1960); TIME FOR KILLING, A(1967); GREAT NORTHFIELD, MINNESOTA RAID, THE(1972)
Dan Curtis
HOUSE OF DARK SHADOWS(1970), p&d; NIGHT OF DARK SHADOWS(1971), p, d, w; BURNT OFFERINGS(1976), p, d
David Curtis
27A(1974, Aus.)
Dick Curtis
KING KONG(1933); CODE OF THE MOUNTED(1935); NORTHERN FRONTIER(1935); RACING LUCK(1935); TRAILS OF THE WILD(1935); WESTERN COURAGE(1935); WESTERN FRONTIER(1935); WILDERNESS MAIL(1935); CROOKED TRAIL, THE(1936); GHOST PATROL(1936); LION'S DEN, THE(1936); PHANTOM PATROL(1936); TRAITOR, THE(1936); BAR Z BAD MEN(1937); BOOTHILL BRIGADE(1937); GAMBLING TERROR, THE(1937); GAME THAT KILLS, THE(1937); GUNS IN THE DARK(1937); HEADLINE CRASHER(1937); LAWMAN IS BORN, A(1937); MOONLIGHT ON THE RANGE(1937); OLD WYOMING TRAIL, THE(1937); ONE MAN JUSTICE(1937); PAID TO DANCE(1937); SHADOW, THE(1937); SINGING BUCKAROO(1937); TRAIL OF VENGEANCE(1937); TWO GUN LAW(1937); WILD HORSE ROUND-UP(1937); ADVENTURE IN SAHARA(1938); CALL OF THE ROCKIES(1938); COLORADO TRAIL(1938); CRASHIN' THRU DANGER(1938); JUVENILE COURT(1938); LAW OF THE PLAINS(1938); LONE WOLF IN PARIS(1938); MAIN EVENT, THE(1938); OUTLAWS OF THE PRAIRIE(1938); PENITENTIARY(1938); RAWHIDE(1938); SOUTH OF ARIZONA(1938); SQUADRON OF HONOR(1938); THERE'S THAT WOMAN AGAIN(1938); WEST OF CHEYENNE(1938); WEST OF SANTA FE(1938); WHO KILLED GAIL PRESTON?(1938); WOMEN IN PRISON(1938); YOU CAN'T TAKE IT WITH YOU(1938); BEHIND PRISON GATES(1939); HOMICIDE BUREAU(1939); LET US LIVE(1939); LONE WOLF SPY HUNT, THE(1939); MAN THEY COULD NOT HANG, THE(1939); OUTPOST OF THE MOUNTIES(1939); OUTSIDE THESE WALLS(1939); RIDERS OF BLACK RIVER(1939); RIO GRANDE(1939); SPOILERS OF THE RANGE(1939); TAMING OF THE WEST, THE(1939); THUNDERING WEST, THE(1939); WESTERN CARAVANS(1939); BLAZING SIX SHOOTERS(1940); BLONDIE ON A BUDGET(1940); BOOM TOWN(1940); BULLETS FOR RUSTLERS(1940); MEN WITHOUT SOULS(1940); MY SON IS GUILTY(1940); PIONEERS OF THE FRONTIER(1940); RAGTIME COWBOY JOE(1940); STRANGER FROM TEXAS, THE(1940); TEXAS STAGECOACH(1940); THREE MEN FROM TEXAS(1940); TWO-FISTED RANGERS(1940); WYOMING(1940); ACROSS THE SIERRAS(1941); ARIZONA CYCLONE(1941); BILLY THE KID(1941); I WAS A PRISONER ON DEVIL'S ISLAND(1941); MYSTERY SHIP(1941); ROUNDUP, THE(1941); CITY OF SILENT MEN(1942); JACKASS MAIL(1942); MEN OF SAN QUENTIN(1942); PARDON MY GUN(1942); SHUT MY BIG MOUTH(1942); TOMBSTONE, THE TOWN TOO TOUGH TO DIE(1942); TWO YANKS IN TRINIDAD(1942); COWBOY IN THE CLOUDS(1943); JACK LONDON(1943); RIDERS OF THE NORTHWEST MOUNTED(1943); SALUTE TO THE MARINES(1943); COWBOY CANTEEN(1944); SPOOK TOWN(1944); GREAT JOHN L. THE(1945); SCARLET STREET(1945); ABILENE TOWN(1946); BANDIT OF SHERWOOD FOREST,

THE(1946); LAWLESS BREED, THE(1946); RENEGADE GIRL(1946); SANTA FE UPRISING(1946); SONG OF ARIZONA(1946); TRAFFIC IN CRIME(1946); WILD BEAUTY(1946); WYOMING(1947); NAVAJO TRAIL RAIDERS(1949); SHERIFF OF WICHITA(1949); COVERED WAGON RAID(1950); JACKPOT, THE(1950); VANISHING WESTERNER, THE(1950); CHICAGO CALLING(1951); LORNA DOONE(1951); RAWHIDE(1951); RED BADGE OF COURAGE, THE(1951); WHIRLWIND(1951); MY SIX CONVICTS(1952); ROSE OF CIMARRON(1952); WAGON WHEELS WESTWARD(1956); SUPPORT YOUR LOCAL GUNFIGHTER(1971); MOTEL HELL(1980)
Misc. Talkies
VALLEY OF TERROR(1937); VENGEANCE OF THE WEST(1942)

Don Curtis
SON OF DAVY CROCKETT, THE(1941)
Misc. Talkies
TORNADO IN THE SADDLE, A(1942)

Donald Curtis
NORTHWEST MOUNTED POLICE(1940); TEXAS RANGERS RIDE AGAIN(1940); CRIMINALS WITHIN(1941); ROYAL MOUNTED PATROL, THE(1941); SECRET EVIDENCE(1941); THUNDER OVER THE PRAIRIE(1941); CODE OF THE OUTLAW(1942); IN OLD CALIFORNIA(1942); INVISIBLE AGENT(1942); JOAN OF OZARK(1942); TOMBSTONE, THE TOWN TOO TOUGH TO DIE(1942); WESTWARD HO(1942); BATAAN(1943); CROSS OF LORRAINE, THE(1943); LAW OF THE NORTHWEST(1943); SALUTE TO THE MARINES(1943); SWING SHIFT MAISIE(1943); MEET ME IN ST. LOUIS(1944); NATIONAL VELVET(1944); SEE HERE, PRIVATE HARGROVE(1944); THIRTY SECONDS OVER TOKYO(1944); LETTER FOR EVIE, A(1945); SON OF LASSIE(1945); SPELLBOUND(1945); THEY WERE EXPENDABLE(1945); THIS MAN'S NAVY(1945); THRILL OF A ROMANCE(1945); WITHOUT LOVE(1945); BAD BASCOMB(1946); BLUE SIERRA(1946); COURAGE OF LASSIE(1946); GALLANT BESS(1946); WHITE TIE AND TAILS(1946); DANGEROUS YEARS(1947); I LOVE TROUBLE(1947); NIGHT SONG(1947); FULLER BRUSH MAN(1948); SPIRITUALIST, THE(1948); STAMPEDE(1949); PHFFFT!(1954); ALL THAT HEAVEN ALLOWS(1955); FLAME OF THE ISLANDS(1955); IT CAME FROM BENEATH THE SEA(1955); EARTH VS. THE FLYING SAUCERS(1956); SEVENTH CAVALRY(1956); TEN COMMANDMENTS, THE(1956); NIGHT PASSAGE(1957); WARNING SHOT(1967)

Dorothy Curtis
CONFESSIONS OF BOSTON BLACKIE(1941); FIRST YANK INTO TOKYO(1945); DEADLINE AT DAWN(1946); LOCKET, THE(1946); BUFFALO BILL RIDES AGAIN(1947); LIKELY STORY, A(1947)

Douglas Curtis
HAZING, THE(1978), p, d
1984
PHILADELPHIA EXPERIMENT, THE(1984), p

E. Curtis
DEVIL'S PIPELINE, THE(1940), ed

Ed Curtis
FRESHMAN YEAR(1938), ed; SECRETS OF A NURSE(1938), ed; GAMBLING SHIP(1939), ed; SKI PATROL(1940), ed; MUG TOWN(1943), ed

Edward Curtis
CRIMINAL CODE(1931), ed; BITTER TEA OF GENERAL YEN, THE(1933), ed; TODAY WE LIVE(1933), ed; I GIVE MY LOVE(1934), ed; BARBARY COAST(1935), ed; MYSTERY OF EDWIN DROOD, THE(1935), ed; I STOLE A MILLION(1939), ed; ONE HOUR TO LIVE(1939), ed; RAWHIDE RANGERS(1941), ed; STRICTLY IN THE GROOVE(1942), ed; CALAMITY JANE AND SAM BASS(1949), ed

Edward D. Curtis
SCARFACE(1932), ed

Edward S. Curtis
Silents
TEN COMMANDMENTS, THE(1923), ph

Elaine Curtis
CHINA DOLL(1958)

Elinor Curtis
Silents
SHOULD A WIFE WORK?(1922)

Floyd Curtis
SUNRISE AT CAMPOBELLO(1960)

Gabriel Curtis
MUTINY IN OUTER SPACE(1965)

Gene Curtis
LOVE BUG, THE(1968)

Gloria Curtis
HUSTLER, THE(1961)

Gonz Curtis
ZIG-ZAG(1975, Fr/Ital.)

Howard Curtis
PAJAMA PARTY(1964); 36 HOURS(1965); SPLIT, THE(1968); GREAT WALDO PEPPER, THE(1975), stunts; DEEP, THE(1977), stunts

J. Curtis
FLESH EATERS, THE(1964), d

Jack Curtis
LOVE RACKET, THE(1929); PHANTOM IN THE HOUSE, THE(1929); HOLD EVERYTHING(1930); LOVE TRADER(1930); MAMMY(1930); MOBY DICK(1930); UNDER A TEXAS MOON(1930); DAWN TRAIL, THE(1931); DEADLINE, THE(1932); CHEYENNE KID, THE(1933), w; FRISCO KID(1935); LAWLESS RANGE(1935); CHARGE OF THE LIGHT BRIGADE, THE(1936); IT HAD TO HAPPEN(1936); TRAIL OF THE LONESOME PINE, THE(1936); WESTWARD HO(1936); SONG OF THE SARONG(1945); MAGNIFICENT DOLL(1946); RUSTLER'S ROUNDUP(1946); EXILE, THE(1947); X THE UNKNOWN(1957, Brit.), spec eff; FLESH EATERS, THE(1964), p; UNSATISFIED, THE(1964, Span.), ed; HEAT(1970, Arg.), d
Silents
SECRET LOVE(1916); GREATER LAW, THE(1917); PEST, THE(1919); BIG PUNCH, THE(1921); SEA LION, THE(1921); STEELHEART(1921); TORRENT, THE(1921); LONG CHANCE, THE(1922); SILENT VOW, THE(1922); STRANGER'S BANQUET(1922); RENO(1923); FIGHTER'S PARADISE(1924); GREED(1925); WEDDING SONG, THE(1925); HEARTS AND FISTS(1926); JAWS OF STEEL(1927); WOLF'S CLOTHING(1927); SCARLET SEAS(1929)
Misc. Silents
END OF THE RAINBOW, THE(1916); WOMAN'S LAW, THE(1916); BROADWAY ARIZONA(1917); MUTINY(1917); SOUTHERN JUSTICE(1917); GOLDEN FLEECE, THE(1918); HARD ROCK BREED, THE(1918); LITTLE RED DECIDES(1918); MARKED CARDS(1918); MY HUSBAND'S FRIEND(1918); UNTIL THEY GET ME(1918); WOLVES OF THE BORDER(1918); COMING OF THE LAW, THE(1919);

MAN'S DESIRE(1919); COURAGE OF MARGE O'DOONE, THE(1920); SEEDS OF VENGEANCE(1920); SERVANT IN THE HOUSE, THE(1920); BEACH OF DREAMS(1921); CAUGHT BLUFFING(1922); BAREE, SON OF KAZAN(1925); THROUGH THICK AND THIN(1927)

Jackie Curtis
UNDERGROUND U.S.A.(1980)

James Curtis
FUGITIVE LADY(1934); MANHATTAN MELODRAMA(1934); THEY DRIVE BY NIGHT(1938, Brit.), w; THERE AIN'T NO JUSTICE(1939, Brit.), w; MISSING TEN DAYS(1941, Brit.), w; DEVIL ON HORSEBACK(1954, Brit.), w

James [Tony] Curtis
CRISS CROSS(1949)

Jamie Lee Curtis
HALLOWEEN(1978); FOG, THE(1980); PROM NIGHT(1980); TERROR TRAIN(1980, Can.); HALLOWEEN II(1981); ROAD GAMES(1981, Aus.); LOVE LETTERS(1983); TRADING PLACES(1983)
1984
ADVENTURES OF BUCKAROO BANZAI: ACROSS THE 8TH DIMENSION, THE(1984); GRANDVIEW, U.S.A.(1984)

Jo Ann Curtis
Misc. Talkies
STRANGER FROM SANTA FE(1945)

Joan Curtis
HOT RHYTHM(1944)
Misc. Talkies
WHERE TRAILS END(1942)

Joe Curtis
SLAUGHTER IN SAN FRANCISCO(1981), m

John Curtis
TRAIL RIDERS(1942); TWO FISTED JUSTICE(1943)

Judy Curtis
HAPPY BIRTHDAY, DAVY(1970)

Keene Curtis
MACBETH(1948); BLADE(1973); WRONG DAMN FILM, THE(1975); HEAVEN CAN WAIT(1978); RABBIT TEST(1978)
1984
BUDDY SYSTEM, THE(1984)

Kelly Curtis
TRADING PLACES(1983)

Ken Curtis
COWBOY BLUES(1946); OUT OF THE DEPTHS(1946); STALLION CANYON(1949); RIO GRANDE(1950); QUIET MAN, THE(1952); LONG GRAY LINE, THE(1955); MISTER ROBERTS(1955); SEARCHERS, THE(1956); SPRING REUNION(1957); WINGS OF EAGLES, THE(1957); LAST HURRAH, THE(1958); MISSOURI TRAVELER, THE(1958); ESCORT WEST(1959); GIANT GILA MONSTER, THE(1959), p; HORSE SOLDIERS, THE(1959); KILLER SHREWS, THE(1959), a, p; YOUNG LAND, THE(1959); ALAMO, THE(1960); FRECKLES(1960); MY DOG, BUDDY(1960), a, p; TWO RODE TOGETHER(1961); HOW THE WEST WAS WON(1962); CHEYENNE AUTUMN(1964); ROBIN HOOD(1973); PONY EXPRESS RIDER(1976)
Misc. Talkies
RHYTHM ROUND-UP(1945); SONG OF THE PRAIRIE(1945); LONE STAR MOONLIGHT(1946); SINGING ON THE TRAIL(1946); THAT TEXAS JAMBOREE(1946); THROW A SADDLE ON A STAR(1946); OVER THE SANTA FE TRAIL(1947); CALL OF THE FOREST(1949); RIDERS OF THE PONY EXPRESS(1949); LEGEND OF THE WILD(1981); LOST(1983)

King Curtis
PRIDE OF THE FORCE, THE(1933, Brit.)

Leslie Curtis
LAST TYCOON, THE(1976)
Silents
EYES RIGHT(1926), w; WESTERN COURAGE(1927), w

Liane Curtis
BABY, IT'S YOU(1983)
1984
BROTHER FROM ANOTHER PLANET, THE(1984); HARD CHOICES(1984); SIXTEEN CANDLES(1984)

Lizie Curtis
TERROR IN THE JUNGLE(1968)

Lucile Curtis
IT'S A BIG COUNTRY(1951); INVITATION(1952); NORTH BY NORTHWEST(1959); THIRD VOICE, THE(1960)

Lucille Curtis
HOODLUM SAINT, THE(1946); GREEN DOLPHIN STREET(1947); FATHER OF THE BRIDE(1950); MYSTERY STREET(1950); FLESH AND FURY(1952); LOVE IS BETTER THAN EVER(1952); HANGMAN, THE(1959); SHOCK CORRIDOR(1963)

Lucinda Curtis
NOTHING BUT THE BEST(1964, Brit.); RICHARD'S THINGS(1981, Brit.)

Lynn Curtis
SHAKEDOWN, THE(1960, Brit.)

Madeline Curtis
EYES OF A STRANGER(1980)

Marilyn Curtis
UP THE SANDBOX(1972)

Martin Curtis
BRANDY FOR THE PARSON(1952, Brit.), ph; SECRET CAVE, THE(1953, Brit.), ph; FUSS OVER FEATHERS(1954, Brit.), ph; PACIFIC DESTINY(1956, Brit.), ph; NEVER PUT IT IN WRITING(1964), ph; SILENT PLAYGROUND, THE(1964, Brit.), ph; CITY OF FEAR(1965, Brit.), ph; MOZAMBIQUE(1966, Brit.), ph

Mary Ann Curtis
NASHVILLE REBEL(1966), cos

Mary Curtis
SABOTEUR(1942)

Mary Jo Curtis
RAT PFINK AND BOO BOO(1966)

Mel Curtis
URANIUM BOOM(1956); ZOMBIES OF MORA TAU(1957); PHANTOM PLANET, THE(1961)

Mickey Curtis
FIRES ON THE PLAIN(1962, Jap.); OPERATION X(1963, Jap.)
Nat Curtis
JACK AND THE BEANSTALK(1952), w
Nathaniel Curtis
TIME OF YOUR LIFE, THE(1948), w; HARVEY GIRLS, THE(1946), w; PLEASE BELIEVE ME(1950), w
Neil Curtis
Silents
DAUGHTER IN REVOLT, A(1927, Brit.)
Oren Curtis
BLACK ZOO(1963)
Patrick Curtis
SORCERERS, THE(1967, Brit.), p; HANNIE CALDER(1971, Brit.), p
Paulette Rubenstein Curtis
HEAT(1970, Arg.), w
Percy Curtis
ELECTRA GLIDE IN BLUE(1973)
Peter Curtis
GUILT IS MY SHADOW(1950, Brit.), w; DEVIL'S OWN, THE(1967, Brit.), w
Ray Curtis
BIG CITY BLUES(1932), ed; MISS PINKERTON(1932), ed; THREE ON A MATCH(1932), ed; PARACHUTE JUMPER(1933), ed; BLACK CAT, THE(1934), ed; HARMONY LANE(1935), ed; SOUTH OF PAGO PAGO(1940), ed
Raymond Curtis
GIFT OF GAB(1934), ed; I'VE BEEN AROUND(1935), ed
Rex Curtis
GUILT(1930, Brit.); TWO HEARTS IN HARMONY(1935, Brit.)
Richard Curtis
SHOOTING STRAIGHT(1930); WILDCAT TROOPER(1936); CRIME IN THE STREETS(1956)
Robert Curtis
WITCH, THE(1969, Ital.), ch
Robin Curtis
GHOST STORY(1981)
1984
STAR TREK III: THE SEARCH FOR SPOCK(1984)
Ronald Curtis
NIGHT AND DAY(1933, Brit.)
Roxanne Curtis
LIGHTNIN'(1930)
Sam Curtis
THOSE WERE THE DAYS(1934, Brit.)
Sammy Curtis
STARS IN YOUR EYES(1956, Brit.)
Sid Curtis
BLACK WHIP, THE(1956)
Sonny Curtis
GIRLS ON THE BEACH(1965)
Terry Curtis
FLESH EATERS, THE(1964), p
Tom Curtis
SANDPIPER, THE(1965)
Tony Curtis
TAKE ONE FALSE STEP(1949); KANSAS RAIDERS(1950); PRINCE WHO WAS A THIEF, THE(1951); FLESH AND FURY(1952); MEET DANNY WILSON(1952); NO ROOM FOR THE GROOM(1952); SON OF ALI BABA(1952); ALL-AMERICAN, THE(1953); FORBIDDEN(1953); HOUDINI(1953); BEACHHEAD(1954); BLACK SHIELD OF FALWORTH, THE(1954); JOHNNY DARK(1954); SO THIS IS PARIS(1954); PURPLE MASK, THE(1955); SIX BRIDGES TO CROSS(1955); SQUARE JUNGLE, THE(1955); RAWHIDE YEARS, THE(1956); TRAPEZE(1956); MIDNIGHT STORY, THE(1957); MISTER CORY(1957); SWEET SMELL OF SUCCESS(1957); DEFIANT ONES, THE(1958); KINGS GO FORTH(1958); PERFECT FURLOUGH, THE(1958); VIKINGS, THE(1958); OPERATION PETTICOAT(1959); SOME LIKE IT HOT(1959); GREAT IMPOSTOR, THE(1960); PEPE(1960); RAT RACE, THE(1960); SPARTACUS(1960); WHO WAS THAT LADY?(1960); FORTY POUNDS OF TROUBLE(1962); OUTSIDER, THE(1962); TARAS BULBA(1962); CAPTAIN NEWMAN, M.D.(1963); LIST OF ADRIAN MESSENGER, THE(1963); GOODBYE CHARLIE(1964); PARIS WHEN IT SIZZLES(1964); SEX AND THE SINGLE GIRL(1964); WILD AND WONDERFUL(1964); BOEING BOEING(1965); GREAT RACE, THE(1965); ARRIVEDERCI, BABY!(1966, Brit.); CHAMBER OF HORRORS(1966); NOT WITH MY WIFE, YOU DON'T(1966); DON'T MAKE WAVES(1967); SORCERERS, THE(1967, Brit.), art d; CHASTITY BELT, THE(1968, Ital.); ROSEMARY'S BABY(1968); THE BOSTON STRANGLER, THE(1968); TOMCAT, THE(1968, Brit.), art d; THANK YOU ALL VERY MUCH(1969, Brit.); THOSE DARING YOUNG MEN IN THEIR JAUNTY JALOPIES(1969, Fr./Brit./ Ital.); SUPPOSE THEY GAVE A WAR AND NOBODY CAME?(1970); YOU CAN'T WIN 'EM ALL(1970, Brit.); HOUSE THAT DRIPPED BLOOD, THE(1971, Brit.), art d; ASYLUM(1972, Brit.), art d; TALES FROM THE CRYPT(1972, Brit.), art d; WHAT BECAME OF JACK AND JILL?(1972, Brit.), art d; AND NOW THE SCREAMING STARTS(1973, Brit.), art d; VAULT OF HORROR, THE(1973, Brit.), art d; MADHOUSE(1974, Brit.), art d; LEPKE(1975, U.S./Israel); COUNT OF MONTE CRISTO(1976, Brit.); LAST TYCOON(1976); BAD NEWS BEARS GO TO JAPAN, THE(1978); MANITOU, THE(1978); ODD JOB, THE(1978, Brit.), prod d; SEXTETTE(1978); SOME LIKE IT COOL(1979, Ger./Aust./Ital./Fr.); GODSEND, THE(1980, Can.), art d; LITTLE MISS MARKER(1980); MIRROR CRACK'D, THE(1980, Brit.); MONSTER CLUB, THE(1981, Brit.), art d; TITLE SHOT(1982, Can.); VENOM(1982, Brit.), art d; BRAINWAVES(1983)
1984
WHERE IS PARSIFAL?(1984, Brit.)
Misc. Talkies
IT RAINED ALL NIGHT THE DAY I LEFT(1978); MISSION: MONTE CARLO(1981, Brit.)
V. Curtis
YOU GOTTA STAY HAPPY(1948), makeup
Walt Curtis
PROPERTY(1979)
Wanda Curtis
KING DINOSAUR(1955)

Willa Curtis
TOY WIFE, THE(1938)
Willa Pearl Curtis
VALLEY OF DECISION, THE(1945); VARIETY GIRL(1947); LAWTON STORY, THE(1949); MATING SEASON, THE(1951); QUEEN BEE(1955)
Willy Curtis
INCREDIBLE MELTING MAN, THE(1978), ph
Yvette Curtis
WARM DECEMBER, A(1973, Brit.); CLAUDINE(1974)
The Curtis Mayfield Experience
SUPERFLY(1972)
Carol Curtis-Brown
SUSPICION(1941); THIS ABOVE ALL(1942)
Robert Curtis-Brown
TRADING PLACES(1983)
Dorita Curtis-Hayward
STRANGER'S MEETING(1957, Brit.)
Dorothy Curtiss
SUNSET PASS(1946)
Ed Curtiss
GENTLEMAN FROM ARIZONA, THE(1940), ed; MA, HE'S MAKING EYES AT ME(1940), ed; MY LITTLE CHICKADEE(1940), ed; WHEN THE DALTONS RODE(1940), ed; LUCKY DEVILS(1941), ed
Edward Curtiss
FOR THE LOVE O'LIL(1930), ed; GOOD BAD GIRL, THE(1931), ed; GREAT EXPECTATIONS(1934), ed; UNCERTAIN LADY(1934), ed; STRANGE WIVES(1935), ed; COME AND GET IT(1936), ed; ROAD TO GLORY, THE(1936), ed; SWING THAT CHEER(1938), ed; TOWER OF LONDON(1939), ed; TRAIL OF THE VIGILANTES(1940), ed; PARIS CALLING(1941), ed; THIS WOMAN IS MINE(1941), ed; ALMOST MARRIED(1942), ed; HALF WAY TO SHANGHAI(1942), ed; INVISIBLE AGENT(1942), ed; SIN TOWN(1942), ed; UNSEEN ENEMY(1942), ed; CORVETTE K-225(1943), ed; FRANKENSTEIN MEETS THE WOLF MAN(1943), ed; GOOD MORNING, JUDGE(1943), ed; HI BEAUTIFUL(1944), ed; PARDON MY RHYTHM(1944), ed; SINGING SHERIFF, THE(1944), ed; SWINGTIME JOHNNY(1944), ed; WEEKEND PASS(1944), ed; FRISCO SAL(1945), ed; PILLOW OF DEATH(1945), ed; RENEGADES OF THE RIO GRANDE(1945), ed; SHADY LADY(1945), ed; SWING OUT, SISTER(1945), ed; WOMAN IN GREEN, THE(1945), ed; BLONDE ALIBI(1946), ed; HER ADVENTUROUS NIGHT(1946), ed; SWELL GUY(1946), ed; TANGIER(1946), ed; BRUTE FORCE(1947), ed; BUCK PRIVATES COME HOME(1947), ed; CASBAH(1948), ed; COUNTESS OF MONTE CRISTO, THE(1948), ed; FEUDIN', FUSSIN' AND A-FIGHTIN'(1948), ed; ABANDONED(1949), ed; ABBOTT AND COSTELLO MEET THE KILLER, BORIS KARLOFF(1949), ed; ILLEGAL ENTRY(1949), ed; STORY OF MOLLY X, THE(1949), ed; ABBOTT AND COSTELLO IN THE FOREIGN LEGION(1950), ed; OUTSIDE THE WALL(1950), ed; WINCHESTER '73(1950), ed; WYOMING MAIL(1950), ed; CAVE OF OUTLAWS(1951), ed; COMIN' ROUND THE MOUNTAIN(1951), ed; PRINCE WHO WAS A THIEF, THE(1951), ed; STRANGE DOOR, THE(1951), ed; BRONCO BUSTER(1952), ed; RED BALL EXPRESS(1952), ed; SALLY AND SAINT ANNE(1952), ed; ALL-AMERICAN, THE(1953), ed; CITY BENEATH THE SEA(1953), ed; FORBIDDEN(1953), ed; GREAT SIOUX UPRISING, THE(1953), ed; MISSISSIPPI GAMBLER, THE(1953), ed; DAWN AT SOCORRO(1954), ed; JOHNNY DARK(1954), ed; RIDE CLEAR OF DIABLO(1954), ed; YELLOW MOUNTAIN, THE(1954), ed; ABBOTT AND COSTELLO MEET THE KEYSTONE KOPS(1955), ed; RUNNING WILD(1955), ed; TO HELL AND BACK(1955), ed; CREATURE WALKS AMONG US, THE(1956), ed; KETTLES IN THE OZARKS, THE(1956), ed; RED SUNDOWN(1956), ed; UNGUARDED MOMENT, THE(1956), ed; GUN FOR A COWARD(1957), ed; KETTLES ON OLD MACDONALD'S FARM, THE(1957), ed; MAN IN THE SHADOW(1957), ed; MISTER CORY(1957), ed; TATTERED DRESS, THE(1957), ed; BIG BEAT, THE(1958), ed; GIRLS ON THE LOOSE(1958), ed; LIVE FAST, DIE YOUNG(1958), ed; RIDE A CROOKED TRAIL(1958), ed; THING THAT COULDN'T DIE, THE(1958), ed; MOUNTAIN ROAD, THE(1960), ed; DONDI(1961), ed; CONFESSIONS OF AN OPIUM EATER(1962), ed
Jacqueline Curtiss
FIRE MAIDENS FROM OUTER SPACE(1956, Brit.); LADY OF VENGEANCE(1957, Brit)
Joseph Curtiss
LITTLE EGYPT(1951), ed
Ray Curtiss
RED HOT SPEED ½(1929), ed; SCANDAL(1929), ed; YOUNG NOWHERES(1929), ed; BACK PAY(1930), ed; DAWN PATROL, THE(1930), ed; WAY OF ALL MEN, THE(1930), ed; CHANCES(1931), ed; LITTLE CAESAR(1931), ed; KEYHOLE, THE(1933), ed; MARY STEVENS, M.D.(1933), ed; FURY OF THE JUNGLE(1934), ed; WATERFRONT LADY(1935), ed; $1,000 A MINUTE(1935), ed; GO WEST, YOUNG MAN(1936), ed; LOVE ON TOAST(1937), ed; ON SUCH A NIGHT(1937), ed; EVERY DAY'S A HOLIDAY(1938), ed; CRASH DIVE(1943), ed; GANG'S ALL HERE, THE(1943), ed; FOUR JILLS IN A JEEP(1944), ed; RECKLESS AGE(1944), ed; FOREVER YOURS(1945), ed
Silents
GOOSE WOMAN, THE(1925), ed; RED LIPS(1928), ed; 13 WASHINGTON SQUARE(1928), ed
Ray F. Curtiss
MIDNIGHT MADONNA(1937), ed; OUTCAST(1937), ed
Thomas Quinn Curtiss
ICEMAN COMETH, THE(1973), w
Ursula Curtiss
I SAW WHAT YOU DID(1965), w; WHAT EVER HAPPENED TO AUNT ALICE?(1969), w
Willa Pearl Curtiss
NATIVE SON(1951, U.S., Arg.)
David Curtiz
ROMANCE ON THE HIGH SEAS(1948), spec eff
Gabor Curtiz
INTERRUPTED MELODY(1955); GIRL IN THE KREMLIN, THE(1957)
Gabriel Curtiz
JUGGLER, THE(1953); DEATH OF A SCOUNDREL(1956); FUNNY FACE(1957)
Maryon Curtiz
CEILNG ZERO(1935)

Michael Curtiz
NOAH'S ARK(1928), d; TENDERLOIN(1928), d; GAMBLERS, THE(1929), d; GLAD RAG DOLL, THE(1929), d; HEARTS IN EXILE(1929), d; MADONNA OF AVENUE A(1929), d; MAMMY(1930), d; MATRIMONIAL BED, THE(1930), d; UNDER A TEXAS MOON(1930), d; BRIGHT LIGHTS(1931), d; GOD'S GIFT TO WOMEN(1931), d; MAD GENIUS, THE(1931), d; RIVER'S END(1931), d; SOLDIER'S PLAYTHING, A(1931), d; CABIN IN THE COTTON(1932), d; DOCTOR X(1932), d; WOMAN FROM MONTE CARLO, THE(1932), d; FEMALE(1933), d; GOODBYE AGAIN(1933), d; KENNEL MURDER CASE, THE(1933), d; KEYHOLE, THE(1933), d; MYSTERY OF THE WAX MUSEUM, THE(1933), d; PRIVATE DETECTIVE 62(1933), d; 20,000 YEARS IN SING SING(1933), d; BRITISH AGENT(1934), d; JIMMY THE GENT(1934), d; KEY, THE(1934), d; MANDALAY(1934), d; BLACK FURY(1935), d; CAPTAIN BLOOD(1935), d; FRONT PAGE WOMAN(1935), d; LITTLE BIG SHOT(1935), d; CHARGE OF THE LIGHT BRIGADE, THE(1936), d; WALKING DEAD, THE(1936), d; KID GALAHAD(1937), d; MOUNTAIN JUSTICE(1937), d; PERFECT SPECIMEN, THE(1937), d; STOLEN HOLIDAY(1937), d; ADVENTURES OF ROBIN HOOD, THE(1938), d; ANGELS WITH DIRTY FACES(1938), d; FOUR DAUGHTERS(1938), d; FOUR'S A CROWD(1938), d; GOLD IS WHERE YOU FIND IT(1938), d; DAUGHTERS COURAGEOUS(1939), d; DODGE CITY(1939), d; FOUR WIVES(1939), d; PRIVATE LIVES OF ELIZABETH AND ESSEX, THE(1939), d; SANTA FE TRAIL(1940), d; SEA HAWK, THE(1940), d; VIRGINIA CITY(1940), d; DIVE BOMBER(1941), d; SEA WOLF, THE(1941), d; CAPTAINS OF THE CLOUDS(1942), d; CASABLANCA(1942), d; MISSION TO MOSCOW(1943), d; THIS IS THE ARMY(1943), d; JANIE(1944), d; PASSAGE TO MARSEILLE(1944), d; MILDRED PIERCE(1945), d; ROUGHLY SPEAKING(1945), d; NIGHT AND DAY(1946), d; LIFE WITH FATHER(1947), d; UNSUSPECTED, THE(1947), d; ROMANCE ON THE HIGH SEAS(1948), d; FLAMINGO ROAD(1949), d; IT'S A GREAT FEELING(1949); LADY TAKES A SAILOR, THE(1949), d; MY DREAM IS YOURS(1949), p&d; BREAKING POINT, THE(1950), d; BRIGHT LEAF(1950), d; YOUNG MAN WITH A HORN(1950), d; FORCE OF ARMS(1951), d; I'LL SEE YOU IN MY DREAMS(1951), d; JIM THORPE–ALL AMERICAN(1951), d; STORY OF WILL ROGERS, THE(1952), d; JAZZ SINGER, THE(1953), d; TROUBLE ALONG THE WAY(1953), d; BOY FROM OKLAHOMA, THE(1954), d; EGYPTIAN, THE(1954), d; WHITE CHRISTMAS(1954), d; WE'RE NO ANGELS(1955), d; BEST THINGS IN LIFE ARE FREE, THE(1956), d; SCARLET HOUR, THE(1956), p&d; VAGABOND KING, THE(1956), d; KING CREOLE(1958), d; PROUD REBEL, THE(1958), d; HANGMAN, THE(1959), d; HELEN MORGAN STORY, THE(1959), d; MAN IN THE NET, THE(1959), d; ADVENTURES OF HUCKLEBERRY FINN, THE(1960), d; BREATH OF SCANDAL, A(1960), d; FRANCIS OF ASSISI(1961), d
Silents
THIRD DEGREE, THE(1926), d
Misc. Silents
ATLANTIS(1913, Ger./Den.); DESIRED WOMAN, THE(1927), d; GOOD TIME CHARLEY(1927), d; MILLION BID, A(1927), d; MOON OF ISRAEL(1927, Aust.), d

Michael Curtiz [Mikhaly Kertesz]
STRANGE LOVE OF MOLLY LOUVAIN, THE(1932), d

Ray Curtiz
GREAT DIVIDE, THE(1930), ed

Guido Curto
ROTHSCHILD(1938, Fr.), m

Curtois
Misc. Silents
L'AUBERGE ROUGE(1923, Fr.)

Jorga Curtright
WHISTLE STOP(1946)

Jorja Curtright
LOVE IS A MANY-SPLENDORED THING(1955)

Patricia Curts
I WAS A MALE WAR BRIDE(1949)

Jorja Curtwright
M(1951); REVOLT OF MAMIE STOVER, THE(1956)

Michael Curtz
CASE OF THE CURIOUS BRIDE, THE(1935), d

Alfred Curven
GHOST STORY(1981)

Patric Curwen
RINGER, THE(1932, Brit.); LOYALTIES(1934, Brit.); DEPARTMENT STORE(1935, Brit.); HEARTS OF HUMANITY(1936, Brit.); MEN OF YESTERDAY(1936, Brit.); THERE WAS A YOUNG MAN(1937, Brit.); RETURN TO YESTERDAY(1940, Brit.); LAMP STILL BURNS, THE(1943, Brit.); SHIPBUILDERS(1943, Brit.); DON'T TAKE IT TO HEART(1944, Brit.); GIVE ME THE STARS(1944, Brit.); IT HAPPENED ONE SUNDAY(1944, Brit.); YELLOW CANARY, THE(1944, Brit.); ECHO MURDERS, THE(1945, Brit.); STRAWBERRY ROAN(1945, Brit.); THEY KNEW MR. KNIGHT(1945, Brit.); GAY INTRUDERS, THE(1946, Brit.); GREEN FINGERS(1947); NOTHING VENTURE(1948, Brit.)

Patrick Curwen
MAN IN GREY, THE(1943, Brit.); GRAND ESCAPADE, THE(1946, Brit.)

James Curwood
WILD HORSE ROUND-UP(1937), w

James Oliver Curwood
RIVER'S END(1931), w; TRAIL BEYOND, THE(1934), w; CODE OF THE MOUNTED(1935), w; FIGHTING TROOPER, THE(1935), w; HIS FIGHTING BLOOD(1935), w; NORTHERN FRONTIER(1935), w; RED BLOOD OF COURAGE(1935), w; TRAILS OF THE WILD(1935), w; WILDERNESS MAIL(1935), w; CARYL OF THE MOUNTAINS(1936), w; PHANTOM PATROL(1936), w; SONG OF THE TRAIL(1936), w; TIMBER WAR(1936), w; WILDCAT TROOPER(1936), w; FIGHTING TEXAN(1937), w; GALLOPING DYNAMITE(1937), w; GOD'S COUNTRY AND THE WOMAN(1937), w; ROARING SIX GUNS(1937), w; ROUGH RIDIN' RHYTHM(1937), w; SILVER TRAIL, THE(1937), w; WHISTLING BULLETS(1937), w; CALL OF THE YUKON(1938), w; SKULL AND CROWN(1938), w; RIVER'S END(1940), w; LAW OF THE TIMBER(1941), w; DAWN ON THE GREAT DIVIDE(1942), w; GOD'S COUNTRY(1946), w; KAZAN(1949), w; TRAIL OF THE YUKON(1949), w; WOLF HUNTERS, THE(1949), w; CALL OF THE KLONDIKE(1950), w; SNOW DOG(1950), w; TIMBER FURY(1950), w; YUKON MANHUNT(1951), w; NORTHWEST TERRITORY(1952), w; YUKON GOLD(1952), w; BACK TO GOD'S COUNTRY(1953), w; FANGS OF THE ARCTIC(1953), w; NORTHERN PATROL(1953), w; YUKON VENGEANCE(1954), w; NIKKI, WILD DOG OF THE NORTH(1961, U.S./Can.), w
Silents
HER FIGHTING CHANCE(1917), w; MAN HATER, THE(1917), w; ISOBEL(1920), w; NOMADS OF THE NORTH(1920), w; VALLEY OF SILENT MEN, THE(1922), w; GOLD MADNESS(1923), w; JACQUELINE, OR BLAZING BARRIERS(1923), w;

ALASKAN, THE(1924), w; ANCIENT HIGHWAY, THE(1925), w; CAPTAIN'S COURAGE, A(1926), w; OLD CODE, THE(1928), w

Maurice Cury
FIVE WILD GIRLS(1966, Fr.), w; HEAT OF MIDNIGHT(1966, Fr.), w; ROAD TO SALINA(1971, Fr./Ital.), w

Pierre Curzi
SUZANNE(1980, Can.)

Ann Curzon
WHITE CLIFFS OF DOVER, THE(1944)

Charlotte Curzon
JOKERS, THE(1967, Brit.)

Fiona Curzon
LOVE IS A SPLENDID ILLUSION(1970, Brit.); FRIGHTMARE(1974, Brit.)
Misc. Talkies
LICENSED TO LOVE AND KILL(1979, Brit.)

George Curzon
ESCAPE(1930, Brit.); BOAT FROM SHANGHAI(1931, Brit.); AFTER THE BALL(1932, Brit.); HER FIRST AFFAIRE(1932, Brit.); MURDER AT COVENT GARDEN(1932, Brit.); WOMAN IN CHAINS(1932, Brit.); STRANGE EVIDENCE(1933, Brit.); TROUBLE(1933, Brit.); WIDOW'S MIGHT(1934, Brit.); ADMIRALS ALL(1935, Brit.); JAVA HEAD(1935, Brit.); LORNA DOONE(1935, Brit.); MAN WHO KNEW TOO MUCH, THE(1935, Brit.); SEXTON BLAKE AND THE BEARDED DOCTOR(1935, Brit.); SEXTON BLAKE AND THE MADEMOISELLE(1935, Brit.); TWO HEARTS IN HARMONY(1935, Brit.); LIVING DEAD, THE(1936, Brit.); WHITE ANGEL, THE(1936); ROYAL DIVORCE, A(1938, Brit.); SEXTON BLAKE AND THE HOODED TERROR(1938, Brit.); STRANGE BOARDERS(1938, Brit.); YOUNG AND INNOCENT(1938, Brit.); CLOUDS OVER EUROPE(1939, Brit.); JAMAICA INN(1939, Brit.); MOZART(1940, Brit.); MYSTERIOUS MR. REEDER, THE(1940, Brit.); FOR THEM THAT TRESPASS(1949, Brit.); IF THIS BE SIN(1950, Brit.); INHERITANCE, THE(1951, Brit.); SING ALONG WITH ME(1952, Brit.); CRUEL SEA, THE(1953); HARRY BLACK AND THE TIGER(1958, Brit.); WOMAN OF STRAW(1964, Brit.)

Jill Curzon
80,000 SUSPECTS(1963, Brit.); SPYLARKS(1965, Brit.); DALEKS–INVASION EARTH 2155 A.D.(1966, Brit.)

Cyril Cusack
LATE EXTRA(1935, Brit.); MAIL TRAIN(1941, Brit.); ONCE A CROOK(1941, Brit.); ODD MAN OUT(1947, Brit.); ESCAPE(1948, Brit.); ESTHER WATERS(1948, Brit.); ALL OVER THE TOWN(1949, Brit.); BLUE LAGOON, THE(1949, Brit.); HOUR OF GLORY(1949, Brit.); FIGHTING PIMPERNEL, THE(1950, Brit.); BLUE VEIL, THE(1951); MANIACS ON WHEELS(1951, Brit.); SECRET OF CONVICT LAKE(1951); SOLDIERS THREE(1951); WILD HEART, THE(1952, Brit.); SAADIA(1953); DESTINATION MILAN(1954, Brit.); LAST MOMENT, THE(1954, Brit.); PASSAGE HOME(1955, Brit.); JACQUELINE(1956, Brit.); MAN WHO NEVER WAS, THE(1956, Brit.); MARCH HARE, THE(1956, Brit.); MAN IN THE ROAD, THE(1957, Brit.); MIRACLE IN SOHO(1957, Brit.); SPANISH GARDENER, THE(1957, Span.); FLOODS OF FEAR(1958, Brit.); NIGHT AMBUSH(1958, Brit.); GIDEON OF SCOTLAND YARD(1959, Brit.); NIGHT FIGHTERS, THE(1960); I THANK A FOOL(1962, Brit.); WALTZ OF THE TOREADORS(1962, Brit.); 80,000 SUSPECTS(1963, Brit.); JOHNNY NOBODY(1965, Brit.); SPY WHO CAME IN FROM THE COLD, THE(1965, Brit.); WHERE THE SPIES ARE(1965, Brit.); FAHRENHEIT 451(1966, Brit.); TIME LOST AND TIME REMEMBERED(1966, Brit.); TAMING OF THE SHREW, THE(1967, U.S./Ital.); GALILEO(1968, Ital./Bul.); OEDIPUS THE KING(1968, Brit.); BROTHERLY LOVE(1970, Brit.); DAVID COPPERFIELD(1970, Brit.); HAROLD AND MAUDE(1971); KING LEAR(1971, Brit./Den.); SACCO AND VANZETTI(1971, Ital./Fr.); DEVIL'S WIDOW, THE(1972, Brit.); ALL THE WAY, BOYS(1973, Ital.); DAY OF THE JACKAL, THE(1973, Brit./Fr.); HOMECOMING, THE(1973); ITALIAN CONNECTION, THE(1973, U.S./Ital./Ger.); ABDICATION, THE(1974, Brit.); CHILDREN OF RAGE(1975, Brit.-Israeli); POITIN(1979, Irish); TRUE CONFESSIONS(1981); WAGNER(1983, Brit./Hung./Aust.)
1984
1984(1984, Brit.)
Misc. Talkies
RUN, RUN, JOE!(1974); KINGFISHER, THE(1982)
Silents
KNOCKNAGOW(1918, Ireland)

Dick Cusack
CLASS(1983)

Frank Cusack
O. HENRY'S FULL HOUSE(1952)

Joan Cusack
MY BODYGUARD(1980); CLASS(1983)
1984
GRANDVIEW, U.S.A.(1984); SIXTEEN CANDLES(1984)

John Cusack
CLASS(1983)
1984
GRANDVIEW, U.S.A.(1984); SIXTEEN CANDLES(1984)

Maureen Cusack
ODD MAN OUT(1947, Brit.); RISING OF THE MOON, THE(1957, Ireland); VON RICHTHOFEN AND BROWN(1970)

Noel Cusack
CONVICTED(1938)

Richard Cusack
MY BODYGUARD(1980)

Sinead Cusack
DAVID COPPERFIELD(1970, Brit.); HOFFMAN(1970, Brit.); TERROR FROM UNDER THE HOUSE(1971, Brit.); DEVIL'S WIDOW, THE(1972, Brit.); LAST REMAKE OF BEAU GESTE, THE(1977)

Sorcha Cusack
HITCH IN TIME, A(1978, Brit.)

Joseph Cusanelli
HOODLUM PRIEST, THE(1961)

Pete Cusanelli
UP IN ARMS(1944)

Peter Cusanelli
KISMET(1944); BELL FOR ADANO, A(1945); DAKOTA(1945); SARATOGA TRUNK(1945); SONG TO REMEMBER, A(1945); TAHITI NIGHTS(1945); TREE GROWS IN BROOKLYN, A(1945); DARK CORNER, THE(1946); IDEA GIRL(1946); CALCUTTA(1947); LADY FROM SHANGHAI, THE(1948); LOVES OF CARMEN, THE(1948)

Isabel Cushin
UNION STATION(1950); SON OF PALEFACE(1952)
Bartley Cushing
Misc. Silents
FALL OF A NATION, THE(1916), d
Catherine Chisholm Cushing
PRINCE AND THE PAUPER, THE(1937), w
Silents
POLLYANNA(1920), w; DON'T CALL ME LITTLE GIRL(1921), w
Harry Cushing
LADY FRANKENSTEIN(1971, Ital.), p
Peter Cushing
MAN IN THE IRON MASK, THE(1939); CHUMP AT OXFORD, A(1940); LAD-DIE(1940); VIGIL IN THE NIGHT(1940); WOMEN IN WAR(1940); HAMLET(1948, Brit.); MOULIN ROUGE(1952); BLACK KNIGHT, THE(1954); END OF THE AFFAIR, THE(1955, Brit.); ALEXANDER THE GREAT(1956); MAGIC FIRE(1956); ABOMINA-BLE SNOWMAN OF THE HIMALAYAS, THE(1957, Brit.); CURSE OF FRANKEN-STEIN, THE(1957, Brit.); TIME WITHOUT PITY(1957, Brit.); HORROR OF DRACULA, THE(1958, Brit.); REVENGE OF FRANKENSTEIN, THE(1958, Brit.); VIOLENT PLAYGROUND(1958, Brit.); HOUND OF THE BASKERVILLES, THE(1959, Brit.); JOHN PAUL JONES(1959); MUMMY, THE(1959, Brit.); BRIDES OF DRACULA, THE(1960, Brit.); MANIA(1961, Brit.); NAKED EDGE, THE(1961); RISK, THE(1961, Brit.); SWORD OF SHERWOOD FOREST(1961, Brit.); TROUBLE IN THE SKY(1961, Brit.); CASH ON DEMAND(1962, Brit.); NIGHT CREATURES(1962, Brit.); FURY AT SMUGGLERS BAY(1963, Brit.); HELLFIRE CLUB, THE(1963, Brit.); EVIL OF FRAN-KENSTEIN, THE(1964, Brit.); GORGON, THE(1964, Brit.); DR. TERROR'S HOUSE OF HORRORS(1965, Brit.); DR. WHO AND THE DALEKS(1965, Brit.); FRANKENSTEIN CREATED WOMAN(1965, Brit.); SHE(1965, Brit.); SKULL, THE(1965, Brit.); DALEKS–INVASION EARTH 2155 A.D.(1966, Brit.); BLOOD BEAST TERROR, THE(1967, Brit.); ISLAND OF TERROR(1967, Brit.); MAN WHO FINALLY DIED, THE(1967, Brit.); SOME MAY LIVE(1967, Brit.); CORRUPTION(1968, Brit.); TORTURE GARDEN(1968, Brit.); FRANKENSTEIN MUST BE DESTROYED!(1969, Brit.); INCENSE FOR THE DAMNED(1970, Brit.); ONE MORE TIME(1970, Brit.); SCREAM AND SCREAM AGAIN(1970, Brit.); VAMPIRE LOVERS, THE(1970, Brit.); HOUSE THAT DRIPPED BLOOD, THE(1971, Brit.); I, MONSTER(1971, Brit.); ISLAND OF THE BURNING DAMNED(1971, Brit.); TWINS OF EVIL(1971, Brit.); ASYLUM(1972, Brit.); DOCTOR PHIBES RISES AGAIN(1972, Brit.); DRACULA A.D. 1972(1972, Brit.); FEAR IN THE NIGHT(1972, Brit.); HORROR EXPRESS(1972, Span./Brit.); TALES FROM THE CRYPT(1972, Brit.); AND NOW THE SCREAMING STARTS(1973, Brit.); CREEPING FLESH,THE(1973, Brit.); BEAST MUST DIE, THE(1974, Brit.); FRANKENSTEIN AND THE MONSTER FROM HELL(1974, Brit.); FROM BEYOND THE GRAVE(1974, Brit.); MADHOUSE(1974, Brit.); GHOUL, THE(1975, Brit.); NOTHING BUT THE NIGHT(1975, Brit.); AT THE EARTH'S CORE(1976, Brit.); CALL HIM MR. SHAT-TER(1976, Hong Kong); DIRTY KNIGHT'S WORK(1976, Brit.); LAND OF THE MINOTAUR(1976, Gr.); SHOCK WAVES(1977); STAR WARS(1977); UNCANNY, THE(1977, Brit./Can.); COUNT DRACULA AND HIS VAMPIRE BRIDE(1978, Brit.); DRACULA AND THE SEVEN GOLDEN VAMPIRES(1978, Brit./Chi.); ARABIAN ADVENTURE(1979, Brit.); MONSTER ISLAND(1981, Span./U.S.); HOUSE OF LONG SHADOWS, THE(1983, Brit.)
1984
SWORD OF THE VALIANT(1984, Brit.); TOP SECRET!(1984)
Misc. Talkies
LEGEND OF THE WEREWOLF(1974); TENDER DRACULA OR CONFESSIONS OF A BLOOD DRINKER(1974, Fr.)
Roy Cushing
Silents
EASY GOING GORDON(1925)
Tom Cushing
SOUTH SEA ROSE(1929), w
Silents
ANNEXING BILL(1918), w; BLOOD AND SAND(1922), w; LAUGH, CLOWN, LAUGH(1928), w
Winifred Cushing
LITTLE FUGITIVE, THE(1953)
Elinor Cushingham
PAT AND MIKE(1952)
Jack Cushingham
TENDER FLESH(1976), p
John H. Cushingham
EXTRAORDINARY SEAMAN, THE(1969), p; QUACKSER FORTUNE HAS A COUS-IN IN THE BRONX(1970), p
Clarissa Fairchild Cushman
YOUNG WIDOW(1946), w
Dan Cushman
TIMBERJACK(1955), w; STAY AWAY, JOE(1968), w
Nancy Cushman
SWIMMER, THE(1968)
Ralph Cushman
SECRET FILE: HOLLYWOOD(1962), d; VARAN THE UNBELIEVABLE(1962, U.S./Jap.), ed; MOONWOLF(1966, Fin./Ger.), ed
Scott Cushman
ENDLESS LOVE(1981)
Stephanie Cushna
DEMONS OF LUDLOW, THE(1983)
Fay Cusic
Misc. Silents
CHIMES, THE(1914)
Dorian Cusick
WAY WE WERE, THE(1973)
Fay Cusick
Misc. Silents
YELLOW TRAFFIC, THE(1914)
Faye Cusick
Misc. Silents
MYSTERY OF EDWIN DROOD, THE(1914)
Jeannie Cusick
LEGACY OF BLOOD(1978)
Misc. Talkies
LEGACY OF HORROR(1978)

Peter Cusick
LONG DARK HALL, THE(1951, Brit.), p; PARDON MY FRENCH(1951, U.S./Fr.), p
George Cusin
CONFESSIONS OF A ROGUE(1948, Fr.)
Georges Cusin
BACK TO THE WALL(1959, Fr.)
Ricardo Cusiolla
BORSALINO AND CO.(1974, Fr.)
Louise Cussing
Misc. Silents
VIRGIN'S SACRIFICE, A(1922)
Clive Cussler
RAISE THE TITANIC(1980, Brit.), w
Danielle Cusson
STILL OF THE NIGHT(1982)
Bob Custer
COVERED WAGON TRAILS(1930); HEADIN' FOR TROUBLE(1931); LAW OF THE RIO GRANDE(1931); SON OF THE PLAINS(1931); UNDER TEXAS SKIES(1931); SCARLET BRAND(1932); AMBUSH VALLEY(1936)
Misc. Talkies
QUICK TRIGGER LEE(1931); MARK OF THE SPUR(1932); VENGEANCE OF RANNAH(1936); SANTA FE RIDES(1937)
Silents
MAN OF NERVE, A(1925); DUDE COWBOY, THE(1926); FIGHTING BOOB, THE(1926); HAIR TRIGGER BAXTER(1926); VALLEY OF BRAVERY, THE(1926); BULLDOG PLUCK(1927); TERROR OF BAR X, THE(1927); ARIZONA DAYS(1928); LAW OF THE MOUNTED(1928); MANHATTAN COWBOY(1928); ON THE DIVI-DE(1928); WEST OF SANTA FE(1928); FIGHTING TERROR, THE(1929); HEADIN' WESTWARD(1929); LAST ROUNDUP, THE(1929); OKLAHOMA KID, THE(1929); RIDERS OF THE RIO GRANDE(1929)
Misc. Silents
FLASHING SPURS(1924); TRIGGER FINGER(1924); BLOODHOUND, THE(1925); GALLOPING VENGENCE(1925); NO MAN'S LAW(1925); RANGE TERROR, THE(1925); RIDIN' STREAK, THE(1925); TEXAS BEARCAT, THE(1925); THAT MAN JACK!(1925); BEYOND THE ROCKIES(1926); BORDER WHIRLWIND, THE(1926); DEAD LINE, THE(1926); DEVIL'S GULCH, THE(1926); MAN RUSTLIN'(1926); CAC-TUS TRAILS(1927); FIGHTING HOMBRE, THE(1927); GALLOPING THUNDER(1927); SILENT TRAIL(1928); TEXAS TOMMY(1928); CODE OF THE WEST(1929); COVERED WAGON TRAILS(1930); O'MALLEY RIDES ALONE(1930); PARTING OF THE TRAILS(1930)
Bob Custer [Raymond Glenn]
RIDERS OF THE NORTH(1931)
Donnabella Custer
Silents
GOLD RUSH, THE(1925)
Edward Custiss
FAT MAN, THE(1951), ed
Ana Maria Custodio
GUNFIGHTERS OF CASA GRANDE(1965, U.S./Span.)
Mario Custudio
Misc. Talkies
BLACK PEARL, THE(1977)
Peter Custulovich
HAPPY DAYS(1930)
Rudolph Cusumano
SECRET FILE: HOLLYWOOD(1962), p; WILD ONES ON WHEELS(1967), d
C. J. Cutcliffe-Hyne
Silents
ADVENTURES OF CAPTAIN KETTLE, THE(1922, Brit.), w
Lou Cutell
FRANKENSTEIN MEETS THE SPACE MONSTER(1965); LITTLE BIG MAN(1970); EVERY LITTLE CROOK AND NANNY(1972); RHINOCEROS(1974); YOUNG FRAN-KENSTEIN(1974); WORLD'S GREATEST LOVER, THE(1977); SHOOT THE MOON(1982)
Count Cutelli
OBLIGING YOUNG LADY(1941)
Louis Cutelli
SHE'S WORKING HER WAY THROUGH COLLEGE(1952)
Rene Cutford
QUEEN'S GUARDS, THE(1963, Brit.)
Phil Cuthbert
ROBERTA(1935)
Tony Cuthbert
YELLOW SUBMARINE(1958, Brit.), animation
Winslow Cuthbert
CHARTROOSE CABOOSE(1960)
Allan Cuthberton
BRAIN, THE(1965, Ger./Brit.); BODY STEALERS, THE(1969)
Alan Cuthbertson
ASSAULT(1971, Brit.)
Allan Cuthbertson
HELL, HEAVEN OR HOBOKEN(1958, Brit.); COURT MARTIAL(1954, Brit.); DOU-BLE CROSS(1956, Brit.); EYEWITNESS(1956, Brit.); MAN WHO NEVER WAS, THE(1956, Brit.); POSTMARK FOR DANGER(1956, Brit.); NOVEL AFFAIR, A(1957, Brit.); OPERATION CONSPIRACY(1957, Brit.); DESERT ATTACK(1958, Brit.); LAW AND DISORDER(1958, Brit.); CROWNING TOUCH, THE(1959, Brit.); ROOM AT THE TOP(1959, Brit.); SHAKE HANDS WITH THE DEVIL(1959, Ireland); KILLERS OF KILIMANJARO(1960, Brit.); STRANGLERS OF BOMBAY, THE(1960, Brit.); TUNES OF GLORY(1960, Brit.); GUNS OF NAVARONE, THE(1961); MAN AT THE CARLTON TOWER(1961, Brit.); ON THE DOUBLE(1961); BOYS, THE(1962, Brit.); FREUD(1962); TERM OF TRIAL(1962, Brit.); BITTER HARVEST(1963, Brit.); FAST LADY, THE(1963, Brit.); MOUSE ON THE MOON, THE(1963, Brit.); NINE HOURS TO RAMA(1963, U.S./Brit.); RUNNING MAN, THE(1963, Brit.); SEVENTH DAWN, THE(1964); TAMA-HINE(1964, Brit.); GAME FOR THREE LOSERS(1965, Brit.); LIFE AT THE TOP(1965, Brit.); OPERATION CROSSBOW(1965, U.S./Ital.); UNDERWORLD INFORMERS(1965, Brit.); CAST A GIANT SHADOW(1966); PRESS FOR TIME(1966, Brit.); SOLO FOR SPARROW(1966, Brit.); HALF A SIXPENCE(1967, Brit.); MALPAS MYSTERY, THE(1967, Brit.); THOSE FANTASTIC FLYING FOOLS(1967, Brit); CAPTAIN NEMO AND THE UNDERWATER CITY(1969, Brit.); SINFUL DAVEY(1969, Brit.); TRYGON FACTOR, THE(1969, Brit.); ADVENTURERS, THE(1970); FIRECHASERS, THE(1970,

Brit.); ONE MORE TIME(1970, Brit.); HOPSCOTCH(1980); MIRROR CRACK'D, THE(1980, Brit.); OUTSIDER, THE(1980); SEA WOLVES, THE(1981, Brit.)

Iain Cuthbertson
RAILWAY CHILDREN, THE(1971, Brit.)

Adele Cutler
WORDS AND MUSIC(1929)

Barry Cutler
LASERBLAST(1978)
1984
BAD MANNERS(1984)

Bernie Cutler
SMOKEY AND THE BANDIT II(1980), art d; PENNIES FROM HEAVEN(1981), art d; D.C. CAB(1983), art d

Brian Cutler
CONCORDE, THE–AIRPORT '79(; CATALINA CAPER, THE(1967); TOP OF THE HEAP(1972); FURTHER ADVENTURES OF THE WILDERNESS FAMILY–PART TWO(1978)

Bunty Cutler
NEW MOON(1940); POSSESSED(1947); UNSUSPECTED, THE(1947); VOICE OF THE TURTLE, THE(1947)

Cheryl Cutler
1984
REPO MAN(1984), set d

Eddie Cutler
COVER GIRL(1944); EASY TO LOOK AT(1945); ON STAGE EVERYBODY(1945); WONDER MAN(1945); KID FROM BOOKLYN, THE(1946)

Edward Cutler
TAKE ME OUT TO THE BALL GAME(1949)

Ian Cutler
WICKER MAN, THE(1974, Brit.)

Ivor Cutler
IT'S ALL OVER TOWN(1963, Brit.)

Jon Cutler
NEW YORK, NEW YORK(1977); HOMETOWN U.S.A.(1979)

Julie Cutler
HARD KNOCKS(1980, Aus.), cos

Kate Cutler
DARK RED ROSES(1930, Brit.); SUCH IS THE LAW(1930, Brit.); GREAT GAY ROAD, THE(1931, Brit.); WEDDING REHEARSAL(1932, Brit.); LORD OF THE MANOR(1933, Brit.); THAT'S A GOOD GIRL(1933, Brit.); BLACK MASK(1935, Brit.); COME OUT OF THE PANTRY(1935, Brit.); I STAND CONDEMNED(1936, Brit.); ACTION FOR SLANDER(1937, Brit.); PERFECT CRIME, THE(1937, Brit.); PYGMALION(1938, Brit.); WHEN KNIGHTS WERE BOLD(1942, Brit.)

Kenneth Cutler
WEEKEND AT THE WALDORF(1945); LADY GAMBLES, THE(1949)

Lester Cutler
GALLANT LADY(1942), p; NIGHT FOR CRIME, A(1942), p; PANTHER'S CLAW, THE(1942), p; PRISON GIRL(1942), p; YANKS ARE COMING, THE(1942), p; MAN OF COURAGE(1943), p; SWEETHEARTS OF THE U.S.A.(1944), p

Ron Cutler
WILLIE DYNAMITE(1973), w

Vic Cutler
CANYON PASSAGE(1946); MAN FROM TEXAS, THE(1948)

Victor Cutler
CAUGHT IN THE DRAFT(1941); MADEMOISELLE FIFI(1944); MY PAL, WOLF(1944); WALK IN THE SUN, A(1945); BEST YEARS OF OUR LIVES, THE(1946); KID FROM BOOKLYN, THE(1946); T-MEN(1947); CANON CITY(1948)

Wendy Cutler
GOODBYE GIRL, THE(1977); I'M DANCING AS FAST AS I CAN(1982)

Sid Cutner
GUNSMOKE IN TUCSON(1958), m

Sidney B. Cutner
HOLD BACK TOMORROW(1955), m

Sidney Cutner
CITY STREETS(1931), m; RIDERS OF THE WHISTLING SKULL(1937), m; HOLIDAY(1938), m; GUN CRAZY(1949), md; THOSE REDHEADS FROM SEATTLE(1953), m

Joel Cutrara
1984
SCREAM FOR HELP(1984)

Vic Cutrier
HOT CARS(1956)

Claudio Cutry
SALAMANDER, THE(1983, U.S./Ital./Brit.), ed
1984
HUNDRA(1984, Ital.), ed; YELLOW HAIR AND THE FORTRESS OF GOLD(1984), ed

Mike Cutt
Misc. Talkies
NIGHT OF THE DEMON(1980)

Tim Cutt
NEW YEAR'S EVIL(1980)
1984
ALLEY CAT(1984)

Lou Cuttell
BLACK MARBLE, THE(1980)

Frank Cutter
Silents
WEB OF THE LAW, THE(1923)

Fred Cutter
SATAN'S MISTRESS(1982), art d

Murray Cutter
MARA MARU(1952), md; SPRINGFIELD RIFLE(1952), md; MAJORITY OF ONE, A(1961), md

Rex Cutter
HARRY'S WAR(1981)

B. Cutterr
POCKET MONEY(1972)

Dick [Richard H.] Cutting
LAW AND ORDER(1953); CHICAGO SYNDICATE(1955); GUN THAT WON THE WEST, THE(1955); YOU'RE NEVER TOO YOUNG(1955); WORLD WAS HIS JURY, THE(1958)

Justine Cutting
Misc. Silents
MAN'S WOMAN(1917); SELF MADE WIDOW(1917); WOMAN ALONE, A(1917)

Richard Cutting
YOU CAN'T RUN AWAY FROM IT(1956); CITY OF BAD MEN(1953); GREAT JESSE JAMES RAID, THE(1953); WAR PAINT(1953); BLACK WIDOW(1954); DRIVE A CROOKED ROAD(1954); DRUM BEAT(1954); LAW VS. BILLY THE KID, THE(1954); SHIELD FOR MURDER(1954); GOOD MORNING, MISS DOVE(1955); LEFT HAND OF GOD, THE(1955); PRINCE OF PLAYERS(1955); SEMINOLE UPRISING(1955); SHOTGUN(1955); EDDY DUCHIN STORY, THE(1956); ATTACK OF THE CRAB MONSTERS(1957); GIRL IN BLACK STOCKINGS(1957); MONOLITH MONSTERS, THE(1957); NIGHT RUNNER, THE(1957); ROCK ALL NIGHT(1957); STORY OF MANKIND, THE(1957); TEENAGE DOLL(1957); TOP SECRET AFFAIR(1957); WAR DRUMS(1957); LAST OF THE FAST GUNS, THE(1958); RIDE A CROOKED TRAIL(1958); SOUTH PACIFIC(1958); HORSE SOLDIERS, THE(1959); GUNFIGHTERS OF ABILENE(1960); RAIDERS, THE(1964); RIDE TO HANGMAN'S TREE, THE(1967)

Richard H. Cutting
MAGNIFICENT OBSESSION(1954); TAZA, SON OF COCHISE(1954); PRIVATE WAR OF MAJOR BENSON, THE(1955); MOUNTAIN, THE(1956); OUTSIDE THE LAW(1956); SHOWDOWN AT ABILENE(1956); FEMALE ANIMAL, THE(1958)

Dale Cutts
DOVE, THE(1974, Brit.); SPOTS ON MY LEOPARD, THE(1974, S. Africa); KILLER FORCE(1975, Switz./Ireland)

Graham Cutts
RETURN OF THE RAT, THE(1929, Brit.), d; LOOKING ON THE BRIGHT SIDE(1932, Brit.), d; LOVE ON THE SPOT(1932, Brit.), d; SIGN OF FOUR, THE(1932, Brit.), d; THREE MEN IN A BOAT(1933, Brit.), d; CAR OF DREAMS(1935, Brit.), d; OH DADDY!(1935, Brit.), d; AREN'T MEN BEASTS?(1937, Brit.), d; LET'S MAKE A NIGHT OF IT(1937, Brit.), d; OVER SHE GOES(1937, Brit.), d; JUST WILLIAM(1939, Brit.), d
Silents
FLAMES OF PASSION(1922, Brit.), d; PADDY, THE NEXT BEST THING(1923, Brit.), d; PASSIONATE ADVENTURE, THE(1924, Brit.), d; PRUDES FALL, THE(1924, Brit.), d; RAT, THE(1925, Brit.), d&w
Misc. Silents
WHILE LONDON SLEEPS(1922, Brit.), d; WOMAN TO WOMAN(1923, Brit.), d; WHITE SHADOWS(1924, Brit.), d; SEA URCHIN, THE(1926, Brit.), d; TRIUMPH OF THE RAT, THE(1926, Brit.), d; CONFETTI(1927, Brit.), d; FORBIDDEN LOVE(1927, Brit.), d; ROLLING ROAD, THE(1927), d; GLORIOUS YOUTH(1928, Brit.), d; GOD'S CLAY(1928, Brit.), d

John Cutts
LAST AMERICAN HERO, THE(1973), p; GOIN' COCONUTS(1978), p

Olan Soule Cutts
NORTH BY NORTHWEST(1959)

Patricia Cutts
JUST WILLIAM'S LUCK(1948, Brit.); ADVENTURES OF PC 49, THE(1949, Brit.); MADNESS OF THE HEART(1949, Brit.); THOSE PEOPLE NEXT DOOR(1952, Brit.); GENIE, THE(1953, Brit.); HAPPINESS OF THREE WOMEN, THE(1954, Brit.); MAN WHO LOVED REDHEADS, THE(1955, Brit.); MERRY ANDREW(1958); BATTLE OF THE CORAL SEA(1959); TINGLER, THE(1959)

Cutty
FREUD(1962)

Charley Cuva
PUT UP OR SHUT UP(1968, Arg.), m; PUTNEY SWOPE(1969), m

Frank Cuva
HAREM BUNCH; OR WAR AND PIECE, THE(1969)
Misc. Talkies
PSYCHO LOVER(1969, Brit.)

Marcel Cuvelier
DOULOS–THE FINGER MAN(1964, Fr./Ital.); LA GUERRE EST FINIE(1967, Fr./Swed.); WANDERER, THE(1969, Fr.); CONFESSION, THE(1970, Fr.)

Yvette Cuvelier
GERVAISE(1956, Fr.)

Marcel Cuvilier
KAMOURASKA(1973, Can./Fr.)

Marcel Cuvillier
STAVISKY(1974, Fr.)

Andre Cuyas
MESSAGE TO GARCIA, A(1936); THAT NIGHT IN RIO(1941)

Frances Cuyler
Silents
PEEP BEHIND THE SCENES, A(1929, Brit.)
Misc. Silents
BONDMAN, THE(1929, Brit.); WOMAN FROM CHINA, THE(1930, Brit.)

Sam Cuzelin
LEFT-HANDED WOMAN, THE(1980, Ger.)

Matt Cvetic
I WAS A COMMUNIST FOR THE F.B.I.(1951), w

Svetozar Cvetkovic
MONTENEGRO(1981, Brit./Swed.)

Jiri Cvrcek
CLOSELY WATCHED TRAINS(1967, Czech.), set d

Miroslav Cvrk
INTIMATE LIGHTING(1969, Czech.)

Victor Cwai
PENNYWHISTLE BLUES, THE(1952, South Africa)

M. Cwinklinska
BORDER STREET(1950, Pol.)

Charles Cybbers
VIGILANTE FORCE(1976)

Christine Cybelle
TORTURE ME KISS ME(1970)

Roxanne Cybelle
1984
 NIGHT PATROL(1984)
Zbigniew Cybulski
 EIGHTH DAY OF THE WEEK, THE(1959, Pol./Ger.); ASHES AND DIAMONDS(1961, Pol.); DOLL, THE(1962, Fr.); LOVE AT TWENTY(1963, Fr./Ital./Jap./Pol./Ger.); TO LOVE(1964, Swed.); SALTO(1966, Pol.); JOVITA(1970, Pol.); SARAGOSSA MANUSCRIPT, THE(1972, Pol.)
Cyclone
Silents
 LITTLE WILD GIRL, THE(1928)
Cyclone the Horse
 WILD HORSE RODEO(1938)
Maria Cyliakus
 LES ENFANTS TERRIBLES(1952, Fr.)
Cynthia Cypert
 STING II, THE(1983)
Chuck Cypher
 TRUCK TURNER(1974)
John Cypher
 FOOD OF THE GODS, THE(1976)
Jon Cypher
 BELIEVE IN ME(1971); VALDEZ IS COMING(1971); BLADE(1973); LADY ICE(1973); MEMORY OF US(1974); KINGFISH CAPER, THE(1976, South Africa)
Charles Cyphers
 ASSAULT ON PRECINCT 13(1976); MAC ARTHUR(1977); COMING HOME(1978); HALLOWEEN(1978); FORCE OF ONE, A(1979); BORDERLINE(1980); FOG, THE(1980); ESCAPE FROM NEW YORK(1981); HALLOWEEN II(1981); DEATH WISH II(1982); HONKYTONK MAN(1982)
Rose Cypress
 STUDENT TEACHERS, THE(1973)
A. Cyran
 LOVE WAGER, THE(1933, Brit.), d
Cyrielle
 BEAUTIFUL PRISONER, THE(1983, Fr.)
Andrea Cyrill
 THIS IS ELVIS(1982)
The Cyrkle
 MINX, THE(1969)
Tony Cyrus
 LIGHT AT THE EDGE OF THE WORLD, THE(1971, U.S./Span./Lichtenstein); TOWN CALLED HELL, A(1971, Span./Brit.)
1984
 SCREAM FOR HELP(1984)
Morris Cytron
Silents
 PENNINGTON'S CHOICE(1915)
Shirley Cytron
 MAJORITY OF ONE, A(1961); TWO FOR THE SEESAW(1962)
Nancy Czar
 WILD GUITAR(1962); WHAT'S UP FRONT(1964); WINTER A GO-GO(1965); WILD SCENE, THE(1970)
Czarmiak
 DEAR DETECTIVE(1978, Fr.)
Henri Czarniak
 LADY IN THE CAR WITH GLASSES AND A GUN, THE(1970, U.S./Fr.); LEGEND OF FRENCHIE KING, THE(1971, Fr./Ital./Span./Brit.)
Henry Czarniak
 BIRDS COME TO DIE IN PERU(1968, Fr.); VERY CURIOUS GIRL, A(1970, Fr.); LOVE AND DEATH(1975)
Mieczyslaw Czechowicz
 YELLOW SLIPPERS, THE(1965, Pol.); TIN DRUM, THE(1979, Ger./Fr./Yugo./Pol.)
Tadeusz Czechowski
 CONDUCTOR, THE(1981, Pol.)
P. Czeike
 VIENNA WALTZES(1961, Aust.)
Andrzej Czekalski
 EVE WANTS TO SLEEP(1961, Pol.), w
Eva Czemeys
 WOMEN IN CELL BLOCK 7(1977, Ital./U.S.)
Margit Czenki
 GERMAN SISTERS, THE(1982, Ger.)
F. Czepa
 VIENNA WALTZES(1961, Aust.)
Friedl Czepa
 EPISODE(1937, Aust.)
Henry Czerniak
 OPERATION THUNDERBOLT(1978, ISRAEL)
Edward Czerniuk
 ROCKET ATTACK, U.S.A.(1961)
Fr. Czerny
 INSPECTOR GENERAL, THE(1937, Czech.)
Ludwig Czerny
Misc. Silents
 BEYOND THE RIVER(1922, Ger.), d
Peter Czerski
1984
 HEY BABE!(1984, Can.), ph
Czerwonsky
 TRUNKS OF MR. O.F., THE(1932, Ger.), set d
Erich Czerwonsky
 TRUNKS OF MR. O.F., THE(1932, Ger.), art d
Prof. Czettell
 PYGMALION(1938, Brit.), cos
Peter Czeyke
 NO TIME FOR FLOWERS(1952)
Cynthia Czigeti
1984
 REPO MAN(1984)

Gustave Czimeg
Silents
 PASSION(1920, Ger.)
Zsuzsa Czinkoczi
1984
 DIARY FOR MY CHILDREN(1984, Hung.)
Paul Czinner
 WAY OF LOST SOULS, THE(1929, Brit.), d; WOMAN HE SCORNED, THE(1930, Brit.), d, w; ARIANE(1931, Ger.), d, w; ARIANE, RUSSIAN MAID(1932, Fr.), d&w; CATHERINE THE GREAT(1934, Brit.), d; ESCAPE ME NEVER(1935, Brit.), d; AS YOU LIKE IT(1936, Brit.), d; DREAMING LIPS(1937, Brit.), p, d; STOLEN LIFE(1939, Brit.), d; DON GIOVANNI(1955, Brit.), p, d; DREADING LIPS(1958, Ger.), w; ROMEO AND JULIET(1966, Brit.), p&d
Henryk Czyz
 EVE WANTS TO SLEEP(1961, Pol.), m
Elzbieta Czyzewska
 IDENTIFICATION MARKS: NONE(1969, Pol.); PUTNEY SWOPE(1969); WALKOVER(1969, Pol.); PASSENGER, THE(1970, Pol.); SARAGOSSA MANUSCRIPT, THE(1972, Pol.)
Stefan Czyzewski
 CAMERA BUFF(1983, Pol.)

D

Berta Dominguez D.
MAYA(1982), w
1984
WHERE IS PARSIFAL?(1984, Brit.), w
Harry D'Abbadie
Misc. Silents
SERENADE(1927), d; DRY MARTINI(1928), d
Ingram d'Abbes
BLUE SMOKE(1935, Brit.), w; LATE EXTRA(1935, Brit.), w; SPORTING LOVE(1936, Brit.), w; TERROR ON TIPTOE(1936, Brit.), w; BIG FELLA(1937, Brit.), w; LEAVE IT TO ME(1937, Brit.), w; AROUND THE TOWN(1938, Brit.), w; I'VE GOT A HORSE(1938, Brit.), w; SONG OF FREEDOM(1938, Brit.), w; HOME FROM HOME(1939, Brit.), w; LAUGHING LADY, THE(1950, Brit.), w
Guy D'Ablon
GREEN ROOM, THE(1979, Fr.)
Maryam D'Abo
XTRO(1983, Brit.)
1984
UNTIL SEPTEMBER(1984)
Mike D'Abo
THERE'S A GIRL IN MY SOUP(1970, Brit.), m
Olivia d'Abo
1984
BOLERO(1984); CONAN THE DESTROYER(1984)
Luciano D'Achille
TAKE A HARD RIDE(1975, U.S./Ital.), spec eff
Antonino D'Acquisto
STATUE, THE(1971, Brit.)
Francesco D'Adda
BREAD AND CHOCOLATE(1978, Ital.)
Michael D'Agosta
1984
RED DAWN(1984)
Al D'Agostino
FINISHING SCHOOL(1934), art d
Silents
SALVATION NELL(1921), art d; RAMONA(1928), art d
Albert D'Agostino
TODAY(1930), art d; GREAT EXPECTATIONS(1934), art d; DRACULA'S DAUGHTER(1936), art d; LOVE BEFORE BREAKFAST(1936), art d; GREAT GAMBINI, THE(1937), art d; SHE ASKED FOR IT(1937), art d; GLADIATOR, THE(1938), art d; PROFESSOR BEWARE(1938), art d; HIGHWAYS BY NIGHT(1942), art d; MEXICAN SPITFIRE SEES A GHOST(1942), art d; MEXICAN SPITFIRE'S ELEPHANT(1942), art d; FALLEN SPARROW, THE(1943), art d; GANGWAY FOR TOMORROW(1943), art d; I WALKED WITH A ZOMBIE(1943), art d; LEOPARD MAN, THE(1943), art d; TENDER COMRADE(1943), art d; FALCON IN HOLLYWOOD, THE(1944), art d; GILDERSLEEVE'S GHOST(1944), art d; MADEMOISELLE FIFI(1944), art d; MARINE RAIDERS(1944), art d; MASTER RACE, THE(1944), art d; NEVADA(1944), art d; MAN ALIVE(1945), art d; DEADLINE AT DAWN(1946), art d; DICK TRACY VS. CUEBALL(1946), art d; DING DONG WILLIAMS(1946), art d; FALCON'S ADVENTURE, THE(1946), art d; HONEYMOON(1947), art d; IF YOU KNEW SUSIE(1948), art d; INDIAN AGENT(1948), art d; ROUGHSHOD(1949), art d; WALK SOFTLY, STRANGER(1950), art d; WHITE TOWER, THE(1950), art d; WOMAN ON PIER 13, THE(1950), art d; HARD, FAST, AND BEAUTIFUL(1951), art d; HOT LEAD(1951), art d; ON THE LOOSE(1951), art d; OVERLAND TELEGRAPH(1951), art d; THING, THE(1951), art d; BIG SKY, THE(1952), art d; DEVIL'S CANYON(1953), art d; SPLIT SECOND(1953), art d; GLORY(1955), art d; GREAT DAY IN THE MORNING(1956), art d; UNHOLY WIFE, THE(1957), art d; YOUNG STRANGER, THE(1957), art d; PROFESSIONALS, THE(1966), art d
Albert S. D'Agostino
WITHOUT RESERVATIONS(1946), art d; THEY WON'T BELIEVE ME(1947), art d; SHE GOES TO WAR(1929), art d; MYSTERY OF EDWIN DROOD, THE(1935), art d; RAVEN, THE(1935), art d; WEREWOLF OF LONDON, THE(1935), art d; THE INVISIBLE RAY(1936), art d; TWO IN A CROWD(1936), art d; UNEXPECTED UNCLE(1941), art d; FALCON TAKES OVER, THE(1942), art d; FALCON'S BROTHER, THE(1942), art d; GREAT GILDERSLEEVE, THE(1942), art d; JOAN OF PARIS(1942), art d; JOURNEY INTO FEAR(1942), art d; MY FAVORITE SPY(1942), art d; ONCE UPON A HONEYMOON(1942), art d; PIRATES OF THE PRAIRIE(1942), art d; POWDER TOWN(1942), art d; SEVEN DAYS LEAVE(1942), art d; SEVEN MILES FROM ALCATRAZ(1942), art d; SYNCOPATION(1942), art d; AROUND THE WORLD(1943), art d; FALCON AND THE CO-EDS, THE(1943), art d; FALCON IN DANGER, THE(1943), art d; FALCON STRIKES BACK, THE(1943), art d; FIGHTING FRONTIER(1943), art d; FLIGHT FOR FREEDOM(1943), art d; FOREVER AND A DAY(1943), art d; GHOST SHIP, THE(1943), art d; GILDERSLEEVE ON BROADWAY(1943), art d; GILDERSLEEVE'S BAD DAY(1943), art d; GOVERNMENT GIRL(1943), art d; HIGHER AND HIGHER(1943), art d; IRON MAJOR, THE(1943), art d; LADIES' DAY(1943), art d; LADY TAKES A CHANCE, A(1943), art d; MEXICAN SPITFIRE'S BLESSED EVENT(1943), art d; MR. LUCKY(1943), art d; PETTICOAT LARCENY(1943), art d; ROOKIES IN BURMA(1943), art d; SEVENTH VICTIM, THE(1943), art d; SKY'S THE LIMIT, THE(1943), art d; THIS LAND IS MINE(1943), art d; EXPERIMENT PERILOUS(1944), art d; FALCON IN MEXICO, THE(1944), art d; FALCON OUT WEST, THE(1944), art d; GIRL RUSH(1944), art d; HEAVENLY DAYS(1944), art d; MUSIC IN MANHATTAN(1944), art d; MY PAL, WOLF(1944), art d; NIGHT OF ADVENTURE, A(1944), art d; NONE BUT THE LONELY HEART(1944), art d; PASSPORT TO DESTINY(1944), art d; SEVEN DAYS ASHORE(1944), art d; SHOW BUSINESS(1944), art d; STEP LIVELY(1944), art d; TALL IN THE SADDLE(1944), art d; YOUTH RUNS WILD(1944), art d; BACK TO BATAAN(1945), art d; BETRAYAL FROM THE EAST(1945), art d; BODY SNATCHER, THE(1945), art d; CHINA SKY(1945), art d; CORNERED(1945), art d; DICK TRACY(1945), art d; ENCHANTED COTTAGE, THE(1945), art d; FIRST YANK INTO TOKYO(1945), art d; GAME OF DEATH, A(1945), art d; GEORGE WHITE'S SCANDALS(1945), art d; HAVING WONDERFUL CRIME(1945), art d; ISLE OF THE DEAD(1945), art d; JOHNNY ANGEL(1945), art d; MAMA LOVES PAPA(1945), art d; MURDER, MY SWEET(1945), art d; RADIO STARS ON PARADE(1945), art d; SING YOUR WAY HOME(1945), art d; SPANISH MAIN, THE(1945), art d; THOSE ENDEARING YOUNG CHARMS(1945), art d; WANDERER OF THE WASTELAND(1945), art d; WEST OF THE PECOS(1945), art d; WHAT A BLONDE(1945), art d; ZOMBIES ON BROADWAY(1945), art d; BEDLAM(1946), art d; CRACK-UP(1946), art d; FALCON'S ALIBI, THE(1946), art d; FROM THIS DAY FORWARD(1946), art d; GENIUS AT WORK(1946), art d; LADY LUCK(1946), art d; LOCKET, THE(1946), art d; NOCTURNE(1946), art d; NOTORIOUS(1946), art d; RIVERBOAT RHYTHM(1946), art d; SISTER KENNY(1946), art d; SPIRAL STAIRCASE, THE(1946), art d; STEP BY STEP(1946), art d; SUNSET PASS(1946), art d; TILL THE END OF TIME(1946), art d; TRUTH ABOUT MURDER, THE(1946), art d; BACHELOR AND THE BOBBY-SOXER, THE(1947), art d; CROSSFIRE(1947), art d; DESPERATE(1947), art d; DICK TRACY MEETS GRUESOME(1947), art d; DICK TRACY'S DILEMMA(1947), art d; MOURNING BECOMES ELECTRA(1947), art d; NIGHT SONG(1947), art d; OUT OF THE PAST(1947), art d; RIFFRAFF(1947), art d; SEVEN KEYS TO BALDPATE(1947), art d; SINBAD THE SAILOR(1947), art d; THUNDER MOUNTAIN(1947), art d; TRAIL STREET(1947), art d; TYCOON(1947), art d; UNDER THE TONTO RIM(1947), art d; WILD HORSE MESA(1947), art d; WOMAN ON THE BEACH, THE(1947), art d; BERLIN EXPRESS(1948), art d; EVERY GIRL SHOULD BE MARRIED(1948), art d; FIGHTING FATHER DUNNE(1948), art d; I REMEMBER MAMA(1948), art d; MR. BLANDINGS BUILDS HIS DREAM HOUSE(1948), art d; RACE STREET(1948), art d; RACHEL AND THE STRANGER(1948), art d; RETURN OF THE BADMEN(1948), art d; STATION WEST(1948), art d; WESTERN HERITAGE(1948), art d; BRIDE FOR SALE(1949), art d; DANGEROUS PROFESSION, A(1949), art d; EASY LIVING(1949), art d; FOLLOW ME QUIETLY(1949), art d; HOLIDAY AFFAIR(1949), art d; JUDGE STEPS OUT, THE(1949), art d; MASKED RAIDERS(1949), art d; MYSTERIOUS DESPERADO, THE(1949), art d; RIDERS OF THE RANGE(1949), art d; RUSTLERS(1949), art d; SET-UP, THE(1949), art d; STAGECOACH KID(1949), art d; STRANGE BARGAIN(1949), art d; THEY LIVE BY NIGHT(1949), art d; THREAT, THE(1949), art d; WOMAN'S SECRET, A(1949), art d; DOUBLE DEAL(1950), art d; DYNAMITE PASS(1950), art d; GAMBLING HOUSE(1950), art d; HUNT THE MAN DOWN(1950), art d; LAW OF THE BADLANDS(1950), art d; NEVER A DULL MOMENT(1950), art d; RIDER FROM TUCSON(1950), art d; SECRET FURY, THE(1950), art d; STORM OVER WYOMING(1950), art d; WHERE DANGER LIVES(1950), art d; DOUBLE DYNAMITE(1951), art d; FLYING LEATHERNECKS(1951), art d; GUNPLAY(1951), art d; HIS KIND OF WOMAN(1951), art d; MY FORBIDDEN PAST(1951), art d; ON DANGEROUS GROUND(1951), art d; PAYMENT ON DEMAND(1951), art d; PISTOL HARVEST(1951), art d; RACKET, THE(1951), art d; ROADBLOCK(1951), art d; SADDLE LEGION(1951), art d; SEALED CARGO(1951), art d; TWO TICKETS TO BROADWAY(1951), art d; CLASH BY NIGHT(1952), art d; GIRL IN EVERY PORT, A(1952), art d; HALF-BREED, THE(1952), art d; LAS VEGAS STORY, THE(1952), art d; LUSTY MEN, THE(1952), art d; MACAO(1952), art d; NARROW MARGIN, THE(1952), art d; ONE MINUTE TO ZERO(1952), art d; PACE THAT THRILLS, THE(1952), art d; ROAD AGENT(1952), art d; TARGET(1952), art d; TRAIL GUIDE(1952), art d; ANGEL FACE(1953), art d; HITCH-HIKER, THE(1953), art d; SECOND CHANCE(1953), art d; DANGEROUS MISSION(1954), art d; FRENCH LINE, THE(1954), art d; SHE COULDN'T SAY NO(1954), art d; SON OF SINBAD(1955), art d; FIRST TRAVELING SALESLADY, THE(1956), art d; TENSION AT TABLE ROCK(1956), art d; GIRL MOST LIKELY, THE(1957), art d; JET PILOT(1957), art d; PUBLIC PIGEON NO. 1(1957), art d; RUN OF THE ARROW(1957), art d; I MARRIED A WOMAN(1958), art d
Alberto D'Agostino
DATE WITH THE FALCON, A(1941), art d; DEVIL THUMBS A RIDE, THE(1947), art d
Alberto S. D'Agostino
LIKELY STORY, A(1947), art d
Antonella D'Agostino
1984
JOKE OF DESTINY LYING IN WAIT AROUND THE CORNER LIKE A STREETBANDIT, A(1984, Ital.)
Bruno D'Agostino
SINGING TAXI DRIVER(1953, Ital.), w
Frank D'Agostino
QUICK AND THE DEAD, THE(1963)
Jean D'Agostino
RETURN OF THE JEDI(1983)
A. d'Aguiar
GOLGOTHA(1937, Fr.), p
Thelma d'Aguiar
CHASE A CROOKED SHADOW(1958, Brit.); MALAGA(1962, Brit.)
A. D'Aguilar
FORBIDDEN FRUIT(1959, Fr.), p
Pedro d'Aguillon
LIVING COFFIN, THE(1965, Mex.)
Thelma D'Aguir
ROMAN SPRING OF MRS. STONE, THE(1961, U.S./Brit.)
Cedric d'Ailly
LYDIA(1964, Can.), d
Alessandro D'Alatie
GARDEN OF THE FINZI-CONTINIS, THE(1976, Ital./Ger.)
Delia D'Alberti
HERCULES AGAINST THE MOON MEN(1965, Fr./Ital.)
Julian d'Albie
WELCOME, MR. WASHINGTON(1944, Brit.); GIRL IN A MILLION, A(1946, Brit.); SO WELL REMEMBERED(1947, Brit.); ESTHER WATERS(1948, Brit.); EDWARD, MY SON(1949, U.S./Brit.); NOW BARABBAS WAS A ROBBER(1949, Brit.); FIVE ANGLES ON MURDER(1950, Brit.); LADY WITH A LAMP, THE(1951, Brit.); TIME GENTLEMEN PLEASE!(1953, Brit.); SCOTCH ON THE ROCKS(1954, Brit.); ROOM IN THE HOUSE(1955, Brit.); CORRIDORS OF BLOOD(1962, Brit.); MAKE MINE A DOUBLE(1962, Brit.); ONE MORE TIME(1970, Brit.); RULING CLASS, THE(1972, Brit.)
Sid D'Albrook
BANK ALARM(1937); ARSENE LUPIN RETURNS(1938); YOU CAN'T TAKE IT WITH YOU(1938); OUR LEADING CITIZEN(1939); THIRD FINGER, LEFT HAND(1940); I MARRIED AN ANGEL(1942); MRS. MINIVER(1942); TAKE A LETTER, DARLING(1942); DESIRE ME(1947); SEA OF GRASS, THE(1947); JULIA MISBEHAVES(1948)
Sidney D'Albrook
BAT WHISPERS, THE(1930); MIDNIGHT MYSTERY(1930); JEALOUSY(1934); JOURNAL OF A CRIME(1934); TREASURE ISLAND(1934); MAID OF SALEM(1937); PRESCRIPTION FOR ROMANCE(1937); PERILS OF PAULINE, THE(1947); SAINTED SISTERS, THE(1948)

Angelo d'Angelo
BMX BANDITS(1983)

Beverly D'Angelo
ANNIE HALL(1977); FIRST LOVE(1977); SENTINEL, THE(1977); EVERY WHICH WAY BUT LOOSE(1978); HAIR(1979); COAL MINER'S DAUGHTER(1980); HONKY TONK FREEWAY(1981); PATERNITY(1981); NATIONAL LAMPOON'S VACATION(1983)
1984
FINDERS KEEPERS(1984); HIGHPOINT(1984, Can.)

Carlo D'Angelo
DEVIL'S COMMANDMENT, THE(1956, Ital.); HERCULES UNCHAINED(1960, Ital./Fr.); BATTLE OF THE WORLDS(1961, Ital.); DAVID AND GOLIATH(1961, Ital.); GREAT WAR, THE(1961, Fr., Ital.); QUEEN OF THE NILE(1964, Ital.); SECRET AGENT SUPER DRAGON(1966, Fr./Ital./Ger./Monaco)

Darlene D'Angelo
YOUNG WARRIORS(1983)

Gabriele D'Angelo
SUPERARGO VERSUS DIABOLICUS(1966, Ital./Span.), set d; FINE PAIR, A(1969, Ital.), set d

Mirella D'Angelo
SWORD OF THE CONQUEROR(1962, Ital.); HERCULES(1983)

Salvo d'Angelo
FABIOLA(1951, Ital.), p; BEAUTY AND THE DEVIL(1952, Fr./Ital.), p; FATHER'S DILEMMA(1952, Ital.), p

Yvonne D'Angers
MOVE(1970); SEVEN MINUTES, THE(1971)

Yvonne D'Angiers
GROUND ZERO(1973)

Salvo D'Anglo
LA TERRA TREMA(1947, Ital.), p

Frank D'Annibale
MAX DUGAN RETURNS(1983)

Gabriel D'Annunzio
CENTO ANNI D'AMORE(1954, Ital.), w

Gabriele d'Annunzio
INNOCENT, THE(1979, Ital.), w
Silents
CABIRIA(1914, Ital.), w

Lola D'Annunzio
WRONG MAN, THE(1956)

Frank D'Anolfo
SUN VALLEY SERENADE(1941)

Mary D'Antin
LONELY LADY, THE(1983)

Joanne D'Antone
SUMMERSPELL(1983), p

Philip D'Antoni
BULLITT(1968), p; FRENCH CONNECTION, THE(1971), p; SEVEN UPS, THE(1973), p&d

Carmen D'Antonio
DESTRY RIDES AGAIN(1939); ANGELS OVER BROADWAY(1940); LONG VOYAGE HOME, THE(1940); ROAD TO SINGAPORE(1940); ARABIAN NIGHTS(1942); CONEY ISLAND(1943); KISMET(1944); MASK OF DIMITRIOS, THE(1944); GOLDEN GIRL(1951); SALOME(1953); SINS OF JEZEBEL(1953); WORLD FOR RANSOM(1954); MARACAIBO(1958); TANK COMMANDOS(1959); CHEYENNE AUTUMN(1964)

Joanne D'Antonio
SATURDAY THE 14TH(1981), ed

Thelma D'Aquiar
WOMAN'S ANGLE, THE(1954, Brit.)

Diane D'Aquila
LAST CHASE, THE(1981)

Nazzareno D'Aquilio
SERAFINO(1970, Fr./Ital.)

Rossella D'Aquino
SEVEN SEAS TO CALAIS(1963, Ital.); MYTH, THE(1965, Ital.)

Lionel d'Aragon
BLOCKADE(1928, Brit.)
Silents
EUGENE ARAM(1914, Brit.); LONDON'S ENEMIES(1916, Brit.); LILY OF THE ALLEY(1923, Brit.); FLYING FIFTY-FIVE, THE(1924, Brit.); ADVENTUROUS YOUTH(1928, Brit.)
Misc. Silents
WRECKER OF LIVES, THE(1914, Brit.); SECRET SEVEN, THE(1915, Brit.); IN ANOTHER GIRL'S SHOES(1917, Brit.); SORROWS OF SATAN, THE(1917); GREAT IMPOSTER, THE(1918, Brit.); THEN YOU'LL REMEMBER ME(1918, Brit.); FIRST MEN IN THE MOON, THE(1919, Brit.); PALLARD THE PUNTER(1919, Brit.); SWORD OF FATE, THE(1921, Brit.); LOST LEADER, A(1922, Brit.); FAIR MAID OF PERTH, THE(1923, Brit.)

Patti D'Arbanville
L'AMOUR(1973); RANCHO DELUXE(1975); BIG WEDNESDAY(1978); MAIN EVENT, THE(1979); TIME AFTER TIME(1979, Brit.); FIFTH FLOOR, THE(1980); HOG WILD(1980, Can.); MODERN PROBLEMS(1981)

Giselle D'Arc
FOUR GIRLS IN TOWN(1956); JEANNE EAGELS(1957); PAL JOEY(1957); VOODOO WOMAN(1957)

Alex D'Arcy
SOLDIER OF FORTUNE(1955)

Alex D'Arcy
ANOTHER THIN MAN(1939); IRENE(1940); HOW TO MARRY A MILLIONAIRE(1953); MAN ON A TIGHTROPE(1953); VICKI(1953); ABDULLAH'S HAREM(1956, Brit./Egypt.); VICE DOLLS(1961, Fr.); IT'S HOT IN PARADISE(1962, Ger./Yugo.); FANNY HILL: MEMOIRS OF A WOMAN OF PLEASURE zero(1965); WAY...WAY OUT(1966); BLOOD OF DRACULA'S CASTLE(1967); ST. VALENTINE'S DAY MASSACRE, THE(1967); SEVEN MINUTES, THE(1971); DEAD PIGEON ON BEETHOVEN STREET(1972, Ger.)

Alexander D'Arcy
CARNIVAL IN FLANDERS(1936, Fr.); AWFUL TRUTH, THE(1937); PRISONER OF ZENDA, THE(1937); STOLEN HOLIDAY(1937); FLIGHT TO FAME(1938); SHE MARRIED AN ARTIST(1938); FIFTH AVENUE GIRL(1939); GOOD GIRLS GO TO PARIS(1939); THREE SONS(1939); TOPPER TAKES A TRIP(1939); CITY OF

CHANCE(1940); BLONDE FROM SINGAPORE, THE(1941); MARRIAGE IS A PRIVATE AFFAIR(1944)
Silents
PARADISE(1928, Brit.)

Alexandre D'Arcy
ROMANCE OF SEVILLE, A(1929, Brit.); A NOUS LA LIBERTE(1931, Fr.)

Andre d'Arcy
DREAM WIFE(1953); MA AND PA KETTLE ON VACATION(1953)

Camille D'Arcy
Misc. Silents
DAUGHTER OF THE CITY, A(1915); WHITE SISTER, THE(1915); PRINCE CHAP, THE(1916)

Emery D'Arcy
WHEN YOU'RE IN LOVE(1937)

Gene D'Arcy
MIAMI STORY, THE(1954); SARACEN BLADE, THE(1954); RACERS, THE(1955)

George D'Arcy
WHEN LONDON SLEEPS(1934, Brit.)

Harry D'Arcy
THEY WON'T BELIEVE ME(1947)

Jake D'Arcy
GREGORY'S GIRL(1982, Brit.)

Jan D'Arcy
WHY WOULD I LIE(1980)

Jeanne d'Arcy
JOY RIDE(1935, Brit.)

Jim D'Arcy
EXPLOSIVE GENERATION, THE(1961)

John D'Arcy
GRANDAD RUDD(1935, Aus.)

Margaret D'Arcy
SIEGE OF SIDNEY STREET, THE(1960, Brit.)

Pat D'Arcy
SON OF SINBAD(1955)

Peter D'Arcy
EASY MONEY(1983)

Robert D'Arcy
MAX DUGAN RETURNS(1983)

Roy D'Arcy
BLACK WATCH, THE(1929); LAST WARNING, THE(1929); BROADWAY TO CHEYENNE(1932); DISCARDED LOVERS(1932); FILE 113(1932); GAY BUCKAROO, THE(1932); LOVE BOUND(1932); SHERLOCK HOLMES(1932); FLYING DOWN TO RIO(1933); MAN FROM HELL, THE(1934); ORIENT EXPRESS(1934); SING AND LIKE IT(1934); KENTUCKY BLUE STREAK(1935); OUTLAWED GUNS(1935); CAPTAIN CALAMITY(1936); HOLLYWOOD BOULEVARD(1936); REVOLT OF THE ZOMBIES(1936); LEGION OF MISSING MEN(1937); UNDER STRANGE FLAGS(1937); CHASING DANGER(1939); STORY OF VERNON AND IRENE CASTLE, THE(1939)
Silents
MERRY WIDOW, THE(1925); PRETTY LADIES(1925); BEVERLY OF GRAUSTARK(1926); TEMPTRESS, THE(1926); ADAM AND EVIL(1927); ON ZE BOULEVARD(1927); ACTRESS, THE(1928); GIRLS GONE WILD(1929)
Misc. Silents
GRAUSTARK(1925); MASKED BRIDE, THE(1925); BARDELYS THE MAGNIFICENT(1926); MONTE CARLO(1926); VALENCIA(1926); ROAD TO ROMANCE, THE(1927); WINNERS OF THE WILDERNESS(1927); BEWARE OF BLONDES(1928); BEYOND THE SIERRAS(1928); DOMESTIC MEDDLERS(1928); RIDERS OF THE DARK(1928); WOMAN FROM HELL, THE(1929)

William D'Arcy
ONE OF OUR AIRCRAFT IS MISSING(1942, Brit.)

Yvonne D'Arcy
FRIENDS AND LOVERS(1931)

Nora d'Argel
TALKING FEET(1937, Brit.)

Ted D'Arms
JOYRIDE(1977); DOUBLES(1978); THE RUNNER STUMBLES(1979)

David D'Arnal
1984
IRRECONCILABLE DIFFERENCES(1984)

David D'Arnel
BOOGEYMAN II(1983)

Albert d'Arno
ARTISTS AND MODELS ABROAD(1938); MISSION TO MOSCOW(1943); THEY CAME TO BLOW UP AMERICA(1943); THIS LAND IS MINE(1943); 13 RUE MADELEINE(1946); FLIGHT TO TANGIER(1953); FUNNY FACE(1957); MR. SARDONICUS(1961)

Gustavo D'Arpe
SEDUCED AND ABANDONED(1964, Fr./Ital.); SERAFINO(1970, Fr./Ital.)

Harry D'Abbadie D'Arrast
LAUGHTER(1930), d, w; RAFFLES(1930), d; DIE MANNER UM LUCIE(1931), w; TOPAZE(1933), d
Silents
MAGNIFICENT FLIRT, THE(1928), d, w
Misc. Silents
GENTLEMAN OF PARIS, A(1927), d

Harry D'Arrast
Misc. Silents
SERVICE FOR LADIES(1927), d

Alfonso D'Artega
CARNEGIE HALL(1947)

D'Artega All-Girl Orchestra
YOU CAN'T RATION LOVE(1944)

Lena D'Arvil
Silents
INNOCENCE OF RUTH, THE(1916)

Collette d'Arville
TANGO BAR(1935)

Roger D'Ashelbe
ALGIERS(1938), w

Detective Roger d'Ashelbe [Henri La Barthe]
PEPE LE MOKO(1937, Fr.), w
Rocco D'Assunta
ANNA(1951, Ital.); SEDUCED AND ABANDONED(1964, Fr./Ital.); VERY HANDY MAN, A(1966, Fr./Ital.)
Solveig D'Assunta
VERY HANDY MAN, A(1966, Fr./Ital.)
Irene D'Astrea
DAY THE HOTLINE GOT HOT, THE(1968, Fr./Span.)
Giacomo D'Attino
Silents
WHITE SISTER, THE(1923)
Jean Gabriel d'Aubonne
BLOOD OF A POET, THE(1930, Fr.), art d
Denis d'Auborn
CHARGE OF THE LIGHT BRIGADE, THE(1936)
Denis d'Auburn
CAPTAIN BLOOD(1935); MARIE ANTOINETTE(1938); SUEZ(1938); RULERS OF THE SEA(1939); HUDSON'S BAY(1940)
Silents
KING OF KINGS, THE(1927)
Dennis d'Auburn
BODY AND SOUL(1931); UNFAITHFUL(1931); LOST HORIZON(1937); WATERLOO BRIDGE(1940)
Carrie D'Aumery
Silents
FORBIDDEN PARADISE(1924); LADY WINDERMERE'S FAN(1925)
Jacques D'Auray
Silents
FOUR HORSEMEN OF THE APOCALYPSE, THE(1921); MY AMERICAN WIFE(1923)
Rene D'Auriac
HUSBANDS(1970), art d; LADY LIBERTY(1972, Ital./Fr.), art d; GLORIA(1980), prod d
Massimo D'Avack
DETECTIVE BELLI(1970, Ital.), w
Andre D'Avant-Cour
RETURN OF MARTIN GUERRE, THE(1983, Fr.)
Alberto D'Aversa
VOICE IN YOUR HEART, A(1952, Ital.), d, w
Guy D'Avout
SECRET WORLD(1969, Fr.)
Jo D'Avra
LONGEST DAY, THE(1962)
Yola D'Avril
HOUSE OF HORROR(1929); LOVE PARADE, THE(1929); SHANGHAI LADY(1929); SHE GOES TO WAR(1929); ALL QUIET ON THE WESTERN FRONT(1930); BAD ONE, THE(1930); BORN RECKLESS(1930); FOX MOVIETONE FOLLIES OF 1930(1930); HOT FOR PARIS(1930); JUST LIKE HEAVEN(1930); THOSE THREE FRENCH GIRLS(1930); TRUTH ABOUT YOUTH, THE(1930); COMMON LAW, THE(1931); GOD'S GIFT TO WOMEN(1931); JUST A GIGOLO(1931); RIGHT OF WAY, THE(1931); SUICIDE FLEET(1931); WOMEN GO ON FOREVER(1931); BEAUTY AND THE BOSS(1932); COCK OF THE AIR(1932); MAN FROM YESTERDAY, THE(1932); PARISIAN ROMANCE, A(1932); PASSPORT TO HELL(1932); SCARLET DAWN(1932); SKY DEVILS(1932); GLAMOUR(1934); MONTE CARLO NIGHTS(1934); CAPTAIN BLOOD(1935); STRAIGHT FROM THE HEART(1935); UNGUARDED HOUR, THE(1936); I MET HIM IN PARIS(1937); GREEN HELL(1940); LADY HAS PLANS, THE(1942); NIGHT IN NEW ORLEANS, A(1942); NOW, VOYAGER(1942); RHAPSODY IN BLUE(1945); CLOAK AND DAGGER(1946); LITTLE BOY LOST(1953)
Silents
AMERICAN BEAUTY(1927); SMILE, BROTHER, SMILE(1927); TENDER HOUR, THE(1927); WAR HORSE, THE(1927); AWAKENING, THE(1928); LADY BE GOOD(1928); NOOSE, THE(1928); VAMPING VENUS(1928)
Misc. Silents
THREE-RING MARRIAGE(1928)
D'Dee
FIVE DAYS ONE SUMMER(1982), ch
1984
LE BAL(1984, Fr./Ital./Algeria), ch
D'Eaubonne
LA RONDE(1954, Fr.), set d
A.J. d'Eaubonne
RELUCTANT DEBUTANTE, THE(1958), art d
Jean D'Eaubonne
JUST ME(1950, Fr.), set d; ORPHEUS(1950, Fr.), art d; TALE OF FIVE WOMEN, A(1951, Brit.), art d; EARRINGS OF MADAME DE..., THE(1954, Fr.), set d; LE PLAISIR(1954, Fr.), art d; LOLA MONTES(1955, Fr./Ger.), art d; CRACK IN THE MIRROR(1960), art d; BIG GAMBLE, THE(1961), art d; DOUBLE DECEPTION(1963, Fr.), art d; LOVE IS A BALL(1963), art d; MADAME(1963, Fr./Ital./Span.), art d; MAGNIFICENT SINNER(1963, Fr.), art d; PARIS WHEN IT SIZZLES(1964), art d; LADY L(1965, Fr./Ital.), art d; MAN FROM THE CUSTER OF THE WEST(1968, U.S., Span.), art d; GIRL ON A MOTORCYCLE, THE(1968, Fr./Brit.), art d; JOHNNY BANCO(1969, Fr./Ital./Ger.), art d; ROAD TO SALINA(1971, Fr./Ital.), art d
Alan d'Egville
HIGHLAND FLING(1936, Brit.), w
Geraldo d'el Rey
GIVEN WORD, THE(1964, Braz.)
Henri D'Elba
Silents
ALIAS MARY BROWN(1918), d
Misc. Silents
MARKED CARDS(1918), d
Guy D'Emmery
MARIE ANTOINETTE(1938)
Adolphe D'Ennery
Silents
CELEBRATED CASE, A(1914), w

Frederick Guy D'Ennery
WIFE VERSUS SECRETARY(1936)
Guy D'Ennery
LIGHTS OF NEW YORK(1928); STAR WITNESS(1931); ANNA KARENINA(1935); ESPIONAGE(1937); FIREFLY, THE(1937); MAYTIME(1937); UNDER SUSPICION(1937); RAINS CAME, THE(1939); TRAPPED IN THE SKY(1939); COVERED WAGON DAYS(1940); EDISON, THE MAN(1940); MARK OF ZORRO, THE(1940); MEET THE WILDCAT(1940); MASKED RIDER, THE(1941); PRAIRIE PIONEERS(1941); CROSSROADS(1942); DRUMS OF FU MANCHU(1943); MADAME CURIE(1943); WHITE CLIFFS OF DOVER, THE(1944); WILSON(1944)
Silents
SILVER THREADS AMONG THE GOLD(1915)
June D'Eon
Silents
IS YOUR DAUGHTER SAFE?(1927)
Giovanni D'Eramo
300 SPARTANS, THE(1962), w
Didi D'Errico
1984
GARBO TALKS(1984)
Mimi d'Estee
WHISPERING CITY(1947, Can.)
Angel d'Esteffani
CURSE OF THE AZTEC MUMMY, THE(1965, Mex.); ROBOT VS. THE AZTEC MUMMY, THE(1965, Mex.)
Lisa d'Esterre
KNIGHT WITHOUT ARMOR(1937, Brit.)
Mme. d'Esterre
Silents
INNOCENT(1921, Brit.)
Mme. d'Esterre
Silents
PRESUMPTION OF STANLEY HAY, MP, THE(1925, Brit.)
Roberta D'Esti
MYSTERY SUBMARINE(1963, Brit.)
Tamara d'Etter
ROYAL DIVORCE, A(1938, Brit.)
Robert D'Ettore
TENTACLES(1977, Ital.), ph
Roberto D'Ettore
STARCRASH(1979), ph
Saverio D'Eugenio
PIRATE OF THE BLACK HAWK, THE(1961, Fr./Ital.), art d; LAST OF THE VIKINGS, THE(1962, Fr./Ital.), art d; KILL OR BE KILLED(1967, Ital.), art d; PAYMENT IN BLOOD(1968, Ital.), art d
Alessandro D'Eva
NUDE ODYSSEY(1962, Fr./Ital.), ph
Sandro D'Eva
LET'S TALK ABOUT WOMEN(1964, Fr./Ital.), ph; ONE MILLION DOLLARS(1965, Ital.), ph; MATCHLESS(1967, Ital.), ph; TIGER AND THE PUSSYCAT, THE(1967, U.S., Ital.), ph
Alfred D'Eyncourt
LITTLE MISS SOMEBODY(1937, Brit.), p
Walter d'Eyncourt
JACK OF DIAMONDS, THE(1949, Brit.), p
Louis d'Helo
ANGEL AND SINNER(1947, Fr.), w
d'Hennequin and Veber
CONFESSIONS OF A NEWLYWED(1941, Fr.), w
Lillian D'Honau
PENNIES FROM HEAVEN(1981)
Marilyn D'Honau
NIGHT THEY RAIDED MINSKY'S, THE(1968)
Danica D'Hondt
LIVING VENUS(1961); HOUSE IS NOT A HOME, A(1964); WILD AND WONDERFUL(1964); VERY SPECIAL FAVOR, A(1965); MOTHER GOOSE A GO-GO(1966)
Denis d'Ines
RASPUTIN(1939, Fr.)
Dennis D'Ines
MADAME DU BARRY(1954 Fr./Ital.)
Ron D'Ippolito
MR. SYCAMORE(1975)
Greg D'Jah
Misc. Talkies
CHEERING SECTION(1977)
Fanny D'Morgal
Silents
JUST OFF BROADWAY(1929), w
d'Oberfeld
CONFESSIONS OF A NEWLYWED(1941, Fr.), m
Valeria D'Obici
MASOCH(1980, Ital.); PASSION OF LOVE(1982, Ital./Fr.)
Andrea D'Odorico
1984
DEMONS IN THE GARDEN(1984, Span.), prod d
Philip D'Oench
Silents
KID, THE(1921)
Sergio d'Offizi
TODAY IT'S ME...TOMORROW YOU!(1968, Ital.), ph; RUTHLESS FOUR, THE(1969, Ital./Ger.), ph; SQUEEZE, THE(1980, Ital.), ph
Jack D'Oise
Misc. Silents
FLYING BUCKAROO, THE(1928)
Wendy D'Olive
CATCH-22(1970); DEAD ARE ALIVE, THE(1972, Yugo./Ger./Ital.)
Lien d'Oliveyra
SPY IN THE SKY(1958), ed

Erminio d'Olivo
LOYALTY OF LOVE(1937, Ital.); BALL AT THE CASTLE(1939, Ital.)

Lien d'Olliveyra
LAST BLITZKRIEG, THE(1958), ed

Vincent D'Onofrio
1984
FIRST TURN-ON!, THE(1984)

Tarquini d'Or
CONGRESS DANCES(1932, Ger.)

Daisy d'Ora
Silents
PANDORA'S BOX(1929, Ger.)

Pier Luigi D'Orazio
DEAD ARE ALIVE, THE(1972, Yugo./Ger./Ital.)

Cot d'Ordan
MR. SATAN(1938, Brit.); SAILING ALONG(1938, Brit.); STOLEN LIFE(1939, Brit.); NEUTRAL PORT(1941, Brit.); CANDLELIGHT IN ALGERIA(1944, Brit.)

Philippe D'Orleans
LET JOY REIGN SUPREME(1977, Fr.), m

Fifi D'Orsay
THEY HAD TO SEE PARIS(1929); ON THE LEVEL(1930); THOSE THREE FRENCH GIRLS(1930); WOMEN EVERYWHERE(1930); WOMEN OF ALL NATIONS(1931); YOUNG AS YOU FEEL(1931); GIRL FROM CALGARY(1932); GOING HOLLYWOOD(1933); LIFE OF JIMMY DOLAN, THE(1933); THEY JUST HAD TO GET MARRIED(1933); WONDER BAR(1934); THREE LEGIONNAIRES, THE(1937); SUBMARINE BASE(1943); DELINQUENT DAUGHTERS(1944); NABONGA(1944); DIXIE JAMBOREE(1945); GANGSTER, THE(1947); WHAT A WAY TO GO(1964); WILD AND WONDERFUL(1964); ART OF LOVE, THE(1965)

Ghislaine d'Orsay
DIARY OF A SCHIZOPHRENIC GIRL(1970, Ital.)

Jacqueline D'Orsay
Misc. Talkies
FOR MEMBERS ONLY(1960)

Lawrence D'Orsay
Silents
EARL OF PAWTUCKET, THE(1915); SIDESHOW OF LIFE, THE(1924); MISS BLUEBEARD(1925); SORROWS OF SATAN(1926)
Misc. Silents
RUGGLES OF RED GAP(1918); BOND BOY, THE(1922)

Pam D'Orsay
NOW THAT APRIL'S HERE(1958, Can.)

Ugo D'Orsi
SNOW WHITE AND THE SEVEN DWARFS(1937), anim; FANTASIA(1940), anim

Umberto D'Orsi
LET'S TALK ABOUT WOMEN(1964, Fr./Ital.); TWELVE-HANDED MEN OF MARS, THE(1964, Ital./Span.); HOURS OF LOVE, THE(1965, Ital.); LITTLE NUNS, THE(1965, Ital.); LOVE AND MARRIAGE(1966, Ital.); SPIRITS OF THE DEAD(1969, Fr./Ital.); TIN GIRL, THE(1970, Ital.)

Jacques d'Orvidio
VERY HAPPY ALEXANDER(1969, Fr.), art d&set d

Victoria D'Orzai
Misc. Talkies
HURRAY FOR BETTY BOOP(1980)

Clara d'Ovar
SEASON FOR LOVE, THE(1963, Fr.), p

Jacques d'Ovidio
GIRL WITH THE GOLDEN EYES, THE(1962, Fr.), art d; GREAT SPY CHASE, THE(1966, Fr.), art d; LAST ADVENTURE, THE(1968, Fr./Ital.), art d; Z(1969, Fr./Algeria), art d; MAN WITH CONNECTIONS, THE(1970, Fr.), art d; BLANCHE(1971, Fr.), art d; STATE OF SIEGE(1973, Fr./U.S./Ital./Ger.), prod d, art d

Dante D'Paulo
SWEET CHARITY(1969)

Anita D'Ray
MYSTERY AT THE BURLESQUE(1950, Brit.); OLD MOTHER RILEY'S JUNGLE TREASURE(1951, Brit.)

Orlando D'Ubaldo
SERAFINO(1970, Fr./Ital.)

Arnaud d'Usseau
ONE CROWDED NIGHT(1940), w; LADY SCARFACE(1941), w; REPENT AT LEISURE(1941), w; JUST OFF BROADWAY(1942), w; MAN WHO WOULDN'T DIE, THE(1942), w; WHO IS HOPE SCHUYLER?(1942), w; TOMORROW THE WORLD(1944), w; HORROR EXPRESS(1972, Span./Brit.), w; PSYCHOMANIA(1974, Brit.), w

Leon D'Usseau
GIRL FROM CALGARY(1932), d, w; WINE, WOMEN, AND SONG(1934), w
Silents
RANGER OF THE NORTH(1927), w; ONE MAN DOG, THE(1929), d
Misc. Silents
FURY OF THE WILD(1929), d

Juan D'Vega
TANGO BAR(1935)

Didier d'Yd
RED, INN, THE(1954, Fr.)

Jean d'Yd
END OF THE WORLD, THE(1930, Fr.); ROTHSCHILD(1938, Fr.); ENTENTE CORDIALE(1939, Fr.); ETERNAL RETURN, THE(1943, Fr.); LES DERNIERES VACANCES(1947, Fr.); ROOM UPSTAIRS, THE(1948, Fr.)
Silents
NAPOLEON(1927, Fr.); PASSION OF JOAN OF ARC, THE(1928, Fr.)
Misc. Silents
LE CHANT DE L'AMOUR TRIOMPHANT(1923, Fr.)

Julie da Costa
DON QUIXOTE(1973, Aus.)

Morton Da Costa
AUNTIE MAME(1958), d

Philip Da Costa
SCROOGE(1970, Brit.); ATCH ME A SPY(1971, Brit./Fr.)

Donald Da Gradi
SLEEPING BEAUTY(1959), prod d

Janna Da Loos
ADAM'S RIB(1949)

Banda Da Lua
THAT NIGHT IN RIO(1941); SPRINGTIME IN THE ROCKIES(1942); GREENWICH VILLAGE(1944)

Bardo da Mart
Silents
PAGES OF LIFE(1922, Brit.)

Maria Da Matteis
SON OF THE RED CORSAIR(1963, Ital.), cos

Lorenzo da Ponte
DON GIOVANNI(1955, Brit.), w; DON JUAN(1956, Aust.), w; MARRIAGE OF FIGARO, THE(1970, Ger.), w; DON GIOVANNI(1979, Fr./Ital./Ger.), w

Bill Da Prato
PIE IN THE SKY(1964)

William Da Prato
ANDERSON TAPES, THE(1971)

Louis Da Pron
MELODY LANE(1941); SWEETHEART OF THE CAMPUS(1941), ch; SWING IT SOLDIER(1941); ALWAYS A BRIDESMAID(1943), ph; FOLLOW THE BAND(1943), ch; HE'S MY GUY(1943); HOW'S ABOUT IT?(1943); MOONLIGHT IN VERMONT(1943), ch; MR. BIG(1943), ch; SHE'S FOR ME(1943), a, ch; TOP MAN(1943), ch; WHEN JOHNNY COMES MARCHING HOME(1943), ch; MERRY MONAHANS, THE(1944), ch; SINGING SHERIFF, THE(1944); THIS IS THE LIFE(1944), ch; HER LUCKY NIGHT(1945), ch; GIRL ON THE SPOT(1946), ch; SLIGHTLY SCANDALOUS(1946); ARE YOU WITH IT?(1948), a, ch; THERE'S A GIRL IN MY HEART(1949), ch; YES SIR, THAT'S MY BABY(1949), ch; ONE TOO MANY(1950); WALKING MY BABY BACK HOME(1953), ch

Eraldo Da Roma
PAISAN(1948, Ital.), ed; BICYCLE THIEF, THE(1949, Ital.), ed; GERMANY, YEAR ZERO(1949, Ger.), ed; MIRACLE IN MILAN(1951, Ital.), ed; INDISCRETION OF AN AMERICAN WIFE(1954, U.S./Ital.), ed; LOVE SPECIALIST, THE(1959, Ital.), ed; FAST AND SEXY(1960, Fr./Ital.), ed; LAST DAYS OF POMPEII, THE(1960, Ital.), ed; L'AVVENTURA(1960, Ital.), ed; SAVAGE INNOCENTS, THE(1960, Brit.), ed; COLOSSUS OF RHODES, THE(1961, Ital., Fr., Span.), ed; LA NOTTE(1961, Fr./Ital.), ed; REVOLT OF THE SLAVES, THE(1961, Ital./Span./Ger.), ed; ECLIPSE(1962, Fr./Ital.), ed; IL GRIDO(1962, U.S./Ital.), ed; LE AMICHE(1962, Ital.), ed; LOVE AND LARCENY(1963, Fr./Ital.), ed; MADAME(1963, Fr./Ital./Span.), ed; GOLIATH AND THE VAMPIRES(1964, Ital.), ed; OF WAYWARD LOVE(1964, Ital./Ger.), ed; AMERICAN WIFE, AN(1965, Ital.), ed; LOVE A LA CARTE(1965, Ital.), ed; MAGNIFICENT CUCKOLD, THE(1965, Fr./Ital.), ed; RED DESERT(1965, Fr./Ital.), ed; THREE FACES OF A WOMAN(1965, Ital.), ed; LA VISITA(1966, Ital./Fr.), ed; RUN FOR YOUR WIFE(1966, Fr./Ital.), ed; ARABELLA(1969, U.S./Ital.), ed; DEATH RIDES A HORSE(1969, Ital.), ed

Evaldo da Roma
GOLD OF NAPLES(1957, Ital.), ed

Eliana Da Sabata
EVIL EYE(1964 Ital.), w

Ademir Da Silva
WILD PACK, THE(1972)

Adhemar da Silva
BLACK ORPHEUS(1959 Fr./Ital./Braz.)

Bryan Da Silva
SWEET CHARITY(1969)

Carlos Da Silva
CLOPORTES(1966, Fr., Ital.)

Fernando Ramos da Silva
PIXOTE(1981, Braz.)

Henry Da Silva
BRAZIL(1944)

Howard Da Silva
ABE LINCOLN IN ILLINOIS(1940); I'M STILL ALIVE(1940); BAD MEN OF MISSOURI(1941); BLUES IN THE NIGHT(1941); NAVY BLUES(1941); NINE LIVES ARE NOT ENOUGH(1941); SEA WOLF, THE(1941); SERGEANT YORK(1941); STEEL AGAINST THE SKY(1941); STRANGE ALIBI(1941); BIG SHOT, THE(1942); BULLET SCARS(1942); JUKE GIRL(1942); KEEPER OF THE FLAME(1942); NATIVE LAND(1942); OMAHA TRAIL, THE(1942); REUNION IN FRANCE(1942); WILD BILL HICKOK RIDES(1942); TONIGHT WE RAID CALAIS(1943); DUFFY'S TAVERN(1945); LOST WEEKEND, THE(1945); BLUE DAHLIA, THE(1946); TWO YEARS BEFORE THE MAST(1946); BLAZE OF NOON(1947); UNCONQUERED(1947); VARIETY GIRL(1947); BORDER INCIDENT(1949); GREAT GATSBY, THE(1949); THEY LIVE BY NIGHT(1949); THREE HUSBANDS(1950); TRIPOLI(1950); WHIPPED, THE(1950); WYOMING MAIL(1950); FOURTEEN HOURS(1951); M(1951); DAVID AND LISA(1962); IT'S A MAD, MAD, MAD, MAD WORLD(1963); OUTRAGE, THE(1964); NEVADA SMITH(1966); 1776(1972); GREAT GATSBY, THE(1974); PRIVATE FILES OF J. EDGAR HOOVER, THE(1978); MOMMIE DEAREST(1981)
1984
GARBO TALKS(1984)

Lopes da Silva
KILL OR BE KILLED(1950)

Maria Luisa Da Silva
MY SEVEN LITTLE SINS(1956, Fr./Ital.)

Monica M. da Silva
1984
FOOTLOOSE(1984)

Walter da Silveira
GIVEN WORD, THE(1964, Braz.)

Antonio Vaz da Silver
IN THE WHITE CITY(1983, Switz./Portugal), p

Elena Da Vinci
GHOST DIVER(1957); GIRL IN THE KREMLIN, THE(1957); HELL ON DEVIL'S ISLAND(1957)

Clyde Da Vinna
AIR CADET(1951), ph

Hyatt Daab
NIGHT PARADE(1929, Brit.), w

Mary Daair
TOP OF THE TOWN(1937)
Renee Daalder
MASSACRE AT CENTRAL HIGH(1976), d&w
Erik Daarstad
HELL SQUAD(1958), ph; EXILES, THE(1966), ph, ed
Eddie Daas
STUDENT TOUR(1934)
Jean-Loup Dabadie
TALES OF PARIS(1962, Fr./Ital.), w; DOUBLE BED, THE(1965, Fr./Ital.), w; THINGS OF LIFE, THE(1970, Fr./Ital./Switz.), w; CESAR AND ROSALIE(1972, Fr.), w; SUCH A GORGEOUS KID LIKE ME(1973, Fr.), w; SAVAGE, THE(1975, Fr.), w
1984
WOMAN IN RED, THE(1984), w
Grisha M. Dabat
DANIELLA BY NIGHT(1962, Fr/Ger.), w; SWEET ECSTASY(1962, Fr.), w; SIN ON THE BEACH(1964, Fr.), w
Brenda Dabbs
"EQUUS"(1977), cos; PEOPLE THAT TIME FORGOT, THE(1977, Brit.), cos
Jack Dabdoub
LADY LIBERTY(1972, Ital./Fr.)
Joe Dabenigno
NIGHTHAWKS(1981); DANIEL(1983)
Hugh Dabernon-Stoke
Misc. Silents
GOD'S GOOD MAN(1921, Brit.)
Ethel Dabey
RED FORK RANGE(1931), ed
Ardella Dabney
Misc. Talkies
THIRTY YEARS LATER(1938)
Misc. Silents
THIRTY YEARS LATER(1928)
Ardelle Dabney
Misc. Silents
BROKEN VIOLIN, THE(1927)
Augusta Dabney
THAT NIGHT(1957); HEARTBREAK KID, THE(1972); FIRE SALE(1977); COLD RIVER(1982)
Charlotte Dabney
TRUE CONFESSION(1937)
James Dabney, Jr.
STALAG 17(1953)
Kathleen Dabney
ALICE'S RESTAURANT(1969)
Virginia Dabney
FOLIES DERGERE(1935); BULLETS OR BALLOTS(1936); GOLD DIGGERS OF 1937(1936); DAUGHTER OF SHANGHAI(1937); EASY LIVING(1937); KID GALAHAD(1937); KING OF ALCATRAZ(1938); PRISON FARM(1938); DISBARRED(1939); MAGNIFICENT FRAUD, THE(1939); WOMEN WITHOUT NAMES(1940)
Jane Dabon
HAREM BUNCH; OR WAR AND PIECE, THE(1969)
David Dabov
YOUNG LIONS, THE(1958)
Marek Dabrowski
CONDUCTOR, THE(1981, Pol.)
Murielle Dabrule
1984
CHEECH AND CHONG'S THE CORSICAN BROTHERS(1984)
Judith Daby
JESUS CHRIST, SUPERSTAR(1973)
Pierre Dac
LA BELLE AMERICAINE(1961, Fr.); DEADLY DECOYS, THE(1962, Fr.); COUNTERFEIT CONSTABLE, THE(1966, Fr.); DON'T PLAY WITH MARTIANS(1967, Fr.)
Stephen Dach
MOONSHINE COUNTY EXPRESS(1977)
M. Dacheux
Silents
NAPOLEON(1927, Fr.)
Dacia
Silents
WEAVERS OF FORTUNE(1922, Brit.)
Jolanda Dacic
KAYA, I'LL KILL YOU(1969, Yugo./Fr.)
Corinne Dacla
PEPPERMINT SODA(1979, Fr.)
Jeremy Dacon
IT HAPPENED HERE(1966, Brit.)
Morton DaCosta
MUSIC MAN, THE(1962), p&d; ISLAND OF LOVE(1963), p&d
Jacques Dacqmine
CAROLINE CHERIE(1951, Fr.); MICHAEL STROGOFF(1960, Fr./Ital./Yugo.); GAME OF TRUTH, THE(1961, Fr.); WEB OF PASSION(1961, Fr.); BACK STREETS OF PARIS(1962, Fr.); ROAD TO SHAME, THE(1962, Fr.); WHERE THE TRUTH LIES(1962, Fr.); EXTERMINATORS, THE(1965 Fr.)
Michel Dacquin
DIARY OF A CHAMBERMAID(1964, Fr./Ital.); CLOPORTES(1966, Fr., Ital.); MILKY WAY, THE(1969, Fr./Ital.)
Don Dacus
HAIR(1979)
Robert Dadashian
CHILD, THE(1977), p
Hisao Dadayu
TORA-SAN PART 2(1970, Jap.)
Virgilio Daddi
1984
BIZET'S CARMEN(1984, Fr./Ital.)

Anthony Daddio
SYNANON(1965)
Frances Dade
GRUMPY(1930); HE KNEW WOMEN(1930); RAFFLES(1930); DAUGHTER OF THE DRAGON(1931); DRACULA(1931); RANGE LAW(1931); SEED(1931); SHE-WOLF, THE(1931); BIG TOWN(1932)
Francis Dade
PLEASURE(1933)
Stephen Dade
CROOKED ROAD, THE(, ph; SAILOR'S DON'T CARE(1940, Brit.), ph; BOB'S YOUR UNCLE(1941, Brit.), ph; DANNY BOY(1941, Brit.), ph; FACING THE MUSIC(1941, Brit.), ph; GERT AND DAISY'S WEEKEND(1941, Brit.), ph; BALLOON GOES UP, THE(1942, Brit.), ph; FRONT LINE KIDS(1942, Brit.), ph; GERT AND DAISY CLEAN UP(1942, Brit.), ph; MISSING MILLION, THE(1942, Brit.), ph; SOMEWHERE IN CAMP(1942, Brit.), ph; WE'LL MEET AGAIN(1942, Brit.), ph; GET CRACKING(1943, Brit.), ph; UP WITH THE LARK(1943, Brit.), ph; DEMOBBED(1944, Brit.), ph; PLACE OF ONE'S OWN, A(1945, Brit.), ph; CARAVAN(1946, Brit.), ph; DEAR MURDERER(1947, Brit.), ph; ROOT OF ALL EVIL, THE(1947, Brit.), ph; BROTHERS, THE(1948, Brit.), ph; BAD LORD BYRON, THE(1949, Brit.), ph; CHRISTOPHER COLUMBUS(1949, Brit.), ph; DON'T EVER LEAVE ME(1949, Brit.), ph; SNOWBOUND(1949, Brit.), ph; DANCING YEARS, THE(1950, Brit.), ph; GOOD TIME GIRL(1950, Brit.), ph; THIRD VISITOR, THE(1951, Brit.), ph; APPOINTMENT IN LONDON(1953, Brit.), ph; KNIGHTS OF THE ROUND TABLE(1953), ph; SEA SHALL NOT HAVE THEM, THE(1955, Brit.), ph; FLESH IS WEAK, THE(1957, Brit.), ph; ANGRY HILLS, THE(1959, Brit.), ph; QUESTION OF ADULTERY, A(1959, Brit.), ph; BLUEBEARD'S TEN HONEYMOONS(1960, Brit.), ph; NIGHT FIGHTERS, THE(1960), ph; DOUBLE BUNK(1961, Brit.), ph; DR. BLOOD'S COFFIN(1961), ph; SNAKE WOMAN, THE(1961, Brit.), ph; THREE ON A SPREE(1961, Brit.), ph; BAY OF SAINT MICHEL, THE(1963, Brit.), ph; GET ON WITH IT(1963, Brit.), ph; ZULU(1964, Brit.), ph; BLOOD BEAST FROM OUTER SPACE(1965, Brit.), ph; CITY UNDER THE SEA(1965, Brit.), ph; COAST OF SKELETONS(1965, Brit.), ph; DATELINE DIAMONDS(1966, Brit.), ph; MAN WHO FINALLY DIED, THE(1967, Brit.), ph; VIKING QUEEN, THE(1967, Brit.), ph; VULTURE, THE(1967, U.S./Brit./Can.), ph
Robert Dadies
ONE SINGS, THE OTHER DOESN'T(1977, Fr.)
Leon E. Dadmum
Silents
LURE OF LOVE, THE(1924), d
Leon E. Dadmun
Misc. Silents
PEARL OF LOVE, THE(1925), d
Suzanne Dadolle
NEW KIND OF LOVE, A(1963)
Frank Dae
WITHOUT RESERVATIONS(1946); IN OLD CHICAGO(1938); LITTLE MISS BROADWAY(1938); PRIVATE DETECTIVE(1939); STANLEY AND LIVINGSTONE(1939); SLIGHTLY HONORABLE(1940); NOW, VOYAGER(1942); TALES OF MANHATTAN(1942); SONG OF BERNADETTE, THE(1943); DALTONS RIDE AGAIN, THE(1945); DON'T GAMBLE WITH STRANGERS(1946); LADY LUCK(1946); NIGHT AND DAY(1946); NIGHT EDITOR(1946); O.S.S.(1946); SHE WROTE THE BOOK(1946); UNDERCURRENT(1946); LADY IN THE LAKE(1947); PANHANDLE(1948); ROMANCE ON THE HIGH SEAS(1948); SECRET BEYOND THE DOOR, THE(1948); WINNER'S CIRCLE, THE(1948); JOHNNY ALLEGRO(1949); KISS IN THE DARK, A(1949); SURRENDER(1950); PAINTING THE CLOUDS WITH SUNSHINE(1951); GIRL WHO HAD EVERYTHING, THE(1953)
Anne-Marie Daehli
EDVARD MUNCH(1976, Norway/Swed.)
Van Daele
GOLGOTHA(1937, Fr.)
Misc. Silents
LA MONTEE VERS L'ACROPOLE(1920, Fr.); NARAYANA(1920, Fr.); FIEVRE(1921, Fr.); L'INONDATION(1924, Fr.); NENE(1924, Fr.); MADAME RECAMIER(1928, Fr.); SABLES(1928, Fr.)
Marie Daems
JOURNEY, THE(1959, U.S./Aust.); CRIME DOES NOT PAY(1962, Fr.); ONE NIGHT STAND(1976, Fr.)
C. I. Dafau
IN CALIENTE(1935)
Felix Dafauce
AWFUL DR. ORLOFF, THE(1964, Span./Fr.); FLAME OVER VIETNAM(1967, Span./Ger.); WITCH WITHOUT A BROOM, A(1967, U.S./Span.)
The Daffodil Girls
STAR!(1968)
Dr. Allan Dafoe
COUNTRY DOCTOR, THE(1936), tech adv
Willem Dafoe
HUNGER, THE(1983)
1984
NEW YORK NIGHTS(1984); ROADHOUSE 66(1984); STREETS OF FIRE(1984)
William Dafoe
LOVELESS, THE(1982)
Iran Dafteri
INVINCIBLE SIX, THE(1970, U.S./Iran)
Gavriel Dagan
THEY WERE TEN(1961, Israel), a, w
Hans Dagelet
LIFT, THE(1983, Neth.)
Dagenham Girl Pipers
TALKING FEET(1937, Brit.); SCHOOL FOR SECRETS(1946, Brit.); WHO DONE IT?(1956, Brit.)
Carl Dagenhart
SQUIRM(1976)
Lo Dagerman
LOVING COUPLES(1966, Swed.)
Stig Halvard Dagerman
SWEDISH WEDDING NIGHT(1965, Swed.), w
William Dagg
TOGETHER BROTHERS(1974)

Margaret Daggett
SOULS AT SEA(1937)
Rae Daggett
BROADWAY TO CHEYENNE(1932); MOTH, THE(1934); EARLY TO BED(1936)
Thomas Daggett
1984
FIRSTBORN(1984)
K. T. Daggott
SQUARE ROOT OF ZERO, THE(1964)
Jiairo Daghini
JONAH–WHO WILL BE 25 IN THE YEAR 2000(1976, Switz.)
Sergio Dagliana
NIGHT OF THE SHOOTING STARS, THE(1982, Ital.)
R. Daglish
DAY THE WAR ENDED, THE(1961, USSR)
Florence Dagmar
Silents
CALL OF THE NORTH, THE(1914); CIRCUS MAN, THE(1914); MAN FROM HOME, THE(1914); READY MONEY(1914); CHIMMIE FADDEN OUT WEST(1915); KINDLING(1915)
Misc. Silents
COUNTRY BOY, THE(1915); CLOWN, THE(1916)
Jack Dagmar
FRIGHTMARE(1974, Brit.)
Jeanette Dagna
COCK-EYED WORLD, THE(1929)
Ernest A. Dagnall
SYMPHONY IN TWO FLATS(1930, Brit.)
Ernest Dagnall
Silents
OUT TO WIN(1923, Brit.)
Albert Dagnat
FANTOMAS STRIKES BACK(1965, Fr./Ital.)
Robert Dagny
WATERMELON MAN(1970); ANDERSON TAPES, THE(1971)
Lil Dagover
ELISABETH OF AUSTRIA(1931, Ger.); BARBERINA(1932, Ger.); CONGRESS DANCES(1932, Ger.); WOMAN FROM MONTE CARLO, THE(1932); FINAL CHORD, THE(1936, Ger.); DAY WILL COME, A(1960, Ger.); PEDESTRIAN, THE(1974, Ger.); END OF THE GAME(1976, Ger./Ital.)
Silents
CABINET OF DR. CALIGARI, THE(1921, Ger.); TARTUFFE(1927, Ger.)
Misc. Silents
GOLDEN SEA, THE(1919, Ger.); HARAKIRI(1919, Ger.); SPIDERS, THE(1919, Ger.); DESTINY(1921, Ger.); PHANTOM, THE(1922, Ger.); CHRONICLES OF THE GRAY HOUSE, THE(1923, Ger.); LE TOURBILLON DE PARIS(1928, Fr.); MONTE-CRISTO(1929, Fr.)
Don DaGradi
SON OF FLUBBER(1963), w; MARY POPPINS(1964), w; BLACKBEARD'S GHOST(1968), w; LOVE BUG, THE(1968), w; BEDKNOBS AND BROOMSTICKS(1971), w; SCANDALOUS JOHN(1971), w
Donald DaGradi
LADY AND THE TRAMP(1955), w; LT. ROBIN CRUSOE, U.S.N.(1966), w
Jean-Claude Dague
HEAT OF MIDNIGHT(1966, Fr.); PLAYMATES(1969, Fr./Ital.), d&w
Misc. Talkies
PLAYMATES(1971), d
Roswell Dague
Silents
JAMESTOWN(1923), w
Andre Daguenet
RISE OF LOUIS XIV, THE(1970, Fr.)
Jose Dagumboy
RAVAGERS, THE(1965, U.S./Phil.); PASSIONATE STRANGERS, THE(1968, Phil.)
Bill Dagwell
SONS O' GUNS(1936)
Armand Dahan
GOD TOLD ME TO(1976); NEXT MAN, THE(1976); SOPHIE'S CHOICE(1982)
1984
MOSCOW ON THE HUDSON(1984)
Michael Dahan
1984
CHEECH AND CHONG'S THE CORSICAN BROTHERS(1984)
Bob Dahdah
WAY WE WERE, THE(1973); YOUNG DOCTORS, THE(1961); SUPERMAN(1978)
Robert Dahdah
LILITH(1964); THREE DAYS OF THE CONDOR(1975)
John Daheim
TWO YANKS IN TRINIDAD(1942); THIS IS THE ARMY(1943); WHIPLASH(1948); WHERE THE SIDEWALK ENDS(1950); COLORADO SUNDOWN(1952); WILD HORSE AMBUSH(1952); WINGS OF THE HAWK(1953); I DIED A THOUSAND TIMES(1955); ONE DESIRE(1955); SHENANDOAH(1965); DUEL AT DIABLO(1966); MAN COULD GET KILLED, A(1966), stunts; TOBRUK(1966), stunts; PINK JUNGLE, THE(1968), stunts; LOST MAN, THE(1969); MAN CALLED GANNON, A(1969), stunts; TELL THEM WILLIE BOY IS HERE(1969), stunts
Johnny Daheim
WILDCAT OF TUCSON(1941)
John Dahein
STRANGE BEDFELLOWS(1965)
Alice Dahl
PHANTOM EXPRESS, THE(1932); DEADWOOD PASS(1933); BABES IN TOYLAND(1934); JEALOUSY(1934)
Misc. Talkies
WHIRLWIND, THE(1933); TWISTED RAILS(1935)
Arlene Dahl
LIFE WITH FATHER(1947); MY WILD IRISH ROSE(1947); BRIDE GOES WILD, THE(1948); SOUTHERN YANKEE, A(1948); BLACK BOOK, THE(1949); SCENE OF THE CRIME(1949); AMBUSH(1950); OUTRIDERS, THE(1950); THREE LITTLE WORDS(1950); WATCH THE BIRDIE(1950); INSIDE STRAIGHT(1951); NO QUESTIONS ASKED(1951); CARIBBEAN(1952); DESERT LEGION(1953); DIAMOND

QUEEN, THE(1953); HERE COME THE GIRLS(1953); JAMAICA RUN(1953); SANGAREE(1953); BENGAL BRIGADE(1954); WOMAN'S WORLD(1954); SLIGHTLY SCARLET(1956); PORTRAIT IN SMOKE(1957, Brit.); SHE PLAYED WITH FIRE(1957, Brit.); JOURNEY TO THE CENTER OF THE EARTH(1959); KISSES FOR MY PRESIDENT(1964); LAND RAIDERS(1969)
Misc. Talkies
OUTRIDERS, THE(1950)
Arvid O. Dahl
YANK IN LONDON, A(1946, Brit.)
Carsten Dahl
GOLDEN MOUNTAINS(1958, Den.), ed
Helen Dahl
COYOTE TRAILS(1935)
Silents
GOD'S HALF ACRE(1916); MICE AND MEN(1916)
Misc. Silents
MOLLY MAKE-BELIEVE(1916); SLEEPING FIRES(1917); FLOOR BELOW, THE(1918)
Pat Dahl
ERRAND BOY, THE(1961); IT'S ONLY MONEY(1962)
Roald Dahl
36 HOURS(1965), d&w; YOU ONLY LIVE TWICE(1967, Brit.), w; CHITTY CHITTY BANG BANG(1968, Brit.), w; NIGHT DIGGER, THE(1971, Brit.), w; WILLY WONKA AND THE CHOCOLATE FACTORY(1971), w
Sonja Dahl
SALT OF THE EARTH(1954), prod d
Sophus Dahl
ONLY ONE NIGHT(1942, Swed.)
Steve Dahl
1984
GRANDVIEW, U.S.A.(1984)
Tessa Dahl
HAPPY MOTHER'S DAY... LOVE, GEORGE(1973); SLIPPER AND THE ROSE, THE(1976, Brit.)
Eva Dahlbeck
VILLAGE, THE(1953, Brit./Switz.); SMILES OF A SUMMER NIGHT(1957, Swed.); BRINK OF LIFE(1960, Swed.); DREAMS(1960, Swed.); LESSON IN LOVE, A(1960, Swed.); MATTER OF MORALS, A(1961, U.S./Swed.); SECRETS OF WOMEN(1961, Swed.); COUNTERFEIT TRAITOR, THE(1962); ALL THESE WOMEN(1964, Swed.); LOVING COUPLES(1966, Swed.); HAGBARD AND SIGNE(1968, Den./Iceland/Swed.); WOMAN OF DARKNESS(1968, Swed.), w; LES CREATURES(1969, Fr./Swed.); PEOPLE MEET AND SWEET MUSIC FILLS THE HEART(1969, Den./Swed.)
Camilla Dahlberg
Silents
ONE OF OUR GIRLS(1914); ONE MILLION DOLLARS(1915)
Gilda Dahlberg
EVA(1962, Fr./Ital.); 8 ½(1963, Ital.); WOMAN OF STRAW(1964, Brit.); POPPY IS ALSO A FLOWER, THE(1966)
Lasse Dahlberg
GRASS IS SINGING, THE(1982, Brit./Swed.), m
Galen Keith Dahle
NEW KIND OF LOVE, A(1963)
Keith Dahle
THEY SAVED HITLER'S BRAIN(1964)
Armin Dahlen
DIVIDED HEART, THE(1955, Brit.)
David Dahlgren
1984
TIGHTROPE(1984)
Nils Dahlgren
DOLLAR(1938, Swed.); TORMENT(1947, Swed.); PORT OF CALL(1963, Swed.)
Tom Dahlgren
CANDIDATE, THE(1972); GODFATHER, THE, PART II(1974); ONE FROM THE HEART(1982); NEVER CRY WOLF(1983)
Richard Dahlia
I, THE JURY(1982)
Patricia Dahling
NIGHT OF EVIL(1962)
Paul Dahlke
LONG IS THE ROAD(1948, Ger.); CONFESSIONS OF FELIX KRULL, THE(1957, Ger.); HEAD, THE(1961, Ger.); ENCOUNTERS IN SALZBURG(1964, Ger.); SITUATION HOPELESS–BUT NOT SERIOUS(1965); MOONWOLF(1966, Fin./Ger.); RED DRAGON(1967, Ital./Ger./US)
Gregor Dahlman
SHAME(1968, Swed.)
Jerry Dahlman
DETROIT 9000(1973)
Rynol Dahlman
YANK IN VIET-NAM, A(1964), cos
Gunilla Dahlmann
MY FATHER'S MISTRESS(1970, Swed.)
Jerry Dahlmann
BLUE COLLAR(1978)
Ake Dahlquist
COUNT OF THE MONK'S BRIDGE, THE(1934, Swed.), ph; SWEDENHIELMS(1935, Swed.), ph; ON THE SUNNYSIDE(1936, Swed.), ph; INTERMEZZO(1937, Swed.), ph; DOLLAR(1938, Swed.), ph; WOMAN'S FACE, A(1939, Swed.), ph; NIGHT IN JUNE, A(1940, Swed.), ph; AFFAIRS OF A MODEL(1952, Swed.), ph; DOLL, THE(1964, Swed.), ph
Kay Dahlquist
WILD GYPSIES(1969)
Valdemar Dahlquist
COUNT OF THE MONK'S BRIDGE, THE(1934, Swed.)
Gus Dahlstrom
FANNY AND ALEXANDER(1983, Swed./Fr./Ger.)
Dorothy Dahm
Silents
ON THE STROKE OF THREE(1924)

Josef Dahmen
LOST ONE, THE(1951, Ger.); GIRL OF THE MOORS, THE(1961, Ger.)
Joseph Dahmen
THEY WERE SO YOUNG(1955)
Gail Dahms
SILENT PARTNER, THE(1979, Can.)
Misc. Talkies
TOMORROW MAN, THE(1979)
Felix Dahn
FIGHT FOR ROME(1969, Ger./Rum.), w
J.J. Dahner
WAR IS HELL(1964)
Lin Dai
MADAME WHITE SNAKE(1963, Hong Kong); LAST WOMAN OF SHANG, THE(1964, Hong Kong)
Alan Daiches
HEROSTRATUS(1968, Brit.), w, d&w
Louis Daige
LINEUP, THE(1958), set d
Marga Daighton
STAGECOACH(1939)
Melanie Daigle
FOND MEMORIES(1982, Can.)
Michel Daigle
FOND MEMORIES(1982, Can.)
Thomas Peter Daikos
WORLD ACCORDING TO GARP, The(1982)
Akira Daikubara
MAGIC BOY(1960, Jap.), d; PANDA AND THE MAGIC SERPENT(1961, Jap.), anim
Alexander Daikun
MC CABE AND MRS. MILLER(1971)
Allen Dailey
DISCARDED LOVERS(1932); INVASION OF THE STAR CREATURES(1962)
Dan Dailey
SUSAN AND GOD(1940); MOTHER WORE TIGHTS(1947); CHICKEN EVERY SUNDAY(1948); GIVE MY REGARDS TO BROADWAY(1948); WHEN MY BABY SMILES AT ME(1948); YOU WERE MEANT FOR ME(1948); YOU'RE MY EVERYTHING(1949); I'LL GET BY(1950); MY BLUE HEAVEN(1950); TICKET TO TOMAHAWK(1950); WHEN WILLIE COMES MARCHING HOME(1950); CALL ME MISTER(1951); I CAN GET IT FOR YOU WHOLESALE(1951); MEET ME AT THE FAIR(1952); PRIDE OF ST. LOUIS, THE(1952); WHAT PRICE GLORY?(1952); GIRL NEXT DOOR, THE(1953); KID FROM LEFT FIELD, THE(1953); TAXI(1953); THERE'S NO BUSINESS LIKE SHOW BUSINESS(1954); IT'S ALWAYS FAIR WEATHER(1955); BEST THINGS IN LIFE ARE FREE, THE(1956); MEET ME IN LAS VEGAS(1956); OH, MEN! OH, WOMEN!(1957); WAYWARD BUS, THE(1957); WINGS OF EAGLES, THE(1957); UNDERWATER WARRIOR(1958); PEPE(1960); ADVENTURES OF A YOUNG MAN(1962); PRIVATE FILES OF J. EDGAR HOOVER, THE(1978)
Dan Dailey, Jr.
CAPTAIN IS A LADY, THE(1940); DULCY(1940); HULLABALOO(1940); MORTAL STORM, THE(1940); DOWN IN SAN DIEGO(1941); GET-AWAY, THE(1941); KEEPING COMPANY(1941); LADY BE GOOD(1941); MOON OVER HER SHOULDER(1941); WASHINGTON MELODRAMA(1941); WILD MAN OF BORNEO, THE(1941); ZIEGFELD GIRL(1941); GIVE OUT, SISTERS(1942); MOKEY(1942); PANAMA HATTIE(1942); SUNDAY PUNCH(1942); TIMBER(1942)
Elizabeth Dailey
MAISIE GOES TO RENO(1944)
Irene Dailey
DARING GAME(1968); NO WAY TO TREAT A LADY(1968); FIVE EASY PIECES(1970); GRISSOM GANG, THE(1971); AMITYVILLE HORROR, THE(1979)
J. Hammond Dailey
COUNSELLOR-AT-LAW(1933)
Jack Dailey
NORA PRENTISS(1947)
Joseph Dailey
Silents
AVENGING TRAIL, THE(1918)
Mike Dailey
MAN FROM O.R.G.Y., THE(1970)
Ray Dailey
MANCHURIAN CANDIDATE, THE(1962)
Bernard Daillencourt
BEAST, THE(1975, Fr.), ph; COUSINS IN LOVE(1982), ph
Magdeleine Dailloux
ADOPTION, THE(1978, Fr.), w
Bill Daily
BAREFOOT EXECUTIVE, THE(1971)
Elizabeth Daily
MARRIAGE IS A PRIVATE AFFAIR(1944); ESCAPE ARTIST, THE(1982); STREET MUSIC(1982); FUNNY MONEY(1983, Brit.); ONE DARK NIGHT(1983); VALLEY GIRL(1983); WACKO(1983)
1984
NO SMALL AFFAIR(1984); STREETS OF FIRE(1984)
Margaret Daily
DEVOTION(1931)
Mary Daily
Misc. Talkies
HANDS ACROSS THE ROCKIES(1941)
Masaki Daimon
GODZILLA VERSUS THE COSMIC MONSTER(1974, Jap.)
Edward Dain
OPERATION DIPLOMAT(1953, Brit.)
Neil Dainard
WHEN TOMORROW DIES(1966, Can.); IF YOU COULD SEE WHAT I HEAR(1982)
1984
AMERICAN NIGHTMARE(1984)
Misc. Talkies
AMERICAN NIGHTMARE(1981, Can.)

Ella Daincourt
SHE WAS ONLY A VILLAGE MAIDEN(1933, Brit.)
Lesley Daine
FAMILY WAY, THE(1966, Brit.)
Lois Daine
HELL IS A CITY(1960, Brit.); CASH ON DEMAND(1962, Brit.); WUTHERING HEIGHTS(1970, Brit.); CAPTAIN KRONOS: VAMPIRE HUNTER(1974, Brit.)
Marie Daine
SONG AT EVENTIDE(1934, Brit.)
Tony Daines
SEASIDE SWINGERS(1965, Brit.)
Susan Dains
DON QUIXOTE(1973, Aus.)
Dora Dainton
VISITING HOURS(1982, Can.); STRANGE BREW(1983)
Joanne Dainton
FIRECHASERS, THE(1970, Brit.)
Leonard Dainton
MAN FROM CHICAGO, THE(1931, Brit.)
Noel Dainton
NEW HOTEL, THE(1932, Brit.); REUNION(1932, Brit.); THIRD CLUE, THE(1934, Brit.); MURDER IN THE OLD RED BARN(1936, Brit.); 13 MEN AND A GUN(1938, Brit.); NEUTRAL PORT(1941, Brit.); SOMEWHERE ON LEAVE(1942, Brit.); IT'S IN THE BAG(1943, Brit.); OLD MOTHER RILEY, DETECTIVE(1943, Brit.); SAINT MEETS THE TIGER, THE(1943, Brit.); DEMOBBED(1944, Brit.); DREAMING(1944, Brit.); KISS THE BRIDE GOODBYE(1944, Brit.); TIME FLIES(1944, Brit.); TWILIGHT HOUR(1944, Brit.); ECHO MURDERS, THE(1945, Brit.); RANDOLPH FAMILY, THE(1945, Brit.)
Patricia Dainton
DANCING WITH CRIME(1947, Brit.); LOVE IN WAITING(1948, Brit.); DON'T EVER LEAVE ME(1949, Brit.); DANCING YEARS, THE(1950, Brit.); CASTLE IN THE AIR(1952, Brit.); HAMMER THE TOFF(1952, Brit.); PAUL TEMPLE RETURNS(1952, Brit.); TREAD SOFTLY(1952, Brit.); OPERATION DIPLOMAT(1953, Brit.); AT THE STROKE OF NINE(1957, Brit.); NO ROAD BACK(1957, Brit.); NOVEL AFFAIR, A(1957, Brit.); WITNESS IN THE DARK(1959, Brit.); HOUSE IN MARSH ROAD, THE(1960, Brit.); THIRD ALIBI, THE(1961, Brit.); TICKET TO PARADISE(1961, Brit.)
Misc. Talkies
BOMBAY WATERFRONT(1952, Brit.)
Frances Dair
Misc. Silents
DANGER ZONE, THE(1925)
Johan Daisne
ONE NIGHT... A TRAIN(1968, Fr./Bel.), w
Amleto Daisse
PRETTY BUT WICKED(1965, Braz.), ph; TRAIN ROBBERY CONFIDENTIAL(1965, Braz.), ph
Daisy
FREAKS(1932); BLONDIE(1938); BLONDIE BRINGS UP BABY(1939); BLONDIE TAKES A VACATION(1939); BLONDIE HAS SERVANT TROUBLE(1940); BLONDIE ON A BUDGET(1940); BLONDIE PLAYS CUPID(1940); BLONDIE GOES LATIN(1941); BLONDIE IN SOCIETY(1941); BLONDIE FOR VICTORY(1942); BLONDIE GOES TO COLLEGE(1942); BLONDIE'S BLESSED EVENT(1942); FOLLOW THE BOYS(1944); LEAVE IT TO BLONDIE(1945); BLONDIE'S LUCKY DAY(1946); BLONDIE IN THE DOUGH(1947); BLONDIE'S BIG MOMENT(1947); BLONDIE'S SECRET(1948); FIGHTING BACK(1948); BLONDIE HITS THE JACKPOT(1949); BLONDIE'S HERO(1950); BADMAN'S GOLD(1951)
Daisy the Cow
1984
TOP SECRET!(1984)
Daisy the Dog
FOOTLIGHT GLAMOUR(1943); IT'S A GREAT LIFE(1943); LIFE WITH BLONDIE(1946); RED STALLION, THE(1947)
Daisy the Wonder Dog
VALIANT HOMBRE, THE(1948)
Diane Daives
LOVING(1970)
Didier Daix
HOW TO MURDER A RICH UNCLE(1957, Brit.), w; LA BELLE AMERICAINE(1961, Fr.)
Irene Daix
THIEF OF PARIS, THE(1967, Fr./Ital.)
Evalds Dajevskis
HANSEL AND GRETEL(1954), set d
Guy Dakar
TIME BOMB(1961, Fr./Ital.); DAY AND THE HOUR, THE(1963, Fr./Ital.); WOMEN AND WAR(1965, Fr.)
Ruby Dake
CACTUS IN THE SNOW(1972)
Andre Daker
NEVER TAKE CANDY FROM A STRANGER(1961, Brit.)
Dave Daker
STARDUST(1974, Brit.)
David Daker
O LUCKY MAN!(1973, Brit.); OPTIMISTS, THE(1973, Brit.); BLACK WINDMILL, THE(1974, Brit.); ACES HIGH(1977, Brit.); THAT SUMMER(1979, Brit.)
Vicki Dakil
PERSONALS, THE(1982)
Gay Ellen Dakin
BROADWAY LIMITED(1941)
Philip Dakin
GREAT EXPECTATIONS(1934); WAKE UP AND DREAM(1934)
John Dako
DAKOTA LIL(1950)
Dakshinamoorthy
JUNGLE, THE(1952), m
Daksnamurti
HINDU, THE(1953, Brit.), m

Nino Dal Fabbro
ENGAGEMENT ITALIANO(1966, Fr./Ital.)
Paul Dal Porto
SERIAL(1980), set d
John Dala
CRIME DOCTOR'S COURAGE, THE(1945), art d
Jacques Dalafontaine
1984
SWANN IN LOVE(1984, Fr.Ger.)
Max Dalban
PANIQUE(1947, Fr.); INNOCENTS IN PARIS(1955, Brit.); FRENCH CANCAN(1956, Fr.); BOUDU SAVED FROM DROWNING(1967, Fr.); TONI(1968, Fr.); LA CHIENNE(1975, Fr.)
Robert Dalban
JENNY LAMOUR(1948, Fr.); WALLS OF MALAPAGA, THE(1950, Fr./Ital.); DAUGHTERS OF DESTINY(1954, Fr./Ital.); OBSESSION(1954, Fr./Ital.); COUNTERFEITERS OF PARIS, THE(1962, Fr., Ital.); LOVE ON A PILLOW(1963, Fr./Ital.); PARIS PICK-UP(1963, Fr./Ital.); OF FLESH AND BLOOD(1964, Fr./Ital.); SEVENTH JUROR, THE(1964, Fr.); FANTOMAS STRIKES BACK(1965, Fr./Ital.); HIGHWAY PICK-UP(1965, Fr./Ital.); PROSTITUTION(1965, Fr.); FANTOMAS(1966, Fr./Ital.); GREAT SPY CHASE, THE(1966, Fr.); MAN FROM COCODY(1966, Fr/Ital.); BRAIN, THE(1969, Fr./US); TALL BLOND MAN WITH ONE BLACK SHOE, THE(1973, Fr.); DAYDREAMER, THE(1975, Fr.)
1984
LES COMPERES(1984, Fr.)
Camilla Dalberg
Misc. Silents
WOMAN NEXT DOOR, THE(1915)
Lydia Dalbert
CATHERINE & CO.(1976, Fr.)
Suzannae Dalbert
MY FAVORITE SPY(1951)
Suzanne Dalbert
SORRY, WRONG NUMBER(1948); ACCUSED, THE(1949); TRAIL OF THE YUKON(1949); BREAKTHROUGH(1950); MARK OF THE GORILLA(1950); LADY AND THE BANDIT, THE(1951); TARGET UNKNOWN(1951); THUNDERBIRDS(1952); FORTY-NINTH MAN, THE(1953)
Alberto Dalbes
DIABOLICAL DR. Z, THE(1966 Span./Fr.); 100 RIFLES(1969); DRACULA VERSUS FRANKENSTEIN(1972, Span.)
Julian Dalbie [d'Albie]
GAY ADVENTURE, THE(1953, Brit.)
Dalbon
DANGER IS A WOMAN(1952, Fr.)
Sid Dalbrook
JACK LONDON(1943)
Madam Dalburg
Silents
SEVEN SISTERS, THE(1915)
Amy Dalby
QUIET WEDDING(1941, Brit.); GREAT MR. HANDEL, THE(1942, Brit.); GENTLE SEX, THE(1943, Brit.); MILLIONS LIKE US(1943, Brit.); RANDOLPH FAMILY, THE(1945, Brit.); WICKED LADY, THE(1946, Brit.); MY SISTER AND I(1948, Brit.); WATERLOO ROAD(1949, Brit.); HOME TO DANGER(1951, Brit.); STRAW MAN, THE(1953, Brit.); MAN UPSTAIRS, THE(1959, Brit.); LAMP IN ASSASSIN MEWS, THE(1962, Brit.); HAUNTING, THE(1963); TOPKAPI(1964); SPY WITH A COLD NOSE, THE(1966, Brit.); WHO KILLED THE CAT?(1966, Brit.); SMASHING TIME(1967 Brit.)
Edmund Dalby
LEND ME YOUR WIFE(1935, Brit.), w; CHICK(1936, Brit.); MAN WITH 100 FACES, THE(1938, Brit.); OH BOY!(1938, Brit.); TAKE OFF THAT HAT(1938, Brit.), w
Edward Dalby
BROWN WALLET, THE(1936, Brit.)
John Dalby
STORIES FROM A FLYING TRUNK(1979, Brit.); BIDDY(1983, Brit.)
Lynn Dalby
Misc. Talkies
LEGEND OF THE WEREWOLF(1974)
Stephen Dalby
SECRET FOUR, THE(1940, Brit.), ed
W. Barrington Dalby
MAGIC CHRISTIAN, THE(1970, Brit.)
Dick Dalduzzi
1984
JOHNNY DANGEROUSLY(1984)
Alan Dale
DON'T KNOCK THE ROCK(1956)
Allan Dale
Silents
REDHEADS PREFERRED(1926), d; PRINCESS FROM HOBOKEN, THE(1927), d
Allen Dale
Silents
JOY STREET(1929)
Misc. Silents
TIRED BUSINESS MAN, THE(1927), d
Bill Dale
FRISCO KID(1935)
Bobbie Dale
JEALOUSY(1934)
Carlo Dale
TWO NIGHTS WITH CLEOPATRA(1953, Ital.); BAREFOOT CONTESSA, THE(1954); WAR AND PEACE(1956, Ital./U.S.)
Charles Dale
MANHATTAN PARADE(1931); NOB HILL(1945); TWO TICKETS TO BROADWAY(1951)
Charlie Dale
HEART OF NEW YORK(1932)
Cicely Dale
KISENGA, MAN OF AFRICA(1952, Brit.)

Cynthia Dale
MY BLOODY VALENTINE(1981, Can.)
Dana Dale
LADIES MUST LIVE(1940); MAN WHO TALKED TOO MUCH, THE(1940); TUGBOAT ANNIE SAILS AGAIN(1940); CITY, FOR CONQUEST(1941)
Daphne Dale
INVITATION TO THE DANCE(1956)
Dick Dale
MUSCLE BEACH PARTY(1964)
Donna Dale
INSIDE THE MAFIA(1959); PIER 5, HAVANA(1959)
Duchess Dale
SUNSHINE BOYS, THE(1975)
E.L. Dale
WHO KILLED GAIL PRESTON?(1938)
Eileen Dale
LAST DAYS OF DOLWYN, THE(1949, Brit.)
Ellis Dale
IF ...(1968, Brit.); INADMISSIBLE EVIDENCE(1968, Brit.); POOR COW(1968, Brit.); MAN WHO HAD POWER OVER WOMEN, THE(1970, Brit.); SUNDAY BLOODY SUNDAY(1971, Brit.); EYE OF THE NEEDLE(1981); PINK FLOYD–THE WALL(1982, Brit.); EUREKA(1983, Brit.)
1984
BLOODBATH AT THE HOUSE OF DEATH(1984, Brit.)
Ernest Dale
WHEN YOU COME HOME(1947, Brit.)
Esther Dale
CRIME WITHOUT PASSION(1934); CURLY TOP(1935); GREAT IMPERSONATION, THE(1935); I DREAM TOO MUCH(1935); I LIVE MY LIFE(1935); IN OLD KENTUCKY(1935); MARY BURNS, FUGITIVE(1935); PRIVATE WORLDS(1935); WEDDING NIGHT, THE(1935); CASE AGAINST MRS. AMES, THE(1936); FARMER IN THE DELL, THE(1936); FURY(1936); HOLLYWOOD BOULEVARD(1936); LADY OF SECRETS(1936); MAGNIFICENT BRUTE, THE(1936); TIMOTHY'S QUEST(1936); AWFUL TRUTH, THE(1937); DAMAGED GOODS(1937); DEAD END(1937); EASY LIVING(1937); ON SUCH A NIGHT(1937); OUTCAST(1937); WILD MONEY(1937); CONDEMNED WOMEN(1938); DRAMATIC SCHOOL(1938); GIRLS ON PROBATION(1938); OF HUMAN HEARTS(1938); PRISON FARM(1938); STOLEN HEAVEN(1938); BAD LITTLE ANGEL(1939); BIG TOWN CZAR(1939); BLACKMAIL(1939); BROADWAY SERENADE(1939); MADE FOR EACH OTHER(1939); SERGEANT MADDEN(1939); SWANEE RIVER(1939); TELL NO TALES(1939); WOMEN, THE(1939); 6000 ENEMIES(1939); AND ONE WAS BEAUTIFUL(1940); ARISE, MY LOVE(1940); BLONDIE HAS SERVANT TROUBLE(1940); CHILD IS BORN, A(1940); CONVICTED WOMAN(1940); LADDIE(1940); MORTAL STORM, THE(1940); OPENED BY MISTAKE(1940); UNTAMED(1940); VILLAGE BARN DANCE(1940); WOMEN WITHOUT NAMES(1940); ALL-AMERICAN CO-ED(1941); ALOMA OF THE SOUTH SEAS(1941); BACK STREET(1941); MR. AND MRS. SMITH(1941); THERE'S MAGIC IN MUSIC(1941); UNFINISHED BUSINESS(1941); BLONDIE GOES TO COLLEGE(1942); DANGEROUSLY THEY LIVE(1942); I MARRIED AN ANGEL(1942); TEN GENTLEMEN FROM WEST POINT(1942); WRECKING CREW(1942); YOU'RE TELLING ME(1942); AMAZING MRS. HOLLIDAY(1943); HELLO, FRISCO, HELLO(1943); MURDER IN TIMES SQUARE(1943); NORTH STAR, THE(1943); OLD ACQUAINTANCE(1943); SWING YOUR PARTNER(1943); BEDSIDE MANNER(1945); BEHIND CITY LIGHTS(1945); ON STAGE EVERYBODY(1945); OUT OF THIS WORLD(1945); MARGIE(1946); MY REPUTATION(1946); SMOKY(1946); STOLEN LIFE, A(1946); EGG AND I, THE(1947); THIS TIME FOR KEEPS(1947); UNFINISHED DANCE,THE(1947); SONG IS BORN, A(1948); HOLIDAY AFFAIR(1949); MA AND PA KETTLE(1949); MA AND PA KETTLE GO TO TOWN(1950); NO MAN OF HER OWN(1950); SURRENDER(1950); WALK SOFTLY, STRANGER(1950); ON MOONLIGHT BAY(1951); TOO YOUNG TO KISS(1951); MA AND PA KETTLE AT THE FAIR(1952); MONKEY BUSINESS(1952); BETRAYED WOMEN(1955); MA AND PA KETTLE AT WAIKIKI(1955); OKLAHOMAN, THE(1957); NORTH TO ALASKA(1960)
Esther Dale [Elaine May]
SUCH GOOD FRIENDS(1971), w
Frances Dale
Silents
LOVER'S LANE(1924); KING OF KINGS, THE(1927); SENSATION SEEKERS(1927)
Frank Dale
CAROLINA MOON(1940)
Fred Dale
FATHER WAS A FULLBACK(1949); HALLS OF MONTEZUMA(1951); HOUSE OF BAMBOO(1955); 80 STEPS TO JONAH(1969)
Grover Dale
WAY WE WERE, THE(1973), ch; UNSINKABLE MOLLY BROWN, THE(1964); HALF A SIXPENCE(1967, Brit.); YOUNG GIRLS OF ROCHEFORT, THE(1968, Fr.); LANDLORD, THE(1970); SO FINE(1981), ch
Highland Dale
BLACK BEAUTY(1946); RETURN OF WILDFIRE, THE(1948)
Jack Dale
SWEET SUBSTITUTE(1964, Can.), m; WHEN TOMORROW DIES(1966, Can.), m
James Dale
VICTORIA THE GREAT(1937, Brit.); CASE OF GABRIEL PERRY, THE(1935, Brit.), w; MURDER AT MONTE CARLO(1935, Brit.); I, JANE DOE(1948); SONS OF ADVENTURE(1948); HOUR OF GLORY(1949, Brit.); SERGEANT WAS A LADY, THE(1961)
Jane Dale
Silents
LOST BRIDEGROOM, THE(1916)
Jean Dale
MISSING WITNESSES(1937)
Jennifer Dale
STONE COLD DEAD(1980, Can.); SUZANNE(1980, Can.); TICKET TO HEAVEN(1981); OF UNKNOWN ORIGIN(1983, Can.)
Misc. Talkies
LOVE AND LARCENY(1983)
Jim Dale
6.5 SPECIAL(1958, Brit.); ROOMMATES(1962, Brit.); CARRY ON CABBIE(1963, Brit.); CARRY ON JACK(1963, Brit.); SWINGIN' MAIDEN, THE(1963, Brit.); CARRY ON CLEO(1964, Brit.); CARRY ON SPYING(1964, Brit.); NURSE ON WHEELS(1964, Brit.); BIG JOB, THE(1965, Brit.); CARRY ON COWBOY(1966, Brit.); CARRY ON SCREAMING(1966, Brit.); DON'T LOSE YOUR HEAD(1967, Brit.); FOLLOW THAT CAMEL(1967, Brit.); PLANK, THE(1967, Brit.); CARRY ON DOCTOR(1968, Brit.);

WINTER'S TALE, THE(1968, Brit.), a, m; CARRY ON AGAIN, DOCTOR(1969, Brit.); LOCK UP YOUR DAUGHTERS(1969, Brit.); ADOLF HITLER-MY PART IN HIS DOWNFALL(1973, Brit.); NATIONAL HEALTH, OR NURSE NORTON'S AFFAIR, THE(1973, Brit.); DIGBY, THE BIGGEST DOG IN THE WORLD(1974, Brit.); JOSEPH ANDREWS(1977, Brit.); PETE'S DRAGON(1977); HOT LEAD AND COLD FEET(1978); UNIDENTIFIED FLYING ODDBALL, THE(1979, Brit.)
1984
SCANDALOUS(1984)
Jimmy Dale
ON AN ISLAND WITH YOU(1948); SQUAD CAR(1961); B.S. I LOVE YOU(1971), m
Joan Dale
LADY OF BURLESQUE(1943); SUMMER STOCK(1950); ALICE IN WONDER-LAND(1951, Fr.)
Joane Dale
ROYAL WEDDING(1951)
Joanne Dale
WHEN MY BABY SMILES AT ME(1948); PRODIGAL, THE(1955)
Johnny Dale
NAKED CITY, THE(1948)
Laurie Dale
VIRGIN AND THE GYPSY, THE(1970, Brit.)
Little Buck Dale
Misc. Talkies
GALLOPING KID, THE(1932)
Margaret Dale
MAN WITH TWO FACES, THE(1934)
Silents
ONE EXCITING NIGHT(1922); SECOND YOUTH(1924)
Misc. Silents
DISRAELI(1921)
Marjorie Dale
DEAD MEN TELL NO TALES(1939, Brit.)
Michael Dale
EAST OF SUMATRA(1953); MISSISSIPPI GAMBLER, THE(1953); NIGHT FREIGHT(1955); ISTANBUL(1957); OUTCASTS OF THE CITY(1958)
Mike Dale
I'VE LIVED BEFORE(1956)
Moira Dale
LOVE WAGER, THE(1933, Brit.), a, w
Nova Dale
SHOW BOAT(1951)
Paul Dale
IT'S A SMALL WORLD(1950)
Philip Dale
EYE WITNESS(1950, Brit.); MYSTERY JUNCTION(1951, Brit.); WOODEN HORSE, THE(1951); TRAIN OF EVENTS(1952, Brit.); THREE CASES OF MURDER(1955, Brit.)
Rex Dale
KILLERS, THE(1946); BRUTE FORCE(1947); SENATOR WAS INDISCREET, THE(1947)
Robert Dale
10 TO MIDNIGHT(1983), cos
Sam Dale
BROTHERS AND SISTERS(1980, Brit.)
Sandra Dale
SATAN IN HIGH HEELS(1962)
Shirley Dale
BEGGAR STUDENT, THE(1931,Brit.)
Stan Dale
SOMETHING WEIRD(1967)
Suzan Dale
RHYTHM OF THE RIO GRANDE(1940)
Ted Dale
ZERO HOUR!(1957), m; DANGEROUS CHARTER(1962), m
Virginia Dale
NO TIME TO MARRY(1938); START CHEERING(1938); ALL WOMEN HAVE SECRETS(1939); DEATH OF A CHAMPION(1939); IDIOT'S DELIGHT(1939); KID FROM TEXAS, THE(1939); BUCK BENNY RIDES AGAIN(1940); DANCING ON A DIME(1940); LOVE THY NEIGHBOR(1940); PAROLE FIXER(1940); QUARTERBACK, THE(1940); KISS THE BOYS GOODBYE(1941); LAS VEGAS NIGHTS(1941); SINGING HILL, THE(1941); WORLD PREMIERE(1941); HOLIDAY INN(1942); HEADIN' FOR GOD'S COUNTRY(1943); FALL GUY(1947); HUCKSTERS, THE(1947); DOCKS OF NEW ORLEANS(1948); STRIKE IT RICH(1948); DANGER ZONE(1951); DRAG-NET(1974)
Silents
GAY OLD BIRD, THE(1927), w
Misc. Silents
SHADOWS OF THE WEST(1921)
William Dale
Silents
RACE, THE(1916)
Laara Dalen
SKIP TRACER, THE(1979, Can.), p
Zale Dalen
SKIP TRACER, THE(1979, Can.), d; HOUNDS... OF NOTRE DAME, THE(1980, Can.), d
Arthur Dales
SHERIFF OF FRACTURED JAW, THE(1958, Brit.), w; WE JOINED THE NA-VY(1962, Brit.), w
N. Dalesky
BOUNTIFUL SUMMER(1951, USSR), w
Amy Daley
TERROR HOUSE(1942, Brit.)
Bill Daley
PUT UP OR SHUT UP(1968, Arg.), spec eff; PUTNEY SWOPE(1969), spec eff
Blythe Daley
THAT'S GRATITUDE(1934)
Cass Daley
FLEET'S IN, THE(1942); STAR SPANGLED RHYTHM(1942); CRAZY HOUSE(1943); RIDING HIGH(1943); DUFFY'S TAVERN(1945); OUT OF THIS WORLD(1945); LA-DIES' MAN(1947); VARIETY GIRL(1947); HERE COMES THE GROOM(1951); RED

GARTERS(1954); SPIRIT IS WILLING, THE(1967); NORWOOD(1970); PHYNX, THE(1970)
Harry Daley
NATURAL ENEMIES(1979)
Jack Daley
SAP FROM SYRACUSE, THE(1930); O'SHAUGHNESSY'S BOY(1935); SHE COULDN'T TAKE IT(1935); FURY(1936); KLONDIKE ANNIE(1936); NEXT TIME WE LOVE(1936); SWORN ENEMY(1936); BORN TO THE WEST(1937); EXCLUSIVE(1937); GIRL WITH IDEAS, A(1937); MAN WHO CRIED WOLF, THE(1937); SWING HIGH, SWING LOW(1937); THUNDER TRAIL(1937); GOODBYE BROADWAY(1938); LITTLE TOUGH GUY(1938); GOOD GIRLS GO TO PARIS(1939); LUCKY NIGHT(1939); MUTINY IN THE BIG HOUSE(1939); TELL NO TALES(1939); I LOVE YOU AGAIN(1940); STRAWBERRY BLONDE, THE(1941); DOWN TEXAS WAY(1942); NAZI AGENT(1942); POWERS GIRL, THE(1942); WEST OF THE LAW(1942); SIX GUN GOSPEL(1943); SHINE ON, HARVEST MOON(1944); WITHIN THESE WALLS(1945); DEADLINE AT DAWN(1946); HOODLUM SAINT, THE(1946); MAN I LOVE, THE(1946); CHICKEN EVERY SUNDAY(1948); TENSION(1949); SUMMER STOCK(1950); TEA FOR TWO(1950); PAINTING THE CLOUDS WITH SUN-SHINE(1951); TEXAS CARNIVAL(1951); LOAN SHARK(1952); SCARLET AN-GEL(1952); I'LL CRY TOMORROW(1955); INSIDE THE MAFIA(1959)
Jeff Daley
ENEMY BELOW, THE(1957); OUTLAW'S SON(1957)
Jerome Daley
GIRL HABIT(1931)
Marcelle Daley
Misc. Silents
LEAVE IT TO ME(1920)
Oscar Daley
PASSION STREET, U.S.A.(1964), p, d
Ray Daley
OUTSIDER, THE(1962); THIN RED LINE, THE(1964)
Robert Daley
PLAY MISTY FOR ME(1971), p; BREEZY(1973), p; HIGH PLAINS DRIFTER(1973), p; MAGNUM FORCE(1973), p; THUNDERBOLT AND LIGHTFOOT(1974), p; EIGER SANCTION, THE(1975), p; ENFORCER, THE(1976), p; OUTLAW JOSEY WALES, THE(1976), p; GAUNTLET, THE(1977), p; EVERY WHICH WAY BUT LOOSE(1978), p; PRINCE OF THE CITY(1981), w
Selby Daley
SHINBONE ALLEY(1971), anim
Tom Daley
ON STAGE EVERYBODY(1945); THREE BRAVE MEN(1957)
William Daley
HI, MOM!(1970)
Alice Dalgarno
SINFUL DAVEY(1969, Brit.), ch
Fabienne Dali
DOULOS-THE FINGER MAN(1964, Fr./Ital.); KILL BABY KILL(1966, Ital.); MAYERLING(1968, Brit./Fr.)
Gisela Dali
EXECUTIONER, THE(1970, Brit.)
Salvador Dali
L'AGE D'OR(1979, Fr.), w
Nathalie Dalian
DIVA(1982, Fr.)
Yannis Dalianidis
SPOILED ROTTEN(1968, Gr.), d; STEFANIA(1968, Gr.), d, w
Dalibert
RED, INN, THE(1954, Fr.)
A. Dalibert
KNOCK(1955, Fr.)
Andre Dalibert
TIME BOMB(1961, Fr./Ital.); MONKEY IN WINTER, A(1962, Fr.)
Dalida
$100 A NIGHT(1968, Ger.)
David DaLie
VIRGIN SACRIFICE(1959), a, w; MIGHTY JUNGLE, THE(1965, U.S./Mex.), a, d, w; SWAMP COUNTRY(1966), a, w; TENDER WARRIOR, THE(1971), w
Charles Dalin
EROTIQUE(1969, Fr.)
Dalio
GRAND ILLUSION(1938, Fr.); AFFAIR LAFONT, THE(1939, Fr.); CURTAIN RISES, THE(1939, Fr.); KISS OF FIRE, THE(1940, Fr.); DAMNED, THE(1948, Fr.); DE-DEE(1949, Fr.); LOVER'S NET(1957, Fr.); BEAST, THE(1975, Fr.)
Marcel Dalio
LIFE AND LOVES OF BEETHOVEN, THE(1937, Fr.); PEPE LE MOKO(1937, Fr.); RULES OF THE GAME, THE(1939, Fr.); ONE NIGHT IN LISBON(1941); SHANGHAI GESTURE, THE(1941); UNHOLY PARTNERS(1941); CASABLANCA(1942); FLIGHT LIEUTENANT(1942); PIED PIPER, THE(1942); CONSTANT NYMPH, THE(1943); DESERT SONG, THE(1943); FLESH AND FANTASY(1943); SONG OF BERNADETTE, THE(1943); TONIGHT WE RAID CALAIS(1943); ACTION IN ARABIA(1944); CON-SPIRATORS, THE(1944); PIN UP GIRL(1944); TO HAVE AND HAVE NOT(1944); WILSON(1944); BELL FOR ADANO, A(1945); SNOWBOUND(1949, Brit.); TEMPTA-TION HARBOR(1949, Brit.); LOVERS OF VERONA, THE(1951, Fr.); ON THE RIVE-RA(1951); RICH, YOUNG AND PRETTY(1951); CAPTAIN BLACK JACK(1952, U.S./Fr.); HAPPY TIME, THE(1952); LOVELY TO LOOK AT(1952); MERRY WIDOW, THE(1952); SNOWS OF KILIMANJARO, THE(1952); FLIGHT TO TANGIER(1953); GENTLEMEN PREFER BLONDES(1953); LUCKY ME(1954); SABRINA(1954); JUMP INTO HELL(1955); MIRACLE IN THE RAIN(1956); CHINA GATE(1957); SUN ALSO RISES, THE(1957); TEN THOUSAND BEDROOMS(1957); TIP ON A DEAD JOCK-EY(1957); LAFAYETTE ESCADRILLE(1958); PERFECT FURLOUGH, THE(1958); MAN WHO UNDERSTOOD WOMEN, THE(1959); PILLOW TALK(1959); CAN-CAN(1960); SONG WITHOUT END(1960); DEVIL AT FOUR O'CLOCK, THE(1961); CARTOUCHE(1962, Fr./Ital.); JESSICA(1962, U.S./Ital./Fr.); DONOVAN'S REEF(1963); LIST OF ADRIAN MESSENGER, THE(1963); WILD AND WONDER-FUL(1964); LADY L(1965, Fr./Ital.); MALE COMPANION(1965, Fr./Ital.); HOW TO STEAL A MILLION(1966); MADE IN PARIS(1966); TENDER SCOUNDREL(1967, Fr./Ital.); 25TH HOUR, THE(1967, Fr./Ital./Yugo.); HOW SWEET IT IS(1968); OLDEST PROFESSION, THE(1968, Fr./Ital./Ger.); JUSTINE(1969); CATCH-22(1970); GREAT WHITE HOPE, THE(1970); MAD ADVENTURES OF RABBI JACOB, THE(1973, Fr.)

Marcel Dalip
PARIS AFTER DARK(1943)
John Dalk
BAD CHARLESTON CHARLIE(1973)
Ray Dalke
1984
KILLPOINT(1984)
Elynore Dalkhart
GREAT GOD GOLD(1935), w
Christine Dall
DOZENS, THE(1981), p&d, w, ed
Evelyn Dall
SING AS YOU SWING(1937, Brit.); HE FOUND A STAR(1941, Brit.); KING ARTHUR WAS A GENTLEMAN(1942, Brit.); PLAYBOY, THE(1942, Brit.); MISS LONDON LTD.(1943, Brit.); TIME FLIES(1944, Brit.)
John Dall
CORN IS GREEN, THE(1945); SOMETHING IN THE WIND(1947); ANOTHER PART OF THE FOREST(1948); ROPE(1948); GUN CRAZY(1949); MAN WHO CHEATED HIMSELF, THE(1951); SPARTACUS(1960); ATLANTIS, THE LOST CONTINENT(1961)
Lucio Dalla
SUBVERSIVES, THE(1967, Ital.); LADY LIBERTY(1972, Ital./Fr.), m; GOODNIGHT, LADIES AND GENTLEMEN(1977, Ital.), m
Simeon Dallaire
MY UNCLE ANTOINE(1971, Can.)
Peppino Dallalic
SHE COULDN'T TAKE IT(1935)
Masimo Dallamano
MYSTERY OF THE BLACK JUNGLE(1955), ph
Massimo Dallamano
DESERT DESPERADOES(1959), ph; COSSACKS, THE(1960, It.), ph; HEROD THE GREAT(1960, Ital.), ph; NIGHTS OF LUCRETIA BORGIA, THE(1960, Ital.), ph; CONSTANTINE AND THE CROSS(1962, Ital.), ph; LOVE AND LARCENY(1963, Fr./Ital.), ph; QUEEN OF THE NILE(1964, Ital.), ph; FOR A FEW DOLLARS MORE(1967, Ital./Ger./Span.), ph; PONTIUS PILATE(1967, Fr./Ital.), ph; GIRL GAME(1968, Braz./Fr./Ital.), ph; BLACK VEIL FOR LISA, A(1969 Ital./Ger.), d, w; DORIAN GRAY(1970, Ital./Brit./Ger./Liechtenstein), d, w; NIGHT CHILD(1975, Brit./Ital.), w
Misc. Talkies
MAFIA JUNCTION(1977), d
Max Dallamano
NIGHT CHILD(1975, Brit./Ital.), d
Charlene Dallas
RANCHO DELUXE(1975); GREAT BANK HOAX, THE(1977)
Gertrude Dallas
Misc. Silents
WOMAN IN WHITE, THE(1917)
Ian Dallas
8 ½(1963, Ital.)
Jean Dallas
HAND, THE(1960, Brit.)
Jimmy Dallas
STAND UP AND CHEER(1934 80m FOX bw)
Julian Dallas
NIGHT BOAT TO DUBLIN(1946, Brit.); BUT NOT IN VAIN(1948, Brit.); THIS WAS A WOMAN(1949, Brit.); MRS. FITZHERBERT(1950, Brit.)
Lorna Dallas
INSIDE OUT(1975, Brit.)
Philip Dallas
TENTACLES(1977, Ital.)
Roland Dallas
TOM BROWN'S SCHOOLDAYS(1951, Brit.)
Trixie Dallas
DEVIL DOLL(1964, Brit.)
John Dalleen
OUTBACK(1971, Aus.)
Emilia Dallenbach
LAS VEGAS LADY(1976)
Walter Dallenbach
LAS VEGAS LADY(1976), w
Walter C. Dallenbach
PSYCHOPATH, THE(1973), w
Joe Dallesandro
BLACK MOON(1975, Fr.); SEEDS OF EVIL(1981)
1984
COTTON CLUB, THE(1984)
Misc. Talkies
HEAT(1972); ANDY WARHOL'S DRACULA(1974); ANDY WARHOL'S FRANKENSTEIN(1974)
Maurice Dallimore
TENDER IS THE NIGHT(1961); LAD: A DOG(1962); THREE STOOGES GO AROUND THE WORLD IN A DAZE, THE(1963); MY FAIR LADY(1964); COLLECTOR, THE(1965); STRANGE BEDFELLOWS(1965); NOT WITH MY WIFE, YOU DON'T(1966); JOHNNY GOT HIS GUN(1971); HOW TO SEDUCE A WOMAN(1974)
Howard Dallin
PARALLELS(1980, Can.)
Jacques Dallin
ALIBI, THE(1939, Fr.), m
Nat Dallinger
SHAKEDOWN(1950), w
Susan Dallison
WESTMINSTER PASSION PLAY–BEHOLD THE MAN, THE(1951, Brit), p
Marcel Dallo
CONFLICT(1939, Fr.)
Frank Dallone
THERE IS STILL ROOM IN HELL(1963, Ger.), m
Towyna Dally
STORY OF THREE LOVES, THE(1953)

Jean Dalmain
TIGHT SKIRTS, LOOSE PLEASURES(1966, Fr.); VIOLETTE(1978, Fr.)
Claudine Dalmas
YOUNG REBEL, THE(1969, Fr./Ital./Span.)
Etta Dalmas
Misc. Talkies
FLYING LARIATS(1931)
Herbert Dalmas
SADDLEMATES(1941), w; SAILORS ON LEAVE(1941), w; ADDRESS UNKNOWN(1944), w; AMERICAN ROMANCE, AN(1944), w; LAST OF THE REDMEN(1947), w; ADVENTURES OF DON JUAN(1949), w; STAR OF INDIA(1956, Brit.), w
Jack Dalmas
GRINGO(1963, Span./Ital.), ph
Jack Dalmas [Massimo Dallamano]
BUFFALO BILL, HERO OF THE FAR WEST(1962, Ital.), ph; FISTFUL OF DOLLARS, A(1964, Ital./Ger./Span.), ph
Michael Dalmatoff
WONDER BAR(1934); ONCE IN A BLUE MOON(1936); FOR WHOM THE BELL TOLLS(1943); IRISH EYES ARE SMILING(1944); UTOPIA(1952, Fr./Ital.)
Malcolm Dalmayne
MINE OWN EXECUTIONER(1948, Brit.)
John Dalmer
GUN BATTLE AT MONTEREY(1957)
Mony Dalmes
LOVE IS A BALL(1963); DON'T TEMPT THE DEVIL(1964, Fr./Ital.); MAYERLING(1968, Brit./Fr.)
The Dalmora Can-Can Dancers
SHE SHALL HAVE MUSIC(1935, Brit.)
Aimee Dalmores
Misc. Silents
ON-THE-SQUARE GIRL, THE(1917); SCANDAL(1917)
Francois Dalou
CLOPORTES(1966, Fr., Ital.)
Roger Dalphin
GERVAISE(1956, Fr.)
Harry Dalroy
Silents
STORMY SEAS(1923)
Rube Dalroy
CODE OF THE CACTUS(1939)
Andrew Angus Dalrymple
QUIET DAY IN BELFAST, A(1974, Can.), w
Ian Dalrymple
TAXI FOR TWO(1929, Brit.), w; HOUND OF THE BASKERVILLES(1932, Brit.), ed; MICHAEL AND MARY(1932, Brit.), ed; OFFICE GIRL, THE(1932, Brit.), ed; CUCKOO IN THE NEST, THE(1933, Brit.), p; GOOD COMPANIONS(1933, Brit.), w; MAN THEY COULDN'T ARREST, THE(1933, Brit.), ed; NIGHT AND DAY(1933, Brit.), ed; CHANNEL CROSSING(1934, Brit.), p; EVERGREEN(1934, Brit.), ed; GHOUL, THE(1934, Brit.), ed; WOMAN IN COMMAND, THE(1934 Brit.), ed; HER LAST AFFAIRE(1935, Brit.), w; BROWN WALLET, THE(1936, Brit.), w; JURY'S EVIDENCE(1936, Brit.), w; RADIO LOVER(1936, Brit.), w; STORM IN A TEACUP(1937, Brit.), d, w; CITADEL, THE(1938, Brit.), w; DIVORCE OF LADY X. THE(1938, Brit.), w; PYGMALION(1938, Brit.), w; SOUTH RIDING(1938, Brit.), w; CHEER BOYS CHEER(1939, Brit.), w; CLOUDS OVER EUROPE(1939, Brit.), w; FRENCH WITHOUT TEARS(1939, Brit.), w; LION HAS WINGS, THE(1940, Brit.), w; OLD BILL AND SON(1940, Brit.), d, w; LADY IN DISTRESS(1942, Brit.), w; PIMPERNEL SMITH(1942, Brit.), w; ESTHER WATERS(1948, Brit.), p, d; ALL OVER THE TOWN(1949, Brit.), p; DEAR MR. PROHACK(1949, Brit.), p; WOMAN IN THE HALL, THE(1949, Brit.), p, w; MANIACS ON WHEELS(1951, Brit.), p; WOODEN HORSE, THE(1951), p; HEART OF THE MATTER, THE(1954, Brit.), p, w; THREE CASES OF MURDER(1955, Brit.), p; HELL IN KOREA(1956, Brit.), w; ADMIRABLE CRICHTON, THE(1957, Brit.), p; RAISING A RIOT(1957, Brit.), p, w; CRY FROM THE STREET, A(1959, Brit.), p; HUNTED IN HOLLAND(1961, Brit.), p, w; MIX ME A PERSON(1962, Brit.), w; CALAMITY THE COW(1967, Brit.), p
Jean Dalrymple
IT HAPPENED IN NEW YORK(1935), w
Leona Dalrymple
DANGEROUS NUMBER(1937), w
Joanne Dalsass
IMPASSE(1969)
1984
LONELY GUY, THE(1984)
Dr. Frederick Dalsheim
WAJAN(1938, South Bali), p
Abby Dalton
ROCK ALL NIGHT(1957); SAGA OF THE VIKING WOMEN AND THEIR VOYAGE TO THE WATERS OF THE GREAT SEA SERPENT, THE(1957); COLE YOUNGER, GUNFIGHTER(1958); GIRLS ON THE LOOSE(1958); STAKEOUT ON DOPE STREET(1958); PLAINSMAN, THE(1966); WHALE OF A TALE, A(1977)
Alan Dalton
NICHOLAS AND ALEXANDRA(1971, Brit.)
Anne Dalton
YOUNG CASSIDY(1965, U.S./Brit.)
Annie Dalton
RYAN'S DAUGHTER(1970, Brit.)
Audrey Dalton
MY COUSIN RACHEL(1952); GIRLS OF PLEASURE ISLAND, THE(1953); TITANIC(1953); CASANOVA'S BIG NIGHT(1954); DRUM BEAT(1954); PRODIGAL, THE(1955); DEADLIEST SIN, THE(1956, Brit.); HOLD BACK THE NIGHT(1956); MONSTER THAT CHALLENGED THE WORLD, THE(1957); SEPARATE TABLES(1958); THUNDERING JETS(1958); LONE TEXAN(1959); THIS OTHER EDEN(1959, Brit.); MR. SARDONICUS(1961); KITTEN WITH A WHIP(1964); BOUNTY KILLER, THE(1965)
Charles Dalton
Silents
FIGHTING ODDS(1917); ETERNAL MAGDALENE, THE(1919)
Misc. Silents
WAKEFIELD CASE, THE(1921)

Christopher Dalton
CLOWN MURDERS, THE(1976, Can.), p; POWER PLAY(1978, Brit./Can.), p

Clark Dalton [Walter Enstine]
MISSION STARDUST(1968, Ital./Span./Ger.), w

Danie-Wade Dalton
STING II, THE(1983)

Darren Dalton
OUTSIDERS, THE(1983)
1984
JOY OF SEX(1984); RED DAWN(1984)

Deborah Dalton
TWO OF A KIND(1983)
1984
WOMAN IN RED, THE(1984)

Dorothy Dalton
Silents
PIERRE OF THE PLAINS(1914); CAPTIVE GOD, THE(1916); JUNGLE CHILD, THE(1916); CHICKEN CASEY(1917); DARK ROAD, THE(1917); FEMALE OF THE SPECIES(1917); PRICE MARK, THE(1917); KAISER'S SHADOW, THE(1918); QUICK-SANDS(1918); EXTRAVAGANCE(1919); DARK MIRROR, THE(1920); GUILTY OF LOVE(1920); IDOL OF THE NORTH, THE(1921); CRIMSON CHALLENGE(1922); MORAN OF THE LADY LETTY(1922); ON THE HIGH SEAS(1922); SIREN CALL, THE(1922); WOMAN WHO WALKED ALONE, THE(1922); LAW OF THE LAWLESS, THE(1923)
Misc. Silents
DISCIPLE, THE(1915); CIVILIZATION'S CHILD(1916); D'ARTAGNAN(1916); GAMBLE IN SOULS, A(1916); RAIDERS, THE(1916); VAGABOND PRINCE, THE(1916); BACK OF THE MAN(1917); FLAME OF THE YUKON, THE(1917); LOVE LETTERS(1917); TEN OF DIAMONDS(1917); WEAKER SEX, THE(1917); WILD WINSHIP'S WIDOW(1917); FLARE-UP SAL(1918); GREEN EYES(1918); LOVE ME(1918); MATING OF MARCELLA, THE(1918); TYRANT FEAR(1918); VIVE LA FRANCE(1918); HARD BOILED(1919); HOMEBREAKER, THE(1919); L' APACHE(1919); LADY OF RED BUTTE, THE(1919); MARKET OF SOULS, THE(1919); OTHER MEN'S WIVES(1919); BLACK IS WHITE(1920); HALF AN HOUR(1920); HIS WIFE'S FRIEND(1920); ROMANTIC ADVENTURESS, A(1920); BEHIND MASKS(1921); FOOL'S PARADISE(1921); DARK SECRETS(1923); FOG BOUND(1923); LONE WOLF, THE(1924); MORAL SINNER, THE(1924)

Emmet Dalton
DEVIL'S AGENT, THE(1962, Brit.), p

Emmett Dalton
WHEN THE DALTONS RODE(1940), w; WEBSTER BOY, THE(1962, Brit.), p
Misc. Silents
BEYOND THE LAW(1918)

Eric Dalton
Silents
OAKDALE AFFAIR, THE(1919)

Fred Dalton
Misc. Silents
WELCOME TO OUR CITY(1922)

Hugh Dalton
BIG BLOCKADE, THE(1942, Brit.)

Jackie Dalton
JUST OUT OF REACH(1979, Aus.)

James Dalton
PRODUCERS, THE(1967), set d

Jeff Dalton
I WALK THE LINE(1970)

John Dalton
FIREBALL JUNGLE(1968), ed

Ken Dalton
1984
HARDBODIES(1984), p

Lacy J. Dalton
TAKE THIS JOB AND SHOVE IT(1981)

Ninkey Dalton
IMPROPER CHANNELS(1981, Can.), art d
1984
CHAMPIONS(1984), set d; CITY GIRL, THE(1984), art d; SAVAGE STREETS(1984), art d

Patti Dalton
GREAT MUPPET CAPER, THE(1981)

Patty Dalton
EXPRESSO BONGO(1959, Brit.); SHAKEDOWN, THE(1960, Brit.)

Phyllis Dalton
ROB ROY, THE HIGHLAND ROGUE(1954, Brit.), cos; JOHN PAUL JONES(1959), cos; OUR MAN IN HAVANA(1960, Brit.), cos; LAWRENCE OF ARABIA(1962, Brit.), cos; FURY AT SMUGGLERS BAY(1963, Brit.), cos; DOCTOR ZHIVAGO(1965), cos; OLIVER!(1968, Brit.), cos; FRAGMENT OF FEAR(1971, Brit.), cos; HIRELING, THE(1973, Brit.), cos; MOHAMMAD, MESSENGER OF GOD(1976, Lebanon/Brit.), cos; VOYAGE OF THE DAMNED(1976, Brit.), cos; UNIDENTIFIED FLYING ODDBALL, THE(1979, Brit.), cos; WATER BABIES, THE(1979, Brit.), cos; AWAKENING, THE(1980), cos; MIRROR CRACK'D, THE(1980, Brit.), cos

Phyllus Dalton
LORD JIM(1965, Brit.), cos

Robert Dalton
LIFE BEGINS AT 40(1935); UNDER YOUR SPELL(1936); GIRL WITH IDEAS, A(1937); HARD TRAIL(1969)

Sam Dalton
1984
FOOTLOOSE(1984)

Sue Dalton
MS. 45(1981), spec eff

Susanna Dalton
PATERNITY(1981); LITTLE SEX, A(1982)

Timothy Dalton
LION IN WINTER, THE(1968, Brit.); CROMWELL(1970, Brit.); WUTHERING HEIGHTS(1970, Brit.); MARY, QUEEN OF SCOTS(1971, Brit.); PERMISSION TO KILL(1975, U.S./Aust.); SEXTETTE(1978); AGATHA(1979, Brit.); FLASH GORDON(1980); CHANEL SOLITAIRE(1981)

Tony Dalton
DEMOBBED(1944, Brit.); HONEYMOON HOTEL(1946, Brit.)

Valda Dalton
RABID(1976, Can.)

Vera Dalton
ODYSSEY OF THE PACIFIC(1983, Can./Fr.)

Roger Daltrey
LISZTOMANIA(1975, Brit.); TOMMY(1975, Brit.), a, a, m; LEGACY, THE(1979, Brit.); MC VICAR(1982, Brit.), p

Nancy Dalunde
LOVING COUPLES(1966, Swed.)

Robert Dalva
LIONS LOVE(1969), ed; BLACK STALLION, THE(1979), ed; BLACK STALLION RETURNS, THE(1983), d

Alberto Dalves
HUNCHBACK OF THE MORGUE, THE(1972, Span.)

Don Dalvin
GANG, THE(1938, Brit.)

Arnold Daly
Silents
PORT OF MISSING MEN(1914); KING'S GAME, THE(1916), w; IN BORROWED PLUMES(1926)
Misc. Silents
AFFAIR OF THREE NATIONS, AN(1915), a, d; HOUSE OF FEAR, THE(1915), a, d; MY OWN UNITED STATES(1918)

Barbara Daly
CLOCKWORK ORANGE, A(1971, Brit.), makeup

Blythe Daly
HER MAN(1930); STAR IS BORN, A(1954)

Brian Daly
STORY OF WILL ROGERS, THE(1952)
Silents
FLYING FROM JUSTICE(1915, Brit.); NEW CLOWN, THE(1916, Brit.)

Carroll John Daly
TICKET TO CRIME(1934), w

Cindy Daly
COACH(1978); DEATH WISH II(1982)

Esther Lynd Daly
BEGGARS IN ERMINE(1934), w

Frank Daly
OLD IRON(1938, Brit.)

George Daly
LITTLE CAESAR(1931); PUBLIC ENEMY, THE(1931); PICTURE SNATCHER(1933); G-MEN(1935); EXCUSE MY GLOVE(1936, Brit.)

Hazel Daly
Silents
SKINNER'S DRESS SUIT(1917); STOP THIEF(1920); BEATING THE GAME(1921)
Misc. Silents
BROWN IN HARVARD(1917); FILLING HIS OWN SHOES(1917); SATAN'S PRIVATE DOOR(1917); SKINNER'S BABY(1917); SKINNER'S BUBBLE(1917); LITTLE ROWDY, THE(1919); WILD GOOSE CHASE(1919); GAY LORD QUEX, THE(1920)

Jack Daly
PAROLE RACKET(1937); KATHLEEN(1938, Ireland); I DIDN'T DO IT(1945, Brit.); SEARCH FOR DANGER(1949); CHAMPAGNE FOR CAESAR(1950); FOR HEAVEN'S SAKE(1950); MISTER 880(1950); ONCE A THIEF(1950); BADMAN'S GOLD(1951); LOVE NEST(1951); PICKUP(1951); NO ROOM FOR THE GROOM(1952); LAW AND ORDER(1953); PHANTOM FROM SPACE(1953); BIG CHASE, THE(1954); KILLERS FROM SPACE(1954); SNOW CREATURE, THE,(1954); TOBOR THE GREAT(1954); ABBOTT AND COSTELLO MEET THE KEYSTONE KOPS(1955); BIG BLUFF, THE(1955); HARDER THEY FALL, THE(1956); MEET ME IN LAS VEGAS(1956); RAINTREE COUNTY(1957); SPIRIT OF ST. LOUIS, THE(1957); NORTH BY NORTHWEST(1959); RETURN OF THE FLY(1959); LAD: A DOG(1962); DEAR BRIGETTE(1965)

Jacqueline Daly
BATHING BEAUTY(1944)

James Daly
SLEEPING CITY, THE(1950); COURT-MARTIAL OF BILLY MITCHELL, THE(1955); YOUNG STRANGER, THE(1957); I AIM AT THE STARS(1960); PLANET OF THE APES(1968); BIG BOUNCE, THE(1969); FOUR RODE OUT(1969, US/Span.); FIVE MAN ARMY, THE(1970, Ital.); RESURRECTION OF ZACHARY WHEELER, THE(1971)
Silents
FORTUNE HUNTER, THE(1914)

James J. Daly
Misc. Silents
OGRE AND THE GIRL, THE(1915)

Jane Daly
MYSTERIOUS ISLAND(1929); CHILDREN SHOULDN'T PLAY WITH DEAD THINGS(1972); NORTH DALLAS FORTY(1979); AMY(1981)
Silents
WEST OF ZANZIBAR(1928)

Joe Daly
Misc. Silents
LORDS OF HIGH DECISION, THE(1916)

John Daly
SUNBURN(1979), p
1984
BREED APART, A(1984), p

Jonathan Daly
OUT OF SIGHT(1966); YOUNG WARRIORS, THE(1967); SUPERDAD(1974); SHAGGY D.A., THE(1976); AMY(1981)

Jonathon Daly
RASCAL(1969); $1,000,000 DUCK(1971)

Ken Daly
1984
KARATE KID, THE(1984)

Marcella Daly
Silents
WEST OF CHICAGO(1922); ARIZONA ROMEO, THE(1925); NON-STOP FLIGHT, THE(1926); ARIZONA WILDCAT(1927); LONE EAGLE, THE(1927); MARRIED ALI-

VE(1927); MIDNIGHT WATCH, THE(1927); TWO LOVERS(1928)
Misc. Silents
  PRINCE OF PEP, THE(1925)

Mark Daly
  BEGGAR STUDENT, THE(1931,Brit.); EAST LYNNE ON THE WESTERN FRONT(1931, Brit.); THIRD STRING, THE(1932, Brit.); CUCKOO IN THE NEST, THE(1933, Brit.); DOSS HOUSE(1933, Brit.); UP FOR THE DERBY(1933, Brit.); BYPASS TO HAPPINESS(1934, Brit.); MUSIC HALL(1934, Brit.); RIVER WOLVES, THE(1934, Brit.); SAY IT WITH FLOWERS(1934, Brit.); FLOOD TIDE(1935, Brit.); JUBILEE WINDOW(1935, Brit.); REAL BLOKE, A(1935, Brit.); SCANDALS OF PARIS(1935, Brit.); SMALL MAN, THE(1935, Brit.); THAT'S MY UNCLE(1935, Brit.); CAPTAIN'S TABLE, THE(1936, Brit.); GHOST GOES WEST, THE(1936, Brit.); HEARTS OF HUMANITY(1936, Brit.); MURDER AT THE CABARET(1936, Brit.); SHIPMATES O' MINE(1936, Brit.); CAPTAIN'S ORDERS(1937, Brit.); COMMAND PERFORMANCE(1937, Brit.); MAN WHO COULD WORK MIRACLES, THE(1937, Brit.); WANTED(1937, Brit.); WHERE THERE'S A WILL(1937, Brit.); WINGS OF THE MORNING(1937, Brit.); BREAK THE NEWS(1938, Brit.); FOLLOW YOUR STAR(1938, Brit.); LASSIE FROM LANCASHIRE(1938, Brit.); HOOTS MON!(1939, Brit.); FARMER'S WIFE, THE(1941, Brit.); BONNIE PRINCE CHARLIE(1948, Brit.); NAUGHTY ARLETTE(1951, Brit.); ALF'S BABY(1953, Brit.); DELAVINE AFFAIR, THE(1954, Brit.); DON'T BLAME THE STORK(1954, Brit.); LEASE OF LIFE(1954, Brit.); DYNAMITERS, THE(1956, Brit.); GENTLE TOUCH, THE(1956, Brit.); KEEP IT CLEAN(1956, Brit.); ROCK AROUND THE WORLD(1957, Brit.); YOU PAY YOUR MONEY(1957, Brit.); SOAPBOX DERBY(1958, Brit.)

Michael K. Daly
  HOW TO BEAT THE HIGH COST OF LIVING(1980)

Orlando Daly
Misc. Silents
  BETTER MAN, THE(1915); RUNAWAY WIFE, THE(1915)

Pat Daly
  SLIGHT CASE OF MURDER, A(1938); EDUCATING RITA(1983)

Paul Daly
  FOURTEEN, THE(1973, Brit.); CLASS OF MISS MAC MICHAEL, THE(1978, Brit./U.S.)

Peter-Hugo Daly
  BREAKING GLASS(1980, Brit.)
1984
  OXFORD BLUES(1984)

Rad Daly
  10(1979)

Rad Daly, Jr.
  NORTH DALLAS FORTY(1979)

Ray Daly
  FIVE PENNIES, THE(1959)

Robert Daly
Silents
  PARDON MY NERVE!(1922); YELLOW STAIN, THE(1922); HELD TO ANSWER(1923)
Misc. Silents
  ROOF TREE, THE(1921)

Sefton Daly
  WHEREVER SHE GOES(1953, Aus.)

Timothy Daly
  DINER(1982)
1984
  JUST THE WAY YOU ARE(1984)

Tom Daly
  MY GAL LOVES MUSIC(1944); I'LL TELL THE WORLD(1945); SCARLET STREET(1945); SPIDER WOMAN STRIKES BACK, THE(1946); DOWN TO EARTH(1947); GOG(1954); JET PILOT(1957); THREE BRAVE MEN(1957); 27TH DAY, THE(1957); FRONTIER GUN(1958); ANGRY RED PLANET, THE(1959); MIRACLE OF THE HILLS, THE(1959); THIRD VOICE, THE(1960); FIREBRAND, THE(1962); WOMAN HUNT(1962); CYCLE SAVAGES(1969); PROLOGUE(1970, Can.), p

Tyne Daly
  JOHN AND MARY(1969); ANGEL UNCHAINED(1970); PLAY IT AS IT LAYS(1972); ENTERTAINER, THE(1975); ENFORCER, THE(1976); TELEFON(1977); SPEEDTRAP(1978); ZOOT SUIT(1981)
Misc. Talkies
  ADULTERESS, THE(1976)

William Daly
  AIR MAIL(1932); OKAY AMERICA(1932)

William Robert Daly
Silents
  FORGIVEN, OR THE JACK O'DIAMONDS(1914), d; UNCLE TOM'S CABIN(1914), d; SAWDUST(1923); RIDE FOR YOUR LIFE(1924)
Misc. Silents
  AT PINEY RIDGE(1916), d

Jacqueline Dalya
  HONEYMOON IN BALI(1939); GAY CABALLERO, THE(1940); ONE MILLION B.C.(1940); PRIMROSE PATH(1940); BLOOD AND SAND(1941); CHARLIE CHAN IN RIO(1941); LADY FROM LOUISIANA(1941); I MARRIED AN ANGEL(1942); BEHIND PRISON WALLS(1943); FLESH AND FANTASY(1943); MISSION TO MOSCOW(1943); MYSTERY OF THE 13TH GUEST(1943); SO'S YOUR UNCLE(1943); SUBMARINE BASE(1943); VOICE IN THE WIND(1944); SONG OF MEXICO(1945); QUEEN OF BURLESQUE(1946); MYSTERY IN MEXICO(1948); SMUGGLERS' COVE(1948); TREASURE OF THE SIERRA MADRE, THE(1948); WABASH AVENUE(1950)

Jackie Dalyea
Misc. Talkies
  MISS MELODY JONES(1973)

John Dalz
  ER LOVE A STRANGER(1958)

Arch R. Dalzell
  TOWER OF LONDON(1962), ph; APACHE RIFLES(1964), ph; GIRLS ON THE BEACH(1965), ph; MUTINY IN OUTER SPACE(1965), ph; WOMEN OF THE PREHISTORIC PLANET(1966), ph; TRIP, THE(1967), ph; MINI-SKIRT MOB, THE(1968), ph

Archie Dalzell
  DALTON GANG, THE(1949), ph; THE HYPNOTIC EYE(1960), ph; LITTLE SHOP OF HORRORS(1961), ph

Archie R. Dalzell
  SUNSET BOULEVARD(1950)

Dennis Dalzell
  SIDEWINDER ONE(1977), ph; SPEEDTRAP(1978), ph; BUSTIN' LOOSE(1981), ph; HARD COUNTRY(1981), ph

Lyda Dalzell
Misc. Silents
  FILLING HIS OWN SHOES(1917)

William Dalzell
  LES MISERABLES(1952)

Marjorie Dalziel
  BROTHERLY LOVE(1970, Brit.)

Stassa Damacus
  STORY OF RUTH, THE(1960)

Cathryn Daman
  FIRST TIME, THE(1983)

Gerhard Damann
  JOHNNY STEALS EUROPE(1932, Ger.); MAID HAPPY(1933, Brit.)

Andree Damant
  IT ONLY HAPPENS TO OTHERS(1971, Fr./Ital.)

Susan Damante
  STUDENT TEACHERS, THE(1973)

Germaine Damar
  SCHLAGER-PARADE(1953); BIMBO THE GREAT(1961, Ger.)

Shoshana Damari
  HILL 24 DOESN'T ANSWER(1955, Israel)

Stasa Damascus
  LAST MOMENT, THE(1966); DREAM OF KINGS, A(1969)

A. Th. Damaskinos
  APOLLO GOES ON HOLIDAY(1968, Ger./Swed.), p

Th. A. Damaskinos
  MADALENA(1965, Gr.), p

Theophanis A. Damaskinos
  RED LANTERNS(1965, Gr.), p; FEAR, THE(1967, Gr.), p; LOVE CYCLES(1969, Gr.), p; SISTERS, THE(1969, Gr.), p

Sandra Damato
  DREAM OF KINGS, A(1969)

G. Dambakare
  TAKE ME AWAY, MY LOVE(1962, Gr.), p

William Dambrosi
  FRENCH LEAVE(1948)

Nathan Dambuza
  TWO GENTLEMEN SHARING(1969, Brit.)

Beverly Dame
  MEDIUM, THE(1951)

Josef Damen
  M(1933, Ger.); TESTAMENT OF DR. MABUSE, THE(1943, Ger.)

Sam Damen
Silents
  SOULS FOR SALE(1923)

Frank Damer
  UNDER THE RED ROBE(1937, Brit.)

Margaret Damer
  HIGH SOCIETY(1932, Brit.); ILLEGAL(1932, Brit.); TIN GODS(1932, Brit.); OUT OF THE PAST(1933, Brit.); CITY OF BEAUTIFUL NONSENSE, THE(1935, Brit.); MR. WHAT'S-HIS-NAME(1935, Brit.); FAREWELL TO CINDERELLA(1937, Brit.); FIRST NIGHT(1937, Brit.); LANCASHIRE LUCK(1937, Brit.); WARNING TO WANTONS, A(1949, Brit.)

Donna Damerel
  MYRT AND MARGE(1934)

Stanley Damerell
  CHARMING DECEIVER, THE(1933, Brit.), m/l

Lisa Dameron
  NIGHT OF BLOODY HORROR zero(1969)

Lilo Damert
  CROSS OF LORRAINE, THE(1943), w

Damia
  HUNCHBACK OF NOTRE DAME, THE(1957, Fr.)

Maryse Damia
Silents
  NAPOLEON(1927, Fr.)

Michael Damian
  WIND AND THE LION, THE(1975); YOUNG DOCTORS IN LOVE(1982)

Damiano Damiani
  GODDESS OF LOVE, THE(1960, Ital./Fr.), w; HEROD THE GREAT(1960, Ital.), w; ARTURO'S ISLAND(1963, Ital.), d, w; CLEOPATRA'S DAUGHTER(1963, Fr., Ital.), w; EMPTY CANVAS, THE(1964, Fr./Ital.), d, w; LIPSTICK(1965, Fr./Ital.), d, w; BULLET FOR THE GENERAL, A(1967, Ital.), d; DAY OF THE OWL, THE(1968, Ital./Fr.), d, w; MAFIA(1969, Fr./Ital.), d, w; WITCH, THE(1969, Ital.), d, w; CONFESSIONS OF A POLICE CAPTAIN(1971, Ital.), d, w; TEMPTER, THE(1974, Ital./Brit.), d&w; DEVIL IS A WOMAN, THE(1975, Brit./Ital.), d, w; GENIUS, THE(1976, Ital./Fr./Ger.), d, w; AMITYVILLE II: THE POSSESSION(1982), d

Donatella Damiani
  CITY OF WOMEN(1980, Ital./Fr.)

Luciano Damiani
  MAN OF LA MANCHA(1972), art d, cos

Simon Damiani
  FANTASTIC PLANET(1973, Fr./Czech.), p

Tilde Damiani
  PLAYGIRLS AND THE VAMPIRE(1964, Ital.)

Gerard Damiano
Misc. Talkies
  LEGACY OF SATAN(1973), d

Jenny Damianopoulou
  OEDIPUS THE KING(1968, Brit.)

Alexis Damianos
  FEAR, THE(1967, Gr.)

Cleanthis Damianos
300 SPARTANS, THE(1962), tech adv
Mario Damicelli
DESERT WARRIOR(1961 Ital./Span.), ph
Pedro Damieari
EAGLE'S WING(1979, Brit.)
Eva Damien
FRUIT IS RIPE, THE(1961, Fr./Ital.)
Madeleine Damien
DIARY OF A CHAMBERMAID(1964, Fr./Ital.); THIEF OF PARIS, THE(1967, Fr./Ital.); CHRISTMAS TREE, THE(1969, Fr.); VERY HAPPY ALEXANDER(1969, Fr.); QUIET PLACE IN THE COUNTRY, A(1970, Ital./Fr.); HERBIE GOES TO MONTE CARLO(1977)
Pedro Damien
RETURN OF A MAN CALLED HORSE, THE(1976)
John Damier
D-DAY, THE SIXTH OF JUNE(1956)
Salvatore Damino
STARLIGHT OVER TEXAS(1938)
Lili Damita
MATCH KING, THE(1932); GOLDIE GETS ALONG(1933); MAN STOLEN(1934, Fr.); BREWSTER'S MILLIONS(1935, Brit.); DEVIL ON HORSEBACK, THE(1936)
Misc. Silents
FORBIDDEN LOVE(1927, Brit.)
Lily Damita
BRIDGE OF SAN LUIS REY, THE(1929); COCK-EYED WORLD, THE(1929); FIGHTING CARAVANS(1931); FRIENDS AND LOVERS(1931); WOMAN BETWEEN(1931); THIS IS THE NIGHT(1932); FRISCO KID(1935)
Silents
RESCUE, THE(1929)
Misc. Silents
SCANDAL IN PARIS(1929, Ger.)
John Damler
I WAS AN AMERICAN SPY(1951); ATOMIC CITY, THE(1952); IT GROWS ON TREES(1952); CHARGE AT FEATHER RIVER, THE(1953); SOUTH SEA WOMAN(1953); DRIVE A CROOKED ROAD(1954); LONG WAIT, THE(1954); ROSE MARIE(1954); TENNESSEE CHAMP(1954); BETRAYED WOMEN(1955); FIGHTING CHANCE, THE(1955); LOVE ME OR LEAVE ME(1955); MARAUDERS, THE(1955); PRODIGAL, THE(1955); ACCUSED OF MURDER(1956); LAST OF THE BADMEN(1957); LEGION OF THE DOOMED(1958); PARTY GIRL(1958); NORTH BY NORTHWEST(1959); RAYMIE(1960); GUN FIGHT(1961); HOW THE WEST WAS WON(1962); SAM WHISKEY(1969)
Anna Dammann
HIS MAJESTY, KING BALLYHOO(1931, Ger.)
Gerhard Dammann
WORLD WITHOUT A MASK, THE(1934, Ger.)
Sarah Dammann
WHEN A STRANGER CALLS(1979)
Blackie Dammett
NATIONAL LAMPOON'S CLASS REUNION(1982); DOCTOR DETROIT(1983)
1984
MEATBALLS PART II(1984)
Gail Damms
STONE COLD DEAD(1980, Can.)
Jack Damn
TEST PILOT(1938), makeup
Bob Damon
Misc. Talkies
LEGEND OF ALFRED PACKER, THE(1979)
Bruno Damon
I DRINK YOUR BLOOD(1971)
1984
ALPHABET CITY(1984)
Cathryn Damon
HOW TO BEAT THE HIGH COST OF LIVING(1980)
Dwayne Damon
M(1970)
Kenny Damon
ADDING MACHINE, THE(1969)
Mark Damon
INSIDE DETROIT(1955); BETWEEN HEAVEN AND HELL(1956); SCREAMING EAGLES(1956); YOUNG AND DANGEROUS(1957); LIFE BEGINS AT 17(1958); PARTY CRASHERS, THE(1958); HOUSE OF USHER(1960); THIS REBEL BREED(1960); LONGEST DAY, THE(1962); RELUCTANT SAINT, THE(1962, U.S./Ital.); BEAUTY AND THE BEAST(1963); BLACK SABBATH(1963, Ital.); YOUNG RACERS, THE(1963); RINGO AND HIS GOLDEN PISTOL(1966, Ital.); JOHNNY YUMA(1967, Ital.); ANZIO(1968, Ital.); YOUNG, THE EVIL AND THE SAVAGE, THE(1968, Ital.); ARENA, THE(1973), p; CRYPT OF THE LIVING DEAD zero(1973); DEVIL'S WEDDING NIGHT, THE(1973, Ital.); LITTLE MOTHER(1973, U.S./Yugo./Ger.); THERE IS NO 13(1977)
Misc. Talkies
LIONS OF ST. PETERSBURG, THE(1971); AGE OF PISCES(1972); HANNAH-QUEEN OF THE VAMPIRES(1972); SCALAWAG BUNCH, THE(1976)
Peter Damon
SKY HIGH(1952); FALL OF THE ROMAN EMPIRE, THE(1964); CRACK IN THE WORLD(1965)
Stuart Damon
YOUNG DOCTORS IN LOVE(1982); STAR 80(1983)
Misc. Talkies
LEGEND OF CHAMPIONS(1983)
Renee Damonde
ALL QUIET ON THE WESTERN FRONT(1930)
Vic Damone
RICH, YOUNG AND PRETTY(1951); STRIP, THE(1951); ATHENA(1954); DEEP IN MY HEART(1954); HIT THE DECK(1955); KISMET(1955); MEET ME IN LAS VEGAS(1956); HELL TO ETERNITY(1960)
James Damore
HAIL THE CONQUERING HERO(1944)

Claude Dampier
NO MONKEY BUSINESS(1935, Brit.); RADIO FOLLIES(1935, Brit.); SHE SHALL HAVE MUSIC(1935, Brit.); SO YOU WON'T TALK?(1935, Brit.); WHITE LILAC(1935, Brit.); ALL IN(1936, Brit.); BOYS WILL BE BOYS(1936, Brit.); KING OF THE CASTLE(1936, Brit.); PUBLIC NUISANCE NO. 1(1936, Brit.); SHE KNEW WHAT SHE WANTED(1936, Brit.); SUCH IS LIFE(1936, Brit.); MR. STRINGFELLOW SAYS NO(1937, Brit.); RIDING HIGH(1937, Brit.); SING AS YOU SWING(1937, Brit.); WANTED(1937, Brit.); DON'T TAKE IT TO HEART(1944, Brit.); STICK 'EM UP(1950, Brit.); MEET MR. MALCOLM(1954, Brit.)
Delano Damron
GROUND ZERO(1973), m
Roy Damron
THIEVES' HIGHWAY(1949); SHOW BOAT(1951); UNDERWATER CITY, THE(1962)
Walter Damrosch
STAR MAKER, THE(1939); CARNEGIE HALL(1947)
Mel Damski
YELLOWBEARD(1983), d
Froeydis Damslora
TERRORISTS, THE(1975, Brit.)
Brian Damude
SUDDEN FURY(1975, Can.), d&w; I, MAUREEN(1978, Can.)
Jane Damvell
CRAIG'S WIFE(1936)
Allen Dan
PAISAN(1948, Ital.)
Debbie Dan
LAST AFFAIR, THE(1976)
Ikuma Dan
SAMURAI(PART III)** (1967, Jap.), m, m; SAMURAI(1955, Jap.), m; RICKSHAW MAN, THE(1960, Jap.), m; I BOMBED PEARL HARBOR(1961, Jap.), m; LIFE OF A COUNTRY DOCTOR(1961, Jap.), m; MADAME AKI(1963, Jap.), m; YOUTH AND HIS AMULET, THE(1963, Jap.), m; SAGA OF THE VAGABONDS(1964, Jap.), m; RABBLE, THE(1965, Jap.), m; WE WILL REMEMBER(1966, Jap.), w, m
Judy Dan
PAL JOEY(1957); SPIRAL ROAD, THE(1962); STAGECOACH TO DANCER'S PARK(1962); WAR IS HELL(1964); KILL A DRAGON(1967)
Kazuo Dan
MAGIC BOY(1960, Jap.), w
Reiko Dan
DANGEROUS KISS, THE(1961, Jap.); DIPLOMAT'S MANSION, THE(1961, Jap.); EARLY AUTUMN(1962, Jap.); SANJURO(1962, Jap.); STAR OF HONG KONG(1962, Jap.); WISER AGE(1962, Jap.); MY HOBO(1963, Jap.); WHEN A WOMAN ASCENDS THE STAIRS(1963, Jap.); NAKED GENERAL, THE(1964, Jap.); DON'T CALL ME A CON MAN(1966, Jap.); FORT GRAVEYARD(1966, Jap.); RED BEARD(1966, Jap.); THREE DOLLS FROM HONG KONG(1966, Jap.); DAPHNE, THE(1967)
Uri Dan
ESCAPE TO THE SUN(1972, Fr./Ger./Israel), w
Dana
FLIGHT OF THE DOVES(1971)
Barbara Dana
INSPECTOR CLOUSEAU(1968, Brit.); P.J.(1968); MONITORS, THE(1969); POPI(1969); WRONG DAMN FILM, THE zero(1975); FIRE SALE(1977); IN-LAWS, THE(1979); CHU CHU AND THE PHILLY FLASH(1981), a, w
Bill Dana
BUSYBODY, THE(1967); HARRAD SUMMER, THE(1974); NUDE BOMB, THE(1980), a, w
Misc. Talkies
I WONDER WHO'S KILLING HER NOW(1975)
Dick Dana
TOP BANANA(1954)
Fred Dana
Silents
APACHE RAIDER, THE(1928)
Frederick Dana
WAGON MASTER, THE(1929)
Misc. Silents
DON DESPERADO(1927); LONG LOOP ON THE PECOS, THE(1927); TWO-GUN OF THE TUMBLEWEED(1927)
Gregory Dana
TILL DEATH(1978), w
Jamie Dana
DRAGONWYCH(1946)
Jeanette Dana
SHOCK CORRIDOR(1963)
Justin Dana
INCREDIBLE SHRINKING WOMAN, THE(1981)
Leona Dana
AMITYVILLE 3-D(1983)
Leora Dana
3:10 TO YUMA(1957); KINGS GO FORTH(1958); SOME CAME RUNNING(1959); POLLYANNA(1960); GATHERING OF EAGLES, A(1963); GROUP, THE(1966); THE BOSTON STRANGLER, THE(1968); CHANGE OF HABIT(1969); TORA! TORA! TORA!(1970, U.S./Jap.); WILD ROVERS(1971); SHOOT THE MOON(1982); BABY, IT'S YOU(1983)
Mark Dana
DESERT SONG, THE(1953); THUNDER OVER THE PLAINS(1953); KING RICHARD AND THE CRUSADERS(1954); HOT CARS(1956); HOT SHOTS(1956); PHARAOH'S CURSE(1957); BIG FISHERMAN, THE(1959); HERE COME THE JETS(1959); TIMBUKTU(1959); TARZAN GOES TO INDIA(1962, U.S./Brit./Switz.)
Michael Dana
MOVING FINGER, THE(1963)
Mike Dana
KILLER'S KISS(1955)
Mordo Dana
LAST AMERICAN VIRGIN, THE(1982)
Muriel Dana
Misc. Silents
FOOL THERE WAS, A(1922); CAN A WOMAN LOVE TWICE?(1923)

Muriel Frances Dana
Silents
WHITE HANDS(1922); SUNSHINE TRAIL, THE(1923); COMPROMISE(1925); MIKE(1926)
Misc. Silents
FAST WORKER, THE(1924)
Patricia Dana
ZIEGFELD GIRL(1941)
Richard Henry Dana, Jr.
TWO YEARS BEFORE THE MAST(1946), w
Rod Dana
HOW TO MAKE A MONSTER(1958); HORNET'S NEST(1970)
Rodd Dana
CAST A GIANT SHADOW(1966)
Rudi Dana
WESTBOUND(1959)
Vic Dana
DON'T KNOCK THE TWIST(1962)
Viola Dana
Silents
GLADIOLA(1915); HOUSE OF THE LOST CORD, THE(1915); INNOCENCE OF RUTH, THE(1916); ALADDIN'S OTHER LAMP(1917); GIRL WITHOUT A SOUL, THE(1917); FALSE EVIDENCE(1919); CHORUS GIRL'S ROMANCE, A(1920); DANGEROUS TO MEN(1920); HOME STUFF(1921); LIFE'S DARN FUNNY(1921); OFFSHORE PIRATE, THE(1921); JUNE MADNESS(1922); SEEING'S BELIEVING(1922); CRINOLINE AND ROMANCE(1923); HER FATAL MILLIONS(1923); IN SEARCH OF A THRILL(1923); NOISE IN NEWBORO, A(1923); SOCIAL CODE, THE(1923); ALONG CAME RUTH(1924); MERTON OF THE MOVIES(1924); OPEN ALL NIGHT(1924); REVELATION(1924); AS MAN DESIRES(1925); FORTY WINKS(1925); GREAT LOVE, THE(1925); NECESSARY EVIL, THE(1925); ICE FLOOD, THE(1926); SILENT LOVER, THE(1926); WILD OATS LANE(1926); HOME STRUCK(1927); NAUGHTY NANETTE(1927); SALVATION JANE(1927); ONE SPLENDID HOUR(1929)
Misc. Silents
CHILDREN OF EVE, THE(1915); COHEN'S LUCK(1915); ON DANGEROUS PATHS(1915); SLAVEY STUDENT, THE(1915); COSSACK WHIP, THE(1916); FLOWER OF NO MAN'S LAND, THE(1916); GATES OF EDEN, THE(1916); LIGHT OF HAPPINESS, THE(1916); BLUE JEANS(1917); GOD'S LAW AND MAN'S(1917); LADY BARNACLE(1917); MORTAL SIN, THE(1917); THREADS OF FATE(1917); BREAKERS AHEAD(1918); FLOWER OF THE DUSK(1918); ONLY ROAD, THE(1918); OPPORTUNITY(1918); RIDERS OF THE NIGHT(1918); WINDING TRAIL, THE(1918); GOLD CURE, THE(1919); JEANNE OF THE GUTTER(1919); MICROBE, THE(1919); PARISIAN TIGRESS, THE(1919); PLEASE GET MARRIED(1919); SATAN JUNIOR(1919); SOME BRIDE(1919); BLACKMAIL(1920); CINDERELLA'S TWIN(1920); WILLOW TREE, THE(1920); MATCH-BREAKER, THE(1921); PUPPETS OF FATE(1921); THERE ARE NO VILLAINS(1921); FIVE DOLLAR BABY, THE(1922); FOURTEENTH LOVER, THE(1922); GLASS HOUSES(1922); LOVE IN THE DARK(1922); THEY LIKE 'EM ROUGH(1922); ROUGED LIPS(1923); BEAUTY PRIZE, THE(1924); DON'T DOUBT YOUR HUSBAND(1924); HEART BANDIT, THE(1924); WINDS OF CHANCE(1925); BIGGER THAN BARNUM'S(1926); BRED IN OLD KENTUCKY(1926); KOSHER KITTY KELLY(1926); LURE OF THE NIGHT CLUB, THE(1927); THAT CERTAIN THING(1928); TWO SISTERS(1929)
Nicholas Danaev
Silents
BY WHOSE HAND?(1916)
Theo Danagger
MOZART STORY, THE(1948, Aust.)
S. Danalis
CANNON AND THE NIGHTINGALE, THE(1969, Gr.), ph
Malcolm Danare
CHRISTINE(1983); FLASHDANCE(1983); LORDS OF DISCIPLINE, THE(1983)
Gaetano Danaro
HORNET'S NEST(1970)
Vincenzo Danaro
MORE THAN A MIRACLE(1967, Ital./Fr.); HORNET'S NEST(1970)
Alex Danaroff
ANYTHING CAN HAPPEN(1952)
Alexander Danaroff
BLACK MAGIC(1949)
Elsie Danbric
Silents
CHASING THE MOON(1922)
Ruby Danbridge
TISH(1942)
Jan Danby
MONSIGNOR(1982)
P. J. Danby
Silents
CAMPUS KNIGHTS(1929)
Marija Danc
TWILIGHT TIME(1983, U.S./Yugo.), cos
Bill Dance
WILD PARTY, THE(1975)
Charles Dance
FOR YOUR EYES ONLY(1981)
Patsy Dance
HOUSEHOLDER, THE(1963, US/India); NED KELLY(1970, Brit.)
Reginald Dance
DREYFUS CASE, THE(1931, Brit.)
Linda Danceil
JUBILEE TRAIL(1954)
Nancy Dancer
MARDI GRAS MASSACRE(1978)
Mazzone-Abbott Dancers
ABBOTT AND COSTELLO MEET THE MUMMY(1955)
Dancers from the London Casino
EASY MONEY(1948, Brit.)
Dancers of the Australian Ballet
DON QUIXOTE(1973, Aus.)

"Boley" Dancewicz
TRIPLE THREAT(1948)
William Danch
MONSTER FROM THE OCEAN FLOOR, THE(1954), w
Aaron Danches
OKEFENOKEE(1960), p
L. Danchishin
MOTHER AND DAUGHTER(1965, USSR)
Georges Danciger
EAGLE WITH TWO HEADS(1948, Fr.), p; LUCRECE BORGIA(1953, Ital./Fr.), p; LAW IS THE LAW, THE(1959, Fr.), p; LIVE FOR LIFE(1967, Fr./Ital.), p; MAGNIFICENT ONE, THE(1974, Fr./Ital.), p
Liz Danciger
OTHER SIDE OF THE UNDERNEATH, THE(1972, Brit.)
Georges Dancigers
THAT MAN FROM RIO(1964, Fr./Ital.), p; UP TO HIS EARS(1966, Fr./Ital.), p; LES GAULOISES BLEUES(1969, Fr.), p; LIFE LOVE DEATH(1969, Fr./Ital.), p; LOVE IS A FUNNY THING(1970, Fr./Ital.), p; ANOTHER MAN, ANOTHER CHANCE(1977 Fr./US), p; INCORRIGIBLE(1980, Fr.), p; INQUISITOR, THE(1982, Fr.), p; LA BALANCE(1983, Fr.), p
Oscar Dancigers
LOS OLVIDADOS(1950, Mex.), p; BRUTE, THE(1952, Mex.), p; ADVENTURES OF ROBINSON CRUSOE, THE(1954), p; EL(1955, Mex.), p; GINA(1961, Fr./Mex.), p; VIVA MARIA(1965, Fr./Ital.), p; DAUGHTER OF DECEIT(1977, Mex.), p; DEATH IN THE GARDEN(1977, Fr./Mex.), p
Veronique Dancigers
LIKE A TURTLE ON ITS BACK(1981, Fr.)
Oscar Dancingers
PEARL, THE(1948, U.S./Mex.), p
Bill Dancy
INFORMATION RECEIVED(1962, Brit.)
Jeanette Dancy
FOX MOVIETONE FOLLIES(1929)
C.H. Dand
BELLS, THE(1931, Brit.), w; FAREWELL TO LOVE(1931, Brit.), w; M'BLIMEY(1931, Brit.), w
Nick Dandau
Silents
SKYROCKET, THE(1926)
Jean Dandeny
JE T'AIME, JE T'AIME(1972, Fr./Swed.), m
Sandy Danders
COW TOWN(1950)
Susanne Dando
OCTOPUSSY(1983, Brit.)
Giusi Raspani Dandolo
MAIDEN FOR A PRINCE, A(1967, Fr./Ital.); LOVE FACTORY(1969, Ital.)
Armba Dandridge
NIGHT AND DAY(1946)
Don Dandridge
TRAIN RIDE TO HOLLYWOOD(1975)
Dorothy Dandridge
BAHAMA PASSAGE(1941); LADY FROM LOUISIANA(1941); SUN VALLEY SERENADE(1941); SUNDOWN(1941); DRUMS OF THE CONGO(1942); LUCKY JORDAN(1942); HIT PARADE OF 1943(1943); ATLANTIC CITY(1944); SINCE YOU WENT AWAY(1944); PILLOW TO POST(1945); HARLEM GLOBETROTTERS, THE(1951); TARZAN'S PERIL(1951); BRIGHT ROAD(1953); REMAINS TO BE SEEN(1953); CARMEN JONES(1954); ISLAND IN THE SUN(1957); DECKS RAN RED, THE(1958); PORGY AND BESS(1959); TAMANGO(1959, Fr.); MALAGA(1962, Brit.)
Misc. Talkies
CONDEMNED MEN(1940); JUNGLE QUEEN(1946); FLAMINGO(1947)
Putney Dandridge
HARLEM IS HEAVEN(1932)
Robert Dandridge
FATHER'S SON(1931); PENROD AND SAM(1931)
Ruby Dandridge
GALLANT LADY(1942); NIGHT FOR CRIME, A(1942); PRISON GIRL(1942); CABIN IN THE SKY(1943); CORREGIDOR(1943); MELODY PARADE(1943); NEVER A DULL MOMENT(1943); LADIES OF WASHINGTON(1944); JUNIOR MISS(1945); SARATOGA TRUNK(1945); HOME IN OKLAHOMA(1946); INSIDE JOB(1946); THREE LITTLE GIRLS IN BLUE(1946); ARNELO AFFAIR, THE(1947); DEAD RECKONING(1947); MY WILD IRISH ROSE(1947); TAP ROOTS(1948); FATHER IS A BACHELOR(1950); HOLE IN THE HEAD, A(1959)
Vivian Dandridge
I WALKED WITH A ZOMBIE(1943)
The Dandridge Sisters
IRENE(1940)
Dominique Dandrieux
BELLE DE JOUR(1968, Fr.)
Evelyne Dandry
SELLERS OF GIRLS(1967, Fr.); COUSINS IN LOVE(1982)
Jim Dandy
SGT. PEPPER'S LONELY HEARTS CLUB BAND(1978)
Ned Dandy
HONOLULU LU(1941), w; SWEETHEART OF THE FLEET(1942), w; TRAMP, TRAMP, TRAMP(1942), w; LAUGH YOUR BLUES AWAY(1943), w
Texas Dandy
BOY FROM INDIANA(1950)
Alexandra Dane
CARRY ON DOCTOR(1968, Brit.); CARRY ON, UP THE KHYBER(1968, Brit.); CORRUPTION(1968, Brit.); DON'T RAISE THE BRIDGE, LOWER THE RIVER(1968, Brit.); JABBERWOCKY(1977, Brit.)
Bonnie Irma Dane
STORK PAYS OFF, THE(1941)
Bruce Dane
PORT OF HATE(1939); WAGON TRAIN(1940)
Clemence Dane
MURDER(1930, Brit.), w; BILL OF DIVORCEMENT, A(1932), w; ANNA KARENINA(1935), w; TRANSATLANTIC TUNNEL(1935, Brit.), w; AMATEUR GENTLEMAN(1936, Brit.), w; FIRE OVER ENGLAND(1937, Brit.), w; TROOPSHIP(1938,

Brit.), w; BILL OF DIVORCEMENT(1940), w; SIDEWALKS OF LONDON(1940, Brit.), w; SALUTE JOHN CITIZEN(1942, Brit.), w; VACATION FROM MARRIAGE(1945, Brit.), w; BONNIE PRINCE CHARLIE(1948, Brit.), w; BRIDE OF VENGEANCE(1949), w

Constance Dane
HOUSE IS NOT A HOME, A(1964)

Cyril Dane
Silents
OLD BILL THROUGH THE AGES(1924, Brit.)

Doris Dane
1,000 SHAPES OF A FEMALE(1963)

Edward Dane
DEADLIEST SIN, THE(1956, Brit.)

Faith Dane
GYPSY(1962)

Frank Dane
Silents
KENT, THE FIGHTING MAN(1916, Brit.); BLIND BOY, THE(1917, Brit.); DEMOCRACY(1918, Brit.); FATE'S PLAYTHING(1920, Brit.); INNOCENT(1921, Brit.); CREATION(1922, Brit.); SILENT EVIDENCE(1922, Brit.)
Misc. Silents
FURTHER EXPLOITS OF SEXTON BLAKE, THE - MYSTERY OF THE S.S. OLYMPIC, THE(1919, Brit.); BLACK TULIP, THE(1921, Brit.); BLOOD MONEY(1921, Brit.); I'PAGLIACCI(1923, Brit.); HOOSIER SCHOOLMASTER, THE(1924)

Frank H. Dane
Misc. Silents
DAUGHTER OF ENGLAND, A(1915, Brit.)

Karl Dane
ALIAS JIMMY VALENTINE(1928); MYSTERIOUS ISLAND(1929); BIG HOUSE, THE(1930); BILLY THE KID(1930); FREE AND EASY(1930); MONTANA MOON(1930); NAVY BLUES(1930)
Misc. Talkies
BROTHERLY LOVE(1928)
Silents
MY FOUR YEARS IN GERMANY(1918); BIG PARADE, THE(1925); HIS SECRETARY(1925); SCARLET LETTER, THE(1926); SON OF THE SHEIK(1926); WAR PAINT(1926); ENEMY, THE(1927); RED MILL, THE(1927); SLIDE, KELLY, SLIDE(1927); BABY MINE(1928); SHOW PEOPLE(1928); DUKE STEPS OUT, THE(1929); TRAIL OF '98, THE(1929)
Misc. Silents
MONTE CARLO(1926); ROOKIES(1927); CIRCUS ROOKIES(1928); DETECTIVES(1928); ALL AT SEA(1929); CHINA BOUND(1929); SPEEDWAY(1929); VOICE OF THE STORM, THE(1929)

Lawrence Dane
ONLY GOD KNOWS(1974, Can.); IT SEEMED LIKE A GOOD IDEA AT THE TIME(1975, Can.); CLOWN MURDERS, THE(1976, Can.); RUNNING(1979, Can.); BEAR ISLAND(1980, Brit.-Can.); CREEPER, THE(1980, Can.), a, p; NOTHING PERSONAL(1980, Can.); HAPPY BIRTHDAY TO ME(1981, Can.); HEAD ON(1981, Can.); SCANNERS(1981, Can.); OF UNKNOWN ORIGIN(1983, Can.)

Lawrence Z. Dane
ROWDYMAN, THE(1973, Can.), p; ONLY GOD KNOWS(1974, Can.), p, w

Lois Dane
LINDA(1960, Brit.)

Olga Dane
NIGHT AT THE OPERA, A(1935)

Pat Dane
ARE YOU WITH IT?(1948); ROAD TO BALI(1952); HARDER THEY FALL, THE(1956)

Patricia Dane
LIFE BEGINS FOR ANDY HARDY(1941); GRAND CENTRAL MURDER(1942); JOHNNY EAGER(1942); NORTHWEST RANGERS(1942); RIO RITA(1942); SOMEWHERE I'LL FIND YOU(1942); I DOOD IT(1943); FIGHTING MAD(1948)

Penny Dane
PRELUDE TO FAME(1950, Brit.); GENTLEMEN MARRY BRUNETTES(1955)

Peter Dane
ENEMY BELOW, THE(1957); AL CAPONE(1959); PLANETS AGAINST US, THE(1961, Ital./Fr.); COBRA, THE(1968); FINE PAIR, A(1969, Ital.); FAMILY, THE(1974, Fr./Ital.); MIDNIGHT MAN, THE(1974); AT LONG LAST LOVE(1975); ONE DOWN TWO TO GO(1982)

Rick Dane
MINI-AFFAIR, THE(1968, Brit.)

Robert Dane
GIRL ON THE BRIDGE, THE(1951); WE'RE NOT MARRIED(1952); SEMINOLE(1953); BAMBOO SAUCER, THE(1968)

Stephen Dane
1984
ADVENTURES OF BUCKAROO BANZAI: ACROSS THE 8TH DIMENSION, THE(1984), art d

Sylvia Daneel
SEVEN WOMEN FROM HELL(1961)

Theodore Danegger
ROYAL WALTZ, THE(1936); LITTLE MELODY FROM VIENNA(1948, Aust.)

Georgi Danelia
AUTUMN MARATHON(1982, USSR), d

Georgiy Daneliya
SUMMER TO REMEMBER, A(1961, USSR), d, w; MEET ME IN MOSCOW(1966, USSR), d

Ileana Danelli
DAVID AND GOLIATH(1961, Ital.)

Paul Daneman
FUN AT ST. FANNY'S(1956, Brit.); PERIL FOR THE GUY(1956, Brit.); TIME WITHOUT PITY(1957, Brit.); CLUE OF THE NEW PIN, THE(1961, Brit.); FOURTH SQUARE, THE(1961, Brit.); LOCKER 69(1962, Brit.); ZULU(1964, Brit.); HOW I WON THE WAR(1967, Brit.); OH! WHAT A LOVELY WAR(1969, Brit.)

James Danen
GIDGET GOES HAWAIIAN(1961)

Julio Daneri
VAMPIRE, THE(1968, Mex.)

Harry Danes
Silents
BALLET GIRL, THE(1916)

Shera Danese
NEW YORK, NEW YORK(1977); RISKY BUSINESS(1983)

Alfredo Danesi
BEN HUR(1959)

Arturo Danesi
STRANGER RETURNS, THE(1968, U.S./Ital./Ger./Span.)

Giovanni Danesi
L'AVVENTURA(1960, Ital.)

Roberto Danesi
LA NOTTE(1961, Fr./Ital.)

Jean Danet
DIARY OF A COUNTRY PRIEST(1954, Fr.); HUNCHBACK OF NOTRE DAME, THE(1957, Fr.); GAMBLER, THE(1958, Fr.)

Leila Danette
1984
GARBO TALKS(1984)

Nena Danevic
1984
AMADEUS(1984), ed

Dianne Danford
WEEKEND OF FEAR(1966)

Joe Danford
WEEKEND OF FEAR(1966), p,d&w, ed

Carolyn Danforth
NORMA RAE(1979)

Dan Danforth
1984
IMPULSE(1984)

Jim Danforth
JACK THE GIANT KILLER(1962), spec eff; SEVEN FACES OF DR. LAO(1964), spec eff; EQUINOX(1970), spec eff; WHEN DINOSAURS RULED THE EARTH(1971, Brit.), spec eff

Logan N. Danforth
CROSS COUNTRY(1983, Can.), w

William Danforth
GIRL SAID NO, THE(1937)
Misc. Silents
SEVEN SWANS, THE(1918)

Henry Dangar
STIR(1980, Aus.), ed; WINTER OF OUR DREAMS(1982, Aus.), ed

Linda Dangcil
EL DORADO(1967); LAST WORD, THE(1979)

Linda Dangell
ESCAPE FROM RED ROCK(1958)

Bru Danger
STORY ON PAGE ONE, THE(1959)

Dean Danger
RAT PFINK AND BOO BOO(1966)

Diana Dangerfield
INN OF THE DAMNED(1974, Aus.)

Elma Dangerfield
RADIO LOVER(1936, Brit.), w

George Dangerfield
Silents
BAR SINISTER, THE(1917)

Ogden Dangerfield
NOTORIOUS LANDLADY, THE(1962)

Rodney Dangerfield
PROJECTIONIST, THE(1970); CADDY SHACK(1980); EASY MONEY(1983), a, w

Sebastian Dangerfield [Stefan Peters]
GIRL GRABBERS, THE(1968)

Yves Dangerfield
1984
LA PETIT SIRENE(1984, Fr.), w

Anita Dangler
FOR LOVE OF IVY(1968); POPI(1969); PEOPLE NEXT DOOR, THE(1970); LAW AND DISORDER(1974); GOODBYE GIRL, THE(1977); SLOW DANCING IN THE BIG CITY(1978); HERO AT LARGE(1980); HONKY TONK FREEWAY(1981)

David Dangler
UNCOMMON VALOR(1983)

Dani
DAY FOR NIGHT(1973, Fr.); LOVE ON THE RUN(1980, Fr.)

Buster Danials
SUGARLAND EXPRESS, THE(1974)

Starr Danias
TURNING POINT, THE(1977)

Leo Daniderff
BOUDU SAVED FROM DROWNING(1967, Fr.), m

Daniel
WIND FROM THE EAST(1970, Fr./Ital./Ger.)

Allyson Daniel
CLARENCE, THE CROSS-EYED LION(1965)

Ann Daniel
ISLAND OF THE BLUE DOLPHINS(1964)

Bill Daniel
ALAMO, THE(1960)

Billy Daniel
DUFFY'S TAVERN(1945), ch; IMPERFECT LADY, THE(1947), ch; PALEFACE, THE(1948), ch; LOVE HAPPY(1949), ch; RED, HOT AND BLUE(1949), a, ch; WABASH AVENUE(1950), a, ch; WITH A SONG IN MY HEART(1952), ch; DANGEROUS WHEN WET(1953), ch; POWDER RIVER(1953), ch; FRENCH LINE, THE(1954), a, ch; JOURNEY TO THE LOST CITY(1960, Ger./Fr./Ital.), ch

Carmel Daniel
AMAZING TRANSPARENT MAN, THE(1960)

Chuck Daniel
FIREBALL JUNGLE(1968); AIRPORT(1970); BLACK GUNN(1972); POLICEWOMAN(1974)
Misc. Talkies
FOX STYLE(1973)
Dany Daniel
Misc. Talkies
TEENAGE TEASERS(1982)
Elaine Daniel
BEYOND AND BACK(1978)
Elek Daniel
FATHER(1967, Hung.)
Eliot Daniel
FUN AND FANCY FREE(1947), m; MELODY TIME(1948), md; POWDER RIVER(1953), md
Elsa Daniel
END OF INNOCENCE(1960, Arg.); HAND IN THE TRAP, THE(1963, Arg./Span.); GAMES MEN PLAY, THE(1968, Arg.)
Elwyn Daniel
LONG JOHN SILVER(1954, Aus.)
Gabi Daniel
RED AND THE WHITE, THE(1969, Hung./USSR)
George M. Daniel
Misc. Silents
ONE EIGHTH APACHE(1922)
Henry Daniel
DRESSED TO KILL(1941)
Jay Daniel
TARGETS(1968)
Jennifer Daniel
CLUE OF THE SILVER KEY, THE(1961, Brit.); KISS OF EVIL(1963, Brit.); RETURN TO SENDER(1963, Brit.); REPTILE, THE(1966, Brit.); MARRIAGE OF CONVENIENCE(1970, Brit.)
Joshua Daniel
NATIONAL LAMPOON'S ANIMAL HOUSE(1978); WHERE THE BUFFALO ROAM(1980); ZAPPED!(1982)
Lana Daniel
PAPER MOON(1973)
Leslie Daniel
BRAIN THAT WOULDN'T DIE, THE(1959); JOHNNY YUMA(1967, Ital.)
Mickey Daniel
GREAT ZIEGFELD, THE(1936)
Paul Daniel
FORCE OF IMPULSE(1961); WE SHALL RETURN(1963); SHIP OF FOOLS(1965); APACHE UPRISING(1966); JOHNNY RENO(1966); LAST OF THE SECRET AGENTS?, THE(1966)
Roberta Daniel
IMPERFECT LADY, THE(1947)
Roger Daniel
BOY SLAVES(1938); KING OF THE TURF(1939); HER FIRST ROMANCE(1940); LIFE BEGINS FOR ANDY HARDY(1941); WE'VE NEVER BEEN LICKED(1943)
Roland Daniel
WIFE OR TWO, A(1935, Brit.), w; MAN WITH THE MAGNETIC EYES, THE(1945, Brit.), w
Susan Daniel
1984
BIZET'S CARMEN(1984, Fr./Ital.)
Tom Daniel
PUT UP OR SHUT UP(1968, Arg.), spec eff; PUTNEY SWOPE(1969), spec eff
Trudik Daniel
CASTLE, THE(1969, Ger.)
Viora Daniel
Silents
THOU ART THE MAN(1920)
Daniel Daniele
MAHOGANY(1975)
Graciela Daniele
PIRATES OF PENZANCE, THE(1983), ch
Tad Danielewski
NO EXIT(1962, U.S./Arg.), d; GUIDE, THE(1965, U.S./India), p&d, w
Emma Danieli
GUNS OF THE BLACK WITCH(1961, Fr./Ital.); LAST MAN ON EARTH, THE(1964, U.S./Ital.)
Isa Danieli
ALL SCREWED UP(1976, Ital.)
Luciana Danieli
FUGITIVE LADY(1951)
Allison Daniell
MY FAIR LADY(1964)
Allyson Daniell
NEW KIND OF LOVE, A(1963); SHOCK CORRIDOR(1963)
Athalie Daniell
MODEL AND THE MARRIAGE BROKER, THE(1951)
David Daniell
1984
STARMAN(1984)
Henry Daniell
AWFUL TRUTH, THE(1929); JEALOUSY(1929); LAST OF THE LONE WOLF(1930); PATH OF GLORY, THE(1934, Brit.); UNGUARDED HOUR, THE(1936); CAMILLE(1937); FIREFLY, THE(1937); MADAME X(1937); THIRTEENTH CHAIR, THE(1937); UNDER COVER OF NIGHT(1937); HOLIDAY(1938); MARIE ANTOINETTE(1938); PRIVATE LIVES OF ELIZABETH AND ESSEX, THE(1939); WE ARE NOT ALONE(1939); ALL THIS AND HEAVEN TOO(1940); GREAT DICTATOR, THE(1940); PHILADELPHIA STORY, THE(1940); SEA HAWK, THE(1940); FEMININE TOUCH, THE(1941); FOUR JACKS AND A JILL(1941); WOMAN'S FACE(1941); CASTLE IN THE DESERT(1942); GREAT IMPERSONATION, THE(1942); NIGHTMARE(1942); RANDOM HARVEST(1942); REUNION IN FRANCE(1942); SHERLOCK HOLMES AND THE VOICE OF TERROR(1942); MISSION TO MOSCOW(1943); SHERLOCK HOLMES IN WASHINGTON(1943); WATCH ON THE RHINE(1943); JANE EYRE(1944); SUSPECT, THE(1944); BODY SNATCHER, THE(1945); CHICAGO

KID, THE(1945); HOTEL BERLIN(1945); WOMAN IN GREEN, THE(1945); BANDIT OF SHERWOOD FOREST, THE(1946); EXILE, THE(1947); SONG OF LOVE(1947); SIREN OF ATLANTIS(1948); SECRET OF ST. IVES, THE(1949); WAKE OF THE RED WITCH(1949); BUCCANEER'S GIRL(1950); EGYPTIAN. THE(1954); DIANE(1955); PRODIGAL, THE(1955); LUST FOR LIFE(1956); MAN IN THE GREY FLANNEL SUIT, THE(1956); LES GIRLS(1957); MISTER CORY(1957); STORY OF MANKIND, THE(1957); SUN ALSO RISES, THE(1957); WITNESS FOR THE PROSECUTION(1957); FROM THE EARTH TO THE MOON(1958); FOUR SKULLS OF JONATHAN DRAKE, THE(1959); COMANCHEROS, THE(1961); VOYAGE TO THE BOTTOM OF THE SEA(1961); CHAPMAN REPORT, THE(1962); FIVE WEEKS IN A BALLOON(1962); MADISON AVENUE(1962); MUTINY ON THE BOUNTY(1962); NOTORIOUS LANDLADY, THE(1962); MY FAIR LADY(1964)
Suzanne Danielle
CARRY ON EMANUELLE(1978, Brit.); ARABIAN ADVENTURE(1979, Brit.); GOLDEN LADY, THE(1979, Brit.); FLASH GORDON(1980); SIR HENRY AT RAWLINSON END(1980, Brit.); LONG SHOT(1981, Brit.)
Adelaide Danielli
MY UNCLE(1958, Fr.)
Wendy Danielli
PORT OF ESCAPE(1955, Brit.)
Lisa Danielly
CURSE OF THE VOODOO(1965, Brit.)
Alex Daniels
1984
STARMAN(1984)
Ann Daniels
YOUNG LIONS, THE(1958)
Anne Daniels
TALK OF THE DEVIL(1937, Brit.)
Anthony Daniels
STAR WARS(1977); EMPIRE STRIKES BACK, THE(1980); RETURN OF THE JEDI(1983)
Bebe Daniels
RIO RITA(1929); ALIAS FRENCH GERTIE(1930); DIXIANA(1930); LAWFUL LARCENY(1930); LOVE COMES ALONG(1930); HONOR OF THE FAMILY(1931); MALTESE FALCON, THE(1931); MY PAST(1931); REACHING FOR THE MOON(1931); SILVER DOLLAR(1932); COCKTAIL HOUR(1933); COUNSELLOR-AT-LAW(1933); SOUTHERN MAID, A(1933, Brit.); 42ND STREET(1933); REGISTERED NURSE(1934); SONG YOU GAVE ME, THE(1934, Brit.); MUSIC IS MAGIC(1935); RETURN OF CAROL DEANE(1938, Brit.); TREACHERY ON THE HIGH SEAS(1939, Brit.); HI, GANG!(1941, Brit.), a, w; FAMILY AFFAIR(1954, Brit.), a, w; LYONS IN PARIS, THE(1955, Brit.), a, w
Silents
MALE AND FEMALE(1919); OH, LADY, LADY(1920); AFFAIRS OF ANATOL, THE(1921); DUCKS AND DRAKES(1921); ONE WILD WEEK(1921); SPEED GIRL, THE(1921); NANCY FROM NOWHERE(1922); NICE PEOPLE(1922); NORTH OF THE RIO GRANDE(1922); SINGED WINGS(1922); EXCITERS, THE(1923); ARGENTINE LOVE(1924); DARING YOUTH(1924); MONSIEUR BEAUCAIRE(1924); SINNERS IN HEAVEN(1924); MISS BLUEBEARD(1925); CAMPUS FLIRT, THE(1926); MISS BREWSTER'S MILLIONS(1926); VOLCANO(1926); SHE'S A SHEIK(1927); FIFTY-FIFTY GIRL, THE(1928); HOT NEWS(1928); TAKE ME HOME(1928); WHAT A NIGHT!(1928)
Misc. Silents
DANCIN' FOOL, THE(1920); FOURTEENTH MAN, THE(1920); SICK ABED(1920); WHY CHANGE YOUR WIFE?(1920); YOU NEVER CAN TELL(1920); MARCH HARE, THE(1921); SHE COULDN'T HELP IT(1921); TWO WEEKS WITH PAY(1921); GAME CHICKEN, THE(1922); PINK GODS(1922); GLIMPSES OF THE MOON, THE(1923); HIS CHILDREN'S CHILDREN(1923); WORLD'S APPLAUSE, THE(1923); DANGEROUS MONEY(1924); HERITAGE OF THE DESERT, THE(1924); UNGUARDED WOMEN(1924); CROWED HOUR, THE(1925); LOVERS IN QUARANTINE(1925); MANICURE GIRL, THE(1925); WILD, WILD SUSAN(1925); PALM BEACH GIRL, THE(1926); SPLENDID CRIME, THE(1926); STRANDED IN PARIS(1926); KISS IN A TAXI, A(1927); SENORITA(1927); SWIM, GIRL, SWIM(1927); FEEL MY PULSE(1928)
Ben Daniels
DESPERATE WOMEN, THE(?)
Bette Daniels
SAN ANTONE AMBUSH(1949)
Betty Daniels
TOAST OF NEW ORLEANS, THE(1950)
Billy Daniels
HOLD 'EM NAVY!(1937); THRILL OF A LIFETIME(1937); SAY IT IN FRENCH(1938); MIDNIGHT(1939); FRENCHMAN'S CREEK(1944); LADY IN THE DARK(1944), a, ch; THREE CABALLEROS, THE(1944), ch; KITTY(1945), ch; MASQUERADE IN MEXICO(1945), a, ch; STORK CLUB, THE(1945), ch; MONSIEUR BEAUCAIRE(1946), ch; DREAM GIRL(1947), ch; GOLDEN EARRINGS(1947), ch; LADIES' MAN(1947), ch; PERILS OF PAULINE, THE(1947), ch; ROAD TO RIO(1947), ch; SEPIA CINDERELLA(1947); TROUBLE WITH WOMEN, THE(1947), ch; VARIETY GIRL(1947), ch; EMPEROR WALTZ, THE(1948), ch; ENCHANTMENT(1948), ch; ONE TOUCH OF VENUS(1948), ch; ROGUES' REGIMENT(1948), ch; MY BLUE HEAVEN(1950); WHEN YOU'RE SMILING(1950); SUNNY SIDE OF THE STREET(1951); RAINBOW 'ROUND MY SHOULDER(1952); CRUISIN' DOWN THE RIVER(1953); SCARED STIFF(1953), ch; BEAT GENERATION, THE(1959); BIG OPERATOR, THE(1959); NIGHT OF THE QUARTER MOON(1959)
Carol Ann Daniels
QUICK, LET'S GET MARRIED(1965); PSYCHOPATH, THE(1973)
Carolan Daniels
MARLOWE(1969)
D.W.L. Daniels
QUIET WEEKEND(1948, Brit.), art d
Danice Daniels
MAGIC SPECTACLES(1961)
Danny Daniels
PASSIONATE SUMMER(1959, Brit.); WOMAN OF STRAW(1964, Brit.); PREHISTORIC WOMEN(1967, Brit.); DARK OF THE SUN(1968, Brit.); NIGHT THEY RAIDED MINSKY'S, THE(1968), ch; OBLONG BOX, THE(1969, Brit.); ONE PLUS ONE(1969, Brit.); TOM SAWYER(1973); PENNIES FROM HEAVEN(1981), ch; PIAF-THE EARLY YEARS(1982, U.S./Fr.), ch; ZELIG(1983), ch

THAN DESIRE(1939), ph; MORTAL STORM, THE(1940), ph; NEW MOON(1940), ph; SHOP AROUND THE CORNER, THE(1940), ph; BACK STREET(1941), ph; DESIGN FOR SCANDAL(1941), ph; DR. KILDARE'S VICTORY(1941), ph; SHADOW OF THE THIN MAN(1941), ph; SO ENDS OUR NIGHT(1941), ph; THEY MET IN BOMBAY(1941), ph; FOR ME AND MY GAL(1942), ph; KEEPER OF THE FLAME(1942), ph; GIRL CRAZY(1943), ph; BRUTE FORCE(1947), ph; LURED(1947), ph; BECAUSE OF EVE(1948), p; FAMILY HONEYMOON(1948), ph; FOR THE LOVE OF MARY(1948), ph; NAKED CITY, THE(1948), ph; ABANDONED(1949), ph; GAL WHO TOOK THE WEST, THE(1949), ph; ILLEGAL ENTRY(1949), ph; LIFE OF RILEY, THE(1949), ph; WOMAN IN HIDING(1949), ph; DEPORTED(1950), ph; HARVEY(1950), ph; WINCHESTER '73(1950), ph; BRIGHT VICTORY(1951), ph; THUNDER ON THE HILL(1951), ph; GLORY ALLEY(1952), ph; NEVER WAVE AT A WAC(1952), ph; PAT AND MIKE(1952), ph; PLYMOUTH ADVENTURE(1952), ph; WHEN IN ROME(1952), ph; FORBIDDEN(1953), ph; GLENN MILLER STORY, THE(1953), ph; THUNDER BAY(1953), ph; WAR ARROW(1953), ph; FAR COUNTRY, THE(1955), ph; FOXFIRE(1955), ph; GIRL RUSH, THE(1955), ph; SHRIKE, THE(1955), ph; SIX BRIDGES TO CROSS(1955), ph; STRATEGIC AIR COMMAND(1955), ph; AWAY ALL BOATS(1956), ph; BENNY GOODMAN STORY, THE(1956), ph; UNGUARDED MOMENT, THE(1956), ph; INTERLUDE(1957), ph; ISTANBUL(1957), ph; MY MAN GODFREY(1957), ph; NIGHT PASSAGE(1957), ph; CAT ON A HOT TIN ROOF(1958), ph; VOICE IN THE MIRROR(1958), ph; STRANGER IN MY ARMS(1959), ph; COME SEPTEMBER(1961), ph; HOW THE WEST WAS WON(1962), ph; LADYBUG, LADYBUG(1963); PRIZE, THE(1963), ph; THOUSAND CLOWNS, A(1965); GRADUATE, THE(1967); PRESIDENT'S ANALYST, THE(1967); TWO FOR THE ROAD(1967, Brit.); MARLOWE(1969); MOVE(1970), ph; 1776(1972); PARALLAX VIEW, THE(1974); LONG NIGHT, THE(1976), m; BLACK SUNDAY(1977); OH, GOD!(1977); ONE AND ONLY, THE(1978); SUNBURN(1979); BLUE LAGOON, THE(1980); ALL NIGHT LONG(1981); REDS(1981)
Silents
FOOLISH WIVES(1920), ph; MERRY-GO-ROUND(1923), ph; HELEN'S BABIES(1924), ph; MERRY WIDOW, THE(1925), ph; FLESH AND THE DEVIL(1926), ph; TEMPTRESS, THE(1926), ph; TORRENT, THE(1926), ph; ALTARS OF DESIRE(1927), ph; CAPTAIN SALVATION(1927), ph; LOVE(1927), ph; ON ZE BOULEVARD(1927), ph; TILLIE THE TOILER(1927), ph; ACTRESS, THE(1928), ph; LATEST FROM PARIS, THE(1928), ph; MYSTERIOUS LADY, THE(1928), ph; TELLING THE WORLD(1928), ph; WOMAN OF AFFAIRS, A(1928), ph; KISS, THE(1929), ph; WILD ORCHIDS(1929), ph

William H. Daniels
OCEAN BREAKERS(1949, Swed.), ph; LADY PAYS OFF, THE(1951), ph; HOLE IN THE HEAD, A(1959), ph; NEVER SO FEW(1959), ph; SOME CAME RUNNING(1959), ph; ALL THE FINE YOUNG CANNIBALS(1960), ph; CAN-CAN(1960), ph; OCEAN'S ELEVEN(1960), ph; JUMBO(1962), ph; COME BLOW YOUR HORN(1963), ph; ROBIN AND THE SEVEN HOODS(1964), ph; MARRIAGE ON THE ROCKS(1965), p, ph; VON RYAN'S EXPRESS(1965), ph; ASSAULT ON A QUEEN(1966), ph; IN LIKE FLINT(1967), ph; VALLEY OF THE DOLLS(1967), ph; IMPOSSIBLE YEARS, THE(1968), ph; MALTESE BIPPY, THE(1969), ph; MARLOWE(1969), ph
Silents
GREED(1925), ph

Cliff Danielson
DR. KILDARE GOES HOME(1940); DOWN IN SAN DIEGO(1941); SHADOW OF THE THIN MAN(1941); TRIAL OF MARY DUGAN, THE(1941); TWO-FACED WOMAN(1941); EYES IN THE NIGHT(1942); JOHNNY EAGER(1942); KEEPER OF THE FLAME(1942); NAZI AGENT(1942); SEVEN SWEETHEARTS(1942); PILOT NO. 5(1943); THOUSANDS CHEER(1943)

Tage Danielsson
ADVENTURES OF PICASSO, THE(1980, Swed.), d, w

Lisa Daniely
LILLI MARLENE(1951, Brit.); HOLIDAY WEEK(1952, Brit.); OPERATION DIPLOMAT(1953, Brit.); WEDDING OF LILLI MARLENE, THE(1953, Brit.); MAN IN THE ROAD, THE(1957, Brit.); ROCK AROUND THE WORLD(1957, Brit.); CROSS-UP(1958); CIRCLE, THE(1959, Brit.); HIGH JUMP(1959, Brit.); HONOURABLE MURDER, AN(1959, Brit.); DANGER TOMORROW(1960, Brit.); MAN WHO WAS NOBODY, THE(1960, Brit.); MIDDLE COURSE, THE(1961, Brit.); TWO WIVES AT ONE WEDDING(1961, Brit.); INVITATION TO MURDER(1962, Brit.); LAMP IN ASSASSIN MEWS, THE(1962, Brit.); COP-OUT(1967, Brit.)

Leonteen Danies
SON OF SINBAD(1955)

Danika
WOMAN ON FIRE, A(1970, Ital.)

G.P. Danilevski
BETRAYAL(1939, Fr.), w

A. Danilova
DAY THE WAR ENDED, THE(1961, USSR); MUMU(1961, USSR); LAST GAME, THE(1964, USSR)

A.S. Danilova
ALEXANDER NEVSKY(1939)

Alexandra Danilova
TURNING POINT, THE(1977)

Will Danin
DEEP END(1970 Ger./U.S.)

Make Daning
TERROR BENEATH THE SEA(1966, Jap.)

Mike Daning
GIRARA(1967, Jap.)

Daninos
MARTIAN IN PARIS, A(1961, Fr.), w

Jean-Daniel Daninos
MARTIAN IN PARIS, A(1961, Fr.), d

Pierre Daninos
FRENCH, THEY ARE A FUNNY RACE, THE(1956, Fr.), w

Danio
SLAVE OF THE CANNIBAL GOD(1979, Ital.), p

Danique
1984
SUPERGIRL(1984)

Pierre Danis
Silents
NAPOLEON(1927, Fr.)

John Danischewsky
RUN WILD, RUN FREE(1969, Brit.), p

M. Danischewsky
BITTER SPRINGS(1950, Aus.), w

Monja Danischewsky
UNDERGROUND GUERRILLAS(1944, Brit.), w; GALLOPING MAJOR, THE(1951, Brit.), p, w; MEET MR. LUCIFER(1953, Brit.), p, w; LOVE LOTTERY, THE(1954, Brit.), p; MAD LITTLE ISLAND(1958, Brit.), w; BATTLE OF THE SEXES, THE(1960, Brit.), w; TWO AND TWO MAKE SIX(1962, Brit.), p, w; TOPKAPI(1964), w; MISTER MOSES(1965), w

Eli Danker
JESUS(1979)
1984
LITTLE DRUMMER GIRL, THE(1984)

Betty Danko
HAZARD(1948)

Edward Danko
STATUE, THE(1971, Brit.)

Indira Danks
WICKED, WICKED(1973)

Jeff Danks
MY BLOODY VALENTINE(1981, Can.)

John Dankworth
SATURDAY NIGHT AND SUNDAY MORNING(1961, Brit.), m, md; SERVANT, THE(1964, Brit.), a, m, md; DARLING(1965, Brit.), m; RETURN FROM THE ASHES(1965, U.S./Brit.), m; SANDS OF THE KALAHARI(1965, Brit.), m; IDOL, THE(1966, Brit.), m, md; MODESTY BLAISE(1966, Brit.), m; MORGAN!(1966, Brit.), m; FATHOM(1967), m; LAST SAFARI, THE(1967, Brit.), m; MAGUS, THE(1968, Brit.), m, md; SALT & PEPPER(1968, Brit.), m; LAST GRENADE, THE(1970, Brit.), m; PERFECT FRIDAY(1970, Brit.), m, md; 10 RILLINGTON PLACE(1971, Brit.), m, md

Johnny Dankworth
6.5 SPECIAL(1958, Brit.); ALL NIGHT LONG(1961, Brit.); CONCRETE JUNGLE, THE(1962, Brit.), m; ACCIDENT(1967, Brit.), m

Jan Danley-Smith
RUNAWAY RAILWAY(1965, Brit.), d

Leon Danmun
Misc. Silents
PHANTOM HONEYMOON, THE(1919)

Asher Dann
SEPTEMBER STORM(1960)

Judy Dann
DESTINATION GOBI(1953)

Larry Dann
CARRY ON TEACHER(1962, Brit.); WHAT A CRAZY WORLD(1963, Brit.); GHOST STORY(1974, Brit.); CARRY ON ENGLAND(1976, Brit.); CARRY ON EMANUELLE(1978, Brit.)

Roger Dann
CRIME DOCTOR'S GAMBLE(1947); VARIETY GIRL(1947); I, JANE DOE(1948); I CONFESS(1953); TWO FOR THE ROAD(1967, Brit.); TAMARIND SEED, THE(1974, Brit.)

Ron Dann
HANK WILLIAMS: THE SHOW HE NEVER GAVE(1982, Can.)

Frederic Dannay
DESPERATE CHANCE FOR ELLERY QUEEN, A(1942), w; ENEMY AGENTS MEET ELLERY QUEEN(1942), w

Francoise Dannel
FRUIT IS RIPE, THE(1961, Fr./Ital.)

Don Dannemann
MINX, THE(1969), m

Karl Dannemann
MOSCOW SHANGHAI(1936, Ger.); PILLARS OF SOCIETY(1936, Ger.)

Blythe Danner
TO KILL A CLOWN(1972); 1776(1972); LOVIN' MOLLY(1974); HEARTS OF THE WEST(1975); FUTUREWORLD(1976); GREAT SANTINI, THE(1979); MAN, WOMAN AND CHILD(1983)

Frederick Danner
PRIVILEGE(1967, Brit.); GLADIATORS, THE(1970, Swed.)

Walther Dannerfjord
HAGBARD AND SIGNE(1968, Den./Iceland/Swed.), art d; HUNGER(1968, Den./Norway/Swed.), art d

Sylvia G. L. Dannet
UNDERCOVER WOMAN, THE(1946), w

Erika Dannhoff
REBEL, THE(1933, Ger.)

Faye Dannick
IF EVER I SEE YOU AGAIN(1978)

Joseph Danning
NORTH OF SHANGHAI(1939)

Sybil Danning
CONCORDE, THE–AIRPORT '79(; SAM'S SONG(1971); BLUEBEARD(1972); THREE MUSKETEERS, THE(1974, Panama); GOD'S GUN(1977); CROSSED SWORDS(1978); NIGHT OF THE ASKARI(1978, Ger./South African); OPERATION THUNDERBOLT(1978, ISRAEL); METEOR(1979); BATTLE BEYOND THE STARS(1980); CUBA CROSSING(1980); HOW TO BEAT THE HIGH COST OF LIVING(1980); MAN WITH BOGART'S FACE, THE(1980); SEPARATE WAYS(1981); JULIE DARLING(1982, Can./Ger.); CHAINED HEAT(1983 U.S./Ger.); HERCULES(1983); SALAMANDER, THE(1983, U.S./Ital./Brit.)
1984
JUNGLE WARRIORS(1984, U.S./Ger./Mex.); THEY'RE PLAYING WITH FIRE(1984)
Misc. Talkies
NAUGHTY NYMPHS(1974); RUN, RUN, JOE!(1974); ALBINO(1980)

Genevieve Danninger
Silents
DARING CHANCES(1924)

Dannio
DON QUIXOTE(1935, Fr.)

Ray Dannis
AIR PATROL(1962); YOUNG SWINGERS, THE(1963); RAIDERS FROM BENEATH THE SEA(1964); AGENT FOR H.A.R.M.(1966); LAST OF THE SECRET AGENTS?, THE(1966); UNDERTAKER AND HIS PALS, THE(1966); CORPSE GRINDERS,

THE(1972)

Eddie Danno
SAVAGE SEVEN, THE(1968)

Jacqueline Danno
MURDER AT 45 R.P.M.(1965, Fr.)

Jacques Dannoville
PICNIC ON THE GRASS(1960, Fr.)

Pierre Danny
LES CREATURES(1969, Fr./Swed.)

Danny and the Juniors
LET'S ROCK(1958)

Albert Dano
STAGE DOOR CANTEEN(1943), cos

Anita Dano
REVOLT OF MAMIE STOVER, THE(1956)

Dick Dano
WILD PARTY, THE(1975)

Ellen Dano
EFFECT OF GAMMA RAYS ON MAN-IN-THE-MOON MARIGOLDS, THE(1972)

Linda Dano
WISHBONE CUTTER(1978)

Richard Dano
1984
SPLASH(1984)

Royal Dano
UNDERCOVER GIRL(1950); FLAME OF ARABY(1951); RED BADGE OF COURAGE, THE(1951); UNDER THE GUN(1951); CARRIE(1952); JOHNNY GUITAR(1954); FAR COUNTRY, THE(1955); TROUBLE WITH HARRY, THE(1955); MOBY DICK(1956, Brit.); SANTIAGO(1956); TENSION AT TABLE ROCK(1956); TRIBUTE TO A BAD-MAN(1956); ALL MINE TO GIVE(1957); CRIME OF PASSION(1957); MAN IN THE SHADOW(1957); TROOPER HOOK(1957); HANDLE WITH CARE(1958); MAN OF THE WEST(1958); SADDLE THE WIND(1958); BOY AND THE BRIDGE, THE(1959, Brit.); FACE OF FIRE(1959, U.S./Brit.); HOUND-DOG MAN(1959); NEVER STEAL ANY-THING SMALL(1959); THESE THOUSAND HILLS(1959); ADVENTURES OF HUCK-LEBERRY FINN, THE(1960); CIMARRON(1960); KING OF KINGS(1961); POSSE FROM HELL(1961); SAVAGE SAM(1963); SEVEN FACES OF DR. LAO(1964); GUN-POINT(1966); LAST CHALLENGE, THE(1967); WELCOME TO HARD TIMES(1967); DAY OF THE EVIL GUN(1968); IF HE HOLLERS, LET HIM GO(1968); BACK-TRACK(1969); DEATH OF A GUNFIGHTER(1969); UNDEFEATED, THE(1969); MA-CHISMO-40 GRAVES FOR 40 GUNS(1970); MR. MAGOO'S HOLIDAY FESTIVAL(1970); CHANDLER(1971); CULPEPPER CATTLE COMPANY, THE(1972); GREAT NORTHFIELD, MINNESOTA RAID, THE(1972); ACE ELI AND RODGER OF THE SKIES(1973); CAHILL, UNITED STATES MAR-SHAL(1973); ELECTRA GLIDE IN BLUE(1973); HOWZER(1973); BIG BAD MA-MA(1974); DEAD PEOPLE(1974); CAPONE(1975); WILD PARTY, THE(1975); DRUM(1976); KILLER INSIDE ME, THE(1976); OUTLAW JOSEY WALES, THE(1976); ONE MAN JURY(1978); IN SEARCH OF HISTORIC JESUS(1980); TAKE THIS JOB AND SHOVE IT(1981); HAMMETT(1982); RIGHT STUFF, THE(1983); SOMETHING WICKED THIS WAY COMES(1983)
1984
TEACHERS(1984)
Misc. Talkies
SLINGSHOT(1971); BAD GEORGIA ROAD(1977); HUGHES AND HARLOW: AN-GELS IN HELL(1978)

Steve Dano
INVISIBLE AVENGER, THE(1958)

Ambra Danon
LA CAGE AUX FOLLES(1979, Fr./Ital.), cos; LA CAGE AUX FOLLES II(1981, Ital./Fr.), cos

Marcello Danon
BLACK BELLY OF THE TARANTULA, THE(1972, Ital.), p, w; LA CAGE AUX FOLLES(1979, Fr./Ital.), p, w; LA CAGE AUX FOLLES II(1981, Ital./Fr.), p, w

Raymond Danon
OF FLESH AND BLOOD(1964, Fr./Ital.), p; BLONDE FROM PEKING, THE(1968, Fr.), p; LEATHER AND NYLON(1969, Fr./Ital.), p; LADY IN THE CAR WITH GLASSES AND A GUN, THE(1970, U.S./Fr.), p; SOMEONE BEHIND THE DOOR(1971, Fr./Brit.), p; MR. KLEIN(1976, Fr.), p; MADAME ROSA(1977, Fr.), p; FIRST TIME, THE(1978, Fr.), p; JUDGE AND THE ASSASSIN, THE(1979, Fr.), p

Cesare Danova
CROSSED SWORDS(1954); DON JUAN(1956, Aust.); MAN WHO UNDERSTOOD WOMEN, THE(1959); TARZAN, THE APE MAN(1959); TENDER IS THE NIGHT(1961); VALLEY OF THE DRAGONS(1961); CLEOPATRA(1963); GIDGET GOES TO RO-ME(1963); VIVA LAS VEGAS(1964); BOY, DID I GET A WRONG NUMBER!(1966); CHAMBER OF HORRORS(1966); CHE!(1969); MEAN STREETS(1973); SCOR-CHY(1976); TENTACLES(1977, Ital.); NATIONAL LAMPOON'S ANIMAL HOUSE(1978)
1984
INVISIBLE STRANGLER(1984)
Misc. Talkies
CATCH ME IF YOU CAN(1959)

Barbara Danphy
RUNNING BRAVE(1983, Can.), art d

Paul Danquah
TASTE OF HONEY, A(1962, Brit.); MAROC 7(1967, Brit.); SMASHING TIME(1967 Brit.); THAT RIVIERA TOUCH(1968, Brit.)

David Dans
B.S. I LOVE YOU(1971), ph

Lee Danser
THIS STUFF'LL KILL YA!(1971)

Jean Dansereau
FOND MEMORIES(1982, Can.), p

Herbert Dansey
Misc. Silents
LOST AND WON(1915, Brit.)

Herbert Danska
SWEET LOVE, BITTER(1967), d, w

Jack Danskin
MINNIE AND MOSKOWITZ(1971)

Linda Danson
COMBAT SQUAD(1953); DRIVE A CROOKED ROAD(1954); PRODIGAL, THE(1955)

Randy Danson
KING OF THE GYPSIES(1978); LOCAL COLOR(1978); SCENIC ROUTE, THE(1978); IMPOSTORS(1979)

Ted Danson
ONION FIELD, THE(1979); BODY HEAT(1981); CREEPSHOW(1982)

Charles Dant
SUBMARINE BASE(1943), m, md

Fanny Dant
BOLERO(1982, Fr.)

Dantalion's Chariot
POPDOWN(1968, Brit.)

Andre Dantan
FANNY(1948, Fr.), ph

Nelson Dantas
1984
BLAME IT ON RIO(1984)

Dante
BUNCO SQUAD(1950); GOLDEN COACH, THE(1953, Fr./Ital.)

Anthony Dante
WALK IN THE SUN, A(1945); LOVES OF CARMEN, THE(1948)

Jean Dante
DEEP IN MY HEART(1954)

Jeanne Dante
FOUR DAYS WONDER(1936)

Joe Dante
TWO WEEKS IN ANOTHER TOWN(1962); ARENA, THE(1973), ed; CANNON-BALL(1976, U.S./Hong Kong); HOLLYWOOD BOULEVARD(1976), d, ed; PIRAN-HA(1978), d, ed; ROCK 'N' ROLL HIGH SCHOOL(1979), w; HOWLING, THE(1981), d, ed; SLUMBER PARTY MASSACRE, THE(1982); TWILIGHT ZONE-THE MOVIE(1983), d
1984
GREMLINS(1984), d

Joseph Dante
JOKER IS WILD, THE(1957); GRAND THEFT AUTO(1977), ed

Joseph J. Dante
TIDAL WAVE(1975, U.S./Jap.)

Michael Dante
JEANNE EAGELS(1957); FORT DOBBS(1958); WESTBOUND(1959); SEVEN THIEVES(1960); KID GALAHAD(1962); OPERATION BIKINI(1963); APACHE RI-FLES(1964); NAKED KISS, THE(1964); ARIZONA RAIDERS(1965); HARLOW(1965); WILLARD(1971); THAT'S THE WAY OF THE WORLD(1975); WINTERHAWK(1976); FARMER, THE(1977); BEYOND EVIL(1980); BIG SCORE, THE(1983)
Misc. Talkies
CRUISE MISSILE(1978)

Tony Dante
CLASH BY NIGHT(1952); HOODLUM EMPIRE(1952); FIGHTER ATTACK(1953); TEN COMMANDMENTS, THE(1956)

Claude Dantes
BLOOD AND BLACK LACE(1965, Ital.)

Henri Dantes
CIRCUS WORLD(1964)

Raul Dantes
PROSTITUTION(1965, Fr.); NAZARIN(1968, Mex.)

Roger Dantes
1984
MISSING IN ACTION(1984)

Renee Danti
Misc. Silents
WEST VS. EAST(1922)

Helmut Dantine
INTERNATIONAL SQUADRON(1941); CASABLANCA(1942); DESPERATE JOUR-NEY(1942); MRS. MINIVER(1942); NAVY COMES THROUGH, THE(1942); PIED PIPER, THE(1942); TO BE OR NOT TO BE(1942); EDGE OF DARKNESS(1943); MISSION TO MOSCOW(1943); NORTHERN PURSUIT(1943); WATCH ON THE RHINE(1943); HOLLYWOOD CANTEEN(1944); PASSAGE TO MARSEILLE(1944); ESCAPE IN THE DESERT(1945); HOTEL BERLIN(1945); SHADOW OF A WO-MAN(1946); WHISPERING CITY(1947, Can.); CALL ME MADAM(1953); GUERRILLA GIRL(1953); STRANGER FROM VENUS, THE(1954, Brit.); ALEXANDER THE GREAT(1956); WAR AND PEACE(1956, Ital./U.S.); HELL ON DEVIL'S ISLAND(1957); STORY OF MANKIND, THE(1957); FRAULEIN(1958); TEMPEST(1958, Ital./Yugo./ Fr.); THUNDERING JETS(1958), d; OPERATION CROSSBOW(1965, U.S./Ital.); BRING ME THE HEAD OF ALFREDO GARCIA(1974); KILLER ELITE, THE(1975); WILBY CONSPIRACY, THE(1975, Brit.); BEHIND THE IRON MASK(1977)

Niki Dantine
CONCRETE JUNGLE, THE(1982)

Donna Danton
NOT WITH MY WIFE, YOU DON'T!(1966); HURRY SUNDOWN(1967)

Geoffrey Danton
SNAKE WOMAN, THE(1961, Brit.)

Joan Danton
KNOCK ON ANY DOOR(1949)

Ray Danton
CHIEF CRAZY HORSE(1955); I'LL CRY TOMORROW(1955); LOOTERS, THE(1955); SPOILERS, THE(1955); OUTSIDE THE LAW(1956); NIGHT RUNNER, THE(1957); ONIONHEAD(1958); TARAWA BEACHHEAD(1958); TOO MUCH, TOO SOON(1958); BEAT GENERATION, THE(1959); BIG OPERATOR, THE(1959); YELLOWSTONE KELLY(1959); ICE PALACE(1960); RISE AND FALL OF LEGS DIAMOND, THE(1960); FEVER IN THE BLOOD, A(1961); GEORGE RAFT STORY, THE(1961); MAJORITY OF ONE, A(1961); PORTRAIT OF A MOBSTER(1961); CHAPMAN REPORT, THE(1962); LONGEST DAY, THE(1962); FBI CODE 98(1964); SECRET AGENT SUPER DRA-GON(1966, Fr./Ital./Ger./Monaco); LAST MERCENARY, THE(1969, Ital./Span./Ger.); DEATHMASTER, THE(1972), d; CRYPT OF THE LIVING DEAD zero(1973), d; PUR-SUIT(1975)
Misc. Talkies
TRIANGLE(1971); BALLAD OF BILLIE BLUE(1972); HANNAH-QUEEN OF THE VAMPIRES(1972), d; SAGITTARIUS MINE, THE(1972); CENTERFOLD GIRLS, THE(1974)

Raymond Danton
PSYCHIC KILLER(1975), d, w; SIX PACK ANNIE(1975)
Maria Danube
CASTLE KEEP(1969)
Richard Christian Danus
XANADU(1980), w
Charles Danvers
Silents
NO. 5 JOHN STREET(1921, Brit.)
Ivor Danvers
DICK BARTON–SPECIAL AGENT(1948, Brit.); GIVE A DOG A BONE(1967, Brit.)
Minnie Danvers
Silents
CUPID BY PROXY(1918)
Michael Danvers-Walker
NIGHT WATCH(1973, Brit.)
Yvonne Dany
CHANEL SOLITAIRE(1981)
Bob Danyla
1984
NIGHT PATROL(1984), art d
Edgar Danz
1984
QUESTION OF SILENCE(1984, Neth.)
Renate Danz
SCHLAGER-PARADE(1953)
Tony Danza
HOLLYWOOD KNIGHTS, THE(1980); GOING APE!(1981)
1984
CANNONBALL RUN II(1984)
Martin Danzig
DON'T DRINK THE WATER(1969)
Allen Danziger
TEXAS CHAIN SAW MASSACRE, THE(1974)
Edward Danziger
FINAL COLUMN, THE(1955, Brit.), p; WOMAN OF MYSTERY, A(1957, Brit.), p
Edward J. Danziger
JIGSAW(1949), p; SO YOUNG, SO BAD(1950), p; ST. BENNY THE DIP(1951), p; BABES IN BAGDAD(1952), p; DEVIL GIRL FROM MARS(1954, Brit.), p; STAR OF MY NIGHT(1954, Brit.), p; THREE CORNERED FATE(1954, Brit.), p; YELLOW ROBE, THE(1954, Brit.), p; COUNT OF TWELVE(1955, Brit.), p; ONE JUST MAN(1955, Brit.), p; ALIAS JOHN PRESTON(1956), p; SATELLITE IN THE SKY(1956), p; DEPRAVED, THE(1957, Brit.), p; SON OF A STRANGER(1957, Brit.), p; THREE SUNDAYS TO LIVE(1957, Brit.), p; LINKS OF JUSTICE(1958), p; MOMENT OF INDISCRETION(1958, Brit.), p; ON THE RUN(1958, Brit.), p; THREE CROOKED MEN(1958, Brit.), p; WOMAN POSSESSED, A(1958, Brit.), p; CHILD AND THE KILLER, THE(1959, Brit.), p; CRASH DRIVE(1959, Brit.), p; HIGH JUMP(1959, Brit.), p; HONOURABLE MURDER, AN(1959, Brit.), p; INNOCENT MEETING(1959, Brit.), p; MAN ACCUSED(1959), p; NO SAFETY AHEAD(1959, Brit.), p; TOP FLOOR GIRL(1959, Brit.), p; WEB OF SUSPICION(1959, Brit.), p; WOMAN'S TEMPTATION, A(1959, Brit.), p; DATE AT MIDNIGHT(1960, Brit.), p; IDENTITY UNKNOWN(1960, Brit.), p; NIGHT TRAIN FOR INVERNESS(1960, Brit.), p; SENTENCED FOR LIFE(1960, Brit.), p; SPIDER'S WEB, THE(1960, Brit.), p; HIGHWAY TO BATTLE(1961, Brit.), p; TELL-TALE HEART, THE(1962, Brit.), p; GREAT VAN ROBBERY, THE(1963, Brit.), p
Harry Danziger
HIGH JUMP(1959, Brit.), p
Harry Lee Danziger
JIGSAW(1949), p; SO YOUNG, SO BAD(1950), p; ST. BENNY THE DIP(1951), p; BABES IN BAGDAD(1952), p; DEVIL GIRL FROM MARS(1954, Brit.), p; STAR OF MY NIGHT(1954, Brit.), p; TALE OF THREE WOMEN, A(1954, Brit.), p; THREE CORNERED FATE(1954, Brit.), p; YELLOW ROBE, THE(1954, Brit.), p; FINAL COLUMN, THE(1955, Brit.), p; ONE JUST MAN(1955, Brit.), p; ALIAS JOHN PRESTON(1956), p; SATELLITE IN THE SKY(1956), p; DEPRAVED, THE(1957, Brit.), p; SON OF A STRANGER(1957, Brit.), p; THREE SUNDAYS TO LIVE(1957, Brit.), p; WOMAN OF MYSTERY, A(1957, Brit.), p; LINKS OF JUSTICE(1958), p; MOMENT OF INDISCRETION(1958, Brit.), p; ON THE RUN(1958, Brit.), p; THREE CROOKED MEN(1958, Brit.), p; WOMAN POSSESSED, A(1958, Brit.), p; CHILD AND THE KILLER, THE(1959, Brit.), p; CRASH DRIVE(1959, Brit.), p; HONOURABLE MURDER, AN(1959, Brit.), p; INNOCENT MEETING(1959, Brit.), p; MAN ACCUSED(1959), p; NO SAFETY AHEAD(1959, Brit.), p; TOP FLOOR GIRL(1959, Brit.), p; WEB OF SUSPICION(1959, Brit.), p; WOMAN'S TEMPTATION, A(1959, Brit.), p; DATE AT MIDNIGHT(1960, Brit.), p; IDENTITY UNKNOWN(1960, Brit.), p; NIGHT TRAIN FOR INVERNESS(1960, Brit.), p; SENTENCED FOR LIFE(1960, Brit.), p; SPIDER'S WEB, THE(1960, Brit.), p; HIGHWAY TO BATTLE(1961, Brit.), p; TELL-TALE HEART, THE(1962, Brit.), p; GREAT VAN ROBBERY, THE(1963, Brit.), p
Henry Danziger
SUNDAY BLOODY SUNDAY(1971, Brit.)
Howard Danziger
DELTA FACTOR, THE(1970), m
Isaac Danziger
MY FATHER'S HOUSE(1947, Palestine)
Kenneth Danziger
YELLOWBEARD(1983)
Larry Lee Danziger
COUNT OF TWELVE(1955, Brit.), p
Maia Danziger
HONKY(1971); KIRLIAN WITNESS, THE(1978); MAGICIAN OF LUBLIN, THE(1979, Israel/Ger.); DR. HECKYL AND MR. HYPE(1980)
Linda Danzil
YOUNG SAVAGES, THE(1961)
Edward J. Danzinger
TALE OF THREE WOMEN, A(1954, Brit.), p; OPERATION MURDER(1957, Brit.), p
Harry Lee Danzinger
OPERATION MURDER(1957, Brit.), p; BETRAYAL, THE(1958, Brit.), p. Edward J. Danziger
Hoang Dao
SHANGHAI DRAMA, THE(1945, Fr.)

Halima Daoud
1984
MISUNDERSTOOD(1984)
Gerard Daoudal
1984
LES COMPERES(1984, Fr.), prod d
Dap Sugar Willie
GETTING OVER(1981)
James Daplyn
FAKE, THE(1953, Brit.), w
Ronnie Dapo
OCEAN'S ELEVEN(1960); MUSIC MAN, THE(1962); KISSES FOR MY PRESIDENT(1964); FOLLOW ME, BOYS!(1966)
Carlo Dapporto
ANGELS OF DARKNESS(1956, Ital.)
William Daprato
Misc. Talkies
FAKING OF THE PRESIDENT, THE(1976)
Louis DaPron
BIG BROADCAST OF 1937, THE(1936); COLLEGE HOLIDAY(1936); THREE CHEERS FOR LOVE(1936); ALL-AMERICAN SWEETHEART(1937); HIDEAWAY GIRL(1937); GO WEST, YOUNG LADY(1941), ch; ROOKIES ON PARADE(1941); SAN ANTONIO ROSE(1941); HOW'S ABOUT IT?(1943), ch; NIGHT CLUB GIRL(1944), ch; PATRICK THE GREAT(1945), ch; PENTHOUSE RHYTHM(1945); THAT NIGHT WITH YOU(1945), ch; FEUDIN', FUSSIN' AND A-FIGHTIN'(1948); KETTLES IN THE OZARKS, THE(1956)
Louis Daquin
PORTRAIT OF INNOCENCE(1948, Fr.), d
Henry Dar Boggia
FOREVER FEMALE(1953); SALOME(1953); 36 HOURS(1965)
Henry Dar-Boggia
LAST OF THE SECRET AGENTS?, THE(1966)
Enzo Dara
BARBER OF SEVILLE, THE(1973, Ger./Fr.)
Robert Darane
SWEET ECSTASY(1962, Fr.)
Jean Darbaud
TRIAL OF JOAN OF ARC(1965, Fr.)
Howard Darbeen
LAS VEGAS STORY, THE(1952)
Pigeon Darbo
WORLD IS JUST A 'B' MOVIE, THE(1971)
Francois Darbon
ROAD TO SHAME, THE(1962, Fr.); ELUSIVE CORPORAL, THE(1963, Fr.); LOVE AT TWENTY(1963, Fr./Ital./Jap./Pol./Ger.); DON'T TEMPT THE DEVIL(1964, Fr./Ital.); STOLEN KISSES(1969, Fr.)
Alal Darby
LOCAL HERO(1983, Brit.)
Cecilia Darby
OH! WHAT A LOVELY WAR(1969, Brit.)
James Darby
Silents
GOLD RUSH, THE(1925)
Jane Darby
VAMPIRE CIRCUS(1972, Brit.); MARRIAGE, A(1983)
Ken Darby
MELODY TIME(1948), md; SOUTH PACIFIC(1958), md; PORGY AND BESS(1959), md; HOW THE WEST WAS WON(1962), m
Kim Darby
BUS RILEY'S BACK IN TOWN(1965); RESTLESS ONES, THE(1965); KARATE KILLERS, THE(1967); GENERATION(1969); TRUE GRIT(1969); NORWOOD(1970); STRAWBERRY STATEMENT, THE(1970); GRISSOM GANG, THE(1971); ONE AND ONLY, THE(1978)
Mary Darby
LAS VEGAS STORY, THE(1952)
Rhy Darby
Silents
MALE AND FEMALE(1919)
Ron Darby
INSIDE AMY(1975)
Susan Jane Darby
FLIGHT(1960)
Ted Darby
CAT, THE(1966)
Iris Darbyshire
BARNACLE BILL(1935, Brit.)
Misc. Silents
SWEENEY TODD(1928, Brit.)
Michael Darbyshire
VENGEANCE IS MINE(1948, Brit.); CHITTY CHITTY BANG BANG(1968, Brit.); LOCK UP YOUR DAUGHTERS(1969, Brit.)
Katherine Darc
HOW SWEET IT IS(1968); WILD SCENE, THE(1970)
Mireille Darc
PLEASE, NOT NOW!(1963, Fr./Ital.); MONSIEUR(1964, Fr.); MALE HUNT(1965, Fr./Ital.); GALIA(1966, Fr./Ital.); GREAT SPY CHASE, THE(1966, Fr.); UPPER HAND, THE(1967, Fr./Ital./Ger.); BLONDE FROM PEKING, THE(1968, Fr.); FEMMINA(1968 Fr./Ital./Ger.); WEEKEND(1968, Fr./Ital.); THOSE DARING YOUNG MEN IN THEIR JAUNTY JALOPIES(1969, Fr./Brit./ Ital.); MADLY(1970, Fr.); TALL BLOND MAN WITH ONE BLACK SHOE, THE(1973, Fr.)
Jean Darcante
ROOM UPSTAIRS, THE(1948, Fr.)
Denise Darcel
BATTLEGROUND(1949); THUNDER IN THE PINES(1949); TARZAN AND THE SLAVE GIRL(1950); WESTWARD THE WOMEN(1951); YOUNG MAN WITH IDEAS(1952); DANGEROUS WHEN WET(1953); FLAME OF CALCUTTA(1953); VERA CRUZ(1954); SEVEN WOMEN FROM HELL(1961)

JOE(1936); TROUBLE FOR TWO(1936); UNDERCOVER MAN(1936); WEDDING PRESENT(1936); JIM HANVEY, DETECTIVE(1937); LIFE OF EMILE ZOLA, THE(1937); ON THE AVENUE(1937); THAT CERTAIN WOMAN(1937); TOAST OF NEW YORK, THE(1937); TRAPPED BY G-MEN(1937); CASSIDY OF BAR 20(1938); JEZEBEL(1938); LOVE FINDS ANDY HARDY(1938); PRISON BREAK(1938); WESTERN JAMBOREE(1938); DARK VICTORY(1939); LONG SHOT, THE(1939); PANAMA PATROL(1939); SABOTAGE(1939); STAND UP AND FIGHT(1939); TWO THOROUGHBREDS(1939); WHEN TOMORROW COMES(1939); ARIZONA(1940); DOCTOR TAKES A WIFE(1940); GRAPES OF WRATH(1940); LILLIAN RUSSELL(1940); ARKANSAS JUDGE(1941); BLOSSOMS IN THE DUST(1941); HELLZAPOPPIN'(1941); SIS HOPKINS(1941); UNDER FIESTA STARS(1941); GAY SISTERS, THE(1942); HURRICANE SMITH(1942); JACKASS MAIL(1942); JUKE GIRL(1942); ROXIE HART(1942); TALES OF MANHATTAN(1942); GANG'S ALL HERE, THE(1943); HELLO, FRISCO, HELLO(1943); OLD ACQUAINTANCE(1943); OUTLAW, THE(1943); GENTLE ANNIE(1944); TALL IN THE SADDLE(1944); KISS AND TELL(1945); BAD BASCOMB(1946); CLAUDIA AND DAVID(1946); FABULOUS SUZANNE, THE(1946); MY REPUTATION(1946); SECRET HEART, THE(1946); DOWN TO EARTH(1947); HIGH WALL, THE(1947); MAGIC TOWN(1947); SEA OF GRASS, THE(1947); WOMAN ON THE BEACH, THE(1947); MR. BLANDINGS BUILDS HIS DREAM HOUSE(1948); YOU GOTTA STAY HAPPY(1948); FLYING SAUCER, THE(1950); WHIP HAND, THE(1951)

George Darien
THIEF OF PARIS, THE(1967, Fr./Ital.), w

N. Daries
BAKER'S WIFE, THE(1940, Fr.), ph

Robert Darieux
ORGY OF THE DEAD(1965), cos

Bobby Darin
PEPE(1960); COME SEPTEMBER(1961); HELL IS FOR HEROES(1962); IF A MAN ANSWERS(1962); PRESSURE POINT(1962); STATE FAIR(1962); TOO LATE BLUES(1962); CAPTAIN NEWMAN, M.D.(1963); LIVELY SET, THE(1964), m; THAT FUNNY FEELING(1965), a, m; GUNFIGHT IN ABILENE(1967), a, m; HAPPY MOTHER'S DAY... LOVE, GEORGE(1973)

Robert Darin
HELLER IN PINK TIGHTS(1960); PLEASE DON'T EAT THE DAISIES(1960); HAPPY ENDING, THE(1969)

Thelia Darin
MOVIE STUNTMEN(1953)
Misc. Talkies
HOLLYWOOD THRILL-MAKERS(1954)

Jack Daring [Percy Moran]
Silents
JACK, SAM AND PETE(1919, Brit.), d

K. Mason Daring
RETURN OF THE SECAUCUS SEVEN(1980), m

Mason Daring
LIANNA(1983), m
1984
BROTHER FROM ANOTHER PLANET, THE(1984), m

Dario
YO YO(1967, Fr.)

Sascha Dario
ATLAS(1960)

Tony Dario
DIRTY HARRY(1971); ESCAPE FROM ALCATRAZ(1979)

Frank Darion
BIG BUSINESS GIRL(1931)

Joe Darion
SHINBONE ALLEY(1971), w

James Daris
WRECKING CREW, THE(1968)

Elizabeth Darius
CASTLE KEEP(1969)

Bobby Dark
DEADLY BLESSING(1981)

Carol Dark
TALES OF A SALESMAN(1965)

Chris Dark
BABY FACE NELSON(1957)

Christopher Dark
SEPTEMBER AFFAIR(1950); RAIDERS OF THE SEVEN SEAS(1953); STEEL LADY, THE(1953); SUDDENLY(1954); DIANE(1955); JOHNNY CONCHO(1956); WORLD WITHOUT END(1956); HALLIDAY BRAND, THE(1957); DAY OF THE BAD MAN(1958); WILD HERITAGE(1958); RABBIT TRAP, THE(1959); PLATINUM HIGH SCHOOL(1960); HOW THE WEST WAS WON(1962); NONE BUT THE BRAVE(1965, U.S./Jap.); PRIVATE NAVY OF SGT. O'FARRELL, THE(1968); SCANDALOUS JOHN(1971)

Danny Dark
TUNNELVISION(1976); MELVIN AND HOWARD(1980)

Dorothy Dark
LOYAL HEART(1946, Brit.)

Gregory Dark
MISSILE FROM HELL(1960, Brit.)

Jennie Dark
MANIAC(1934)

John Dark
WIND OF CHANGE, THE(1961, Brit.), p; LAND THAT TIME FORGOT, THE(1975, Brit.), p; AT THE EARTH'S CORE(1976, Brit.), p; PEOPLE THAT TIME FORGOT, THE(1977, Brit.), p; WARLORDS OF ATLANTIS(1978, Brit.), p; ARABIAN ADVENTURE(1979, Brit.), p
1984
SLAYGROUND(1984, Brit.), p

Johnny Dark
Misc. Talkies
RIP OFF(1977)

Michael Dark
Silents
ON THE HIGH SEAS(1922); TAILOR MADE MAN, A(1922); BEAU BRUMMEL(1924); BROADWAY AFTER DARK(1924); GIRL ON THE STAIRS, THE(1924); REGULAR FELLOW, A(1925)

Misc. Silents
COUNT OF LUXEMBOURG, THE(1926)

John Darkcloud
Misc. Silents
JOHN ERMINE OF THE YELLOWSTONE(1917)

Dorothy Darke
OLD MOTHER RILEY, HEADMISTRESS(1950, Brit.); EIGHT O'CLOCK WALK(1954, Brit.)

Rebecca Darke
WAY WE LIVE NOW, THE(1970); KING OF THE GYPSIES(1978)

Otchere Darko
1984
WHITE ELEPHANT(1984, Brit.)

Toni Darko
1984
WHITE ELEPHANT(1984, Brit.)

Eva Darlan
BANZAI(1983, Fr.)

Jean Darle
ZITA(1968, Fr.)

Gigi Darlene
1,000 SHAPES OF A FEMALE(1963); "RENT-A-GIRL"(1965)

Bert Darley
Silents
LAUGHTER AND TEARS(1921, Brit.); WHEN GREEK MEETS GREEK(1922, Brit.); FLYING FIFTY-FIVE, THE(1924, Brit.)

Brian Darley
Silents
ROMANCE OF THE AIR, A(1919); RULING PASSION, THE(1922)

Anne Darling
HUMAN SIDE, THE(1934)

Candy Darling
SOME OF MY BEST FRIENDS ARE...(1971); LADY LIBERTY(1972, Ital./Fr.); SILENT NIGHT, BLOODY NIGHT(1974)

Dick Darling
C.H.O.M.P.S.(1979), ed

Dot Darling
WORDS AND MUSIC(1929)

Erin Darling
1984
REPO MAN(1984)

Glenville Darling
SAINTS AND SINNERS(1949, Brit.)

Grace Darling
Silents
AMAZING LOVERS(1921); EVERYMAN'S PRICE(1921)
Misc. Silents
FALSE GODS(1919); VIRTUOUS MEN(1919); COMMON SIN, THE(1920); DISCARDED WOMAN, THE(1920); EVEN AS EVE(1920)

Granville Darling
MINSTREL BOY, THE(1937, Brit.)

Gretchen Darling
MISSISSIPPI RHYTHM(1949), w

Helen Darling
UP IN ARMS(1944)

Ida Darling
LOVE IN THE DESERT(1929); LUMMOX(1930); HERE COMES THE NAVY(1934); GIRL WHO CAME BACK, THE(1935)
Silents
NIGHTINGALE, THE(1914); MASQUERADERS, THE(1915); LOST BRIDEGROOM, THE(1916); SHE LOVES AND LIES(1920); WHISPERS(1920); NOBODY(1921); SOCIETY SNOBS(1921); DESTINY'S ISLE(1922); RULING PASSION, THE(1922); EXCITERS, THE(1923); IRENE(1926); SINGED(1927)
Misc. Silents
HYPOCRISY(1916); BY RIGHT OF PURCHASE(1918); LIFE'S GREATEST PROBLEM(1919); MAROONED HEARTS(1920); WEDDING BELLS(1921)

Jamie Darling
Silents
OLD CURIOSITY SHOP, THE(1913, Brit.); JUSTICE(1914, Brit.)
Misc. Silents
CLOISTER AND THE HEARTH, THE(1913, Brit.)

Jane Darling
YOUNG GIRLS OF ROCHEFORT, THE(1968, Fr.); SONG OF NORWAY(1970)

Jean Darling
BABES IN TOYLAND(1934); JANE EYRE(1935)

Jennifer Darling
UP THE SANDBOX(1972); TRENCHCOAT(1983)

Jill Darling
MOVIE STAR, AMERICAN STYLE, OR, LSD I HATE YOU!(1966)

Joan Darling
TROUBLEMAKER, THE(1964); FEARLESS FRANK(1967); PRESIDENT'S ANALYST, THE(1967); UP IN THE CELLAR(1970); FIRST LOVE(1977), d; SUNNYSIDE(1979)

Joseph Darling
1984
NO SMALL AFFAIR(1984)

Kenneth Darling
STAGECOACH TO DANCER'S PARK(1962), w

Marian Darling
OLD MAN RHYTHM(1935)

Murphy Darling
Silents
KING, QUEEN, JOKER(1921), ph; DAUGHTERS WHO PAY(1925), ph

Nadine Darling
STARTING OVER(1979); TEMPEST(1982)
1984
GARBO TALKS(1984)

Patricia Darling
1,000 SHAPES OF A FEMALE(1963)
Romere Darling
MRS. MIKE(1949)
Ruth Darling
Silents
INTOLERANCE(1916); MANHATTAN MADNESS(1916)
Misc. Silents
FIFTY-FIFTY(1916); HIDDEN WOMAN, THE(1922)
Sally Darling
Misc. Talkies
GUNS FOR HIRE(1932); FIVE BAD MEN(1935)
Sam Darling
ULTIMATE THRILL, THE(1974)
Scott Darling
BORROWED WIVES(1930), w; GOLD(1932), w; POCATELLO KID(1932), w; CONFIDENTIAL(1935), w; FORCED LANDING(1935), w; CHARLIE CHAN AT THE OPERA(1936), w; RETURN OF JIMMY VALENTINE, THE(1936), w; ADVENTURE'S END(1937), w; ATLANTIC FLIGHT(1937), w; BOY OF THE STREETS(1937), w; CALIFORNIA STRAIGHT AHEAD(1937), w; TELEPHONE OPERATOR(1938), w; STUNT PILOT(1939), w; FATAL HOUR, THE(1940), w; HE MARRIED HIS WIFE(1940), w; I'M NOBODY'S SWEETHEART NOW(1940), w; BODY DISAPPEARS, THE(1941), w; DOUBLE DATE(1941), w; GHOST OF FRANKENSTEIN, THE(1942), w; JITTERBUGS(1943), w; BIG NOISE, THE(1944), w; BORN TO SPEED(1947), w; LOUISIANA(1947), w; TOO MANY WINNERS(1947), w; BLACK MIDNIGHT(1949), w; LAWTON STORY, THE(1949), w; PRINCE OF PEACE, THE(1951), w
Silents
ON ZE BOULEVARD(1927), w
Todd Darling
1984
REPO MAN(1984)
W. Scott Darling
TAXI 13(1928), w; NOISY NEIGHBORS(1929), w; CAUGHT CHEATING(1931), w; MURDER AT MIDNIGHT(1931), w; SOUL OF THE SLUMS(1931), w; DRAGNET PATROL(1932), w; DYNAMITE DENNY(1932), w; HER NIGHT OUT(1932, Brit.), w; HIGH SOCIETY(1932, Brit.), w; LUCKY LADIES(1932, Brit.), w; NIGHT BEAT(1932), w; RIVER HOUSE GHOST, THE(1932, Brit.), w; BERMONDSEY KID, THE(1933, Brit.), w; I ADORE YOU(1933, Brit.), w; NAUGHTY CINDERELLA(1933, Brit.), w; OUTLAW JUSTICE(1933), w; TOO MANY WIVES(1933, Brit.), w; CHURCH MOUSE, THE(1934, Brit.), w; GUEST OF HONOR(1934, Brit.), w; NO ESCAPE(1934, Brit.), w; WITHOUT YOU(1934, Brit.), w; OLD HOMESTEAD, THE(1935), w; SWEEPSTAKE ANNIE(1935), w; UNKNOWN WOMAN(1935), w; FRONTIER JUSTICE(1936), w; KING OF THE SIERRAS(1938), w; MR. WONG IN CHINATOWN(1939), w; MYSTERY OF MR. WONG, THE(1939), w; MARGIE(1940), w; CRACKED NUTS(1941), w; GREAT IMPERSONATION, THE(1942), w; SHERLOCK HOLMES AND THE SECRET WEAPON(1942), w; SIN TOWN(1942), w; DANCING MASTERS, THE(1943), w; BERMUDA MYSTERY(1944), w; COBRA WOMAN(1944), w; WEIRD WOMAN(1944), w; BULLFIGHTERS, THE(1945), w; CARIBBEAN MYSTERY, THE(1945), w; SPIDER, THE(1945), w; BEHIND GREEN LIGHTS(1946), w; CHINESE RING, THE(1947), w; DOCKS OF NEW ORLEANS(1948), w; KIDNAPPED(1948), w; MYSTERY OF THE GOLDEN EYE, THE(1948), w; SHANGHAI CHEST, THE(1948), w; FORGOTTEN WOMEN(1949), w; TUNA CLIPPER(1949), w; WOLF HUNTERS, THE(1949), w; BLUE GRASS OF KENTUCKY(1950), w; COUNTY FAIR(1950), w; ACCORDING TO MRS. HOYLE(1951), w; BLUE BLOOD(1951), w; MEET ME AFTER THE SHOW(1951), w; DESERT PURSUIT(1952), w
Silents
WATCH HIM STEP(1922), w; MEDDLER, THE(1925), w; SCARLET SEAS(1929), w
William Darling
SONG OF KENTUCKY(1929), art d; DEVIL WITH WOMEN, A(1930), art d; LAST OF THE DUANES(1930), art d; MEN WITHOUT WOMEN(1930), art d; RENEGADES(1930), set d; WOMEN EVERYWHERE(1930), set d; PASSPORT TO HELL(1932), art d; BERKELEY SQUARE(1933), set d; BEST OF ENEMIES(1933), set d; FACE IN THE SKY(1933), set d; HELLO SISTER!(1933), art d; MR. SKITCH(1933), art d; PILGRIMAGE(1933), art d; JUDGE PRIEST(1934), art d; WORLD MOVES ON, THE(1934), art d; CHARLIE CHAN IN EGYPT(1935), art d; DANTE'S INFERNO(1935), art d; FOLIES DERGERE(1935), art d; IN OLD KENTUCKY(1935), art d; IT'S A SMALL WORLD(1935), art d; LITTLEST REBEL, THE(1935), art d; STEAMBOAT ROUND THE BEND(1935), art d; WAY DOWN EAST(1935), art d; DIMPLES(1936), art d; LADIES IN LOVE(1936), art d; MESSAGE TO GARCIA, A(1936), art d; POOR LITTLE RICH GIRL(1936), art d; PRISONER OF SHARK ISLAND, THE(1936), art d; STOWAWAY(1936), art d; ON THE AVENUE(1937), art d; SEVENTH HEAVEN(1937), art d; WEE WILLIE WINKIE(1937), art d; IN OLD CHICAGO(1938), art d; SUBMARINE PATROL(1938), art d; JESSE JAMES(1939), art d; RAINS CAME, THE(1939), art d; STANLEY AND LIVINGSTONE(1939), art d; BRIGHAM YOUNG–FRONTIERSMAN(1940), art d; HANGMEN ALSO DIE(1943), art d; SONG OF BERNADETTE, THE(1943), art d; KEYS OF THE KINGDOM, THE(1944), art d; ANNA AND THE KING OF SIAM(1946), m
Silents
HER MAD BARGAIN(1921), art d; QUESTION OF HONOR, A(1922), set d
William S. Darling
SEVEN FACES(1929), set d; SOUTH SEA ROSE(1929), set d; MAN TROUBLE(1930), set d; LLOYDS OF LONDON(1936), art d
Marian Darlington
OBLIGING YOUNG LADY(1941)
Marion Darlington
SNOW WHITE AND THE SEVEN DWARFS(1937)
W.A. Darlington
ALF'S CARPET(1929, Brit.), w; ALF'S BUTTON(1930, Brit.), w; ALF'S BUTTON AFLOAT(1938, Brit.), w
Silents
ALF'S BUTTON(1920, Brit.), w
Darlowe
FIRE IN THE STRAW(1943), ed
Jan Darlyn
GARMENT JUNGLE, THE(1957)
Jann Darlyn
GUYS AND DOLLS(1955)

John Darlys
GREYFRIARS BOBBY(1961, Brit.), anim
Aryel Darma
Silents
SHOW GIRL, THE(1927)
Misc. Silents
SMOKE EATERS, THE(1926)
Charles Darmanin
TRENCHCOAT(1983)
Hughes Darmois
FANTASTICA(1980, Can./Fr.), ed; BOLERO(1982, Fr.), ed
Hugues Darmois
1984
EDITH AND MARCEL(1984, Fr.), ed
Gerard Darmon
DIVA(1982, Fr.)
Frank Darmond
Misc. Silents
GREAT JEWEL ROBBERY, THE(1925)
Grace Darmond
Silents
IN THE BALANCE(1917); AMERICAN LIVE WIRE, AN(1918); OTHER MAN, THE(1918); BEAUTIFUL GAMBLER, THE(1921); WHITE AND UNMARRIED(1921); HANDLE WITH CARE(1922); SONG OF LIFE, THE(1922); GOLD MADNESS(1923); ALIMONY(1924); FLATTERY(1925); MARRIAGE CLAUSE, THE(1926); NIGHT PATROL, THE(1926)
Misc. Silents
BLACK SHEEP, A(1915); HOUSE OF A THOUSAND CANDLES, THE(1915); MILLIONAIRE BABY, THE(1915); TEXAS STEER, A(1915); CRUCIBLE OF LIFE, THE(1918); DIPLOMATIC MISSION, A(1918); GULF BETWEEN, THE(1918); MAN WHO WOULDN'T TELL, THE(1918); SEAL OF SILENCE, THE(1918); HIGHEST TRUMP, THE(1919); VALLEY OF THE GIANTS, THE(1919); WHAT EVERY WOMAN WANTS(1919); BELOW THE SURFACE(1920); INVISIBLE DIVORCE, THE(1920); SO LONG LETTY(1920); SEE MY LAWYER(1921); DANGEROUS ADVENTURE, A(1922); I CAN EXPLAIN(1922); DAYTIME WIVES(1923); MIDNIGHT GUEST, THE(1923); DISCONTENTED HUSBANDS(1924); FLATTERY(1925); GREAT JEWEL ROBBERY, THE(1925); WHERE THE WORST BEGINS(1925); HER BIG ADVENTURE(1926); HER MAN O'WAR(1926); MIDNIGHT THIEVES(1926); HOUR OF RECKONING, THE(1927); WAGES OF CONSCIENCE(1927); WIDE OPEN(1927)
Larry Darmont
RECKLESS RANGER(1937), p
The Darmora Ballet
GASLIGHT(1940)
Larry Darmour
GOLD(1932), p; LAW AND LAWLESS(1932), p; GUN LAW(1933), p; OUTLAW JUSTICE(1933), p; VIA PONY EXPRESS(1933), p; FIRETRAP, THE(1935), p; MOTIVE FOR REVENGE(1935), p; MUTINY AHEAD(1935), p; NIGHT ALARM(1935), p; PERFECT CLUE, THE(1935), p; RECKLESS ROADS(1935), p; WESTERN COURAGE(1935), p; WESTERN FRONTIER(1935), p; AVENGING WATERS(1936), p; FUGITIVE SHERIFF, THE(1936), p; HEIR TO TROUBLE(1936), p; HEROES OF THE RANGE(1936), p; LAWLESS RIDERS(1936), p; UNKNOWN RANGER, THE(1936), p; LAW OF THE RANGER(1937), p; NORTH OF NOME(1937), p; RANGER COURAGE(1937), p; RANGERS STEP IN, THE(1937), p; RIO GRANDE RANGER(1937), p; ROARING TIMBER(1937), p; SHADOWS OF THE ORIENT(1937), p; TRAPPED BY G-MEN(1937), p; TROUBLE IN MOROCCO(1937), p; UNDER SUSPICION(1937), p; IN EARLY ARIZONA(1938), p; PHANTOM GOLD(1938), p; PIONEER TRAIL(1938), p; REFORMATORY(1938), p; ROLLING CARAVANS(1938), p; STAGECOACH DAYS(1938), p; FRONTIERS OF '49(1939), p; FUGITIVE AT LARGE(1939), p; HIDDEN POWER(1939), p; LAW COMES TO TEXAS, THE(1939), p; LONE STAR PIONEERS(1939), p; TRAPPED IN THE SKY(1939), p; WHISPERING ENEMIES(1939), p; ELLERY QUEEN. MASTER DETECTIVE(1940), p; FUGITIVE FROM A PRISON CAMP(1940), p; GREAT PLANE ROBBERY, THE(1940), p; OUTSIDE THE 3-MILE LIMIT(1940), p; ELLERY QUEEN AND THE MURDER RING(1941), p; ELLERY QUEEN AND THE PERFECT CRIME(1941), p; ELLERY QUEEN'S PENTHOUSE MYSTERY(1941), p; GREAT SWINDLE, THE(1941), p; CLOSE CALL FOR ELLERY QUEEN, A(1942), p; DESPERATE CHANCE FOR ELLERY QUEEN, A(1942), p; ENEMY AGENTS MEET ELLERY QUEEN(1942), p
Larry J. Darmour
MYSTERY TRAIN(1931), p
Ray Darmour
BEHIND THE HIGH WALL(1956)
Roy Darmour
DARK ANGEL, THE(1935); SMART GUY(1943); FOLLOW THE BOYS(1944); MAN FROM FRISCO(1944); MY BUDDY(1944); EASY TO LOOK AT(1945); SUDAN(1945); I RING DOORBELLS(1946); MASK OF DIIJON, THE(1946); I, JANE DOE(1948); UNDERCOVER MAN, THE(1949); LAS VEGAS STORY, THE(1952); FIRST TRAVELING SALESLADY, THE(1956); INVASION OF THE SAUCER MEN(1957); YOUNG AND DANGEROUS(1957)
Yvette Darnac
RADIO FOLLIES(1935, Brit.)
Anthony Darnborough
GIRL IN THE PAINTING, THE(1948, Brit.), p; BOYS IN BROWN(1949, Brit.), p; HELTER SKELTER(1949, Brit.), p; QUARTET(1949, Brit.), p; ASTONISHED HEART, THE(1950, Brit.), d; HIGHLY DANGEROUS(1950, Brit.), p; TRIO(1950, Brit.), p; ENCORE(1951, Brit.), p; TRAVELLER'S JOY(1951, Brit.), p; PROJECT M7(1953, Brit.), p; PERSONAL AFFAIR(1954, Brit.), p; BABY AND THE BATTLESHIP, THE(1957, Brit.), p
Antony Darnborough
MY BROTHER'S KEEPER(1949, Brit.), p; ONCE UPON A DREAM(1949, Brit.), p; SO LONG AT THE FAIR(1951, Brit.), d; TO PARIS WITH LOVE(1955, Brit.), p
Hermione Darnborough
WINGS OF THE MORNING(1937, Brit.)
August Darnell
1984
AGAINST ALL ODDS(1984)
Deborah Darnell
COUNT YORGA, VAMPIRE(1970)

Denise Darnell
MICKEY ONE(1965)
Diane Darnell
DIRTY HARRY(1971)
Jason Darnell
TOWN THAT DREADED SUNDOWN, THE(1977)
Larry Darnell
DOGS(1976)
Linda Darnell
DAY-TIME WIFE(1939); HOTEL FOR WOMEN(1939); BRIGHAM YOUNG–FRON-TIERSMAN(1940); CHAD HANNA(1940); MARK OF ZORRO, THE(1940); STAR DUST(1940); BLOOD AND SAND(1941); RISE AND SHINE(1941); LOVES OF EDGAR ALLAN POE, THE(1942); CITY WITHOUT MEN(1943); SONG OF BERNADETTE, THE(1943); BUFFALO BILL(1944); IT HAPPENED TOMORROW(1944); SUMMER STORM(1944); SWEET AND LOWDOWN(1944); FALLEN ANGEL(1945); GREAT JOHN L. THE(1945); HANGOVER SQUARE(1945); ANNA AND THE KING OF SIAM(1946); CENTENNIAL SUMMER(1946); MY DARLING CLEMENTINE(1946); FOREVER AMBER(1947); LETTER TO THREE WIVES, A(1948); UNFAITHFULLY YOURS(1948); WALLS OF JERICHO(1948); EVERYBODY DOES IT(1949); SLAT-TERY'S HURRICANE(1949); NO WAY OUT(1950); TWO FLAGS WEST(1950); GUY WHO CAME BACK, THE(1951); LADY PAYS OFF, THE(1951); THIRTEENTH LET-TER, THE(1951); BLACKBEARD THE PIRATE(1952); ISLAND OF DESIRE(1952, Brit.); NIGHT WITHOUT SLEEP(1952); SECOND CHANCE(1953); THIS IS MY LOVE(1954); ANGELS OF DARKNESS(1956, Ital.); DAKOTA INCIDENT(1956); ZERO HOUR!(1957); CASTILIAN, THE(1963, Span./U.S.); BLACK SPURS(1965)
Misc. Talkies
HOMEWARD BORNE(1957)
James Darnley
SMITH'S WIVES(1935, Brit.), w
Louis Darnley
GYPSY MELODY(1936, Brit.); DR. SIN FANG(1937, Brit.)
Jan Darnley-Smith
GO KART GO(1964, Brit.), d; HOVERBUG(1970, Brit.), d; HITCH IN TIME, A(1978, Brit.), d
Misc. Talkies
GHOST OF A CHANCE, A(1968, Brit.), d; FERN, THE RED DEER(1977, Brit.), d
Mina Darno
WHAT DID YOU DO IN THE WAR, DADDY?(1966)
George Darnoux
BOUDU SAVED FROM DROWNING(1967, Fr.)
Charles Darnton
Silents
IRON HORSE, THE(1924), t; DICK TURPIN(1925), w; DESERT'S PRICE, THE(1926), w; MAN FOUR-SQUARE, A(1926), w
Ginette Darnys
Misc. Silents
LE ROI DE LA MER(1917, Fr.)
Ann Daro
HELL BOUND(1957)
Eraldo Daroma
HIS LAST TWELVE HOURS(1953, Ital.), ed
Jacques Daroy
GENERALS WITHOUT BUTTONS(1938, Fr.), d
Laurence Darpy
DIVA(1982, Fr.)
Capt. Darr
TANGA-TIKA(1953)
Cherie Darr
1984
THIS IS SPINAL TAP(1984)
Mary Darr
JULIUS CAESAR(1952)
Vendell Darr
STRIKE UP THE BAND(1940)
Vondell Darr
ON TRIAL(1928); DUMMY, THE(1929); THAT CERTAIN AGE(1938)
Silents
PONY EXPRESS, THE(1925)
Misc. Silents
BORDER VENGENCE(1925)
William Darr
METEOR(1979)
Jean-Pierre Darras
YOUNG WORLD, A(1966, Fr./Ital.)
Steve Darrel
COW TOWN(1950)
Charles Darrell
WHEN LONDON SLEEPS(1932, Brit.), w
Dorothy Darrell
BUCK PRIVATES(1941); CRACKED NUTS(1941); HELLO SUCKER(1941); KEEP 'EM FLYING(1941); MOB TOWN(1941)
J. Stevan Darrell
TEN COMMANDMENTS, THE(1956)
James Darrell
HOODLUM SAINT, THE(1946); POSTMAN ALWAYS RINGS TWICE, THE(1946); TILL THE CLOUDS ROLL BY(1946)
Maisie Darrell
P.C. JOSSER(1931, Brit.)
Maj. Fred Darrell
O.S.S.(1946)
Michael Darrell
E.T. THE EXTRA-TERRESTRIAL(1982)
Pam Darrell
LOOKS AND SMILES(1982, Brit.)
Robert Darrell
HERO FOR A DAY(1939)
Stevan Darrell
ANGELS WITH DIRTY FACES(1938); CODE OF THE SECRET SERVICE(1939)

Steve Darrell
I'LL WAIT FOR YOU(1941); THEY DIED WITH THEIR BOOTS ON(1942); NOTHING BUT TROUBLE(1944); LIGHTNING RAIDERS(1945); DON'T GAMBLE WITH STRAN-GERS(1946); GENTLEMEN WITH GUNS(1946); HELLDORADO(1946); ROLL ON TEXAS MOON(1946); TERRORS ON HORSEBACK(1946); ON THE OLD SPANISH TRAIL(1947); PRAIRIE EXPRESS(1947); SONG OF MY HEART(1947); UNDER COLORADO SKIES(1947); CARSON CITY RAIDERS(1948); I WOULDN'T BE IN YOUR SHOES(1948); MARK OF THE LASH(1948); NIGHT TIME IN NEVADA(1948); PARTNERS OF THE SUNSET(1948); SON OF GOD'S COUNTRY(1948); TIMBER TRAIL, THE(1948); WEST OF SONORA(1948); ABANDONED(1949); BLAZING TRAIL, THE(1949); CHALLENGE OF THE RANGE(1949); CRASHING THRU(1949); EL DORADO PASS(1949); GAL WHO TOOK THE WEST, THE(1949); OUTCASTS OF THE TRAIL(1949); RIDERS IN THE SKY(1949); ARIZONA COWBOY, THE(1950); BLAZING SUN, THE(1950); DAVID HARDING, COUNTERSPY(1950); FRONTIER OUT-POST(1950); I WAS A SHOPLIFTER(1950); UNDER MEXICALI STARS(1950); WIN-CHESTER '73(1950); PECOS RIVER(1951); ROUGH RIDERS OF DURANGO(1951); JUNCTION CITY(1952); SNIPER, THE(1952); THUNDER OVER THE PLAINS(1953); CANNIBAL ATTACK(1954); DANGEROUS MISSION(1954); LAW VS. BILLY THE KID, THE(1954); GIRL IN THE RED VELVET SWING, THE(1955); GOOD MORNING, MISS DOVE(1955); I DIED A THOUSAND TIMES(1955); PRINCE OF PLAYERS(1955); TARANTULA(1955); TREASURE OF RUBY HILLS(1955); PROUD ONES, THE(1956); RED SUNDOWN(1956); JOE DAKOTA(1957); MONOLITH MONSTERS, THE(1957); UTAH BLAINE(1957); GHOST OF ZORRO(1959); THESE THOUSAND HILLS(1959); TIMBUKTU(1959)
Misc. Talkies
RIDERS OF THE LONE STAR(1947)
Steven Darrell
WOMEN IN THE WIND(1939); FUGITIVE FROM JUSTICE, A(1940); BULLFIGHT-ERS, THE(1945); SWORD OF MONTE CRISTO, THE(1951); TALL MEN, THE(1955)
Eva Darren
BRIDES OF BLOOD(1968, US/Phil.)
James Darren
RUMBLE ON THE DOCKS(1956); BROTHERS RICO, THE(1957); OPERATION MAD BALL(1957); TIJUANA STORY, THE(1957); GUNMAN'S WALK(1958); GENE KRUPA STORY, THE(1959); GIDGET(1959); ALL THE YOUNG MEN(1960); BECAUSE THEY'RE YOUNG(1960); LET NO MAN WRITE MY EPITAPH(1960); GUNS OF NAVARONE, THE(1961); DIAMOND HEAD(1962); GIDGET GOES TO ROME(1963); FOR THOSE WHO THINK YOUNG(1964); HEY THERE, IT'S YOGI BEAR(1964); LIVELY SET, THE(1964); VENUS IN FURS(1970, Ital./Brit./Ger.); BOSS'S SON, THE(1978)
Misc. Talkies
ALIENS FROM ANOTHER PLANET(1967); LOST WORLD OF LIBRA, THE(1968)
Patrick Darren
BAY OF SAINT MICHEL, THE(1963, Brit.)
Sonia Darren
BIG SLEEP, THE(1946)
Bill Darrid
THAT NIGHT(1957); VIOLATORS, THE(1957)
Ron Darrier
1984
SPLATTER UNIVERSITY(1984), makeup
Gerard Darrieu
END OF DESIRE(1962 Fr./Ital.); ELUSIVE CORPORAL, THE(1963, Fr.); MADEMOI-SELLE(1966, Fr./Brit.); WEEKEND AT DUNKIRK(1966, Fr./Ital.); Z(1969, Fr./Alg-eria); CONFESSION, THE(1970, Fr.); MON ONCLE D'AMERIQUE(1980, Fr.)
Danielle Darrieux
MAYERLING(1937, Fr.); ABUSED CONFIDENCE(1938, Fr. ABUS DE CONFIANCE); COUNSEL FOR ROMANCE(1938, Fr.); RAGE OF PARIS, THE(1938); HER FIRST AFFAIR(1947, Fr.); RUY BLAS(1948, Fr.); RICH, YOUNG AND PRETTY(1951); FIVE FINGERS(1952); EARRINGS OF MADAME DE..., THE(1954, Fr.); LA RONDE(1954, Fr.); LE PLAISIR(1954, Fr.); RED AND THE BLACK, THE(1954, Fr./Ital.); NAPOLE-ON(1955, Fr.); ADORABLE CREATURES(1956, Fr.); ALEXANDER THE GREAT(1956); IF PARIS WERE TOLD TO US(1956, Fr.); LADY CHATTERLEY'S LOVER(1959, Fr.); LOSS OF INNOCENCE(1961, Brit.); NIGHT AFFAIR(1961, Fr.); CRIME DOES NOT PAY(1962, Fr.); DEVIL AND THE TEN COMMANDMENTS, THE(1962, Fr.); LAND-RU(1963, Fr./Ital.); FRIEND OF THE FAMILY(1965, Fr./Ital.); MURDER AT 45 R.P.M.(1965, Fr.); BIRDS COME TO DIE IN PERU(1968, Fr.); YOUNG GIRLS OF ROCHEFORT, THE(1968, Fr.); 24 HOURS IN A WOMAN'S LIFE(1968, Fr./Ger.)
Jessa Darrieux
MOTHER AND THE WHORE, THE(1973, Fr.)
Olivier Darrieux
PANIQUE(1947, Fr.)
Bobby Darrin
COP-OUT(1967, Brit.)
Camille Darrin
FREEWHEELIN'(1976)
Deanna Darrin
EXECUTIVE ACTION(1973)
Diana Darrin
CRUEL TOWER, THE(1956); GIRLS IN PRISON(1956); AMAZING COLOSSAL MAN, THE(1957); INCREDIBLE SHRINKING MAN, THE(1957); NIGHT RUNNER, THE(1957); REFORM SCHOOL GIRL(1957); BLOOD ARROW(1958); HIGH SCHOOL CONFIDENTIAL(1958); UNWED MOTHER(1958); LITTLE SHEPHERD OF KING-DOM COME(1961); BROKEN LAND, THE(1962); SLITHER(1973)
Michael Darrin
MEET ME AFTER THE SHOW(1951); FOREVER FEMALE(1953); HIDDEN GUNS(1956)
Pat Darrin
FREEWHEELIN'(1976), ph
Sonia Darrin
BURY ME DEAD(1947); I, JANE DOE(1948); CAUGHT(1949); FEDERAL AGENT AT LARGE(1950)
Frankie Darro
CIRCUS KID, THE(1928); RAINBOW MAN(1929); BLAZE O' GLORY(1930); MAD GENIUS, THE(1931); PUBLIC ENEMY, THE(1931); SIN OF MADELON CLAUDET, THE(1931); AMATEUR DADDY(1932); CHEYENNE CYCLONE, THE(1932); THREE ON A MATCH(1932); WAY BACK HOME(1932); LAUGHING AT LIFE(1933); MAYOR OF HELL, THE(1933); TUGBOAT ANNIE(1933); WILD BOYS OF THE ROAD(1933); BIG RACE, THE(1934); MERRY FRINKS, THE(1934); NO GREATER GLORY(1934); LITTLE MEN(1935); PAYOFF, THE(1935); RED HOT TIRES(1935); STRANDED(1935);

THREE KIDS AND A QUEEN(1935); UNWELCOME STRANGER(1935); CHARLIE CHAN AT THE RACE TRACK(1936); ANYTHING FOR A THRILL(1937); DAY AT THE RACES, A(1937); HEADLINE CRASHER(1937); MIND YOUR OWN BUSINESS(1937); SARATOGA(1937); THOROUGHBREDS DON'T CRY(1937); TOUGH TO HANDLE(1937); YOUNG DYNAMITE(1937); BORN TO FIGHT(1938); JUVENILE COURT(1938); RACING BLOOD(1938); REFORMATORY(1938); WANTED BY THE POLICE(1938); BOY'S REFORMATORY(1939); IRISH LUCK(1939); TOUGH KID(1939); CHASING TROUBLE(1940); LAUGHING AT DANGER(1940); ON THE SPOT(1940); PINOCCHIO(1940); UP IN THE AIR(1940); GANG'S ALL HERE(1941); LET'S GO COLLEGIATE(1941); TUXEDO JUNCTION(1941); YOU'RE OUT OF LUCK(1941); FREDDIE STEPS OUT(1946); HIGH SCHOOL HERO(1946); JUNIOR PROM(1946); SARGE GOES TO COLLEGE(1947); THAT'S MY MAN(1947); VACATION DAYS(1947); ANGELS ALLEY(1948); HEART OF VIRGINIA(1948); SMART POLITICS(1948); TROUBLE MAKERS(1948); FIGHTING FOOLS(1949); HOLD THAT BABY!(1949); SONS OF NEW MEXICO(1949); LIFE OF HER OWN, A(1950); RIDING HIGH(1950); WYOMING MAIL(1950); ACROSS THE WIDE MISSOURI(1951); PRIDE OF MARYLAND(1951); SELLOUT, THE(1951); PAT AND MIKE(1952); LAWLESS RIDER, THE(1954); LIVING IT UP(1954); RACING BLOOD(1954); TEN COMMANDMENTS, THE(1956); PERFECT FURLOUGH, THE(1958); OPERATION PETTICOAT(1959); CARPETBAGGERS, THE(1964)
Misc. Talkies
MEN OF ACTION(1935); VALLEY OF WANTED MEN(1935)
Silents
JUDGMENT OF THE STORM(1924); RACING FOR LIFE(1924); ROARING RAILS(1924); SIGNAL TOWER, THE(1924); CARNIVAL GIRL, THE(1926); KIKI(1926); MEMORY LANE(1926); MIKE(1926); OUT OF THE WEST(1926); TOM AND HIS PALS(1926); CYCLONE OF THE RANGE(1927); JUDGMENT OF THE HILLS(1927); LIGHTNING LARIATS(1927); LONG PANTS(1927); AVENGING RIDER, THE(1928); DESERT PIRATE, THE(1928); PHANTOM OF THE RANGE(1928); GUN LAW(1929); IDAHO RED(1929)
Misc. Silents
FIGHTING THE FLAMES(1925); PEOPLE VS. NANCY PRESTON, THE(1925); PHANTOM EXPRESS, THE(1925); ARIZONA STREAK(1926); COWBOY COP, THE(1926); RED HOT HOOFS(1926); MOULDERS OF MEN(1927); TOM'S GANG(1927); TERROR MOUNTAIN(1928); TEXAS TORNADO, THE(1928); TYRANT OF RED GULCH(1928); WHEN THE LAW RIDES(1928); TRAIL OF THE HORSE THIEVES, THE(1929)

Angus Darrock
MONKEY'S PAW, THE(1933)

Barbara Darrow
FRENCH LINE, THE(1954); SUSAN SLEPT HERE(1954); DIANE(1955); MOUNTAIN, THE(1956); MONSTER THAT CHALLENGED THE WORLD, THE(1957); QUEEN OF OUTER SPACE(1958); TALL STORY(1960)

Charlene Darrow
DEER HUNTER, THE(1978)

Frankie Darrow
BROADWAY BILL(1934)
Silents
SO BIG(1924); FEARLESS LOVER, THE(1925)
Misc. Silents
WOMEN AND GOLD(1925); WILD TO GO(1926); LITTLE MICKEY GROGAN(1927)

Henry Darrow
CANCEL MY RESERVATION(1972); BADGE 373(1973); WALK PROUD(1979); ST. HELENS(1981); LOSIN' IT(1983)
Misc. Talkies
WHERE'S WILLIE?(1978)

John Darrow
ARGYLE CASE, THE(1929); CHEER UP AND SMILE(1930); HELL'S ANGELS(1930); BARGAIN, THE(1931); EVERYTHING'S ROSIE(1931); FANNY FOLEY HERSELF(1931); LADY REFUSES, THE(1931); TEN NIGHTS IN A BARROOM(1931); ALIAS MARY SMITH(1932); ALL-AMERICAN, THE(1932); FORBIDDEN COMPANY(1932); MIDNIGHT LADY(1932); PROBATION(1932); BIG CHANCE, THE(1933); MIDSHIPMAN JACK(1933); STRANGE PEOPLE(1933); BIG RACE, THE(1934); FLIRTATION WALK(1934); I GIVE MY LOVE(1934); I LIKE IT THAT WAY(1934); MONTE CARLO NIGHTS(1934); CURTAIN FALLS, THE(1935); EIGHT BELLS(1935); NOTORIOUS GENTLEMAN, A(1935); SYMPHONY OF LIVING(1935); CRIME OVER LONDON(1936, Brit.)
Misc. Talkies
SQUARE SHOOTER(1935)
Silents
AVALANCHE(1928); PREP AND PEP(1928); RACKET, THE(1928); GIRLS GONE WILD(1929)
Misc. Silents
HIGH SCHOOL HERO(1927)

Madeline Darrow
GARMENT JUNGLE, THE(1957)

Madelyn Darrow
GUYS AND DOLLS(1955)

Paul Darrow
LONG AGO, TOMORROW(1971, Brit.)

Susannah Darrow
SAVAGE SEVEN, THE(1968); DEATH WISH II(1982)

Cid Darrows
TULIPS(1981, Can)

Daniel Dean Darst
1984
SWING SHIFT(1984)

Pierre Darteuil
CALL, THE(1938, Fr.)

Gail Dartez
OUT(1982)

Robert Darthez
BONNE CHANCE(1935, Fr.)

Elizabeth Dartmoor
I NEVER PROMISED YOU A ROSE GARDEN(1977)

Stephen Dartnell
OSCAR WILDE(1960, Brit.); CIRCLE OF DECEPTION(1961, Brit.)

Robert Dartres
ARTHUR(1931, Fr.)

Gitty Daruga
DIE FASTNACHTSBEICHTE(1962, Ger.)

Barry Darval
THUNDER IN DIXIE(1965)

Jean-Claude Darval
IMMORAL MOMENT, THE(1967, Fr.)

Ivan Darvas
ADRIFT(1971, Czech.); LOVE(1972, Hung.)

Lili Darvas
AFFAIRS OF MAUPASSANT(1938, Aust.); MEET ME IN LAS VEGAS(1956); CIMARRON(1960); LOVE(1972, Hung.)

Teddy Darvas
ROTTEN TO THE CORE(1956, Brit.), ed; HEAVENS ABOVE!(1963, Brit.), ed; GUTTER GIRLS(1964, Brit.), ed; BANG, BANG, YOU'RE DEAD(1966), ed; WOMAN TIMES SEVEN(1967, U.S./Fr./Ital.), ed; ASSASSINATION BUREAU, THE(1969, Brit.), ed; MAN WHO HAUNTED HIMSELF, THE(1970, Brit.), ed; RAILWAY CHILDREN, THE(1971, Brit.), ed; TALES FROM THE CRYPT(1972, Brit.), ed; BAXTER(1973, Brit.), ed; DARK PLACES(1974, Brit.), ed; BLACK PANTHER, THE(1977, Brit.), ed

Christine Darvel
CROSS OF THE LIVING(1963, Fr.)

Evelyn Darvell
DUMMY TALKS, THE(1943, Brit.); MADONNA OF THE SEVEN MOONS(1945, Brit.); SHOWTIME(1948, Brit.)

Bella Darvi
EGYPTIAN. THE(1954); HELL AND HIGH WATER(1954); RACERS, THE(1955); GORILLA GREETS YOU, THE(1958, Fr.); LIPSTICK(1965, Fr./Ital.)

Jeanne Darville
WELCOME TO THE CLUB(1971)

Darville & Shires
LAUGH IT OFF(1940, Brit.)

Jane Darwell
TOM SAWYER(1930); FIGHTING CARAVANS(1931); HUCKLEBERRY FINN(1931); BACK STREET(1932); HOT SATURDAY(1932); LADIES OF THE BIG HOUSE(1932); NO ONE MAN(1932); AIR HOSTESS(1933); ANN VICKERS(1933); BEFORE DAWN(1933); BONDAGE(1933); CHILD OF MANHATTAN(1933); DESIGN FOR LIVING(1933); EMERGENCY CALL(1933); JENNIE GERHARDT(1933); ONE SUNDAY AFTERNOON(1933); ONLY YESTERDAY(1933); PAST OF MARY HOLMES, THE(1933); ROMAN SCANDALS(1933); WOMEN WON'T TELL(1933); BLIND DATE(1934); BRIGHT EYES(1934); CHANGE OF HEART(1934); DESIRABLE(1934); EMBARRASSING MOMENTS(1934); FASHIONS OF 1934(1934); FINISHING SCHOOL(1934); HAPPINESS AHEAD(1934); HE COULDN'T TAKE IT(1934); HEAT LIGHTNING(1934); JOURNAL OF A CRIME(1934); LET'S TALK IT OVER(1934); MILLION DOLLAR RANSOM(1934); MOST PRECIOUS THING IN LIFE(1934); ONCE TO EVERY WOMAN(1934); ONE NIGHT OF LOVE(1934); SCARLET EMPRESS, THE(1934); WAKE UP AND DREAM(1934); WHITE PARADE, THE(1934); WONDER BAR(1934); CAPTAIN JANUARY(1935); CURLY TOP(1935); LIFE BEGINS AT 40(1935); MC FADDEN'S FLATS(1935); ONE MORE SPRING(1935); PADDY O'DAY(1935); TOMORROW'S YOUTH(1935); COUNTRY DOCTOR, THE(1936); FIRST BABY(1936); LITTLE MISS NOBODY(1936); NAVY WIFE(1936); POOR LITTLE RICH GIRL(1936); PRIVATE NUMBER(1936); RAMONA(1936); STAR FOR A NIGHT(1936); WE'RE ONLY HUMAN(1936); WHITE FANG(1936); DANGEROUSLY YOURS(1937); FIFTY ROADS TO TOWN(1937); GREAT HOSPITAL MYSTERY, THE(1937); LAUGHING AT TROUBLE(1937); LOVE IS NEWS(1937); NANCY STEELE IS MISSING(1937); SINGING MARINE, THE(1937); SLAVE SHIP(1937); WIFE, DOCTOR AND NURSE(1937); BATTLE OF BROADWAY(1938); CHANGE OF HEART(1938); FIVE OF A KIND(1938); JURY'S SECRET, THE(1938); LITTLE MISS BROADWAY(1938); THREE BLIND MICE(1938); TIME OUT FOR MURDER(1938); UP THE RIVER(1938); GONE WITH THE WIND(1939); GRAND JURY SECRETS(1939); INSIDE STORY(1939); JESSE JAMES(1939); RAINS CAME, THE(1939); UNEXPECTED FATHER(1939); ZERO HOUR, THE(1939); 20,000 MEN A YEAR(1939); BRIGHAM YOUNG–FRONTIERSMAN(1940); CHAD HANNA(1940); GRAPES OF WRATH(1940); MIRACLE ON MAIN STREET, A(1940); UNTAMED(1940); YOUTH WILL BE SERVED(1940); DEVIL AND DANIEL WEBSTER, THE(1941); PRIVATE NURSE(1941); SMALL TOWN DEB(1941); THIEVES FALL OUT(1941); ALL THROUGH THE NIGHT(1942); GREAT GILDERSLEEVE, THE(1942); HIGHWAYS BY NIGHT(1942); IT HAPPENED IN FLATBUSH(1942); LOVES OF EDGAR ALLAN POE, THE(1942); MEN OF TEXAS(1942); ON THE SUNNY SIDE(1942); YOUNG AMERICA(1942); GILDERSLEEVE'S BAD DAY(1943); GOVERNMENT GIRL(1943); OX-BOW INCIDENT, THE(1943); STAGE DOOR CANTEEN(1943); TENDER COMRADE(1943); IMPATIENT YEARS, THE(1944); MUSIC IN MANHATTAN(1944); RECKLESS AGE(1944); SHE'S A SWEETHEART(1944); SUNDAY DINNER FOR A SOLDIER(1944); CAPTAIN TUGBOAT ANNIE(1945); DARK HORSE, THE(1946); MY DARLING CLEMENTINE(1946); THREE WISE FOOLS(1946); YANK IN LONDON, A(1946, Brit.); KEEPER OF THE BEES(1947); RED STALLION, THE(1947); THREE GODFATHERS, THE(1948); TRAIN TO ALCATRAZ(1948); RED CANYON(1949); CAGED(1950); DAUGHTER OF ROSIE O'GRADY, THE(1950); FATHER'S WILD GAME(1950); REDWOOD FOREST TRAIL(1950); SECOND FACE, THE(1950); SURRENDER(1950); THREE HUSBANDS(1950); WAGONMASTER(1950); EXCUSE MY DUST(1951); JOURNEY INTO LIGHT(1951); LEMON DROP KID, THE(1951); WE'RE NOT MARRIED(1952); AFFAIR WITH A STRANGER(1953); BIGAMIST,THE(1953); IT HAPPENS EVERY THURSDAY(1953); SUN SHINES BRIGHT, THE(1953); HIT THE DECK(1955); GIRLS IN PRISON(1956); THERE'S ALWAYS TOMORROW(1956); LAST HURRAH, THE(1958); HOUND-DOG MAN(1959); MARY POPPINS(1964)
Misc. Talkies
BEAUTY'S DAUGHTER(1935)
Silents
MASTER MIND, THE(1914); ONLY SON, THE(1914); READY MONEY(1914); ROSE OF THE RANCHO(1914); AFTER FIVE(1915); GOOSE GIRL, THE(1915)

Margaret Darwin
Misc. Silents
PATH OF DARKNESS, THE(1916)

Salah Darwish
JERUSALEM FILE, THE(1972, U.S./Israel)

Max Darwyn
STORY OF VERNON AND IRENE CASTLE, THE(1939)

Rene Dary
MOULIN ROUGE(1944, Fr.); DANIELLA BY NIGHT(1962, Fr/Ger.)

I. Daryalov
QUEEN OF SPADES(1961, USSR)

Jacqueline Daryl
SUMMER HOLIDAY(1963, Brit.)

Lauria Daryl
PARDON MY FRENCH(1951, U.S./Fr.)

Natalie Daryll
GIRL IN THE KREMLIN, THE(1957)

Ananta Das
1984
HOME AND THE WORLD, THE(1984, India), makeup

Eddie Das
LIVES OF A BENGAL LANCER(1935); RAZOR'S EDGE, THE(1946); CALCUTTA(1947); MAN-EATER OF KUMAON(1948)

Edward Das
SUNDOWN(1941)

DAS Associates
PLEASURE PLANTATION(1970), m

Xan Das Bolas
BACKFIRE(1965, Fr.); RUN LIKE A THIEF(1968, Span.)

Aparna Das Gupta
TWO DAUGHTERS(1963, India)

Bandana Das Gupta
MARK, THE(1961, Brit.); TERROR OF THE TONGS, THE(1961, Brit.); BRAIN, THE(1965, Ger./Brit.)

Andrew Dasburg
REDS(1981)

Fred Dash
NIGHT AND DAY(1946)

Pauly Dash
LADY IN CEMENT(1968)

Sarah Dash
SGT. PEPPER'S LONELY HEARTS CLUB BAND(1978)

David Dashev
FISH THAT SAVED PITTSBURGH, THE(1979), p, w; SMOKEY AND THE BANDIT-PART 3(1983), w

Willard Dashiell
CHEAT, THE(1931)
Silents
JOAN OF PLATTSBURG(1918)

Williard Dashiell
WAR IS A RACKET(1934)
Silents
MY FOUR YEARS IN GERMANY(1918)

Ann Dashner
Misc. Talkies
FORBID THEM NOT(1961)

Steve Daskawisz
FRIDAY THE 13TH PART II(1981); NIGHTHAWKS(1981); FRIDAY THE 13TH PART III(1982)
1984
FRIDAY THE 13TH-THE FINAL CHAPTER(1984)

Pat Dasko
1984
PHILADELPHIA EXPERIMENT, THE(1984)

Darm Daskorn
S.T.A.B.(1976, Hong Kong/Thailand)

Kitti Daskorn
1 2 3 MONSTER EXPRESS(1977, Thai.)

Danni Dassa
STORY OF RUTH, THE(1960), ch

Evelyne Dassas
PROSTITUTION(1965, Fr.)

Luce Dassas
LETTERS FROM MY WINDMILL(1955, Fr.)

Stella Dassas
HIROSHIMA, MON AMOUR(1959, Fr./Jap.)

Joseph Dassin
TOPKAPI(1964); LADY L(1965, Fr./Ital.)

Jules Dassin
AFFAIRS OF MARTHA, THE(1942), d; NAZI AGENT(1942), d; REUNION IN FRANCE(1942), d; YOUNG IDEAS(1943), d; CANTERVILLE GHOST, THE(1944), d; LETTER FOR EVIE, A(1945), d; TWO SMART PEOPLE(1946), d; BRUTE FORCE(1947), d; NAKED CITY, THE(1948), d; THIEVES' HIGHWAY(1949), d; NIGHT AND THE CITY(1950, Brit.), d; RIFIFI(1956, Fr.), d, w; NEVER ON SUNDAY(1960, Gr.), a, p,d&w; WHERE THE HOT WIND BLOWS(1960, Fr., Ital.), d, w; PHAEDRA(1962, U.S./Gr./Fr.), a, p&d, w; TOPKAPI(1964), p&d; FRIEND OF THE FAMILY(1965, Fr./Ital.); 10:30 P.M. SUMMER(1966, U.S./Span.), p, d, w; UPTIGHT(1968), p&d, w; PROMISE AT DAWN(1970, U.S./Fr.), p,d&w; DREAM OF PASSION, A(1978, Gr.), p,d&w; CIRCLE OF TWO(1980, Can.), d

Julie Dassin
SHOCK TROOPS(1968, Ital./Fr.); PROMISE AT DAWN(1970, U.S./Fr.)

Peter Dassinger
DROWNING POOL, THE(1975)

Edouard Daste
GRAND ILLUSION(1938, Fr.)

Jean Daste
CRIME OF MONSIEUR LANGE, THE(1936, Fr.); CROISIERES SIDERALES(1941, Fr.); L'ATALANTE(1947, Fr.); MURIEL(1963, Fr./Ital.); SKY ABOVE HEAVEN(1964, Fr./Ital.); BOUDU SAVED FROM DROWNING(1967, Fr.); LA GUERRE EST FINIE(1967, Fr./Swed.); Z(1969, Fr./Algeria); WILD CHILD, THE(1970, Fr.); MAN WHO LOVED WOMEN, THE(1977, Fr.); GREEN ROOM, THE(1979, Fr.); MON ONCLE D'AMERIQUE(1980, Fr.); LIKE A TURTLE ON ITS BACK(1981, Fr.)

Marie-Helene Daste
ANGELS OF THE STREETS(1950, Fr.); GYPSY FURY(1950, Fr.); END OF DESIRE(1962 Fr./Ital.); CLOPORTES(1966, Fr., Ital.); CHANEL SOLITAIRE(1981)

Sam Dastor
MADE(1972, Brit.)

Roger Dattaler
HARD STEEL(1941, Brit.), w

Stephen Date
OBSESSED(1951, Brit.), ph

Alan Dater
GOSPEL ROAD, THE(1973)

Fred Datig, Jr.
O.S.S.(1946); SWEETHEART OF SIGMA CHI(1946); WELCOME STRANGER(1947); STRIP, THE(1951); SOMETHING FOR THE BIRDS(1952)

Agnes Datin
MICHELLE(1970, Fr.)

Datlowe
OPEN ROAD, THE(1940, Fr.), ed

John Datlowe
MILL ON THE FLOSS(1939, Brit.), ed

Samuel Datlowe
FOLLIES GIRL(1943), ed

Stephen Dattner
2,000 WEEKS(1970, Aus.)

John Datu
SHADOWS IN THE NIGHT(1944), art d; SONG FOR MISS JULIE, A(1945), art d

John Datul
MARK OF THE WHISTLER, THE(1944), art d

Gustl Datz
AMERICAN SOLDIER, THE(1970 Ger.)

Ewald Daub
JOHNNY STEALS EUROPE(1932, Ger.), ph; CAPTAIN FROM KOEPENICK(1933, Ger.), ph; WORLD WITHOUT A MASK, THE(1934, Ger.), ph; MASTER OF THE WORLD(1935, Ger.), ph

Belle Daube
OPERATOR 13(1934); IT'S A SMALL WORLD(1935); DANCING IN THE DARK(1949); MY DREAM IS YOURS(1949)

Harda Belle Daube
Misc. Silents
VIRTUOUS VAMP, A(1919)

D. Daubeney
VAMPYRES, DAUGHTERS OF DRACULA(1977, Brit.), w

Diana Daubeney
HOUSE THAT VANISHED, THE(1974, Brit.), p

Dany Dauberson
TALE OF FIVE WOMEN, A(1951, Brit.); UPPER HAND, THE(1967, Fr./Ital./Ger.)

Lise Daubigny
LES ABYSSES(1964, Fr.)

Robert Ciriez Daubigny
LOVERS ON A TIGHTROPE(1962, Fr.), p

Jean-Jacques Daubin
RISE OF LOUIS XIV, THE(1970, Fr.)

Alphonse Daudet
INSPIRATION(1931), w; LETTERS FROM MY WINDMILL(1955, Fr.), w
Silents
ETERNAL SAPHO, THE(1916), w

Delese Daudet
GANGSTER, THE(1947)

Dominique Daudon
FIRST TIME, THE(1978, Fr.), ed

Dominique Daudre
GUINGUETTE(1959, Fr.), w

Frank T. Daugherty
Silents
BANTAM COWBOY, THE(1928), t; DRIFTIN' SANDS(1928), t

Herschel Daugherty
LIFE WITH FATHER(1947), d; RED, HOT AND BLUE(1949); WHERE DANGER LIVES(1950); LIGHT IN THE FOREST, THE(1958), d; RAIDERS, THE(1964), d

Jack Daugherty
Silents
CHAIN LIGHTNING(1922); MEDDLER, THE(1925); ARIZONA BOUND(1927); DOWN THE STRETCH(1927); INTO NO MAN'S LAND(1928)
Misc. Silents
RUNAWAY EXPRESS, THE(1926); LURE OF THE NIGHT CLUB, THE(1927); BODY PUNCH, THE(1929)

Larry Daugherty
1984
HARD TO HOLD(1984)

Robert Daugherty
HARRY'S WAR(1981)

Frank Daughterty
ONCE A DOCTOR(1937), w

Stanley W. Daughtery
CHARTROOSE CABOOSE(1960), p

James Daughton
REVENGERS, THE(1972, U.S./Mex.); MALIBU BEACH(1978); NATIONAL LAMPOON'S ANIMAL HOUSE(1978); BEACH GIRLS(1982)
1984
BLIND DATE(1984)
Misc. Talkies
SWIM TEAM(1979)

Harriet Daughtry
DRUMS O' VOODOO(1934)

Jerry Daugirda
GONE IN 60 SECONDS(1974)

Anatole Dauman
MURIEL(1963, Fr./Ital.), p; MOUCHETTE(1970, Fr.), p; TIN DRUM, THE(1979, Ger./Fr./Yugo./Pol.), p

Carrie Daumery
HEARTS IN EXILE(1929); LAST WARNING, THE(1929); GRAND CANARY(1934); RUGGLES OF RED GAP(1935); SHE COULDN'T TAKE IT(1935); STRANGE WIVES(1935); ESPIONAGE(1937); I'LL TAKE ROMANCE(1937)

Silents
ROSE OF PARIS, THE(1924)
Misc. Silents
DOROTHY VERNON OF HADDON HALL(1924)
John Daumery
ROUGH WATERS(1930), d; BLIND SPOT(1932, Brit.), d; HELP YOURSELF(1932, Brit.), d; CALL ME MAME(1933, Brit.), d; HEAD OF THE FAMILY(1933, Brit.), d; LITTLE MISS NOBODY(1933, Brit.), d; MEET MY SISTER(1933, Brit.), d; MR. QUINCEY OF MONTE CARLO(1933, Brit.), d; NAUGHTY CINDERELLA(1933, Brit.), d; THIRTEENTH CANDLE, THE(1933, Brit.), d; THIS ACTING BUSINESS(1933, Brit.), d; OVER THE GARDEN WALL(1934, Brit.), d; WITHOUT YOU(1934, Brit.), d
Mme. Daumery
GENERAL CRACK(1929); CAMEO KIRBY(1930)
Sophie Daumier
AMELIE OR THE TIME TO LOVE(1961, Fr.); SWEET AND SOUR(1964, Fr./Ital.); HOW NOT TO ROB A DEPARTMENT STORE(1965, Fr./Ital.); TASTE FOR WOMEN, A(1966, Fr./Ital.)
William Daunt
VARIETY(1935, Brit.); SUCH IS LIFE(1936, Brit.)
Claude Dauphin
SLIPPER EPISODE, THE(1938, Fr); AFFAIR LAFONT, THE(1939, Fr.); CONFLICT(1939, Fr.); CURTAIN RISES, THE(1939, Fr.); LE MONDE TREMBLERA(1939, Fr.); HER MAN GILBEY(1949, Brit.); DEPORTED(1950); APRIL IN PARIS(1953); LITTLE BOY LOST(1953); LE PLAISIR(1954, Fr.); PHANTOM OF THE RUE MORGUE(1954); INNOCENTS IN PARIS(1955, Brit.); CASQUE D'OR(1956, Fr.); QUIET AMERICAN, THE(1958); STOP ME BEFORE I KILL!(1961, Brit.); DEVIL AND THE TEN COMMANDMENTS, THE(1962, Fr.); TIARA TAHITI(1962, Brit.); LA BONNE SOUPE(1964, Fr./Ital.); VISIT, THE(1964, Ger./Fr./Ital./U.S.); LADY L(1965, Fr./Ital.); SYMPHONY FOR A MASSACRE(1965, Fr./Ital.); GRAND PRIX(1966); IS PARIS BURNING?(1966, U.S./Fr.); SLEEPING CAR MURDER THE(1966, Fr.); OTHER ONE, THE(1967,Fr.); TWO FOR THE ROAD(1967, Brit.); BARBARELLA(1968, Fr./Ital.); HARD CONTRACT(1969); MADWOMAN OF CHAILLOT, THE(1969); MOST WONDERFUL EVENING OF MY LIFE, THE(1972, Ital./Fr.); MAIN THING IS TO LOVE, THE(1975, Ital./Fr.); ROSEBUD(1975); TENANT, THE(1976, Fr.); MADAME ROSA(1977, Fr.)
Jean-Claude Dauphin
DRACULA AND SON(1976, Fr.); CHOICE OF ARMS(1983, Fr.)
Claude Dauphine
EGLANTINE(1972, Fr.)
Daurand
BATTLE OF THE RAILS(1949, Fr.)
Jean Daurand
PALACE OF NUDES(1961, Fr./Ital.); TIME BOMB(1961, Fr./Ital.)
Gianna Dauro
BIGGEST BUNDLE OF THEM ALL, THE(1968); MR. BILLION(1977)
Jean Dautremay
L'ETOILE DU NORD(1983, Fr.)
Dirk Dautzenberg
GREAT BRITISH TRAIN ROBBERY, THE(1967, Ger.)
Marise Dauvray
Misc. Silents
J'ACCUSE(1919, Fr.)
Maryse Dauvray
Misc. Silents
MARYSE(1917, Fr.)
Dick Davalos
ALL THE YOUNG MEN(1960); CABINET OF CALIGARI, THE(1962); PIT STOP(1969); HOT STUFF(1979); DEATH HUNT(1981)
Dominique Davalos
WOMAN UNDER THE INFLUENCE, A(1974)
1984
LOVE STREAMS(1984)
Ellen Davalos
INTERNS, THE(1962); TARAS BULBA(1962); WOMAN UNDER THE INFLUENCE, A(1974)
Elyssa Davalos
APPLE DUMPLING GANG RIDES AGAIN, THE(1979); HERBIE GOES BANANAS(1980)
Richard Davalos
EAST OF EDEN(1955); I DIED A THOUSAND TIMES(1955); COOL HAND LUKE(1967); KELLY'S HEROES(1970, U.S./Yugo.); LEGACY OF BLOOD(1973); SOMETHING WICKED THIS WAY COMES(1983)
Misc. Talkies
BROTHER, CRY FOR ME(1970)
Richard "Dick" Davalos
SEA CHASE, THE(1955)
Andre Davan
Misc. Silents
STOLEN MOMENTS(1920)
Domenico Forges Davanzanti
SENSO(1968, Ital.), p
Domenico Forges Davanzati
LADY WITHOUT CAMELLIAS, THE(1981, Ital.), p
Fiore Davanzati
HEART AND SOUL(1950, Ital.)
Mario Forges Davanzati
LOVE AND MARRIAGE(1966, Ital.), ed
Cia Dave
TWO FOR THE SEESAW(1962)
Dave Apollon and His Orchestra
MERRY-GO-ROUND OF 1938(1937)
Dave Appell and His Applejacks
DON'T KNOCK THE ROCK(1956)
The Dave Clark Five
GET YOURSELF A COLLEGE GIRL(1964)
Alan Daveau
SCREWBALLS(1983)

Marie Pascale Daveau
ZITA(1968, Fr.)
Zelda Davees
THOSE PEOPLE NEXT DOOR(1952, Brit.), w
Andre Daven
HEART OF PARIS(1939, Fr.), p; PARIS AFTER DARK(1943), p; TONIGHT WE RAID CALAIS(1943), p; HOME IN INDIANA(1944), p; NOB HILL(1945), p; GATES OF PARIS(1958, Fr./Ital.), p
Misc. Silents
LA FEMME DE NULLE PART(1922, Fr.)
A. Bromley Davenport
AMERICAN PRISONER, THE(1929 Brit.); CAPTIVATION(1931, Brit); GLAMOUR(1931, Brit.); MISCHIEF(1931, Brit.); FACE AT THE WINDOW, THE(1932, Brit.); LORD CAMBER'S LADIES(1932, Brit.); MARRIAGE BOND, THE(1932, Brit.); MONEY MEANS NOTHING(1932, Brit.); RETURN OF RAFFLES, THE(1932, Brit.); SELF-MADE LADY(1932, Brit.); WHEN LONDON SLEEPS(1932, Brit.); ENEMY OF THE POLICE(1933, Brit.); IRON STAIR, THE(1933, Brit.); LITTLE MISS NOBODY(1933, Brit.); MAN WHO WON, THE(1933, Brit.); MELODY MAKER, THE(1933, Brit.); SHOT IN THE DARK, A(1933, Brit.); WISHBONE, THE(1933, Brit.); LOVE, LIFE AND LAUGHTER(1934, Brit.); POINTING FINGER, THE(1934, Brit.); WARREN CASE, THE(1934, Brit.); SO YOU WON'T TALK?(1935, Brit.); VINTAGE WINE(1935, Brit.); CARDINAL, THE(1936, Brit.); CROUCHING BEAST, THE(1936, U. S./Brit.); MYSTERIOUS MR. DAVIS, THE(1936, Brit.); CRIME OF PETER FRAME, THE(1938, Brit.); MURDER IN THE FAMILY(1938, Brit.); TO THE VICTOR(1938, Brit.); JAMAICA INN(1939, Brit.); SECOND MR. BUSH, THE(1940, Brit.); FARMER'S WIFE, THE(1941, Brit.); OLD MOTHER RILEY'S GHOSTS(1941, Brit.); THOSE KIDS FROM TOWN(1942, Brit.); YOUNG MR. PITT, THE(1942, Brit.); WHEN WE ARE MARRIED(1943, Brit.); LOVE ON THE DOLE(1945, Brit.); WAY AHEAD, THE(1945, Brit.)
Silents
BIGAMIST, THE(1921, Brit.); FOX FARM(1922, Brit.); RUNNING WATER(1922, Brit.); FAKE, THE(1927, Brit.); ROSES OF PICARDY(1927, Brit.); SISTER TO ASSIST 'ER, A(1927, Brit.)
Misc. Silents
BOY WOODBURN(1922, Brit.); PERSISTENT LOVERS, THE(1922, Brit.); STARLIT GARDEN, THE(1923, Brit.); BLUE PETER, THE(1928, Brit.); SPANGLES(1928, Brit.)
Adele Davenport
LOST HONEYMOON(1947)
Alice Davenport
DUDE WRANGLER, THE(1930)
Silents
TILLIE'S PUNCTURED ROMANCE(1914); LEGEND OF HOLLYWOOD, THE(1924)
Blanche Davenport
Silents
CRIMSON DOVE, THE(1917); PECK'S BAD GIRL(1918); BAB'S CANDIDATE(1920); MADONNAS AND MEN(1920); IF WOMEN ONLY KNEW(1921); LOYAL LIVES(1923); DOWN UPON THE SUWANNEE RIVER(1925)
Misc. Silents
AMERICA - THAT'S ALL(1917); MARRIAGE FOR CONVENIENCE(1919); LOST BATTALION, THE(1921); UNRESTRAINED YOUTH(1925)
Bromley Davenport
BRIDE OF THE LAKE(1934, Brit.); SCARLET PIMPERNEL, THE(1935, Brit.)
Charles E. Davenport
Silents
GOVERNOR'S BOSS, THE(1915), d
Misc. Silents
BROKEN BARRIERS(1919), d
Claire Davenport
RETURN OF THE PINK PANTHER, THE(1975, Brit.); ELEPHANT MAN, THE(1980, Brit.); RETURN OF THE JEDI(1983)
Danny Davenport
BIG LIFT, THE(1950); I'LL GET BY(1950); KOREA PATROL(1951); QUEEN FOR A DAY(1951)
David Davenport
IT TAKES A THIEF(1960, Brit.); THAT KIND OF GIRL(1963, Brit.); CARRY ON CLEO(1964, Brit.); SECRET OF MY SUCCESS, THE(1965, Brit.); CARRY ON HENRY VIII(1970, Brit.); DARWIN ADVENTURE, THE(1972, Brit.)
Delbert F. Davenport
Silents
SMILES ARE TRUMPS(1922), w
Devvy Davenport
FRENCH LINE, THE(1954)
Doris Davenport
KID MILLIONS(1934); THIN ICE(1937); WESTERNER, THE(1940); BEHIND THE NEWS(1941)
Dorothy Davenport
Silents
EVERY WOMAN'S PROBLEM(1921)
Misc. Silents
MR. GREX OF MONTE CARLO(1915); UNKNOWN, THE(1915); BARRIERS OF SOCIETY(1916); BLACK FRIDAY(1916); DEVIL'S BOND WOMAN, THE(1916); DR. NEIGHBOR(1916); MIRACLE OF LOVE, A(1916); UNATTAINABLE, THE(1916); WAY OF THE WORLD, THE(1916); YOKE OF GOLD, A(1916); GIRL AND THE CRISIS, THE(1917); MOTHERS OF MEN(1917); SCARLET CRYSTAL, THE(1917); SQUAW MAN'S SON, THE(1917); TREASON(1917); FIGHTING CHANCE, THE(1920)
E. L. Davenport
I, JANE DOE(1948)
Silents
HIS LAST DOLLAR(1914); THIEF, THE(1915)
Edgar Davenport
Silents
LITTLE GRAY LADY, THE(1914)
Edgar J. L. Davenport
Silents
SALAMANDER, THE(1915)
Edgar L. Davenport
Silents
SIMON THE JESTER(1915)
Misc. Silents
SAMSON(1915); BLINDNESS OF LOVE, THE(1916); DORIAN'S DIVORCE(1916); UPHEAVAL, THE(1916)

Gail Davenport
SWING HOSTESS(1944), w; ROCKIN' IN THE ROCKIES(1945), w

Gloria Davenport
Silents
MOLLY O'(1921); STEP ON IT!(1922); MAN'S MAN, A(1929)

Gwen Davenport
SITTING PRETTY(1948), w; MR. BELVEDERE GOES TO COLLEGE(1949), w; MR. BELVEDERE RINGS THE BELL(1951), w

Harris Davenport
REAR WINDOW(1954)

Harry Bromley Davenport
HAUNTING OF JULIA, THE(1981, Brit./Can.), w; XTRO(1983, Brit.), d, w, m

Harry Davenport
THAT UNCERTAIN FEELING(1941); HIS WOMAN(1931); MY SIN(1931); SCOUNDREL, THE(1935); CASE OF THE BLACK CAT, THE(1936); KING OF HOCKEY(1936); THREE MEN ON A HORSE(1936); ARMORED CAR(1937); AS GOOD AS MARRIED(1937); FIRST LADY(1937); FIT FOR A KING(1937); FLY-AWAY BABY(1937); GREAT GARRICK, THE(1937); HER HUSBAND'S SECRETARY(1937); LIFE OF EMILE ZOLA, THE(1937); MAYTIME(1937); MOUNTAIN JUSTICE(1937); MR. DODD TAKES THE AIR(1937); PARADISE EXPRESS(1937); PERFECT SPECIMEN, THE(1937); THEY WON'T FORGET(1937); UNDER COVER OF NIGHT(1937); WELLS FARGO(1937); WHITE BONDAGE(1937); COWBOY AND THE LADY, THE(1938); FIRST 100 YEARS, THE(1938); GOLD IS WHERE YOU FIND IT(1938); HIGGINS FAMILY, THE(1938); MARIE ANTOINETTE(1938); RAGE OF PARIS, THE(1938); RECKLESS LIVING(1938); SALESLADY(1938); SISTERS, THE(1938); YOU CAN'T TAKE IT WITH YOU(1938); YOUNG FUGITIVES(1938); COVERED TRAILER, THE(1939); DEATH OF A CHAMPION(1939); EXILE EXPRESS(1939); GONE WITH THE WIND(1939); HUNCHBACK OF NOTRE DAME, THE(1939); JUAREZ(1939); LONG SHOT, THE(1939); MADE FOR EACH OTHER(1939); MY WIFE'S RELATIVES(1939); ORPHANS OF THE STREET(1939); SHOULD HUSBANDS WORK?(1939); STORY OF ALEXANDER GRAHAM BELL, THE(1939); TAIL SPIN(1939); ALL THIS AND HEAVEN TOO(1940); DR. EHRLICH'S MAGIC BULLET(1940); EARL OF PUDDLESTONE(1940); FOREIGN CORRESPONDENT(1940); GRANDPA GOES TO TOWN(1940); GRANNY GET YOUR GUN(1940); I WANT A DIVORCE(1940); LUCKY PARTNERS(1940); MONEY TO BURN(1940); TOO MANY HUSBANDS(1940); BRIDE CAME C.O.D., THE(1941); I WANTED WINGS(1941); MEET JOHN DOE(1941); ONE FOOT IN HEAVEN(1941); HURRICANE SMITH(1942); KING'S ROW(1942); LARCENY, INC.(1942); SON OF FURY(1942); TALES OF MANHATTAN(1942); TEN GENTLEMEN FROM WEST POINT(1942); AMAZING MRS. HOLLIDAY(1943); GANGWAY FOR TOMORROW(1943); GOVERNMENT GIRL(1943); HEADIN' FOR GOD'S COUNTRY(1943); JACK LONDON(1943); OX-BOW INCIDENT, THE(1943); PRINCESS O'-ROURKE(1943); SHANTYTOWN(1943); WE'VE NEVER BEEN LICKED(1943); IMPATIENT YEARS, THE(1944); KISMET(1944); MEET ME IN ST. LOUIS(1944); MUSIC FOR MILLIONS(1944); THIN MAN GOES HOME, THE(1944); ADVENTURE(1945); ENCHANTED FOREST, THE(1945); PARDON MY PAST(1945); SHE WOULDN'T SAY YES(1945); THIS LOVE OF OURS(1945); TOO YOUNG TO KNOW(1945); BLUE SIERRA(1946); BOY, A GIRL, AND A DOG, A(1946); CLAUDIA AND DAVID(1946); COURAGE OF LASSIE(1946); FAITHFUL IN MY FASHION(1946); G.I. WAR BRIDES(1946); LADY LUCK(1946); THREE WISE FOOLS(1946); BACHELOR AND THE BOBBY-SOXER, THE(1947); FABULOUS TEXAN, THE(1947); FARMER'S DAUGHTER, THE(1947); KEEPER OF THE BEES(1947); SPORT OF KINGS(1947); STALLION ROAD(1947); THAT HAGEN GIRL(1947); DECISION OF CHRISTOPHER BLAKE, THE(1948); FOR THE LOVE OF MARY(1948); MAN FROM TEXAS, THE(1948); THAT LADY IN ERMINE(1948); THREE DARING DAUGHTERS(1948); DOWN TO THE SEA IN SHIPS(1949); LITTLE WOMEN(1949); TELL IT TO THE JUDGE(1949); THAT FORSYTE WOMAN(1949); RIDING HIGH(1950)
Silents
ISLAND OF REGENERATION, THE(1915), d; FALSE FRIEND, THE(1917), d; TILLIE WAKES UP(1917), d
Misc. Silents
C.O.D.(1915); MAKING OVER OF GEOFFREY MANNING, THE(1915), d; FOR A WOMAN'S FAIR NAME(1916), d; SUPREME TEMPTATION, THE(1916), d; MAN'S LAW, A(1917), d; MILLIONAIRE'S DOUBLE, THE(1917), d; SON OF THE HILLS, A(1917), d; WOMAN ALONE, A(1917), d; DAWN(1919), d; GIRL AT BAY, A(1919); UNKNOWN QUANTITY, THE(1919)

Havis Davenport
SCANDAL INCORPORATED(1956)

Jane Davenport
MADLY(1970, Fr.)

John Davenport
GREAT DAY(1945, Brit.), w; HOTEL RESERVE(1946, Brit.), w; FABIAN OF THE YARD(1954, Brit.), w

Kenneth Davenport
Silents
NUT, THE(1921), w

Leslie Davenport
JUST MY LUCK(1957, Brit.)

Marcia Davenport
VALLEY OF DECISION, THE(1945), w; EAST SIDE, WEST SIDE(1949), w

Mary Davenport
COURAGEOUS DR. CHRISTIAN, THE(1940); THIS GUN FOR HIRE(1942); SISTERS(1973); HOME MOVIES(1979); DRESSED TO KILL(1980)

Michael Davenport
Misc. Talkies
69 MINUTES(1977)

Mildred Davenport
Silents
ELOPE IF YOU MUST(1922)

Milla Davenport
MERRILY WE GO TO HELL(1932); IN LOVE WITH LIFE(1934); WEDDING NIGHT, THE(1935); HUMAN CARGO(1936)
Silents
BRAT, THE(1919); DADDY LONG LEGS(1919); FAITH(1920); FORBIDDEN WOMAN, THE(1920); RED LANE, THE(1920); PATSY(1921); RIP VAN WINKLE(1921); DULCY(1923); HEY! HEY! COWBOY(1927); KING OF KINGS, THE(1927)

Mills Davenport
HERE COMES COOKIE(1935)

Mrs. Davenport
Silents
RAMONA(1916)

Ned Davenport
MIRACLE OF THE BELLS, THE(1948); STORM WARNING(1950); LAWLESS BREED, THE(1952); MONTANA BELLE(1952)

Nigel Davenport
LOOK BACK IN ANGER(1959); DESERT MICE(1960, Brit.); PEEPING TOM(1960, Brit.); LUNCH HOUR(1962, Brit.); IN THE COOL OF THE DAY(1963); RETURN TO SENDER(1963, Brit.); LADIES WHO DO(1964, Brit.); THIRD SECRET, THE(1964, Brit.); VERDICT, THE(1964, Brit.); HIGH WIND IN JAMAICA, A(1965); LIFE AT THE TOP(1965, Brit.); SANDS OF THE KALAHARI(1965, Brit.); WHERE THE SPIES ARE(1965, Brit.); MAN FOR ALL SEASONS, A(1966, Brit.); SEBASTIAN(1968, Brit.); STRANGE AFFAIR, THE(1968, Brit.); PLAY DIRTY(1969, Brit.); ROYAL HUNT OF THE SUN, THE(1969, Brit.); SINFUL DAVEY(1969, Brit.); MIND OF MR. SOAMES, THE(1970, Brit.); NO BLADE OF GRASS(1970, Brit.); VIRGIN SOLDIERS, THE(1970, Brit.); LAST VALLEY, THE(1971, Brit.); MARY, QUEEN OF SCOTS(1971, Brit.); VILLAIN(1971, Brit.); LIVING FREE(1972, Brit.); CHARLEY-ONE-EYE(1973, Brit.); PHASE IV(1974); ISLAND OF DR. MOREAU, THE(1977); STAND UP VIRGIN SOLDIERS(1977, Brit.); ZULU DAWN(1980, Brit.); CHARRIOTS OF FIRE(1981, Brit.); NIGHTHAWKS(1981)
1984
GREYSTOKE: THE LEGEND OF TARZAN, LORD OF THE APES(1984)
Misc. Talkies
BLACK TRASH(1978)

Verne Davenport
WHISTLE AT EATON FALLS(1951)

William Davenport
HERE COME THE NELSONS(1952), w

Jose Davert
Misc. Silents
LA BRIERE(1925, Fr.); LE FANTOME DU MOULIN ROUGE(1925, Fr.); VERDUN, VISIONS D'HISTOIRE(1929, Fr.)

Deborah Daves
DESTINATION TOKYO(1944); DARK PASSAGE(1947)

Delmar Daves
BISHOP MURDER CASE, THE(1930); NO MORE WOMEN(1934), w; PAGE MISS GLORY(1935), w; SHIPMATES FOREVER(1935), w; DARK PASSAGE(1947), d, w; RED HOUSE, THE(1947), d&w

Delmer Daves
3:10 TO YUMA(1957), d; SO THIS IS COLLEGE(1929), a, w; GOOD NEWS(1930); SHIPMATES(1931), w; DIVORCE IN THE FAMILY(1932), w; DAMES(1934), w; FLIRTATION WALK(1934), w; STRANDED(1935), w; PETRIFIED FOREST, THE(1936), w; GO-GETTER, THE(1937), w; SINGING MARINE, THE(1937), w; PROFESSOR BEWARE(1938), w; SHE MARRIED AN ARTIST(1938), w; LOVE AFFAIR(1939), w, w; $1,000 A TOUCHDOWN(1939), w; FARMER'S DAUGHTER, THE(1940), w; SAFARI(1940), w; NIGHT OF JANUARY 16TH(1941), w; UNEXPECTED UNCLE(1941), w; YOU WERE NEVER LOVELIER(1942), w; STAGE DOOR CANTEEN(1943), w; DESTINATION TOKYO(1944), d, w; HOLLYWOOD CANTEEN(1944), d&w; VERY THOUGHT OF YOU, THE(1944), w; PRIDE OF THE MARINES(1945), d; TO THE VICTOR(1948), d; KISS IN THE DARK, A(1949), d; TASK FORCE(1949), d&w; BROKEN ARROW(1950), d; BIRD OF PARADISE(1951), p,d&w; RETURN OF THE TEXAN(1952), d; NEVER LET ME GO(1953, U.S./Brit.), d; TREASURE OF THE GOLDEN CONDOR(1953), d&w; DEMETRIUS AND THE GLADIATORS(1954), d; WHITE FEATHER(1955), w; JUBAL(1956), d; LAST WAGON, THE(1956), d, w; AFFAIR TO REMEMBER, AN(1957), w; BADLANDERS, THE(1958), d; COWBOY(1958), d; KINGS GO FORTH(1958), d; HANGING TREE, THE(1959), d; SUMMER PLACE, A(1959), p,d&w; PARRISH(1961), p&d; SUSAN SLADE(1961), p&d; ROME ADVENTURE(1962), p,d&w; SPENCER'S MOUNTAIN(1963), p&d; YOUNGBLOOD HAWKE(1964), p,d; BATTLE OF THE VILLA FIORITA, THE(1965, Brit.), p,d&w; PROFESSIONALS, THE(1966), w

Michael Daves
DESTINATION TOKYO(1944); DARK PASSAGE(1947)

Michelle Daves
SPENCER'S MOUNTAIN(1963)

Michel Davet
LOVE STORY(1949, Fr.), w

Allen Davey
SWEETHEARTS(1938), ph; BITTER SWEET(1940), ph; HELLO, FRISCO, HELLO(1943), ph; DUEL IN THE SUN(1946), ph
Silents
SOUTH OF SUVA(1922), ph; TILLIE(1922), ph; RAILROADED(1923), ph; SAWDUST(1923), ph; GOLD AND THE GIRL(1925), ph; MAN OF NERVE, A(1925), ph; EYES RIGHT(1926), ph; CHEATERS(1927), ph; BULLET MARK, THE(1928), ph

Allen M. Davey
VALLEY OF THE GIANTS(1938), ph; HOLLYWOOD CAVALCADE(1939), ph; MOON OVER MIAMI(1941), ph; WESTERN UNION(1941), ph; DESPERADOES, THE(1943), ph; COVER GIRL(1944), ph; SONG TO REMEMBER, A(1945), ph

Arthur Davey
JOSEPH ANDREWS(1977, Brit.), cos

Bert Davey
TIME IS MY ENEMY(1957, Brit.), art d; TRAITORS, THE(1963, Brit.), art d; CARRY ON CLEO(1964, Brit.), art d; STITCH IN TIME, A(1967, Brit.), art d; BATTLE OF BRITAIN, THE(1969, Brit.), art d; TOOMORROW(1970, Brit.), art d; ZEPPELIN(1971, Brit.), art d; HENNESSY(1975, Brit.), art d; LAND THAT TIME FORGOT, THE(1975, Brit.), art d; AT THE EARTH'S CORE(1976, Brit.), art d; SLIPPER AND THE ROSE, THE(1976, Brit.), art d; PEOPLE THAT TIME FORGOT, THE(1977, Brit.), art d; GREAT TRAIN ROBBERY, THE(1979, Brit.), art d; DOGS OF WAR, THE(1980, Brit.), art d; FFOLKES(1980, Brit.), art d; EYE OF THE NEEDLE(1981), art d

Ethel Davey
TRAILS OF DANGER(1930), ed; HURRICANE HORSEMAN(1931), ed; CHEYENNE CYCLONE, THE(1932), ed; RACING STRAIN, THE(1933), ed; GUILTY PARENTS(1934), ed

Frances Davey
MAROONED(1933, Brit.)

Horace Davey
Misc. Silents
LION'S BREATH, THE(1916), d; SAGEBRUSH LADY, THE(1925), d

John Davey
LATE SHOW, THE(1977); THREE WOMEN(1977)
Leon Davey
SHE SHALL HAVE MURDER(1950, Brit.); NORMAN CONQUEST(1953, Brit.)
Nuna Davey
BRIEF ENCOUNTER(1945, Brit.); UPTURNED GLASS, THE(1947, Brit.); ESTHER WATERS(1948, Brit.); GAY DOG, THE(1954, Brit.)
Pamela Ann Davey
CHANGE PARTNERS(1965, Brit.)
Perry Davey
VICTOR/VICTORIA(1982)
Scott Davey
NOTORIOUS LANDLADY, THE(1962)
Jana Davi
GUN FEVER(1958); RAWHIDE TRAIL, THE(1958); GUNMEN FROM LAREDO(1959)
Jane Davi
FORT BOWIE(1958)
Robert Davi
1984
CITY HEAT(1984)
Allen Daviau
E.T. THE EXTRA-TERRESTRIAL(1982), ph; HARRY TRACY-DESPERADO(1982, Can.), ph; TWILIGHT ZONE-THE MOVIE(1983), ph
David
JONAH-WHO WILL BE 25 IN THE YEAR 2000(1976, Switz.)
Alain David
DEAR DETECTIVE(1978, Fr.)
Alan David
GONKS GO BEAT(1965, Brit.)
Allan David
MAGIC FOUNTAIN, THE(1961), p&d; TWIST ALL NIGHT(1961), p&d
Andy David
COOL BREEZE(1972), ph
Angel David
1984
MIXED BLOOD(1984)
Ann David
SEVEN ALONE(1975)
Art David
GAY PURR-EE(1962), anim
Baruch David
NOT MINE TO LOVE(1969, Israel)
Boyd David
YOU'RE TELLING ME(1942)
Brad David
EAT MY DUST!(1976); HAZING, THE(1978)
Bud David
WILLARD(1971), spec eff
Charles David
REBEL SON, THE ½(1939, Brit.), p; LADY ON A TRAIN(1945), d; RIVER GANG(1945), p&d; LA CHIENNE(1975, Fr.), p
Chet David
EYE CREATURES, THE(1965)
Clifford David
STREET OF SINNERS(1957); LAST MILE, THE(1959); INVITATION TO A GUN-FIGHTER(1964); PARTY'S OVER, THE(1966, Brit.); RIOT(1969); BETSY, THE(1978); RESURRECTION(1980); FORT APACHE, THE BRONX(1981)
Constantin J. David
ALIMONY(1949), p; PAROLE, INC.(1949), p
Misc. Silents
BERLIN AFTER DARK(1929, Ger.), d
David David
PRAISE MARX AND PASS THE AMMUNITION(1970, Brit.)
Davilia David
1984
BLOODBATH AT THE HOUSE OF DEATH(1984, Brit.)
Edward David
Silents
KILDARE OF STORM(1918)
Eleanor David
PINK FLOYD-THE WALL(1982, Brit.)
1984
COMFORT AND JOY(1984, Brit.)
Filip David
TWILIGHT TIME(1983, U.S./Yugo.), w
Franck David
LES MISERABLES(1982, Fr.)
Fredrick David
LOST, LONELY AND VICIOUS(1958), m
Gadie David
TIME AFTER TIME(1979, Brit.), stunts
George David
CHARGE OF THE LIGHT BRIGADE, THE(1936); TEMPTATION(1946); SIDE STREET(1950)
Graydon F. David
SIX PACK ANNIE(1975), d
Hal David
TWO GALS AND A GUY(1951), m/l
Hubert W. David
BIG BUSINESS(1930, Brit.), w
Hugh David
SUPREME SECRET, THE(1958, Brit.)
Hugh Gray Charles David
RIVER GANG(1945), w
Jacques David
THIEF OF PARIS, THE(1967, Fr./Ital.); JULIA(1977)
James David
Misc. Talkies
CAREER BED(1972)

Jean David
UNHOLY ROLLERS(1972); BANG THE DRUM SLOWLY(1973)
Jeff David
SOME OF MY BEST FRIENDS ARE...(1971); TELEFON(1977); KING OF COMEDY, THE(1983)
Joanna David
ONE PLUS ONE(1969, Brit.)
Johnny David
EASY RIDER(1969)
Judy David
HEATWAVE(1983, Aus.)
Karen David
HOUSE OF WHIPCORD(1974, Brit.)
Karl David
MIGHTY JOE YOUNG(1949)
Keith David
THING, THE(1982)
Kristina David
Misc. Talkies
KNOCKING AT HEAVEN'S DOOR(1980)
Larry David
CAN SHE BAKE A CHERRY PIE?(1983); SECOND THOUGHTS(1983)
Liliane David
ROAD TO SHAME, THE(1962, Fr.); OPHELIA(1964, Fr.)
Lou David
BURNING, THE(1981)
1984
OVER THE BROOKLYN BRIDGE(1984)
Mario David
WEB OF PASSION(1961, Fr.); ELUSIVE CORPORAL, THE(1963, Fr.); LANDRU(1963, Fr./Ital.); UP TO HIS EARS(1966, Fr./Ital.); BORSALINO(1970, Fr.); MAGNIFICENT ONE, THE(1974, Fr./Ital.)
Mary Ellen David
1984
SPLATTER UNIVERSITY(1984)
Michael David
MYSTERY OF THE HOODED HORSEMEN, THE(1937), m; INN OF THE SIXTH HAPPINESS, THE(1958); LET'S MAKE LOVE(1960); WIZARD OF BAGHDAD, THE(1960); CAPTURE THAT CAPSULE(1961); FIERCEST HEART, THE(1961); SNOW WHITE AND THE THREE STOOGES(1961); LISA(1962, Brit.); STARFIGHTERS, THE(1964), ed; TO THE SHORES OF HELL(1966), ed; ROBBERY(1967, Brit.)
Michele David
SEVENTH JUROR, THE(1964, Fr.), ed; WOMEN AND WAR(1965, Fr.), ed; GALIA(1966, Fr./Ital.), ed; FEMMINA(1968 Fr./Ital./Ger.), ed; ROAD TO SALINA(1971, Fr./Ital.), ed
Monica David
ROAD HUSTLERS, THE(1968)
Nina David
FAT ANGELS(1980, U.S./Span.)
Pauline David
JOSEPHINE AND MEN(1955, Brit.)
Peggy David
RIGHT STUFF, THE(1983)
Regina David
SURVIVORS, THE(1983)
Ricardo M. David
WONDER WOMEN(1973, Phil.), ph
Richard David
ARSON, INC.(1949)
Roger David
ADAM'S RIB(1949)
Ronnie David
PAJAMA PARTY(1964)
Ryan David
WORLD ACCORDING TO GARP, The(1982)
Sam David
DAN'S MOTEL(1982)
Saul David
VON RYAN'S EXPRESS(1965), p; FANTASTIC VOYAGE(1966), p; OUR MAN FLINT(1966), p; IN LIKE FLINT(1967), p; SKULLDUGGERY(1970), a, p; LOGAN'S RUN(1976), p
Thayer David
BABY FACE NELSON(1957); TIME TO LOVE AND A TIME TO DIE, A(1958); WOLF LARSEN(1958); JOURNEY TO THE CENTER OF THE EARTH(1959); STORY OF RUTH, THE(1960); HOUSE OF DARK SHADOWS(1970); LITTLE BIG MAN(1970); NIGHT OF DARK SHADOWS(1971); SAVAGES(1972); STOOLIE, THE(1972); HAPPY MOTHER'S DAY... LOVE, GEORGE(1973); SAVE THE TIGER(1973); EIGER SANCTION, THE(1975); HEARTS OF THE WEST(1975); PEEPER(1975); DUCHESS AND THE DIRTWATER FOX, THE(1976); ROCKY(1976); FUN WITH DICK AND JANE(1977); HOUSE CALLS(1978)
Tissa David
RAGGEDY ANN AND ANDY(1977), anim
Vivian David
SATIN MUSHROOM, THE(1969)
Wil David
SIX PACK ANNIE(1975), w
William B. David
NORTHWEST TRAIL(1945), p; WILDFIRE(1945), p; FLIGHT TO NOWHERE(1946), p; GOD'S COUNTRY(1946), p; SCARED TO DEATH(1947), p
William David
Silents
ARMS AND THE GIRL(1917)
Misc. Silents
GIRL PROBLEM, THE(1919); OUTCAST(1922); RECEIVED PAYMENT(1922)
Zorro David
REFLECTIONS IN A GOLDEN EYE(1967)
Raquel Davida
HIS WOMAN(1931)

Davide
Misc. Silents
WITCH'S LURE, THE(1921)
A. Davidescu
FINAL TERROR, THE(1983), ph
Margaret Davidge
CLAIRVOYANT, THE(1935, Brit.); FIGHTING STOCK(1935, Brit.); DOMMED CARGO(1936, Brit.); KING OF HEARTS(1936, Brit.); MAN WITH 100 FACES, THE(1938, Brit.); VILLIERS DIAMOND, THE(1938, Brit.)
John Davidison
Misc. Silents
CHEATED LOVE(1921)
Raquel Davido
MY OLD KENTUCKY HOME(1938)
Alex Davidoff
CROSSROADS(1942); ONCE UPON A HONEYMOON(1942); SENATOR WAS INDISCREET, THE(1947); LARCENY(1948); TRAPPED(1949)
Alexis Davidoff
DISHONORED(1931); GUNFIRE AT INDIAN GAP(1957), cos; SPOILERS OF THE FOREST(1957), cos; CROOKED CIRCLE, THE(1958), cos; MAN OR GUN(1958), cos; MAN WHO DIED TWICE, THE(1958), cos; NOTORIOUS MR. MONKS, THE(1958), cos; YOUNG AND WILD(1958), cos; EXPLOSIVE GENERATION, THE(1961), cos; HOODLUM PRIEST, THE(1961), cos; HOUSE OF WOMEN(1962), cos; PT 109(1963), cos
Jo Davidon
EYEWITNESS(1981)
Basil Davidovich
ARISTOCATS, THE(1970), anim
Paul Davidovsky
1984
MOSCOW ON THE HUDSON(1984)
Kenneth Davidow
DAWN OF THE DEAD(1979), ed
Norma Davids
HOT STUFF(1979); LOVE CHILD(1982)
Ben Davidson
M(1970); BLACK SIX, THE(1974); HARRY AND WALTER GO TO NEW YORK(1976); CONAN THE BARBARIAN(1982)
Bert Davidson
HIGH BARBAREE(1947); FORCE OF EVIL(1948); MIRACLE OF THE BELLS, THE(1948); SAXON CHARM, THE(1948); WALK A CROOKED MILE(1948); ADAM'S RIB(1949); TENSION(1949); MYSTERY STREET(1950); SHAKEDOWN(1950); THREE LITTLE WORDS(1950); STRIP, THE(1951); BRAVE WARRIOR(1952); HOLD THAT LINE(1952); EXECUTIVE SUITE(1954)
Bill Davidson
NAUGHTY BUT NICE(1939); SAN DIEGO, I LOVE YOU(1944); BLONDE RANSOM(1945); SWING OUT, SISTER(1945)
Bing Davidson
MOVE OVER, DARLING(1963)
Boaz Davidson
SEED OF INNOCENCE(1980), d; HOSPITAL MASSACRE(1982), d; LAST AMERICAN VIRGIN, THE(1982), d&w
1984
HOSPITAL MASSACRE(1984), d
Bruria Davidson
LAST AMERICAN VIRGIN, THE(1982), ed
C. Lawford Davidson
Misc. Silents
SQUANDERED LIVES(1920, Brit.)
Carson Davidson
FLESH EATERS, THE(1964), ph; WRONG DAMN FILM, THE zero(1975), p,d&w, ed
Cindy Davidson
1984
LOVE STREAMS(1984)
Claire Davidson
OUR MOTHER'S HOUSE(1967, Brit.)
Cliff Davidson
Misc. Silents
TWO-FISTED SHERIFF, A(1925)
Clifford Davidson
Misc. Silents
ACE OF CACTUS RANGE(1924)
Davey Davidson
NO DRUMS, NO BUGLES(1971)
Diana Davidson
DIRTY HARRY(1971); SCARED TO DEATH(1981)
Dore Davidson
Silents
LIGHT IN THE DARK, THE(1922); SUCCESS(1923); GRIT(1924); WELCOME STRANGER(1924); "THAT ROYLE GIRL"(1925)
Misc. Silents
HUMORESQUE(1920); GOOD PROVIDER, THE(1922); BROADWAY BROKE(1923); NONE SO BLIND(1923); EAST SIDE, WEST SIDE(1927)
Douglas Davidson
FRATERNITY ROW(1977)
E. Roy Davidson
COUNTERFEIT(1936), ph; MR. DEEDS GOES TO TOWN(1936), spec eff; LOST HORIZON(1937), spec eff; NORTHERN PURSUIT(1943), spec eff; PASSAGE TO MARSEILLE(1944), spec eff; UNCERTAIN GLORY(1944), spec eff; BIG SLEEP, THE(1946), spec eff; STOLEN LIFE, A(1946), spec eff
Eileen Davidson
HOUSE ON SORORITY ROW, THE(1983)
Geoff Davidson
SHOUT AT THE DEVIL(1976, Brit.)
Gordon Davidson
TRIAL OF THE CATONSVILLE NINE, THE(1972), d
Grace Davidson
Misc. Silents
WHEN DESTINY WILLS(1921)

Howard Davidson
FINAL CUT, THE(1980, Aus.), m
Jack Davidson
CONFESSION(1937); EASY TO LOOK AT(1945); SMOOTH AS SILK(1946); SUDDENLY IT'S SPRING(1947); HALF ANGEL(1951); FRONT, THE(1976); SHOCK WAVES(1977); TATTOO(1981); I, THE JURY(1982); BABY, IT'S YOU(1983); REUBEN, REUBEN(1983); TRADING PLACES(1983)
Silents
ALIEN, THE(1915)
Jack [Jon] Davidson
GRAND THEFT AUTO(1977), p
James Davidson
TIME FOR KILLING, A(1967); MECHANIC, THE(1972); PARASITE(1982)
James R. Davidson
BULLET FOR PRETTY BOY, A(1970), ph
Jan Davidson
PLAYGIRLS AND THE BELLBOY, THE(1962,Ger.)
Jess Davidson
WHEN HELL BROKE LOOSE(1958), spec eff
Jim Davidson
MOUNTAIN FAMILY ROBINSON(1979)
Jimmy Davidson
SILENT PARTNER, THE(1979, Can.)
John B. Davidson
SCARLET EMPRESS, THE(1934)
John Davidson
CONCORDE, THE–AIRPORT '79(; KID GLOVES(1929); QUEEN OF THE NIGHTCLUBS(1929); SKIN DEEP(1929); TIME, THE PLACE AND THE GIRL, THE(1929); LIFE OF THE PARTY, THE(1930); THIRTEENTH CHAIR, THE(1930); ARSENE LUPIN(1932); DOCKS OF SAN FRANCISCO(1932); GRAND HOTEL(1932); SIX HOURS TO LIVE(1932); DEVIL'S IN LOVE, THE(1933); DINNER AT EIGHT(1933); MAD GAME, THE(1933); BOMBAY MAIL(1934); HOLD THAT GIRL(1934); HOLLYWOOD MYSTERY(1934); MOONSTONE, THE(1934); MURDER IN TRINIDAD(1934); STAND UP AND CHEER(1934 80m FOX bw); VIVA VILLA!(1934); BEHIND GREEN LIGHTS(1935); CHARLIE CHAN IN EGYPT(1935); LAST DAYS OF POMPEII, THE(1935); LIGHTNING STRIKES TWICE(1935); RECKLESS(1935); SHOT IN THE DARK, A(1935); TALE OF TWO CITIES, A(1935); DEATH FROM A DISTANCE(1936); LIVE, LOVE AND LEARN(1937); MR. MOTO TAKES A VACATION(1938); ARREST BULLDOG DRUMMOND(1939, Brit.); MIRACLES FOR SALE(1939); MR. MOTO'S LAST WARNING(1939); DEVIL BAT, THE(1941); CALL OF THE JUNGLE(1944); CHINESE CAT, THE(1944); WHERE DO WE GO FROM HERE?(1945); SENTIMENTAL JOURNEY(1946); SHOCK(1946); DAISY KENYON(1947); BUNGALOW 13(1948); IRON CURTAIN, THE(1948); LETTER TO THREE WIVES, A(1948); LUCK OF THE IRISH(1948); DANCING IN THE DARK(1949); OH, YOU BEAUTIFUL DOLL(1949); SLATTERY'S HURRICANE(1949); SWORD OF MONTE CRISTO, THE(1951); THUNDER IN THE EAST(1953); PRINCE VALIANT(1954); HAPPIEST MILLIONAIRE, THE(1967); ONE AND ONLY GENUINE ORIGINAL FAMILY BAND, THE(1968)
Silents
DANGER SIGNAL, THE(1915); SENTIMENTAL LADY, THE(1915); BRAND OF COWARDICE, THE(1916); AWAKENING, THE(1917); POWER OF DECISION, THE(1917); BRONZE BELL, THE(1921); IDLE RICH, THE(1921); NO WOMAN KNOWS(1921); SATURDAY NIGHT(1922); WOMAN WHO WALKED ALONE, THE(1922); MONSIEUR BEAUCAIRE(1924); RAMSHACKLE HOUSE(1924); RESCUE, THE(1929)
Misc. Silents
PAWN OF FATE, THE(1916); ROMEO AND JULIET(1916); WALL BETWEEN, THE(1916); SOULS ADRIFT(1917); SPURS OF SYBIL, THE(1918); THROUGH THE TOILS(1919); GREAT LOVER, THE(1920); TIGER'S CUB(1920); UNDER TWO FLAGS(1922)
Jon Davidson
1984
TOP SECRET!(1984), p
Joost Davidson
GAS(1981, Can.)
L.W. Davidson
HANDS OF THE RIPPER(1971, Brit.), w
Lawford Davidson
LOVE DOCTOR, THE(1929); STUDIO MURDER MYSTERY, THE(1929); HER PRIVATE AFFAIR(1930); LADIES LOVE BRUTES(1930); VAGABOND KING, THE(1930)
Silents
GARDEN OF RESURRECTION, THE(1919, Brit.); CRIMSON CIRCLE, THE(1922, Brit.); GLORIOUS ADVENTURE, THE(1922, U.S./Brit.); HALF A TRUTH(1922, Brit.); PASSIONATE FRIENDS, THE(1922, Brit.); ROGUE IN LOVE, A(1922, Brit.); RUNNING WATER(1922, Brit.); LITTLE DOOR INTO THE WORLD, THE(1923, Brit.); BRIGHT LIGHTS(1925); COLLEGE DAYS(1926); TONY RUNS WILD(1926); CHEATERS(1927); LITTLE JOURNEY, A(1927); DAREDEVIL'S REWARD(1928); OVERLAND TELEGRAPH, THE(1929)
Misc. Silents
TESTIMONY(1920, Brit.); GRASS ORPHAN, THE(1922, Brit.); TRUANTS, THE(1922, Brit.); THROUGH FIRE AND WATER(1923, Brit.); MIAMI(1924); NEGLECTED WOMEN(1924, Brit.); BACK TO LIFE(1925); GOLDEN STRAIN, THE(1925); GOLDEN WEB, THE(1926); SIN CARGO(1926); BLOOD WILL TELL(1927); MARRIAGE(1927); PATENT LEATHER KID, THE(1927); GEORGE WASHINGTON COHEN(1928); THREE-RING MARRIAGE(1928)
Lawrence Davidson
MYSTERIOUS DR. FU MANCHU, THE(1929); DOGS OF WAR, THE(1980, Brit.); CURSE OF THE PINK PANTHER(1983)
Silents
PLAYTHINGS OF DESIRE(1924)
Lenny Davidson
HAVING A WILD WEEKEND(1965, Brit.)
Lewis Davidson
ACT OF MURDER(1965, Brit.), w
Lillian Davidson
LORDS OF FLATBUSH, THE(1974)
Lionel Davidson
AGENT 8 3/4(1963, Brit.), w

Marsella Davidson
MOTHER'S DAY(1980)
Martin Davidson
LORDS OF FLATBUSH, THE(1974), a, d, w; ALMOST SUMMER(1978), d, w; IF EVER I SEE YOU AGAIN(1978), w; HERO AT LARGE(1980), d; EDDIE AND THE CRUISERS(1983), d, w
Max Davidson
SO THIS IS COLLEGE(1929); LOTTERY BRIDE, THE(1930); DARING DANGER(1932); DOCKS OF SAN FRANCISCO(1932); WORLD GONE MAD, THE(1933); FARMER TAKES A WIFE, THE(1935); EXCLUSIVE(1937); GIRL SAID NO, THE(1937); ROGUE OF THE RANGE(1937); ROSALIE(1937); UNION PACIFIC(1939); KITTY FOYLE(1940); MORTAL STORM, THE(1940); GREAT COMMANDMENT, THE(1941)
Misc. Talkies
ROAMIN' WILD(1936)
Silents
INTOLERANCE(1916); HUN WITHIN, THE(1918); HOODLUM THE(1919); IDLE RICH, THE(1921); NO WOMAN KNOWS(1921); RIGHT THAT FAILED, THE(1922); SECOND HAND ROSE(1922); EXTRA GIRL, THE(1923); RENDEZVOUS, THE(1923); JUSTICE OF THE FAR NORTH(1925); OLD CLOTHES(1925); RAG MAN, THE(1925); JOHNSTOWN FLOOD, THE(1926); CHEATERS(1927)
Misc. Silents
DON QUIXOTE(1916); DAUGHTER OF THE POOR, A(1917); HEIRESS AT "COFFEE DAN'S", THE(1917); SUNSHINE OF PARADISE ALLEY(1926); HOTEL IMPERIAL(1927); PLEASURE BEFORE BUSINESS(1927)
Michael Davidson
ARTISTS AND MODELS(1955), w
Muriel Davidson
STAGECOACH(1966)
Patricia Davidson
WARNING TO WANTONS, A(1949, Brit.)
Paul Davidson
LAST CHASE, THE(1981), spec eff; SMORGASBORD(1983)
Peter Davidson
ELEPHANT MAN, THE(1980, Brit.)
Phillamore Davidson
TWO GENTLEMEN SHARING(1969, Brit.)
Ray Davidson
RHAPSODY IN BLUE(1945), spec eff
Richard Davidson
BREAKING POINT(1976)
1984
VARIETY(1984)
Rick Davidson
BATTLE BEYOND THE STARS(1980)
Robert Davidson
GHOST, THE(1965, Ital.), w
Robert W. Davidson
Misc. Talkies
CRY TO THE WIND(1979), d
Robin Davidson
1984
SOLE SURVIVOR(1984)
Ronald Davidson
HI-YO SILVER(1940), w; DRUMS OF FU MANCHU(1943), w; CAESAR AND CLEOPATRA(1946, Brit.); CYCLOTRODE X(1946), p; COURTIN' TROUBLE(1948), w; COWBOY CAVALIER(1948), w; DAREDEVILS OF THE CLOUDS(1948), w; FIGHTING RANGER, THE(1948), w; RANGE RENEGADES(1948), w; ACROSS THE RIO GRANDE(1949), w; RANGE JUSTICE(1949), w; ROARING WESTWARD(1949), w; BLACK HILLS AMBUSH(1952), w; SATAN'S SATELLITES(1958), w; YOUNG AND THE BRAVE, THE(1963), w
Ross Davidson
PIRATES OF PENZANCE, THE(1983)
Roy Davidson
ONLY ANGELS HAVE WINGS(1939), spec eff; AIR FORCE(1943), spec eff; OUTLAW, THE(1943), spec eff; TO HAVE AND HAVE NOT(1944), spec eff; GOD IS MY CO-PILOT(1945), spec eff; HUMORESQUE(1946), spec eff; MY REPUTATION(1946), spec eff; FIGHTER SQUADRON(1948), spec eff; LADY TAKES A SAILOR, THE(1949), spec eff; TASK FORCE(1949), spec eff; WHITE HEAT(1949), spec eff
Sandra Davidson
COAST TO COAST(1980), cos; HERO AT LARGE(1980), cos
Tito Davidson
BIG CUBE, THE(1969), d, w
Vernon Davidson
Silents
ODDS AGAINST HER, THE(1919, Brit.)
W. B. Davidson
HELL'S ANGELS(1930)
Wilford Davidson
THIRTEENTH LETTER, THE(1951)
William B. Davidson
CARNATION KID(1929); PAINTED FACES(1929); WOMAN TRAP(1929); FOR THE DEFENSE(1930); HOOK, LINE AND SINKER(1930); MAN FROM WYOMING, A(1930); MEN ARE LIKE THAT(1930); OH, FOR A MAN!(1930); PLAYBOY OF PARIS(1930); SCARLET PAGES(1930); SILVER HORDE, THE(1930); DISHONORED(1931); NO LIMIT(1931); SECRET CALL, THE(1931); VICE SQUAD, THE(1931); GUILTY AS HELL(1932); HER MAD NIGHT(1932); INTRUDER, THE(1932); MENACE, THE(1932); SKY DEVILS(1932); THIRTEENTH GUEST, THE(1932); I'M NO ANGEL(1933); MEET THE BARON(1933); SITTING PRETTY(1933); TORCH SINGER(1933); DRAGON MURDER CASE, THE(1934); FOG OVER FRISCO(1934); IMITATION OF LIFE(1934); LAUGHING BOY(1934); LEMON DROP KID, THE(1934); SUCCESS AT ANY PRICE(1934); TWENTY MILLION SWEETHEARTS(1934); UPPER WORLD(1934); BORDERTOWN(1935); CRUSADES, THE(1935); DEVIL DOGS OF THE AIR(1935); IN CALIENTE(1935); IN PERSON(1935); MAN WHO RECLAIMED HIS HEAD, THE(1935); NIGHT AT THE RITZ, A(1935); OIL FOR THE LAMPS OF CHINA(1935); ROBERTA(1935); SECRET BRIDE, THE(1935); SHOW THEM NO MERCY(1935); SPECIAL AGENT(1935); STRAIGHT FROM THE HEART(1935); SWEET MUSIC(1935); WOMAN IN RED, THE(1935); WOMAN WANTED(1935); LOVE ON A BET(1936); MURDER BY AN ARISTOCRAT(1936); ROAD GANG(1936); AFFAIRS OF CAPPY RICKS(1937); EASY LIVING(1937); EVER SINCE EVE(1937); HOLLYWOOD HOTEL(1937); HURRICANE, THE(1937); IT HAPPENED IN HOLLYWOOD(1937); LET THEM LIVE(1937); MARKED WOMAN(1937); MARRY THE GIRL(1937); MIDNIGHT COURT(1937); MIND YOUR OWN BUSINESS(1937); PARADISE ISLE(1937); ROAD BACK,THE(1937); SOMETHING TO SING ABOUT(1937); BLOCKADE(1938); COWBOY FROM BROOKLYN(1938); ILLEGAL TRAFFIC(1938); JURY'S SECRET, THE(1938); LETTER OF INTRODUCTION(1938); MR. DOODLE KICKS OFF(1938); RACKET BUSTERS(1938); SERGEANT MURPHY(1938); TEXANS, THE(1938); YOU AND ME(1938); HIDDEN POWER(1939); HONEYMOON IN BALI(1939); OFF THE RECORD(1939); ON TRIAL(1939); PRIVATE DETECTIVE(1939); SMASHING THE MONEY RING(1939); SUDDEN MONEY(1939); THEY MADE ME A CRIMINAL(1939); WHEN TOMORROW COMES(1939); WINGS OF THE NAVY(1939); FLORIAN(1940); LILLIAN RUSSELL(1940); MARYLAND(1940); MY LITTLE CHICKADEE(1940); MY LOVE CAME BACK(1940); NIGHT AT EARL CARROLL'S, A(1940); ON THEIR OWN(1940); SAILOR'S LADY(1940); SANDY GETS HER MAN(1940); THREE CHEERS FOR THE IRISH(1940); TIN PAN ALLEY(1940); HIGHWAY WEST(1941); IN THE NAVY(1941); KEEP 'EM FLYING(1941); LADY FROM CHEYENNE(1941); REMEMBER THE DAY(1941); SAN FRANCISCO DOCKS(1941); THIEVES FALL OUT(1941); THREE SONS O'GUNS(1941); WEEKEND IN HAVANA(1941); AFFAIRS OF MARTHA, THE(1942); CAREFUL, SOFT SHOULDERS(1942); GENTLEMAN JIM(1942); JUKE GIRL(1942); OVER MY DEAD BODY(1942); YANKEE DOODLE DANDY(1942); GOOD FELLOWS, THE(1943); HAPPY GO LUCKY(1943); HERS TO HOLD(1943); LET'S FACE IT(1943); MISSION TO MOSCOW(1943); MURDER ON THE WATERFRONT(1943); TRUCK BUSTERS(1943); GREENWICH VILLAGE(1944); IMPOSTER, THE(1944); IN SOCIETY(1944); NIGHT CLUB GIRL(1944); SHINE ON, HARVEST MOON(1944); SONG OF NEVADA(1944); CIRCUMSTANTIAL EVIDENCE(1945); MAN WHO WALKED ALONE, THE(1945); SARATOGA TRUNK(1945); SEE MY LAWYER(1945); TELL IT TO A STAR(1945); THEY WERE EXPENDABLE(1945); YOU CAME ALONG(1945); ZIEGFELD FOLLIES(1945); HOODLUM SAINT, THE(1946); IN OLD SACRAMENTO(1946); MY DARLING CLEMENTINE(1946); NOTORIOUS LONE WOLF, THE(1946); PLAINSMAN AND THE LADY(1946); DICK TRACY'S DILEMMA(1947); FARMER'S DAUGHTER, THE(1947); MY WILD IRISH ROSE(1947); THAT HAGEN GIRL(1947); THAT'S MY MAN(1947)
Silents
AMERICAN MAID(1917); MODERN CINDERELLA, A(1917); PERSUASIVE PEGGY(1917); IMPOSSIBLE CATHERINE(1919); PARTNERS OF THE NIGHT(1920); DESTINY'S ISLE(1922); STORM DAUGHTER, THE(1924); RECOMPENSE(1925); LOVE MAKES 'EM WILD(1927)
Misc. Silents
CALL OF HER PEOPLE, THE(1917); GREATEST POWER, THE(1917); LADY BARNACLE(1917); LIFTED VEIL, THE(1917); MAGDALENE OF THE HILLS, A(1917); HER SECOND HUSBAND(1918); OTHER WOMAN, THE(1918); GOLD CURE, THE(1919); LURE OF AMBITION(1919); WOMAN THERE WAS, A(1919); CAPITOL, THE(1920); CONCEIT(1921); GIRL FROM NOWHERE, THE(1921)
William C. Davidson
LAST OF THE SECRET AGENTS?, THE(1966), prod d
William Davidson
QUEEN OF THE NIGHTCLUBS(1929); BLAZE O' GLORY(1930); SUNNY(1930); CAPTAIN APPLEJACK(1931); GRAFT(1931); DANGEROUSLY YOURS(1933); HELLO, EVERYBODY(1933); LADY KILLER(1933); FRIENDS OF MR. SWEENEY(1934); ST. LOUIS KID, THE(1934); GO INTO YOUR DANCE(1935); BIG NOISE, THE(1936); DANGEROUS(1936); EARTHWORM TRACTORS(1936); GOLD DIGGERS OF 1937(1936); SINGING KID, THE(1936); BEHIND THE MIKE(1937); LOVE ON TOAST(1937); COCOANUT GROVE(1938); DUST BE MY DESTINY(1939); EACH DAWN I DIE(1939); HONEYMOON'S OVER, THE(1939); INDIANAPOLIS SPEEDWAY(1939); GIRL IN 313(1940); GRANNY GET YOUR GUN(1940); HIRED WIFE(1940); INVISIBLE STRIPES(1940); LADY WITH RED HAIR(1940); SEVEN SINNERS(1940); MAN MADE MONSTER(1941); SUN VALLEY SERENADE(1941); IN THIS OUR LIFE(1942); LARCENY, INC.(1942); MAGNIFICENT DOPE(1942); MALE ANIMAL, THE(1942); ALLERGIC TO LOVE(1943); AND THE ANGELS SING(1944); UP IN ARMS(1944); CAT CREEPS, THE(1946); DING DONG WILLIAMS(1946); NOW THAT APRIL'S HERE(1958, Can.), p, d; SHAPE OF THINGS TO COME, THE(1979, Can.), p
Misc. Talkies
IVY LEAGUE KILLERS(1962, Can.), d
Silents
PRETENDERS, THE(1916); OUR LITTLE WIFE(1918); CHILD FOR SALE, A(1920); NOBODY(1921); ADAM AND EVA(1923); SALOMY JANE(1923); PORTS OF CALL(1925); LAST TRAIL, THE(1927)
Misc. Silents
HER DEBT OF HONOR(1916); PRICE OF MALICE, THE(1916); MARY LAWSON'S SECRET(1917); WHIRLPOOL, THE(1918); WHY I WOULD NOT MARRY(1918); HEARTS AND SPURS(1925); WOMEN AND GOLD(1925)
William F. Davidson
TENNESSEE JOHNSON(1942)
William H. Davidson
HALF A SINNER(1940); HOLD THAT GHOST(1941)
Williams B. Davidson
SINCE YOU WENT AWAY(1944)
Wynne Davidson
Misc. Silents
BULLDOGS OF THE TRAIL, THE(1915)
Col. Paul Davidson, USA/Ret.
THEY CAME TO CORDURA(1959), tech adv
Petter Davidsson
JOE HILL(1971, Swed./U.S.), ph
Cedric Thorpe Davie
BROTHERS, THE(1948, Brit.), m; BAD LORD BYRON, THE(1949, Brit.), m; SNOWBOUND(1949, Brit.), m; ADVENTURERS, THE(1951, Brit.), m; ROB ROY, THE HIGHLAND ROGUE(1954, Brit.), m; JACQUELINE(1956, Brit.), m; GREEN MAN, THE(1957, Brit.), m; OEDIPUS REX(1957, Can.), m; MAD LITTLE ISLAND(1958, Brit.), m; BRIDAL PATH, THE(1959, Brit.), m; KIDNAPPED(1960), m
Fiona Davie
ROCKETS IN THE DUNES(1960, Brit.)
George W. Davie
CORKY(1972), art d
Richard Davie
SAN ANTONIO ROSE(1941)

Shirley Davien
CHANCE MEETING(1960, Brit.)
Acton Davies
Silents
TILLIE'S TOMATO SURPRISE(1915), w
Albert Davies
LADY JANE GREY(1936, Brit.)
Alex Davies
WE'RE GOING TO BE RICH(1938, Brit.)
Amanda Davies
KNIGHTRIDERS(1981)
Anne Marie Davies
AMERICAN WEREWOLF IN LONDON, AN(1981)
Arthur Davies
LOOKS AND SMILES(1982, Brit.)
Batty Davies
HOUSE OF DARKNESS(1948, Brit.), w
Bernard Davies
WALLET, THE(1952, Brit.); SCARLET SPEAR, THE(1954, Brit.), ph; ESCAPE IN THE SUN(1956, Brit.), ph
Betty Davies
MY OLD DUCHESS(1933, Brit.); DEATH AT A BROADCAST(1934, Brit.); HEIGHTS OF DANGER(1962, Brit.), w
Betty Ann Davies
YOUTHFUL FOLLY(1934, Brit.); PLAY UP THE BAND(1935, Brit.); CHICK(1936, Brit.); EXCUSE MY GLOVE(1936, Brit.); RADIO LOVER(1936, Brit.); SHE KNEW WHAT SHE WANTED(1936, Brit.); TROPICAL TROUBLE(1936, Brit.); LUCKY JADE(1937, Brit.); MERRY COMES TO STAY(1937, Brit.); UNDER A CLOUD(1937, Brit.); MOUNTAINS O'MOURNE(1938, Brit.); SILVER TOP(1938, Brit.); REMARKABLE MR. KIPPS(1942, Brit.); ESCAPE(1948, Brit.); HISTORY OF MR. POLLY, THE(1949, Brit.); IT ALWAYS RAINS ON SUNDAY(1949, Brit.); NOW BARABBAS WAS A ROBBER(1949, Brit.); ONE WOMAN'S STORY(1949, Brit.); BLUE LAMP, THE(1950, Brit.); TRIO(1950, Brit.); HER PANELLED DOOR(1951, Brit.); OUTCAST OF THE ISLANDS(1952, Brit.); SLASHER, THE(1953, Brit.); TONIGHT AT 8:30(1953, Brit.); BELLES OF ST. TRINIAN'S, THE(1954, Brit.); BLACKOUT(1954, Brit.); CHILDREN GALORE(1954, Brit.); WICKED WIFE(1955, Brit.)
Betty Anne Davies
MAN IN BLACK, THE(1950, Brit.); ALIAS JOHN PRESTON(1956)
Betty [Anne] Davies
JOY RIDE(1935, Brit.)
Bill Davies
Misc. Talkies
LEGEND OF HORROR(1972), d
Blair Davies
RENDEZVOUS(1935); MAYTIME(1937); PICK A STAR(1937); GREAT SIOUX MASSACRE, THE(1965)
Brenda Davies
KISENGA, MAN OF AFRICA(1952, Brit.)
Brian Davies
BEDFORD INCIDENT, THE(1965, Brit.); UP FROM THE BEACH(1965); CONVOY(1978); AMERICAN GIGOLO(1980)
Camille Davies
MELODY(1971, Brit.)
Christopher Davies
CITY LOVERS(1982, S. African), p
Clem Davies
APPLE, THE(1980 U.S./Ger.)
Daniel Davies
ROCK 'N' ROLL HIGH SCHOOL(1979)
David Davies
HELL, HEAVEN OR HOBOKEN(1958, Brit.); THREE WEIRD SISTERS, THE(1948, Brit.); LAST DAYS OF DOLWYN, THE(1949, Brit.); RUN FOR YOUR MONEY, A(1950, Brit.); TREASURE ISLAND(1950, Brit.); LAVENDER HILL MOB, THE(1951, Brit.); MYSTERY JUNCTION(1951, Brit.); STORY OF ROBIN HOOD, THE(1952, Brit.); MR. DENNING DRIVES NORTH(1953, Brit.); THIRD KEY, THE(1957, Brit.); BEN HUR(1959); TIGER BAY(1959, Brit.); STORY OF DAVID, A(1960, Brit.); FRIGHTENED CITY, THE(1961, Brit.); KING OF KINGS(1961); SECRET OF MONTE CRISTO, THE(1961, Brit.); GANG WAR(1962, Brit.); ONLY TWO CAN PLAY(1962, Brit.); POT CARRIERS, THE(1962, Brit.); MASQUE OF THE RED DEATH, THE(1964, U.S./Brit.); HEROES OF TELEMARK, THE(1965, Brit.); UNDER MILK WOOD(1973, Brit.)
Deddie Davies
RAILWAY CHILDREN, THE(1971, Brit.)
Delmar Davies
Silents
DUKE STEPS OUT, THE(1929)
Desmond Davies
BEHEMOTH, THE SEA MONSTER(1959, Brit.), ph; MYSTERY SUBMARINE(1963, Brit.); EAST OF SUDAN(1964, Brit.); SMASHING TIME(1967 Brit.)
Dilys Davies
PROUD VALLEY, THE(1941, Brit.)
Dix Davies
OLD SWIMMIN' HOLE, THE(1941)
Eddie Davies
MR. QUILP(1975, Brit.)
Edgar D. Davies
SCREAM AND SCREAM AGAIN(1970, Brit.)
Edna Davies
HATE SHIP, THE(1930, Brit.); LOOSE ENDS(1930, Brit.); SONG OF SOHO(1930, Brit.); SPANISH EYES(1930, Brit.); SOMETIMES GOOD(1934, Brit.); SIDE STREET ANGEL(1937, Brit.)
Misc. Silents
COTTON AND CATTLE(1921)
Edward Davies
MAGNET, THE(1950, Brit.); MY WAY(1974, South Africa)
Emlen Davies
WAC FROM WALLA WALLA, THE(1952); STORM CENTER(1956); STRANGE ADVENTURE, A(1956); YOUNG AND WILD(1958)

Eric Davies
WORM'S EYE VIEW(1951, Brit.)
Ernest Davies
SEVENTH VEIL, THE(1946, Brit.)
Escott Davies
EAST LYNNE ON THE WESTERN FRONT(1931, Brit.)
Fletcher Davies
TRADER HORNEE(1970)
Freeman Davies
SOUTHERN COMFORT(1981), ed; 48 HOURS(1982), ed; BRAINSTORM(1983), ed
1984
STREETS OF FIRE(1984), ed
Freeman Davies, Jr.
JAWS II(1978), ed
Freeman A. Davies
WHEN TIME RAN OUT(1980), ed
Gail Davies
STUDENT TEACHERS, THE(1973)
Gary Davies
Misc. Talkies
DEADLY HARVEST(1972)
Gavin Davies
SMILEY(1957, Brit.)
Geoffrey Davies
OH! WHAT A LOVELY WAR(1969, Brit.); VAULT OF HORROR, THE(1973, Brit.)
George Davies
HISTORY IS MADE AT NIGHT(1937); ON OUR MERRY WAY(1948)
Gilbert Davies
CONDEMNED TO DEATH(1932, Brit.)
Glenda Davies
TEARS FOR SIMON(1957, Brit.)
Glyn Davies
DISCOVERIES(1939, Brit.); MOUSE AND THE WOMAN, THE(1981, Brit.)
Griffith Davies
SPARROWS CAN'T SING(1963, Brit.); MODEL MURDER CASE, THE(1964, Brit.); RULING CLASS, THE(1972, Brit.); UNDER MILK WOOD(1973, Brit.); BAWDY ADVENTURES OF TOM JONES, THE(1976, Brit.)
Gron Davies
GREAT GILBERT AND SULLIVAN, THE(1953, Brit.); THE CREEPING UNKNOWN(1956, Brit.)
Gwen Davies
GOLDEN EARRINGS(1947); OPEN THE DOOR AND SEE ALL THE PEOPLE(1964)
Gwen Ffrangcon Davies
LEO THE LAST(1970, Brit.)
Gwenlliam Davies
1984
YR ALCOHOLIG LION(1984, Brit.)
Harry Parr Davies
LET'S MAKE UP(1955, Brit.), m
Henry Davies
ROOMMATES(1962, Brit.); SECRET OF BLOOD ISLAND, THE(1965, Brit.)
Hilda Davies
MILLIONS LIKE US(1943, Brit.)
Howard Davies
YOU CAN'T TAKE IT WITH YOU(1938); MY SON, MY SON!(1940); GUY NAMED JOE, A(1943); LASSIE, COME HOME(1943); THANK YOUR LUCKY STARS(1943); DEVOTION(1946)
Silents
KILMENY(1915); CODE OF MARCIA GRAY(1916); PARSON OF PANAMINT, THE(1916); IT'S A BEAR(1919); AVENGING SHADOW, THE(1928)
Misc. Silents
YANKEE GIRL, THE(1915); AMERICAN BEAUTY, THE(1916); INTRIGUE(1916); MAKING OF MADDALENA, THE(1916); HER OWN PEOPLE(1917); BOSTON BLACKIE'S LITTLE PAL(1918); HEARTS OR DIAMONDS?(1918); HIS BIRTHRIGHT(1918); SPREADING EVIL, THE(1919); DICE OF DESTINY(1920); WHITE OUTLAW, THE(1929)
Hubert Henry Davies
STRICTLY MODERN(1930), w; GIRL FROM TENTH AVENUE, THE(1935), w
Silents
OUTCAST(1928), w; SINGLE MAN, A(1929), w
Hunter Davies
HERE WE GO ROUND THE MULBERRY BUSH(1968, Brit.), w
Ionette Lloyd Davies
MOUSE AND THE WOMAN, THE(1981, Brit.)
Irving Davies
INVITATION TO THE DANCE(1956); AS LONG AS THEY'RE HAPPY(1957, Brit.), ch; VALUE FOR MONEY(1957, Brit.), a, ch
Iva Davies
1984
RAZORBACK(1984, Aus.), m
J. Trevor Davies
FLAW, THE(1955, Brit.)
Jack Davies
COMING-OUT PARTY, A(, w; MISTER CINDERS(1934, Brit.), w; MUSIC HATH CHARMS(1935, Brit.), w; SOMEONE AT THE DOOR(1936, Brit.), w; STAR FELL FROM HEAVEN, A(1936, Brit.), w; WEEKEND MILLIONAIRE(1937, Brit.), w; CONVICT 99(1938, Brit.), w; TROUBLE IN THE AIR(1948, Brit.), w; LAUGHTER IN PARADISE(1951, Brit.), w; CURTAIN UP(1952, Brit.), w; TONIGHT'S THE NIGHT(1954, Brit.), w; DOCTOR AT SEA(1955, Brit.), w; JUMPING FOR JOY(1956, Brit.), w; ALLIGATOR NAMED DAISY, AN(1957, Brit.), w; HIGH FLIGHT(1957, Brit.), w; TRUE AS A TURTLE(1957, Brit.), w; UP IN THE WORLD(1957, Brit.), w; I ONLY ASKED!(1958, Brit.), w; SQUARE PEG, THE(1958, Brit.), w; DON'T PANIC CHAPS!(1959, Brit.), w; FOLLOW A STAR(1959, Brit.), w; UGLY DUCKLING, THE(1959, Brit.), w; BULLDOG BREED, THE(1960, Brit.), w; IT STARTED IN NAPLES(1960), w; NEARLY A NASTY ACCIDENT(1962, Brit.), w; ON THE BEAT(1962, Brit.), w; SEVEN KEYS(1962, Brit.), w; CROOKS ANONYMOUS(1963, Brit.), w; FAST LADY, THE(1963, Brit.), w; FATHER CAME TOO(1964, Brit.), w; EARLY BIRD, THE(1965, Brit.), w; THOSE MAGNIFICENT MEN IN THEIR FLYING MACHINES; OR HOW I FLEW FROM LONDON TO PARIS IN 25 HOURS AND 11 MINUTES(1965, Brit.), w; GAMBIT(1966), w; CARNABY, M.D.(1967, Brit.), w; STITCH IN TIME,

A(1967, Brit.), w; DOCTOR IN TROUBLE(1970, Brit.), w; SOME WILL, SOME WON'T(1970, Brit.), w; PAPER TIGER(1975, Brit.), w; SHEBA BABY(1975), ed; FFOLKES(1980, Brit.), w

Jack Davies, Jr.
DANCE BAND(1935, Brit.), w; MIMI(1935, Brit.), w; RADIO FOLLIES(1935, Brit.), w; HEART'S DESIRE(1937, Brit.), w

Jack Dies Davies
GIRL THIEF, THE(1938), w

Jackson Davies
MAN, A WOMAN, AND A BANK, A(1979, Can.)
1984
RUNAWAY(1984)

James Davies
EASY COME, EASY GO(1947); I WALK ALONE(1948); NIGHT HAS A THOUSAND EYES(1948); ALIAS NICK BEAL(1949); RED, HOT AND BLUE(1949); SORROWFUL JONES(1949); STREETS OF LAREDO(1949); FURIES, THE(1950); CARRIE(1952); PONY EXPRESS(1953); THREE RING CIRCUS(1954); GUNFIGHT AT THE O.K. CORRAL(1957)

Jane Gill Davies
BONNIE PRINCE CHARLIE(1948, Brit.); FIGHTING PIMPERNEL, THE(1950, Brit.); WINSLOW BOY, THE(1950)

Janet Davies
INTERLUDE(1968, Brit.); WHAT'S NEXT?(1975, Brit.)

Jim Davies
FORCE OF EVIL(1948); CHICAGO DEADLINE(1949); FILE ON THELMA JORDAN, THE(1950); HAPPIEST DAYS OF YOUR LIFE(1950, Brit.); HI-JACKED(1950); HIS KIND OF WOMAN(1951); BLAZING FOREST, THE(1952); WAR OF THE WORLDS, THE(1953)

Joan C. Davies
NIGHT EVELYN CAME OUT OF THE GRAVE, THE(1973, Ital.)

John Davies
LONG GOODBYE, THE(1973); ACCEPTABLE LEVELS(1983, Brit.), d, w

John Howard Davies
ROCKING HORSE WINNER, THE(1950, Brit.); OLIVER TWIST(1951, Brit.); TOM BROWN'S SCHOOLDAYS(1951, Brit.); MAGIC BOX, THE(1952, Brit.)

Joseph E. Davies
MISSION TO MOSCOW(1943), w

Jules Davies
PAL JOEY(1957)

Kathy Davies
OCTOPUSSY(1983, Brit.)

L.P. Davies
GROUNDSTAR CONSPIRACY, THE(1972, Can.), w

Lane Davies
1984
BODY DOUBLE(1984)

Leslie P. Davies
PROJECT X(1968), w

Libba Davies
1984
PLOUGHMAN'S LUNCH, THE(1984, Brit.)

Lilian Hall Davies
Misc. Silents
TOMMY ATKINS(1928, Brit.)

Lillian Hall Davies
Misc. Silents
FAITHFUL HEART, THE(1922, Brit.)

Lloyd G. Davies
RED MENACE, THE(1949)

Lulu Davies
VIRGIN AND THE GYPSY, THE(1970, Brit.)

Lynn Davies
BLONDE DYNAMITE(1950); ANNE OF THE INDIES(1951)

Maria Thompson Davies
Silents
OUT OF A CLEAR SKY(1918), w

Marian Davies
Silents
FAIR CO-ED, THE(1927)

Marion Davies
MARIANNE(1929); FLORODORA GIRL, THE(1930); NOT SO DUMB(1930); BACHELOR FATHER(1931); FIVE AND TEN(1931); IT'S A WISE CHILD(1931); BLONDIE OF THE FOLLIES(1932), a, p; POLLY OF THE CIRCUS(1932); GOING HOLLYWOOD(1933); PEG O' MY HEART(1933); OPERATOR 13(1934); PAGE MISS GLORY(1935); CAIN AND MABEL(1936); HEARTS DIVIDED(1936); EVER SINCE EVE(1937)
Silents
GETTING MARY MARRIED(1919); BURIED TREASURE(1921); ENCHANTMENT(1921); WHEN KNIGHTHOOD WAS IN FLOWER(1922); ADAM AND EVA(1923); JANICE MEREDITH(1924); ZANDER THE GREAT(1925); BEVERLY OF GRAUSTARK(1926); QUALITY STREET(1927); RED MILL, THE(1927); TILLIE THE TOILER(1927); SHOW PEOPLE(1928)
Misc. Silents
RUNAWAY ROMANY(1917); BURDEN OF PROOF, THE(1918); CECILIA OF THE PINK ROSES(1918); BELLE OF NEW YORK, THE(1919); DARK STAR, THE(1919); CINEMA MURDER, THE(1920); RESTLESS SEX, THE(1920); BEAUTY'S WORTH(1922); BRIDE'S PLAY, THE(1922); YOUNG DIANA, THE(1922); LITTLE OLD NEW YORK(1923); YOLANDA(1924); LIGHTS OF OLD BROADWAY(1925); CARDBOARD LOVER, THE(1928); PATSY, THE(1928)

Marjorie Davies
KEEP YOUR POWDER DRY(1945); THEY WERE EXPENDABLE(1945)

Martha Thompson Davies
Silents
ALTARS OF DESIRE(1927), w

Meg Davies
FINAL OPTION, THE(1983, Brit.)

Morgan Davies
LISBON STORY, THE(1946, Brit.)

Muggins Davies
SUNNY(1941)

Nicola Davies
GUNS IN THE HEATHER(1968, Brit.)

Noel Davies
ISADORA(1968, Brit.)

Pat Davies
LIFE OF HER OWN, A(1950)

Paul Davies
LOVING COUPLES(1966, Swed.), ed; NIGHT GAMES(1966, Swed.), ed; OEDIPUS THE KING(1968, Brit.), ed; VIRGIN AND THE GYPSY, THE(1970, Brit.), ed; STRAW DOGS(1971, Brit.), ed; GOT IT MADE(1974, Brit.), ed; PRIEST OF LOVE(1981, Brit.), ed; BMX BANDITS(1983), p
Misc. Talkies
JACKPOT(1982)

Peter Davies
WATERLOO(1970, Ital./USSR); STARSTRUCK(1982, Aus.); OCTOPUSSY(1983, Brit.), ed

Peter Maxwell Davies
BOY FRIEND, THE(1971, Brit.), md

Petra Davies
FOUR DAYS(1951, Brit.); GIRDLE OF GOLD(1952, Brit.); THEY CAN'T HANG ME(1955, Brit.); SILENT INVASION, THE(1962, Brit.); TWO LETTER ALIBI(1962)

Piers Davies
CARS THAT ATE PARIS, THE(1974, Aus,), w; SKIN DEEP(1978, New Zealand), w

Ray Davies
PERCY(1971, Brit.), m

Raymond Davies
ZULU DAWN(1980, Brit.)

Raymond Douglas Davies
VIRGIN SOLDIERS, THE(1970, Brit.), m

Redd Davies
SPECIAL EDITION(1938, Brit.), p&d

Renie Davies
Misc. Silents
SIN WOMAN, THE(1917)

Lt. Col. Rhys Davies ret.
SAFECRACKER, THE(1958, Brit.), w

Richard Davies
DON'T GET PERSONAL(1941); ROAD AGENT(1941); UNFINISHED BUSINESS(1941); BEHIND THE EIGHT BALL(1942); EAGLE SQUADRON(1942); GIVE OUT, SISTERS(1942); MAD DOCTOR OF MARKET STREET, THE(1942); PRIVATE BUCKAROO(1942); STRICTLY IN THE GROOVE(1942); TOP SERGEANT(1942); FALCON IN DANGER, THE(1943); HI'YA, CHUM(1943); IRON MAJOR, THE(1943); SKY'S THE LIMIT, THE(1943); WHEN JOHNNY COMES MARCHING HOME(1943); JUNGLE WOMAN(1944); SWINGIN' ON A RAINBOW(1945); NIGHT MY NUMBER CAME UP, THE(1955, Brit.); MARRIED TOO YOUNG(1962); ZULU(1964, Brit.); IF ...(1968, Brit.); OH! WHAT A LOVELY WAR(1969, Brit.); TWISTED NERVE(1969, Brit.); PLEASE SIR(1971, Brit.); UNDER MILK WOOD(1973, Brit.); MUTATIONS, THE(1974, Brit.)

Rita Davies
INCIDENT IN SHANGHAI(1937, Brit.); MONTY PYTHON AND THE HOLY GRAIL(1975, Brit.)

Robert Davies
GIVE A DOG A BONE(1967, Brit.)

Rosemary Davies
SECRETS(1971), w; NEITHER THE SEA NOR THE SAND(1974, Brit.), w
Misc. Silents
MAD MARRIAGE, THE(1925)

Ross Davies
SMASH PALACE(1982, New Zealand)

Rupert Davies
PRIVATE ANGELO(1949, Brit.); WARRIORS, THE(1955); ACCURSED, THE(1958, Brit.); KEY, THE(1958, Brit.); BOBBIKINS(1959, Brit.); DEVIL'S BAIT(1959, Brit.); IDOL ON PARADE(1959, Brit.); JOHN PAUL JONES(1959); LIFE IN EMERGENCY WARD 10(1959, Brit.); SAPPHIRE(1959, Brit.); SEA FURY(1959, Brit.); DANGER TOMORROW(1960, Brit.); CONCRETE JUNGLE, THE(1962, Brit.); SPY WHO CAME IN FROM THE COLD, THE(1965, Brit.); BRIDES OF FU MANCHU, THE(1966, Brit.); UNCLE, THE(1966, Brit.); VIOLENT MOMENT(1966, Brit.); FIVE GOLDEN DRAGONS(1967, Brit.); CONQUEROR WORM, THE(1968, Brit.); DRACULA HAS RISEN FROM HIS GRAVE(1968, Brit.); OBLONG BOX, THE(1969, Brit.); SUMARINE X-1(1969, Brit.); FIRECHASERS, THE(1970, Brit.); NIGHT VISITOR, THE(1970, Swed./U.S.); WATERLOO(1970, Ital./USSR); ZEPPELIN(1971, Brit.); FRIGHTMARE(1974, Brit.)

Ruth Davies
1984
FOREVER YOUNG(1984, Brit.)

Ryan Davies
UNDER MILK WOOD(1973, Brit.)

Sarah Davies
MEN ARE CHILDREN TWICE(1953, Brit.)

Scott Lloyd Davies
WILD RIDERS(1971), ph

Sid Davies
WITHOUT RESERVATIONS(1946)

Simon Lutton Davies
ISADORA(1968, Brit.)

Stacy Davies
ALL THINGS BRIGHT AND BEAUTIFUL(1979, Brit.)

Stanley Davies
1,000 CONVICTS AND A WOMAN(1971, Brit.)

Stephen Davies
HEART BEAT(1979)
1984
RAZOR'S EDGE, THE(1984)

Sylva Davies
NEVER PUT IT IN WRITING(1964)

Tessa Davies
OMEN, THE(1976), set d; JULIA(1977), set d; YENTL(1983), set d
1984
KILLING FIELDS, THE(1984, Brit.), set d

Tudor Davies
MOZART(1940, Brit.); YOUNG GIRLS OF ROCHEFORT, THE(1968, Fr.)

Tyrell Davies
SMITH'S WIVES(1935, Brit.)

Valentine Davies
SYNCOPATION(1942), w; MIRACLE ON 34TH STREET, THE(1947), w; CHICKEN EVERY SUNDAY(1948), w; YOU WERE MEANT FOR ME(1948), w; IT HAPPENS EVERY SPRING(1949), w; ON THE RIVERA(1951), w; GLENN MILLER STORY, THE(1953), w; SAILOR OF THE KING(1953, Brit.), w; BRIDGES AT TOKO-RI, THE(1954), w; STRATEGIC AIR COMMAND(1955), w; BENNY GOODMAN STORY, THE(1956), d&w; IT STARTED WITH A KISS(1959), w; BACHELOR IN PARADIS-E(1961), w

William Davies
LIFE IN DANGER(1964, Brit.), m, md; HEAD ON(1971), ph

Windsor Davies
MURDER MOST FOUL(1964, Brit.); FRANKENSTEIN MUST BE DE-STROYED!(1969, Brit.); ADOLF HITLER–MY PART IN HIS DOWNFALL(1973, Brit.); MR. QUILP(1975, Brit.); CARRY ON ENGLAND(1976, Brit.)

Maria Thompson Daviess
Silents
LITTLE MISS HOOVER(1918), w

Diana Davila
PLAY IT AGAIN, SAM(1972)

Lolla Davila
SIERRA BARON(1958)

Luis Davila
VISCOUNT, THE(1967, Fr./Span./Ital./Ger.); MISSION STARDUST(1968, Ital./Span./Ger.); EAGLE OVER LONDON(1973, Ital.)

Raul Davila
COUNTERPLOT(1959); HEROINA(1965)

Serge Davin
CASE OF DR. LAURENT(1958, Fr.)

Elena DaVinci
BADLANDS OF MONTANA(1957); ESCAPE FROM RED ROCK(1958); LONE TEX-AN(1959)

Alex Davion
SONG WITHOUT END(1960); PLAGUE OF THE ZOMBIES, THE(1966, Brit.); IN-CENSE FOR THE DAMNED(1970, Brit.); CHARLEY-ONE-EYE(1973, Brit.)

Alexander Davion
GOOD DIE YOUNG, THE(1954, Brit.); RICHARD III(1956, Brit.); MAN IN THE DARK(1963, Brit.); PARANOIAC(1963, Brit.); RATTLE OF A SIMPLE MAN(1964, Brit.); VALLEY OF THE DOLLS(1967); THUNDERBIRDS ARE GO(1968, Brit.); ROYAL HUNT OF THE SUN, THE(1969, Brit.)

Gordon Daviot
YOUTHFUL FOLLY(1934, Brit.), w

Davis
IT'S A BIG COUNTRY(1951), d

A. Anthony Davis
TOAST TO LOVE(1951, Mex.), w

A. Byron Davis
Silents
FOOLS OF FORTUNE(1922), d

Aaron Davis
GOLDEN CALF, THE(1930), w

Alan Davis
FRISCO KID(1935); MAGNIFICENT OBSESSION(1935); UNDER YOUR SPELL(1936); BARRIER, THE(1937); LOVE IS NEWS(1937); MARKED WOMAN(1937); GOLD IS WHERE YOU FIND IT(1938); OVER THE WALL(1938); SWING, SISTER, SWING(1938); I AM NOT AFRAID(1939); KING OF THE UNDERWORLD(1939); WINGS OF THE NAVY(1939); ARISE, MY LOVE(1940); MURDER IN THE AIR(1940); THEY DRIVE BY NIGHT(1940); MOONSHINER'S WOMAN(1968)

Alana Davis
BELL JAR, THE(1979)

Alfred Davis
TILL WE MEET AGAIN(1936), w

Allan Davis
PENROD AND SAM(1937); ROGUE'S MARCH(1952), d; CLUE OF THE NEW PIN, THE(1961, Brit.), d; FOURTH SQUARE, THE(1961, Brit.), d; CLUE OF THE TWISTED CANDLE(1968, Brit.), d

Altovise Davis
PIPE DREAMS(1976); KINGDOM OF THE SPIDERS(1977); CAN'T STOP THE MUSIC(1980)

Andrew Davis
HIT MAN(1972), ph; PRIVATE PARTS(1972), ph; SLAMS, THE(1973), ph; LEP-KE(1975, U.S./Israel), ph; MANSION OF THE DOOMED(1976), ph; STONY IS-LAND(1978), p, d, w; OVER THE EDGE(1979), ph; FINAL TERROR, THE(1983), d
Misc. Talkies
CAMPSITE MASSACRE(1981), d

Andy Davis
JOURNEY TO THE CENTER OF TIME(1967); WHAT AM I BID?(1967)
1984
ANGEL(1984), ph; BEAT STREET(1984), w

Angelina "Pepper" Davis
CHELSEA GIRLS, THE(1967)

Ann B. Davis
PEPE(1960); ALL HANDS ON DECK(1961); LOVER COME BACK(1961)

Ann Davis
MAN CALLED PETER, THE(1955)

Anne Davis
CAESAR AND CLEOPATRA(1946, Brit.)

Annette Davis
WHAT'S THE MATTER WITH HELEN?(1971)

Anthony M. Davis
WATUSI(1959)

Art Davis
SAGEBRUSH TROUBADOR(1935); ROOTIN' TOOTIN' RHYTHM(1937); SPRING-TIME IN THE ROCKIES(1937); IN EARLY ARIZONA(1938); PHANTOM GOLD(1938); PIONEER TRAIL(1938); CODE OF THE CACTUS(1939); SIX-GUN RHYTHM(1939); PRAIRIE PALS(1942); RAIDERS OF THE WEST(1942); ROLLING DOWN THE GREAT DIVIDE(1942); TEXAS MAN HUNT(1942); BUGS BUNNY'S THIRD MOVIE–1001 RABBIT TALES(1982), d
Misc. Talkies
ALONG THE SUNDOWN TRAIL(1942); TUMBLEWEED TRAIL(1942)

Arthur L. Davis
DEATH IN SMALL DOSES(1957), w

Athalie Davis
Misc. Silents
MASTER OF GRAY, THE(1918, Brit.); BARNABY(1919, Brit.); UNCLE DICK'S DARLING(1920, Brit.)

Audrey Davis
SINGING COWBOY, THE(1936)

Audry Davis
GUNS AND GUITARS(1936)

Austin Davis
ROWDYMAN, THE(1973, Can.)

B. J. Davis
1984
LIES(1984, Brit.); SAVAGE STREETS(1984), stunts

Barbara Davis
PAYMENT ON DEMAND(1951); SWEET LOVE, BITTER(1967); FRONT PAGE, THE(1974)

Bart Davis
1984
IMPULSE(1984), w

Becki Davis
1984
TIGHTROPE(1984)

Becky Davis
STERILE CUCKOO, THE(1969)

Ben Davis
1984
NIGHTSONGS(1984), ph

Benjamin Davis
MARRIAGE, A(1983), ph; SLEEPAWAY CAMP(1983), ph
1984
ACT, THE(1984), ph

Beryl Davis
MERRY-GO-ROUND(1948, Brit.); MY HEART GOES CRAZY(1953, Brit.)

Bette Davis
WATERLOO BRIDGE(1931); BAD SISTER(1931); SEED(1931); CABIN IN THE COT-TON(1932); DARK HORSE, THE(1932); HELL'S HOUSE(1932); MAN WHO PLAYED GOD, THE(1932); MENACE, THE(1932); RICH ARE ALWAYS WITH US, THE(1932); SO BIG(1932); THREE ON A MATCH(1932); WAY BACK HOME(1932); BUREAU OF MISSING PERSONS(1933); EX-LADY(1933); PARACHUTE JUMPER(1933); WORK-ING MAN, THE(1933); 20,000 YEARS IN SING SING(1933); BIG SHAKEDOWN, THE(1934); FASHIONS OF 1934(1934); FOG OVER FRISCO(1934); HOUSEWIFE(1934); JIMMY THE GENT(1934); OF HUMAN BONDAGE(1934); BORDERTOWN(1935); FRONT PAGE WOMAN(1935); GIRL FROM TENTH AVENUE, THE(1935); SPECIAL AGENT(1935); DANGEROUS(1936); GOLDEN ARROW, THE(1936); PETRIFIED FOR-EST, THE(1936); SATAN MET A LADY(1936); IT'S LOVE I'M AFTER(1937); KID GALAHAD(1937); MARKED WOMAN(1937); THAT CERTAIN WOMAN(1937); JEZE-BEL(1938); SISTERS, THE(1938); DARK VICTORY(1939); JUAREZ(1939); OLD MAID, THE(1939); PRIVATE LIVES OF ELIZABETH AND ESSEX, THE(1939); ALL THIS AND HEAVEN TOO(1940); LETTER, THE(1940); BRIDE CAME C.O.D., THE(1941); GREAT LIE, THE(1941); LITTLE FOXES, THE(1941); IN THIS OUR LIFE(1942); MAN WHO CAME TO DINNER, THE(1942); NOW, VOYAGER(1942); OLD ACQUAINT-ANCE(1943); THANK YOUR LUCKY STARS(1943); WATCH ON THE RHINE(1943); HOLLYWOOD CANTEEN(1944); MR. SKEFFINGTON(1944); CORN IS GREEN, THE(1945); DECEPTION(1946); STOLEN LIFE, A(1946), a, p; JUNE BRIDE(1948); WINTER MEETING(1948); BEYOND THE FOREST(1949); ALL ABOUT EVE(1950); PAYMENT ON DEMAND(1951); ANOTHER MAN'S POISON(1952, Brit.); PHONE CALL FROM A STRANGER(1952); STAR, THE(1953); VIRGIN QUEEN, THE(1955); CATERED AFFAIR, THE(1956); STORM CENTER(1956); JOHN PAUL JONES(1959); SCAPEGOAT, THE(1959, Brit.); POCKETFUL OF MIRACLES(1961); WHATEVER HAPPENED TO BABY JANE?(1962); DEAD RINGER(1964); EMPTY CANVAS, THE(1964, Fr./Ital.); HUSH... HUSH, SWEET CHARLOTTE(1964); WHERE LOVE HAS GONE(1964); NANNY, THE(1965, Brit.); ANNIVERSARY, THE(1968, Brit.); BUNNY O'HARE(1971); CONNECTING ROOMS(1971, Brit.); SCIENTIFIC CARDPLAYER, THE(1972, Ital.); BURNT OFFERINGS(1976); DEATH ON THE NILE(1978, Brit.); RETURN FROM WITCH MOUNTAIN(1978); WATCHER IN THE WOODS, THE(1980, Brit.)

Betty Davis
Silents
OUTWITTED(1925), ed; DREAM MELODY, THE(1929), ed; ONE SPLENDID HOUR(1929), ed

Beverly Dunn Davis
DREAMER(1979)

Bill C. Davis
1984
MASS APPEAL(1984), w

Bill Davis
CHEYENNE SOCIAL CLUB, THE(1970)

Boyd B. Davis
SENATOR WAS INDISCREET, THE(1947)

Boyd Davis
TWO LATINS FROM MANHATTAN(1941); YOU'LL NEVER GET RICH(1941); HARVARD, HERE I COME(1942); MAD DOCTOR OF MARKET STREET, THE(1942); MEET THE STEWARTS(1942); ONCE UPON A HONEYMOON(1942); RIDE 'EM COWBOY(1942); STAR SPANGLED RHYTHM(1942); STRANGE CASE OF DR. RX, THE(1942); SWEETHEART OF THE FLEET(1942); GHOST SHIP, THE(1943); JUNIOR ARMY(1943); REVEILLE WITH BEVERLY(1943); SO PROUDLY WE HAIL(1943); STANDING ROOM ONLY(1944); CAPTAIN EDDIE(1945); COLONEL EFFINGHAM'S RAID(1945); DOLL FACE(1945); EVE KNEW HER APPLES(1945); HOLD THAT BLONDE(1945); YOUTH ON TRIAL(1945); PERFECT MARRIAGE, THE(1946); SE-

CRET HEART, THE(1946); SMOOTH AS SILK(1946); TERROR BY NIGHT(1946); UNKNOWN, THE(1946); BLONDIE IN THE DOUGH(1947); HIGH WALL, THE(1947); MY FAVORITE BRUNETTE(1947); FOREIGN AFFAIR, A(1948); MA AND PA KETTLE(1949); RECKLESS MOMENTS, THE(1949); SAMSON AND DELILAH(1949); THEY LIVE BY NIGHT(1949); EMERGENCY WEDDING(1950); FATHER OF THE BRIDE(1950); GIRLS' SCHOOL(1950); LET'S DANCE(1950); PERFECT STRANGERS(1950); AT SWORD'S POINT(1951); BORN TO THE SADDLE(1953)

Brad Davis
MIDNIGHT EXPRESS(1978, Brit.); SMALL CIRCLE OF FRIENDS, A(1980); CHARRIOTS OF FIRE(1981, Brit.); QUERELLE(1983, Ger./Fr.)
Misc. Talkies
OLD TESTAMENT(1963, Ital.)

Brian Davis
1984
KARATE KID, THE(1984)

Brownlee Davis
WOLFMAN(1979)

Bryn Davis
HELLER IN PINK TIGHTS(1960)

Bud Davis
TOWN THAT DREADED SUNDOWN, THE(1977), a, stunts; JEKYLL AND HYDE..
.TOGETHER AGAIN(1982)
1984
AGAINST ALL ODDS(1984)

Buster Davis
MOVIE MOVIE(1978), m

C. J. Davis
Silents
POLICE PATROL, THE(1925), ph

Camille Davis
1984
SCRUBBERS(1984, Brit.)

Carl Davis
GAMBLING HOUSE(1950); BOFORS GUN, THE(1968, Brit.), m; ONLY WAY, THE(1970, Panama/Den./U.S.), m; PRAISE MARX AND PASS THE AMMUNITION(1970, Brit.), a, m; UP THE CHASTITY BELT(1971, Brit.), m; LOVERS, THE(1972, Brit.), m; RENTADICK(1972, Brit.), m; WHAT BECAME OF JACK AND JILL?(1972, Brit.), m; NATIONAL HEALTH, OR NURSE NORTON'S AFFAIR, THE(1973, Brit.), m; MAN FRIDAY(1975, Brit.), m; WHAT'S NEXT?(1975, Brit.), m; SAILOR'S RETURN, THE(1978, Brit.), m; FRENCH LIEUTENANT'S WOMAN, THE(1981), m; PRAYING MANTIS(1982, Brit.), m; WEATHER IN THE STREETS, THE(1983, Brit.), m
1984
CHAMPIONS(1984), m

Carole Davis
PIRANHA II: THE SPAWNING(1981, Neth.)

Carole R. Davis
1984
FLAMINGO KID, THE(1984)

Cathy Davis
PRIVATE FILES OF J. EDGAR HOOVER, THE(1978), prod d
Misc. Talkies
GUY FROM HARLEM, THE(1977)

Cedric Thorpe Davis
NIGHT FIGHTERS, THE(1960), m

Charles Belmont Davis
Silents
WOMAN'S BUSINESS, A(1920), w; HANDLE WITH CARE(1922), w

Charles Davis
DOWN THE WYOMING TRAIL(1939); MAN FROM PLANET X, THE(1951); ROGUE'S MARCH(1952); DESERT RATS, THE(1953); STUDENT PRINCE, THE(1954); SOLDIER OF FORTUNE(1955); FIVE STEPS TO DANGER(1957); OH, MEN! OH, WOMEN!(1957); YOUNG STRANGER, THE(1957); WRECK OF THE MARY DEAR, THE(1959); GET OUTTA TOWN(1960), p, d, ed; VIOLENT ONES, THE(1967), w; HAPPY AS THE GRASS WAS GREEN(1973), d&w; HAZEL'S PEOPLE(1978), d&w
Silents
ROAD TO LONDON, THE(1921, Brit.), ph; SINGLE TRACK, THE(1921), ph; DAUGHTERS WHO PAY(1925), ph

Charley Davis
SAVAGE WILD, THE(1970)

Cherry Davis
MAN FROM YESTERDAY, THE(1949, Brit.); I NEVER PROMISED YOU A ROSE GARDEN(1977)

Ches Davis
YES SIR, MR. BONES(1951)

Chet Davis
MARS NEEDS WOMEN(1966)
Misc. Talkies
DEAD MEN DON'T MAKE SHADOWS(1970)

Chick Davis
CYCLONE OF THE SADDLE(1935)

Chip Davis
CONVOY(1978), m

Christopher Davis
BAY OF SAINT MICHEL, THE(1963, Brit.), w

Chuck Davis
STARLIGHT OVER TEXAS(1938)

Clark Davis
TEEN-AGE STRANGLER(1967), p, w

Clayton Davis
Misc. Silents
HIDDEN CODE, THE(1920)

Clifton Davis
TOGETHER FOR DAYS(1972); LOST IN THE STARS(1974); SCOTT JOPLIN(1977)
Misc. Talkies
TOGETHER FOR DAYS(1972)

Clyde Brion Davis
ADVENTURE(1945), w

Clyde Davis
SCARLET EMPRESS, THE(1934); LET'S GET MARRIED(1937)

Connie Davis
PROPER TIME, THE(1959)

"Cyclone" Davis
MONEY FOR SPEED(1933, Brit.)

Cynthia Davis
COOLEY HIGH(1975)

D'Mitch Davis
MEAN STREETS(1973)

Dale Davis
BEACH GIRLS AND THE MONSTER, THE(1965), a, ph

Dan Davis
SUPERFLY T.N.T.(1973)

Daniel Davis [Edward D. Wood, Jr.]
GLEN OR GLENDA(1953)

Dave Davis
RAGGEDY MAN(1981)

David Davis
DOUBLE STOP(1968), m; HOOK, LINE AND SINKER(1969), w; H.O.T.S.(1979), m

Debbie Davis
DOGS(1976)

Delmon Davis
ROBERTA(1935)

Derna Wong Davis
KILLING OF A CHINESE BOOKIE, THE(1976)

Desmond Davis
INSPECTOR CALLS, AN(1954, Brit.), w; GIRL WITH GREEN EYES(1964, Brit.), d; TIME LOST AND TIME REMEMBERED(1966, Brit.), d, w; UNCLE, THE(1966, Brit.), d, w; SMASHING TIME(1967 Brit.), d; NICE GIRL LIKE ME, A(1969, Brit.), d, w; CLASH OF THE TITANS(1981), d; SIGN OF FOUR, THE(1983, Brit.), d
1984
ORDEAL BY INNOCENCE(1984, Brit.), d
Misc. Talkies
BORN FOR TROUBLE(1955), d

DeWitt Davis
DRUMS O' VOODOO(1934)

Diane Davis
Misc. Talkies
MEATEATER(1979)

Dick Davis
FEVER HEAT(1968)

Dilys Davis
CITADEL, THE(1938)

Dix Davis
TEST PILOT(1938); SINGING COWGIRL, THE(1939); I LOVE YOU AGAIN(1940); OUR TOWN(1940)

Dolly Davis
Misc. Silents
PARIS(1924, Fr.); LE VOYAGE IMAGINAIRE(1926, Fr.); PARIS EN CINQ JOURS(1926, Fr.)

Don Davis
SAN DIEGO, I LOVE YOU(1944); FOR LOVE AND MONEY(1967), p&d; GOLDEN BOX, THE(1970), p&d

Donald Davis
DANGEROUS CURVES(1929), w; ROUGH ROMANCE(1930), w; DAMAGED LIVES(1937), w; HELLO ANNAPOLIS(1942), w; CITY WITHOUT MEN(1943), w; ONE DANGEROUS NIGHT(1943), w; TENDER COMRADE(1943); LITTLE MISS BIG(1946); OEDIPUS REX(1957, Can.); JOY IN THE MORNING(1965); AGENCY(1981, Can.)
Silents
TWO FLAMING YOUTHS(1927), w

Donna Davis
PROWLER, THE(1981)

Dorothy Davis
VAGABOND KING, THE(1930); LITTLE GIRL WHO LIVES DOWN THE LANE, THE(1977, Can.)

Dorothy Patrick Davis
VIEW FROM POMPEY'S HEAD, THE(1955)

Dorrance Davis
VIRTUOUS HUSBAND(1931), w

Douglas Davis
1984
BEAT STREET(1984)

Drew Davis
1984
BAD MANNERS(1984); HOLLYWOOD HIGH PART II(1984)

Dyke Davis
THUNDER AND LIGHTNING(1977), cos

Ed Davis
1984
ALL OF ME(1984), w
Misc. Talkies
NOW OR NEVER(1935)

Eddie Davis
SHIP CAFE(1935); BLONDE TROUBLE(1937); ARTISTS AND MODELS ABROAD(1938); RADIO CITY REVELS(1938), w; HOUSE OF ERRORS(1942), w; LEAVE IT TO THE IRISH(1944), w; RANGE LAND(1949), p; RIDERS OF THE DUSK(1949), p; WESTERN RENEGADES(1949), p; WEST OF WYOMING(1950), p; CHITTY CHITTY BANG BANG(1968, Brit.); PANIC IN THE CITY(1968), d, w; COLOR ME DEAD(1969, Aus.), p&d, prod d; IT TAKES ALL KINDS(1969, U.S./Aus.), p&d, w
Misc. Talkies
RACKETEER ROUND-UP(1934); FIGHTING PILOT, THE(1935); GUNNERS AND GUNS(1935)

Eddie M. Davis
TOO MANY WOMEN(1942), w

Edward Davis
LOVE RACKET, THE(1929); TEN LAPS TO GO(1938)
Silents
CHARMER, THE(1925)

Misc. Silents
STRENGTH OF THE WEAK, THE(1916)
Edward S. Davis
Misc. Silents
DELUXE ANNIE(1918)
Edwards Davis
SONG OF KENTUCKY(1929); LOVE IN THE ROUGH(1930); MADAME SATAN(1930); HELLO, EVERYBODY(1933)
Silents
KNIFE, THE(1918); NEW YORK IDEA, THE(1920); RIGHT WAY, THE(1921); SHAMS OF SOCIETY(1921); SILVER LINING, THE(1921); HOOK AND LADDER(1924); ON THE STROKE OF THREE(1924); ONLY WOMAN, THE(1924); FLATTERY(1925); JOANNA(1925); NOT SO LONG AGO(1925); SPLENDID ROAD, THE(1925); AMATEUR GENTLEMAN, THE(1926); TRAMP, TRAMP, TRAMP(1926); SINGED(1927); POWER OF THE PRESS, THE(1928)
Misc. Silents
LOVE CHEAT, THE(1919); PLAYTHING OF BROADWAY, THE(1921); STOLEN SECRETS(1924); TAINTED MONEY(1924); BEST PEOPLE, THE(1925); MY NEIGHBOR'S WIFE(1925); PART TIME WIFE, THE(1925); HERO ON HORSEBACK, A(1927); WINDS OF THE PAMPAS(1927)
Edwin Davis
GEORGE WHITE'S SCANDALS(1945); DRAGONWYCH(1946)
Eileen Davis
DAWN OVER IRELAND(1938, Irish)
Elaine Davis
ATOMIC KID, THE(1954); LAST TIME I SAW ARCHIE, THE(1961)
Eleanore Davis
RAINBOW 'ROUND MY SHOULDER(1952)
Elizabeth Davis
GRUESOME TWOSOME(1968)
Misc. Talkies
HOW TO MAKE A DOLL(1967)
Elliot Davis
INDEPENDENCE DAY(1976), ph; BROKEN ENGLISH(1981), ph
Elmer Davis
FRIENDS OF MR. SWEENEY(1934), w; MY AMERICAN WIFE(1936), w; DAY THE EARTH STOOD STILL, THE(1951)
Elmer Holmes Davis
Silents
WHITE PANTS WILLIE(1927), w
Elvera Davis
MAN CALLED ADAM, A(1966)
Esther Davis
NOTHING BUT A MAN(1964)
Esty F. Davis, Jr.
PREACHERMAN(1971)
Evan Davis
DAN'S MOTEL(1982)
Evans Davis
VICE RAID(1959)
Evelyn Davis
SHAFT'S BIG SCORE(1972)
Fay Davis
Misc. Silents
ENOCH ARDEN(1914, Brit.)
Fitzroy Davis
HEAT'S ON, THE(1943), w
Forrest Davis
SMASHING THE RACKETS(1938), w
Frances Davis
PARTY, THE(1968); DEVIL'S WEDDING NIGHT, THE(1973, Ital.)
Frank Davis
COHENS AND KELLYS IN AFRICA, THE(1930); ONE NEW YORK NIGHT(1935), w; DEVIL IS A SISSY, THE(1936), p; PETTICOAT FEVER(1936), p; CHASER, THE(1938), p; LORD JEFF(1938), p; IT'S A WONDERFUL WORLD(1939), p; DANCE, GIRL, DANCE(1940), w; REMEMBER THE DAY(1941), w; ARE HUSBANDS NECESSARY?(1942), w; TREE GROWS IN BROOKLYN, A(1945), w; WOMAN ON THE BEACH, THE(1947), w; FIGHTING FATHER DUNNE(1948), w; JIM THORPE–ALL AMERICAN(1951), w; TEN TALL MEN(1951), w; SPRINGFIELD RIFLE(1952), w; STORY OF WILL ROGERS, THE(1952), w; JAZZ SINGER, THE(1953), w; BOY FROM OKLAHOMA, THE(1954), w; INDIAN FIGHTER, THE(1955), w; TEENAGE MONSTER(1958); NIGHT OF THE QUARTER MOON(1959), w; TRAIN, THE(1965, Fr./Ital./U.S.), w
Silents
HIS SECRETARY(1925), ed; BROWN OF HARVARD(1926), ed; CALIFORNIA(1927), w
Frank Foster Davis
Silents
HIS MASTER'S VOICE(1925), w
Misc. Silents
PHANTOM OF THE FOREST, THE(1926)
Fred C. Davis
LADY IN THE DEATH HOUSE(1944), w
Frederick C. Davis
DOUBLE ALIBI(1940), w
Gail Davis
BRAND OF FEAR(1949); DEATH VALLEY GUNFIGHTER(1949); FAR FRONTIER, THE(1949); FRONTIER INVESTIGATOR(1949); LAW OF THE GOLDEN WEST(1949); SONS OF NEW MEXICO(1949); SOUTH OF DEATH VALLEY(1949); THEY LIVE BY NIGHT(1949); COW TOWN(1950); INDIAN TERRITORY(1950); WEST OF WYOMING(1950); FLYING LEATHERNECKS(1951); OPERATION PACIFIC(1951); OVERLAND TELEGRAPH(1951); SILVER CANYON(1951); TAKE CARE OF MY LITTLE GIRL(1951); TEXANS NEVER CRY(1951); VALLEY OF FIRE(1951); WHIRLWIND(1951); YUKON MANHUNT(1951); BLUE CANADIAN ROCKIES(1952); OLD WEST, THE(1952); WAGON TEAM(1952); GOLDTOWN GHOST RIDERS(1953); ON TOP OF OLD SMOKY(1953); PACK TRAIN(1953); WINNING OF THE WEST(1953); ALIAS JESSE JAMES(1959); RACE FOR YOUR LIFE, CHARLIE BROWN(1977)
Misc. Talkies
SIX GUN MESA(1950); TRAIL OF THE RUSTLERS(1950); WHIRLWIND(1951)

Garry Davis
PANIC(1966, Brit.)
Gary Davis
SIDEWINDER ONE(1977), stunts; STUNTS(1977); VIVA KNIEVEL!(1977), stunts; KNIGHTRIDERS(1981), stunts
1984
AGAINST ALL ODDS(1984)
Gayle Davis
SMOKEY AND THE BANDIT II(1980); SHARKY'S MACHINE(1982)
Misc. Talkies
HOLLYWOOD 90028(1973)
Geena Davis
TOOTSIE(1982)
1984
FLETCH(1984)
Gene Davis
CRUISING(1980); NIGHT GAMES(1980); 10 TO MIDNIGHT(1983)
George Davis
BROADWAY(1929); DEVIL MAY CARE(1929); FOUR DEVILS(1929); LADY TO LOVE, A(1930); MEN OF THE NORTH(1930); NOT SO DUMB(1930); JUST A GIGOLO(1931); LAUGH AND GET RICH(1931); PRIVATE LIVES(1931); STRANGERS MAY KISS(1931); ARSENE LUPIN(1932); LOVE ME TONIGHT(1932); MAN FROM YESTERDAY, THE(1932); MEN OF CHANCE(1932); ONE HOUR WITH YOU(1932); UNDER-COVER MAN(1932); BLACK CAT, THE(1934); CAT'S PAW, THE(1934); GAY DIVORCEE, THE(1934); SCARLET EMPRESS, THE(1934); GOOD FAIRY, THE(1935); IN PERSON(1935); MAN WHO RECLAIMED HIS HEAD, THE(1935); DESIRE(1936); FATAL LADY(1936); HIS BROTHER'S WIFE(1936); LIBELED LADY(1936); LOVE ON THE RUN(1936); NEXT TIME WE LOVE(1936); SUZY(1936); WEDDING PRESENT(1936); ANGEL(1937); CHARLIE CHAN AT MONTE CARLO(1937); CONQUEST(1937); EMPEROR'S CANDLESTICKS, THE(1937); ESPIONAGE(1937); I MET HIM IN PARIS(1937); MAYTIME(1937); THERE GOES MY GIRL(1937); THIN ICE(1937); WE HAVE OUR MOMENTS(1937); YOU CAN'T HAVE EVERYTHING(1937); ALWAYS GOODBYE(1938); ARSENE LUPIN RETURNS(1938); ARTISTS AND MODELS ABROAD(1938); BARONESS AND THE BUTLER, THE(1938); HUNTED MEN(1938); SAY IT IN FRENCH(1938); THERE'S ALWAYS A WOMAN(1938); CHARLIE CHAN IN THE CITY OF DARKNESS(1939); EVERYTHING HAPPENS AT NIGHT(1939); NINOTCHKA(1939); TOPPER TAKES A TRIP(1939); ARISE, MY LOVE(1940); CHAD HANNA(1940); LADY IN QUESTION, THE(1940); HELLZAPOPPIN'(1941); MILLION DOLLAR BABY(1941); NEW YORK TOWN(1941); THAT HAMILTON WOMAN(1941); UNFINISHED BUSINESS(1941); CROSSROADS(1942); GHOST AND MRS. MUIR, THE(1942), art d; I MARRIED AN ANGEL(1942); PIED PIPER, THE(1942); TOO MANY WOMEN(1942); ABOVE SUSPICION(1943); MADAME CURIE(1943); MISSION TO MOSCOW(1943); PARIS AFTER DARK(1943); MRS. PARKINGTON(1944); NIGHT CLUB GIRL(1944); ONCE UPON A TIME(1944); 'TILL WE MEET AGAIN(1944); WHITE CLIFFS OF DOVER, THE(1944); DANGEROUS PARTNERS(1945); THIS LOVE OF OURS(1945); WITHOUT LOVE(1945); IF I'M LUCKY(1946); LOVER COME BACK(1946); RAZOR'S EDGE, THE(1946); THE CATMAN OF PARIS(1946); CRIME DOCTOR'S GAMBLE(1947); DAISY KENYON(1947), art d; MOTHER WORE TIGHTS(1947); NIGHTMARE ALLEY(1947); JOAN OF ARC(1948); THAT WONDERFUL URGE(1948), art d; EVERYBODY DOES IT(1949); MADAME BOVARY(1949); IN A LONELY PLACE(1950); TOAST OF NEW ORLEANS, THE(1950); AMERICAN IN PARIS, AN(1951); DAVID AND BATHSHEBA(1951), art d; LADY SAYS NO, THE(1951); ON THE RIVERA(1951); SECRETS OF MONTE CARLO(1951); SNOWS OF KILIMANJARO, THE(1952); GENTLEMEN PREFER BLONDES(1953); LILI(1953); SCANDAL AT SCOURIE(1953); 10 NORTH FREDERICK(1958); LIVE A LITTLE, LOVE A LITTLE(1968), art d; DIRTY DINGUS MAGEE(1970), art d
Silents
HE WHO GETS SLAPPED(1924); SHERLOCK, JR.(1924); AWAKENING, THE(1928); CIRCUS, THE(1928); KISS, THE(1929); SIN SISTER, THE(1929)
George D. Davis
GIRL HAPPY(1965), art d
George H. Davis
Silents
WASTED LIVES(1925), p
George K. Davis
TREASURE OF MONTE CRISTO(1949)
George S. Davis
RAWHIDE(1951), art d
George W. Davis
TWO WEEKS IN ANOTHER TOWN(1962), art d; TROUBLE WITH GIRLS(AND HOW TO GET INTO IT), THE*1/2 (1969), art d; DEEP WATERS(1948), art d; DANCING IN THE DARK(1949), art d; HOUSE OF STRANGERS(1949), art d; ALL ABOUT EVE(1950), art d; MISTER 880(1950), art d; NO WAY OUT(1950), art d; TICKET TO TOMAHAWK(1950), art d; PEOPLE WILL TALK(1951), art d; FIVE FINGERS(1952), art d; WHAT PRICE GLORY?(1952), set d; ROBE, THE(1953), art d; TONIGHT WE SING(1953), art d; DEMETRIUS AND THE GLADIATORS(1954), art d; EGYPTIAN. THE(1954), art d; LOVE IS A MANY-SPLENDORED THING(1955), art d; SEVEN YEAR ITCH, THE(1955), art d; VIOLENT SATURDAY(1955), art d; ESCAPADE IN JAPAN(1957), art d; FUNNY FACE(1957), art d; GIRL MOST LIKELY, THE(1957), art d; IN LOVE AND WAR(1958), art d; DIARY OF ANNE FRANK, THE(1959), art d; GAZEBO, THE(1959), art d; THIS EARTH IS MINE(1959), art d; ADVENTURES OF HUCKLEBERRY FINN, THE(1960), art d; ALL THE FINE YOUNG CANNIBALS(1960), art d; BELLS ARE RINGING(1960), art d; BUTTERFIELD 8(1960), art d; CIMARRON(1960), art d; HOME FROM THE HILL(1960), art d; KEY WITNESS(1960), art d; PLEASE DON'T EAT THE DAISIES(1960), art d; SUBTERRANEANS, THE(1960), art d; TIME MACHINE, THE(1960; Brit./U.S.), art d; WHERE THE BOYS ARE(1960), art d; ADA(1961), art d; ATLANTIS, THE LOST CONTINENT(1961), art d; GO NAKED IN THE WORLD(1961), art d; HONEYMOON MACHINE, THE(1961), art d; THUNDER OF DRUMS, A(1961), art d; TWO LOVES(1961), art d; ALL FALL DOWN(1962), art d; FOUR HORSEMEN OF THE APOCALYPSE, THE(1962), art d; HOOK, THE(1962), art d; HORIZONTAL LIEUTENANT, THE(1962), art d; HOW THE WEST WAS WON(1962), art d; JUMBO(1962), art d; MUTINY ON THE BOUNTY(1962), art d; PERIOD OF ADJUSTMENT(1962), art d; RIDE THE HIGH COUNTRY(1962), art d; SWEET BIRD OF YOUTH(1962), art d; WONDERFUL WORLD OF THE BROTHERS ERIMM, THE(1962), art d; COURTSHIP OF EDDY'S FATHER, THE(1963), art d; DRUMS OF AFRICA(1963), art d; HOOTENANNY HOOT(1963), art d; IT HAPPENED AT THE WORLD'S FAIR(1963), art d; PRIZE, THE(1963), art d; SUNDAY IN NEW YORK(1963), art d; TICKLISH AFFAIR, A(1963), art d; TWILIGHT OF HONOR(1963), art d; WHEELER DEALERS,

THE(1963), art d; ADVANCE TO THE REAR(1964), art d; GET YOURSELF A COLLEGE GIRL(1964), art d; GLOBAL AFFAIR, A(1964), art d; GUNS OF DIABLO(1964), art d; HONEYMOON HOTEL(1964), art d; KISSIN' COUSINS(1964), art d; LOOKING FOR LOVE(1964), art d; MAIL ORDER BRIDE(1964), art d; OUTRAGE, THE(1964), art d; QUICK, BEFORE IT MELTS(1964), art d; SEVEN FACES OF DR. LAO(1964), art d; SIGNPOST TO MURDER(1964), art d; UNSINKABLE MOLLY BROWN, THE(1964), art d; VIVA LAS VEGAS(1964), art d; YOUR CHEATIN' HEART(1964), art d; CINCINNATI KID, THE(1965), art d; CLARENCE, THE CROSS-EYED LION(1965), art d; HARUM SCARUM(1965), art d; JOY IN THE MORNING(1965), art d; ONCE A THIEF(1965), art d; PATCH OF BLUE, A(1965), art d; ROUNDERS, THE(1965), art d; SANDPIPER, THE(1965), art d; WHEN THE BOYS MEET THE GIRLS(1965), art d; ZEBRA IN THE KITCHEN(1965), art d; 36 HOURS(1965), art d; GLASS BOTTOM BOAT, THE(1966), art d; HOLD ON(1966), art d; MADE IN PARIS(1966), art d; MISTER BUDDWING(1966), art d; MONEY TRAP, THE(1966), art d; ONE OF OUR SPIES IS MISSING(1966), art d; ONE SPY TOO MANY(1966), art d; PENELOPE(1966), art d; SEVEN WOMEN(1966), art d; SINGING NUN, THE(1966), art d; SPINOUT(1966), art d; SPY IN THE GREEN HAT, THE(1966), art d; SPY WITH MY FACE, THE(1966), art d; TO TRAP A SPY(1966), art d; DOCTOR, YOU'VE GOT TO BE KIDDING(1967), art d; DON'T MAKE WAVES(1967), art d; DOUBLE TROUBLE(1967), art d; FASTEST GUITAR ALIVE, THE(1967), art d; HOT RODS TO HELL(1967), art d; KARATE KILLERS, THE(1967), art d; LAST CHALLENGE, THE(1967), art d; LOVE-INS, THE(1967), art d; POINT BLANK(1967), art d; RIOT ON SUNSET STRIP(1967), art d; VENETIAN AFFAIR, THE(1967), art d; WELCOME TO HARD TIMES(1967), art d; DAY OF THE EVIL GUN(1968), art d; FOR SINGLES ONLY(1968), art d; ICE STATION ZEBRA(1968), art d; IMPOSSIBLE YEARS, THE(1968), art d; LEGEND OF LYLAH CLARE, THE(1968), art d; POWER, THE(1968), art d; SHOES OF THE FISHERMAN, THE(1968), art d; SOL MADRID(1968), art d; SPEEDWAY(1968), art d; SPLIT, THE(1968), art d; STAY AWAY, JOE(1968), art d; TIME TO SING, A(1968), art d; WHERE WERE YOU WHEN THE LIGHTS WENT OUT?(1968), art d; YOUNG RUNAWAYS, THE(1968), art d; EXTRAORDINARY SEAMAN, THE(1969), art d; GYPSY MOTHS, THE(1969), art d; HEAVEN WITH A GUN(1969), art d; MALTESE BIPPY, THE(1969), art d; MARLOWE(1969), art d; BREWSTER McCLOUD(1970), art d; MOONSHINE WAR, THE(1970), art d; PHANTOM TOLLBOOTH, THE(1970), art d; STRAWBERRY STATEMENT, THE(1970), art d; ...TICK...TICK...TICK...(1970), art d; TRAVELING EXECUTIONER, THE(1970), art d; ZIGZAG(1970), art d; PRETTY MAIDS ALL IN A ROW(1971), art d; WILD ROVERS(1971), art d

Georgia Davis
SOMEONE TO REMEMBER(1943); STORM OVER LISBON(1944)

Gerry Davis
FINAL COUNTDOWN, THE(1980), w

Gilbert Davis
RESERVED FOR LADIES(1932, Brit.); SIGN OF FOUR, THE(1932, Brit.); GOING STRAIGHT(1933, Brit.); GOOD COMPANIONS(1933, Brit.); LOVE TEST, THE(1935, Brit.); SMITH'S WIVES(1935, Brit.); AMATEUR GENTLEMAN(1936, Brit.); MEET MR. PENNY(1938, Brit.); MURDER AT THE BASKERVILLES(1941, Brit.); FRIEDA(1947, Brit.); LOVES OF JOANNA GODDEN, THE(1947, Brit.); AGAINST THE WIND(1948, Brit.); IT ALWAYS RAINS ON SUNDAY(1949, Brit.); PASSPORT TO PIMLICO(1949, Brit.); SNOWBOUND(1949, Brit.); GALLOPING MAJOR, THE(1951, Brit.); GREEN GROW THE RUSHES(1951, Brit.); MADE IN HEAVEN(1952, Brit.); ENEMY FROM SPACE(1957, Brit.); DESERT MICE(1960, Brit.); ENTERTAINER, THE(1960, Brit.)

Glenn Davis
SPIRIT OF WEST POINT, THE(1947)

Gordon Davis
Misc. Talkies
UNDER THE TABLE YOU MUST GO(1969)

Griffiths Davis
V.I.P.s, THE(1963, Brit.)

Gunner Davis
HEADIN' NORTH(1930)

Gunnis Davis
BULLDOG DRUMMOND STRIKES BACK(1934); ONE MORE RIVER(1934); DARK ANGEL, THE(1935); RIGHT TO LIVE, THE(1935); WOMAN IN RED, THE(1935); LOVE ON THE RUN(1936); MOON'S OUR HOME, THE(1936); WE HAVE OUR MOMENTS(1937)

Guy Davis
1984
BEAT STREET(1984)

Gwen Davis
WHAT A WAY TO GO(1964), w; RICH AND FAMOUS(1981)

Hal Davis
Silents
BANDIT'S SON, THE(1927)

Harold Davis
WITHOUT RESERVATIONS(1946); CAREER GIRL(1960), d

Harry Davis
DANGEROUSLY YOURS(1937), ph; ONE WILD NIGHT(1938), ph; AMERICA, AMERICA(1963); FORTUNE COOKIE, THE(1966); ONE OF OUR SPIES IS MISSING(1966); TONY ROME(1967); WATERHOLE NO. 3(1967); MAN CALLED GANNON, A(1969); SOME KIND OF A NUT(1969); BROTHER JOHN(1971); GANG THAT COULDN'T SHOOT STRAIGHT, THE(1971); ROLLERCOASTER(1977)
Silents
OLD CLOTHES(1925), ph; LIGHTNING REPORTER(1926), ph; RUNAWAY GIRLS(1928), ph

Helen Davis
DOCTOR TAKES A WIFE(1940)

Helene Davis
SECRET DOCUMENT – VIENNA(1954, Fr.), p

Henry Davis
MAD MEN OF EUROPE(1940, Brit.), ph

Herbert "Red" Davis
Misc. Silents
BELLS OF ST. MARY'S, THE(1928, Brit.), d

Herman Davis
ROCKERS(1980)

Howard Davis
YANK IN THE R.A.F., A(1941); CODE 7, VICTIM 5(1964, Brit.)
Silents
EVIDENCE(1918)

Howell Davis
MEN ARE CHILDREN TWICE(1953, Brit.)

Hubert H. Davis
Silents
SINGLE MAN, THE(1919, Brit.), w

Humphrey Davis
SPELL OF THE HYPNOTIST(1956); ANNIE HALL(1977)

Ilah Davis
HARDCORE(1979)

Irving Davis
GOOD COMPANIONS, THE(1957, Brit.)

Irving Kaye Davis
WOMAN BETWEEN(1931), w

Ivan Davis
HUNGER, THE(1983), w

J. Charles Davis
WEST OF THE ROCKIES(1929), p
Silents
ON THE DIVIDE(1928), sup
Misc. Silents
SHADOW, THE(1921), d

J. Edwards Davis
MADONNA OF THE STREETS(1930)

J. Gunnis Davis
EAST LYNNE(1931)
Silents
SECRET OF THE HILLS, THE(1921); JEALOUS HUSBANDS(1923); LORD JIM(1925); LUCKY HORSESHOE, THE(1925); NOTORIOUS LADY, THE(1927)
Misc. Silents
CHASTITY(1923); REFUGE(1923); TROUBLE SHOOTER, THE(1924)

J. Raleigh Davis
NO DEFENSE(1929), w

J. Trevor Davis
CURSE OF FRANKENSTEIN, THE(1957, Brit.)

J.C. Davis
CHARLIE CHAN CARRIES ON(1931)

Jack Davis
HOODLUM SAINT, THE(1946); NIGHT EDITOR(1946); SECRET OF THE WHISTLER(1946); SHADOWED(1946); SOMEWHERE IN THE NIGHT(1946); STRANGE TRIANGLE(1946); TALK ABOUT A LADY(1946); UP GOES MAISIE(1946); BLONDIE'S BIG MOMENT(1947); HIGH WALL, THE(1947); LADY IN THE LAKE(1947); SEA OF GRASS, THE(1947); SILVER RIVER(1948); TAP ROOTS(1948); TENSION(1949); MALAYA(1950); GUY WHO CAME BACK, THE(1951); MR. POTTS GOES TO MOSCOW(1953, Brit.), w; CAVERN, THE(1965, Ital./Ger.), w; GNOME-MOBILE, THE(1967); MAD MONSTER PARTY(1967), puppetee; THOSE DARING YOUNG MEN IN THEIR JAUNTY JALOPIES(1969, Fr./Brit./ Ital.), w; BIG DOLL HOUSE, THE(1971)

Jackie Davis
CADDY SHACK(1980); SMOKEY AND THE BANDIT–PART 3(1983)

James Davis
DRUMS O' VOODOO(1934); HARLEM ON THE PRAIRIE(1938); SAFARI(1940); TENNESSEE JOHNSON(1942); PILOT NO. 5(1943); SALUTE TO THE MARINES(1943); SWING SHIFT MAISIE(1943); WHAT NEXT, CORPORAL HARGROVE?(1945); UP GOES MAISIE(1946); WINTER MEETING(1948); RED STALLION IN THE ROCKIES(1949); PEGGY(1950)
Silents
PEG OF THE PIRATES(1918)
Misc. Silents
LITTLE DUCHESS, THE(1917)

James Edmiston Chester Davis
WINK OF AN EYE(1958), w

James [Jim] Davis
FRONTIER UPRISING(1961)

Jan Davis
PUFNSTUF(1970); EVEL KNIEVEL(1971)

Janeen Davis
OSTERMAN WEEKEND, THE(1983)

Jean Davis
MOONLIGHT IN VERMONT(1943); SING A JINGLE(1943); PATRICK THE GREAT(1945); OTHELLO(1955, U.S./Fr./Ital.); VOODOO WOMAN(1957)

Jeff Davis
SOHO CONSPIRACY(1951, Brit.), ph; FOLIES BERGERE(1958, Fr.), m; ROOM 43(1959, Brit.), m; HOT MONEY GIRL(1962, Brit./Ger.), m
Misc. Silents
BRIDGE OF SIGHS, THE(1915)

Jerome "Jerry" Davis
GIRL RUSH, THE(1955), w

Jerri Lynn Davis
1984
WHERE THE BOYS ARE '84(1984)

Jerry Davis
DUCHESS OF IDAHO, THE(1950), w; PAGAN LOVE SONG(1950), w; KIND LADY(1951), w; APACHE WAR SMOKE(1952), w; DEVIL MAKES THREE, THE(1952), w; SLIGHT CASE OF LARCENY, A(1953), w; CULT OF THE COBRA(1955), w; PARDNERS(1956), w; ROBIN AND THE SEVEN HOODS(1964)

Jesse Davis
HAWMPS!(1976)

Jessie Davis
FOUR FOR THE MORGUE(1962)

Jim Davis
GALLANT BESS(1946); FABULOUS TEXAN, THE(1947); ROMANCE OF ROSY RIDGE, THE(1947); BRIMSTONE(1949); HELLFIRE(1949); YES SIR, THAT'S MY BABY(1949); CALIFORNIA PASSAGE(1950); CARIBOO TRAIL, THE(1950); SAVAGE HORDE, THE(1950); SHOWDOWN, THE(1950); CAVALRY SCOUT(1951); LITTLE BIG HORN(1951); OH! SUSANNA(1951); SEA HORNET, THE(1951); SILVER CANYON(1951); THREE DESPERATE MEN(1951); BIG SKY, THE(1952); RIDE THE MAN DOWN(1952); ROSE OF CIMARRON(1952); WOMAN OF THE NORTH COUNTRY(1952); PRESIDENT'S LADY, THE(1953); WOMAN THEY ALMOST LYNCHED, THE(1953); BIG CHASE, THE(1954); JUBILEE TRAIL(1954); OUTCAST, THE(1954); OUTLAW'S DAUGHTER, THE(1954); HELL'S OUTPOST(1955); LAST COMMAND,

THE(1955); TIMBERJACK(1955); VANISHING AMERICAN, THE(1955); BLONDE BAIT(1956, U.S./Brit.); BOTTOM OF THE BOTTLE, THE(1956); FRONTIER GAMBLER(1956); LAST OF THE DESPERADOES(1956); MAVERICK QUEEN, THE(1956); WILD DAKOTAS, THE(1956); APACHE WARRIOR(1957); BADGE OF MARSHAL BRENNAN, THE(1957); DUEL AT APACHE WELLS(1957); LAST STAGECOACH WEST, THE(1957); QUIET GUN, THE(1957); RAIDERS OF OLD CALIFORNIA(1957); RESTLESS BREED, THE(1957); FLAMING FRONTIER(1958, Can.); MONSTER FROM THE GREEN HELL(1958); TOUGHEST GUN IN TOMBSTONE(1958); WOLF DOG(1958, Can.); ALIAS JESSE JAMES(1959); 1001 ARABIAN NIGHTS(1959), anim; NOOSE FOR A GUNMAN(1960); GAMBLER WORE A GUN, THE(1961); IRON ANGEL(1964); ZEBRA IN THE KITCHEN(1965); JESSE JAMES MEETS FRANKENSTEIN'S DAUGHTER(1966); EL DORADO(1967); FORT UTAH(1967); ROAD HUSTLERS, THE(1968); THEY RAN FOR THEIR LIVES(1968); GUN RIDERS, THE(1969); ICE HOUSE, THE(1969); MONTE WALSH(1970); RIO LOBO(1970); BIG JAKE(1971); BAD COMPANY(1972); HONKERS, THE(1972); ONE LITTLE INDIAN(1973); PARALLAX VIEW, THE(1974); CHOIRBOYS, THE(1977); COMES A HORSEMAN(1978); DAY TIME ENDED, THE(1980, Span.)
Misc. Talkies
LUST TO KILL(1960); BORDER LUST(1967)

Jimmie Davis
STRICTLY IN THE GROOVE(1942); LOUISIANA(1947); MISSISSIPPI RHYTHM(1949)

Jimmy Davis
KING OF THE ZOMBIES(1941); CYCLONE PRAIRIE RANGERS(1944); ANY NUMBER CAN WIN(1963 Fr.)
1984
ICE PIRATES, THE(1984)

Joan Davis
LITTLE FRIEND(1934, Brit.); MILLIONS IN THE AIR(1935); BUNKER BEAN(1936); ANGEL'S HOLIDAY(1937); GREAT HOSPITAL MYSTERY, THE(1937); HOLY TERROR, THE(1937); LIFE BEGINS IN COLLEGE(1937); LOVE AND HISSES(1937); ON THE AVENUE(1937); SING AND BE HAPPY(1937); THIN ICE(1937); TIME OUT FOR ROMANCE(1937); WAKE UP AND LIVE(1937); YOU CAN'T HAVE EVERYTHING(1937); HOLD THAT CO-ED(1938); JOSETTE(1938); JUST AROUND THE CORNER(1938); MY LUCKY STAR(1938); SALLY, IRENE AND MARY(1938); DAYTIME WIFE(1939); TAIL SPIN(1939); TOO BUSY TO WORK(1939); FREE, BLONDE AND 21(1940); MANHATTAN HEARTBEAT(1940); SAILOR'S LADY(1940); FOR BEAUTY'S SAKE(1941); HOLD THAT GHOST(1941); SUN VALLEY SERENADE(1941); TWO LATINS FROM MANHATTAN(1941); SWEETHEART OF THE FLEET(1942); YOKEL BOY(1942); AROUND THE WORLD(1943); HE'S MY GUY(1943); TWO SENORITAS FROM CHICAGO(1943); BEAUTIFUL BUT BROKE(1944); KANSAS CITY KITTY(1944); SHOW BUSINESS(1944); GEORGE WHITE'S SCANDALS(1945); SHE GETS HER MAN(1945); SHE WROTE THE BOOK(1946); IF YOU KNEW SUSIE(1948); LOVE THAT BRUTE(1950); TRAVELING SALESWOMAN(1950); GROOM WORE SPURS, THE(1951); HAREM GIRL(1952)

Joanna Davis
NIGHTHAWKS(1978, Brit.), ph

Joe Davis
ODDO(1967), d
1984
MICKI AND MAUDE(1984)

Joe W. Davis
1984
STAR TREK III: THE SEARCH FOR SPOCK(1984)

Joel Davis
LIFE BEGINS WITH LOVE(1937); NOBODY'S CHILDREN(1940); IRON MAJOR, THE(1943); TWO FISTED JUSTICE(1943); CURSE OF THE CAT PEOPLE, THE(1944); HEAVENLY DAYS(1944); SPELLBOUND(1945)

John Davis
LAWLESS, THE(1950); FROM HERE TO ETERNITY(1953); MURDER AT 3 A.M.(1953, Brit.); PARSON AND THE OUTLAW, THE(1957); DAYLIGHT ROBBERY(1964, Brit.), p; MODEL MURDER CASE, THE(1964, Brit.), p; CRY WOLF(1968, Brit.), d, w; LOVING COUPLES(1980)
1984
ELLIE(1984), ed

John Walter Davis
JUST TELL ME WHAT YOU WANT(1980)
1984
ADVENTURES OF BUCKAROO BANZAI: ACROSS THE 8TH DIMENSION, THE(1984); STARMAN(1984)

Johnnie Davis
OVER THE GOAL(1937); BROTHER RAT(1938); COWBOY FROM BROOKLYN(1938); GARDEN OF THE MOON(1938); MEN ARE SUCH FOOLS(1938); MR. CHUMP(1938); SWEEPSTAKES WINNER(1939); CHILD IS BORN, A(1940)

Johnnie "Scat" Davis
KNICKERBOCKER HOLIDAY(1944); YOU CAN'T RATION LOVE(1944)

Johnny Davis
VARSITY SHOW(1937)

Johnny "Scat" Davis
HOLLYWOOD HOTEL(1937); SARONG GIRL(1943)

Joshua Davis
CAR, THE(1977)

Joyce Davis
LAUGH AND GET RICH(1931); ROSEMARY'S BABY(1968); WHEN THE LEGENDS DIE(1972); HINDENBURG, THE(1975)

Judy Davis
HIGH ROLLING(1977, Aus.); MY BRILLIANT CAREER(1980, Aus.); HOODWINK(1981, Aus.); WINTER OF OUR DREAMS(1982, Aus.); FINAL OPTION, THE(1983, Brit.)
1984
PASSAGE TO INDIA, A(1984, Brit.)

Jules Davis
JEANNE EAGELS(1957)

Karl Davis
FINGERPRINTS DON'T LIE(1951); MASK OF THE DRAGON(1951); YOUNG MAN WITH IDEAS(1952); SIREN OF BAGDAD(1953); DEMETRIUS AND THE GLADIATORS(1954); EGYPTIAN. THE(1954); CREATURE WITH THE ATOM BRAIN(1955); PIRATES OF TRIPOLI(1955); ROAD TO DENVER, THE(1955); TIMBERJACK(1955); APACHE WARRIOR(1957); ZOMBIES OF MORA TAU(1957); BONNIE PARKER STORY, THE(1958); MAN OR GUN(1958)

Karl "Killer" Davis
RECKLESS MOMENTS, THE(1949); FLESH AND FURY(1952); SALOME(1953)

Kathleen Davis
DEBT OF HONOR(1936, Brit.)

Keith Davis
SOAPBOX DERBY(1958, Brit.); DEATH COLLECTOR(1976); SHORT EYES(1977)
Misc. Talkies
FAMILY ENFORCER(1978)

Kenn Davis
NIGHTMARE IN BLOOD(1978), p, w

Kenny Davis
1984
GREMLINS(1984)

Kevin Davis
HOAX, THE(1972), w

L.J. Davis
DESPERATE CHARACTERS(1971)

Lee Davis
VILLAIN, THE(1979)

Len Davis
I'LL TAKE ROMANCE(1937)

Leo Davis
COLONEL MARCH INVESTIGATES(1952,Brit.), w

Leslie Davis
SQUARE ROOT OF ZERO, THE(1964)

Lew Davis
ONLY ANGELS HAVE WINGS(1939); MEET JOHN DOE(1941); TALK OF THE TOWN(1942)

Lilian Hall Davis
Silents
ADMIRABLE CRICHTON, THE(1918, Brit.); ERNEST MALTRAVERS(1920, Brit.); GAME OF LIFE, THE(1922, Brit.); HOTEL MOUSE, THE(1923, Brit.); KNOCKOUT, THE(1923, Brit.); ELEVENTH COMMANDMENT, THE(1924, Brit.); PASSIONATE ADVENTURE, THE(1924, Brit.)
Misc. Silents
ERNEST MALTRAVERS(1920, Brit.); HONEYPOT, THE(1920, Brit.); RIGHT TO STRIKE, THE(1923); ROYAL DIVORCE, A(1923, Brit.); BLIGHTY(1927, Brit.); WHITE SHEIK, THE(1928, Brit.)

Lillian Davis
JUST FOR A SONG(1930, Brit.)

Lillian Hall Davis
Silents
IF FOUR WALLS TOLD(1922, Brit.)
Misc. Silents
STABLE COMPANIONS(1922, Brit.); MAISIE'S MARRIAGE(1923, Brit.); SHOULD A DOCTOR TELL?(1923, Brit.); QUO VADIS?(1925, Ital.); LA PROIE DU VENT(1927, Fr.)

Lina Davis
FURY AT GUNSIGHT PASS(1956)

Linda Davis
MIDNIGHT COWBOY(1969)

Lindy Davis
SON OF FLUBBER(1963); REIVERS, THE(1969)

Lisa Davis
GLORY(1955); LONG GRAY LINE, THE(1955); VIRGIN QUEEN, THE(1955); SPY CHASERS(1956); BABY FACE NELSON(1957); DALTON GIRLS, THE(1957); QUEEN OF OUTER SPACE(1958); ONE HUNDRED AND ONE DALMATIANS(1961)

Liz Davis
QUACKSER FORTUNE HAS A COUSIN IN THE BRONX(1970)

Lori Davis
BEYOND AND BACK(1978)

Lorrie Davis
GANG THAT COULDN'T SHOOT STRAIGHT, THE(1971); HOSPITAL, THE(1971)

Lou Davis
GIRL WHO CAME BACK, THE(1935); LITTLE RED SCHOOLHOUSE(1936); YOU CAN'T TAKE IT WITH YOU(1938); LONE WOLF SPY HUNT, THE(1939); MEXICAN SPITFIRE AT SEA(1942); GILDERSLEEVE'S BAD DAY(1943); ALONG CAME JONES(1945)

Luther Davis
MAYOR OF 44TH STREET, THE(1942), w; HUCKSTERS, THE(1947), w; B. F.'S DAUGHTER(1948), w; BLACK HAND, THE(1950), w; LION IS IN THE STREETS, A(1953), w; NEW FACES(1954), w; KISMET(1955), w; KISS THEM FOR ME(1957), w; GIFT OF LOVE, THE(1958), w; HOLIDAY FOR LOVERS(1959), w; WONDERS OF ALADDIN, THE(1961, Fr./Ital.), w; LADY IN A CAGE(1964), p, w; ACROSS 110TH STREET(1972), w

Lynn Davis
HOLIDAY RHYTHM(1950)

Mac Davis
NORTH DALLAS FORTY(1979); CHEAPER TO KEEP HER(1980); STING II, THE(1983)

Madelyn Davis
YOURS, MINE AND OURS(1968), w

Marc Davis
SONG OF THE SOUTH(1946), anim; FUN AND FANCY FREE(1947), anim; PETER PAN(1953), anim; ONE HUNDRED AND ONE DALMATIANS(1961), anim

Marcia Davis
P.O.W., THE(1973)

Margaret Davis
THROWBACK, THE(1935); LOVE IS ON THE AIR(1937)

Marianne Davis
SEZ O'REILLY TO MACNAB(1938, Brit.); THURSDAY'S CHILD(1943, Brit.)

Mark Davis
WHICH WAY IS UP?(1977), m; CHEECH AND CHONG'S NEXT MOVIE(1980), m; BUSTIN' LOOSE(1981), m

Marlene Davis
PRESSURE(1976, Brit.)

Martha Davis
SMART POLITICS(1948)

Marvin Aubrey Davis
WESTWARD HO THE WAGONS!(1956), art d; SIGN OF ZORRO, THE(1960), art d; BON VOYAGE(1962), art d; MOON PILOT(1962), art d; SAVAGE SAM(1963), art d; TIGER WALKS, A(1964), art d; FOLLOW ME, BOYS!(1966), art d; UGLY DACHSHUND, THE(1966), art d

Marvin Davis
IN THE MEANTIME, DARLING(1944); SULLIVANS, THE(1944); TOMORROW THE WORLD(1944); SCANDAL IN PARIS, A(1946)

Mary B. Davis
Silents
AMATEUR WIDOW, AN(1919)

Mary Davis
MARK OF THE WITCH(1970), p, w; SCUM OF THE EARTH(1976), w

Maufy Davis
HAPPINESS OF THREE WOMEN, THE(1954, Brit.), w

Maureen Davis
TO PARIS WITH LOVE(1955, Brit.); THIRD KEY, THE(1957, Brit.); TICKET TO PARADISE(1961, Brit.)

Maurice Davis
RACE STREET(1948), w

McClure Davis
TIMBER FURY(1950), art d

Melissa Davis
1984
RIVER RAT, THE(1984)

Michael Davis
ALL THE YOUNG MEN(1960); LET NO MAN WRITE MY EPITAPH(1960); MATTER OF CHOICE, A(1963, Brit.); BALLAD OF A GUNFIGHTER(1964); MOON-SPINNERS, THE(1964); PRODUCERS, THE(1967); FOOLS(1970); MUPPET MOVIE, THE(1979); MARIGOLDS IN AUGUST(1980, South Africa), ph; LONG SHOT(1981, Brit.), ph
1984
MARIGOLDS IN AUGUST(1984, S. Africa), ph

Mike Davis
DOGS(1976); PRESSURE(1976, Brit.), ph

Lt. Col. Mike Davis
THREE STRIPES IN THE SUN(1955)

Mildred Davis
Silents
ALL WRONG(1919); SAILOR-MADE MAN, A(1921); DOCTOR JACK(1922); GRANDMA'S BOY(1922); SAFETY LAST(1923); TEMPORARY MARRIAGE(1923)
Misc. Silents
CONDEMNED(1923); TOO MANY CROOKS(1927)

Miles Davis
FRANTIC(1961, Fr.), m

Mimi Davis
COMMITMENT, THE(1976); S.O.B.(1981)

Monica Davis
DEAD ONE, THE(1961); ROCKET ATTACK, U.S.A.(1961); 1,000 SHAPES OF A FEMALE(1963)

Morgan Davis
Silents
ON THE GO(1925)

Morris C. Davis
SINS OF THE FATHERS(1948, Can.), m

Murray Davis
FREDDIE STEPS OUT(1946); JUNIOR PROM(1946)

Nancy Davis
DOCTOR AND THE GIRL, THE(1949); EAST SIDE, WEST SIDE(1949); SHADOW ON THE WALL(1950); IT'S A BIG COUNTRY(1951); NIGHT INTO MORNING(1951); SHADOW IN THE SKY(1951); TALK ABOUT A STRANGER(1952); DONOVAN'S BRAIN(1953); HELLCATS OF THE NAVY(1957); CRASH LANDING(1958)

Nathan Davis
STONY ISLAND(1978); ON THE RIGHT TRACK(1981); THIEF(1981); RISKY BUSINESS(1983)
1984
WINDY CITY(1984)

Nawana Davis
CISCO PIKE(1971); HAMMER(1972)

Neil Davis
MC MASTERS, THE(1970); GUNFIGHT, A(1971); THOMASINE AND BUSHROD(1974)

Niva Davis
ANGELS HARD AS THEY COME(1971)

Noel Davis
FAHRENHEIT 451(1966, Brit.); TWO A PENNY(1968, Brit.); CLEGG(1969, Brit.); TOUCH OF THE OTHER, A(1970, Brit.); MACBETH(1971, Brit.); YOUNG WINSTON(1972, Brit.)

Oscar Davis
LEGEND OF FRENCHIE KING, THE(1971, Fr./Ital./Span./Brit.); LIGHT AT THE EDGE OF THE WORLD, THE(1971, U.S./Span./Lichtenstein)

Ossie Davis
NO WAY OUT(1950); FOURTEEN HOURS(1951); JOE LOUIS STORY, THE(1953); CARDINAL, THE(1963); GONE ARE THE DAYS(1963), a, w; SHOCK TREATMENT(1964); HILL, THE(1965, Brit.); MAN CALLED ADAM, A(1966); SCALPHUNTERS, THE(1968); SAM WHISKEY(1969); SLAVES(1969); COTTON COMES TO HARLEM(1970), d, w; KONGI'S HARVEST(1971, U.S./Nigeria), d; BLACK GIRL(1972), d; GORDON'S WAR(1973), d; LET'S DO IT AGAIN(1975); COUNTDOWN AT KUSINI(1976, Nigerian), a, d, w; HOT STUFF(1979)
1984
HARRY AND SON(1984); HOUSE OF GOD, THE(1984)
Misc. Talkies
HOUSE OF GOD, THE(1979)

Owen Davis
HAUNTED HOUSE, THE(1928), w; DONOVAN AFFAIR, THE(1929), w; TONIGHT AT TWELVE(1929), w, titles; ONLY SAPS WORK(1930), w; SPRING IS HERE(1930), w; WHOOPEE(1930), w; CONNECTICUT YANKEE, A(1931), w; GIRL HABIT(1931), w; MY SIN(1931), w; LASH, THE(1934, Brit.), w; NINE FORTY-FIVE(1934, Brit.), w; MR. AND MRS. NORTH(1941), w; UP IN ARMS(1944), w; GREAT GATSBY, THE(1949), w; GREAT GATSBY, THE(1974), w

Silents
LOLA(1914), w; WISHING RING, THE(1914), w; FAMILY CUPBOARD, THE(1915), w; SENTIMENTAL LADY, THE(1915), w; BROADWAY AFTER DARK(1924), w; ICEBOUND(1924), w; LIGHTHOUSE BY THE SEA, THE(1924), w; NELLIE, THE BEAUTIFUL CLOAK MODEL(1924), w; LAZYBONES(1925), w; FOREVER AFTER(1926), w; NERVOUS WRECK, THE(1926), w; BLIND ALLEYS(1927), w; EASY COME, EASY GO(1928), w; HOLD 'EM YALE!(1928), w

Owen Davis, Jr.
THEY HAD TO SEE PARIS(1929); ALL QUIET ON THE WESTERN FRONT(1930); GOOD INTENTIONS(1930); BUNKER BEAN(1936); GRAND JURY(1936); MURDER ON A BRIDLE PATH(1936); PLOT THICKENS, THE(1936); SPECIAL INVESTIGATOR(1936); IT COULD HAPPEN TO YOU(1937); LUCK OF ROARING CAMP, THE(1937); WOMAN I LOVE, THE(1937); TOUCHDOWN, ARMY(1938); HENRY GOES ARIZONA(1939); THESE GLAMOUR GIRLS(1939); THOU SHALT NOT KILL(1939); KNUTE ROCKNE–ALL AMERICAN(1940)

Owen Davis, Sr.
THEY HAD TO SEE PARIS(1929), w; SO THIS IS LONDON(1930), w; THREE MARRIED MEN(1936), w

Pamela Davis
VALUE FOR MONEY(1957, Brit.); TOO HOT TO HANDLE(1961, Brit.), ch; DREAM MAKER, THE(1963, Brit.), ch

Pat Davis
MIRACLE OF THE BELLS, THE(1948)

Patricia Davis
CURSE OF THE PINK PANTHER(1983)
Misc. Talkies
RAISING THE ROOF(1971, Brit.)

Patrick Davis
THEY WERE EXPENDABLE(1945)

Paul Davis
WAR AND PEACE(1956, Ital./U.S.); CHILDREN OF RAGE(1975, Brit.-Israeli), ed; SHE DANCES ALONE(1981, Aust./U.S.), w

Paula Earlette Davis
D.C. CAB(1983)

Peggy Davis
Silents
NET, THE(1923)

Pepper Davis
GEORGE RAFT STORY, THE(1961); WHEN THE BOYS MEET THE GIRLS(1965)

Percy Davis
CHANGE OF SEASONS, A(1980)

Peter Davis
JUST WILLIAM'S LUCK(1948, Brit.)

Peter S. Davis
STEEL(1980), p, w; O'HARA'S WIFE(1983), p; OSTERMAN WEEKEND, THE(1983), p

Philip Davis
MR. QUILP(1975, Brit.); QUADROPHENIA(1979, Brit.); PINK FLOYD–THE WALL(1982, Brit.)
1984
BOUNTY, THE(1984)

Phyllis Davis
LAST OF THE SECRET AGENTS?, THE(1966); LIVE A LITTLE, LOVE A LITTLE(1968); DAY OF THE DOLPHIN, THE(1973); TERMINAL ISLAND(1973); CHOIRBOYS, THE(1977)

Phyllis E. Davis
TRAIN RIDE TO HOLLYWOOD(1975)

Phyllis Elizabeth Davis
SWEET SUGAR(1972)

R. J. Davis
RIGHT TO LIVE, THE(1933, Brit.), w; BADGER'S GREEN(1934, Brit.), w; ROLLING IN MONEY(1934, Brit.), w

Ray Davis
SIERRA SUE(1941); HALF A SIXPENCE(1967, Brit.)

Raymond Davis
CUP FEVER(1965, Brit.)

Red Davis
SARUMBA(1950)

Redd Davis
HERE'S GEORGE(1932, Brit.), d; ASK BECCLES(1933, Brit.), d; EXCESS BAGGAGE(1933, Brit.), d; MEDICINE MAN, THE(1933, Brit.), d; UMBRELLA, THE(1933, Brit.), d; EASY MONEY(1934, Brit.), p&d; GIRL IN THE FLAT, THE(1934, Brit.), p&d; SEEING IS BELIEVING(1934, Brit.), d; HANDLE WITH CARE(1935, Brit.), d; SAY IT WITH DIAMONDS(1935, Brit.), p&d; EVERYTHING OKAY(1936, Brit.), d; EXCUSE MY GLOVE(1936, Brit.), d; KING OF THE CASTLE(1936, Brit.), d; BITER BIT, THE(1937, Brit.), d; SING AS YOU SWING(1937, Brit.), d; UNDERNEATH THE ARCHES(1937, Brit.), d; VARIETY HOUR(1937, Brit.), d; DISCOVERIES(1939, Brit.), d, w; THAT'S THE TICKET(1940, Brit.), d; BALLOON GOES UP, THE(1942, Brit.), d

Rex Davis
Silents
HOUSE OF TEMPERLEY, THE(1913, Brit.); PRIDE OF THE FANCY, THE(1920, Brit.); WON BY A HEAD(1920, Brit.); ALL SORTS AND CONDITIONS OF MEN(1921, Brit.); CRIMSON CIRCLE, THE(1922, Brit.); LION'S MOUSE, THE(1922, Brit.); KNOCKOUT, THE(1923, Brit.); EVERY MOTHER'S SON(1926, Brit.)
Misc. Silents
FOR HER PEOPLE(1914, Brit.); SHEPHERD LASSIE OF ARGYLE, THE(1914, Brit.); CRIMSON CIRCLE, THE(1922, Brit.); COUPLE OF DOWN AND OUTS, A(1923, Brit.); MAISIE'S MARRIAGE(1923, Brit.); REMEMBRANCE(1927, Brit.)

Richard Davis
HAT CHECK HONEY(1944); CHINA'S LITTLE DEVILS(1945), w; MAGIC WORLD OF TOPO GIGIO, THE(1961, Ital.), p; SOME PEOPLE(1964, Brit.); MIDSUMMER NIGHT'S DREAM, A(1966), p; NEW HOUSE ON THE LEFT, THE(1978, Brit.); STONY ISLAND(1978)
Misc. Talkies
BLANCHEVILLE MONSTER(1963); LAST STOP ON THE NIGHT TRAIN(1976)

Richard Harding Davis
BAR SINISTER, THE(1955), w
Silents
MAN WHO COULD NOT LOSE, THE(1914), w; LAST CHAPTER, THE(1915), w; RANSON'S FOLLY(1915), w; DICTATOR, THE(1922), w; EXILES, THE(1923), w;

SCARLET CAR, THE(1923), w; STEPHEN STEPS OUT(1923), w; RANSON'S FOLLY(1926), w; LET 'ER GO GALLEGHER(1928), w; FUGITIVES(1929), w

Rick Davis
SAM WHISKEY(1969)

Robert Davis
POSTAL INSPECTOR(1936); CONFESSIONS OF A NAZI SPY(1939); NAZI AGENT(1942); LONG NIGHT, THE(1947); IN A LONELY PLACE(1950); NO WAY OUT(1950); HE RAN ALL THE WAY(1951); LION HUNTERS, THE(1951); RED BALL EXPRESS(1952); FEMALE JUNGLE, THE(1955); LIONHEART(1968, Brit.)

Robert A. Davis
KNOCK ON ANY DOOR(1949); GLENN MILLER STORY, THE(1953); JAMAICA RUN(1953)

Robert H. Davis
MIRACLE MAN, THE(1932), w
Silents
STAIN, THE(1914), w

Robert O. Davis
ESCAPE TO PARADISE(1939); ESPIONAGE AGENT(1939); FOUR SONS(1940); GREAT DICTATOR, THE(1940); MEET THE WILDCAT(1940); DANGEROUS GAME, A(1941); DOWN IN SAN DIEGO(1941); UNDERGROUND(1941); DESPERATE JOURNEY(1942); GREAT IMPERSONATION, THE(1942); PHANTOM PLAINSMEN, THE(1942); RIDERS OF THE NORTHLAND(1942); SHERLOCK HOLMES AND THE SECRET WEAPON(1942); SHERLOCK HOLMES AND THE VOICE OF TERROR(1942); TO BE OR NOT TO BE(1942); JUNIOR ARMY(1943); THEY GOT ME COVERED(1943); TONIGHT WE RAID CALAIS(1943)

Robert O. Davis [Rudolph Anders]
KNUTE ROCKNE–ALL AMERICAN(1940); MORTAL STORM, THE(1940); WATCH ON THE RHINE(1943)

Robert P. Davis
PILOT, THE(1979), w, prod d

Robert-Hartford Davis
BLACK GUNN(1972), w

Robin Davis
BLOOD ON SATAN'S CLAW, THE(1970, Brit.)

Rocky Davis
IN MACARTHUR PARK(1977), m

Roger Davis
ARE YOU THERE?(1930); THAT CERTAIN WOMAN(1937); YOUTH TAKES A FLING(1938); BELLE OF NEW YORK, THE(1952); RIDE THE WILD SURF(1964); HOUSE OF DARK SHADOWS(1970); FLASH AND THE FIRECAT(1976); NEW GIRL IN TOWN(1977); RUBY(1977)
1984
ACT, THE(1984)
Silents
SOCIAL CELEBRITY, A(1926)

Rosemary Davis
IDOL ON PARADE(1959, Brit.)

Roy Davis
Misc. Talkies
SURABAYA CONSPIRACY(1975), d

Roy Milton Davis
SOLDIER, THE(1982)

Rufe Davis
BIG BROADCAST OF 1938, THE(1937); BLOSSOMS ON BROADWAY(1937); MOUNTAIN MUSIC(1937); THIS WAY PLEASE(1937); COCOANUT GROVE(1938); DR. RHYTHM(1938); AMBUSH(1939); SOME LIKE IT HOT(1939); BARNYARD FOLLIES(1940); LONE STAR RAIDERS(1940); TRAIL BLAZERS, THE(1940); UNDER TEXAS SKIES(1940); GANGS OF SONORA(1941); GAUCHOS OF EL DORADO(1941); OUTLAWS OF THE CHEROKEE TRAIL(1941); PALS OF THE PECOS(1941); PRAIRIE PIONEERS(1941); SADDLEMATES(1941); WEST OF CIMARRON(1941); CODE OF THE OUTLAW(1942); PHANTOM PLAINSMEN, THE(1942); RAIDERS OF THE RANGE(1942); WESTWARD HO(1942); JAMBOREE(1944); GEORGE WHITE'S SCANDALS(1945); RADIO STARS ON PARADE(1945); STRAWBERRY ROAN, THE(1948); JOE PALOOKA IN TRIPLE CROSS(1951); ANGEL IN MY POCKET(1969)

Rupert Davis
CRIMSON CULT, THE(1970, Brit.)

Russell Davis
MEDIUM COOL(1969)

Sal Davis
SYNDICATE, THE(1968, Brit.)

Sally Davis
HARPOON(1948)

Sammy Davis, Jr.
ANNA LUCASTA(1958); PORGY AND BESS(1959); OCEAN'S ELEVEN(1960); PEPE(1960); CONVICTS FOUR(1962); SERGEANTS 3(1962); JOHNNY COOL(1963); THREE PENNY OPERA(1963, Fr./Ger.); NIGHTMARE IN THE SUN(1964); ROBIN AND THE SEVEN HOODS(1964); MAN CALLED ADAM, A(1966); SALT & PEPPER(1968, Brit.); SWEET CHARITY(1969); ONE MORE TIME(1970, Brit.); SAMMY STOPS THE WORLD zero(1978); CANNONBALL RUN, THE(1981); HEIDI'S SONG(1982)
1984
CANNONBALL RUN II(1984)
Misc. Talkies
GONE WITH THE WEST(1976)

Samuel Davis
ROCKY II(1979)

Scott R. Davis
1984
FIRESTARTER(1984)

Shelly Davis
LOVE GOD?, THE(1969)

Shirley Davis
PRINCE OF THE PLAINS(1949)

Sian Davis
POOR COW(1968, Brit.)

Sid Davis
V.D.(1961), p

Simon Davis
INTERLUDE(1968, Brit.); 2001: A SPACE ODYSSEY(1968, U.S./Brit.)

Skeeter Davis
FORTY ACRE FEUD(1965); COUNTRY BOY(1966); GOLD GUITAR, THE(1966)

Sol Davis
HOODLUM SAINT, THE(1946)

Sonny Carl Davis
1984
LAST NIGHT AT THE ALAMO(1984)

Sonny Davis
WHOLE SHOOTIN' MATCH, THE(1979); MELVIN AND HOWARD(1980); ROADIE(1980); WHERE THE BUFFALO ROAM(1980); WHY WOULD I LIE(1980); FAST TIMES AT RIDGEMONT HIGH(1982); WACKO(1983)

Spencer Davis
WRONG MAN, THE(1956); PIE IN THE SKY(1964)

Stanley Davis
HERE COMES ELMER(1943), w; HAT CHECK HONEY(1944), w; MURDER IN THE BLUE ROOM(1944), w; SLIGHTLY TERRIFIC(1944), w; SEE MY LAWYER(1945), w

Stanley Davis, Jr.
FAST TIMES AT RIDGEMONT HIGH(1982)

Stephen Davis
LONG GOOD FRIDAY, THE(1982, Brit.)

Steve Davis
ROSE BOWL STORY, THE(1952); BATTLE BEYOND THE STARS(1980); SWORD AND THE SORCERER, THE(1982)

Stratford Davis
VIOLENT STRANGER(1957, Brit.), w

Stringer Davis
MIRANDA(1949, Brit.); HAPPIEST DAYS OF YOUR LIFE(1950, Brit.); CASTLE IN THE AIR(1952, Brit.); CURTAIN UP(1952, Brit.); MAD ABOUT MEN(1954, Brit.); RUNAWAY BUS, THE(1954, Brit.); INNOCENTS IN PARIS(1955, Brit.); MARCH HARE, THE(1956, Brit.); JUST MY LUCK(1957, Brit.); SMALLEST SHOW ON EARTH, THE(1957, Brit.); I'M ALL RIGHT, JACK(1959, Brit.); MURDER SHE SAID(1961, Brit.); MOUSE ON THE MOON, THE(1963, Brit.); MURDER AT THE GALLOP(1963, Brit.); V.I.P.s, THE(1963, Brit.); MURDER AHOY(1964, Brit.); MURDER MOST FOUL(1964, Brit.)

Susan Davis
WARGAMES(1983)

Sylvia Davis
ALICE'S RESTAURANT(1969)

T. Battle Davis
NINTH CONFIGURATION, THE(1980), ed

Teo Davis
LONG SHOT(1981, Brit.), ph

Terry Davis
MARS NEEDS WOMEN(1966)

Tess Davis
REDS(1981)

Tim Davis
RIDERS OF THE DAWN(1937); TEX RIDES WITH THE BOY SCOUTS(1937); GAMBLING SHIP(1939); OUR TOWN(1940); BAMBI(1942)

Tom Davis
TUNNELVISION(1976); TRADING PLACES(1983)

Tommy Davis
NOTORIOUS CLEOPATRA, THE(1970); BLACK GUNN(1972)

Tony Davis
GUNS OF THE MAGNIFICENT SEVEN(1969)

Tudor Davis
LOST CHORD, THE(1937, Brit.)

Tyrell Davis
HIS GLORIOUS NIGHT(1929); DANCERS, THE(1930); LOVE IN THE ROUGH(1930); PAID(1930); STRICTLY UNCONVENTIONAL(1930); GOD'S GIFT TO WOMEN(1931); MURDER AT MIDNIGHT(1931); ROAD TO SINGAPORE(1931); UNEXPECTED FATHER(1932); BLIND ADVENTURE(1933); DANGEROUSLY YOURS(1933); OUR BETTERS(1933); PEG O' MY HEART(1933); DESIGNING WOMEN(1934, Brit.); FREEDOM OF THE SEAS(1934, Brit.); ALL AT SEA(1935, Brit.); UNDER PROOF(1936, Brit.); DINNER AT THE RITZ(1937, Brit.); SECOND BEST BED(1937, Brit.); STRANGE BOARDERS(1938, Brit.)

Tyrrel Davis
Misc. Talkies
LOVE IN HIGH GEAR(1932)

Tyrrell Davis
LUCKY IN LOVE(1929); MOTHER'S BOY(1929); LET US BE GAY(1930); PRINCE OF DIAMONDS(1930); RAIN OR SHINE(1930); CHANCES(1931); MAGNIFICENT LIE(1931)

Ulysses Davis
Misc. Silents
IRON HAND, THE(1916), d; SOUL'S CYCLE, THE(1916), d

Ursula Davis
Misc. Talkies
TERROR IN THE CRYPT(1963, Span./Ital.); ANGEL FOR SATAN, AN(1966, Ital.)

Valentine Davis
THREE LITTLE GIRLS IN BLUE(1946), w

Vance Davis
FORTUNE AND MEN'S EYES(1971, U.S./Can.); CAHILL, UNITED STATES MARSHAL(1973); FINAL CHAPTER–WALKING TALL zero(1977)

Vic Davis
HARD TRAIL(1969), ed

Vince Davis
MOUSE AND HIS CHILD, THE(1977), anim

Violet Davis
Silents
SALAMANDER, THE(1915)

Virginia Davis
STREET SCENE(1931); THREE ON A MATCH(1932)

Viveka Davis
SHOOT THE MOON(1982)

W. Terry Davis
H.O.T.S.(1979), p

W.H. Davis
IT'S A SMALL WORLD(1935); STORMY(1935)

Walt Davis
CHEYENNE SOCIAL CLUB, THE(1970); SUBSTITUTION(1970), p&d; SHAGGY
D.A., THE(1976); MR. BILLION(1977)

Walter Davis
THIS COULD BE THE NIGHT(1957)
Misc. Silents
WHISPERING WOMEN(1921)

Warwick Davis
RETURN OF THE JEDI(1983)

Wee Willie Davis
SHADOW OF THE THIN MAN(1941); GENTLEMAN JIM(1942); JOHNNY COME
LATELY(1943); GHOST CATCHERS(1944); PURSUIT TO ALGIERS(1945); WILD-
FIRE(1945); NIGHT IN PARADISE, A(1946); FOXES OF HARROW, THE(1947);
MIGHTY JOE YOUNG(1949); RED PONY, THE(1949); ABBOTT AND COSTELLO IN
THE FOREIGN LEGION(1950); BODYHOLD(1950); SON OF PALEFACE(1952);
WORLD IN HIS ARMS, THE(1952); TO CATCH A THIEF(1955)

"Wee Willie" Davis
ARABIAN NIGHTS(1942)

Wee Willie [William] Davis
REAP THE WILD WIND(1942)

Will Davis
Misc. Silents
CURIOUS CONDUCT OF JUDGE LEGARDE, THE(1915), d

Will H. Davis
Silents
THOU SHALT NOT(1914), d&w

Will S. Davis
Silents
IN THE STRETCH(1914), w; DESTRUCTION(1915), d&w
Misc. Silents
THROUGH DANTE'S FLAMES(1914); AVALANCHE, THE(1915), d; DR. RA-
MEAU(1915), d; FAMILY STAIN, THE(1915), d; MODERN MAGDALEN, A(1915), d;
FOOL'S REVENGE, THE(1916), d; JEALOUSY(1916), d; SLANDER(1916), d;
STRAIGHT WAY, THE(1916), d; TORTURED HEART, A(1916), d; VICTIM,
THE(1916), d; MOTHER'S ORDEAL, A(1917), d; IN JUDGEMENT OF(1918), d; NO
MAN'S LAND(1918), d

William Davis
ASPHALT JUNGLE, THE(1950)
Misc. Silents
ETERNAL MOTHER, THE(1921), d; INDISCRETION(1921), d

William B. Davis
DEATH VALLEY(1946), p

William S. Davis
Silents
ALIAS MRS. JESSOP(1917), d
Misc. Silents
BRASS CHECK, THE(1918), d; UNDER SUSPICION(1918), d; WITH NEATNESS
AND DISPATCH(1918), d

William "Wee Willie" Davis
ABOVE SUSPICION(1943); HAVING WONDERFUL CRIME(1945); BOWERY BOMB-
SHELL(1946); FOOL'S GOLD(1946); SAMSON AND DELILAH(1949)

Willie Davis
WHICH WAY TO THE FRONT?(1970)

Windsor Davis
ARRIVEDERCI, BABY!(1966, Brit.)

Winifred Davis
SPELL OF AMY NUGENT, THE(1945, Brit.)

Wray Davis
HELL'S HORIZON(1955), a, p; YANK IN VIET-NAM, A(1964), p
Misc. Talkies
DEADLY GAME, THE(1974), d

Yvette Davis
THERE'S ALWAYS A THURSDAY(1957, Brit.)

Zala Davis
Silents
MEASURE OF A MAN, THE(1924)

Zoe Davis
RIVERSIDE MURDER, THE(1935, Brit.)

Davis and Johnson
CASA MANANA(1951)

Sammy Davis, Sr.
BENNY GOODMAN STORY, THE(1956)

Dona Davis-Steckling
DOCTOR DETROIT(1983)

Bert Davison
RIGHT CROSS(1950)

Betty Davison
Misc. Talkies
GHOST OF CROSSBONES CANYON, THE(1952)

Bruce Davison
LAST SUMMER(1969); STRAWBERRY STATEMENT, THE(1970); WILLARD(1971);
JERUSALEM FILE, THE(1972, U.S./Israel); ULZANA'S RAID(1972); MAME(1974);
MOTHER, JUGS & SPEED(1976); BEEN DOWN SO LONG IT LOOKS LIKE UP TO
ME(1977); SHORT EYES(1977); BRASS TARGET(1978); FRENCH QUARTER(1978);
HIGH RISK(1981)
1984
CRIMES OF PASSION(1984); LIES(1984, Brit.)
Misc. Talkies
GRAND JURY(1977); KISS MY GRITS(1982); LIES(1983)

Burke Davison
TORCH SINGER(1933)

D. E. Davison [Alan Davis]
MOONSHINER'S WOMAN(1968), p&d

Davey Davison
STRANGLER, THE(1964); MARRIAGE ON THE ROCKS(1965); WAR PARTY(1965);
ANGEL, ANGEL, DOWN WE GO(1969)

Donn Davison
BEYOND THE DOOR(1975, Ital./U.S.), spec eff; FORCE BEYOND, THE(1978), p, w

Dore Davison
Silents
JOAN OF THE WOODS(1918)

Doris Davison
CASE OF CHARLES PEACE, THE(1949, Brit.), w

Grace Davison
Silents
SPLENDID LIE, THE(1922)
Misc. Silents
SUSPICION(1918); ATONEMENT(1920); HIDDEN CODE, THE(1920); MAN'S PLAY-
THING(1920); LOVE, HATE AND A WOMAN(1921)

Jess Davison
MONSTER FROM THE GREEN HELL(1958), spec eff

John Davison
WHITE DOG(1982), p

John Porter Davison
KNACK ... AND HOW TO GET IT, THE(1965, Brit.); GIRL GETTERS, THE(1966,
Brit.); HANNIBAL BROOKS(1969, Brit.)

Jon Davison
HOLLYWOOD BOULEVARD(1976), p; PIRANHA(1978), p; AIRPLANE!(1980), p

Martin Davison
MOON ZERO TWO(1970, Brit.), w

Michelle Davison
INDEPENDENCE DAY(1976); BOSS'S SON, THE(1978); ENDANGERED SPE-
CIES(1982)
1984
HEARTBREAKERS(1984)

Nancy Davison
WHO SAYS I CAN'T RIDE A RAINBOW!(1971)

Philip Davison
CRIMINAL CONVERSATION(1980, Ireland), w

Steve Davison
KING OF THE MOUNTAIN(1981)

Tito Davison
MUSHROOM EATER, THE(1976, Mex.), w

Tito H. Davison
STAMBOUL QUEST(1934)

John Davisson
ONCE BEFORE I DIE(1967, U.S./Phil.), ed

Steve Davita
NOCTURNA(1979), art d

Hal Davitt
CAPTAIN THUNDER(1931), w

Theodora Davitt
BUCCANEER, THE(1958); PARTY CRASHERS, THE(1958); BEST OF EVERY-
THING, THE(1959); ERRAND BOY, THE(1961)

Jose Marco Davo
NIGHT HEAVEN FELL, THE(1958, Fr.); SPANISH AFFAIR(1958, Span.); MAN WHO
WAGGED HIS TAIL, THE(1961, Ital./Span.); DEVIL MADE A WOMAN, THE(1962,
Span.); INVINCIBLE GLADIATOR, THE(1963, c.u. Ital./Span.); SOFT SKIN ON
BLACK SILK(1964, Fr./Span.); REDEEMER, THE(1965, Span.); EVERY DAY IS A
HOLIDAY(1966, Span.)

Marco Davo
THUNDERSTORM(1956)

Amos Davoli
SEVEN HILLS OF ROME, THE(1958); EMPTY CANVAS, THE(1964, Fr./Ital.);
HORNET'S NEST(1970)

Ivano Davoli
THREE FACES OF A WOMAN(1965, Ital.)

Ninetto Davoli
HAWKS AND THE SPARROWS, THE(1967, Ital.); TEOREMA(1969, Ital.); WITCHES,
THE(1969, Fr./Ital.); FRANKENSTEIN-ITALIAN STYLE(1977, Ital.); ARABIAN
NIGHTS(1980, Ital./Fr.)

Pietro Davoli
HAWKS AND THE SPARROWS, THE(1967, Ital.)

Dominique Davray
CASQUE D'OR(1956, Fr.); BIG CHIEF, THE(1960, Fr.); CLEO FROM 5 TO 7(1961, Fr.);
ANY NUMBER CAN WIN(1963 Fr.); HOW NOT TO ROB A DEPARTMENT STO-
RE(1965, Fr./Ital.); FLEA IN HER EAR, A(1968, Fr.); PARIS IN THE MONTH OF
AUGUST(1968, Fr.); GOING PLACES(1974, Fr.)

Dominque Davray
TO CATCH A THIEF(1955)

Jo Davray
BITTER VICTORY(1958, Fr.)

Denise Davreux
MILLION EYES OF SU-MURU, THE(1967, Brit.)

Serge Davri
SHOOT THE PIANO PLAYER(1962, Fr.); ARMY GAME, THE(1963, Fr.); SIX IN
PARIS(1968, Fr.)

Ann Davy
MORE DEADLY THAN THE MALE(1961, Brit.)

Hope Davy
C.O.D.(1932, Brit.); HOUSE OF TRENT, THE(1933, Brit.); TROUBLE(1933, Brit.);
ADMIRAL'S SECRET, THE(1934, Brit.); JOSSER ON THE FARM(1934, Brit.); RIVER
WOLVES, THE(1934, Brit.); SORRELL AND SON(1934, Brit.); NIGHT MAIL(1935,
Brit.); THAT'S MY UNCLE(1935, Brit.); SHE KNEW WHAT SHE WANTED(1936, Brit.);
THEY DIDN'T KNOW(1936, Brit.)

Jean Davy
CARNIVAL OF SINNERS(1947, Fr.); NAKED WOMAN, THE(1950, Fr.); GIRL FROM
LORRAINE, A(1982, Fr./Switz.)

Jean-Francois Davy
EROTIQUE(1969, Fr.), d, w

Pamela Ann Davy
AMSTERDAM AFFAIR, THE(1968 Brit.)

Peter Davy
LORD OF THE FLIES(1963, Brit.)

Anatoly Davydov
GORKY PARK(1983)

Rostislav Davydov
KATERINA IZMAILOVA(1969, USSR), ph

Carolyn Davys
GUNMEN OF THE RIO GRANDE(1965, Fr./Ital./Span.)

Evelyn Daw
SOMETHING TO SING ABOUT(1937); PANAMINT'S BAD MAN(1938); PALS OF THE SILVER SAGE(1940)

Jonathan Daw
2001: A SPACE ODYSSEY(1968, U.S./Brit.)

Majorie Daw
Silents
HEADIN' SOUTH(1918)

Marjorie Daw
Silents
CAPTIVE, THE(1915); PUPPET CROWN, THE(1915); SECRET ORCHARD(1915); JOAN THE WOMAN(1916); MODERN MUSKETEER, A(1917); REBECCA OF SUNNY-BROOK FARM(1917); ARIZONA(1918); MR. FIX-IT(1918); SAY! YOUNG FEL-LOW(1918); HIS MAJESTY THE AMERICAN(1919); KNICKERBOCKER BUCKAROO, THE(1919); DINTY(1920); BOB HAMPTON OF PLACER(1921); CHEAT-ED HEARTS(1921); FIFTY CANDLES(1921); PATSY(1921); LONG CHANCE, THE(1922); LOVE IS AN AWFUL THING(1922); LYING TRUTH, THE(1922); PEN-ROD(1922); PRIDE OF PALOMAR, THE(1922); RUPERT OF HENTZAU(1923); GAM-BLING WIVES(1924); HUMAN DESIRES(1924, Brit.); PASSIONATE ADVENTURE, THE(1924, Brit.); REVELATION(1924); HIS MASTER'S VOICE(1925); IN BORROWED PLUMES(1926); REDHEADS PREFERRED(1926); OUTLAWS OF RED RIVER(1927)
Misc. Silents
GOLDEN GODDESS, THE(1916); CONSCIENCE(1917); JAGUAR'S CLAWS(1917); HE COMES UP SMILING(1918); DON'T EVER MARRY(1920); GREAT REDEEMER, THE(1920); RIVER'S END, THE(1920); BUTTERFLY GIRL, THE(1921); EXPERIEN-CE(1921); LONE HAND, THE(1922); SAGEBRUSH TRAIL, THE(1922); BAREFOOT BOY, THE(1923); CALL OF THE CANYON, THE(1923); WANDERING DAUGHT-ERS(1923); GREATER THAN MARRIAGE(1924); NOTCH NUMBER ONE(1924); VIR-GINIAN OUTCAST(1924); FEAR-BOUND(1925); ONE WAY STREET(1925); HIGHBINDERS, THE(1926); SPOILERS OF THE WEST(1927)

Pamela Dawber
WEDDING, A(1978)

David R. Dawdy
NAKED ANGELS(1969), p; SKI BUM, THE(1971), p

Cedric Dawe
FREEDOM OF THE SEAS(1934, Brit.), art d; OLD CURIOSITY SHOP, THE(1935, Brit.), art d; HEART'S DESIRE(1937, Brit.), set d; TEMPTATION HARBOR(1949, Brit.), art d; ANOTHER MAN'S POISON(1952, Brit.), art d; LIMPING MAN, THE(1953, Brit.), art d; STAR OF INDIA(1956, Brit.), art d; TEARS FOR SIMON(1957, Brit.), art d; FLOODS OF FEAR(1958, Brit.), art d; DAY OF THE TRIFFIDS, THE(1963), art d; WHERE'S JACK?(1969, Brit.), prod d

Jack Dawe
GIRDLE OF GOLD(1952, Brit.), w

Kathryn Dawe
EGGHEAD'S ROBOT(1970, Brit.)

Ray Dawe
AMAZING DR. CLITTERHOUSE, THE(1938); LET'S GO NAVY(1951)

Rex Dawe
WHEREVER SHE GOES(1953, Aus.)

Anthony Dawes
EMERGENCY(1962, Brit.); DREAM MAKER, THE(1963, Brit.); BARRY LYN-DON(1975, Brit.)
1984
CHAMPIONS(1984)

Darlene Dawes
RAVAGER, THE(1970)

Deborah Dawes
HISTORY OF THE WORLD, PART 1(1981)

Dorothy Dawes
MURDER AT THE VANITIES(1934)

Harry Dawes
OLD FAITHFUL(1935, Brit.), w

Tom Dawes
MINX, THE(1969), m

Richard Dawking
MONTY PYTHON'S THE MEANING OF LIFE(1983, Brit.), art d
1984
ELECTRIC DREAMS(1984), art d

Henry B. Dawkins
BEING THERE(1979)

Monica Dawkins
OUTBACK(1971, Aus.), makeup

Paul Dawkins
FAR FROM THE MADDING CROWD(1967, Brit.); CONQUEROR WORM, THE(1968, Brit.); HOT MILLIONS(1968, Brit.); WORK IS A FOUR LETTER WORD(1968, Brit.); LOCK UP YOUR DAUGHTERS(1969, Brit.); WALK A CROOKED PATH(1969, Brit.); LAST GRENADE, THE(1970, Brit.); MY LOVER, MY SON(1970, Brit.); O LUCKY MAN!(1973, Brit.)

Bert Dawley
Silents
AS A MAN LIVES(1923), ph; HAS THE WORLD GONE MAD!(1923), ph

J. Searle Dawley
Silents
GOOD LITTLE DEVIL, A(1914), d; MRS. BLACK IS BACK(1914), d; MYSTERY OF THE POISON POOL, THE(1914), w; PRIDE OF JENNICO, THE(1914), d; SALOMY JANE(1914), d; FOUR FEATHERS(1915), d&w; STILL WATERS(1915), d; MICE AND MEN(1916), d; OUT OF THE DRIFTS(1916), d; RAINBOW PRINCESS, THE(1916), d; BAB'S BURGLAR(1917), d; BAB'S DIARY(1917), d; BEYOND PRICE(1921), d; AS A MAN LIVES(1923), d; HAS THE WORLD GONE MAD!(1923), d

Misc. Silents
CAPRICE(1913), d; IN THE BISHOP'S CARRIAGE(1913), d; LADY OF QUALITY, A(1913), d; LEAH KLESCHNA(1913), d; PORT OF DOOM, THE(1913), d; AMERICAN CITIZEN, AN(1914), d; IN THE NAME OF THE PRINCE OF PEACE(1914), d; MARTA OF THE LOWLANDS(1914), d; ONE OF MILLIONS(1914), d; WOMAN'S TRIUMPH, A(1914), d; ALWAYS IN THE WAY(1915), d; DAUGHTER OF THE PEOPLE, A(1915), d; HELENE OF THE NORTH(1915), d; LITTLE LADY EILEEN(1916), d; MISS GEORGE WASHINGTON(1916), d; MOLLY MAKE-BELIEVE(1916), d; SILKS AND SATINS(1916), d; BAB'S MATINEE IDOL(1917), d; MYSTERIOUS MISS TERRY, THE(1917), d; SNOW WHITE(1917), d; VALENTINE GIRL, THE(1917), d; DEATH DANCE, THE(1918), d; LIE, THE(1918), d; RICH MAN, POOR MAN(1918), d; SEVEN SWANS, THE(1918), d; UNCLE TOM'S CABIN(1918), d; PHANTOM HONEYMOON, THE(1919), d; TWILIGHT(1919), d; HARVEST MOON, THE(1920), d; VIRGIN PARA-DISE, A(1921), d; WHO ARE MY PARENTS?(1922), d; BROADWAY BROKE(1923), d

Janet Dawley
Misc. Silents
MARTYRDOM OF PHILLIP STRONG, THE(1916)

April Dawn
LORD OF THE MANOR(1933, Brit.); YOUNG WARRIORS(1983)

Bob Dawn
SPY CHASERS(1956), makeup; MARNIE(1964), makeup; PAJAMA PARTY(1964), makeup; 2000 YEARS LATER(1969), makeup; BLACK SUNDAY(1977), makeup

Consuelo Dawn
Misc. Talkies
TWO GUN CABALLERO(1931)

Doreen Dawn
CONSTANT HUSBAND, THE(1955, Brit.); EXTRA DAY, THE(1956, Brit.); ROOM AT THE TOP(1959, Brit.); MASQUE OF THE RED DEATH, THE(1964, U.S./Brit.)

Dorothy Dawn
Silents
PERILS OF THE COAST GUARD(1926); OBEY YOUR HUSBAND(1928); OUT WITH THE TIDE(1928)

Dorren Dawn
SECOND FIDDLE(1957, Brit.)

Gloria Dawn
THEY'RE A WEIRD MOB(1966, Aus.); MANGO TREE, THE(1981, Aus.)

Hazel Dawn
YOUNGEST PROFESSION, THE(1943); MARGIE(1946)
Silents
ONE OF OUR GIRLS(1914); MASQUERADERS, THE(1915); NIOBE(1915); MY LADY INCOG(1916)
Misc. Silents
GAMBLER'S ADVOCATE(1915); HEART OF JENNIFER, THE(1915); FEUD GIRL, THE(1916); SALESLADY, THE(1916); UNDER COVER(1916); LONE WOLF, THE(1917); DEVOTION(1921)

Isabel Dawn
IF I HAD A MILLION(1932), w; DON'T BET ON BLONDES(1935), w; MOON'S OUR HOME, THE(1936), w; WINGS OVER HONOLULU(1937), w; GIRL OF THE GOLDEN WEST, THE(1938), w; BEHIND THE NEWS(1941), w; ICE-CAPADES(1941), w; LADY FOR A NIGHT(1941), w; MAN BETRAYED, A(1941), w; REMEMBER PEARL HAR-BOR(1942), w; TRAGEDY AT MIDNIGHT, A(1942), w; YOKEL BOY(1942), w; GOOD-NIGHT SWEETHEART(1944), w; SINGIN' IN THE CORN(1946), w; FRENCH LINE, THE(1954), w; FEMALE ANIMAL, THE(1958)

Isobel Dawn
UP IN MABEL'S ROOM(1944), w

Jack Dawn
MARK OF THE VAMPIRE(1935), makeup; RECKLESS(1935), makeup; PICK A STAR(1937), makeup; WAY OUT WEST(1937), makeup; MARIE ANTOINETTE(1938), makeup; MIRACLES FOR SALE(1939), makeup; NINOTCHKA(1939), makeup; WIZ-ARD OF OZ, THE(1939), makeup; EDISON, THE MAN(1940), makeup; LITTLE NELLIE KELLY(1940), makeup; MAN FROM DAKOTA, THE(1940), makeup; MOR-TAL STORM, THE(1940), makeup; NEW MOON(1940), makeup; NORTHWEST PAS-SAGE(1940), makeup; PHILADELPHIA STORY, THE(1940), makeup; PRIDE AND PREJUDICE(1940), makeup; STRIKE UP THE BAND(1940), makeup; DR. JEKYLL AND MR. HYDE(1941), makeup; SMILIN' THROUGH(1941), makeup; ZIEGFELD GIRL(1941), makeup; FOR ME AND MY GAL(1942), makeup; I MARRIED AN ANGEL(1942), makeup; KEEPER OF THE FLAME(1942), makeup; TORTILLA FLAT(1942), makeup; WHITE CARGO(1942), makeup; WOMAN OF THE YEAR(1942), makeup; GUY NAMED JOE, A(1943), makeup; MADAME CURIE(1943), makeup; DRAGON SEED(1944), makeup; MARRIAGE IS A PRIVATE AFFAIR(1944), makeup; SEVENTH CROSS, THE(1944), makeup; WHITE CLIFFS OF DOVER, THE(1944), makeup; WITHOUT LOVE(1945), makeup; YOLANDA AND THE THIEF(1945), makeup; ZIEGFELD FOLLIES(1945), makeup; POSTMAN ALWAYS RINGS TWICE, THE(1946), makeup; TILL THE CLOUDS ROLL BY(1946), makeup; UNDERCUR-RENT(1946), makeup; GOOD NEWS(1947), makeup; GREEN DOLPHIN STREET(1947), makeup; HIGH WALL(1947), makeup; LADY IN THE LA-KE(1947), makeup; SEA OF GRASS, THE(1947), makeup; SONG OF LOVE(1947), makeup; EASTER PARADE(1948), makeup; HOMECOMING(1948), makeup; JULIA MISBEHAVES(1948), makeup; KISSING BANDIT, THE(1948), makeup; PIRATE, THE(1948), makeup; SOUTHERN YANKEE, A(1948), makeup; SUMMER HOLI-DAY(1948), makeup; THREE DARING DAUGHTERS(1948), makeup; GREAT SIN-NER, THE(1949), makeup; INTRUDER IN THE DUST(1949), makeup; LITTLE WOMEN(1949), makeup; MADAME BOVARY(1949), makeup; NEPTUNE'S DAUGH-TER(1949), makeup; ON THE TOWN(1949), makeup; SCENE OF THE CRIME(1949), makeup; SECRET GARDEN, THE(1949), makeup; STRATTON STORY, THE(1949), makeup; TAKE ME OUT TO THE BALL GAME(1949), makeup; THAT FORSYTE WOMAN(1949), makeup; CRISIS(1950), makeup; MYSTERY STREET(1950), makeup; SIDE STREET(1950), makeup
Misc. Silents
DESPERATE MOMENT, A(1926), d

Janet Dawn
Misc. Silents
BEYOND THE TRAIL(1926)

Jefferson Dawn
1984
TERMINATOR, THE(1984), makeup

Katherine Dawn
Silents
LURE OF THE YUKON(1924); JUSTICE OF THE FAR NORTH(1925)

Lili Dawn
VIOLATED(1953)

Marpessa Dawn
BLACK ORPHEUS(1959 Fr./Ital./Braz.); WOMAN EATER, THE(1959, Brit.)

Michelle Dawn
Misc. Talkies
YUM-YUM GIRLS(1976)

Norman Dawn
TUNDRA(1936), d, w, ph; ORPHANS OF THE NORTH(1940), p,d,w&ph; ARCTIC FURY(1949), d, w, ph; TWO LOST WORLDS(1950), d

Silents
WHITE YOUTH(1920), d; SON OF THE WOLF, THE(1922), d; LURE OF THE YUKON(1924), d&w; AFTER MARRIAGE(1925), d&w; JUSTICE OF THE FAR NORTH(1925), d&w

Misc. Silents
LASCA(1919), d; ADORABLE SAVAGE, THE(1920), d; TOKIO SIREN, A(1920), d; FIRE CAT, THE(1921), d; THUNDER ISLAND(1921), d; WOLVES OF THE NORTH(1921), d; FIVE DAYS TO LIVE(1922), d; VERMILION PENCIL, THE(1922), d; TYPHOON LOVE(1926), d

Sugar Dawn
PALS OF THE SILVER SAGE(1940); DYNAMITE CANYON(1941); RIDING THE SUNSET TRAIL(1941); WANDERERS OF THE WEST(1941); LONE STAR LAW MEN(1942)

Vincent Dawn [Bruno Mattei]
ZOMBIE CREEPING FLESH(1981, Ital./Span.), d
1984
CAGED WOMEN(1984, Ital./Fr.), d

Wes Dawn
UP IN SMOKE(1978), makeup; NIGHT OF THE LEPUS(1972), makeup; SIDEWINDER ONE(1977), makeup

Jean Dawnay
WONDERFUL THINGS!(1958, Brit.)

Doreen Dawne
MAN OF THE MOMENT(1955, Brit.); DEADLY RECORD(1959, Brit.); SON OF ROBIN HOOD(1959, Brit.)

Allen C. Dawson
WILLIE AND PHIL(1980)

Angela Dawson
FATE IS THE HUNTER(1964)

Anna Dawson
O LUCKY MAN!(1973, Brit.)
1984
BLOODBATH AT THE HOUSE OF DEATH(1984, Brit.)

Anthony Dawson
JOHNNY IN THE CLOUDS(1945, Brit.); SCHOOL FOR SECRETS(1946, Brit.); QUEEN OF SPADES(1948, Brit.); FIVE ANGLES ON MURDER(1950, Brit.); LONG DARK HALL, THE(1951, Brit.); THEY WERE NOT DIVIDED(1951, Brit.); WOODEN HORSE, THE(1951); VALLEY OF EAGLES(1952, Brit.); DIAL M FOR MURDER(1954); THAT LADY(1955, Brit.); HOUR OF DECISION(1957, Brit.); HAUNTED STRANGLER, THE(1958, Brit.); SNORKEL, THE(1958, Brit.), w; LIBEL(1959, Brit.); TIGER BAY(1959, Brit.); MIDNIGHT LACE(1960); CURSE OF THE WEREWOLF, THE(1961); OFFBEAT(1961, Brit.), w; DR. NO(1962, Brit.); SEVEN SEAS TO CALAIS(1963, Ital.); AMOROUS ADVENTURES OF MOLL FLANDERS, THE(1965); CHANGE PARTNERS(1965, Brit.); HELL IS EMPTY(1967, Brit./Ital); ROVER, THE(1967, Ital.); VENGEANCE(1968, Ital./Ger.), w; YOUNG, THE EVIL AND THE SAVAGE, THE(1968, Ital.), w; DEATH RIDES A HORSE(1969, Ital.); BATTLE OF THE NERETVA(1971, Yugo./Ital./Ger.); DIRTY HEROES(1971, Ital./Fr./Ger.); RED SUN(1972, Fr./Ital./Span.); COUNT OF MONTE CRISTO(1976, Brit.); INCHON(1981)

Anthony M. Dawson [Antonio Margheriti]
BATTLE OF THE WORLDS(1961, Ital.), d; FALL OF ROME, THE(1963, Ital.), d, w; HORROR CASTLE(1965, Ital.), d; LIGHTNING BOLT(1967, Ital./Sp.), d; OPERATION KID BROTHER(1967, Ital.); WILD, WILD PLANET, THE(1967, Ital.), d; VENGEANCE(1968, Ital./Ger.), d; YOUNG, THE EVIL AND THE SAVAGE, THE(1968, Ital.), d; WAR BETWEEN THE PLANETS(1971, Ital.), d; VALACHI PAPERS, THE(1972, Ital./Fr.), d; WEB OF THE SPIDER(1972, Ital./Fr./Ger.), d; BLOOD MONEY(1974, U.S./Hong Kong/Ital./Span.), d; MR. SUPERINVISIBLE(1974, Ital./Span./Ger.), d; TAKE A HARD RIDE(1975, U.S./Ital.), d; DEATH RACE(1978, Ital.), d; HUMANOID, THE(1979, Ital.), d, spec eff; KILLER FISH(1979, Ital./Braz.), d; SQUEEZE, THE(1980, Ital.), d; YOR, THE HUNTER FROM THE FUTURE(1983, Ital.), d, w
1984
HUNTERS OF THE GOLDEN COBRA, THE(1984, Ital.), d; LAST HUNTER, THE(1984, Ital.), d

Misc. Talkies
INVASION OF THE FLESH HUNTERS(1981), d

Basil Dawson
DEVIL'S DAFFODIL, THE(1961, Brit./Ger.), w

Beatrice Dawson
NIGHT BEAT(1948, Brit.), cos; DEAR MR. PROHACK(1949, Brit.), cos; PANDORA AND THE FLYING DUTCHMAN(1951, Brit.), cos; IMPORTANCE OF BEING EARNEST, THE(1952, Brit.), cos; PICKWICK PAPERS, THE(1952, Brit.), cos; PENNY PRINCESS(1953, Brit.), cos; FOOTSTEPS IN THE FOG(1955, Brit.), cos; SVENGALI(1955, Brit.), cos; WICKED WIFE(1955, Brit.), cos; PRINCE AND THE SHOWGIRL, THE(1957, Brit.), cos; STOWAWAY GIRL(1957, Brit.), cos; TALE OF TWO CITIES, A(1958, Brit.), cos; WIND CANNOT READ, THE(1958, Brit.), cos; EXPRESSO BONGO(1959, Brit.), cos; DAY THE EARTH CAUGHT FIRE, THE(1961, Brit.), cos; STOP ME BEFORE I KILL!(1961, Brit.), cos; L-SHAPED ROOM, THE(1962, Brit.), cos; TERM OF TRIAL(1962, Brit.), cos; WALTZ OF THE TOREADORS(1962, Brit.), cos; I COULD GO ON SINGING(1963), cos; MACBETH(1963), cos; OF HUMAN BONDAGE(1964, Brit.), cos; SERVANT, THE(1964, Brit.), cos; WOMAN OF STRAW(1964, Brit.), cos; LIFE AT THE TOP(1965, Brit.), cos; MASQUERADE(1965, Brit.), cos; WHERE THE SPIES ARE(1965, Brit.), cos; MODESTY BLAISE(1966, Brit.), cos; PROMISE HER ANYTHING(1966, Brit.), cos; ACCIDENT(1967, Brit.), cos; MRS. BROWN, YOU'VE GOT A LOVELY DAUGHTER(1968, Brit.), cos; ONLY WHEN I LARF(1968, Brit.), cos; ASSASSINATION BUREAU, THE(1969, Brit.), cos; LAST GRENADE, THE(1970, Brit.), cos; MAN WHO HAUNTED HIMSELF, THE(1970, Brit.), cos; DEVIL'S WIDOW, THE(1972, Brit.), cos; X Y & ZEE(1972, Brit.), cos; DOLL'S HOUSE, A(1973), cos; THREE SISTERS(1974, Brit.), cos; BAWDY ADVENTURES OF TOM JONES, THE(1976, Brit.), cos

Billy Dawson
DISPATCH FROM REUTERS, A(1940); FATHER IS A PRINCE(1940); KNUTE ROCKNE–ALL AMERICAN(1940); LADIES MUST LIVE(1940); ADVENTURE IN WASHINGTON(1941); FATHER'S SON(1941); HERE COMES MR. JORDAN(1941); NINE LIVES ARE NOT ENOUGH(1941); NOTHING BUT THE TRUTH(1941); REMEMBER THE DAY(1941); MAJOR AND THE MINOR, THE(1942); NOBODY'S DARLING(1943); LADY IN THE DARK(1944); SWEET AND LOWDOWN(1944)

Blase M. Dawson
EASY RIDER(1969)

Bob Dawson
NORWOOD(1970), spec eff; PANDEMONIUM(1982), spec eff; STAR TREK II: THE WRATH OF KHAN(1982), spec eff

Bumble Dawson
ROMAN SPRING OF MRS. STONE, THE(1961, U.S./Brit.), cos

Coningsby Dawson
GIRL FROM SCOTLAND YARD, THE(1937), w

Curt Dawson
MARDI GRAS MASSACRE(1978)

Diana Dawson
TEN TALL MEN(1951); STRANGER WORE A GUN, THE(1953); DRIVE A CROOKED ROAD(1954); MIRACLE IN THE RAIN(1956)

Dick Dawson
SILENT RUNNING(1972), makeup

Donald D. Dawson
RAGE(1972), cos

Doris Dawson
LITTLE WILDCAT, THE(1928); BROADWAY SCANDALS(1929); HOT STUFF(1929); MAN AND THE MOMENT, THE(1929); SILVER STREAK, THE(1935)

Silents
ARIZONA WILDCAT(1927); DO YOUR DUTY(1928); HEART TROUBLE(1928); NAUGHTY BABY(1929)

Misc. Silents
GOLD FROM WEEPAH(1927)

Douglas Dawson
HURRICANE HORSEMAN(1931), w

Forbes Dawson
Silents
AUDACIOUS MR. SQUIRE, THE(1923, Brit.)

Frank Dawson
LADY AND GENT(1932); DOUBLE DOOR(1934); FLIRTATION WALK(1934); BROADWAY HOSTESS(1935); LAST OUTPOST, THE(1935); NO MORE LADIES(1935); SECRET BRIDE, THE(1935); LADIES IN LOVE(1936); MY MARRIAGE(1936); PRIVATE NUMBER(1936); RHYTHM ON THE RANGE(1936); SUZY(1936); DAY AT THE RACES, A(1937); HOTEL HAYWIRE(1937); ARSENE LUPIN RETURNS(1938); FOUR MEN AND A PRAYER(1938); I'LL GIVE A MILLION(1938); ADVENTURES OF SHERLOCK HOLMES, THE(1939); BEAU GESTE(1939); CAFE SOCIETY(1939); SCOTLAND YARD(1941); UNHOLY PARTNERS(1941); THEY ALL KISSED THE BRIDE(1942); CRASH DIVE(1943); WHAT A WOMAN!(1943); WILSON(1944); MINISTRY OF FEAR(1945); WOMAN IN THE WINDOW, THE(1945); DEVOTION(1946); SHOCKING MISS PILGRIM, THE(1947)

Freddie Dawson
1984
WOMAN IN RED, THE(1984)

George Dawson
GREY FOX, THE(1983, Can.)
1984
BIG MEAT EATER(1984, Can.)

Geri Dawson
EUREKA(1983, Brit.)

Gladys Dawson
MORE THAN A MIRACLE(1967, Ital./Fr.); POOR COW(1968, Brit.); UP THE JUNCTION(1968, Brit.); WORK IS A FOUR LETTER WORD(1968, Brit.)

Gordon Dawson
RIDE BEYOND VENGEANCE(1966), cos; BRING ME THE HEAD OF ALFREDO GARCIA(1974), w

Hal Dawson
ANOTHER LANGUAGE(1933); EASY LIVING(1937); FLEET'S IN, THE(1942); GIRL RUSH, THE(1955); TOP SECRET AFFAIR(1957)

Hal K. Dawson
FIREBIRD, THE(1934); DR. SOCRATES(1935); MUSIC IS MAGIC(1935); PADDY O'DAY(1935); CHINA CLIPPER(1936); EVERYBODY'S OLD MAN(1936); LIBELED LADY(1936); MY AMERICAN WIFE(1936); PUBLIC ENEMY'S WIFE(1936); WEDDING PRESENT(1936); CAFE METROPOLE(1937); DANGER–LOVE AT WORK(1937); LIFE BEGINS IN COLLEGE(1937); LOVE AND HISSES(1937); ON AGAIN–OFF AGAIN(1937); SECOND HONEYMOON(1937); VOGUES OF 1938(1937); WELLS FARGO(1937); WE'RE ON THE JURY(1937); WIFE, DOCTOR AND NURSE(1937); BOY MEETS GIRL(1938); INTERNATIONAL SETTLEMENT(1938); JUST AROUND THE CORNER(1938); KEEP SMILING(1938); SWEETHEARTS(1938); YOU AND ME(1938); BLACKMAIL(1939); FOR LOVE OR MONEY(1939); GREAT VICTOR HERBERT, THE(1939); HOTEL FOR WOMEN(1939); I STOLE A MILLION(1939); ICE FOLLIES OF 1939(1939); LADY'S FROM KENTUCKY, THE(1939); ROSE OF WASHINGTON SQUARE(1939); STORY OF VERNON AND IRENE CASTLE, THE(1939); TWO BRIGHT BOYS(1939); BLONDIE ON A BUDGET(1940); DOCTOR TAKES A WIFE(1940); GREAT PROFILE, THE(1940); LILLIAN RUSSELL(1940); PUBLIC DEB NO. 1(1940); STAR DUST(1940); TIN PAN ALLEY(1940); TWO GIRLS ON BROADWAY(1940); WE WHO ARE YOUNG(1940); CRACKED NUTS(1941); GIRL, A GUY AND A GOB, A(1941); HELLZAPOPPIN'(1941); OBLIGING YOUNG LADY(1941); SAN ANTONIO ROSE(1941); WASHINGTON MELODRAMA(1941); WEEKEND IN HAVANA(1941); YOU'LL NEVER GET RICH(1941); BABY FACE MORGAN(1942); LIFE BEGINS AT 8:30(1942); MAD MARTINDALES, THE(1942); MAGNIFICENT DOPE, THE(1942); MY FAVORITE SPY(1942); SONG OF THE ISLANDS(1942); CONEY ISLAND(1943); HI DIDDLE DIDDLE(1943); MR. LUCKY(1943); RIDING HIGH(1943); SWEET ROSIE O'GRADY(1943); WHAT A WOMAN!(1943); GREENWICH VILLAGE(1944); HENRY ALDRICH'S LITTLE SECRET(1944); DIAMOND HORSESHOE(1944); DOLL FACE(1945); GUEST WIFE(1945); KID FROM BOOKLYN, THE(1946); ONE MORE TOMORROW(1946); BLONDIE'S BIG MOMENT(1947); FABULOUS DORSEYS, THE(1947); LIKELY STORY, A(1947); SHOCKING MISS PILGRIM, THE(1947); VARIETY GIRL(1947); APARTMENT FOR PEGGY(1948); B. F.'S DAUGHTER(1948); CHICKEN EVERY SUNDAY(1948); FLAME, THE(1948); LET'S LIVE A LITTLE(1948); MR. BLANDINGS BUILDS HIS DREAM HOUSE(1948); THAT WON-

DERFUL URGE(1948); YOU GOTTA STAY HAPPY(1948); SLIGHTLY FRENCH(1949); YOU'RE MY EVERYTHING(1949); DALLAS(1950); TO PLEASE A LADY(1950); WABASH AVENUE(1950); DOUBLE DYNAMITE(1951); RHUBARB(1951); SUPERMAN AND THE MOLE MEN(1951); CAPTIVE CITY(1952); IT GROWS ON TREES(1952); PARK ROW(1952); GLENN MILLER STORY, THE(1953); COUNTRY GIRL, THE(1954); YELLOW MOUNTAIN, THE(1954); FOXFIRE(1955); LAWLESS STREET, A(1955); THREE FOR THE SHOW(1955); LOVING YOU(1957); TIN STAR, THE(1957); CATTLE EMPIRE(1958); LAST HURRAH, THE(1958); ALLIGATOR PEOPLE, THE(1959); FACE OF A FUGITIVE(1959); RAT RACE, THE(1960)

Ian Dawson
HUE AND CRY(1950, Brit.)

Ingard Dawson
IRON GLOVE, THE(1954)

Irmgard Dawson
T-MEN(1947); GOOD SAM(1948); NOOSE HANGS HIGH, THE(1948)

Ivo Dawson
HATE SHIP, THE(1930, Brit.); WHITE ENSIGN(1934, Brit.)
Silents
KEEPER OF THE DOOR(1919, Brit.); OTHER PERSON, THE(1921, Brit.); GREEN CARAVAN, THE(1922, Brit.); OUT TO WIN(1923, Brit.); AFTER THE VERDICT(1929, Brit.)
Misc. Silents
FOOTLIGHTS AND SHADOWS(1920); STRAWS IN THE WIND(1924, Brit.)

Jack Dawson
FOREIGN CORRESPONDENT(1940)

Jan Dawson
STORY OF ADELE H., THE(1975, Fr.), w

John Dawson
SMART GUY(1943); MAN WHO HAUNTED HIMSELF, THE(1970, Brit.)

Jon Dawson
MYSTERY OF THE 13TH GUEST, THE(1943); OUTLAWS OF STAMPEDE PASS(1943); DELINQUENT DAUGHTERS(1944)

Jonathan Dawson
FINAL CUT, THE(1980, Aus.), w

Julie Dawson
CHANT OF JIMMIE BLACKSMITH, THE(1980, Aus.)

June Dawson
FLAW, THE(1955, Brit.)

Juno Dawson
HEY, GOOD LOOKIN'(1982)

Len Dawson
PERSONAL BEST(1982)

Lloyd Dawson
NOCTURNE(1946); WINDOW, THE(1949)

Marian Dawson
LAST COUPON, THE(1932, Brit.); SAVE A LITTLE SUNSHINE(1938, Brit.)

Marion Dawson
HIS WIFE'S MOTHER(1932, Brit.); LOVE NEST, THE(1933, Brit.); POLITICAL PARTY, A(1933, Brit.)

Mark Dawson
DETECTIVE, THE(1968); CROSS AND THE SWITCHBLADE, THE(1970); HOT ROCK, THE(1972); LADY LIBERTY(1972, Ital./Fr.)

Martine Dawson
WHITE DOG(1982)

Merv Dawson
DEVIL'S BEDROOM, THE(1964)

Nancy Juno Dawson
ICEMAN COMETH, THE(1973)

Patrick Dawson
GUNS IN THE HEATHER(1968, Brit.); BARRY LYNDON(1975, Brit.)
1984
JIGSAW MAN, THE(1984, Brit.)

Paul Dawson
NIGHT OF EVIL(1962)

Peter Dawson
OKAY FOR SOUND(1937, Brit.); CHIPS(1938. Brit.); FACE OF A FUGITIVE(1959), w; DON'T KNOCK THE TWIST(1962); THREE STOOGES IN ORBIT, THE(1962); VON RICHTHOFEN AND BROWN(1970), spec eff; NATE AND HAYES(1983, U.S./New Zealand), spec eff

Ralph Dawson
CAUGHT IN THE FOG(1928), ed; SINGING FOOL, THE(1928), ed; TENDERLOIN(1928), ed; DESERT SONG, THE(1929), ed; GIRL IN THE GLASS CAGE, THE(1929), d; STARK MAD(1929), ed; OUTWARD BOUND(1930), ed; UNDER A TEXAS MOON(1930), ed; BLONDE CRAZY(1931), ed; HER MAJESTY LOVE(1931), ed; MAD GENIUS, THE(1931), ed; MY PAST(1931), ed; HIGH PRESSURE(1932), ed; JEWEL ROBBERY(1932), ed; ONE WAY PASSAGE(1932), ed; TAXI!(1932), ed; BERMONDSEY KID, THE(1933, Brit.), d; GIRL MISSING(1933), ed; SHE HAD TO SAY YES(1933), ed; FIREBIRD, THE(1934), ed; LIFE OF THE PARTY(1934, Brit.), d; DR. SOCRATES(1935), ed; MIDSUMMER'S NIGHT'S DREAM, A(1935), ed; ANTHONY ADVERSE(1936), ed; STORY OF LOUIS PASTEUR, THE(1936), ed; THREE MEN ON A HORSE(1936), ed; ANOTHER DAWN(1937), ed; FIRST LADY(1937), ed; PRINCE AND THE PAUPER, THE(1937), ed; SCHOONER GANG, THE(1937, Brit.), a, w; ADVENTURES OF ROBIN HOOD, THE(1938), ed; DANCE OF DEATH, THE(1938, Brit.), w; DAWN PATROL, THE(1938), ed; FOUR DAUGHTERS(1938), ed; DAUGHTERS COURAGEOUS(1939), ed; ESPIONAGE AGENT(1939), ed; FOUR WIVES(1939), ed; YES, MY DARLING DAUGHTER(1939), ed; KNUTE ROCKNE–ALL AMERICAN(1940), ed; 'TIL WE MEET AGAIN(1940), ed; FOUR MOTHERS(1941), ed; GREAT LIE, THE(1941), ed; MANPOWER(1941), ed; GEORGE WASHINGTON SLEPT HERE(1942), ed; KING'S ROW(1942), ed; LARCENY, INC.(1942), ed; ADVENTURES OF MARK TWAIN, THE(1944), ed; EXPERIMENT PERILOUS(1944), ed; MR. SKEFFINGTON(1944), ed; SARATOGA TRUNK(1945), ed; SPANISH MAIN, THE(1945), ed; LADY LUCK(1946), ed; HONEYMOON(1947), ed; IVY(1947), ed; RIDE THE PINK HORSE(1947), ed; ACT OF MURDER, AN(1948), ed; ALL MY SONS(1948), ed; ROGUES' REGIMENT(1948), ed; FREE FOR ALL(1949), ed; ONCE MORE, MY DARLING(1949), ed; UNDERTOW(1949), ed; DEPORTED(1950), ed; HARVEY(1950), ed; PEGGY(1950), ed; SEALED CARGO(1951), ed; SOHO CONSPIRACY(1951, Brit.), w; BLACKBEARD THE PIRATE(1952), ed; GIRL IN EVERY PORT, A(1952), ed; LUSTY MEN, THE(1952), ed; HONDO(1953), ed; ISLAND IN THE SKY(1953), ed; HIGH AND THE MIGHTY, THE(1954), ed; BOSS, THE(1956), ed; FLIGHT TO HONG KONG(1956), ed

Silents
LADY OF THE NIGHT(1925), ed; IF I WERE SINGLE(1927), ed

Richard Dawson
KING RAT(1965); MUNSTER, GO HOME(1966); DEVIL'S BRIGADE, THE(1968)

Rico Dawson
BINGO LONG TRAVELING ALL-STARS AND MOTOR KINGS, THE(1976)

Robert Dawson
MY HANDS ARE CLAY(1948, Irish); PROPHECY(1979), spec eff

Robert N. Dawson
MR. MAJESTYK(1974), spec eff

Ron Dawson
BLUE COLLAR(1978), cos; GO TELL THE SPARTANS(1978), cos

Ronald Dawson
MAD DOG COLL(1961)

Rufus Dawson
INADMISSIBLE EVIDENCE(1968, Brit.)

Sheila Dawson
DOCTOR FAUSTUS(1967, Brit.)

Steve Dawson
LILITH(1964); SIDELONG GLANCES OF A PIGEON KICKER, THE(1970)

Ted Dawson
COACH(1978)

Thomas S. Dawson
MOUNTAIN MEN, THE(1980), cos

Tom Dawson
GUADALCANAL DIARY(1943); SINCE YOU WENT AWAY(1944); THEY CAME TO CORDURA(1959), cos; MAJOR DUNDEE(1965), cos; DOCTOR DEATH: SEEKER OF SOULS(1973), cos; BAKER'S HAWK(1976), cos; CHOIRBOYS, THE(1977), cos; TWILIGHT'S LAST GLEAMING(1977, U.S./Ger.), cos; CASEY'S SHADOW(1978)

Tony Dawson
ACTION OF THE TIGER(1957)

Vicki Dawson
PROWLER, THE(1981)

Vicky Dawson
CARBON COPY(1981)

Wendy Dawson
OH, HEAVENLY DOG!(1980)

Donna Dax
TOPPER(1937); SING FOR YOUR SUPPER(1941); PARACHUTE NURSE(1942); SHADOWS OF DEATH(1945); JOLSON STORY, THE(1946); SECRET LIFE OF WALTER MITTY, THE(1947)

Jacqueline Dax
ZAZA(1939)

Jean Dax
ACCUSED–STAND UP(1930, Fr.); CONGRESS DANCES(1932, Ger.); MAYERLING(1937, Fr.); GLORY OF FAITH, THE(1938, Fr.); SLIPPER EPISODE, THE(1938, Fr)

Micheline Dax
LOVE AND THE FRENCHWOMAN(1961, Fr.); TENDER SCOUNDREL(1967, Fr./Ital.); SIX IN PARIS(1968, Fr.)

Roger Dax
LES CREATURES(1969, Fr./Swed.)

Daxely
LETTERS FROM MY WINDMILL(1955, Fr.)

Arius Daxely
CASE OF DR. LAURENT(1958, Fr.)

Albert Day
Misc. Silents
HAUNTED HOUSE, THE(1917)

Alexandra Day
1984
BODY DOUBLE(1984)
Misc. Talkies
BOARDING HOUSE(1984)

Alfred Day
BLUE, WHITE, AND PERFECT(1941), ed; A-HAUNTING WE WILL GO(1942), ed; MANILA CALLING(1942), ed; SECRET AGENT OF JAPAN(1942), ed; TIME TO KILL(1942), ed; CHETNIKS(1943), ed

Alice Day
DRAG(1929); IS EVERYBODY HAPPY?(1929); LOVE RACKET, THE(1929); RED HOT SPEED ½(1929); SKIN DEEP(1929); TIMES SQUARE(1929); IN THE NEXT ROOM(1930); LADIES IN LOVE(1930); LITTLE JOHNNY JONES(1930); MELODY MAN(1930); VIENNESE NIGHTS(1930); LADY FROM NOWHERE(1931); GOLD(1932); TWO-FISTED LAW(1932)
Silents
NIGHT LIFE(1927); PHYLLIS OF THE FOLLIES(1928); SMART SET, THE(1928); WAY OF THE STRONG, THE(1928)
Misc. Silents
TEMPLE OF VENUS, THE(1923); HIS NEW YORK WIFE(1926); GORILLA, THE(1927); SEE YOU IN JAIL(1927)

Ambrose Day
SONG OF THE FORGE(1937, Brit.); ON VELVET(1938, Brit.); SKY RAIDERS, THE(1938, Brit.); OUTSIDER, THE(1949, Brit.)

Annette Day
DOUBLE TROUBLE(1967)

Asher Day
KID FOR TWO FARTHINGS, A(1956, Brit.)

Baybi Day
DRILLER KILLER(1979)

Carol Day
VALUE FOR MONEY(1957, Brit.)

Clarence Day, Jr.
LIFE WITH FATHER(1947), w

Claude Day
VERY PRIVATE AFFAIR, A(1962, Fr./Ital.)

Clayton Day
DEEP IN THE HEART(1983)

Cora Lee Day
FUN WITH DICK AND JANE(1977)
Cynthia Day
Silents
WOMAN AND WINE(1915)
Danielle Day
HOMECOMING(1948)
Daphne Day
CAESAR AND CLEOPATRA(1946, Brit.); LATE AT NIGHT(1946, Brit.); WOMAN TO WOMAN(1946, Brit.); ESCAPE DANGEROUS(1947, Brit.)
Dennis Day
BUCK BENNY RIDES AGAIN(1940); POWERS GIRL, THE(1942); SLEEPY LAGOON(1943); MUSIC IN MANHATTAN(1944); MELODY TIME(1948); I'LL GET BY(1950); GOLDEN GIRL(1951); GIRL NEXT DOOR, THE(1953); WON TON TON, THE DOG WHO SAVED HOLLYWOOD(1976)
Diana Day
BELLES OF ST. TRINIAN'S, THE(1954, Brit.); SECRET OF THE FOREST, THE(1955, Brit.); STORY OF ESTHER COSTELLO, THE(1957, Brit.); STOLEN AIRLINER, THE(1962, Brit.)
Diane Day
HISTORY OF THE WORLD, PART 1(1981)
Donna Day
IN OLD NEW MEXICO(1945); MY FAIR LADY(1964)
Doris Day
SAGA OF DEATH VALLEY(1939); THOU SHALT NOT KILL(1939); VILLAGE BARN DANCE(1940); FEDERAL FUGITIVES(1941); LADY BE GOOD(1941); WOMAN'S FACE(1941); MR. CELEBRITY(1942); THIS TIME FOR KEEPS(1942); THEY GOT ME COVERED(1943); ROMANCE ON THE HIGH SEAS(1948); IT'S A GREAT FEELING(1949); MY DREAM IS YOURS(1949); STORM WARNING(1950); TEA FOR TWO(1950); WEST POINT STORY, THE(1950); YOUNG MAN WITH A HORN(1950); I'LL SEE YOU IN MY DREAMS(1951); LULLABY OF BROADWAY, THE(1951); ON MOONLIGHT BAY(1951); STARLIFT(1951); WINNING TEAM, THE(1952); APRIL IN PARIS(1953); BY THE LIGHT OF THE SILVERY MOON(1953); CALAMITY JANE(1953); LUCKY ME(1954); LOVE ME OR LEAVE ME(1955); YOUNG AT HEART(1955); JULIE(1956); MAN WHO KNEW TOO MUCH, THE(1956); PAJAMA GAME, THE(1957); TEACHER'S PET(1958); TUNNEL OF LOVE, THE(1958); IT HAPPENED TO JANE(1959); PILLOW TALK(1959); MIDNIGHT LACE(1960); PLEASE DON'T EAT THE DAISIES(1960); LOVER COME BACK(1961); JUMBO(1962); THAT TOUCH OF MINK(1962); MOVE OVER, DARLING(1963); THRILL OF IT ALL, THE(1963); SEND ME NO FLOWERS(1964); DO NOT DISTURB(1965); GLASS BOTTOM BOAT, THE(1966); CAPRICE(1967); BALLAD OF JOSIE(1968); WHERE WERE YOU WHEN THE LIGHTS WENT OUT?(1968); WITH SIX YOU GET EGGROLL(1968)
Dorothy Day
VOGUES OF 1938(1937); HAVING WONDERFUL TIME(1938)
Dulce Day
KID FROM BOOKLYN, THE(1946); CHICAGO DEADLINE(1949)
Dulcie Day
JEALOUSY(1934); RACKET, THE(1951)
Dulcy Day
HOLLOW TRIUMPH(1948)
Dwane Day
THAT CERTAIN WOMAN(1937)
Edith Day
Silents
ROMANCE OF THE AIR, A(1919)
Misc. Silents
CHILDREN NOT WANTED(1920)
Edmund Day
ROUNDUP, THE(1941), w
Silents
ROUND UP, THE(1920), w
Elida Day
NIGHT THEY KILLED RASPUTIN, THE(1962, Fr./Ital.)
Emmett Day
TRAIL DUST(1936)
Ernest Day
MADE(1972, Brit.), ph; RUNNING SCARED(1972, Brit.), ph; VISIT TO A CHIEF'S SON(1974), ph; GREEN ICE(1981, Brit.), d; SPHINX(1981), ph; WALTZ ACROSS TEXAS(1982), d
1984
PASSAGE TO INDIA, A(1984, Brit.), ph
Ernie Day
REVENGE OF THE PINK PANTHER(1978), ph
Frances Day
BIG BUSINESS(1930, Brit.); SUCH IS THE LAW(1930, Brit.); FIRST MRS. FRASER, THE(1932, Brit.); TWO HEARTS IN WALTZ TIME(1934, Brit.); OH DADDY!(1935, Brit.); TEMPTATION(1935, Brit.); DREAMS COME TRUE(1936, Brit.); GIRL FROM MAXIM'S, THE(1936, Brit.); PUBLIC NUISANCE NO. 1(1936, Brit.); YOU MUST GET MARRIED(1936, Brit.); GIRL IN THE TAXI(1937, Brit.); WHO'S YOUR LADY FRIEND?(1937, Brit.); ROOM FOR TWO(1940, Brit.); PLAYBOY, THE(1942, Brit.); FIDDLERS THREE(1944, Brit.); TREAD SOFTLY(1952, Brit.); THERE'S ALWAYS A THURSDAY(1957, Brit.)
Misc. Silents
PRICE OF DIVORCE, THE(1928, Brit.)
Gabrielle Day
TWILIGHT HOUR(1944, Brit.)
Gary Day
CROSSTALK(1982, Aus.); DUET FOR FOUR(1982, Aus.)
Misc. Talkies
NIGHT NURSE, THE(1977)
Gerry Day
STORY OF DAVID, A(1960, Brit.), w; BLACK HOLE, THE(1979), w
Holman Day
Silents
RED LANE, THE(1920), w
Holman F. Day
Silents
KING SPRUCE(1920), w

Holman Francis Day
Silents
ALONG CAME RUTH(1924), w
J.D. Day
STRAWBERRY STATEMENT, THE(1970), spec eff
Jacqueline Day
Misc. Talkies
ASTROLOGER, THE(1975)
Jane Day
1,000 SHAPES OF A FEMALE(1963)
Jennie Day
DRUMS O' VOODOO(1934)
Jerry Day
MAD MAX(1979, Aus.)
Jill Day
ALWAYS A BRIDE(1954, Brit.); ALL FOR MARY(1956, Brit.)
Joe Day
GALLOPING MAJOR, THE(1951, Brit.); LEGEND OF NIGGER CHARLEY, THE(1972), spec eff; NIGHT MOVES(1975), spec eff; 92 IN THE SHADE(1975, U.S./Brit.), spec eff; TELEFON(1977), spec eff; COMA(1978), spec eff; HURRICANE(1979), spec eff; LOOKER(1981), spec eff
Joel Day
Silents
CAPRICE OF THE MOUNTAINS(1916); PRIDE OF THE CLAN, THE(1917); CHALLENGE ACCEPTED, THE(1918); WATCH YOUR STEP(1922)
Misc. Silents
RED COURAGE(1921)
John Day
BROADWAY(1942); CHAMPION(1949); KISS TOMORROW GOODBYE(1950); ABBOTT AND COSTELLO MEET THE INVISIBLE MAN(1951); MEET DANNY WILSON(1952); CITY OF BAD MEN(1953); MAN FROM THE ALAMO, THE(1953); SEMINOLE(1953); 99 RIVER STREET(1953); NAKED ALIBI(1954); YANKEE PASHA(1954); SQUARE JUNGLE, THE(1955); STAR IN THE DUST(1956); TOWARD THE UNKNOWN(1956); JAILHOUSE ROCK(1957); NIGHT PASSAGE(1957); BADLANDERS, THE(1958); WESTBOUND(1959); MISFITS, THE(1961), stunts; UGLY AMERICAN, THE(1963); ADVANCE TO THE REAR(1964); VON RYAN'S EXPRESS(1965); TELL THEM WILLIE BOY IS HERE(1969); SILVER STREAK(1976); IN-LAWS, THE(1979)
Johnny Day
CAFE SOCIETY(1939); DANCING CO-ED(1939); SKY PATROL(1939); STUNT PILOT(1939); IT'S A DATE(1940); SADDLE PALS(1947); RACKET, THE(1951); LOVE ME OR LEAVE ME(1955)
Jonathan Day
SAVAGE WEEKEND(1983), ed
Josette Day
LUCREZIA BORGIA(1937, Fr.); MAN OF THE HOUR, THE(1940, Fr.); WELL-DIGGER'S DAUGHTER, THE(1946, Fr.); BEAUTY AND THE BEAST(1947, Fr.); FOUR DAYS LEAVE(1950, Switz.); LES PARENTS TERRIBLES(1950, Fr.)
Juliette Day
Misc. Silents
BETTY AND THE BUCCANEERS(1917); CALENDER GIRL, THE(1917); RAINBOW GIRL, THE(1917)
Lambert Day
CANDIDATE, THE(1964), set d
Laraine Day
STELLA DALLAS(1937); CALLING DR. KILDARE(1939); SECRET OF DR. KILDARE, THE(1939); SERGEANT MADDEN(1939); TARZAN FINDS A SON!(1939); AND ONE WAS BEAUTIFUL(1940); DR. KILDARE GOES HOME(1940); DR. KILDARE'S CRISIS(1940); DR. KILDARE'S STRANGE CASE(1940); FOREIGN CORRESPONDENT(1940); I TAKE THIS WOMAN(1940); MY SON, MY SON!(1940); BAD MAN, THE(1941); DR. KILDARE'S WEDDING DAY(1941); KATHLEEN(1941); PEOPLE VS. DR. KILDARE, THE(1941); TRIAL OF MARY DUGAN, THE(1941); UNHOLY PARTNERS(1941); FINGERS AT THE WINDOW(1942); JOURNEY FOR MARGARET(1942); YANK ON THE BURMA ROAD, A(1942); MR. LUCKY(1943); BRIDE BY MISTAKE(1944); STORY OF DR. WASSELL, THE(1944); KEEP YOUR POWDER DRY(1945); THOSE ENDEARING YOUNG CHARMS(1945); LOCKET, THE(1946); TYCOON(1947); MY DEAR SECRETARY(1948); WITHOUT HONOR(1949); WOMAN ON PIER 13, THE(1950); HIGH AND THE MIGHTY, THE(1954); THREE FOR JAMIE DAWN(1956); TOY TIGER(1956); THIRD VOICE, THE(1960)
Lawrence S. Day
1984
AMERICAN NIGHTMARE(1984)
Misc. Talkies
AMERICAN NIGHTMARE(1981, Can.)
Lillian Day
PERSONAL MAID'S SECRET(1935), w; OUR WIFE(1941), w; YOUNGEST PROFESSION, THE(1943), w
Lt. Richard Day
UP IN ARMS(1944), tech adv
Lucille Day
WORDS AND MUSIC(1929)
Lynda Day
GENTLE RAIN, THE(1966, Braz.); CHISUM(1970)
Lynda Day [George]
OUTSIDER, THE(1962)
Marceline Day
WILD PARTY, THE(1929); JAZZ AGE, THE(1929); PARADISE ISLAND(1930); SUNNY SKIES(1930); TEMPLE TOWER(1930); MAD PARADE, THE(1931); MYSTERY TRAIN(1931); SKY RAIDERS(1931); ARM OF THE LAW(1932); BROADWAY TO CHEYENNE(1932); CRUSADER, THE(1932); FIGHTING FOOL, THE(1932); KING MURDER, THE(1932); POCATELLO KID(1932); BY APPOINTMENT ONLY(1933); FIGHTING PARSON, THE(1933); FLAMING SIGNAL(1933); TELEGRAPH TRAIL, THE(1933); VIA PONY EXPRESS(1933); DAMAGED LIVES(1937)
Misc. Talkies
FROM BROADWAY TO CHEYENNE(1932)
Silents
SPLENDID ROAD, THE(1925); WHITE OUTLAW, THE(1925); BARRIER, THE(1926); COLLEGE DAYS(1926); LOOKING FOR TROUBLE(1926); BELOVED ROGUE, THE(1927); CAPTAIN SALVATION(1927); LONDON AFTER MIDNIGHT(1927); BIG CITY, THE(1928); CAMERAMAN, THE(1928); FREEDOM OF THE PRESS(1928);

SINGLE MAN, A(1929)
Misc. Silents
RENEGADE HOLMES, M.D.(1925); TAMING OF THE WEST, THE(1925); WALL STREET WHIZ, THE(1925); BOY FRIEND, THE(1926); FOOLS OF FASHION(1926); GAY DECEIVER, THE(1926); THAT MODEL FROM PARIS(1926); WESTERN PLUCK(1926); RED CLAY(1927); ROAD TO ROMANCE, THE(1927); ROOKIES(1927); CERTAIN YOUNG MAN, A(1928); DETECTIVES(1928); DRIFTWOOD(1928); REST-LESS YOUTH(1928); STOLEN LOVE(1928); UNDER THE BLACK EAGLE(1928); ONE WOMAN IDEA, THE(1929); TRENT'S LAST CASE(1929)

Marceline [Alice] Day
HOT CURVES(1930)

Marie Day
STORM OVER LISBON(1944)
Silents
TIMOTHY'S QUEST(1922); RAGGED EDGE, THE(1923)

Marilyn Day
MOONLIGHT IN VERMONT(1943)

Marjorie Day
FACING THE MUSIC(1941, Brit.)
Silents
GLORIOUS ADVENTURE, THE(1922, U.S./Brit.)
Misc. Silents
DAMAGED GOODS(1919, Brit.)

Marjory Day
Silents
NEW CLOWN, THE(1916, Brit.)

Max Day
FURTHER UP THE CREEK!(1958, Brit.)

Molly O' Day
Misc. Silents
HARD BOILED HAGGERTY(1927)

Morris Day
1984
PURPLE RAIN(1984)

Mrs. Clarence Day
LIFE WITH FATHER(1947), tech adv

Norman Day
SELF-PORTRAIT(1973, U.S./Chile)

Olga Day
Misc. Silents
CASANOVA(1927, Fr.)

Percy Day
SECRET MISSION(1944, Brit.), spec eff; VACATION FROM MARRIAGE(1945, Brit.), spec eff; OUTCAST OF THE ISLANDS(1952, Brit.), spec eff

Price Day
LADY AND THE MOB, THE(1939), w

Raymond Day
1984
NUMBER ONE(1984, Brit.), p

Regina Day
HOLIDAY RHYTHM(1950)

Richard Day
ARROWSMITH(1931), set d; FRONT PAGE, THE(1931), art d; ONE HEAVENLY NIGHT(1931), art d; PALMY DAYS(1931), art d; STREET SCENE(1931), art d; UNHO-LY GARDEN, THE(1931), art d; GREEKS HAD A WORD FOR THEM(1932), art d; KID FROM SPAIN, THE(1932), art d; RAIN(1932), art d; BOWERY, THE(1933), art d; HALLELUJAH, I'M A BUM(1933), art d; MASQUERADER, THE(1933), art d; ROMAN SCANDALS(1933), art d; BORN TO BE BAD(1934), art d; GALLANT LADY(1934), ed; KID MILLIONS(1934), art d; LOOKING FOR TROUBLE(1934), art d; NANA(1934), art d; WE LIVE AGAIN(1934), art d; DARK ANGEL, THE(1935), art d; SPLEN-DOR(1935), art d; WEDDING NIGHT, THE(1935), art d; COME AND GET IT(1936), art d; DODSWORTH(1936), art d; GAY DESPERADO, THE(1936), art d; ONE RAINY AFTERNOON(1936), art d; STRIKE ME PINK(1936), art d; THESE THREE(1936), art d; DEAD END(1937), art d; HURRICANE, THE(1937), art d; STELLA DALLAS(1937), art d; WOMAN CHASES MAN(1937), art d; ADVENTURES OF MARCO POLO, THE(1938), art d; COWBOY AND THE LADY, THE(1938), art d; GOLDWYN FOL-LIES, THE(1938), art d; DAY-TIME WIFE(1939), art d; DRUMS ALONG THE MO-HAWK(1939), art d; FRONTIER MARSHAL(1939), art d; GORILLA, THE(1939), art d; HOLLYWOOD CAVALCADE(1939), art d; HOUND OF THE BASKERVILLES, THE(1939), art d; MR. MOTO IN DANGER ISLAND(1939), art d; PACK UP YOUR TROUBLES(1939), art d; ROSE OF WASHINGTON SQUARE(1939), art d; SECOND FIDDLE(1939), art d; SWANEE RIVER(1939), art d; WIFE, HUSBAND AND FRIEND(1939), art d; YOUNG MR. LINCOLN(1939), art d; CHAD HANNA(1940), art d; DOWN ARGENTINE WAY(1940), art d; FOUR SONS(1940), art d; GIRL FROM AVENUE A(1940), art d; GIRL IN 313(1940), art d; GRAPES OF WRATH(1940), art d; GREAT PROFILE, THE(1940), art d; HE MARRIED HIS WIFE(1940), art d; HUD-SON'S BAY(1940), art d; I WAS AN ADVENTURESS(1940), art d; JOHNNY APOL-LO(1940), art d; LILLIAN RUSSELL(1940), art d; LITTLE OLD NEW YORK(1940), art d; MARK OF ZORRO, THE(1940), art d; MARYLAND(1940), art d; PIER 13(1940), art d; RETURN OF FRANK JAMES, THE(1940), art d; SHOOTING HIGH(1940), art d; STREET OF MEMORIES(1940), art d; TIN PAN ALLEY(1940), art d; YESTERDAY'S HEROES(1940), art d; YOUNG PEOPLE(1940), art d; BLOOD AND SAND(1941), art d; CHARLEY'S AUNT(1941), art d; GREAT AMERICAN BROADCAST, THE(1941), art d; GREAT GUNS(1941), art d; HOW GREEN WAS MY VALLEY(1941), art d; LAST OF THE DUANES(1941), art d; MAN HUNT(1941), art d; MOON OVER MIAMI(1941), art d; PERFECT SNOB, THE(1941), art d; REMEMBER THE DAY(1941), art d; SUN VALLEY SERENADE(1941), art d; THAT NIGHT IN RIO(1941), art d; TOBACCO ROAD(1941), art d; VERY YOUNG LADY, A(1941), art d; WEEKEND IN HAVA-NA(1941), art d; WESTERN UNION(1941), art d; YANK IN THE R.A.F.(1941), art d; A-HAUNTING WE WILL GO(1942), art d; BLACK SWAN, THE(1942), art d; FOOTLIGHT SERENADE(1942), art d; GHOST AND MRS. MUIR, THE(1942), art d; GIRL TROUBLE(1942), art d; I WAKE UP SCREAMING(1942), art d; ICELAND(1942), art d; IT HAPPENED IN FLATBUSH(1942), art d; JUST OFF BROADWAY(1942), art d; LIFE BEGINS AT 8:30(1942), art d; LITTLE TOKYO, U.S.A.(1942), art d; LONE STAR RANGER(1942), art d; LOVES OF EDGAR ALLAN POE(1942), art d; MAGNIFICENT DOPE, THE(1942), art d; MAN IN THE TRUNK, THE(1942), art d; MAN WHO WOULDN'T DIE, THE(1942), art d; MANILA CALLING(1942), art d; MOONTIDE(1942), art d; MY GAL SAL(1942), art d; ORCHESTRA WIVES(1942), art d; PIED PIPER, THE(1942), art d; POSTMAN DIDN'T RING, THE(1942), art d; QUIET PLEASE, MURDER(1942), art d; RINGS ON HER FINGERS(1942), art d; ROXIE

HART(1942), art d; SON OF FURY(1942), art d; SPRINGTIME IN THE ROCK-IES(1942), art d; TALES OF MANHATTAN(1942), art d; TEN GENTLEMEN FROM WEST POINT(1942), art d; THAT OTHER WOMAN(1942), art d; THIS ABOVE ALL(1942), art d; THRU DIFFERENT EYES(1942), art d; THUNDER BIRDS(1942), art d; TIME TO KILL(1942), art d; UNDYING MONSTER, THE(1942), art d; WHIS-PERING GHOSTS(1942), art d; CRASH DIVE(1943), art d; DIXIE DUGAN(1943), art d; HE HIRED THE BOSS(1943), art d; IMMORTAL SERGEANT, THE(1943), art d; MARGIN FOR ERROR(1943), art d; MEANEST MAN IN THE WORLD, THE(1943), art d; MY FRIEND FLICKA(1943), art d; OX-BOW INCIDENT, THE(1943), art d; TONIGHT WE RAID CALAIS(1943), art d; RAZOR'S EDGE, THE(1946), art d; CAP-TAIN FROM CASTILE(1947), art d; I WONDER WHO'S KISSING HER NOW(1947), art d; MIRACLE ON 34TH STREET, THE(1947), art d; MOSS ROSE(1947), art d; MOTHER WORE TIGHTS(1947), art d; FORCE OF EVIL(1948), art d; JOAN OF ARC(1948), art d; MY FOOLISH HEART(1949), art d; EDGE OF DOOM(1950), art d; OUR VERY OWN(1950), art d; CRY DANGER(1951), art d; I WANT YOU(1951), art d; STREETCAR NAMED DESIRE, A(1951), art d; HANS CHRISTIAN ANDER-SEN(1952), art d; ON THE WATERFRONT(1954), art d; ER LOVE A STRAN-GER(1958), p, w; EXODUS(1960), art d; SOMETHING WILD(1961), art d; CHEYENNE AUTUMN(1964), art d; GOODBYE CHARLIE(1964), art d; GREATEST STORY EVER TOLD, THE(1965), art d; CHASE, THE(1966), prod d; HAPPENING, THE(1967), prod d; VALLEY OF THE DOLLS(1967), art d; SWEET RIDE, THE(1968), art d; THE BOSTON STRANGLER, THE(1968), art d; TORA! TORA! TORA!(1970, U.S./Jap.), art d; TRIBES(1970), art d
Silents
MERRY-GO-ROUND(1923), set d, cos; BRIGHT LIGHTS(1925), set d; HIS SECRE-TARY(1925), art d; MERRY WIDOW, THE(1925), cos; BEVERLY OF GRAUS-TARK(1926), art d; ADAM AND EVIL(1927), art d; AFTER MIDNIGHT(1927), set d; ENEMY, THE(1927), set d; MR. WU(1927), set d; TEA FOR THREE(1927), set d; WEDDING MARCH, THE(1927), art d

Capt. Richard Day
DEVIL TO PAY, THE(1930), art d; WHOOPEE(1930), art d
Silents
GREED(1925), prod d

Robert Day
SILENT DUST(1949, Brit.), ph; NEVER TAKE NO FOR AN ANSWER(1952, Brit./ Ital.), ph; SNIPER, THE(1952); GREEN MAN, THE(1957, Brit.), d; STRANGER'S MEETING(1957, Brit.), d; HAUNTED STRANGLER, THE(1958, Brit.), d; BOB-BIKINS(1959, Brit.), d; FIRST MAN INTO SPACE(1959, Brit.), d; LIFE IN EMERGEN-CY WARD 10(1959, Brit.), d; TARZAN THE MAGNIFICENT(1960, Brit.), d, w; CALL ME GENIUS(1961, Brit.), d; TWO-WAY STRETCH(1961, Brit.), d; CORRIDORS OF BLOOD(1962, Brit.), d; OPERATION SNATCH(1962, Brit.), d; TARZAN'S THREE CHALLENGES(1963), d, w; SHE(1965, Brit.), d; TARZAN AND THE VALLEY OF GOLD(1966 U.S./Switz.), d; TARZAN AND THE GREAT RIVER(1967, U.S./Switz.), d; TARZAN AND THE JUNGLE BOY(1968, US/Switz.), p; BIG GAME, THE(1972), d&w; ELEPHANT MAN, THE(1980, Brit.), d; MAN WITH BOGART'S FACE, THE(1980), d
Silents
QUEEN KELLY(1929), art d

Roy Day
MAKE-UP(1937, Brit.), ph; LONG WEEKEND(1978, Aus.)

Ruth Day
FOLIES DERGERE(1935)

Sally Day
ROBBERY WITH VIOLENCE(1958, Brit.)

Shannon Day
WORLDLY GOODS(1930); BIG TOWN(1932); HOTEL VARIETY(1933); TRAMP, TRAMP, TRAMP(1942), w
Silents
AFFAIRS OF ANATOL, THE(1921); AFTER THE SHOW(1921); NORTH OF THE RIO GRANDE(1922); ONE CLEAR CALL(1922); ORDEAL, THE(1922); ALL THE BROTH-ERS WERE VALIANT(1923); GIRL ON THE STAIRS, THE(1924); BARRIER, THE(1926); STRANDED(1927)
Misc. Silents
MAN WHO HAD EVERYTHING, THE(1920); CAPTAIN FLY-BY-NIGHT(1922); HONOR FIRST(1922); SILENT PAL(1925); GYPSY ROMANCE, THE(1926)

Sharon Day
CHEECH AND CHONG'S NICE DREAMS(1981), cos

Susan Day
BIG MOUTH, THE(1967)

Terry Day
LITTLE OF WHAT YOU FANCY, A(1968, Brit.)

Valerie Day
SWEETHEARTS(1938)

Venecia Day
CRAZE(1974, Brit.)

Vera Day
HELL, HEAVEN OR HOBOKEN(1958, Brit.); CROWDED DAY, THE(1954, Brit.); DANCE LITTLE LADY(1954, Brit.); FUN AT ST. FANNY'S(1956, Brit.); IT'S A GREAT DAY(1956, Brit.); KID FOR TWO FARTHINGS, A(1956, Brit.); STARS IN YOUR EYES(1956, Brit.); ENEMY FROM SPACE(1957, Brit.); FLESH IS WEAK, THE(1957, Brit.); PRINCE AND THE SHOWGIRL, THE(1957, Brit.); HAUNTED STRANGLER, THE(1958, Brit.); HELL DRIVERS(1958, Brit.); THEM NICE AMERICANS(1958, Brit.); UP THE CREEK(1958, Brit.); TOO MANY CROOKS(1959, Brit.); WOMAN EATER, THE(1959, Brit.); AND THE SAME TO YOU(1960, Brit.); TRUNK, THE(1961, Brit.); WATCH IT, SAILOR!(1961, Brit.); IN TROUBLE WITH EVE(1964, Brit.); SATURDAY NIGHT OUT(1964, Brit.); STITCH IN TIME, A(1967, Brit.)

Vicki Day
GUMSHOE(1972, Brit.)

W. Percy Day
MAN ABOUT THE HOUSE, A(1947, Brit.), spec eff; ANNA KARENINA(1948, Brit.), spec eff; IDEAL HUSBAND, AN(1948, Brit.), spec eff; MINE OWN EXECUTION-ER(1948, Brit.), spec eff; FALLEN IDOL, THE(1949, Brit.), spec eff; BLACK ROSE, THE(1950), spec eff; FIGHTING PIMPERNEL, THE(1950), spec eff; MUDLARK, THE(1950, Brit.), spec. eff
Silents
NAPOLEON(1927, Fr.)

Warren Day
BIRDS DO IT(1966)

William Day
WAYWARD(1932), w
Yvonne Day
Silents
DON JUAN(1926)
Daniel Day-Lewis
1984
BOUNTY, THE(1984)
Assaf Dayan
DAY THE FISH CAME OUT, THE(1967. Brit./Gr.); WALK WITH LOVE AND
DEATH, A(1969); PROMISE AT DAWN(1970, U.S./Fr.); SABRA(1970, Fr./Ital./Israel);
SELL OUT, THE(1976); OPERATION THUNDERBOLT(1978, ISRAEL)
Daniel Dayan
ZAPPED!(1982)
David Dayan
1984
AGAINST ALL ODDS(1984)
Bernard Dayde
PORTRAIT OF INNOCENCE(1948, Fr.)
Liane Dayde
MAYERLING(1968, Brit./Fr.)
Billy Daye
Misc. Silents
LOVE'S PAY DAY(1918)
Dulce Daye
MR. SMITH GOES TO WASHINGTON(1939); THEY SHALL HAVE MUSIC(1939);
THAT NIGHT WITH YOU(1945); GIRL ON THE SPOT(1946); JACKPOT, THE(1950);
CARRIE(1952); SOMETHING TO LIVE FOR(1952); FOREVER FEMALE(1953); DEEP
IN MY HEART(1954)
Gabrielle Daye
SAINTS AND SINNERS(1949, Brit.); LITTLE BIG SHOT(1952, Brit.); SUNDAY
BLOODY SUNDAY(1971, Brit.); 10 RILLINGTON PLACE(1971, Brit.); IN CELEBRA-
TION(1975, Brit.)
Harold Daye
VERBOTEN!(1959)
June Daye
Misc. Silents
HEARTACHES(1915); HER WAYWARD SISTER(1916); SORROWS OF HAP-
PINESS(1916); DERELICT, THE(1917); TROOPER 44(1917)
Loretta Daye
PRINCESS AND THE PIRATE, THE(1944); WONDER MAN(1945)
Margery Daye
GALS, INCORPORATED(1943)
Ruth Daye
YOUTH ON PARADE(1943)
Tamara Daykarhanova
DREAM OF KINGS, A(1969); THREE SISTERS, THE(1977)
Tamara Daykarhonova
ANDY(1965)
Ellis Dayle
MADHOUSE(1974, Brit.)
Les Dayman
GALLIPOLI(1981, Aus.)
Don Daynard
PORKY'S(1982)
Marjorie Dayne
HOW SWEET IT IS(1968); CYCLE SAVAGES(1969); DEVIL'S 8, THE(1969)
Robert Dayne
NORTHERN PURSUIT(1943)
Robert Dayo
SINGIN' IN THE RAIN(1952); FRENCH LINE, THE(1954)
Charles Dayton
BRIDE OF VENGEANCE(1949); DEAR WIFE(1949); SAMSON AND DELILAH(1949);
MY FRIEND IRMA GOES WEST(1950); NO MAN OF HER OWN(1950); SUNSET
BOULEVARD(1950); UNION STATION(1950); MATING SEASON, THE(1951); PLACE
IN THE SUN, A(1951); WARPATH(1951); SOMETHING TO LIVE FOR(1952)
Dan Dayton
AT WAR WITH THE ARMY(1950); NO QUESTIONS ASKED(1951); TURNING
POINT, THE(1952); GUYS AND DOLLS(1955)
Danny Dayton
WHICH WAY TO THE FRONT?(1970); LOVE AT FIRST BITE(1979); LOOSE
SHOES(1980); STING II, THE(1983)
Dorothy Dayton
COCOANUT GROVE(1938); YOU AND ME(1938); CAFE SOCIETY(1939); ZAZA(1939);
$1,000 A TOUCHDOWN(1939); THANK YOUR LUCKY STARS(1943)
Ethel Dayton [Ethel Corcoran]
Misc. Silents
END OF THE TOUR, THE(1917)
Frank Dayton
Misc. Silents
CORNER IN COTTON, A(1916)
Fred Dayton
Misc. Silents
SHACKLES OF FEAR(1924)
Howard Dayton
DINOSAURUS(1960); VAN, THE(1977); SPACE RAIDERS(1983)
James Dayton
Silents
SCARLET SIN, THE(1915), w; SUBURBAN, THE(1915), w
June Dayton
TWILIGHT OF HONOR(1963); ONE MAN'S WAY(1964); TORA! TORA! TORA!(1970,
U.S./Jap.); OTHER SIDE OF THE MOUNTAIN–PART 2, THE(1978)
Katharine Dayton
FIRST LADY(1937), w
Lewis Dayton
Silents
RANK OUTSIDER(1920, Brit.); MYSTERY OF MR. BERNARD BROWN(1921, Brit.);
SLANDER THE WOMAN(1923); YESTERDAY'S WIFE(1923); WHAT FOOLS
MEN(1925)

Misc. Silents
SHADOW BETWEEN, THE(1920, Brit.); MARRIAGE LINES, THE(1921, Brit.); WAY
OF A MAN, THE(1921, Brit.); WIFE'S ROMANCE, A(1923); COST OF BEAUTY,
THE(1924, Brit.); WHO IS THE MAN?(1924, Brit.); S.O.S.(1928, Brit.); SPANGLES(1928,
Brit.); CELESTIAL CITY, THE(1929, Brit.); SACRIFICE(1929, Brit.)
Lyman D. Dayton
AGAINST A CROOKED SKY(1975), p; SEVEN ALONE(1975), p; BAKER'S
HAWK(1976), p&d
Lyman Dayton
WHERE THE RED FERN GROWS(1974), p; PONY EXPRESS RIDER(1976), w
Ron Dayton
ROBIN AND THE SEVEN HOODS(1964)
Ronnie Dayton
PAJAMA PARTY(1964); HOW TO STUFF A WILD BIKINI(1965); SKI PARTY(1965);
DEVIL'S ANGELS(1967); MARYJANE(1968); HELL'S BELLES(1969)
Hisao Dazai
NONE BUT THE BRAVE(1965, U.S./Jap.)
C. T. Dazey
Silents
ALIEN, THE(1915), w
Charles T. Dazey
IN OLD KENTUCKY(1935), w
Silents
MANHATTAN MADNESS(1916), w; NIGHT OUT, A(1916), w; IN OLD KENTUCK-
Y(1920), w; PRINCE OF AVENUE A., THE(1920), w; KENTUCKY DERBY, THE(1922),
w; SIGN OF THE ROSE, THE(1922), w; IN OLD KENTUCKY(1927), w
Frank Dazey
Silents
HOME STUFF(1921), w; RICH MEN'S WIVES(1922), w; SHADOWS OF THE
SEA(1922), w; GOLD DIGGERS, THE(1923), ed; MOTHERS-IN-LAW(1923), w; POOR
MEN'S WIVES(1923), w
Frank M. Dazey
UNDER EIGHTEEN(1932), w; WHEN A MAN'S A MAN(1935), w; NOBODY'S
FOOL(1936), w
Silents
POLLY OF THE STORM COUNTRY(1920), w; PRINCE OF AVENUE A., THE(1920),
Frank Mitchell Dazey
DEVIL IS DRIVING, THE(1932), w; HELLDORADO(1935), w; KLONDIKE AN-
NIE(1936), w; THIRTEEN HOURS BY AIR(1936), w
Grace Dazey
CARNATION KID(1929), ed
Charles T. Dazy
Silents
SUBURBAN, THE(1915), w
Micaela Dazzi
EMPTY CANVAS, THE(1964, Fr./Ital.)
Pierre Dduan
YELLOW HAT, THE(1966, Brit.)
David De
HORSEMEN, THE(1971)
Tony De Aarraga
BURY ME AN ANGEL(1972), ed
Mario De Abros
1984
YELLOW HAIR AND THE FORTRESS OF GOLD(1984)
Fabio de Agostini
NIGHTMARE CASTLE(1966, Ital.), w
Pedro de Aguillon
ORLAK, THE HELL OF FRANKENSTEIN(1960, Mex.)
Gino De Agustino
THIS EARTH IS MINE(1959); BLACK KLANSMAN, THE(1966)
Kerstin De Ahna
1984
LITTLE DRUMMER GIRL, THE(1984)
Edit De Ak
OFFENDERS, THE(1980)
Pedro de Alacon
MILLER'S WIFE, THE(1957, Ital.), w
Juan Luis de Alarcon
POLITICAL ASYLUM(1975, Mex./Guatemalan), w
Aurora de Alba
NARCO MEN, THE(1969, Span./Ital.)
Felipe de Alba
STRONGHOLD(1952, Mex.); ADVENTURES OF ROBINSON CRUSOE, THE(1954)
Luana de Alcaniz
FRONTIERS OF '49(1939)
Ferdinando De Aldisio
ROMAN HOLIDAY(1953)
Rodolfo De Alejandre
1984
UNDER THE VOLCANO(1984)
Iracema de Alencar
BRASIL ANNO 2,000(1968, Braz.)
Rudolfo de Alexandre
HIGH RISK(1981)
Abilio Pereira de Almeida
GIRL GAME(1968, Braz./Fr./Ital.), p
Acacio de Almeida
IN THE WHITE CITY(1983, Switz./Portugal), ph
Joaquim De Almeida
BEYOND THE LIMIT(1983)
Jose de Almeyda
GAY ADVENTURE, THE(1953, Brit.)
Raquel de Alva
SONG OF MEXICO(1945)
Luciano De Ambrosis
LITTLE MARTYR, THE(1947, Ital.); HEART AND SOUL(1950, Ital.)

Edmondo De Amicia
CARMELA(1949, Ital.), w
Angelo de Amicio
GUNMEN OF THE RIO GRANDE(1965, Fr./Ital./Span.), art d
Alberto De Amicis
SWINDLE, THE(1962, Fr./Ital.); PASSIONATE THIEF, THE(1963, Ital.)
Edmondo De Amicis
HEART AND SOUL(1950, Ital.), w
Miguel de Anda
SULLIVAN'S EMPIRE(1967)
Mike de Anda
GUNS OF DIABLO(1964); PORTNOY'S COMPLAINT(1972)
Peter De Anda
COOL WORLD, THE(1963); COME BACK CIHARLESTON BLUE(1972); NEW CENTURIONS, THE(1972)
Raul de Anda
LEGEND OF A BANDIT, THE(1945, Mex.)
Robert De Anda
FUN IN ACAPULCO(1963); CANDIDATE, THE(1972)
Rodolfo De Anda
1984
TOY SOLDIERS(1984)
Nato De Angeles
DEVIL WITHIN HER, THE(1976, Brit.), p, w
Remo De Angeles
STREET PEOPLE(1976, U.S./Ital.), stunts
Richard de Angeles
FIRST MONDAY IN OCTOBER(1981)
Fabrizio de Angelis
ZOMBIE(1980, Ital.), p; DR. BUTCHER, M.D.(1982, Ital.), w; NEW BARBARIANS, THE(1983, Ital.), p; 1990: THE BRONX WARRIORS(1983, Ital.), p
1984
HOUSE BY THE CEMETERY, THE(1984, Ital.), p; WARRIORS OF THE WASTELAND(1984, Ital.), p
Guido De Angelis
TRINITY IS STILL MY NAME(1971, Ital.), m; ALL THE WAY, BOYS(1973, Ital.), m; MAN FROM THE EAST, A(1974, Ital./Fr.), m; MIDNIGHT PLEASURES(1975, Ital.), m; CHINO(1976, Ital., Span., Fr.), m; KILLER FISH(1979, Ital./Braz.), m; YOR, THE HUNTER FROM THE FUTURE(1983, Ital.), m
Jefferson de Angelis
Silents
HER GREAT CHANCE(1918)
Mario De Angelis
VARIETY LIGHTS(1965, Ital.)
Maurizio De Angelis
TRINITY IS STILL MY NAME(1971, Ital.), m; ALL THE WAY, BOYS(1973, Ital.), m; MAN FROM THE EAST, A(1974, Ital./Fr.), m; MIDNIGHT PLEASURES(1975, Ital.), m; CHINO(1976, Ital., Span., Fr.), m; KILLER FISH(1979, Ital./Braz.), m; YOR, THE HUNTER FROM THE FUTURE(1983, Ital.), m
Remo De Angelis
WITCH'S CURSE, THE(1963, Ital.); GLASS SPHINX, THE(1968, Egypt/Ital./Span.); LONG RIDE FROM HELL, A(1970, Ital.), stunts; MERCENARY, THE(1970, Ital./Span.); DESERTER, THE(1971 Ital./Yugo.), stunts; MAN CALLED SLEDGE, A(1971, Ital.), a, stunts; GREAT ADVENTURE, THE(1976, Span./Ital.)
Rosemary De Angelis
1984
NOTHING LASTS FOREVER(1984)
Paul De Angelo
SLEEPAWAY CAMP(1983)
Robert de Ansorena
Silents
NAPOLEON(1927, Fr.)
Maria De Aragon
BLOOD MANIA(1971); WONDER WOMEN(1973, Phil.)
Jose Teixeira de Araujo
GIVEN WORD, THE(1964, Braz.), art d
Jaime de Arminan
NEST, THE(1982, Span.), d&w
1984
IT'S NEVER TOO LATE(1984, Span.), d, w
Jesus Maria de Arozamena
DEVIL MADE A WOMAN, THE(1962, Span.), w
Lex De Azevdo
WHERE THE RED FERN GROWS(1974), m
Lex De Azevedo
AGAINST A CROOKED SKY(1975), m; BAKER'S HAWK(1976), m
Jean de Baer
GIRLFRIENDS(1978)
1984
FLASH OF GREEN, A(1984)
Patrice de Bailliencourt
LA COLLECTIONNEUSE(1971, Fr.)
Libertad de Baiza
VIOLATED LOVE(1966, Arg.), cos
Honore de Balzac
HONOR OF THE FAMILY(1931), w; COLONEL CHABERT(1947, Fr.), w; LOVABLE CHEAT, THE(1949), w; TRUE AND THE FALSE, THE(1955, Swed.), w; GIRL WITH THE GOLDEN EYES, THE(1962, Fr.), w
Silents
CONQUERING POWER, THE(1921), w; IF WOMEN ONLY KNEW(1921), w; SLAVE OF DESIRE(1923), w
Brenda de Banzie
LONG DARK HALL, THE(1951, Brit.); NEVER LOOK BACK(1952, Brit.); PRIVATE INFORMATION(1952, Brit.); DAY TO REMEMBER, A(1953, Brit.); I BELIEVE IN YOU(1953, Brit.); DON'T BLAME THE STORK(1954, Brit.); HAPPINESS OF THREE WOMEN, THE(1954, Brit.); HOBSON'S CHOICE(1954, Brit.); PURPLE PLAIN, THE(1954, Brit.); WHAT EVERY WOMAN WANTS(1954, Brit.); DOCTOR AT SEA(1955, Brit.); KID FOR TWO FARTHINGS, A(1956, Brit.); MAN WHO KNEW TOO MUCH, THE(1956); AS LONG AS THEY'RE HAPPY(1957, Brit.); TRIPLE DECEPTION(1957, Brit.); ROOM 43(1959, Brit.); TOO MANY CROOKS(1959, Brit.); ENTER-

TAINER, THE(1960, Brit.); THIRTY NINE STEPS, THE(1960, Brit.); COME SEPTEMBER(1961); FLAME IN THE STREETS(1961, Brit.); MARK, THE(1961, Brit.); I THANK A FOOL(1962, Brit.); PAIR OF BRIEFS, A(1963, Brit.); PINK PANTHER, THE(1964); MATTER OF INNOCENCE, A(1968, Brit.)
Lois de Banzie
TOOTSIE(1982); SUDDEN IMPACT(1983)
1984
MASS APPEAL(1984)
Andre de Baranger
Misc. Silents
BEAUTY AND THE BAD MAN(1925)
Jeanne De Bard
VERY IDEA, THE(1929)
Pascale De Bardlet
BON VOYAGE, CHARLIE BROWN(AND DON'T COME BACK)*** (1980)
Audoin de Bardot
SPIRITS OF THE DEAD(1969, Fr./Ital.)
Irene De Bari
WALK PROUD(1979)
Jacques De Baroncelli
FRENCH WAY, THE(1952, Fr.), p&d
Misc. Silents
LA NOUVELLE ANTIGONE(1916, Fr.), d; LE ROI DE LA MER(1917, Fr.), d; LE RETOUR AUX CHAMPS(1918, Fr.), d; LE SCANDALE(1918, Fr.), d; LE SIEGE DES TROIS(1918, Fr.), d; RAMUNTCHO(1919, Fr.), d; FLIPOTTE(1920, Fr.), d; LA RAFALE(1920, Fr.), d; LE SECRET DU 'LONE STAR'(1920, Fr.), d; CHAMPI TORTU(1921, Fr.), d; LA PERE GORIOT(1921, Fr.), d; LE REVE(1921, Fr.), d; LE CARILLON DE MINUIT(1922, Fr.), d; ROGER LA HONTE(1922, Fr.), d; LA FEMME INCONNUE(1923, Fr.), d; LA LEGENDE DE SOEUR BEATRIX(1923, Fr.), d; LA FLAMBEE DE REVES(1924, Fr.), d; NENE(1924, Fr.), d; PECHEUR D'ISLANDE(1924, Fr.), d; LE REVEIL(1925, Fr.), d; VEILLE D'ARMES(1925, Fr.), d; NITCHEVO(1926, Fr.), d; FEU(1927, Fr.), d; DUEL(1928, Fr.), d; LE PASSAGER(1928, Fr.), d; LA FEMME ET LE PANTIN(1929, Fr.), d; LA FEMME SU VOISIN(1929, Fr.), d; LA TENTATION(1929, Fr.), d
Estella De Barr
Silents
LOVES OF RICARDO, THE(1926)
Lilita De Barros
RECKONING, THE(1971, Brit.)
Mario De Barros
ALEXANDER THE GREAT(1956); GUNFIGHTERS OF CASA GRANDE(1965, U.S./Span.); LOST COMMAND, THE(1966); VALLEY OF GWANGI, THE(1969)
Eric de Bayser
TAKE IT ALL(1966, Can.), ed
Rene De Beau
ORGY OF THE DEAD(1965)
Pierre-Augustin Caron de Beaumarchais
MARRIAGE OF FIGARO, THE(1963, Fr.), w
Mme. Leprince de Beaumont
BEAUTY AND THE BEAST(1947, Fr.), w; BEAUTY AND THE BEAST(1963), w
Carlo Ponti De Beauregard
DOULOS–THE FINGER MAN(1964, Fr./Ital.), p
George De Beauregard
CLEO FROM 5 TO 7(1961, Fr.), p
Georges de Beauregard
BREATHLESS(1959, Fr.), p; LOLA(1961, Fr./Ital.), p; WOMAN IS A WOMAN, A(1961, Fr./Ital.), p; CONTEMPT(1963, Fr./Ital.), p; LANDRU(1963, Fr./Ital.), p; THIRD LOVER, THE(1963, Fr./Ital.), p; LE PETIT SOLDAT(1965, Fr.), a, p; MADE IN U.S.A.(1966, Fr.), p; OBJECTIVE 500 MILLION(1966, Fr.), p; LES CARABINIERS(1968, Fr./Ital.), p; PIERROT LE FOU(1968, Fr./Ital.), p; NUN, THE(1971, Fr.), p; HORSE OF PRIDE(1980, Fr.), p
1984
LE CRABE TAMBOUR(1984, Fr.), p
Michael De Beausset
HONEYMOON OF HORROR(1964); DEVIL'S SISTERS, THE(1966); HOOKED GENERATION, THE(1969)
Joseph de Beauvolers
ARTISTS AND MODELS ABROAD(1938)
Billy De Beck
HILLBILLY BLITZKRIEG(1942), w; SNUFFY SMITH, YARD BIRD(1942), w
George De Beck
Misc. Silents
CAVEMAN, THE(1915)
Marian De Beck
Silents
ONE A MINUTE(1921)
Dorothy Daniels de Becker
THIS ABOVE ALL(1942)
Haldor de Becker
GOLDEN EARRINGS(1947)
Harold de Becker
EAGLE SQUADRON(1942); NIGHTMARE(1942); SHERLOCK HOLMES AND THE SECRET WEAPON(1942); THIS ABOVE ALL(1942); MADAME CURIE(1943); MYSTERIOUS DOCTOR, THE(1943); SHERLOCK HOLMES FACES DEATH(1943); TWO TICKETS TO LONDON(1943); LODGER, THE(1944); PEARL OF DEATH, THE(1944); TWO O'CLOCK COURAGE(1945); WOMAN IN GREEN(1945)
Marie De Becker
MRS. MINIVER(1942); DOUGHGIRLS, THE(1944); NONE BUT THE LONELY HEART(1944); SHERLOCK HOLMES AND THE SPIDER WOMAN(1944)
Reggie de Beer
WISHBONE, THE(1933, Brit.)
Marguerite de Belabre
Misc. Silents
WOMAN AND OFFICER 26, THE(1920, Brit.)
Kristine De Bell
BIG BRAWL, THE(1980)
Joe De Bella
ONE MAN'S WAY(1964), makeup

Joseph De Bella
MURDER BY DEATH(1976), makeup
Frederick de Belleville
Misc. Silents
DAUGHTER OF THE PEOPLE, A(1915)
John De Bello
ATTACK OF THE KILLER TOMATOES(1978), p, d, w
Aldo de Benedetti
MY WIDOW AND I(1950, Ital.), w; SINGING TAXI DRIVER(1953, Ital.), w; MY
SEVEN LITTLE SINS(1956, Fr./Ital.), w; RICE GIRL(1963, Fr./Ital.), w; DROP DEAD,
MY LOVE(1968, Italy), w
Gianni De Benedetto
BLOOD AND ROSES(1961, Fr./Ital.); BARABBAS(1962, Ital.)
Tony De Benedetto
SHORT EYES(1977)
Burr De Benning
BEACH RED(1967)
Misc. Talkies
J.C.(1972)
Andre de Beranger
Silents
ASHES OF VENGEANCE(1923); BAT, THE(1926); MISS BREWSTER'S MIL-
LIONS(1926); SO THIS IS PARIS(1926)
Misc. Silents
TIGER ROSE(1923); MAN IN BLUE, THE(1925); EAGLE OF THE SEA, THE(1926);
FIG LEAVES(1926)
Joanna De Bergh
DOCTOR AND THE GIRL, THE(1949)
Joanne de Bergh
CALL NORTHSIDE 777(1948)
Farnesio De Bernal
DOMINO PRINCIPLE, THE(1977); EAGLE'S WING(1979, Brit.)
Pero de Bernardi
CLARETTA AND BEN(1983, Ital., Fr.), w
Piero De Bernardi
GIRL WITH A SUITCASE(1961, Fr./Ital.), w; IMPERIAL VENUS(1963, Ital./Fr.), w;
FRIENDS FOR LIFE(1964, Ital.), w; MARRIAGE–ITALIAN STYLE(1964, Fr./Ital.), w;
ITALIAN SECRET SERVICE(1968, Ital.), w; GHOSTS, ITALIAN STYLE(1969, Ital./
Fr.), w; SERAFINO(1970, Fr./Ital.), w; ALFREDO, ALFREDO(1973, Ital.), w; GOOD-
NIGHT, LADIES AND GENTLEMEN(1977, Ital.), d&w
1984
MISUNDERSTOOD(1984), w; ONCE UPON A TIME IN AMERICA(1984), w
Austin de Besche
RETURN OF THE SECAUCUS SEVEN(1980), ph; LIANNA(1983), ph
Caroline De Beus
1984
FOURTH MAN, THE(1984, Neth.)
David De Beyer
MY WAY(1974, South Africa), ed
Violet de Biccari
Silents
BATTLE OF LIFE, THE(1916); LIFE WITHOUT SOUL(1916)
Manuel De Blas
BULLET FOR SANDOVAL, A(1970, Ital./Span.); HORROR OF THE ZOMBIES(1974,
Span.); GREAT ADVENTURE, THE(1976, Span./Ital.)
Manuyel de Blas
CAULDRON OF BLOOD(1971, Span.)
Virgile De Blasi
LEGIONS OF THE NILE(1960, Ital.), p
Virgilio De Blasi
WARRIOR AND THE SLAVE GIRL, THE(1959, Ital.), p; CON MEN, THE(1973,
Ital.,Span.), p
Giuseppe De Blasio
LIGHTNING BOLT(1967, Ital./Sp.), p; YOUNG, THE EVIL AND THE SAVAGE,
THE(1968, Ital.), p
Madeleine De Blonay
EXPOSED(1983)
William De Boar
Silents
KING OF KINGS, THE(1927)
Madame de Bodamere
Silents
LITTLE LORD FAUNTLEROY(1921); TESS OF THE STORM COUNTRY(1922)
Mme. de Bodamere
Silents
ROSITA(1923)
Lodewijk De Boer
1984
QUESTION OF SILENCE(1984, Neth.), m
Albina de Boisrouvray
WOMAN AT HER WINDOW, A(1978, Fr./Ital./Ger.), p
Pascale De Boisson
MADLY(1970, Fr.)
Birdie De Bolt
HAWAII CALLS(1938)
Jan de Bont
PRIVATE LESSONS(1981), ph; ROAR(1981), ph; I'M DANCING AS FAST AS I
CAN(1982), ph
1984
BAD MANNERS(1984), ph; FOURTH MAN, THE(1984, Neth.), ph
Peter De Bont
SOLDIER OF ORANGE(1979, Dutch), ph
Maria De Booy
GIRL WITH THE RED HAIR, THE(1983, Neth.)
Sharon De Bord
THAT TENNESSEE BEAT(1966)
Armand de Bordes
WHITE COCKATOO(1935)

Gianfranco de Bosio
MOSES(1976, Brit./Ital.), d, w
H. W. de Bouille
CORRUPTION(1933), ed
Barry De Boulay
SWORD OF SHERWOOD FOREST(1961, Brit.)
Princess De Bourbon
Silents
JANICE MEREDITH(1924)
Princess Marie de Bourbon
Silents
NEVER THE TWAIN SHALL MEET(1925)
Marie-France de Bourges
QUARTET(1981, Brit./Fr.)
Mary De Bow
SEA GOD, THE(1930)
Pascale de Boysson
LES ABYSSES(1964, Fr.); MODERATO CANTABILE(1964, Fr./Ital.); SHAMELESS
OLD LADY, THE(1966, Fr.); TESS(1980, Fr./Brit.)
Bob de Bragelonne
Z(1969, Fr./Algeria)
Jean de Braic
MISSION TO MOSCOW(1943)
Muguette De Braie
INTERLUDE(1968, Brit.)
Harry de Bray
MOUSE THAT ROARED, THE(1959, Brit.)
Henry De Bray
TRAITORS, THE(1963, Brit.)
Sybil de Bray
Misc. Silents
FIVE NIGHTS(1915, Brit.)
Yvonne de Bray
ETERNAL RETURN, THE(1943, Fr.); LES PARENTS TERRIBLES(1950, Fr.); CARO-
LINE CHERIE(1951, Fr.)
Astrid De Brea
ART OF LOVE, THE(1965)
Christian de Bresson
QUESTION 7(1961, U.S./Ger.)
Martine de Breteuil
GENDARME OF ST. TROPEZ, THE(1966, Fr./Ital.)
Claire De Brey
DOUBLE DYNAMITE(1951)
Charles De Briac
Silents
HIGH HEELS(1921)
Jean De Briac
BEHIND THE MAKEUP(1930); MIDNIGHT CLUB(1933); UNDER THE PAMPAS
MOON(1935); PRINCESS COMES ACROSS, THE(1936); CAFE METROPOLE(1937); I
MET HIM IN PARIS(1937); SHALL WE DANCE(1937); WHEN YOU'RE IN LO-
VE(1937); WISE GIRL(1937); BULLDOG DRUMMOND IN AFRICA(1938); SUEZ(1938);
SWISS MISS(1938); ESPIONAGE AGENT(1939); ARISE, MY LOVE(1940); ENEMY
AGENT(1940); I TAKE THIS WOMAN(1940); MOONLIGHT IN HAWAII(1941); PIED
PIPER, THE(1942); BACKGROUND TO DANGER(1943); SONG OF BERNADETTE,
THE(1943); NOTHING BUT TROUBLE(1944); TO HAVE AND HAVE NOT(1944); NOB
HILL(1945); MONSIEUR BEAUCAIRE(1946); RAZOR'S EDGE, THE(1946); UNFAITH-
FUL, THE(1947); HALF PAST MIDNIGHT(1948); SAIGON(1948); DOUBLE DYNA-
MITE(1951); GENTLEMEN PREFER BLONDES(1953); MA AND PA KETTLE ON
VACATION(1953); SO THIS IS PARIS(1954); PURPLE MASK, THE(1955); SEA CHASE,
THE(1955); TENDER IS THE NIGHT(1961)
Silents
HIGH HEELS(1921); LOVE LIGHT, THE(1921); OVER THE BORDER(1922); EAGLE,
THE(1925); LADYBIRD, THE(1927); DIVINE WOMAN, THE(1928)
Misc. Silents
BUTTERFLY GIRL, THE(1921)
Raymond De Briac
Silents
HIGH HEELS(1921)
De Briac Twins
Silents
DON'T TELL EVERYTHING(1921)
Mons. le Marquis de Brissac
RISE OF LOUIS XIV, THE(1970, Fr.)
Michelle de Broca
LET JOY REIGN SUPREME(1977, Fr.), p
Philippe de Broca
BREATHLESS(1959, Fr.); JOKER, THE(1961, Fr.), d, w; CARTOUCHE(1962, Fr./
Ital.), a, d, w; SEVEN CAPITAL SINS(1962, Fr./Ital.), d; THAT MAN FROM RI-
O(1964, Fr./Ital.), d, w; MALE COMPANION(1965, Fr./Ital.), d, w; UP TO HIS
EARS(1966, Fr./Ital.), d, w; DON'T PLAY WITH MARTIANS(1967, Fr.), w; KING OF
HEARTS(1967, Fr./Ital.), p&d; OLDEST PROFESSION, THE(1968, Fr./Ital./Ger.), d;
VOYAGE OF SILENCE(1968, Fr.), p; DEVIL BY THE TAIL, THE(1969, Fr./Ital.), d;
GIVE HER THE MOON(1970, Fr./Ital.), d, w; MAGNIFICENT ONE, THE(1974,
Fr./Ital.), d, w; DEAR DETECTIVE(1978, Fr.), d, w; INCORRIGIBLE(1980, Fr.), d;
AFRICAN, THE(1983, Fr.), d, w
1984
LOUISIANE(1984, Fr./Can.), d
Michel de Broin
TWO ENGLISH GIRLS(1972, Fr.), art d; DAYDREAMER, THE(1975, Fr.), art d
Michel de Bronin
LA GRANDE BOUFFE(1973, Fr.), art d
George de Brook
SKY RAIDERS, THE(1938, Brit.)
N. De Brouillet
Silents
DUMB GIRL OF PORTICI(1916)
Lee De Broux
RUN, ANGEL, RUN(1969); TELL THEM WILLIE BOY IS HERE(1969); EVEL
KNIEVEL(1971); SOMETIMES A GREAT NOTION(1971); WILD ROVERS(1971);
COFFY(1973); HAWMPS!(1976); BACK ROADS(1981)

Robert De Bruce
PHILADELPHIA STORY, THE(1940); SCOTLAND YARD(1941)
Celia de Brugh
GETTING OF WISDOM, THE(1977, Aus.)
Lex de Bruijn
LA CHINOISE(1967, Fr.)
Delight De Bruine
Misc. Talkies
DAY IT CAME TO EARTH, THE(1979)
Nigel De Brulier
NOAH'S ARK(1928); IRON MASK, THE(1929); THRU DIFFERENT EYES(1929); WHEEL OF LIFE, THE(1929); GOLDEN DAWN(1930); GREEN GODDESS, THE(1930); MOBY DICK(1930); REDEMPTION(1930); SON OF INDIA(1931); MISS PINKERTON(1932); I'M NO ANGEL(1933); LIFE IN THE RAW(1933); VIVA VILLA!(1934); CHARLIE CHAN IN EGYPT(1935); TALE OF TWO CITIES, A(1935); THREE MUSKETEERS, THE(1935); DOWN TO THE SEA(1936); GARDEN OF ALLAH, THE(1936); HALF ANGEL(1936); MARY OF SCOTLAND(1936); WHITE LEGION, THE(1936); CALIFORNIAN, THE(1937); HOUND OF THE BASKERVILLES, THE(1939); MAN IN THE IRON MASK, THE(1939); MUTINY IN THE BIG HOUSE(1939); TOWER OF LONDON(1939); MAD EMPRESS, THE(1940); ONE MILLION B.C.(1940); VIVA CISCO KID(1940); WRECKING CREW(1942); TONIGHT WE RAID CALAIS(1943)
Silents
RAMONA(1916); KAISER, BEAST OF BERLIN, THE(1918); SAHARA(1919); FLAMES OF THE FLESH(1920); FOUR HORSEMEN OF THE APOCALYPSE, THE(1921); THREE MUSKETEERS, THE(1921); SALOME(1922); ELEVENTH HOUR, THE(1923); HUNCHBACK OF NOTRE DAME, THE(1923); RUPERT OF HENTZAU(1923); ST. ELMO(1923); ANCIENT MARINER, THE(1925); BEN-HUR(1925); REGULAR FELLOW, A(1925); DON JUAN(1926); YELLOW FINGERS(1926); BELOVED ROGUE, THE(1927); SOFT CUSHIONS(1927); WINGS(1927); GAUCHO, THE(1928); TWO LOVERS(1928)
Misc. Silents
GHOSTS(1915); PURITY(1916); BOND BETWEEN, THE(1917); FORBIDDEN FIRE(1919); MOTHER OF HIS CHILDREN, THE(1920); DEVIL WITHIN, THE(1921); THAT SOMETHING(1921); DOLL'S HOUSE, A(1922); OMAR THE TENTMAKER(1922); BOY OF FLANDERS, A(1924); WILD ORANGES(1924); SURRENDER(1927); DIVINE SINNER(1928)
Louis De Bulger
Misc. Silents
GUNSAULUS MYSTERY, THE(1921)
Celia De Burgh
1984
PHAR LAP(1984, Aus.)
Shirley de Burgh
FOUR GIRLS IN TOWN(1956)
Gayle de Camp
THIS IS THE ARMY(1943)
Rosemary De Camp
HOLD BACK THE DAWN(1941); JUNGLE BOOK(1942); YANKEE DOODLE DANDY(1942); BOWERY TO BROADWAY(1944); MERRY MONAHANS, THE(1944); PRACTICALLY YOURS(1944); BLOOD ON THE SUN(1945); PRIDE OF THE MARINES(1945); RHAPSODY IN BLUE(1945); NIGHT UNTO NIGHT(1949); STORY OF SEABISCUIT, THE(1949); NIGHT INTO MORNING(1951); TREASURE OF LOST CANYON, THE(1952); MAIN STREET TO BROADWAY(1953); SO THIS IS LOVE(1953); THIRTEEN GHOSTS(1960); SATURDAY THE 14TH(1981)
Javier de Campos
SUPERSONIC MAN(1979, Span.)
Tommy De Canio
LITTLE FUGITIVE, THE(1953)
Pierre de Canolle
Silents
NAPOLEON(1927, Fr.)
Maurice de Canonge
DAY THE HOTLINE GOT HOT, THE(1968, Fr./Span.); YOUNG REBEL, THE(1969, Fr./Ital./Span.)
Grace de Capitani
1984
DOG DAY(1984, Fr.); MY NEW PARTNER(1984, Fr.)
Natalia de Capua
SILHOUETTES(1982)
Francis de Carco
MARKED GIRLS(1949, Fr.), a, d&w
Paula de Cardo
ARTISTS AND MODELS ABROAD(1938); SAY IT IN FRENCH(1938); YOU AND ME(1938); HOTEL IMPERIAL(1939); LADY'S FROM KENTUCKY, THE(1939); $1,000 A TOUCHDOWN(1939); THOSE WERE THE DAYS(1940)
Petro de Cardoba
Silents
DARK MIRROR, THE(1920)
Aldo De Carellis
YOUNG, THE EVIL AND THE SAVAGE, THE(1968, Ital.); SECRET OF SANTA VITTORIA, THE(1969); STATUE, THE(1971, Brit.)
Len De Carl
YOU'RE A BIG BOY NOW(1966)
Nancy De Carl
GUIDE FOR THE MARRIED MAN, A(1967)
Phil De Carla
LIAR'S DICE(1980)
Louise De Carlo
SOMBRERO(1953); WHAT DID YOU DO IN THE WAR, DADDY?(1966); WILLARD(1971)
Phil de Carlo
MICROWAVE MASSACRE(1983)
Toni De Carlo
SAUL AND DAVID(1968, Ital./Span.), p
Vinnie De Carlo
HUNTERS, THE(1958)
Yvonne De Carlo
TRUE TO LIFE(1943); HARVARD, HERE I COME(1942); LUCKY JORDAN(1942); ROAD TO MOROCCO(1942); THIS GUN FOR HIRE(1942); CRYSTAL BALL, THE(1943); DEERSLAYER(1943); LET'S FACE IT(1943); RHYTHM PARADE(1943);

SALUTE FOR THREE(1943); SO PROUDLY WE HAIL(1943); YOUTH ON PARADE(1943); KISMET(1944); PRACTICALLY YOURS(1944); RAINBOW ISLAND(1944); STANDING ROOM ONLY(1944); STORY OF DR. WASSELL, THE(1944); FRONTIER GAL(1945); SALOME, WHERE SHE DANCED(1945); BRUTE FORCE(1947); SLAVE GIRL(1947); SONG OF SCHEHERAZADE(1947); CASBAH(1948); RIVER LADY(1948); CALAMITY JANE AND SAM BASS(1949); CRISS CROSS(1949); GAL WHO TOOK THE WEST, THE(1949); BUCCANEER'S GIRL(1950); DESERT HAWK, THE(1950); HOTEL SAHARA(1951); SILVER CITY(1951); TOMAHAWK(1951); HURRICANE SMITH(1952); SAN FRANCISCO STORY, THE(1952); SCARLET ANGEL(1952); CAPTAIN'S PARADISE, THE(1953, Brit.); FORT ALGIERS(1953); SEA DEVILS(1953); SOMBRERO(1953); BORDER RIVER(1954); PASSION(1954); TONIGHT'S THE NIGHT(1954, Brit.); FLAME OF THE ISLANDS(1955); SHOTGUN(1955); DEATH OF A SCOUNDREL(1956); MAGIC FIRE(1956); RAW EDGE(1956); TEN COMMANDMENTS, THE(1956); BAND OF ANGELS(1957); TIMBUKTU(1959); MC LINTOCK!(1963); LAW OF THE LAWLESS(1964); MUNSTER, GO HOME(1966); HOSTILE GUNS(1967); ARIZONA BUSHWHACKERS(1968); POWER, THE(1968); DELTA FACTOR, THE(1970); SEVEN MINUTES, THE(1971); WON TON TON, THE DOG WHO SAVED HOLLYWOOD(1976); SATAN'S CHEERLEADERS(1977); NOCTURNA(1979); GUYANA, CULT OF THE DAMNED zero(1980, Mex./Span./Panama); SILENT SCREAM(1980); PLAY DEAD(1981)
Misc. Talkies
HOUSE OF SHADOWS(1977, Arg.); VULTURES IN PARADISE(1984)
John de Carlos
HAMMER(1972)
George De Carlton
Silents
CAPTAIN SWIFT(1914); GREYHOUND, THE(1914); ORDEAL, THE(1914); THIEF, THE(1915); LIFE WITHOUT SOUL(1916); AMERICAN VENUS, THE(1926); NEW KLONDIKE, THE(1926)
Misc. Silents
TO HIM THAT HATH(1918)
Grace De Carlton
Misc. Silents
BETRAYED!(1916)
Renato De Carmine
TORPEDO BAY(1964, Ital./Fr.)
Lucio De Caro
GIORDANO BRUNO(1973, Ital.), w
Cinzia De Carolis
CAT O'NINE TAILS(1971, Ital./Ger./Fr.)
Grace De Carolis
WORLD'S GREATEST SINNER, THE(1962)
J.P. de Carvalho
PRETTY BUT WICKED(1965, Braz.), d
Jose de Carvalho
1984
THREE CROWNS OF THE SAILOR(1984, Fr.)
Rafael de Carvalho
EARTH ENTRANCED(1970, Braz.)
Denise de Casabianca
PARIS BELONGS TO US(1962, Fr.), ed; LES ABYSSES(1964, Fr.), ed; MORE(1969, Luxembourg), ed; NUN, THE(1971, Fr.), ed; MOTHER AND THE WHORE, THE(1973, Fr.), ed; RETURN OF MARTIN GUERRE, THE(1983, Fr.), ed
Jeanne de Casalis
CHARLEY'S(BIG-HEARTED) AUNT*1/2 (1940); KNOWING MEN(1930, Brit.); NINE TILL SIX(1932, Brit.); MIXED DOUBLES(1933, Brit.); NELL GWYN(1935, Brit.); GIRL WHO FORGOT, THE(1939, Brit.); JAMAICA INN(1939, Brit.); JUST LIKE A WOMAN(1939, Brit.); THREE COCKEYED SAILORS(1940, Brit.); BOMBSIGHT STOLEN(1941, Brit.); THOSE KIDS FROM TOWN(1942, Brit.); THEY MET IN THE DARK(1945, Brit.); GAY INTRUDERS, THE(1946, Brit.); THIS MAN IS MINE(1946 Brit.); TURNERS OF PROSPECT ROAD, THE(1947, Brit.); WOMAN HATER(1949, Brit.); TWENTY QUESTIONS MURDER MYSTERY, THE(1950, Brit.)
Silents
ARCADIANS, THE(1927, Brit.); ZERO(1928, Brit.)
Misc. Silents
SETTLED OUT OF COURT(1925, Brit.)
Ben de Casseres
Silents
NOSFERATU, THE VAMPIRE(1922, Ger.), t
Rosa de Castilla
ORLAK, THE HELL OF FRANKENSTEIN(1960, Mex.)
Babette De Castro
HELEN MORGAN STORY, THE(1959)
Cheri De Castro
HELEN MORGAN STORY, THE(1959)
J.L. Bermuder De Castro
HORROR OF THE ZOMBIES(1974, Span.), p
Jerry de Castro
CORNERED(1945); RIDE THE PINK HORSE(1947); LOVES OF CARMEN, THE(1948)
Julio Alejandro de Castro
EMPTY STAR, THE(1962, Mex.), w; YOUNG AND EVIL(1962, Mex.), w
Peggy De Castro
HELEN MORGAN STORY, THE(1959)
Christina de Cattani
10 VIOLENT WOMEN(1982)
Countess De Cella
Silents
ROWDY, THE(1921)
Carrado De Cenzo
BALL AT THE CASTLE(1939, Ital.)
Ferruccio De Ceresa
SUBVERSIVES, THE(1967, Ital.)
Miguel de Cervantes
DON QUIXOTE(1935, Fr.), w; DON QUIXOTE(1961, USSR), w; DULCINEA(1962, Span.), d&w
Silents
DON QUIXOTE(1923, Brit.), w

Alba De Cespedes
LE AMICHE(1962, Ital.), w
Mons. le Vicomte de Chabot
RISE OF LOUIS XIV, THE(1970, Fr.)
Christian de Chalonge
MALEVIL(1981, Fr./Ger.), d, w
Christian de Chalonges
VOYAGE OF SILENCE(1968, Fr.), d, w
Pauline de Chalus
MILL ON THE FLOSS(1939, Brit.)
Louise de Champfleury
1984
LOVE ON THE GROUND(1984,Fr.), ed
Roland de Chaudenay
1984
SWANN IN LOVE(1984, Fr.Ger.)
Andree De Chauveron
WOULD-BE GENTLEMAN, THE(1960, Fr.)
Segundo de Chomon
Silents
CABIRIA(1914, Ital.), ph
Pat De Cicco
NIGHT LIFE OF THE GODS(1935)
Richard De Cinces
SMOKEY AND THE BANDIT II(1980), set d
William D. De Cinces
GAMES(1967), art d; YOU'LL LIKE MY MOTHER(1972), art d
Isabel Jimines de Cisneros
FITZCARRALDO(1982)
Patrizia de Clara
WHITE SISTER(1973, Ital./Span./Fr.)
Kuulei De Clercq
WAIKIKI WEDDING(1937)
Nalani De Clercq
WAIKIKI WEDDING(1937)
James De Closs
CINDERELLA LIBERTY(1973)
Ennio De Cocini
MY SON, THE HERO(1963, Ital./Fr.), w
Linda De Coff
HURRY UP OR I'LL BE 30(1973)
Lisa De Cohen
LITTLE NIGHT MUSIC, A(1977, Aust./U.S./Ger.)
Ligio De Colonda
Misc. Silents
BRAND OF COWARDICE(1925)
A.B. De Comatheire
Misc. Silents
MIDNIGHT ACE, THE(1928); THIRTY YEARS LATER(1928)
Richard De Combray
TENDER IS THE NIGHT(1961)
Giuseppe De Compo
Silents
ARAB, THE(1924)
Ennio De Concini
WANDERING JEW, THE(1948, Ital.), w; APPOINTMENT FOR MURDER(1954, Ital.), w; HELL RAIDERS OF THE DEEP(1954, Ital.), w; SENSUALITA(1954, Ital.), w; MAMBO(1955, Ital.), w; ULYSSES(1955, Ital.), w; QUEEN OF BABYLON, THE(1956, Ital.), w; WAR AND PEACE(1956, Ital./U.S.), w; MILLER'S WIFE, THE(1957, Ital.), w; HERCULES(1959, Ital.), w; HOUSE OF INTRIGUE, THE(1959, Ital.), w; LOVE SPECIALIST, THE(1959, Ital.), w; WARRIOR AND THE SLAVE GIRL, THE(1959, Ital.), w; GIANT OF MARATHON, THE(1960, Ital.), w; HERCULES UNCHAINED(1960, Ital./Fr.), w; LAST DAYS OF POMPEII, THE(1960, Ital.), w; LEGIONS OF THE NILE(1960, Ital.), w; CARTHAGE IN FLAMES(1961, Fr./Ital.), w; COLOSSUS OF RHODES, THE(1961, Ital./Fr./Span.), w; WARRIOR EMPRESS, THE(1961, Ital./Fr.), w; CONSTANTINE AND THE CROSS(1962, Ital.), w; IL GRIDO(1962, U.S./Ital.), w; MARCO POLO(1962, Fr./Ital.), w; SIEGE OF SYRACUSE(1962, Fr./Ital.), w; SON OF SAMSON(1962, Fr./Ital./Yugo.), w; STORY OF JOSEPH AND HIS BRETHREN THE(1962, Ital.), w; MADAME(1963, Fr./Ital./Span.), w; RICE GIRL(1963, Fr./Ital.), w; RUN WITH THE DEVIL(1963, Fr./Ital.), w; SHIP OF CONDEMNED WOMEN, THE(1963, ITAL.), w; WITCH'S CURSE, THE(1963, Ital.), w; DUEL OF CHAMPIONS(1964 Ital./Span.), w; EVIL EYE(1964 Ital.), w; FACTS OF MURDER, THE(1965, Ital.), w; ITALIANO BRAVA GENTE(1965, Ital./USSR), w; RAILROAD MAN, THE(1965, Ital.), w; LOVE AND MARRIAGE(1966, Ital.), w; THE DIRTY GAME(1966, Fr./Ital./Ger.), w; ROSE FOR EVERYONE, A(1967, Ital.), w; WEEKEND, ITALIAN STYLE(1967, Fr./Ital./Span.), w; OPERATION ST. PETER'S(1968, Ital.), w; TREASURE OF SAN GENNARO(1968, Fr./Ital./Ger.), w; BETTER A WIDOW(1969, Ital.), w; GIRL WHO COULDN'T SAY NO, THE(1969, Ital.), w; PLACE FOR LOVERS, A(1969, Ital./Fr.), w; SONS OF SATAN(1969, Ital./Fr./Ger.), w; RED TENT, THE(1971, Ital./USSR), w; THAT SPLENDID NOVEMBER(1971, Ital./Fr.), w; HITLER: THE LAST TEN DAYS(1973, Brit./Ital.), d, w; TWIST, THE(1976, Fr.), w; JUST A GIGOLO(1979, Ger.), w
1984
CORRUPT(1984, Ital.), w
Syn De Conde
Silents
GIRL WHO STAYED AT HOME, THE(1919); OUT OF THE SHADOW(1919)
Misc. Silents
REVELATION(1918); ROUGE AND RICHES(1920)
Ennio De Coneine
BLACK SUNDAY(1961, Ital.), w
Destournelles De Constant
Silents
JOY STREET(1929)
Ryk De Cooyer
WILBY CONSPIRACY, THE(1975, Brit.)
Theodosia De Coppett [Theda Bara]
Silents
STAIN, THE(1914)

Pedro De Corboda
CONDEMNED TO LIVE(1935)
Silents
FIRES OF FATE(1923, Brit.)
Paul de Corday
EMPEROR WALTZ, THE(1948); LIGHT TOUCH, THE(1951)
Leander de Cordoba
FEAR IN THE NIGHT(1947)
Luisa De Cordoba
SON OF CAPTAIN BLOOD, THE(1964, U.S./Ital./Span.)
Mercedes de Cordoba
Silents
OUT OF A CLEAR SKY(1918)
Pedro De Cordoba
TIME OF YOUR LIFE, THE(1948); CAPTAIN BLOOD(1935); CRUSADES, THE(1935); DEVIL DOLL, THE(1936); GARDEN OF ALLAH, THE(1936); HIS BROTHER'S WIFE(1936); MOONLIGHT MURDER(1936); PROFESSIONAL SOLDIER(1936); RAMONA(1936); ROSE OF THE RANCHO(1936); TROUBLE FOR TWO(1936); DAMAGED GOODS(1937); FIREFLY, THE(1937); GIRL LOVES BOY(1937); MAID OF SALEM(1937); HEART OF THE NORTH(1938); INTERNATIONAL SETTLEMENT(1938); KEEP SMILING(1938); STORM OVER BENGAL(1938); CHARLIE CHAN IN THE CITY OF DARKNESS(1939); CHASING DANGER(1939); ESCAPE TO PARADISE(1939); JUAREZ(1939); LAW OF THE PAMPAS(1939); LIGHT THAT FAILED, THE(1939); MAN OF CONQUEST(1939); BEFORE I HANG(1940); DEVIL'S ISLAND(1940); EARTHBOUND(1940); GHOST BREAKERS, THE(1940); MARK OF ZORRO, THE(1940); MY FAVORITE WIFE(1940); SEA HAWK, THE(1940); SOUTH OF PAGO PAGO(1940); BLOOD AND SAND(1941); CORSICAN BROTHERS, THE(1941); MILLION DOLLAR BABY(1941); PARIS CALLING(1941); PHANTOM SUBMARINE, THE(1941); ROMANCE OF THE RIO GRANDE(1941); SABOTEUR(1942); SHUT MY BIG MOUTH(1942); SON OF FURY(1942); BACKGROUND TO DANGER(1943); FOR WHOM THE BELL TOLLS(1943); SONG OF BERNADETTE, THE(1943); TARZAN TRIUMPHS(1943); WHITE SAVAGE(1943); FALCON IN MEXICO, THE(1944); KISMET(1944); ONCE UPON A TIME(1944); UNCERTAIN GLORY(1944); ADVENTURE(1945); IN OLD NEW MEXICO(1945); SAN ANTONIO(1945); SON OF LASSIE(1945); TAHITI NIGHTS(1945); CLUB HAVANA(1946); CUBAN PETE(1946); NIGHT IN PARADISE, A(1946); SCANDAL IN PARIS, A(1946); SWAMP FIRE(1946); CARNIVAL IN COSTA RICA(1947); MEXICAN HAYRIDE(1948); DARING CABALLERO, THE(1949); OMOO OMOO, THE SHARK GOD(1949); SAMSON AND DELILAH(1949); COMMANCHE TERRITORY(1950); CRISIS(1950); LAWLESS, THE(1950); CUBAN FIREBALL(1951); WHEN THE REDSKINS RODE(1951); SAIL INTO DANGER(1957, Brit.); THUNDER IN THE SUN(1959), a, ch
Misc. Talkies
ROBIN HOOD OF MONTEREY(1947)
Silents
CARMEN(1915); TEMPTATION(1915); ONE LAW FOR BOTH(1917); NEW MOON, THE(1919); SIN THAT WAS HIS, THE(1920); INNER CHAMBER, THE(1921); JUST A SONG AT TWILIGHT(1922); WHEN KNIGHTHOOD WAS IN FLOWER(1922); ENEMIES OF WOMEN, THE(1923); NEW COMMANDMENT, THE(1925)
Misc. Silents
MARIA ROSA(1916); BARBARY SHEEP(1917); RUNAWAY ROMANY(1917); WORLD AND HIS WIFE, THE(1920); PURPLE HIGHWAY, THE(1923); SWORDS AND THE WOMAN(1923, Brit.); DESERT SHEIK, THE(1924)
Senorita de Cordoba
Misc. Silents
NATURE GIRL, THE(1919)
Arturo de Cordova
FOR WHOM THE BELL TOLLS(1943); HOSTAGES(1943); FRENCHMAN'S CREEK(1944); DUFFY'S TAVERN(1945); INCENDIARY BLONDE(1945); MASQUERADE IN MEXICO(1945); MEDAL FOR BENNY, A(1945); NEW ORLEANS(1947); ADVENTURES OF CASANOVA(1948); STRONGHOLD(1952, Mex.); EL(1955, Mex.); INVISIBLE MAN, THE(1958, Mex.); VIOLENT AND THE DAMNED, THE(1962, Braz.)
Fred De Cordova
KING OF COMEDY, THE(1983)
Frederick de Cordova
TOO YOUNG TO KNOW(1945), d; HER KIND OF MAN(1946), d; ALWAYS TOGETHER(1947), d; LOVE AND LEARN(1947), d; THAT WAY WITH WOMEN(1947), d; COUNTESS OF MONTE CRISTO, THE(1948), d; FOR THE LOVE OF MARY(1948), d; WALLFLOWER(1948), d; GAL WHO TOOK THE WEST, THE(1949), d; ILLEGAL ENTRY(1949), d; BUCCANEER'S GIRL(1950), d; DESERT HAWK, THE(1950), d; PEGGY(1950), d; FINDERS KEEPERS(1951), d; KATIE DID IT(1951), d; LITTLE EGYPT(1951), d; BONZO GOES TO COLLEGE(1952), d; HERE COME THE NELSONS(1952), d; YANKEE BUCCANEER(1952), d; COLUMN SOUTH(1953), d; FRANKIE AND JOHNNY(1966), d
Joseph de Cordova
NO MAN IS AN ISLAND(1962); SECRET OF THE SACRED FOREST, THE(1970)
Leader De Cordova
DOUBLE LIFE, A(1947)
Leander de Cordova
PENAL CODE, THE(1933); MIDNIGHT(1939); TORTURE SHIP(1939); LARAMIE TRAIL, THE(1944); GAY SENORITA, THE(1945); GILDA(1946); CASBAH(1948); TOUGH ASSIGNMENT(1949); ACCORDING TO MRS. HOYLE(1951)
Misc. Talkies
TRAILS OF THE GOLDEN WEST(1931), d
Silents
LOVE, HONOR AND OBEY(1920), d
Misc. Silents
SCREAM IN THE NIGHT, A(1919), d; POLLY WITH A PAST(1920), d; SHE(1925, Brit.), d
Lucila de Cordova
LOS INVISIBLES(1961, Mex.)
Pedro de Cordova
WINNER TAKE ALL(1939); DAUGHTER OF THE WEST(1949)
Misc. Silents
DAUGHTER OF THE OLD SOUTH, A(1918)
Rafael de Cordova
EVERY DAY IS A HOLIDAY(1966, Span.)
Rienzi de Cordova
Misc. Silents
FLAME OF PASSION, THE(1915)

Eduardo De Fillipo
GHOSTS, ITALIAN STYLE(1969, Ital./Fr.), w
Don De Fina
STREET MUSIC(1982), art d
Danielle De Flavis
FIEND(
Phil De Flavis
FIEND(
R. De Flers
ROYAL AFFAIR, A(1950), w
Robert de Flers
BEAUTIFUL ADVENTURE(1932, Ger.), w
Felipe De Flores
SOMBRERO(1953)
Annette De Foe
Silents
ONE CLEAR CALL(1922)
Caroline De Fonseca
MIDAS RUN(1969)
Anthony De Fonte
1984
BEVERLY HILLS COP(1984)
Don De Fore
RIGHT TO THE HEART(1942); GUY WHO CAME BACK, THE(1951)
Marian De Forest
Silents
ERSTWHILE SUSAN(1919), w
Marie De Forest
PENITENTE MURDER CASE, THE(1936); ARTISTS AND MODELS ABROAD(1938); TRADE WINDS(1938)
Patsy De Forest
Misc. Silents
NIGHT IN NEW ARABIA, A(1917)
Pituka De Foronda
PASSION ISLAND(1943, Mex.)
Charles De Forrest
Misc. Silents
BLACK CROOK, THE(1916)
Patsy De Forrest
Misc. Silents
SQUARE SHOOTER, THE(1920); SUNSET SPRAGUE(1920)
Germaine de France
IS PARIS BURNING?(1966, U.S./Fr.)
Stephen De France
NIGHT OF THE LEPUS(1972)
Piero De Franceschi
QUIET PLACE IN THE COUNTRY, A(1970, Ital./Fr.)
Aldo De Francesco
SPY IN YOUR EYE(1966, Ital.)
Louis de Francesco
WILD GIRL(1932), md; BERKELEY SQUARE(1933), m; FACE IN THE SKY(1933), md; HOOPLA(1933), m; POWER AND THE GLORY, THE(1933), m, md; WORST WOMAN IN PARIS(1933), m; CHANGE OF HEART(1934), m; GEORGE WHITE'S SCANDALS(1934), md; MUSIC IN THE AIR(1934), md; WHITE PARADE, THE(1934), md; WORLD MOVES ON, THE(1934), m; GEORGE WHITE'S 1935 SCANDALS(1935), m; HERE'S TO ROMANCE(1935), m; UNDER PRESSURE(1935), m; RAMPARTS WE WATCH, THE(1940), m
Silents
WEDDING MARCH, THE(1927), m
Aldo De Franchi
CARTOUCHE(1957, Ital./US)
Antonita de Franco
I'M NOBODY'S SWEETHEART NOW(1940)
Felix De Franco
TRAPPED IN TANGIERS(1960, Ital./Span.)
Jose de Franco
I'M NOBODY'S SWEETHEART NOW(1940)
Mark de Frani
NEW YEAR'S EVIL(1980)
Lauri De Frece
Silents
LABOUR LEADER, THE(1917, Brit.); ONCE UPON A TIME(1918, Brit.)
Lauri de Freece
Silents
ALL THE SAD WORLD NEEDS(1918, Brit.)
Carlo de Fries
AZURE EXPRESS(1938, Hung.), m
Fernando de Fuentes
RANCHO GRANDE(1938, Mex.), d; FACE OF THE SCREAMING WEREWOLF(1959, Mex.), w
Louis de Funes
SEVEN DEADLY SINS, THE(1953, Fr./Ital.); GAME OF LOVE, THE(1954, Fr.); FROU-FROU(1955, Fr.); INNOCENTS IN PARIS(1955, Brit.); FOUR BAGS FULL(1957, Fr./Ital.); LA BELLE AMERICAINE(1961, Fr.); PEEK-A-BOO(1961, Fr.); CANDIDE(1962, Fr.); CRIME DOES NOT PAY(1962, Fr.); DEVIL AND THE TEN COMMANDMENTS, THE(1962, Fr.); FANTOMAS STRIKES BACK(1965, Fr./Ital.); FANTOMAS(1966, Fr./Ital.); GENDARME OF ST. TROPEZ, THE(1966, Fr./Ital.); SUCKER, THE(1966, Fr./Ital.); DON'T LOOK NOW(1969, Brit./Fr.); DELUSIONS OF GRANDEUR(1971 Fr.); MAD ADVENTURES OF RABBI JACOB, THE(1973, Fr.); LE GENDARME ET LES EXTRATERRESTRES(1978, Fr.)
Afred De Gaetano
RAW DEAL(1948), ed
Al De Gaetano
BIG TIME(1929), ed; LOVE, LIVE AND LAUGH(1929), ed; ARE YOU THERE?(1930), ed; OH, FOR A MAN!(1930), ed; BLACK CAMEL, THE(1931), ed; CHARLIE CHAN CARRIES ON(1931), ed; BACHELOR'S AFFAIRS(1932), ed; GAY CABALLERO, THE(1932), ed; I BELIEVED IN YOU(1934), ed; CHARLIE CHAN IN EGYPT(1935), ed; SONG AND DANCE MAN, THE(1936), ed; CHARLIE CHAN ON BROADWAY(1937), ed; DANGEROUSLY YOURS(1937), ed; LADY ESCAPES, THE(1937), ed; MIDNIGHT TAXI(1937), ed; TIME OUT FOR ROMANCE(1937), ed; WILD AND

WOOLLY(1937), ed; MICHAEL SHAYNE, PRIVATE DETECTIVE(1940), ed; YESTERDAY'S HEROES(1940), ed; JENNIE(1941), ed; SCOTLAND YARD(1941), ed
Alfred De Gaetano
BEHIND THAT CURTAIN(1929), ed; STEAMBOAT ROUND THE BEND(1935), ed; RAMONA(1936), ed; OUT OF THE BLUE(1947), ed; HE WALKED BY NIGHT(1948), ed
Silents
CHASER, THE(1928), ed; HEART TROUBLE(1928), ed
Michael De Gaetano
HAUNTED(1976), p,d,&w
Michael A. de Gaetano
UFO: TARGET EARTH(1974), p&d
Alexis de Galien
LOSER TAKES ALL(1956, Brit.)
Alex de Gallier
FLAME AND THE FLESH(1954)
Sol De Garda
TWO GIRLS AND A SAILOR(1944)
Adele De Garde
Silents
MR. BARNES OF NEW YORK(1914); LIGHTS OF NEW YORK, THE(1916)
Misc. Silents
GREEN STOCKINGS(1916); BOTTOM OF THE WELL(1917); WITHIN THE LAW(1917); TRIUMPH OF THE WEAK, THE(1918)
Harold De Garro
IT AIN'T HAY(1943); KNICKERBOCKER HOLIDAY(1944); TWO SMART PEOPLE(1946); PEGGY(1950)
Ronald De Gastro
Silents
OLYMPIC HERO, THE(1928), w
Guy de Gastyne
HEART OF A NATION, THE(1943, Fr.), art d; LES PARENTS TERRIBLES(1950, Fr.), art d; ROYAL AFFAIR, A(1950), prod d
Marco De Gastyne
ROTHSCHILD(1938, Fr.), d
Misc. Silents
INCH'ALLAH(1922, Fr.), d; L'AVENTURE(1923, Fr.), d; A L'HORIZON DU SUD(1924, Fr.), d; LA BLESSURE(1925, Fr.), d; LA CHATELAINE DU LIBAN(1926, Fr.), d; MON COEUR AU RALENTI(1928, Fr.), d; LA MERVELILLEUSE VIE DE JEANNE D'ARC(1929, Fr.), d
Bernard de Gautier
CAESAR AND CLEOPATRA(1946, Brit.)
Boyce De Gaw
IF I HAD A MILLION(1932), w; WINGS OVER HONOLULU(1937), w; BEHIND THE NEWS(1941), w
Fiorella de Gennaro
LA BALANCE(1983, Fr.)
Elsa de Giorgi
LOYALTY OF LOVE(1937, Ital.)
Americo De Giorgio
Silents
NERO(1922, U.S./Ital.)
Gastone De Giovanni
TIN GIRL, THE(1970, Ital.), ph
Franco de Girolama
1984
BLACK CAT, THE(1984, Ital./Brit.), makeup
Hubert de Givenchy
FUNNY FACE(1957), cos; LOVE IN THE AFTERNOON(1957), cos; V.I.P.s, THE(1963, Brit.), cos; PARIS WHEN IT SIZZLES(1964), cos; HOW TO STEAL A MILLION(1966), cos
Claude de Givray
ARMY GAME, THE(1963, Fr.), d, w; TIGHT SKIRTS, LOOSE PLEASURES(1966, Fr.), d, w; STOLEN KISSES(1969, Fr.), w; BED AND BOARD(1971, Fr.), w
Georges de Givray
SOFT SKIN, THE(1964, Fr.)
Joseph Arthur de Gobineau
FINO A FARTI MALE(1969, Fr./Ital.), w
Marie De Goer
ADALEN 31(1969, Swed.)
Constantin De Goguel
MC KENZIE BREAK, THE(1970); THERE'S A GIRL IN MY SOUP(1970, Brit.); DIAMONDS ARE FOREVER(1971, Brit.); TAMARIND SEED, THE(1974, Brit.); ALFIE DARLING(1975, Brit.); INSIDE OUT(1975, Brit.); RUSSIAN ROULETTE(1975, Brit.); EMILY(1976, Brit.); TO THE DEVIL A DAUGHTER(1976, Brit./Ger.); CLASS OF MISS MAC MICHAEL, THE(1978, Brit./U.S.); MEETINGS WITH REMARKABLE MEN(1979, Brit.); STUD, THE(1979, Brit.); ENTER THE NINJA(1982)
Jack de Golconda
CALCUTTA(1947), set d
Gilbert de Goldschmidt
SPECIAL DELIVERY(1955, Ger.), p; GIRL WITH THE GOLDEN EYES, THE(1962, Fr.), p; NUDE IN HIS POCKET(1962, Fr.), p; THREE FABLES OF LOVE(1963, Fr./Ital./Span.), p; YOUNG GIRLS OF ROCHEFORT, THE(1968, Fr.), p; WANDERER, THE(1969, Fr.), p; HOA-BINH(1971, Fr.), p; GIFT, THE(1983, Fr./Ital.), p
Georges de Gombert
ARTISTS AND MODELS ABROAD(1938)
Rijk De Gooyer
SOLDIER OF ORANGE(1979, Dutch); OUTSIDER IN AMSTERDAM(1983, Neth.)
Ryk De Gooyer
BRAINWASHED(1961, Ger.); NOSFERATU, THE VAMPIRE(1979, Fr./Ger.)
Jean-Claude de Goros
ENTRE NOUS(1983, Fr.)
Jean-Claude de Gorros
JUDGE AND THE ASSASSIN, THE(1979, Fr.)
Fred De Gorter
DAYTON'S DEVILS(1968), w
Fred de Gortner
PHANTOM PLANET, THE(1961), w

Jack De Govia
THIEVES LIKE US(1974), cons
Jackson de Govia
1984
RED DAWN(1984), prod d
Manfred De Graaf
LIFT, THE(1983, Neth.)
Marina de Graaf
OUTSIDER IN AMSTERDAM(1983, Neth.)
Joseph De Graf
WILBY CONSPIRACY, THE(1975, Brit.)
Alfred De Graff
LA COLLECTIONNEUSE(1971, Fr.)
Manfred De Graff
LITTLE ARK, THE(1972)
Ton De Graff
GIRL WITH THE RED HAIR, THE(1983, Neth.), ed
E. de Graffenried
RACERS, THE(1955), tech adv
Tom de Graffenried
TIGHT SPOT(1955)
Joe de Graft
HAMILE(1965, Ghana), p
Charles de Grandcourt
VICTORIA THE GREAT(1937, Brit.), w; SIXTY GLORIOUS YEARS(1938, Brit.), w;
EARL OF CHICAGO, THE(1940), w
James De Graot
LITTLE NIGHT MUSIC, A(1977, Aust./U.S./Ger.)
Joseph De Grasse
Silents
GILDED SPIDER, THE(1916), d; ANTHING ONCE(1917), d; BROADWAY SCAN-
DAL(1918), d; ROUGH LOVER, THE(1918), d; NINETEEN AND PHYLLIS(1920), d;
OLD SWIMMIN' HOLE, THE(1921), d; TAILOR MADE MAN, A(1922), d; FLOWING
GOLD(1924), d; SO BIG(1924)
Misc. Silents
FATHER AND THE BOYS(1915), d; BOBBIE OF THE BALLET(1916), d; GRASP OF
GREED, THE(1916), d; GRIP OF JEALOUSY, THE(1916), d; IF MY COUNTRY
SHOULD CALL(1916), d; MARK OF CAIN, THE(1916), a, d; PLACE BEYOND THE
WINDS, THE(1916), a, d; PRICE OF SILENCE, THE(1916), d; DOLL'S HOUSE,
A(1917), d; GIRL IN THE CHECKERED COAT, THE(1917), d; HELL MORGAN'S
GIRL(1917), d; PAY ME(1917), d; PIPER'S PRICE, THE(1917), d; TRIUMPH(1917), d;
WINGED MYSTERY, THE(1917), d; AFTER THE WAR(1918), d; FIGHTING GRIN,
THE(1918), d; SCARLET CAR, THE(1918), d; L' APACHE(1919), d; MARKET OF
SOULS, THE(1919), d; WILD CAT OF PARIS, THE(1919), d; BONNIE MAY(1920), d;
BRAND OF LOPEZ, THE(1920), d; HIS WIFE'S FRIEND(1920), d; MIDLANDERS,
THE(1920), d; 45 MINUTES FROM BROADWAY(1920), d; GIRL I LOVED, THE(1923),
d; THUNDERGATE(1923), d; HIDDEN WAY, THE(1926), d
Robert de Grasse
NINE TILL SIX(1932, Brit.), ph; SIGN OF FOUR, THE(1932, Brit.), ph; WATER
GYPSIES, THE(1932, Brit.), ph; ALICE ADAMS(1935), ph; BREAK OF HEARTS(1935),
ph; FRECKLES(1935), ph; SEVEN KEYS TO BALDPATE(1935), ph; CHATTER-
BOX(1936), ph; LOVE ON A BET(1936), ph; M'LISS(1936), ph; WANTED: JANE
TURNER(1936), ph; WITNESS CHAIR, THE(1936), ph; WOMAN REBELS, A(1936),
ph; OUTCASTS OF POKER FLAT, THE(1937), ph; QUALITY STREET(1937), ph;
STAGE DOOR(1937), ph; CAREFREE(1938), ph; HAVING WONDERFUL TIME(1938),
ph; VIVACIOUS LADY(1938), ph; BACHELOR MOTHER(1939), ph; FIFTH AVENUE
GIRL(1939), ph; STORY OF VERNON AND IRENE CASTLE, THE(1939), ph; KITTY
FOYLE(1940), ph; LUCKY PARTNERS(1940), ph; VIGIL IN THE NIGHT(1940), ph;
DATE WITH THE FALCON, A(1941), ph; FATHER TAKES A WIFE(1941), ph;
FOOTLIGHT FEVER(1941), ph; UNEXPECTED UNCLE(1941), ph; HIGHWAYS BY
NIGHT(1942), ph; MAYOR OF 44TH STREET, THE(1942), ph; MY FAVORITE
SPY(1942), ph; PITTSBURGH(1942), ph; SEVEN DAYS LEAVE(1942), ph; SEVEN
MILES FROM ALCATRAZ(1942), ph; FOREVER AND A DAY(1943), ph; HIGHER
AND HIGHER(1943), ph; IRON MAJOR, THE(1943), ph; LADY OF BURLES-
QUE(1943), ph; LEOPARD MAN, THE(1943), ph; SHOW BUSINESS(1944), ph; STEP
LIVELY(1944), ph; TALL IN THE SADDLE(1944), ph; BODY SNATCHER, THE(1945),
ph; FLAME OF THE BARBARY COAST(1945), ph; GEORGE WHITE'S SCAN-
DALS(1945), ph; BADMAN'S TERRITORY(1946), ph; CRACK-UP(1946), ph; GENIUS
AT WORK(1946), ph; RIVERBOAT RHYTHM(1946), ph; BACHELOR AND THE
BOBBY-SOXER, THE(1947), ph; BORN TO KILL(1947), ph; BODYGUARD(1948), ph;
MIRACLE OF THE BELLS, THE(1948), ph; ADVENTURE IN BALTIMORE(1949), ph;
CLAY PIGEON, THE(1949), ph; DANGEROUS PROFESSION, A(1949), ph; FOLLOW
ME QUIETLY(1949), ph; HOME OF THE BRAVE(1949), ph; JUDGE STEPS OUT,
THE(1949), ph; KISS FOR CORLISS, A(1949), ph; MEN, THE(1950), ph; CHICAGO
CALLING(1951), ph; DOUBLE DYNAMITE(1951), ph; FIRST LEGION, THE(1951),
ph; MARRY ME AGAIN(1953), ph
Silents
KICK BACK, THE(1922), ph; CRASHIN' THRU(1923), ph; BREED OF THE SUN-
SETS(1928), ph; FANGS OF THE WILD(1928), ph; ONE MAN DOG, THE(1929), ph
Sam De Grasse
LAST PERFORMANCE, THE(1929); WALL STREET(1929); CAPTAIN OF THE
GUARD(1930)
Silents
BIRTH OF A NATION, THE(1915); MAN AND HIS MATE, A(1915); MARTYRS OF
THE ALAMO, THE(1915); ACQUITTED(1916); GOOD BAD MAN, THE(1916); INNO-
CENT MAGDALENE, AN(1916); INTOLERANCE(1916); ANTHING ONCE(1917);
WILD AND WOOLLY(1917); NARROW PATH, THE(1918); BLIND HUSBANDS(1919);
DEVIL'S PASSKEY, THE(1920); MOON MADNESS(1920); CHEATER REFORMED,
THE(1921); COURAGE(1921); WIFE'S AWAKENING, A(1921); ROBIN HOOD(1922);
CIRCUS DAYS(1923); COURTSHIP OF MILES STANDISH, THE(1923); SLIPPY
MCGEE(1923); PAINTED PEOPLE(1924); ONE YEAR TO LIVE(1925); BLACK PI-
RATE, THE(1926); BROKEN HEARTS OF HOLLYWOOD(1926); LOVE'S BLIND-
NESS(1926); MIKE(1926); CAPTAIN SALVATION(1927); KING OF KINGS, THE(1927);
MAN WHO LAUGHS, THE(1927); DOG LAW(1928), ph; OUR DANCING DAUGH-
TERS(1928); RACKET, THE(1928); SILKS AND SADDLES(1929)
Misc. Silents
CHILD OF GOD, A(1915); CROSS CURRENTS(1916); DIANA OF THE FOL-
LIES(1916); HALF BREED, THE(1916); HER OFFICAL FATHERS(1917); OLD FASH-
IONED YOUNG MAN, AN(1917); HOPE CHEST, THE(1918); MORTGAGED WIFE,
THE(1918); SIX-SHOOTER ANDY(1918); SMASHING THROUGH(1918); EXQUISIT

THIEF, THE(1919); SILK-LINED BURGLAR, THE(1919); SIS HOPKINS(1919); BROK-
EN GATE, THE(1920); LITTLE GREY MOUSE, THE(1920); SKYWAYMAN, THE(1920);
UNCHARTED CHANNELS(1920); UNSEEN FORCES(1920); FORSAKING ALL OTH-
ERS(1922); DANCER OF THE NILE, THE(1923); VIRGIN, THE(1924); SUN-UP(1925);
EAGLE OF THE SEA, THE(1926); HER SECOND CHANCE(1926); COUNTRY DOC-
TOR, THE(1927); FIGHTING EAGLE, THE(1927); WHEN A MAN LOVES(1927);
WRECK OF THE HESPERUS, THE(1927)
William De Grasse
Silents
NOBODY(1921)
Dario De Grassi
SEVEN GOLDEN MEN(1969, Fr./Ital./Span.)
Gabriel de Gravone
Misc. Silents
L'APPEL DU SANG(1920, Fr.); LA ROUE(1923, Fr.)
Gabriel de Gravonne
Misc. Silents
MICHEL STROGOFF(1926, Fr.)
Denton De Gray
HEART WITHIN, THE(1957, Brit.); IT HAPPENED IN ATHENS(1962)
Sidney De Gray
JUST IMAGINE(1930)
Silents
ALIAS MARY BROWN(1918); ALMOST A HUSBAND(1919); KING OF THE WILD
HORSES, THE(1924); AMATEUR GENTLEMAN, THE(1926); NAUGHTY NANET-
TE(1927)
Misc. Silents
ROUGED LIPS(1923)
Alfonso de Grazia
VIOLATED LOVE(1966, Arg.)
Peter de Greeff
CHAMPAGNE CHARLIE(1944, Brit.)
Jennifer de Greenlaw
LAST WAVE, THE(1978, Aus.)
Mario De Grenet
LA DOLCE VITA(1961, Ital./Fr.)
Fred De Gresac
HELL HARBOR(1930), w; ESCAPE FROM DEVIL'S ISLAND(1935), w
Silents
MARRIAGE OF KITTY, THE(1915), w; SON OF THE SHEIK(1926), w; CAMIL-
LE(1927), w
Mme. Fred De Gresac
SHE GOES TO WAR(1929), w
Silents
ETERNAL TEMPTRESS, THE(1917), w; AFRAID TO LOVE(1927), w
Sidney De Grey
THREE SISTERS, THE(1930); GAY BUCKAROO, THE(1932); UPPER WORLD(1934)
Silents
RECKONING DAY, THE(1918); CHORUS GIRL'S ROMANCE, A(1920); MARK OF
ZORRO(1920); BLOOD AND SAND(1922)
Misc. Silents
ONE WONDERFUL NIGHT(1922); AMERICAN PLUCK(1925); STELLE OF THE
ROYAL MOUNTED(1925); CLOSED GATES(1927)
Slim de Grey
THEY'RE A WEIRD MOB(1966, Aus.); DEMONSTRATOR(1971, Aus.); OUT-
BACK(1971, Aus.)
Etta De Groff
Silents
JOHN GLAYDE'S HONOR(1915)
Carl de Groof
LAST BRIDGE, THE(1957, Aust.), m
Andrew De Groot
1984
STRIKEBOUND(1984, Aus.), ph
Frederik de Groot
OUTSIDER IN AMSTERDAM(1983, Neth.)
1984
QUESTION OF SILENCE(1984, Neth.)
Hugo De Groot
LAST BLITZKRIEG, THE(1958), m; SPY IN THE SKY(1958), m, md
Myra De Groot
NORMAN LOVES ROSE(1982, Aus.)
Roland De Groot
SOLDIER OF ORANGE(1979, Dutch), art d; OUTSIDER IN AMSTERDAM(1983,
Neth.), art d
1984
FOURTH MAN, THE(1984, Neth.), prod d
Sara de Groot
Silents
GENERAL POST(1920, Brit.)
Anatole De Grunwald
DISCOVERIES(1939, Brit.), w; FRENCH WITHOUT TEARS(1939, Brit.), w; SPY FOR
A DAY(1939, Brit.), w; BOMBSIGHT STOLEN(1941, Brit.), w; COURAGEOUS MR.
PENN, THE(1941, Brit.), w; GIRL IN DISTRESS(1941, Brit.), w; MAJOR BAR-
BARA(1941, Brit.), w; QUIET WEDDING(1941, Brit.), w; VOICE IN THE NIGHT,
A(1941, Brit.), w; AVENGERS, THE(1942, Brit.), w; PIMPERNEL SMITH(1942, Brit.),
w; UNPUBLISHED STORY(1942, Brit.), w; AT DAWN WE DIE(1943, Brit.), w; SPIT-
FIRE(1943, Brit.), w; ADVENTURE FOR TWO(1945, Brit.), p&w; JOHNNY IN THE
CLOUDS(1945, Brit.), w; THEY MET IN THE DARK(1945, Brit.), w; BOND
STREET(1948, Brit.), p, w; QUEEN OF SPADES(1948, Brit.), p; HER MAN GIL-
BEY(1949, Brit.), p, w; LAST DAYS OF DOLWYN, THE(1949, Brit.), p; NOW BARAB-
BAS WAS A ROBBER(1949, Brit.), p; WHILE THE SUN SHINES(1950, Brit.), p, w;
WINSLOW BOY, THE(1950), p, w; FLESH AND BLOOD(1951, Brit.), p, w; TREAS-
URE HUNT(1952, Brit.), w; GAY ADVENTURE, THE(1953, Brit.), p, w; MURDER
ON MONDAY(1953, Brit.), w; TWILIGHT WOMEN(1953, Brit.), w; HOLLY AND THE
IVY, THE(1954, Brit.), p, w; INNOCENTS IN PARIS(1955, Brit.), p, w; DOCTOR'S
DILEMMA, THE(1958, Brit.), p, w; LIBEL(1959, Brit.), p, w; I THANK A FOOL(1962,
Brit.), p; COME FLY WITH ME(1963), p; V.I.P.s, THE(1963, Brit.), p; YELLOW
ROLLS-ROYCE, THE(1965, Brit.), p

SANTIAGO(1956); WHITE SQUAW, THE(1956); RUN OF THE ARROW(1957); APACHE TERRITORY(1958); APPOINTMENT WITH A SHADOW(1958); COWBOY(1958); MACHINE GUN KELLY(1958); TEENAGE CAVEMAN(1958); RISE AND FALL OF LEGS DIAMOND, THE(1960); PORTRAIT OF A MOBSTER(1961); FOLLOW THAT DREAM(1962); SCARFACE MOB, THE(1962); THOSE CALLOWAYS(1964); GREATEST STORY EVER TOLD, THE(1965); WILD COUNTRY, THE(1971); MECHANIC, THE(1972); DON IS DEAD, THE(1973); FRASIER, THE SENSUOUS LION(1973); SLAMS, THE(1973); HEY, GOOD LOOKIN'(1982)
Misc. Talkies
APPOINTMENT WITH A SHADOW(1957)

Roger De Koven
UP FRONT(1951); SEIZURE(1974)

Victor de Kowa
DEVIL'S GENERAL, THE(1957, Ger.); EMBEZZLED HEAVEN(1959,Ger.); ENCOUNTERS IN SALZBURG(1964, Ger.)

Paul de Kruif
YELLOW JACK(1938), w

Jean de Kuharski
Silents
EMERALD OF THE EAST(1928, Brit.), a, d&w

Beatrice de L'Etang
PARIS OOH-LA-LA!(1963, U.S./Fr.)

Pedro Calderon de la Barca
Silents
NIGHT OF LOVE, THE(1927), w

Guy De la Berg
OBSESSION(1968, Swed.)

Stig de la Berg
LOVING COUPLES(1966, Swed.)

Marcel De La Bross
JOHNNY ANGEL(1945)

Marcel De La Brosse
GARDEN OF ALLAH, THE(1936); ARISE, MY LOVE(1940); TO HAVE AND HAVE NOT(1944); PARIS UNDERGROUND(1945); IN FAST COMPANY(1946); RAZOR'S EDGE, THE(1946); MY FOOLISH HEART(1949); TO PLEASE A LADY(1950); WHEN WORLDS COLLIDE(1951); SOMETHING TO LIVE FOR(1952); MISSISSIPPI GAMBLER, THE(1953); SO THIS IS PARIS(1954); WHITE CHRISTMAS(1954); FUNNY FACE(1957); TENDER IS THE NIGHT(1961); DEAR BRIGETTE(1965)

Simon De La Brosse
PAULINE AT THE BEACH(1983, Fr.)

Jose Revueltas de la Cabada
ILLUSION TRAVELS BY STREETCAR, THE(1977, Mex.), w

Marthe de la Chevrotiere
TI-CUL TOUGAS(1977, Can.), ed

Zedra de la Conde
MOONLIGHT IN HAVANA(1942)

Mme. de la Croix
Silents
SCANDAL, THE(1923, Brit.)

Raven De La Croix
SCREWBALLS(1983)

Carmelo de la Cruz
PIE IN THE SKY(1964)

Joe De La Cruz
LAW AND LAWLESS(1932); FOUR FRIGHTENED PEOPLE(1934); FRONTIERS OF '49(1939); WESTERNER, THE(1940)

Jose de la Cruz
TRAILING THE KILLER(1932)

Juan De La Cruz
SUZY(1936); MEET THE WILDCAT(1940); MISS V FROM MOSCOW(1942); DELINQUENT DAUGHTERS(1944); SHAKE HANDS WITH MURDER(1944); SPANISH MAIN, THE(1945)
Silents
ADVENTURE IN HEARTS, AN(1919)
Misc. Silents
FLIRT, THE(1916); HOUSE OF LIES, THE(1916); GENTLEMAN'S AGREEMENT, A(1918)

Jimmy De La Cruze
FLIGHT(1929)

Joe De La Cruze
LAWLESS BORDER(1935)

Jean de La Fontaine
THREE FABLES OF LOVE(1963, Fr./Ital./Span.), w; DOUBLE BED, THE(1965, Fr./Ital.), w

Victor De La Fosse
BEN HUR(1959)

Georges de la Fouchardiere
SCARLET STREET(1945), w

Georges de la Fouchardiere
LA CHIENNE(1975, Fr.), w

Alfred De La Fuente
EASY MONEY(1983)

Eduardo Torre de la Fuente
LAZARILLO(1963, Span.), art d; THAT MAN GEORGE!(1967, Fr./Ital./Span.), art d; NARCO MEN, THE(1969, Span./Ital.), art d

Armand de La Garza
MADE FOR EACH OTHER(1971)

Dorothy de La Garza
MADE FOR EACH OTHER(1971)

Georges de la Grandiere
BERNADETTE OF LOURDES(1962, Fr.), p

Viscount George de la Grandiere
MONSIEUR VINCENT(1949, Fr.), p

Jose A. De La Guerra
WIDOWS' NEST(1977, U.S./Span.), art d

Jose Antonio de la Guerra
CASTILIAN, THE(1963, Span./U.S.), art d; MOMENT OF TRUTH, THE(1965, Ital./Span.), set d; NOT ON YOUR LIFE(1965, Ital./Span.), art d; CHIMES AT MIDNIGHT(1967, Span.,Switz.), art d

Leon de la Guignaraye
1984
SUGAR CANE ALLEY(1984, Fr.)

Ina De La Haye
SALT TO THE DEVIL(1949, Brit.); MOULIN ROUGE(1952); MR. POTTS GOES TO MOSCOW(1953, Brit.); NIGHT WITHOUT STARS(1953, Brit.); TOP OF THE FORM(1953, Brit.); DANCE LITTLE LADY(1954, Brit.); ROB ROY, THE HIGHLAND ROGUE(1954, Brit.); I AM A CAMERA(1955, Brit.); ANASTASIA(1956); SPANISH GARDENER, THE(1957, Span.); VILLAGE OF DAUGHTERS(1962, Brit.); ISADORA(1968, Brit.); PRIVATE LIFE OF SHERLOCK HOLMES, THE(1970, Brit.)

Ina de la Hye
BEDEVILLED(1955)

Eloy De La Iglesia
Misc. Talkies
APARTMENT ON THE THIRTEENTH FLOOR(1973), d

Lisarao de la Inglesia
ROYAL HUNT OF THE SUN, THE(1969, Brit.)

Antonio de la Loma
GRAND SLAM(1968, Ital., Span., Ger.), w

Jose Antonio de la Loma
SOFT SKIN ON BLACK SILK(1964, Fr./Span.), d, w; SUNSCORCHED(1966, Span./Ger.), w; TEXICAN, THE(1966, U.S./Span.), w; LIGHTNING BOLT(1967, Ital./Sp.), w; SEA PIRATE, THE(1967, Fr./Span./Ital.), w; BOLDEST JOB IN THE WEST, THE(1971, Ital.), d&w

Jose Antonio de la Loma, Sr.
1984
CONQUEST(1984, Ital./Span./Mex.), w

Joe Antonio de la Loma Hernandez
FIVE GIANTS FROM TEXAS(1966, Ital./Span.), w

Roberto de la Madrid
YOUNG LAND, THE(1959)

Victor Gil de la Madrid
OLIVER'S STORY(1978)

Mary De La Mare
Misc. Talkies
KNOCKING AT HEAVEN'S DOOR(1980)

Antonio de la Mogueis
NO MAN IS AN ISLAND(1962)

Francois de La mothe
KING OF HEARTS(1967, Fr./Ital.), art d

Leon De La Mothe
Silents
NORTHERN CODE(1925), d
Misc. Silents
DESERT HAWK, THE(1924), d; DESPERATE CHANCE(1926); PAINTED TRAIL(1928); TRAILIN' BACK(1928)

Leon De La Motte
Misc. Silents
RIDIN' WILD(1925), d

Marguerite de la Motte
IRON MASK, THE(1929); SHADOW RANCH(1930)
Misc. Talkies
WOMAN'S MAN, A(1934)
Silents
ARIZONA(1918); MARK OF ZORRO(1920); NUT, THE(1921); TEN DOLLAR RAISE, THE(1921); THREE MUSKETEERS, THE(1921); FOOLS OF FORTUNE(1922); JILT, THE(1922); SHATTERED IDOLS(1922); SCARS OF JEALOUSY(1923); EAST OF BROADWAY(1924); DAUGHTERS WHO PAY(1925); FLATTERY(1925); OFF THE HIGHWAY(1925); HEARTS AND FISTS(1926); RED DICE(1926); HELD BY THE LAW(1927); KID SISTER, THE(1927); RAGTIME(1927)
Misc. Silents
DANGEROUS WATERS(1919); IN WRONG(1919); PAGAN GOD, THE(1919); SAGE BRUSH HAMLET, A(1919); BROKEN GATE, THE(1920); HOPE, THE(1920); SAGEBRUSHER, THE(1920); TRUMPET ISLAND(1920); U.P. TRAIL, THE(1920); DESIRE(1923); FAMOUS MRS. FAIR, THE(1923); MAN OF ACTION, THE(1923); RICHARD, THE LION-HEARTED(1923); WANDERING DAUGHTERS(1923); WHAT A WIFE LEARNED(1923); BEHOLD THIS WOMAN(1924); BELOVED BRUTE, THE(1924); CLEAN HEART, THE(1924); IN LOVE WITH LOVE(1924); THOSE WHO DARE(1924); WHEN A MAN'S A MAN(1924); CHEAPER TO MARRY(1925); CHILDREN OF THE WHIRLWIND(1925); FLATTERY(1925); PEOPLE VS. NANCY PRESTON(1925); FIFTH AVENUE(1926); LAST FRONTIER, THE(1926); MEET THE PRINCE(1926); PALS IN PARADISE(1926); UNKNOWN SOLDIER, THE(1926); BROADWAY MADNESS(1927); FINAL EXTRA, THE(1927); MONTMARTE ROSE(1929)

Margueritte de la Motte
REG'LAR FELLERS(1941)

Maurguerite De La Motte
Silents
SHADOWS(1922)

Mischa de la Motte
FERRY ACROSS THE MERSEY(1964, Brit.); RETURN FROM THE ASHES(1965, U.S./Brit.); ONE MORE TIME(1970, Brit.)

Jean de la Muir
PARISIAN, THE(1931, Fr.), d

L. de la Parelle
Misc. Silents
STRIPPED FOR A MILLION(1919), d

Javier de la Parra
ILLUSION TRAVELS BY STREETCAR, THE(1977, Mex.)

Denys de La Patelliere
TAXI FOR TOBRUK(1965, Fr./Span./Ger.), p&d, w; MARCO THE MAGNIFICENT(1966, Ital./Fr./Yugo./Egypt/Afghanistan), d, w; UPPER HAND, THE(1967, Fr./Ital./Ger.), d, w; CAROLINE CHERIE(1968, Fr.), d; SABRA(1970, Fr./Ital./Israel), d

Danny De La Paz
CUBA(1979); BARBAROSA(1982)

George De La Pena
NIJINSKY(1980, Brit.); PERSONAL BEST(1982)

Gilbert De La Pena
  TRACKDOWN(1976)
Antonella De La Porta
  TWO WOMEN(1961, Ital./Fr.)
Jean Pierre Mahot de la Querantonnais
  QUARTET(1981, Brit./Fr.), p
Amelia De La Rama
  STEEL CLAW, THE(1961)
Mazo de la Roche
  JALNA(1935), w
Pierre de la Salle
  DUFFY(1968, Brit.), w
Maurice de la Serna
  ILLUSION TRAVELS BY STREETCAR, THE(1977, Mex.), w
Carlos Ruiz de la Tejera
  DEATH OF A BUREAUCRAT(1979, Cuba)
Raf De La Terre
  MARY, QUEEN OF SCOTS(1971, Brit.)
Enrique de la Torre
  HEROINA(1965), w
Raf de la Torre
  PICKWICK PAPERS, THE(1952, Brit.); PENNY PRINCESS(1953, Brit.); PORTRAIT IN SMOKE(1957, Brit.); FEMALE FIENDS(1958, Brit.); MANIA(1961, Brit.); THERE'S A GIRL IN MY SOUP(1970, Brit.); S(1974)
Luis Rojas de la Torres
  MAN HUNTERS OF THE CARIBBEAN(1938), p
Andrew De La Tour
1984
  LOOSE CONNECTIONS(1984, Brit.)
Charles de la Tour
  IMPULSE(1955, Brit.), d
Frances De La Tour
  BROTHERLY LOVE(1970, Brit.); OUR MISS FRED(1972, Brit.); TO THE DEVIL A DAUGHTER(1976, Brit./Ger.); WOMBLING FREE(1977, Brit.); RISING DAMP(1980, Brit.); TIME BANDITS(1981, Brit.)
John De La Vega
  POLYESTER(1981)
Billie de la Volta
  AVENGING HAND, THE(1936, Brit.); EVERYBODY DANCE(1936, Brit.)
Caridad de Laberdesque
  L'AGE D'OR(1979, Fr.)
Francisca Lopes de Laboriel
  SLAUGHTER(1972)
Marcelle De LaBrosse
  WOMAN'S SECRET, A(1949)
Leigh De Lacey
  YOUNGEST PROFESSION, THE(1943)
Leona De Lacey
Silents
  IDAHO RED(1929), ed
Philippe de Lacey
  SINS OF THE CHILDREN(1930)
Silents
  PETER PAN(1924); DON JUAN(1926); WAY OF ALL FLESH, THE(1927); ROYAL RIDER, THE(1929)
Phillipe de Lacey
Silents
  ROSITA(1923)
Ralph De Lacey
  THOSE WE LOVE(1932), art d; IMPORTANT WITNESS, THE(1933), art d
Robert De Lacey
Silents
  LIGHTNING LARIATS(1927), d; SPLITTING THE BREEZE(1927), d; IDAHO RED(1929), d
Misc. Silents
  LET'S GO GALLAGHER(1925), d; WYOMING WILDCAT, THE(1925), d; COWBOY COP, THE(1926), d; MASQUERADE BANDIT, THE(1926), d; RED HOT HOOFS(1926), d; WILD TO GO(1926), d
Pierre Ambroise Francois Choderlos de Laclos
  LES LIAISONS DANGEREUSES(1961, Fr./Ital.), w
Juan De LaCrux
Silents
  HOP, THE DEVIL'S BREW(1916)
Joe De LaCruz
  DEVIL WITH WOMEN, A(1930); HIDDEN VALLEY(1932); OKLAHOMA FRONTIER(1939); TULSA KID, THE(1940)
Jose De LaCruz
  HELL'S HEROES(1930)
Bob De Lacy
Silents
  CYCLONE OF THE RANGE(1927), d
Jack De Lacy
Silents
  EARLY BIRD, THE(1925)
Leigh De Lacy
  THUNDER AFLOAT(1939); HOUSE OF THE SEVEN GABLES, THE(1940)
May De Lacy
Silents
  GILDED CAGE, THE(1916); ROMEO AND JULIET(1916); ARMS AND THE GIRL(1917); TILLIE WAKES UP(1917); LES MISERABLES(1918)
Philippe De Lacy
  MARRIAGE PLAYGROUND, THE(1929); REDEEMING SIN, THE(1929); SQUARE SHOULDERS(1929); ONE ROMANTIC NIGHT(1930); SARAH AND SON(1930)
Silents
  LOVER'S OATH, A(1925); IS ZAT SO?(1927); LOVE(1927); FOUR FEATHERS(1929)
Misc. Silents
  MAGIC GARDEN, THE(1927); TIGRESS, THE(1927); MOTHER MACHREE(1928)

Phillip De Lacy
Silents
  DIVORCE(1923)
Ralph de Lacy
  BORDER ROMANCE(1930), set d; BORROWED WIVES(1930), set d; THIRD ALARM, THE(1930), set d; THOROUGHBRED, THE(1930), set d; UNDER MONTANA SKIES(1930), set d
Silents
  CONNECTICUT YANKEE AT KING ARTHUR'S COURT, A(1921), art d
Ralph M. De Lacy
  STRANGERS OF THE EVENING(1932), set d
Robert De Lacy
  PARDON MY GUN(1930), d
Silents
  BOY OF MINE(1923), ed; GIRL OF THE GOLDEN WEST, THE(1923), ed; OUT OF THE WEST(1926), d; TOM AND HIS PALS(1926), d; SONORA KID, THE(1927), d
Misc. Silents
  COWBOY MUSKETEER, THE(1925), d; ARIZONA STREAK, THE(1926), d; BORN TO BATTLE(1926), d; CHEROKEE KID, THE(1927), d; FLYING U RANCH, THE(1927), d; TOM'S GANG(1927), d; KING COWBOY(1928), d; RED RIDERS OF CANADA(1928), d; TYRANT OF RED GULCH(1928), d; WHEN THE LAW RIDES(1928), d; DRIFTER, THE(1929), d; TRAIL OF THE HORSE THIEVES, THE(1929), d
Loulou De LaFalaise
  PILGRIMAGE(1972)
Alfredo de Lafeld
  8 ½(1963, Ital.)
Marcel De Lage
  MAFIA GIRLS, THE(1969)
Marguerite De Lain
  SWEET CHARITY(1969)
Diane De Laire
  CELL 2455, DEATH ROW(1955)
Elenor De Lamater
  HOT WATER(1937), w
Marlene De Lamater
  STRIPPER, THE(1963)
Francois de Lamoth
  AFRICAN, THE(1983, Fr.), art d
Francois de Lamothe
  CARTOUCHE(1962, Fr./Ital.), art d; DEVIL AND THE TEN COMMANDMENTS, THE(1962, Fr.), art d; THREE FACES OF SIN(1963, Fr./Ital.), art d; CIRCLE OF LOVE(1965, Fr.), art d; HIGHWAY PICKUP(1965, Fr./Ital.), art d; MALE HUNT(1965, Fr./Ital.), art d; UP TO HIS EARS(1966, Fr./Ital.), art d; 24 HOURS IN A WOMAN'S LIFE(1968, Fr./Ger.), art d; BORSALINO(1970, Fr.), art d; MADLY(1970, Fr.), art d; START THE REVOLUTION WITHOUT ME(1970), art d; MAGNIFICENT ONE, THE(1974, Fr./Ital.), art d; AND NOW MY LOVE(1975, Fr.), art d; CATHERINE & CO.(1976, Fr.), art d; LITTLE ROMANCE, A(1979, U.S./Fr.), art d; LES MISERABLES(1982, Fr.), art d
1984
  JUST THE WAY YOU ARE(1984), art d; LE BON PLAISIR(1984, Fr.), art d
Shirley De Lancey
  BLOOD OF DRACULA(1957)
Juan De Landa
  BRIEF RAPTURE(1952, Ital.); BEAT THE DEVIL(1953); DEVOTION(1953, Ital.); OSSESSIONE(1959, Ital.); MAN WHO WAGGED HIS TAIL, THE(1961, Ital./Span.)
Norma De Landa
  DESERT HAWK, THE(1950)
Juan De Lando
  KING'S JESTER, THE(1947, Ital.)
Jacques de Lane Lea
  NO LOVE FOR JUDY(1955, Brit.), d&w; IT'S ALL OVER TOWN(1963, Brit.), p
William De Lane Lea
  CARTHAGE IN FLAMES(1961, Fr./Ital.), w
Bob De Lange
  SPY IN THE SKY(1958)
David De Lange
1984
  KARATE KID, THE(1984)
Eddie de Lange
  HALF SHOT AT SUNRISE(1930)
Sann De Lange
  AFTER YOU, COMRADE(1967, S. Afr.)
Frank De Langton
  13 RUE MADELEINE(1946)
Glorya De Lani
  HUMAN TORNADO, THE(1976)
Stella De Lanti
Silents
  SWORD OF VALOR, THE(1924); DON Q, SON OF ZORRO(1925)
Hubert de LaParrent
  GERVAISE(1956, Fr.)
Hubert De Lapparent
  FOUR BAGS FULL(1957, Fr./Ital.); HUNCHBACK OF NOTRE DAME, THE(1957, Fr.); PARIS DOES STRANGE THINGS(1957, Fr./Ital.); DAY AND THE HOUR, THE(1963, Fr./ Ital.); CHECKERBOARD(1969, Fr.)
Gemze de Lappe
  KING AND I, THE(1956); JUSTINE(1969), ch
Frederic de Lara
  WATCH BEVERLY(1932, Brit.)
Frederick de Lara
Misc. Silents
  CHARLATAN, THE(1916, Brit.)
Hattie De Lara
Misc. Silents
  HEIGHTS OF HAZARDS, THE(1915)
Leslie De Larenzo
  HAREM BUNCH; OR WAR AND PIECE, THE(1969)

Ramon De Larrocha
  BITTER VICTORY(1958, Fr.)
Shirley De Las Alas
  BIG DOLL HOUSE, THE(1971)
Alexander Dembo de Lasta
  TREACHERY ON THE HIGH SEAS(1939, Brit.), p
Raf De LaTerre
  GOLDEN COACH, THE(1953, Fr./Ital.)
Anthony de Laune
  NIGHT OF THE WITCHES(1970), ed
Alfredo De Laurentiis
  SHIP OF CONDEMNED WOMEN, THE(1963, ITAL.), p
Dino De Laurentiis
  BITTER RICE(1950, Ital.), p; ANNA(1951, Ital.), p; ULYSSES(1955, Ital.), p; LA STRADA(1956, Ital.), p; WAR AND PEACE(1956, Ital./U.S.), p; GOLD OF NAPLES(1957, Ital.), p; MILLER'S WIFE, THE(1957, Ital.), p; NIGHTS OF CABIRIA(1957, Ital.), p; ATTILA(1958, Ital.), p; TEMPEST(1958, Ital./Yugo./Fr.), p; THIS ANGRY AGE(1958, Ital./Fr.), p; UNDER TEN FLAGS(1960, U.S./Ital.), p; GREAT WAR, THE(1961, Fr., Ital.), p; BARABBAS(1962, Ital.), p; BEST OF ENEMIES, THE(1962), p; HUNCHBACK OF ROME, THE(1963, Ital.), p; AND SUDDENLY IT'S MURDER!(1964, Ital.), p; FLYING SAUCER, THE(1964, Ital.), p; DAY IN COURT, A(1965, Ital.), p; BIBLE...IN THE BEGINNING, THE(1966), p; KISS THE GIRLS AND MAKE THEM DIE(1967, U.S./Ital.), p; STRANGER, THE(1967, Algeria/Fr./Ital.), p; BARBARELLA(1968, Fr./Ital.), p; DANGER: DIABOLIK(1968, Ital./Fr.), p; VIOLENT FOUR, THE(1968, Ital.), p; FRAULEIN DOKTOR(1969, Ital./Yugo.), p; WITCHES, THE(1969, Fr./Ital.), p; WATERLOO(1970, Ital./USSR), p; MAN CALLED SLEDGE, A(1971, Ital.), p; VALACHI PAPERS, THE(1972, Ital./Fr.), p; THREE TOUGH GUYS(1974, U.S./Ital.), p; KING KONG(1976), p; RAGTIME(1981), p
Federico De Laurentiis
  KING OF THE GYPSIES(1978), p
Rafaella De Laurentiis
1984
  DUNE(1984), p
Raffaella De Laurentiis
  CONAN THE BARBARIAN(1982), p
1984
  CONAN THE DESTROYER(1984), p
Veronica De Laurentiis
  WATERLOO(1970, Ital./USSR)
Daniel De Laurentis
  HIS KIND OF WOMAN(1951)
Dino de Laurentis
  MAMBO(1955, Ital.), p; HURRICANE(1979), p
Luigi De Laurentis
  HELL RAIDERS OF THE DEEP(1954, Ital.), p
Robert de Laurentis
  GREEN ICE(1981, Brit.), w
Dino De Laurentiis
  EVERYBODY GO HOME!(1962, Fr./Ital.), p
Charles De Lautour
  LIMPING MAN, THE(1953, Brit.), d
Carmen de Lavallade
  LYDIA BAILEY(1952); ABBOTT AND COSTELLO MEET DR. JEKYLL AND MR. HYDE(1954); DEMETRIUS AND THE GLADIATORS(1954); EGYPTIAN. THE(1954); ODDS AGAINST TOMORROW(1959)
Yvonne De Lavallade
  MOLE PEOPLE, THE(1956)
Carol De Lay
  HUSH... HUSH, SWEET CHARLOTTE(1964)
Kay De Lay
Silents
  GOLD RUSH, THE(1925)
Melville De Lay
  LAW OF THE SADDLE(1944), d
Sebastiano De Leandro
  8 ½(1963, Ital.)
Virginia De Lee
  HELL BOUND(1957)
Kitty de Legh
  THEY DRIVE BY NIGHT(1938, Brit.); HIS BROTHER'S KEEPER(1939, Brit.)
Alfred De Leo
  RING AROUND THE CLOCK(1953, Ital.)
Angela De Leo
  ROMA(1972, Ital./Fr.)
Don De Leo
  DESERT FOX, THE(1951); MOB, THE(1951); SALOME(1953); HUSTLER, THE(1961); NIGHT OF EVIL(1962)
Rosy De Leo
  SAMSON AND THE SLAVE QUEEN(1963, Ital.)
Sandro de Leo
  GREATEST LOVE, THE(1954, Ital.), w
Antonio de Leon
  BOY WHO STOLE A MILLION, THE(1960, Brit.), w
Chavo De Leon
  PARIS AFTER DARK(1943); EASY TO WED(1946)
Enandine Diaz De Leon
  PEARL, THE(1948, U.S./Mex.)
Enedina Diaz de Leon
  RUN FOR THE SUN(1956)
Galvan De Leon
  SOUTH PACIFIC(1958)
Geraldo de Leon
  MAD DOCTOR OF BLOOD ISLAND, THE(1969, Phil./U.S.), d
Gerardo de Leon
  MORO WITCH DOCTOR(1964, U.S./Phil.), d; WALLS OF HELL, THE(1964, U.S./Phil.), d; BLOOD DRINKERS, THE(1966, U.S./Phil.), d; BRIDES OF BLOOD(1968, US/Phil.), d; CURSE OF THE VAMPIRES(1970, Phil., U.S.), d

Gerry De Leon
  TERROR IS A MAN(1959, U.S./Phil.), d
Misc. Talkies
  WOMEN IN CAGES(1972), d
Isobel De Leon
Silents
  IRON MAN, THE(1925)
Jack de Leon
  GABLES MYSTERY, THE(1931, Brit.), w; CRIME ON THE HILL(1933, Brit.), w; LINE ENGAGED(1935, Brit.), w; JURY'S EVIDENCE(1936, Brit.), w; GABLES MYSTERY, THE(1938, Brit.), w
Misc. Talkies
  LINDA LOVELACE FOR PRESIDENT(1975)
Jacques De Leon
  DOULOS-THE FINGER MAN(1964, Fr./Ital.)
Loolee de Leon
  ONE FROM THE HEART(1982)
Luis de Leon
  CREATURE OF THE WALKING DEAD(1960, Mex.), prod d
Pedro De Leon
Silents
  JOYOUS TROUBLEMAKERS, THE(1920)
Raoul De Leon
  THIRD VOICE, THE(1960); PLEASURE SEEKERS, THE(1964)
Walter De Leon
  BIG MONEY(1930), w; NIGHT WORK(1930), w; UNION DEPOT(1932), w; TILLIE AND GUS(1933), w; YOU'RE TELLING ME(1934), w; CAT AND THE CANARY, THE(1939), w; GHOST BREAKERS, THE(1940), w; TUGBOAT ANNIE SAILS AGAIN(1940), w; POT O' GOLD(1941), w; RIDING HIGH(1943), w; TIME OF THEIR LIVES, THE(1946), w; SCARED STIFF(1953), w
Silents
  SCHOOL DAYS(1921), w; RAGS TO RICHES(1922), w
Francesco De Leone
  GUNS OF THE BLACK WITCH(1961, Fr./Ital.); PRISONER OF THE IRON MASK(1962, Fr./Ital.); AFTER THE FOX(1966, U.S./Brit./Ital.)
Francoise de Leu
1984
  MY NEW PARTNER(1984, Fr.), art d
Ray de Leeuw
  CHARLEY AND THE ANGEL(1973), ed; SUPERDAD(1974), ed; HOT LEAD AND COLD FEET(1978), ed
Raymond A. de Leeuw
  DEVIL AND MAX DEVLIN, THE(1981), ed
Marietta de Leyse
Silents
  LONDON'S ENEMIES(1916, Brit.)
Misc. Silents
  HOW MEN LOVE WOMEN(1915, Brit.); PARTED BY THE SWORD(1915, Brit.)
Marisa De Leza
  ALEXANDER THE GREAT(1956)
Rina de Ligoure
Misc. Silents
  MYSTIC MIRROR, THE(1928, Ger.)
Countess De Liguoro
  MADAME SATAN(1930); ROMANCE(1930)
Eugenio De Liguoro
  STOP THAT CAB(1951), d
Rina De Liguoro
  LEOPARD, THE(1963, Ital.)
Misc. Silents
  MESSALINA(1924, Ital.); CASANOVA(1927, Fr.)
C. A. de Lima
Silents
  HER GREAT CHANCE(1918)
Charles de Lima
Silents
  AMERICAN ARISTOCRACY(1916)
Jose Augusto de Lima
  DOVE, THE(1974, Brit.)
Josette De Lima
  BILL OF DIVORCEMENT, A(1932), cos; WESTWARD PASSAGE(1932), cos
Luis de Lima
  WAGES OF FEAR, THE(1955, Fr./Ital.)
Count Jean de Limur
Silents
  ARAB, THE(1924)
Jean De Limur
  JEALOUSY(1929), d; LETTER, THE(1929), d, ed; RUNAWAY LADIES(1935, Brit.), d; SLIPPER EPISODE, THE(1938, Fr), d
Silents
  MAGNIFICENT FLIRT, THE(1928), w; THREE SINNERS(1928), w
Ilsa De Lindt
Silents
  CRIMSON RUNNER, THE(1925)
Anna De Linsky
  DEATH TAKES A HOLIDAY(1934)
Silents
  KING OF KINGS, THE(1927)
Victor De Linsky
  STRANGE WIVES(1935)
Silents
  KING OF KINGS, THE(1927)
Derek De Lint
  SOLDIER OF ORANGE(1979, Dutch)
Fritz de Lint
Misc. Silents
  WHAT WILL PEOPLE SAY(1915); SOUL MARKET, THE(1916)

Carmen de Lirio
GOLIATH AGAINST THE GIANTS(1963, Ital./Span.); BACKFIRE(1965, Fr.)

Andre De Lise
1984
DELIVERY BOYS(1984)

Marie de Lisle
Misc. Silents
SLAVE, THE(1918, Brit.)

Monte de Lisle
BALL AT SAVOY(1936, Brit.)

Elizabeth de Lisser
CHILDREN OF BABYLON(1980, Jamaica)

Johnny De Little
DREAM MAKER, THE(1963, Brit.)

Antonio Ramirez de Loayra
BAD MAN'S RIVER(1972, Span.), ed

Rene de Loffre
LITTLE BOY LOST(1953)

Gertrude de Lolsky
LOVE WALTZ, THE(1930, Ger.)

Ines de Lonchamps
LEFT-HANDED WOMAN, THE(1980, Ger.)

Anthony De Longis
CIRCLE OF IRON(1979, Brit.)

Janna De Loos
LAKE PLACID SERENADE(1944); O.S.S.(1946); BUCK PRIVATES COME HO-ME(1947)

Carl De Lora
CORNERED(1945)

Andre de Lorde
DIARY OF A CHAMBERMAID(1946), w

Claire De Lorez
Silents
JOYOUS TROUBLEMAKERS, THE(1920); FOUR HORSEMEN OF THE APOCA-LYPSE, THE(1921); QUEEN OF SHEBA, THE(1921); NET, THE(1923); BEAU BRUM-MEL(1924); COBRA(1925); NORTHERN CODE(1925)
Misc. Silents
BRIGHT LIGHTS OF BROADWAY(1923); SIREN OF SEVILLE, THE(1924); COAST PATROL, THE(1925); RANGE TERROR, THE(1925); MORGANE, THE ENCHANT-RESS(1929, Fr.)

Al de Lory
OUT OF SIGHT(1966), m; NORWOOD(1970), m; DEVIL'S RAIN, THE(1975, U.S./Mex.), m

Consuelo De Los Angeles
HAPPY DAYS(1930)

Luis de los Arcos
CASTILIAN, THE(1963, Span./U.S.), w; PYRO(1964, U.S./Span.), w; FINGER ON THE TRIGGER(1965, US/Span.), w; OPERATION DELILAH(1966, U.S./Span.), d, w

Waldo de los Rios
SAVAGE PAMPAS(1967, Span./Arg.), m; HOUSE THAT SCREAMED, THE(1970, Span.), m; MURDERS IN THE RUE MORGUE(1971), m&md; TOWN CALLED HELL, A(1971, Span./Brit.), m, md; BAD MAN'S RIVER(1972, Span.), m; ISLAND OF THE DAMNED(1976, Span.), m; CORRUPTION OF CHRIS MILLER, THE(1979, Span.), m

Christine Hopf_de Loup
MARRIAGE OF MARIA BRAUN, THE(1979, Ger.)

Shane De Louvres
LIVING FREE(1972, Brit.)

Claudine De Luc
ONCE UPON A HONEYMOON(1942)

Costantino De Luca
QUIET PLACE IN THE COUNTRY, A(1970, Ital./Fr.)

Giovanni De Luca
WAKE UP AND DIE(1967, Fr./Ital.)

Julio De Luca
LITTLE MISS DEVIL(1951, Egypt), ph

Lorella De Luca
SIGN OF THE GLADIATOR(1959, Fr./Ger./Ital.); SWINDLE, THE(1962, Fr./Ital.); LOVE ON THE RIVIERA(1964, Fr./Ital.); THREE TOUGH GUYS(1974, U.S./Ital.)

Paul De Luca
WIRE SERVICE(1942), d

Pepino De Luca
DEAD OF SUMMER(1970 Ital./Fr.), m

Pupo De Luca
TRINITY IS STILL MY NAME(1971, Ital.)

Rudy De Luca
CAVEMAN(1981), w

Alfonso de Lucas
SOFT SKIN ON BLACK SILK(1964, Fr./Span.), art d

Paul De Lucca
LOST HORIZON(1973)

Paco de Lucia
SABINA, THE(1979, Span./Swed.), m; CARMEN(1983, Span.), a, m

Francois de Lucy
CIRCLE OF TWO(1980, Can.), art d

Milton De Lugg
GONG SHOW MOVIE, THE(1980), m

Rene de Luguro
MAD EMPRESS, THE(1940)

Gianni De Luigi
LOVE PROBLEMS(1970, Ital.)

Dom De Luise
GLASS BOTTOM BOAT, THE(1966); WHAT'S SO BAD ABOUT FEELING GOOD?(1968); NORWOOD(1970); END, THE(1978)

Giorgio De Lullo
HEART AND SOUL(1950, Ital.)

Alvaro de Luna
GUNMEN OF THE RIO GRANDE(1965, Fr./Ital./Span.); KID RODELO(1966, U.S./Span.); THAT MAN IN ISTANBUL(1966, Fr./Ital./Span.); HELLBENDERS, THE(1967, U.S./Ital./Span.); NAVAJO JOE(1967, Ital./Span.); VISCOUNT, THE(1967, Fr./Span./Ital./Ger.); CHRISTMAS KID, THE(1968, U.S., Span.); MERCENARY, THE(1970,

Ital./Span.); SONNY AND JED(1974, Ital.)

Consuelo Guerrero de Luna
FACE OF THE SCREAMING WEREWOLF(1959, Mex.); LITTLE RED RIDING HOOD AND HER FRIENDS(1964, Mex.)

Margarito De Luna
LAST SUNSET, THE(1961)

Salvador Ruiz de Luna
LAZARILLO(1963, Span.), ed

Toni de Lungo
HOUSE OF THE ARROW, THE(1930, Brit.); SLEEPING CAR TO TRIESTE(1949, Brit.)

Tony de Lungo
LOOKING ON THE BRIGHT SIDE(1932, Brit.); LOVE ON WHEELS(1932, Brit.); CONSTANT NYMPH, THE(1933, Brit.); CAMELS ARE COMING, THE(1934, Brit.); TO BE A LADY(1934, Brit.); OH DADDY!(1935, Brit.); VINTAGE WINE(1935, Brit.); BALL AT SAVOY, THE(1938, Brit.); BELOVED IMPOSTER(1936, Brit.); MAN WITH 100 FACES, THE(1938, Brit.)

Paul De Lussanet
MYSTERIES(1979, Neth.), d&w

Michel De Lutry
KNIGHTS OF THE ROUND TABLE(1953)

Mike De Lutry
HIPPODROME(1961, Aust./Ger.), ch

Monte de Lyle
SECRET VOICE, THE(1936, Brit.); BOMBS OVER LONDON(1937, Brit.); GIVE US THE MOON(1944, Brit.); NIGHT COMES TOO SOON(1948, Brit.); SILK NOOSE, THE(1950, Brit.)

Monti de Lyle
UNDERCOVER AGENT(1935, Brit.); GYPSY MELODY(1936, Brit.); PHANTOM SHIP(1937, Brit.); HEATWAVE(1954, Brit.); DYNAMITERS, THE(1956, Brit.); AR-RIVEDERCI, BABY!(1966, Brit.); CHITTY CHITTY BANG BANG(1968, Brit.)

Tuff de Lyle
BLIND MAN'S BLUFF(1936, Brit.)

Michelle de Lys
LISBON STORY, THE(1946, Brit.)

Tei de Maal
HANNIBAL BROOKS(1969, Brit.)

Nick De Maggi
YOUTH WILL BE SERVED(1940), ed

Nick De Maggio
CHAMPAGNE CHARLIE(1936), ed; CHARLIE CHAN AT THE RACE TRACK(1936), ed; CHARLIE CHAN'S SECRET(1936), ed; CHARLIE CHAN AT MONTE CAR-LO(1937), ed; HOLY TERROR, THE(1937), ed; HOT WATER(1937), ed; THANK YOU, MR. MOTO(1937), ed; ALWAYS IN TROUBLE(1938), ed; CHARLIE CHAN IN HONOLULU(1938), ed; INTERNATIONAL SETTLEMENT(1938), ed; MR. MOTO TAKES A CHANCE(1938), ed; ONE WILD NIGHT(1938), ed; PASSPORT HUS-BAND(1938), ed; SHARPSHOOTERS(1938), ed; CISCO KID AND THE LADY, THE(1939), ed; IT COULD HAPPEN TO YOU(1939), ed; NEWS IS MADE AT NIGHT(1939), ed; PACK UP YOUR TROUBLES(1939), ed; ON THEIR OWN(1940), ed; SHOOTING HIGH(1940), ed; STREET OF MEMORIES(1940), ed; LAST OF THE DUANES(1941), ed; RIDERS OF THE PURPLE SAGE(1941), ed; LONE STAR RANG-ER(1942), ed; MAD MARTINDALES, THE(1942), ed; SUNDOWN JIM(1942), ed; PA-RIS AFTER DARK(1943), ed; THEY CAME TO BLOW UP AMERICA(1943), ed; THUNDERHEAD-SON OF FLICKA(1945), ed; SAND(1949), ed; THIEVES' HIGH-WAY(1949), ed; NIGHT AND THE CITY(1950, Brit.), ed; FIXED BAYONETS(1951), ed; HOUSE ON TELEGRAPH HILL(1951), ed; KANGAROO(1952), ed; PICKUP ON SOUTH STREET(1953), ed

Vanni De Maigret
ARTURO'S ISLAND(1963, Ital.)

Gordon De Main
MARRIAGE PLAYGROUND, THE(1929); YOUNG EAGLES(1930); MATA HA-RI(1931); SHIPS OF HATE(1931); HEART PUNCH(1932); CHAINED(1934); PALOO-KA(1934); WONDER BAR(1934); BEHIND THE EVIDENCE(1935); ESPIONAGE(1937); ACROSS THE PACIFIC(1942)
Silents
TOLL OF MAMON(1914)
Misc. Silents
PATH FORBIDDEN, THE(1914); WHEN FATE LEADS TRUMP(1914)

Betty de Malero
HOUSE OF THE ARROW, THE(1930, Brit.)

Derrick de Mamey
CAFE MASCOT(1936, Brit.)

Andre Pieyre de Mandiargues
GIRL ON A MOTORCYCLE, THE(1968, Fr./Brit.), w

Charles de Mansan
Misc. Silents
L'ASSOMOIR(1921, Fr.), d

Aime de March
JULIE THE REDHEAD(1963, Fr.); DOULOS-THE FINGER MAN(1964, Fr./Ital.); IS PARIS BURNING?(1966, U.S./Fr.); BLONDE FROM PEKING, THE(1968, Fr.)

Laura De Marchi
CHINA IS NEAR(1968, Ital.)

Carlo De Marchis
TREASURE OF THE FOUR CROWNS(1983, Span./U.S.), spec eff

Marcella De Marchis
TEOREMA(1969, Ital.), cos

Anthony De Marco
TRACKDOWN(1976), ed

Arlene de Marco
DEATH OVER MY SHOULDER(1958, Brit.)

Dina de Marco
WITCH'S MIRROR, THE(1960, Mex.)

Frank De Marco
DON'T WORRY, WE'LL THINK OF A TITLE(1966), spec eff

Renee de Marco
SWORD OF VENUS(1953)

Sally De Marco
GREENWICH VILLAGE(1944)

Tony De Marco
SHINING HOUR, THE(1938); GREENWICH VILLAGE(1944)

The De Marco Sisters
SKIRTS AHOY!(1952)

Jean de Marguenat
STREET SINGER, THE(1937, Brit.), d, w

Anthony De Mario
FLIGHT TO TANGIER(1953); KID FROM LEFT FIELD, THE(1953); LET'S DO IT AGAIN(1953)

Donna De Mario
LOST MOMENT, THE(1947)

Donna de Mario [Martell]
MEXICAN HAYRIDE(1948)

Tony De Mario
DREAMBOAT(1952); THREE COINS IN THE FOUNTAIN(1954)

Merrill De Maris
SNOW WHITE AND THE SEVEN DWARFS(1937), w

Denis De Marne
MAN WITH TWO HEADS, THE(1972)

Derrick de Marnek
VICTORIA THE GREAT(1937, Brit.)

Derrick de Marney
SHADOWS(1931, Brit.); STRANGLEHOLD(1931, Brit.); MUSIC HALL(1934, Brit.); IMMORTAL GENTLEMAN(1935, Brit.); ONCE IN A NEW MOON(1935, Brit.); SCARLET PIMPERNEL, THE(1935, Brit.); WINDFALL(1935, Brit.); FORBIDDEN MUSIC(1936, Brit.); THINGS TO COME(1936, Brit.); BLOND CHEAT(1938); PEARLS OF THE CROWN(1938, Fr.); SIXTY GLORIOUS YEARS(1938, Brit.); YOUNG AND INNOCENT(1938, Brit.); FLYING FIFTY-FIVE(1939, Brit.); LION HAS WINGS, THE(1940, Brit.); SECOND MR. BUSH, THE(1940, Brit.); SPIDER, THE(1940, Brit.); THREE SILENT MEN(1940, Brit.); SUICIDE SQUADRON(1942, Brit.); GENTLE SEX, THE(1943, Brit.), p; SPITFIRE(1943, Brit.); FRENZY(1946, Brit.), a, p; NO WAY BACK(1949, Brit.), p, w; SLEEPING CAR TO TRIESTE(1949, Brit.); SHE SHALL HAVE MURDER(1950, Brit.), a, p; INHERITANCE, THE(1951, Brit.); MEET MR. CALLAGHAN(1954, Brit.), a, p; MARCH HARE, THE(1956, Brit.); PRIVATE'S PROGRESS(1956, Brit.); DOOMSDAY AT ELEVEN(1963 Brit.); PROJECTED MAN, THE(1967, Brit.)
Silents
ADVENTUROUS YOUTH(1928, Brit.)

Terence de Marney
ETERNAL FEMININE, THE(1931, Brit.); EYES OF FATE(1933, Brit.); UNHOLY QUEST, THE(1934, Brit.); IMMORTAL GENTLEMAN(1935, Brit.); BORN THAT WAY(1937, Brit.); PHANTOM SHIP(1937, Brit.); THUNDER IN THE CITY(1937, Brit.); WHO IS GUILTY?(1940, Brit.); WANTED FOR MURDER(1946, Brit.), w; DUAL ALIBI(1947, Brit.); NO WAY BACK(1949, Brit.); SILVER CHALICE, THE(1954); TARGET ZERO(1955); 23 PACES TO BAKER STREET(1956); PHARAOH'S CURSE(1957); WRECK OF THE MARY DEAR, THE(1959); SECRET OF THE PURPLE REEF, THE(1960); SPARTACUS(1960); DIE, MONSTER, DIE(1965, Brit.); LOVE IS A WOMAN(1967, Brit.); HAND OF NIGHT, THE(1968, Brit.); SEPARATION(1968, Brit.); STRANGE AFFAIR, THE(1968, Brit.); ALL NEAT IN BLACK STOCKINGS(1969, Brit.)

Terrence De Marney
MY GUN IS QUICK(1957); ON THE DOUBLE(1961)

Joan de Marrais
1984
GARBO TALKS(1984)

Charles de Marsan
Misc. Silents
RENONCEMENT(1917, Fr.), d; LA MASCOTTE DES POILUS(1918, Fr.), d; LA BOURASQUE(1920, Fr.), d; LE DROIT DE TUER(1920, Fr.), d; LE LYS ROUGE(1920, Fr.), d; LA FIANCEE DU DISPARU(1921, Fr.), d; LE MERCHANT HOMME(1921, Fr.), d; LE TALISON(1921, Fr.), d; L'INCONNU(1921, Fr.), d; UN AVENTUERIER(1921, Fr.), d; SERGE PANIN(1922, Fr.), d; L'HOMME DU TRAIN 117(1923, Fr.), d; ROCAMBOLE(1923, Fr.), d; LES AMOURS DE ROCAMBOLE(1924, Fr.), d; LES PREMIERES ARMES DE ROCAMBOLE(1924, Fr.), d

Eric de Marsan
L'ARMEE DES OMBRES(1969, Fr./Ital.), m

Wilkie de Martel
SAY ONE FOR ME(1959)

Countess De Martimprey
Misc. Silents
TOO FAT TO FIGHT(1918)

Vito de Martini
VIOLATED LOVE(1966, Arg.), w

Alberto De Martino
INVINCIBLE GLADIATOR, THE(1963, c.u. Ital./Span.), p; GLADIATORS 7(1964, Span./Ital.), w; HERCULES VS THE GIANT WARRIORS(1965 Fr./Ital.), d; HE WHO SHOOTS FIRST(1966, Ital.), d, w; SECRET SEVEN, THE(1966, Ital/Span.), d, w; OPERATION KID BROTHER(1967, Ital.), d; CHOSEN, THE(1978, Brit./Ital.), d

Ferruccio De Martino
AIDA(1954, Ital.), p; WAR OF THE ZOMBIES, THE(1965 Ital.), p, w

Peppino de Martino
PASSIONATE THIEF, THE(1963, Ital.); FACTS OF MURDER, THE(1965, Ital.)

Romolo De Martino
THIEF OF BAGHDAD, THE(1961, Ital./Fr.), makeup

Inigo de Martino Noriega
TORCH, THE(1950), w

Sloane De Masber
Silents
ROSE OF THE WORLD(1918)

Francesco De Masi
SULEIMAN THE CONQUEROR(1963, Ital.), m; GOLIATH AND THE SINS OF BABYLON(1964, Ital.), m; HERCULES VS THE GIANT WARRIORS(1965 Fr./Ital.), m; INVASION 1700(1965, Fr./Ital./Yugo.), m; REVENGE OF THE GLADIATORS(1965, Ital.), m; SEVEN SLAVES AGAINST THE WORLD(1965, Ital.), m; HYPNOSIS(1966, Ger./Sp./Ital.), m; SERENADE FOR TWO SPIES(1966, Ital./Ger.), m; TIKO AND THE SHARK(1966, U.S./Ital./Fr.), m; PAYMENT IN BLOOD(1968, Ital.), m; KILL THEM ALL AND COME BACK ALONE(1970, Ital./Span.), m; WEEKEND MURDERS, THE(1972, Ital.), m; ARENA, THE(1973), m; EAGLE OVER LONDON(1973, Ital.), m; LONE WOLF McQUADE(1983), m

1984
RUSH(1984, Ital.), m

Franceso de Masi
JOHNNY HAMLET(1972, Ital.), m

Louis De Masure
SPUTNIK(1960, Fr.), p

Louise de Masure
JOURNEY TO THE LOST CITY(1960, Ger./Fr./Ital.), p

Maria de Matteis
OTHELLO(1955, U.S./Fr./Ital.), cos; WAR AND PEACE(1956, Ital./U.S.), cos; TEMPEST(1958, Ital./Yugo./Fr.), cos; THIS ANGRY AGE(1958, Ital./Fr.), cos; NEOPOLITAN CAROUSEL(1961, Ital.), cos; RELUCTANT SAINT, THE(1962, U.S./Ital.), cos; SON OF SAMSON(1962, Fr./Ital./Yugo.), cos; STORY OF JOSEPH AND HIS BRETHREN THE(1962, Ital.), cos; BIBLE...IN THE BEGINNING, THE(1966), cos; GIRL AND THE GENERAL, THE(1967, Fr./Ital.), cos; KISS THE GIRLS AND MAKE THEM DIE(1967, U.S./Ital.), cos; FRAULEIN DOKTOR(1969, Ital./Yugo.), cos; WATERLOO(1970, Ital./USSR), cos

Pierre De Matteis
Silents
ETERNAL TEMPTRESS, THE(1917)

Henri De Maublanc
DEVIL PROBABLY, THE(1977, FR.)

Guy de Maupassant
MADEMOISELLE FIFI(1944), w; ANGEL AND SINNER(1947, Fr.), w; PRIVATE AFFAIRS OF BEL AMI, THE(1947), w; WAYS OF LOVE(1950, Ital./Fr.), w; PRIZE, THE(1952, Fr.), w; LE PLAISIR(1954, Fr.), w; TRUE AND THE FALSE, THE(1955, Swed.), w; END OF DESIRE(1962 Fr./Ital.), w; GREH(1962, Ger./Yugo.), d&w; DIARY OF A MADMAN(1963), w; MASCULINE FEMININE(1966, Fr./Swed.), w
Silents
DIAMOND NECKLACE, THE(1921, Brit.), w

Christiane de Maurin
2,000 WOMEN(1944, Brit.)

Jack De Mave
BLINDFOLD(1966); 1776(1972)

Mons. de Max
Misc. Silents
MILADY(1923, Fr.)

Isabelle Canto de Maya
QUARTET(1981, Brit./Fr.)

Rod De Medici
CORNERED(1945); UP IN CENTRAL PARK(1948)

Win de Meijer
1984
QUESTION OF SILENCE(1984, Neth.)

Carlo De Mejo
TEOREMA(1969, Ital.); DEAD ARE ALIVE, THE(1972, Yugo./Ger./Ital.); OUTSIDE MAN, THE(1973, U.S./FR.); STATELINE MOTEL(1976, Ital.); CASSANDRA CROSSING, THE(1977); GATES OF HELL, THE zero(1983, U.S./Ital.)

Oscar De Mejo
RENT CONTROL(1981), m

Alberto De Mello
MIGHTY MOUSE IN THE GREAT SPACE CHASE(1983), art d

Anais De Mello
1984
EVIL THAT MEN DO, THE(1984)

Susana De Mello
OPEN THE DOOR AND SEE ALL THE PEOPLE(1964)

Yeda De Mellow Lewinsohn
1984
BLAME IT ON RIO(1984), set d

Anais de Melo
CAVEMAN(1981)

Alberto de Mendoza
ADVENTURES OF SCARAMOUCHE, THE(1964, Fr.); THAT MAN GEORGE!(1967, Fr./Ital./Span.); DESPERATE ONES, THE(1968 U.S./Span.); VENGEANCE IS MINE(1969, Ital./Span.); DELUSIONS OF GRANDEUR(1971 Fr.); NEXT!(1971, Ital./Span.); PSYCHOUT FOR MURDER(1971, Arg./Ital.); HORROR EXPRESS(1972, Span./Brit.); TEN LITTLE INDIANS(1975, Ital./Fr./Span./Ger.)

Carlos De Mendoza
PRIDE AND THE PASSION, THE(1957)

Alberto De Mendozo
BULLET FOR SANDOVAL, A(1970, Ital./Span.)

John De Menil
MAIDSTONE(1970)

Joe De Meo
HOMEBODIES(1974)

Julian de Meriche
CURSE OF THE AZTEC MUMMY, THE(1965, Mex.); ROBOT VS. THE AZTEC MUMMY, THE(1965, Mex.)

Julien De Meriche
EL TOPO(1971, Mex.)

Michael De Mesa
STRYKER(1983, Phil.)

Mae De Mets
Silents
DIMPLES(1916)

Danielle De Metz
RETURN OF THE FLY(1959); VALLEY OF THE DRAGONS(1961); MAGIC SWORD, THE(1962); GIDGET GOES TO ROME(1963); KARATE KILLERS, THE(1967); PARTY, THE(1968); RAID ON ROMMEL(1971)

Baroness De Meyer
Silents
DEVIL'S PASSKEY, THE(1920), w

Adriano De Micheli
MOTIVE WAS JEALOUSY, THE(1970 Ital./Span.), p; ROCCO PAPALEO(1974, Ital./Fr.), p; VIVA ITALIA(1978, Ital.), p; TILL MARRIAGE DO US PART(1979, Ital.), p

Andriano de Micheli
PIZZA TRIANGLE, THE(1970, Ital./Span.), p; SCENT OF A WOMAN(1976, Ital.), p

Giancomino De Michelis
VALACHI PAPERS, THE(1972, Ital./Fr.)
Agnes De Mille
ROMEO AND JULIET(1936), ch; CAROUSEL(1956), ch
Cecil De Mille
Silents
ROMANCE OF THE REDWOODS, A(1917), w
Cecil B. De Mille
GODLESS GIRL, THE(1929), p&d
Silents
ROMANCE OF THE REDWOODS, A(1917), d
Misc. Silents
HEART OF NORA FLYNN, THE(1916), d; SQUAW MAN, THE(1918), d; FOR
BETTER, FOR WORSE(1919), d; FOOL'S PARADISE(1921), d; FORBIDDEN
FRUIT(1921), d; HOLLYWOOD(1923), d; FEET OF CLAY(1924), d; GOLDEN BED,
THE(1925), d; ROAD TO YESTERDAY, THE(1925), d
Cecilia De Mille
GODLESS GIRL, THE(1929)
Henry C. De Mille
Silents
WOMAN, THE(1915), w
Katherine De Mille
TRUMPET BLOWS, THE(1934); VIVA VILLA!(1934); BLACK ROOM, THE(1935);
CRUSADES, THE(1935); ROMEO AND JULIET(1936); CHARLIE CHAN AT THE
OLYMPICS(1937); LOVE UNDER FIRE(1937); UNDER SUSPICION(1937); BLOCK-
ADE(1938); TRAPPED IN THE SKY(1939)
Nelson de Mille
1984
SILENT MADNESS(1984), w
William De Mille
THIS MAD WORLD(1930), d; CAPTAIN FURY(1939), w
Silents
BEDROOM WINDOW, THE(1924), d; ICEBOUND(1924), d
Misc. Silents
GRUMPY(1923), d; MARRIAGE MAKER, THE(1923), d; WORLD'S APPLAUSE,
THE(1923), d; FAST SET, THE(1924), d; MEN AND WOMEN(1925), d; FOR ALIMONY
ONLY(1926), d; LITTLE ADVENTURESS, THE(1927), d
William C. de Mille
TWO KINDS OF WOMEN(1932), d
Silents
SECRET ORCHARD(1915), w; WOMAN, THE(1915), w; SECRET GAME, THE(1917),
d; ONE MORE AMERICAN(1918), d, w; MIDSUMMER MADNESS(1920), d; ONLY
38(1923), d; CRAIG'S WIFE(1928), d
Misc. Silents
CLOWN, THE(1916), d; COMMON GROUND(1916), d; HEIR TO THE HOORAH,
THE(1916), d; SOWERS, THE(1916), d; GHOST HOUSE, THE(1917), d; HASHIMURA
TOGO(1917), d; HONOR OF HIS HOUSE, THE(1918), d; MIRANDY SMILES(1918), d;
MYSTERY OF A GIRL, THE(1918), d; WIDOW'S MIGHT, THE(1918), d; PEG O' MY
HEART(1919), d; CONRAD IN QUEST OF HIS YOUTH(1920), d; PRINCE CHAP,
THE(1920), d; TREE OF KNOWLEDGE, THE(1920), d; LOST ROMANCE, THE(1921),
d; MISS LULU BETT(1921), d; BOUGHT AND PAID FOR(1922), d; CLARENCE(1922),
d; DON'T CALL IT LOVE(1924), d; LOST - A WIFE(1925), d; SPLENDID CRIME,
THE(1926), d; FORBIDDEN WOMAN, THE(1927), d; TENTH AVENUE(1928), d
William Churchill De Mille
Silents
TELEPHONE GIRL, THE(1927), w
Adonis De Milo
THIS EARTH IS MINE(1959)
Renee De Milo
GIRL ON THE RUN(1961)
Denise De Mirjian
OTHER SIDE OF MIDNIGHT, THE(1977)
Leonardo De Mitri
VERGINITA(1953, Ital.), d, w
Olga De Mojean
Silents
WHITE YOUTH(1920)
Tursio de Molina
DON JUAN(1956, Aust.), w
Laurence De Monaghan
CLAIRE'S KNEE(1971, Fr.); CHLOE IN THE AFTERNOON(1972, Fr.); IMPOSSIBLE
OBJECT(1973, Fr.)
Guy De Monceau
PARATROOPER(1954, Brit.)
Albert De Mond
IT CAN BE DONE(1929), w; LOVE TRAP, THE(1929), w; RED HOT SPEED ½(1929),
w; SHAKEDOWN, THE(1929), w; SKINNER STEPS OUT(1929), w; DAMES
AHOY(1930), w; ABOVE THE CLOUDS(1934), w; LOUDSPEAKER, THE(1934), w;
SHADOWS OF SING SING(1934), w; TWO HEADS ON A PILLOW(1934), w; PERFECT
CLUE, THE(1935), w; WOMEN IN THE WIND(1939), w; OUTSIDE THE 3-MILE
LIMIT(1940), w; RIDIN' DOWN THE CANYON(1942), w
Silents
IRRESISTIBLE LOVER, THE(1927), t; PAINTING THE TOWN(1927), t; COHENS
AND THE KELLYS IN PARIS, THE(1928), t; GATE CRASHER, THE(1928), t;
HONEYMOON FLATS(1928), t; LOVE ME AND THE WORLD IS MINE(1928), t;
PHYLLIS OF THE FOLLIES(1928), t; SPEEDY(1928), t; KID'S CLEVER, THE(1929),
t; SILKS AND SADDLES(1929), t
Henry De Mond
HOLD BACK TOMORROW(1955), ed
Arthur De Montalembert
LANCELOT OF THE LAKE(1975, Fr.)
Idanna Pucci De Montalembert
PILGRIMAGE(1972)
Alejandro de Montenegro
WHITE ORCHID, THE(1954)
Rico de Montez
DOWN MEXICO WAY(1941); MASKED RIDER, THE(1941); SIX LESSONS FROM
MADAME LA ZONGA(1941); MADAME SPY(1942); MOONLIGHT IN HAVANA(1942);
RHYTHM OF THE ISLANDS(1943); BRAZIL(1944); CUBAN PETE(1946)

Guido de Moor
AMSTERDAM AFFAIR, THE(1968 Brit.)
Harry De Moore
Misc. Silents
EMPTY CAB, THE(1918)
Bob De Mora
JINXED!(1982), cos
Robert De Mora
MARATHON MAN(1976), cos; EXORCIST II: THE HERETIC(1977), cos; WANDER-
ERS, THE(1979), cos; TIMES SQUARE(1980), cos; GREASE 2(1982), cos; RISKY BUSI-
NESS(1983), cos
Julio De Moraes
VEILED WOMAN, THE(1929), w
Vinicius de Moraes
BLACK ORPHEUS(1959 Fr./Ital./Braz.), w
Don Jaime de Moray Aragon
LOVE AND PAIN AND THE WHOLE DAMN THING(1973)
Harry De More
Misc. Silents
PEOPLE VS. JOHN DOE, THE(1916); PLOW WOMAN, THE(1917)
Ninos Cantoros De Morelia
SUN ALSO RISES, THE(1957)
Patricia De Morelos
EXTERMINATING ANGEL, THE(1967, Mex.)
William de Morgan
Silents
SOMEHOW GOOD(1927, Brit.), w
Marguerite de Morlaye
LADIES OF THE PARK(1964, Fr.)
Camille de Morlhon
Misc. Silents
FILLE D'ARTISTE(1916, Fr.), d; L'ORAGE(1917, Fr.), d; MARYSE(1917, Fr.), d;
MISERICORDE(1917, Fr.), d; EXPIATION(1918, Fr.), d; SIMONE(1918, Fr.), d;
ELIANE(1919, Fr.), d; L'IBIS BLEU(1919, Fr.), d; FABIENNE(1920, Fr.), d; LA FILLE
DU PEUPLE(1920, Fr.), d; UNE FLEUR DANS LES RONCES(1921, Fr.), d
Rebecca De Mornay
RISKY BUSINESS(1983)
Derra de Moroda
Misc. Silents
PRODIGAL DAUGHTER, THE(1916, Brit.)
Derra de Morods
LILAC DOMINO, THE(1940, Brit.), ch
Harry De Mors
Silents
GOLD RUSH, THE(1925)
Ulises Petit de Murat
MAN AND THE BEAST, THE(1951, Arg.), w; SAVAGE PAMPAS(1967, Span./Arg.),
w
Enzo De Muro Lomanto
ROSSINI(1948, Ital.)
Charles De Muth
1984
SPLASH(1984), cos
Emile de Najac
THAT UNCERTAIN FEELING(1941), w
Silents
KISS ME AGAIN(1925), w
Luciano De Nardi
LAST MERCENARY, THE(1969, Ital./Span./Ger.), art d; YOUNG REBEL, THE(1969,
Fr./Ital./Span.), art d
Gustavo De Nardo
NAKED MAJA, THE(1959, Ital./U.S.); ANGEL WORE RED, THE(1960); LOST
SOULS(1961, Ital.); IT HAPPENED IN ATHENS(1962)
Giovanni de Nari
1984
HOUSE BY THE CEMETERY, THE(1984, Ital.)
Don De Natale
WILD PARTY, THE(1975); ROSELAND(1977)
Jud de Naut
PETE KELLY'S BLUES(1955)
Igor de Navrotzki
CUBAN PETE(1946)
Germaine De Nec
COMING OUT PARTY(1934)
Germaine De Neel
SUNRISE TRAIL(1931)
Giuliani De Negri
PADRE PADRONE(1977, Ital.), p; NIGHT OF THE SHOOTING STARS, THE(1982,
Ital.), p, w
Robert de Nesle
JUDEX(1966, Fr./Ital.), p
Yvonne Sassinot de Nesle
DANTON(1983), cos
1984
SUNDAY IN THE COUNTRY, A(1984, Fr.), cos; SWANN IN LOVE(1984, Fr.Ger.), cos
Lucille De Never
MEN OF THE NIGHT(1934)
Lucille De Nevers
Silents
SKINNER'S DRESS SUIT(1926)
Francesco de Nicola
SHOE SHINE(1947, Ital.)
Joseph De Nicola
ST. IVES(1976)
Petra de Nieva
HUNCHBACK OF THE MORGUE, THE(1972, Span.), ed
Domenico De Ninno
MONSTER OF THE ISLAND(1953, Ital.)

Robert De Niro
WEDDING PARTY, THE(1969); BLOODY MAMA(1970); HI, MOM!(1970); BORN TO
WIN(1971); GANG THAT COULDN'T SHOOT STRAIGHT, THE(1971); JENNIFER ON
MY MIND(1971); SAM'S SONG(1971); BANG THE DRUM SLOWLY(1973); MEAN
STREETS(1973); GODFATHER, THE, PART II(1974); LAST TYCOON, THE(1976);
TAXI DRIVER(1976); 1900(1976, Ital.); NEW YORK, NEW YORK(1977); DEER HUNT-
ER, THE(1978); RAGING BULL(1980); TRUE CONFESSIONS(1981); KING OF COME-
DY, THE(1983)
1984
FALLING IN LOVE(1984); ONCE UPON A TIME IN AMERICA(1984)
William De Niro
SOLDIER, THE(1982)
Le Vicomte de Noailles
L'AGE D'OR(1979, Fr.), p
Alphonse de Noble
NIGHT OF THE ZOMBIES(1981)
George De Normand
TARZAN THE FEARLESS(1933); MELODY TRAIL(1935); HOMICIDE BU-
REAU(1939); GHOST SHIP, THE(1943); FALCON IN HOLLYWOOD, THE(1944);
YOUTH RUNS WILD(1944); SATAN'S CRADLE(1949); GUNSLINGERS(1950);
JEANNE EAGELS(1957); THIS EARTH IS MINE(1959); UNDERWATER CITY,
THE(1962); MONEY JUNGLE, THE(1968); SEVEN MINUTES, THE(1971)
Italia De Nublia
ROYAL WEDDING(1951); RIDE, VAQUERO!(1953); SALOME(1953)
Jerome De Nuccio
SUEZ(1938); NO TIME FOR LOVE(1943)
Marguerite De Ochoa
MAIN STREET(1956, Span.), ed
Aloysio de Oliveira
WILD PACK, THE(1972)
Lourdes de Oliveira
BLACK ORPHEUS(1959 Fr./Ital./Braz.)
Lucia De Oliveira
LOVES AND TIMES OF SCARAMOUCHE, THE(1976, Ital.)
Ubiracy de Oliveira
THAT MAN FROM RIO(1964, Fr./Ital.)
Sergio De Oliveira
CURUCU, BEAST OF THE AMAZON(1956)
Juan de Orduna
MAD QUEEN, THE(1950, Span.), d
Maria L. de Ossio
OLLY, OLLY, OXEN FREE(1978), w
Amando De Ossorie
Misc. Talkies
NIGHT OF THE SORCERORS(1970), d
Armando De Ossorio
BLIND DEAD, THE(1972, Span.), d&w; MALENKA, THE VAMPIRE(1972, Span./
Ital.), d&w; HORROR OF THE ZOMBIES(1974, Span.), d&w; PEOPLE WHO OWN
THE DARK(1975, Span.), d
Armondo De Ossorio
DEMON WITCH CHILD(1974, Span.), d
Luis de Pablo
SOUND OF HORROR(1966, Span.), m; HUNT, THE(1967, Span.), m; SPIRIT OF THE
BEEHIVE, THE(1976, Span.), m
Maurice de Packh
STORM OVER LISBON(1944), m
Dolores de Padilla
EIGHT GIRLS IN A BOAT(1932, Ger.)
Norman de Palm
1984
DESIREE(1984, Neth.), p, w
Brian de Palma
MURDER A LA MOD(1968), d,w&ed; WEDDING PARTY, THE(1969), p,d&w, ed; HI,
MOM!(1970), d&w; SISTERS(1973), d, w; PHANTOM OF THE PARADISE(1974),
d&w; CARRIE(1976), d; OBSESSION(1976), d, w; FURY, THE(1978), d; DRESSED TO
KILL(1980), d&w; BLOW OUT(1981), d&w; SCARFACE(1983), d
1984
BODY DOUBLE(1984), p&d, w
Cameron De Palma
CARRIE(1976)
Pietro de Palma
JOAN AT THE STAKE(1954$c Ital./Fr.)
Ralph De Palma
Silents
RACING FOR LIFE(1924)
Walter De Palma
HOLLYWOOD COWBOY(1937); YOU ONLY LIVE ONCE(1937); RHYTHM OF THE
SADDLE(1938); KISMET(1944)
Alessio de Paola
CHASTITY(1969), d
Valerio de Paolis
CHINA 9, LIBERTY 37(1978, Ital.), p
Dante De Paolo
BLOOD AND BLACK LACE(1965, Ital.)
Yanik de Pardos
ISLAND OF LOVE(1963)
Jean De Parva
HAPPY DAYS(1930)
Ugo de Pascale
ANGELO IN THE CROWD(1952, Ital.); ROMAN HOLIDAY(1953)
Frederic de Pasquale
GIRL WITH THE GOLDEN EYES, THE(1962, Fr.), a, art d; DON'T PLAY WITH
MARTIANS(1967, Fr.); LE VIOL(1968, Fr./Swed.); YOU ONLY LIVE ONCE(1969, Fr.);
FRENCH CONNECTION, THE(1971); BLOOD IN THE STREETS(1975, Ital./Fr.)
Suzanne De Passe
LADY SINGS THE BLUES(1972), w
David De Paul
SAD HORSE, THE(1959)

Gene De Paul
ADVENTURES OF ICHABOD AND MR. TOAD(1949), m/l Don Raye
Dante De Paulo
CHA-CHA-CHA BOOM(1956)
Starletta De Paur
GAMBLER, THE(1974)
Sylvio de Pedrelli
Misc. Silents
L'EPERVIER(1924, Fr.)
Sylvo de Pedrelli
Misc. Silents
LA SULTANE DE L'AMOUR(1919, Fr.)
Sylvio de Pedrelli Delaitre
AMOUR, AMOUR(1937, Fr.)
Sylvie de Pedrillo
TESTAMENT OF DR. MABUSE, THE(1943, Ger.)
Jaime de Pedro
COMMANDO(1962, Ital., Span., Bel., Ger.)
Adrian De Perio
1984
DEATHSTALKER, THE(1984)
Tiziano De Persio
SPECIAL DAY, A(1977, Ital./Can.)
Deirdre de Peyer
LADY GODIVA RIDES AGAIN(1955, Brit.)
Julia De Peyer
NUTCRACKER(1982, Brit.)
Adrian De Piero
DEATHSTALKER(1983, Arg./U.S.)
Mario de Pietro
ON THE AIR(1934, Brit.)
Manuel De Pina
MAC ARTHUR(1977)
Oscar Ortiz de Pinedo
FACE OF THE SCREAMING WEREWOLF(1959, Mex.)
Tullio De Piscopo
GUN, THE(1978, Ital.), m
D'Arlette De Pitray
CRAZY FOR LOVE(1960, Fr.), w
Carl de Planta
Silents
GOOD-BYE, BILL(1919)
Charles De Planta
Misc. Silents
COME ON IN(1918)
Manitas de Plata
CARAVAN TO VACCARES(1974, Brit./Fr)
Leo de Pokorny
CROOKS TOUR(1940, Brit.); PETERVILLE DIAMOND, THE(1942, Brit.); OLD
MOTHER RILEY, DETECTIVE(1943, Brit.); LISBON STORY, THE(1946, Brit.);
AGAINST THE WIND(1948, Brit.); PAUL TEMPLE'S TRIUMPH(1951, Brit.)
Dorothy De Poliolo
L'AVVENTURA(1960, Ital.)
Felix De Pomes
PRIDE AND THE PASSION, THE(1957); KING OF KINGS(1961); REDEEMER,
THE(1965, Span.); LOST COMMAND, THE(1966)
Fleixes De Pomes
THUNDERSTORM(1956)
Isabel De Pomes
THUNDERSTORM(1956); MAN WHO WAGGED HIS TAIL, THE(1961, Ital./Span.)
Leo de Porkony
LADY FROM LISBON(1942, Brit.)
Leo de [von] Porkony
ROOM FOR TWO(1940, Brit.)
Marquis de Portago
SANDERS OF THE RIVER(1935, Brit.)
Marcello de Prato
GIANT OF MARATHON, THE(1960, Ital.), art d
Fulvia de Priamo
MAN ABOUT THE HOUSE, A(1947, Brit.)
Ed De Priest
HARD ROAD, THE(1970), p
Louis De Pron
CHIP OFF THE OLD BLOCK(1944), ch
Luis De Pron
BOWERY TO BROADWAY(1944), ch
Lya de Putti
INFORMER, THE(1929, Brit.)
Silents
VARIETY(1925, Ger.); SORROWS OF SATAN(1926); SCARLET LADY, THE(1928)
Misc. Silents
PHANTOM, THE(1922, Ger.); GOD GAVE ME TWENTY CENTS(1926); MANON
LESCAUT(1926, Ger.); PRINCE OF TEMPTERS, THE(1926); HEART THIEF,
THE(1927); BUCK PRIVATES(1928); MIDNIGHT ROSE(1928)
Beryl de Querton
THARK(1932, Brit.); FACES(1934, Brit.); BLUE SMOKE(1935, Brit.); SMITH'S
WIVES(1935, Brit.)
P. De Quevedo
HORSEMEN, THE(1971)
Pedro Rodriguez de Quevedo
WEEKEND, ITALIAN STYLE(1967, Fr./Ital./Span.)
Bonnie De Rahm
PILOT, THE(1979), set d
Whitney de Rahm
WHITE HEAT(1934)
P de Ramey
CROSSROADS(1938, Fr.)

Pierre De Ramey
SINNERS IN THE SUN(1932)
Silents
TIME TO LOVE(1927)
Mickey De Rauch
ONE MILLION YEARS B.C.(1967, Brit./U.S.)
Charles De Ravenne
ARTISTS AND MODELS ABROAD(1936); HOUSE OF A THOUSAND CANDLES, THE(1936); CAFE METROPOLE(1937); ARISE, MY LOVE(1940); THAT NIGHT IN RIO(1941); ABOVE SUSPICION(1943); MADAME BOVARY(1949); GENTLEMEN PREFER BLONDES(1953)
Ray de Ravenne
ARTISTS AND MODELS ABROAD(1938); REUNION IN FRANCE(1942); MASK OF DIMITRIOS, THE(1944); PARIS UNDERGROUND(1945); RAZOR'S EDGE, THE(1946); MISTER 880(1950); JOHNNY BANCO(1969$c Fr./Ital./Ger.)
Raymond de Ravenne
PERILS OF PAULINE, THE(1947)
Ward De Ravet
Misc. Talkies
LOVE COMES QUIETLY(1974)
Michel de Re
DOLL, THE(1962, Fr.); SUNDAYS AND CYBELE(1962, Fr.); EMPIRE OF NIGHT, THE(1963, Fr.); VICE AND VIRTUE(1965, Fr./Ital.); PARIS IN THE MONTH OF AUGUST(1968, Fr.); LACEMAKER, THE(1977, Fr.)
Joe de Reda
FLIGHT FROM ASHIYA(1964, U.S./Jap.); 36 HOURS(1965)
Frits de Rek
SPLITTING UP(1981, Neth.)
Ruby De Remer
Silents
AUCTION BLOCK, THE(1917)
Rubye de Remer
GORGEOUS HUSSY, THE(1936)
Silents
TILLIE WAKES UP(1917); DUST OF DESIRE(1919); DON'T MARRY FOR MONEY(1923)
Misc. Silents
PALS FIRST(1918); WE SHOULD WORRY(1918); FOR FREEDOM(1919); GREAT ROMANCE, THE(1919); LIFE'S GREATEST PROBLEM(1919); FOOL AND HIS MONEY, A(1920); HIS TEMPORARY WIFE(1920); WAY WOMEN LOVE, THE(1920); LUXURY(1921); PILGRIMS OF THE NIGHT(1921); UNCONQUERED WOMAN(1922)
Claudio De Renzi
SAILOR FROM GIBRALTAR, THE(1967, Brit.)
Alex de Renzy
Misc. Talkies
LITTLE SISTERS(1972), d
Charles De Revenna
Misc. Silents
THUNDERING HOOFS(1924)
Whitney de Rhan
OF MICE AND MEN(1939)
Luca De Rico
MAGIC WORLD OF TOPO GIGIO, THE(1961, Ital.), d
Vonk De Ridder
KIMBERLEY JIM(1965, South Africa)
Max de Rieux
CROSS OF THE LIVING(1963, Fr.)
Louise de Rigney
Misc. Silents
MAID OF BELGIUM, THE(1917); STOLEN HOURS(1918)
Arpad De Riso
LAST OF THE VIKINGS, THE(1962, Fr./Ital.), w; CAESAR THE CONQUEROR(1963, Ital.), w; GOLIATH AGAINST THE GIANTS(1963, Ital./Span.), w; TIGER OF THE SEVEN SEAS(1964, Fr./Ital.), w; HERCULES AGAINST THE MOON MEN(1965, Fr./Ital.), w; MYSTERY OF THUG ISLAND, THE(1966, Ital./Ger.), w; LION OF ST. MARK(1967, Ital.), w; JUSTINE(1969, Ital./Span.), w
"Curly Joe" De Rita
THREE STOOGES IN ORBIT, THE(1962); THREE STOOGES MEET HERCULES, THE(1962)
Joe De Rita
THANK YOUR LUCKY STARS(1943); DOUGHGIRLS, THE(1944); BRAVADOS, THE(1958); HAVE ROCRET, WILL TRAVEL(1959); THREE STOOGES GO AROUND THE WORLD IN A DAZE, THE(1963); OUTLAWS IS COMING, THE(1965)
Massimo De Rita
BLACK SUNDAY(1961, Ital.), p; WAR OF THE ZOMBIES, THE(1965 Ital.), p; VIOLENT FOUR, THE(1968, Ital.), w; COMPANEROS(1970 Ital./Span./Ger.), w; DON'T TURN THE OTHER CHEEK(1974, Ital./Ger./Span.), w; FAMILY, THE(1974, Fr./Ital.), w; BLOOD IN THE STREETS(1975, Ital./Fr.), w; CHINO(1976, Ital., Span., Fr.), w
Francesco de Robertis
ANGELO(1951, Ital.), d&w
Adriana De Roberto
LOST HAPPINESS(1948, Ital.)
Rosanna De Rocco
BIBLE...IN THE BEGINNING, THE(1966)
Charles De Roche
Silents
LAW OF THE LAWLESS, THE(1923); TEN COMMANDMENTS, THE(1923)
Misc. Silents
CHEAT, THE(1923); MARRIAGE MAKER, THE(1923); LOVE AND GLORY(1924); SHADOWS OF PARIS(1924); WHITE MOTH, THE(1924); MADAME SANS-GENE(1925)
Everett De Roche
LONG WEEKEND(1978, Aus.), w; PATRICK(1979, Aus.), w
1984
TREASURE OF THE YANKEE ZEPHYR(1984), w
Charles de Rochefort
Misc. Silents
SPANISH JADE(1922, Brit.)

Louis de Rochemont
RAMPARTS WE WATCH, THE(1940), p&d; HOUSE ON 92ND STREET, THE(1945), p; 13 RUE MADELEINE(1946), p; BOOMERANG(1947), p; LOST BOUNDARIES(1949), p; WALK EAST ON BEACON(1952), p; MARTIN LUTHER(1953), p; MAN ON A STRING(1960), p; ROMAN SPRING OF MRS. STONE, THE(1961, U.S./Brit.), p
Louis de Rochemont III
RAMPARTS WE WATCH, THE(1940)
Lorenzo de Rodas
SURVIVE!(1977, Mex.)
Bebe De Roland
CARNIVAL(1946, Brit.)
Paul De Rolf
SEVEN LITTLE FOYS, THE(1955); JEANNE EAGELS(1957)
Eraldo De Roma
CHILDREN OF CHANCE(1950, Ital.), ed; WOMAN OF ROME(1956, Ital.), ed
Dr. D. W. De Roos
MISTER 880(1950)
Adrien de Rooy
TRAFFIC(1972, Fr.), art d
Felix de Rooy
1984
DESIREE(1984, Neth.), d
A. De Rosa
Silents
SAINTED DEVIL, A(1924)
Alberto de Rosa
HAPPY BIRTHDAY, GEMINI(1980)
Arianna De Rosa
IDENTIFICATION OF A WOMAN(1983, Ital.)
Francesco de Rosa
1984
LE BAL(1984, Fr./Ital./Algeria)
Franco De Rosa
RINGO AND HIS GOLDEN PISTOL(1966, Ital.); YOUNG, THE EVIL AND THE SAVAGE, THE(1968, Ital.); STUD, THE(1979, Brit.)
Enrique de Rosas
TANGO BAR(1935); TE QUIERO CON LOCURA(1935); WHEN YOU'RE IN LOVE(1937)
Peter de Rose
BIRD OF PARADISE(1932), song
Teresa De Rose
WHAT'S THE MATTER WITH HELEN?(1971)
Rex De Roselli
Silents
REPUTATION(1921); LAZY LIGHTNING(1926)
Misc. Silents
MAN TAMER, THE(1921)
D. de Roseville
BELLE DE JOUR(1968, Fr.)
Alain de Rosnay
LOVERS, THE(1959, Fr.), m
Geza de Rosner
HIGH CONQUEST(1947); SEALED CARGO(1951)
Rex De Rosselli
Misc. Silents
WINE GIRL, THE(1918)
Alberto De Rossi
NUN'S STORY, THE(1959), makeup; WHITE NIGHTS(1961, Ital./Fr.), makeup; CLEOPATRA(1963), makeup; LEOPARD, THE(1963, Ital.), makeup; HOW TO STEAL A MILLION(1966), makeup; TAMING OF THE SHREW, THE(1967, U.S./Ital.), makeup; TWO FOR THE ROAD(1967, Brit.), makeup; WOMAN TIMES SEVEN(1967, U.S./Fr./Ital.), makeup; ONCE UPON A TIME IN THE WEST(1969, U.S./Ital.), makeup; STAIRCASE(1969 U.S./Brit./Fr.), makeup; WATERLOO(1970, Ital./USSR), makeup; LAST VALLEY, THE(1971, Brit.), makeup; RED SUN(1972, Fr./Ital./Span.), makeup
G. De Rossi
PIRANHA II: THE SPAWNING(1981, Neth.), spec eff
Gianette De Rossi
1984
HOUSE BY THE CEMETERY, THE(1984, Ital.), makeup
Gianetto De Rossi
VALACHI PAPERS, THE(1972, Ital./Fr.), makeup; CANNIBALS IN THE STREETS(1982, Ital./Span.), makeup
Giannetto De Rossi
HOURS OF LOVE, THE(1965, Ital.), makeup; ROSE FOR EVERYONE, A(1967, Ital.), makeup; TAMING OF THE SHREW, THE(1967, U.S./Ital.), makeup; INVINCIBLE SIX, THE(1970, U.S./Iran), makeup; ZOMBIE(1980, Ital.), spec eff
1984
CONAN THE DESTROYER(1984), makeup
Gino de Rossi
GATES OF HELL, THE(1983, U.S./Ital.), spec eff
Massimo De Rossi
PAYMENT IN BLOOD(1968, Ital.), makeup
Philippe de Rothschild
LADY CHATTERLEY'S LOVER(1959, Fr.), d&w
Francois de Roubaix
BLONDE FROM PEKING, THE(1968, Fr.), m; LAST ADVENTURE, THE(1968, Fr./Ital.), m; ZITA(1968, Fr.), m; WISE GUYS(1969, Fr./Ital.), m; GODSON, THE(1972, Ital./Fr.), m
Francoise de Roubaix
FAREWELL, FRIEND(1968, Fr./Ital.), m
Francois De Roubiax
DAUGHTERS OF DARKNESS(1971, Bel./ Fr./ Ger./ Ital.), m
Jackie De Rouen
1984
ANGEL(1984)
Reed de Rouen
YOU CAN'T FOOL AN IRISHMAN(1950, Ireland); SIX MEN, THE(1951, Brit.), a, w; MISS ROBIN HOOD(1952, Brit.), w; SCOTLAND YARD INSPECTOR(1952, Brit.); MR. POTTS GOES TO MOSCOW(1953, Brit.); SEA DEVILS(1953); SHERIFF OF FRAC-

TURED JAW, THE(1958, Brit.); MURDER AT SITE THREE(1959, Brit.); NAKED FURY(1959, Brit.); HAND, THE(1960, Brit.); TRAITORS, THE(1963, Brit.); MAN WHO COULDN'T WALK, THE(1964, Brit.); PLEASURE LOVERS, THE(1964, Brit.); REVOLUTIONARY, THE(1970, Brit.); YOU CAN'T WIN 'EM ALL(1970, Brit.)

Nicole de Rouves
ABUSED CONFIDENCE(1938, Fr. ABUS DE CONFIANCE)

Clay De Roy
SHUT MY BIG MOUTH(1942)

Harry De Roy
Silents
HAUNTED PAJAMAS(1917); BIG TOWN IDEAS(1921); WILD HONEY(1922)

Jan Kees De Roy
ALSINO AND THE CONDOR(1983, Nicaragua)

Antoine de Rudder
YOUNG WORLD, A(1966, Fr./Ital.)

Baby De Rue
Silents
BREWSTER'S MILLIONS(1914); SQUAW MAN, THE(1914)

Carmen De Rue
Silents
ACQUITTED(1916); GRETCHEN, THE GREENHORN(1916); LITTLE SCHOOL MA'AM, THE(1916)
Misc. Silents
BABES IN THE WOODS(1917); FAN FAN(1918)

Eugene De Rue
Misc. Silents
THRILL HUNTER, THE(1926), d

Emile de Ruelle
BLACKMAIL(1929, Brit.), ed; JUNO AND THE PAYCOCK(1930, Brit.), ed; MURDER(1930, Brit.), ed; UNDER THE GREENWOOD TREE(1930, Brit.), ed; YELLOW MASK, THE(1930, Brit.), ed
Silents
DRESS PARADE(1927), art d

Nicholas De Ruiz
Silents
MORALS(1921); SLAVE OF DESIRE(1923)

Nick De Ruiz
RIO RITA(1929); GOLDEN DAWN(1930); ISLE OF ESCAPE(1930); WINGS OF ADVENTURE(1930); VIVA VILLA!(1934); LOVE BEFORE BREAKFAST(1936)
Silents
SHARK MASTER, THE(1921); ALTAR STAIRS, THE(1922); EAST IS WEST(1922); WOLF LAW(1922); WONDERFUL WIFE, A(1922); HUNCHBACK OF NOTRE DAME, THE(1923); FORBIDDEN PARADISE(1924); LORD JIM(1925); OLD IRONSIDES(1926); MAN WHO LAUGHS, THE(1927); UNKNOWN, THE(1927)
Misc. Silents
HONOR BOUND(1920); ANOTHER MAN'S SHOES(1922); MAN IN BLUE, THE(1925)

Emil De Rulle
MIDDLE WATCH, THE(1930, Brit.), ed

Emile De Rulle
FLAME OF LOVE, THE(1930, Brit.), ed; TWO WORLD(1930, Brit.), ed

Gilbert De Rush
Misc. Talkies
GAME SHOW MODELS(1977)

Col. John H. De Russy
TWELVE O'CLOCK HIGH(1949), tech adv

Alfredo De Sa
BRAZIL(1944); NOTORIOUS(1946)

Eliana De Sabata
MARCO POLO(1962, Fr./Ital.), w; LOVE AND MARRIAGE(1966, Ital.), w

Ana De Sade
RETURN OF A MAN CALLED HORSE, THE(1976); CAVEMAN(1981); HIGH RISK(1981); SORCERESS(1983); TRIUMPHS OF A MAN CALLED HORSE(1983, US/Mex.)

Marquis de Sade
JUSTINE(1969, Ital./Span.), w

Paul de Saint-Andre
WOMAN OF SIN(1961, Fr.), p

Antoine de Saint-Exupery
NIGHT FLIGHT(1933), w; ANNE-MARIE(1936, Fr.), w; COURRIER SUD(1937, Fr.), w; LITTLE PRINCE, THE(1974, Brit.), w

Paul de Sainte-Colombe
I MARRIED A SPY(1938), w; OUTPOST IN MOROCCO(1949), w

Francis de Sales
PORTLAND EXPOSE(1957); LINEUP, THE(1958); NO TIME FOR SERGEANTS(1958); RETURN TO WARBOW(1958); REVOLT IN THE BIG HOUSE(1958); SENIOR PROM(1958); FACE OF A FUGITIVE(1959); PSYCHO(1960); FLIGHT THAT DISAPPEARED, THE(1961); MAJORITY OF ONE, A(1961); POLICE DOG STORY, THE(1961); WHEN THE CLOCK STRIKES(1961); FBI CODE 98(1964); GLOBAL AFFAIR, A(1964); OUTFIT, THE(1973); MOVING VIOLATION(1976)

Richard De Salle
DON'T WORRY, WE'LL THINK OF A TITLE(1966), m

Anne De Salvo
STARTING OVER(1979)
1984
BAD MANNERS(1984)

Brian De Salvo
GREAT TRAIN ROBBERY, THE(1979, Brit.)

Jeanne de Salzmann,Peter Brook
MEETINGS WITH REMARKABLE MEN(1979, Brit.), w

Jose De San
MONDAY'S CHILD(1967, U.S., Arg.)

Jose de San Anton
HARBOR LIGHTS(1963); THUNDER ISLAND(1963); HEROINA(1965)

Gino de Sanctis
ATOM AGE VAMPIRE(1961, Ital.), w

Marcel De Sano
PEACOCK ALLEY(1930), d

Silents
GIRL WHO WOULDN'T WORK, THE(1925), d
Misc. Silents
BEAUTIFULLY TRIMMED(1920), d; DANGEROUS MOMENT, THE(1921), d; BLARNEY(1926), d

Gaspar de Santelices
DEATH OF A BUREAUCRAT(1979, Cuba)

Claudio De Santis
RETURN OF SABATA(1972, Ital./Fr./Ger.), set d, cos; YETI(1977, Ital.), art d

Dina De Santis
CENTURION, THE(1962, Fr./Ital.); 8 ½(1963, Ital.); JULIET OF THE SPIRITS(1965, Fr./Ital./W.Ger.)

Gino De Santis
ROMMEL'S TREASURE(1962, Ital.), w; WARRIORS FIVE(1962), w; RED SHEIK, THE(1963, Ital.), w; TERROR OF THE BLACK MASK(1967, Fr./Ital.), w

Giuseppe De Santis
BITTER RICE(1950, Ital.), d; OSSESSIONE(1959, Ital.), w

Guiseppe De Santis
BITTER RICE(1950, Ital.), w

Irma de Santis
LAST MERCENARY, THE(1969, Ital./Span./Ger.)

Joe De Santis
MAN WITH A CLOAK, THE(1951); JEANNE EAGELS(1957); UNHOLY WIFE, THE(1957); BUCHANAN RIDES ALONE(1958); I WANT TO LIVE!(1958); AL CAPONE(1959); FLYING FONTAINES, THE(1959); COLD WIND IN AUGUST(1961); GEORGE RAFT STORY, THE(1961); AND NOW MIGUEL(1966); BEAU GESTE(1966); PROFESSIONALS, THE(1966); VENETIAN AFFAIR, THE(1967); BLUE(1968); BROTHERHOOD, THE(1968); CHUBASCO(1968); LITTLE CIGARS(1973)

Joseph De Santis
DEADLINE–U.S.A.(1952)

Joseph [Joe] De Santis
SLATTERY'S HURRICANE(1949)

Lucio de Santis
WAR AND PEACE(1956, Ital./U.S.); ROVER, THE(1967, Ital.)

Luisa De Santis
THANK YOU, AUNT(1969, Ital.); IN SEARCH OF GREGORY(1970, Brit./Ital.)

Nanda De Santis
FACTS OF MURDER, THE(1965, Ital.)

Orchidea De Santis
WEEKEND MURDERS, THE(1972, Ital.)

Pasquale De Santis
MOMENT OF TRUTH, THE(1965, Ital./Span.), ph; MORE THAN A MIRACLE(1967, Ital./Fr.), ph; LISTEN, LET'S MAKE LOVE(1969, Fr./Ital.), ph; PLACE FOR LOVERS, A(1969, Ital./Fr.), ph; DEATH IN VENICE(1971, Ital./Fr.), ph

Pasquale [Pasqualino] De Santis
ROMEO AND JULIET(1968, Brit./Ital.), ph

Pasqualine De Santis
DEVIL PROBABLY, THE(1977, FR.), ph

Pasqualino de Santis
LANCELOT OF THE LAKE(1975, Fr.), ph; SPECIAL DAY, A(1977, Ital./Can.), ph; INNOCENT, THE(1979, Ital.), ph; EBOLI(1980, Ital.), ph; IMMORTAL BACHELOR, THE(1980, Ital.), ph
1984
BIZET'S CARMEN(1984, Fr./Ital.), ph; L'ARGENT(1984, Fr./Switz.), ph; SHEENA(1984), ph

Pasquel De Santis
ASSASSINATION OF TROTSKY, THE(1972 Fr./Ital.), ph

Patrick De Santis
1984
PHILADELPHIA EXPERIMENT, THE(1984)

Riccardo Freda De Santis
WHITE WARRIOR, THE(1961, Ital./Yugo.), d

Rolando De Santis
MAN OF LA MANCHA(1972)

Tony de Santis
FLASHDANCE(1983)

Miguel de Santos
Misc. Silents
LA VIRGEN DE LA CARIDAD(1930, Cuba)

Francesca De Sapio
PORTNOY'S COMPLAINT(1972); MASOCH(1980, Ital.)

Peter de Sarigny
MALTA STORY(1954, Brit.), p, w; SIMBA(1955, Brit.), p; TRUE AS A TURTLE(1957, Brit.), p; NEVER LET GO(1960, Brit.), p, w; WALTZ OF THE TOREADORS(1962, Brit.), p

Marie De Sarlabous
Silents
PRINCE IN A PAWNSHOP, A(1916), w

Sir Cecil De Sausmarez
STORY OF ADELE H., THE(1975, Fr.)

Guillaume de Sax
CARNIVAL OF SINNERS(1947, Fr.)

Gulliaume De Sax
CLANDESTINE(1948, Fr.)

Rudy De Saxe
TEXAN MEETS CALAMITY JANE, THE(1950), a, m

Francesca de Scaffa
TENDER HEARTS(1955); EDGE OF HELL(1956)

Francesco de Scaffa
RACERS, THE(1955)

Franchesca De Scaffa
ON THE RIVERA(1951)

Linda De Scenna
STAR TREK: THE MOTION PICTURE(1979), set d
1984
ADVENTURES OF BUCKAROO BANZAI: ACROSS THE 8TH DIMENSION, THE(1984), set d

Gladys de Segonzac
LITTLE BOY LOST(1953); WHAT'S NEW, PUSSYCAT?(1965, U.S./Fr.), cos; HARD CONTRACT(1969), cos

Andre de Segurola
MY MAN(1928)
Silents
PRINCE IN A PAWNSHOP, A(1916), w
Misc. Silents
BEHIND CLOSED DOORS(1929)

Andrea de Segurola
GENERAL CRACK(1929)

Andreas De Segurola
WE'RE RICH AGAIN(1934)

Andres de Segurola
MAMBA(1930); ONE NIGHT OF LOVE(1934); TWO AND ONE TWO(1934); GOIN' TO TOWN(1935); PUBLIC OPINION(1935)

Lorraine de Selle
STORY WITHOUT WORDS(1981, Ital.)
1984
CAGED WOMEN(1984, Ital./Fr.)

Paul De Senneville
1984
IRRECONCILABLE DIFFERENCES(1984), m

Martial de Serrand
ARTISTS AND MODELS ABROAD(1938)

Vittorio De Seta
BANDITS OF ORGOSOLO(1964, Ital.), p&d, w, ph

William De Seta
SOMETHING SHORT OF PARADISE(1979), art d

Catherine de Seynes
MURIEL(1963, Fr./Ital.); LA GUERRE EST FINIE(1967, Fr./Swed.)

Jackie De Shannon
SURF PARTY(1964)

Kyrill de Shishmareff
EXPENSIVE HUSBANDS(1937), w

Christian De Sica
ALMOST PERFECT AFFAIR, AN(1979)

Manuel De Sica
PLACE FOR LOVERS, A(1969, Ital./Fr.), m; VOYAGE, THE(1974, Ital.), m; BRIEF VACATION, A(1975, Ital.), m; CAGLIOSTRO(1975, Ital.), m; GARDEN OF THE FINZI-CONTINIS, THE(1976, Ital./Ger.), m; AGE OF THE MEDICI, THE(1979, Ital.), m; SUNDAY LOVERS(1980, Ital./Fr.), m

Victoria De Sica
VOYAGE, THE(1974, Ital.), d

Vittorio De Sica
CUCKOO CLOCK, THE(1938, Ital.); LITTLE MARTYR, THE(1947, Ital.), d, w; SHOE SHINE(1947, Ital.), d, w; BICYCLE THIEF, THE(1949, Ital.), p&d; PEDDLIN' IN SOCIETY(1949, Ital.); HEART AND SOUL(1950, Ital.); MY WIDOW AND I(1950, Ital.); DOCTOR BEWARE(1951, Ital.), a, d, w; MIRACLE IN MILAN(1951, Ital.), p&d, w; BREAD, LOVE AND DREAMS(1953, Ital.); TIMES GONE BY(1953, Ital.); CENTO ANNI D'AMORE(1954, Ital.); EARRINGS OF MADAME DE..., THE(1954, Fr.); HELLO, ELEPHANT(1954, Ital.), a, p; INDISCRETION OF AN AMERICAN WIFE(1954, U.S./Ital.), p&d; SECRETS D'ALCOVE(1954, Fr./Ital.); TOO BAD SHE'S BAD(1954, Ital.); FRISKY(1955, Ital.); GRAN VARIETA(1955, Ital.); SIGN OF VENUS, THE(1955, Ital.); UMBERTO D(1955, Ital.), p&d, w; CASINO DE PARIS(1957, Fr./Ger.); FAREWELL TO ARMS, A(1957); GOLD OF NAPLES(1957, Ital.), a, d, w; MILLER'S WIFE, THE(1957, Ital.); MONTE CARLO STORY, THE(1957, Ital.); SCANDAL IN SORRENTO(1957, Ital./Fr.); ANNA OF BROOKLYN(1958, Ital.), a, m; ANATOMY OF LOVE(1959, Ital.); IT HAPPENED IN ROME(1959, Ital.); ALWAYS VICTORIOUS(1960, Ital.); ANGEL WORE RED, THE(1960); AUSTERLITZ(1960, Fr./Ital./Yugo.); FAST AND SEXY(1960, Fr./Ital.), a, m; GENERALE DELLA ROVERE(1960, Ital./Fr.); HERCULES' PILLS(1960, Ital.); IT STARTED IN NAPLES(1960); MILLIONAIRESS, THE(1960, Brit.); TWO WOMEN(1961, Ital./Fr.), d, w; WONDERS OF ALADDIN, THE(1961, Fr./Ital.); BOCCACCIO '70(1962/Ital./Fr.), d; EVA(1962, Fr./Ital.); NERO'S MISTRESS(1962, Ital.); LADY DOCTOR, THE(1963, Fr./Ital./Span.); LAFAYETTE(1963, Fr.); MARRIAGE–ITALIAN STYLE(1964, Fr./Ital.), d; MORALIST, THE(1964, Ital.); YESTERDAY, TODAY, AND TOMORROW(1964, Ital./Fr.), d; AMOROUS ADVENTURES OF MOLL FLANDERS, THE(1965); AFTER THE FOX(1966, U.S./Brit./Ital.), d; YOUNG WORLD, A(1966, Fr./Ital.), d; MY WIFE'S ENEMY(1967, Ital.); WOMAN TIMES SEVEN(1967, U.S./Fr./Ital.), d; BIGGEST BUNDLE OF THEM ALL, THE(1968); CAROLINE CHERIE(1968, Fr.); SHOES OF THE FISHERMAN, THE(1968); IF IT'S TUESDAY, THIS MUST BE BELGIUM(1969); PLACE FOR LOVERS, A(1969, Ital./Fr.), d, w; WITCHES, THE(1969, Fr./Ital.), d; SUNFLOWER(1970, Fr./Ital.), d; TWELVE PLUS ONE(1970, Fr./Ital.); SNOW JOB(1972); BRIEF VACATION, A(1975, Ital.), d; GARDEN OF THE FINZI-CONTINIS, THE(1976, Ital./Ger.), d

Aura De Silva
SUTTER'S GOLD(1936)

Enrico de Silva
SHOE SHINE(1947, Ital.)

Fred De Silva
Silents
EXCITEMENT(1924); RAINBOW TRAIL, THE(1925)
Misc. Silents
THUNDER ISLAND(1921); DURAND OF THE BAD LANDS(1925)

Henry De Silva
IN CALIENTE(1935)

Marcia de Silva
ELEPHANT BOY(1937, Brit.), w

Michael de Silva
EYES OF A STRANGER(1980)

Sid Albina de Silva
OUT OF THE BLUE(1982)

Stany De Silva
1984
INDIANA JONES AND THE TEMPLE OF DOOM(1984)

Mario De Silvio
DEATH IN VENICE(1971, Ital./Fr.), makeup

John De Simone
HOODLUM, THE(1951); MILLION DOLLAR PURSUIT(1951); PUSHOVER(1954)

Mario De Simone
HERCULES, SAMSON & ULYSSES(1964, Ital.); ROMEO AND JULIET(1968, Ital./Span.)

Roberto De Simone
BAMBOLE!(1965, Ital.); BIGGEST BUNDLE OF THEM ALL, THE(1968)

Tom De Simone
TERROR IN THE JUNGLE(1968), d
Misc. Talkies
CHATTERBOX(1977), d

Maria De Sisti
FELLINI SATYRICON(1969, Fr./Ital.)

Johan De Slaa
LITTLE ARK, THE(1972)

Michel de Slubicki
END OF DESIRE(1962 Fr./Ital.)

Emilio de Solar
1984
THREE CROWNS OF THE SAILOR(1984, Fr.), w

Marie de Solla
Silents
JUSTICE(1914, Brit.)

Rachel de Solla
Silents
EAST LYNNE(1913, Brit.); GRIT OF A JEW, THE(1917, Brit.)
Misc. Silents
DIANA OF DOBSON'S(1917, Brit.)

Filipe de Solms
COUNTRY DOCTOR, THE(1963, Portuguese), p

Ignacio de Soroa
THE EAVESDROPPER(1966, U.S./Arg.)

Henri De Soto
SOMEONE TO REMEMBER(1943); SCARLET STREET(1945); DARK HORSE, THE(1946); SOMEWHERE IN THE NIGHT(1946)

Henrique de Sousa
VOYAGE OF SILENCE(1968, Fr.)

Aubrey De Souza
THAT'S THE WAY OF THE WORLD(1975)

Edward De Souza
PHANTOM OF THE OPERA, THE(1962, Brit.); KISS OF EVIL(1963, Brit.); MAIN CHANCE, THE(1966, Brit.); THOSE FANTASTIC FLYING FOOLS(1967, Brit); SPY WHO LOVED ME, THE(1977, Brit.); THIRTY NINE STEPS, THE(1978, Brit.); GOLDEN LADY, THE(1979, Brit.); RETURN OF THE SOLDIER, THE(1983, Brit.)

Ivan de Souza
EARTH ENTRANCED(1970, Braz.)

Jackson de Souza
VIOLENT AND THE DAMNED, THE(1962, Braz.)
1984
MEMOIRS OF PRISON(1984, Braz.)

Modesto de Souza
EARTH ENTRANCED(1970, Braz.)

Ruth de Souza
MACUMBA LOVE(1960); TRAIN ROBBERY CONFIDENTIAL(1965, Braz.)

Steve de Souza
RETURN OF CAPTAIN INVINCIBLE, THE(1983, Aus./U.S.), w
Misc. Talkies
ARNOLD'S WRECKING CO.(1973), d

Steven E. de Souza
48 HOURS(1982), w

Waldetar de Souza
BLACK ORPHEUS(1959 Fr./Ital./Braz.)

Antoine de St. Exupery
CONQUEST OF THE AIR(1940), w

Ed De Stefane
YOUNG WARRIORS(1983)

Joe De Stefani
LET US LIVE(1939)

Josef De Stefani
THERE'S ALWAYS A WOMAN(1938)

Joseph de Stefani
BEAU IDEAL(1931); G-MEN(1935); MAN WHO BROKE THE BANK AT MONTE CARLO, THE(1935); SEVENTH HEAVEN(1937); TOAST OF NEW YORK, THE(1937); I AM THE LAW(1938); SMASHING THE RACKETS(1938); EVERYTHING HAPPENS AT NIGHT(1939); HOMICIDE BUREAU(1939); MIDNIGHT(1939); NURSE EDITH CAVELL(1939); RANCHO GRANDE(1940)

Vitale De Stefano
Silents
CABIRIA(1914, Ital.)

Joseph De Stephani
EXCLUSIVE(1937); MAN TO REMEMBER, A(1938); MAN THEY COULD NOT HANG, THE(1939); TWELVE CROWDED HOURS(1939)

Angelo De Stiffney
SEVEN CITIES OF GOLD(1955)

Joe De Sue
BLACKENSTEIN(1973)

Marion de Sydow
STORY OF DR. WASSELL, THE(1944)

B.G. De Sylva [Buddy]
SUNNY SIDE UP(1929), w; JUST IMAGINE(1930), p, w; MY WEAKNESS(1933), p, w; LITTLE COLONEL, THE(1935), p; UNDER THE PAMPAS MOON(1935), p; YOU'RE A SWEETHEART(1937), p; RAGE OF PARIS, THE(1938), p; ALOMA OF THE SOUTH SEAS(1941), p; PANAMA HATTIE(1942), w; DU BARRY WAS A LADY(1943), w; STORK CLUB, THE(1945), p; GOOD NEWS(1947), w

Edith Perez De Tagle
CRY FREEDOM(1961, Phil.), p

Vito De Taranto
ROSSINI(1948, Ital.)

Vito de Tarranto
BARBER OF SEVILLE, THE(1947, Ital.)
Antonio De Teffe
SODOM AND GOMORRAH(1962, U.S./Fr./Ital.); STRANGER'S GUNDOWN, THE(1974, Ital.), w
Misc. Talkies
ANGEL FOR SATAN, AN(1966, Ital.)
Charles De Temple
WAR LOVER, THE(1962, U.S./Brit.); VICTORS, THE(1963)
Gillian De Terville
OCTOPUSSY(1983, Brit.)
Christian de Tiliere
ARMY GAME, THE(1963, Fr.); THIEF OF PARIS, THE(1967, Fr./Ital.); WANDERER, THE(1969, Fr.); BORSALINO(1970, Fr.); BED AND BOARD(1971, Fr.); JULIA(1977)
1984
AMERICAN DREAMER(1984)
Christian de Tillere
VERY PRIVATE AFFAIR, A(1962, Fr./Ital.)
Arthur De Titta
Silents
SORROWS OF SATAN(1926), ph
George De Titta
THOUSAND CLOWNS, A(1965), set d; COME BACK CIHARLESTON BLUE(1972), set; DEATH WISH(1974), set d; THREE DAYS OF THE CONDOR(1975), set d; THIEVES(1977), set d; HAIR(1979), set d
Gaston de Tolignac [Griffith]
Silents
ORPHANS OF THE STORM(1922), w
M. Gaston de Tolignac [D.W. Griffith]
Silents
HEARTS OF THE WORLD(1918), w
Lola De Tolly
NORTHWEST OUTPOST(1947)
Inga De Toro
ONE, TWO, THREE(1961)
Andre De Toth
DARK WATERS(1944), d; NONE SHALL ESCAPE(1944), d; OTHER LOVE, THE(1947), d; RAMROD(1947), d; SLATTERY'S HURRICANE(1949), d; GUNFIGHTER, THE(1950), w; MAN IN THE SADDLE(1951), d; CARSON CITY(1952), d; LAST OF THE COMANCHES(1952), d; SPRINGFIELD RIFLE(1952), d; HOUSE OF WAX(1953), d; STRANGER WORE A GUN, THE(1953), d; THUNDER OVER THE PLAINS(1953), d; BOUNTY HUNTER, THE(1954), d; RIDING SHOTGUN(1954), d; TANGANYIKA(1954), d; INDIAN FIGHTER, THE(1955), d; HIDDEN FEAR(1957), d, w; MONKEY ON MY BACK(1957), d; DAY OF THE OUTLAW(1959), d; TWO-HEADED SPY, THE(1959, Brit.), d; MAN ON A STRING(1960), d; MORGAN THE PIRATE(1961, Fr./Ital.), d, w; GOLD FOR THE CAESARS(1964), d; MONGOLS, THE(1966, Fr./Ital.), d; PLAY DIRTY(1969, Brit.), d; EL CONDOR(1970), p
Irene de Trebert
LACOMBE, LUCIEN(1974), a, m
Rosita de Triana
STRANGERS IN THE CITY(1962)
Suzanne de Troeye
CESAR(1936, Fr.), ed; LA BETE HUMAINE(1938, Fr.), ed; BAKER'S WIFE, THE(1940, Fr.), ed; PLEASE! MR. BALZAC(1957, Fr.), ed; MIDNIGHT FOLLY(1962, Fr.), ed; HIGHWAY PICKUP(1965, Fr./Ital.), ed
Suzanne de Troye
TONI(1968, Fr.), ed
Charlotte de Turckeim
1984
TO CATCH A COP(1984, Fr.)
Charlotte de Turckheim
1984
SWANN IN LOVE(1984, Fr.Ger.)
Charlotte de Turkheim
1984
EDITH AND MARCEL(1984, Fr.)
Pedro de Urdimales
LOS PLATILLOS VOLADORES(1955, Mex.), w
Frederico de Urnutia
VENGEANCE IS MINE(1969, Ital./Span.), w
Miryan de Urquijo
GAMES MEN PLAY, THE(1968, Arg.)
Frederic De Urratia
BULLET FOR SANDOVAL, A(1970, Ital./Span.), w
Federico de Urrutia
UNSATISFIED, THE(1964, Span.), w; MAN WHO KILLED BILLY THE KID, THE(1967, Span./Ital.), w; FEW BULLETS MORE, A(1968, Ital./Span.), w
Frederico de Urrutia
MISSION STARDUST(1968, Ital./Span./Ger.), w; NUN AT THE CROSSROADS, A(1970, Ital./Span.), w
Jean De Val
LIFE WITH FATHER(1947)
Ludio de Val
GAMES MEN PLAY, THE(1968, Arg.)
Mercedes De Valasco
BEHIND THAT CURTAIN(1929)
Carlos de Valdez
LITTLE MAN, WHAT NOW?(1934); VIVA VILLA!(1934); PRESCOTT KID, THE(1936); CONQUEST(1937); DRUMS OF DESTINY(1937); MEN IN EXILE(1937); BLOCKADE(1938); OLD LOUISIANA(1938); ROMANCE IN THE DARK(1938); JUAREZ(1939); MIDNIGHT(1939); BRITISH INTELLIGENCE(1940); LLANO KID, THE(1940)
Carlos J. de Valdez
PARIS INTERLUDE(1934); NIGHT IS YOUNG, THE(1935); ESPIONAGE(1937); LANCER SPY(1937); SUEZ(1938)
M. Rodolpho de Valentina
Misc. Silents
ALL NIGHT(1918)

Regina de Valet
HIS DOUBLE LIFE(1933)
Jaime De Valle
LINEUP, THE(1958), p
Ninelle De Valois
AS YOU LIKE IT(1936, Brit.), ch
Isabelle De Valvert
COUNT OF MONTE CRISTO(1976, Brit.)
Eleanor De Van
PAROLED FROM THE BIG HOUSE(1938)
Chris de Varga
AMERICAN GUERRILLA IN THE PHILIPPINES, AN(1950)
Val De Vargas
TREASURE OF MATECUMBE(1976)
Valentin de Vargas
GIRL MOST LIKELY, THE(1957); TOUCH OF EVIL(1958); FIREBRAND, THE(1962); HATARI!(1962); NUN AND THE SERGEANT, THE(1962); HELLFIGHTERS(1968)
E. J. De Varney
GAMBLING(1934)
Emile J. de Varney
Misc. Silents
FRUITS OF PASSION(1919)
E.J. De Varnie
Silents
AWAKENING, THE(1917), w
Hugo De Varnier
WHOLE TRUTH, THE(1958, Brit.)
Emil De Varny
Silents
TIGER WOMAN, THE(1917)
William De Vaull
Silents
BIRTH OF A NATION, THE(1915); BIG TREMAINE(1916); HAUNTED PAJAMAS(1917); BLIND HUSBANDS(1919); POOR RELATIONS(1919); KENTUCKY DAYS(1923)
Misc. Silents
BETTER TIMES(1919)
Renee De Vaux
RHODES(1936, Brit.); CAVALIER OF THE STREETS, THE(1937, Brit.)
Mario de Vecchi
VITELLONI(1956, Ital./Fr.), p
Sergio De Vecchi
LONG RIDE FROM HELL, A(1970, Ital.)
Jose De Vega
WEST SIDE STORY(1961); COVENANT WITH DEATH, A(1966); ASH WEDNESDAY(1973); ROME WANTS ANOTHER CAESAR(1974, Ital.)
Gianni De Venanzo
JULIET OF THE SPIRITS(1965, Fr./Ital./W.Ger.), ph
P.J. de Venloo
ANNE-MARIE(1936, Fr.), p
Harry De Vere
Silents
END OF THE TRAIL, THE(1916); NE'ER-DO-WELL, THE(1916); TALE OF TWO CITIES, A(1917); JOYOUS TROUBLEMAKERS, THE(1920); ALTAR STAIRS, THE(1922); JILT, THE(1922); HUNCHBACK OF NOTRE DAME, THE(1923)
Misc. Silents
I'M GLAD MY BOY GREW TO BE A SOLDIER(1915); DAVY CROCKETT(1916); HIGHWAY OF HOPE, THE(1917); HIS SWEETHEART(1917); ROADSIDE IMPRESARIO, A(1917); LAST OF THE DUANES, THE(1919)
Horace de Vere
Silents
BULLDOG DRUMMOND(1923, Brit.)
Hugo De Vernier
HOT MILLIONS(1968, Brit.); LIMBO LINE, THE(1969, Brit.); KELLY'S HEROES(1970, U.S./Yugo.); TALES FROM THE CRYPT(1972, Brit.)
Frank De Vernon
Silents
ALL FOR A GIRL(1915); WAY OF A WOMAN(1919); MAN WORTH WHILE, THE(1921)
Misc. Silents
CONCEALED TRUTH, THE(1915); LOVELY MARY(1916); SOULS ADRIFT(1917); WOMAN BENEATH, THE(1917); PALS FIRST(1918); UNBELIEVER, THE(1918)
Vina de Vesci
RHYTHM IN THE AIR(1936, Brit.), w; DOMINANT SEX, THE(1937, Brit.), w
Guy de Vestal
SECRET OF ST. IVES, THE(1949); SOUTH SEA WOMAN(1953)
Robert De Vestal
HIRED HAND, THE(1971), set d
Robert De Veste
FOR SINGLES ONLY(1968), set d
Guy De Vestel
TO CATCH A THIEF(1955); WILD AND WONDERFUL(1964)
Robert De Vestel
COVER ME BABE(1970), set d; SIMON, KING OF THE WITCHES(1971), set d; NECROMANCY(1972), set d; UP THE SANDBOX(1972), set d; HUCKLEBERRY FINN(1974), set d; UPTOWN SATURDAY NIGHT(1974), set d; LOGAN'S RUN(1976), set d; ST. IVES(1976), set d; EVERY WHICH WAY BUT LOOSE(1978), set d; ISLAND, THE(1980), set d; JAZZ SINGER, THE(1980), set d; FIRST MONDAY IN OCTOBER(1981), set d
Pietro De Vico
GLADIATOR OF ROME(1963, Ital.); RED SHEIK, THE(1963, Ital.)
Anne De Vigier
HOT MILLIONS(1968, Brit.); DECLINE AND FALL... OF A BIRD WATCHER(1969, Brit.)
Jean-Luis de Vilallonga
BURGLARS, THE(1972, Fr./Ital.)
Jose Luis de Vilallonga
NAKED AUTUMN(1963, Fr.); HIRED KILLER, THE(1967, Fr./Ital.); MAIDEN FOR A PRINCE, A(1967, Fr./Ital.)

Jose-Luis de Vilallonga
TALES OF PARIS(1962, Fr./Ital.); DON'T TEMPT THE DEVIL(1964, Fr./Ital.); JULIET OF THE SPIRITS(1965, Fr./Ital./W.Ger.); MAGNIFICENT CUCKOLD, THE(1965, Fr./Ital.); SUCKER, THE(1966, Fr./Ital.)

Robert De Vilbiss
Silents
RENO(1923); SIX DAYS(1923)

Nestor De Villa
SURRENDER-HELL!(1959)

Jose de Villalonga
THREE FACES OF A WOMAN(1965, Ital.)

Jose-Luis de Villalonga
LOVERS, THE(1959, Fr.); CLEO FROM 5 TO 7(1961, Fr.)

Jose' Luis De Villalonga
DARLING(1965, Brit.)

Martha de Villalonga
1984
A NOS AMOURS(1984, Fr.), cos

Annette De Villiers
RIDER IN THE NIGHT, THE(1968, South Africa)

Duc de Villiers
NEW MOON(1940)

John De Villiers
LAST SAFARI, THE(1967, Brit.); SYNDICATE, THE(1968, Brit.)

Nantando de Villiers
CAESAR AND CLEOPATRA(1946, Brit.)

Louise de Vilmorin
EARRINGS OF MADAME DE..., THE(1954, Fr.), w; JULIETTA(1957, Fr.), w; LOVERS, THE(1959, Fr.), w; AMELIE OR THE TIME TO LOVE(1961, Fr.), w; LOVE AND THE FRENCHWOMAN(1961, Fr.), w; SECRET OF MAGIC ISLAND, THE(1964, Fr./Ital.), w; IMMORTAL STORY, THE(1969, Fr.), w

Father Amando de Vincenzo
MECHANIC, THE(1972)

Janet De Vine
JUST IMAGINE(1930)

Clyde De Vinna
WHITE SHADOWS IN THE SOUTH SEAS(1928), ph; PAGAN, THE(1929), ph; POLITICS(1931), ph; TRADER HORN(1931), ph; BIRD OF PARADISE(1932), ph; TARZAN AND HIS MATE(1934), ph; AH, WILDERNESS!(1935), ph; LAST OF THE PAGANS(1936), ph; OLD HUTCH(1936), ph; BAD MAN OF BRIMSTONE(1938), ph; GIRL DOWNSTAIRS, THE(1938), ph; BLACKMAIL(1939), ph; BRIDAL SUITE(1939), ph; PHANTOM RAIDERS(1940), ph; BAD MAN, THE(1941), ph; BARNACLE BILL(1941), ph; BUGLE SOUNDS, THE(1941), ph; PEOPLE VS. DR. KILDARE, THE(1941), ph; TARZAN'S SECRET TREASURE(1941), ph; JACKASS MAIL(1942), ph; WHISTLING IN DIXIE(1942), ph; IMMORTAL SERGEANT, THE(1943), ph; CARIBBEAN MYSTERY, THE(1945), ph; IT'S A JOKE, SON!(1947), ph; SWORD OF THE AVENGER(1948), ph; JUNGLE, THE(1952), ph
Silents
CAPTIVE GOD, THE(1916), ph; CIVILIZATION(1916), ph; CORNER IN COLLEENS, A(1916), ph; ADELE(1919), ph; ALL WRONG(1919), ph; CHEATER REFORMED, THE(1921), ph; BEN-HUR(1925), ph; WAR PAINT(1926), ph; CALIFORNIA(1927), ph; FOREIGN DEVILS(1927), ph; ADVENTURER, THE(1928), ph; LAW OF THE RANGE, THE(1928), ph

Chet De Vito
BALL OF FIRE(1941)

Danny De Vito
DREAMS OF GLASS(1969); HURRY UP OR I'LL BE 30(1973); ONE FLEW OVER THE CUCKOO'S NEST(1975); GOING APE!(1981)
1984
ROMANCING THE STONE(1984)

Frank De Voe
IT HAD TO HAPPEN(1936); WHIPSAW(1936)

Theo de Voe
ROAD TO MOROCCO(1942)

Carl de Vogt
NUMBER SEVENTEEN(1928, Brit./Ger.)
Misc. Silents
GOLDEN SEA, THE(1919, Ger.); HALFBREED(1919, Ger.); MASTER OF LOVE, THE(1919, Ger.)

Carl de Voigt
INVISIBLE DR. MABUSE, THE(1965, Ger.)

adapted by Frank De Vol
DOC SAVAGE... THE MAN OF BRONZE(1975), m

Frank De Vol
PARDNERS(1956), md; JOHNNY TROUBLE(1957), m, md; RIDE BACK, THE(1957), m; MURDER, INC.(1960), m; FOR LOVE OR MONEY(1963), m; MC LINTOCK!(1963), m; THRILL OF IT ALL, THE(1963), m; WHEELER DEALERS, THE(1963), m; HUSH... HUSH, SWEET CHARLOTTE(1964), m; FLIGHT OF THE PHOENIX, THE(1965), m; GLASS BOTTOM BOAT, THE(1966), m; GUESS WHO'S COMING TO DINNER(1967), m; LEGEND OF LYLAH CLARE, THE(1968), m; WHAT'S SO BAD ABOUT FEELING GOOD?(1968), m; KRAKATOA, EAST OF JAVA(1969), m; HERBIE GOES TO MONTE CARLO(1977), m; HERBIE GOES BANANAS(1980), m; ...ALL THE MARBLES(1981), m

Fred de Vol
RIDE BACK, THE(1957), md

Gordon De Vol
1776(1972)

Chester De Vonde
Silents
WEST OF ZANZIBAR(1928), w
Misc. Silents
EVEN AS EVE(1920), d; VOICES(1920), d

Adele De Vore
Silents
FANGS OF JUSTICE(1926), w

Christopher De Vore
1984
DUNE(1984), w

Russell De Vorkin
PERFECT STRANGERS(1950)

Jess De Vorska
LAST PARADE, THE(1931)

Jesse de Vorska
SPIDER, THE(1931); TRANSATLANTIC(1931); WOMEN OF ALL NATIONS(1931)

Barry De Vorzon
BLESS THE BEASTS AND CHILDREN(1971), m; WARRIORS, THE(1979), m

Peter de Vos
GIRL WITH THE RED HAIR, THE(1983, Neth.), w

Beppi De Vries
GET OUTTA TOWN(1960)

Bernard de Vries
FRAULEIN DOKTOR(1969, Ital./Yugo.)

Charles de Vries
SHIP OF FOOLS(1965)
1984
LONELY GUY, THE(1984)

Dolf De Vries
SOLDIER OF ORANGE(1979, Dutch)
1984
QUESTION OF SILENCE(1984, Neth.)

George De Vries
GAVILAN(1968)

Hans De Vries
SHALAKO(1968, Brit.); SUMARINE X-1(1969, Brit.)

Henri de Vries
MURDER AT COVENT GARDEN(1932, Brit.); SCARAB MURDER CASE, THE(1936, Brit.)
Misc. Silents
NIGHT HAWK, THE(1921, Brit.)

Henry de Vries
WHITE CARGO(1930, Brit.); STRANGE EXPERIMENT(1937, Brit.)
Misc. Silents
WOMAN WHO OBEYED, THE(1923, Brit.); MASTER AND MAN(1929, Brit.)

Mark De Vries
WILD PACK, THE(1972)

Peter De Vries
HOW DO I LOVE THEE?(1970), w; PETE 'N' TILLIE(1972), w

Theun De Vries
GIRL WITH THE RED HAIR, THE(1983, Neth.), w

Larry De Waay
1984
ELECTRIC DREAMS(1984), p

Anders de Wahl
Misc. Silents
EROTIKON(1920, Swed.)

Adeline de Walt
SINCE YOU WENT AWAY(1944)

Adeline de Walt Reynolds
TUTTLES OF TAHITI(1942); HUMAN COMEDY, THE(1943); TREE GROWS IN BROOKLYN, A(1945); HERE COMES THE GROOM(1951); TEN COMMANDMENTS, THE(1956)

Gloria De Ward
GIRL MOST LIKELY, THE(1957)

Simon de Wardener
GIRL IS MINE, THE(1950, Brit.)

George de Warfaz
WARM CORNER, A(1930, Brit.); CAPTIVATION(1931, Brit); FRENCH LEAVE(1931, Brit.); GENTLEMAN OF PARIS, A(1931); NINE TILL SIX(1932, Brit.); IT'S A KING(1933, Brit.); DEATH AT A BROADCAST(1934, Brit.); SILENT PASSENGER, THE(1935, Brit.); MADNESS OF THE HEART(1949, Brit.); SLEEPING CAR TO TRIESTE(1949, Brit.); FIGHTING PIMPERNEL, THE(1950, Brit.); LAUGHING LADY, THE(1950, Brit.); BEAU BRUMMELL(1954)

Karel De Wet
WILD SEASON(1968, South Africa)

Brandon De Wilde
MEMBER OF THE WEDDING, THE(1952); SHANE(1953); GOODBYE, MY LADY(1956); NIGHT PASSAGE(1957); MISSOURI TRAVELER, THE(1958); BLUE DENIM(1959); ALL FALL DOWN(1962); HUD(1963); THOSE CALLOWAYS(1964); IN HARM'S WAY(1965); DESERTER, THE(1971 Ital./Yugo.); BLACK JACK(1973)

David De Wilde
BLACK GUNN(1972), ed

Arione de Winter
CAT PEOPLE(1982)

David De Winter
Silents
PINK TIGHTS(1920)

Jo de Winter
1984
BREAKIN' 2: ELECTRIC BOOGALOO(1984)

Orion De Winter
RIVERRUN(1968)

Vera de Winter
TENDER IS THE NIGHT(1961)

Agnes de Winton
Silents
LOVE(1916, Brit.)

Albert De Winton
LOVE PARADE, THE(1929)

Alice de Winton
Silents
DEMOCRACY(1918, Brit.); SINGLE MAN, THE(1919, Brit.); BACHELORS' CLUB, THE(1921, Brit.)
Misc. Silents
DEAD HEART, THE(1914, Brit.); CINEMA GIRL'S ROMANCE, A(1915, Brit.); VAGABOND'S REVENGE, A(1915, Brit.); FAIR IMPOSTER, A(1916, Brit.); SALLY BISHOP(1916, Brit.); MY LADY'S DRESS(1917, Brit.); MEG O' THE WOODS(1918, Brit.); HER CROSS(1919, Brit.)

Dora de Winton
Silents
IN THE HANDS OF THE LONDON CROOKS(1913, Brit.); LOVE(1916, Brit.); JO THE CROSSING SWEEPER(1918, Brit.); MANCHESTER MAN, THE(1920, Brit.); PRESUMPTION OF STANLEY HAY, MP, THE(1925, Brit.)
Misc. Silents
CHAINS OF BONDAGE(1916, Brit.); WHAT WOULD A GENTLEMAN DO?(1918, Brit.); FLAME, THE(1920, Brit.); MR. GILFIL'S LOVE STORY(1920, Brit.)

Jacqueline De Wit
LEOPARD MAN, THE(1943); DRAGON SEED(1944); MOONLIGHT AND CACTUS(1944); I'LL REMEMBER APRIL(1945); MEN IN HER DIARY(1945); SWING OUT, SISTER(1945); THAT NIGHT WITH YOU(1945); WEEKEND AT THE WALDORF(1945); CUBAN PETE(1946); LITTLE GIANT(1946); WILD BEAUTY(1946); LONE WOLF IN MEXICO, THE(1947); SOMETHING IN THE WIND(1947); SNAKE PIT, THE(1948); CHINATOWN AT MIDNIGHT(1949); IT'S A GREAT FEELING(1949); DAMNED DON'T CRY, THE(1950); GREAT JEWEL ROBBER, THE(1950); NEVER A DULL MOMENT(1950); ON THE ISLE OF SAMOA(1950); CARRIE(1952); SHE'S BACK ON BROADWAY(1953); PLAYGIRL(1954); LAY THAT RIFLE DOWN(1955); TEA AND SYMPATHY(1956); TOY TIGER(1956); TWICE TOLD TALES(1963); HARPER(1966)

Alan De Witt
ONE DESIRE(1955); ANGELS DIE HARD(1970); ENTERTAINER, THE(1975)

Claire De Witt
SON OF SINBAD(1955)

Elina De Witt
KILL OR BE KILLED(1967, Ital.)

Elizabeth De Witt
Misc. Silents
COWBOY KING, THE(1922)

Fay de Witt
PATSY, THE(1964); I'LL TAKE SWEDEN(1965); RELUCTANT ASTRONAUT, THE(1967); HOW TO FRAME A FIGG(1971)

Jack De Witt
LOUISIANA(1947), w; RETURN OF RIN TIN TIN, THE(1947), w; BATTLES OF CHIEF PONTIAC(1952), w; CELL 2455, DEATH ROW(1955), w; TOGETHER BROTHERS(1974), w

Jacqueline De Witt
ALL THAT HEAVEN ALLOWS(1955)

Louis De Witt
NIGHT OF THE HUNTER, THE(1955), spec eff; VOODOO ISLAND(1957), spec eff

De Witt Jennings
THIS IS MY AFFAIR(1937)

Louis de Wohl
CRIME OVER LONDON(1936, Brit.), w; MR. EMMANUEL(1945, Brit.); CAESAR AND CLEOPATRA(1946, Brit.); FRANCIS OF ASSISI(1961), w

Karen de Wold
BY CANDLELIGHT(1934), w

Francis de Wolf
DEVIL DOLL(1964, Brit.)

Karen De Wolf
COUNTESS OF MONTE CRISTO, THE(1934), w; LOVE CAPTIVE, THE(1934), w; CHECKERS(1937), w; HOT WATER(1937), w; ALWAYS IN TROUBLE(1938), w; PASSPORT HUSBAND(1938), w; BLONDIE BRINGS UP BABY(1939), w; BLONDIE TAKES A VACATION(1939), w; EVERYBODY'S BABY(1939), w; BLONDIE PLAYS CUPID(1940), w; PIONEERS OF THE WEST(1940), w; BLONDIE GOES LATIN(1941), w; BLONDIE IN SOCIETY(1941), w; BLONDIE FOR VICTORY(1942), w; BLONDIE'S BLESSED EVENT(1942), w; DARING YOUNG MAN, THE(1942), w; SHUT MY BIG MOUTH(1942), w; IT'S A GREAT LIFE(1943), w; BURY ME DEAD(1947), w; ADVENTURES OF CASANOVA(1948), w; COUNT THE HOURS(1953), w

De Wolfe
FALL OF THE HOUSE OF USHER, THE(1952, Brit.), m; IMPERSONATOR, THE(1962, Brit.), m; SKIN GAME, THE(1965, Brit.), m; TOMCAT, THE(1968, Brit.), m

Billy de Wolfe
DIXIE(1943); DUFFY'S TAVERN(1945); MISS SUSIE SLAGLE'S(1945); OUR HEARTS WERE GROWING UP(1946); PERILS OF PAULINE, THE(1947); VARIETY GIRL(1947); ISN'T IT ROMANTIC?(1948); DEAR WIFE(1949); TEA FOR TWO(1950); DEAR BRAT(1951); LULLABY OF BROADWAY, THE(1951); CALL ME MADAM(1953)

Francis de Wolfe
FIRE OVER ENGLAND(1937, Brit.)

Karen De Wolfe
SOCIETY FEVER(1935), w; STEPCHILD(1947), w; APPOINTMENT IN HONDURAS(1953), w; SILVER LODE(1954), w

Marie de Wolfe
Misc. Silents
KINGDOM OF YOUTH, THE(1918)

Thomas De Wolfe
ALICE'S RESTAURANT(1969)

De Wolfe Hopper
CALLING PHILO VANCE(1940)

Francis de Wolff
FLAME IN THE HEATHER(1935, Brit.); GAY LADY, THE(1949, Brit.); UNDER CAPRICORN(1949); SHE SHALL HAVE MURDER(1950, Brit.); TREASURE ISLAND(1950, Brit.); TOM BROWN'S SCHOOLDAYS(1951, Brit.); MISS ROBIN HOOD(1952, Brit.); MOULIN ROUGE(1952); MASTER OF BALLANTRAE, THE(1953, U.S./Brit.); DIAMOND WIZARD, THE(1954, Brit.); LITTLE KIDNAPPERS, THE(1954, Brit.); KING'S RHAPSODY(1955, Brit.); LAND OF FURY(1955 Brit.); NAKED HEART, THE(1955, Brit.); MOBY DICK(1956, Brit.); ODONGO(1956, Brit.); WEE GEORDIE(1956, Brit.); SAINT JOAN(1957); SMALLEST SHOW ON EARTH, THE(1957, Brit.); ROOTS OF HEAVEN, THE(1958); HOUND OF THE BASKERVILLES, THE(1959, Brit.); MAN WHO COULD CHEAT DEATH, THE(1959, Brit.); SEA FURY(1959, Brit.); TOMMY THE TOREADOR(1960, Brit.); HOUSE OF FRIGHT(1961); CORRIDORS OF BLOOD(1962, Brit.); DURANT AFFAIR, THE(1962, Brit.); SILENT INVASION, THE(1962, Brit.); FROM RUSSIA WITH LOVE(1963, Brit.); SIEGE OF THE SAXONS(1963, Brit.); THREE LIVES OF THOMASINA, THE(1963, U.S./Brit.); CARRY ON CLEO(1964, Brit.); BLACK TORMENT, THE(1965, Brit.); PUSSYCAT ALLEY(1965, Brit.); SECOND BEST SECRET AGENT IN THE WHOLE WIDE WORLD, THE(1965, Brit.); TRIPLE CROSS(1967, Fr./Brit.); FIXER, THE(1968); GIRL GAME(1968, Braz./Fr./Ital.); GHOSTS, ITALIAN STYLE(1969, Ital./Fr.); SINFUL DAVEY(1969, Brit.); THREE MUSKETEERS, THE(1974, Panama)

Francois De Wolff
SAVAGE INNOCENTS, THE(1960, Brit.)

Lorraine De Wood
BULLFIGHTERS, THE(1945)

Joe De Yong
PLAINSMAN, THE(1937), cos; NORTHWEST MOUNTED POLICE(1940), set d, cos

Cliff de Young
PILGRIMAGE(1972); BLUE COLLAR(1978)
1984
PROTOCOL(1984); RECKLESS(1984)

Frances De Young
BETRAYAL, THE(1948)

Joe De Young
SHANE(1953), tech adv

Moss De Young
EXCUSE MY GLOVE(1936, Brit.)

Tina de Yzarduy
Misc. Silents
LA TERRE PROMISE(1925, Fr.)

Herbert de Zaltza
MAIS OU ET DONC ORNICAR(1979, Fr.), p

Antonio Mateos De Zarate
CUSTER OF THE WEST(1968, U.S., Span.), set d

Laure De Zarate
BATTLE OF THE BULGE(1965), cos; CRACK IN THE WORLD(1965), cos; KRAKATOA, EAST OF JAVA(1969), cos

Tony de Zarraga
ANGELS DIE HARD(1970), ed; COUNT YORGA, VAMPIRE(1970), ed; BEWARE! THE BLOB(1972), ed; PAT GARRETT AND BILLY THE KID(1973), ed; KILLER ELITE, THE(1975), ed; GREAT GUNDOWN, THE(1977), ed

Carolyn De Zurik
BARNYARD FOLLIES(1940)

Mary Jane De Zurik
BARNYARD FOLLIES(1940)

Lysandre de-la-Haye
DARK PLACES(1974, Brit.)

Murray De'Atley
THIS IS NOT A TEST(1962), p

A. Dea
GUNMEN OF THE RIO GRANDE(1965, Fr./Ital./Span.), art d

Gloria Dea
STORY OF DR. WASSELL, THE(1944); SOMETHING TO LIVE FOR(1952); PRODIGAL, THE(1955); SEA CHASE, THE(1955)

Jay Dea
SWEET BEAT(1962, Brit.), ed

Marie Dea
PERSONAL COLUMN(1939, Fr.); DEVIL'S ENVOYS, THE(1947, Fr.); FOOLISH HUSBANDS(1948, Fr.); ORPHEUS(1950, Fr.); CAROLINE CHERIE(1951, Fr.); GREEN MARE, THE(1961, Fr./Ital.); TWO ARE GUILTY(1964, Fr.)

Robert Deac
LADY IN THE CAR WITH GLASSES AND A GUN, THE(1970, U.S./Fr.)

Brian Deacon
TRIPLE ECHO, THE(1973, Brit.); VAMPYRES, DAUGHTERS OF DRACULA(1977, Brit.); JESUS(1979); NELLY'S VERSION(1983, Brit.)
Misc. Talkies
AND THE WALL CAME TUMBLING DOWN(1984)

Don Deacon
BORN FREE(1966), ed; CORRUPTION(1968, Brit.), ed; LIVING FREE(1972, Brit.), ed; SCHOOL FOR UNCLAIMED GIRLS(1973, Brit.), ed

Harold Deacon
Silents
LIKENESS OF THE NIGHT, THE(1921, Brit.)

Kim Deacon
GETTING OF WISDOM, THE(1977, Aus.); HOODWINK(1981, Aus.); CROSSTALK(1982, Aus.); WINTER OF OUR DREAMS(1982, Aus.)

L.S. Deacon
OLD MOTHER RILEY OVERSEAS(1943, Brit.), w

Mai Deacon
Silents
OLD CURIOSITY SHOP, THE(1913, Brit.)

Michael Deacon
KIND OF LOVING, A(1962, Brit.); SINISTER MAN, THE(1965, Brit.)

Pamela Deacon
NO ROOM AT THE INN(1950, Brit.)

Richard Deacon
DESIREE(1954); ROGUE COP(1954); THEM!(1954); ABBOTT AND COSTELLO MEET THE MUMMY(1955); BLACKBOARD JUNGLE, THE(1955); GOOD MORNING, MISS DOVE(1955); LAY THAT RIFLE DOWN(1955); MY SISTER EILEEN(1955); THIS ISLAND EARTH(1955); CAROUSEL(1956); FRANCIS IN THE HAUNTED HOUSE(1956); HOT BLOOD(1956); INVASION OF THE BODY SNATCHERS(1956); KETTLES IN THE OZARKS, THE(1956); POWER AND THE PRIZE, THE(1956); PROUD ONES, THE(1956); SCARLET HOUR, THE(1956); SOLID GOLD CADILLAC, THE(1956); WHEN GANGLAND STRIKES(1956); AFFAIR IN RENO(1957); DECISION AT SUNDOWN(1957); KISS THEM FOR ME(1957); MY MAN GODFREY(1957); SPIRIT OF ST. LOUIS, THE(1957); SPRING REUNION(1957); LAST HURRAH, THE(1958); NICE LITTLE BANK THAT SHOULD BE ROBBED, A(1958); REMARKABLE MR. PENNYPACKER, THE(1959); SUMMER PLACE, A(1959); YOUNG PHILADELPHIANS, THE(1959); NORTH TO ALASKA(1960); EVERYTHING'S DUCKY(1961); LOVER COME BACK(1961); THAT TOUCH OF MINK(1962); BIRDS, THE(1963); CRITIC'S CHOICE(1963); WHO'S MINDING THE STORE?(1963); DEAR HEART(1964); DISORDERLY ORDERLY, THE(1964); JOHN GOLDFARB, PLEASE COME HOME(1964); PATSY, THE(1964); RAIDERS, THE(1964); BILLIE(1965); THAT DARN CAT(1965); DON'T WORRY, WE'LL THINK OF A TITLE(1966); ENTER LAUGHING(1967); GNOME-MOBILE, THE(1967); KING'S PIRATE(1967); LADY IN CEMENT(1968); ONE AND ONLY GENUINE ORIGINAL FAMILY BAND, THE(1968); NARCO MEN, THE(1969, Span./Ital.); PIRANHA(1978); HAPPY HOOKER GOES TO HOLLYWOOD, THE(1980)
1984
BAD MANNERS(1984)

Derek Deadman
DARWIN ADVENTURE, THE(1972, Brit.); WHAT'S NEXT?(1975, Brit.); BIG SLEEP, THE½(1978, Brit.); APPLE, THE(1980 U.S./Ger.); TIME BANDITS(1981, Brit.); FUNNY MONEY(1983, Brit.); NEVER SAY NEVER AGAIN(1983)

Vince Deadrick
OPERATION PETTICOAT(1959); APPLE DUMPLING GANG RIDES AGAIN, THE(1979); TRON(1982)

Vince Deadrick, Jr.
1984
STREETS OF FIRE(1984); THIEF OF HEARTS(1984)

Vincent Deadrick
ENEMY BELOW, THE(1957); LOVE WITH THE PROPER STRANGER(1963); DIRTY HARRY(1971)

Vincent Deadrick, Jr.
1984
CITY HEAT(1984)

Vince Deadrick, Sr.
1984
BREAKIN' 2: ELECTRIC BOOGALOO(1984); ROMANCING THE STONE(1984)

Vincent P. Deadrick
DIRTY HARRY(1971)

Jean Deady
CRY OF THE BANSHEE(1970, Brit.)

Deagneaux
BATTLE OF THE RAILS(1949, Fr.)

Roger Deakins
ANOTHER TIME, ANOTHER PLACE(1983, Brit.), ph
1984
1984(1984, Brit.), ph

Borden Deal
WILD RIVER(1960), w

Randall Deal
DELIVERANCE(1972)

Francis Deale
THIN RED LINE, THE(1964)

Nancy Deale
SHADOWS(1960)

Joaquim DeAlmeida
SOLDIER, THE(1982)

Franco DeAlto
SHE DANCES ALONE(1981, Aust./U.S.)

Phillip Deamer
OFFICE PICNIC, THE(1974, Aus.)

A. J. "Man Mountain" Dean
MAN OF THE MOMENT(1955, Brit.); WOMAN FOR JOE, THE(1955, Brit.); JUMPING FOR JOY(1956, Brit.)

Alan Dean
MELODY IN THE DARK(1948, Brit.); DR. FRANKENSTEIN ON CAMPUS(1970, Can.); CROWD INSIDE, THE(1971, Can.)

Alfie Dean
CARDBOARD CAVALIER, THE(1949, Brit.); MY HEART GOES CRAZY(1953, Brit.)

Alfred Dean
DENTIST IN THE CHAIR(1960, Brit.)

Alice Dean
Misc. Silents
IN THE SPIDER'S WEB(1924)

Angie Dean
ENTERTAINER, THE(1960, Brit.)

Barney Dean
THANKS FOR THE MEMORY(1938); STAR SPANGLED RHYTHM(1942); DUFFY'S TAVERN(1945); VARIETY GIRL(1947)

Barry Dean
WHISTLE DOWN THE WIND(1961, Brit.)

Basil Dean
ESCAPE(1930, Brit.), p&d, w; PERFECT ALIBI, THE(1931, Brit.), p&d, w; SALLY IN OUR ALLEY(1931, Brit.), p; FOOTSTEPS IN THE NIGHT(1932, Brit.), p, w; LOOKING ON THE BRIGHT SIDE(1932, Brit.), p, d, w; LOVE ON THE SPOT(1932, Brit.), p; NINE TILL SIX(1932, Brit.), p&d; WATER GYPSIES, THE(1932, Brit.), p, w; WOMAN IN CHAINS(1932, Brit.), p&d; CONSTANT NYMPH, THE(1933, Brit.), d, w; THREE MEN IN A BOAT(1933, Brit.), p; AUTUMN CROCUS(1934, Brit.), p, d; LOVE, LIFE AND LAUGHTER(1934, Brit.), p; LOYALTIES(1934, Brit.), p&d; SING AS WE GO(1934, Brit.), p&d; JAVA HEAD(1935, Brit.), p; LOOK UP AND LAUGH(1935, Brit.), p&d; LORNA DOONE(1935, Brit.), p&d; NO LIMIT(1935, Brit.), p; KEEP YOUR SEATS PLEASE(1936, Brit.), p; LABURNUM GROVE(1936, Brit.), p; QUEEN OF HEARTS(1936, Brit.), p; RETURN OF SHERLOCK HOLMES(1936), d, w; SENSATION(1936, Brit.), w; FEATHER YOUR NEST(1937, Brit.), p; KEEP FIT(1937, Brit.), p; SCOTLAND YARD COMMANDS(1937, Brit.), p; SHOW GOES ON, THE(1937, Brit.), p&d, w; I SEE ICE(1938), p; PENNY PARADISE(1938, Brit.), p; IT'S IN THE AIR(1940, Brit.), p; MOZART(1940, Brit.), p&d; TWENTY-ONE DAYS TOGETHER(1940, Brit.), d, w; MEN OF THE SEA(1951, Brit.), p

Beth Dean
COBRA WOMAN(1944)

Bill Dean
FAMILY LIFE(1971, Brit.); NIGHT WATCH(1973, Brit.)
1984
SLAYGROUND(1984, Brit.)

Billy Dean
I KILLED WILD BILL HICKOK(1956); KES(1970, Brit.); GUMSHOE(1972, Brit.)

Brian E. Dean
RAGTIME(1981)

Charles Dean
Silents
MAN AND HIS WOMAN(1920)

Claudia Dean
Misc. Talkies
CURSE OF THE HEADLESS HORSEMAN(1972)

Dale Dean
DANCING LADY(1933)

David Dean
RAMPARTS WE WATCH, THE(1940); HOWZER(1973)
1984
SCARRED(1984)

Debbie Dean
ENTERTAINER, THE(1960, Brit.)

Derry Dean
NEW FACES OF 1937(1937)

Diana Dean
MAYTIME(1937)

Dink Dean
OPERATION HAYLIFT(1950)

Dinky Dean
Silents
PILGRIM, THE(1923)
Misc. Silents
PRINCE OF A KING, A(1923)

Dixie Dean
STUDENT TOUR(1934)

Don Dean
NATIVE SON(1951, U.S., Arg.)

Donya Dean
ALIAS NICK BEAL(1949)

Dora Dean
Silents
SILVER THREADS AMONG THE GOLD(1915); EYES RIGHT(1926)
Misc. Silents
TIME LOCK NO. 776(1915)

Dorothy Dean
CHELSEA GIRLS, THE(1967)

Douglas Dean
LADY IS WILLING, THE(1942), ch; TAKE A LETTER, DARLING(1942)

E. Brian Dean
NIGHTHAWKS(1981); ROLLOVER(1981); WOLFEN(1981); TOUCHED(1983)

Eddie Dean
WESTERN JAMBOREE(1938); LAW OF THE PAMPAS(1939); RANGE WAR(1939); RENEGADE TRAIL(1939); GOLDEN TRAIL, THE(1940); HIDDEN GOLD(1940); KNIGHTS OF THE RANGE(1940); LIGHT OF WESTERN STARS, THE(1940); LLANO KID, THE(1940); OKLAHOMA RENEGADES(1940); SANTA FE MARSHAL(1940); STAGECOACH WAR(1940); DOWN MEXICO WAY(1941); KANSAS CYCLONE(1941); PALS OF THE PECOS(1941); ROLLIN' HOME TO TEXAS(1941); SIERRA SUE(1941); TRAIL OF THE SILVER SPURS(1941); LONE RIDER AND THE BANDIT, THE(1942); RAIDERS OF THE WEST(1942); STAGECOACH EXPRESS(1942); KING OF THE COWBOYS(1943); SONG OF OLD WYOMING(1945); WILDFIRE(1945); CARAVAN TRAIL, THE(1946); COLORADO SERENADE(1946); DOWN MISSOURI WAY(1946); DRIFTIN' RIVER(1946); ROMANCE OF THE WEST(1946); STARS OVER TEXAS(1946); TUMBLEWEED TRAIL(1946); WILD WEST(1946); RANGE BEYOND THE BLUE(1947); SHADOW VALLEY(1947); WEST TO GLORY(1947); WHITE STALLION(1947); WILD COUNTRY(1947); BLACK HILLS(1948); CHECK YOUR GUNS(1948); HAWK OF POWDER RIVER, THE(1948); PRAIRIE OUTLAWS(1948); TIOGA KID, THE(1948); TORNADO RANGE(1948); WESTWARD TRAIL, THE(1948)

Edward Dean
MANHATTAN LOVE SONG(1934)

Fabian Dean
FALLGUY(1962); RELUCTANT ASTRONAUT, THE(1967); RIDE TO HANGMAN'S TREE, THE(1967); CANDY(1968, Ital./Fr.); SINGLE ROOM FURNISHED(1968); SPLIT, THE(1968); COMPUTER WORE TENNIS SHOES, THE(1970); BAREFOOT EXECUTIVE, THE(1971)

Faxon Dean
LITTLE JOHNNY JONES(1930), ph; TEXAS PIONEERS(1932), ph; BREED OF THE BORDER(1933), ph; DIAMOND TRAIL(1933), ph; ONE YEAR LATER(1933), ph
Silents
ALL SOULS EVE(1921), ph; HER WINNING WAY(1921), ph; MAKING A MAN(1922), ph; STEPHEN STEPS OUT(1923), ph; LORD JIM(1925), ph; BABY MINE(1928), ph; JAZZLAND(1928), ph; OLYMPIC HERO, THE(1928), ph; TRAGEDY OF YOUTH, THE(1928), ph

Faxon M. Dean
Silents
CUMBERLAND ROMANCE, A(1920), ph; DON'T CALL ME LITTLE GIRL(1921), ph; LITTLE CLOWN, THE(1921), ph; NORTH OF THE RIO GRANDE(1922), ph; WHILE SATAN SLEEPS(1922), ph; GENTLEMAN OF LEISURE, A(1923), ph; SIXTY CENTS AN HOUR(1923), ph; TIGER'S CLAW, THE(1923), ph; STRANGER, THE(1924), ph

Felicity Dean
CROSSED SWORDS(1978)
1984
SUCCESS IS THE BEST REVENGE(1984, Brit.)

Floy Dean
FOOLS(1970); BLACK EYE(1974)

Foxon M. Dean
Silents
WINGS(1927), ph

Frances Dean
JEWEL, THE(1933, Brit.); MEET MY SISTER(1933, Brit.)

Gerald Dean
Silents
BULLDOG DRUMMOND(1923, Brit.)

Gertrude Dean
PASSION HOLIDAY(1963)

Gillian Dean
TEMPORARY WIDOW, THE(1930, Ger./Brit.)
Silents
HONEYMOON AHEAD(1927, Brit.); EMERALD OF THE EAST(1928, Brit.)

Hannah Dean
WORLD'S GREATEST LOVER, THE(1977)

Harriet Dean
KNICKERBOCKER HOLIDAY(1944)

Harry Dean
REAP THE WILD WIND(1942)

Sheila Dean
GETTING OVER(1981)

Sidney Dean
Silents
WARRENS OF VIRGINIA, THE(1915); ONCE A PLUMBER(1920); TREASURE ISLAND(1920)
Misc. Silents
DOLL'S HOUSE, A(1917); FIELD OF HONOR, THE(1917); MIDNIGHT TRAIL, THE(1918)

Susan Dean
DIARY OF A BACHELOR(1964)
1984
SAVAGE STREETS(1984)

Sydney Dean
Misc. Silents
WIFE HE BOUGHT, THE(1918)

Terri Dean
TALES OF A SALESMAN(1965)

Vaughan M. Dean
HOUSE OF THE ARROW, THE(1953, Brit.), p

Vaughan N. Dean
BAD BOY(1938, Brit.), p; MEN ARE CHILDREN TWICE(1953, Brit.), p; MOBY DICK(1956, Brit.), p

Vaughn N. Dean
GIRLS AT SEA(1958, Brit.), p

Wallace Dean
DRAGONWYCH(1946)

Wally Dean
TOAST OF NEW YORK, THE(1937); GOVERNMENT GIRL(1943)

William Dean
JOAN OF OZARK(1942); PANIC IN THE STREETS(1950)

Mike H. deAnda
LAST OF THE SECRET AGENTS?, THE(1966)

Peter DeAnda
LADY LIBERTY(1972, Ital./Fr.)

Raymond DeAnda
TALISMAN, THE(1966)

Charles Deane
SALUTE JOHN CITIZEN(1942, Brit.); CAESAR AND CLEOPATRA(1946, Brit.); DEVIL'S HARBOR(1954, Brit.), p, w; BLONDE BLACKMAILER(1955, Brit.), p,d&w

Dacia Deane
Silents
PASSION ISLAND(1927, Brit.); DAWN(1928, Brit.)

Darcia Deane
Silents
EASY VIRTUE(1927, Brit.)

Dorris Deane
Silents
SHARK MASTER, THE(1921)

Douglas Deane
FAMILY JEWELS, THE(1965); WHAT'S THE MATTER WITH HELEN?(1971)

Elaine Deane
NATION AFLAME(1937)

Hamilton Deane
DRACULA(1931), w; SILVER DARLINGS, THE(1947, Brit.); TRIAL OF MADAM X, THE(1948, Brit.)

Hazel Deane
Silents
SOUTH OF NORTHERN LIGHTS(1922); SEVEN CHANCES(1925); GALLANT FOOL, THE(1926)
Misc. Silents
BUTTERFLY RANGE(1922); SECRET OF THE PUEBLO, THE(1923); DEVIL'S GULCH, THE(1926); FIGHTING JACK(1926); SPEEDY SMITH(1927)

Howard Deane
GOOD GUYS AND THE BAD GUYS, THE(1969), ed

Howard S. Deane
INTERVAL(1973, Mex./U.S.), ed

Jean Deane
CHICAGO CONFIDENTIAL(1957)

Joanne Helen Deane
RABBIT, RUN(1970)

Lee Deane
CATALINA CAPER, THE(1967)

LeRoy Deane
PALM SPRINGS WEEKEND(1963), art d; INCREDIBLE MR. LIMPET, THE(1964), art d; ROBIN AND THE SEVEN HOODS(1964), art d; MARRIAGE ON THE ROCKS(1965), art d; MY BLOOD RUNS COLD(1965), art d; NONE BUT THE BRAVE(1965, U.S./Jap.), art d; COOL ONES THE(1967), art d; HEART IS A LONELY HUNTER, THE(1968), art d; LADY IN CEMENT(1968), art d

LeRoy G. Deane
ONE LITTLE INDIAN(1973), art d

Lesley Deane
DEADLY NIGHTSHADE(1953, Brit.)

Linda Deane
IT'S A DATE(1940); GIRL CRAZY(1943); MARRIAGE IS A PRIVATE AFFAIR(1944); MEET THE PEOPLE(1944)

Marjorie Deane
FRESHMAN YEAR(1938); GOLDWYN FOLLIES, THE(1938); NEW YORK TOWN(1941)

Martin Deane
FARMER TAKES A WIFE, THE(1953)

Palmer Deane
STILL OF THE NIGHT(1982)

Patricia Deane
GAY LADY, THE(1949, Brit.)

Richard Deane
NURSE EDITH CAVELL(1939); SWAMP WOMAN(1941); TONIGHT AND EVERY NIGHT(1945)

Shirley Deane
BACK TO NATURE(1936); CHARLIE CHAN AT THE CIRCUS(1936); EDUCATING FATHER(1936); FIRST BABY(1936); GIRLS' DORMITORY(1936); KING OF BURLESQUE(1936); ONE IN A MILLION(1936); BIG BUSINESS(1937); BORROWING TROUBLE(1937); HOT WATER(1937); NANCY STEELE IS MISSING(1937); OFF TO THE RACES(1937); LOVE ON A BUDGET(1938); PRAIRIE MOON(1938); SAFETY IN NUMBERS(1938); TRIP TO PARIS, A(1938); EVERYBODY'S BABY(1939); UNDERCOVER AGENT(1939); YOU PAY YOUR MONEY(1957, Brit.)

Sidney Deane
Silents
CALL OF THE NORTH, THE(1914); ROSE OF THE RANCHO(1914); GIRL OF THE GOLDEN WEST, THE(1915); GOOSE GIRL, THE(1915); MALE AND FEMALE(1919)

Sydney Deane
Silents
BREWSTER'S MILLIONS(1914); READY MONEY(1914); VIRGINIAN, THE(1914); ARAB, THE(1915); SECRET ORCHARD(1915); LAST OF THE MOHICANS, THE(1920); MISSING MILLIONS(1922); AMERICA(1924)
Misc. Silents
WHAT'S HIS NAME?(1914); STOLEN GOODS(1915); HER OWN STORY(1922); BROKEN VIOLIN, THE(1923)

Terence F. Deane
I NEVER PROMISED YOU A ROSE GARDEN(1977), p

Tessa Deane
VARIETY(1935, Brit.); VARIETY JUBILEE(1945, Brit.)

Uel Deane
10 RILLINGTON PLACE(1971, Brit.)

Verna Deane
LADY LIES, THE(1929)

Mercie Deane-Johns
WINTER OF OUR DREAMS(1982, Aus.)

Gina DeAngelis
DEATH VENGEANCE(1982)
1984
BROADWAY DANNY ROSE(1984)

Guido DeAngelis
CHARLESTON(1978, Ital.), m; TWO SUPER COPS(1978, Ital.), m; IMMORTAL BACHELOR, THE(1980, Ital.), m

Maurizio DeAngelis
CHARLESTON(1978, Ital.), m; TWO SUPER COPS(1978, Ital.), m

Remo DeAngelis
MONSIGNOR(1982)

Rosemary DeAngelis
WANDERERS, THE(1979)

Joe DeAngelo
SERENADE(1956)

Marjorie Deanne
TRUE TO LIFE(1943); DESIGN FOR SCANDAL(1941); WEST POINT WIDOW(1941); STAR SPANGLED RHYTHM(1942); CRYSTAL BALL, THE(1943); FOR WHOM THE BELL TOLLS(1943); SALUTE FOR THREE(1943)

Herbert Deans
BAL TABARIN(1952); MAN BEHIND THE GUN, THE(1952); ROGUE'S MARCH(1952); HOW TO MARRY A MILLIONAIRE(1953); TITANIC(1953); ABBOTT AND COSTELLO MEET DR. JEKYLL AND MR. HYDE(1954); FIRST TRAVELING SALESLADY, THE(1956)

Marjorie Deans
CATHERINE THE GREAT(1934, Brit.), w; GREAT DEFENDER, THE(1934, Brit.), w; DRAKE THE PIRATE(1935, Brit.), w; REGAL CAVALCADE(1935, Brit.), w; GIVE HER A RING(1936, Brit.), w; LIVING DANGEROUSLY(1936, Brit.), w; SENSATION(1936, Brit.), w; SOMEONE AT THE DOOR(1936, Brit.), w; STAR FELL FROM HEAVEN, A(1936, Brit.), w; AREN'T MEN BEASTS?(1937, Brit.), w; TENTH MAN, THE(1937, Brit.), w; KATHLEEN(1938, Ireland), w; TALK ABOUT JACQUELINE(1942, Brit.), w; RHYTHM SERENADE(1943, Brit.), w; CAESAR AND CLEOPATRA(1946, Brit.), w; GIRL WHO COULDN'T QUITE, THE(1949, Brit.), w; GIRL IS MINE, THE(1950, Brit.), d, w

Pearl Deans
1984
COMFORT AND JOY(1984, Brit.)

Billy Dear
WRATH OF JEALOUSY(1936, Brit.)

Buck Dear
1984
STONE BOY, THE(1984)

Clay Dear
VERDICT, THE(1982)

Elizabeth Dear
LOSS OF INNOCENCE(1961, Brit.); NIGHTMARE(1963, Brit.); PUMPKIN EATER, THE(1964, Brit.); BATTLE OF THE VILLA FIORITA, THE(1965, Brit.); CALAMITY THE COW(1967, Brit.)

Frank L. Dear
Misc. Silents
AT THE OLD CROSSED ROADS(1914), d

Leslie Dear
CAT GANG, THE(1959, Brit.), ph; FLYING SORCERER, THE(1974, Brit.), ph

Liz Dear
MILESTONES(1975)

Michael Dear
CURE FOR LOVE, THE(1950, Brit.); OLIVER TWIST(1951, Brit.); STEEL BAYONET, THE(1958, Brit.)

Peter Dear
Silents
ROYAL OAK, THE(1923, Brit.)

Susan Dear
TIMERIDER(1983)

William Dear
NORTHVILLE CEMETERY MASSACRE, THE(1976), p,d&ph; TIMERIDER(1983), a, d, w

Robert Dearberg
DARWIN ADVENTURE, THE(1972, Brit.), ed; HOUSE OF LONG SHADOWS, THE(1983, Brit.), ed

Robert Dearburg
FRIGHTMARE(1974, Brit.), ed
Anthony Dearden
SCARLET COAT, THE(1955)
Basil Dearden
THIS MAN IS NEWS(1939, Brit.), w; LET GEORGE DO IT(1940, Brit.), w; SPARE A COPPER(1940, Brit.), p, w; BLACK SHEEP OF WHITEHALL, THE(1941 Brit.), d; TURNED OUT NICE AGAIN(1941, Brit.), p, w; GOOSE STEPS OUT, THE(1942, Brit.), d; BELLS GO DOWN, THE(1943, Brit.), d; MY LEARNED FRIEND(1943, Brit.), d; THEY CAME TO A CITY(1944, Brit.), d, w; FRIEDA(1947, Brit.), d; CAPTIVE HEART, THE(1948, Brit.), d; SARABAND(1949, Brit.), d; BLUE LAMP, THE(1950, Brit.), d; CAGE OF GOLD(1950, Brit.), d; POOL OF LONDON(1951, Brit.), d; GENTLE GUNMAN, THE(1952, Brit.), p&d; TRAIN OF EVENTS(1952, Brit.), w; I BELIEVE IN YOU(1953, Brit.), p&d, w; RAINBOW JACKET, THE(1954, Brit.), d; SQUARE RING, THE(1955, Brit.), p&d; SHIP THAT DIED OF SHAME, THE(1956, Brit.), p&d, w; WHO DONE IT?(1956, Brit.), d; OUT OF THE CLOUDS(1957, Brit.), p, d; SMALLEST SHOW ON EARTH, THE(1957, Brit.), d; DAVY(1958, Brit.), p; MAD LITTLE ISLAND(1958, Brit.), p; VIOLENT PLAYGROUND(1958, Brit.), d; SAPPHIRE(1959, Brit.), d; DESERT MICE(1960, Brit.), p; ALL NIGHT LONG(1961, Brit.), d; LEAGUE OF GENTLEMEN, THE(1961, Brit.), d; MAN IN THE MOON(1961, Brit.), d; SECRET PARTNER, THE(1961, Brit.), d; VICTIM(1961, Brit.), d; MIND BENDERS, THE(1963, Brit.), d; PLACE TO GO, A(1964, Brit.), d; WOMAN OF STRAW(1964, Brit.), d; MASQUERADE(1965, Brit.), d; KHARTOUM(1966, Brit.), d; WALK IN THE SHADOW(1966, Brit.), d; ONLY WHEN I LARF(1968, Brit.), d; ASSASSINATION BUREAU, THE(1969, Brit.), d; MAN WHO HAUNTED HIMSELF, THE(1970, Brit.), d, w
Harold Dearden
INTERFERENCE(1928), w; WOMAN IN CHAINS(1932, Brit.), w; WIVES BEWARE(1933, Brit.), w; WITHOUT REGRET(1935), w
Julia Dearden
1984
CAL(1984, Ireland)
Basil Deardeu
HALF-WAY HOUSE, THE(1945, Brit.), d
Morgan Deare
1984
SCREAM FOR HELP(1984)
Ashton Dearholt
NEW ADVENTURES OF TARZAN(1935), p; TARZAN AND THE GREEN GODDESS(1938), p
Silents
BRIDE'S SILENCE, THE(1917); BRIDE'S AWAKENING, THE(1918); GIRL IN THE DARK, THE(1918); CABARET GIRL, THE(1919); OUT OF THE STORM(1920); IMPULSE(1922); AT DEVIL'S GORGE(1923), a, d; STING OF THE SCORPION, THE(1923); LASH OF THE WHIP(1924); WEST OF THE LAW(1926); RACING ROMEO(1927)
Misc. Silents
CALENDER GIRL, THE(1917); HIGH PLAY(1917); TWO-SOUL WOMAN, THE(1918); SILK-LINED BURGLAR, THE(1919); YANKEE GO-GETTER, A(1921); PRICE OF YOUTH, THE(1922); COWBOY PRINCE, THE(1924); CUPID'S RUSTLER(1924); LASH OF PINTO PETE, THE(1924); WESTERN YESTERDAYS(1924)
Ray Dearholt
DATE WITH DEATH, A(1959)
Ann Dearing
Silents
MY FOUR YEARS IN GERMANY(1918)
Dorothy Dearing
UP THE RIVER(1938); HOTEL FOR WOMEN(1939); WIFE, HUSBAND AND FRIEND(1939); BLUE BIRD, THE(1940); FREE, BLONDE AND 21(1940); GIRL IN 313(1940); GREAT PROFILE, THE(1940); HUDSON'S BAY(1940); GREAT AMERICAN BROADCAST, THE(1941); THAT NIGHT IN RIO(1941); I WAKE UP SCREAMING(1942); MY GAL SAL(1942)
Ed Dearing
STAR WITNESS(1931); THIRTY-DAY PRINCESS(1934); SHE COULDN'T TAKE IT(1935); STOLEN HARMONY(1935); AFTER THE THIN MAN(1936); ROSE MARIE(1936); THANK YOU, JEEVES(1936); THANKS FOR EVERYTHING(1938); REMEMBER THE DAY(1941); MY GAL SAL(1942); JOHNNY ANGEL(1945); NOCTURNE(1946); SORROWFUL JONES(1949); RIGHT CROSS(1950); AS YOU WERE(1951); MY WIFE'S BEST FRIEND(1952)
Edgar Dearing
JAZZ AGE, THE(1929); LOCKED DOOR, THE(1929); FREE AND EASY(1930); MILLION DOLLAR LEGS(1932); CLEOPATRA(1934); CRUSADES, THE(1935); RAINMAKERS, THE(1935); RENDEZVOUS(1935); BRIDE WALKS OUT, THE(1936); BUNKER BEAN(1936); END OF THE TRAIL(1936); SKY PARADE(1936); SKY TIME(1936); AWFUL TRUTH, THE(1937); BIG CITY(1937); CHINA PASSAGE(1937); IT HAPPENED IN HOLLYWOOD(1937); MARRIED BEFORE BREAKFAST(1937); PLAINSMAN, THE(1937); SARATOGA(1937); THAT GIRL FROM PARIS(1937); THERE GOES MY GIRL(1937); THEY GAVE HIM A GUN(1937); AMAZING DR. CLITTERHOUSE, THE(1938); BORDER G-MAN(1938); CITY GIRL(1938); EVERY DAY'S A HOLIDAY(1938); HARD TO GET(1938); MAID'S NIGHT OUT(1938); THREE LOVES HAS NANCY(1938); VIVACIOUS LADY(1938); HONOLULU(1939); NICK CARTER, MASTER DETECTIVE(1939); ROSE OF WASHINGTON SQUARE(1939); SOME LIKE IT HOT(1939); TORCHY PLAYS WITH DYNAMITE(1939); CHILD IS BORN, A(1940); DOCTOR TAKES A WIFE(1940); KNUTE ROCKNE–ALL AMERICAN(1940); LITTLE ORVIE(1940); LUCKY PARTNERS(1940); MANHATTAN HEARTBEAT(1940); NO TIME FOR COMEDY(1940); ONE NIGHT IN THE TROPICS(1940); QUEEN OF THE MOB(1940); SAILOR'S LADY(1940); THOSE WERE THE DAYS(1940); WE WHO ARE YOUNG(1940); WHEN THE DALTONS RODE(1940); WYOMING(1940); CAUGHT IN THE DRAFT(1941); DESIGN FOR SCANDAL(1941); HOLD THAT GHOST(1941); KISSES FOR BREAKFAST(1941); MAISIE WAS A LADY(1941); POT O' GOLD(1941); SHADOW OF THE THIN MAN(1941); SULLIVAN'S TRAVELS(1941); GENTLEMAN AFTER DARK, A(1942); HENRY ALDRICH, EDITOR(1942); MISS ANNIE ROONEY(1942); MY FAVORITE BLONDE(1942); NAVY COMES THROUGH, THE(1942); TRUE TO THE ARMY(1942); WINGS FOR THE EAGLE(1942); HENRY ALDRICH HAUNTS A HOUSE(1943); AND THE ANGELS SING(1944); BIG NOISE, THE(1944); DESTINY(1944); GHOST CATCHERS(1944); GYPSY WILDCAT(1944); IN SOCIETY(1944); SEVEN DOORS TO DEATH(1944); STRANGE AFFAIR(1944); WEEK-END PASS(1944); ABBOTT AND COSTELLO IN HOLLYWOOD(1945); DON'T FENCE ME IN(1945); HER LUCKY NIGHT(1945); ROAD TO UTOPIA(1945); SCARLET STREET(1945); SWING OUT, SISTER(1945); SHE WROTE THE BOOK(1946); MAGIC

TOWN(1947); UNCONQUERED(1947); VARIETY GIRL(1947); WHERE THERE'S LIFE(1947); WILD HARVEST(1947); OUT OF THE STORM(1948); PALEFACE, THE(1948); RETURN OF THE WHISTLER, THE(1948); BOSTON BLACKIE'S CHINESE VENTURE(1949); PRISON WARDEN(1949); SAMSON AND DELILAH(1949); FANCY PANTS(1950); LIGHTNING GUNS(1950); RAIDERS OF TOMAHAWK CREEK(1950); UNION STATION(1950); PECOS RIVER(1951); RIDIN' THE OUTLAW TRAIL(1951); SANTA FE(1951); SILVER CANYON(1951); KID FROM BROKEN GUN, THE(1952); IT CAME FROM OUTER SPACE(1953); LONG, LONG TRAILER, THE(1954); MA AND PA KETTLE AT HOME(1954); TARANTULA(1955); POLLYANNA(1960)
Henry Edgar Dearing
GOOD FELLOWS, THE(1943)
Peter Dearing
NAKED IN THE SUN(1957)
R. E. Dearing
MAN WHO LIVED AGAIN, THE(1936, Brit.), ed; DOCTOR SYN(1937, Brit.), ed; WINDBAG THE SAILOR(1937, Brit.), ed; LADY VANISHES, THE(1938, Brit.), ed; TO THE VICTOR(1938, Brit.), ed; NIGHT TRAIN(1940, Brit.), ed; THEY CAME BY NIGHT(1940, Brit.), ed; GIRL IN THE NEWS(1941, Brit.), ed; MAIL TRAIN(1941, Brit.), ed; REMARKABLE MR. KIPPS(1942, Brit.), ed; YOUNG MR. PITT, THE(1942, Brit.), ed; MAN IN GREY, THE(1943, Brit.), ed; WE DIVE AT DAWN(1943, Brit.), ed; UNCENSORED(1944, Brit.), ed; MAN OF EVIL(1948, Brit.), ed
Sayre Dearing
WORDS AND MUSIC(1929); NONE BUT THE LONELY HEART(1944); ADVENTURE(1945); DON'T GAMBLE WITH STRANGERS(1946); STRANGE LOVE OF MARTHA IVERS, THE(1946); DEAD RECKONING(1947); HOLLOW TRIUMPH(1948); LET'S DANCE(1950); MY FAVORITE SPY(1951); JUBILEE TRAIL(1954)
Edgar Dearling
CROSS COUNTRY ROMANCE(1940)
Jack Dearlove
RAIDERS OF THE LOST ARK(1981)
Max Dearly
AZAIS(1931, Fr.); LE DENIER MILLIARDAIRE(1934, Fr.); LES MISERABLES(1936, Fr.)
Glyn Dearman
HIDEOUT(1948, Brit.); CHRISTMAS CAROL, A(1951, Brit.); TOM BROWN'S SCHOOLDAYS(1951, Brit.); FOUR SIDED TRIANGLE(1953, Brit.)
Jennifer Dearman
MR. H. C. ANDERSEN(1950, Brit.); FOUR SIDED TRIANGLE(1953, Brit.)
A.P. Dearsley
FLY AWAY PETER(1948, Brit.), w; COME BACK PETER(1952, Brit.), w; ALF'S BABY(1953, Brit.), w; AND THE SAME TO YOU(1960, Brit.), w
Joyce Dearsley
Silents
GENERAL POST(1920, Brit.); ADVENTURES OF MR. PICKWICK, THE(1921, Brit.)
Misc. Silents
DIVINE GIFT, THE(1918, Brit.); BEYOND THE DREAMS OF AVARICE(1920, Brit.); CHAPPY - THAT'S ALL(1924, Brit.)
Bill Dearth
48 HOURS(1982)
1984
RHINESTONE(1984)
John Dearth
MAILBAG ROBBERY(1957, Brit.); DANGEROUS EXILE(1958, Brit.); LOOK BACK IN ANGER(1959); WRECK OF THE MARY DEAR, THE(1959); CIRCLE OF DECEPTON(1961, Brit.); SHADOW OF THE CAT, THE(1961, Brit.); ROAD TO HONG KONG, THE(1962, U.S./Brit.); STRONGROOM(1962, Brit.); RUNAWAY, THE(1964, Brit.)
Lynn Dearth
SWEENEY 2(1978, Brit.)
Tony Deary
PIRATE MOVIE, THE(1982, Aus.); ROAD WARRIOR, THE(1982, Aus.)
Henry Deas
TWO-MINUTE WARNING(1976)
Lialani Deas
Silents
RED WINE(1928)
John Dease
SMITHY(1946, Aus.); PACIFIC ADVENTURE(1947, Aus.); NED KELLY(1970, Brit.); NEWSFRONT(1979, Aus.)
Paul Deason
TRUCK STOP WOMEN(1974), w
Ted Deason
CARAVAN TO VACCARES(1974, Brit./Fr), ph
Seamus Deasy
POITIN(1979, Irish), ph
Donna Death
GEEK MAGGOT BINGO(1983), a, set d
Aaron Deaton
WILD REBELS, THE(1967)
Emil Deaton
WILD REBELS, THE(1967); HOOKED GENERATION, THE(1969)
George Deaton
ONE MAN JURY(1978); TOOLBOX MURDERS, THE(1978), m
Tom Deaton
MOONSHINE COUNTY EXPRESS(1977)
Bob Deats
Misc. Talkies
RIO GRANDE(1949)
Jean dEaubonne
CHARADE(1963), art d
Emile DeAuelle
LOOSE ENDS(1930, Brit.), ed
Sheryl Deauville
IRMA LA DOUCE(1963)
Nancy Deaver
Misc. Silents
CHIVALROUS CHARLEY(1921); MOHICAN'S DAUGHTER, THE(1922); SOLOMON IN SOCIETY(1922); WOLF'S FANGS, THE(1922); CIRCUS CYCLONE, THE(1925); FIGHTING FATE(1925); TRAIL RIDER, THE(1925)

Ada Deaves
Silents
MICE AND MEN(1916)
Peter Deb
PRECIOUS JEWELS(1969)
Jean DeBaer
FAN, THE(1981)
Jeanne DeBaer
WORLD ACCORDING TO GARP, The(1982)
Henri Debain
LA MATERNELLE(1933, Fr.)
Misc. Silents
LE PETIT CAFE(1919, Fr.); LE SECRET DE ROSETTE LAMBERT(1920, Fr.); LA MAISON VIDE(1921, Fr.); TRIPLEPATTE(1922, Fr.); MARQUITTA(1927, Fr.)
Henry Debain
Misc. Silents
MICHEL STROGOFF(1926, Fr.)
John DeBallo
SURVIVORS, THE(1983)
Lois DeBanzie
SO FINE(1981); ANNIE(1982)
Andree Debar
GUILTY?(1956, Brit.)
Jacques Debary
THIEF OF PARIS, THE(1967, Fr./Ital.); THAT OBSCURE OBJECT OF DESIRE(1977, Fr./Span.)
Jumoke Debayo
BUSHBABY, THE(1970); CRY OF THE PENGUINS(1972, Brit.)
Jumoko Debayo
NATIONAL HEALTH, OR NURSE NORTON'S AFFAIR, THE(1973, Brit.)
Kymoke Debayo
O LUCKY MAN!(1973, Brit.)
Peter DeBear
SIDE STREET(1950); PRODIGAL, THE(1955)
Michael DeBeausset
MISSION MARS(1968); DARKER THAN AMBER(1970)
Harold DeBecker
FLESH AND FANTASY(1943); CLUNY BROWN(1946); NIGHT AND DAY(1946)
Harold deBecker, Jr.
NATIONAL VELVET(1944)
Marie deBecker
DEVOTION(1946)
Marie deBecker
HOUR BEFORE THE DAWN, THE(1944)
Baron DeBeer
BANANAS(1971)
Gerritt Debeer
1984
ONCE UPON A TIME IN AMERICA(1984)
Frantisek Debelka
FIREMAN'S BALL, THE(1968, Czech.)
Christine DeBell
BLOODBROTHERS(1978)
Kristine DeBell
I WANNA HOLD YOUR HAND(1978); MAIN EVENT, THE(1979); MEAT-BALLS(1979, Can.); WILLIE AND PHIL(1980); T.A.G.: THE ASSASSINATION GAME(1982)
Misc. Talkies
LIFE POD(1980)
John Debello
1984
DELIVERY BOYS(1984)
Frank DeBenedett
BULLET FOR PRETTY BOY, A(1970)
Dick DeBenedictis
EARTHLING, THE(1980), m
Dick DeBenedictus
MANCHU EAGLE MURDER CAPER MYSTERY, THE(1975), m
Cecily Debenham
Misc. Silents
SOME ARTIST(1919, Brit.)
Burr DeBenning
SWEET NOVEMBER(1968); ST. IVES(1976); INCREDIBLE MELTING MAN, THE(1978); WOLFEN(1981)
Misc. Talkies
ALIEN ZONE(1978)
Jeff DeBenning
FIVE GUNS TO TOMBSTONE(1961); HOW TO SUCCEED IN BUSINESS WITHOUT REALLY TRYING(1976)
Chantal Deberg
SWORD OF EL CID, THE(1965, Span./Ital.)
Emmanuelle Debever
DANTON(1983)
Allen DeBevoise
1984
BREAKIN'(1984), p, w; BREAKIN' 2: ELECTRIC BOOGALOO(1984), w
Edward DeBlasio
LEGEND OF LYLAH CLARE, THE(1968), w
Birdie DeBolt
PAGAN LOVE SONG(1950)
The Debonaires
PRIORITIES ON PARADE(1942)
Jan DeBont
ALL THE RIGHT MOVES(1983), ph; CUJO(1983), ph
Michel Deborb
MASCULINE FEMININE(1966, Fr./Swed.)
Levirne DeBord
GENTLE GIANT(1967)

Sharon DeBord
CHEYENNE SOCIAL CLUB, THE(1970); HOAX, THE(1972)
Jean-Jacques Debout
MASCULINE FEMININE(1966, Fr./Swed.), m; MATTER OF DAYS, A(1969, Fr./Czech.), m; EGLANTINE(1972, Fr.), m
Michel Debrane
DIVA(1982, Fr.)
Michel Debranne
RISE OF LOUIS XIV, THE(1970, Fr.)
Eddy Debray
RULES OF THE GAME, THE(1939, Fr.)
Hal Debrett
SHADOW OF FEAR(1956, Brit.), w
Andre Debreuil
I LOVE YOU, I KILL YOU(1972, Ger.), ph
Jean DeBriac
LLOYDS OF LONDON(1936); WATCH ON THE RHINE(1943); DECEPTION(1946); GILDA(1946); MY FAVORITE SPY(1951); CARRIE(1952); LUCKY ME(1954)
Lee DeBroux
DIRT GANG, THE(1972); CHINATOWN(1974); NICKEL RIDE, THE(1974); TERMINAL MAN, THE(1974); NORMA RAE(1979); FRANCES(1982)
Helen Debroy
COLONEL BLIMP(1945, Brit.)
Debroy Somers and his Band
PICCADILLY(1932, Brit.); KENTUCKY MINSTRELS(1934, Brit.); MUSIC HALL(1934, Brit.); REGAL CAVALCADE(1935, Brit.)
Nigel DeBrulier
MONKEY'S PAW, THE(1933); SAN FRANCISCO(1936); MARIE ANTOINETTE(1938); FOR BEAUTY'S SAKE(1941)
Elaine Debry
ONCE YOU KISS A STRANGER(1969)
Jean Debucourt
LIFE AND LOVES OF BEETHOVEN, THE(1937, Fr.); MAYERLING(1937, Fr.); EAGLE WITH TWO HEADS(1948, Fr.); IDIOT, THE(1948, Fr.); DEVIL IN THE FLESH, THE(1949, Fr.); LOVE STORY(1949, Fr.); MONSIEUR VINCENT(1949, Fr.); WOMAN WHO DARED(1949, Fr.); GOLDEN COACH, THE(1953, Fr./Ital.); SEVEN DEADLY SINS, THE(1953, Fr./Ital.); DESPERATE DECISION(1954, Fr.); EARRINGS OF MADAME DE..., THE(1954, Fr.); DOCTORS, THE(1956, Fr.); LE CIEL EST A VOUS(1957, Fr.); LIGHT ACROSSS THE STREET, THE(1957, Fr.); NANA(1957, Fr./Ital.); MAIGRET LAYS A TRAP(1958, Fr.)
Misc. Silents
FALL OF THE HOUSE OF USHER, THE(1928, Fr.)
Shirley DeBurgh
PEPE(1960)
Chuck Debus
PERSONAL BEST(1982)
Debussy
ALLEGRO NON TROPPO(1977, Ital.), m; L'AGE D'OR(1979, Fr.), m
Achille Claude Debussy
1984
BASILEUS QUARTET(1984, Ital.), m
Claude Debussy
FLOWER THIEF, THE(1962), m; LA VIACCIA(1962, Fr./Ital.), m
The Debutantes
TWENTY MILLION SWEETHEARTS(1934)
B. Dec
WALKOVER(1969, Pol.)
Henri Decae
LES ENFANTS TERRIBLES(1952, Fr.), ph; COUSINS, THE(1959, Fr.), ph; FOUR HUNDRED BLOWS, THE(1959), ph; LE BEAU SERGE(1959, Fr.), ph; LOVERS, THE(1959, Fr.), ph; FRANTIC(1961, Fr.), ph; PURPLE NOON(1961, Fr./Ital.), ph; WEB OF PASSION(1961, Fr.), ph; SEVEN CAPITAL SINS(1962, Fr./Ital.), ph; SUNDAYS AND CYBELE(1962, Fr.), ph; VERY PRIVATE AFFAIR, A(1962, Fr./Ital.), ph; DAY AND THE HOUR, THE(1963, Fr./ Ital.), ph; JOY HOUSE(1964, Fr.), ph; SWEET AND SOUR(1964, Fr./Ital.), ph; CIRCLE OF LOVE(1965, Fr.), ph; VIVA MARIA(1965, Fr./Ital.), ph; HOTEL PARADISO(1966, U.S./Brit.), ph; SUCKER, THE(1966, Fr./Ital.), ph; WEEKEND AT DUNKIRK(1966, Fr./Ital.), ph; COMEDIANS, THE(1967), ph; NIGHT OF THE GENERALS, THE(1967, Brit./Fr.), ph; THIEF OF PARIS, THE(1967, Fr./Ital.), ph; DIABOLICALLY YOURS(1968, Fr.), ph; CASTLE KEEP(1969), ph; HELLO-GOODBYE(1970), ph; ONLY GAME IN TOWN, THE(1970), ph; SICILIAN CLAN, THE(1970, Fr.), ph; DELUSIONS OF GRANDEUR(1971 Fr.), ph; LIGHT AT THE EDGE OF THE WORLD, THE(1971, U.S./Span./Lichtenstein), ph; GODSON, THE(1972, Ital./Fr.), ph; ADVENTURES OF RABBI JACOB, THE(1973, Fr.), ph; TWO PEOPLE(1973), ph; OPERATION DAYBREAK(1976, U.S./Brit./Czech.), ph; SEVEN NIGHTS IN JAPAN(1976, Brit./Fr.), ph; BOBBY DEERFIELD(1977), ph; ALMOST PERFECT AFFAIR, AN(1979), ph; ISLAND, THE(1980), ph; EXPOSED(1983), ph
Marie Decaitre
OLIVE TREES OF JUSTICE, THE(1967, Fr.)
Rosemary DeCamp
CHEERS FOR MISS BISHOP(1941); COMMANDOS STRIKE AT DAWN, THE(1942); EYES IN THE NIGHT(1942); THIS IS THE ARMY(1943); DANGER SIGNAL(1945); TOO YOUNG TO KNOW(1945); WEEKEND AT THE WALDORF(1945); FROM THIS DAY FORWARD(1946); NORA PRENTISS(1947); LIFE OF RILEY, THE(1949); LOOK FOR THE SILVER LINING(1949); BIG HANGOVER, THE(1950); ON MOONLIGHT BAY(1951); SCANDAL SHEET(1952); BY THE LIGHT OF THE SILVERY MOON(1953); MANY RIVERS TO CROSS(1955); STRATEGIC AIR COMMAND(1955)
Victor DeCamp
HARMONY LANE(1935)
Paula DeCardo
THRILL OF A LIFETIME(1937); TROPIC HOLIDAY(1938); ROAD TO SINGAPORE(1940)
Walton DeCardo
SENATOR WAS INDISCREET, THE(1947)
Joseph DeCardova
Misc. Talkies
ETHAN(1971)
Nancy Ann DeCarl
REMARKABLE MR. PENNYPACKER, THE(1959)

Nancy DeCarl
PRINCESS AND THE MAGIC FROG, THE(1965)
Kitty DeCarlo
10(1979)
Louise DeCarlo
HARRY AND WALTER GO TO NEW YORK(1976)
Vinnie DeCarlo
HARDER THEY FALL, THE(1956); HIDE IN PLAIN SIGHT(1980)
Yvonne DeCarlo
FOR WHOM THE BELL TOLLS(1943); HERE COME THE WAVES(1944); BLACK BART(1948); GLOBAL AFFAIR, A(1964); IT SEEMED LIKE A GOOD IDEA AT THE TIME(1975, Can.); MAN WITH BOGART'S FACE, THE(1980); LIAR'S MOON(1982)
Misc. Talkies
BLAZING STEWARDESSES(1975)
Juan DeCarlos
UP THE SANDBOX(1972)
Carol DeCastro
GENERAL DIED AT DAWN, THE(1936)
Gwen DeCastro
ETERNAL SUMMER(1961)
Jerry DeCastro
GILDA(1946)
Travis DeCastro
IN SEARCH OF HISTORIC JESUS(1980)
Alain Decaux
LES MISERABLES(1982, Fr.), w
Philippe Decaux
OPERATION LOVEBIRDS(1968, Den.)
Yves Decaux
STORY OF A THREE DAY PASS, THE(1968, Fr.), set d
Pierre Decazes
SHAMELESS OLD LADY, THE(1966, Fr.); LA GUERRE EST FINIE(1967, Fr./Swed.); CONFESSION, THE(1970, Fr.); LACOMBE, LUCIEN(1974)
Claudia Decea
1984
ALLEY CAT(1984)
Ronald Decent
FERRY TO HONG KONG(1959, Brit.)
Stojan Decermic
25TH HOUR, THE(1967, Fr./Ital./Yugo.)
Paul-Edmond Decharme
MANON(1950, Fr.), p; BACKFIRE(1965, Fr.), p; TENDER SCOUNDREL(1967, Fr./Ital.), p
Paul-Edmonde DeCharme
BANANA PEEL(1965, Fr.), p
Laure Dechasnel
COUSINS IN LOVE(1982)
Conrad Dechert
AMERICAN SUCCESS COMPANY, THE(1980)
Eunice Dechert
AMERICAN SUCCESS COMPANY, THE(1980)
Miki Decima
SHOW FLAT(1936, Brit.)
William D. DeCinces
SWORD OF ALI BABA, THE(1965), art d; LET'S KILL UNCLE(1966), art d; PLAINSMAN, THE(1966), art d; TEXAS ACROSS THE RIVER(1966), art d; GUNFIGHT IN ABILENE(1967), art d; RELUCTANT ASTRONAUT, THE(1967), art d; EYE OF THE CAT(1969), art d
William DeCinces
DON'T JUST STAND THERE(1968), art d
Hamilton Deck
MYSTERY SUBMARINE(1963, Brit.)
Kathy Deckard
1984
HIGHPOINT(1984, Can.)
Simon Deckard
ALICE'S RESTAURANT(1969); NIGHT MOVES(1975); STEPFORD WIVES, THE(1975)
Diana Decker
FIDDLERS THREE(1944, Brit.); MEET ME AT DAWN(1947, Brit.); ROOT OF ALL EVIL, THE(1947, Brit.); SAN DEMETRIO, LONDON(1947, Brit.); WHEN YOU COME HOME(1947, Brit.); MAN'S AFFAIR, A(1949, Brit.); MYSTERY AT THE BURLESQUE(1950, Brit.); ISLAND OF DESIRE(1952, Brit.); IS YOUR HONEYMOON REALLY NECESSARY?(1953, Brit.); BAREFOOT CONTESSA, THE(1954); LOVERS, HAPPY LOVERS!(1955, Brit.); WILL ANY GENTLEMAN?(1955, Brit.); YANK IN ERMINE, A(1955, Brit.); BETRAYAL, THE(1958, Brit.); LOLITA(1962); DEVILS OF DARKNESS, THE(1965, Brit.)
Duane Decker
YOU'RE TELLING ME(1942), w
Geraldine Decker
HARRY AND WALTER GO TO NEW YORK(1976); LA TRAVIATA(1982)
Harry Decker
GALLANT DEFENDER(1935), p; REVENGE RIDER, THE(1935), p; MYSTERIOUS AVENGER, THE(1936), p; SHAKEDOWN(1936), p; OLD WYOMING TRAIL, THE(1937), p; TRAPPED(1937), p; TWO-FISTED SHERIFF(1937), p; COLORADO TRAIL(1938), p; LAW OF THE PLAINS(1938), p; SOUTH OF ARIZONA(1938), p; RIO GRANDE(1939), p; TEXAS STAMPEDE(1939), p
Silents
ALIAS JULIUS CAESAR(1922), ed; KID'S CLEVER, THE(1929), sup
Harry L. Decker
SCANDAL(1929), p; IT CAN'T LAST FOREVER(1937), p; CALL OF THE ROCKIES(1938), p; OUTLAWS OF THE PRAIRIE(1938), p; SPOILERS OF THE RANGE(1939), p; STRANGER FROM TEXAS, THE(1940), p
Silents
TAILOR MADE MAN, A(1922), ed; GATE CRASHER, THE(1928), sup
Henry L. Decker
CATTLE RAIDERS(1938), p

Kathryn Brown Decker
Misc. Silents
FIFTH COMMANDMENT, THE(1915)
Kathryn Browne Decker
Silents
PRIDE OF THE CLAN, THE(1917)
Misc. Silents
PRIMA DONNA'S HUSBAND, THE(1916)
Larry L. Decker
Silents
OLD SWIMMIN' HOLE, THE(1921), ed
Marge Decker
TO PLEASE A LADY(1950), w
Melvin Decker
STREET OF SINNERS(1957)
Michael Decker
IF EVER I SEE YOU AGAIN(1978)
William Decker
Silents
CRIMSON RUNNER, THE(1925), ed
Eugene Deckers
WOMAN TO WOMAN(1946, Brit.); DUAL ALIBI(1947, Brit.); AGAINST THE WIND(1948, Brit.); PRINCE OF FOXES(1949); SLEEPING CAR TO TRIESTE(1949, Brit.); FIGHTING PIMPERNEL, THE(1950, Brit.); GOLDEN SALAMANDER(1950, Brit.); HIGHLY DANGEROUS(1950, Brit.); MADELEINE(1950, Brit.); MRS. FITZHERBERT(1950, Brit.); HOTEL SAHARA(1951, Brit.); LAVENDER HILL MOB, THE(1951, Brit.); SO LONG AT THE FAIR(1951, Brit.); NIGHT WITHOUT STARS(1953, Brit.); DETECTIVE, THE(1954, Qit.); LOVE LOTTERY, THE(1954, Brit.); COLDITZ STORY, THE(1955, Brit.); DOCTOR AT SEA(1955, Brit.); MAN OF THE MOMENT(1955, Brit.); PORT AFRIQUE(1956, Brit.); LET'S BE HAPPY(1957, Brit.); TRIPLE DECEPTION(1957, Brit.); BEASTS OF MARSEILLES, THE(1959, Brit.); CRACK IN THE MIRROR(1960); FLAME OVER INDIA(1960, Brit.); WEEKEND WITH LULU, A(1961, Brit.); LONGEST DAY, THE(1962); LADY L(1965, Fr./Ital.); HELL IS EMPTY(1967, Brit./Ital); LAST SAFARI, THE(1967, Brit.); ASSASSINATION BUREAU, THE(1969, Brit.); LIMBO LINE, THE(1969, Brit.)
Gene Deckers
FOREIGN INTRIGUE(1956)
John DeClair
MR. BELVEDERE RINGS THE BELL(1951), art d
Kuulei DeClercq
HURRICANE, THE(1937)
Madeleine Declercq
FIRE WITHIN, THE(1964, Fr./Ital.)
James DeCloss
HARRY AND WALTER GO TO NEW YORK(1976); HIDE IN PLAIN SIGHT(1980)
Jim DeCloss
LOOKIN' TO GET OUT(1982)
Linda DeCoff
BEEN DOWN SO LONG IT LOOKS LIKE UP TO ME(1977)
Henri Decoin
DRAGNET NIGHT(1931, Fr.), w; HER FIRST AFFAIR(1947, Fr.), p,d&w; DEVIL'S DAUGHTER(1949, Fr.), p, w; STRANGERS IN THE HOUSE(1949, Fr.), d; LOVERS OF TOLEDO, THE(1954, Fr./Span./Ital.), d; SECRETS D'ALCOVE(1954, Fr./Ital.), d; FOLIES BERGERE(1958, Fr.), d; CAT, THE(1959, Fr.), d, w; NATHALIE, AGENT SECRET(1960, Fr.), d; LOVE AND THE FRENCHWOMAN(1961, Fr.), d; WHERE THE TRUTH LIES(1962, Fr.), d, w
Misc. Talkies
ATOMIC AGENT(1959, Fr.), d
Henry Decoin
ABUSED CONFIDENCE(1938, Fr. ABUS DE CONFIANCE), d, w; FOLIES BERGERE(1958, Fr.), w
Dick Decoit
TO BE FREE(1972)
Misc. Talkies
IMAGO(1970)
Eddie DeComa
THIRTEEN WOMEN(1932)
Guy Decombie
JOUR DE FETE(1952, Fr.); COUSINS, THE(1959, Fr.)
Guy Decomble
CRIME OF MONSIEUR LANGE, THE(1936, Fr.); LA BETE HUMAINE(1938, Fr.); WE ARE ALL MURDERERS(1957, Fr.); MAIGRET LAYS A TRAP(1958, Fr.); FOUR HUNDRED BLOWS, THE(1959)
Ennio DeConcini
ATTILA(1958, Ital.), w; DIVORCE, ITALIAN STYLE(1962, Ital.), w; JESSICA(1962, U.S./Ital./Fr.), w; NUDE ODYSSEY(1962, Fr./Ital.), w; DUEL OF THE TITANS(1963, Ital.), w
Jean-Marie DeConinck
ZAZIE(1961, Fr.)
Pedro DeCordoba
BEAST WITH FIVE FINGERS, THE(1946); TWO YEARS BEFORE THE MAST(1946)
Frederick DeCordova
BEDTIME FOR BONZO(1951), d; I'LL TAKE SWEDEN(1965), d
Leander DeCordova
AFTER THE FOG(1930), d; MYSTERIOUS DESPERADO, THE(1949)
Ted DeCorsia
RIDE, VAQUERO!(1953); CONQUEROR, THE(1956); BLOOD ON THE ARROW(1964)
Frank C. Decot
MACK, THE(1973), ed; THOMASINE AND BUSHROD(1974), ed
Dayson Decourcy
PROMISES IN THE DARK(1979)
F. DeCroisset
Silents
AFRAID TO LOVE(1927), w
Etienne Decroux
CHILDREN OF PARADISE(1945, Fr.)
Maxmilien Decroux
LES GAULOISES BLEUES(1969, Fr.)

Ernest Decsey
  KING STEPS OUT, THE(1936), w
Cecile Decugis
  BREATHLESS(1959, Fr.), ed; SHOOT THE PIANO PLAYER(1962, Fr.), ed; SMUG-
  GLERS, THE(1969, Fr.), ed; MY NIGHT AT MAUD'S(1970, Fr.), ed; CHLOE IN THE
  AFTERNOON(1972, Fr.), ed; AVIATOR'S WIFE, THE(1981, Fr.), ed; LE BEAU MA-
  RIAGE(1982, Fr.), ed; PAULINE AT THE BEACH(1983, Fr.), ed
Don DeCuir
  MODEL AND THE MARRIAGE BROKER, THE(1951), art d
John DeCuir
  HALF ANGEL(1951), art d; HOUSE ON TELEGRAPH HILL(1951), art d; DI-
  PLOMATIC COURIER(1952), art d; SOUTH PACIFIC(1958), art d; ONCE IS NOT
  ENOUGH(1975), prod d; DEAD MEN DON'T WEAR PLAID(1982), prod d
  1984
  GHOSTBUSTERS(1984), prod d
John DeCuir, Jr.
  1984
  GHOSTBUSTERS(1984), art d
John F. DeCuir
  BRUTE FORCE(1947), art d; TIME OUT OF MIND(1947), art d; NAKED CITY,
  THE(1948), art d; RAISE THE TITANIC(1980, Brit.), prod d
John F. DeCuir, Jr.
  RAISE THE TITANIC(1980, Brit.), art d
Cecile Decujis
  1984
  FULL MOON IN PARIS(1984, Fr.), ed
Duana Dedda
  WORLD'S GREATEST SINNER, THE(1962)
Samra Dedes
  CAST A GIANT SHADOW(1966)
Yann Dedet
  TWO ENGLISH GIRLS(1972, Fr.), ed; DAY FOR NIGHT(1973, Fr.), ed; SUCH A
  GORGEOUS KID LIKE ME(1973, Fr.), ed; STORY OF ADELE H., THE(1975, Fr.), ed;
  SMALL CHANGE(1976, Fr.), ed; LOULOU(1980, Fr.), ed; CONFIDENTIALLY
  YOURS(1983, Fr.); SNOW(1983, Fr.), ed
  1984
  A NOS AMOURS(1984, Fr.), ed
Eldon Dedini
  FUN AND FANCY FREE(1947), w
A. Dedintsev
  Misc. Silents
  HEIR TO JENGHIS-KHAN, THE(1928, USSR)
L. Dediseff
  Silents
  STORM OVER ASIA(1929, USSR)
Richard Dedmon
  WOLFMAN(1979)
Chris Dedrick
  SIDELONG GLANCES OF A PIGEON KICKER, THE(1970), m; HAPPINESS CAGE,
  THE(1972), m
Ann Dee
  THOROUGHLY MODERN MILLIE(1967); DIAMOND STUD(1970)
Blanche Dee
  HALLELUJAH THE HILLS(1963)
Buffy Dee
  LADY ICE(1973); MURPH THE SURF(1974); PEEPER(1975); MAKO: THE JAWS OF
  DEATH(1976); HARDLY WORKING(1981)
Candy Dee
  PSYCHO FROM TEXAS(1982)
Frances Dee
  MONTE CARLO(1930); PLAYBOY OF PARIS(1930); TRUE TO THE NAVY(1930);
  ALONG CAME YOUTH(1931); AMERICAN TRAGEDY, AN(1931); CAUGHT(1931);
  JUNE MOON(1931); RICH MAN'S FOLLY(1931); WORKING GIRLS(1931); CASE OF
  CLARA DEANE, THE(1932); IF I HAD A MILLION(1932); LOVE IS A RACKET(1932);
  NICE WOMAN(1932); NIGHT OF JUNE 13(1932); STRANGE CASE OF CLARA
  DEANE, THE(1932); THIS RECKLESS AGE(1932); BLOOD MONEY(1933); CRIME OF
  THE CENTURY, THE(1933); HEADLINE SHOOTER(1933); KING OF THE JUN-
  GLE(1933); LITTLE WOMEN(1933); ONE MAN'S JOURNEY(1933); SILVER
  CORD(1933); COMING OUT PARTY(1934); FINISHING SCHOOL(1934); KEEP 'EM
  ROLLING(1934); OF HUMAN BONDAGE(1934); BECKY SHARP(1935); GAY DECEP-
  TION, THE(1935); HALF ANGEL(1936); SOULS AT SEA(1937); IF I WERE KING(1938);
  COAST GUARD(1939); MAN BETRAYED, A(1941); SO ENDS OUR NIGHT(1941);
  MEET THE STEWARTS(1942); HAPPY LAND(1943); I WALKED WITH A ZOM-
  BIE(1943); PATRICK THE GREAT(1945); PRIVATE AFFAIRS OF BEL AMI,
  THE(1947); FOUR FACES WEST(1948); PAYMENT ON DEMAND(1951); REUNION IN
  RENO(1951); BECAUSE OF YOU(1952); MR. SCOUTMASTER(1953); GYPSY
  COLT(1954)
Frank Dee
  COVERED TRAILER, THE(1939)
George Dee
  CASABLANCA(1942); JOAN OF ARC(1948); LIGHT TOUCH, THE(1951); OPERA-
  TION SECRET(1952); FORTY-NINTH MAN, THE(1953); GENTLEMEN PREFER
  BLONDES(1953); WE'RE NO ANGELS(1955); FUNNY FACE(1957); WRECK OF THE
  MARY DEAR, THE(1959); WHO'S GOT THE ACTION?(1962); 36 HOURS(1965)
Jasmine Dee
  WALKING ON AIR(1946, Brit.); LADY CRAVED EXCITEMENT, THE(1950, Brit.)
Joey Dee
  HEY, LET'S TWIST!(1961); TWO TICKETS TO PARIS(1962)
John Dee
  TRIBUTE(1980, Can.)
  1984
  MRS. SOFFEL(1984)
Marlene Ann Dee
  LADY GODIVA RIDES AGAIN(1955, Brit.)
Maurice Dee
  1984
  KIPPERBANG(1984, Brit.)

Protacio Dee
  1984
  HUNTERS OF THE GOLDEN COBRA, THE(1984, Ital.); MISSING IN ACTION(1984)
Ruby Dee
  JACKIE ROBINSON STORY, THE(1950); NO WAY OUT(1950); TALL TARGET,
  THE(1951); GO, MAN, GO!(1954); EDGE OF THE CITY(1957); ST. LOUIS BLUES(1958);
  TAKE A GIANT STEP(1959); VIRGIN ISLAND(1960, Brit.); RAISIN IN THE SUN,
  A(1961); BALCONY, THE(1963); GONE ARE THE DAYS(1963); INCIDENT, THE(1967);
  UPTIGHT(1968), a, w; BLACK GIRL(1972); BUCK AND THE PREACHER(1972);
  COUNTDOWN AT KUSINI(1976, Nigerian); CAT PEOPLE(1982)
  Misc. Talkies
  FIGHT NEVER ENDS, THE(1947); THAT MAN OF MINE(1947)
Sandra Dee
  UNTIL THEY SAIL(1957); RELUCTANT DEBUTANTE, THE(1958); RESTLESS
  YEARS, THE(1958); GIDGET(1959); IMITATION OF LIFE(1959); SNOW QUEEN,
  THE(1959, USSR); STRANGER IN MY ARMS(1959); SUMMER PLACE, A(1959); WILD
  AND THE INNOCENT, THE(1959); PORTRAIT IN BLACK(1960); COME SEPTEM-
  BER(1961); ROMANOFF AND JULIET(1961); TAMMY, TELL ME TRUE(1961); IF A
  MAN ANSWERS(1962); TAKE HER, SHE'S MINE(1963); TAMMY AND THE DOC-
  TOR(1963); I'D RATHER BE RICH(1964); THAT FUNNY FEELING(1965); MAN
  COULD GET KILLED, A(1966); DOCTOR, YOU'VE GOT TO BE KIDDING(1967);
  ROSIE!(1967); DUNWICH HORROR, THE(1970)
  Misc. Talkies
  LOST(1983)
Simon Dee
  ITALIAN JOB, THE(1969, Brit.); DOCTOR IN TROUBLE(1970, Brit.)
Vincent Dee
  RAIDERS, THE(1964), cos; DARK INTRUDER(1965), cos; TEXAS ACROSS THE
  RIVER(1966), cos
Felix Deebank
  MY BROTHER JONATHAN(1949, Brit.)
Marjorie Deebe
  DRAGNET PATROL(1932)
Josette Deegan
  B. F.'S DAUGHTER(1948); CASBAH(1948); SOMETHING TO LIVE FOR(1952);
  FLIGHT TO TANGIER(1953); LAST TIME I SAW PARIS, THE(1954)
Kaie Deei
  TIME LIMIT(1957)
Deek Watson and his Brown Dots
  BOY! WHAT A GIRL(1947); SEPIA CINDERELLA(1947)
Rose Ann Deel
  SHEBA BABY(1975)
Sandra Deel
  JUNIOR BONNER(1972)
Ben Deeley
  Silents
  PATCHWORK GIRL OF OZ, THE(1914); ACQUITTAL, THE(1923); NEVER THE
  TWAIN SHALL MEET(1925)
  Misc. Silents
  KAZAN(1921)
Michael Deeley
  AT THE STROKE OF NINE(1957, Brit.), w; CROSSTRAP(1962, Brit.), p; ROB-
  BERY(1967, Brit.), p; ITALIAN JOB, THE(1969, Brit.), p; MURPHY'S WAR(1971,
  Brit.), p; CONDUCT UNBECOMING(1975, Brit.), p; MAN WHO FELL TO EARTH,
  THE(1976, Brit.), p; DEER HUNTER, THE(1978), p; BLADE RUNNER(1982), p
Ben Deely
  Silents
  EAST LYNNE(1916); FLAMES OF THE FLESH(1920); MOLLY O'(1921)
  Misc. Silents
  SISTER TO SALOME, A(1920); TATTLERS, THE(1920); WOULD YOU FOR-
  GIVE?(1920); CROSSROADS OF NEW YORK, THE(1922)
Michael Deely
  ONE WAY PENDULUM(1965, Brit.), p
Lola Deem
  PIRATE, THE(1948)
Ed Deemer
  JOE KIDD(1972)
Marianne Deeming
  THIRD TIME LUCKY(1950, Brit.); LOSER TAKES ALL(1956, Brit.); ACROSS THE
  BRIDGE(1957, Brit.); VICTORS, THE(1963); SPY WHO CAME IN FROM THE COLD,
  THE(1965, Brit.)
Pamela Deeming
  DANGEROUS ASSIGNMENT(1950, Brit.); GIRL IS MINE, THE(1950, Brit.); MYS-
  TERY AT THE BURLESQUE(1950, Brit.); PICKWICK PAPERS, THE(1952, Brit.)
Von Deeming
  SUPER VAN(1977), stunts
Douglas Deems
  HEROES OF THE SADDLE(1940); PUBLIC ENEMIES(1941)
Mickey Deems
  DIARY OF A BACHELOR(1964); HOLD ON(1966); BUSYBODY, THE(1967); GUIDE
  FOR THE MARRIED MAN, A(1967); SPIRIT IS WILLING, THE(1967); ST. VALEN-
  TINE'S DAY MASSACRE, THE(1967); WHO'S MINDING THE MINT?(1967); WITH
  SIX YOU GET EGGROLL(1968)
Nicky Deems
  1984
  GOODBYE PEOPLE, THE(1984)
Richard Deems
  FRANCIS JOINS THE WACS(1954); WILL SUCCESS SPOIL ROCK HUNTER?(1957)
Jo Ann Deen
  SUSPENSE(1946)
Kamalo Deen
  INDEPENDENCE DAY(1976)
Carol Deene
  DREAM MAKER, THE(1963, Brit.)
James Deenen
  1984
  MISSION, THE(1984)

Catherine Deeney
DIAMONDS ARE FOREVER(1971, Brit.)

Harry Deep
VIOLENCE(1947)

Deep Roy
FLASH GORDON(1980)

Warwick Deeping
KITTY(1929, Brit.), w; SORRELL AND SON(1934, Brit.), w; TWO SINNERS(1935), w
Silents
UNREST(1920, Brit.), w; FOX FARM(1922, Brit.), w

Don Deer [Murray]
HOODLUM PRIEST, THE(1961), w

Gary Mule Deer
GONG SHOW MOVIE, THE(1980)

Carol Deere
OUT OF THIS WORLD(1945); OUR HEARTS WERE GROWING UP(1946)

George Deere
ESCAPE TO BURMA(1955)

Ann Deering
Misc. Silents
BEWARE OF THE LAW(1922)

Dee Dee Deering
1984
WHERE THE BOYS ARE '84(1984)

DeeDee Deering
SMOKEY AND THE BANDIT–PART 3(1983)

Don Deering
LOVE IS ON THE AIR(1937)

Ed Deering
MAN FROM WYOMING, A(1930); LOVE IS NEWS(1937); NANCY STEELE IS MISSING(1937); MY FAVORITE SPY(1942)

Edgar Deering
ABRAHAM LINCOLN(1930); LIGHTNING STRIKES TWICE(1935); LITTLE BIT OF HEAVEN, A(1940); HOUSE ON 92ND STREET, THE(1945)

Elizabeth Deering
FACES(1968); MINNIE AND MOSKOWITZ(1971); WOMAN UNDER THE INFLUENCE, A(1974); KILLING OF A CHINESE BOOKIE, THE(1976)

Jeanette Deering
1984
PRODIGAL, THE(1984)

Joan Deering
MR. CHEDWORTH STEPS OUT(1939, Aus.)

John Deering
FORGOTTEN COMMANDMENTS(1932); CONFESSIONS OF A NAZI SPY(1939); ROARING TWENTIES, THE(1939); MURDER IN THE AIR(1940); SLIGHTLY HONORABLE(1940)

M.B. Deering
PARADISE ISLAND(1930), w

Marda Deering
NIGHT LIFE OF THE GODS(1935)

Olive Deering
GENTLEMAN'S AGREEMENT(1947); AIR HOSTESS(1949); SAMSON AND DELILAH(1949); CAGED(1950); TEN COMMANDMENTS, THE(1956); SHOCK TREATMENT(1964); HOWZER(1973)

Patricia Deering
LADY LIES, THE(1929)

Rex Deering
OVER THE ODDS(1961, Brit.)

Sayre Deering
MYSTERY PLANE(1939); LADY LUCK(1946); GREAT SINNER, THE(1949)

Jackson Deerson
TWO-LANE BLACKTOP(1971), ph

Jacque Deerson
DARK SIDE OF TOMORROW, THE(1970), d&w, ph

Alfred Deery
Misc. Silents
MADAME SHERRY(1917)

Jack Deery
DISRAELI(1929); DARK ANGEL, THE(1935); TWO FOR TONIGHT(1935); MAID OF SALEM(1937); THREE HEARTS FOR JULIA(1943); EXPERIMENT PERILOUS(1944); ZIEGFELD FOLLIES(1945)

Mary Dees
SARATOGA(1937); SHOPWORN ANGEL(1938)

Maxwell Dees
GET CARTER(1971, Brit.)

Rick Dees
RECORD CITY(1978)
1984
BEST DEFENSE(1984), stunts

Oscar Deesee
BRIDES OF BLOOD(1968, US/Phil.)

Jasper Deeter
4D MAN(1959)

Jim Deeth
1984
STARMAN(1984)

Nancy Deever
Misc. Silents
LAW OF THE YUKON, THE(1920)

Ed Deezen
ZAPPED!(1982)

Eddie Deezen
GREASE(1978); I WANNA HOLD YOUR HAND(1978); LASERBLAST(1978); 1941(1979); MIDNIGHT MADNESS(1980); GREASE 2(1982); WARGAMES(1983)
1984
ROSEBUD BEACH HOTEL(1984); SURF II(1984)

Martin Defalco
COLD JOURNEY(1975, Can.), d

Christopher DeFaria
BOY NAMED CHARLIE BROWN, A(1969)

Walt deFaria
MOUSE AND HIS CHILD, THE(1977), p; NUTCRACKER FANTASY(1979), p

Walt deFarla
DON'T CRY, IT'S ONLY THUNDER(1982), p

Felix Defauce
55 DAYS AT PEKING(1963)

J.M. Defaye
ARMY GAME, THE(1963, Fr.), m

Sam DeFazio
DEVIL'S EXPRESS(1975)

James DeFelice
WHY SHOOT THE TEACHER(1977, Can.), w

Frank DeFelitta
ENTITY, THE(1982), w

Jo Ella Defenbaugh
ADAM AT 6 A.M.(1970)

U.S. Defense Department
NOBODY'S PERFECT(1968), tech adv

Joella Deffenbaugh
SHOOT IT: BLACK, SHOOT IT: BLUE(1974)

Dino DeFilippi
CROSS AND THE SWITCHBLADE, THE(1970)

Jose DeFillippo
REDS(1981)

Don DeFina
NORTHERN LIGHTS(1978)
1984
HOT DOG...THE MOVIE(1984), art d; SIGNAL 7(1984)

Jeanne DeFlorio
LILITH(1964)

Annette DeFoe
Silents
FAME AND FORTUNE(1918)

Daniel Defoe
ROBINSON CRUSOE ON MARS(1964), w; AMOROUS ADVENTURES OF MOLL FLANDERS, THE(1965), w; MAN FRIDAY(1975, Brit.), w
Silents
ROBINSON CRUSOE(1927, Brit.), w

Luis Bunuel Daniel Defoe
ADVENTURES OF ROBINSON CRUSOE, THE(1954), w

Carolynn DeFonseca
LONELY LADY, THE(1983)

Jane Deford
PHANTOM OF THE PARADISE(1974)

Don DeFore
WITHOUT RESERVATIONS(1946); KID GALAHAD(1937); SUBMARINE D-1(1937); FRESHMAN YEAR(1938); MALE ANIMAL, THE(1942); WINGS FOR THE EAGLE(1942); YOU CAN'T ESCAPE FOREVER(1942); GUY NAMED JOE, A(1943); HUMAN COMEDY, THE(1943); THIRTY SECONDS OVER TOKYO(1944); AFFAIRS OF SUSAN(1945); STORK CLUB, THE(1945); YOU CAME ALONG(1945); IT HAPPENED ON 5TH AVENUE(1947); RAMROD(1947); ONE SUNDAY AFTERNOON(1948); ROMANCE ON THE HIGH SEAS(1948); MY FRIEND IRMA(1949); TOO LATE FOR TEARS(1949); DARK CITY(1950); SOUTHSIDE 1-1000(1950); GIRL IN EVERY PORT, A(1952); JUMPING JACKS(1952); NO ROOM FOR THE GROOM(1952); SHE'S WORKING HER WAY THROUGH COLLEGE(1952); BATTLE HYMN(1957); TIME TO LOVE AND A TIME TO DIE, A(1958); FACTS OF LIFE, THE(1960)
1984
RARE BREED(1984)
Misc. Talkies
AND NOW TOMORROW(1952)

Don Deforest [Defore]
WE GO FAST(1941)

Daniele Deforme
CROOK, THE(1971, Fr.)

Michael DeForrest
CAMILLE 2000(1969), w

Marina Defosse
1984
CHEECH AND CHONG'S THE CORSICAN BROTHERS(1984)

Gilberte Defoucault
PARDON MY FRENCH(1951, U.S./Fr.)

Mark Defrain
1984
ALLEY CAT(1984)

Steve DeFrance
IN SEARCH OF HISTORIC JESUS(1980)

L. E. DeFrancesco
WARRIOR'S HUSBAND, THE(1933), md

Louis DeFrancesco
MR. SKITCH(1933), md; STATE FAIR(1933), md; ALL MEN ARE ENEMIES(1934), m; DAVID HARUM(1934), md; SPRINGTIME FOR HENRY(1934), m; DRESSED TO THRILL(1935), md

Sebastian DeFrancesco
WHOSE LIFE IS IT ANYWAY?(1981)

Tom DeFranco
DEADLY SPAWN, THE(1983)

Bob DeFrank
DRILLER KILLER(1979)

Rolf Defrank
TINDER BOX, THE(1968, E. Ger.)

Jami DeFrates
BLOOD WATERS OF DOCTOR Z(1982), m

Guy Defresne
ORDERS, THE(1977, Can.), w

Cornelius Defries
BLACK SPIDER, THE(1983, Swit.), spec eff

Henry Defries
FRENCH LEAVE(1931, Brit.), p
George Dega
LAST OF THE SECRET AGENTS?, THE(1966); MADAME X(1966); MARATHON MAN(1976)
Igor Dega
MY WILD IRISH ROSE(1947); SORRY, WRONG NUMBER(1948)
Al DeGaetano
LET'S GO PLACES(1930), ed; ON THE LEVEL(1930), ed; SPIDER, THE(1931), ed; WOMAN IN ROOM 13, THE(1932), ed; MAN WHO DARED, THE(1933), ed; MURDER IN TRINIDAD(1934), ed; FIRST BABY(1936), ed; LITTLE MISS NOBODY(1936), ed; BIG BUSINESS(1937), ed; WOMAN-WISE(1937), ed; GREAT GUNS(1941), ed; PRIVATE NURSE(1941), ed; GAS HOUSE KIDS IN HOLLYWOOD(1947), ed
Alfred DeGaetano
DANTE'S INFERNO(1935), ed; PADDY O'DAY(1935), ed; UNDER THE PAMPAS MOON(1935), ed; BIG FIX, THE(1947), ed; REPEAT PERFORMANCE(1947), ed; STEPCHILD(1947), ed; IN THIS CORNER(1948), ed; MAN FROM TEXAS, THE(1948), ed; TRAPPED(1949), ed
Michael DeGaetano
Misc. Talkies
SCORING(1980), d
Marc Degagne
HAPPY BIRTHDAY TO ME(1981)
Filippo Degara
INVESTIGATION OF A CITIZEN ABOVE SUSPICION(1970, Ital.); LION OF THE DESERT(1981, Libya/Brit.)
Harold DeGarro
DESTRY RIDES AGAIN(1939)
B. Degas
SUMMERTIME KILLER(1973), w
Brian Degas
BARBARELLA(1968, Fr./Ital.), w; DANGER: DIABOLIK(1968, Ital./Fr.), w
Boyce DeGaw
DON'T BET ON BLONDES(1935), w; MOON'S OUR HOME, THE(1936), w; GIRL OF THE GOLDEN WEST, THE(1938), w; ICE-CAPADES(1941), w; LADY FOR A NIGHT(1941), w
Ursul DeGeer
1984
FOURTH MAN, THE(1984, Neth.)
Michael Degen
1984
BEYOND GOOD AND EVIL(1984, Ital./Fr./Ger.)
Jerry DeGennaro
SCREAM, BABY, SCREAM(1969)
Dominique Degeorge
1984
CHEECH AND CHONG'S THE CORSICAN BROTHERS(1984)
John Degerberg
PIMPERNEL SVENSSON(1953, Swed.)
Pia Degermark
ELVIRA MADIGAN(1967, Swed.); LOOKING GLASS WAR, THE(1970, Brit.)
Guy Deghy
MR. EMMANUEL(1945, Brit.); FAKE, THE(1953, Brit.); COMPANIONS IN CRIME(1954, Brit.); CONSTANT HUSBAND, THE(1955, Brit.); TEARS FOR SIMON(1957, Brit.); HOUSE OF THE SEVEN HAWKS, THE(1959); MOUSE THAT ROARED, THE(1959, Brit.); DANGER TOMORROW(1960, Brit.), w; FOLLOW THAT HORSE!(1960, Brit.); SURPRISE PACKAGE(1960); MATTER OF WHO, A(1962, Brit.); MOUSE ON THE MOON, THE(1963, Brit.); DEVIL DOLL(1964, Brit.); BOY TEN FEET TALL, A(1965, Brit.); YELLOW ROLLS-ROYCE, THE(1965, Brit.); ONE-EYED SOLDIERS(1967, U.S./Brit./Yugo.); DARK OF THE SUN(1968, Brit.); DUFFY(1968, Brit.); BEFORE WINTER COMES(1969, Brit.); SUBTERFUGE(1969, US/Brit.); WALK WITH LOVE AND DEATH, A(1969); CRY OF THE BANSHEE(1970, Brit.); KREMLIN LETTER, THE(1970); LOOKING GLASS WAR, THE(1970, Brit.); MARCH OR DIE(1977, Brit.); GREEK TYCOON, THE(1978)
Guy Stephen Deghy
DIVIDED HEART, THE(1955, Brit.)
Tom Degidon
EYES OF LAURA MARS(1978); IN-LAWS, THE(1979); NIGHTHAWKS(1981); TRADING PLACES(1983)
Vilma Degischer
EMBEZZLED HEAVEN(1959,Ger.); FOREVER MY LOVE(1962); CARDINAL, THE(1963); UNCLE TOM'S CABIN(1969, Fr./Ital./Ger./Yugo.)
Christa Degler
CHRONICLE OF ANNA MAGDALENA BACH(1968, Ital., Ger.)
Piera Degli Esposti
1984
JOKE OF DESTINY LYING IN WAIT AROUND THE CORNER LIKE A STREET-BANDIT, A(1984, Ital.)
Claude Degliame
LES GAULOISES BLEUES(1969, Fr.)
Guy Degny
1984
SUCCESS IS THE BEST REVENGE(1984, Brit.)
Mary DeGolyer
RED MENACE, THE(1949)
Rijk DeGooyer
LUCKY STAR, THE(1980, Can.)
Jack Degovia
LEPKE(1975, U.S./Israel), prod d; BUTCH AND SUNDANCE: THE EARLY DAYS(1979), art d; IT'S MY TURN(1980), prod d
Jackson DeGovia
BOULEVARD NIGHTS(1979), prod d; MY BODYGUARD(1980), prod d; SPACEHUNTER: ADVENTURES IN THE FORBIDDEN ZONE(1983), prod d
Julea DeGrace
VIOLATED LOVE(1966, Arg.)
Jean Degrave
ROAD TO SHAME, THE(1962, Fr.); LAFAYETTE(1963, Fr.); JUDEX(1966, Fr./Ital.); TIGHT SKIRTS, LOOSE PLEASURES(1966, Fr.); DISCREET CHARM OF THE BOURGEOISIE, THE(1972, Fr.)

Fred DeGresac
SWEETHEARTS(1938), w
Sidney DeGrey
HOTEL HAYWIRE(1937)
Slim DeGrey
YOU CAN'T SEE 'ROUND CORNERS(1969, Aus.); STONE(1974, Aus.)
Carl DeGroof
LULU(1962, Aus.), m
Fred DeGrote
LUCKY STAR, THE(1980, Can.)
A. Degtyar
WAR AND PEACE(1968, USSR)
Nicolas Deguy
DEVIL PROBABLY, THE(1977, FR.)
Hadj Hadi Dehali
Misc. Silents
GIRL FROM CARTHAGE, THE(1924, Tunisia)
Judith DeHart
SHOCK TREATMENT(1964)
Carter DeHaven
SENIORS, THE(1978), p
Carter DeHaven III
DEAD HEAT ON A MERRY-GO-ROUND(1966), p; CARBON COPY(1981), p
Carter DeHaven, Jr.
BLONDIE'S HOLIDAY(1947), md
Gloria DeHaven
PENALTY, THE(1941); BEST FOOT FORWARD(1943); THOUSANDS CHEER(1943); BETWEEN TWO WOMEN(1944); BROADWAY RHYTHM(1944); STEP LIVELY(1944); THIN MAN GOES HOME, THE(1944); TWO GIRLS AND A SAILOR(1944); SUMMER HOLIDAY(1948); YES SIR, THAT'S MY BABY(1949); SUMMER STOCK(1950); THREE LITTLE WORDS(1950); YELLOW CAB MAN, THE(1950); WON TON TON, THE DOG WHO SAVED HOLLYWOOD(1976)
Penny DeHaven
Misc. Talkies
VALLEY OF BLOOD(1973)
Richard DeHaven
1984
SAVAGE STREETS(1984)
Robert DeHaven
GALLANT JOURNEY(1946)
Rose DeHaven
ISN'T IT ROMANTIC?(1948)
Richard DeHavilland
VICE GIRLS, LTD.(1964)
Alain DeHay
SUPERMAN II(1980)
Madelaine Deheco
MINNESOTA CLAY(1966, Ital./Fr./Span.)
John Dehelly
Misc. Silents
SAHARA LOVE(1926, Brit.)
Paula Dehelly
ANGELS OF THE STREETS(1950, Fr.); GIGOT(1962); UP FROM THE BEACH(1965); TENDER SCOUNDREL(1967, Fr./Ital.); RISE OF LOUIS XIV, THE(1970, Fr.)
Suzanne Dehelly
CINDERELLA(1937, Fr.); CROISIERES SIDERALES(1941, Fr.); HER FIRST AFFAIR(1947, Fr.); PRIZE, THE(1952, Fr.)
Roberta Deherrera
WINDWALKER(1980)
Katherine DeHetre
PROMISE, THE(1979); LOOKER(1981)
Gladys Dehl
SMILING ALONG(1938, Brit.)
Dorothy Dehn
SO THIS IS COLLEGE(1929); MADAME SATAN(1930); MERRY WIDOW, THE(1934); STAND UP AND CHEER(1934 80m FOX bw)
Paul Dehn
SEVEN DAYS TO NOON(1950, Brit.), w; ORDERS TO KILL(1958, Brit.), w; GOLDFINGER(1964, Brit.), w; SPY WHO CAME IN FROM THE COLD, THE(1965, Brit.), w; DEADLY AFFAIR, THE(1967, Brit.), w; NIGHT OF THE GENERALS, THE(1967, Brit./Fr.), w; TAMING OF THE SHREW, THE(1967, U.S./Ital.), w; BENEATH THE PLANET OF THE APES(1970), w; ESCAPE FROM THE PLANET OF THE APES(1971), w; FRAGMENT OF FEAR(1971, Brit.), w; CONQUEST OF THE PLANET OF THE APES(1972), w; BATTLE FOR THE PLANET OF THE APES(1973), w; MURDER ON THE ORIENT EXPRESS(1974, Brit.), w
Ronald Dehne
ESCAPE FROM EAST BERLIN(1962)
John Dehner
RELUCTANT DRAGON, THE(1941); LAKE PLACID SERENADE(1944); CHRISTMAS IN CONNECTICUT(1945); SHE WENT TO THE RACES(1945); STATE FAIR(1945); LAST CROOKED MILE, THE(1946); O.S.S.(1946); OUT CALIFORNIA WAY(1946); RENDEZVOUS 24(1946); THE CATMAN OF PARIS(1946); UNDERCOVER WOMAN, THE(1946); BLONDE SAVAGE(1947); DREAM GIRL(1947); GOLDEN EARRINGS(1947); VIGILANTES OF BOOMTOWN(1947); HE WALKED BY NIGHT(1948); LET'S LIVE A LITTLE(1948); BARBARY PIRATE(1949); KAZAN(1949); MARY RYAN, DETECTIVE(1949); PREJUDICE(1949); SECRET OF ST. IVES, THE(1949); TULSA(1949); BODYHOLD(1950); CAPTIVE GIRL(1950); COUNTERSPY MEETS SCOTLAND YARD(1950); DAVID HARDING, COUNTERSPY(1950); DESTINATION MURDER(1950); DYNAMITE PASS(1950); HORSEMEN OF THE SIERRAS(1950); LAST OF THE BUCCANEERS(1950); ROGUES OF SHERWOOD FOREST(1950); TEXAS DYNAMO(1950); AL JENNINGS OF OKLAHOMA(1951); BANDITS OF EL DORADO(1951); CHINA CORSAIR(1951); CORKY OF GASOLINE ALLEY(1951); FORT SAVAGE RAIDERS(1951); HOT LEAD(1951); LORNA DOONE(1951); TEN TALL MEN(1951); TEXAS RANGERS, THE(1951); WHEN THE REDSKINS RODE(1951); ALADDIN AND HIS LAMP(1952); CALIFORNIA CONQUEST(1952); CRIPPLE CREEK(1952); DESERT PASSAGE(1952); HAREM GIRL(1952); JUNCTION CITY(1952); PLYMOUTH ADVENTURE(1952); SCARAMOUCHE(1952); FORT ALGIERS(1953); GUN BELT(1953); MAN ON A TIGHTROPE(1953); POWDER RIVER(1953); STEEL LADY, THE(1953); VICKI(1953); APACHE(1954); BOWERY BOYS MEET THE MONSTERS, THE(1954); SOUTHWEST

PASSAGE(1954); DUEL ON THE MISSISSIPPI(1955); KING'S THIEF, THE(1955); MAN FROM BITTER RIDGE, THE(1955); PRODIGAL, THE(1955); SCARLET COAT, THE(1955); TALL MAN RIDING(1955); TOP GUN(1955); CAROUSEL(1956); DAY OF FURY, A(1956); FASTEST GUN ALIVE(1956); PLEASE MURDER ME(1956); TENSION AT TABLE ROCK(1956); TERROR AT MIDNIGHT(1956); GIRL IN BLACK STOCKINGS(1957); IRON SHERIFF, THE(1957); REVOLT AT FORT LARAMIE(1957); TROOPER HOOK(1957); APACHE TERRITORY(1958); LEFT-HANDED GUN, THE(1958); MAN OF THE WEST(1958); CAST A LONG SHADOW(1959); TIMBUKTU(1959); SIGN OF ZORRO, THE(1960); CANADIANS, THE(1961, Brit.); CHAPMAN REPORT, THE(1962); CRITIC'S CHOICE(1963); YOUNGBLOOD HAWKE(1964); HALLELUJAH TRAIL, THE(1965); STILETTO(1969); CHEYENNE SOCIAL CLUB, THE(1970); DIRTY DINGUS MAGEE(1970); TIGER BY THE TAIL(1970); SUPPORT YOUR LOCAL GUNFIGHTER(1971); SLAUGHTERHOUSE-FIVE(1972); DAY OF THE DOLPHIN, THE(1973); KILLER INSIDE ME, THE(1976); FUN WITH DICK AND JANE(1977); GUARDIAN OF THE WILDERNESS(1977); LINCOLN CONSPIRACY, THE(1977); BOYS FROM BRAZIL, THE(1978); AIRPLANE II: THE SEQUEL(1982)

Kent Deigaard
DEAD MEN DON'T WEAR PLAID(1982)

Glenn Deigan
FRATERNITY ROW(1977)

Mary Deighan
NAKED FURY(1959, Brit.)

Howard Deighton
SHE SHALL HAVE MUSIC(1935, Brit.), ch

Len Deighton
IPCRESS FILE, THE(1965, Brit.), w; FUNERAL IN BERLIN(1966, Brit.), w; BILLION DOLLAR BRAIN(1967, Brit.), w; ONLY WHEN I LARF(1968, Brit.), p, w; OH! WHAT A LOVELY WAR(1969, Brit.), p, w

Marga Ann Deighton
SCOTLAND YARD(1941); YANKS AHOY(1943)

Martina Deignan
LONG RIDERS, THE(1980)

Karlheinz Deikert
SWEET SMELL OF LOVE(1966, Ital./Ger.), w

Edward Dein
BABY FACE MORGAN(1942), w; BOSS OF BIG TOWN(1943), w; CALLING DR. DEATH(1943), w; FALCON STRIKES BACK, THE(1943), w; GALS, INCORPORATED(1943), w; LEOPARD MAN, THE(1943), w; PAYOFF, THE(1943), w; PISTOL PACKIN' MAMA(1943), w; JUNGLE WOMAN(1944), w; SLIGHTLY TERRIFIC(1944), w; SOUL OF A MONSTER, THE(1944), w; BOSTON BLACKIE'S RENDEZVOUS(1945), w; FIGHTING GUARDSMAN, THE(1945), w; SWING OUT, SISTER(1945), w; CAT CREEPS, THE(1946), w; NOTORIOUS LONE WOLF, THE(1946), w; GALLANT BLADE, THE(1948), w; LONE WOLF AND HIS LADY, THE(1949), w; SHACK OUT ON 101(1955), d, w; CALYPSO JOE(1957), d, w; SEVEN GUNS TO MESA(1958), d, w; CURSE OF THE UNDEAD(1959), d, w; LEECH WOMAN, THE(1960), d; SWEET SMELL OF LOVE(1966, Ital./Ger.), w

Edward Dein [Ubaldo Ragona]
SWEET SMELL OF LOVE(1966, Ital./Ger.), d

Mildred Dein
SHACK OUT ON 101(1955), w; CALYPSO JOE(1957); SEVEN GUNS TO MESA(1958), w; CURSE OF THE UNDEAD(1959), w

Ursula Deinert
FINAL CHORD, THE(1936, Ger.)

Diane Deininger
PSYCHIC KILLER(1975)

Ed Deitch
WATCHED(1974), ed

Gene Deitch
Misc. Talkies
ALICE OF WONDERLAND IN PARIS(1966), d

Louise Deitch
ZELIG(1983)

Richard Deitsch
HEIDI(1968, Aust.), p

Nenad Dejanovic
TWILIGHT TIME(1983, U.S./Yugo.)

Predrag Dejanovic
TWILIGHT TIME(1983, U.S./Yugo.)

Steven DeJarnatt
STRANGE BREW(1983), w

Bill DeJarnette
CARNIVAL OF SOULS(1962), ed

Elizabeth Dejeans
Silents
CRASHIN' THRU(1923), w

Louie DeJesus
BLOODSUCKING FREAKS(1982)

Luchi DeJesus
BAD CHARLESTON CHARLIE(1973), m; DETROIT 9000(1973), m

George DeJitta, Sr.
KING OF COMEDY, THE(1983), set d

Daniel DeJohghe
GREAT SINNER, THE(1949)

Denise DeJon
WIZ, THE(1978)

David DeKeyser
LEO THE LAST(1970, Brit.); YENTL(1983)

Vasiliy Dekhteryov
OPTIMISTIC TRAGEDY, THE(1964, USSR), m; THREE SISTERS, THE(1969, USSR), m

Alan Dekkar
RATTLERS(1976)

Albert Dekker
GREAT GARRICK, THE(1937); LAST WARNING, THE(1938); MARIE ANTOINETTE(1938); BEAU GESTE(1939); HOTEL IMPERIAL(1939); MAN IN THE IRON MASK, THE(1939); NEVER SAY DIE(1939); DR. CYCLOPS(1940); RANGERS OF FORTUNE(1940); SEVEN SINNERS(1940); STRANGE CARGO(1940); AMONG THE LIVING(1941); BLONDE INSPIRATION(1941); BUY ME THAT TOWN(1941); GREAT COMMANDMENT, THE(1941); HONKY TONK(1941); REACHING FOR THE SUN(1941); YOU'RE THE ONE(1941); FOREST RANGERS, THE(1942); IN OLD CALIFORNIA(1942); LADY HAS PLANS, THE(1942); NIGHT IN NEW ORLEANS, A(1942); ONCE UPON A HONEYMOON(1942); STAR SPANGLED RHYTHM(1942); WAKE ISLAND(1942); YOKEL BOY(1942); BUCKSKIN FRONTIER(1943); IN OLD OKLAHOMA(1943); KANSAN, THE(1943); WOMAN OF THE TOWN, THE(1943); EXPERIMENT PERILOUS(1944); HOLD THAT BLONDE(1945); INCENDIARY BLONDE(1945); SALOME, WHERE SHE DANCED(1945); CALIFORNIA(1946); FRENCH KEY, THE(1946); KILLERS, THE(1946); SUSPENSE(1946); TWO YEARS BEFORE THE MAST(1946); CASS TIMBERLANE(1947); FABULOUS TEXAN, THE(1947); GENTLEMAN'S AGREEMENT(1947); PRETENDER, THE(1947); SLAVE GIRL(1947); WYOMING(1947); FURY AT FURNACE CREEK(1948); LULU BELLE(1948); BRIDE OF VENGEANCE(1949); SEARCH FOR DANGER(1949); TARZAN'S MAGIC FOUNTAIN(1949); DESTINATION MURDER(1950); FURIES, THE(1950); KID FROM TEXAS, THE(1950); AS YOUNG AS YOU FEEL(1951); WAIT 'TIL THE SUN SHINES, NELLIE(1952); EAST OF EDEN(1955); ILLEGAL(1955); KISS ME DEADLY(1955); SHE DEVIL(1957); MACHETE(1958); MIDDLE OF THE NIGHT(1959); SOUND AND THE FURY, THE(1959); SUDDENLY, LAST SUMMER(1959, Brit.); THESE THOUSAND HILLS(1959); WONDERFUL COUNTRY, THE(1959); GAMERA THE INVINCIBLE(1966, Jap.); COME SPY WITH ME(1967); WILD BUNCH, THE(1969)

Desmond Dekker
HARDER THEY COME, THE(1973, Jamaica), m

Truss Dekker
LITTLE ARK, THE(1972)

Fannie Belle DeKnight
HALLELUJAH(1929)

Rene DeKnight
GUN RUNNER(1969), m&md

Maurice Dekobra
MASK OF KOREA(1950, Fr.), w; HELL IS SOLD OUT(1951, Brit.), w; SECRET DOCUMENT – VIENNA(1954, Fr.), w

Alain Dekock
CARTOUCHE(1962, Fr./Ital.)

Mare Dekock
BIG CHIEF, THE(1960, Fr.)

Richard DeKoker
JUGGERNAUT(1974, Brit.), p, w

Wera Dekormos
RUN WITH THE DEVIL(1963, Fr./Ital.)

Frank DeKova
HOLIDAY FOR SINNERS(1952); ALL THE BROTHERS WERE VALIANT(1953); DESERT SONG, THE(1953); FIGHTER ATTACK(1953); KING OF THE KHYBER RIFLES(1953); RAIDERS OF THE SEVEN SEAS(1953); THEY RODE WEST(1954); TEN COMMANDMENTS, THE(1956); RIDE OUT FOR REVENGE(1957); BROTHERS KARAMAZOV, THE(1958); DAY OF THE OUTLAW(1959); JAYHAWKERS, THE(1959); ATLANTIS, THE LOST CONTINENT(1961); SWORD OF ALI BABA, THE(1965); AMERICAN POP(1981)
Misc. Talkies
BABY NEEDS A NEW PAIR OF SHOES(1974); HEAVY TRAFFIC(1974); JOHNNY FIRECLOUD(1975); JIVE TURKEY(1976)

Roger Dekoven
SOMETHING WILD(1961)

Arthur DeKuh
BABY FACE(1933); LIFE OF JIMMY DOLAN, THE(1933)

Pablo Del Amo
LEONOR(1977, Fr./Span./Ital.), ed; BLOOD WEDDING(1981, Sp.), ed

Pablo G. del Amo
SPIRIT OF THE BEEHIVE, THE(1976, Span.), ed; THAT HOUSE IN THE OUTSKIRTS(1980, Span.), ed

Pablo Gonzalez del Amo
HAND IN THE TRAP, THE(1963, Arg./Span.), ed; HUNT, THE(1967, Span.), ed

Gianni Del Balzo
LOVE AND MARRIAGE(1966, Ital.)

Liana Del Balzo
THIEF OF VENICE, THE(1952); LUXURY GIRLS(1953, Ital.); SODOM AND GOMORRAH(1962, U.S./Fr./Ital.)

Paulette del Baye
Silents
FRAILTY(1921, Brit.)
Misc. Silents
WOMAN WITH THE FAN, THE(1921, Brit.)

Alfred Del Cambre
WAGON WHEELS(1934); YOU'RE TELLING ME(1934)

Cesar Del Campo
EXTERMINATING ANGEL, THE(1967, Mex.)

Manuel Del Campo
CODE OF SCOTLAND YARD)(1948), ed; NO ORCHIDS FOR MISS BLANDISH(1948, Brit.), ed; NO HIGHWAY IN THE SKY(1951, Brit.), ed; BLACK ROSE, THE(1950), ed; HIS MAJESTY O'KEEFE(1953), ed; LOVES OF THREE QUEENS, THE(1954, Ital./Fr.), ed; BABY AND THE BATTLESHIP, THE(1957, Brit.), ed; TRUE AS A TURTLE(1957, Brit.), ed; ROBBERY UNDER ARMS(1958, Brit.), ed; THEN THERE WERE THREE(1961), ed; RELUCTANT SAINT, THE(1962, U.S./Ital.), ed; CONDEMNED OF ALTONA, THE(1963), ed

Mike Del Campo
LONG JOHN SILVER(1954, Aus.), ed

Oscar del Campo
TEXICAN, THE(1966, U.S./Span.)

Rudy Del Campo
WEST SIDE STORY(1961)

Herlinda Del Carmen
CHUKA(1967)

Maria del Carmen Duque
HOUSE THAT SCREAMED, THE(1970, Span.)

Hugo del Carril
DARK RIVER(1956, Arg.), a, p&d

Eric del Castillo
EXTERMINATING ANGEL, THE(1967, Mex.)

Guadalupe Del Castillo
PORTRAIT OF MARIA(1946, Mex.)

Miguel Del Castillo
KID RODELO(1966, U.S./Span.); GRAND SLAM(1968, Ital., Span., Ger.)

Josefina del Cid
1984
IT'S NEVER TOO LATE(1984, Span.)

Cleofe Del Cile
PLUCKED(1969, Fr./Ital.)

Ugo Del Colle
Misc. Silents
NOBODY'S CHILDREN(1926, Ital.), d

Ken Del Conte
WHAT DID YOU DO IN THE WAR, DADDY?(1966); SOL MADRID(1968); YOUNG RUNAWAYS, THE(1968); WORKING GIRLS, THE(1973)

Alfredo del Cuelo
DEATH OF A BUREAUCRAT(1979, Cuba), w

Alfredo del Diestro
NADA MAS QUE UNA MUJER(1934)

Cino Del Duca
L'AVVENTURA(1960, Ital.), p

Nino Del Fabbro
LADY WITHOUT CAMELLIAS, THE(1981, Ital.)

Iolanda Del Fabro
VOICE IN YOUR HEART, A(1952, Ital.)

Lino Del Fra
WARRIORS FIVE(1962), w

Patricia del Frate
MINNESOTA CLAY(1966, Ital./Fr./Span.)

Renato del Frate
APPOINTMENT FOR MURDER(1954, Ital.), ph; ROMMEL'S TREASURE(1962, Ital.), ph

Ramon Del Gado
SWORD OF THE AVENGER(1948)

Lenny Del Genio
1984
GHOSTBUSTERS(1984)

Filippo Del Giudice
HENRY V(1946, Brit.), p

Gaetano Del Grande
PIRANHA II: THE SPAWNING(1981, Neth.)

Louis Del Grande
ATLANTIC CITY(1981, U.S./Can.); HAPPY BIRTHDAY TO ME(1981); OF UNKNOWN ORIGIN(1983, Can.)

Eugenie Del Greco
1984
ALMOST YOU(1984), cos

Luciano Del Greco
SPY IN YOUR EYE(1966, Ital.), art d

Velia Del Greco
SINGLE ROOM FURNISHED(1968)

Louis Del Grende
SECOND WIND(1976, Can.)

Remigio Del Grosso
NEOPOLITAN CAROUSEL(1961, Ital.), w; PHAROAH'S WOMAN, THE(1961, Ital.), w; 300 SPARTANS, THE(1962), w; MILL OF THE STONE WOMEN(1963, Fr./Ital.), w; RED SHEIK, THE(1963, Ital.), w; CONQUEST OF MYCENE(1965, Ital., Fr.), w; SECRET AGENT SUPER DRAGON(1966, Fr./Ital./Ger./Monaco), w

Cecil del Gue
Silents
ANGEL ESQUIRE(1919, Brit.)

Ann Del Guercio
BACHELOR FLAT(1962)

Daniele Del Guidice
TAKE ALL OF ME(1978, Ital.), w

Filippo del Guidice
SPITFIRE(1943, Brit.)

Emilio del Haro
1984
EL NORTE(1984)

Pablo del Hoyo
TO BEGIN AGAIN(1982, Span.)

Alicia del Lago
BRAVADOS, THE(1958); SIERRA BARON(1958); GINA(1961, Fr./Mex.); LA CUCARACHA(1961, Mex.); SCALPHUNTERS, THE(1968); DEATH IN THE GARDEN(1977, Fr./Mex.)
1984
EL NORTE(1984)

Dolores Del Mar
LAST DAYS OF MAN ON EARTH, THE(1975, Brit.)

Marcia Del Mar
1984
BODY DOUBLE(1984)

Norman Del Mar
RELUCTANT WIDOW, THE(1951, Brit.), md

Michael Del Medico
CHILDRENS GAMES(1969)

Nick Del Negro
JOY HOUSE(1964, Fr.)

Joseph Del Nostro, Jr.
DIARY OF A MADMAN(1963)

Mike Del Piano
INVASION OF THE STAR CREATURES(1962)

Rosario del Pilar
CURSE OF THE VAMPIRES(1970, Phil., U.S.)

Maria del Pilar Armesto
HAND IN THE TRAP, THE(1963, Arg./Span.)

Carla Del Poggio
BANDIT, THE(1949, Ital.); WITHOUT PITY(1949, Ital.); VARIETY LIGHTS(1965, Ital.)

Angel Del Pozo
CASTILIAN, THE(1963, Span./U.S.); OPERATION DELILAH(1966, U.S./Span.); PLACE CALLED GLORY, A(1966, Span./Ger.); SAVAGE PAMPAS(1967, Span./Arg.); GLASS SPHINX, THE(1968, Egypt/Ital./Span.); YOUNG REBEL, THE(1969, Fr./Ital./Span.); TREASURE ISLAND(1972, Brit./Span./Fr./Ger.); MAN CALLED NOON, THE(1973, Brit.); DEMON WITCH CHILD(1974, Span.); THREE MUSKETEERS, THE(1974, Panama); PANCHO VILLA(1975, Span.); PASSENGER, THE(1975, Ital.); LEONOR(1977, Fr./Span./Ital.); WIDOWS' NEST(1977, U.S./Span.)

Enzo del Prato
MATCHLESS(1967, Ital.), art d

Vincenzo Del Prato
MAN WHO CAME FOR COFFEE, THE(1970, Ital.), art d; WHITE SISTER(1973, Ital./Span./Fr.), art d

Diulio Del Prete
GIFT, THE(1983, Fr./Ital.)

Duilio Del Prete
ASSASSINATION OF TROTSKY, THE(1972 Fr./Ital.); ALFREDO, ALFREDO(1973, Ital.); AT LONG LAST LOVE(1975); DEVIL IS A WOMAN, THE(1975, Brit./Ital.); REDNECK(1975, Ital./Span.); DIVINE NYMPH, THE(1979, Ital.)

Dulio Del Prete
DAISY MILLER(1974)

Isobel del Puerto
CAPTAIN SCARLETT(1953)

Barry Del Rae
INCIDENT, THE(1967); TAKING OFF(1971)

John Del Ragno
KING OF THE GYPSIES(1978)

Pilar Del Ray
FLIGHT TO TANGIER(1953)

Artie Del Rey
FURIES, THE(1950)

Nita Del Rey
FABULOUS SENORITA, THE(1952)

Paquita del Rey
DOWN MEXICO WAY(1941)

Pedro del Rey
IMPORTANT MAN, THE(1961, Mex.), ed; SAVAGE GUNS, THE(1962, U.S./Span.), ed; VIRIDIANA(1962, Mex./Span.), ed; SEVEN GOLDEN MEN(1969, Fr./Ital./Span.), ed; TRISTANA(1970, Span./Ital./Fr.), ed; SUPERSONIC MAN(1979, Span.), ed; CARMEN(1983, Span.), ed

Pilar Del Rey
KID FROM TEXAS, THE(1950); NAKED JUNGLE, THE(1953); SOMBRERO(1953); TROPIC ZONE(1953); BLACK HORSE CANYON(1954); JUBILEE TRAIL(1954); SIEGE AT RED RIVER, THE(1954); GIANT(1956); FLAME BARRIER, THE(1958); AND NOW MIGUEL(1966)

Diana Del Rio
REMEMBER PEARL HARBOR(1942); SECRETS OF A CO-ED(1942)

Dolores Del Rio
EVANGELINE(1929); BAD ONE, THE(1930); BIRD OF PARADISE(1932); GIRL OF THE RIO(1932); FLYING DOWN TO RIO(1933); MADAME DU BARRY(1934); WONDER BAR(1934); I LIVE FOR LOVE(1935); IN CALIENTE(1935); ACCUSED(1936, Brit.); WIDOW FROM MONTE CARLO, THE(1936); DEVIL'S PLAYGROUND(1937); LANCER SPY(1937); INTERNATIONAL SETTLEMENT(1938); MAN FROM DAKOTA, THE(1940); JOURNEY INTO FEAR(1942); PORTRAIT OF MARIA(1946, Mex.); FUGITIVE, THE(1947); FLAMING STAR(1960); LA CUCARACHA(1961, Mex.); CHEYENNE AUTUMN(1964); MORE THAN A MIRACLE(1967, Ital./Fr.); CHILDREN OF SANCHEZ, THE(1978, U. S./Mex.)
Silents
JOANNA(1925); WHAT PRICE GLORY(1926); GATEWAY OF THE MOON, THE(1928); RAMONA(1928); EVANGELINE(1929); TRAIL OF '98, THE(1929)
Misc. Silents
PALS FIRST(1926); LOVES OF CARMEN(1927); RESURRECTION(1927); REVENGE(1928)

Dora Del Rio
Misc. Talkies
TRAIL TO MEXICO(1946)

Emmy del Rio
TROPIC HOLIDAY(1938)

Evelyn Del Rio
YOU CAN'T CHEAT AN HONEST MAN(1939); BANK DICK, THE(1940); ALOMA OF THE SOUTH SEAS(1941)

Jack Del Rio
GILDA(1946); PERILOUS HOLIDAY(1946); HEADING FOR HEAVEN(1947); LOVABLE CHEAT, THE(1949); BETWEEN MIDNIGHT AND DAWN(1950); MISSISSIPPI GAMBLER, THE(1953); WE'RE NO ANGELS(1955); TATTERED DRESS, THE(1957); ST. VALENTINE'S DAY MASSACRE, THE(1967)

Manuela del Rio
Silents
LIFE(1928, Brit.)

Pedro Del Rio
1984
DEMONS IN THE GARDEN(1984, Span.)

Rafael del Rio
INVASION OF THE VAMPIRES, THE(1961, Mex.)

Teresa Del Rio
ALEXANDER THE GREAT(1956)

Tony Del Rio
SLAVE GIRL(1947)

Vivian Del Rio
TOUCH OF HER FLESH, THE(1967)

Dolores Del Rioo
Silents
NO OTHER WOMAN(1928)

Laura Del Rivo
WEST 11(1963, Brit.), w

Jaime Del Rosario
GHOST OF THE CHINA SEA(1958)

Rosa Del Rosario
BORDER BANDITS(1946); AMERICAN GUERRILLA IN THE PHILIPPINES, AN(1950)

Xochitl del Rosario
HIGH RISK(1981)

Guy Del Russo
JOHNNY TIGER(1966), makeup; HOW DO I LOVE THEE?(1970), makeup; LIMBO(1972), makeup; SMOKEY AND THE BANDIT(1977), makeup; THUNDER AND LIGHTNING(1977), makeup

Marie Del Russo
WILD REBELS, THE(1967), makeup; STANLEY(1973), makeup

Hampton Del Ruth
MIDNIGHT DADDIES(1929), w; DEFENDERS OF THE LAW(1931), w; MYSTERY TRAIN(1931), w; AIR EAGLES(1932), w; STRANGE ADVENTURE(1932), d; GOODBYE LOVE(1934), w
Silents
TILLIE'S PUNCTURED ROMANCE(1914), w; INVISIBLE FEAR, THE(1921), w; FRIENDLY HUSBAND, A(1923), w
Misc. Silents
SKIRTS(1921), d; MARRIAGE CHANCE, THE(1922), d; BLONDES BY CHOICE(1927), d; NAUGHTY(1927), d

Roy Del Ruth
TERROR, THE(1928), d; AVIATOR, THE(1929), d; CONQUEST(1929), d; DESERT SONG, THE(1929), d; GOLD DIGGERS OF BROADWAY(1929), d; HOTTENTOT, THE(1929), d; HOLD EVERYTHING(1930), d; LIFE OF THE PARTY, THE(1930), d; SECOND FLOOR MYSTERY, THE(1930), d; THREE FACES EAST(1930), d; BLONDE CRAZY(1931), d; DIVORCE AMONG FRIENDS(1931), d; MALTESE FALCON, THE(1931), d; MY PAST(1931), d; BEAUTY AND THE BOSS(1932), d; BLESSED EVENT(1932), d; TAXI!(1932), d; WINNER TAKE ALL(1932), p; BUREAU OF MISSING PERSONS(1933), d; CAPTURED(1933), d; EMPLOYEE'S ENTRANCE(1933), d; LADY KILLER(1933), d; LITTLE GIANT, THE(1933), d; MIND READER, THE(1933), d; BULLDOG DRUMMOND STRIKES BACK(1934), d; KID MILLIONS(1934), d; UPPER WORLD(1934), d; BROADWAY MELODY OF 1936(1935), d; FOLIES DERGERE(1935), d; THANKS A MILLION(1935), d; BORN TO DANCE(1936), d; IT HAD TO HAPPEN(1936), d; PRIVATE NUMBER(1936), d; BROADWAY MELODY OF '38(1937), d; ON THE AVENUE(1937), d; HAPPY LANDING(1938), d; MY LUCKY STAR(1938), d; HERE I AM A STRANGER(1939), d; STAR MAKER, THE(1939), d; TAIL SPIN(1939), d; HE MARRIED HIS WIFE(1940), d; TOPPER RETURNS(1941), d; MAISIE GETS HER MAN(1942), d; BARBARY COAST GENT(1944), d; BROADWAY RHYTHM(1944), d; ZIEGFELD FOLLIES(1945), d; IT HAPPENED ON 5TH AVENUE(1947), p&d; BABE RUTH STORY, THE(1948), d; ALWAYS LEAVE THEM LAUGHING(1949), d; RED LIGHT(1949), p&d; WEST POINT STORY, THE(1950), d; ON MOONLIGHT BAY(1951), d; THREE SAILORS AND A GIRL(1953), d; PHANTOM OF THE RUE MORGUE(1954), d; ALLIGATOR PEOPLE, THE(1959), d; WHY MUST I DIE?(1960), d
Misc. Talkies
BEWARE OF BACHELORS(1928), d
Silents
EVE'S LOVER(1925), d; ACROSS THE PACIFIC(1926), d; LITTLE IRISH GIRL, THE(1926), d; HAM AND EGGS AT THE FRONT(1927), d; IF I WERE SINGLE(1927), d; WOLF'S CLOTHING(1927), d; POWDER MY BACK(1928), d
Misc. Silents
HOGAN'S ALLEY(1925), d; THREE WEEKS IN PARIS(1925), d; FOOTLOOSE WIDOWS(1926), d; MAN UPSTAIRS, THE(1926), d; FIRST AUTO, THE(1927), d; FIVE AND TEN CENT ANNIE(1928), d

Thomas Del Ruth
MOTEL HELL(1980), ph; GET CRAZY(1983), ph
1984
IMPULSE(1984), ph

Tom Del Ruth
DEATH WISH II(1982), ph

Camillo Del Signore
MYSTERY OF THUG ISLAND, THE(1966, Ital./Ger.), set d; TRAMPLERS, THE(1966, Ital.), set d

Laura del Sol
CARMEN(1983, Span.)

Maria del Sol
UNSATISFIED, THE(1964, Span.)

The Del Tones
MUSCLE BEACH PARTY(1964)

Mario Del Vago
ROMA(1972, Ital./Fr.)

Jean Del Val
SEA LEGS(1930); MAGNIFICENT LIE(1931); WOMEN MEN MARRY(1931); PASSIONATE PLUMBER(1932); EVERYTHING HAPPENS AT NIGHT(1939); FLYING DEUCES, THE(1939); ARISE, MY LOVE(1940); HOUSE ACROSS THE BAY, THE(1940); HUDSON'S BAY(1940); MARK OF ZORRO, THE(1940); MYSTERY SEA RAIDER(1940); OUTLAWS OF THE DESERT(1941); PARIS CALLING(1941); RAGE IN HEAVEN(1941); SERGEANT YORK(1941); THAT NIGHT IN RIO(1941); CROSSROADS(1942); DR. RENAULT'S SECRET(1942); GENTLEMAN JIM(1942); LADY HAS PLANS, THE(1942); PIED PIPER, THE(1942); REUNION IN FRANCE(1942); SECRET AGENT OF JAPAN(1942); TAKE A LETTER, DARLING(1942); FOR WHOM THE BELL TOLLS(1943); MISSION TO MOSCOW(1943); PARIS AFTER DARK(1943); SONG OF BERNADETTE, THE(1943); WINTERTIME(1943); PASSAGE TO MARSEILLE(1944); TAMPICO(1944); CORNERED(1945); MOLLY AND ME(1945); GILDA(1946); MONSIEUR BEAUCAIRE(1946); RAZOR'S EDGE, THE(1946); RETURN OF MONTE CRISTO, THE(1946); SO DARK THE NIGHT(1946); DOWN TO EARTH(1947); PRIVATE AFFAIRS OF BEL AMI, THE(1947); I WALK ALONE(1948); JULIA MISBEHAVES(1948); GREAT SINNER, THE(1949); SECRET OF ST. IVES, THE(1949); LAST OF THE BUCCANEERS(1950); UNDER MY SKIN(1950); IRON MISTRESS, THE(1952); FORTY-NINTH MAN, THE(1953); GENTLEMEN PREFER BLONDES(1953); HITCH-HIKER, THE(1953); LITTLE BOY LOST(1953); DUEL ON THE MISSISSIPPI(1955); PIRATES OF TRIPOLI(1955); FUNNY FACE(1957); SAD SACK, THE(1957); WRECK OF THE MARY DEAR, THE(1959); DEVIL AT FOUR O'CLOCK, THE(1961); FANTASTIC VOYAGE(1966); WAIT UNTIL DARK(1967)
Silents
SAINTED DEVIL, A(1924); IRON MAN, THE(1925)
Misc. Silents
BACK TO LIBERTY(1927)

Jena Del Val
O.S.S.(1946)

Jenn Del Val
SPIDER, THE(1945)

Maria Del Val
AMERICAN GUERRILLA IN THE PHILIPPINES, AN(1950)

Fernando Del Valle
CRISIS(1950); BRAVE BULLS, THE(1951)

Gabrile Del Valle
TALL MEN, THE(1955)

Goya Del Valle
PAN-AMERICANA(1945)

Juan Del Valle
1984
POWER, THE(1984)

Raul del Valle
DARK RIVER(1956, Arg.)

Amapola Del Vando
CRISIS(1950); SOMBRERO(1953); OUTSIDE THE LAW(1956); COWBOY(1958); JUSTINE(1969)

Ampola del Vando
MARACAIBO(1958)

Poppy del Vando
CONQUEST OF COCHISE(1953)

Poppy A. del Vando
GOLDEN HAWK, THE(1952)

Mauro Del Vecchio
MYTH, THE(1965, Ital.)

Michael Del Viscovo, Jr.
PLEASANTVILLE(1976)

The Del-Aires
HORROR OF PARTY BEACH, THE(1964)

Leni Del-Genio
SILVER BEARS(1978)

Jean Del-Val
DRUMS OF THE DESERT(1940)

Alberto Del'Acqua
MINUTE TO PRAY, A SECOND TO DIE, A(1968, Ital.)

Gene Del'Mace
PIRATE MOVIE, THE(1982, Aus.)

Celso dela Cruz
1984
MISSING IN ACTION(1984), set d

The Delacardos
UP THE JUNCTION(1968, Brit.)

Leigh DeLacey
GOOD GIRLS GO TO PARIS(1939)

Philippe DeLacey
FOUR DEVILS(1929)

Ralph M. DeLacey
DEATH KISS, THE(1933), art d; DELUGE(1933), set d

Delacorta
DIVA(1982, Fr.), w

Joe Delacruzo
SUNSET OF POWER(1936)

Ralph DeLacy
LAST MILE, THE(1932), set d; YOUNG FUGITIVES(1938), art d; FRONTIER BADMEN(1943), art d

Ralph M. DeLacy
DRUMS OF JEOPARDY(1931), art d; MURDER AT MIDNIGHT(1931), art d; TOMBSTONE CANYON(1932), art d; STUDY IN SCARLET, A(1933), art d; PARDON MY RHYTHM(1944), art d; SCARLET CLAW, THE(1944), art d

E. M. Delafield
CRIME ON THE HILL(1933, Brit.), w; MOONLIGHT SONATA(1938, Brit.), w

Miguel Delagado
ZOOT SUIT(1981)

Jean-Pierre Delage
PARIS BELONGS TO US(1962, Fr.)

Agnes Delahaie
END OF DESIRE(1962 Fr./Ital.), p; TRIAL OF JOAN OF ARC(1965, Fr.), p

France Delahalle
ROYAL AFFAIRS IN VERSAILLES(1957, Fr.); PLAYTIME(1973, Fr.)

Michel Delahaye
ALPHAVILLE, A STRANGE CASE OF LEMMY CAUTION(1965, Fr.); BAND OF OUTSIDERS(1966, Fr.); WINTER WIND(1970, Fr./Hung.); SUCH A GORGEOUS KID LIKE ME(1973, Fr.); EXPOSED(1983)

Agnes Delahie
PICKPOCKET(1963, Fr.), p

Heather Delaine
HUE AND CRY(1950, Brit.)

Yvonne Delaine
SUPERFLY(1972)

Suzy Delair
MURDERER LIVES AT NUMBER 21, THE(1947, Fr.); CONFESSIONS OF A ROGUE(1948, Fr.); JENNY LAMOUR(1948, Fr.); UTOPIA(1952, Fr./Ital.); GERVAISE(1956, Fr.); FERNANDEL THE DRESSMAKER(1957, Fr.); ROCCO AND HIS BROTHERS(1961, Fr./Ital.); IS PARIS BURNING?(1966, U.S./Fr.); MAD ADVENTURES OF RABBI JACOB, THE(1973, Fr.)

Diane DeLaire
HUMAN DESIRE(1954); LONG GRAY LINE, THE(1955); WOMEN'S PRISON(1955); GARMENT JUNGLE, THE(1957)

Delaitre
CRIME AND PUNISHMENT(1935, Fr.); J'ACCUSE(1939, Fr.); MR. ORCHID(1948, Fr.); ROYAL AFFAIR, A(1950)

Marcel Delaitre
RAVEN, THE(1948, Fr.)

Aimee Delamain
SECRET, THE(1955, Brit.); LONG AGO, TOMORROW(1971, Brit.); WHO IS KILLING THE GREAT CHEFS OF EUROPE?(1978, US/Ger.)

1984
OXFORD BLUES(1984)
Mickey Delamar
RACE FOR LIFE, A(1955, Brit.), p; BREAK IN THE CIRCLE, THE(1957, Brit.), p; IMMORAL CHARGE(1962, Brit.), p, w
Gil Delamare
THAT MAN FROM RIO(1964, Fr./Ital.), spec eff; HOW TO STEAL A MILLION(1966); MAN FROM COCODY(1966, Fr/Ital.), spec eff; UP TO HIS EARS(1966, Fr./Ital.), spec eff, stunts
Glen Delamare
MAVERICK QUEEN, THE(1956), spec eff
Jean-Philippe Delamare
MAN ESCAPED, A(1957, Fr.)
Lise Delamare
LA MARSEILLAISE(1938, Fr.); SYMPHONIE FANTASTIQUE(1947, Fr.); MONSIEUR VINCENT(1949, Fr.); LOLA MONTES(1955, Fr./Ger.); GRAND MANEUVER, THE(1956, Fr.); NATHALIE(1958, Fr.); BERNADETTE OF LOURDES(1962, Fr.)
Rosine Delamare
HEART OF A NATION, THE(1943, Fr.), cos; FRENCH CANCAN(1956, Fr.), cos; GRAND MANEUVER, THE(1956, Fr.), cos; PARIS DOES STRANGE THINGS(1957, Fr./Ital.), cos; ROOTS OF HEAVEN, THE(1958), cos; GREEN MARE, THE(1961, Fr./Ital.), cos; WONDERS OF ALADDIN, THE(1961, Fr./Ital.), cos; MAXIME(1962, Fr.), cos; MOST WANTED MAN, THE(1962, Fr./Ital.), cos; STORY OF THE COUNT OF MONTE CRISTO, THE(1962, Fr./Ital.), cos; NIGHT OF THE GENERALS, THE(1967, Brit./Fr.), cos; 25TH HOUR, THE(1967, Fr./Ital./Yugo.), cos; MADWOMAN OF CHAILLOT, THE(1969), cos; HELLO—GOODBYE(1970), cos; RIDER ON THE RAIN(1970, Fr./Ital.), cos; DAY OF THE JACKAL, THE(1973, Brit./Fr.), cos; LITTLE ROMANCE, A(1979, U.S./Fr.), cos; CHANEL SOLITAIRE(1981), cos; PIAF–THE EARLY YEARS(1982, U.S./Fr.), cos
Gil Delamere
EXTERMINATORS, THE(1965 Fr.)
Rosine Delamere
RED AND THE BLACK, THE(1954, Fr./Ital.), cos
Junior Delameter
Misc. Silents
WHILE JUSTICE WAITS(1922)
Maurice Delamore
NORTH TO ALASKA(1960)
Francois DeLamothe
PIAF–THE EARLY YEARS(1982, U.S./Fr.), art d
Jean-Pierre Delamour
GLADIATORS, THE(1970, Swed.)
Joyanne Delancey
HALF A SIXPENCE(1967, Brit.)
John deLancie
LOVING COUPLES(1980)
Charles Deland
Misc. Silents
THIRTEENTH HOUR, THE(1927)
Edmond Deland
DANGEROUS MEDICINE(1938, Brit.), w
Margaret Delane
FINAL RECKONING, THE(1932, Brit.); GAME OF CHANCE, A(1932, Brit.); THOROUGHBRED(1932, Brit.)
Silents
PARADISE ALLEY(1931, Brit.)
Misc. Silents
LAST TIDE, THE(1931, Brit.)
Barry Delaney
Misc. Talkies
PHANTOM KID, THE(1983)
Barry F. Delaney
WARGAMES(1983), cos
Bernard Delaney
Misc. Silents
SMALL TOWN GIRL, A(1917)
Bert Delaney
Silents
NET, THE(1916)
Charles Delaney
AIR CIRCUS, THE(1928); RIVER WOMAN, THE(1928); SHOW GIRL(1928); BROADWAY BABIES(1929); GIRL FROM WOOLWORTH'S, THE(1929); HARD TO GET(1929); KATHLEEN MAVOURNEEN(1930); LONESOME TRAIL, THE(1930); MAN HUNTER, THE(1930); AIR POLICE(1931); HELL BENT FOR 'FRISCO(1931); MILLIE(1931); SUICIDE FLEET(1931); HEARTS OF HUMANITY(1932); MIDNIGHT MORALS(1932); CORRUPTION(1933); ELMER THE GREAT(1933); IMPORTANT WITNESS, THE(1933); OFFICER 13(1933); BIG TIME OR BUST(1934); MURDER MAN(1935); TRAILS OF THE WILD(1935); WHAT PRICE CRIME?(1935); BELOW THE DEADLINE(1936); MILLIONAIRE KID(1936); BANK ALARM(1937); GOLD RACKET, THE(1937); TEN LAPS TO GO(1938); BLONDE RANSOM(1945); KANSAS RAIDERS(1950); HALF-BREED, THE(1952); WINNING OF THE WEST(1953); RUNNING TARGET(1956); BEATNIKS, THE(1960)
Misc. Talkies
AROUND THE CORNER(1930); BIG TIMER(1932); CAPTURED IN CHINATOWN(1935)
Silents
DEVIL'S PARTNER, THE(1923); ENEMIES OF YOUTH(1925); COLLEGE DAYS(1926); NIGHT WATCH, THE(1926); SILENT POWER, THE(1926); HUSBAND HUNTERS(1927); LOVELORN, THE(1927); ADVENTURER, THE(1928); AFTER THE STORM(1928); COHENS AND THE KELLYS IN PARIS, THE(1928); DO YOUR DUTY(1928)
Misc. Silents
SOLOMON IN SOCIETY(1922); EMBLEMS OF LOVE(1924); ACCUSED(1925); FLAMING FURY(1926); SKY PIRATE, THE(1926); MAIN EVENT, THE(1927); MOUNTAINS OF MANHATTAN(1927); SILENT AVENGER, THE(1927); BRANDED MAN(1928); HOME JAMES(1928); OUTCAST SOULS(1928); STOOL PIGEON(1928); WOMEN WHO DARE(1928); CLEAN-UP, THE(1929); FAKER, THE(1929); RIVER WOMAN(1929)

Charles E. Delaney
FRONT PAGE WOMAN(1935); COLLEEN(1936)
Charlie Delaney
FIGHTING TROOPER, THE(1935)
Delvane Delaney
END PLAY(1975, Aus.)
Gloria Delaney
PENITENTIARY(1979)
Iris Delaney
Silents
IF(1916, Brit.)
J.C. Delaney
BUTTERFIELD 8(1960), set d; FAIL SAFE(1964), set d
Jack Delaney
Silents
TWO FLAMING YOUTHS(1927)
Jere Delaney
LIGHTS OF NEW YORK(1928)
Joan Delaney
PRESIDENT'S ANALYST, THE(1967); DON'T DRINK THE WATER(1969); ALEX IN WONDERLAND(1970); BUNNY O'HARE(1971)
Larry Delaney
WESTWORLD(1973)
Leo Delaney
Silents
ISLAND OF REGENERATION, THE(1915)
Misc. Silents
RETURN OF MAURICE DONNELLY, THE(1915); SUPRISES OF AN EMPTY HOTEL, THE(1916); SUSIE SNOWFLAKE(1916); WHOSO TAKETH A WIFE(1916); SLACKER, THE(1917); CIRCUMSTANTIAL EVIDENCE(1920)
Leon Delaney
WARRIORS, THE(1979)
Maureen Delaney
CAPTAIN BOYCOTT(1947, Brit.); ANOTHER SHORE(1948, Brit.); MARK OF CAIN, THE(1948, Brit.); SAINTS AND SINNERS(1949, Brit.); NIGHT AND THE CITY(1950, Brit.); JACQUELINE(1956, Brit.); MARCH HARE, THE(1956, Brit.); RISING OF THE MOON, THE(1957, Ireland); STORY OF ESTHER COSTELLO, THE(1957, Brit.); THIRD KEY, THE(1957, Brit.); STRANGE AFFECTION(1959, Brit.)
Pat Delaney
GREAT LOCOMOTIVE CHASE, THE(1956), set d; MARS NEEDS WOMEN(1966); BAT PEOPLE, THE(1974); GREAT BRAIN, THE(1978); HOMETOWN U.S.A.(1979)
Misc. Talkies
CREATURE OF DESTRUCTION(1967); HALF A HOUSE(1979)
Patricia Delaney
ZONTAR, THE THING FROM VENUS(1966)
Pauline Delaney
INNOCENT SINNERS(1958, Brit.); ROONEY(1958, Brit.); YOUNG CASSIDY(1965, U.S./Brit.)
Shelagh Delaney
TASTE OF HONEY, A(1962, Brit.), w; CHARLIE BUBBLES(1968, Brit.), w
Tom Delaney
CATTLE ANNIE AND LITTLE BRITCHES(1981)
Tom J. Delaney
SCREAMERS(1978, Ital.); COAST TO COAST(1980)
Toni Delaney
VON RICHTHOFEN AND BROWN(1970), makeup; IMAGES(1972, Ireland), makeup
Trevor Delaney
CUL-DE-SAC(1966, Brit.); SPY WITH A COLD NOSE, THE(1966, Brit.)
Delaney & Bonnie & Friends
VANISHING POINT(1971)
Lena Delanne
SHAMELESS OLD LADY, THE(1966, Fr.)
Henriette Delannoy
AZAIS(1931, Fr.)
Jean Delannoy
ETERNAL RETURN, THE(1943, Fr.), d; LES JEUX SONT FAITS(1947, Fr.), d, w; SYMPHONIE PASTORALE(1948, Fr.), d, w; MASK OF KOREA(1950, Fr.), p; DAUGHTERS OF DESTINY(1954, Fr./Ital.), d; OBSESSION(1954, Fr./Ital.), d; SECRETS D'ALCOVE(1954, Fr./Ital.), d; HUNCHBACK OF NOTRE DAME, THE(1957, Fr.), d; MAIGRET LAYS A TRAP(1958, Fr.), d, w; GUINGUETTE(1959, Fr.), d, w; LOVE AND THE FRENCHWOMAN(1961, Fr.), d; IMPERIAL VENUS(1963, Ital./Fr.), d, w; DOUBLE BED, THE(1965, Fr./Ital.), d; THIS SPECIAL FRIENDSHIP(1967, Fr.), d; LEATHER AND NYLON(1969, Fr./Ital.), d, w
Marcel Delannoy
VOLPONE(1947, Fr.), m
Sylvine Delannoy
FRENCH CANCAN(1956, Fr.); ZAZIE(1961, Fr.); BRIDE WORE BLACK, THE(1968, Fr./Ital.); TWO OF US, THE(1968, Fr.)
Clotilde Delano
Silents
SCARAMOUCHE(1923)
Diane Delano
HEART LIKE A WHEEL(1983)
Edith Barnard Delano
Silents
RAGS(1915), w; STILL WATERS(1915), w; PRODIGAL WIFE, THE(1918), w
Laura DeLano
WARRIORS, THE(1979)
Lee DeLano
PROJECT X(1968); LATE LIZ, THE(1971); EXECUTIVE ACTION(1973); REPORT TO THE COMMISSIONER(1975); SILENT MOVIE(1976); HIGH ANXIETY(1977); HISTORY OF THE WORLD, PART 1(1981)
1984
SPLASH(1984)
Michael Delano
CATLOW(1971, Span.); NEW CENTURIONS, THE(1972)
Sal Delano
SHINBONE ALLEY(1971)

Ronn Delanor
BOUNTY KILLER, THE(1965); REQUIEM FOR A GUNFIGHTER(1965)

Cathleen Delany
MY HANDS ARE CLAY(1948, Irish)

Dana Delany
FAN, THE(1981)
1984
ALMOST YOU(1984)

Maureen Delany
HIS FAMILY TREE(1936); ODD MAN OUT(1947, Brit.); UNDER CAPRICORN(1949); HOLLY AND THE IVY, THE(1954, Brit.); DOCTOR'S DILEMMA, THE(1958, Brit.); TREAD SOFTLY STRANGER(1959, Brit.)

Pat Delany
FLAREUP(1969); NOW YOU SEE HIM, NOW YOU DON'T(1972); CHARLEY AND THE ANGEL(1973)

Pati Delany
Misc. Talkies
J.C.(1972)

Patrick Delany
I WALK ALONE(1948), set d

Pauline Delany
QUESTION OF SUSPENSE, A(1961, Brit.); AMBUSH IN LEOPARD STREET(1962, Brit.); QUARE FELLOW, THE(1962, Brit.); NOTHING BUT THE BEST(1964, Brit.); PERCY(1971, Brit.); TRENCHCOAT(1983)

Robert Delapp
1984
LOVELINES(1984)

Bron Delar
I KILLED WILD BILL HICKOK(1956)

Harriet Delaro
Silents
ETERNAL SAPHO, THE(1916)

Hattie Delaro
Silents
KENNEDY SQUARE(1916); RAGGED EDGE, THE(1923); JANICE MEREDITH(1924)
Misc. Silents
NIGHT IN NEW ARABIA, A(1917)

Hatty Delaro
Silents
CARDIGAN(1922)

Christine Delaroche
DEFECTOR, THE(1966, Ger./Fr.); YOUNG WORLD, A(1966, Fr./Ital.)

Gerard Delaroche
LOLA(1961, Fr./Ital.)

Callie Delatorre
Silents
RISE OF JENNIE CUSHING, THE(1917)

Ed DeLatte
BENJI(1974)

Chantal Delattre
OTHER ONE, THE(1967,Fr.), ed; TWO OR THREE THINGS I KNOW ABOUT HER(1970, Fr.), ed

Bob DeLauer
PEGGY(1950)

Virgine Delaunay-Belleville
1984
SUGAR CANE ALLEY(1984, Fr.)

Dino DeLaurentiis
TWO NIGHTS WITH CLEOPATRA(1953, Ital.), p; FIVE BRANDED WOMEN(1960), p; UNFAITHFULS, THE(1960, Ital.), p; ANZIO(1968, Ital.), p; MANDINGO(1975), p; MEAN FRANK AND CRAZY TONY(1976, Ital.), p; SERPENT'S EGG, THE(1977, Ger./U.S.), p; FLASH GORDON(1980), p

Frederico DeLaurentiis
SHE DANCES ALONE(1981, Aust./U.S.), p

Daniel DeLaurentis
MY FORBIDDEN PAST(1951)

Robert DeLaurentis
LITTLE SEX, A(1982), p, w

Madeleine Delavaivre
GENDARME OF ST. TROPEZ, THE(1966, Fr./Ital.)

Mario DeLaval
GREAT CARUSO, THE(1951)

Pierre Delaval
CONFESSION, THE(1970, Fr.)

April Delavanti
GUN FEVER(1958)

Cyril Delavanti
JOURNEY FOR MARGARET(1942); MINISTRY OF FEAR(1945); GREATEST STORY EVER TOLD, THE(1965); OH DAD, POOR DAD, MAMA'S HUNG YOU IN THE CLOSET AND I'M FEELIN' SO SAD(1967)

Dot Delavine
NIGHT OF MAGIC, A(1944, Brit.)

Mel Delay
COME OUT FIGHTING(1945), prod d

Melville DeLay
MYSTIC HOUR, THE(1934), d

Mme. Claude Delay
CHANEL SOLITAIRE(1981), w

Germaine Delbat
DAY TO REMEMBER, A(1953, Brit.); LOLA MONTES(1955, Fr./Ger.); FOUR BAGS FULL(1957, Fr./Ital.); GIGOT(1962); UP FROM THE BEACH(1965); LA PRISONNIERE(1969, Fr./Ital.)
1984
CHEECH AND CHONG'S THE CORSICAN BROTHERS(1984)

Robert Delbert
DESPERATE CHARACTERS(1971); TITLE SHOT(1982, Can.)

Enza Delbi
CARMELA(1949, Ital.)

Jean Jacques Delbo
CONFESSIONS OF A ROGUE(1948, Fr.)

Jean-Jacques Delbo
ROYAL AFFAIRS IN VERSAILLES(1957, Fr.); DAY THE SKY EXPLODED, THE(1958, Fr./Ital.); BIG CHIEF, THE(1960, Fr.); THOUSAND EYES OF DR. MABUSE, THE(1960, Fr./Ital./Ger.); BERNADETTE OF LOURDES(1962, Fr.); STORY OF THE COUNT OF MONTE CRISTO, THE(1962, Fr./Ital.); ERIK THE CONQUEROR(1963, Fr./Ital.); LAFAYETTE(1963, Fr.); HIGHWAY PICKUP(1965, Fr./Ital.); WITHOUT APPARENT MOTIVE(1972, Fr.)

Alfred Delcambre
WHARF ANGEL(1934); CAR 99(1935); FOUR HOURS TO KILL(1935); HOME ON THE RANGE(1935); ONE HOUR LATE(1935); SO RED THE ROSE(1935); WANDERER OF THE WASTELAND(1935); WINGS IN THE DARK(1935)

Delcassan
JOUR DE FETE(1952, Fr.)

Stephane Delcher
ONCE IN PARIS(1978)

R.F. Delderfield
ALL OVER THE TOWN(1949, Brit.), w; WORM'S EYE VIEW(1951, Brit.), w; WHERE THERE'S A WILL(1955, Brit.), w; HOME AND AWAY(1956, Brit.), w; NOW AND FOREVER(1956, Brit.), w; OPERATION SNAFU(1965, Brit.), w

Francoise Deldick
HOT HOURS(1963, Fr.)

Guy Delecluse
MATCHLESS(1967, Ital.), spec eff; MYSTERIOUS ISLAND OF CAPTAIN NEMO, THE(1973, Fr./Ital. 87m Span./Cameroon), ph

Grazia Deledda
DEVOTION(1953, Ital.), w

Bob Delegall
HANGUP(1974)

Robert W. Delegall
SPARKLE(1976)

Don DeLeo
INCIDENT, THE(1967)

Ed DeLeo
1984
POPE OF GREENWICH VILLAGE, THE(1984)

Lia DeLeo
QUO VADIS(1951)

Catherine DeLeon
DOZENS, THE(1981)

Edwin DeLeon
BUSTIN' LOOSE(1981)

Jack Deleon
SILENT WITNESS, THE(1932), w; TRAIN RIDE TO HOLLYWOOD(1975); CHOIRBOYS, THE(1977); LITTLE MISS MARKER(1980)
Misc. Talkies
CARHOPS(1980)

Raoul DeLeon
ADVISE AND CONSENT(1962)

Sonia DeLeon
BARBAROSA(1982)

Walter DeLeon
BIG NEWS(1929), w; SOPHOMORE, THE(1929), w; RED HOT RHYTHM(1930), w; BIG GAMBLE, THE(1931), w; LONELY WIVES(1931), w; MEET THE WIFE(1931), w; SPIRIT OF NOTRE DAME, THE(1931), w; GIRL CRAZY(1932), w; HOLD'EM JAIL(1932), w; IF I HAD A MILLION(1932), w; MAKE ME A STAR(1932), w; PHANTOM PRESIDENT, THE(1932), w; HER BODYGUARD(1933), w; INTERNATIONAL HOUSE(1933), w; LADY'S PROFESSION, A(1933), w; COLLEGE RHYTHM(1934), w; SIX OF A KIND(1934), w; YOU BELONG TO ME(1934), w; BIG BROADCAST OF 1936, THE(1935), w; RUGGLES OF RED GAP(1935), w; BIG BROADCAST OF 1937, THE(1936), w; COLLEGIATE(1936), w; PRINCESS COMES ACROSS, THE(1936), w; RHYTHM ON THE RANGE(1936), w; STRIKE ME PINK(1936), w; ARTISTS AND MODELS(1937), w; BIG BROADCAST OF 1938, THE(1937), w; WAIKIKI WEDDING(1937), w; COLLEGE SWING(1938), w; MEET THE MAYOR(1938), w; UNION PACIFIC(1939), w; ZENOBIA(1939), w; MAN WHO TALKED TOO MUCH, THE(1940), w; BIRTH OF THE BLUES(1941), w; FLEET'S IN, THE(1942), w; HAPPY GO LUCKY(1943), w; RAINBOW ISLAND(1944), w; DELIGHTFULLY DANGEROUS(1945), w; HOLD THAT BLONDE(1945), w; OUT OF THIS WORLD(1945), w; LITTLE GIANT(1946), w

Georges Delerue
GET OUT YOUR HANDKERCHIEFS(1978, Fr.), m

George Delerue
LOVE AND THE FRENCHWOMAN(1961, Fr.), m; PLAYTIME(1963, Fr.), m; BROKEN ENGLISH(1981), m

Georges Delerue
HIROSHIMA, MON AMOUR(1959, Fr./Jap.), m; JOKER, THE(1961, Fr.), m; CARTOUCHE(1962, Fr./Ital.), m; CRIME DOES NOT PAY(1962, Fr.), m; JULES AND JIM(1962, Fr.), m; LONG ABSENCE, THE(1962, Fr./Ital.), m; NUDE IN HIS POCKET(1962, Fr.), m; PASSION OF SLOW FIRE, THE(1962, Fr.), m; SHOOT THE PIANO PLAYER(1962, Fr.), m; CONTEMPT(1963, Fr./Ital.), m; LOVE AT TWENTY(1963, Fr./Ital./Jap./Pol./Ger.), m; PARIS PICK-UP(1963, Fr./Ital.), m; RIFIFI IN TOKYO(1963, Fr./Ital.), m; SEASON FOR LOVE, THE(1963, Fr.), m; FRENCH DRESSING(1964, Brit.), m; MISTRESS FOR THE SUMMER, A(1964, Fr./Ital.), m; PUMPKIN EATER, THE(1964, Brit.), m; SOFT SKIN, THE(1964, Fr.), m; THAT MAN FROM RIO(1964, Fr./Ital.), m; GREED IN THE SUN(1965, Fr./ Ital.), m; HIGHWAY PICK-UP(1965, Fr./Ital.), m; MALE COMPANION(1965, Fr./Ital.), m; MATA HARI(1965, Fr./Ital.), m; RAPTURE(1965), m; VIVA MARIA(1965, Fr./Ital.), m; WOMEN AND WAR(1965, Fr.), m; MAN FOR ALL SEASONS, A(1966, Brit.), m, md; SUCKER, THE(1966, Fr./Ital.), m; UP TO HIS EARS(1966, Fr./Ital.), m; IMMORAL MOMENT, THE(1967, Fr.), m; KING OF HEARTS(1967, Fr./Ital.), m; OUR MOTHER'S HOUSE(1967, Brit.), m; 25TH HOUR, THE(1967, Fr./Ital./Yugo.), m; HIGH COMMISSIONER, THE(1968, U.S./Brit.), m, md; INTERLUDE(1968, Brit.), m; TWO OF US, THE(1968, Fr.), m; UNINHIBITED, THE(1968, Fr./Ital./Span.), m; ANNE OF THE THOUSAND DAYS(1969, Brit.), m; BRAIN, THE(1969, Fr./US), m; DEVIL BY THE TAIL, THE(1969, Fr./Ital.), m; L'IMMORTELLE(1969, Fr./Ital./Turkey), m; WALK WITH LOVE AND DEATH, A(1969), m, md; GIVE HER THE MOON(1970, Fr./Ital.), m; PROMISE AT DAWN(1970, U.S./Fr.), m; CONFORMIST, THE(1971, Ital., Fr), m; HORSEMEN, THE(1971), m; MALPERTIUS(1972, Bel./Fr.), m; TWO ENGLISH GIRLS(1972, Fr.), a, m; DAY FOR NIGHT(1973, Fr.), m; DAY OF THE DOLPHIN,

THE(1973), m; DAY OF THE JACKAL, THE(1973, Brit./Fr.), m; SUCH A GORGEOUS KID LIKE ME(1973, Fr.), m; MAIN THING IS TO LOVE, THE(1975, Ital./Fr.), m; POLICE PYTHON 357(1976, Fr.), m; JULIA(1977), m, md; DEAR DETECTIVE(1978, Fr.), m; ALMOST PERFECT AFFAIR, AN(1979), m; LITTLE ROMANCE, A(1979, U.S./Fr.), m; CASE AGAINST FERRO, THE(1980, Fr.), m; INCORRIGIBLE(1980, Fr.), m; LOVE ON THE RUN(1980, Fr.), m; WILLIE AND PHIL(1980), m; LAST METRO, THE(1981, Fr.), m; RICH AND FAMOUS(1981), m; RICHARD'S THINGS(1981, Brit.), m; TRUE CONFESSIONS(1981), m; WOMAN NEXT DOOR, THE(1981, Fr.), m; ESCAPE ARTIST, THE(1982), m; INQUISITOR, THE(1982, Fr.), m; LA VIE CONTINUE(1982, Fr.), m; LITTLE SEX, A(1982), m; PARTNERS(1982), m; AFRICAN, THE(1983, Fr.), m; BLACK STALLION RETURNS, THE(1983), m; CONFIDENTIALLY YOURS(1983, Fr.), m; EXPOSED(1983), m; LA PASSANTE(1983, Fr./Ger.), m; MAN, WOMAN AND CHILD(1983), m; SILKWOOD(1983), m
1984
LE BON PLAISIR(1984, Fr.), m; ONE DEADLY SUMMER(1984, Fr.), m

Georges Delerve
TIGHT SKIRTS, LOOSE PLEASURES(1966, Fr.), m; WOMEN IN LOVE(1969, Brit.), m, md

Jacqueline Delessert
OF LOVE AND DESIRE(1963), w

Francoise Deleu
1984
PERILS OF GWENDOLINE, THE(1984, Fr.), prod d

Claude Deleusse
FIRE WITHIN, THE(1964, Fr./Ital.)

Ray deLeuw
APPLE DUMPLING GANG, THE(1975), ed

Anne Deleuze
SOLO(1970, Fr.)

Cyril Delevanti
DEVOTION(1931); DISPATCH FROM REUTERS, A(1940); MAN HUNT(1941); NIGHT MONSTER(1942); PHANTOM OF THE OPERA(1943); SON OF DRACULA(1943); LODGER, THE(1944); CAPTAIN TUGBOAT ANNIE(1945); DALTONS RIDE AGAIN, THE(1945); HOUSE OF FEAR, THE(1945); JADE MASK, THE(1945); KITTY(1945); PHANTOM OF 42ND STREET, THE(1945); THIS LOVE OF OURS(1945); DECEPTION(1946); SHADOW RETURNS, THE(1946); FOREVER AMBER(1947); I'LL BE YOURS(1947); MONSIEUR VERDOUX(1947); EMPEROR WALTZ, THE(1948); D-DAY, THE SIXTH OF JUNE(1956); LES GIRLS(1957); RIDE OUT FOR REVENGE(1957); TROOPER HOOK(1957); I BURY THE LIVING(1958); TEACHER'S PET(1958); BYE BYE BIRDIE(1963); DEAD RINGER(1964); MARY POPPINS(1964); NIGHT OF THE IGUANA, THE(1964); COUNTERPOINT(1967); MACHO CALLAHAN(1970); SOYLENT GREEN(1973); BLACK EYE(1974)

Winifred Delevanti
Misc. Silents
MAN IN POSSESSION, THE(1915, Brit.); ONLY MAN, THE(1915, Brit.)

Harry Delf
HARMONY AT HOME(1930), w; STOP, LOOK, AND LOVE(1939), w

Peter Delfgou
REMEMBRANCE(1982, Brit.), ed
1984
REAL LIFE(1984, Brit.), ed

Carlo Delfini
MAGIC WORLD OF TOPO GIGIO, THE(1961, Ital.)

Frank Delfino
COURT JESTER, THE(1956); PRINCESS AND THE MAGIC FROG, THE(1965); MOVIE STAR, AMERICAN STYLE, OR, LSD I HATE YOU!(1966); LITTLE CIGARS(1973); HUNTER, THE(1980)

Mildred Delfino
Misc. Silents
FRAMING FRAMERS(1918)

Sallie Delfino
WHAT'S THE MATTER WITH HELEN?(1971)

Jacques Delfosse
1984
SMURFS AND THE MAGIC FLUTE, THE(1984, Fr./Belg.), ph

Raoul Delfosse
BITTER VICTORY(1958, Fr.); TRIAL, THE(1963, Fr./Ital./Ger.); TASTE FOR WOMEN, A(1966, Fr./Ital.); WEEKEND AT DUNKIRK(1966, Fr./Ital.); 25TH HOUR, THE(1967, Fr./Ital./Yugo.); HOUSE OF CARDS(1969); MILKY WAY, THE(1969, Fr./Ital.); LADY IN THE CAR WITH GLASSES AND A GUN, THE(1970, U.S./Fr.); SICILIAN CLAN, THE(1970, Fr.); LEGEND OF FRENCHIE KING, THE(1971, Fr./Ital./Span./Brit.); BURGLARS, THE(1972, Fr./Ital.); FRENCH CONNECTION 11(1975); HERBIE GOES TO MONTE CARLO(1977)

Nick Delgadi
FRANCHETTE; LES INTRIGUES(1969)

Alfonso Maria Delgado
1984
YELLOW HAIR AND THE FORTRESS OF GOLD(1984)

Camilo Delgado
STRANGERS IN THE CITY(1962)

Henry Delgado
CAGE OF EVIL(1960); SNIPER'S RIDGE(1961)

James Delgado
MAD AT THE WORLD(1955)

Jason Delgado
PATERNITY(1981)

John Delgado
ROBIN AND THE SEVEN HOODS(1964)

Johnny Delgado
JAGUAR(1980, Phil.)

Juan Garcia Delgado
CEREMONY, THE(1963, U.S./Span.)
1984
YELLOW HAIR AND THE FORTRESS OF GOLD(1984)

Kim Delgado
BOARDWALK(1979); FORT APACHE, THE BRONX(1981)

Lucy Delgado
SHE-DEVIL ISLAND(1936, Mex.); TOAST TO LOVE(1951, Mex.)

Luis Delgado
36 HOURS(1965); CASTAWAY COWBOY, THE(1974)

Marcel Delgado
KING KONG(1933), spec eff; SON OF KONG(1933), spec eff; MIGHTY JOE YOUNG(1949), spec eff

Marie Delgado
GREEN FIRE(1955)

Marissa Delgado
1984
BONA(1984, Phil.)
Misc. Talkies
BAMBOO GODS AND IRON MEN(1974)

Miguel Delgado
SUN ALSO RISES, THE(1957), ch; POR MIS PISTOLAS(1969, Mex.), d

Miguel M. Delgado
CHIQUITO PERO PICOSO(1967, Mex.), d; SANTO CONTRA LA HIJA DE FRANKENSTEIN(1971, Mex.), d

Roberta Delgado
ZOOT SUIT(1981)

Roger Delgado
CAPTAIN'S PARADISE, THE(1953, Brit.); DEADLY GAME, THE(1955, Brit.); PURSUIT OF THE GRAF SPEE(1957, Brit.); STOWAWAY GIRL(1957, Brit.); VIOLENT STRANGER(1957, Brit.); MARK OF THE PHOENIX(1958, Brit.); FIRST MAN INTO SPACE(1959, Brit.); SEA FURY(1959, Brit.); STRANGLERS OF BOMBAY, THE(1960, Brit.); SINGER NOT THE SONG, THE(1961, Brit.); TERROR OF THE TONGS, THE(1961, Brit.); IN SEARCH OF THE CASTAWAYS(1962, Brit.); AGENT 8 3/4(1963, Brit.); MIND BENDERS, THE(1963, Brit.); RUNNING MAN, THE(1963, Brit.); MASQUERADE(1965, Brit.); MUMMY'S SHROUD, THE(1967, Brit.); ASSASSINATION BUREAU, THE(1969, Brit.); UNDERGROUND(1970, Brit.); ANTONY AND CLEOPATRA(1973, Brit.)

Jeff Delgar
1984
ON THE LINE(1984, Span.)

John Delgar
HOTHEAD(1963)

Domenick Delgarde
TOUCH OF EVIL(1958)

Dominick Delgarde
VON RYAN'S EXPRESS(1965)

Henry Delgardo
THIRD VOICE, THE(1960)

Roger Delgardo
STORM OVER THE NILE(1955, Brit.); ROAD TO HONG KONG, THE(1962, U.S./Brit.)

Robert Delhez
GIRL WITH THE RED HAIR, THE(1983, Neth.)

Sanders Delhomme
CASEY'S SHADOW(1978)

Jean-Paul Delhumeau
MAN ESCAPED, A(1957, Fr.)

Joe Delia
MS. 45(1981), m

Joseph Delia
DRILLER KILLER(1979), m

Russell P. Delia
DAMIEN–OMEN II(1978)

Tony DeLia
1984
WEEKEND PASS(1984)

Clement Delibes
DR. COPPELIUS(1968, U.S./Span.), d&w, m

Leo Delibes
MYSTERIOUS HOUSE OF DR. C., THE(1976), m

Miguel Delibes
1984
HOLY INNOCENTS, THE(1984, Span.), w

Djurdjica Delic
NINTH CIRCLE, THE(1961, Yugo.)

Stipe Delic
SULEIMAN THE CONQUEROR(1963, Ital.), w

Michel Deligne
THREE HOURS(1944, Fr.), w

Delilah
SWEET BEAT(1962, Brit.); PUTNEY SWOPE(1969)

Jany Delille
LA MATERNELLE(1933, Fr.)

Jean DeLimur
LETTER, THE(1929), w

Bert Deling
PURE S(1976, Aus.), d, w

Anna Delinsky
DESIRE(1936)

Madame Delinsky
I CONQUER THE SEA(1936)

Vic DeLinsky
Silents
KAISER'S FINISH, THE(1918)

Victor Delinsky
ROYAL SCANDAL, A(1945)

Georges Delisle
FOND MEMORIES(1982, Can.)

Monte DeLisle
TOO MANY HUSBANDS(1938, Brit.)

Debra Deliso
SLUMBER PARTY MASSACRE, THE(1982)

Christine Delit
ADVENTURERS, THE(1970)

Frederick Delius
YEARLING, THE(1946), m

Denny Delk
MORE AMERICAN GRAFFITI(1979)

Joe Delk
PUT UP OR SHUT UP(1968, Arg.)

Dell
MARVIN AND TIGE(1983), w

Bozo Dell
LADYBUG, LADYBUG(1963)

Budd Dell
CAIN'S WAY(1969), p; WILD WHEELS(1969), p

Charlie Dell
BULLET FOR PRETTY BOY, A(1970); SCUM OF THE EARTH(1976)

Claudia Dell
BIG BOY(1930); SWEET KITTY BELLAIRS(1930); BACHELOR APARTMENT(1931); CONFESSIONS OF A CO-ED(1931); FIFTY MILLION FRENCHMEN(1931); LEFTOVER LADIES(1931); SIT TIGHT(1931); SPORTING CHANCE(1931); DESTRY RIDES AGAIN(1932); HEARTS OF HUMANITY(1932); MIDNIGHT LADY(1932); MIDNIGHT WARNING, THE(1932); SCANDAL FOR SALE(1932); BIG BLUFF, THE(1933); CLEOPATRA(1934); LADY IN SCARLET, THE(1935); GHOST PATROL(1936); YELLOW CARGO(1936); BOOTS OF DESTINY(1937); BRIDE FOR HENRY, A(1937); WE'RE IN THE LEGION NOW(1937); ALGIERS(1938); MAD EMPRESS, THE(1940); SPEED LIMITED(1940); SPOTLIGHT SCANDALS(1943); CALL OF THE JUNGLE(1944); CHARLIE CHAN IN BLACK MAGIC(1944)
Misc. Talkies
GUILTY OR NOT GUILTY(1932); WOMAN CONDEMNED(1934); MIDNIGHT PHANTOM, THE(1935); TRAIL'S END(1935)

David Dell
BALTIC DEPUTY(1937, USSR), w

Dorothea Dell
TROUBLE IN THE GLEN(1954, Brit.)

Dorothy Dell
LITTLE MISS MARKER(1934); SHOOT THE WORKS(1934); WHARF ANGEL(1934)

Edith Dell
SATELLITE IN THE SKY(1956), w; DEPRAVED, THE(1957, Brit.), w

Ethel M. Dell
HIGH TREASON(1937, Brit.), w
Silents
WAY OF AN EAGLE, THE(1918, Brit.), w; KEEPER OF THE DOOR(1919, Brit.), w; QUESTION OF TRUST, A(1920, Brit.), w; PLACE OF HONOUR, THE(1921, Brit.), w; DEBT OF HONOR(1922, Brit.), w; ELEVENTH HOUR, THE(1922, Brit.), w; EXPERIMENT, THE(1922, Brit.), w

Ethel May Dell
Silents
HER OWN FREE WILL(1924), w

Floyd Dell
LITTLE ACCIDENT(1930), w; LITTLE ACCIDENT(1939), w; CASANOVA BROWN(1944), w

Gabriel Dell
DEAD END(1937); ANGELS WITH DIRTY FACES(1938); CRIME SCHOOL(1938); LITTLE TOUGH GUY(1938); ANGELS WASH THEIR FACES(1939); DEAD END KIDS ON DRESS PARADE(1939); HELL'S KITCHEN(1939); THEY MADE ME A CRIMINAL(1939); GIVE US WINGS(1940); YOU'RE NOT SO TOUGH(1940); HIT THE ROAD(1941); MOB TOWN(1941); LET'S GET TOUGH(1942); MR. WISE GUY(1942); 'NEATH BROOKLYN BRIDGE(1942); SMART ALECKS(1942); TOUGH AS THEY COME(1942); KEEP 'EM SLUGGING(1943); KID DYNAMITE(1943); MR. MUGGS STEPS OUT(1943); MUG TOWN(1943); BLOCK BUSTERS(1944); BOWERY CHAMPS(1944); FOLLOW THE LEADER(1944); MILLION DOLLAR KID(1944); COME OUT FIGHTING(1945); MR. HEX(1946); SPOOK BUSTERS(1946); BOWERY BUCKAROOS(1947); HARD BOILED MAHONEY(1947); NEWS HOUNDS(1947); ANGELS ALLEY(1948); JINX MONEY(1948); SMUGGLERS' COVE(1948); TROUBLE MAKERS(1948); ANGELS IN DISGUISE(1949); FIGHTING FOOLS(1949); HOLD THAT BABY!(1949); MASTER MINDS(1949); BLONDE DYNAMITE(1950); BLUES BUSTERS(1950); LUCKY LOSERS(1950); TRIPLE TROUBLE(1950); ESCAPE FROM TERROR(1960); WHO IS HARRY KELLERMAN AND WHY IS HE SAYING THOSE TERRIBLE THINGS ABOUT ME?(1971); 300 YEAR WEEKEND(1971); EARTHQUAKE(1974); FRAMED(1975); MANCHU EAGLE MURDER CAPER MYSTERY, THE(1975), a, w; ESCAPE ARTIST, THE(1982)

Gabe [Gabriel] Dell
WHEN THE GIRLS TAKE OVER(1962)

Jeffery Dell
AS THE SEA RAGES(1960 Ger.), w; MAN IN A COCKED HAT(1960, Bri.), d&w

Jeffrey Dell
FIREBIRD, THE(1934), w; SANDERS OF THE RIVER(1935, Brit.), w; MAKEUP(1937, Brit.), w; KATE PLUS TEN(1938, Brit.), w; NIGHT ALONE(1938, Brit.), w; SPIES OF THE AIR(1940, Brit.), w; FOOTSTEPS IN THE DARK(1941), w; VOICE IN THE NIGHT, A(1941, Brit.), w; FLEMISH FARM, THE(1943, Brit.), d, w; DON'T TAKE IT TO HEART(1944, Brit.), d&w; THUNDER ROCK(1944, Brit.), w; IT'S HARD TO BE GOOD(1950, Brit.), d&w; DARK MAN, THE(1951, Brit.), d&w; ROTTEN TO THE CORE(1956, Brit.), w; BROTHERS IN LAW(1957, Brit.), w; LUCKY JIM(1957, Brit.), w; HAPPY IS THE BRIDE(1958, Brit.), w; RISK, THE(1961, Brit.), w; HOT MONEY GIRL(1962, Brit./Ger.), w; FAMILY WAY, THE(1966, Brit.), w

Jeffrey F. Dell
PAYMENT DEFERRED(1932), w

Jeffry Dell
SAINT'S VACATION, THE(1941, Brit.), w

Jill Craigie Dell
FLEMISH FARM, THE(1943, Brit.), w

Myrna Dell
ZIEGFELD GIRL(1941); ARIZONA WHIRLWIND(1944); RAIDERS OF RED GAP(1944); SHOW BUSINESS(1944); THIRTY SECONDS OVER TOKYO(1944); UP IN ARMS(1944); FALCON IN SAN FRANCISCO, THE(1945); MAN ALIVE(1945); DEADLINE AT DAWN(1946); FALCON'S ADVENTURE, THE(1946); FALCON'S ALIBI, THE(1946); LADY LUCK(1946); LOCKET, THE(1946); NOCTURNE(1946); SPIRAL STAIRCASE, THE(1946); STEP BY STEP(1946); VACATION IN RENO(1946); FIGHTING FATHER DUNNE(1948); GAL WHO TOOK THE WEST, THE(1949); GIRL FROM JONES BEACH, THE(1949); JUDGE STEPS OUT, THE(1949); LOST TRIBE, THE(1949); LUST FOR GOLD(1949); ROSE OF THE YUKON(1949); ROUGHSHOD(1949); SEARCH FOR DANGER(1949); DESTINATION MURDER(1950); FURIES, THE(1950); JOE PALOOKA IN THE SQUARED CIRCLE(1950); RADAR SECRET SERVICE(1950); NEVER TRUST A GAMBLER(1951); REUNION IN RE-

NO(1951); STRIP, THE(1951); BUSHWHACKERS, THE(1952); HERE COME THE MARINES(1952); NIGHT FREIGHT(1955); TOUGHEST MAN ALIVE(1955); LAST OF THE DESPERADOES(1956); NAKED HILLS, THE(1956); MA BARKER'S KILLER BROOD(1960); ONE MAN JURY(1978); BUDDY BUDDY(1981)

Paula Dell
1984
JOHNNY DANGEROUSLY(1984)

Ralph Dell
VIOLATED LOVE(1966, Arg.), ed

Sylvia Dell
TWO SISTERS(1938)

Wanda Dell
PRIZE FIGHTER, THE(1979), p; PRIVATE EYES, THE(1980), p; MARVIN AND TIGE(1983), p

Norma Dell-Agnese
CIRCLE OF TWO(1980, Can.)

Giuliano Dell-Ovo
DUEL OF THE TITANS(1963, Ital.)

Camillo Mariani dell' Anguillara
DEFEAT OF HANNIBAL, THE(1937, Ital.), w

Alberto Dell'Acqua
KILL THEM ALL AND COME BACK ALONE(1970, Ital./Span.)

Ottaviano Dell'Acqua
MINUTE TO PRAY, A SECOND TO DIE, A(1968, Ital.)

Norma Dell'Agnese
MEATBALLS(1979, Can.); ATLANTIC CITY(1981, U.S./Can.)
1984
MRS. SOFFEL(1984)

Norma Dell'Agnesi
MIDDLE AGE CRAZY(1980, Can.)

Len Dell'Amico
KIRLIAN WITNESS, THE(1978), ed

Consalvo Dell'Arti
REBEL GLADIATORS, THE(1963, Ital.); HORROR CASTLE(1965, Ital.)

Gaetano Dell'Era
EMBALMER, THE(1966, Ital.)

Sandro Dell'Orco
KILL BABY KILL(1966, Ital.), art d

Sandro dell'Orco
MOON IN THE GUTTER, THE(1983, Fr./Ital.), prod d

Jay Della
SIMON, KING OF THE WITCHES(1971)

Lorna Della
Silents
ODDS AGAINST HER, THE(1919, Brit.)

Vittorio Della Balle
MONTE CASSINO(1948, Ital.), ph

Lisa della Casa
DON GIOVANNI(1955, Brit.)

Blanca della Corte
SCHOOLGIRL DIARY(1947, Ital.)

Francesco Della Noce
PSYCHOUT FOR MURDER(1971, Arg./Ital.), art d

Luisa Della Noce
RAILROAD MAN, THE(1965, Ital.)

Donatella Della Nora
LA DOLCE VITA(1961, Ital./Fr.)

Carlo Della Posta
BALL AT THE CASTLE(1939, Ital.), w

Bruno Della Santina
PAY OR DIE(1960)

Joe Della Sorte
PSYCHIC KILLER(1975)

Joseph Della Sorte
LAS VEGAS LADY(1976)

Eliso della Vedova
NEVER TAKE NO FOR AN ANSWER(1952, Brit./Ital.)

Jean Dellannoy
BLIND DESIRE(1948, Fr.), d, w

Mel Dellar
JOHNNY BELINDA(1948), md

Alan Dellay
SOME OF MY BEST FRIENDS ARE...(1971); BLOODSUCKING FREAKS(1982); I, THE JURY(1982); TRADING PLACES(1983)

Allan Dellay
MINX, THE(1969)

Tonino delle Colli
TILL MARRIAGE DO US PART(1979, Ital.), ph

Carlo Delle Piane
GREAT HOPE, THE(1954, Ital.)

Antonella Delle Port
OPERATION ST. PETER'S(1968, Ital.)

Tonino Delli
SPIRITS OF THE DEAD(1969, Fr./Ital.), ph

Franco Delli Colli
SEVEN HILLS OF ROME, THE(1958), ph; LAST MAN ON EARTH, THE(1964, U.S./Ital.), ph

Tinino Delli Colli
PURPLE TAXI, THE(1977, Fr./Ital./Ireland), ph

Tomino Delli Colli
ONCE UPON A TIME IN THE WEST(1969, U.S./Ital.), ph; BLOOD FEUD(1979, Ital.), ph

Tonino Delli Colli
CITY OF PAIN(1951, Ital.), ph; SEVEN HILLS OF ROME, THE(1958), ph; MORGAN THE PIRATE(1961, Fr./Ital.), ph; WONDERS OF ALADDIN, THE(1961, Fr./Ital.), ph; MAMMA ROMA(1962, Ital.), ph; NOT ON YOUR LIFE(1965, Ital./Span.), ph; GOSPEL ACCORDING TO ST. MATTHEW, THE(1966, Fr., Ital.), ph; GOOD, THE BAD, AND THE UGLY, THE(1967, Ital./Span.), ph; HAWKS AND THE SPARROWS, THE(1967, Ital.), ph; CHINA IS NEAR(1968, Ital.), ph; NO ROSES FOR OSS 117(1968, Fr.), ph; GHOSTS, ITALIAN STYLE(1969, Ital./Fr.), ph; MAFIA(1969, Fr./Ital.), ph; PUS-

SYCAT, PUSSYCAT, I LOVE YOU(1970), ph; COMETOGETHER(1971), ph; MASTER TOUCH, THE(1974, Ital./Ger.), ph; SUNDAY LOVERS(1980, Ital./Fr.), ph; LOVERS AND LIARS(1981, Ital.), ph

Tonio Delli Colli
SWORDSMAN OF SIENA, THE(1962, Fr./Ital.), ph

Tonion Delli Colli
LOVE IN 4 DIMENSIONS(1965 Fr./Ital.), ph

Dorthy Dells
EYE FOR AN EYE, AN(1981)

Louis Delluc
Misc. Silents
FIEVRE(1921, Fr.), d; LE CHEMIN D'ERONA(1921, Fr.), d; LE TONNERRE(1921, Fr.), d; LA FEMME DE NULLE PART(1922, Fr.), d; L'INONDATION(1924, Fr.), d

Delly
Silents
ROSE OF PARIS, THE(1924), w

Barry Delmaine
GOLDEN RABBIT, THE(1962, Brit.), p

Howard Delman
BIG RED ONE, THE(1980)

Jeff Delman
STUCK ON YOU(1983), w

Roxann Delman
CAT WOMEN OF THE MOON(1953)

Roxanne Delman
SON OF SINBAD(1955)

Armand Delmar
OUT OF TOWNERS, THE(1970), makeup

Delores Delmar
HUSBANDS(1970)

Elaine Delmar
MAHLER(1974, Brit.)

Frank Delmar
JEOPARDY(1953), cos

Gary Delmar
THEY WERE EXPENDABLE(1945)

Kenny Delmar
IT'S A JOKE, SON!(1947); STRANGERS IN THE CITY(1962)
Silents
ORPHANS OF THE STORM(1922)

Peter Delmar
2001: A SPACE ODYSSEY(1968, U.S./Brit.); BOYS OF PAUL STREET, THE(1969, Hung./US)

Roxann Delmar
VERTIGO(1958)

Thomas Delmar
Silents
MAN WHO COULD NOT LOSE, THE(1914); GIRL OF THE GOLDEN WEST, THE(1923); RAINBOW TRAIL, THE(1925); RUGGED WATER(1925)
Misc. Silents
LASH, THE(1916); VICTORY OF CONSCIENCE, THE(1916); BROADWAY COWBOY, THE(1920); ACROSS THE DIVIDE(1921)

Tom Delmar
Misc. Silents
LAW OF THE YUKON, THE(1920)

Vina Delmar
DANCE HALL(1929), w; PLAYING AROUND(1930), w; BAD GIRL(1931), w; SOLDIER'S PLAYTHING, A(1931), w; UPTOWN NEW YORK(1932), w; CHANCE AT HEAVEN(1933), w; PICK-UP(1933), w; WOMAN ACCUSED(1933), w; SADIE MCKEE(1934), w; BAD BOY(1935), w; HANDS ACROSS THE TABLE(1935), w; KING OF BURLESQUE(1936), w; AWFUL TRUTH, THE(1937), w; MAKE WAY FOR TOMORROW(1937), w; MANHATTAN HEARTBEAT(1940), w; GREAT MAN'S LADY, THE(1942), w; CYNTHIA(1947), w; ABOUT MRS. LESLIE(1954), w

Fred Delmare
NAKED AMONG THE WOLVES(1967, Ger.)

Etta Delmas
RIDERS OF THE CACTUS(1931)

Herbert Delmas
PALS OF THE PECOS(1941), w

Suzanne Delmas
Misc. Silents
RASPUTIN(1929, USSR)

Michael Delmatoff
SHANGHAI GESTURE, THE(1941)

Olive Delmer
ON VELVET(1938, Brit.)

Carlo Delmi
WAR AND PEACE(1956, Ital./U.S.); REBEL GLADIATORS, THE(1963, Ital.)

Jean-Pierre Delmon
CHILDREN OF PARADISE(1945, Fr.)

Delmont
ANGELE(1934 Fr.); ALI BABA(1954, Fr.); LETTERS FROM MY WINDMILL(1955, Fr.)

E. Delmont
THREE HOURS(1944, Fr.)

Edouard Delmont
MARIUS(1933, Fr.); CESAR(1936, Fr.); LA MARSEILLAISE(1938, Fr.); PORT OF SHADOWS(1938, Fr.); HARVEST(1939, Fr.); FANNY(1948, Fr.); PASSION FOR LIFE(1951, Fr.); TONI(1968, Fr.)

Gene Delmont
JOHNNY O'CLOCK(1947); WHIPLASH(1948); FIGHTING FOOLS(1949); SET-UP, THE(1949)

David Delmonte
DISCOVERIES(1939, Brit.)

Richard Delmonte
SCARFACE(1983)
1984
LONELY GUY, THE(1984)

Arthur Delmore
Silents
ALWAYS THE WOMAN(1922)

Herbert Delmore
Silents
BROKEN CHAINS(1916)

Ralph Delmore
Silents
SINS OF SOCIETY(1915); FRUITS OF DESIRE, THE(1916); MAN WHO FORGOT, THE(1917)
Misc. Silents
HAND OF PERIL, THE(1916)

Michael Delnao
NINE TO FIVE(1980)

Ken Delo
DESTINATION INNER SPACE(1966)

Zachary DeLoach
INDEPENDENCE DAY(1983)

Genevieve Deloir
RED(1970, Can.); CROWD INSIDE, THE(1971, Can.); DRACULA VERSUS FRANKENSTEIN(1972, Span.)

Alain Delon
CONCORDE, THE–AIRPORT '79(; CHRISTINE(1959, Fr.); PURPLE NOON(1961, Fr./Ital.); ROCCO AND HIS BROTHERS(1961, Fr./Ital.); DEVIL AND THE TEN COMMANDMENTS, THE(1962, Fr.); ECLIPSE(1962, Fr./Ital.); ANY NUMBER CAN WIN(1963 Fr.); LEOPARD, THE(1963, Ital.); JOY HOUSE(1964, Fr.); ONCE A THIEF(1965); YELLOW ROLLS-ROYCE, THE(1965, Brit.); IS PARIS BURNING?(1966, U.S./Fr.); LOST COMMAND, THE(1966); TEXAS ACROSS THE RIVER(1966); DIABOLICALLY YOURS(1968, Fr.); FAREWELL, FRIEND(1968, Fr./Ital.); GIRL ON A MOTORCYCLE, THE(1968, Fr./Brit.); LAST ADVENTURE, THE(1968, Fr./Ital.); SPIRITS OF THE DEAD(1969, Fr./Ital.); BORSALINO(1970, Fr.), a, p; MADLY(1970, Fr.), a, p; SICILIAN CLAN, THE(1970, Fr.); ASSASSINATION OF TROTSKY, THE(1972 Fr./Ital.); GODSON, THE(1972, Ital./Fr.); RED SUN(1972, Fr./Ital./Span.); COP, A(1973, Fr.); SCORPIO(1973); SHOCK TREATMENT(1973, Fr.); TWO MEN IN TOWN(1973, Fr.); BORSALINO AND CO.(1974, Fr.), a, p; NO WAY OUT(1975, Ital./Fr.); MR. KLEIN(1976, Fr.), a, p; DIRTY MONEY(1977, Fr.); ATTENTION, THE KIDS ARE WATCHING(1978, Fr.); THREE MEN TO DESTROY(1980, Fr.), a, p
1984
SWANN IN LOVE(1984, Fr.Ger.)

Andre Delon
RETURN OF MARTIN GUERRE, THE(1983, Fr.)

Nathalie Delon
WHEN EIGHT BELLS TOLL(1971, Brit.); BLUEBEARD(1972); GODSON, THE(1972, Ital./Fr.); ROMANTIC ENGLISHWOMAN, THE(1975, Brit./Fr.)
Misc. Talkies
EYES BEHIND THE STARS(1972)

Roland DeLong
LIST OF ADRIAN MESSENGER, THE(1963)

Anthony DeLongis
JAGUAR LIVES(1979); IN SEARCH OF HISTORIC JESUS(1980); KING OF THE MOUNTAIN(1981); SWORD AND THE SORCERER, THE(1982)

Delonnel-Garnier
RULES OF THE GAME, THE(1939, Fr.), m

Chantal Delor
PARIS OOH-LA-LA!(1963, U.S./Fr.)

Carl DeLord
PASSPORT TO SUEZ(1943)

Jacques Delord
STOLEN KISSES(1969, Fr.)

Daniele Delorme
DESPERATE DECISION(1954, Fr.); DEADLIER THAN THE MALE(1957, Fr.); ROYAL AFFAIRS IN VERSAILLES(1957, Fr.); WAR OF THE BUTTONS(1963 Fr.), p; SEVENTH JUROR, THE(1964, Fr.); VERY HAPPY ALEXANDER(1969, Fr.), p

Danielle Delorme
CLEO FROM 5 TO 7(1961, Fr.); HOA-BINH(1971, Fr.)

Gaye Delorme
THINGS ARE TOUGH ALL OVER(1982), m

Guy Delorme
DEAD RUN(1961, Fr./Ital./Ger.); OSS 117–MISSION FOR A KILLER(1966, Fr./Ital.); SUCKER, THE(1966, Fr./Ital.); FAREWELL, FRIEND(1968, Fr./Ital.); LAST ADVENTURE, THE(1968, Fr./Ital.); SOUTHERN STAR, THE(1969, Fr./Brit.)

Noel Delorme
VOICE OF THE TURTLE, THE(1947)

Noelle DeLorme
GANGWAY FOR TOMORROW(1943)

Carl Deloro
SPANISH MAIN, THE(1945); MALAYA(1950)

Al DeLory
JORY(1972), m

Dominique Delouche
24 HOURS IN A WOMAN'S LIFE(1968, Fr./Ger.), d, w

Carl DeLoue
TWO-FISTED JUSTICE(1931)

Raoul Delpard
THINGS OF LIFE, THE(1970, Fr./Ital./Switz.)

John Delph
EASY MONEY(1983)

Delphin
CARNIVAL IN FLANDERS(1936, Fr.); DEVIL IS AN EMPRESS, THE(1939, Fr.)

Emile Delpierre
LE BEAU SERGE(1959, Fr.), m

Yvan Delporte
1984
SMURFS AND THE MAGIC FLUTE, THE(1984, Fr./Belg.), w

Albert Delpy
BLUE COUNTRY, THE(1977, Fr.)

Hal Delrich
EVIL DEAD, THE(1983)

Irene Delroy
LIFE OF THE PARTY, THE(1930); OH! SAILOR, BEHAVE!(1930); DIVORCE AMONG FRIENDS(1931); MEN OF THE SKY(1931)
Maly Delschaft
ECHO OF A DREAM(1930, Ger.); AFFAIR BLUM, THE(1949, Ger.)
Silents
VARIETY(1925, Ger.)
Misc. Silents
ALL FOR A WOMAN(1921, Ger.)
Mary Delschaft
Silents
LAST LAUGH, THE(1924, Ger.)
Gerald Delsol
CHILDREN OF THE DAMNED(1963, Brit.)
Paule Delsol
HEAT OF THE SUMMER(1961, Fr.), w
Gloria Delson
WONDER MAN(1945)
Susan Delson
1984
FAR FROM POLAND(1984), p&d
Delta Rhythm Boys
CRAZY HOUSE(1943); HI' YA, SAILOR(1943); SO'S YOUR UNCLE(1943); HI, GOOD-LOOKIN'(1944); NIGHT CLUB GIRL(1944); RECKLESS AGE(1944); EASY TO LOOK AT(1945)
The Delta Rhythm Boys
FOLLOW THE BOYS(1944); WEEKEND PASS(1944)
Joseph Delteil
Silents
PASSION OF JOAN OF ARC, THE(1928, Fr.), w
Rene Deltgen
MOZART STORY, THE(1948, Aust.); TROMBA, THE TIGER MAN(1952, Ger.); SPECIAL DELIVERY(1955, Ger.); HOUSE OF INTRIGUE, THE(1959, Ital.); JOURNEY TO THE LOST CITY(1960, Ger./Fr./Ital.)
Vince Deltito
NEXT OF KIN(1983, Aus.)
Dahl Delu
WARM IN THE BUD(1970), ph
Poppy Deluando
SARACEN BLADE, THE(1954)
Jacqueline Delubac
BONNE CHANCE(1935, Fr.); PEARLS OF THE CROWN(1938, Fr.); STORY OF A CHEAT, THE(1938, Fr.); VOLPONE(1947, Fr.)
Al DeLuca
SMOKEY AND THE BANDIT-PART 3(1983)
Claudio Deluca
SMALL CHANGE(1976, Fr.)
Dangio Nando DeLuca
BLOOD FEUD(1979, Ital.), m
Franck Deluca
SMALL CHANGE(1976, Fr.)
Neal Deluca
ECHOES(1983), art d
Peppino DeLuca
DORIAN GRAY(1970, Ital./Brit./Ger./Liechtenstein), m
Rudy DeLuca
RETURN OF COUNT YORGA, THE(1971); SILENT MOVIE(1976), a, w; HIGH ANXIETY(1977), a, w; HISTORY OF THE WORLD, PART 1(1981)
Steve DeLuca
1984
ALMOST YOU(1984)
Virginia DeLuce
NEW FACES(1954)
Anne Delugg
SLEEPING BEAUTY(1965, Ger.), m/l
Milton Delugg
LET'S DANCE(1950); SLEEPING BEAUTY(1965, Ger.), m/l
Carol DeLuise
HOT STUFF(1979)
David DeLuise
HOT STUFF(1979)
Dom DeLuise
DIARY OF A BACHELOR(1964); FAIL SAFE(1964); BUSYBODY, THE(1967); TWELVE CHAIRS, THE(1970); WHO IS HARRY KELLERMAN AND WHY IS HE SAYING THOSE TERRIBLE THINGS ABOUT ME?(1971); EVERY LITTLE CROOK AND NANNY(1972); BLAZING SADDLES(1974); ADVENTURES OF SHERLOCK HOLMES' SMARTER BROTHER, THE(1975, Brit.); SILENT MOVIE(1976); CHEAP DETECTIVE, THE(1978); SEXTETTE(1978); HOT STUFF(1979), a, d; MUPPET MOVIE, THE(1979); FATSO(1980); LAST MARRIED COUPLE IN AMERICA, THE(1980); SMOKEY AND THE BANDIT II(1980); WHOLLY MOSES(1980); CANNONBALL RUN, THE(1981); HISTORY OF THE WORLD, PART 1(1981); BEST LITTLE WHOREHOUSE IN TEXAS, THE(1982); SECRET OF NIMH, THE(1982)
1984
CANNONBALL RUN II(1984); JOHNNY DANGEROUSLY(1984)
Don DeLuise
WORLD'S GREATEST LOVER, THE(1977)
Michael DeLuise
HOT STUFF(1979)
Peter DeLuise
HOT STUFF(1979)
Yannick Delulle
COLD SWEAT(1974, Ital., Fr.)
Giorgio DeLullo
VERONA TRIAL, THE(1963, Ital.)
Michael DeLuna
LOOKIN' TO GET OUT(1982)
Gabe DeLutri
DRAGSTRIP RIOT(1958); JAILBREAKERS, THE(1960)

Delores DeLuxe
1984
REPO MAN(1984)
Mady Deluz
JONAH-WHO WILL BE 25 IN THE YEAR 2000(1976, Switz.)
Rosita Delva
LOVES OF CARMEN, THE(1948)
Yvonne Delva
Misc. Silents
THIRTEENTH CHAIR, THE(1919)
Jean Delval
CRIME DOCTOR'S GAMBLE(1947)
Liliane Delval
1984
LE BAL(1984, Fr./Ital./Algeria)
Andre Delvaux
ONE NIGHT... A TRAIN(1968, Fr./Bel.), d&w; BENVENUTA(1983, Fr.), d&w
Lucas Delvaux
TROUT, THE(1982, Fr.)
Simone Delve
ACCUSED-STAND UP(1930, Fr.)
Lya Delvelez
Silents
EMERALD OF THE EAST(1928, Brit.)
Rainer Delventhal
SISTERS, OR THE BALANCE OF HAPPINESS(1982, Ger.)
Lea Delworth
Silents
JAZZ GIRL, THE(1926)
Christiane Delyne
CINDERELLA(1937, Fr.); LE MONDE TREMBLERA(1939, Fr.)
Max Delys
L'AMOUR(1973); BREAD AND CHOCOLATE(1978, Ital.)
Alice Delysia
EVENSONG(1934, Brit.)
Misc. Silents
SHE(1916, Brit.)
Minister Dem
SUPERFLY T.N.T.(1973)
Nick DeMaggio
THANK YOU, JEEVES(1936), ed; ANGEL'S HOLIDAY(1937), ed; GREAT HOSPITAL MYSTERY, THE(1937), ed; LAUGHING AT TROUBLE(1937), ed; UP THE RIVER(1938), ed; HONEYMOON'S OVER, THE(1939), ed; STOP, LOOK, AND LOVE(1939), ed; WINNER TAKE ALL(1939), ed; FOR BEAUTY'S SAKE(1941), ed; CAREFUL, SOFT SHOULDERS(1942), ed; POSTMAN DIDN'T RING, THE(1942), ed; GREEN GRASS OF WYOMING(1948), ed; LOVE THAT BRUTE(1950), ed; NIGHT WITHOUT SLEEP(1952), ed
Live Demaigret
CHINA SEAS(1935)
Gordon DeMain
WHY LEAVE HOME?(1929); HEADIN' NORTH(1930); MEN ARE LIKE THAT(1930); GOD'S COUNTRY AND THE MAN(1931); RIDER OF THE PLAINS(1931); SON OF THE PLAINS(1931); NO LIVING WITNESS(1932); WHAT PRICE HOLLYWOOD?(1932); COWBOY COUNSELOR(1933); DEVIL'S MATE(1933); DUDE BANDIT, THE(1933); FIGHTING TEXANS(1933); FUGITIVE, THE(1933); HIGH GEAR(1933); RAINBOW RANCH(1933); STRANGE PEOPLE(1933); GAY BRIDE, THE(1934); LUCKY TEXAN, THE(1934); MYSTERY LINER(1934); WE LIVE AGAIN(1934); FIGHTING TROOPER, THE(1935); PORT OF LOST DREAMS(1935); WHOLE TOWN'S TALKING, THE(1935); INTERNATIONAL LADY(1941); THUNDERING HOOFS(1941); I MARRIED A WITCH(1942); KING OF THE STALLIONS(1942); LADY BODYGUARD(1942); MAD MONSTER, THE(1942); WEST OF TOMBSTONE(1942); CHATTERBOX(1943)
Misc. Talkies
WESTERN CODE(1932)
Nicole DeMaio
NUNZIO(1978)
Robert Deman
JUD(1971); PAPILLON(1973)
Paul Demange
CRIME OF MONSIEUR LANGE, THE(1936, Fr.); CHILDREN OF PARADISE(1945, Fr.); MAN ABOUT TOWN(1947, Fr.); SYLVIA AND THE PHANTOM(1950, Fr.); PARIS DOES STRANGE THINGS(1957, Fr./Ital.); MAIDEN, THE(1961, Fr.); NIGHTS OF SHAME(1961, Fr.); PALACE OF NUDES(1961, Fr./Ital.); VICE DOLLS(1961, Fr.); BACK STREETS OF PARIS(1962, Fr.); PLEASURES AND VICES(1962, Fr.); SEVEN CAPITAL SINS(1962, Fr./Ital.); RAVISHING IDIOT, A(1966, Ital./Fr.)
Ferdinand W. "Fred" Demara
THE HYPNOTIC EYE(1960)
Kent DeMarche
1984
OH GOD! YOU DEVIL(1984)
Laura DeMarchi
1984
NOSTALGHIA(1984, USSR/Ital.)
Carlo DeMarchis
1984
YELLOW HAIR AND THE FORTRESS OF GOLD(1984), spec eff
Frank DeMarco
FIREBALL 590(1966), spec eff
John DeMarco
BEST HOUSE IN LONDON, THE(1969, Brit.)
Richard DeMarco
THAT SINKING FEELING(1979, Brit.); LONG SHOT(1981, Brit.)
Sally DeMarco
CRAZY HOUSE(1943)
Tony DeMarco
SHINING HOUR, THE(1938), ch; CRAZY HOUSE(1943); GANG'S ALL HERE, THE(1943)

Fred Demare
LOST FACE, THE(1965, Czech.)
Jacques Demarecaux
I DRINK YOUR BLOOD(1971), ph
Ralph Demaree
HAPPY DAYS(1930)
Bill Demarest
DIAMOND JIM(1935)
Drew Demarest
BROADWAY MELODY, THE(1929); LORD BYRON OF BROADWAY(1930); ONCE A GENTLEMAN(1930); TODAY(1930); GIRL WITH IDEAS, A(1937); SARATOGA(1937); JURY'S SECRET, THE(1938); RECKLESS LIVING(1938); I STOLE A MILLION(1939); YOU CAN'T CHEAT AN HONEST MAN(1939); 6000 ENEMIES(1939); MEN OF SAN QUENTIN(1942); NAZI AGENT(1942); SPOILERS, THE(1942); STRANGE CASE OF DR. RX, THE(1942); STRICTLY IN THE GROOVE(1942); SECRET HEART, THE(1946)
Rich Demarest
TWILIGHT'S LAST GLEAMING(1977, U.S./Ger.)
Rube Demarest
GIRL, A GUY AND A GOB, A(1941)
Wiliam Demarest
SULLIVAN'S TRAVELS(1941)
William Demarest
TRUE TO LIFE(1943); JAZZ SINGER, THE(1927); FOG OVER FRISCO(1934); FUGITIVE LADY(1934); MANY HAPPY RETURNS(1934); BRIGHT LIGHTS(1935); CASINO MURDER CASE, THE(1935); HANDS ACROSS THE TABLE(1935); MURDER MAN(1935); WHITE LIES(1935); CHARLIE CHAN AT THE OPERA(1936); GREAT ZIEGFELD, THE(1936); LOVE ON THE RUN(1936); WEDDING PRESENT(1936); BIG CITY(1937); BLONDE TROUBLE(1937); DON'T TELL THE WIFE(1937); EASY LIVING(1937); GREAT GAMBINI, THE(1937); GREAT HOSPITAL MYSTERY, THE(1937); HIT PARADE, THE(1937); MIND YOUR OWN BUSINESS(1937); OH DOCTOR(1937); ROSALIE(1937); TIME OUT FOR ROMANCE(1937); WAKE UP AND LIVE(1937); JOSETTE(1938); ONE WILD NIGHT(1938); PECK'S BAD BOY WITH THE CIRCUS(1938); REBECCA OF SUNNYBROOK FARM(1938); ROMANCE ON THE RUN(1938); WHILE NEW YORK SLEEPS(1938); COWBOY QUARTERBACK(1939); GRACIE ALLEN MURDER CASE(1939); GREAT MAN VOTES, THE(1939); KING OF THE TURF(1939); LAUGH IT OFF(1939); MIRACLES FOR SALE(1939); MR. SMITH GOES TO WASHINGTON(1939); CHRISTMAS IN JULY(1940); COMIN' ROUND THE MOUNTAIN(1940); FARMER'S DAUGHTER, THE(1940); GOLDEN FLEECING, THE(1940); GREAT McGINTY, THE(1940); LITTLE MEN(1940); WOLF OF NEW YORK(1940); COUNTRY FAIR(1941); DEVIL AND MISS JONES, THE(1941); DRESSED TO KILL(1941); GLAMOUR BOY(1941); LADY EVE, THE(1941); RIDE ON VAQUERO(1941); ROOKIES ON PARADE(1941); ALL THROUGH THE NIGHT(1942); BEHIND THE EIGHT BALL(1942); LIFE BEGINS AT 8:30(1942); MY FAVORITE SPY(1942); PALM BEACH STORY, THE(1942); PARDON MY SARONG(1942); TRUE TO THE ARMY(1942); DANGEROUS BLONDES(1943); JOHNNY DOUGHBOY(1943); STAGE DOOR CANTEEN(1943); GREAT MOMENT, THE(1944); HAIL THE CONQUERING HERO(1944); MIRACLE OF MORGAN'S CREEK, THE(1944); NINE GIRLS(1944); ONCE UPON A TIME(1944); ALONG CAME JONES(1945); PARDON MY PAST(1945); SALTY O'ROURKE(1945); JOLSON STORY, THE(1946); OUR HEARTS WERE GROWING UP(1946); PERILS OF PAULINE, THE(1947); VARIETY GIRL(1947); NIGHT HAS A THOUSAND EYES(1948); ON OUR MERRY WAY(1948); SAINTED SISTERS, THE(1948); WHISPERING SMITH(1948); JOLSON SINGS AGAIN(1949); RED, HOT AND BLUE(1949); SORROWFUL JONES(1949); HE'S A COCKEYED WONDER(1950); NEVER A DULL MOMENT(1950); RIDING HIGH(1950); WHEN WILLIE COMES MARCHING HOME(1950); BEHAVE YOURSELF(1951); EXCUSE MY DUST(1951); FIRST LEGION, THE(1951); STRIP, THE(1951); BLAZING FOREST, THE(1952); WHAT PRICE GLORY?(1952); DANGEROUS WHEN WET(1953); ESCAPE FROM FORT BRAVO(1953); HERE COME THE GIRLS(1953); LADY WANTS MINK, THE(1953); YELLOW MOUNTAIN, THE(1954); FAR HORIZONS(1955); JUPITER'S DARLING(1955); LUCY GALLANT(1955); PRIVATE WAR OF MAJOR BENSON, THE(1955); SINCERELY YOURS(1955); HELL ON FRISCO BAY(1956); MOUNTAIN, THE(1956); RAWHIDE YEARS, THE(1956); PEPE(1960); KING OF THE ROARING TWENTIES–THE STORY OF ARNOLD ROTHSTEIN(1961); TWENTY PLUS TWO(1961); IT'S A MAD, MAD, MAD, MAD WORLD(1963); SON OF FLUBBER(1963); VIVA LAS VEGAS(1963); THAT DARN CAT(1965); WILD McCULLOCHS, THE(1975); WON TON TON, THE DOG WHO SAVED HOLLYWOOD(1976)
Silents
GAY OLD BIRD, THE(1927); MATINEE LADIES(1927); SAILOR'S SWEETHEART, A(1927); WHAT HAPPENED TO FATHER(1927); ESCAPE, THE(1928); SHARP SHOOTERS(1928)
Misc. Silents
BUSH LEAGUER, THE(1927); SIMPLE SIS(1927); BUTTER AND EGG MAN, THE(1928); CRASH, THE(1928); FIVE AND TEN CENT ANNIE(1928); PAY AS YOU ENTER(1928)
Al Demaret
FOLLOW THE SUN(1951)
James Demaret
FOLLOW THE SUN(1951)
Andree Demarez
MAN WITH CONNECTIONS, THE(1970, Fr.), cos
Donna DeMario
APACHE ROSE(1947); WOMAN FROM TANGIER, THE(1948)
Tony DeMario
LOVE NEST(1951); ISLAND IN THE SKY(1953); BLACK WIDOW(1954)
Ovid Demaris
GANG WAR(1958), w
Terence deMarney
DESERT SANDS(1955)
Terence DeMarney
MIDNIGHT LACE(1960); CONFESSIONS OF AN OPIUM EATER(1962)
Eric Demarsen
1984
HEAT OF DESIRE(1984, Fr.), m
Albert Demartino
Misc. Talkies
PUMA MAN, THE(1980), d
Alberto DeMartino
DIRTY HEROES(1971, Ital./Fr./Ger.), d, w; CRIME BOSS(1976, Ital.), d; TEMPTER, THE(1978, Ital.), d, w

Misc. Talkies
BANDITS IN ROME(1967, Ital.), d
Andy DeMartino
SUPER VAN(1977), m
Peppino Demartino
LIGHT IN THE PIAZZA(1962)
Romolo Demartino
SECRET SEVEN, THE(1966, Ital./Span.), makeup
Carole Demas
300 YEAR WEEKEND(1971)
Jean-Michel Demase
TERM OF TRIAL(1962, Brit.), m
Maria DeMatteis
BARABBAS(1962, Ital.), cos
Ed DeMattia
PHANTOM TOLLBOOTH, THE(1970), anim
The DeMattiazzis
LULLABY OF BROADWAY, THE(1951)
Edna Demaurey
Silents
CONQUERING POWER, THE(1921)
Josette Demay
PRICE OF FLESH, THE(1962, Fr.)
Sally DeMay
LADY LIBERTY(1972, Ital./Fr.); LOOKING UP(1977)
Orane Demazis
MARIUS(1933, Fr.); CESAR(1936, Fr.); LES MISERABLES(1936, Fr.); HARVEST(1939, Fr.); FIRE IN THE STRAW(1943); FANNY(1948, Fr.); CASE OF DR. LAURENT(1958, Fr.)
Orane Demaziz
ANGELE(1934 Fr.)
Boris Demb
WELCOME KOSTYA!(1965, USSR)
Doris Dembow
MAID TO ORDER(1932), w
Dani Dembrosky
CARNY(1980)
Maurice Dembsky
COUNTRY BOY(1966); THAT TENNESSEE BEAT(1966); TRACK OF THUNDER(1967)
Emanuel Demby
INVISIBLE AVENGER, THE(1958), p
Luci Drudi Demby
1984
MISUNDERSTOOD(1984), m
Lucia Dridi Demby
THAT SPLENDID NOVEMBER(1971, Ital./Fr.), w
William Demby
COMMANDO(1962, Ital., Span., Bel., Ger.), w; EYE OF THE NEEDLE, THE(1965, Ital./Fr.), w
Paul Demel
IT HAPPENED ONE SUNDAY(1944, Brit.); LATE AT NIGHT(1946, Brit.); MAN FROM MOROCCO, THE(1946, Brit.); PASSPORT TO PIMLICO(1949, Brit.); HUE AND CRY(1950, Brit.); MINIVER STORY, THE(1950, Brit./U.S.); GREAT MANHUNT, THE(1951, Brit.); LAVENDER HILL MOB, THE(1951, Brit.); HIS EXCELLENCY(1952, Brit.)
Angelo DeMeo
DEAD AND BURIED(1981)
Joseph DeMeo
SOME CALL IT LOVING(1973)
Drew Demerest
VIOLENCE(1947)
Jacques Demers
QUEST FOR FIRE(1982, Fr./Can.)
Rene Demers
MY UNCLE ANTOINE(1971, Can.), makeup
V. Demert
Misc. Silents
DOUBLE, THE(1916, USSR), d
Anthony Demery
CONRACK(1974)
Catherine Demesmaeker
MALEVIL(1981, Fr./Ger.), makeup
Georges Demestre
LES GAULOISES BLEUES(1969, Fr.)
Nina Demestre
MAN WITH CONNECTIONS, THE(1970, Fr.)
Johanna Demetrakas
NUNZIO(1978), ed
Johanna Demetrakis
RENEGADE GIRLS(1974), ed
Ann Demetrio
BORN TO BE WILD(1938)
Anna Demetrio
TOO MUCH HARMONY(1933); CRUSADES, THE(1935); MC FADDEN'S FLATS(1935); NEXT TIME WE LOVE(1936); BRIDE WORE RED, THE(1937); MAYTIME(1937); IN OLD MEXICO(1938); TEXANS, THE(1938); TROPIC HOLIDAY(1938); ESCAPE TO PARADISE(1939); LAW OF THE PAMPAS(1939); IT'S A DATE(1940); LLANO KID, THE(1940); YOUNG BUFFALO BILL(1940); LAW OF THE TROPICS(1941); MISS V FROM MOSCOW(1942); SUBMARINE BASE(1943); CALL OF THE SOUTH SEAS(1944); DRAGON SEED(1944); KISMET(1944); BELL FOR ADANO, A(1945); CARNIVAL IN COSTA RICA(1947); BANDIT QUEEN(1950); SEPTEMBER AFFAIR(1950)
Irene Demetrion
ROBE, THE(1953)
Sgt. Demetrios
THREE STRIPES IN THE SUN(1955)

Cristos Demetriou
PRIVATE RIGHT, THE(1967, Brit.)
Theodore Demetriou
ELECTRA(1962, Gr.)
Nicholas Demetroules
TEENAGE MOTHER(1967), p, d&w; STATELINE MOTEL(1976, Ital.), p
George Demetru
STEPS TO THE MOON(1963, Rum.)
Danielle DeMetz
JESSICA(1962, U.S./Ital./Fr.)
Demicheli
DEVIL MADE A WOMAN, THE(1962, Span.), w
Tuilio Demicheli
GUNMEN OF THE RIO GRANDE(1965, Fr./Ital./Span.), w
Tulio Demicheli
DEVIL MADE A WOMAN, THE(1962, Span.), d; SON OF CAPTAIN BLOOD, THE(1964, U.S./Ital./Span.), d; GUNMEN OF THE RIO GRANDE(1965, Fr./Ital./Span.), d; ASSIGNMENT TERROR(1970, Ger./Span./Ital.), d; CAULDRON OF DEATH, THE(1979, Ital.), d
Irene Demick
Misc. Talkies
TIFFANY MEMORANDUM(1966)
Irina Demick
LONGEST DAY, THE(1962); VISIT, THE(1964, Ger./Fr./Ital./U.S.); MALE COMPANION(1965, Fr./Ital.); THOSE MAGNIFICENT MEN IN THEIR FLYING MACHINES; OR HOW I FLEW FROM LONDON TO PARIS IN 25 HOURS AND 11 MINUTES(1965, Brit.); UP FROM THE BEACH(1965); CLOPORTES(1966, Fr., Ital.); PRUDENCE AND THE PILL(1968, Brit.); SICILIAN CLAN, THE(1970, Fr.)
Alexandra Demidova
STALKER(1982, USSR), p
V. Demidovskiy
OPTIMISTIC TRAGEDY, THE(1964, USSR)
Ruby DeMiel
1984
INDIANA JONES AND THE TEMPLE OF DOOM(1984)
Agnes DeMille
OKLAHOMA(1955), ch
Beatrice C. DeMille
Silents
EACH PEARL A TEAR(1916), w
C. B. DeMille
Silents
CARMEN(1915), ed
Cecil B DeMille
Silents
KINDLING(1915), w
Cecil B. DeMille
DYNAMITE(1930), p&d; FREE AND EASY(1930); MADAME SATAN(1930), p&d; SQUAW MAN, THE(1931), p&d; SIGN OF THE CROSS, THE(1932), p&d; THIS DAY AND AGE(1933), p&d; CLEOPATRA(1934), p&d; FOUR FRIGHTENED PEOPLE(1934), p&d; CRUSADES, THE(1935), p&d; LAST TRAIN FROM MADRID, THE(1937); PLAINSMAN, THE(1937), p&d; BUCCANEER, THE(1938), p&d; UNION PACIFIC(1939), p&d; NORTHWEST MOUNTED POLICE(1940), p&d; REAP THE WILD WIND(1942), p&d; STAR SPANGLED RHYTHM(1942); STORY OF DR. WASSELL, THE(1944), p&d; UNCONQUERED(1947), p&d; VARIETY GIRL(1947); SAMSON AND DELILAH(1949), p&d; SUNSET BOULEVARD(1950); GREATEST SHOW ON EARTH, THE(1952), p&d; SON OF PALEFACE(1952); TEN COMMANDMENTS, THE(1956), p&d; BUSTER KEATON STORY, THE(1957)
Silents
BREWSTER'S MILLIONS(1914), d; CALL OF THE NORTH, THE(1914), d&w; CIRCUS MAN, THE(1914), w; MAN FROM HOME, THE(1914), d, w; READY MONEY(1914), w; ROSE OF THE RANCHO(1914), d, w; SQUAW MAN, THE(1914), p,d&w; VIRGINIAN, THE(1914), d&w; AFTER FIVE(1915), w; ARAB, THE(1915), p&d, w, ed; CAPTIVE, THE(1915), d, w, ed; CARMEN(1915), p&d; CHIMMIE FADDEN(1915), d, w, ed; CHIMMIE FADDEN OUT WEST(1915), p&d, w, ed; GIRL OF THE GOLDEN WEST, THE(1915), d&w; GOLDEN CHANCE, THE(1915), d; KINDLING(1915), d; SNOBS(1915), w; TEMPTATION(1915), d; WARRENS OF VIRGINIA, THE(1915), d; WILD GOOSE CHASE, THE(1915), d; OLD WIVES FOR NEW(1918), d; MALE AND FEMALE(1919), d; SOMETHING TO THINK ABOUT(1920), d; AFFAIRS OF ANATOL(1921), p&d; SATURDAY NIGHT(1922), d; ADAM'S RIB(1923), p&d; TEN COMMANDMENTS, THE(1923), p&d; COMING OF AMOS, THE(1925), p; FORTY WINKS(1925), w; NIGHT CLUB, THE(1925), w; WEDDING SONG, THE(1925), sup; VOLGA BOATMAN, THE(1926), d; KING OF KINGS, THE(1927), p&d
Misc. Silents
MAN ON THE BOX, THE(1914), d; WHAT'S HIS NAME?(1914), d; CHEAT, THE(1915), d; UNAFRAID, THE(1915), d; DREAM GIRL, THE(1916), d; MARIA ROSA(1916), d; TEMPTATION(1916), d; TRAIL OF THE LONESOME PINE, THE(1916), d; DEVIL STONE, THE(1917), d; LITTLE AMERICAN, THE(1917), d; WOMAN GOD FORGOT, THE(1917), d; 'TILL I COME BACK TO YOU(1918), d; WE CAN'T HAVE EVERYTHING(1918), d; WHISPERING CHORUS, THE(1918), d; DON'T CHANGE YOUR HUSBAND(1919), d; WHY CHANGE YOUR WIFE?(1920), d; MANSLAUGHTER(1922), d; TRIUMPH(1924), d
Katherine DeMille
MADAME SATAN(1930); BELLE OF THE NINETIES(1934); ALL THE KING'S HORSES(1935); CALL OF THE WILD(1935); BANJO ON MY KNEE(1936); DRIFT FENCE(1936); RAMONA(1936); SKY PARADE(1936); CALIFORNIAN, THE(1937); IN OLD CALIENTE(1939); DARK STREETS OF CAIRO(1940); ELLERY QUEEN. MASTER DETECTIVE(1940); ISLE OF DESTINY(1940); ALOMA OF THE SOUTH SEAS(1941); BLACK GOLD(1947); UNCONQUERED(1947); JUDGE, THE(1949); MAN FROM DEL RIO(1956)
William B. DeMille
Silents
WARRENS OF VIRGINIA, THE(1915), w
William C. DeMille
DOCTOR'S SECRET(1929), p,d,&w; SECRET CALL, THE(1931), w; EMPEROR JONES, THE(1933), p
Silents
CLASSMATES(1914), w; MASTER MIND, THE(1914), sup; ONLY SON, THE(1914), sup; ROSE OF THE RANCHO(1914); AFTER FIVE(1915), w; CARMEN(1915), w;

GOOSE GIRL, THE(1915), w; WILD GOOSE CHASE, THE(1915), w; ANTON THE TERRIBLE(1916), d; JACK STRAW(1920), d; AFTER THE SHOW(1921), d; WHAT EVERY WOMAN KNOWS(1921), d; CLASSMATES(1924), w; WARRENS OF VIRGINIA, THE(1924), w; NIGHT CLUB, THE(1925), w; RUNAWAY, THE(1926), d
Misc. Silents
BLACKLIST(1916), d
William DeMille
IDLE RICH, THE(1929), d; PASSION FLOWER(1930), d
Silents
PUPPET CROWN, THE(1915), w; NICE PEOPLE(1922), d; NEW BROOMS(1925), d
Adonis DeMilo
PASSPORT TO SUEZ(1943)
Tony DeMilo
OCEAN'S ELEVEN(1960)
Peter Demin
Misc. Talkies
ADVENTURES OF YOUNG ROBIN HOOD(1983)
Fred Deming
NIGHT AND DAY(1946)
Mark Deming
GORP(1980)
Mark R. Deming
WEDDING, A(1978)
Millicent Deming
TWO TICKETS TO BROADWAY(1951); GARMENT JUNGLE, THE(1957)
Norman Deming
RIDERS OF BLACK RIVER(1939), d; TAMING OF THE WEST, THE(1939), d; BIRDS, THE(1963), prod d
Pat Deming
GIRLS ON THE BEACH(1965)
Richard Deming
ARRIVEDERCI, BABY!(1966, Brit.), p,d&w
Von Deming
LOSERS, THE(1970)
W.R. Deming
QUIET PLEASE, MURDER(1942)
Walter Deming
Silents
PASSIONATE YOUTH(1925)
V. Deminskiy
TRAIN GOES TO KIEV, THE(1961, USSR), spec eff; KIEV COMEDY, A(1963, USSR), spec eff; SONG OF THE FOREST(1963, USSR), spec eff
Caroly DeMirjian
BLADE RUNNER(1982)
Denise DeMirjian
BITTERSWEET LOVE(1976)
Erol Demiroz
1984
HORSE, THE(1984, Turk.)
Katherine Demise
LA DOLCE VITA(1961, Ital./Fr.)
Ann Demitri
APPOINTMENT WITH MURDER(1948)
Leonardo DeMitri
ANGELO IN THE CROWD(1952, Ital.), d
Nick Demitri
HARLOW(1965)
Milan Demjanenko
1984
AMADEUS(1984)
Ronald Demko
DOUBLE-BARRELLED DETECTIVE STORY, THE(1965)
Jonathan Demme
ANGELS HARD AS THEY COME(1971), p, w; HOT BOX, THE(1972, U.S./Phil.), p; BLACK MAMA, WHITE MAMA(1973), w; RENEGADE GIRLS(1974), d&w; CRAZY MAMA(1975), d; FIGHTING MAD(1976), d, w; CITIZENS BAND(1977), d; LAST EMBRACE(1979), a, d; MELVIN AND HOWARD(1980), d
1984
SWING SHIFT(1984), d
Jonathon Demme
HOT BOX, THE(1972, U.S./Phil.), w; INCREDIBLE MELTING MAN, THE(1978)
John Demmitt
ON THE YARD(1978)
Al DeMond
STORM OVER THE ANDES(1935), w
Albert DeMond
CLEAR THE DECKS(1929), w; GIVE AND TARE(1929), w; MODERN LOVE(1929), w; COHENS AND KELLYS IN SCOTLAND, THE(1930), w; SPHINX, THE(1933), w; HOUSE OF MYSTERY(1934), w; TAKE THE STAND(1934), w; DEATH FLIES EAST(1935), w; LOST IN THE STRATOSPHERE(1935), w; NO RANSOM(1935), w; SCHOOL FOR GIRLS(1935), w; SECRET OF THE CHATEAU(1935), w; SPANISH CAPE MYSTERY(1935), w; UNKNOWN WOMAN(1935), w; LEAVENWORTH CASE, THE(1936), w; NAVY BORN(1936), w; GIRLS CAN PLAY(1937), w; NORTH OF NOME(1937), w; WOMAN IN DISTRESS(1937), w; BLONDES AT WORK(1938), w; LITTLE MISS THOROUGHBRED(1938), w; TORCHY GETS HER MAN(1938), w; SWEEPSTAKES WINNER(1939), w; FUGITIVE FROM A PRISON CAMP(1940), w; GREAT PLANE ROBBERY, THE(1940), w; PASSPORT TO ALCATRAZ(1940), w; GANGS OF SONORA(1941), w; GAUCHOS OF EL DORADO(1941), w; GREAT SWINDLE, THE(1941), w; OUTLAWS OF THE CHEROKEE TRAIL(1941), w; SADDLEMATES(1941), w; WEST OF CIMARRON(1941), w; RAIDERS OF THE RANGE(1942), w; VALLEY OF HUNTED MEN(1942), w; RIDERS OF THE RIO GRANDE(1943), w; BENEATH WESTERN SKIES(1944), w; CALL OF THE SOUTH SEAS(1944), w; CODE OF THE PRAIRIE(1944), w; SHADOW OF SUSPICION(1944), w; TRAIL OF KIT CARSON(1945), w; SHOCK(1946), w; BLACKMAIL(1947), w; CODE OF THE SADDLE(1947), w; WILD FRONTIER, THE(1947), w; HOMICIDE FOR THREE(1948), w; KING OF THE GAMBLERS(1948), w; MADONNA OF THE DESERT(1948), w; ALIAS THE CHAMP(1949), w; DUKE OF CHICAGO(1949), w; FLAME OF YOUTH(1949), w; PRINCE OF THE PLAINS(1949), w; RED MENACE, THE(1949), w; FEDERAL AGENT AT LARGE(1950), w; TRIAL WITHOUT JURY(1950), w; UNMASKED(1950), w; MILLION DOLLAR PURSUIT(1951), w; BORDER SADDLE-

MATES(1952), w; DESPERADOES OUTPOST(1952), w; OLD OKLAHOMA PLAINS(1952), w; PALS OF THE GOLDEN WEST(1952), w; MARSHAL OF CEDAR ROCK(1953), w

Albert E. DeMond
SKYWAY(1933), w; SWEETHEART OF SIGMA CHI(1933), w; SENSATION HUNT-ERS(1934), w; FLIRTING WITH DANGER(1935), w

Alfred DeMond
CYCLOTRODE X(1946), w

Henry DeMond
SIX-GUN LAW(1948), ed

Catherine Demongeot
WOMAN IS A WOMAN, A(1961, Fr./Ital.); ZAZIE(1961, Fr.)

Mylene Demongeot
BONJOUR TRISTESSE(1958); GIANT OF MARATHON, THE(1960, Ital.); UNDER TEN FLAGS(1960, U.S./Ital.); SINGER NOT THE SONG, THE(1961, Brit.); TIME BOMB(1961, Fr./Ital.); UPSTAIRS AND DOWNSTAIRS(1961, Brit.); LA NOTTE BRAVA(1962, Fr./Ital.); DOCTOR IN DISTRESS(1963, Brit.); GOLD FOR THE CAE-SARS(1964); FANTOMAS STRIKES BACK(1965, Fr./Ital.); FANTOMAS(1966, Fr./Ital.); OSS 117-MISSION FOR A KILLER(1966, Fr./Ital.); TENDER SCOUN-DREL(1967, Fr./Ital.); GIRL GAME(1968, Braz./Fr./Ital.); HOW TO SEDUCE A PLAYBOY(1968, Aust./Fr./Ital.); PRIVATE NAVY OF SGT. O'FARRELL, THE(1968); UNCLE TOM'S CABIN(1969, Fr./Ital./Ger./Yugo.); TWELVE PLUS ONE(1970, Fr./Ital.)

Harry Demopoulas
SUDDEN IMPACT(1983)

Harry Demopoulos, M.D.
1984
CITY HEAT(1984)

Bob DeMora
NIGHTHAWKS(1981), cos

Robert Demora
DIFFERENT STORY, A(1978), cos; AMERICAN SUCCESS COMPANY, THE(1980), cos; CRUISING(1980), cos; SOUP FOR ONE(1982), cos

Don Demore
VOYAGE TO THE END OF THE UNIVERSE(1963, Czech.), cos

Drew Demorest
SUZY(1936); FIREFLY, THE(1937)

Robert Demorget
CHILDREN OF CHAOS(1950, Fr.)

Hermine Demoriane
JUBILEE(1978, Brit.)

Rebecca DeMornay
TESTAMENT(1983)

Pierre DeMoro
SAVANNAH SMILES(1983), d

Darcy DeMoss
1984
HARDBODIES(1984)

Susan Demott
CANDIDATE, THE(1972)

Vic Demourelle
MEXICALI ROSE(1939)

Vic Demourelle, Jr.
TIP-OFF GIRLS(1938); MAN FROM TEXAS, THE(1939)

Al Dempsey
STING OF DEATH(1966), w

Bob Dempsey
EXPERIMENT IN TERROR(1962)

Clifford Dempsey
GHOST TALKS, THE(1929); SALUTE(1929); VALIANT, THE(1929); HAPPY DAYS(1930); ONLY SAPS WORK(1930); EVERYTHING'S ROSIE(1931); SOB SIS-TER(1931); TOO MANY COOKS(1931); BLONDE VENUS(1932); GUILTY AS HELL(1932)

Daniel Dempsey
HORNET'S NEST(1970)

George Dempsey
TURNING POINT, THE(1952)

Jack Dempsey
PRIZEFIGHTER AND THE LADY, THE(1933); SWEET SURRENDER(1935); BIG CITY(1937); OFF LIMITS(1953); DAMN CITIZEN(1958); REQUIEM FOR A HEAVY-WEIGHT(1962)
Misc. Silents
MANHATTAN MADNESS(1925)

James Dempsey
NAKED ALIBI(1954), m

Janet Dempsey
TARNISHED ANGEL(1938); ALOMA OF THE SOUTH SEAS(1941); FOREST RANG-ERS, THE(1942)

Janey Dempsey
REG'LAR FELLERS(1941)

Jerome Dempsey
MALATESTA'S CARNIVAL(1973); NETWORK(1976)

Marion Dempsey
CAROUSEL(1956)

Mark Dempsey
VALLEY OF THE DRAGONS(1961); PALM SPRINGS WEEKEND(1963); OH! CAL-CUTTA!(1972)
1984
PRODIGAL, THE(1984)

Martin Dempsey
ULYSSES(1967, U.S./Brit.); MC KENZIE BREAK, THE(1970); WEDDING NIGHT(1970, Ireland)

Patrick Dempsey
Misc. Silents
DEATHLOCK, THE(1915)

Pauline Dempsey
Silents
AMATEUR WIDOW, AN(1919); BROADWAY ROSE(1922); DESTINY'S ISLE(1922); MODERN MARRIAGE(1923)

Ray Dempsey
ALL NIGHT LONG(1961, Brit.)

Rosemarie Dempsey
ARABIAN NIGHTS(1942)

Sandy Dempsey
J.W. COOP(1971)
Misc. Talkies
LITTLE MISS INNOCENCE(1973); AMAZING LOVE SECRET(1975)

Sean Dempsey
NORAH O'NEALE(1934, Brit.); KATHLEEN(1938, Ireland)

Tom Dempsey
ELMER AND ELSIE(1934)

Al Dempster
JUNGLE BOOK, THE(1967), art d; ARISTOCATS, THE(1970), anim

Albert Dempster
THREE CABALLEROS, THE(1944), art d; LADY AND THE TRAMP(1955), art d; SLEEPING BEAUTY(1959), art d; ONE HUNDRED AND ONE DALMATIANS(1961), art d; SWORD IN THE STONE, THE(1963), art d

Austin Dempster
MAYTIME IN MAYFAIR(1952, Brit.), ph; BEDAZZLED(1967, Brit.), ph; OT-LEY(1969, Brit.), ph; LOOKING GLASS WAR, THE(1970, Brit.), ph; LOOT(1971, Brit.), ph; PETER RABBIT AND TALES OF BEATRIX POTTER(1971, Brit.), ph; SEVERED HEAD, A(1971, Brit.), ph; LITTLE ARK, THE(1972), ph; TOUCH OF CLASS, A(1973, Brit.), ph

Carol Dempster
Silents
GREATEST THING IN LIFE, THE(1918); GIRL WHO STAYED AT HOME, THE(1919); ROMANCE OF HAPPY VALLEY, A(1919); SCARLET DAYS(1919); LOVE FLOWER, THE(1920); DREAM STREET(1921); ONE EXCITING NIGHT(1922); SHER-LOCK HOLMES(1922); WHITE ROSE, THE(1923); AMERICA(1924); ISN'T LIFE WONDERFUL(1924); "THAT ROYLE GIRL"(1925); SALLY OF THE SAWDUST(1925); SORROWS OF SATAN(1926)

Hugh Dempster
LORD BABS(1932, Brit.); MUSIC HATH CHARMS(1935, Brit.); SCARLET PIMPER-NEL, THE(1935, Brit.); STUDENT'S ROMANCE, THE(1936, Brit.); APRIL BLOS-SOMS(1937, Brit.); MARIGOLD(1938, Brit.); ME AND MY PAL(1939, Brit.); GARRISON FOLLIES(1940, Brit.); THREE SILENT MEN(1940, Brit.); BELL-BOTTOM GEOR-GE(1943, Brit.); CANDLES AT NINE(1944, Brit.); HE SNOOPS TO CONQUER(1944, Brit.); HEAVEN IS ROUND THE CORNER(1944, Brit.); JOHNNY IN THE CLOUDS(1945, Brit.); SCHOOL FOR SECRETS(1946, Brit.); TROJAN BROTHERS, THE(1946); WALTZ TIME(1946, Brit.); ANNA KARENINA(1948, Brit.); VICE VER-SA(1948, Brit.); FAN, THE(1949); WHILE THE SUN SHINES(1950, Brit.); WINSLOW BOY, THE(1950); CHRISTMAS CAROL, A(1951, Brit.); FLESH AND BLOOD(1951, Brit.); HAPPY GO LOVELY(1951, Brit.); PAUL TEMPLE'S TRIUMPH(1951, Brit.); BABES IN BAGDAD(1952); FRIGHTENED BRIDE, THE(1952, Brit.); MOULIN ROUGE(1952); DETECTIVE, THE(1954, Qit.); HEATWAVE(1954, Brit.); EXTRA DAY, THE(1956, Brit.); CURSE OF FRANKENSTEIN, THE(1957, Brit.)

Jeff DeMunn
RAGTIME(1981)

Jeffrey DeMunn
FIRST DEADLY SIN, THE(1980); RESURRECTION(1980); FRANCES(1982); I'M DANCING AS FAST AS I CAN(1982)
1984
WINDY CITY(1984)

Fumio Demura
ISLAND OF DR. MOREAU, THE(1977)

Ryuzo Demura
GEISHA BOY, THE(1958)

M. DeMuro
SUBWAY RIDERS(1981)

Norman Demuth
PINK STRING AND SEALING WAX(1950, Brit.), m

Daniel Demutski
Silents
EARTH(1930, USSR), ph

D. Demutsky
SECRET MISSION(1949, USSR), ph

Danylo Demutsky
Silents
ARSENAL(1929, USSR), ph

Jacques Demy
FOUR HUNDRED BLOWS, THE(1959); LOLA(1961, Fr./Ital.), d&w; PARIS BE-LONGS TO US(1962, Fr.); SEVEN CAPITAL SINS(1962, Fr./Ital.), d, w; BAY OF ANGELS(1964, Fr.), d&w; UMBRELLAS OF CHERBOURG, THE(1964, Fr./Ger.), d&w; YOUNG GIRLS OF ROCHEFORT, THE(1968, Fr.), d&w; MODEL SHOP, THE(1969), p,d, w; PIED PIPER, THE(1972, Brit.), d, w; DONKEY SKIN(1975, Fr.), d&w; LADY OSCAR(1979, Fr./Jap.), d, w

Lincoln Demyan
MAN'S FAVORITE SPORT(?)(1964); MARRIED TOO YOUNG(1962); I'D RATHER BE RICH(1964); GUNN(1967); WHITE LIGHTNING(1973)

A. Demyanenko
NIGHT BEFORE CHRISTMAS, A(1963, USSR)

Aleksandr Demyanenko
GROWN-UP CHILDREN(1963, USSR); PEACE TO HIM WHO ENTERS(1963, USSR)

Edward O. DeNault
1984
LAST STARFIGHTER, THE(1984), p

Brenda DeNaut
TOO YOUNG, TOO IMMORAL!(1962)

Yves-Claude Denaux
SIN ON THE BEACH(1964, Fr.), w

Al Denava
MAIN EVENT, THE(1979)

Igor DeNavrotsky
THANK YOUR LUCKY STARS(1943)

D.M. Denawake
1984
INDIANA JONES AND THE TEMPLE OF DOOM(1984)

Grace Denbeigh-Russell
MY BROTHER JONATHAN(1949, Brit.); FINGER OF GUILT(1956, Brit.); DEVIL'S DAFFODIL, THE(1961, Brit./Ger.)

Arthur Denberg
WAGNER(1983, Brit./Hung./Aust.)

Susan Denberg
FRANKENSTEIN CREATED WOMAN(1965, Brit.); AMERICAN DREAM, AN(1966)

Grace Denbigh-Russell
GREAT EXPECTATIONS(1946, Brit.); HIDEOUT(1948, Brit.); THINGS HAPPEN AT NIGHT(1948, Brit.); WARNING TO WANTONS, A(1949, Brit.); DISTANT TRUM-PET(1952, Brit.)

Jack Denbo
SKYJACKED(1972); PAPILLON(1973)

Susan Denbo
Misc. Talkies
GREAT LESTER BOGGS, THE(1975)

Edwin Denby
CAGE OF NIGHTINGALES, A(1947, Fr.), titles

Jerry Denby
TEENAGE GANG DEBS(1966), p; WHIP'S WOMEN(1968), d; PLEASURE PLANTA-TION(1970), d

Maggie Dence
OUTBACK(1971, Aus.)

Bertram Dench
MUSIC HALL(1934, Brit.); STRAUSS' GREAT WALTZ(1934, Brit.); FLOOD TI-DE(1935, Brit.)

Judi Dench
THIRD SECRET, THE(1964, Brit.); FOUR IN THE MORNING(1965, Brit.); HE WHO RIDES A TIGER(1966, Brit.); STUDY IN TERROR, A(1966, Brit./Ger.); MIDSUMMER NIGHT'S DREAM, A(1969, Brit.); LUTHER(1974)
Misc. Talkies
DEAD CERT(1974, Brit.)

Sydney Dench
MOUNTAIN, THE(1935, Brit.)

Dench and Stewart
ICE-CAPADES(1941); ICE-CAPADES REVUE(1942)

Merrill Dendoff
RUNNING BRAVE(1983, Can.)

R. Dendy
IT ALWAYS RAINS ON SUNDAY(1949, Brit.), spec eff

Carmen Dene
GENGHIS KHAN(U.S./Brit./Ger./Yugo); DEADFALL(1968, Brit.); SUBTER-FUGE(1969, US/Brit.)

Graham Dene
1984
GIVE MY REGARDS TO BROAD STREET(1984, Brit.)

Terence Dene
HOMER(1970), p

Terry Dene
INBETWEEN AGE, THE(1958, Brit.)

Zulema Dene
PIRATES OF PENZANCE, THE(1983)

Margie Denecke
MAN WHO LOVED WOMEN, THE(1983)

Mr. Denecke
Silents
CAMPBELLS ARE COMING, THE(1915)

Germaine DeNeel
GOIN' TO TOWN(1935)

Margie Deneke
GOING BERSERK(1983)

Carol Denell
BATTLE OF THE WORLDS(1961, Ital.)

Stephen Denenberg
JESUS CHRIST, SUPERSTAR(1973)

Babe Denetdeel
UNTAMED(1940)

George Deneubourg
Silents
RIGHT TO LIE, THE(1919)
Misc. Silents
TARNISHED REPUTATIONS(1920)

Catherine Deneuve
TALES OF PARIS(1962, Fr./Ital.); UMBRELLAS OF CHERBOURG, THE(1964, Fr./Ger.); MALE COMPANION(1965, Fr./Ital.); MALE HUNT(1965, Fr./Ital.); REPUL-SION(1965, Brit.); VICE AND VIRTUE(1965, Fr./Ital.); BEAUTIFUL SWINDLERS, THE(1967, Fr./Ital./Jap./Neth.); LA VIE DE CHATEAU(1967, Fr.); BELLE DE JOUR(1968, Fr.); BENJAMIN(1968, Fr.); MANON 70(1968, Fr.); MAYERLING(1968, Brit./Fr.); YOUNG GIRLS OF ROCHEFORT, THE(1968, Fr.); APRIL FOOLS, THE(1969); LES CREATURES(1969, Fr./Swed.); MISSISSIPPI MERMAID(1970, Fr./ Ital.); TRISTANA(1970, Span./Ital./Fr.); IT ONLY HAPPENS TO OTHERS(1971, Fr./Ital.); COP, A(1973, Fr.); DON'T TOUCH WHITE WOMEN!(1974, Fr.); DONKEY SKIN(1975, Fr.); DRAMA OF THE RICH(1975, Ital./Fr.); HUSTLE(1975, Fr.); SAVAGE, THE(1975, Fr.); ZIG-ZAG(1975, Fr/Ital.); LIZA(1976, Fr./Ital.); DIRTY MONEY(1977, Fr.); LA GRANDE BOURGEOISE(1977, Ital.); MARCH OR DIE(1977, Brit.); WOMAN WITH RED BOOTS, THE(1977, Fr./Span.); LAST METRO, THE(1981, Fr.); AFRICAN, THE(1983, Fr.); CHOICE OF ARMS(1983, Fr.); HUNGER, THE(1983)
1984
LE BON PLAISIR(1984, Fr.)

Marco Denevi
SECRET CEREMONY(1968, Brit.), w

Charles Deney
HAIR(1979)

Lea Denfield
SQUEEZE A FLOWER(1970, Aus.)

Dennis Dengate
ROGUES' REGIMENT(1948); SWORD IN THE DESERT(1949); PREHISTORIC WOM-EN(1950); THREE SAILORS AND A GIRL(1953); CRIME WAVE(1954); HANG'EM HIGH(1968)

Mike Dengate
RACERS, THE(1955)

Jake Dengel
SOMETHING WICKED THIS WAY COMES(1983)
1984
BEST DEFENSE(1984)

Fred Denger
RAMPAGE AT APACHE WELLS(1966, Ger./Yugo.), w; FLAMING FRONTIER(1968, Ger./Yugo.), w; UNCLE TOM'S CABIN(1969, Fr./Ital./Ger./Yugo.), w; MARK OF THE DEVIL II(1975, Ger./Brit.), w

Christopher Denham
MAN OUTSIDE, THE(1968, Brit.)

Maurice Denham
CAPTAIN BOYCOTT(1947, Brit.); END OF THE RIVER, THE(1947, Brit.); HOLIDAY CAMP(1947, Brit.); I BECAME A CRIMINAL(1947); UPTURNED GLASS, THE(1947, Brit.); BLANCHE FURY(1948, Brit.); BLIND GODDESS, THE(1948, Brit.); DAY-DREAK(1948, Brit.); DULCIMER STREET(1948, Brit.); EASY MONEY(1948, Brit.); ESCAPE(1948, Brit.); HERE COME THE HUGGETTS(1948, Brit.); JASSY(1948, Brit.); LOOK BEFORE YOU LOVE(1948, Brit.); SMUGGLERS, THE(1948, Brit.); TAKE MY LIFE(1948, Brit.); BLUE LAGOON, THE(1948, Brit.); BOY, A GIRL AND A BIKE, A(1949 Brit.); DON'T EVER LEAVE ME(1949, Brit.); IT'S NOT CRICKET(1949, Brit.); MADNESS OF THE HEART(1949, Brit.); MIRANDA(1949, Brit.); MY BROTHER'S KEEPER(1949, Brit.); ONCE UPON A DREAM(1949, Brit.); POET'S PUB(1949, Brit.); NO HIGHWAY IN THE SKY(1951, Brit.); OLIVER TWIST(1951, Brit.); TRAVELLER'S JOY(1951, Brit.); SPIDER AND THE FLY, THE(1952, Brit.); BOTH SIDES OF THE LAW(1953, Brit.); LANDFALL(1953, Brit.); PROJECT M7(1953, Brit.); TERROR ON A TRAIN(1953); COURT MARTIAL(1954, Brit.); EIGHT O'CLOCK WALK(1954, Brit.); MALTA STORY(1954, Brit.); MAN WITH A MILLION(1954, Brit.); PURPLE PLAIN, THE(1954, Brit.); ANIMAL FARM(1955, Brit.); DOCTOR AT SEA(1955, Brit.); SIMON AND LAURA(1956, Brit.); 23 PACES TO BAKER STREET(1956); CHECKPOINT(1957, Brit.); ALL AT SEA(1958, Brit.); CURSE OF THE DEMON(1958); CAPTAIN'S TABLE, THE(1960, Brit.); OUR MAN IN HAVANA(1960, Brit.); SINK THE BISMARCK!(1960, Brit.); INVASION QUARTET(1961, Brit.); LOSS OF INNOCENCE(1961, Brit.); MARK, THE(1961, Brit.); TWO-WAY STRETCH(1961, Brit.); DAMN THE DEFIANT!(1962, Brit.); PARANOIAC(1963, Brit.); SET-UP, THE(1963, Brit.); VERY EDGE, THE(1963, Brit.); DOWNFALL(1964, Brit.); SEVENTH DAWN, THE(1964); BLOOD BEAST FROM OUTER SPACE(1965, Brit.); HEROES OF TELEMARK, THE(1965, Brit.); HYS-TERIA(1965, Brit.); NANNY, THE(1965, Brit.); OPERATION CROSSBOW(1965, U.S./ Ital.); THOSE MAGNIFICENT MEN IN THEIR FLYING MACHINES; OR HOW I FLEWFROM LONDON TO PARIS IN 25 HOURS AND 11 MINUTES(1965, Brit.); AFTER THE FOX(1966, U.S./Brit./Ital.); ALPHABET MURDERS, THE(1966); UNCLE, THE(1966, Brit.); LONG DUEL, THE(1967, Brit.); ATTACK ON THE IRON COAST(1968, U.S./Brit.); DANGER ROUTE(1968, Brit.); NEGATIVES(1968, Brit.); TORTURE GARDEN(1968, Brit.); BEST HOUSE IN LONDON, THE(1969, Brit.); MIDAS RUN(1969); SOME GIRLS DO(1969, Brit.); THANK YOU ALL VERY MUCH(1969, Brit.); NICHOLAS AND ALEXANDRA(1971, Brit.); VIRGIN AND THE GYPSY, THE(1970, Brit.); SUNDAY BLOODY SUNDAY(1971, Brit.); COUNTESS DRACULA(1972, Brit.); DAY OF THE JACKAL, THE(1973, Brit./Fr.); LUTHER(1974); SHOUT AT THE DEVIL(1976, Brit.); JULIA(1977)

Phillippe Denham
1984
MICKI AND MAUDE(1984)

Reginald Denham
STAMBOUL(1931, Brit.), w; EBB TIDE(1932, Brit.), w; JEWEL, THE(1933, Brit.), d; BORROW A MILLION(1934, Brit.), d; BRIDES TO BE(1934, Brit.), p&d; DEATH AT A BROADCAST(1934, Brit.), d; LUCKY LOSER(1934, Brit.), d; PRIMROSE PATH, THE(1934, Brit.), p&d; LIEUTENANT DARING, RN(1935, Brit.), d; LUCKY DAYS(1935, Brit.), d; PRICE OF WISDOM, THE(1935, Brit.), d; SILENT PASSENGER, THE(1935, Brit.), d; VILLAGE SQUIRE, THE(1935, Brit.), d; CALLING THE TU-NE(1936, Brit.), d; CRIMSON CIRCLE, THE(1936, Brit.), d; DREAMS COME TRUE(1936, Brit.), d; HOUSE OF THE SPANIARD(1936, Brit.), d; KATE PLUS TEN(1938, Brit.), d; BLIND FOLLY(1939, Brit.), d; FLYING FIFTY-FIVE(1939, Brit.), d; DESIGN FOR MURDER(1940, Brit.), w; LADIES IN RETIREMENT(1941), w; WALLFLOWER(1948), w; ANNA OF BROOKLYN(1958, Ital.), d; FAST AND SEX-Y(1960, Fr./Ital.), d; MAD ROOM, THE(1969), w

Christian Denhez
GERVAISE(1956, Fr.); GATES OF PARIS(1958, Fr./Ital.)

Yves Deniaud
CRIME OF MONSIEUR LANGE, THE(1936, Fr.); MONSEIGNEUR(1950, Fr.); SIM-PLE CASE OF MONEY, A(1952, Fr.); KNOCK(1955, Fr.); ROYAL AFFAIRS IN VERSAILLES(1957, Fr.); WOMAN OF SIN(1961, Fr.)

Miomir Denic
FRAGRANCE OF WILD FLOWERS, THE(1979, Yugo.), art d

Joseph DeNicola
STEEL(1980); EYE FOR AN EYE, AN(1981)

Christina Maire Denihan
1984
ALPHABET CITY(1984)

Terry Denim
SLEEPING CITY, THE(1950)

Joseph R. Denini
SLENDER THREAD, THE(1965)

William DeNino
THEY ALL LAUGHED(1981)

Raphael DeNiro
1984
LOVE STREAMS(1984)

Armand Denis
Misc. Talkies
GOONA-GOONA(1932), d

Jacques Denis
CLOCKMAKER, THE(1976, Fr.); JONAH-WHO WILL BE 25 IN THE YEAR 2000(1976, Switz.); QUESTION, THE(1977, Fr.)

Jean Denis
DEPUTY DRUMMER, THE(1935, Brit.)

Jean-Michael Denis
1984
FIRST NAME: CARMEN(1984, Fr.)

Jean-Peirre Denis
BIRD WATCH, THE(1983, Fr.), d, w
Maria Denis
PRIVATE ANGELO(1949, Brit.)
Trevor Denis
WE'LL SMILE AGAIN(1942, Brit.)
Denise Denise
LADY SINGS THE BLUES(1972); DOCTOR DEATH: SEEKER OF SOULS(1973)
Misc. Talkies
FOX STYLE(1973)
Patricia Denise
EASY TO WED(1946); SINGIN' IN THE RAIN(1952); KNOCK ON WOOD(1954); MARJORIE MORNINGSTAR(1958)
Denishawn Dancers
Silents
NIGHT LIFE IN HOLLYWOOD(1922)
John Denison
GREEK TYCOON, THE(1978)
Leslie Denison
CHARLIE CHAN IN RIO(1941); INTERNATIONAL SQUADRON(1941); YANK IN THE R.A.F., A(1941); BOMBS OVER BURMA(1942); COUNTER-ESPIONAGE(1942); DANGEROUSLY THEY LIVE(1942); INVISIBLE AGENT(1942); MY FAVORITE BLONDE(1942); SECRET AGENT OF JAPAN(1942); SHERLOCK HOLMES AND THE SECRET WEAPON(1942); SHERLOCK HOLMES AND THE VOICE OF TERROR(1942); WIFE TAKES A FLYER, THE(1942); FIRST COMES COURAGE(1943); FIVE GRAVES TO CAIRO(1943); MURDER IN TIMES SQUARE(1943); TONIGHT WE RAID CALAIS(1943); FOLLOW THE BOYS(1944); FRENCHMAN'S CREEK(1944); HOUR BEFORE THE DAWN, THE(1944); PEARL OF DEATH, THE(1944); RETURN OF THE VAMPIRE, THE(1944); HANGOVER SQUARE(1945); HER LUCKY NIGHT(1945); HOUSE OF FEAR, THE(1945); MOLLY AND ME(1945); SHE GETS HER MAN(1945); BANDIT OF SHERWOOD FOREST, THE(1946); DANGEROUS MONEY(1946); HOW DO YOU DO?(1946); O.S.S.(1946); RENDEZVOUS 24(1946); THREE STRANGERS(1946); DOUBLE LIFE, A(1947); GOLDEN EARRINGS(1947); KISS THE BLOOD OFF MY HANDS(1948); MY OWN TRUE LOVE(1948); FIGHTING O'FLYNN, THE(1949); TWELVE O'CLOCK HIGH(1949); THREE CAME HOME(1950); SON OF DR. JEKYLL, THE(1951); BRAVE WARRIOR(1952); LES MISERABLES(1952); MILLION DOLLAR MERMAID(1952); ROGUE'S MARCH(1952); SALOME(1953); BENGAL BRIGADE(1954); SNOW CREATURE, THE,(1954); FLAME OF THE ISLANDS(1955); SCARLET COAT, THE(1955); SOMETHING OF VALUE(1957); IN THE MONEY(1958); SIGNPOST TO MURDER(1964)
Michael Denison
TILLY OF BLOOMSBURY(1940, Brit.); HUNGRY HILL(1947, Brit.); MY BROTHER JONATHAN(1949, Brit.); GLASS MOUNTAIN, THE(1950, Brit); FRANCHISE AFFAIR, THE(1952, Brit.); FRIGHTENED BRIDE, THE(1952, Brit.); IMPORTANCE OF BEING EARNEST, THE(1952, Brit.); MAGIC BOX, THE(1952, Brit.); LANDFALL(1953, Brit.); THERE WAS A YOUNG LADY(1953, Brit.); ANGELS ONE FIVE(1954, Brit.); CONTRABAND SPAIN(1955, Brit.); TRUTH ABOUT WOMEN, THE(1958, Brit.); FACES IN THE DARK(1960, Brit.)
Muriel Denison
SUSANNAH OF THE MOUNTIES(1939), w
Robert Denison
Misc. Talkies
SOUTHERN DOUBLE CROSS(1973)
Susan Denison
SPRING BREAK(1983), cos
V. Denisov
HOUSE ON THE FRONT LINE, THE(1963, USSR)
A. Denisova
MUMU(1961, USSR); GIRL AND THE BUGLER, THE(1967, USSR)
Mimi Denissi
GREEK TYCOON, THE(1978)
Hermanos Deniz
OUR MAN IN HAVANA(1960, Brit.), m
Gerard Denizot
CATHERINE & CO.(1976, Fr.)
Foster Denker
ONE FROM THE HEART(1982)
Henry Denker
TIME LIMIT(1957), w; HOOK, THE(1962), w; TWILIGHT OF HONOR(1963), w; GREATEST STORY EVER TOLD, THE(1965), w
Marty Denkin
ROCKY III(1982); STING II, THE(1983)
Yves Denlaud
BLIND DESIRE(1948, Fr.)
Wilton Denmark
CAIN'S WAY(1969), w
Clint Denn
SHARK'S TREASURE(1975)
Marie Denn
WILD GUITAR(1962); BURY ME AN ANGEL(1972); MOONCHILD(1972); DIFFERENT STORY, A(1978)
Albert Dennable
MUGGER, THE(1958)
Tee Dennard
OFFICER AND A GENTLEMAN, AN(1982)
Carol Denne
BAND OF THIEVES(1962, Brit.)
Max Denne
KID FOR TWO FARTHINGS, A(1956, Brit.)
Olive Denneccio
Misc. Talkies
AMAZING TRANSPLANT, THE(1970)
Brian Dennehy
SEMI-TOUGH(1977); F.I.S.T.(1978); FOUL PLAY(1978); 10(1979); LITTLE MISS MARKER(1980); FIRST BLOOD(1982); SPLIT IMAGE(1982); GORKY PARK(1983); NEVER CRY WOLF(1983)
1984
FINDERS KEEPERS(1984); RIVER RAT, THE(1984)

Barbara Dennek
PLAYTIME(1973, Fr.)
Barry Dennem
KENTUCKY FRIED MOVIE, THE(1977)
Barry Dennen
FIDDLER ON THE ROOF(1971); JESUS CHRIST, SUPERSTAR(1973); MADHOUSE(1974, Brit.); BRANNIGAN(1975, Brit.); SHINING, THE(1980); SHOCK TREATMENT(1981); DARK CRYSTAL, THE(1982, Brit.); SUPERMAN III(1983); TRADING PLACES(1983)
1984
MEMED MY HAWK(1984, Brit.); NOT FOR PUBLICATION(1984)
Bob Denner
PATSY, THE(1964)
Charles Denner
LANDRU(1963, Fr./Ital); LIFE UPSIDE DOWN(1965, Fr.); MATA HARI(1965, Fr./Ital.); SLEEPING CAR MURDER THE(1966, Fr.); THIEF OF PARIS, THE(1967, Fr./Ital.); BRIDE WORE BLACK, THE(1968, Fr./Ital.); TWO OF US, THE(1968, Fr.); DIANE'S BODY(1969, Fr./Czech.); Z(1969, Fr./Algeria); CROOK, THE(1971, Fr.); SUCH A GORGEOUS KID LIKE ME(1973, Fr.); AND NOW MY LOVE(1975, Fr.); MAN WHO LOVED WOMEN, THE(1977, Fr.); FIRST TIME, THE(1978, Fr.)
John Denner
RIGHT STUFF, THE(1983)
Joyce Denner
BEHIND LOCKED DOORS(1976, S. Africa)
Misc. Talkies
ANY BODY...ANY WAY(1968)
Adolphe Philippe Dennery
Silents
ORPHANS OF THE STORM(1922), w; ROSITA(1923), w
Eileen Dennes
Silents
ALF'S BUTTON(1920, Brit.); ONCE ABOARD THE LUGGER(1920, Brit.); MR. JUSTICE RAFFLES(1921, Brit.); PIPES OF PAN, THE(1923, Brit.)
Misc. Silents
HER SISTER(1917); TINTED VENUS, THE(1921, Brit.); TIT FOR TAT(1922, Brit.); COMIN' THRO' THE RYE(1923, Brit.); SINS YE DO, THE(1924, Brit.); SQUIRE OF LONG HADLEY, THE(1925, Brit.)
Irving Dennes
OLD FAITHFUL(1935, Brit.), w
Jill Dennett
TENDERFOOT, THE(1932); TWO SECONDS(1932); PICTURE SNATCHER(1933); SING SINNER, SING(1933); MERRY WIDOW, THE(1934); SHOOT THE WORKS(1934); WHARF ANGEL(1934); DEVIL IS A WOMAN, THE(1935)
Barbara Denney
KID FOR TWO FARTHINGS, A(1956, Brit.)
Charles Denney
ZELIG(1983)
Craig Denney
Misc. Talkies
ASTROLOGER, THE(1975), a, d
Dirty Denney
WILD RIDERS(1971)
Dodo Denney
WHO'S MINDING THE MINT?(1967); I WALK THE LINE(1970)
Julie Denney
CAT PEOPLE(1982)
Nora Denney
1984
SPLASH(1984)
Ava Denning
OLGA'S GIRLS(1964)
Charles Denning
1984
RENO AND THE DOC(1984, Can.)
Glen Denning
BATTLE FLAME(1955)
Glenn Denning
STOP THAT CAB(1951); STRATEGIC AIR COMMAND(1955)
Katherine Denning
NATIONAL LAMPOON'S ANIMAL HOUSE(1978)
Richard Denning
AIR STRIKE(1955); HOLD'EM NAVY!(1937); BUCCANEER, THE(1938); CAMPUS CONFESSIONS(1938); COLLEGE SWING(1938); HER JUNGLE LOVE(1938); ILLEGAL TRAFFIC(1938); KING OF ALCATRAZ(1938); SAY IT IN FRENCH(1938); TEXANS, THE(1938); YOU AND ME(1938); DISPUTED PASSAGE(1939); GERONIMO(1939); GRACIE ALLEN MURDER CASE(1939); GRAND JURY SECRETS(1939); I'M FROM MISSOURI(1939); KING OF CHINATOWN(1939); MILLION DOLLAR LEGS(1939); NIGHT OF NIGHTS, THE(1939); OUR NEIGHBORS–THE CARTERS(1939); SOME LIKE IT HOT(1939); STAR MAKER, THE(1939); SUDDEN MONEY(1939); TELEVISION SPY(1939); UNION PACIFIC(1939); EMERGENCY SQUAD(1940); FARMER'S DAUGHTER, THE(1940); GOLDEN GLOVES(1940); LOVE THY NEIGHBOR(1940); NORTHWEST MOUNTED POLICE(1940); PAROLE FIXER(1940); QUEEN OF THE MOB(1940); SEVENTEEN(1940); THOSE WERE THE DAYS(1940); ADAM HAD FOUR SONS(1941); WEST POINT WIDOW(1941); BEYOND THE BLUE HORIZON(1942); GLASS KEY, THE(1942); ICE-CAPADES REVUE(1942); QUIET PLEASE, MURDER(1942); BLACK BEAUTY(1946); FABULOUS SUZANNE, THE(1946); SEVEN WERE SAVED(1947); CAGED FURY(1948); DISASTER(1948); LADY AT MIDNIGHT(1948); UNKNOWN ISLAND(1948); DOUBLE DEAL(1950); HARBOR OF MISSING MEN(1950); NO MAN OF HER OWN(1950); INSURANCE INVESTIGATOR(1951); WEEKEND WITH FATHER(1951); HANGMAN'S KNOT(1952); OKINAWA(1952); SCARLET ANGEL(1952); TARGET HONG KONG(1952); FORTY-NINTH MAN, THE(1953); GLASS WEB, THE(1953); BATTLE OF ROGUE RIVER(1954); CREATURE FROM THE BLACK LAGOON(1954); JIVARO(1954); TARGET EARTH(1954); CREATURE WITH THE ATOM BRAIN(1955); CROOKED WEB, THE(1955); GUN THAT WON THE WEST, THE(1955); MAGNIFICENT MATADOR, THE(1955); DAY THE WORLD ENDED, THE(1956); GIRLS IN PRISON(1956); OKLAHOMA WOMAN, THE(1956); AFFAIR TO REMEMBER, AN(1957); BLACK SCORPION, THE(1957); BUCKSKIN LADY, THE(1957); FLAME OF STAMBOUL(1957); NAKED PARADISE(1957); DESERT HELL(1958); LADY TAKES A FLYER, THE(1958); MILLION DOLLAR MANHUNT(1962, Brit.); TWICE TOLD

TALES(1963); I SAILED TO TAHITI WITH AN ALL GIRL CREW(1969); MARY, QUEEN OF SCOTS(1971, Brit.)

Ruth Denning
WEAK AND THE WICKED, THE(1954, Brit.)

Sara Denning
SPRING BREAK(1983), cos

Wade Denning
RAIN FOR A DUSTY SUMMER(1971, U.S./Span.), m

Al Everett Dennis
NAKED FLAME, THE(1970, Can.), w

Alex Dennis
SAVAGE WILD, THE(1970)

Alfred Dennis
SWEET CHARITY(1969); SHOOTIST, THE(1976); DEMON SEED(1977)

Amy Dennis
Misc. Silents
YORK STATE FOLKS(1915); BARKER, THE(1917); SOONER OR LATER(1920)

Beverly Dennis
TAKE CARE OF MY LITTLE GIRL(1951); WESTWARD THE WOMEN(1951)

Bob Dennis
LIFE BEGINS AT 17(1958); PARADISE ALLEY(1962)

C.J. Dennis
HIS ROYAL HIGHNESS(1932, Aus.), w

Charles Dennis
THIRSTY DEAD, THE(1975), w; DOUBLE NEGATIVE(1980, Can.), w
1984
COVERGIRL(1984, Can.), a, w; FINDERS KEEPERS(1984), w; RENO AND THE DOC(1984, Can.), d&w

Claire Dennis
PETTY GIRL, THE(1950)

Danny Dennis
BLACKBOARD JUNGLE, THE(1955); STREET OF SINNERS(1957)

Donald C. Dennis
WICKED DIE SLOW, THE(1968), p

Eddie Dennis
Silents
GILDED DREAM, THE(1920); RAINBOW RANGERS(1924)

Emmett Dennis III
UNCOMMON VALOR(1983)

Farley Dennis
NIGHT OF BLOODY HORROR zero(1969)

Frances Dennis
RED, WHITE AND BLACK, THE(1970), cos

Francis Dennis
SLUMBER PARTY '57(1977), cos

Fred Dennis
DOC(1971); TRUE CONFESSIONS(1981); STING II, THE(1983)

G.G. Dennis
GREAT JEWEL ROBBER, THE(1950), w

Geoffrey Dennis
MURDER IN REVERSE(1946, Brit.); UNEARTHLY, THE(1957), w

Gil Dennis
KID FROM BOOKLYN, THE(1946); DESPERATE SEARCH(1952)

Gordon Dennis
Misc. Silents
IDOL OF PARIS, THE(1914, Brit.)

Hal Dennis
THIS IS NOT A TEST(1962), ed

Harold J. Dennis
TRAUMA(1962), ed; TIME TRAVELERS, THE(1964), ed

Irene Dennis
MORGAN'S MARAUDERS(1929)

Irving Dennis
SUNSCORCHED(1966, Span./Ger.), w

Jack Dennis
VALIANT, THE(1929), ed; BIG TRAIL, THE(1930), ed; DOUBLE CROSS ROADS(1930), ed; SO THIS IS LONDON(1930), ed; DOCTORS' WIVES(1931), ed; WICKED(1931), ed; WOMEN OF ALL NATIONS(1931), ed; FINAL EDITION(1932), ed; LOVE AFFAIR(1932), ed; THAT'S MY BOY(1932), ed; THREE WISE GIRLS(1932), ed; COCKTAIL HOUR(1933), ed; WAGON WHEELS(1934), ed; WITCHING HOUR, THE(1934), ed; HOLD'EM YALE(1935), ed; HOME ON THE RANGE(1935), ed; LAST OUTPOST, THE(1935), ed; ROCKY MOUNTAIN MYSTERY(1935), ed; LAST OF THE MOHICANS, THE(1936), ed; NEVADA(1936), ed; TIMOTHY'S QUEST(1936), ed; MURDER ON DIAMOND ROW(1937, Brit.), ed; SOUTH RIDING(1938, Brit.), ed; TROOPSHIP(1938, Brit.), ed; BARRICADE(1939), ed; FLYING DEUCES, THE(1939), ed; THREE MUSKETEERS, THE(1939), ed; SECOND CHORUS(1940), ed; ISLE OF MISSING MEN(1942), ed; KLONDIKE FURY(1942), ed; RUBBER RACKETEERS(1942), ed
Silents
WHITE GOLD(1927), ed; NOOSE, THE(1928), ed

Jackie Dennis
6.5 SPECIAL(1958, Brit.)

Jake Dennis
FINAL COUNTDOWN, THE(1980)

Jan Dennis
FORCE OF EVIL(1948)

Joe Dennis
LOST BATTALION(1961, U.S./Phil.)

John Dennis
FIRE OVER ENGLAND(1937, Brit.), ed; FROM HERE TO ETERNITY(1953); BATTLE TAXI(1955); CONQUEST OF SPACE(1955); NAKED STREET, THE(1955); PETE KELLY'S BLUES(1955); RETURN OF JACK SLADE, THE(1955); TARGET ZERO(1955); CALLING HOMICIDE(1956); MY GUN IS QUICK(1957); FRANKENSTEIN 1970(1958); REVOLT IN THE BIG HOUSE(1958); TOO MUCH, TOO SOON(1958); VIOLENT ROAD(1958); BY LOVE POSSESSED(1961), w; CONVICTS FOUR(1962); QUICK, BEFORE IT MELTS(1964); TICKLE ME(1965); 36 HOURS(1965); LT. ROBIN CRUSOE, U.S.N.(1966); MISTER BUDDWING(1966); OSCAR, THE(1966); NEVER A DULL MOMENT(1968); FANDANGO(1970); KINFOLK(1970); CONQUEST OF THE PLANET OF THE APES(1972); GARDEN OF THE DEAD(1972); TOMB OF THE UNDEAD(1972); UP THE SANDBOX(1972); SLAMS, THE(1973); SOYLENT GREEN(1973); EARTHQUAKE(1974); YOUNG FRANKENSTEIN(1974); PSYCHIC KILLER(1975)

Joseph Dennis
COOL WORLD, THE(1963)

Judy Dennis
Misc. Talkies
BLOOD THIRST(1965 Phil./U.S.)

Laddie Dennis
SUNDAY IN THE COUNTRY(1975, Can.)

Marjean Dennis
FLASHDANCE(1983)

Mark Dennis
MILLERSON CASE, THE(1947); SPORT OF KINGS(1947); 13TH HOUR, THE(1947); SECRET BEYOND THE DOOR, THE(1948); RUSTY'S BIRTHDAY(1949); PAGAN ISLAND(1961), ph; TARGETS(1968); NICKELODEON(1976)
Misc. Talkies
RETURN OF RUSTY, THE(1946)

Matt Dennis
SMASH-UP, THE STORY OF A WOMAN(1947); BIGAMIST,THE(1953); JENNIFER(1953)

Nick Dennis
DOUBLE LIFE, A(1947); SIROCCO(1951); STREETCAR NAMED DESIRE, A(1951); TEN TALL MEN(1951); ANYTHING CAN HAPPEN(1952); EIGHT IRON MEN(1952); IRON MISTRESS, THE(1952); GLORY BRIGADE, THE(1953); MAN IN THE DARK(1953); BIG KNIFE, THE(1955); EAST OF EDEN(1955); KISS ME DEADLY(1955); TOP OF THE WORLD(1955); HOT BLOOD(1956); SLAUGHTER ON TENTH AVENUE(1957); ALASKA PASSAGE(1959); SPARTACUS(1960); TOO LATE BLUES(1962); FOUR FOR TEXAS(1963); GUNPOINT(1966); LEGEND OF LYLAH CLARE, THE(1968); GOOD GUYS AND THE BAD GUYS, THE(1969)

Patricia Dennis
AUNTIE MAME(1958), w

Patrick Dennis
MRS. POLLIFAX-SPY(1971); MAME(1974), w

Paul Dennis
Silents
DOUBLING WITH DANGER(1926)

Peter Dennis
CONFESSIONS OF A WINDOW CLEANER(1974, Brit.)
1984
SCANDALOUS(1984)

Reid Dennis
CAYMAN TRIANGLE, THE(1977)

Rick Dennis
WILD GUITAR(1962); WHAT'S UP FRONT(1964)

Robert C. Dennis
CRIME AGAINST JOE(1956), w; MAN IS ARMED, THE(1956), w; REVOLT AT FORT LARAMIE(1957), w; MY WORLD DIES SCREAMING(1958), w; DATE WITH DEATH, A(1959), w

Robert Dennis
RAW FORCE(1982)
1984
ALLEY CAT(1984)

Russell Dennis
BRIGHT VICTORY(1951)

Sandy Dennis
SPLENDOR IN THE GRASS(1961); WHO'S AFRAID OF VIRGINIA WOOLF?(1966); FOX, THE(1967); UP THE DOWN STAIRCASE(1967); SWEET NOVEMBER(1968); THANK YOU ALL VERY MUCH(1969, Brit.); THAT COLD DAY IN THE PARK(1969, U.S./Can.); OUT OF TOWNERS, THE(1970); MR. SYCAMORE(1975); GOD TOLD ME TO(1976); NASTY HABITS(1976, Brit.); THREE SISTERS, THE(1977); FOUR SEASONS, THE(1981); COME BACK TO THE 5 & DIME, JIMMY DEAN, JIMMY DEAN(1982)
Misc. Talkies
ONLY WAY OUT IS DEAD, THE(1970)

Susan Dennis
Misc. Silents
BLACK CARGOES OF THE SOUTH SEAS(1929); BLACK HILLS(1929)

Trevor Dennis
MAYTIME IN MAYFAIR(1952, Brit.)

Vincent Dennis
ROGUES' TAVERN, THE(1936); TOO MUCH BEEF(1936)

William Dennis
Silents
IS YOUR DAUGHTER SAFE?(1927)

Winifred Dennis
ONE PLUS ONE(1961, Can.); DIE, DIE, MY DARLING(1965, Brit.)
Silents
HER HERITAGE(1919, Brit.)

Winston Dennis
TIME BANDITS(1981, Brit.)

Patrick Dennis-Leigh
DEADHEAD MILES(1982)

Marian Dennish
DESERT HAWK, THE(1950); MILKMAN, THE(1950)

Edwin Dennison
Misc. Silents
BATTLER, THE(1919)

Eva Dennison
HIS GLORIOUS NIGHT(1929); LIGHTNIN'(1930); SQUAW MAN, THE(1931); ALMOST MARRIED(1932); PASSPORT TO HELL(1932); IT HAPPENED ONE NIGHT(1934); MAN WHO BROKE THE BANK AT MONTE CARLO, THE(1935); MOON'S OUR HOME, THE(1936); PRINCESS COMES ACROSS, THE(1936); LADY EVE, THE(1941); I MARRIED AN ANGEL(1942); PRIDE OF THE YANKEES, THE(1942)

Jo Carroll Dennison
PREHISTORIC WOMEN(1950); MILLIONAIRE FOR CHRISTY, A(1951); PICK-UP(1951)

Jo Dennison
BEYOND THE PURPLE HILLS(1950)
Jo-Carroll Dennison
LADIES OF WASHINGTON(1944); WINGED VICTORY(1944); STATE FAIR(1945); JOLSON STORY, THE(1946); MISSING LADY, THE(1946)
Leslie Dennison
ESCAPE TO GLORY(1940); THEY RAID BY NIGHT(1942); TO BE OR NOT TO BE(1942); CORNERED(1945); GREEN DOLPHIN STREET(1947); FEATHERED SERPENT, THE(1948); HOMECOMING(1948); JOHNNY STOOL PIGEON(1949); COURT JESTER, THE(1956)
Michael Dennison
BLIND GODDESS, THE(1948, Brit.)
William Dennison
Silents
KING OF DIAMONDS, THE(1918)
Dusty Dennison
PURPLE HAZE(1982), ed
Bill Denniston
Misc. Talkies
CAMERONS, THE(1974)
Reynolds Denniston
LOVE LETTERS OF A STAR(1936); LOVE ON THE RUN(1936)
Ray Dennus
BLACK KLANSMAN, THE(1966)
Barbara Denny
FOUR MEN AND A PRAYER(1938); LIGHT THAT FAILED, THE(1939); ONE NIGHT IN LISBON(1941)
Cynthia Denny
Misc. Talkies
DANDY(1973)
Dodo Denny
WILLY WONKA AND THE CHOCOLATE FACTORY(1971)
Drew Denny
PLAYERS(1979)
Ernest Denny
LAZYBONES(1935, Brit.), w; OH, WHAT A NIGHT(1935), d; VANITY(1935), d&w
Silents
SIDESHOW OF LIFE, THE(1924), w
Harry Denny
LOVES OF EDGAR ALLAN POE, THE(1942); SECRET AGENT OF JAPAN(1942); GOVERNMENT GIRL(1943); SONG OF BERNADETTE, THE(1943); HOODLUM SAINT, THE(1946); MAGNIFICENT DOLL(1946); TILL THE CLOUDS ROLL BY(1946); DEAD RECKONING(1947); SECRET BEYOND THE DOOR, THE(1948); UP IN CENTRAL PARK(1948); LET'S MAKE IT LEGAL(1951); CARRIE(1952); HELL AND HIGH WATER(1954); LONG GRAY LINE, THE(1955); OH, MEN! OH, WOMEN!(1957)
Irene Denny
MRS. MINIVER(1942)
John Denny
ESCAPE DANGEROUS(1947, Brit.), p
Malcolm Denny
Silents
ANY WOMAN(1925); KING OF KINGS, THE(1927)
Misc. Silents
DRUG STORE COWBOY(1925)
Martin Denny
FORBIDDEN ISLAND(1959)
Mary Kate Denny
GIRLS ON THE BEACH(1965)
Reginald Denny
CLEAR THE DECKS(1929); HIS LUCKY DAY(1929); RED HOT SPEED ½(1929); EMBARRASSING MOMENTS(1930); LADY'S MORALS, A(1930); MADAME SATAN(1930); OH, FOR A MAN!(1930); ONE HYSTERICAL NIGHT(1930), a, w, ed; THOSE THREE FRENCH GIRLS(1930); WHAT A MAN(1930); KIKI(1931); PARLOR, BEDROOM AND BATH(1931); PRIVATE LIVES(1931); STRANGE JUSTICE(1932); BARBARIAN, THE(1933); BIG BLUFF, THE(1933), a, d&w; IRON MASTER, THE(1933); ONLY YESTERDAY(1933); DANCING MAN(1934); FOG(1934); LITTLE MINISTER, THE(1934); LOST PATROL, THE(1934); OF HUMAN BONDAGE(1934); ONE MORE RIVER(1934); RICHEST GIRL IN THE WORLD, THE(1934); WE'RE RICH AGAIN(1934); WORLD MOVES ON, THE(1934); ANNA KARENINA(1935); HERE'S TO ROMANCE(1935); LADY IN SCARLET, THE(1935); LOTTERY LOVER(1935); NO MORE LADIES(1935); REMEMBER LAST NIGHT(1935); VAGABOND LADY(1935); IT COULDN'T HAVE HAPPENED--BUT IT DID(1936); MORE THAN A SECRETARY(1936); PENTHOUSE PARTY(1936); PREVIEW MURDER MYSTERY(1936); ROMEO AND JULIET(1936); TWO IN A CROWD(1936); BEG, BORROW OR STEAL(1937); BULLDOG DRUMMOND COMES BACK(1937); BULLDOG DRUMMOND ESCAPES(1937); BULLDOG DRUMMOND'S REVENGE(1937); GREAT GAMBINI, THE(1937); JOIN THE MARINES(1937); LET'S GET MARRIED(1937); WE'RE IN THE LEGION NOW(1937); WOMEN OF GLAMOUR(1937); BLOCKADE(1938); BULLDOG DRUMMOND IN AFRICA(1938); BULLDOG DRUMMOND'S PERIL(1938); FOUR MEN AND A PRAYER(1938); ARREST BULLDOG DRUMMOND(1939, Brit.); BULLDOG DRUMMOND'S BRIDE(1939); EVERYBODY'S BABY(1939); REBECCA(1940); SEVEN SINNERS(1940); SPRING PARADE(1940); APPOINTMENT FOR LOVE(1941); ONE NIGHT IN LISBON(1941); CAPTAINS OF THE CLOUDS(1942); EYES IN THE NIGHT(1942); OVER MY DEAD BODY(1942); SHERLOCK HOLMES AND THE VOICE OF TERROR(1942); THUNDER BIRDS(1942); CRIME DOCTOR'S STRANGEST CASE(1943); SONG OF THE OPEN ROAD(1944); LOVE LETTERS(1945); LOCKET, THE(1946); TANGIER(1946); CHRISTMAS EVE(1947); ESCAPE ME NEVER(1947); MACOMBER AFFAIR, THE(1947); MY FAVORITE BRUNETTE(1947); SECRET LIFE OF WALTER MITTY, THE(1947); MR. BLANDINGS BUILDS HIS DREAM HOUSE(1948); IROQUOIS TRAIL(1950); FORT VENGEANCE(1953); HINDU, THE(1953, Brit.); ABBOTT AND COSTELLO MEET DR. JEKYLL AND MR. HYDE(1954); WORLD FOR RANSOM(1954); ESCAPE TO BURMA(1955); AROUND THE WORLD IN 80 DAYS(1956); CAT BALLOU(1965); ASSAULT ON A QUEEN(1966); BATMAN(1966)
Misc. Talkies
STEPPING OUT(1931); MIDNIGHT PHANTOM, THE(1935)
Silents
OAKDALE AFFAIR, THE(1919); KENTUCKY DERBY, THE(1922); SHERLOCK HOLMES(1922); ABYSMAL BRUTE, THE(1923); OH, DOCTOR(1924); RECKLESS AGE, THE(1924); ROLLING HOME(1926); SKINNER'S DRESS SUIT(1926); TAKE IT

FROM ME(1926); WHAT HAPPENED TO JONES(1926); OUT ALL NIGHT(1927)
Misc. Silents
BRINGING UP BETTY(1919); DARK LANTERN, A(1920); 39 EAST(1920); FOOTLIGHTS(1921); IRON TRAIL, THE(1921); PRICE OF POSSESSION, THE(1921); TROPICAL LOVE(1921); FAST WORKER, THE(1924); SPORTING YOUTH(1924); CALIFORNIA STRAIGHT AHEAD(1925); I'LL SHOW YOU THE TOWN(1925); WHERE WAS I?(1925); CHEERFUL FRAUD, THE(1927); FAST AND FURIOUS(1927); ON YOUR TOES(1927); GOOD MORNING JUDGE(1928); NIGHT BIRD, THE(1928); THAT'S MY DADDY(1928); CLEAR THE DECKS(1929)
Steve Denny
NORSEMAN, THE(1978)
Susan Denny
SHERIFF OF FRACTURED JAW, THE(1958, Brit.); PURSUERS, THE(1961, Brit.); TOO HOT TO HANDLE(1961, Brit.); UNSTOPPABLE MAN, THE(1961, Brit.); SICILIANS, THE(1964, Brit.); 20,000 POUNDS KISS, THE(1964, Brit.); TALES FROM THE CRYPT(1972, Brit.)
Victor Denny
GREAT SINNER, THE(1949)
Alphonso DeNoble
ALICE, SWEET ALICE(1978)
Bill Denochelle
GRAND THEFT AUTO(1977)
Jacques Denoel
STRANGERS IN THE HOUSE(1949, Fr.)
Sam Denoff
SERIAL(1980)
Nick Denoia
SOME OF MY BEST FRIENDS ARE...(1971)
John W. DeNoria
GLASS KEY, THE(1942)
Georg DeNormand
WRITTEN ON THE WIND(1956)
George DeNormand
LONE WOLF SPY HUNT, THE(1939); STARDUST ON THE SAGE(1942); WEST OF THE LAW(1942); CLANCY STREET BOYS(1943); LAW OF THE VALLEY(1944); NEVADA(1944); GAY AMIGO, THE(1949); LOST TRIBE, THE(1949); FENCE RIDERS(1950); LAW OF THE PANHANDLE(1950); OUTLAW GOLD(1950); OUTLAWS OF TEXAS(1950); SILVER RAIDERS(1950); OKLAHOMA JUSTICE(1951); CANYON AMBUSH(1952); PAL JOEY(1957); RAISIN IN THE SUN, A(1961)
John Denos
DREAMS OF GLASS(1969); ONLY THING YOU KNOW, THE(1971, Can.); WANDA NEVADA(1979)
Tom Denove
TIME TO DIE, A(1983), ph
1984
LAST HORROR FILM, THE(1984), ph
Denny Densham
DEVIL ON HORSEBACK(1954, Brit.), ph; MAKE ME AN OFFER(1954, Brit.), ph
R. Densham
SOHO CONSPIRACY(1951, Brit.), ph
Ray Densham
EYES THAT KILL(1947, Brit.), ph; NIGHT COMES TOO SOON(1948, Brit.), ph
Patsy Densitt
ALFIE DARLING(1975, Brit.)
Gene Densmore
GAL YOUNG UN(1979)
1984
FLASH OF GREEN, A(1984)
John Densmore
GET CRAZY(1983)
Alan Dent
HENRY V(1946, Brit.), w; HAMLET(1948, Brit.), w; RICHARD III(1956, Brit.), w; WHERE'S JACK?(1969, Brit.), tech adv
Arthur Dent
OLD MOTHER RILEY, DETECTIVE(1943, Brit.); COMIN' THRU' THE RYE(1947, Brit.), p; BLESS 'EM ALL(1949, Brit.), w
Charles Dent
PAYOFF, THE(1943), md
David Dent
SKIMPY IN THE NAVY(1949, Brit.), p; MY DEATH IS A MOCKERY(1952, Brit.), p; MY WIFE'S LODGER(1952, Brit.), p; DISOBEDIENT(1953, Brit.), p; GREAT GAME, THE(1953, Brit.), p; IS YOUR HONEYMOON REALLY NECESSARY?(1953, Brit.), p; CROWDED DAY, THE(1954, Brit.), p; DON'T BLAME THE STORK(1954, Brit.), p; HAPPINESS OF THREE WOMEN, THE(1954, Brit.), p; WHAT EVERY WOMAN WANTS(1954, Brit.), p; YOU LUCKY PEOPLE(1955, Brit.), p; FUN AT ST. FANNY'S(1956, Brit.), p; STARS IN YOUR EYES(1956, Brit.), p
Liz Dent
LINCOLN CONSPIRACY, THE(1977)
Vernon Dent
TRUE TO LIFE(1943); MIDNIGHT DADDIES(1929); BUSINESS AND PLEASURE(1932); DARING DANGER(1932); DRAGNET PATROL(1932); MILLION DOLLAR LEGS(1932); RIDING TORNADO, THE(1932); TEXAS CYCLONE(1932); MANHATTAN MELODRAMA(1934); PAINTED VEIL, THE(1934); YOU'RE TELLING ME(1934); FUGITIVE SHERIFF, THE(1936); SAN FRANCISCO(1936); AWFUL TRUTH, THE(1937); EASY LIVING(1937); SHADOW, THE(1937); JUVENILE COURT(1938); OUTLAWS OF THE PRAIRIE(1938); THANKS FOR THE MEMORY(1938); VIVACIOUS LADY(1938); WHO KILLED GAIL PRESTON?(1938); YOU CAN'T TAKE IT WITH YOU(1938); BEASTS OF BERLIN(1939); LONE WOLF SPY HUNT, THE(1939); MR. SMITH GOES TO WASHINGTON(1939); ONLY ANGELS HAVE WINGS(1939); STANLEY AND LIVINGSTONE(1939); DOCTOR TAKES A WIFE(1940); HE STAYED FOR BREAKFAST(1940); LADY IN QUESTION, THE(1940); MEET JOHN DOE(1941); MISBEHAVING HUSBANDS(1941); GLASS KEY, THE(1942); HOUSE OF ERRORS(1942); MY FAVORITE BLONDE(1942); JAM SESSION(1944); MRS. PARKINGTON(1944); ONCE UPON A TIME(1944); SAN DIEGO, I LOVE YOU(1944); ROCKIN' IN THE ROCKIES(1945); SHE GETS HER MAN(1945); COWBOY BLUES(1946); HARVEY GIRLS, THE(1946); IT'S GREAT TO BE YOUNG(1946); NIGHT EDITOR(1946); RENEGADES(1946); IT HAD TO BE YOU(1947); SEA OF GRASS, THE(1947); SECRET LIFE OF WALTER MITTY, THE(1947); WILD HARVEST(1947); MAKE BELIEVE BALLROOM(1949); BONANZA TOWN(1951)

Silents
EXTRA GIRL, THE(1923); SOUL OF THE BEAST(1923); CAMERAMAN, THE(1928)
Misc. Silents
HIS FIRST FLAME(1927)
Keith Dentice
ANNIE HALL(1977)
Ludovico Dentice
DETECTIVE BELLI(1970, Ital.), w
Marco Dentici
SUPER FUZZ(1981), prod d; BLOW TO THE HEART(1983, Ital.), art d
Edward Dentith
MOONRAKER, THE(1958, Brit.); FOLLOW THAT HORSE!(1960, Brit.); HUMAN FACTOR, THE(1979, Brit.); SEA WOLVES, THE(1981, Brit.)
Marion Dentler
Silents
CLARION, THE(1916)
Arthur Denton
SAILING ALONG(1938, Brit.); FOR FREEDOM(1940, Brit.); SHEEPDOG OF THE HILLS(1941, Brit.); REMARKABLE MR. KIPPS(1942, Brit.); DUMMY TALKS, THE(1943, Brit.); MILLIONS LIKE US(1943, Brit.); GIVE US THE MOON(1944, Brit.); UNCENSORED(1944, Brit.); RANDOLPH FAMILY, THE(1945, Brit.); GRAND ESCAPADE, THE(1946, Brit.); I'LL TURN TO YOU(1946, Brit.); NOTHING VENTURE(1948, Brit.); ONCE UPON A DREAM(1949, Brit.); PASSPORT TO PIMLICO(1949, Brit.); WATERLOO ROAD(1949, Brit.); HUE AND CRY(1950, Brit.); GALLOPING MAJOR, THE(1951, Brit.); I'LL NEVER FORGET YOU(1951)
Christa Denton
1984
MICKI AND MAUDE(1984)
Coby Denton
OUT OF SIGHT(1966); WILD ANGELS, THE(1966); 80 STEPS TO JONAH(1969)
Crahan Denton
GREAT ST. LOUIS BANK ROBBERY, THE(1959); PARENT TRAP, THE(1961); YOUNG ONE, THE(1961, Mex.); BIRDMAN OF ALCATRAZ(1962); WALK ON THE WILD SIDE(1962); HUD(1963); BUS RILEY'S BACK IN TOWN(1965)
Crehan Denton
TO KILL A MOCKINGBIRD(1962); CAPTAIN NEWMAN, M.D.(1963)
Donna Denton
NASHVILLE(1975)
Gentle Roy Denton
DARWIN ADVENTURE, THE(1972, Brit.)
Geoffrey Denton
ADAM AND EVELYNE(1950, Brit.); ISLAND RESCUE(1952, Brit.); PROJECT M7(1953, Brit.); NAKED FURY(1959, Brit.); WITNESS, THE(1959, Brit.); LIFE IS A CIRCUS(1962, Brit.); TOUCH OF DEATH(1962, Brit.); GREAT ARMORED CAR SWINDLE, THE(1964); DANDY IN ASPIC, A(1968, Brit.); NOTHING BUT THE NIGHT(1975, Brit.)
Jack Denton
HELLCATS, THE(1968)
1984
SPLASH(1984)
Silents
FLYING FROM JUSTICE(1915, Brit.); LASS O' THE LOOMS, A(1919, Brit.), d; ERNEST MALTRAVERS(1920, Brit.), d; BACHELORS' CLUB, THE(1921, Brit.); GAY CORINTHIAN, THE(1924); NOTORIOUS MRS. CARRICK, THE(1924, Brit.); OLD BILL THROUGH THE AGES(1924, Brit.)
Misc. Silents
BARNABY(1919, Brit.), d; HEART OF A ROSE, THE(1919, Brit.), d; ERNEST MALTRAVERS(1920, Brit.), d; LADY AUDLEY'S SECRET(1920, Brit.), d; TWELVE POUND LOOK, THE(1920, Brit.), d; SYBIL(1921, Brit.), d
Kit Denton
DEMONSTRATOR(1971, Aus.), w
Morris Denton
HUCKLEBERRY FINN(1974)
Paul A. Denton
ROSEMARY'S BABY(1968)
Paul Denton
CATERED AFFAIR, THE(1956); SHOCK TREATMENT(1964)
J. Denton-Thompson
Silents
MAN'S SHADOW, A(1920, Brit.)
Misc. Silents
BY BERWIN BANKS(1920, Brit.); TWO LITTLE WOODEN SHOES(1920, Brit.)
Erika Dentzler
PLAYTIME(1973, Fr.)
Italia DeNubila
IMMORTAL SERGEANT, THE(1943); MUSIC IN MANHATTAN(1944); WEST OF THE PECOS(1945)
Maurice Denuziere
1984
LOUISIANE(1984, Fr./Can.), w
Bob Denver
FOR THOSE WHO THINK YOUNG(1964); WHO'S MINDING THE MINT?(1967); DID YOU HEAR THE ONE ABOUT THE TRAVELING SALESLADY?(1968); SWEET RIDE, THE(1968); WACKIEST WAGON TRAIN IN THE WEST, THE(1976)
Joan Denver
WARNING TO WANTONS, A(1949, Brit.)
John Denver
OH, GOD!(1977)
Karl Denver
JUST FOR FUN(1963, Brit.)
Lucille Denver
WOMEN IN THE WIND(1939)
Mary Esther Denver
BORN TO BE LOVED(1959)
Maryesther Denver
UNDER THE YUM-YUM TREE(1963); FORTUNE COOKIE, THE(1966); PROJECT X(1968); FRASIER, THE SENSUOUS LION(1973); WICKED, WICKED(1973)

Megan Denver
HIRED HAND, THE(1971)
Robert Denver
TAKE HER, SHE'S MINE(1963)
Robert [Bob] Denver
PRIVATE'S AFFAIR, A(1959)
Barry Denville
RELUCTANT WIDOW, THE(1951, Brit.)
Jay Denyer
FINGER OF GUILT(1956, Brit.)
Geoffrey Denys
WALLET, THE(1952, Brit.); MAKE MINE A DOUBLE(1962, Brit.)
Eumir Deodato
ONION FIELD, THE(1979), m
Bart DePalma
HI, MOM!(1970)
Brian DePalma
GET TO KNOW YOUR RABBIT(1972), d; HOME MOVIES(1979), p, d, w
Walter DePalma
DOUGHGIRLS, THE(1944)
Gerard Depardieu
NATHALIE GRANGER(1972, Fr.); GOING PLACES(1974, Fr.); BAROCCO(1976, Fr.); 1900(1976, Ital.); BYE BYE MONKEY(1978, Ital/Fr.); GET OUT YOUR HANDKERCHIEFS(1978, Fr.); LEFT-HANDED WOMAN, THE(1980, Ger.); LOULOU(1980, Fr.); MON ONCLE D'AMERIQUE(1980, Fr.); LAST METRO, THE(1981, Fr.); WOMAN NEXT DOOR, THE(1981, Fr.); CHOICE OF ARMS(1983, Fr.); DANTON(1983); MOON IN THE GUTTER, THE(1983, Fr./Ital.); RETURN OF MARTIN GUERRE, THE(1983, Fr.)
1984
LES COMPERES(1984, Fr.)
Dave DePate
NARCOTICS STORY, THE(1958), ed
David H. DePatie
TRAIL OF THE PINK PANTHER, THE(1982), w
Dave DePaul
WALK TALL(1960)
Ernest Depew
BRIDE OF THE DESERT(1929), ph
Silents
LIGHT IN THE WINDOW, THE(1927), ph; DEVIL'S TOWER(1929), ph
Gary DePew
1984
ICE PIRATES, THE(1984)
Hap Depew
HANDCUFFED(1929), ph; SHOULD A GIRL MARRY?(1929), ph; NEAR THE RAINBOW'S END(1930), ph; DEVIL'S BROTHER, THE(1933), ph
Silents
GYPSY OF THE NORTH(1928), ph; ISLE OF LOST MEN(1928), ph; MAN FROM HEADQUARTERS(1928), ph; MY HOME TOWN(1928), ph; ANNE AGAINST THE WORLD(1929), ph; DEVIL'S CHAPLAIN(1929), ph; FIGHTING TERROR, THE(1929), ph; INVADERS, THE(1929), ph; LAST ROUNDUP, THE(1929), ph; LONE HORSEMAN, THE(1929), ph; OKLAHOMA KID, THE(1929), ph; RIDERS OF THE RIO GRANDE(1929), ph
Joe Depew
QUEEN OF THE NIGHTCLUBS(1929)
Joseph Depew
Silents
TIMOTHY'S QUEST(1922); JACQUELINE, OR BLAZING BARRIERS(1923); STEADFAST HEART, THE(1923); GRIT(1924); ICEBOUND(1924)
Misc. Silents
FIFTH HORSEMAN, THE(1924)
Patrick Depeyrat
INQUISITOR, THE(1982, Fr.)
Albert DePina
JOE PALOOKA, CHAMP(1946), w
Manuel DePina
BLACK GUNN(1972); SWASHBUCKLER(1976)
Philippe Deplanche
1984
THREE CROWNS OF THE SAILOR(1984, Fr.)
Jay DePland
SILENT RAGE(1982)
Pierrette Deplanque
ME(1970, Fr.)
Don DePollo
TOWING(1978)
Harry Depp
ONE HOUR LATE(1935); COLLEEN(1936); DESIRE(1936); FATAL LADY(1936); LONE WOLF RETURNS, THE(1936); ROSE BOWL(1936); FIND THE WITNESS(1937); GO-GETTER, THE(1937); LOVE IS NEWS(1937); PALS OF THE SADDLE(1938); EAST SIDE OF HEAVEN(1939); LITTLE ACCIDENT(1939); MADE FOR EACH OTHER(1939); TELL NO TALES(1939); DANGER AHEAD(1940); FOREIGN CORRESPONDENT(1940); I'M NOBODY'S SWEETHEART NOW(1940); MAN I MARRIED, THE(1940); MORTAL STORM, THE(1940); REMEMBER THE NIGHT(1940); CONFESSIONS OF BOSTON BLACKIE(1941); HONOLULU LU(1941); LADY EVE, THE(1941); PAPER BULLETS(1941); RICHEST MAN IN TOWN(1941); BROADWAY BIG SHOT(1942); HEART OF THE RIO GRANDE(1942); LIVING GHOST, THE(1942); MAGNIFICENT DOPE, THE(1942); PHANTOM KILLER(1942); GIRL CRAZY(1943); CHARLIE CHAN IN BLACK MAGIC(1944); EVER SINCE VENUS(1944); JOHNNY DOESN'T LIVE HERE ANY MORE(1944); LADIES OF WASHINGTON(1944); LADY AND THE MONSTER, THE(1944); PORT OF 40 THIEVES, THE(1944); CAPTAIN TUGBOAT ANNIE(1945); FASHION MODEL(1945); ROAD TO ALCATRAZ(1945); STATE FAIR(1945); THERE GOES KELLY(1945); WONDER MAN(1945); DO YOU LOVE ME?(1946); LADY LUCK(1946); LEAVE HER TO HEAVEN(1946); SHADOWS OVER CHINATOWN(1946); TWO SMART PEOPLE(1946); SECRET LIFE OF WALTER MITTY, THE(1947)
Silents
LOVE GIRL, THE(1916); SAVING THE FAMILY NAME(1916); NOBODY'S MONEY(1923); INEZ FROM HOLLYWOOD(1924); WHEN THE WIFE'S AWAY(1926)

Misc. Silents
STRANGE WOMAN, THE(1918); HIS LAST RACE(1923)

Johnny Depp
1984
NIGHTMARE ON ELM STREET, A(1984)

Gordon Deppe
1984
LISTEN TO THE CITY(1984, Can.), m

Hans Deppe
ETERNAL LOVE(1960, Ger.), d

Harry Depps
IN OLD NEW MEXICO(1945)

Bill DePrato
BLAST OF SILENCE(1961); LADY LIBERTY(1972, Ital./Fr.)

William DePrato
JUKE BOX RACKET(1960)

Xavier Depraz
BUTTERFLY ON THE SHOULDER, A(1978, Fr.)

Jeffrey Deprend
Silents
SLANDER THE WOMAN(1923), w

Ed DePriest
KILL, THE(1968), p; MANTIS IN LACE(1968), spec eff

James E. dePriest
KENNY AND CO.(1976)

Louis DePron
BABES ON SWING STREET(1944), ch

Lena Deptula
EVE WANTS TO SLEEP(1961, Pol.), ed; LOTNA(1966, Pol.), ed

Wesley E. Depue
THIRSTY DEAD, THE(1975), p

Julia Depyer
OUTLAND(1981)

Thomas DeQuincey
CONFESSIONS OF AN OPIUM EATER(1962), w

Ricky Der
TARZAN'S THREE CHALLENGES(1963)

Veith der Furstenberg
ALICE IN THE CITIES(1974, W. Ger.), w

Van der Veer
EXORCIST II: THE HERETIC(1977), spec eff

Phae Dera
THAT TENDER TOUCH(1969)

Lynne Deragon
RABID(1976, Can.)

Clif DeRaita
FAN, THE(1981)

Margaret Deramee
STATE FAIR(1962)

Theda Deramus
1984
REPO MAN(1984), cos

Jacques Deray
RIFIFI IN TOKYO(1963, Fr./Ital.), d, w; SYMPHONY FOR A MASSACRE(1965, Fr./Ital.), d, w; THAT MAN GEORGE!(1967, Fr./Ital./Span.), d, w; BORSALINO(1970, Fr.), d, w; OUTSIDE MAN, THE(1973, U.S./FR.), d, w; BORSALINO AND CO.(1974, Fr.), d, w; BUTTERFLY ON THE SHOULDER, A(1978, Fr.), d; THREE MEN TO DESTROY(1980, Fr.), d, w

Mimi Derba
SANTA(1932, Mex.)

Vadim Derbenev
SANDU FOLLOWS THE SUN(1965, USSR), ph

Vadim Derbenyov
LULLABY(1961, USSR), ph

Brown Derby
QUEEN OF SPADES(1948, Brit.); SUSPENDED ALIBI(1957, Brit.)

Ted Derby
MARLOWE(1969)

Delia Derbyshire
LEGEND OF HELL HOUSE, THE(1973, Brit.), m

Jacques Dercourt
LES MAITRES DU TEMPS(1982, Fr./Switz./Ger.), p

Ann Dere
STREETCAR NAMED DESIRE, A(1951); TAXI(1953)

Colette Dereal
HAPPY ROAD, THE(1957)

Collette Dereal
LITTLE BOY LOST(1953)

Rosine Derean
BARRANCO(1932, Fr.); SACRIFICE OF HONOR(1938, Fr.); STORY OF A CHEAT, THE(1938, Fr.)

Mario Derecchi
SWINDLE, THE(1962, Fr./Ital.), p

Bo Derek
ORCA(1977); 10(1979); CHANGE OF SEASONS, A(1980); FANTASIES(1981); TARZAN, THE APE MAN(1981), a, p
1984
BOLERO(1984), a, p

John Derek
I'LL BE SEEING YOU(1944); DOUBLE LIFE, A(1947); ALL THE KING'S MEN(1949); KNOCK ON ANY DOOR(1949); ROGUES OF SHERWOOD FOREST(1950); FAMILY SECRET, THE(1951); MASK OF THE AVENGER(1951); SATURDAY'S HERO(1951); SCANDAL SHEET(1952); THUNDERBIRDS(1952); AMBUSH AT TOMAHAWK GAP(1953); LAST POSSE, THE(1953); MISSION OVER KOREA(1953); PRINCE OF PIRATES(1953); SEA OF LOST SHIPS(1953); ADVENTURES OF HAJJI BABA(1954); OUTCAST, THE(1954); ANNAPOLIS STORY, AN(1955); PRINCE OF PLAYERS(1955); RUN FOR COVER(1955); LEATHER SAINT, THE(1956); TEN COMMANDMENTS, THE(1956); FLESH IS WEAK, THE(1957, Brit.); FURY AT SHOWDOWN(1957); OMAR KHAYYAM(1957); HIGH HELL(1958); EXODUS(1960); PRISONER OF THE VOLGA(1960, Fr./Ital.); NIGHTMARE IN THE SUN(1964), a, p; ONCE BEFORE I DIE(1967, U.S./Phil.), a, p&d; BOY...A GIRL, A(1969), d,w&ph; CHILDISH THINGS(1969), d, ph; FANTASIES(1981), d,w&ph; TARZAN, THE APE MAN(1981), d, ph
1984
BOLERO(1984), d,w&ph

Misc. Talkies
CONFESSIONS OF TOM HARRIS(1972), d

Maya Deren
MAEVA(1961), w

Susan Derendorf
BABY, IT'S YOU(1983)

Claude Derepp
1984
THREE CROWNS OF THE SAILOR(1984, Fr.)

David Dereszke
THUNDER AT THE BORDER(1966, Ger./Yugo.), w

Alexander Derevitsky
NIGHTS OF LUCRETIA BORGIA, THE(1960, Ital.), m

Alexandre Derevitsky
LOVES OF SALAMMBO, THE(1962, Fr./Ital.), m

Philip S. Derfler
STERILE CUCKOO, THE(1969)

Dianne Derfner
1984
WINDY CITY(1984)

Dana Derfus
LOVE BUG, THE(1968); BLACK OAK CONSPIRACY(1977); ESCAPE FROM ALCATRAZ(1979)

Robert DeRise
HAIL(1973), ed

Joe DeRita
FRENCH KEY, THE(1946); HIGH SCHOOL HERO(1946)

Jacqueline DeRiver
COURAGEOUS DR. CHRISTIAN, THE(1940)

Jacques Derives
ROYAL AFFAIRS IN VERSAILLES(1957, Fr.)

K.N. Derjavin
HOUSE OF GREED(1934, USSR), w

Paul J. Derkum
Silents
RACING FOR LIFE(1924)

August Derleth
SHUTTERED ROOM, THE(1968, Brit.), w

Lucy Derleth
WEREWOLF IN A GIRL'S DORMITORY(1961, Ital./Aust.)

Dominique Derly
MY UNCLE(1958, Fr.)

Max Derly
THEY MET ON SKIS(1940, Fr.)

Bruce Derm
WILD ANGELS, THE(1966)

Edouard Dermit
ORPHEUS(1950, Fr.); LES ENFANTS TERRIBLES(1952, Fr.); TESTAMENT OF ORPHEUS, THE(1962, Fr.)

Drew Dermorest
HIGH BARBAREE(1947)

Anton Dermota
LIFE AND LOVES OF MOZART, THE(1959, Ger.)

Anton Dermots
DON GIOVANNI(1955, Brit.)

Germaine Dermoz
MONSIEUR VINCENT(1949, Fr.); PRIZE, THE(1952, Fr.)

Bruce Dern
WILD RIVER(1960); HUSH... HUSH, SWEET CHARLOTTE(1964); MARNIE(1964); ST. VALENTINE'S DAY MASSACRE, THE(1967); TRIP, THE(1967); WAR WAGON, THE(1967); WATERHOLE NO. 3(1967); HANG'EM HIGH(1968); PSYCH-OUT(1968); WILL PENNY(1968); CASTLE KEEP(1969); CYCLE SAVAGES(1969); NUMBER ONE(1969); SUPPORT YOUR LOCAL SHERIFF(1969); THEY SHOOT HORSES, DON'T THEY?(1969); BLOODY MAMA(1970); REBEL ROUSERS(1970); DRIVE, HE SAID(1971); INCREDIBLE TWO-HEADED TRANSPLANT, THE(1971); COWBOYS, THE(1972); KING OF MARVIN GARDENS, THE(1972); SILENT RUNNING(1972); THUMB TRIPPING(1972); LAUGHING POLICEMAN, THE(1973); GREAT GATSBY, THE(1974); POSSE(1975); SMILE(1975); FAMILY PLOT(1976); TWIST, THE(1976, Fr.); WON TON TON, THE DOG WHO SAVED HOLLYWOOD(1976); BLACK SUNDAY(1977); COMING HOME(1978); DRIVER, THE(1978); MIDDLE AGE CRAZY(1980, Can.); TATTOO(1981); HARRY TRACY–DESPERADO(1982, Can.); THAT CHAMPIONSHIP SEASON(1982)

Laura Dern
FOXES(1980); LADIES AND GENTLEMEN, THE FABULOUS STAINS(1982)
1984
TEACHERS(1984)

Derna-Hazell
DUMMY TALKS, THE(1943, Brit.)

Georges Dernier
CHILDREN OF CHAOS(1950, Fr.), p

Alain Derobe
PARIS OOH-LA-LA!(1963, U.S./Fr.), ph; VOYAGE OF SILENCE(1968, Fr.), ph; MAN WITH CONNECTIONS, THE(1970, Fr.), ph; EGLANTINE(1972, Fr.), ph; 1★2?(1975, Fr.), ph; ONE NIGHT STAND(1976, Fr.), ph

Chris DeRoche
DAY AFTER HALLOWEEN, THE(1981, Aus.), w

Darrell DeRoche
1984
PRODIGAL, THE(1984)

Everett DeRoche
HARLEQUIN(1980, Aus.), w; DAY AFTER HALLOWEEN, THE(1981, Aus.), w; ROAD GAMES(1981, Aus.), w
1984
RAZORBACK(1984, Aus.), w

Louis deRochemont
WHISTLE AT EATON FALLS(1951), p

Georges Derocles
OLIVE TREES OF JUSTICE, THE(1967, Fr.), p

Thierry Derocles
CHOICE OF ARMS(1983, Fr.), ed

Julien Derode
VISIT, THE(1964, Ger./Fr./Ital./U.S.), p; MALE COMPANION(1965, Fr./Ital.), p; SYMPHONY FOR A MASSACRE(1965, Fr./Ital.), p; SLEEPING CAR MURDER THE(1966, Fr.), p; DAY OF THE JACKAL, THE(1973, Brit./Fr.), p

Al DeRogatis
HEAVEN CAN WAIT(1978)

Paul DeRolf
TEN COMMANDMENTS, THE(1956); 1941(1979), ch

Lorraine DeRome
SECRET LIFE OF WALTER MITTY, THE(1947)

Edward DeRoo
HELL BOUND(1957)

Dore DeRosa
EVERY MAN FOR HIMSELF(1980, Fr.)

Franco DeRosa
RETURN FROM THE ASHES(1965, U.S./Brit.); ARRIVEDERCI, BABY!(1966, Brit.); JOURNEY TO THE FAR SIDE OF THE SUN(1969, Brit.); RICHARD'S THINGS(1981, Brit.)

Justin Derosa
1984
FEAR CITY(1984)

Rob DeRosa
VOICES(1979)

Enrique DeRosas
HI GAUCHO!(1936); SANDFLOW(1937); SWING HIGH, SWING LOW(1937)
Misc. Talkies
TIMBERESQUE(1937)

Franco Derossa
THAT LUCKY TOUCH(1975, Brit.)

Gianetto DeRossi
DON'T OPEN THE WINDOW(1974, Ital.), spec eff
1984
DUNE(1984), makeup

Bernard Deroux
NIGHT AND DAY(1946); FOXES OF HARROW, THE(1947); VOICE OF THE TURTLE, THE(1947)

Harry DeRoy
Silents
CHIMMIE FADDEN(1915); PARADISE GARDEN(1917)

Richard DeRoy
TWO PEOPLE(1973), w

Scott DeRoy
SOMETHING WICKED THIS WAY COMES(1983)

Albert Derr
MANHATTAN ANGEL(1948), w; FOR SINGLES ONLY(1968), w

Celia Derr
PHANTOM OF THE PARADISE(1974)

E. B. Derr
HOLIDAY(1930), p; NIGHT WORK(1930), p; PARDON MY GUN(1930), p; SIN TAKES A HOLIDAY(1930), p; SWING HIGH(1930), p; PAINTED DESERT, THE(1931), p; BATTLE OF GREED(1934), p; DRUMS OF DESTINY(1937), p; GLORY TRAIL, THE(1937), p; RAW TIMBER(1937), p; UNDER STRANGE FLAGS(1937), p; BAREFOOT BOY(1938), p; FEMALE FUGITIVE(1938), p; GANG BULLETS(1938), p; LAW COMMANDS, THE(1938), p; MY OLD KENTUCKY HOME(1938), p; OLD LOUISIANA(1938), p; REBELLION(1938), p; CONVICT'S CODE(1939), p; GIRL FROM RIO, THE(1939), p; I AM A CRIMINAL(1939), p; SHOULD A GIRL MARRY?(1939), p; STAR REPORTER(1939), p; UNDERCOVER AGENT(1939), p; CRIMINALS WITHIN(1941), p; SECRET EVIDENCE(1941), p; DEERSLAYER(1943), p, w

E. R. Derr
COUNTY FAIR(1937), p

E.D. Derr
BEYOND VICTORY(1931), p

Richard Derr
CHARLIE CHAN IN RIO(1941); MAN AT LARGE(1941); CASTLE IN THE DESERT(1942); COMMANDOS STRIKE AT DAWN, THE(1942); GENTLEMAN AT HEART, A(1942); JUST OFF BROADWAY(1942); MAN WHO WOULDN'T DIE, THE(1942); TEN GENTLEMEN FROM WEST POINT(1942); TONIGHT WE RAID CALAIS(1943); SECRET HEART, THE(1946); BRIDE GOES WILD, THE(1948); JOAN OF ARC(1948); LUXURY LINER(1948); GUILTY OF TREASON(1950); WHEN WORLDS COLLIDE(1951); SOMETHING TO LIVE FOR(1951); INVISIBLE AVENGER, THE(1958); TERROR IS A MAN(1959, U.S./Phil.); ROSIE!(1967); THREE IN THE ATTIC(1968); ADAM AT 6 A.M.(1970); DROWNING POOL, THE(1975); AMERICAN GIGOLO(1980); FIREFOX(1982)
Misc. Talkies
BOURBON ST. SHADOWS(1962)

Dickie Derrel
MADAME BOVARY(1949); DOUBLE DYNAMITE(1951)

George Derrick
STORM OVER LISBON(1944); JEOPARDY(1953); SOMBRERO(1953)

Michael Derrick
GIRL IN GOLD BOOTS(1968)

William Derrick
OCTOPUSSY(1983, Brit.)

Cleavant Derricks
FORT APACHE, THE BRONX(1981)
1984
MOSCOW ON THE HUDSON(1984)

Jacques Derrida
1984
GHOST DANCE(1984, Brit.)

Marcelle Derrien
MAN ABOUT TOWN(1947, Fr.)

Bill Derringer
GOODBYE COLUMBUS(1969)

Rick Derringer
SGT. PEPPER'S LONELY HEARTS CLUB BAND(1978)

William Derringer
DARK, THE(1979)

Robert C. Dertano
BLONDE PICKUP(1955), d; JOURNEY TO FREEDOM(1957), d, ed

Chantal Deruaz
DIVA(1982, Fr.); RETURN OF MARTIN GUERRE, THE(1983, Fr.)

Carmen Fay DeRue
Silents
JACK AND THE BEANSTALK(1917)

Michel Deruel
LADY L(1965, Fr./Ital.), makeup

Michel Deruelle
IS PARIS BURNING?(1966, U.S./Fr.), makeup; LIVE FOR LIFE(1967, Fr./Ital.), makeup; SERGEANT, THE(1968), makeup; LA PRISONNIERE(1969, Fr./Ital.), makeup; MISSISSIPPI MERMAID(1970, Fr./Ital.), makeup; SICILIAN CLAN, THE(1970, Fr.), makeup

Michele Deruelle
IN THE FRENCH STYLE(1963, U.S./Fr.), makeup

John Derum
SIDECAR RACERS(1975, Aus.); TRESPASSERS, THE(1976, Aus.); NIGHT OF THE PROWLER, THE(1979, Aus.)

Jacqueline Derval
BATTLE OF THE WORLDS(1961, Ital.); DUEL OF CHAMPIONS(1964 Ital./Span.)

Michel Dervelle
SECRET WORLD(1969, Fr.), makeup

Frank Dervieux
JE T'AIME(1974, Can.), m

Joseph Dervim
FAST COMPANY(1953), ed

Joseph Dervin
DESIRE ME(1947), ed; NO QUESTIONS ASKED(1951), ed; DESPERATE SEARCH(1952), ed; BRIGHT ROAD(1953), ed; SPY IN THE GREEN HAT, THE(1966), ed; SPY WITH MY FACE, THE(1966), ed; BRIGHTY OF THE GRAND CANYON(1967), ed

Charles Dervis
Silents
RED MARK, THE(1928)

Clarence Derwent
NIGHT ANGEL, THE(1931); STANLEY AND LIVINGSTONE(1939); STORY OF VERNON AND IRENE CASTLE, THE(1939); WE ARE NOT ALONE(1939); BRITISH INTELLIGENCE(1940); UNCLE VANYA(1958)

Hal Derwin
SMASH-UP, THE STORY OF A WOMAN(1947); EVERYBODY'S DANCIN'(1950)

Jordan Derwin
I'M DANCING AS FAST AS I CAN(1982)

Tibor Dery
LOVE(1972, Hung.), w

Lenochka Derzhavina
THERE WAS AN OLD COUPLE(1967, USSR)

Van Des Autels
HOW TO MARRY A MILLIONAIRE(1953); ROBE, THE(1953); CROOKED WEB, THE(1955)

Michael Des Barres
TO SIR, WITH LOVE(1967, Brit.)

Guy Des Cars
GREEN SCARF, THE(1954, Brit.), w

Guillaume Des Forets
FOUR NIGHTS OF A DREAMER(1972, Fr.)

Simon Des Innocents
LE BEAU MARIAGE(1982, Fr.), m

Ghislaine Des Jonqueres
LE MANS(1971), ed

Francoise des Ligneris
PSYCHE 59(1964, Brit.), w

Ines Des Longchamps
STARDUST(1974, Brit.)

Jean Des Vallieres
MY SEVEN LITTLE SINS(1956, Fr./Ital.), w

Alfredo DeSa
WE'VE NEVER BEEN LICKED(1943); ANGEL ON THE AMAZON(1948)

Ana DeSade
Misc. Talkies
SORCERESS(1983)

Jacques Desagneau
DEAD RUN(1961, Fr./Ital./Ger.), ed; LOVE AND THE FRENCHWOMAN(1961, Fr.), ed; DON'T TEMPT THE DEVIL(1964, Fr./Ital.), ed; MAN FROM COCODY(1966, Fr./Ital.), ed

Jacques Desagneaux
MADAME DU BARRY(1954 Fr./Ital.), ed; ADORABLE CREATURES(1956, Fr.), ed; NANA(1957, Fr./Ital.), ed; NATHALIE(1958, Fr.), ed; LAW IS THE LAW, THE(1959, Fr.), ed; BABETTE GOES TO WAR(1960, Fr.), ed; DYNAMITE JACK(1961, Fr.), ed; MADAME(1963, Fr./Ital./Span.), ed

Jean Desagneaux
GYPSY FURY(1950, Fr.), ed; FANFAN THE TULIP(1952, Fr.), ed

Anang Desai
GANDHI(1982)

Chandrakant Desai
GLADIATORS, THE(1970, Swed.)

Kanu Desai
TIGER AND THE FLAME, THE(1955, India), cos

Shelley Desai
IMPOSTORS(1979)

Shelly Desai
Q(1982)

Vasant Desai
MONSOON(1953), m; TIGER AND THE FLAME, THE(1955, India), m; TWO EYES, TWELVE HANDS(1958, India), m

Claude Desailly
TONIGHT THE SKIRTS FLY(1956, Fr.), w; FIRE IN THE FLESH(1964, Fr.), w

Jean Desailly
SYMPHONIE PASTORALE(1948, Fr.); JUST A BIG, SIMPLE GIRL(1949, Fr.); SYLVIA AND THE PHANTOM(1950, Fr.); GRAND MANEUVER, THE(1956, Fr.); ROYAL AFFAIRS IN VERSAILLES(1957, Fr.); MAIGRET LAYS A TRAP(1958, Fr.); PASSION OF SLOW FIRE, THE(1962, Fr.); FINGERMAN, THE(1963, Fr.); DOULOS– THE FINGER MAN(1964, Fr./Ital.); SOFT SKIN, THE(1964, Fr.); 25TH HOUR, THE(1967, Fr./Ital./Yugo.); ASSASSINATION OF TROTSKY, THE(1972 Fr./Ital.); COP, A(1973, Fr.); DIRTY MONEY(1977, Fr.)

Nicole Desailly
MATA HARI(1965, Fr./Ital.)

Paul Desailly
SEVEN CAPITAL SINS(1962, Fr./Ital.)

Frank DeSal
BOOK OF NUMBERS(1973)

Francis DeSales
TERROR AT MIDNIGHT(1956); ALL MINE TO GIVE(1957); JAILHOUSE ROCK(1957); WAYWARD GIRL, THE(1957); APACHE TERRITORY(1958); TOO MUCH, TOO SOON(1958); LET NO MAN WRITE MY EPITAPH(1960); SUNRISE AT CAMPOBELLO(1960); SERGEANT RYKER(1968)

Peter DeSalis
WILD DUCK, THE(1983, Aus.)

Gerard Desalles
WE ARE ALL NAKED(1970, Can./Fr.)

Ann DeSalvo
STARDUST MEMORIES(1980)

Anne DeSalvo
ARTHUR(1981); I'M DANCING AS FAST AS I CAN(1982); MY FAVORITE YEAR(1982); D.C. CAB(1983); LOVESICK(1983)

Rolfe Desan
CHARLIE CHAN IN THE CITY OF DARKNESS(1939)

Gino DeSanotis
PONTIUS PILATE(1967, Fr./Ital.), w

Dina DeSantis
LOVE AND LARCENY(1963, Fr./Ital.)

Giuseppe DeSantis
ITALIANO BRAVA GENTE(1965, Ital./USSR), d, w

Joe DeSantis
FULL OF LIFE(1956); LAST HUNT, THE(1956); TENSION AT TABLE ROCK(1956); DINO(1957); CRY TOUGH(1959); AMERICAN DREAM, AN(1966); MADAME X(1966)

Pasquale DeSantis
MIDNIGHT PLEASURES(1975, Ital.), ph

Pasqualino DeSantis
THREE BROTHERS(1982, Ital.), ph
1984
MISUNDERSTOOD(1984), ph

Tony DeSantis
RITZ, THE(1976)

Michael DeSanto
D.C. CAB(1983)

Francesca deSapio
GODFATHER, THE, PART II(1974)

Serge Desarnauds
PASSION(1983, Fr./Switz.)

Raul DeSarro
ANTHONY OF PADUA(1952, Ital.), w

Lorraine DeSart
ROBERTA(1935)

Gerard Desarthe
LET JOY REIGN SUPREME(1977, Fr.)
1984
LOVE IN GERMANY, A(1984, Fr./Ger.)

Rudy DeSaxe
LAWLESS RIDER, THE(1954), m

Peter Desbarats
DON'T LET THE ANGELS FALL(1969, Can.)

Helene Desbiez
1984
UNTIL SEPTEMBER(1984)

Sylvie Desbois
VISITING HOURS(1982, Can.)

Jean Desbordes
BLOOD OF A POET, THE(1930, Fr.)

Philip Desborough
SCARLET PIMPERNEL, THE(1935, Brit.)

Francois Descamps
Misc. Silents
PERILOUS VALLEY(1920)

Marie-Jo Descas
1984
SUGAR CANE ALLEY(1984, Fr.)

France Descaut
AMAZING MONSIEUR FABRE, THE(1952, Fr.)

Linda DeScenna
FATSO(1980), set d; SECOND THOUGHTS(1983), set d
1984
LONELY GUY, THE(1984), set d

Charles Deschamps
LADY ON A TRAIN(1945); LOVERS OF VERONA, THE(1951, Fr.); GAME OF LOVE, THE(1954, Fr.); INNOCENTS IN PARIS(1955, Brit.)

Claude Deschamps
FIRE WITHIN, THE(1964, Fr./Ital.)

Hubert Deschamps
FRENCH CANCAN(1956, Fr.); FRANTIC(1961, Fr.); ZAZIE(1961, Fr.); LOVERS ON A TIGHTROPE(1962, Fr.); FIRE WITHIN, THE(1964, Fr./Ital.); FRIEND OF THE FAMILY(1965, Fr./Ital.); MALE COMPANION(1965, Fr./Ital.); MURDER AT 45

R.P.M.(1965, Fr.); MAGNIFICENT ONE, THE(1974, Fr./Ital.); ZIG-ZAG(1975, Fr./Ital.); DEAR DETECTIVE(1978, Fr.)

Jacques Deschamps
GODSON, THE(1972, Ital./Fr.)

Josiane Deschamps
1984
LOUISIANE(1984, Fr./Can.), makeup

Josianne Deschamps
1984
BAY BOY(1984, Can.), makeup

Yves Deschamps
MOON IN THE GUTTER, THE(1983, Fr./Ital.), ed

Caleb Deschanel
BEING THERE(1979), ph; BLACK STALLION, THE(1979), ph; MORE AMERICAN GRAFFITI(1979), ph; ESCAPE ARTIST, THE(1982), d; BLACK STALLION RETURNS, THE(1983), ph; RIGHT STUFF, THE(1983), ph
1984
NATURAL, THE(1984), ph

Mary Jo Deschanel
RIGHT STUFF, THE(1983)
1984
2010(1984)

Sandra Descher
COBWEB, THE(1955); INTERRUPTED MELODY(1955); PRODIGAL, THE(1955)

Sandy Descher
IT GROWS ON TREES(1952); MY PAL GUS(1952); LAST TIME I SAW PARIS, THE(1954); THEM!(1954); THREE RING CIRCUS(1954); BOTTOM OF THE BOTTLE, THE(1956); MAN IN THE GREY FLANNEL SUIT, THE(1956); OPPOSITE SEX, THE(1956); THREE BRAVE MEN(1957); SPACE CHILDREN, THE(1958)
Misc. Talkies
GIFT FOR HEIDI, A(1958)

Frank Deschon
Silents
GIRL IN THE DARK, THE(1918)

Colette Descombes
FIRST TASTE OF LOVE(1962, Fr.); UNSATISFIED, THE(1964, Span.)

Paul Descombies
GUINGUETTE(1959, Fr.)

Anne Marie Descott
SORCERER(1977)

George Descrieres
WOULD-BE GENTLEMAN, THE(1960, Fr.)

Georges Descrieres
LOVERS ON A TIGHTROPE(1962, Fr.); MARRIAGE OF FIGARO, THE(1963, Fr.); TWO FOR THE ROAD(1967, Brit.); FLEA IN HER EAR, A(1968, Fr.)

Edouard DeSegonzac
CATHERINE & CO.(1976, Fr.), w

Gladys DeSegonzac
LOVE AND DEATH(1975), cos

Andre DeSegurola
SONG O' MY HEART(1930)

Andres DeSegurola
Misc. Silents
CARDBOARD LOVER, THE(1928)

William DeSeta
SCALPEL(1976), prod d; SOLDIER, THE(1982), prod d

William F. DeSeta
TERROR EYES(1981), prod d

Maurice Desfassiaux
Silents
ITALIAN STRAW HAT, AN(1927, Fr.), ph

Angelos Desfia
DARK MOUNTAIN(1944)

Angelos Desfis
GANGWAY FOR TOMORROW(1943)

Delphine Desfons
LA CHINOISE(1967, Fr.), ed

Henri Desfontaines
Silents
QUEEN ELIZABETH(1912, Fr.), d
Misc. Silents
LES BLEUS DE L'AMOUR(1918, Fr.), d; LA SUPREME EPOEE(1919, Fr.), d; SA GOSSE(1919, Fr.), d; AUTOUR DU MYSTERE(1920, Fr.), d; LA MARSEILLAISE(1920, Fr.), d; CHICHINETTE ET CLE(1921, Fr.), d; LA FILLE DES CHIFFONNIERS(1922, Fr.), d; L'INSIGNE MYSTERIEUX(1922, Fr.), d; CHATEAU HISTORIQUE(1923, Fr.), d; L'ESPIONE(1923, Fr.), d; L'OEILLET BLANC(1923, Fr.), d; MADAME FLIRT(1923, Fr.), d; VERS ABECHER LA MYSTERIEUSE(1924, Fr.), d; L'ESPIONE AUX YEUX NOIRS(1926, Fr.), d

Henri Desforges
Silents
MOTHER(1914)

Eric Desfosses
EVERY MAN FOR HIMSELF(1980, Fr.)

Jean-Pierre Desganat
NO ROSES FOR OSS 117(1968, Fr.), w

Jackie DeShannon
INTIMACY(1966); C'MON, LET'S LIVE A LITTLE(1967)

A. Deshe
EVERY BASTARD A KING(1968, Israel), p

Jack DeShields
BLACK GUNN(1972), art d; MARATHON MAN(1976), art d; PANDEMONI- UM(1982), prod d

Willard Deshielle
Misc. Silents
MAN AND HIS ANGEL(1916)

Florence Deshon
Silents
AUCTION BLOCK, THE(1917); DESIRED WOMAN, THE(1918); OTHER MAN, THE(1918); DOLLARS AND SENSE(1920)

Misc. Silents
JAFFERY(1915); BACHELOR'S CHILDREN, A(1918); CLUTCH OF CIRCUM-
STANCE, THE(1918); GOLDEN GOAL, THE(1918); LOVE WATCHES(1918); ONE
THOUSAND DOLLARS(1918); DEEP WATERS(1920); ROOF TREE, THE(1921)
Frank Deshon
Misc. Silents
BORDER RAIDERS, THE(1918)
Nancy DeShon
TOMBSTONE TERROR(1935); TRAIL OF TERROR(1935)
Misc. Talkies
WOLF RIDERS(1935)
Peter Desiante
HOWZER(1973)
Vittorio DeSica
CONDEMNED OF ALTONA, THE(1963), d
Danilo Desideri
SHOOT LOUD, LOUDER... I DON'T UNDERSTAND(1966, Ital.), ph
Gioia Desideri
PIZZA TRIANGLE, THE(1970, Ital./Span.)
Giorgio Desideri
WONDERS OF ALADDIN, THE(1961, Fr./Ital.), cos; GLADIATOR OF ROME(1963,
Ital.), cos; GOLDEN ARROW, THE(1964, Ital.), cos; TORPEDO BAY(1964, Ital./Fr.),
cos; KILL OR BE KILLED(1967, Ital.), cos; PAYMENT IN BLOOD(1968, Ital.), cos;
VALACHI PAPERS, THE(1972, Ital./Fr.), cos; CAGLIOSTRO(1975, Ital.), art d; CLASH
OF THE TITANS(1981), art d; LION OF THE DESERT(1981, Libya/Brit.), art d;
TEMPEST(1982), set d
1984
CONAN THE DESTROYER(1984), set d; DUNE(1984), set d
Osvaldo Desideri
PASSENGER, THE(1975, Ital.), set d
Robert Desiderio
1984
OH GOD! YOU DEVIL(1984)
Dress Designer
OPERATION CONSPIRACY(1957, Brit.)
David DeSilva
FAME(1980), p
Nico DeSilva
1984
FLETCH(1984)
B.J. DeSimone
LILITH(1964)
Bob DeSimone
1984
SAVAGE STREETS(1984)
Bonnie DeSimone
RODEO KING AND THE SENORITA(1951)
John DeSimone
WOMAN FROM HEADQUARTERS(1950)
Pat DeSimone
DINO(1957)
Robert DeSimone
SEDUCTION, THE(1982)
Roberto DeSimone
END OF THE WORLD(in Our Usual Bed In a Night Full of Rain), THE*1/2 (1978,
Ital.), m
Tom DeSimone
HELL NIGHT(1981), d; CONCRETE JUNGLE, THE(1982), d
Desire
1984
SUPERGIRL(1984)
M. Desjardins
Misc. Silents
SOUL OF FRANCE(1929, Fr.)
Maxime Desjardins
Misc. Silents
J'ACCUSE(1919, Fr.)
Ghislaine Desjonqueres
TALL BLOND MAN WITH ONE BLACK SHOE, THE(1973, Fr.), ed
Andrew Deskin
1984
AMERICAN NIGHTMARE(1984), art d
Robert Deslandes
WEEKEND AT DUNKIRK(1966, Fr./Ital.)
Jean Deslauriers
WHISPERING CITY(1947, Can.), m
Nicole Deslauriers
MARATHON MAN(1976)
Kay Desleys
YOU CAN'T TAKE IT WITH YOU(1938)
Silents
GOLD RUSH, THE(1925)
Jackie Deslonde
BLACK KLANSMAN, THE(1966)
Gaby Deslys
Misc. Silents
BOUCLETTE(1918, Fr.); LE DIEU DU HASARD(1919, Fr.)
Kay Deslys
DANCE OF LIFE, THE(1929); TAKE THE HEIR(1930); FRIENDS AND LO-
VERS(1931); DEVIL'S BROTHER, THE(1933); BELLE OF THE NINETIES(1934);
TREASURE ISLAND(1934); SYLVIA SCARLETT(1936); MURDER BY INVITA-
TION(1941); NEVER GIVE A SUCKER AN EVEN BREAK(1941); FOREVER AND A
DAY(1943); CASANOVA BROWN(1944); WHITE CLIFFS OF DOVER, THE(1944);
STRANGE LOVE OF MARTHA IVERS, THE(1946); PAT AND MIKE(1952)
Silents
LEOPARD LADY, THE(1928)
Sophie Desmaretes
LOVE AND THE FRENCHWOMAN(1961, Fr.)

Jacqueline Desmarets
HER FIRST AFFAIR(1947, Fr.)
Sophie Desmarets
JUST ME(1950, Fr.); ROYAL AFFAIR, A(1950); IF PARIS WERE TOLD TO US(1956,
Fr.); TONIGHT THE SKIRTS FLY(1956, Fr.); SWEET AND SOUR(1964, Fr./Ital.);
SECOND WIND, A(1978, Fr.)
Pierre Desmet
LA CAGE AUX FOLLES II(1981, Ital./Fr.)
Carol Desmond
CRY OF THE BANSHEE(1970, Brit.)
Cleo Desmond
SPIRIT OF YOUTH(1937); AM I GUILTY?(1940); MOKEY(1942)
Misc. Silents
MILLIONARE, THE(1927)
Dagmar Desmond
Silents
MAN AND MAID(1925)
Danny Desmond
LOUISIANA HAYRIDE(1944); SHE'S A SWEETHEART(1944); THEY LIVE IN
FEAR(1944); YOUTH RUNS WILD(1944); WALK IN THE SUN, A(1945)
Dick Desmond
ENTER THE NINJA(1982), w
Dino Desmond
TRAMPLERS, THE(1966, Ital.)
Dona Desmond
BLACK GESTAPO, THE(1975)
Misc. Talkies
TENDER LOVING CARE(1974); FUGITIVE GIRLS(1975)
Eric Desmond
Misc. Silents
DAVID COPPERFIELD(1913, Brit.)
Florence Desmond
ROAD TO FORTUNE, THE(1930, Brit.); SALLY IN OUR ALLEY(1931, Brit.); HIGH
SOCIETY(1932, Brit.); MARRIAGE BOND, THE(1932, Brit.); MURDER ON THE
SECOND FLOOR(1932, Brit.); NINE TILL SIX(1932, Brit.); RIVER HOUSE GHOST,
THE(1932, Brit.); MR. SKITCH(1933); MY LUCKY STAR(1933, Brit.); I AM SUZAN-
NE(1934); NO LIMIT(1935, Brit.); ACCUSED(1936, Brit.); GAY LOVE(1936, Brit.); KEEP
YOUR SEATS PLEASE(1936, Brit.); HOOTS MON!(1939, Brit.); PLAYBOY, THE(1942,
Brit.); THREE CAME HOME(1950); CHARLEY MOON(1956, Brit.); SOME GIRLS
DO(1969, Brit.)
Grace Desmond
Misc. Silents
GIRL IN HIS HOUSE, THE(1918)
Jim Desmond
MAIDSTONE(1970), ph
John Desmond
NIGHT COMES TOO SOON(1948, Brit.)
Johnny Desmond
CALYPSO HEAT WAVE(1957); ESCAPE FROM SAN QUENTIN(1957); CHINA
DOLL(1958); DESERT HELL(1958); BUBBLE, THE(1967)
Lino Desmond
WILD, WILD PLANET, THE(1967, Ital.); MID-DAY MISTRESS(1968)
Lola Desmond
PROPERTY(1979)
Lorrae Desmond
STOCK CAR(1955, Brit.)
Lucile Desmond
Silents
RECKONING DAY, THE(1918)
Marc Desmond
NAME OF THE GAME IS KILL, THE(1968)
Marian Desmond
S(1974)
Mark Desmond
ORGY OF THE DEAD(1965), ch
Mary Jo Desmond
MAD MISS MANTON, THE(1938)
Patric Desmond
THOUSAND AND ONE NIGHTS, A(1945)
Patrick Desmond
FRENCHMAN'S CREEK(1944)
Misc. Talkies
TRAILING DANGER(1947)
Robert Desmond
OUTSIDER, THE(1949, Brit.); COCKLESHELL HEROES, THE(1955); DANGEROUS
YOUTH(1958, Brit.); LADY IS A SQUARE, THE(1959, Brit.); UGLY DUCKLING,
THE(1959, Brit.); TOO YOUNG TO LOVE(1960, Brit.); BEST OF ENEMIES, THE(1962);
GAOLBREAK(1962, Brit.); GREAT ESCAPE, THE(1963)
Roy Desmond
MACBETH(1971, Brit.)
Shaun Desmond
SCARAB MURDER CASE, THE(1936, Brit.); SONG OF THE FORGE(1937, Brit.);
IRISH AND PROUD OF IT(1938, Ireland)
Stanley Desmond
MAJOR AND THE MINOR, THE(1942)
William Desmond
NO DEFENSE(1929); MURDER ON THE ROOF(1930); FIRST AID(1931); HELL
BENT FOR 'FRISCO(1931); OKLAHOMA JIM(1931); SCARLET WEEKEND, A(1932);
FARGO EXPRESS(1933); LAUGHING AT LIFE(1933); RUSTLERS' ROUNDUP(1933);
STRAWBERRY ROAN(1933); FRONTIER DAYS(1934); WAY OF THE WEST,
THE(1934); COWBOY AND THE BANDIT, THE(1935); CYCLONE OF THE SAD-
DLE(1935); FRISCO KID(1935); GHOST RIDER, THE(1935); NAUGHTY MARIET-
TA(1935); POWDERSMOKE RANGE(1935); ROUGH RIDING RANGER(1935);
TIMBER TERRORS(1935); HOLLYWOOD BOULEVARD(1936); NEVADA(1936);
SONG OF THE GRINGO(1936); SONG OF THE SADDLE(1936); TREACHERY RIDES
THE RANGE(1936); ARIZONA DAYS(1937); HEADIN' FOR THE RIO GRANDE(1937);
LITTLE BIT OF HEAVEN, A(1940); YOUNG BILL HICKOK(1940); BURY ME NOT ON
THE LONE PRAIRIE(1941); DOWN RIO GRANDE WAY(1941); RAIDERS OF THE
WEST(1942); SILVER BULLET, THE(1942); LONE STAR TRAIL, THE(1943); PHAN-
TOM OF THE OPERA(1943); GYPSY WILDCAT(1944); MARSHAL OF GUNS-

MOKE(1944); OKLAHOMA RAIDERS(1944); OLD TEXAS TRAIL, THE(1944); TALL IN THE SADDLE(1944); FRONTIER GAL(1945); NAUGHTY NINETIES, THE(1945); SONG OF THE SARONG(1945)

Misc. Talkies
RAWHIDE TERROR, THE(1934); BORN TO BATTLE(1935); COURAGE OF THE NORTH(1935); DEFYING THE LAW(1935); DEVIL'S CANYON(1935); FIVE BAD MEN(1935); GUNFIRE(1935); PHANTOM COWBOY, THE(1935)

Silents
KILMENY(1915); LIEUT. DANNY, U.S.A.(1916); NOT MY SISTER(1916); PEG-GY(1916); ICED BULLET, THE(1917); LAST OF THE INGRAHAMS, THE(1917); PAWS OF THE BEAR(1917); TWIN BEDS(1920); NIGHT LIFE IN HOLLYWOOD(1922); EXTRA GIRL, THE(1923); MEASURE OF A MAN, THE(1924); BARRIERS OF THE LAW(1925); MEDDLER, THE(1925); OUTWITTED(1925)

Misc. Silents
MAJESTY OF THE LAW, THE(1915); BULLETS AND BROWN EYES(1916); CRIMI-NAL, THE(1916); DAWN MAKER, THE(1916); GAMBLE IN SOULS, A(1916); PAY-MENT, THE(1916); SORROWS OF LOVE, THE(1916); WAIFS, THE(1916); BLOOD WILL TELL(1917); FIGHTING BACK(1917); FLYING COLORS(1917); MARRIED IN NAME ONLY(1917); MASTER OF HIS HOME(1917); PADDY O'HARA(1917); SUDDEN GENTLEMAN, THE(1917); TIME LOCKS AND DIAMONDS(1917); BEYOND THE SHADOWS(1918); CAPTAIN OF HIS SOUL(1918); CLOSIN' IN(1918); DEUCE DUN-CAN(1918); HELL'S END(1918); HONEST MAN, AN(1918); OLD HARTWELL'S CUB(1918); PRETENDER, THE(1918); SEA PANTHER, THE(1918); SOCIETY FOR SALE(1918); WILD LIFE(1918); BARE-FISTED GALLAGHER(1919); BLUE BANDAN-NA, THE(1919); DANGEROUS WATERS(1919); HER CODE OF HONOR(1919); LIFE'S A FUNNY PROPOSITION(1919); MINTS OF HELL, THE(1919); PRINCE AND BETTY, THE(1919); PRODIGAL LIAR, THE(1919); SAGE BRUSH HAMLET, A(1919); BROAD-WAY COWBOY, THE(1920); DANGEROUS TOYS(1921); FIGHTIN' MAD(1921); PAR-ISH PRIEST, THE(1921); WOMEN MEN LOVE(1921); MCGUIRE OF THE MOUNTED(1923); SHADOWS OF THE NORTH(1923); BIG TIMBER(1924); BREATH-LESS MOMENT, THE(1924); SUNSET TRAIL, THE(1924); BLOOD AND STEEL(1925); BURNING TRAIL, THE(1925); DUPED(1925); RIDIN' PRETTY(1925); STRAIGHT THROUGH(1925); RED CLAY(1927); TONGUES OF SCANDAL(1927)

Brian Desmond-Hurst
RIVER OF UNREST(1937, Brit.), p&d

Jerry Desmonde
CARDBOARD CAVALIER, THE(1949, Brit.); ALF'S BABY(1953, Brit.); MY HEART GOES CRAZY(1953, Brit.); MALTA STORY(1954, Brit.); MAN OF THE MOMENT(1955, Brit.); TROUBLE IN STORE(1955, Brit.); ANGEL WHO PAWNED HER HARP, THE(1956, Brit.); RAMSBOTTOM RIDES AGAIN(1956, Brit.); KING IN NEW YORK, A(1957, Brit.); UP IN THE WORLD(1957, Brit.); FOLLOW A STAR(1959, Brit.); CARRY ON REGARDLESS(1961, Brit.); KIND OF LOVING, A(1962, Brit.); STOLEN HOURS(1963); SWITCH, THE(1963, Brit.); EARLY BIRD, THE(1965, Brit.); GONKS GO BEAT(1965, Brit.); BEAUTY JUNGLE, THE(1966, Brit.); STITCH IN TIME, A(1967, Brit.)

Mercedes Desmore
MR. H. C. ANDERSEN(1950, Brit.)

Geory Desmouceaux
SMALL CHANGE(1976, Fr.)

Victor Desney
WEST POINT STORY, THE(1950)

Tamara Desni
FALLING FOR YOU(1933, Brit.); BYPASS TO HAPPINESS(1934, Brit.); DIPLOMAT-IC LOVER, THE(1934, Brit.); BLUE SMOKE(1935, Brit.); DARK WORLD(1935, Brit.); HELL'S CARGO(1935, Brit.); JACK AHOY!(1935, Brit.); LOVE IN EXILE(1936, Brit.); FIRE OVER ENGLAND(1937, Brit.); MURDER ON DIAMOND ROW(1937, Brit.); FORBIDDEN TERRITORY(1938, Brit.); HIS BROTHER'S KEEPER(1939, Brit.); TOR-SO MURDER MYSTERY, THE(1940, Brit.); FLIGHT FROM FOLLY(1945, Brit.); SEND FOR PAUL TEMPLE(1946, Brit.); HILLS OF DONEGAL, THE(1947, Brit.); DICK BARTON AT BAY(1950, Brit.)

Victory Desni
STORY OF THREE LOVES, THE(1953)

Xeni Desni
Misc. Silents
LEAP INTO LIFE(1924, Ger.)

Xenia Desni
Silents
DECAMERON NIGHTS(1924, Brit.)

Sergiusz Desnitsky
TEST OF PILOT PIRX, THE(1978, Pol./USSR)

Ivan Desny
MADELEINE(1950, Brit.); LOLA MONTES(1955, Fr./Ger.); ANASTASIA(1956); GIVE ME MY CHANCE(1958, Fr.); MIRROR HAS TWO FACES, THE(1959, Fr.); SONG WITHOUT END(1960); BON VOYAGE(1962); DANIELLA BY NIGHT(1962, Fr/Ger.); END OF DESIRE(1962 Fr./Ital.); NUMBER SIX(1962, Brit.); SHERLOCK HOLMES AND THE DEADLY NECKLACE(1962, Ger.); WHITE SLAVE SHIP(1962, Fr./Ital.); GOLDEN PLAGUE, THE(1963, Ger.); INVISIBLE MAN, THE(1963, Ger.); LOVE, THE ITALIAN WAY(1964, Ital.); MYSTERY OF THUG ISLAND, THE(1966, Ital./Ger.); TENDER SCOUNDREL(1967, Fr./Ital.); GUNS FOR SAN SEBASTIAN(1968, U.S./Fr./Mex./Ital.); MAYERLING(1968, Brit./Fr.); ADVENTURES OF GERARD, THE(1970, Brit.); LITTLE MOTHER(1973, U.S./Yugo./Ger.); TOUCH ME NOT(1974, Brit.); PAPER TIGER(1975, Brit.); WHO?(1975, U.S./Ger.); MARRIAGE OF MARIA BRAUN, THE(1979, Ger.); I HATE BLONDES(1981, Ital.); LADY WITHOUT CAMELLIAS, THE(1981, Ital.); LOLA(1982, Ger.); MALOU(1983)

Victor Desny
MISTER 880(1950); SEPTEMBER AFFAIR(1950)

Finita DeSopia
Misc. Silents
THROWN TO THE LIONS(1916)

Joao Desordi
GIVEN WORD, THE(1964, Braz.)

Desormes
RULES OF THE GAME, THE(1939, Fr.), m

Desormier
GYPSY FURY(1950, Fr.), md

Roger Desormieres
LA MARSEILLAISE(1938, Fr.), m; RULES OF THE GAME, THE(1939, Fr.), md

Alfredo DeSoto
KILLER SHREWS, THE(1959)

Edouard DeSoto
1984
CRACKERS(1984)

Henri DeSoto
SKY'S THE LIMIT, THE(1943); THANK YOUR LUCKY STARS(1943); ONE MORE TOMORROW(1946)

Henry DeSoto
SEVEN DAYS LEAVE(1942); NIGHT AND DAY(1946)

Rosana DeSoto
BALLAD OF GREGORIO CORTEZ, THE(1983)

Herbert DeSouza
BOOLOO(1938)

Aileen Despard
SUCH IS THE LAW(1930, Brit.); THREADS(1932, Brit.)

Olivier Despax
DARK OF THE SUN(1968, Brit.)

Jean Despeaux
CARNIVAL OF SINNERS(1947, Fr.); MURDERER LIVES AT NUMBER 21, THE(1947, Fr.)

Suzanne Despers
SHANGHAI DRAMA, THE(1945, Fr.)

Gerard Despierre
DEATH OF MARIO RICCI, THE(1983, Ital.)

Joseph Despins
MOON OVER THE ALLEY(1980, Brit.), d, ed

Despo
PROMISE AT DAWN(1970, U.S./Fr.); SOMETHING FOR EVERYONE(1970); GANG THAT COULDN'T SHOOT STRAIGHT, THE(1971); HORSEMEN, THE(1971); MADE FOR EACH OTHER(1971)

Veljko Despotovic
I EVEN MET HAPPY GYPSIES(1968, Yugo.), art d; GAMBLERS, THE(1969), art d
1984
MEMED MY HAWK(1984, Brit.), art d

Nada Despotovich
SMITHEREENS(1982)

Philippe Desprats
SOPHIE'S WAYS(1970, Fr.)

Suzanne Despres
LOUISE(1940, Fr.)
Misc. Silents
LE CARNIVAL DES VERITES(1920, Fr.); L'OMBRE DECHIREE(1921, Fr.); LE TORNOI(1928, Fr.)

Robert Desroches
APPRENTICESHIP OF DUDDY KRAVITZ, THE(1974, Can.)

Bente Dessau
WEEKEND(1964, Den.)

Masja Dessau
WEEKEND(1964, Den.)

Paul Dessau
S.O.S. ICEBERG(1933), m; IT HAPPENED IN GIBRALTAR(1943, Fr.), m; WIFE OF MONTE CRISTO, THE(1946), md; PRETENDER, THE(1947), md; RUTHLESS(1948), md; VICIOUS CIRCLE, THE(1948), md

Bandes Dessinees
KILLING GAME, THE(1968, Fr.), ph

Ed Dessisso
SUPER SPOOK(1975), p, w

Angelo Dessy
ISLAND OF PROCIDA, THE(1952, Ital.); MAN FROM CAIRO, THE(1953)

Betty Dessy
1990: THE BRONX WARRIORS(1983, Ital.)

Jo Dest
DAMNED, THE(1948, Fr.); WAGES OF FEAR, THE(1955, Fr./Ital.)

Joe Dest
LE PLAISIR(1954, Fr.)

Pierre Destailles
PERFECTIONIST, THE(1952, Fr.)

Robert Destain
FERNANDEL THE DRESSMAKER(1957, Fr.); LA BELLE AMERICAINE(1961, Fr.); COUNTERFEIT CONSTABLE, THE(1966, Fr.)

Luli Deste
THUNDER IN THE CITY(1937, Brit.); SHE MARRIED AN ARTIST(1938); SKI PATROL(1940); SOUTH TO KARANGA(1940); CASE OF THE BLACK PARROT, THE(1941); OUTLAWS OF THE DESERT(1941)

Joe DeStefani
FIVE LITTLE PEPPERS AT HOME(1940)

Joseph DeStefani
BAR 20 JUSTICE(1938); JUVENILE COURT(1938)

Jacques Destoop
TIGHT SKIRTS, LOOSE PLEASURES(1966, Fr.)

Manos Destounis
OEDIPUS THE KING(1968, Brit.)

Blanche Destournelles
LA MARSEILLAISE(1938, Fr.)

Robert Destrain
MY SEVEN LITTLE SINS(1956, Fr./Ital.)

Jimmy Destri
ROADIE(1980)

Robert Destri
PSYCHO II(1983)

Irene DeStrozzi
INNOCENTS IN PARIS(1955, Brit.)

C. Desty
LOVE CONTRACT, THE(1932, Brit.), w

Pierre Destys
LA CHIENNE(1975, Fr.)

Maurice Desvallieres
HOTEL PARADISO(1966, U.S./Brit.), w
Victor Desy
TAKE IT ALL(1966, Can.), a, w; RABID(1976, Can.); JACOB TWO-TWO MEETS THE
HOODED FANG(1979, Can.); SCANNERS(1981, Can.)
B.G. "Buddy" DeSylva
FOLLOW THE LEADER(1930), w; FOLLOW THRU(1930), w; GOOD NEWS(1930), w;
HOLD EVERYTHING(1930), w; INDISCREET(1931), p, w; TAKE A CHANCE(1933),
w; BOTTOMS UP(1934), p, w; DOUBTING THOMAS(1935), p; LITTLEST REBEL,
THE(1935), p; WELCOME HOME(1935), p; BORN TO DANCE(1936), w; LADIES IN
LOVE(1936), p; STOWAWAY(1936), p; MERRY-GO-ROUND OF 1938(1937), p;
BACHELOR MOTHER(1939), p; BIRTH OF THE BLUES(1941), p; CAUGHT IN THE
DRAFT(1941), p; LOUISIANA PURCHASE(1941), p, w; FRENCHMAN'S
CREEK(1944), p; HITLER GANG, THE(1944), p
Hoskins Deterly
HUCKLEBERRY FINN(1974)
E. Dethorey
DOLLAR(1938, Swed.)
David Detiege
MAN FROM BUTTON WILLOW, THE(1965), d&w; SHINBONE ALLEY(1971), prod
d; BUGS BUNNY'S THIRD MOVIE–1001 RABBIT TALES(1982), d, w; DAFFY
DUCK'S MOVIE: FANTASTIC ISLAND(1983), w
Phyllis Bounds Detiege
MAN FROM BUTTON WILLOW, THE(1965), p
George Detitta
SATURDAY NIGHT FEVER(1977), set d; NUNZIO(1978), set d; FAME(1980), set d;
LORDS OF DISCIPLINE, THE(1983), set d
George DeTitta, Jr.
TRADING PLACES(1983), set d
1984
BEAT STREET(1984), set d
George DeTitta, Sr.
DEATHTRAP(1982), set d; TRADING PLACES(1983), set d
1984
POPE OF GREENWICH VILLAGE, THE(1984), set d
John Detlie
SARATOGA(1937), art d; TEST PILOT(1938), art d
John S. Detlie
EDISON, THE MAN(1940), art d; STRIKE UP THE BAND(1940), art d; LADY BE
GOOD(1941), art d; CROSSROADS(1942), art d; I MARRIED AN ANGEL(1942), art d
Maruschka Detmers
1984
FIRST NAME: CARMEN(1984, Fr.)
Lala DeTolly
LOVES OF CARMEN, THE(1948)
Andre DeToth
PASSPORT TO SUEZ(1943), d; PITFALL(1948), d; CRIME WAVE(1954), d
Babe DeTreest
OUTLAWED GUNS(1935)
Dena Detrich
ON THE AIR LIVE WITH CAPTAIN MIDNIGHT(1979)
Bruce Detrick
INVASION OF THE BLOOD FARMERS(1972)
Detroit Lions Coaching Staff and Team
PAPER LION(1968)
Nathaniel Dett
WHITE ZOMBIE(1932), m
Loredana Detto
SOUND OF TRUMPETS, THE(1963, Ital.)
Helen Dettweiler
PAT AND MIKE(1952)
Karl Detzer
CAR 99(1935), w; CRASH DONOVAN(1936), w
Robert Deubel
1984
GIRLS NIGHT OUT(1984), d
Deuce Spriggins and his Band
COWBOY BLUES(1946)
Aime Deude
BEAUTIFUL PRISONER, THE(1983, Fr.), prod d
Clarisse Deudon
MOON IN THE GUTTER, THE(1983, Fr./Ital.)
Geoffrey Deuel
CHISUM(1970); TERMINAL ISLAND(1973)
Peter Deuel
W.I.A.(WOUNDED IN ACTION)*1/2 (1966); HELL WITH HEROES, THE(1968)
Ralph E. Deuhr
1984
COUNTRY(1984)
Constance Deumar
Misc. Silents
BRAMBLE BUSH, THE(1919)
Carl Deurell
NIGHT IN JUNE, A(1940, Swed.)
Derek Deurvorst
MC CABE AND MRS. MILLER(1971)
Benny Deus
REQUIEM FOR A SECRET AGENT(1966, Ital.)
Beny Deus
CASTILIAN, THE(1963, Span./U.S.); GUNMEN OF THE RIO GRANDE(1965, Fr./
Ital./Span.); DRUMS OF TABU, THE(1967, Ital./Span.)
Adolph Deutch
RACKET BUSTERS(1938), m
David Deutch
PLAY IT COOL(1963, Brit.), p
Helen Deutch
VALLEY OF THE DOLLS(1967), w

Kent Deuters
SCREWBALLS(1983)
Deutsch
TORCH SONG(1953), md
Adolph Deutsch
FOLLOW THE LEADER(1930), m; SMILING LIEUTENANT, THE(1931), md;
GREAT GARRICK, THE(1937), m; MR. DODD TAKES THE AIR(1937), m; THEY
WON'T FORGET(1937), m; SWING YOUR LADY(1938), m; OFF THE RECORD(1939),
m; FIGHTING 69TH, THE(1940), m; THEY DRIVE BY NIGHT(1940), md; TORRID
ZONE(1940), m; GREAT MR. NOBODY, THE(1941), m; HIGH SIERRA(1941), m;
MALTESE FALCON, THE(1941), m; MANPOWER(1941), m; UNDERGROUND(1941),
m; ACROSS THE PACIFIC(1942), m; ALL THROUGH THE NIGHT(1942), m; BIG
SHOT, THE(1942), m; JUKE GIRL(1942), m; LARCENY, INC.(1942), m; LUCKY
JORDAN(1942), md; ACTION IN THE NORTH ATLANTIC(1943), m; NORTHERN
PURSUIT(1943), m; DOUGHGIRLS, THE(1944), m; MASK OF DIMITRIOS,
THE(1944), m; UNCERTAIN GLORY(1944), m; DANGER SIGNAL(1945), m; ESCAPE
IN THE DESERT(1945), m; NOBODY LIVES FOREVER(1946), m; SHADOW OF A
WOMAN(1946), m; THREE STRANGERS(1946), m; BLAZE OF NOON(1947), m; RAM-
ROD(1947), m; JULIA MISBEHAVES(1948), m; WHISPERING SMITH(1948), m; IN-
TRUDER IN THE DUST(1949), m; LITTLE WOMEN(1949), m; STRATTON STORY,
THE(1949), md; TAKE ME OUT TO THE BALL GAME(1949), md; ANNIE GET YOUR
GUN(1950), md; BIG HANGOVER, THE(1950), m; FATHER OF THE BRIDE(1950), m;
MRS. O'MALLEY AND MR. MALONE(1950), m; PAGAN LOVE SONG(1950), md;
STARS IN MY CROWN(1950), m; IT'S A BIG COUNTRY(1951), m; SHOW BOAT(1951),
md; SOLDIERS THREE(1951), m; BELLE OF NEW YORK, THE(1952), md; MILLION
DOLLAR MERMAID(1952), md; BAND WAGON, THE(1953), md; TORCH
SONG(1953), a, m; DEEP IN MY HEART(1954), md; LONG, LONG TRAILER,
THE(1954), m; SEVEN BRIDES FOR SEVEN BROTHERS(1954), md; INTERRUPTED
MELODY(1955), m, md; OKLAHOMA(1955), md; RACK, THE(1956), m, md; TEA
AND SYMPATHY(1956), m; FUNNY FACE(1957), md; LES GIRLS(1957), md; LONE-
LYHEARTS(1958), md; MATCHMAKER, THE(1958), m; SOME LIKE IT HOT(1959),
m; APARTMENT, THE(1960), m; GO NAKED IN THE WORLD(1961), m
Armand Deutsch
AMBUSH(1950), p; MAGNIFICENT YANKEE, THE(1950), p; RIGHT CROSS(1950),
p; KIND LADY(1951), p; THREE GUYS NAMED MIKE(1951), p; CARBINE WIL-
LIAMS(1952), p; GIRL IN WHITE, THE(1952), p; GIRL WHO HAD EVERYTHING,
THE(1953), p; GREEN FIRE(1955), p; SLANDER(1956), p; SADDLE THE
WIND(1958), p
David Deutsch
NOTHING BUT THE BEST(1964, Brit.), p; HAVING A WILD WEEKEND(1965,
Brit.), p; INTERLUDE(1968, Brit.), p; LOCK UP YOUR DAUGHTERS(1969, Brit.), p;
DAY IN THE DEATH OF JOE EGG, A(1972, Brit.), p; DAY OF THE JACKAL,
THE(1973, Brit./Fr.), p
1984
REFLECTIONS(1984, Brit.), p
Davis Deutsch
CHANCE MEETING(1960, Brit.), p
Ernest Deutsch
PRISONER OF CORBAL(1939, Brit.); TRIAL, THE(1948, Aust.)
Ernst Deutsch
NURSE EDITH CAVELL(1939); MAN I MARRIED, THE(1940); SO ENDS OUR
NIGHT(1941); THIRD MAN, THE(1950, Brit.)
Silents
GOLEM: HOW HE CAME INTO THE WORLD, THE(1920, Ger.)
Helen Deutsch
NATIONAL VELVET(1944), w; SEVENTH CROSS, THE(1944), w; GOLDEN EAR-
RINGS(1947), w; LOVES OF CARMEN, THE(1948), w; SHOCKPROOF(1949), p, w;
KIM(1950), w; KING SOLOMON'S MINES(1950), w; IT'S A BIG COUNTRY(1951), w;
PLYMOUTH ADVENTURE(1952), w; LILI(1953), w; FLAME AND THE FLESH(1954),
w; GLASS SLIPPER, THE(1955), w; I'LL CRY TOMORROW(1955), w; FOREVER
DARLING(1956), w; UNSINKABLE MOLLY BROWN, THE(1964), w
Jordan Arthur Deutsch
KAREN, THE LOVEMAKER(1970), w
Mildred Deutsch
LORDS OF FLATBUSH, THE(1974)
Nikolaus Deutsch
MONEY ON THE STREET(1930, Aust.), p
Patti Deutsch
MR. MOM(1983)
Ron Deutsch
ZAPPED!(1982)
Stephen Deutsch
SOMEWHERE IN TIME(1980), p; ALL THE RIGHT MOVES(1983), p
Satan Deutscher
GERMAN SISTERS, THE(1982, Ger.)
Clara Deutschmann
SINGING BLACKSMITH(1938)
Janet Deutschmann
SINGING BLACKSMITH(1938)
F. Deutschmeister
GUILTY MELODY(1936, Brit.), p; LOST ON THE WESTERN FRONT(1940, Brit.), p
Peppino Dev-Luca
GIRL WITH A PISTOL, THE(1968, Ital.), m
Louis Devaivre
JULIE THE REDHEAD(1963, Fr.), ed; SOFT SKIN ON BLACK SILK(1964, Fr./
Span.), ed
Jacques Deval
PASSIONATE PLUMBER(1932), w; JOURNAL OF A CRIME(1934), w; MARIE
GALANTE(1934), w; CAFE METROPOLE(1937), w; TOVARICH(1937), w; SAY IT IN
FRENCH(1938), w; BALALAIKA(1939), w; NEW MOON(1940), w; HER CARDBOARD
LOVER(1942), w; SEVEN DAYS ASHORE(1944), w; MISS TATLOCK'S MIL-
LIONS(1948), w
Marguerite Deval
MAN OF THE HOUR, THE(1940, Fr.); MARKED GIRLS(1949, Fr.); SPICE OF
LIFE(1954, Fr.)
Francois B. DeValdes
MESSAGE TO GARCIA, A(1936), tech adv

Louis Devalvre
ALERT IN THE SOUTH(1954, Fr.), ed
Eleanor DeVan
LADY IN THE DARK(1944)
William Devane
IN THE COUNTRY(1967); GLORY BOY(1971); MC CABE AND MRS. MILLER(1971); PURSUIT OF HAPPINESS, THE(1971); 300 YEAR WEEKEND(1971), a, w; LADY LIBERTY(1972, Ital./Fr.); IRISH WHISKEY REBELLION(1973); REPORT TO THE COMMISSIONER(1975); FAMILY PLOT(1976); MARATHON MAN(1976); BAD NEWS BEARS IN BREAKING TRAINING, THE(1977); ROLLING THUNDER(1977); DARK, THE(1979); YANKS(1979); HONKY TONK FREEWAY(1981); TESTAMENT(1983)
1984
HADLEY'S REBELLION(1984)
John Devaney
NIGHTHAWKS(1981)
D. Forges Devanzati
HEART AND SOUL(1950, Ital.), p
Jose DeVarga
BLUE HAWAII(1961)
Val DeVargas
BEARS AND I, THE(1974)
Donna DeVarona
DEATH VENGEANCE(1982)
Joanna DeVarona
Misc. Talkies
A(1976, U.S./Korea)
Ginette Devaud
300 SPARTANS, THE(1962), cos
Carolotta A. DeVaughn
WITHOUT A TRACE(1983)
William DeVaull
Silents
INNOCENT MAGDALENE, AN(1916)
Jack Deveau
Misc. Talkies
LEFT-HANDED(1972), d
Jean Deveaux
PARIS EXPRESS, THE(1953, Brit.)
David Deveen
WOMAN IN COMMAND, THE(1934 Brit.)
Ashik Devello
MIND BENDERS, THE(1963, Brit.)
Carrie Deven
BLUEBEARD(1944)
Don Devendorf
HOUSE ON SKULL MOUNTAIN, THE(1974)
Myrtle Devenish
TIME BANDITS(1981, Brit.)
Ross Devenish
GUEST AT STEENKAMPSKRAAL, THE(1977, South Africa), d; MARIGOLDS IN AUGUST(1980, South Africa), d
1984
GUEST, THE(1984, Brit.), d; MARIGOLDS IN AUGUST(1984, S. Africa), d
Misc. Talkies
BOESMAN AND LENA(1976), d
Ed Deveraux
COMING-OUT PARTY, A(; PRESSURE(1976, Brit.)
Felicity Deveraux
GREEN FINGERS(1947)
Jack Deveraux
Misc. Silents
SUPERSTITION(1922)
Arthur Devere
CARNIVAL IN FLANDERS(1936, Fr.); CAFE DE PARIS(1938, Fr.); END OF A DAY, THE(1939, Fr.); DAYBREAK(1940, Fr.); IT HAPPENED AT THE INN(1945, Fr.); LE PLAISIR(1954, Fr.)
Gertrude DeVere
Misc. Silents
ME UND GOTT(1918)
Harry DeVere
Silents
FRUITS OF DESIRE, THE(1916); SHOCK, THE(1923)
Harry T. DeVere
Misc. Silents
PATH OF DARKNESS, THE(1916)
Henry DeVere
Silents
CODE OF MARCIA GRAY(1916)
Lillian Devere
Misc. Silents
FRIEND WILSON'S DAUGHTER(1915)
Audrey Devereau
BRAIN THAT WOULDN'T DIE, THE(1959)
Ed Devereaux
FLOODS OF FEAR(1958, Brit.); SAVAGE INNOCENTS, THE(1960, Brit.); MAN IN THE MOON(1961, Brit.); WATCH YOUR STERN(1961, Brit.); MIX ME A PERSON(1962, Brit.); PASSWORD IS COURAGE, THE(1962, Brit.); THERE WAS A CROOKED MAN(1962, Brit.); CARRY ON JACK(1963, Brit.); WRONG ARM OF THE LAW, THE(1963, Brit.); LADIES WHO DO(1964, Brit.); NEVER PUT IT IN WRITING(1964); SING AND SWING(1964, Brit.); THEY'RE A WEIRD MOB(1966, Aus.); NICKEL QUEEN, THE(1971, Aus.); BARRY MC KENZIE HOLDS HIS OWN(1975, Aus.); MONEY MOVERS(1978, Aus.)
Helen Devereaux
SCARLET CLUE, THE(1945)
Jack Devereaux
Silents
SENTIMENTAL LADY, THE(1915); MAN WHO MADE GOOD, THE(1917)
Misc. Silents
AMERICA - THAT'S ALL(1917); GRAFTERS(1917); HER FATHER'S KEEPER(1917); JINX JUMPER, THE(1917); SUCCESSFUL FAILURE, A(1917)

John Devereaux
GET OFF MY FOOT(1935, Brit.)
Marie Devereaux
MARK, THE(1961, Brit.)
Ora Devereaux
Silents
ENTER MADAME(1922)
Misc. Silents
PEDDLER OF LIES, THE(1920)
Rex Devereaux
OCEAN'S ELEVEN(1960)
Shawn Devereaux
FANDANGO(1970)
Thorp Devereaux
GIRL ON THE PIER, THE(1953, Brit.)
Helen Deverell
BOSS OF HANGTOWN MESA(1942); STRICTLY IN THE GROOVE(1942)
Misc. Talkies
BLOCKED TRAIL, THE(1943)
John Deverell
CHILDREN OF CHANCE(1930, Brit.); ALIBI(1931, Brit.); NIGHT IN MONTMARTE, A(1931, Brit.); KING OF PARIS, THE(1934, Brit.); PATH OF GLORY, THE(1934, Brit.); DIVINE SPARK, THE(1935, Brit./Ital.); MARRY THE GIRL(1935, Brit.); EVERYTHING IN LIFE(1936, Brit.); THEY DIDN'T KNOW(1936, Brit.); GIRL IN THE TAXI(1937, Brit.); INCIDENT IN SHANGHAI(1937, Brit.); STREET SINGER, THE(1937, Brit.)
Spencer Deverell
TWO OF A KIND(1983), art d
Marie Devereux
GIRLS AT SEA(1958, Brit.); I ONLY ASKED!(1958, Brit.); BRIDES OF DRACULA, THE(1960, Brit.); STRANGLERS OF BOMBAY, THE(1960, Brit.); CALL ME GENIUS(1961, Brit.); HIS AND HERS(1961, Brit.); WEEKEND WITH LULU, A(1961, Brit.); HOT MONEY GIRL(1962, Brit./Ger.); PIRATES OF BLOOD RIVER, THE(1962, Brit.); YOUNG, WILLING AND EAGER(1962, Brit.); CLEOPATRA(1963); SHOCK CORRIDOR(1963); NAKED KISS, THE(1964)
Thorp Devereux
TWO-HEADED SPY, THE(1959, Brit.)
Nat C. Deverich
Misc. Silents
INVISIBLE DIVORCE, THE(1920), d
Nat Deverich
Silents
HIS LAST DOLLAR(1914)
Misc. Silents
POWER OF LOVE, THE(1922), d; FORBIDDEN LOVER(1923), d
Herbert Spencer Deverill
FISH THAT SAVED PITTSBURGH, THE(1979), art d
Spencer Deverill
HEAVEN'S GATE(1980), art d; JAZZ SINGER, THE(1980), art d
Hugo DeVernier
CONFESSIONS OF A WINDOW CLEANER(1974, Brit.)
Michael Devery
FLYING LEATHERNECKS(1951)
Guy DeVestal
TOAST OF NEW ORLEANS, THE(1950)
Robert DeVestel
DIRTY HARRY(1971), set d; TOM SAWYER(1973), set d; YOUNG FRANKENSTEIN(1974), setd; NEW YORK, NEW YORK(1977), set d
Bopha Devi
DRAGON SKY(1964, Fr.)
Chitra Devi
JUNGLE, THE(1952)
Chunibala Devi
PATHER PANCHALI(1958, India)
Kamala Devi
HARRY BLACK AND THE TIGER(1958, Brit.); GERONIMO(1962); LOVES OF SALAMMBO, THE(1962, Fr./Ital.); BRASS BOTTLE, THE(1964)
Padma Devi
MUSIC ROOM, THE(1963, India)
Reva Devi
PATHER PANCHALI(1958, India)
Seeta Devi
Misc. Silents
THROW OF THE DICE(1930, Brit.)
Shymala Devi
LONG DUEL, THE(1967, Brit.)
Devi Dja and Her Balinese Dancers
PICTURE OF DORIAN GRAY, THE(1945)
Andre Devigny
MAN ESCAPED, A(1957, Fr.), d&w
the Devil Horse
MAN FROM MONTEREY, THE(1933)
Jose DeVilallonga
ANY NUMBER CAN WIN(1963 Fr.)
Andy DeVilla
Silents
HOT WATER(1924)
Joe deVillard
WATCH ON THE RHINE(1943)
Joseph DeVillard
NIGHT FOR CRIME, A(1942); LEAVE IT TO THE IRISH(1944)
Francoise Deville
RISE OF LOUIS XIV, THE(1970, Fr.)
Michel Deville
ADORABLE LIAR(1962, Fr.), d, w; BENJAMIN(1968, Fr.), d, w; BYE BYE BARBARA(1969, Fr.), d, w; FRENCH WAY, THE(1975, Fr.), d
Paul C.R. Deville
LAST OF THE SECRET AGENTS?, THE(1966)

Rene Devillers
BLUE VEIL, THE(1947, Fr.)
Renee Devillers
J'ACCUSE(1939, Fr.); MAN OF THE HOUR, THE(1940, Fr.); LES DERNIERES VACANCES(1947, Fr.); FRENCH TOUCH, THE(1954, Fr.); GAME OF LOVE, THE(1954, Fr.); ROYAL AFFAIRS IN VERSAILLES(1957, Fr.); THERESE(1963, Fr.)
Catherine Devilliers
Misc. Silents
DEAD MAN, THE(1914, USSR)
Dirk DeVilliers
KINGFISH CAPER, THE(1976, South Africa), d
Renee Devilliers
HEART OF A NATION, THE(1943, Fr.); PERFECTIONIST, THE(1952, Fr.)
Marilyn Devin
FIRST TO FIGHT(1967); MONEY JUNGLE, THE(1968); TIGER BY THE TAIL(1970)
Richard Devin
WOMEN OF PITCAIRN ISLAND, THE(1957)
Devine
FEMALE TROUBLE(1975)
Andy Devine
YELLOW JACK(1938); HOT STUFF(1929); CRIMINAL CODE(1931); SPIRIT OF NOTRE DAME, THE(1931); ALL-AMERICAN, THE(1932); DESTRY RIDES AGAIN(1932); FAST COMPANIONS(1932); IMPATIENT MAIDEN(1932); LAW AND ORDER(1932); MAN FROM YESTERDAY, THE(1932); MAN WANTED(1932); RADIO PATROL(1932); THREE WISE GIRLS(1932); TOM BROWN OF CULVER(1932); BIG CAGE, THE(1933); CHANCE AT HEAVEN(1933); COHENS AND KELLYS IN TROUBLE, THE(1933); DR. BULL(1933); HORSEPLAY(1933); MIDNIGHT MARY(1933); SATURDAY'S MILLIONS(1933); SONG OF THE EAGLE(1933); GIFT OF GAB(1934); HELL IN THE HEAVENS(1934); LET'S TALK IT OVER(1934); MILLION DOLLAR RANSOM(1934); POOR RICH, THE(1934); PRESIDENT VANISHES, THE(1934); STINGAREE(1934); UPPER WORLD(1934); WAKE UP AND DREAM(1934); CHINATOWN SQUAD(1935); CORONADO(1935); FARMER TAKES A WIFE, THE(1935); FIGHTING YOUTH(1935); HOLD'EM YALE(1935); STRAIGHT FROM THE HEART(1935); WAY DOWN EAST(1935); BIG GAME, THE(1936); FLYING HOSTESS(1936); ROMEO AND JULIET(1936); SMALL TOWN GIRL(1936); YELLOWSTONE(1936); DOUBLE OR NOTHING(1937); MYSTERIOUS CROSSING(1937); ROAD BACK,THE(1937); STAR IS BORN, A(1937); YOU'RE A SWEETHEART(1937); DR. RHYTHM(1938); IN OLD CHICAGO(1938); MEN WITH WINGS(1938); PERSONAL SECRETARY(1938); STORM, THE(1938); STRANGE FACES(1938); SWING THAT CHEER(1938); GERONIMO(1939); LEGION OF LOST FLYERS(1939); MUTINY ON THE BLACKHAWK(1939); NEVER SAY DIE(1939); SPIRIT OF CULVER, THE(1939); STAGECOACH(1939); TROPIC FURY(1939); BLACK DIAMONDS(1940); BUCK BENNY RIDES AGAIN(1940); DANGER ON WHEELS(1940); DEVIL'S PIPELINE, THE(1940); HOT STEEL(1940); LEATHER-PUSHERS, THE(1940); LITTLE OLD NEW YORK(1940); MAN FROM MONTREAL, THE(1940); MARGIE(1940); TORRID ZONE(1940); TRAIL OF THE VIGILANTES(1940); WHEN THE DALTONS RODE(1940); BADLANDS OF DAKOTA(1941); DANGEROUS GAME, A(1941); FLAME OF NEW ORLEANS, THE(1941); KID FROM KANSAS, THE(1941); LUCKY DEVILS(1941); MEN OF THE TIMBERLAND(1941); MUTINY IN THE ARCTIC(1941); RAIDERS OF THE DESERT(1941); ROAD AGENT(1941); SOUTH OF TAHITI(1941); BETWEEN US GIRLS(1942); DANGER IN THE PACIFIC(1942); ESCAPE FROM HONG KONG(1942); NORTH TO THE KLONDIKE(1942); SIN TOWN(1942); TIMBER(1942); TOP SERGEANT(1942); UNSEEN ENEMY(1942); CORVETTE K-225(1943); CRAZY HOUSE(1943); FRONTIER BADMEN(1943); RHYTHM OF THE ISLANDS(1943); ALI BABA AND THE FORTY THIEVES(1944); BABES ON SWING STREET(1944); BOWERY TO BROADWAY(1944); GHOST CATCHERS(1944); FRISCO SAL(1945); FRONTIER GAL(1945); SUDAN(1945); THAT'S THE SPIRIT(1945); CANYON PASSAGE(1946); BELLS OF SAN ANGELO(1947); FABULOUS TEXAN, THE(1947); MICHIGAN KID, THE(1947); ON THE OLD SPANISH TRAIL(1947); SLAVE GIRL(1947); SPRINGTIME IN THE SIERRAS(1947); VIGILANTES RETURN, THE(1947); EYES OF TEXAS(1948); GALLANT LEGION, THE(1948); GAY RANCHERO, THE(1948); GRAND CANYON TRAIL(1948); NIGHT TIME IN NEVADA(1948); OLD LOS ANGELES(1948); UNDER CALIFORNIA STARS(1948); FAR FRONTIER, THE(1949); LAST BANDIT, THE(1949); NEVER A DULL MOMENT(1950); TRAVELING SALESWOMAN(1950); NEW MEXICO(1951); RED BADGE OF COURAGE, THE(1951); SLAUGHTER TRAIL(1951); MONTANA BELLE(1952); ISLAND IN THE SKY(1953); THUNDER PASS(1954); PETE KELLY'S BLUES(1955); AROUND THE WORLD IN 80 DAYS(1956); ADVENTURES OF HUCKLEBERRY FINN, THE(1960); TWO RODE TOGETHER(1961); HOW THE WEST WAS WON(1962); MAN WHO SHOT LIBERTY VALANCE, THE(1962); IT'S A MAD, MAD, MAD, MAD WORLD(1963); ZEBRA IN THE KITCHEN(1965); BALLAD OF JOSIE(1968); ROAD HUSTLERS, THE(1968); RIDE A NORTHBOUND HORSE(1969); PHYNX, THE(1970); ROBIN HOOD(1973); WON TON TON, THE DOG WHO SAVED HOLLYWOOD(1976); MOUSE AND HIS CHILD, THE(1977); WHALE OF A TALE, A(1977)
Misc. Talkies
IN OLD LOS ANGELES(1948); BEHIND SOUTHERN LINES(1952); GHOST OF CROSSBONES CANYON, THE(1952); TRAIL OF THE ARROW(1952); YELLOW HAIRED KID, THE(1952); BORDER CITY RUSTLERS(1953); SECRET OF OUTLAW FLATS(1953); SIX-GUN DECISION(1953); MARSHALS IN DISGUISE(1954); OUTLAW'S SON(1954); TROUBLE ON THE TRAIL(1954)
Silents
RED LIPS(1928); NAUGHTY BABY(1929)
Delores Devine
SUNBURN(1979)
Dennis Devine
CANYON PASSAGE(1946); LAFAYETTE ESCADRILLE(1958)
George Devine
CONTINENTAL EXPRESS(1939, Brit.); PROMOTER, THE(1952, Brit.); BEGGAR'S OPERA, THE(1953); MAN WITH A MILLION(1954, Brit.); TIME WITHOUT PITY(1957, Brit.); LOOK BACK IN ANGER(1959); TOM JONES(1963, Brit.)
Harriet Devine
SERVANT, THE(1964, Brit.)
Jerry Devine
MAD GAME, THE(1933)
Silents
OVER THE HILL TO THE POORHOUSE(1920); CLAY DOLLARS(1921); HUSH MONEY(1921); SHERLOCK HOLMES(1922); WIDE-OPEN TOWN, A(1922); STEADFAST HEART, THE(1923)

Misc. Silents
REMORSELESS LOVE(1921); CUSTARD CUP, THE(1923); DAMAGED HEARTS(1924)
Jim Devine
EYES OF LAURA MARS(1978)
Kathleen Devine
NIGHT THEY ROBBED BIG BERTHA'S, THE(1975)
Liewellyn Devine
GORGON, THE(1964, Brit.), w
Marty Devine
1,000 SHAPES OF A FEMALE(1963)
Michael D. Devine
WHERE THE RED FERN GROWS(1974), prod d
Richard Devine
PARTY GIRL(1958)
Sophie Devine
INNOCENTS, THE(1961, U.S./Brit.), cos; THIS SPORTING LIFE(1963, Brit.), cos
Tad Devine
CANYON PASSAGE(1946)
Clyde DeVinna
SHIPMATES(1931), ph; TARZAN, THE APE MAN(1932), ph; TREASURE ISLAND(1934), ph; WEST POINT OF THE AIR(1935), ph; GOOD OLD SOAR, THE(1937), ph; FAST COMPANY(1938), ph; OF HUMAN HEARTS(1938), ph; THEY ALL COME OUT(1939), ph; TWENTY MULE TEAM(1940), ph; WYOMING(1940), ph; WITHIN THESE WALLS(1945), ph
David Devir
JESUS CHRIST, SUPERSTAR(1973)
Rachel Devirys
BOMBARDMENT OF MONTE CARLO, THE(1931, Ger.); ARIANE, RUSSIAN MAID(1932, Fr.); GERVAISE(1956, Fr.)
Misc. Silents
MORGANE, THE ENCHANTRESS(1929, Fr.)
James Devis
THERE GOES THE BRIDE(1980, Brit.), ph; DEATH HUNT(1981), ph; TAKE THIS JOB AND SHOVE IT(1981), ph
Pam Devis
UP JUMPED A SWAGMAN(1965, Brit.), ch
Pamela Devis
PERFECT WOMAN, THE(1950, Brit.)
Danny Devito
LADY LIBERTY(1972, Ital./Fr.); SCALAWAG(1973, Yugo.); VAN, THE(1977); WORLD'S GREATEST LOVER, THE(1977); GOIN' SOUTH(1978); TERMS OF ENDEARMENT(1983)
1984
JOHNNY DANGEROUSLY(1984)
Ralph DeVito
DEATH COLLECTOR(1976), d&w
Misc. Talkies
FAMILY ENFORCER(1978), d
Francis Devlaeminck
SMALL CHANGE(1976, Fr.)
Laurent Devlaeminck
SMALL CHANGE(1976, Fr.)
Alan Devlin
MOUSE AND THE WOMAN, THE(1981, Brit.); ANGEL(1982, Irish); LONG GOOD FRIDAY, THE(1982, Brit.)
Brigid Devlin
SKATETOWN, U.S.A.(1979)
Cory Devlin
TWELVE TO THE MOON(1960)
Dean Devlin
MY BODYGUARD(1980)
1984
WILD LIFE, THE(1984)
Don Devlin
CATERED AFFAIR, THE(1956); RUMBLE ON THE DOCKS(1956); THREE VIOLENT PEOPLE(1956); BLOOD OF DRACULA(1957); ESCAPE FROM SAN QUENTIN(1957); YOUNG AND DANGEROUS(1957); TANK BATTALION(1958); OPERATION DAMES(1959); ANATOMY OF A PSYCHO(1961); THUNDER ISLAND(1963), w; LOVING(1970), p, w; FORTUNE, THE(1975), p; HARRY AND WALTER GO TO NEW YORK(1976), p; MY BODYGUARD(1980), p
Donald Devlin
SWELL GUY(1946)
J. C. Devlin
COMEDY MAN, THE(1964); INNOCENT BYSTANDERS(1973, Brit.)
J.G. Devlin
RISING OF THE MOON, THE(1957, Ireland); DARBY O'GILL AND THE LITTLE PEOPLE(1959); ATTEMPT TO KILL(1961, Brit.); BIG GAMBLE, THE(1961); FRIGHTENED CITY, THE(1961, Brit.); I THANK A FOOL(1962, Brit.); JOHNNY NOBODY(1965, Brit.); GUNS IN THE HEATHER(1968, Brit.); RECKONING, THE(1971, Brit.); OUTSIDER, THE(1980); SIR HENRY AT RAWLINSON END(1980, Brit.)
James Devlin
CAPTAIN LIGHTFOOT(1955); JACQUELINE(1956, Brit.)
Jane Devlin
SINCE YOU WENT AWAY(1944)
Jay Devlin
CROSS AND THE SWITCHBLADE, THE(1970); THREE DAYS OF THE CONDOR(1975)
Joe A. Devlin
ANGELS WITH DIRTY FACES(1938); SWEETHEARTS(1938)
Joe Devlin
GANGSTER'S BOY(1938); PAROLED FROM THE BIG HOUSE(1938); ADVENTURES OF JANE ARDEN(1939); ANOTHER THIN MAN(1939); HELL'S KITCHEN(1939); KING OF THE UNDERWORLD(1939); NO PLACE TO GO(1939); OKLAHOMA KID, THE(1939); PANAMA LADY(1939); ROARING TWENTIES, THE(1939); TORCHY RUNS FOR MAYOR(1939); FUGITIVE FROM JUSTICE, A(1940); HALF A SINNER(1940); INVISIBLE STRIPES(1940); STRIKE UP THE BAND(1940); THEY DRIVE BY NIGHT(1940); FLAME OF NEW ORLEANS(1941); HONKY TONK(1941); MAN BETRAYED, A(1941); MANPOWER(1941); SHADOW OF THE THIN MAN(1941); SIS HOPKINS(1941); WHISTLING IN THE DARK(1941); DEVIL

WITH HITLER, THE(1942); LARCENY, INC.(1942); SHEPHERD OF THE OZARKS(1942); THEY DIED WITH THEIR BOOTS ON(1942); HI DIDDLE DIDDLE(1943); LADY OF BURLESQUE(1943); SLIGHTLY DANGEROUS(1943); THAT NAZTY NUISANCE(1943); THEY GOT ME COVERED(1943); DELINQUENT DAUGHTERS(1944); MIRACLE OF MORGAN'S CREEK, THE(1944); MR. SKEFFINGTON(1944); MY BUDDY(1944); SEE HERE, PRIVATE HARGROVE(1944); SENSATIONS OF 1945(1944); SWEETHEARTS OF THE U.S.A.(1944); BEDSIDE MANNER(1945); BOSTON BLACKIE'S RENDEZVOUS(1945); DIXIE JAMBOREE(1945); SCARLET STREET(1945); SHANGHAI COBRA, THE(1945); WITHOUT LOVE(1945); WOMAN IN THE WINDOW, THE(1945); BRINGING UP FATHER(1946); CRIMINAL COURT(1946); HOODLUM SAINT, THE(1946); SAN QUENTIN(1946); BODY AND SOUL(1947); SHOOT TO KILL(1947); THAT WAY WITH WOMEN(1947); ON OUR MERRY WAY(1948); SONG IS BORN, A(1948); KISS IN THE DARK, A(1949); NIGHT UNTO NIGHT(1949); DOUBLE DYNAMITE(1951); ON DANGEROUS GROUND(1951); STOP THAT CAB(1951); BITTER CREEK(1954); SILVER LODE(1954); ABBOTT AND COSTELLO MEET THE KEYSTONE KOPS(1955); TENNESSEE'S PARTNER(1955); SHAKE, RATTLE, AND ROCK!(1957); UP IN SMOKE(1957); DECKS RAN RED, THE(1958); IN THE MONEY(1958); LAST OF THE SECRET AGENTS?, THE(1966); GOOD TIMES(1967)
Misc. Talkies
LAST THREE(1942)
John Devlin
GREAT GATSBY, THE(1974)
1984
MASS APPEAL(1984)
Joseph Devlin
ENCHANTED VALLEY, THE(1948)
Nancy Devlin
FOUR BOYS AND A GUN(1957)
Tony Devlin
PREHISTORIC WOMEN(1950)
William Devlin
CONCERNING MR. MARTIN(1937, Brit.); I MET A MURDERER(1939, Brit.); JAMAICA INN(1939, Brit.); MILL ON THE FLOSS(1939, Brit.); MUTINY OF THE ELSINORE, THE(1939, Brit.); TREASURE ISLAND(1950, Brit.); BLOOD OF THE VAMPIRE(1958, Brit.); OSCAR WILDE(1960, Brit.); JOKERS, THE(1967, Brit.); SHUTTERED ROOM, THE(1968, Brit.)
Jim Devney
MALIBU HIGH(1979)
Devo
HUMAN HIGHWAY(1982), m
Devo's Nuclear Garbagemen
HUMAN HIGHWAY(1982)
Leon DeVoe
WHIRLWIND(1951)
DeVol
TEXAS ACROSS THE RIVER(1966), m
Frank DeVol
WORLD FOR RANSOM(1954), m; BIG KNIFE, THE(1955), m; FRESH FROM PARIS(1955), md; KISS ME DEADLY(1955), m; PARIS FOLLIES OF 1956(1955), md; ATTACK!(1956), m; PILLOW TALK(1959), m; LOVER COME BACK(1961), m; PARENT TRAP, THE(1961), m; BOYS' NIGHT OUT(1962), m; WHATEVER HAPPENED TO BABY JANE?(1962), m; UNDER THE YUM-YUM TREE(1963), m; GOOD NEIGHBOR SAM(1964), m; SEND ME NO FLOWERS(1964), m; CAT BALLOU(1965), m; VERY SPECIAL FAVOR, A(1965); BIG MOUTH, THE(1967); CAPRICE(1967), m; DIRTY DOZEN, THE(1967, Brit.), m; BALLAD OF JOSIE(1968), m; ULZANA'S RAID(1972), m; EMPEROR OF THE NORTH POLE(1973), m; LONGEST YARD, THE(1974), m; HUSTLE(1975), m; CHOIRBOYS, THE(1977), m; FRISCO KID, THE(1979), m
Gordon Devol
HAROLD AND MAUDE(1971); REFLECTION OF FEAR, A(1973); NO LONGER ALONE(1978)
Misc. Talkies
KILLING AT OUTPOST ZETA, THE(1980)
Norman Devol
MAKING THE GRADE(1929), ph
Silents
OUTLAWED(1929), ph
Laura Devon
GOODBYE CHARLIE(1964); RED LINE 7000(1965); CHAMBER OF HORRORS(1966); COVENANT WITH DEATH, A(1966); GUNN(1967)
Richard Devon
PRODIGAL, THE(1955); BLOOD OF DRACULA(1957); ESCAPE FROM SAN QUENTIN(1957); SAGA OF THE VIKING WOMEN AND THEIR VOYAGE TO THE WATERS OF THE GREAT SEA SERPENT, THE(1957); TEENAGE DOLL(1957); UNDEAD, THE(1957); BADMAN'S COUNTRY(1958); MACHINE GUN KELLY(1958); MONEY, WOMEN AND GUNS(1958); WAR OF THE SATELLITES(1958); BATTLE OF BLOOD ISLAND(1960); GUNFIGHTERS OF ABILENE(1960); COMANCHEROS, THE(1961); KID GALAHAD(1962); CATTLE KING(1963); THREE STOOGES GO AROUND THE WORLD IN A DAZE, THE(1963); SILENCERS, THE(1966); THREE GUNS FOR TEXAS(1968)
Misc. Talkies
SCORCHING FURY(1952)
Tony Devon
KING OF COMEDY, THE(1983); WITHOUT A TRACE(1983)
Chester DeVonde
KONGO(1932), w
Felicity Devonshire
Misc. Talkies
NAUGHTY WIVES(1974); WHOSE CHILD AM I?(1976)
Donald Devor
FROM THE MIXED-UP FILES OF MRS. BASIL E. FRANKWEILER(1973), m
Christopher DeVore
ELEPHANT MAN, THE(1980, Brit.), w; FRANCES(1982), w
Dorothy Devore
TAKE THE HEIR(1930)
Silents
WHEN ODDS ARE EVEN(1923); NARROW STREET, THE(1924); PRAIRIE WIFE, THE(1925); GILDED HIGHWAY, THE(1926); SOCIAL HIGHWAYMAN, THE(1926); NO BABIES WANTED(1928)

Misc. Silents
45 MINUTES FROM BROADWAY(1920); MAGNIFICENT BRUTE, THE(1921); HOLD YOUR BREATH(1924); TOMBOY, THE(1924); BROADWAY BUTTERFLY, A(1925); FIGHTING THE FLAMES(1925); HIS MAJESTY BUNKER BEAN(1925); HOW BAXTER BUTTED IN(1925); MIDNIGHT FLYER, THE(1925); THREE WEEKS IN PARIS(1925); WHO CARES(1925); MAN UPSTAIRS, THE(1926); MONEY TO BURN(1926); SENOR DAREDEVIL(1926); BETTER DAYS(1927); FIRST NIGHT, THE(1927); MOUNTAINS OF MANHATTAN(1927); WRONG MR. WRIGHT, THE(1927); TAKE THE HEIR(1930)
Frank Devore
DEER HUNTER, THE(1978)
Gary DeVore
DOGS OF WAR, THE(1980, Brit.), w; BACK ROADS(1981), w
Mary Lou Devore
WOMEN'S PRISON(1955)
Sy Devore
YELLOW CANARY, THE(1963), cos; WRECKING CREW, THE(1968), cos
Heather Devore-Haase
1984
HARD TO HOLD(1984)
Jess Devorska
SO IT'S SUNDAY(1932)
Silents
JAKE THE PLUMBER(1927)
Jesse DeVorska
GOLDIE(1931)
Barry DeVorzon
R.P.M.(1970), m; DILLINGER(1973), m; HARD TIMES(1975), m; BOBBIE JO AND THE OUTLAW(1976), m; ROLLING THUNDER(1977), m; NINTH CONFIGURATION, THE(1980), m; XANADU(1980), m; LOOKER(1981), m; TATTOO(1981), m; JEKYLL AND HYDE...TOGETHER AGAIN(1982), m
Jacques Devos
PROSTITUTION(1965, Fr.)
Louis Devos
MOSES AND AARON(1975, Ger./Fr./Ital.)
Raymond Devos
PIERROT LE FOU(1968, Fr./Ital.)
Bernard DeVoto
ACROSS THE WIDE MISSOURI(1951), w
Ian deVoy
WHY ROCK THE BOAT?(1974, Can.)
Blanche Devreaux
STING OF DEATH(1966)
Frederic Devreese
BENVENUTA(1983, Fr.), m
Charles DeVries
MORITURI(1965)
Dolf DeVries
1984
FOURTH MAN, THE(1984, Neth.)
George DeVries
AROUND THE WORLD UNDER THE SEA(1966); MISSION MARS(1968); EYES OF A STRANGER(1980)
Jon DeVries
LIANNA(1983)
Peter DeVries
TUNNEL OF LOVE, THE(1958), w; REUBEN, REUBEN(1983), w
Elaine DeVry
MAN-TRAP(1961); DIARY OF A MADMAN(1963); GUIDE FOR THE MARRIED MAN, A(1967); WITH SIX YOU GET EGGROLL(1968); CHEYENNE SOCIAL CLUB, THE(1970); BLESS THE BEASTS AND CHILDREN(1971); BOY WHO CRIED WEREWOLF, THE(1973); HERBIE RIDES AGAIN(1974)
Paul Devry
PEGGY(1950)
Ed Dew
MOB TOWN(1941)
Eddie Dew
PROFESSOR BEWARE(1938); CYCLONE ON HORSEBACK(1941); DEVIL AND DANIEL WEBSTER, THE(1941); PARIS CALLING(1941); SUNSET IN WYOMING(1941); ACROSS THE PACIFIC(1942); ARMY SURGEON(1942); MY FAVORITE BLONDE(1942); PIRATES OF THE PRAIRIE(1942); RIDING THE WIND(1942); SHADOWS ON THE SAGE(1942); STAR SPANGLED RHYTHM(1942); BEYOND THE LAST FRONTIER(1943); DESTROYER(1943); FIGHTING FRONTIER(1943); FLIGHT FOR FREEDOM(1943); HI, BUDDY(1943); LADIES' DAY(1943); MEXICAN SPITFIRE'S BLESSED EVENT(1943); RAIDERS OF SUNSET PASS(1943); RED RIVER ROBIN HOOD(1943); SALUTE FOR THREE(1943); SIX GUN GOSPEL(1943); OLD TEXAS TRAIL, THE(1944); RIDERS OF THE SANTA FE(1944); TRAIL TO GUNSIGHT(1944); TRIGGER TRAIL(1944); BEYOND THE PECOS(1945); RENEGADES OF THE RIO GRANDE(1945); SUNSET BOULEVARD(1950); SCARLET ANGEL(1952); THEM!(1954)
Edward Dew
FIGHTING 69TH, THE(1940); MILITARY ACADEMY(1940); LET'S FACE IT(1943); SO PROUDLY WE HAIL(1943); NAKED GUN, THE(1956), d; PAGAN ISLAND(1961); WINGS OF CHANCE(1961, Can.), d
Simon Christopher Dew
QUIET DAY IN BELFAST, A(1974, Can.), ed
Larry DeWaay
DOGS OF WAR, THE(1980, Brit.), p
Patrick Dewaere
GOING PLACES(1974, Fr.); CATHERINE & CO.(1976, Fr.); BEST WAY, THE(1978, Fr.); GET OUT YOUR HANDKERCHIEFS(1978, Fr.); BEAU PERE(1981, Fr.); PARADISE POUR TOUS(1982, Fr.)
1984
HEAT OF DESIRE(1984, Fr.)
Aubrey Dewar
SEPARATION(1968, Brit.), ph; OTHER SIDE OF THE UNDERNEATH, THE(1972, Brit.), ph
Dicky Dewar
RING AROUND THE MOON(1936)

Donald Dewar
RETURN OF THE VAMPIRE, THE(1944); TONIGHT AND EVERY NIGHT(1945); SECRET HEART, THE(1946); LARCENY(1948); YOU GOTTA STAY HAPPY(1948)

Frank Dewar
ALCATRAZ ISLAND(1937), ed; FUGITIVE IN THE SKY(1937), ed; GUNS OF THE PECOS(1937), ed; PUBLIC WEDDING(1937), ed; WEST OF SHANGHAI(1937), ed; WHITE BONDAGE(1937), ed; HE COULDN'T SAY NO(1938), ed; PENROD AND HIS TWIN BROTHER(1938), ed; PENROD'S DOUBLE TROUBLE(1938), ed; KING OF THE UNDERWORLD(1939), ed; NANCY DREW-REPORTER(1939), ed; PRIDE OF THE BLUEGRASS(1939), ed

Ian Dewar
MIND BENDERS, THE(1963, Brit.); HUNCH, THE(1967, Brit.)

John DeWar
SATIN MUSHROOM, THE(1969)

Kash Dewar
PUMPKIN EATER, THE(1964, Brit.)

Edmund Deward
WILD INNOCENCE(1937, Aus.), w

Ted DeWayne
VARIETY GIRL(1947); JULIA MISBEHAVES(1948)

Bonnie Dewberry
POINT BLANK(1967)

Jack Dewees
LOVE ON THE RUN(1936)

Bill DeWeese
EDDIE MACON'S RUN(1983)

Michael Dewell
RICH AND FAMOUS(1981)

Jean Dewever
LIFE UPSIDE DOWN(1965, Fr.); KILLING GAME, THE(1968, Fr.)

Anna Dewey
MIRACLE IN THE RAIN(1956)

Arthur Dewey
WHOOPEE(1930)
Silents
INNER MAN, THE(1922); AMERICA(1924)

Christopher C. Dewey
JUMP(1971), p; SAM'S SONG(1971), p

Diane Dewey
U-TURN(1973, Can.); MIDDLE AGE CRAZY(1980, Can.)
Misc. Talkies
GIRL IN BLUE, THE(1974)

Earl Dewey
PETTICOAT LARCENY(1943); LOUISIANA HAYRIDE(1944); ROGUES GAL-LERY(1945); DECEPTION(1946)

Earl S. Dewey
STATE FAIR(1945)

Earle Dewey
H.M. PULHAM, ESQ.(1941); THIS GUN FOR HIRE(1942); DOUGHGIRLS, THE(1944); HONEYMOON AHEAD(1945)

Earle S. Dewey
IN OLD MISSOURI(1940); I MARRIED AN ANGEL(1942); SHADOW OF A DOUBT(1943)

Edward Dewey
TAKE MY LIFE(1942), w

Elmer Dewey
Silents
BRING HIM IN(1921); GIRLS DON'T GAMBLE(1921); TAKING CHANCES(1922)
Misc. Silents
SHADOWS OF CHINATOWN(1926)

George Dewey
Silents
NO MOTHER TO GUIDE HER(1923)

Jane Dewey
WELLS FARGO(1937); MEN WITH WINGS(1938); YOU AND ME(1938); RULERS OF THE SEA(1939)

Mike Dewey
GREAT WALDO PEPPER, THE(1975), stunts

Mr. Dewey
Silents
LOVE IN A HURRY(1919)

Mrs. Charles Dewey
Silents
AMATEUR WIFE, THE(1920)

John Dewey-Carter
BUCK ROGERS IN THE 25TH CENTURY(1979)

Colleen Dewhurst
TRIBUTE(1980, Can.); NUN'S STORY, THE(1959); MAN ON A STRING(1960); FINE MADNESS, A(1966); LAST RUN, THE(1971); COWBOYS, THE(1972); MC Q(1974); ANNIE HALL(1977); ICE CASTLES(1978); THIRD WALKER, THE(1978, Can.); WHEN A STRANGER CALLS(1979); FINAL ASSIGNMENT(1980, Can.); DEAD ZONE, THE(1983)

Dorothy Dewhurst
FULL SPEED AHEAD(1936, Brit.); GRAND FINALE(1936, Brit.); LOVE AT SEA(1936, Brit.); TWO ON A DOORSTEP(1936, Brit.); MR. SMITH CARRIES ON(1937, Brit.); PASSENGER TO LONDON(1937, Brit.); BEDTIME STORY(1938, Brit.); OLD MOTHER RILEY JOINS UP(1939, Brit.); STOLEN LIFE(1939, Brit.); MYSTERIOUS MR. REEDER, THE(1940, Brit.); FACING THE MUSIC(1941, Brit.); STRANGER AT MY DOOR(1950, Brit.); RAISING A RIOT(1957, Brit.)

Eve Dewhurst
OLD MOTHER RILEY, HEADMISTRESS(1950, Brit.)

George Dewhurst
SISTER TO ASSIST'ER, A(1930, Brit.), d&w; NEVER TROUBLE TROUBLE(1931, Brit.), a, w; NO LADY(1931, Brit.), w; ADVENTURE LIMITED(1934, Brit.), w; GET YOUR MAN(1934, Brit.), w; PRICE OF WISDOM, THE(1935, Brit.), w; KING OF THE CASTLE(1936, Brit.), w; LOVE AT SEA(1936, Brit.); WEDNESDAY'S LUCK(1936, Brit.); SISTER TO ASSIST'ER, A(1938, Brit.), d, w; SISTER TO ASSIST'ER, A(1948, Brit.), d&w

Silents
DEAD CERTAINTY, A(1920, Brit.), d; NARROW VALLEY, THE(1921, Brit.); CRIMSON CIRCLE, THE(1922, Brit.); SISTER TO ASSIST 'ER, A(1922, Brit.), d&w; LITTLE DOOR INTO THE WORLD, THE(1923, Brit.), w; UNINVITED GUEST, THE(1923, Brit.), p,d&w; PIPES OF PAN, THE(1923, Brit.), w; MOTORING(1927, Brit.), d; SISTER TO ASSIST 'ER, A(1927, Brit.), d&w

Misc. Silents
IT'S NEVER TOO LATE TO MEND(1917, Brit.); MAN WHO MADE GOOD, THE(1917, Brit.); QUICKSANDS(1917); GREAT COUP, A(1919, Brit.), d; HOMEMAKER, THE(1919, Brit.), d; TOILERS, THE(1919, Brit.); HELEN OF FOUR GATES(1920, Brit.); SHADOW BETWEEN, THE(1920, Brit.), d; DOLLARS IN SURREY(1921, Brit.), d; TINTED VENUS, THE(1921, Brit.); WILD HEATHER(1921, Brit.); WHAT THE BUTLER SAW(1924, Brit.), d; RISING GENERATION, THE(1928, Brit.), d

George W. Dewhurst
Silents
NARROW VALLEY, THE(1921, Brit.), w

William Dewhurst
VICTORIA THE GREAT(1937, Brit.); TOILERS OF THE SEA(1936, Brit.); BULLDOG DRUMMOND AT BAY(1937, Brit.); DARK JOURNEY(1937, Brit.); DINNER AT THE RITZ(1937, Brit.); NON-STOP NEW YORK(1937, Brit.); SABOTAGE(1937, Brit.); WIND-MILL, THE(1937, Brit.); SAILING ALONG(1938, Brit.); TWENTY-ONE DAYS TOGETHER(1940, Brit.)

Sheila DeWindt
CONCORDE, THE-AIRPORT '79(; GOLDENGIRL(1979)

Jo DeWinter
DIRTY HARRY(1971)

Roslyn DeWinter
INTERLUDE(1968, Brit.)

Alan Dewit
TALES OF TERROR(1962)

Jacqueline DeWit
CHARLIE CHAN IN BLACK MAGIC(1944); SARATOGA TRUNK(1945); SHE WROTE THE BOOK(1946)

Alan DeWitt
LUV(1967); BURY ME AN ANGEL(1972); WAR BETWEEN MEN AND WOMEN, THE(1972)

Angela DeWitt
RENDEZVOUS 24(1946)

Elaine DeWitt
Misc. Talkies
TEN MILLION DOLLAR GRAB(1966, Ital.)

Fay DeWitt
SHAKIEST GUN IN THE WEST, THE(1968)
Misc. Talkies
KITTY CAN'T HELP IT(1975)

Faye Dewitt
HARPER VALLEY, P.T.A.(1978)

George DeWitt
HOLE IN THE HEAD, A(1959); LENNY(1974)

Jack DeWitt
INTERNATIONAL LADY(1941), w; BEYOND THE BLUE HORIZON(1942), w; DON RICARDO RETURNS(1946), w; BELLS OF SAN FERNANDO(1947), w; ROCKY(1948), w; BOMBA THE JUNGLE BOY(1949), W; CANADIAN PACIFIC(1949), w; HIGH-WAYMAN, THE(1951), w; LADY AND THE BANDIT, THE(1951), w; FARGO(1952), w; GUN BELT(1953), w; SON OF BELLE STARR(1953), w; KHYBER PATROL(1954), w; SITTING BULL(1954), w; BAMBOO PRISON, THE(1955), w; WOMEN'S PRISON(1955), w; BEAST OF HOLLOW MOUNTAIN, THE(1956), w; RUMBLE ON THE DOCKS(1956), w; PORTLAND EXPOSE(1957), w; ROCK ALL NIGHT(1957); OREGON PASSAGE(1958), w; WOLF LARSEN(1958), w; PURPLE GANG, THE(1960), w; FIVE GUNS TO TOMBSTONE(1961), w; JACK OF DIAMONDS(1967, U.S./Ger.), w; ONE STEP TO HELL(1969, U.S./Ital./Span.), w; MAN CALLED HORSE, A(1970), w; MAN IN THE WILDERNESS(1971, U.S./Span.), w; NEPTUNE FACTOR, THE(1973, Can.), w; RETURN OF A MAN CALLED HORSE, THE(1976), w; SKY RIDERS(1976, U.S./Gr.), w; TRIUMPHS OF A MAN CALLED HORSE(1983, US/Mex.), w

Jacqueline DeWitt
FOG ISLAND(1945); FIRST LEGION, THE(1951)

Lew DeWitt
SMOKEY AND THE BANDIT II(1980)

Louis DeWitt
HELL BOUND(1957), spec eff; INVISIBLE BOY, THE(1957), spec eff; KRO-NOS(1957), p, spec eff; DESERT HELL(1958), spec eff; FORT BOWIE(1958), spec eff; MACABRE(1958), spec eff; MONSTER FROM THE GREEN HELL(1958), spec eff; MURDER BY CONTRACT(1958), spec eff; WAR OF THE SATELLITES(1958), spec eff; THIRTY FOOT BRIDE OF CANDY ROCK, THE(1959), spec eff; ATOMIC SUBMA-RINE, THE(1960), spec eff

Roger DeWitt
HEIDI'S SONG(1982)

Al Dewlen
TWILIGHT OF HONOR(1963), w

Al Dewlin
RIDE BEYOND VENGEANCE(1966), w

David Dewlow
FIGHT FOR YOUR LIFE(1977)

Karen DeWoff
GO WEST, YOUNG LADY(1941), w

Grete deWolf
COCKEYED MIRACLE, THE(1946)

Guy deWolf
COCKEYED MIRACLE, THE(1946)

Jack DeWolf
WITHOUT WARNING(1980), prod d; WORM EATERS, THE(1981), prod d

Karen DeWolf
CONDEMNED TO LIVE(1935), w; NOTORIOUS GENTLEMAN, A(1935), w; PUBLIC OPINION(1935), w; DOUGHNUTS AND SOCIETY(1936), w; RIDE, RANGER, RI-DE(1936), w; BORROWING TROUBLE(1937), w; DANGEROUS HOLIDAY(1937), d&w; LOVE IN A BUNGALOW(1937), w; SAFETY IN NUMBERS(1938), w; WALKING DOWN BROADWAY(1938), w; SAGA OF DEATH VALLEY(1939), w; HER FIRST BEAU(1941), w; SADDLEMATES(1941), w; TILLIE THE TOILER(1941), w; MEET THE STEWARTS(1942), w; NINE GIRLS(1944), w; COCKEYED MIRACLE, THE(1946), w; IT'S GREAT TO BE YOUNG(1946), w; RETURN OF OCTOBER,

THE(1948), w; HOLIDAY IN HAVANA(1949), w; JOHNNY ALLEGRO(1949), w; MAKE BELIEVE BALLROOM(1949), w; SLIGHTLY FRENCH(1949), w

DeWolfe
MONTY PYTHON AND THE HOLY GRAIL(1975, Brit.), m

Billy DeWolfe
BLUE SKIES(1946); BILLIE(1965); WORLD'S GREATEST ATHLETE, THE(1973)

Jack DeWolfe
HOLLYWOOD BOULEVARD(1976), art d

Karen DeWolfe
FOOTLIGHT GLAMOUR(1943), w; GETTING GERTIE'S GARTER(1945), w; WHEN YOU'RE SMILING(1950), W

Dorothy DeWolff
Misc. Silents
VOICES FROM THE PAST(1915)

Francis DeWolff
CLUE OF THE TWISTED CANDLE(1968, Brit.)

Edward Dewsbury
WINTER'S TALE, THE(1968, Brit.)

Ralph Dewsbury
Silents
GREATER NEED, THE(1916, Brit.), d
Misc. Silents
HIS VINDICATION(1915, Brit.), d; MAN IN THE ATTIC, THE(1915, Brit.), d; WHOSO DIGGETH A PIT(1915, Brit.), d; HIS DAUGHTER'S DILEMMA(1916, Brit.), d; MAN IN MOTLEY, THE(1916, Brit.), d; PARTNERS AT LAST(1916, Brit.), d; GOLDEN DAWN, THE(1921, Brit.), d

Alan Dexter
CITY OF BAD MEN(1953); FORBIDDEN(1953); IT CAME FROM OUTER SPACE(1953); MISSISSIPPI GAMBLER, THE(1953); DOWN THREE DARK STREETS(1954); PUSHOVER(1954); ENEMY BELOW, THE(1957); TIME LIMIT(1957); I MARRIED A MONSTER FROM OUTER SPACE(1958); STEP DOWN TO TERROR(1958); VOICE IN THE MIRROR(1958); OPERATION PETTICOAT(1959); BRASS BOTTLE, THE(1964); KISS ME, STUPID(1964); PAINT YOUR WAGON(1969)

Anthony Dexter
THOROUGHLY MODERN MILLIE(1967); VALENTINO(1951); BRIGAND, THE(1952); CAPTAIN JOHN SMITH AND POCAHONTAS(1953); BLACK PIRATES, THE(1954, Mex.); CAPTAIN KIDD AND THE SLAVE GIRL(1954); FIRE MAIDENS FROM OUTER SPACE(1956, Brit.); HE LAUGHED LAST(1956); PARSON AND THE OUTLAW, THE(1957); STORY OF MANKIND, THE(1957); TWELVE TO THE MOON(1960); PHANTOM PLANET, THE(1961); MARRIED TOO YOUNG(1962); SATURDAY NIGHT IN APPLE VALLEY(1965)

Aubrey Dexter
RICH AND STRANGE(1932, Brit.); OUT OF THE PAST(1933, Brit.); LOYALTIES(1934, Brit.); CROSS CURRENTS(1935, Brit.); LOVE TEST, THE(1935, Brit.); PRIVATE SECRETARY, THE(1935, Brit.); IT'S IN THE BAG(1936, Brit.); PLEASE TEACHER(1937, Brit.); SHOW GOES ON, THE(1937, Brit.); SIXTY GLORIOUS YEARS(1938, Brit.); HIS BROTHER'S KEEPER(1939, Brit.); CASTLE OF CRIMES(1940, Brit.); GASLIGHT(1940, Brit.); OLD MOTHER RILEY IN SOCIETY(1940, Brit.); SALOON BAR(1940, Brit.); YOUNG MAN'S FANCY(1943, Brit.); DULCIMER STREET(1948, Brit.); ROOM TO LET(1949, Brit.); NIGHT AND THE CITY(1950, Brit.); STARS IN YOUR EYES(1956, Brit.); COUNTERFEIT PLAN, THE(1957, Brit.); PRINCE AND THE SHOWGIRL, THE(1957, Brit.)

Bob Dexter
Silents
AS A MAN LIVES(1923), w

Brad Dexter
ASPHALT JUNGLE, THE(1950); FOURTEEN HOURS(1951); LAS VEGAS STORY, THE(1952); MACAO(1952); 99 RIVER STREET(1953); HOUSE OF BAMBOO(1955); UNTAMED(1955); VIOLENT SATURDAY(1955); BETWEEN HEAVEN AND HELL(1956); BOTTOM OF THE BOTTLE, THE(1956); OKLAHOMAN, THE(1957); RUN SILENT, RUN DEEP(1958); LAST TRAIN FROM GUN HILL(1959); VICE RAID(1959); MAGNIFICENT SEVEN, THE(1960); THIRTEEN FIGHTING MEN(1960); GEORGE RAFT STORY, THE(1961); TWENTY PLUS TWO(1961); X-15(1961); TARAS BULBA(1962); JOHNNY COOL(1963); KINGS OF THE SUN(1963); INVITATION TO A GUNFIGHTER(1964); BUS RILEY'S BACK IN TOWN(1965); NONE BUT THE BRAVE(1965, U.S./Jap.); VON RYAN'S EXPRESS(1965); BLINDFOLD(1966); NAKED RUNNER, THE(1967, Brit.), p; LAWYER, THE(1969), p; JORY(1972); SHAMPOO(1975); VIGILANTE FORCE(1976); HOUSE CALLS(1978); PRIVATE FILES OF J. EDGAR HOOVER, THE(1978); WINTER KILLS(1979)

Elliot Dexter
Silents
DAPHNE AND THE PIRATE(1916); ETERNAL TEMPTRESS, THE(1917); DON'T TELL EVERYTHING(1921); ENTER MADAME(1922)

Elliott Dexter
Silents
MASQUERADERS, THE(1915); PLOW GIRL, THE(1916); RISE OF JENNIE CUSHING, THE(1917); ROMANCE OF THE REDWOODS, A(1917); OLD WIVES FOR NEW(1918); SOMETHING TO THINK ABOUT(1920); AFFAIRS OF ANATOL, THE(1921); WITCHING HOUR, THE(1921); ADAM'S RIB(1923); COMMON LAW, THE(1923); ONLY 38(1923); SOULS FOR SALE(1923); SPITFIRE, THE(1924); STELLA MARIS(1925); WASTED LIVES(1925)
Misc. Silents
AMERICAN BEAUTY, THE(1916); DIPLOMACY(1916); HEART OF NORA FLYNN, THE(1916); INTERNATIONAL MARRIAGE, AN(1916); LASH, THE(1916); VICTORY OF CONSCIENCE, THE(1916); CASTLES FOR TWO(1917); INNER SHRINE, THE(1917); LOST AND WON(1917); STRANDED IN ARCADY(1917); TIDES OF BARNEGAT, THE(1917); GIRL WHO CAME BACK, THE(1918); SQUAW MAN, THE(1918); VENGEANCE IS MINE(1918); WE CAN'T HAVE EVERYTHING(1918); WHISPERING CHORUS, THE(1918); WOMAN AND WIFE(1918); WOMAN'S WEAPONS(1918); DAUGHTER OF THE WOLF, A(1919); DON'T CHANGE YOUR HUSBAND(1919); FOR BETTER, FOR WORSE(1919); MAGGIE PEPPER(1919); BEHOLD MY WIFE!(1920); GRAND LARCENY(1922); HANDS OF NARA, THE(1922); FLAMING YOUTH(1923); OLD SWEETHEART OF MINE, AN(1923); AGE OF INNOCENCE, THE(1924); BY DIVINE RIGHT(1924); FAST SET, THE(1924); FOR WOMAN'S FAVOR(1924); TRIFLERS, THE(1924); CAPITAL PUNISHMENT(1925)

Frank Dexter, Sr.
PAPER BULLETS(1941), art d

Gayne Dexter
SILENCE OF DEAN MAITLAND, THE(1934, Aus.), w

Helen Dexter
FLASHDANCE(1983)

Jean Dexter
I NEVER SANG FOR MY FATHER(1970)

Jerry Dexter
PATSY, THE(1964); DOWNHILL RACER(1969)

Johm Dexter
VIRGIN SOLDIERS, THE(1970, Brit.), d

John Dexter
LAURA(1944); BUFFALO BILL RIDES AGAIN(1947); SIDELONG GLANCES OF A PIGEON KICKER, THE(1970), d; I WANT WHAT I WANT(1972, Brit.), d

Mary Dexter
MARYJANE(1968), w

Maury Dexter
ONE EXCITING WEEK(1946); HIGH-POWERED RIFLE, THE(1960), p&d; THIRD VOICE, THE(1960), p; WALK TALL(1960), p&d; LITTLE SHEPHERD OF KINGDOM COME(1961), p; PURPLE HILLS, THE(1961), p&d; AIR PATROL(1962), p, d; FIRE-BRAND, THE(1962), p&d; WOMAN HUNT(1962), p&d; DAY MARS INVADED EARTH, THE(1963), p&d; HARBOR LIGHTS(1963), p&d; HOUSE OF THE DAMNED(1963), p&d; POLICE NURSE(1963), p&d; YELLOW CANARY, THE(1963), p; YOUNG GUNS OF TEXAS(1963), p&d; YOUNG SWINGERS, THE(1963), p&d; RAIDERS FROM BENEATH THE SEA(1964), p&d; SURF PARTY(1964), p&d; NAKED BRIGADE, THE(1965, U.S./Gr.), d; WILD ON THE BEACH(1965), p&d; BORN WILD(1968), p&d; MARYJANE(1968), p&d; MINI-SKIRT MOB, THE(1968), p&d; HELL'S BELLES(1969), p&d

Peggy Dexter
WE'LL SMILE AGAIN(1942, Brit.); THEATRE ROYAL(1943, Brit.); THEY MET IN THE DARK(1945, Brit.)

Rit Dexter
TOUCH OF HER FLESH, THE(1967)

Ron Dexter
GAS-S-S-S!(1970), ph

Rosemarie Dexter
CASANOVA '70(1965, Ital.); MALE COMPANION(1965, Fr./Ital.); ALL THE OTHER GIRLS DO!(1967, Ital.); ROMEO AND JULIET(1968, Ital./Span.); SHOES OF THE FISHERMAN, THE(1968); DIRTY OUTLAWS, THE(1971, Ital.)

Rosemary Dexter
OMICRON(1963, Ital.); FOR A FEW DOLLARS MORE(1967, Ital./Ger./Span.); HOUSE OF CARDS(1969); COMETOGETHER(1971)

Sharon Dexter
BUFFALO BILL IN TOMAHAWK TERRITORY(1952); OTHER WOMAN, THE(1954)

Tony "Anthony" Dexter
THREE BLONDES IN HIS LIFE(1961)

Van Dexter
TINGLER, THE(1959), m

Von Dexter
HOUSE ON HAUNTED HILL(1958), m; THIRTEEN GHOSTS(1960), m; MR. SARDONICUS(1961), m

William Dexter
KNACK ... AND HOW TO GET IT, THE(1965, Brit.); LOVE IS A WOMAN(1967, Brit.); HAND OF NIGHT, THE(1968, Brit.); MY LOVER, MY SON(1970, Brit.); YOUNG WINSTON(1972, Brit.)

Gita Dey
TWO DAUGHTERS(1963, India)

Howard L. Dey
NEW ORLEANS UNCENSORED(1955)

Shelagh Dey
UGLY DUCKLING, THE(1959, Brit.)

Susan Dey
SKYJACKED(1972); FIRST LOVE(1977); LOOKER(1981)

Peter Deyell
MASSACRE AT CENTRAL HIGH(1976), makeup

Lien Deyers
DIE MANNER UM LUCIE(1931); GOLD(1934, Ger.)
Silents
SPIES(1929, Ger.)

Serge Deyglun
RED(1970, Can.)

Rudolf Deyl
ECSTACY OF YOUNG LOVE(1936, Czech.); LEMONADE JOE(1966, Czech.)

Rudolif Deyl
SKELETON ON HORSEBACK(1940, Czech.)

Rudolf Deyl, Jr.
WISHING MACHINE(1971, Czech.)

Kazimierz Deyna
VICTORY(1981)

Cliff DeYoung
HARRY AND TONTO(1974); SHOCK TREATMENT(1981); HUNGER, THE(1983); INDEPENDENCE DAY(1983)

Gypsi DeYoung
DIFFERENT STORY, A(1978)

Al Dezel
VICE RACKET(1937), p

Al Dezer
WEST OF THE ROCKIES(1931), p

Barbara DeZonia
REAL LIFE(1979)

Dudley DeZonia
REAL LIFE(1979)

Laszlo Dezsoffy
BLUE IDOL, THE(1931, Hung.)

Karam Dhaliwal
KING OF THE KHYBER RIFLES(1953)

Anandi Dhalwani
CALCUTTA(1947)

Buruminy Dhamarrandji
MANGANINNIE(1982, Aus.)
Alice Dhanifu
NEW YEAR'S EVIL(1980)
Krishna Dhawan
GUIDE, THE(1965, U.S./India)
Prem Dhawan
KENNER(1969), m
Arne Dhean
HARD TRAIL(1969)
France Dhelia
Misc. Silents
LA SULTANE DE L'AMOUR(1919, Fr.); LA MONTEE VERS L'ACROPOLE(1920, Fr.);
NENE(1924, Fr.)
Bernard Dheran
DOCTORS, THE(1956, Fr.); ROYAL AFFAIRS IN VERSAILLES(1957, Fr.); LA BELLE
AMERICAINE(1961, Fr.); STORY OF THE COUNT OF MONTE CRISTO, THE(1962,
Fr./Ital.); MAGNIFICENT SINNER(1963, Fr.)
Jean Dhermay
MILKY WAY, THE(1969, Fr./Ital.)
Andre Dheron
MAN WHO BROKE THE BANK AT MONTE CARLO, THE(1935)
Guy Dhers
LA BALANCE(1983, Fr.)
Jacques Dhery
LOSS OF INNOCENCE(1961, Brit.)
Robert Dhery
CHILDREN OF PARADISE(1945, Fr.); LA BELLE AMERICAINE(1961, Fr.), a, d, w;
PEEK-A-BOO(1961, Fr.), a, w; COUNTERFEIT CONSTABLE, THE(1966, Fr.), a, d, w;
TIME FOR LOVING, A(1971, Brit.); MALEVIL(1981, Fr./Ger.)
Hattah Dhib
1984
MISUNDERSTOOD(1984)
Khigh Dhieg
GOIN' COCONUTS(1978)
Khigh Dhiegh
MANCHURIAN CANDIDATE, THE(1962); THIRTEEN FRIGHTENED GIRLS(1963);
SECONDS(1966); DESTRUCTORS, THE(1968); HAWAIIANS, THE(1970); MEPHISTO
WALTZ, THE(1971)
Max Dhlamini
CRY, THE BELOVED COUNTRY(1952, Brit.)
Ribbon Dhlamini
CRY, THE BELOVED COUNTRY(1952, Brit.)
Sylvain Dhomme
SEVEN CAPITAL SINS(1962, Fr./Ital.), d; OLIVE TREES OF JUSTICE, THE(1967,
Fr.), w; JE T'AIME, JE T'AIME(1972, Fr./Swed.)
Desmond Dhooge
GIANT GILA MONSTER, THE(1959); MY DOG, BUDDY(1960); BULLET FOR
PRETTY BOY, A(1970); PAPER MOON(1973); SILENT RAGE(1982)
Moncef Dhouib
1984
MISUNDERSTOOD(1984)
Frankie Di
MORE AMERICAN GRAFFITI(1979)
Tung Di
GRAND SUBSTITUTION, THE(1965, Hong Kong); MERMAID, THE(1966, Hong
Kong)
Otto Di Amant
FEARLESS VAMPIRE KILLERS, OR PARDON ME BUT YOUR TEETH ARE IN MY
NECK, THE(1967)
Maria Di Aragon
CREMATORS, THE(1972)
Andrea Di Bari
NIGHT OF THE SHOOTING STARS, THE(1982, Ital.)
Dina Di Bari
DIVORCE, ITALIAN STYLE(1962, Ital.), cos
Fausto di Bella
LA NUIT DE VARENNES(1983, Fr./Ital.)
Joe Di Bella
OTHER, THE(1972), makeup
Joseph Di Bella
DON'T KNOCK THE TWIST(1962), makeup; ZOTZ!(1962), makeup; GUESS WHO'S
COMING TO DINNER(1967), makeup; GLORY BOY(1971), makeup
Edda di Benedetta
DRUMMER OF VENGEANCE(1974, Brit.)
Aldo di Benedetti
SHADOW OF THE PAST(1950, Brit.), w
Gianni Di Benedetto
EVIL EYE(1964 Ital.); HERCULES, SAMSON & ULYSSES(1964, Ital.); ROVER,
THE(1967, Ital.); GIRL WHO COULDN'T SAY NO, THE(1969 Ital.); SEVEN GOLDEN
MEN(1969, Fr./Ital./Span.)
Maria di Benedetto
THAT SPLENDID NOVEMBER(1971, Ital./Fr.)
Tony Di Benedetto
EXTERMINATOR, THE(1980); WINDOWS(1980)
Anselmo di Biagio
UNDER THE SUN OF ROME(1949, Ital.)
Louis Di Bianco
1984
HOTEL NEW HAMPSHIRE, THE(1984)
Paul Di Bionde
WHO'S THAT KNOCKING AT MY DOOR?(1968)
Dominic Di Bona
GOOD GUYS AND THE BAD GUYS, THE(1969), cos
Antonio Faa Di Bruno
DEAF SMITH AND JOHNNY EARS(1973, Ital.)
Nicia Di Bruno
TIMBER FURY(1950)

Vincenza Di Capua
MARRIAGE–ITALIAN STYLE(1964, Fr./Ital.)
Paula Di Cardo
DAUGHTER OF SHANGHAI(1937)
Erika Di Centa
PLAYGIRLS AND THE VAMPIRE(1964, Ital.); MYTH, THE(1965, Ital.)
George Di Cerzo
CHOIRBOYS, THE(1977)
Bobby Di Cicco
1984
PHILADELPHIA EXPERIMENT, THE(1984); SPLASH(1984)
Pat Di Cicco
AVALANCHE(1946), p
Giovanni Di Clemente
CRIME AT PORTA ROMANA(1980, Ital.), p
1984
CONQUEST(1984, Ital./Span./Mex.), p, w
Ennio Di Concini
BLUEBEARD(1972), w
Bruno di Cosmi
GROUP, THE(1966)
Paolo Di Credico
DEVIL IN LOVE, THE(1968, Ital.)
Pietro Di Donato
OPEN CITY(1946, Ital.), titles; SALT TO THE DEVIL(1949, Brit.), w
Francesco di Ecaffa
CAPTAIN JOHN SMITH AND POCAHONTAS(1953)
Marcello di Falco
AMARCORD(1974, Ital.)
Tony Di Falco
IN-LAWS, THE(1979)
Renata Di Faveri
IT HAPPENED IN CANADA(1962, Can.)
Linda Di Felice
IF IT'S TUESDAY, THIS MUST BE BELGIUM(1969)
Giancarlo di Fonzo
MASOCH(1980, Ital.), p
Adelmo Di Fraia
CONQUERED CITY(1966, Ital.); MADE IN ITALY(1967, Fr./Ital.)
Jim Di Gangi
STEAGLE, THE(1971), p
Jimmy Di Gangi
YOUNG DOCTORS, THE(1961), art d
Franco di Giacomo
NIGHT OF THE SHOOTING STARS, THE(1982, Ital.), ph
Raniero Di Giovanbattista
RUN FOR YOUR WIFE(1966, Fr./Ital.)
Altiero Di Giovanni
MAN CALLED SLEDGE, A(1971, Ital.)
Augusto Di Giovanni
MERCHANT OF SLAVES(1949, Ital.)
Gastone Di Giovanni
THEN THERE WERE THREE(1961), ph; EVERYBODY GO HOME!(1962, Fr./Ital.),
ph
Franco Di Girolamo
SLAVE, THE(1963, Ital.), makeup
John Di Giso, Jr.
NUNZIO(1978)
Umberto Di Grazia
VIOLENT FOUR, THE(1968, Ital.); QUIET PLACE IN THE COUNTRY, A(1970,
Ital./Fr.)
Umberto Di Grazie
SUNFLOWER(1970, Fr./Ital.)
Gennaro Di Gregario
YESTERDAY, TODAY, AND TOMORROW(1964, Ital./Fr.)
Piero Di Jorio
DIVINE NYMPH, THE(1979, Ital.)
Angela Tommasi di Lampedusa
L'AVVENTURA(1960, Ital.)
Giuseppe Tomasi di Lampedusa
LEOPARD, THE(1963, Ital.), w
Stella Di Lanti
Silents
ONLY WOMAN, THE(1924)
Orlando Di Lasso
EVERY MAN FOR HIMSELF AND GOD AGAINST ALL(1975, Ger.), m
Dalila di Lazzaro
Misc. Talkies
ANDY WARHOL'S FRANKENSTEIN(1974)
Loretta Di Lelio
THIS WINE OF LOVE(1948, Ital.)
Accursio Di Leo
1984
BIZET'S CARMEN(1984, Fr./Ital.)
Anna Di Leo
JOURNEY TO LOVE(1953, Ital.)
Fernando Di Leo
RETURN OF RINGO, THE(1966, Ital./Span.), w; HATE FOR HATE(1967, Ital.), w;
JOHNNY YUMA(1967, Ital.), w; NAVAJO JOE(1967, Ital./Span.), w; BRUTE AND
THE BEAST, THE(1968, Ital.), w; WOMAN ON FIRE, A(1970, Ital.), d, w; SLAUGH-
TER HOTEL(1971, Ital.), d, w; ITALIAN CONNECTION, THE(1973, U.S./Ital./Ger.),
d, w
Misc. Talkies
MISTER SCARFACE(1977), d
Lia di Leo
EARRINGS OF MADAME DE..., THE(1954, Fr.)
Mario Di Leo
GENTLE RAIN, THE(1966, Braz.), ph; 2000 YEARS LATER(1969), ph; BREAKER!
BREAKER!(1977), ph; EVIL, THE(1978), ph

1984
GIMME AN 'F'(1984), ph
Serafina Di Leo
CURSE OF THE WEREWOLF, THE(1961); SINGER NOT THE SONG, THE(1961, Brit.)
Jean di Limur
Silents
HUMAN DESIRES(1924, Brit.)
Edward Di Lorenzo
PLACE CALLED GLORY, A(1966, Span./Ger.), w; LADY FRANKENSTEIN(1971, Ital.), w; IDOLMAKER, THE(1980), w
Rossana di Lorenzo
CLARETTA AND BEN(1983, Ital., Fr.)
1984
LE BAL(1984, Fr./Ital./Algeria)
Dino Di Luca
MERCHANT OF SLAVES(1949, Ital.); HEY, LET'S TWIST!(1961); CARDINAL, THE(1963)
Dino Di Lucca
SPIRIT AND THE FLESH, THE(1948, Ital.)
Monte di Lyle
HAMMER THE TOFF(1952, Brit.)
Carlo Di Maggio
LA DOLCE VITA(1961, Ital./Fr.)
Nick Di Maggio
SMOKY(1946), ed
Ross Di Maggio
PURPLE HEART DIARY(1951), md; SNAKE RIVER DESPERADOES(1951), md; CHARGE OF THE LANCERS(1953), md; CHINA VENTURE(1953), m; SKY COMMANDO(1953), m; DON'T KNOCK THE ROCK(1956), md; CALYPSO HEAT WAVE(1957), m; MAN WHO TURNED TO STONE, THE(1957), m, md; UTAH BLAINE(1957), m
Lorenzo di Marco
UNDER THE SUN OF ROME(1949, Ital.)
Nina Di Marco
CONCRETE JUNGLE, THE(1982), ed
Nino di Marco
CHAINED HEAT(1983 U.S./Ger.), ed
Tony Di Marco
MISSION BATANGAS(1968), ed; SECRET OF THE SACRED FOREST, THE(1970), ed; HELL NIGHT(1981), ed
Raffaelle Di Mario
NEST OF VIPERS(1979, Ital.)
Aldo Di Martino
CHOSEN, THE(1978, Brit./Ital.), w
Grazia di Marza
THAT SPLENDID NOVEMBER(1971, Ital./Fr.); MALICIOUS(1974, Ital.)
Luciano Di Mauro
MORE THAN A MIRACLE(1967, Ital./Fr.)
Robert Di Milia
HE KNOWS YOU'RE ALONE(1980), p
Cardella Di Milo
BLACKENSTEIN(1973)
Tony Di Milo
HANG'EM HIGH(1968)
Pasquale Di Napoli
MORE THAN A MIRACLE(1967, Ital./Fr.)
Stephane Di Napoli
LA FEMME INFIDELE(1969, Fr./Ital.); THIS MAN MUST DIE(1970, Fr./Ital.)
Mario Di Nardo
SONS OF SATAN(1969, Ital./Fr./Ger.), w; UNHOLY FOUR, THE(1969, Ital.), w
Maurizio di Nardo
TIMES GONE BY(1953, Ital.)
Olimpia Di Nardo
CRIME AT PORTA ROMANA(1980, Ital.)
Shara Di Nepi
LUNA(1979, Ital.)
Gene di Novi
CAVERN, THE(1965, Ital./Ger.), m
Piero Di Orio
SEVEN BEAUTIES(1976, Ital.)
Carlo Di Palma
ASSASSIN, THE(1961, Ital./Fr.), ph; OMICRON(1963, Ital.), ph; THREE FABLES OF LOVE(1963, Fr./Ital./Span.), ph; NAKED HOURS, THE(1964, Ital.), ph; LOVE IN 4 DIMENSIONS(1965 Fr./Ital.), ph; RED DESERT(1965, Ital.), ph; THREE FACES OF A WOMAN(1965, Ital.), ph; BLOW-UP(1966, Brit.), ph; VERY HANDY MAN, A(1966, Fr./Ital.), ph; TERROR-CREATURES FROM THE GRAVE(1967, U.S./Ital.), ph; CHASTITY BELT, THE(1968, Ital.), ph; GIRL WITH A PISTOL, THE(1968, Ital.), ph; APPOINTMENT, THE(1969), ph; MOTIVE WAS JEALOUSY, THE(1970 Ital./Span.), ph; PIZZA TRIANGLE, THE(1970, Ital./Span.), ph; IDENTIFICATION OF A WOMAN(1983, Ital.), ph
1984
GABRIELA(1984, Braz.), ph
Dario Di Palma
DUEL OF THE TITANS(1963$c Hal.), ph; LOVE IN 4 DIMENSIONS(1965 Fr./Ital.), ph; QUEENS, THE(1968, Ital./Fr.), ph; DROP THEM OR I'LL SHOOT(1969, Fr./Ger./Span.), ph; PLUCKED(1969, Fr./Ital.), ph
Maurizio Di Paolantonio
SPECIAL DAY, A(1977, Ital./Can.)
Dante Di Paolo
STORY OF JOSEPH AND HIS BRETHREN THE(1962, Ital.); ATLAS AGAINST THE CYCLOPS(1963, Ital.); SAMSON AND THE SEVEN MIRACLES OF THE WORLD(1963, Fr./Ital.); EVIL EYE(1964 Ital.); PONTIUS PILATE(1967, Fr./Ital.)
Marcello di Paolo
1984
CAGED WOMEN(1984, Ital./Fr.), makeup
James di Pasquale
FAST BREAK(1979), m

Gerald Di Pego
W(1974), w; SHARKY'S MACHINE(1982), w
Guadenzio Di Pietro
YOUNG REBEL, THE(1969, Fr./Ital./Span.)
Rosi Di Pietro
BATTLE OF THE VILLA FIORITA, THE(1965, Brit.)
Rosy Di Pietro
EL GRECO(1966, Ital., Fr.)
Danti di Pinto
OMICRON(1963, Ital.)
Prince Eugenio Ruspoli di Poggio Suasa
LA DOLCE VITA(1961, Ital./Fr.)
Settimo Di Porto
GOSPEL ACCORDING TO ST. MATTHEW, THE(1966, Fr., Ital.)
Florence Di Re
DIFFERENT STORY, A(1978)
Joe di Reda
SCREAMING EAGLES(1956); ENEMY BELOW, THE(1957); TIME LIMIT(1957); IN LOVE AND WAR(1958); JUVENILE JUNGLE(1958); BIG FISHERMAN, THE(1959); BLACK ORCHID(1959); EMPEROR OF THE NORTH POLE(1973); HINDENBURG, THE(1975); SPECIAL DELIVERY(1976)
Joseph Di Reda
TRUE STORY OF JESSE JAMES, THE(1957); SAND PEBBLES, THE(1966); CACTUS IN THE SNOW(1972)
Rosanna Di Rocco
HAWKS AND THE SPARROWS, THE(1967, Ital.)
Rossana Di Rocco
GOSPEL ACCORDING TO ST. MATTHEW, THE(1966, Fr., Ital.)
Eraldo di Roma
UMBERTO D(1955, Ital.), ed
Anibal Di Salvo
MAFIA, THE(1972, Arg.), ph
Elaine di Sangro
Misc. Silents
FABIOLA(1923, Ital.)
Elena Di Sangro
Misc. Silents
QUO VADIS?(1925, Ital.)
Francesca Di Sapio
THAT'S THE WAY OF THE WORLD(1975)
Giorgio Di Segni
DAY OF ANGER(1970, Ital./Ger.)
Rosella di Sepio
JULIET OF THE SPIRITS(1965, Fr./Ital./W.Ger.)
Moe Di Sesso
WILLARD(1971), animal t
Nora Di Sesso
WILLARD(1971), animal t
Rino Di Silvestro
LEGEND OF THE WOLF WOMAN, THE(1977, Span.), d&w; WOMEN IN CELL BLOCK 7(1977, Ital./U.S.), d&w
Anna Di Silvio
ORGANIZER, THE(1964, Fr./Ital./Yugo.)
Antonio Di Silvio
ORGANIZER, THE(1964, Fr./Ital./Yugo.)
Di Stefano brothers
DIFFICULT YEARS(1950, Ital.)
Angel Di Steffano
KINGS OF THE SUN(1963)
Gianni Di Stolfo
NAVAJO JOE(1967, Ital./Span.)
Rodolpho di Valentina [Rudolph Valentino]
Misc. Silents
MARRIED VIRGIN, THE(1918)
Gianni di Venanzio
LA NOTTE(1961, Fr./Ital.), ph
Gianni Di Venanzo
LAW IS THE LAW, THE(1959, Fr.), ph; ECLIPSE(1962, Fr./Ital.), ph; EVA(1962, Fr./Ital.), ph; LE AMICHE(1962, Ital.), ph; 8 ½(1963, Ital.), ph; BEBO'S GIRL(1964, Ital.), ph; HIGH INFIDELITY(1965, Fr./Ital.), ph; MOMENT OF TRUTH, THE(1965, Ital./Span.), ph; TENTH VICTIM, THE(1965, Fr./Ital.), ph; TIME OF INDIFFERENCE(1965, Fr./Ital.), ph; SALVATORE GIULIANO(1966, Ital.), ph; HONEY POT, THE(1967, Brit.), ph; MY WIFE'S ENEMY(1967, Ital.), ph; KISS THE OTHER SHEIK(1968, Fr./Ital.), ph
Rosita Di Vera Cruz
LA VIACCIA(1962, Fr./Ital.)
Gianni Di Veranzo
IL GRIDO(1962, U.S./Ital.), ph
Elene Di Vinci
NAKED GUN, THE(1956)
Makoura Dia
CEDDO(1978, Nigeria)
Antonio Diabelli
MODERATO CANTABILE(1964, Fr./Ital.), m
Louis Diage
EADIE WAS A LADY(1945), set d; EVE KNEW HER APPLES(1945), set d; OVER 21(1945), set d; JOLSON STORY, THE(1946), set d; CRIME DOCTOR'S GAMBLE(1947), set d; DEAD RECKONING(1947), set d; TRAPPED BY BOSTON BLACKIE(1948), set d; SHOCKPROOF(1949), set d; WE WERE STRANGERS(1949), set d; KILLER THAT STALKED NEW YORK, THE(1950), set d; FOUR POSTER, THE(1952), set d; MISS SADIE THOMPSON(1953), set d; WILD ONE, THE(1953), set d; VIOLENT MEN, THE(1955), set d; WOMEN'S PRISON(1955), set d; FULL OF LIFE(1956), set d; JUBAL(1956), set d; NIGHTFALL(1956), set d; SOLID GOLD CADILLAC, THE(1956), set d; PAL JOEY(1957), set d; BELL, BOOK AND CANDLE(1958), set d; FACE OF A FUGITIVE(1959), set d; IT HAPPENED TO JANE(1959), set d; STRANGERS WHEN WE MEET(1960), set d; DEVIL AT FOUR O'CLOCK, THE(1961), set d; RAISIN IN THE SUN, A(1961), set d; NOTORIOUS LANDLADY, THE(1962), set d

Jack Diagilaitis
CIRCLE OF DECEIT(1982, Fr./Ger.)

Ismaila Diagne
CEDDO(1978, Nigeria)

Rodney Diak
FIRE MAIDENS FROM OUTER SPACE(1956, Brit.); DUNKIRK(1958, Brit.)

Alex Diakun
FIREBIRD 2015 AD(1981)

B. H. Dial
FLY NOW, PAY LATER(1969), p&d, ph

Bill Dial
LINCOLN CONSPIRACY, THE(1977)

Carl Dial
WORDS AND MUSIC(1929)

Diana Dial
ROSE BOWL STORY, THE(1952)

Patterson Dial
Silents
TOL'ABLE DAVID(1921); SEVENTH DAY, THE(1922); SONNY(1922); RENO(1923); SILENT PARTNER, THE(1923); MARRIED FLIRTS(1924)
Misc. Silents
SECRETS(1924)

Tim Dial
HARDCORE(1979)

Rudolph Dial [Rudolf Deyl]
VOYAGE TO THE END OF THE UNIVERSE(1963, Czech.)

George Dialegmenos
OEDIPUS THE KING(1968, Brit.); THANOS AND DESPINA(1970, Fr./Gr.)

Rika Dialina
BLACK SABBATH(1963, Ital.); DR. MABUSE'S RAYS OF DEATH(1964, Ger./Fr./Ital.); OPIATE '67(1967, Fr./Ital.); SUMMER LOVERS(1982)

Makhete Diallo
BROKEN ENGLISH(1981)

Marilyn Dialon
PLACE IN THE SUN, A(1951)

Henri Diamand-Berger
AMAZING MONSIEUR FABRE, THE(1952, Fr.), d

Catherine Diamant
NUN, THE(1971, Fr.)

Henri Diamant
Misc. Silents
FIFTY-FIFTY(1925), d

Otto Diamant
PRAISE MARX AND PASS THE AMMUNITION(1970, Brit.); FIDDLER ON THE ROOF(1971); SAVAGE MESSIAH(1972, Brit.); MAHLER(1974, Brit.)

Sherry Lynn Diamant
TODD KILLINGS, THE(1971)

Henri Diamant-Berger
WHIRLWIND OF PARIS(1946, Fr.), d; LA BELLE AMERICAINE(1961, Fr.), p; THANK HEAVEN FOR SMALL FAVORS(1965, Fr.), p; COUNTERFEIT CONSTABLE, THE(1966, Fr.), p
Silents
LOVER'S ISLAND(1925), p&d
Misc. Silents
GONZAQUE(1923, Fr.), d; L'AFFAIRE DE LA RUE DE LOUREINE(1923, Fr.), d; LE MAUVAIS GARCON(1923, Fr.), d; LE ROI DE LA VITESSE(1923, Fr.), d; MILADY(1923, Fr.), d; LA MARCHE DU DESTIN(1924, Fr.), d; L'EMPRISE(1924, Fr.), d; UNFAIR SEX, THE(1926), d; EDUCATION DE PRINCE(1927, Fr.), d; RUE DE LA PAIX(1927, Fr.), d

Saverio Diamanti
MOSES AND AARON(1975, Ger./Fr./Ital.), ph

Despo Diamantidou
NEVER ON SUNDAY(1960, Gr.); TOPKAPI(1964); RED LANTERNS(1965, Gr.); STEFANIA(1968, Gr.); LOVE CYCLES(1969, Gr.); SISTERS, THE(1969, Gr.); LOVE AND DEATH(1975); DREAM OF PASSION, A(1978, Gr.)

Basile Diamantopoulos
CONFESSION, THE(1970, Fr.)

Joe Diamini
NAKED PREY, THE(1966, U.S./South Africa)

Arnold Diamond
WOMAN IN HIDING(1953, Brit.); GOLDEN MASK, THE(1954, Brit.); CONSTANT HUSBAND, THE(1955, Brit.); DUKE WORE JEANS, THE(1958, Brit.); REVENGE OF FRANKENSTEIN, THE(1958, Brit.); BOBBIKINS(1959, Brit.); CARRY ON SERGEANT(1959, Brit.); HAND IN HAND(1961, Brit.); BREAKING POINT(1961, Brit.); FRIGHTENED CITY, THE(1961, Brit.); RING-A-DING RHYTHM(1962, Brit. 73m Amicus/COL bw (G.B: IT'S TRAD, DAD!); MANIAC(1963, Brit.); SWITCH, THE(1963, Brit.); GREAT ARMORED CAR SWINDLE, THE(1964); HANDS OF ORLAC(1964, Brit./Fr.); RETURN FROM THE ASHES(1965, U.S./Brit.); MAN COULD GET KILLED, A(1966); SPY WITH A COLD NOSE, THE(1966, Brit.); VULTURE, THE(1967, U.S./Brit./Can.); ANNIVERSARY, THE(1968, Brit.); GIRL ON A MOTORCYCLE, THE(1968, Fr./Brit.); ISADORA(1968, Brit.); BEST HOUSE IN LONDON, THE(1969, Brit.); ITALIAN JOB, THE(1969, Brit.); FIDDLER ON THE ROOF(1971); ZEPPELIN(1971, Brit.); BAWDY ADVENTURES OF TOM JONES, THE(1976, Brit.); MARCH OR DIE(1977, Brit.); FINAL CONFLICT, THE(1981); VENOM(1982, Brit.)

Art Diamond
AIRBORNE(1962), p; MAGIC VOYAGE OF SINBAD, THE(1962, USSR), p

Barry Diamond
HEARTBEEPS(1981); NATIONAL LAMPOON'S CLASS REUNION(1982); GET CRAZY(1983)

Bobby Diamond
YOUNG MAN WITH IDEAS(1952); LADY WANTS MINK, THE(1953); SILVER WHIP, THE(1953); UNTAMED(1955); AIRBORNE(1962); BILLIE(1965)

Dana Diamond
POINT OF TERROR(1971)

Daniel Diamond
HANSEL AND GRETEL(1954), anim

David Diamond
AFFAIR OF SUSAN(1935), p; RAVEN, THE(1935), p; SHE GETS HER MAN(1935), p, w; DON'T GET PERSONAL(1936), p; ADVENTUROUS BLONDE(1937), w. Robertson White; SWING IT SAILOR(1937), p, w; I WAS AN AMERICAN SPY(1951), p; BULLET

FOR JOEY, A(1955), p; PHENIX CITY STORY, THE(1955), p; SCREAMING EAGLES(1956), p; REVOLT IN THE BIG HOUSE(1958), p; BEHEMOTH, THE SEA MONSTER(1959, Brit.), p; KING OF THE ROARING TWENTIES–THE STORY OF ARNOLD ROTHSTEIN(1961), p; OPERATION EICHMANN(1961), p; MODERN MARRIAGE, A(1962), p; STRANGLER, THE(1964), p

Don Diamond
BORDERLINE(1950); RAIDERS OF OLD CALIFORNIA(1957); STORY OF RUTH, THE(1960); SWINGIN' ALONG(1962); IRMA LA DOUCE(1963); HOW SWEET IT IS(1968); VIVA MAX!(1969); MRS. POLLIFAX-SPY(1971); HIT MAN(1972); BREEZY(1973); HERBIE GOES BANANAS(1980)

Donald Diamond
OLD MAN AND THE SEA, THE(1958)

Gary Diamond
GOOD MORNING, MISS DOVE(1955); UNTAMED(1955)

Henry Diamond
SORCERER(1977)

I.A.L. Diamond
MURDER IN THE BLUE ROOM(1944), w; NEVER SAY GOODBYE(1946), w; ALWAYS TOGETHER(1947), w; LOVE AND LEARN(1947), w; ROMANCE ON THE HIGH SEAS(1948), w; TWO GUYS FROM TEXAS(1948), w; GIRL FROM JONES BEACH, THE(1949), w; IT'S A GREAT FEELING(1949), w; LET'S MAKE IT LEGAL(1951), w; LOVE NEST(1951), w; MONKEY BUSINESS(1952), w; SOMETHING FOR THE BIRDS(1952), w; THAT CERTAIN FEELING(1956), w; LOVE IN THE AFTERNOON(1957), w; MERRY ANDREW(1958), w; SOME LIKE IT HOT(1959), w; APARTMENT, THE(1960), w; ONE, TWO, THREE(1961), w; IRMA LA DOUCE(1963), w; KISS ME, STUPID(1964), w; FORTUNE COOKIE, THE(1966), w; CACTUS FLOWER(1969), w; PRIVATE LIFE OF SHERLOCK HOLMES, THE(1970, Brit.), w; AVANTI!(1972), w; FRONT PAGE, THE(1974), w; FEDORA(1978, Ger./Fr.), w; ONE-TRICK PONY(1980), w

Jack Diamond
SIDE STREET(1950); TAXI(1953); BOWERY BOYS MEET THE MONSTERS, THE(1954); BATTLE STATIONS(1956); TERROR FROM THE YEAR 5,000(1958)

James Diamond
NIGHT RIDER, THE(1932), ph; THEY NEVER COME BACK(1932), ph; HER SPLENDID FOLLY(1933), ph; SUCKER MONEY(1933), ph; MURDER IN THE MUSEUM(1934), ph; ROAD TO RUIN(1934), ph; TEXAS TORNADO(1934), ph; CIRCLE OF DEATH(1935), ph; OUTLAW DEPUTY, THE(1935), ph; MAN FROM GUN TOWN, THE(1936), ph; DEATH IN THE SKY(1937), ph; MILLION TO ONE, A(1938), ph
Silents
JANE EYRE(1921), ph; JOURNEY'S END, THE(1921), ph; NOTORIETY(1922), ph; KEEP SMILING(1925), ph; PRAIRIE WIFE, THE(1925), ph; RED KIMONO(1925), ph; WHITE PANTS WILLIE(1927), ph

Jeff Diamond
GAS(1981, Can.)

Marcia Diamond
CLASS OF '44(1973); DERANGED(1974, Can.); MOURNING SUIT, THE(1975, Can.); TICKET TO HEAVEN(1981)

Margaret Diamond
ESTHER WATERS(1948, Brit.); WEAK AND THE WICKED, THE(1954, Brit.); HOSTAGE, THE(1956, Brit.); VICTIM(1961, Brit.)

Marian Diamond
SUBTERFUGE(1969, US/Brit.)

Marion Diamond
GOODBYE GEMINI(1970, Brit.)

Matthew Diamond
1984
SPLITZ(1984), ch

Neil Diamond
JONATHAN LIVINGSTON SEAGULL(1973), m; JAZZ SINGER, THE(1980), a, m

Paul Diamond
O.S.S.(1946); CHICKEN CHRONICLES, THE(1977), w

Peter Diamond
PSYCHOPATH, THE(1966, Brit.); STAR WARS(1977), stunts; NATE AND HAYES(1983, U.S./New Zealand); RETURN OF THE JEDI(1983), stunts

Reed Diamond
TWO-MINUTE WARNING(1976)

Rex Diamond
TAKE A POWDER(1953, Brit.), w

Robert Diamond
1984
BIRDY(1984)

Robert LeRoy Diamond
THREE RING CIRCUS(1954)

Ron Diamond
CAT PEOPLE(1982); TO BE OR NOT TO BE(1983)

Selma Diamond
IT'S A MAD, MAD, MAD, MAD WORLD(1963); BANG THE DRUM SLOWLY(1973); MY FAVORITE YEAR(1982); LOVESICK(1983); TWILIGHT ZONE–THE MOVIE(1983)
1984
ALL OF ME(1984)

Tessa Diamond
LIFE IN EMERGENCY WARD 10(1959, Brit.), w

Diamond Brothers
GIVE HER A RING(1936, Brit.); HE'S MY GUY(1943)

Diamond's Solid-Aires
STRICTLY IN THE GROOVE(1942)

Herbert Diamonds
WEREWOLF IN A GIRL'S DORMITORY(1961, Ital./Aust.)

Laure Diana
CHEAT, THE(1950, Fr.)

The Diana Nellis Dancers
SHE DEMONS(1958)

O. Diancoli
BANDIT, THE(1949, Ital.), w

Dolores Diane
GIRLS' TOWN(1942); HI, BUDDY(1943); MOONLIGHT IN VERMONT(1943); PATRICK THE GREAT(1945)

Ric DiAngelo
  HUNTER, THE(1980); TWO OF A KIND(1983)
Dianik
  BANG BANG KID, THE(1968 U.S./Span./Ital.)
John Diar
  YELLOWBEARD(1983)
Nils Diarberg
  BREAD OF LOVE, THE(1954, Swed.)
Jennie Dias
  TOUCH OF EVIL(1958)
Maria Helena Dias
  GENTLE RAIN, THE(1966, Braz.); LOLLIPOP(1966, Braz.)
Selma Caz Dias
  BLUEBEARD'S TEN HONEYMOONS(1960, Brit.)
Romy Diax
  DEVIL WOMAN(1976, Phil.)
Alicia Diaz
  SONG OF BERNADETTE, THE(1943)
Andre Diaz
  NIGHTMARES(1983)
Anthony Diaz
  SANTA CLAUS(1960, Mex.), md
Arnaldo L. Diaz
1984
  FEAR CITY(1984)
Emilia Diaz
  JUNGLE PRINCESS, THE(1936)
George Diaz
  VERY NATURAL THING, A(1974)
Hazel Diaz
Misc. Talkies
  SWING(1938)
Horace Diaz
  NEW LIFE STYLE, THE(1970, Ger.), m
Juan L. Diaz
  CARMEN(1949, Span.)
Lario Diaz
  BLOOD WEDDING(1981, Sp.)
Leody M. Diaz
  BIONIC BOY, THE(1977, Hong Kong/Phil.), d
Manolito Diaz
  DOLORES(1949, Span.)
Manuel Diaz
  JUAREZ(1939)
Oliverio Maciel Diaz
  BEYOND THE REEF(1981)
Paulino Rodrigo Diaz
  CASTILIAN, THE(1963, Span./U.S.), w
Rafael Diaz
1984
  DEMONS IN THE GARDEN(1984, Span.)
Ramon Pere Diaz
  DEVIL'S GODMOTHER, THE(1938, Mex.)
Ricardo Diaz
  EVE(1968, Brit./Span.)
Rudi Diaz
  FLAP(1970)
Rudy Diaz
  BANDOLERO!(1968); COOGAN'S BLUFF(1968); HELLFIGHTERS(1968); CHE!(1969);
  MACKENNA'S GOLD(1969); UNDEFEATED, THE(1969); PIECES OF DREAMS(1970);
  CHARLEY VARRICK(1973); ONE LITTLE INDIAN(1973); WINDWALKER(1980)
Tom R. Diaz
  LEGEND OF THE LONE RANGER, THE(1981)
Vic Diaz
  SCAVENGERS, THE(1959, U.S./Phil.); MORO WITCH DOCTOR(1964, U.S./Phil.);
  OPERATION CIA(1965); RAVAGERS, THE(1965, U.S./Phil.); FLIGHT TO FURY(1966,
  U.S./Phil.); MISSION BATANGAS(1968); PASSIONATE STRANGERS, THE(1968,
  Phil.); IMPASSE(1969); LOSERS, THE(1970); DAUGHTERS OF SATAN(1972); SUPER-
  BEAST(1972); BLACK MAMA, WHITE MAMA(1973); TASTE OF HELL, A(1973);
  WONDER WOMEN(1973, Phil.); NIGHT OF THE COBRA WOMAN(1974, U.S./Phil.);
  PROJECT: KILL(1976); BOYS IN COMPANY C, THE(1978, U.S./Hong Kong); FIRE-
  CRACKER(1981); RAW FORCE(1982)
Misc. Talkies
  BLOOD THIRST(1965 Phil./U.S.); BEAST OF THE YELLOW NIGHT(1971, U.S./Phil.);
  SAVAGE!(1973); TOO HOT TO HANDLE(1976)
Antonio Diaz Conde
  SPIRITISM(1965, Mex.), m
Felipe Diazgarza
  EL TOPO(1971, Mex.)
Manu Dibango
  COUNTDOWN AT KUSINI(1976, Nigerian), m; CEDDO(1978, Nigeria), m; FORTY
  DEUCE(1982), m
Daphne Dibble
  JAWS II(1978)
Arthur Dibbs
  LITTLE BIG SHOT(1952, Brit.)
Kem Dibbs
  BIGAMIST,THE(1953); DANGEROUS MISSION(1954); RIDING SHOTGUN(1954);
  ABBOTT AND COSTELLO MEET THE MUMMY(1955); HIGH SOCIETY(1955); TWIN-
  KLE IN GOD'S EYE, THE(1955); TEN COMMANDMENTS, THE(1956); TERROR AT
  MIDNIGHT(1956); DANIEL BOONE, TRAIL BLAZER(1957); OMAR
  KHAYYAM(1957); PATHS OF GLORY(1957); PARTY GIRL(1958); FATE IS THE
  HUNTER(1964)
Ken Dibbs
  RIDERS TO THE STARS(1954); SUDDENLY(1954); SPOILERS OF THE FO-
  REST(1957); HOW THE WEST WAS WON(1962)
Kim Dibbs
  UNTAMED(1955)

George Dibdin-Pitt
  DEMON BARBER OF FLEET STREET, THE(1939, Brit.), w
Joe DiBella
  THREE STOOGES GO AROUND THE WORLD IN A DAZE, THE(1963), makeup;
  KING RAT(1965), makeup; OUTLAWS IS COMING, THE(1965), makeup; TRAIN
  ROBBERS, THE(1973), makeup
Joseph DiBella
  THIRTEEN FRIGHTENED GIRLS(1963), makeup; MURDERERS' ROW(1966),
  makeup
Sam Dibello
Misc. Talkies
  TWO CATCH TWO(1979); KNOCKING AT HEAVEN'S DOOR(1980)
Tony DiBenedetto
1984
  SPLASH(1984)
Tony DiBenedetto
  NUNZIO(1978); FORT APACHE, THE BRONX(1981); PATERNITY(1981); PRINCE
  OF THE CITY(1981); DEATHTRAP(1982); MY FAVORITE YEAR(1982)
1984
  GARBO TALKS(1984); POPE OF GREENWICH VILLAGE, THE(1984)
Luigi Diberti
  SERPENT, THE(1973, Fr./Ital./Ger.); ALL SCREWED UP(1976, Ital.); VIVA ITA-
  LIA(1978, Ital.)
Jose Luis Dibildos
  DOS COSMONAUTAS A LA FUERZA(1967, Span./*Ital.), w
Mary Dibley
Silents
  ADMIRABLE CRICHTON, THE(1918, Brit.); RED POTTAGE(1918, Brit.); WAY OF
  AN EAGLE, THE(1918, Brit.); AS HE WAS BORN(1919, Brit.); GARDEN OF RESUR-
  RECTION, THE(1919, Brit.); NATURE OF THE BEAST, THE(1919, Brit.); AYL-
  WIN(1920, Brit.); LONDON PRIDE(1920, Brit.); UNREST(1920, Brit.); AUTUMN OF
  PRIDE, THE(1921, Brit.); UNWANTED, THE(1924, Brit.); HIS HOUSE IN OR-
  DER(1928, Brit.)
Misc. Silents
  CHRISTIAN, THE(1915, Brit.); DERBY WINNER, THE(1915, Brit.); HEART OF A
  CHILD, THE(1915, Brit.); MAN OF HIS WORD, A(1915, Brit.); SHULMATE, THE(1915);
  WHOSO DIGGETH A PIT(1915, Brit.); SALLY IN OUR ALLEY(1916, Brit.); SILVER
  GREYHOUND, THE(1919, Brit.); THUNDERCLOUD, THE(1919, Brit.); WOMEN WHO
  WIN(1919, Brit.); BARGAIN, THE(1921, Brit.); FRUITFUL VINE, THE(1921, Brit.);
  SHADOW OF EVIL(1921, Brit.); WOMAN OF HIS DREAM, THE(1921, Brit.); CARD,
  THE(1922, Brit.); SIMPLE SIMON(1922, Brit.); STRANGLING THREADS(1923, Brit.);
  BLUE PETER, THE(1928, Brit.)
Henry Dibling
  TATTOO(1981)
Mary Dibly
Silents
  APPEARANCES(1921)
Martin Dibner
  DEEP SIX, THE(1958), w
Nam Dibot
  FOLIES DERGERE(1935)
V. Dibrov
  FAREWELL, DOVES(1962, USSR)
Olena Dibrova
  GIRL FROM POLTAVA(1937)
George DiCaprio
1984
  DUBEAT-E-O(1984), art d
Joacquim Dicenta
Silents
  LIFE(1928, Brit.), w
George DiCenzo
  GOING HOME(1971); SHOOT IT: BLACK, SHOOT IT: BLUE(1974); LAS VEGAS
  LADY(1976); CLOSE ENCOUNTERS OF THE THIRD KIND(1977); NINTH CONFIGU-
  RATION, THE(1980)
George Ralph DiCenzo
  FRISCO KID, THE(1979)
Igor Dicga
  BACHELOR'S DAUGHTERS, THE(1946)
Fernand Dichamps
  BLOOD OF A POET, THE(1930, Fr.)
Arik Dichner
  DIAMONDS(1975, U.S./Israel)
Bobby DiCicco
  I WANNA HOLD YOUR HAND(1978); TOWING(1978); 1941(1979); BIG RED ONE,
  THE(1980); NIGHT SHIFT(1982)
Thomas DiCillo
  PERMANENT VACATION(1982), ph
Tom DiCillo
  UNDERGROUND U.S.A.(1980), ph
1984
  STRANGER THAN PARADISE(1984, U.S./Ger.), ph; VARIETY(1984), ph
Alistair Dick
  WRONG BOX, THE(1966, Brit.)
Dewey Dick
  BOOTS MALONE(1952)
Diane Dick
  ANNIE GET YOUR GUN(1950)
Douglas Dick
  SEARCHING WIND, THE(1946); CASBAH(1948); ROPE(1948); SAIGON(1948); AC-
  CUSED, THE(1949); HOME OF THE BRAVE(1949); RED BADGE OF COURAGE,
  THE(1951); IRON MISTRESS, THE(1952); SOMETHING TO LIVE FOR(1952); YANK
  IN INDO-CHINA, A(1952); SO THIS IS LOVE(1953); GAMBLER FROM NATCHEZ,
  THE(1954); FOOTSTEPS IN THE NIGHT(1957); OKLAHOMAN, THE(1957); FLAMING
  STAR(1960); NORTH TO ALASKA(1960)
Gina Dick
  MY SIDE OF THE MOUNTAIN(1969); MIDDLE AGE CRAZY(1980, Can.); SUZAN-
  NE(1980, Can.); HAPPY BIRTHDAY TO ME(1981); MY BLOODY VALENTINE(1981,
  Can.); TICKET TO HEAVEN(1981)

THE(1973, U.S./FR.); BIG BAD MAMA(1974); ANGRY MAN, THE(1979 Fr./Can.); DRESSED TO KILL(1980); KLONDIKE FEVER(1980); CHARLIE CHAN AND THE CURSE OF THE DRAGON QUEEN(1981); DEATH HUNT(1981)

Misc. Talkies
SCORPIO SCARAB, THE(1972); JIG SAW(1979)

Christine Dickinson
HISTORY OF THE WORLD, PART 1(1981)

David Dickinson
GLAMOUR(1934)

Desmond Dickinson
SUCH IS THE LAW(1930, Brit.), ph; GREAT GAY ROAD, THE(1931, Brit.), ph; HOUSE OF UNREST, THE(1931, Brit.), ph; OTHER PEOPLE'S SINS(1931, Brit.), ph; HERE'S GEORGE(1932, Brit.), ph; DAUGHTERS OF TODAY(1933, Brit.), ph; DICK TURPIN(1933, Brit.), ph; LOVE'S OLD SWEET SONG(1933, Brit.), ph; DANNY BOY(1934, Brit.), ph; SONG AT EVENTIDE(1934, Brit.), ph; CITY OF BEAUTIFUL NONSENSE, THE(1935, Brit.), ph; REAL BLOKE, A(1935, Brit.), ph; SMALL MAN, THE(1935, Brit.), ph; VARIETY(1935, Brit.), ph; KING OF HEARTS(1936, Brit.), ph; HOLIDAY'S END(1937, Brit.), ph; SONG OF THE FORGE(1937, Brit.), ph; CHIPS(1938. Brit.), ph; SCRUFFY(1938, Brit.), ph; TAKE OFF THAT HAT(1938, Brit.), ph; ARSENAL STADIUM MYSTERY, THE(1939, Brit.), ph; CHAMBER OF HORRORS(1941, Brit.), ph; THURSDAY'S CHILD(1943, Brit.), ph; SECRET MISSION(1944, Brit.), spec eff; HUNGRY HILL(1947, Brit.), ph; HAMLET(1948, Brit.), ph; HISTORY OF MR. POLLY, THE(1949, Brit.), ph; MADNESS OF THE HEART(1949, Brit.), ph; FIVE ANGLES ON MURDER(1950, Brit.), ph; ROCKING HORSE WINNER, THE(1950, Brit.), ph; BROWNING VERSION, THE(1951, Brit.), ph; ENCORE(1951, Brit.), ph; OPERATION DISASTER(1951, Brit.), ph; IMPORTANCE OF BEING EARNEST, THE(1952, Brit.), ph; KISENGA, MAN OF AFRICA(1952, Brit.), ph; MAN BETWEEN, THE(1953, Brit.), ph; MEET MR. LUCIFER(1953, Brit.), ph; PROJECT M7(1953, Brit.), ph; TONIGHT AT 8:30(1953, Brit.), ph; COURT MARTIAL(1954, Brit.), ph; LOVES OF THREE QUEENS, THE(1954, Ital./Fr.), ph; GENTLEMEN MARRY BRUNETTES(1955), ph; BLACK TENT, THE(1956, Brit.), ph; LAST MAN TO HANG, THE(1956, Brit.), ph; FIRE DOWN BELOW(1957, U.S./Brit.), ph; INTENT TO KILL(1958, Brit.), ph; ORDERS TO KILL(1958, Brit.), ph; HORRORS OF THE BLACK MUSEUM(1959, U.S./Brit.), ph; FOXHOLE IN CAIRO(1960, Brit.), ph; HORROR HOTEL(1960, Brit.), w; DEVIL'S DAFFODIL, THE(1961, Brit./Ger.), ph; FRIGHTENED CITY, THE(1961, Brit.), ph; KONGA(1961, Brit.), ph; MARY HAD A LITTLE(1961, Brit.), ph; MALAGA(1962, Brit.), ph; TWO AND TWO MAKE SIX(1962, Brit.), ph; CAIRO(1963, Brit.), ph; SPARROWS CAN'T SING(1963, Brit.), ph; HANDS OF ORLAC, THE(1964, Brit./Fr.), ph; MURDER AHOY(1964, Brit.), ph; MURDER MOST FOUL(1964, Brit.), ph; ALPHABET MURDERS, THE(1966), ph; STUDY IN TERROR, A(1966, Brit./Ger.), ph; BERSERK(1967), ph; BABY LOVE(1969, Brit.), ph; DECLINE AND FALL... OF A BIRD WATCHER(1969, Brit.), ph; SOPHIE'S PLACE(1970), ph; TROG(1970, Brit.), ph; WHO SLEW AUNTIE ROO?(1971, U.S./Brit.), ph; BURKE AND HARE(1972, Brit.), ph; BEYOND THE FOG(1981, Brit.), ph

Dick Dickinson
FIGHTING MARSHAL, THE(1932); HIDDEN VALLEY(1932); HIGH SPEED(1932); MAN FROM HELL'S EDGES(1932); MASON OF THE MOUNTED(1932); TEXAS BUDDIES(1932); FUGITIVE, THE(1933); RANGER'S CODE, THE(1933); WEST OF THE DIVIDE(1934); DESERT TRAIL(1935); TRAIL DUST(1936); BLACK BANDIT(1938); SILVER ON THE SAGE(1939); YOU CAN'T CHEAT AN HONEST MAN(1939); LIGHTNING STRIKES WEST(1940); HOUSE OF FRANKENSTEIN(1944); HOUSE OF DRACULA(1945); LOST TRAIL, THE(1945); SUDAN(1945); GIRL ON THE SPOT(1946); MAGNIFICENT DOLL(1946); TANGIER(1946); PIRATES OF MONTEREY(1947); TAP ROOTS(1948); FAR COUNTRY, THE(1955); VILLAIN, THE(1979)

Misc. Talkies
TRAILING NORTH(1933)

Edmund Dickinson
ACTION OF THE TIGER(1957), ph

Eva Dickinson
F.J. HOLDEN, THE(1977, Aus.)

Geoffrey Dickinson
SCOTT OF THE ANTARCTIC(1949, Brit.), spec eff; MAN IN THE WHITE SUIT, THE(1952), spec eff

Homer Dickinson
TOAST OF NEW YORK, THE(1937); YOU CAN'T TAKE IT WITH YOU(1938); SUDDEN MONEY(1939); TOO MANY GIRLS(1940); KNOCK ON ANY DOOR(1949); GAMBLING HOUSE(1950); ON DANGEROUS GROUND(1951); SON OF PALEFACE(1952)

Howard Dickinson
SWEET ADELINE(1935)

Jim Dickinson
1984
PARIS, TEXAS(1984, Ger./Fr.), m

Joanna Dickinson
HILL 24 DOESN'T ANSWER(1955, Israel), ed

M.A. Dickinson
Misc. Silents
SOME MOTHER'S BOY(1929)

Milton A. Dickinson
THREE RING CIRCUS(1954)

Milton Dickinson
STREET ANGEL(1928)

Sandra Dickinson
LONELY LADY, THE(1983); SUPERMAN III(1983)
1984
SUPERGIRL(1984)

T. Dickinson
TILLY OF BLOOMSBURY(1931, Brit.), ed

Thorold Dickinson
PERFECT UNDERSTANDING(1933, Brit.), ed; HIGH COMMAND(1938, Brit.), d; ARSENAL STADIUM MYSTERY, THE(1939, Brit.), d, w; GASLIGHT(1940), d; PRIME MINISTER, THE(1941, Brit.), d; NEXT OF KIN(1942, Brit.), d, w; QUEEN OF SPADES(1948, Brit.), d; MEN OF THE SEA(1951, Brit.), p; KISENGA, MAN OF AFRICA(1952, Brit.), d, w; SECRET PEOPLE(1952, Brit.), d, w; MALTA STORY(1954, Brit.), w; HILL 24 DOESN'T ANSWER(1955, Israel), p, d, ed

W. Dickinson
Silents
ARE YOU A MASON?(1915)

Jon Dickman
HOW TO BEAT THE HIGH COST OF LIVING(1980)

Jacinta Dicks
CAPTAIN'S PARADISE, THE(1953, Brit.)

John Dicks
FLAME(1975, Brit.); EMPIRE STRIKES BACK, THE(1980)

Ted Dicks
30 IS A DANGEROUS AGE, CYNTHIA(1968, Brit.); VIRGIN WITCH, THE(1973, Brit.), m

Dickson
DOLLAR(1938, Swed.)

Barbara Dickson
SGT. PEPPER'S LONELY HEARTS CLUB BAND(1978)

Bettina Dickson
BAD BLONDE(1953, Brit.)

Brenda Dickson
DEATHMASTER, THE(1972); TAXI DRIVER(1976)

Carter Dickson
COLONEL MARCH INVESTIGATES(1952,Brit.), w

Charles Dickson
Silents
LITTLE MISS BROWN(1915); AMERICAN WIDOW, AN(1917); GOOD NIGHT, PAUL(1918), w

Curtis Dickson
GRAY LADY DOWN(1978), spec eff; I WANNA HOLD YOUR HAND(1978), spec eff

David Dickson
KNUTE ROCKNE–ALL AMERICAN(1940)

Donald Dickson
UP IN ARMS(1944)

Dorothy Dickson
ROAD IS FINE, THE(1930, Fr.); CHANNEL CROSSING(1934, Brit.); DANNY BOY(1934, Brit.); SWORD OF HONOUR(1938, Brit.)
Silents
SILVER LINING, THE(1921)
Misc. Silents
HEADIN' NORTH(1921); PAYING THE PIPER(1921)

Florine Dickson
GEORGE WHITE'S 1935 SCANDALS(1935)

Forrest Dickson
STORY OF DR. WASSELL, THE(1944); SENATOR WAS INDISCREET, THE(1947)

Frank Dickson
STELLA DALLAS(1937)

Gloria Dickson
THEY WON'T FORGET(1937); GOLD DIGGERS IN PARIS(1938); HEART OF THE NORTH(1938); RACKET BUSTERS(1938); SECRETS OF AN ACTRESS(1938); COWBOY QUARTERBACK(1939); NO PLACE TO GO(1939); ON YOUR TOES(1939); PRIVATE DETECTIVE(1939); THEY MADE ME A CRIMINAL(1939); WATERFRONT(1939); I WANT A DIVORCE(1940); KING OF THE LUMBERJACKS(1940); TEAR GAS SQUAD(1940); THIS THING CALLED LOVE(1940); BIG BOSS, THE(1941); MERCY ISLAND(1941); CRIME DOCTOR'S STRANGEST CASE(1943); LADY OF BURLESQUE(1943); POWER OF THE PRESS(1943); RATIONING(1944)

Helen Dickson
THEY WON'T BELIEVE ME(1947); LADIES THEY TALK ABOUT(1933); MAN ON THE FLYING TRAPEZE, THE(1935); SHE GETS HER MAN(1935); LADIES IN LOVE(1936); MOON'S OUR HOME, THE(1936); HOTEL HAYWIRE(1937); MAKE WAY FOR TOMORROW(1937); WHEN YOU'RE IN LOVE(1937); MEN WITH WINGS(1938); OUR LEADING CITIZEN(1939); CAPTAIN IS A LADY, THE(1940); THIRD FINGER, LEFT HAND(1940); HONOLULU LU(1941); LADY EVE, THE(1941); GIRL CRAZY(1943); PRACTICALLY YOURS(1944); SEVEN DAYS ASHORE(1944); LOST WEEKEND, THE(1945); THOSE ENDEARING YOUNG CHARMS(1945); TWO SMART PEOPLE(1946); SEA OF GRASS, THE(1947); SUDDENLY IT'S SPRING(1947); GAL WHO TOOK THE WEST, THE(1949); PAULA(1952); SOMETHING TO LIVE FOR(1952); EASY TO LOVE(1953)

Hugh Dickson
DEATHLINE(1973, Brit.)

Izek Dickson
LITTLE MISS DEVIL(1951, Egypt), ch

Jeanette Dickson
JOAN OF OZARK(1942)

Lamont Dickson
ALMOST A HONEYMOON(1930, Brit.)

Laura Dickson
1984
RENO AND THE DOC(1984, Can.)

Leone Dickson
MANGANINNIE(1982, Aus.)

Lydia Dickson
Silents
DON'T MARRY(1928)

Muriel Dickson
DEVILS OF DARKNESS, THE(1965, Brit.), cos

Patricia Dickson
GIRL IS MINE, THE(1950, Brit.)

Paul Dickson
STAR OF MY NIGHT(1954, Brit.), d; TALE OF THREE WOMEN, A(1954, Brit.), d; SATELLITE IN THE SKY(1956), d; DEPRAVED, THE(1957, Brit.), d; WOMAN OF MYSTERY, A(1957, Brit.); MATTER OF WHO, A(1962, Brit.), w

Ted Dickson
RICH PEOPLE(1929), set d; SWING HIGH(1930), set d

Theodore Dickson
OFFICER O'BRIEN(1930), set d

Vernon Dickson
PRELUDE TO FAME(1950, Brit.), set d

Wendy Dickson
BREAK OF DAY(1977, Aus.), prod d

Dickson/Vasu
RACE FOR YOUR LIFE, CHARLIE BROWN(1977), ph

Sol Dickstein
Misc. Talkies
GREATER ADVISOR, THE(1940)
Tricky Dicky
WHAT A CRAZY WORLD(1963, Brit.)
Abdoulaye Dico
COUP DE TORCHON(1981, Fr.)
William Dicterle
DR. EHRLICH'S MAGIC BULLET(1940), d
Bo Diddley
TRADING PLACES(1983)
Francis Didelot
SEVENTH JUROR, THE(1964, Fr.), w
R.F. Didelot
LE MONDE TREMBLERA(1939, Fr.), w
Denis Diderot
LADIES OF THE PARK(1964, Fr.), w; NUN, THE(1971, Fr.), w
Evelyne Didi
1984
ONE DEADLY SUMMER(1984, Fr.)
Arlette Didier
MY BABY IS BLACK!(1965, Fr.)
Jean Didier
DAMNED, THE(1948, Fr.)
Tony Didio
TOOLBOX MURDERS, THE(1978), p
Joan Didion
PANIC IN NEEDLE PARK(1971), w; PLAY IT AS IT LAYS(1972), w; STAR IS BORN, A(1976), w; TRUE CONFESSIONS(1981), w
George Diditta
GANG THAT COULDN'T SHOOT STRAIGHT, THE(1971), set d
Cilly Didzoneit
MAEDCHEN IN UNIFORM(1965, Ger./Fr.), makeup
Nicole Die
JONAH–WHO WILL BE 25 IN THE YEAR 2000(1976, Switz.)
Leonard Diebold
CITY THAT NEVER SLEEPS(1953)
Henry Dieckoff
HAROLD AND MAUDE(1971)
John Diedrich
DEVIL'S PLAYGROUND, THE(1976, Aus.); DAWN(1979, Aus.)
Samuel Diege
KING OF THE SIERRAS(1938), d; RIDE 'EM COWGIRL(1939), d; SINGING COW-GIRL, THE(1939), d; WATER RUSTLERS(1939), d
Wilhelm Diegelmann
BLUE ANGEL, THE(1930, Ger.)
Misc. Silents
PIED PIPER OF HAMELIN, THE(1917, Ger.)
Albert Diego
LOVE HUNGER(1965, Arg.), w
Dan Diego
Misc. Talkies
THREE WAY WEEKEND(1979)
Emilio Diego
PLEASURE SEEKERS, THE(1964)
Juan Diego
PIZZA TRIANGLE, THE(1970, Ital./Span.)
1984
HOLY INNOCENTS, THE(1984, Span.)
Carlos Diegues
BYE-BYE BRASIL(1980, Braz.), d&w; XICA(1982, Braz.), d, w
Manuel Zecena Dieguez
POLITICAL ASYLUM(1975, Mex./Guatemalan), p&d, w
Carl Ludwig Diehl
RASPUTIN(1932, Ger.); SECRET AGENT(1933, Brit.); CITY OF SECRETS(1963, Ger.)
Fred Diehl
NOW THAT APRIL'S HERE(1958, Can.)
Jac Diehl
COURT CONCERT, THE(1936, Ger.)
James Diehl
RANGERS RIDE, THE(1948)
Jim Diehl
LONE HAND TEXAN, THE(1947); HAWK OF WILD RIVER, THE(1952)
Misc. Talkies
SOUTH OF THE CHISHOLM TRAIL(1947); STRANGER FROM PONCA CITY, THE(1947)
John Diehl
STRIPES(1981); D.C. CAB(1983); JOYSTICKS(1983); NATIONAL LAMPOON'S VA-CATION(1983)
1984
ANGEL(1984)
Karl Ludwig Diehl
COPPER, THE(1930, Brit.); LOVE WALTZ, THE(1930, Ger.); SHOT AT DAWN, A(1934, Ger.); EPISODE(1937, Aust.); STORY OF VICKIE, THE(1958, Aust.)
William Diehl
SHARKY'S MACHINE(1982), a, w
William Diehl, Jr.
Misc. Talkies
NAKED RIVER(1977), d
Marie-Helene Diekmann
SISTERS, OR THE BALANCE OF HAPPINESS(1982, Ger.)
Kurt Diell
CELESTE(1982, Ger.), art d
Frank Dielsi
WHEN A STRANGER CALLS(1979)
1984
UNFAITHFULLY YOURS(1984)

Baruch Dienar
THEY WERE TEN(1961, Israel), p&d, w
Arpad Diener
I AIM AT THE STARS(1960)
Jean Diener
CHILDREN OF PARADISE(1945, Fr.)
Mildred Dienstag
YEAR OF THE HORSE, THE(1966), p
Phong Diep
GO TELL THE SPARTANS(1978)
Wynne Dieppe
DON'T CRY, IT'S ONLY THUNDER(1982)
Charles Diercep
HUSTLER, THE(1961)
Richard A. Diercks
IT AIN'T EASY(1972), p
Dan Dierdorf
STUCKEY'S LAST STAND(1980)
Hugh Dierker
Misc. Silents
OTHER SIDE, THE(1922), d; CAUSE FOR DIVORCE(1923), d; CAMILLE OF THE BARBARY COAST(1925), d; WRONG DOERS, THE(1925), d; BROKEN HOMES(1926), d; FALSE PRIDE(1926), d; THINGS WIVES TELL(1926), d
John Dierkes
MACBETH(1948); THREE HUSBANDS(1950); RED BADGE OF COURAGE, THE(1951); SELLOUT, THE(1951); SILVER CITY(1951); THING, THE(1951); LES MISERABLES(1952); PLYMOUTH ADVENTURE(1952); MOONLIGHTER, THE(1953); NAKED JUNGLE, THE(1953); PERILOUS JOURNEY, A(1953); SHANE(1953); VAN-QUISHED, THE(1953); ABBOTT AND COSTELLO MEET DR. JEKYLL AND MR. HYDE(1954); DESPERADO, THE(1954); PASSION(1954); PRINCE VALIANT(1954); RAID, THE(1954); SILVER LODE(1954); BETRAYED WOMEN(1955); HELL'S OUT-POST(1955); VANISHING AMERICAN, THE(1955); JUBAL(1956); BUCKSKIN LADY, THE(1957); DAUGHTER OF DR. JEKYLL(1957); DUEL AT APACHE WELLS(1957); HALLIDAY BRAND, THE(1957); VALERIE(1957); BLOOD ARROW(1958); BUCCA-NEER, THE(1958); LEFT-HANDED GUN, THE(1958); RAWHIDE TRAIL, THE(1958); HANGING TREE, THE(1959); OREGON TRAIL, THE(1959); ALAMO, THE(1960); COMANCHEROS, THE(1961); ONE-EYED JACKS(1961); PREMATURE BURIAL, THE(1962); HAUNTED PALACE, THE(1963); JOHNNY COOL(1963); OMEGA MAN, THE(1971); RAGE(1972); OKLAHOMA CRUDE(1973)
Nuella Dierking
SEDUCERS, THE(1962)
Charles Dierkof
GUNN(1967)
Charles Dierkop
ST. VALENTINE'S DAY MASSACRE, THE(1967); SWEET RIDE, THE(1968); BUTCH CASSIDY AND THE SUNDANCE KID(1969); 1,000 PLANE RAID, THE(1969); AN-GELS HARD AS THEY COME(1971); HOT BOX, THE(1972, U.S./Phil.); STING, THE(1973); STUDENT TEACHERS, THE(1973)
1984
SILENT NIGHT, DEADLY NIGHT(1984)
Christine Diersch
PRIEST OF ST. PAULI, THE(1970, Ger.)
Gustav Diesel
MISTRESS OF ATLANTIS, THE(1932, Ger.); MOSCOW SHANGHAI(1936, Ger.); TESTAMENT OF DR. MABUSE, THE(1943, Ger.)
Misc. Silents
THAT MURDER IN BERLIN(1929, Ger.)
Linda Diesem
NO MORE EXCUSES(1968)
Gustav Diessl
KOLBERG(1945, Ger.); TRIAL, THE(1948, Aust.)
Silents
PANDORA'S BOX(1929, Ger.)
Misc. Silents
LIVING CORPSE, A(1931, USSR)
Yvonne Diessner
FLOWERS FOR THE MAN IN THE MOON(1975, Ger.)
Edith Diestel
Silents
KING LEAR(1916)
George Diestel
ATTACK OF THE PUPPET PEOPLE(1958); VOYAGE TO THE BOTTOM OF THE SEA(1961)
Monroe Diestel
DREAMER(1979)
Ursula Diestel
HELDINNEN(1962, Ger.)
Jochen Diestelmann
DECISION BEFORE DAWN(1951); HANSEL AND GRETEL(1965, Ger.)
Burnell Dietch
COURT JESTER, THE(1956)
Ralph Dieterle
RIGHT TO ROMANCE(1933), ed
Wilhelm Dieterle [William Dieterle]
LAST FLIGHT, THE(1931), d; DEVIL'S IN LOVE, THE(1933), d
Silents
FAUST(1926, Ger.)
Misc. Silents
BACKSTAIRS(1921, Ger.); MAN BY THE ROADSIDE, THE(1923, Ger.), a, d; WAX-WORKS(1924, Ger.); AT THE EDGE OF THE WORLD(1929, Ger.); BEHIND THE ALTAR(1929, Ger.), a, d; RUSSIA(1929, Ger.)
William Dieterle
HER MAJESTY LOVE(1931), d; JEWEL ROBBERY(1932), d; MAN WANTED(1932), d; SCARLET DAWN(1932), d; SIX HOURS TO LIVE(1932), d; THE CRASH(1932), d; ADORABLE(1933), d; FEMALE(1933), d; FROM HEADQUARTERS(1933), d; GRAND SLAM(1933), d; LAWYER MAN(1933), d; FASHIONS OF 1934(1934), d; FOG OVER FRISCO(1934), d; MADAME DU BARRY(1934), d; DR. SOCRATES(1935), d; MID-SUMMER'S NIGHT'S DREAM, A(1935), d; SECRET BRIDE, THE(1935), d; SATAN MET A LADY(1936), d; STORY OF LOUIS PASTEUR, THE(1936), d; WHITE ANGEL, THE(1936), d; ANOTHER DAWN(1937), d; GREAT O'MALLEY, THE(1937), d; LIFE

OF EMILE ZOLA, THE(1937), d; BLOCKADE(1938), d; JUAREZ(1939), d; DISPATCH FROM REUTERS, A(1940), d; DEVIL AND DANIEL WEBSTER, THE(1941), p&d; SYNCOPATION(1942), p&d; TENNESSEE JOHNSON(1942), d; I'LL BE SEEING YOU(1944), d; KISMET(1944), d; LOVE LETTERS(1945), d; THIS LOVE OF OURS(1945), d; SEARCHING WIND, THE(1946), d; ACCUSED, THE(1949), d; PORTRAIT OF JENNIE(1949), d; ROPE OF SAND(1949), d; DARK CITY(1950), d; PAID IN FULL(1950), d; SEPTEMBER AFFAIR(1950), d; PEKING EXPRESS(1951), d; RED MOUNTAIN(1951), d; BOOTS MALONE(1952), d; TURNING POINT, THE(1952), d; SALOME(1953), d; VOLCANO(1953, Ital.), p&d; ELEPHANT WALK(1954), d; MAGIC FIRE(1956), p&d; OMAR KHAYYAM(1957), d; MISTRESS OF THE WORLD(1959, Ital./Fr./Ger.), p&d; DIE FASTNACHTSBEICHTE(1962, Ger.), d; QUICK, LET'S GET MARRIED(1965), d

Misc. Talkies
CONFESSION, THE(1964), d

William S. Dieterle
HUNCHBACK OF NOTRE DAME, THE(1939), d

Anton Diether
NIGHT GAMES(1980), w

Harald Dietl
DOWNHILL RACER(1969); LAST ESCAPE, THE(1970, Brit.)

Robert Dietl
MIRACLE OF THE WHITE STALLIONS(1963); FIVE DAYS ONE SUMMER(1982)

Shauna Dietlien
NO RETURN ADDRESS(1961)

Homer Dietmeier
JULIUS CAESAR(1952)

Bruno Dietrich
CORPSE OF BEVERLY HILLS, THE(1965, Ger.); TERROR AFTER MIDNIGHT(1965, Ger.)

Carrie Dietrich
REVENGE OF THE CHEERLEADERS(1976)

Cindi Dietrich
MAN WHO LOVED WOMEN, THE(1983)

Daniel Dietrich
MALATESTA'S CARNIVAL(1973)

Misc. Talkies
GIRLS OF 42ND STREET(1974)

Dena Dietrich
CRAZY WORLD OF JULIUS VROODER, THE(1974); WILD PARTY, THE(1975); NORTH AVENUE IRREGULARS, THE(1979); HISTORY OF THE WORLD, PART 1(1981)

Hans J. Dietrich
PLAYGIRLS AND THE BELLBOY, THE(1962,Ger.)

Marlene Dietrich
BLUE ANGEL, THE(1930, Ger.); MOROCCO(1930); DISHONORED(1931); BLONDE VENUS(1932); SHANGHAI EXPRESS(1932); SONG OF SONGS(1933); SCARLET EMPRESS, THE(1934); DEVIL IS A WOMAN, THE(1935); DESIRE(1936); GARDEN OF ALLAH, THE(1936); ANGEL(1937); KNIGHT WITHOUT ARMOR(1937, Brit.); DESTRY RIDES AGAIN(1939); SEVEN SINNERS(1940); FLAME OF NEW ORLEANS, THE(1941); MANPOWER(1941); LADY IS WILLING, THE(1942); PITTSBURGH(1942); SPOILERS, THE(1942); FOLLOW THE BOYS(1944); KISMET(1944); GOLDEN EARRINGS(1947); FOREIGN AFFAIR, A(1948); ROOM UPSTAIRS, THE(1948, Fr.); JIGSAW(1949); NO HIGHWAY IN THE SKY(1951, Brit.); STAGE FRIGHT(1950, Brit.); RANCHO NOTORIOUS(1952); AROUND THE WORLD IN 80 DAYS(1956); MONTE CARLO STORY, THE(1957, Ital.); WITNESS FOR THE PROSECUTION(1957); TOUCH OF EVIL(1958); JUDGMENT AT NUREMBERG(1961); PARIS WHEN IT SIZZLES(1964); JUST A GIGOLO(1979, Ger.)

Misc. Silents
CAFE ELECTRIC(1927, Aust.); IMAGINARY BARON, THE(1927, Ger.); DANGERS OF THE ENGAGEMENT PERIOD(1929, Ger.); SHIP OF LOST MEN, THE(1929, Ger.); THREE LOVES(1931, Ger.)

Monica Dietrich
CARRY ON HENRY VIII(1970, Brit.)

Monika Dietrich
DANDY IN ASPIC, A(1968, Brit.)

Ralph Dietrich
UNDER TWO FLAGS(1936), ed; FOX MOVIETONE FOLLIES(1929), ed; MASQUERADE(1929), ed; SKY HAWK(1929), ed; CHEER UP AND SMILE(1930), ed; CRAZY THAT WAY(1930), ed; LAST OF THE DUANES(1930), ed; DADDY LONG LEGS(1931), ed; FAIR WARNING(1931), ed; ONCE A SINNER(1931), ed; SOB SISTER(1931), ed; THREE GIRLS LOST(1931), ed; GOLDEN WEST, THE(1932), ed; REBECCA OF SUNNYBROOK FARM(1932), ed; TRIAL OF VIVIENNE WARE, THE(1932), ed; DEVIL'S IN LOVE, THE(1933), ed; FACE IN THE SKY(1933), ed; HAT, COAT AND GLOVE(1934), ed; LET'S TRY AGAIN(1934), ed; RAINBOW'S END(1935), ed; SUNSET RANGE(1935), ed; KING OF BURLESQUE(1936), ed; LADIES IN LOVE(1936), ed; TO MARY–WITH LOVE(1936), ed; CHARLIE CHAN AT THE WAX MUSEUM(1940), p; GAY CABALLERO, THE(1940), p; ACCENT ON LOVE(1941), p; COWBOY AND THE BLONDE, THE(1941), p; DEAD MEN TELL(1941), p; GOLDEN HOOFS(1941), p; MAN AT LARGE(1941), p; MURDER AMONG FRIENDS(1941), p; CASTLE IN THE DESERT(1942), p; NIGHT BEFORE THE DIVORCE, THE(1942), p; POSTMAN DIDN'T RING, THE(1942), p; QUIET PLEASE, MURDER(1942), p; MARGIN FOR ERROR(1943), p; MY FRIEND FLICKA(1943), p; UNDERTOW(1949), p; MYSTERY SUBMARINE(1950), p, w; PEGGY(1950), p; SPY HUNT(1950), p; UNDER THE GUN(1951), p

Silents
PLAY GIRL, THE(1928), ed

Ruth Dietrich
FATHER TAKES A WIFE(1941); LADY SCARFACE(1941); REPENT AT LEISURE(1941)

Leo Dietrichstein
GREAT LOVER, THE(1931), w

Silents
DIVORCE GAME, THE(1917), w

Veronique Dietschy
1984
SWANN IN LOVE(1984, Fr.Ger.)

George Dietsel
NIGHT OF EVIL(1962)

Alfred Dietz
YOUNG TORLESS(1968, Fr./Ger.)

Bill Dietz
TOWN THAT DREADED SUNDOWN, THE(1977)

Charles Dietz
Silents
SYLVIA GRAY(1914)

Eileen Dietz
DAVID HOLZMAN'S DIARY(1968); YOU LIGHT UP MY LIFE(1977)

Howard Dietz
HOLLYWOOD PARTY(1934), p, w; DANCING IN THE DARK(1949), w

Jack Dietz
BLACK DRAGONS(1942), p; BOWERY AT MIDNIGHT(1942), p; CORPSE VANISHES, THE(1942), p; LET'S GET TOUGH(1942), p; MR. WISE GUY(1942), p; 'NEATH BROOKLYN BRIDGE(1942), p; SMART ALECKS(1942), p, w; APE MAN, THE(1943), p; CLANCY STREET BOYS(1943), p; GHOSTS ON THE LOOSE(1943), p; KID DYNAMITE(1943), p; MR. MUGGS STEPS OUT(1943), p; SPOTLIGHT SCANDALS(1943), p; BLOCK BUSTERS(1944), p; BOWERY CHAMPS(1944), p; FOLLOW THE LEADER(1944), p; MILLION DOLLAR KID(1944), p; RETURN OF THE APE MAN(1944), p; VOODOO MAN(1944), p; COME OUT FIGHTING(1945), p; DOCKS OF NEW YORK(1945), p; MR. MUGGS RIDES AGAIN(1945), p; BEAST FROM 20,000 FATHOMS, THE(1953), p; BLACK SCORPION, THE(1957), p

Patty Dietz
BABY MAKER, THE(1970)

Robert Dietz
GUN RIDERS, THE(1969), set d

William Dietz
BORDER DEVILS(1932), ph

Max Dietze
Silents
METROPOLIS(1927, Ger.)

Albert Dieudonne
Silents
NAPOLEON(1927, Fr.)

Misc. Silents
SON CRIME(1921, Fr.), d; GLOIRE ROUGE(1923, Fr.), d; CATHERINE(1924, Fr.), a, d

Francois Dieudonne
LA DOLCE VITA(1961, Ital./Fr.)

Helene Dieudonne
LA BELLE AMERICAINE(1961, Fr.); PARIS BLUES(1961); COUNTERFEITERS OF PARIS, THE(1962, Fr., Ital.); MONKEY IN WINTER, A(1962, Fr.); THERESE(1963, Fr.); RAVISHING IDIOT, A(1966, Ital./Fr.); DON'T CRY WITH YOUR MOUTH FULL(1974, Fr.)

Nicole Dieudonne
CHECKERBOARD(1969, Fr.)

Yvette Dieudonne
Silents
NAPOLEON(1927, Fr.)

Marcel-Louis Dieulot
PICNIC ON THE GRASS(1960, Fr.), set d

Don DiFaure
SINCE YOU WENT AWAY(1944), ed

Philip Diferman
HELL'S BLOODY DEVILS(1970)

Mike Diffenderfer
MUSCLE BEACH PARTY(1964)

Anton Diffring
HIGHLY DANGEROUS(1950, Brit.); GREAT MANHUNT, THE(1951, Brit.); HOTEL SAHARA(1951, Brit.); ISLAND RESCUE(1952, Brit.); ALBERT, R.N.(1953, Brit.); NEVER LET ME GO(1953, U.S./Brit.); NORMAN CONQUEST(1953, Brit.); OPERATION DIPLOMAT(1953, Brit.); BETRAYED(1954); WOMAN'S ANGLE, THE(1954, Brit.); COLDITZ STORY, THE(1955, Brit.); I AM A CAMERA(1955, Brit.); SEA SHALL NOT HAVE THEM, THE(1955, Brit.); BLACK TENT, THE(1956, Brit.); DOUBLE CROSS(1956, Brit.); CROOKED SKY, THE(1957, Brit.); LADY OF VENGEANCE(1957, Brit); REACH FOR THE SKY(1957, Brit.); TRIPLE DECEPTION(1957, Brit.); ACCURSED, THE(1958, Brit.); MARK OF THE PHOENIX(1958, Brit.); BEASTS OF MARSEILLES, THE(1959, Brit.); MAN WHO COULD CHEAT DEATH, THE(1959, Brit.); QUESTION OF ADULTERY, A(1959, Brit.); CIRCUS OF HORRORS(1960, Brit.); ENTER INSPECTOR DUVAL(1961, Brit.); HEROES OF TELEMARK, THE(1965, Brit.); BLUE MAX, THE(1966); FAHRENHEIT 451(1966, Brit.); INCIDENT AT MIDNIGHT(1966, Brit.); COUNTERPOINT(1967); DOUBLE MAN, THE(1967); WHERE EAGLES DARE(1968, Brit.); ZEPPELIN(1971, Brit.); DEAD PIGEON ON BEETHOVEN STREET(1972, Ger.); LITTLE MOTHER(1973, U.S./Yugo.); BEAST MUST DIE, THE(1974, Brit.); MARK OF THE DEVIL II(1975, Ger./Brit.); NO WAY OUT(1975, Ital./Fr.); CALL HIM MR. SHATTER(1976, Hong Kong); OPERATION DAYBREAK(1976, U.S./Brit./Czech.); SWISS CONSPIRACY, THE(1976, U.S./Ger.); VALENTINO(1977, Brit.); TUSK(1980, Fr.); VICTORY(1981)

Marcello DiFolco
FELLINI SATYRICON(1969, Fr./Ital.)

Darren DiFonzo
THIRD WALKER, THE(1978, Can.)

Louis J. DiFonzo
NEWMAN'S LAW(1974)

Barbara DiFrenza
1984
LOVE STREAMS(1984)

John Difusco
BREAKER! BREAKER!(1977)

Diga Valery Gypsies
LOVE IN THE AFTERNOON(1957)

Joe DiGaetano
WARGAMES(1983), spec eff

Uschi Digaid
WORLD IS JUST A 'B' MOVIE, THE(1971)

Jayne DiGalano
NIGHT AND DAY(1946)

Uschi Digart
SCAVENGERS, THE(1969); SUPERCHICK(1973); FANTASM(1976, Aus.)
Ushi Digart
INSIDE AMY(1975)
Delia Digby
UNEASY TERMS(1948, Brit.)
Helena Digby
JACK THE RIPPER(1959, Brit.)
Elizabeth Digby-Smith
COURT MARTIAL(1954, Brit.); INTRUDER, THE(1955, Brit.)
Randy Digeronimo
RIVALS(1972)
Peter DiGesu
1984
AMADEUS(1984)
Dudley Digges
CONDEMNED(1929); OUTWARD BOUND(1930); ALEXANDER HAMILTON(1931); DEVOTION(1931); MALTESE FALCON, THE(1931); RULING VOICE, THE(1931); CASE OF CLARA DEANE, THE(1932); FIRST YEAR, THE(1932); HATCHET MAN, THE(1932); ROAR OF THE DRAGON(1932); STRANGE CASE OF CLARA DEANE, THE(1932); TESS OF THE STORM COUNTRY(1932); BEFORE DAWN(1933); BISHOP MISBEHAVES, THE(1933); EMPEROR JONES, THE(1933); INVISIBLE MAN, THE(1933); KING'S VACATION, THE(1933); MAYOR OF HELL, THE(1933); NARROW CORNER, THE(1933); SILK EXPRESS, THE(1933); CARAVAN(1934); FURY OF THE JUNGLE(1934); MASSACRE(1934); WHAT EVERY WOMAN KNOWS(1934); WORLD MOVES ON, THE(1934); CHINA SEAS(1935); I AM A THIEF(1935); KIND LADY(1935); MUTINY ON THE BOUNTY(1935); NOTORIOUS GENTLEMAN, A(1935); THREE LIVE GHOSTS(1935); GENERAL DIED AT DAWN, THE(1936); UNGUARDED HOUR, THE(1936); VALIANT IS THE WORD FOR CARRIE(1936); VOICE OF BUGLE ANN(1936); LOVE IS NEWS(1937); LIGHT THAT FAILED, THE(1939); SON OF FURY(1942); SEARCHING WIND, THE(1946)
Mae Digges
SAN FRANCISCO(1936)
Richard H. Digges, Jr.
BURNING UP(1930), ed; ONLY THE BRAVE(1930), w
Cliff Diggins
INNOCENT BYSTANDERS(1973, Brit.)
Clifford Diggins
SHUTTERED ROOM, THE(1968, Brit.)
Eddie Diggins
Silents
GOAT GETTER(1925); ONE PUNCH O'DAY(1926)
Peggy Diggins
NAVY BLUES(1941); STRAWBERRY BLONDE, THE(1941); YOU'RE IN THE ARMY NOW(1941); LADY GANGSTER(1942); MAN WHO CAME TO DINNER, THE(1942); TRUCK BUSTERS(1943)
Donald Diggs
RED, WHITE AND BLACK, THE(1970)
Dudley Diggs
RAFFLES(1939)
John Diggs
CORVETTE K-225(1943)
Kenneth Dight
ROTTEN TO THE CORE(1956, Brit.)
Mark Dightam
BOY WHO TURNED YELLOW, THE(1972, Brit.)
Myrtis Dightman
J.W. COOP(1971)
John Dighton
ROMA RIVUOLE CESARE, (w; HAIL AND FAREWELL(1936, Brit.), w; COMPULSORY WIFE, THE(1937, Brit.), w; EVERYTHING HAPPENS TO ME(1938, Brit.), w; IT'S IN THE BLOOD(1938, Brit.), w; MANY TANKS MR. ATKINS(1938, Brit.), w; THANK EVANS(1938, Brit.), w; VIPER, THE(1938, Brit.), w; GOOD OLD DAYS, THE(1939, Brit.), w; HOOTS MON!(1939, Brit.), w; BRIGGS FAMILY, THE(1940, Brit.), w; LET GEORGE DO IT(1940, Brit.), w; SALOON BAR(1940, Brit.), w; THAT'S THE TICKET(1940, Brit.), w; THREE COCKEYED SAILORS(1940, Brit.), w; BLACK SHEEP OF WHITEHALL, THE(1941 Brit.), w; GHOST OF ST. MICHAEL'S. THE(1941, Brit.), w; TURNED OUT NICE AGAIN(1941, Brit.), w; GOOSE STEPS OUT, THE(1942, Brit.), w; NEXT OF KIN(1942, Brit.), w; MY LEARNED FRIEND(1943, Brit.), w; SOMEWHERE IN FRANCE(1943, Brit.), w; CHAMPAGNE CHARLIE(1944, Brit.), w; UNDERGROUND GUERRILLAS(1944, Brit.), w; 48 HOURS(1944, Brit.), w; NICHOLAS NICKLEBY(1947, Brit.), w; KIND HEARTS AND CORONETS(1949, Brit.), w; SARABAND(1949, Brit.), w; HAPPIEST DAYS OF YOUR LIFE(1950, Brit.), w; BRANDY FOR THE PARSON(1952, Brit.), w; MAN IN THE WHITE SUIT, THE(1952), w; PASSIONATE SENTRY, THE(1952, Brit.), w; FOLLY TO BE WISE(1953), w; SWAN, THE(1956), w; BARRETTS OF WIMPOLE STREET, THE(1957), w; DEVIL'S DISCIPLE, THE(1959), w; SEASON OF PASSION(1961, Aus./Brit.), w
Mary Ann Dighton
THIRD OF A MAN(1962)
Franco DiGiacomo
DUCH IN ORANGE SAUCE(1976, Ital.), ph; AMITYVILLE II: THE POSSESSION(1982), ph; DEATH VENGEANCE(1982), ph
Gastone DiGiovanni
NIGHT EVELYN CAME OUT OF THE GRAVE, THE(1973, Ital.), ph
Joseph DiGiroloma
VICE SQUAD(1982)
Enrico DiGiuseppe
FOUL PLAY(1978)
Mark Digman
EYES OF ANNIE JONES, THE(1963, Brit.)
Alex Dignam
OF HUMAN BONDAGE(1964, Brit.)
Arthur Dignam
PETERSEN(1974, Aus.); DEVIL'S PLAYGROUND, THE(1976, Aus.); SUMMER OF SECRETS(1976, Aus.); CATHY'S CHILD(1979, Aus.); DEAD KIDS(1981 Aus./New Zealand); GRENDEL GRENDEL GRENDEL(1981, Aus.); WE OF THE NEVER NEVER(1983, Aus.); WILD DUCK, THE(1983, Aus.)

Basil Dignam
LADY WITH A LAMP, THE(1951, Brit.); HAMMER THE TOFF(1952, Brit.); HIS EXCELLENCY(1952, Brit.); ISLAND RESCUE(1952, Brit.); THERE WAS A YOUNG LADY(1953, Brit.); COURT MARTIAL(1954, Brit.); LIGHT TOUCH, THE(1955, Brit.); PORT OF ESCAPE(1955, Brit.); THEY CAN'T HANG ME(1955, Brit.); BATTLE HELL(1956, Brit.); FINGER OF GUILT(1956, Brit.); NARROWING CIRCLE, THE(1956, Brit.); PRIVATE'S PROGRESS(1956, Brit.); ROTTEN TO THE CORE(1956, Brit.); BROTHERS IN LAW(1957, Brit.); DEPRAVED, THE(1957, Brit.); SON OF A STRANGER(1957, Brit.); THREE SUNDAYS TO LIVE(1957, Brit.); VIOLENT STRANGER(1957, Brit.); WEAPON, THE(1957, Brit.); YOU PAY YOUR MONEY(1957, Brit.); FURTHER UP THE CREEK!(1958, Brit.); SAFECRACKER, THE(1958, Brit.); SPANIARD'S CURSE, THE(1958, Brit.); THEM NICE AMERICANS(1958, Brit.); UP THE CREEK(1958, Brit.); CARRY ON SERGEANT(1959, Brit.); I'M ALL RIGHT, JACK(1959, Brit.); ROOM AT THE TOP(1959, Brit.); MAN IN A COCKED HAT(1960, Bri.); SENTENCED FOR LIFE(1960, Brit.); SPIDER'S WEB, THE(1960, Brit.); COURT MARTIAL OF MAJOR KELLER, THE(1961, Brit.); FOURTH SQUARE, THE(1961, Brit.); GORGO(1961, Brit.); RISK, THE(1961, Brit.); SECRET PARTNER, THE(1961, Brit.); CORRIDORS OF BLOOD(1962, Brit.); FATE TAKES A HAND(1962, Brit.); HEAVENS ABOVE!(1963, Brit.); SEVEN SEAS TO CALAIS(1963, Ital.); 80,000 SUSPECTS(1963, Brit.); MASTER SPY(1964, Brit.); RING OF SPIES(1964, Brit.); AMOROUS ADVENTURES OF MOLL FLANDERS, THE(1965); CUCKOO PATROL(1965, Brit.); JOEY BOY(1965, Brit.); WHERE THE SPIES ARE(1965, Brit.); EXORCISM AT MIDNIGHT(1966, Brit. revised 1973, U.S.); WALK IN THE SHADOW(1966, Brit.); I'LL NEVER FORGET WHAT'S 'IS NAME(1967, Brit.); JOKERS, THE(1967, Brit.); ASSIGNMENT K(1968, Brit.); TWISTED NERVE(1969, Brit.); GAMES, THE(1970); GREAT WHITE HOPE, THE(1970); 10 RILLINGTON PLACE(1971, Brit.); YOUNG WINSTON(1972, Brit.)
Mark Dignam
MURDER IN THE CATHEDRAL(1952, Brit.); TRAIN OF EVENTS(1952, Brit.); BEAU BRUMMELL(1954); COURT MARTIAL(1954, Brit.); DOCTOR IN THE HOUSE(1954, Brit.); LEASE OF LIFE(1954, Brit.); PASSING STRANGER, THE(1954, Brit.); THREE CORNERED FATE(1954, Brit.); ESCAPADE(1955, Brit.); PRISONER, THE(1955, Brit.); CONSCIENCE BAY(1960, Brit.); SINK THE BISMARCK!(1960, Brit.); PURE HELL OF ST. TRINIAN'S, THE(1961, Brit.); IN SEARCH OF THE CASTAWAYS(1962, Brit.); SIEGE OF THE SAXONS(1963, Brit.); SWORD OF LANCELOT(1963, Brit.); TOM JONES(1963, Brit.); JOLLY BAD FELLOW, A(1964, Brit.); ESCAPE BY NIGHT(1965, Brit.); GAME FOR THREE LOSERS(1965, Brit.); TAMING OF THE SHREW, THE(1967, U.S./Ital.); CHARGE OF THE LIGHT BRIGADE, THE(1968, Brit.); ISADORA(1968, Brit.); HAMLET(1969, Brit.); THERE'S A GIRL IN MY SOUP(1970, Brit.); MACBETH(1971, Brit.); MEMOIRS OF A SURVIVOR(1981, Brit.)
Misc. Talkies
DEAD CERT(1974, Brit.)
Rebecca Dignam
CONSPIRACY OF HEARTS(1960, Brit.); SANDS OF THE DESERT(1960, Brit.); THESE ARE THE DAMNED(1965, Brit.)
Teresa Dignan
CHARRIOTS OF FIRE(1981, Brit.)
Edmond Dignon
AMERICAN PRISONER, THE(1929 Brit.)
Edward Dignon
ASK BECCLES(1933, Brit.), w; ADMIRAL'S SECRET, THE(1934, Brit.), w; RIVER WOLVES, THE(1934, Brit.), w; SEXTON BLAKE AND THE BEARDED DOCTOR(1935, Brit.); WHITE LILAC(1935, Brit.); SOMEONE AT THE DOOR(1936, Brit.)
Randy DiGrazio
1984
HARDBODIES(1984), ch
Jan Dijkgraaf
ROMAN HOLIDAY(1953)
Alan Dijon
ASSIGNMENT OUTER SPACE(1960, Ital.); LA DOLCE VITA(1961, Ital./Fr.); TERROR OF DR. MABUSE, THE(1965, Ger.)
Rene Dijon
MAIN EVENT, THE(1979)
Anatoliy Dikan
MAGIC WEAVER, THE(1965, USSR), set d
Phil Dike
SNOW WHITE AND THE SEVEN DWARFS(1937), anim
Aleksandr Dikhtyar
NIGHT BEFORE CHRISTMAS, A(1963, USSR), art d
Loek Dikker
1984
FOURTH MAN, THE(1984, Neth.), m
Alexi Dikki
ADMIRAL NAKHIMOV(1948, USSR)
Michael Dikova
SCAVENGERS, THE(1969)
Raffaella DiLaurentiis
BEYOND THE REEF(1981), p
Dalila DiLazzaro
THREE MEN TO DESTROY(1980, Fr.)
Frankl Dilbert
NIGHTHAWKS(1978, Brit.)
Mary Dilby
Silents
GREATER NEED, THE(1916, Brit.)
Richard Dilello
BAD BOYS(1983), w
Accursio DiLeo
THREE BROTHERS(1982, Ital.)
Fernando DiLeo
BEYOND THE LAW(1967, Ital.), w; RUTHLESS FOUR, THE(1969, Ital./Ger.), w
Mario DiLeo
CONQUEST OF THE EARTH(1980), ph; NIGHTMARES(1983), ph
Tom Dileo
KNIGHTRIDERS(1981)
Larry Dilg
1984
GHOSTBUSTERS(1984)

Douglas Dilge
  THEY ALL LAUGHED(1981), m
1984
  STRANGERS KISS(1984), p
Larry Dilge
1984
  STRANGERS KISS(1984)
Jeanette Dilger
Misc. Talkies
  HOLLYWOOD 90028(1973)
Irasema Dilian
  SCHOOLGIRL DIARY(1947, Ital.); RETURN OF THE BLACK EAGLE(1949, Ital.)
Raphael Diligent
  L'ATALANTE(1947, Fr.)
Bill Dill
  YOU CAN'T TAKE IT WITH YOU(1938); THREE HEARTS FOR JULIA(1943)
Frank Dill
Silents
  FOOLS OF FORTUNE(1922)
J. Webster Dill
Misc. Silents
  ONE-WAY TRAIL, THE(1920)
Jack Dill
Silents
  FAME AND FORTUNE(1918)
Misc. Silents
  FOLLOW THE GIRL(1917)
Jim Dill
  MISSISSIPPI RHYTHM(1949)
Marcel Dill
  NONE BUT THE LONELY HEART(1944)
Max Dill
Misc. Silents
  MILLION FOR MARY, A(1916); GLORY(1917)
Max M. Dill
Misc. Silents
  BLUFF(1916); LONESOME TOWN(1916); PECK O' PICKLES(1916); THREE PALS(1916); BELOVED ROGUES(1917)
Michael Dill
  MOONRISE(1948); SUN COMES UP, THE(1949)
Stefan Dillan
  GLADIATORS, THE(1970, Swed.)
Art Dillard
  RAINBOW VALLEY(1935); RED BLOOD OF COURAGE(1935); FUGITIVE SHERIFF, THE(1936); GHOST PATROL(1936); BAR Z BAD MEN(1937); GAMBLING TERROR, THE(1937); OLD WYOMING TRAIL, THE(1937); ROGUE OF THE RANGE(1937); YODELIN' KID FROM PINE RIDGE(1937); GOLD MINE IN THE SKY(1938); GUNSMOKE TRAIL(1938); PALS OF THE SADDLE(1938); RIDERS OF THE BLACK HILLS(1938); WILD HORSE RODEO(1938); SAGA OF DEATH VALLEY(1939); CARSON CITY KID(1940); PIONEERS OF THE WEST(1940); RANGER AND THE LADY, THE(1940); TULSA KID, THE(1940); PHANTOM COWBOY, THE(1941); PIONEERS, THE(1941); SHERIFF OF TOMBSTONE(1941); SIERRA SUE(1941); WYOMING WILDCAT(1941); HEART OF THE GOLDEN WEST(1942); MAN FROM CHEYENNE(1942); PRAIRIE PALS(1942); RIDIN' DOWN THE CANYON(1942); DAYS OF OLD CHEYENNE(1943); MOJAVE FIREBRAND(1944); SANTA FE UPRISING(1946); WILD FRONTIER, THE(1947); RENEGADES OF SONORA(1948); VIGILANTE HIDEOUT(1950); LEADVILLE GUNSLINGER(1952)
Bert Dillard
  DAWN RIDER(1935); RAINBOW VALLEY(1935); TEXAS TERROR(1935); BILLY THE KID TRAPPED(1942); DEVIL RIDERS(1944); GHOST OF HIDDEN VALLEY(1946); NAVAJO KID, THE(1946); THREE DESPERATE MEN(1951)
Mimi Dillard
  MANCHURIAN CANDIDATE, THE(1962); LIVING BETWEEN TWO WORLDS(1963); MY SIX LOVES(1963); LOOKING FOR LOVE(1964); STRANGLER, THE(1964); MAN CALLED DAGGER, A(1967); MAN FROM O.R.G.Y., THE(1970)
R. H. W. Dillard
  FRANKENSTEIN MEETS THE SPACE MONSTER(1965), w
Denise Dillaway
Misc. Talkies
  CHEERLEADERS, THE(1973)
Don Dillaway
  CIPHER BUREAU(1938); I'M STILL ALIVE(1940); JUKE BOX JENNY(1942); MAD MARTINDALES, THE(1942); MAGNIFICENT AMBERSONS, THE(1942); OVER MY DEAD BODY(1942); FLIGHT FOR FREEDOM(1943); GANGWAY FOR TOMORROW(1943); MARGIN FOR ERROR(1943); MUSIC IN MANHATTAN(1944); DANGEROUS PROFESSION, A(1949); HOLIDAY AFFAIR(1949); GUNMEN OF ABILENE(1950); STORM WARNING(1950); ON DANGEROUS GROUND(1951); PEOPLE AGAINST O'HARA, THE(1951); RACKET, THE(1951); SEALED CARGO(1951); NARROW MARGIN, THE(1952); I DIED A THOUSAND TIMES(1955); TARANTULA(1955); EVERYTHING BUT THE TRUTH(1956); SUNRISE AT CAMPOBELLO(1960); PARRISH(1961)
Donald Dillaway
  MIN AND BILL(1930); BODY AND SOUL(1931); MR. LEMON OF ORANGE(1931); PLATINUM BLONDE(1931); SKYLINE(1931); YOUNG AS YOU FEEL(1931); ANIMAL KINGDOM, THE(1932); CROSS-EXAMINATION(1932); LADY WITH A PAST(1932); MISS PINKERTON(1932); NIGHT MAYOR, THE(1932); PACK UP YOUR TROUBLES(1932); SHE WANTED A MILLIONAIRE(1932); IMPORTANT WITNESS, THE(1933); LITTLE GIANT, THE(1933); MEN MUST FIGHT(1933); MIND READER, THE(1933); ONE YEAR LATER(1933); SING SINNER, SING(1933); UNDER SECRET ORDERS(1933); MARRIAGE ON APPROVAL(1934); NOTORIOUS BUT NICE(1934); DYNAMITE DELANEY(1938); FRONTIER PONY EXPRESS(1939); GOOD GIRLS GO TO PARIS(1939); SOMETHING TO LIVE FOR(1952); DREAM WIFE(1953); OPPOSITE SEX, THE(1956)
Rusty Dillen
  TIMERIDER(1983)
George P. Dillenback
Silents
  PRICE FOR FOLLY, A(1915), w

Donna Dillenschneider
  GUNFIGHT, A(1971)
Leo Dillenschneider
  MC MASTERS, THE(1970)
Paula Dillenschneider
  GUNFIGHT, A(1971)
C.H. Diller
  SERGEANT BERRY(1938, Ger.), w
Marie Diller
Silents
  SAINTED DEVIL, A(1924)
Phyllis Diller
  MANIAC(1934); SPLENDOR IN THE GRASS(1961); BOY, DID I GET A WRONG NUMBER!(1966); FAT SPY(1966); EIGHT ON THE LAM(1967); MAD MONSTER PARTY(1967); DID YOU HEAR THE ONE ABOUT THE TRAVELING SALESLADY?(1968); PRIVATE NAVY OF SGT. O'FARRELL, THE(1968); ADDING MACHINE, THE(1969); SUNSHINE BOYS, THE(1975); PINK MOTEL(1983)
Silents
  OVER THE HILL TO THE POORHOUSE(1920)
Leigh Dilley
  EAGLE HAS LANDED, THE(1976, Brit.)
Les Dilley
  LAST REMAKE OF BEAU GESTE, THE(1977), art d
Leslie Dilley
  STAR WARS(1977), art d; EMPIRE STRIKES BACK, THE(1980), art d; AMERICAN WEREWOLF IN LONDON, AN(1981), art d; RAIDERS OF THE LOST ARK(1981), art d; NEVER SAY NEVER AGAIN(1983), art d
Irasema Dillian
  DOCTOR BEWARE(1951, Ital.)
Mildred Dilling
Misc. Talkies
  ADVENTURE IN MUSIC(1944)
Chris Dillinger
  MOONRAKER(1979, Brit.)
Howard Dillinger
  MAN'S COUNTRY(1938), ed; PAINTED TRAIL, THE(1938), ed; DRIFTING WESTWARD(1939), ed; TRIGGER SMITH(1939), ed; WILD HORSE CANYON(1939), ed; CRIMINALS WITHIN(1941), ed
Charles Dillingham
  GLORIFYING THE AMERICAN GIRL(1930)
Victor Dillingham
Silents
  BLUE STREAK, THE(1926); NIGHT PATROL, THE(1926)
John W. Dillion
Silents
  JOAN OF PLATTSBURG(1918)
John Webb Dillion
  LEATHERNECKS HAVE LANDED, THE(1936)
Robert Dillion
  BIKINI BEACH(1964), w
Bradford Dillman
  WAY WE WERE, THE(1973); CERTAIN SMILE, A(1958); IN LOVE AND WAR(1958); COMPULSION(1959); CRACK IN THE MIRROR(1960); CIRCLE OF DECEPTON(1961, Brit.); FRANCIS OF ASSISI(1961); SANCTUARY(1961); RAGE TO LIVE, A(1965); PLAINSMAN, THE(1966); HELICOPTER SPIES, THE(1968); JIGSAW(1968); SERGEANT RYKER(1968); BRIDGE AT REMAGEN, THE(1969); SUPPOSE THEY GAVE A WAR AND NOBODY CAME?(1970); BROTHER JOHN(1971); ESCAPE FROM THE PLANET OF THE APES(1971); MEPHISTO WALTZ, THE(1971); RESURRECTION OF ZACHARY WHEELER, THE(1971); ICEMAN COMETH, THE(1973); CHOSEN SURVIVORS(1974 U.S.-Mex.); GOLD(1974, Brit.); 99 AND 44/100% DEAD(1974); BUG(1975); ENFORCER, THE(1976); LINCOLN CONSPIRACY, THE(1977); MASTERMIND(1977); AMSTERDAM KILL, THE(1978, Hong Kong); PIRANHA(1978); SWARM, THE(1978); LOVE AND BULLETS(1979, Brit.); GUYANA, CULT OF THE DAMNED zero(1980, Mex./Span./Panama); SUDDEN IMPACT(1983)
Misc. Talkies
  ONE AWAY(1980); RUNNING SCARED(1980); TREASURE OF THE AMAZON(1983)
Dean Dillman, Jr.
  ATOMIC BRAIN, THE(1964), p, w
Hugh Dillman
Silents
  AMATEUR WIDOW, AN(1919)
Max Dillman
  BANDIDOS(1967, Ital.), d
Andrea Dillon
  MY BODYGUARD(1980)
Basil Dillon
  WHO KILLED JOHN SAVAGE?(1937, Brit.), w; DARK STAIRWAY, THE(1938, Brit.), w; IT'S IN THE BLOOD(1938, Brit.), w; SIMPLY TERRIFIC(1938, Brit.), w; 13 MEN AND A GUN(1938, Brit.), w
Bob Dillon
  I'LL REMEMBER APRIL(1945), w
Bobby Dillon
  FORCED LANDING(1941); GREAT STAGECOACH ROBBERY(1945); THIS LOVE OF OURS(1945)
Brandon Dillon
  FLAMING FRONTIER(1958, Can.)
Brendan Dillon
  HERO'S ISLAND(1962); PREMATURE BURIAL, THE(1962); UNSINKABLE MOLLY BROWN, THE(1964); MOLLY MAGUIRES, THE(1970); ISLAND AT THE TOP OF THE WORLD, THE(1974)
Brendon Dillon
  MY FAIR LADY(1964)
Carmen Dillon
  SECRET MISSION(1944, Brit.), art d; ADVENTURE FOR TWO(1945, Brit.), art d; JOHNNY IN THE CLOUDS(1945, Brit.), art d; HIGH FURY(1947, Brit.), art d; HAMLET(1948, Brit.), art d; VICE VERSA(1948, Brit.), art d; WOMAN HATER(1949, Brit.), art d; FIVE ANGLES ON MURDER(1950, Brit.), art d; ROCKING HORSE WINNER, THE(1950, Brit.), art d; RELUCTANT WIDOW, THE(1951, Brit.), art d; IMPORTANCE OF BEING EARNEST, THE(1952, Brit.), art d; STORY OF ROBIN HOOD, THE(1952, Brit.), art d; SWORD AND THE ROSE, THE(1953), art d; DOCTOR

Costa Dillon (continued)

IN THE HOUSE(1954, Brit.), art d; ROB ROY, THE HIGHLAND ROGUE(1954, Brit.), prod d; DOCTOR AT SEA(1955, Brit.), art d; IRON PETTICOAT, THE(1956, Brit.), art d; RICHARD III(1956, Brit.), art d; SIMON AND LAURA(1956, Brit.), art d; TALE OF TWO CITIES, A(1958, Brit.), art d; SAPPHIRE(1959, Brit.), art d; CARRY ON CONSTABLE(1960, Brit.), art d; KIDNAPPED(1960), art d; NAKED EDGE, THE(1961), art d; WATCH YOUR STERN(1961, Brit.), art d; ROOMMATES(1962, Brit.), art d; SWINGIN' MAIDEN, THE(1963, Brit.), art d; CHALK GARDEN, THE(1964, Brit.), art d; BATTLE OF THE VILLA FIORITA, THE(1965, Brit.), art d; GYPSY GIRL(1966, Brit.), art d; ACCIDENT(1967, Brit.), art d; DANDY IN ASPIC, A(1968, Brit.), art d; OTLEY(1969, Brit.), art d; SINFUL DAVEY(1969, Brit.), art d; RISE AND RISE OF MICHAEL RIMMER, THE(1970, Brit.), art d; CATCH ME A SPY(1971, Brit./Fr.), art d; GO-BETWEEN, THE(1971, Brit.), art d; LADY CAROLINE LAMB(1972, Brit./Ital.), art d; NELSON AFFAIR, THE(1973, Brit.), prod d; BUTLEY(1974, Brit.), art d; OMEN, THE(1976), art d; JULIA(1977), prod d

Costa Dillon
ATTACK OF THE KILLER TOMATOES(1978), w

Dan Dillon
Silents
KID, THE(1921)

Denny Dillon
SATURDAY NIGHT FEVER(1977)
1984
GARBO TALKS(1984)

Dickie Dillon
IT'S A GREAT LIFE(1943); SHERIFF OF LAS VEGAS(1944); CORPUS CHRISTI BANDITS(1945); GREAT STAGECOACH ROBBERY(1945); SHERIFF OF CIMARRON(1945); TRAIL OF KIT CARSON(1945)

Ed Dillon
GOLDEN WEST, THE(1932)

Eddie Dillon
HOT FOR PARIS(1930); CISCO KID(1931); IRON MAN, THE(1931); SOB SISTER(1931); SHERLOCK HOLMES(1932); TRIAL OF VIVIENNE WARE, THE(1932); WHILE PARIS SLEEPS(1932); JUST MY LUCK(1957, Brit.)
Silents
JUDITH OF BETHULIA(1914); SKYROCKET, THE(1926)
Misc. Silents
REJUVINATION OF AUNT MARY, THE(1914), d; BRED IN OLD KENTUCKY(1926), d

Edward Dillon
BROADWAY MELODY, THE(1929); LOCKED DOOR, THE(1929); CAUGHT SHORT(1930)
Silents
HOME SWEET HOME(1914); INTOLERANCE(1916); ANTICS OF ANN, THE(1917), d; EMBARRASSMENT OF RICHES, THE(1918), d; OUR LITTLE WIFE(1918), d; LUCK AND PLUCK(1919), d; NEVER SAY QUIT(1919), d; WINNING STROKE, THE(1919), d; AMATEUR WIFE, THE(1920), d; EDUCATION OF ELIZABETH, THE(1921), d; LILAC TIME(1928)
Misc. Silents
DON QUIXOTE(1916), d; MR. GOODE, THE SAMARITAN(1916), a, d; SUNSHINE DAD(1916), d; DAUGHTER OF THE POOR, A(1917), d; HEIRESS AT "COFFEE DAN'S", THE(1917), d; MIGHT AND THE MAN(1917), d; HELP! HELP! POLICE!(1919), d; PUTTING ONE OVER(1919), d; FRISKY MRS. JOHNSON, THE(1920), d; PARLOR, BEDROOM AND BATH(1920), d; HEART TO LET(1921), d; SHELTERED DAUGHTERS(1921), d; BEAUTY SHOP, THE(1922), d; WOMEN MEN MARRY(1922), d; BROADWAY GOLD(1923), d; DRUMS OF JEOPARDY, THE(1923), d; DANGER GIRL, THE(1926), d; FLAME OF THE ARGENTINE(1926), d; DICE WOMAN, THE(1927), d

Edward F. Dillon
GHOST STORY(1981)

Forrest Dillon
DAYS OF JESSE JAMES(1939); OX-BOW INCIDENT, THE(1943)

Forrest H. Dillon
MAN FROM SUNDOWN, THE(1939)

George Dillon
I'M AN EXPLOSIVE(1933, Brit.); IRISH FOR LUCK(1936, Brit.); MUDLARK, THE(1950, Brit.)

Henry Dillon
Misc. Talkies
COME ONE, COME ALL(1970)

J. Francis Dillon
Misc. Silents
KEY TO YESTERDAY, THE(1914)

Jack Dillon
Silents
GANGSTERS OF NEW YORK, THE(1914); LOST BRIDEGROOM, THE(1916); ALL WOMAN(1918); LOVE SWINDLE(1918), d; NANCY COMES HOME(1918), d; FOLLIES GIRL, THE(1919), d; SUDS(1920), d; CAPPY RICKS(1921); CHILDREN OF THE NIGHT(1921), d; JOURNEY'S END, THE(1921); CUB REPORTER, THE(1922), d; GLEAM O'DAWN(1922), d; YELLOW STAIN, THE(1922), d; SMILE, BROTHER, SMILE(1927)
Misc. Silents
CASE AT LAW, A(1917); INDISCREET CORINNE(1917), d; BEANS(1918), d; BETTY TAKES A HAND(1918), d; HEIRESS FOR A DAY(1918), d; LIMOUSINE LIFE(1918), d; BURGLAR BY PROXY(1919), a, d; LOVE'S PRISONER(1919), d; SHE HIRED A HUSBAND(1919), d; SILK-LINED BURGLAR, THE(1919), d; TASTE OF LIFE, A(1919), d; BLACKBIRDS(1920), d; RIGHT OF WAY, THE(1920), d; PLAYTHING OF BROADWAY, THE(1921), d; CALVERT'S VALLEY(1922), d; BROKEN VIOLIN, THE(1923), d; SELF-MADE WIFE, THE(1923), d

James Dillon
TEX TAKES A HOLIDAY(1932)

John Dillon
IN OLD ARIZONA(1929)
Silents
HOME SWEET HOME(1914); MARTYRS OF THE ALAMO, THE(1915); BY WHOSE HAND?(1916); EMBARRASSMENT OF RICHES, THE(1918)
Misc. Silents
FOR HIS SAKE(1922); TIGER THOMPSON(1924); MIDNIGHT MOLLY(1925)

John Frances Dillon
Silents
NOOSE, THE(1928), d

John Francis Dillon
CAREERS(1929), d; FAST LIFE(1929), d; SALLY(1929), d; BRIDE OF THE REGIMENT(1930), d; GIRL OF THE GOLDEN WEST(1930), d; KISMET(1930), d; ONE NIGHT AT SUSIE'S(1930), d; SPRING IS HERE(1930), d; FINGER POINTS, THE(1931), d; MILLIE(1931), d; PAGAN LADY(1931), d; RECKLESS HOUR, THE(1931), d; YOUR NUMBER'S UP(1931), d; BEHIND THE MASK(1932), d; CALL HER SAVAGE(1932), d; COHENS, AND KELLYS IN HOLLYWOOD, THE(1932), d; MAN ABOUT TOWN(1932), d; HUMANITY(1933), d; BIG SHAKEDOWN, THE(1934), d
Silents
IF I MARRY AGAIN(1925), d; LOVE'S BLINDNESS(1926), d; CRYSTAL CUP, THE(1927), d; MAN CRAZY(1927), d; SEA TIGER, THE(1927), d; SMILE, BROTHER, SMILE(1927), d; HEART OF A FOLLIES GIRL, THE(1928), d; SCARLET SEAS(1929), d
Misc. Silents
ROOF TREE, THE(1921), d; MAN WANTED(1922), d; FLAMING YOUTH(1923), d; FLIRTING WITH LOVE(1924), d; LILLIES OF THE FIELD(1924), d; PERFECT FLAPPER, THE(1924), d; CHICKIE(1925), d; HALF-WAY GIRL, THE(1925), d; ONE WAY STREET(1925), d; WE MODERNS(1925), d; DON JUAN'S THREE NIGHTS(1926), d; MIDNIGHT LOVERS(1926), d; TOO MUCH MONEY(1926), d; PRINCE OF HEADWAITERS, THE(1927), d; CHILDREN OF THE RITZ(1929), d

John T. "Jack" Dillon
FRISCO KID(1935)

John W. Dillon
Misc. Silents
WHY I WOULD NOT MARRY(1918)

John Webb Dillon
GIRL OF THE PORT(1930); CROSS-EXAMINATION(1932); SALLY OF THE SUBWAY(1932); DIAMOND TRAIL(1933); CAROLINA(1934); LIFE BEGINS AT 40(1935); ON PROBATION(1935); SHE COULDN'T TAKE IT(1935); TRADE WINDS(1938); SERGEANT MADDEN(1939); THIRD FINGER, LEFT HAND(1940); SECRET HEART, THE(1946); LADY IN THE LAKE(1947)
Silents
ONE DAY(1916); ROMEO AND JULIET(1916); DARLING OF PARIS, THE(1917); TIGER WOMAN, THE(1917); INNER CHAMBER, THE(1921); JANE EYRE(1921); EXILES, THE(1923); NO MOTHER TO GUIDE HER(1923); AIR MAIL, THE(1925); DEVIL'S CARGO, THE(1925); BOWERY CINDERELLA(1927); WOLF'S CLOTHING(1927)
Misc. Silents
HYPOCRISY(1916); ALMA, WHERE DO YOU LIVE?(1917); PRIMITIVE CALL, THE(1917); RICH MAN'S PLAYTHING, A(1917); SCREAM IN THE NIGHT, A(1919); SEVENTH BANDIT, THE(1926)

Joseph Dillon
ESTHER WATERS(1948, Brit.)

Josephine Dillon
LADY AND THE MONSTER, THE(1944)

Kim Dillon
WAY OF A GAUCHO(1952)

Lauri Dillon
FRENCH CONNECTION 11(1975), w

Maria Dillon
TRICK OR TREATS(1982)

Matt Dillon
OVER THE EDGE(1979); LITTLE DARLINGS(1980); MY BODYGUARD(1980); LIAR'S MOON(1982); TEX(1982); OUTSIDERS, THE(1983); RUMBLE FISH(1983)
1984
FLAMINGO KID, THE(1984)

Melinda Dillon
APRIL FOOLS, THE(1969); BOUND FOR GLORY(1976); CLOSE ENCOUNTERS OF THE THIRD KIND(1977); SLAP SHOT(1977); F.I.S.T.(1978); ABSENCE OF MALICE(1981)
1984
SONGWRITER(1984)

Mellinda Dillon
CHRISTMAS STORY, A(1983)

Michael Dillon
GORGO(1961, Brit.)

Mick Dillon
HOW I WON THE WAR(1967, Brit.)
1984
CHAMPIONS(1984)

Pat Dillon
SONG OF BERNADETTE, THE(1943)

Patricia Dillon
TORTURE DUNGEON(1970)

Richard Dillon
IRON MAJOR, THE(1943)

Robert Dillon
ORCHIDS TO YOU(1935), w; WILDERNESS MAIL(1935), w; PAROLE(1936), w; CITY OF FEAR(1959), w; SAFE AT HOME(1962), w; "X"–THE MAN WITH THE X-RAY EYES(1963), w; OLD DARK HOUSE, THE(1963, Brit.), w; THIRTEEN FRIGHTENED GIRLS(1963), w; MUSCLE BEACH PARTY(1964), p, w; PRIME CUT(1972), w; 99 AND 44/100% DEAD(1974), s; FRENCH CONNECTION 11(1975), w
1984
RIVER, THE(1984), w
Silents
LAMPLIGHTER, THE(1921), w; FORTUNE HUNTER, THE(1927), w; HAM AND EGGS AT THE FRONT(1927), w; RANGE RIDERS, THE(1927), w

Robert A. Dillon
CRUSADE AGAINST RACKETS(1937), w
Silents
MAN WHO COULD NOT LOSE, THE(1914), w; LAST OF THE MOHICANS, THE(1920), w

Thomas Dillon
THIN MAN GOES HOME, THE(1944); DUEL IN THE SUN(1946); KISS TOMORROW GOODBYE(1950); MILLION DOLLAR MERMAID(1952); CLOWN, THE(1953); OKLAHOMA WOMAN, THE(1956)

Thomas P. Dillon
WOMAN IN THE WINDOW, THE(1945); BLACK BEAUTY(1946); EXILE, THE(1947); KISS THE BLOOD OFF MY HANDS(1948); WOMAN ON THE RUN(1950); REMAINS TO BE SEEN(1953); SEARCH FOR BRIDEY MURPHY, THE(1956)

Tom Dillon
WHISTLING IN BROOKLYN(1943); GOING MY WAY(1944); DANGEROUS PARTNERS(1945); MILDRED PIERCE(1945); NOB HILL(1945); PURSUIT TO ALGIERS(1945); SCARLET STREET(1945); THOSE ENDEARING YOUNG CHARMS(1945); BEAUTIFUL CHEAT, THE(1946); BLUE DAHLIA, THE(1946); HOODLUM SAINT, THE(1946); POSTMAN ALWAYS RINGS TWICE, THE(1946); STRANGE LOVE OF MARTHA IVERS, THE(1946); WELL-GROOMED BRIDE, THE(1946); DEAD RECKONING(1947); MY FAVORITE BRUNETTE(1947); MY GIRL TISA(1948); SAINTS AND SINNERS(1949, Brit.); ENFORCER, THE(1951); KANSAS CITY CONFIDENTIAL(1952); NORTH TO ALASKA(1960); NOTORIOUS LANDLADY, THE(1962); NIGHT TIDE(1963)

Tom P. Dillon
DRESSED TO KILL(1946); UP IN CENTRAL PARK(1948); EAST SIDE, WEST SIDE(1949)

Jean Carmen Dillow
Misc. Talkies
PAWN, THE(1968), a, d

Donald Dilloway
CIMARRON(1931); MEN IN HER LIFE(1931); ATTORNEY FOR THE DEFENSE(1932); STRANGE LOVE OF MOLLY LOUVAIN, THE(1932)

The Dills
UP IN SMOKE(1978)

William Dills
Misc. Silents
CHECHAHCOS, THE(1924)

Clyde Dillson
LET 'EM HAVE IT(1935)

Dorothy Dilly
FIFTH AVENUE GIRL(1939)

Brenden Dilon
BUG(1975)

Oscar DiLorenzo
THIEF(1981)

Clyde Dilson
UNMASKED(1929); STAND UP AND CHEER(1934 80m FOX bw); KING SOLOMON OF BROADWAY(1935); MEN WITHOUT NAMES(1935); FLORIDA SPECIAL(1936); THIRTEEN HOURS BY AIR(1936); UNDER YOUR SPELL(1936); YOU MAY BE NEXT(1936); DUKE COMES BACK, THE(1937); GAME THAT KILLS, THE(1937); MIDNIGHT MADONNA(1937); THERE GOES MY GIRL(1937); UNDER SUSPICION(1937); SECRETS OF A NURSE(1938); MR. SMITH GOES TO WASHINGTON(1939); UP IN THE AIR(1940)

John Dilson
GIRL WHO CAME BACK, THE(1935); HAPPINESS C.O.D.(1935); I FOUND STELLA PARISH(1935); MURDER MAN(1935); SILVER STREAK, THE(1935); SPECIAL AGENT(1935); CHARLIE CHAN AT THE CIRCUS(1936); DEATH FROM A DISTANCE(1936); EASY MONEY(1936); EX-MRS. BRADFORD, THE(1936); GREAT GUY(1936); HITCH HIKE TO HEAVEN(1936); IT HAD TO HAPPEN(1936); NEXT TIME WE LOVE(1936); PIGSKIN PARADE(1936); THREE OF A KIND(1936); UNDER YOUR SPELL(1936); WE'RE ONLY HUMAN(1936); EASY LIVING(1937); ESCAPE BY NIGHT(1937); LOVE IS NEWS(1937); THEY WON'T FORGET(1937); ANGELS WITH DIRTY FACES(1938); DOWN IN ARKANSAW(1938); MY LUCKY STAR(1938); THERE'S THAT WOMAN AGAIN(1938); WHO KILLED GAIL PRESTON?(1938); WOMEN IN PRISON(1938); EACH DAWN I DIE(1939); FIXER DUGAN(1939); IN NAME ONLY(1939); LAUGH IT OFF(1939); ON TRIAL(1939); RACKETEERS OF THE RANGE(1939); STAND UP AND FIGHT(1939); TROUBLE IN SUNDOWN(1939); WHEN TOMORROW COMES(1939); WOMAN IS THE JUDGE, A(1939); WOMEN IN THE WIND(1939); CHARLIE CHAN'S MURDER CRUISE(1940); DANGER AHEAD(1940); DARK COMMAND, THE(1940); FIVE LITTLE PEPPERS AT HOME(1940); GIRLS UNDER TWENTY-ONE(1940); HOLD THAT WOMAN(1940); I LOVE YOU AGAIN(1940); LEGION OF THE LAWLESS(1940); MAN WITH NINE LIVES, THE(1940); MARKED MEN(1940); NO, NO NANETTE(1940); PHANTOM OF CHINATOWN(1940); PIONEERS OF THE WEST(1940); PUBLIC DEB NO. 1(1940); SCANDAL SHEET(1940); THUNDERING FRONTIER(1940); ACROSS THE SIERRAS(1941); ANDY HARDY'S PRIVATE SECRETARY(1941); CYCLONE ON HORSEBACK(1941); DEADLY GAME, THE(1941); DESIGN FOR SCANDAL(1941); FACE BEHIND THE MASK, THE(1941); FATHER'S SON(1941); FOOTSTEPS IN THE DARK(1941); INTERNATIONAL LADY(1941); MAN MADE MONSTER(1941); NAVAL ACADEMY(1941); OBLIGING YOUNG LADY(1941); SHADOW OF THE THIN MAN(1941); SUNSET IN WYOMING(1941); THEY MEET AGAIN(1941); TWO LATINS FROM MANHATTAN(1941); UNHOLY PARTNERS(1941); WAGONS ROLL AT NIGHT, THE(1941); WHISTLING IN THE DARK(1941); FALCON'S BROTHER, THE(1942); FLY BY NIGHT(1942); FOOTLIGHT SERENADE(1942); JOHNNY EAGER(1942); MADAME SPY(1942); QUEEN OF BROADWAY(1942); SABOTAGE SQUAD(1942); SHIP AHOY(1942); THEY ALL KISSED THE BRIDE(1942); TRAMP, TRAMP, TRAMP(1942); WILDCAT(1942); YOU CAN'T ESCAPE FOREVER(1942); DR. GILLESPIE'S CRIMINAL CASE(1943); DRUMS OF FU MANCHU(1943); HAPPY LAND(1943); IRON MAJOR, THE(1943); LEOPARD MAN, THE(1943); MISSION TO MOSCOW(1943); PILOT NO. 5(1943); PRINCESS O'ROURKE(1943); SONG OF BERNADETTE, THE(1943); SO'S YOUR UNCLE(1943); SWEET ROSIE O'GRADY(1943); THIS LAND IS MINE(1943); YOU'RE A LUCKY FELLOW, MR. SMITH(1943); BEAUTIFUL BUT BROKE(1944); BUFFALO BILL(1944); COVER GIRL(1944); JAM SESSION(1944); ONCE UPON A TIME(1944); YELLOW ROSE OF TEXAS, THE(1944)
Misc. Talkies
CITY LIMITS(1941)

John H. Dilson
EVERY NIGHT AT EIGHT(1935); CHEERS OF THE CROWD(1936); WESTERNER, THE(1936); MONSTER AND THE GIRL, THE(1941); LADY BODYGUARD(1942); MAYOR OF 44TH STREET, THE(1942); NIGHT TO REMEMBER, A(1942); SHE HAS WHAT IT TAKES(1943)

Dickie Dilton
CHATTERBOX(1943)

Charles Diltz
DAUGHTER OF THE TONG(1939), ed; KILLERS OF THE WILD(1940), w
Silents
OUT ALL NIGHT(1927), w

Carol Dilworth
HORROR HOUSE(1970, Brit.)

Gordon Dilworth
FLIPPER'S NEW ADVENTURE(1964)

C. DiMaggio
MAN COULD GET KILLED, A(1966)

Joe DiMaggio
MANHATTAN MERRY-GO-ROUND(1937)

Nick DiMaggio
MR. MOTO'S GAMBLE(1938), ed; LADIES OF WASHINGTON(1944), ed; O. HENRY'S FULL HOUSE(1952), ed

Rose DiMaggio
INDIAN UPRISING(1951), m

Ross DiMaggio
DOUBLE TROUBLE(1941), md; REG'LAR FELLERS(1941), m; TOUGHER THEY COME, THE(1950), m; FORT SAVAGE RAIDERS(1951), md; YANK IN KOREA, A(1951), md; YANK IN INDO-CHINA, A(1952), md; AMBUSH AT TOMAHAWK GAP(1953), m; MAN IN THE DARK(1953), md; NEBRASKAN, THE(1953), md; DRIVE A CROOKED ROAD(1954), md; CHICAGO SYNDICATE(1955), md; GUN THAT WON THE WEST, THE(1955), md; FLAME OF STAMBOUL(1957), m, md; NIGHT THE WORLD EXPLODED, THE(1957), md

Rossi DiMaggio
BANDITS OF EL DORADO(1951), m

Pol Dimalanta
STRYKER(1983, Phil.), prod d

David Dimanna
FLASHDANCE(1983)

Tony DiMarco
CALYPSO HEAT WAVE(1957), ed; GIANT CLAW, THE(1957), ed; 80 STEPS TO JONAH(1969), ed; DAUGHTERS OF SATAN(1972), ed; SUPERBEAST(1972), ed; DOCTOR DEATH: SEEKER OF SOULS(1973), ed; SEDUCTION, THE(1982), ed

Tony DiMario
BIG TIP OFF, THE(1955)

Ray Dimas
LITTLE BIG MAN(1970); ONE MORE TRAIN TO ROB(1971)

Richard Dimbleby
TWENTY QUESTIONS MURDER MYSTERY, THE(1950, Brit.); JOHN AND JULIE(1957, Brit.); MAD LITTLE ISLAND(1958, Brit.); LIBEL(1959, Brit.)

James Dime
PROFESSOR BEWARE(1938); SUDAN(1945)
Silents
KING OF KINGS, THE(1927); SPEEDY(1928); STAND AND DELIVER(1928)

Jimmie Dime
WHITE WOMAN(1933)

Jimmy Dime
FRENCHMAN'S CREEK(1944); JET PILOT(1957)
Silents
GOLD RUSH, THE(1925)

Johnny Dime
ONCE UPON A HONEYMOON(1942)

John Dimech
KILLERS OF KILIMANJARO(1960, Brit.); LAWRENCE OF ARABIA(1962, Brit.); DEADLY AFFAIR, THE(1967, Brit.)

Luisa DiMeo
SEVEN HILLS OF ROME, THE(1958)

Fiseha Dimetros
EXORCIST II: THE HERETIC(1977)

Bernard Dimey
PRICE OF FLESH, THE(1962, Fr.), w

Danny DiMinno
NEW LIFE STYLE, THE(1970, Ger.), m

Dimitri
NAKED HEART, THE(1955, Brit.)

Michele Dimitri
POURQUOI PAS!(1979, Fr.), p

Nick Dimitri
ISLAND OF LOVE(1963); LAST MOMENT, THE(1966); STUDENT TEACHERS, THE(1973); HARD TIMES(1975); SCORCHY(1976); DRIVER, THE(1978); 48 HOURS(1982); SUDDEN IMPACT(1983)
1984
CITY HEAT(1984)

Nicola Dimitri
N. P.(1971, Ital.), ph

Richard Dimitri
WORLD'S GREATEST LOVER, THE(1977)
1984
JOHNNY DANGEROUSLY(1984)

Mikica Dimitrijevic
MEETINGS WITH REMARKABLE MEN(1979, Brit.)

Slobodan Dimitrijevic
TREASURE OF SILVER LAKE(1965, Fr./Ger./Yugo.); RAMPAGE AT APACHE WELLS(1966, Ger./Yugo.)

Theodore Dimitriou
ATLAS(1960); AUNT FROM CHICAGO(1960, Gr.)

Antonin Dimitrov
HEAD ON(1981, Can.), prod d

Olga Dimitrov
IN PRAISE OF OLDER WOMEN(1978, Can.), cos; AGENCY(1981, Can.), cos; DEATH HUNT(1981), cos; SILENCE OF THE NORTH(1981, Can.), cos

Blaga Dimitrova
DETOUR, THE(1968, Bulgarian), w

Vanya Dimitrova
PEKING EXPRESS(1951)

Kathleen Dimmick
WILD PARTY, THE(1975)

Guy "Buz" Dillow
Misc. Talkies
PAWN, THE(1968)

Walter Dimmick
SQUIRM(1976)

Joseph Dimmitt
GREAT LOCOMOTIVE CHASE, THE(1956), cos; SILENT CALL, THE(1961), cos; RIDER ON A DEAD HORSE(1962), cos; WILD ON THE BEACH(1965), cos; WINTER A GO-GO(1965), cos; 40 GUNS TO APACHE PASS(1967), cos

Joe DiMona
INCREDIBLE MR. LIMPET, THE(1964), w

Jack Dimond
FIVE AGAINST THE HOUSE(1955)

Dino Dimopoulos
ASTERO(1960, Gr.), d

Dinos Dimopoulos
MADALENA(1965, Gr.), d; RAPE, THE(1965, Gr.), d, w

Stephen Dimopoulos
FIRST BLOOD(1982)

Stephen Dimopoulous
1984
BIG MEAT EATER(1984, Can.)

Howard Dimsdale
LIVING GHOST, THE(1942), w; PENTHOUSE RHYTHM(1945), w; SENORITA FROM THE WEST(1945), w; LOVE LAUGHS AT ANDY HARDY(1946), w; SOMEWHERE IN THE NIGHT(1946), w; KISS FOR CORLISS, A(1949), w; CURTAIN CALL AT CACTUS CREEK(1950), w; LADY WITHOUT PASSPORT, A(1950), w; TRAVELING SALESWOMAN(1950), w; ABBOTT AND COSTELLO MEET CAPTAIN KIDD(1952), w; ALADDIN AND HIS LAMP(1952), w; CAPTAIN SCARLETT(1953), p, w

Ross Dimsey
FANTASM(1976, Aus.), w; FINAL CUT, THE(1980, Aus.), d, w
1984
SECOND TIME LUCKY(1984, Aus./New Zealand), w

Dennis Dimster
OLLY, OLLY, OXEN FREE(1978)

The Dimtrievitch Gypsy Orchestra
LOVE AND DEATH(1975)

Gilbert Wright Jalal Din
MAYA(1966), w

Nella Dina
CRAZY JOE(1974)

Wissia Dina
THEY MET ON SKIS(1940, Fr.)

Pino Dinaggio
CARRIE(1976), m

Dinah
SWISS MISS(1938)

Dinah the Mule
WAY OUT WEST(1937)

Dinan
FOUR IN A JEEP(1951, Switz.)

Albert Dinan
INNOCENTS IN PARIS(1955, Brit.); LAW IS THE LAW, THE(1959, Fr.); WOMAN OF SIN(1961, Fr.); COUNTERFEITERS OF PARIS, THE(1962, Fr., Ital.); DANIELLA BY NIGHT(1962, Fr/Ger.); GIGOT(1962); MAGNIFICENT TRAMP, THE(1962, Fr./Ital.); SWEET ECSTASY(1962, Fr.); FIRE IN THE FLESH(1964, Fr.)

Marc DiNapoli
THIS MAN MUST DIE(1970, Fr./Ital.)

Monette Dinay
FOUR BAGS FULL(1957, Fr./Ital.)

Audrey Dineen
Misc. Talkies
SCORCHING FURY(1952)

Joseph Dineen
SIX BRIDGES TO CROSS(1955), w

Joseph F. Dineen
LET US LIVE(1939), w

Mike Dineen
1984
REAL LIFE(1984, Brit.), p

Dimitri Dineff
MY LIFE TO LIVE(1963, Fr.)

Alan Dinehart
BRAT, THE(1931); SOB SISTER(1931); WICKED(1931); ALMOST MARRIED(1932); BACHELOR'S AFFAIRS(1932); DEVIL IS DRIVING, THE(1932); DISORDERLY CONDUCT(1932); OKAY AMERICA(1932); STREET OF WOMEN(1932); TRIAL OF VIVIENNE WARE, THE(1932); WASHINGTON MERRY-GO-ROUND(1932); AS THE DEVIL COMMANDS(1933); BUREAU OF MISSING PERSONS(1933); DANCE, GIRL, DANCE(1933); HER BODYGUARD(1933); I HAVE LIVED(1933); LAWYER MAN(1933); NO MARRIAGE TIES(1933); SIN OF NORA MORAN(1933); STUDY IN SCARLET, A(1933); SUPERNATURAL(1933); SWEEPINGS(1933); WORLD CHANGES, THE(1933); BABY, TAKE A BOW(1934); CAT'S PAW, THE(1934); CROSBY CASE, THE(1934); CROSS COUNTRY CRUISE(1934); FURY OF THE JUNGLE(1934); JIMMY THE GENT(1934); LOVE CAPTIVE, THE(1934); VERY HONORABLE GUY, A(1934); DANTE'S INFERNO(1935); IN OLD KENTUCKY(1935); LOTTERY LOVER(1935); PAYOFF, THE(1935); REDHEADS ON PARADE(1935); THANKS A MILLION(1935); YOUR UNCLE DUDLEY(1935); $10 RAISE(1935); BORN TO DANCE(1936); CHARLIE CHAN AT THE RACE TRACK(1936); COUNTRY BEYOND, THE(1936); CRIME OF DR. FORBES(1936); EVERYBODY'S OLD MAN(1936); HUMAN CARGO(1936); IT HAD TO HAPPEN(1936); KING OF THE ROYAL MOUNTED(1936); PAROLE(1936); REUNION(1936); STAR FOR A NIGHT(1936); ALI BABA GOES TO TOWN(1937); BIG TOWN GIRL(1937); DANGER–LOVE AT WORK(1937); DANGEROUSLY YOURS(1937); FIFTY ROADS TO TOWN(1937); MIDNIGHT TAXI(1937); STEP LIVELY, JEEVES(1937); THIS IS MY AFFAIR(1937); WOMAN-WISE(1937); FIRST 100 YEARS, THE(1938); LOVE ON A BUDGET(1938); REBECCA OF SUNNYBROOK FARM(1938); UP THE RIVER(1938); EVERYTHING HAPPENS AT NIGHT(1939); FAST AND LOOSE(1939); HOTEL FOR WOMEN(1939); HOUSE OF FEAR(1939); KING OF THE TURF(1939); SECOND FIDDLE(1939); TWO BRIGHT BOYS(1939); SLIGHTLY HONORABLE(1940); GIRL TROUBLE(1942); FIRED WIFE(1943); HEAT'S ON, THE(1943); IT'S A GREAT LIFE(1943); SWEET ROSIE O'GRADY(1943); JOHNNY DOESN'T LIVE HERE ANY MORE(1944); MINSTREL MAN(1944); MOON OVER LAS VEGAS(1944); OH, WHAT A NIGHT(1944); SEVEN DAYS ASHORE(1944); WAVE, A WAC AND A MARINE, A(1944); WHISTLER, THE(1944)

Alan Dinehart III
BLONDIE'S BIG DEAL(1949); EASY LIVING(1949); SUN COMES UP, THE(1949); COPPER CANYON(1950); HAPPY YEARS, THE(1950); NEVER A DULL MOMENT(1950); CARELESS YEARS, THE(1957); JET PILOT(1957)

Allan Dinehart
GIRLS ABOUT TOWN(1931); GOOD SPORT(1931); RACKETY RAX(1932)

Mason Alan Dinehart
HOT ANGEL, THE(1958)

Mason Alan Dinehart, Jr.
ROADRACERS(1959)

Mason Allan Dinehart
PLATINUM HIGH SCHOOL(1960)

Peter Dineley
IT HAPPENED HERE(1966, Brit.)

Mel Dinelli
SPIRAL STAIRCASE, THE(1946), w; RECKLESS MOMENTS, THE(1949), w; WINDOW, THE(1949), w; HOUSE BY THE RIVER(1950), w; CAUSE FOR ALARM(1951), w; BEWARE, MY LOVELY(1952), w; JEOPARDY(1953), w; LIZZIE(1957), w; STEP DOWN TO TERROR(1958), w

Denis Dines
ANGEL AND SINNER(1947, Fr.)

Gordon Dines
DREAMS COME TRUE(1936, Brit.), ph; KEEP FIT(1937, Brit.), ph; I SEE ICE(1938), ph; PENNY PARADISE(1938, Brit.), ph; LET'S BE FAMOUS(1939, Brit.), ph; PHANTOM STRIKES, THE(1939, Brit.), ph; IT'S IN THE AIR(1940, Brit.), ph; TURNED OUT NICE AGAIN(1941, Brit.), ph; ZOMBIES ON BROADWAY(1945), d; FRIEDA(1947, Brit.), ph; NICHOLAS NICKLEBY(1947, Brit.), ph; BLUE LAMP, THE(1950, Brit.), ph; POOL OF LONDON(1951, Brit.), ph; GENTLE GUNMAN, THE(1952, Brit.), ph; SECRET PEOPLE(1952, Brit.), ph; TRAIN OF EVENTS(1952, Brit.), ph; CRUEL SEA, THE(1953), ph; I BELIEVE IN YOU(1953, Brit.), ph; CROWDED DAY, THE(1954, Brit.), ph; HIGH AND DRY(1954, Brit.), ph; COLDITZ STORY, THE(1955, Brit.), ph; SQUARE RING, THE(1955, Brit.), ph; YOU LUCKY PEOPLE(1955, Brit.), ph; SHIP THAT DIED OF SHAME, THE(1956, Brit.), ph; THIRD KEY, THE(1957, Brit.), ph; DANGEROUS YOUTH(1958, Brit.), ph; MAN WHO WOULDN'T TALK, THE(1958, Brit.), ph; WONDERFUL THINGS!(1958, Brit.), ph; LADY IS A SQUARE, THE(1959, Brit.), ph; NAVY LARK, THE(1959, Brit.), ph; FOUR DESPERATE MEN(1960, Brit.), ph; IT TAKES A THIEF(1960, Brit.), ph; BOMB IN THE HIGH STREET(1961, Brit.), ph; CIRCLE OF DECEPTON(1961, Brit.), ph

Karen Dines
NO LONGER ALONE(1978)

Isak Dinesen [Karen Blixen]
IMMORTAL STORY, THE(1969, Fr.), w

Pat Dinga
HOUSE OF USHER(1960), spec eff; PIT AND THE PENDULUM, THE(1961), spec eff; PANIC IN YEAR ZERO!(1962), spec eff; PREMATURE BURIAL, THE(1962), spec eff; TALES OF TERROR(1962), spec eff; RAVEN, THE(1963), spec eff; WAR IS HELL(1964), spec eff

Norbert Dingeldein
IT HAPPENED HERE(1966, Brit.)

Mark Dingham
HIGH AND DRY(1954, Brit.)

Charles Dingle
ONE THIRD OF A NATION(1939); LITTLE FOXES, THE(1941); UNHOLY PARTNERS(1941); ARE HUSBANDS NECESSARY?(1942); CALLING DR. GILLESPIE(1942); GEORGE WASHINGTON SLEPT HERE(1942); JOHNNY EAGER(1942); SOMEWHERE I'LL FIND YOU(1942); TALK OF THE TOWN(1942); TENNESSEE JOHNSON(1942); EDGE OF DARKNESS(1943); LADY OF BURLESQUE(1943); SHE'S FOR ME(1943); SOMEONE TO REMEMBER(1943); SONG OF BERNADETTE, THE(1943); HOME IN INDIANA(1944); NATIONAL BARN DANCE(1944); TOGETHER AGAIN(1944); GUEST WIFE(1945); HERE COME THE CO-EDS(1945); MEDAL FOR BENNY, A(1945); BEAST WITH FIVE FINGERS, THE(1946); CENTENNIAL SUMMER(1946); CINDERELLA JONES(1946); DUEL IN THE SUN(1946); SISTER KENNY(1946); THREE WISE FOOLS(1946); WIFE OF MONTE CRISTO, THE(1946); MY FAVORITE BRUNETTE(1947); ROMANCE OF ROSY RIDGE, THE(1947); WELCOME STRANGER(1947); IF YOU KNEW SUSIE(1948); SOUTHERN YANKEE, A(1948); STATE OF THE UNION(1948); BIG JACK(1949); NEVER WAVE AT A WAC(1952); CALL ME MADAM(1953); HALF A HERO(1953); PRESIDENT'S LADY, THE(1953); COURT-MARTIAL OF BILLY MITCHELL, THE(1955)

Christine Dingle
NICE GIRL LIKE ME, A(1969, Brit.); BARTLEBY(1970, Brit.)

Kay Dingle
MR. MOM(1983)

Tony Dingman
ONE FROM THE HEART(1982)

May Dington
ADVENTURE IN MANHATTAN(1936), w

John Dingwall
SUNDAY TOO FAR AWAY(1975, Aus.), w; BUDDIES(1983, Aus.), p, w

George Dinica
Misc. Talkies
OIL(1977, Ital.)

Veveldo Diniz
GIVEN WORD, THE(1964, Braz.)

Dinke
HALF PINT, THE(1960)

Craig Dinkel
1984
ALLEY CAT(1984)

Joseph F. Dinneen
UNDERWORLD U.S.A.(1961), p,d&w

June Dinneen
HITCH-HIKER, THE(1953)

Jannice Dinnen
SMILEY GETS A GUN(1959, Brit.)

William Dinner
OBSESSED(1951, Brit.), w

Dinning Sisters
STRICTLY IN THE GROOVE(1942); NATIONAL BARN DANCE(1944)

The Dinning Sisters
FUN AND FANCY FREE(1947); MELODY TIME(1948)

Andre Dino
MY UNCLE(1958, Fr.); LE BEAU SERGE(1959, Fr.); WEB OF PASSION(1961, Fr.)

Ralph Dino
VIVA MAX!(1969), m

Dino, Desi & Billy
MURDERERS' ROW(1966)

Anna Dinokhovskaya
COUNTRY BRIDE(1938, USSR)

Lou Dinos
FUNNY FARM, THE(1982, Can.)

Abe Dinovich
SPANISH MAIN, THE(1945); HIGH WALL, THE(1947)

Abe Dinovitch
LADY BY CHOICE(1934); BEASTS OF BERLIN(1939); SHADOW OF THE THIN MAN(1941); STRAWBERRY BLONDE, THE(1941); DR. BROADWAY(1942); COLONEL EFFINGHAM'S RAID(1945); EVE KNEW HER APPLES(1945); LOVE FROM A STRANGER(1947); NORTHWEST OUTPOST(1947); CALL NORTHSIDE 777(1948); SET-UP, THE(1949); SECRET FURY, THE(1950); TEA FOR TWO(1950); PAINTING THE CLOUDS WITH SUNSHINE(1951); O. HENRY'S FULL HOUSE(1952); EXECUTIVE SUITE(1954)

A.T. Dinsdale
UNDERCOVER AGENT(1935, Brit.), ph; FOOL AND THE PRINCESS, THE(1948, Brit.), ph; TRAPPED BY THE TERROR(1949, Brit.), ph

Howard Dinsdale
BABES ON SWING STREET(1944), w

Reece Dinsdale
1984
WINTER FLIGHT(1984, Brit.)

Dinty
Silents
NO BABIES WANTED(1928)

Mira Dinulovic
KAPO(1964, Ital./Fr./Yugo.)

Abe Dinvitch
LET'S MAKE IT LEGAL(1951)

John Dinwoodie
1984
MAJDHAR(1984, Brit.), ed

Franco Diogene
TENTACLES(1977, Ital.); MIDNIGHT EXPRESS(1978, Brit.)

Richard Dioguardi
ROSE, THE(1979); KING OF COMEDY, THE(1983)

Dion
TEENAGE MILLIONAIRE(1961); TWIST AROUND THE CLOCK(1961)

Aurie Dion
RED(1970, Can.)

Debbie Dion
1984
SCARRED(1984)

Dennis Dion
SATAN'S MISTRESS(1982), spec eff

Hector Dion
Silents
FORGIVEN, OR THE JACK O'DIAMONDS(1914); $5,000,000 COUNTERFEITING PLOT, THE(1914); KING LEAR(1916); ONE MORE AMERICAN(1918)
Misc. Silents
SHEPHERD LASSIE OF ARGYLE, THE(1914, Brit.); SAINT, DEVIL AND WOMAN(1916); FIGHTING MAD(1917); PAINTED LIPS(1918)

Rose Dione
HEARTS IN EXILE(1929); ONE STOLEN NIGHT(1929); ISLE OF ESCAPE(1930); ON YOUR BACK(1930); WOMEN EVERYWHERE(1930); SALVATION NELL(1931); FREAKS(1932); KING MURDER, THE(1932)
Silents
SUDS(1920); BLUSHING BRIDE, THE(1921); LITTLE LORD FAUNTLEROY(1921); SALOME(1922); FRENCH DOLL, THE(1923); SCARAMOUCHE(1923); INEZ FROM HOLLYWOOD(1924); ROSE OF PARIS, THE(1924); ONE YEAR TO LIVE(1925); LOVE'S BLINDNESS(1926); BELOVED ROGUE, THE(1927); CAMILLE(1927); RAGTIME(1927); RED MARK, THE(1928); NAUGHTY BABY(1929)
Misc. Silents
IT HAPPENED IN PARIS(1919); SILK HOSIERY(1920); BE MY WIFE(1921); SILENT YEARS(1921); GOLDEN DREAMS(1922); DUCHESS OF BUFFALO, THE(1926); HIS TIGER LADY(1928)

Mario Dionisi
STRANGER RETURNS, THE(1968, U.S./Ital./Ger./Span.)

Sylvia Dionisio
YOUNG, THE EVIL AND THE SAVAGE, THE(1968, Ital.)

Paola Dionisotti
SAILOR'S RETURN, THE(1978, Brit.)

Margot Dionne
TICKET TO HEAVEN(1981)

Dionne Quintuplets
REUNION(1936); FIVE OF A KIND(1938)

The Dionne Quintuplets
COUNTRY DOCTOR, THE(1936)

Philippe Dionnet
YO YO(1967, Fr.)

Baye Macoumba Diop
BLACK AND WHITE IN COLOR(1976, Fr.)

Omar Diop
LA CHINOISE(1967, Fr.)

Christian Dior
MAN ABOUT TOWN(1947, Fr.), cos; NO HIGHWAY IN THE SKY(1951, Brit.), cos; STAGE FRIGHT(1950, Brit.), cos; INDISCRETION OF AN AMERICAN WIFE(1954, U.S./Ital.), cos; GENTLEMEN MARRY BRUNETTES(1955), cos; AMBASSADOR'S DAUGHTER, THE(1956), cos; LITTLE HUT, THE(1957), cos; LIBEL(1959, Brit.), cos; GRASS IS GREENER, THE(1960), cos; CHEATERS, THE(1961, Fr.), cos; GOODBYE AGAIN(1961), cos; LIGHT IN THE PIAZZA(1962), cos; NEW KIND OF LOVE, A(1963), cos; PARIS WHEN IT SIZZLES(1964), cos; WOMAN OF STRAW(1964, Brit.), cos; YESTERDAY, TODAY, AND TOMORROW(1964, Ital./Fr.), cos; DOUBLE MAN, THE(1967), cos; SECRET CEREMONY(1968, Brit.), cos; YOU ONLY LIVE ONCE(1969, Fr.), cos; LADY IN THE CAR WITH GLASSES AND A GUN, THE(1970, U.S./Fr.), cos

Kathy Dior
MONEY MOVERS(1978, Aus.)

Pierre Dios
LOVE ON THE RUN(1980, Fr.)

Enrique Diosdade
DOLORES(1949, Span.)

Enrique A. Diosdado
MAN WHO WAGGED HIS TAIL, THE(1961, Ital./Span.)

Yu. Dioshi
WAR AND PEACE(1968, USSR)

Daniel Diot
TIME OF THE WOLVES(1970, Fr.), ph

Francois Diot
RAPTURE(1965), ed

Francoise Diot
PRICE OF FLESH, THE(1962, Fr.), ed; VISIT, THE(1964, Ger./Fr./Ital./U.S.), ed; SERGEANT, THE(1968), ed

Moussa Diouf
MANDABI(1970, Fr./Senegal)

Mamadou Dioum
CEDDO(1978, Nigeria); COUP DE TORCHON(1981, Fr.)

Carlo DiPalma
TRAGEDY OF A RIDICULOUS MAN, THE(1982, Ital.), ph; BLACK STALLION RETURNS, THE(1983), ph

Dante Dipaolo
MEET ME AT THE FAIR(1952); SEVEN BRIDES FOR SEVEN BROTHERS(1954)

Richard DiPaolo
ROUSTABOUT(1964)

Dick Dipling
IT'S IN THE AIR(1935)

Joseph V. DiPrima
TIMERIDER(1983)

Luc-Antoine Diquero
LA BALANCE(1983, Fr.)

Etienne Dirand
DAY AND THE HOUR, THE(1963, Fr./ Ital.)

Doug Dirken
DIRTY LITTLE BILLY(1972)

Sen. Everett Dirksen
MONITORS, THE(1969)

Debbie Dirkson
KING OF THE MOUNTAIN(1981)

Doug Dirkson
GATOR BAIT(1974)

Douglas Dirkson
HOPSCOTCH(1980); HARRY'S WAR(1981); KING OF THE MOUNTAIN(1981)
1984
FOOTLOOSE(1984)
Misc. Talkies
BEYOND REASON(1977)

Zora Dirnbach
NINTH CIRCLE, THE(1961, Yugo.), w

Willy Dirtl
DIE FLEDERMAUS(1964, Aust.), ch; $100 A NIGHT(1968, Ger.), ch

Disa
Silents
NOTORIOUS MRS. CARRICK, THE(1924, Brit.)

Anthony DiSabantino
TRADING PLACES(1983)

John Disanti
HOT STUFF(1979); EYES OF A STRANGER(1980); ABSENCE OF MALICE(1981); HARDLY WORKING(1981); NOBODY'S PERFEKT zero(1981); STAR CHAMBER, THE(1983)
Misc. Talkies
KING FRAT(1979)

Giuseppe DiSantis
OUTCRY(1949, Ital.), w

Nick Discenza
GODFATHER, THE, PART II(1974); SORCERER(1977)

Discovery
WINNER'S CIRCLE, THE(1948)

Bob Dishy
TIGER MAKES OUT, THE(1967); BIG BUS, THE(1976); FIRST FAMILY(1980); LAST MARRIED COUPLE IN AMERICA, THE(1980); AUTHOR! AUTHOR!(1982)
Misc. Talkies
I WONDER WHO'S KILLING HER NOW(1975)

Robert Dishy
LOVERS AND OTHER STRANGERS(1970)

David Disick
OKAY BILL(1971), p

George Diskant
WOMAN'S SECRET, A(1949), ph; DAVY CROCKETT, INDIAN SCOUT(1950), ph; FACE TO FACE(1952), ph; BIGAMIST,THE(1953), ph

George B. Diskant
TRAVELING SALESWOMAN(1950), ph

George E. Diskant
DICK TRACY VS. CUEBALL(1946), ph; VACATION IN RENO(1946), ph; BANJO(1947), ph; DESPERATE(1947), ph; RIFFRAFF(1947), ph; FIGHTING FATHER DUNNE(1948), ph; GUNS OF HATE(1948), ph; MASKED RAIDERS(1949), ph; PORT OF NEW YORK(1949), ph; THEY LIVE BY NIGHT(1949), ph; BETWEEN MIDNIGHT AND DAWN(1950), ph; DAVID HARDING, COUNTERSPY(1950), ph; FORTUNES OF CAPTAIN BLOOD(1950), ph; LAW OF THE BADLANDS(1950), ph; ON DANGEROUS GROUND(1951), ph; RACKET, THE(1951), ph; SEALED CARGO(1951), ph; BEWARE, MY LOVELY(1952), ph; KANSAS CITY CONFIDENTIAL(1952), ph; NARROW MARGIN, THE(1952), ph; STORM OVER TIBET(1952), ph; BANDITS OF CORSICA,

THE(1953), ph
George S. Diskant
EVERY GIRL SHOULD BE MARRIED(1948), ph
Joe Diskay
ONCE UPON A HONEYMOON(1942)
Joseph Diskay
BLACK WATCH, THE(1929)
Jane Colette Disko
DEER HUNTER, THE(1978)
Alberta Dismon
INTRUDER IN THE DUST(1949)
Doris Miles Disney
STELLA(1950), d&w; FUGITIVE LADY(1951), w; STRAW MAN, THE(1953, Brit.), p,d&w
Walt Disney
HOLLYWOOD PARTY(1934); SNOW WHITE AND THE SEVEN DWARFS(1937), p; FANTASIA(1940), p; PINOCCHIO(1940), p; DUMBO(1941), p; RELUCTANT DRAGON, THE(1941), p; BAMBI(1942), p; SONG OF THE SOUTH(1946), p; FUN AND FANCY FREE(1947), p; MELODY TIME(1948), p; ADVENTURES OF ICHABOD AND MR. TOAD(1949), p; SO DEAR TO MY HEART(1949), p; CINDERELLA(1950), p; ALICE IN WONDERLAND(1951), p; PETER PAN(1953), p; 20,000 LEAGUES UNDER THE SEA(1954), p; LADY AND THE TRAMP(1955), p; JOHNNY TREMAIN(1957), p; OLD YELLER(1957), p; LIGHT IN THE FOREST, THE(1958), p; DARBY O'GILL AND THE LITTLE PEOPLE(1959), p; SHAGGY DOG, THE(1959), p; SLEEPING BEAUTY(1959), p; KIDNAPPED(1960), p; POLLYANNA(1960), p; SIGN OF ZORRO, THE(1960), p; TEN WHO DARED(1960), p; ABSENT-MINDED PROFESSOR, THE(1961), p; BABES IN TOYLAND(1961), p; GREYFRIARS BOBBY(1961, Brit.), p; NIKKI, WILD DOG OF THE NORTH(1961, U.S./Can.), p; ONE HUNDRED AND ONE DALMATIANS(1961), p; BIG RED(1962), p; BON VOYAGE(1962), p; IN SEARCH OF THE CASTAWAYS(1962, Brit.), p; INCREDIBLE JOURNEY, THE(1963), p; MIRACLE OF THE WHITE STALLIONS(1963), p; SUMMER MAGIC(1963), p; EMIL AND THE DETECTIVES(1964), p; MARY POPPINS(1964), p; THOSE CALLOWAYS(1964), p; TIGER WALKS, A(1964), p; MONKEY'S UNCLE, THE(1965), p; FIGHTING PRINCE OF DONEGAL, THE(1966, Brit.), p; FOLLOW ME, BOYS!(1966), p; UGLY DACHSHUND, THE(1966), p; ADVENTURES OF BULLWHIP GRIFFIN, THE(1967), p; CHARLIE, THE LONESOME COUGAR(1967), p; GNOME-MOBILE, THE(1967), p; HAPPIEST MILLIONAIRE, THE(1967), p; JUNGLE BOOK, THE(1967), p; MONKEYS, GO HOME!(1967), p; DR. SYN, ALIAS THE SCARECROW(1975), p
Will Disney
THE CRAZIES(1973)
Rosana DiSota
CANNERY ROW(1982)
Disraeli the English Bulldog
SPY WITH A COLD NOSE, THE(1966, Brit.)
Eileen Diss
DOLL'S HOUSE, A(1973, Brit.), art d; SWEET WILLIAM(1980, Brit.), prod d; BETRAYAL(1983, Brit.), prod d; SIGN OF FOUR, THE(1983, Brit.), art d
1984
SECRET PLACES(1984, Brit.), prod d
Michel Dissart
SMALL CHANGE(1976, Fr.)
Werner Dissel
NAKED AMONG THE WOLVES(1967, Ger.)
Dan Dist
HEIST, THE(1979, Ital.), ph
Dominic "Pee Wee" Distarce
TO PLEASE A LADY(1950)
Ronald Distefano
1984
BIRDY(1984)
Tony DiStefano
Misc. Talkies
ONE CHANCE TO WIN(1976)
Sacha Distel
SEVEN CAPITAL SINS(1962, Fr./Ital.), m; LA BONNE SOUPE(1964, Fr./Ital.); CROOK, THE(1971, Fr.); WITHOUT APPARENT MOTIVE(1972, Fr.)
Jean Distinghin
PLAYMATES(1969, Fr./Ital.)
Louis Diswarte
YOUNG MR. PITT, THE(1942, Brit.)
Ann Ditchburn
SIX WEEKS(1982), a, ch
Anne Ditchburn
SLOW DANCING IN THE BIG CITY(1978), a, ch; CURTAINS(1983, Can.)
Zdenek Dite
DIVINE EMMA, THE(1983, Czech,)
Larry Ditillio
LAST PORNO FLICK, THE(1974), w
George Dititta, Jr.
AMITYVILLE II: THE POSSESSION(1982), set d
S. Ditlovich
DIARY OF A NAZI(1943, USSR)
Stanislav Ditrich
FIREMAN'S BALL, THE(1968, Czech.)
Leo Ditrichstein
ARE YOU A MASON?(1934, Brit.), w
Silents
HOW MOLLY MADE GOOD(1915)
Harry Ditson
NASTY HABITS(1976, Brit.); YANKS(1979); IMPROPER CHANNELS(1981, Can.); RAGTIME(1981); REDS(1981); SENDER, THE(1982, Brit.)
1984
TOP SECRET!(1984)
Josephine Ditt
Silents
DAMAGED GOODS(1915)
Harry Dittmar
Silents
RAINBOW(1921), w; SINGLE TRACK, THE(1921), w; ANGEL OF CROOKED STREET, THE(1922), w; STORMY WATERS(1928), w

Hans Dittmer
VIBRATION(1969, Swed.), ph
Ray Dittrich
SORCERER(1977); KING OF COMEDY, THE(1983)
1984
ONCE UPON A TIME IN AMERICA(1984)
Scott Dittrich
FREEWHEELIN'(1976), p&d
Ivan Diubeznov
COUNTRY BRIDE(1938, USSR)
David Divad
Silents
LITTLE WILDCAT(1922), d
Misc. Silents
GIRL'S DESIRE, A(1922), d
Sonja Divak
FRAGRANCE OF WILD FLOWERS, THE(1979, Yugo.)
Tom Diventi
POLYESTER(1981)
Alison Diver
MEATBALLS(1979, Can.)
Roy Dividson
ROUGHLY SPEAKING(1945), spec eff
Vaclav Divina
STRANGE FASCINATION(1952), m; ONE GIRL'S CONFESSION(1953), m; BAIT(1954), m
Divine
MONDO TRASHO(1970); POLYESTER(1981)
David Divine
BOY ON A DOLPHIN(1957), w; DUNKIRK(1958, Brit.), w
Julian Divivier
PANIQUE(1947, Fr.), d
Jesse Divorsky
WINE, WOMEN, AND SONG(1934)
Bob Divorsney
WORLD'S GREATEST SINNER, THE(1962)
Belynda Dix
9/30/55(1977)
Beulah Marie Dix
GIRL OF THE PORT(1930), w; MIDNIGHT MYSTERY(1930), w; THREE WHO LOVED(1931), w; EVER IN MY HEART(1933), w; LIFE OF JIMMY DOLAN, THE(1933), w; COLLEGE SCANDAL(1935), w; THEY MADE ME A CRIMINAL(1939), w; SWEATER GIRL(1942), w
Silents
NAN OF MUSIC MOUNTAIN(1917), w; ON RECORD(1917), w; AFFAIRS OF ANATOL, THE(1921), w; EASY ROAD, THE(1921), w; CRIMSON CHALLENGE, THE(1922), w; NOBODY'S MONEY(1923), w; LEOPARD LADY, THE(1928), w; GIRLS GONE WILD(1929), w; NED MCCOBB'S DAUGHTER(1929), w
Bill Dix
WILD DAKOTAS, THE(1956)
Billie Dix
HAPPY DAYS ARE HERE AGAIN(1936, Brit.)
Billy Dix
SONG OF THE SIERRAS(1946); WEST OF THE ALAMO(1946); RAIDERS OF THE SOUTH(1947); RAINBOW OVER THE ROCKIES(1947); FRONTIER REVENGE(1948); SIX-GUN LAW(1948); KID FROM GOWER GULCH, THE(1949); SCENE OF THE CRIME(1949); SILVER BANDIT, THE(1950); CALLAWAY WENT THATAWAY(1951); LION AND THE HORSE, THE(1952); ROSE MARIE(1954); TRIBUTE TO A BADMAN(1956); LONELY MAN, THE(1957); SHE DEMONS(1958)
Bob Dix
DIANE(1955); I'LL CRY TOMORROW(1955); KING'S THIEF, THE(1955); FORBIDDEN PLANET(1956); SCREAMING EAGLES(1956)
Buelah Marie Dix
Silents
ORDEAL, THE(1922), w
Dan Dix
VIVA VILLA!(1934); OX-BOW INCIDENT, THE(1943)
Dorothy Dix
FIRST MRS. FRASER, THE(1932, Brit.); DRUM TAPS(1933); WHEELS OF DESTINY(1934); DANTE'S INFERNO(1935); MUSIC IS MAGIC(1935); GUNS AND GUITARS(1936); SUNSET OF POWER(1936)
Misc. Talkies
NEVADA BUCKAROO, THE(1931)
Edward Marion Dix
PAST OF MARY HOLMES, THE(1933), w
Franklin Dix
FALL GUY(1947)
Holmes Dix
LIGHTNING STRIKES TWICE(1935), w
Kenny Dix
WHIRLWIND HORSEMAN(1938)
Marian Dix
BEFORE DAWN(1933), w; EVERYTHING IS THUNDER(1936, Brit.), w; FORBIDDEN MUSIC(1936, Brit.), w
Marion Dix
MEN ARE LIKE THAT(1930), w; SAFETY IN NUMBERS(1930), w; SEA LEGS(1930), w; TWO AGAINST THE WORLD(1932), w; WORST WOMAN IN PARIS(1933), w; DOWN TO THEIR LAST YACHT(1934), w; SING AND LIKE IT(1934), w; THEIR BIG MOMENT(1934), w; LIGHTNING STRIKES TWICE(1935), w; IT'S LOVE AGAIN(1936, Brit.), w; CLIMBING HIGH(1938, Brit.), w
Mary Lou Dix
KID MILLIONS(1934); CEILNG ZERO(1935); MR. DEEDS GOES TO TOWN(1936); LOST HORIZON(1937)
Peter Dix
CAPTAIN LIGHTFOOT(1955)
Richard Dix
LOVE DOCTOR, THE(1929); NOTHING BUT THE TRUTH(1929); WHEEL OF LIFE, THE(1929); LOVIN' THE LADIES(1930); SEVEN KEYS TO BALDPATE(1930); SHOOTING STRAIGHT(1930); CIMARRON(1931); PUBLIC DEFENDER, THE(1931); SECRET SERVICE(1931); YOUNG DONOVAN'S KID(1931); CONQUERORS, THE(1932);

HELL'S HIGHWAY(1932); LOST SQUADRON, THE(1932); ROAR OF THE DRAGON(1932); ACE OF ACES(1933); DAY OF RECKONING(1933); GREAT JASPER, THE(1933); NO MARRIAGE TIES(1933); HIS GREATEST GAMBLE(1934); STINGAREE(1934); ARIZONIAN, THE(1935); TRANSATLANTIC TUNNEL(1935, Brit.); WEST OF THE PECOS(1935); DEVIL'S SQUADRON(1936); SPECIAL INVESTIGATOR(1936); YELLOW DUST(1936); DEVIL IS DRIVING, THE(1937); DEVIL'S PLAYGROUND(1937); IT HAPPENED IN HOLLYWOOD(1937); BLIND ALIBI(1938); SKY GIANT(1938); HERE I AM A STRANGER(1939); MAN OF CONQUEST(1939); RENO(1939); TWELVE CROWDED HOURS(1939); CHEROKEE STRIP(1940); MARINES FLY HIGH, THE(1940); MEN AGAINST THE SKY(1940); BADLANDS OF DAKOTA(1941); ROUNDUP, THE(1941); AMERICAN EMPIRE(1942); TOMBSTONE, THE TOWN TOO TOUGH TO DIE(1942); BUCKSKIN FRONTIER(1943); EYES OF THE UNDERWORLD(1943); GHOST SHIP, THE(1943); KANSAN, THE(1943); TOP MAN(1943); MARK OF THE WHISTLER, THE(1944); WHISTLER, THE(1944); POWER OF THE WHISTLER, THE(1945); VOICE OF THE WHISTLER(1945); MYSTERIOUS INTRUDER(1946); SECRET OF THE WHISTLER(1946); 13TH HOUR, THE(1947); BLACK MARBLE, THE(1980)
Silents
ONE OF MANY(1917); ALL'S FAIR IN LOVE(1921); NOT GUILTY(1921); POVERTY OF RICHES, THE(1921); WALL FLOWER, THE(1922); RACING HEARTS(1923); SOULS FOR SALE(1923); TEN COMMANDMENTS, THE(1923); TO THE LAST MAN(1923); ICEBOUND(1924); MANHATTAN(1924); SINNERS IN HEAVEN(1924); STRANGER, THE(1924); WOMANHANDLED(1925); LET'S GET MARRIED(1926); QUARTERBACK, THE(1926); KNOCKOUT REILLY(1927); EASY COME, EASY GO(1928); SPORTING GOODS(1928); WARMING UP(1928)
Misc. Silents
DANGEROUS CURVE AHEAD(1921); BONDED WOMAN, THE(1922); FOOLS FIRST(1922); GLORIOUS FOOL, THE(1922); SIN FLOOD, THE(1922); YELLOW MEN AND GOLD(1922); CALL OF THE CANYON, THE(1923); CHRISTIAN, THE(1923); QUICKSANDS(1923); WOMAN WITH FOUR FACES, THE(1923); UNGUARDED WOMEN(1924); LUCKY DEVIL(1925); MAN MUST LIVE, THE(1925); MEN AND WOMEN(1925); SHOCK PUNCH, THE(1925); TOO MANY KISSES(1925); VANISHING AMERICAN, THE(1925); SAY IT AGAIN(1926); GAY DEFENDER, THE(1927); MAN POWER(1927); PARADISE FOR TWO(1927); SHANGHAI BOUND(1927); MORAN OF THE MARINES(1928); REDSKIN(1929)

Robert Dix
SCARLET COAT, THE(1955); FORTY GUNS(1957); FRANKENSTEIN'S DAUGHTER(1958); THUNDERING JETS(1958); LONE TEXAN(1959); THIRTEEN FIGHTING MEN(1960); YOUNG JESSE JAMES(1960); LITTLE SHEPHERD OF KINGDOM COME(1961); AIR PATROL(1962); DEADWOOD'76(1965); BLOOD OF DRACULA'S CASTLE(1967); ROAD HUSTLERS, THE(1968); CAIN'S WAY(1969); GUN RIDERS, THE(1969), a, w; SATAN'S SADISTS(1969); WILD WHEELS(1969); HELL'S BLOODY DEVILS(1970); HORROR OF THE BLOOD MONSTERS zero(1970, U.S./Phil.); REBEL ROUSERS(1970); RED, WHITE AND BLACK, THE(1970)

Rollo Dix
RENDEZVOUS(1935); BULLDOG DRUMMOND IN AFRICA(1938)

Rolls Dix
Misc. Talkies
HAWK, THE(1935)

Tom Dix
UNDER A TEXAS MOON(1930)

Tommy Dix
BEST FOOT FORWARD(1943); ANDY HARDY'S BLONDE TROUBLE(1944)

William Dix
NANNY, THE(1965, Brit.); DOCTOR DOLITTLE(1967)

Henry E. Dixey
Misc. Silents
FATHER AND SON(1916)

Phyllis Dixey
LOVE UP THE POLE(1936, Brit.); DUAL ALIBI(1947, Brit.)

Dixie Jubilee Singers
HALLELUJAH(1929)

Adela Dixon
BANANA RIDGE(1941, Brit.)

Adele Dixon
UNEASY VIRTUE(1931, Brit.); CALLING THE TUNE(1936, Brit.); WOMAN TO WOMAN(1946, Brit.)

Aileen Dixon
MISSISSIPPI RHYTHM(1949)

Billie Dixon
LIONS LOVE(1969); LADY IN THE CAR WITH GLASSES AND A GUN, THE(1970, U.S./Fr.)

Campbell Dixon
SECRET AGENT, THE(1936, Brit.), w

Carol Dixon
MAN FROM THE DINERS' CLUB, THE(1963)

Charles Dixon
Silents
ARE YOU A MASON?(1915)

Conway Dixon
TRIUMPH OF SHERLOCK HOLMES, THE(1935, Brit.); WANDERING JEW, THE(1935, Brit.); MUTINY OF THE ELSINORE, THE(1939, Brit.)

David Dixon
YOUNG GRADUATES, THE(1971), w; MISSIONARY, THE(1982)

Debbie Dixon
RETURN OF THE JEDI(1983)

Deborah E. Dixon
1984
PHILADELPHIA EXPERIMENT, THE(1984)

Denver Dixon [Victor Adamson, George Kesterson, Art Mix]
FIGHTING COWBOY(1933), d; FIGHTING RANGER, THE(1934); LIGHTNING RANGE(1934); ARIZONA TRAILS(1935); DESERT MESA(1935); GHOST RIDER, THE(1935); GUNS AND GUITARS(1936); WAY OUT WEST(1937); DANGER VALLEY(1938); HEROES OF THE ALAMO(1938); STARLIGHT OVER TEXAS(1938); WHERE THE BUFFALO ROAM(1938); FEUD OF THE RANGE(1939); TONTO BASIN OUTLAWS(1941); PARDON MY GUN(1942); LONE STAR TRAIL, THE(1943); SAN ANTONIO(1945); UNCONQUERED(1947); RIDERS IN THE SKY(1949); ROARING WESTWARD(1949); STORY OF WILL ROGERS, THE(1952); GUN RIDERS, THE(1969)

Misc. Silents
LONE RIDER, THE(1922), a, d; ACE OF CACTUS RANGE(1924), d

Dick Dixon
RED, WHITE AND BLACK, THE(1970), ed

Donna Dixon
DOCTOR DETROIT(1983); TWILIGHT ZONE–THE MOVIE(1983)

Dori Dixon
MELINDA(1972)

Dwight Dixon
1984
PERFECT STRANGERS(1984), m

Eileen Dixon
SON OF BILLY THE KID(1949)

Ernest Dixon
SIX PACK(1982)

Florence Dixon
Silents
NEVER SAY QUIT(1919); ANNA ASCENDS(1922); BACK HOME AND BROKE(1922); IT IS THE LAW(1924)
Misc. Silents
TOO FAT TO FIGHT(1918); CAPTAIN SWIFT(1920); SILENT BARRIER, THE(1920); WOMEN MEN MARRY(1922)

Floyd Dixon
INVASION OF THE SAUCER MEN(1957)

Floyd Hugh Dixon
COURT JESTER, THE(1956)

G.C. Dixon
ISLE OF ESCAPE(1930), w

Gale Dixon
TREE, THE(1969)

George Dixon
LAW AND ORDER(1932); CLAY(1964 Aus.)

Glenn Dixon
DALTON GIRLS, THE(1957); JUNGLE HEAT(1957); UNTAMED YOUTH(1957); VOODOO ISLAND(1957); BAREFOOT EXECUTIVE, THE(1971)

Gordon C. Dixon
NIGHT OF THE ZOMBIES(1981)

Guy Dixon
SHIPMATES O' MINE(1936, Brit.)

Harland Dixon
SOMETHING TO SING ABOUT(1937), a, ch

Helen Dixon
JUVENILE COURT(1938)

Henry Dixon
PENNY SERENADE(1941)

Henry P. Dixon
Silents
MAN WHO MADE GOOD, THE(1917)

Humphrey Dixon
ROSELAND(1977), ed; EUROPEANS, THE(1979, Brit.), ed; HULLABALOO OVER GEORGIE AND BONNIE'S PICTURES(1979, Brit.), ed; QUARTET(1981, Brit./Fr.), ed; HEAT AND DUST(1983, Brit.), ed

Ivan Dixon
SOMETHING OF VALUE(1957); PORGY AND BESS(1959); BATTLE AT BLOODY BEACH(1961); RAISIN IN THE SUN, A(1961); NOTHING BUT A MAN(1964); PATCH OF BLUE, A(1965); TO TRAP A SPY(1966); WHERE'S JACK?(1969, Brit.); SUPPOSE THEY GAVE A WAR AND NOBODY CAME?(1970); CLAY PIGEON(1971); TROUBLE MAN(1972), d; SPOOK WHO SAT BY THE DOOR, THE(1973), p, d; CARWASH(1976)

Jack Dixon
FAR COUNTRY, THE(1955)

James Dixon
BLACK CAESAR(1973); YOUR THREE MINUTES ARE UP(1973), a, w; IT'S ALIVE(1974); GOD TOLD ME TO(1976); IT LIVES AGAIN(1978); Q(1982)

Jean Dixon
LADY LIES, THE(1929); KISS BEFORE THE MIRROR, THE(1933); SADIE MCKEE(1934); I'LL LOVE YOU ALWAYS(1935); MR. DYNAMITE(1935); SHE MARRIED HER BOSS(1935); MAGNIFICENT BRUTE, THE(1936); MY MAN GODFREY(1936); TO MARY–WITH LOVE(1936); SWING HIGH, SWING LOW(1937); YOU ONLY LIVE ONCE(1937); HOLIDAY(1938); JOY OF LIVING(1938)

Jennifer Dixon
1984
MIKE'S MURDER(1984)

Jill Dixon
HIGH TIDE AT NOON(1957, Brit.); JUST MY LUCK(1957, Brit.); UP IN THE WORLD(1957, Brit.); NIGHT TO REMEMBER, A(1958, Brit.); WITCHCRAFT(1964, Brit.)

Jim Dixon
ICE STATION ZEBRA(1968)

Joan Dixon
BUNCO SQUAD(1950); EXPERIMENT ALCATRAZ(1950); LAW OF THE BADLANDS(1950); GUNPLAY(1951); HOT LEAD(1951); PISTOL HARVEST(1951); ROADBLOCK(1951); DESERT PASSAGE(1952)

John Dixon
MAN FROM SNOWY RIVER, THE(1983, Aus.), w

Larry Dixon
DANNY BOY(1946)

Lee Dixon
GOLD DIGGERS OF 1937(1936); READY, WILLING AND ABLE(1937); SINGING MARINE, THE(1937); VARSITY SHOW(1937); ANGEL AND THE BADMAN(1947)

Leonard Dixon
RUNAWAY, THE(1964, Brit.); SEABO(1978)

Mac Intyre Dixon
ALICE'S RESTAURANT(1969)

MacIntyre Dixon
THIEVES(1977)

MacIntyre Dixon
FIRE SALE(1977); KING OF THE GYPSIES(1978); STARTING OVER(1979); POPEYE(1980); PATERNITY(1981); REDS(1981)

Malcolm Dixon
FLASH GORDON(1980); TIME BANDITS(1981, Brit.)
Malcom Dixon
RETURN OF THE JEDI(1983)
Marion Dixon
LADIES OF THE JURY(1932), w
McIntyre Dixon
FRONT, THE(1976)
Mel Dixon
CHICAGO 70(1970)
Mort Dixon
HOUSEWIFE(1934), m
Ole Dixon
OPERATION CAMEL(1961, Den.)
Pat Dixon
NIGHT COMES TOO SOON(1948, Brit.), w
Paul Dixon
DISC JOCKEY(1951)
Peggy Dixon
DRAGONSLAYER(1981), ch
Peter Dixon
DOWN THE WYOMING TRAIL(1939), w; HIGH FLIGHT(1957, Brit.); ATTENTION, THE KIDS ARE WATCHING(1978, Fr.), w
R. G. Dixon
Silents
ABRAHAM LINCOLN(1924)
Ralph Dixon
AIR CIRCUS, THE(1928), ed; WORDS AND MUSIC(1929), ed, ed; HOLY TERROR, A(1931), ed; MR. LEMON OF ORANGE(1931), ed; YOUNG SINNERS(1931), ed; DOCKS OF SAN FRANCISCO(1932), ed; SHE WANTED A MILLIONAIRE(1932), ed; DANCING FEET(1936), ed; DANIEL BOONE(1936), ed; HEARTS IN BONDAGE(1936), ed; HOUSE OF A THOUSAND CANDLES, THE(1936), ed; GREAT COMMANDMENT, THE(1941), ed; HELLO SUCKER(1941), ed; HILLBILLY BLITZKRIEG(1942), ed; MAD DOCTOR OF MARKET STREET, THE(1942), ed; HOOSIER HOLIDAY(1943), ed; MAN FROM THE RIO GRANDE, THE(1943), ed; WHISPERING FOOTSTEPS(1943), ed; GOODNIGHT SWEETHEART(1944), ed; LIGHTS OF OLD SANTA FE(1944), ed; MY BEST GAL(1944), ed; ROSIE THE RIVETER(1944), ed; SAN FERNANDO VALLEY(1944), ed; SILENT PARTNER(1944), ed; SING, NEIGHBOR, SING(1944), ed; CHICAGO KID, THE(1945), ed; FATAL WITNESS, THE(1945), ed; SANTA FE SADDLEMATES(1945), ed; SPORTING CHANCE, A(1945), ed; THOROUGHBREDS(1945), ed; TRAIL OF KIT CARSON(1945), ed; BRINGING UP FATHER(1946), ed; SHADOWS OVER CHINATOWN(1946), ed; SHERIFF OF REDWOOD VALLEY(1946), ed; SONG OF THE SIERRAS(1946), ed; RAINBOW OVER THE ROCKIES(1947), ed
Silents
GIRL IN EVERY PORT, A(1928), ed; HOMESICK(1928), ed; WOMAN WISE(1928), ed
Ralph H. Dixon
Silents
SOUL OF THE BEAST(1923), w
Reg Dixon
LOVE IN PAWN(1953, Brit.); NO SMOKING(1955, Brit.)
Richard Dixon
Misc. Talkies
FAKING OF THE PRESIDENT, THE(1976)
Richard M. Dixon
RICHARD(1972); TOP OF THE HEAP(1972); WHERE THE BUFFALO ROAM(1980)
Steve Dixon
PRIVATES ON PARADE(1982)
Thomas Dixon
NATION AFLAME(1937), w
Misc. Silents
MARK OF THE BEAST(1923), d
Thomas Dixon, Jr.
Silents
BIRTH OF A NATION, THE(1915), w; BRING HIM IN(1921), w; WHERE MEN ARE MEN(1921), w; WING TOY(1921), w; THELMA(1922), w; CHAMPION OF LOST CAUSES(1925), w
Tommy Dixon
ANGELS OVER BROADWAY(1940); BLONDIE PLAYS CUPID(1940); BLONDIE IN SOCIETY(1941)
Vernon Dixon
IRON PETTICOAT, THE(1956, Brit.), set d; GYPSY AND THE GENTLEMAN, THE(1958, Brit.), set d; CARRY ON CONSTABLE(1960, Brit.), set d; GRASS IS GREENER, THE(1960), set d; KIDNAPPED(1960), set d; GREYFRIARS BOBBY(1961, Brit.), set d; NAKED EDGE, THE(1961), set d; IN SEARCH OF THE CASTAWAYS(1962, Brit.), set d; THREE LIVES OF THOMASINA, THE(1963, U.S./Brit.), set d; FUNERAL IN BERLIN(1966, Brit.), set d; LOST COMMAND, THE(1966), set d; COUNTESS FROM HONG KONG, A(1967, Brit.), set d; OLIVER!(1968, Brit.), set d; NICHOLAS AND ALEXANDRA(1971, Brit.), set d; ADVENTURERS, THE(1970), set d; LADY CAROLINE LAMB(1972, Brit./Ital.), set d; NELSON AFFAIR, THE(1973, Brit.), set d; BARRY LYNDON(1975, Brit.), set d; DEEP, THE(1977), set d; GREEK TYCOON, THE(1978), set d; FOR YOUR EYES ONLY(1981), set d
Bunch Dixon-Spain
HANGMAN WAITS, THE(1947, Brit.), ed
Bill Dixson
SYNDICATE, THE(1968, Brit.)
Eleanor Dixson
WORLD IS JUST A 'B' MOVIE, THE(1971)
Jesse Dizon
MAC ARTHUR(1977)
Misc. Talkies
PRISONERS(1975)
Devi Dja
THREE CAME HOME(1950)
Mostepha Djadjam
1984
THREE CROWNS OF THE SAILOR(1984, Fr.)

Mikhail Djagafarov
ROAD TO LIFE(1932, USSR)
Sandro Djaliashvili
Misc. Silents
SABA(1929, USSR)
Gitti Djamal
DESPAIR(1978, Ger.)
Gitty Djamal
THREE MUSKETEERS, THE(1974, Panama)
Andre Djaoui
LADY CHATTERLEY'S LOVER(1981, Fr./Brit.), p
Djauan
JEDDA, THE UNCIVILIZED(1956, Aus.)
Yannis Djiotis
LOVE CYCLES(1969, Gr.), w
Jabo Djohansjan
YEAR OF LIVING DANGEROUSLY, THE(1982, Aus.)
Badja Djola
PENITENTIARY(1979); NIGHT SHIFT(1982)
Badja Medu Djola
MAIN EVENT, THE(1979)
Milivoje Djordjevic
I EVEN MET HAPPY GYPSIES(1968, Yugo.)
Bengt Djurberg
Misc. Silents
CHARLES XII, PARTS 1 & 2(1927, Swed.)
Milan Djurdjevic
STEPPE, THE(1963, Fr./Ital.)
Dusan Djuric
FRAULEIN DOKTOR(1969, Ital./Yugo.)
Rada Djuricin
TWELVE CHAIRS, THE(1970)
Rada Djuriein
OPERATION CROSS EAGLES(1969, U.S./Yugo.)
George Djurkovic
PIED PIPER, THE(1972, Brit.), art d; GREAT MCGONAGALL, THE(1975, Brit.), prod d
George Djurovic
MAGIC CHRISTIAN, THE(1970, Brit.), art d
Maroussia Dmitravitch
QUEEN OF SPADES(1948, Brit.)
A. Dmitriev
Misc. Silents
RIVALS(1933, USSR), d
I. Dmitriev
HAMLET(1966, USSR)
Igor Dmitriev
AND QUIET FLOWS THE DON(1960 USSR)
Yu. Dmitriyev
LAST GAME, THE(1964, USSR)
Mariusz Dmochowski
EROICA(1966, Pol.); GOLEM(1980, Pol.); WAR OF THE WORLDS–NEXT CENTURY, THE(1981, Pol.)
Anna Dmokhovskava
Misc. Silents
CHILDREN – FLOWERS OF LIFE(1919, USSR)
Anna Dmokhovskaya
Misc. Silents
CIGARETTE GIRL FROM MOSSELPROM(1924, USSR)
Edward Dmtryk
LOVE AFFAIR(1939), ed
Henri Alain Dmurtal
WANDERER, THE(1969, Fr.)
Edward Dmytryk
ONLY SAPS WORK(1930), ed; ROYAL FAMILY OF BROADWAY, THE(1930), ed; RUGGLES OF RED GAP(1935), ed; EASY TO TAKE(1936), ed; THREE CHEERS FOR LOVE(1936), ed; TOO MANY PARENTS(1936), ed; DOUBLE OR NOTHING(1937), ed; HOLD'EM NAVY!(1937), ed; MURDER GOES TO COLLEGE(1937), ed; TURN OFF THE MOON(1937), ed; BULLDOG DRUMMOND'S PERIL(1938), ed; PRISON FARM(1938), ed; MILLION DOLLAR LEGS(1939), d; SOME LIKE IT HOT(1939), ed; TELEVISION SPY(1939), d; ZAZA(1939), ed; EMERGENCY SQUAD(1940), d; GOLDEN GLOVES(1940), d; HER FIRST ROMANCE(1940), d; MYSTERY SEA RAIDER(1940), d; BLONDE FROM SINGAPORE, THE(1941), d; CONFESSIONS OF BOSTON BLACKIE(1941), d; DEVIL COMMANDS, THE(1941), d; SECRETS OF THE LONE WOLF(1941), d; SWEETHEART OF THE CAMPUS(1941), d; UNDER AGE(1941), d; COUNTER-ESPIONAGE(1942), d; HITLER'S CHILDREN(1942), d; SEVEN MILES FROM ALCATRAZ(1942), d; BEHIND THE RISING SUN(1943), d; CAPTIVE WILD WOMAN(1943), d; FALCON STRIKES BACK, THE(1943), d; TENDER COMRADE(1943), d; BACK TO BATAAN(1945), d; CORNERED(1945), d; MURDER, MY SWEET(1945), d; TILL THE END OF TIME(1946), d; CROSSFIRE(1947), d; SO WELL REMEMBERED(1947, Brit.), d; HIDDEN ROOM, THE(1949, Brit.), d; SALT TO THE DEVIL(1949, Brit.), p, d; EIGHT IRON MEN(1952), d; MUTINY(1952), d; SNIPER, THE(1952), d; JUGGLER, THE(1953), d; BROKEN LANCE(1954), d; CAINE MUTINY, THE(1954), d; END OF THE AFFAIR, THE(1955, Brit.), d; LEFT HAND OF GOD, THE(1955), d; SOLDIER OF FORTUNE(1955), d; MOUNTAIN, THE(1956), p&d; RAINTREE COUNTY(1957), d; YOUNG LIONS, THE(1958), d; BLUE ANGEL, THE(1959), d; WARLOCK(1959), p&d; RELUCTANT SAINT, THE(1962, U.S./Ital.), p&d; WALK ON THE WILD SIDE(1962), d; CARPETBAGGERS, THE(1964), d; WHERE LOVE HAS GONE(1964), d; MIRAGE(1965), d; ALVAREZ KELLY(1966), d; ANZIO(1968, Ital.), d; SHALAKO(1968, Brit.), d; BLUEBEARD(1972), d, w; HUMAN FACTOR, THE(1975), d
Misc. Talkies
HAWK, THE(1935), d; TRAIL OF THE HAWK(1935), d; HE IS MY BROTHER(1976), d
Madeleine Dmytryk
MASTER RACE, THE(1944), d
Michael Dmytryk
Misc. Talkies
KINGS OF THE HILL(1976), d

Sabu do Brasil
THAT MAN FROM RIO(1964, Fr./Ital.)
Jorge Brum do Canto
COUNTRY DOCTOR, THE(1963, Portuguese), d, w
Eduardo do Gregorio
CELINE AND JULIE GO BOATING(1974, Fr.), w
Francesci do Masi
COUNTERFEIT COMMANDOS(1981, Ital.), m
Mauricio do Vale
1984
GABRIELA(1984, Braz.)
Mauricio do Valle
ANTONIO DAS MORTES(1970, Braz.); EARTH ENTRANCED(1970, Braz.)
"Mr. and Mrs. Doaks"
MARKED WOMAN(1937), m/l
Frank Doak
NIGHT OF THE LIVING DEAD(1968)
Conrad Doan
1984
COUNTRY(1984)
Doane
CAVALIER, THE(1928), ed
Frank Doane
Silents
TRUTH, THE(1920)
Samantha Doane
GAUNTLET, THE(1977)
Anne Doat
SEVENTH JUROR, THE(1964, Fr.); SWEET AND SOUR(1964, Fr./Ital.); WOMEN AND WAR(1965, Fr.)
Wayne Doba
FUNHOUSE, THE(1981); SCARFACE(1983)
Peter Dobai
MEPHISTO(1981, Ger.), w
Joel Dobart
1984
CHEECH AND CHONG'S THE CORSICAN BROTHERS(1984)
Henri Dobb
Silents
ITALIAN STRAW HAT, AN(1927, Fr.), ed
Diana Dobbelman
1984
QUESTION OF SILENCE(1984, Neth.)
Anneliese Dobbertin
1984
LOOSE CONNECTIONS(1984, Brit.)
John Dobbie
GONE TO THE DOGS(1939, Aus.)
Claire Dobbin
DIMBOOLA(1979, Aus.)
Barbara Dobbins
FRENCH LINE, THE(1954)
Ben Dobbins
LIFE AND TIMES OF JUDGE ROY BEAN, THE(1972); WHITE BUFFALO, THE(1977), stunts
Bennie Dobbins
RIDE LONESOME(1959); BARQUERO(1970); SOMETIMES A GREAT NOTION(1971); WILD ROVERS(1971); 99 AND 44/100% DEAD(1974); DUCHESS AND THE DIRTWATER FOX, THE(1976); MOUNTAIN MEN, THE(1980); LEGEND OF THE LONE RANGER, THE(1981); 48 HOURS(1982)
Bennie E. Dobbins
DIRTY HARRY(1971)
Earl Dobbins
LONE TEXAS RANGER(1945)
Charlie Dobbs
SUGARLAND EXPRESS, THE(1974)
Frank Q. Dobbs
Misc. Talkies
DISCIPLES OF DEATH(1975), d; HOTWIRE(1980), d
Fred C. Dobbs
GREAT SIOUX MASSACRE, THE(1965), w
George Dobbs
FOOTLIGHT SERENADE(1942); LADY HAS PLANS, THE(1942); MAN WITH TWO LIVES, THE(1942); GANG'S ALL HERE, THE(1943); COVER GIRL(1944); SONG OF THE OPEN ROAD(1944), ch
Heidi Dobbs
ADIOS AMIGO(1975)
Misc. Talkies
DEATH JOURNEY(1976)
James Dobbs
MAN I LOVE, THE(1946); NIGHT AND DAY(1946); IMPULSE(1975)
Johnny Dobbs
ROCK BABY, ROCK IT(1957)
Quail Dobbs
J.W. COOP(1971)
Randolph Dobbs
YOUNG FRANKENSTEIN(1974); WORLD'S GREATEST LOVER, THE(1977)
H. Dobelaere
PINOCCHIO IN OUTER SPACE(1965, U.S./Bel.), m
Alan Doberman
1984
NEW YORK NIGHTS(1984), ph
Josef Dobes
ECSTACY OF YOUNG LOVE(1936, Czech.), m
Alan Dobie
SEVEN KEYS(1962, Brit.); COMEDY MAN, THE(1964); CHARGE OF THE LIGHT BRIGADE, THE(1968, Brit.); LONG DAY'S DYING, THE(1968, Brit.); ALFRED THE GREAT(1969, Brit.); CHAIRMAN, THE(1969); DR. SYN, ALIAS THE SCARECROW(1975)

Laurence Dobie
YOUNG AND WILLING(1964, Brit.), w
Pat Dobie
GREASER'S PALACE(1972), makeup
L. Dobkevich
GORDEYEV FAMILY, THE(1961, U.S.S.R.)
Larry Dobkin
NOT WANTED(1949); WHIRLPOOL(1949); FRENCHIE(1950); NEVER FEAR(1950); CHAIN OF CIRCUMSTANCE(1951); MOB, THE(1951); PEOPLE WILL TALK(1951); DEADLINE-U.S.A.(1952); FIVE FINGERS(1952); LOAN SHARK(1952); RED SKIES OF MONTANA(1952); WASHINGTON STORY(1952); ABOVE AND BEYOND(1953); HINDU, THE(1953, Brit.); MA AND PA KETTLE ON VACATION(1953); SILVER CHALICE, THE(1954); PORTLAND EXPOSE(1957); RAIDERS OF OLD CALIFORNIA(1957); GERONIMO(1962); LIKE A CROW ON A JUNE BUG(1972), d
Lawrence Dobkin
TWELVE O'CLOCK HIGH(1949); ON THE LOOSE(1951); JULIUS CAESAR(1953); REMAINS TO BE SEEN(1953); RIDERS TO THE STARS(1954); THEM!(1954); ILLEGAL(1955); JUMP INTO HELL(1955); KISS OF FIRE(1955); TEN COMMANDMENTS, THE(1956); THAT CERTAIN FEELING(1956); BADGE OF MARSHAL BRENNAN, THE(1957); SWEET SMELL OF SUCCESS(1957); DEFIANT ONES, THE(1958); WILD HERITAGE(1958); GENE KRUPA STORY, THE(1959); NORTH BY NORTHWEST(1959); TOKYO AFTER DARK(1959); CABINET OF CALIGARI, THE(1962); JOHNNY YUMA(1967, Ital.); PATTON(1970); TARZAN'S DEADLY SILENCE(1970), d; UNDERGROUND(1970, Brit.); LIFE AND TIMES OF GRIZZLY ADAMS, THE(1974), w; MIDNIGHT MAN, THE(1974); IN SEARCH OF HISTORIC JESUS(1980)
Frances Doble
DARK RED ROSES(1930, Brit.); NINE TILL SIX(1932, Brit.); WATER GYPSIES, THE(1932, Brit.)
Silents
VORTEX, THE(1927, Brit.)
Misc. Silents
CONSTANT NYMPH, THE(1928, Brit.)
Shirley Doble
MY REPUTATION(1946)
Doblin
M(1933, Ger.)
Bruce Dobos
1984
HOLLYWOOD HIGH PART II(1984)
Paul Dobov
SET-UP, THE(1949); MAD AT THE WORLD(1955)
Nich Dobree
CIRCLE OF DECEIT(1982, Fr./Ger.)
Nadejda Dobrev
ORGY OF THE DEAD(1965)
Josef Dobrichovsky
VOYAGE TO THE END OF THE UNIVERSE(1963, Czech.), ed
Donna Dobrijevic
SILENCE OF THE NORTH(1981, Can.)
Yulius Dobringer
LAUGHING LADY, THE(1950, Brit.)
Benny Dobrofsky
WANDA NEVADA(1979)
Neal Dobrofsky
WANDA NEVADA(1979), p
I. Dobrolyubov
NINE DAYS OF ONE YEAR(1964, USSR)
Fyodor Dobronavov
DERSU UZALA(1976, Jap./USSR), ph
A. Dobronravov
MUMU(1961, USSR)
Fyodor Dobronravov
THREE SISTERS, THE(1969, USSR), ph
N. Dobronravov
Misc. Silents
DOMESTIC-AGITATOR(1920, USSR)
M. Dobrovolskaya
WAR AND PEACE(1968, USSR)
Ya. Dobrovolskaya
SONG OF THE FOREST(1963, USSR), cos
V. Dobrovolski
SKY CALLS, THE(1959, USSR)
V. Dobrovolsky
SECRET MISSION(1949, USSR); BOUNTIFUL SUMMER(1951, USSR)
Akin Dobrynin
WE LIVE AGAIN(1934)
Count Ivenda Dobrzensky
LA DOLCE VITA(1961, Ital./Fr.)
Lyubov Dobrzhanskaya
UNCOMMON THIEF, AN(1967, USSR)
Arlette Dobson
DOUBLE, THE(1963, Brit)
Fred Dobson
Silents
TONGUES OF MEN, THE(1916), ph
James Dobson
WEST POINT STORY, THE(1950); FLYING LEATHERNECKS(1951); TANKS ARE COMING, THE(1951); FOR MEN ONLY(1952); I DREAM OF JEANIE(1952); OKINAWA(1952); ROSE BOWL STORY, THE(1952); CULT OF THE COBRA(1955); FRIENDLY PERSUASION(1956); STORM RIDER, THE(1957); TALL STRANGER, THE(1957); JET ATTACK(1958); ARMORED COMMAND(1961); CAPTAIN SINDBAD(1963); COME FLY WITH ME(1963); HARLOW(1965); MUTINY IN OUTER SPACE(1965); COUNTRY BOY(1966); TRACK OF THUNDER(1967); DREAM OF KINGS, A(1969); UNDEFEATED, THE(1969); WHAT'S THE MATTER WITH HELEN?(1971)
Jimmy Dobson
BOOMERANG(1947); THEY LIVE BY NIGHT(1949); ON MOONLIGHT BAY(1951)

John Dobson
DELINQUENT DAUGHTERS(1944)
Kevin Dobson
MIDWAY(1976); ALL NIGHT LONG(1981); MANGO TREE, THE(1981, Aus.), d
1984
SQUIZZY TAYLOR(1984, Aus.), d
Misc. Talkies
DEMOLITION(1977, d; IMAGE OF DEATH(1977, Brit.), d
Laurie Dobson
LONELY HEARTS(1983, Aus.)
Miles Dobson
Silents
ARE YOU LEGALLY MARRIED?(1919), w
Ned Dobson, Jr.
HAPPY LAND(1943)
Robert Dobson
ROARING TWENTIES, THE(1939); DIAL M FOR MURDER(1954)
Tamara Dobson
CLEOPATRA JONES(1973); CLEOPATRA JONES AND THE CASINO OF
GOLD(1975 U. S. Hong Kong); NORMAN...IS THAT YOU?(1976); CHAINED
HEAT(1983 U.S./Ger.)
Viki Dobson
CATCH AS CATCH CAN(1937, Brit.)
W. S. Dobson
Silents
GOLD RUSH, THE(1925)
Vernon Dobtcheff
IDOL, THE(1966, Brit.); TAMING OF THE SHREW, THE(1967, U.S./Ital.); DANDY IN
ASPIC, A(1968, Brit.); ANNE OF THE THOUSAND DAYS(1969, Brit.); ASSASSINA-
TION BUREAU, THE(1969, Brit.); NICHOLAS AND ALEXANDRA(1971, Brit.); DAR-
LING LILI(1970); BEAST IN THE CELLAR, THE(1971, Brit.); FIDDLER ON THE
ROOF(1971); HORSEMEN, THE(1971); MARY, QUEEN OF SCOTS(1971, Brit.); DAY
OF THE JACKAL, THE(1973, Brit./Fr.); DESTRUCTORS, THE(1974, Brit.); MURDER
ON THE ORIENT EXPRESS(1974, Brit.); UNDERCOVERS HERO(1975, Brit.); OPERA-
TION DAYBREAK(1976, U.S./Brit./Czech.); MARCH OR DIE(1977, Brit.); SPY WHO
LOVED ME, THE(1977, Brit.); NIJINSKY(1980, Brit.); CONDORMAN(1981); NUT-
CRACKER(1982, Brit.); LA NUIT DE VARENNES(1983, Fr./Ital.); WAGNER(1983,
Brit./Hung./Aust.)
1984
PERILS OF GWENDOLINE, THE(1984, Fr.)
Valerie Dobuzinsky
MODERATO CANTABILE(1964, Fr./Ital.)
Dan Doby
REUBEN, REUBEN(1983)
Kathryn Doby
NIGHT THEY RAIDED MINSKY'S, THE(1968); SWEET CHARITY(1969); CABA-
RET(1972); ALL THAT JAZZ(1979)
Larry Doby
KID FROM CLEVELAND, THE(1949)
Michael Doby
SPRING FEVER(1983, Can.)
John Docherty
1984
EVERY PICTURE TELLS A STORY(1984, Brit.)
Rudy Dochtermann
FIENDISH PLOT OF DR. FU MANCHU, THE(1980), w
Tom Docillo
1984
STRANGER THAN PARADISE(1984, U.S./Ger.)
Van Dock
VARIETY(1935, Brit.)
Ronald L. Docken
SLAP SHOT(1977)
Ericka Dockery
1984
HARDBODIES(1984)
Bob Docking
SONG OF THE SIERRAS(1946)
E. Dockson
MEET JOHN DOE(1941)
Evellyn Dockson
COME ON DANGER(1942)
Evelyn Dockson
GREAT ZIEGFELD, THE(1936); HEAVENLY BODY, THE(1943); LET'S FACE
IT(1943); VALLEY OF DECISION, THE(1945); CAGED(1950)
George Dockstader
RECKLESS MOMENTS, THE(1949); SWORD IN THE DESERT(1949); JACKIE
ROBINSON STORY, THE(1950); KANSAS CITY CONFIDENTIAL(1952); SNIPER,
THE(1952); JALOPY(1953); PRIVATE HELL 36(1954); HELL'S OUTPOST(1955);
DRAGSTRIP GIRL(1957); GHOST OF DRAGSTRIP HOLLOW(1959); MA BARKER'S
KILLER BROOD(1960); FATE IS THE HUNTER(1964); ELECTRA GLIDE IN
BLUE(1973)
Lew Dockstader
Silents
DAN(1914)
Scott Dockstader
ELECTRA GLIDE IN BLUE(1973)
Tod Dockstader
FELLINI SATYRICON(1969, Fr./Ital.), m
Efrem Dockter
HITCHHIKERS, THE(1972)
Michal Docolomansky
ADELE HASN'T HAD HER SUPPER YET(1978, Czech.)
E.L. Doctorow
WELCOME TO HARD TIMES(1967), w; RAGTIME(1981), w; DANIEL(1983), w
Daniel Dod
SOLDIER, THE(1982)

Carol Doda
HEAD(1968)
Barbara Dodd
BABY BLUE MARINE(1976)
Bo Dodd
INTRUDER, THE(1962)
Claire Dodd
IT'S A DEAL(1930); OUR BLUSHING BRIDES(1930); WHOOPEE(1930); GIRLS
ABOUT TOWN(1931); SECRET CALL, THE(1931); WORKING GIRLS(1931); ALIAS
THE DOCTOR(1932); BROKEN WING, THE(1932); CROONER(1932); DANCERS IN
THE DARK(1932); GUILTY AS HELL(1932); MAN WANTED(1932); MATCH KING,
THE(1932); THIS IS THE NIGHT(1932); TWO KINDS OF WOMEN(1932); UNDER
EIGHTEEN(1932); ANN CARVER'S PROFESSION(1933); BLONDIE JOHNSON(1933);
ELMER THE GREAT(1933); EX-LADY(1933); FOOTLIGHT PARADE(1933); HARD TO
HANDLE(1933); LAWYER MAN(1933); MY WOMAN(1933); PARACHUTE JUM-
PER(1933); BABBITT(1934); GAMBLING LADY(1934); I SELL ANYTHING(1934);
JOURNAL OF A CRIME(1934); MASSACRE(1934); PERSONALITY KID, THE(1934);
SMARTY(1934); CASE OF THE CURIOUS BRIDE, THE(1935); DON'T BET ON
BLONDES(1935); GLASS KEY, THE(1935); GOOSE AND THE GANDER, THE(1935);
PAYOFF, THE(1935); ROBERTA(1935); SECRET OF THE CHATEAU(1935); CASE OF
THE VELVET CLAWS, THE(1936); MURDER BY AN ARISTOCRAT(1936); NAVY
BORN(1936); SINGING KID, THE(1936); TWO AGAINST THE WORLD(1936); WOM-
EN MEN MARRY, THE(1937); CHARLIE CHAN IN HONOLULU(1938); FAST COM-
PANY(1938); ROMANCE IN THE DARK(1938); THREE LOVES HAS NANCY(1938);
WOMAN DOCTOR(1939); IF I HAD MY WAY(1940); SLIGHTLY HONORABLE(1940);
BLACK CAT, THE(1941); IN THE NAVY(1941); DARING YOUNG MAN, THE(1942);
MAD DOCTOR OF MARKET STREET, THE(1942); MISSISSIPPI GAMBLER(1942)
Everett Dodd
OVER THE GOAL(1937), ed; BLONDES AT WORK(1938), ed; DAREDEVIL DRIV-
ERS(1938), ed; LITTLE MISS THOROUGHBRED(1938), ed; TORCHY RUNS FOR
MAYOR(1939), ed; LADIES MUST LIVE(1940), ed; SINGAPORE WOMAN(1941), ed;
STEEL CAGE, THE(1954), ed; FRANKENSTEIN'S DAUGHTER(1958), ed; MISSILE
TO THE MOON(1959), ed
Father Dodd
HOLD'EM YALE(1935)
Father Neal Dodd
STRANGE WIVES(1935); THEY ALL KISSED THE BRIDE(1942)
Frank Dodd
LIVING ON VELVET(1935)
J. Douglas Dodd
1984
BIG MEAT EATER(1984, Can.), m
James [Jimmy] Dodd
HI BEAUTIFUL(1944)
James Dodd
LAW AND ORDER(1940); THOSE WERE THE DAYS(1940); FLYING TIGERS(1942);
CRIMSON CANARY(1945); NIGHT AND DAY(1946); WINNING TEAM, THE(1952)
Jimmie Dodd
HILLBILLY BLITZKRIEG(1942); SHADOWS ON THE SAGE(1942); SNUFFY
SMITH, YARD BIRD(1942); VALLEY OF HUNTED MEN(1942); RIDERS OF THE RIO
GRANDE(1943); SANTA FE SCOUTS(1943); THUNDERING TRAILS(1943); TWI-
LIGHT ON THE PRAIRIE(1944); YOUNG WIDOW(1946); BUCK PRIVATES COME
HOME(1947); SONG OF MY HEART(1947); TENDER YEARS, THE(1947); DAREDE-
VILS OF THE CLOUDS(1948); INCIDENT(1948); FLAMING FURY(1949); POST
OFFICE INVESTIGATOR(1949); TOO LATE FOR TEARS(1949); CONVICTED(1950);
SINGING GUNS(1950); AL JENNINGS OF OKLAHOMA(1951); PHFFFT!(1954)
Misc. Talkies
BLOCKED TRAIL, THE(1943)
Jimmy Dodd
CAUGHT IN THE DRAFT(1941); RICHEST MAN IN TOWN(1941); MY FAVORITE
BLONDE(1942); KEEP 'EM SLUGGING(1943); JANIE(1944); MOON OVER LAS
VEGAS(1944); SINCE YOU WENT AWAY(1944); WING AND A PRAYER(1944);
CHINA'S LITTLE DEVILS(1945); PENTHOUSE RHYTHM(1945); EASTER PARA-
DE(1948); LET'S LIVE A LITTLE(1948); NOOSE HANGS HIGH, THE(1948); SLEEP,
MY LOVE(1948); WHIPLASH(1948); YOU GOTTA STAY HAPPY(1948); KISS IN THE
DARK, A(1949); G.I. JANE(1951); SECOND WOMAN, THE(1951); UNKNOWN MAN,
THE(1951); IT GROWS ON TREES(1952); LUSTY MEN, THE(1952)
Kathryn Dodd
Misc. Talkies
FOX AFFAIR, THE(1978)
Lee Wilson Dodd
BUNKER BEAN(1936), w
Maria Dodd
SUNSET PASS(1946); TWO SMART PEOPLE(1946)
Marie Dodd
WOMAN ON THE BEACH, THE(1947)
Mimi Lee Dodd
BOOK OF NUMBERS(1973)
Mollie Dodd
VERTIGO(1958)
Molly Dodd
MY SIX LOVES(1963); WHAT'S THE MATTER WITH HELEN?(1971); HARPER
VALLEY, P.T.A.(1978)
Neal Dodd
EMPLOYEE'S ENTRANCE(1933)
Patrick Dodd
THEY CAME FROM WITHIN(1976, Can.), ed; GAS(1981, Can.), ed
Rev. Neal Dodd
UNCLE HARRY(1945); MERRILY WE GO TO HELL(1932); GAMBLING LADY(1934);
YOU BELONG TO ME(1934); SANTA FE TRAIL(1940); UNFINISHED BUSI-
NESS(1941); MARRIAGE IS A PRIVATE AFFAIR(1944); SCARLET STREET(1945);
KILLERS, THE(1946); LOUISA(1950); HERE COMES THE GROOM(1951)
Silents
ONLY WOMAN, THE(1924)
Reverend Neal Dodd
MAN WHO CRIED WOLF, THE(1937); SHE'S DANGEROUS(1937)
Richard Dodd
DR. COPPELIUS(1968, U.S./Span.), ch

Steve Dodd
GALLIPOLI(1981, Aus.)
Terry Dodd
1984
SOLDIER'S STORY, A(1984)
Tona Dodd
CANNERY ROW(1982)
Edward K. Dodds
MANCHU EAGLE MURDER CAPER MYSTERY, THE(1975), p
Father Dodds
IT HAPPENED ONE NIGHT(1934)
Larry Dodds
RAFFLES(1939)
Malcolm Dodds
LAWYER, THE(1969), m
Michael Dodds
LONG SHOT(1981, Brit.), ph
Phil Dodds
CLOSE ENCOUNTERS OF THE THIRD KIND(1977)
Philip Dodds
CLOSE ENCOUNTERS OF THE THIRD KIND(1977)
Steve Dodds
CHANT OF JIMMIE BLACKSMITH, THE(1980, Aus.)
Vivian Dodds
SUNSCORCHED(1966, Span./Ger.)
Bohuslav Dodek
FIFTH HORSEMAN IS FEAR, THE(1968, Czech.)
Kurt Dodenhoff
BELIEVE IN ME(1971)
Joop Doderer
HUMAN FACTOR, THE(1979, Brit.)
Fred Doderlein
TRUNKS OF MR. O.F., THE(1932, Ger.)
Anna Dodge
Silents
DEVIL DODGER, THE(1917); FLAMES OF CHANCE, THE(1918); NANCY COMES
HOME(1918); DARLING MINE(1920); JACK KNIFE MAN, THE(1920)
Misc. Silents
ROSARY, THE(1915); LONELY WOMAN, THE(1918); SHOES THAT DANCED,
THE(1918)
David Dodge
PLUNDER OF THE SUN(1953), w; TO CATCH A THIEF(1955), w
Estelle Dodge
MAN-EATER OF KUMAON(1948)
Henry Irving Dodge
SKINNER STEPS OUT(1929), w
Silents
SKINNER'S DRESS SUIT(1917), w; SKINNER'S DRESS SUIT(1926), w; SKINNER'S
BIG IDEA(1928), w
Mike Dodge
FOLLOW ME, BOYS!(1966)
Richard Dodge
JUBILEE TRAIL(1954)
Roye Dodge
THIS ANGRY AGE(1958, Ital./Fr.), ch
Sam Dodge
1984
RED DAWN(1984)
Warren L. Dodge
INDIAN PAINT(1965)
David Dodimead
HONEY POT, THE(1967, Brit.); JULIUS CAESAR(1970, Brit.); BEAST IN THE
CELLAR, THE(1971, Brit.)
Dodo From Hamburg
PARIS OOH-LA-LA!(1963, U.S./Fr.)
Marji Dodril
WEDNESDAY CHILDREN, THE(1973)
Gillian Dods
ROCKY HORROR PICTURE SHOW, THE(1975, Brit.), cos
John Dods
NIGHTBEAST(1982), spec eff; DEADLY SPAWN, THE(1983), d&w, spec eff
Larry Dods
OX-BOW INCIDENT, THE(1943); THEY WERE EXPENDABLE(1945)
Marcus Dods
TIME WITHOUT PITY(1957, Brit.), md; TARZAN'S THREE CHALLENGES(1963),
md; UNEARTHLY STRANGER, THE(1964, Brit.), md; LIFE AT THE TOP(1965,
Brit.), md; ONE WAY PENDULUM(1965, Brit.), md; YOUNG CASSIDY(1965, U.S./
Brit.), md; 24 HOURS TO KILL(1966, Brit.), md; FAR FROM THE MADDING
CROWD(1967, Brit.), md; REFLECTIONS IN A GOLDEN EYE(1967), md; SECRET
CEREMONY(1968, Brit.), md; FIGURES IN A LANDSCAPE(1970, Brit.), md; GOOD-
BYE GEMINI(1970, Brit.), md; DAY IN THE DEATH OF JOE EGG, A(1972, Brit.), m;
LADY CAROLINE LAMB(1972, Brit./Ital.), md; MURDER ON THE ORIENT EX-
PRESS(1974, Brit.), md; GET CHARLIE TULLY(1976, Brit.), md; RIDE A WILD
PONY(1976, U.S./Aus.), md; DARK CRYSTAL, THE(1982, Brit.), md
Angela Dodson
1984
UNDER THE VOLCANO(1984), cos
Bert Dodson
RIDERS OF THE WHISTLING PINES(1949); INDIAN TERRITORY(1950); WAGON
TEAM(1952); ON TOP OF OLD SMOKY(1953)
Eric Dodson
NIGHT TRAIN FOR INVERNESS(1960, Brit.); SENTENCED FOR LIFE(1960, Brit.);
TRIAL AND ERROR(1962, Brit.); MIRROR CRACK'D, THE(1980, Brit.)
Jack Dodson
MUNSTER, GO HOME(1966); ANGEL IN MY POCKET(1969); GETAWAY,
THE(1972); PAT GARRETT AND BILLY THE KID(1973); THUNDERBOLT AND
LIGHTFOOT(1974); SOMETHING WICKED THIS WAY COMES(1983)

Kay Dodson
GOLDEN EARRINGS(1947), cos
Kenneth M. Dodson
AWAY ALL BOATS(1956), w
Mary Dodson
THIEF(1981), art d
Mary K. Dodson
SAXON CHARM, THE(1948), cos
Mary Kay Dodson
MONSIEUR BEAUCAIRE(1946), cos; SUDDENLY IT'S SPRING(1947), cos; PALE-
FACE, THE(1948), cos; SEALED VERDICT(1948), cos; ALIAS NICK BEAL(1949), cos;
CHICAGO DEADLINE(1949), cos; SORROWFUL JONES(1949), cos; STREETS OF
LAREDO(1949), cos; TOP O' THE MORNING(1949), cos; UNION STATION(1950), cos
Betty Dodsworth
Misc. Silents
TROOPER 44(1917)
John Dodsworth
HERE COMES THE SUN(1945, Brit.); NOTORIOUS GENTLEMAN(1945, Brit.);
ROGUE'S MARCH(1952); SINGIN' IN THE RAIN(1952); SNOWS OF KILIMANJARO,
THE(1952); STORM OVER TIBET(1952); BWANA DEVIL(1953); CHARADE(1953);
LOOSE IN LONDON(1953); MAGNETIC MONSTER, THE(1953); MAZE, THE(1953);
TITANIC(1953); BENGAL BRIGADE(1954); ESCAPE TO BURMA(1955); UN-
TAMED(1955); MOLE PEOPLE, THE(1956); 27TH DAY, THE(1957); IN THE MO-
NEY(1958); WHO KILLED VAN LOON?(1984, Brit.)
Charles Doe
GREAT MR. HANDEL, THE(1942, Brit.); LET THE PEOPLE SING(1942, Brit.); WE'LL
SMILE AGAIN(1942, Brit.); OLD MOTHER RILEY, DETECTIVE(1943, Brit.); WHEN
WE ARE MARRIED(1943, Brit.); UNCENSORED(1944, Brit.); DON CHICAGO(1945,
Brit.); STRAWBERRY ROAN(1945, Brit.); LOYAL HEART(1946, Brit.); WALTZ TI-
ME(1946, Brit.); THINGS HAPPEN AT NIGHT(1948, Brit.)
Karen Doe
YOICKS!(1932, Brit.)
Scott Doebler
ORDINARY PEOPLE(1980)
Alfred Doeblin
BERLIN ALEXANDERPLATZ(1933, Ger.), w
Fred Doederlein
1984
HOTEL NEW HAMPSHIRE, THE(1984)
Charles Doehrer
THAT'S RIGHT–YOU'RE WRONG(1939)
Frances Doel
BIG BAD MAMA(1974), w; AVALANCHE(1978), w; DEATHSPORT(1978), w
Francis Doel
CRAZY MAMA(1975), w
Franz Doelle
BOCCACCIO(1936, Ger.), m; ROYAL WALTZ, THE(1936), m
Marc Doelnitz
ROOTS OF HEAVEN, THE(1958); ZAZIE(1961, Fr.), a, cos; CIRCLE OF LOVE(1965,
Fr.), cos; VICE AND VIRTUE(1965, Fr./Ital.), cos
Michel Doen
PURPLE TAXI, THE(1977, Fr./Ital./Ireland), w
Kitty Jefferson Doepken
FOOLS' PARADE(1971)
Craig Doerge
PERFECT COUPLE, A(1979); RICH KIDS(1979), m
Kent O. Doering
TWILIGHT'S LAST GLEAMING(1977, U.S./Ger.)
Felix Doermann
SMILING LIEUTENANT, THE(1931), w
Christian Doermer
ESCAPE TO BERLIN(1962, U.S./Switz./Ger.); TERROR AFTER MIDNIGHT(1965,
Ger.); JOANNA(1968, Brit.); SYNDICATE, THE(1968, Brit.); THAT WOMAN(1968,
Ger.); DOWNHILL RACER(1969); OH! WHAT A LOVELY WAR(1969, Brit.)
James Doerr
SAVAGE WEEKEND(1983)
Adrian Doeshou
NIGHT AND DAY(1946)
Millie Doff
FRENCH LINE, THE(1954)
Red Doff
ANDY HARDY COMES HOME(1958), p; BIG OPERATOR, THE(1959), p; PLATI-
NUM HIGH SCHOOL(1960), p; EVERYTHING'S DUCKY(1961), p; PRIVATE LIVES
OF ADAM AND EVE, THE(1961), p
The Dog Wolf
MARKED MEN(1940)
Ulvi Dogan
DRY SUMMER(1967, Turkey), a, p
Ed Dogans
1984
TERMINATOR, THE(1984)
Robert Doggan
FATE IS THE HUNTER(1964)
Norma Doggett
SEVEN BRIDES FOR SEVEN BROTHERS(1954)
Marlene Dogherty
AMIN–THE RISE AND FALL(1982, Kenya)
Duccio Dogone
PRIEST OF LOVE(1981, Brit.)
Peter Dohanos
FOR LOVE OF IVY(1968), a, prod d; SWIMMER, THE(1968), art d; LAST SUM-
MER(1969), art d; TRUMAN CAPOTE'S TRILOGY(1969), prod d; DIARY OF A MAD
HOUSEWIFE(1970), a, prod d; TO FIND A MAN(1972), prod d; SUMMER WISHES,
WINTER DREAMS(1973), prod d; ONE SUMMER LOVE(1976), art d
John Doheim
SILENCERS, THE(1966)
Lawrence F. Doheny
TEENAGE MILLIONAIRE(1961), d, w

Charla Doherty
TAKE HER, SHE'S MINE(1963); VILLAGE OF THE GIANTS(1965); IN THE YEAR 2889(1966)
Charles Doherty
TOAST OF NEW YORK, THE(1937); UP FROM THE DEPTHS(1979, Phil.)
Chuck Doherty
BOYS IN COMPANY C, THE(1978, U.S./Hong Kong)
Edward Doherty
MURDER ON THE ROOF(1930), w; PAST OF MARY HOLMES, THE(1933), w; SULLIVANS, THE(1944), w
Edward J. Doherty
UNDER PRESSURE(1935), w
Ethel Doherty
MANHATTAN COCKTAIL(1928), w; INNOCENTS OF PARIS(1929), w; RIVER OF ROMANCE(1929), w; SATURDAY NIGHT KID, THE(1929), w; STUDIO MURDER MYSTERY, THE(1929), w; IT PAYS TO ADVERTISE(1931), w; MEN ARE SUCH FOOLS(1933), w; SAILOR BE GOOD(1933), w; HOME ON THE RANGE(1935), w; ROCKY MOUNTAIN MYSTERY(1935), w
Silents
BEHIND THE FRONT(1926), w; ROUGH HOUSE ROSIE(1927), w; FIFTY-FIFTY GIRL, THE(1928), w; TAKE ME HOME(1928), w
James Doherty
LADY TAKES A FLYER, THE(1958)
Kate Doherty
DRAUGHTSMAN'S CONTRACT, THE(1983, Brit.)
Shannen Doherty
NIGHT SHIFT(1982); SECRET OF NIMH, THE(1982)
Tom Doherty
DEATH HUNT(1981), art d
Don Dohler
FIEND(, d&w, ph, ed; NIGHTBEAST(1982), p,d&w, ed
1984
ALIEN FACTOR, THE(1984)
Misc. Talkies
TERROR FROM THE UNKNOWN(1983), d
Donald M. Dohler
1984
ALIEN FACTOR, THE(1984), d&w, ed
Misc. Talkies
ALIEN FACTOR, THE(1978), d
Greg Dohler
FIEND(; NIGHTBEAST(1982)
Kim Dohler
FIEND(; NIGHTBEAST(1982)
Hazel Dohlman
YOUNGEST PROFESSION, THE(1943); TWO GIRLS AND A SAILOR(1944)
Gaby Dohm
SERPENT'S EGG, THE(1977, Ger./U.S.); FROM THE LIFE OF THE MARIONETTES(1980, Ger.)
Will Dohm
BARCAROLE(1935, Ger.)
Will Dohn
CRUISER EMDEN(1932, Ger.)
Keiko Doi
THREE WEEKS OF LOVE(1965)
Lee Doig
SUICIDE MISSION(1956, Brit.), ed; THUNDERSTORM(1956), ed; BEHEMOTH, THE SEA MONSTER(1959, Brit.), ed; ROOM 43(1959, Brit.), ed; SWORD OF SHERWOOD FOREST(1961, Brit.), ed; INFORMATION RECEIVED(1962, Brit.), ed; DR. CRIPPEN(1963, Brit.), ed
Pavlik Dojdev
UNIVERSITY OF LIFE(1941, USSR)
Mona Dol
CHEAT, THE(1950, Fr.); FIRE WITHIN, THE(1964, Fr./Ital.)
Bobby Dolan, Jr.
GOOD SAM(1948)
Chuck Dolan
1984
GRANDVIEW, U.S.A.(1984), spec eff
Cindy Dolan
SCHIZOID(1980)
Dennis Dolan
THINGS ARE TOUGH ALL OVER(1982), ed; WOLFEN(1981), ed; CLASS(1983), ed
1984
REPO MAN(1984), ed
Dennis E. Dolan
BRING ME THE HEAD OF ALFREDO GARCIA(1974), ed
Des Dolan
1984
DON'T OPEN TILL CHRISTMAS(1984, Brit.), a, m
Don Dolan
FM(1978)
1984
PHILADELPHIA EXPERIMENT, THE(1984)
Ed Dolan
1984
SCANDALOUS(1984)
Frank Dolan
AMATEUR DADDY(1932), w; MAN OF THE PEOPLE(1937), w; STREET OF MISSING MEN(1939), w; FEELIN' GOOD(1966); CHARLY(1968)
Jack Dolan
1984
STRANGERS KISS(1984)
James Dolan
PLOT THICKENS, THE(1936)
Joann Dolan
EVE OF ST. MARK, THE(1944); DOUBLE LIFE, A(1947)

Judy Dolan
OUTSIDER, THE(1980), cos
Katie Dolan
VAMPIRE HOOKERS, THE(1979, Phil.)
Larry Dolan
FORBIDDEN(1932)
Leo Dolan
STAND UP VIRGIN SOLDIERS(1977, Brit.); THIRTY NINE STEPS, THE(1978, Brit.)
Lindsay Dolan
SUMMER HOLIDAY(1963, Brit.); YOUNG GIRLS OF ROCHEFORT, THE(1968, Fr.)
Mary Jane Dolan
HAVING WONDERFUL CRIME(1945)
Maureen Dolan
NIGHTHAWKS(1978, Brit.)
Michael Dolan
SAINTS AND SINNERS(1949, Brit.); CAPTAIN HORATIO HORNBLOWER(1951, Brit.); CHRISTMAS CAROL, A(1951, Brit.); YOU CAN'T BEAT THE IRISH(1952, Brit.)
Nan Dolan
GOOD MORNING, MISS DOVE(1955); BIGGER THAN LIFE(1956); CRIME OF PASSION(1957)
Robert Emmet Dolan
GOOD SAM(1948), m; MY SON, JOHN(1952), m
Robert Emmett Dolan
BIRTH OF THE BLUES(1941), m; HENRY ALDRICH GETS GLAMOUR(1942), m; HOLIDAY INN(1942), md; MAJOR AND THE MINOR, THE(1942), m; ONCE UPON A HONEYMOON(1942), m; STAR SPANGLED RHYTHM(1942), m, md; DIXIE(1943), md; HAPPY GO LUCKY(1943), md; LET'S FACE IT(1943), md; GOING MY WAY(1944), md; HERE COME THE WAVES(1944), m; I LOVE A SOLDIER(1944), m; LADY IN THE DARK(1944), m, md; STANDING ROOM ONLY(1944), m; BELLS OF ST. MARY'S, THE(1945), m; BRING ON THE GIRLS(1945), md; DUFFY'S TAVERN(1945), m; INCENDIARY BLONDE(1945), m; MURDER, HE SAYS(1945), m; ROAD TO UTOPIA(1945), md; SALTY O'ROURKE(1945), m; STORK CLUB, THE(1945), md; BLUE SKIES(1946), m; CROSS MY HEART(1946), m; MONSIEUR BEAUCAIRE(1946), m, md; DEAR RUTH(1947), m; MY FAVORITE BRUNETTE(1947), m, md; PERILS OF PAULINE, THE(1947), m; ROAD TO RIO(1947), md; TROUBLE WITH WOMEN, THE(1947), m; WELCOME STRANGER(1947), md; MR. PEABODY AND THE MERMAID(1948), m; MY OWN TRUE LOVE(1948), m; SAIGON(1948), m, md; GREAT GATSBY, THE(1949), m; SORROWFUL JONES(1949), m; TOP O' THE MORNING(1949), md; LET'S DANCE(1950), md; AARON SLICK FROM PUNKIN CRICK(1952), md; WHITE CHRISTMAS(1954), p; ANYTHING GOES(1956), p; THREE FACES OF EVE, THE(1957), m; MAN WHO UNDERSTOOD WOMEN, THE(1959), m; GREAT GATSBY, THE(1974), m
Trent Dolan
GUN RUNNER(1969); TWO-MINUTE WARNING(1976); DAMNATION ALLEY(1977); DIFFERENT STORY, A(1978); SWARM, THE(1978); WHEN A STRANGER CALLS(1979); RAISE THE TITANIC(1980, Brit.)
1984
DREAMSCAPE(1984); HIGHPOINT(1984, Can.)
Claude Dolbert
BARBER OF SEVILLE(1949, Fr.), p
Eric Dolbert
WILD CHILD, THE(1970, Fr.)
Frederique Dolbert
WILD CHILD, THE(1970, Fr.)
Amy Dolby
SECRET OF MY SUCCESS, THE(1965, Brit.)
Donnah Dolce
Misc. Talkies
DEATH MAY BE YOUR SANTA CLAUS(1969)
Ignazio Dolce
COLOSSUS OF RHODES, THE(1961, Ital., Fr., Span.); MAGIC WORLD OF TOPO GIGIO, THE(1961, Ital.); THIEF OF BAGHDAD, THE(1961, Ital./Fr.); EVA(1962, Fr./Ital.); SON OF SAMSON(1962, Fr./Ital./Yugo.); SWORDSMAN OF SIENA, THE(1962, Fr./Ital.); GOLIATH AGAINST THE GIANTS(1963, Ital./Span.); GREEN TREE, THE(1965, Ital.); LA FUGA(1966, Ital.); JOURNEY BENEATH THE DESERT(1967, Fr./Ital.)
Ray Dolciame
GAS HOUSE KIDS GO WEST(1947); I WOULDN'T BE IN YOUR SHOES(1948)
Klaus Doldinger
DAS BOOT(1982), m
1984
NEVERENDING STORY, THE(1984, Ger.), m
Bert Dole
SALOME, WHERE SHE DANCED(1945)
Emily Dole
PERSONAL BEST(1982)
Marianne Dole
BOXCAR BERTHA(1972)
Orlando Dole
TATTOO(1981)
Bretislav Dolejsi
LEMONADE JOE(1966, Czech.)
Guy Doleman
ALWAYS ANOTHER DAWN(1948, Aus.); KANGAROO KID, THE(1950, Aus./U.S.); KANGAROO(1952); HIS MAJESTY O'KEEFE(1953); DIAL M FOR MURDER(1954); SMILEY(1957, Brit.); ON THE BEACH(1959); CAPTAIN SINDBAD(1963); IPCRESS FILE, THE(1965, Brit.); THUNDERBALL(1965, Brit.); FUNERAL IN BERLIN(1966, Brit.); GIRL GETTERS, THE(1966, Brit.); IDOL, THE(1966, Brit.); PARTNER, THE(1966, Brit.); BILLION DOLLAR BRAIN(1967, Brit.); DEADLY BEES,THE(1967, Brit.); TWIST OF SAND, A(1968, Brit.)
Jay Dolen
CONTENDER, THE(1944), w
Jim Dolen
FALL OF ROME, THE(1963, Ital.); GIDGET GOES TO ROME(1963); EVIL EYE(1964 Ital.); HORROR CASTLE(1965, Ital.)
Vera Dolen
CAST A GIANT SHADOW(1966); WAR BETWEEN THE PLANETS(1971, Ital.)

Elisa Dolenko
MAX DUGAN RETURNS(1983)
Vasiliy Dolenko
STEPCHILDREN(1962, USSR), ed; FATHER OF A SOLDIER(1966, USSR), ed
George Dolenz
UNEXPECTED UNCLE(1941); TAKE A LETTER, DARLING(1942); FIRED WIFE(1943); MOONLIGHT IN VERMONT(1943); NO TIME FOR LOVE(1943); SHE'S FOR ME(1943); STRANGE DEATH OF ADOLF HITLER, THE(1943); YOUNG IDEAS(1943); BOWERY TO BROADWAY(1944); CLIMAX, THE(1944); ENTER ARSENE LUPIN(1944); IN SOCIETY(1944); EASY TO LOOK AT(1945); SONG OF THE SARONG(1945); GIRL ON THE SPOT(1946); IDEA GIRL(1946); NIGHT IN PARADISE, A(1946); SONG OF SCHEHERAZADE(1947); VENDETTA(1950); MY COUSIN RACHEL(1952); SCARED STIFF(1953); WINGS OF THE HAWK(1953); LAST TIME I SAW PARIS, THE(1954); SIGN OF THE PAGAN(1954); BULLET FOR JOEY, A(1955); PURPLE MASK, THE(1955); RACERS, THE(1955); SAD SACK, THE(1957); TIMBUKTU(1959); LOOK IN ANY WINDOW(1961); FOUR HORSEMEN OF THE APOCALYPSE, THE(1962)
Mickey Dolenz
HEAD(1968); NIGHT OF THE STRANGLER(1975)
Misc. Talkies
KEEP OFF! KEEP OFF!(1975); LINDA LOVELACE FOR PRESIDENT(1975)
Herta Dolezel
LITTLE MELODY FROM VIENNA(1948, Aust.)
Donna Jean Dolfer
LET'S MAKE MUSIC(1940)
Fioretto Dolfi
LADY IS FICKLE, THE(1948, Ital.)
Giorgio Dolfin
DEAF SMITH AND JOHNNY EARS(1973, Ital.)
Giorgio Dolfini
SACCO AND VANZETTI(1971, Ital./Fr.)
Larry Dolgin
HOT ROD RUMBLE(1957); SERPENT, THE(1973, Fr./Ital./Ger.)
Sol Dolgin
WHEN HELL BROKE LOOSE(1958), p
Volf Dolgiy
DIMKA(1964, USSR), w
Mikhail Dolgopolov
SPRINGTIME ON THE VOLGA(1961, USSR), w
Igor Dolgoruki
PURPLE HEART, THE(1944); CORNERED(1945); NORTHWEST OUTPOST(1947)
L. Dolgorukova
SANDU FOLLOWS THE SUN(1965, USSR)
O. Dolgova
SUN SHINES FOR ALL, THE(1961, USSR)
N. Dolidze
Misc. Silents
MURDER OF GENERAL GRYAZNOV, THE(1921, USSR)
S. Dolidze
DRAGONFLY, THE(1955 USSR), d
Anton Dolin
DARK RED ROSES(1930, Brit.); CHU CHIN CHOW(1934, Brit.), ch; INVITATION TO THE WALTZ(1935, Brit.); FORBIDDEN TERRITORY(1938, Brit.); SONG FOR MISS JULIE, A(1945); NEVER LET ME GO(1953, U.S./Brit.); GIRL FROM PETROVKA, THE(1974); NIJINSKY(1980, Brit.)
Tom Dolin
Misc. Silents
PASSING OF THE OKLAHOMA OUTLAWS, THE(1915)
Larissa Dolina
1984
JAZZMAN(1984, USSR)
Ivan Doline
Misc. Silents
BURNT FINGERS(1927)
Andrei Dolinin
THIRTEEN, THE(1937, USSR)
Voytck Dolinski
BLUE ANGEL, THE(1959)
Meyer Dolinsky
HOT ROD RUMBLE(1957), w; AS YOUNG AS WE ARE(1958), w; FIFTH FLOOR, THE(1980), w
Voytek Dolinsky
VILLAGE, THE(1953, Brit./Switz.)
Don Dolittle
CREATION OF THE HUMANOIDS(1962)
Lia Dolitzkaya
MY MARGO(1969, Israel)
Louis Dolivet
MR. ARKADIN(1962, Brit./Fr./Span.), p; CUSTER OF THE WEST(1968, U.S., Span.), p
Dixie Doll
Misc. Silents
PAYING HIS DEBT(1918)
Dora Doll
PARDON MY FRENCH(1951, U.S./Fr.); FRENCH CANCAN(1956, Fr.); MAIN STREET(1956, Span.); NANA(1957, Fr./Ital.); PARIS DOES STRANGE THINGS(1957, Fr./Ital.); YOUNG LIONS, THE(1958); MAIDEN, THE(1961, Fr.); MAGNIFICENT TRAMP, THE(1962, Fr./Ital.); PLEASURES AND VICES(1962, Fr.); ANY NUMBER CAN WIN(1963 Fr.); BLACK AND WHITE IN COLOR(1976, Fr.); CATHERINE & CO.(1976, Fr.); JULIA(1977); PEPPERMINT SODA(1979, Fr.); LA NUIT DE VARENNES(1983, Fr./Ital.)
1984
AVE MARIA(1984, Fr.)
Lawrence Doll
1984
PHILADELPHIA EXPERIMENT, THE(1984)
Tanja Doll
GOLEM, THE(1937, Czech./Fr.)

Bill Dollar
STROKER ACE(1983)
Roger Dollarhide
VELVET VAMPIRE, THE(1971), m
Ross Dollarhyde
HONKERS, THE(1972)
Mikhail Doller
GENERAL SUVOROV(1941, USSR), d
Pierre Dolley
PALACE OF NUDES(1961, Fr./Ital.), ph
Dollie
Silents
MATING OF MARCUS, THE(1924, Brit.)
Jeff Dollison
1984
BODY ROCK(1984)
Edward Dolly
ARE YOU THERE?(1930), ch
Roszika Dolly
Misc. Silents
MILLION DOLLAR DOLLIES, THE(1918)
Rozsika Dolly
Silents
LILY AND THE ROSE, THE(1915)
Tonyna Micky Dolly
LADY POSSESSED(1952)
Yancsi Dolly
Misc. Silents
CALL OF THE DANCE, THE(1915); MILLION DOLLAR DOLLIES, THE(1918)
Guy Dolman
PHANTOM STOCKMAN, THE(1953, Aus.); SMILEY GETS A GUN(1959, Brit.)
Martin Dolman
1984
AFTER THE FALL OF NEW YORK(1984, Ital./Fr.), d, w
Ralph Dolman
GLORIA(1980)
Richard Dolman
LOOKING ON THE BRIGHT SIDE(1932, Brit.); LOVE ON THE SPOT(1932, Brit.); GOOD COMPANIONS(1933, Brit.); LUCKY LOSER(1934, Brit.); MAN WHO CHANGED HIS NAME, THE(1934, Brit.); KING OF HEARTS(1936, Brit.); SOUTHERN ROSES(1936, Brit.); THIS GREEN HELL(1936, Brit.); LILAC DOMINO, THE(1940, Brit.)
Marc Dolnitz
STRANGERS IN THE HOUSE(1949, Fr.)
Christine Dolny
PURSUIT OF D.B. COOPER, THE(1981)
Jean Dolores
Misc. Silents
LONE PATROL, THE(1928)
Sue Doloria
FANTASM(1976, Aus.)
Garda Dolotskova
Silents
LOVE'S TOLL(1916)
Sue Dolph
TIME WALKER(1982), makeup
Hal Dolphe
RICH AND STRANGE(1932, Brit.), m
Giorgio Dolphin
BLACK BELLY OF THE TARANTULA, THE(1972, Ital.)
Peter Dolphin
DEADLY RECORD(1959, Brit.)
W. Dolphin
VARIETY(1935, Brit.)
Neige Dolsky
INVITATION, THE(1975, Fr./Switz.); DEATH OF MARIO RICCI, THE(1983, Ital.); RETURN OF MARTIN GUERRE, THE(1983, Fr.)
P. Dolzhanov
SUN SHINES FOR ALL, THE(1961, USSR); MEET ME IN MOSCOW(1966, USSR)
Dorith Dom
SKI FEVER(1969, U.S./Aust./Czech.)
Andre Domage
SCHEHERAZADE(1965, Fr./Ital./Span.), ph; HORSEMEN, THE(1971), ph
1984
PAR OU T'ES RENTRE? ON T'A PAS VUE SORTIR(1984, Fr./Tunisia), ph; PERILS OF GWENDOLINE, THE(1984, Fr.), ph
Eric Domain
MAN COULD GET KILLED, A(1966)
Ingrid Domann
1984
LOOSE CONNECTIONS(1984, Brit.)
Antonina Domanska
YELLOW SLIPPERS, THE(1965, Pol.), w
Jacek Domanski
MAN OF MARBLE(1979, Pol.)
Jean Domarchi
BREATHLESS(1959, Fr.)
Marta Domasheva
BALTIC DEPUTY(1937, USSR)
Dolores Domasin
SUBMARINE SEAHAWK(1959); BOUNTY KILLER, THE(1965)
Larry Domasin
DIME WITH A HALO(1963); FUN IN ACAPULCO(1963); ISLAND OF THE BLUE DOLPHINS(1964); RARE BREED, THE(1966); RIDE BEYOND VENGEANCE(1966); VALLEY OF MYSTERY(1967)
Adam Domb
WITHOUT A HOME(1939, Pol.)

Arielle Dombasle
TESS(1980, Fr./Brit.); LE BEAU MARIAGE(1982, Fr.); PAULINE AT THE BEACH(1983, Fr.)

James Dombek
9/30/55(1977)

Regina Dombek
SO THIS IS PARIS(1954)

Claudio Domberger
NOT RECONCILED, OR "ONLY VIOLENCE HELPS WHERE IT RULES"(1969, Ger.)

Barbara Dombre
HEAVEN WITH A GUN(1969)

Andrea Domburg
SPY IN THE SKY(1958)

Andrea Domburh
SOLDIER OF ORANGE(1979, Dutch)

B. Domchovsky
NO GREATER LOVE(1944, USSR)

Zsolt Dome
ANNA(1981, Fr./Hung.), m
1984
DIARY FOR MY CHILDREN(1984, Hung.), m

Jan Domela
WAR OF THE WORLDS, THE(1953), spec eff

Jan Domels
CONQUEST OF SPACE(1955), spec eff

Joseph Domenchini
DEAD ZONE, THE(1983)

Anton Gino Domeneghini
SINGING PRINCESS, THE(1967, Ital.), p&d

Cassandra Domenica "Berta Dominguez D."
1984
WHERE IS PARSIFAL?(1984, Brit.)

Riccardo Domenici
SLAVE, THE(1963, Ital.), set d; HORROR CASTLE(1965, Ital.), art d

Myrtle Domerel
BUCKET OF BLOOD, A(1959)

Faith Domergue
YOUNG WIDOW(1946); VENDETTA(1950); WHERE DANGER LIVES(1950); DUEL AT SILVER CREEK, THE(1952); GREAT SIOUX UPRISING, THE(1953); THIS IS MY LOVE(1954); ATOMIC MAN, THE(1955, Brit.); CULT OF THE COBRA(1955); IT CAME FROM BENEATH THE SEA(1955); SANTA FE PASSAGE(1955); THIS ISLAND EARTH(1955); SPIN A DARK WEB(1956, Brit.); VIOLENT STRANGER(1957, Brit.); ESCORT WEST(1959); CALIFORNIA(1963); VOYAGE TO THE PREHISTORIC PLANET(1965); TRACK OF THUNDER(1967); GAMBLERS, THE(1969); LEGACY OF BLOOD(1973); HOUSE OF SEVEN CORPSES, THE(1974)
Misc. Talkies
MAN WITH THE ICY EYES, THE(1971); PSYCHO SISTERS(1972)

Anna Dometrio
FORCE OF ARMS(1951)

Friedrich Domin
LOLA MONTES(1955, Fr./Ger.); CAPTAIN FROM KOEPENICK, THE(1956, Ger.); TRAPP FAMILY, THE(1961, Ger.); DIE FASTNACHTSBEICHTE(1962, Ger.); MAN WHO WALKED THROUGH THE WALL, THE(1964, Ger.)

Anni Domingo
OUTLAND(1981)

Antoine Domingo
DUCK, YOU SUCKER!(1972, Ital.)

Eddie Domingo
DINGAKA(1965, South Africa), m; KIMBERLEY JIM(1965, South Africa)

Eugenio Domingo
LOVE IN A HOT CLIMATE(1958, Fr./Span.)

J.S. Domingo
STRYKER(1983, Phil.), spec eff

Placido Domingo
LA TRAVIATA(1982)
1984
BIZET'S CARMEN(1984, Fr./Ital.)

Norris Domingue
1984
HOTEL NEW HAMPSHIRE, THE(1984)
Misc. Talkies
ENTER THE DEVIL(1975)

Beatrice Domingues
Misc. Silents
SUNDOWN TRAIL, THE(1919)

Joe Domingues
RED SALUTE(1935); GERONIMO(1939); BULLFIGHTERS, THE(1945)

L. Domingues
POCKET MONEY(1972)

Adriano Dominguez
NIGHT HEAVEN FELL, THE(1958, Fr.); RUNNING MAN, THE(1963, Brit.); TRISTANA(1970, Span./Ital./Fr.)

Beatrice Dominguez
Silents
LIGHT OF VICTORY(1919); FOUR HORSEMEN OF THE APOCALYPSE, THE(1921)

Bertha Dominguez
LIGHT AT THE EDGE OF THE WORLD, THE(1971, U.S./Span./Lichtenstein), w

Bobby Dominguez
GYPSY COLT(1954); GREEN FIRE(1955)

Chazz Dominguez
1984
THIS IS SPINAL TAP(1984)

Columba Dominguez
DEVOTION(1953, Ital.); IMPORTANT MAN, THE(1961, Mex.)

Danilo Dominguez
1984
PURPLE HEARTS(1984), spec eff

Ernest Dominguez
THEY WERE EXPENDABLE(1945)

Estevan Dominguez
BRAVE BULLS, THE(1951)

Frances Dominguez
BIG CARNIVAL, THE(1951); JUBILEE TRAIL(1954); GREEN FIRE(1955)

Francisco Dominguez
PORTRAIT OF MARIA(1946, Mex.), m

Joe Dominguez
SUICIDE FLEET(1931); MASON OF THE MOUNTED(1932); RIDERS OF THE DESERT(1932); UNDER THE PAMPAS MOON(1935); TEXAS RANGERS, THE(1936); WHEN YOU'RE IN LOVE(1937); GIRL OF THE GOLDEN WEST, THE(1938); OUTLAW EXPRESS(1938); MEXICALI ROSE(1939); GAUCHO SERENADE(1940); NEW MOON(1940); OUTLAWS OF THE RIO GRANDE(1941); UNDERCOVER MAN(1942); LEOPARD MAN, THE(1943); STORY OF DR. WASSELL, THE(1944); PERILOUS HOLIDAY(1946); THRILL OF BRAZIL, THE(1946); TYCOON(1947); MEXICAN HAYRIDE(1948); STREETS OF LAREDO(1949); BANDIT QUEEN(1950); FURIES, THE(1950); RANCHO NOTORIOUS(1952); HITCH-HIKER, THE(1953); RIDE, VAQUERO!(1953); SON OF BELLE STARR(1953); GYPSY COLT(1954); JUBILEE TRAIL(1954); GREEN FIRE(1955); BROKEN STAR, THE(1956); RIDE BACK, THE(1957); MAN OF THE WEST(1958); ONE-EYED JACKS(1961); I LOVE YOU, ALICE B. TOKLAS!(1968)

Jose Dominguez
KISSING BANDIT, THE(1948); CRISIS(1950); DALLAS(1950); ONE WAY STREET(1950); SECOND CHANCE(1953)

Joseph Dominguez
YELLOW JACK(1938)

Nestor Dominguez
SCALPHUNTERS, THE(1968)

Raul Dominguez
SNAKE PEOPLE, THE(1968, Mex./U.S.), ph; INCREDIBLE INVASION, THE(1971, Mex./U.S.), ph; RUN FOR THE ROSES(1978), ph

Robert Dominguez
FANCY PANTS(1950)

Tino Dominguez
HOLLYWOOD HIGH(1977)

Luis Miguel Dominguin
AROUND THE WORLD IN 80 DAYS(1956)

Luis-Miguel Dominguin
TESTAMENT OF ORPHEUS, THE(1962, Fr.)

Paola Dominguin
IDENTIFICATION OF A WOMAN(1983, Ital.)

Alebtor Domini
CUCKOO CLOCK, THE(1938, Ital.), w

Jose Dominiani
MAFIA, THE(1972, Arg.), w

A.J. Dominic
JUNGLE, THE(1952), art d

Arturo Dominici
HERCULES(1959, Ital.); GOLIATH AND THE BARBARIANS(1960, Ital.); BLACK SUNDAY(1961, Ital.); LOST SOULS(1961, Ital.); THIEF OF BAGHDAD, THE(1961, Ital./Fr.); STORY OF JOSEPH AND HIS BRETHREN THE(1962, Ital.); TROJAN HORSE, THE(1962, Fr./Ital.); SEVEN SEAS TO CALAIS(1963, Ital.); CONQUEST OF MYCENE(1965, Ital., Fr.); INVESTIGATION OF A CITIZEN ABOVE SUSPICION(1970, Ital.); LOVE IS A FUNNY THING(1970, Fr./Ital.); CONFESSIONS OF A POLICE CAPTAIN(1971, Ital.)

Franca Dominici
FIVE BRANDED WOMEN(1960); KILL BABY KILL(1966, Ital.)

Germana Dominici
BLACK SUNDAY(1961, Ital.)

Mario Dominici
FOX MOVIETONE FOLLIES(1929); IF I WERE FREE(1933); FOLIES DERGERE(1935); CAFE METROPOLE(1937)

Riccardo Dominici
BLACK SABBATH(1963, Ital.), set d

David J. Dominick
1984
TANK(1984)

Rex Dominick
NEVER A DULL MOMENT(1968)

Norris Dominigue
GAS(1981, Can.)

Dominique
LIFE BEGINS TOMORROW(1952, Fr.)

Antoine Dominique
GORILLA GREETS YOU, THE(1958, Fr.), w; DEADLY DECOYS, THE(1962, Fr.), w

Pierre Dominique
WITHOUT APPARENT MOTIVE(1972, Fr.)

Domino
LA DOLCE VITA(1961, Ital./Fr.); RUMBLE FISH(1983)

Fats Domino
GIRL CAN'T HELP IT, THE(1956); JAMBOREE(1957); SHAKE, RATTLE, AND ROCK!(1957)

Dominot
MATTER OF TIME, A(1976, Ital./U.S.)

Berta Dominquez
CROSSED SWORDS(1978), w

Joe Dominquez
BROKEN WING, THE(1932); BLACKMAIL(1939)

The Dominquez Brothers
TROPIC HOLIDAY(1938)

Ernest Dominy
WALK THE DARK STREET(1956)

Melissa Domke
1984
GRANDVIEW, U.S.A.(1984)

Peter Dompe
HAVE A NICE WEEKEND(1975)

Antiqua Domsa
MAYA(1982), p
Carl Don
ROMANOFF AND JULIET(1961); ZOTZ!(1962); SANTA CLAUS CONQUERS THE MARTIANS(1964)
Dominique Don
GENGHIS KHAN(U.S./Brit./Ger./Yugo)
Jack Don
GUNS AND GUITARS(1936)
R.G. Don
Misc. Silents
UNWELCOME WIFE, THE(1915)
Don Cossack Chorus
HOTEL IMPERIAL(1939)
The Don Cossack Chorus
MAYTIME(1937)
Don Post Studios
SPACE MONSTER(1965), m
The Don Randi Trio Plus One
FIREBALL 590(1966)
Don Rendell's Six
INBETWEEN AGE, THE(1958, Brit.)
Don Sollash and His Rockin' Horses
ROCK YOU SINNERS(1957, Brit.)
Don Strawn's Calypso Band
I EAT YOUR SKIN(1971)
Don the Dog
Silents
NO MORE WOMEN(1924)
Arsenia Dona
RAIDERS OF LEYTE GULF(1963 U.S./Phil.), ph
David Donable
STOP THE WORLD-I WANT TO GET OFF(1966, Brit.), w
Ron Donachie
1984
COMFORT AND JOY(1984, Brit.)
Giulio Donadio
DISILLUSION(1949, Ital.)
Pino Donaggio
DON'T LOOK NOW(1973, Brit./Ital.), m; PIRANHA(1978), m; HOME MOVIES(1979), m; DESIRE, THE INTERIOR LIFE(1980, Ital./Ger.), m; DRESSED TO KILL(1980), m; BLOW OUT(1981), m; FAN, THE(1981), m; HOWLING, THE(1981), m; TEX(1982), m; HERCULES(1983), m
1984
BLACK CAT, THE(1984, Ital./Brit.), m; BODY DOUBLE(1984), m; OVER THE BROOKLYN BRIDGE(1984), m
Frank Donaghue
ESPIONAGE AGENT(1939), w
Michael Donaghue
SILENT PARTNER, THE(1979, Can.); HAPPY BIRTHDAY, GEMINI(1980)
Pip Donaghy
1984
1984(1984, Brit.)
Zora Donahoo
CARIBBEAN(1952)
Archie Donahue
RAGGEDY MAN(1981)
Bill Donahue
THEY WERE EXPENDABLE(1945)
Edward Donahue
MY LIFE WITH CAROLINE(1941), ed
Elinor Donahue
HER FIRST ROMANCE(1951); LOVE IS BETTER THAN EVER(1952); GIRLS' TOWN(1959); GOING BERSERK(1983)
Frank Donahue
THEY WERE EXPENDABLE(1945); FROGMEN, THE(1951)
Jack Donahue
UNDER THE PAMPAS MOON(1935), ch; SONS O' GUNS(1936), w; PRIORITIES ON PARADE(1942), ch; EASY TO WED(1946), ch; CLOSE-UP(1948), w; ON AN ISLAND WITH YOU(1948), ch; NEPTUNE'S DAUGHTER(1949), ch
Jean Donahue
SING WHILE YOU DANCE(1946); DOWN TO EARTH(1947)
Jerry Donahue
FINAL OPTION, THE(1983, Brit.), m
Jill Donahue
FACE OF FIRE(1959, U.S./Brit.); WINTER A GO-GO(1965)
Joe Donahue
SUNNY(1930); EXPENSIVE WOMEN(1931); PARTY HUSBAND(1931); RECKLESS HOUR, THE(1931)
Marc Donahue
FINAL OPTION, THE(1983, Brit.), m
1984
LIES(1984, Brit.), m
Mary Donahue
HARD TRAIL(1969)
Mary Eleanor Donahue
HONEYMOON LODGE(1943); UNFINISHED DANCE,THE(1947); OLD-FASHIONED GIRL, AN(1948); THREE DARING DAUGHTERS(1948); TEA FOR TWO(1950)
Mary Eleanore Donahue
WINTER WONDERLAND(1947)
Mike Donahue
KILL SQUAD(1982), stunts
Pat Donahue
MY GUN IS QUICK(1957)
Patrica Donahue
PAPER TIGER(1975, Brit.)
Patricia Donahue
IN THE MONEY(1958); BOY TEN FEET TALL, A(1965, Brit.); FASTEST GUITAR ALIVE, THE(1967); CUTTER AND BONE(1981)

Patrick G. Donahue
KILL SQUAD(1982), p, d&w
Troy Donahue
TARNISHED ANGELS, THE(1957); LIVE FAST, DIE YOUNG(1958); MONSTER ON THE CAMPUS(1958); PERFECT FURLOUGH, THE(1958); SUMMER LOVE(1958); THIS HAPPY FEELING(1958); VOICE IN THE MIRROR(1958); WILD HERITAGE(1958); IMITATION OF LIFE(1959); SUMMER PLACE, A(1959); CROWDED SKY, THE(1960); PARRISH(1961); SUSAN SLADE(1961); ROME ADVENTURE(1962); PALM SPRINGS WEEKEND(1963); DISTANT TRUMPET, A(1964); MY BLOOD RUNS COLD(1965); COME SPY WITH ME(1967); THOSE FANTASTIC FLYING FOOLS(1967, Brit); GODFATHER, THE, PART II(1974); SEIZURE(1974); BORN TO KILL(1975); TIN MAN(1983)
1984
GRANDVIEW, U.S.A.(1984)
Misc. Talkies
SWEET SAVIOR(1971); LEGEND OF FRANK WOODS, THE(1977)
Vincent Donahue
BEYOND GLORY(1948); JOAN OF ARC(1948); STREET WITH NO NAME, THE(1948)
William "Red" Donahue
LITTLE GIANT(1946)
Donald
YOUNG DR. KILDARE(1938)
Archer Mac Donald
AFFAIRS OF DOBIE GILLIS, THE(1953)
Dorothy Donald
Misc. Silents
RIDING FOOL(1924); DESPERATE ODDS(1925); FANGS OF FATE(1925); FLASHING STEEDS(1925); EYES OF THE DESERT(1926); JUST TRAVELIN'(1927)
Elsie Donald
CHILDRENS GAMES(1969)
Henry Donald
ADVENTURES OF HAL 5, THE(1958, Brit.), d&w,Don Sharp
Ian Mac Donald
ACCUSED OF MURDER(1956)
James Donald
IN WHICH WE SERVE(1942, Brit.); MISSING MILLION, THE(1942, Brit.); WAY AHEAD, THE(1945, Brit.); SAN DEMETRIO, LONDON(1947, Brit.); BROKEN JOURNEY(1948, Brit.); HIDEOUT(1948, Brit.); EDWARD, MY SON(1949, U.S./Brit.); GAY LADY, THE(1949, Brit.); CAGE OF GOLD(1950, Brit.); BRANDY FOR THE PARSON(1952, Brit.); GLORY AT SEA(1952, Brit.); PICKWICK PAPERS, THE(1952, Brit.); WHITE CORRIDORS(1952, Brit.); PROJECT M7(1953, Brit.); BEAU BRUMMELL(1954); LUST FOR LIFE(1956); BRIDGE ON THE RIVER KWAI, THE(1957); VIKINGS, THE(1958); THIRD MAN ON THE MOUNTAIN(1959); GREAT ESCAPE, THE(1963); KING RAT(1965); CAST A GIANT SHADOW(1966); JOKERS, THE(1967, Brit.); FIVE MILLION YEARS TO EARTH(1968, Brit.); HANNIBAL BROOKS(1969, Brit.); ROYAL HUNT OF THE SUN, THE(1969, Brit.); DAVID COPPERFIELD(1970, Brit.); CONDUCT UNBECOMING(1975, Brit.); BIG SLEEP, THE½(1978, Brit.)
Juliana Donald
1984
MUPPETS TAKE MANHATTAN, THE(1984)
Pamela Donald
GONKS GO BEAT(1965, Brit.)
Shirley May Donald
NED KELLY(1970, Brit.)
Terry Donald
RABID(1976, Can.)
Val Donald
Misc. Talkies
BOESMAN AND LENA(1976)
Donald Heywood's Band
EXILE, THE(1931)
Andrew W. Donaldson
WHISTLE AT EATON FALLS(1951)
Arthur Donaldson
Silents
WISE HUSBANDS(; MOTH AND THE FLAME, THE(1915); SALAMANDER, THE(1915), d; BABBLING TONGUES(1917); CAPTAIN'S CAPTAIN, THE(1919); MISS DULCIE FROM DIXIE(1919); GREATER THAN FAME(1920); MODERN SALOME, A(1920); SILVER LINING, THE(1921); WHEN KNIGHTHOOD WAS IN FLOWER(1922); AMERICA(1924); DOWN UPON THE SUWANNEE RIVER(1925)
Misc. Silents
HEARTS OF MEN(1915); FADED FLOWER, THE(1916); SHOULD A BABY DIE?(1916); WOMAN'S HONOR, A(1916); DANGER TRAIL, THE(1917); ENLIGHTEN THY DAUGHTER(1917); FOR FRANCE(1917); I WILL REPAY(1917); WHO GOES THERE?(1917); FIND THE WOMAN(1918); GOLDEN GOAL, THE(1918); GREEN GOD, THE(1918); HIS OWN PEOPLE(1918); OVER THE TOP(1918); ABC OF LOVE, THE(1919); COAX ME(1919); DARING HEARTS(1919); FIGHTING DESTINY(1919); ME AND CAPTAIN KID(1919); HIDDEN LIGHT(1920); ORPHANS OF THE GHETTO(1922); SCHOOL FOR WIVES(1925); BROADWAY DRIFTER, THE(1927); WINNING OAR, THE(1927)
Arthur W. Donaldson
Silents
STORMY SEAS(1923), w
Bert Donaldson
COOL WORLD, THE(1963)
Cass Donaldson
SLEEPING DOGS(1977, New Zealand)
David Donaldson
GUN FIGHT(1961)
Dick Donaldson
Misc. Silents
GOOD LOSER, THE(1918), d
Gil Donaldson
DALLAS(1950); TREASURE OF THE GOLDEN CONDOR(1953)
Jack Donaldson
THREE LOVES HAS NANCY(1938)
Jeff Donaldson
MEDIUM COOL(1969)

Lesleh Donaldson
RUNNING(1979, Can.); HAPPY BIRTHDAY TO ME(1981); DEADLY EYES(1982); FUNERAL HOME(1982, Can.); CURTAINS(1983, Can.)

Lyn Donaldson
Misc. Silents
EMPRESS, THE(1917)

Melissa Donaldson
SLEEPING DOGS(1977, New Zealand)

Mona Donaldson
RANGLE RIVER(1939, Aus.), ed

Norma Donaldson
ACROSS 110TH STREET(1972); WILLIE DYNAMITE(1973); NINE TO FIVE(1980); STAYING ALIVE(1983)

Roger Donaldson
SLEEPING DOGS(1977, New Zealand), p&d; SMASH PALACE(1982, New Zealand), p&d, w
1984
BOUNTY, THE(1984), d

Ted Donaldson
MR. WINKLE GOES TO WAR(1944); ONCE UPON A TIME(1944); ADVENTURES OF RUSTY(1945); GUY, A GAL AND A PAL, A(1945); TREE GROWS IN BROOKLYN, A(1945); PERSONALITY KID(1946); FOR THE LOVE OF RUSTY(1947); RED STALLION, THE(1947); DECISION OF CHRISTOPHER BLAKE, THE(1948); MY DOG RUSTY(1948); RUSTY LEADS THE WAY(1948); GREEN PROMISE, THE(1949); RUSTY SAVES A LIFE(1949); RUSTY'S BIRTHDAY(1949); PHONE CALL FROM A STRANGER(1952)
Misc. Talkies
RETURN OF RUSTY, THE(1946); SON OF RUSTY, THE(1947)

Walter Donaldson
WHOOPEE(1930), w

William B. Donaldson
Misc. Silents
POOR, DEAR MARGARET KIRBY(1921)

Andrew Donally
PSYCHOMANIA(1974, Brit.), p; CONDUCT UNBECOMING(1975, Brit.), p; DOMINIQUE(1978, Brit.), p; PRIEST OF LOVE(1981, Brit.), p

Martin Donan [Mario Donen]
SECRET AGENT FIREBALL(1965, Fr./Ital.), d

Jean Donarinou
VINTAGE, THE(1957), art d

John Donat
THIS LAND IS MINE(1943)

Lucas Donat
DAMIEN–OMEN II(1978)

Misha Donat
CHARLIE BUBBLES(1968, Brit.), m

Peter Donat
LOST LAGOON(1958); GLORY BOY(1971); GODFATHER, THE, PART II(1974); HINDENBURG, THE(1975); RUSSIAN ROULETTE(1975); DIFFERENT STORY, A(1978); F.I.S.T.(1978); CHINA SYNDROME, THE(1979); LADIES AND GENTLEMEN, THE FABULOUS STAINS(1982)
1984
BAY BOY(1984, Can.); HIGHPOINT(1984, Can.); MASSIVE RETALIATION(1984); MIRRORS(1984)
Misc. Talkies
MIRRORS(1978)

Richard Donat
HOUSE BY THE LAKE, THE(1977, Can.); TOMORROW NEVER COMES(1978, Brit./Can.); CITY ON FIRE(1979 Can.); GAS(1981, Can.)

Robert Donat
OVERNIGHT(1933, Brit.); PRIVATE LIFE OF HENRY VIII, THE(1933); COUNT OF MONTE CRISTO, THE(1934); FOR LOVE OR MONEY(1934, Brit.); MEN OF TOMORROW(1935, Brit.); 39 STEPS, THE(1935, Brit.); GHOST GOES WEST, THE(1936); KNIGHT WITHOUT ARMOR(1937, Brit.); CITADEL, THE(1938); GOODBYE MR. CHIPS(1939, Brit.); YOUNG MR. PITT, THE(1942, Brit.); ADVENTURES OF TARTU(1943, Brit.); VACATION FROM MARRIAGE(1945, Brit.); CAPTAIN BOYCOTT(1947, Brit.); CURE FOR LOVE, THE(1950, Brit.), a, p,d,&w; WINSLOW BOY, THE(1950); MAGIC BOX, THE(1952, Brit.); LEASE OF LIFE(1954, Brit.); INN OF THE SIXTH HAPPINESS, THE(1958)

Sandra Donat
SIN OF MONA KENT, THE(1961)

Sergio Donate
ONCE UPON A TIME IN THE WEST(1969, U.S./Ital.), w

Mauro Donatella
WITCH'S CURSE, THE(1963, Ital.)

Doug Donatelli
1984
MICKI AND MAUDE(1984)

Roberta Donatelli
ADVENTURERS, THE(1970)

Donatello
DIARY OF AN ITALIAN(1972, Ital.)

Louis Donath
HANGMEN ALSO DIE(1943); THIS LAND IS MINE(1943)

Louis [Ludwig] Donath
ENEMY AGENTS MEET ELLERY QUEEN(1942); LADY FROM CHUNG-KING(1943); MASTER RACE, THE(1944)

Ludwig Donath
MARGIN FOR ERROR(1943); STRANGE DEATH OF ADOLF HITLER, THE(1943); HITLER GANG, THE(1944); STORY OF DR. WASSELL, THE(1944); TAMPICO(1944); COUNTER-ATTACK(1945); PRISON SHIP(1945); BLONDIE KNOWS BEST(1946); DEVIL'S MASK, THE(1946); GILDA(1946); JOLSON STORY, THE(1946); RENEGADES(1946); RETURN OF MONTE CRISTO, THE(1946); CIGARETTE GIRL(1947); SEALED VERDICT(1948); TO THE ENDS OF THE EARTH(1948); FIGHTING O'FLYNN, THE(1949); GREAT SINNER, THE(1949); JOLSON SINGS AGAIN(1949); LOVABLE CHEAT, THE(1949); THERE'S A GIRL IN MY HEART(1949); KILLER THAT STALKED NEW YORK, THE(1950); MYSTERY SUBMARINE(1950); GREAT CARUSO, THE(1951); JOURNEY INTO LIGHT(1951); SIROCCO(1951); MY PAL GUS(1952); SINS OF JEZEBEL(1953); VEILS OF BAGDAD, THE(1953); SPY IN THE GREEN HAT, THE(1966); TORN CURTAIN(1966); TOO MANY THIEVES(1968)

Aldo Donati
STORY WITHOUT WORDS(1981, Ital.)

Danilo Donati
EL GRECO(1966, Ital., Fr.), cos; GOSPEL ACCORDING TO ST. MATTHEW, THE(1966, Fr., Ital.), cos; MANDRAGOLA(1966 Fr./Ital.), cos; HAWKS AND THE SPARROWS, THE(1967, Ital.), cos; CHASTITY BELT, THE(1968, Ital.), cos; ROMEO AND JULIET(1968, Brit./Ital.), cos; FELLINI SATYRICON(1969, Fr./Ital.), prod d, cos; LADY OF MONZA, THE(1970, Ital.), cos; ROMA(1972, Ital./Fr.), prod d, cos; AMARCORD(1974, Ital.), art d & cos; CASANOVA(1976, Ital.), art d, cos; HURRICANE(1979), prod d, set d & cos; FLASH GORDON(1980), prod d, set d, cos

Donatella Donati
1984
BURIED ALIVE(1984, Ital.), art d

Ermanno Donati
DEVIL'S COMMANDMENT, THE(1956, Ital.), p; IT HAPPENED IN ROME(1959, Ital.), p; MARCO POLO(1962, Fr./Ital.), p; SON OF SAMSON(1962, Fr./Ital./Yugo.), p; STORY OF JOSEPH AND HIS BRETHREN THE(1962, Ital.), p; ATLAS AGAINST THE CYCLOPS(1963, Ital.), p; SAMSON AND THE SEVEN MIRACLES OF THE WORLD(1963, Fr./Ital.), p; SON OF THE RED CORSAIR(1963, Ital.), p; WITCH'S CURSE, THE(1963, Ital.), p; HORRIBLE DR. HICHCOCK, THE(1964, Ital.), p; GHOST, THE(1965, Ital.), p; LOVE AND MARRIAGE(1966, Ital.), p; HILLS RUN RED, THE(1967, Ital.), p; MATCHLESS(1967, Ital.), p, w; NAVAJO JOE(1967, Ital./Span.), p; DAY OF THE OWL, THE(1968, Ital./Fr.), p; MAFIA(1969, Fr./Ital.), p

Maria Donati
ANGELINA(1948, Ital.)

Sergio Donati
REQUIEM FOR A SECRET AGENT(1966, Ital.), w; WEB OF VIOLENCE(1966, Ital./Span.), w; BIG GUNDOWN, THE(1968, Ital.), w; MISSION STARDUST(1968, Ital./Span./Ger.), w; NARCO MEN, THE(1969, Span./Ital.), w; DUCK, YOU SUCKER!(1972, Ital.), w; WEEKEND MURDERS, THE(1972, Ital.), w; ORCA(1977), w; CHOSEN, THE(1978, Brit./Ital.), w; SCREAMERS(1978, Ital.), w

Donatien
Misc. Silents
UNE HISTOIRE DE BRIGANDS(1920, Fr.), d; LA SIN-VENTURA(1922, Fr.), d; LA CHEVAUCHE BLANCHE(1923, Fr.), d; L'ILE DE LA MORT(1923, Fr.), d; NANTAS(1924, Fr.), d; PIERRE ET JEAN(1924, Fr.), d; PRINCESSE LULU(1924, Fr.), d; MON CURE CHEZ LES PAUVRES(1925, Fr.), d; MON CURE CHEZ LES RICHES(1925, Fr.), d; UN CHATEAU DE LA MORT LENTE(1925, Fr.), d; FLORINE LA FLEUR DU VALOIS(1926, Fr.), d; SIMONE(1926, Fr.), d; LA MARTYRE DE STE. MAXENCE(1927, Fr.), d; MISS EDITH, DUCHESSE(1928, Fr.), d; L'ARPETE(1929, Fr.), d

Frank Donato
BLACK ANGELS, THE(1970); GUESS WHAT HAPPENED TO COUNT DRACULA(1970)

Magda Donato
LITTLE RED RIDING HOOD AND THE MONSTERS(1965, Mex.)

Stephen Donato
BABY, IT'S YOU(1983)

A. Donatov
TSAR'S BRIDE, THE(1966, USSR), w

Maura Donatt
TWO TICKETS TO BROADWAY(1951)

Renee Donatt
MADONNA OF THE DESERT(1948); MOONRISE(1948); TOO LATE FOR TEARS(1949)

Danilo Donatti
TAMING OF THE SHREW, THE(1967, U.S./Ital.), cos

Hobart Donavan
ESCAPE TO BURMA(1955), w

John Donavan
BLACK ANGELS, THE(1970)

King Donavan
RIGHT CROSS(1950); COME FILL THE CUP(1951); COWBOY(1958)

Hebe Donay
REDEEMER, THE(1965, Span.)

John Doncetto
BURNING CROSS, THE(1947)

Len Doncheff
STRANGE BREW(1983)
1984
MRS. SOFFEL(1984)

Kiril Donchev
WITH LOVE AND TENDERNESS(1978, Bulgaria), m

Antonio Diaz Donde
DOCTOR OF DOOM(1962, Mex.), m

Manuel Donde
TREASURE OF THE SIERRA MADRE, THE(1948); GARDEN OF EVIL(1954); EL(1955, Mex.); LAST FRONTIER, THE(1955); TOM THUMB(1967, Mex.)

Ada Dondini
SCHOOLGIRL DIARY(1947, Ital.)

Anna Dondini
HONEYMOON DEFERRED(1951, Brit.)

Donegal
WORK IS A FOUR LETTER WORD(1968, Brit.)

Dorothy Donegan
SENSATIONS OF 1945(1944)

Lonnie Donegan
LIGHT FINGERS(1957, Brit.), a, m; 6.5 SPECIAL(1958, Brit.)

Vincent J. Donehue
LONELYHEARTS(1958), d; SUNRISE AT CAMPOBELLO(1960), d

Frances Donelan
ZIEGFELD FOLLIES(1945); HOODLUM SAINT, THE(1946)

Lou Donelan
LAST MOVIE, THE(1971)

Carol Donell
LOCKET, THE(1946); NOCTURNE(1946); WOMAN ON THE BEACH, THE(1947)

Claudia Donelly
DARK INTRUDER(1965)

Bertha Donn
LOVE KISS, THE(1930)
Carl Donn
HAMMERSMITH IS OUT(1972)
Jorge Donn
BOLERO(1982, Fr.)
Brian Oswald Donn-Byrne
Silents
WOMAN GOD CHANGED, THE(1921), w; STRANGER'S BANQUET(1922), w
Dorothea Donn-Byrne
ENTER MADAME(1935), w
Christine Donna
CONFESSIONS OF A WINDOW CLEANER(1974, Brit.)
La Donna
SATAN'S MISTRESS(1982)
Bernard Donnadieu
TENANT, THE(1976, Fr.)
Bernard Pierre Donnadieu
DEATH OF MARIO RICCI, THE(1983, Ital.); RETURN OF MARTIN GUERRE, THE(1983, Fr.)
Pino Donnagio
TOURIST TRAP, THE(1979), m
Kelly Donnally
THEY ALL LAUGHED(1981)
George Donnan
SOMEWHERE IN CIVVIES(1943, Brit.)
Carol Donne
DECOY(1946); VIOLENCE(1947)
Carole Donne
DECOY(1946); APPOINTMENT WITH MURDER(1948); ARGYLE SECRETS, THE(1948); MIRACULOUS JOURNEY(1948); AMAZON QUEST(1949); NOT WANTED(1949); STATE DEPARTMENT–FILE 649(1949)
Jim Donnegan
DON'T GO IN THE HOUSE(1980)
Anna Pace Donnela
PULP(1972, Brit.)
Jeff Donnell
BOOGIE MAN WILL GET YOU, THE(1942); MY SISTER EILEEN(1942); NIGHT TO REMEMBER, A(1942); DOUGHBOYS IN IRELAND(1943); THERE'S SOMETHING ABOUT A SOLDIER(1943); WHAT'S BUZZIN COUSIN?(1943); CAROLINA BLUES(1944); COWBOY CANTEEN(1944); MR. WINKLE GOES TO WAR(1944); NINE GIRLS(1944); ONCE UPON A TIME(1944); STARS ON PARADE(1944); 3 IS A FAMILY(1944); DANCING IN MANHATTAN(1945); EADIE WAS A LADY(1945); OVER 21(1945); POWER OF THE WHISTLER, THE(1945); COWBOY BLUES(1946); IT'S GREAT TO BE YOUNG(1946); MR. DISTRICT ATTORNEY(1946); NIGHT EDITOR(1946); PHANTOM THIEF, THE(1946); TARS AND SPARS(1946); UNKNOWN, THE(1946); EASY LIVING(1949); OUTCASTS OF THE TRAIL(1949); POST OFFICE INVESTIGATOR(1949); ROUGHSHOD(1949); STAGECOACH KID(1949); BIG TIMBER(1950); FULLER BRUSH GIRL, THE(1950); HOEDOWN(1950); IN A LONELY PLACE(1950); REDWOOD FOREST TRAIL(1950); WALK SOFTLY, STRANGER(1950); THREE GUYS NAMED MIKE(1951); BECAUSE YOU'RE MINE(1952); FIRST TIME, THE(1952); SKIRTS AHOY!(1952); THIEF OF DAMASCUS(1952); BLUE GARDENIA, THE(1953); FLIGHT NURSE(1953); SO THIS IS LOVE(1953); MASSACRE CANYON(1954); MAGNIFICENT ROUGHNECKS(1956); DESTINATION 60,000(1957); GUNS OF FORT PETTICOAT, THE(1957); MY MAN GODFREY(1957); SWEET SMELL OF SUCCESS(1957); FORCE OF IMPULSE(1961); GIDGET GOES HAWAIIAN(1961); GIDGET GOES TO ROME(1963); SWINGIN' MAIDEN, THE(1963, Brit.); COMIC, THE(1969); TORA! TORA! TORA!(1970, U.S./Jap.); STAND UP AND BE COUNTED(1972)
Misc. Talkies
SONG OF THE PRAIRIE(1945); SINGING ON THE TRAIL(1946); THAT TEXAS JAMBOREE(1946); THROW A SADDLE ON A STAR(1946)
Don Donnellan
LILITH(1964)
Barry Donnelly
WALKABOUT(1971, Aus./U.S.); SUMMERFIELD(1977, Aus.)
Ben Donnelly
LAST RITES(1980), w
Bill Donnelly
DOUBLE DANGER(1938); FLYING MISSILE(1950)
Bob Donnelly
MA AND PA KETTLE AT THE FAIR(1952); MEET DANNY WILSON(1952)
Budd Donnelly
JESSIE'S GIRLS(1976), w; SUNSET COVE(1978), w
Deirdre Donnelly
CRIMINAL CONVERSATION(1980, Ireland)
Dennis Donnelly
NIGHT UNTO NIGHT(1949); TOOLBOX MURDERS, THE(1978), d
Donal Donnelly
RISING OF THE MOON, THE(1957, Ireland); GIDEON OF SCOTLAND YARD(1959, Brit.); I'M ALL RIGHT, JACK(1959, Brit.); SHAKE HANDS WITH THE DEVIL(1959, Ireland); KNACK ... AND HOW TO GET IT, THE(1965, Brit.); UP JUMPED A SWAGMAN(1965, Brit.); YOUNG CASSIDY(1965, U.S./Brit.); MIND OF MR. SOAMES, THE(1970, Brit.); WATERLOO(1970, Ital./USSR)
Dorothy Donnelly
POPPY(1936), w; STUDENT PRINCE, THE(1954), w
Silents
SEALED VALLEY, THE(1915); THIEF, THE(1915); SALLY OF THE SAWDUST(1925), w
Misc. Silents
MADAME X(1916)
Edmund Donnelly
FEMALE RESPONSE, THE(1972)
Edward Donnelly
Silents
EMBARRASSMENT OF RICHES, THE(1918)
James Donnelly
SEA DEVILS(1931); THEY CAME FROM BEYOND SPACE(1967, Brit.); SWAPPERS, THE(1970, Brit.); SUBURBAN WIVES(1973, Brit.); GIRO CITY(1982, Brit.)

Silents
BLACK BEAUTY(1921); CITY LIGHTS(1931)
James H. Donnelly
FROM HELL IT CAME(1957), spec eff
Jamie Donnelly
GREASE(1978)
Jennifer Donnelly
1984
ONCE UPON A TIME IN AMERICA(1984)
Kerry Donnelly
SO BIG(1953)
Leo Donnelly
ROADHOUSE NIGHTS(1930)
Nicholas Donnelly
VENOM(1982, Brit.)
Nick Donnelly
THAT SUMMER(1979, Brit.)
Patrice Donnelly
PERSONAL BEST(1982)
Ruth Donnelly
SPIDER, THE(1931); TRANSATLANTIC(1931); WICKED(1931); BLESSED EVENT(1932); JEWEL ROBBERY(1932); MAKE ME A STAR(1932); RAINBOW TRAIL(1932); BUREAU OF MISSING PERSONS(1933); CONVENTION CITY(1933); EMPLOYEE'S ENTRANCE(1933); EVER IN MY HEART(1933); FEMALE(1933); FOOTLIGHT PARADE(1933); GOODBYE AGAIN(1933); HARD TO HANDLE(1933); HAVANA WIDOWS(1933); LADIES THEY TALK ABOUT(1933); LILLY TURNER(1933); PRIVATE DETECTIVE 62(1933); SING SINNER, SING(1933); HAPPINESS AHEAD(1934); HEAT LIGHTNING(1934); HOUSEWIFE(1934); MANDALAY(1934); MERRY WIVES OF RENO, THE(1934); ROMANCE IN THE RAIN(1934); WONDER BAR(1934); ALIBI IKE(1935); HANDS ACROSS THE TABLE(1935); MAYBE IT'S LOVE(1935); METROPOLITAN(1935); PERSONAL MAID'S SECRET(1935); RED SALUTE(1935); TRAVELING SALESLADY, THE(1935); WHITE COCKATOO(1935); CAIN AND MABEL(1936); FATAL LADY(1936); MORE THAN A SECRETARY(1936); MR. DEEDS GOES TO TOWN(1936); SONG AND DANCE MAN, THE(1936); THIRTEEN HOURS BY AIR(1936); PORTIA ON TRIAL(1937); ROARING TIMBER(1937); AFFAIRS OF ANNABEL(1938); ANNABEL TAKES A TOUR(1938); ARMY GIRL(1938); MEET THE GIRLS(1938); PERSONAL SECRETARY(1938); SLIGHT CASE OF MURDER, A(1938); AMAZING MR. WILLIAMS(1939); FAMILY NEXT DOOR, THE(1939); MR. SMITH GOES TO WASHINGTON(1939); MEET THE MISSUS(1940); MY LITTLE CHICKADEE(1940); SCATTERBRAIN(1940); GAY VAGABOND, THE(1941); MODEL WIFE(1941); PETTICOAT POLITICS(1941); RISE AND SHINE(1941); ROUNDUP, THE(1941); SAILORS ON LEAVE(1941); YOU BELONG TO ME(1941); JOHNNY DOUGHBOY(1943); SLEEPY LAGOON(1943); THANK YOUR LUCKY STARS(1943); THIS IS THE ARMY(1943); BELLS OF ST. MARY'S, THE(1945); PILLOW TO POST(1945); CINDERELLA JONES(1946); CROSS MY HEART(1946); IN OLD SACRAMENTO(1946); FABULOUS TEXAN, THE(1947); GHOST GOES WILD, THE(1947); LITTLE MISS BROADWAY(1947); FIGHTING FATHER DUNNE(1948); SNAKE PIT, THE(1948); WHERE THE SIDEWALK ENDS(1950); I'D CLIMB THE HIGHEST MOUNTAIN(1951); SECRET OF CONVICT LAKE, THE(1951); WILD BLUE YONDER, THE(1952); LAWLESS STREET, A(1955); SPOILERS, THE(1955); AUTUMN LEAVES(1956); WAY TO THE GOLD, THE(1957)
Thomas Michael Donnelly
DEFIANCE(1980), w
Tim Donnelly
SECRET OF SANTA VITTORIA, THE(1969); TOOLBOX MURDERS, THE(1978); CLONUS HORROR, THE(1979)
William Donnelly
GAL WHO TOOK THE WEST, THE(1949)
Bernard Donnenfield
LADY OF VENGEANCE(1957, Brit), p
Bart Donner
DAY THE EARTH FROZE, THE(1959, Fin./USSR), art d
Bob Donner
VANISHING POINT(1971); SANTEE(1973); LAST HARD MEN, THE(1976)
Bob [Robert] Donner
SPIRIT IS WILLING, THE(1967)
Clive Donner
CHRISTMAS CAROL, A(1951, Brit.), ed; PROMOTER, THE(1952, Brit.), ed; GENEVIEVE(1953, Brit.), ed; MAN WITH A MILLION(1954, Brit.), ed; PURPLE PLAIN, THE(1954, Brit.), ed; I AM A CAMERA(1955, Brit.), ed; HEART OF A CHILD(1958, Brit.), d; SECRET PLACE, THE(1958, Brit.), d; GUEST, THE(1963, Brit.), d; NOTHING BUT THE BEST(1964, Brit.), d; SOME PEOPLE(1964, Brit.), d; SINISTER MAN, THE(1965, Brit.), d; WHAT'S NEW, PUSSYCAT?(1965, U.S./Fr.), d; LUV(1967), d; HERE WE GO ROUND THE MULBERRY BUSH(1968, Brit.), p&d; ALFRED THE GREAT(1969, Brit.), d; MARRIAGE OF CONVENIENCE(1970, Brit.), d; OLD DRACULA(1975, Brit.), d; NUDE BOMB, THE(1980), d; CHARLIE CHAN AND THE CURSE OF THE DRAGON QUEEN(1981), d
Jack Donner
HAND OF DEATH(1962); MAN IN THE WATER, THE(1963); HOTEL(1967)
Jorn Donner
TO LOVE(1964, Swed.), d&w
1984
AFTER THE REHEARSAL(1984, Swed.), p
Judith Donner
SEANCE ON A WET AFTERNOON(1964 Brit.)
Kenneth Donner
MEET ME IN ST. LOUIS(1944)
Maurice Donner
ENEMY BELOW, THE(1957)
Otto Donner
TIME OF ROSES(1970, Fin.), m
Ral Donner
THIS IS ELVIS(1982)
Richard Donner
LOLA(1971, Brit./Ital.), d; OMEN, THE(1976), d; SUPERMAN(1978), d; INSIDE MOVES(1980), d; TOY, THE(1982), d
Richard D. Donner
X-15(1961), d; SALT & PEPPER(1968, Brit.), d

Robert Donner
RED LINE 7000(1965); AGENT FOR H.A.R.M.(1966); CATALINA CAPER, THE(1967); COOL HAND LUKE(1967); EL DORADO(1967); PRIVATE NAVY OF SGT. O'FARRELL, THE(1968); SKIDOO(1968); UNDEFEATED, THE(1969); CHISUM(1970); RIO LOBO(1970); ZIGZAG(1970); FOOLS' PARADE(1971); MRS. POLLIFAX-SPY(1971); ONE MORE TRAIN TO ROB(1971); SOMETHING BIG(1971); PICKUP ON 101(1972); HIGH PLAINS DRIFTER(1973); MAN WHO LOVED CAT DANCING, THE(1973); BITE THE BULLET(1975); TAKE A HARD RIDE(1975, U.S./Ital.); DAMNATION ALLEY(1977); FIVE DAYS FROM HOME(1978); UNDER THE RAINBOW(1981); HYSTERICAL(1983)

Mary Donnet
TOOTSIE(1982)

Giulio Donnini
ISLAND OF PROCIDA, THE(1952, Ital.); CAESAR THE CONQUEROR(1963, Ital.); HERCULES AGAINST THE SONS OF THE SUN(1964, Span./Ital.); EL GRECO(1966, Ital., Fr.); MATCHLESS(1967, Ital.); DANGER: DIABOLIK(1968, Ital./Fr.); PLUCKED(1969, Fr./Ital.); PULP(1972, Brit.)

Guilio Donnini
BEAT THE DEVIL(1953)

Rene Donnio
BARRANCO(1932, Fr.)

Eddie Donno
LAST OF THE SECRET AGENTS?, THE(1966); LAST MOVIE, THE(1971); I'M DANCING AS FAST AS I CAN(1982); TWILIGHT ZONE–THE MOVIE(1983)

Eddy Donno
GREEN BERETS, THE(1968); KID BLUE(1973); CLEOPATRA JONES AND THE CASINO OF GOLD(1975 U. S. Hong Kong); GUMBALL RALLY, THE(1976), stunts; HARRY AND WALTER GO TO NEW YORK(1976); TRACKDOWN(1976), stunts; VAN, THE(1977), stunts; NORTH AVENUE IRREGULARS, THE(1979), stunts; HIDE IN PLAIN SIGHT(1980); OSTERMAN WEEKEND, THE(1983)
1984
LOVE STREAMS(1984); STAR TREK III: THE SEARCH FOR SPOCK(1984)

Edward Donno
RUBY(1977)

Mary Agnes Donoghue
1984
BUDDY SYSTEM, THE(1984), w

Steve Donoghue
WINGS OF THE MORNING(1937, Brit.)

David Donoho
NIGHTBEAST(1982), makeup

Brenda Donohue
MOURNING SUIT, THE(1975, Can.); PLAGUE(1978, Can.)

Jack Donohue
MUSIC IN THE AIR(1934), ch; CAPTAIN JANUARY(1935), ch; CURLY TOP(1935), ch; DRESSED TO THRILL(1935), ch; LIFE BEGINS AT 40(1935), ch; MUSIC IS MAGIC(1935), ch; RHYTHM IN THE AIR(1936, Brit.), a, w; MAYFAIR MELODY(1937, Brit.), ch; VARIETY HOUR(1937, Brit.); GAIETY GIRLS THE(1938, Brit.), ch; SMILING ALONG(1938, Brit.); SALUTE FOR THREE(1943), ch; MEET THE PEOPLE(1944), ch; TWO SISTERS FROM BOSTON(1946), ch; IT HAPPENED IN BROOKLYN(1947), md, ch; ROMANCE OF ROSY RIDGE, THE(1947), ch; CLOSE-UP(1948), d; MADAME BOVARY(1949), ch; DUCHESS OF IDAHO, THE(1950), ch; WATCH THE BIRDIE(1950), d; YELLOW CAB MAN, THE(1950), d; CALAMITY JANE(1953), ch; LUCKY ME(1954), d; BABES IN TOYLAND(1961), d; MARRIAGE ON THE ROCKS(1965), d; ASSAULT ON A QUEEN(1966), d

Jill Donohue
NOBODY'S PERFECT(1968)

Jim Donohue
BANG THE DRUM SLOWLY(1973)

Joe Donohue
Silents
OVER THE HILL TO THE POORHOUSE(1920)

Lucy Donohue
Silents
LOVE LETTER, THE(1923)

Nancy Donohue
FIREBALL JUNGLE(1968)

Thomas Donohue
WHY ROCK THE BOAT?(1974, Can.)

Jackie Donoro
FLIGHT OF THE LOST BALLOON(1961)

John J. Donough
Silents
DIMPLES(1916)

Donovan
CHAPPAQUA(1967); POOR COW(1968, Brit.), m; IF IT'S TUESDAY, THIS MUST BE BELGIUM(1969); PIED PIPER, THE(1972, Brit.), a, m; BROTHER SUN, SISTER MOON(1973, Brit./Ital.), m; SGT. PEPPER'S LONELY HEARTS CLUB BAND(1978)
Misc. Talkies
ALIENS FROM SPACESHIP EARTH(1977)

Arlene Donovan
STILL OF THE NIGHT(1982), p
1984
PLACES IN THE HEART(1984), p

Arthur Donno
PITTSBURGH KID, THE(1941)

Bill Donovan
Misc. Silents
RIDIN' COMET(1925)

Casey Donovan
GAL YOUNG UN(1979)

Dan Donovan
MUSIC HATH CHARMS(1935, Brit.); LET'S MAKE A NIGHT OF IT(1937, Brit.)

David Donovan
HARVEY MIDDLEMAN, FIREMAN(1965), ed

Dixie Donovan
NOTORIOUS CLEOPATRA, THE(1970)

Elaine Donovan
OTHER SIDE OF THE UNDERNEATH, THE(1972, Brit.)

Erin Donovan
HOMEWORK(1982)

Frank Donovan
Misc. Silents
SILAS MARNER(1922), d

Frank P. Donovan
Silents
BULLIN' THE BULLSHEVIKI(1919), d&w
Misc. Silents
MAD MARRIAGE, THE(1925), d

Gloria Donovan
YOUTH RUNS WILD(1944); STORK CLUB, THE(1945); I'VE ALWAYS LOVED YOU(1946); LOCKET, THE(1946)

Gregg Donovan
DESERT RAVEN, THE(1965)

Gwen Donovan
NOB HILL(1945); SENORITA FROM THE WEST(1945); LOVER COME BACK(1946); BEHIND LOCKED DOORS(1948)

Jack Donovan
Misc. Talkies
OUTLAWS' HIGHWAY(1934); TWISTED RAILS(1935)
Silents
SPITFIRE, THE(1924); BULLET MARK, THE(1928), a, ed; CAPTAIN CARELESS(1928)
Misc. Silents
HOOF MARKS(1927)

James Seay Donovan
WHEN WORLDS COLLIDE(1951)

John Donovan
SUPERCHICK(1973)

King Donovan
MAN FROM TEXAS, THE(1948); OPEN SECRET(1948); SHOCKPROOF(1949); CARGO TO CAPETOWN(1950); KISS TOMORROW GOODBYE(1950); MYSTERY STREET(1950); ONE WAY STREET(1950); REDHEAD AND THE COWBOY, THE(1950); SIDE STREET(1950); STORM WARNING(1950); SUN SETS AT DAWN, THE(1950); ANGELS IN THE OUTFIELD(1951); ENFORCER, THE(1951); LITTLE BIG HORN(1951); PRINCE WHO WAS A THIEF, THE(1951); SCARF, THE(1951); TAKE CARE OF MY LITTLE GIRL(1951); UNKNOWN MAN, THE(1951); MERRY WIDOW, THE(1952); SALLY AND SAINT ANNE(1952); SINGIN' IN THE RAIN(1952); SOMETHING TO LIVE FOR(1952); BEAST FROM 20,000 FATHOMS, THE(1953); EASY TO LOVE(1953); FOREVER FEMALE(1953); HALF A HERO(1953); KID FROM LEFT FIELD, THE(1953); MAGNETIC MONSTER, THE(1953); MISSISSIPPI GAMBLER, THE(1953); THREE SAILORS AND A GIRL(1953); TUMBLEWEED(1953); BROKEN LANCE(1954); PRIVATE HELL 36(1954); RIDERS TO THE STARS(1954); BAMBOO PRISON, THE(1955); SEVEN LITTLE FOYS, THE(1955); INVASION OF THE BODY SNATCHERS(1956); IRON SHERIFF, THE(1957); DEFIANT ONES, THE(1958); PERFECT FURLOUGH, THE(1958); HANGING TREE, THE(1959); PROMISES, PROMISES(1963), d; BIRDS AND THE BEES, THE(1965)

Linda Donovan
CURSE OF THE LIVING CORPSE, THE(1964)

Lydia Donovan
WOMAN TO WOMAN(1946, Brit.)

Maria Donovan
JACK LONDON(1943), cos; D.O.A.(1950), cos; PROWLER, THE(1951), cos; SECOND WOMAN, THE(1951), cos

Maria P. Donovan
DESTINATION MURDER(1950), cos

Martin Donovan
LOVING COUPLES(1980), w
1984
HARD CHOICES(1984)

Mary Donovan
VIOLENCE(1947)

Michael Donovan
SIEGE(1983, Can.), p
Silents
AMERICA(1924)

Michael Patrick Donovan
MYSTERY STREET(1950)

Mike Donovan
RETURN OF THE APE MAN(1944); SHINE ON, HARVEST MOON(1944); KILLERS, THE(1946); SEA OF GRASS, THE(1947); JOAN OF ARC(1948); DALLAS(1950)

Mike P Donovan
CARRIE(1952)

Mike P. Donovan
DARK CITY(1950); UNION STATION(1950); WHITE CHRISTMAS(1954)

Mike Pat Donovan
SHE GETS HER MAN(1935); MURDER WITH PICTURES(1936); LITTLE TOUGH GUY(1938); CONFESSIONS OF BOSTON BLACKIE(1941); JOHNNY EAGER(1942); BRINGING UP FATHER(1946); DEADLINE AT DAWN(1946); IN FAST COMPANY(1946); HIGH BARBAREE(1947); JINX MONEY(1948); FIGHTING FOOLS(1949); IMPACT(1949); PLACE IN THE SUN, A(1951)

P. Donovan
SIEGE(1983, Can.), d, w

Paul Donovan
GOOD DAY FOR A HANGING(1958); SIEGE(1983, Can.), p

Robert Donovan
1984
PROTOCOL(1984)

Spatz Donovan
NIGHT IN HEAVEN, A(1983)

Sue Donovan
WHERE THE BULLETS FLY(1966, Brit.)

Susan Donovan
USED CARS(1980)

Tate Donovan
1984
NO SMALL AFFAIR(1984)
Terence Donovan
YELLOW DOG(1973, Brit.), p&d; GETTING OF WISDOM, THE(1977, Aus.); MONEY MOVERS(1978, Aus.); BREAKER MORANT(1980, Aus.); SMASH PALACE(1982, New Zealand); MAN FROM SNOWY RIVER, THE(1983, Aus.)
Warde Donovan
DID YOU HEAR THE ONE ABOUT THE TRAVELING SALESLADY?(1968); MAC ARTHUR(1977); HOT LEAD AND COLD FEET(1978); HERBIE GOES BANANAS(1980)
Wilfred Donovan
Silents
SOCIETY SCANDAL, A(1924)
William Donovan
PHANTOM OF THE PARADISE(1974)
Silents
MASKED AVENGER, THE(1922); SON OF THE SHEIK(1926)
Donovan & Byl
HOME SWEET HOME(1945, Brit.)
Donovan Sisters
Silents
ARCADIANS, THE(1927, Brit.)
Terry Donovan-Smith
CUJO(1983)
Kurt Donsbach
WEEKEND OF FEAR(1966)
Irina Donskaya
SONS AND MOTHERS(1967, USSR), w
Mark Donskoi
CHILDHOOD OF MAXIM GORKY(1938, Russ.), d; ON HIS OWN(1939, USSR), d
Mark Donskoy
UNIVERSITY OF LIFE(1941, USSR), d, w; DIARY OF A NAZI(1943, USSR), d; HEROES ARE MADE(1944, USSR), p,d&w; RAINBOW, THE(1944, USSR), d; TARAS FAMILY, THE(1946, USSR), d; GORDEYEV FAMILY, THE(1961, U.S.S.R.), d, w; SONS AND MOTHERS(1967, USSR), d
Joel Donte
MOST DANGEROUS MAN ALIVE, THE(1961)
Joseph Donte
DADDY-O(1959)
G. Donyagin
MARRIAGE OF BALZAMINOV, THE(1966, USSR)
Donzetti
DREAM OF BUTTERFLY, THE(1941, Ital.), m
N. C. Doo
MARK OF THE HAWK, THE(1958)
Eleonore Doodt
INDECENT(1962, Ger.)
Graham Doody
MANIACS ON WHEELS(1951, Brit.)
James Doody
KISS OF DEATH(1947)
James Doogue
KANGAROO(1952)
Anita Doohan
EMBRYO(1976), p, w
James Doohan
36 HOURS(1965); ONE OF OUR SPIES IS MISSING(1966); JIGSAW(1968); MAN IN THE WILDERNESS(1971, U.S./Span.); PRETTY MAIDS ALL IN A ROW(1971); STAR TREK: THE MOTION PICTURE(1979); STAR TREK II: THE WRATH OF KHAN(1982)
1984
STAR TREK III: THE SEARCH FOR SPOCK(1984)
Charles Doolan
WARRIORS, THE(1979)
Joe Doolan
ARTHUR(1981)
John Doolan
ARTHUR(1981)
Michael Doolan
OF HUMAN BONDAGE(1964, Brit.)
Toby Doolan
PICTURE OF DORIAN GRAY, THE(1945)
Bill Dooley
FUGITIVE LADY(1934)
Billy Dooley
MANHATTAN TOWER(1932); NAUGHTY MARIETTA(1935); ONE HOUR LATE(1935); ANYTHING GOES(1936); DOUBLE WEDDING(1937); LIVE, LOVE AND LEARN(1937); STAR IS BORN, A(1937); CALL OF THE YUKON(1938); GO CHASE YOURSELF(1938); MARINES ARE HERE, THE(1938)
Johnny Dooley
Silents
WHEN KNIGHTHOOD WAS IN FLOWER(1922)
Misc. Silents
SKINNING SKINNERS(1921)
Paul Dooley
OUT OF TOWNERS, THE(1970); UP THE SANDBOX(1972); RAGGEDY ANN AND ANDY(1977); SLAP SHOT(1977); WEDDING, A(1978); BREAKING AWAY(1979); PERFECT COUPLE, A(1979); RICH KIDS(1979); HEALTH(1980), a, w; POPEYE(1980); PATERNITY(1981); ENDANGERED SPECIES(1982); KISS ME GOODBYE(1982); GOING BERSERK(1983); STRANGE BREW(1983)
1984
SIXTEEN CANDLES(1984)
Ray Dooley
HONEYMOON LANE(1931)
Trish Doolin
TATTOO(1981)
Lucinda Dooling
1941(1979)
1984
SURF II(1984)

Misc. Talkies
ALCHEMIST, THE(1981); LOVELY BUT DEADLY(1983)
Amy Doolittle
VISITOR, THE(1973, Can.)
Gardner Doolittle
1984
ICE PIRATES, THE(1984)
John Doolittle
MISSING(1982)
1984
OH GOD! YOU DEVIL(1984)
Joyce Doolittle
VISITOR, THE(1973, Can.)
Sgt. Wm. Dooms, USAF
OPERATION HAYLIFT(1950)
Anthony Doonan
TOM BROWN'S SCHOOLDAYS(1951, Brit.); BLIND MAN'S BLUFF(1952, Brit.); DAM BUSTERS, THE(1955, Brit.); LIBEL(1959, Brit.)
Denis Doonan
SET, THE(1970, Aus.)
George Doonan
ENTERTAINER, THE(1960, Brit.); SHADOW OF THE CAT, THE(1961, Brit.)
Patric Doonan
ALL OVER THE TOWN(1949, Brit.); BLACKOUT(1950, Brit.); HIGHLY DANGEROUS(1950, Brit.); RUN FOR YOUR MONEY, A(1950, Brit.); HIGH TREASON(1951, Brit.); LAVENDER HILL MOB, THE(1951, Brit.); MANIACS ON WHEELS(1951, Brit.); GLORY AT SEA(1952, Brit.); I'M A STRANGER(1952, Brit.); ISLAND RESCUE(1952, Brit.); MAN IN THE WHITE SUIT, THE(1952); TRAIN OF EVENTS(1952, Brit.); PROJECT M7(1953, Brit.); WHEEL OF FATE(1953, Brit.); CREST OF THE WAVE(1954, Brit.); PARATROOPER(1954, Brit.); WHAT EVERY WOMAN WANTS(1954, Brit.); JOHN AND JULIE(1957, Brit.)
Patrick Doonan
BLUE LAMP, THE(1950, Brit.); CALLING BULLDOG DRUMMOND(1951, Brit.); GENTLE GUNMAN, THE(1952, Brit.)
Tony Doonan
FUSS OVER FEATHERS(1954, Brit.); DYNAMITERS, THE(1956, Brit.); HOUSE IN THE WOODS, THE(1957, Brit.); HIGH JUMP(1959, Brit.); INNOCENT MEETING(1959, Brit.); NO SAFETY AHEAD(1959, Brit.); COVER GIRL KILLER(1960, Brit.); OSCAR WILDE(1960, Brit.); CIRCLE OF DECEPTON(1961, Brit.); PURSUERS, THE(1961, Brit.); UNSTOPPABLE MAN, THE(1961, Brit.); GREAT VAN ROBBERY, THE(1963, Brit.); SPACEFLIGHT IC-1(1965, Brit.)
Holly Doone
LIFT, THE(1965, Brit./Can.)
Lester Door
FOG OVER FRISCO(1934)
William Door
MIDNIGHT COWBOY(1969)
Mikandor Dooraff
SINBAD THE SAILOR(1947)
Van Dooren
SOUTHERN STAR, THE(1969, Fr./Brit.)
Richard Doorish
SLENDER THREAD, THE(1965)
Jacques Dopagne
I SPIT ON YOUR GRAVE(1962, Fr.), w
Dopey the Dog
RODEO RHYTHM(1941)
Yolande Doquette
Silents
MAN AND THE WOMAN, A(1917)
Bob Doqui
FORTUNE COOKIE, THE(1966); MAN, THE(1972)
Robert DoQui
TAFFY AND THE JUNGLE HUNTER(1965); UPTIGHT(1968); DEVIL'S 8, THE(1969); RED, WHITE AND BLACK, THE(1970); TARZAN'S DEADLY SILENCE(1970); COFFY(1973); NASHVILLE(1975); WALKING TALL, PART II(1975); BUFFALO BILL AND THE INDIANS, OR SITTING BULL'S HISTORY LESSON(1976); TREASURE OF MATECUMBE(1976); CARNY(1980); GUYANA, CULT OF THE DAMNED zero(1980, Mex./Span./Panama); I'M DANCING AS FAST AS I CAN(1982)
1984
CLOAK AND DAGGER(1984)
Christiane Dor
POIL DE CAROTTE(1932, Fr.)
Karen Dor
Misc. Talkies
FOUR AGAINST THE DESERT(1979)
Karin Dor
PLAYGIRLS AND THE BELLBOY, THE(1962,Ger.); FACE OF FU MANCHU, THE(1965, Brit.); INVISIBLE DR. MABUSE, THE(1965, Ger.); LAST TOMAHAWK, THE(1965, Ger./Ital./Span.); TREASURE OF SILVER LAKE(1965, Fr./Ger./Yugo.); LAST OF THE RENEGADES(1966, Fr./Ital./Ger./Yugo.); BLOOD DEMON(1967, Ger.); YOU ONLY LIVE TWICE(1967, Brit.); TOPAZ(1969, Brit.); ASSIGNMENT TERROR(1970, Ger./Span./Ital.)
Misc. Talkies
SECRET OF THE BLACK WIDOW(1964); WARHEAD(1974)
Louis Dor
NIGHTS OF SHAME(1961, Fr.), makeup; VICE DOLLS(1961, Fr.), makeup; TRIAL, THE(1963, Fr./Ital./Ger.), makeup; WISE GUYS(1969, Fr./Ital.), makeup
Meira Attia Dor
SITTING DUCKS(1979), p
Josephine Dora
TRUNKS OF MR. O.F., THE(1932, Ger.); BURG THEATRE(1936, Ger.)
Mickey Dora
MUSCLE BEACH PARTY(1964); SURF PARTY(1964); HOW TO STUFF A WILD BIKINI(1965); SKI PARTY(1965)
Dora Stratou Dance Ensemble
GIRL OF THE MOUNTAINS(1958, Gr.)

Eleanor Dorado
TOUCH OF EVIL(1958)
Lucy Doraine
Misc. Silents
GOOD AND EVIL(1921)
Dorak Film Services
SWAPPERS, THE(1970, Brit.), ed
Doraldina
Misc. Silents
WOMAN UNTAMED, THE(1920); PASSION FRUIT(1921)
Mlle. Doraldina
Silents
NAULAHKA, THE(1918)
May Doram
BREACH OF PROMISE(1942, Brit.)
Alec Doran
MC KENZIE BREAK, THE(1970); PADDY(1970, Irish)
Ann Doran
TRUE TO LIFE(1943); SERVANTS' ENTRANCE(1934); MARY BURNS, FUGITI-VE(1935); NIGHT LIFE OF THE GODS(1935); ONE EXCITING ADVENTURE(1935); WAY DOWN EAST(1935); LET'S SING AGAIN(1936); LITTLE RED SCHOOL-HOUSE(1936); MISSING GIRLS(1936); MR. DEEDS GOES TO TOWN(1936); PALM SPRINGS(1936); RING AROUND THE MOON(1936); DEVIL'S PLAYGROUND(1937); GIRLS CAN PLAY(1937); GO-GETTER, THE(1937); NOTHING SACRED(1937); PAID TO DANCE(1937); RED LIGHTS AHEAD(1937); SHADOW, THE(1937); STELLA DALLAS(1937); WHEN YOU'RE IN LOVE(1937); BLONDIE(1938); EXTORTION(1938); HIGHWAY PATROL(1938); LADY OBJECTS, THE(1938); PENITENTIARY(1938); WOMEN IN PRISON(1938); YOU CAN'T TAKE IT WITH YOU(1938); BLIND AL-LEY(1939); GOOD GIRLS GO TO PARIS(1939); HOMICIDE BUREAU(1939); LET US LIVE(1939); MAN THEY COULD NOT HANG, THE(1939); MR. SMITH GOES TO WASHINGTON(1939); RIO GRANDE(1939); SMASHING THE SPY RING(1939); FIVE LITTLE PEPPERS AT HOME(1940); GIRLS OF THE ROAD(1940); GLAMOUR FOR SALE(1940); MANHATTAN HEARTBEAT(1940); UNTAMED(1940); BLUE, WHITE, AND PERFECT(1941); CRIMINALS WITHIN(1941); DIVE BOMBER(1941); DR. KIL-DARE'S WEDDING DAY(1941); ELLERY QUEEN'S PENTHOUSE MYSTERY(1941); KID FROM KANSAS, THE(1941); MEET JOHN DOE(1941); NEW YORK TOWN(1941); PENNY SERENADE(1941); SING ANOTHER CHORUS(1941); SUN VALLEY SERE-NADE(1941); BEYOND THE BLUE HORIZON(1942); HARD WAY, THE(1942); MR. WISE GUY(1942); MY SISTER EILEEN(1942); STREET OF CHANCE(1942); THEY ALL KISSED THE BRIDE(1942); GILDERSLEEVE ON BROADWAY(1943); MORE THE MERRIER, THE(1943); OLD ACQUAINTANCE(1943); SLIGHTLY DAN-GEROUS(1943); SO PROUDLY WE HAIL(1943); HENRY ALDRICH'S LITTLE SE-CRET(1944); HERE COME THE WAVES(1944); I LOVE A SOLDIER(1944); MR. SKEFFINGTON(1944); STORY OF DR. WASSELL, THE(1944); PRIDE OF THE MARINES(1945); ROUGHLY SPEAKING(1945); OUR HEARTS WERE GROWING UP(1946); PERFECT MARRIAGE, THE(1946); STRANGE LOVE OF MARTHA IVERS, THE(1946); CRIMSON KEY, THE(1947); FEAR IN THE NIGHT(1947); FOR THE LOVE OF RUSTY(1947); MAGIC TOWN(1947); MY FAVORITE BRUNETTE(1947); ROAD TO THE BIG HOUSE(1947); SECOND CHANCE(1947); SEVEN WERE SAVED(1947); VARIETY GIRL(1947); HAZARD(1948); HE WALKED BY NIGHT(1948); MY DOG RUSTY(1948); NO MINOR VICES(1948); PITFALL(1948); RETURN OF THE WHIS-TLER, THE(1948); RUSTY LEADS THE WAY(1948); SEALED VERDICT(1948); SNAKE PIT, THE(1948); WALLS OF JERICHO(1948); ACCUSED, THE(1949); AIR HOSTESS(1949); CALAMITY JANE AND SAM BASS(1949); FOUNTAINHEAD, THE(1949); HOLIDAY IN HAVANA(1949); KID FROM CLEVELAND, THE(1949); ONE LAST FLING(1949); RUSTY SAVES A LIFE(1949); RUSTY'S BIRTHDAY(1949); GAMBLING HOUSE(1950); JACKPOT, THE(1950); LONELY HEARTS BAN-DITS(1950); NEVER A DULL MOMENT(1950); NO SAD SONGS FOR ME(1950); HER FIRST ROMANCE(1951); PAINTED HILLS, THE(1951); PEOPLE AGAINST O'HARA, THE(1951); STARLIFT(1951); TOMAHAWK(1951); HERE COME THE NEL-SONS(1952); LOVE IS BETTER THAN EVER(1952); PAULA(1952); RODEO(1952); ROSE BOWL STORY, THE(1952); EDDIE CANTOR STORY, THE(1953); ISLAND IN THE SKY(1953); SO THIS IS LOVE(1953); BOB MATHIAS STORY, THE(1954); CITY STORY(1954); HIGH AND THE MIGHTY, THE(1954); THEM!(1954); DESPERATE HOURS, THE(1955); REBEL WITHOUT A CAUSE(1955); BAND OF ANGELS(1957); MAN WHO TURNED TO STONE, THE(1957); SHOOT-OUT AT MEDICINE BEND(1957); TWO GROOMS FOR A BRIDE(1957); YOUNG AND DANGEROUS(1957); DAY OF THE BAD MAN(1958); DEEP SIX, THE(1958); FEMALE ANIMAL, THE(1958); IT! THE TERROR FROM BEYOND SPACE(1958); JOY RIDE(1958); LIFE BEGINS AT 17(1958); RAWHIDE TRAIL, THE(1958); STEP DOWN TO TERROR(1958); VIOLENT ROAD(1958); VOICE IN THE MIRROR(1958); CAST A LONG SHADOW(1959); FBI STORY, THE(1959); RIOT IN JUVENILE PRISON(1959); SUMMER PLACE, A(1959); WARLOCK(1959); CAPTAIN NEWMAN, M.D.(1963); BRASS BOTTLE, THE(1964); CARPETBAGGERS, THE(1964); KITTEN WITH A WHIP(1964); WHERE LOVE HAS GONE(1964); HOSTAGE, THE(1966); NOT WITH MY WIFE, YOU DON'T!(1966); ROSIE!(1967); ONCE YOU KISS A STRANGER(1969); THERE WAS A CROOKED MAN(1970); HIRED HAND, THE(1971); FIRST MONDAY IN OCTOBER(1981)
Misc. Talkies
SON OF RUSTY, THE(1947); RAWHIDE TRAIL, THE(1950)
Charles Doran
MY WIFE'S FAMILY(1962, Brit.)
Douglas Doran
GUNFIGHT, A(1971); SECOND THOUGHTS(1983)
Elaine Doran
SLEEPING CAR TO TRIESTE(1949, Brit.)
James Doran
IPCRESS FILE, THE(1965, Brit.), w
Jesse Doran
STAYING ALIVE(1983)
Jesus Doran
REVENGERS, THE(1972, U.S./Mex.), spec eff
Johnny Doran
FROM THE MIXED-UP FILES OF MRS. BASIL E. FRANKWEILER(1973); TREAS-URE OF MATECUMBE(1976)
Mary Doran
RIVER WOMAN, THE(1928); BROADWAY MELODY, THE(1929); GIRL IN THE SHOW, THE(1929); LUCKY BOY(1929); NEW YORK NIGHTS(1929); THEIR OWN DESIRE(1929); TONIGHT AT TWELVE(1929); TRIAL OF MARY DUGAN, THE(1929); DIVORCEE, THE(1930); OUR BLUSHING BRIDES(1930); REMOTE CONTROL(1930); SINS OF THE CHILDREN(1930); THEY LEARNED ABOUT WOMEN(1930); THIRD

ALARM, THE(1930); CRIMINAL CODE(1931); EX-BAD BOY(1931); FIFTY FATHOMS DEEP(1931); IRON MAN, THE(1931); MIRACLE WOMAN, THE(1931); PARTY HUS-BAND(1931); BEAUTY AND THE BOSS(1932); FINAL EDITION(1932); LOVE ME TONIGHT(1932); MISS PINKERTON(1932); MOVIE CRAZY(1932); RIDIN' FOR JUS-TICE(1932); SILVER LINING(1932); STRANGE LOVE OF MOLLY LOUVAIN, THE(1932); THREE ON A MATCH(1932); UNDER EIGHTEEN(1932); UNION DE-POT(1932); GRAND SLAM(1933); HARD TO HANDLE(1933); SATURDAY'S MIL-LIONS(1933); MISS PACIFIC FLEET(1935); MURDER IN THE FLEET(1935); NAUGHTY MARIETTA(1935); SING SING NIGHTS(1935); SUNSET RANGE(1935); BORDER PATROLMAN, THE(1936); KID GALAHAD(1937)
1984
ELECTRIC DREAMS(1984)
Misc. Talkies
EXPOSURE(1932)
Silents
HALF A BRIDE(1928)
Peter Doran
EXPERIENCE PREFERRED... BUT NOT ESSENTIAL(1983, Brit.)
Richard Doran
HARRAD SUMMER, THE(1974); HOLLYWOOD BOULEVARD(1976)
Robert Doran
GUILTY PARENTS(1934), ph; SINGING BUCKAROO, THE(1937), ph; I DEMAND PAYMENT(1938), ph; RACING BLOOD(1938), ph; KILLERS OF THE WILD(1940), ph; JUST YOU AND ME, KID(1979); PROMISES IN THE DARK(1979); LAST AMERICAN VIRGIN, THE(1982)
Takayo Doran
ROLLERCOASTER(1977); WHEN TIME RAN OUT(1980)
Veronica Doran
HORROR HOUSE(1970, Brit.)
Irma Dorantes
ORLAK, THE HELL OF FRANKENSTEIN(1960, Mex.)
Raniero Dorascienzi
FINE PAIR, A(1969, Ital.)
Charles Dorat
GOLEM, THE(1937, Czech./Fr.); THEY WERE FIVE(1938, Fr.); PANIQUE(1947, Fr.); DEADLIER THAN THE MALE(1957, Fr.), w
Maria Doray
ARTISTS AND MODELS ABROAD(1938)
Therese Doray
COGNASSE(1932, Fr.)
Lele Dorazio
ELVIS! ELVIS!(1977, Swed.)
Anna Dorbert
FIEND(
The Dorchester Girls
HOT NEWS(1936, Brit.)
Adrienne Dore
WILD PARTY, THE(1929); POINTED HEELS(1930); ALIAS THE DOCTOR(1932); EXPERT, THE(1932); FAMOUS FERGUSON CASE, THE(1932); PLAY GIRL(1932); RICH ARE ALWAYS WITH US, THE(1932); STREET OF WOMEN(1932); THIR-TEENTH GUEST, THE(1932); UNION DEPOT(1932); LOVE, HONOR, AND OH BABY!(1933)
Misc. Talkies
UNDERCOVER MEN(1935)
Misc. Silents
BEYOND LONDON LIGHTS(1928)
Alexander Dore
UGLY DUCKLING, THE(1959, Brit.); WIND OF CHANGE, THE(1961, Brit.), w; JUNGLE STREET GIRLS(1963, Brit.), w; CHITTY CHITTY BANG BANG(1968, Brit.)
Anne Dore
LAS VEGAS STORY, THE(1952); SON OF PALEFACE(1952); SIREN OF BAG-DAD(1953); PSYCHO(1960); EXPLOSIVE GENERATION, THE(1961); MY FAIR LA-DY(1964)
Anne Marie Dore
SHOW BOAT(1951)
Ben Dore
MONSTER WALKS, THE(1932), art d; TANGLED DESTINIES(1932), art d
Bill Dore
THE RUNNER STUMBLES(1979)
Charlie Dore
1984
PLOUGHMAN'S LUNCH, THE(1984, Brit.)
Edna Dore
MORE DEADLY THAN THE MALE(1961, Brit.); JUNGLE STREET GIRLS(1963, Brit.)
Gladys Dore
Silents
MODERN MONTE CRISTO, A(1917)
Jane Dore
VALUE FOR MONEY(1957, Brit.)
Nadine Dore
GOOD SPORT(1931); PALMY DAYS(1931); LAW OF THE NORTH(1932); PARISIAN ROMANCE, A(1932); STRANGE ADVENTURE(1932); SHE COULDN'T TAKE IT(1935); WOMEN OF GLAMOUR(1937)
Sandy Dore
FRASIER, THE SENSUOUS LION(1973), w
Bob Dorel
JUDGE AND THE ASSASSIN, THE(1979, Fr.)
Johnny Dorell
BREAD AND CHOCOLATE(1978, Ital.)
Allen Doremus
HOMER(1970)
Nica Doret
DEATH RIDES THE PLAINS(1944)
Charles Dorety
PARDON US(1931); PACK UP YOUR TROUBLES(1932); LUCKY NIGHT(1939); BENEATH WESTERN SKIES(1944); ABBOTT AND COSTELLO MEET THE KEY-STONE KOPS(1955)

Paula Dorety
CAPTIVE WOMEN(1952)
Reubin Dorey
STORY OF ADELE H., THE(1975, Fr.)
Marta Dorff
GYPSY FURY(1950, Fr.); LOVING COUPLES(1966, Swed.)
Steve Dorff
HONKYTONK MAN(1982), m; WALTZ ACROSS TEXAS(1982), m
Franz Dorfler
MADAME CURIE(1943); SEA OF GRASS, THE(1947)
Walter Dorfler
PLAYGIRLS AND THE BELLBOY, THE(1962,Ger.), art d
Annie Dorfman
END OF DESIRE(1962 Fr./Ital.), p
Arnold Dorfman
GOLD GUITAR, THE(1966)
Edmund I. Dorfman
PREJUDICE(1949), p
Nat Dorfman
ATLANTIC ADVENTURE(1935), w
Robert Dorfman
FORBIDDEN GAMES(1953, Fr.), p; MY WIFE'S HUSBAND(1965, Fr./Ital.), p; DON'T LOOK NOW(1969, Brit./Fr.), p; LA PRISONNIERE(1969, Fr./Ital.), p; DEADLY TRAP, THE(1972, Fr./Ital.), p; COP, A(1973, Fr.), p; PAPILLON(1973), p
Ron Dorfman
DEAR, DEAD DELILAH(1972), ed; NIGHT OF THE ZOMBIES(1981), a, ph
Stanley Dorfman
SWINGER'S PARADISE(1965, Brit.), prod d
Annie Dorfmann
GERVAISE(1956, Fr.), p
Jacques Dorfmann
MAYERLING(1968, Brit./Fr.); QUEST FOR FIRE(1982, Fr./Can.), p
Robert Dorfmann
CHEATERS, THE(1961, Fr.), p; MAYERLING(1968, Brit./Fr.), p; CHRISTMAS TREE, THE(1969, Fr.), p; CONFESSION, THE(1970, Fr.), p; ROAD TO SALINA(1971, Fr./Ital.), p; TRAFFIC(1972, Fr.), p; COLD SWEAT(1974, Ital., Fr.), p; DIRTY MONEY(1977, Fr.), p
Roland Dorgeles
ROAD TO GLORY, THE(1936), w
Robert Dorhelm
SHE DANCES ALONE(1981, Aust./U.S.), w
Sandro Dori
WHITE, RED, YELLOW, PINK(1966, Ital.); KISS THE GIRLS AND MAKE THEM DIE(1967, U.S./Ital.); LOVE FACTORY(1969, Ital.)
Doria
LOVES OF HERCULES, THE(1960), w
Bianca Doria
ANNA(1951, Ital.)
Blanca Doria
STORMBOUND(1951, Ital.)
Daniela Doria
GATES OF HELL, THE zero(1983, U.S./Ital.)
E.F. Doria
TENTACLES(1977, Ital.), p
Enzo Doria
HEAD OF A TYRANT(1960, Fr./Ital.); LA DOLCE VITA(1961, Ital./Fr.); ERIK THE CONQUEROR(1963, Fr./Ital.); THANK YOU, AUNT(1969, Ital.), p; CANNIBALS, THE(1970, Ital.), p
Franco Doria
WILD, WILD PLANET, THE(1967, Ital.)
Jaime Doria
OPEN SEASON(1974, U.S./Span.)
Jorge Doria
TRAIN ROBBERY CONFIDENTIAL(1965, Braz.); LOLLIPOP(1966, Braz.)
Max Doria
COUNTERFEITERS OF PARIS, THE(1962, Fr., Ital.)
Oswaldo Doria
UNDER FIRE(1983)
Sergio Doria
RUTHLESS FOUR, THE(1969, Ital./Ger.)
Vera Doria
Silents
PAIR OF SILK STOCKINGS, A(1918)
Misc. Silents
MADCAP, THE(1916); LADY'S NAME, A(1918); SAUCE FOR THE GOOSE(1918); WOMAN'S WEAPONS(1918); LIFE'S A FUNNY PROPOSITION(1919); VEILED ADVENTURE, THE(1919)
Angela Dorian
CHUKA(1967); ROSEMARY'S BABY(1968)
Charles Dorian
TWO-FACED WOMAN(1941), d
Silents
ALL NIGHT(1918); ANSWER, THE(1918)
Misc. Silents
RED-HAIRED CUPID, A(1918); SOCIETY FOR SALE(1918); SEALED ENVELOPE, THE(1919)
Elsa Dorian
NO EXIT(1962, U.S./Arg.)
Ernest Dorian
ENEMY AGENTS MEET ELLERY QUEEN(1942); NIGHT PLANE FROM CHUNGKING(1942); PRISONER OF JAPAN(1942); REUNION IN FRANCE(1942); MOON IS DOWN, THE(1943)
Ernst Dorian
ISLE OF THE DEAD(1945)
Leon Dorian
SPY IN THE SKY(1958)
Marion Dorian
VOLPONE(1947, Fr.)

Reine Dorian
FRENCH WAY, THE(1952, Fr.), ed; GIVEN WORD, THE(1964, Braz.), titles
Martin Doric
IMPACT(1949); MATING SEASON, THE(1951); CARRIE(1952)
Eddie Dorie
KILL AND KILL AGAIN(1981)
Dori Dorika
PASSIONATE THIEF, THE(1963, Ital.); WHITE SISTER(1973, Ital./Span./Fr.)
Phoebe Dorin
RIVALS(1972); MAKING LOVE(1982)
Misc. Talkies
DISCO FEVER(1978)
Arturo R. Doring
UNDER FIRE(1983)
Edda Dorini
WIDOWS' NEST(1977, U.S./Span.), set d
Daniela Dorio
1984
BLACK CAT, THE(1984, Ital./Brit.)
Luciano Dorio
ISLAND OF PROCIDA, THE(1952, Ital.), p
Doris
CLARENCE, THE CROSS-EYED LION(1965)
Dainty Doris
WOMAN OBSESSED(1959)
Pierre Doris
JULIE THE REDHEAD(1963, Fr.); COUNTERFEIT CONSTABLE, THE(1966, Fr.); STORY OF A THREE DAY PASS, THE(1968, Fr.); SLOGAN(1970, Fr.)
John Dorish
ONE DOWN TWO TO GO(1982)
Rosemary Dorken
FLIGHT FROM SINGAPORE(1962, Brit.); HAUNTING, THE(1963); V.I.P.s, THE(1963, Brit.)
Nikolai Dorkhin
DEFENSE OF VOLOTCHAYEVSK, THE(1938, USSR)
Barry Dorking
MERRY CHRISTMAS MR. LAWRENCE(1983, Jap./Brit.)
Jean Dorl
LONERS, THE(1972)
Francoise Dorleac
GENGHIS KHAN(U.S./Brit./Ger./Yugo); GIRL WITH THE GOLDEN EYES, THE(1962, Fr.); SOFT SKIN, THE(1964, Fr.); THAT MAN FROM RIO(1964, Fr./Ital.); CIRCLE OF LOVE(1965, Fr.); MALE HUNT(1965, Fr./Ital.); WHERE THE SPIES ARE(1965, Brit.); CUL-DE-SAC(1966, Brit.); BILLION DOLLAR BRAIN(1967, Brit.); YOUNG GIRLS OF ROCHEFORT, THE(1968, Fr.)
Jean Pierre Dorleac
NATIONAL LAMPOON'S CLASS REUNION(1982), cos
Jean-Pierre Dorleac
BUCK ROGERS IN THE 25TH CENTURY(1979), cos; BLUE LAGOON, THE(1980), cos; SOMEWHERE IN TIME(1980), cos
Martha Dorlon
FOXY LADY(1971, Can.), set d
John Dorman
DEAD TO THE WORLD(1961)
Julie Dorman
WHICH WAY IS UP?(1977)
Shirley Dorman
Misc. Silents
ONE WOMAN IDEA, THE(1929)
V. Dorman
THREE TALES OF CHEKHOV(1961, USSR), ed
Veniamin Dorman
SPRINGTIME ON THE VOLGA(1961, USSR), d
Genevieve Dormann
COUP DE GRACE(1978, Ger./Fr.), w
Norman Dorme
INSPECTOR CLOUSEAU(1968, Brit.), art d; SUNDAY BLOODY SUNDAY(1971, Brit.), art d; ALICE'S ADVENTURES IN WONDERLAND(1972, Brit.), art d; POPE JOAN(1972, Brit.), art d; SATURN 3(1980), art d; FRENCH LIEUTENANT'S WOMAN, THE(1981), art d; GANDHI(1982), art d; KRULL(1983), art d
1984
GREYSTOKE: THE LEGEND OF TARZAN, LORD OF THE APES(1984), art d
Charles Dormer
CHILDREN OF CHANCE(1930, Brit.); HATE SHIP, THE(1930, Brit.); VAGABOND QUEEN, THE(1931, Brit.)
Silents
VIRGINIA'S HUSBAND(1928, Brit.)
Daisy Dormer
CITY OF BEAUTIFUL NONSENSE, THE(1935, Brit.)
Edmee Dormeuil
Silents
ODDS AGAINST HER, THE(1919, Brit.)
Roger Dormoy
TALE OF FIVE WOMEN, A(1951, Brit.), ph
Annette Dorn
SISTERS, OR THE BALANCE OF HAPPINESS(1982, Ger.), ed
Blake Dorn
GANGWAY(1937, Brit.); NIGHT RIDE(1937, Brit.); NO PARKING(1938, Brit.)
Delores Dorn
Misc. Talkies
CANDY SNATCHERS, THE(1974)
Dody Dorn
TUNNELVISION(1976)
Dolores Dorn
BOUNTY HUNTER, THE(1954); LUCKY ME(1954); PHANTOM OF THE RUE MORGUE(1954); UNDERWORLD U.S.A.(1961); THIRTEEN WEST STREET(1962); TRUCK STOP WOMEN(1974); TELL ME A RIDDLE(1980)

Doris Dorn
Silents
ROARING RAILS(1924), w
Philip Dorn
DIAMOND FRONTIER(1940); ENEMY AGENT(1940); ESCAPE(1940); SKI PATROL(1940); TARZAN'S SECRET TREASURE(1941); UNDERGROUND(1941); ZIEGFELD GIRL(1941); CALLING DR. GILLESPIE(1942); RANDOM HARVEST(1942); REUNION IN FRANCE(1942); CHETNIKS(1943); PARIS AFTER DARK(1943); BLONDE FEVER(1944); PASSAGE TO MARSEILLE(1944); ESCAPE IN THE DESERT(1945); I'VE ALWAYS LOVED YOU(1946); I REMEMBER MAMA(1948); FIGHTING KENTUCKIAN, THE(1949); SPY HUNT(1950); SEALED CARGO(1951)
Ray Dorn
DR. TERROR'S GALLERY OF HORRORS(1967), p, art d; JOURNEY TO THE CENTER OF TIME(1967), p; CYCLE SAVAGES(1969), p; INCREDIBLE TWO-HEADED TRANSPLANT, THE(1971), spec eff
Rudi Dorn
TAKE HER BY SURPRISE(1967, Can.), d
Susan Dorn
ZOTZ!(1962)
Veronicka Dorn
PARSIFAL(1983, Fr.), cos
Dolores Dorn-Heft [Dorn]
UNCLE VANYA(1958)
David Dornack
SHADOW OF THE THIN MAN(1941)
Jane Dornacker
RIGHT STUFF, THE(1983)
Robert Dornam
X-15(1961)
Robert Dornan
STARFIGHTERS, THE(1964); TO THE SHORES OF HELL(1966); HELL ON WHEELS(1967)
Sallie Dornan
SERGEANT DEADHEAD(1965)
Sallie H. Dornan
MONEY TRAP, THE(1966)
Siegfried Dornbusch
ONE, TWO, THREE(1961)
Sandra Dorne
EYES THAT KILL(1947, Brit.); ALL OVER THE TOWN(1949, Brit.); DON'T EVER LEAVE ME(1949, Brit.); MARRY ME!(1949, Brit.); SARABAND(1949, Brit.); CLOUDED YELLOW, THE(1950, Brit.); DON'T SAY DIE(1950, Brit.); HAPPY GO LOVELY(1951, Brit.); MANIACS ON WHEELS(1951, Brit.); TRAVELLER'S JOY(1951, Brit.); HOLIDAY WEEK(1952, Brit.); 13 EAST STREET(1952, Brit.); ALF'S BABY(1953, Brit.); BEGGAR'S OPERA, THE(1953); GAY ADVENTURE, THE(1953, Brit.); MARILYN(1953, Brit.); WHEEL OF FATE(1953, Brit.); YELLOW BALLOON, THE(1953, Brit.); GOOD DIE YOUNG, THE(1954, Brit.); WEAK AND THE WICKED, THE(1954, Brit.); FINAL COLUMN, THE(1955, Brit.); POLICE DOG(1955, Brit.); ALIAS JOHN PRESTON(1956); DYNAMITERS, THE(1956, Brit.); IRON PETTICOAT, THE(1956, Brit.); OPERATION MURDER(1957, Brit.); THREE SUNDAYS TO LIVE(1957, Brit.); BANK RAIDERS, THE(1958, Brit.); ORDERS TO KILL(1958, Brit.); HOUSE IN MARSH ROAD, THE(1960, Brit.); NOT A HOPE IN HELL(1960, Brit.); DEVIL DOLL(1964, Brit.); SECRET DOOR, THE(1964); AMOROUS MR. PRAWN, THE(1965, Brit.); MALPAS MYSTERY, THE(1967, Brit.)
Brigitte Dornes
FINO A FARTI MALE(1969, Fr./Ital.), ed
Gypsey Dorney
NORMAN LOVES ROSE(1982, Aus.)
Roger Dorney
FIREFOX(1982), spec eff
Robert Dornhelm
SHE DANCES ALONE(1981, Aust./U.S.), d
Robert Dorning
SCOTLAND YARD INSPECTOR(1952, Brit.); LINKS OF JUSTICE(1958); MOMENT OF INDISCRETION(1958, Brit.); SECRET MAN, THE(1958, Brit.); INNOCENT MEETING(1959, Brit.); MAN ACCUSED(1959); NO SAFETY AHEAD(1959, Brit.); TOP FLOOR GIRL(1959, Brit.); MAN WHO WAS NOBODY, THE(1960, Brit.); DIE, DIE, MY DARLING(1965, Brit.); CUL-DE-SAC(1966, Brit.); SALT & PEPPER(1968, Brit.); SCHOOL FOR SEX(1969, Brit.); CONFESSIONS OF A POP PERFORMER(1975, Brit.); HUMAN FACTOR, THE(1979, Brit.); RAGTIME(1981); EVIL UNDER THE SUN(1982, Brit.)
Stacey Dorning
VICTOR FRANKENSTEIN(1975, Swed./Ireland)
Stacy Dorning
CROMWELL(1970, Brit.)
William Dornisch
BROTHERS(1977), ed
William P. Dornisch
JOHNNY GOT HIS GUN(1971), ed; STAR TREK II: THE WRATH OF KHAN(1982), ed
Therese Dorny
ABUSED CONFIDENCE(1938, Fr. ABUS DE CONFIANCE); DEVIL'S DAUGHTER(1949, Fr.); DIABOLIQUE(1955, Fr.)
Marie Doro
Silents
OLIVER TWIST(1916); 12-10(1919, Brit.)
Misc. Silents
COMMON GROUND(1916); DIPLOMACY(1916); HEART OF NORA FLYNN, THE(1916); LASH, THE(1916); WOOD NYMPH, THE(1916); CASTLES FOR TWO(1917); HEART'S DESIRE(1917); LOST AND WON(1917); MIDNIGHT GAMBOLS(1919, Brit.); SALLY BISHOP(1923, Brit.)
Mino Doro
TWO WEEKS IN ANOTHER TOWN(1962); BANDIT, THE(1949, Ital.); MAN FROM CAIRO, THE(1953); WAR AND PEACE(1956, Ital./U.S.); BEN HUR(1959); LAST DAYS OF POMPEII, THE(1960, Ital.); LEGIONS OF THE NILE(1960, Ital.); LA DOLCE VITA(1961, Ital./Fr.); EVERYBODY GO HOME!(1962, Fr./Ital.); HERCULES AND THE CAPTIVE WOMEN(1963, Fr./Ital.); 8 ½(1963, Ital.); DUEL OF CHAMPIONS(1964 Ital./Span.); HERCULES IN THE HAUNTED WORLD(1964, Ital.); WAR OF THE ZOMBIES, THE(1965 Ital.); ROVER, THE(1967, Ital.); UPPER HAND, THE(1967, Fr./Ital./Ger.); FEMMINA(1968 Fr./Ital./Ger.); GUILT IS NOT MINE(1968, Ital.);

LEATHER AND NYLON(1969, Fr./Ital.); HORNET'S NEST(1970)
Peggy Doro
THREE STEPS NORTH(1951)
Virginia Doro
EVIL EYE(1964 Ital.)
V. Dorofeyev
SECRET BRIGADE, THE(1951 USSR); BRIDE WITH A DOWRY(1954, USSR)
Vladimar Dorofeyev
SPRINGTIME ON THE VOLGA(1961, USSR)
Gyorgyi Dorogi
CONFIDENCE(1980, Hung.)
Z. Dorogova
LADY WITH THE DOG, THE(1962, USSR)
N. Dorokhin
UNIVERSITY OF LIFE(1941, USSR)
Nikolai Dorokhin
LAST HILL, THE(1945, USSR)
I. Doromin
CONCENTRATION CAMP(1939, USSR)
Mikhail Doronin
Misc. Silents
WHEN WILL WE DEAD AWAKEN?(1918, USSR)
V. Doronin
BRIDE WITH A DOWRY(1954, USSR)
Dina Doronne
CLOUDS OVER ISRAEL(1966, Israel)
R. Doroshenko
SONG OF THE FOREST(1963, USSR)
Jack Doroshow
ANDERSON TAPES, THE(1971)
Jackie Doroshow
MAKE A FACE(1971)
Dorothee
LOVE ON THE RUN(1980, Fr.); MON ONCLE D'AMERIQUE(1980, Fr.)
Bob Dorough
FAT ANGELS(1980, U.S./Span.), m
Adolph Dorr
MUSIC IN THE AIR(1934)
Dorothy Dorr
Silents
LEGEND OF HOLLYWOOD, THE(1924); QUICKER'N LIGHTNIN'(1925)
Lester Dorr
RIDERS OF THE PURPLE SAGE(1931); IF I HAD A MILLION(1932); BOWERY, THE(1933); LITTLE GIANT, THE(1933); DAMES(1934); JIMMY THE GENT(1934); SMARTY(1934); UPPER WORLD(1934); FRONT PAGE WOMAN(1935); RED SALUTE(1935); SHE GETS HER MAN(1935); SHOW THEM NO MERCY(1935); GREAT GUY(1936); LOVE BEFORE BREAKFAST(1936); PHANTOM PATROL(1936); RIDE 'EM COWBOY(1936); SNOWED UNDER(1936); SPENDTHRIFT(1936); CAPTAINS COURAGEOUS(1937); CRIMINALS OF THE AIR(1937); FIREFLY, THE(1937); HOLLYWOOD COWBOY(1937); WAY OUT WEST(1937); COMET OVER BROADWAY(1938); I AM THE LAW(1938); IN EARLY ARIZONA(1938); JUVENILE COURT(1938); MAIN EVENT, THE(1938); PENITENTIARY(1938); SPY RING, THE(1938); SWEETHEARTS(1938); SWISS MISS(1938); TEST PILOT(1938); THREE LOVES HAS NANCY(1938); YOU CAN'T TAKE IT WITH YOU(1938); GONE WITH THE WIND(1939); HOMICIDE BUREAU(1939); RIDE 'EM COWGIRL(1939); SOCIETY LAWYER(1939); STRONGER THAN DESIRE(1939); DANGER AHEAD(1940); MEXICAN SPITFIRE OUT WEST(1940); NO, NO NANETTE(1940); RETURN OF FRANK JAMES, THE(1940); SAILOR'S LADY(1940); TWO GIRLS ON BROADWAY(1940); I WANTED WINGS(1941); RELUCTANT DRAGON, THE(1941); SOUTH OF PANAMA(1941); SUNSET MURDER CASE(1941); THREE GIRLS ABOUT TOWN(1941); TWO LATINS FROM MANHATTAN(1941); UNFINISHED BUSINESS(1941); UNHOLY PARTNERS(1941); WHISTLING IN THE DARK(1941); YOU BELONG TO ME(1941); YOU'LL NEVER GET RICH(1941); GENTLEMAN JIM(1942); LADY IN A JAM(1942); MEET THE MOB(1942); MYSTERY OF MARIE ROGET, THE(1942); SABOTAGE SQUAD(1942); SLEEPYTIME GAL(1942); SPIRIT OF STANFORD, THE(1942); DESTROYER(1943); HITLER'S MADMAN(1943); ENEMY OF WOMEN(1944); FOUR JILLS IN A JEEP(1944); LADY IN THE DARK(1944); SHADOW OF SUSPICION(1944); DUFFY'S TAVERN(1945); JADE MASK, THE(1945); NOB HILL(1945); BOWERY BOMBSHELL(1946); DEADLINE FOR MURDER(1946); KID FROM BOOKLYN, THE(1946); NOTORIOUS(1946); SHADOW RETURNS, THE(1946); CASS TIMBERLANE(1947); PURSUED(1947); ROBIN OF TEXAS(1947); BIG CLOCK, THE(1948); COUNTESS OF MONTE CRISTO, THE(1948); JOAN OF ARC(1948); NIGHT HAS A THOUSAND EYES(1948); ON AN ISLAND WITH YOU(1948); SILVER RIVER(1948); VICIOUS CIRCLE, THE(1948); ON THE TOWN(1949); RED, HOT AND BLUE(1949); ROSEANNA McCOY(1949); TELL IT TO THE JUDGE(1949); WITHOUT HONOR(1949); BLONDE BANDIT, THE(1950); COVERED WAGON RAID(1950); WHERE DANGER LIVES(1950); BIG CARNIVAL, THE(1951); FOLLOW THE SUN(1951); NIGHT RIDERS OF MONTANA(1951); STRIP, THE(1951); TWO TICKETS TO BROADWAY(1951); GREATEST SHOW ON EARTH, THE(1952); SOMEBODY LOVES ME(1952); KILLERS FROM SPACE(1954); THREE RING CIRCUS(1954); GIRL RUSH, THE(1955); FIRST TRAVELING SALESLADY, THE(1956); HOT ROD GANG(1958); MARJORIE MORNINGSTAR(1958); ARSON FOR HIRE(1959); VICE RAID(1959); HOTEL(1967); AT LONG LAST LOVE(1975)
Sabi Dorr
1984
LITTLE DRUMMER GIRL, THE(1984)
Lucy Dorraine
CHRISTINA(1929)
Silents
ADORATION(1928)
Ethel Dorrance
Silents
HIS ROBE OF HONOR(1918), w
James Dorrance
Silents
HIS ROBE OF HONOR(1918), w
Thea Dorree
EIGHT GIRLS IN A BOAT(1932, Ger.)

Artie Dorrell
  BODY AND SOUL(1947)
Dick Dorrell
  BORDER WOLVES(1938); IN EARLY ARIZONA(1938)
Don Dorrell
  GAMBLER WORE A GUN, THE(1961); TAMMY, TELL ME TRUE(1961); ENSIGN
  PULVER(1964); NONE BUT THE BRAVE(1965, U.S./Jap.); THAT DARN CAT(1965)
Carlos Dorremochea
  1984
  MIDSUMMER NIGHT'S DREAM, A(1984, Brit./Span.), art d
V. Dorrer
  OTHELLO(1960, U.S.S.R.), art d
Petar Dorric
  SON OF SAMSON(1962, Fr./Ital./Yugo.)
Dorrie
  LUPE(1967)
Clint Dorrington
  FOREST RANGERS, THE(1942); STORY OF DR. WASSELL, THE(1944); TWO
  YEARS BEFORE THE MAST(1946); HURRICANE SMITH(1952)
Eve Dorrington
  Misc. Silents
  YOUR WIFE AND MINE(1919)
Hildra Dorrington
  IT ISN'T DONE(1937, Aus.)
Lucile Dorrington
  Misc. Silents
  INEVITABLE, THE(1917); LITTLE MISS FORTUNE(1917); LITTLE SAMARITAN,
  THE(1917)
Wayne Dorris
  TEX(1982)
Diana Dors
  DANCING WITH CRIME(1947, Brit.); CALENDAR, THE(1948, Brit.); HERE COME
  THE HUGGETTS(1948, Brit.); MY SISTER AND I(1948, Brit.); VOTE FOR HUG-
  GETT(1948, Brit.); BOY, A GIRL AND A BIKE, A(1949 Brit.); DIAMOND CITY(1949,
  Brit.); IT'S NOT CRICKET(1949, Brit.); DANCE HALL(1950, Brit.); GOOD TIME
  GIRL(1950, Brit.); OLIVER TWIST(1951, Brit.); WORM'S EYE VIEW(1951, Brit.); MAN
  BAIT(1952, Brit.); MY WIFE'S LODGER(1952, Brit.); GREAT GAME, THE(1953, Brit.);
  IS YOUR HONEYMOON REALLY NECESSARY?(1953, Brit.); IT'S A GRAND LI-
  FE(1953, Brit.); SAINT'S GIRL FRIDAY, THE(1954, Brit.); WEAK AND THE WICKED,
  THE(1954, Brit.); LADY GODIVA RIDES AGAIN(1955, Brit.); MISS TULIP STAYS
  THE NIGHT(1955, Brit.); BLONDE SINNER(1956, Brit.); KID FOR TWO FARTHINGS,
  A(1956, Brit.); ALLIGATOR NAMED DAISY, AN(1957, Brit.); AS LONG AS THEY'RE
  HAPPY(1957, Brit.); LONG HAUL, THE(1957, Brit.); UNHOLY WIFE, THE(1957);
  VALUE FOR MONEY(1957, Brit.); I MARRIED A WOMAN(1958); LOVE SPECIALIST,
  THE(1959, Ital.); ROOM 43(1959, Brit.); TREAD SOFTLY STRANGER(1959, Brit.);
  SCENT OF MYSTERY(1960); KING OF THE ROARING TWENTIES–THE STORY OF
  ARNOLD ROTHSTEIN(1961); ON THE DOUBLE(1961); MRS. GIBBONS' BOYS(1962,
  Brit.); WEST 11(1963, Brit.); COUNTERFEIT CONSTABLE, THE(1966, Fr.); SAND-
  WICH MAN, THE(1966, Brit.); BERSERK(1967); DANGER ROUTE(1968); HAM-
  MERHEAD(1968); BABY LOVE(1969, Brit.); DEEP END(1970 Ger./U.S.); THERE'S A
  GIRL IN MY SOUP(1970, Brit.); HANNIE CALDER(1971, Brit.); PIED PIPER,
  THE(1972, Brit.); AMAZING MR. BLUNDEN, THE(1973, Brit.); THEATRE OF
  BLOOD(1973, Brit.); CRAZE(1974, Brit.); FROM BEYOND THE GRAVE(1974, Brit.);
  NOTHING BUT THE NIGHT(1975, Brit.)
  Misc. Talkies
  GROOVE ROOM, THE(1974, Brit.)
Biddle Dorsay
  PERFECT SNOB, THE(1941)
Fifi Dorsay
  HOT FOR PARIS(1930); MR. LEMON OF ORANGE(1931)
Robert Dorsay
  LIFE BEGINS ANEW(1938, Ger.)
Robert Dorsen
  PANIC IN THE STREETS(1950)
Charles B. Dorsett
  FOOLS(1970)
Charles Dorsett
  DIRTY HARRY(1971); AMERICAN GRAFFITI(1973)
Chuck Dorsett
  PICKUP ON 101(1972); DIE LAUGHING(1980)
  1984
  IMPULSE(1984)
Curtis Dorsett
  Misc. Talkies
  FRONTIER WOMAN(1956)
Bob Dorsey
  IN A YEAR OF THIRTEEN MOONS(1980, Ger.)
Diane Dorsey
  PILLOW TO POST(1945)
Don Dorsey
  Misc. Talkies
  LOVE AND KISSES(?), d
Jack Dorsey
  VISITOR, THE(1980, Ital./U.S.)
Jimmy Dorsey
  FABULOUS DORSEYS, THE(1947); MUSIC MAN(1948); MAKE BELIEVE BALL-
  ROOM(1949)
Joe A. Dorsey
  LINCOLN CONSPIRACY, THE(1977); NORMA RAE(1979)
Joe Dorsey
  HOPSCOTCH(1980); BRAINSTORM(1983); WARGAMES(1983)
  1984
  PHILADELPHIA EXPERIMENT, THE(1984)
Joseph Dorsey
  LONGEST YARD, THE(1974); GRIZZLY(1976)
Kenneth Dorsey
  OTHER SIDE OF THE MOUNTAIN, THE(1975)

Kim Dorsey
  TOGETHER BROTHERS(1974)
Lee Dorsey
  Misc. Talkies
  ROBIN(1979)
Maggie Dorsey
  TALES OF MANHATTAN(1942)
Michael Dorsey
  1984
  BIG MEAT EATER(1984, Can.), spec eff
Mike Dorsey
  LITTLE JUNGLE BOY(1969, Aus.)
Reginald Dorsey
  BOOK OF NUMBERS(1973)
Sandra Dorsey
  NORMA RAE(1979)
Tommy Dorsey
  FABULOUS DORSEYS, THE(1947); DISC JOCKEY(1951)
Ellen Dorsher
  HOUSE ON SORORITY ROW, THE(1983)
Nathaniel Dorsky
  REVENGE OF THE CHEERLEADERS(1976), p, w, ph
Judith Dorsman
  CADDIE(1976, Aus.), cos; RIDE A WILD PONY(1976, U.S./Aus.), cos; IRISHMAN,
  THE(1978, Aus.), cos
Judy Dorsman
  PICNIC AT HANGING ROCK(1975, Aus.), cos; PICTURE SHOW MAN, THE(1980,
  Aus.), cos
Richard J. Dorso
  SIERRA STRANGER(1957), w
David Dortort
  CLASH BY NIGHT(1952), w; LUSTY MEN, THE(1952), w; CRY IN THE NIGHT,
  A(1956), w; REPRISAL(1956), w; BIG LAND, THE(1957), w
Erdmann Dortschy
  NOT RECONCILED, OR "ONLY VIOLENCE HELPS WHERE IT RULES"(1969, Ger.)
Dorville
  COURIER OF LYONS(1938, Fr.); ENTENTE CORDIALE(1939, Fr.); SHANGHAI
  DRAMA, THE(1945, Fr.)
Edgar Dorwell
  HARLEM IS HEAVEN(1932), m
Mlle. Doryans
  LA CHIENNE(1975, Fr.)
Avraham Doryon
  DREAM NO MORE(1950, Palestine)
Gabrielle Dorziat
  COURRIER SUD(1937, Fr.); MAYERLING(1937, Fr.); END OF A DAY, THE(1939, Fr.);
  HATRED(1941, Fr.); SHANGHAI DRAMA, THE(1945, Fr.); HER FIRST AFFAIR(1947,
  Fr.); RUY BLAS(1948, Fr.); JUST A BIG, SIMPLE GIRL(1949, Fr.); MONSIEUR
  VINCENT(1949, Fr.); BALLERINA(1950, Fr.); LES PARENTS TERRIBLES(1950, Fr.);
  MANON(1950, Fr.); FRENCH WAY, THE(1952, Fr.); ACT OF LOVE(1953); LITTLE BOY
  LOST(1953); SO LITTLE TIME(1953, Brit.); MADAME DU BARRY(1954 Fr./Ital.);
  GIGOT(1962); MONKEY IN WINTER, A(1962, Fr.); MAGNIFICENT SINNER(1963, Fr.)
Joao Felicio dos Santos
  XICA(1982, Braz.), a, w
Jorge dos Santos
  BLACK ORPHEUS(1959 Fr./Ital./Braz.)
Jose Nilson dos Santos
  PIXOTE(1981, Braz.)
Nelson Pereira dos Santos
  1984
  MEMOIRS OF PRISON(1984, Braz.), d&w
Susana Dosamantes
  RIO LOBO(1970)
Susana Dosamates
  Misc. Talkies
  TARGET EAGLE(1982)
Fred Dosch
  TO HAVE AND HAVE NOT(1944)
Michel Doset
  1984
  LE DERNIER COMBAT(1984, Fr.)
Charles Dosinan
  WANDA(1971)
Andrea Dosne
  WATERLOO(1970, Ital./USSR)
Leonard Doss
  YOU'RE MY EVERYTHING(1949), m
Sharon Doss
  1984
  PHILADELPHIA EXPERIMENT, THE(1984)
Tommy Doss
  RIO GRANDE(1950)
Chappell Dossett
  MADAME X(1929); MYSTERIOUS DR. FU MANCHU, THE(1929); TALE OF TWO
  CITIES, A(1935)
  Silents
  JUDGE NOT(1920, Brit.); NAME THE WOMAN(1928)
  Misc. Silents
  CHARITY ANN(1915, Brit.); PARTNERS AT LAST(1916, Brit.)
Curtis Dossett
  NATCHEZ TRACE(1960)
Jane Dossick
  P.O.W., THE(1973), p
Joanna Lee Dossick
  P.O.W., THE(1973)
Philip H. Dossick
  P.O.W., THE(1973), d&w, ed

Karel Dostal
SKELETON ON HORSEBACK(1940, Czech.); BOHEMIAN RAPTURE(1948, Czech); KRAKATIT(1948, Czech.)

Kathryn Reve Doster
STUDENT BODIES(1981)

Vojislav Dostic
INNOCENCE UNPROTECTED(1971, Yugo.), m

Feodor Dostoevski
HOUSE OF DEATH(1932, USSR), w

Fedor Mikhailovich Dostoyevsky
WHITE NIGHTS(1961, Ital./Fr.), w

Feodor Dostoyevsky
CRIME AND PUNISHMENT(1935, Fr.), w, w; CRIME AND PUNISHMENT(1948, Swed.), w; IDIOT, THE(1948, Fr.), w; GREAT SINNER, THE(1949), w; GAMBLER, THE(1958, Fr.), w; CRIME AND PUNISHMENT, U.S.A.(1959), w; IDIOT, THE(1960, USSR), d&w; CRIME AND PUNISHMENT(1975, USSR), w

Feodor Mikhailovich Dostoyevsky
IDIOT, THE(1963, Jap.), w

Fyodor Dostoyevsky
KARAMAZOV(1931, Ger.), w; ETERNAL HUSBAND, THE(1946, Fr.), w; BROTHERS KARAMAZOV, THE(1958), w; PICKPOCKET(1963, Fr.), w; GENTLE CREATURE, A(1971, Fr.), w; FOUR NIGHTS OF A DREAMER(1972, Fr.), w
Silents
CRIME AND PUNISHMENT(1917), w

Dot and Dash
TEMPTATION(1936)

Dvora Dotan
EVERY BASTARD A KING(1968, Israel)

Karen Dotrice
THREE LIVES OF THOMASINA, THE(1963, U.S./Brit.); MARY POPPINS(1964); GNOME-MOBILE, THE(1967); JOSEPH ANDREWS(1977, Brit.); THIRTY NINE STEPS, THE(1978, Brit.)

Kay Dotrice
1984
CHEECH AND CHONG'S THE CORSICAN BROTHERS(1984)

Michele Dotrice
DEVIL'S OWN, THE(1967, Brit.); AND SOON THE DARKNESS(1970, Brit.); BLOOD ON SATAN'S CLAW, THE(1970, Brit.); JANE EYRE(1971, Brit.)

Roy Dotrice
CONCRETE JUNGLE, THE(1962, Brit.); HEROES OF TELEMARK, THE(1965, Brit.); TWIST OF SAND, A(1968, Brit.); LOCK UP YOUR DAUGHTERS(1969, Brit.); NICHOLAS AND ALEXANDRA(1971, Brit.); TOOMORROW(1970, Brit.); BUTTERCUP CHAIN, THE(1971, Brit.); TALES FROM THE CRYPT(1972, Brit.)
1984
AMADEUS(1984); CHEECH AND CHONG'S THE CORSICAN BROTHERS(1984)
Misc. Talkies
ONE OF THOSE THINGS(1974, Brit.)

Alyosha Dotsenko
SUMMER TO REMEMBER, A(1961, USSR)

Ernest Dotson
GOOD MORNING, MISS DOVE(1955)

Ernie Dotson
OUTLAW'S SON(1957)

Rhonda Dotson
1984
SONGWRITER(1984)

Elizabeth Dott
HOUND OF THE BASKERVILLES, THE(1959, Brit.)

Attilio Dottesio
SAMSON AND THE SLAVE QUEEN(1963, Ital.); LET'S TALK ABOUT WOMEN(1964, Fr./Ital.)

Carlo Dotto
VERTIGO(1958)

Douglas Z. Dotty
Silents
DRESS PARADE(1927), w

Carlotta Doty
Misc. Silents
LION AND THE MOUSE, THE(1914)

Douglas Doty
COLLEGE LOVERS(1930), w; LAUGHTER(1930), w; DIE MANNER UM LUCIE(1931), w; SILENT WITNESS, THE(1932), w; IMPORTANT WITNESS, THE(1933), w; RACETRACK(1933), w; GALLANT LADY(1934), w; THREE ON A HONEYMOON(1934), w; ALWAYS GOODBYE(1938), w
Silents
HER WINNING WAY(1921), w; KISS IN TIME, A(1921), w; SHAM(1921), w; SPEED GIRL, THE(1921), w; NANCY FROM NOWHERE(1922), w; BROADWAY AFTER DARK(1924), w; AFTER BUSINESS HOURS(1925), w; UNCHASTENED WOMAN(1925), w; WEDDING SONG, THE(1925), w; RED DICE(1926), w; NOBODY'S WIDOW(1927), w; VANITY(1927), w

Douglas Z. Doty
PLEASURE CRAZED(1929), w; VEILED WOMAN, THE(1929), w
Silents
MAN BAIT(1926), w; MASKED EMOTIONS(1929), t

Margaret Doty
1984
HIGHPOINT(1984, Can.)

Alain Douarinou
LA MARSEILLAISE(1938, Fr.), ph

Jacqueline Douarinou
NIGHT AFFAIR(1961, Fr.), ed

Jean Douarinou
CANDIDE(1962, Fr.), art d; TEMPTATION(1962, Fr.), art d; VISCOUNT, THE(1967, Fr./Span./Ital./Ger.), art d

Steve Doubet
SILENT SCREAM(1980)

Harold Double
Silents
ALL THE WORLD'S A STAGE(1917, Brit.), p

Frank Doubleday
FIRST NUDIE MUSICAL, THE(1976); BIG FIX, THE(1978)

Kay Doubleday
MAD DOG COLL(1961); ACROSS THE RIVER(1965); SLENDER THREAD, THE(1965)

Anthony Doublin
CREATURE WASN'T NICE,THE(1981), spec eff

Albert Doubrava
Silents
DOWN TO THE SEA IN SHIPS(1923), ph

Marie Doucemetier
Misc. Silents
SOLD APPETITE, THE(1928, USSR)

Catharine Doucet
PARTY'S OVER, THE(1934); WAKE UP AND DREAM(1934); AGE OF INDISCRETION(1935); EIGHT BELLS(1935); MILLIONS IN THE AIR(1935); RENDEZVOUS AT MIDNIGHT(1935); GOLDEN ARROW, THE(1936); LONGEST NIGHT, THE(1936); JIM HANVEY, DETECTIVE(1937); IT STARTED WITH EVE(1941); NOTHING BUT THE TRUTH(1941); THERE'S ONE BORN EVERY MINUTE(1942)

Catherine Doucet
AS HUSBANDS GO(1934); LITTLE MAN, WHAT NOW?(1934); SERVANTS' ENTRANCE(1934); ACCENT ON YOUTH(1935); LUCKIEST GIRL IN THE WORLD, THE(1936); POPPY(1936); THESE THREE(1936); MAN OF THE PEOPLE(1937); OH DOCTOR(1937); WHEN YOU'RE IN LOVE(1937); DUDE GOES WEST, THE(1948); FAMILY HONEYMOON(1948); HOLLOW TRIUMPH(1948); DETECTIVE STORY(1951)

Elaina Doucet
CARNY(1980)

Paul Doucet
Silents
FAIR PRETENDER, THE(1918); KNIFE, THE(1918); AMERICA(1924)
Misc. Silents
DEVIL'S DAUGHTER, THE(1915); JAFFERY(1915); JUDGEMENT HOUSE, THE(1917); DANGER GAME, THE(1918); HEART OF A SIREN(1925)

Greg Doucette
VERDICT, THE(1982)

Jeff Doucette
1984
SPLASH(1984)

John A. Doucette
TRAIN TO ALCATRAZ(1948)

John Doucette
RIDE THE PINK HORSE(1947); ROAD TO THE BIG HOUSE(1947); CANON CITY(1948); I WOULDN'T BE IN YOUR SHOES(1948); IN THIS CORNER(1948); ROGUES' REGIMENT(1948); STATION WEST(1948); BLACK BOOK, THE(1949); CRISS CROSS(1949); CROOKED WAY, THE(1949); FIGHTING O'FLYNN, THE(1949); FOUNTAINHEAD, THE(1949); BORDER TREASURE(1950); BREAKING POINT, THE(1950); BROKEN ARROW(1950); CONVICTED(1950); COUNTERSPY MEETS SCOTLAND YARD(1950); CUSTOMS AGENT(1950); FULLER BRUSH GIRL, THE(1950); IROQUOIS TRAIL, THE(1950); LOVE THAT BRUTE(1950); SIERRA(1950); VICIOUS YEARS, THE(1950); WINCHESTER '73(1950); BANDITS OF EL DORADO(1951); CAVALRY SCOUT(1951); CORKY OF GASOLINE ALLEY(1951); FIXED BAYONETS(1951); LADY PAYS OFF, THE(1951); STRANGERS ON A TRAIN(1951); TALES OF ROBIN HOOD(1951); TEXAS RANGERS, THE(1951); THUNDER IN GOD'S COUNTRY(1951); YUKON MANHUNT(1951); BUGLES IN THE AFTERNOON(1952); DEADLINE–U.S.A.(1952); DESERT PURSUIT(1952); HIGH NOON(1952); PHONE CALL FROM A STRANGER(1952); PRIDE OF ST. LOUIS, THE(1952); RANCHO NOTORIOUS(1952); SAN FRANCISCO STORY, THE(1952); TOUGHEST MAN IN ARIZONA(1952); TREASURE OF LOST CANYON, THE(1952); WOMAN IN THE DARK(1952); AMBUSH AT TOMAHAWK GAP(1953); BIG HEAT, THE(1953); CITY OF BAD MEN(1953); FLIGHT TO TANGIER(1953); GOLDTOWN GHOST RIDERS(1953); JULIUS CAESAR(1953); ROBE, THE(1953); WAR PAINT(1953); BEACHHEAD(1954); CRY VENGEANCE(1954); DESTRY(1954); EXECUTIVE SUITE(1954); FORTYNINERS, THE(1954); LAST TIME I SAW PARIS, THE(1954); RETURN FROM THE SEA(1954); RIVER OF NO RETURN(1954); THERE'S NO BUSINESS LIKE SHOW BUSINESS(1954); ANNAPOLIS STORY, AN(1955); FAR COUNTRY, THE(1955); HOUSE OF BAMBOO(1955); NEW YORK CONFIDENTIAL(1955); SEA CHASE, THE(1955); SEVEN CITIES OF GOLD(1955); DAKOTA INCIDENT(1956); FASTEST GUN ALIVE(1956); GHOST TOWN(1956); MAVERICK QUEEN, THE(1956); QUINCANNON, FRONTIER SCOUT(1956); THUNDER OVER ARIZONA(1956); GUNFIRE AT INDIAN GAP(1957); KISS THEM FOR ME(1957); LAST OF THE BADMEN(1957); LAWLESS EIGHTIES, THE(1957); LONELY MAN, THE(1957); PEYTON PLACE(1957); PHANTOM STAGECOACH, THE(1957); SABU AND THE MAGIC RING(1957); TRUE STORY OF JESSE JAMES, THE(1957); CROOKED CIRCLE, THE(1958); GANG WAR(1958); HUNTERS, THE(1958); TOO MUCH, TOO SOON(1958); HERE COME THE JETS(1959); CLEOPATRA(1963); SEVEN FACES OF DR. LAO(1964); SONS OF KATIE ELDER, THE(1965); NEVADA SMITH(1966); PARADISE, HAWAIIAN STYLE(1966); FASTEST GUITAR ALIVE, THE(1967); JOURNEY TO SHILOH(1968); TRUE GRIT(1969); PATTON(1970); BIG JAKE(1971); ONE MORE TRAIN TO ROB(1971); ONE LITTLE INDIAN(1973); FIGHTING MAD(1976)
Misc. Talkies
GHOST OF CROSSBONES CANYON, THE(1952)

Pamela Doucette
1984
PHILADELPHIA EXPERIMENT, THE(1984)

Rudy Doucette
LOVE BUG, THE(1968)

Jean Douchet
SIX IN PARIS(1968, Fr.), d, w

Earle Doud
RACQUET(1979), w

Gil Doud
FORBIDDEN(1953), w; THUNDER BAY(1953), w; SASKATCHEWAN(1954), w; PORT OF HELL(1955), w; TO HELL AND BACK(1955), w; WALK THE PROUD LAND(1956), w; HELL TO ETERNITY(1960), w

Jack Doud
Silents
OH, LADY, LADY(1920)

A. Douda
Silents
STRANGER THAN FICTION(1921), art d
Solo Doudauz
DEAD MARCH, THE(1937)
Salo Douday
HOUSE ON 92ND STREET, THE(1945); SIDELONG GLANCES OF A PIGEON
KICKER, THE(1970)
Lorena Doude
SHAME OF THE SABINE WOMEN, THE(1962, Mex.)
Teresa Doude
SHAME OF THE SABINE WOMEN, THE(1962, Mex.)
Van Doude
HAPPY ROAD, THE(1957); LOVE IN THE AFTERNOON(1957); BREATHLESS(1959,
Fr.); MAXIME(1962, Fr.); PASSION OF SLOW FIRE, THE(1962, Fr.); BRIDE WORE
BLACK, THE(1968, Fr./Ital.); Z(1969, Fr./Algeria); JE T'AIME, JE T'AIME(1972,
Fr./Swed.); DAY OF THE JACKAL, THE(1973, Brit./Fr.)
Clement Douenias
CROSSROADS(1938, Fr.), titles; ALIBI, THE(1939, Fr.), titles
Robin Douet
1984
WINTER FLIGHT(1984, Brit.), p
Peter Douett
ADULTEROUS AFFAIR(1966), art d
Bernard Dougall
LET'S MAKE MUSIC(1940), w
Vikki Dougan
TUNNEL OF LOVE, THE(1958); HERE COME THE JETS(1959); REBEL SET,
THE(1959); HOOTENANNY HOOT(1963)
Doughboy
Silents
WELCOME CHILDREN(1921)
Chuck Dougherty
1984
PURPLE HEARTS(1984)
Dick Dougherty
TOMORROW(1972)
Herschel Dougherty
TEA FOR TWO(1950); LULLABY OF BROADWAY, THE(1951)
Jack Dougherty
CHARLIE CHAN ON BROADWAY(1937); DOUBLE WEDDING(1937); GAME THAT
KILLS, THE(1937); YODELIN' KID FROM PINE RIDGE(1937); PENITENTIARY(1938)
Silents
IMPULSE(1922); SECOND HAND ROSE(1922); MONEY! MONEY! MONEY!(1923);
SPECIAL DELIVERY(1927); GYPSY OF THE NORTH(1928)
Misc. Silents
GREATER CLAIM, THE(1921)
Joe Dougherty
KNOCK ON ANY DOOR(1949); SHAKEDOWN(1950)
Kathleen Dougherty
1984
NOTHING LASTS FOREVER(1984), ed
Priscilla Dougherty
1984
SONGWRITER(1984)
Richard Dougherty
MADIGAN(1968), w
Terry Dougherty
LONG SHOT(1981, Brit.), m
John Doughten
FEVER HEAT(1968)
Russell S. Doughton
HOSTAGE, THE(1966), p&d
Russell S. Doughten, Jr.
FEVER HEAT(1968), p&d
Carol Doughty
TRACK OF THUNDER(1967)
Chuck Doughty
COUNTRY BOY(1966); TRACK OF THUNDER(1967)
Elsie Doughty
THERE'S ALWAYS VANILLA(1972)
Harold Doughty
FANTASIA(1940), art d
Henry Doughty
Silents
AUCTION MART, THE(1920, Brit.); POTTER'S CLAY(1922, Brit.)
Neal Doughty
FM(1978)
Peter Doughty
NOW BARABBAS WAS A ROBBER(1949, Brit.)
Richard Doughty
DANDY, THE ALL AMERICAN GIRL(1976)
Yvonne Doughty
WILD ONE, THE(1953)
Dougie Millings & Son
HARD DAY'S NIGHT, A(1964, Brit.), cos
Alan Douglas
DANGEROUS MONEY(1946); SUNNYSIDE(1979), m
Alicia Douglas
1,000 SHAPES OF A FEMALE(1963)
Alistair Douglas
1984
PALLET ON THE FLOOR(1984, New Zealand)
Allan Douglas
SAIGON(1948); DARLING, HOW COULD YOU!(1951); LITTLE BOY LOST(1953);
COUNTRY GIRL, THE(1954)
Angela Douglas
FEET OF CLAY(1960, Brit.); SHAKEDOWN, THE(1960, Brit.); GENTLE TERROR,
THE(1962, Brit.); MURDER IN EDEN(1962, Brit.); DREAM MAKER, THE(1963, Brit.);
COMEDY MAN, THE(1964); JOHN GOLDFARB, PLEASE COME HOME(1964); SOME

PEOPLE(1964, Brit.); CARRY ON COWBOY(1966, Brit.); CARRY ON SCREA-
MING(1966, Brit.); FOLLOW THAT CAMEL(1967, Brit.); MAROC 7(1967, Brit.); CARRY
ON, UP THE KHYBER(1968, Brit.); DIGBY, THE BIGGEST DOG IN THE
WORLD(1974, Brit.)
Anita Douglas
I AM A CAMERA(1955, Brit.)
Ann Douglas
WIDOW FROM MONTE CARLO, THE(1936)
Anne Douglas
SCALAWAG(1973, Yugo.), p
Barbara Douglas
RANDOLPH FAMILY, THE(1945, Brit.); TO BE FREE(1972); YOUR THREE MI-
NUTES ARE UP(1973); CRAZY WORLD OF JULIUS VROODER, THE(1974)
Misc. Talkies
IMAGO(1970)
Beth Douglas
LIFE OF HER OWN, A(1950)
Betty Douglas
NOTHING SACRED(1937); VOGUES OF 1938(1937); GOLDWYN FOLLIES,
THE(1938)
Bill Douglas
MY CHILDHOOD(1972, Brit.), d&w; MY AIN FOLK(1974, Brit.), d&w; MY WAY
HOME(1978, Brit.), d&w
Bob W. Douglas
1984
RIVER, THE(1984)
Buddy Douglas
PUFNSTUF(1970); CALIFORNIA SUITE(1978)
Burt Douglas
HANDLE WITH CARE(1958); HIGH SCHOOL CONFIDENTIAL(1958); LAW AND
JAKE WADE, THE(1958); PARTY GIRL(1958); PLEASE DON'T EAT THE DAI-
SIES(1960); RESTLESS ONES, THE(1965)
Byron Douglas
DRAKE CASE, THE(1929)
Silents
WINNING STROKE, THE(1919); BEYOND PRICE(1921); KNOW YOUR MEN(1921);
NET, THE(1923); SILENT COMMAND, THE(1923); IT IS THE LAW(1924); COWARD,
THE(1927); DEAD MAN'S CURVE(1928); SPEEDY(1928)
Misc. Silents
PLUNGER, THE(1920); THAT DEVIL QUEMADO(1925); RED CLAY(1927); BORN TO
THE SADDLE(1929); MAN, WOMAN AND WIFE(1929)
Carlos Douglas
HOT MILLIONS(1968, Brit.)
Carol Douglas
PEPE(1960); STRANGERS WHEN WE MEET(1960)
Carole Douglas
BIG SLEEP, THE(1946)
Cathy Douglas
Misc. Talkies
RIDERS OF THE PONY EXPRESS(1949)
Charles Douglas
MISTER BROWN(1972)
Silents
RING AND THE MAN, THE(1914)
Chet Douglas
CRY FOR HAPPY(1961); TWO RODE TOGETHER(1961); UNDERWATER CITY,
THE(1962); REQUIEM FOR A GUNFIGHTER(1965)
Chloe Douglas
GIVE US THIS NIGHT(1936)
Chuck Douglas, Jr.
SWEET JESUS, PREACHER MAN(1973)
Colin Douglas
DICK BARTON–SPECIAL AGENT(1948, Brit.); GHOST SHIP(1953, Brit.); HORNET'S
NEST, THE(1955, Brit.); MIRACLE IN SOHO(1957, Brit.); CRAWLING EYE, THE(1958,
Brit.); NIGHT CREATURES(1962, Brit.); VALIANT, THE(1962, Brit./Ital.); DON'T
RAISE THE BRIDGE, LOWER THE RIVER(1968, Brit.)
Craig Douglas
RING-A-DING RHYTHM(1962, Brit. 73m Amicus/COL bw (G.B: IT'S TRAD, DAD!);
MURDER CAN BE DEADLY(1963, Brit.)
Damon Douglas
BABY BLUE MARINE(1976); FROM NOON TO THREE(1976); MASSACRE AT
CENTRAL HIGH(1976); OUR WINNING SEASON(1978); SKATEBOARD(1978); REUB-
EN, REUBEN(1983)
Debbie Douglas
TRADER HORNEE(1970)
Deon Douglas
OUT OF SIGHT(1966)
Devon Douglas
WHERE ANGELS GO...TROUBLE FOLLOWS(1968)
Diana Douglas
DAMES(1934); KEEPER OF THE FLAME(1942); LATE GEORGE APLEY, THE(1947);
LET'S LIVE AGAIN(1948); SIGN OF THE RAM, THE(1948); HOUSE OF STRAN-
GERS(1949); WHISTLE AT EATON FALLS(1951); STORM OVER TIBET(1952); MON-
SOON(1953); INDIAN FIGHTER, THE(1955); LOVING(1970); ANOTHER MAN,
ANOTHER CHANCE(1977 Fr./US); JAWS OF SATAN(1980); STAR CHAMBER,
THE(1983)
Don Douglas
GREAT GABBO, THE(1929); JIMMY THE GENT(1934); OPERATOR 13(1934); CON-
VICTED(1938); JUDGE HARDY'S CHILDREN(1938); LAW OF THE TEXAN(1938);
TEST PILOT(1938); DEAD END KIDS ON DRESS PARADE(1939); FUGITIVE AT
LARGE(1939); I AM NOT AFRAID(1939); JESSE JAMES(1939); MR. MOTO IN
DANGER ISLAND(1939); MYSTERIOUS MISS X, THE(1939); ORPHANS OF THE
STREET(1939); SABOTAGE(1939); SECOND FIDDLE(1939); SMASHING THE
MONEY RING(1939); SPECIAL INSPECTOR(1939); WINGS OF THE NAVY(1939);
ZERO HOUR, THE(1939); CHARLIE CHAN IN PANAMA(1940); ISLAND OF
DOOMED MEN(1940); DEAD MEN TELL(1941); GET-AWAY, THE(1941); GREAT
SWINDLE, THE(1941); HOLD BACK THE DAWN(1941); MELODY LANE(1941);
MERCY ISLAND(1941); MURDER AMONG FRIENDS(1941); SLEEPERS WEST(1941);
WHISTLING IN THE DARK(1941); DARING YOUNG MAN, THE(1942); JUKE BOX
JENNY(1942); LITTLE TOKYO, U.S.A.(1942); NOW, VOYAGER(1942); ON THE SUN-

NY SIDE(1942); TALES OF MANHATTAN(1942); ACTION IN THE NORTH ATLANTIC(1943); APPOINTMENT IN BERLIN(1943); BEHIND THE RISING SUN(1943); HE'S MY GUY(1943); MEANEST MAN IN THE WORLD, THE(1943); MORE THE MERRIER, THE(1943); WINTERTIME(1943); FALCON OUT WEST, THE(1944); HEAVENLY DAYS(1944); SHOW BUSINESS(1944); TALL IN THE SADDLE(1944); GRISSLY'S MILLIONS(1945); MURDER, MY SWEET(1945); ROYAL SCANDAL, A(1945); STRANGE MR. GREGORY, THE(1945); TARZAN AND THE AMAZONS(1945); TOKYO ROSE(1945); CLUB HAVANA(1946); GILDA(1946); TRUTH ABOUT MURDER, THE(1946); SPELL OF THE HYPNOTIST(1956); UNDERWORLD U.S.A.(1961)

Donald Douglas

TONIGHT AT TWELVE(1929); HE COULDN'T TAKE IT(1934); LAZY RIVER(1934); MEN IN WHITE(1934); HEADIN' EAST(1937); NAVY BLUE AND GOLD(1937); ALEXANDER'S RAGTIME BAND(1938); CROWD ROARS, THE(1938); FAST COMPANY(1938); GLADIATOR, THE(1938); SMASHING THE RACKETS(1938); HOUSE OF FEAR, THE(1939); MANHATTAN SHAKEDOWN(1939); SERGEANT MADDEN(1939); STRONGER THAN DESIRE(1939); WITHIN THE LAW(1939); CALLING PHILO VANCE(1940); EDISON, THE MAN(1940); FLIGHT COMMAND(1940); FUGITIVE FROM JUSTICE, A(1940); GALLANT SONS(1940); I LOVE YOU AGAIN(1940); QUEEN OF THE MOB(1940); ANDY HARDY'S PRIVATE SECRETARY(1941); CHEERS FOR MISS BISHOP(1941); NIGHT OF JANUARY 16TH(1941); SERGEANT YORK(1941); SHOT IN THE DARK, THE(1941); CRYSTAL BALL, THE(1943); TUNES OF GLORY(1960, Brit.); RECKONING, THE(1971, Brit.)
1984
GIVE MY REGARDS TO BROAD STREET(1984, Brit.)

Donald A. Douglas

HEY THERE, IT'S YOGI BEAR(1964), ed

Donna Douglas

CAREER(1959); LOVER COME BACK(1961); FRANKIE AND JOHNNY(1966)

Dorothy Douglas

OUT OF THE BLUE(1947); DUCHESS OF IDAHO, THE(1950)

Earl Douglas

FIGHTING CABALLERO(1935); PAROLED FROM THE BIG HOUSE(1938); SWISS MISS(1938); CRASHING THRU(1939); DOWN THE WYOMING TRAIL(1939); TRIGGER PALS(1939); WILD HORSE CANYON(1939); DANGER AHEAD(1940); MURDER ON THE YUKON(1940); RHYTHM OF THE RIO GRANDE(1940); YUKON FLIGHT(1940); GUN MAN FROM BODIE, THE(1941); LAS VEGAS NIGHTS(1941)
Misc. Talkies
RIDERS OF THE SAGE(1939)
Misc. Silents
HERE HE COMES(1926); SEE YOU LATER(1928)

Earle Douglas

CRIME AFLOAT(1937); MILE A MINUTE LOVE(1937); RIDING THE SUNSET TRAIL(1941)
Misc. Silents
KEEP GOING(1926); I'LL BE THERE(1927)

Edward Douglas

Silents
ADAM AND EVA(1923)

Eleanora Douglas

EDUCATION OF SONNY CARSON, THE(1974)

Eric Douglas

GUNFIGHT, A(1971)
1984
FLAMINGO KID, THE(1984)

Ernest A. Douglas

Silents
GREAT GAME, THE(1918, Brit.); ERNEST MALTRAVERS(1920, Brit.); SHOEBLACK OF PICCADILLY, THE(1920, Brit.); OUT TO WIN(1923, Brit.)
Misc. Silents
CALL OF THE PIPES, THE(1917, Brit.); MASTER OF GRAY, THE(1918, Brit.); MATT(1918, Brit.)

Ethel Douglas

Silents
FATHER O'FLYNN(1919, Brit.)

Eve Douglas

MAN, WOMAN AND CHILD(1983)

Everett Douglas

STRAIGHT FROM THE SHOULDER(1936), ed; EMERGENCY SQUAD(1940), ed; AMONG THE LIVING(1941), ed; MONSTER AND THE GIRL, THE(1941), ed; HENRY ALDRICH, EDITOR(1942), ed; HENRY AND DIZZY(1942), ed; HENRY ALDRICH HAUNTS A HOUSE(1943), ed; HENRY ALDRICH, BOY SCOUT(1944), ed; HENRY ALDRICH PLAYS CUPID(1944), ed; HENRY ALDRICH'S LITTLE SECRET(1944), ed; NATIONAL BARN DANCE(1944), ed; VIRGINIAN, THE(1946), ed; LADIES' MAN(1947), ed; WELCOME STRANGER(1947), ed; MISS TATLOCK'S MILLIONS(1948), ed; MR. MUSIC(1950), ed; JENNIFER(1953), ed; NAKED JUNGLE, THE(1953), ed; THUNDER IN THE EAST(1953), ph; WAR OF THE WORLDS, THE(1953), ed; CONQUEST OF SPACE(1955), ed; SCARLET HOUR, THE(1956), ed; JOKER IS WILD, THE(1957), ed; OMAR KHAYYAM(1957), ed; AS YOUNG AS WE ARE(1958), ed; MARACAIBO(1958), ed; PARTY CRASHERS, THE(1958), ed; JAYHAWKERS, THE(1959), ed; TRAP, THE(1959), ed

F.E. Douglas

BAR L RANCH(1930), p; BEYOND THE RIO GRANDE(1930), p; CANYON HAWKS(1930), p; FIREBRAND JORDAN(1930), p; PHANTOM OF THE DESERT(1930), p; RIDIN' LAW(1930), p; TRAILS OF DANGER(1930), p.; LAW OF THE RIO GRANDE(1931), p; WESTWARD BOUND(1931), p

Felicity Douglas

IT'S NEVER TOO LATE(1958, Brit.), w; TEENAGE BAD GIRL(1959, Brit.), w

Flora E. Douglas

Silents
PHANTOM OF THE NORTH(1929), w

Frank Douglas

KILLER FORCE(1975, Switz./Ireland)

Gale Douglas

DARK ROAD, THE(1948, Brit.); MEET THE DUKE(1949, Brit.)

George Douglas

ARSENE LUPIN RETURNS(1938); PALS OF THE SADDLE(1938); REBELLIOUS DAUGHTERS(1938); YOUNG FUGITIVES(1938); GOOD GIRLS GO TO PARIS(1939); KANSAS TERRORS, THE(1939); LET US LIVE(1939); NIGHT RIDERS, THE(1939); CITY OF CHANCE(1940); COVERED WAGON DAYS(1940); HOLD THAT WOMAN(1940); LONE STAR RAIDERS(1940); TULSA KID, THE(1940); SUNSET MUR-

DER CASE(1941); HOME IN WYOMIN'(1942); RIDERS OF THE SANTA FE(1944); DOUBLE LIFE, A(1947); HER HUSBAND'S AFFAIRS(1947); HAZARD(1948); MY OWN TRUE LOVE(1948); UNDERCOVER MAN, THE(1949); WOMAN'S SECRET, A(1949); MY FORBIDDEN PAST(1951); SNOW CREATURE, THE,(1954); ATTACK OF THE 50 FOOT WOMAN(1958); SHOWDOWN AT BOOT HILL(1958)

Gilbert Douglas

Silents
DULCY(1923)
Misc. Silents
FIVE THOUSAND AN HOUR(1918); GOOD GRACIOUS ANNABELLE(1919)

Gordon Douglas

PARDON US(1931); KELLY THE SECOND(1936), w; GENERAL SPANKY(1937), d; HOUSEKEEPER'S DAUGHTER(1939), w; ZENOBIA(1939), d; SAPS AT SEA(1940), d; BROADWAY LIMITED(1941), d; ROAD SHOW(1941), d; TOPPER RETURNS(1941), w; DEVIL WITH HITLER, THE(1942), d; GREAT GILDERSLEEVE, THE(1942), d; GILDERSLEEVE ON BROADWAY(1943), d; GILDERSLEEVE'S BAD DAY(1943), d; FALCON IN HOLLYWOOD, THE(1944), d; GILDERSLEEVE'S GHOST(1944), d; GIRL RUSH(1944), d; NIGHT OF ADVENTURE, A(1944), d; FIRST YANK INTO TOKYO(1945), d; BLACK ARROW(1948), d; WALK A CROOKED MILE(1948), d; DOOLINS OF OKLAHOMA, THE(1949), d; MR. SOFT TOUCH(1949), d; BETWEEN MIDNIGHT AND DAWN(1950), d; FORTUNES OF CAPTAIN BLOOD(1950), d; GREAT MISSOURI RAID, THE(1950), d; KISS TOMORROW GOODBYE(1950), d; NEVADAN, THE(1950), d; ROGUES OF SHERWOOD FOREST(1950), d; COME FILL THE CUP(1951), d; I WAS A COMMUNIST FOR THE F.B.I.(1951), d; ONLY THE VALIANT(1951), d; IRON MISTRESS, THE(1952), d; MARA MARU(1952), d; CHARGE AT FEATHER RIVER, THE(1953), d; SHE'S BACK ON BROADWAY(1953), d; SO THIS IS LOVE(1953), d; THEM!(1954), d; MC CONNELL STORY, THE(1955), d; SINCERELY YOURS(1955), d; YOUNG AT HEART(1955), d; SANTIAGO(1956), d; BIG LAND, THE(1957), d; BOMBERS B-52(1957), d; FIEND WHO WALKED THE WEST, THE(1958), d; FORT DOBBS(1958), d; UP PERISCOPE(1959), d; YELLOWSTONE KELLY(1959), d; SINS OF RACHEL CADE, THE(1960), d; CLAUDELLE INGLISH(1961), d; GOLD OF THE SEVEN SAINTS(1961), d; FOLLOW THAT DREAM(1962), d; CALL ME BWANA(1963, Brit.), d; RIO CONCHOS(1964), d; ROBIN AND THE SEVEN HOODS(1964), d; HARLOW(1965), d; SYLVIA(1965), d; STAGECOACH(1966), d; WAY...WAY OUT(1966), d; CHUKA(1967), d; IN LIKE FLINT(1967), d; TONY ROME(1967), d; DETECTIVE, THE(1968), d; LADY IN CEMENT(1968), d; BARQUERO(1970), d; SKULLDUGGERY(1970), d; THEY CALL ME MISTER TIBBS(1970), d; SLAUGHTER'S BIG RIP-OFF(1973), d; VIVA KNIEVEL!(1977), d

Gordon M. Douglas

DICK TRACY VS. CUEBALL(1946), d; SAN QUENTIN(1946), d; IF YOU KNEW SUSIE(1948), d

Graham Douglas

Misc. Silents
CHASE ME CHARLIE(1918, Brit.)

Haldane Douglas

MR. MOTO'S GAMBLE(1938), art d; ONE WILD NIGHT(1938), art d; BARRICADE(1939), art d; GLAMOUR BOY(1941), art d; NIGHT OF JANUARY 16TH(1941), art d; WEST POINT WIDOW(1941), art d; GLASS KEY, THE(1942), art d; HENRY AND DIZZY(1942), art d; LADY BODYGUARD(1942), art d; MY HEART BELONGS TO DADDY(1942), art d; NIGHT IN NEW ORLEANS, A(1942), art d; PRIORITIES ON PARADE(1942), art d; STREET OF CHANCE(1942), art d; FOR WHOM THE BELL TOLLS(1943), art d; GOOD FELLOWS, THE(1943), art d; HENRY ALDRICH HAUNTS A HOUSE(1943), art d; SALUTE FOR THREE(1943), art d; RAINBOW ISLAND(1944), art d; OUT OF THIS WORLD(1945), art d; SALTY O'ROURKE(1945), art d; O.S.S.(1946), art d; OUR HEARTS WERE GROWING UP(1946), art d; EASY COME, EASY GO(1947), art d; WILD HARVEST(1947), art d

Harry Douglas

ONE PLUS ONE(1969, Brit.)

Howard Douglas

DEATH AT A BROADCAST(1934, Brit.); HIS MAJESTY AND CO(1935, Brit.); NO LIMIT(1935, Brit.); BIG NOISE, THE(1936, Brit.); HEARTS OF HUMANITY(1936, Brit.); BRIEF ECSTASY(1937, Brit.); FIRE OVER ENGLAND(1937, Brit.); LAST ADVENTURERS, THE(1937, Brit); DANGEROUS SECRETS(1938, Brit.); WIFE OF GENERAL LING, THE(1938, Brit.); CHALLENGE, THE(1939, Brit.); MEN WITHOUT HONOUR(1939, Brit.); WORLD OWES ME A LIVING, THE(1944, Brit.); ECHO MURDERS, THE(1945, Brit.); HOME SWEET HOME(1945, Brit.); NOTORIOUS GENTLEMAN(1945, Brit.); GRAND ESCAPADE, THE(1946, Brit.); DEAR MURDERER(1947, Brit.); GREEN FINGERS(1947, Brit.); JOURNEY AHEAD(1947, Brit.); UPTURNED GLASS, THE(1947, Brit.); MR. PERRIN AND MR. TRAILL(1948, Brit.); NIGHT COMES TOO SOON(1948, Brit.); NOTHING VENTURE(1948, Brit.); AGITATOR, THE(1949); MAN ON THE RUN(1949, Brit.); MIRANDA(1949, Brit.); MY BROTHER JONATHAN(1949, Brit.); HUE AND CRY(1950, Brit.); MUDLARK, THE(1950, Brit.); SECOND MATE, THE(1950, Brit.); SILK NOOSE, THE(1950, Brit.); TREASURE ISLAND(1950, Brit.); TWENTY QUESTIONS MURDER MYSTERY, THE(1950, Brit.); GREAT MANHUNT, THE(1951, Brit.); NAUGHTY ARLETTE(1951, Brit.); SPIDER AND THE FLY, THE(1952, Brit.); STOLEN FACE(1952, Brit.); MEET MR. CALLAGHAN(1954, Brit.); ROB ROY, THE HIGHLAND ROGUE(1954, Brit.); WHISTLE DOWN THE WIND(1961, Brit.); JUNGLE STREET GIRLS(1963, Brit.); CROOKS IN CLOISTERS(1964, Brit.); HEROES OF TELEMARK, THE(1965, Brit.); PLANK, THE(1967, Brit.)

Hugh Douglas

BLOCKADE(1928, Brit.); HELL ON EARTH(1934, Ger.)
1984
LONELY GUY, THE(1984)

Irving Douglas

COURT JESTER, THE(1956)

J. B. Douglas

M(1970); BAREFOOT EXECUTIVE, THE(1971)

J. Ian Douglas

FORT BOWIE(1958)

J. McGregor Douglas

EARLY BIRD, THE(1936, Brit.), d&w

Jack Douglas

HE STAYED FOR BREAKFAST(1940); NEARLY A NASTY ACCIDENT(1962, Brit.); CARRY ON ENGLAND(1976, Brit.); CARRY ON EMANUELLE(1978, Brit.); SHILLINGBURY BLOWERS, THE(1980, Brit.); BLOODY KIDS(1983, Brit.)

James Douglas

UNTIL THEY SAIL(1957); TIME LIMIT(1957); G.I. BLUES(1960); THUNDER OF DRUMS, A(1961); SWEET BIRD OF YOUTH(1962); DRYLANDERS(1963, Can.); CHANGELING, THE(1980, Can.)

James B. Douglas-

Silents
LADY OF THE LAKE, THE(1928, Brit.)
James B. Douglas
GONG SHOW MOVIE, THE(1980); DEADLY EYES(1982)
Janice Douglas
KINFOLK(1970)
Jean Douglas
VAGABOND KING, THE(1930)
Jerry Douglas
BLAST OF SILENCE(1961); BLACK ZOO(1963); GUNN(1967); LOOKER(1981); MOMMIE DEAREST(1981)
Jo Douglas
6.5 SPECIAL(1958, Brit.)
Jo Robert Douglas
CHINESE DEN, THE(1940, Brit.)
Joan Douglas
EVERYBODY DOES IT(1949); YOUNG LIONS, THE(1958); MANCHURIAN CANDIDATE, THE(1962)
Joanna Douglas
DIAMOND SAFARI(1958)
Jodi Douglas
I, THE JURY(1982)
Joel Douglas
1984
TORCHLIGHT(1984), p
Johanna Douglas
JACKTOWN(1962)
John Douglas
WAR AND PEACE(1956, Ital./U.S.); THUNDERING JETS(1958); CRACK IN THE WORLD(1965), m; MILESTONES(1975), a, d,w&ed, ph
Misc. Silents
VICAR OF WAKEFIELD, THE(1913, Brit.), d
John M. Douglas
BRUTE AND THE BEAST, THE(1968, Ital.)
John O. Douglas
MISS TULIP STAYS THE NIGHT(1955, Brit.), p, w
Johnny Douglas
BAY OF SAINT MICHEL, THE(1963, Brit.), m, md; TRAITORS, THE(1963, Brit.), m; CODE 7, VICTIM 5(1964, Brit.), m; CITY OF FEAR(1965, Brit.), m; GUNFIGHTERS OF CASA GRANDE(1965, U.S./Span.), m&md; DATELINE DIAMONDS(1966, Brit.), m; KID RODELO(1966, U.S./Span.), m; MOZAMBIQUE(1966, Brit.), m; PSYCHO-CIRCUS(1967, Brit.), m; RUN LIKE A THIEF(1968, Span.), m; DULCIMA(1971, Brit.), m; RAILWAY CHILDREN, THE(1971, Brit.), m
Josephine Douglas
SCOTLAND YARD INSPECTOR(1952, Brit.); THREE CORNERED FATE(1954, Brit.); WILL ANY GENTLEMAN?(1955, Brit.); 6.5 SPECIAL(1958, Brit.); LEFT, RIGHT AND CENTRE(1959); DRACULA A.D. 1972(1972, Brit.), p; OUR MISS FRED(1972, Brit.), p
Karen Douglas
LOCAL HERO(1983, Brit.)
Katya Douglas
STOP ME BEFORE I KILL!(1961, Brit.); KILL OR CURE(1962, Brit.); ROAD TO HONG KONG, THE(1962, U.S./Brit.); DAY OF THE TRIFFIDS, THE(1963); MURDER AT THE GALLOP(1963, Brit.)
Kay Douglas
TARGETS(1968)
Keith Douglas
AFFECTIONATELY YOURS(1941); BRIDE CAME C.O.D., THE(1941); NURSE'S SECRET, THE(1941); PASSAGE FROM HONG KONG(1941)
Kent Douglas
WATERLOO BRIDGE(1931); HOUSE DIVIDED, A(1932)
Kirk Douglas
TWO WEEKS IN ANOTHER TOWN(1962); STRANGE LOVE OF MARTHA IVERS, THE(1946); MOURNING BECOMES ELECTRA(1947); OUT OF THE PAST(1947); I WALK ALONE(1948); LETTER TO THREE WIVES, A(1948); MY DEAR SECRETARY(1948); WALLS OF JERICHO(1948); CHAMPION(1949); GLASS MENAGERIE, THE(1950); YOUNG MAN WITH A HORN(1950); ALONG THE GREAT DIVIDE(1951); BIG CARNIVAL, THE(1951); DETECTIVE STORY(1951); BAD AND THE BEAUTIFUL, THE(1952); BIG SKY, THE(1952); BIG TREES, THE(1952); ACT OF LOVE(1953); JUGGLER, THE(1953); STORY OF THREE LOVES, THE(1953); 20,000 LEAGUES UNDER THE SEA(1954); INDIAN FIGHTER, THE(1955); MAN WITHOUT A STAR(1955); RACERS, THE(1955); ULYSSES(1955, Ital.); LUST FOR LIFE(1956); GUNFIGHT AT THE O.K. CORRAL(1957); PATHS OF GLORY(1957); TOP SECRET AFFAIR(1957); VIKINGS, THE(1958); DEVIL'S DISCIPLE, THE(1959); LAST TRAIN FROM GUN HILL(1959); SPARTACUS(1960); STRANGERS WHEN WE MEET(1960); LAST SUNSET, THE(1961); TOWN WITHOUT PITY(1961, Ger./Switz./U.S.); HOOK, THE(1962); LONELY ARE THE BRAVE(1962); FOR LOVE OR MONEY(1963); LIST OF ADRIAN MESSENGER, THE(1963); SEVEN DAYS IN MAY(1964); HEROES OF TELEMARK, THE(1965, Brit.); IN HARM'S WAY(1965); CAST A GIANT SHADOW(1966); IS PARIS BURNING?(1966, U.S./Fr.); WAR WAGON, THE(1967); WAY WEST, THE(1967); BROTHERHOOD, THE(1968), a, p; LOVELY WAY TO DIE, A(1968); ARRANGEMENT, THE(1969); THERE WAS A CROOKED MAN(1970); CATCH ME A SPY(1971, Brit./Fr.); GUNFIGHT, A(1971); LIGHT AT THE EDGE OF THE WORLD, THE(1971, U.S./Span./Lichtenstein), a, p; SUMMERTREE(1971), p; SCALAWAG(1973, Yugo.), a, d; MASTER TOUCH, THE(1974, Ital./Ger.); ONCE IS NOT ENOUGH(1975); POSSE(1975), a, p&d; CHOSEN, THE(1978, Brit./Ital.); FURY, THE(1978); HOME MOVIES(1979); VILLAIN, THE(1979); FINAL COUNTDOWN, THE(1980); SATURN 3(1980); EDDIE MACON'S RUN(1983); MAN FROM SNOWY RIVER, THE(1983, Aus.)
Lamont Douglas
REBEL ANGEL(1962), d
Lantz Douglas
1984
CALIFORNIA GIRLS(1984)
Laurie Douglas
WHEN LOVE IS YOUNG(1937); FLEET'S IN, THE(1942); YOUNG AND WILLING(1943); SMASH-UP, THE STORY OF A WOMAN(1947)
Lawrence Douglas
LITTLE BIG SHOT(1952, Brit.); KIDNAPPED(1971, Brit.)

Leal Douglas
Silents
LURE OF LONDON, THE(1914, Brit.); UNINVITED GUEST, THE(1923, Brit.); EVERY MOTHER'S SON(1926, Brit.); PASSION ISLAND(1927, Brit.)
Misc. Silents
LAMP OF DESTINY(1919, Brit.)
Lilian Douglas
Silents
MASTER OF CRAFT, A(1922, Brit.); PADDY, THE NEXT BEST THING(1923, Brit.)
Misc. Silents
LITTLE MOTHER, THE(1922, Brit.); SPORTING INSTINCT, THE(1922, Brit.)
Lillian Douglas
Silents
WHEN GREEK MEETS GREEK(1922, Brit.); IN THE BLOOD(1923, Brit.); JUNGLE WOMAN, THE(1926, Brit.); PEARL OF THE SOUTH SEAS(1927, Brit.)
Misc. Silents
SPORTING DOUBLE, A(1922, Brit.); HYPOCRITES, THE(1923, Brit.)
Linda Douglas
TARGET(1952)
Linda Douglas [Mary Jo Tarola]
TRAIL GUIDE(1952)
Lloyd C. Douglas
MAGNIFICENT OBSESSION(1935), w; GREEN LIGHT(1937), w; WHITE BANNERS(1938), w; DISPUTED PASSAGE(1939), w; ROBE, THE(1953), w. Philip Dunne; DEMETRIUS AND THE GLADIATORS(1954), w; MAGNIFICENT OBSESSION(1954), w; BIG FISHERMAN, THE(1959), w
Louis Douglas
HELL ON EARTH(1934, Ger.)
Malcolm Douglas
EDUCATING RITA(1983)
Marian Douglas
ALOHA(1931)
Silents
SIOUX BLOOD(1929)
Misc. Silents
BUSHRANGER, THE(1928); DEVIL'S TRADEMARK, THE(1928); POWER OF SILENCE, THE(1928); UPLAND RIDER, THE(1928); WAGON SHOW, THE(1928)
Mark Douglas
SNIPER'S RIDGE(1961); MOONSHINE MOUNTAIN(1964); TWO THOUSAND MANIACS!(1964)
Mary Douglas
RIDING THE WIND(1942)
Melvin Douglas
CHANGELING, THE(1980, Can.)
Melvyn Douglas
THAT UNCERTAIN FEELING(1941); TONIGHT OR NEVER(1931); AS YOU DESIRE ME(1932); BROKEN WING, THE(1932); OLD DARK HOUSE, THE(1932); PRESTIGE(1932); WISER SEX, THE(1932); COUNSELLOR-AT-LAW(1933); NAGANA(1933); VAMPIRE BAT, THE(1933); WOMAN IN THE DARK(1934); ANNIE OAKLEY(1935); DANGEROUS CORNER(1935); MARY BURNS, FUGITIVE(1935); PEOPLE'S ENEMY, THE(1935); SHE MARRIED HER BOSS(1935); AND SO THEY WERE MARRIED(1936); GORGEOUS HUSSY, THE(1936); LONE WOLF RETURNS, THE(1936); THEODORA GOES WILD(1936); ANGEL(1937); CAPTAINS COURAGEOUS(1937); I MET HIM IN PARIS(1937); I'LL TAKE ROMANCE(1937); WOMEN OF GLAMOUR(1937); ARSENE LUPIN RETURNS(1938); FAST COMPANY(1938); SHINING HOUR, THE(1938); THAT CERTAIN AGE(1938); THERE'S ALWAYS A WOMAN(1938); THERE'S THAT WOMAN AGAIN(1938); TOY WIFE, THE(1938); AMAZING MR. WILLIAMS(1939); GOOD GIRLS GO TO PARIS(1939); NINOTCHKA(1939); TELL NO TALES(1939); HE STAYED FOR BREAKFAST(1940); THIRD FINGER, LEFT HAND(1940); THIS THING CALLED LOVE(1940); TOO MANY HUSBANDS(1940); OUR WIFE(1941); TWO-FACED WOMAN(1941); WOMAN'S FACE(1941); THEY ALL KISSED THE BRIDE(1942); WE WERE DANCING(1942); THREE HEARTS FOR JULIA(1943); GUILT OF JANET AMES, THE(1947); SEA OF GRASS, THE(1947); MR. BLANDINGS BUILDS HIS DREAM HOUSE(1948); MY OWN TRUE LOVE(1948); GREAT SINNER, THE(1949); WOMAN'S SECRET, A(1949); MY FORBIDDEN PAST(1951); ON THE LOOSE(1951); BILLY BUDD(1962); HUD(1963); ADVANCE TO THE REAR(1964); AMERICANIZATION OF EMILY, THE(1964); RAPTURE(1965); HOTEL(1967); I NEVER SANG FOR MY FATHER(1970); CANDIDATE, THE(1972); ONE IS A LONELY NUMBER(1972); TENANT, THE(1976, Fr.); TWILIGHT'S LAST GLEAMING(1977, U.S./Ger.); BEING THERE(1979); SEDUCTION OF JOE TYNAN, THE(1979); TELL ME A RIDDLE(1980); GHOST STORY(1981)
Michael Douglas
HAIL, HERO!(1969); WHERE'S JACK?(1969, Brit.); ADAM AT 6 A.M.(1970); SUMMERTREE(1971); NAPOLEON AND SAMANTHA(1972); ONE FLEW OVER THE CUCKOO'S NEST(1975), p; COMA(1978); CHINA SYNDROME, THE(1979), a, p; RUNNING(1979, Can.); IT'S MY TURN(1980); STAR CHAMBER, THE(1983)
1984
ROMANCING THE STONE(1984), a, p
Mickey Douglas
YOUR NUMBER'S UP(1931), stunts
Mike Douglas
LAST VALLEY, THE(1971, Brit.); GATOR(1976); NASTY HABITS(1976, Brit.)
Milton Douglas
VIENNESE NIGHTS(1930); JANIE(1944)
Nathan E. Douglas
DEFIANT ONES, THE(1958), w; INHERIT THE WIND(1960), w
Patricia Ann Douglas
DOCTOR DETROIT(1983); GOING BERSERK(1983)
Paul Douglas
LETTER TO THREE WIVES, A(1948); EVERYBODY DOES IT(1949); IT HAPPENS EVERY SPRING(1949); BIG LIFT, THE(1950); LOVE THAT BRUTE(1950); PANIC IN THE STREETS(1950); ANGELS IN THE OUTFIELD(1951); FOURTEEN HOURS(1951); GUY WHO CAME BACK, THE(1951); RHUBARB(1951); CLASH BY NIGHT(1952); NEVER WAVE AT A WAC(1952); WE'RE NOT MARRIED(1952); WHEN IN ROME(1952); FOREVER FEMALE(1953); EXECUTIVE SUITE(1954); HIGH AND DRY(1954, Brit.); GREEN FIRE(1955); JOE MACBETH(1955); GAMMA PEOPLE, THE(1956); LEATHER SAINT, THE(1956); SOLID GOLD CADILLAC, THE(1956); BEAU JAMES(1957); THIS COULD BE THE NIGHT(1957); MATING GAME, THE(1959)

Peggy Douglas
TONS OF MONEY(1931, Brit.)
Peter Douglas
FINAL COUNTDOWN, THE(1980)
1984
FLETCH(1984), p
Peter Vincent Douglas
FINAL COUNTDOWN, THE(1980), p; SOMETHING WICKED THIS WAY CO-MES(1983), p
Phyllis Douglas
UNTIL THEY SAIL(1957); RAINTREE COUNTY(1957); GIRLS' TOWN(1959)
R. H. Douglas
WOLVES OF THE UNDERWORLD(1935, Brit.), w
Ralph Douglas
VERDICT, THE(1982)
Rita Douglas
JUNGLE MAN(1941), w
Robert Douglas
MANY WATERS(1931, Brit.); P.C. JOSSER(1931, Brit.); BLARNEY KISS(1933, Brit.); DEATH DRIVES THROUGH(1935, Brit.); GIRLS IN THE STREET(1937, Brit.); GIRL IN THE STREET(1938, Brit.); CHALLENGE, THE(1939, Brit.); TORPEDOED!(1939); LION HAS WINGS, THE(1940, Brit.); OVER THE MOON(1940, Brit.); DICK TRA-CY(1945); END OF THE RIVER, THE(1947, Brit.); DECISION OF CHRISTOPHER BLAKE, THE(1948); ADVENTURES OF DON JUAN(1949); FOUNTAINHEAD, THE(1949); HOMICIDE(1949); LADY TAKES A SAILOR, THE(1949); BAR-RICADE(1950); BUCCANEER'S GIRL(1950); FLAME AND THE ARROW, THE(1950); KIM(1950); MYSTERY SUBMARINE(1950); SPY HUNT(1950); THIS SIDE OF THE LAW(1950); AT SWORD'S POINT(1951); TARGET UNKNOWN(1951); THUNDER ON THE HILL(1951); IVANHOE(1952, Brit.); PRISONER OF ZENDA, THE(1952); DESERT RATS, THE(1953); FAIR WIND TO JAVA(1953); FLIGHT TO TANGIER(1953); KING RICHARD AND THE CRUSADERS(1954); SASKATCHEWAN(1954); GOOD MORN-ING, MISS DOVE(1955); SCARLET COAT, THE(1955); VIRGIN QUEEN, THE(1955); HELEN OF TROY(1956, Ital); TARZAN, THE APE MAN(1959); YOUNG PHILADEL-PHIANS, THE(1959); NIGHT TRAIN TO PARIS(1964, Brit.), d; SECRET CEREMO-NY(1968, Brit.)
Misc. Talkies
LAWBREAKERS, THE(1960)
Ron Douglas
TOP OF THE HEAP(1972)
Rowland Douglas
NEUTRAL PORT(1941, Brit.)
Roy Douglas
BELLS GO DOWN, THE(1943, Brit.), m; CANDLELIGHT IN ALGERIA(1944, Brit.), m
Sally Douglas
GENGHIS KHAN(U.S./Brit./Ger./Yugo); WEEKEND WITH LULU, A(1961, Brit.); CARRY ON COWBOY(1966, Brit.); CONQUEROR WORM, THE(1968, Brit.)
Sam Douglas
1984
RAZOR'S EDGE, THE(1984)
Sarah Douglas
LAST DAYS OF MAN ON EARTH, THE(1975, Brit.); PEOPLE THAT TIME FORGOT, THE(1977, Brit.); SUPERMAN(1978); SUPERMAN II(1980)
1984
CONAN THE DESTROYER(1984)
Scott Douglas
BUNDLE OF JOY(1956); FIRST TEXAN, THE(1956); PARDNERS(1956); TURNING POINT, THE(1977)
Shaft Douglas
SCALAWAG(1973, Yugo.)
Sharon Douglas
GENTLEMAN AFTER DARK, A(1942); NAVY WAY, THE(1944); FOG ISLAND(1945); OUR HEARTS WERE GROWING UP(1946)
Shirley Douglas
JOE MACBETH(1955); LOLITA(1962)
Susan Douglas
PRIVATE AFFAIRS OF BEL AMI, THE(1947); LOST BOUNDARIES(1949); FORBID-DEN JOURNEY(1950, Can.); FIVE(1951); TARGETS(1968)
Tom Douglas
ROAD TO RENO(1931); BROKEN LULLABY(1932); PHANTOM OF CRESTWOOD, THE(1932); SKY BRIDE(1932); WEST OF SINGAPORE(1933)
Misc. Talkies
GUILTY OR NOT GUILTY(1932)
Misc. Silents
BLINKEYES(192?); FOOTFALLS(1921); FREE AIR(1922)
Tony Douglas
SHOWDOWN AT BOOT HILL(1958)
Trevor Douglas
ROCKERS(1980)
W.A. Douglas
Misc. Silents
BEWARE OF THE LAW(1922), d
Wallace Douglas
LOVE WAGER, THE(1933, Brit.); MUSIC HATH CHARMS(1935, Brit.); DON'T RUSH ME(1936, Brit.); BREAK THE NEWS(1938, Brit.); CHINESE DEN, THE(1940, Brit.); SPIES OF THE AIR(1940, Brit.); SPIDER AND THE FLY, THE(1952, Brit.)
Warren Douglas
FIRST OFFENDERS(1939); SKI PATROL(1940), p; ZANZIBAR(1940), p; ADVEN-TURES IN IRAQ(1943); AIR FORCE(1943); MISSION TO MOSCOW(1943); MURDER ON THE WATERFRONT(1943); NORTHERN PURSUIT(1943); DESTINATION TOKYO(1944); GOD IS MY CO-PILOT(1945); PRIDE OF THE MARINES(1945); BELOW THE DEADLINE(1946); INNER CIRCLE, THE(1946); MAGNIFICENT ROGUE, THE(1946); MAN I LOVE, THE(1946); CHINESE RING, THE(1947); HIGH CON-QUEST(1947); PILGRIM LADY, THE(1947); TRESPASSER, THE(1947); HOMICIDE FOR THREE(1948); INCIDENT(1948); LIGHTNIN' IN THE FOREST(1948); FORGOT-TEN WOMEN(1949); HOMICIDE(1949); POST OFFICE INVESTIGATOR(1949); TASK FORCE(1949); COUNTY FAIR(1950); GREAT JEWEL ROBBER, THE(1950); SQUARE DANCE KATY(1950); CUBAN FIREBALL(1951); SECRETS OF MONTE CARLO(1951); YELLOW FIN(1951); NORTHWEST TERRITORY(1952); FANGS OF THE ARC-TIC(1953), a, w; JACK SLADE(1953), w; NORTHERN PATROL(1953), w; TORPEDO

ALLEY(1953), w; CRY VENGEANCE(1954), a, w; LOOPHOLE(1954), w; FINGER MAN(1955), w; RETURN OF JACK SLADE, THE(1955), w; COME ON, THE(1956), w; CRUEL TOWER, THE(1956), w; STRANGE INTRUDER(1956), w; DRAGON WELLS MASSACRE(1957), a, w; DEEP SIX, THE(1958); NIGHT OF THE GRIZZLY, THE(1966), w
Wayne Douglas
TERROR IN THE JUNGLE(1968)
William Douglas
FORBIDDEN(1949, Brit.); PT 109(1963)
William O. Douglas
INTERNS, THE(1962)
Douglas Scott and his Debonair Boys
HAPPY GO LOVELY(1951, Brit.)
William Douglas-Home
UNDER TEN FLAGS(1960, U.S./Ital.), w
Amy Douglass
PLEASE DON'T EAT THE DAISIES(1960); UNSINKABLE MOLLY BROWN, THE(1964)
Bess Douglass
Misc. Talkies
PICK-UP(1975)
C. H. Douglass
VERY NATURAL THING, A(1974), ph
Charles Douglass
GETTING TOGETHER(1976)
Misc. Talkies
FEELIN' UP(1983)
Diane Douglass
STRANGE BREW(1983)
Don Douglass
THREE CABALLEROS, THE(1944), art d
Everett Douglass
WANDERER OF THE WASTELAND(1935), ed; LAST TRAIN FROM MADRID, THE(1937), ed; SAINTED SISTERS, THE(1948), ed
Judie Douglass
1984
CONSTANCE(1984, New Zealand)
Kent Douglass
PAID(1930); DAYBREAK(1931); FIVE AND TEN(1931)
Pi Douglass
JESUS CHRIST, SUPERSTAR(1973)
Robyn Douglass
BREAKING AWAY(1979); CONQUEST OF THE EARTH(1980); PARTNERS(1982); ROMANTIC COMEDY(1983)
1984
LONELY GUY, THE(1984)
Stuart Douglass
SCARLET WEB, THE(1954, Brit.); BOYS, THE(1962, Brit.), w
Allan Douglaus
DARLING, HOW COULD YOU!(1951)
France Dougnac
LEGEND OF FRENCHIE KING, THE(1971, Fr./Ital./Span./Brit.)
Bill Doukas
FEEDBACK(1979), a, p,d&w
Susan Doukas
BELIEVE IN ME(1971); LIQUID SKY(1982)
Douking
CARNIVAL OF SINNERS(1947, Fr.); JOY HOUSE(1964, Fr.); WHAT'S NEW, PUS-SYCAT?(1965, U.S./Fr.); MADEMOISELLE(1966, Fr./Brit.); MILKY WAY, THE(1969, Fr./Ital.); SPIRITS OF THE DEAD(1969, Fr./Ital.)
Anna Douking
JUST BEFORE NIGHTFALL(1975, Fr./Ital.)
George Douking
DISCREET CHARM OF THE BOURGEOISIE, THE(1972, Fr.)
Georges Douking
CRIME AND PUNISHMENT(1935, Fr.); DAYBREAK(1940, Fr.); HUNCHBACK OF NOTRE DAME, THE(1957, Fr.); CHARGE OF THE LIGHT BRIGADE, THE(1968, Brit.)
Gabrielle Doulcet
HOW NOT TO ROB A DEPARTMENT STORE(1965, Fr./Ital.); THINGS OF LIFE, THE(1970, Fr./Ital./Switz.)
John Doumanian
ANNIE HALL(1977); MANHATTAN(1979); ZELIG(1983)
1984
BROADWAY DANNY ROSE(1984)
Doumel
CESAR(1936, Fr.)
Sonia Doumen
IF IT'S TUESDAY, THIS MUST BE BELGIUM(1969)
Clement Douneias
SPIRIT AND THE FLESH, THE(1948, Ital.), ed
Renee Dounis
Misc. Silents
L'ATRE(1923, Fr.)
Marie-Claude Douquet
LA CAGE AUX FOLLES II(1981, Ital./Fr.)
Brad Dourif
ONE FLEW OVER THE CUCKOO'S NEST(1975); EYES OF LAURA MARS(1978); WISE BLOOD(1979, U.S./Ger.); RAGTIME(1981)
Brad Douriff
1984
DUNE(1984)
Mohamed Dous
1984
MISUNDERSTOOD(1984)
Christianna Dousnard
JOY(1983, Fr./Can.)
Mara Dousse
BALL AT THE CASTLE(1939, Ital.), ch

Alain Doutey
BIG RED ONE, THE(1980)
Jacques Douy
CASTLE KEEP(1969), art d
Max Douy
RULES OF THE GAME, THE(1939, Fr.), set d; LUMIERE D'ETE(1943, Fr.), art d; JENNY LAMOUR(1948, Fr.), set d; MANON(1950, Fr.), set d; ADVENTURES OF CAPTAIN FABIAN(1951), set d; RED AND THE BLACK, THE(1954, Fr./Ital.), art d; RED, INN, THE(1954, Fr.), art d; FRENCH CANCAN(1956, Fr.), set d; FOUR BAGS FULL(1957, Fr./Ital.), prod d; LE CIEL EST A VOUS(1957, Fr.), art d; LOVE IS MY PROFESSION(1959, Fr.), art d; GREEN MARE, THE(1961, Fr./Ital.), art d; PHAE-DRA(1962, U.S./Gr./Fr.), art d; SEVEN CAPITAL SINS(1962, Fr./Ital.), d; STORY OF THE COUNT OF MONTE CRISTO, THE(1962, Fr./Ital.), art d; LADIES OF THE PARK(1964, Fr.), art d; TOPKAPI(1964), art d; FRIEND OF THE FAMILY(1965, Fr./Ital.), set d; ENOUGH ROPE(1966, Fr./Ital./Ger.), art d; YOUNG WORLD, A(1966, Fr./Ital.), art d; OLDEST PROFESSION, THE(1968, Fr./Ital./Ger.), art d; CASTLE KEEP(1969), art d; BLACK AND WHITE IN COLOR(1976, Fr.), art d; MOON-RAKER(1979, Brit.), art d; MALEVIL(1981, Fr./Ger.), art d
Ben Dova
MARATHON MAN(1976)
Capt. Dove
FOR FREEDOM(1940, Brit.)
Andrew Dove
ONE OF OUR DINOSAURS IS MISSING(1975, Brit.)
Bille Dove
Silents
YOUTH TO YOUTH(1922)
Billie Dove
CAREERS(1929); HER PRIVATE LIFE(1929); MAN AND THE MOMENT, THE(1929); PAINTED ANGEL, THE(1929); NOTORIOUS AFFAIR, A(1930); ONE NIGHT AT SUSIE'S(1930); OTHER TOMORROW, THE(1930); SWEETHEARTS AND WIVES(1930); AGE FOR LOVE, THE(1931); LADY WHO DARED, THE(1931); BLONDIE OF THE FOLLIES(1932); COCK OF THE AIR(1932)
Silents
AT THE STAGE DOOR(1921); ALL THE BROTHERS WERE VALIANT(1923); MADNESS OF YOUTH(1923); ON TIME(1924); ROUGHNECK, THE(1924); AIR MAIL, THE(1925); ANCIENT HIGHWAY, THE(1925); LUCKY HORSESHOE, THE(1925); BLACK PIRATE, THE(1926); KID BOOTS(1926); MARRIAGE CLAUSE, THE(1926); AFFAIR OF THE FOLLIES, AN(1927); AMERICAN BEAUTY(1927); SENSATION SEEKERS(1927); STOLEN BRIDE, THE(1927); TENDER HOUR, THE(1927); ADORA-TION(1928); HEART OF A FOLLIES GIRL, THE(1928); NIGHT WATCH, THE(1928)
Misc. Silents
BEYOND THE RAINBOW(1922); LONE STAR RANGER, THE(1923); SOFT BOI-LED(1923); THRILL CHASER, THE(1923); FOLLY OF VANITY, THE(1924); TRY AND GET IT(1924); YANKEE MADNESS(1924); FIGHTING HEART, THE(1925); LIGHT OF THE WESTERN STARS, THE(1925); WILD HORSE MESA(1925); LONE WOLF RETURNS, THE(1926); LOVE MART, THE(1927); YELLOW LILY, THE(1928)
Jock Dove
THE RUNNER STUMBLES(1979)
Walter Dove
FOOLS' PARADE(1971)
The Dovells
DON'T KNOCK THE TWIST(1962)
Arnold Dover
TOP OF THE HEAP(1972)
Katherine Dover
CREATURE WASN'T NICE,THE(1981), cos
Nancy Dover
SCANDAL(1929); DYNAMITE(1930); THOROUGHBRED, THE(1930); BIG BUSI-NESS GIRL(1931); CIMARRON(1931)
Nita Dover
QUEEN OF SHEBA(1953, Ital.)
Nyta Dover
RED CLOAK, THE(1961, Ital./Fr.)
Robert Dover
INDIAN UPRISING(1951)
Robert Foster Dover
BROKEN ARROW(1950)
William B. Dover
YOU SAID A MOUTHFUL(1932), w
Alice Dovey
Silents
COMMANDING OFFICER, THE(1915)
Misc. Silents
ROMANTIC JOURNEY, THE(1916)
L. Dovgvillo
DAY THE EARTH FROZE, THE(1959, Fin./USSR), spec eff
Dovima
FUNNY FACE(1957)
Alexander Dovshenko
Silents
EARTH(1930, USSR), d&w, ed
Dovzhenko
Silents
ARSENAL(1929, USSR), d&w, ed
Elizabeth Dow
PARACHUTE NURSE(1942)
Graham Dow
STORM BOY(1976, Aus.); GALLIPOLI(1981, Aus.)
Herb Dow
CALIFORNIA DREAMING(1979), ed
Herbert H. Dow
SUNNYSIDE(1979), ed
Ivan Dow
ROBERTA(1935)
J. Donald Dow
ISABEL(1968, Can.)

Maree Dow
1984
MUPPETS TAKE MANHATTAN, THE(1984)
Mary Dow
Silents
SEA HORSES(1926)
Mindy Dow
EARTHBOUND(1981)
Nancy Dow
ICE HOUSE, THE(1969)
Peggy Dow
UNDERTOW(1949); WOMAN IN HIDING(1949); HARVEY(1950); SHAKE-DOWN(1950); SLEEPING CITY, THE(1950); BRIGHT VICTORY(1951); I WANT YOU(1951); REUNION IN RENO(1951); YOU NEVER CAN TELL(1951)
R.A. Dow
SQUIRM(1976)
Richard Dow
EASY MONEY(1983)
T.J. Dow
Misc. Silents
VANDERHOFF AFFAIR, THE(1915)
Tony Dow
KENTUCKY FRIED MOVIE, THE(1977)
Francine Dowd
NIGHT ANGEL, THE(1931)
John Dowd
KID MILLIONS(1934); ILLIAC PASSION, THE(1968)
Judith Dowd
DAMIEN–OMEN II(1978)
Kay Dowd
THEY LIVE IN FEAR(1944)
Kaye Dowd
ANGEL COMES TO BROOKLYN, AN(1945)
M'el Dowd
300 YEAR WEEKEND(1971)
Mel Dowd
WRONG MAN, THE(1956)
Nancy Dowd
SLAP SHOT(1977), w; COMING HOME(1978), w; LOVE(1982$c Can.), d, w
Nancy N. Dowd
SLAP SHOT(1977)
Neal Dowd
GREAT SINNER, THE(1949)
Ned Dowd
SLAP SHOT(1977), a, stunts; POPEYE(1980); SOUTHERN COMFORT(1981); EN-DANGERED SPECIES(1982); 48 HOURS(1982)
1984
PLACES IN THE HEART(1984)
Ross Dowd
JOURNEY INTO FEAR(1942), set d; JANE EYRE(1944), set d; YOUTH RUNS WILD(1944), set d; VARIETY GIRL(1947), set d; BIG CLOCK, THE(1948), set d; FOREIGN AFFAIR, A(1948), set d; MISS TATLOCK'S MILLIONS(1948), set d; MY OWN TRUE LOVE(1948), set d; ALIAS NICK BEAL(1949), set d; CHICAGO DEAD-LINE(1949), set d; RED, HOT AND BLUE(1949), set d; HIS KIND OF WOMAN(1951), set d; WHEN WORLDS COLLIDE(1951), set d; FOREVER FEMALE(1953), set d; LITTLE BOY LOST(1953), set d; AROUND THE WORLD IN 80 DAYS(1956), set d
Russ Dowd
ROAD TO BALI(1952), set d; SOMEBODY LOVES ME(1952), set d
Jim Dowdall
OCTOPUSSY(1983, Brit.), stunts
Jim Dowdell
SUPERMAN II(1980)
Robert Dowdell
MACHO CALLAHAN(1970)
1984
INITIATION, THE(1984)
Frank Dowding
ROCKERS(1980)
John Dowding
RAW DEAL(1977, Aus.), art d
Jon Dowding
MAD MAX(1979, Aus.), art d; THIRST(1979, Aus.), art d; DAY AFTER HAL-LOWEEN, THE(1981, Aus.), art d; ROAD GAMES(1981, Aus.), prod d&art d
1984
MELVIN, SON OF ALVIN(1984, Aus.), prod d
Liana Dowding
BABES IN TOYLAND(1961)
Llana Dowding
AIRPORT(1970)
Anthony Dowell
ROMEO AND JULIET(1966, Brit.); VALENTINO(1977, Brit.)
Carol Dowell
MOUSE ON THE MOON, THE(1963, Brit.)
Doug Dowell
CHANGES(1969)
George B. Dowell
GOIN' TO TOWN(1935), w; KLONDIKE ANNIE(1936), w
Lee Dowell
WHO SAYS I CAN'T RIDE A RAINBOW!(1971)
Robin Dowell
PRELUDE TO FAME(1950, Brit.); TOM BROWN'S SCHOOLDAYS(1951, Brit.); TWILIGHT WOMEN(1953, Brit.)
Garrick Dowhen
1984
JUST THE WAY YOU ARE(1984)
Freda Dowie
SUBTERFUGE(1969, US/Brit.)

Bernice Dowis
ZELIG(1983)
William C. Dowlan
Silents
CHORUS GIRL'S ROMANCE, A(1920), d; DANGEROUS TO MEN(1920), d
Misc. Silents
RICHELIEU(1914); DRUGGED WATERS(1916), a, d; LIGHT, THE(1916), d; MAD-CAP, THE(1916), d; ROSE OF THE ALLEY(1916), d; YOUTH'S ENDEARING CHARM(1916), d; OUTSIDER, THE(1917), d; COMMON PROPERTY(1919), d; COW-ARDICE COURT(1919), d; LOOT(1919), d; RESTLESS SOULS(1919), d; UNDER SUS-PICION(1919), d; LOCKED LIPS(1920), d; PEDDLER OF LIES, THE(1920), d
William Dowlan
Silents
ALIAS MARY BROWN(1918), d; ATOM, THE(1918), d
Misc. Silents
DAUGHTER ANGELE(1918), d; IRISH EYES(1918), d
William Dowlin
Misc. Silents
COLLEGE ORPHAN, THE(1915), d
Alison Dowling
MEMOIRS OF A SURVIVOR(1981, Brit.); REMEMBRANCE(1982, Brit.)
Bairbre Dowling
ZARDOZ(1974, Brit)
Barbara Dowling
DEMENTIA 13(1963)
Catherine Dowling
DOWN ARGENTINE WAY(1940)
Constance Dowling
KNICKERBOCKER HOLIDAY(1944); UP IN ARMS(1944); BLACK ANGEL(1946); BOSTON BLACKIE AND THE LAW(1946); WELL-GROOMED BRIDE, THE(1946); FLAME, THE(1948); CITY OF PAIN(1951, Ital.); STORMBOUND(1951, Ital.); VOICE IN YOUR HEART, A(1952, Ital.); DUEL WITHOUT HONOR(1953, Ital.); GOG(1954)
Misc. Talkies
BLIND SPOT(1947)
Dan Dowling
GOD IS MY CO-PILOT(1945); MY REPUTATION(1946)
Silents
LILAC TIME(1928)
Danny Dowling
STALLION ROAD(1947); TATTERED DRESS, THE(1957)
Denis Dowling
OH ROSALINDA(1956, Brit.)
Doris Dowling
LOST WEEKEND, THE(1945); BLUE DAHLIA, THE(1946); CRIMSON KEY, THE(1947); EMPEROR WALTZ, THE(1948); BITTER RICE(1950, Ital.); SARUM-BA(1950); OTHELLO(1955, U.S./Fr./Ital.); RUNNING TARGET(1956); PARTY CRASH-ERS, THE(1958); WINK OF AN EYE(1958); BIRDS DO IT(1966); CAR, THE(1977); SEPARATE WAYS(1981)
Eddie Dowling
RAINBOW MAN(1929), a, w; BLAZE O' GLORY(1930); HONEYMOON LANE(1931), a, w
Edward Dowling
SALLY, IRENE AND MARY(1938), w
Helen Dowling
FIXER, THE(1968)
J.J. Dowling
Silents
ICED BULLET, THE(1917); WOODEN SHOES(1917)
Misc. Silents
BULLETS AND BROWN EYES(1916); THOROUGHBRED, THE(1916); PADDY O'-HARA(1917); KITTY KELLY, M.D.(1919)
Joan Dowling
BOND STREET(1948, Brit.); FOR THEM THAT TRESPASS(1949, Brit.); MAN'S AFFAIR, A(1949, Brit.); HUE AND CRY(1950, Brit.); NO ROOM AT THE INN(1950, Brit.); MURDER WITHOUT CRIME(1951, Brit.); POOL OF LONDON(1951, Brit.); MAGIC BOX, THE(1952, Brit.); TRAIN OF EVENTS(1952, Brit.); AFFAIR IN MONTE CARLO(1953, Brit.); LANDFALL(1953, Brit.); TWILIGHT WOMEN(1953, Brit.)
Joe Dowling
OUTSIDER, THE(1980)
Misc. Silents
BAWBS O' BLUE RIDGE(1916)
Joseph Dowling
Silents
AND A STILL, SMALL VOICE(1918); ADELE(1919); ALL OF A SUDDEN NOR-MA(1919); MAN IN THE OPEN, A(1919); EVERYBODY'S SWEETHEART(1920); LITTLE LORD FAUNTLEROY(1921); IF YOU BELIEVE IT, IT'S SO(1922); ONE CLEAR CALL(1922); PRIDE OF PALOMAR, THE(1922); COURTSHIP OF MILES STANDISH, THE(1923); DOLLAR DEVILS(1923); ENEMIES OF CHILDREN(1923); LAW FORBIDS, THE(1924); LORD JIM(1925); NEW LIVES FOR OLD(1925); LITTLE IRISH GIRL, THE(1926); RAINMAKER, THE(1926)
Misc. Silents
BRINK, THE(1915); YANKEE WAY, THE(1917); HER PURCHASE PRICE(1919); JOSSELYN'S WIFE(1919); MAN'S COUNTRY, A(1919); HOUSE OF WHISPERS, THE(1920); U.P. TRAIL, THE(1920); HIS NIBS(1921); GIRL WHO RAN WILD, THE(1922); INFIDEL, THE(1922); TIGER ROSE(1923); THOSE WHO DARE(1924); FLOWER OF NIGHT(1925); TWO-GUN MAN, THE(1926)
Joseph J. Dowling
Silents
APOSTLE OF VENGEANCE, THE(1916); HOME(1916); PINCH HITTER, THE(1917); ALIEN ENEMY, AN(1918); CARMEN OF THE KLONDIKE(1918); HIS ROBE OF HONOR(1918); MORE TROUBLE(1918); JOYOUS LIAR, THE(1919); LORD LOVES THE IRISH, THE(1919); MIRACLE MAN, THE(1919); DEVIL TO PAY, THE(1920); RIDERS OF THE DAWN(1920); BEAUTIFUL LIAR(1921); BREAKING POINT, THE(1921); SIN OF MARTHA QUEED, THE(1921); DANGER POINT, THE(1922); TRAIL OF THE AXE, THE(1922); SPIDER AND THE ROSE, THE(1923); TESS OF THE D'URBERVILLES(1924)
Misc. Silents
CRIMINAL, THE(1916); GUNFIGHTER, THE(1917); MADAM WHO?(1917); MASTER OF HIS HOME(1917); SQUARE DEAL MAN, THE(1917); SUDDEN JIM(1917); BELLS, THE(1918); BLINDFOLDED(1918); GODDESS OF LOST LAKE, THE(1918); HONOR'S

CROSS(1918); LITTLE SISTER OF EVERYBODY, A(1918); FALSE CODE, THE(1919); MASTER MAN, THE(1919); BECKONING ROADS(1920); KENTUCKY COLONEL, THE(1920); LURE OF EGYPT, THE(1921); SPENDERS, THE(1921); GAIETY GIRL, THE(1924); UNSEEN HANDS(1924)
Kathryn Dowling
DINER(1982)
Marion Dowling
MELODY TRAIL(1935)
Mary Louise Dowling
PROUD AND THE PROFANE, THE(1956), tech adv
Silents
DIMPLES(1916), w
Maryan Dowling
FOLIES DERGERE(1935)
Patrick Dowling
SECRET VENTURE(1955, Brit.)
Sydell Dowling
Misc. Silents
TEMPTATION AND THE MAN(1916)
Thomas Dowling
DOWN ARGENTINE WAY(1940)
Vincent Dowling
BOYD'S SHOP(1960, Brit.); YOUNG CASSIDY(1965, U.S./Brit.); GUNS IN THE HEATHER(1968, Brit.)
William Dowling
Silents
LOST WORLD, THE(1925), d
Allison Louise Down
BLOOD FEAST(1963), w
Angela Down
LOOKING GLASS WAR, THE(1970, Brit.); WHAT BECAME OF JACK AND JILL?(1972, Brit.); MAHLER(1974, Brit.)
John Down
Silents
TRAIL OF '98, THE(1929)
Lesley Anne Down
BRANNIGAN(1975, Brit.)
Lesley-Anne Down
ASSAULT(1971, Brit.); COUNTESS DRACULA(1972, Brit.); POPE JOAN(1972, Brit.); SCALAWAG(1973, Yugo.); SCHOOL FOR UNCLAIMED GIRLS(1973, Brit.); FROM BEYOND THE GRAVE(1974, Brit.); PINK PANTHER STRIKES AGAIN, THE(1976, Brit.); LITTLE NIGHT MUSIC, A(1977, Aust./U.S./Ger.); BETSY, THE(1978); GREAT TRAIN ROBBERY, THE(1979, Brit.); HANOVER STREET(1979, Brit.); ROUGH CUT(1980, Brit.); SPHINX(1981)
Leslie-Ann Down
ALL THE RIGHT NOISES(1973, Brit.)
Martyn Down
BUDDIES(1983, Aus.), ed
Maurice Down
PROJECT: KILL(1976)
Louise Downe
GIRL, THE BODY, AND THE PILL, THE(1967), w; GRUESOME TWOSOME(1968), w; SHE-DEVILS ON WHEELS(1968), w
Don Downen
FRISCO KID(1935); PUBLIC ENEMY'S WIFE(1936); EVER SINCE EVE(1937)
Donald Downen
STRANDED(1935)
Donn Downen, Jr.
THAT CERTAIN WOMAN(1937)
David Downer
NORMAN LOVES ROSE(1982, Aus.); ROAD WARRIOR, THE(1982, Aus.); KILLING OF ANGEL STREET, THE(1983, Aus.)
Herb Downer
1984
BROTHER FROM ANOTHER PLANET, THE(1984); EXTERMINATOR 2(1984)
Katherine Downer
Silents
NO MOTHER TO GUIDE HER(1923)
Cathy Downes
WINTER OF OUR DREAMS(1982, Aus.); MONKEY GRIP(1983, Aus.)
Donald C. Downes
ORDERS TO KILL(1958, Brit.), w
Donald Downes
PIGEON THAT TOOK ROME, THE(1962), w
Jane Downes
DARLING(1965, Brit.)
Maurice Downes
SHEBA BABY(1975)
Olin Downes
CARNEGIE HALL(1947)
Sandra Downes
SPRING AND PORT WINE(1970, Brit.)
Terry Downes
STUDY IN TERROR, A(1966, Brit./Ger.); FEARLESS VAMPIRE KILLERS, OR PARDON ME BUT YOUR TEETH ARE IN MY NECK, THE(1967); SINGAPORE, SINGAPORE(1969, Fr./Ital.)
Bob Downey
YOU'VE GOT TO WALK IT LIKE YOU TALK IT OR YOU'LL LOSE THAT BEAT(1971)
Dorothy Downey
LIKE FATHER LIKE SON(1961); YOUNG SINNER, THE(1965)
Elsie Downey
CHAFED ELBOWS(1967); GREASER'S PALACE(1972)
Gary Downey
ICE STATION ZEBRA(1968)
Helen Downey
THUNDER IN CAROLINA(1960)

John Downey
LAST OF THE PONY RIDERS(1953)
Kenneth Downey
DULCIMER STREET(1948, Brit.); HAPPIEST DAYS OF YOUR LIFE(1950, Brit.);
OLIVER TWIST(1951, Brit.); GREAT GILBERT AND SULLIVAN, THE(1953, Brit.)
Morton Downey
LUCKY IN LOVE(1929); MOTHER'S BOY(1929); SYNCOPATION(1929); DEVIL'S
HOLIDAY, THE(1930); GHOST CATCHERS(1944)
Robert Downey
CHAFED ELBOWS(1967), p,d,&w; NO MORE EXCUSES(1968), a, d&w; PUT UP OR
SHUT UP(1968, Arg.), d&w; PUTNEY SWOPE(1969), d&w; GREASER'S PALA-
CE(1972), d&w; GONG SHOW MOVIE, THE(1980), w; UP THE ACADEMY(1980), d
1984
FIRSTBORN(1984)
Misc. Talkies
BABO 73(1964), d; TWO TONS OF TURQUOISE TO TAOS(1967), d
Robert Downey, Jr.
BABY, IT'S YOU(1983)
Roy Downey
EMPIRE OF THE ANTS(1977), spec eff; WHITE BUFFALO, THE(1977), spec eff
Roy L. Downey
DEATH VALLEY(1982), spec eff
1984
MICKI AND MAUDE(1984), spec eff
Downey Sisters
HIGH HAT(1937)
The Downey Sisters
GIFT OF GAB(1934)
Heather Downham
2001: A SPACE ODYSSEY(1968, U.S./Brit.)
Andrew Downie
YOU'RE ONLY YOUNG TWICE(1952, Brit.); HIGH AND DRY(1954, Brit.); TUNES
OF GLORY(1960, Brit.); TWO-WAY STRETCH(1961, Brit.); SPACEFLIGHT IC-1(1965,
Brit.); THIRTY NINE STEPS, THE(1978, Brit.)
Penny Downie
CROSSTALK(1982, Aus.)
Barry Downing
CAVALCADE OF THE WEST(1936); GARDEN OF ALLAH, THE(1936); PHANTOM
GOLD(1938); LIGHT THAT FAILED(1939); MY GAL SAL(1942)
Barry Noble Downing
THAT CERTAIN WOMAN(1937)
Betty Downing
INCREDIBLY STRANGE CREATURES WHO STOPPED LIVING AND BECAME
CRAZY MIXED-UP ZOMBIES, THE(1965)
Connie Downing
SKATETOWN, U.S.A.(1979)
David Downing
UP THE SANDBOX(1972); GORDON'S WAR(1973); BEEN DOWN SO LONG IT
LOOKS LIKE UP TO ME(1977)
Frank Downing
COMA(1978)
George Downing
GREAT TRAIN ROBBERY, THE(1979, Brit.)
Helen Downing
GIRL WITH A PISTOL, THE(1968, Ital.); VIRGIN WITCH, THE(1973, Brit.)
Silents
IVANHOE(1913)
Joe Downing
ANGELS WITH DIRTY FACES(1938); RACKET BUSTERS(1938); ANOTHER THIN
MAN(1939); EACH DAWN I DIE(1939); SMASHING THE MONEY RING(1939);
TORCHY RUNS FOR MAYOR(1939); DOUBLE DATE(1941); SAN FRANCISCO
DOCKS(1941); SEALED LIPS(1941); STRANGE ALIBI(1941); LEGACY OF
BLOOD(1978)
John Downing
TIME OF HIS LIFE, THE(1955, Brit.); HIGH FLIGHT(1957, Brit.); BOBBIKINS(1959,
Brit.)
Joseph Downing
CASE OF THE LUCKY LEGS, THE(1935); DR. SOCRATES(1935); BORROWING
TROUBLE(1937); DEVIL'S PARTY, THE(1938); I AM THE LAW(1938); LADY IN THE
MORGUE(1938); NIGHT HAWK, THE(1938); SLIGHT CASE OF MURDER, A(1938);
WIDE OPEN FACES(1938); FORGOTTEN WOMAN, THE(1939); MISSING EVI-
DENCE(1939); YOU CAN'T GET AWAY WITH MURDER(1939); CASTLE ON THE
HUDSON(1940); INVISIBLE STRIPES(1940); OH JOHNNY, HOW YOU CAN LO-
VE!(1940); SANDY IS A LADY(1940); SECRET SEVEN, THE(1940); BELLE
STARR(1941); UNHOLY PARTNERS(1941); BIG SHOT, THE(1942); JOHNNY EA-
GER(1942); LARCENY, INC.(1942); LUCKY JORDAN(1942); YOU CAN'T ESCAPE
FOREVER(1942); LAS VEGAS SHAKEDOWN(1955); FIGHTING TROUBLE(1956)
Maryan Downing
DESERT JUSTICE(1936)
Michael Downing
WILD, FREE AND HUNGRY(1970)
Pam Downing
TALK OF THE DEVIL(1937, Brit.)
Patrick Downing
PULP(1972, Brit.), prod d, set d
Rex Downing
BLACK BANDIT(1938); ESCAPE, THE(1939); NURSE EDITH CAVELL(1939);
WUTHERING HEIGHTS(1939); ADVENTURE IN DIAMONDS(1940); BLOOD AND
SAND(1941); MAYOR OF 44TH STREET, THE(1942); GAS HOUSE KIDS(1946);
GANGSTER, THE(1947); CALL NORTHSIDE 777(1948); HE WALKED BY
NIGHT(1948)
Rupert Downing
FOOTSTEPS IN THE NIGHT(1932, Brit.), w; GHOUL, THE(1934, Brit.), w
Terence Downing
EVERYTHING IS THUNDER(1936, Brit.); SKIMPY IN THE NAVY(1949, Brit.)
Tom Downing
STAKEOUT!(1962), m

Verno Downing
GUY NAMED JOE, A(1943)
Vernon Downing
BARRETTS OF WIMPOLE STREET, THE(1934); TREASURE ISLAND(1934); CLIVE
OF INDIA(1935); I FOUND STELLA PARISH(1935); LES MISERABLES(1935); MUTI-
NY ON THE BOUNTY(1935); ROMEO AND JULIET(1936); EMPEROR'S CANDLES-
TICKS, THE(1937); MARIE ANTOINETTE(1938); WUTHERING HEIGHTS(1939);
PRIDE AND PREJUDICE(1940); SUSPICION(1941); WIFE TAKES A FLYER,
THE(1942); SHERLOCK HOLMES FACES DEATH(1943); SHERLOCK HOLMES AND
THE SPIDER WOMAN(1944); CLOAK AND DAGGER(1946); TIME OF THEIR LIVES,
THE(1946); FOREVER AMBER(1947); GOLDEN EARRINGS(1947); MACOMBER AF-
FAIR, THE(1947); HOMECOMING(1948); MILLION DOLLAR MERMAID(1952)
Vernon P. Downing
DARK ANGEL, THE(1935)
Vincent Downing
MY WIFE'S LODGER(1952, Brit.)
Virginia Downing
BUTTERFIELD 8(1960)
Walter Downing
ARROWSMITH(1931); MARY BURNS, FUGITIVE(1935); ONE MORE SPRING(1935);
ONE MAN JUSTICE(1937); TWO-FISTED SHERIFF(1937)
Wilfred Downing
IT'S GREAT TO BE YOUNG(1956, Brit.); SHAKE HANDS WITH THE DEVIL(1959,
Ireland); HEIGHTS OF DANGER(1962, Brit.); SHE DIDN'T SAY NO!(1962, Brit.)
Wilfrid Downing
FINGER OF GUILT(1956, Brit.); NIGHT FIGHTERS, THE(1960)
Alena Downs
1984
THIEF OF HEARTS(1984)
Anson Downs
URBAN COWBOY(1980)
Cathy Downs
DARK CORNER, THE(1946); MY DARLING CLEMENTINE(1946); FOR YOU I
DIE(1947); NOOSE HANGS HIGH, THE(1948); PANHANDLE(1948); MASSACRE
RIVER(1949); SHORT GRASS(1950); SUNDOWNERS, THE(1950); JOE PALOOKA IN
TRIPLE CROSS(1951); GOBS AND GALS(1952); BANDITS OF THE WEST(1953); BIG
TIP OFF, THE(1955); KENTUCKY RIFLE(1956); OKLAHOMA WOMAN, THE(1956);
PHANTOM FROM 10,000 LEAGUES, THE(1956); SHE-CREATURE, THE(1956);
AMAZING COLOSSAL MAN, THE(1957); CURFEW BREAKERS(1957); MISSILE TO
THE MOON(1959)
Misc. Talkies
FLAMING URGE, THE(1953)
Charles Downs
CATSKILL HONEYMOON(1950), ph
Silents
JACQUELINE, OR BLAZING BARRIERS(1923), ph
Charlie Downs
RAGGEDY ANN AND ANDY(1977), anim; HEIDI'S SONG(1982), anim
Deedee Downs
HOMEWORK(1982)
Dermott Downs
ESCAPE TO WITCH MOUNTAIN(1975); FREAKY FRIDAY(1976)
Fred Downs
BUG(1975)
Frederic Downs
TERROR FROM THE YEAR 5,000(1958); EXPERIMENT IN TERROR(1962); HELL-
CATS, THE(1968); I LOVE MY WIFE(1970); 1776(1972)
Frederick Downs
I, THE JURY(1982)
Frederick Downs, Jr.
1984
COTTON CLUB, THE(1984)
Hugh Downs
LITTLE ANGEL(1961, Mex.); GLOBAL AFFAIR, A(1964); OH GOD! BOOK II(1980)
Jack Downs
BATTLE FLAME(1955)
Jane Downs
NIGHT TO REMEMBER, A(1958, Brit.)
Jimmy Downs
Silents
OUTLAWS OF RED RIVER(1927)
Johnny Downs
BABES IN TOYLAND(1934); COLLEGE SCANDAL(1935); CORONADO(1935); SO
RED THE ROSE(1935); VIRGINIA JUDGE, THE(1935); ARIZONA RAIDERS,
THE(1936); COLLEGE HOLIDAY(1936); EVERYBODY'S OLD MAN(1936); FIRST
BABY(1936); PIGSKIN PARADE(1936); BLONDE TROUBLE(1937); CLARENCE(1937);
THRILL OF A LIFETIME(1937); TURN OFF THE MOON(1937); ALGIERS(1938);
HOLD THAT CO-ED(1938); HUNTED MEN(1938); SWING, SISTER, SWING(1938);
BAD BOY(1939); FIRST OFFENDERS(1939); HAWAIIAN NIGHTS(1939); LAUGH IT
OFF(1939); PARENTS ON TRIAL(1939); CHILD IS BORN, A(1940); I CAN'T GIVE YOU
ANYTHING BUT LOVE, BABY(1940); MELODY AND MOONLIGHT(1940); SING,
DANCE, PLENTY HOT(1940); SLIGHTLY TEMPTED(1940); ADAM HAD FOUR
SONS(1941); ALL-AMERICAN CO-ED(1941); HONEYMOON FOR THREE(1941);
MOONLIGHT IN HAWAII(1941); REDHEAD(1941); SING ANOTHER CHORUS(1941);
BEHIND THE EIGHT BALL(1942); FRECKLES COMES HOME(1942); MAD MON-
STER, THE(1942); CAMPUS RHYTHM(1943); HARVEST MELODY(1943); TROCADE-
RO(1944); TWILIGHT ON THE PRAIRIE(1944); WHAT A MAN!(1944); FOREVER
YOURS(1945); RHAPSODY IN BLUE(1945); KID FROM BOOKLYN, THE(1946);
SQUARE DANCE JUBILEE(1949); HILLS OF OKLAHOMA(1950); COLUMN
SOUTH(1953); CRUISIN' DOWN THE RIVER(1953); GIRLS OF PLEASURE ISLAND,
THE(1953); HERE COME THE GIRLS(1953)
Margaret Downs
MAN OF THE MOMENT(1955, Brit.); IT'S A GREAT DAY(1956, Brit.)
Mike Downs
TOWN THAT DREADED SUNDOWN, THE(1977)
Sandra Downs
NEW KIND OF LOVE, A(1963)

Watson Downs
DOUBLE LIFE, A(1947); SENATOR WAS INDISCREET, THE(1947); SECRET BEYOND THE DOOR, THE(1948); MY FORBIDDEN PAST(1951); YOU NEVER CAN TELL(1951); LAW AND ORDER(1953); MAGNETIC MONSTER, THE(1953); OKLAHOMAN, THE(1957); ROCKABILLY BABY(1957)

Watson H. Downs
HOT SPELL(1958)

Bill Dowson
MARIE-ANN(1978, Can.)

Filippi Dowson
Silents
SHIPS THAT PASS IN THE NIGHT(1921, Brit.)

Ralph Dowson
DANCE OF DEATH, THE(1938, Brit.)

Henry Payson Dowst
Silents
ON THE STROKE OF THREE(1924), w

B. E. Doxat-Pratt
Silents
AS GOD MADE HER(1920, Brit.), d&w; FATE'S PLAYTHING(1920, Brit.), d; JOHN HERIOT'S WIFE(1920, Brit.), d&w; LAUGHTER AND TEARS(1921, Brit.), d; OTHER PERSON, THE(1921, Brit.), d; MY LORD THE CHAUFFEUR(1927, Brit.), d
Misc. Silents
LITTLE HOUR OF PETER WELLS, THE(1920, Brit.), d; SKIN GAME, THE(1920, Brit.), d; CIRCUS JIM(1921, Brit.), d

C. B. Doxat-Pratt
Silents
BULLDOG DRUMMOND(1923, Brit.), w

Norman Doxat-Pratt
Misc. Silents
CIRCUS JIM(1921, Brit.)

Jacqueline Doyen
ZAZIE(1961, Fr.); VERY PRIVATE AFFAIR, A(1962, Fr./Ital.); NO TIME FOR BREAKFAST(1978, Fr.); ENTRE NOUS(1983, Fr.)

Leon Doyen
PLAYTIME(1973, Fr.)

Truuk Doyer
PASSIONATE DEMONS, THE(1962, Norway)

A. Conan Doyle
FIRES OF FATE(1932, Brit.), w

Adalyn Doyle
FINISHING SCHOOL(1934); SHE MARRIED HER BOSS(1935)

Arthur Conan Doyle
HOUND OF THE BASKERVILLES(1932, Brit.), w; ADVENTURES OF SHERLOCK HOLMES, THE(1939), w; HOUND OF THE BASKERVILLES, THE(1939), w; HOUND OF THE BASKERVILLES, THE(1959, Brit.), w; ADVENTURES OF GERARD, THE(1970, Brit.), w; HOUND OF THE BASKERVILLES, THE(1980, Brit.), w; HOUND OF THE BASKERVILLES, THE(1983, Brit.), w
Silents
HOUSE OF TEMPERLEY, THE(1913, Brit.), w; FIRM OF GIRDLESTONE, THE(1915, Brit.), w; FIRES OF FATE(1923, Brit.), w

Sir Arthur Conan Doyle
SHERLOCK HOLMES' FATAL HOUR(1931, Brit.), w; SPECKLED BAND, THE(1931, Brit.), w; MISSING REMBRANDT, THE(1932, Brit.), w; SHERLOCK HOLMES(1932), w; SIGN OF FOUR, THE(1932, Brit.), w; STUDY IN SCARLET, A(1933), w; TRIUMPH OF SHERLOCK HOLMES, THE(1935, Brit.), w; RETURN OF SHERLOCK HOLMES(1936), w; MURDER AT THE BASKERVILLES(1941, Brit.), w; SHERLOCK HOLMES AND THE VOICE OF TERROR(1942), w; SHERLOCK HOLMES FACES DEATH(1943), w; SHERLOCK HOLMES IN WASHINGTON(1943), w; PEARL OF DEATH, THE(1944), w; SCARLET CLAW, THE(1944), w; SHERLOCK HOLMES AND THE SPIDER WOMAN(1944), w; HOUSE OF FEAR, THE(1945), w; PURSUIT TO ALGIERS(1945), w; DRESSED TO KILL(1946), w; TERROR BY NIGHT(1946), w; LOST WORLD, THE(1960), w; SHERLOCK HOLMES AND THE DEADLY NECKLACE(1962, Ger.), w; STUDY IN TERROR, A(1966, Brit./Ger.), w; MURDER BY DECREE(1979, Brit.), w; SIGN OF FOUR, THE(1983, Brit.), w
Silents
SHERLOCK HOLMES(1922), w; LOST WORLD, THE(1925), w

Barbara Doyle
1984
SUBURBIA(1984)

Barc Doyle
LAST PICTURE SHOW, THE(1971)

Betty Doyle
Misc. Silents
BLEAK HOUSE(1922, Brit.)

Bobby Doyle
Silents
JOHNNY GET YOUR HAIR CUT(1927); SUNSET DERBY, THE(1927)

Brenda Doyle
ULYSSES(1967, U.S./Brit.)

Buddy Doyle
GREAT ZIEGFELD, THE(1936)

Bunny Doyle
FACING THE MUSIC(1941, Brit.)

Col. Thomas Doyle
SO PROUDLY WE HAIL(1943), tech adv

David Doyle
ACT ONE(1964); TIGER MAKES OUT, THE(1967); NO WAY TO TREAT A LADY(1968); PAPER LION(1968); APRIL FOOLS, THE(1969); SOME KIND OF A NUT(1969); LOVING(1970); SIDELONG GLANCES OF A PIGEON KICKER, THE(1970); MAKING IT(1971); NEW LEAF, A(1971); PURSUIT OF HAPPINESS, THE(1971); WHO KILLED MARY WHAT'SER NAME?(1971); LADY LIBERTY(1972, Ital./Fr.); PARADES(1972); VIGILANTE FORCE(1976); CAPRICORN ONE(1978); COMEBACK, THE(1982, Brit.); LINE, THE(1982)
Misc. Talkies
PARADES(1972)

David F. Doyle
COOGAN'S BLUFF(1968)

Deidre Doyle
OLIVER TWIST(1951, Brit.)

Deirdre Doyle
PROMOTER, THE(1952, Brit.); WHITE CORRIDORS(1952, Brit.)

Denise Doyle
NAKED CITY, THE(1948)

Desmond Doyle
ROMEO AND JULIET(1966, Brit.)

Frank Doyle
FROM THIS DAY FORWARD(1946), ed; SINBAD THE SAILOR(1947), ed; TYCOON(1947), ed; BOY WITH THE GREEN HAIR, THE(1949), ed; KISS FOR CORLISS, A(1949), ed; RUSTLERS(1949), ed; OUTCASTS OF THE CITY(1958), ed

Henry Doyle
Misc. Silents
CHILDREN OF COURAGE(1921, Brit.)

Jack Doyle
HELL'S CARGO(1935, Brit.); NAVY SPY(1937)

James H. Doyle
LITTLE GIANT, THE(1933)

Jim Doyle
THE RUNNER STUMBLES(1979)
1984
NIGHTMARE ON ELM STREET, A(1984), spec eff

John T. Doyle
MOTHER'S BOY(1929); HIS WOMAN(1931); GAMBLING(1934)

Johnny Doyle
Silents
WITHOUT HOPE(1914)

Julian Doyle
MONTY PYTHON'S LIFE OF BRIAN(1979, Brit.), ed; TIME BANDITS(1981, Brit.), ed; MONTY PYTHON'S THE MEANING OF LIFE(1983, Brit.), ed

Kathleen Doyle
CANNERY ROW(1982)

Laird Doyle
PHANTOM EXPRESS, THE(1932), w; HELL BELOW(1933), w; BRITISH AGENT(1934), w; FINISHING SCHOOL(1934), w; JIMMY THE GENT(1934), w; KEY, THE(1934), w; SING AND LIKE IT(1934), w; BORDERTOWN(1935), w; FRONT PAGE WOMAN(1935), w; OIL FOR THE LAMPS OF CHINA(1935), w; SPECIAL AGENT(1935), w; CAIN AND MABEL(1936), w; DANGEROUS(1936), w; HEARTS DIVIDED(1936), w; THREE MEN ON A HORSE(1936), w; ANOTHER DAWN(1937), w; PRINCE AND THE PAUPER, THE(1937), w; STRANGERS ON A HONEYMOON(1937, Brit.), w; SINGAPORE WOMAN(1941), w; NORTHWEST OUTPOST(1947), w

Lee Doyle
JANE AUSTEN IN MANHATTAN(1980)
1984
BOSTONIANS, THE(1984)

Lee H. Doyle
JUST TELL ME WHAT YOU WANT(1980); I, THE JURY(1982)

Len Doyle
DEAD TO THE WORLD(1961)

Lording Doyle
RAIDERS OF THE LOST ARK(1981), anim

Maggie Doyle
CLUB, THE(1980, Aus.)

Martin Doyle
HOG WILD(1980, Can.)

Mary Doyle
MARKED WOMAN(1937); TALENT SCOUT(1937); BELOVED BRAT(1938); YOUNG NURSES, THE(1973); LINE, THE(1982)
Silents
BAR SINISTER, THE(1917)
Misc. Silents
GOLDEN GOD, THE(1917)

Maxine Doyle
BABBITT(1934); KANSAS CITY PRINCESS(1934); KEY, THE(1934); SIX-DAY BIKE RIDER(1934); STUDENT TOUR(1934); BORN TO GAMBLE(1935); CONDEMNED TO LIVE(1935); MYSTERY MAN, THE(1935); PUT ON THE SPOT(1936); RIO GRANDE ROMANCE(1936); COME ON, COWBOYS(1937); ROUNDUP TIME IN TEXAS(1937); TAMING THE WILD(1937); THANKS FOR LISTENING(1937); FURY BELOW(1938); OVERLAND MAIL ROBBERY(1943); RAIDERS OF SUNSET PASS(1943); LADY AND THE MONSTER, THE(1944); MAN FROM FRISCO(1944); SAN FERNANDO VALLEY(1944); SING, NEIGHBOR, SING(1944)

Michael Doyle
MARINES COME THROUGH, THE(1943)
1984
FLASH OF GREEN, A(1984)

Mimi Doyle
DRAMATIC SCHOOL(1938); KITTY FOYLE(1940); MARRIED BACHELOR(1941); PENALTY, THE(1941); SLIGHTLY DANGEROUS(1943); SO PROUDLY WE HAIL(1943); PRACTICALLY YOURS(1944); MASQUERADE IN MEXICO(1945); DANGEROUS YEARS(1947); GOOD SAM(1948); HOMECOMING(1948); EXECUTIVE SUITE(1954); LONG GRAY LINE, THE(1955); MISTER ROBERTS(1955); SPRING REUNION(1957); LAST HURRAH, THE(1958); PAY OR DIE(1960); INCIDENT IN AN ALLEY(1962); BABY MAKER, THE(1970)

Monte Doyle
SIGNPOST TO MURDER(1964), w

Pat Doyle
CHARRIOTS OF FIRE(1981, Brit.)

Patricia Doyle
WUTHERING HEIGHTS(1970, Brit.)

Patsy Doyle
STAGECOACH(1939); DEVIL AND DANIEL WEBSTER, THE(1941)

Peggy Doyle
1984
FLETCH(1984)

Ramsaye Doyle
DEVIL TIGER(1934)

FEMALE ON THE BEACH(1955); TO HELL AND BACK(1955); PRICE OF FEAR, THE(1956); WALK THE PROUD LAND(1956); JEANNE EAGELS(1957); STEP DOWN TO TERROR(1958); NO NAME ON THE BULLET(1959); BACK STREET(1961); TAMMY, TELL ME TRUE(1961); SHOWDOWN(1963); DEAR HEART(1964); LIVELY SET, THE(1964); THIRD DAY, THE(1965); VALLEY OF THE DOLLS(1967); COUNTERFEIT KILLER, THE(1968); MONEY JUNGLE, THE(1968); SWIMMER, THE(1968); ARRANGEMENT, THE(1969); HAIL, HERO!(1969); SEVEN MINUTES, THE(1971)

Charlie Drake
GOLDEN LINK, THE(1954, Brit.); SANDS OF THE DESERT(1960, Brit.), a, w; PETTICOAT PIRATES(1961, Brit.), a, w; CRACKSMAN, THE(1963, Brit.), a, w; MISTER TEN PERCENT(1967, Brit.)

Chauncey M. Drake
HANDS ACROSS THE TABLE(1935)

Chris Drake
FALCON IN HOLLYWOOD, THE(1944); MUSIC IN MANHATTAN(1944); MY PAL, WOLF(1944); YOUTH RUNS WILD(1944); DELIGHTFULLY DANGEROUS(1945); TOKYO ROSE(1945); TWO O'CLOCK COURAGE(1945); WALK IN THE SUN, A(1945); FEAR IN THE NIGHT(1947); LOST MOMENT, THE(1947); THIS TIME FOR KEEPS(1947); FATHER OF THE BRIDE(1950); AS YOU WERE(1951); HALLS OF MONTEZUMA(1951); PIER 23(1951); FOR MEN ONLY(1952); THEM!(1954)

Claudia Drake
REUNION IN FRANCE(1942); BORDER PATROL(1943); CAMPUS RHYTHM(1943); FALSE COLORS(1943); ENEMY OF WOMEN(1944); BEDSIDE MANNER(1945); CRIMSON CANARY(1945); DETOUR(1945); LADY CONFESSES, THE(1945); WHY GIRLS LEAVE HOME(1945); FACE OF MARBLE(1946); GENTLEMAN FROM TEXAS(1946); LAWLESS BREED, THE(1946); LIVE WIRES(1946); RENEGADE GIRL(1946); RETURN OF RIN TIN TIN, THE(1947); INDIAN AGENT(1948); LADY AT MIDNIGHT(1948); COWBOY AND THE INDIANS, THE(1949); PACE THAT THRILLS, THE(1952); NORTHERN PATROL(1953); CALYPSO JOE(1957)
Misc. Talkies
LONE STAR MOONLIGHT(1946)

Colin Drake
ONCE MORE, WITH FEELING(1960); WHAT'S NEW, PUSSYCAT?(1965, U.S./Fr.); MISTER FREEDOM(1970, Fr.); INN OF THE DAMNED(1974, Aus.); GREAT MACARTHY, THE(1975, Aus.)

Colleen Drake
QUEEN OF OUTER SPACE(1958)

Dan Drake
SOME OF MY BEST FRIENDS ARE...(1971); WHO SAYS I CAN'T RIDE A RAINBOW!(1971)

Danny Drake
KID FROM BOOKLYN, THE(1946)

Dennis Drake
1984
PREPPIES(1984)

Dick Drake
HAWMPS!(1976)

Dodie Drake
DIARY OF A HIGH SCHOOL BRIDE(1959)

Dona Drake
WITHOUT RESERVATIONS(1946); ALOMA OF THE SOUTH SEAS(1941); LOUISIANA PURCHASE(1941); ROAD TO MOROCCO(1942); STAR SPANGLED RHYTHM(1942); LET'S FACE IT(1943); SALUTE FOR THREE(1943); HOT RHYTHM(1944); DANGEROUS MILLIONS(1946); ANOTHER PART OF THE FOREST(1948); SO THIS IS NEW YORK(1948); BEYOND THE FOREST(1949); DOOLINS OF OKLAHOMA, THE(1949); GIRL FROM JONES BEACH, THE(1949); FORTUNES OF CAPTAIN BLOOD(1950); VALENTINO(1951); KANSAS CITY CONFIDENTIAL(1952); BANDITS OF CORSICA, THE(1953); DOWN LAREDO WAY(1953); SON OF BELLE STARR(1953); PRINCESS OF THE NILE(1954)

Donna Leigh Drake
TRACK OF THE MOONBEAST(1976)

Dorothy Drake
KISS AND MAKE UP(1934); YOUNG AND BEAUTIFUL(1934)
Misc. Silents
UNDER THE RED ROBE(1915, Brit.); SAINTLY SINNER, THE(1917)

Douglass Drake [Johnny Mitchell]
LAUGH YOUR BLUES AWAY(1943); LAW OF THE NORTHWEST(1943); ROBIN HOOD OF THE RANGE(1943); THERE'S SOMETHING ABOUT A SOLDIER(1943); REDHEAD FROM MANHATTAN(1954)

Ellis Drake
SEZ O'REILLY TO MACNAB(1938, Brit.)

Eugenia Drake
Misc. Silents
THAT SOMETHING(1921)

Fabia Drake
MEET MR. PENNY(1938, Brit.); DULCIMER STREET(1948, Brit.); ALL OVER THE TOWN(1949, Brit.); POET'S PUB(1949, Brit.); HOUR OF THIRTEEN, THE(1952); WHITE CORRIDORS(1952, Brit.); ISN'T LIFE WONDERFUL!(1953, Brit.); FAST AND LOOSE(1954, Brit.); YOUNG WIVES' TALE(1954, Brit.); ALL FOR MARY(1956, Brit.); GOOD COMPANIONS, THE(1957, Brit.); NOT WANTED ON VOYAGE(1957, Brit.); VIOLENT STRANGER(1957, Brit.); GIRLS AT SEA(1958, Brit.); WHAT A WHOPPER(1961, Brit.); MY WIFE'S FAMILY(1962, Brit.); SEVEN KEYS(1962, Brit.); OPERATION BULLSHINE(1963, Brit.); NICE GIRL LIKE ME, A(1969, Brit.); DEVIL'S WIDOW, THE(1972, Brit.); GOT IT MADE(1974, Brit.)

Frances Drake
BOLERO(1934); LADIES SHOULD LISTEN(1934); TRUMPET BLOWS, THE(1934); FORSAKING ALL OTHERS(1935); LES MISERABLES(1935); MAD LOVE(1935); TRANSIENT LADY(1935); WITHOUT REGRET(1935); AND SUDDEN DEATH(1936); FLORIDA SPECIAL(1936); I'D GIVE MY LIFE(1936); PREVIEW MURDER MYSTERY(1936); THE INVISIBLE RAY(1936); LOVE UNDER FIRE(1937); MIDNIGHT TAXI(1937); LONE WOLF IN PARIS, THE(1938); SHE MARRIED AN ARTIST(1938); THERE'S ALWAYS A WOMAN(1938); IT'S A WONDERFUL WORLD(1939); I TAKE THIS WOMAN(1940); AFFAIRS OF MARTHA, THE(1942)

Gabrielle Drake
MAN OUTSIDE, THE(1968, Brit.); CROSSPLOT(1969, Brit.); THERE'S A GIRL IN MY SOUP(1970, Brit.); CONNECTING ROOMS(1971, Brit.); SUBURBAN WIVES(1973, Brit.)
Misc. Talkies
AU PAIR GIRLS(1973); COMMUTER HUSBANDS(1974)

Geoffrey Drake
TARZAN AND THE LOST SAFARI(1957, Brit.), art d; INN OF THE SIXTH HAPPINESS, THE(1958), art d; KEY, THE(1958, Brit.), art d; MOUSE THAT ROARED, THE(1959, Brit.), art d; JASON AND THE ARGONAUTS(1963, Brit.), prod d; VICTORS, THE(1963), prod d; LORD JIM(1965, Brit.), prod d; MACKENNA'S GOLD(1969), prod d, art d, spec eff; YOUNG WINSTON(1972, Brit.), prod d; INTERNECINE PROJECT, THE(1974, Brit.), prod d; SINBAD AND THE EYE OF THE TIGER(1977, U.S./Brit.), prod d; FORCE 10 FROM NAVARONE(1978, Brit.), prod d; ALL THINGS BRIGHT AND BEAUTIFUL(1979, Brit.), prod d

Geofrey Drake
GUNS OF NAVARONE, THE(1961), prod d

Gerald Drake
LOOSE ENDS(1975)

Herbert Drake
JOURNEY INTO FEAR(1942)

Hilary Drake
1984
SUCCESS IS THE BEST REVENGE(1984, Brit.)

James Drake
SAILOR OF THE KING(1953, Brit.)

James H. Drake
IF HE HOLLERS, LET HIM GO(1968)

Jim Drake
TARGET EARTH(1954); THERE'S ALWAYS VANILLA(1972), m

Jodie Drake
MELANIE(1982, Can.)

John Drake
MYSTERY ON BIRD ISLAND(1954, Brit.); FIND THE LADY(1956, Brit.); DATE WITH DISASTER(1957, Brit.); LINKS OF JUSTICE(1958); SONG OF THE LOON(1970)

Josephine Drake
Silents
SOCIAL CELEBRITY, A(1926)
Misc. Silents
BOUGHT AND PAID FOR(1916); PALM BEACH GIRL, THE(1926)

Judith Drake
TALES OF ORDINARY MADNESS(1983, Ital.)

Karen Drake
MALE SERVICE(1966)

Ken Drake
I BURY THE LIVING(1958); CRIME AND PUNISHMENT, U.S.A.(1959); NEW INTERNS, THE(1964)

Kenneth Drake
BIGAMIST,THE(1953)

Larry Drake
THIS STUFF'LL KILL YA!(1971)
1984
KARATE KID, THE(1984)
Misc. Talkies
TRUCKIN' MAN(1975)

Lisa Drake
RAT RACE, THE(1960)

Marcie Drake
JACKSON COUNTY JAIL(1976)

Marciee Drake
TOOLBOX MURDERS, THE(1978)

Margot Drake
Silents
BACHELORS' CLUB, THE(1921, Brit.)
Misc. Silents
HEADMASTER, THE(1921, Brit.); MONEY(1921); STREET OF ADVENTURE, THE(1921, Brit.); WONDERFUL YEAR, THE(1921, Brit.)

Marsha Drake
SHE FREAK(1967)

Maurice Drake
Silents
NETS OF DESTINY(1924, Brit.), w

Melissa Drake
CONJUGAL BED, THE(1963, Ital.)

Mervyn Drake
1984
RAZORBACK(1984, Aus.)

Michael Drake
RETURN OF CAROL DEANE, THE(1938, Brit.); DESIGN FOR MURDER(1940, Brit.)

Michele Drake
HISTORY OF THE WORLD, PART 1(1981)

Miller Drake
CANNONBALL(1976, U.S./Hong Kong); HOLLYWOOD BOULEVARD(1976)

Milton Drake
GLAMOUR FOR SALE(1940), m/l Oakland

Oliver Drake [John Wesley Patterson]
DEADWOOD PASS(1933), w

Oliver Drake
ROGUE OF THE RIO GRANDE(1930), w; HURRICANE HORSEMAN(1931), w; LAW OF THE TONG(1931), w; WEST OF CHEYENNE(1931), w; BATTLING BUCKAROO(1932), w; CHEYENNE CYCLONE, THE(1932), w; DRIFTER, THE(1932), w; LAW AND LAWLESS(1932), w; SADDLE BUSTER, THE(1932), w; SINISTER HANDS(1932), w; GUN LAW(1933), w; OUTLAW JUSTICE(1933), w; VIA PONY EXPRESS(1933), w; WAR OF THE RANGE(1933), w; WHEN A MAN RIDES ALONE(1933), w; TEXAS TORNADO(1933), p,d&w; CYCLONE RANGER(1935), w; SAGEBRUSH TROUBADOR(1935), w; SINGING VAGABOND, THE(1935), w; COMIN' ROUND THE MOUNTAIN(1936), w; GHOST TOWN GOLD(1937), w; GUNSMOKE RANCH(1937), w; HEART OF THE ROCKIES(1937), w; HIT THE SADDLE(1937), w; NATION AFLAME(1937), w; OH, SUSANNA(1937), w; PUBLIC COWBOY NO. 1(1937), w; RIDERS OF THE WHISTLING SKULL(1937), w; ROARIN' LEAD(1937), w; ROUNDUP TIME IN TEXAS(1937), w; TRIGGER TRIO, THE(1937), w; BORDER G-MAN(1938), w; GUN LAW(1938), w; LAWLESS VALLEY(1938), w; PAINTED DESERT, THE(1938), w; PURPLE VIGILANTES, THE(1938), w; RENEGADE RANGER(1938), w; WILD HORSE RODEO(1938), w; ARIZONA LEGION(1939), w; COWBOYS FROM TEXAS(1939), w; FIGHTING GRINGO, THE(1939), w; RACKETEERS OF THE RANGE(1939), w; TROUBLE IN SUNDOWN(1939), w; TRAILING

DOUBLE TROUBLE(1940), w; TULSA KID, THE(1940), W; CITY OF MISSING GIRLS(1941), w; FORBIDDEN TRAILS(1941), w; FUGITIVE VALLEY(1941), w; HARD GUY(1941), w; KANSAS CYCLONE(1941), w; LONE RIDER AMBUSHED, THE(1941), w; PALS OF THE PECOS(1941), w; ROBBERS OF THE RANGE(1941), w; BILLY THE KID TRAPPED(1942), w; BOSS OF HANGTOWN MESA(1942), p, w; DEEP IN THE HEART OF TEXAS(1942), p, w; LITTLE JOE, THE WRANGLER(1942), p; LONE RIDER IN CHEYENNE, THE(1942), w; RAIDERS OF THE WEST(1942), w; SHUT MY BIG MOUTH(1942), w; SILVER BULLET, THE(1942), p, w; TODAY I HANG(1942), d, w; ARIZONA TRAIL(1943), p; BORDER BUCKAROOS(1943), d, w; CHEYENNE ROUNDUP(1943), p; FIGHTING VALLEY(1943), d&w; FRONTIER LAW(1943), p; LONE STAR TRAIL, THE(1943), p, w; OLD CHISHOLM TRAIL(1943), p; RAIDERS OF SAN JOAQUIN(1943), p; TENTING TONIGHT ON THE OLD CAMP GROUND(1943), p; WEST OF TEXAS(1943), d&w; MARSHAL OF GUNSMOKE(1944), p; MUMMY'S CURSE, THE(1944), p; OKLAHOMA RAIDERS(1944), p; OLD TEXAS TRAIL, THE(1944), p; PRIDE OF THE PLAINS(1944), p; RIDERS OF THE SANTA FE(1944), p; TRAIL OF TERROR(1944), d&w; TRAIL TO GUNSIGHT(1944), p; TRIGGER TRAIL(1944), p; WEIRD WOMAN(1944), p; BEYOND THE PECOS(1945), p; RENEGADES OF THE RIO GRANDE(1945), p; RIDERS OF THE DAWN(1945), p&d; SONG OF THE SIERRAS(1946), p&d, w; WEST OF THE ALAMO(1946), p&d; GINGER(1947), d, w; RAINBOW OVER THE ROCKIES(1947), p&d, w; DEADLINE(1948), p, d&w; FEATHERED SERPENT, THE(1948), w; ACROSS THE RIO GRANDE(1949), d; BRAND OF FEAR(1949), d; KID FROM GOWER GULCH(1949), d; LAWLESS CODE(1949), d; ROARING WESTWARD(1949), d; SKY DRAGON(1949), w; TRAIL OF THE YUKON(1949), w; BATTLING MARSHAL(1950), d; OUTLAW TREASURE(1955), d; DRAGON WELLS MASSACRE(1957), w; PARSON AND THE OUTLAW, THE(1957), d, w

Misc. Talkies

LONESOME TRAIL(1945), d; SADDLE SERENADE(1945), d; SPRINGTIME IN TEXAS(1945), d; MOON OVER MONTANA(1946), d; TRAIL TO MEXICO(1946), d; FIGHTING MUSTANG(1948), d; SUNSET CARSON RIDES AGAIN(1948), d

Silents

CYCLONE OF THE RANGE(1927), w; BREED OF THE SUNSETS(1928), w; DESERT PIRATE, THE(1928), w; DRIFTIN' SANDS(1928), w, ed; ORPHAN OF THE SAGE(1928), w; PHANTOM OF THE RANGE(1928), w; DESERT RIDER, THE(1929), w; GUN LAW(1929), w; PALS OF THE PRAIRIE(1929), w

Pat Drake
VENGEANCE IS MINE(1948, Brit.)

Patsy Drake
LOVE IN WAITING(1948, Brit.); TROUBLE IN THE AIR(1948, Brit.)

Paul Drake
MILLIONS LIKE US(1943, Brit.); SUDDEN IMPACT(1983)

1984

BEVERLY HILLS COP(1984); CRACKERS(1984)

Paula Drake
NIGHT CLUB GIRL(1944)

Pauline Drake
FATAL HOUR, THE(1940); LADY EVE, THE(1941); UNDER FIESTA STARS(1941); HI, NEIGHBOR(1942); SECRETS OF THE UNDERGROUND(1943); HAIL THE CONQUERING HERO(1944); JAM SESSION(1944); ONCE UPON A TIME(1944); RACKET MAN, THE(1944); CAGED(1950); ILLEGAL(1955); MY FAIR LADY(1964); WILLARD(1971)

Misc. Talkies

HER UNBORN CHILD(1933)

Peggy Drake
TUTTLES OF TAHITI(1942)

Pete Drake
SECOND FIDDLE TO A STEEL GUITAR(1965)

Peter Drake
THAT TENNESSEE BEAT(1966)

Richard Drake
MEMENTO MEI(1963)

Roger Drake
FIREFLY, THE(1937); HURRICANE, THE(1937)

Ronald Drake
KILLER WALKS, A(1952, Brit.), p,d&w

Steve Drake
PIONEER JUSTICE(1947); BLACK HILLS(1948); GALLANT LEGION, THE(1948); WESTWARD TRAIL, THE(1948)

T.Y. Drake
TERROR TRAIN(1980, Can.), w

Tom Drake
HOWARDS OF VIRGINIA, THE(1940); MAISIE GOES TO RENO(1944); MARRIAGE IS A PRIVATE AFFAIR(1944); MEET ME IN ST. LOUIS(1944); MRS. PARKINGTON(1944); TWO GIRLS AND A SAILOR(1944); WHITE CLIFFS OF DOVER, THE(1944); THIS MAN'S NAVY(1945); BLUE SIERRA(1946); COURAGE OF LASSIE(1946); FAITHFUL IN MY FASHION(1946); GREEN YEARS, THE(1946); BEGINNING OR THE END, THE(1947); CASS TIMBERLANE(1947); I'LL BE YOURS(1947); ALIAS A GENTLEMAN(1948); HILLS OF HOME(1948); MR. BELVEDERE GOES TO COLLEGE(1949); SCENE OF THE CRIME(1949); GREAT RUPERT, THE(1950); DISC JOCKEY(1951); FBI GIRL(1951); NEVER TRUST A GAMBLER(1951); SANGAREE(1953); BETRAYED WOMEN(1955); SUDDEN DANGER(1955); CYCLOPS(1957); DATE WITH DISASTER(1957, Brit.); RAINTREE COUNTY(1957); MONEY, WOMEN AND GUNS(1958); WARLOCK(1959); BRAMBLE BUSH, THE(1960); HOUSE OF THE BLACK DEATH(1965); SANDPIPER, THE(1965); JOHNNY RENO(1966); SINGING NUN, THE(1966); RED TOMAHAWK(1967); WARKILL(1968, U.S./Phil.); SPECTRE OF EDGAR ALLAN POE, THE(1974); SAVAGE ABDUCTION(1975); KEEPER, THE(1976, Can.), d&w

Virgil Drake
RENEGADES OF THE RIO GRANDE(1945)

William Drake
ADVENTURES OF SHERLOCK HOLMES, THE(1939), w

William A. Drake
GRAND HOTEL(1932), w; STRANGE JUSTICE(1932), w; THREE MUSKETEERS, THE(1939), w

Bebe Drake-Hooks
WHICH WAY IS UP?(1977); LAST MARRIED COUPLE IN AMERICA, THE(1980)

Bebe Drake-Massey
FIRST MONDAY IN OCTOBER(1981)

The Dramatics
DARKTOWN STRUTTERS(1975)

Sam Drane
Misc. Silents
CRISIS, THE(1915)

Leontine Dranet
Silents
PATCHWORK GIRL OF OZ, THE(1914)

George Draney
PARTY GIRL(1930), w; EX-FLAME(1931), w

D. Dranizin
THEY CALL ME ROBERT(1967, USSR)

Robert Dranko
1001 ARABIAN NIGHTS(1959), prod d; WAR BETWEEN MEN AND WOMEN, THE(1972), anim

L. Dranovskaya
LAST GAME, THE(1964, USSR)

Lydia Dranovskaya
TRAIN GOES EAST, THE(1949, USSR)

Barry Dransfield
1984
BOUNTY, THE(1984)

Colleen Drape
CALIFORNIA SUITE(1978)

Dewey Drapeau
GREAT SIOUX UPRISING, THE(1953)

Alice Draper
MOONLIGHT IN VERMONT(1943); SO'S YOUR UNCLE(1943)

Billy Draper
NAVAJO(1952)

David Draper
LORD LOVE A DUCK(1966); WALK, DON'T RUN(1966); DON'T MAKE WAVES(1967)

Don Draper
CHECKMATE(1973)

Emily Draper
1984
MAKING THE GRADE(1984), cos

Forrest Draper
SEND ME NO FLOWERS(1964)

Fred Draper
FACES(1968); HUSBANDS(1970); DIRTY HARRY(1971); WOMAN UNDER THE INFLUENCE, A(1974); OPENING NIGHT(1977)

Frederick Draper
CHILD IS WAITING, A(1963)

Golda Draper
NIGHT WAITRESS(1936), w

Grace Draper
SECRET PEOPLE(1952, Brit.)

Jack Draper
MYSTERY IN MEXICO(1948), ph; TARZAN AND THE MERMAIDS(1948), ph; BULLFIGHTER AND THE LADY(1951), ph; PLUNDER OF THE SUN(1953), ph; ROBBER'S ROOST(1955), ph; DANIEL BOONE, TRAIL BLAZER(1957), ph

Joe Draper
CITY ACROSS THE RIVER(1949)

John Draper
THIS IS THE ARMY(1943); SILENT INVASION, THE(1962, Brit.), p

Josef Draper
JOE LOUIS STORY, THE(1953); WRONG MAN, THE(1956)

Lauren A. Draper
Silents
PONY EXPRESS RIDER(1926), ph; JAZZLAND(1928), ph

Lauron Draper
SHE-DEVIL ISLAND(1936, Mex.), ph

Malcolm Draper
YELLOW SUBMARINE(1958, Brit.), animation

Margaret Draper
VIOLATORS, THE(1957)

Mary Draper
Misc. Talkies
GIRL TROUBLE(1933)

Natalie Draper
DU BARRY WAS A LADY(1943); GIRL CRAZY(1943); HITLER'S MADMAN(1943); THOUSANDS CHEER(1943); THREE HEARTS FOR JULIA(1943); MEET THE PEOPLE(1944); RATIONING(1944); PICTURE OF DORIAN GRAY, THE(1945); ZIEGFELD FOLLIES(1945); FOREVER AMBER(1947)

Paul Draper
TIME OF YOUR LIFE, THE(1948); COLLEEN(1936)

Peter Draper
GIRL GETTERS, THE(1966, Brit.), w; I'LL NEVER FORGET WHAT'S 'IS NAME(1967, Brit.), w; BUTTERCUP CHAIN, THE(1971, Brit.), w

T. Wain-Cogan Draper
Silents
PRICE FOR FOLLY, A(1915)

Thalia Draper
MYSTERY IN MEXICO(1948)

W.J. Draper
Silents
ROYAL FAMILY, A(1915)

B. Drapinska
LAST STOP, THE(1949, Pol.)

Richard Drasin
BEN(1972)

Boro Draskovic
HOROSCOPE(1950, Yugo.), d, w

Milton Drasner
HOLD'EM YALE(1935), ph

Robert Drasnin
HOT ANGEL, THE(1958), md; PICTURE MOMMY DEAD(1966), m; RIDE IN THE WHIRLWIND(1966), m; KREMLIN LETTER, THE(1970), m, md

Patricia Dratel
FORT APACHE, THE BRONX(1981)

Jim Dratfield
Misc. Talkies
LEGEND OF ALFRED PACKER, THE(1979)

Jay Dratler
GIRLS UNDER TWENTY-ONE(1940), w; LA CONGA NIGHTS(1940), w; CONFESSIONS OF BOSTON BLACKIE(1941), w; MEET BOSTON BLACKIE(1941), w; WHERE DID YOU GET THAT GIRL?(1941), w; FLY BY NIGHT(1942), w; GET HEP TO LOVE(1942), w; WIFE TAKES A FLYER, THE(1942), w; HIGHER AND HIGHER(1943), w; IT COMES UP LOVE(1943), w; LAURA(1944), w; IT'S IN THE BAG(1945), w; DARK CORNER, THE(1946), w; CALL NORTHSIDE 777(1948), w; PITFALL(1948), w; THAT WONDERFUL URGE(1948), w; DANCING IN THE DARK(1949), w; IMPACT(1949), w; LAS VEGAS STORY, THE(1952), w; WE'RE NOT MARRIED(1952), w; I AIM AT THE STARS(1960), w

Doris Draught
SILVER LINING(1932), ed

Jean-Pierre Dravei
QUARTET(1981, Brit./Fr.)

Vicki Draves
TROUBLE WITH ANGELS, THE(1966)

Milena Dravic
HOROSCOPE(1950, Yugo.); ADRIFT(1971, Czech.); BATTLE OF THE NERETVA(1971, Yugo./Ital./Ger.)

James W. Drawbell
WHO GOES NEXT?(1938, Brit.), w; LADY SURRENDERS, A(1947, Brit.), w

Albert Dray
LA BALANCE(1983, Fr.)

Douglas Dray
BODY AND SOUL(1931)

John Dray
SQUADRON 633(1964, U.S./Brit.)

Magali Dray
HORSE OF PRIDE(1980, Fr.), cos

Patrick Dray
Misc. Talkies
LEGEND OF ALFRED PACKER, THE(1979)

Alfred Drayton
SQUEAKER, THE(1930, Brit.); "W" PLAN, THE(1931, Brit.); BROWN SUGAR(1931, Brit.); HAPPY ENDING, THE(1931, Brit.); LORD BABS(1932, Brit.); FALLING FOR YOU(1933, Brit.); LITTLE DAMOZEL, THE(1933, Brit.); FRIDAY THE 13TH(1934, Brit.); IT'S A BOY(1934, Brit.); LADY IN DANGER(1934, Brit.); STRIKE!(1934, Brit.); DICTATOR, THE(1935, Brit./Ger.); FIRST A GIRL(1935, Brit.); JACK AHOY!(1935, Brit.); LOOK UP AND LAUGH(1935, Brit.); ME AND MARLBOROUGH(1935, Brit.); OH DADDY!(1935, Brit.); RADIO FOLLIES(1935, Brit.); CRIMSON CIRCLE, THE(1936, Brit.); TROPICAL TROUBLE(1936, Brit.); AREN'T MEN BEASTS?(1937, Brit.); SPOT OF BOTHER, A(1938, Brit.); SO THIS IS LONDON(1940, Brit.); BANANA RIDGE(1941, Brit.); BIG BLOCKADE, THE(1942, Brit.); WOMEN AREN'T ANGELS(1942, Brit.); DON'T TAKE IT TO HEART(1944, Brit.); HALF-WAY HOUSE, THE(1945, Brit.); THEY KNEW MR. KNIGHT(1945, Brit.); NICHOLAS NICKLEBY(1947, Brit.); THINGS HAPPEN AT NIGHT(1948, Brit.)
Silents
IRON JUSTICE(1915, Brit.)

Lewis Drayton
PERSONAL MAID(1931)

Noel Drayton
UNDER MY SKIN(1950); BLACKBEARD THE PIRATE(1952); PLYMOUTH ADVENTURE(1952); BOTANY BAY(1953); ELEPHANT WALK(1954); KNOCK ON WOOD(1954); SEVEN LITTLE FOYS, THE(1955); VIRGIN QUEEN, THE(1955); COURT JESTER, THE(1956); ZERO HOUR!(1957); HONG KONG CONFIDENTIAL(1958); WRECK OF THE MARY DEAR, THE(1959); PUBLIC AFFAIR, A(1962); PRIZE, THE(1963); WRECKING CREW, THE(1968)

Julie Drazen
INCREDIBLE MELTING MAN, THE(1978)

Jaroslav Drbohlav
OPERATION DAYBREAK(1976, U.S./Brit./Czech.)

Jana Drchalova
CAPRICIOUS SUMMER(1968, Czech.)

Helen Dream
CONFESSOR(1973)

Rinse Dream
Misc. Talkies
CAFE FLESH(1982), d

Tangerine Dream
KEEP, THE(1983), m; WAVELENGTH(1983), m

J. P. Drean
CHECKERBOARD(1969, Fr.)

Sammy Drechsel
24-HOUR LOVER(1970, Ger.)

Michael Drechsler
LIQUID SKY(1982)

Anneli Marian Drecker
CHILDREN OF GOD'S EARTH(1983, Norwegian)

Alan Dreeban
OKINAWA(1952)

A.V. Dreeson
JUST FOR THE HELL OF IT(1968)

A.V. Dreeson, Sr.
JUST FOR THE HELL OF IT(1968)

Martin Dreffke
LINCOLN CONSPIRACY, THE(1977), ed; DARK, THE(1979), ed

Carl Dreher
CRIME OF DR. HALLET(1938), w; STRANGE CONQUEST(1946), w
1984
SOLDIER'S STORY, A(1984)

Lea Drehgorn
SLIPPER AND THE ROSE, THE(1976, Brit.)

A. Drehle
Misc. Silents
OH MARY BE CAREFUL(1921)

Alex Dreier
THE BOSTON STRANGLER, THE(1968); CHANDLER(1971); CAREY TREATMENT, THE(1972); LONERS, THE(1972)
1984
INVISIBLE STRANGLER(1984)
Misc. Talkies
LADY COCOA(1975)

Hans Dreier
TRUE TO LIFE(1943), art d; PATRIOT, THE(1928), set d; INNOCENTS OF PARIS(1929), art d; LOVE PARADE, THE(1929), art d & set d; THUNDERBOLT(1929), art d; MONTE CARLO(1930), set d; MOROCCO(1930), art d; PLAYBOY OF PARIS(1930), art d; VAGABOND KING, THE(1930), art d; AMERICAN TRAGEDY, AN(1931), art d; CONFESSIONS OF A CO-ED(1931), art d; DISHONORED(1931), art d; SMILING LIEUTENANT, THE(1931), art d; BROKEN LULLABY(1932), set d; DR. JEKYLL AND MR. HYDE(1932), art d; FAREWELL TO ARMS, A(1932), art d; LOVE ME TONIGHT(1932), art d; MIRACLE MAN, THE(1932), art d; ONE HOUR WITH YOU(1932), art d; SHANGHAI EXPRESS(1932), prod d; TROUBLE IN PARADISE(1932), art d; DESIGN FOR LIVING(1933), art d; DUCK SOUP(1933), art d; I'M NO ANGEL(1933), art d; ONE SUNDAY AFTERNOON(1933), art d; SONG OF SONGS(1933), art d; TILLIE AND GUS(1933), art d; WAY TO LOVE, THE(1933), art d; WHITE WOMAN(1933), art d; BELLE OF THE NINETIES(1934), art d; DEATH TAKES A HOLIDAY(1934), art d; IT'S A GIFT(1934), art d; KISS AND MAKE UP(1934), art d; LADIES SHOULD LISTEN(1934), art d; MRS. WIGGS OF THE CABBAGE PATCH(1934), art d; NOTORIOUS SOPHIE LANG, THE(1934), art d; NOW AND FOREVER(1934), art d; SCARLET EMPRESS, THE(1934), art d; SHOOT THE WORKS(1934), art d; SIX OF A KIND(1934), art d; THIRTY-DAY PRINCESS(1934), art d; WE'RE NOT DRESSING(1934), art d; YOU'RE TELLING ME(1934), art d; DEVIL IS A WOMAN, THE(1935), art d; ENTER MADAME(1935), art d; GOIN' TO TOWN(1935), art d; LAST OUTPOST, THE(1935), art d; LIVES OF A BENGAL LANCER(1935), art d; MISSISSIPPI(1935), art d; PARIS IN SPRING(1935), art d; PETER IBBETSON(1935), art d; RUGGLES OF RED GAP(1935), art d; RUMBA(1935), art d; SO RED THE ROSE(1935), art d; STOLEN HARMONY(1935), art d; WINGS IN THE DARK(1935), art d; ANYTHING GOES(1936), art d; ARIZONA MAHONEY(1936), art d; BRIDE COMES HOME(1936), art d; DESERT GOLD(1936), art d; DESIRE(1936), art d; F MAN(1936), art d; GENERAL DIED AT DAWN, THE(1936), art d; GIRL OF THE OZARKS(1936), art d; HOLLYWOOD BOULEVARD(1936), art d; KLONDIKE ANNIE(1936), art d; LADY BE CAREFUL(1936), art d; MILKY WAY, THE(1936), art d; MURDER WITH PICTURES(1936), art d; POPPY(1936), art d; PREVIEW MURDER MYSTERY(1936), art d; PRINCESS COMES ACROSS, THE(1936), art d; RHYTHM ON THE RANGE(1936), art d; TEXAS RANGERS, THE(1936), art d; THIRTEEN HOURS BY AIR(1936), art d; TIMOTHY'S QUEST(1936), art d; TRAIL OF THE LONESOME PINE, THE(1936), art d; WEDDING PRESENT(1936), art d; YOURS FOR THE ASKING(1936), art d; ANGEL(1937), art d; BIG BROADCAST OF 1938, THE(1937), art d; DAUGHTER OF SHANGHAI(1937), art d; EASY LIVING(1937), art d; HIGH, WIDE AND HANDSOME(1937), art d; HOLD'EM NAVY!(1937), art d; I MET HIM IN PARIS(1937), art d; INTERNES CAN'T TAKE MONEY(1937), art d; KING OF GAMBLERS(1937), art d; MAID OF SALEM(1937), art d; MAKE WAY FOR TOMORROW(1937), art d; MOUNTAIN MUSIC(1937), art d; NIGHT CLUB SCANDAL(1937), art d; PARTNERS IN CRIME(1937), art d; PLAINSMAN, THE(1937), art d; SOULS AT SEA(1937), art d; SWING HIGH, SWING LOW(1937), art d; THIS WAY PLEASE(1937), art d; THRILL OF A LIFETIME(1937), art d; TRUE CONFESSION(1937), art d; TURN OFF THE MOON(1937), art d; WELLS FARGO(1937), art d; ARTISTS AND MODELS ABROAD(1938), art d; BULLDOG DRUMMOND IN AFRICA(1938), art d; DANGEROUS TO KNOW(1938), art d; GIVE ME A SAILOR(1938), art d; HER JUNGLE LOVE(1938), art d; HUNTED MEN(1938), art d; IF I WERE KING(1938), art d; ILLEGAL TRAFFIC(1938), art d; KING OF ALCATRAZ(1938), art d; PRISON FARM(1938), art d; SING YOU SINNERS(1938), art d; SONS OF THE LEGION(1938), art d; SPAWN OF THE NORTH(1938), art d; STOLEN HEAVEN(1938), art d; THANKS FOR THE MEMORY(1938), art d; TIP-OFF GIRLS(1938), art d; YOU AND ME(1938), art d; BEAU GESTE(1939), art d; CAFE SOCIETY(1939), art d; CAT AND THE CANARY, THE(1939), art d; DISBARRED(1939), art d; DISPUTED PASSAGE(1939), art d; GERONIMO(1939), art d; GRACIE ALLEN MURDER CASE(1939), art d; GRAND JURY SECRETS(1939), art d; GREAT VICTOR HERBERT, THE(1939), art d; INVITATION TO HAPPINESS(1939), art d; ISLAND OF LOST MEN(1939), art d; KING OF CHINATOWN(1939), art d; LIGHT THAT FAILED, THE(1939), art d; MAN ABOUT TOWN(1939), art d; NEVER SAY DIE(1939), art d; OUR LEADING CITIZEN(1939), art d; OUR NEIGHBORS—THE CARTERS(1939), art d; PARIS HONEYMOON(1939), art d; PERSONS IN HIDING(1939), art d; RULERS OF THE SEA(1939), art d; ST. LOUIS BLUES(1939), art d; STAR MAKER, THE(1939), art d; TELEVISION SPY(1939), art d; UNION PACIFIC(1939), art d; UNMARRIED(1939), art d; WHAT A LIFE(1939), art d; ZAZA(1939), art d; $1,000 A TOUCHDOWN(1939), art d; ARISE, MY LOVE(1940), art d; DR. CYCLOPS(1940), art d; EMERGENCY SQUAD(1940), art d; GHOST BREAKERS, THE(1940), art d; GOLDEN GLOVES(1940), art d; GREAT McGINTY, THE(1940), art d; I WANT A DIVORCE(1940), art d; MYSTERY SEA RAIDER(1940), art d; NIGHT AT EARL CARROLL'S, A(1940), art d; NORTHWEST MOUNTED POLICE(1940), art d; OPENED BY MISTAKE(1940), art d; PAROLE FIXER(1940), art d; QUEEN OF THE MOB(1940), art d; RANGERS OF FORTUNE(1940), art d; REMEMBER THE NIGHT(1940), art d; RHYTHM ON THE RIVER(1940), art d; ROAD TO SINGAPORE(1940), art d; SAFARI(1940), art d; SEVENTEEN(1940), art d; TEXAS RANGERS RIDE AGAIN(1940), art d; THOSE WERE THE DAYS(1940), art d; TYPHOON(1940), art d; UNTAMED(1940), art d; VICTORY(1940), art d; WOMEN WITHOUT NAMES(1940), art d; BIRTH OF THE BLUES(1941), art d; GLAMOUR BOY(1941), art d; HENRY ALDRICH FOR PRESIDENT(1941), art d; HOLD BACK THE DAWN(1941), art d; I WANTED WINGS(1941), art d; LADY EVE, THE(1941), art d; LAS VEGAS NIGHTS(1941), art d; LOUISIANA PURCHASE(1941), art d; MIDNIGHT ANGEL(1941), art d; NEW YORK TOWN(1941), art d; NIGHT OF JANUARY 16TH(1941), art d; NOTHING BUT THE TRUTH(1941), art d; ONE NIGHT IN LISBON(1941), art d; ROAD TO ZANZIBAR(1941), art d; SHEPHERD OF THE HILLS, THE(1941), art d; SKYLARK(1941), art d; SULLIVAN'S TRAVELS(1941), art d; THERE'S MAGIC IN MUSIC(1941), art d; VIRGINIA(1941), art d; WEST POINT WIDOW(1941), art d; BEYOND THE BLUE HORIZON(1942), art d; DR. BROADWAY(1942), art d; FOREST RANGERS, THE(1942), art d; GLASS KEY, THE(1942), art d; GREAT MAN'S LADY, THE(1942), art d; HENRY ALDRICH, EDITOR(1942), art d; HENRY ALDRICH GETS GLAMOUR(1942), art d; HENRY AND DIZZY(1942), art

d; HOLIDAY INN(1942), art d; I MARRIED A WITCH(1942), art d; LADY BODY-
GUARD(1942), art d; LUCKY JORDAN(1942), art d; MAJOR AND THE MINOR,
THE(1942), art d; MRS. WIGGS OF THE CABBAGE PATCH(1942), art d; MY FAVOR-
ITE BLONDE(1942), art d; MY HEART BELONGS TO DADDY(1942), art d; NIGHT IN
NEW ORLEANS, A(1942), art d; NIGHT PLANE FROM CHUNGKING(1942), art d;
PALM BEACH STORY, THE(1942), art d; PRIORITIES ON PARADE(1942), art d;
REAP THE WILD WIND(1942), art d; ROAD TO MOROCCO(1942), art d; STAR
SPANGLED RHYTHM(1942), art d; STREET OF CHANCE(1942), art d; TAKE A
LETTER, DARLING(1942), art d; THIS GUN FOR HIRE(1942), art d; TRUE TO THE
ARMY(1942), art d; WAKE ISLAND(1942), art d; CRYSTAL BALL, THE(1943), art d;
FIVE GRAVES TO CAIRO(1943), art d; FOR WHOM THE BELL TOLLS(1943), art d;
GOOD FELLOWS, THE(1943), art d; HAPPY GO LUCKY(1943), art d; HENRY
ALDRICH HAUNTS A HOUSE(1943), art d; HENRY ALDRICH SWINGS IT(1943), art
d; HOSTAGES(1943), art d; LET'S FACE IT(1943), art d; NO TIME FOR LOVE(1943),
art d; RIDING HIGH(1943), art d; SALUTE FOR THREE(1943), art d; SO PROUDLY
WE HAIL(1943), art d; YOUNG AND WILLING(1943), art d; AND THE ANGELS
SING(1944), art d; DOUBLE INDEMNITY(1944), art d; FRENCHMAN'S
CREEK(1944), art d; GOING MY WAY(1944), art d; GREAT MOMENT, THE(1944), art
d; HAIL THE CONQUERING HERO(1944), art d; HENRY ALDRICH, BOY
SCOUT(1944), art d; HENRY ALDRICH PLAYS CUPID(1944), art d; HENRY AL-
DRICH'S LITTLE SECRET(1944), art d; HERE COME THE WAVES(1944), art d;
HITLER GANG, THE(1944), art d; HOUR BEFORE THE DAWN, THE(1944), art d; I
LOVE A SOLDIER(1944), art d; LADY IN THE DARK(1944), art d; MAN IN HALF-
MOON STREET, THE(1944), art d; MIRACLE OF MORGAN'S CREEK, THE(1944), art
d; NATIONAL BARN DANCE(1944), art d; OUR HEARTS WERE YOUNG AND
GAY(1944), art d; PRACTICALLY YOURS(1944), art d; RAINBOW ISLAND(1944), art
d; STANDING ROOM ONLY(1944), art d; STORY OF DR. WASSELL, THE(1944), art
d; 'TILL WE MEET AGAIN(1944), art d; UNINVITED, THE(1944), art d; YOU CAN'T
RATION LOVE(1944), art d; BRING ON THE GIRLS(1945), art d; DUFFY'S TA-
VERN(1945), art d; HOLD THAT BLONDE(1945), art d; INCENDIARY BLON-
DE(1945), art d; KITTY(1945), art d; LOST WEEKEND, THE(1945), art d; LOVE
LETTERS(1945), art d; MASQUERADE IN MEXICO(1945), art d; MEDAL FOR BEN-
NY, A(1945), art d; MINISTRY OF FEAR(1945), art d; MISS SUSIE SLAGLE'S(1945),
art d; MURDER, HE SAYS(1945), art d; OUT OF THIS WORLD(1945), art d; ROAD TO
UTOPIA(1945), art d; SALTY O'ROURKE(1945), art d; STORK CLUB, THE(1945), art
d; UNSEEN, THE(1945), art d; YOU CAME ALONG(1945), art d; BLUE DAHLIA,
THE(1946), art d; BRIDE WORE BOOTS, THE(1946), art d; CALIFORNIA(1946), art d;
MONSIEUR BEAUCAIRE(1946), art d; O.S.S.(1946), art d; OUR HEARTS WERE
GROWING UP(1946), art d; SEARCHING WIND, THE(1946), art d; STRANGE LOVE
OF MARTHA IVERS, THE(1946), art d; TO EACH HIS OWN(1946), art d; TWO YEARS
BEFORE THE MAST(1946), art d; VIRGINIAN, THE(1946), art d; WELL-GROOMED
BRIDE, THE(1946), art d; CALCUTTA(1947), art d; DEAR RUTH(1947), art d; DREAM
GIRL(1947), art d; EASY COME, EASY GO(1947), art d; GOLDEN EARRINGS(1947),
art d; IMPERFECT LADY, THE(1947), art d; LADIES' MAN(1947), art d; MY FAVOR-
ITE BRUNETTE(1947), art d; PERILS OF PAULINE, THE(1947), art d; ROAD TO
RIO(1947), art d; SUDDENLY IT'S SPRING(1947), art d; TROUBLE WITH WOMEN,
THE(1947), art d; UNCONQUERED(1947), art d; VARIETY GIRL(1947), art d; WEL-
COME STRANGER(1947), art d; WHERE THERE'S LIFE(1947), art d; WILD HAR-
VEST(1947), art d; BIG CLOCK, THE(1948), art d; EMPEROR WALTZ, THE(1948), art
d; FOREIGN AFFAIR, A(1948), art d; HAZARD(1948), art d; I WALK ALONE(1948),
art d; ISN'T IT ROMANTIC?(1948), art d; MISS TATLOCK'S MILLIONS(1948), art d;
MY OWN TRUE LOVE(1948), art d; NIGHT HAS A THOUSAND EYES(1948), art d;
PALEFACE, THE(1948), art d; SAIGON(1948), art d; SAINTED SISTERS, THE(1948),
art d; SEALED VERDICT(1948), art d; SORRY, WRONG NUMBER(1948), art d;
WHISPERING SMITH(1948), art d; ACCUSED, THE(1949), art d; ALIAS NICK
BEAL(1949), art d; BRIDE OF VENGEANCE(1949), art d; CONNECTICUT YANKEE
IN KING ARTHUR'S COURT, A(1949), art d; DEAR WIFE(1949), art d; GREAT
GATSBY, THE(1949), art d; GREAT LOVER, THE(1949), art d; MY FRIEND IR-
MA(1949), art d; RED, HOT AND BLUE(1949), art d; ROPE OF SAND(1949), art d;
SAMSON AND DELILAH(1949), art d; SONG OF SURRENDER(1949), art d; SOR-
ROWFUL JONES(1949), art d; STREETS OF LAREDO(1949), art d; TOP O' THE
MORNING(1949), art d; COPPER CANYON(1950), art d; DARK CITY(1950), art d;
FANCY PANTS(1950), art d; FILE ON THELMA JORDAN, THE(1950), art d; FURIES,
THE(1950), art d; LET'S DANCE(1950), art d; MR. MUSIC(1950), art d; MY FRIEND
IRMA GOES WEST(1950), art d; NO MAN OF HER OWN(1950), art d; PAID IN
FULL(1950), art d; RIDING HIGH(1950), art d; SEPTEMBER AFFAIR(1950), art d;
SUNSET BOULEVARD(1950), art d; UNION STATION(1950), art d; PLACE IN THE
SUN, A(1951), art d; GREAT GATSBY, THE(1974), art d
Silents
FORBIDDEN PARADISE(1924), set d; UNDERWORLD(1927), art d & set d; DRAG-
NET, THE(1928), set d; LAST COMMAND, THE(1928), set d; STREET OF SIN,
THE(1928), set d
Hans J. Dreier
LEMON DROP KID, THE(1934), art d
Rose Dreifus
1984
ALLEY CAT(1984)
Arthur Dreifuss
HATS OFF(1937), ch; RIDE 'EM COWGIRL(1939), p; REG'LAR FELLERS(1941), d,
w; BABY FACE MORGAN(1942), d; BOSS OF BIG TOWN(1943), d; CAMPUS
RHYTHM(1943), d; MELODY PARADE(1943), d; NEARLY EIGHTEEN(1943), d;
PAYOFF, THE(1943), d; SARONG GIRL(1943), d; SULTAN'S DAUGHTER,
THE(1943), d; EVER SINCE VENUS(1944), d, w; BOSTON BLACKIE BOOKED ON
SUSPICION(1945), d; BOSTON BLACKIE'S RENDEZVOUS(1945), d; EADIE WAS A
LADY(1945), d; GAY SENORITA, THE(1945), d; PRISON SHIP(1945), d; BETTY
CO-ED(1946), d, w; FREDDIE STEPS OUT(1946), d; HIGH SCHOOL HERO(1946), d,
w; JUNIOR PROM(1946), d; GLAMOUR GIRL(1947), d; LITTLE MISS BROAD-
WAY(1947), d, w; TWO BLONDES AND A REDHEAD(1947), d; VACATION
DAYS(1947), d; I SURRENDER DEAR(1948), d; MANHATTAN ANGEL(1948), d;
MARY LOU(1948), d; OLD-FASHIONED GIRL, AN(1948), p&d, w; SHAMROCK
HILL(1949), p&d; THERE'S A GIRL IN MY HEART(1949), p&d; LAST BLITZKRIEG,
THE(1958), d; LIFE BEGINS AT 17(1958), d; JUKE BOX RHYTHM(1959), d; QUARE
FELLOW, THE(1962, Brit.), d, w; LOVE-INS, THE(1967), d, w; RIOT ON SUNSET
STRIP(1967), d; FOR SINGLES ONLY(1968), d, w; TIME TO SING, A(1968), d;
YOUNG RUNAWAYS, THE(1968), d
Misc. Talkies
DOUBLE DEAL(1939), d; MYSTERY IN SWING(1940), d; MURDER ON LENOX
AVENUE(1941), d; SUNDAY SINNERS(1941), d; SWEET GENEVIEVE(1947), d; AS-
SIGNMENT ABROAD(1955), d

Hans Dreir
CHICAGO DEADLINE(1949), art d
Jeffrey Dreisbach
1984
SPLASH(1984)
Theodore Dreiser
AMERICAN TRAGEDY, AN(1931), w; JENNIE GERHARDT(1933), w; MY GAL
SAL(1942), w; PLACE IN THE SUN, A(1951), w; PRINCE WHO WAS A THIEF,
THE(1951), w; CARRIE(1952), w
Jean Drejac
FRIEND OF THE FAMILY(1965, Fr./Ital.), m/l Hubert Rostaing
Jane Drennan
SEED OF INNOCENCE(1980)
Edna Dreon
KENTUCKY JUBILEE(1951)
Gracia Dreon
KENTUCKY JUBILEE(1951)
Fran Drescher
SATURDAY NIGHT FEVER(1977); AMERICAN HOT WAX(1978); HOLLYWOOD
KNIGHTS, THE(1980); RAGTIME(1981)
1984
ROSEBUD BEACH HOTEL(1984); THIS IS SPINAL TAP(1984)
Franc Drescher
DOCTOR DETROIT(1983)
Frank Drescher
GORP(1980)
Sandy Drescher
FRENCH LINE, THE(1954)
Sonia Dresdel
WORLD OWES ME A LIVING, THE(1944, Brit.); WHILE I LIVE(1947, Brit.); FALLEN
IDOL, THE(1949, Brit.); THIS WAS A WOMAN(1949, Brit.); CLOUDED YELLOW,
THE(1950, Brit.); THIRD VISITOR, THE(1951, Brit.); NOW AND FOREVER(1956,
Brit.); SECRET TENT, THE(1956, Brit.); DEATH OVER MY SHOULDER(1958, Brit.);
MAN WITH THE GREEN CARNATION, THE(1960, Brit.); BREAK, THE(1962, Brit.);
LADY CAROLINE LAMB(1972, Brit./Ital.)
Albert Dresden
COCK-EYED WORLD, THE(1929)
Silents
JUST OFF BROADWAY(1929)
Curley Dresden
LAWLESS NINETIES, THE(1936); OLD WYOMING TRAIL, THE(1937); RANGE
DEFENDERS(1937); ROARING SIX GUNS(1937); ROOTIN' TOOTIN' RHYTHM(1937);
ROUGH RIDIN' RHYTHM(1937); GUN PACKER(1938); HEROES OF THE
HILLS(1938); OUTLAWS OF SONORA(1938); OUTLAWS OF THE PRAIRIE(1938);
OVERLAND STAGE RAIDERS(1938); PALS OF THE SADDLE(1938); RHYTHM OF
THE SADDLE(1938); ROLLING CARAVANS(1938); SANTA FE STAMPEDE(1938);
TWO-GUN JUSTICE(1938); UNDER WESTERN STARS(1938); IN OLD MON-
TEREY(1939); NEW FRONTIER(1939); ONLY ANGELS HAVE WINGS(1939); SOUTH
OF THE BORDER(1939); SOUTHWARD HO!(1939); WYOMING OUTLAW(1939);
ARIZONA GANGBUSTERS(1940); CARSON CITY KID(1940); GHOST VALLEY RAID-
ERS(1940); MELODY RANCH(1940); ONE MAN'S LAW(1940); RIDE, TENDERFOOT,
RIDE(1940); UNDER TEXAS SKIES(1940); BILLY THE KID IN SANTA FE(1941);
BILLY THE KID WANTED(1941); BILLY THE KID'S FIGHTING PALS(1941); DEATH
VALLEY OUTLAWS(1941); GANGS OF SONORA(1941); IN OLD COLORADO(1941);
JESSE JAMES AT BAY(1941); LONE RIDER CROSSES THE RIO, THE(1941); LONE
RIDER IN GHOST TOWN, THE(1941); PRAIRIE PIONEERS(1941); SON OF DAVY
CROCKETT, THE(1941); TWO GUN SHERIFF(1941); UNDER FIESTA STARS(1941);
WYOMING WILDCAT(1941); BILLY THE KID TRAPPED(1942); LONE RIDER AND
THE BANDIT, THE(1942); MISSOURI OUTLAW, A(1942); PRAIRIE PALS(1942);
RAIDERS OF THE WEST(1942); ROLLING DOWN THE GREAT DIVIDE(1942);
SHADOWS ON THE SAGE(1942); SHERIFF OF SAGE VALLEY(1942); SOMBRERO
KID, THE(1942); WESTWARD HO(1942); BEYOND THE LAST FRONTIER(1943);
CARSON CITY CYCLONE(1943); DEATH VALLEY MANHUNT(1943); FIGHTING
VALLEY(1943); KID RIDES AGAIN, THE(1943); MAN FROM THUNDER RIVER,
THE(1943); SANTA FE SCOUTS(1943); WAGON TRACKS WEST(1943); LAST HORSE-
MAN, THE(1944); LAW OF THE SADDLE(1944); WESTWARD BOUND(1944)
Curly Dresden
KANSAS TERRORS, THE(1939)
John Dresden
DARK, THE(1979); RAW FORCE(1982); TWO OF A KIND(1983)
Beatrice A. Dresher
PASSION(1954), w
Hal Dresner
APRIL FOOLS, THE(1969), w; EXTRAORDINARY SEAMAN, THE(1969), w;
SSSSSSSS(1973), w; EIGER SANCTION, THE(1975), w; ZORRO, THE GAY BLA-
DE(1981), w
Julie Dresner
1984
PREY, THE(1984), cos
Julie Starr Dresner
1984
RED DAWN(1984), cos
Leila Dresner
CITY OF PLAY(1929, Brit.)
Evelyne Dress
LA NUIT DE VARENNES(1983, Fr./Ital.)
1984
LA PETIT SIRENE(1984, Fr.)
Michael Dress
ROTTEN TO THE CORE(1956, Brit.), m; THANK YOU ALL VERY MUCH(1969,
Brit.), m, md; MIND OF MR. SOAMES, THE(1970, Brit.), m, md; QUACKSER FOR-
TUNE HAS A COUSIN IN THE BRONX(1970), m; HOUSE THAT DRIPPED BLOOD,
THE(1971, Brit.), m
Danny Dresser
PIE IN THE SKY(1964)
Louise Dresser
AIR CIRCUS, THE(1928); MOTHER KNOWS BEST(1928); MADONNA OF AVENUE
A(1929); NOT QUITE DECENT(1929); LIGHTNIN'(1930); MAMMY(1930); THIS MAD
WORLD(1930); THREE SISTERS, THE(1930); CAUGHT(1931); STEPPING SIS-
TERS(1932); CRADLE SONG(1933); DR. BULL(1933); SONG OF THE EAGLE(1933);

STATE FAIR(1933); DAVID HARUM(1934); GIRL OF THE LIMBERLOST(1934); SCARLET EMPRESS, THE(1934); SERVANTS' ENTRANCE(1934); WORLD MOVES ON, THE(1934); COUNTY CHAIRMAN, THE(1935); MAID OF SALEM(1937)
Silents
BURNING SANDS(1922); ENTER MADAME(1922); FOG, THE(1923); RUGGLES OF RED GAP(1923); SALOMY JANE(1923); EAGLE, THE(1925); GOOSE WOMAN, THE(1925); BLIND GODDESS, THE(1926); BROKEN HEARTS OF HOLLYWOOD(1926); THIRD DEGREE, THE(1926); MR. WU(1927); WHITE FLANNELS(1927)
Misc. Silents
TO THE LADIES(1923); WOMAN-PROOF(1923); CITY THAT NEVER SLEEPS, THE(1924); WHAT SHALL I DO?(1924); PERCY(1925); EVERYBODY'S ACTING(1926); FIFTH AVENUE(1926); GIGOLO(1926); PADLOCKED(1926); GARDEN OF EDEN, THE(1928); SHIP COMES IN, A(1928)

Paul Dresser
Silents
ON THE BANKS OF THE WABASH(1923), w

Susie Dresser
PIE IN THE SKY(1964)

David Dressler
CRIME DOCTOR'S DIARY, THE(1949), w

Lieux Dressler
GRAVE OF THE VAMPIRE(1972); TRUCK STOP WOMEN(1974); KINGDOM OF THE SPIDERS(1977)

Marie Dressler
VAGABOND LOVER(1929); ANNA CHRISTIE(1930); CAUGHT SHORT(1930); CHASING RAINBOWS(1930); GIRL SAID NO, THE(1930); LET US BE GAY(1930); MIN AND BILL(1930); ONE ROMANTIC NIGHT(1930); POLITICS(1931); REDUCING(1931); EMMA(1932); PROSPERITY(1932); CHRISTOPHER BEAN(1933); DINNER AT EIGHT(1933); TUGBOAT ANNIE(1933)
Misc. Talkies
DIVINE LADY, THE(1929)
Silents
TILLIE'S PUNCTURED ROMANCE(1914); TILLIE'S TOMATO SURPRISE(1915); TILLIE WAKES UP(1917); CALLAHANS AND THE MURPHYS, THE(1927); JOY GIRL, THE(1927)
Misc. Silents
BRINGING UP FATHER(1928); PATSY, THE(1928)

Roger Dressler
GROUNDSTAR CONSPIRACY, THE(1972, Can.)

Rachel Dretzin
BABY, IT'S YOU(1983)

Philippe Dreux
TRIAL OF JOAN OF ARC(1965, Fr.)

Jean Dreville
DEVIL IS AN EMPRESS, THE(1939, Fr.), d, w; LA FERME DU PENDU(1946, Fr.), d; CAGE OF NIGHTINGALES, A(1947, Fr.), d; SEVEN DEADLY SINS, THE(1953, Fr./Ital.), d; SPICE OF LIFE(1954, Fr.), d; SPUTNIK(1960, Fr.), d; LAFAYETTE(1963, Fr.), d, w

Valerie Dreville
1984
FIRST NAME: CARMEN(1984, Fr.)

Ann Drew
Silents
SILENT VOICE, THE(1915)
Misc. Silents
RED RAIDERS, THE(1927)

Barbara Drew
SPRING REUNION(1957); SOME LIKE IT HOT(1959)

Bob Drew
FADE TO BLACK(1980)

Clay Drew
GAY BRIDE, THE(1934)

Cora Drew
Silents
OPENED SHUTTERS, THE(1914); IT'S NO LAUGHING MATTER(1915); LILY AND THE ROSE, THE(1915); NINETEEN AND PHYLLIS(1920); POLLY OF THE STORM COUNTRY(1920); PRINCE OF AVENUE A., THE(1920); WHAT'S A WIFE WORTH?(1921)
Misc. Silents
SOUTHERN PRIDE(1917); GO STRAIGHT(1921)

Cora Rankin Drew
Misc. Silents
MORAL LAW, THE(1918)

David Drew
SOME OF MY BEST FRIENDS ARE...(1971)
Misc. Talkies
FUN AND GAMES(1973)

Donna Drew
BIG COMBO, THE(1955); RETURN OF JACK SLADE, THE(1955)
Silents
MADAME SPY(1918)
Misc. Silents
'49 - '17(1917)

Dorothy Drew
Misc. Silents
ACCUSED(1925); DEFEND YOURSELF(1925); PURSUED(1925); PAY OFF, THE(1926)

Eddie Drew
DUDE COWBOY(1941)

Ellen Drew
COLLEGE HOLIDAY(1936); MOUNTAIN MUSIC(1937); THIS WAY PLEASE(1937); COCOANUT GROVE(1938); IF I WERE KING(1938); SING YOU SINNERS(1938); YOU AND ME(1938); FRENCH WITHOUT TEARS(1939, Brit.); GERONIMO(1939); GRACIE ALLEN MURDER CASE(1939); LADY'S FROM KENTUCKY, THE(1939); BUCK BENNY RIDES AGAIN(1940); CHRISTMAS IN JULY(1940); TEXAS RANGERS RIDE AGAIN(1940); WOMEN WITHOUT NAMES(1940); MAD DOCTOR, THE(1941); MONSTER AND THE GIRL, THE(1941); NIGHT OF JANUARY 16TH(1941); OUR WIFE(1941); PARSON OF PANAMINT, THE(1941); REACHING FOR THE SUN(1941); ICE-CAPADES REVUE(1942); MY FAVORITE SPY(1942); NIGHT PLANE FROM

CHUNGKING(1942); REMARKABLE ANDREW, THE(1942); STAR SPANGLED RHYTHM(1942); DARK MOUNTAIN(1944); IMPOSTER, THE(1944); THAT'S MY BABY(1944); CHINA SKY(1945); ISLE OF THE DEAD(1945); MAN ALIVE(1945); CRIME DOCTOR'S MAN HUNT(1946); SING WHILE YOU DANCE(1946); JOHNNY O'CLOCK(1947); SWORDSMAN, THE(1947); MAN FROM COLORADO(1948); CROOKED WAY, THE(1949); BARON OF ARIZONA, THE(1950); CARGO TO CAPETOWN(1950); DAVY CROCKETT, INDIAN SCOUT(1950); GREAT MISSOURI RAID, THE(1950); STARS IN MY CROWN(1950); MAN IN THE SADDLE(1951); OUTLAW'S SON(1957)

Ellen Drew [Terry Ray]
INTERNES CAN'T TAKE MONEY(1937)

Florence Drew
Silents
COME ON OVER(1922); NEAR LADY, THE(1923)
Misc. Silents
DENNY FROM IRELAND(1918)

Frank Drew
GEORGE IN CIVVY STREET(1946, Brit.)

Gene Drew
STEEL ARENA(1973); TRUCK STOP WOMEN(1974); BOBBIE JO AND THE OUTLAW(1976)
Misc. Talkies
SWEET GEORGIA(1972)

Geoffrey Drew
PARTY PARTY(1983, Brit.)

Gloria Drew
GREATEST SHOW ON EARTH, THE(1952)

Irene Drew
Silents
SINGLE MAN, THE(1919, Brit.); GENERAL POST(1920, Brit.)

Jerry Drew
PAINTED FACES(1929); PAINTED DESERT, THE(1931); INTERNATIONAL HOUSE(1933)
Misc. Silents
POWER(1928)

Lillian Drew
MILLIONS IN THE AIR(1935); MAN FROM MUSIC MOUNTAIN(1938)
Misc. Silents
VULTURES OF SOCIETY(1916)

Lowell Drew
GREENE MURDER CASE, THE(1929); LES MISERABLES(1935); TRAIL OF THE LONESOME PINE, THE(1936); HOTEL HAYWIRE(1937); SOULS AT SEA(1937); GUN PACKER(1938); LONG VOYAGE HOME, THE(1940); LONE STAR VIGILANTES, THE(1942)

Mark Drew
EDUCATING RITA(1983)

Michael Drew
1984
SCANDALOUS(1984)

Mr. Sidney Drew
Misc. Silents
PLAYING DEAD(1915); PAY DAY(1918), a, d

Mrs. Cora Drew
Silents
HONOR SYSTEM, THE(1917)

Mrs. Sidney Drew
Misc. Silents
PLAYING DEAD(1915); PAY DAY(1918), a, d; COUSIN KATE(1921), d

Norma Drew
OUR BLUSHING BRIDES(1930); WHAT A MAN(1930); FORBIDDEN COMPANY(1932); DOCTOR MONICA(1934); MAGNIFICENT OBSESSION(1935)

Paddy Drew
FACING THE MUSIC(1941, Brit.)

Paula Drew
NIGHT AND DAY(1946); SLIGHTLY SCANDALOUS(1946); VIGILANTES RETURN, THE(1947); WATCH THE BIRDIE(1950); DANGER ZONE(1951)

Philip Yale Drew
Misc. Silents
ROOT OF EVIL, THE(1919)

Robert Drew
TRAIL DUST(1936)

Robert L. Drew
Misc. Talkies
STORM SIGNAL(1966), d

Roland Drew
EVANGELINE(1929); RACKETEER, THE(1929); LOVE TRADER(1930); EX-FLAME(1931); GREAT GAMBINI, THE(1937); SHE ASKED FOR IT(1937); SOME BLONDES ARE DANGEROUS(1937); THUNDER IN THE CITY(1937, Brit.); GOLDWYN FOLLIES, THE(1938); LADY IN THE MORGUE(1938); LAST WARNING, THE(1938); BEASTS OF BERLIN(1939); MYSTERY OF THE WHITE ROOM(1939); INVISIBLE KILLER, THE(1940); SAINT TAKES OVER, THE(1940); WILDCAT BUS(1940); BULLETS FOR O'HARA(1941); LAW OF THE TROPICS(1941); MANPOWER(1941); SERGEANT YORK(1941); SMILING GHOST, THE(1941); UNDERGROUND(1941); ACROSS THE PACIFIC(1942); BIG SHOT, THE(1942); BULLET SCARS(1942); CAPTAINS OF THE CLOUDS(1942); DANGEROUSLY THEY LIVE(1942); HIDDEN HAND, THE(1942); I WAS FRAMED(1942); LADY GANGSTER(1942); LARCENY, INC.(1942); MAN WHO CAME TO DINNER, THE(1942); MURDER IN THE BIG HOUSE(1942); SECRET ENEMIES(1942); SPY SHIP(1942); PRINCESS O'ROURKE(1943); ADVENTURES OF MARK TWAIN, THE(1944); BERMUDA MYSTERY(1944); CONTENDER, THE(1944); SILENT PARTNER(1944); TWO O'CLOCK COURAGE(1945)
Silents
RAMONA(1928); EVANGELINE(1929)
Misc. Silents
LADY RAFFLES(1928); BROADWAY FEVER(1929)

S. Rankin Drew
Silents
MR. BARNES OF NEW YORK(1914); ISLAND OF REGENERATION, THE(1915)

Misc. Silents
  THOU ART THE MAN(1915), a, d; WHO KILLED JOE MERRION?(1915); DARING OF DIANA, THE(1916), d; HUNTED WOMAN, THE(1916), a, d; SUSPECT, THE(1916), a, d; THOU ART THE MAN(1916), a, d; VITAL QUESTION, THE(1916), d; WHO'S YOUR NEIGHBOR?(1917), d; BELLE OF THE SEASON, THE(1919), a, d

S. Ranklin Drew
Misc. Silents
  GIRL PHILIPPA, THE(1917), d

Sidney Drew
Silents
  FLORIDA ENCHANTMENT, A(1914), a, d; RAGGED EDGE, THE(1923)
Misc. Silents
  PLAYING DEAD(1915), d

Sidney Rankin Drew
Misc. Silents
  GIRL PHILIPPA, THE(1917)

Urban Drew
  YANK IN VIET-NAM, A(1964)

Katja Drewanz
  CHRONICLE OF ANNA MAGDALENA BACH(1968, Ital., Ger.)

Raymond Drewe
  JUST JOE(1960, Brit.), w; NOT A HOPE IN HELL(1960, Brit.), w

Norman Drewes
  FLASH GORDON(1936), spec eff

Sande Drewes
  MARK OF THE WITCH(1970)

Pauline Drewett
  SECOND MATE, THE(1950, Brit.); GAMMA PEOPLE, THE(1956); TRUE AS A TURTLE(1957, Brit.)

Pauline Drewitt
  BELLES OF ST. TRINIAN'S, THE(1954, Brit.)

Josef Drewniak
  NORMAN LOVES ROSE(1982, Aus.)

Mark Drewry
  REMEMBRANCE(1982, Brit.)

Berta Drews
  IT HAPPENED IN BROAD DAYLIGHT(1960, Ger./Switz.); GIRL OF THE MOORS, THE(1961, Ger.); COURT MARTIAL(1962, Ger.); DIE FASTNACHTSBEICHTE(1962, Ger.); TIN DRUM, THE(1979, Ger./Fr./Yugo./Pol.)

Carl Drews
  PILLARS OF SOCIETY(1936, Ger.), ph

Karl Drews
  DREAM OF SCHONBRUNN(1933, Aus.), ph

Nancy Drexel
  FOUR DEVILS(1929); MAN FROM HELL'S EDGES(1932); MASON OF THE MOUNTED(1932); PARTNERS(1932); SPEED MADNESS(1932); TEXAS BUDDIES(1932)
Misc. Talkies
  LAW OF THE WEST(1932)
Silents
  BREED OF THE SUNSETS(1928); ESCAPE, THE(1928); PREP AND PEP(1928); RILEY THE COP(1928)

Ruth Drexel
  JAIL BAIT(1977, Ger.)

Steve Drexel
  TARNISHED ANGELS, THE(1957); BIG BEAT, THE(1958); HOT ROD GANG(1958); TERRIFIED!(1963); MOVIE STAR, AMERICAN STYLE, OR, LSD I HATE YOU!(1966); RED, WHITE AND BLACK, THE(1970); SUPERCHICK(1973)
Misc. Talkies
  BROTHER, CRY FOR ME(1970)

Rosalyn Drexler
  BELOW THE BELT(1980), w

Emmanuelle Drey
  SHAMELESS OLD LADY, THE(1966, Fr.)

Anita Dreyer
  THANK YOU, AUNT(1969, Ital.)

Carl Dreyer
  DAY OF WRATH(1948, Den.), p&d, w

Carl Theodor Dreyer
  VAMPYR(1932, Fr./Ger.), p, d, w; ORDET(1957, Den.), p,d&w
Silents
  PASSION OF JOAN OF ARC, THE(1928, Fr.), d&w, ed

Carl Theodore Dreyer
  GERTRUD(1966, Den.), d&w

Carl-Theodor Dreyer
Misc. Silents
  PRESIDENT, THE(1918, Den.), d; PARSON'S WIDOW, THE(1920, Den.), d; CHAINED(1927, Ger.), d

Carl-Theodore Dreyer
Misc. Silents
  LEAVES FROM SATAN'S BOOK(1921, Den.), d; LOVE ONE ANOTHER(1922, Den.), d; ONCE UPON A TIME(1922, Den.), d; MICHAEL(1924, Ger.), d; MASTER OF THE HOUSE(1925, Den.), d

Charles Dreyer
Silents
  SILENT CALL, THE(1921), ph

David Dreyer
  FUZZ(1972)

Fred Dreyer
1984
  CANNONBALL RUN II(1984)

Gunni Dreyer
  EIGHT GIRLS IN A BOAT(1932, Ger.)

Luise Dreyer-Sachsenberg
  TROMBA, THE TIGER MAN(1952, Ger.), ed

George Dreyfus
  LET THE BALLOON GO(1977, Aus.), m; DIMBOOLA(1979, Aus.), m; TENDER MERCIES(1982), m

Jean-Claude Dreyfus
1984
  CHEECH AND CHONG'S THE CORSICAN BROTHERS(1984); DOG DAY(1984, Fr.)

Mme. Jean-Paul Dreyfus
  LA MARSEILLAISE(1938, Fr.), w

N. Martel Dreyfus
  LA MARSEILLAISE(1938, Fr.), w

Randy Dreyfus
  MAN, WOMAN AND CHILD(1983)

Jack J. Dreyfus, Jr.
  LONG DAY'S JOURNEY INTO NIGHT(1962), p

Jean-Claude Dreyfuss
  FITZCARRALDO(1982)

Justin Dreyfuss
  CLOSE ENCOUNTERS OF THE THIRD KIND(1977)

Lorin Dreyfuss
  SKATETOWN, U.S.A.(1979), p, w

Michael Dreyfuss
  PATTERNS(1956)

Randolph Dreyfuss
  NATIONAL LAMPOON'S VACATION(1983)
1984
  JOY OF SEX(1984)

Randy Dreyfuss
  LOVE CHILD(1982)

Richard Dreyfuss
  GRADUATE, THE(1967); YOUNG RUNAWAYS, THE(1968); HELLO DOWN THERE(1969); AMERICAN GRAFFITI(1973); DILLINGER(1973); APPRENTICESHIP OF DUDDY KRAVITZ, THE(1974, Can.); SECOND COMING OF SUZANNE, THE(1974); JAWS(1975); CLOSE ENCOUNTERS OF THE THIRD KIND(1977); GOODBYE GIRL, THE(1977); BIG FIX, THE(1978), a, p; COMPETITION, THE(1980); WHOSE LIFE IS IT ANYWAY?(1981)
1984
  BUDDY SYSTEM, THE(1984)

Michel Drhey
  VICTORY(1981)

London Dri
  DARK SIDE OF TOMORROW, THE(1970), m

Jean Driant
  TRIPLE DECEPTION(1957, Brit.); WHOLE TRUTH, THE(1958, Brit.); UGLY DUCKLING, THE(1959, Brit.); RETURN FROM THE ASHES(1965, U.S./Brit.)

Tom Driberg
  TELL ME LIES(1968, Brit.)

Hans Drier
  GIVE US THIS NIGHT(1936), art d

Moosie Drier
  UP THE SANDBOX(1972); WAR BETWEEN MEN AND WOMEN, THE(1972); OH, GOD!(1977); AMERICAN HOT WAX(1978)

Peggy Drier
  BEGUILED, THE(1971)

Paul Driessen
  YELLOW SUBMARINE(1958, Brit.), animation

Burkhard Driest
  QUERELLE(1983, Ger./Fr.)

Burkhardt Driest
  CROSS OF IRON(1977, Brit., Ger.)

Simone Drieu
  TRUTH, THE(1961, Fr./Ital.), w

Don Driggers
  PIRATES OF MONTEREY(1947)

John Drimmer
1984
  ICEMAN(1984), w

Keith Drinkel
  BRIDGE TOO FAR, A(1977, Brit.)

Carol Drinkwater
  CLOCKWORK ORANGE, A(1971, Brit.); SHOUT, THE(1978, Brit.)

John Drinkwater
  SALLY BISHOP(1932, Brit.), w; KING OF PARIS, THE(1934, Brit.), w; CLOWN MUST LAUGH, A(1936, Brit.), w; APRIL BLOSSOMS(1937, Brit.), w; MILL ON THE FLOSS(1939, Brit.), w

Ros Drinkwater
  SONG OF NORWAY(1970)

Ralph Drischell
  TAPS(1981)

Bobby Driscoll
  BIG BONANZA, THE(1944); LOST ANGEL(1944); SULLIVANS, THE(1944); SUNDAY DINNER FOR A SOLDIER(1944); IDENTITY UNKNOWN(1945); FROM THIS DAY FORWARD(1946); O.S.S.(1946); SO GOES MY LOVE(1946); SONG OF THE SOUTH(1946); IF YOU KNEW SUSIE(1948); MELODY TIME(1948); SO DEAR TO MY HEART(1949); WINDOW, THE(1949); TREASURE ISLAND(1950, Brit.); WHEN I GROW UP(1951); HAPPY TIME, THE(1952); PETER PAN(1953); SCARLET COAT, THE(1955); PARTY CRASHERS, THE(1958)

Christopher Driscoll
  HOPSCOTCH(1980); LONG GOOD FRIDAY, THE(1982, Brit.)

Frank Driscoll
  JOHNNY, YOU'RE WANTED(1956, Brit.), w

Halleck H. Driscoll
  INCREDIBLE JOURNEY, THE(1963), animal sup

Harry Driscoll
Silents
  $5,000,000 COUNTERFEITING PLOT, THE(1914)

Julie Driscoll
  POPDOWN(1968, Brit.)

Lawrason Driscoll
  ROLLING THUNDER(1977); GRAY LADY DOWN(1978)

Lawrie Driscoll
  FEMALE RESPONSE, THE(1972); SPECIAL DELIVERY(1976)

Loren Driscoll
  YOUNG LORD, THE(1970, Ger.)
Michael R. Driscoll
Misc. Talkies
  TEENAGE GRAFFITI(1977)
Mike Driscoll
  RULERS OF THE SEA(1939)
Patricia Driscoll
  CHARLEY MOON(1956, Brit.); CHILD AND THE KILLER, THE(1959, Brit.); WOMAN'S TEMPTATION, A(1959, Brit.); WACKIEST SHIP IN THE ARMY, THE(1961)
Peter Driscoll
  WILBY CONSPIRACY, THE(1975, Brit.), w
R. C. Driscoll
  NO BLADE OF GRASS(1970, Brit.)
Robert Miller Driscoll
  I LOVE YOU, ALICE B. TOKLAS!(1968); TRADER HORN(1973); HARRY AND WALTER GO TO NEW YORK(1976)
Sam Wallace Driscoll
  MUTINY ON THE BOUNTY(1935)
Ted Driscoll
  MARRIED TOO YOUNG(1962), set d; TERRIFIED!(1963), set d
Tex Driscoll
  NAUGHTY MARIETTA(1935); PLAINSMAN, THE(1937); WAY OUT WEST(1937); SWING YOUR LADY(1938); SWISS MISS(1938); STAGECOACH(1939); OX-BOW INCIDENT, THE(1943); GIANT(1956)
Silents
  MAN FROM HOME, THE(1914); VIRGINIAN, THE(1914); CAPTIVE, THE(1915); CARMEN(1915); CHIMMIE FADDEN(1915); GIRL OF THE GOLDEN WEST, THE(1915); KINDLING(1915); TEMPTATION(1915); WILD GOOSE CHASE, THE(1915)
William L. Driscoll
  MUTINY ON THE BOUNTY(1962), w
James Driskill
  YOUR THREE MINUTES ARE UP(1973)
William Driskill
  ROCKABILLY BABY(1957), w; SEVEN(1979), w
Gus Drisse
  THE BEACHCOMBER(1938, Brit.), ph; FLYING FORTRESS(1942, Brit.), ph; MR. EMMANUEL(1945, Brit.), ph; SHOWTIME(1948, Brit.), ph; LAST DAYS OF DOLWYN, THE(1949, Brit.), ph
Guy Drisse
  GAY ADVENTURE, THE(1953, Brit.), ph
K. Drista
  TAKE ME AWAY, MY LOVE(1962, Gr.), p
K. Dritsa
  TAKE ME AWAY, MY LOVE(1962, Gr.), w
Robert Drivas
  COOL HAND LUKE(1967); ILLUSTRATED MAN, THE(1969); WHERE IT'S AT(1969); ROAD MOVIE(1974); GOD TOLD ME TO(1976)
Ada Belle Driver
  COWBOY AND THE BANDIT, THE(1935)
Adabelle Driver
Silents
  DREAM MELODY, THE(1929); FIGHTING TERROR, THE(1929); LAST ROUNDUP, THE(1929)
Betty Driver
  BOOTS! BOOTS!(1934, Brit.); PENNY PARADISE(1938, Brit.); LET'S BE FAMOUS(1939, Brit.); FACING THE MUSIC(1941, Brit.)
Donald Driver
  NAKED APE, THE(1973), d&w
Edgar Driver
  COUNTY FAIR(1933, Brit.); DOSS HOUSE(1933, Brit.); ADMIRAL'S SECRET, THE(1934, Brit.); DESIGNING WOMEN(1934, Brit.); KENTUCKY MINSTRELS(1934, Brit.); MUSIC HALL(1934, Brit.); RIVER WOLVES, THE(1934, Brit.); SAY IT WITH FLOWERS(1934, Brit.); WHITE ENSIGN(1934, Brit.); FLOOD TIDE(1935, Brit.); JIMMY BOY(1935, Brit.); MAD HATTERS, THE(1935, Brit.); RADIO PIRATES(1935, Brit.); REAL BLOKE, A(1935, Brit.); SMALL MAN, THE(1935, Brit.); HEARTS OF HUMANITY(1936, Brit.); MEN OF YESTERDAY(1936, Brit.); LAST CHANCE, THE(1937, Brit.); OLD MOTHER RILEY(1937, Brit.); SONG OF THE ROAD(1937, Brit.); TALKING FEET(1937, Brit.); LILY OF LAGUNA(1938, Brit.); STEPPING TOES(1938, Brit.); OLD MOTHER RILEY IN BUSINESS(1940, Brit.); SUICIDE LEGION(1940, Brit.); OLD MOTHER RILEY'S CIRCUS(1941, Brit.); PLAYBOY, THE(1942, Brit.); WE'LL SMILE AGAIN(1942, Brit.); OLD MOTHER RILEY, DETECTIVE(1943, Brit.); DEMOBBED(1944, Brit.); YELLOW CANARY, THE(1944, Brit.); GRAND ESCAPADE, THE(1946, Brit.); AGITATOR, THE(1949); DARK SECRET(1949, Brit.); JUDGMENT DEFERRED(1952, Brit.); TIME OF HIS LIFE, THE(1955, Brit.); FIND THE LADY(1956, Brit.); SCOTLAND YARD DRAGNET(1957, Brit.); MISSING NOTE, THE(1961, Brit.)
Frances Driver
  PLACE IN THE SUN, A(1951); BLACK WIDOW(1954); VIEW FROM POMPEY'S HEAD, THE(1955); JEANNE EAGELS(1957); DIAMOND SAFARI(1958)
Linda Driver
  BLOODTHIRSTY BUTCHERS(1970)
Sara Driver
  PERMANENT VACATION(1982)
1984
  STRANGER THAN PARADISE(1984, U.S./Ger.), a, p
Teddy Driver
  MIRACLE ON 34TH STREET, THE(1947); CHEAPER BY THE DOZEN(1950); BELLES ON THEIR TOES(1952)
Bozidar Drnic
  NINTH CIRCLE, THE(1961, Yugo.)
Bozidar Drnie
  ONE-EYED SOLDIERS(1967, U.S./Brit./Yugo.)
Romuald Drobaczynski
  GUESTS ARE COMING(1965, Pol.), p&d
Squadron Ldr. B. Drobinski
  BATTLE OF BRITAIN, THE(1969, Brit.), tech adv
Nina Drobysheva
  CLEAR SKIES(1963, USSR)

Martin Droch
1984
  SWANN IN LOVE(1984, Fr.Ger.)
Adrian Droeshout
  NOBODY LIVES FOREVER(1946)
Leszek Drogosz
  BOXER(1971, Pol.)
Evelyn Drogue
  FOR YOUR EYES ONLY(1981)
Benny Drohan
  WINTER CARNIVAL(1939)
Ed Drohan
  SIMON(1980), spec eff
1984
  MUPPETS TAKE MANHATTAN, THE(1984), spec eff
H. Drohocka
  LAST STOP, THE(1949, Pol.)
George Dromgold
  GERALDINE(1929), w; SQUARE SHOULDERS(1929), w
Silents
  LYING TRUTH, THE(1922); PENROD(1922); RAGTIME(1927), w, t; HOLD 'EM YALE!(1928), w; MARKED MONEY(1928), w
Misc. Silents
  IN WRONG(1919)
Patrick Dromgoole
  DEAD MAN'S CHEST(1965, Brit.), d; DIAGNOSIS: MURDER(1974, Brit.), p
Andrea Dromm
  RUSSIANS ARE COMING, THE RUSSIANS ARE COMING, THE(1966); COME SPY WITH ME(1967)
Ben Dronen
  MAKO: THE JAWS OF DEATH(1976)
Sydney Droshin
  HILDUR AND THE MAGICIAN(1969)
Oliver Dross
  WEEKEND AT THE WALDORF(1945)
Tom Drossis
  NO MAN'S LAND(1964)
Martin Droste
  INVISIBLE DR. MABUSE, THE(1965, Ger.)
Richard Drosten
  ETERNAL LOVE(1960, Ger.)
Jean-Marie Drot
  MATA HARI(1965, Fr./Ital.)
Cecilia Drott
  PASSION OF ANNA, THE(1970, Swed.), makeup
Cilla Drott
  TOUCH, THE(1971, U.S./Swed.), makeup
Michel Drouet
  QUEST FOR FIRE(1982, Fr./Can.)
Amos Droughan
Misc. Talkies
  GO DOWN DEATH(1944)
Doris Drought
  MANHATTAN COCKTAIL(1928), ed; BEHIND THE MAKEUP(1930), ed; BENSON MURDER CASE, THE(1930), ed; BORDER LEGION, THE(1930), ed; HER WEDDING NIGHT(1930), ed; ONLY THE BRAVE(1930), ed; SEA LEGS(1930), ed; TRUE TO THE NAVY(1930), ed; HONEYMOON LANE(1931), ed; CRIMSON ROMANCE(1934), ed
Silents
  RED HAIR(1928), ed; WHAT A NIGHT!(1928), ed
James Drought
  GYPSY MOTHS, THE(1969), w
Yves Drouhet
  MISSISSIPPI MERMAID(1970, Fr./Ital.)
Jose Germain Drouilly
Silents
  MAGNIFICENT FLIRT, THE(1928), w
Claire Drouot
  LE BONHEUR(1966, Fr.)
Jean Claude Drouot
  LIGHT AT THE EDGE OF THE WORLD, THE(1971, U.S./Span./Lichtenstein)
Jean-Claude Drouot
  LE BONHEUR(1966, Fr.); NICHOLAS AND ALEXANDRA(1971, Brit.); MISTER FREEDOM(1970, Fr.)
Oliver Drouot
  LE BONHEUR(1966, Fr.)
Pierre Drouot
  DAUGHTERS OF DARKNESS(1971, Bel./ Fr./ Ger./ Ital.), w
Sandrine Drouot
  LE BONHEUR(1966, Fr.)
Francesca Drown
  STRAIGHT TIME(1978)
Hope Drown
Misc. Silents
  HOLLYWOOD(1923)
Richard Drown
1984
  CITY HEAT(1984); MICKI AND MAUDE(1984); ROMANCING THE STONE(1984)
Yu. Drozdov
  FATHER OF A SOLDIER(1966, USSR)
M. Drozdovskaya
  THERE WAS AN OLD COUPLE(1967, USSR)
Jean Droze
  I SPIT ON YOUR GRAVE(1962, Fr.); SUCKER, THE(1966, Fr./Ital.); EROTIQUE(1969, Fr.)
Joanne Dru
  ABIE'S IRISH ROSE(1946); RED RIVER(1948); ALL THE KING'S MEN(1949); SHE WORE A YELLOW RIBBON(1949); WAGONMASTER(1950); 711 OCEAN DRIVE(1950); MR. BELVEDERE RINGS THE BELL(1951); VENGEANCE VALLEY(1951); MY PAL GUS(1952); PRIDE OF ST. LOUIS, THE(1952); RETURN OF THE TEXAN(1952); FORBIDDEN(1953); HANNAH LEE(1953); THUNDER BAY(1953); DAY OF

TRIUMPH(1954); DUFFY OF SAN QUENTIN(1954); SIEGE AT RED RIVER, THE(1954); SOUTHWEST PASSAGE(1954); THREE RING CIRCUS(1954); SINCERELY YOURS(1955); WARRIORS, THE(1955); HELL ON FRISCO BAY(1956); DRANGO(1957); LIGHT IN THE FOREST, THE(1958); WILD AND THE INNOCENT, THE(1959); SEPTEMBER STORM(1960); SYLVIA(1965); SUPER FUZZ(1981)

Diane Drube
Misc. Talkies
BOD SQUAD, THE(1976)

Herbert Druce
LAUGHING LADY, THE(1930)

Hubert Druce
NIGHT ANGEL, THE(1931); RETURN OF SHERLOCK HOLMES(1936)
Misc. Silents
PLEASE HELP EMILY(1917); MY WIFE(1918)

Jeffry Druce
IN SEARCH OF HISTORIC JESUS(1980)

David Drucker
WACKO(1983)

Harry Drucker
OCEAN'S ELEVEN(1960)

Nichole Drucker
HALLOWEEN II(1981)

Lucia Drudi
DEAF SMITH AND JOHNNY EARS(1973, Ital.), w

Vera Drudi
VERY HANDY MAN, A(1966, Fr./Ital.)

Don Druick
WOLFPEN PRINCIPLE, THE(1974, Can.), m

Matt Druker
HOUSE OF THE LIVING DEAD(1973, S. Afr.), p

James Drum
UNDERCOVER MAN, THE(1949); STUDS LONIGAN(1960); SSSSSSSS(1973)

Jim Drum
FORCE OF EVIL(1948); JOAN OF ARC(1948); VELVET TOUCH, THE(1948); HUMPHREY TAKES A CHANCE(1950); MAGNIFICENT YANKEE, THE(1950); ON DANGEROUS GROUND(1951); RISE AND FALL OF LEGS DIAMOND, THE(1960)

Rupert Drum
Silents
GOING THE LIMIT(1925)

Bob Drumbeller
COTTON COMES TO HARLEM(1970), set d

Douglass Drumbrille
FAST COMPANY(1938)

George Drumgold
SHOW FOLKS(1928), w

Bob Drumheller
STILETTO(1969), set d; SIDELONG GLANCES OF A PIGEON KICKER, THE(1970), set d

Robert Drumheller
INCIDENT, THE(1967), set d; DIARY OF A MAD HOUSEWIFE(1970), set d; SHAFT(1971), set d; HOT ROCK, THE(1972), set d; SHAFT'S BIG SCORE(1972), set d; GORDON'S WAR(1973), set d; EDUCATION OF SONNY CARSON, THE(1974), set d; DOG DAY AFTERNOON(1975), set d; STEPFORD WIVES, THE(1975), set d; FRONT, THE(1976), set d; NEXT MAN, THE(1976), set d; ANNIE HALL(1977), set d; KING OF THE GYPSIES(1978), set d; MANHATTAN(1979), set d; FOUR FRIENDS(1981), set d; WORLD ACCORDING TO GARP, The(1982), set d
1984
GHOSTBUSTERS(1984), set d; MUPPETS TAKE MANHATTAN, THE(1984), set d

Jack Drumier
Silents
$5,000,000 COUNTERFEITING PLOT, THE(1914); ADVENTURES OF CAROL, THE(1917); DANCER'S PERIL, THE(1917); FALSE FRIEND, THE(1917); APPEARANCE OF EVIL(1918); JOURNEY'S END(1918); JUST SYLVIA(1918); MAN HUNT, THE(1918); AMATEUR WIDOW, AN(1919); PRAISE AGENT, THE(1919); SHADOWS OF THE SEA(1922); SPLENDID LIE, THE(1922); ENEMIES OF YOUTH(1925)
Misc. Silents
MADNESS OF HELEN, THE(1916); BELOVED ADVENTURESS, THE(1917); LITTLE DUCHESS, THE(1917); BY HOOK OR CROOK(1918); LOVE NET, THE(1918); ROAD TO FRANCE, THE(1918); WHIMS OF SOCIETY, THE(1918); WITCH WOMAN, THE(1918); BLACK CIRCLE, THE(1919); FOREST RIVALS(1919); HIT OR MISS(1919); HOME WANTED(1919); GIRL FROM PORCUPINE, THE(1921); EMBLEMS OF LOVE(1924); PINCH HITTER, THE(1925)

John Drumier
Silents
DIVORCE GAME, THE(1917)

Jim Drumm
HIGH WALL, THE(1947); NIGHT HAS A THOUSAND EYES(1948)

Richard Drumm
MADEMOISELLE FIFI(1944)

Alice Drummond
WHERE'S POPPA?(1970); MAN ON A SWING(1974); THIEVES(1977); HIDE IN PLAIN SIGHT(1980); EYEWITNESS(1981); BEST LITTLE WHOREHOUSE IN TEXAS, THE(1982)
1984
GHOSTBUSTERS(1984)

David Drummond
TRIAL AND ERROR(1962, Brit.); CROOKS ANONYMOUS(1963, Brit.)

Fred Drummond
Silents
KENT, THE FIGHTING MAN(1916, Brit.)

Harry Drummond
Silents
IT'S HAPPINESS THAT COUNTS(1918, Brit.)
Misc. Silents
MEG O' THE WOODS(1918, Brit.)

Jane Drummond
SUSAN AND GOD(1940); FARGO KID, THE(1941)

Keith Drummond
YOUNG GIRLS OF ROCHEFORT, THE(1968, Fr.)

Margaret Drummond
THURSDAY'S CHILD(1943, Brit.)

Paul Drummond
PIRANHA II: THE SPAWNING(1981, Neth.)

Reed Drummond
MIDDLETON FAMILY AT THE N.Y. WORLD'S FAIR(1939), w

Reginald Drummond
SLEEPING CAR TO TRIESTE(1949, Brit.); TREASURE ISLAND(1950, Brit.)

Vivienne Drummond
GENTLE TOUCH, THE(1956, Brit.)

Robert Drunheller
LOVIN' MOLLY(1974), set d

Maurice Druon
MATTER OF TIME, A(1976, Ital./U.S.), w

Allen Drury
ADVISE AND CONSENT(1962), w

David Drury
1984
FOREVER YOUNG(1984, Brit.), d

Ellen Drury
YOICKS!(1932, Brit.)

James Drury
DIANE(1955); LOVE ME OR LEAVE ME(1955); TENDER TRAP, THE(1955); FORBIDDEN PLANET(1956); LAST WAGON, THE(1956); LOVE ME TENDER(1956); BERNARDINE(1957); GOOD DAY FOR A HANGING(1958); POLLYANNA(1960); TEN WHO DARED(1960); TOBY TYLER(1960); RIDE THE HIGH COUNTRY(1962); THIRD OF A MAN(1962); YOUNG WARRIORS, THE(1967); BACKTRACK(1969)

Joe Drury
SCALPHUNTERS, THE(1968), cos

Jon Drury
YOUNG WARRIORS, THE(1967); ONE MORE TRAIN TO ROB(1971)

Ken Drury
1984
PLOUGHMAN'S LUNCH, THE(1984, Brit.)

Morley Drury
TOUCHDOWN!(1931)

Norma Drury
STAGE DOOR(1937); PARIS CALLING(1941); THAT HAMILTON WOMAN(1941); UNFINISHED BUSINESS(1941); GET HEP TO LOVE(1942); MADAME SPY(1942); MYSTERY OF MARIE ROGET, THE(1942); SABOTEUR(1942); SKY'S THE LIMIT, THE(1943); SONG TO REMEMBER, A(1945); SPANISH MAIN, THE(1945)

Patrick Drury
AWAKENING, THE(1980)
1984
LAUGHTER HOUSE(1984, Brit.)

Peter Drury
DR. MORELLE-THE CASE OF THE MISSING HEIRESS(1949, Brit.); I'LL NEVER FORGET YOU(1951)

Sarah Drury
HAPPY IS THE BRIDE(1958, Brit.)

Roy Drusky
FORTY ACRE FEUD(1965); GOLD GUITAR, THE(1966); LAS VEGAS HILLBILLYS(1966)

Dena Drute
GREEN FIELDS(1937)

Irving Drutman
BEAUTY AND THE BEAST(1947, Fr.), titles

Svetlana Druzhinina
HOUSE ON THE FRONT LINE, THE(1963, USSR)

Vladimir Druzhnikov
SYMPHONY OF LIFE(1949, USSR); SECRET BRIGADE, THE(1951 USSR); DUEL, THE(1964, USSR); THREE SISTERS, THE(1969, USSR); WATERLOO(1970, Ital./USSR)

Mojmir Drvota
DISTANT JOURNEY(1950, Czech.), w

Ellen Dryden
L-SHAPED ROOM, THE(1962, Brit.)

Ernest Dryden
KING STEPS OUT, THE(1936), cos; LOST HORIZON(1937), cos; PRISONER OF ZENDA, THE(1937), cos

Jane Dryden
Silents
MAN WITHOUT DESIRE, THE(1923, Brit.)

Jeremy Craig Dryden
RUN WITH THE WIND(1966, Brit.), w

John Dryden
HILLS OF DONEGAL, THE(1947, Brit.), w

Leo Dryden
Silents
LADY OF THE LAKE, THE(1928, Brit.)

Noel Dryden
THREE WITNESSES(1935, Brit.); LATE AT NIGHT(1946, Brit.)

Norman Dryden
BUCKET OF BLOOD(1934, Brit.)

Raymond M. Dryden
ATTIC, THE(1979), p

Richard Dryden
MAN ON A SWING(1974)

Robert Dryden
FOUR BOYS AND A GUN(1957); TAKING OFF(1971)

Wheeler Dryden
LIMELIGHT(1952)
Silents
PENROD(1922)
Misc. Silents
SKIRTS(1928, Brit.), d

Carl-Theodor Dryer
Misc. Silents
BRIDE OF GLOMDAL, THE(1925, Nor.), d
Dave Dryer
COUNTRY MUSIC HOLIDAY(1958), md
David Dryer
NEVER SAY NEVER AGAIN(1983), spec eff
Janice Dryer
JUD(1971)
Robert Dryer
HEARTBREAKER(1983)
1984
SAVAGE STREETS(1984)
Sally Dryer
BOY NAMED CHARLIE BROWN, A(1969)
Edward Dryhurst
DANGEROUS SEAS(1931, Brit.), d&w; COMMISSIONAIRE(1933, Brit.), d; END OF THE ROAD, THE(1936, Brit.), w; FIND THE LADY(1936, Brit.), w; JENIFER HALE(1937, Brit.), w; STRANGE EXPERIMENT(1937, Brit.), w; CLAYDON TREASURE MYSTERY, THE(1938, Brit.), w; CASE OF THE FRIGHTENED LADY, THE(1940. Brit.), w; CRIMES AT THE DARK HOUSE(1940, Brit.), w; ATLANTIC FERRY(1941, Brit.), w; FLYING FORTRESS(1942, Brit.), w; THIS WAS PARIS(1942, Brit.), w; BELL-BOTTOM GEORGE(1943, Brit.), w; NIGHT INVADER, THE(1943, Brit), w; RHYTHM SERENADE(1943, Brit.), w; MAN FROM MOROCCO, THE(1946, Brit.), w; MASTER OF BANKDAM, THE(1947, Brit.), p, w; PATIENT VANISHES, THE(1947, Brit.), w; WHILE I LIVE(1947, Brit.), p; AGITATOR, THE(1949), w; SILK NOOSE, THE(1950, Brit.), p; NAUGHTY ARLETTE(1951, Brit.), p, w; CASTLE IN THE AIR(1952, Brit.), p, w; HOUSE OF THE ARROW, THE(1953, Brit.), w; STRANGER IN TOWN(1957, Brit.), w; IT'S NEVER TOO LATE(1958, Brit.), w
Misc. Silents
DIZZY LIMIT, THE(1930, Brit.), d; WOMAN FROM CHINA, THE(1930, Brit.), d
Michael Dryhurst
Misc. Talkies
HARD WAY, THE(1980, Brit.), d
Sarah Drylie
GAL YOUNG UN(1979)
Jeanne Dryman
THEY'RE A WEIRD MOB(1966, Aus.)
Jeanie Drynan
TOUCH AND GO(1955); 2,000 WEEKS(1970, Aus.); MONEY MOVERS(1978, Aus.)
1984
FANTASY MAN(1984, Aus.)
Jeannie Drynan
DON'S PARTY(1976, Aus.); PICTURE SHOW MAN, THE(1980, Aus.)
Judith Drynan
FAHRENHEIT 451(1966, Brit.)
Peter Drynan
SUNSET BOULEVARD(1950)
Bill Drysdale
MACBETH(1971, Brit.)
Denise Drysdale
DAY AFTER HALLOWEEN, THE(1981, Aus.); LAST OF THE KNUCKLEMEN, THE(1981, Aus.)
Don Michael Drysdale
HOODLUM EMPIRE(1952)
Tim Drysdale
WHEREVER SHE GOES(1953, Aus.)
Wieslaw Drzewica
GOLEM(1980, Pol.)
Wieslaw Drzewicz
MAN OF MARBLE(1979, Pol.)
Emile Dtain
ANTOINE ET ANTOINETTE(1947 Fr.)
Lambool Dtangpaibool
1984
KILLING FIELDS, THE(1984, Brit.)
Alphonse Du Bois
MAN WHO BROKE THE BANK AT MONTE CARLO, THE(1935)
Diane Du Bois
DAKOTA INCIDENT(1956); FUNNY FACE(1957)
Gladys Du Bois
DANCE OF LIFE, THE(1929)
Helen Du Bois
Silents
ICEBOUND(1924)
Misc. Silents
PRINCESS JONES(1921)
Hope Du Bois
SANCTUARY(1961)
Lucille Du Bois
Misc. Silents
PHANTOM SHADOWS(1925); SCARLET AND GOLD(1925)
Marta Du Bois
BOULEVARD NIGHTS(1979)
Philip Du Bois
Silents
BLOT, THE(1921), ph
Raoul Pene Du Bois
DIXIE(1943), cos; FRENCHMAN'S CREEK(1944), cos; LADY IN THE DARK(1944), art d, cos
Wilson Du Bois
Silents
EVERY WOMAN'S PROBLEM(1921)
Paul Du Bov
SNIPER, THE(1952)
J. A. Du Bray
Silents
OCCASIONALLY YOURS(1920), ph

Clair Du Brey
LIFE BEGINS AT 40(1935)
Claire Du Brey
FOR THE LOVE O'LIL(1930); THIS SIDE OF HEAVEN(1934); DEVIL DOLL, THE(1936); NOTHING SACRED(1937); MEN WITH WINGS(1938); EVERYBODY'S BABY(1939); JESSE JAMES(1939); WHEN TOMORROW COMES(1939); ALL THIS AND HEAVEN TOO(1940); BLUE BIRD, THE(1940); BRIGHAM YOUNG-FRONTIERSMAN(1940); HIGH SCHOOL(1940); YOUTH WILL BE SERVED(1940); PRIVATE NURSE(1941); GAY SISTERS, THE(1942); MAGNIFICENT DOPE, THE(1942); NOW, VOYAGER(1942); LIGHTS OF OLD SANTA FE(1944); CLOAK AND DAGGER(1946); HOMESTRETCH, THE(1947); IVY(1947); ABBOTT AND COSTELLO MEET THE KILLER, BORIS KARLOFF(1949)
Silents
PEGGY(1916); ANTHING ONCE(1917); RESCUE, THE(1917); MADAME SPY(1918); PRISONER OF THE PINES(1918); RISKY ROAD, THE(1918); MAN IN THE OPEN, A(1919); OLD MAID'S BABY, THE(1919); GREEN FLAME, THE(1920); BRONZE BELL, THE(1921); ONLY A SHOP GIRL(1922); ORDEAL, THE(1922); TO HAVE AND TO HOLD(1922); EXQUISITE SINNER, THE(1926); MISS NOBODY(1926)
Misc. Silents
FIGHTING GRINGO, THE(1917); FOLLOW THE GIRL(1917); REWARD OF THE FAITHLESS, THE(1917); WINGED MYSTERY, THE(1917); BRACE UP(1918); MAGIC EYE, THE(1918); SPITE BRIDE, THE(1919); WISHING RING MAN, THE(1919); DANGEROUS HOURS(1920); LIFE'S TWIST(1920); LIGHT WOMAN, A(1920); PERILOUS VALLEY(1921); I AM GUILTY(1921); WHEN LOVE COMES(1922); YOU NEVER KNOW(1922); TWO SISTERS(1929)
Alma Du Bus
CITIZEN SAINT(1947); HOMEBODIES(1974)
Diana Du Cane
BROKEN MELODY(1938, Aus.)
Countess Du Cello
Silents
HONOR SYSTEM, THE(1917)
Mary Du Cello
Misc. Silents
GIRL OF LOST LAKE, THE(1916)
Walter Du Cloux
INTERRUPTED MELODY(1955), md
Robert du Couedic
LOVE ON THE RUN(1936); ESPIONAGE(1937); ARTISTS AND MODELS ABROAD(1938)
George Du Count
GAY DESPERADO, THE(1936)
Tote Du Crow
Silents
AMERICANO, THE(1917); MARK OF ZORRO(1920); PRIDE OF PALOMAR, THE(1922); THIEF OF BAGDAD, THE(1924); DON Q, SON OF ZORRO(1925); SPOOK RANCH(1925); BLUE STREAK, THE(1926)
Misc. Silents
BETTY AND THE BUCCANEERS(1917)
Frank Du Frane
LOVE ON THE RUN(1936); ROSALIE(1937)
L. du Garde Peach
MAN OF AFFAIRS(1937, Brit.), w
Cecil du Gue
Silents
AUTUMN OF PRIDE, THE(1921, Brit.); IN HIS GRIP(1921, Brit.); SILENT EVIDENCE(1922, Brit.)
Misc. Silents
GREEN TERROR, THE(1919, Brit.); WAY OF A MAN, THE(1921, Brit.)
Pierre Du Kane
MY THIRD WIFE GEORGE(1968), set d
Robert Du Laine
TELL THEM WILLIE BOY IS HERE(1969)
Holly Du Marreck
LAST VALLEY, THE(1971, Brit.)
Gerald du Mauier
Misc. Silents
JUSTICE(1917, Brit.)
Daphne du Maurier
JAMAICA INN(1939, Brit.), w; REBECCA(1940), w; FRENCHMAN'S CREEK(1944), w; HUNGRY HILL(1947, Brit.), w; YEARS BETWEEN, THE(1947, Brit.), w; MY COUSIN RACHEL(1952); SCAPEGOAT, THE(1959, Brit.), w; BIRDS, THE(1963), w; DON'T LOOK NOW(1973, Brit./Ital.), w
George du Maurier
SVENGALI(1931), w; PETER IBBETSON(1935), w; SVENGALI(1955, Brit.), d&w
Silents
TRILBY(1915), w
Gerald Du Maurier
BULLDOG DRUMMOND(1929), w; DANCERS, THE(1930), w; LORD CAMBER'S LADIES(1932, Brit.); CATHERINE THE GREAT(1934, Brit.); I WAS A SPY(1934, Brit.); POWER(1934, Brit.); LIVING DEAD, THE(1936, Brit.)
Misc. Silents
MASKS AND FACES(1917, Brit.); UNMARRIED(1920, Brit.)
Guy du Maurier
MAD MEN OF EUROPE(1940, Brit.), w
Sir Gerald du Maurier
ESCAPE(1930, Brit.)
Rob Du Mee
ZERO IN THE UNIVERSE(1966)
Guy du Monceau
ENCORE(1951, Brit.); INNOCENTS IN PARIS(1955, Brit.); PORT AFRIQUE(1956, Brit.)
Magasin du Nord
HIDDEN FEAR(1957), cos
E. B. Du Par
Silents
COUNTRY KID, THE(1923), ph

Ed Du Par
QUEEN OF THE NIGHTCLUBS(1929), ph
Silents
BETTER 'OLE, THE(1926), ph; NIGHT CRY, THE(1926), ph; DOG OF THE REGI-
MENT(1927), ph; FORTUNE HUNTER, THE(1927), ph; IF I WERE SINGLE(1927), ph;
WHITE FLANNELS(1927), ph
Edwin Du Par
LIGHTS OF NEW YORK(1928), ph; TOO YOUNG TO KNOW(1945), spec eff; TASK
FORCE(1949), spec eff; LION AND THE HORSE, THE(1952), ph; SPRINGFIELD
RIFLE(1952), ph; SYSTEM, THE(1953), ph; FRESH FROM PARIS(1955), ph; RE-
DEEMER, THE(1965, Span.), ph
Edwin A. Du Par
SHINE ON, HARVEST MOON(1944), spec eff
Edwin B. Du Par
PASSAGE TO MARSEILLE(1944), spec eff
Nilda du Piessy
Misc. Silents
L'EPERVIER(1924, Fr.)
Johan Du Plooy
KIMBERLEY JIM(1965, South Africa); WILD SEASON(1968, South Africa)
E. A. du Pont
LADIES MUST LOVE(1933), d
Michael Du Pont
HANDS OF A STRANGER(1962), p; SECRET OF THE SACRED FOREST, THE(1970),
d
Misc. Talkies
BLOODLESS VAMPIRE, THE(1965), d
Miss Du Pont
Silents
FOOLISH WIVES(1920); RAGE OF PARIS, THE(1921); WONDERFUL WIFE, A(1922);
COMMON LAW, THE(1923); RAFFLES, THE AMATEUR CRACKSMAN(1925); GOOD
AND NAUGHTY(1926); WHEEL OF DESTINY, THE(1927)
Misc. Silents
FALSE KISSES(1921); GOLDEN GALLOWS, THE(1922); BROKEN WING,
THE(1923); DEFEND YOURSELF(1925)
Miss Du Pont [Patricia Hannon]
Misc. Silents
SHATTERED DREAMS(1922); WHAT THREE MEN WANTED(1924)
Norman Du Pont
NUN AND THE SERGEANT, THE(1962)
John Du Prez
BULLSHOT(1983), m; MONTY PYTHON'S THE MEANING OF LIFE(1983, Brit.), m
Andre Du Rona
MONDAY'S CHILD(1967, U.S., Arg.), p, w
Carmen Du Sautoy
PRAYING MANTIS(1982, Brit.)
Harry A. Du Souchet
Silents
LET'S GET MARRIED(1926), w
Josh Du Toit
KILLER FORCE(1975, Switz./Ireland), spec eff
Marie Du Toit
WILD SEASON(1968, South Africa); MY WAY(1974, South Africa)
Danielle du Tombe
CONFIDENCE(1980, Hung.)
Roland Guinier du Vignaud
FIRST TASTE OF LOVE(1962, Fr.), w
Deborah du'Lacey
HELP!(1965, Brit.)
David Duack
JESUS CHRIST, SUPERSTAR(1973)
Doris Duane
THAT'S MY BABY(1944)
Georgette Duane
COME TO THE STABLE(1949)
Jessie Holladay Duane
MARCH ON PARIS 1914–OF GENERALOBERST ALEXANDER VON KLUCK–AND
HIS MEMORY OF JESSIE HOLLADAY(1977), a, m
John Duane
FOLLOW THE BOYS(1944)
Michael Duane
CITY WITHOUT MEN(1943); DANGEROUS BLONDES(1943); DR. GILLESPIE'S
CRIMINAL CASE(1943); IS EVERYBODY HAPPY?(1943); DEVIL'S MASK,
THE(1946); PERSONALITY KID(1946); SECRET OF THE WHISTLER(1946); SHAD-
OWED(1946); GLAMOUR GIRL(1947); KEEPER OF THE BEES(1947); SWORDSMAN,
THE(1947); GALLANT BLADE, THE(1948); PRINCE OF THIEVES, THE(1948); RE-
TURN OF THE WHISTLER, THE(1948); WOMAN FROM TANGIER(1948);
REDHEAD FROM MANHATTAN(1954)
Misc. Talkies
ALIAS MR. TWILIGHT(1946)
Duane Eddy and The Rebels
BECAUSE THEY'RE YOUNG(1960)
Anselmo Duarte
GIVEN WORD, THE(1964, Braz.), d, w
Armando Duarte
ZORRO, THE GAY BLADE(1981)
Felix Duarte
MUTATIONS, THE(1974, Brit.)
Jose Duarte
FUNHOUSE, THE(1981), art d
Radoslav Dubansky
OPERATION DAYBREAK(1976, U.S./Brit./Czech.)
Denise Dubarry
SKATEBOARD(1978); BEING THERE(1979); DEVIL AND MAX DEVLIN, THE(1981)
Y. Dubasov
HUNTING IN SIBERIA(1962, USSR)
Ahley DuBay
BOOGEYMAN II(1983)

Agnese Dubbini
ANGELINA(1948, Ital.); JOAN AT THE STAKE(1954, Ital./Fr.)
Don Dubbins
FROM HERE TO ETERNITY(1953); CAINE MUTINY, THE(1954); THESE WILDER
YEARS(1956); TRIBUTE TO A BADMAN(1956); D.I., THE(1957); ENCHANTED IS-
LAND(1958); FROM THE EARTH TO THE MOON(1958); PRIZE, THE(1963); GUN-
FIGHT IN ABILENE(1967); ILLUSTRATED MAN, THE(1969); LEARNING TREE,
THE(1969); HOAX, THE(1972); DEATH WISH II(1982)
Arthur R. Dubbs
ADVENTURES OF THE WILDERNESS FAMILY, THE(1975), p
A. Dubchak
TRAIN GOES TO KIEV, THE(1961, USSR), makeup
Cyprien P. R. Dube
JAWS(1975)
Pandit S.R. Dube
TIGER AND THE FLAME, THE(1955, India), w
Stanley Dubens
MODESTY BLAISE(1966, Brit.), w
Axel Duberg
MAGICIAN, THE(1959, Swed.); DEVIL'S EYE, THE(1960, Swed.); VIRGIN SPRING,
THE(1960, Swed.); SHAME(1968, Swed.); TIME IN THE SUN, A(1970, Swed.)
Roland Dubillard
BEAUTIFUL PRISONER, THE(1983, Fr.)
Al Dubin
BRIDE OF THE REGIMENT(1930), m; HOLD EVERYTHING(1930), m; 42ND
STREET(1933); VERY HONORABLE GUY, A(1934); GO INTO YOUR DANCE(1935);
MARKED WOMAN(1937), m/l
Alexis Dubin
MADMAN(1982)
Charles Dubin
MISTER ROCK AND ROLL(1957), d
Charles S. Dubin
MOVING VIOLATION(1976), d
Gary Dubin
APRIL FOOLS, THE(1969); ARISTOCATS, THE(1970); DIAMONDS ARE FORE-
VER(1971, Brit.); JAWS II(1978)
Joseph Dubin
ATLANTIC CITY(1944), m; CODE OF THE PRAIRIE(1944), md; FIREBRANDS OF
ARIZONA(1944), md; MARSHAL OF RENO(1944), m; SAN ANTONIO KID,
THE(1944), m; SHERIFF OF SUNDOWN(1944), m; SILVER CITY KID(1944), m;
STAGECOACH TO MONTEREY(1944), m; TUCSON RAIDERS(1944), m; VIGI-
LANTES OF DODGE CITY(1944), m; GIRLS OF THE BIG HOUSE(1945), m; HOME IN
OKLAHOMA(1946), m; LAST CROOKED MILE, THE(1946), m; MADONNA'S SE-
CRET, THE(1946), m; RENDEZVOUS WITH ANNIE(1946), m; GHOST GOES WILD,
THE(1947), m; TRAIL TO SAN ANTONE(1947), m
Sid Dubin
ADAM'S RIB(1949)
Sidney Dubin
KNOCK ON ANY DOOR(1949); UNDERCOVER MAN, THE(1949); PERFECT
STRANGERS(1950); 711 OCEAN DRIVE(1950)
Josef Dubin-Behrman
AMSTERDAM AFFAIR, THE(1968 Brit.)
J.A.B. Dubin-Behrmann
SECOND BEST SECRET AGENT IN THE WHOLE WIDE WORLD, THE(1965, Brit.);
NAKED RUNNER, THE(1967, Brit.)
Kay Dubinski
DINGAKA(1965, South Africa), art d
Miss Dubinsky
Misc. Silents
FIFTH COMMANDMENT, THE(1927)
Yudel Dubinsky
TWO SISTERS(1938)
Misc. Talkies
AMERICAN MATCHMAKER(1940); LIVE AND LAUGH(1933); DOBBIN, THE(1939)
Beverley Dublin
BABYLON(1980, Brit.)
Darren Dublin
WILD ONE, THE(1953); I DIED A THOUSAND TIMES(1955)
1984
FLETCH(1984)
Florence Dublin
DESIREE(1954)
Jessica Dublin
FRAGMENT OF FEAR(1971, Brit.); LAST REBEL, THE(1971); TRINITY IS STILL
MY NAME(1971, Ital.)
Daniele Dublino
BLACK BELLY OF THE TARANTULA, THE(1972, Ital.); DON'T TOUCH WHITE
WOMEN!(1974, Fr.)
Yudel Dublinsky
SINGING BLACKSMITH(1938)
Laura Dubman
SONG OF LOVE(1947), tech adv
Mirtha Dubner
HAND IN THE TRAP, THE(1963, Arg./Span.); TERRACE, THE(1964, Arg.)
Jane Duboc
1984
BLAME IT ON RIO(1984)
Albert Dubois
LOVE HUNGER(1965, Arg.), d, w
Alphonse Dubois
TO HAVE AND HAVE NOT(1944)
Andre Dubois
MR. HULOT'S HOLIDAY(1954, Fr.)
Daniel Dubois
RISE OF LOUIS XIV, THE(1970, Fr.)
Diane Dubois
AMAZING MRS. HOLLIDAY(1943); PASSAGE TO MARSEILLE(1944); 'TILL WE
MEET AGAIN(1944); GIRL IN THE RED VELVET SWING, THE(1955); PURPLE
MASK, THE(1955)

Gladys DuBois
BATTLE OF PARIS, THE(1929)
Ilse Dubois
SITUATION HOPELESS–BUT NOT SERIOUS(1965), cos; UNWILLING AGENT(1968, Ger.), cos
Ja'Net Dubois
FIVE ON THE BLACK HAND SIDE(1973)
Janet DuBois
PIECE OF THE ACTION, A(1977)
Jeanette DuBois
MAN CALLED ADAM, A(1966); DIARY OF A MAD HOUSEWIFE(1970)
Julien Dubois
LOVE ON THE RUN(1980, Fr.)
Marie Dubois
WOMAN IS A WOMAN, A(1961, Fr./Ital.); JULES AND JIM(1962, Fr.); SHOOT THE PIANO PLAYER(1962, Fr.); CIRCLE OF LOVE(1965, Fr.); MALE HENRI(1965, Fr./Ital.); MATA HARI(1965, Fr./Ital.); WEEKEND AT DUNKIRK(1966, Fr./Ital.); THIEF OF PARIS, THE(1967, Fr./Ital.); DAY THE HOTLINE GOT HOT, THE(1968, Fr./Span.); MARRIAGE CAME TUMBLING DOWN, THE(1968, Fr.); DON'T LOOK NOW(1969, Brit./Fr.); THOSE DARING YOUNG MEN IN THEIR JAUNTY JALOPIES(1969, Fr./Brit./ Ital.); WISE GUYS(1969, Fr./Ital.); SERPENT, THE(1973, Fr./Ital./Ger.); INNOCENT, THE(1979, Ital.); MON ONCLE D'AMERIQUE(1980, Fr.)
1984
LA PETIT SIRENE(1984, Fr.)
Philip R. Dubois
Silents
LAST OF THE MOHICANS, THE(1920), ph
Raoul Pene DuBois
KITTY(1945), set d&cos
Raoul Rene DuBois
HAPPY GO LUCKY(1943), art d
Richard DuBois
1984
MUPPETS TAKE MANHATTAN, THE(1984)
Vivian DuBois
I MARRIED AN ANGEL(1942)
William DuBois
PAGAN LADY(1931), w; I LOVED YOU WEDNESDAY(1933), w
Dubosc
DARK EYES(1938, Fr.)
Andre Dubosc
MAYERLING(1937, Fr.)
Andre Dubose
ACCUSED–STAND UP(1930, Fr.)
Phil J. Duboski
ROSE BOWL(1936)
Jean Dubost
MY UNCLE ANTOINE(1971, Can.)
Paulet Dubost
MAIGRET LAYS A TRAP(1958, Fr.)
Paulette Dubost
RULES OF THE GAME, THE(1939, Fr.); NAKED WOMAN, THE(1950, Fr.); FOUR IN A JEEP(1951, Switz.); LE PLAISIR(1954, Fr.); HOLIDAY FOR HENRIETTA(1955, Fr.); LOLA MONTES(1955, Fr./Ger.); PICNIC ON THE GRASS(1960, Fr.); LOVE AND THE FRENCHWOMAN(1961, Fr.); SEVEN CAPITAL SINS(1962, Fr./Ital.); PLAYTIME(1963, Fr.); MAEDCHEN IN UNIFORM(1965, Ger./Fr.); VIVA MARIA(1965, Fr./Ital.); WOMEN AND WAR(1965, Fr.); ENOUGH ROPE(1966, Fr./Ital./Ger.); LAST METRO, THE(1981, Fr.); LA VIE CONTINUE(1982, Fr.)
Anne Dubot
MY NIGHT AT MAUD'S(1970, Fr.)
A. Dubov
CLEAR SKIES(1963, USSR)
D. Dubov
BRIDE WITH A DOWRY(1954, USSR)
Paul Dubov
LITTLE TOUGH GUY(1938); BOMBAY CLIPPER(1942); DANGER IN THE PACIFIC(1942); ESCAPE FROM HONG KONG(1942); GIRLS' TOWN(1942); MYSTERY OF MARIE ROGET, THE(1942); NORTH TO THE KLONDIKE(1942); WHO DONE IT?(1942); BOSS OF BIG TOWN(1943); FOLLOW THE BAND(1943); IT AIN'T HAY(1943); MUG TOWN(1943); WE'VE NEVER BEEN LICKED(1943); STRANGE HOLIDAY(1945); CYRANO DE BERGERAC(1950); PERFECT STRANGERS(1950); TRIPLE TROUBLE(1950); YOUNG MAN WITH A HORN(1950); MOB, THE(1951); SUNNY SIDE OF THE STREET(1951); DEADLINE–U.S.A.(1952); HIGH NOON(1952); KANSAS CITY CONFIDENTIAL(1952); GLASS WEB, THE(1953); I, THE JURY(1953); ABBOTT AND COSTELLO MEET THE KEYSTONE KOPS(1955); APACHE WOMAN(1955); CELL 2455, DEATH ROW(1955); SIX BRIDGES TO CROSS(1955); DAY THE WORLD ENDED, THE(1956); HE LAUGHED LAST(1956); SHE-CREATURE, THE(1956); THAT CERTAIN FEELING(1956); BROTHERS RICO, THE(1957); CHINA GATE(1957); FORTY GUNS(1957); SHAKE, RATTLE, AND ROCK!(1957); CRIMSON KIMONO, THE(1959); TOKYO AFTER DARK(1959); VERBOTEN!(1959); ATOMIC SUBMARINE, THE(1960); MA BARKER'S KILLER BROOD(1960); PURPLE GANG, THE(1960); UNDERWORLD U.S.A.(1961); SCARFACE MOB, THE(1962); UNDERWATER CITY, THE(1962); IRMA LA DOUCE(1963); SHOCK CORRIDOR(1963); WITH SIX YOU GET EGGROLL(1968), w
I. Dubravim
Misc. Silents
WANDERING STARS(1927, USSR)
Claire DuBray
INVISIBLE INFORMER(1946); HOT ROD GANG(1958)
Joseph A. Dubray
Silents
KISMET(1920), ph; IF I WERE QUEEN(1922), ph; AWFUL TRUTH, THE(1925), ph; REDHEADS PREFERRED(1926), ph; BACKSTAGE(1927), ph; CHEATERS(1927), ph; ENCHANTED ISLAND, THE(1927), ph; HUSBAND HUNTERS(1927), ph
Joseph Dubray
Silents
WIFE'S AWAKENING, A(1921), w, ph; ALIMONY(1924), ph; PRINCESS FROM HOBOKEN, THE(1927), ph

Raymond Dubreil
Misc. Silents
L'INVITATION AU VOYAGE(1927, Fr.)
Alain Dubreuil
MUSIC LOVERS, THE(1971, Brit.)
Andre Dubreuil
BLANCHE(1971, Fr.), ph
Claire DuBrey
BROADWAY TO HOLLYWOOD(1933); EVER IN MY HEART(1933); GABRIEL OVER THE WHITE HOUSE(1933); SIN OF NORA MORAN(1933); AMONG THE MISSING(1934); SHADOWS OF SING SING(1934); JANE EYRE(1935); RAMONA(1936); MOUNTAIN JUSTICE(1937); WIFE, DOCTOR AND NURSE(1937); BARONESS AND THE BUTLER, THE(1938); LITTLE MISS BROADWAY(1938); THAT CERTAIN AGE(1938); FORGOTTEN WOMAN, THE(1939); SOUTH OF THE BORDER(1939); STORY OF ALEXANDER GRAHAM BELL, THE(1939); STRANGE CASE OF DR. MEADE(1939); TELL NO TALES(1939); CHARLIE CHAN'S MURDER CRUISE(1940); SHOP AROUND THE CORNER, THE(1940); RISE AND SHINE(1941); BELLS OF CAPISTRANO(1942); CLOSE CALL FOR ELLERY QUEEN, A(1942); JUKE BOX JENNY(1942); HEAVEN CAN WAIT(1943); DRAGON SEED(1944); OH, WHAT A NIGHT(1944); DAKOTA(1945); RHAPSODY IN BLUE(1945); SONG TO REMEMBER, A(1945); DON RICARDO RETURNS(1946); SECRET OF THE WHISTLER(1946); BELLS OF SAN FERNANDO(1947); UNCONQUERED(1947); EVERY GIRL SHOULD BE MARRIED(1948); FRENCH LEAVE(1948); LIGHTNIN' IN THE FOREST(1948); LOVES OF CARMEN, THE(1948); OUT OF THE STORM(1948); WHO KILLED "DOC" ROBBIN?(1948); DEAR WIFE(1949); SAMSON AND DELILAH(1949); STREETS OF SAN FRANCISCO(1949); CINDERELLA(1950); DESTINATION BIG HOUSE(1950); RAIDERS OF THE SEVEN SEAS(1953); FRONTIER GUN(1958); ESCORT WEST(1959)
Silents
DEVIL'S TRAIL, THE(1919)
Misc. Silents
SAWDUST DOLL, THE(1919); WHEN FATE DECIDES(1919)
F. Dubrovskiy
TRAIN GOES TO KIEV, THE(1961, USSR)
Donna Dubrow
WATERMELON MAN(1970)
Arthur Dubs
FURTHER ADVENTURES OF THE WILDERNESS FAMILY–PART TWO(1978), p, w
Arthur R. Dubs
ACROSS THE GREAT DIVIDE(1976), p; MOUNTAIN FAMILY ROBINSON(1979), p, w; WINDWALKER(1980), p
1984
MYSTERY MANSION(1984), p; SACRED GROUND(1984), p
Adolph Dubsky
JUMBO(1962)
Mario Dubuc
MY UNCLE ANTOINE(1971, Can.)
Marie-Sophie Dubus
JESSICA(1962, U.S./Ital./Fr.), ed; POSSESSION(1981, Fr./Ger.), ed
1984
LES COMPERES(1984, Fr.), ed
Isabelle Duby
LITTLE ROMANCE, A(1979, U.S./Fr.); CHANEL SOLITAIRE(1981)
Jacques Duby
ADULTERESS, THE(1959, Fr.); CHRISTINE(1959, Fr.); LOVE AND THE FRENCHWOMAN(1961, Fr.); OLDEST PROFESSION, THE(1968, Fr./Ital./Ger.); THOSE DARING YOUNG MEN IN THEIR JAUNTY JALOPIES(1969, Fr./Brit./ Ital.); SICILIAN CLAN, THE(1970, Fr.); PIAF–THE EARLY YEARS(1982, U.S./Fr.)
Satya Dev Duby
GUIDE, THE(1965, U.S./India)
Helene Duc
PICNIC ON THE GRASS(1960, Fr.); MALE HUNT(1965, Fr./Ital.)
Jacqueline Duc
PROMISE AT DAWN(1970, U.S./Fr.)
Jean Bernard Duc
DOCTEUR LAENNEC(1949, Fr.), w
Loi Lam Duc
1984
PERILS OF GWENDOLINE, THE(1984, Fr.)
Michelle Ducasse
SO THIS IS PARIS(1954)
Annie Ducaux
LIFE AND LOVES OF BEETHOVEN, THE(1937, Fr.); AFFAIR LAFONT, THE(1939, Fr.); CONFLICT(1939, Fr.); TWO WOMEN(1940, Fr.); ROYAL AFFAIR, A(1950); LA BELLE AMERICAINE(1961, Fr.)
Gerard Ducaux-Rupp
WEB OF FEAR(1966, Fr./Span.), p
Duccio
HERCULES AND THE CAPTIVE WOMEN(1963, Fr./Ital.), w
Jerri Duce
BUFFALO BILL AND THE INDIANS, OR SITTING BULL'S HISTORY LESSON(1976)
Joy Duce
BUFFALO BILL AND THE INDIANS, OR SITTING BULL'S HISTORY LESSON(1976)
Richard Duce
MAIN STREET AFTER DARK(1944), art d; ROMANCE OF ROSY RIDGE, THE(1947), art d
Sharon Duce
TAMARIND SEED, THE(1974, Brit.); ABSOLUTION(1981, Brit.); OUTLAND(1981)
Jean Duceppe
ACT OF THE HEART(1970, Can.); MY UNCLE ANTOINE(1971, Can.); JE T'AIME(1974, Can.); ALIEN THUNDER(1975, US/Can.)
Pierre Duceppe
JE T'AIME(1974, Can.), d, w
Paul Ducet
Misc. Silents
BLACK PANTHER'S CUB, THE(1921)

Lillian Ducey
Silents
BROKEN DOLL, A(1921), w; ENEMIES OF CHILDREN(1923), d&w; LULLABY, THE(1924), w; WARNING, THE(1927), w; DEVIL'S APPLE TREE(1929), w

Marcel Duchamp
DREAMS THAT MONEY CAN BUY(1948), w

Camille Ducharme
THIRTEENTH LETTER, THE(1951)

Connie Ducharme
PAJAMA PARTY(1964); ROUSTABOUT(1964)

Rejean Ducharme
FOND MEMORIES(1982, Can.), w

Yvan Ducharme
VISITING HOURS(1982, Can.)

Renee Duchateau
SUNDAYS AND CYBELE(1962, Fr.)

Michel Duchaussoy
KILLING GAME, THE(1968, Fr.); BYE BYE BARBARA(1969, Fr.); LA FEMME INFIDELE(1969, Fr./Ital.); SOPHIE'S WAYS(1970, Fr.); THIS MAN MUST DIE(1970, Fr./Ital.); MAN WITH THE TRANSPLANTED BRAIN, THE(1972, Fr./Ital./Ger.); SHOCK TREATMENT(1973, Fr.); NADA GANG, THE(1974, Fr./Ital.)

Louis Duchesne
SOFT SKIN ON BLACK SILK(1964, Fr./Span.), d

Roger Duchesne
GOLEM, THE(1937, Czech./Fr.); AFFAIR LAFONT, THE(1939, Fr.); CONFLICT(1939, Fr.); LE MONDE TREMBLERA(1939, Fr.); IT HAPPENED IN GIBRALTAR(1943, Fr.); SAVAGE BRIGADE(1948, Fr.); SELLERS OF GIRLS(1967, Fr.)

Roger Duchet
MAN FROM COCODY(1966, Fr./Ital.), p; SOUTHERN STAR, THE(1969, Fr./Brit.), p

Peter Duchin
WORLD OF HENRY ORIENT, THE(1964)

Gigi Duckett
KAMOURASKA(1973, Can./Fr.)

Lucinda Duckett
SQUEEZE, THE(1977, Brit.)

Luke Duckett
BIDDY(1983, Brit.)

Cordett Duckie
CHILDREN OF BABYLON(1980, Jamaica)

Maria Esther Duckse
TERRACE, THE(1964, Arg.)

Dorothea Duckworth
RACHEL, RACHEL(1968); ME, NATALIE(1969)

Dortha Duckworth
HONEYMOON KILLERS, THE(1969)
1984
PROTOCOL(1984)

Tania Duckworth
FELLINI SATYRICON(1969, Fr./Ital.)

Todd Duckworth
1984
RUNAWAY(1984)

David Duclon
GRASSHOPPER, THE(1970)

Pierre Duclos
LAFAYETTE(1963, Fr.), m

Rick Ducommun
1984
NO SMALL AFFAIR(1984)

Flavie Ducorps
1984
LIFE IS A BED OF ROSES(1984, Fr.)

Jean-Pierre Ducos
GREEN ROOM, THE(1979, Fr.); LOVE ON THE RUN(1980, Fr.)

George Ducount
UNDER TWO FLAGS(1936); WHITE FANG(1936); GUNGA DIN(1939)

Marguerite Ducouret
CARNIVAL IN FLANDERS(1936, Fr.); DR. KNOCK(1936, Fr.); CAGE OF NIGHTINGALES, A(1947, Fr.)

Louis Ducreux
1984
SUNDAY IN THE COUNTRY, A(1984, Fr.), a, m

Yvette Ducreux
PLAYTIME(1973, Fr.)

Michel Ducrocq
MATTER OF DAYS, A(1969, Fr./Czech.)

Peter Ducrow
CHILDREN OF CHANCE(1949, Brit.); WHERE THE BULLETS FLY(1966, Brit.)

Roger Duculot
FIRST TASTE OF LOVE(1962, Fr.), ph; FIVE WILD GIRLS(1966, Fr.), ph; YOU ONLY LIVE ONCE(1969, Fr.), ph

Gernot Duda
TOWN WITHOUT PITY(1961, Ger./Switz./U.S.); BASHFUL ELEPHANT, THE(1962, Aust.); UNWILLING AGENT(1968, Ger.)
1984
LOVE IN GERMANY, A(1984, Fr./Ger.)

Pierre Dudan
LYONS IN PARIS, THE(1955, Brit.); TOUCH OF THE SUN, A(1956, Brit.); ROOTS OF HEAVEN, THE(1958)

Bohumil Dudar
VOYAGE TO THE END OF THE UNIVERSE(1963, Czech.), art d

G. Dudarev
THREE SISTERS, THE(1969, USSR)

Ludmilla Dudarova
FATHER'S DILEMMA(1952, Ital.); ULYSSES(1955, Ital.); KREMLIN LETTER, THE(1970)

V. Dudarova
LULLABY(1961, USSR), md; SOUND OF LIFE, THE(1962, USSR), md; OPTIMISTIC TRAGEDY, THE(1964, USSR), md

Bruno Duday
WHITE DEMON, THE(1932, Ger.), p; COURT CONCERT, THE(1936, Ger.), p; FINAL CHORD, THE(1936, Ger.), p; LA HABANERA(1937, Ger.), p; LIFE BEGINS ANEW(1938, Ger.).

Klaus Dudenhoefer
CAPTAIN FROM KOEPENICK, THE(1956, Ger.), ed; CITY OF SECRETS(1963, Ger.), ed

Klaus Dudenhofer
DIE GANS VON SEDAN(1962, Fr./Ger.), ed; GLASS OF WATER, A(1962, Cgr.), ed; WILLY(1963, U.S./Ger.), ed; CAVE OF THE LIVING DEAD(1966, Yugo./Ger.), ed

Elspeth Dudgeon
MOONSTONE, THE(1934); STAND UP AND CHEER(1934 80m FOX bw); BECKY SHARP(1935); I FOUND STELLA PARISH(1935); LAST OUTPOST, THE(1935); NIGHT IS YOUNG, THE(1935); VANESSA, HER LOVE STORY(1935); GIVE ME YOUR HEART(1936); SHOW BOAT(1936); SUZY(1936); SYLVIA SCARLETT(1936); GREAT GARRICK, THE(1937); PRINCE AND THE PAUPER, THE(1937); SH! THE OCTOPUS(1937); FOOLS FOR SCANDAL(1938); MYSTERY HOUSE(1938); RAFFLES(1939); STORY OF VERNON AND IRENE CASTLE, THE(1939); FOREIGN CORRESPONDENT(1940); NIGHTMARE(1942); NOW, VOYAGER(1942); HEAVENLY BODY, THE(1943); DEVOTION(1946); TILL THE CLOUDS ROLL BY(1946); IF WINTER COMES(1947); YANKEE FAKIR(1947); JULIA MISBEHAVES(1948); GREAT SINNER, THE(1949); LUST FOR GOLD(1949)

H.N. Dudgeon
Misc. Silents
UNTAMED(1918)

John [Elspeth] Dudgeon
OLD DARK HOUSE, THE(1932)

Robert Dudich
CASEY'S SHADOW(1978)

Marc Dudicourt
MADE IN U.S.A.(1966, Fr.); KING OF HEARTS(1967, Fr./Ital.); LA VIE DE CHATEAU(1967, Fr.); THIEF OF PARIS, THE(1967, Fr./Ital.)

Michael Dudikoff
BLACK MARBLE, THE(1980); I OUGHT TO BE IN PICTURES(1982); MAKING LOVE(1982); UNCOMMON VALOR(1983)

Michael J. Dudikoff II
TRON(1982)

Natalia Dudinskaya
SLEEPING BEAUTY, THE(1966, USSR)

A. Dudko
TIGER GIRL(1955, USSR), ph

Apollinari Dudko
DEFENSE OF VOLOTCHAYEVSK, THE(1938, USSR), ph

Apollinarily Dudko
SLEEPING BEAUTY, THE(1966, USSR), d

Apollinariy Dudko
DON QUIXOTE(1961, USSR), ph; MORNING STAR(1962, USSR), w

Apollinary Dudko
MORNING STAR(1962, USSR), ph

Alan Dudley
CHARRIOTS OF FIRE(1981, Brit.)

Bernard Dudley
REUNION(1932, Brit.)
Silents
BRENDA OF THE BARGE(1920, Brit.); GIRL OF LONDON, A(1925, Brit.)
Misc. Silents
GREAT IMPOSTER, THE(1918, Brit.); RILKA(1918, Brit.); LADS OF THE VILLAGE, THE(1919, Brit.); MAN WHO FORGOT, THE(1919, Brit.); LOVE IN THE WELSH HILLS(1921, Brit.), d; MEN WHO FORGET(1923)

Bill Dudley
TRIPLE THREAT(1948)

Carl Dudley
TOBOR THE GREAT(1954), w

Charles Dudley
Silents
SOLD AT AUCTION(1917); STEELHEART(1921); WHERE MEN ARE MEN(1921); SILENT VOW, THE(1922)
Misc. Silents
BOOTS AND SADDLES(1916); SULTANA, THE(1916); BIT OF KINDLING, A(1917); SECRET OF BLACK MOUNTAIN, THE(1917); PETTICOATS AND POLITICS(1918); WHATEVER THE COST(1918)

Cuddly Dudley
GIRLS OF LATIN QUARTER(1960, Brit.)

Doris Dudley
WOMAN REBELS, A(1936); MOON AND SIXPENCE, THE(1942); SECRET FURY, THE(1950)

Doug Dudley
GETAWAY, THE(1972)

E. Lawrence Dudley
VOLTAIRE(1933), W

Ernest Dudley
CONCERNING MR. MARTIN(1937, Brit.), w; LASSIE FROM LANCASHIRE(1938, Brit.), w; DR. MORELLE–THE CASE OF THE MISSING HEIRESS(1949, Brit.), w; ARMCHAIR DETECTIVE, THE(1952, Brit.), a, w; HARASSED HERO, THE(1954, Brit.), w; GUILTY?(1956, Brit.), w

Florence A. Dudley
OUR LEADING CITIZEN(1939)

Florence Dudley
BROADWAY(1929); PARTY GIRL(1930); ROGUE OF THE RIO GRANDE(1930); I HAVE LIVED(1933); PICK-UP(1933); GOOD DAME(1934); WHARF ANGEL(1934); G-MEN(1935); MILLIONS IN THE AIR(1935); EASY LIVING(1937); VICE RACKET(1937); YOU CAN'T TAKE IT WITH YOU(1938); ST. LOUIS BLUES(1939); MY FAVORITE WIFE(1940); MONSTER AND THE GIRL, THE(1941)
Silents
MAKING THE VARSITY(1928)
Misc. Silents
HOUSE OF SHAME, THE(1928); PACE THAT KILLS, THE(1928)

George Dudley
JESSE JAMES(1939), art d; RAINS CAME, THE(1939), art d; STANLEY AND LIVINGSTONE(1939), art d; STREET OF MEMORIES(1940), art d; LAUGHING LADY, THE(1950, Brit.)

James Dudley
1984
C.H.U.D.(1984)

Janet Dudley
SLENDER THREAD, THE(1965)

Jean Dudley
JEALOUSY(1934)

Joanne Dudley
HOLLYWOOD BOULEVARD(1936)

John Dudley
LOVE UP THE POLE(1936, Brit.); WILD RIVER(1960)

Lesley Dudley
JOHN AND JULIE(1957, Brit.); GUTTER GIRLS(1964, Brit.)

Marjorie Dudley
I ACCUSE MY PARENTS(1945), w

Paul Dudley
MONKEY ON MY BACK(1957), w; TIMBUKTU(1959), w

Raymond Dudley
SOAPBOX DERBY(1958, Brit.)

Robert Dudley
UNCLE HARRY(1945); WIDE OPEN(1930); REUNION(1932, Brit.); THREE WISE GIRLS(1932); FRISCO KID(1935); GOIN' TO TOWN(1935); PADDY O'DAY(1935); PRISONER OF SHARK ISLAND, THE(1936); SPRINGTIME IN THE ROCKIES(1937); TOAST OF NEW YORK, THE(1937); ZENOBIA(1939); HOUSE OF THE SEVEN GABLES, THE(1940); LUCKY PARTNERS(1940); STRANGER ON THE THIRD FLOOR(1940); WHEN THE DALTONS RODE(1940); DEVIL AND DANIEL WEBSTER, THE(1941); LADY EVE, THE(1941); SKYLARK(1941); SULLIVAN'S TRAVELS(1941); PALM BEACH STORY, THE(1942); FOLLOW THE BAND(1943); GHOST AND THE GUEST(1943); HAPPY LAND(1943); HONEYMOON LODGE(1943); SON OF DRACULA(1943); BIG NOISE, THE(1944); CASANOVA BROWN(1944); GREAT MOMENT, THE(1944); I'LL BE SEEING YOU(1944); MIRACLE OF MORGAN'S CREEK, THE(1944); COLONEL EFFINGHAM'S RAID(1945); LADY ON A TRAIN(1945); SINGIN' IN THE CORN(1946); STOLEN LIFE, A(1946); MAGIC TOWN(1947); RACE STREET(1948); SONG IS BORN, A(1948); STRIKE IT RICH(1948); PORTRAIT OF JENNIE(1949); JACKPOT, THE(1950); MAD WEDNESDAY(1950); BANANAS(1971)
Silents
OUT OF A CLEAR SKY(1918); MAKING A MAN(1922); NINETY AND NINE, THE(1922); NOBODY'S BRIDE(1923); SIXTY CENTS AN HOUR(1923); NIGHT FLYER, THE(1928); SKINNER'S BIG IDEA(1928)

Roy Dudley
PIRATE MOVIE, THE(1982, Aus.)

Russ Dudley
PAINTED FACES(1929)

Sherman H. Dudley, Jr.
Misc. Silents
SIMP, THE(1921); EASY MONEY(1922); RECKLESS MONEY(1926)

Susan Dudley
NAUGHTY ARLETTE(1951, Brit.); TONY DRAWS A HORSE(1951, Brit.)

William Dudley
FATHER TAKES A WIFE(1941)

Dudley and his Midgets
HERE COMES THE SUN(1945, Brit.)

Dudley Moore Trio
30 IS A DANGEROUS AGE, CYNTHIA(1968, Brit.)

Penelope Dudley-Ward
ESCAPE ME NEVER(1935, Brit.); WAY AHEAD, THE(1945, Brit.)

D. Dudnikov
NEW HORIZONS(1939, USSR)

Slatan Dudow
OUR DAILY BREAD(1950, Ger.), d, w

Jean-Charles Dudrumet
LOVERS ON A TIGHTROPE(1962, Fr.), d, w

Pierre Dudry
NUMBER TWO(1975, Fr.)

Pete Duel
CANNON FOR CORDOBA(1970)

Peter Duel
GENERATION(1969)

Randall Duell
CHASER, THE(1938), art d; NINOTCHKA(1939), art d; SERGEANT MADDEN(1939), art d; WOMAN OF THE YEAR(1942), art d; ABOVE SUSPICION(1943), art d; MRS. PARKINGTON(1944), art d; WHITE CLIFFS OF DOVER, THE(1944), art d; ANCHORS AWEIGH(1945), art d; POSTMAN ALWAYS RINGS TWICE, THE(1946), art d; UNDERCURRENT(1946), art d; SONG OF THE THIN MAN(1947), art d; THIS TIME FOR KEEPS(1947), art d; HOMECOMING(1948), art d; KISSING BANDIT, THE(1948), art d; SOUTHERN YANKEE, A(1948), art d; EAST SIDE, WEST SIDE(1949), art d; IN THE GOOD OLD SUMMERTIME(1949), art d; INTRUDER IN THE DUST(1949), art d; SUN COMES UP, THE(1949), art d; ASPHALT JUNGLE, THE(1950); PAGAN LOVE SONG(1950), art d; EXCUSE MY DUST(1951), art d; SHADOW IN THE SKY(1951), art d; UNKNOWN MAN, THE(1951), art d; EVERYTHING I HAVE IS YOURS(1952), art d; SINGIN' IN THE RAIN(1952), art d; GIRL WHO HAD EVERYTHING, THE(1953), art d; LAST TIME I SAW PARIS, THE(1954), art d; PRODIGAL, THE(1955), art d; TRIAL(1955), art d; GREAT AMERICAN PASTIME, THE(1956), art d; INVITATION TO THE DANCE(1956), art d; SWAN, THE(1956), art d; SILK STOCKINGS(1957), art d; TEN THOUSAND BEDROOMS(1957), art d; HIGH COST OF LOVING, THE(1958), art d; PARTY GIRL(1958), art d; TUNNEL OF LOVE, THE(1958), art d

Randell Duell
JAILHOUSE ROCK(1957), art d; COUNT YOUR BLESSINGS(1959), art d

William Duell
1776(1972); HAPPY HOOKER, THE(1975); ONE FLEW OVER THE CUCKOO'S NEST(1975); KING OF THE GYPSIES(1978); DEADHEAD MILES(1982); WITHOUT A TRACE(1983)

1984
MRS. SOFFEL(1984); POPE OF GREENWICH VILLAGE, THE(1984); ULTIMATE SOLUTION OF GRACE QUIGLEY, THE(1984)

Stanislaw Duelz
SIGNALS-AN ADVENTURE IN SPACE(1970, E. Ger./Pol.), spec eff

Caroline Duer
Silents
LADY IN LOVE, A(1920), w

Shoshana Duer
NOT MINE TO LOVE(1969, Israel)

Carl Duering
PARATROOPER(1954, Brit.); COLDITZ STORY, THE(1955, Brit.); DIVIDED HEART, THE(1955, Brit.); LET'S BE HAPPY(1957, Brit.); BEASTS OF MARSEILLES, THE(1959, Brit.); ELECTRONIC MONSTER. THE(1960, Brit.); MISSILE FROM HELL(1960, Brit.); STRIP TEASE MURDER(1961, Brit.); MAIN ATTRACTION, THE(1962, Brit.); GREAT VAN ROBBERY, THE(1963, Brit.); ARABESQUE(1966); DUFFY(1968, Brit.); DARLING LILI(1970); UNDERGROUND(1970, Brit.); CLOCKWORK ORANGE, A(1971, Brit.); OPERATION DAYBREAK(1976, U.S./Brit./Czech.); BOYS FROM BRAZIL, THE(1978); POSSESSION(1981, Fr./Ger.); MALOU(1983)

Karl Duering
GOLD(1974, Brit.)

Annemarie Dueringer
ETERNAL WALTZ, THE(1959, Ger.)

Friedrich Duerrenmatt
IT HAPPENED IN BROAD DAYLIGHT(1960, Ger./Switz.), w; MOST WONDERFUL EVENING OF MY LIFE, THE(1972, Ital./Fr.), w; END OF THE GAME(1976, Ger./Ital.), a, w

Benny Dues
FINGER ON THE TRIGGER(1965, US/Span.)

C.R. Dufau
LAND OF MISSING MEN, THE(1930)

George Dufaux
FOND MEMORIES(1982, Can.), ph

Georges Dufaux
ISABEL(1968, Can.), ph; FORTUNE AND MEN'S EYES(1971, U.S./Can.), ph

Maxime Dufeu
1984
UNTIL SEPTEMBER(1984)

Amanda Duff
IT'S A DEAL(1930); JUST AROUND THE CORNER(1938); ESCAPE, THE(1939); HOTEL FOR WOMEN(1939); MR. MOTO IN DANGER ISLAND(1939); CITY OF CHANCE(1940); DEVIL COMMANDS, THE(1941)e

Bridget Duff
PRIVATE HELL 36(1954)

Christopher Duff
OLIVER!(1968, Brit.)

Harry Duff
TOM BROWN'S SCHOOL DAYS(1940)

Howard Duff
BRUTE FORCE(1947); ALL MY SONS(1948); NAKED CITY, THE(1948); CALAMITY JANE AND SAM BASS(1949); ILLEGAL ENTRY(1949); JOHNNY STOOL PIGEON(1949); RED CANYON(1949); WOMAN IN HIDING(1949); SHAKEDOWN(1950); SPY HUNT(1950); LADY FROM TEXAS, THE(1951); MODELS, INC.(1952); STEEL TOWN(1952); JENNIFER(1953); ROAR OF THE CROWD(1953); SPACEWAYS(1953, Brit.); PRIVATE HELL 36(1954); TANGANYIKA(1954); YELLOW MOUNTAIN, THE(1954); FLAME OF THE ISLANDS(1955); WOMEN'S PRISON(1955); BLACKJACK KETCHUM, DESPERADO(1956); BROKEN STAR, THE(1956); WHILE THE CITY SLEEPS(1956); SIERRA STRANGER(1957); BOYS' NIGHT OUT(1962); PANIC IN THE CITY(1968); LATE SHOW, THE(1977); WEDDING, A(1978); KRAMER VS. KRAMER(1979); DOUBLE NEGATIVE(1980, Can.)
Misc. Talkies
DEADLY AUGUST(1966)

Norwich Duff
EMPIRE STRIKES BACK, THE(1980)

Norwick Duff
SUPERMAN(1978)

Patricia Duff
D.C. CAB(1983)

Utpal Duff
BOMBAY TALKIE(1970, India)

Warren B. Duff
HOTEL CONTINENTAL(1932), w; LENA RIVERS(1932), w; STRANGERS OF THE EVENING(1932), w; UPTOWN NEW YORK(1932), w; DELUGE(1933), w

Warren Duff
X MARKS THE SPOT(1931), w; CROSBY CASE, THE(1934), w; FASHIONS OF 1934(1934), w; FRIENDS OF MR. SWEENEY(1934), w; HEAT LIGHTNING(1934), w; I'VE GOT YOUR NUMBER(1934), w; MIDNIGHT ALIBI(1934), w; ST. LOUIS KID, THE(1934), w; TWENTY MILLION SWEETHEARTS(1934), w; BROADWAY GONDOLIER(1935), w; FRISCO KID(1935), w; IN CALIENTE(1935), w; SWEET MUSIC(1935), w; GOLD DIGGERS OF 1937(1936), w; SINGING KID, THE(1936), w; STAGE STRUCK(1936), w; BACK IN CIRCULATION(1937), w; READY, WILLING AND ABLE(1937), w; STOLEN HOLIDAY(1937), w; SUBMARINE D-1(1937), w; VARSITY SHOW(1937), w; ANGELS WITH DIRTY FACES(1938), w; GOLD DIGGERS IN PARIS(1938), w; GOLD IS WHERE YOU FIND IT(1938), w; EACH DAWN I DIE(1939), w; ESPIONAGE AGENT(1939), w; OKLAHOMA KID, THE(1939), w; INVISIBLE STRIPES(1940), w; 'TIL WE MEET AGAIN(1940), w; LADY FROM CHEYENNE(1941), w; FALLEN SPARROW, THE(1943), w; IRON MAJOR, THE(1943), w; NO TIME FOR LOVE(1943), w; EXPERIMENT PERILOUS(1944), w; MARINE RAIDERS(1944), w; STEP LIVELY(1944), w; LADY LUCK(1946), p; HONEYMOON(1947), p; OUT OF THE PAST(1947), p; CHICAGO DEADLINE(1949), w; DANGEROUS PROFESSION, A(1949), w; GAMBLING HOUSE(1950), p; APPOINTMENT WITH DANGER(1951), w; TURNING POINT, THE(1952), w; MAKE HASTE TO LIVE(1954), w; LAST COMMAND, THE(1955), w

William Duff
SEALED CARGO(1951), p

Cara Duff-MacCormick
ALL THE PRESIDENT'S MEN(1976)

Bea Duffell
STRANGER AT MY DOOR(1950, Brit.); WONDERWALL(1969, Brit.)

Bee Duffell
TREASURE HUNT(1952, Brit.); DUEL IN THE JUNGLE(1954, Brit.); NIGHT TO REMEMBER, A(1958, Brit.); TOO YOUNG TO LOVE(1960, Brit.); VICTORS, THE(1963); TAMAHINE(1964, Brit.); FAHRENHEIT 451(1966, Brit.); DOUBLE MAN, THE(1967); ON THE RUN(1967, Brit.); BATTLE BENEATH THE EARTH(1968, Brit.); FIVE MILLION YEARS TO EARTH(1968, Brit.); MONTY PYTHON AND THE HOLY GRAIL(1975, Brit.)

Peter Duffell
HOUSE THAT DRIPPED BLOOD, THE(1971, Brit.), d; ENGLANO MADE ME(1973, Brit.), d, w; INSIDE OUT(1975, Brit.), d; EXPERIENCE PREFERRED... BUT NOT ESSENTIAL(1983, Brit.), d
Misc. Talkies
PARTNERS IN CRIME(1961, Brit.), d

Paul Dufficey
TOMMY(1975, Brit.), set d

Duffield
MACBETH(1948)

Brainard Duffield
JIGSAW(1949)

Brainerd Duffield
MACBETH(1948)

Harry Duffield
Silents
WISE FOOL, A(1921)
Misc. Silents
FACE OF THE WORLD(1921)

Lee Ann Duffield
PATERNITY(1981)

Michael Duffield
ROCK YOU SINNERS(1957, Brit.); 2,000 WEEKS(1970, Aus.); LAST WAVE, THE(1978, Aus.); LAST OF THE KNUCKLEMEN, THE(1981, Aus.)

Tom Duffield
HEART LIKE A WHEEL(1983), a, set d

Shay Duffin
WHITE BUFFALO, THE(1977); FRISCO KID, THE(1979); MAIN EVENT, THE(1979); BALTIMORE BULLET, THE(1980); 10 TO MIDNIGHT(1983)

J. Patrick Duffner
CRIMINAL CONVERSATION(1980, Ireland), ed

Pat Duffner
ANGEL(1982, Irish), ed

Daisy Dufford
NAUGHTY BUT NICE(1939)

Stanley R. Dufford
TAKE THE MONEY AND RUN(1969), makeup; PLAY IT AGAIN, SAM(1972), makeup

Barrie Duffus
PUFNSTUF(1970)

Albert Duffy
HUNTED MEN(1938), w; BEWARE SPOOKS(1939), w; BLIND ALLEY(1939), w; COAST GUARD(1939), w; BLONDIE HAS SERVANT TROUBLE(1940), w; GAY CABALLERO, THE(1940), w; LONE WOLF STRIKES, THE(1940), w; DOWN MEXICO WAY(1941), w; ROAR OF THE PRESS(1941), w; TWO LATINS FROM MANHATTAN(1941), w; HARVARD, HERE I COME(1942), w; SLEEPYTIME GAL(1942), w; SWEETHEART OF THE FLEET(1942), w; REVEILLE WITH BEVERLY(1943), w; DARK PAST, THE(1948), w; MAKE BELIEVE BALLROOM(1949), w; THREE STRIPES IN THE SUN(1955), w

Beatrice Duffy
Misc. Silents
STREETS OF LONDON, THE(1929, Brit.)

Bill Duffy
DRIVE, HE SAID(1971); CALIFORNIA SPLIT(1974)

Bob Duffy
STREET OF SINNERS(1957)

Sir Brandon Duffy
TRADER HORNEE(1970)

Brian Duffy
ONLY WHEN I LARF(1968, Brit.), p; OH! WHAT A LOVELY WAR(1969, Brit.), p

Clinton T. Duffy
DUFFY OF SAN QUENTIN(1954), d&w; STEEL CAGE, THE(1954), w

Dan Duffy
Silents
ETERNAL LOVE(1917)

Dana Duffy
1984
STONE BOY, THE(1984)

Dee Duffy
MURDERERS' ROW(1966); HELLCATS, THE(1968)

Dorothy Duffy
GNOME-MOBILE, THE(1967)

Farrel Levy Duffy
MARRIAGE, A(1983), art d

Frank Duffy
Silents
IN OLD KENTUCKY(1920)

Gerald Duffy
MEN OF IRELAND(1938, Ireland)
Silents
ARGENTINE LOVE(1924), w; TRAMP, TRAMP, TRAMP(1926), w; HEAD MAN, THE(1928), t

Gerald C. Duffy
Silents
DOLLARS AND SENSE(1920), w; WHAT HAPPENED TO ROSA?(1921), w; SURE FIRE FLINT(1922), w; SPIDER AND THE ROSE, THE(1923), w; HER OWN FREE WILL(1924), w; RECOIL, THE(1924), w; ROULETTE(1924), w; CRYSTAL CUP, THE(1927), w; HEART OF A FOLLIES GIRL, THE(1928), w

J. A. Duffy
CATTLE THIEF, THE(1936), w

Jack Duffy
SALLY(1929); HEAVEN ON EARTH(1931); ALICE IN WONDERLAND(1933); SHE COULDN'T TAKE IT(1935); TEXAS TERROR(1935); WILD BRIAN KENT(1936); SILENT PARTNER, THE(1979, Can.); NOTHING PERSONAL(1980, Can.); TITLE SHOT(1982, Can.)
Misc. Talkies
DIVORCE MADE EASY(1929)
Silents
RECKLESS ROMANCE(1924); ELLA CINDERS(1926); NO CONTROL(1927); HAROLD TEEN(1928)
Misc. Silents
BRASS BOWL, THE(1924)

James Duffy
Silents
OUR HOSPITALITY(1923)
Misc. Silents
THAT'S GOOD(1919)

Jesse Duffy
LAW OF THE RANGER(1937), w; RANGERS STEP IN, THE(1937), w; RECKLESS RANGER(1937), w; RIDERS OF THE FRONTIER(1939), w; CYCLOTRODE X(1946), w

Jim Duffy
1984
IMPULSE(1984), set d

John Duffy
MEN OF IRELAND(1938, Ireland), w; WOMAN INSIDE, THE(1981), ed

Julia Duffy
BATTLE BEYOND THE STARS(1980); CUTTER AND BONE(1981); WACKO(1983)

Kate Duffy
HOODWINK(1981, Aus.), cos

Patrick Duffy
1984
VAMPING(1984)

Ron Duffy
VILLAIN, THE(1979)

Sean Duffy
SMASH PALACE(1982, New Zealand)
1984
UTU(1984, New Zealand)

Thomas Duffy
DEATH WISH II(1982)

Wally Duffy
THEM!(1954)

William Duffy
ROUND TRIP(1967), w; LOVING(1970); NO BLADE OF GRASS(1970, Brit.)

Jacques Dufilho
SAADIA(1953); HUNCHBACK OF NOTRE DAME, THE(1957, Fr.); LOVE IN A HOT CLIMATE(1958, Fr./Span.); NATHALIE(1958, Fr.); ZAZIE(1961, Fr.); DOLL, THE(1962, Fr.); MAXIME(1962, Fr.); JULIE THE REDHEAD(1963, Fr.); WAR OF THE BUTTONS(1963 Fr.); SWEET AND SOUR(1964, Fr./Ital.); VISIT, THE(1964, Ger./Fr./Ital./U.S.); LADY L(1965, Fr./Ital.); UNKNOWN MAN OF SHANDIGOR, THE(1967, Switz.); BENJAMIN(1968, Fr.); BLACK AND WHITE IN COLOR(1976, Fr.); NOSFERATU, THE VAMPIRE(1979, Fr./Ger.); HORSE OF PRIDE(1980, Fr.)
1984
LE CRABE TAMBOUR(1984, Fr.)

J. Duflio
HAPPY ROAD, THE(1957)

Hugette Duflos
Misc. Silents
TRAVAIL(1920, Fr.); MADEMOISELLE DE LA SEIGLIERE(1921, Fr.); YASMINA(1926, Fr.)

Huguette Duflos
JUPITER(1952, Fr.)
Misc. Silents
L'AMI FRITZ(1920, Fr.); KOENIGSMARK(1923, Fr.)

Alphonse Dufort
Silents
HEARTS OF THE WORLD(1918)

Marie-Claire Dufour
CHARLES, DEAD OR ALIVE(1972, Switz.)

Val DuFour
UNDEAD, THE(1957)

Yvon Dufour
RED(1970, Can.); ANGELA(1977, Can.); KING SOLOMON'S TREASURE(1978, Can.); LUCKY STAR, THE(1980, Can.)

Frank DuFrance
LARCENY ON THE AIR(1937)

Frank Dufrane
GOING HIGHBROW(1935); I LIVE FOR LOVE(1935); TEST PILOT(1938)

Jacqueline Dufranne
LOULOU(1980, Fr.)

Jane Dufrayne
CITIZEN SAINT(1947)

Jean-V Dufresne
CAT IN THE SACK, THE(1967, Can.)

William Dufty
LADY SINGS THE BLUES(1972), w

Alberta Dugan
Misc. Talkies
SENOR JIM(1936)

Dennis Dugan
NIGHT CALL NURSES(1974); DAY OF THE LOCUST, THE(1975); NIGHT MOVES(1975); SMILE(1975); HARRY AND WALTER GO TO NEW YORK(1976); NORMAN...IS THAT YOU?(1976); UNIDENTIFIED FLYING ODDBALL, THE(1979, Brit.); HOWLING, THE(1981)

Dorothy Dugan
STRIKE ME PINK(1936)

Ed Dugan
FALLGUY(1962)
Fritzi Dugan
JUST ACROSS THE STREET(1952)
Irvin Dugan
REFLECTIONS IN A GOLDEN EYE(1967)
James Dugan
Silents
DESERT PIRATE, THE(1928), d; PHANTOM OF THE RANGE(1928), d; WARMING UP(1928)
Misc. Silents
HER SUMMER HERO(1928), d
Jim Dugan
ISLAND IN THE SKY(1953)
Jimmie Dugan
DEVIL AND THE DEEP(1932)
Jimmy Dugan
NORTHERN PURSUIT(1943)
John Dugan
TEXAS CHAIN SAW MASSACRE, THE(1974)
Mary Dugan
Misc. Talkies
SWING THE WESTERN WAY(1947)
Michael Dugan
LUXURY LINER(1948); THREE GODFATHERS, THE(1948); RANGE LAND(1949); SHE WORE A YELLOW RIBBON(1949); YES SIR, THAT'S MY BABY(1949); NO QUESTIONS ASKED(1951); PEOPLE AGAINST O'HARA, THE(1951); SHOW BOAT(1951); TEXAS CARNIVAL(1951); DESPERATE SEARCH(1952); DANGEROUS WHEN WET(1953); ESCAPE FROM FORT BRAVO(1953); JUPITER'S DARLING(1955); KING'S THIEF, THE(1955); MARAUDERS, THE(1955); TRIAL(1955); FASTEST GUN ALIVE(1956); GHOST DIVER(1957); GUN GLORY(1957); MONSTER THAT CHALLENGED THE WORLD, THE(1957); RAINTREE COUNTY(1957); PARTY GIRL(1958); THUNDER ALLEY(1967); DESTRUCTORS, THE(1968); MAUSOLEUM(1983), d
Misc. Talkies
SUPER SEAL(1976), d
Michael J. Dugan
IRON CURTAIN, THE(1948)
Mike Dugan
HE WALKED BY NIGHT(1948); BEN HUR(1959)
Sue Dugan
TRADING PLACES(1983); TWILIGHT ZONE–THE MOVIE(1983)
Thom Dugan
WHEN TOMORROW COMES(1939)
Thomas Dugan
LAUGHING AT LIFE(1933), w; AFFAIR OF SUSAN(1935); ANOTHER FACE(1935), w
Thomas "Tom" Dugan
WE GO FAST(1941)
Thomas J. Dugan
PICK A STAR(1937), w
Tom Dugan
LIGHTS OF NEW YORK(1928); BROADWAY BABIES(1929); DRAG(1929); DRAKE CASE, THE(1929); HEARTS IN EXILE(1929); BAD ONE, THE(1930); NIGHT WORK(1930); THEY LEARNED ABOUT WOMEN(1930); BRIGHT LIGHTS(1931); HOT HEIRESS(1931); STAR WITNESS(1931); WOMAN HUNGRY(1931); BIG CITY BLUES(1932); BLESSED EVENT(1932); BY WHOSE HAND?(1932); DOCTOR X(1932); DON'T BET ON LOVE(1933); GRAND SLAM(1933); SKYWAY(1933); SWEETHEART OF SIGMA CHI(1933); TRICK FOR TRICK(1933); CAT'S PAW, THE(1934); LET'S TALK IT OVER(1934); NO MORE WOMEN(1934); PALOOKA(1934); CHINATOWN SQUAD(1935); GILDED LILY, THE(1935); I LIVE MY LIFE(1935); MURDER IN THE FLEET(1935); PRINCESS O'HARA(1935); RED SALUTE(1935); RENDEZVOUS(1935); THREE KIDS AND A QUEEN(1935); DON'T GET PERSONAL(1936); MISTER CINDERELLA(1936); PENNIES FROM HEAVEN(1936); SAN FRANCISCO(1936); MARRIED BEFORE BREAKFAST(1937); NOBODY'S BABY(1937); PICK A STAR(1937); SHE HAD TO EAT(1937); TRUE CONFESSION(1937); FOUR DAUGHTERS(1938); SING YOU SINNERS(1938); SONS OF THE LEGION(1938); THERE'S ALWAYS A WOMAN(1938); THERE'S THAT WOMAN AGAIN(1938); HOUSE OF FEAR, THE(1939); HOUSEKEEPER'S DAUGHTER(1939); I'M FROM MISSOURI(1939); LADY AND THE MOB, THE(1939); LAUGH IT OFF(1939); LONE WOLF SPY HUNT, THE(1939); LOVE AFFAIR(1939); MILLION DOLLAR LEGS(1939); MISSING EVIDENCE(1939); MYSTERY OF THE WHITE ROOM(1939); NAUGHTY BUT NICE(1939); THEY MADE ME A CRIMINAL(1939); YOU CAN'T GET AWAY WITH MURDER(1939); $1,000 A TOUCHDOWN(1939); CROSS COUNTRY ROMANCE(1940); FARMER'S DAUGHTER, THE(1940); FIGHTING 69TH, THE(1940); GHOST BREAKERS, THE(1940); HALF A SINNER(1940); ISLE OF DESTINY(1940); JOHNNY APOLLO(1940); LITTLE BIT OF HEAVEN, A(1940); LUCKY PARTNERS(1940); SO YOU WON'T TALK(1940); STAR DUST(1940); TOO MANY HUSBANDS(1940); VIRGINIA CITY(1940); WHO KILLED AUNT MAGGIE?(1940); DANGEROUS GAME, A(1941); DIVE BOMBER(1941); ELLERY QUEEN AND THE MURDER RING(1941); ELLERY QUEEN'S PENTHOUSE MYSTERY(1941); MONSTER AND THE GIRL, THE(1941); NAVY BLUES(1941); RICHEST MAN IN TOWN(1941); RINGSIDE MAISIE(1941); SWING IT SOLDIER(1941); TIGHT SHOES(1941); UNEXPECTED UNCLE(1941); WHERE DID YOU GET THAT GIRL?(1941); YOU'RE THE ONE(1941); CAPTAINS OF THE CLOUDS(1942); GLASS KEY, THE(1942); MAJOR AND THE MINOR, THE(1942); MEET THE STEWARTS(1942); MOONLIGHT IN HAVANA(1942); MOONTIDE(1942); STAR SPANGLED RHYTHM(1942); THEY ALL KISSED THE BRIDE(1942); TO BE OR NOT TO BE(1942); YANKEE DOODLE DANDY(1942); YOKEL BOY(1942); BATAAN(1943); CRYSTAL BALL, THE(1943); FLIGHT FOR FREEDOM(1943); HAPPY GO LUCKY(1943); JOHNNY COME LATELY(1943); NO PLACE FOR A LADY(1943); GHOST CATCHERS(1944); GREENWICH VILLAGE(1944); HI BEAUTIFUL(1944); HOME IN INDIANA(1944); IN SOCIETY(1944); MOON OVER LAS VEGAS(1944); NIGHT CLUB GIRL(1944); ONCE UPON A TIME(1944); SWINGTIME JOHNNY(1944); THIN MAN GOES HOME, THE(1944); UP IN ARMS(1944); DON JUAN QUILLIGAN(1945); EADIE WAS A LADY(1945); EARL CARROLL'S VANITIES(1945); KID SISTER, THE(1945); LADY ON A TRAIN(1945); MAN WHO WALKED ALONE, THE(1945); SHE WOULDN'T SAY YES(1945); TELL IT TO A STAR(1945); TRAIL OF KIT CARSON(1945); ACCOMPLICE(1946); BRINGING UP FATHER(1946); CROSS MY HEART(1946); EASY TO WED(1946); HOODLUM SAINT, THE(1946); IT SHOULDN'T HAPPEN TO A DOG(1946); JOHNNY COMES FLYING HOME(1946); SHADOW

RETURNS, THE(1946); FABULOUS DORSEYS, THE(1947); GOOD NEWS(1947); PERILS OF PAULINE, THE(1947); PILGRIM LADY, THE(1947); SENATOR WAS INDISCREET, THE(1947); SONG OF THE THIN MAN(1947); GOOD SAM(1948); HALF PAST MIDNIGHT(1948); TEXAS, BROOKLYN AND HEAVEN(1948); ALIAS NICK BEAL(1949); DEAR WIFE(1949); IT'S A GREAT FEELING(1949); ON THE TOWN(1949); TAKE ME OUT TO THE BALL GAME(1949); TULSA(1949); FATHER TAKES THE AIR(1951); LEMON DROP KID, THE(1951); PAINTING THE CLOUDS WITH SUNSHINE(1951); BELLE OF NEW YORK, THE(1952); MEET DANNY WILSON(1952); CRASHOUT(1955)
Misc. Talkies
NEIGHBORHOOD HOUSE(1936)
Silents
BY WHOSE HAND?(1927); KID SISTER, THE(1927); SWELL-HEAD, THE(1927); SHADOWS OF THE NIGHT(1928); SHARP SHOOTERS(1928)
Tommy [Tom] Dugan
MELODY OF LOVE, THE(1928); MIDNIGHT TAXI, THE(1928); KID GLOVES(1929); MILLION DOLLAR COLLAR, THE(1929); SONNY BOY(1929); MEDICINE MAN, THE(1930); PRIDE OF THE LEGION, THE(1932); PRESIDENT VANISHES, THE(1934); CASE OF THE MISSING MAN, THE(1935); GIRL O' MY DREAMS(1935); ONE NEW YORK NIGHT(1935); DAN MATTHEWS(1936); WIFE VERSUS SECRETARY(1936); GAMBLER'S CHOICE(1944); THOSE ENDEARING YOUNG CHARMS(1945)
Misc. Talkies
BIG TIMER(1932)
Vicki Dugan
GREAT MAN, THE(1957)
William Dugan
CLANCY IN WALL STREET(1930), w
Phyllis Duganne
NICE GIRL?(1941), w
Silents
SWEET SIXTEEN(1928), w
Oscar Roy Dugas
Misc. Silents
MIDNIGHT ACE, THE(1928)
Yvette Dugay
GREAT IMPERSONATION, THE(1942); HEAVENLY DAYS(1944); CIMARRON KID, THE(1951); HIAWATHA(1952); FRANCIS COVERS THE BIG TOWN(1953); CATTLE QUEEN OF MONTANA(1954); SHANGHAI STORY, THE(1954); TENNESSEE CHAMP(1954); DOMINO KID(1957)
A. Duges
Misc. Silents
SOUL OF FRANCE(1929, Fr.), d
Andrew Duggan
DECISION AT SUNDOWN(1957); DOMINO KID(1957); THREE BRAVE MEN(1957); BRAVADOS, THE(1958); RETURN TO WARBOW(1958); WESTBOUND(1959); CHAPMAN REPORT, THE(1962); HOUSE OF WOMEN(1962); MERRILL'S MARAUDERS(1962); PALM SPRINGS WEEKEND(1963); FBI CODE 98(1964); INCREDIBLE MR. LIMPET, THE(1964); SEVEN DAYS IN MAY(1964); GLORY GUYS, THE(1965); IN LIKE FLINT(1967); SECRET WAR OF HARRY FRIGG, THE(1968); SKIN GAME(1971); BEARS AND I, THE(1974); IT'S ALIVE(1974); IT LIVES AGAIN(1978); PRIVATE FILES OF J. EDGAR HOOVER, THE(1978); DOCTOR DETROIT(1983)
Misc. Talkies
BONE(1972); ONE LAST RIDE(1980)
Ann Duggan
DEVIL AT FOUR O'CLOCK, THE(1961)
Bob Duggan
I'D RATHER BE RICH(1964)
Cal Duggan
MARS NEEDS WOMEN(1966)
G. Thomas Duggan
VAGABOND KING, THE(1956)
Gerry Duggan
FOUR DESPERATE MEN(1960, Brit.); SUNDOWNERS, THE(1960); L-SHAPED ROOM, THE(1962, Brit.); SERVANT, THE(1964, Brit.); NED KELLY(1970, Brit.); DEVIL'S PLAYGROUND, THE(1976, Aus.); SINGER AND THE DANCER, THE(1977, Aus.); LAST OF THE KNUCKLEMEN, THE(1981, Aus.); MANGO TREE, THE(1981, Aus.)
Jack Duggan
1984
MYSTERY MANSION(1984), w
Jan Duggan
OLD-FASHIONED WAY, THE(1934); WAGON WHEELS(1934); COUNTY CHAIRMAN, THE(1935); I LIVE MY LIFE(1935); MISSISSIPPI(1935); DRIFT FENCE(1936); EASY TO TAKE(1936); PRISONER OF SHARK ISLAND, THE(1936); DAMSEL IN DISTRESS, A(1937); MOUNTAIN MUSIC(1937); WIFE, DOCTOR AND NURSE(1937); KENTUCKY MOONSHINE(1938); MIDNIGHT INTRUDER(1938); ONE WILD NIGHT(1938); SCANDAL STREET(1938); THANKS FOR EVERYTHING(1938); HERE I AM A STRANGER(1939); HOUSE OF FEAR, THE(1939); INSIDE STORY(1939); STORY OF ALEXANDER GRAHAM BELL, THE(1939); YOU CAN'T CHEAT AN HONEST MAN(1939); BANK DICK, THE(1940); MANHATTAN HEARTBEAT(1940); MY LITTLE CHICKADEE(1940); RICHEST MAN IN TOWN(1941); DUDES ARE PRETTY PEOPLE(1942); MEANEST MAN IN THE WORLD, THE(1943)
Jerry Duggan
ON THE BEACH(1959)
Pat Duggan
JUST FOR YOU(1952), p; FOREVER FEMALE(1953), p; RED GARTERS(1954), p; WE'RE NO ANGELS(1955), p; SEARCH FOR BRIDEY MURPHY, THE(1956), p; VAGABOND KING, THE(1956), p; LONELY MAN, THE(1957), p; YOUNG SAVAGES, THE(1961), p
Patrick Duggan
1984
DEATHSTALKER, THE(1984)
Richard Duggan
Q(1982)
Misc. Talkies
BEACH HOUSE(1982)

Terry Duggan
POOR COW(1968, Brit.); 2001: A SPACE ODYSSEY(1968, U.S./Brit.); NICE GIRL LIKE ME, A(1969, Brit.); SCHIZO(1977, Brit.)

Thomas Duggan
TARZAN THE MAGNIFICENT(1960, Brit.); GORGO(1961, Brit.)

Tom Duggan
GENIE, THE(1953, Brit.); HEAR ME GOOD(1957); ANDY HARDY COMES HOME(1958); FRANKENSTEIN 1970(1958); BORN RECKLESS(1959); BUT NOT FOR ME(1959); BLUEPRINT FOR ROBBERY(1961); PARADISE ALLEY(1962); FURY AT SMUGGLERS BAY(1963, Brit.); WHY BOTHER TO KNOCK(1964, Brit.); REVOLUTIONARY, THE(1970, Brit.)

Tommy Duggan
FLYING FORTRESS(1942, Brit.); THUNDER ROCK(1944, Brit.); TIME FLIES(1944, Brit.); BONNIE PRINCE CHARLIE(1948, Brit.); FIGHTING PIMPERNEL, THE(1950, Brit.); YOU CAN'T FOOL AN IRISHMAN(1950, Ireland), a, w; THERE WAS A YOUNG LADY(1953, Brit.); DEATH OF MICHAEL TURBIN, THE(1954, Brit.); DESTINATION MILAN(1954, Brit.); TONIGHT'S THE NIGHT(1954, Brit.); LADY GODIVA RIDES AGAIN(1955, Brit.); DEAD MAN'S EVIDENCE(1962, Brit.); ADDING MACHINE, THE(1969); OMEN, THE(1976); SUPERMAN II(1980); FINAL CONFLICT, THE(1981)

Florrie Dugger
BUGSY MALONE(1976, Brit.)

Jacques Dugied
FAREWELL, FRIEND(1968, Fr./Ital.), art d; SECRET WORLD(1969, Fr.), art d; MISTER FREEDOM(1970, Fr.), art d; JE T'AIME, JE T'AIME(1972, Fr./Swed.), art d; TOUT VA BIEN(1973, Fr.), set d; DONKEY SKIN(1975, Fr.), art d
1984
DOG DAY(1984, Fr.), art d

Ern Dugo
VOODOO HEARTBEAT(1972)

Norma Dugo
SWEET SKIN(1965, Fr./Ital.); GENDARME OF ST. TROPEZ, THE(1966, Fr./Ital.)

Joe Dugonics
MARCO POLO JUNIOR(1973, Aus.), ph

Christian Duguay
1984
MEMOIRS(1984, Can.), ph

Yvette Duguay
TORTILLA FLAT(1942); ALI BABA AND THE FORTY THIEVES(1944); 'TILL WE MEET AGAIN(1944); GREAT CARUSO, THE(1951); PEOPLE AGAINST O'HARA, THE(1951)

Francis Duguid
Silents
PRINCE AND THE BEGGARMAID, THE(1921, Brit.)

Peter Duguid
LONELINESS OF THE LONG DISTANCE RUNNER, THE(1962, Brit.); THIS SPORTING LIFE(1963, Brit.)

Terri Duhaime
FAN, THE(1981)

Terry DuHaime
SOMEBODY KILLED HER HUSBAND(1978)

Yvon Duhaime
CITY ON FIRE(1979 Can.), cos

Antoine Duhamel
SAILOR FROM GIBRALTAR, THE(1967, Brit.), m; PIERROT LE FOU(1968, Fr./Ital.), m; WEEKEND(1968, Fr./Ital.), m; DIANE'S BODY(1969, Fr./Czech.), m; SECRET WORLD(1969, Fr.), m; SINGAPORE, SINGAPORE(1969, Fr./Ital.), m; STOLEN KISSES(1969, Fr.), m; MISSISSIPPI MERMAID(1970, Fr./Ital.), m; QUESTION, THE(1977, Fr.), m; MAIS OU ET DONC ORNICAR(1979, Fr.), m; DEATHWATCH(1980, Fr./Ger.), m

Claire Duhamel
PERFECTIONIST, THE(1952, Fr.); STOLEN KISSES(1969, Fr.); BED AND BOARD(1971, Fr.); JE T'AIME, JE T'AIME(1972, Fr./Swed.)

Francois Duhamel
1984
LOVE STREAMS(1984)

Herve Duhamel
LE BEAU MARIAGE(1982, Fr.)

Joseph E. Duhamel
I'M GOING TO GET YOU ... ELLIOT BOY(1971, Can.), w

M. Duhamel
BIZARRE BIZARRE(1939, Fr.)

Marcel Duhamel
CRIME OF MONSIEUR LANGE, THE(1936, Fr.)

Simone Duhart
GAME OF LOVE, THE(1954, Fr.); GERVAISE(1956, Fr.)

Brian Duhig
MANGANINNIE(1982, Aus.)

Clement Duhour
CROSSROADS OF PASSION(1951, Fr.); NAPOLEON(1955, Fr.); IF PARIS WERE TOLD TO US(1956, Fr.); CANDIDE(1962, Fr.), p

John Duigan
TRESPASSERS, THE(1976, Aus.), p,d&w; MOUTH TO MOUTH(1978, Aus.), p, d&w; DIMBOOLA(1979, Aus.), d

Virginia Duigan
WINTER OF OUR DREAMS(1982, Aus.)

John Duigen
WINTER OF OUR DREAMS(1982, Aus.), d&w

Nancy Duiguid
REDS(1981)

Warren Duit
1984
COUNTRY(1984)

Galia Dujardin
LA BALANCE(1983, Fr.)

John Dukakis
JAWS II(1978); KING OF THE MOUNTAIN(1981); MAKING LOVE(1982); SPLIT IMAGE(1982)

1984
HOUSE WHERE DEATH LIVES, THE(1984)
Misc. Talkies
HOUSE WHERE DEATH LIVES, THE(1982)

Olympia Dukakis
LILITH(1964); TWICE A MAN(1964); JOHN AND MARY(1969); MADE FOR EACH OTHER(1971); RICH KIDS(1979); WANDERERS, THE(1979); IDOLMAKER, THE(1980)

James Dukas
GREAT ST. LOUIS BANK ROBBERY, THE(1959); DETECTIVE, THE(1968); GOD TOLD ME TO(1976); BRUBAKER(1980)

Jim Dukas
PRETTY BOY FLOYD(1960); NO WAY TO TREAT A LADY(1968)

Paul Dukas
FANTASIA(1940), w

Duke
MAN FROM MONTEREY, THE(1933)

Duke the horse
BIG STAMPEDE, THE(1932)

Duke the Devil Horse
RIDE HIM, COWBOY(1932); RIDERS OF DESTINY(1933)

Duke the Miracle Horse
SOMEWHERE IN SONORA(1933)

Bill Duke
CARWASH(1976); AMERICAN GIGOLO(1980)

Darryl Duke
MR. HOBBS TAKES A VACATION(1962)

Daryl Duke
PAYDAY(1972), d; SILENT PARTNER, THE(1979, Can.), d
Misc. Talkies
HARD FEELINGS(1981), d

Edward Duke
SILVER BEARS(1978); FRENCH LIEUTENANT'S WOMAN, THE(1981)

Forrest Duke
VOODOO HEARTBEAT(1972)

Ivy Duke
KNIGHT IN LONDON, A(1930, Brit./Ger.)
Silents
DOUBLE LIFE OF MR. ALFRED BURTON, THE(1919, Brit.); FANCY DRESS(1919, Brit.); GARDEN OF RESURRECTION, THE(1919, Brit.); MARCH HARE, THE(1919, Brit.); BIGAMIST, THE(1921, Brit.); FOX FARM(1922, Brit.); DECAMERON NIGHTS(1924, Brit.)
Misc. Silents
I WILL(1919, Brit.); LURE OF CROONING WATER, THE(1920, Brit.); SQUANDERED LIVES(1920, Brit.); TESTIMONY(1920, Brit.); BOY WOODBURN(1922, Brit.); PERSISTENT LOVERS, THE(1922, Brit.); STARLIT GARDEN, THE(1923, Brit.); GREAT PRINCE SHAN, THE(1924, Brit.)

John Duke
NEVER STEAL ANYTHING SMALL(1959); PAY OR DIE(1960); FOLLOW THAT DREAM(1962)

Maurice Duke
DISC JOCKEY(1951), p; ATOMIC KID, THE(1954), p; JAGUAR(1956), p; SABU AND THE MAGIC RING(1957), p; TWIST ALL NIGHT(1961), p; CANDIDATE, THE(1964), p

Nancy Duke
MY FAVORITE SPY(1951); CLASH BY NIGHT(1952); MAN IN THE VAULT(1956)

Nigel Duke
FACTS OF LOVE(1949, Brit.), ph

Patty Duke
COUNTRY MUSIC HOLIDAY(1958); GODDESS, THE(1958); HAPPY ANNIVERSARY(1959); 4D MAN(1959); MIRACLE WORKER, THE(1962); BILLIE(1965); DAYDREAMER, THE(1966); VALLEY OF THE DOLLS(1967); ME, NATALIE(1969); YOU'LL LIKE MY MOTHER(1972)

Robert Duke
ANGEL COMES TO BROOKLYN, AN(1945)
Misc. Talkies
TIME RUNNING OUT(1950)

Stan Duke
LOVE BUG, THE(1968)

Tony Duke
MAIDSTONE(1970)

Vernon Duke
CABIN IN THE SKY(1943), w; SHE'S WORKING HER WAY THROUGH COLLEGE(1952), m

Duke Ellington and Band
HIT PARADE, THE(1937)

Duke Ellington and His Orchestra
MURDER AT THE VANITIES(1934); REVEILLE WITH BEVERLY(1943)

Duke Ellington and Orchestra
CABIN IN THE SKY(1943)

Duke Kahanamoku International Surfing Champions
I SAILED TO TAHITI WITH AN ALL GIRL CREW(1969)

Duke of Bedford
NOTHING BARRED(1961, Brit.); SWINGIN' MAIDEN, THE(1963, Brit.)

Duke of Iron
CALYPSO JOE(1957)

The Duke of Paducah
LAS VEGAS HILLBILLYS(1966)

Duke of York's School Boys
STEPPING TOES(1938, Brit.)

Ashley Dukes
PATRIOT, THE(1928), w; ABDUL THE DAMNED(1935, Brit.), w; VINTAGE WINE(1935, Brit.), w

David Dukes
STRAWBERRY STATEMENT, THE(1970); WILD PARTY, THE(1975); LITTLE ROMANCE, A(1979, U.S./Fr.); FIRST DEADLY SIN, THE(1980); ONLY WHEN I LAUGH(1981); WITHOUT A TRACE(1983)

Leroy Dukes
1984
HARRY AND SON(1984)
Lulu Dukes
WOMAN TO WOMAN(1946, Brit.)
Pauline Dukes
SHAKEDOWN, THE(1960, Brit.)
Robert Dukes
Misc. Talkies
LOST CITY, THE(1982), d
The Dukes of Dixieland
RING-A-DING RHYTHM(1962, Brit. 73m Amicus/COL bw (G.B: IT'S TRAD, DAD!)
V. Dukhina
RESURRECTION(1963, USSR)
Bernard Dukore
GRASS EATER, THE(1961)
Lawrence DuKore
GREASED LIGHTNING(1977), w
B. Duksht
GORDEYEV FAMILY, THE(1961, U.S.S.R.), set d
Arthur Dulac
ARTISTS AND MODELS ABROAD(1938); I MARRIED AN ANGEL(1942); BERLIN EXPRESS(1948); MISTER 880(1950); LITTLE BOY LOST(1953); FRENCH LINE, THE(1954); FLY, THE(1958)
Germaine Dulac
Misc. Silents
GEO, LE MYSTERIEUX(1917, Fr.), d; LES SOEURS ENNEMIES(1917, Fr.), d; VENUS VICTRIX(1917, Fr.), d; LA CIGARETTE(1919, Fr.), d; LA FETE ESPAG-NOLE(1919, Fr.), d; LE BONHEUR DES AUTRES(1919, Fr.), d; LA BELLE DAME SANS MERCI(1920, Fr.), d; MALENCONTRE(1920, Fr.), d; LA MORT DU SO-LEIL(1922, Fr.), d; AME D'ARTISTE(1925, Fr.), d; LA FOLIE DES VAILLANTS(1925, Fr.), d; LE DIABLE DANS LA VILLE(1925, Fr.), d; ANTOINETTE SABRIER(1927, Fr.), d; LA CINEMA AU SERVICE DE L'HISTOIRE(1927, Fr.), d; L'INVITATION AU VOYAGE(1927, Fr.), d; LA CIQUILLE ET LE CLERGYMAN(1928, Fr.), d; LA PRIN-CESSE MANDANE(1928, Fr.), d
Yvonne Dulac
SAILING ALONG(1938, Brit.)
Robert Dulaine
STRIPES(1981)
Arthur Dulay
MRS. FITZHERBERT(1950, Brit.)
Boris Dulenkov
DAY THE WAR ENDED, THE(1961, USSR), art d; SONS AND MOTHERS(1967, USSR), art d
Susanne Dulier
TANGO BAR(1935)
Suzanne Dulier
JEZEBEL(1938); VOICE OF THE TURTLE, THE(1947)
Orville Dull
Silents
BRONCHO TWISTER(1927), d
Orville O. Dull
VACATION FROM LOVE(1938), p; EDISON, THE MAN(1940), p; WHEN LADIES MEET(1941), p; STAND BY FOR ACTION(1942), p; TISH(1942), p; WE WERE DANC-ING(1942), p; MAN FROM DOWN UNDER, THE(1943), p; BARBARY COAST GENT(1944), p; RATIONING(1944), p; BAD BASCOMB(1946), p; LITTLE MISTER JIM(1946), p
Misc. Silents
FLYING HORSEMAN, THE(1926), d; BLACK JACK(1927), d
Paul Dullac
MARIUS(1933, Fr.); CESAR(1936, Fr.); LA MARSEILLAISE(1938, Fr.); HAR-VEST(1939, Fr.)
John Dullaghan
THING WITH TWO HEADS, THE(1972); TOMB OF THE UNDEAD(1972)
Keir Dullea
HOODLUM PRIEST, THE(1961); DAVID AND LISA(1962); MAIL ORDER BRI-DE(1964); NAKED HOURS, THE(1964, Ital.); THIN RED LINE, THE(1964); BUNNY LAKE IS MISSING(1965); MADAME X(1966); FOX, THE(1967); 2001: A SPACE ODYSSEY(1968, U.S./Brit.); DE SADE(1969); POPE JOAN(1972, Brit.); PAPERBACK HERO(1973, Can.); BLACK CHRISTMAS(1974, Can.); PAUL AND MICHELLE(1974, Fr./Brit.); FULL CIRCLE(1977, Brit./Can.); WELCOME TO BLOOD CITY(1977, Brit./Can.); LEOPARD IN THE SNOW(1979, Brit./Can.); HAUNTING OF JULIA, THE(1981, Brit./Can.); NEXT ONE, THE(1982, U.S./Gr.); BRAINWAVES(1983)
1984
BLIND DATE(1984); 2010(1984)
Brainerd Dullfield
TREASURE OF LOST CANYON, THE(1952), w
Charles Dullin
LES MISERABLES(1936, Fr.); COURIER OF LYONS(1938, Fr.); LES JEUX SONT FAITS(1947, Fr.); VOLPONE(1947, Fr.); JENNY LAMOUR(1948, Fr.)
Misc. Silents
LE SECRET DE ROSETTE LAMBERT(1920, Fr.); MIRACLE OF WOLVES, THE(1925, Fr.); MALDONE(1928, Fr.); CHESS PLAYER, THE(1930, Fr.)
George Dullin
Misc. Silents
CAGLIOSTRO(1928, Fr.)
Jane Dulo
ROUSTABOUT(1964); DID YOU HEAR THE ONE ABOUT THE TRAVELING SALESLADY?(1968); PUFNSTUF(1970); SOYLENT GREEN(1973)
1984
OH GOD! YOU DEVIL(1984)
Bruno DuLouvat
LA NUIT DE VARENNES(1983, Fr./Ital.)
Yvonne Dulquette
Silents
LADY NOGGS-PEERESS(1929, Brit.)
James Dultz
YOUNGBLOOD(1978), art d

Jim Dultz
TAKE THIS JOB AND SHOVE IT(1981), art d; LAST AMERICAN VIRGIN, THE(1982), art d
Jim Dulz
1984
BAD MANNERS(1984), art d
Kenneth DuMain
FIRST MONDAY IN OCTOBER(1981)
Andre Dumaitre
PASSION FOR LIFE(1951, Fr.), ph
Wade Duman
VIEW FROM POMPEY'S HEAD, THE(1955)
Roberto Dumant
UNDER FIRE(1983)
Jean Dumar
Misc. Silents
GRELL MYSTERY, THE(1917)
Louis Dumar
Silents
GOLDEN GIFT, THE(1922); SALOME(1922)
Philippe Dumarcay
SWEET HUNTERS(1969, Panama), w; GOING PLACES(1974, Fr.), w
William Dumaresq
MOON OVER THE ALLEY(1980, Brit.), w
Alexander Dumas
BRIGAND, THE(1952), w; BLADES OF THE MUSKETEERS(1953), w; STORY OF THE COUNT OF MONTE CRISTO, THE(1962, Fr./Ital.), w; CAMILLE 2000(1969), w
Alexandre Dumas
IRON MASK, THE(1929), w; ROYAL BOX, THE(1930), w; COUNT OF MONTE CRISTO, THE(1934), w; THREE MUSKETEERS, THE(1935), w; BLACK TULIP, THE(1937, Brit.), w; CAMILLE(1937), w; MAN IN THE IRON MASK, THE(1939), w; THREE MUSKETEERS, THE(1939), w; FIGHTING GUARDSMAN, THE(1945), w; PRINCE OF THIEVES, THE(1948), w; THREE MUSKETEERS, THE(1948), w; BLACK MAGIC(1949), w; MASK OF THE AVENGER(1951), w; SWORD OF MONTE CRISTO, THE(1951), w; LADY IN THE IRON MASK(1952), w; COUNT OF MONTE-CRIS-TO(1955, Fr., Ital.), w; PRISONER OF THE IRON MASK(1962, Fr./Ital.), w; YOU CAME TOO LATE(1962, Gr.), w; LA TRAVIATA(1968, Ital.), w; LADY HAMIL-TON(1969, Ger./Ital./Fr.), w; THREE MUSKETEERS, THE(1974, Panama), w; FOUR MUSKETEERS, THE(1975), w; COUNT OF MONTE CRISTO(1976, Brit.), w; BEHIND THE IRON MASK(1977), w; LA TRAVIATA(1982), w
Silents
CLEMENCEAU CASE, THE(1915), w; KING'S DAUGHTER, THE(1916, Brit.), w; CAMILLE(1927), w
Andre Dumas
FANTOMAS(1966, Fr./Ital.); FAREWELL, FRIEND(1968, Fr./Ital.); RISE OF LOUIS XIV, THE(1970, Fr.)
C.R. Dumas
LE MONDE TREMBLERA(1939, Fr.), w
Charles Robert Dumas
AMONG HUMAN WOLVES(1940 Brit.), w
Francois Dumas
Silents
REPUTATION(1921); TWO MINUTES TO GO(1921)
Misc. Silents
TRACKS(1922)
Jean Dumas
99 WOUNDS(1931)
Silents
OUR HOSPITALITY(1923)
Misc. Silents
PRAIRIE PIRATE, THE(1925)
Jebidiah R. Dumas
NATIONAL LAMPOON'S ANIMAL HOUSE(1978)
Jennifer Dumas
DIFFERENT STORY, A(1978)
John Dumas
NEWMAN'S LAW(1974), ed; BUCK ROGERS IN THE 25TH CENTURY(1979), ed
Monique Dumas
ROYAL AFFAIRS IN VERSAILLES(1957, Fr.), cos
Richard Dumas
FAMILY HONEYMOON(1948); MOTHER IS A FRESHMAN(1949)
Robert Dumas
STAR IS BORN, A(1954)
Roger Dumas
CROSS OF THE LIVING(; CARNIVAL OF SINNERS(1947, Fr.), m; BRIDE IS MUCH TOO BEAUTIFUL, THE(1958, Fr.); DEADLY DECOYS, THE(1962, Fr.); THAT MAN FROM RIO(1964, Fr./Ital.); DEAR DETECTIVE(1978, Fr.)
Roland Dumas
WAY OF A GAUCHO(1952)
Valerie Dumas
COUSINS IN LOVE(1982)
Wade Dumas
HARLEM RIDES THE RANGE(1939); NO WAY OUT(1950); TEENAGE REBEL(1956); PARRISH(1961)
Philippe Dumat
SOFT SKIN, THE(1964, Fr.)
Dezma DuMay
Silents
OLD CURIOSITY SHOP, THE(1921, Brit.)
Pierre Dumayet
VERDICT(1975, Fr./Ital.), w; MALEVIL(1981, Fr./Ger.), w
Helen Dumbar
Silents
ALL WRONG(1919); FIGHTING COWARD, THE(1924)
Betty Dumbries
ROBERTA(1935)
Douglas Dumbrille
HIS WOMAN(1931); BLONDIE OF THE FOLLIES(1932); I AM A FUGITIVE FROM A CHAIN GANG(1932); THAT'S MY BOY(1932); WISER SEX, THE(1932); BABY FACE(1933); ELMER THE GREAT(1933); FEMALE(1933); HARD TO HANDLE(1933);

HEROES FOR SALE(1933); KING OF THE JUNGLE(1933); LADY KILLER(1933); LAUGHTER IN HELL(1933); MAN WHO DARED, THE(1933); RUSTLERS' ROUND-UP(1933); SILK EXPRESS, THE(1933); VOLTAIRE(1933); WAY TO LOVE, THE(1933); WORKING MAN, THE(1933); WORLD CHANGES, THE(1933); BROADWAY BILL(1934); FOG OVER FRISCO(1934); HAROLD TEEN(1934); HI, NELLIE!(1934); HIDE-OUT(1934); JOURNAL OF A CRIME(1934); MASSACRE(1934); OPERATOR 13(1934); STAMBOUL QUEST(1934); TREASURE ISLAND(1934); AIR HAWKS(1935); CARDINAL RICHELIEU(1935); CRIME AND PUNISHMENT(1935); LIVES OF A BENGAL LANCER(1935); LOVE ME FOREVER(1935); NAUGHTY MARIETTA(1935); PETER IBBETSON(1935); PUBLIC MENACE(1935); SECRET BRIDE, THE(1935); UNKNOWN WOMAN(1935); DAN MATTHEWS(1936); END OF THE TRAIL(1936); LONE WOLF RETURNS, THE(1936); M'LISS(1936); MR. DEEDS GOES TO TOWN(1936); MUSIC GOES ROUND, THE(1936); PRINCESS COMES ACROSS, THE(1936); WITNESS CHAIR, THE(1936); YOU MAY BE NEXT(1936); ALI BABA GOES TO TOWN(1937); COUNTERFEIT LADY(1937); DAY AT THE RACES, A(1937); EMPEROR'S CANDLESTICKS, THE(1937); FIREFLY, THE(1937); WOMAN IN DIS-TRESS(1937); BUCCANEER, THE(1938); CRIME TAKES A HOLIDAY(1938); KEN-TUCKY(1938); MYSTERIOUS RIDER, THE(1938); SHARPSHOOTERS(1938); STOLEN HEAVEN(1938); STORM OVER BENGAL(1938); CAPTAIN FURY(1939); CHARLIE CHAN AT TREASURE ISLAND(1939); CHARLIE CHAN IN THE CITY OF DARK-NESS(1939); MR. MOTO IN DANGER ISLAND(1939); ROVIN' TUMBLEWEEDS(1939); TELL NO TALES(1939); THREE MUSKETEERS, THE(1939); THUNDER AFLOAT(1939); MICHAEL SHAYNE, PRIVATE DETECTIVE(1940); SLIGHTLY HON-ORABLE(1940); SOUTH OF PAGO PAGO(1940); VIRGINIA CITY(1940); BIG STORE, THE(1941); ELLERY QUEEN AND THE PERFECT CRIME(1941); MURDER AMONG FRIENDS(1941); ROAD TO ZANZIBAR(1941); ROUNDUP, THE(1941); WASHINGTON MELODRAMA(1941); CASTLE IN THE DESERT(1942); GENTLEMAN AFTER DARK, A(1942); I MARRIED AN ANGEL(1942); RIDE 'EM COWBOY(1942); STAND BY FOR ACTION(1942); TEN GENTLEMEN FROM WEST POINT(1942); DU BARRY WAS A LADY(1943); FALSE COLORS(1943); FORTY THIEVES(1944); GYPSY WILD-CAT(1944); JUNGLE WOMAN(1944); LOST IN A HAREM(1944); LUMBER-JACK(1944); UNCERTAIN GLORY(1944); DALTONS RIDE AGAIN, THE(1945); FLAME OF THE WEST(1945); FROZEN GHOST, THE(1945); MEDAL FOR BENNY, A(1945); PARDON MY PAST(1945); ROAD TO UTOPIA(1945); CAT CREEPS, THE(1946); MONSIEUR BEAUCAIRE(1946); NIGHT IN PARADISE, A(1946); SPOOK BUSTERS(1946); THE CATMAN OF PARIS(1946); UNDER NEVADA SKIES(1946); BLONDE SAVAGE(1947); CHRISTMAS EVE(1947); DISHONORED LADY(1947); FABULOUS TEXAN, THE(1947); IT'S A JOKE, SON!(1947); DYNAMITE(1948); LAST OF THE WILD HORSES(1948); ALIMONY(1949); JOE PALOOKA IN THE COUNTER-PUNCH(1949); LONE WOLF AND HIS LADY, THE(1949); RIDERS OF THE WHIS-TLING PINES(1949); TELL IT TO THE JUDGE(1949); ABBOTT AND COSTELLO IN THE FOREIGN LEGION(1950); BUCCANEER'S GIRL(1950); KANGAROO KID, THE(1950, Aus./U.S.); RAPTURE(1950, Ital.); RIDING HIGH(1950); SAVAGE HORDE, THE(1950); MILLIONAIRE FOR CHRISTY, A(1951); APACHE WAR SMOKE(1952); SCARAMOUCHE(1952); SKY FULL OF MOON(1952); SON OF PALEFACE(1952); CAPTAIN JOHN SMITH AND POCAHONTAS(1953); JULIUS CAESAR(1953); PLUN-DER OF THE SUN(1953); LAWLESS RIDER, THE(1954); WORLD FOR RAN-SOM(1954); JUPITER'S DARLING(1955); DAVY CROCKETT AND THE RIVER PIRATES(1956); MOBS INC(1956); TEN COMMANDMENTS, THE(1956); SHAKE, RATTLE, AND ROCK!(1957); BUCCANEER, THE(1958); AIR PATROL(1962); JOHN-NY COOL(1963); SHOCK TREATMENT(1964); DRAGNET(1974)

Misc. Talkies
SMOKE LIGHTNING(1933); CALLING OF DAN MATTHEWS, THE(1936)

Erwin Dumbrille
HELLO DOWN THERE(1969), ed; HAPPY AS THE GRASS WAS GREEN(1973), ed; HAZEL'S PEOPLE(1978), ed

Irwin Dumbrille
BIRDS DO IT(1966), ed

Ernst Dumcke
CASE VAN GELDERN(1932, Ger.)

Jacques Dumensil
PLEASE! MR. BALZAC(1957, Fr.)

Jean Dumercier
Silents
HEARTS OF THE WORLD(1918)

Dumesnil
LUCREZIA BORGIA(1937, Fr.)

Jacques Dumesnil
TWO WOMEN(1940, Fr.); ANNA(1951, Ital.); NAPOLEON(1955, Fr.); ULYSSES(1955, Ital.)

Ralph Dumke
LUCKY JORDAN(1942); ALL THE KING'S MEN(1949); BREAKING POINT, THE(1950); FIREBALL, THE(1950); MYSTERY STREET(1950); WHERE DANGER LIVES(1950); LAW AND THE LADY, THE(1951); MOB, THE(1951); WHEN I GROW UP(1951); BOOTS MALONE(1952); CARBINE WILLIAMS(1952); HOLIDAY FOR SINNERS(1952); HURRICANE SMITH(1952); WE'RE NOT MARRIED(1952); HAN-NAH LEE(1953); LILI(1953); MISSISSIPPI GAMBLER, THE(1953); PRESIDENT'S LADY, THE(1953); WAR OF THE WORLDS, THE(1953); ALASKA SEAS(1954); IT SHOULD HAPPEN TO YOU(1954); MASSACRE CANYON(1954); RAILS INTO LARA-MIE(1954); SHE COULDN'T SAY NO(1954); THEY RODE WEST(1954); DADDY LONG LEGS(1955); HELL'S ISLAND(1955); VIOLENT SATURDAY(1955); FOREVER DAR-LING(1956); FRANCIS IN THE HAUNTED HOUSE(1956); INVASION OF THE BODY SNATCHERS(1956); SOLID GOLD CADILLAC, THE(1956); WHEN GANGLAND STRIKES(1956); BUSTER KEATON STORY, THE(1957); LOVING YOU(1957); WAKE ME WHEN IT'S OVER(1960); ALL IN A NIGHT'S WORK(1961)

Ralph E. Dumke
SAN FRANCISCO STORY, THE(1952)

Melvin E. Dummar
MELVIN AND HOWARD(1980)

Audrey Dummett
KING OF COMEDY, THE(1983)

Evelyn Dumo
Silents
SYLVIA GRAY(1914); LOVE LIGHT, THE(1921)
Misc. Silents
MY MADONNA(1916)

Guy DuMonceau
PORTRAIT IN SMOKE(1957, Brit.)

Alan Dumont
Misc. Talkies
HILARY'S BLUES(1983)

Charles Dumont
TRAFFIC(1972, Fr.), m

Danielle Dumont
HUNCHBACK OF NOTRE DAME, THE(1957, Fr.)

Ghislaine Dumont
PICNIC ON THE GRASS(1960, Fr.)

Gordon Dumont
HOODLUM SAINT, THE(1946)

Guy Dumont
BOYS FROM BRAZIL, THE(1978)

J. M. Dumont
Silents
THOU ART THE MAN(1920); WEALTH(1921)
Misc. Silents
DOLLAR-A-YEAR MAN, THE(1921)

J. Monte Dumont
Silents
ALWAYS AUDACIOUS(1920)

Jean Dumont
Silents
STRANGER THAN FICTION(1921)

Jean M. Dumont
Silents
MIRACLE MAN, THE(1919)

Jean Montague Dumont
Silents
MIDNIGHT ROMANCE, A(1919)

Jean Monte Dumont
Silents
JACK STRAW(1920)

Joseh Dumont
1984
MEMOIRS OF PRISON(1984, Braz.)

Margaret Dumont
COCOANUTS, THE(1929); ANIMAL CRACKERS(1930); GIRL HABIT(1931); DUCK SOUP(1933); FIFTEEN WIVES(1934); GRIDIRON FLASH(1935); KENTUCKY KER-NELS(1935); NIGHT AT THE OPERA, A(1935); RECKLESS(1935); RENDEZ-VOUS(1935); ANYTHING GOES(1936); SONG AND DANCE MAN, THE(1936); DAY AT THE RACES, A(1937); HIGH FLYERS(1937); LIFE OF THE PARTY, THE(1937); WISE GIRL(1937); YOUTH ON PAROLE(1937); DRAMATIC SCHOOL(1938); AT THE CIR-CUS(1939); WOMEN, THE(1939); BIG STORE, THE(1941); FOR BEAUTY'S SA-KE(1941); NEVER GIVE A SUCKER AN EVEN BREAK(1941); ABOUT FACE(1942); BORN TO SING(1942); SING YOUR WORRIES AWAY(1942); DANCING MASTERS, THE(1943); RHYTHM PARADE(1943); BATHING BEAUTY(1944); SEVEN DAYS ASHORE(1944); UP IN ARMS(1944); DIAMOND HORSESHOE(1945); HORN BLOWS AT MIDNIGHT, THE(1945); SUNSET IN EL DORADO(1945); MAGNIFICENT FRAUD, THE(1943) ... LITTLE GIANT(1946); SUSIE STEPS OUT(1946); STOP, YOU'RE KILLING ME(1952); THREE FOR BED-ROOM C(1952); SHAKE, RATTLE, AND ROCK!(1957); ZOTZ!(1962); WHAT A WAY TO GO(1964)

Paul Dumont
MADE FOR EACH OTHER(1971)

Robert Dumont
DR. TARR'S TORTURE DUNGEON(1972, Mex.)

Roberto Dumont
ZORRO, THE GAY BLADE(1981)

Sky Dumont
LION OF THE DESERT(1981, Libya/Brit.); NIGHT CROSSING(1982)

Michele Dumontier
FIRST TASTE OF LOVE(1962, Fr.)

Albert Dumortier
PATTON(1970)

Alain Dumoulin
FIRST TASTE OF LOVE(1962, Fr.)

Jean-Claude Dumoutier
CROSS OF THE LIVING(1963, Fr.), p, w

Dump and Tony
DISCOVERIES(1939, Brit.)

Baby Dumpling [Larry Simms]
MR. SMITH GOES TO WASHINGTON(1939)

Dumplings
Silents
WELCOME CHILDREN(1921)

Michel Dumur
DIABOLIQUE(1955, Fr.)

Eddie Dun
SLEEP, MY LOVE(1948)

Steffi Duna
INDISCRETIONS OF EVE(1932, Brit.); IRON STAIR, THE(1933, Brit.); MAN OF TWO WORLDS(1934); ONE NEW YORK NIGHT(1935); RED MORNING(1935); ANTHONY ADVERSE(1936); CLOWN MUST LAUGH, A(1936, Brit.); DANCING PIRATE(1936); HI GAUCHO!(1936); I CONQUER THE SEA(1936); ESCAPE BY NIGHT(1937); FLIRTING WITH FATE(1938); RASCALS(1938); BEASTS OF BERLIN(1939); GIRL AND THE GAMBLER, THE(1939); LAW OF THE PAMPAS(1939); MAGNIFICENT FRAUD, THE(1939); PANAMA LADY(1939); WAY DOWN SOUTH(1939); GIRL FROM HAVA-NA(1940); GREAT McGINTY, THE(1940); MARINES FLY HIGH, THE(1940); PHAN-TOM RAIDERS(1940); RIVER'S END(1940); WATERLOO BRIDGE(1940)

Teri Duna
KOREA PATROL(1951)

Nicholas A. Dunaev
Silents
SIBERIA(1926), w

Nicholas Dunaew
Silents
KISMET(1920)
Misc. Silents
FLOWER OF DOOM, THE(1917); CHEATING CHEATERS(1919)

Deanna Dunagan
1984
NAKED FACE, THE(1984)

Donnie Dunagan
MOTHER CAREY'S CHICKENS(1938); FORGOTTEN WOMAN, THE(1939); SON OF FRANKENSTEIN(1939); TOWER OF LONDON(1939); BAMBI(1942)

Tamas Dunai
ANGI VERA(1980, Hung.); CONFIDENCE(1980, Hung.)

Monique Dunan
PICNIC ON THE GRASS(1960, Fr.), cos

Alex Dunand
RETURN TO PEYTON PLACE(1961)

Ronald S. Dunas
ABOMINABLE DR. PHIBES, THE(1971, Brit.), p

Don Carlos Dunaway
LADY LIBERTY(1972, Ital./Fr.), w; CUJO(1983), w
1984
IMPULSE(1984), w

Faye Dunaway
BONNIE AND CLYDE(1967); HAPPENING, THE(1967); HURRY SUNDOWN(1967); THOMAS CROWN AFFAIR, THE(1968); ARRANGEMENT, THE(1969); EXTRAORDINARY SEAMAN, THE(1969); PLACE FOR LOVERS, A(1969, Ital./Fr.); LITTLE BIG MAN(1970); PUZZLE OF A DOWNFALL CHILD(1970); DOC(1971); DEADLY TRAP, THE(1972, Fr./Ital.); OKLAHOMA CRUDE(1973); CHINATOWN(1974); THREE MUSKETEERS, THE(1974, Panama); TOWERING INFERNO, THE(1974); FOUR MUSKETEERS, THE(1975); THREE DAYS OF THE CONDOR(1975); NETWORK(1976); VOYAGE OF THE DAMNED(1976, Brit.); EYES OF LAURA MARS(1978); CHAMP, THE(1979); FIRST DEADLY SIN, THE(1980); MOMMIE DEAREST(1981); WICKED LADY, THE(1983, Brit.)
1984
ORDEAL BY INNOCENCE(1984, Brit.); SUPERGIRL(1984)

Michael Dunaway
REPENT AT LEISURE(1941)

S. Angelece Dunaway
1984
IMPULSE(1984)

Steven Dunaway
1984
OH GOD! YOU DEVIL(1984)

Isaac O. Dunayevsky
COUNTRY BRIDE(1938, USSR), m

Issac Dunayevsky
SPRING(1948, USSR), m

Anton Dunaysky
RAINBOW, THE(1944, USSR)

Bill Dunbar
WHERE THE RED FERN GROWS(1974); APPLE DUMPLING GANG, THE(1975)

Bob Dunbar
TIMERIDER(1983)

Charles Dunbar
WHAT! NO BEER?(1933); MANHATTAN MELODRAMA(1934); NAUGHTY MARIETTA(1935); STABLEMATES(1938)

Dave Dunbar
MRS. MINIVER(1942); JOAN OF ARC(1948); DALLAS(1950); MILKMAN, THE(1950); YOUNG MAN WITH A HORN(1950); SOLDIERS THREE(1951); SON OF DR. JEKYLL, THE(1951)

David Dunbar
RETURN OF DR. FU MANCHU, THE(1930); SHOCK(1934); GREAT IMPERSONATION, THE(1935); DRACULA'S DAUGHTER(1936); RULERS OF THE SEA(1939); EARL OF CHICAGO, THE(1940); KISS THE BLOOD OFF MY HANDS(1948); THAT FORSYTE WOMAN(1949)
Silents
NORTH OF 36(1924); FAIR PLAY(1925); MAN OF NERVE, A(1925); RIDIN' THE WIND(1925); NON-STOP FLIGHT, THE(1926); BOY RIDER, THE(1927); KING OF KINGS, THE(1927); PLUNGING HOOFS(1929)
Misc. Silents
TRAIL DUST(1924); 40TH DOOR, THE(1924); BLOODHOUND, THE(1925); COWBOY MUSKETEER, THE(1925); BEYOND THE ROCKIES(1926); ARIZONA WHIRLWIND, THE(1927); FIGHTING HOMBRE, THE(1927); DOWNSTREAM(1929, Brit.); HUMAN CARGO(1929, Brit.); SECOND MATE, THE(1929); STREETS OF LONDON, THE(1929, Brit.)

Dixie Dunbar
GEORGE WHITE'S SCANDALS(1934); BACK TO NATURE(1936); EDUCATING FATHER(1936); FIRST BABY(1936); GIRLS' DORMITORY(1936); KING OF BURLESQUE(1936); ONE IN A MILLION(1936); PIGSKIN PARADE(1936); PROFESSIONAL SOLDIER(1936); SING, BABY, SING(1936); LIFE BEGINS IN COLLEGE(1937); SING AND BE HAPPY(1937); ALEXANDER'S RAGTIME BAND(1938); FRESHMAN YEAR(1938); LOVE ON A BUDGET(1938); REBECCA OF SUNNYBROOK FARM(1938); WALKING DOWN BROADWAY(1938)

Dorothy Dunbar
Silents
AMATEUR GENTLEMAN, THE(1926); LIGHTNING LARIATS(1927)
Misc. Silents
FLAMING CRISIS, THE(1924); MASQUERADE BANDIT, THE(1926); RED HOT HOOFS(1926)

Helen Dunbar
Silents
PENNINGTON'S CHOICE(1915); SECOND IN COMMAND, THE(1915); SILENT VOICE, THE(1915); MOLLY ENTANGLED(1917); INSIDE THE LINES(1918); MORE TROUBLE(1918); GOD'S OUTLAW(1919); JANE GOES A' WOOING(1919); HER WINNING WAY(1921); LITTLE CLOWN, THE(1921); SHAM(1921); BEYOND THE ROCKS(1922); HOMESPUN VAMP, A(1922); IMPOSSIBLE MRS. BELLEW, THE(1922); THIRTY DAYS(1922); WORLD'S CHAMPION, THE(1922); COMPROMISE(1925); LADY WINDERMERE'S FAN(1925); NEW LIVES FOR OLD(1925); RECKLESS SEX, THE(1925); ROSE OF THE WORLD(1925); FINE MANNERS(1926); HIS JAZZ BRIDE(1926)
Misc. Silents
IN THE DIPLOMATIC SERVICE(1916); PRICE OF MALICE, THE(1916); HITTING THE HIGH SPOTS(1918); PUPPY LOVE(1919); YOU NEVER CAN TELL(1920); YOUNG MRS. WINTHROP(1920); SACRED AND PROFANE LOVE(1921); MAN

UPSTAIRS, THE(1926)

Hooper Dunbar
BERNARDINE(1957)

John Dunbar
HELL, HEAVEN OR HOBOKEN(1958, Brit.); DEVIL'S HARBOR(1954, Brit.); BLONDE BLACKMAILER(1955, Brit.); TWO-HEADED SPY, THE(1959, Brit.); NEVER LET GO(1960, Brit.); PEEPING TOM(1960, Brit.); INVASION QUARTET(1961, Brit.); PUNCH AND JUDY MAN, THE(1963, Brit.); NEVER PUT IT IN WRITING(1964); TOMORROW AT TEN(1964, Brit.); WITCHCRAFT(1964, Brit.); AMOROUS MR. PRAWN, THE(1965, Brit.); MURDER GAME, THE(1966, Brit.); PRIME OF MISS JEAN BRODIE, THE(1969, Brit.)

Louise Dunbar
Misc. Silents
GREEN-EYED MONSTER, THE(1921)

Olive Dunbar
WAR BETWEEN MEN AND WOMEN, THE(1972); HEARSE, THE(1980); FIRST MONDAY IN OCTOBER(1981)

Robert Dunbar
FAMILY AFFAIR(1954, Brit.), p, w; DEADLY GAME, THE(1955, Brit.), p; LYONS IN PARIS, THE(1955, Brit.), p; SECOND FIDDLE(1957, Brit.), p, w; SUSPENDED ALIBI(1957, Brit.), p; SOLITARY CHILD, THE(1958, Brit.), w; MAN UPSTAIRS, THE(1959, Brit.), p, w; DEAD LUCKY(1960, Brit.), p; MODEL FOR MURDER(1960, Brit.), p, w; PIPER'S TUNE, THE(1962, Brit.), p; NIGHTWING(1979)
Silents
PUTTING IT OVER(1919); ALIAS JIMMY VALENTINE(1920); HIGH HEELS(1921); KID, THE(1921)
Misc. Silents
THIRD DEGREE, THE(1914)

Robert N. Dunbar
Silents
GOOSE GIRL, THE(1915)
Misc. Silents
ME UND GOTT(1918)

Vivyen Dunbar
STOP THE WORLD–I WANT TO GET OFF(1966, Brit.)

Duncan
CASINO ROYALE(1967, Brit.)

Alex Duncan
IN THE DOGHOUSE(1964, Brit.), w

Alistair Duncan
DEMONSTRATOR(1971, Aus.)

Andrew Duncan
VIRGIN PRESIDENT, THE(1968); RAIN PEOPLE, THE(1969); LOVE STORY(1970); LOVING(1970); HOSPITAL, THE(1971); PARADES(1972); I COULD NEVER HAVE SEX WITH ANY MAN WHO HAS SO LITTLE REGARD FOR MY HUSBAND(1973); CRAZY WORLD OF JULIUS VROODER, THE(1974); FOREPLAY(1975); SLAP SHOT(1977); UNMARRIED WOMAN, AN(1978); FIREPOWER(1979, Brit.); LAST EMBRACE(1979); LITTLE ROMANCE, A(1979, U.S./Fr.); USED CARS(1980); LINE, THE(1982)

Angus Duncan
HIGH TIME(1960); MAGIC SWORD, THE(1962); STAY AWAY, JOE(1968); YOUNG RUNAWAYS, THE(1968); MARLOWE(1969); SIMON, KING OF THE WITCHES(1971); SWEET SUGAR(1972); HOW TO SEDUCE A WOMAN(1974); GOING APE!(1981); SEPARATE WAYS(1981)
Misc. Talkies
HALF A HOUSE(1979)

Ann Duncan
FORCE OF EVIL(1948); KNOCK ON ANY DOOR(1949)

Anna Duncan
DINNER AT EIGHT(1933); BLACK CAT, THE(1934); SCARLET EMPRESS, THE(1934)

Archie Duncan
UNDERCOVER AGENT(1935, Brit.); DEVIL'S PLOT, THE(1948, Brit.); OPERATION DIAMOND(1948, Brit.); BAD LORD BYRON, THE(1949, Brit.); FLOODTIDE(1949, Brit.); GORBALS STORY, THE(1950, Brit.); FLESH AND BLOOD(1951, Brit.); GREEN GROW THE RUSHES(1951, Brit.); LAVENDER HILL MOB, THE(1951, Brit.); BRAVE DON'T CRY, THE(1952, Brit.); CASTLE IN THE AIR(1952, Brit.); HOT ICE(1952, Brit.); STORY OF ROBIN HOOD, THE(1952, Brit.); YOU'RE ONLY YOUNG TWICE(1952, Brit.); TWICE UPON A TIME(1953, Brit.); ROB ROY, THE HIGHLAND ROGUE(1954, Brit.); SCOTCH ON THE ROCKS(1954, Brit.); TROUBLE IN THE GLEN(1954, Brit.); DEVIL'S PASS, THE(1957, Brit.); SAINT JOAN(1957); X THE UNKNOWN(1957, Brit.); HARRY BLACK AND THE TIGER(1958, Brit.); JOHN PAUL JONES(1959); BOY AND THE PIRATES, THE(1960); TESS OF THE STORM COUNTRY(1961); WHAT A WHOPPER(1961, Brit.); POSTMAN'S KNOCK(1962, Brit.); MOUSE ON THE MOON, THE(1963, Brit.); SWORD OF LANCELOT(1963, Brit.); HORROR OF IT ALL, THE(1964, Brit.); MAN OUTSIDE, THE(1968, Brit.); RING OF BRIGHT WATER(1969, Brit.); WILBY CONSPIRACY, THE(1975, Brit.)

Arletta Duncan
FRANKENSTEIN(1931); BACK STREET(1932); NIGHT WORLD(1932); FIGHTING CHAMP(1933); MENACE(1934); UNKNOWN BLONDE(1934); CRIME AFLOAT(1937); DAMAGED GOODS(1937); MILE A MINUTE LOVE(1937)

Artletta Duncan
GALLANT FOOL, THE(1933)

Betty Duncan
HOT MILLIONS(1968, Brit.); NEITHER THE SEA NOR THE SAND(1974, Brit.)

Bob Duncan
FLAMING BULLETS(1945); NORTHWEST TRAIL(1945); CARAVAN TRAIL, THE(1946); COLORADO SERENADE(1946); TUMBLEWEED TRAIL(1946); WILD WEST(1946); BORDER FEUD(1947); RANGE BEYOND THE BLUE(1947); PRAIRIE OUTLAWS(1948); WESTWARD TRAIL, THE(1948); OUTLAW COUNTRY(1949); SON OF BILLY THE KID(1949); FIGHTING REDHEAD, THE(1950); LAW OF THE PANHANDLE(1950); NEW MEXICO(1951); MARSHAL'S DAUGHTER, THE(1953), a, w; PARSON AND THE OUTLAW, THE(1957); BLACK GOLD(1963), w

Brenda Duncan
INSPECTOR CALLS, AN(1954, Brit.)

Bud Duncan
HILLBILLY BLITZKRIEG(1942); SNUFFY SMITH, YARD BIRD(1942)

Carmen Duncan
TOUCH AND GO(1955); STRANGE HOLIDAY(1969, Aus.); YOU CAN'T SEE 'ROUND CORNERS(1969, Aus.); HARLEQUIN(1980, Aus.); ESCAPE 2000(1983, Aus.); NOW AND FOREVER(1983, Aus.)
Misc. Talkies
MAMA'S GONE A-HUNTING(1976)
Charles Duncan
LITTLE TOUGH GUYS IN SOCIETY(1938); CODE OF THE STREETS(1939); NEWSBOY'S HOME(1939); OPERATION EICHMANN(1961), spec eff; SHOCK CORRIDOR(1963), spec eff; SLIME PEOPLE, THE(1963), spec eff; TERRIFIED!(1963), spec eff
Silents
ALL MAN(1916)
Cornett Wood Philip Duncan
FANTASIA(1940), anim
Craig Duncan
HOW THE WEST WAS WON(1962)
Dan Duncan
SO THIS IS WASHINGTON(1943)
Danny Duncan
INSIDE THE LAW(1942); LUCKY JORDAN(1942); TWO WEEKS TO LIVE(1943); GOIN' TO TOWN(1944); PARTNERS IN TIME(1946); SECRET BEYOND THE DOOR, THE(1948); MARSHAL'S DAUGHTER, THE(1953)
David Duncan
SANGAREE(1953), w; JIVARO(1954), w; WHITE ORCHID, THE(1954), w; BLACK SCORPION, THE(1957), w; MONSTER THAT CHALLENGED THE WORLD, THE(1957), w; MONSTER ON THE CAMPUS(1958), w; THING THAT COULDN'T DIE, THE(1958), w; LEECH WOMAN, THE(1960), w; TIME MACHINE, THE(1960; Brit./U.S.), w; FANTASTIC VOYAGE(1966), w
Diana Duncan
1984
THIS IS SPINAL TAP(1984)
Fiona Duncan
THESE ARE THE DAMNED(1965, Brit.); TO SIR, WITH LOVE(1967, Brit.)
Frank Duncan
MOUSE ON THE MOON, THE(1963, Brit.); FAR FROM THE MADDING CROWD(1967, Brit.)
1984
GIVE MY REGARDS TO BROAD STREET(1984, Brit.)
Harry Duncan
TRUE CONFESSIONS(1981)
Harry "Slim" Duncan
FIRECREEK(1968)
Isadora Duncan
ISADORA(1968, Brit.), w
Jennifer Duncan
CHEER THE BRAVE(1951, Brit.)
John Duncan
MYSTERY OF THE 13TH GUEST, THE(1943); HEAVENLY DAYS(1944); TRAIL TO SAN ANTONE(1947); STREET CORNER(1948); WOMAN ON PIER 13, THE(1950); DAVID AND BATHSHEBA(1951); PRIDE OF ST. LOUIS, THE(1952); MISS SADIE THOMPSON(1953)
Johnny Duncan
CAMPUS RHYTHM(1943); CLANCY STREET BOYS(1943); DELINQUENT DAUGHTERS(1944); JIVE JUNCTION(1944); MILLION DOLLAR KID(1944); COME OUT FIGHTING(1945); MR. MUGGS RIDES AGAIN(1945); FIGHTING FOOLS(1949)
Julie Duncan
TEXAS TERRORS(1940); DESPERATE CARGO(1941); FUGITIVE VALLEY(1941); WYOMING WILDCAT(1941); OVERLAND STAGECOACH(1942); TEXAS MAN HUNT(1942); COWBOY IN THE CLOUDS(1943); HAUNTED RANCH, THE(1943); YOUTH AFLAME(1945)
Misc. Talkies
ALONG THE SUNDOWN TRAIL(1942); TEXAS TROUBLE SHOOTERS(1942); BULLETS AND SADDLES(1943)
Ken Duncan
RIDING THE SUNSET TRAIL(1941); DATE WITH DEATH, A(1959)
Kenne Duncan
NO LIMIT(1931); COLORADO KID(1938); FIGHTING THOROUGHBREDS(1939); FLAMING LEAD(1939); FRONTIER SCOUT(1939); MAN FROM TEXAS(1939); NORTH OF THE YUKON(1939); TRIGGER FINGERS ½(1939); FRONTIER CRUSADER(1940); KID FROM SANTA FE, THE(1940); LAND OF THE SIX GUNS(1940); MURDER ON THE YUKON(1940); PINTO CANYON(1940); SAGEBRUSH FAMILY TRAILS WEST, THE(1940); SKY BANDITS, THE(1940); TRAILING DOUBLE TROUBLE(1940); WESTBOUND STAGE(1940); BILLY THE KID IN SANTA FE(1941); DYNAMITE CANYON(1941); OUTLAWS OF THE RIO GRANDE(1941); BILLY THE KID TRAPPED(1942); CODE OF THE OUTLAW(1942); LAW AND ORDER(1942); LONE RIDER AND THE BANDIT, THE(1942); LONE RIDER IN CHEYENNE, THE(1942); MAN WITH TWO LIVES, THE(1942); MISSOURI OUTLAW, A(1942); RAIDERS OF THE WEST(1942); SOMBRERO KID, THE(1942); SUNDOWN KID, THE(1942); TEXAS MAN HUNT(1942); TEXAS TO BATAAN(1942); TRAIL RIDERS(1942); VALLEY OF HUNTED MEN(1942); WESTWARD HO(1942); BORDER BUCKAROOS(1943); CANYON CITY(1943); DAYS OF OLD CHEYENNE(1943); FUGITIVE FROM SONORA(1943); KID RIDES AGAIN, THE(1943); MAN FROM THE RIO GRANDE, THE(1943); OVERLAND MAIL ROBBERY(1943); RAIDERS OF SUNSET PASS(1943); RED RIVER ROBIN HOOD(1943); SANTA FE SCOUTS(1943); WAGON TRACKS WEST(1943); WILD HORSE STAMPEDE(1943); WOLVES OF THE RANGE(1943); BENEATH WESTERN SKIES(1944); CHEYENNE WILDCAT(1944); END OF THE ROAD(1944); HIDDEN VALLEY OUTLAWS(1944); LARAMIE TRAIL, THE(1944); MAN FROM FRISCO(1944); MARSHAL OF RENO(1944); MOJAVE FIREBRAND(1944); OUTLAWS OF SANTA FE(1944); PRIDE OF THE PLAINS(1944); SECRETS OF SCOTLAND YARD(1944); SHERIFF OF LAS VEGAS(1944); SHERIFF OF SUNDOWN(1944); SONG OF NEVADA(1944); STAGECOACH TO MONTEREY(1944); STORM OVER LISBON(1944); TRAIL OF TERROR(1944); TUCSON RAIDERS(1944); VIGILANTES OF DODGE CITY(1944); CHICAGO KID, THE(1945); CORPUS CHRISTI BANDITS(1945); OREGON TRAIL(1945); ROAD TO ALCATRAZ(1945); ROUGH RIDERS OF CHEYENNE(1945); SANTA FE SADDLEMATES(1945); SPORTING CHANCE, A(1945); THOROUGHBREDS(1945); TRAIL OF KIT CARSON(1945); CONQUEST OF CHEYENNE(1946); CYCLOTRODE X(1946); HOME ON THE RANGE(1946); MAN FROM RAINBOW VALLEY, THE(1946); MY PAL TRIGGER(1946); MYSTERIOUS MR. VALENTINE, THE(1946); NIGHT TRAIN TO MEMPHIS(1946); RAINBOW OVER TEXAS(1946); RED RIVER RENEGADES(1946); RIO GRANDE RAIDERS(1946); ROLL ON TEXAS MOON(1946); SANTA FE UPRISING(1946); SHERIFF OF REDWOOD VALLEY(1946); SIOUX CITY SUE(1946); SUN VALLEY CYCLONE(1946); TWILIGHT ON THE RIO GRANDE(1947); SUNDOWN IN SANTA FE(1948); ACROSS THE RIO GRANDE(1949); CRASHING THRU(1949); DEPUTY MARSHAL(1949); GUN RUNNER(1949); HIDDEN DANGER(1949); LAW OF THE WEST(1949); LAWLESS CODE(1949); RANGE JUSTICE(1949); RANGE LAND(1949); RIDERS IN THE SKY(1949); ROARING WESTWARD(1949); SHADOWS OF THE WEST(1949); SONS OF NEW MEXICO(1949); STAMPEDE(1949); WEST OF EL DORADO(1949); BLAZING SUN, THE(1950); CODE OF THE SILVER SAGE(1950); INDIAN TERRITORY(1950); LIFE OF HER OWN, A(1950); MULE TRAIN(1950); RADAR SECRET SERVICE(1950); SURRENDER(1950); BADMAN'S GOLD(1951); HILLS OF UTAH(1951); NEVADA BADMEN(1951); OKLAHOMA JUSTICE(1951); SILVER CANYON(1951); WHIRLWIND(1951); FRONTIER PHANTOM, THE(1952); ON TOP OF OLD SMOKY(1953); PACK TRAIN(1953); LAWLESS RIDER, THE(1954); HELL'S HORIZON(1955); WAGON WHEELS WESTWARD(1956); FLESH AND THE SPUR(1957); REVOLT AT FORT LARAMIE(1957); ASTOUNDING SHE-MONSTER, THE(1958); NIGHT OF THE GHOULS(1959); NATCHEZ TRACE(1960); SINISTER URGE, THE(1961)
Misc. Talkies
TEXAS RENEGADES(1940); OUTLAW QUEEN(1957)
Kenneth Duncan
CROSS MY HEART(1937, Brit.); LAST CURTAIN, THE(1937, Brit.); MAKE-UP(1937, Brit.); CHEYENNE KID, THE(1940); EMERGENCY SQUAD(1940); ISLE OF MISSING MEN(1942); AVENGING RIDER, THE(1943); DAVY CROCKETT, INDIAN SCOUT(1950)
Misc. Talkies
UNDERCOVER MEN(1935)
Kenneth [Kenne] Duncan
ROLL, WAGONS, ROLL(1939)
Kenny Duncan
ARIZONA GANGBUSTERS(1940)
Kirk Duncan
PSYCHO A GO-GO!(1965); SECONDS(1966)
Lanny Duncan
SEED OF INNOCENCE(1980); HOSPITAL MASSACRE(1982)
1984
HOSPITAL MASSACRE(1984)
Lee Duncan
HOLLYWOOD CAVALCADE(1939); HIT(1973); MACK, THE(1973)
Lindsay Duncan
1984
LOOSE CONNECTIONS(1984, Brit.)
Lola Duncan
SELF-MADE LADY(1932, Brit.); ONCE A THIEF(1935, Brit.); BONNIE PRINCE CHARLIE(1948, Brit.)
Malcolm Duncan
Silents
SPENDTHRIFT, THE(1915); SCARLET ROAD, THE(1916)
Misc. Silents
WILD OATS(1916)
Margaret Duncan
FLAME IN THE HEATHER(1935, Brit.)
Margie Duncan
HOW SWEET IT IS(1968); SINGLE ROOM FURNISHED(1968)
Martin Duncan
1984
FOREVER YOUNG(1984, Brit.)
Mary David Duncan
JAWS 3-D(1983)
Mary Davis Duncan
1984
INITIATION, THE(1984)
Mary Duncan
RIVER, THE(1928); FOUR DEVILS(1929); ROMANCE OF THE RIO GRANDE(1929); THRU DIFFERENT EYES(1929); BOUDOIR DIPLOMAT(1930); CITY GIRL(1930); KISMET(1930); AGE FOR LOVE, THE(1931); FIVE AND TEN(1931); MEN CALL IT LOVE(1931); PHANTOM OF CRESTWOOD, THE(1932); THIRTEEN WOMEN(1932); MORNING GLORY(1933)
Misc. Silents
VERY CONFIDENTIAL(1927); SOFT LIVING(1928)
Norman Duncan
Silents
MEASURE OF A MAN, THE(1916), w; MEASURE OF A MAN, THE(1924), w
Pamela Duncan
WHISTLING HILLS(1951); CONFIDENCE GIRL(1952); LAWLESS COWBOYS(1952); DRAGONFLY SQUADRON(1953); SARACEN BLADE, THE(1954); JULIE(1956); SEVEN MEN FROM NOW(1956); ATTACK OF THE CRAB MONSTERS(1957); GUN BATTLE AT MONTEREY(1957); MY GUN IS QUICK(1957); UNDEAD, THE(1957); SUMMER AND SMOKE(1961)
Patrick Duncan
BEACH GIRLS(1982), w
Paul Duncan
1984
STRANGERS KISS(1984)
Peter Duncan
STARDUST(1974, Brit.); MR. QUILP(1975, Brit.); FLASH GORDON(1980)
Phil Duncan
MAKE MINE MUSIC(1946), anim; FUN AND FANCY FREE(1947), anim; 1001 ARABIAN NIGHTS(1959), anim; GAY PURR-EE(1962), anim
Philip Duncan
WATERSHIP DOWN(1978, Brit.), anim
Renault Duncan
DON RICARDO RETURNS(1946), w; BELLS OF SAN FERNANDO(1947), w; HIGHWAYMAN, THE(1951), w
Renee Duncan
VERY CURIOUS GIRL, A(1970, Fr.); CHARLES AND LUCIE(1982, Fr.)

Rita Duncan
INVISIBLE WALL, THE(1947); TRUE STORY OF LYNN STUART, THE(1958); STUDS LONIGAN(1960)

Robert Duncan
ONE OF OUR AIRCRAFT IS MISSING(1942, Brit.); RASPUTIN–THE MAD MONK(1966, Brit.); UNCLE, THE(1966, Brit.); EYE OF THE DEVIL(1967, Brit.)

Ronald Duncan
GIRL ON A MOTORCYCLE, THE(1968, Fr./Brit.), w

Rosetta Duncan
IT'S A GREAT LIFE(1930)
Misc. Silents
TOPSY AND EVA(1927)

Sam Duncan
WHITE HUNTER(1936), w; SUEZ(1938), w; TRAGEDY AT MIDNIGHT, A(1942), w; CIRCUMSTANTIAL EVIDENCE(1945), w

Sam G. Duncan
WHITE FANG(1936), w

Sandy Duncan
STAR SPANGLED GIRL(1971); $1,000,000 DUCK(1971); CAT FROM OUTER SPACE, THE(1978); FOX AND THE HOUND, THE(1981)

Slim Duncan
BLAZING TRAIL, THE(1949); FRONTIER OUTPOST(1950); TEXAS DYNAMO(1950); BONANZA TOWN(1951); DESPERADOES OUTPOST(1952); SOUTH PACIFIC TRAIL(1952); LADY WANTS MINK, THE(1953)

Capt. T. E. Duncan
Silents
TUMBLEWEEDS(1925)

Taylor Duncan
Silents
SUDS(1920); BELOW THE LINE(1925); RANSON'S FOLLY(1926); AIR PATROL, THE(1928)

Taylor E. Duncan
SOLDIER, THE(1982)

Ted Duncan
EASY TO WED(1946), md; LOVE BUG, THE(1968); WHAT'S UP, DOC?(1972); DANDY, THE ALL AMERICAN GIRL(1976), stunts; STUNTS(1977); METEOR(1979); NIGHT SCHOOL(1981), stunts; TERROR EYES(1981); SWAMP THING(1982), stunts

Todd Duncan
SYNCOPATION(1942); UNCHAINED(1955)

Tom Duncan
1984
STONE BOY, THE(1984)

Trevor Duncan
CASE OF THE RED MONKEY(1955, Brit.), m; FINGER OF GUILT(1956, Brit.), m; LONG HAUL, THE(1957, Brit.), m; SCOTLAND YARD DRAGNET(1957, Brit.), m

Victor Duncan
GREAT ST. LOUIS BANK ROBBERY, THE(1959), ph; SECOND FIDDLE TO A STEEL GUITAR(1965), d

Vivian Duncan
IT'S A GREAT LIFE(1930)
Misc. Silents
TOPSY AND EVA(1927)

Wanda Duncan
BLACK GOLD(1963), w

William Duncan
RANGE LAW(1931); NEVADA(1936); THREE ON THE TRAIL(1936); FORLORN RIVER(1937); HOPALONG RIDES AGAIN(1937); THUNDER TRAIL(1937); FRONTIERSMAN, THE(1938); LAW OF THE PAMPAS(1939); FARMER'S DAUGHTER, THE(1940); QUEEN OF THE MOB(1940); TEXAS RANGERS RIDE AGAIN(1940)
Silents
ALADDIN FROM BROADWAY(1917); MONEY MAGIC(1917); STEELHEART(1921), a, d; WHERE MEN ARE MEN(1921), a, d; SILENT VOW, THE(1922), a, d; PLAYING IT WILD(1923), a, d
Misc. Silents
CHALICE OF COURAGE, THE(1915); GOD'S COUNTRY AND THE WOMAN(1916); LAST MAN, THE(1916); THROUGH THE WALL(1916); DEAD-SHOT BAKER(1917), a, d; TENDERFOOT, THE(1917), a, d; NO DEFENSE(1921), a, d; FIGHTING GUIDE, THE(1922), a, d; WHEN DANGER SMILES(1922), a, d; SMASHING BARRIERS(1923), a, d

Duncan Sisters
Silents
TWO FLAMING YOUTHS(1927)

David Dundas
PRUDENCE AND THE PILL(1968, Brit.); MOSQUITO SQUADRON(1970, Brit.); PRIVATE ROAD(1971, Brit.), m

Jennie Dundas
1984
HOTEL NEW HAMPSHIRE, THE(1984); MRS. SOFFEL(1984)

Nick Dundas
TORTURE ME KISS ME(1970)
Misc. Talkies
BED OF VIOLENCE(1967)

Stella Dundas
ILLIAC PASSION, THE(1968)

James Dundea
WHERE THERE'S LIFE(1947)

James Dundee
DR. SOCRATES(1935); IT HAD TO HAPPEN(1936); NORTHWEST MOUNTED POLICE(1940); ANGEL ON MY SHOULDER(1946); SUDDENLY IT'S SPRING(1947); DARK CITY(1950)

Jim Dundee
STAR MAKER, THE(1939); WHERE DANGER LIVES(1950)

Jimmie Dundee
LADY BY CHOICE(1934); HIDEAWAY GIRL(1937); YOU AND ME(1938); EMERGENCY SQUAD(1940); LUCKY CISCO KID(1940); SULLIVAN'S TRAVELS(1941); GOING MY WAY(1944); HAIL THE CONQUERING HERO(1944); I LOVE A SOLDIER(1944); DUFFY'S TAVERN(1945); INCENDIARY BLONDE(1945); MEDAL FOR BENNY, A(1945); O.S.S.(1946); NIGHT HAS A THOUSAND EYES(1948); SAINTED SISTERS, THE(1948); WHISPERING SMITH(1948); RED, HOT AND BLUE!(1949); AT WAR WITH THE ARMY(1950); FANCY PANTS(1950); MY FRIEND IRMA GOES

WEST(1950); NO MAN OF HER OWN(1950); PAID IN FULL(1950); DARLING, HOW COULD YOU!(1951); MY FAVORITE SPY(1951); SAILOR BEWARE(1951); MY SON, JOHN(1952); SOMEBODY LOVES ME(1952); WAR OF THE WORLDS, THE(1953)

Jimmy Dundee
WEDDING PRESENT(1936); FLEET'S IN, THE(1942); HERE COME THE WAVES(1944); ROAD TO UTOPIA(1945); STORK CLUB, THE(1945); BLUE DAHLIA, THE(1946); MIGHTY MCGURK, THE(1946); FORCE OF EVIL(1948); SAIGON(1948); MY FRIEND IRMA(1949); SCENE OF THE CRIME(1949); MILKMAN, THE(1950); TWO TICKETS TO BROADWAY(1951)

Dave Dundon
ETERNAL SUMMER(1961); WILD HARVEST(1962)

Vuka Dundzerovic
BOY CRIED MURDER, THE(1966, Ger./Brit./Yugo.)

Justine Duney
MADAME CURIE(1943)

Susan Dunfee
TRUMAN CAPOTE'S TRILOGY(1969)

Andrew Dungan
GOODBYE PORK PIE(1981, New Zealand)

Charles Dungan
Silents
AS YE SOW(1914)
Misc. Silents
WHAT WILL PEOPLE SAY(1915); BEHIND THE MASK(1917); SILENCE SELLERS, THE(1917); T'OTHER DEAR CHARMER(1918)

John Dungan
Silents
MAN HUNT, THE(1918)

Sebastian Dungan
MAN, WOMAN AND CHILD(1983)

Tony Dungan
MISSION BATANGAS(1968)

Kymm Dungy
1984
FINDERS KEEPERS(1984)

Art Dunham
JUDGMENT AT NUREMBERG(1961), md

"By" Dunham
I'LL TAKE SWEDEN(1965), m; BOY, DID I GET A WRONG NUMBER!(1966), m

Duwayne Dunham
RETURN OF THE JEDI(1983), ed

George Dunham
SAND CASTLE, THE(1961)

Gladys Dunham
BIRDS OF A FEATHER(1931, Brit.); DANGEROUS SEAS(1931, Brit.)
Misc. Silents
RECKLESS GAMBLE, A(1928, Brit.)

Joanna Dunham
BREAKING POINT, THE(1961, Brit.); DANGEROUS AFTERNOON(1961, Brit.); GREAT ARMORED CAR SWINDLE, THE(1964); GREATEST STORY EVER TOLD, THE(1965); HOUSE THAT DRIPPED BLOOD, THE(1971, Brit.)

Katharine Dunham
GREEN MANSIONS(1959), ch

Katherine Dunham
PARDON MY SARONG(1942), ch; STAR SPANGLED RHYTHM(1942); CASBAH(1948); MAMBO(1955, Ital.), a, ch; BIBLE...IN THE BEGINNING, THE(1966), ch

Maud Dunham
GENTLE SEX, THE(1943, Brit.)

Maude Dunham
Misc. Silents
BEETLE, THE(1919, Brit.)

Maudie Dunham
Silents
ALL THE WINNERS(1920, Brit.); LAUGHTER AND TEARS(1921, Brit.); SHEER BLUFF(1921); WINNING GOAL, THE(1929, Brit.)
Misc. Silents
LADS OF THE VILLAGE, THE(1919, Brit.); LOVE IN THE WILDERNESS(1920, Brit.); NIGHT RIDERS, THE(1920, Brit.); TEMPORARY GENTLEMAN, A(1920, Brit.); UGLY DUCKLING, THE(1920, Brit.); LOVE MAGGY(1921, Brit.); MR. PIM PASSES BY(1921, Brit.); SINISTER STREET(1922, Brit.)

Phil Dunham
TOM BROWN OF CULVER(1932); FIGHTING PARSON, THE(1933); FUGITIVE, THE(1933); RAINBOW RANCH(1933), a, w; SATURDAY'S MILLIONS(1933); DOWN TO THEIR LAST YACHT(1934); JEALOUSY(1934); SEARCH FOR BEAUTY(1934); SIX OF A KIND(1934); POWDERSMOKE RANGE(1935); CASE AGAINST MRS. AMES, THE(1936); CAVALCADE OF THE WEST(1936); FEUD OF THE WEST(1936), w; ROMANCE RIDES THE RANGE(1936); STORMY TRAILS(1936), w; ACES WILD(1937); BANK ALARM(1937); GHOST TOWN(1937); IDAHO KID(1937); NAVY SPY(1937); SPECIAL AGENT K-7(1937), w; TRAILING TROUBLE(1937); DUKE IS THE TOPS, THE(1938), w; FURY BELOW(1938), a, w; LET US LIVE(1939); OUR LEADING CITIZEN(1939); $1,000 A TOUCHDOWN(1939); WEST OF PINTO BASIN(1940); WESTBOUND STAGE(1940); CODE OF THE OUTLAW(1942); DUFFY'S TAVERN(1945); SUDAN(1945); HOODLUM SAINT, THE(1946); TWO SMART PEOPLE(1946); UNDERCURRENT(1946); HIGH BARBAREE(1947); HIGH WALL, THE(1947); HOMECOMING(1948); MAN WITH A CLOAK, THE(1951)
Misc. Talkies
HAIR-TRIGGER CASEY(1936)
Silents
ROMANCE OF TARZAN, THE(1918)

Philip Dunham
SHE GETS HER MAN(1935); TWO-GUN TROUBADOR(1939), w

Phillip Dunham
Silents
TWO MINUTES TO GO(1921); ALIAS JULIUS CAESAR(1922)
Misc. Silents
DEUCE OF SPADES, THE(1922)

Robert Dunham
GREEN SLIME, THE(1969)

Ron Dunham
HAIR(1979)

Rosemarie Dunham
GET CARTER(1971, Brit.); SOMETHING TO HIDE(1972, Brit.); INCREDIBLE SARAH, THE(1976, Brit.)

Rosemary Dunham
Misc. Talkies
MISTRESS PAMELA(1974)

Claire Dunhamel
LA GUERRE EST FINIE(1967, Fr./Swed.)

Ford Dunhill
THIS EARTH IS MINE(1959); THIRTEEN FIGHTING MEN(1960); VIVA LAS VEGAS(1964)

John Dunhill
OH! WHAT A LOVELY WAR(1969, Brit.)

Steve Dunhill
DUEL IN THE SUN(1946); OUTLAW COUNTRY(1949); DALLAS(1950); ROCKY MOUNTAIN(1950)

John Dunigan
FIRM MAN, THE(1975, Aus.), p,d,&w

George Duning
YOU CAN'T RUN AWAY FROM IT(1956), m; 3:10 TO YUMA(1957), m; TOYS IN THE ATTIC(1963), m; EADIE WAS A LADY(1945), m; DOWN TO EARTH(1947), m; GUILT OF JANET AMES, THE(1947), m; JOHNNY O'CLOCK(1947), m; DARK PAST, THE(1948), m; GALLANT BLADE, THE(1948), m; MAN FROM COLORADO, THE(1948), m; RETURN OF OCTOBER, THE(1948), m; JOHNNY ALLEGRO(1949), m; JOLSON SINGS AGAIN(1949), m; LUST FOR GOLD(1949), m; SHOCKPROOF(1949), m; SLIGHTLY FRENCH(1949), m; UNDERCOVER MAN, THE(1949), m; BETWEEN MIDNIGHT AND DAWN(1950), m; CARGO TO CAPETOWN(1950), m; CONVICTED(1950), m; FLYING MISSILE(1950), m; HARRIET CRAIG(1950), m; NO SAD SONGS FOR ME(1950), m; BAREFOOT MAILMAN, THE(1951), m; FAMILY SECRET, THE(1951), m; LADY AND THE BANDIT, THE(1951), m; LORNA DOONE(1951), m; MOB, THE(1951), m; SUNNY SIDE OF THE STREET(1951), md; TWO OF A KIND(1951), m; AFFAIR IN TRINIDAD(1952), m; ASSIGNMENT-PARIS(1952), m; CAPTAIN PIRATE(1952), m; LAST OF THE COMANCHES(1952), m; PAULA(1952), m; RAINBOW 'ROUND MY SHOULDER(1952), md; SCANDAL SHEET(1952), m; SOUND OFF(1952), m; FROM HERE TO ETERNITY(1953), m; LET'S DO IT AGAIN(1953), m; MISS SADIE THOMPSON(1953), m; SALOME(1953), m; COUNT THREE AND PRAY(1955), m; FIVE AGAINST THE HOUSE(1955), m; MAN FROM LARAMIE, THE(1955), m; MY SISTER EILEEN(1955), m; PICNIC(1955), m; QUEEN BEE(1955), m; THREE FOR THE SHOW(1955), m; THREE STRIPES IN THE SUN(1955), m; TIGHT SPOT(1955), m; EDDY DUCHIN STORY, THE(1956), m; NIGHTFALL(1956), m; STORM CENTER(1956), m; BROTHERS RICO, THE(1957), m; JEANNE EAGELS(1957), m; OPERATION MAD BALL(1957), m; SHADOW ON THE WINDOW, THE(1957), m; BELL, BOOK AND CANDLE(1958), m; COWBOY(1958), m; GUNMAN'S WALK(1958), m; HOUSEBOAT(1958), m, md; ME AND THE COLONEL(1958), m; IT HAPPENED TO JANE(1959), m; LAST ANGRY MAN, THE(1959), m; WRECK OF THE MARY DEAR, THE(1959), m; 1001 ARABIAN NIGHTS(1959), m; ALL THE YOUNG MEN(1960), m; MAN ON A STRING(1960), m; STRANGERS WHEN WE MEET(1960), m; WORLD OF SUZIE WONG, THE(1960), m; CRY FOR HAPPY(1961), m; DEVIL AT FOUR O'CLOCK, THE(1961), m; GIDGET GOES HAWAIIAN(1961), m; SAIL A CROOKED SHIP(1961), m; TWO RODE TOGETHER(1961), m; WACKIEST SHIP IN THE ARMY, THE(1961), m; NOTORIOUS LANDLADY, THE(1962), m; THAT TOUCH OF MINK(1962), m; WHO'S GOT THE ACTION?(1962), m, md; CRITIC'S CHOICE(1963), m; ISLAND OF LOVE(1963), m; WHO'S BEEN SLEEPING IN MY BED?(1963), m; ENSIGN PULVER(1964), m; BRAINSTORM(1965), m; DEAR BRIGETTE(1965), m; MY BLOOD RUNS COLD(1965), m; ANY WEDNESDAY(1966), m; ARNOLD(1973), m; TERROR IN THE WAX MUSEUM(1973), m; MAN WITH BOGART'S FACE, THE(1980), m

Albert Dunk
CLASS OF 1984(1982, Can.), ph

Albert J. Dunk
INCUBUS, THE(1982, Can.), ph

Bert Dunk
KLONDIKE FEVER(1980), ph
1984
HIGHPOINT(1984, Can.), ph

John A. Dunkel
TIGER WOMAN, THE(1945), w

Yvonne Dunkerley
INTERNES CAN'T TAKE MONEY(1937)

Claude Dunkin
AT SWORD'S POINT(1951); GREATEST SHOW ON EARTH, THE(1952); OPERATION SECRET(1952); RED PLANET MARS(1952)

William Dunkin
BAR 20 JUSTICE(1938)

Harry Dunkinson
TILLIE AND GUS(1933); FEROCIOUS PAL(1934); STAND UP AND CHEER(1934 80m FOX bw); GEORGE WHITE'S 1935 SCANDALS(1935); LIFE BEGINS AT 40(1935); NEVADA(1936)
Silents
SLIM PRINCESS, THE(1915); SKINNER'S DRESS SUIT(1917); BLUSHING BRIDE, THE(1921); LAST TRAIL(1921); GENTLE JULIA(1923); STING OF THE SCORPION, THE(1923); LASH OF THE WHIP(1924); DESERT'S PRICE, THE(1926); DOUBLING WITH DANGER(1926); SILVER VALLEY(1927); SMILE, BROTHER, SMILE(1927)
Misc. Silents
BLINDNESS OF VIRTUE, THE(1915); SELFISH YATES(1918); SOUL FOR SALE, A(1918); CHASING RAINBOWS(1919); FORBIDDEN ROOM, THE(1919); BEWARE OF THE BRIDE(1920); HUSBAND HUNTER, THE(1920); MOLLY AND I(1920); OFFICER 666(1920); WILLOW TREE, THE(1920); BIG TOWN ROUND-UP(1921); PRIMAL LAW, THE(1921); WHY TRUST YOUR HUSBAND?(1921); MULHALL'S GREAT CATCH(1926)

Doretta Dunkler
FLASH GORDON(1980)

Dorothy Dunkley
SQUATTER'S DAUGHTER(1933, Aus.)

Harry Dunkminson
DESIGN FOR LIVING(1933)

Al Dunlap
MADIGAN(1968); DIRTY HARRY(1971); POINT OF TERROR(1971); CHARLEY VARRICK(1973); SLITHER(1973); ESCAPE TO WITCH MOUNTAIN(1975); RATTLERS(1976); TELEFON(1977)

Kenne Duncan, Jr.
CODE OF THE SADDLE(1947)

Charles Dunlap
CRUISING(1980)

Dawn Dunlap
FORBIDDEN WORLD(1982); NIGHT SHIFT(1982); HEARTBREAKER(1983)

Jack Dunlap
PURSUIT OF D.B. COOPER, THE(1981)
1984
FLESHBURN(1984)

Louise Dunlap
Silents
TESS OF THE STORM COUNTRY(1914)

Pamela Dunlap
BLOODY MAMA(1970)

Paul Dunlap
BARON OF ARIZONA, THE(1950), m; HI-JACKED(1950), m; CRY DANGER(1951), m; JOURNEY INTO LIGHT(1951), m; LITTLE BIG HORN(1951), m; LOST CONTINENT(1951), m; STEEL HELMET, THE(1951), m; HELLGATE(1952), m; PARK ROW(1952), m; SAN FRANCISCO STORY, THE(1952), m; COMBAT SQUAD(1953), m; DRAGONFLY SQUADRON(1953), m; FORT VENGEANCE(1953), m; JACK SLADE(1953), m, md; ROYAL AFRICAN RIFLES, THE(1953), m; CRY VENGEANCE(1954), m; DUFFY OF SAN QUENTIN(1954), m; FANGS OF THE WILD(1954), m; LOOPHOLE(1954), m; SHIELD FOR MURDER(1954), m; BIG HOUSE, U.S.A.(1955), m; BLACK TUESDAY(1955), m; DESERT SANDS(1955), m, md; FINGER MAN(1955), m; FORT YUMA(1955), m; RETURN OF JACK SLADE, THE(1955), m; ROBBER'S ROOST(1955), m; SHACK OUT ON 101(1955), m; STRANGER ON HORSEBACK(1955), m; BRASS LEGEND, THE(1956), m; BROKEN STAR, THE(1956), m; COME ON, THE(1956), m; CRIME AGAINST JOE(1956), m; CRUEL TOWER, THE(1956), m; DANCE WITH ME, HENRY(1956), m; EMERGENCY HOSPITAL(1956), m; GHOST TOWN(1956), m; LAST OF THE DESPERADOS(1956), m; MAGNIFICENT ROUGHNECKS(1956), m, md; STAGECOACH TO FURY(1956), m; STRANGE INTRUDER(1956), m, md; THREE BAD SISTERS(1956), m, md; WALK THE DARK STREET(1956), m, m; APACHE WARRIOR(1957), m; BLOOD OF DRACULA(1957), m; CRIME OF PASSION(1957), m; DRAGON WELLS MASSACRE(1957), m; GOD IS MY PARTNER(1957), m&md; I WAS A TEENAGE WEREWOLF(1957), m; LURE OF THE SWAMP(1957), m; PORTLAND EXPOSE(1957), m, md; QUIET GUN, THE(1957), m; ROCKABILLY BABY(1957), m, md; UNDER FIRE(1957), m; WOMEN OF PITCAIRN ISLAND, THE(1957), m; YOUNG AND DANGEROUS(1957), m&md; FRANKENSTEIN 1970(1958), m, set d; FRONTIER GUN(1958), m; GANG WAR(1958), m, md; GUN FEVER(1958), m; HOW TO MAKE A MONSTER(1958), m; I WAS A TEENAGE FRANKENSTEIN(1958), m, md; OREGON PASSAGE(1958), m; TOUGHEST GUN IN TOMBSTONE(1958), m; WOLF LARSEN(1958), m; ANGRY RED PLANET, THE(1959), m; FIVE GATES TO HELL(1959), m; FOUR SKULLS OF JONATHAN DRAKE, THE(1959), m; HERE COME THE JETS(1959), m; LONE TEXAN(1959), m; OREGON TRAIL, THE(1959), m; REBEL SET, THE(1959), m; ROOKIE, THE(1959), m; CROWNING EXPERIENCE, THE(1960), md; DESIRE IN THE DUST(1960), m; GUNFIGHTERS OF ABILENE(1960), m; PURPLE GANG, THE(1960), m; TWELVE HOURS TO KILL(1960), m; WALK LIKE A DRAGON(1960), m; SEVEN WOMEN FROM HELL(1961), m; THREE STOOGES IN ORBIT, THE(1962), m; THREE STOOGES MEET HERCULES, THE(1962), m; BLACK ZOO(1963), m; SHOCK CORRIDOR(1963), m; THREE STOOGES GO AROUND THE WORLD IN A DAZE, THE(1963), m; NAKED KISS, THE(1964), m; STAGE TO THUNDER ROCK(1964), m; OPERATION CIA(1965), m; OUTLAWS IS COMING, THE(1965), m; YOUNG FURY(1965), m; CYBORG 2087(1966), m; DESTINATION INNER SPACE(1966), m; DIMENSION 5(1966), m; CASTLE OF EVIL(1967), m; DESTRUCTORS, THE(1968), m; MONEY JUNGLE, THE(1968), m; PANIC IN THE CITY(1968), m; SMITHEREENS(1982)

Robert Dunlap
COVENANT WITH DEATH, A(1966); THEY SHOOT HORSES, DON'T THEY?(1969)

Scott Dunlap
DRIFTING WESTWARD(1939), p
Silents
HER ELEPHANT MAN(1920), d; CHEATER REFORMED, THE(1921), d, w; PAWN TICKET 210(1922), d; WEST OF CHICAGO(1922), d; SKID PROOF(1923), d; BLUE BLOOD(1925), d; FEARLESS LOVER, THE(1925), w; SMOKE BELLEW(1929), d
Misc. Silents
BLUEBEARD, JR.(, d; BE A LITTLE SPORT(1919), d; LOST PRINCESS, THE(1919), d; LOVE IS LOVE(1919), d; VAGABOND LUCK(1919), d; WORDS AND MUSIC BY...(1919), d; CHALLENGE OF THE LAW, THE(1920), d; FORBIDDEN TRAILS(1920), d; HELL SHIP, THE(1920), d; IRON RIDER, THE(1920), d; TWINS OF SUFFERING CREEK(1920), d; WOULD YOU FORGIVE?(1920), d; TOO MUCH MARRIED(1921), d; BELLS OF SAN JUAN(1922), d; TROOPER O'NEIL(1922), d; WESTERN SPEED(1922), d; BOSTON BLACKIE(1923), d; FOOTLIGHT RANGER, THE(1923), d; SNOWDRIFT(1923), d; FATAL MISTAKE, THE(1924), d; ONE GLORIOUS NIGHT(1924), d; TRAFFIC IN HEARTS(1924), d; WINNING THE FUTURITY(1926), d; GOOD AS GOLD(1927), d

Scott E. Dunlap
Silents
MIDNIGHT LIFE(1928), ed

Scott R. Dunlap
ONE STOLEN NIGHT(1929), d; LUCK OF ROARING CAMP, THE(1937), p; MARINES ARE HERE, THE(1938), p; MR. WONG, DETECTIVE(1938), p; IRISH LUCK(1939), p; MR. WONG IN CHINATOWN(1939), p; MYSTERY OF MR. WONG, THE(1939), p; TOUGH KID(1939), p; APE, THE(1940), p; QUEEN OF THE YUKON(1940), p; ARIZONA BOUND(1941), p; FORBIDDEN TRAILS(1941), p; GUN MAN FROM BODIE, THE(1941), p; OLD SWIMMIN' HOLE, THE(1941), p; ROAR OF THE PRESS(1941), p; BELOW THE BORDER(1942), p; DAWN ON THE GREAT DIVIDE(1942), p; DOWN TEXAS WAY(1942), p; GHOST TOWN LAW(1942), p; RIDERS OF THE WEST(1942), p; ROAD TO HAPPINESS(1942), p; WEST OF THE LAW(1942), p; OUTLAWS OF STAMPEDE PASS(1943), p; SIX GUN GOSPEL(1943), p; STRANGER FROM PECOS, THE(1943), p; LADY, LET'S DANCE(1944), p, w; OH, WHAT A NIGHT(1944), p; PARTNERS OF THE TRAIL(1944), p; RAIDERS OF THE BORDER(1944), p; TEXAS KID, THE(1944), p; FLAME OF THE WEST(1945), p;

SUNBONNET SUE(1945), p; BEAUTY AND THE BANDIT(1946), p; BORDER BANDITS(1946), p; DRIFTING ALONG(1946), p; GENTLEMAN FROM TEXAS(1946), p; UNDER ARIZONA SKIES(1946), p; RAIDERS OF THE SOUTH(1947), p; HUNTED, THE(1948), p; STAMPEDE(1949), p; SHORT GRASS(1950), p; COW COUNTRY(1953), p; RETURN FROM THE SEA(1954), p; JOHNNY ROCCO(1958), p; MAN FROM GOD'S COUNTRY(1958), p
Silents
DOUBLING WITH DANGER(1926), d; MIDNIGHT LIFE(1928), d; OBJECT–ALIMONY(1929), d
Misc. Silents
BEYOND THE BORDER(1925), d; SILENT SANDERSON(1925), d; TEXAS TRAIL, THE(1925), d; WRECKAGE(1925), d; BETTER MAN, THE(1926), d; DESERT VALLEY(1926), d; DRIFTIN' THRU(1926), d; FRONTIER TRAIL, THE(1926), d; SEVENTH BANDIT, THE(1926), d; WHISPERING SAGE(1927), d

Vic Dunlap
1984
NIGHT PATROL(1984)
Victor Dunlap
JUD(1971)
Paul Dunlay
BREAKDOWN(1953), m
James Dunleavy
WAY OUT(1966)
Terry Dunleavy
RETURN TO PARADISE(1953)
Yvonne Dunleavy
HAPPY HOOKER, THE(1975), w
Jim Dunlevy
HOT MONEY GIRL(1962, Brit./Ger.), cos
James Dunlin
WINGS OVER AFRICA(1939), ph
Charles Dunlop
IMPROPER CHANNELS(1981, Can.), art d
1984
SURROGATE, THE(1984, Can.), art d
Dave Dunlop
YOUNG FURY(1965)
Ewart Dunlop
MUSIC MAN, THE(1962)
Frank Dunlop
NIGHT COMES TOO SOON(1948, Brit.); THREE WEIRD SISTERS, THE(1948, Brit.); LAST DAYS OF DOLWYN, THE(1949, Brit.); WINTER'S TALE, THE(1968, Brit.), d
G. Thomas Dunlop
JAWS II(1978)
Jack Dunlop
FREE, WHITE AND 21(1963)
Lesley Dunlop
LITTLE NIGHT MUSIC, A(1977, Aust./U.S./Ger.); ELEPHANT MAN, THE(1980, Brit.); MONSTER CLUB, THE(1981, Brit.)
Marissa Dunlop
1984
SECRET PLACES(1984, Brit.)
Peter Dunlop
MADNESS OF THE HEART(1949, Brit.); RELUCTANT WIDOW, THE(1951, Brit.); WILD HEART, THE(1952, Brit.)
Scott Dunlop
1984
LAST STARFIGHTER, THE(1984)
Sian Dunlop
1984
SECRET PLACES(1984, Brit.)
Van Dunlop
SPOTS ON MY LEOPARD, THE(1974, S. Africa)
Vic Dunlop
SKATETOWN, U.S.A.(1979); DEVIL AND MAX DEVLIN, THE(1981); LUNCH WAGON(1981)
1984
MEATBALLS PART II(1984)
Beatrice Dunmore
WIZ, THE(1978)
James Dunmore
HI-DE-HO(1947)
Louis Dunmyre
Silents
CHILD FOR SALE, A(1920), ph; MAN FROM BEYOND, THE(1922), ph; CLOTHES MAKE THE PIRATE(1925), ph
Alla Dunn
EXILE, THE(1947)
Benny Dunn
MICKEY ONE(1965)
Bill Dunn
NOTHING SACRED(1937)
Billy Dunn
BABES ON SWING STREET(1944); NIGHT CLUB GIRL(1944)
Bobbie Dunn
RACKETEER, THE(1929); PARADE OF THE WEST(1930)
Misc. Silents
PARTING OF THE TRAILS(1930)
Bobby Dunn
WAGON MASTER, THE(1929); CANYON HAWKS(1930); CANYON OF MISSING MEN, THE(1930); TRAILS OF DANGER(1930); PARDON US(1931); LAST RIDE, THE(1932); MILLION DOLLAR LEGS(1932); BOWERY, THE(1933); TERROR ABOARD(1933); WHEELS OF DESTINY(1934); ONE MORE SPRING(1935); OUR RELATIONS(1936); SLAVE SHIP(1937); WAY OUT WEST(1937)
Silents
WHEN THE WIFE'S AWAY(1926); SPEEDY(1928); ROYAL RIDER, THE(1929)
Misc. Silents
CODE OF THE WEST(1929); RIDERS OF THE STORM(1929)

Bridgett Dunn
PHANTOM OF THE PARADISE(1974)
Cal Dunn
DESERT RAVEN, THE(1965), p
Cara Dunn
GREASED LIGHTNING(1977)
Cathy Dunn
LOVERS AND LOLLIPOPS(1956)
Charles Dunn
Misc. Silents
HAPPINESS(1917)
Clara Dunn
PAYDAY(1972)
Clive Dunn
WHAT A WHOPPER(1961, Brit.); HOT MONEY GIRL(1962, Brit./Ger.); FAST LADY, THE(1963, Brit.); MAID FOR MURDER(1963, Brit.); MOUSE ON THE MOON, THE(1963, Brit.); YOU MUST BE JOKING!(1965, Brit.); JUST LIKE A WOMAN(1967, Brit.); MINI-AFFAIR, THE(1968, Brit.); 30 IS A DANGEROUS AGE, CYNTHIA(1968, Brit.); MAGIC CHRISTIAN, THE(1970, Brit.); SOPHIE'S PLACE(1970); DAD'S ARMY(1971, Brit.); FIENDISH PLOT OF DR. FU MANCHU, THE(1980)
Conrad Dunn
STRIPES(1981)
David Dunn
CHEER THE BRAVE(1951, Brit.)
Donald "Duck" Dunn
BLUES BROTHERS, THE(1980)
Dorothy Dunn
MY FAVORITE SPY(1942)
Eddie Dunn
SATURDAY NIGHT KID, THE(1929); HEADIN' NORTH(1930); TRUE TO THE NAVY(1930); GANG BUSTER, THE(1931); PARDON US(1931); RIDERS OF THE NORTH(1931); SUNRISE TRAIL(1931); MILLION DOLLAR LEGS(1932); SOUTH OF SANTA FE(1932); WHAT PRICE HOLLYWOOD?(1932); PRIVATE DETECTIVE 62(1933); ANNIE OAKLEY(1935); CAR 99(1935); G-MEN(1935); GILDED LILY, THE(1935); POWDERSMOKE RANGE(1935); RUMBA(1935); STOLEN HARMONY(1935); BRIDE COMES HOME(1936); BRIDE WALKS OUT, THE(1936); GO WEST, YOUNG MAN(1936); HOLLYWOOD BOULEVARD(1936); MILKY WAY, THE(1936); MURDER WITH PICTURES(1936); PREVIEW MURDER MYSTERY(1936); PRINCESS COMES ACROSS, THE(1936); CHINA PASSAGE(1937); INTERNES CAN'T TAKE MONEY(1937); MARRIED BEFORE BREAKFAST(1937); SLAVE SHIP(1937); THERE'S ALWAYS A WOMAN(1938); CAFE SOCIETY(1939); DAY THE BOOKIES WEPT, THE(1939); FRONTIER MARSHAL(1939); I STOLE A MILLION(1939); LET FREEDOM RING(1939); OF MICE AND MEN(1939); YOU CAN'T CHEAT AN HONEST MAN(1939); BANK DICK, THE(1940); GREAT DICTATOR, THE(1940); GREAT PROFILE, THE(1940); MEN AGAINST THE SKY(1940); MEXICAN SPITFIRE OUT WEST(1940); ONE NIGHT IN THE TROPICS(1940); BILLY THE KID(1941); DATE WITH THE FALCON, A(1941); DESIGN FOR SCANDAL(1941); FOUR JACKS AND A JILL(1941); GAY FALCON, THE(1941); IN THE NAVY(1941); PARACHUTE BATTALION(1941); SAINT IN PALM SPRINGS, THE(1941); FALCON'S BROTHER, THE(1942); I WAKE UP SCREAMING(1942); INVISIBLE AGENT(1942); LADY IN A JAM(1942); MEXICAN SPITFIRE AT SEA(1942); MISSISSIPPI GAMBLER(1942); NIGHT TO REMEMBER, A(1942); RIDE 'EM COWBOY(1942); DIXIE DUGAN(1943); FALCON IN DANGER, THE(1943); HELLO, FRISCO, HELLO(1943); HERS TO HOLD(1943); HIT THE ICE(1943); LET'S FACE IT(1943); MARGIN FOR ERROR(1943); NEVER A DULL MOMENT(1943); SHE HAS WHAT IT TAKES(1943); SO'S YOUR UNCLE(1943); STRANGER IN TOWN, A(1943); ARMY WIVES(1944); COVER GIRL(1944); DEAD MAN'S EYES(1944); GREENWICH VILLAGE(1944); GYPSY WILDCAT(1944); HAT CHECK HONEY(1944); HENRY ALDRICH'S LITTLE SECRET(1944); I LOVE A SOLDIER(1944); LOST IN A HAREM(1944); MOON OVER LAS VEGAS(1944); NIGHT CLUB GIRL(1944); NOTHING BUT TROUBLE(1944); STANDING ROOM ONLY(1944); WEEKEND PASS(1944); DANGEROUS PARTNERS(1945); FRONTIER GAL(1945); LADY ON A TRAIN(1945); PATRICK THE GREAT(1945); SALOME, WHERE SHE DANCED(1945); TWO O'CLOCK COURAGE(1945); WONDER MAN(1945); ZIEGFELD FOLLIES(1945); BOWERY BOMBSHELL(1946); CENTENNIAL SUMMER(1946); CLOAK AND DAGGER(1946); DARK HORSE, THE(1946); HOODLUM SAINT, THE(1946); LADY LUCK(1946); DEEP VALLEY(1947); I WONDER WHO'S KISSING HER NOW(1947); SLAVE GIRL(1947); BIG PUNCH, THE(1948); CALL NORTHSIDE 777(1948); CHECKERED COAT, THE(1948); FLAME, THE(1948); HOLLOW TRIUMPH(1948); HOMICIDE FOR THREE(1948); INCIDENT(1948); LIGHTNIN' IN THE FOREST(1948); I SHOT JESSE JAMES(1949); MOTHER IS A FRESHMAN(1949); WHIRLPOOL(1949); LONELY HEARTS BANDITS(1950); SECRET FURY, THE(1950); SUMMER STOCK(1950)
Misc. Silents
BLOOD BARRIER, THE(1920)
Eddy Dunn
HIGH WALL, THE(1947)
Edward Dunn
LAND OF MISSING MEN, THE(1930); RASCALS(1938); BOSTON BLACKIE AND THE LAW(1946)
Edward "Eddie" Dunn
TEN GENTLEMEN FROM WEST POINT(1942)
Edward F. Dunn
PHANTOM THIEF, THE(1946); MARY RYAN, DETECTIVE(1949)
Eileen Dunn
DON'T GO IN THE HOUSE(1980)
Elizabeth Dunn
MEET THE STEWARTS(1942), w
Emma Dunn
SIDE STREET(1929); MANSLAUGHTER(1930); TEXAN, THE(1930); BAD COMPANY(1931); BAD SISTER(1931); COMPROMISED(1931); MORALS FOR WOMEN(1931); PRODIGAL, THE(1931); THIS MODERN AGE(1931); TOO YOUNG TO MARRY(1931); BROKEN LULLABY(1932); COHENS, AND KELLYS IN HOLLYWOOD, THE(1932); HELL'S HOUSE(1932); IT'S TOUGH TO BE FAMOUS(1932); LETTY LYNTON(1932); UNDER EIGHTEEN(1932); WET PARADE, THE(1932); ELMER THE GREAT(1933); GRAND SLAM(1933); HARD TO HANDLE(1933); IT'S GREAT TO BE ALIVE(1933); MAN OF SENTIMENT, A(1933); PRIVATE JONES(1933); DARK HAZARD(1934); DOCTOR MONICA(1934); QUITTERS, THE(1934); ANOTHER FACE(1935); CRUSADES, THE(1935); GEORGE WHITE'S 1935 SCANDALS(1935); GLASS KEY, THE(1935); KEEPER OF THE BEES(1935); LADIES CRAVE EXCITEMENT(1935); LITTLE BIG SHOT(1935); SEVEN KEYS TO BALDPATE(1935); THIS IS THE LI-

FE(1935); HARVESTER, THE(1936); MR. DEEDS GOES TO TOWN(1936); PIGSKIN PARADE(1936); SECOND WIFE(1936); CIRCUS GIRL(1937); EMPEROR'S CANDLESTICKS, THE(1937); HIDEAWAY(1937); MADAME X(1937); VARSITY SHOW(1937); WAIKIKI WEDDING(1937); WHEN YOU'RE IN LOVE(1937); COWBOY AND THE LADY, THE(1938); COWBOY FROM BROOKLYN(1938); DUKE OF WEST POINT, THE(1938); LORD JEFF(1938); THANKS FOR THE MEMORY(1938); THREE LOVES HAS NANCY(1938); YOUNG DR. KILDARE(1938); CALLING DR. KILDARE(1939); EACH DAWN I DIE(1939); HERO FOR A DAY(1939); SECRET OF DR. KILDARE, THE(1939); SON OF FRANKENSTEIN(1939); DANCE, GIRL, DANCE(1940); DR. KILDARE GOES HOME(1940); DR. KILDARE'S CRISIS(1940); DR. KILDARE'S STRANGE CASE(1940); GREAT DICTATOR, THE(1940); HALF A SINNER(1940); HIGH SCHOOL(1940); LITTLE ORVIE(1940); LLANO KID, THE(1940); ONE CROWDED NIGHT(1940); YESTERDAY'S HEROES(1940); YOU CAN'T FOOL YOUR WIFE(1940); BABES ON BROADWAY(1941); DR. KILDARE'S WEDDING DAY(1941); LADIES IN RETIREMENT(1941); MONSTER AND THE GIRL, THE(1941); MR. AND MRS. SMITH(1941); PENALTY, THE(1941); RISE AND SHINE(1941); SCATTERGOOD BAINES(1941); SCATTERGOOD MEETS BROADWAY(1941); SCATTERGOOD PULLS THE STRINGS(1941); I MARRIED A WITCH(1942); MAD MARTINDALES, THE(1942); POSTMAN DIDN'T RING, THE(1942); TALK OF THE TOWN(1942); HOOSIER HOLIDAY(1943); MINESWEEPER(1943); NORTH STAR, THE(1943); WHEN JOHNNY COMES MARCHING HOME(1943); ARE THESE OUR PARENTS?(1944); BRIDGE OF SAN LUIS REY, THE(1944); IT HAPPENED TOMORROW(1944); MY BUDDY(1944); HORN BLOWS AT MIDNIGHT, THE(1945); HOODLUM SAINT, THE(1946); NIGHT TRAIN TO MEMPHIS(1946); LIFE WITH FATHER(1947); MOURNING BECOMES ELECTRA(1947); WOMAN IN WHITE, THE(1948)

Misc. Talkies
BROKEN DISHES(1930)
Silents
MOTHER(1914)
Misc. Silents
OLD LADY 31(1920); PIED PIPER MALONE(1924)

Frank Dunn
TREASURE ISLAND(1934); MAN WHO BROKE THE BANK AT MONTE CARLO, THE(1935); IT ISN'T DONE(1937, Aus.)

Frank G. Dunn
BOLERO(1934); ENTER MADAME(1935)

Geoffrey Dunn
POET'S PUB(1949, Brit.); WHILE THE SUN SHINES(1950, Brit.); QUO VADIS(1951); GHOST SHIP(1953, Brit.); I AM A CAMERA(1955, Brit.); DOOMSDAY AT ELEVEN(1963 Brit.); SWORD OF LANCELOT(1963, Brit.); FATHER CAME TOO(1964, Brit.); LEATHER BOYS, THE(1965, Brit.)

George Dunn
HOW TO MARRY A MILLIONAIRE(1953); DADDY LONG LEGS(1955); GOOD MORNING, MISS DOVE(1955); PRINCE OF PLAYERS(1955); JOE DAKOTA(1957); KETTLES ON OLD MACDONALD'S FARM, THE(1957); LONG, HOT SUMMER, THE(1958); OPERATION PETTICOAT(1959); SILENT WITNESS, THE(1962); BABY, THE RAIN MUST FALL(1965)

Harvey B. Dunn
KETTLES ON OLD MACDONALD'S FARM, THE(1957); REMARKABLE MR. PENNYPACKER, THE(1959); TEENAGERS FROM OUTER SPACE(1959)

Harvey Dunn
VENGEANCE VALLEY(1951); DRAGON'S GOLD(1954); SABRINA(1954); BRIDE OF THE MONSTER(1955); I KILLED WILD BILL HICKOK(1956); MY FAIR LADY(1964)

Hurschel G. Dunn
INDEPENDENCE DAY(1983)

J. Allen Dunn
Silents
NO MAN'S GOLD(1926), w

J. Malcolm Dunn
SAP FROM SYRACUSE, THE(1930)
Silents
DR. JEKYLL AND MR. HYDE(1920)

J. Malcom Dunn
Silents
ARMS AND THE GIRL(1917)

J. Norton Dunn
MARGIN FOR ERROR(1943)

Jack Dunn
Silents
GREAT ADVENTURE, THE(1918)

James Dunn
BAD GIRL(1931); OVER THE HILL(1931); SOB SISTER(1931); DANCE TEAM(1932); HANDLE WITH CARE(1932); SOCIETY GIRL(1932); ARIZONA TO BROADWAY(1933); GIRL IN 419(1933); HELLO SISTER!(1933); HOLD ME TIGHT(1933); JIMMY AND SALLY(1933); SAILOR'S LUCK(1933); TAKE A CHANCE(1933); BABY, TAKE A BOW(1934); BRIGHT EYES(1934); CHANGE OF HEART(1934); HAVE A HEART(1934); HOLD THAT GIRL(1934); STAND UP AND CHEER(1934 80m FOX bw); 365 NIGHTS IN HOLLYWOOD(1934); BAD BOY(1935); DARING YOUNG MAN, THE(1935); GEORGE WHITE'S 1935 SCANDALS(1935); PAYOFF, THE(1935); WELCOME HOME(1935); COME CLOSER, FOLKS(1936); DON'T GET PERSONAL(1936); HEARTS IN BONDAGE(1936); TWO-FISTED GENTLEMAN(1936); LIVING ON LOVE(1937); MYSTERIOUS CROSSING(1937); VENUS MAKES TROUBLE(1937); WE HAVE OUR MOMENTS(1937); SHADOWS OVER SHANGHAI(1938); PRIDE OF THE NAVY(1939); HOLD THAT WOMAN(1940); MERCY PLANE(1940); SON OF THE NAVY(1940); LIVING GHOST, THE(1942); GHOST AND THE GUEST(1943); GOVERNMENT GIRL(1943); LEAVE IT TO THE IRISH(1944); CARIBBEAN MYSTERY, THE(1945); TREE GROWS IN BROOKLYN, A(1945); THAT BRENNAN GIRL(1946); KILLER McCOY(1947); TEXAS, BROOKLYN AND HEAVEN(1948); GOLDEN GLOVES STORY, THE(1950); BRAMBLE BUSH, THE(1960); ADVENTURES OF A YOUNG MAN(1962); OSCAR, THE(1966)

Jan Dunn
AMERICAN GRAFFITI(1973); SHOOT THE MOON(1982)
1984
NO SMALL AFFAIR(1984)

Jim Dunn
ONE FROM THE HEART(1982)

Jimmy Dunn
SCENE OF THE CRIME(1949)

Jody Dunn
HOLD THAT BABY!(1949)

John Dunn
ACROSS THE WIDE MISSOURI(1951), ed; GROUND ZERO(1973); BUGS BUNNY'S THIRD MOVIE–1001 RABBIT TALES(1982), w; DAFFY DUCK'S MOVIE: FANTASTIC ISLAND(1983), w
Silents
CHARITY?(1916)
Misc. Silents
SOUL OF A CHILD, THE(1916)

John E. Dunn
SLEEPAWAY CAMP(1983)

Johnny Dunn
GUY NAMED JOE, A(1943)

Josephine Dunn
SINGING FOOL, THE(1928); BIG TIME(1929); MELODY LANE(1929); MOST IMMORAL LADY, A(1929); OUR MODERN MAIDENS(1929); MADONNA OF THE STREETS(1930); RED HOT RHYTHM(1930); SAFETY IN NUMBERS(1930); AIR POLICE(1931); SECOND HONEYMOON(1931); BETWEEN FIGHTING MEN(1932); BIG CITY BLUES(1932); FIGHTING GENTLEMAN, THE(1932); FORBIDDEN COMPANY(1932); MURDER AT DAWN(1932); ONE HOUR WITH YOU(1932); TWO KINDS OF WOMEN(1932); BIRTH OF A BABY(1938)
Silents
IT'S THE OLD ARMY GAME(1926); SORROWS OF SATAN(1926); FIREMAN, SAVE MY CHILD(1927); SHE'S A SHEIK(1927); EXCESS BAGGAGE(1928); MILLION FOR LOVE, A(1928); MAN'S MAN, A(1929); OUR MODERN MAIDENS(1929); SIN SISTER, THE(1929)
Misc. Silents
GET YOUR MAN(1927); LOVE'S GREATEST MISTAKE(1927); SWIM, GIRL, SWIM(1927); ALL AT SEA(1929); BLACK MAGIC(1929); CHINA BOUND(1929); SECOND HONEYMOON(1930)

Judy Ann Dunn
RAWHIDE(1951)

Judy Dunn
HOLD THAT BABY!(1949)

Kathy Dunn
THIRTEEN FRIGHTENED GIRLS(1963)

Katie Dunn
CLOWN AND THE KIDS, THE(1968, U.S./Bulgaria)

Larry Dunn
STUNTS(1977); STUNT MAN, THE(1980)

Liam Dunn
CATCH-22(1970); GREAT NORTHFIELD, MINNESOTA RAID, THE(1972); WHAT'S UP, DOC?(1972); CHARLEY AND THE ANGEL(1973); EMPEROR OF THE NORTH POLE(1973); PAPILLON(1973); REFLECTION OF FEAR, A(1973); WORLD'S GREATEST ATHLETE, THE(1973); BANK SHOT(1974); BLAZING SADDLES(1974); HERBIE RIDES AGAIN(1974); YOUNG FRANKENSTEIN(1974); AT LONG LAST LOVE(1975); PEEPER(1975); SHAGGY D.A., THE(1976); SILENT MOVIE(1976)

Linwood Dunn
MONKEY'S PAW, THE(1933), spec eff; MIGHTY JOE YOUNG(1949), spec eff; THING, THE(1951), spec eff; FORTY GUNS(1957), spec eff

Linwood G. Dunn
IT'S A MAD, MAD, MAD, MAD WORLD(1963), spec eff; HAWAII(1966), spec eff; DARLING LILI(1970), spec eff

Lorna Dunn
MOON'S OUR HOME, THE(1936); CONFESSIONS OF BOSTON BLACKIE(1941); FATHER TAKES A WIFE(1941); LADY IS WILLING, THE(1942); PRIDE OF THE YANKEES, THE(1942); SEVENTH VICTIM, THE(1943); CASANOVA BROWN(1944)

Louise Dunn
SATURDAY NIGHT AND SUNDAY MORNING(1961, Brit.); WAR LOVER, THE(1962, U.S./Brit.); LIQUIDATOR, THE(1966, Brit.)

Lynn Dunn
SHOCK CORRIDOR(1963), spec eff

Marie Dunn
Misc. Silents
DOUBLE-DYED DECIEVER, A(1920)

Mary Dunn
RIDERS OF THE GOLDEN GULCH(1932); LITTLE MISS SOMEBODY(1937, Brit.), w; MYSTERY ON BIRD ISLAND(1954, Brit.), w

Matthew Dunn
1984
GIRLS NIGHT OUT(1984)

Maxwell Dunn
RUGGED O'RIORDANS, THE(1949, Aus.), w

Michael Dunn
WITHOUT EACH OTHER(1962); SHIP OF FOOLS(1965); YOU'RE A BIG BOY NOW(1966); BOOM!(1968); MADIGAN(1968); NO WAY TO TREAT A LADY(1968); FIGHT FOR ROME(1969, Ger./Rum.); JUSTINE(1969); MURDERS IN THE RUE MORGUE(1971); HOUSE OF FREAKS(1973, Ital.); WEREWOLF OF WASHINGTON(1973); ABDICATION, THE(1974, Brit.); MUTATIONS, THE(1974, Brit.)
Misc. Talkies
PITY ME NOT(1960)

Murphy Dunn
HONKY TONK FREEWAY(1981)

Nancy Dunn
SON OF SINBAD(1955)

Nell Dunn
POOR COW(1968, Brit.), w; UP THE JUNCTION(1968, Brit.), w

O.G. Dunn
WOMAN UNDER THE INFLUENCE, A(1974)

Pat Dunn
RODEO RHYTHM(1941)

Patricia Dunn
KISMET(1955)

Paul Dunn
HIGH BARBAREE(1947); TRAIL STREET(1947); WISTFUL WIDOW OF WAGON GAP, THE(1947); FIGHTING FATHER DUNNE(1948); MA AND PA KETTLE(1949); MA AND PA KETTLE GO TO TOWN(1950)

Peter Dunn
MONSTER OF PIEDRAS BLANCAS, THE(1959)
Philip Dunn
SATAN'S BED(1965)
Ralph A. Dunn
PLACE IN THE SUN, A(1951)
Ralph Dunn
CROWD ROARS, THE(1932); CHINA CLIPPER(1936); PUBLIC ENEMY'S WIFE(1936); GAME THAT KILLS, THE(1937); KID GALAHAD(1937); NIGHT KEY(1937); SAN QUENTIN(1937); SINGING MARINE, THE(1937); SUBMARINE D-1(1937); ACCIDENTS WILL HAPPEN(1938); ALEXANDER'S RAGTIME BAND(1938); CITY GIRL(1938); COME ON, LEATHERNECKS(1938); KING OF THE NEWSBOYS(1938); MR. MOTO TAKES A VACATION(1938); MR. MOTO'S GAMBLE(1938); NEXT TIME I MARRY(1938); PATIENT IN ROOM 18, THE(1938); SLIGHT CASE OF MURDER, A(1938); TENTH AVENUE KID(1938); ANOTHER THIN MAN(1939); DESPERATE TRAILS(1939); I STOLE A MILLION(1939); NEWSBOY'S HOME(1939); ONE HOUR TO LIVE(1939); ROSE OF WASHINGTON SQUARE(1939); SMASHING THE MONEY RING(1939); BRIGHAM YOUNG–FRONTIERSMAN(1940); FIGHTING 69TH, THE(1940); GRAPES OF WRATH(1940); HIS GIRL FRIDAY(1940); INVISIBLE STRIPES(1940); NEW MOON(1940); PUBLIC DEB NO. 1(1940); SAINT'S DOUBLE TROUBLE, THE(1940); SON OF ROARING DAN(1940); WE WHO ARE YOUNG(1940); YOU'RE NOT SO TOUGH(1940); CONFESSIONS OF BOSTON BLACKIE(1941); IN THE NAVY(1941); INTERNATIONAL LADY(1941); LADY FROM CHEYENNE(1941); MANPOWER(1941); MR. AND MRS. SMITH(1941); SAN FRANCISCO DOCKS(1941); SUN VALLEY SERENADE(1941); TWO LATINS FROM MANHATTAN(1941); WESTERN UNION(1941); BOSTON BLACKIE GOES HOLLYWOOD(1942); I MARRIED A WITCH(1942); I WAKE UP SCREAMING(1942); LUCKY JORDAN(1942); MOONTIDE(1942); MY SISTER EILEEN(1942); NAVY COMES THROUGH, THE(1942); SABOTEUR(1942); SEVEN DAYS LEAVE(1942); SHIP AHOY(1942); STREET OF CHANCE(1942); STRICTLY IN THE GROOVE(1942); TALK OF THE TOWN(1942); TRUE TO THE ARMY(1942); YOU'RE TELLING ME(1942); GOVERNMENT GIRL(1943); HANGMEN ALSO DIE(1943); HE HIRED THE BOSS(1943); MOONLIGHT IN VERMONT(1943); MUG TOWN(1943); THANK YOUR LUCKY STARS(1943); THEY GOT ME COVERED(1943); DARK MOUNTAIN(1944); EVER SINCE VENUS(1944); FOLLOW THE BOYS(1944); GYPSY WILDCAT(1944); HAIRY APE, THE(1944); IN SOCIETY(1944); LAURA(1944); PRINCESS AND THE PIRATE, THE(1944); ROGER TOUHY, GANGSTER!(1944); SHOW BUSINESS(1944); TOGETHER AGAIN(1944); WILSON(1944); ALONG CAME JONES(1945); ANGEL COMES TO BROOKLYN, AN(1945); CIRCUMSTANTIAL EVIDENCE(1945); COLONEL EFFINGHAM'S RAID(1945); CONFLICT(1945); DICK TRACY(1945); ESCAPE IN THE FOG(1945); HOLD THAT BLONDE(1945); LOVE, HONOR AND GOODBYE(1945); MURDER, MY SWEET(1945); SARATOGA TRUNK(1945); SCARLET STREET(1945); SENORITA FROM THE WEST(1945); WHERE DO WE GO FROM HERE?(1945); WITHIN THESE WALLS(1945); WOMAN IN THE WINDOW, THE(1945); WONDER MAN(1945); BANDIT OF SHERWOOD FOREST, THE(1946); CALIFORNIA(1946); DARK CORNER, THE(1946); DEADLINE AT DAWN(1946); DICK TRACY VS. CUEBALL(1946); FROM THIS DAY FORWARD(1946); GAS HOUSE KIDS(1946); GENIUS AT WORK(1946); KID FROM BROOKLYN, THE(1946); LADY CHASER(1946); LARCENY IN HER HEART(1946); LITTLE GIANT(1946); MISSING LADY, THE(1946); MURDER IS MY BUSINESS(1946); NOBODY LIVES FOREVER(1946); STEP BY STEP(1946); TILL THE CLOUDS ROLL BY(1946); DEEP VALLEY(1947); I WONDER WHO'S KISSING HER NOW(1947); LADY IN THE LAKE(1947); NEWS HOUNDS(1947); NORA PRENTISS(1947); POSSESSED(1947); ROAD TO RIO(1947); SECRET LIFE OF WALTER MITTY, THE(1947); THREE ON A TICKET(1947); TOO MANY WINNERS(1947); BIG CLOCK, THE(1948); CANON CITY(1948); FIGHTING FATHER DUNNE(1948); FORCE OF EVIL(1948); INCIDENT(1948); JINX MONEY(1948); KING OF THE GAMBLERS(1948); LADY AT MIDNIGHT(1948); MYSTERY OF THE GOLDEN EYE, THE(1948); TRAIN TO ALCATRAZ(1948); TREASURE OF THE SIERRA MADRE, THE(1948); LOST TRIBE, THE(1949); MARY RYAN, DETECTIVE(1949); THEY LIVE BY NIGHT(1949); GREAT PLANE ROBBERY(1950); NO WAY OUT(1950); SECRET FURY, THE(1950); SINGING GUNS(1950); SURRENDER(1950); ABBOTT AND COSTELLO MEET THE INVISIBLE MAN(1951); ENFORCER, THE(1951); TAXI(1953); CROWDED PARADISE(1956); PAJAMA GAME, THE(1957); FROM THE TERRACE(1960); DRAGNET(1974)
Red Dunn
PANHANDLE(1948), m
Richard Dunn
FIVE ANGLES ON MURDER(1950, Brit.); ACROSS THE BRIDGE(1957, Brit.)
Rita Dunn
FOLIES DERGERE(1935); OUR RELATIONS(1936); KEEP YOUR POWDER DRY(1945)
Robert Dunn
BREATHLESS(1983)
Rev. Robert Dunn
LOST BOUNDARIES(1949); WALK EAST ON BEACON(1952)
Rev. Robert A. Dunn
WHISTLE AT EATON FALLS(1951)
Roger Dunn
DEAD ZONE, THE(1983); STRANGE BREW(1983)
1984
POLICE ACADEMY(1984)
Shirley Dunn
GOODBYE PORK PIE(1981, New Zealand)
Stephen Dunn
NORSEMAN, THE(1978), ed
Stephen P. Dunn
BLUE COLLAR(1978); HARDCORE(1979)
Steve Dunn
CHA-CHA-CHA BOOM(1956)
Tay Dunn
WITHOUT RESERVATIONS(1946); CRAZY KNIGHTS(1944); DANNY BOY(1946); HIGH WALL, THE(1947)
Valentine Dunn
HIS LORDSHIP REGRETS(1938, Brit.); WEDDINGS ARE WONDERFUL(1938, Brit.); BANANA RIDGE(1941, Brit.); QUIET WEDDING(1941, Brit.); SALUTE JOHN CITIZEN(1942, Brit.); HAPPIDROME(1943, Brit.); MILLIONS LIKE US(1943, Brit.); OLD MOTHER RILEY, DETECTIVE(1943, Brit.); GREAT DAY(1945, Brit.); LOYAL HEART(1946, Brit.); SONG FOR TOMORROW, A(1948, Brit.); PAPER GALLOWS(1950, Brit.); WILD HEART, THE(1952, Brit.); MEN ARE CHILDREN TWICE(1953, Brit.)

Violet Dunn
BLACK CAMEL, THE(1931); DOCTORS' WIVES(1931); RACHEL, RACHEL(1968)
William Dunn
ROBERTA(1935); STANLEY AND LIVINGSTONE(1939); SUNDOWN(1941)
Silents
JUGGERNAUT, THE(1915); ON HER WEDDING NIGHT(1915); ARTIE, THE MILLIONAIRE KID(1916); REDEEMING SIN, THE(1925); VANISHING HOOFS(1926); PAINTED PONIES(1927)
Misc. Silents
MAN BEHIND THE CURTAIN, THE(1916); BABETTE(1917); I WILL REPAY(1917); PRINCESS OF PARK ROW, THE(1917); HIS OWN PEOPLE(1918); WOOING OF PRINCESS PAT, THE(1918)
William H. Dunn
NAGANA(1933)
William R. Dunn
Silents
I WANT TO FORGET(1918)
Misc. Silents
BLOOD BARRIER, THE(1920); FORBIDDEN VALLEY(1920); RESPECTABLE BY PROXY(1920)
Winifred Dunn
FREE LOVE(1930), w; MAMBA(1930), w; SHE-WOLF, THE(1931), w; IMPATIENT MAIDEN(1932), w; I HAVE LIVED(1933), w; RAINBOW OVER BROADWAY(1933), w
Silents
EAGLE'S FEATHER, THE(1923), w; FOG, THE(1923), w; HELD TO ANSWER(1923), w; IN SEARCH OF A THRILL(1923), w; STORMSWEPT(1923), w; ALONG CAME RUTH(1924), w; SPARROWS(1926), w; TWINKLETOES(1926), w; DROPKICK, THE(1927), w; TENDER HOUR, THE(1927), w; ADORATION(1928), w
Bill Dunnagan
MEAL, THE(1975)
Stephanie Dunnam
PLAY DEAD(1981); SILENT RAGE(1982)
Virginia Dunnam
PIRANHA(1978)
David Dunnard
INDEPENDENCE DAY(1983)
Brendan Dunne
PADDY(1970, Irish)
Brian Dunne
WARNING SHOT(1967)
Burt Dunne
NIGHT OF THE GRIZZLY, THE(1966), p
Carole Dunne
JOE PALOOKA, CHAMP(1946)
Clare Dunne
THEY'RE A WEIRD MOB(1966, Aus.)
Corinne Dunne
HUMAN FACTOR, THE(1975)
Dominick Dunne
PANIC IN NEEDLE PARK(1971), p; PLAY IT AS IT LAYS(1972), p; ASH WEDNESDAY(1973), p
Dominique Dunne
POLTERGEIST(1982)
Edward Dunne
SIDELONG GLANCES OF A PIGEON KICKER, THE(1970)
Eithne Dunne
NO RESTING PLACE(1952, Brit.); EIGHT O'CLOCK WALK(1954, Brit.); SHAKE HANDS WITH THE DEVIL(1959, Ireland); SHE DIDN'T SAY NO!(1962, Brit.); DEMENTIA 13(1963); MUTATIONS, THE(1974, Brit.)
Elizabeth Dunne
FIRST LADY(1937); STAGE DOOR(1937); FOOLS FOR SCANDAL(1938); BLONDIE TAKES A VACATION(1939); NAUGHTY BUT NICE(1939); CAT PEOPLE(1942); SOMEONE TO REMEMBER(1943); DOUBLE LIFE, A(1947); ANGEL ON THE AMAZON(1948); SURRENDER(1950)
Finley Peter Dunne
MAGNIFICENT OBSESSION(1935), w; MAGNIFICENT OBSESSION(1954), w
Finley Peter Dunne, Jr.
WE WENT TO COLLEGE(1936), w; BREEZING HOME(1937), w
George Dunne
GIANT(1956)
Griffin Dunne
OTHER SIDE OF THE MOUNTAIN, THE(1975); AMERICAN WEREWOLF IN LONDON, AN(1981); FAN, THE(1981); CHILLY SCENES OF WINTER(1982), a, p; BABY, IT'S YOU(1983), p
1984
ALMOST YOU(1984); COLD FEET(1984); JOHNNY DANGEROUSLY(1984)
Harvey Dunne
SINISTER URGE, THE(1961)
Irene Dunne
LEATHERNECKING(1930); BACHELOR APARTMENT(1931); CIMARRON(1931); CONSOLATION MARRIAGE(1931); GREAT LOVER, THE(1931); BACK STREET(1932); SYMPHONY OF SIX MILLION(1932); THIRTEEN WOMEN(1932); ANN VICKERS(1933); IF I WERE FREE(1933); NO OTHER WOMAN(1933); SECRET OF MADAME BLANCHE, THE(1933); SILVER CORD(1933); AGE OF INNOCENCE(1934); STINGAREE(1934); THIS MAN IS MINE(1934); MAGNIFICENT OBSESSION(1935); ROBERTA(1935); SWEET ADELINE(1935); SHOW BOAT(1936); THEODORA GOES WILD(1936); AWFUL TRUTH, THE(1937); HIGH, WIDE AND HANDSOME(1937); JOY OF LIVING(1938); INVITATION TO HAPPINESS(1939); LOVE AFFAIR(1939); WHEN TOMORROW COMES(1939); MY FAVORITE WIFE(1940); PENNY SERENADE(1941); UNFINISHED BUSINESS(1941); LADY IN A JAM(1942); GUY NAMED JOE, A(1943); TOGETHER AGAIN(1944); WHITE CLIFFS OF DOVER, THE(1944); OVER 21(1945); ANNA AND THE KING OF SIAM(1946); LIFE WITH FATHER(1947); I REMEMBER MAMA(1948); MUDLARK, THE(1950, Brit.); NEVER A DULL MOMENT(1950); IT GROWS ON TREES(1952)
James Dunne
ECHOES(1983)

James C. Dunne
PASSION STREET, U.S.A.(1964), p
Joe Dunne
PUPPET ON A CHAIN(1971, Brit.), stunts; 1,000 CONVICTS AND A WOMAN(1971, Brit.); REVENGE OF THE PINK PANTHER(1978), stunts; PRISONER OF ZENDA, THE(1979)
1984
MICKI AND MAUDE(1984), stunts; POLICE ACADEMY(1984)
John Dunne
PACIFIC ADVENTURE(1947, Aus.); GREAT TRAIN ROBBERY, THE(1979, Brit.)
John Gregory Dunne
PANIC IN NEEDLE PARK(1971), w; PLAY IT AS IT LAYS(1972), w; STAR IS BORN, A(1976), w; TRUE CONFESSIONS(1981), w
Lee Dunne
PADDY(1970, Irish), w; WEDDING NIGHT(1970, Ireland), w
Michael Dunne
COLONEL EFFINGHAM'S RAID(1945); DOLL FACE(1945); JUNIOR MISS(1945); GENTLE GUNMAN, THE(1952, Brit.)
Michael [Stephen] Dunne
SHOCK(1946); MOTHER WORE TIGHTS(1947)
Murphy Dunne
BIG BUS, THE(1976); HIGH ANXIETY(1977); MAIN EVENT, THE(1979); BLUES BROTHERS, THE(1980); LAST MARRIED COUPLE IN AMERICA, THE(1980); LOOSE SHOES(1980), a, m; PATERNITY(1981); GOING BERSERK(1983)
1984
BAD MANNERS(1984)
Peter Dunne
I ESCAPED FROM THE GESTAPO(1943); ONCE A THIEF(1950)
Philip Dunne
COUNT OF MONTE CRISTO, THE(1934), w; STUDENT TOUR(1934), w; MELODY LINGERS ON, THE(1935), w; LAST OF THE MOHICANS, THE(1936), w; BREEZING HOME(1937), w; LANCER SPY(1937), w; SUEZ(1938), w; RAINS CAME, THE(1939), w; STANLEY AND LIVINGSTONE(1939), w; SWANEE RIVER(1939), w; JOHNNY APOLLO(1940), w; HOW GREEN WAS MY VALLEY(1941), w; GHOST AND MRS. MUIR, THE(1942), w; SON OF FURY(1942), w; FOREVER AMBER(1947), w; LATE GEORGE APLEY, THE(1947), w; ESCAPE(1948, Brit.), w; LUCK OF THE IRISH(1948), w; PINKY(1949), w; ANNE OF THE INDIES(1951), w; DAVID AND BATH-SHEBA(1951), w; LYDIA BAILEY(1952), w; WAY OF A GAUCHO(1952), p, w; DEMETRIUS AND THE GLADIATORS(1954), w; EGYPTIAN. THE(1954), w; PRINCE OF PLAYERS(1955), p&d; VIEW FROM POMPEY'S HEAD, THE(1955), p,d&w; HILDA CRANE(1956), d&w; THREE BRAVE MEN(1957), d&w; IN LOVE AND WAR(1958), d; 10 NORTH FREDERICK(1958), d&w; BLUE DENIM(1959), d, w; WILD IN THE COUNTRY(1961), d; LISA(1962, Brit.), d; AGONY AND THE ECSTASY, THE(1965), w; BLINDFOLD(1966), d, w
Stephen Dunne
WHEN A GIRL'S BEAUTIFUL(1947); DARK PAST, THE(1948); RETURN OF OCTOBER, THE(1948); WOMAN FROM TANGIER, THE(1948); BIG SOMBRERO, THE(1949); CRIME DOCTOR'S DIARY, THE(1949); KAZAN(1949); LAW OF THE BARBARY COAST(1949); MISS GRANT TAKES RICHMOND(1949); RUSTY SAVES A LIFE(1949); WHIPPED, THE(1950); LADY POSSESSED(1952); WAC FROM WALLA WALLA, THE(1952); ABOVE AND BEYOND(1953)
Misc. Talkies
SON OF RUSTY, THE(1947)
Steve Dunne
TEN THOUSAND BEDROOMS(1957); HOME BEFORE DARK(1958); I MARRIED A WOMAN(1958); EXPLOSIVE GENERATION, THE(1961); HAND OF DEATH(1962); LATE LIZ, THE(1971); SUPERDAD(1974)
Tay Dunne
STRIP, THE(1951); UNKNOWN MAN, THE(1951)
Tom Dunne
IRELAND'S BORDER LINE(1939, Ireland)
John Dunne-Hill
WELCOME TO THE CLUB(1971)
Teresa Dunnien
IT STARTED IN PARADISE(1952, Brit.)
James P. Dunnigan
SOMEWHERE IN TIME(1980)
Alfred Dunning
DANCE LITTLE LADY(1954, Brit.), w
Burton Dunning
Misc. Talkies
HOT CHILD(1974); NYMPH(1974)
Decla Dunning
HAIRY APE, THE(1944), w; STRANGER THE(1946), w; TARS AND SPARS(1946), w; I, JANE DOE(1948), w; SLEEP, MY LOVE(1948), w
Don Dunning
UNION STATION(1950); FLAMING FEATHER(1951); MY FAVORITE SPY(1951); SILVER CITY(1951); SUBMARINE COMMAND(1951); HURRICANE SMITH(1952); SON OF PALEFACE(1952); FLIGHT TO TANGIER(1953); COUNTRY GIRL, THE(1954); THREE VIOLENT PEOPLE(1956)
Frances Dunning
WOMAN RACKET, THE(1930), w
Fred Dunning
Misc. Silents
ONLY MAN, THE(1915, Brit.)
G.T. Dunning
Misc. Silents
LAST CHALLENGE, THE(1916, Brit.)
George Dunning
CORPSE CAME C.O.D., THE(, m; CRUISIN' DOWN THE RIVER(1953), md; FULL OF LIFE(1956), m; YELLOW SUBMARINE(1958, Brit.), d; LET NO MAN WRITE MY EPITAPH(1960), m
Jessica Dunning
BURN WITCH BURN(1962)
John Dunning
CASS TIMBERLANE(1947), ed; THIS TIME FOR KEEPS(1947), ed; HOMECOMING(1948), ed; JULIA MISBEHAVES(1948), ed; BATTLEGROUND(1949), ed; HAPPY YEARS, THE(1950), ed; SHOW BOAT(1951), ed; MY MAN AND I(1952), ed; WASHINGTON STORY(1952), ed; WILD NORTH, THE(1952), ed; JULIUS CAESAR(1953), ed; TAKE THE HIGH GROUND(1953), ed; BETRAYED(1954), ed; LAST

TIME I SAW PARIS, THE(1954), ed; RHAPSODY(1954), ed; BAR SINISTER, THE(1955), ed; INTERRUPTED MELODY(1955), ed; TENDER TRAP, THE(1955), ed; SWAN, THE(1956), ed; RAINTREE COUNTY(1957), ed; BROTHERS KARAMAZOV, THE(1958), ed; BEN HUR(1959), ed; CIMARRON(1960), ed; RABID(1976, Can.), p; BLACKOUT(1978, Fr./Can.), p; YESTERDAY(1980, Can.), p, w; HAPPY BIRTHDAY TO ME(1981), p; MY BLOODY VALENTINE(1981, Can.), p; SPACEHUNTER: ADVENTURES IN THE FORBIDDEN ZONE(1983), p
1984
SURROGATE, THE(1984, Can.), p
Nick Dunning
REMEMBRANCE(1982, Brit.)
Philip Dunning
SHOW FOLKS(1928), w; BROADWAY(1929), w; WOMAN RACKET, THE(1930), w; LILLY TURNER(1933), w; PAGE MISS GLORY(1935), w; REMEMBER THE DAY(1941), w; BROADWAY(1942), w
Ruth Dunning
SAVE A LITTLE SUNSHINE(1938, Brit.); WOMAN IN THE HALL, THE(1949, Brit.); DISOBEDIENT(1953, Brit.); MAN OF THE MOMENT(1955, Brit.); IT'S A GREAT DAY(1956, Brit.); AND WOMEN SHALL WEEP(1960, Brit.); SONS AND LOVERS(1960, Brit.); URGE TO KILL(1960, Brit.); DANGEROUS AFTERNOON(1961, Brit.); THREE LIVES OF THOMASINA, THE(1963, U.S./Brit.); HOFFMAN(1970, Brit.); BLACK PANTHER, THE(1977, Brit.)
Mildred Dunnock
CORN IS GREEN, THE(1945); KISS OF DEATH(1947); I WANT YOU(1951); DEATH OF A SALESMAN(1952); GIRL IN WHITE, THE(1952); VIVA ZAPATA!(1952); JAZZ SINGER, THE(1953); BAD FOR EACH OTHER(1954); HANSEL AND GRETEL(1954); TROUBLE WITH HARRY, THE(1955); BABY DOLL(1956); LOVE ME TENDER(1956); PEYTON PLACE(1957); NUN'S STORY, THE(1959); STORY ON PAGE ONE, THE(1959); SOMETHING WILD(1961); SWEET BIRD OF YOUTH(1962); BEHOLD A PALE HORSE(1964); YOUNGBLOOD HAWKE(1964); SEVEN WOMEN(1966); WHAT EVER HAPPENED TO AUNT ALICE?(1969); SPIRAL STAIRCASE, THE(1975, Brit.); ONE SUMMER LOVE(1976)
Jean Dunot
PRIZE, THE(1952, Fr.); FOUR BAGS FULL(1957, Fr./Ital.)
Francois Dunoyer
SPERMULA(1976, Fr.)
Barbara Dunphy
DEAD ZONE, THE(1983), art d
1984
LISTEN TO THE CITY(1984, Can.), art d
Don Dunphy
BANANAS(1971); GREATEST, THE(1977, U.S./Brit.); MATILDA(1978)
Jerry Dunphy
PRIZE, THE(1963); GOODBYE CHARLIE(1964); KITTEN WITH A WHIP(1964); WARNING SHOT(1967); LOVE MACHINE, THE,(1971); NIGHT OF THE LEPUS(1972)
Brenda Dunrich
INTENT TO KILL(1958, Brit.)
Virginia Dunsaith
SWEET SUBSTITUTE(1964, Can.)
Lord Dunsany
IT HAPPENED TOMORROW(1944), w
John Dunsford
UGLY DUCKLING, THE(1959, Brit.), ed; HELL IS A CITY(1960, Brit.), ed; CRIMSON BLADE, THE(1964, Brit.), ed; SKIN GAME, THE(1965, Brit.), ed
Lisa Dunsheath
PROWLER, THE(1981); THEY ALL LAUGHED(1981); LITTLE SEX, A(1982); EDDIE MACON'S RUN(1983)
Yuliy Dunskiy
THERE WAS AN OLD COUPLE(1967, USSR), w
Erich Dunskus
GIRL FROM THE MARSH CROFT, THE(1935, Ger.); PRIZE OF GOLD, A(1955)
John Dunsmuir
ENEMIES OF THE LAW(1931)
Cliff Dunstan
ROOM SERVICE(1938)
Clifford Dunstan
WOMAN IN THE DARK(1934)
Eric Dunstan
DEATH AT A BROADCAST(1934, Brit.)
Joy Dunstan
20TH CENTURY OZ(1977, Aus.)
Shirley Dunstead
WILD BOYS OF THE ROAD(1933)
Eddie Dunstedter
DONOVAN'S BRAIN(1953), m
David Dunstone
NIGHT OF EVIL(1962)
Dean Dunstone
PUBERTY BLUES(1983, Aus.)
J. Dunsyevshy
CAPTAIN GRANT'S CHILDREN(1939, USSR), m
A. Dunsysky
HEROES ARE MADE(1944, USSR)
John Dunton
Silents
AMERICA(1924)
G. Dunts
DAY THE WAR ENDED, THE(1961, USSR); HOUSE ON THE FRONT LINE, THE(1963, USSR)
Roma Dunville
CONSTANT HUSBAND, THE(1955, Brit.)
Don Dunwell
WRONG IS RIGHT(1982)
James Dupam
NIGHT PARADE(1929, Brit.)
E. B. DuPar
Silents
LITTLE CHURCH AROUND THE CORNER(1923), ph

Ed DuPar
PARIS FOLLIES OF 1956(1955), ph
Edward DuPar
GIRL FROM JONES BEACH, THE(1949), spec eff
Edwin DuPar
MY DREAM IS YOURS(1949), spec eff
Edwin A. DuPar
DAWN PATROL, THE(1938), spec eff; BODY DISAPPEARS, THE(1941), spec eff; BUSSES ROAR(1942), spec eff; SECRET ENEMIES(1942), spec eff
Edwin B. DuPar
KID GALAHAD(1937), spec eff; ROARING TWENTIES, THE(1939), spec eff; IT ALL CAME TRUE(1940), spec eff; THEY DRIVE BY NIGHT(1940), spec eff; ACTION IN THE NORTH ATLANTIC(1943), spec eff; WATCH ON THE RHINE(1943), spec eff; Jack Holden; CLOAK AND DAGGER(1946), spec eff; ALWAYS TOGETHER(1947), spec eff; RING OF FEAR(1954), ph; FROM THE EARTH TO THE MOON(1958), ph
Edwin DuPar
PERFECT SPECIMEN, THE(1937), spec eff; DESPERATE JOURNEY(1942), spec eff; DANGER SIGNAL(1945), spec eff; GOD IS MY CO-PILOT(1945), spec eff; OBJECTIVE, BURMA!(1945), spec eff; MAN I LOVE, THE(1946), spec eff; SHADOW OF A WOMAN(1946), spec eff; THREE STRANGERS(1946), spec eff; NORA PRENTISS(1947), spec eff; VOICE OF THE TURTLE, THE(1947), spec eff; JOHNNY BELINDA(1948), spec eff; SILVER RIVER(1948), spec eff; WHIPLASH(1948), spec eff; FOUNTAIN-HEAD, THE(1949), spec eff; BREAKTHROUGH(1950), ph; WEST POINT STORY, THE(1950), spec eff; I WAS A COMMUNIST FOR THE F.B.I.(1951), ph; INSIDE THE WALLS OF FOLSOM PRISON(1951), ph; TANKS ARE COMING, THE(1951), ph; MIRACLE OF OUR LADY OF FATIMA, THE(1952), ph; EDDIE CANTOR STORY, THE(1953), ph; SHE'S BACK ON BROADWAY(1953), ph; BOUNTY HUNTER, THE(1954), ph; LONE RANGER, THE(1955), ph; TARGET ZERO(1955), ph
Jean-Francois Dupas
VIOLETTE(1978, Fr.)
Ralph Dupas
NEW ORLEANS UNCENSORED(1955)
E.B. DuPax
ROYAL BOX, THE(1930), ph
Anne Duperey
1984
LES COMPERES(1984, Fr.)
Annie Duperey
BLOOD ROSE, THE(1970, Fr.); FROM HELL TO VICTORY(1979, Fr./Ital./Span.)
Anny Duperey
SPIRITS OF THE DEAD(1969, Fr./Ital.); TWO OR THREE THINGS I KNOW ABOUT HER(1970, Fr.); STAVISKY(1974, Fr.); BOBBY DEERFIELD(1977)
A. Duperoux
GOODBYE AGAIN(1961)
Annie Duperoux
LOLA(1961, Fr./Ital.)
Humberto Dupeyron
PUSS 'N' BOOTS(1964, Mex.)
Jose Dupeyron
MACARIO(1961, Mex.)
Cleve Dupin
1984
SONGWRITER(1984)
Joan Dupius
WITHOUT HONOR(1949)
Michel Duplaix
CLOPORTES(1966, Fr., Ital.); FANTOMAS(1966, Fr./Ital.)
Daniel DuPlessis
KILL OR BE KILLED(1980)
Art Dupois
WHIP HAND, THE(1951)
Patrick Dupond
SHE DANCES ALONE(1981, Aust./U.S.)
Colyer Dupont
FOLLOW ME, BOYS!(1966)
E.A. Dupont
ATLANTIC(1929 Brit.), p&d; TWO WORLD(1930, Brit.), p&d, w; LOVE STORM, THE(1931, Brit.), p&d, w; PICCADILLY(1932, Brit.), p&d; TRAPEZE(1932, Ger.), d; BISHOP MISBEHAVES, THE(1933), d; FORGOTTEN FACES(1936), d; SON COMES HOME, A(1936), d; LOVE ON TOAST(1937), d; NIGHT OF MYSTERY(1937), d; ON SUCH A NIGHT(1937), d; HELL'S KITCHEN(1939), d; SCARF, THE(1951), d&w; NEANDERTHAL MAN, THE(1953), d; PROBLEM GIRLS(1953), d; STEEL LADY, THE(1953), d; RETURN TO TREASURE ISLAND(1954), d; MAGIC FIRE(1956), w
Silents
VARIETY(1925, Ger.), d&w; MADAME POMPADOUR(1927, Brit.), p, w; LOVE ME AND THE WORLD IS MINE(1928), d, w; MOULIN ROUGE(1928, Brit.), p,d&w
Elaine Dupont
SON OF SINBAD(1955); GHOST OF DRAGSTRIP HOLLOW(1959); BEACH GIRLS AND THE MONSTER, THE(1965)
Greti DuPont
STREET CORNER(1948)
Gretl Dupont
MAJOR AND THE MINOR, THE(1942); BOMBER'S MOON(1943); WATCH ON THE RHINE(1943); DAYS OF GLORY(1944)
Jacques Dupont
LOVERS OF TERUEL, THE(1962, Fr.), set d&cos; HOTEL PARADISO(1966, U.S./Brit.), cos
Lawrence DuPont
MARK OF THE WITCH(1970)
Max Dupont
EXTRAVAGANCE(1930), ph; HOT CURVES(1930), ph; JUST LIKE HEAVEN(1930), ph; MEDICINE MAN, THE(1930), ph; PARADISE ISLAND(1930), ph; THIRD ALARM, THE(1930), ph; THOROUGHBRED, THE(1930), ph; CAUGHT CHEATING(1931), ph; MORALS FOR WOMEN(1931), ph; SINGLE SIN(1931), ph; MR. ROBINSON CRUSOE(1932), ph
Silents
JUDGMENT OF THE STORM(1924), ph

Michael duPont
HANDS OF A STRANGER(1962)
Norman Dupont
JUMP INTO HELL(1955); RISE AND FALL OF LEGS DIAMOND, THE(1960)
Renald Dupont
FRENCH LINE, THE(1954)
Rene Dupont
UNCANNY, THE(1977, Brit./Can.), p; MURDER BY DECREE(1979, Brit.), p; SILVER DREAM RACER(1982, Brit.), p; CHRISTMAS STORY, A(1983), p
Reynold DuPont
STORY OF DR. WASSELL, THE(1944)
Robert Dupont [Armand Mestral]
FIRE IN THE FLESH(1964, Fr.)
Francois Dupont-Midy
DOUBLE BED, THE(1965, Fr./Ital.), d
Catherine Duport
SOFT SKIN, THE(1964, Fr.)
Catherine-Isabelle Duport
MASCULINE FEMININE(1966, Fr./Swed.)
Gaston Dupray
AZAIS(1931, Fr.); STORY OF A CHEAT, THE(1938, Fr.)
Pierre Dupray
ONCE IN PARIS(1978)
Dupraz
PICNIC ON THE GRASS(1960, Fr.)
George Dupre
Silents
AVALANCHE, THE(1919)
Peter DuPre
EYES OF A STRANGER(1980)
Rene Dupre
LAST METRO, THE(1981, Fr.)
Roland Dupre
JULIA MISBEHAVES(1948)
Vanda Dupre
GIRL IN THE KREMLIN, THE(1957)
Dupree
KILLER SHREWS, THE(1959)
George Dupree
Misc. Silents
BACHELOR APARTMENTS(1920)
Judge Dupree
MY DOG, BUDDY(1960)
Lee Dupree
CLAUDINE(1974)
Linda Dupree
STRIPES(1981)
Minnie Dupree
YOUNG IN HEART, THE(1938); ANNE OF WINDY POPLARS(1940)
Roland Dupree
YOU CAN'T TAKE IT WITH YOU(1938); ZIS BOOM BAH(1941); COLLEGE SWEET-HEARTS(1942); MISS ANNIE ROONEY(1942); MOONLIGHT IN HAVANA(1942); IRON MAJOR, THE(1943); YOUNGEST PROFESSION, THE(1943); AND THE ANGELS SING(1944); MAISIE GOES TO RENO(1944); OUR HEARTS WERE YOUNG AND GAY(1944); YOU CAN'T RATION LOVE(1944); OUR HEARTS WERE GROWING UP(1946); BIG TOWN SCANDAL(1948); FIGHTING FOOLS(1949); JOE PALOOKA IN THE COUNTERPUNCH(1949); PANAMA SAL(1957), ch; HELL TO ETERNITY(1960), ch; GIDGET GOES HAWAIIAN(1961), ch
William Dupree
INCHON(1981)
Lynette Dupret
LIFE STUDY(1973)
Rene Dupreyon
LOVE HAS MANY FACES(1965)
Frank Duprez
LASCA OF THE RIO GRANDE(1931), w
Fred Duprez
MY WIFE'S FAMILY(1932, Brit.), w; MEET MY SISTER(1933, Brit.); MY OLD DUCHESS(1933, Brit.); DANNY BOY(1934, Brit.); LOVE, LIFE AND LAUGHTER(1934, Brit.); WITHOUT YOU(1934, Brit.); DANCE BAND(1935, Brit.); DARK WORLD(1935, Brit.); LEND ME YOUR WIFE(1935, Brit.), w; NO MONKEY BUSINESS(1935, Brit.); WIFE OR TWO, A(1935, Brit.); ALL THAT GLITTERS(1936, Brit.); BALL AT SAVOY(1936, Brit.); BIG NOISE, THE(1936, Brit.); GYPSY MELODY(1936, Brit.); HEARTS OF HUMANITY(1936, Brit.); QUEEN OF HEARTS(1936, Brit.); REASONABLE DOUBT(1936, Brit.); YOU MUST GET MARRIED(1936, Brit.); CAFE COLETTE(1937, Brit.); HEAD OVER HEELS IN LOVE(1937, Brit.); KNIGHTS FOR A DAY(1937, Brit.); OKAY FOR SOUND(1937, Brit.); HEY! HEY! U.S.A.(1938, Brit.); KATHLEEN(1938, Ireland); PEARLS OF THE CROWN(1938, Fr.); TAKE OFF THAT HAT(1938, Brit.); MY WIFE'S FAMILY(1941, Brit.), w; MY WIFE'S FAMILY(1962, Brit.), w
Hatton Duprez
DULCIMER STREET(1948, Brit.); GUNMAN HAS ESCAPED, A(1948, Brit.)
Joey Duprez
FINDERS KEEPERS, LOVERS WEEPERS(1968)
John DuPrez
1984
OXFORD BLUES(1984), m
June Duprez
CARDINAL, THE(1936, Brit.); CRIMSON CIRCLE, THE(1936, Brit.); FOUR FEATHERS, THE(1939, Brit.); U-BOAT 29(1939, Brit.); LION HAS WINGS, THE(1940, Brit.); THIEF OF BAGHDAD, THE(1940, Brit.); LITTLE TOKYO, U.S.A.(1942); THEY RAID BY NIGHT(1942); FOREVER AND A DAY(1943); TIGER FANGS(1943); NONE BUT THE LONELY HEART(1944); AND THEN THERE WERE NONE(1945); BRIGHTON STRANGLER, THE(1945); THAT BRENNAN GIRL(1946); CALCUTTA(1947); ONE PLUS ONE(1961, Can.)
Annette Dupuis
MAN, A WOMAN, AND A BANK, A(1979, Can.)

Art Dupuis
MESSAGE TO GARCIA, A(1936); LOVE IS NEWS(1937); STRANGE CARGO(1940); RAGE IN HEAVEN(1941); JOAN OF ARC(1948); MIRACLE OF THE BELLS, THE(1948); FOLLOW ME QUIETLY(1949); GAMBLING HOUSE(1950); NEVER A DULL MOMENT(1950); WHERE DANGER LIVES(1950); ENFORCER, THE(1951); ON DANGEROUS GROUND(1951); RACKET, THE(1951); SEALED CARGO(1951); CLASH BY NIGHT(1952); MACAO(1952)

Claudine Dupuis
JENNY LAMOUR(1948, Fr.); SEVEN DEADLY SINS, THE(1953, Fr./Ital.); MAIDEN, THE(1961, Fr.); FIRE IN THE FLESH(1964, Fr.)

Jean L. Dupuis
SYMPTOMS(1976, Brit.), p

Jean-Michel Dupuis
DEATH OF MARIO RICCI, THE(1983, Ital.)
1984
LIFE IS A BED OF ROSES(1984, Fr.)

Joan Dupuis
INVASION OF THE SAUCER MEN(1957)

Paul Dupuis
JOHNNY FRENCHMAN(1946, Brit.); BAD SISTER(1947, Brit.); AGAINST THE WIND(1948, Brit.); MADNESS OF THE HEART(1949, Brit.); PASSPORT TO PIMLICO(1949, Brit.); SLEEPING CAR TO TRIESTE(1949, Brit.); LAUGHING LADY, THE(1950, Brit.); NAUGHTY ARLETTE(1951, Brit.); RELUCTANT WIDOW, THE(1951, Brit.)

Renee DuPuis
RAINBOW ISLAND(1944)

Stephan Dupuis
OF UNKNOWN ORIGIN(1983, Can.), makeup; STRANGE INVADERS(1983), spec eff

Stephen Dupuis
VISITING HOURS(1982, Can.), makeup; SPASMS(1983, Can.), makeup

Candace Dupuy
PEACE KILLERS, THE(1971)

Philip Dupuy
1984
ANOTHER COUNTRY(1984, Brit.)

Rene Dupuy
FIRE WITHIN, THE(1964, Fr./Ital.)

H. Dupuy-Mazuel
DEVIL IS AN EMPRESS, THE(1939, Fr.), w

Henri Dupuy-Mazuel
Misc. Silents
CHESS PLAYER, THE(1930, Fr.), d

Antonio Duque
DESPERATE ONES, THE(1968 U.S./Span.); THAT OBSCURE OBJECT OF DESIRE(1977, Fr./Span.)

Adrien Duquesne
RETURN OF MARTIN GUERRE, THE(1983, Fr.)

Pierre Duquesne
MALE COMPANION(1965, Fr./Ital.), art d

Tony Duquette
KISMET(1955), cos

Luc-Antoine Duquiero
1984
LES COMPERES(1984, Fr.)

Poldy Dur
MARGIN FOR ERROR(1943); THEY CAME TO BLOW UP AMERICA(1943); HITLER GANG, THE(1944)

Dennis Durack
VIRGIN WITCH, THE(1973, Brit.), p

Darlene Duralia
INCREDIBLE TWO-HEADED TRANSPLANT, THE(1971)
Misc. Talkies
OUTLAW RIDERS(1971)

Ann Duran
WEDDING OF LILLI MARLENE, THE(1953, Brit.)

Claude Duran
WEEKEND AT DUNKIRK(1966, Fr./Ital.), ed

Edna Duran
DRIFTING WESTWARD(1939)

Elana Duran
ONLY ANGELS HAVE WINGS(1939)

Elena Duran
Misc. Talkies
IRISH GRINGO, THE(1935)

Elsie Duran
TUNDRA(1936)

Giustino Duran
LUCKY TO BE A WOMAN(1955, Ital.)

Gloria Duran
IRON MAJOR, THE(1943)

Jesus Duran
SUNBURN(1979), spec eff; UNDER FIRE(1983), spec eff

Jim Duran
EQUINOX(1970)

Jorge Duran
PIXOTE(1981, Braz.), w

Joseph Duran
MC MASTERS, THE(1970)

Larry Duran
FLAME BARRIER, THE(1958); ONE-EYED JACKS(1961); HALLELUJAH TRAIL, THE(1965); LAST OF THE SECRET AGENTS?, THE(1966); GOOD TIMES(1967); DIRTY HARRY(1971); LADY SINGS THE BLUES(1972); LOST HORIZON(1973); BUCK ROGERS IN THE 25TH CENTURY(1979); CHAMP, THE(1979); METEOR(1979); TIME AFTER TIME(1979, Brit.), stunts; KIDNAPPING OF THE PRESIDENT, THE(1980, Can.); CHARLIE CHAN AND THE CURSE OF THE DRAGON QUEEN(1981)

Laurence Duran
HAWAII CALLS(1938)

Lilia Duran
TERROR IS A MAN(1959, U.S./Phil.)

Liza Duran
Misc. Talkies
CAREER BED(1972)

Michael Duran
I WAS AN ADVENTURESS(1940), w

Michel Duran
FRIC FRAC(1939, FR.), w; HE STAYED FOR BREAKFAST(1940), w; HEARTBEAT(1946), w; MALE HUNT(1965, Fr./Ital.), w

Nellie Duran
SOUTH OF PAGO PAGO(1940)

Pat Duran
SUBSTITUTION(1970)

Rafael Duran
LEGIONS OF THE NILE(1960, Ital.); CASTILIAN, THE(1963, Span./U.S.)

Rich Duran
STUDENT TEACHERS, THE(1973)

Ruben Duran
HAWAII CALLS(1938)

Rudy Duran
WEIRD ONES, THE(1962)

Steven Duran
1984
REVENGE OF THE NERDS(1984)

Thomas Duran
MACHISMO–40 GRAVES FOR 40 GUNS(1970)

Tommy Duran
SEVEN LITTLE FOYS, THE(1955); TEN COMMANDMENTS, THE(1956)

Val Duran
GENERAL DIED AT DAWN, THE(1936); JOIN THE MARINES(1937)

Angeles Durand
5 SINNERS(1961, Ger.); PLAYGIRLS AND THE BELLBOY, THE(1962,Ger.)

Carlos Durand
Silents
SCARLET DOVE, THE(1928)

Claude Durand
FOLIES BERGERE(1958, Fr.), ed; NATHALIE, AGENT SECRET(1960, Fr.), ed; LOVE AND THE FRENCHWOMAN(1961, Fr.), ed; MARRIAGE OF FIGARO, THE(1963, Fr.), ed; GREED IN THE SUN(1965, Fr./ Ital.), ed; UPPER HAND, THE(1967, Fr./Ital./Ger.), ed; CAROLINE CHERIE(1968, Fr.), ed; SABRA(1970, Fr./ Ital./Israel), ed

Dave Durand
KEEP 'EM SLUGGING(1943); KID DYNAMITE(1943); MR. MUGGS STEPS OUT(1943); FOLLOW THE LEADER(1944); MILLION DOLLAR KID(1944)

David Durand
INNOCENTS OF PARIS(1929); SONG OF LOVE, THE(1929); JAZZ CINDERELLA(1930); LADIES LOVE BRUTES(1930); BAD SISTER(1931); FORBIDDEN COMPANY(1932); PROBATION(1932); SILVER DOLLAR(1932); GREAT JASPER, THE(1933); JENNIE GERHARDT(1933); LIFE OF JIMMY DOLAN, THE(1933); SON OF THE BORDER(1933); BAND PLAYS ON, THE(1934); HAT, COAT AND GLOVE(1934); VIVA VILLA!(1934); WEDNESDAY'S CHILD(1934); LITTLE MEN(1935); ANGELS WITH DIRTY FACES(1938); BOY'S REFORMATORY(1939); OFF THE RECORD(1939); STREETS OF NEW YORK(1939); EAST SIDE KIDS(1940); GHOST BREAKERS, THE(1940); GOLDEN GLOVES(1940); TULSA KID, THE(1940); NAVAL ACADEMY(1941)
1984
RUNAWAY(1984), spec eff,

Edouard Durand
Silents
BRANDED WOMAN, THE(1920)

Edward Durand
Silents
CONSPIRACY, THE(1914)

Fernand Durand
TI-CUL TOUGAS(1977, Can.), art d

Jean Durand
JENNY LAMOUR(1948, Fr.); HOUSE ON SKULL MOUNTAIN, THE(1974)
Misc. Silents
LA CHAUSSEE DES GEANTS(1926, Fr.), d; PALACES(1927, Fr.), d; L'ILE D'AMOUR(1928, Fr.), d; LA FEMME REVEE(1929, Fr.), d

Jean M. Durand
THX 1138(1971)

Judi Durand
1984
STAR TREK III: THE SEARCH FOR SPOCK(1984)

Lud Durand
YOUNG GIRLS OF ROCHEFORT, THE(1968, Fr.), makeup

Paul Durand
FOREIGN INTRIGUE(1956), m; CASINO DE PARIS(1957, Fr./Ger.), m; COW AND I, THE(1961, Fr., Ital., Ger.), m

Rudy Durand
TILT(1979), p&d, w

Val Durand
LOST HORIZON(1937)

David Durand, Jr.
RICH MAN'S FOLLY(1931)

Giustino Durano
QUEEN OF THE PIRATES(1961, Ital./Ger.); GOLDEN ARROW, THE(1964, Ital.); MALE COMPANION(1965, Fr./Ital.); BOBO, THE(1967, Brit.); BANG BANG KID, THE(1968 U.S./Span./Ital.)

Giustino Durano
RAGE OF THE BUCCANEERS(1963, Ital.)

Allan Durant
Misc. Silents
MARRIAGE(1927)

Don Durant
SHE-GODS OF SHARK REEF(1958)

Fred W. Durant
Misc. Silents
TEMPORARY GENTLEMAN, A(1920, Brit.), d

H. R. Durant
Silents
MAN AND HIS MATE, A(1915), w

Harold Riggs Durant
Silents
HEART RAIDER, THE(1923), w

Henry Durant
WHAT PRICE DECENCY?(1933)

Jack Durant
SHE LEARNED ABOUT SAILORS(1934); STAND UP AND CHEER(1934 80m FOX bw); 365 NIGHTS IN HOLLYWOOD(1934); MUSIC IS MAGIC(1935); SPRING TO-NIC(1935); SINGING KID, THE(1936); FOUR JACKS AND A JILL(1941); JOURNEY INTO FEAR(1942); TRAMP, TRAMP, TRAMP(1942); NO ORCHIDS FOR MISS BLAN-DISH(1948, Brit.)

John Durant
WASHINGTON STORY(1952), ed; TWIST ALL NIGHT(1961), ed

M. Durant
Silents
PEACOCK ALLEY(1922)

Marjorie Durant
FRIENDLY PERSUASION(1956); QUEEN OF OUTER SPACE(1958); SUMMER LOVE(1958); GREAT NORTHFIELD, MINNESOTA RAID, THE(1972)

Mary Durant
STATE FAIR(1962)

Maurice Durant
MURDER REPORTED(1958, Brit.); PEEPING TOM(1960, Brit.)

Michel Durant
THIS, THAT AND THE OTHER(1970, Brit.)

Ted Durant
NIGHT WALKER, THE(1964); HUMAN DUPLICATORS, THE(1965)

Thomas C. Durant
Silents
IRON HORSE, THE(1924)

Tim Durant
RED BADGE OF COURAGE, THE(1951); RETURN TO PEYTON PLACE(1961); LIST OF ADRIAN MESSENGER, THE(1963)

V. Durant
WHAT PRICE DECENCY?(1933)

Will Durant
FALL OF THE ROMAN EMPIRE, THE(1964), cons; REDS(1981)

Anita Durante
WHITE VOICES(1965, Fr./Ital.); MADE IN ITALY(1967, Fr./Ital.)

Catherine Durante
LES CARABINIERS(1968, Fr./Ital.)

Checco Durante
DISHONORED(1950, Ital.); ISLAND OF PROCIDA, THE(1952, Ital.); VARIETY LIGHTS(1965, Ital.)

Doris Durante
CARMELA(1949, Ital.)

Jean Durante
HOLLYWOOD PARTY(1934)

Jimmy Durante
ROADHOUSE NIGHTS(1930); CUBAN LOVE SONG,THE(1931); NEW ADVEN-TURES OF GET-RICH-QUICK WALLINGFORD, THE(1931); BLONDIE OF THE FOLLIES(1932); PASSIONATE PLUMBER(1932); PHANTOM PRESIDENT, THE(1932); SPEAK EASILY(1932); WET PARADE, THE(1932); BROADWAY TO HOLLYWOOD(1933); HELL BELOW(1933); MEET THE BARON(1933); WHAT! NO BEER?(1933); GEORGE WHITE'S SCANDALS(1934); HOLLYWOOD PARTY(1934); PALOOKA(1934); STRICTLY DYNAMITE(1934); STUDENT TOUR(1934); CAR-NIVAL(1935); FORBIDDEN MUSIC(1936, Brit.); LITTLE MISS BROADWAY(1938); SALLY, IRENE AND MARY(1938); START CHEERING(1938); MELODY RANCH(1940); YOU'RE IN THE ARMY NOW(1941); MAN WHO CAME TO DINNER, THE(1942); MUSIC FOR MILLIONS(1944); TWO GIRLS AND A SAILOR(1944); TWO SISTERS FROM BOSTON(1946); IT HAPPENED IN BROOKLYN(1947); THIS TIME FOR KEEPS(1947); ON AN ISLAND WITH YOU(1948); GREAT RUPERT, THE(1950); MILKMAN, THE(1950); PEPE(1960); JUMBO(1962); IT'S A MAD, MAD, MAD, MAD WORLD(1963)

Vito Durante
TOP BANANA(1954)

Doris Duranti
KING'S JESTER, THE(1947, Ital.); COUNTERFEITERS, THE(1953, Ital.)

Robert Duranton
BURGLARS, THE(1972, Fr./Ital.)

Ludmilla Durarowa
PRINCE OF FOXES(1949)

Marguerite Duras
THIS ANGRY AGE(1958, Ital./Fr.), w; HIROSHIMA, MON AMOUR(1959, Fr./Jap.), w; LONG ABSENCE, THE(1962, Fr./Ital.), w; MODERATO CANTABILE(1964, Fr./Ital.), w; 10:30 P.M. SUMMER(1966, U.S./Span.), w; SAILOR FROM GIBRALTAR, THE(1967, Brit.), w; DESTROY, SHE SAID(1969, Fr.), d&w; NATHALIE GRAN-GER(1972, Fr.), d&w, m

L. Durasov
MAN OF MUSIC(1953, USSR)

M. Durasova
Misc. Silents
YEKATERINA IVANOVNA(1915, USSR)

Bill Duray
SUNSET MURDER CASE(1941); DESK SET(1957)

Ethel Duray
Misc. Silents
BACK PAY(1922)

William Duray
STRANGE LOVE OF MARTHA IVERS, THE(1946); HOT SPELL(1958)

John Durban
1984
TERMINATOR, THE(1984)

Deanna Durbin
THREE SMART GIRLS(1937); 100 MEN AND A GIRL(1937); MAD ABOUT MU-SIC(1938); THAT CERTAIN AGE(1938); FIRST LOVE(1939); THREE SMART GIRLS GROW UP(1939); IT'S A DATE(1940); SPRING PARADE(1940); IT STARTED WITH EVE(1941); NICE GIRL?(1941); AMAZING MRS. HOLLIDAY(1943); HERS TO HOLD(1943); HIS BUTLER'S SISTER(1943); CAN'T HELP SINGING(1944); CHRIST-MAS HOLIDAY(1944); LADY ON A TRAIN(1945); BECAUSE OF HIM(1946); I'LL BE YOURS(1947); SOMETHING IN THE WIND(1947); FOR THE LOVE OF MARY(1948); UP IN CENTRAL PARK(1948)

Roy Durbin
FIDDLER ON THE ROOF(1971)

Francis Durbridge
SEND FOR PAUL TEMPLE(1946, Brit.), w; CALLING PAUL TEMPLE(1948, Brit.), w; PAUL TEMPLE'S TRIUMPH(1951, Brit.), w; PAUL TEMPLE RETURNS(1952, Brit.), w; BROKEN HORSESHOE, THE(1953, Brit.), w; OPERATION DI-PLOMAT(1953, Brit.), w; TECKMAN MYSTERY, THE(1955, Brit), w; POSTMARK FOR DANGER(1956, Brit.), w; CIRCLE, THE(1959, Brit.), w

Joy Durden
MY BODY HUNGERS(1967)

Richard Durden
SCARS OF DRACULA, THE(1970, Brit.)

Richard Durden-Smith
DOCTOR FAUSTUS(1967, Brit.)

Memed Durdu
TARGET: HARRY(1980)

Durec
Misc. Silents
LE CHEMIN D'ERONA(1921, Fr.)

Gianpaolo Duregon
GARDEN OF THE FINZI-CONTINIS, THE(1976, Ital./Ger.)

Marina Durell
UP THE SANDBOX(1972); BADGE 373(1973)

Emile Durelle
TOAST OF NEW YORK, THE(1937)

Frenchy Durelle
DON'T TURN'EM LOOSE(1936)

Larry Duren
NAKED IN THE SUN(1957), art d

Edwin Durer
ALL IN(1936, Brit.)

Otto Durer
LULU(1962, Aus.), p

Marc Duret
FIVE DAYS ONE SUMMER(1982)

Jacques Durette
APPRENTICESHIP OF DUDDY KRAVITZ, THE(1974, Can.)

Peter DuRey
FIREFLY, THE(1937)

Duke Durfee
1984
FLAMINGO KID, THE(1984), art d

Minta Durfee
ROLLIN' HOME TO TEXAS(1941); MIRACLE KID(1942); EVE KNEW HER AP-PLES(1945); WILL SUCCESS SPOIL ROCK HUNTER?(1957)
Silents
TILLIE'S PUNCTURED ROMANCE(1914); CABARET, THE(1918); MICKEY(1919)

Ross Durfee
DESPERATE WOMEN, THE(?); TWO-MINUTE WARNING(1976); OTHER SIDE OF THE MOUNTAIN–PART 2, THE(1978)

Gian Paolo Durgar
MEDEA(1971, Ital./Fr./Ger.)

Rosa Elena Durgel
EMPTY STAR, THE(1962, Mex.); YOUNG AND EVIL(1962, Mex.); EXTERMINAT-ING ANGEL, THE(1967, Mex.)

Augusta Durgeon
RAMPARTS WE WATCH, THE(1940)

Bob Durham
NIGHT OF EVIL(1962)

Earl Durham
FEAR NO MORE(1961), p

G.A. Durham
OKLAHOMA JIM(1931), w

Inez Durham
SOUNDER(1972)

Louis Durham
Silents
ICED BULLET, THE(1917); ONE SHOT ROSS(1917); PINCH HITTER, THE(1917)
Misc. Silents
LAW UNTO HIMSELF, A(1916); HELL'S END(1918)

Lowell Durham
MAGNIFICENT OBSESSION(1935)

Marcel Durham
JULIA(1977), ed

Marilyn Durham
MAN WHO LOVED CAT DANCING, THE(1973), w

Richard Durham
WRONG MAN, THE(1956); GREATEST, THE(1977, U.S./Brit.), w

Branko Duric
DAY THAT SHOOK THE WORLD, THE(1977, Yugo./Czech.)

Tilla Durieurx
Silents
WOMAN ON THE MOON, THE(1929, Ger.)

Gilles Durieux
1984
EDITH AND MARCEL(1984, Fr.), w; L'ARGENT(1984, Fr./Switz.)

Tilla Durieux
LAST BRIDGE, THE(1957, Aust.)

Pierre Durin
VICE AND VIRTUE(1965, Fr./Ital.), spec eff
Anne Marie Duringer
LACEMAKER, THE(1977, Fr.)
Annearie Duringer
DEVIL STRIKES AT NIGHT, THE(1959, Ger.)
Annemarie Duringer
COUNT FIVE AND DIE(1958, Brit.); VOR SONNENUNTERGANG(1961, Ger); CITY OF SECRETS(1963, Ger.); YOU ARE THE WORLD FOR ME(1964, Aust.); VERONIKA VOSS(1982, Ger.)
Frank Durk
WHO SAYS I CAN'T RIDE A RAINBOW!(1971)
William Durkee
UNHOLY WIFE, THE(1957, w
Bernard Durkin
RECAPTURED LOVE(1930)
Billy Durkin
SEVEN MINUTES, THE(1971); FINAL COMEDOWN, THE(1972)
Douglas Durkin
UNION DEPOT(1932), w
Eddie Durkin
SPEED CRAZY(1959)
Grace Durkin
MAN WHO PLAYED GOD, THE(1932); CLEOPATRA(1934); MAN BETRAYED, A(1937); THIRTEENTH MAN, THE(1937)
James Durkin
DERELICT(1930); SHADOW OF THE LAW(1930); ALEXANDER HAMILTON(1931); CONQUERING HORDE, THE(1931); GUN SMOKE(1931); HUCKLEBERRY FINN(1931); VICE SQUAD, THE(1931); NICE WOMAN(1932); SHOPWORN(1932); SOUTH OF THE RIO GRANDE(1932); WILD GIRL(1932); DEVIL'S MATE(1933); HEAT LIGHTNING(1934); THIS SIDE OF HEAVEN(1934); UNCERTAIN LADY(1934); UPPER WORLD(1934)
Silents
INCORRIGIBLE DUKANE, THE(1915), d; BY WHOSE HAND?(1916), d; CLARION, THE(1916), d; RED WIDOW, THE(1916), d
Misc. Silents
MUMMY AND THE HUMMINGBIRD, THE(1915), d
Junior Durkin
RECAPTURED LOVE(1930); SANTA FE TRAIL, THE(1930); TOM SAWYER(1930); HELL'S HOUSE(1932); MAN HUNT(1933); LITTLE MEN(1935)
Mary Ann Durkin
THESE THREE(1936)
Mary Anne Durkin
SINCE YOU WENT AWAY(1944)
Mary Durkin
CURTAINS(1983, Can.)
Pat Durkin
STICK UP, THE(1978, Brit.)
Patrick Durkin
PLEASE TURN OVER(1960, Brit.); CARRY ON SPYING(1964, Brit.); MAN WHO HAD POWER OVER WOMEN, THE(1970, Brit.); BIG SLEEP, THE½(1978, Brit.); RAIDERS OF THE LOST ARK(1981)
Trent Durkin
BIG HEARTED HERBERT(1934); CHASING YESTERDAY(1935)
Trent [Junior] Durkin
READY FOR LOVE(1934)
Otto Durkoltz
SILENT ENEMY, THE(1930), ph
Jay Durkus
GOING APE!(1981)
Jaye Durkus
PROPHECY(1979)
Arthur Durlam
YOUNG DYNAMITE(1937), w; FRONTIER CRUSADER(1940), w
Arthur G. Durlam
SWAMP WOMAN(1941), w
G. A. Durlam
CODE OF HONOR(1930), w; LONESOME TRAIL, THE(1930), w, ed; IN THE LINE OF DUTY(1931), w; MONTANA KID, THE(1931), w; NEAR THE TRAIL'S END(1931), w; PARTNERS OF THE TRAIL(1931), w; RIDERS OF THE NORTH(1931), p, w; UNDER TEXAS SKIES(1931), w; SOUTH OF SANTA FE(1932), w
G. Arthur Durlam
TWO-FISTED JUSTICE(1931), d&w
George Arthur Durlam
MAN FROM DEATH VALLEY, THE(1931), w; LIGHTNING BILL CARSON(1936), d
Arthur Durlan
ACES AND EIGHTS(1936), w
Frank Durlauf
DEEP VALLEY(1947), art d; CANON CITY(1948), art d; HOLLOW TRIUMPH(1948), art d; SPIRITUALIST, THE(1948), art d; BIG CAT, THE(1949), art d; TRAPPED(1949), art d; FOR MEN ONLY(1952), art d
E. V. Durling
Silents
MANHATTAN MADNESS(1916), w; ALMOST MARRIED(1919), w; REPORTED MISSING(1922), t
Doris Durnati
DIVINE NYMPH, THE(1979, Ital.)
Allen Durnell
Silents
CRAZY TO MARRY(1921)
Margaret Durnell
DEVIL DOLL(1964, Brit.)
Dennis Durney
MOLLY AND LAWLESS JOHN(1972), p
Charles Durnham
HI, MOM!(1970)
Bernard Durning
Silents
DIANE OF STAR HOLLOW(1921)

Misc. Silents
BLACKIE'S REDEMPTION(1919); UNWRITTEN CODE, THE(1919), d; WHEN BEARCAT WENT DRY(1919); GIFT SUPREME, THE(1920); SEEDS OF VENGEANCE(1920); DEVIL WITHIN, THE(1921); PARTNERS OF FATE(1921), d; STRAIGHT FROM THE SHOULDER(1921), d
Bernard J. Durning
Silents
OATH-BOUND(1922), d; ELEVENTH HOUR, THE(1923), d
Misc. Silents
DEVIL WITHIN, THE(1921), d; ONE-MAN TRAIL, THE(1921), d; PRIMAL LAW, THE(1921), d; TO A FINISH(1921), d; FAST MAIL, THE(1922), d; IRON TO GOLD(1922), d; STRANGE IDOLS(1922), d; WHILE JUSTICE WAITS(1922), d; YOSEMITE TRAIL, THE(1922), d
Charles Durning
HARVEY MIDDLEMAN, FIREMAN(1965); I WALK THE LINE(1970); DEALING: OR THE BERKELEY-TO-BOSTON FORTY-BRICK LOST-BAG BLUES(1971); PURSUIT OF HAPPINESS, THE(1971); SISTERS(1973); STING, THE(1973); FRONT PAGE, THE(1974); DOG DAY AFTERNOON(1975); HINDENBURG, THE(1975); BREAKHEART PASS(1976); HARRY AND WALTER GO TO NEW YORK(1976); CHOIRBOYS, THE(1977); TWILIGHT'S LAST GLEAMING(1977, U.S./Ger.); ENEMY OF THE PEOPLE, AN(1978); FURY, THE(1978); GREEK TYCOON, THE(1978); NORTH DALLAS FORTY(1979); STARTING OVER(1979); TILT(1979); WHEN A STRANGER CALLS(1979); DIE LAUGHING(1980); FINAL COUNTDOWN, THE(1980); TRUE CONFESSIONS(1981); BEST LITTLE WHOREHOUSE IN TEXAS, THE(1982); DEADHEAD MILES(1982); SHARKY'S MACHINE(1982); TOOTSIE(1982); TO BE OR NOT TO BE(1983); TWO OF A KIND(1983)
1984
HADLEY'S REBELLION(1984); MASS APPEAL(1984)
Manfred Durniok
CATAMOUNT KILLING, THE(1975, Ger.), p; MEPHISTO(1981, Ger.), p
Annie Duroc
TIGHT SKIRTS, LOOSE PLEASURES(1966, Fr.)
Chris Durocher
MAIN STREET TO BROADWAY(1953)
Leo Durocher
MAIN STREET TO BROADWAY(1953)
Dick Durock
COAST TO COAST(1980); SWAMP THING(1982)
Antoine Durousseau
PORGY AND BESS(1959)
L. Durov
NINE DAYS OF ONE YEAR(1964, USSR); MEET ME IN MOSCOW(1966, USSR)
Lev Durov
ARMED AND DANGEROUS(1977, USSR)
Paul Durov
VOODOO WOMAN(1957)
Lida Durova
THEY WON'T BELIEVE ME(1947); SINBAD THE SAILOR(1947)
Ratko Durovic
BATTLE OF THE NERETVA(1971, Yugo./Ital./Ger.), w
Tracy Durphy
PORKY'S II: THE NEXT DAY(1983)
Fred Durr
TOWN WITHOUT PITY(1961, Ger./Switz./U.S.); LONGEST DAY, THE(1962); PHONY AMERICAN, THE(1964, Ger.); STOP TRAIN 349(1964, Fr./Ital./Ger.)
Storm Durr
FOXHOLE IN CAIRO(1960, Brit.)
Durra
HELP!(1965, Brit.)
Val Durran
Misc. Talkies
BEAST OF BORNEO(1935)
Edward Durrand
Silents
ANNA ASCENDS(1922)
Nathalie Durrand
LIFE LOVE DEATH(1969, Fr./Ital.)
Fred W. Durrant
Silents
PICTURE OF DORIAN GRAY, THE(1916, Brit.), d; WHAT EVERY WOMAN KNOWS(1917, Brit.), d; EDGE O'BEYOND(1919, Brit.), d
Misc. Silents
MRS. CASSELL'S PROFESSION(1915, Brit.), d; MILL-OWNER'S DAUGHTER, THE(1916, Brit.), d; STRANGE CASE OF PHILIP KENT, THE(1916, Brit.), d; WOMEN WHO WIN(1919, Brit.), d; HUSBAND HUNTER, THE(1920, Brit.), d
Theo Durrant [Terry Adler]
MACABRE(1958), w
Lloyd Durre
SHEPHERD OF THE HILLS, THE(1964)
Bill Durrell
SIX PACK(1982), set d
Dianne Durrell
GUN RUNNER(1969)
Don Durrell
WHEN THE GIRLS TAKE OVER(1962)
Gioia Durrell
LOVE AND MARRIAGE(1966, Ital.)
Lawrence Durrell
JUDITH(1965), w; JUSTINE(1969), w
Michel Durrell
AMERICAN SUCCESS COMPANY, THE(1980)
Rusty Durrell
CHRISTIAN LICORICE STORE, THE(1971)
William Durrell, Jr.
YES, GIORGIO(1982), set d
William Joseph Durrell
CHRISTINE(1983), art d

William Joseph Durrell, Jr.
CHRISTINE(1983), set d
John Durren
OPERATION BOTTLENECK(1961); ROOMMATES, THE(1973), a, w; LEPKE(1975, U.S./Israel); BOBBIE JO AND THE OUTLAW(1976); GUMBALL RALLY, THE(1976); JESSIE'S GIRLS(1976); SUNSET COVE(1978)
Friedrich Durrenmatt
VISIT, THE(1964, Ger./Fr./Ital./U.S.), w
Dick Durrier
CRAZY KNIGHTS(1944), ed
Edward L. Durst
DAYS OF GLORY(1944)
Eric Durst
STAR IS BORN, A(1954), ph
John Durst
SECRET CAVE, THE(1953, Brit.), d; ONE WISH TOO MANY(1956, Brit.), d
Paul Durst
UNDERWORLD INFORMERS(1965, Brit.), w
David Durston
DRY SUMMER(1967, Turkey), d; I DRINK YOUR BLOOD(1971), d&w
David E. Durston
STIGMA(1972), d&w
Misc. Talkies
BLUE SEXTET(1972), d
Alain Durtal
ROYAL AFFAIRS IN VERSAILLES(1957, Fr.)
Durthal
ARIANE, RUSSIAN MAID(1932, Fr.)
Frederic Duru
DON'T CRY WITH YOUR MOUTH FULL(1974, Fr.)
Alan Durusissean
BY DESIGN(1982)
Ian Dury
1984
NUMBER ONE(1984, Brit.)
Monique Dury
DAY FOR NIGHT(1973, Fr.), cos; SUCH A GORGEOUS KID LIKE ME(1973, Fr.), cos; SMALL CHANGE(1976, Fr.), cos; MAN WHO LOVED WOMEN, THE(1977, Fr.); GREEN ROOM, THE(1979, Fr.); LOVE ON THE RUN(1980, Fr.)
1984
L'ARGENT(1984, Fr./Switz.), cos
Yael Duryanoff
JERUSALEM FILE, THE(1972, U.S./Israel)
Dan Duryea
BALL OF FIRE(1941); LITTLE FOXES, THE(1941); PRIDE OF THE YANKEES, THE(1942); THAT OTHER WOMAN(1942); SAHARA(1943); MAIN STREET AFTER DARK(1944); MAN FROM FRISCO(1944); MRS. PARKINGTON(1944); NONE BUT THE LONELY HEART(1944); ALONG CAME JONES(1945); GREAT FLAMARION, THE(1945); LADY ON A TRAIN(1945); MINISTRY OF FEAR(1945); SCARLET STREET(1945); VALLEY OF DECISION, THE(1945); WOMAN IN THE WINDOW, THE(1945); BLACK ANGEL(1946); WHITE TIE AND TAILS(1946); ANOTHER PART OF THE FOREST(1948); BLACK BART(1948); LARCENY(1948); RIVER LADY(1948); CRISS CROSS(1949); JOHNNY STOOL PIGEON(1949); TOO LATE FOR TEARS(1949); ONE WAY STREET(1950); WHIPPED, THE(1950); WINCHESTER '73(1950); AL JENNINGS OF OKLAHOMA(1951); CHICAGO CALLING(1951); SKY COMMANDO(1953); TERROR STREET(1953); THUNDER BAY(1953); RAILS INTO LARAMIE(1954); RIDE CLEAR OF DIABLO(1954); SILVER LODE(1954); THIS IS MY LOVE(1954); WORLD FOR RANSOM(1954); FOXFIRE(1955); MARAUDERS, THE(1955); BURGLAR, THE(1956); STORM FEAR(1956); BATTLE HYMN(1957); NIGHT PASSAGE(1957); SLAUGHTER ON TENTH AVENUE(1957); KATHY O'(1958); PLATINUM HIGH SCHOOL(1960); SIX BLACK HORSES(1962); HE RIDES TALL(1964); TAGGART(1964); WALK A TIGHTROPE(1964, U.S./Brit.); BOUNTY KILLER, THE(1965); FLIGHT OF THE PHOENIX, THE(1965); INCIDENT AT PHANTOM HILL(1966); FIVE GOLDEN DRAGONS(1967, Brit.); HILLS RUN RED, THE(1967, Ital.); BAMBOO SAUCER, THE(1968)
Misc. Talkies
DO YOU KNOW THIS VOICE?(1964)
Don Duryea
MANHANDLED(1949)
George Duryea [Tom Keene]
GODLESS GIRL, THE(1929); HONKY TONK(1929); IN OLD CALIFORNIA(1929); BEAU BANDIT(1930); DUDE WRANGLER, THE(1930); NIGHT WORK(1930); PARDON MY GUN(1930); TOL'ABLE DAVID(1930)
Silents
MARKED MONEY(1928); THUNDER(1929)
Misc. Silents
TIDE OF EMPIRE(1929)
Peter Duryea
CARPETBAGGERS, THE(1964); TAGGART(1964); BOUNTY KILLER, THE(1965); LT. ROBIN CRUSOE, U.S.N.(1966); CATALINA CAPER, THE(1967); IS THIS TRIP REALLY NECESSARY?(1970)
Misc. Talkies
BLOOD OF THE IRON MAIDEN(1969)
Debra Dusay
1984
CHOOSE ME(1984)
Marj Dusay
SWEET NOVEMBER(1968); PENDULUM(1969); BREEZY(1973); MAC ARTHUR(1977)
Anna Duse
FOLLY TO BE WISE(1953), cos; DEEP BLUE SEA, THE(1955, Brit.), cos; LADY GODIVA RIDES AGAIN(1955, Brit.), cos.; WEE GEORDIE(1956, Brit.), cos; LET'S BE HAPPY(1957, Brit.), cos; TARZAN AND THE LOST SAFARI(1957, Brit.), cos; THAT RIVIERA TOUCH(1968, Brit.), cos; CHAIRMAN, THE(1969), cos; DECLINE AND FALL... OF A BIRD WATCHER(1969, Brit.), cos
Anne Duse
KID FOR TWO FARTHINGS, A(1956, Brit.), cos

Carlo Duse
ADVENTURE OF SALVATOR ROSA, AN(1940, Ital.); UNA SIGNORA DELL'OVEST(1942, Ital); BEFORE HIM ALL ROME TREMBLED(1947, Ital.); MONSTER OF THE ISLAND(1953, Ital.)
Vittorio Duse
OUTCRY(1949, Ital.); OSSESSIONE(1959, Ital.); LEOPARD, THE(1963, Ital.); STRANGER, THE(1967, Algeria/Fr./Ital.); INVESTIGATION OF A CITIZEN ABOVE SUSPICION(1970, Ital.)
Ann Dusenberry
GOODBYE FRANKLIN HIGH(1978); JAWS II(1978); CUTTER AND BONE(1981)
1984
LIES(1984, Brit.)
Misc. Talkies
LIES(1983)
Anne Dusenberry
HEART BEAT(1979)
Phil Dusenberry
HAIL(1973), w
1984
NATURAL, THE(1984), w
Jack Dusick
MAVERICK QUEEN, THE(1956), makeup
Nancy Dusina
OPERATION BIKINI(1963)
G. Dusmatas
MAN COULD GET KILLED, A(1966)
Robert C. DuSoe
TWENTY MULE TEAM(1940), w; DEVIL THUMBS A RIDE, THE(1947), d&w
Rene Dussaq
O.S.S.(1946); WHERE THERE'S LIFE(1947)
Ghislain Dussart
SAND CASTLE, THE(1961)
Philippe Dussart
BAND OF OUTSIDERS(1966, Fr.), p; MAN WITH THE TRANSPLANTED BRAIN, THE(1972, Fr./Ital./Ger.), p; ADOLESCENT, THE(1978, Fr./W.Ger.), p; MON ONCLE D'AMERIQUE(1980, Fr.), p
1984
LIFE IS A BED OF ROSES(1984, Fr.), p
Phillipe Dussart
CONTEMPT(1963, Fr./Ital.), prod d
Nancy Dussault
IN-LAWS, THE(1979)
Andre Dussolier
1984
LIFE IS A BED OF ROSES(1984, Fr.)
Andre Dussollier
SUCH A GORGEOUS KID LIKE ME(1973, Fr.); AND NOW MY LOVE(1975, Fr.); ALICE, OR THE LAST ESCAPADE(1977, Fr.); LE BEAU MARIAGE(1982, Fr.)
1984
JUST THE WAY YOU ARE(1984); LOVE ON THE GROUND(1984,Fr.)
R. J. Dustin
Silents
ABRAHAM LINCOLN(1924)
Deborah Dutch
1984
PROTOCOL(1984)
Jack Dutch
THERE'S ALWAYS VANILLA(1972)
Guy Dute
TESTAMENT OF ORPHEUS, THE(1962, Fr.)
John Duthie
HIGH COUNTRY, THE(1981, Can.)
Michael Duthie
SHOUT AT THE DEVIL(1976, Brit.), ed
Michael J. Duthie
REVENGE OF THE NINJA(1983), ed
1984
CALIFORNIA GIRLS(1984), ed; NIGHT SHADOWS(1984), ed; NINJA III–THE DOMINATION(1984), ed; SAHARA(1984), ed
Laure Duthilleul
DIVA(1982, Fr.)
Robert Dutil
I AM THE CHEESE(1983)
Jose Dutillieu
1984
SMURFS AND THE MAGIC FLUTE, THE(1984, Fr./Belg.), p, d
Janine Dutivitski
MISSIONARY, THE(1982)
Eddie Dutko
WALK TALL(1960), ed
Eddy Dutko
BLACK PIRATES, THE(1954, Mex.); TESS OF THE STORM COUNTRY(1961), ed
Edward Dutko
HIGH-POWERED RIFLE, THE(1960), ed; WAR HUNT(1962), ed; PROMISES, PROMISES(1963), ed
Josh DuToit
COAST OF SKELETONS(1965, Brit.)
Roger Dutoit
PIERROT LE FOU(1968, Fr./Ital.)
John Dutra
ROCKETSHIP X-M(1950); NO WAY TO TREAT A LADY(1968)
Mortie Dutra
MONEY FROM HOME(1953)
Edward Dutreil
INVISIBLE AVENGER, THE(1958), md
P. Dutrelli
GREEN TREE, THE(1965, Ital.)

Edward Dutriel
FOUR FOR THE MORGUE(1962), ed
Paul Dutron
YOUNG GIRLS OF WILKO, THE(1979, Pol./Fr.)
Jacques Dutronc
MAIN THING IS TO LOVE, THE(1975, Ital./Fr.); EVERY MAN FOR HIMSELF(1980, Fr.); MALEVIL(1981, Fr./Ger.); PARADISE POUR TOUS(1982, Fr.)
Nikolaus Dutsch
I LOVE YOU, I KILL YOU(1972, Ger.)
Dilip Dutt
GUIDE, THE(1965, U.S./India)
Dulal Dutt
1984
HOME AND THE WORLD, THE(1984, India), ed
Santosh Dutt
TWO DAUGHTERS(1963, India)
Utpal Dutt
SHAKESPEARE WALLAH(1966, India); GURU, THE(1969, U.S./India)
Dulal Dutta
PATHER PANCHALI(1958, India), ed; WORLD OF APU, THE(1960, India), ed; GODDESS, THE(1962, India), ed; MUSIC ROOM, THE(1963, India), ed; TWO DAUGH-TERS(1963, India), ed; KANCHENJUNGHA(1966, India), ed; ADVERSARY, THE(1973, Ind.), ed; CHESS PLAYERS, THE(1978, India), ed
Dulala Dutta
APARAJITO(1959, India), ed
John Duttine
FINAL OPTION, THE(1983, Brit.)
Clement Dutto
SAILING ALONG(1938, Brit.)
Anthony Dutton
PERMISSION TO KILL(1975, U.S./Aust.)
Deborah Dutton
1984
HOT DOG...THE MOVIE(1984)
Evelyn Dutton
FOR LOVE OR MONEY(1963); PUFNSTUF(1970)
Evelyn J. Dutton
WHICH WAY IS UP?(1977)
George Dutton
SO PROUDLY WE HAIL(1943), spec eff
Laura Deane Dutton
IDEA GIRL(1946)
Simon Dutton
1984
MEMED MY HAWK(1984, Brit.)
Syd Dutton
PSYCHO II(1983), spec eff
Guy Duty
WHILE PARIS SLEEPS(1932), cos
Guy S. Duty
DISORDERLY CONDUCT(1932), cos
Al Duval
SAFARI(1940); SUNDOWN(1941)
B. C. Duval
Silents
BLUEBEARD'S SEVEN WIVES(1926)
Charles Duval
NIGHTHAWKS(1981)
Claire Duval
LUMIERE(1976, Fr.), p
Dominie Duval
RAINS CAME, THE(1939)
Hedi Duval
WRITTEN ON THE WIND(1956)
Henry Duval
BACK DOOR TO HELL(1964); WARKILL(1968, U.S./Phil.); SECRET OF THE SA-CRED FOREST, THE(1970)
Misc. Talkies
KILL, THE(1973)
Jacqueline Duval
FATHER OF THE BRIDE(1950); WATCH THE BIRDIE(1950); RED BALL EX-PRESS(1952); SOUTH SEA WOMAN(1953); RHAPSODY(1954)
Jacques-Henri Duval
THREE FACES OF SIN(1963, Fr./Ital.)
Joan Duval
KING'S ROW(1942)
Joe Duval
GIRL ON THE BRIDGE, THE(1951); THY NEIGHBOR'S WIFE(1953); I'LL CRY TOMORROW(1955)
John Duval
MESSAGE TO GARCIA, A(1936)
Jose Duval
CARDINAL, THE(1963); BADGE 373(1973)
Juan Duval
FLYING DOWN TO RIO(1933); ON THE GREAT WHITE TRAIL(1938); ARISE, MY LOVE(1940); RHYTHM OF THE RIO GRANDE(1940); LAW OF THE TROPICS(1941); RAZOR'S EDGE, THE(1946); LOVES OF CARMEN, THE(1948); DAUGHTER OF THE WEST(1949), m; NEPTUNE'S DAUGHTER(1949); CRISIS(1950); PALOMINO, THE(1950); SOMBRERO(1953)
LaRayne DuVal
HIS LUCKY DAY(1929)
Malila Saint Duval
AIRPORT(1970)
Maria Duval
LIVING COFFIN, THE(1965, Mex.); VAMPIRES, THE(1969, Mex.); PERMANENT VACATION(1982)
Mme. Duval
THINGS OF LIFE, THE(1970, Fr./Ital./Switz.)

Nikki Duval
QUEBEC(1951)
Pat DuVal
SUDDEN IMPACT(1983)
Paulette Duval
Silents
NERO(1922, U.S./Ital.); HE WHO GETS SLAPPED(1924); MONSIEUR BEAUCAI-RE(1924); MY HUSBAND'S WIVES(1924); MAN AND MAID(1925); BEVERLY OF GRAUSTARK(1926); EXQUISITE SINNER, THE(1926); SKYROCKET, THE(1926); TWELVE MILES OUT(1927); DIVINE WOMAN, THE(1928); NO OTHER WO-MAN(1928)
Misc. Silents
CHEAPER TO MARRY(1925); SPORTING LIFE(1925); BLARNEY(1926); BEWARE OF WINDOWS(1927); BREAKFAST AT SUNRISE(1927)
Pierre Duval
NIGHT AND DAY(1946)
Roland Duval
DON'T CRY WITH YOUR MOUTH FULL(1974, Fr.), w
Thomas Duval
1984
SUNDAY IN THE COUNTRY, A(1984, Fr.)
Veronique Duval
MARRIED WOMAN, THE(1965, Fr.); YOUNG GIRLS OF ROCHEFORT, THE(1968, Fr.)
Yvonne Duval
ARTISTS AND MODELS ABROAD(1938); TROPIC HOLIDAY(1938); YOU AND ME(1938)
Duvaleix
PRIZE, THE(1952, Fr.); ROYAL AFFAIRS IN VERSAILLES(1957, Fr.)
Christian Duvaleix
DRY ROT(1956, Brit.); ISADORA(1968, Brit.); MADWOMAN OF CHAILLOT, THE(1969); SOLO(1970, Fr.)
Maurine Duvalier
ISLAND WOMEN(1958)
Christian Duvaliex
THREE MEN IN A BOAT(1958, Brit.)
Henry Duvall
1984
PHAR LAP(1984, Aus.)
John Duvall
ANGELO MY LOVE(1983)
Paulette Duvall
Silents
ALIAS THE LONE WOLF(1927)
Robed Duvall
EAGLE HAS LANDED, THE(1976, Brit.)
Robert Duvall
TO KILL A MOCKINGBIRD(1962); CAPTAIN NEWMAN, M.D.(1963); NIGHTMARE IN THE SUN(1964); CHASE, THE(1966); BULLITT(1968); COUNTDOWN(1968); DE-TECTIVE, THE(1968); RAIN PEOPLE, THE(1969); TRUE GRIT(1969); M(1970); REVO-LUTIONARY, THE(1970, Brit.); LAWMAN(1971); THX 1138(1971); GODFATHER, THE(1972); GREAT NORTHFIELD, MINNESOTA RAID, THE(1972); JOE KIDD(1972); TOMORROW(1972); BADGE 373(1973); LADY ICE(1973); OUTFIT, THE(1973); CON-VERSATION, THE(1974); GODFATHER, THE, PART II(1974); BREAKOUT(1975); KILLER ELITE, THE(1975); NETWORK(1976); GREATEST, THE(1977, U.S./Brit.); SEVEN-PER-CENT SOLUTION, THE(1977, Brit.); BETSY, THE(1978); APOCALYPSE NOW(1979); GREAT SANTINI, THE(1979); PURSUIT OF D.B. COOPER, THE(1981); TRUE CONFESSIONS(1981); TENDER MERCIES(1982), a, p; ANGELO MY LO-VE(1983), d&w
1984
NATURAL, THE(1984); STONE BOY, THE(1984)
Misc. Talkies
ALIENS FROM ANOTHER PLANET(1967)
Roxanne Duvall
1984
ALLEY CAT(1984)
Shelley Duvall
BREWSTER McCLOUD(1970); MC CABE AND MRS. MILLER(1971); NASHVIL-LE(1975); BUFFALO BILL AND THE INDIANS, OR SITTING BULL'S HISTORY LESSON(1976); ANNIE HALL(1977); THREE WOMEN(1977); POPEYE(1980); SHIN-ING, THE(1980); TIME BANDITS(1981, Brit.)
Shelly Duvall
THIEVES LIKE US(1974)
Susan Duvall
SECOND THOUGHTS(1983)
William Duvall
ANGELO MY LOVE(1983)
Christian Duvalleix
NOUS IRONS A PARIS(1949, Fr.)
Frederic Duvalles
PARIS DOES STRANGE THINGS(1957, Fr./Ital.)
Christian Duvallex
PARIS WHEN IT SIZZLES(1964)
The Duvals
WHIP'S WOMEN(1968), m
Juan Duvan
FEATHERED SERPENT, THE(1948)
Jean Duvane
Silents
MARRY IN HASTE(1924), w
Lorna Duveen
Silents
KNOCKOUT, THE(1925); UNGUARDED HOUR, THE(1925)
Misc. Silents
SECOND MATE, THE(1929, Brit.)
Anita Duvel
GIRL FROM THE MARSH CROFT, THE(1935, Ger.)

Arthur C. Duvel
Silents
MY FOUR YEARS IN GERMANY(1918)
Albert Duverger
L'AGE D'OR(1979, Fr.), ph
Pierre Duverger
GERVAISE(1956, Fr.); PARIS DOES STRANGE THINGS(1957, Fr./Ital.)
Henri Duvernois
MAXIME(1962, Fr.), w
Henry Duvernois
APRES L'AMOUR(1948, Fr.), w
Claude Duvernoy
SCHIZOID(1980)
Janine Duvitski
DRACULA(1979); GREAT TRAIN ROBBERY, THE(1979, Brit.); BREAKING
GLASS(1980, Brit.)
Julien Duvivier
CAPTAIN BLACK JACK(1952, U.S./Fr.), w
Julian Duvivier
DESTINY(1944), d; PANIQUE(1947, Fr.), w
Julien Duvivier
DAVID GOLDER(1932, Fr.), d&w; POIL DE CAROTTE(1932, Fr.), d&w; GOLEM,
THE(1937, Czech./Fr.), d, w; GOLGOTHA(1937, Fr.), d; PEPE LE MOKO(1937, Fr.), d,
w; GREAT WALTZ, THE(1938), d; MARIE ANTOINETTE(1938), d; THEY WERE
FIVE(1938, Fr.), d, w; UN CARNET DE BAL(1938, Fr.), d, w; END OF A DAY,
THE(1939, Fr.), d, w; ESCAPE FROM YESTERDAY(1939, Fr.), d, w; MAN OF THE
HOUR, THE(1940, Fr.), p&d, w; LYDIA(1941), d, w; TALES OF MANHATTAN(1942),
d; FLESH AND FANTASY(1943), p, d; HEART OF A NATION, THE(1943, Fr.), d, w;
IMPOSTER, THE(1944), p&d, w; ANNA KARENINA(1948, Brit.), d, w; CAPTAIN
BLACK JACK(1952, U.S./Fr.), p&d; LITTLE WORLD OF DON CAMILLO, THE(1953, Fr.), d, w; LIT-
TLE WORLD OF DON CAMILLO, THE(1953, Fr./Ital.), d, w; HOLIDAY FOR HEN-
RIETTA(1955, Fr.), d, w; DEADLIER THAN THE MALE(1957, Fr.), d, w; FEMALE,
THE(1960, Fr.), d; DEVIL AND THE TEN COMMANDMENTS, THE(1962, Fr.), d, w;
PARIS WHEN IT SIZZLES(1964), w; HIGHWAY PICKUP(1965, Fr./Ital.), d, w;
DIABOLICALLY YOURS(1968, Fr.), d, w
Misc. Silents
HACELDAMA(1919, Fr.), d; LES ROQUEVILLARD(1922, Fr.), d; L'OURAGAN SUR
LA MONTAGE(1922, Fr.), d; COEURS FAROUCHES(1923, Fr.), d; LE REFLET DE
CLAUDE MERCOEUR(1923, Fr.), d; L'AGONIE CONSTANTIN(1925, Fr.), d; L'AGONIE
DE JERUSALEM(1926, Fr.), d; POIL DE CAROTTE(1926, Fr.), d; LE MARIAGE DE
MADEMOISELLE BEULEMANS(1927, Fr.), d; LE MYSTERE DE LA TOUR EIF-
FEL(1927, Fr.), d; L'HOMME A L'HISPANO(1927, Fr.), d; LA DIVINE CROISIE-
RE(1928, Fr.), d; LE TOURBILLON DE PARIS(1928, Fr.), d; AU BONHEUR DES
DAMES(1929, Fr.), d; LA VIE MIRACULEUSE DE THERESE MARTIN(1929, Fr.), d;
MAMAN COLIBRI(1929, Fr.), d
Yvette Duvosin
Silents
HEARTS OF THE WORLD(1918)
Eckard Dux
HAMLET(1962, Ger.)
Eckart Dux
MERRY WIVES OF WINDSOR, THE(1952, Ger.)
Francis Dux
TROUBLEMAKER, THE(1964); COUNTESS FROM HONG KONG, A(1967, Brit.)
Margarethe Dux
MIRACLE OF THE WHITE STALLIONS(1963)
Pierre Dux
LES DERNIERES VACANCES(1947, Fr.); DOCTEUR LAENNEC(1949, Fr.); MON-
SIEUR VINCENT(1949, Fr.); GRAND MANEUVER, THE(1956, Fr.); GORILLA
GREETS YOU, THE(1958, Fr.); GOODBYE AGAIN(1961); DAY AND THE HOUR,
THE(1963, Fr./ Ital.); FRIEND OF THE FAMILY(1965, Fr./Ital.); IS PARIS BURN-
ING?(1966, U.S./Fr.); Z(1969, Fr./Algeria); THREE MEN TO DESTROY(1980, Fr.); LA
VIE CONTINUE(1982, Fr.)
Elspeth Duxbury
MAKE MINE MINK(1960, Brit.); GREAT ST. TRINIAN'S TRAIN ROBBERY,
THE(1966, Brit.); YELLOW HAT, THE(1966, Brit.)
George Duxbury
SEVEN AGAINST THE SUN(1968, South Africa), adv
Pierre Duxx
1984
HEAT OF DESIRE(1984, Fr.)
Allen Duzak
SOLDIER, THE(1982)
N. Dvigubsky
UNCLE VANYA(1972, USSR), art d
Z. Dvizhkova
WAR AND PEACE(1968, USSR)
Russ Dvonch
ROCK 'N' ROLL HIGH SCHOOL(1979), w
Dvorak
ALLEGRO NON TROPPO(1977, Ital.), m
Ann Dvorak
GUARDSMAN, THE(1931); JUST A GIGOLO(1931); CROONER(1932); CROWD
ROARS, THE(1932); LOVE IS A RACKET(1932); SCARFACE(1932); SKY DE-
VILS(1932); STRANGE LOVE OF MOLLY LOUVAIN, THE(1932); THREE ON A
MATCH(1932); COLLEGE COACH(1933); WAY TO LOVE, THE(1933); FRIENDS OF
MR. SWEENEY(1934); GENTLEMEN ARE BORN(1934); HEAT LIGHTNING(1934);
HOUSEWIFE(1934); I SELL ANYTHING(1934); MASSACRE(1934); MIDNIGHT
ALIBI(1934); MURDER IN THE CLOUDS(1934); SIDE STREETS(1934); BRIGHT
LIGHTS(1935); DR. SOCRATES(1935); G-MEN(1935); SWEET MUSIC(1935); THANKS
A MILLION(1935); CASE OF THE STUTTERING BISHOP, THE(1937); MANHATTAN
MERRY-GO-ROUND(1937); MIDNIGHT COURT(1937); RACING LADY(1937); SHE'S
NO LADY(1937); WE WHO ARE ABOUT TO DIE(1937); GANGS OF NEW YORK(1938);
MERRILY WE LIVE(1938); BLIND ALLEY(1939); STRONGER THAN DESIRE(1939);
CAFE HOSTESS(1940); GIRLS OF THE ROAD(1940); THIS WAS PARIS(1942, Brit.);
ESCAPE TO DANGER(1943, Brit.); SQUADRON LEADER X(1943, Brit.); FLAME OF
THE BARBARY COAST(1945); MASQUERADE IN MEXICO(1945); ABILENE
TOWN(1946); BACHELOR'S DAUGHTERS, THE(1946); LONG NIGHT, THE(1947);
OUT OF THE BLUE(1947); PRIVATE AFFAIRS OF BEL AMI, THE(1947); WALLS OF
JERICHO(1948); LIFE OF HER OWN, A(1950); MRS. O'MALLEY AND MR. MALO-
NE(1950); OUR VERY OWN(1950); RETURN OF JESSE JAMES, THE(1950); I WAS AN
AMERICAN SPY(1951); SECRET OF CONVICT LAKE, THE(1951)
Anton Dvorak
DUET FOR CANNIBALS(1969, Swed.), m
Frantisek A. Dvorak
DEVIL'S TRAP, THE(1964, Czech.), w
Geraldine Dvorak
MONTE CARLO(1930); MOONLIGHT AND PRETZELS(1933); SARATOGA(1937)
Paula Dvorak
MERRY WIVES OF WINDSOR, THE(1966, Aust.), ed
Reggie Dvorak
D-DAY, THE SIXTH OF JUNE(1956)
Rosemary Dvorak
GREATEST SHOW ON EARTH, THE(1952)
Zandra Dvorak
FOLIES DERGERE(1935)
A. Dvoretsky
Misc. Silents
DRUNKENNESS AND ITS CONSEQUENCES(1913, USSR), d
Vladislav Dvorjetzki
SOLARIS(1972, USSR)
Ann Dvork
STRANGER IN TOWN(1932)
Boris Dvornik
NINTH CIRCLE, THE(1961, Yugo.); EVENT, AN(1970, Yugo.); BATTLE OF THE
NERETVA(1971, Yugo./Ital./Ger.)
Eva Dvorska
LITTLE NIGHT MUSIC, A(1977, Aust./U.S./Ger.)
Milena Dvorska
NIGHTS OF PRAGUE, THE(1968, Czech.); LAST ACT OF MARTIN WESTON,
THE(1970, Can./Czech.)
A. Dvorsky
INSPECTOR GENERAL, THE(1937, Czech.)
Alois Dvorsky
LEMONADE JOE(1966, Czech.)
Peter Dvorsky
VIDEODROME(1983, Can.)
Vaclav Dvorzetski
CHEREZ TERNII K SVEZDAM(1981 USSR)
Hal Dwain
FREE, WHITE AND 21(1963), w
Allan Dwan
FROZEN JUSTICE(1929), d; IRON MASK, THE(1929), d; SOUTH SEA ROSE(1929),
p&d; WHAT A WIDOW(1930), d; CHANCES(1931), d; MAN TO MAN(1931), d;
WICKED(1931), d; HER FIRST AFFAIRE(1932, Brit.), d; WHILE PARIS
SLEEPS(1932), d; COUNSEL'S OPINION(1933, Brit.), d; I SPY(1933, Brit.), d, w;
HOLLYWOOD PARTY(1934), d; BLACK SHEEP(1935), d, w; FIFTEEN MAIDEN
LANE(1936), d; HIGH TENSION(1936), d; HUMAN CARGO(1936), d; NAVY WI-
FE(1936), d; SONG AND DANCE MAN, THE(1936), d; HEIDI(1937), d; ONE MILE
FROM HEAVEN(1937), d; THAT I MAY LIVE(1937), d; WOMAN-WISE(1937), d;
JOSETTE(1938), d; REBECCA OF SUNNYBROOK FARM(1938), d; SUEZ(1938), d;
FRONTIER MARSHAL(1939), d; GORILLA, THE(1939), d; THREE MUSKETEERS,
THE(1939), d; SAILOR'S LADY(1940), d; TRAIL OF THE VIGILANTES(1940), p&d;
YOUNG PEOPLE(1940), d; LOOK WHO'S LAUGHING(1941), p&d; RISE AND
SHINE(1941), d; FRIENDLY ENEMIES(1942), d; HERE WE GO AGAIN(1942), p&d;
AROUND THE WORLD(1943), p&d; UP IN MABEL'S ROOM(1944), d; BREWSTER'S
MILLIONS(1945), d; GETTING GERTIE'S GARTER(1945), d, w; RENDEZVOUS
WITH ANNIE(1946), p&d; CALENDAR GIRL(1947), p&d; DRIFTWOOD(1947), d;
NORTHWEST OUTPOST(1947), d; ANGEL IN EXILE(1948), d; INSIDE STORY,
THE(1948), d; SANDS OF IWO JIMA(1949), d; SURRENDER(1950), d; BELLE LE
GRAND(1951), d; I DREAM OF JEANIE(1952), d; MONTANA BELLE(1952), d; WILD
BLUE YONDER, THE(1952), d; FLIGHT NURSE(1953), d; SWEETHEARTS ON
PARADE(1953), d; WOMAN THEY ALMOST LYNCHED, THE(1953), p&d; CATTLE
QUEEN OF MONTANA(1954), d; PASSION(1954), d; SILVER LODE(1954), d; ES-
CAPE TO BURMA(1955), d; PEARL OF THE SOUTH PACIFIC(1955), d; TENNES-
SEE'S PARTNER(1955), d; HOLD BACK THE NIGHT(1956), d; SLIGHTLY
SCARLET(1956), d; RESTLESS BREED, THE(1957), d; RIVER'S EDGE(1957), d;
ENCHANTED ISLAND(1958), d; MOST DANGEROUS MAN ALIVE, THE(1961), d
Misc. Talkies
BEAUTY'S DAUGHTER(1935), d
Silents
CONSPIRACY, THE(1914), d; COUNTY CHAIRMAN, THE(1914), d&w; DAMON
AND PYTHIAS(1914), w; STRAIGHT ROAD, THE(1914), d; COMMANDING OFFIC-
ER, THE(1915), d; DAVID HARUM(1915), d&w; JORDAN IS A HARD ROAD(1915), d,
w; MAY BLOSSOM(1915), d; PRETTY SISTER OF JOSE(1915), d; GOOD BAD MAN,
THE(1916), d; HABIT OF HAPPINESS, THE(1916), d, w; INNOCENT MAGDALENE,
AN(1916), d; MANHATTAN MADNESS(1916), d; CASSIDY(1917), sup; FIGHTING
ODDS(1917), d; MAN HATER, THE(1917), w; MAN WHO MADE GOOD, THE(1917),
sup; MODERN MUSKETEER, A(1917), d&w; HEADIN' SOUTH(1918), sup&w; MR.
FIX-IT(1918), d&w; GETTING MARY MARRIED(1919), d; SAHARA(1919), sup;
BROKEN DOLL, A(1921), d, w; PERFECT CRIME, THE(1921), d&w; SIN OF MARTHA
QUEED, THE(1921), d&w; ROBIN HOOD(1922), d; LAWFUL LARCENY(1923), d;
ARGENTINE LOVE(1924), d; SOCIETY SCANDAL, A(1924), p&d; NIGHT LIFE OF
NEW YORK(1925), d; SEA HORSES(1926), d; SUMMER BACHELORS(1926), d; TIN
GODS(1926), d; FRENCH DRESSING(1927), p&d; JOY GIRL, THE(1927), d; HAROLD
TEEN(1928), p; WHIP WOMAN, THE(1928), p; FAR CALL, THE(1929), d
Misc. Silents
FORBIDDEN ROOM, THE(1914), d; RICHELIEU(1914), d; UNWELCOME MRS.
HATCH, THE(1914), d; WILDFLOWER(1914), d; DANCING GIRL, THE(1915), d;
LOVE ROUTE, THE(1915), d; BETTY OF GRAYSTONE(1916), d; FIFTY-FIFTY(1916),
d; HALF BREED, THE(1916), d; PANTHEA(1917), d; BOUND IN MOROCCO(1918),
d; HE COMES UP SMILING(1918), d; CHEATING CHEATERS(1919), d; DARK STAR,
THE(1919), d; SOLDIERS OF FORTUNE(1919), d; FORBIDDEN THING,
THE(1919), d; IN THE HEART OF A FOOL(1920), d; LUCK OF THE IRISH, THE(1920),
d; SCOFFER, THE(1920), d; HIDDEN WOMAN, THE(1922), d; SUPERSTITION(1922), d;
BIG BROTHER(1923), d; GLIMPSES OF THE MOON, THE(1923), d; ZAZA(1923), d;
HER LOVE STORY(1924), d; MANHANDLED(1924), d; WAGES OF VIRTUE(1924), d;
COAST OF FOLLY, THE(1925), d; STAGE STRUCK(1925), d; PADLOCKED(1926), d;
EAST SIDE, WEST SIDE(1927), d; MUSIC MASTER, THE(1927), d; BIG NOISE,
THE(1928), d; TIDE OF EMPIRE(1929), d

Dorothy Dwan
FIGHTING LEGION, THE(1930); HIDE-OUT, THE(1930)
Silents
SILENT VOW, THE(1922); BASHFUL BUCCANEER(1925); WIZARD OF OZ, THE(1925); CAPTAIN'S COURAGE, A(1926); GREAT K & A TRAIN ROBBERY, THE(1926); HILLS OF KENTUCKY(1927); SILVER VALLEY(1927); SPUDS(1927); TUMBLING RIVER(1927); PEACOCK FAN(1929)
Misc. Silents
BREED OF THE BORDER, THE(1924); PERFECT CLOWN, THE(1925); CALL OF THE KLONDIKE, THE(1926); CANYON OF LIGHT, THE(1926); DANGEROUS DUDE, THE(1926); STOP, LOOK, AND LISTEN(1926); LAND BEYOND THE LAW, THE(1927); PRINCESS OF BROADWAY, THE(1927); RIDERS OF THE DARK(1928); SQUARE CROOKS(1928); CALIFORNIA MAIL, THE(1929); DRIFTER, THE(1929)

Isabel Dwan
SEA CHASE, THE(1955)

Isabelle Dwan
THERE'S NO BUSINESS LIKE SHOW BUSINESS(1954); PATSY, THE(1964); SINGLE ROOM FURNISHED(1968)

Norman Dwan
Misc. Silents
BLACK CARGOES OF THE SOUTH SEAS(1929), d; BLACK HILLS(1929), d

Sue Dwiggens
ATOMIC BRAIN, THE(1964), w

Jay Dwiggins
Silents
HIS MAJESTY THE AMERICAN(1919); IN FOR THIRTY DAYS(1919); MAN WHO TURNED WHITE, THE(1919)

David Dwight
GIRL IN BLACK STOCKINGS(1957)

Howard Dwight
Misc. Silents
DANCER AND THE KING, THE(1914)

Marguerita Dwight
Misc. Silents
DANCER AND THE KING, THE(1914)

Earl Dwire
DUGAN OF THE BAD LANDS(1931); BROADWAY TO CHEYENNE(1932); MAN FROM HELL'S EDGES(1932); MASON OF THE MOUNTED(1932); SON OF OKLAHOMA(1932); FUGITIVE, THE(1933); GALLOPING ROMEO(1933); RIDERS OF DESTINY(1933); BLUE STEEL(1934); DUDE RANGER, THE(1934); LUCKY TEXAN, THE(1934); MAN FROM UTAH, THE(1934); 'NEATH THE ARIZONA SKIES(1934); RANDY RIDES ALONE(1934); SAGEBRUSH TRAIL(1934); STAR PACKER, THE(1934); TRAIL BEYOND, THE(1934); WEST OF THE DIVIDE(1934); ALIAS JOHN LAW(1935); BETWEEN MEN(1935); COURAGEOUS AVENGER, THE(1935); FIGHTING PIONEERS(1935); JUSTICE OF THE RANGE(1935); LAST OF THE CLINTONS, THE(1935); LAWLESS FRONTIER, THE(1935); NEW ADVENTURES OF TARZAN(1935); NEW FRONTIER, THE(1935); NO MAN'S RANGE(1935); PARADISE CANYON(1935); RIDER OF THE LAW, THE(1935); SMOKEY SMITH(1935); TOMBSTONE TERROR(1935); WAGON TRAIL(1935); CARYL OF THE MOUNTAINS(1936); CAVALCADE OF THE WEST(1936); CROOKED TRAIL, THE(1936); DESERT JUSTICE(1936); KID RANGER, THE(1936); KING OF THE PECOS(1936); MILLIONAIRE KID(1936); RED RIVER VALLEY(1936); SONG OF THE GRINGO(1936); STORMY TRAILS(1936); TOLL OF THE DESERT(1936); TUNDRA(1936); ARIZONA DAYS(1937); DOOMED AT SUNDOWN(1937); EMPTY HOLSTERS(1937); GALLOPING DYNAMITE(1937); GAMBLING TERROR, THE(1937); GHOST TOWN(1937); GUN RANGER, THE(1937); HEADIN' FOR THE RIO GRANDE(1937); HITTIN' THE TRAIL(1937); IDAHO KID, THE(1937); LAW AND LEAD(1937); LIGHTNIN' CRANDALL(1937); MYSTERY OF THE HOODED HORSEMEN, THE(1937); OH, SUSANNA(1937); PINTO RUSTLERS(1937); RIDERS OF THE DAWN(1937); RIDERS OF THE ROCKIES(1937); RIDING ON(1937); SANTA FE BOUND(1937); STARS OVER ARIZONA(1937); SUNDOWN SAUNDERS(1937); THEY WON'T FORGET(1937); TOAST OF NEW YORK, THE(1937); TROUBLE AT MIDNIGHT(1937); TROUBLE IN TEXAS(1937); TRUSTED OUTLAW, THE(1937); ACCIDENTS WILL HAPPEN(1938); ANGELS WITH DIRTY FACES(1938); DANGER VALLEY(1938); DAREDEVIL DRIVERS(1938); GOLD MINE IN THE SKY(1938); MAN FROM MUSIC MOUNTAIN(1938); MYSTERIOUS RIDER, THE(1938); OLD BARN DANCE, THE(1938); OUTLAWS OF SONORA(1938); PURPLE VIGILANTES, THE(1938); ROMANCE OF THE ROCKIES(1938); SIX SHOOTIN' SHERIFF(1938); TWO-GUN JUSTICE(1938); ARIZONA KID, THE(1939); EACH DAWN I DIE(1939); ON TRIAL(1939); PRIVATE DETECTIVE(1939); STAR MAKER, THE(1939); TIMBER STAMPEDE(1939); TROUBLE IN SUNDOWN(1939); DEVIL'S ISLAND(1940); HIS GIRL FRIDAY(1940); KING OF THE LUMBERJACKS(1940)
Misc. Talkies
LAW OF THE WEST(1932); BIG CALIBRE(1935); BORN TO BATTLE(1935); SADDLE ACES(1935); UNCONQUERED BANDIT(1935); WOLF RIDERS(1935); RIDIN' ON(1936)

Earle Dwire
LAWLESS RANGE(1935); SPEED REPORTER(1936); GIT ALONG, LITTLE DOGIES(1937); UNDER WESTERN STARS(1938)

William Dwire
HONOR OF THE MOUNTED(1932)

Otto Dworak
WALK WITH LOVE AND DEATH, A(1969)

Ida Dworkin
Misc. Talkies
LIVING ORPHAN, THE(1939)

Patty Dworkin
MR. MOM(1983)
1984
GHOSTBUSTERS(1984)

Zofia Dwornik
PARTINGS(1962, Pol.), ed; PASSENGER, THE(1970, Pol.), ed

Lois Dworshak
ICE-CAPADES(1941)

Lola Dworshak
ICE-CAPADES REVUE(1942)

Steve Dwoskin
Misc. Talkies
HINDERED(1974), d

Bill Dwyer
CRY MURDER(1936)

Bobbie Dwyer
GRAND ESCAPADE, THE(1946, Brit.)

Earl Dwyer
Silents
KINGFISHER'S ROOST, THE(1922)

Elmer Dwyer
ONLY ANGELS HAVE WINGS(1939), ph

Ethel Dwyer
Misc. Silents
COWBOY ACE, A(1921)

Hilary Dwyer
CONQUEROR WORM, THE(1968, Brit.); BODY STEALERS, THE(1969); FILE OF THE GOLDEN GOOSE, THE(1969, Brit.); OBLONG BOX, THE(1969, Brit.); TWO GENTLEMEN SHARING(1969, Brit.); CRY OF THE BANSHEE(1970, Brit.); WUTHERING HEIGHTS(1970, Brit.)

James Francis Dwyer
Silents
BRIDE OF THE STORM(1926), w

John Dwyer
MIDWAY(1976), set d; GRAY LADY DOWN(1978), set d; I WANNA HOLD YOUR HAND(1978), set d; OTHER SIDE OF THE MOUNTAIN-PART 2, THE(1978), set d; THING, THE(1982), set d
Silents
OVER THE HILL TO THE POORHOUSE(1920)

John M. Dwyer
VALLEY OF MYSTERY(1967), set d; THIS SAVAGE LAND(1969), set d; JAWS(1975), set d; TWO-MINUTE WARNING(1976), set d; WHICH WAY IS UP?(1977), set d; COAL MINER'S DAUGHTER(1980), set d
1984
BEVERLY HILLS COP(1984), set d; ICE PIRATES, THE(1984), set d; TEACHERS(1984), set d

John T. Dwyer
Silents
JACK O'HEARTS(1926)

Kerry Dwyer
DEMONSTRATOR(1971, Aus.); DIMBOOLA(1979, Aus.)

Leslie Dwyer
IN WHICH WE SERVE(1942, Brit.); WINGS AND THE WOMAN(1942, Brit.); YOUNG MR. PITT, THE(1942, Brit.); LAMP STILL BURNS, THE(1943, Brit.); YELLOW CANARY, THE(1944, Brit.); GREAT DAY(1945, Brit.); VACATION FROM MARRIAGE(1945, Brit.); WAY AHEAD, THE(1945, Brit.); NIGHT BOAT TO DUBLIN(1946, Brit.); THIS MAN IS MINE(1946 Brit.); WHEN THE BOUGH BREAKS(1947, Brit.); BOND STREET(1948, Brit.); CALENDAR, THE(1948, Brit.); PICCADILLY INCIDENT(1948, Brit.); BAD LORD BYRON, THE(1949, Brit.); BOY, A GIRL AND A BIKE, A(1949 Brit.); IT'S NOT CRICKET(1949, Brit.); NOW BARABBAS WAS A ROBBER(1949, Brit.); POET'S PUB(1949, Brit.); TEMPTATION HARBOR(1949, Brit.); LAUGHTER IN PARADISE(1951, Brit.); LILLI MARLENE(1951, Brit.); LITTLE BALLERINA, THE(1951, Brit.); MIDNIGHT EPISODE(1951, Brit.); SMART ALEC(1951, Brit.); HOLIDAY WEEK(1952, Brit.); HOUR OF THIRTEEN, THE(1952); JUDGMENT DEFERRED(1952, Brit.); MY WIFE'S LODGER(1952, Brit.); ACT OF LOVE(1953); DOUBLE CONFESSION(1953, Brit.); MARILYN(1953, Brit.); BLACK RIDER, THE(1954, Brit.); GOOD DIE YOUNG, THE(1954, Brit.); ROOM IN THE HOUSE(1955, Brit.); WHERE THERE'S A WILL(1955, Brit.); EYEWITNESS(1956, Brit.); NOT SO DUSTY(1956, Brit.); OPERATION CONSPIRACY(1957, Brit.); MENACE IN THE NIGHT(1958, Brit.); STORMY CROSSING(1958, Brit.); LEFT, RIGHT AND CENTRE(1959); THIRTY NINE STEPS, THE(1960, Brit.); SEVENTY DEADLY PILLS(1964, Brit.); DIE, MONSTER, DIE(1965, Brit.); I'VE GOTTA HORSE(1965, Brit.); LIONHEART(1968, Brit.); UP IN THE AIR(1969, Brit.); SOPHIE'S PLACE(1970)

Mario Dwyer
SHORT GRASS(1950)

Marla Dwyer
HER FIRST ROMANCE(1940)

Marlo Dwyer
FOOTLIGHT PARADE(1933); SECRETS OF THE LONE WOLF(1941); MAN WITH TWO LIVES, THE(1942); TOO MANY WOMEN(1942); CROSSFIRE(1947); FOLLOW ME QUIETLY(1949); CAGED(1950); PRISONERS IN PETTICOATS(1950); WALK SOFTLY, STRANGER(1950); WOMAN FROM HEADQUARTERS(1950); MISSING WOMEN(1951); SNIPER, THE(1952); DANGEROUS MISSION(1954)

Mo Dwyer
POOR COW(1968, Brit.)

Nina Dwyer
TOMCAT, THE(1968, Brit.)

Nornie Dwyer
GRAND ESCAPADE, THE(1946, Brit.)

P. Dwyer
UNCIVILISED(1937, Aus.)

Paul Dwyer
THREE DAYS OF THE CONDOR(1975)

Roger Dwyer
TAMANGO(1959, Fr.), ed

Ruth Dwyer
MANNEQUIN(1937); FATHER TAKES A WIFE(1941); UNFINISHED BUSINESS(1941)
Silents
CLAY DOLLARS(1921); SECOND HAND LOVE(1923); AFTER A MILLION(1924); COVERED TRAIL, THE(1924); DARK STAIRWAYS(1924); JACK O' CLUBS(1924); RECKLESS AGE, THE(1924); GOING THE LIMIT(1925); SEVEN CHANCES(1925); STEPPING ALONG(1926); LOST LIMITED, THE(1927); NEST, THE(1927); WHITE PANTS WILLIE(1927); ALEX THE GREAT(1928)
Misc. Silents
HIS MYSTERY'S GIRL(1923); BROADWAY OR BUST(1924); CANVAS KISSER, THE(1925); CRACK O'DAWN(1925); FEAR FIGHTER, THE(1925); WHITE FANG(1925); BROWN DERBY, THE(1926); MAN OF QUALITY, A(1926); PATENT LEATHER PUG, THE(1926); RACING FOOL, THE(1927); PERFECT GENTLEMAN, A(1928)

Samuel Dwyer
OTHER SIDE OF THE MOUNTAIN, THE(1975)
William Dwyer
CHARLY(1968)
John Dwyre
VALACHI PAPERS, THE(1972, Ital./Fr.), ed
Johnny Dwyre
CHRISTMAS TREE, THE(1969, Fr.), ed; RED SUN(1972, Fr./Ital./Span.), ed; COLD
SWEAT(1974, Ital., Fr.), ed
Robert Dwyre
KILL! KILL! KILL!(1972, Fr./Ger./Ital./Span.), ed
Roger Dwyre
DAMNED, THE(1948, Fr.), ed; JUST ME(1950, Fr.), ed; ROYAL AFFAIR, A(1950),
ed; FORBIDDEN GAMES(1953, Fr.), ed; AMBASSADOR'S DAUGHTER, THE(1956),
ed; RIFIFI(1956, Fr.), ed; CRACK IN THE MIRROR(1960), ed; NEVER ON SUN-
DAY(1960, Gr.), ed; BIG GAMBLE, THE(1961), ed; PARIS BLUES(1961), ed; CRIME
DOES NOT PAY(1962, Fr.), ed; GIGOT(1962), ed; PHAEDRA(1962, U.S./Gr./Fr.), ed;
TOPKAPI(1964), ed; LADY L(1965, Fr./Ital.), ed; DEFECTOR, THE(1966, Ger./Fr.),
ed; 10:30 P.M. SUMMER(1966, U.S./Span.), ed; TRIPLE CROSS(1967, Fr./Brit.), ed;
MADWOMAN OF CHAILLOT, THE(1969), ed; AND HOPE TO DIE(1972 Fr/US), ed;
DAY THAT SHOOK THE WORLD, THE(1977, Yugo./Czech.), ed
Valentine Dyafl
CAESAR AND CLEOPATRA(1946, Brit.)
Alexander Dyakov
WITH LOVE AND TENDERNESS(1978, Bulgaria)
H. Kaye Dyal
MEMORY OF US(1974), d; LONE WOLF McQUADE(1983), w
Franklin Dyall
ATLANTIC(1929 Brit.); LIMPING MAN, THE(1931, Brit.); NIGHT IN MONTMARTE,
A(1931, Brit.); SAFE AFFAIR, A(1931, Brit.), a, p; MEN OF STEEL(1932, Brit.);
RINGER, THE(1932, Brit.); CALLED BACK(1933, Brit.); CASE OF GABRIEL PERRY,
THE(1935, Brit.); IRON DUKE, THE(1935, Brit.); LEAVE IT TO ME(1937, Brit.); MR.
STRINGFELLOW SAYS NO(1937, Brit.); MR. SATAN(1938, Brit.); ALL AT SEA(1939,
Brit.); CONQUEST OF THE AIR(1940); YELLOW CANARY, THE(1944, Brit.)
Silents
GARDEN OF RESURRECTION, THE(1919, Brit.); EASY VIRTUE(1927, Brit.)
Misc. Silents
SQUANDERED LIVES(1920, Brit.), d
Franklyn Dyall
ALIBI(1931, Brit.); PRIVATE LIFE OF HENRY VIII, THE(1933); CAPTAIN'S OR-
DERS(1937, Brit.); BONNIE PRINCE CHARLIE(1948, Brit.)
Valentine Dyall
MUCH TOO SHY(1942, Brit.); YELLOW CANARY, THE(1944, Brit.); BRIEF EN-
COUNTER(1945, Brit.); COLONEL BLIMP(1945, Brit.); SILVER FLEET, THE(1945,
Brit.); FRENZY(1946, Brit.); HENRY V(1946, Brit.); HOTEL RESERVE(1946, Brit.);
NIGHT BOAT TO DUBLIN(1946, Brit.); BAD SISTER(1947, Brit.); I KNOW WHERE
I'M GOING(1947, Brit.); CORRIDOR OF MIRRORS(1948, Brit.); NIGHT COMES TOO
SOON(1948, Brit.); QUEEN OF SPADES(1948, Brit.); STORY OF SHIRLEY YORKE,
THE(1948, Brit.); VENGEANCE IS MINE(1948, Brit.); CASE OF CHARLES PEACE,
THE(1949, Brit.); DR. MORELLE–THE CASE OF THE MISSING HEIRESS(1949, Brit.);
FOR THEM THAT TRESPASS(1949, Brit.); HELTER SKELTER(1949, Brit.); MAN ON
THE RUN(1949, Brit.); MY BROTHER'S KEEPER(1949, Brit.); ROOM TO LET(1949,
Brit.); WOMAN HATER(1949, Brit.); BODY SAID NO!, THE(1950, Brit.); GOLDEN
SALAMANDER(1950, Brit.); MAN IN BLACK, THE(1950, Brit.); MISS PILGRIM'S
PROGRESS(1950, Brit.); PINK STRING AND SEALING WAX(1950, Brit.); STRANGER
AT MY DOOR(1950, Brit.); HAMMER THE TOFF(1952, Brit.); IVANHOE(1952, Brit.);
PAUL TEMPLE RETURNS(1952, Brit.); SALUTE THE TOFF(1952, Brit.); FINAL TEST,
THE(1953, Brit.); DEVIL'S JEST, THE(1954, Brit.); JOHNNY ON THE SPOT(1954,
Brit.); SUSPENDED ALIBI(1957, Brit.); HORROR HOTEL(1960, Brit.); IDENTITY
UNKNOWN(1960, Brit.); NIGHT TRAIN FOR INVERNESS(1960, Brit.); FATE TAKES
A HAND(1962, Brit.); HAUNTING, THE(1963); HORROR OF IT ALL, THE(1964, Brit.);
WRONG BOX, THE(1966, Brit.); NAKED WORLD OF HARRISON MARKS, THE(1967,
Brit.); GREAT MCGONAGALL, THE(1975, Brit.); SLIPPER AND THE ROSE,
THE(1976, Brit.)
Elmer Dyar
CLIPPED WINGS(1938), ph
Ralph E. Dyar
Silents
VOICE IN THE DARK(1921), w
David Dyas
Misc. Silents
TIMBER WOLF(1925)
James Dybas
PRIVATE BENJAMIN(1980)
Hamilton Dyce
WHISTLE DOWN THE WIND(1961, Brit.); DOUBLE, THE(1963, Brit); BECKET(1964,
Brit.); MASTER SPY(1964, Brit.); KING RAT(1965); GYPSY GIRL(1966, Brit.); TWO
GENTLEMEN SHARING(1969, Brit.); UNMAN, WITTERING AND ZIGO(1971, Brit.);
PIED PIPER, THE(1972, Brit.)
Doris Dyck
OUT OF THE BLUE(1982), ed
Van Dycke
Silents
PRICE OF SILENCE, THE(1920, Brit.)
Cameron Dye
VALLEY GIRL(1983)
1984
BODY ROCK(1984); JOY OF SEX(1984); LAST STARFIGHTER, THE(1984)
Debi Dye
HAIR(1979)
Diane Dye
EMPEROR OF THE NORTH POLE(1973)
Florence Dye
Silents
MONEY MAGIC(1917)
Misc. Silents
TENDERFOOT, THE(1917)

George Dye
TOUCHDOWN!(1931)
John Dye
1984
MAKING THE GRADE(1984)
Leighton Dye
Silents
COLLEGE(1927)
Marjorie Durant Dye
J.W. COOP(1971)
Hamilton Dyee
WRONG BOX, THE(1966, Brit.)
Alec Dyer
MEIN KAMPF–MY CRIMES(1940, Brit.), w
Ann Dyer
BATTLE BEYOND THE STARS(1980), w
Anson Dyer
VICAR OF BRAY, THE(1937, Brit.), w; SECOND MATE, THE(1950, Brit.), w
Misc. Silents
DOLLARS IN SURREY(1921, Brit.), d
Bernard Victor Dyer
PORT AFRIQUE(1956, Brit.), w
Bill Dyer
GUN JUSTICE(1934); FOLLOW THE BOYS(1944); SEVEN DAYS ASHORE(1944);
TOMORROW IS FOREVER(1946); THREE STOOGES IN ORBIT, THE(1962)
Misc. Silents
MAN'S DESIRE(1919); TRIGGER FINGER(1924); SPURS AND SADDLES(1927);
THUNDER RIDERS(1928)
Bob Dyer
SUNSET PASS(1946)
Charles Dyer
RATTLE OF A SIMPLE MAN(1964, Brit.), a, w; KNACK ... AND HOW TO GET IT,
THE(1965, Brit.); HOW I WON THE WAR(1967, Brit.); STAIRCASE(1969 U.S./Brit./
Fr.), w
Denise Dyer
DIRTY HARRY(1971)
Diane Dyer
NONE BUT THE LONELY HEART(1944); DIRTY HARRY(1971)
Eddy Dyer
EMMA MAE(1976)
Eddie C. Dyer
DIFFERENT STORY, A(1978)
Eddy C. Dyer
STAR CHAMBER, THE(1983)
Elmer Dyer
FLIGHT(1929), ph; HELL'S ANGELS(1930), ph; BRANDED(1931), ph; DIRIGI-
BLE(1931), ph; LOST SQUADRON, THE(1932), ph; NIGHT FLIGHT(1933), ph; WEST
POINT OF THE AIR(1935), ph; SPECIAL AGENT K-7(1937), ph; DAUGHTER OF THE
TONG(1939), ph; FLYING DEUCES, THE(1939), aer ph; TWO-GUN TROUBA-
DOR(1939), ph; WINGS OF THE NAVY(1939), ph; LIGHTNING STRIKES
WEST(1940), ph; MURDER ON THE YUKON(1940), ph; DIVE BOMBER(1941), aerial
ph; KEEP 'EM FLYING(1941), ph; GALLANT JOURNEY(1946), ph; WINNER'S CIR-
CLE, THE(1948), ph; TIMBER FURY(1950), ph; CATTLE QUEEN(1951), ph; KOREA
PATROL(1951), ph; BUFFALO BILL IN TOMAHAWK TERRITORY(1952), ph; MOV-
IE STUNTMEN(1953), ph; SPRING AFFAIR(1960), ph
Elmer G. Dyer
HOT ANGEL, THE(1958), ph
Silents
WEB OF THE LAW, THE(1923), ph; LONE WAGON, THE(1924), ph
Ernest Anson Dyer
FLOOD TIDE(1935, Brit.), w
Fred Dyer
Silents
LOST PATROL, THE(1929, Brit.)
Gary L. Dyer
CHEAP DETECTIVE, THE(1978)
George Dyer
FOG OVER FRISCO(1934), w; SPY SHIP(1942), w
Jack Dyer
Silents
FAMILY SKELETON, THE(1918)
James Dyer
SECRET FILE: HOLLYWOOD(1962), p
Capt. James Dyer, USN
TASK FORCE(1949), tech adv
Jeane Dyer
TWO TICKETS TO BROADWAY(1951)
Lee Dyer
SOMETHING WICKED THIS WAY COMES(1983), spec eff
Linda Dyer
LITTLE BIG MAN(1970)
Lorely Dyer
LISBON STORY, THE(1946, Brit.)
Lou Dyer
STORMY CROSSING(1958, Brit.), w
Marion Dyer
Misc. Silents
YOU NEVER KNOW YOUR LUCK(1919)
Marlo Dyer
WOMAN ON PIER 13, THE(1950)
Percy Dyer
Silents
FROM THE MANGER TO THE CROSS(1913)
Pete Dyer
WOLFEN(1981)
Raymond Dyer
LONELINESS OF THE LONG DISTANCE RUNNER, THE(1962, Brit.)

Wayne Dyer
FOURTEEN, THE(1973, Brit.)
William Dyer
CODE OF HONOR(1930); TEXAS BUDDIES(1932); WOMAN IN THE WINDOW, THE(1945)
Silents
ANTHING ONCE(1917); ALL NIGHT(1918); SILENT CALL, THE(1921); SCARA-MOUCHE(1923); MARRY IN HASTE(1924); SINGER JIM MCKEE(1924); LOOKING FOR TROUBLE(1926)
Misc. Silents
LAW OF THE GREAT NORTHWEST, THE(1918); LITTLE WHITE SAVAGE, THE(1919); LOVE CALL, THE(1919); WHO WILL MARRY ME?(1919); SHERIFF OF HOPE ETERNAL, THE(1921); DON'T SHOOT(1922); WOLVES OF THE BOR-DER(1923); MARTYR SEX, THE(1924)
William Dyer, Jr.
MY PAL GUS(1952)
William J. Dyer
OVERLAND BOUND(1929)
Silents
MEASURE OF A MAN, THE(1924)
Misc. Silents
TRIUMPH(1917); DESERT OF THE LOST, THE(1927)
Lien Dyers
NUMBER SEVENTEEN(1928, Brit./Ger.)
Stanislaw Dygat
PARTINGS(1962, Pol.), w; JOVITA(1970, Pol.), w
John Hart Dyke
ASSASSIN(1973, Brit.)
Thomas L. Dyke
NORTHVILLE CEMETERY MASSACRE, THE(1976), p,d&ph
Jack Dykeman
TWO(1975)
Jimmy Dykes
STRATTON STORY, THE(1949)
Bozena Dykiel
MAN OF IRON(1981, Pol.); WAR OF THE WORLDS–NEXT CENTURY, THE(1981, Pol.); CONTRACT, THE(1982, Pol.)
Alexei Dykki
1812(1944, USSR)
Joan Dykman
1984
LOVE STREAMS(1984); WEEKEND PASS(1984)
John Dykstra
SILENT RUNNING(1972), spec eff; STAR WARS(1977), ph, spec eff; AVALANCHE EXPRESS(1979), spec eff; STAR TREK: THE MOTION PICTURE(1979), spec eff; FIREFOX(1982), spec eff
Bob Dylan
PAT GARRETT AND BILLY THE KID(1973), a, m; RENALDO AND CLARA(1978), a, d, w, ed
Sara Dylan
RENALDO AND CLARA(1978)
Amentha Dymally
HONKY(1971); SWEET JESUS, PREACHER MAN(1973)
Lionel Dymoke
MRS. PYM OF SCOTLAND YARD(1939, Brit.)
Frankie Dymon, Jr.
SOME PEOPLE(1964, Brit.); ONE PLUS ONE(1969, Brit.)
Misc. Talkies
DEATH MAY BE YOUR SANTA CLAUS(1969), d
Ossip Dymow
RASPUTIN(1932, Ger.), w; SINS OF MAN(1936), w; OVERTURE TO GLORY(1940), a, w
Dynam
DOCTEUR LAENNEC(1949, Fr.); JUST ME(1950, Fr.)
Jacques Dynam
FANTOMAS STRIKES BACK(1965, Fr./Ital.); MALE COMPANION(1965, Fr./Ital.); MALE HUNT(1965, Fr./Ital.); FANTOMAS(1966, Fr./Ital.); SLEEPING CAR MURDER THE(1966, Fr.); SELLERS OF GIRLS(1967, Fr.); LE PETIT THEATRE DE JEAN RENOIR(1974, Fr.); FRENCH CONNECTION 11(1975)
1984
ONE DEADLY SUMMER(1984, Fr.)
Dynamite
RED STALLION IN THE ROCKIES(1949)
Misc. Silents
FANGS OF DESTINY(1927); CALL OF THE HEART(1928); FOUR-FOOTED RANG-ER, THE(1928); HOUND OF THE SILVER CREEK, THE(1928)
Dynamite the Horse
Silents
OLD CLOTHES(1925); RAG MAN, THE(1925)
"Dynamite" the Wonder Horse
TIMBER TERRORS(1935)
Eugene Dynarski
MORITURI(1965); IN ENEMY COUNTRY(1968)
Gene Dynarski
EARTHQUAKE(1974); ALL THE PRESIDENT'S MEN(1976); CLOSE ENCOUNTERS OF THE THIRD KIND(1977)
1984
BEST DEFENSE(1984)
Aminta Dyne
HOUR BEFORE THE DAWN, THE(1944); MAN IN HALF-MOON STREET, THE(1944); MINISTRY OF FEAR(1945); MOLLY AND ME(1945); TONIGHT AND EVERY NIGHT(1945); CALCUTTA(1947); KISS THE BLOOD OFF MY HANDS(1948); SONG OF INDIA(1949); DANGEROUS WHEN WET(1953)
Michael Dyne
HANGOVER SQUARE(1945); KITTY(1945); WHITE PONGO(1945); CLUNY BROWN(1946); HOMESTRETCH, THE(1947); IMPERFECT LADY, THE(1947); MOSS ROSE(1947); MOON-SPINNERS, THE(1964), w

Peter Dyneley
LAUGHING IN THE SUNSHINE(1953, Brit./Swed.); BEAU BRUMMELL(1954); CHANCE MEETING(1954, Brit.); HELL BELOW ZERO(1954, Brit.); YOU KNOW WHAT SAILORS ARE(1954, Brit.); DEADLY GAME, THE(1955, Brit.); FEMALE FIENDS(1958, Brit.); INBETWEEN AGE, THE(1958, Brit.); WHOLE TRUTH, THE(1958, Brit.); DEADLY RECORD(1959, Brit.); OCTOBER MOTH(1960, Brit.); HOUSE OF MYSTERY(1961, Brit.); ROMAN SPRING OF MRS. STONE, THE(1961, U.S./Brit.); MANSTER, THE(1962, Jap.); STOLEN AIRLINER, THE(1962, Brit.); CALL ME BWANA(1963, Brit.); THUNDERBIRD 6(1968, Brit.); THUNDERBIRDS ARE GO(1968, Brit.); EXECUTIONER, THE(1970, Brit.); CHATO'S LAND(1972)
Misc. Talkies
THUNDERBIRDS 6(1968); BLACK TRASH(1978)
Dennis Dynsley
GREAT WALL OF CHINA, THE(1970, Brit.)
George M. Dyott
SAVAGE GOLD(1933), a, p, w, ph; MANHUNT IN THE JUNGLE(1958), w
Francois Dyreck
JUDGE AND THE ASSASSIN, THE(1979, Fr.)
Gilles Dyreck
JUDGE AND THE ASSASSIN, THE(1979, Fr.)
Marcus Dyrector
DRAGSTRIP RIOT(1958)
Francois Dyrek
QUESTION, THE(1977, Fr.); PIAF–THE EARLY YEARS(1982, U.S./Fr.)
Dr. Harold Dyrenforth
PRIZE, THE(1963); MORITURI(1965)
Harald Dyrenforth
STORM OVER TIBET(1952)
Harold Dyrenforth
CARNEGIE HALL(1947); CROOKED WEB, THE(1955); JUMP INTO HELL(1955); CONGO CROSSING(1956); AS YOUNG AS WE ARE(1958); WATUSI(1959); 36 HOURS(1965)
Howard Dyrenforth
MAGNIFICENT OBSESSION(1954)
James Dyrenforth
MAYFAIR MELODY(1937, Brit.), w; SINGING COP, THE(1938, Brit.), w; FIEND WITHOUT A FACE(1958); FLOODS OF FEAR(1958, Brit.); NIGHT TO REMEMBER, A(1958, Brit.); MAN IN A COCKED HAT(1960, Bri.); NEVER TAKE CANDY FROM A STRANGER(1961, Brit.); LOLITA(1962); GIRL HUNTERS, THE(1963, Brit.); SECRET DOOR, THE(1964); REVOLUTIONARY, THE(1970, Brit.)
Jacqueline Dyris
GODLESS GIRL, THE(1929)
Silents
MAN WHO SAW TOMORROW, THE(1922)
Bill Dysart
HOW I WON THE WAR(1967, Brit.)
Richard A. Dysart
CRAZY WORLD OF JULIUS VROODER, THE(1974); TERMINAL MAN, THE(1974); DAY OF THE LOCUST, THE(1975); HINDENBURG, THE(1975); ENEMY OF THE PEOPLE, AN(1978); METEOR(1979)
Richard Dysart
LOVE WITH THE PROPER STRANGER(1963); PETULIA(1968, U.S./Brit.); LOST MAN, THE(1969); HOSPITAL, THE(1971); SPORTING CLUB, THE(1971); BEING THERE(1979); PROPHECY(1979); THING, THE(1982)
Tommy Dysart
MAN FROM SNOWY RIVER, THE(1983, Aus.); NEXT OF KIN(1983, Aus.)
William Dysart
RICOCHET(1966, Brit.); DEADLY AFFAIR, THE(1967, Brit.); LAST SHOT YOU HEAR, THE(1969, Brit.); SUMARINE X-1(1969, Brit.)
1984
NEW YORK NIGHTS(1984)
Ann Dyson
YANKS(1979)
Anne Dyson
LONG AGO, TOMORROW(1971, Brit.); PRIEST OF LOVE(1981, Brit.)
1984
SACRED HEARTS(1984, Brit.)
Bobby Dyson
COUNTRY BOY(1966)
Hugo Dyson
DARLING(1965, Brit.)
Katherine Dyson
MIKADO, THE(1967, Brit.)
Noel Dyson
EIGHT O'CLOCK WALK(1954, Brit.); THREE CROOKED MEN(1958, Brit.); PLEASE TURN OVER(1960, Brit.); SILENT INVASION, THE(1962, Brit.); CARRY ON CAB-BIE(1963, Brit.); GUTTER GIRLS(1964, Brit.); PRESS FOR TIME(1966, Brit.); MISTER TEN PERCENT(1967, Brit.)
1984
CHAMPIONS(1984)
Reginald Dyson
ROOM TO LET(1949, Brit.)
Ronald Dyson
PUTNEY SWOPE(1969)
Ronnie Dyson
HAIR(1979)
Will Dyson
Silents
SQUIBS, MP(1923, Brit.), w
Richard Dyszel
NIGHTBEAST(1982)
1984
ALIEN FACTOR, THE(1984)
Misc. Talkies
ALIEN FACTOR, THE(1978)
Revas Dzhaparidze
STEPCHILDREN(1962, USSR), w

V. Dzheneyeva
Misc. Silents
  FATHER SERGIUS(1918, USSR)
Julian Dziedzina
  BOXER(1971, Pol.), d
Arie Dzierlatka
  CHLOE IN THE AFTERNOON(1972, Fr.), m; MON ONCLE D'AMERIQUE(1980,
Fr.), m; GIRL FROM LORRAINE, A(1982, Fr./Switz.), m; LIGHT YEARS AWAY(1982,
Fr./Switz.), m; DEATH OF MARIO RICCI, THE(1983, Ital.), m
H. Dzieszynski
  LOTNA(1966, Pol.)
Edward Dziewonski
  EROICA(1966, Pol.)
Sz. Dzigan
  WITHOUT A HOME(1939, Pol.)
Ahmed Dziri
Misc. Silents
  GIRL FROM CARTHAGE, THE(1924, Tunisia)
Anulka Dziubinska
  LISZTOMANIA(1975, Brit.)
Joe Dzizmba
  DEER HUNTER, THE(1978)
Zuko Dzumhur
  HOROSCOPE(1950, Yugo.), w
George Dzunda
  HAPPY HOOKER, THE(1975)
George Dzundza
  DEER HUNTER, THE(1978); HONKY TONK FREEWAY(1981); STREAMERS(1983)
1984
  BEST DEFENSE(1984)
A. Dzyubina
Misc. Silents
  MABUL(1927, USSR)
I. Dzyura
  SHADOWS OF FORGOTTEN ANCESTORS(1967, USSR)

E

Chen E-hsin
GRAND SUBSTITUTION, THE(1965, Hong Kong), w

Eva Eacott
WHAT A CARRY ON!(1949, Brit.); STICK 'EM UP(1950, Brit.)

Eve Eacott
YOU CAN'T FOOL AN IRISHMAN(1950, Ireland)

Bessie Eade
Silents
GOLD RUSH, THE(1925)

Margaret Eaden
TOWN LIKE ALICE, A(1958, Brit.)

Tony Eades
Misc. Talkies
SINFUL DWARF, THE(1973)

Wilfred Eades
YOU CAN'T ESCAPE(1955, Brit.), d; SMALL HOTEL(1957, Brit.), w; GORGO(1961, Brit.), p; VIOLENT ENEMY, THE(1969, Brit.), p

Wilfrid Eades
MOONRAKER, THE(1958, Brit.), w

Dennis Eadie
Misc. Silents
MAN WHO STAYED AT HOME, THE(1915, Brit.); DISRAELI(1916, Brit.)

Mark Eadie
LORDS OF DISCIPLINE, THE(1983)

Paul Eads
FAN, THE(1981), art d; SO FINE(1981), art d; HIT AND RUN(1982), prod d; TEMPEST(1982), art d; JAWS 3-D(1983), art d

David Eady
CRY, THE BELOVED COUNTRY(1952, Brit.), ed; THREE CASES OF MURDER(1955, Brit.), d; HEART WITHIN, THE(1957, Brit.), d; ZOO BABY(1957, Brit.), d; DUBLIN NIGHTMARE(1958, Brit.), p; BOY AND THE BRIDGE, THE(1959, Brit.), p; CROWNING TOUCH, THE(1959, Brit.), d; MAN WHO LIKED FUNERALS, THE(1959, Brit.), d; FACES IN THE DARK(1960, Brit.), d; IN THE WAKE OF A STRANGER(1960, Brit.), d; VERDICT, THE(1964, Brit.), d; OPERATION THIRD FORM(1966, Brit.), d, w; SCRAMBLE(1970, Brit.), d

Alberta Stedman Eagan
THEY CALL IT SIN(1932), w

Beverli Eagan
KISS ME GOODBYE(1982), set d

Jeanne Eagels
JEALOUSY(1929); LETTER, THE(1929)
Misc. Silents
MAN, WOMAN AND SIN(1927)

Virginia Eagels
THAT NIGHT WITH YOU(1945)

Keith Eager
ROLLOVER(1981)

Victoria Eagger
1984
MAN OF FLOWERS(1984, Aus.)

Eagle Eye
Silents
LAMB, THE(1915); PRIDE OF PALOMAR, THE(1922); LURE OF THE YUKON(1924)

Arnold Eagle
DREAMS THAT MONEY CAN BUY(1948), ph

Bill Eagle
Misc. Talkies
BLONDE GODDESS(1982), d

Billy Eagle
MISTER CORY(1957)

Brave Eagle
RAMRODDER, THE(1969)

Charles White Eagle
ALTERED STATES(1980)

Gordon Eagle
WOLFEN(1981)

James Eagle
HALF-MARRIAGE(1929); WHEN WILLIE COMES MARCHING HOME(1950)
Silents
HEY RUBE!(1928)

Oscar Eagle
Silents
COTTON KING, THE(1915), d&w; LITTLE MADEMOISELLE, THE(1915), d; SINS OF SOCIETY(1915), d; FRUITS OF DESIRE, THE(1916), d
Misc. Silents
ROYAL BOX, THE(1914), d; CHARLOTTE(1917), d; FROZEN WARNING, THE(1918), d

S.P. Eagle [Sam Spiegel]
TALES OF MANHATTAN(1942), p; STRANGER THE(1946), p; WE WERE STRANGERS(1949), p; AFRICAN QUEEN, THE(1951, U.S./Brit.), p; PROWLER, THE(1951), p; WHEN I GROW UP(1951), p; MELBA(1953, Brit.), p

Vincent Eagle [Enzo Dell'Aquila]
UP THE MACGREGORS(1967, Ital./Span.), w; SEVEN GUNS FOR THE MACGREGORS(1968, Ital./Span.), w

White Eagle
OKLAHOMA JIM(1931)

Charles Eagle Eye
Silents
INTOLERANCE(1916)

William Eagle Eye
Silents
HONOR SYSTEM, THE(1917); SON OF THE WOLF, THE(1922)

Misc. Silents
FIRE CAT, THE(1921)

Ben Eagleman
MAN CALLED HORSE, A(1970)

Paul Eagler
REAL GLORY, THE(1939), spec eff; WESTERNER, THE(1940), spec eff; NOTORIOUS(1946), spec eff; PORTRAIT OF JENNIE(1949), spec eff; KISS TOMORROW GOODBYE(1950), spec eff
Silents
PARTNERS OF THE TIDE(1921), ph; ROBIN HOOD(1922), spec eff; TESS OF THE STORM COUNTRY(1922), ph; BEN-HUR(1925), ph

James Eagles
SON OF THE GODS(1930); PARISIAN ROMANCE, A(1932); YOU SAID A MOUTHFUL(1932); PENAL CODE, THE(1933); STORY OF TEMPLE DRAKE, THE(1933); TO THE LAST MAN(1933); HE WAS HER MAN(1934); MASSACRE(1934); CHARLIE CHAN IN EGYPT(1935); I'D GIVE MY LIFE(1936); MURDER AT GLEN ATHOL(1936); SONS O' GUNS(1936); HIDEAWAY GIRL(1937); HEROES OF THE HILLS(1938); EAGLE SQUADRON(1942); FLIGHT FOR FREEDOM(1943); NEVER A DULL MOMENT(1943)

Jeanne Eagles
Misc. Silents
WORLD AND THE WOMAN, THE(1916); FIRES OF YOUTH(1917); UNDER FALSE COLORS(1917); CROSS BEARER, THE(1918)

Jimmie Eagles
RACING BLOOD(1938)

Jimmy Eagles
ABRAHAM LINCOLN(1930); GAMBLING SEX(1932); DOWN THE STRETCH(1936); ALL-AMERICAN SWEETHEART(1937); PAINTED TRAIL, THE(1938)

Seymour Eaglespeaker
RUNNING BRAVE(1983, Can.)

Ron Eagleton
DOUBLE, THE(1963, Brit)

John Eagown
Silents
GOLD RUSH, THE(1925)

June Ealey
ARABIAN NIGHTS(1942)

Clare Eames
Silents
NEW COMMANDMENT, THE(1925)

David Eames
BY DESIGN(1982), w

John Eames
PUZZLE OF A DOWNFALL CHILD(1970); FAREWELL, MY LOVELY(1975)

Kathryn Eames
BIG HEAT, THE(1953)

Virginia Eames
Misc. Silents
RAILROADER, THE(1919)

Joni Eareckson
JONI(1980), a, w

Earl of Chichester
FUGITIVE LOVERS(1934)

Earl of Huntington
ROGUES OF SHERWOOD FOREST(1950)

A. Earl
Silents
SALVATION NELL(1921)

Clifford Earl
ATTEMPT TO KILL(1961, Brit.); FATHER CAME TOO(1964, Brit.); INCIDENT AT MIDNIGHT(1966, Brit.); SUBTERFUGE(1969, US/Brit.); HORROR HOUSE(1970, Brit.); SCREAM AND SCREAM AGAIN(1970, Brit.); DIAMONDS ARE FOREVER(1971, Brit.); TALES FROM THE CRYPT(1972, Brit.); HUMAN FACTOR, THE(1979, Brit.); SEA WOLVES, THE(1981, Brit.)

David Earl
1984
KIPPERBANG(1984, Brit.), m

Eddie Earl
Silents
CAPTAIN'S COURAGE, A(1926)

Elizabeth Earl
LETTER, THE(1940); RIVER'S END(1940)

Else Earl
PORKY'S II: THE NEXT DAY(1983)

Frederick Earl
RAINBOW BOYS, THE(1973, Can.)

Ilse Earl
EMPIRE OF THE ANTS(1977); ABSENCE OF MALICE(1981); PORKY'S(1982)

Jane Earl
IRMA LA DOUCE(1963)

John Earl
HAND, THE(1960, Brit.), art d; DURING ONE NIGHT(1962, Brit.), art d; YOUNG, WILLING AND EAGER(1962, Brit.), art d; GREAT ARMORED CAR SWINDLE, THE(1964), art d; IN TROUBLE WITH EVE(1964, Brit.), art d; MAN WHO COULDN'T WALK, THE(1964, Brit.), art d; DEVILS OF DARKNESS, THE(1965, Brit.), art d

John G. Earl
SNAKE WOMAN, THE(1961, Brit.), art d

Josephine Earl
BARNYARD FOLLIES(1940), ch; SWING YOUR PARTNER(1943), ch; MONSIEUR BEAUCAIRE(1946), ch; IMPERFECT LADY, THE(1947), ch; SON OF PALEFACE(1952), ch; CASANOVA'S BIG NIGHT(1954), ch; CALYPSO HEAT WAVE(1957), ch; JOKER IS WILD, THE(1957), ch; HOUND-DOG MAN(1959), ch; FLAMING STAR(1960), ch; NORTH TO ALASKA(1960), ch; ONE-EYED JACKS(1961), ch; RIGHT APPROACH, THE(1961), ch

Kenneth Earl
LOVE ON A BET(1936), w; WHITE HUNTER(1936), w; OPENED BY MISTAKE(1940), w; STAR DUST(1940), w; BRIDE CAME C.O.D., THE(1941), w; SHE KNEW ALL THE ANSWERS(1941), w; FOOTLIGHT SERENADE(1942), w; SEVEN DAYS LEAVE(1942), w; TWIN BEDS(1942), w; BATHING BEAUTY(1944), w; CAROLINA BLUES(1944), w; WHIPLASH(1948), w; BIG TREES, THE(1952), w; TWO-

HEADED SPY, THE(1959, Brit.)
Laurence Earl
 BATTLE HELL(1956, Brit.), w
Max Earl
 ONE WOMAN'S STORY(1949, Brit.)
Paris Earl
 HALLS OF ANGER(1970)
Misc. Talkies
 BLACKJACK(1978)
Paris Nathan Earl
 SKIN GAME(1971)
Robert Earl
 SECRET OF THE PURPLE REEF, THE(1960)
Ruth Earl
 IRMA LA DOUCE(1963)
Wallace Earl
 VARIETY GIRL(1947)
Wally Earl
 ANNA LUCASTA(1958)
Wiley Earl
 1984
 FALLING IN LOVE(1984)
Earl Bartlett's Biltmore Trio
 FOOTLIGHTS AND FOOLS(1929)
Earl Burtnett's Biltmore Orchestra and Trio
 PARTY GIRL(1930)
Earl Grant Trio
 JUKE BOX RHYTHM(1959)
Earl Royce and the Olympics
 FERRY ACROSS THE MERSEY(1964, Brit.)
Rosita Earlan
 UNDER TWO FLAGS(1936)
Earle
 BREEZY(1973)
Dr. Craig E. Earle
 START CHEERING(1938)
Darien Earle
Misc. Talkies
 ASTROLOGER, THE(1975)
Dick Earle
 THANK YOUR LUCKY STARS(1943); THRILL OF A ROMANCE(1945); NIGHT AND DAY(1946); TILL THE CLOUDS ROLL BY(1946); UNDERCURRENT(1946); SECRET LIFE OF WALTER MITTY, THE(1947)
Dorothy Earle
Silents
 OUT ALL NIGHT(1927)
Misc. Silents
 PIONEERS OF THE WEST(1927)
Eddie Earle
 CAPTAIN TUGBOAT ANNIE(1945)
Edna Earle
 GIRLS PLEASE!(1934, Brit.)
Silents
 EAGLE, THE(1918)
Misc. Silents
 MODEL'S CONFESSION, THE(1918); STUDIO GIRL, THE(1918)
Edward Earle
 WIND, THE(1928); HOTTENTOT, THE(1929); KID GLOVES(1929); SMILING IRISH EYES(1929); IN THE NEXT ROOM(1930); PHANTOM OF THE DESERT(1930); SECOND HONEYMOON(1931); WOMAN OF EXPERIENCE, A(1931); FORGOTTEN WOMEN(1932); ALIMONY MADNESS(1933); REVENGE AT MONTE CARLO(1933); HERE COMES THE NAVY(1934); LITTLE MISS MARKER(1934); STAND UP AND CHEER(1934 80m FOX bw); TICKET TO CRIME(1934); WHITE PARADE, THE(1934); CHINATOWN SQUAD(1935); MAGNIFICENT OBSESSION(1935); MUTINY AHEAD(1935); RENDEZVOUS(1935); REVENGE RIDER, THE(1935); CASE AGAINST MRS. AMES, THE(1936); LOVE BEFORE BREAKFAST(1936); RETURN OF SOPHIE LANG, THE(1936); SAN FRANCISCO(1936); ARTISTS AND MODELS(1937); FIND THE WITNESS(1937); FRAME-UP(1937); HEADLINE CRASHER(1937); LIVE, LOVE AND LEARN(1937); LOVE IN A BUNGALOW(1937); ROSALIE(1937); DUKE OF WEST POINT, THE(1938); GIVE ME A SAILOR(1938); HER JUNGLE LOVE(1938); JUDGE HARDY'S CHILDREN(1938); KENTUCKY(1938); MARINES ARE HERE, THE(1938); MEN WITH WINGS(1938); MR. MOTO'S GAMBLE(1938); RIDERS OF THE BLACK HILLS(1938); SAY IT IN FRENCH(1938); SWEETHEARTS(1938); WHEN G-MEN STEP IN(1938); YOU CAN'T TAKE IT WITH YOU(1938); BURIED ALIVE(1939); EAST SIDE OF HEAVEN(1939); HEADLEYS AT HOME, THE(1939); HOTEL FOR WOMEN(1939); I AM A CRIMINAL(1939); ICE FOLLIES OF 1939(1939); IN OLD MONTEREY(1939); MIRACLES FOR SALE(1939); NEWSBOY'S HOME(1939); WHEN TOMORROW COMES(1939); ANGELS OVER BROADWAY(1940); DARK COMMAND, THE(1940); DOCTOR TAKES A WIFE(1940); EDISON, THE MAN(1940); I LOVE YOU AGAIN(1940); I WANT A DIVORCE(1940); MANHATTAN HEARTBEAT(1940); NOBODY'S CHILDREN(1940); SAILOR'S LADY(1940); SEVENTEEN(1940); SUED FOR LIBEL(1940); BLUE, WHITE, AND PERFECT(1941); BORDER VIGILANTES(1941); MEET JOHN DOE(1941); RICHEST MAN IN TOWN(1941); RIDE, KELLY, RIDE(1941); SCATTERGOOD BAINES(1941); SHE KNEW ALL THE ANSWERS(1941); SUN VALLEY SERENADE(1941); JOHNNY EAGER(1942); LUCKY JORDAN(1942); PACIFIC RENDEZVOUS(1942); SLEEPYTIME GAL(1942); SUNDAY PUNCH(1942); WAKE ISLAND(1942); ALASKA HIGHWAY(1943); BORDERTOWN GUNFIGHTERS(1943); CHATTERBOX(1943); DANCING MASTERS, THE(1943); GOOD FELLOWS, THE(1943); GOOD MORNING, JUDGE(1943); HEAT'S ON, THE(1943); JACK LONDON(1943); LAUGH YOUR BLUES AWAY(1943); SLIGHTLY DANGEROUS(1943); SO PROUDLY WE HAIL(1943); SOMEONE TO REMEMBER(1943); SUBMARINE ALERT(1943); SWEET ROSIE O'GRADY(1943); TWO WEEKS TO LIVE(1943); WHAT A WOMAN!(1943); YOUTH ON PARADE(1943); CALIFORNIA JOE(1944); CHARLIE CHAN IN BLACK MAGIC(1944); DETECTIVE KITTY O'DAY(1944); GHOST CATCHERS(1944); KANSAS CITY KITTY(1944); KNICKERBOCKER HOLIDAY(1944); MAISIE GOES TO RENO(1944); MY BUDDY(1944); PRACTICALLY YOURS(1944); STORY OF DR. WASSELL, THE(1944); UP IN ARMS(1944); I ACCUSE MY PARENTS(1945); I'LL TELL THE WORLD(1945); IN OLD NEW MEXICO(1945); IT'S A PLEASURE(1945); ACCOMPLICE(1946); DARK ALIBI(1946); DEVIL'S MASK, THE(1946); HARVEY GIRLS, THE(1946); MIGHTY MCGURK(1946); POSTMAN ALWAYS

RINGS TWICE, THE(1946); HOMESTRETCH, THE(1947); RIDE THE PINK HORSE(1947); COMMAND DECISION(1948); DARK PAST, THE(1948); NIGHT HAS A THOUSAND EYES(1948); RIVER LADY(1948); GAL WHO TOOK THE WEST, THE(1949); THAT MIDNIGHT KISS(1949); BLONDIE'S HERO(1950); KEY TO THE CITY(1950); MRS. O'MALLEY AND MR. MALONE(1950); WHEN YOU'RE SMILING(1950); FLIGHT TO MARS(1951); TEXAS RANGERS, THE(1951); HANGMAN'S KNOT(1952); LAWLESS BREED, THE(1952); MERRY WIDOW, THE(1952); IT HAPPENS EVERY THURSDAY(1953); MISSISSIPPI GAMBLER, THE(1953); STRANGER WORE A GUN, THE(1953); THREE HOURS TO KILL(1954); MAN CALLED PETER, THE(1955); ONE DESIRE(1955); FRANCIS IN THE HAUNTED HOUSE(1956); NEVER SAY GOODBYE(1956); TEN COMMANDMENTS, THE(1956)
Misc. Talkies
 FIGHTING LADY(1935)
Silents
 EUGENE ARAM(1915); RANSON'S FOLLY(1915); INNOCENCE OF RUTH, THE(1916); MAN WHO PLAYED GOD, THE(1922); STREETS OF NEW YORK, THE(1922); FAMILY SECRET, THE(1924); GAMBLING WIVES(1924); LURE OF LOVE, THE(1924); SPLENDID ROAD, THE(1925); IRENE(1926); TWELVE MILES OUT(1927); RUNAWAY GIRLS(1928); SPITE MARRIAGE(1929)
Misc. Silents
 GREATER THAN ART(1915); GATES OF EDEN, THE(1916); BEAUTIFUL LIE, THE(1917); FOR FRANCE(1917); BLIND ADVENTURE, THE(1918); LITTLE RUNAWAY, THE(1918); ONE THOUSAND DOLLARS(1918); HIS BRIDAL NIGHT(1919); HIGH SPEED(1920); LAW OF THE YUKON, THE(1920); EAST LYNNE(1921); PASSION FRUIT(1921); FALSE FRONTS(1922); NONE SO BLIND(1923); DANGEROUS FLIRT, THE(1924); WOMAN'S HEART, A(1926); SECOND HONEYMOON(1930)
Edward C. Earle
Silents
 BAR SINISTER, THE(1917), ph
Edwin Earle
 HELLO, FRISCO, HELLO(1943)
Eyvind Earle
 LADY AND THE TRAMP(1955), art d
Ferdinand P. Earle
Silents
 BEN-HUR(1925), d; LOVER'S OATH, A(1925), d
Frank Earle
Silents
 DEVIL'S TOWER(1929)
Misc. Silents
 LIGHTNIN' SHOT(1928)
Freddie Earle
 RITZ, THE(1976)
H. Hamilton Earle
 ROOM TO LET(1949, Brit.)
Jenny Earle
Silents
 LADY NOGGS-PEERESS(1929, Brit.)
Jessie Earle
Silents
 ALL MEN ARE LIARS(1919, Brit.)
Josephine Earle
 RAISE THE ROOF(1930); HOOSIER HOLIDAY(1943), ch
Silents
 TWO-EDGED SWORD, THE(1916); AWAKENING, THE(1917); WALLS OF PREJUDICE(1920, Brit.); HOTEL MOUSE, THE(1923, Brit.); KNOCKOUT, THE(1923, Brit.)
Misc. Silents
 BRANDED(1920, Brit.); EDGE OF YOUTH, THE(1920, Brit.); FALL OF A SAINT, THE(1920, Brit.); SERVING TWO MASTERS(1921); WOMAN TO WOMAN(1923, Brit.); UNTO EACH OTHER(1929, Brit.)
Josphine Earle
Misc. Silents
 WAY OF A MAN, THE(1921, Brit.)
June Earle
 JOAN OF OZARK(1942); UNION STATION(1950)
Madelyn Earle
 GEORGE WHITE'S 1935 SCANDALS(1935)
Marilee Earle
 HOT CARS(1956); STREET OF SINNERS(1957); FEARMAKERS, THE(1958); ISLAND WOMEN(1958); LOST MISSILE, THE(1958, U.S./Can.); TERROR IN A TEXAS TOWN(1958)
Mary Earle
 MILLION DOLLAR MERMAID(1952)
Max Earle
 DUMMY TALKS, THE(1943, Brit.); LAMP STILL BURNS, THE(1943, Brit.)
Merie Earle
 GAILY, GAILY(1969); NORWOOD(1970); SUMMER SCHOOL TEACHERS(1977); GOING APE!(1981)
Merle Earle
 CRAZY MAMA(1975)
Robert Earle
 DESIRE IN THE DUST(1960); TOY, THE(1982)
William P.S. Earle
Silents
 WHISPERS(1920), d; WAY OF A MAID, THE(1921), d; DESTINY'S ISLE(1922), d
Misc. Silents
 LAW DECIDES, THE(1916), d; WHOM THE GODS DESTROY(1916), d; COURAGE OF SILENCE, THE(1917), d; I WILL REPAY(1917), d; MARY JANE'S PA(1917), d; WHO GOES THERE?(1917), d; WITHIN THE LAW(1917), d; HEREDITY(1918), d; HIS OWN PEOPLE(1918), d; LITTLE MISS NO-ACCOUNT(1918), d; LITTLE RUNAWAY, THE(1918), d; T'OTHER DEAR CHARMER(1918), d; WOOING OF PRINCESS PAT, THE(1918), d; BETTER WIFE, THE(1919), d; LONE WOLF'S DAUGHTER, THE(1919), d; LOVE HUNGER, THE(1919), d; BROKEN MELODY, THE(1920), d; DANGEROUS PARADISE, THE(1920), d; ROAD OF AMBITION, THE(1920), d; WOMAN GAME, THE(1920), d; GILDED LIES(1921), d; LAST DOOR, THE(1921), d; POOR, DEAR MARGARET KIRBY(1921), d; LOVE'S MASQUERADE(1922), d; DANCER OF THE NILE, THE(1923), d

Harold Earle-Fishbacher
GHOST GOES WEST, THE(1936), ed
Daisy Earles
FREAKS(1932)
Harry Earles
UNHOLY THREE, THE(1930); FREAKS(1932)
Silents
UNHOLY THREE, THE(1925); THAT'S MY BABY(1926)
Freddie Earlle
MAGIC CHRISTIAN, THE(1970, Brit.)
C. Gregory Earls
PILOT, THE(1979), p
Claude Earls
MARS NEEDS WOMEN(1966)
David Early
DAWN OF THE DEAD(1979); KNIGHTRIDERS(1981); CREEPSHOW(1982)
Dora Early
MUSIC GOES ROUND, THE(1936)
Dudley Early
Silents
ISLE OF LOST MEN(1928), t
Dwayne Early
DON'T DRINK THE WATER(1969)
J. W. Early
Silents
UNKNOWN, THE(1921)
Margaret Early
STAGE DOOR(1937); JEZEBEL(1938); SWING THAT CHEER(1938); YOUNG IN HEART, THE(1938); JUDGE HARDY AND SON(1939); FORTY LITTLE MOTHERS(1940); STRIKE UP THE BAND(1940); ANDY HARDY'S PRIVATE SECRETARY(1941); SMALL TOWN DEB(1941); TO THE SHORES OF TRIPOLI(1942); STAGE DOOR CANTEEN(1943); 3 IS A FAMILY(1944); CINDERELLA JONES(1946)
Margo Early
STUDENT TOUR(1934)
Mary Jane Early
Misc. Talkies
HEADLESS EYES, THE(1983)
Pearl Early
IN OLD CALIFORNIA(1942); THIS LOVE OF OURS(1945)
Steve Early
STARFIGHTERS, THE(1964)
Dale Earnhardt
STROKER ACE(1983)
Fenton Earnshaw
KILLER AT LARGE(1947), w; SAVAGE DRUMS(1951), w
Franklyn Earnum
PAGE MISS GLORY(1935)
Earth, Wind and Fire
THAT'S THE WAY OF THE WORLD(1975), a, m; SGT. PEPPER'S LONELY HEARTS CLUB BAND(1978)
Tommy Earwood
LAST HURRAH, THE(1958)
Brian Easdale
BLACK NARCISSUS(1947, Brit.), m; RED SHOES, THE(1948, Brit.), m; HOUR OF GLORY(1949, Brit.), m; FIGHTING PIMPERNEL, THE(1950, Brit.), m; OUTCAST OF THE ISLANDS(1952, Brit.), m; WILD HEART, THE(1952, Brit.), m; GREEN SCARF, THE(1954, Brit.), m&md; MIRACLE IN SOHO(1957, Brit.), m; PURSUIT OF THE GRAF SPEE(1957, Brit.), m; PEEPING TOM(1960, Brit.), m, md; QUEEN'S GUARDS, THE(1963, Brit.), m
Jessica Easley
COAL MINER'S DAUGHTER(1980)
Richard Easley
OUTRAGEOUS!(1977, Can.)
Richert Easley
HAPPY BIRTHDAY, GEMINI(1980)
B. Reaves Eason
MURDER ON THE WATERFRONT(1943), d
Silents
JOHNNY GET YOUR HAIR CUT(1927), d
Reaves Eason
Silents
PARDON MY NERVE!(1922), d; BEN-HUR(1925), d; ROUGH SHOD(1925), d; LARIAT KID, THE(1929), d
Misc. Silents
PAY DIRT(1916), d; NINE-TENTHS OF THE LAW(1918), a, d; TWO KINDS OF LOVE(1920), a, d; COLORADO(1921), d; FIRE EATER, THE(1921), d; RED COURAGE(1921), d; GALLOPING FURY(1927), d; FLYIN' COWBOY, THE(1928), d; RIDING FOR FAME(1928), d
B. Reeves Eason
ROARING RANCH(1930), d&w; SPURS(1930), d&w; TRIGGER TRICKS(1930), d&w; TROOPERS THREE(1930), d; CORNERED(1932), d; SUNSET TRAIL(1932), d; ALIMONY MADNESS(1933), d; DARKEST AFRICA(1936), d; RED RIVER VALLEY(1936), p&d; KID COMES BACK, THE(1937), d; LAND BEYOND THE LAW(1937), d; LAW FOR TOMBSTONE(1937), d; PRAIRIE THUNDER(1937), d; ARMY GIRL(1938), d; CALL OF THE YUKON(1938), d; DAREDEVIL DRIVERS(1938), d; SERGEANT MURPHY(1938), d; BLUE MONTANA SKIES(1939), d; MOUNTAIN RHYTHM(1939), d; MURDER IN THE BIG HOUSE(1942), d; SPY SHIP(1942), d; TRUCK BUSTERS(1943), d; RIMFIRE(1949), d
Silents
WHEN EAST COMES WEST(1922), d; CLEARING THE TRAIL(1928), d
Misc. Silents
TIGER THOMPSON(1924), d; TEXAS BEARCAT, THE(1925), d; TEST OF DONALD NORTON, THE(1926), d; DENVER DUDE, THE(1927), d
B. Reeves "Breezy" Eason
Misc. Talkies
EVIL EYE OF KALINOR, THE(1934), d
Breezy Eason
HEART PUNCH(1932), d; BEHIND JURY DOORS(1933, Brit.), d; REVENGE AT MONTE CARLO(1933), d; HOLLYWOOD MYSTERY(1934), d

Breezy Eason, Jr.
Misc. Silents
BLUE STREAK MCCOY(1920); BIG ADVENTURE, THE(1921); SURE FIRE(1921)
Joanne Eason
BLACK RODEO(1972)
Lorraine Eason
Silents
RIDIN' MAD(1924); GREY DEVIL, THE(1926); BOY RIDER, THE(1927)
Misc. Silents
BORDER RIDER, THE(1924); CIRCUS LURE(1924); NORTH OF ALASKA(1924); FIGHTING DEMON, THE(1925); MUST WE MARRY?(1928)
Myles Eason
SARABAND(1949, Brit.); PORTRAIT OF A SINNER(1961, Brit.)
Reeves Eason
DANCE MALL HOSTESS(1933), d; NEIGHBORS' WIVES(1933), d; EMPTY HOLSTERS(1937), d
Silents
HUMAN STUFF(1920), d, w; PINK TIGHTS(1920), d; NEW CHAMPION(1925), d; PAINTED PONIES(1927), d
Misc. Silents
HELL HATH NO FURY(1917); BLUE STREAK MCCOY(1920), d; BIG ADVENTURE, THE(1921), d; LONE HAND, THE(1922), d; HIS LAST RACE(1923), d; FLASHING SPURS(1924), d; TRIGGER FINGER(1924), d; WOMEN FIRST(1924), d; BORDER JUSTICE(1925), d; FIGHT TO THE FINISH, A(1925), d; FIGHTING THE FLAMES(1925), d; FIGHTING YOUTH(1925), d; SHADOW ON THE WALL, THE(1925), d; LONE HAND SAUNDERS(1926), d; SIGN OF THE CLAW, THE(1926), d; PRAIRIE KING, THE(1927), d; THROUGH THICK AND THIN(1927), d; DANGER RIDER, THE(1928), d; TRICK OF HEARTS, A(1928), d; WINGED HORSEMAN, THE(1929), d
Reeves Eason, Jr.
Silents
PINK TIGHTS(1920)
Reeves "Breezy" Eason
HONOR OF THE PRESS(1932), d; HER RESALE VALUE(1933), d
Roy Eason
36 HOURS(1965)
Ben East
SILENCE OF THE NORTH(1981, Can.), w
Carlos East
BLUE(1968); FEAR CHAMBER, THE(1968, US/Mex.); BIG CUBE, THE(1969); GUYANA, CULT OF THE DAMNED zero(1980, Mex./Span./Panama)
Charles East
SNAKE PEOPLE, THE(1968, Mex./U.S.)
Ed East
STOP THAT CAB(1951)
Henry East
ON MOONLIGHT BAY(1951)
Jeff East
TOM SAWYER(1973); HUCKLEBERRY FINN(1974); HAZING, THE(1978); SUPERMAN(1978); KLONDIKE FEVER(1980); DEADLY BLESSING(1981)
1984
UP THE CREEK(1984)
John East
SHOOT TO KILL(1961, Brit.)
Silents
GLORIOUS ADVENTURE, THE(1922, U.S./Brit.)
John M. East
Silents
HOUSE OF TEMPERLEY, THE(1913, Brit.); LITTLE LORD FAUNTLEROY(1914, Brit.); KIPPS(1921, Brit.)
Leonard East
DANGER WOMAN(1946); MICHIGAN KID, THE(1947); SONG OF SCHEHERAZADE(1947)
Robert East
FIGURES IN A LANDSCAPE(1970, Brit.); BROTHERS AND SISTERS(1980, Brit.)
Roger East
THREE STEPS IN THE DARK(1953, Brit.), w
Steward East
MOUNTAIN MEN, THE(1980)
Susanna East
SAVAGE MESSIAH(1972, Brit.)
Therese East
RESURRECTION(1980)
Howard Eastbrook
Silents
FOUR FEATHERS(1929), w
David Easter
MUSIC MACHINE, THE(1979, Brit.)
1984
GIVE MY REGARDS TO BROAD STREET(1984, Brit.)
Robert Easter
SUPER VAN(1977), w; TOOLBOX MURDERS, THE(1978), w
Susan Easter
ROCKABILLY BABY(1957); GOING STEADY(1958)
Esme Easterbrook
DECISION AGAINST TIME(1957, Brit.)
Leslie Easterbrook
JUST TELL ME WHAT YOU WANT(1980)
1984
POLICE ACADEMY(1984)
Richard Eastham
SIX MEN, THE(1951, Brit.), w; THERE'S NO BUSINESS LIKE SHOW BUSINESS(1954); MAN ON FIRE(1957); TOBY TYLER(1960); THAT DARN CAT(1965); MURDERERS' ROW(1966); NOT WITH MY WIFE, YOU DON'T!(1966); BATTLE FOR THE PLANET OF THE APES(1973); TOM SAWYER(1973); MC Q(1974)
Ida Easthope
Silents
EYES OF JULIA DEEP, THE(1918)

Steve Eastin
CHANGE OF SEASONS, A(1980)
William Eastlake
CASTLE KEEP(1969), w
Brad Eastman
SAVAGE WILD, THE(1970), ph
Carole Eastman
FUNNY FACE(1957)
Charles Eastman
LITTLE FAUSS AND BIG HALSY(1970), w; SHOOTING, THE(1971); ALL-AMERI-CAN BOY, THE(1973), d&w; SECOND-HAND HEARTS(1981), w
David Eastman
CALAMITY THE COW(1967, Brit.), d, w; GREAT GUNDOWN, THE(1977)
Donald Eastman
LULU(1978), art d
Elaine Eastman
Misc. Silents
FIGHTING ROMEO, THE(1925)
George Eastman
CAMEO KIRBY(1930), ph; SUCH MEN ARE DANGEROUS(1930), ph; NO ROSES FOR OSS 117(1968, Fr.); CALL OF THE WILD(1972, Ger./ Span./Ital./Fr.); SCALA-WAG(1973, Yugo.); GRIM REAPER, THE(1981, Ital.); NEW BARBARIANS, THE(1983, Ital.); 1990: THE BRONX WARRIORS(1983, Ital.)
1984
AFTER THE FALL OF NEW YORK(1984, Ital./Fr.); WARRIORS OF THE WASTE-LAND(1984, Ital.)
Silents
SIN SISTER, THE(1929), ph
Gordon Eastman
SAVAGE WILD, THE(1970), a, p,d&w, ph, m/l Title song
Janet Eastman
MR. DEEDS GOES TO TOWN(1936)
Kerry Eastman
CALAMITY THE COW(1967, Brit.), w
Lynn Eastman
PHANTASM(1979)
Maria Eastman
SAVAGE WILD, THE(1970)
Marilyn Eastman
NIGHT OF THE LIVING DEAD(1968), a, makeup
Monk Eastman
PARK ROW(1952)
Orio Eastman
Silents
KAISER, BEAST OF BERLIN, THE(1918)
Peter Paul Eastman
WHAT'S UP, DOC?(1972)
Rod Eastman
SAVAGE WILD, THE(1970), ph
Spencer Eastman
HIDE IN PLAIN SIGHT(1980), w
Bob Easton
UNION STATION(1950); COMIN' ROUND THE MOUNTAIN(1951); HAVANA RO-SE(1951); SAVAGE DRUMS(1951); DREAMBOAT(1952); FEUDIN' FOOLS(1952); CITY OF BAD MEN(1953); JALOPY(1953); SERPENT OF THE NILE(1953); WHITE LIGHT-NING(1953); BITTER CREEK(1954); FRENCH LINE, THE(1954); PURPLE MASK, THE(1955); SON OF SINBAD(1955); BROTHERS RICO, THE(1957); JET PILOT(1957)
Jay Easton
LOVE BEFORE BREAKFAST(1936)
Jock Easton
CIRCUS BOY(1947, Brit.)
Jon Easton
ARISE, MY LOVE(1940)
Joyce Easton
MEMORY OF US(1974); SPARKLE(1976); BIG FIX, THE(1978); FURY, THE(1978)
Miller Easton
TOLL OF THE DESERT(1936), w
Philip Easton
FAREWELL TO LOVE(1931, Brit.)
Rick Easton
YOUNG WARRIORS(1983)
Robert Easton
WHEN YOU COMIN' BACK, RED RYDER?(1979); UNDERTOW(1949); CALL ME MISTER(1951); CAUSE FOR ALARM(1951); DRUMS IN THE DEEP SOUTH(1951); BELLES ON THEIR TOES(1952); O. HENRY'S FULL HOUSE(1952); COMBAT SQUAD(1953); NEANDERTHAL MAN, THE(1953); DEEP IN MY HEART(1954); HIGH AND THE MIGHTY, THE(1954); FIRST TRAVELING SALESLADY, THE(1956); KETTLES IN THE OZARKS, THE(1956); SOMEBODY UP THERE LIKES ME(1956); WHEN HELL BROKE LOOSE(1958); VOYAGE TO THE BOTTOM OF THE SEA(1961); NUN AND THE SERGEANT, THE(1962); WAR LOVER, THE(1962, U.S./Brit.); COME FLY WITH ME(1963); LOVED ONE, THE(1965); ONE OF OUR SPIES IS MIS-SING(1966); PAINT YOUR WAGON(1969); JOHNNY GOT HIS GUN(1971); GIANT SPIDER INVASION, THE(1975), a, w; MR. SYCAMORE(1975); PETE'S DRA-GON(1977)

Samuelle Easton
1984
PREPPIES(1984)
Sid Easton
OUANGA(1936, Brit.)
Sidney Easton
HIS WOMAN(1931); WAYWARD(1932)
Wallas Easton
ALIVE ON SATURDAY(1957, Brit.)
Lori Eastside
GET CRAZY(1983)
1984
FEAR CITY(1984)
John Eastway
1984
MELVIN, SON OF ALVIN(1984, Aus.), d
Alison Eastwood
1984
TIGHTROPE(1984)
Clint Eastwood
FRANCIS IN THE NAVY(1955); LADY GODIVA(1955); REVENGE OF THE CREA-TURE(1955); TARANTULA(1955); FIRST TRAVELING SALESLADY, THE(1956); NEVER SAY GOODBYE(1956); STAR IN THE DUST(1956); ESCAPADE IN JA-PAN(1957); AMBUSH AT CIMARRON PASS(1958); LAFAYETTE ESCADRILLE(1958); FISTFUL OF DOLLARS, A(1964, Ital./Ger./Span.); FOR A FEW DOLLARS MO-RE(1967, Ital./Ger./Span.); GOOD, THE BAD, AND THE UGLY, THE(1967, Ital./Span.); COOGAN'S BLUFF(1968); HANG'EM HIGH(1968); WHERE EAGLES DARE(1968, Brit.); PAINT YOUR WAGON(1969); WITCHES, THE(1969, Fr./Ital.); KELLY'S HEROES(1970, U.S./Yugo.); TWO MULES FOR SISTER SARA(1970); BEGUILED, THE(1971); DIRTY HARRY(1971); PLAY MISTY FOR ME(1971), a, d; JOE KIDD(1972); BREEZY(1973), d; HIGH PLAINS DRIFTER(1973), a, d; MAGNUM FORCE(1973); THUNDERBOLT AND LIGHTFOOT(1974); EIGER SANCTION, THE(1975), a, d; ENFORCER, THE(1976); OUTLAW JOSEY WALES, THE(1976), a, d; GAUNTLET, THE(1977), a, d; EVERY WHICH WAY BUT LOOSE(1978); ESCAPE FROM ALCATRAZ(1979); ANY WHICH WAY YOU CAN(1980); BRONCO BIL-LY(1980), a, d; FIREFOX(1982), a, p&d; HONKYTONK MAN(1982), a, p&d; SUD-DEN IMPACT(1983), a, p&d
1984
CITY HEAT(1984); TIGHTROPE(1984), a, p
Gini Eastwood
Misc. Talkies
PICK-UP(1975)
James Eastwood
DEVIL GIRL FROM MARS(1954, Brit.), w; TALE OF THREE WOMEN, A(1954, Brit.), w; THREE CORNERED FATE(1954, Brit.), w; YELLOW ROBE, THE(1954, Brit.), w; CASE OF THE RED MONKEY(1955, Brit.), w; FINAL COLUMN, THE(1955, Brit.), w; ONE JUST MAN(1955, Brit.), w; BEYOND MOMBASA(1957), w; COUNTER-FEIT PLAN, THE(1957, Brit.), w; DESPERATE MAN, THE(1959, Brit.), w; WRONG NUMBER(1959, Brit.), w; MAN WHO WAS NOBODY, THE(1960, Brit.), w; URGE TO KILL(1960, Brit.), w; FOURTH SQUARE, THE(1961, Brit.), w; TRANSATLAN-TIC(1961, Brit.), w
Jane Eastwood
TOMORROW NEVER COMES(1978, Brit./Can.)
Jayne Eastwood
GOIN' DOWN THE ROAD(1970, Can.); ONE MAN(1979, Can.); VIDEODROME(1983, Can.)
1984
FINDERS KEEPERS(1984)
Misc. Talkies
MY PLEASURE IS MY BUSINESS(1974, Can.)
Kyle Eastwood
HONKYTONK MAN(1982)
Larry Eastwood
LONG WEEKEND(1978, Aus.), art d; DIMBOOLA(1979, Aus.), art d; NEWS-FRONT(1979, Aus.), art d
Laurence Eastwood
1984
PHAR LAP(1984, Aus.), prod d
The Easy Riders
CALYPSO JOE(1957)
Barbara Eather
SMILEY GETS A GUN(1959, Brit.)
Lou Eather
TOO HOT TO HANDLE(1961, Brit.)
Al Eaton
DARK END OF THE STREET, THE(1981)
Bekka Eaton
1984
SIXTEEN CANDLES(1984)
Charles Eaton
GHOST TALKS, THE(1929); HARMONY AT HOME(1930); ENLIGHTEN THY DAUGHTER(1934); BLONDES FOR DANGER(1938, Brit.); LIGHTNING CONDUC-TOR(1938, Brit.); SWORD OF HONOUR(1938, Brit.); WHO GOES NEXT?(1938, Brit.); PHANTOM STRIKES, THE(1939, Brit.); SONS OF THE SEA(1939, Brit.)
Don Eaton
1984
SPLATTER UNIVERSITY(1984)
Doris Eaton
VERY IDEA, THE(1929)
Silents
AT THE STAGE DOOR(1921); CALL OF THE EAST, THE(1922, Brit.)
Misc. Silents
BROADWAY PEACOCK, THE(1922); HIS SUPREME SACRIFICE(1922, Brit.)
Elwin Eaton
Silents
ROMEO AND JULIET(1916)
Evelyn Eaton
ADVENTURES OF GALLANT BESS(1948); WHERE ARE YOUR CHILDREN?(1943); FIGHTING FOOLS(1949)

Mary Eberle
Misc. Silents
DEVIL'S CONFESSION, THE(1921)
Ray Eberle
SUN VALLEY SERENADE(1941); FOLLOW THE BAND(1943); HONEYMOON LODGE(1943); MR. BIG(1943)
Robert Eberlein
NAKED ANGELS(1969), ph
Jane Eberling
VIVACIOUS LADY(1938)
Bob Eberly
FLEET'S IN, THE(1942); I DOOD IT(1943); FABULOUS DORSEYS, THE(1947)
Eugene Eberly
MISSION TO MOSCOW(1943)
Erich Ebermayer
DREAMER, THE(1936, Ger.), w; CANARIS(1955, Ger.), w
Horst Ebersberg
36 HOURS(1965); AGENT FOR H.A.R.M.(1966); SECRET WAR OF HARRY FRIGG, THE(1968); BOB AND CAROL AND TED AND ALICE(1969)
Christine Ebersole
TOOTSIE(1982)
1984
AMADEUS(1984); THIEF OF HEARTS(1984)
Drew Eberson
OVERLAND EXPRESS, THE(1938), d
William R. Eberson
BEST MAN, THE(1964)
Erich Ebert
DECISION BEFORE DAWN(1951)
Fritz Ebert
COMPANEROS(1970 Ital./Span./Ger.), w
Gunter Ebert
DORIAN GRAY(1970, Ital./Brit./Ger./Liechtenstein), w
Joyce Ebert
1984
MRS. SOFFEL(1984)
Michael Ebert
HAMLET(1964); NIGHT MOVES(1975); COUNTDOWN AT KUSINI(1976, Nigerian)
Walter Ebert
MAN BETWEEN, THE(1953, Brit.), w; YOUNG GO WILD, THE(1962, Ger.), w
Wolfgang Ebert
I LOVE YOU, I KILL YOU(1972, Ger.)
John Eberts
CORNERED(1932); BORDERTOWN(1935); UNDER THE PAMPAS MOON(1935); DANCING PIRATE(1936); LAW OF THE TROPICS(1941); TYCOON(1947)
Johnny Eberts
LAST MAN(1932)
Blandine Ebinger
BEAUTIFUL ADVENTURE(1932, Ger.); TALES OF THE UNCANNY(1932, Ger.); FRAULEIN(1958); MAEDCHEN IN UNIFORM(1965, Ger./Fr.)
Robert Ebinger
STUDENT BODIES(1981), ph; BEING, THE(1983), ph
1984
LIES(1984, Brit.), ph
Gene Eblen
SIERRA SUE(1941)
Marcia Ebs
TRIAL, THE(1948, Aust.)
Alix Ebsen
SILVER CITY BONANZA(1951)
Buddy Ebsen
YELLOW JACK(1938); BROADWAY MELODY OF 1936(1935); CAPTAIN JANUARY(1935); BANJO ON MY KNEE(1936); BORN TO DANCE(1936); BROADWAY MELODY OF '38(1937); GIRL OF THE GOLDEN WEST, THE(1938); MY LUCKY STAR(1938); FOUR GIRLS IN WHITE(1939); KID FROM TEXAS, THE(1939); PARACHUTE BATTALION(1941); THEY MET IN ARGENTINA(1941); SING YOUR WORRIES AWAY(1942); UNDER MEXICALI STARS(1950); RODEO KING AND THE SENORITA(1951); SILVER CITY BONANZA(1951); THUNDER IN GOD'S COUNTRY(1951); UTAH WAGON TRAIN(1951); NIGHT PEOPLE(1954); RED GARTERS(1954); DAVY CROCKETT, KING OF THE WILD FRONTIER(1955); ATTACK!(1956); BETWEEN HEAVEN AND HELL(1956); DAVY CROCKETT AND THE RIVER PIRATES(1956); BREAKFAST AT TIFFANY'S(1961); INTERNS, THE(1962); MAIL ORDER BRIDE(1964); ONE AND ONLY GENUINE ORIGINAL FAMILY BAND, THE(1968)
Vilma Ebsen
BROADWAY MELODY OF 1936(1935)
Maude Eburn
PRINCESS AND THE PIRATE, THE(1944)
Maude Eburne
BAT WHISPERS, THE(1930); BLONDE CRAZY(1931); BOUGHT(1931); GUARDSMAN, THE(1931); HER MAJESTY LOVE(1931); INDISCREET(1931); LONELY WIVES(1931); MAN IN POSSESSION, THE(1931); FIRST YEAR, THE(1932); JAZZ BABIES(1932); PANAMA FLO(1932); PASSIONATE PLUMBER(1932); POLLY OF THE CIRCUS(1932); STRANGER IN TOWN(1932); THIS RECKLESS AGE(1932); TRIAL OF VIVIENNE WARE, THE(1932); UNDER EIGHTEEN(1932); WOMAN FROM MONTE CARLO, THE(1932); BIG EXECUTIVE(1933); EAST OF FIFTH AVE.(1933); HAVANA WIDOWS(1933); HELL BELOW(1933); LADIES MUST LOVE(1933); LADIES THEY TALK ABOUT(1933); MY LIPS BETRAY(1933); ROBBERS' ROOST(1933); SHANGHAI MADNESS(1933); VAMPIRE BAT, THE(1933); WARRIOR'S HUSBAND, THE(1933); FOG(1934); LAZY RIVER(1934); LOVE BIRDS(1934); RETURN OF THE TERROR(1934); WHEN STRANGERS MEET(1934); DON'T BET ON BLONDES(1935); HAPPINESS C.O.D.(1935); MAYBE IT'S LOVE(1935); PARTY WIRE(1935); RUGGLES OF RED GAP(1935); DOUGHNUTS AND SOCIETY(1936); LEAVENWORTH CASE, THE(1936); MAN HUNT(1936); POPPY(1936); REUNION(1936); VALIANT IS THE WORD FOR CARRIE(1936); CHAMPAGNE WALTZ(1937); FIGHT FOR YOUR LADY(1937); HOLLYWOOD COWBOY(1937); LIVE, LOVE AND LEARN(1937); PARADISE EXPRESS(1937); WHEN'S YOUR BIRTHDAY?(1937); RIDERS OF THE BLACK HILLS(1938); VIVACIOUS LADY(1938); CONVICT'S CODE(1939); COVERED TRAILER, THE(1939); EXILE EXPRESS(1939); MEET DR. CHRISTIAN; MOUNTAIN RHYTHM(1939); MY WIFE'S RELATIVES(1939); SABOTAGE(1939); UNDERCOVER

AGENT(1939); BORDER LEGION, THE(1940); COLORADO(1940); COURAGEOUS DR. CHRISTIAN, THE(1940); DR. CHRISTIAN MEETS THE WOMEN(1940); AMONG THE LIVING(1941); MELODY FOR THREE(1941); REMEDY FOR RICHES(1941); THEY MEET AGAIN(1941); WEST POINT WIDOW(1941); YOU BELONG TO ME(1941); ALMOST MARRIED(1942); BOOGIE MAN WILL GET YOU, THE(1942); HENRY ALDRICH, EDITOR(1942); HENRY AND DIZZY(1942); I MARRIED AN ANGEL(1942); LADY BODYGUARD(1942); THERE'S ONE BORN EVERY MINUTE(1942); TO BE OR NOT TO BE(1942); CRYSTAL BALL, THE(1943); REVEILLE WITH BEVERLY(1943); BOWERY TO BROADWAY(1944); GOODNIGHT SWEETHEART(1944); HENRY ALDRICH PLAYS CUPID(1944); I'M FROM ARKANSAS(1944); ROSIE THE RIVETER(1944); SUSPECT, THE(1944); HITCHHIKE TO HAPPINESS(1945); LEAVE IT TO BLONDIE(1945); MAN FROM OKLAHOMA, THE(1945); TOWN WENT WILD, THE(1945); MOTHER WORE TIGHTS(1947); SECRET LIFE OF WALTER MITTY, THE(1947); PLUNDERERS, THE(1948); SLIPPY MCGEE(1948); ARSON, INC.(1949); LAWTON STORY, THE(1949); PRINCE OF PEACE, THE(1951)
Silents
PAIR OF SIXES, A(1918)
Misc. Silents
TAXI(1919)
Earl Eby
RENDEZVOUS(1935); LOVE BEFORE BREAKFAST(1936); SINGING COWBOY, THE(1936); LAW OF THE TIMBER(1941)
Lois Eby
TOO MANY WIVES(1937), w; HI-YO SILVER(1940), w
Rick Eby
NATIONAL LAMPOON'S ANIMAL HOUSE(1978)
Helen Eby-Rock
ANN VICKERS(1933); CRIME OF HELEN STANLEY(1934); HOODLUM SAINT, THE(1946); UNDERCURRENT(1946); HIGH BARBAREE(1947); HIGH WALL, THE(1947); FORCE OF EVIL(1948); CAGED(1950); SIDE STREET(1950); CALLAWAY WENT THATAWAY(1951); MAN WITH A CLOAK, THE(1951); PAT AND MIKE(1952)
Aimee Eccles
ULZANA'S RAID(1972); MARCO(1973); PARADISE ALLEY(1978); CONCRETE JUNGLE, THE(1982)
1984
LOVELINES(1984)
Misc. Talkies
GROUP MARRIAGE(1972)
Amy Eccles
NO MORE EXCUSES(1968); LITTLE BIG MAN(1970); PRETTY MAIDS ALL IN A ROW(1971)
David Eccles
ROUGH CUT(1980, Brit.)
Donald Eccles
TASTE OF MONEY, A(1960, Brit.); MIDSUMMER NIGHT'S DREAM, A(1969, Brit.); WICKER MAN, THE(1974, Brit.); DRESSER, THE(1983)
Jane Eccles
LOOK BACK IN ANGER(1959); ROOM AT THE TOP(1959, Brit.)
Jeremy Eccles
DOCTOR FAUSTUS(1967, Brit.)
Lila Eccles
PHANTOM OF THE DESERT(1930)
Robin Eccles
HORSE IN THE GRAY FLANNEL SUIT, THE(1968)
Ted Eccles
HONKERS, THE(1972)
Teddy Eccles
MY SIX LOVES(1963); IN COLD BLOOD(1967); MY SIDE OF THE MOUNTAIN(1969); PHYNX, THE(1970)
Louis Ecclesia
1984
AFTER THE FALL OF NEW YORK(1984, Ital./Fr.)
Paul Ecenta
SCREAM BLOODY MURDER(1972)
Josefina Echanove
MISSING(1982)
Margaret Echard
LIGHTNING STRIKES TWICE(1951), w
Fritz Echardt
ALMOST ANGELS(1962)
Alfredo Echegaray
MAD QUEEN, THE(1950, Span.), w
Anacani Echeverria
ZOOT SUIT(1981)
Dr. Gerald Echeverria
RAZOR'S EDGE, THE(1946)
Raquel Echeverria
WAIKIKI WEDDING(1937)
Josephina Echinova
HIGH RISK(1981)
Edward Echols
SEPARATE PEACE, A(1972)
Jill Echols
HOUSE OF 1,000 DOLLS(1967, Ger./Span./Brit.)
Kermit Echols
WAIT 'TIL THE SUN SHINES, NELLIE(1952); DELINQUENTS, THE(1957); GRIZZLY(1976)
Randy Echols
Misc. Talkies
HITCHHIKE TO HELL(1978)
Joe Echovar
FINGER ON THE TRIGGER(1965, US/Span.), makeup
Hildegard Echtler
1984
SACRED HEARTS(1984, Brit.), art d
Johnny Eck
FREAKS(1932)

Max Eckard
WOZZECK(1962, E. Ger.); FAUST(1963, Ger.)
Hans-Eckardt Eckardt
KAMIKAZE '89(1983, Ger.)
Steve Eckardt
FAREWELL, FRIEND(1968, Fr./Ital.); BURGLARS, THE(1972, Fr./Ital.)
Jean Eckart
PAJAMA GAME, THE(1957), cos; DAMN YANKEES(1958), prod d, cos; NIGHT THEY RAIDED MINSKY'S, THE(1968), prod d
Norma Jean Eckart
HOUDINI(1953)
William Eckart
DAMN YANKEES(1958), prod d, cos; NIGHT THEY RAIDED MINSKY'S, THE(1968), prod d
Hanns Eckelkamp
JIMMY ORPHEUS(1966, Ger.), p
Raymond D. Eckel
1984
TANK(1984)
Ted Eckelberry
YOUNG MAN WITH A HORN(1950); KISS ME KATE(1953)
Tener Eckelberry
DEADLY TRAP, THE(1972, Fr./Ital.)
Thomas Eckelmann
I LOVE YOU, I KILL YOU(1972, Ger.)
Allan Eckelund
PIPPI IN THE SOUTH SEAS(1974, Swed./Ger.), p
Agneta Eckemyr
BLINDMAN(1972, Ital.); ISLAND AT THE TOP OF THE WORLD, THE(1974)
John Eckert
TEXANS, THE(1938); STAGECOACH(1939)
John M. Eckert
INCUBUS, THE(1982, Can.), p
S.B. Eckert
WAKAMBA!(1955), ph
E. Eckert-Lundin
RAILROAD WORKERS(1948, Swed.), m; AFFAIRS OF A MODEL(1952, Swed.), m; WILD STRAWBERRIES(1959, Swed.), md; SECRETS OF WOMEN(1961, Swed.), md
Robert Eckertt
NO TIME FOR FLOWERS(1952)
Jack Eckes
1001 ARABIAN NIGHTS(1959), ph
Fritz Eckhardt
MIRACLE OF THE WHITE STALLIONS(1963); MAN WHO WALKED THROUGH THE WALL, THE(1964, Ger.)
Hermann Eckhardt
NAKED AMONG THE WOLVES(1967, Ger.)
Oliver Eckhardt
CAVALIER, THE(1928); LONE STAR RANGER, THE(1930); FORBIDDEN(1932); IT HAPPENED ONE NIGHT(1934); MEN WITHOUT NAMES(1935); SHE MARRIED HER BOSS(1935); DESIRE(1936); I AM THE LAW(1938); YOU CAN'T TAKE IT WITH YOU(1938)
Silents
LAST TRAIL, THE(1927)
Sara Eckhardt
STUDENT BODIES(1981)
Wes Eckhardt
1984
FIRESTARTER(1984), cos
Alan Eckhart
PEER GYNT(1965)
Frederick Eckhart
Silents
MAN WORTH WHILE, THE(1921)
Lois Eckhart
GEORGE WHITE'S 1935 SCANDALS(1935)
Oliver Eckhart
COWBOY AND THE KID,THE(1936); EMPTY SADDLES(1937)
Sylvia Eckhausen
ORDET(1957, Den.)
Eckhof
M(1933, Ger.)
James Eckhouse
TRADING PLACES(1983)
Ecki
CLEOPATRA(1934)
Jane Eckland
THIS LOVE OF OURS(1945)
Tener Riggs Eckleberry
HAIL MAFIA(1965, Fr./Ital.)
Daphne Eckler
1984
CITY HEAT(1984)
Lew Eckles
HOUSE ON 92ND STREET, THE(1945); CALL NORTHSIDE 777(1948)
Carl Ecklund
ADVENTURERS, THE(1970)
Britta Eckman
PRIZE, THE(1963)
Gosta Eckman
Misc. Silents
LOVE'S CRUCIBLE(1922, Swed.)
Agneta Eckmyr
WINTER KILLS(1979)
K.M. Eckstein
THREE MOVES TO FREEDOM(1960, Ger.), ed
Klaus Eckstein
GREH(1962, Ger./Yugo.), ed

Billy Eckstine
SKIRTS AHOY!(1952); LET'S DO IT AGAIN(1975)
Misc. Talkies
FLICKER UP(1946)
Ronnie Eckstine
LOVE-INS, THE(1967)
Carl Eckstrom
Misc. Silents
DERELICT, THE(1917)
Annie Ecleston
Silents
RIGHT WAY, THE(1921)
Peter Eco
LEGEND OF NIGGER CHARLEY, THE(1972), ph
James Ecoffey
MOUNTAIN MEN, THE(1980)
Chris Economaki
SIX PACK(1982); STROKER ACE(1983)
George Economides
WITHOUT RESERVATIONS(1946); THEY WERE EXPENDABLE(1945); IT'S A BIG COUNTRY(1951)
James Economides
SLAUGHTER IN SAN FRANCISCO(1981)
Michael Economides
WITHOUT RESERVATIONS(1946); THEY WERE EXPENDABLE(1945)
Georges Economou
IPHIGENIA(1977, Gr.)
Michael Economou
DEADLY TRACKERS(1973), ed; FIVE ON THE BLACK HAND SIDE(1973), ed; NAKED APE, THE(1973), ed; TRIAL OF BILLY JACK, THE(1974), ed; FOUR SEASONS, THE(1981), ed
Nicholas Economou
FRIENDS AND HUSBANDS(1983, Ger.), m
Nicolas Economou
GERMAN SISTERS, THE(1982, Ger.), m
Michael Economu
HARPER VALLEY, P.T.A.(1978), ed
Carl Ed
HAROLD TEEN(1934), w
Silents
HAROLD TEEN(1928), w
Barbara Eda-Young
SERPICO(1973)
Gilbert Edard
SUNDAYS AND CYBELE(1962, Fr.); LE PETIT SOLDAT(1965, Fr.)
Bonnie Kay Eddie
WINNING TEAM, THE(1952)
The Eddie Beal Trio
JUKE BOX JENNY(1942)
Eddie Calver and Band
SIMCHON FAMILY, THE(1969, Israel)
Eddie Carroll and His Band
LET'S MAKE A NIGHT OF IT(1937, Brit.)
Eddie Dean Trio
FIGHTING BILL FARGO(1942)
Eddie Dolly Dance Troupe
Silents
NETS OF DESTINY(1924, Brit.)
Eddie Duchin Orchestra
CORONADO(1935)
Eddie Durant and his Rhumba band
HARD GUY(1941), m
Eddie Durant's Rhumba Orchestra
TIME OUT FOR RHYTHM(1941)
Eddie Heywood & Orchestra
DARK CORNER, THE(1946)
Eddie Heywood Orchestra
JUNIOR PROM(1946)
Eddie Le Baron and his Rhumba Orchestra
SHE'S FOR ME(1943)
The Eddie Le Baron Orchestra
TROCADERO(1944); CASA MANANA(1951)
Eddie LeBaron and his Continental Orchestra
PERILOUS HOLIDAY(1946)
Eddie LeBaron Orchestra
HARVEST MELODY(1943)
Eddie Phyfe Jazz Ensemble
DEAD TO THE WORLD(1961), m
Eddie Rio and Brothers
NEW FACES OF 1937(1937)
Eddie the Pigeon
CAN SHE BAKE A CHERRY PIE?(1983)
Malek Eddine
L'ETOILE DU NORD(1983, Fr.)
Ruth Edding
PALMY DAYS(1931)
Laurence Eddinger
Silents
TOL'ABLE DAVID(1921)
Wallace Eddinger
Misc. Silents
GREAT DIAMOND ROBBERY, THE(1914)
Ruth Eddings
WHOOPEE(1930); 42ND STREET(1933); DAMES(1934)
Harry E. Eddington
LUCKY PARTNERS(1940), p
May Eddington
FALSE MADONNA(1932), w

Paul Eddington
MAN WHO WAS NOBODY, THE(1960, Brit.); JET STORM(1961, Brit.); DEVIL'S BRIDE, THE(1968, Brit.); BAXTER(1973, Brit.)

Beverly Eddins
KISS OF THE TARANTULA(1975)

Rebecca Eddins
KISS OF THE TARANTULA(1975)

Robert Eddison
VICE VERSA(1948, Brit.); ANGEL WHO PAWNED HER HARP, THE(1956, Brit.); BOY WHO TURNED YELLOW, THE(1972, Brit.)

Eddie Eddon
SAFECRACKER, THE(1958, Brit.)

Sadie Eddon
SECRETS OF A WINDMILL GIRL(1966, Brit.)

William Eddritt
MIDNIGHT(1939); HOODLUM SAINT, THE(1946); UNDERCURRENT(1946); THAT FORSYTE WOMAN(1949)

Hank Edds
SHENANDOAH(1965), makeup; RELUCTANT ASTRONAUT, THE(1967), makeup; WRECKING CREW, THE(1968), makeup; FOOLS' PARADE(1971), makeup; LOVE MACHINE, THE,(1971), makeup; SOMETHING BIG(1971), makeup; CHINATOWN(1974), makeup

Bonnie Eddy
GLENN MILLER STORY, THE(1953)

Bonnie Kay Eddy
WINCHESTER '73(1950); MA AND PA KETTLE AT WAIKIKI(1955)

Buck Eddy
KENTUCKY JUBILEE(1951)

Cecile Eddy
ROYAL AFFAIRS IN VERSAILLES(1957, Fr.)

Chickie Eddy
KENTUCKY JUBILEE(1951)

Danni Eddy
INSIDE LOOKING OUT(1977, Aus.)

Duane Eddy
THUNDER OF DRUMS, A(1961); WILD WESTERNERS, THE(1962); KONA COAST(1968); SAVAGE SEVEN, THE(1968)

Helen Eddy
Silents
TONGUES OF MEN, THE(1916); JULES OF THE STRONG HEART(1918)
Misc. Silents
RED VIRGIN, THE(1915)

Helen Jerome Eddy
MIDSTREAM(1929); WAR NURSE(1930); GIRLS DEMAND EXCITEMENT(1931); GREAT, MEADOW, THE(1931); MATA HARI(1931); REACHING FOR THE MOON(1931); SKIPPY(1931); SOOKY(1931); IMPATIENT MAIDEN(1932); MADAME BUTTERFLY(1932); MAKE ME A STAR(1932); NIGHT OF JUNE 13(1932); NO GREATER LOVE(1932); PARISIAN ROMANCE, A(1932); BITTER TEA OF GENERAL YEN, THE(1933); BROADWAY THROUGH A KEYHOLE(1933); FRISCO JENNY(1933); MAN'S CASTLE, A(1933); MASQUERADER, THE(1933); STRICTLY PERSONAL(1933); TORCH SINGER(1933); DOCTOR MONICA(1934); GIRL OF THE LIMBERLOST(1934); RIP TIDE(1934); UNKNOWN BLONDE(1934); GIRL FROM TENTH AVENUE, THE(1935); HELLDORADO(1935); KEEPER OF THE BEES(1935); RENDEZVOUS AT MIDNIGHT(1935); SHOT IN THE DARK, A(1935); COUNTRY DOCTOR, THE(1936); GARDEN OF ALLAH, THE(1936); KLONDIKE ANNIE(1936); SHOW BOAT(1936); STOWAWAY(1936); WINTERSET(1936); JIM HANVEY, DETECTIVE(1937); WOMEN MEN MARRY, THE(1937); CITY STREETS(1938); BLONDIE BRINGS UP BABY(1939); GOOD GIRLS GO TO PARIS(1939); STRANGE CASE OF DR. MEADE(1939); STRIKE UP THE BAND(1940)
Silents
CODE OF MARCIA GRAY(1916); AS MEN LOVE(1917); REBECCA OF SUNNYBROOK FARM(1917); OLD WIVES FOR NEW(1918); ONE MORE AMERICAN(1918); MISS HOBBS(1920); POLLYANNA(1920); TEN DOLLAR RAISE(1921); FLIRT, THE(1922); COUNTRY KID, THE(1923); DARK ANGEL, THE(1925); CAMILLE(1927); QUALITY STREET(1927); CHICAGO AFTER MIDNIGHT(1928); TWO LOVERS(1928); 13 WASHINGTON SQUARE(1928)
Misc. Silents
HER FATHER'S SON(1916); PASQUALE(1916); COOK OF CANYON CAMP, THE(1917); HIS SWEETHEART(1917); LOST IN TRANSIT(1917); MARCELLINI MILLIONS, THE(1917); WAX MODEL, THE(1917); WINNER TAKES ALL(1918); BLINDING TRAIL, THE(1919); BOOMERANG, THE(1919); MAN BENEATH, THE(1919); TONG MAN, THE(1919); TREMBLING HOUR, THE(1919); COUNTY FAIR, THE(1920); FORBIDDEN THING, THE(1920); HOUSE OF TOYS, THE(1920); LIGHT WOMAN, A(1920); FIRST BORN, THE(1921); ONE MAN IN A MILLION(1921); OTHER WOMAN, THE(1921); WHEN LOVE COMES(1922); OLD SWEETHEART OF MINE, AN(1923); TO THE LADIES(1923); DARK ANGEL, THE(1925); MARRY ME(1925); PADLOCKED(1926)

Jan Eddy
VILLAIN, THE(1979)

Jean Eddy
JEALOUSY(1934)

Ken Eddy
KILLER FORCE(1975, Switz./Ireland), ph

Lorraine Eddy
CARNATION KID(1929); CHARMING SINNERS(1929)

Michael Alan Eddy
1984
BEDROOM EYES(1984, Can.), w

Nelson Eddy
BROADWAY TO HOLLYWOOD(1933); DANCING LADY(1933); STUDENT TOUR(1934); NAUGHTY MARIETTA(1935); ROSE MARIE(1936); MAYTIME(1937); ROSALIE(1937); GIRL OF THE GOLDEN WEST, THE(1938); SWEETHEARTS(1938); BALALAIKA(1939); LET FREEDOM RING(1939); BITTER SWEET(1940); NEW MOON(1940); CHOCOLATE SOLDIER, THE(1941); I MARRIED AN ANGEL(1942); PHANTOM OF THE OPERA(1943); KNICKERBOCKER HOLIDAY(1944); MAKE MINE MUSIC(1946); NORTHWEST OUTPOST(1947)

Robert Eddy
Silents
ACTION GALORE(1925), d; HANDSOME BRUTE, THE(1925), d; LONG PANTS(1927), w; THREE'S A CROWD(1927), w; CHASER, THE(1928), w

Misc. Silents
GALLOPING JINX(1925), d; HURRICANE HORSEMAN(1925), d; READIN"RITIN'-'RITHMETIC(1926), d; STACKED CARDS(1926), d

Eddy Duchin and Band
HIT PARADE, THE(1937)

Beryl Ede
HAPPIEST DAYS OF YOUR LIFE(1950, Brit.)

Francois Ede
1984
THREE CROWNS OF THE SAILOR(1984, Fr.), w

George Ede
FUNNYMAN(1967); SERPICO(1973); WORLD ACCORDING TO GARP, The(1982)

H. S. Ede
SAVAGE MESSIAH(1972, Brit.), w

Janet Ede
CONFESSIONS FROM A HOLIDAY CAMP(1977, Brit.)

Robert Ede
LIAR'S DICE(1980)

Aud Edege-Nissen
Misc. Silents
STREET, THE(1927, Ger.)

A.D. Edel
TRAPP FAMILY, THE(1961, Ger.)

Alfred Edel
OUR HITLER, A FILM FROM GERMANY(1980, Ger.)

Velma Edele
Misc. Silents
SHADOWS OF CHINATOWN(1926)

Yvette Edelhart
1984
DELIVERY BOYS(1984)

Dana Edelman
HOME MOVIES(1979), w

Herb Edelman
WAY WE WERE, THE(1973); IN LIKE FLINT(1967); WAR BETWEEN MEN AND WOMEN, THE(1972); YAKUZA, THE(1975, U.S./Jap.); CHARGE OF THE MODEL-T'S(1979); ON THE RIGHT TRACK(1981); SMORGASBORD(1983)

Herbert Edelman
BAREFOOT IN THE PARK(1967); I LOVE YOU, ALICE B. TOKLAS!(1968); ODD COUPLE, THE(1968); P.J.(1968); FRONT PAGE, THE(1974); HEARTS OF THE WEST(1975); CALIFORNIA SUITE(1978); GOIN' COCONUTS(1978)

Lou Edelman
SHIPMATES(1931), w; FLIRTATION WALK(1934), w; HERE COMES THE NAVY(1934), p; KANSAS CITY PRINCESS(1934), p; DEVIL DOGS OF THE AIR(1935), p; G-MEN(1935), p; WALKING DEAD, THE(1936), p; MARKED WOMAN(1937), p; SINGING MARINE, THE(1937), p; SUBMARINE D-1(1937), p; VARSITY SHOW(1937), p; VALLEY OF THE GIANTS(1938), p; DUST BE MY DESTINY(1939), p; ESPIONAGE AGENT(1939), p; WINGS OF THE NAVY(1939), p

Louis Edelman
GARDEN OF THE MOON(1938), p; ONCE UPON A TIME(1944), p

Louis F. Edelman
BULLETS OR BALLOTS(1936), p; INVISIBLE STRIPES(1940), p; YOU WERE NEVER LOVELIER(1942), p; DESTROYER(1943), p; HOTEL BERLIN(1945), p; SONG TO REMEMBER, A(1945), p; WHITE HEAT(1949), p; WEST POINT STORY, THE(1950), p; I'LL SEE YOU IN MY DREAMS(1951), p, w; OPERATION PACIFIC(1951), p; BIG TREES, THE(1952), p; SPRINGFIELD RIFLE(1952), p; STOP, YOU'RE KILLING ME(1952), p; JAZZ SINGER, THE(1953), p; ADAM'S WOMAN(1972, Austral.), p

Randy Edelman
EXECUTIVE ACTION(1973), m; SGT. PEPPER'S LONELY HEARTS CLUB BAND(1978)

Rosemary Edelman
CAREY TREATMENT, THE(1972)

Heinz Edelmann
YELLOW SUBMARINE(1958, Brit.), art d

Otto Edelmann
DON GIOVANNI(1955, Brit.)

Harry Edelson
TOUCHDOWN!(1931)

William Edelson
CRAWLING HAND, THE(1963), w

Robert Edelstein
SALLY'S HOUNDS(1968), a, p,d,w&ph, ed

Alice Eden
CAREER(1939)

Barbara Eden
WAYWARD GIRL, THE(1957); PRIVATE'S AFFAIR, A(1959); FLAMING STAR(1960); FROM THE TERRACE(1960); TWELVE HOURS TO KILL(1960); ALL HANDS ON DECK(1961); VOYAGE TO THE BOTTOM OF THE SEA(1961); FIVE WEEKS IN A BALLOON(1962); SWINGIN' ALONG(1962); WONDERFUL WORLD OF THE BROTHERS ERIMM, THE(1962); YELLOW CANARY, THE(1963); BRASS BOTTLE, THE(1964); NEW INTERNS, THE(1964); RIDE THE WILD SURF(1964); SEVEN FACES OF DR. LAO(1964); QUICK, LET'S GET MARRIED(1965); AMAZING DOBERMANS, THE(1976); HARPER VALLEY, P.T.A.(1978); JAWS 3-D(1983)
1984
CHATTANOOGA CHOO CHOO(1984)
Misc. Talkies
CONFESSION, THE(1964)

Carole Eden
ZERO HOUR!(1957)

Chana Eden
WIND ACROSS THE EVERGLADES(1958)

Daniel Eden
FEAR NO EVIL(1981)

Diana Eden
PRODUCERS, THE(1967)
Misc. Talkies
BROTHER ON THE RUN(1973)

Elana Eden
STORY OF RUTH, THE(1960); TRUNK TO CAIRO(1966, Israel/Ger.)

Eve Eden
NAKED FURY(1959, Brit.); WEEKEND WITH LULU, A(1961, Brit.); YOUNG, WILLING AND EAGER(1962, Brit.); OPERATION BULLSHINE(1963, Brit.); HELP!(1965, Brit.)

Hugh Eden
ROMANCE OF SEVILLE, A(1929, Brit.); DARK RED ROSES(1930, Brit.)

Jack Eden
1984
NUMBER ONE(1984, Brit.)

Jerome Eden
BLOOD FEAST(1963); TWO THOUSAND MANIACS!(1964); COLOR ME BLOOD RED(1965)

Jill Eden
THIRST(1979, Aus.), art d; DAY AFTER HALLOWEEN, THE(1981, Aus.), art d

Jonathan Eden
VIVA MARIA(1965, Fr./Ital.)

Keith Eden
ON THE BEACH(1959)

M. V. Eden
FREUD(1962)

Marc Eden
OPERATION BOTTLENECK(1961)

Mark Eden
L-SHAPED ROOM, THE(1962, Brit.); PASSWORD IS COURAGE, THE(1962, Brit.); HEAVENS ABOVE!(1963, Brit.); MAN IN THE DARK(1963, Brit.); SEANCE ON A WET AFTERNOON(1964 Brit.); DOCTOR ZHIVAGO(1965); GAME FOR THREE LO-SERS(1965, Brit.); PSYCHO A GO-GO!(1965), w; PARTNER, THE(1966, Brit.); PLEAS-URE GIRLS, THE(1966, Brit.); I'LL NEVER FORGET WHAT'S 'IS NAME(1967, Brit.); ATTACK ON THE IRON COAST(1968, U.S./Brit.); LITTLE OF WHAT YOU FANCY, A(1968, Brit.); CRIMSON CULT, THE(1970, Brit.); RICHARD'S THINGS(1981, Brit.)

Michael Eden
COME SEPTEMBER(1961)

Rob Eden
DANCING FEET(1936), w; I DEMAND PAYMENT(1938), w

Rod Eden
JENIFER HALE(1937, Brit.), w

Rolf Eden
TERROR OF DR. MABUSE, THE(1965, Ger.); NEW LIFE STYLE, THE(1970, Ger.)

Sandy Eden
Misc. Talkies
AMAZING TRANSPLANT, THE(1970)

Sidney Eden
SPOOK WHO SAT BY THE DOOR, THE(1973)

Dennis Edenfield
PUFNSTUF(1970)

Alric Edens
MINNIE AND MOSKOWITZ(1971), ph; ONE MORE TRAIN TO ROB(1971), ph

Olive Edens
HOUSE DIVIDED, A(1932), w

Robert Edens
TAKE ME OUT TO THE BALL GAME(1949), m

Roger Edens
ICE FOLLIES OF 1939(1939), m; SOCIETY LAWYER(1939), md; LITTLE NELLIE KELLY(1940), m; CABIN IN THE SKY(1943), m; ZIEGFELD FOLLIES(1945), w; TILL THE CLOUDS ROLL BY(1946), m; ON THE TOWN(1949), m, md; DEEP IN MY HEART(1954), p; INVITATION TO THE DANCE(1956), m; FUNNY FACE(1957), p, m

Lieselotte Eder
MARRIAGE OF MARIA BRAUN, THE(1979, Ger.)

Liselotte Eder
FEAR EATS THE SOUL(1974, Ger.); DESPAIR(1978, Ger.)

Gertrude Ederle
Misc. Silents
SWIM, GIRL, SWIM(1927)

Arjan Ederveen
STILL SMOKIN'(1983)

Arthur Edeson
WATERLOO BRIDGE(1931), ph; COCK-EYED WORLD, THE(1929), ph; IN OLD ARIZONA(1929), ph; ROMANCE OF THE RIO GRANDE(1929), ph; ALL QUIET ON THE WESTERN FRONT(1930), ph; BIG TRAIL, THE(1930), ph; DOCTORS' WI-VES(1931), ph; FRANKENSTEIN(1931), ph; MAN WHO CAME BACK, THE(1931), ph; FAST COMPANIONS(1932), ph; FLESH(1932), ph; IMPATIENT MAIDEN(1932), ph; LAST MILE, THE(1932), ph; OLD DARK HOUSE, THE(1932), ph; STRANGERS OF THE EVENING(1932), ph; THOSE WE LOVE(1932), ph; BIG BRAIN, THE(1933), ph; HIS DOUBLE LIFE(1933), ph; INVISIBLE MAN, THE(1933), ph; LIFE OF JIMMY DOLAN, THE(1933), ph; STUDY IN SCARLET, A(1933), ph; HERE COMES THE NAVY(1934), ph; MERRY FRINKS, THE(1934), ph; PALOOKA(1934), ph; CEILNG ZERO(1935), ph; DEVIL DOGS OF THE AIR(1935), ph; DINKY(1935), ph; MAYBE IT'S LOVE(1935), ph; MUTINY ON THE BOUNTY(1935), ph; WHILE THE PATIENT SLEPT(1935), ph; CHINA CLIPPER(1936), ph; GOLD DIGGERS OF 1937(1936), ph; GOLDEN ARROW, THE(1936), ph; HOT MONEY(1936), ph; SATAN MET A LA-DY(1936), ph; FOOTLOOSE HEIRESS, THE(1937), ph; GO-GETTER, THE(1937), ph; KID COMES BACK, THE(1937), ph; MR. DODD TAKES THE AIR(1937), ph; SUBMA-RINE D-1(1937), ph; THEY WON'T FORGET(1937), ph; COWBOY FROM BROOK-LYN(1938), ph; MR. CHUMP(1938), ph; RACKET BUSTERS(1938), ph; SWING YOUR LADY(1938), ph; EACH DAWN I DIE(1939), ph; KID NIGHTINGALE(1939), ph; NANCY DREW-REPORTER(1939), ph; NO PLACE TO GO(1939), ph; SWEEPSTAKES WINNER(1939), ph; CASTLE ON THE HUDSON(1940), ph; LADY WITH RED HAIR(1940), ph; THEY DRIVE BY NIGHT(1940), ph; TUGBOAT ANNIE SAILS AGAIN(1940), ph; KISSES FOR BREAKFAST(1941), ph; MALTESE FALCON, THE(1941), ph; ACROSS THE PACIFIC(1942), ph; CASABLANCA(1942), ph; MALE ANIMAL, THE(1942), ph; THANK YOUR LUCKY STARS(1943), ph; CONSPIRA-TORS, THE(1944), ph; MASK OF DIMITRIOS, THE(1944), ph; SHINE ON, HARVEST MOON(1944), ph; NOBODY LIVES FOREVER(1946), ph; THREE STRANGERS(1946), ph; TIME, THE PLACE AND THE GIRL, THE(1946), ph; MY WILD IRISH RO-SE(1947), ph; STALLION ROAD(1947), ph; TWO GUYS FROM TEXAS(1948), ph; FIGHTING O'FLYNN, THE(1949), ph

Silents
GILDED CAGE, THE(1916), ph; BABY MINE(1917), ph; JACK SPURLOCK, PRODI-GAL(1918), ph; FORBIDDEN WOMAN, THE(1920), ph; THREE MUSKETEERS, THE(1921), ph; ROBIN HOOD(1922), ph; INEZ FROM HOLLYWOOD(1924), ph; THIEF OF BAGDAD, THE(1924), ph; LOST WORLD, THE(1925), ph; STELLA DAL-LAS(1925), ph; BAT, THE(1926), ph; PARTNERS AGAIN(1926), ph; DROPKICK, THE(1927), ph; GIRLS GONE WILD(1929), ph

Robert Edeson
HOME TOWNERS, THE(1928); LITTLE WILDCAT, THE(1928); MARRIAGE BY CONTRACT(1928); DOCTOR'S SECRET(1929); MARIANNE(1929); MOST IMMORAL LADY, A(1929); ROMANCE OF THE RIO GRANDE(1929); BIG MONEY(1930); CAMEO KIRBY(1930); DANGER LIGHTS(1930); DEVIL WITH WOMEN, A(1930); DYNAMI-TE(1930); LASH, THE(1930); LITTLE JOHNNY JONES(1930); KEEP SMILING(1930); PARDON MY GUN(1930); SWING HIGH(1930); WAY OF ALL MEN, THE(1930); ALOHA(1931)
Silents
CALL OF THE NORTH, THE(1914); MASTER MIND, THE(1914); WHERE THE TRAIL DIVIDES(1914); ABSENTEE-NRA, THE(1915); HOW MOLLY MADE GOOD(1915); MAN'S PREROGATIVE, A(1915); PRISONER OF ZENDA, THE(1922); SURE FIRE FLINT(1922); HAS THE WORLD GONE MAD!(1923); SILENT PARTNER, THE(1923); SOULS FOR SALE(1923); TEN COMMANDMENTS, THE(1923); TIE THAT BINDS, THE(1923); TO THE LAST MAN(1923); BEDROOM WINDOW, THE(1924); WELCOME STRANGER(1924); KEEP SMILING(1925); RAG MAN, THE(1925); VOLGA BOATMAN, THE(1926); WHISPERING SMITH(1926); ALTARS OF DESIRE(1927); KING OF KINGS, THE(1927); NIGHT BRIDE, THE(1927); CHICAGO(1928); POWER OF THE PRESS, THE(1928); WALKING BACK(1928)
Misc. Silents
CAVEMAN, THE(1915); GIRL I LEFT BEHIND ME, THE(1915); MORTMAIN(1915); ON THE NIGHT STAGE(1915); BIG JIM GARRITY(1916); FATHERS OF MEN(1916); FOR A WOMAN'S FAIR NAME(1916); LIGHT THAT FAILED, THE(1916); PUBLIC DEFENDER(1917); SEALED HEARTS(1919); EXTRAVAGANCE(1921); ANY NIGHT(1922); SPOILERS, THE(1923); YOU ARE GUILTY(1923); FEET OF CLAY(1924); MEN(1924); BLOOD AND STEEL(1925); BRAVEHEART(1925); DANGER SIGNAL, THE(1925); HELL'S HIGHROAD(1925); SCARLET WEST, THE(1925); BLUE EAGLE, THE(1926); CLINGING VINE, THE(1926); EVE'S LEAVES(1926); HEART THIEF, THE(1927); BEWARE OF BLONDES(1928); GEORGE WASHINGTON CO-HEN(1928); MARRIAGE BY CONRACT(1928)

Katarina Edfeldt
LOVING COUPLES(1966, Swed.); HERE'S YOUR LIFE(1968, Swed.)

Avril Edgar
SHE ALWAYS GETS THEIR MAN(1962, Brit.)

Craig Edgar
WORLD'S GREATEST LOVER, THE(1977), set d; RIGHT STUFF, THE(1983), set d; TO BE OR NOT TO BE(1983), set d

George Edgar
Silents
KENT, THE FIGHTING MAN(1916, Brit.), w; PRIDE OF THE FANCY, THE(1920, Brit.), w

Graham Edgar
DEADLY STRANGERS(1974, Brit.), ph; WHAT CHANGED CHARLEY FARTH-ING?(1976, Brit.), ph

Hindle Edgar
PRIVATE LIFE OF DON JUAN, THE(1934, Brit.); STRAUSS' GREAT WALTZ(1934, Brit.); SCARLET PIMPERNEL, THE(1935, Brit.); STAR FELL FROM HEAVEN, A(1936, Brit.); TENTH MAN, THE(1937, Brit.); PERIL FOR THE GUY(1956, Brit.), p; RESCUE SQUAD, THE(1963, Brit.), p; OPERATION THIRD FORM(1966, Brit.), p, w

Kenneth Allan Edgar
EDDIE MACON'S RUN(1983)

Margaret Edgar
THRESHOLD(1983, Can.)

Marriott Edgar
CHARLEY'S(BIG-HEARTED) AUNT*1/2(1940), w; HERE'S GEORGE(1932, Brit.), a, w; HELLO SWEETHEART(1935, Brit.); OH, MR. PORTER!(1937, Brit.), w; OKAY FOR SOUND(1937, Brit.), w; WINDBAG THE SAILOR(1937, Brit.), w; ALF'S BUTTON AFLOAT(1938, Brit.), w; CONVICT 99(1938, Brit.), w; HEY! HEY! U.S.A.(1938, Brit.), w; OLD BONES OF THE RIVER(1938, Brit.), w; SEZ O'REILLY TO MACNAB(1938, Brit.), w; ASK A POLICEMAN(1939, Brit.), w; FROZEN LIMITS, THE(1939, Brit.), w; WHERE'S THAT FIRE?(1939, Brit.), w; BAND WAGGON(1940, Brit.), w; GAS-BAGS(1940, Brit.), w; GHOST TRAIN, THE(1941, Brit.), w; HI, GANG!(1941, Brit.), w; I THANK YOU(1941, Brit.), w; BACK ROOM BOY(1942, Brit.), w; KING ARTHUR WAS A GENTLEMAN(1942, Brit.), w; MISS LONDON LTD.(1943, Brit.), w; BEES IN PARADISE(1944, Brit.), w; TOP OF THE FORM(1953, Brit.), w

P. Hindle Edgar
SALVAGE GANG, THE(1958, Brit.), p

Wayne Edgar
EXORCIST II: THE HERETIC(1977), spec eff

William Edgar
STACEY!(1973), w

Toni Edgar-Bruce
FOUR AGAINST FATE(1952, Brit.)

Lewis Edgard
Misc. Silents
IN THE PALACE OF THE KING(1915)

Louis Edgard
Silents
FALSE FRIEND, THE(1917)

Marriott Edgard
WHERE THERE'S A WILL(1937, Brit.), w

James Edgcomb
UNCOMMON VALOR(1983)

Debbie Edge
THIS IS ELVIS(1982)

Francis Edge
HOME TO DANGER(1951, Brit.), w; PROFILE(1954, Brit.), p; ONE WAY OUT(1955, Brit.), p; FIND THE LADY(1956, Brit.), p; HIDEOUT, THE(1956, Brit.), p; ACCOUNT RENDERED(1957, Brit.), p; BIG CHANCE, THE(1957, Brit.), p

Tony Edge
NUTCRACKER(1982, Brit.)

Edmundo Ros' Conga Band
WHAT DO WE DO NOW?(1945, Brit.)

Ann Edmunds
SHE COULDN'T SAY NO(1941)

Bill Edmunds
IT'S A WONDERFUL LIFE(1946)

Billy Edmunds
GERONIMO(1939); TONIGHT WE RAID CALAIS(1943)

Bob Edmunds
MAD MEN OF EUROPE(1940, Brit.), w

Dave Edmunds
STARDUST(1974, Brit.), a, m

Elizabeth Edmunds
RETURN OF THE SOLDIER, THE(1983, Brit.)

Fella Edmunds
STOLEN AIRLINER, THE(1962, Brit.)

Frank Edmunds
SWING TIME(1936)

Jerre Edmunds
LIQUID SKY(1982)

Michael Edmunds
TIME GENTLEMEN PLEASE!(1953, Brit.)

Mike Edmunds
TIME BANDITS(1981, Brit.)

Molly Edmunds
GLAMOUR(1931, Brit.)

Pamela Edmunds
STOLEN PLANS, THE(1962, Brit.)

Robert Edmunds
MEDICINE MAN, THE(1933, Brit.), w; LOVE, LIFE AND LAUGHTER(1934, Brit.), w; GET OFF MY FOOT(1935, Brit.), w; MY HEART IS CALLING(1935, Brit.), w; MY SONG FOR YOU(1935, Brit.), w; PRINCESS CHARMING(1935, Brit.), w; TWO HEARTS IN HARMONY(1935, Brit.), w; BOYS WILL BE BOYS(1936, Brit.), w; EDUCATED EVANS(1936, Brit.), w; PUBLIC NUISANCE NO. 1(1936, Brit.), w; WHERE THERE'S A WILL(1936, Brit), w; FEATHER YOUR NEST(1937, Brit.), w; TELEVISION TALENT(1937, Brit.), d&w; WINDBAG THE SAILOR(1937, Brit.), w; LAMBETH WALK, THE(1940, Brit.), w

Tony Edmunds
MAD DOCTOR OF BLOOD ISLAND, THE(1969, Phil./U.S.)

William Edmunds
ANGELS WITH DIRTY FACES(1938); EVERYTHING HAPPENS AT NIGHT(1939); FIXER DUGAN(1939); IDIOT'S DELIGHT(1939); JUAREZ(1939); RAINS CAME, THE(1939); GIRL FROM HAVANA(1940); GIRLS UNDER TWENTY-ONE(1940); HE MARRIED HIS WIFE(1940); MARK OF ZORRO, THE(1940); MORTAL STORM, THE(1940); SHOP AROUND THE CORNER, THE(1940); STRANGE CARGO(1940); STRANGER ON THE THIRD FLOOR(1940); BARNACLE BILL(1941); KNOCK-OUT(1941); MAN AT LARGE(1941); MR. AND MRS. SMITH(1941); PARIS CALLING(1941); BIG SHOT, THE(1942); CASABLANCA(1942); CROSSROADS(1942); JUKE GIRL(1942); PIED PIPER, THE(1942); REUNION IN FRANCE(1942); WIFE TAKES A FLYER, THE(1942); BACKGROUND TO DANGER(1943); CAPTIVE WILD WOMAN(1943); DEERSLAYER(1943); DESERT SONG, THE(1943); EDGE OF DARKNESS(1943); FALLEN SPARROW, THE(1943); FOR WHOM THE BELL TOLLS(1943); MADAME CURIE(1943); CLIMAX, THE(1944); DANGEROUS PASSAGE(1944); HOUSE OF FRANKENSTEIN(1944); ONE BODY TOO MANY(1944); SECRETS OF SCOTLAND YARD(1944); TILL WE MEET AGAIN(1944); BELL FOR ADANO, A(1945); THIS LOVE OF OURS(1945); ANNA AND THE KING OF SIAM(1946); BEAST WITH FIVE FINGERS, THE(1946); MAN I LOVE, THE(1946); NOBODY LIVES FOREVER(1946); SWAMP FIRE(1946); CARNIVAL IN COSTA RICA(1947); LOST MOMENT, THE(1947); THAT HAGEN GIRL(1947); WHERE THERE'S LIFE(1947); THIRTEEN LEAD SOLDIERS(1948); THREE MUSKETEERS, THE(1948); BIG SOMBRERO, THE(1949); MR. SOFT TOUCH(1949); RINGSIDE(1949); LAWLESS, THE(1950); DOUBLE DYNAMITE(1951); CADDY, THE(1953)

Williams Edmunds
BERLIN CORRESPONDENT(1942)

Al Edmundsen
Silents
FOOLISH WIVES(1920); MERRY-GO-ROUND(1923)

Mr. Edmundsen
Silents
JUST JIM(1915)

Audie Edmundson
TIMERIDER(1983)

Buddy Edmundson
TIMERIDER(1983)

Joan Yale Edmundson
SIX WEEKS(1982)

Sandy Edmundson
MY FAIR LADY(1964)

Beatrice Edney
DAY AT THE BEACH, A(1970)

Benjamin Edney
DESPERADOS, THE(1969)

Sylvia Edney
Misc. Silents
KINGDOM OF HUMAN HEARTS, THE(1921)

Michael Edols
OFFICE PICNIC, THE(1974, Aus.), ph; 27A(1974, Aus.), ph

Mike Edols
IN SEARCH OF ANNA(1978, Aus.), ph

Farciot Edouart
ALICE IN WONDERLAND(1933), spec eff; PRINCESS COMES ACROSS, THE(1936), spec eff; THIRTEEN HOURS BY AIR(1936), spec eff; ANGEL(1937), spec eff; EASY LIVING(1937), spec eff; I MET HIM IN PARIS(1937), spec eff; PLAINSMAN, THE(1937), spec eff; SWING HIGH, SWING LOW(1937), spec eff; WAIKIKI WEDDING(1937), spec eff; ARTISTS AND MODELS ABROAD(1938), spec eff; RIDE A CROOKED MILE(1938), spec eff; SPAWN OF THE NORTH(1938), spec eff; GERONIMO(1939), spec eff; NEVER SAY DIE(1939), spec eff; UNION PACIFIC(1939), spec eff; DR. CYCLOPS(1940), spec eff; GHOST BREAKERS(1940), spec eff; NORTHWEST MOUNTED POLICE(1940), spec eff; ROAD TO SINGAPORE(1940), spec eff; SULLIVAN'S TRAVELS(1941), spec eff; REAP THE WILD WIND(1942), spec eff;

CHINA(1943), ph; NO TIME FOR LOVE(1943), spec eff; SO PROUDLY WE HAIL(1943), spec eff; AND NOW TOMORROW(1944), ph; DOUBLE INDEMNITY(1944), ph; FRENCHMAN'S CREEK(1944), ph; LADY IN THE DARK(1944), ph; PRACTICALLY YOURS(1944), spec eff; STORY OF DR. WASSELL, THE(1944), spec eff; TILL WE MEET AGAIN(1944), ph; UNINVITED, THE(1944), ph; DUFFY'S TAVERN(1945), ph; INCENDIARY BLONDE(1945), spec eff; ROAD TO UTOPIA(1945), spec eff; SALTY O'ROURKE(1945), spec eff; STORK CLUB, THE(1945), ph; YOU CAME ALONG(1945), ph; BLUE SKIES(1946), spec eff; MONSIEUR BEAUCAIRE(1946), spec eff; O.S.S.(1946), spec eff; SEARCHING WIND, THE(1946), spec eff; STRANGE LOVE OF MARTHA IVERS, THE(1946), spec eff; TO EACH HIS OWN(1946), spec eff; IMPERFECT LADY, THE(1947), spec eff; SUDDENLY IT'S SPRING(1947), spec eff; UNCONQUERED(1947), spec eff; VARIETY GIRL(1947), spec eff; WILD HARVEST(1947), ph; PALEFACE, THE(1948), spec eff; SEALED VERDICT(1948), process ph; WHISPERING SMITH(1948), spec eff; CONNECTICUT YANKEE IN KING ARTHUR'S COURT, A(1949), spec eff; MR. MUSIC(1950), spec eff; NO MAN OF HER OWN(1950), spec eff; RIDING HIGH(1950), spec eff; SUNSET BOULEVARD(1950), spec eff; DETECTIVE STORY(1951), ph; SON OF PALEFACE(1952), spec eff; TURNING POINT, THE(1952), spec eff; NAKED JUNGLE, THE(1953), spec eff; ELEPHANT WALK(1954), ph; SABRINA(1954), spec eff; DESPERATE HOURS, THE(1955), spec eff; RUN FOR COVER(1955), spec eff; TO CATCH A THIEF(1955), ph; PROUD AND THE PROFANE, THE(1956), spec eff; THREE VIOLENT PEOPLE(1956), spec eff; OMAR KHAYYAM(1957), spec eff; WILD IS THE WIND(1957), spec eff; TEACHER'S PET(1958), spec eff; VERTIGO(1958), ph; YOUNG CAPTIVES, THE(1959), spec eff; VISIT TO A SMALL PLANET(1960), spec eff; ON THE DOUBLE(1961), spec eff; ONE-EYED JACKS(1961), spec eff; POCKETFUL OF MIRACLES(1961), spec eff; IT'S ONLY MONEY(1962), spec eff; PIGEON THAT TOOK ROME, THE(1962), spec eff; DISORDERLY ORDERLY, THE(1964), spec eff; ROUSTABOUT(1964), process ph; RED LINE 7000(1965), spec eff; SHIP OF FOOLS(1965), spec eff; EL DORADO(1967), ph; OH DAD, POOR DAD, MAMA'S HUNG YOU IN THE CLOSET AND I'M FEELIN' SO SAD(1967), spec eff; SPIRIT IS WILLING, THE(1967), spec eff; ROSEMARY'S BABY(1968), spec eff

Dagmar Edqvist
NIGHT IS MY FUTURE(1962, Swed.), w

William Edritt
GOOD MORNING, JUDGE(1943)

Paul Eds
1984
MUPPETS TAKE MANHATTAN, THE(1984), art d

Elsa Edsman
DESERT LEGION(1953)

Eric Edson
SOGGY BOTTOM U.S.A.(1982), w

Gus Edson
DONDI(1961), p

John Edson
NIGHT THE LIGHTS WENT OUT IN GEORGIA, THE(1981)

John Edson, Jr.
JAWS 3-D(1983)

John P. Edson, Jr.
1984
CLOAK AND DAGGER(1984)

Mark Edson
TOUGH ENOUGH(1983)

Richard Edson
VORTEX(1982), m
1984
STRANGER THAN PARADISE(1984, U.S./Ger.)

Anton Edthofer
Misc. Silents
FOUR AROUND THE WOMAN(1921, Ger.)

The Eduardini
SILENCE, THE(1964, Swed.)

Allan Edwall
DEVIL'S EYE, THE(1960, Swed.); VIRGIN SPRING, THE(1960, Swed.); WINTER LIGHT, THE(1963, Swed.); ALL THESE WOMEN(1964, Swed.); HERE'S YOUR LIFE(1968, Swed.); SHORT IS THE SUMMER(1968, Swed.); EMIGRANTS, THE(1972, Swed.); NEW LAND, THE(1973, Swed.); ELVIS! ELVIS!(1977, Swed.); FANNY AND ALEXANDER(1983, Swed./Fr./Ger.)

Edward
LADY LUCK(1946), cos

Aaron Edward
Silents
GOLD RUSH, THE(1925)

Alan Edward
SHOW-OFF, THE(1934)

Albert Edward
Misc. Silents
WHY NOT MARRY?(1922)

J. Edward
Misc. Talkies
BOOTS TURNER(1973), d

Marion Edward
ROAD GAMES(1981, Aus.); WILD DUCK, THE(1983, Aus.)
1984
STRIKEBOUND(1984, Aus.)

Owen Edward
Misc. Talkies
PINOCCHIO'S STORYBOOK ADVENTURES(1979)

Rory Edward
1984
SUCCESS IS THE BEST REVENGE(1984, Brit.)

Sarah Edward
HOODLUM SAINT, THE(1946)

George Edwardes
Silents
ONE OF THE BEST(1927, Brit.), w

Kenneth Edwardes
MAN ACCUSED(1959)

Olga Edwardes
DOMINANT SEX, THE(1937, Brit.); CAESAR AND CLEOPATRA(1946, Brit.); CHRISTMAS CAROL, A(1951, Brit.); SIX MEN, THE(1951, Brit.)
Misc. Talkies
BLACK ORCHID(1952)
George Edwardes-Hall
Silents
ETERNAL SIN, THE(1917), w; KICK BACK, THE(1922), w
Aaron Edwards
ARE WE CIVILIZED?(1934)
Silents
FLY GOD, THE(1918)
Misc. Silents
MEDICINE MAN, THE(1917); SHIP OF DOOM, THE(1917); WOLF LOWRY(1917); WORLD OF FOLLY, A(1920)
Alan Edwards
CLEAR ALL WIRES(1933); LIFE IN THE RAW(1933); STAGE MOTHER(1933); WHITE SISTER, THE(1933); FRONTIER MARSHAL(1934); HOLD THAT GIRL(1934); WOMEN MUST DRESS(1935); FORGOTTEN FACES(1936); IF YOU COULD ONLY COOK(1936); MAKE WAY FOR A LADY(1936); RING AROUND THE MOON(1936); FORTY NAUGHTY GIRLS(1937); LITTLE TOUGH GUY(1938); FOR LOVE OR MONEY(1939); FORGOTTEN WOMAN, THE(1939); LAUGH IT OFF(1939); SOUTH OF THE BORDER(1939); THEY SHALL HAVE MUSIC(1939); MR. DISTRICT ATTORNEY(1941); MEN ON HER MIND(1944); JUNIOR MISS(1945); SALOME, WHERE SHE DANCED(1945); THOROUGHBREDS(1945); MR. ACE(1946); LONE WOLF IN MEXICO, THE(1947); GENTLE TRAP, THE(1960, Brit.); UNSTOPPABLE MAN, THE(1961, Brit.); NIGHT WITHOUT PITY(1962, Brit.); DOOMSDAY AT ELEVEN(1963 Brit.)
Misc. Talkies
DO YOU KNOW THIS VOICE?(1964)
Misc. Silents
VIRGIN PARADISE, A(1921)
Allen Edwards
Misc. Silents
GIRL BY THE ROADSIDE, THE(1918)
Anne Edwards
QUANTEZ(1957), w; QUESTION OF ADULTERY, A(1959, Brit.), w
Anthony Edwards
FAST TIMES AT RIDGEMONT HIGH(1982); HEART LIKE A WHEEL(1983)
1984
REVENGE OF THE NERDS(1984)
Antoinette Edwards
MARRIED COUPLE, A(1969, Can.)
Becca Edwards
1984
SLAPSTICK OF ANOTHER KIND(1984)
Ben Edwards
LOVERS AND OTHER STRANGERS(1970), prod d; JENNIFER ON MY MIND(1971), art d; LAST OF THE RED HOT LOVERS(1972), art d; CLASS OF '44(1973), prod d; FORT APACHE, THE BRONX(1981), prod d; HANKY-PANKY(1982), prod d
Bernard Edwards
RAINBOW BOYS, THE(1973, Can.); SOUP FOR ONE(1982), m
Bill Edwards
STRANGE FACES(1938); GAY SISTERS, THE(1942); NOW, VOYAGER(1942); YANKEE DOODLE DANDY(1942); YOU CAN'T ESCAPE FOREVER(1942); ADVENTURES IN IRAQ(1943); MURDER ON THE WATERFRONT(1943); PRINCESS O'ROURKE(1943); HAIL THE CONQUERING HERO(1944); OUR HEARTS WERE YOUNG AND GAY(1944); YOU CAN'T RATION LOVE(1944); DUFFY'S TAVERN(1945); MISS SUSIE SLAGLE'S(1945); CHASE, THE(1946), cos; OUR HEARTS WERE GROWING UP(1946); VIRGINIAN, THE(1946); DANGER STREET(1947); LADIES OF THE CHORUS(1948); TRAIL OF THE YUKON(1949); BORDER OUTLAWS(1950); FIGHTING STALLION, THE(1950); FIRST LEGION, THE(1951); STAR, THE(1953), cos; FLOODS OF FEAR(1958, Brit.); THEM NICE AMERICANS(1958, Brit.); YOUR PAST IS SHOWING(1958, Brit.); FIRST MAN INTO SPACE(1959, Brit.); MOUSE THAT ROARED, THE(1959, Brit.); SUBWAY IN THE SKY(1959, Brit.); BIG NIGHT, THE(1960), cos; CLOWN AND THE KID, THE(1961), cos; UPSTAIRS AND DOWNSTAIRS(1961, Brit.); PRIMITIVES, THE(1962, Brit.); MOUSE ON THE MOON, THE(1963, Brit.)
Misc. Talkies
HOME IN SAN ANTONE(1949); PLOTTERS, THE(1966)
Billy Edwards
TWO AND TWO MAKE SIX(1962, Brit.); WAR LOVER, THE(1962, U.S./Brit.); MARRIED COUPLE, A(1969, Can.); NEON PALACE, THE(1970, Can.)
Blake Edwards
TEN GENTLEMEN FROM WEST POINT(1942); GUY NAMED JOE, A(1943); EVE OF ST. MARK, THE(1944); IN THE MEANTIME, DARLING(1944); LADIES COURAGEOUS(1944); MARINE RAIDERS(1944); MARSHAL OF RENO(1944); MY BUDDY(1944); SEE HERE, PRIVATE HARGROVE(1944); THIRTY SECONDS OVER TOKYO(1944); WING AND A PRAYER(1944); STRANGLER OF THE SWAMP(1945); THEY WERE EXPENDABLE(1945); THIS MAN'S NAVY(1945); TOKYO ROSE(1945); STRANGE LOVE OF MARTHA IVERS, THE(1946); TILL THE END OF TIME(1946); LEATHER GLOVES(1948); PANHANDLE(1948), a, p, w; STAMPEDE(1949), p, w; RAINBOW 'ROUND MY SHOULDER(1952), w; SOUND OFF(1952), w; ALL ASHORE(1953), w; CRUISIN' DOWN THE RIVER(1953), w; ATOMIC KID, THE(1954), w; DRIVE A CROOKED ROAD(1954), w; BRING YOUR SMILE ALONG(1955), d&w; MY SISTER EILEEN(1955), w; HE LAUGHED LAST(1956), d&w; MISTER CORY(1957), d, w; OPERATION MAD BALL(1957), w; PERFECT FURLOUGH, THE(1958), d&w; THIS HAPPY FEELING(1958), d&w; OPERATION PETTICOAT(1959), d; HIGH TIME(1960), d; BREAKFAST AT TIFFANY'S(1961), d; COUCH, THE(1962), w; DAYS OF WINE AND ROSES(1962), d; EXPERIMENT IN TERROR(1962), p&d; NOTORIOUS LANDLADY, THE(1962), w; SOLDIER IN THE RAIN(1963), w; PINK PANTHER, THE(1964), d, w; SHOT IN THE DARK, A(1964), p&d, w; GREAT RACE, THE(1965), d, w; WHAT DID YOU DO IN THE WAR, DADDY?(1966), p&d, w; GUNN(1967), a, w; INSPECTOR CLOUSEAU(1968, Brit.), w; PARTY, THE(1968), p&d, w; DARLING LILI(1970), p&d, w; WILD ROVERS(1971), p, d&w; CAREY TREATMENT, THE(1972), d; TAMARIND SEED, THE(1974, Brit.), d&w; RETURN OF THE PINK PANTHER, THE(1975, Brit.), p&d, w; PINK PANTHER STRIKES AGAIN, THE(1976, Brit.), p&d, w; REVENGE OF THE PINK PANTHER(1978), p, d, w; 10(1979), p, d&w; S.O.B.(1981), p, d&w; TRAIL OF THE PINK PANTHER, THE(1982), p, d, w; VICTOR/VICTORIA(1982), p, d&w; CURSE OF THE PINK PANTHER(1983), p, d, w; MAN WHO LOVED WOMEN, THE(1983), p, d, w

1984
MICKI AND MAUDE(1984), d
Bob Edwards
JULIET OF THE SPIRITS(1965, Fr./Ital./W.Ger.); DIAGNOSIS: MURDER(1974, Brit.), ph
Bogart Edwards
MARRIED COUPLE, A(1969, Can.)
Bruce Edwards
MARRY THE BOSS' DAUGHTER(1941); SMALL TOWN DEB(1941); SUN VALLEY SERENADE(1941); HITLER–DEAD OR ALIVE(1942); MOONTIDE(1942); FALCON IN DANGER, THE(1943); FALLEN SPARROW, THE(1943); GANGWAY FOR TOMORROW(1943); GOVERNMENT GIRL(1943); IRON MAJOR, THE(1943); BRIDE BY MISTAKE(1944); MY PAL, WOLF(1944); BETRAYAL FROM THE EAST(1945); DICK TRACY(1945); FIRST YANK INTO TOKYO(1945); WEST OF THE PECOS(1945); BELOW THE DEADLINE(1946); DANGEROUS MONEY(1946); SO GOES MY LOVE(1946); QUEEN OF THE AMAZONS(1947); DENVER KID, THE(1948); POWDER RIVER RUSTLERS(1949); PREJUDICE(1949); SANDS OF IWO JIMA(1949); FORT DODGE STAMPEDE(1951); OKLAHOMA JUSTICE(1951); CONFIDENCE GIRL(1952); LAWLESS COWBOYS(1952); STORY OF THREE LOVES, THE(1953); COOL WORLD, THE(1963)
Misc. Talkies
MONTANA INCIDENT(1952)
Buck Edwards
LOVE ME DEADLY(1972), p
Buddy Edwards
HIGH HAT(1937)
Carl Edwards
THEY SAVED HITLER'S BRAIN(1964), p
Cecil Edwards
Misc. Silents
CANVAS KISSER, THE(1925)
Charles Edwards
FLAMING TEEN-AGE, THE(1956), p&d
Silents
MASTER MIND, THE(1920)
Misc. Silents
CLOUDED NAME, THE(1919)
Cliff Edwards
MARIANNE(1929); SO THIS IS COLLEGE(1929); DOUGH BOYS(1930); GOOD NEWS(1930); LORD BYRON OF BROADWAY(1930); MONTANA MOON(1930); THOSE THREE FRENCH GIRLS(1930); WAY OUT WEST(1930); DANCE, FOOLS, DANCE(1931); GREAT LOVER, THE(1931); LAUGHING SINNERS(1931); PARLOR, BEDROOM AND BATH(1931); PRODIGAL, THE(1931); SHIPMATES(1931); SIDEWALKS OF NEW YORK(1931); SIN OF MADELON CLAUDET, THE(1931); FAST LIFE(1932); HELL DIVERS(1932); YOUNG BRIDE(1932); FLYING DEVILS(1933); TAKE A CHANCE(1933); GEORGE WHITE'S SCANDALS(1934); GEORGE WHITE'S 1935 SCANDALS(1935); RED SALUTE(1935); MAN I MARRY, THE(1936); BAD GUY(1937); BETWEEN TWO WOMEN(1937); SARATOGA(1937); THEY GAVE HIM A GUN(1937); WOMEN MEN MARRY, THE(1937); BAD MAN OF BRIMSTONE(1938); GIRL OF THE GOLDEN WEST, THE(1938); LITTLE ADVENTURESS, THE(1938); MAISIE(1939); SMUGGLED CARGO(1939); FLOWING GOLD(1940); FRIENDLY NEIGHBORS(1940); HIGH SCHOOL(1940); HIS GIRL FRIDAY(1940); MILLIONAIRES IN PRISON(1940); PINOCCHIO(1940); DUMBO(1941); INTERNATIONAL SQUADRON(1941); KNOCKOUT(1941); MONSTER AND THE GIRL, THE(1941); POWER DIVE(1941); PRAIRIE STRANGER(1941); SHE COULDN'T SAY NO(1941); AMERICAN EMPIRE(1942); BAD MEN OF THE HILLS(1942); LAWLESS PLAINSMEN(1942); RIDERS OF THE NORTHLAND(1942); SEVEN MILES FROM ALCATRAZ(1942); SUNDOWN JIM(1942); WEST OF TOMBSTONE(1942); FALCON STRIKES BACK, THE(1943); FIGHTING FRONTIER(1943); SALUTE FOR THREE(1943); FUN AND FANCY FREE(1947); MAN FROM BUTTON WILLOW, THE(1965)
Misc. Talkies
STEPPING OUT(1931); OVERLAND TO DEADWOOD(1942)
Cliff Edwards
GONE WITH THE WIND(1939)
Cliff "Ukelele Ike" Edwards
RIDERS OF THE BADLANDS(1941); THUNDER OVER THE PRAIRIE(1941); BANDIT RANGER(1942); PIRATES OF THE PRAIRIE(1942); AVENGING RIDER, THE(1943); RED RIVER ROBIN HOOD(1943); SAGEBRUSH LAW(1943)
Darryl Edwards
FORT APACHE, THE BRONX(1981)
1984
BROTHER FROM ANOTHER PLANET, THE(1984)
Daryl Edwards
1984
ALMOST YOU(1984); SPLASH(1984)
David Edwards
TWO GENTLEMEN SHARING(1969, Brit.)
Dennis Edwards
PRINCE AND THE SHOWGIRL, THE(1957, Brit.); MYSTERY SUBMARINE(1963, Brit.)
Dennis W. Edwards
1984
HARRY AND SON(1984)
Dickie Edwards
CARNIVAL(1931, Brit.)
Dorothy Edwards
INTERNATIONAL VELVET(1978, Brit.), cos
Eddie Edwards
MAN I LOVE, THE(1946), set d
Edgar Edwards
HIS BROTHER'S WIFE(1936); COMET OVER BROADWAY(1938); CONVICTED(1938), a, w; SISTERS, THE(1938); WOMAN AGAINST THE WORLD(1938), a, w; ADVENTURES OF JANE ARDEN(1939); CODE OF THE SECRET SERVICE(1939); DARK VICTORY(1939); DEATH GOES NORTH(1939); MANHATTAN SHAKEDOWN(1939), w; MURDER IS NEWS(1939), w; NANCY DREW, TROUBLE SHOOTER(1939); ON TRIAL(1939); PRIDE OF THE BLUEGRASS(1939); SECRET SERVICE OF THE AIR(1939); SPECIAL INSPECTOR(1939), a, w; WINGS OF THE NAVY(1939); FIGHTING 69TH, THE(1940); ONE MILLION B.C.(1940); BROADWAY LIMITED(1941)

Elaine Edwards
DANCING IN THE DARK(1949); OLD OKLAHOMA PLAINS(1952); HARDER THEY FALL, THE(1956); CURSE OF THE FACELESS MAN(1958); GUNS, GIRLS AND GANGSTERS(1958); BAT, THE(1959); BATTLE CRY(1959); INSIDE THE MAFIA(1959); PURPLE GANG, THE(1960); THREE BLONDES IN HIS LIFE(1961); YOU HAVE TO RUN FAST(1961); CURIOUS FEMALE, THE(1969); FIDDLER ON THE ROOF(1971)

Elizabeth Edwards
TUNNELVISION(1976)

Ella Edwards
FOR PETE'S SAKE!(1966); NOBODY'S PERFECT(1968); SWEET SUGAR(1972); DETROIT 9000(1973); MR. RICCO(1975)

Enrique Edwards
LITTLE RED RIDING HOOD AND HER FRIENDS(1964, Mex.)

Eric Edwards
PROPERTY(1979), ph
1984
AMERICAN TABOO(1984), ph

Eric A. Edwards
1984
LAST NIGHT AT THE ALAMO(1984), a, ph

Ethan Edwards
STUCKEY'S LAST STAND(1980), ed

Ethel Edwards
KILLER WALKS, A(1952, Brit.)

Frank Edwards
MODIGLIANI OF MONTPARNASSE(1961, Fr./Ital.); PROLOGUE(1970, Can.); PICTURES(1982, New Zealand)

Fred L. Edwards
SILVER TRAILS(1948)

Gail Edwards
GET CRAZY(1983)

Goeff Edwards
WUSA(1970)

Geoffrey Edwards
WILD ROVERS(1971); TRAIL OF THE PINK PANTHER, THE(1982), w; CURSE OF THE PINK PANTHER(1983), w; MAN WHO LOVED WOMEN, THE(1983), w

George Edwards
MONKEY'S PAW, THE(1933); VOYAGE TO THE PREHISTORIC PLANET(1965), p; NAVY VS. THE NIGHT MONSTERS, THE(1966), p; QUEEN OF BLOOD(1966), p; WOMEN OF THE PREHISTORIC PLANET(1966), p; GAMES(1967), p, w; WHAT'S THE MATTER WITH HELEN?(1971), p; FROGS(1972), p; OUTSIDE IN(1972), p; KILLING KIND, THE(1973), p, w; RUBY(1977), p, w; HARPER VALLEY, P.T.A.(1978), p, w; ATTIC, THE(1979), d, w
1984
CHATTANOOGA CHOO CHOO(1984), p

Gloria Edwards
BLACK GIRL(1972); WHICH WAY IS UP?(1977)

Glyn Edwards
HEART WITHIN, THE(1957, Brit.); ROBBERY(1967, Brit.); FRAGMENT OF FEAR(1971, Brit.)

Glynn Edwards
HI-JACKERS, THE(1963, Brit.); SPARROWS CAN'T SING(1963, Brit.); SMOKESCREEN(1964, Brit.); ZULU(1964, Brit.); IPCRESS FILE, THE(1965, Brit.); BLOOD BEAST TERROR, THE(1967, Brit.); GET CARTER(1971, Brit.); BURKE AND HARE(1972, Brit.); SHAFT IN AFRICA(1973); UNDER MILK WOOD(1973, Brit.); 11 HARROWHOUSE(1974, Brit.); STICK UP, THE(1978, Brit.); RISING DAMP(1980, Brit.); RED MONARCH(1983, Brit.)

Gordon Edwards
DUMMY TALKS, THE(1943, Brit.); IT'S IN THE BAG(1943, Brit.); MILLIONS LIKE US(1943, Brit.); WALKING ON AIR(1946, Brit.); WALTZ TIME(1946, Brit.); HELL SQUAD(1958)
Misc. Silents
LOVE LETTERS(1924)

Graveley Edwards
OLIVER TWIST(1951, Brit.)

Gus Edwards
STAR MAKER, THE(1939), w
1984
GO TELL IT ON THE MOUNTAIN(1984), w

Guy Edwards
WEEKEND WITH THE BABYSITTER(1970)

H. P. Edwards
WILD, FREE AND HUNGRY(1970), d

Harry Edwards
Silents
LITTLE LORD FAUNTLEROY(1914, Brit.); TRAMP, TRAMP, TRAMP(1926), d
Misc. Silents
HIS PAJAMA GIRL(1921); HIS FIRST FLAME(1927), d

Henry Edwards
CALL OF THE SEA, THE(1930, Brit.), a, p; HOUSE OF THE ARROW, THE(1930, Brit.), p; LORD RICHARD IN THE PANTRY(1930, Brit.), p; MYSTERY AT THE VILLA ROSE(1930, Brit.), a, p&d, w; STRANGLEHOLD(1931, Brit.), p&d; BARTON MYSTERY, THE(1932, Brit.), d; BROTHER ALFRED(1932, Brit.), d, w; FLAG LIEUTENANT, THE(1932, Brit.), a, d; ANNE ONE HUNDRED(1933, Brit.), d; DISCORD(1933, Brit.), d; GENERAL JOHN REGAN(1933, Brit.), a, d; LORD OF THE MANOR(1933, Brit.), d; ONE PRECIOUS YEAR(1933, Brit.), d&w; PURSE STRINGS(1933, Brit.), d; ARE YOU A MASON?(1934, Brit.), d; LASH, THE(1934, Brit.), d; LORD EDGEWARE DIES(1934, Brit.), d; MAN WHO CHANGED HIS NAME, THE(1934, Brit.), d; LAD, THE(1935, Brit.), d; PRIVATE SECRETARY, THE(1935, Brit.), d; SCROOGE(1935, Brit.), d; SQUIBS(1935, Brit.), d; VINTAGE WINE(1935, Brit.), d; ELIZA COMES TO STAY(1936, Brit.), d; IN THE SOUP(1936, Brit.), d; BEAUTY AND THE BARGE(1937, Brit.), d; CAPTAIN'S ORDERS(1937, Brit.), d; HIGH TREASON(1937, Brit.), d; JUGGERNAUT(1937, Brit.), d; SONG OF THE FORGE(1937, Brit.), d; VICAR OF BRAY, THE(1937, Brit.), d; CAPTAIN MOONLIGHT(1940, Brit.), d; SPRING MEETING(1941, Brit.), d; STRANGLER, THE(1941, Brit.); GREEN FOR DANGER(1946, Brit.); MAGIC BOW, THE(1947, Brit.); SARGE GOES TO COLLEGE(1947), w; DULCIMER STREET(1948, Brit.); TAKE MY LIFE(1948, Brit.); DEAR MR. PROHACK(1949, Brit.); QUARTET(1949, Brit.); WOMAN HATER(1949, Brit.); GOLDEN SALAMANDER(1950, Brit.); MADELEINE(1950, Brit.);

ROSSITER CASE, THE(1950, Brit.); TRIO(1950, Brit.); LADY WITH A LAMP, THE(1951, Brit.); LUCKY MASCOT, THE(1951, Brit.); OLIVER TWIST(1951, Brit.); MAGIC BOX, THE(1952, Brit.); NEVER LOOK BACK(1952, Brit.); SOMETHING MONEY CAN'T BUY(1952, Brit.); WHITE CORRIDORS(1952, Brit.); DOUBLE CONFESSION(1953, Brit.); LONG MEMORY, THE(1953, Brit.); SGT. PEPPER'S LONELY HEARTS CLUB BAND(1978), w
Silents
ALONE IN LONDON(1915, Brit.); FAR FROM THE MADDING CROWD(1915, Brit.); MY OLD DUTCH(1915, Brit.); WELSH SINGER, A(1915, Brit.), a, d, w; DOORSTEPS(1916, Brit.), a, d, w; EAST IS EAST(1916, Brit.), a, d&w; HANGING JUDGE, THE(1918, Brit.), a, d&w; POSSESSION(1919, Brit.), a, d; AYLWIN(1920, Brit.), a, d; TEMPORARY VAGABOND, A(1920, Brit.), a, d&w; LILY OF THE ALLEY(1923, Brit.), a, d&w; OWD BOB(1924, Brit.), d; GIRL OF LONDON, A(1925, Brit.), d; KING OF THE CASTLE(1925, Brit.), d; FLAG LIEUTENANT, THE(1926, Brit.); ONE COLUMBO NIGHT(1926, Brit.), d; FAKE, THE(1927, Brit.); FURTHER ADVENTURES OF THE FLAG LIEUTENANT(1927, Brit.)
Misc. Silents
LOST AND WON(1915, Brit.); GRIM JUSTICE(1916, Brit.); BROKEN THREADS(1917, Brit.), a, d; COBWEB, THE(1917, Brit.); DICK CARSON WINS THROUGH(1917, Brit.), a, d; MERELY MRS. STUBBS(1917, Brit.), a, d; NEARER MY GOD TO THEE(1917, Brit.); TOUCH OF A CHILD, THE(1918, Brit.); TOWARDS THE LIGHT(1918, Brit.), a, d; CITY OF BEAUTIFUL NONSENSE, THE(1919), a, d; HIS DEAREST POSSESSION(1919, Brit.), a, d; KINSMAN, THE(1919, Brit.), a, d; JOHN FORREST FINDS HIMSELF(1920, Brit.), a, d; BARGAIN, THE(1921, Brit.), a, d; LUNATIC AT LARGE, THE(1921), a, d; SIMPLE SIMON(1922, Brit.), a, d; TIT FOR TAT(1922, Brit.), a, d; BODEN'S BOY(1923, Brit.), a, d; ISLAND OF DESPAIR, THE(1926, Brit.), d; RINGING THE CHANGES(1929, Brit.); THREE KINGS, THE(1929, Brit.)

Henryetta Edwards
SHE SHALL HAVE MURDER(1950, Brit.); GENTLE TOUCH, THE(1956, Brit.)

Hilton Edwards
CALL OF THE BLOOD(1948, Brit.); OTHELLO(1955, U.S./Fr./Ital.); CAT AND MOUSE(1958, Brit); THIS OTHER EDEN(1959, Brit.); NIGHT FIGHTERS, THE(1960); VICTIM(1961, Brit.); QUARE FELLOW, THE(1962, Brit.); SHE DIDN'T SAY NO!(1962, Brit.); WRONG BOX, THE(1966, Brit.); HALF A SIXPENCE(1967, Brit.)

Hubert Edwards
WARRIORS, THE(1979)

Hubert J. Edwards
WILLIE AND PHIL(1980)

Hugh Edwards
LORD OF THE FLIES(1963, Brit.)

J. Gordon Edwards
Silents
SONG OF HATE, THE(1915), d; ROMEO AND JULIET(1916), d; DARLING OF PARIS, THE(1917), d; TIGER WOMAN, THE(1917), d; WHEN A WOMAN SINS(1918), d; JOYOUS TROUBLEMAKERS, THE(1920), d; QUEEN OF SHEBA, THE(1921), d; NERO(1922, U.S./Ital.), d; NET, THE(1923), d; SILENT COMMAND, THE(1923), d; IT IS THE LAW(1924), d
Misc. Silents
BLINDNESS OF DEVOTION(1915), d; CELEBRATED SCANDAL, A(1915), d; GALLEY SLAVE, THE(1915), d; SHOULD A MOTHER TELL?(1915), d; UNFAITHFUL WIFE, THE(1915), d; GREEN-EYED MONSTER, THE(1916), d; HER DOUBLE LIFE(1916), d; SPIDER AND THE FLY, THE(1916), d; UNDER TWO FLAGS(1916), d; VIXEN, THE(1916), d; WIFE'S SACRIFICE, A(1916), d; CAMILLE(1917), d; CLEOPATRA(1917), d; HEART AND SOUL(1917), d; HER GREATEST LOVE(1917), d; ROSE OF BLOOD, THE(1917), d; TANGLED LIVES(1917), d; FORBIDDEN PATH, THE(1918), d; MADAME DUBARRY(1918), d; SHE DEVIL, THE(1918), d; SOUL OF BUDDHA, THE(1918), d; UNDER THE YOKE(1918), d; LAST OF THE DUANES, THE(1919), d; LIGHT, THE(1919), d; LONE STAR RANGER, THE(1919), d; SALOME(1919), d; SIREN'S SONG, THE(1919), d; WHEN MEN DESIRE(1919), d; WINGS OF THE MORNING, THE(1919), d; WOLVES OF THE NIGHT(1919), d; WOMAN THERE WAS, A(1919), d; ADVENTURER, THE(1920), d; DRAG HARLAN(1920), d; HEART STRINGS(1920), d; IF I WERE KING(1920), d; ORPHAN, THE(1920), d; SCUTTLERS, THE(1920), d; HIS GREATEST SACRIFICE(1921), d; SHEPHERD KING, THE(1923), d

J. Gordon Edwards, Jr.
Silents
PLASTIC AGE, THE(1925)

J. Harrison Edwards
Misc. Silents
FIGHTING KENTUCKIANS, THE(1920), d

J. Steven Edwards
MIDNIGHT AT THE WAX MUSEUM(1936, Brit.), p, w
Silents
BROKEN ROMANCE, A(1929, Brit.), d&w; PRIDE OF DONEGAL, THE(1929, Brit.), d
Misc. Silents
HUMAN CARGO(1929, Brit.), d; SECOND MATE, THE(1929, Brit.), d

J. Stevens Edwards
TWIN FACES(1937, Brit.), p

Jack Edwards
BOYS OF THE CITY(1940); EAST SIDE KIDS(1940); GHOST BREAKERS, THE(1940)

Jack Edwards, Jr.
CROSS OF LORRAINE, THE(1943); WE'VE NEVER BEEN LICKED(1943); ROAD HOUSE(1948)

James Edwards
HOME OF THE BRAVE(1949); SET-UP, THE(1949); BRIGHT VICTORY(1951); STEEL HELMET, THE(1951); MEMBER OF THE WEDDING, THE(1952); JOE LOUIS STORY, THE(1953); CAINE MUTINY, THE(1954); AFRICAN MANHUNT(1955); PHENIX CITY STORY, THE(1955); SEVEN ANGRY MEN(1955); THUNDER OVER SANGOLAND(1955); KILLING, THE(1956); BATTLE HYMN(1957); MEN IN WAR(1957); ANNA LUCASTA(1958); FRAULEIN(1958); TARZAN'S FIGHT FOR LIFE(1958); BLOOD AND STEEL(1959); NIGHT OF THE QUARTER MOON(1959); PORK CHOP HILL(1959); MANCHURIAN CANDIDATE, THE(1962); SANDPIPER, THE(1965); COOGAN'S BLUFF(1968); YOUNG RUNAWAYS, THE(1968); PATTON(1970)

James G. Edwards [James William MacQueen]
MYSTERY OF THE WHITE ROOM(1939), w

James Steven Edwards
FEAR SHIP, THE(1933, Brit.), p,d&w

Jay Edwards
NOTORIOUS CLEOPATRA, THE(1970)

Jeilo Edwards
MEMOIRS OF A SURVIVOR(1981, Brit.)

Jennifer Edwards
HOOK, LINE AND SINKER(1969); CAREY TREATMENT, THE(1972); S.O.B.(1981); MAN WHO LOVED WOMEN, THE(1983)

Jimmie Edwards
I AM A GROUPIE(1970, Brit.)

Jimmy Edwards
TROUBLE IN THE AIR(1948, Brit.); HELTER SKELTER(1949, Brit.); MYSTERY AT THE BURLESQUE(1950, Brit.); TREASURE HUNT(1952, Brit.); INNOCENTS IN PARIS(1955, Brit.); THREE MEN IN A BOAT(1958, Brit.); BOTTOMS UP(1960, Brit.); NEARLY A NASTY ACCIDENT(1962, Brit.); PLANK, THE(1967, Brit.); LION-HEART(1968, Brit.)
Misc. Talkies
GHOST OF A CHANCE, A(1968, Brit.)

Joan Edwards
HIT PARADE OF 1947(1947)

Joaquin Edwards
EMERGENCY LANDING(1941); PANTHER'S CLAW, THE(1942)

John Edwards
FOOLS' PARADE(1971)

Judy Edwards
MERMAIDS OF TIBURON, THE(1962)

Julie Edwards
GUN RIDERS, THE(1969); STONE(1974, Aus.)

Kaye Edwards
Misc. Talkies
TROUBLE BUSTERS(1933)

Keith Edwards
1984
SUPERGIRL(1984)

Kenneth Edwards
STAR OF MY NIGHT(1954, Brit.); STRANGER FROM VENUS, THE(1954, Brit.); THREE CROOKED MEN(1958, Brit.); THUNDERING JETS(1958); HONOURABLE MURDER, AN(1959, Brit.); STRANGE AFFECTION(1959, Brit.); IDENTITY UN-KNOWN(1960, Brit.)

Kyle Edwards
HOUSE BY THE LAKE, THE(1977, Can.)

L.S. Edwards
ROCKY MOUNTAIN(1950), set d

Lee Edwards
INVISIBLE AVENGER, THE(1958)
Misc. Talkies
BOURBON ST. SHADOWS(1962)

Leo Edwards
IT COMES UP LOVE(1943), m

Leslie Edwards
ROMEO AND JULIET(1966, Brit.); PETER RABBIT AND TALES OF BEATRIX POTTER(1971, Brit.)

Lloyd Edwards
COOL WORLD, THE(1963)

Lorraine Edwards
SING WHILE YOU DANCE(1946), w

Marcelle Edwards
MY WEAKNESS(1933)

Marianne Edwards
LOVE IS ON THE AIR(1937)

Mark Edwards
GOLDEN BOX, THE(1970); BOLDEST JOB IN THE WEST, THE(1971, Ital.); LAST VALLEY, THE(1971, Brit.); BLOOD FROM THE MUMMY'S TOMB(1972, Brit.); BEYOND THE FOG(1981, Brit.)

Mark W. Edwards
TERROR IN THE WAX MUSEUM(1973)

Marshall Edwards
WHERE THE RED FERN GROWS(1974)

Marvis Edwards
MORGAN!(1966, Brit.)

Mary Ann Edwards
SON OF SINBAD(1955); GIANT(1956)

Mary Edwards
VARIETY GIRL(1947)

Mattie Edwards
GIVE US THIS NIGHT(1936)

Maudie Edwards
FLYING DOCTOR, THE(1936, Aus.); MY LEARNED FRIEND(1943, Brit.); SHIP-BUILDERS, THE(1943, Brit.); I'LL BE YOUR SWEETHEART(1945, Brit.); MURDER IN REVERSE(1946, Brit.); WALKING ON AIR(1946, Brit.); SCHOOL FOR RANDLE(1949, Brit.); PINK STRING AND SEALING WAX(1950, Brit.); GIRDLE OF GOLD(1952, Brit.); TAKE A POWDER(1953, Brit.); KEY MAN, THE(1957, Brit.); UGLY DUCKLING, THE(1959, Brit.); BAND OF THIEVES(1962, Brit.); ONLY TWO CAN PLAY(1962, Brit.); UNDER MILK WOOD(1973, Brit.)

Megan Edwards
THAT CERTAIN SOMETHING(1941, Aus.)

Meredith Edwards
MAGNET, THE(1950, Brit.); RUN FOR YOUR MONEY, A(1950, Brit.); LAVENDER HILL MOB, THE(1951, Brit.); MIDNIGHT EPISODE(1951, Brit.); GAMBLER AND THE LADY, THE(1952, Brit.); GIRDLE OF GOLD(1952, Brit.); GLORY AT SEA(1952, Brit.); IVORY HUNTER(1952, Brit.); MAN BAIT(1952, Brit.); CRUEL SEA, THE(1953, Brit.); DAY TO REMEMBER, A(1953, Brit.); GREAT GAME, THE(1953, Brit.); BURNT EVIDEN-CE(1954, Brit.); DEVIL ON HORSEBACK(1954, Brit.); FINAL APPOINTMENT(1954, Brit.); MAD ABOUT MEN(1954, Brit.); MEET MR. MALCOLM(1954, Brit.); RED DRESS, THE(1954, Brit.); RACE FOR LIFE, A(1955, Brit.); CASH ON DELIVERY(1956, Brit.); PERIL FOR THE GUY(1956, Brit.); TEARS FOR SIMON(1957, Brit.); THIRD KEY, THE(1957, Brit.); TOWN ON TRIAL(1957, Brit.); DUNKIRK(1958, Brit.); LAW AND DISORDER(1958, Brit.); SUPREME SECRET, THE(1958, Brit.); TIGER BAY(1959, Brit.); DOCTOR IN LOVE(1960, Brit.); ELECTRONIC MONSTER. THE(1960, Brit.);

MAN WITH THE GREEN CARNATION, THE(1960, Brit.); FLAME IN THE STREETS(1961, Brit.); CIRCUS FRIENDS(1962, Brit.); MIX ME A PERSON(1962, Brit.); ONLY TWO CAN PLAY(1962, Brit.); THIS IS MY STREET(1964, Brit.); GREAT ST. TRINIAN'S TRAIN ROBBERY, THE(1966, Brit.); GULLIVER'S TRAVELS(1977, Brit., Bel.)

Michael Edwards
MOMMIE DEAREST(1981)

Mike Edwards
PAYDAY(1972); PLAY IT AS IT LAYS(1972)

Milton Edwards
CAPTAIN LIGHTFOOT(1955)

Nate H. Edwards
ESCORT WEST(1959), p; JESSICA(1962, U.S./Ital./Fr.), prod d
Silents
ANYTHING ONCE(1925), w

Neeley Edwards
SUTTER'S GOLD(1936); SIN TOWN(1942); STRICTLY IN THE GROOVE(1942)

Neely Edwards
GOLD DIGGERS OF BROADWAY(1929); SHOW BOAT(1929); DYNAMITE(1930); SCARLET PAGES(1930); OKAY AMERICA(1932); DIPLOMANIACS(1933); LOVE, HONOR, AND OH BABY!(1933); FOR LOVE OR MONEY(1939); MEXICAN SPIT-FIRE'S ELEPHANT(1942); GEORGE WHITE'S SCANDALS(1945); PATRICK THE GREAT(1945)
Silents
BREWSTER'S MILLIONS(1921); LITTLE CLOWN, THE(1921); EXCESS BAG-GAGE(1928)
Misc. Silents
GREEN TEMPTATION, THE(1922)

Norman Edwards
WRONG NUMBER(1959, Brit.), w

Olga Edwards
ANGEL WITH THE TRUMPET, THE(1950, Brit.)

Paddi Edwards
TO BE OR NOT TO BE(1983)

Paddie Edwards
HALLOWEEN III: SEASON OF THE WITCH(1982)

Paddy Edwards
INN FOR TROUBLE(1960, Brit.)

Pat Edwards
10(1979), cos

Patricia Edwards
SWEET JESUS, PREACHER MAN(1973); STIR CRAZY(1980), cos; TARZAN, THE APE MAN(1981), cos; TRAIL OF THE PINK PANTHER, THE(1982), cos; CURSE OF THE PINK PANTHER(1983), cos

Patty Edwards
NEW HOUSE ON THE LEFT, THE(1978, Brit.)
Misc. Talkies
LAST STOP ON THE NIGHT TRAIN(1976)

Paul Edwards
OFFICER 13(1933), w; TRACKDOWN(1976), w; HIGH-BALLIN'(1978), w

Paul Edwards, Jr.
NO MAN IS AN ISLAND(1962); MORO WITCH DOCTOR(1964, U.S./Phil.); WALLS OF HELL, THE(1964, U.S./Phil.); WARKILL(1968, U.S./Phil.)

Penny Edwards
MY WILD IRISH ROSE(1947); THAT HAGEN GIRL(1947); FEUDIN', FUSSIN' AND A-FIGHTIN'(1948); TWO GUYS FROM TEXAS(1948); TUCSON(1949); NORTH OF THE GREAT DIVIDE(1950); SUNSET IN THE WEST(1950); TRAIL OF ROBIN HOOD(1950); HEART OF THE ROCKIES(1951); IN OLD AMARILLO(1951); MILLION DOLLAR PURSUIT(1951); MISSING WOMEN(1951); SPOILERS OF THE PLAINS(1951); STREET BANDITS(1951); UTAH WAGON TRAIN(1951); CAPTIVE OF BILLY THE KID(1952); PONY SOLDIER(1952); WILD BLUE YONDER, THE(1952); WOMAN IN THE DARK(1952); POWDER RIVER(1953); DALTON GIRLS, THE(1957); RIDE A VIOLENT MILE(1957)

Percy Edwards
RISE AND RISE OF MICHAEL RIMMER, THE(1970, Brit.); DARK CRYSTAL, THE(1982, Brit.)

Peter Edwards
RUN FOR YOUR MONEY, A(1950, Brit.); CONSTANT HUSBAND, THE(1955, Brit.)

Powell Edwards
ROYAL DEMAND, A(1933, Brit.)

Ralph Edwards
GEORGE WASHINGTON CARVER(1940); BAMBOO BLONDE, THE(1946); BEAT THE BAND(1947); I'LL CRY TOMORROW(1955)

Ralph G. Edwards
DEVIL'S BEDROOM, THE(1964)
Misc. Talkies
YOUNG MAN'S BRIDE, THE(1968)

Randall Edwards
1984
POPE OF GREENWICH VILLAGE, THE(1984)

Raymond S. Edwards
OH! WHAT A LOVELY WAR(1969, Brit.)

Rebecca Edwards
S.O.B.(1981)

Rick Edwards
SKATETOWN, U.S.A.(1979)

Robert Edwards
THUNDER IN THE PINES(1949), d; THEM NICE AMERICANS(1958, Brit.)

Robert Gordon Edwards
NIGHT PORTER, THE(1974, Ital./U.S.), p
1984
BEYOND GOOD AND EVIL(1984, Ital./Fr./Ger.), p

Roland G. Edwards
Misc. Silents
DARING LOVE(1924), d

Ronald Edwards
WOMEN OF DESIRE(1968)

Ronnie Claire Edwards
ALL THE WAY HOME(1963); FIVE DAYS FROM HOME(1978)
Rory Edwards
EYE OF THE NEEDLE(1981)
Rowland G. Edwards
MAN FROM YESTERDAY, THE(1932), w
Sally Edwards
HARPER(1966), cos
Misc. Silents
CALL OF THE HILLS, THE(1923)
Sam Edwards
EAST SIDE KIDS(1940); BAMBI(1942); RUBBER RACKETEERS(1942); LAR-CENY(1948); STREET WITH NO NAME, THE(1948); TWELVE O'CLOCK HIGH(1949); JACKPOT, THE(1950); SUN SETS AT DAWN, THE(1950); FLYING LEATHER-NECKS(1951); OPERATION PACIFIC(1951); WITNESS TO MURDER(1954); GANG BUSTERS(1955); REVOLT IN THE BIG HOUSE(1958); PRIZE, THE(1963); SCANDAL-OUS JOHN(1971); ESCAPE TO WITCH MOUNTAIN(1975); POSTMAN ALWAYS RINGS TWICE, THE(1981)
Misc. Silents
CHAMBER OF MYSTERY, THE(1920)
Sam G. Edwards
SUPPOSE THEY GAVE A WAR AND NOBODY CAME?(1970)
Sara Edwards
GLASS MENAGERIE, THE(1950)
Sarah Edwards
GLORIFYING THE AMERICAN GIRL(1930); SMARTY(1934); DARK ANGEL, THE(1935); MAN ON THE FLYING TRAPEZE, THE(1935); RUGGLES OF RED GAP(1935); STARS OVER BROADWAY(1935); TWO FISTED(1935); WELCOME HOME(1935); WORLD ACCUSES, THE(1935); COLLEEN(1936); EARLY TO BED(1936); EARTHWORM TRACTORS(1936); GENERAL DIED AT DAWN, THE(1936); GREAT ZIEGFELD, THE(1936); PALM SPRINGS(1936); STAGE STRUCK(1936); THEODORA GOES WILD(1936); HOLLYWOOD HOTEL(1937); IT'S LOVE I'M AFTER(1937); LIFE BEGINS IN COLLEGE(1937); MAYTIME(1937); PUBLIC WEDDING(1937); SECOND HONEYMOON(1937); WE'RE ON THE JURY(1937); FOOLS FOR SCANDAL(1938); GOLD IS WHERE YOU FIND IT(1938); SHINING HOUR, THE(1938); THREE LOVES HAS NANCY(1938); WOMEN ARE LIKE THAT(1938); BOY TROUBLE(1939); ESPION-AGE AGENT(1939); MEET DR. CHRISTIAN(1939); ARISE, MY LOVE(1940); LITTLE MEN(1940); NEW MOON(1940); SHOP AROUND THE CORNER, THE(1940); STRIKE UP THE BAND(1940); YOUNG PEOPLE(1940); DEVIL AND DANIEL WEBSTER, THE(1941); FACE BEHIND THE MASK, THE(1941); FOOTSTEPS IN THE DARK(1941); INVISIBLE WOMAN, THE(1941); MEET JOHN DOE(1941); MR. DIS-TRICT ATTORNEY(1941); ONE FOOT IN HEAVEN(1941); SUNSET IN WYO-MING(1941); THREE GIRLS ABOUT TOWN(1941); TOM, DICK AND HARRY(1941); YOU BELONG TO ME(1941); DUDES ARE PRETTY PEOPLE(1942); FOREST RANG-ERS, THE(1942); GAY SISTERS, THE(1942); MY FAVORITE BLONDE(1942); RINGS ON HER FINGERS(1942); SCATTERGOOD SURVIVES A MURDER(1942); ALL BY MYSELF(1943); DIXIE DUGAN(1943); GIRL CRAZY(1943); HAPPY GO LUCKY(1943); SHADOW OF A DOUBT(1943); WHERE ARE YOUR CHILDREN?(1943); HENRY ALDRICH PLAYS CUPID(1944); HENRY ALDRICH'S LITTLE SECRET(1944); STORM OVER LISBON(1944); STORY OF DR. WASSELL, THE(1944); THIN MAN GOES HOME, THE(1944); GIRLS OF THE BIG HOUSE(1945); LADY ON A TRAIN(1945); SARATOGA TRUNK(1945); TWO O'CLOCK COURAGE(1945); EASY TO WED(1946); GIRL ON THE SPOT(1946); IT'S A WONDERFUL LIFE(1946); SHAD-OWED(1946); SONG OF ARIZONA(1946); UNDERCURRENT(1946); BISHOP'S WIFE, THE(1947); MAIN STREET KID, THE(1947); THAT HAGEN GIRL(1947); VOICE OF THE TURTLE, THE(1947); CALIFORNIA FIREBRAND(1948); FAMILY HONEY-MOON(1948); GOOD SAM(1948); ISN'T IT ROMANTIC?(1948); FULLER BRUSH GIRL, THE(1950); PETTY GIRL, THE(1950); HONEYCHILE(1951)
Saundra Edwards
FEVER IN THE BLOOD, A(1961); PARRISH(1961)
Sherman Edwards
1776(1972), w, m
Snitz Edwards
DANGEROUS WOMAN(1929); MYSTERIOUS ISLAND(1929); PHANTOM OF THE OPERA, THE(1929); PUBLIC ENEMY, THE(1931); RIGHT OF WAY, THE(1931); SIT TIGHT(1931)
Silents
KEEP MOVING(1915); MARK OF ZORRO(1920); CHARM SCHOOL, THE(1921); NO WOMAN KNOWS(1921); JUNE MADNESS(1922); LOVE IS AN AWFUL THING(1922); RAGS TO RICHES(1922); RED HOT ROMANCE(1922); HUNTRESS, THE(1923); ROSITA(1923); SOULS FOR SALE(1923); IN FAST COMPANY(1923); INEZ FROM HOLLYWOOD(1924); THIEF OF BAGDAD, THE(1924); LOVER'S OATH, A(1925); PHANTOM OF THE OPERA, THE(1925); SEVEN CHANCES(1925); WOMAN WHO SINNED, A(1925); APRIL FOOL(1926); BATTLING BUTLER(1926); VOLCANO(1926); COLLEGE(1927); NIGHT LIFE(1927); OLD SHOES(1927); RED MILL, THE(1927)
Misc. Silents
TORNADO, THE(1924); CRUISE OF THE JASPER B, THE(1926); SEA WOLF, THE(1926)
Sonny Edwards
HIGH HAT(1937)
Stephanie Edwards
MAURIE(1973)
Stephen Edwards
WILL PENNY(1968)
Ted Edwards
MANIAC(1934); WAY TO THE GOLD, THE(1957)
Misc. Silents
FIRES OF YOUTH(1924)
Teddy Edwards
THEY SHOOT HORSES, DON'T THEY?(1969)
Thornton Edwards
GRAPES OF WRATH(1940); MEN AGAINST THE SKY(1940); THREE MEN FROM TEXAS(1940); DESPERATE CARGO(1941); DOWN MEXICO WAY(1941); FORCED LANDING(1941); LONE RIDER CROSSES THE RIO, THE(1941); OUTLAWS OF THE RIO GRANDE(1941); SILVER STALLION(1941); MADAME SPY(1942); MIRACLE KID(1942); DRIFTING ALONG(1946); CHINESE RING, THE(1947); STATE OF THE UNION(1948)
Silents
EYE OF THE NIGHT, THE(1916); LIEUT. DANNY, U.S.A.(1916); FALSE FA-CES(1919)

Thorton Edwards
RIDERS OF THE DUSK(1949)
Tony Edwards
1984
STARMAN(1984)
Vince Edwards
ROGUE COP(1954); CELL 2455, DEATH ROW(1955); NIGHT HOLDS TERROR, THE(1955); KILLING, THE(1956); SERENADE(1956); HIRED GUN, THE(1957); HIT AND RUN(1957); RIDE OUT FOR REVENGE(1957); ISLAND WOMEN(1958); MUR-DER BY CONTRACT(1958); CITY OF FEAR(1959); SCAVENGERS, THE(1959, U.S./ Phil.); DEVIL'S BRIGADE, THE(1968); HAMMERHEAD(1968); DESPERADOS, THE(1969); MAD BOMBER, THE(1973); MISSION GALACTICA: THE CYLON AT-TACK(1979), d; SEDUCTION, THE(1982); DEAL OF THE CENTURY(1983); SPACE RAIDERS(1983)
Vincent Edwards
MR. UNIVERSE(1951); SAILOR BEWARE(1951); HIAWATHA(1952); I AM A CAM-ERA(1955, Brit.); OUTSIDER, THE(1962); TOO LATE BLUES(1962); VICTORS, THE(1963)
Virginia Edwards
SILVER DOLLAR(1932); NOCTURNE(1946)
Vivian Edwards
GOING IN STYLE(1979)
Misc. Silents
MODERN ENOCH ARDEN, A(1916)
Waldo Edwards
UNMASKED(1929)
Misc. Talkies
UNMASKED(1929)
Walter C. Edwards
Misc. Silents
FINAL CLOSEUP, THE(1919), d
Walter Edwards
Silents
BATTLE OF GETTYSBURG(1914); CIVILIZATION(1916), d; DIVIDEND, THE(1916), d; EYE OF THE NIGHT, THE(1916), d; JUNGLE CHILD, THE(1916), d; LIEUT. DANNY, U.S.A.(1916), d; ASHES OF HOPE(1917), d; BRIDE OF HATE, THE(1917), d; CRAB, THE(1917), d; LAST OF THE INGRAHAMS, THE(1917), d; EVIDENCE(1918), d; GOOD NIGHT, PAUL(1918), d; I LOVE YOU(1918), d; PAIR OF SILK STOCKINGS, A(1918), d; REAL FOLKS(1918), d; ROMANCE AND ARABELLA(1919), d; EASY TO GET(1920), d; LADY IN LOVE, A(1920), d
Misc. Silents
BRINK, THE(1915), d; MAN FROM OREGON, THE(1915), d; WINGED IDOL, THE(1915), d; BECKONING FLAME, THE(1916), d; CORNER, THE(1916), d; DES-ERTER, THE(1916), d; GAMBLE IN SOULS, A(1916), d; HONOR'S ALTAR(1916), d; NO-GOOD GUY, THE(1916), d; SIN YE DO, THE(1916), d; WOLF WOMAN, THE(1916), d; FUEL OF LIFE(1917), d; IDOLATORS(1917), d; LOVE OR JUSTICE(1917), d; MASTER OF HIS HOME(1917), d; PADDY O'HARA(1917), d; TIME LOCKS AND DIAMONDS(1917), d; GYPSY TRAIL, THE(1918), d; LADY'S NAME, A(1918), d; MAN FROM FUNERAL RANGE, THE(1918), d; MRS. LEFFINGWELL'S BOOTS(1918), d; SAUCE FOR THE GOOSE(1918), d; VIVIETTE(1918), d; GIRLS(1919), d; HAPPINESS A LA MODE(1919), d; LUCK IN PAWN(1919), d; RESCUING ANGEL, THE(1919), d; VEILED ADVENTURE, THE(1919), d; WHO CARES?(1919), d; WIDOW BY PROX-Y(1919), d; ALL OF A SUDDEN PEGGY(1920), d; GIRL NAMED MARY, A(1920), d; YOUNG MRS. WINTHROP(1920), d
Wes Edwards
1984
BODY DOUBLE(1984)
Weston Edwards
'NEATH THE ARIZONA SKIES(1934); LAST OF THE CLINTONS, THE(1935), w; RUSTLER'S PARADISE(1935), w; WILD MUSTANG(1935), w; GHOST TOWN(1937), w; SIX SHOOTIN' SHERIFF(1938), w
William Edwards
DRACULA(THE DIRTY OLD MAN) (1969), p,d&w; RIDING HIGH(1943); FEDERAL MAN(1950)
William S. Edwards
MY WORLD DIES SCREAMING(1958), p; DATE WITH DEATH, A(1959), p
Wilson Edwards
TEXAS MARSHAL, THE(1941)
Winifred Edwards
Silents
SLEEPWALKER, THE(1922)
Marian Edwards-Greene
SING ALONG WITH ME(1952, Brit.)
Grace Edwin
CUCKOO IN THE NEST, THE(1933, Brit.)
J.H. Edwin
JIMMY BOY(1935, Brit.); IRELAND'S BORDER LINE(1939, Ireland)
Walter Edwin
Silents
SPENDTHRIFT, THE(1915), d
Misc. Silents
MUTE APPEAL, A(1917), d
Alfred Edyvean
JULIUS CAESAR(1952)
Christine Edzard
ROMEO AND JULIET(1968, Brit./Ital.), set d; PETER RABBIT AND TALES OF BEATRIX POTTER(1971, Brit.), w, prod d, cos; STORIES FROM A FLYING TRUNK(1979, Brit.), d&w; BIDDY(1983, Brit.), d&w
G. Edzhubov
WAR AND PEACE(1968, USSR)
Liselotte Eeer
FOX AND HIS FRIENDS(1976, Ger.)
Suesie Eejima
SOYLENT GREEN(1973)
Pedro Efe
IN THE WHITE CITY(1983, Switz./Portugal)
Karel Effa
WHO KILLED JESSIE?(1965, Czech.); LEMONADE JOE(1966, Czech.); WISHING MACHINE(1971, Czech.)

Camera Effects
HORROR PLANET(1982, Brit.), spec eff
Modern Film Effects
JOURNEY TO THE CENTER OF TIME(1967), spec eff; CYCLE SAVAGES(1969), spec eff
Effects Associates
HAWK THE SLAYER(1980, Brit.), spec eff
Keith Wilson Effects Associates
MEMOIRS OF A SURVIVOR(1981, Brit.), prod d
Harry Effertz
STUDENT BODY, THE(1976)
Robert Efford
BOYS OF PAUL STREET, THE(1969, Hung./US)
Cherie Effron
FAST TIMES AT RIDGEMONT HIGH(1982)
Eric Effron
DRAMATIC SCHOOL(1938)
Marshall Effron
1984
BAD MANNERS(1984)
R. Ben Efraim
MITCHELL(1975), p; PRIVATE LESSONS(1981), p; PRIVATE SCHOOL(1983), p
Ram Ben Efraim
JERUSALEM FILE, THE(1972, U.S./Israel), p
Laura Efrikian
CRIME DOES NOT PAY(1962, Fr.)
Eric Efron
NEWSBOY'S HOME(1939)
Marshall Efron
FUNNYMAN(1967); DOC(1971); THX 1138(1971); BANG THE DRUM SLOWLY(1973); BLADE(1973); BABY BLUE MARINE(1976); CALIFORNIA DREAMING(1979); FIRST TIME, THE(1983); TWICE UPON A TIME(1983)
Misc. Talkies
IS THERE SEX AFTER DEATH(1971); FAKING OF THE PRESIDENT, THE(1976)
Yehuda Efroni
ESCAPE TO THE SUN(1972, Fr./Ger./Israel); DIAMONDS(1975, U.S./Israel); DR. HECKYL AND MR. HYPE(1980); HERCULES(1983); NANA(1983, Ital.)
Yehudah Efroni
KAZABLAN(1974, Israel)
Sam Efrus
ON PROBATION(1935), p
R&B Efx
AMERICAN POP(1981), ph
Babs Egan
SUBWAY RIDERS(1981)
Beresford Egan
SILVER FLEET, THE(1945, Brit.); FRENZY(1946, Brit.); ESCAPE DANGEROUS(1947, Brit.); GHOSTS OF BERKELEY SQUARE(1947, Brit.), cos; MAN OF EVIL(1948, Brit.); TERROR SHIP(1954, Brit.); JOE MACBETH(1955); STRICTLY CONFIDENTIAL(1959, Brit.)
Bernard Egan
PLAGUE OF THE ZOMBIES, THE(1966, Brit.)
Betty Egan
Silents
MAN IN HOBBLES, THE(1928)
Beverli Egan
FIRST MONDAY IN OCTOBER(1981), set d
Eddie Egan
FRENCH CONNECTION, THE(1971); PRIME CUT(1972); BADGE 373(1973)
Eric Egan
RIDE THE HIGH WIND(1967, South Africa)
Gina Egan
LADY GODIVA RIDES AGAIN(1955, Brit.)
Jack Egan
BROADWAY HOOFER, THE(1929); BROADWAY SCANDALS(1929); IT CAN BE DONE(1929); GILDED LILY, THE(1935); OUR RELATIONS(1936); PICK A STAR(1937); TOAST OF NEW YORK, THE(1937); WINGS OVER HONOLULU(1937); WHO KILLED GAIL PRESTON?(1938); MR. SMITH GOES TO WASHINGTON(1939); NEWSBOY'S HOME(1939); BLONDIE ON A BUDGET(1940); WOMEN WITHOUT NAMES(1940); NOTHING BUT THE TRUTH(1941)
Silents
POTTERS, THE(1927); HAROLD TEEN(1928)
Jenny Egan
POLLYANNA(1960); THEY MIGHT BE GIANTS(1971)
Jim Egan
WOMEN AND BLOODY TERROR(1970)
Martin Egan
P.O.W., THE(1973), m
Michael Egan
DOMINANT SEX, THE(1937, Brit.), w; SQUARE ROOT OF ZERO, THE(1964); NEXT STOP, GREENWICH VILLAGE(1976)
Misc. Talkies
NIGHT TO DISMEMBER, A(1983)
Mishka Egan
MY SON, JOHN(1952)
Miska Egan
HOODLUM SAINT, THE(1946)
Pat Egan
AVALANCHE(1978)
Patrick Egan
BUTCH AND SUNDANCE: THE EARLY DAYS(1979)
Peter Egan
ONE BRIEF SUMMER(1971, Brit.); HIRELING, THE(1973, Brit.); CALLAN(1975, Brit.); HENNESSY(1975, Brit.); CHARRIOTS OF FIRE(1981, Brit.)
Reubin Egan
SHEPHERD OF THE HILLS, THE(1964)
Richard Egan
DAMNED DON'T CRY, THE(1950); GOOD HUMOR MAN, THE(1950); HIGHWAY 301(1950); KANSAS RAIDERS(1950); KILLER THAT STALKED NEW YORK, THE(1950); UNDERCOVER GIRL(1950); WYOMING MAIL(1950); BRIGHT VIC-

TORY(1951); FLAME OF ARABY(1951); GOLDEN HORDE, THE(1951); HOLLYWOOD STORY(1951); UP FRONT(1951); BATTLE AT APACHE PASS, THE(1952); BLACK-BEARD THE PIRATE(1952); CRIPPLE CREEK(1952); DEVIL MAKES THREE, THE(1952); ONE MINUTE TO ZERO(1952); GLORY BRIGADE, THE(1953); KID FROM LEFT FIELD, THE(1953); SPLIT SECOND(1953); WICKED WOMAN(1953); DEMETRIUS AND THE GLADIATORS(1954); GOG(1954); KHYBER PATROL(1954); SEVEN CITIES OF GOLD(1955); UNDERWATER!(1955); UNTAMED(1955); VIEW FROM POMPEY'S HEAD, THE(1955); VIOLENT SATURDAY(1955); LOVE ME TENDER(1956); TENSION AT TABLE ROCK(1956); SLAUGHTER ON TENTH AVENUE(1957); HUNTERS, THE(1958); VOICE IN THE MIRROR(1958); SUMMER PLACE, A(1959); THESE THOUSAND HILLS(1959); ESTHER AND THE KING(1960, U.S./Ital.); POLLYANNA(1960); 300 SPARTANS, THE(1962); VALLEY OF MYSTERY(1967); CHUBASCO(1968); DESTRUCTORS, THE(1968); BIG CUBE, THE(1969); MOONFIRE(1970); DAY OF THE WOLVES(1973); AMSTERDAM KILL, THE(1978, Hong Kong); SWEET CREEK COUNTY WAR, THE(1979)
Misc. Talkies
LEFT HAND OF GEMINI, THE(1972); KINO, THE PADRE ON HORSEBACK(1977)
Terence Egan
HOME, SWEET HOME(1933, Brit.), w; RIVER WOLVES, THE(1934, Brit.), w; SHADOW, THE(1936, Brit.), w
Ureo Egawa
ESCAPADE IN JAPAN(1957)
Albert Egbert
Silents
FURTHER ADVENTURES OF THE FLAG LIEUTENANT(1927, Brit.)
Seth Egbert
Silents
FURTHER ADVENTURES OF THE FLAG LIEUTENANT(1927, Brit.)
Henrik N. Ege
LET'S MAKE A NIGHT OF IT(1937, Brit.), w
Julie Ege
ON HER MAJESTY'S SECRET SERVICE(1969, Brit.); THINK DIRTY(1970, Brit.); CREATURES THE WORLD FORGOT(1971, Brit.); MAGNIFICENT SEVEN DEADLY SINS, THE(1971, Brit.); UP POMPEII(1971, Brit.); RENTADICK(1972, Brit.); CRAZE(1974, Brit.); MUTATIONS, THE(1974, Brit.); LAST DAYS OF MAN ON EARTH, THE(1975, Brit.); NOT NOW DARLING(1975, Brit.); DRACULA AND THE SEVEN GOLDEN VAMPIRES(1978, Brit./Chi.); IT'S NOT THE SIZE THAT COUNTS(1979, Brit.)
Misc. Talkies
GO FOR A TAKE(1972, Brit.)
Oscar Egede-Nissen
WHALERS, THE(1942, Swed.)
Jan Egelson
DARK END OF THE STREET, THE(1981), d&w
George Egeniou
NIGHT AMBUSH(1958, Brit.)
Dennis Eger
Q(1982), makeup
R. Eger
UTOPIA(1952, Fr./Ital.), p
Raymond Eger
LOVERS OF TOLEDO, THE(1954, Fr./Span./Ital.), p; PLEASE! MR. BALZAC(1957, Fr.), p; BLOOD AND ROSES(1961, Fr./Ital.), p; CHAMPAGNE MURDERS, THE(1968, Fr.), p
Carla Egerer
FRIENDS AND HUSBANDS(1983, Ger.)
Mark Egerton
CROSSTALK(1982, Aus.), d, w; YEAR OF LIVING DANGEROUSLY, THE(1982, Aus.)
Samantha Eggar
DOCTOR IN DISTRESS(1963, Brit.); DR. CRIPPEN(1963, Brit.); PSYCHE 59(1964, Brit.); YOUNG AND WILLING(1964, Brit.); COLLECTOR, THE(1965); RETURN FROM THE ASHES(1965, U.S./Brit.); WALK, DON'T RUN(1966); DOCTOR DOLITTLE(1967); LADY IN THE CAR WITH GLASSES AND A GUN, THE(1970, U.S./Fr.); MOLLY MAGUIRES, THE(1970); NAME FOR EVIL, A(1970); WALKING STICK, THE(1970, Brit.); LIGHT AT THE EDGE OF THE WORLD, THE(1971, U.S./Span./Lichtenstein); DEAD ARE ALIVE, THE(1972, Yugo./Ger./Ital.); SEVEN-PER-CENT SOLUTION, THE(1977, Brit.); UNCANNY, THE(1977, Brit./Can.); WELCOME TO BLOOD CITY(1977, Brit./Can.); WHY SHOOT THE TEACHER(1977, Can.); BROOD, THE(1979, Can.); EXTERMINATOR, THE(1980); DEMONOID(1981); CURTAINS(1983, Can.)
Misc. Talkies
UNKNOWN POWERS(1979)
David Eggby
MAD MAX(1979, Aus.), ph; DEAD MAN'S FLOAT(1980, Aus.), ph; BUDDIES(1983, Aus.), ph
K.V. Egge
Misc. Silents
MARRIAGE OF THE BEAR, THE(1928, USSR), d
Axel Eggebrecht
LOST ONE, THE(1951, Ger.), w
Albert Eggen
1984
RUNAWAY(1984)
Fern Eggen
DATE WITH JUDY, A(1948); HOMECOMING(1948); JULIA MISBEHAVES(1948); WHITE HEAT(1949)
Joe Eggenton
BLACK DRAGONS(1942)
Joseph Eggenton
DOCTOR TAKES A WIFE(1940); RANGERS OF FORTUNE(1940); YOU'LL FIND OUT(1940); BANDIT TRAIL, THE(1941); DOWN RIO GRANDE WAY(1942)
Jack Egger
STELLA DALLAS(1937)
Jose Egger
FOR A FEW DOLLARS MORE(1967, Ital./Ger./Span.)
Josef Egger
FOREVER MY LOVE(1962); FISTFUL OF DOLLARS, A(1964, Ital./Ger./Span.)

Marianne Eggerick
CARAVAN TO VACCARES(1974, Brit./Fr)
Marianne Eggerikx
EASY LIFE, THE(1971, Fr.); MAN WITH THE TRANSPLANTED BRAIN, THE(1972, Fr./Ital./Ger.)
Fred Eggers
HIGHWAY DRAGNET(1954), w; THUNDER PASS(1954), w; PORT OF HELL(1955), w; TREASURE OF RUBY HILLS(1955), w; LEGION OF THE DOOMED(1958), w; RETURN OF MR. MOTO, THE(1965, Brit.), w
Lillian Eggers
THAT NIGHT IN RIO(1941); I MARRIED AN ANGEL(1942); POWERS GIRL, THE(1942)
Almut Eggert
QUESTION 7(1961, U.S./Ger.)
K.V. Eggert
Misc. Silents
MARRIAGE OF THE BEAR, THE(1928, USSR)
Konstantin Eggert
Misc. Silents
BEAR'S WEDDING, THE(1926, USSR), a, d; AELITA(1929, USSR)
Nicole Eggert
RICH AND FAMOUS(1981)
1984
HAMBONE AND HILLIE(1984)
Roy Eggert, Jr.
PEER GYNT(1965)
Marta Eggerth
WHERE IS THIS LADY?(1932, Brit.); DIVINE SPARK, THE(1935, Brit./Ital.); MY HEART IS CALLING(1935, Brit.); FOR ME AND MY GAL(1942); PRESENTING LILY MARS(1943)
Martha Eggerth
DREAM OF SCHONBRUNN(1933, Aus.); COURT CONCERT, THE(1936, Ger.); UNFINISHED SYMPHONY, THE(1953, Aust./Brit.)
Joseph Eggerton
FIGHTING BILL FARGO(1942)
John Eggett
YOUNG WARRIORS(1983), spec eff
Allen Eggleston
GAL YOUNG UN(1979), cos
Charles Eggleston
WELL-GROOMED BRIDE, THE(1946)
Clark Eggleston
BLUE DAHLIA, THE(1946)
Colin Eggleston
LONG WEEKEND(1978, Aus.), d
Misc. Talkies
LITTLE FELLER, THE(1979), d
Edward Eggleston
HOOSIER SCHOOLMASTER(1935), w; HOOSIER SCHOOLBOY(1937), w
Silents
HOOSIER SCHOOLMASTER(1914), w
Mrs. Eggleston
Silents
WANTED FOR MURDER(1919)
Parker Eggleston
KISS IN THE DARK, A(1949)
Carlo Egidi
ASSASSIN, THE(1961, Ital./Fr.), set d; FROM A ROMAN BALCONY(1961, Fr./Ital.), art d; BELL' ANTONIO(1962, Ital.), art d; EVERYBODY GO HOME!(1962, Fr./Ital.), art d; LA NOTTE BRAVA(1962, Fr./Ital.), art d; MAFIOSO(1962, Ital.), art d; FIASCO IN MILAN(1963, Fr./Ital.), art d; EMPTY CANVAS, THE(1964, Fr./Ital.), art d; MARRIAGE–ITALIAN STYLE(1964, Fr./Ital.), art d; SEDUCED AND ABAN-DONED(1964, Fr./Ital.), art d, cos; FACTS OF MURDER, THE(1965, Ital.), art d; RAILROAD MAN, THE(1965, Ital.), art d; SALVATORE GIULIANO(1966, Ital.), art d; CLIMAX, THE(1967, Fr., Ital.), prod d; HEAD OF THE FAMILY(1967, Ital./Fr.), art d; ITALIAN SECRET SERVICE(1968, Ital.), art d; MAN WITH THE BALLOONS, THE(1968, Ital./Fr.), art d; SERAFINO(1970, Fr./Ital.), art d; ALFREDO, AL-FREDO(1973, Ital.), set d
Antonina Egina
DUEL, THE(1964, USSR), ph
Charles Eglee
DEADLY EYES(1982), p, w
J. Egleson
BILLY IN THE LOWLANDS(1979), ed
Jan Egleson
FRIENDS OF EDDIE COYLE, THE(1973); BILLY IN THE LOWLANDS(1979), d&w
Nick Egleson
BILLY IN THE LOWLANDS(1979), p
Clive Egleton
BLACK WINDMILL, THE(1974, Brit.), w
Andre Eglevsky
LIMELIGHT(1952), a, ch
Red Egner
SHADOWS OF THE WEST(1949)
Bertha Egnos
DINGAKA(1965, South Africa), m
Sandra Ego
TRIAL OF BILLY JACK, THE(1974)
Mary Egoff
POLYESTER(1981)
Maria Egri
FATHER(1967, Hung.)
Lucien Egrot
Misc. Silents
EARLY BIRDS(1923, Brit.), d
Tony Egry
COCKTAIL MOLOTOV(1980, Fr.), art d

Juan Carlos Eguillor
1984
IT'S NEVER TOO LATE(1984, Span.), w
Lenke Egyed
SUN SHINES, THE(1939, Hung.)
Zoltan Egyed
DRAMATIC SCHOOL(1938), w
Michael Egyes
1984
BAY BOY(1984, Can.)
Little Egypt
SEVEN(1979)
The Egyptian Folklore Group
SPY WHO LOVED ME, THE(1977, Brit.)
Tatsuyoshi Ehara
SANJURO(1962, Jap.); RED BEARD(1966, Jap.)
Al Ehen
BLACK EAGLE(1948)
William Ehfe
Silents
BIG TREMAINE(1916)
Misc. Silents
BEST MAN, THE(1917)
William Ramon Ehfe
Misc. Silents
DAUGHTER OF THE DON, THE(1917)
Beth Ehlers
HUNGER, THE(1983)
Christl Ehlers
Misc. Silents
PEOPLE ON SUNDAY(1929, Ger.)
Corky Ehlers
ABBY(1974), ed; RETURN TO MACON COUNTY(1975), ed; FOOD OF THE GODS, THE(1976), ed; STUNTS(1977), ed
Gerd Ehlers
NAKED AMONG THE WOLVES(1967, Ger.)
Paul Ehlers
MADMAN(1982)
Walter D. Ehlers
LONG GRAY LINE, THE(1955)
Kald Ehmann
APRIL 1, 2000(1953, Aust.)
Karl Ehmann
VIENNA WALTZES(1961, Aust.)
George Ehmig
PANIC IN THE STREETS(1950)
Jacques Ehrem
TESTAMENT OF DR. MABUSE, THE(1943, Ger.)
Frances Ehren
RAILROADED(1947), cos; T-MEN(1947), cos; BEHIND LOCKED DOORS(1948), cos; CANON CITY(1948), cos; NORTHWEST STAMPEDE(1948), cos; SPIRITUALIST, THE(1948), cos
Heinz Ehrenfreund
ODESSA FILE, THE(1974, Brit./Ger.); CRIME AND PASSION(1976, U.S., Ger.)
Sidney Ehrenreich
HIDE IN PLAIN SIGHT(1980)
Barbara Jean Ehrhardt
Misc. Talkies
DANNY(1979)
Bess Ehrhardt
ICE FOLLIES OF 1939(1939)
Herman Ehrhardt
MAGIC FACE, THE(1951, Aust.)
Horst Ehrhardt
NUDE BOMB, THE(1980)
Eddie Ehrhart
YOU GOTTA STAY HAPPY(1948); GUNFIGHTER, THE(1950)
Maggie Ehrig
1984
SUBURBIA(1984)
John Ehrin
COURAGE OF BLACK BEAUTY(1957), ed
Misc. Talkies
FORBID THEM NOT(1961)
Johnny Ehrin
FROM HELL TO TEXAS(1958), ed
Gerald Ehrlich
PENNYWHISTLE BLUES, THE(1952, South Africa), ed
Henry Ehrlich
ADVENTURES OF ROBINSON CRUSOE, THE(1954), p
Jean Ehrlich
VOICES(1979)
Jesse Ehrlich
FRIGHTMARE(1983)
Karl Ehrlich
ONE APRIL 2000(1952, Aust.), p; VIENNA WALTZES(1961, Aust.), p; GOOD SOL-DIER SCHWEIK, THE(1963, Ger.), p; YOU ARE THE WORLD FOR ME(1964, Aust.), p
Lynne Ehrlich
SIERRA BARON(1958)
Max Ehrlich
VIENNA, CITY OF SONGS(1931, Ger.); NAKED EDGE, THE(1961), w; Z.P.G.(1972), w; SAVAGE IS LOOSE, THE(1974), w; REINCARNATION OF PETER PROUD, THE(1975), w
Max Simon Ehrlich
GLASS WEB, THE(1953), w
Peter Ehrlich
EMIL AND THE DETECTIVES(1964); BLACK SPIDER, THE(1983, Swit.)

Monica Ehrling
WILD STRAWBERRIES(1959, Swed.)
Sixten Ehrling
SEVENTH SEAL, THE(1958, Swed.), md
Jean-Daniel Ehrmann
MILKY WAY, THE(1969, Fr./Ital.)
Else Ehser
M(1933, Ger.); PRIVATE LIFE OF LOUIS XIV(1936, Ger.); GLASS TOWER, THE(1959, Ger.); DAY WILL COME, A(1960, Ger.); CASTLE, THE(1969, Ger.)
Istvan Eiben
SPRING SHOWER(1932, Hung.), ph
Adolfo Eibenstein
ONE MILLION DOLLARS(1965, Ital.)
Franz Eicchorn
RIO 70(1970, U.S./Ger./Span.), w
Carl Eich
PROSTITUTION(1965, Fr.)
Diana Eichbauer
1984
GABRIELA(1984, Braz.), cos
Helio Eichbauer
1984
GABRIELA(1984, Braz.), art d
Richard Eichberg
COPPER, THE(1930, Brit.), p&d; FLAME OF LOVE, THE(1930, Brit.), p, d; NIGHT BIRDS(1931, Brit.), p&d; BRIDEGROOM FOR TWO(1932, Brit.), p&d
Misc. Silents
MONNA VANNA(1923, Ger.), d; WASTED LOVE(1930, Brit.), d
Willy Eichberger
BURG THEATRE(1936, Ger.); LOLA MONTES(1955, Fr./Ger.)
Wolfgang Eichberger
HANSEL AND GRETEL(1965, Ger.)
Edmundo Eichelbaum
THE EAVESDROPPER(1966, U.S./Arg.), w
Mickey Eichen
APPRENTICESHIP OF DUDDY KRAVITZ, THE(1974, Can.)
Paul Eichenberg
MC MASTERS, THE(1970)
Renate Eichholz
SNOW WHITE(1965, Ger.)
Eichhorn
STRANGE WORLD(1952), w
Bernard Eichhorn
CAPTAIN FROM KOEPENICK, THE(1956, Ger.), m; GLASS OF WATER, A(1962, Cgr.), m
Bernhard Eichhorn
FILM WITHOUT A NAME(1950, Ger.), m; DIE GANS VON SEDAN(1962, Fr/Ger.), m; GOOD SOLDIER SCHWEIK, THE(1963, Ger.), m
Edgar Eichhorn
STRANGE WORLD(1952), ph
Franz Eichhorn
STRANGE WORLD(1952), d
Lisa Eichhorn
EUROPEANS, THE(1979, Brit.); YANKS(1979); WHY WOULD I LIE(1980); CUTTER AND BONE(1981); WEATHER IN THE STREETS, THE(1983, Brit.)
Werner Eichhorn
LOST HONOR OF KATHARINA BLUM, THE(1975, Ger.); FRIENDS AND HUSBANDS(1983, Ger.)
Bernd Eichinger
WILD DUCK, THE(1977, Ger./Aust.), p; OUR HITLER, A FILM FROM GERMANY(1980, Ger.), p
1984
NEVERENDING STORY, THE(1984, Ger.), p
Edna Eichor
Silents
ROUGHNECK, THE(1924)
Bernard Eichorn
HOUSE OF LIFE(1953, Ger.), m
Franz Eichorn
VIOLENT YEARS, THE(1956), d
Elke Eichwede
ORDERED TO LOVE(1963, Ger.)
Van Eicken
EVA(1962, Fr./Ital.)
Brad Eide
TIME AFTER TIME(1979, Brit.), stunts
Carey Eidel
1984
C.H.U.D.(1984)
Paul Eiding
PERSONALS, THE(1982)
1984
BEST DEFENSE(1984)
Alma Eidnea
DISPUTED PASSAGE(1939)
Jack Eigen
I SURRENDER DEAR(1948); HOODLUM PRIEST, THE(1961)
S. M. Eiger
1984
SHEENA(1984), w
Eight Black Streaks
KENTUCKY MINSTRELS(1934, Brit.)
The Eight Black Streaks
NIGHT CLUB QUEEN(1934, Brit.)
Misc. Talkies
SWANEE SHOWBOAT(1939)
The Eight Buckaroos
TWILIGHT ON THE PRAIRIE(1944)

Eight Master Singers
SOMEWHERE IN ENGLAND(1940, Brit.)
The Eight Rhythmeers
SLIGHTLY TERRIFIC(1944)
Go Eiji
YAKUZA, THE(1975, U.S./Jap.)
Okada Eiji
YAKUZA, THE(1975, U.S./Jap.)
Jill Eikenberry
BETWEEN THE LINES(1977); UNMARRIED WOMAN, AN(1978); BUTCH AND SUNDANCE: THE EARLY DAYS(1979); RICH KIDS(1979); HIDE IN PLAIN SIGHT(1980); ARTHUR(1981)
1984
ULTIMATE SOLUTION OF GRACE QUIGLEY, THE(1984)
Yona Eilan
Misc. Talkies
LAST WINTER, THE(1983)
Kenneth S. Eiland
SOME KIND OF HERO(1982)
Cindy Eilbacher
BIG BOUNCE, THE(1969); SHANKS(1974)
Lisa Eilbacher
WAR BETWEEN MEN AND WOMEN, THE(1972); RUN FOR THE ROSES(1978); ON THE RIGHT TRACK(1981); OFFICER AND A GENTLEMAN, AN(1982); 10 TO MIDNIGHT(1983)
1984
BEVERLY HILLS COP(1984)
Eileen Idare Ltd.
THAT'S A GOOD GIRL(1933,Brit.), cos
Janet Eilber
WHOSE LIFE IS IT ANYWAY?(1981); ROMANTIC COMEDY(1983)
1984
HARD TO HOLD(1984)
Barbara Eiler
DEEP SIX, THE(1958); BUBBLE, THE(1967)
Virginia Eiler
EXECUTIVE SUITE(1954)
Joe Eilers
RESTLESS ONES, THE(1965)
Kurt Eilers
LAST TEN DAYS, THE(1956, Ger.)
Sally Eilers
BROADWAY BABIES(1929); LONG, LONG TRAIL, THE(1929); SAILORS' HOLIDAY(1929); DOUGH BOYS(1930); LET US BE GAY(1930); ROARING RANCH(1930); SHE COULDN'T SAY NO(1930); TRIGGER TRICKS(1930); BAD GIRL(1931); BLACK CAMEL, THE(1931); CLEARING THE RANGE(1931); HOLY TERROR, A(1931); OVER THE HILL(1931); PARLOR, BEDROOM AND BATH(1931); QUICK MILLIONS(1931); REDUCING(1931); DANCE TEAM(1932); DISORDERLY CONDUCT(1932); HAT CHECK GIRL(1932); CENTRAL AIRPORT(1933); HOLD ME TIGHT(1933); I SPY(1933, Brit.); MADE ON BROADWAY(1933); SAILOR'S LUCK(1933); SECOND HAND WIFE(1933); STATE FAIR(1933); WALLS OF GOLD(1933); SHE MADE HER BED(1934); THREE ON A HONEYMOON(1934); ALIAS MARY DOW(1935); CARNIVAL(1935); PURSUIT(1935); REMEMBER LAST NIGHT(1935); DON'T GET PERSONAL(1936); FLORIDA SPECIAL(1936); STRIKE ME PINK(1936); WITHOUT ORDERS(1936); DANGER PATROL(1937); LADY BEHAVE(1937); TALK OF THE DEVIL(1937, Brit.); WE HAVE OUR MOMENTS(1937); CONDEMNED WOMEN(1938); EVERYBODY'S DOING IT(1938); NURSE FROM BROOKLYN(1938); TARNISHED ANGEL(1938); FULL CONFESSION(1939); THEY MADE HER A SPY(1939); I WAS A PRISONER ON DEVIL'S ISLAND(1941); WAVE, A WAC AND A MARINE, A(1944); STRANGE ILLUSION(1945); CORONER CREEK(1948); STAGE TO TUCSON(1950)
Silents
SLIGHTLY USED(1927); SUNRISE–A SONG OF TWO HUMANS(1927); GOOD-BYE KISS, THE(1928)
Misc. Silents
DRY MARTINI(1928); TRAIL MARRIAGE(1929)
Al Eilks
THUNDER IN THE CITY(1937, Brit.), ph
John Eiman
OCEAN'S ELEVEN(1960)
Donald Ein
PRIZE, THE(1963)
Ellie Ein
PRIZE, THE(1963)
Felda Ein
PRIZE, THE(1963)
Cory Einbinder
KING OF THE GYPSIES(1978)
Erich Einegg
SOMEWHERE IN BERLIN(1949, E. Ger.), m
Bob Einer
INVASION OF THE SAUCER MEN(1957)
Robert Einer
WHEN WILLIE COMES MARCHING HOME(1950)
Richard Einfeld
GHOST DIVER(1957), p, d&w; OREGON TRAIL, THE(1959), p; YOUNG GUNS OF TEXAS(1963), ed
Richard Einfield
POLICE NURSE(1963), ed
Beth Noreen Einhorn
1984
FLAMINGO KID, THE(1984)
Daphna Einhorn
STORY OF RUTH, THE(1960)
Richard Einhorn
SHOCK WAVES(1977), m; DON'T GO IN THE HOUSE(1980), m; EYES OF A STRANGER(1980), m; PROWLER, THE(1981), m
Arik Einstein
SALLAH(1965, Israel)

Bob Einstein
GET TO KNOW YOUR RABBIT(1972); MODERN ROMANCE(1981)
Carl Einstein
TONI(1968, Fr.), w
Charles Einstein
WHILE THE CITY SLEEPS(1956), w
Cliff Einstein
MODERN ROMANCE(1981)
Clifford Einstein
REAL LIFE(1979)
Harold Einstein
REAL LIFE(1979)
Karen Einstein
REAL LIFE(1979)
Mandy Einstein
REAL LIFE(1979)
Parkyakardus "Harry" Einstein
SWEETHEARTS OF THE U.S.A.(1944)
E. Eis
PRISON WITHOUT BARS(1939, Brit.), w
Egon Eis
TRAPEZE(1932, Ger.), w; SHOT AT DAWN, A(1934, Ger.), w
Elizabeth Eis
DEAR, DEAD DELILAH(1972)
Maria Eis
ETERNAL WALTZ, THE(1959, Ger.)
O. Eis
PRISON WITHOUT BARS(1939, Brit.), w
Otto Eis
SHOT AT DAWN, A(1934, Ger.), w
Werner Eisbrenner
RATS, THE(1955, Ger.), m; AS LONG AS YOU'RE NEAR ME(1956, Ger.), m; GLASS TOWER, THE(1959, Ger.), m; KING IN SHADOW(1961, Ger.), m; VOR SONNENUN-TERGANG(1961, Ger), m; COURT MARTIAL(1962, Ger.), m
Mihaly Eisemann
HIPPOLYT, THE LACKEY(1932, Hung.), m
David Eisen
MICKEY ONE(1965)
Harry Eisen
BLACK VEIL FOR LISA, A(1969 Ital./Ger.), ed
Robert Eisen
BIG COMBO, THE(1955), ed; TENDER HEARTS(1955), ed; EDGE OF HELL(1956), ed; PARATROOP COMMAND(1959), ed
Robert S. Eisen
BAIT(1954), ed; OTHER WOMAN, THE(1954), ed; INVASION OF THE BODY SNATCHERS(1956), ed; SCREAMING EAGLES(1956), ed; SHAKE, RATTLE, AND ROCK!(1957), ed; JET ATTACK(1958), ed; SUICIDE BATTALION(1958), ed; LEGEND OF TOM DOOLEY, THE(1959), ed; CONFESSIONS OF AN OPIUM EATER(1962), ed; STRANGLER, THE(1964), ed; DESTINATION INNER SPACE(1966), ed; DIMENSION 5(1966), ed; CASTLE OF EVIL(1967), ed; DESTRUCTORS, THE(1968), ed
John Eisenbach
NASHVILLE REBEL(1966), ph
Ned Eisenberg
BURNING, THE(1981); SOLDIER, THE(1982)
1984
SLAYGROUND(1984, Brit.)
David Eisenbise
CHINA SYNDROME, THE(1979)
Gary Eisencraft
HIGH(1968, Can.)
Seymour A. Eisenfeld
WILD REBELS, THE(1967)
Jo Eisenger
BEDEVILLED(1955), w
Tim Eisenhart
REVENGE OF THE NINJA(1983)
Allan Eisenman
TWO-MINUTE WARNING(1976)
Elizabeth Eisenman
SUMMERDOG(1977)
Christopher Eisenmann
TWILIGHT ZONE–THE MOVIE(1983)
Chuck Eisenmann
MY DOG, BUDDY(1960)
Ike Eisenmann
ESCAPE TO WITCH MOUNTAIN(1975); RETURN FROM WITCH MOUN-TAIN(1978); FORMULA, THE(1980); STAR TREK II: THE WRATH OF KHAN(1982); CROSS CREEK(1983)
Allan Eisennman
BELL JAR, THE(1979)
Sergei Eisenstein
IVAN THE TERRIBLE(Part I, 1947, USSR), p,d&w; ALEXANDER NEVSKY(1939), d, w; SEEDS OF FREEDOM(1943, USSR), w
Silents
BATTLESHIP POTEMKIN, THE(1925, USSR), a, d&w, ed
Misc. Silents
STRIKE(1925, USSR), d; OCTOBER(1928, USSR), d; OLD AND NEW(1930, USSR), d
Sergei M. Eisenstein
Silents
TEN DAYS THAT SHOOK THE WORLD(1927, USSR), d, w
Yulia Eisenstein
Silents
BATTLESHIP POTEMKIN, THE(1925, USSR)
Victor Eisimont
ONCE THERE WAS A GIRL(1945, USSR), d
Irene Eisinger
YOUNG MAN'S FANCY(1943, Brit.)

Jo Eisinger
SPIDER, THE(1945), w; GILDA(1946), w; WALLS CAME TUMBLING DOWN, THE(1946), w; SLEEPING CITY, THE(1950), w; SYSTEM, THE(1953), w; BIG BOO-DLE, THE(1957), w; CRIME OF PASSION(1957), w; HOUSE OF THE SEVEN HAWKS, THE(1959), w; AS THE SEA RAGES(1960 Ger.), w; OSCAR WILDE(1960, Brit.), w; POPPY IS ALSO A FLOWER, THE(1966), w; THE DIRTY GAME(1966, Fr./Ital./Ger.), w; ROVER, THE(1967, Ital.), w; THEY CAME TO ROB LAS VEGAS(1969, Fr./Ital./Span./Ger.), w
1984
JIGSAW MAN, THE(1984, Brit.), w
Joe Eisinger
NIGHT AND THE CITY(1950, Brit.), w
Hanns Eisler
HELL ON EARTH(1934, Ger.), m; ABDUL THE DAMNED(1935, Brit.), m; NONE BUT THE LONELY HEART(1944), m; JEALOUSY(1945), m; SPANISH MAIN, THE(1945), m; DEADLINE AT DAWN(1946), m; SCANDAL IN PARIS, A(1946), m, md; SO WELL REMEMBERED(1947, Brit.), m; WOMAN ON THE BEACH, THE(1947), m; OUR DAILY BREAD(1950, Aust.), m; FIDELIO(1961, Aust.), w; LOVE AFFAIR; OR THE CASE OF THE MISSING SWITCHBOARD OPERATOR(1968, Yugo.), m
Hans Eisler
CLOWN MUST LAUGH, A(1936, Brit.), md; HANGMEN ALSO DIE(1943), m; GALILEO(1975, Brit.), m
Anthony Eisley
PORTRAIT OF A MOBSTER(1961); NAKED KISS, THE(1964); ONE WAY WAHI-NI(1965); FRANKIE AND JOHNNY(1966); NAVY VS. THE NIGHT MONSTERS, THE(1966); JOURNEY TO THE CENTER OF TIME(1967); LIGHTNING BOLT(1967, Ital./Sp.); STAR!(1968); THEY RAN FOR THEIR LIVES(1968); MIGHTY GORGA, THE(1969); WITCHMAKER, THE(1969); BLOOD OF FRANKENSTEIN(1970); DOLL SQUAD, THE(1973); MONSTER(1979)
Fred [Anthony] Eisley
WASP WOMAN, THE(1959)
Larry Eisley
HARD RIDE, THE(1971)
Tony Eisley
OPERATION SECRET(1952)
Joey Eisnach
SWARM, THE(1978)
David Eisner
PHOBIA(1980, Can.); HAPPY BIRTHDAY TO ME(1981)
Gretchen Eisner
MOONSHINE MOUNTAIN(1964)
Hannelore Eisner
ENDLESS NIGHT, THE(1963, Ger.)
June Eisner
DEADLINE–U.S.A.(1952)
Will Eisner
1984
SHEENA(1984), w
Mickey Eissa
OUTLAWS OF THE DESERT(1941); RIDERS OF THE TIMBERLINE(1941); STICK TO YOUR GUNS(1941)
John Eitel
1984
DELIVERY BOYS(1984)
Marta Eitler
PIRATES OF PENZANCE, THE(1983)
Dan Eitner
UNTIL THEY SAIL(1957)
Don Eitner
THIS REBEL BREED(1960); QUEEN OF BLOOD(1966); SOFI(1967), w
Donald Eitner
KRONOS(1957)
Karoly Eizler
RED AND THE WHITE, THE(1969, Hung./USSR)
Charlotte Eizlini
UP FROM THE BEACH(1965)
the Eje Thelin Quintet
TO LOVE(1964, Swed.)
Ingemar Ejve
FACE OF FIRE(1959, U.S./Brit.), ed; DOLL, THE(1964, Swed.), ed; SWEDISH WED-DING NIGHT(1965, Swed.), ed; HUGS AND KISSES(1968, Swed.), ed; HYS-TERICAL(1983), ed
Anders Ek
JOHANSSON GETS SCOLDED(1945, Swed.); NAKED NIGHT, THE(1956, Swed.); SEVENTH SEAL, THE(1958, Swed.); RITUAL, THE(1970, Swed.)
Malin Ek
PASSION OF ANNA, THE(1970, Swed.)
M. Ekaterinsky
NEW TEACHER, THE(1941, USSR)
Misc. Talkies
HALF A HOUSE(1979)
Anita Ekberg
ABBOTT AND COSTELLO GO TO MARS(1953); GOLDEN BLADE, THE(1953); MISSISSIPPI GAMBLER, THE(1953); TAKE ME TO TOWN(1953); ARTISTS AND MODELS(1955); BLOOD ALLEY(1955); BACK FROM ETERNITY(1956); HOLLY-WOOD OR BUST(1956); MAN IN THE VAULT(1956); WAR AND PEACE(1956, Ital./U.S.); ZARAK(1956, Brit.); PICKUP ALLEY(1957, Brit.); VALERIE(1957); MAN INSIDE, THE(1958, Brit.); PARIS HOLIDAY(1958); SCREAMING MIMI(1958); LA DOLCE VITA(1961, Ital./Fr.); BOCCACCIO '70(1962/Ital./Fr.); CALL ME BWA-NA(1963, Brit.); FOUR FOR TEXAS(1963); ALPHABET MURDERS, THE(1966); MON-GOLS, THE(1966, Fr./Ital.); WAY...WAY OUT(1966); WHITE, RED, YELLOW, PINK(1966, Ital.); COBRA, THE(1968); GLASS SPHINX, THE(1968, Egypt/Ital./Span.); IF IT'S TUESDAY, THIS MUST BE BELGIUM(1969); LOVE FACTORY(1969, Ital.); MALENKA, THE VAMPIRE(1972, Span./Ital.)
Misc. Talkies
NORTHEAST TO SEOUL(1974)
Carl Ekberg
FOREIGN CORRESPONDENT(1940); MAN HUNT(1941); MEET JOHN DOE(1941); DESPERATE JOURNEY(1942); ONCE UPON A HONEYMOON(1942); REUNION IN FRANCE(1942); WIFE TAKES A FLYER, THE(1942); SECRETS OF SCOTLAND

YARD(1944); TAMPICO(1944); UNWRITTEN CODE, THE(1944); O.S.S.(1946); WHAT DID YOU DO IN THE WAR, DADDY?(1966)

Monika Ekberg
BRINK OF LIFE(1960, Swed.)

Victor Ekberg
WRATH OF GOD, THE(1972)

Anita Ekbery
WOMAN TIMES SEVEN(1967, U.S./Fr./Ital.)

Monica Ekblad
10 TO MIDNIGHT(1983)

Stina Ekblad
FANNY AND ALEXANDER(1983, Swed./Fr./Ger.)

Lars Ekborg
MAGICIAN, THE(1959, Swed.); YOUNG PHILADELPHIANS, THE(1959); SWEDISH WEDDING NIGHT(1965, Swed.); DUET FOR CANNIBALS(1969, Swed.)

Allan Ekelund
ILLICIT INTERLUDE(1954, Swed.), p; SMILES OF A SUMMER NIGHT(1957, Swed.), p; SEVENTH SEAL, THE(1958, Swed.), p; DEVIL'S EYE, THE(1960, Swed.), p; VIRGIN SPRING, THE(1960, Swed.), p; SECRETS OF WOMEN(1961, Swed.), p; THROUGH A GLASS DARKLY(1962, Swed.), p; PORT OF CALL(1963, Swed.), p; SILENCE, THE(1964, Swed.), p

Allen Ekelund
WILD STRAWBERRIES(1959, Swed.), p

Bengt Ekerot
SEVENTH SEAL, THE(1958, Swed.); MAGICIAN, THE(1959, Swed.); HERE'S YOUR LIFE(1968, Swed.)

Alexander Ekert
Silents
PASSION(1920, Ger.)

Harry Ekezian
ISLAND OF LOST SOULS(1933); MAN ON THE FLYING TRAPEZE, THE(1935)

Bud Ekins
LOVE BUG, THE(1968); HELL'S ANGELS '69(1969); SORCERER(1977), stunts; MOVIE MOVIE(1978); NATIONAL LAMPOON'S ANIMAL HOUSE(1978); DEADLY FORCE(1983)
1984
CITY HEAT(1984)

Mike Ekiss
GUNFIGHTERS OF CASA GRANDE(1965, U.S./Span.)

Nikolai Ekk
ROAD TO LIFE(1932, USSR), d, w

Britt Ekland
AFTER THE FOX(1966, U.S./Brit./Ital.); BOBO, THE(1967, Brit.); DOUBLE MAN, THE(1967); NIGHT THEY RAIDED MINSKY'S, THE(1968); TOO MANY THIEVES(1968); STILETTO(1969); CANNIBALS, THE(1970, Ital.); MACHINE GUN McCAIN(1970, Ital.); ENDLESS NIGHT(1971, Brit.); GET CARTER(1971, Brit.); NIGHT HAIR CHILD(1971, Brit.); PERCY(1971, Brit.); TIME FOR LOVING, A(1971, Brit.); ASYLUM(1972, Brit.); BAXTER(1973, Brit.); MAN WITH THE GOLDEN GUN, THE(1974, Brit.); ULTIMATE THRILL, THE(1974); WICKER MAN, THE(1974, Brit.); ROYAL FLASH(1975, Brit.); HIGH VELOCITY(1977); SLAVERS(1977, Ger.); KING SOLOMON'S TREASURE(1978, Can.); SOME LIKE IT COOL(1979, Ger./Aust./Ital./Fr.); MONSTER CLUB, THE(1981, Brit.); SATAN'S MISTRESS(1982)
Misc. Talkies
DARK EYES(1980)

John Eklof
ONLY ONE NIGHT(1942, Swed.)

Bengt Eklund
RAILROAD WORKERS(1948, Swed.); MAKE WAY FOR LILA(1962, Swed./Ger.); NIGHT IS MY FUTURE(1962, Swed.); PORT OF CALL(1963, Swed.); DOLL, THE(1964, Swed.); SHAME(1968, Swed.)

Britt-Marie Eklund
SHORT IS THE SUMMER(1968, Swed.)

Kay Eklund
GETTING OF WISDOM, THE(1977, Aus.)

Nils Eklund
TO LOVE(1964, Swed.)

Britta Ekman [Britt Ekland]
HAPPY THIEVES, THE(1962); ADVANCE TO THE REAR(1964)

Gosta Ekman
SWEDENHIELMS(1935, Swed.); INTERMEZZO(1937, Swed.); FACE TO FACE(1976, Swed.); ADVENTURES OF PICASSO, THE(1980, Swed.), a, w
Silents
FAUST(1926, Ger.)
Misc. Silents
CHARLES XII, PARTS 1 & 2(1927, Swed.)

Gosta Ekman, Jr.
JUST ONCE MORE(1963, Swed.), a, p; WOMAN OF DARKNESS(1968, Swed.); DUET FOR CANNIBALS(1969, Swed.)

Hakke Ekman
NAKED NIGHT, THE(1956, Swed.)

Hans Ekman
INTERMEZZO(1937, Swed.)

Hasse Ekman
NIGHT IN JUNE, A(1940, Swed.); DEVIL'S WANTON, THE(1962, Swed.)

Stefan Ekman
Misc. Talkies
AWOL(1973)

Agneta Ekmanner
HUGS AND KISSES(1968, Swed.); DUET FOR CANNIBALS(1969, Swed.)

Bruno Ekmar
SALVATORE GIULIANO(1966, Ital.)

Emy Eko
TOMB OF TORTURE(1966, Ital.)

Juri Ekonomzev
RED TENT, THE(1971, Ital./USSR), set d

Kerstin Ekwall
NIGHT IN JUNE, A(1940, Swed.)

Walter J. Ekwert
SQUARE JUNGLE, THE(1955)

Walter "Whitey" Ekwart
IRON MAN, THE(1951)

Sam El
DRAGON SKY(1964, Fr.)

Farid El Atrache
LITTLE MISS DEVIL(1951, Egypt), a, p, m

Abd el Aziz
Misc. Silents
STAMPEDE(1930, Sudan)

Hassan el Baroudi
EGYPT BY THREE(1953)

El Chicote
LEGEND OF A BANDIT, THE(1945, Mex.)

Enrique El Cojo
1984
BIZET'S CARMEN(1984, Fr./Ital.)

El Cordobes
LIFE LOVE DEATH(1969, Fr./Ital.)

El Duce
1984
DUBEAT-E-O(1984), w

Ibrahim El Hadish
LEGEND OF THE LOST(1957, U.S./Panama/Ital.)

Chirine El Khadem
FOREIGNER, THE(1978), a, ph

Chririne El Khadem
SMITHEREENS(1982), ph

Paco El Laberinto
PRIDE AND THE PASSION, THE(1957)

Mahmoud el Miligui
EGYPT BY THREE(1953)

Allel El Mouhib
Z(1969, Fr./Algeria)

Abd el Nebi
Misc. Silents
STAMPEDE(1930, Sudan)

Khaled el Saeid
CIRCLE OF DECEIT(1982, Fr./Ger.)

Kamel El Sheik
GLASS SPHINX, THE(1968, Egypt/Ital./Span.), d

Ahmed El Shenawi
MIDNIGHT EXPRESS(1978, Brit.)
1984
ELEMENT OF CRIME, THE(1984, Den.)

Kamal El Shennawy
CAIRO(1963)

Cuy El Tsosie
SHOOTING, THE(1971)

Nameer El-Kadi
QUEST FOR FIRE(1982, Fr./Can.)

Ahmed El-Shenawi
1984
INDIANA JONES AND THE TEMPLE OF DOOM(1984)

Elaine
MAN WITH TWO HEADS, THE(1972), art d; RATS ARE COMING! THE WEREWOLVES ARE HERE!, THE(1972), set d

Lynne Elaine
MY BREAKFAST WITH BLASSIE(1983)

Sylbil Elaine
PEOPLE'S ENEMY, THE(1935)

Elaine & Derek
GONKS GO BEAT(1965, Brit.)

Greg Elam
FIRE AND ICE(1983)
1984
SOLDIER'S STORY, A(1984), stunts

Jack Elam
WILD WEED(1949); AMERICAN GUERRILLA IN THE PHILIPPINES, AN(1950); HIGH LONESOME(1950); KEY TO THE CITY(1950); ONE WAY STREET(1950); SUNDOWNERS, THE(1950); TICKET TO TOMAHAWK(1950); BIRD OF PARADISE(1951); FINDERS KEEPERS(1951); RAWHIDE(1951); BATTLE AT APACHE PASS, THE(1952); BUSHWHACKERS, THE(1952); HIGH NOON(1952); KANSAS CITY CONFIDENTIAL(1952); LURE OF THE WILDERNESS(1952); MONTANA TERRITORY(1952); MY MAN AND I(1952); RANCHO NOTORIOUS(1952); RING, THE(1952); APPOINTMENT IN HONDURAS(1953); COUNT THE HOURS(1953); GUN BELT(1953); MOONLIGHTER, THE(1953); RIDE, VAQUERO!(1953); CATTLE QUEEN OF MONTANA(1954); JUBILEE TRAIL(1954); PRINCESS OF THE NILE(1954); RIDE CLEAR OF DIABLO(1954); VERA CRUZ(1954); ARTISTS AND MODELS(1955); FAR COUNTRY, THE(1955); KISMET(1955); KISS ME DEADLY(1955); MAN FROM LARAMIE, THE(1955); MAN WITHOUT A STAR(1955); MOONFLEET(1955); TARZAN'S HIDDEN JUNGLE(1955); WICHITA(1955); JUBAL(1956); PARDNERS(1956); THUNDER OVER ARIZONA(1956); BABY FACE NELSON(1957); DRAGON WELLS MASSACRE(1957); GUNFIGHT AT THE O.K. CORRAL(1957); LURE OF THE SWAMP(1957); NIGHT PASSAGE(1957); GUN RUNNERS, THE(1958); EDGE OF ETERNITY(1959); GIRL IN LOVER'S LANE, THE(1960); COMANCHEROS, THE(1961); LAST SUNSET, THE(1961); POCKETFUL OF MIRACLES(1961); FOUR FOR TEXAS(1963); NIGHT OF THE GRIZZLY, THE(1966); RARE BREED, THE(1966); LAST CHALLENGE, THE(1967); WAY WEST, THE(1967); FIRECREEK(1968); NEVER A DULL MOMENT(1968); ONCE UPON A TIME IN THE WEST(1969, U.S./Ital.); RIDE A NORTHBOUND HORSE(1969); SUPPORT YOUR LOCAL SHERIFF(1969); COCKEYED COWBOYS OF CALICO COUNTY, THE(1970); DIRTY DINGUS MAGEE(1970); RIO LOBO(1970); HANNIE CALDER(1971, Brit.); LAST REBEL, THE(1971); SUPPORT YOUR LOCAL GUNFIGHTER(1971); WILD COUNTRY, THE(1971); PAT GARRETT AND BILLY THE KID(1973); CREATURE FROM BLACK LAKE, THE(1976); HAWMPS!(1976); PONY EXPRESS RIDER(1976); GRAYEAGLE(1977); HOT LEAD AND COLD FEET(1978); NORSEMAN, THE(1978); APPLE DUMPLING GANG RIDES AGAIN, THE(1979); VILLAIN, THE(1979); CANNONBALL RUN, THE(1981); JINXED!(1982); SOGGY BOTTOM U.S.A.(1982)

1984
CANNONBALL RUN II(1984); SACRED GROUND(1984)
Misc. Talkies
KNIFE FOR THE LADIES, A(1973); WINDS OF AUTUMN, THE(1976); LOST(1983)
Paulette Elambert
LA MATERNELLE(1933, Fr.); CRIME AND PUNISHMENT(1935, Fr.); MAN OF THE HOUR, THE(1940, Fr.)
Joan Elan
HELL IS SOLD OUT(1951, Brit.); GIRLS OF PLEASURE ISLAND, THE(1953); KING'S THIEF, THE(1955); DARBY'S RANGERS(1958)
Chris Eland
HELL ON WHEELS(1967)
Michael Eland
HELL IS EMPTY(1967, Brit./Ital.), p
Carol Elasz
Misc. Talkies
ROGUE AND GRIZZLY, THE(1982)
Ruth Elbaum
Misc. Talkies
MIRELE EFROS(1939)
Jan Elbein
CAPTURE THAT CAPSULE(1961), w
Istovn Elben
HIPPOLYT, THE LACKEY(1932, Hung.), ph
Istvan Elben
BLUE IDOL, THE(1931, Hung.), ph
Ed Elbert
PINK MOTEL(1983), p
Max Elbeze
GERVAISE(1956, Fr.)
Peter Elbing
WORLD'S GREATEST LOVER, THE(1977)
Peter Elbling
PRIVATE LESSONS(1981); DOCTOR DETROIT(1983); MAN WITH TWO BRAINS, THE(1983)
Yehuda Elboy
1984
SAHARA(1984)
Ed Elby
TILL THE CLOUDS ROLL BY(1946)
Dana Elcar
FAIL SAFE(1964); FOOL KILLER, THE(1965); LOVELY WAY TO DIE, A(1968); THE BOSTON STRANGLER, THE(1968); LEARNING TREE, THE(1969); MALTESE BIPPY, THE(1969); PENDULUM(1969); ADAM AT 6 A.M.(1970); SOLDIER BLUE(1970); ZIGZAG(1970); GUNFIGHT, A(1971); MRS. POLLIFAX-SPY(1971); GREAT NORTH-FIELD, MINNESOTA RAID, THE(1972); STING, THE(1973); REPORT TO THE COMMISSIONER(1975); BABY BLUE MARINE(1976); ST. IVES(1976); W.C. FIELDS AND ME(1976); CHAMP, THE(1979); GOOD LUCK, MISS WYCKOFF(1979); LAST FLIGHT OF NOAH'S ARK, THE(1980); NUDE BOMB, THE(1980); BUDDY BUDDY(1981); CONDORMAN(1981); BLUE SKIES AGAIN(1983)
1984
ALL OF ME(1984); JUNGLE WARRIORS(1984, U.S./Ger./Mex.); 2010(1984)
Misc. Talkies
METAMORPHOSIS(1951)
Ann Elder
ONE OF OUR SPIES IS MISSING(1966); DON'T MAKE WAVES(1967); FOR SINGLES ONLY(1968)
Boris Elder
TIGER GIRL(1955, USSR)
Charles Elder
CHANGE OF MIND(1969)
Silents
CAROLYN OF THE CORNERS(1919)
Misc. Silents
YANKEE WAY, THE(1917)
Clarence Elder
ABDUL THE DAMNED(1935, Brit.), art d; APRIL BLOSSOMS(1937, Brit.), set d; HEART'S DESIRE(1937, Brit.), art d; SILVER DARLINGS, THE(1947, Brit.), d, w
Jane Elder
FINGERS(1978)
John Elder
PHANTOM OF THE OPERA, THE(1962, Brit.), w; EVIL OF FRANKENSTEIN, THE(1964, Brit.), w; DRACULA-PRINCE OF DARKNESS(1966, Brit.), w; DRACULA HAS RISEN FROM HIS GRAVE(1968, Brit.), w; TASTE THE BLOOD OF DRACULA(1970, Brit.), w; GHOUL, THE(1975, Brit.), w
John Elder [Anthony Hinds]
CURSE OF THE WEREWOLF, THE(1961), w; KISS OF EVIL(1963, Brit.), w; FRANKENSTEIN CREATED WOMAN(1965, Brit.), w; PLAGUE OF THE ZOMBIES, THE(1966, Brit.), w; RASPUTIN-THE MAD MONK(1966, Brit.), w; REPTILE, THE(1966, Brit.), w; MUMMY'S SHROUD, THE(1967, Brit.), d&w; SCARS OF DRACULA, THE(1970, Brit.), w; FRANKENSTEIN AND THE MONSTER FROM HELL(1974, Brit.), w
Judyann Elder
MELINDA(1972)
Kevin Elder
FAHRENHEIT 451(1966, Brit.)
Lonne Elder
MELINDA(1972)
Lonne Elder III
MELINDA(1972), w; SOUNDER(1972), w; SOUNDER, PART 2(1976), w; BUSTIN' LOOSE(1981), w
Mary Elder
Misc. Silents
WINGED HORSEMAN, THE(1929)
Michael Elder
STAR PILOT(1977, Ital.), w
Patti Elder
ICE CASTLES(1978)

Patty Elder
RARE BREED, THE(1966); WHAT'S UP, DOC?(1972); TWO-MINUTE WARNING(1976)
Ray Elder
LAND OF THE OUTLAWS(1944); SONG OF OLD WYOMING(1945)
Ruth Elder
Misc. Silents
MORAN OF THE MARINES(1928)
Thomas Coutts Elder
Silents
BROKEN MELODY, THE(1929, Brit.), w
William Elder
HURRY SUNDOWN(1967)
Elder Lovelies
SQUARE DANCE JUBILEE(1949)
The Elderbloom Chorus
IT ALL CAME TRUE(1940)
Kevin Elders
1984
PURPLE HEARTS(1984)
Jim Elderton
TERROR(1979, Brit.), ed
J. Elderwills
PERFECT WOMAN, THE(1950, Brit.), art d
Gene Eldman
HI, MOM!(1970)
Gabi Eldor
JERUSALEM FILE, THE(1972, U.S./Israel)
Tom Eldred
TEENAGE GANG DEBS(1966)
Florence Eldredge
THIRTEEN WOMEN(1932); GREAT JASPER, THE(1933)
Frank Eldredge
YEARLING, THE(1946); GUN FIGHT(1961)
George Eldredge
HIS BROTHER'S WIFE(1936); SPECIAL AGENT K-7(1937); PAROLED FROM THE BIG HOUSE(1938); STAR MAKER, THE(1939); NORTHWEST PASSAGE(1940); GHOST OF FRANKENSTEIN, THE(1942); JOAN OF OZARK(1942); LIVING GHOST, THE(1942); SHERLOCK HOLMES AND THE SECRET WEAPON(1942); SILVER QUEEN(1942); THEY DIED WITH THEIR BOOTS ON(1942); CALLING DR. DEATH(1943); FRONTIER BADMEN(1943); FRONTIER LAW(1943); LONE STAR TRAIL, THE(1943); RAIDERS OF SAN JOAQUIN(1943); FOLLOW THE BOYS(1944); JAM SESSION(1944); OLD TEXAS TRAIL, THE(1944); ONCE UPON A TIME(1944); STORY OF DR. WASSELL, THE(1944); TRIGGER TRAIL(1944); FRONTIER GAL(1945); GREAT JOHN L. THE(1945); HONEYMOON AHEAD(1945); THERE GOES KELLY(1945); BANDIT OF SHERWOOD FOREST, THE(1946); BELOW THE DEAD-LINE(1946); DARK ALIBI(1946); DEVIL'S PLAYGROUND, THE(1946); HER ADVEN-TUROUS NIGHT(1946); IN FAST COMPANY(1946); LIVE WIRES(1946); SHADOWS OVER CHINATOWN(1946); DEAD RECKONING(1947); UNSUSPECTED, THE(1947); CAMPUS SLEUTH(1948); JINX MONEY(1948); SHANGHAI CHEST, THE(1948); QUICK ON THE TRIGGER(1949); SKY DRAGON(1949); CHAIN GANG(1950); FEDER-AL MAN(1950); HI-JACKED(1950); LOUISA(1950); ONE TOO MANY(1950); ROOKIE FIREMAN(1950); FINGERPRINTS DON'T LIE(1951); FURY OF THE CONGO(1951); SIERRA PASSAGE(1951); BRAVE WARRIOR(1952); CALIFORNIA CONQUEST(1952); DUEL AT SILVER CREEK, THE(1952); FLESH AND FURY(1952); JUNGLE JIM IN THE FORBIDDEN LAND(1952); JUST ACROSS THE STREET(1952); LOAN SHARK(1952); MEET DANNY WILSON(1952); MONKEY BUSINESS(1952); MY SIX CONVICTS(1952); NO HOLDS BARRED(1952); PHONE CALL FROM A STRAN-GER(1952); SPRINGFIELD RIFLE(1952); IT CAME FROM OUTER SPACE(1953); MAN FROM THE ALAMO, THE(1953); PICKUP ON SOUTH STREET(1953); VALLEY OF THE HEADHUNTERS(1953); DEMETRIUS AND THE GLADIATORS(1954); OVER-LAND PACIFIC(1954); RIDERS TO THE STARS(1954); WOMAN'S WORLD(1954); DIAL RED O(1955); MISTER CORY(1957); GANG WAR(1958); LIFE BEGINS AT 17(1958); LINEUP, THE(1958); ROOKIE, THE(1959); VICE RAID(1959); THIRD VOICE, THE(1960); AIR PATROL(1962)
Misc. Talkies
SONG OF THE RANGE(1944)
John Eldredge
FLIRTATION WALK(1934); MAN WITH TWO FACES, THE(1934); DR. SO-CRATES(1935); GIRL FROM TENTH AVENUE, THE(1935); GOOSE AND THE GANDER, THE(1935); MAN OF IRON(1935); OIL FOR THE LAMPS OF CHINA(1935); WHITE COCKATOO(1935); WOMAN IN RED, THE(1935); DANGEROUS(1936); FOL-LOW YOUR HEART(1936); MURDER BY AN ARISTOCRAT(1936); MURDER OF DR. HARRIGAN, THE(1936); SNOWED UNDER(1936); CHARLIE CHAN AT THE OLYM-PICS(1937); FAIR WARNING(1937); HOLY TERROR, THE(1937); MR. DODD TAKES THE AIR(1937); MYSTERIOUS CROSSING(1937); ONE MILE FROM HEAVEN(1937); SH! THE OCTOPUS(1937); WOMEN ARE LIKE THAT(1938); BLIND ALLEY(1939); KING OF THE UNDERWORLD(1939); PERSONS IN HIDING(1939); PRIVATE DE-TECTIVE(1939); TELEVISION SPY(1939); UNDERCOVER DOCTOR(1939); ALWAYS A BRIDE(1940); DEVIL'S PIPELINE, THE(1940); DR. KILDARE'S STRANGE CA-SE(1940); MARINES FLY HIGH, THE(1940); SON OF ROARING DAN(1940); BLACK CAT, THE(1941); BLOSSOMS IN THE DUST(1941); FLIGHT FROM DESTINY(1941); HIGH SIERRA(1941); HORROR ISLAND(1941); LIFE BEGINS FOR ANDY HAR-DY(1941); MAD DOCTOR OF MARKET STREET, THE(1942); MADAME SPY(1942); SABOTEUR(1942); TOUGH AS THEY COME(1942); SWING OUT THE BLUES(1943); BEAUTIFUL BUT BROKE(1944); BERMUDA MYSTERY(1944); DANGEROUS PAS-SAGE(1944); SONG OF NEVADA(1944); BAD MEN OF THE BORDER(1945); CIRCUM-STANTIAL EVIDENCE(1945); DANGEROUS PARTNERS(1945); EVE KNEW HER APPLES(1945); DARK ALIBI(1946); FRENCH KEY, THE(1946); I RING DOOR-BELLS(1946); LITTLE MISS BIG(1946); LIVE WIRES(1946); PASSKEY TO DAN-GER(1946); SWING PARADE OF 1946(1946); TEMPTATION(1946); UP GOES MAISIE(1946); CARTER CASE, THE(1947); SECOND CHANCE(1947); SEVEN WERE SAVED(1947); ANGELS ALLEY(1948); JINX MONEY(1948); SEALED VER-DICT(1948); SMART WOMAN(1948); WHISPERING SMITH(1948); SKY DRA-GON(1949); SQUARE DANCE JUBILEE(1949); STAMPEDE(1949); TOP O' THE MORNING(1949); CHAMPAGNE FOR CAESAR(1950); LONELY HEARTS BAN-DITS(1950); RUSTLERS ON HORSEBACK(1950); UNMASKED(1950); INSURANCE INVESTIGATOR(1951); LAW AND THE LADY, THE(1951); NIGHT INTO MOR-NING(1951); STREET BANDITS(1951); SCARAMOUCHE(1952); SNIPER, THE(1952); INVADERS FROM MARS(1953); MA AND PA KETTLE ON VACATION(1953);

LOOPHOLE(1954); RACING BLOOD(1954); TOUGHEST MAN ALIVE(1955); SOME-
BODY UP THERE LIKES ME(1956); RAINTREE COUNTY(1957); I MARRIED A
MONSTER FROM OUTER SPACE(1958); FIVE GUNS TO TOMBSTONE(1961)
Misc. Talkies
ALL THAT I HAVE(1951)
Freddy Eldrett
REACH FOR GLORY(1963, Brit.)
Anthony Eldridge
HUSTLE(1975)
Charles Eldridge
Silents
WHEELS OF JUSTICE(1915); AS IN A LOOKING GLASS(1916); PRETENDERS,
THE(1916); HIS FATHER'S SON(1917); POLLY OF THE CIRCUS(1917); CHALLENGE
ACCEPTED, THE(1918); EYE FOR EYE(1918); ASHAMED OF PARENTS(1921); MADE
IN HEAVEN(1921); NO TRESPASSING(1922)
Misc. Silents
MAN WHO COULD'T BEAT GOD, THE(1915); SPORTING LIFE(1918); BIRTH OF A
SOUL, THE(1920)
E.M. Eldridge
Misc. Silents
FORBIDDEN GRASS(1928), d
Florence Eldridge
CHARMING SINNERS(1929); GREENE MURDER CASE, THE(1929); STUDIO MUR-
DER MYSTERY, THE(1929); DIVORCEE, THE(1930); MATRIMONIAL BED,
THE(1930); DANGEROUSLY YOURS(1933); STORY OF TEMPLE DRAKE, THE(1933);
MODERN HERO, A(1934); LES MISERABLES(1935); MARY OF SCOTLAND(1936);
ACT OF MURDER, AN(1948); ANOTHER PART OF THE FOREST(1948); CHRISTO-
PHER COLUMBUS(1949, Brit.); INHERIT THE WIND(1960)
Misc. Silents
SIX CYLINDER LOVE(1923)
Francis Eldridge
Silents
ARE CHILDREN TO BLAME?(1922)
Frank Eldridge
THEY WERE EXPENDABLE(1945); YOUNG BESS(1953)
George Eldridge
CORPSE VANISHES, THE(1942); TENTING TONIGHT ON THE OLD CAMP
GROUND(1943); OKLAHOMA RAIDERS(1944); OUTLAW TRAIL(1944); RETURN OF
THE APE MAN(1944); SONORA STAGECOACH(1944); FALSE PARADISE(1948);
MOM AND DAD(1948); LET'S GO NAVY(1951); PSYCHO(1960)
Misc. Talkies
BUZZY RIDES THE RANGE(1940); TAKE ME BACK TO OKLAHOMA(1940);
RUSTLERS OF THE BADLANDS(1945)
James Henry Eldridge
SKULLDUGGERY(1970)
John Eldridge
GO-GETTER, THE(1937); BACKLASH(1947); POOL OF LONDON(1951, Brit.), w;
BRANDY FOR THE PARSON(1952, Brit.), d; FUSS OVER FEATHERS(1954, Brit.), d;
SCOTCH ON THE ROCKS(1954, Brit.), d, w; FIRST TRAVELING SALESLADY,
THE(1956); ONE WISH TOO MANY(1956, Brit.), w; DECISION AGAINST TIME(1957,
Brit.), w; KID FROM CANADA, THE(1957, Brit.), w; OUT OF THE CLOUDS(1957,
Brit.), w; SMALLEST SHOW ON EARTH, THE(1957, Brit.), w; CAT GANG, THE(1959,
Brit.), w; BOY WHO STOLE A MILLION, THE(1960, Brit.), w; FRECKLES(1960);
OPERATION AMSTERDAM(1960, Brit.), w; SOME PEOPLE(1964, Brit.), w
Nick Eldridge
NORTHERN LIGHTS(1978)
Phyllis Eldridge
TRUMAN CAPOTE'S TRILOGY(1969)
Arnold Eldus
WRONG DAMN FILM, THE(1975), m
Mary Eleanor [Elinor Donahue]
MR. BIG(1943)
Electric Chairs
JUBILEE(1978, Brit.), m
Joseph Elena
DREAM NO MORE(1950, Palestine), ed
N. Elenbogen
SONG OVER MOSCOW(1964, USSR), makeup
Suesie Elene
Misc. Talkies
DAMIEN'S ISLAND(1976)
Susie Elene
REVENGE OF THE CHEERLEADERS(1976)
Erika Eleniak
E.T. THE EXTRA-TERRESTRIAL(1982)
John Elerick
EARTHQUAKE(1974); EMBRYO(1976)
Minnie Elerick
URBAN COWBOY(1980)
Bela Eles
CONFIDENCE(1980, Hung.)
Sandor Eles
CALL ME GENIUS(1961, Brit.); NAKED EDGE, THE(1961); GUNS OF DARK-
NESS(1962, Brit.); EVIL OF FRANKENSTEIN, THE(1964, Brit.); FRENCH DRESS-
ING(1964, Brit.); MAGNIFICENT TWO, THE(1967, Brit.); AND SOON THE
DARKNESS(1970, Brit.); KREMLIN LETTER, THE(1970); 1,000 CONVICTS AND A
WOMAN(1971, Brit.); COUNTESS DRACULA(1972, Brit.); SCORPIO(1973); LOVE AND
DEATH(1975); GREEK TYCOON, THE(1978)
Zev Eletheriou
PIRATE MOVIE, THE(1982, Aus.)
Martin Elfand
DOG DAY AFTERNOON(1975), p; IT'S MY TURN(1980), p; OFFICER AND A
GENTLEMAN, AN(1982), p
Marty Elfand
KANSAS CITY BOMBER(1972), p
Clifford S. Elfelt
Silents
UNDER FIRE(1926), d

Misc. Silents
BIG STAKES(1922), d; FLAMING HEARTS(1922), d; DANGER(1923), d; $50,000
Reward(1924), d; FIGHTING COURAGE(1925), d
Conrad Elfers
FUNERAL IN BERLIN(1966, Brit.), m
Konrad Elfers
INSIDE OUT(1975, Brit.), m
David Elfick
NEWSFRONT(1979, Aus.), p; PALM BEACH(1979, Aus.); CHAIN REACTION(1980,
Aus.), p; STARSTRUCK(1982, Aus.), p
Danny Elfman
HOT TOMORROWS(1978); FORBIDDEN ZONE(1980), m
Marie Elfman
HOT TOMORROWS(1978)
Marie-Pascale Elfman
FORBIDDEN ZONE(1980), a, prod d
Richard Elfman
FORBIDDEN ZONE(1980), p&d
Owen Elford
ALL IN A NIGHT'S WORK(1961), w
John Elfstrom
RAILROAD WORKERS(1948, Swed.); LESSON IN LOVE, A(1960, Swed.); NIGHT IS
MY FUTURE(1962, Swed.)
Katherine Elfstrom
PEER GYNT(1965)
Robert Elfstrom
HI, MOM!(1970), ph; GOSPEL ROAD, THE(1973), a, d, ph
Robert Elfstrom, Jr.
GOSPEL ROAD, THE(1973)
Kerstin Elg
VICTOR FRANKENSTEIN(1975, Swed./Ireland), makeup
Taina Elg
DIANE(1955); PRODIGAL, THE(1955); GABY(1956); LES GIRLS(1957); IMITATION
GENERAL(1958); WATUSI(1959); THIRTY NINE STEPS, THE(1960, Brit.); BAC-
CHANTES, THE(1963, Fr./Ital.)
Tania Elg
HERCULES IN NEW YORK(1970)
Otto Elg-Lundberg
Misc. Silents
SAGA OF GOSTA BERLING, THE(1924, Fr.)
Anthony Elgar
ROOM AT THE TOP(1959, Brit.)
Avril Elgar
ROOM AT THE TOP(1959, Brit.); LADIES WHO DO(1964, Brit.); SPRING AND PORT
WINE(1970, Brit.); MEDUSA TOUCH, THE(1978, Brit.)
Harold Elgar
BREAKING AWAY(1979)
Peter Elgar
MY FATHER'S HOUSE(1947, Palestine), ed
Sir Edward Elgar
YOUNG WINSTON(1972, Brit.), m
Les Elgart
SENIOR PROM(1958)
Ingrid Elhardt
DAY THE EARTH FROZE, THE(1959, Fin./USSR)
Kay Elhardt
DR. GOLDFOOT AND THE BIKINI MACHINE(1965)
Kaye Elhardt
CRIMSON KIMONO, THE(1959); PSYCHOMANIA(1964)
John Elhert
NATIVE SON(1951, U.S., Arg.), m
Lovie Eli
1984
ICEMAN(1984)
Valeria Elia
THRESHOLD(1983, Can.)
Jona Elian
DIAMONDS(1975, U.S./Israel)
Yona Elian
JERUSALEM FILE, THE(1972, U.S./Israel)
Alix Elias
JOHN AND MARY(1969); CITIZENS BAND(1977); FISH THAT SAVED PITTS-
BURGH, THE(1979); ROCK 'N' ROLL HIGH SCHOOL(1979); PANDEMONIUM(1982);
NIGHT IN HEAVEN, A(1983)
Arie Elias
JERUSALEM FILE, THE(1972, U.S./Israel); KAZABLAN(1974, Israel)
Buddy Elias
MAGICIAN OF LUBLIN, THE(1979, Israel/Ger.)
Cesar Elias
MIRAGE(1972, Peru)
Cyrus Elias
FIVE BRANDED WOMEN(1960); FRANCIS OF ASSISI(1961); ECLIPSE(1962, Fr./
Ital.); HERCULES, SAMSON & ULYSSES(1964, Ital.); PULP(1972, Brit.); PRIEST OF
LOVE(1981, Brit.); HANNAH K.(1983, Fr.); LONELY LADY, THE(1983)
Hector Elias
BANG THE DRUM SLOWLY(1973); MASTER GUNFIGHTER, THE(1975); HERO-
ES(1977); DEADLY FORCE(1983); LOSIN' IT(1983)
Jeannie Elias
BY DESIGN(1982)
Misc. Talkies
PIT, THE(1984)
John Elias
COMPANY OF KILLERS(1970), ed
Jonathan Elias
1984
ALMOST YOU(1984), m; CHILDREN OF THE CORN(1984), m
Louie Elias
TICKLE ME(1965); POSSE(1975); APPLE DUMPLING GANG RIDES AGAIN,
THE(1979)

Louis Elias
STILETTO(1969); VANISHING POINT(1971), stunts; NIGHT MOVES(1975)
Luiz Elias
PIXOTE(1981, Braz.), ed
Michael Elias
FRISCO KID, THE(1979), w; JERK, THE(1979), w; SERIAL(1980), w; YOUNG DOCTORS IN LOVE(1982), w
Michael T. Elias
JAWS II(1978), ed
Mike Elias
NIGHT THEY RAIDED MINSKY'S, THE(1968); APPLE DUMPLING GANG RIDES AGAIN, THE(1979)
Mike M. Elias
1984
BEAR, THE(1984)
Mirjam Elias
TWO WORLD(1930, Brit.)
Robert Elias
MEXICAN HAYRIDE(1948)
Stacie Elias
APPLE DUMPLING GANG RIDES AGAIN, THE(1979)
William Elias
1984
JOY OF SEX(1984), ed
K. Eliasberg
SUN SHINES FOR ALL, THE(1961, USSR), md
Joyce Eliason
TELL ME A RIDDLE(1980), w
Garth Eliassen
HEART BEAT(1979)
E. Eliazaroff
Silents
HIS HOUR(1924)
Josip Elic
MURDER, INC.(1960); CONVICTS FOUR(1962); THIRD OF A MAN(1962); SANTA CLAUS CONQUERS THE MARTIANS(1964); PRODUCERS, THE(1967); FOR LOVE OF IVY(1968); TRUMAN CAPOTE'S TRILOGY(1969); WHO IS HARRY KELLERMAN AND WHY IS HE SAYING THOSE TERRIBLE THINGS ABOUT ME?(1971); DIRTY LITTLE BILLY(1972); STOOLIE, THE(1972); ONE FLEW OVER THE CUCKOO'S NEST(1975)
Josip Elie
WORLD'S GREATEST LOVER, THE(1977)
Willie P. Elie
FINGER ON THE TRIGGER(1965, US/Span.); NUN AT THE CROSSROADS, A(1970, Ital./Span.)
Lise Elina
RULES OF THE GAME, THE(1939, Fr.)
Mary Eline
Silents
UNCLE TOM'S CABIN(1914)
Carli D. Elinor
WOMEN OF ALL NATIONS(1931), md
Carli Elinor
BRIDGE OF SAN LUIS REY, THE(1929), m; MY FAVORITE SPY(1942); THRILL OF A ROMANCE(1945); WEEKEND AT THE WALDORF(1945); GILDA(1946); MALAYA(1950); MA AND PA KETTLE ON VACATION(1953)
Carlie Elinor
Silents
HEARTS OF THE WORLD(1918), m
Irving Elinson
SHOW BUSINESS(1944), w; BELLE OF NEW YORK, THE(1952), w; BY THE LIGHT OF THE SILVERY MOON(1953), w; LUCKY ME(1954), w
Lawrence Elion
RECOMMENDATION FOR MERCY(1975, Can.)
Nicholas Eliopoulous
BEST LITTLE WHOREHOUSE IN TEXAS, THE(1982), ed
Tom Elios
UNMARRIED WOMAN, AN(1978)
Alex Eliot
WILD WHEELS(1969); HARD ROAD, THE(1970)
Arthur Eliot
Silents
BETTER 'OLE, THE(1926), w
George Eliot
MILL ON THE FLOSS(1939, Brit.), w
Silents
ADAM BEDE(1918, Brit.), w; ROMOLA(1925), w
Helen Eliot
SNIPER, THE(1952); PAL JOEY(1957)
John Eliot
SECRETS OF SEX(1970, Brit.), w
Kathleen Eliot
PAROLED-TO DIE(1938); WEST OF RAINBOW'S END(1938)
Maj. George F. Eliot
FEDERAL BULLETS(1937), w
Rosemary Eliot
WILD AND THE INNOCENT, THE(1959); UP THE ACADEMY(1980)
T. S. Eliot
MURDER IN THE CATHEDRAL(1952, Brit.), a, w
Terry Eliot
WHISPERERS, THE(1967, Brit.)
Dick Eliott
CHINA PASSAGE(1937)
Gerald Eliott
SONS OF THE SEA(1939, Brit.), w
John Eliott
MARRYING KIND, THE(1952)

Peter Eliott
Misc. Talkies
DIRTIEST GIRL I EVER MET, THE(1973)
Tim Eliott
SHIRLEY THOMPSON VERSUS THE ALIENS(1968, Aus.)
Daniel Elis
1984
PERILS OF GWENDOLINE, THE(1984, Fr.), cos
Paul Elis
IN OLD CALIFORNIA(1929)
Elisaveta
ELVIS! ELVIS!(1977, Swed.)
Edward Eliscu
PROFESSIONAL SWEETHEART(1933), m; MUSIC IS MAGIC(1935), w; PADDY O'DAY(1935), w; SILK HAT KID(1935), w; EVERY SATURDAY NIGHT(1936), w; HIGH TENSION(1936), w; LITTLE MISS NOBODY(1936), w; HIS EXCITING NIGHT(1938), w; LITTLE TOUGH GUYS IN SOCIETY(1938), w; SIS HOPKINS(1941), w; SOMETHING TO SHOUT ABOUT(1943), w; HEY, ROOKIE(1944), w; GAY SENORITA, THE(1945), w; OUT OF THE BLUE(1947), w; THREE HUSBANDS(1950), w; ALICE IN WONDERLAND(1951, Fr.), w
Fernanda Eliscu
WINTERSET(1936); SONG OF BERNADETTE, THE(1943); GILDA(1946); DESIRE ME(1947); DOUBLE LIFE, A(1947); UNCONQUERED(1947); HARBOR OF MISSING MEN(1950); VIVA ZAPATA!(1952); CHARGE OF THE LANCERS(1953)
Fernanda Eliscuo
REMAINS TO BE SEEN(1953)
Elise-Anne
SATAN'S MISTRESS(1982)
Catherine Elison
DOCTOR ZHIVAGO(1965)
Elizabeth
FEMALE TROUBLE(1975)
Elizabeth of Toro
1984
SHEENA(1984)
"Elizabeth" [Mary Annette Beauchamp Russell]
ENCHANTED APRIL(1935), w; MR. SKEFFINGTON(1944), w
Joaquin Elizando
HOLLOW TRIUMPH(1948)
Elias Elizaroff
Silents
GOLD RUSH, THE(1925)
Joaquin Elizonda
LOVES OF CARMEN, THE(1948)
Evangelina Elizondo
LOS PLATILLOS VOLADORES(1955, Mex.); CASTLE OF THE MONSTERS(1958, Mex.); CHIQUTTO PERO PICOSO(1967, Mex.)
Fernando Elizondo
UNDER FIRE(1983)
Hector Elizondo
TAKING OF PELHAM ONE, TWO, THREE, THE(1974); VIXENS, THE(1969); LANDLORD, THE(1970); BORN TO WIN(1971); VALDEZ IS COMING(1971); POCKET MONEY(1972); STAND UP AND BE COUNTED(1972); REPORT TO THE COMMISSIONER(1975); THIEVES(1977); CUBA(1979); AMERICAN GIGOLO(1980); FAN, THE(1981); DEADHEAD MILES(1982); YOUNG DOCTORS IN LOVE(1982)
1984
FLAMINGO KID, THE(1984)
Humberton Elizondo
1984
ERENDIRA(1984, Mex./Fr./Ger.)
Joaquin Elizondo
CORNERED(1945); TWILIGHT ON THE RIO GRANDE(1947); STREETS OF LAREDO(1949)
Rene Elizondo
1984
BODY ROCK(1984)
Ben Black Elk
HOW THE WEST WAS WON(1962)
Jim Elk
WAVELENGTH(1983)
Lois Red Elk
ONE LITTLE INDIAN(1973); JOE PANTHER(1976)
Edward Elkas
Silents
ALADDIN'S OTHER LAMP(1917); JOAN OF PLATTSBURG(1918); LES MISERABLES(1918); PRUNELLA(1918); OAKDALE AFFAIR, THE(1919); SAINTED DEVIL, A(1924)
Misc. Silents
MORTMAIN(1915); DOLLAR AND THE LAW, THE(1916); PHANTOM FORTUNES, THE(1916); MONEY MILL, THE(1917); MORAL COURAGE(1917); HOUSE OF THE TOLLING BELLS, THE(1920)
Mahmoud Abu Elkhair
1984
LITTLE DRUMMER GIRL, THE(1984)
Bob Elkin
GEEK MAGGOT BINGO(1983)
Clifford Elkin
LISA(1962, Brit.); CRIMSON BLADE, THE(1964, Brit.)
Elkin/Universal
SSSSSSSS(1973), spec eff
Mort W. Elkind
INTERNECINE PROJECT, THE(1974, Brit.), w
Rachel Elkind
SHINING, THE(1980), m
Bud Elkins
THING WITH TWO HEADS, THE(1972), stunts
Don Elkins
FORCE BEYOND, THE(1978)

Flora Elkins
DOUBLE-BARRELLED DETECTIVE STORY, THE(1965)
Hillard Elkins
ALICE'S RESTAURANT(1969), p; DOLL'S HOUSE, A(1973), p
Jack Elkins
CAPE FEAR(1962)
Judy Elkins
RAIDERS OF THE LOST ARK(1981), anim
Liston Elkins
TENDER WARRIOR, THE(1971)
Michael Elkins
ESTHER AND THE KING(1960, U.S./Ital.), w; DOG EAT DOG(1963, U.S./Ger./Ital.), w
Mignon Elkins
LIES MY FATHER TOLD ME(1975, Can.); LOVE AT FIRST SIGHT(1977, Can.); IN PRAISE OF OLDER WOMEN(1978, Can.)
Peter Elkins
IT HAPPENED HERE(1966, Brit.)
Richard Elkins
NUMBER ONE(1969); ...TICK...TICK...TICK...(1970)
Robert Elkins
COAL MINER'S DAUGHTER(1980)
Roy Elkins
MARINES COME THROUGH, THE(1943)
Saul Elkins
CRIME OF DR. FORBES(1936), w; STAR FOR A NIGHT(1936), w; UNDER YOUR SPELL(1936), w; TARNISHED ANGEL(1938), w; WOMEN IN PRISON(1938), w; OFF THE RECORD(1939), w; PRIDE OF THE NAVY(1939), w; BIG PUNCH, THE(1948), p; EMBRACEABLE YOU(1948), p; SMART GIRLS DON'T TALK(1948), p; FLAXY MARTIN(1949), p; HOMICIDE(1949), p; HOUSE ACROSS THE STREET, THE(1949), p; ONE LAST FLING(1949), p; YOUNGER BROTHERS, THE(1949), p; BARRICADE(1950), p; COLT .45(1950), p; RETURN OF THE FRONTIERSMAN(1950), p; THIS SIDE OF THE LAW(1950), p; RATON PASS(1951), p; SUGARFOOT(1951), p
Stanley Elkins
ALEX AND THE GYPSY(1976), w
Aina Elkman
DOLLAR(1938, Swed.)
Jack Elkubi
SUPERSONIC MAN(1979, Span.), spec eff
Coco Ellacott
BEYOND THE REEF(1981), ch
Joan Ellacott
SNOWBOUND(1949, Brit.), cos; UP TO HIS NECK(1954, Brit.), cos; DOCTOR AT SEA(1955, Brit.), cos; SUDDENLY, LAST SUMMER(1959, Brit.), cos; CAPTAIN'S TABLE, THE(1960, Brit.), cos; PICCADILLY THIRD STOP(1960, Brit.), cos; BEWARE OF CHILDREN(1961, Brit.), cos; CARRY ON REGARDLESS(1961, Brit.), cos; CIRCLE OF DECEPTON(1961, Brit.), cos; LEAGUE OF GENTLEMEN, THE(1961, Brit.), cos; UPSTAIRS AND DOWNSTAIRS(1961, Brit.), cos; WATCH YOUR STERN(1961, Brit.), cos; CARRY ON CABBIE(1963, Brit.), cos; SWINGIN' MAIDEN, THE(1963, Brit.), cos; IN THE DOGHOUSE(1964, Brit.), cos; STITCH IN TIME, A(1967, Brit.), cos
Alan Elledge
WATERLOO(1970, Ital./USSR)
Barbara Ellen
Misc. Talkies
MAN OUTSIDE(1965)
Cliff Ellen
PETERSEN(1974, Aus.)
Jack Ellen
HEADLESS GHOST, THE(1959, Brit.)
Vera Ellen
LET'S BE HAPPY(1957, Brit.)
Harrison Ellenshaw
WATCHER IN THE WOODS, THE(1980, Brit.), prod d; TRON(1982), spec eff
Paul Ellenshaw
MAN WHO FELL TO EARTH, THE(1976, Brit.), spec eff
Peter Ellenshaw
TREASURE ISLAND(1950, Brit.), art d; 20,000 LEAGUES UNDER THE SEA(1954), art d; JOHNNY TREMAIN(1957), prod d; DARBY O'GILL AND THE LITTLE PEOPLE(1959), spec eff; KIDNAPPED(1960), spec eff; ABSENT-MINDED PROFESSOR, THE(1961), spec eff; IN SEARCH OF THE CASTAWAYS(1962, Brit.), spec eff; SON OF FLUBBER(1963), spec eff; SUMMER MAGIC(1963), spec eff; MARY POPPINS(1964), spec eff; FIGHTING PRINCE OF DONEGAL, THE(1966, Brit.), spec eff; LT. ROBIN CRUSOE, U.S.N.(1966), spec eff; HAPPIEST MILLIONAIRE, THE(1967), spec eff; BLACKBEARD'S GHOST(1968), art d; LOVE BUG, THE(1968), spec eff; BEDKNOBS AND BROOMSTICKS(1971), art d; ISLAND AT THE TOP OF THE WORLD, THE(1974), prod d; BLACK HOLE, THE(1979), prod d
David Ellenstein
VAN, THE(1977)
Peter Ellenstein
LAST AMERICAN VIRGIN, THE(1982)
1984
WEEKEND PASS(1984)
Robert Ellenstein
3:10 TO YUMA(1957); ROGUE COP(1954); ILLEGAL(1955); GARMENT JUNGLE, THE(1957); TOO MUCH, TOO SOON(1958); YOUNG LIONS, THE(1958); GAZEBO, THE(1959); NORTH BY NORTHWEST(1959); PAY OR DIE(1960); KING OF THE ROARING TWENTIES–THE STORY OF ARNOLD ROTHSTEIN(1961); DEATHWATCH(1966); LEGEND OF LYLAH CLARE, THE(1968); LOVE AT FIRST BITE(1979)
Elliott Ellentuck
1984
NINJA III–THE DOMINATION(1984), art d
Carl Eller
OUTFIT, THE(1973); BLACK SIX, THE(1974)
Henry Eller
OPERATION DELILAH(1966, U.S./Span.), p
Kermit Eller
SCARED TO DEATH(1981)

Mary Eller
MR. SUPERINVISIBLE(1974, Ital./Span./Ger.), w
Robert Eller
DEVIL TIGER(1934)
Harry Ellerbe
MISLEADING LADY, THE(1932); SO RED THE ROSE(1935); MAGNETIC MONSTER, THE(1953); YOUNG LIONS, THE(1958); MAN WHO UNDERSTOOD WOMEN, THE(1959); HOUSE OF USHER(1960)
Harry Ellerbee
MURDER ON A HONEYMOON(1935); DESK SET(1957)
Harry Ellerby
HAUNTED PALACE, THE(1963)
Tina Ellers
BOCCACCIO(1936, Ger.)
Sid Ellery
UNDER THE GREENWOOD TREE(1930, Brit.)
Fred Elles
MRS. PYM OF SCOTLAND YARD(1939, Brit.), d, w
Nick Ellesworth
REMEMBRANCE(1982, Brit.)
Roy Ellett
CAESAR AND CLEOPATRA(1946, Brit.)
Mickey Elley
EASY COME, EASY GO(1967)
Frank Elli
RIOT(1969), w
Yvonne Elliman
JESUS CHRIST, SUPERSTAR(1973); SGT. PEPPER'S LONELY HEARTS CLUB BAND(1978)
Stanley Ellin
BIG NIGHT, THE(1951), w; WEB OF PASSION(1961, Fr.), w; NOTHING BUT THE BEST(1964, Brit.), w; SUNBURN(1979), w
Tom Elling
1984
ELEMENT OF CRIME, THE(1984, Den.), ph
William Ellingford
Silents
ONE SHOT ROSS(1917); LORD LOVES THE IRISH, THE(1919); CYCLONE, THE(1920)
Misc. Silents
CACTUS CRANDALL(1918); PAYING HIS DEBT(1918); ONCE TO EVERY WOMAN(1920); ROAD TO DIVORCE, THE(1920)
Dave Ellingson
Misc. Talkies
LEGEND OF ALFRED PACKER, THE(1979)
Hester Ellingsworth
YOICKS!(1932, Brit.)
Duke Ellington
ANATOMY OF A MURDER(1959), a, m; PARIS BLUES(1961), m; ASSAULT ON A QUEEN(1966), m; CHANGE OF MIND(1969), m; ROUGH CUT(1980, Brit.), m; CITY NEWS(1983), m
E.A. Ellington
IRISH EYES ARE SMILING(1944), w; GILDA(1946), w
Elmer Ellingwood
PURSUED(1947)
Helmert Ellingwood
OBJECTIVE, BURMA!(1945)
Tom Ellingwood
LATE LIZ, THE(1971), makeup; DILLINGER(1973), makeup; SMOKEY AND THE BANDIT(1977), makeup
1984
CITY HEAT(1984), makeup
Dick Ellioit
HOLD THAT HYPNOTIST(1957)
John Ellioit
HOLD THAT CO-ED(1938)
Elliot
ONCE UPON A SCOUNDREL(1973), p
Adelaide Elliot
Silents
ANN'S FINISH(1918)
Alice Elliot
Misc. Silents
SLEEPING LION, THE(1919); SUNDOWN TRAIL, THE(1919)
Beda Elliot
SO FINE(1981)
Biff Elliot
I, THE JURY(1953); HOUSE OF BAMBOO(1955); BETWEEN HEAVEN AND HELL(1956); ENEMY BELOW, THE(1957); TRUE STORY OF JESSE JAMES, THE(1957); PORK CHOP HILL(1959); STORY ON PAGE ONE, THE(1959); HARD RIDE, THE(1971); KOTCH(1971); FRONT PAGE, THE(1974)
Bill Elliot
DESIRABLE(1934); BROADWAY GONDOLIER(1935); GOOSE AND THE GANDER, THE(1935); LIVING ON VELVET(1935); SOLDIER, SAILOR(1944, Brit.)
Clyde E. Elliot
BOOLOO(1938), p&d, w
Courtenay Elliot
ASSAULT(1971, Brit.), cos
Dick Elliot
SCATTERGOOD SURVIVES A MURDER(1942); DEADLINE AT DAWN(1946); HOT CARGO(1946); DUDE GOES WEST, THE(1948); ROSE OF THE YUKON(1949)
Duncan Elliot
GENTLEMEN MARRY BRUNETTES(1955)
Edythe Elliot
DICK TRACY(1945)
Francis Perry Elliot
Silents
HAUNTED PAJAMAS(1917), w

Frank Elliot
BULLDOG DRUMMOND ESCAPES(1937); ZIS BOOM BAH(1941); EMPEROR WALTZ, THE(1948); FUNNY THING HAPPENED ON THE WAY TO THE FORUM, A(1966)
Silents
JOHN NEEDHAM'S DOUBLE(1916); MARRIAGE OF WILLIAM ASHE, THE(1921); GARRISON'S FINISH(1923); LOVE'S WILDERNESS(1924); DARK ANGEL, THE(1925); LADY FROM HELL, THE(1926); EASY VIRTUE(1927, Brit.)
Misc. Silents
HIGH ROAD, THE(1915)
George Elliot
Misc. Silents
RANCHERS, THE(1923)
Gertrude Elliot
Silents
HAMLET(1913, Brit.)
Gordon Elliott
BROADWAY SCANDALS(1929); GREAT DIVIDE, THE(1930); NIGHT AFTER NIGHT(1932); HERE COMES THE NAVY(1934); REGISTERED NURSE(1934); MAN OF IRON(1935); PERSONAL MAID'S SECRET(1935); CASE OF THE BLACK CAT, THE(1936); DOWN THE STRETCH(1936); MOONLIGHT ON THE PRAIRIE(1936); MURDER BY AN ARISTOCRAT(1936); MURDER OF DR. HARRIGAN, THE(1936); STORY OF LOUIS PASTEUR, THE(1936); BOOTS AND SADDLES(1937); BOY OF THE STREETS(1937); FUGITIVE IN THE SKY(1937); MELODY FOR TWO(1937); MID-NIGHT COURT(1937); SWING IT, PROFESSOR(1937)
Silents
ARIZONA WILDCAT(1927)
Misc. Silents
BEYOND LONDON LIGHTS(1928); PASSION SONG, THE(1928)
Gordon [Bill] Elliot
EAST IS WEST(1930); JEWEL ROBBERY(1932); KEYHOLE, THE(1933); DOCTOR MONICA(1934); HOUSEWIFE(1934); TWENTY MILLION SWEETHEARTS(1934); WONDER BAR(1934); ALIBI IKE(1935); CEILNG ZERO(1935); DEVIL DOGS OF THE AIR(1935); DR. SOCRATES(1935); G-MEN(1935); GIRL FROM TENTH AVENUE, THE(1935); I FOUND STELLA PARISH(1935); I LIVE FOR LOVE(1935); PAGE MISS GLORY(1935); SECRET BRIDE, THE(1935); STARS OVER BROADWAY(1935); TRAV-ELING SALESLADY, THE(1935); WOMAN IN RED, THE(1935); BULLETS OR BALLOTS(1936); CHINA CLIPPER(1936); DANGEROUS(1936); POLO JOE(1936); TRAILIN' WEST(1936); GUNS OF THE PECOS(1937); LOVE TAKES FLIGHT(1937); SPEED TO SPARE(1937); WIFE, DOCTOR AND NURSE(1937); YOU CAN'T HAVE EVERYTHING(1937); DEVIL'S PARTY, THE(1938); LADY IN THE MORGUE(1938); LETTER OF INTRODUCTION(1938); ROLL ALONG, COWBOY(1938)
Misc. Talkies
IN OLD LOS ANGELES(1948)
Greg Elliot
ROLLERCOASTER(1977)
Jane Elliot
CHANGE OF HABIT(1969); ONE IS A LONELY NUMBER(1972)
Jerry Elliot
LIFE OF RILEY, THE(1949)
Jill Elliot
Misc. Talkies
ENDGAME(1984)
John Elliot
DUGAN OF THE BAD LANDS(1931); AVENGING WATERS(1936); BARS OF HATE(1936); DEATH IN THE SKY(1937); RIO GRANDE RANGER(1937); LAND OF THE OPEN RANGE(1941); TWO FISTED JUSTICE(1943); FIGHTING VIGILANTES, THE(1947); WIZARD OF GORE, THE(1970)
Misc. Talkies
NO DIAMONDS FOR URSULA(1967)
Silents
ARE ALL MEN ALIKE?(1920); HER WINNING WAY(1921); EAGLE'S FEATHER, THE(1923)
Kathleen Elliot
STARS OVER ARIZONA(1937)
Laura Elliot
SAMSON AND DELILAH(1949); SPECIAL AGENT(1949); GIRLS' SCHOOL(1950); PAID IN FULL(1950); UNION STATION(1950); HERE COMES THE GROOM(1951); PLACE IN THE SUN, A(1951); SILVER CITY(1951); WHEN WORLDS COLLIDE(1951); DENVER AND RIO GRANDE(1952); SOMETHING TO LIVE FOR(1952); JAMAICA RUN(1953); FRENCH LINE, THE(1954)
Lillian Elliot
TRUMPET BLOWS, THE(1934); BOY'S REFORMATORY(1939); HEROES IN BLUE(1939); ON THE SPOT(1940)
Silents
LAVENDER AND OLD LACE(1921)
Marianna Elliot
BLUE THUNDER(1983), cos
Mark Elliot
PRIVATES ON PARADE(1982)
1984
PRIVATES ON PARADE(1984, Brit.)
Maxine Elliot
Silents
ETERNAL MAGDALENE, THE(1919)
Monty Elliot
ARNOLD(1973), art d
Nell Elliot
MODEL SHOP, THE(1969)
Patricia Elliot
GREEN SLIME, THE(1969)
Paul Elliot
SIGN OF AQUARIUS(1970)
Peter Elliot
WRONG NUMBER(1959, Brit.); COOL IT, CAROL!(1970, Brit.); LAST ESCAPE, THE(1970, Brit.), ed
1984
GREYSTOKE: THE LEGEND OF TARZAN, LORD OF THE APES(1984), ch

Ramblin' Jack Elliot
ROADIE(1980)
Richard Elliot
HENRY ALDRICH PLAYS CUPID(1944)
Rita Elliot
ROBBY(1968)
Robert Elliot
ROARING TWENTIES, THE(1939); HALF A SINNER(1940); CAPTAIN TUGBOAT ANNIE(1945)
Misc. Silents
RESURRECTION(1918)
Rosalind Elliot
TOMCAT, THE(1968, Brit.); BARTLEBY(1970, Brit.); SCREAM AND SCREAM AGAIN(1970, Brit.); MURDERS IN THE RUE MORGUE(1971)
Ross Elliot
CHICAGO CALLING(1951); CHAIN OF EVIDENCE(1957); ACT OF VENGEAN-CE(1974)
Shawn Elliot
1984
BEAT STREET(1984)
Stephen Elliot
STREET OF SINNERS(1957)
Susan Elliot
WHY WOULD I LIE(1980)
Tamar Elliot
Misc. Talkies
BOD SQUAD, THE(1976)
Tim Elliot
JOURNEY AMONG WOMEN(1977, Aus.)
1984
UTU(1984, New Zealand)
William Elliot
WHERE DOES IT HURT?(1972)
Silents
FORTUNE HUNTER, THE(1914)
William J. Elliot
Silents
EXPERIMENT, THE(1922, Brit.), w
Yves Elliot
BLONDE FROM PEKING, THE(1968, Fr.)
Alan F. Elliott
MOUNTAIN, THE(1935, Brit.)
Alice Clair Elliott
Misc. Silents
SOCIAL HIGHWAYMAN, THE(1916)
Alice Claire Elliott
Misc. Silents
BETTER MAN, THE(1914)
Ann Elliott
Misc. Silents
DEFINITE OBJECT, THE(1920, Brit.); TWELVE POUND LOOK, THE(1920, Brit.); SCALLYWAG, THE(1921, Brit.)
Art Elliott
FANTASIA(1940), anim
Arthur Elliott
FOREVER AMBER(1947)
B. Ron Elliott
SMELL OF HONEY, A SWALLOW OF BRINE! A(1966), d
Misc. Talkies
ACID EATERS, THE(1968), d
Bernice Elliott
SECOND HONEYMOON(1931)
Misc. Silents
SECOND HONEYMOON(1930)
Betty Elliott
HAT CHECK GIRL(1932)
Biff Elliott
GOOD MORNING, MISS DOVE(1955); PT 109(1963); DESTINATION INNER SPA-CE(1966); SAVE THE TIGER(1973); DARK, THE(1979)
Bill Elliott
BORN TO LOVE(1931); CITY STREETS(1931); PLATINUM BLONDE(1931); LADY WITH A PAST(1932); MERRILY WE GO TO HELL(1932); ONE HOUR WITH YOU(1932); RICH ARE ALWAYS WITH US, THE(1932); DANCING LADY(1933); GOLD DIGGERS OF 1933(1933); LITTLE GIANT, THE(1933); PRIVATE DETECTIVE 62(1933); GOLDEN ARROW, THE(1936); WALKING DEAD, THE(1936); FRONTIERS OF '49(1939); LAW COMES TO TEXAS, THE(1939); LONE STAR PIONEERS(1939); TAMING OF THE WEST, THE(1939); MAN FROM TUMBLEWEEDS, THE(1940); PIONEERS OF THE FRONTIER(1940); RETURN OF WILD BILL, THE(1940); ACROSS THE SIERRAS(1941); BEYOND THE SACRAMENTO(1941); KING OF DODGE CI-TY(1941); NORTH FROM LONE STAR(1941); RETURN OF DANIEL BOONE, THE(1941); SON OF DAVY CROCKETT, THE(1941); WILDCAT OF TUCSON(1941); DEVIL'S TRAIL, THE(1942); LONE STAR VIGILANTES, THE(1942); CALLING WILD BILL ELLIOTT(1943); CHEYENNE WILDCAT(1944); HIDDEN VALLEY OUT-LAWS(1944); MARSHAL OF RENO(1944); MOJAVE FIREBRAND(1944); SAN AN-TONIO KID, THE(1944); COLORADO PIONEERS(1945); GREAT STAGECOACH ROBBERY(1945); LONE TEXAS RANGER(1945); MARSHAL OF LAREDO(1945); PHANTOM OF THE PLAINS(1945); CONQUEST OF CHEYENNE(1946); SUN VAL-LEY CYCLONE(1946); FARGO(1952); DIAL RED O(1955); SUDDEN DANGER(1955); CALLING HOMICIDE(1956); CHAIN OF EVIDENCE(1957); FOOTSTEPS IN THE NIGHT(1957); CHANGE OF HABIT(1969)
Misc. Talkies
HANDS ACROSS THE ROCKIES(1941); ROARING FRONTIERS(1941); BULLETS FOR BANDITS(1942); NORTH OF THE ROCKIES(1942); PRAIRIE GUNSMOKE(1942); VENGEANCE OF THE WEST(1942); CALIFORNIA GOLD RUSH(1946)
Billy Jack Elliott
WHERE DID YOU GET THAT GIRL?(1941)
Bob Elliott
COLD TURKEY(1971); AUTHOR! AUTHOR!(1982)

Cecil Elliott
ONE TOO MANY(1950); SURRENDER(1950); MARSHAL'S DAUGHTER, THE(1953); BIG TIP OFF, THE(1955); MIRACLE OF THE HILLS, THE(1959); FROM THE TERRACE(1960); THREE STOOGES MEET HERCULES, THE(1962); CHINA-TOWN(1974); DROWNING POOL, THE(1975); SUMMER SCHOOL TEACHERS(1977)

Cecile Elliott
SECRET OF THE CHATEAU(1935); HONEYCHILE(1951)

Chick Elliott
ASKING FOR TROUBLE(1942, Brit.)

Christopher Elliott
LIANNA(1983)

Clive Elliott
PIED PIPER, THE(1972, Brit.)

Clyde E. Elliott
DEVIL TIGER(1934), d

Clyde Elliott
CITIZEN SAINT(1947), p

Courtenay Elliott
DOUBLE MAN, THE(1967), cos; CARRY ON HENRY VIII(1970, Brit.), cos; CARRY ON LOVING(1970, Brit.), cos; CARRY ON UP THE JUNGLE(1970, Brit.), cos; DOCTOR IN TROUBLE(1970, Brit.), cos; TERROR FROM UNDER THE HOUSE(1971, Brit.), cos; CARRY ON EMANUELLE(1978, Brit.), cos

David Elliott
POSSESSION OF JOEL DELANEY, THE(1972); JAWS II(1978)

Dean Elliott
SEX KITTENS GO TO COLLEGE(1960), m; PHANTOM TOLLBOOTH, THE(1970), m; GREAT AMERICAN BUGS BUNNY-ROAD RUNNER CHASE(1979), m
1984
BEAT STREET(1984)

Del Elliott
DESERT SONG, THE(1929)

Denholm Elliott
DEAR MR. PROHACK(1949, Brit.); BREAKING THE SOUND BARRIER(1952); CRUEL SEA, THE(1953); RINGER, THE(1953, Brit.); HEART OF THE MATTER, THE(1954, Brit.); HOLLY AND THE IVY, THE(1954, Brit.); LEASE OF LIFE(1954, Brit.); THEY WHO DARE(1954, Brit.); MAN WHO LOVED REDHEADS, THE(1955, Brit.); NIGHT MY NUMBER CAME UP, THE(1955, Brit.); PACIFIC DESTINY(1956, Brit.); SCENT OF MYSTERY(1960); NOTHING BUT THE BEST(1964, Brit.); STATION SIX-SAHARA(1964, Brit./Ger.); YOU MUST BE JOKING!(1965, Brit.); ALFIE(1966, Brit.); MC GUIRE, GO HOME!(1966, Brit.); SPY WITH A COLD NOSE, THE(1966, Brit.); MAROC 7(1967, Brit.); HERE WE GO ROUND THE MULBERRY BUSH(1968, Brit.); NIGHT THEY RAIDED MINSKY'S, THE(1968); SEA GULL, THE(1968); RISE AND RISE OF MICHAEL RIMMER, THE(1970, Brit.); TOO LATE THE HERO(1970); HOUSE THAT DRIPPED BLOOD, THE(1971, Brit.); PERCY(1971, Brit.); QUEST FOR LOVE(1971, Brit.); DOLL'S HOUSE, A(1973); VAULT OF HORROR, THE(1973, Brit.); APPRENTICESHIP OF DUDDY KRAVITZ, THE(1974, Can.); RUSSIAN ROULETTE(1975); PARTNERS(1976, Can.); ROBIN AND MARIAN(1976, Brit.); TO THE DEVIL A DAUGHTER(1976, Brit./Ger.); VOYAGE OF THE DAMNED(1976, Brit.); BOYS FROM BRAZIL, THE(1978); SWEENEY 2(1978, Brit.); WATERSHIP DOWN(1978, Brit.); CUBA(1979); IT'S NOT THE SIZE THAT COUNTS(1979, Brit.); SAINT JACK(1979); GAME FOR VULTURES, A(1980, Brit.); HOUND OF THE BASKERVILLES, THE(1980, Brit.); RISING DAMP(1980, Brit.); SUNDAY LOVERS(1980, Ital./Fr.); ZULU DAWN(1980, Brit.); RAIDERS OF THE LOST ARK(1981); BRIMSTONE AND TREACLE(1982, Brit.); MISSIONARY, THE(1982); HOUND OF THE BASKERVILLES, THE(1983, Brit.); TRADING PLACES(1983); WICKED LADY, THE(1983, Brit.)
1984
RAZOR'S EDGE, THE(1984)
Misc. Talkies
RISE AND RISE OF MICHAEL RIMMER, THE(1970, Brit.); TWO FACES OF EVIL, THE(1981, Brit.)

Dick Elliott
PICTURE SNATCHER(1933); WE'RE RICH AGAIN(1934); DR. SOCRATES(1935); IT HAPPENED IN NEW YORK(1935); RECKLESS(1935); BRILLIANT MARRIAGE(1936); GO WEST, YOUNG MAN(1936); HER MASTER'S VOICE(1936); PRINCESS COMES ACROSS, THE(1936); PRISONER OF SHARK ISLAND, THE(1936); OUTCASTS OF POKER FLAT, THE(1937); VOGUES OF 1938(1937); EVERY DAY'S A HOLIDAY(1938); MAN FROM MUSIC MOUNTAIN(1938); NEXT TIME I MARRY(1938); PENITENTIARY(1938); PRISON FARM(1938); QUICK MONEY(1938); UNDER WESTERN STARS(1938); ANOTHER THIN MAN(1939); BOY TROUBLE(1939); DISBARRED(1939); I STOLE A MILLION(1939); LET US LIVE(1939); LONE WOLF SPY HUNT, THE(1939); MR. SMITH GOES TO WASHINGTON(1939); NANCY DREW AND THE HIDDEN STAIRCASE(1939); STORY OF ALEXANDER GRAHAM BELL, THE(1939); STORY OF VERNON AND IRENE CASTLE, THE(1939); SUDDEN MONEY(1939); FLORIAN(1940); LI'L ABNER(1940); MELODY RANCH(1940); MORTAL STORM, THE(1940); ONE MAN'S LAW(1940); UP IN THE AIR(1940); WOMEN WITHOUT NAMES(1940); YOUNG BILL HICKOK(1940); BEHIND THE NEWS(1941); MAN BETRAYED, A(1941); ONE FOOT IN HEAVEN(1941); PITTSBURGH KID, THE(1941); SHE KNEW ALL THE ANSWERS(1941); SUNSET IN WYOMING(1941); THREE GIRLS ABOUT TOWN(1941); TOP SERGEANT MULLIGAN(1941); TWO LATINS FROM MANHATTAN(1941); ANTHONY ALDRICH GETS GLAMOUR(1942); I MARRIED AN ANGEL(1942); KEEPER OF THE FLAME(1942); MAN FROM HEADQUARTERS(1942); MY FAVORITE BLONDE(1942); SWEETHEART OF THE FLEET(1942); WE WERE DANCING(1942); YOU CAN'T ESCAPE FOREVER(1942); AFTER MIDNIGHT WITH BOSTON BLACKIE(1943); LAUGH YOUR BLUES AWAY(1943); OUTLAW, THE(1943); SO'S YOUR UNCLE(1943); SWING OUT THE BLUES(1943); THANK YOUR LUCKY STARS(1943); THREE HEARTS FOR JULIA(1943); WINTERTIME(1943); ADVENTURES OF KITTY O'DAY(1944); GIRL IN THE CASE(1944); GOIN' TO TOWN(1944); HI BEAUTIFUL(1944); SILENT PARTNER(1944); WHEN STRANGERS MARRY(1944); CHRISTMAS IN CONNECTICUT(1945); CLOCK, THE(1945); GANGS OF THE WATERFRONT(1945); MAN WHO WALKED ALONE, THE(1945); SARATOGA TRUNK(1945); WHERE DO WE GO FROM HERE?(1945); BLUE DAHLIA, THE(1946); DANGEROUS MONEY(1946); DARK HORSE, THE(1946); DECOY(1946); HIGH SCHOOL HERO(1946); LADY LUCK(1946); MY REPUTATION(1946); PARTNERS IN TIME(1946); RAINBOW OVER TEXAS(1946); DESPERATE(1947); FOR THE LOVE OF RUSTY(1947); GINGER(1947); HEADING FOR HEAVEN(1947); LIKELY STORY, A(1947); MAGIC TOWN(1947); MAIN STREET KID, THE(1947); SINGAPORE(1947); GOOD SAM(1948); HOMICIDE FOR THREE(1948); PALEFACE, THE(1948); SAINTED SISTERS, THE(1948); SLIPPY MCGEE(1948); NIGHT UNTO NIGHT(1949); TRAIL OF THE YUKON(1949); ACROSS THE BAD-

LANDS(1950); LUCKY LOSERS(1950); ROCK ISLAND TRAIL(1950); SEPTEMBER AFFAIR(1950); SURRENDER(1950); UNION STATION(1950); WESTERN PACIFIC AGENT(1950); FORT DEFIANCE(1951); HONEYCHILE(1951); HIGH NOON(1952); MONTANA BELLE(1952); PARK ROW(1952); RANCHO NOTORIOUS(1952); WAC FROM WALLA WALLA, THE(1952); WITNESS TO MURDER(1954); DON'T KNOCK THE ROCK(1956); WHEN GANGLAND STRIKES(1956); JOKER IS WILD, THE(1957); LOOKING FOR DANGER(1957); UP IN SMOKE(1957); IN THE MONEY(1958); MODERN MARRIAGE, A(1962); WEEKEND WITH THE BABYSITTER(1970), ed

Don Elliott
HAPPY HOOKER, THE(1975), m

Dorothy Elliott
WHERE'S JACK?(1969, Brit.), set d

Duncan Elliott
DAUGHTER OF THE SANDS(1952, Fr.); ROMMEL'S TREASURE(1962, Ital.), w; THIEF OF PARIS, THE(1967, Fr./Ital.)

Edythe Elliott
SHOW THEM NO MERCY(1935); I MARRIED A DOCTOR(1936); STELLA DALLAS(1937); DOUBLE DANGER(1938); DANCING CO-ED(1939); FIXER DUGAN(1939); NOBODY'S CHILDREN(1940); FATHER TAKES A WIFE(1941); MEDICO OF PAINTED SPRINGS, THE(1941); RICHEST MAN IN TOWN(1941); LUCKY JORDAN(1942); VALLEY OF HUNTED MEN(1942); GANGWAY FOR TOMORROW(1943); SEVENTH VICTIM, THE(1943); SONG OF BERNADETTE, THE(1943); COWBOY CANTEEN(1944); GREAT MIKE, THE(1944); STARS ON PARADE(1944); PHANTOM OF 42ND STREET, THE(1945); FREDDIE STEPS OUT(1946); HIGH SCHOOL HERO(1946); PERSONALITY KID(1946); SANTA FE UPRISING(1946); THAT BRENNAN GIRL(1946); UNDERCOVER WOMAN, THE(1946); FABULOUS TEXAN, THE(1947); GINGER(1947); HER HUSBAND'S AFFAIRS(1947); HOMESTEADERS OF PARADISE VALLEY(1947); VACATION DAYS(1947); LADY FROM SHANGHAI, THE(1948); MESSENGER OF PEACE(1950); RAINBOW 'ROUND MY SHOULDER(1952); REDHEAD FROM MANHATTAN(1954)

Eileen Elliott
CRIME WAVE(1954); DR. COPPELIUS(1968, U.S./Span.); MYSTERIOUS HOUSE OF DR. C., THE(1976)

Eric Elliott
AWAKENING, THE(1938, Brit.)

Erica Elliott
CREATION OF THE HUMANOIDS(1962)

Faith Elliott
GO, MAN, GO!(1954), ed

Frank Elliott
PLAYBOY OF PARIS(1930); TAKE THE HEIR(1930); LAST OUTPOST, THE(1935); WIFE VERSUS SECRETARY(1936); MAYTIME(1937); DR. RHYTHM(1938); MARIE ANTOINETTE(1938); NEW MOON(1940); COLLEGE SWEETHEARTS(1942); GLASS KEY, THE(1942); LODGER, THE(1944); OUR HEARTS WERE YOUNG AND GAY(1944); STORY OF DR. WASSELL, THE(1944); LIFE WITH FATHER(1947); JOAN OF ARC(1948); FAN, THE(1949); GREAT SINNER, THE(1949); DARLING, HOW COULD YOU!(1951); PRISONER OF ZENDA, THE(1952); MONTE CARLO STORY, THE(1957, Ital.)
Silents
NEARLY A LADY(1915); SCARLET SIN, THE(1915); SPEED GIRL, THE(1921); IMPOSSIBLE MRS. BELLEW, THE(1922); GENTLE JULIA(1923); RED LIGHTS(1923); RUGGLES OF RED GAP(1923); GOLDFISH, THE(1924); TENDER HOUR, THE(1927)
Misc. Silents
MR. GREX OF MONTE CARLO(1915); SCHOOL FOR HUSBANDS, A(1917); CRY OF THE WEAK, THE(1919); HOME(1919); LOVE THAT DARES, THE(1919); SCARLET SHADOW, THE(1919); WINGS OF THE MORNING, THE(1919); HOPE, THE(1920); WHAT WOULD YOU DO?(1920); LADYFINGERS(1921); LAST CARD, THE(1921); THIS WOMAN(1924); TORRENT, THE(1924); SPEED WILD(1925); TEARING THROUGH(1925)

G.H. Elliott
MUSIC HALL(1934, Brit.); THOSE WERE THE DAYS(1934, Brit.)

Gerald Elliott
GREAT, MEADOW, THE(1931), w; BIRDS OF A FEATHER(1935, Brit.), w; CROSS CURRENTS(1935, Brit.), w; JUBILEE WINDOW(1935, Brit.), w; LIEUTENANT DARING, RN(1935, Brit.), w; CAFE MASCOT(1936, Brit.), w; FULL SPEED AHEAD(1936, Brit.), w; MEN OF YESTERDAY(1936, Brit.), w; PAY BOX ADVENTURE(1936, Brit.), w; STAR FELL FROM HEAVEN, A(1936, Brit.), w; STRANGE CARGO(1936, Brit.), w; TWO ON A DOORSTEP(1936, Brit.), w; DOUBLE EXPOSURES(1937, Brit.), w; FATAL HOUR, THE(1937, Brit.), w; FROG, THE(1937, Brit.), w; HOLIDAY'S END(1937, Brit.), w; MUSEUM MYSTERY(1937, Brit.), w; TWIN FACES(1937, Brit.), w; BLONDES FOR DANGER(1938, Brit.), w; NO PARKING(1938, Brit.), w; RETURN OF THE FROG, THE(1938, Brit.), w; SILVER TOP(1938, Brit.), w; SWORD OF HONOUR(1938, Brit.), w; ALL AT SEA(1939, Brit.), w; INSPECTOR HORNLEIGH(1939, Brit.), w; TORPEDOED!(1939, Brit.), w; GREAT MR. HANDEL, THE(1942, Brit.), w

Grace Elliott
MAID TO ORDER(1932), w

Heenan Elliott
LADY FROM SHANGHAI, THE(1948)

Helen Elliott
ADDING MACHINE, THE(1969)

Herbert Elliott
GHOST BREAKERS, THE(1940)

Jack Elliott
APACHE ROSE(1947), m; FLAME OF THE ISLANDS(1955), m; HAPPIEST MILLIONAIRE, THE(1967), md; VALLEY OF MYSTERY(1967), m; COMIC, THE(1969), m; WHERE'S POPPA?(1970), m; SUPPORT YOUR LOCAL GUNFIGHTER(1971), m; T.R. BASKIN(1971), m; GET TO KNOW YOUR RABBIT(1972), m; OH, GOD!(1977), m; RENALDO AND CLARA(1978); JERK, THE(1979), m; JUST YOU AND ME, KID(1979), m

James Elliott
SEEDS OF FREEDOM(1943, USSR); NED KELLY(1970, Brit.); NO. 96(1974, Aus.); MONEY MOVERS(1978, Aus.)

James S. Elliott
IT HAPPENED IN ATHENS(1962), p

Jane Elliott
Silents
ONCE A PLUMBER(1920)

Janice Elliott
BUTTERCUP CHAIN, THE(1971, Brit.), w
1984
SECRET PLACES(1984, Brit.), w
Janis Elliott
SOUTH OF SANTA FE(1932)
Jean Elliott
1984
OVER THE BROOKLYN BRIDGE(1984)
Jerry Elliott
JOAN OF ARC(1948); TATTERED DRESS, THE(1957)
John Elliott
PHANTOM IN THE HOUSE, THE(1929); FOR THE DEFENSE(1930); LET'S GO NATIVE(1930); RAMPANT AGE, THE(1930); WIDOW FROM CHICAGO, THE(1930); CONQUERING HORDE, THE(1931); GOD'S COUNTRY AND THE MAN(1931); MONTANA KID, THE(1931); MOTHER AND SON(1931); OKLAHOMA JIM(1931); SECRET MENACE(1931); TWO-FISTED JUSTICE(1931); BROADWAY TO CHEYENNE(1932); CORNERED(1932); GALLOPING THRU(1932); HIDDEN VALLEY(1932); RIDERS OF THE DESERT(1932); SINGLE-HANDED SANDERS(1932); TEXAS PIONEERS(1932); TRIAL OF VIVIENNE WARE, THE(1932); WEEK-ENDS ONLY(1932); GALLANT FOOL, THE(1933); LUCKY LARRIGAN(1933); SONS OF THE DESERT(1933); CAROLINA(1934); COWBOY HOLIDAY(1934); FIFTEEN WIVES(1934); GREEN EYES(1934); I SELL ANYTHING(1934); KEY, THE(1934); LOST LADY, A(1934); MURDER IN THE MUSEUM(1934); OPERATOR 13(1934); TICKET TO CRIME(1934); UPPER WORLD(1934); DANGER AHEAD(1935); DANGER TRAILS(1935); FIGHTING PIONEERS(1935); FRISCO KID(1935); LAWLESS BORDER(1935); RAINBOW'S END(1935); RED HOT TIRES(1935); RIDER OF THE LAW, THE(1935); SUNSET RANGE(1935); TOMBSTONE TERROR(1935); TRAILS OF THE WILD(1935); VAGABOND LADY(1935); WAGON TRAIL(1935); WHAT PRICE CRIME?(1935); FACE IN THE FOG, A(1936); FRONTIER JUSTICE(1936); FUGITIVE SHERIFF, THE(1936); KELLY OF THE SECRET SERVICE(1936); MILLIONAIRE KID(1936); PRISON SHADOWS(1936); RIP ROARIN' BUCKAROO(1936); ROARIN' GUNS(1936); ROGUES' TAVERN, THE(1936); SATAN MET A LADY(1936); SNOWED UNDER(1936); TOLL OF THE DESERT(1936); TRAIL DUST(1936); HEADIN' EAST(1937); HEART OF THE WEST(1937); RIDING ON(1937); SMOKE TREE RANGE(1937); SUBMARINE D-1(1937); CASSIDY OF BAR 20(1938); FRONTIER TOWN(1938); HEART OF ARIZONA(1938); HUNTED MEN(1938); KENTUCKY(1938); ORPHAN OF THE PECOS(1938); PHANTOM OF THE RANGE, THE(1938); SKULL AND CROWN(1938); CHARLIE CHAN AT TREASURE ISLAND(1939); FIGHTING RENEGADE(1939); JESSE JAMES(1939); MESQUITE BUCKAROO(1939); PORT OF HATE(1939); TRIGGER FINGERS ½(1939); DEATH RIDES THE RANGE(1940); GUN CODE(1940); LIGHTNING STRIKES WEST(1940); LONE STAR RAIDERS(1940); PHANTOM RANCHER(1940); TULSA KID, THE(1940); YOUNG BILL HICKOK(1940); APACHE KID, THE(1941); GENTLEMAN FROM DIXIE(1941); KID'S LAST RIDE, THE(1941); SADDLE MOUNTAIN ROUNDUP(1941); TEXAS MARSHAL, THE(1941); TUMBLEDOWN RANCH IN ARIZONA(1941); UNDERGROUND RUSTLERS(1941); COME ON DANGER(1942); MAD MONSTER, THE(1942); MAGNIFICENT AMBERSONS, THE(1942); OVERLAND STAGECOACH(1942); RAIDERS OF THE WEST(1942); ROCK RIVER RENEGADES(1942); ROLLING DOWN THE GREAT DIVIDE(1942); CALLING DR. DEATH(1943); CATTLE STAMPEDE(1943); FIGHTING VALLEY(1943); HEAVENLY BODY, THE(1943); RAIDERS OF SAN JOAQUIN(1943); SAGEBRUSH LAW(1943); TENTING TONIGHT ON THE OLD CAMP GROUND(1943); YOU'RE A LUCKY FELLOW, MR. SMITH(1943); DEATH RIDES THE PLAINS(1944); EXPERIMENT PERILOUS(1944); FUZZY SETTLES DOWN(1944); GYPSY WILDCAT(1944); HEAVENLY DAYS(1944); LAW OF THE SADDLE(1944); MARINE RAIDERS(1944); OKLAHOMA RAIDERS(1944); WILD HORSE PHANTOM(1944); HOLLYWOOD AND VINE(1945); DARK CORNER, THE(1946); DEADLINE AT DAWN(1946); DEVIL'S MASK, THE(1946); CRY WOLF(1947); LAW OF THE LASH(1947); NORA PRENTISS(1947); UNFAITHFUL, THE(1947); WOMAN ON THE BEACH, THE(1947); COUNTESS OF MONTE CRISTO, THE(1948); LADY FROM SHANGHAI, THE(1948); FLAXY MARTIN(1949); SMOKY MOUNTAIN MELODY(1949); ARIZONA COWBOY, THE(1950); PEACE KILLERS, THE(1971), makeup; BIG FOOT(1973), makeup
Misc. Talkies
MAN FROM ARIZONA, THE(1932); VANISHING MEN(1932); BIG CALIBRE(1935); BULLDOG COURAGE(1935); TRIGGER TOM(1935); UNCONQUERED BANDIT(1935); RIDIN' ON(1936); VENGEANCE OF RANNAH(1936)
Silents
MASTER STROKE, A(1920); WHAT HAPPENED TO JONES(1926)
Misc. Silents
RACING BLOOD(1926); HORSE SHOES(1927)
John H. Elliott
ONLY THE BRAVE(1930); LOVE IS ON THE AIR(1937); YOUNG AS YOU FEEL(1940); PIRATES OF THE PRAIRIE(1942); FIRST COMES COURAGE(1943); ESCAPE IN THE FOG(1945); NEWS HOUNDS(1947); I WOULDN'T BE IN YOUR SHOES(1948); SMART WOMAN(1948)
Misc. Silents
HELD IN TRUST(1920)
John M. Elliott
SMOKY(1966), art d
John M. Elliott, Jr
JEKYLL AND HYDE...TOGETHER AGAIN(1982), makeup
John R. Elliott
1984
BEST DEFENSE(1984), spec eff; JOY OF SEX(1984), spec eff
John Wesley Elliott, Jr.
BRONCO BILLY(1980)
Jonathan Elliott
MANGANINNIE(1982, Aus.)
Keenan Elliott
HELLFIRE(1949)
Ken Elliott
MODERN MARRIAGE, A(1962)
Kirk Elliott
ISLAND OF LOVE(1963)
Lang Elliott
BILLION DOLLAR HOBO, THE(1977), p; THEY WENT THAT-A-WAY AND THAT-A-WAY(1978), p; PRIZE FIGHTER, THE(1979), p; PRIVATE EYES, THE(1980), p, d

Laud Elliott
CHICAGO DEADLINE(1949)
Laura Elliott
FILE ON THELMA JORDAN, THE(1950); NO MAN OF HER OWN(1950); PAID IN FULL(1950); TWO LOST WORLDS(1950); MATING SEASON, THE(1951); MY FAVORITE SPY(1951); STRANGERS ON A TRAIN(1951); ABOUT MRS. LESLIE(1954)
Leonard Elliott
OVERTURE TO GLORY(1940); BUCK PRIVATES(1941); IT STARTED WITH EVE(1941); WEDDINGS AND BABIES(1960); GHOST, THE(1965, Ital.); DIARY OF A MAD HOUSEWIFE(1970)
Lillian Elliott
HER WEDDING NIGHT(1930); LILIOM(1930); SWELLHEAD, THE(1930); SINGLE SIN(1931); BROKEN LULLABY(1932); EVENINGS FOR SALE(1932); POLLY OF THE CIRCUS(1932); MRS. WIGGS OF THE CABBAGE PATCH(1934); JURY'S SECRET, THE(1938); WANTED BY THE POLICE(1938); IRISH LUCK(1939); TOUGH KID(1939); WHEN TOMORROW COMES(1939); CHASING TROUBLE(1940); EMERGENCY SQUAD(1940); LAUGHING AT DANGER(1940); WOMEN WITHOUT NAMES(1940); ROAD TO HAPPINESS(1942)
Silents
OLD CLOTHES(1925); PROUD FLESH(1925); PARTNERS AGAIN(1926); ANKLES PREFERRED(1927); KING OF KINGS, THE(1927)
Misc. Silents
CHORUS LADY, THE(1924); CITY, THE(1926); FAMILY UPSTAIRS, THE(1926)
Lorraine Elliott
HELLO, FRISCO, HELLO(1943)
Marianna Elliott
WHOSE LIFE IS IT ANYWAY?(1981), cos
Marietta Elliott
HIS KIND OF WOMAN(1951); ROYAL WEDDING(1951); SHOW BOAT(1951); HALF-BREED, THE(1952)
Marjorie Elliott
LYDIA BAILEY(1952)
Mary Elliott
GIRL CRAZY(1943); GUY NAMED JOE, A(1943); SLIGHTLY DANGEROUS(1943); OUT OF THIS WORLD(1945)
Maxine Elliott
Silents
FIGHTING ODDS(1917)
Neil Elliott
1984
ALL OF ME(1984)
Pat Elliott
1984
BRADY'S ESCAPE(1984, U.S./Hung.)
Patricia Elliott
BIRCH INTERVAL(1976); SOMEBODY KILLED HER HUSBAND(1978); NATURAL ENEMIES(1979)
Peggy Elliott
COME BACK CIHARLESTON BLUE(1972), w
Peter Elliott
PICKUP ALLEY(1957, Brit.); CURSE OF THE DEMON(1958); NOBODY IN TOYLAND(1958, Brit.); SECRET MAN, THE(1958, Brit.); LEFT, RIGHT AND CENTRE(1959); WEB OF SUSPICION(1959, Brit.); MALAGA(1962, Brit.); GREAT VAN ROBBERY, THE(1963, Brit.); MODEL MURDER CASE, THE(1964, Brit.); SECRET DOOR, THE(1964); VULTURE, THE(1967, U.S./Brit./Can.); BATTLE BENEATH THE EARTH(1968, Brit.); TORTURE GARDEN(1968, Brit.), ed; SCREAM AND SCREAM AGAIN(1970, Brit.), ed; QUEST FOR FIRE(1982, Fr./Can.)
Peter J. Elliott
1,000 CONVICTS AND A WOMAN(1971, Brit.), a, m; SAFARI 3000(1982)
Richard Elliott
GIFT OF GAB(1934); FLIGHT ANGELS(1940); WAGONS ROLL AT NIGHT, THE(1941); SILVER BANDIT, THE(1950)
Robert Elliott
LIGHTS OF NEW YORK(1928); LONE WOLF'S DAUGHTER, THE(1929); THUNDERBOLT(1929); DIVORCEE, THE(1930); DOORWAY TO HELL(1930); HIDE-OUT, THE(1930); KATHLEEN MAVOURNEEN(1930); MEN OF THE NORTH(1930); SWEET MAMA(1930); CAPTAIN THUNDER(1931); FINGER POINTS, THE(1931); FIVE STAR FINAL(1931); MALTESE FALCON, THE(1931); MURDER AT MIDNIGHT(1931); RULING VOICE, THE(1931); STAR WITNESS(1931); BEHIND STONE WALLS(1932); MADISON SQUARE GARDEN(1932); MIDNIGHT PATROL, THE(1932); PHANTOM OF CRESTWOOD, THE(1932); WHITE EAGLE(1932); CRIME OF THE CENTURY, THE(1933); HEROES FOR SALE(1933); LADY KILLER(1933); MY MOTHER(1933); RETURN OF CASEY JONES(1933); GAMBLING LADY(1934); TRANSATLANTIC MERRY-GO-ROUND(1934); TWIN HUSBANDS(1934); PORT OF LOST DREAMS(1935); TIMES SQUARE LADY(1935); WORLD ACCUSES, THE(1935); I'D GIVE MY LIFE(1936); TRADE WINDS(1938); GONE WITH THE WIND(1939); I STOLE A MILLION(1939); MICKEY, THE KID(1939); SAINT STRIKES BACK, THE(1939); SHOULD A GIRL MARRY?(1939); INVISIBLE STRIPES(1940); 'TIL WE MEET AGAIN(1940); DEVIL'S PLAYGROUND, THE(1946); STUDENT BODY, THE(1976); NATIONAL LAMPOON'S ANIMAL HOUSE(1978)
Misc. Talkies
SELF DEFENSE(1933)
Silents
JOAN OF PLATTSBURG(1918); WITHOUT FEAR(1922); OBEY YOUR HUSBAND(1928); PROTECTION(1929)
Misc. Silents
LIFE'S SHADOWS(1916); MISS PETTICOATS(1916); MARY MORELAND(1917); MIRROR, THE(1917); MOTHERHOOD(1917); MRS. BALFANE(1917); FOR THE FREEDOM OF THE EAST(1918); CHECKERS(1919); L' APACHE(1919); UNKNOWN LOVE, THE(1919); WOMAN THERE WAS, A(1919); EMPIRE OF DIAMONDS, THE(1920); LONELY HEART(1921); MONEY MANIAC, THE(1921); VIRGIN PARADISE, A(1921); BROKEN SILENCE, THE(1922); FAIR LADY(1922); PASTEBOARD CROWN, A(1922); ROMANCE OF THE UNDERWORLD(1928)
Rosaline Elliott
ALFIE DARLING(1975, Brit.)
Ross Elliott
THIS IS THE ARMY(1943); ANGEL ON THE AMAZON(1948); CHINATOWN AT MIDNIGHT(1949); GAL WHO TOOK THE WEST, THE(1949); DYNAMITE PASS(1950); TYRANT OF THE SEA(1950); WOMAN ON THE RUN(1950); DESERT OF LOST MEN(1951); HOT LEAD(1951); I CAN GET IT FOR YOU WHOLESALE(1951); AFFAIR

IN TRINIDAD(1952); LOAN SHARK(1952); WOMAN IN THE DARK(1952); BEAST FROM 20,000 FATHOMS, THE(1953); PROBLEM GIRLS(1953); TUMBLEWEED(1953); MA AND PA KETTLE AT HOME(1954); MASSACRE CANYON(1954); AFRICAN MANHUNT(1955); CAROLINA CANNONBALL(1955); TARANTULA(1955); TOUGHEST MAN ALIVE(1955); WOMEN'S PRISON(1955); D-DAY, THE SIXTH OF JUNE(1956); INDESTRUCTIBLE MAN, THE(1956); AS YOUNG AS WE ARE(1958); MONSTER ON THE CAMPUS(1958); NEVER SO FEW(1959); TAMMY, TELL ME TRUE(1961); CRAWLING HAND, THE(1963); FBI CODE 98(1964); LIVELY SET, THE(1964); WILD SEED(1965); DAY OF THE EVIL GUN(1968); KELLY'S HEROES(1970, U.S./Yugo.); SKYJACKED(1972); TOWERING INFERNO, THE(1974); GABLE AND LOMBARD(1976)

Sam Elliott
BUTCH CASSIDY AND THE SUNDANCE KID(1969); GAMES, THE(1970); FROGS(1972); MOLLY AND LAWLESS JOHN(1972); LIFEGUARD(1976); LEGACY, THE(1979, Brit.)

Scott Elliott
KISS AND TELL(1945); WHERE DO WE GO FROM HERE?(1945); DRAGONWYCH(1946); SONG OF MY HEART(1947); LAW OF THE GOLDEN WEST(1949); FRENCH LINE, THE(1954); LAST OF THE SECRET AGENTS?, THE(1966)

Shawn Elliott
SHORT EYES(1977)

Stephen Elliott
THREE HOURS TO KILL(1954); CANYON CROSSROADS(1955); HOSPITAL, THE(1971); DEATH WISH(1974); HINDENBURG, THE(1975); REPORT TO THE COMMISSIONER(1975); ARTHUR(1981); CUTTER AND BONE(1981); KISS ME GOODBYE(1982)
1984
BEVERLY HILLS COP(1984); ROADHOUSE 66(1984)

Steven Elliott
GENE AUTRY AND THE MOUNTIES(1951)

Sumner Locke Elliott
1984
CAREFUL, HE MIGHT HEAR YOU(1984, Aus.), w

Susan Elliott
GOODBYE GIRL, THE(1977)

Suzanne Elliott
WHERE THE BUFFALO ROAM(1980)

Ted Elliott
STAMPEDE(1949)

Tim Elliott
FAN, THE(1981)

Tom Elliott
WARGAMES(1983), stunts
Misc. Silents
WIN THAT GIRL(1928)

Tommy Elliott
PASSWORD IS COURAGE, THE(1962, Brit.)

Violet Elliott
Misc. Silents
EDGE OF YOUTH, THE(1920, Brit.)

"Wild Bill" Elliott
IN EARLY ARIZONA(1938); PRAIRIE SCHOONERS(1940); BORDERTOWN GUN-FIGHTERS(1943); DEATH VALLEY MANHUNT(1943); MAN FROM THUNDER RIVER, THE(1943); OVERLAND MAIL ROBBERY(1943); WAGON TRACKS WEST(1943); SHERIFF OF LAS VEGAS(1944); TUCSON RAIDERS(1944); VIGILANTES OF DODGE CITY(1944); BELLS OF ROSARITA(1945); SHERIFF OF REDWOOD VALLEY(1946); HELLFIRE(1949); LONGHORN, THE(1951); KANSAS TERRITORY(1952); MAVERICK, THE(1952); WACO(1952); HOMESTEADERS, THE(1953); REBEL CITY(1953); TOPEKA(1953); VIGILANTE TERROR(1953); BITTER CREEK(1954); FORTYNINERS, THE(1954); WAGON WHEELS WESTWARD(1956)

William Elliott
IN OLD SACRAMENTO(1946); PLAINSMAN AND THE LADY(1946); FABULOUS TEXAN, THE(1947); WYOMING(1947); GALLANT LEGION, THE(1948); OLD LOS ANGELES(1948); LAST BANDIT, THE(1949); SAVAGE HORDE, THE(1950); SHOWDOWN, THE(1950), a, p; NIGHT OF THE LEPUS(1972); COFFY(1973); HANGUP(1974); PIRATES OF PENZANCE, THE(1983), md
Silents
LIGHTNING CONDUCTOR, THE(1914); WOMAN AND WINE(1915); HEARTS OF THE WORLD(1918)
Misc. Silents
COMRADE JOHN(1915); WHEN WE WERE TWENTY-ONE(1915)

William J. Elliott
Silents
GENERAL JOHN REGAN(1921, Brit.), w; INNOCENT(1921, Brit.), w; PLACE OF HONOUR, THE(1921, Brit.), w

John Elliotte
FANTASIA(1940), anim; PINOCCHIO(1940), anim

Judith Elliotte
MISTER BROWN(1972); SCREAM BLACULA SCREAM(1973)

Michael Elliotte
MISTER BROWN(1972)

Paul Elliotts [Gianfranco Baldanello]
GREAT ADVENTURE, THE(1976, Span./Ital.), d

Ada Ellis
SOMEONE TO REMEMBER(1943)

Adrianne Ellis
NEW INTERNS, THE(1964)

Albert Ellis
Silents
BIG TREMAINE(1916)

Anderson Ellis
MORTAL STORM, THE(1940), w

Anita Ellis
THREE LITTLE WORDS(1950); JOE LOUIS STORY, THE(1953)
1984
NOTHING LASTS FOREVER(1984)

Anthony Ellis
TO EACH HIS OWN(1946)

Antonia Ellis
BOY FRIEND, THE(1971, Brit.); PERCY(1971, Brit.); MAHLER(1974, Brit.)

Antony Ellis
RIDE BACK, THE(1957), w

Arden Ellis
CANYON OF MISSING MEN, THE(1930)

Art Ellis
TWIST ALL NIGHT(1961), ed

Arthur Ellis
HIS WOMAN(1931), ed; PERSONAL MAID(1931), ed; WAYWARD(1932), ed; HIS DOUBLE LIFE(1933), ed; SCOUNDREL, THE(1935), ed

Bette Ellis
Misc. Talkies
METAMORPHOSIS(1951)

Bob Ellis
PRISONER OF WAR(1954); NEWSFRONT(1979, Aus.), w; FATTY FINN(1980, Aus.), w
1984
MAN OF FLOWERS(1984, Aus.), a, w

Bobby Ellis
BABE RUTH STORY, THE(1948); EL PASO(1949); TEA AND SYMPATHY(1956)

Bruce E. Ellis
STRIPES(1981)

Butch Ellis
ROSE, THE(1979)

Byron Ellis
ROPE OF SAND(1949)

Carlyle Ellis
Misc. Silents
HOME-KEEPING HEARTS(1921), d

Charles Ellis
VICE RAID(1959), w; EDEN CRIED(1967), p

Christopher Ellis
FLOOD, THE(1963, Brit.); MIND BENDERS, THE(1963, Brit.); NIGHT COMERS, THE(1971, Brit.)

Christophr Ellis
PUMPKIN EATER, THE(1964, Brit.)

Clive Ellis
1984
GIVE MY REGARDS TO BROAD STREET(1984, Brit.)

Dave Ellis
1984
ALIEN FACTOR, THE(1984), a, ed

David Ellis
MAYTIME IN MAYFAIR(1952, Brit.); LAST RHINO, THE(1961, Brit.); HEROES(1977); KING OF THE MOUNTAIN(1981), stunts

David Graham Ellis
NIGHTHAWKS(1978, Brit.), m

Debbie Ellis
GIRLS UNDER TWENTY-ONE(1940)

Desmond Walter Ellis
CARRY ON ADMIRAL(1957, Brit.); HELLFIRE CLUB, THE(1963, Brit.); GREAT ST. TRINIAN'S TRAIN ROBBERY, THE(1966, Brit.); PADDY(1970, Irish)

Diane Ellis
HIGH VOLTAGE(1929); LEATHERNECK, THE(1929); LAUGHTER(1930)

Dione Ellis
Silents
HOOK AND LADDER NO. 9(1927); IS ZAT SO?(1927)
Misc. Silents
CHAIN LIGHTING(1927)

Dolan Ellis
PEACE FOR A GUNFIGHTER(1967), m

Don Ellis
FRENCH CONNECTION, THE(1971), m, md; CORPSE GRINDERS, THE(1972); KANSAS CITY BOMBER(1972), m; SEVEN UPS, THE(1973), m; FRENCH CONNECTION 11(1975), m; MANIAC!(1977), m; RUBY(1977), m; NATURAL ENEMIES(1979), m

Earl Ellis
Silents
HIGH HEELS(1921), ph; ROWDY, THE(1921), ph

Edith Ellis
IDLE RICH, THE(1929), w; EASIEST WAY, THE(1931), w; AFFAIRS OF A GENTLE-MAN(1934), w; RICH MAN, POOR GIRL(1938), Jerome Chodorov

Edward Ellis
I AM A FUGITIVE FROM A CHAIN GANG(1932); AFTER TONIGHT(1933); FROM HEADQUARTERS(1933); GIRL MISSING(1933); STRICTLY PERSONAL(1933); AFFAIRS OF A GENTLEMAN(1934), w; HI, NELLIE!(1934); LAST GENTLEMAN, THE(1934); NINTH GUEST, THE(1934); PRESIDENT VANISHES, THE(1934); THIN MAN, THE(1934); TRUMPET BLOWS, THE(1934); RETURN OF PETER GRIMM, THE(1935); TRANSIENT LADY(1935); VILLAGE TALE(1935); WANDERER OF THE WASTELAND(1935); CHATTERBOX(1936); FURY(1936); LADY CONSENTS, THE(1936); TEXAS RANGERS, THE(1936); WINTERSET(1936); LET THEM LIVE(1937); MAID OF SALEM(1937); MAN IN BLUE, THE(1937); MIDNIGHT MADONNA(1937); LITTLE MISS BROADWAY(1938); MAN TO REMEMBER, A(1938); CAREER(1939); MAIN STREET LAWYER(1939); MAN OF CONQUEST(1939); THREE SONS(1939); MAN BETRAYED, A(1941); STEEL AGAINST THE SKY(1941); OMAHA TRAIL, THE(1942); EAST OF SUDAN(1964, Brit.)
Silents
OUT YONDER(1920)
Misc. Silents
GREAT BRADLEY MYSTERY, THE(1917); LAW THAT FAILED, THE(1917); FRONTIER OF THE STARS, THE(1921)

Edwin Ellis
EAST LYNNE ON THE WESTERN FRONT(1931, Brit.); EYES OF FATE(1933, Brit.); PARIS PLANE(1933, Brit.); JOSSER ON THE FARM(1934, Brit.); SAY IT WITH FLOWERS(1934, Brit.); LIEUTENANT DARING, RN(1935, Brit.); BELOVED IMPOSTER(1936, Brit.); HANGMAN WAITS, THE(1947, Brit.); WOMAN FOR JOE, THE(1955, Brit.); MAN WITHOUT A BODY, THE(1957, Brit.)

Evelyn Ellis
LADY FROM SHANGHAI, THE(1948); JOE LOUIS STORY, THE(1953); INTERRUPTED MELODY(1955); MEAT CLEAVER MASSACRE(1977)

Frank Ellis
CHEYENNE KID, THE(1930); SHADOW RANCH(1930); TRAILS OF DANGER(1930); AVENGER, THE(1931); RANGE FEUD, THE(1931); 99 WOUNDS(1931); BIG STAMPEDE, THE(1932); SUNSET TRAIL(1932); TEXAS GUN FIGHTER(1932); WHISTLIN' DAN(1932); COWBOY COUNSELOR(1933); DUDE BANDIT, THE(1933); COWBOY HOLIDAY(1934); FIDDLIN' BUCKAROO, THE(1934); FIGHTING RANGER, THE(1934); GUN JUSTICE(1934); TRAIL DRIVE, THE(1934); DESERT TRAIL(1935); GALLANT DEFENDER(1935); IN OLD SANTA FE(1935); JUSTICE OF THE RANGE(1935); POWDERSMOKE RANGE(1935); RAINBOW VALLEY(1935); WESTERN FRONTIER(1935); FUGITIVE SHERIFF, THE(1936); LAWLESS RIDERS(1936); LIGHTNING BILL CARSON(1936); ROARIN' GUNS(1936); TEXAS RANGERS, THE(1936); THUNDERBOLT(1936); TOO MUCH BEEF(1936); TREACHERY RIDES THE RANGE(1936); BOOTHILL BRIGADE(1937); GAMBLING TERROR, THE(1937); GIT ALONG, LITTLE DOGIES(1937); GUN LORDS OF STIRRUP BASIN(1937); GUNS IN THE DARK(1937); HOPALONG RIDES AGAIN(1937); OLD WYOMING TRAIL, THE(1937); ONE MAN JUSTICE(1937); PHANTOM OF SANTA FE(1937); PRAIRIE THUNDER(1937); PUBLIC COWBOY NO. 1(1937); RANGE DEFENDERS(1937); RIDERS OF THE WHISTLING SKULL(1937); RIO GRANDE RANGER(1937); SPRINGTIME IN THE ROCKIES(1937); TRAIL OF VENGEANCE(1937); TWO-FISTED SHERIFF(1937); BORDER WOLVES(1938); GHOST TOWN RIDERS(1938); IN EARLY ARIZONA(1938); LAST STAND, THE(1938); OUTLAWS OF THE PRAIRIE(1938); ROMANCE OF THE ROCKIES(1938); SUNSET TRAIL(1938); WESTERN JAMBOREE(1938); DESPERATE TRAILS(1939); FRONTIERS OF '49(1939); IN OLD MONTEREY(1939); LAW COMES TO TEXAS, THE(1939); LONE STAR PIONEERS(1939); MAN FROM SUNDOWN, THE(1939); MARSHAL OF MESA CITY, THE(1939); NEW FRONTIER(1939); RIDE 'EM COWGIRL(1939); ROLL, WAGONS, ROLL(1939); ROUGH RIDERS' ROUNDUP(1939); ROVIN' TUMBLEWEEDS(1939); SIX-GUN RHYTHM(1939); SOUTHWARD HO!(1939); SUNDOWN ON THE PRAIRIE(1939); TEXAS WILDCATS(1939); ARIZONA GANGBUSTERS(1940); CHIP OF THE FLYING U(1940); FRONTIER CRUSADER(1940); LAW AND ORDER(1940); MY LITTLE CHICKADEE(1940); PRAIRIE LAW(1940); WEST OF ABILENE(1940); WESTBOUND STAGE(1940); YOUNG BILL HICKOK(1940); BANDIT TRAIL, THE(1941); BILLY THE KID IN SANTA FE(1941); BILLY THE KID WANTED(1941); BOSS OF BULLION CITY(1941); BURY ME NOT ON THE LONE PRAIRIE(1941); KID'S LAST RIDE, THE(1941); LAND OF THE OPEN RANGE(1941); LONE RIDER CROSSES THE RIO, THE(1941); LONE RIDER FIGHTS BACK, THE(1941); LONE RIDER IN GHOST TOWN, THE(1941); MAN FROM MONTANA(1941); OUTLAWS OF THE RIO GRANDE(1941); PALS OF THE PECOS(1941); PHANTOM COWBOY, THE(1941); PINTO KID, THE(1941); PRAIRIE PIONEERS(1941); RAWHIDE RANGERS(1941); SHERIFF OF TOMBSTONE(1941); SON OF DAVY CROCKETT, THE(1941); STICK TO YOUR GUNS(1941); TEXAS MARSHAL, THE(1941); THUNDERING HOOFS(1941); TRAIL OF THE SILVER SPURS(1941); TUMBLEDOWN RANCH IN ARIZONA(1941); TWILIGHT ON THE TRAIL(1941); WRANGLER'S ROOST(1941); WYOMING WILDCAT(1941); ARIZONA STAGECOACH(1942); BANDIT RANGER(1942); DEEP IN THE HEART OF TEXAS(1942); IN OLD CALIFORNIA(1942); MYSTERIOUS RIDER, THE(1942); PHANTOM KILLER(1942); PRAIRIE PALS(1942); RAIDERS OF THE WEST(1942); ROCK RIVER RENEGADES(1942); SONS OF THE PIONEERS(1942); STAGECOACH BUCKAROO(1942); STARDUST ON THE SAGE(1942); TEXAS MAN HUNT(1942); TEXAS TO BATAAN(1942); TRAIL RIDERS(1942); UNDERCOVER MAN(1942); BLACK MARKET RUSTLERS(1943); CATTLE STAMPEDE(1943); OVERLAND MAIL ROBBERY(1943); TWO FISTED JUSTICE(1943); WAGON TRACKS WEST(1943); WESTERN CYCLONE(1943); WILD HORSE RUSTLERS(1943); ARIZONA WHIRLWIND(1944); BLAZING FRONTIER(1944); CHEYENNE WILDCAT(1944); CODE OF THE PRAIRIE(1944); DEATH RIDES THE PLAINS(1944); DEVIL RIDERS(1944); FIREBRANDS OF ARIZONA(1944); LAW OF THE SADDLE(1944); MOJAVE FIREBRAND(1944); OKLAHOMA RAIDERS(1944); OUTLAW TRAIL(1944); RAIDERS OF RED GAP(1944); SONORA STAGECOACH(1944); TRAIL OF TERROR(1944); WESTWARD BOUND(1944); WILD HORSE PHANTOM(1944); CORPUS CHRISTI BANDITS(1945); ENEMY OF THE LAW(1945); FRONTIER FUGITIVES(1945); SHADOWS OF DEATH(1945); SUNSET IN EL DORADO(1945); THREE IN THE SADDLE(1945); WILDFIRE(1945); AMBUSH TRAIL(1946); GENTLEMEN WITH GUNS(1946); OVERLAND RIDERS(1946); PRAIRIE BADMEN(1946); SANTA FE UPRISING(1946); TERRORS ON HORSEBACK(1946); TUMBLEWEED TRAIL(1946); RETURN OF THE LASH(1947); STAGE TO MESA CITY(1947); DEADLINE(1948); VALIANT HOMBRE, THE(1948); WESTWARD TRAIL, THE(1948); LAW OF THE WEST(1949); BEYOND THE PURPLE HILLS(1950); INDIAN TERRITORY(1950); WHISTLING HILLS(1951); CANYON AMBUSH(1952); FRONTIER PHANTOM, THE(1952); JUNCTION CITY(1952); MONTANA BELLE(1952); OLD WEST, THE(1952); PACK TRAIN(1953); STRANGER WORE A GUN, THE(1953); SILVER LODE(1954); WAGON WHEELS WESTWARD(1956); EVEL KNIEVEL(1971)
Misc. Talkies
BIG BOY RIDES AGAIN(1935)
Silents
KING'S CREEK LAW(1923); ACE OF ACTION(1926); VANISHING HOOFS(1926); LAW OF THE MOUNTED(1928)
Misc. Silents
DESERT DEMON, THE(1925); FIGHTING SHERIFF, THE(1925)

Capt. Fred F. Ellis, BMM/ret.
UNCONQUERED(1947), tech adv

Gary Ellis
GROUND ZERO(1973)

George Ellis
GODLESS GIRL, THE(1929); LEGEND OF BLOOD MOUNTAIN, THE(1965); GOLD GUITAR, THE(1966); MOONRUNNERS(1975); NIGHT THEY ROBBED BIG BERTHA'S, THE(1975)
Misc. Talkies
LEGEND OF BLOOD MOUNTAIN, THE(1965); SHANTYTOWN HONEYMOON(1972)

Georgia Ellis
DRAGNET(1954)

Glenn Ellis
MALAY NIGHTS(1933), w

Herb Ellis
DRAGNET(1954); PETE KELLY'S BLUES(1955); TOO MUCH, TOO SOON(1958); FORTUNE COOKIE, THE(1966); WHAT DID YOU DO IN THE WAR, DADDY?(1966); HANG'EM HIGH(1968); PARTY, THE(1968)

Herbert Ellis
ROGUE COP(1954)

Ian Ellis
DAY THE EARTH CAUGHT FIRE, THE(1961, Brit.); FLOOD, THE(1963, Brit.); SKY BIKE, THE(1967, Brit.)

J. Breckenridge Ellis
Silents
STORK'S NEST, THE(1915), w

J. Ellis
DESIREE(1954)

Jack Ellis
EAST SIDE SADIE(1929); HOLIDAY CAMP(1947, Brit.); NORA PRENTISS(1947); CANON CITY(1948); SMOKY MOUNTAIN MELODY(1949); LONG GRAY LINE, THE(1955)
Misc. Silents
NATURAL LAW, THE(1917)

Jacqueline Ellis
ACCIDENTAL DEATH(1963, Brit.); HI-JACKERS, THE(1963, Brit.); TRAITORS, THE(1963, Brit.); GUTTER GIRLS(1964, Brit.); SINISTER MAN, THE(1965, Brit.); NEVER BACK LOSERS(1967, Brit.)

James Ellis
WHERE THE BULLETS FLY(1966, Brit.)

Jeanne Ellis
GIRL OF THE GOLDEN WEST, THE(1938)

John Ellis
BEASTS OF BERLIN(1939); SKI PATROL(1940); DEVIL BAT, THE(1941); FOR BEAUTY'S SAKE(1941); MEN OF THE TIMBERLAND(1941)

Julie Ellis
LADIES LOVE DANGER(1935), w
1984
BEST DEFENSE(1984)

June C. Ellis
I NEVER PROMISED YOU A ROSE GARDEN(1977)

June Ellis
DEVIL-SHIP PIRATES, THE(1964, Brit.); MISADVENTURES OF MERLIN JONES, THE(1964); GYPSY GIRL(1966, Brit.); FIVE MILLION YEARS TO EARTH(1968, Brit.); ANNE OF THE THOUSAND DAYS(1969, Brit.); RING OF BRIGHT WATER(1969, Brit.); MELODY(1971, Brit.); YANKS(1979)

Juney Ellis
GLASS WALL, THE(1953); PROBLEM GIRLS(1953); DRAGON'S GOLD(1954); LONG, LONG TRAILER, THE(1954); COUNT THREE AND PRAY(1955); GIANT(1956); JUBAL(1956); LAST WAGON, THE(1956); JEANNE EAGELS(1957); JOE DAKOTA(1957); VALERIE(1957); LEGEND OF TOM DOOLEY, THE(1959)

Junie Ellis
BLUE DENIM(1959)

Katharine Ellis
VIVACIOUS LADY(1938)

Kathleen Ellis
FLIGHT FOR FREEDOM(1943); PAYMENT ON DEMAND(1951); SEALED CARGO(1951)

Kenneth M. Ellis
TRIAL OF VIVIENNE WARE, THE(1932), w

Leanne Ellis
FIGHTING BACK(1983, Brit.)

Lena Ellis
BIG SWITCH, THE(1970, Brit.)

Lillian Ellis
Misc. Silents
STRAUSS, THE WALTZ KING(1929, Ger.)

Lloyd Ellis
LOUISIANA(1947)

Marie Edith Ellis
Misc. Silents
MY PARTNER(1916)

Marvin Ellis
INDESTRUCTIBLE MAN, THE(1956)

Mary Ellis
BELLA DONNA(1934, Brit.); ALL THE KING'S HORSES(1935); PARIS IN SPRING(1935); FATAL LADY(1936); GLAMOROUS NIGHT(1937, Brit.); MAGIC BOX, THE(1952, Brit.); THREE WORLDS OF GULLIVER, THE(1960, Brit.)

Mary Jo Ellis
MAKE WAY FOR A LADY(1936); STRIKE UP THE BAND(1940); LIFE BEGINS FOR ANDY HARDY(1941); UNFINISHED BUSINESS(1941); JOAN OF OZARK(1942); MEET ME IN ST. LOUIS(1944); HARVEY GIRLS, THE(1946); B. F.'S DAUGHTER(1948); PIRATE, THE(1948)

Mary Joe Ellis
HOMECOMING(1948)

Maurice Ellis
LOST BOUNDARIES(1949)

Mel Ellis
WILD HORSE HANK(1979, Can.), w

Michael Ellis
DEATHWATCH(1980, Fr./Ger.), ed; GODSEND, THE(1980, Can.), ed; BRITTANIA HOSPITAL(1982, Brit.), ed; LORDS OF DISCIPLINE, THE(1983), ed
1984
COMFORT AND JOY(1984, Brit.), ed

Mike Ellis
CROSS OF IRON(1977, Brit., Ger.), ed

Mirco Ellis
LADY HAMILTON(1969, Ger./Ital./Fr.)

Mirko Ellis
STORMBOUND(1951, Ital.); DAUGHTERS OF DESTINY(1954, Fr./Ital.); MELODY OF LOVE(1954, Ital.); RED AND THE BLACK, THE(1954, Fr./Ital.); PARIS DOES STRANGE THINGS(1957, Fr./Ital.); HANNIBAL(1960, Ital.); BUFFALO BILL, HERO OF THE FAR WEST(1962, Ital.); WHITE SLAVE SHIP(1962, Fr./Ital.); GLADIATOR OF ROME(1963, Ital.); ARIZONA COLT(1965, It./Fr./Span.); WEB OF VIOLENCE(1966, Ital./Span.); HATE FOR HATE(1967, Ital.); MISSION BLOODY MARY(1967, Fr./Ital./Span.); NARCO MEN, THE(1969, Span./Ital.); DON'T TURN THE OTHER CHEEK(1974, Ital./Ger./Span.)

Patricia Ellis
CENTRAL PARK(1932); THREE ON A MATCH(1932); CONVENTION CITY(1933); ELMER THE GREAT(1933); KING'S VACATION, THE(1933); NARROW CORNER, THE(1933); PICTURE SNATCHER(1933); WORLD CHANGES, THE(1933); 42ND STREET(1933); AFFAIRS OF A GENTLEMAN(1934); BIG HEARTED HERBERT(1934); CIRCUS CLOWN(1934); EASY TO LOVE(1934); HAROLD TEEN(1934); HERE COMES THE GROOM(1934); LET'S BE RITZY(1934); ST. LOUIS KID, THE(1934); BRIGHT LIGHTS(1935); CASE OF THE LUCKY LEGS, THE(1935); HOLD'EM YALE(1935); NIGHT AT THE RITZ, A(1935); PAYOFF, THE(1935); STRANDED(1935); WHILE THE PATIENT SLEPT(1935); BOULDER DAM(1936); DOWN THE STRETCH(1936); FRESHMAN LOVE(1936); LOVE BEGINS AT TWENTY(1936); POSTAL INSPECTOR(1936); SING ME A LOVE SONG(1936); SNOWED UNDER(1936); MELODY FOR TWO(1937); RHYTHM IN THE CLOUDS(1937); STEP LIVELY, JEEVES(1937); VENUS MAKES TROUBLE(1937); BLOCKHEADS(1938); GAIETY GIRLS, THE(1938, Brit.); LADY IN THE MORGUE(1938); ROMANCE ON THE RUN(1938); FUGITIVE AT LARGE(1939)

Patti Marie Ellis
BRIGHT ROAD(1953)

Paul Ellis
BRIDGE OF SAN LUIS REY, THE(1929); COMMON LAW, THE(1931); NO MAN OF HER OWN(1933); SECRET SINNERS(1933); UNDER SECRET ORDERS(1933); MERRY WIDOW, THE(1934); ONE NIGHT OF LOVE(1934); FIGHTING CABALLERO(1935); PUBLIC OPINION(1935); RIP ROARING RILEY(1935); WOMEN MUST DRESS(1935); HOUSE OF A THOUSAND CANDLES, THE(1936); MURDER AT GLEN ATHOL(1936); WIFE VERSUS SECRETARY(1936); HEROES OF THE ALAMO(1938); NICK CARTER, MASTER DETECTIVE(1939); BLOOD AND SAND(1941); SIX LESSONS FROM MADAME LA ZONGA(1941); THEY MET IN ARGENTINA(1941); WHISTLING IN THE DARK(1941)
Misc. Talkies
PAPA SOLTERO(1939)
Silents
PACE THAT THRILLS, THE(1925); PRETTY LADIES(1925)
Misc. Silents
BITTER APPLES(1927); THREE HOURS(1927); CHARGE OF THE GAUCHOS, THE(1928)

Peter Ellis
LORD JEFF(1938); REMEMBRANCE(1982, Brit.)

Ray Ellis
CAULDRON OF BLOOD(1971, Span.), m

Raymond Ellis
LOVE AT SEA(1936, Brit.); JENIFER HALE(1937, Brit.); KNIGHTS FOR A DAY(1937, Brit.)
Silents
REST CURE, THE(1923, Brit.)

Robert Ellis
VARSITY(1928); BROADWAY(1929); LOVE TRAP, THE(1929); NIGHT PARADE(1929, Brit.); TONIGHT AT TWELVE(1929); SQUEALER, THE(1930); UNDERTOW(1930); WHAT MEN WANT(1930); ALOHA(1931); CAUGHT CHEATING(1931); DANCING DYNAMITE(1931); DESERT VENGEANCE(1931); FIGHTING SHERIFF, THE(1931); GOOD BAD GIRL, THE(1931); IS THERE JUSTICE?(1931); LAST PARADE, THE(1931); MOUNTED FURY(1931); MURDER AT MIDNIGHT(1931); AMERICAN MADNESS(1932); BEHIND STONE WALLS(1932); BROADWAY TO CHEYENNE(1932); COME ON DANGER!(1932); DARING DANGER(1932); DEADLINE, THE(1932); DEVIL PAYS, THE(1932); FIGHTING FOOL, THE(1932); LAST MAN(1932); MAN'S LAND, A(1932); MONSTER WALKS, THE(1932), w; ONE-MAN LAW(1932); PHANTOM EXPRESS, THE(1932); WHITE EAGLE(1932); BY APPOINTMENT ONLY(1933), w; DANCE, GIRL, DANCE(1933), w; IMPORTANT WITNESS, THE(1933); MAN OF SENTIMENT, A(1933), w; OFFICER 13(1933); ONLY YESTERDAY(1933); PENAL CODE, THE(1933); POLICE CALL(1933); REFORM GIRL(1933); SLIGHTLY MARRIED(1933); SOLDIERS OF THE STORM(1933), w; SPHINX, THE(1933); THRILL HUNTER, THE(1933); WOMEN WON'T TELL(1933); DANCING MAN(1934); FUGITIVE ROAD(1934), w; GIRL OF THE LIMBERLOST(1934); IN LOVE WITH LIFE(1934), w; IN THE MONEY(1934), w; I'VE GOT YOUR NUMBER(1934); KID MILLIONS(1934); MADAME SPY(1934); NOTORIOUS BUT NICE(1934); QUITTERS, THE(1934), w; TWIN HUSBANDS(1934), w; CHARLIE CHAN IN EGYPT(1935), w; HAPPINESS C.O.D.(1935), w; LADY IN SCARLET, THE(1935), w; ONE IN A MILLION(1935), w; PORT OF LOST DREAMS(1935), w; BACK TO NATURE(1936), w; CHARLIE CHAN AT THE CIRCUS(1936), w; CHARLIE CHAN AT THE RACE TRACK(1936), w; CHARLIE CHAN'S SECRET(1936), w; HERE COMES TROUBLE(1936), w; HITCH HIKE TO HEAVEN(1936), w; BIG BUSINESS(1937), w; BIG TOWN GIRL(1937), w; BORN RECKLESS(1937), w; CHARLIE CHAN AT MONTE CARLO(1937), w; CHARLIE CHAN AT THE OLYMPICS(1937), w; CHARLIE CHAN ON BROADWAY(1937), w; LAUGHING AT TROUBLE(1937), w; OFF TO THE RACES(1937), w; DOWN ON THE FARM(1938), w; LOVE ON A BUDGET(1938), w; RASCALS(1938), w; ROAD DEMON(1938), w; SHARPSHOOTERS(1938), w; SPEED TO BURN(1938), w; TRIP TO PARIS, A(1938), w; CHARLIE CHAN IN THE CITY OF DARKNESS(1939), w; CHASING DANGER(1939), w; ESCAPE, THE(1939), w; PARDON OUR NERVE(1939), w; SUSANNAH OF THE MOUNTIES(1939), w; TOO BUSY TO WORK(1939), w; HIGH SCHOOL(1940), w; LUCKY CISCO KID(1940), w; MAN WHO WOULDN'T TALK, THE(1940), w; STAR DUST(1940), w; TIN PAN ALLEY(1940), w; GREAT AMERICAN BROADCAST, THE(1941), w; SUN VALLEY SERENADE(1941), w; FOOTLIGHT SERENADE(1942), w; ICELAND(1942), w; SONG OF THE ISLANDS(1942), w; HELLO, FRISCO, HELLO(1943), w; FOUR JILLS IN A JEEP(1944), w; PIN UP GIRL(1944), w; SOMETHING FOR THE BOYS(1944), w; DO YOU LOVE ME?(1946), w; IF I'M LUCKY(1946), w; THREE LITTLE GIRLS IN BLUE(1946), w; APRIL SHOWERS(1948); EASY LIVING(1949); GREEN PROMISE, THE(1949); KISS FOR CORLISS, A(1949); I'LL GET BY(1950), w; WALK SOFTLY, STRANGER(1950); CALL ME MISTER(1951); NIAGARA(1953); LONG GRAY LINE, THE(1955); MC CONNELL STORY, THE(1955); PILLARS OF THE SKY(1956); SPACE MASTER X-7(1958); GIDGET(1959)
1984
REPO MAN(1984)
Misc. Talkies
FROM BROADWAY TO CHEYENNE(1932); SPEED DEMON(1933); TREASON(1933); CAPTURED IN CHINATOWN(1935)
Silents
IN FOR THIRTY DAYS(1919); LOUISIANA(1919); DAUGHTER PAYS, THE(1920), a, d; ANNA ASCENDS(1922); TAILOR MADE MAN, A(1922), art d; WILD HONEY(1922); WOMAN WHO FOOLED HERSELF, THE(1922), a, d; WANTERS, THE(1923); LAW FORBIDS, THE(1924); LOVER'S LANE(1924); ON PROBA-

TION(1924); LADY ROBINHOOD(1925); NORTHERN CODE(1925); RAGTIME(1927); FREEDOM OF THE PRESS(1928); MARRY THE GIRL(1928)
Misc. Silents
APACHES OF PARIS, THE(1915), a, d; SECRET ROOM, THE(1915); CHILD OF DESTINY, THE(1916); CUSTOMARY TWO WEEKS, THE(1917); FRINGE OF SOCIETY, THE(1918), d; PEGGY DOES HER DARNDEST(1919); SPITE BRIDE, THE(1919); THIRD KISS, THE(1919); FIGUREHEAD, THE(1920), d; FOOL AND HIS MONEY, A(1920), d; IMP, THE(1920), d; CHIVALROUS CHARLEY(1921), d; DIVORCE OF CONVENIENCE, A(1921), d; HANDCUFFS OR KISSES(1921); LADIES MUST LIVE(1921); DANGEROUS LITTLE DEMON, THE(1922); HURRICANE'S GAL(1922); INFIDEL, THE(1922); LOVE'S MASQUERADE(1922); DARK SECRETS(1923); FLAME OF LIFE, THE(1923); MARK OF THE BEAST(1923); WILD PARTY, THE(1923); CAFE IN CAIRO, A(1924); FOR SALE(1924); SILK STOCKING SAL(1924); DEFEND YOURSELF(1925); FORBIDDEN CARGO(1925); PART TIME WIFE, THE(1925); S.O.S. PERILS OF THE SEA(1925); BROODING EYES(1926); DEVIL'S DICE(1926); GIRL FROM MONTMARTRE, THE(1926); LADIES OF LEISURE(1926); WHISPERING CANYON(1926); LURE OF THE NIGHT CLUB, THE(1927); LAW AND THE MAN(1928); LAW'S LASH, THE(1928); RESTLESS YOUTH(1928)

Robin Ellis
EUROPEANS, THE(1979, Brit.)

Sarah Ellis
WINSTANLEY(1979, Brit.), ed

Seger Ellis
ONE RAINY AFTERNOON(1936)

Stephen Ellis
FOUR GIRLS IN TOWN(1956); TARNISHED ANGELS, THE(1957)

Steve Ellis
WORLD IN MY CORNER(1956)

Sue Ellis
TOUCH OF FLESH, THE(1960)

Susan Ellis
LISETTE(1961)

T. Arthur Ellis
STRICTLY ILLEGAL(1935, Brit.)

T.C. Ellis
SWEET JESUS, PREACHER MAN(1973)

Tawn Ellis
SHRIEK OF THE MUTILATED(1974)

Terry Ellis
1984
TEACHERS(1984)

Tom Ellis
MARATHON MAN(1976)

Tony Ellis
CORN IS GREEN, THE(1945); MOLLY AND ME(1945); THIS LOVE OF OURS(1945); GOLDEN EARRINGS(1947)

Vincent Ellis
SAINTS AND SINNERS(1949, Brit.)

Vivian Ellis
NIGHT AND DAY(1933, Brit.), m; MISTER CINDERS(1934, Brit.), m

Von Ellis
MOON ZERO TWO(1970, Brit.), m

Walter Ellis
ALMOST A HONEYMOON(1930, Brit.), w; LET ME EXPLAIN, DEAR(1932), w; HAWLEY'S OF HIGH STREET(1933, Brit.), w; HER LAST AFFAIRE(1935, Brit.), w; ALMOST A HONEYMOON(1938, Brit.), w; BEDTIME STORY(1938, Brit.), d&w

Ward Ellis
STRIP, THE(1951); SECOND GREATEST SEX, THE(1955); WAR DRUMS(1957); THREE NUTS IN SEARCH OF A BOLT(1964), ch

William Ellis
DRACULA A.D. 1972(1972, Brit.)

Ellis Larkins Trio
JOE LOUIS STORY, THE(1953)

George Ellisha
SPLINTERS IN THE AIR(1937, Brit.)

Angela Ellison
CARRY ON SPYING(1964, Brit.)

Art Ellison
CARNIVAL OF SOULS(1962); PAPER MOON(1973); SHOOT IT: BLACK, SHOOT IT: BLUE(1974)

Bob Ellison
BUCKTOWN(1975), w

Burns Ellison
1984
SIGNAL 7(1984)

Catherine Ellison
GRAVEYARD OF HORROR(1971, Span.)

Christopher Ellison
1984
GIVE MY REGARDS TO BROAD STREET(1984, Brit.)

Clint Ellison
PRIME CUT(1972)

Corey Ellison
UNCENSORED(1944, Brit.)

David Ellison
MACBETH(1971, Brit.)

Dorothee Ellison
UNCLE TOM'S CABIN(1969, Fr./Ital./Ger./Yugo.)

Edith Ellison
LADIES OF LEISURE(1930)

Gwen Ellison
LUGGAGE OF THE GODS(1983)

Harlan Ellison
OSCAR, THE(1966), w; BOY AND HIS DOG, A(1975), w

James Ellison
PLAY GIRL(1932); CAROLINA(1934); DEATH OF THE DIAMOND(1934); HOPALONG CASSIDY(1935); RECKLESS(1935); WINNING TICKET, THE(1935); TRAIL DUST(1936); ANNAPOLIS SALUTE(1937); BARRIER, THE(1937); BORDERLAND(1937); PLAINSMAN, THE(1937); 23 ½ HOURS LEAVE(1937); MOTHER CAREY'S CHICKENS(1938); NEXT TIME I MARRY(1938); VIVACIOUS LADY(1938);

ALMOST A GENTLEMAN(1939); FIFTH AVENUE GIRL(1939); HOTEL FOR WOM-EN(1939); SORORITY HOUSE(1939); ZENOBIA(1939); ANNE OF WINDY PO-PLARS(1940); PLAY GIRL(1940); YOU CAN'T FOOL YOUR WIFE(1940); CHARLEY'S AUNT(1941); ICE-CAPADES(1941); THEY MET IN ARGENTINA(1941); ARMY SUR-GEON(1942); CAREFUL, SOFT SHOULDERS(1942); THAT OTHER WOMAN(1942); UNDYING MONSTER, THE(1942); DIXIE DUGAN(1943); GANG'S ALL HERE, THE(1943); I WALKED WITH A ZOMBIE(1943); JOHNNY DOESN'T LIVE HERE ANY MORE(1944); LADY, LET'S DANCE(1944); HOLLYWOOD AND VINE(1945); G.I. WAR BRIDES(1946); CALENDAR GIRL(1947); CARTER CASE, THE(1947); GHOST GOES WILD, THE(1947); LAST OF THE WILD HORSES(1948); I KILLED GERONIMO(1950); TEXAN MEETS CALAMITY JANE, THE(1950); KENTUCKY JUBILEE(1951); OK-LAHOMA JUSTICE(1951); MAN FROM BLACK HILLS, THE(1952)

Jane Ellison
TROCADERO(1944)

Jennie Ellison
Misc. Silents
BY HOOK OR CROOK(1918); HEREDITY(1918); SCAR, THE(1919)

Jimmy Ellison
BAR 20 RIDES AGAIN(1936); CALL OF THE PRAIRIE(1936); EAGLE'S BROOD, THE(1936); HITCH HIKE LADY(1936); LEATHERNECKS HAVE LANDED, THE(1936); THREE ON THE TRAIL(1936); HEART OF THE WEST(1937); COLORADO RANGER(1950); CROOKED RIVER(1950); FAST ON THE DRAW(1950); HOSTILE COUNTRY(1950); MARSHAL OF HELDORADO(1950); TEXAS LAWMEN(1951); DEAD MAN'S TRAIL(1952); TEXAS CITY(1952)
Misc. Talkies
MAN FROM THE BLACK HILLS(1952)

Jimmy [James] Ellison
WEST OF THE BRAZOS(1950); WHISTLING HILLS(1951); WHEN THE GIRLS TAKE OVER(1962)

Jimmy "Shamrock" Ellison
EVERYBODY'S DANCIN'(1950)

John Ellison
SIMON AND LAURA(1956, Brit.)

Joseph Ellison
DON'T GO IN THE HOUSE(1980), d, w

Joy Ellison
SUPERDAD(1974)

Katherine Ellison
CIRCUS WORLD(1964); WITCH WITHOUT A BROOM, A(1967, U.S./Span.)

Margaret Ellison
PERSONAL BEST(1982)

Marjorie Ellison
Silents
RANSON'S FOLLY(1915); GILDED SPIDER, THE(1916)
Misc. Silents
TANGLED HEARTS(1916)

Mark Ellison
Misc. Silents
NOT GUILTY(1915)

Michael Ellison
STOLEN ASSIGNMENT(1955, Brit.)

Sheryl Ellison
STRANGERS WHEN WE MEET(1960)

Stanley Ellison
RIDIN' DOWN THE TRAIL(1947); SIX GUN SERENADE(1947)

Tim Ellison
HOUSE IN THE WOODS, THE(1957, Brit.); BANK RAIDERS, THE(1958, Brit.)

True Ellison
MR. HOBBS TAKES A VACATION(1962); WHEN THE GIRLS TAKE OVER(1962)

Vicki Ellison
UP YOUR TEDDY BEAR(1970)

Violet Ellison
Silents
MOTORING(1927, Brit.)

Daisy Elliston
Misc. Silents
DUCHESS OF SEVEN DIALS, THE(1920)

Grace Elliston
Misc. Silents
BLACK FEAR(1915)

Mark Elliston
Misc. Silents
FIBBERS, THE(1917); SMALL TOWN GUY, THE(1917)

Robert Ellmer
BULLFIGHTERS, THE(1945)

Max Elloy
NOUS IRONS A PARIS(1949, Fr.); FATHER'S DILEMMA(1952, Ital.); UTOPIA(1952, Fr./Ital.)

Eberhard Ellrich
NOT RECONCILED, OR "ONLY VIOLENCE HELPS WHERE IT RULES"(1969, Ger.)

Comdr. Edward Ellsberg
HELL BELOW(1933), w

Effie Ellsler
WOMAN TRAP(1929); LADY OF SCANDAL, THE(1930); SONG O' MY HEART(1930); DADDY LONG LEGS(1931); FRONT PAGE, THE(1931); UP POPS THE DEVIL(1931); CHIEF, THE(1933); DR. BULL(1933); GIRL IN 419(1933); SECOND HAND WIFE(1933); HOLD THAT GIRL(1934); BLACK FURY(1935); WHOLE TOWN'S TALKING, THE(1935); WE'RE ONLY HUMAN(1936)
Silents
OLD IRONSIDES(1926); ACTRESS, THE(1928)

Edna Ellsmere
Misc. Silents
BACHELOR'S CLUB, THE(1929)

Abraham Ellstein
YIDDLE WITH HIS FIDDLE(1937, Pol.), m

Allan Vaughan Ellston
PARADISE ISLE(1937), w

Christine Ellsworth
TOWN THAT DREADED SUNDOWN, THE(1977)

Dave Ellsworth
ROLLOVER(1981)

Elmer Ellsworth
SEA FURY(1929), w; ESCORT WEST(1959), cos

Heinz Ellsworth
FLOWER THIEF, THE(1962)

James Ellsworth
FIVE MINUTES TO LIVE(1961), p

Nick Ellsworth
SPY WHO LOVED ME, THE(1977, Brit.); FORCE 10 FROM NAVARONE(1978, Brit.)
Misc. Talkies
DOLL'S EYE(1982)

Robert E. Ellsworth
PSYCHO II(1983), cos

Robert Ellsworth
Silents
KING OF KINGS, THE(1927)

Scott Ellsworth
H.O.T.S.(1979)

Stephen Ellsworth
SCREAMING MIMI(1958); WILD HERITAGE(1958)

Warren Ellsworth
Silents
OVERALLS(1916)
Misc. Silents
LIFE'S BLIND ALLEY(1916); SIGN OF THE SPADE, THE(1916)

Luis Ellul
CLUE OF THE MISSING APE, THE(1953, Brit.)

Joan Ellum
SOUTH RIDING(1938, Brit.); PRISON WITHOUT BARS(1939, Brit.)

W. T. Ellwanger
COME OUT OF THE PANTRY(1935, Brit.); TOUCH OF THE MOON, A(1936, Brit.); MERRY COMES TO STAY(1937, Brit.)
Silents
ANGEL ESQUIRE(1919, Brit.); IN HIS GRIP(1921, Brit.)
Misc. Silents
GREEN TERROR, THE(1919, Brit.); FALL OF A SAINT, THE(1920, Brit.)

William T. Ellwanger
TROUBLED WATERS(1936, Brit.)

Jean Ellyn
C-MAN(1949)

Mary Ellyn
HOME FREE ALL(1983)

Maura Ellyn
1984
HOME FREE ALL(1984)

Gunilla Elm-Tornkvist
DEVIL, THE(1963)

Eugene Elman
SKATEBOARD(1978)

Gene Elman
WORKING GIRLS, THE(1973); THUNDERBOLT AND LIGHTFOOT(1974)

I. Elman
NO GREATER LOVE(1944, USSR), w

Irving Elman
ACCOMPLICE(1946), w; STRANGE JOURNEY(1946), w; BACKLASH(1947), w; CRIMSON KEY, THE(1947), w; JEWELS OF BRANDENBURG(1947), w; ROSES ARE RED(1947), w; CHALLENGE, THE(1948), w; THIRTEEN LEAD SOLDIERS(1948), w

John Elman
DARK AT THE TOP OF THE STAIRS, THE(1960)

Sarita Elman
VISITING HOURS(1982, Can.)

Ziggy Elman
FABULOUS DORSEYS, THE(1947); BENNY GOODMAN STORY, THE(1956)

Zarubi Elmassian
NAUGHTY MARIETTA(1935)

Edith Elmay
EMBEZZLED HEAVEN(1959,Ger.); HOUSE OF THE THREE GIRLS, THE(1961, Aust.); GOOD SOLDIER SCHWEIK, THE(1963, Ger.); $100 A NIGHT(1968, Ger.)

Don Elmblad
ONE FROM THE HEART(1982)

Garry J. Elmendorf
1984
BUDDY SYSTEM, THE(1984), spec eff; RACING WITH THE MOON(1984), spec eff

Elmer
SMALL WORLD OF SAMMY LEE, THE(1963, Brit.); 1941(1979)

Elmer [Ed Platt]
GUNSMOKE RANCH(1937)

Billy Elmer
KITTY FOYLE(1940); MAGNIFICENT AMBERSONS, THE(1942); REAP THE WILD WIND(1942)
Silents
MASTER MIND, THE(1914); READY MONEY(1914); SQUAW MAN, THE(1914); VIRGINIAN, THE(1914); ARAB, THE(1915); CAPTIVE, THE(1915); CARMEN(1915); GIRL OF THE GOLDEN WEST, THE(1915); KINDLING(1915); FAMILY SKELETON, THE(1918); PLAYING THE GAME(1918); IN SEARCH OF A THRILL(1923)
Misc. Silents
UNAFRAID, THE(1915); BLACKLIST(1916); COUNTESS CHARMING, THE(1917); HER STRANGE WEDDING(1917); PRISON WITHOUT WALLS, THE(1917); COALS OF FIRE(1918); BATTLING MASON(1924)

Clarence Elmer
Silents
CLIMBERS, THE(1915); MAN WHO, THE(1921)
Misc. Silents
MORAL COURAGE(1917)

Clarence J. Elmer
Silents
JOY GIRL, THE(1927)
Jonas Elmer
1984
ZAPPA(1984, Den.)
William Elmer
CONDEMNED(1929)
Silents
ROSE OF THE RANCHO(1914); WOMAN, THE(1915); JOAN THE WOMAN(1916); PLOW GIRL, THE(1916); ALIAS MIKE MORAN(1919)
Misc. Silents
HIS MOTHER'S BOY(1917); CHEATING HERSELF(1919); FORBIDDEN TRAILS(1920); IRON TO GOLD(1922)
Elmer-Clifton
HARD GUY(1941), d
Charles Elmergreen
WITHOUT RESERVATIONS(1946)
Frederick Elmes
BREAKFAST IN BED(1978), ph; VALLEY GIRL(1983), ph
Guy Elmes
UNDERCOVER AGENT(1935, Brit.), w; OUTPOST IN MALAYA(1952, Brit.), w; BAD BLONDE(1953, Brit.), w; WHEEL OF FATE(1953, Brit.), w; BANG! YOU'RE DEAD(1954, Brit.), w; STRANGER'S HAND, THE(1955, Brit.), w; ACROSS THE BRIDGE(1957, Brit.), w; HELLO LONDON(1958, Brit.), w; ELEPHANT GUN(1959, Brit.), w; IMMORAL CHARGE(1962, Brit.), w; STORY OF JOSEPH AND HIS BRETHREN THE(1962, Brit.), w; STRANGLEHOLD(1962, Brit.), w; CAPTIVE CITY, THE(1963, Ital.), w; FACE IN THE RAIN, A(1963), w; CONQUERED CITY(1966, Ital.), w; EL GRECO(1966, Ital., Fr.), w; SUMARINE X-1(1969, Brit.), w; INVINCIBLE SIX, THE(1970, U.S./Iran), w; NIGHT VISITOR, THE(1970, Swed./U.S.), w
Nicole Elmi
NIGHT CHILD(1975, Brit./Ital.)
Nicoletta Elmi
BARON BLOOD(1972, Ital.)
Peeme Elmo
MISSISSIPPI RHYTHM(1949)
Barney Elmore
YOU WERE MEANT FOR ME(1948)
Dick Elmore
O.S.S.(1946); FORCE OF EVIL(1948)
Gilbert Elmore
SHEPHERD OF THE HILLS, THE(1964); PLASTIC DOME OF NORMA JEAN, THE(1966)
Marion Elmore
Misc. Silents
DANGEROUS TOYS(1921)
Otis Elmore
LAST PICTURE SHOW, THE(1971)
Pearl Elmore
Silents
INTOLERANCE(1916); MEDIATOR, THE(1916); PEST, THE(1919)
Misc. Silents
SOLD FOR MARRIAGE(1916)
Richard Elmore
DESERT FOX, THE(1951); ENEMY BELOW, THE(1957)
Albert Elms
MANFISH(1956), m; SATELLITE IN THE SKY(1956), m; BLUEBEARD'S TEN HONEYMOONS(1960, Brit.), m; GREAT VAN ROBBERY, THE(1963, Brit.), m; GREAT ARMORED CAR SWINDLE, THE(1964), m
Frederick Elms
ERASERHEAD(1978), ph
Eloise
NAVY BLUES(1937), cos; TWO WISE MAIDS(1937), cos; WRONG ROAD, THE(1937), cos; YOUTH ON PAROLE(1937), cos
Xabier Elorriaga
1984
ESCAPE FROM SEGOVIA(1984, Span.)
Jose Maria Elorrieta
TREASURE OF MAKUBA, THE(1967, U.S./Span.), w
Jean-Claude Eloy
NUN, THE(1971, Fr.), m
Jeanette Elphick
PHANTOM STOCKMAN, THE(1953, Aus.)
John Elphick
PLACE OF ONE'S OWN, A(1945, Brit.), art d; DEAR MURDERER(1947, Brit.), art d; WHEN THE BOUGH BREAKS(1947, Brit.), art d; SEVEN DAYS TO NOON(1950, Brit.), art d; STRANGER FROM VENUS, THE(1954, Brit.), art d; DYNAMITERS, THE(1956, Brit.), art d; HAUNTED STRANGLER, THE(1958, Brit.), art d; MANIA(1961, Brit.), art d
Kate Elphick
BIDDY(1983, Brit.)
Michael Elphick
FRAULEIN DOKTOR(1969, Ital./Yugo.); HAMLET(1969, Brit.); WHERE'S JACK?(1969, Brit.); CRY OF THE BANSHEE(1970, Brit.); BUTTERCUP CHAIN, THE(1971, Brit.); O LUCKY MAN!(1973, Brit.); STARDUST(1974, Brit.); ODD JOB, THE(1978, Brit.); GREAT TRAIN ROBBERY, THE(1979, Brit.); QUADROPHENIA(1979, Brit.); ELEPHANT MAN, THE(1980, Brit.); PRIVATES ON PARADE(1982); CURSE OF THE PINK PANTHER(1983); GORKY PARK(1983)
1984
ELEMENT OF CRIME, THE(1984, Den.); MEMED MY HAWK(1984, Brit.); ORDEAL BY INNOCENCE(1984, Brit.); PRIVATES ON PARADE(1984, Brit.)
Daphne Elphinstone
GEORGE IN CIVVY STREET(1946, Brit.)
Derek Elphinstone
EAST MEETS WEST(1936, Brit.); FOUR FEATHERS, THE(1939, Brit.); THREE COCKEYED SAILORS(1940, Brit.); IN WHICH WE SERVE(1942, Brit.); NIGHT BOAT TO DUBLIN(1946, Brit.); RED SHOES, THE(1948, Brit.); ARMCHAIR DETECTIVE, THE(1952, Brit.), a, p, w; DISTANT TRUMPET(1952, Brit.), a, p, w; SECRET PEOPLE(1952, Brit.)

John Elrod
KID COURAGEOUS(1935)
Lu Elrod
SEDUCTION OF JOE TYNAN, THE(1979)
Bob Elross
TELL ME A RIDDLE(1980)
1984
SIGNAL 7(1984)
Robert Elross
CUJO(1983); RIGHT STUFF, THE(1983)
Egon Els
COPPER, THE(1930, Brit.), w
Elsa The Lioness
LIVING FREE(1972, Brit.)
Ann Elsden
MEN ARE CHILDREN TWICE(1953, Brit.)
Garrett Elsden
Silents
GAY AND DEVILISH(1922), w
Ann Elsdon
I AM A CAMERA(1955, Brit.)
David Else
Misc. Talkies
PERILOUS JOURNEY(1983)
Jon Else
OFF THE WALL(1977), ph; JOURNEYS FROM BERLIN–1971(1980), ph
James Elsegood
TOO MUCH, TOO SOON(1958)
Robert S. Elsen
HOLD BACK THE NIGHT(1956), ed; HOT ROD GANG(1958), ed
Arnica Elsendoorn
LIFT, THE(1983, Neth.)
Frank B. Elser
FARMER TAKES A WIFE, THE(1953), w
Paula Elser
1984
SIXTEEN CANDLES(1984)
Ian Elsey
ASCENDANCY(1983, Brit.), p
Michael Elsey
Misc. Talkies
CITIZEN SOLDIER(1984), d
Arne Elsholtz
ESCAPE FROM EAST BERLIN(1962)
Peter Elsholtz
FINAL CHORD, THE(1936, Ger.)
Elsie the Cow
LITTLE MEN(1940)
Lily Elsie
Silents
GREAT LOVE, THE(1918)
Misc. Silents
COMRADESHIP(1919, Brit.)
V. Elsky
Misc. Silents
LOVE OF A STATE COUNCILLOR(1915, USSR); ISLE OF OBLIVION(1917, USSR)
Edeltraut Elsner
BRIDGE, THE(1961, Ger.)
Hannelore Elsner
FREDDY UNTER FREMDEN STERNEN(1962, Ger.); LOVE FEAST, THE(1966, Ger.)
Maria Elsner
ALLURING GOAL, THE(1930, Germ.)
Isobel Elsom
OTHER WOMAN, THE(1931, Brit.); STRANGLEHOLD(1931, Brit.); CROOKED LADY, THE(1932, Brit.); ILLEGAL(1932, Brit.); THIRTEENTH CANDLE, THE(1933, Brit.); PRIMROSE PATH, THE(1934, Brit.); LADIES IN RETIREMENT(1941); EAGLE SQUADRON(1942); GHOST AND MRS. MUIR, THE(1942); SEVEN SWEETHEARTS(1942); WAR AGAINST MRS. HADLEY, THE(1942); YOU WERE NEVER LOVELIER(1942); FIRST COMES COURAGE(1943); FOREVER AND A DAY(1943); LAUGH YOUR BLUES AWAY(1943); MY KINGDOM FOR A COOK(1943); BETWEEN TWO WORLDS(1944); CASANOVA BROWN(1944); WHITE CLIFFS OF DOVER, THE(1944); HORN BLOWS AT MIDNIGHT, THE(1945); UNSEEN, THE(1945); OF HUMAN BONDAGE(1946); TWO SISTERS FROM BOSTON(1946); ESCAPE ME NEVER(1947); IVY(1947); LOVE FROM A STRANGER(1947); MONSIEUR VERDOUX(1947); PARADINE CASE, THE(1947); TWO MRS. CARROLLS, THE(1947); SMART WOMAN(1948); SECRET GARDEN, THE(1949); DEEP IN MY HEART(1954); DESIREE(1954); KING'S THIEF, THE(1955); LOVE IS A MANY-SPLENDORED THING(1955); LUST FOR LIFE(1956); OVER-EXPOSED(1956); 23 PACES TO BAKER STREET(1956); GUNS OF FORT PETTICOAT, THE(1957); ROCK-A-BYE BABY(1958); MIRACLE, THE(1959); YOUNG PHILADELPHIANS, THE(1959); ERRAND BOY, THE(1961); SECOND TIME AROUND, THE(1961); WHO'S MINDING THE STORE?(1963); MY FAIR LADY(1964); PLEASURE SEEKERS, THE(1964)
Silents
ONWARD CHRISTIAN SOLDIERS(1918, Brit.); WAY OF AN EAGLE, THE(1918, Brit.); EDGE O'BEYOND(1919, Brit.); MRS. THOMPSON(1919, Brit.); AUNT RACHEL(1920, Brit.); DEBT OF HONOR(1922, Brit.); GAME OF LIFE, THE(1922, Brit.); LAST WITNESS, THE(1925, Brit.)
Misc. Silents
MILESTONES(1916, Brit.); GOD BLESS OUR RED, WHITE AND BLUE(1918, Brit.); MAN WHO WON, THE(1918, Brit.); TINKER, TAILOR, SOLDIER, SAILOR(1918, Brit.); WANTED - A WIFE(1918, Brit.); LINKED BY FATE(1919, Brit.); MEMBER OF THE TATTERSALL'S, A(1919, Brit.); SWEETHEARTS(1919, Brit.); NANCE(1920, Brit.); FOR HER FATHER'S SAKE(1921, Brit.); DICK TURPIN'S RIDE TO YORK(1922, Brit.); HARBOUR LIGHTS, THE(1923, Brit.); SIGN OF FOUR, THE(1923, Brit.); WANDERING JEW, THE(1923, Brit.); LOVE STORY OF ALIETTE BRUNTON, THE(1924, Brit.); WHO IS THE MAN?(1924, Brit.)
Jonathan Elsom
ROUGH CUT(1980, Brit.)

Jonathon Elsom
SMASHING TIME(1967 Brit.)

Alf Elson
DUEL AT DIABLO(1966)

Don Elson
GREAT TEXAS DYNAMITE CHASE, THE(1976)
1984
GREMLINS(1984)

Donald Elson
JULIUS CAESAR(1953); DAY OF THE OUTLAW(1959); DREAMS OF GLASS(1969); ESCAPE FROM THE PLANET OF THE APES(1971); VAN, THE(1977)

Isabel Elson
Misc. Silents
JUST A MOTHER(1923); DANCE MAGIC(1927)

Lee Elson
CRACK-UP(1946); OUT OF THE PAST(1947); HARPOON(1948)

Robert Elson
SCHOOL FOR SECRETS(1946, Brit.)

Else Elster
BLONDE NIGHTINGALE(1931, Ger.)

J.G. Elster
DR. TARR'S TORTURE DUNGEON(1972, Mex.), p

Allan Elston
PARADISE EXPRESS(1937), w

Allan Vaughn Elston
ISLE OF DESTINY(1940), w

Robert Elston
MARK OF THE WITCH(1970)

Tim Elston
Misc. Talkies
BELLAMY: MESSAGE GIRL MURDERS(1980)

Elstree
Silents
RING, THE(1927, Brit.), set d; CHAMPAGNE(1928, Brit.), set d; FARMER'S WIFE, THE(1928, Brit.), set d; MANXMAN, THE(1929, Brit.), set d

Bob Elswit
END OF AUGUST, THE(1982), ph

Robert Elswit
WALTZ ACROSS TEXAS(1982), ph

Warren Elsworth
Silents
SECRET LOVE(1916)

Ruby Elsy
TELL NO TALES(1939)

Anielka Elter
GODLESS GIRL, THE(1929)
Silents
MERRY WIDOW, THE(1925); KING OF KINGS, THE(1927)
Misc. Silents
LAST MOMENT, THE(1928)

Capt. Marco Elter
Silents
JOY STREET(1929)

Julian Eltinge
MAID TO ORDER(1932); IF I HAD MY WAY(1940)
Silents
HOW MOLLY MADE GOOD(1915); CLEVER MRS. CARFAX, THE(1917)
Misc. Silents
COUNTESS CHARMING, THE(1917); WIDOW'S MIGHT, THE(1918); ISLE OF LOVE, THE(1922); MADAME BEHAVE(1925)

Don Eltner
BEGINNING OF THE END(1957)

Arthur Elton
Misc. Silents
RICH SLAVE, THE(1921)

Edmond Elton
SHOULD A GIRL MARRY?(1939)

Edmund Elton
STELLA DALLAS(1937); SPAWN OF THE NORTH(1938); STORY OF ALEXANDER GRAHAM BELL, THE(1939); THOU SHALT NOT KILL(1939); ABE LINCOLN IN ILLINOIS(1940); RETURN OF FRANK JAMES, THE(1940); BACK IN THE SADDLE(1941); HERE COMES MR. JORDAN(1941); PENNY SERENADE(1941); SAINT IN PALM SPRINGS, THE(1941)
Misc. Silents
MYSTERY OF THE YELLOW ROOM, THE(1919)

Eileen Elton
TWICE UPON A TIME(1953, Brit.); LADY OF VENGEANCE(1957, Brit)

Hugh Elton
MAN OUTSIDE, THE(1968, Brit.)

Jack Elton
RIGHT HAND OF THE DEVIL, THE(1963)

John Elton
STRIP TEASE MURDER(1961, Brit.), p

Philip Elton
PURSUERS, THE(1961, Brit.), p; DURANT AFFAIR, THE(1962, Brit.), p

Ray Elton
BLIND GODDESS, THE(1948, Brit.), ph; BOY, A GIRL AND A BIKE, A(1949 Brit.), ph; MARRY ME!(1949, Brit.), ph; QUARTET(1949, Brit.), ph; LAST HOLIDAY(1950, Brit.), ph; FOUR DAYS(1951, Brit.), ph; SMART ALEC(1951, Brit.), ph; SCHOOL FOR BRIDES(1952, Brit.), ph; BACHELOR IN PARIS(1953, Brit.), ph

Raymond Elton
SOLDIER, SAILOR(1944, Brit.), ph; MIRANDA(1949, Brit.), ph

Richard Elton
1984
BOSTONIANS, THE(1984), set d

Guy Eltsosis
DISTANT TRUMPET, A(1964)

Hans Elvenspoeck
BRIDGE, THE(1961, Ger.)

Sonia Elverson [Holm]
SCHOOL FOR SECRETS(1946, Brit.)

Maurice Elvey
HIGH TREASON(1929, Brit.), d; SCHOOL FOR SCANDAL, THE(1930, Brit.), p&d; HER STRANGE DESIRE(1931, Brit.), d; SALLY IN OUR ALLEY(1931, Brit.), d; FOOTSTEPS IN THE NIGHT(1932, Brit.), d; FRAIL WOMEN(1932, Brit.), d; MARRIAGE BOND, THE(1932, Brit.), d; WATER GYPSIES, THE(1932, Brit.), d; I LIVED WITH YOU(1933, Brit.), d; THIS WEEK OF GRACE(1933, Brit.), d; BRIDE OF THE LAKE(1934, Brit.), d; LOVE, LIFE AND LAUGHTER(1934, Brit.), d; ROAD HOUSE(1934, Brit.), d; WOMAN IN COMMAND, THE(1934 Brit.), d; CLAIRVOYANT, THE(1935, Brit.), d; HEAT WAVE(1935, Brit.), d; IN A MONASTERY GARDEN(1935), d; MY SONG FOR YOU(1935, Brit.), d; PHANTOM FIEND, THE(1935, Brit.), d; PRINCESS CHARMING(1935, Brit.), d; TRANSATLANTIC TUNNEL(1935, Brit.), d; WANDERING JEW, THE(1935, Brit.), d; MAN IN THE MIRROR, THE(1936, Brit.), d; CHANGE FOR A SOVEREIGN(1937, Brit.), d; LOST CHORD, THE(1937, Brit.), d; MELODY AND ROMANCE(1937, Brit.), d, w; WHO KILLED JOHN SAVAGE?(1937, Brit.), d; LIGHTNING CONDUCTOR(1938, Brit.), d; RETURN OF THE FROG, THE(1938, Brit.), d; SWORD OF HONOUR(1938, Brit.), p&d; WHO GOES NEXT?(1938, Brit.), d; SONS OF THE SEA(1939, Brit.), d, w; SPY OF NAPOLEON(1939, Brit.), d; LOST ON THE WESTERN FRONT(1940, Brit.), d; ROOM FOR TWO(1940, Brit.), d; SPIDER, THE(1940, Brit.), d; UNDER YOUR HAT(1940, Brit.), d; SALUTE JOHN CITIZEN(1942, Brit.), d; GENTLE SEX, THE(1943, Brit.), d; LAMP STILL BURNS, THE(1943, Brit.), d; STRAWBERRY ROAN(1945, Brit.), d; BEWARE OF PITY(1946, Brit.), d; GAY INTRUDERS, THE(1946, Brit.), d; OBSESSED(1951, Brit.), d; THIRD VISITOR, THE(1951, Brit.), d; MY WIFE'S LODGER(1952, Brit.), d; GREAT GAME, THE(1953, Brit.), d; HOUSE OF BLACKMAIL(1953, Brit.), d; IS YOUR HONEYMOON REALLY NECESSARY?(1953, Brit.), d; GAY DOG, THE(1954, Brit.), d; HAPPINESS OF THREE WOMEN, THE(1954, Brit.), d; HARASSED HERO, THE(1954, Brit.), d; WHAT EVERY WOMAN WANTS(1954, Brit.), d; ROOM IN THE HOUSE(1955, Brit.), d; YOU LUCKY PEOPLE(1955, Brit.), d; DRY ROT(1956, Brit.), d; FUN AT ST. FANNY'S(1956, Brit.), d; LAST MAN TO HANG, THE(1956, Brit.), w; STARS IN YOUR EYES(1956, Brit.), d; SECOND FIDDLE(1957, Brit.), d
Silents
LOVE IN A WOOD(1915, Brit.), d; KING'S DAUGHTER, THE(1916, Brit.), d; PRINCESS OF HAPPY CHANCE, THE(1916, Brit.), d; FLAMES(1917, Brit.), d; GAY LORD QUEX, THE(1917, Brit.), d; GRIT OF A JEW, THE(1917, Brit.), d; ADAM BEDE(1918, Brit.), d; GREATEST WISH IN THE WORLD, THE(1918, Brit.), d; NELSON(1918, Brit.), d; ELUSIVE PIMPERNEL, THE(1919, Brit.), d; KEEPER OF THE DOOR(1919, Brit.), d; MR. WU(1919, Brit.), d; AMATEUR GENTLEMAN, THE(1920, Brit.), d; AT THE VILLA ROSE(1920, Brit.), d; QUESTION OF TRUST, A(1920, Brit.), d; INNOCENT(1921, Brit.), d; DEBT OF HONOR(1922, Brit.), d; PASSIONATE FRIENDS, THE(1922, Brit.), d; RUNNING WATER(1922, Brit.), d; DON QUIXOTE(1923, Brit.), d; ROYAL OAK, THE(1923, Brit.), d; MY HUSBAND'S WIVES(1924), d; SLAVES OF DESTINY(1924, Brit.), d; EVERY MAN'S WIFE(1925), d; FLAG LIEUTENANT, THE(1926, Brit.), d; ARCADIANS, THE(1927, Brit.), p; ROSES OF PICARDY(1927, Brit.), p, d; SISTER TO ASSIST 'ER, A(1927, Brit.), p; PALAIS DE DANSE(1928, Brit.), p, d; PHYSICIAN, THE(1928, Brit.), p; SMASHING THROUGH(1928, Brit.), p; WOMAN TEMPTED, THE(1928, Brit.), p, d
Misc. Silents
IDOL OF PARIS, THE(1914, Brit.), d; LOSS OF THE BIRKENHEAD, THE(1914, Brit.), d; PRICE OF JUSTICE, THE(1914, Brit.), d; SUICIDE CLUB, THE(1914, Brit.), d; CHARITY ANN(1915, Brit.), d; FINE FEATHERS(1915, Brit.), d; FLORENCE NIGHTINGALE(1915, Brit.), d; FROM SHOPGIRL TO DUCHESS(1915, Brit.), d; GRIP(1915, Brit.), d; HER NAMLESS CHILD(1915, Brit.), d; HOME(1915, Brit.), d; WILL OF HER OWN, A(1915, Brit.), d; DESPERATION(1916, Brit.), d; MOTHER-LOVE(1916, Brit.), d; WHEN KNIGHTS WERE BOLD(1916, Brit.), d; DOMBEY AND SON(1917, Brit.), d; JUSTICE(1917, Brit.), d; SMITH(1917, Brit.), d; WOMAN WHO WAS NOTHING, THE(1917, Brit.), d; GOODBYE(1918, Brit.), d; HINDLE WAKES(1918, Brit.), d; LIFE STORY OF DAVID LLOYD GEORGE, THE(1918, Brit.), d; COMRADESHIP(1919, Brit.), d; ROCKS OF VALPRE, THE(1919, Brit.), d; SWINDLER, THE(1919, Brit.), d; BLEAK HOUSE(1920, Brit.), d; HUNDRETH CHANCE, THE(1920, Brit.), d; TAVERN KNIGHT, THE(1920, Brit.), d; FRUITFUL VINE, THE(1921, Brit.), d; GENTLEMAN OF FRANCE, A(1921, Brit.), d; GOD'S GOOD MAN(1921, Brit.), d; HOUND OF THE BASKERVILLES, THE(1921, Brit.), d; ROMANCE OF WASTDALE, A(1921, Brit.), d; DICK TURPIN'S RIDE TO YORK(1922, Brit.), d; GUY FAWKES(1923, Brit.), d; SALLY BISHOP(1923, Brit.), d; SIGN OF FOUR, THE(1923, Brit.), d; WANDERING JEW, THE(1923, Brit.), d; CURLYTOP(1924), d; FOLLY OF VANITY, THE(1924), d; HENRY, KING OF NAVARRE(1924, Brit.), d; LOVE STORY OF ALIETTE BRUNTON, THE(1924, Brit.), d; SHE WOLVES(1925), d; FANNY HAWTHORNE(1927, Brit.), d; FLIGHT COMMANDER, THE(1927, Brit.), d; GLAD EYE, THE(1927, Brit.), d; JAWS OF HELL(1928, Brit.), d; YOU KNOW WHAT SAILORS ARE(1928, Brit.), d

June Elvidge
Silents
CRIMSON DOVE, THE(1917); GIRL'S FOLLY, A(1917); APPEARANCE OF EVIL(1918); CABARET, THE(1918); JOAN OF THE WOODS(1918); OLDEST LAW, THE(1918); FINE FEATHERS(1921); BEYOND THE ROCKS(1922); IMPOSSIBLE MRS. BELLEW, THE(1922); MAN WHO SAW TOMORROW, THE(1922); THELMA(1922); ELEVENTH HOUR, THE(1923); PRISONER, THE(1923); TEMPTATION(1923); PAINTED PEOPLE(1924)
Misc. Silents
ALMIGHTY DOLLAR, THE(1916); FATE'S BOOMERANG(1916); HAND OF PERIL, THE(1916); LA VIE DE BOHEME(1916); LOVE'S CRUCIBLE(1916); WORLD AGAINST HIM, THE(1916); FAMILY HONOR(1917); GUARDIAN, THE(1917); MARRIAGE MARKET, THE(1917); PAGE MYSTERY, THE(1917); PRICE OF PRIDE, THE(1917); RASPUTIN, THE BLACK MONK(1917); RED WOMAN, THE(1917); SHALL WE FORGIVE HER?(1917); SOCIAL LEPER, THE(1917); SQUARE DEAL, A(1917); TENTH CASE, THE(1917); WHIP, THE(1917); YOUTH(1917); BEAUTIFUL MRS. REYNOLDS, THE(1918); BROKEN TIES(1918); POWER AND THE GLORY, THE(1918); STOLEN ORDERS(1918); STRONG WAY, THE(1918); WAY OUT, THE(1918); WOMAN OF REDEMPTION, A(1918); BLUFFER, THE(1919); COAX ME(1919); HIS FATHER'S WIFE(1919); LOVE AND THE WOMAN(1919); LOVE DEFENDER, THE(1919); MORAL DEADLINE, THE(1919); POISON PEN, THE(1919); QUICKENING FLAME, THE(1919); SOCIAL PIRATE, THE(1919); STEEL KING, THE(1919); THREE GREEN EYES(1919); WOMAN OF LIES(1919); BEAUTY'S WORTH(1922); FORSAKING ALL OTHERS(1922); WOMAN CONQUERS, THE(1922); CHALK MARKS(1924); PAGAN PASSIONS(1924)

Arthur Elvin
DESIGN FOR MURDER(1940, Brit.), ph
Joan Elvin
HAUNTED STRANGLER, THE(1958, Brit.)
June Elvin
NICHOLAS NICKLEBY(1947, Brit.); LOOK BEFORE YOU LOVE(1948, Brit.); THINGS HAPPEN AT NIGHT(1948, Brit.); HOUR OF GLORY(1949, Brit.); MR. H. C. ANDERSEN(1950, Brit.); SHE SHALL HAVE MURDER(1950, Brit.); WONDER BOY(1951, Brit./Aust.); JUDGMENT DEFERRED(1952, Brit.); SALUTE THE TOFF(1952, Brit.); TOO HOT TO HANDLE(1961, Brit.)
Violetta Elvin
QUEEN OF SPADES(1948, Brit.); MELBA(1953, Brit.)
Violette Elvin
TWICE UPON A TIME(1953, Brit.)
Elvira
FREAKS(1932)
Elviry
DOWN IN ARKANSAW(1938)
Elviry [June Weaver]
JEEPERS CREEPERS(1939)
Bois Elwell
1984
ALLEY CAT(1984)
Eva Elwen
Silents
MARY LATIMER, NUN(1920, Brit.), w
Lottie Elwen
C-MAN(1949)
Hans Elwenspoek
DIVIDED HEART, THE(1955, Brit.)
Cary Elwes
1984
ANOTHER COUNTRY(1984, Brit.); OXFORD BLUES(1984)
Cassian Elwes
1984
OXFORD BLUES(1984), p
Mark Elwes
BILLION DOLLAR BRAIN(1967, Brit.); MAROC 7(1967, Brit.); DIAMONDS ARE FOREVER(1971, Brit.); GAMEKEEPER, THE(1980, Brit.)
Roger Elwin
LORD OF THE FLIES(1963, Brit.)
Michael Elwyn
DECLINE AND FALL... OF A BIRD WATCHER(1969, Brit.); PRIVATE LIFE OF SHERLOCK HOLMES, THE(1970, Brit.); TOUCH OF CLASS, A(1973, Brit.); FRENCH LIEUTENANT'S WOMAN, THE(1981)
Robert Elwyn
THAT MAN FROM TANGIER(1953), p&d
Bill Ely
THAT CERTAIN AGE(1938), makeup
David Ely
SECONDS(1966), w
Lois Ely
LARCENY(1948), w
Rick Ely
I ESCAPED FROM DEVIL'S ISLAND(1973)
Ron Ely
FIEND WHO WALKED THE WEST, THE(1958); SOUTH PACIFIC(1958); REMARK-ABLE MR. PENNYPACKER, THE(1959); NIGHT OF THE GRIZZLY, THE(1966); ONCE BEFORE I DIE(1967, U.S./Phil.); TARZAN'S DEADLY SILENCE(1970); TAR-ZAN'S JUNGLE REBELLION(1970); DOC SAVAGE... THE MAN OF BRONZE(1975); SLAVERS(1977, Ger.)
Misc. Talkies
HALLELUJAH AND SARTANA, SON OF...GOD(1972)
Kevin Elyot
1984
SCANDALOUS(1984)
Sallee Elyse
DEMENTED(1980); HOME SWEET HOME(1981)
Charles F. Elyston
BOOK OF NUMBERS(1973)
Elzer
M(1933, Ger.)
Ruby Elzy
EMPEROR JONES, THE(1933); TOY WIFE, THE(1938)
Demetris Emanuel
CODE OF THE SECRET SERVICE(1939); BACKGROUND TO DANGER(1943)
Demetrius Emanuel
GIVE ME YOUR HEART(1936); THEY DRIVE BY NIGHT(1940); LAW OF THE TROPICS(1941); SIX LESSONS FROM MADAME LA ZONGA(1941)
Demitris Emanuel
MEN IN EXILE(1937)
Elzie Emanuel
TO HAVE AND HAVE NOT(1944); INTRUDER IN THE DUST(1949); THREE LITTLE WORDS(1950); WELL, THE(1951); SUN SHINES BRIGHT, THE(1953); WHITE WITCH DOCTOR(1953)
Manuel Emanuel
I'LL TAKE ROMANCE(1937)
Phillip Emanuel
WILD DUCK, THE(1983, Aus.), p
Paule Emanuele
SOFT SKIN, THE(1964, Fr.)
Barbara K. Emary
STEPPING TOES(1938, Brit.), w; OLD MOTHER RILEY IN SOCIETY(1940, Brit.), w; COMMON TOUCH, THE(1941, Brit.), w; OLD MOTHER RILEY'S CIRCUS(1941, Brit.), w; LET THE PEOPLE SING(1942, Brit.), w; WE'LL SMILE AGAIN(1942, Brit.), w; OLD MOTHER RILEY, DETECTIVE(1943, Brit.), w; WHEN WE ARE MARRIED(1943, Brit.), w; LOVE ON THE DOLE(1945, Brit.), w; GRAND ESCAPADE, THE(1946, Brit.), w; SECOND MATE, THE(1950, Brit.), w; JUDGMENT DEFER-RED(1952, Brit.), w; YOU'RE ONLY YOUNG TWICE(1952, Brit.), p. John Grierson

Bella Emberg
HISTORY OF THE WORLD, PART 1(1981)
The Embers
GUTTER GIRLS(1964, Brit.)
Caroline Embling
TESS(1980, Fr./Brit.); BLOODY KIDS(1983, Brit.)
John Embling
FIGHTING BACK(1983, Brit.), w
Julia Embree
HOMETOWN U.S.A.(1979)
Coleen Embry
PHOBIA(1980, Can.)
Susan Embry
MYSTIC HOUR, THE(1934), w
Margaret Emden
BRACELETS(1931, Brit.); CALLED BACK(1933, Brit.); LITTLE MISS SOMEBO-DY(1937, Brit.); MR. SMITH CARRIES ON(1937, Brit.); TWILIGHT HOUR(1944, Brit.); SILVER FLEET, THE(1945, Brit.); MAN FROM MOROCCO, THE(1946, Brit.)
Nicholas Emdett
SECRET CAVE, THE(1953, Brit.)
Nicky Emdett
MYSTERY ON BIRD ISLAND(1954, Brit.)
Jac Emel
SLAMS, THE(1973); STUDENT TEACHERS, THE(1973)
Piotr Emelianov
THREE TALES OF CHEKHOV(1961, USSR), ph
Emelka
Silents
PLEASURE GARDEN, THE(1925, Brit./Ger.), set d
V. Emelyanov
IMMORTAL GARRISON, THE(1957, USSR)
Bob Emenegger
PASSION STREET, U.S.A.(1964), m
Robert Emenegger
FRASIER, THE SENSUOUS LION(1973), m
Michael Emer
CROSSROADS(1938, Fr.), m
Michel Emer
ACT OF LOVE(1953), m
Charles Emerald
BLOCKADE(1928, Brit.)
Silents
ONE OF THE BEST(1927, Brit.); BOLIBAR(1928, Brit.); RINGER, THE(1928, Brit.); LOST PATROL, THE(1929, Brit.)
Misc. Silents
BETRAYAL, THE(1929)
Charley Emerald
HATE SHIP, THE(1930, Brit.)
Connie Emerald
SAFE AFFAIR, A(1931, Brit.); BACHELOR'S BABY(1932, Brit.); TWO FOR TO-NIGHT(1935)
Nell Emerald
THIS WEEK OF GRACE(1933, Brit.), w; MURDER AT THE CABARET(1936, Brit.), p; TERROR ON TIPTOE(1936, Brit.), p; DR. SIN FANG(1937, Brit.), a, p; CHINATOWN NIGHTS(1938, Brit.), p; EVERYTHING HAPPENS TO ME(1938, Brit.); DR. O'DOWD(1940, Brit.)
Silents
FIRES OF INNOCENCE(1922, Brit.); GIRL OF LONDON, A(1925, Brit.)
Misc. Silents
GRIP OF IRON, THE(1913, Brit.); BOLD ADVENTURESS, A(1915, Brit.); MAYOR OF CASTERBRIDGE, THE(1921, Brit.)
Gilbert Emergy
RAGE IN HEAVEN(1941)
Bessie Emerick
Misc. Silents
WELCOME TO OUR CITY(1922)
Geoff Emerick
1984
GIVE MY REGARDS TO BROAD STREET(1984, Brit.)
George H. Emerick
Silents
FINNEGAN'S BALL(1927), sup&w
Lucille Emerick
DOLL THAT TOOK THE TOWN, THE(1965, Ital.), p
Robert Emerick
JOE(1970)
Agnes Emerson
Silents
JOHN NEEDHAM'S DOUBLE(1916)
Misc. Silents
WANTED AT HEADQUARTERS(1920)
Allen Emerson
SLENDER THREAD, THE(1965); THOMAS CROWN AFFAIR, THE(1968); WIN-NING(1969)
Baron Emerson
REDHEAD(1941)
Branch Emerson
IF EVER I SEE YOU AGAIN(1978)
Charles Emerson
Misc. Silents
IT HAPPENED TO ADELE(1917)
E. Emerson
Silents
GREAT SHADOW, THE(1920)
Ed Emerson
PARIS CALLING(1941); HARVARD, HERE I COME(1942); WHO DONE IT?(1942)
Eda Emerson
Misc. Silents
CRIMSON SHOALS(1919)

Eddie Spaghetti" Emerson
TOBY TYLER(1960)

Edna Emerson
Misc. Silents
BERLIN VIA AMERICA(1918)

Edward Emerson
MURDER GOES TO COLLEGE(1937); I COVER CHINATOWN(1938); MOB TOWN(1941); ROAD TO MOROCCO(1942); DIXIE(1943); ROAD TO UTOPIA(1945); THERE GOES KELLY(1945)

Emalie Emerson
BIG TRAIL, THE(1930)

Emmett Emerson
HIGH NOON(1952), set d

Eric Emerson
CHELSEA GIRLS, THE(1967); LONESOME COWBOYS(1968)

Faye Emerson
AFFECTIONATELY YOURS(1941); BAD MEN OF MISSOURI(1941); MAN-POWER(1941); NINE LIVES ARE NOT ENOUGH(1941); NURSE'S SECRET, THE(1941); HARD WAY, THE(1942); JUKE GIRL(1942); LADY GANGSTER(1942); MURDER IN THE BIG HOUSE(1942); SECRET ENEMIES(1942); WILD BILL HICKOK RIDES(1942); AIR FORCE(1943); DESERT SONG, THE(1943); FIND THE BLACK-MAILER(1943); BETWEEN TWO WORLDS(1944); CRIME BY NIGHT(1944); DESTI-NATION TOKYO(1944); HOLLYWOOD CANTEEN(1944); MASK OF DIMITRIOS, THE(1944); UNCERTAIN GLORY(1944); VERY THOUGHT OF YOU, THE(1944); DANGER SIGNAL(1945); HOTEL BERLIN(1945); HER KIND OF MAN(1946); NO-BODY LIVES FOREVER(1946); GUILTY BYSTANDER(1950); MAIN STREET TO BROADWAY(1953)

George Emerson
CARNY(1980)

Hope Emerson
CRY OF THE CITY(1948); THAT WONDERFUL URGE(1948); ADAM'S RIB(1949); DANCING IN THE DARK(1949); HOUSE OF STRANGERS(1949); ROSEANNA McCOY(1949); THIEVES' HIGHWAY(1949); CAGED(1950); COPPER CANYON(1950); DOUBLE CROSSBONES(1950); BELLE LE GRAND(1951); WESTWARD THE WOM-EN(1951); CHAMP FOR A DAY(1953); LADY WANTS MINK, THE(1953); PERILOUS JOURNEY, A(1953); CASANOVA'S BIG NIGHT(1954); UNTAMED(1955); ALL MINE TO GIVE(1957); GUNS OF FORT PETTICOAT, THE(1957)

John Emerson
FALL OF EVE, THE(1929), w; CONSPIRACY(1930), Beulah M. Dix; EX-BAD BOY(1931), w; STRUGGLE, THE(1931), w; GIRL FROM MISSOURI, THE(1934), w; SOCIAL REGISTER(1934), w; SAN FRANCISCO(1936), p; MAMA STEPS OUT(1937), p
Silents
CONSPIRACY, THE(1914), a, w; FLYING TORPEDO, THE(1916), a, w; MA-TRIMANIAC, THE(1916), w; SOCIAL SECRETARY, THE(1916), d; AMERICANO, THE(1917), d, w; DOWN TO EARTH(1917), d; IN AGAIN-OUT AGAIN(1917), d; REACHING FOR THE MOON(1917), d, w; WILD AND WOOLLY(1917), d; GETTING MARY MARRIED(1919), w; GOOD-BYE, BILL(1919), d, w; ISLE OF CON-QUEST(1919), w; IN SEARCH OF A SINNER(1920), w; WOMAN'S PLACE(1921), w; RED HOT ROMANCE(1922), w; DULCY(1923), w; LEARNING TO LOVE(1925), w; GENTLEMEN PREFER BLONDES(1928), w
Misc. Silents
BACHELOR'S ROMANCE, THE(1915); FAILURE, THE(1915); GHOSTS(1915), d; OLD HEIDELBERG(1915), d; HIS PICTURE IN THE PAPERS(1916), d; LESS THAN THE DUST(1916), d; MACBETH(1916), d; COME ON IN(1918), d; OH, YOU WO-MEN!(1919), d; POLLY OF THE FOLLIES(1922), d

Karrie Emerson
WHITE DOG(1982)
Misc. Talkies
EVILS OF THE NIGHT(1983)

Kathleen Emerson
Misc. Silents
DREAM LADY, THE(1918)

Keith Emerson
INFERNO(1980, Ital.), m; NIGHTHAWKS(1981), m

Ralph Emerson
MARRIAGE BY CONTRACT(1928); DANCE HALL(1929); HARDBOILED RO-SE(1929); LOTUS LADY(1930); NIGHT AT EARL CARROLL'S, A(1940)
Silents
ENEMY, THE(1927); ALBANY NIGHT BOAT, THE(1928); WEST POINT(1928)
Misc. Silents
CHEER LEADER, THE(1928); MARRIAGE BY CONRACT(1928)

Steve Emerson
BIG SWITCH, THE(1970, Brit.); MAN OF VIOLENCE(1970, Brit.)

Walter Emerson
Misc. Silents
FACE ON THE BARROOM FLOOR, THE(1923); LOVE OF PAQUITA, THE(1927)

Oliver Emert
FRONTIER GAL(1945), set d; THIS LOVE OF OURS(1945), set d; RIDE THE PINK HORSE(1947), set d; SINGAPORE(1947), set d; NAKED CITY, THE(1948), set d; CRISS CROSS(1949), set d; AGAINST ALL FLAGS(1952), set d; BEND OF THE RIVER(1952), set; LAWLESS BREED, THE(1952), set d; YANKEE BUC-CANEER(1952), set d; SIGN OF THE PAGAN(1954), set d; TAZA, SON OF CO-CHISE(1954), set d; CAPTAIN LIGHTFOOT(1955), set d; BATTLE HYMN(1957), set d; TARNISHED ANGELS, THE(1957), set d; LADY TAKES A FLYER(1958), set d; PERFECT FURLOUGH, THE(1958), set d; TONKA(1958), set d; TWILIGHT FOR THE GODS(1958), set d; OPERATION PETTICOAT(1959), set d; THIS EARTH IS MI-NE(1959), set d; MIDNIGHT LACE(1960), set d; LAST SUNSET, THE(1961), set d; LOVER COME BACK(1961), set d; POSSE FROM HELL(1961), set d; CAPE FEAR(1962), set d; OUTSIDER, THE(1962), set d; SIX BLACK HORSES(1962), set d; SPIRAL ROAD, THE(1962), set d; TO KILL A MOCKINGBIRD(1962), set d; LIST OF ADRIAN MESSENGER, THE(1963), set d; SHOWDOWN(1963), set d; UGLY AMERI-CAN, THE(1963), set d; ISLAND OF THE BLUE DOLPHINS(1964), set d; KITTEN WITH A WHIP(1964), set d; SEND ME NO FLOWERS(1964), set d; SHENAN-DOAH(1965), set d; WAR LORD, THE(1965), set d; GHOST AND MR. CHICKEN, THE(1966), set d; GUNPOINT(1966), set d; RARE BREED, THE(1966), set d; TO-BRUK(1966), set d

Ollie Emert
NEVER STEAL ANYTHING SMALL(1959), set d

Renate Emert
BACKFIRE(1965, Fr.)

Roy Emerton
SHADOWS(1931, Brit.); SIGN OF FOUR, THE(1932, Brit.); OVERNIGHT(1933, Brit.); LASH, THE(1934, Brit.); IT HAPPENED IN PARIS(1935, Brit.); JAVA HEAD(1935, Brit.); LORNA DOONE(1935, Brit.); TRIUMPH OF SHERLOCK HOLMES, THE(1935, Brit.); EVERYTHING IS THUNDER(1936, Brit.); LADY JANE GREY(1936, Brit.); POT LUCK(1936, Brit.); BIG FELLA(1937, Brit.); DOCTOR SYN(1937, Brit.); LAST ADVEN-TURERS, THE(1937, Brit); SILENT BARRIERS(1937, Brit.); CONVICT 99(1938, Brit.); DRUMS(1938, Brit.); EVERYTHING HAPPENS TO ME(1938, Brit.); GANG, THE(1938, Brit.); GOOD OLD DAYS, THE(1939, Brit.); HOME FROM HOME(1939, Brit.); CASE OF THE FRIGHTENED LADY, THE(1940. Brit.); THIEF OF BAGHDAD, THE(1940, Brit.); OLD MOTHER RILEY'S CIRCUS(1941, Brit.); YOUNG MR. PITT, THE(1942, Brit.); TIME FLIES(1944, Brit.); WELCOME, MR. WASHINGTON(1944, Brit.); HENRY V(1946, Brit.)

Bob Emery
TAKE A CHANCE(1937, Brit.)

Calvin Emery
WOMAN IN THE WINDOW, THE(1945)

Dick Emery
YELLOW SUBMARINE(1958, Brit.); LIGHT UP THE SKY(1960, Brit.); TASTE OF MONEY, A(1960, Brit.); MRS. GIBBONS' BOYS(1962, Brit.); CROOKS ANONY-MOUS(1963, Brit.); FAST LADY, THE(1963, Brit.); JUST FOR FUN(1963, Brit.); WRONG ARM OF THE LAW, THE(1963, Brit.); BIG JOB, THE(1965, Brit.); BABY LOVE(1969, Brit.); LOOT(1971, Brit.); GET CHARLIE TULLY(1976, Brit.)

Filbert Emery
LIFE OF EMILE ZOLA, THE(1937)

Follie Emery
Silents
BEAUTIFUL KITTY(1923, Brit.)

Gilbert Emery
BEHIND THAT CURTAIN(1929); SKY HAWK(1929); LADY'S MORALS, A(1930); LET US BE GAY(1930); PRINCE OF DIAMONDS(1930); SARAH AND SON(1930); CUBAN LOVE SONG,THE(1931), w; LADIES' MAN(1931); LADY REFUSES, THE(1931); MATA HARI(1931), w; PARTY HUSBAND(1931); RICH MAN'S FOL-LY(1931); ROYAL BED, THE(1931); RULING VOICE, THE(1931); SCANDAL SHEET(1931); FAREWELL TO ARMS, A(1932); MAN CALLED BACK, THE(1932); OKAY AMERICA(1932); ALL OF ME(1934); COMING OUT PARTY(1934); GALLANT LADY(1934), w; GRAND CANARY(1934); HOUSE OF ROTHSCHILD, THE(1934); NOW AND FOREVER(1934); ONE MORE RIVER(1934); WHERE SINNERS MEET(1934); WHOM THE GODS DESTROY(1934); CARDINAL RICHELIEU(1935); CLIVE OF INDIA(1935); GOIN' TO TOWN(1935); HARMONY LANE(1935); LADIES CRAVE EXCITEMENT(1935); LET'S LIVE TONIGHT(1935); MAGNIFICENT OBSES-SION(1935); MAN WHO RECLAIMED HIS HEAD, THE(1935); NIGHT LIFE OF THE GODS(1935); PETER IBBETSON(1935); RECKLESS ROADS(1935); WITHOUT RE-GRET(1935); BULLETS OR BALLOTS(1936); DRACULA'S DAUGHTER(1936); GIRL ON THE FRONT PAGE, THE(1936); LITTLE LORD FAUNTLEROY(1936); WIFE VERSUS SECRETARY(1936); DOUBLE OR NOTHING(1937); SOULS AT SEA(1937); ALWAYS GOODBYE(1938), w; BUCCANEER, THE(1938); LORD JEFF(1938); MAK-ING THE HEADLINES(1938); MAN TO REMEMBER, A(1938); STORM OVER BEN-GAL(1938); LADY'S FROM KENTUCKY, THE(1939); NURSE EDITH CAVELL(1939); RAFFLES(1939); SAINT STRIKES BACK, THE(1939); ANNE OF WINDY PO-PLARS(1940); DISPATCH FROM REUTERS, A(1940); HOUSE OF THE SEVEN GABLES, THE(1940); RIVER'S END(1940); SOUTH OF SUEZ(1940); WATERLOO BRIDGE(1940); ADAM HAD FOUR SONS(1941); NEW WINE(1941); SCOTLAND YARD(1941); SINGAPORE WOMAN(1941); SUNDOWN(1941); THAT HAMILTON WOMAN(1941); WOMAN'S FACE(1941); ESCAPE FROM HONG KONG(1942); LOVES OF EDGAR ALLAN POE, THE(1942); REMARKABLE ANDREW, THE(1942); SHER-LOCK HOLMES IN WASHINGTON(1943); BETWEEN TWO WORLDS(1944); RETURN OF THE VAMPIRE, THE(1944); BRIGHTON STRANGLER, THE(1945); SWELL GUY(1946), w
Silents
ANY WIFE(1922); HERO, THE(1923), w
Misc. Silents
COUSIN KATE(1921)

John Emery
ROAD BACK,THE(1937); CORSICAN BROTHERS, THE(1941); HERE COMES MR. JORDAN(1941); EYES IN THE NIGHT(1942); GEORGE WASHINGTON SLEPT HERE(1942); SHIP AHOY(1942); TWO YANKS IN TRINIDAD(1942); ASSIGNMENT IN BRITTANY(1943); MADEMOISELLE FIFI(1944); BLOOD ON THE SUN(1945); SPANISH MAIN, THE(1945); SPELLBOUND(1945); VOICE OF THE TURTLE, THE(1947); GAY INTRUDERS, THE(1948); JOAN OF ARC(1948); LET'S LIVE AGAIN(1948); WOMAN IN WHITE, THE(1948); DAKOTA LIL(1950); DOUBLE CROSS-BONES(1950); FRENCHIE(1950); ROCKETSHIP X-M(1950); JOE PALOOKA IN TRI-PLE CROSS(1951); MAD MAGICIAN, THE(1954); LAWLESS STREET, A(1955); FOREVER DARLING(1956); GIRL CAN'T HELP IT, THE(1956); KRONOS(1957); 10 NORTH FREDERICK(1958); YOUNGBLOOD HAWKE(1964)

Katherine Emery
EYES IN THE NIGHT(1942); ISLE OF THE DEAD(1945); LOCKET, THE(1946); WALLS CAME TUMBLING DOWN, THE(1946); PRIVATE AFFAIRS OF BEL AMI, THE(1947); CHICKEN EVERY SUNDAY(1948); STRANGE BARGAIN(1949); PAY-MENT ON DEMAND(1951); HIAWATHA(1952); UNTAMED FRONTIER(1952); MAZE, THE(1953)

Lee Emery
VARIETY GIRL(1947)

Louie Emery
RAISE THE ROOF(1930); MISCHIEF(1931, Brit.); SOMETHING ALWAYS HAP-PENS(1934, Brit.); PHANTOM LIGHT, THE(1935, Brit.)

Mary Emery
I'LL TAKE ROMANCE(1937); MAGNIFICENT DOLL(1946); BLONDIE IN THE DOUGH(1947); KNOCK ON ANY DOOR(1949); EMERGENCY WEDDING(1950)

Matt Emery
FUNNY LADY(1975)

Maud Emery
Silents
LITTLE WILDCAT(1922); SILENT VOW, THE(1922)

Misc. Silents
MY WILD IRISH ROSE(1922)
Pat Emery
GANGSTER, THE(1947)
Patricia Emery
GREEN DOLPHIN STREET(1947)
Paul Emery
Misc. Silents
FIGHTING ROMEO, THE(1925)
Pollie Emery
SISTER TO ASSIST'ER, A(1930, Brit.); FOOTSTEPS IN THE NIGHT(1932, Brit.); THIRD STRING, THE(1932, Brit.); GOOD COMPANIONS(1933, Brit.); CRUCIFIX, THE(1934, Brit.); PEG OF OLD DRURY(1936, Brit.); SISTER TO ASSIST'ER, A(1938, Brit.)
Silents
PATRICIA BRENT, SPINSTER(1919, Brit.); IF FOUR WALLS TOLD(1922, Brit.); SISTER TO ASSIST 'ER, A(1922, Brit.); ALLEY OF GOLDEN HEARTS, THE(1924, Brit.); SISTER TO ASSIST 'ER, A(1927, Brit.)
Misc. Silents
WILL AND A WAY, A(1922, Brit.)
Polly Emery
SILVER TOP(1938, Brit.)
Prudence Emery
1984
HOTEL NEW HAMPSHIRE, THE(1984)
Ralph Emery
Misc. Talkies
GIRL FROM TOBACCO ROW, THE(1966)
Richard Emery
BURGLAR, THE(1956)
Robert Emery
GUESS WHAT WE LEARNED IN SCHOOL TODAY?(1970); MY BROTHER HAS BAD DREAMS(1977), p&d
Robert J. Emery
SIGN OF AQUARIUS(1970), d, w; SCREAM BLOODY MURDER(1972), p,d&w; RIDE IN A PINK CAR(1974, Can.), d
Misc. Talkies
WILLIE AND SCRATCH(1975), d
David Emge
DAWN OF THE DEAD(1979)
Robert Emhardt
3:10 TO YUMA(1957); IRON MISTRESS, THE(1952); BADLANDERS, THE(1958); WAKE ME WHEN IT'S OVER(1960); UNDERWORLD U.S.A.(1961); INTRUDER, THE(1962); KID GALAHAD(1962); GROUP, THE(1966); HOSTILE GUNS(1967); WHERE WERE YOU WHEN THE LIGHTS WENT OUT?(1968); CHANGE OF HABIT(1969); RASCAL(1969); SUPPOSE THEY GAVE A WAR AND NOBODY CAME?(1970); LAWMAN(1971); SCORPIO(1973); STONE KILLER, THE(1973); IT'S ALIVE(1974); ALEX AND THE GYPSY(1976); FRATERNITY ROW(1977); SENIORS, THE(1978); FORCED VENGEANCE(1982)
Misc. Talkies
DIE SISTER, DIE(1978)
Sanae Emi
LAKE OF DRACULA(1973, Jap.)
George Emick
UP IN MABEL'S ROOM(1944), spec eff
Jac Emil
NEWMAN'S LAW(1974); TRUCK TURNER(1974)
Michael Emil
TRACKS(1977); SITTING DUCKS(1979); CAN SHE BAKE A CHERRY PIE?(1983)
Emil Pallenberg's "Carmichael"
BUCK BENNY RIDES AGAIN(1940)
Wilbert Emile
Silents
MAN FROM HEADQUARTERS(1928)
William Emile
ARTISTS AND MODELS ABROAD(1938); PLAYMATES(1941)
Daniel Emilfark
GOHA(1958, Tunisia)
Daniel Emilfork
HUNCHBACK OF NOTRE DAME, THE(1957, Fr.); DOLL, THE(1962, Fr.); NUTTY, NAUGHTY CHATEAU(1964, Fr./Ital.); LADY L(1965, Fr./Ital.); WHAT'S NEW, PUSSYCAT?(1965, U.S./Fr.); LIQUIDATOR, THE(1966, Brit.); UNKNOWN MAN OF SHANDIGOR, THE(1967, Switz.); TRANS-EUROP-EXPRESS(1968, Fr.); DEVIL'S NIGHTMARE, THE(1971 Bel./Ital.); KILL! KILL! KILL!(1972, Fr./Ger./Ital./Span.); TRAVELS WITH MY AUNT(1972, Brit.); WHO IS KILLING THE GREAT CHEFS OF EUROPE?(1978, US/Ger.); BEAUTIFUL PRISONER, THE(1983, Fr.)
Emilio
SHE-DEVIL ISLAND(1936, Mex.)
Emilio Colombo Orchestrak
CHARMING DECEIVER, THE(1933, Brit.)
Emilio Colombo's Tzigane Band
GYPSY(1937, Brit.)
Jacques Emin
CONFESSION, THE(1970, Fr.)
Irene Emirza
DREAM OF PASSION, A(1978, Gr.)
Yannis Emirzas
APOLLO GOES ON HOLIDAY(1968, Ger./Swed.), ch
Edward L. Emling, Jr.
PREMONITION, THE(1976)
Fairy Emlyn
Silents
OLD CURIOSITY SHOP, THE(1921, Brit.)
Andrew Emm
Silents
GIRL WHO TOOK THE WRONG TURNING, THE(1915, Brit.)
Emma
ESCAPE TO BURMA(1955)

Sweet Emma
LOVE IS A FUNNY THING(1970, Fr./Ital.)
Takis Emmanouel
ELECTRA(1962, Gr.); YOUNG APHRODITES(1966, Gr.); OEDIPUS THE KING(1968, Brit.); PLAY DIRTY(1969, Brit.)
Benjamin Emmanuel
PAISAN(1948, Ital.)
Dharma Emmanuel
OUTCAST OF THE ISLANDS(1952, Brit.)
Frank Emmanuel
1984
JUST THE WAY YOU ARE(1984)
Ivor Emmanuel
ZULU(1964, Brit.)
Jacques Emmanuel
AMAZING MONSIEUR FABRE, THE(1952, Fr.); LA PARISIENNE(1958, Fr./Ital.), w; NATHALIE(1958, Fr.), w; LAW IS THE LAW, THE(1959, Fr.), w; DYNAMITE JACK(1961, Fr.), w; MAN FROM COCODY(1966, Fr/Ital.), w
Maurice Emmanuel
VICE SQUAD(1982)
Takis Emmanuel
ZORBA THE GREEK(1964, U.S./Gr.); MAGUS, THE(1968, Brit.); CANNON FOR CORDOBA(1970); HELL BOATS(1970, Brit.); GOLDEN VOYAGE OF SINBAD, THE(1974, Brit.); THAT LUCKY TOUCH(1975, Brit.); CADDIE(1976, Aus.); LION OF THE DESERT(1981, Libya/Brit.)
Luigi Emmanuele
THIS MAN CAN'T DIE(1970, Ital.), w
Gilda Emmanuelli
ROOM AT THE TOP(1959, Brit.); PURE HELL OF ST. TRINIAN'S, THE(1961, Brit.)
Emmanuelo
WINGS OF THE MORNING(1937, Brit.)
U. Emmer
FREUD(1962)
Roy Emmerton
MAN IN GREY, THE(1943, Brit.)
Fern Emmet
HENRY ALDRICH'S LITTLE SECRET(1944)
Jesse Emmet
HUGO THE HIPPO(1976, Hung./U.S.)
Katherine Emmet
HOLE IN THE WALL(1929)
Michael Emmet
GUN THE MAN DOWN(1957); NIGHT OF THE BLOOD BEAST(1958); ATTACK OF THE GIANT LEECHES(1959)
Robert Emmet
HEADIN' FOR THE RIO GRANDE(1937), w
Basil Emmett
CONFIDENTIAL LADY(1939, Brit.), ph; GREEN BUDDHA, THE(1954, Brit.), ph; TRACK THE MAN DOWN(1956, Brit.), ph
E.V.H. Emmett
NON-STOP NEW YORK(1937, Brit.), w; SABOTAGE(1937, Brit.), w; WINGS OF THE MORNING(1937, Brit.); WARE CASE, THE(1939, Brit.); FOR FREEDOM(1940, Brit.); LION HAS WINGS, THE(1940, Brit.), w; THREE COCKEYED SAILORS(1940, Brit.); YOUNG MAN'S FANCY(1943, Brit.), w; ON APPROVAL(1944, Brit.); EASY MONEY(1948, Brit.); DANCE HALL(1950, Brit.), w; I'M ALL RIGHT, JACK(1959, Brit.); CARRY ON CLEO(1964, Brit.)
Edna Emmett
FORTY THOUSAND HORSEMEN(1941, Aus.)
Fern Emmett
BAR L RANCH(1930); LAND OF MISSING MEN, THE(1930); RIDIN' LAW(1930); RIDER OF THE PLAINS(1931); SECOND HONEYMOON(1931); TEN NIGHTS IN A BARROOM(1931); WEST OF CHEYENNE(1931); WESTWARD BOUND(1931); DYNAMITE DENNY(1932); FORTY-NINERS, THE(1932); EAST OF FIFTH AVE.(1933); HELLO, EVERYBODY(1933); RIDERS OF DESTINY(1933); VAMPIRE BAT, THE(1933); TRAIL DRIVE, THE(1934); WAGON WHEELS(1934); MELODY TRAIL(1935); MOTIVE FOR REVENGE(1935); RAINBOW VALLEY(1935); SMART GIRL(1935); TEXAS TERROR(1935); $1,000 A MINUTE(1935); BURNING GOLD(1936); DON'T TURN'EM LOOSE(1936); FATAL LADY(1936); HARVESTER, THE(1936); HEIR TO TROUBLE(1936); M'LISS(1936); OREGON TRAIL, THE(1936); SWING TIME(1936); TICKET TO PARADISE(1936); TRAIL OF THE LONESOME PINE, THE(1936); COME ON, COWBOYS(1937); DANGEROUS HOLIDAY(1937); GIRL WITH IDEAS, A(1937); GIRLS CAN PLAY(1937); PARADISE EXPRESS(1937); RIDERS OF THE WHISTLING SKULL(1937); HUNTED MEN(1938); OVERLAND STAGE RAIDERS(1938); YOU AND ME(1938); DESPERATE TRAILS(1939); FRONTIER MARSHAL(1939); LADY'S FROM KENTUCKY, THE(1939); LUCKY NIGHT(1939); MADE FOR EACH OTHER(1939); PIRATES OF THE SKIES(1939); RAINS CAME, THE(1939); SAGA OF DEATH VALLEY(1939); SECOND FIDDLE(1939); ARISE, MY LOVE(1940); HALF A SINNER(1940); HIDDEN ENEMY(1940); LADY IN QUESTION, THE(1940); LITTLE ORVIE(1940); LUCKY PARTNERS(1940); RANGERS OF FORTUNE(1940); SOUTH OF SUEZ(1940); STAR DUST(1940); TRIPLE JUSTICE(1940); GIRL, A GUY AND A GOB, A(1941); JESSE JAMES AT BAY(1941); LOVE CRAZY(1941); MONSTER AND THE GIRL, THE(1941); SCATTERGOOD BAINES(1941); SCATTERGOOD PULLS THE STRINGS(1941); SHE KNEW ALL THE ANSWERS(1941); SHEPHERD OF THE HILLS, THE(1941); SIX GUN GOLD(1941); BROADWAY(1942); CINDERELLA SWINGS IT(1942); GAY SISTERS, THE(1942); GREAT MAN'S LADY, THE(1942); MY HEART BELONGS TO DADDY(1942); POLICE BULLETS(1942); QUIET PLEASE, MURDER(1942); SHUT MY BIG MOUTH(1942); SONS OF THE PIONEERS(1942); SUNDOWN KID, THE(1942); VALLEY OF THE SUN(1942); DEAD MEN WALK(1943); FIRST COMES COURAGE(1943); FRONTIER BADMEN(1943); GILDERSLEEVE'S BAD DAY(1943); IS EVERYBODY HAPPY?(1943); KEEP 'EM SLUGGING(1943); COVER GIRL(1944); JOHNNY DOESN'T LIVE HERE ANY MORE(1944); KNICKERBOCKER HOLIDAY(1944); ONCE UPON A TIME(1944); SAN DIEGO, I LOVE YOU(1944); TOGETHER AGAIN(1944); DALTONS RIDE AGAIN, THE(1945); PILLOW OF DEATH(1945); SONG TO REMEMBER, A(1945); NIGHT AND DAY(1946)
Misc. Talkies
LOSER'S END(1934); TERROR OF THE PLAINS(1934); WEST ON PARADE(1934)
Jay Emmett
JUNGLE BRIDE(1933)

Silents
YOUR WIFE AND MINE(1927)
Katherine Emmett
NIGHT ANGEL, THE(1931)
Silents
ORPHANS OF THE STORM(1922)
Robert Emmett
BADGE OF HONOR(1934), w; MEN OF THE PLAINS(1936), w; OREGON TRAIL, THE(1936), w; GOD'S COUNTRY AND THE MAN(1937), w; HITTIN' THE TRAIL(1937), w; DANGER VALLEY(1938), w; GUN PACKER(1938), w; GUNSMOKE TRAIL(1938), w; ACROSS THE PLAINS(1939), w; DRIFTING WESTWARD(1939), w; TRIGGER SMITH(1939), w; GOLDEN TRAIL, THE(1940), w; RAINBOW OVER THE RANGE(1940), w; RHYTHM OF THE RIO GRANDE(1940), w; RIDING THE SUNSET TRAIL(1941), w; SILVER STALLION(1941), w; DEATH VALLEY RANGERS(1944), w; CARAVAN TRAIL, THE(1946), p&d; BADMAN'S GOLD(1951), w; CATTLE QUEEN(1951), w
Misc. Talkies
GALLOPING KID, THE(1932), d; LONE RIDER, THE(1934), d; SUNDOWN TRAIL, THE(1975), d
Robert Emmett [Tansey]
WAY OF THE WEST, THE(1934), p&d; NEW FRONTIER, THE(1935), w; TIMBER TERRORS(1935), p,d&w; SONG OF THE GRINGO(1936), w; WESTWARD HO(1936), w; RIDERS OF THE DAWN(1937), w; RIDERS OF THE ROCKIES(1937), w; SING, COWBOY, SING(1937), w; TROUBLE IN TEXAS(1937), w; WHERE TRAILS DIVIDE(1937), w; MAN'S COUNTRY(1938), w; MEXICALI KID, THE(1938), w; PAINTED TRAIL, THE(1938), w; ROMANCE OF THE ROCKIES(1938), w; WEST OF RAINBOW'S END(1938), w; WHERE THE BUFFALO ROAM(1938), w; MAN FROM TEXAS, THE(1939), w; OVERLAND MAIL(1939), w; WILD HORSE CANYON(1939), w; COWBOY FROM SUNDOWN(1940), w; WESTBOUND STAGE(1940), w; DRIFTIN' KID, THE(1941), w; ROLLIN' HOME TO TEXAS(1941), w; WANDERERS OF THE WEST(1941), w; LONE STAR LAW MEN(1942), w; WESTERN MAIL(1942), w; SONORA STAGECOACH(1944), w; SONG OF OLD WYOMING(1945), p&d; ROMANCE OF THE WEST(1946), p&d; WHITE STALLION(1947), d
Misc. Talkies
COURAGE OF THE NORTH(1935), d
Sheila Emmett
RIVERRUN(1968)
Cliff Emmich
PAYDAY(1972); TOP OF THE HEAP(1972); THUNDERBOLT AND LIGHTFOOT(1974); TELEFON(1977); BARRACUDA(1978); STINGRAY(1978); HALLOWEEN II(1981)
Clifford Emmich
JACKSON COUNTY JAIL(1976)
Fern Emmitt
DEVIL AND DANIEL WEBSTER, THE(1941)
Buster Emmonds
Silents
JOHN NEEDHAM'S DOUBLE(1916)
Bob Emmons
Silents
COMMANDING OFFICER, THE(1915); HEADIN' SOUTH(1918)
Della Gould Emmons
FAR HORIZONS, THE(1955), w
Louise Emmons
HEAVEN ON EARTH(1931)
Marion Emmons
Silents
MEASURE OF A MAN, THE(1916); HEARTS OF THE WORLD(1918)
Misc. Silents
JESS(1914)
Mary Emmons
FUGITIVE LOVERS(1934)
William Emmons
SASQUATCH(1978)
Basil Emmont
HELL, HEAVEN OR HOBOKEN(1958, Brit.), ph
Basil Emmott
FEATHER, THE(1929, Brit.), ph; TO WHAT RED HELL(1929, Brit.), ph; GREAT GAME, THE(1930), ph; BOAT FROM SHANGHAI(1931, Brit.), ph; FRAIL WOMEN(1932, Brit.), ph; MARRIAGE BOND, THE(1932, Brit.), ph; MISSING REMBRANDT, THE(1932, Brit.), ph; OUT OF THE PAST(1933, Brit.), ph; GLIMPSE OF PARADISE, A(1934, Brit.), ph; SILVER SPOON, THE(1934, Brit.), ph; SOMETHING ALWAYS HAPPENS(1934, Brit.), ph; BLACK MASK(1935, Brit.), ph; CRIME UNLIMITED(1935, Brit.), ph; GET OFF MY FOOT(1935, Brit.), ph; HELLO SWEETHEART(1935, Brit.), ph; IN A MONASTERY GARDEN(1935, Brit.), ph; MAN OF THE MOMENT(1935, Brit.), ph; MR. WHAT'S-HIS-NAME(1935, Brit.), ph; MURDER AT MONTE CARLO(1935, Brit.), ph; PHANTOM FIEND, THE(1935, Brit.), ph; SO YOU WON'T TALK?(1935, Brit.), ph; SOME DAY(1935, Brit.), ph; BROWN WALLET, THE(1936, Brit.), ph; CROWN VS STEVENS(1936), ph; EDUCATED EVANS(1936, Brit.), ph; FAIR EXCHANGE(1936, Brit.), ph; FAITHFUL(1936, Brit.), ph; GAOL BREAK(1936, Brit.), ph; HAIL AND FAREWELL(1936, Brit.), ph; IT'S IN THE BAG(1936, Brit.), ph; MR. COHEN TAKES A WALK(1936, Brit.), ph; TWELVE GOOD MEN(1936, Brit.), ph; WHERE'S SALLY?(1936, Brit.), ph; CHANGE FOR A SOVEREIGN(1937, Brit.), ph; COMPULSORY WIFE, THE(1937, Brit.), ph; DON'T GET ME WRONG(1937, Brit.), ph; IT'S NOT CRICKET(1937, Brit.), ph; MAN WHO MADE DIAMONDS, THE(1937, Brit.), ph; MAYFAIR MELODY(1937, Brit.), ph; PATRICIA GETS HER MAN(1937, Brit.), ph; PERFECT CRIME, THE(1937, Brit.), ph; SIDE STREET ANGEL(1937, Brit.), ph; TAKE IT FROM ME(1937, Brit.), ph; VULTURE, THE(1937, Brit.), ph; WHO KILLED JOHN SAVAGE?(1937, Brit.), ph; YOU LIVE AND LEARN(1937, Brit.), ph; DANGEROUS MEDICINE(1938, Brit.), ph; DARK STAIRWAY, THE(1938, Brit.), ph; DOUBLE OR QUITS(1938, Brit.), ph; EVERYTHING HAPPENS TO ME(1938, Brit.), ph; GLAMOUR GIRL(1938, Brit.), ph; IT'S IN THE BLOOD(1938, Brit.), ph; MANY TANKS MR. ATKINS(1938, Brit.), ph; QUIET PLEASE(1938, Brit.), ph; RETURN OF CAROL DEANE, THE(1938, Brit.), ph; SINGING COP, THE(1938, Brit.), ph; THANK EVANS(1938, Brit.), ph; THEY DRIVE BY NIGHT(1938, Brit.), ph; THISTLEDOWN(1938, Brit.), ph; VIPER, THE(1938, Brit.), ph; GENTLEMAN'S GENTLEMAN, A(1939, Brit.), ph; GOOD OLD DAYS, THE(1939, Brit.), ph; HIS BROTHER'S KEEPER(1939, Brit.), ph; HOOTS MON!(1939, Brit.), ph; MURDER WILL OUT(1939, Brit.), ph; NURSEMAID WHO DISAPPEARED, THE(1939, Brit.), ph; TOO DANGEROUS TO LIVE(1939, Brit.), ph; BRIGGS FAMILY,

THE(1940, Brit.), ph; DR. O'DOWD(1940, Brit.), ph; FINGERS(1940, Brit.), ph; GEORGE AND MARGARET(1940, Brit.), ph; MIDAS TOUCH, THE(1940, Brit.), ph; THAT'S THE TICKET(1940, Brit.), ph; TWO FOR DANGER(1940, Brit.), ph; ATLANTIC FERRY(1941, Brit.), ph; PRIME MINISTER, THE(1941, Brit.), ph; SEVENTH SURVIVOR(1941, Brit.), ph; FLYING FORTRESS(1942, Brit.), ph; PETERVILLE DIAMOND, THE(1942, Brit.), ph; THIS WAS PARIS(1942, Brit.), ph; MISS LONDON LTD.(1943, Brit.), ph; IT HAPPENED ONE SUNDAY(1944, Brit.), ph; TIME FLIES(1944, Brit.), ph; MAN FROM MOROCCO, THE(1946, Brit.), ph; MASTER OF BANKDAM, THE(1947, Brit.), ph; PAPER ORCHID(1949, Brit.), ph; COMPANIONS IN CRIME(1954, Brit.), ph; CROSS CHANNEL(1955, Brit.), ph; JOE MACBETH(1955), ph; SECRET VENTURE(1955, Brit.), ph; WHERE THERE'S A WILL(1955, Brit.), ph; HOME AND AWAY(1956, Brit.), ph; JOHNNY, YOU'RE WANTED(1956, Brit.), ph; SPIN A DARK WEB(1956, Brit.), ph; LONG HAUL, THE(1957, Brit.), ph; PORTRAIT IN SMOKE(1957, Brit.), ph; TOWN ON TRIAL(1957, Brit.), ph; ENEMY GENERAL, THE(1960), ph; MISSILE FROM HELL(1960, Brit.), ph; STRONGROOM(1962, Brit.), ph; YOUNG, WILLING AND EAGER(1962, Brit.), ph; MAN IN THE DARK(1963, Brit.), ph; MURDER CAN BE DEADLY(1963, Brit.), ph; GREAT ARMORED CAR SWINDLE, THE(1964), ph; SING AND SWING(1964, Brit.), ph; TOMORROW AT TEN(1964, Brit.), ph; WALK A TIGHTROPE(1964, U.S./Brit.), ph; BE MY GUEST(1965, Brit.), ph; CURSE OF THE FLY(1965, Brit.), ph; RETURN OF MR. MOTO, THE(1965, Brit.), ph
Fred Emney
BREWSTER'S MILLIONS(1935, Brit.); COME OUT OF THE PANTRY(1935, Brit.); LET'S MAKE A NIGHT OF IT(1937, Brit.); HOLD MY HAND(1938, Brit.); JANE STEPS OUT(1938, Brit.); YES, MADAM?(1938, Brit.); JUST LIKE A WOMAN(1939, Brit.); JUST WILLIAM(1939, Brit.); MIDDLE WATCH, THE(1939, Brit.); SHE COULDN'T SAY NO(1939, Brit.); LILAC DOMINO, THE(1940, Brit.); LET THE PEOPLE SING(1942, Brit.); FUN AT ST. FANNY'S(1956, Brit.), a, w; FAST LADY, THE(1963, Brit.); FATHER CAME TOO(1964, Brit.); BUNNY LAKE IS MISSING(1965); I'VE GOTTA HORSE(1965, Brit.); THOSE MAGNIFICENT MEN IN THEIR FLYING MACHINES; OR HOW I FLEWFROM LONDON TO PARIS IN 25 HOURS AND 11 MINUTES(1965, Brit.); SANDWICH MAN, THE(1966, Brit.); OLIVER!(1968, Brit.); ITALIAN JOB, THE(1969, Brit.); LOCK UP YOUR DAUGHTERS(1969, Brit.); DOCTOR IN TROUBLE(1970, Brit.); MAGIC CHRISTIAN, THE(1970, Brit.); UP THE CHASTITY BELT(1971, Brit.)
Joan Fred Emney
SONG OF FREEDOM(1938, Brit.); NORTH SEA PATROL(1939, Brit.)
E.W. Emo
LITTLE MELODY FROM VIENNA(1948, Aust.), d, w; HELP I'M INVISIBLE(1952, Ger.), d
Maria Emo
GIRL OF THE MOORS, THE(1961, Ger.); HITLER(1962)
Toru Emori
GIRL I ABANDONED, THE(1970, Jap.)
Gilbert Emory
JUAREZ(1939)
Mary Emory
TWO SMART PEOPLE(1946)
Maud Emory
Silents
GREATER LAW, THE(1917)
Maude Emory
Silents
MADAME SPY(1918)
Ralph Emory
HANSEL AND GRETEL(1954), anim
Richard Emory
BANDIT KING OF TEXAS(1949); SOUTH OF DEATH VALLEY(1949); CODE OF THE SILVER SAGE(1950); DESTINATION MURDER(1950); FINGERPRINTS DON'T LIE(1951); GENE AUTRY AND THE MOUNTIES(1951); KOREA PATROL(1951); LITTLE BIG HORN(1951); MASK OF THE DRAGON(1951); BATTLE ZONE(1952); CAPTIVE OF BILLY THE KID(1952); HELLGATE(1952); LAWLESS COWBOYS(1952); RED SNOW(1952); SINGIN' IN THE RAIN(1952); LAST TIME I SAW PARIS, THE(1954); CROOKED WEB, THE(1955); SERGEANT WAS A LADY, THE(1961)
Mike Emperio
YEAR OF LIVING DANGEROUSLY, THE(1982, Aus.)
Arthur Guy Empey
TROOPERS THREE(1930), p, w
Silents
INTO NO MAN'S LAND(1928), d
Misc. Silents
OVER THE TOP(1918); LIQUID GOLD(1919); UNDERCURRENT, THE(1919); MILLIONAIRE FOR A DAY, A(1921)
Marie Empress
Misc. Silents
WHEN WE WERE TWENTY-ONE(1915); WOMAN PAYS, THE(1915); LOVE'S CROSS ROADS(1916); GIRL WHO DOESN'T KNOW, THE(1917)
Emsh
HALLELUJAH THE HILLS(1963)
Ed Emshviller
HALLELUJAH THE HILLS(1963), ph
Ed Emshwiller
TIME OF THE HEATHEN(1962), ph, ed
Henrik Emyl
MID-DAY MISTRESS(1968), p
Nils Emyl
MID-DAY MISTRESS(1968), w
Rolf Emyl
MID-DAY MISTRESS(1968), d
Enakshi
Misc. Silents
SHIRAZ(1929)
Keiko Enami
SANSHO THE BAILIFF(1969, Jap.)
Kyoko Enami
GAMERA VERSUS BARUGON(1966, Jap./U.S.)
Koichi Enatsu
SONG FROM MY HEART, THE(1970, Jap.), p

Yuko Enatsu
FIGHT FOR THE GLORY(1970, Jap.)
Haim Enav
HILL 24 DOESN'T ANSWER(1955, Israel)
Dick Enberg
GUS(1976); TWO-MINUTE WARNING(1976); HEAVEN CAN WAIT(1978)
Lalo Encinas
ONLY THE BRAVE(1930); KID MILLIONS(1934); CALL OF THE WILD(1935); WAIKIKI WEDDING(1937); HURRY, CHARLIE, HURRY(1941); MEXICAN HAY-RIDE(1948)
Silents
HUNTRESS, THE(1923)
Oudy Rachmat Endang
SEVENTH CONTINENT, THE(1968, Czech./Yugo.)
Michael Ende
1984
NEVERENDING STORY, THE(1984, Ger.), w
Vi Endean
INSPECTOR CALLS, AN(1954, Brit.)
Robert A. Endelson
FIGHT FOR YOUR LIFE(1977), p, d, ed
Gernot Endemann
SHOUT AT THE DEVIL(1976, Brit.)
David Endene
1984
GREYSTOKE: THE LEGEND OF TARZAN, LORD OF THE APES(1984)
Chuck Ender
PUTNEY SWOPE(1969)
Eleanor Enderle
WORLD'S GREATEST SINNER, THE(1962)
Liselotte Enderle
SPESSART INN, THE(1961, Ger.), w
David Enders
THAT LUCKY TOUCH(1975, Brit.)
Dusty Enders
RUNAWAY GIRL(1966)
F. A. Enders
Silents
THIS MARRIAGE BUSINESS(1927, Brit.), p
Robert Enders
MALTESE BIPPY, THE(1969), p; HOW DO I LOVE THEE?(1970), p; ZIGZAG(1970), p, w; VOICES(1973, Brit.), p, w; CONDUCT UNBECOMING(1975, Brit.), w; HED-DA(1975, Brit.), p; MAIDS, THE(1975, Brit.), p, w; NASTY HABITS(1976, Brit.), p, w; STEVIE(1978, Brit.), p&d
Robert J. Enders
THUNDER OF DRUMS, A(1961), p
Clive Endersby
GIRL HUNTERS, THE(1963, Brit.); CHARGE OF THE LIGHT BRIGADE, THE(1968, Brit.); WALK A CROOKED PATH(1969, Brit.); CHATO'S LAND(1972)
Ralph Endersby
MY SIDE OF THE MOUNTAIN(1969); HOMER(1970); RIP-OFF(1971, Can.); SUNDAY IN THE COUNTRY(1975, Can.)
C. Raker "Cy" Endfield
SECRET, THE(1955, Brit.), d&w; CHILD IN THE HOUSE(1956, Brit.), d, w; HELL DRIVERS(1958, Brit.), d, w; SEA FURY(1959, Brit.), d, w
Cy Endfield
LIMPING MAN, THE(1953, Brit.), d; IMPULSE(1955, Brit.), d; MYSTERIOUS IS-LAND(1961, U.S./Brit.), d; HIDE AND SEEK(1964, Brit.), d; ZULU(1964, Brit.), p, d, w; SANDS OF THE KALAHARI(1965, Brit.), p, d&w; DE SADE(1969), d; UNIVERSAL SOLDIER(1971, Brit.), d&w; ZULU DAWN(1980, Brit.), w
Cy Raker Endfield
JET STORM(1961, Brit.), d&w, w
Cyril Endfield
JOE PALOOKA, CHAMP(1946), w; MR. HEX(1946), w; ARGYLE SECRETS, THE(1948), d, w; SLEEP, MY LOVE(1948), w; JOE PALOOKA IN THE BIG FIGHT(1949), d, w; JOE PALOOKA IN THE COUNTERPUNCH(1949), w; COLONEL MARCH INVESTIGATES(1952,Brit.), d
Cyril "Cy" Endfield
STORK BITES MAN(1947), d, w; SOUND OF FURY, THE(1950), d; WHIPPED, THE(1950), d, w; TARZAN'S SAVAGE FURY(1952), d
Frances Endfield
SECRET OF CONVICT LAKE, THE(1951)
Lucian Endicott
ON THE BEACH(1959)
Ruth Belmore Endicott
Silents
CAROLYN OF THE CORNERS(1919), w
Gerald Endler
SLEEPER(1973), spec eff
Jerry Endler
SAND PEBBLES, THE(1966), spec eff; MATILDA(1978), spec eff
Michael Endler
EASY MONEY(1983), w
Jipp Endo
KARATE, THE HAND OF DEATH(1961)
Seichi Endo
GIGANTIS(1959, Jap./U.S.), ph
Shusaku Endo
GIRL I ABANDONED, THE(1970, Jap.), a, w
Teppei Endo
GOLDEN DEMON(1956, Jap.)
Chick Endor
TWO HEARTS IN HARMONY(1935, Brit.)
Guy Endore
MAD LOVE(1935), w; MARK OF THE VAMPIRE(1935), w; RUMBA(1935), w; DEVIL DOLL, THE(1936), w; LEAGUE OF FRIGHTENED MEN(1937), w; LADY FROM LOUISIANA(1941), w; SONG OF RUSSIA(1943), w; STORY OF G.I. JOE, THE(1945), w; VICIOUS CIRCLE, THE(1948), w; JOHNNY ALLEGRO(1949), w; WHIRLPOOL(1949), w; HE RAN ALL THE WAY(1951), w; TOMORROW IS ANOTH-ER DAY(1951), w; CURSE OF THE WEREWOLF, THE(1961), w

George Endoso
1984
LOVE STREAMS(1984)
Ken Endoso
METEOR(1979)
Keney Endoso
HERBIE GOES BANANAS(1980)
Kenny Endoso
GREAT BANK ROBBERY, THE(1969); SERIAL(1980)
1984
ICE PIRATES, THE(1984); STAR TREK III: THE SEARCH FOR SPOCK(1984)
Kenny Endosoa
BUCK ROGERS IN THE 25TH CENTURY(1979)
Bela Endre
SUN SHINES, THE(1939, Hung.), m
The Enemies
RIOT ON SUNSET STRIP(1967)
Bob Enescelle, Jr.
SHOOT FIRST, LAUGH LAST(1967, Ital./Ger./U.S.), w
Tsvetana Eneva
WITH LOVE AND TENDERNESS(1978, Bulgaria)
Bob Enevoldsen
SUBTERRANEANS, THE(1960)
Woody Eney
FIREFOX(1982)
Richard Enfeld
HERE COME THE JETS(1959), p
Cyril Enfield
HARD BOILED MAHONEY(1947), w
Hugh Enfield [Craig Reynolds]
I'LL TELL THE WORLD(1934); LOVE BIRDS(1934); FOUR HOURS TO KILL(1935); PARIS IN SPRING(1935); RUMBA(1935)
Norman Enfield
TWIST, THE(1976, Fr.), w
Esther Eng
GOLDEN GATE GIRL(1941), d
Frank Eng
KEYS OF THE KINGDOM, THE(1944)
Ronald Eng
WORLD OF SUZIE WONG, THE(1960)
Lewell Enge
YOUNG MAN WITH A HORN(1950)
William Enge
PATSY, THE(1964)
Olav Engebregtsen
PASSIONATE DEMONS, THE(1962, Norway), ed
Alexander Engel
JUST A GIGOLO(1931), w; VINTAGE WINE(1935, Brit.), w; FINAL CHORD, THE(1936, Ger.); SERGEANT BERRY(1938, Ger.); MERRY WIVES OF WINDSOR, THE(1952, Ger.); TIME TO LOVE AND A TIME TO DIE, A(1958); RETURN OF DR. MABUSE, THE(1961, Ger./Fr./Ital.); MAD EXECUTIONERS, THE(1965, Ger.)
Alezander Engel
HAMLET(1962, Ger.)
Barbara Engel
THAT'S THE WAY OF THE WORLD(1975)
Bill Engel
OUR DAILY BREAD(1934)
Billy Engel
WEDDING PRESENT(1936); MAN WHO LOST HIMSELF, THE(1941)
Christoph Engel
NAKED AMONG THE WOLVES(1967, Ger.)
Erich Engel
KARAMAZOV(1931, Ger.), w; JAZZBAND FIVE, THE(1932, Ger,), d; AFFAIR BLUM, THE(1949, Ger.), d
Francoise Engel
BERNADETTE OF LOURDES(1962, Fr.)
Fred Engel
DUEL AT DIABLO(1966), p; WILL PENNY(1968), p; SUPPOSE THEY GAVE A WAR AND NOBODY CAME?(1970), p
Georgia Engel
TAKING OFF(1971); OUTSIDE MAN, THE(1973, U.S./FR.)
Harry Engel
JUDGE AND THE SINNER, THE(1964, Ger.); GREAT BRITISH TRAIN ROBBERY, THE(1967, Ger.)
Joseph Engel
SILK HAT KID(1935), p; THIS IS THE LIFE(1935), p; $10 RAISE(1935), p
Jules Engel
SHINBONE ALLEY(1971), prod d
Karel Engel
LEMONADE JOE(1966, Czech.)
Lehman Engel
SLEEPING BEAUTY(1965, Ger.), md; SNOW WHITE(1965, Ger.), md
Les Engel
WHERE THE BUFFALO ROAM(1980)
Mark Engel
GOOD MORNING, MISS DOVE(1955)
Mary Engel
HONEYMOON KILLERS, THE(1969)
Morris Engel
LITTLE FUGITIVE, THE(1953), p, d&w, ph; LOVERS AND LOLLIPOPS(1956), p&d, w, ph; WEDDINGS AND BABIES(1960), p&d, w, ph
Olga Engel
CONGRESS DANCES(1932, Ger.)
Paul Engel
GOOD MORNING, MISS DOVE(1955)
Roy Engel
HEAT'S ON, THE(1943); FLYING SAUCER, THE(1950); OUTRAGE(1950); SHAKE-DOWN(1950); CHICAGO CALLING(1951); M(1951); MAN FROM PLANET X, THE(1951); ROGUE RIVER(1951); SELLOUT, THE(1951); WELL, THE(1951); PAU-LA(1952); STRANGE FASCINATION(1952); BAND WAGON, THE(1953); BREAK-

DOWN(1953); MISSISSIPPI GAMBLER, THE(1953); THREE SAILORS AND A GIRL(1953); VICKI(1953); DANGEROUS MISSION(1954); DRAGON'S GOLD(1954); SUDDENLY(1954); LOVE ME OR LEAVE ME(1955); NAKED DAWN, THE(1955); FRONTIER GAMBLER(1956); THREE VIOLENT PEOPLE(1956); TRIBUTE TO A BADMAN(1956); DEATH IN SMALL DOSES(1957); ESCAPE FROM SAN QUENTIN(1957); NOT OF THIS EARTH(1957); STORM RIDER, THE(1957); JOY RIDE(1958); SATAN'S SATELLITES(1958); SOME CAME RUNNING(1959); DOG'S BEST FRIEND, A(1960); FLIGHT THAT DISAPPEARED, THE(1961); SERGEANT WAS A LADY, THE(1961); JUMBO(1962); THREE STOOGES IN ORBIT, THE(1962); IT'S A MAD, MAD, MAD, MAD WORLD(1963); VIVA LAS VEGAS(1964); YOUR CHEATIN' HEART(1964); LAST MOVIE, THE(1971); SKYJACKED(1972); WHEN THE LEGENDS DIE(1972); CHARLEY AND THE ANGEL(1973); KINGDOM OF THE SPIDERS(1977)

Sam Engel
GRAND JURY SECRETS(1939), p

Samuel C. Engel
STREET WITH NO NAME, THE(1948), p

Samuel G. Engel
SINS OF MAN(1936), w; STOWAWAY(1936), w; CRACK-UP, THE(1937), p; LANCER SPY(1937), p; SHE HAD TO EAT(1937), p, w; WE'RE GOING TO BE RICH(1938, Brit.), p; EARTHBOUND(1940), w; JOHNNY APOLLO(1940), w; VIVA CISCO KID(1940), w; BLUE, WHITE, AND PERFECT(1941), w; CHARLIE CHAN IN RIO(1941), w; PRIVATE NURSE(1941), w; RIDE ON VAQUERO(1941), w; ROMANCE OF THE RIO GRANDE(1941), w; SCOTLAND YARD(1941), w; THRU DIFFERENT EYES(1942), w; YOUNG AMERICA(1942), w; MY DARLING CLEMENTINE(1946), w; DEEP WATERS(1948), p; SITTING PRETTY(1948), p; COME TO THE STABLE(1949), p; MR. BELVEDERE GOES TO COLLEGE(1949), p; JACKPOT, THE(1950), p; NIGHT AND THE CITY(1950, Brit.), p; FOLLOW THE SUN(1951), p; FROGMEN, THE(1951), p; RAWHIDE(1951), p; BELLES ON THEIR TOES(1952), p; PONY SOLDIER(1952), p; RED SKIES OF MONTANA(1952), p; SOMETHING FOR THE BIRDS(1952), p; TAXI(1953), p; DADDY LONG LEGS(1955), p; GOOD MORNING, MISS DOVE(1955), p; MAN CALLED PETER, THE(1955), p; BERNARDINE(1957), p; BOY ON A DOLPHIN(1957), p; STORY OF RUTH, THE(1960), p

Susan Engel
INSPECTOR CLOUSEAU(1968, Brit.); KING LEAR(1971, Brit./Den.); BUTLEY(1974, Brit.); ASCENDANCY(1983, Brit.)

Tina Engel
TIN DRUM, THE(1979, Ger./Fr./Yugo./Pol.)

David Engelbach
DEATH WISH II(1982), w

Fred Engelberg
PIER 5, HAVANA(1959); DINOSAURUS(1960)

Mort Engelberg
HOT STUFF(1979), p; VILLAIN, THE(1979), p; HUNTER, THE(1980), p; NOBODY'S PERFEKT(1981), p; SMOKEY AND THE BANDIT–PART 3(1983), p

Engelen
SUPERMAN III(1983), makeup

Paul Engelen
PULP(1972, Brit.), makeup; SPY WHO LOVED ME, THE(1977, Brit.), makeup

Wally Engelhardt
DREAMER(1979); TAKE THIS JOB AND SHOVE IT(1981)

Andrews Engelman
WATER FOR CANITOGA(1939, Ger.)

Leonard Engelman
TOPAZ(1969, Brit.), makeup

Andrews Engelmann
I SPY(1933, Brit.); LOVE IN MOROCCO(1933, Fr.); STORMY WEATHER(1935, Brit.); CROUCHING BEAST, THE(1936, U. S./Brit.); TOILERS OF THE SEA(1936, Brit.)

Franklyn Engelmann
HEAVENS ABOVE!(1963, Brit.)

Heinz Engelmann
U-47 LT. COMMANDER PRIEN(1967, Ger.); MORE(1969, Luxembourg)

Darlette Engelmeier
LOOSE ENDS(1975)

Andy Engels
WARRIORS, THE(1979)

Billy Engels
EXPOSED(1932)

Frank Engels
GURU, THE MAD MONK(1971)

Lehman Engels
ROOGIE'S BUMP(1954), m

Roy Engels
THY NEIGHBOR'S WIFE(1953)

Sam Engels
BIG SHAKEDOWN, THE(1934), w

Susan Engels
HOPSCOTCH(1980)

Virginia Engels
IT'S A DATE(1940); KEEP 'EM FLYING(1941); OBLIGING YOUNG LADY(1941); UNEXPECTED UNCLE(1941); UNFINISHED BUSINESS(1941); ARABIAN NIGHTS(1942); GOOD MORNING, JUDGE(1943); CAGED(1950)

Wera Engels
GREAT JASPER, THE(1933); FUGITIVE ROAD(1934); GREAT IMPERSONATION, THE(1935); HONG KONG NIGHTS(1935); SWEEPSTAKE ANNIE(1935); TOGETHER WE LIVE(1935)

Charles Van Enger
MIRACLE ON MAIN STREET, A(1940), ph

Eva Enger
PRAISE MARX AND PASS THE AMMUNITION(1970, Brit.)

Leif Enger
HUNGER(1968, Den./Norway/Swed.)

Richard L. Van Enger
GALLANT LEGION, THE(1948), ed

William Engesser
GATOR(1976)

Karin Engh
PLACE FOR LOVERS, A(1969, Ital./Fr.)

Harry Engholm
Silents
EAST LYNNE(1913, Brit.), w; JUST A GIRL(1916, Brit.), w; EVERY MOTHER'S SON(1926, Brit.), w; IF YOUTH BUT KNEW(1926, Brit.), w; BATTLES OF THE CORONEL AND FALKLAND ISLANDS, THE(1928, Brit.), w

Erdogan Engin
YOL(1982, Turkey), ph

Olga Engl
EMIL AND THE DETECTIVE(1931, Ger.); REBEL, THE(1933, Ger.)

Sigi Engl
SKI PARTY(1965)

Barry England
FIGURES IN A LANDSCAPE(1970, Brit.), w; CONDUCT UNBECOMING(1975, Brit.), w

Bryan England
1984
WEEKEND PASS(1984), ph

Daisy England
Silents
HEAD OF THE FAMILY, THE(1922, Brit.)

Hal England
HANG'EM HIGH(1968); DIRT GANG, THE(1972)

Jan England
REFORM SCHOOL GIRL(1957)

Jo England
LAST WAVE, THE(1978, Aus.)

John England
2,000 WOMEN(1944, Brit.); LOYAL HEART(1946, Brit.); GREEN FINGERS(1947); DEVIL'S PLOT, THE(1948, Brit.); UNEASY TERMS(1948, Brit.)

Ken England
ARTISTS AND MODELS ABROAD(1938), w

Paul England
I ADORE YOU(1933, Brit.), w; IT'S A KING(1933, Brit.), w; CHARLIE CHAN IN LONDON(1934); LOVE TIME(1934); SHE SHALL HAVE MUSIC(1935, Brit.), w; DISPUTED PASSAGE(1939); EARL OF CHICAGO, THE(1940); INVISIBLE MAN RETURNS, THE(1940); MOSS ROSE(1947); TRIAL OF MADAM X, THE(1948, Brit.), a, d&w; KNOCK ON WOOD(1954)
Silents
JUST A GIRL(1916, Brit.)

Sue England
THIS LOVE OF OURS(1945); DEVIL ON WHEELS, THE(1947); KIDNAPPED(1948); CITY ACROSS THE RIVER(1949); MISSISSIPPI RHYTHM(1949); BOMBA AND THE HIDDEN CITY(1950); HELL'S OUTPOST(1955); TEEN-AGE CRIME WAVE(1955); DEVIL'S HAIRPIN, THE(1957); FUNNY FACE(1957); WOMEN OF PITCAIRN ISLAND, THE(1957); CLAMBAKE(1967)

Alec Englander
ENCHANTED COTTAGE, THE(1945)

Ira Englander
RUNNING BRAVE(1983, Can.), p

Margaret Englander
NEARLY EIGHTEEN(1943), w

Otto Englander
SNOW WHITE AND THE SEVEN DWARFS(1937), w; PINOCCHIO(1940), w; DUMBO(1941), d; BOY FROM INDIANA(1950), w; DIAMOND QUEEN, THE(1953), w

Billy Engle
MILLION DOLLAR LEGS(1932); RIDIN' FOR JUSTICE(1932); TILLIE AND GUS(1933); IT HAPPENED ONE NIGHT(1934); IT'S A GIFT(1934); JEALOUSY(1934); YOU'RE TELLING ME(1934); OUR RELATIONS(1936); LIVE, LOVE AND LEARN(1937); MARIE ANTOINETTE(1938); MIDNIGHT INTRUDER(1938); TEST PILOT(1938); FLYING DEUCES, THE(1939); HERO FOR A DAY(1939); I STOLE A MILLION(1939); OUR NEIGHBORS–THE CARTERS(1939); SUDDEN MONEY(1939); TELL NO TALES(1939); YOU CAN'T CHEAT AN HONEST MAN(1939); MRS. MINIVER(1942); LONE STAR TRAIL, THE(1943); MRS. PARKINGTON(1944); ALONG CAME JONES(1945); FRONTIER GAL(1945); HOODLUM SAINT, THE(1946); WISTFUL WIDOW OF WAGON GAP, THE(1947); PALEFACE, THE(1948); RED, HOT AND BLUE(1949); MY FAVORITE SPY(1951)
Misc. Talkies
NEVADA BUCKAROO, THE(1931)
Silents
CAT AND THE CANARY, THE(1927); WESTERN WHIRLWIND, THE(1927)

Bruno Engle
RACHEL, RACHEL(1968)

Darleen Engle
SOUTH PACIFIC(1958)

Fred Engle
TWIST OF SAND, A(1968, Brit.), p

Paul Engle
GREAT AMERICAN PASTIME, THE(1956); PERSUADER, THE(1957); GUNSMOKE IN TUCSON(1958)

Roy Engle
I WAS A COMMUNIST FOR THE F.B.I.(1951); STRANGERS ON A TRAIN(1951); CONFIDENCE GIRL(1952)

Samuel G. Engle
LION, THE(1962, Brit.), p

Tod Engle
RACHEL, RACHEL(1968)

William Engle
1776(1972)

William F. Engle
BIG BAD MAMA(1974)

Fred Engleberg
LOST MISSILE, THE(1958, U.S./Can.)

Mort Engleberg
SMOKEY AND THE BANDIT(1977), p

Dean Englehardt
NIGHT MOVES(1975)

Ron Englehardt
HE KNOWS YOU'RE ALONE(1980)

Billy Englehart
GONE IN 60 SECONDS(1974)
Andrews Englemann
CITY OF PLAY(1929, Brit.); TWO WORLD(1930, Brit.); WOLVES(1930, Brit.); PRISON BREAKER(1936, Brit.)
Angeline Engler
FAR COUNTRY, THE(1955)
Bruno Engler
LOST AND FOUND(1979)
Joe Engler
PUTNEY SWOPE(1969)
Wolf Englert
DUCK RINGS AT HALF PAST SEVEN, THE(1969, Ger./Ital.), set d
Wolfe Englert
BRAINWASHED(1961, Ger.), art d
Judy Engles
HAROLD AND MAUDE(1971)
Susan Engles
CHARLIE BUBBLES(1968, Brit.)
Lucie Englisch
ALLURING GOAL, THE(1930, Germ.); RENDEZ-VOUS(1932, Ger.)
Lucy Englisch
DREAM OF BUTTERFLY, THE(1941, Ital.)
Arthur English
HI-JACKERS, THE(1963, Brit.); PERCY(1971, Brit.); MALACHI'S COVE(1973, Brit.)
Brad English
ONION FIELD, THE(1979); HANKY-PANKY(1982)
Bradford English
ANDERSON TAPES, THE(1971)
David English
LISZTOMANIA(1975, Brit.); SILVER BEARS(1978)
Doreen English
UNEASY TERMS(1948, Brit.)
Harry English
Misc. Silents
PLAYING DEAD(1915)
Jack English
CLEAR THE DECKS(1929), ed; HOLD YOUR MAN(1929), ed; RED HOT SPEED ½(1929), ed; MEET THE WIFE(1931), ed; CODE OF THE MOUNTED(1935), ed; NORTHERN FRONTIER(1935), ed; RED BLOOD OF COURAGE(1935), d; GHOST PATROL(1936), ed; LIGHTNING BILL CARSON(1936), ed; MARLOWE(1969); INCREDIBLE TWO-HEADED TRANSPLANT, THE(1971)
Jack [John] English
TRAILS OF THE WILD(1935), ed; WILDERNESS MAIL(1935), ed
James English
Silents
FANCY DRESS(1919, Brit.); PRIDE OF THE NORTH, THE(1920, Brit.); GOD IN THE GARDEN, THE(1921, Brit.); POINTING FINGER, THE(1922, Brit.); NETS OF DESTINY(1924, Brit.)
John English
ARIZONA DAYS(1937), d; WHISTLING BULLETS(1937), d; CALL THE MESQUITEERS(1938), d; HI-YO SILVER(1940), d; GANGS OF SONORA(1941), d; CODE OF THE OUTLAW(1942), d; PHANTOM PLAINSMEN, THE(1942), d; RAIDERS OF THE RANGE(1942), d; VALLEY OF HUNTED MEN(1942), d; WESTWARD HO(1942), d; BLACK HILLS EXPRESS(1943), d; DEAD MAN'S GULCH(1943), d; DEATH VALLEY MANHUNT(1943), d; DRUMS OF FU MANCHU(1943), d; MAN FROM THUNDER RIVER, THE(1943), d; OVERLAND MAIL ROBBERY(1943), d; RAIDERS OF SUNSET PASS(1943), d; THUNDERING TRAILS(1943), d; CALL OF THE SOUTH SEAS(1943), d; FACES IN THE FOG(1944), d; LARAMIE TRAIL, THE(1944), d; PORT OF 40 THIEVES, THE(1944), d; SAN FERNANDO VALLEY(1944), d; SILVER CITY KID(1944), d; BEHIND CITY LIGHTS(1945), d; DON'T FENCE ME IN(1945), d; GRISSLY'S MILLIONS(1945), d; PHANTOM SPEAKS, THE(1945), d; UTAH(1945), d; MURDER IN THE MUSIC HALL(1946), d; LAST ROUND-UP, THE(1947), d; TRAIL TO SAN ANTONE(1947), d; LOADED PISTOLS(1948), d; STRAWBERRY ROAN, THE(1948), d; COWBOY AND THE INDIANS, THE(1949), d; RIDERS IN THE SKY(1949), d; RIDERS OF THE WHISTLING PINES(1949), d; RIM OF THE CANYON(1949), d; SONS OF NEW MEXICO(1949), d; BEYOND THE PURPLE HILLS(1950), d; BLAZING SUN, THE(1950), d; COW TOWN(1950), d; INDIAN TERRITORY(1950), d; MULE TRAIN(1950), d; GENE AUTRY AND THE MOUNTIES(1951), d; HILLS OF UTAH(1951), d; SILVER CANYON(1951), d; VALLEY OF FIRE(1951), d; WHIRLWIND(1951), d
Misc. Talkies
FIGHTING DEVIL DOGS(1938), d; WHIRLWIND(1951), d
John W. English
HIS FIGHTING BLOOD(1935), d
Silents
EXQUISITE SINNER, THE(1926), ed; LOVELORN, THE(1927), ed; MOCKERY(1927), ed
Jon English
TOUCH AND GO(1955)
Kay English
LOCKED DOOR, THE(1929); NAUGHTY MARIETTA(1935); HARVEY GIRLS, THE(1946); PAT AND MIKE(1952); PLYMOUTH ADVENTURE(1952); WE'RE NOT MARRIED(1952); RIDE, VAQUERO!(1953); STORY OF THREE LOVES, THE(1953); I'LL CRY TOMORROW(1955); OPPOSITE SEX, THE(1956); LINEUP, THE(1958)
Silents
NOOSE, THE(1928)
Liz English
ARISTOCATS, THE(1970)
Louise English
BUGSY MALONE(1976, Brit.); HOUSE OF LONG SHADOWS, THE(1983, Brit.)
Marla English
LIVING IT UP(1954); REAR WINDOW(1954); SHIELD FOR MURDER(1954); DESERT SANDS(1955); HELL'S HORIZON(1955); SHE-CREATURE, THE(1956); STRANGE ADVENTURE, A(1956); RUNAWAY DAUGHTERS(1957); VOODOO WOMAN(1957)
Pam English
KILL, THE(1968)

Patricia English
TWO AND TWO MAKE SIX(1962, Brit.)
Paul English
HONEYSUCKLE ROSE(1980)
1984
SONGWRITER(1984)
Peter English
WIVES BEWARE(1933, Brit.)
Rachel English
HARD RIDE, THE(1971)
Richard English
BULLDOG EDITION(1936), w; ALL OVER TOWN(1937), w; LARCENY ON THE AIR(1937), w; TOO MANY WIVES(1937), w; HIGGINS FAMILY, THE(1938), w; MR. BOGGS STEPS OUT(1938), w; MILLION DOLLAR LEGS(1939), w; MILITARY ACADEMY(1940), w; CADET GIRL(1941), w; FOLLOW THE BAND(1943), w; BRAZIL(1944), w; SWEET AND LOWDOWN(1944), w; THOUSAND AND ONE NIGHTS, A(1945), w; DING DONG WILLIAMS(1946), w; FABULOUS DORSEYS, THE(1947), w; LEATHER GLOVES(1948), w; LUST FOR GOLD(1949), w; COPPER CANYON(1950), w; FLYING MISSILE(1950), w; 711 OCEAN DRIVE(1950), w; BIG JIM McLAIN(1952), w; BEYOND MOMBASA(1957), w
Robert English
AMERICAN PRISONER, THE(1929 Brit.); KNIGHT IN LONDON, A(1930, Brit./Ger.); CHANCE OF A NIGHT-TIME, THE(1931, Brit); FOOTSTEPS IN THE NIGHT(1932, Brit.); COMMISSIONAIRE(1933, Brit.); HONEYMOON FOR THREE(1935, Brit.); STOKER, THE(1935, Brit.); EDUCATED EVANS(1936, Brit.); GUILTY MELODY(1936, Brit.); HEARTS OF HUMANITY(1936, Brit.); SECRET OF STAMBOUL, THE(1936, Brit.); SAM SMALL LEAVES TOWN(1937, Brit.); SONG OF THE ROAD(1937, Brit.); TALKING FEET(1937, Brit.); MRS. PYM OF SCOTLAND YARD(1939, Brit.); EVERYTHING IS RHYTHM(1940, Brit.)
Silents
CRIMSON CIRCLE, THE(1922, Brit.); OUT TO WIN(1923, Brit.); OWD BOB(1924, Brit.)
Misc. Silents
FRUITFUL VINE, THE(1921, Brit.); LOST LEADER, A(1922, Brit.); STABLE COMPANIONS(1922, Brit.); TRUANTS, THE(1922, Brit.)
Robert Paul English
BARBAROSA(1982)
Susan English
MARK OF CAIN, THE(1948, Brit.)
Bror Englund
EMIGRANTS, THE(1972, Swed.)
Bryan Englund
CRAZY MAMA(1975); PROWLER, THE(1981)
David Englund
MARS NEEDS WOMEN(1966)
Dinah Englund
CRAZY MAMA(1975)
Einar Englund
PRELUDE TO ECSTASY(1963, Fin.), m
George Englund
WORLD, THE FLESH, AND THE DEVIL, THE(1959), p; UGLY AMERICAN, THE(1963), p&d; SIGNPOST TO MURDER(1964), d; DARK OF THE SUN(1968, Brit.), p; SHOES OF THE FISHERMAN, THE(1968), p; ZACHARIAH(1971), p, d; SNOW JOB(1972), d; STONY ISLAND(1978)
Jan Englund
BAIT(1954); OTHER WOMAN, THE(1954); HOLD BACK TOMORROW(1955); EMERGENCY HOSPITAL(1956); HIT AND RUN(1957); INVASION OF THE SAUCER MEN(1957); LIZZIE(1957); SUICIDE BATTALION(1958); PARADISE ALLEY(1962)
Ken Englund
BIG BROADCAST OF 1938, THE(1937), w; THERE'S THAT WOMAN AGAIN(1938), w; GOOD GIRLS GO TO PARIS(1939), w; DOCTOR TAKES A WIFE(1940), w; NO, NO NANETTE(1940), w; SLIGHTLY HONORABLE(1940), w; THIS THING CALLED LOVE(1940), w; NOTHING BUT THE TRUTH(1941), w; RINGS ON HER FINGERS(1942), w; SPRINGTIME IN THE ROCKIES(1942), w; SWEET ROSIE O'GRADY(1943), w; HERE COME THE WAVES(1944), w; UNSEEN, THE(1945), w; SECRET LIFE OF WALTER MITTY, THE(1947), w; GOOD SAM(1948), w; MILLIONAIRE FOR CHRISTY, A(1951), w; ANDROCLES AND THE LION(1952), w; NEVER WAVE AT A WAC(1952), w; CADDY, THE(1953), w; VAGABOND KING, THE(1956), w; HELLO LONDON(1958, Brit.), w; WICKED DREAMS OF PAULA SCHULTZ, THE(1968), w
Pat Englund
DAY OF THE DOLPHIN, THE(1973)
Patricia Englund
STAGE STRUCK(1958)
Robert Englund
HUSTLE(1975); ST. IVES(1976); STAR IS BORN, A(1976); STAY HUNGRY(1976); BIG WEDNESDAY(1978); BLOODBROTHERS(1978); GREAT SMOKEY ROADBLOCK, THE(1978); FIFTH FLOOR, THE(1980); DEAD AND BURIED(1981); GALAXY OF TERROR(1981); DON'T CRY, IT'S ONLY THUNDER(1982)
1984
NIGHTMARE ON ELM STREET, A(1984)
Andy Engman
MAKE MINE MUSIC(1946), anim
Edward D. Engoron
JOURNEY TO THE CENTER OF TIME(1967), art d
Edward Engoron
HOW TO COMMIT MARRIAGE(1969), art d; LEARNING TREE, THE(1969), art d
Stuart Engstrand
BEYOND THE FOREST(1949), w
Birgitta Engstrom
PRIZE, THE(1963)
Charles Engstrom
1984
FLASH OF GREEN, A(1984), m
Elena Engstrom
HELLCATS, THE(1968)
Flora Jean Engstrom
SEARCH FOR BRIDEY MURPHY, THE(1956)

Jean Engstrom
DRIVE A CROOKED ROAD(1954); VOODOO ISLAND(1957); ERRAND BOY, THE(1961); RESTLESS ONES, THE(1965)

Stig Engstrom
DUET FOR CANNIBALS(1969, Swed.); GEORGIA, GEORGIA(1972); GIRLS, THE(1972, Swed.)

Bill Engvall
SPLIT IMAGE(1982)

Annmari Engwall
VIBRATION(1969, Swed.)

Col. Ivar Enhorning
PRISONER OF ZENDA, THE(1937), tech adv

Bo Enivel
JOE(1970)

Werner Enke
DEGREE OF MURDER, A(1969, Ger.)

Darlene Enlow
DIARY OF A BACHELOR(1964)

Guy D. Ennery
KLONDIKE ANNIE(1936)

Bert Ennis
UNMASKED(1929), w; INSIDE INFORMATION(1934), w

Bob Ennis
BABY MAKER, THE(1970)

Charles Ennis
SEPARATE TABLES(1958), ed

E. C. "Skinny" Ennis
COLLEGE SWING(1938)

Ethel Ennis
MAD MONSTER PARTY(1967)

Floyd Ennis
ODDS AGAINST TOMORROW(1959); HANKY-PANKY(1982)

Jack Ennis
ADULTEROUS AFFAIR(1966), p

Linda Ennis
GEORGE WHITE'S SCANDALS(1945)

Lucy Ennis
Misc. Talkies
HOWDY BROADWAY(1929)

Skinnay Ennis
SLEEPYTIME GAL(1942); LET'S GO STEADY(1945)

Brian Eno
LAND OF THE MINOTAUR(1976, Gr.), m; JUBILEE(1978, Brit.), m; EGON SCHIELE-EXCESS AND PUNISHMENT(1981, Ger.), m
1984
DUNE(1984), m

Harry Eno
GOD TOLD ME TO(1976)

Roger Eno
1984
DUNE(1984), m

Russell Enoch
GLORY AT SEA(1952, Brit.); DISOBEDIENT(1953, Brit.); GAY DOG, THE(1954, Brit.); SAINT'S GIRL FRIDAY, THE(1954, Brit.)

Russell Enoch [William Russell]
THEY WHO DARE(1954, Brit.)

Hisao Enoki
KUROENKO(1968, Jap), ed

Toshio Enoki
ISLAND, THE(1962, Jap.), ed; ONIBABA(1965, Jap.), ed

Enric Madriguera Orchestra
THRILL OF BRAZIL, THE(1946)

Enrico
LAST ADVENTURE, THE(1968, Fr./Ital.), w; ZITA(1968, Fr.), w

Robert Enrico
HO(1968, Fr.), d, w; LAST ADVENTURE, THE(1968, Fr./Ital.), d; ZITA(1968, Fr.), d; WISE GUYS(1969, Fr./Ital.), d, w

Robert Enrietto
GIRL, THE BODY, AND THE PILL, THE(1967), set d; JUST FOR THE HELL OF IT(1968), set d; SHE-DEVILS ON WHEELS(1968), set d

Brian Enright
SUMMER SCHOOL TEACHERS(1977)

Don Enright
ACAPULCO GOLD(1978), w; SEARCH AND DESTROY(1981), w; HIT AND RUN(1982), w; PRIVATE SCHOOL(1983), p; SPASMS(1983, Can.), w

Florence Enright
NICE WOMAN(1932); OUT ALL NIGHT(1933); GIFT OF GAB(1934); SIX OF A KIND(1934); YOU'RE TELLING ME(1934)

Kevin Enright
TIGHT SPOT(1955); DALTON GIRLS, THE(1957); THUNDERING JETS(1958); HAND OF DEATH(1962)

Ray Enright
LAND OF THE SILVER FOX(1928), d; LITTLE WILDCAT, THE(1928), d; KID GLOVES(1929), d; SKIN DEEP(1929), d; STOLEN KISSES(1929), d; DANCING SWEETIES(1930), d; GOLDEN DAWN(1930), d; SCARLET PAGES(1930), d; SONG OF THE WEST(1930), d; GOLD DUST GERTIE(1931), d; FIREMAN, SAVE MY CHILD(1932), w; PLAY GIRL(1932), d; TENDERFOOT, THE(1932), d; BLONDIE JOHNSON(1933), d; HAVANA WIDOWS(1933), d; SILK EXPRESS, THE(1933), d; TOMORROW AT SEVEN(1933), d; CIRCUS CLOWN(1934), d; DAMES(1934), d; I'VE GOT YOUR NUMBER(1934), d; ST. LOUIS KID, THE(1934), d; TWENTY MILLION SWEETHEARTS(1934), d; ALIBI IKE(1935), d; MISS PACIFIC FLEET(1935), d; TRAVELING SALESLADY, THE(1935), d; WHILE THE PATIENT SLEPT(1935), d; BACK IN CIRCULATION(1937), d; READY, WILLING AND ABLE(1937), d; SINGING MARINE, THE(1937), d; SLIM(1937), d; GOLD DIGGERS IN PARIS(1938), d; HARD TO GET(1938), d; SWING YOUR LADY(1938), d; ANGELS WASH THEIR FACES(1939), d; GOING PLACES(1939), d; NAUGHTY BUT NICE(1939), d; ON YOUR TOES(1939), d; ANGEL FROM TEXAS, AN(1940), d; BROTHER RAT AND A BABY(1940), d; RIVER'S END(1940), d; BAD MEN OF MISSOURI(1941), d; LAW OF THE TROPICS(1941), d; THIEVES FALL OUT(1941), d; WAGONS ROLL AT NIGHT, THE(1941), d; MEN OF TEXAS(1942), d; SIN TOWN(1942), d; SPOILERS, THE(1942), d; WILD

BILL HICKOK RIDES(1942), d; GOOD LUCK, MR. YATES(1943), d; GUNG HO!(1943), d; IRON MAJOR, THE(1943), d; CHINA SKY(1945), d; MAN ALIVE(1945), d; ONE WAY TO LOVE(1946), d; TRAIL STREET(1947), d; ALBUQUERQUE(1948), d; RETURN OF THE BADMEN(1948), d; SOUTH OF ST. LOUIS(1949), d; KANSAS RAIDERS(1950), d; MONTANA(1950), d; FLAMING FEATHER(1951), d
Silents
GIRL FROM CHICAGO, THE(1927), d; JAWS OF STEEL(1927), d
Misc. Silents
TRACKED BY THE POLICE(1927), d; DOMESTIC TROUBLES(1928), d

Ray H. Enright
MAN FROM CAIRO, THE(1953), d

Raymond Enright
WE'RE IN THE MONEY(1935), d; CHINA CLIPPER(1936), d; EARTHWORM TRACTORS(1936), d; SING ME A LOVE SONG(1936), d; SNOWED UNDER(1936), d

Luis Enriquez
STREET PEOPLE(1976, U.S./Ital.), m

Rene Enriquez
BANANAS(1971); HARRY AND TONTO(1974); NIGHT MOVES(1975); UNDER FIRE(1983)
1984
EVIL THAT MEN DO, THE(1984)

Tito Enriquez
FIEND OF DOPE ISLAND(1961)

G. Enriton
Misc. Silents
PICTURE OF DORIAN GRAY, THE(1915, USSR)

M. Enserro
LOVE WITH THE PROPER STRANGER(1963)

Mike Enserro
ER LOVE A STRANGER(1958); TWO FOR THE SEESAW(1962)

Bob Ensescalle, Jr.
STRANGER RETURNS, THE(1968, U.S./Ital./Ger./Span.), w

Paul Ensia
PALACE OF NUDES(1961, Fr./Ital.)

John Ensign
TEEN-AGE STRANGLER(1967)

Michael Ensign
MIDNIGHT EXPRESS(1978, Brit.); SUPERMAN(1978); BUDDY BUDDY(1981); JEKYLL AND HYDE...TOGETHER AGAIN(1982); KISS ME GOODBYE(1982); PINK FLOYD-THE WALL(1982, Brit.); SIX WEEKS(1982); VICE SQUAD(1982); MAN WHO WASN'T THERE, THE(1983); MR. MOM(1983); STAR CHAMBER, THE(1983); WARGAMES(1983)
1984
ALL OF ME(1984); GHOSTBUSTERS(1984)

Robert Ensiminger
Misc. Silents
FORTUNE'S MASK(1922), d

Michael Ensing
RAISE THE TITANIC(1980, Brit.)

Bert Ensminger
Misc. Silents
CLIMBER, THE(1917); MAINSPRING, THE(1917)

Robert Ensminger
Silents
BRING HIM IN(1921), d; ONE STOLEN NIGHT(1923), d
Misc. Silents
MIDNIGHT BURGLAR, THE(1918), d; WANTED - A BROTHER(1918), d; WHATEVER THE COST(1918), d; RESTLESS SOULS(1922), d; YOU NEVER KNOW(1922), d

Lambert Enson
WINSLOW BOY, THE(1950)

David Ensor
MAN WITH THE GREEN CARNATION, THE(1960, Brit.); INFORMATION RECEIVED(1962, Brit.); POT CARRIERS, THE(1962, Brit.); VALLEY GIRL(1983)

Derek Ensor
GALLOPING MAJOR, THE(1951, Brit.)

Peter Ensor
SPY WHO LOVED ME, THE(1977, Brit.)

Dick Ensslen
LADY LIBERTY(1972, Ital./Fr.)

Howard Enstedt
Silents
ROLLING HOME(1926)

James Enstone
TRAPPED IN A SUBMARINE(1931, Brit.)

Boni Enten
SIDELONG GLANCES OF A PIGEON KICKER, THE(1970)

Joe Enterentree [Bonnie Shefield]
OTHER SIDE OF BONNIE AND CLYDE, THE(1968)

Angna Enters
TENTH AVENUE ANGEL(1948), w

Ezat Entezami
CYCLE, THE(1979, Iran)

Gabriel Enthoven
Silents
QUEST OF LIFE, THE(1916), w

Gregory Enton
1984
EL NORTE(1984)

Jack Entratter
PEPE(1960)

Gale Entrekin
RAZOR'S EDGE, THE(1946)

Harold Entwhistle
TREASURE ISLAND(1934); GOIN' TO TOWN(1935); MUTINY ON THE BOUNTY(1935); MAYTIME(1937)
Misc. Silents
MISS ROBINSON CRUSOE(1917)

Thomas Entwhistle
THIN RED LINE, THE(1964)

H.E. Entwistle
Misc. Silents
BEGGAR OF CAWNPORE, THE(1916)

Harold Entwistle
TWO AGAINST THE WORLD(1932); OUR BETTERS(1933); JIMMY THE
GENT(1934); PARIS IN SPRING(1935); TWO SINNERS(1935); ROMEO AND JU-
LIET(1936); SYLVIA SCARLETT(1936); EASY LIVING(1937); MAID OF SALEM(1937);
MARIE ANTOINETTE(1938); LIGHT THAT FAILED, THE(1939); WUTHERING
HEIGHTS(1939)
Silents
ONE OF MANY(1917)

Howard Entwistle
KITTY FOYLE(1940)

John Entwistle
TOMMY(1975, Brit.), a, w, m; QUADROPHENIA(1979, Brit.), md

Peg Entwistle
THIRTEEN WOMEN(1932)

Stuart Envin
CHAINED(1934)

Robert Enwit
SUMMERSPELL(1983), ph

Stacey Enyeart
ROBBY(1968), p

Erina Enyo
INCREDIBLY STRANGE CREATURES WHO STOPPED LIVING AND BECAME
CRAZY MIXED-UP ZOMBIES, THE(1965); THRILL KILLERS, THE(1965)

Jim Enzel
SOME OF MY BEST FRIENDS ARE...(1971)

Silvestre Enzo
SUNSCORCHED(1966, Span./Ger.), m

Tatsuo Enzo
MAJIN(1968, Jap.)

Capacci Eolo
VICTORY(1981)

Matyas Eorsi
FATHER(1967, Hung.)

Iran Eory
WEB OF VIOLENCE(1966, Ital./Span.)

Mane Eotha
KILL OR BE KILLED(1980), ph

Jules Epailly
FOLLOW THE LEADER(1930); HONOR AMONG LOVERS(1931); BEFORE MORN-
ING(1933); SWEET SURRENDER(1935)

Andros Epaminondas
1984
GIVE MY REGARDS TO BROAD STREET(1984, Brit.), p

Richard Epan
REVOLT OF MAMIE STOVER, THE(1956)

Elisabeth Epf
STORY OF VICKIE, THE(1958, Aust.)

Henry Ephron
BRIDE BY MISTAKE(1944), w; 3 IS A FAMILY(1944), w; ALWAYS TOGE-
THER(1947), w; WALLFLOWER(1948), w; JOHN LOVES MARY(1949), w; LOOK FOR
THE SILVER LINING(1949), w; JACKPOT, THE(1950), w; ON THE RIVERA(1951), w;
BELLES ON THEIR TOES(1952), w; WHAT PRICE GLORY?(1952), w; THERE'S NO
BUSINESS LIKE SHOW BUSINESS(1954), w; DADDY LONG LEGS(1955), w; GIRL
RUSH, THE(1955), w; BEST THINGS IN LIFE ARE FREE, THE(1956), p; CAROU-
SEL(1956), p&w; 23 PACES TO BAKER STREET(1956), p; DESK SET(1957), p, w;
CERTAIN SMILE, A(1958), p; SING, BOY, SING(1958), p&d; CAPTAIN NEWMAN,
M.D.(1963), w; TAKE HER, SHE'S MINE(1963), w

Nora Ephron
SILKWOOD(1983), w

Phoebe Ephron
BRIDE BY MISTAKE(1944), w; 3 IS A FAMILY(1944), w; ALWAYS TOGE-
THER(1947), w; WALLFLOWER(1948), w; JOHN LOVES MARY(1949), w; LOOK FOR
THE SILVER LINING(1949), w; JACKPOT, THE(1950), w; ON THE RIVERA(1951), w;
BELLES ON THEIR TOES(1952), w; WHAT PRICE GLORY?(1952), w; THERE'S NO
BUSINESS LIKE SHOW BUSINESS(1954), w; DADDY LONG LEGS(1955), w; GIRL
RUSH, THE(1955), w; BEST THINGS IN LIFE ARE FREE, THE(1956), w; CAROU-
SEL(1956), w; DESK SET(1957), w; CAPTAIN NEWMAN, M.D.(1963), w; TAKE HER,
SHE'S MINE(1963), w

I. J. Eppel
Silents
IRISH DESTINY(1925, Brit.), p, d, w

Jack Eppel
FORTUNATE FOOL, THE(1933, Brit.), p

Johnny Eppelite
SWEET ADELINE(1935)

Andrew Epper
PHANTOM OF THE PARADISE(1974)

Andy Epper
CUTTER AND BONE(1981)

Gary Epper
ROLLERBALL(1975); NIGHTWING(1979)

Jean Epper
CHEYENNE AUTUMN(1964)

Jeannie Epper
LIFE AND TIMES OF JUDGE ROY BEAN, THE(1972)

John Epper
THEY CAME TO BLOW UP AMERICA(1943); JOAN OF ARC(1948); KING RICHARD
AND THE CRUSADERS(1954); THESE THOUSAND HILLS(1959); SCALPHUNTERS,
THE(1968)

Joseph Epper
SON OF PALEFACE(1952)

Margo Epper
LIFE AND TIMES OF JUDGE ROY BEAN, THE(1972)

Stephanie Epper
CHEYENNE AUTUMN(1964); RARE BREED, THE(1966); LIFE AND TIMES OF
JUDGE ROY BEAN, THE(1972)

Tony Epper
MA AND PA KETTLE AT HOME(1954); SCALPHUNTERS, THE(1968), a, stunts;
GAY DECEIVERS, THE(1969); ULZANA'S RAID(1972); ISLAND OF DR. MOREAU,
THE(1977), stunts; CUTTER AND BONE(1981)
1984
WILD LIFE, THE(1984)

John Eppers
WINNER'S CIRCLE, THE(1948), anim t; BROKEN LANCE(1954)

Jon Eppers
THEY WERE EXPENDABLE(1945)

Toni Eppers
DOC SAVAGE... THE MAN OF BRONZE(1975), stunts

Tony Eppers
VALDEZ IS COMING(1971)

George Eppersen
MIDNIGHT COWBOY(1969)

Don Epperson
FEMALE BUNCH, THE(1969); WILD WHEELS(1969); BIG JAKE(1971)

George Epperson
CHARLOTTE'S WEB(1973), ph

Dieter Eppler
UNDER TEN FLAGS(1960, U.S./Ital.); HEAD, THE(1961, Ger.); FREDDY UNTER
FREMDEN STERNEN(1962, Ger.); I DEAL IN DANGER(1966); BLOOD DEMON(1967,
Ger.); U-47 LT. COMMANDER PRIEN(1967, Ger.); CURSE OF THE BLOOD
GHOULS(1969, Ital.); DEEP END(1970 Ger./U.S.)

Mickey Epps
JOYSTICKS(1983), w

Hans Epskamp
JUDGE AND THE SINNER, THE(1964, Ger.)

Brian Epsom
WILBY CONSPIRACY, THE(1975, Brit.)

Brian Epson
HUMAN FACTOR, THE(1979, Brit.)

Bryan Epson
BORN FREE(1966)

Arthur Epstein
ENDLESS LOVE(1981)

Carol Epstein
HIGH(1968, Can.)

Claire Epstein
DREAM NO MORE(1950, Palestine)

Howard Epstein
DEVIL'S PARTNER, THE(1958), ed; LITTLEST HOBO, THE(1958), ed; THREAT,
THE(1960), ed; DEVIL'S HAND, THE(1961), ed; HELL WITH HEROES, THE(1968),
ed

Howard G. Epstein
COUNTERPOINT(1967), ed

Israela Epstein
MY FATHER'S HOUSE(1947, Palestine)

Jack Epstein
HIGH(1968, Can.)

Jean Epstein
Misc. Silents
PASTEUR(1922, Fr.), d; COEUR FIDELE(1923, Fr.), d; LA BELLE NIVER-
NAISE(1923, Fr.), d; L'AUBERGE ROUGE(1923, Fr.), d; LE LION DES MOGOLS(1924,
Fr.), d; L'AFFICHE(1925, Fr.), d; LE DOUBLE AMOUR(1925, Fr.), d; MAUPRAT(1926,
Fr.), d; 6 ½ X 11(1927, Fr.), d; FALL OF THE HOUSE OF USHER, THE(1928, Fr.), d;
FINNIS TERRAE(1929, Fr.), d; SA TETE(1930, Fr.), d

Jerome Epstein
SEARCH FOR DANGER(1949), w; COUNTESS FROM HONG KONG, A(1967, Brit.),
p; ADDING MACHINE, THE(1969), p,d&w

Jerry Epstein
FOLLOW THAT MAN(1961, Brit.), p, d&w

Jonathan Epstein
1984
ICE PIRATES, THE(1984)

Julius Epstein
LIVING ON VELVET(1935), w; KISS THEM FOR ME(1957), w

Julius J. Epstein
BROADWAY GONDOLIER(1935), w; I LIVE FOR LOVE(1935), w; IN CALIEN-
TE(1935), w; LITTLE BIG SHOT(1935), w; STARS OVER BROADWAY(1935), w; SONS
O' GUNS(1936), w; CONFESSION(1937), w; FOUR DAUGHTERS(1938), w; SECRETS
OF AN ACTRESS(1938), w; DAUGHTERS COURAGEOUS(1939), w; FOUR WI-
VES(1939), w; NO TIME FOR COMEDY(1940), w; SATURDAY'S CHILDREN(1940),
w; BRIDE CAME C.O.D., THE(1941), w; HONEYMOON FOR THREE(1941), w;
STRAWBERRY BLONDE, THE(1941), w; CASABLANCA(1942), w; MALE ANIMAL,
THE(1942), w; MAN WHO CAME TO DINNER, THE(1942), w; ARSENIC AND OLD
LACE(1944), w; MR. SKEFFINGTON(1944), p; ONE MORE TOMORROW(1946), w;
CHICKEN EVERY SUNDAY(1948), w; ROMANCE ON THE HIGH SEAS(1948), w;
MY FOOLISH HEART(1949), w; TAKE CARE OF MY LITTLE GIRL(1951), w; FOREV-
ER FEMALE(1953), w; LAST TIME I SAW PARIS, THE(1954), w; TENDER TRAP,
THE(1955), w; YOUNG AT HEART(1955), w; BROTHERS KARAMAZOV, THE(1958),
w; TAKE A GIANT STEP(1959), p, w; TALL STORY(1960), w; FANNY(1961), w;
LIGHT IN THE PIAZZA(1962), w; RETURN FROM THE ASHES(1965, U.S./Brit.), w;
ANY WEDNESDAY(1966), p, w; PETE 'N' TILLIE(1972), p, w; ONCE IS NOT
ENOUGH(1975), w; CROSS OF IRON(1977, Brit., Ger.), w; HOUSE CALLS(1978), w;
REUBEN, REUBEN(1983), w

Julius V. Epstein
SEND ME NO FLOWERS(1964), w

Marcelo Epstein
1984
BODY ROCK(1984), d

Marie Epstein
LA MATERNELLE(1933, Fr.), d&w
Misc. Silents
AMES D'ENFANTS(1929, Fr.), d; PEAU DE PECHE(1929, Fr.), d

Mel Epstein
GHOST BREAKERS, THE(1940), set d; HAZARD(1948), p; WHISPERING SMITH(1948), p; COPPER CANYON(1950), p; GOLDBERGS, THE(1950), p; BRANDED(1951), p; DEAR BRAT(1951), p; SAVAGE, THE(1953), p; ALASKA SEAS(1954), p; SECRET OF THE INCAS(1954), p

Phil G. Epstein
LOVE ON A BET(1936), w

Phillip Epstein
FM(1978)

Philip C. Epstein
DAUGHTERS COURAGEOUS(1939), w

Philip G. Epstein
GIFT OF GAB(1934), w; BRIDE WALKS OUT, THE(1936), w; GRAND JURY(1936), w; MUMMY'S BOYS(1936), w; NEW FACES OF 1937(1937), w; MAD MISS MANTON, THE(1938), w; THERE'S THAT WOMAN AGAIN(1938), w; FOUR WIVES(1939), w; NO TIME FOR COMEDY(1940), w; SATURDAY'S CHILDREN(1940), w; BRIDE CAME C.O.D., THE(1941), w; STRAWBERRY BLONDE, THE(1941), w; CASABLANCA(1942), w; MALE ANIMAL, THE(1942), w; MAN WHO CAME TO DINNER, THE(1942), w; ARSENIC AND OLD LACE(1944), w; MR. SKEFFINGTON(1944), w; ONE MORE TOMORROW(1946), w; CHICKEN EVERY SUNDAY(1948), w; ROMANCE ON THE HIGH SEAS(1948), w; MY FOOLISH HEART(1949), w; TAKE CARE OF MY LITTLE GIRL(1951), w; FOREVER FEMALE(1953), w; LAST TIME I SAW PARIS, THE(1954), w; BROTHERS KARAMAZOV, THE(1958), w

Pierre Epstein
NOCTURNA(1979); SIMON(1980); SO FINE(1981)
1984
SPLASH(1984)

Lou Epton
Misc. Talkies
CALLIOPE(1971)

Enrique L. Equiluz [Henry L. Egan]
FRANKENSTEIN'S BLOODY TERROR(1968, Span.), d

Arrigo Equini
WANDERING JEW, THE(1948, Ital.), art d; RAPTURE(1950, Ital.), art d; BAREFOOT CONTESSA, THE(1954), art d; CROSSED SWORDS(1954), art d; PHAROAH'S WOMAN, THE(1961, Ital.), art d; NIGHT THEY KILLED RASPUTIN, THE(1962, Fr./Ital.), art d; 300 SPARTANS, THE(1962), art d; CLEOPATRA'S DAUGHTER(1963, Fr., Ital.), art d; MILL OF THE STONE WOMEN(1963, Fr./Ital.), art d; WASTREL, THE(1963, Ital.), art d; SANDOKAN THE GREAT(1964, Fr./Ital./Span.), set d; CONQUEST OF MYCENE(1965, Ital., Fr.), art d; INVASION 1700(1965, Fr./Ital./Yugo.), art d; CAST A GIANT SHADOW(1966), art d; SECRET AGENT SUPER DRAGON(1966, Fr./Ital./Ger./Monaco), set d; BIGGEST BUNDLE OF THEM ALL, THE(1968), art; BUONA SERA, MRS. CAMPBELL(1968, Ital.), art d; SEVEN GOLDEN MEN(1969, Fr./Ital./Span.), art d; HORNET'S NEST(1970), art d; ASSASSINATION OF TROTSKY, THE(1972 Fr./Ital.), art d

Equipoise
WINNER'S CIRCLE, THE(1948)

Tomoslav Erak
APACHE GOLD(1965, Ger.)

Jorges Eras
MEXICO IN FLAMES(1982, USSR/Mex./Ital.), m

Edith Erastoff
Misc. Silents
MAN THERE WAS, A(1917, Swed.); OUTLAW AND HIS WIFE, THE(1918, Swed.)

Brune Erba
STATUE, THE(1971, Brit.)

John Erbe
UTILITIES(1983, Can.), m

Mickey Erbe
HARRY TRACY-DESPERADO(1982, Can.), m

Micky Erbe
IMPROPER CHANNELS(1981, Can.), m; TICKET TO HEAVEN(1981), m; THRESHOLD(1983, Can.), m

Johnny Erben
LOST, LONELY AND VICIOUS(1958)

Nina Erber
NIGHT COMES TOO SOON(1948, Brit.)

Geno Erbisti
THIS IS THE ARMY(1943)

Morris D. Erby
THX 1138(1971)

Morris Erby
MAN CALLED ADAM, A(1966); LOST MAN, THE(1969); FINAL COMEDOWN, THE(1972)

Erckmann and Chatrian
BELLS, THE(1931, Brit.), w

Ercole
MONTE CARLO STORY, THE(1957, Ital.)

Nicoletta Ercole
TALES OF ORDINARY MADNESS(1983, Ital.), cos

Linda Ercoli
SNOOPY, COME HOME(1972)

Luciano Ercoli
NUDE ODYSSEY(1962, Fr./Ital.), p; PISTOL FOR RINGO, A(1966, Ital./Span.), p; RUTHLESS FOUR, THE(1969, Ital./Ger.), p

Tuciano Ercoli
RETURN OF RINGO, THE(1966, Ital./Span.), p

Elizabeth Ercy
PHAEDRA(1962, U.S./Gr./Fr.); VICTORS, THE(1963); CARNABY, M.D.(1967, Brit.); FATHOM(1967); SORCERERS, THE(1967, Brit.)

Julee Erdahl
1984
RHINESTONE(1984)

Daniel Erdelyi
FATHER(1967, Hung.)

Mici Erdelyt
HIPPOLYT, THE LACKEY(1932, Hung.); KIND STEPMOTHER(1936, Hung.)

D. Erdman
Silents
ARSENAL(1929, USSR)

Dick Erdman
HOLLYWOOD CANTEEN(1944); JANIE(1944); DANGER SIGNAL(1945); DECEPTION(1946); JANIE GETS MARRIED(1946); NIGHT AND DAY(1946); NOBODY LIVES FOREVER(1946); WILD HARVEST(1947); EASY LIVING(1949)

Dick [Richard] Erdman
VERY THOUGHT OF YOU, THE(1944); TOO YOUNG TO KNOW(1945); SHADOW OF A WOMAN(1946); THAT WAY WITH WOMEN(1947)

Nikolay Erdman
JACK FROST(1966, USSR), w

Paul E. Erdman
SILVER BEARS(1978), w

Richard Erdman
TIME OF YOUR LIFE, THE(1948); MR. SKEFFINGTON(1944); OBJECTIVE, BURMA!(1945); ADMIRAL WAS A LADY, THE(1950); FOUR DAYS LEAVE(1950, Switz.); MEN, THE(1950); CRY DANGER(1951); YOU'RE IN THE NAVY NOW(1951); ALADDIN AND HIS LAMP(1952); HAPPY TIME, THE(1952); JUMPING JACKS(1952); SAN FRANCISCO STORY, THE(1952); STOOGE, THE(1952); WILD BLUE YONDER, THE(1952); BLUE GARDENIA, THE(1953); MISSION OVER KOREA(1953); STALAG 17(1953); STEEL LADY, THE(1953); BENGAZI(1955); FRANCIS IN THE NAVY(1955); ANYTHING GOES(1956); POWER AND THE PRIZE, THE(1956); RAWHIDE TRAIL, THE(1958); SADDLE THE WIND(1958); FACE OF FIRE(1959, U.S./Brit.); BRASS BOTTLE, THE(1964); NAMU, THE KILLER WHALE(1966); RASCAL(1969); TORA! TORA! TORA!(1970, U.S./Jap.); BROTHERS O'TOOLE, THE(1973), a, d; HEIDI'S SONG(1982)
Misc. Talkies
RAWHIDE TRAIL, THE(1950); TEENAGE TEASE(1983), d

Hans Erdmann
TESTAMENT OF DR. MABUSE, THE(1943, Ger.), m

Iris Erdmann
SHADOWS GROW LONGER, THE(1962, Switz./Ger.)

Otto Erdmann
DAUGHTER OF EVIL(1930, Ger.), art d; SOMEWHERE IN BERLIN(1949, E. Ger.), set d; RETURN OF DR. MABUSE, THE(1961, Ger./Fr./Ital.), art d

Leo Erdody
BABY FACE MORGAN(1942), m; QUEEN OF BROADWAY(1942), m; TOMORROW WE LIVE(1942), m; BOSS OF BIG TOWN(1943), m; CORREGIDOR(1943), m; DEAD MEN WALK(1943), md; GIRLS IN CHAINS(1943), m; ISLE OF FORGOTTEN SINS(1943), m; WESTERN CYCLONE(1943), m; WILD HORSE RUSTLERS(1943), m; JIVE JUNCTION(1944), m; MINSTREL MAN(1944), md; APOLOGY FOR MURDER(1945), md; DETOUR(1945), m; STRANGE ILLUSION(1945), md; WHITE PONGO(1945), md; BLONDE FOR A DAY(1946), md; GAS HOUSE KIDS(1946), m, md; I RING DOORBELLS(1946), m; LARCENY IN HER HEART(1946), md; MURDER IS MY BUSINESS(1946), md; RETURN OF RIN TIN TIN, THE(1947), m; LADY AT MIDNIGHT(1948), m; MONEY MADNESS(1948), md

Ben Erdway
SIN TOWN(1942)

V. Erenberg
HAMLET(1966, USSR)

Vladimir Erenberg
LADY WITH THE DOG, THE(1962, USSR)

Moris Ergas
STEPPE, THE(1963, Fr./Ital.), p; LOVE A LA CARTE(1965, Ital.), p; LA VISITA(1966, Ital./Fr.), p; DESERTER AND THE NOMADS, THE(1969, Czech./Ital.), p

Morris Ergas
GENERALE DELLA ROVERE(1960, Ital./Fr.), p; KAPO(1964, Ital./Fr./Yugo.), p

Raymond Erger
LEGEND OF FRENCHIE KING, THE(1971, Fr./Ital./Span./Brit.), p

Halil Ergun
YOL(1982, Turkey)

Bernard Erhard
FIREFOX(1982); DEATHSTALKER(1983, Arg./U.S.)
1984
DEATHSTALKER, THE(1984)

Herman Erhard
STOLEN IDENTITY(1953)

Heinz Erhardt
RAMPAGE AT APACHE WELLS(1966, Ger./Yugo.)

Kurt Erhardt
AFFAIR BLUM, THE(1949, Ger.)

Tom Erhardt
MICKEY ONE(1965)

Thomas Erhart
GOLDSTEIN(1964); MONITORS, THE(1969); T.R. BASKIN(1971)

Thomas Erhart, Jr.
DOCTOR DETROIT(1983)

Thomas O. Erhart, Jr.
DAMIEN-OMEN II(1978); THIEF(1981)

Tom Erhart
NICKELODEON(1976); SILVER STREAK(1976)

Chiemi Eri
LIFE OF A COUNTRY DOCTOR(1961, Jap.)

Barry Eric
ECHOES(1983)

E.H. Eric
WALL-EYED NIPPON(1963, Jap.)

Fred Eric
Silents
SKID PROOF(1923)
Misc. Silents
DIVORCED(1915); WOMAN AND THE BEAST, THE(1917); COLUMBUS(1923)

James Eric
JESUS TRIP, THE(1971), art d

Kal Eric
VORTEX(1982)

Martin Eric
SUMMER PLACE, A(1959); PARRISH(1961); MY FAIR LADY(1964); BAKER'S HAWK(1976)

Wreckless Eric
RADIO ON(1980, Brit./Ger.), m

Eric Winstone and his Band
DON CHICAGO(1945, Brit.)

Victor Erice
SPIRIT OF THE BEEHIVE, THE(1976, Span.), d, w

Heidi Erich
COMING-OUT PARTY, A(; WEEKEND WITH LULU, A(1961, Brit.); DEVIL DOLL(1964, Brit.); WHERE THE BULLETS FLY(1966, Brit.)

Erick Erichsen
ESCAPE FROM TERROR(1960)

Siv Ericks
FANNY AND ALEXANDER(1983, Swed./Fr./Ger.)

Leon Ericksen
PSYCH-OUT(1968), art d; RAIN PEOPLE, THE(1969), art d; THAT COLD DAY IN THE PARK(1969, U.S./Can.), art d; MC CABE AND MRS. MILLER(1971), prod d; IMAGES(1972, Ireland), prod d; CINDERELLA LIBERTY(1973), art d; CALIFORNIA SPLIT(1974), art d; QUINTET(1979), prod d; LADIES AND GENTLEMEN, THE FABULOUS STAINS(1982), prod d
1984
ICEMAN(1984), art d

A. F. Erickson
LONE STAR RANGER, THE(1930), p&d; ROUGH ROMANCE(1930), d; UNDER SUSPICION(1931), d; THIS SPORTING AGE(1932), d
Misc. Silents
WOMAN FROM HELL, THE(1929), d

A.F "Buddy" Erickson
CITY GIRL(1930)

Bill Erickson
HERBIE GOES TO MONTE CARLO(1977); APPLE DUMPLING GANG RIDES AGAIN, THE(1979); SWAMP THING(1982)

Bob Erickson
Silents
RIDERS OF THE RIO GRANDE(1929)

C.O. Erickson
ZORRO, THE GAY BLADE(1981), p

Carl Erickson
SILVER DOLLAR(1932), w; STRANGER IN TOWN(1932), W; GIRL MISSING(1933), w; MYSTERY OF THE WAX MUSEUM, THE(1933), w; EASY TO LOVE(1934), w; FASHIONS OF 1934(1934), w; SMARTY(1934), w; BLACK FURY(1935), w; STRAND-ED(1935), w; SWEET MUSIC(1935), w

Casey Erickson
1984
SAM'S SON(1984)

Clem Erickson
JUNGLE JIM IN THE FORBIDDEN LAND(1952)

Del Erickson
HOT ROD GIRL(1956); TEA AND SYMPATHY(1956); BLUE ANGEL, THE(1959)

Dell Erickson
TAKE A GIANT STEP(1959)

Delmar Erickson
DIARY OF ANNE FRANK, THE(1959)

Devon Erickson
1984
NIGHT OF THE COMET(1984)

Doc Erickson
CHINATOWN(1974)

Frank Erickson
MAGNIFICENT DOLL(1946)

Glen [Leif] Erickson
WANDERER OF THE WASTELAND(1935); DESERT GOLD(1936); DRIFT FEN-CE(1936); NEVADA(1936)

Harold Erickson
STRANGLER OF THE SWAMP(1945), w

Harry Erickson
ANNE OF THE INDIES(1951), ph

Helen Erickson
CEILNG ZERO(1935)

Helge Erickson
WOODEN HORSE, THE(1951)

Jack Erickson
SKY COMMANDO(1953), spec eff; MIAMI STORY, THE(1954), spec eff; IT CAME FROM BENEATH THE SEA(1955), spec eff; EL CID(1961, U.S./Ital.), spec eff; KOTCH(1971), spec eff

Jim Erickson
1984
RUNAWAY(1984), set d

John Erickson
FIVE GRAVES TO CAIRO(1943)

Johnny Erickson
MY FAVORITE BLONDE(1942)

Jon Christian Erickson
FUN WITH DICK AND JANE(1977)

Judy Erickson
PHANTOM PLANET, THE(1961)

Keith Erickson
Misc. Talkies
LAST TANGO IN ACAPULCO, THE(1975)

Knute Erickson
SQUALL, THE(1929); TWIN BEDS(1929); SPOILERS, THE(1930); DEADLINE, THE(1932); STOWAWAY(1932); BITTER TEA OF GENERAL YEN, THE(1933)
Silents
CONFLICT, THE(1921); GASOLINE GUS(1921); MONSTER, THE(1925); RUGGED WATER(1925); NON-STOP FLIGHT, THE(1926); JOHNNY GET YOUR HAIR CUT(1927); SCARLET SEAS(1929)

Misc. Silents
WATERFRONT(1928)

Lee Erickson
KENTUCKIAN, THE(1955); SEVEN LITTLE FOYS, THE(1955); LONG, HOT SUM-MER, THE(1958)

Leif Erickson
SWEETHEART OF SIGMA CHI(1933); BIG BROADCAST OF 1938, THE(1937); THRILL OF A LIFETIME(1937); WAIKIKI WEDDING(1937); RIDE A CROOKED MILE(1938); ONE THIRD OF A NATION(1939); BLONDE FROM SINGAPORE, THE(1941); H.M. PULHAM, ESQ.(1941); NOTHING BUT THE TRUTH(1941); ARE HUSBANDS NECESSARY?(1942); EAGLE SQUADRON(1942); FLEET'S IN, THE(1942); NIGHT MONSTER(1942); PARDON MY SARONG(1942); BLONDE SAV-AGE(1947); GANGSTER, THE(1947); GAY INTRUDERS, THE(1948); JOAN OF ARC(1948); MISS TATLOCK'S MILLIONS(1948); SNAKE PIT, THE(1948); SORRY, WRONG NUMBER(1948); JOHNNY STOOL PIGEON(1949); LADY GAMBLES, THE(1949); DALLAS(1950); LOVE THAT BRUTE(1950); MOTHER DIDN'T TELL ME(1950); SHOWDOWN, THE(1950); STELLA(1950); THREE SECRETS(1950); CIMAR-RON KID, THE(1951); REUNION IN RENO(1951); SAILOR BEWARE(1951); SHOW BOAT(1951); TALL TARGET, THE(1951); ABBOTT AND COSTELLO MEET CAPTAIN KIDD(1952); CARBINE WILLIAMS(1952); MY WIFE'S BEST FRIEND(1952); NEVER WAVE AT A WAC(1952); WITH A SONG IN MY HEART(1952); BORN TO THE SADDLE(1953); FORT ALGIERS(1953); INVADERS FROM MARS(1953); PARIS MOD-EL(1953); PERILOUS JOURNEY, A(1953); TROUBLE ALONG THE WAY(1953); ON THE WATERFRONT(1954); FASTEST GUN ALIVE(1956); STAR IN THE DUST(1956); TEA AND SYMPATHY(1956); ISTANBUL(1957); KISS THEM FOR ME(1957); VIN-TAGE, THE(1957); ONCE UPON A HORSE(1958); TWILIGHT FOR THE GODS(1958); SHOOT OUT AT BIG SAG(1962); GATHERING OF EAGLES, A(1963); CARPETBAG-GERS, THE(1964); ROUSTABOUT(1964); STRAIT-JACKET(1964); I SAW WHAT YOU DID(1965); MIRAGE(1965); MAN AND BOY(1972); ABDUCTION(1975); WINTER-HAWK(1976); TWILIGHT'S LAST GLEAMING(1977, U.S./Ger.)

Leon Erickson
WILD ANGELS, THE(1966), art d; MEDIUM COOL(1969), art d; LAST MOVIE, THE(1971), art d; MC CABE AND MRS. MILLER(1971), cos; MAHOGANY(1975), art d; HAMMETT(1982), art d

Lisa Erickson
1984
POWER, THE(1984)

Lorna Erickson
WANDERERS, THE(1979)

Louise Erickson
MEET MISS BOBBY SOCKS(1944); ROSIE THE RIVETER(1944); THREE HUS-BANDS(1950)

Mark Erickson
1984
RIVER, THE(1984)

Maude Erickson
EASY TO LOVE(1953)

Melinda Erickson
IN A LONELY PLACE(1950)

Paul Erickson
WHITE FIRE(1953, Brit.), a, w; GILDED CAGE, THE(1954, Brit.), w; GREEN BUD-DHA, THE(1954, Brit.), w; SECRET VENTURE(1955, Brit.), w; SHADOW OF A MAN(1955, Brit.), w; FIND THE LADY(1956, Brit.), w; TRACK THE MAN DOWN(1956, Brit.), w; KILL HER GENTLY(1958, Brit.), w; END OF THE LINE, THE(1959, Brit.), w; NIGHT OF THE PROWLER(1962, Brit.), w; MARKED ONE, THE(1963, Brit.), w

Phil Erickson
UFO: TARGET EARTH(1974)

Rudolf Erickson
SAINTED SISTERS, THE(1948)

Rune Erickson
LOVE MATES(1967, Swed.), ph

Uta Erickson
Misc. Talkies
BACCHANALE(1970)

Annalisa Ericson
ILLICIT INTERLUDE(1954, Swed.)

Christian Ericson
SIDELONG GLANCES OF A PIGEON KICKER, THE(1970)

Devon Ericson
RETURN TO MACON COUNTY(1975)

Doc Ericson
IS PARIS BURNING?(1966, U.S./Fr.)

Erica Ericson
FANNY HILL: MEMOIRS OF A WOMAN OF PLEASURE zero(1965)

Helen Ericson
FOUR MEN AND A PRAYER(1938); ESCAPE, THE(1939); HOTEL FOR WO-MEN(1939); PARDON OUR NERVE(1939); QUICK MILLIONS(1939); TOO BUSY TO WORK(1939); WIFE, HUSBAND AND FRIEND(1939); CHARLIE CHAN IN PANA-MA(1940); FREE, BLONDE AND 21(1940); YOUNG AS YOU FEEL(1940)

John Ericson
TERESA(1951); RHAPSODY(1954); STUDENT PRINCE, THE(1954); BAD DAY AT BLACK ROCK(1955); GREEN FIRE(1955); RETURN OF JACK SLADE, THE(1955); CRUEL TOWER, THE(1956); FORTY GUNS(1957); DAY OF THE BAD MAN(1958); OREGON PASSAGE(1958); PRETTY BOY FLOYD(1960); UNDER TEN FLAGS(1960, U.S./Ital.); SEVEN FACES OF DR. LAO(1964); BAMBOO SAUCER, THE(1968); DESTRUCTORS, THE(1968); MONEY JUNGLE, THE(1968); BEDKNOBS AND BROOMSTICKS(1971); CRASH(1977)
Misc. Talkies
SLAVE GIRL OF BABYLON(1962, Ital.); HUSTLER SQUAD(1976)

June Ericson
THAT TOUCH OF MINK(1962)

Karen Ericson
Misc. Talkies
HUSTLER SQUAD(1976)

Rune Ericson
SWEDISH WEDDING NIGHT(1965, Swed.), ph; DEAR JOHN(1966, Swed.), ph; NIGHT GAMES(1966, Swed.), ph; LE VIOL(1968, Fr./Swed.), ph; GIRLS, THE(1972, Swed.), ph

Sharon Ernster
TAKE THIS JOB AND SHOVE IT(1981); CANNERY ROW(1982)
Bela Erny
JUST A GIGOLO(1979, Ger.)
Bengt Ernyrd
HUGS AND KISSES(1968, Swed.), m
Joseph Erons
ZIEGFELD FOLLIES(1945), w
Gabor Eross
FATHER(1967, Hung.)
Tamas Eross
AGE OF ILLUSIONS(1967, Hung.)
Mario Erpichini
CRAZY JOE(1974); THREE TOUGH GUYS(1974, U.S./Ital.)
Kendall Errair
1984
FOOTLOOSE(1984), cos
Krista Errickson
LITTLE DARLINGS(1980); JEKYLL AND HYDE...TOGETHER AGAIN(1982); FIRST TIME, THE(1983)
Bill Errigo
HOSPITAL MASSACRE(1982)
Leon Errol
ONLY SAPS WORK(1930); FINN AND HATTIE(1931); HER MAJESTY LOVE(1931); ONE HEAVENLY NIGHT(1931); ALICE IN WONDERLAND(1933); CAPTAIN HATES THE SEA, THE(1934); NOTORIOUS SOPHIE LANG, THE(1934); WE'RE NOT DRESSING(1934); CORONADO(1935); PRINCESS O'HARA(1935); GREAT ZIEGFELD, THE(1936); MAKE A WISH(1937); CAREER(1939); DANCING CO-ED(1939); GIRL FROM MEXICO, THE(1939); MEXICAN SPITFIRE(1939); GOLDEN FLEECING, THE(1940); MEXICAN SPITFIRE OUT WEST(1940); POP ALWAYS PAYS(1940); HURRY, CHARLIE, HURRY(1941); MELODY LANE(1941); MEXICAN SPITFIRE'S BABY(1941); NEVER GIVE A SUCKER AN EVEN BREAK(1941); SIX LESSONS FROM MADAME LA ZONGA(1941); WHERE DID YOU GET THAT GIRL?(1941); MEXICAN SPITFIRE AT SEA(1942); MEXICAN SPITFIRE SEES A GHOST(1942); MEXICAN SPITFIRE'S ELEPHANT(1942); STRICTLY IN THE GROOVE(1942); COWBOY IN MANHATTTAN(1943); FOLLOW THE BAND(1943); GALS, INCORPORATED(1943); HIGHER AND HIGHER(1943); MEXICAN SPITFIRE'S BLESSED EVENT(1943); BABES ON SWING STREET(1944); HAT CHECK HONEY(1944); INVISIBLE MAN'S REVENGE(1944); SLIGHTLY TERRIFIC(1944); TWILIGHT ON THE PRAIRIE(1944); MAMA LOVES PAPA(1945); SHE GETS HER MAN(1945); UNDER WESTERN SKIES(1945); WHAT A BLONDE(1945); JOE PALOOKA, CHAMP(1946); RIVERBOAT RHYTHM(1946); FIGHTING MAD(1948); NOOSE HANGS HIGH, THE(1948); JOE PALOOKA IN THE BIG FIGHT(1949); JOE PALOOKA IN THE COUNTERPUNCH(1949); HUMPHREY TAKES A CHANCE(1950); JOE PALOOKA MEETS HUMPHREY(1950)
Misc. Talkies
JOE PALOOKA IN THE KNOCKOUT(1947)
Silents
CLOTHES MAKE THE PIRATE(1925); SALLY(1925)
Misc. Silents
LUNATIC AT LARGE, THE(1927)
Claus Ersbak
WELCOME TO THE CLUB(1971)
V.L. Ersbov
ALEXANDER NEVSKY(1939)
Elsa Ersi
ROYAL BOX, THE(1930)
Chester Erskin
MIDNIGHT(1934), p&d, w; FRANKIE AND JOHNNY(1936), d
Audrey Erskine
FRIGHTENED BRIDE, THE(1952, Brit.), w
Carl Erskine
ROOGIE'S BUMP(1954)
Chester Erskine
MASTER OF MEN(1933), w; SAILOR TAKES A WIFE, THE(1946), w; EGG AND I, THE(1947), p, d; ALL MY SONS(1948), p, w; TAKE ONE FALSE STEP(1949), p&d, w; ANDROCLES AND THE LION(1952), d, w; BELLE OF NEW YORK, THE(1952), w; GIRL IN EVERY PORT, A(1952), d, w; ANGEL FACE(1953), w; SPLIT SECOND(1953), w; WITNESS TO MURDER(1954), p, w; WONDERFUL COUNTRY, THE(1959), p; INVINCIBLE SIX, THE(1970, U.S./Iran), w
Drummond Erskine
LIGHT FANTASTIC(1964)
Eileen Erskine
MIDAS TOUCH, THE(1940, Brit.); THIS HAPPY BREED(1944, Brit.); WAY AHEAD, THE(1945, Brit.); GREAT EXPECTATIONS(1946, Brit.); HILLS OF HOME(1948); LADY POSSESSED(1952)
Elizabeth Erskine
YOU CAN'T BEAT THE IRISH(1952, Brit.)
Howard Erskine
SEMINOLE(1953); ROLLOVER(1981); ZELIG(1983)
John Erskine
LADY SURRENDERS, A(1930), w; BACHELOR OF ARTS(1935), w; PRESIDENT'S MYSTERY, THE(1936), w; SPIRIT AND THE FLESH, THE(1948, Ital.), titles; DIANE(1955), w
Laurie York Erskine
RENFREW OF THE ROYAL MOUNTED(1937), w; ON THE GREAT WHITE TRAIL(1938), w; CRASHING THRU(1939), w; FIGHTING MAD(1939), w; MURDER ON THE YUKON(1940), w; SKY BANDITS, THE(1940), w; YUKON FLIGHT(1940), w
Laurlee Yorke Erskine
DANGER AHEAD(1940), w
Marilyn Erskine
WESTWARD THE WOMEN(1951); GIRL IN WHITE, THE(1952); JUST THIS ONCE(1952); ABOVE AND BEYOND(1953); CONFIDENTIAL CONNIE(1953); EDDIE CANTOR STORY, THE(1953); SLIGHT CASE OF LARCENY, A(1953)
Norman Erskine
OUTBACK(1971, Aus.); SUNSTRUCK(1973, Aus.); CADDIE(1976, Aus.); STARSTRUCK(1982, Aus.)

Wallace Erskine
Silents
RAGGED EDGE, THE(1923)
Misc. Silents
PERJURY(1921)
Audrey Erskine-Lindop
PORTRAIT OF A SINNER(1961, Brit.), w
Tony Erstich
LAND OF FURY(1955 Brit.)
Jacques Ertaud
MAN ESCAPED, A(1957, Fr.)
Susan Ertz
IN THE COOL OF THE DAY(1963), w
Sarah Erukker
HUNCH, THE(1967, Brit.), d&w
Lifla Erulkar
CAESAR AND CLEOPATRA(1946, Brit.)
Diane Ervin
CALCUTTA(1947)
R.D. Ervin
RUN FOR THE HILLS(1953), p
St. John G. Ervine
BOYD'S SHOP(1960, Brit.), w
Julius Erving
FISH THAT SAVED PITTSBURGH, THE(1979)
Ben Erway
MOUNTAIN RHYTHM(1942); KEEP 'EM SLUGGING(1943); MISSION TO MOSCOW(1943); NORTHERN PURSUIT(1943); TAMPICO(1944); DARK MIRROR, THE(1946); LOCKET, THE(1946); NOTORIOUS(1946); BRASHER DOUBLOON, THE(1947); LULU BELLE(1948); JOLSON SINGS AGAIN(1949); RIMFIRE(1949); SAND(1949); SHEP COMES HOME(1949); UNDERCOVER MAN, THE(1949); DARK AT THE TOP OF THE STAIRS, THE(1960)
Antoinette Erwin
Silents
SPREADING DAWN, THE(1917)
Bill Erwin
DOUBLE DYNAMITE(1951); JET PILOT(1957); CRY BABY KILLER, THE(1958); TERROR AT BLACK FALLS(1962); UNDER THE YUM-YUM TREE(1963); CHRISTINE JORGENSEN STORY, THE(1970); SOMEWHERE IN TIME(1980)
Billy Erwin
HAPPY LANDING(1934)
E. L. Erwin
DALTON THAT GOT AWAY(1960), w
Ed Erwin
DATE WITH DEATH, A(1959); VENGEANCE(1964), w
Edward Erwin
AMAZING TRANSPARENT MAN, THE(1960)
Felix Erwin
FIRST NIGHT(1937, Brit.)
Hobe Erwin
DINNER AT EIGHT(1933), set d; LITTLE WOMEN(1933), set d; LITTLE MINISTER, THE(1934), set d; GONE WITH THE WIND(1939), art d
Jacques Erwin
MR. PEEK-A-BOO(1951, Fr.)
John Erwin
THIRTEEN FIGHTING MEN(1960)
Misc. Silents
BARKER, THE(1928)
Jon Erwin
1984
RECKLESS(1984)
Judy Erwin
ERRAND BOY, THE(1961)
Lee Erwin
TARZAN'S DEADLY SILENCE(1970), w
Ralph Erwin
SHANGHAI DRAMA, THE(1945, Fr.), m
Stu Erwin
BIG BROADCAST, THE(1932); HEADING FOR HEAVEN(1947)
Stuart Erwin
MOTHER KNOWS BEST(1928); COCK-EYED WORLD, THE(1929); DANGEROUS CURVES(1929); SPEAKEASY(1929); SWEETIE(1929); THIS THING CALLED LOVE(1929); THRU DIFFERENT EYES(1929); TRESPASSER, THE(1929); DANGEROUS NAN McGREW(1930); HAPPY DAYS(1930); LOVE AMONG THE MILLIONAIRES(1930); MAYBE IT'S LOVE(1930); MEN WITHOUT WOMEN(1930); ONLY SAPS WORK(1930); PLAYBOY OF PARIS(1930); YOUNG EAGLES(1930); ALONG CAME YOUTH(1931); DUDE RANCH(1931); MAGNIFICENT LIE(1931); NO LIMIT(1931); UP POPS THE DEVIL(1931); WORKING GIRLS(1931); MAKE ME A STAR(1932); MISLEADING LADY, THE(1932); STRANGERS IN LOVE(1932); TWO KINDS OF WOMEN(1932); BEFORE DAWN(1933); CRIME OF THE CENTURY, THE(1933); DAY OF RECKONING(1933); FACE IN THE SKY(1933); GOING HOLLYWOOD(1933); HE LEARNED ABOUT WOMEN(1933); HOLD YOUR MAN(1933); INTERNATIONAL HOUSE(1933); STRANGER'S RETURN(1933); UNDER THE TONTO RIM(1933); BACHELOR BAIT(1934); BAND PLAYS ON, THE(1934); HAVE A HEART(1934); PALOOKA(1934); PARTY'S OVER, THE(1934); VIVA VILLA!(1934); AFTER OFFICE HOURS(1935); CEILNG ZERO(1935); ABSOLUTE QUIET(1936); ALL-AMERICAN CHUMP(1936); EXCLUSIVE STORY(1936); PIGSKIN PARADE(1936); WOMEN ARE TROUBLE(1936); CHECKERS(1937); DANCE, CHARLIE, DANCE(1937); I'LL TAKE ROMANCE(1937); SECOND HONEYMOON(1937); SLIM(1937); SMALL TOWN BOY(1937); MR. BOGGS STEPS OUT(1938); PASSPORT HUSBAND(1938); THREE BLIND MICE(1938); BACK DOOR TO HEAVEN(1939); HOLLYWOOD CAVALCADE(1939); HONEYMOON'S OVER, THE(1939); IT COULD HAPPEN TO YOU(1939); LITTLE BIT OF HEAVEN, A(1940); OUR TOWN(1940); SANDY GETS HER MAN(1940); WHEN THE DALTONS RODE(1940); BRIDE CAME C.O.D., THE(1941); CRACKED NUTS(1941); ADVENTURES OF MARTIN EDEN, THE(1942); BLONDIE FOR VICTORY(1942); DRUMS OF THE CONGO(1942); HE HIRED THE BOSS(1943); GREAT MIKE, THE(1944); PILLOW TO POST(1945); HEAVEN ONLY KNOWS(1947); KILLER DILL(1947); STRIKE IT RICH(1948); FATHER IS A BACHELOR(1950); FOR THE LOVE OF MIKE(1960); SON OF FLUBBER(1963); MISADVENTURES OF MERLIN JONES, THE(1964)

Silents
EXALTED FLAPPER, THE(1929); NEW YEAR'S EVE(1929)
Ted Erwin
MARKED MEN(1940); THUNDER IN DIXIE(1965)
Terry Erwin
NED KELLY(1970, Brit.)
William Erwin
VELVET TOUCH, THE(1948); EASY LIVING(1949); MAN FROM DEL RIO(1956); NIGHT RUNNER, THE(1957); GUN FEVER(1958)
Masok Es
WITNESS, THE(1982, Hung.)
R. Esadze
NINE DAYS OF ONE YEAR(1964, USSR)
S. Esadze
Misc. Silents
CONQUEST OF THE CAUCASUS(1913, USSR), d
Esaka
HIROSHIMA, MON AMOUR(1959, Fr./Jap.), prod d
John Esam
CHAPPAQUA(1967)
Barbara Esback
CAGED(1950)
Paul Esberg
SINCE YOU WENT AWAY(1944)
Stig Esbern
Silents
MOCKERY(1927), w
Harold Esboldt
Silents
OLIVER TWIST, JR.(1921)
Henry Escalanate
FRENCHMAN'S CREEK(1944); SECOND CHANCE(1953)
Blackie Escalante
MONTE WALSH(1970)
Harry Escalante
CREATURE FROM THE BLACK LAGOON(1954)
Henry Escalante
CAPTAIN CAREY, U.S.A(1950); HITCH-HIKER, THE(1953); SALOME(1953); ESCAPE TO BURMA(1955); HELL'S ISLAND(1955); THREE OUTLAWS, THE(1956); SOL MADRID(1968)
E.R. Escalmel
ROTHSCHILD(1938, Fr.), w
Francisco Castillo Escalona
SUPERARGO VERSUS DIABOLICUS(1966, Ital./Span.)
Teo Escamilia
1984
IT'S NEVER TOO LATE(1984, Span.), ph
Joel Escamilla
1984
PURPLE HEARTS(1984)
Teo Escamilla
BLOOD WEDDING(1981, Sp.), ph; CARMEN(1983, Span.), ph
1984
ON THE LINE(1984, Span.), ph
Teodoro Escamilla
NEST, THE(1982, Span.), ph
Escande
LUCREZIA BORGIA(1937, Fr.)
Maurice Escande
CINDERELLA(1937, Fr.); CAFE DE PARIS(1938, Fr.); LA MARSEILLAISE(1938, Fr.)
G. Escandon
POCKET MONEY(1972)
Gil Escandon
ULZANA'S RAID(1972)
Stanley Escane
YOUNG MR. PITT, THE(1942, Brit.); FRIEDA(1947, Brit.); HUE AND CRY(1950, Brit.); NO ROOM AT THE INN(1950, Brit.); I BELIEVE IN YOU(1953, Brit.); SLASHER, THE(1953, Brit.); NEXT TO NO TIME(1960, Brit.)
Mabel Escano
OPEN SEASON(1974, U.S./Span.)
Felix Escartefigue
FANNY(1948, Fr.)
Bernard Eschasseriaux
SUNDAYS AND CYBELE(1962, Fr.), w
Don Escobar
SINGAPORE(1947)
Enrique Escobar
UNSATISFIED, THE(1964, Span.), m
Jess Escobar
OUT OF THE PAST(1947)
Mbewe Escobar
FAME(1980)
Mena Escobar
1984
ERENDIRA(1984, Mex./Fr./Ger.)
Jaime Escobedo
BAD NEWS BEARS, THE(1976); BAD NEWS BEARS IN BREAKING TRAINING, THE(1977)
Manuel Escobosa
NEW YORK, NEW YORK(1977)
Marcel Escoffier
LUCRECE BORGIA(1953, Ital./Fr.), cos; LOLA MONTES(1955, Fr./Ger.), cos; MICHAEL STROGOFF(1960, Fr./Ital./Yugo.), cos; BLOOD AND ROSES(1961, Fr./Ital.), cos; MADAME(1963, Fr./Ital./Span.), cos; LA BOHEME(1965, Ital.), cos; LADY L(1965, Fr./Ital.), cos; TIME OF INDIFFERENCE(1965, Fr./Ital.), cos; HEAD OF THE FAMILY(1967, Ital./Fr.), cos; WOMAN TIMES SEVEN(1967, U.S./Fr./Ital.), cos; MAYERLING(1968, Brit./Fr.), cos; SENSO(1968, Ital.), cos; VOYAGE, THE(1974, Ital.), cos

Paul Escoffier
PEPE LE MOKO(1937, Fr.)
Eduardo Escorel
EARTH ENTRANCED(1970, Braz.), ed
Lauro Escorel
ALL NUDITY SHALL BE PUNISHED(1974, Brazil), ph
Ernesto Escoto
TREASURE OF THE SIERRA MADRE, THE(1948)
T.J. Escott
ICE STATION ZEBRA(1968); DIRT GANG, THE(1972)
Eugenia Escriba
TREASURE OF THE FOUR CROWNS(1983, Span./U.S.), cos
Antonio J. Escribano
DIABOLICAL DR. Z, THE(1966 Span./Fr.)
Javier Escriva
TRAVELS WITH MY AUNT(1972, Brit.); THAT HOUSE IN THE OUTSKIRTS(1980, Span.)
Vicanie Escriva
DULCINEA(1962, Span.), d&w
Juan Jesus Escudero
1984
BOLERO(1984), set d
Vicente Escudero
HERE'S TO ROMANCE(1935)
Ernest Esdaile
Silents
KILTIES THREE(1918, Brit.)
Charles Esdale
Silents
SUMMER BACHELORS(1926)
Misc. Silents
SOUL-FIRE(1925)
Micaela Esdra
KILL BABY KILL(1966, Ital.); ADOLESCENTS, THE(1967, Can.)
Anthony Esemplare
NUNZIO(1978)
Nate Esformes
PETULIA(1968, U.S./Brit.); MARLOWE(1969); COMPANY OF KILLERS(1970); BLACK BELT JONES(1974); ULTIMATE WARRIOR, THE(1975); ALL THE PRESIDENT'S MEN(1976); VICE SQUAD(1982)
Faith Esham
1984
BIZET'S CARMEN(1984, Fr./Ital.)
Drew Eshelman
STRAWBERRY STATEMENT, THE(1970); NIGHTMARE IN BLOOD(1978)
Ruth Esherick
BRIGHT VICTORY(1951)
Debebe Eshetu
SHAFT IN AFRICA(1973)
Norman Eshley
LOST CONTINENT, THE(1968, Brit.); CROSSPLOT(1969, Brit.); IMMORTAL STORY, THE(1969, Fr.); SEE NO EVIL(1971, Brit.); CONFESSIONAL, THE(1977, Brit.); GEORGE AND MILDRED(1980, Brit.)
Jo Esinger
MISTRESS OF THE WORLD(1959, Ital./Fr./Ger.), w
Drew Eskenazi
SLENDER THREAD, THE(1965)
Lord Esketh
RAINS CAME, THE(1939)
Carmelita Eskew
TWO TICKETS TO BROADWAY(1951)
Jerry Eskow
UNDERSEA GIRL(1957)
Mike Esky
SCORCHY(1976)
Lemist Esler
WHISTLE AT EATON FALLS(1951), w
Michael A. Esler
BUSTIN' LOOSE(1981)
Henry Eslick
GROUND ZERO(1973)
Roy Eslick
Silents
BANTAM COWBOY, THE(1928), ph
Fred Esmelton
BORN TO LOVE(1931)
Silents
AVALANCHE, THE(1919); THREE WISE FOOLS(1923); LADY OF THE NIGHT(1925); KID BOOTS(1926); SHIELD OF HONOR, THE(1927); MICHIGAN KID, THE(1928); TWO LOVERS(1928)
Misc. Silents
CAN A WOMAN LOVE TWICE?(1923); RED HOT TIRES(1925); SMOOTH AS SATIN(1925)
Frederick Esmelton
Silents
DULCY(1923); RAFFLES, THE AMATEUR CRACKSMAN(1925)
Misc. Silents
LAW OF COMPENSATION, THE(1917); OUT OF THE NIGHT(1918); LAW OF COMPENSATION(1927)
Esmeralda
20,000 LEAGUES UNDER THE SEA(1954)
Andy Esmond
Silents
AFTER THE VERDICT(1929, Brit.)
Annie Esmond
OFFICER'S MESS, THE(1931, Brit.); STAMBOUL(1931, Brit.); TO OBLIGE A LADY(1931, Brit.); EBB TIDE(1932, Brit.); RESERVED FOR LADIES(1932, Brit.); SALLY BISHOP(1932, Brit.); GOOD COMPANIONS(1933, Brit.); HEAD OF THE FAMILY(1933, Brit.); I'LL STICK TO YOU(1933, Brit.); JEWEL, THE(1933, Brit.); OUTSIDER, THE(1933, Brit.); PRINCE OF ARCADIA(1933, Brit.); IT'S A COP(1934, Brit.); LUCKY

LOSER(1934, Brit.); PRIVATE LIFE OF DON JUAN, THE(1934, Brit.); VIRGINIA'S HUSBAND(1934, Brit.); ABDUL THE DAMNED(1935, Brit.); LEND ME YOUR HUSBAND(1935, Brit.); MEN OF TOMORROW(1935, Brit.); REGAL CAVALCADE(1935, Brit.); SILENT PASSENGER, THE(1935, Brit.); ALL THAT GLITTERS(1936, Brit.); GAY OLD DOG(1936, Brit.); IMPROPER DUCHESS, THE(1936, Brit.); PEARLS BRING TEARS(1937, Brit.); THUNDER IN THE CITY(1937, Brit.); WHEN THE DEVIL WAS WELL(1937, Brit.); CLAYDON TREASURE MYSTERY(1938, Brit.); COMING OF AGE(1938, Brit.); HIS LORDSHIP REGRETS(1938, Brit.); MURDER IN THE FAMILY(1938, Brit.); SAVE A LITTLE SUNSHINE(1938, Brit.); STOLEN LIFE(1939, Brit.); SALOON BAR(1940, Brit.); GERT AND DAISY'S WEEKEND(1941, Brit.); LET THE PEOPLE SING(1942, Brit.); RANDOLPH FAMILY, THE(1945, Brit.)
Silents
DAWN(1917, Brit.); WAY OF AN EAGLE, THE(1918, Brit.); POSSESSION(1919, Brit.); INNOCENT(1921, Brit.); MYSTERY OF MR. BERNARD BROWN(1921, Brit.); PASSIONATE FRIENDS, THE(1922, Brit.); ONE COLUMBO NIGHT(1926, Brit.)
Misc. Silents
MAN WHO WON, THE(1918, Brit.)
Carl Esmond
EVENSONG(1934, Brit.); INVITATION TO THE WALTZ(1935, Brit.); APRIL BLOSSOMS(1937, Brit.); DAWN PATROL, THE(1938); THUNDER AFLOAT(1939); SUNDOWN(1941); NAVY COMES THROUGH, THE(1942); PACIFIC RENDEZVOUS(1942); PANAMA HATTIE(1942); SEVEN SWEETHEARTS(1942); FIRST COMES COURAGE(1943); MARGIN FOR ERROR(1943); EXPERIMENT PERILOUS(1944); MASTER RACE, THE(1944); STORY OF DR. WASSELL, THE(1944); HER HIGHNESS AND THE BELLBOY(1945); MINISTRY OF FEAR(1945); THIS LOVE OF OURS(1945); WITHOUT LOVE(1945); LOVER COME BACK(1946); THE CATMAN OF PARIS(1946); SLAVE GIRL(1947); SMASH-UP, THE STORY OF A WOMAN(1947); WALK A CROOKED MILE(1948); DESERT HAWK, THE(1950); MYSTERY SUBMARINE(1950); WORLD IN HIS ARMS, THE(1952); FROM THE EARTH TO THE MOON(1958); THUNDER IN THE SUN(1959); BRUSHFIRE(1962); HITLER(1962); MORITURI(1965); AGENT FOR H.A.R.M.(1966)
Charles [Carl] Esmond
LITTLE MEN(1940); SERGEANT YORK(1941)
Diane Esmond
Misc. Talkies
TWO GUN CABALLERO(1931)
Elsie Esmond
Misc. Silents
CITY, THE(1916); LOTTERY MAN, THE(1916); BLACK STORK, THE(1917)
Frank Esmond
Misc. Silents
WORLD, THE FLESH AND THE DEVIL, THE(1914, Brit.)
Gilbert Esmond
Misc. Silents
HIDDEN HAND, THE(1916, Brit.)
H.V. Esmond
ELIZA COMES TO STAY(1936, Brit.), w
Silents
ONE SUMMER'S DAY(1917, Brit.), w; DANGEROUS TO MEN(1920), w
Misc. Silents
LAW DIVINE, THE(1920, Brit.); SWORD OF DAMOCLES, THE(1920, Brit.)
Henry V. Esmond
TRUTH ABOUT YOUTH, THE(1930), w
Jill Esmond
ONCE A LADY(1931); SKIN GAME, THE(1931, Brit.); IS MY FACE RED?(1932); LADIES OF THE JURY(1932); STATE'S ATTORNEY(1932); THIRTEEN WOMEN(1932); F.P. 1(1933, Brit.); NO FUNNY BUSINESS(1934, Brit.); EAGLE SQUADRON(1942); JOURNEY FOR MARGARET(1942); ON THE SUNNY SIDE(1942); PIED PIPER, THE(1942); RANDOM HARVEST(1942); THIS ABOVE ALL(1942); CASANOVA BROWN(1944); MY PAL, WOLF(1944); WHITE CLIFFS OF DOVER, THE(1944); BANDIT OF SHERWOOD FOREST, THE(1946); BEDELIA(1946, Brit.); ESCAPE(1948, Brit.); PRIVATE INFORMATION(1952, Brit.); NIGHT PEOPLE(1954); MAN CALLED PETER, THE(1955); DON'T LOOK IN THE BASEMENT(1973), makeup
Elsie Esmonde
Silents
PRINCE OF INDIA, A(1914)
John Esmonde
MAGNIFICENT SEVEN DEADLY SINS, THE(1971, Brit.), w; PLEASE SIR(1971, Brit.), w
Mercita Esmonde
Silents
ISLE OF CONQUEST(1919); PERFECT LOVER, THE(1919)
Misc. Silents
THOUGHTLESS WOMEN(1920)
Elsie Esmonds
CAMILLE(1937)
Carl Esmong
ADDRESS UNKNOWN(1944)
Juan Espantaleon
MAD QUEEN, THE(1950, Span.)
Antonio Esparza
HARDCORE(1979)
Montezuma Esparza
ONLY ONCE IN A LIFETIME(1979), p
Oscar Esparza
VIOLATED LOVE(1966, Arg.), ed
Mike Espe
INCREDIBLE TWO-HEADED TRANSPLANT, THE(1971)
Walter Maria Espe
CRIME OF THE CENTURY, THE(1933), w
Bridget Espeet
PLAY DIRTY(1969, Brit.)
Paul Espel
SCARFACE(1983)
Maury Espelin
Misc. Talkies
EVERYDAY(1976)

Dwain Esper
MANIAC(1934), p&d
Misc.
HOW TO UNDRESS IN FRONT OF YOUR HUSBAND(1937), d; NARCOTIC, THE(1937), d
Manuel Esperon
LIVING IDOL, THE(1957), m; DAUGHTER OF DECEIT(1977, Mex.), m
Manuel Esperson
SONG OF MEXICO(1945), md
Claes Esphagen
SWEDISH WEDDING NIGHT(1965, Swed.)
William Gray Espie
KANSAS CITY BOMBER(1972)
Luisa Espinal
DEVIL IS A WOMAN, THE(1935)
Edmundo Espino
LITTLE RED RIDING HOOD AND HER FRIENDS(1964, Mex.)
Espinosa
TESHA(1929, Brit.); PRIVATE LIFE OF HENRY VIII, THE(1933), ch
David Perez Espinosa
FITZCARRALDO(1982)
E. Espinosa
Silents
GOLD RUSH, THE(1925)
Enrique Espinosa
DON'T TURN THE OTHER CHEEK(1974, Ital./Ger./Span.)
Herbert Espinosa
WITHOUT RESERVATIONS(1946)
Jose Espinosa
FURY IN PARADISE(1955, U.S./Mex.); HAMMERSMITH IS OUT(1972)
Jose A. Espinosa
BANDIDO(1956)
Jose Angel Espinosa
RAGE(1966, U.S./Mex.); RIO LOBO(1970); TWO MULES FOR SISTER SARA(1970); SOMETHING BIG(1971)
Jose Angel Espinosa [Ferresquilla]
VIVA MARIA(1965, Fr./Ital.)
Luis Perez Espinosa
MR. ARKADIN(1962, Brit./Fr./Span.), set d; SOUND OF HORROR(1966, Span.), art d; KRAKATOA, EAST OF JAVA(1969), art d
P. Espinosa
POCKET MONEY(1972)
Robert Espinosa
NIGHT IN PARADISE, A(1946); RIDE THE PINK HORSE(1947); SECRET BEYOND THE DOOR, THE(1948); RED LIGHT(1949)
Espinoza
FRENZY(1946, Brit.)
Ferrusquilla [Jose] Espinoza
SIERRA BARON(1958)
James Espinoza
IN MACARTHUR PARK(1977); CALIFORNIA SUITE(1978)
Jose Espinoza
VILLA!(1958); JET OVER THE ATLANTIC(1960)
Jose A. Espinoza
Misc. Talkies
BRIDGE IN THE JUNGLE, THE(1971)
Robert Espinoza
CARGO TO CAPETOWN(1950); KILLER SHARK(1950); ONE WAY STREET(1950)
Daniel Francois Espirit
Silents
DUMB GIRL OF PORTICI(1916), w
Roque Espiritu
BATAAN(1943); PURPLE HEART, THE(1944); STORY OF DR. WASSELL, THE(1944); MALAYA(1950)
Joe Espitallier
OPERATION SECRET(1952)
Emilo Esposito
BEBO'S GIRL(1964, Ital.)
Giancarlo Esposito
RUNNING(1979, Can.); TAPS(1981); TRADING PLACES(1983)
1984
COTTON CLUB, THE(1984)
Giani Esposito
ANATOMY OF A MARRIAGE(MY DAYS WITH JEAN-MARC AND MY NIGHTS WITH FRANCOISE)**1/2 (1964 Fr.); FRENCH CANCAN(1956, Fr.); PARIS BELONGS TO US(1962, Fr.); CROSS OF THE LIVING(1963, Fr.); SEA PIRATE, THE(1967, Fr./Span./Ital.)
Joe Esposito
THIS IS ELVIS(1982)
Nicola Esposito
MAN ABOUT THE HOUSE, A(1947, Brit.)
Tony Esposito
WHITE RAT(1972), m
Piera Degli Esposti
GHOSTS, ITALIAN STYLE(1969, Ital./Fr.)
William Gray Espy
HAUNTS(1977)
Jose Esqueda
VIVA MARIA(1965, Fr./Ital.)
Jean-Pierre Esquenazi
1984
DREAM ONE(1984, Brit./Fr.), w
Esquire All-American Band Winners
CRIMSON CANARY(1945)
The Esquire Trio
TUNNEL OF LOVE, THE(1958)
Gonzalo Esquiroz
MURIETA(1965, Span.); SEA PIRATE, THE(1967, Fr./Span./Ital.); UGLY ONES, THE(1968, Ital./Span.)

Alan Esquivel
ALSINO AND THE CONDOR(1983, Nicaragua)
Hassan Essakali
BANG, BANG, YOU'RE DEAD(1966)
Richard Essame
ITALIAN JOB, THE(1969, Brit.)
Chris Essay
GIRL MOST LIKELY, THE(1957)
Hugh G. Esse
STRANGLEHOLD(1931, Brit.), w
Rudolf Essek
COURT CONCERT, THE(1936, Ger.)
Franz Essel
CANARIS(1955, Ger.)
Viola Essen
SPECTER OF THE ROSE(1946)
Ellen Esser
SISTERS, OR THE BALANCE OF HAPPINESS(1982, Ger.)
1984
LOVE IN GERMANY, A(1984, Fr./Ger.)
Karl Wright Esser
GREAT LOVER, THE(1949)
Paul Esser
MERRY WIVES OF WINDSOR, THE(1952, Ger.); SPESSART INN, THE(1961, Ger.);
ENDLESS NIGHT, THE(1963, Ger.); RESTLESS NIGHT, THE(1964, Ger.); IF IT'S
TUESDAY, THIS MUST BE BELGIUM(1969); NOT RECONCILED, OR "ONLY
VIOLENCE HELPS WHERE IT RULES"(1969, Ger.); DAUGHTERS OF DARK-
NESS(1971, Bel./ Fr./ Ger./ Ital.)
Peter Esser
KING IN SHADOW(1961, Ger.)
Wright Esser
MEMENTO MEI(1963)
George Essery
HANK WILLIAMS: THE SHOW HE NEVER GAVE(1982, Can.)
Robert Essetn
WRONG MAN, THE(1956)
David Essex
EVE OF ST. MARK, THE(1944); ASSAULT(1971, Brit.); OCTAMAN(1971); STAR-
DUST(1974, Brit.); THAT'LL BE THE DAY(1974, Brit.); SILVER DREAM RACER(1982,
Brit.), a, m
Estella Essex
HAPPY DAYS(1930)
Francis Essex
SHILLINGBURY BLOWERS, THE(1980, Brit.), w
H. J. Essex
MAN MADE MONSTER(1941), w
Harry Essex
DESPERATE(1947), w; BODYGUARD(1948), w; HE WALKED BY NIGHT(1948), w;
KILLER THAT STALKED NEW YORK, THE(1950), w; UNDERCOVER GIRL(1950),
w; WYOMING MAIL(1950), w; FAT MAN, THE(1951), w; KANSAS CITY CONFIDEN-
TIAL(1952), w; LAS VEGAS STORY, THE(1952), w; MODELS, INC.(1952), w; DEVIL'S
CANYON(1953), w; FORTY-NINTH MAN, THE(1953), w; I, THE JURY(1953), d, w; IT
CAME FROM OUTER SPACE(1953), w; CREATURE FROM THE BLACK LA-
GOON(1954), w; SOUTHWEST PASSAGE(1954), w; MAD AT THE WORLD(1955),
d&w; TEEN-AGE CRIME WAVE(1955), w; RAW EDGE(1956), w; LONELY MAN,
THE(1957), w; SONS OF KATIE ELDER, THE(1965), w; OCTAMAN(1971), d; CREMA-
TORS, THE(1972), p&d; MAN AND BOY(1972), w; DEAF SMITH AND JOHNNY
EARS(1973, Ital.), w; DRAGNET(1974), w
Harry J. Essex
BOSTON BLACKIE AND THE LAW(1946), w; DANGEROUS BUSINESS(1946), w
Robert Essex
MONEY MOVERS(1978, Aus.)
Stella Essex
Silents
TUMBLING RIVER(1927)
Wilfred Essex
PHANTOM SHIP(1937, Brit.)
Fred Essler
BEHIND THE RISING SUN(1943); MISSION TO MOSCOW(1943); SONG OF BER-
NADETTE, THE(1943); MASK OF DIMITRIOS, THE(1944); PASSAGE TO MAR-
SEILLE(1944); UNWRITTEN CODE(1944); UP IN ARMS(1944); CAPTAIN
EDDIE(1945); ROYAL SCANDAL, A(1945); SARATOGA TRUNK(1945); SCARLET
STREET(1945); WHAT NEXT, CORPORAL HARGROVE?(1945); WHERE DO WE GO
FROM HERE?(1945); FAITHFUL IN MY FASHION(1946); ONE MORE TOMOR-
ROW(1946); TEMPTATION(1946); EVERY GIRL SHOULD BE MARRIED(1948); AD-
MIRAL WAS A LADY, THE(1950); MESSENGER OF PEACE(1950); TOAST OF NEW
ORLEANS, THE(1950); WHITE TOWER, THE(1950); PEOPLE AGAINST O'HARA,
THE(1951); HOUDINI(1953); GIRL IN THE RED VELVET SWING, THE(1955); FIRST
TRAVELING SALESLADY, THE(1956); HOT ROD GIRL(1956); MY MAN GOD-
FREY(1957); 10 NORTH FREDERICK(1958); THAT TOUCH OF MINK(1962); UNSINK-
ABLE MOLLY BROWN, THE(1964); MONEY TRAP, THE(1966)
Gabe Essoe
DEVIL'S RAIN, THE(1975, U.S./Mex.), w
Bruce Estabrook
CORSICAN BROTHERS, THE(1941), w
Christine Estabrook
BELL JAR, THE(1979)
1984
ALMOST YOU(1984)
Edward Estabrook
Silents
ANOTHER MAN'S BOOTS(1922), ph; NONE BUT THE BRAVE(1928), ph
Howard Estabrook
SHOPWORN ANGEL, THE(1928), w; VARSITY(1928), w; SHE GOES TO WAR(1929),
w; VIRGINIAN, THE(1929), w; BAD MAN, THE(1930), w; BEHIND THE MA-
KEUP(1930), w; DOUBLE CROSS ROADS(1930), w; HELL'S ANGELS(1930), w; KIS-
MET(1930), w; SLIGHTLY SCARLET(1930), w; STREET OF CHANCE(1930), w; ARE
THESE OUR CHILDREN?(1931), w; CIMARRON(1931), w; WOMAN BE-
TWEEN(1931), w; WOMAN HUNGRY(1931), w; BILL OF DIVORCEMENT, A(1932),
w; CONQUERORS, THE(1932), w; ROAR OF THE DRAGON(1932), w; BOWERY,

THE(1933), w; DEVIL'S IN LOVE, THE(1933), w; MASQUERADER, THE(1933), w;
SWEEPINGS(1933), w; DAVID COPPERFIELD(1935), w; ORCHIDS TO YOU(1935),
w; WAY DOWN EAST(1935), w; CORSICAN BROTHERS, THE(1941), w; INTERNA-
TIONAL LADY(1941), w; NEW WINE(1941), w; HUMAN COMEDY, THE(1943), w;
BRIDGE OF SAN LUIS REY, THE(1944), w; HEAVENLY DAYS(1944), d, w; DAKO-
TA(1945), w; VIRGINIAN, THE(1946), w; GIRL FROM MANHATTAN(1948), w;
LONE STAR(1952), w; CATTLE QUEEN OF MONTANA(1954), w; PASSION(1954), w;
BIG FISHERMAN, THE(1959), w
Silents
FOUR FEATHERS(1915); ADVENTUROUS SEX, THE(1925), p; PLAY SAFE(1927),
sup
Misc. Silents
OFFICER 666(1914); BUTTERFLY, THE(1915); CLOSING NET, THE(1915);
M'LISS(1915); GIVING BECKY A CHANCE(1917), d; HIGHWAY OF HOPE,
THE(1917), d; WILD GIRL, THE(1917), d
Manuel Estanillo
DEATH OF A BUREAUCRAT(1979, Cuba)
Louis Este
Silents
WINNING STROKE, THE(1919)
Estelita
FABULOUS SENORITA, THE(1952); TROPICAL HEAT WAVE(1952); SWEET-
HEARTS ON PARADE(1953); TROPIC ZONE(1953); JESSE JAMES MEETS FRAN-
KENSTEIN'S DAUGHTER(1966)
Debbie Estell
1984
LASSITER(1984)
Alfonso Estella
CONTRABAND SPAIN(1955, Brit.)
May Estelle
SAFARI(1956)
Juan Estelrich
RUN LIKE A THIEF(1968, Span.), art d
Alrise Estense
LOVE AND MARRIAGE(1966, Ital.)
Roberta Ester
TOGETHER BROTHERS(1974)
Agnes Ester-hazy
Silents
STUDENT OF PRAGUE, THE(1927, Ger.)
Joe Esterhas
FLASHDANCE(1983), w
Andre Esterhazi
NAKED MAJA, THE(1959, Ital./U.S.)
Andre Esterhazy
55 DAYS AT PEKING(1963); NEW LIFE STYLE, THE(1970, Ger.); WATERLOO(1970,
Ital./USSR)
Andrea Esterhazy
ASH WEDNESDAY(1973); OBSESSION(1976)
Bondi Esterhazy
DAISY MILLER(1974)
Bondy Esterhazy
HORNET'S NEST(1970)
Wilhelm Esterhuizen
AFTER YOU, COMRADE(1967, S. Afr.)
Juan Esterlich
ADVENTURERS, THE(1970)
Dick Esterly
MOONSHINE COUNTY EXPRESS(1977)
Carole Estes
MITCHELL(1975)
Franchon Estes
SING FOR YOUR SUPPER(1941)
Frank Estes
OPERATION CIA(1965)
Fred Estes
LITTLE MEN(1940)
Frisco Estes
MACHISMO—40 GRAVES FOR 40 GUNS(1970)
Gene Estes
STAKEOUT ON DOPE STREET(1958)
John Estes
LITTLE TOUGH GUY(1938); STRANGE FACES(1938); GIRL CRAZY(1943); SHE HAS
WHAT IT TAKES(1943); FOLLOW THE BOYS(1944); REDHEAD FROM MANHAT-
TAN(1954)
Enrique Esteve
BLOOD WEDDING(1981, Sp.)
Enrique Esteves
MAN FRIDAY(1975, Brit.), set d; GREAT SCOUT AND CATHOUSE THURSDAY,
THE(1976), set d
Estevez
HURRY SUNDOWN(1967), cos
Emilio Estevez
TEX(1982); OUTSIDERS, THE(1983)
1984
REPO MAN(1984)
Enrique Estevez
BRING ME THE HEAD OF ALFREDO GARCIA(1974), set d; SAVAGE IS LOOSE,
THE(1974), set d; UNDER FIRE(1983), set d
1984
EVIL THAT MEN DO, THE(1984), art d; ROMANCING THE STONE(1984), set d
Luis Estevez
INTERVAL(1973, Mex./U.S.), cos
Ramon Estevez
DEAD ZONE, THE(1983)
Marie-Helene Estienne
1984
SWANN IN LOVE(1984, Fr.Ger.), w

Kathy Estocin
1984
HAMBONE AND HILLIE(1984), cos
Carmen Estrabeau
DONOVAN'S REEF(1963)
Angelina Estrada
UP IN SMOKE(1978); CARBON COPY(1981)
Blanca Estrada
HORROR OF THE ZOMBIES(1974, Span.); MONSTER ISLAND(1981, Span./U.S.)
Carlos Estrada
MASTER OF HORROR(1965, Arg.); ROMEO AND JULIET(1968, Ital./Span.)
Daniel Estrada
DAKOTA LIL(1950)
Erik Estrada
CROSS AND THE SWITCHBLADE, THE(1970); NEW CENTURIONS, THE(1972); PARADES(1972); AIRPORT 1975(1974); MIDWAY(1976); TRACKDOWN(1976); LINE, THE(1982)
1984
WHERE IS PARSIFAL?(1984, Brit.)
Misc. Talkies
BALLAD OF BILLIE BLUE(1972)
Joseph Estrada
FLIGHT TO FURY(1966, U.S./Phil.)
Juan Estrada
NIGHT IN PARADISE, A(1946)
Luis Pico Estrada
MAFIA, THE(1972, Arg.), w
Patrick Estrada-Pox
GERMAN SISTERS, THE(1982, Ger.)
Esther Estrella
LIGHT OF WESTERN STARS, THE(1940); THREE MEN FROM TEXAS(1940); ALOMA OF THE SOUTH SEAS(1941); BLOOD AND SAND(1941); DOWN MEXICO WAY(1941); PRAIRIE PIONEERS(1941); PRAIRIE PALS(1942); TO THE SHORES OF TRIPOLI(1942); UNDERCOVER MAN(1942)
David Estridge
HUSTLE(1975)
Robin Estridge
HOUSE OF DARKNESS(1948, Brit.), w; DAY TO REMEMBER, A(1953, Brit.), w; CHANCE MEETING(1954, Brit.), w; SIMBA(1955, Brit.), w; ABOVE US THE WAVES(1956, Brit.), w; CAMPBELL'S KINGDOM(1957, Brit.), w; CHECKPOINT(1957, Brit.), w; DANGEROUS EXILE(1958, Brit.), w; FLAME OVER INDIA(1960, Brit.), w; BEWARE OF CHILDREN(1961, Brit.), w; ESCAPE FROM ZAHRAIN(1962), w; DRUMS OF AFRICA(1963), w; BOY CRIED MURDER, THE(1966, Ger./Brit./Yugo.), w; EYE OF THE DEVIL(1967, Brit.), w; PERMISSION TO KILL(1975, U.S./Aust.), w
Jonathan Estrin
CINDERELLA LIBERTY(1973)
Patric Estrin
ACT OF VENGEANCE(1974)
Robert Estrin
CANDIDATE, THE(1972), ed; BADLANDS(1974), ed; MEMORY OF US(1974), ed; BREATHLESS(1983), ed
1984
MIRRORS(1984), ed
Robert L. Estrin
PIPE DREAMS(1976), ed
David Estuardo
TWO MULES FOR SISTER SARA(1970)
1984
ON THE LINE(1984, Span.)
Bob Esty
ROLLER BOOGIE(1979), m
Alexander Esway
TAXI FOR TWO(1929, Brit.), d, w; CHILDREN OF CHANCE(1930, Brit.), d; SHADOWS(1931, Brit.), p&d; IT'S A BET(1935, Brit.), d; MUSIC HATH CHARMS(1935, Brit.), d; THUNDER IN THE CITY(1937, Brit.), p; CONQUEST OF THE AIR(1940), d; CROSS OF LORRAINE, THE(1943), w; STEPPIN' IN SOCIETY(1945), d; THEY ARE NOT ANGELS(1948, Fr.), d
Cecilia Esztergalyos
GOLDEN HEAD, THE(1965, Hung., U.S.)
Cecilia Eszterggalyos
AGE OF ILLUSIONS(1967, Hung.)
Joe Eszterhas
F.I.S.T.(1978), w
Andrea Eszterhazy
WAR AND PEACE(1956, Ital./U.S.)
Count Andre Eszterhazy
ROMAN HOLIDAY(1953)
Alvarez et Confortes
JULIE THE REDHEAD(1963, Fr.)
Pierre Etaix
MY UNCLE(1958, Fr.), art d; PICKPOCKET(1963, Fr.); SUITOR, THE(1963, Fr.), a, d, w; THIEF OF PARIS, THE(1967, Fr./Ital.); YO YO(1967, Fr.), a, d, w
Alberto Etchebehere
HAND IN THE TRAP, THE(1963, Arg./Span.), ph; THE EAVESDROPPER(1966, U.S./Arg.), ph; GAMES MEN PLAY, THE(1968, Arg.), ph
Fred Etcheberry
300 SPARTANS, THE(1962), spec eff
Fred Etcheverry
ROOTS OF HEAVEN, THE(1958), spec eff
Michel Etcheverry
HORROR CHAMBER OF DR. FAUSTUS, THE(1962, Fr./Ital.); TOMORROW IS MY TURN(1962, Fr./Ital./Ger.); JULIE THE REDHEAD(1963, Fr.); NIGHT ENCOUNTER(1963, Fr./Ital.); THREE FACES OF SIN(1963, Fr./Ital.); IS PARIS BURNING?(1966, U.S./Fr.); LA PRISONNIERE(1969, Fr./Ital.); MILKY WAY, THE(1969, Fr./Ital.)
Lois Etelman
STING OF DEATH(1966)

Estelle Eterre
WEDDING PRESENT(1936)
Rae Ethelyn
Misc. Silents
TIME, THE COMEDIAN(1925)
Jeanette Etheridge
SHE DANCES ALONE(1981, Aust./U.S.)
Jim Etheridge
GAS-S-S-S!(1970)
Colin Etherington
SUPERMAN(1978)
James Etherington
HILLS OF DONEGAL, THE(1947, Brit.)
Kirsteen Etherington
VIDEODROME(1983, Can.), ch
Mabel Etherington
INSPECTOR CALLS, AN(1954, Brit.)
Alphonse Ethier
DONOVAN AFFAIR, THE(1929); HIS FIRST COMMAND(1929); IN OLD ARIZONA(1929); BIG TRAIL, THE(1930); STORM, THE(1930); HONOR OF THE FAMILY(1931); MATCH KING, THE(1932); WILD GIRL(1932); BABY FACE(1933); EX-LADY(1933); MEN OF AMERICA(1933); BRITISH AGENT(1934); VOICE IN THE NIGHT(1934); BORDERTOWN(1935); CRUSADES, THE(1935); SECRET OF THE CHATEAU(1935); BOSS RIDER OF GUN CREEK(1936); BARONESS AND THE BUTLER, THE(1938); SUNSET TRAIL(1938)
Silents
ROUGH AND READY(1918); OH, JOHNNY(1919); SHADOWS OF THE NIGHT(1928); SMOKE BELLEW(1929)
Misc. Silents
M. LECOQ(1915); PATRIOT AND THE SPY, THE(1915); WOMAN AND THE BEAST, THE(1917); SANDY BURKE OF THE U-BAR-U(1919); MORAL SINNER, THE(1924)
Alphonz Ethier
FAIR WARNING(1931); LAW AND ORDER(1932); REBECCA OF SUNNYBROOK FARM(1932); NO MORE WOMEN(1934); RED MORNING(1935); STORY OF LOUIS PASTEUR, THE(1936)
Silents
I WANT TO FORGET(1918); ALASKAN, THE(1924); GOLD AND THE GIRL(1925); ALIAS THE LONE WOLF(1927); CHEATERS(1927)
Misc. Silents
FRONTIER OF THE STARS, THE(1921); BREED OF THE SEA(1926)
Andrew Ethier
1984
SAM'S SON(1984)
Chris Ethridge
HONEYSUCKLE ROSE(1980)
Ella Ethridge
ANNA KARENINA(1935); I'LL TELL THE WORLD(1945); WEEKEND AT THE WALDORF(1945); UNDERCURRENT(1946); IVY(1947); SUDDENLY IT'S SPRING(1947); FAMILY HONEYMOON(1948); GAL WHO TOOK THE WEST, THE(1949); FATHER OF THE BRIDE(1950); GIANT(1956); PLUNDERERS, THE(1960); PURPLE GANG, THE(1960); DAYS OF WINE AND ROSES(1962)
Samuel Ethridge
OLD-FASHIONED WAY, THE(1934)
Dolores Etienne
TOMORROW NEVER COMES(1978, Brit./Can.)
Hicky Etienne
RUDE BOY(1980, Brit.)
Rafael Etienne
INVASION OF THE VAMPIRES, THE(1961, Mex.)
Roger Etienne
SO THIS IS PARIS(1954); AIN'T MISBEHAVIN'(1955); DESERT HELL(1958); PERFECT FURLOUGH, THE(1958); MARATHON MAN(1976); OTHER SIDE OF MIDNIGHT, THE(1977); PATERNITY(1981); I'M DANCING AS FAST AS I CAN(1982)
Tony Etienne
MARK OF CAIN, THE(1948, Brit.); SLEEPING CAR TO TRIESTE(1949, Brit.)
Henri Etievant
Misc. Silents
ETRE AIME POUR SOI-MEME(1920, Fr.), d; LA POUPEE(1920, Fr.), d; NINE(1920, Fr.), d; CREPUSCULE D'EPOUVANTE(1921, Fr.), d; COEUR DE TITI(1924, Fr.), d; LA NIEGE SUR LE PAS(1924, Fr.), d; LA NUIT DE LA REVANCHE(1924, Fr.), d; LE REVEIL DE MADDALONE(1924, Fr.), d; LA FIN DE MONTE(1927, Fr.), d; LA SIRENE DES TROPIQUES(1928, Fr.), d; FECONDITE(1929, Fr.), d; LA SYMPHONIE PATHETIQUE(1929, Fr.), d
Jean Etievant
DIARY OF A COUNTRY PRIEST(1954, Fr.)
Yvette Etievant
PRIZE, THE(1952, Fr.); WE ARE ALL MURDERERS(1957, Fr.); HORROR CHAMBER OF DR. FAUSTUS, THE(1962, Fr./Ital.); PASSION OF SLOW FIRE, THE(1962, Fr.); BEAR, THE(1963, Fr.); DAY AND THE HOUR, THE(1963, Fr./ Ital.); WAR OF THE BUTTONS(1963 Fr.); LADIES OF THE PARK(1964, Fr.); LA GUERRE EST FINIE(1967, Fr./Swed.); JE T'AIME, JE T'AIME(1972, Fr./Swed.); STATE OF SIEGE(1973, Fr./U.S./ Ital./Ger.)
Karl Etlinger
BOMBARDMENT OF MONTE CARLO, THE(1931, Ger.)
Kan Eto
1984
BALLAD OF NARAYAMA, THE(1984, Jap.)
Peter Eton
QUEST FOR LOVE(1971, Brit.), p
Jack Etra
JAMBOREE(1957), ph; LET'S ROCK(1958), ph
Estella Ettaire
TEST PILOT(1938)
Friedrich Ettel
EIGHT GIRLS IN A BOAT(1932, Ger.); TREMENDOUSLY RICH MAN, A(1932, Ger.); TRUNKS OF MR. O.F., THE(1932, Ger.)
Estelle Ettere
MOON'S OUR HOME, THE(1936); FATHER OF THE BRIDE(1950)

Estelle Etterre
KING OF GAMBLERS(1937); LIFE BEGINS FOR ANDY HARDY(1941); UNHOLY PARTNERS(1941); THREE HEARTS FOR JULIA(1943); WEEKEND AT THE WALDORF(1945); FORCE OF EVIL(1948); JACKPOT, THE(1950); UNKNOWN MAN, THE(1951); WHEN WORLDS COLLIDE(1951); LEATHER SAINT, THE(1956); MANCHURIAN CANDIDATE, THE(1962)

Estelle Etterve
WOMEN, THE(1939)

Ruth Etting
ROMAN SCANDALS(1933); GIFT OF GAB(1934); HIPS, HIPS, HOORAY(1934)

Don Ettinger
HOLD THAT CO-ED(1938), w; SALLY, IRENE AND MARY(1938), w; PUBLIC DEB NO. 1(1940), w

Edward Ettinger
MAN WHO WOULDN'T TALK, THE(1940), w

David Ettinson
THUNDER ROAD(1958), ph

Don Ettlinger
LADY ESCAPES, THE(1937), w; LIFE BEGINS IN COLLEGE(1937), w; MY LUCKY STAR(1938), w; REBECCA OF SUNNYBROOK FARM(1938), w; I WAS AN ADVENTURESS(1940), w; SHIPYARD SALLY(1940, Brit.), w; YOUNG PEOPLE(1940), w; GREAT AMERICAN BROADCAST, THE(1941), w; GUILTY BYSTANDER(1950), w

Herman Ettlinger
ONE PLUS ONE(1961, Can.)

Karl Ettlinger
LOVE WALTZ, THE(1930, Ger.)

Norman Ettlinger
MASK, THE(1961, Can.); NOBODY WAVED GOODBYE(1965, Can.)

Claudye Ettori
BOOM!(1968)

Monika Ettrich
TRAPP FAMILY, THE(1961, Ger.)

Ursula Ettrich
TRAPP FAMILY, THE(1961, Ger.)

The Etude Ethiopian Chorus
PARDON US(1931)

Asa Etula
MOGAMBO(1953)

Roy Etzel
SINAI COMMANDOS: THE STORY OF THE SIX DAY WAR(1968, Israel/Ger.), m

Opal Euard
TWO LITTLE BEARS, THE(1961)

Wolf Euba
CELESTE(1982, Ger.)

Anita Eubank
DID YOU HEAR THE ONE ABOUT THE TRAVELING SALESLADY?(1968); WILD SCENE, THE(1970)

Shari Eubank
CHESTY ANDERSON, U.S. NAVY(1976)

Victoria Eubank
HEARSE, THE(1980)

Bob Eubanks
OUT OF SIGHT(1966)
1984
JOHNNY DANGEROUSLY(1984)

Brian Eubanks
TRENCHCOAT(1983)

Corey Eubanks
STING II, THE(1983)

Ed Eubanks
LIAR'S DICE(1980), p

Joe Eubanks
THUNDER IN CAROLINA(1960)

Terry Eubanks-Makdissy
LIAR'S DICE(1980), a, w

Eubie Blake and His Orchestra
HARLEM IS HEAVEN(1932)

Marcy Eudal
IN MACARTHUR PARK(1977)

Joe Eudemiller
REG'LAR FELLERS(1941), p

Eugene
SHERIFF OF WICHITA(1949)

Billy Eugene
Silents
RENO(1923)

William Eugene
Misc. Silents
GIRL FROM MONTMARTRE, THE(1926); CRASHING THROUGH(1928); GIRL HE DIDN'T BUY, THE(1928)

Eugene Pini and His Tango Orchestra
FLAMINGO AFFAIR, THE(1948, Brit.)

Maria Eugenia
LITTLEST OUTLAW, THE(1955)

Saverio D' Eugenio
DUEL OF THE TITANS(1963, Ital.), art d

George Eugeniou
HELL, HEAVEN OR HOBOKEN(1958, Brit.); MIRACLE IN SOHO(1957, Brit.); KILL ME TOMORROW(1958, Brit.); KITCHEN, THE(1961, Brit.); THAT RIVIERA TOUCH(1968, Brit.)

Bonas Eugevio
LIGHT IN THE PIAZZA(1962)

Al Eugster
SNOW WHITE AND THE SEVEN DWARFS(1937), anim

Bob Euler
MY DOG, BUDDY(1960)

Eunahad the Mule
LITTLE GIANT(1946)

Dale Eunson
ALL WOMEN HAVE SECRETS(1939), w; GUEST IN THE HOUSE(1944), w; ON THE LOOSE(1951), w; HOW TO MARRY A MILLIONAIRE(1953), w; SABRE JET(1953), w; STAR, THE(1953), w; ALL MINE TO GIVE(1957), w; EIGHTEEN AND ANXIOUS(1957), w; GIDGET GOES TO ROME(1963), w; JOE PANTHER(1976), w

Katherine Eunson
ALL MINE TO GIVE(1957), w; EIGHTEEN AND ANXIOUS(1957), w; GIDGET GOES TO ROME(1963), w

Opal Eurard
STUDS LONIGAN(1960)

Tom Eure
CHINA SYNDROME, THE(1979)

Wesley Eure
JENNIFER(1978); TOOLBOX MURDERS, THE(1978); C.H.O.M.P.S.(1979)

Robin Eurich
NATIONAL LAMPOON'S CLASS REUNION(1982)

Maria Euridice
TROPICS(1969, Ital.)

Euripides
PHAEDRA(1962, U.S./Gr./Fr.), w; BACCHANTES, THE(1963, Fr./Ital.), w; MEDEA(1971, Ital./Fr./Ger.), w; TROJAN WOMEN, THE(1971), w; IPHIGENIA(1977, Gr.), w

Clarence Eurist
TEN DAYS TO TULARA(1958), p

Europe's Top Stunt Drivers
HEIST, THE(1979, Ital.)

The Eurythmics
1984
1984(1984, Brit.), m

Engo Eusepi
WHITE NIGHTS(1961, Ital./Fr.), set d

Enzo Eusepi
FRAULEIN DOKTOR(1969, Ital./Yugo.), set d; MAN CALLED SLEDGE, A(1971, Ital.), set d; LUDWIG(1973, Ital./Ger./Fr.), set d
1984
SAHARA(1984), set d

Vincenzo Eusepi
DESERTER, THE(1971 Ital./Yugo.), set d

Col. Harry K. Eustace
WAR IS A RACKET(1934)

David F. Eustace
SOMETHING'S ROTTEN(1979, Can.), p

Fred Eustace
Silents
LITTLE LORD FAUNTLEROY(1914, Brit.)

Jean Eustache
WEEKEND(1968, Fr./Ital.); MOTHER AND THE WHORE, THE(1973, Fr.), d&w, ed; AMERICAN FRIEND, THE(1977, Ger.)

Eugueni Eustigneev
THREE TALES OF CHEKHOV(1961, USSR)

Helen Eustis
FOOL KILLER, THE(1965), w

Rich Eustis
SERIAL(1980), w; YOUNG DOCTORS IN LOVE(1982), w

Antony Eustral
SILVER CHALICE, THE(1954)

Anthony Eustrel
SECOND BUREAU(1937, Brit.); UNDER THE RED ROBE(1937, Brit.); WIFE OF GENERAL LING, THE(1938, Brit.); GASBAGS(1940, Brit.); ADVENTURES OF TARTU(1943, Brit.); YELLOW CANARY, THE(1944, Brit.); SILVER FLEET, THE(1945, Brit.); CAESAR AND CLEOPATRA(1946, Brit.); I KNOW WHERE I'M GOING(1947, Brit.); COUNTER BLAST(1948, Brit.); CAPTAIN JOHN SMITH AND POCAHONTAS(1953); ROBE, THE(1953); LADY GODIVA(1955); SEA CHASE, THE(1955); MIDNIGHT LACE(1960); FOR THOSE WHO THINK YOUNG(1964); UNSINKABLE MOLLY BROWN, THE(1964); WHAT A WAY TO GO(1964)

Antony Eustrel
DEVIL'S PLOT, THE(1948, Brit.); STORY OF ROBIN HOOD, THE(1952, Brit.); EAST OF SUMATRA(1953); TITANIC(1953); KING RICHARD AND THE CRUSADERS(1954); LUST FOR LIFE(1956); NOTORIOUS LANDLADY, THE(1962); THREE STOOGES GO AROUND THE WORLD IN A DAZE, THE(1963); GOODBYE CHARLIE(1964); ONE OF OUR SPIES IS MISSING(1966); FITZWILLY(1967); GAMES(1967)

Suzi Euzaine
MOULIN ROUGE(1952)

Evi Eva
Misc. Silents
CARNIVAL OF CRIME(1929, Ger.)

Reg Evabs
STONE(1974, Aus.)

Janice Evan
FARMER'S OTHER DAUGHTER, THE(1965)

Jeanne Evan
1984
NOT FOR PUBLICATION(1984)

Roy Evan
FUNNY MONEY(1983, Brit.)

Franco Evangeliste
DIFFICULT YEARS(1950, Ital.), w

Evanghelou
INNOCENTS IN PARIS(1955, Brit.)

Linda Evanoff
FLOWER THIEF, THE(1962)

A. Frederic Evans
OUTLAW OF THE PLAINS(1946), w

Adoree Evans
MARINES, LET'S GO(1961)

Alan Evans
PRISONER OF THE IRON MASK(1962, Fr./Ital.)

Aled Evans
1984
YR ALCOHOLIG LION(1984, Brit.), ed

Andy Evans
YELLOWBEARD(1983), spec eff

Angelo Evans
ANGELO MY LOVE(1983)

Art Evans
LEADBELLY(1976); FUN WITH DICK AND JANE(1977); YOUNGBLOOD(1978); APPLE DUMPLING GANG RIDES AGAIN, THE(1979); IN-LAWS, THE(1979); MAIN EVENT, THE(1979); NATIONAL LAMPOON'S CLASS REUNION(1982); WRONG IS RIGHT(1982)
1984
SOLDIER'S STORY, A(1984)
Misc. Talkies
BIG TIME(1977)

Arthur Evans
CLAUDINE(1974)

Barry Evans
HERE WE GO ROUND THE MULBERRY BUSH(1968, Brit.); DIE SCREAMING, MARIANNE(1970, Brit.)

Bertram Evans
Silents
LODGER, THE(1926, Brit.), art d

Bill Evans
BERMONDSEY KID, THE(1933, Brit.), w

Billy Evans
CORN IS GREEN, THE(1945)

Bob Evans
KID GALAHAD(1937); INVITATION TO HAPPINESS(1939); FLAME OF NEW ORLEANS, THE(1941); HEY, ROOKIE(1944); WHERE THE SIDEWALK ENDS(1950); IRON MAN, THE(1951); LYDIA BAILEY(1952)

Bonnie Evans
LADIES MAN, THE(1961)

Brad Evans
TASK FORCE(1949)

Brandon Evans
EMPEROR JONES, THE(1933); WINDJAMMER(1937)

Brook Evans
LOUISIANA PURCHASE(1941); ROAD TO MOROCCO(1942); LET'S FACE IT(1943); BLUE DAHLIA, THE(1946)

Bruce A. Evans
MAN, A WOMAN, AND A BANK, A(1979, Can.), w
1984
STARMAN(1984), w

Bruce Evans
BACK DOOR TO HEAVEN(1939)

C. Middleton Evans
FIGHTING PLAYBOY(1937)

Carolyn Evans
FLASH GORDON(1980)

Cecille Evans
Silents
BLUE BLOOD(1925)
Misc. Silents
HEIR-LOONS(1925)

Charles E. Evans
DISRAELI(1929); GREENE MURDER CASE, THE(1929); HAPPY DAYS(1930); MILLIONAIRE, THE(1931); MAN WHO PLAYED GOD, THE(1932); HERE COMES THE GROOM(1951)

Charles Evans
WITHOUT RESERVATIONS(1946); ALEXANDER HAMILTON(1931); EXPERT, THE(1932); KING'S VACATION, THE(1933); WORKING MAN, THE(1933); HOUSE OF ROTHSCHILD, THE(1934); PECK'S BAD BOY(1934); CLIVE OF INDIA(1935); I FOUND STELLA PARISH(1935); OVER 21(1945); BLACK BEAUTY(1946); DARK MIRROR, THE(1946); JUNIOR PROM(1946); MAN WHO DARED, THE(1946); EXPOSED(1947); HIGH BARBAREE(1947); IT HAD TO BE YOU(1947); KILLER AT LARGE(1947); MONSIEUR VERDOUX(1947); TWILIGHT ON THE RIO GRANDE(1947); BEYOND GLORY(1948); FORCE OF EVIL(1948); ISN'T IT ROMANTIC?(1948); PRAIRIE, THE(1948); RUTHLESS(1948); SEALED VERDICT(1948); WALK A CROOKED MILE(1948); ALIAS NICK BEAL(1949); CROOKED WAY, THE(1949); PRISON WARDEN(1949); RECKLESS MOMENTS, THE(1949); SAMSON AND DELILAH(1949); ACROSS THE BADLANDS(1950); COLT .45(1950); FLYING MISSILE(1950); FURIES, THE(1950); LOVE THAT BRUTE(1950); MAGNIFICENT YANKEE, THE(1950); MY FRIEND IRMA GOES WEST(1950); REFORMER AND THE REDHEAD, THE(1950); SEPTEMBER AFFAIR(1950); STAGE TO TUCSON(1950); WOMAN OF DISTINCTION, A(1950); DESERT FOX, THE(1951); JOURNEY INTO LIGHT(1951); KID FROM AMARILLO(1951); LAST OUTPOST, THE(1951); SANTA FE(1951); BUGLES IN THE AFTERNOON(1952); DESPERADOES OUTPOST(1952); JUMPING JACKS(1952); SINGIN' IN THE RAIN(1952); FORT ALGIERS(1953); PERILOUS JOURNEY, A(1953); SANGAREE(1953); VANQUISHED, THE(1953); BATTLE OF ROGUE RIVER(1954); CANNIBAL ATTACK(1954); DEMETRIUS AND THE GLADIATORS(1954); CREATURE WITH THE ATOM BRAIN(1955); ILLEGAL(1955); MAN CALLED PETER, THE(1955); NEW YORK CONFIDENTIAL(1955); TRIAL(1955); UNTAMED(1955); BEYOND A REASONABLE DOUBT(1956); CHA-CHA-CHA BOOM(1956); EARTH VS. THE FLYING SAUCERS(1956); RACK, THE(1956); RAWHIDE YEARS, THE(1956); THESE WILDER YEARS(1956); NIGHT THE WORLD EXPLODED, THE(1957); SHAKE, RATTLE, AND ROCK!(1957); TOO MUCH, TOO SOON(1958); ALL IN A NIGHT'S WORK(1961); FUN IN ACAPULCO(1963)

Cicely Evans
IMITATION OF LIFE(1959)

Clara Evans
CHILDREN, THE(1980)

Claude Evans
NEW ORLEANS AFTER DARK(1958)

Clifford Evans
RIVER HOUSE MYSTERY, THE(1935, Brit.); CALLING THE TUNE(1936, Brit.); RIVER OF UNREST(1937, Brit.); TENTH MAN, THE(1937, Brit.); 13 MEN AND A GUN(1938, Brit.); HIS BROTHER'S KEEPER(1939, Brit.); MUTINY OF THE EL-

SINORE, THE(1939, Brit.); NORTH SEA PATROL(1939, Brit.); CASTLE OF CRIMES(1940, Brit.); FINGERS(1940, Brit.); COURAGEOUS MR. PENN, THE(1941, Brit.); HOUSE OF MYSTERY(1941, Brit.); PROUD VALLEY, THE(1941, Brit.); VOICE IN THE NIGHT, A(1941, Brit.); FLEMISH FARM, THE(1943, Brit.); SAINT MEETS THE TIGER, THE(1943, Brit.); SOMEWHERE IN FRANCE(1943, Brit.); SUSPECTED PERSON(1943, Brit.); UNDER SECRET ORDERS(1943, Brit.); LOVE ON THE DOLE(1945, Brit.); SILVER DARLINGS, THE(1947, Brit.), a, d; WHILE I LIVE(1947, Brit.); RUN FOR YOUR MONEY, A(1950, Brit.), w; TWENTY QUESTIONS MURDER MYSTERY, THE(1950, Brit.); I'LL GET YOU(1953, Brit.); MEN ARE CHILDREN TWICE(1953, Brit.); STRAW MAN, THE(1953, Brit.); COMPANIONS IN CRIME(1954, Brit.); GILDED CAGE, THE(1954, Brit.); RED DRESS, THE(1954, Brit.); SOLUTION BY PHONE(1954, Brit.); YELLOW ROBE, THE(1954, Brit.); PASSPORT TO TREASON(1956, Brit.); AT THE STROKE OF NINE(1957, Brit.); HEART WITHIN, THE(1957, Brit.); MENACE IN THE NIGHT(1958, Brit.); VIOLENT PLAYGROUND(1958, Brit.); S.O.S. PACIFIC(1960, Brit.); CURSE OF THE WEREWOLF, THE(1961); KISS OF EVIL(1963, Brit.); LONG SHIPS, THE(1964, Brit./Yugo.); TWIST OF SAND, A(1968, Brit.); ONE BRIEF SUMMER(1971, Brit.)
Misc. Talkies
ACCUSED, THE(1953)

Clive Evans
NEGATIVES(1968, Brit.), cos

Colleen Townsend Evans
SOULS IN CONFLICT(1955, Brit.)

Connie Evans
SABOTAGE SQUAD(1942); SECRETS OF THE UNDERGROUND(1943); NOCTURNE(1946); REDHEAD FROM MANHATTAN(1954)
Silents
SEVEN CHANCES(1925)

Conor Evans
MC KENZIE BREAK, THE(1970); UNDERGROUND(1970, Brit.)

Dale Evans
GIRL TROUBLE(1942); HERE COMES ELMER(1943); HOOSIER HOLIDAY(1943); IN OLD OKLAHOMA(1943); SWING YOUR PARTNER(1943); WEST SIDE KID(1943); CASANOVA IN BURLESQUE(1944); COWBOY AND THE SENORITA(1944); LIGHTS OF OLD SANTA FE(1944); SAN FERNANDO VALLEY(1944); SONG OF NEVADA(1944); YELLOW ROSE OF TEXAS, THE(1944); ALONG THE NAVAJO TRAIL(1945); BELLS OF ROSARITA(1945); BIG SHOW-OFF, THE(1945); DON'T FENCE ME IN(1945); HITCHHIKE TO HAPPINESS(1945); MAN FROM OKLAHOMA, THE(1945); SUNSET IN EL DORADO(1945); UTAH(1945); HELLDORADO(1946); HOME IN OKLAHOMA(1946); MY PAL TRIGGER(1946); OUT CALIFORNIA WAY(1946); RAINBOW OVER TEXAS(1946); ROLL ON TEXAS MOON(1946); SONG OF ARIZONA(1946); UNDER NEVADA SKIES(1946); APACHE ROSE(1947); BELLS OF SAN ANGELO(1947); TRESPASSER, THE(1947); SLIPPY MCGEE(1948); DOWN DAKOTA WAY(1949); GOLDEN STALLION, THE(1949); SUSANNA PASS(1949); BELLS OF CORONADO(1950); TRIGGER, JR.(1950); TWILIGHT IN THE SIERRAS(1950); SOUTH OF CALIENTE(1951); PALS OF THE GOLDEN WEST(1952)

Dame Edith Evans
PRUDENCE AND THE PILL(1968, Brit.)

Daniel Evans
UNCERTAIN LADY(1934), w

David Evans
BOOMERANG(1934, Brit.), w; YOU MUST GET MARRIED(1936, Brit.), w; FIVE POUND MAN, THE(1937, Brit.), w; MACUSHLA(1937, Brit.), w; MEMBER OF THE JURY(1937, Brit.), w; PASSENGER TO LONDON(1937, Brit.), w; THERE WAS A YOUNG MAN(1937, Brit.), w; WISE GUYS(1937, Brit.), w; CRIME OF PETER FRAME, THE(1938, Brit.), w; IRISH AND PROUD OF IT(1938, Ireland), w; MURDER IN THE FAMILY(1938, Brit.), w; VILLIERS DIAMOND, THE(1938, Brit.), w; WHO GOES NEXT?(1938, Brit.), w; WHAT WOULD YOU DO, CHUMS?(1939, Brit.), w; HE FOUND A STAR(1941, Brit.), w; BIG BLOCKADE, THE(1942, Brit.), w; ONE OF OUR AIRCRAFT IS MISSING(1942, Brit.); I'LL TURN TO YOU(1946, Brit.), w; THIS MAN IS MINE(1946 Brit.), w; WHEN YOU COME HOME(1947, Brit.), w; GIRL IN THE PAINTING, THE(1948, Brit.), w; THREE WEIRD SISTERS, THE(1948, Brit.), w; SNOWBOUND(1949, Brit.), w; MIDNIGHT EPISODE(1951, Brit.), w; OBSESSED(1951, Brit.), w; THIRD VISITOR, THE(1951, Brit.), w; ONCE A SINNER(1952, Brit.), w; STRANGE INTRUDER(1956), w; STRANGE AFFECTION(1959, Brit.); VICTIM(1961, Brit.); PRODUCERS, THE(1967)

Debbie Evans
ROCK 'N' ROLL HIGH SCHOOL(1979); MOON OVER THE ALLEY(1980, Brit.); ANGELO MY LOVE(1983)

Derek Evans
1984
EXTERMINATOR 2(1984)

Dillon Evans
HAMLET(1964); ARTHUR(1981)

Dirk Evans
COMBAT SQUAD(1953); PROFESSIONALS, THE(1966); SILENCERS, THE(1966)

Don Evans
MANGANINNIE(1982, Aus.)

Doug Evans
PUBLIC COWBOY NO. 1(1937); CRIMSON KEY, THE(1947); LEAVE IT TO THE MARINES(1951); ACTORS AND SIN(1952); SKY HIGH(1952)

Douglas Evans
YOUNG FUGITIVES(1938); MR. SMITH GOES TO WASHINGTON(1939); MAN MADE MONSTER(1941); PARACHUTE BATTALION(1941); HITLER'S CHILDREN(1942); DANGEROUS VENTURE(1947); FARMER'S DAUGHTER, THE(1947); FLASHING GUNS(1947); MAIN STREET KID, THE(1947); CALIFORNIA FIREBRAND(1948); COWBOY CAVALIER(1948); CROSSED TRAILS(1948); GUN TALK(1948); MICHAEL O'HALLORAN(1948); SECRET SERVICE INVESTIGATOR(1948); GOLDEN STALLION, THE(1949); HIDEOUT(1949); POWDER RIVER RUSTLERS(1949); TRAIL'S END(1949); ARIZONA COWBOY, THE(1950); AT WAR WITH THE ARMY(1950); CHAMPAGNE FOR CAESAR(1950); COUNTERSPY MEETS SCOTLAND YARD(1950); LUCKY LOSERS(1950); NO SAD SONGS FOR ME(1950); NORTH OF THE GREAT DIVIDE(1950); RUSTLERS ON HORSEBACK(1950); I WAS A COMMUNIST FOR THE F.B.I.(1951); LET'S GO NAVY(1951); QUEEN FOR A DAY(1951); WELL, THE(1951); CAPTIVE WOMEN(1952); MY SON, JOHN(1952); QUIET MAN, THE(1952); SOUTH PACIFIC TRAIL(1952); WITH A SONG IN MY HEART(1952); CITY OF BAD MEN(1953); EDDIE CANTOR STORY, THE(1953); LET'S DO IT AGAIN(1953); MAGNETIC MONSTER, THE(1953); SO BIG(1953); SHORT CUT TO HELL(1957); FEMALE ANIMAL, THE(1958); MAN IN THE NET, THE(1959); BIRDS AND THE BEES, THE(1965); I SAW WHAT YOU DID(1965); PANIC IN THE

CITY(1968)

E. Eynon Evans
ROOM IN THE HOUSE(1955, Brit.), w; TIGER BAY(1959, Brit.)

Edith Evans
QUEEN OF SPADES(1948, Brit.); IMPORTANCE OF BEING EARNEST, THE(1952, Brit.); LOOK BACK IN ANGER(1959); NUN'S STORY, THE(1959); TOM JONES(1963, Brit.); CHALK GARDEN, THE(1964, Brit.); YOUNG CASSIDY(1965, U.S./Brit.); FITZWILLY(1967); WHISPERERS, THE(1967, Brit.); MADWOMAN OF CHAILLOT, THE(1969); DAVID COPPERFIELD(1970, Brit.); SCROOGE(1970, Brit.); SOPHIE'S PLACE(1970); DOLL'S HOUSE, A(1973); CRAZE(1974, Brit.); NASTY HABITS(1976, Brit.); SLIPPER AND THE ROSE, THE(1976, Brit.)
Silents
WELSH SINGER, A(1915, Brit.); EAST IS EAST(1916, Brit.)

Edward Evans
DULCIMER STREET(1948, Brit.); HIDEOUT(1948, Brit.); SECRET PEOPLE(1952, Brit.); DEADLY NIGHTSHADE(1953, Brit.); MEN ARE CHILDREN TWICE(1953, Brit.); MR. DENNING DRIVES NORTH(1953, Brit.); SLASHER, THE(1953, Brit.); MAN OF THE MOMENT(1955, Brit.); WICKED WIFE(1955, Brit.); ANGEL WHO PAWNED HER HARP, THE(1956, Brit.); IT'S A GREAT DAY(1956, Brit.); TWO AND TWO MAKE SIX(1962, Brit.); MAN IN THE DARK(1963, Brit.); ALF 'N' FAMILY(1968, Brit.); TWO A PENNY(1968, Brit.); ONE MORE TIME(1970, Brit.); SUNDAY BLOODY SUNDAY(1971, Brit.); 10 RILLINGTON PLACE(1971, Brit.); TALES FROM THE CRYPT(1972, Brit.)

Elba Evans
MILLIONS IN THE AIR(1935)

Eleri Evans
1984
YR ALCOHOLIG LION(1984, Brit.)

Ena Evans
Silents
DAUGHTER OF LOVE, A(1925, Brit.)

Erick Ray Evans
1984
SCREAM FOR HELP(1984); SLAYGROUND(1984, Brit.); SUPERGIRL(1984)

Estelle Evans
TO KILL A MOCKINGBIRD(1962); LEARNING TREE, THE(1969)
Silents
DADDY LONG-LEGS(1919); INVISIBLE FEAR, THE(1921)
Misc. Silents
MAN WHO WOKE UP, THE(1918)

Evan Evans
BRANDED(1951), w

Evan S. Evans
HOW GREEN WAS MY VALLEY(1941)

Evans Evans
ALL FALL DOWN(1962); GRAND PRIX(1966); BONNIE AND CLYDE(1967); ICEMAN COMETH, THE(1973); IMPOSSIBLE OBJECT(1973, Fr.); PROPHECY(1979)

Eynon Evans
UNDERGROUND GUERRILLAS(1944, Brit.); HAPPINESS OF THREE WOMEN, THE(1954, Brit.), a, w; PRIVATE'S PROGRESS(1956, Brit.); SHERIFF OF FRACTURED JAW, THE(1958, Brit.); I'M ALL RIGHT, JACK(1959, Brit.); TWO-WAY STRETCH(1961, Brit.); ONLY TWO CAN PLAY(1962, Brit.)

Felix Evans
NAKED EARTH, THE(1958, Brit.), cos; MURDER SHE SAID(1961, Brit.), cos; I LIKE MONEY(1962, Brit.), cos; COP-OUT(1967, Brit.), cos

Foy Evans
OLIVER!(1968, Brit.)

Frank Evans
DOUBLE STOP(1968), art d
Silents
DESTRUCTION(1915); BATTLE OF LIFE, THE(1916); ARGYLE CASE, THE(1917); CONQUERED HEARTS(1918); KNIFE, THE(1918); PEG OF THE PIRATES(1918); OH, JOHNNY(1919); LAST EDITION, THE(1925); ph; BLUE STREAK, THE(1926), ph; THREE'S A CROWD(1927), ph; CHASER, THE(1928), ph; HEART TROUBLE(1928), ph
Misc. Silents
HER MATERNAL RIGHT(1916); UNWELCOME MOTHER, THE(1916); WORLD'S GREAT SNARE, THE(1916); MISS U.S.A.(1917); OPEN DOOR, THE(1919)

Frankie Evans
Silents
MODERN MARRIAGE(1923); KNOCKOUT, THE(1925); POLICE PATROL, THE(1925)
Misc. Silents
BACKBONE(1923)

Fred Evans
RIO GRANDE(1939); MAN OF LA MANCHA(1972); MR. QUILP(1975, Brit.)
Misc. Silents
STOLEN HONOURS(1914, Brit.); PIMPLE'S THREE WEEKS(1915, Brit.)

G. Ewait Evans
CAT GANG, THE(1959, Brit.), w

Gene Evans
UNDER COLORADO SKIES(1947); ASSIGNED TO DANGER(1948); LARCENY(1948); CRISS CROSS(1949); IT HAPPENS EVERY SPRING(1949); MOTHER IS A FRESHMAN(1949); ARMORED CAR ROBBERY(1950); DALLAS(1950); NEVER A DULL MOMENT(1950); STORM WARNING(1950); WYOMING MAIL(1950); BIG CARNIVAL, THE(1951); FIXED BAYONETS(1951); FORCE OF ARMS(1951); I WAS AN AMERICAN SPY(1951); STEEL HELMET, THE(1951); SUGARFOOT(1951); MUTINY(1952); PARK ROW(1952); THUNDERBIRDS(1952); DONOVAN'S BRAIN(1953); GOLDEN BLADE, THE(1953); CATTLE QUEEN OF MONTANA(1954); HELL AND HIGH WATER(1954); LONG WAIT, THE(1954); CRASHOUT(1955); WYOMING RENEGADES(1955); JET PILOT(1957); SAD SACK, THE(1957); BRAVADOS, THE(1958); MONEY, WOMEN AND GUNS(1958); REVOLT IN THE BIG HOUSE(1958); YOUNG AND WILD(1958); BEHEMOTH, THE SEA MONSTER(1959, Brit.); HANGMAN, THE(1959); HELEN MORGAN STORY, THE(1959); OPERATION PETTICOAT(1959); GOLD OF THE SEVEN SAINTS(1961); LIVING BETWEEN TWO WORLDS(1963), ed; SHOCK CORRIDOR(1963); APACHE UPRISING(1966); NEVADA SMITH(1966); WACO(1966); WAR WAGON, THE(1967); SUPPORT YOUR LOCAL SHERIFF(1969); BALLAD OF CABLE HOGUE, THE(1970); THERE WAS A CROOKED MAN(1970); SUPPORT YOUR LOCAL GUNFIGHTER(1971); PAT GARRETT AND BILLY THE KID(1973); WALKING TALL(1973); DEVIL TIMES FIVE(1974); SOURDOUGH(1977)

Misc. Talkies
CAMPER JOHN(1973); KNIFE FOR THE LADIES, A(1973)

Geoffrey Evans
MY CHILDHOOD(1972, Brit.), p

George Ewart Evans
SECRET OF THE FOREST, THE(1955, Brit.), w

Gillian Evans
PRIME OF MISS JEAN BRODIE, THE(1969, Brit.)

Godfrey Evans
FINAL TEST, THE(1953, Brit.)

Gwenda Evans
1984
ORDEAL BY INNOCENCE(1984, Brit.), cos

Gwendoline Evans
KNIGHTS OF THE ROUND TABLE(1953)

Gwylim Evans
Misc. Silents
ROYAL DIVORCE, A(1923, Brit.)

Gwyllum Evans
TRADING PLACES(1983)

Harry Evans
WITHOUT RESERVATIONS(1946); SAPS AT SEA(1940); WISTFUL WIDOW OF WAGON GAP, THE(1947); DESK SET(1957)

Harry H. Evans
JOHNNY STOOL PIGEON(1949)

Harvey Evans
EXPERIMENT IN TERROR(1962); BANK SHOT(1974)

Helena Evans
MY FAVORITE BRUNETTE(1947)

Helena P. Evans
DANGEROUS INTRUDER(1945)

Helena Phillips Evans
ELMER AND ELSIE(1934); I'LL FIX IT(1934); COLLEGE SCANDAL(1935); MY BILL(1938); NANCY DREW–DETECTIVE(1938); 6000 ENEMIES(1939); FOREIGN CORRESPONDENT(1940); FOR BEAUTY'S SAKE(1941); RANDOM HARVEST(1942)

Herb Evans
ON THE NICKEL(1980)

Herbert Evans
SQUAW MAN, THE(1931); GRAND HOTEL(1932); MILLION DOLLAR LEGS(1932); BRIEF MOMENT(1933); ONE YEAR LATER(1933); REUNION IN VIENNA(1933); SECRETS(1933); SLIGHTLY MARRIED(1933); TILLIE AND GUS(1933); GAY BRIDE, THE(1934); RIP TIDE(1934); STUDENT TOUR(1934); GLASS KEY, THE(1935); TWO FOR TONIGHT(1935); AND SUDDEN DEATH(1936); CHARGE OF THE LIGHT BRIGADE, THE(1936); COLLEEN(1936); RETURN OF SOPHIE LANG, THE(1936); WIDOW FROM MONTE CARLO, THE(1936); ANGEL(1937); HIGH FLYERS(1937); LANCER SPY(1937); MAID OF SALEM(1937); DAWN PATROL, THE(1938); EVERYBODY'S DOING IT(1938); GANGSTER'S BOY(1938); HARD TO GET(1938); KID FROM KOKOMO, THE(1939); MAN ABOUT TOWN(1939); RAINS CAME, THE(1939); SUSANNAH OF THE MOUNTIES(1939); FOREIGN CORRESPONDENT(1940); LITTLE OLD NEW YORK(1940); SUSAN AND GOD(1940); WATERLOO BRIDGE(1940); MAN HUNT(1941); ONE NIGHT IN LISBON(1941); SCOTLAND YARD(1941); JOURNEY FOR MARGARET(1942); MRS. MINIVER(1942); FOREVER AND A DAY(1943); ABROAD WITH TWO YANKS(1944); HER PRIMITIVE MAN(1944); LODGER, THE(1944); NONE BUT THE LONELY HEART(1944); UP IN ARMS(1944); WHITE CLIFFS OF DOVER, THE(1944); CORN IS GREEN, THE(1945); PARDON MY PAST(1945); BRINGING UP FATHER(1946); GILDA(1946); NIGHT AND DAY(1946); BANJO(1947); IVY(1947); NIGHT SONG(1947); JIGGS AND MAGGIE IN SOCIETY(1948); JOAN OF ARC(1948); MIRACLE OF THE BELLS, THE(1948); SKY LINER(1949); THAT FORSYTE WOMAN(1949)
Silents
SPEEDY(1928)
Misc. Silents
ALL FOR A HUSBAND(1917); CUSTOMARY TWO WEEKS, THE(1917); DAUGHTER OF FRANCE, A(1918); FIREBRAND, THE(1918); WHO LOVED HIM BEST?(1918); BEYOND LONDON LIGHTS(1928)

J. Willard Evans
RAW WEEKEND(1964), p

J.C. Evans
I WALK THE LINE(1970)

Jack Evans
CORNERED(1932); FIGHTING COWBOY(1933); LIGHTNING RANGE(1934); WHEELS OF DESTINY(1934); CHEYENNE TORNADO(1935); COYOTE TRAILS(1935); FAST BULLETS(1936); GUNS AND GUITARS(1936); LION'S DEN, THE(1936); ROARIN' GUNS(1936); ROMANCE RIDES THE RANGE(1936); VALLEY OF THE LAWLESS(1936); FIGHTING DEPUTY, THE(1937); LEFT-HANDED LAW(1937); MOONLIGHT ON THE RANGE(1937); HEROES OF THE ALAMO(1938); RIDERS FROM NOWHERE(1940); FRONTIER REVENGE(1948); HAND, THE(1981)

Jacqueline Evans
DANIEL BOONE, TRAIL BLAZER(1957); SUN ALSO RISES, THE(1957); BRAVADOS, THE(1958); TARZAN THE MAGNIFICENT(1960, Brit.); SINGER NOT THE SONG, THE(1961, Brit.); MISSING(1982)

Jean Evans
HOT BLOOD(1956), w

Jeanne Evans
SON OF SINBAD(1955); SHE-CREATURE, THE(1956); SPLIT IMAGE(1982)

Jeptha Evans
CHILDREN, THE(1980)

Jerry Evans
HELL'S BLOODY DEVILS(1970), w

Jessie Evans
PICKWICK PAPERS, THE(1952, Brit.); HAPPINESS OF THREE WOMEN, THE(1954, Brit.); EXTRA DAY, THE(1956, Brit.); NO TIME FOR TEARS(1957, Brit.); RAISING A RIOT(1957, Brit.); DOCTOR IN DISTRESS(1963, Brit.); COUNTESS DRACULA(1972, Brit.)

Jill Evans
FOLIES DERGERE(1935); FACTS OF LOVE(1949, Brit.)

Jimmy Evans
DESTINATION TOKYO(1944); HAND, THE(1960, Brit.), makeup; TWO-WAY STRETCH(1961, Brit.), makeup; LONELINESS OF THE LONG DISTANCE RUNNER, THE(1962, Brit.), makeup; SMALL WORLD OF SAMMY LEE, THE(1963, Brit.),

makeup; GUTTER GIRLS(1964, Brit.), makeup; MAN WHO COULDN'T WALK, THE(1964, Brit.), makeup; SATURDAY NIGHT OUT(1964, Brit.), makeup; SALT & PEPPER(1968, Brit.), makeup; SCREAM AND SCREAM AGAIN(1970, Brit.), makeup; TROG(1970, Brit.), makeup; PERSECUTION(1974, Brit.), makeup

Joan Evans
ROSEANNA McCOY(1949); EDGE OF DOOM(1950); OUR VERY OWN(1950); ON THE LOOSE(1951); TWO TICKETS TO BROADWAY(1951); IT GROWS ON TREES(1952); SKIRTS AHOY!(1952); COLUMN SOUTH(1953); OUTCAST, THE(1954); STRANGE ADVENTURE, A(1956); FLYING FONTAINES, THE(1959); NO NAME ON THE BULLET(1959); WALKING TARGET, THE(1960)

Joe Evans
CLOWN, THE(1953); THREE RING CIRCUS(1954); SEVEN LITTLE FOYS, THE(1955); MY FAIR LADY(1964)
Misc. Silents
PEARLS OF DEATH(1914, Brit.), a, d; STOLEN HONOURS(1914, Brit.), a, d

John Evans
THEM NICE AMERICANS(1958, Brit.); PIE IN THE SKY(1964); WELCOME TO BLOOD CITY(1977, Brit./Can.); MOONRAKER(1979, Brit.), spec eff; KRULL(1983), spec eff
1984
SUPERGIRL(1984), spec eff
Misc. Talkies
BLACK GODFATHER, THE(1974), d; BLACKJACK(1978), d

John Morgan Evans
ROOMMATES, THE(1973); SHEILA LEVINE IS DEAD AND LIVING IN NEW YORK(1975)

Jon Evans
SONG OF THE LOON(1970)

Joyce Evans
WHO KILLED FEN MARKHAM?(1937, Brit.)

Julius Evans
SWORD OF THE AVENGER(1948), w; FIRST TRAVELING SALESLADY, THE(1956); GUN FEVER(1958), w; RAIN FOR A DUSTY SUMMER(1971, U.S./Span.), w

June Evans
CRYSTAL BALL, THE(1943); JACKPOT, THE(1950)

Karin Evans
AFFAIR BLUM, THE(1949, Ger.); FANNY HILL: MEMOIRS OF A WOMAN OF PLEASURE zero(1965)

Kendall Evans
HOLD'EM YALE(1935)

Kenneth Evans
WE DIVE AT DAWN(1943, Brit.); LAST DAYS OF DOLWYN, THE(1949, Brit.); GALLOPING MAJOR, THE(1951, Brit.); GIRDLE OF GOLD(1952, Brit.); MEN ARE CHILDREN TWICE(1953, Brit.); NEXT TO NO TIME(1960, Brit.)

Larry Evans
PURSUED(1934), w; JOURNEY TO THE CENTER OF TIME(1967)
Silents
CASSIDY(1917), w; ARE YOU A FAILURE?(1923), w; MONEY! MONEY! MONEY!(1923), w; JUDGMENT OF THE HILLS(1927), w

Linda Evans
TWILIGHT OF HONOR(1963); THOSE CALLOWAYS(1964); BEACH BLANKET BINGO(1965); CHILDISH THINGS(1969); KLANSMAN, THE(1974); MITCHELL(1975); AVALANCHE EXPRESS(1979); TOM HORN(1980)
Misc. Talkies
CONFESSIONS OF TOM HARRIS(1972)

Lindley Evans
UNCIVILISED(1937, Aus.), m

Louise Evans
Silents
QUESTION, THE(1916)

Lyle Evans
CONVICT'S CODE(1930)

Lyn Evans
GIRL IN DISTRESS(1941, Brit.); GEORGE IN CIVVY STREET(1946, Brit.); I BECAME A CRIMINAL(1947); MASTER OF BANKDAM, THE(1947, Brit.); UPTURNED GLASS, THE(1947, Brit.); YEARS BETWEEN, THE(1947, Brit.); DAYDREAK(1948, Brit.); HIDEOUT(1948, Brit.); SMUGGLERS, THE(1948, Brit.); VOTE FOR HUGGETT(1948, Brit.); BLUE LAGOON, THE(1949, Brit.); CHRISTOPHER COLUMBUS(1949, Brit.); DON'T EVER LEAVE ME(1949, Brit.); KIND HEARTS AND CORONETS(1949, Brit.); MARRY ME!(1949, Brit.); MIRANDA(1949, Brit.); MY BROTHER'S KEEPER(1949, Brit.); QUARTET(1949, Brit.); CLOUDBURST(1952, Brit.); GLORY AT SEA(1952, Brit.); MR. LORD SAYS NO(1952, Brit.); PROMOTER, THE(1952, Brit.); WHITE CORRIDORS(1952, Brit.); MR. DENNING DRIVES NORTH(1953, Brit.); LADY GODIVA RIDES AGAIN(1955, Brit.)

M. K. Evans
MANTIS IN LACE(1968)

Madge Evans
GUILTY HANDS(1931); HEARTBREAK(1931); SON OF INDIA(1931); SPORTING BLOOD(1931); WEST OF BROADWAY(1931); ARE YOU LISTENING?(1932); FAST LIFE(1932); GREEKS HAD A WORD FOR THEM(1932); HUDDLE(1932); JAZZ BABIES(1932); LOVERS COURAGEOUS(1932); BEAUTY FOR SALE(1933); BROADWAY TO HOLLYWOOD(1933); DAY OF RECKONING(1933); DINNER AT EIGHT(1933); HALLELUJAH, I'M A BUM(1933); HELL BELOW(1933); MADE ON BROADWAY(1933); MAYOR OF HELL, THE(1933); NUISANCE, THE(1933); DEATH OF THE DIAMOND(1934); FUGITIVE LOVERS(1934); GRAND CANARY(1934); PARIS INTERLUDE(1934); SHOW-OFF, THE(1934); STAND UP AND CHEER(1934 80m FOX bw); WHAT EVERY WOMAN KNOWS(1934); AGE OF INDISCRETION(1935); CALM YOURSELF(1935); DAVID COPPERFIELD(1935); HELLDORADO(1935); MEN WITHOUT NAMES(1935); TRANSATLANTIC TUNNEL(1935, Brit.); EXCLUSIVE STORY(1936); MOONLIGHT MURDER(1936); PENNIES FROM HEAVEN(1936); PICCADILLY JIM(1936); ESPIONAGE(1937); THIRTEENTH CHAIR, THE(1937); ARMY GIRL(1938); SINNERS IN PARADISE(1938)
Silents
SEVEN SISTERS, THE(1915); BROKEN CHAINS(1916); HIDDEN SCAR, THE(1916); ADVENTURES OF CAROL, THE(1917); LITTLE PATRIOT, A(1917); NEIGHBORS(1918); ON THE BANKS OF THE WABASH(1923); CLASSMATES(1924)
Misc. Silents
(; HUSBAND AND WIFE(1916); SEVENTEEN(1916); SUDDEN RICHES(1916); BELOVED ADVENTURESS, THE(1917); BURGLAR, THE(1917); LITTLE DUCHESS,

THE(1917); GATES OF GLADNESS(1918); HEREDITY(1918); LOVE NET, THE(1918); POWER AND THE GLORY, THE(1918); VOLUNTEER, THE(1918); WANTED - A MOTHER(1918); HOME WANTED(1919); LOVE DEFENDER, THE(1919)

Margaret Evans
POPDOWN(1968, Brit.)

Marge Evans
HELL BOUND(1957)

Marguerite Evans
Misc. Silents
STAGE STRUCK(1925)

Mark Evans
C'MON, LET'S LIVE A LITTLE(1967)
Misc. Talkies
ORPHAN, THE(1979)

Mary Beth Evans
1984
LOVELINES(1984); TOY SOLDIERS(1984)

Maureen Evans
YOUNG GIRLS OF ROCHEFORT, THE(1968, Fr.)

Maurice Evans
RAISE THE ROOF(1930); WHITE CARGO(1930, Brit.); SHOULD A DOCTOR TELL?(1931, Brit.); MARRY ME(1932, Brit.); WEDDING REHEARSAL(1932, Brit.); EMPRESS AND I, THE(1933, Ger.); HEART SONG(1933, Brit.); BYPASS TO HAPPINESS(1934, Brit.); PATH OF GLORY, THE(1934, Brit.); CHECKMATE(1935, Brit.); SCROOGE(1935, Brit.); KIND LADY(1951); ANDROCLES AND THE LION(1952); GREAT GILBERT AND SULLIVAN, THE(1953, Brit.); MACBETH(1963); WAR LORD, THE(1965); ONE OF OUR SPIES IS MISSING(1966); JACK OF DIAMONDS(1967, U.S./Ger.); PLANET OF THE APES(1968); ROSEMARY'S BABY(1968); BODY STEALERS, THE(1969); BENEATH THE PLANET OF THE APES(1970); TERROR IN THE WAX MUSEUM(1973); JERK, THE(1979)
Misc. Talkies
OUT OF THIN AIR(1969)
Misc. Silents
WHITE CARGO(1929, Brit.)

Max Evans
ROUNDERS, THE(1965), w; BALLAD OF CABLE HOGUE, THE(1970)

Meredith Evans
WINGS OF CHANCE(1961, Can.), spec eff; NAKED FLAME, THE(1970, Can.), art d

Michael Evans
NO TRACE(1950, Brit.); SIX MEN, THE(1951, Brit.); ISLAND RESCUE(1952, Brit.); BYE BYE BIRDIE(1963); PLAINSMAN, THE(1966); SPY WITH MY FACE, THE(1966); LOVE-INS, THE(1967); RIOT ON SUNSET STRIP(1967); 1,000 PLANE RAID, THE(1969); TIME AFTER TIME(1979, Brit.); SWORD AND THE SORCERER, THE(1982); ANGELO MY LOVE(1983)

Mike Evans
NOW YOU SEE HIM, NOW YOU DON'T(1972); HOUSE ON SKULL MOUNTAIN, THE(1974)

Millicent Evans
Silents
SEATS OF THE MIGHTY, THE(1914)
Misc. Silents
WOMAN IN BLACK, THE(1914); DORA THORNE(1915); FATHER AND SON(1916)

Mina Evans
HIDE IN PLAIN SIGHT(1980)

Mitch Evans
DR. TERROR'S GALLERY OF HORRORS(1967); HAREM BUNCH; OR WAR AND PIECE, THE(1969)

Monica Evans
BE MY GUEST(1965, Brit.); ODD COUPLE, THE(1968); ARISTOCATS, THE(1970); ROBIN HOOD(1973)

Morgan Evans
TO BE FREE(1972)
Misc. Talkies
IMAGO(1970)

Mostyn Evans
EXPERIENCE PREFERRED... BUT NOT ESSENTIAL(1983, Brit.)

Muriel Evans
PACK UP YOUR TROUBLES(1932); BROADWAY TO HOLLYWOOD(1933); FAST WORKERS(1933); PRIZEFIGHTER AND THE LADY, THE(1933); HAVE A HEART(1934); HEAT LIGHTNING(1934); HIDE-OUT(1934); HOLLYWOOD PARTY(1934); MANHATTAN MELODRAMA(1934); WOMEN IN HIS LIFE, THE(1934); NEW FRONTIER, THE(1935); THROWBACK, THE(1935); BOSS RIDER OF GUN CREEK(1936); CALL OF THE PRAIRIE(1936); KING OF THE PECOS(1936); MISSING GIRLS(1936); MR. DEEDS GOES TO TOWN(1936); SILVER SPURS(1936); THREE ON THE TRAIL(1936); UNDER YOUR SPELL(1936); BOSS OF LONELY VALLEY(1937); HEADLINE CRASHER(1937); HOUSE OF SECRETS, THE(1937); LAW FOR TOMBSTONE(1937); SMOKE TREE RANGE(1937); TEN LAPS TO GO(1938); ROLL, WAGONS, ROLL(1939); ROOKIE COP, THE(1939); WESTBOUND STAGE(1940)

Murray Evans
PAYROLL(1962, Brit.); THIS SPORTING LIFE(1963, Brit.); RAPTURE(1965); ATTACK ON THE IRON COAST(1968, U.S./Brit.)

Nancy Evans
MEN OF SAN QUENTIN(1942); MR. WINKLE GOES TO WAR(1944); BOY, A GIRL, AND A DOG, A(1946); MY REPUTATION(1946); STRANGE TRIANGLE(1946); HOMESTRETCH, THE(1947); LIFE WITH FATHER(1947); DESPERADOES ARE IN TOWN, THE(1956); PEACEMAKER, THE(1956)

Nicholas Evans
TOO YOUNG TO LOVE(1960, Brit.)

Nora Evans
TENDER IS THE NIGHT(1961)

Norman Evans
DEMOBBED(1944, Brit.); HONEYMOON HOTEL(1946, Brit.); OVER THE GARDEN WALL(1950, Brit.); BANANAS(1971); THREE THE HARD WAY(1974); AARON LOVES ANGELA(1975)

Osmond Evans
1001 ARABIAN NIGHTS(1959), d

Owen Evans
UNHOLY FOUR, THE(1954, Brit.)

Patrick Evans
HAND, THE(1981)
Paul L. Evans
MELINDA(1972), ed; AMAZING GRACE(1974), ed
Paulette Evans
GIRLS ON PROBATION(1938); SISTERS, THE(1938); DARK VICTORY(1939); MIL-LION DOLLAR BABY(1941); SHE COULDN'T SAY NO(1941); KISS IN THE DARK, A(1949)
Peggy Evans
SCHOOL FOR SECRETS(1946, Brit.); LOOK BEFORE YOU LOVE(1948, Brit.); LOVE IN WAITING(1948, Brit.); BLUE LAMP, THE(1950, Brit.); CALLING BULLDOG DRUMMOND(1951, Brit.); MURDER AT 3 A.M.(1953, Brit.)
Perry Evans
GREAT COMMANDMENT, THE(1941)
Silents
SMALL TOWN IDOL, A(1921), ph
Peter Evans
HEATWAVE(1954, Brit.); SKIN GAME, THE(1965, Brit.); IMPOSTORS(1979); AR-THUR(1981)
R.N.F. Evans
SHIELD OF FAITH, THE(1956, Brit.), w; CROWNING GIFT, THE(1967, Brit.), p
Randy Evans
HAND, THE(1981)
Ray Evans
SUNSET BOULEVARD(1950); LEMON DROP KID, THE(1951), m; AARON SLICK FROM PUNKIN CRICK(1952), m/l Jay Livingston; SPY WHO LOVED ME, THE(1977, Brit.); SUPERMAN(1978)
Reg Evans
MAD MAX(1979, Aus.); ISLAND, THE(1980); GALLIPOLI(1981, Aus.); MANGANIN-NIE(1982, Aus.); KITTY AND THE BAGMAN(1983, Aus.)
1984
STRIKEBOUND(1984, Aus.)
Misc. Talkies
PLAINS OF HEAVEN, THE(1982)
Renee Evans
IVY(1947)
Rex Evans
ALONG CAME SALLY(1934, Brit.); PRINCE AND THE PAUPER, THE(1937); VOGUES OF 1938(1937); WRONG ROAD, THE(1937); FIRST 100 YEARS, THE(1938); ZAZA(1939); ADVENTURE IN DIAMONDS(1940); EARL OF CHICAGO, THE(1940); FIVE LITTLE PEPPERS AT HOME(1940); FIVE LITTLE PEPPERS IN TROU-BLE(1940); I'M NOBODY'S SWEETHEART NOW(1940); OUT WEST WITH THE PEPPERS(1940); PHILADELPHIA STORY, THE(1940); FLAME OF NEW ORLEANS, THE(1941); SHANGHAI GESTURE, THE(1941); SUSPICION(1941); WOMAN'S FA-CE(1941); BROOKLYN ORCHID(1942); GREAT IMPERSONATION, THE(1942); KEEP-ER OF THE FLAME(1942); FRANKENSTEIN MEETS THE WOLF MAN(1943); HEAVENLY BODY, THE(1943); HIGHER AND HIGHER(1943); THAT NAZTY NUI-SANCE(1943); MRS. PARKINGTON(1944); SUMMER STORM(1944); THIN MAN GOES HOME, THE(1944); BRIGHTON STRANGLER, THE(1945); KEEP YOUR POW-DER DRY(1945); PICTURE OF DORIAN GRAY, THE(1945); PURSUIT TO AL-GIERS(1945); SWING OUT, SISTER(1945); WEEKEND AT THE WALDORF(1945); ZIEGFELD FOLLIES(1945); CLUNY BROWN(1946); DANGEROUS MILLIONS(1946); NIGHT IN PARADISE, A(1946); TILL THE CLOUDS ROLL BY(1946); ADAM'S RIB(1949); CAPTAIN PIRATE(1952); JAMAICA RUN(1953); LOOSE IN LON-DON(1953); IT SHOULD HAPPEN TO YOU(1954); KNOCK ON WOOD(1954); STAR IS BORN, A(1954); LUST FOR LIFE(1956); MATCHMAKER, THE(1958); MERRY AN-DREW(1958); MIDNIGHT LACE(1960); ALL IN A NIGHT'S WORK(1961); ON THE DOUBLE(1961); BIRDS AND THE BEES, THE(1965)
Richard Evans
TOO SOON TO LOVE(1960); RETURN OF MR. MOTO, THE(1965, Brit.); SYNA-NON(1965); MACHO CALLAHAN(1970); DIRTY LITTLE BILLY(1972); NICKEL RIDE, THE(1974); ISLANDS IN THE STREAM(1977)
Robert Evans
MILDRED PIERCE(1945); FIEND WHO WALKED THE WEST, THE(1958); BEST OF EVERYTHING, THE(1959); CHINATOWN(1974), p; MARATHON MAN(1976), p; BLACK SUNDAY(1977), p; PLAYERS(1979), p; POPEYE(1980), p; URBAN COW-BOY(1980), p
1984
COTTON CLUB, THE(1984), p
Silents
KISMET(1920)
Robert J. Evans
MAN OF A THOUSAND FACES(1957); SUN ALSO RISES, THE(1957)
Robin Evans
ONE DARK NIGHT(1983)
Roger Evans
1984
YR ALCOHOLIG LION(1984, Brit.), ph
Ron Evans
RAISE THE TITANIC(1980, Brit.)
Ross Evans
FAN, THE(1949), w; COMPETITION, THE(1980)
Roy Evans
HALF A SIXPENCE(1967, Brit.); DECLINE AND FALL... OF A BIRD WATCH-ER(1969, Brit.); DUCK RINGS AT HALF PAST SEVEN, THE(1969, Ger./Ital.), w; WHERE'S JACK?(1969, Brit.); LOVING MEMORY(1970, Brit.); MOON ZERO TWO(1970, Brit.); DR. JEKYLL AND SISTER HYDE(1971, Brit.); SAY HELLO TO YESTERDAY(1971, Brit.); DARK PLACES(1974, Brit.); LITTLEST HORSE THIEVES, THE(1977); ELEPHANT MAN, THE(1980, Brit.)
Rudolph Evans
KISENGA, MAN OF AFRICA(1952, Brit.)
Rupert Evans
SWORD AND THE ROSE, THE(1953); RADIO CAB MURDER(1954, Brit.); ROB ROY, THE HIGHLAND ROGUE(1954, Brit.); HELP!(1965, Brit.); GREAT CATHERINE(1968, Brit.)
Russ Evans
BAND OF ANGELS(1957)

Russell Evans
DETECTIVE STORY(1951); GLORY BRIGADE, THE(1953)
Ruthie Evans
ANGELO MY LOVE(1983)
Sandra Evans
HOUSE ON THE SAND(1967); DIMBOOLA(1979, Aus.)
Sandy Evans
Misc. Talkies
CHEERLEADERS, THE(1973)
Scott Evans
HAND, THE(1981)
Steve Evans
MORE AMERICAN GRAFFITI(1979); HEART LIKE A WHEEL(1983)
Sue Evans
Misc. Talkies
BED OF VIOLENCE(1967)
T.H. Evans
UNDER MILK WOOD(1973, Brit.)
Tenniel Evans
NEVER BACK LOSERS(1967, Brit.); WALK A CROOKED PATH(1969, Brit.); 10 RILLINGTON PLACE(1971, Brit.)
Terry Evans
MONGREL(1982)
Misc. Talkies
CODY(1977)
Tolchard Evans
CHARMING DECEIVER, THE(1933, Brit.), m/l
Tony Evans
ANGELO MY LOVE(1983)
Tookie Evans
FORBIDDEN ISLAND(1959)
Tracie Evans
MANIAC(1980)
Trevor Evans
NINE MEN(1943, Brit.)
Troy Evans
1984
RHINESTONE(1984)
Venida Evans
ONLY WHEN I LAUGH(1981)
Victor Evans
CLASS OF MISS MAC MICHAEL, THE(1978, Brit./U.S.)
Victor Romero Evans
BABYLON(1980, Brit.)
Vincent Evans
CHAIN LIGHTNING(1950), w
Vincent B. Evans
BATTLE HYMN(1957), w
Wilba Evans
HER FIRST ROMANCE(1940)
Wilbur Evans
MAN WITH A MILLION(1954, Brit.)
Will Evans
TONS OF MONEY(1931, Brit.), w
Winifred Evans
THREE MEN IN A BOAT(1933, Brit.)
Silents
PAINTED PICTURES(1930, Brit.)
Misc. Silents
SPLENDID COWARD, THE(1918, Brit.)
Winsome Evans
27A(1974, Aus.), m
Augusta J. Evans-Wilson
Silents
ST. ELMO(1923, Brit.), w
Augusta Jane Evans-Wilson
Silents
ST. ELMO(1923), w
Edith Evanson
LIFE WITH HENRY(1941); GIRL TROUBLE(1942); ORCHESTRA WIVES(1942); REUNION IN FRANCE(1942); WOMAN OF THE YEAR(1942); FALLEN SPARROW, THE(1943); FOUR JILLS IN A JEEP(1944); JADE MASK, THE(1945); DON'T GAMBLE WITH STRANGERS(1946); NOTORIOUS LONE WOLF, THE(1946); FOREVER AM-BER(1947); SINGAPORE(1947); I REMEMBER MAMA(1948); ROPE(1948); YOU GOT-TA STAY HAPPY(1948); MADAME BOVARY(1949); CAGED(1950); DAMNED DON'T CRY, THE(1950); MAGNIFICENT YANKEE, THE(1950); PERFECT STRAN-GERS(1950); REDHEAD AND THE COWBOY, THE(1950); UNION STATION(1950); BIG CARNIVAL, THE(1951); DAY THE EARTH STOOD STILL, THE(1951); ELE-PHANT STAMPEDE(1951); RAWHIDE(1951); BIG HEAT, THE(1953); DOWN AMONG THE SHELTERING PALMS(1953); IT HAPPENS EVERY THURSDAY(1953); SHA-NE(1953); STRANGER WORE A GUN, THE(1953); ABOUT MRS. LESLIE(1954); DESIREE(1954); GIRL IN THE RED VELVET SWING, THE(1955); SILVER STAR, THE(1955); LEATHER SAINT, THE(1956); STORM CENTER(1956); DRANGO(1957); QUIET GUN, THE(1957); YOUNG STRANGER, THE(1957); TOBY TYLER(1960); CLOWN AND THE KID, THE(1961); SWINGIN' ALONG(1962); PRIZE, THE(1963); TWICE TOLD TALES(1963); MARNIE(1964); SPLIT, THE(1968)
Richard Evanson
BLUE LAGOON, THE(1980)
Opan Evard
RIDING SHOTGUN(1954)
Hal Evarts
SANTA FE TRAIL, THE(1930), w
Hal G. Evarts
BIG TRAIL, THE(1930), w
Silents
SILENT CALL, THE(1921), w; TUMBLEWEEDS(1925), w
Roy Evarts
1984
MY KIND OF TOWN(1984, Can.)

Forest Evashevski
HARMON OF MICHIGAN(1941)
Joan Evatt
DAWN(1979, Aus.)
"Eve"
BELLA DONNA(1934, Brit.)
Trevor Eve
DRACULA(1979)
Bernard Evein
FOUR HUNDRED BLOWS, THE(1959), art d; LOVERS, THE(1959, Fr.), prod d; CLEO FROM 5 TO 7(1961, Fr.), art d; LOLA(1961, Fr./Ital.), art d; WEB OF PASSION(1961, Fr.), art d; WOMAN IS A WOMAN, A(1961, Fr./Ital.), art d, cos; ZAZIE(1961, Fr.), art d; LAST YEAR AT MARIENBAD(1962, Fr./Ital.), cos; SEVEN CAPITAL SINS(1962, Fr./Ital.), art d; SUNDAYS AND CYBELE(1962, Fr.), art d; DAY AND THE HOUR, THE(1963, Fr./ Ital.), art d; TIME OUT FOR LOVE(1963, Ital./Fr.), art d; BAY OF ANGELS(1964, Fr.), prod d; FIRE WITHIN, THE(1964, Fr./Ital.), art d; UMBRELLAS OF CHERBOURG, THE(1964, Fr./Ger.), art d; VIVA MARIA(1965, Fr./Ital.), art d; TASTE FOR WOMEN, A(1966, Fr./Ital.), art d; WOMAN TIMES SEVEN(1967, U.S./Fr./Ital.), art d; OLDEST PROFESSION, THE(1968, Fr./Ital./Ger.), art d; PARIS IN THE MONTH OF AUGUST(1968, Fr.), art d; YOUNG GIRLS OF ROCHEFORT, THE(1968, Fr.), set d; SWEET HUNTERS(1969, Panama), art d; CONFESSION, THE(1970, Fr.), art d; LADY OSCAR(1979, Fr./Jap.), art d
Dorothy Eveleigh
SAIGON(1948)
Ruth Eveler
NEW EARTH, THE(1937, Jap./Ger.)
George Eveling
BIRCH INTERVAL(1976)
Evelyn and Her Magic Violin
WHEN JOHNNY COMES MARCHING HOME(1943)
Baby Evelyn
Misc. Silents
GREATEST LOVE OF ALL, THE(1925)
Fay Evelyn
Misc. Silents
HEART OF A GYPSY, THE(1919)
Judith Evelyn
THIRTEENTH LETTER, THE(1951); EGYPTIAN. THE(1954); REAR WINDOW(1954); FEMALE ON THE BEACH(1955); GIANT(1956); HILDA CRANE(1956); BROTHERS KARAMAZOV, THE(1958); TWILIGHT FOR THE GODS(1958); TINGLER, THE(1959)
Mildred Evelyn
Silents
MONTY WORKS THE WIRES(1921, Brit.); PADDY, THE NEXT BEST THING(1923, Brit.)
Charles Evemy
Silents
FOX FARM(1922, Brit.)
Harold N. Even
PHONY AMERICAN, THE(1964, Ger.), p
Wallace Evenett
ARMS AND THE MAN(1932, Brit.); YOU LIVE AND LEARN(1937, Brit.)
Julie Evening Lilly
WOLFEN(1981)
Wallace Evennett
BOMBS OVER LONDON(1937, Brit.); DON'T GET ME WRONG(1937, Brit.); FACE AT THE WINDOW, THE(1939, Brit.); GENTLEMAN'S GENTLEMAN, A(1939, Brit.); WARE CASE, THE(1939, Brit.); SECOND MR. BUSH, THE(1940, Brit.)
Charles S. Evens
COWBOY AND THE INDIANS, THE(1949)
Roger Etienne Everaert
LITTLE BOY LOST(1953)
Barbara Everest
LILY CHRISTINE(1932, Brit.); WHEN LONDON SLEEPS(1932, Brit.); WORLD, THE FLESH, AND THE DEVIL, THE(1932, Brit.); HOME, SWEET HOME(1933, Brit.); LOVE'S OLD SWEET SONG(1933, Brit.); ROOF(1933, Brit.); SHE WAS ONLY A VILLAGE MAIDEN(1933, Brit.); THERE GOES THE BRIDE(1933, Brit.); UMBRELLA, THE(1933, Brit.); PASSING SHADOWS(1934, Brit.); RIVER WOLVES, THE(1934, Brit.); SONG AT EVENTIDE(1934, Brit.); LAD, THE(1935, Brit.); PHANTOM FIEND, THE(1935, Brit.); SCROOGE(1935, Brit.); LOVE IN EXILE(1936, Brit.); MAN BEHIND THE MASK, THE(1936, Brit.); MEN OF YESTERDAY(1936, Brit.); PASSING OF THE THIRD FLOOR BACK, THE(1936, Brit.); DEATH CROONS THE BLUES(1937, Brit.); LOST CHORD, THE(1937, Brit.); OLD MOTHER RILEY(1937, Brit.); WHEN THIEF MEETS THIEF(1937, Brit.); DISCOVERIES(1939, Brit.); INQUEST(1939, Brit.); DESIGN FOR MURDER(1940, Brit.); SECOND MR. BUSH, THE(1940, Brit.); HE FOUND A STAR(1941, Brit.); PRIME MINISTER, THE(1941, Brit.); COMMANDOS STRIKE AT DAWN, THE(1942); MAXWELL ARCHER, DETECTIVE(1942, Brit.); FOREVER AND A DAY(1943); MISSION TO MOSCOW(1943); PHANTOM OF THE OPERA(1943); GASLIGHT(1944); JANE EYRE(1944); UNINVITED, THE(1944); FATAL WITNESS, THE(1945); VALLEY OF DECISION, THE(1945); WANTED FOR MURDER(1946, Brit.); FRIEDA(1947, Brit.); PATIENT VANISHES, THE(1947, Brit.); CHILDREN OF CHANCE(1949, Brit.); MADELEINE(1950, Brit.); TONY DRAWS A HORSE(1951, Brit.); INSPECTOR CALLS, AN(1954, Brit.); ROTTEN TO THE CORE(1956, Brit.); SAFECRACKER, THE(1958, Brit.); DANGEROUS AFTERNOON(1961, Brit.); EL CID(1961, U.S./Ital.); UPSTAIRS AND DOWNSTAIRS(1961, Brit.); NURSE ON WHEELS(1964, Brit.); THESE ARE THE DAMNED(1965, Brit.); MAN WHO FINALLY DIED, THE(1967, Brit.); FRANCHETTE; LES INTRIGUES(1969)
Silents
NOT GUILTY(1919, Brit.); JOYOUS ADVENTURES OF ARISTIDE PUJOL, THE(1920, Brit.); BIGAMIST, THE(1921, Brit.); FOX FARM(1922, Brit.)
Misc. Silents
I BELIEVE(1916, Brit.)
Agnes Everett
Misc. Silents
SINNERS(1920)
Ann Everett
NIGHT IN PARADISE, A(1946)
Arthur Everett
ROARING SIX GUNS(1937), w; ROUGH RIDIN' RHYTHM(1937), w

Chad Everett
CLAUDELLE INGLISH(1961); CHAPMAN REPORT, THE(1962); ROME ADVENTURE(1962); GET YOURSELF A COLLEGE GIRL(1964); JOHNNY TIGER(1966); MADE IN PARIS(1966); SINGING NUN, THE(1966); FIRST TO FIGHT(1967); LAST CHALLENGE, THE(1967); IMPOSSIBLE YEARS, THE(1968); JOURNEY INTO MIDNIGHT(1968, Brit.); FIRECHASERS, THE(1970, Brit.); AIRPLANE II: THE SEQUEL(1982)
D.S. Everett [Donald Shebib]
RUNNING BRAVE(1983, Can.), d
Elaine Everett
YOU'VE GOT TO WALK IT LIKE YOU TALK IT OR YOU'LL LOSE THAT BEAT(1971); WORLD'S GREATEST LOVER, THE(1977)
Francine Everett
Misc. Talkies
KEEP PUNCHING(1939); TALL, TAN AND TERRIFIC(1946); BIG TIMERS(1947)
George Everett
Misc. Silents
CRIMSON CROSS, THE(1921), d
Herbert Everett
Silents
ALL THE WORLD'S A STAGE(1917, Brit.), w
Jane Everett
HALF PAST MIDNIGHT(1948)
Jeff Everett
RED, WHITE AND BLACK, THE(1970)
Kenny Everett
DATELINE DIAMONDS(1966, Brit.)
1984
BLOODBATH AT THE HOUSE OF DEATH(1984, Brit.)
Peter Everett
NEGATIVES(1968, Brit.), w
Richard Everett
IF ...(1968, Brit.); HAMLET(1969, Brit.); CRY OF THE BANSHEE(1970, Brit.); WINDSPLITTER, THE(1971)
Roger Everett
HARD ROAD, THE(1970)
Rupert Everett
1984
ANOTHER COUNTRY(1984, Brit.); REAL LIFE(1984, Brit.)
Silas Everett
MACHISMO–40 GRAVES FOR 40 GUNS(1970)
Skip Everett
HELL'S PLAYGROUND(1967)
Terry Everett
HA' PENNY BREEZE(1950, Brit.)
Timmy Everett
MUSIC MAN, THE(1962)
Todd Everett
WINDFLOWERS(1968); FEMALE RESPONSE, THE(1972)
1984
BUDDY SYSTEM, THE(1984)
Tom Everett
1984
BEVERLY HILLS COP(1984); FRIDAY THE 13TH–THE FINAL CHAPTER(1984)
Everett Hoagland's Band
OKAY AMERICA(1932)
Francinne Everette
Misc. Talkies
DIRTY GERTY FROM HARLEM, USA(1946)
James Evergreen
LOVE BUTCHER, THE(1982), w
Rex Everhardt
SUPERMAN(1978)
Marvim Everhart
DRUMS O' VOODOO(1934)
Rex Everhart
WHO KILLED TEDDY BEAR?(1965); SEVEN UPS, THE(1973); FRIDAY THE 13TH(1980)
1984
FRIDAY THE 13TH–THE FINAL CHAPTER(1984)
Agnes Everitt
Misc. Silents
SAMSON(1915)
Trish Everly
Misc. Talkies
MADHOUSE(1982)
Stacy Everly
VICE SQUAD(1982)
Vaughn Everly
Misc. Talkies
CYCLES SOUTH(1971)
Viviane Everly
SOMEONE BEHIND THE DOOR(1971, Fr./Brit.)
Ann Evers
FORGOTTEN FACES(1936); SON COMES HOME, A(1936); ANYTHING FOR A THRILL(1937); FRONTIER TOWN(1938); IF I WERE KING(1938); MAD MISS MANTON, THE(1938); MARIE ANTOINETTE(1938); RIDERS OF THE BLACK HILLS(1938); BEAUTY FOR THE ASKING(1939); GUNGA DIN(1939); SHE HAS WHAT IT TAKES(1943); SOMEONE TO REMEMBER(1943); CASANOVA BROWN(1944)
Arthur Evers
Silents
STILL WATERS(1915); ONE DAY(1916)
E.P. Evers
Misc. Silents
DRUGGED WATERS(1916)
Ernest Evers
Silents
JUNGLE, THE(1914)

Gayle Evers
  BILL OF DIVORCEMENT, A(1932)
Herb "Jason" Evers
  BRAIN THAT WOULDN'T DIE, THE(1959)
Herbert Evers
  GREENWICH VILLAGE(1944); PRETTY BOY FLOYD(1960)
Jane Evers
  BUNNY LAKE IS MISSING(1965)
Jason Evers
  HOUSE OF WOMEN(1962); GREEN BERETS, THE(1968); P.J.(1968); ILLUSTRATED MAN, THE(1969); MAN CALLED GANNON, A(1969); TARZAN'S JUNGLE REBELLION(1970); ESCAPE FROM THE PLANET OF THE APES(1971); PIECE OF THE ACTION, A(1977); BARRACUDA(1978)
Misc. Talkies
  CLAWS(1977)
Juanita Evers
  FARMER TAKES A WIFE, THE(1953); PRESIDENT'S LADY, THE(1953)
Melissa Evers
Misc. Talkies
  BLUE SUMMER(1973)
Ralph Evers
  TIME IN THE SUN, A(1970, Swed.), ph
Rhett Evers
1984
  BEAR, THE(1984)
Serge Evers
  MY UNCLE ANTOINE(1971, Can.)
Ron Everslage
  AMERICAN GRAFFITI(1973), ph
Margaret Eversole
  HERE COME THE CO-EDS(1945)
Elizabeth Everson
  HIGH FURY(1947, Brit.), w
John Everson
  RITZ, THE(1976)
Roy Everson
  EXPRESSO BONGO(1959, Brit.)
Francis Everth
Misc. Silents
  PRINCE AND THE PAUPER, THE(1929, Aust./Czech.)
Paul Everton
  GREAT GARRICK, THE(1937); LIFE OF EMILE ZOLA, THE(1937); THEY WON'T FORGET(1937); BELOVED BRAT(1938); GUN LAW(1938); LITTLE MISS THOROUGHBRED(1938); MERRILY WE LIVE(1938); MIDNIGHT INTRUDER(1938); REFORMATORY(1938); FIVE LITTLE PEPPERS AND HOW THEY GREW(1939); HOTEL IMPERIAL(1939); JOE AND ETHEL TURP CALL ON THE PRESIDENT(1939); LAW COMES TO TEXAS, THE(1939); MAISIE(1939); ORPHANS OF THE STREET(1939); STAND UP AND FIGHT(1939); STRANGE CASE OF DR. MEADE(1939); TOPPER TAKES A TRIP(1939); TRAPPED IN THE SKY(1939); UNION PACIFIC(1939); WHISPERING ENEMIES(1939); ARISE, MY LOVE(1940); FIVE LITTLE PEPPERS AT HOME(1940); MEN AGAINST THE SKY(1940); MEXICAN SPITFIRE OUT WEST(1940); PRAIRIE LAW(1940); TRIPLE JUSTICE(1940); BORROWED HERO(1941); MEET JOHN DOE(1941); UNFINISHED BUSINESS(1941); SABOTEUR(1942); BEHIND PRISON WALLS(1943); WILSON(1944); NOB HILL(1945); CENTENNIAL SUMMER(1946); LEAVE HER TO HEAVEN(1946); WIFE WANTED(1946)
Misc. Talkies
  OUTSIDE THE LAW(1938)
Silents
  LIFE'S WHIRLPOOL(1917); OUTWITTED(1917); CAPPY RICKS(1921); CITY OF SILENT MEN(1921); SILVER LINING, THE(1921); "THAT ROYLE GIRL"(1925)
Misc. Silents
  BLACK FEAR(1915); QUITTER, THE(1916); DEBT, THE(1917); LAST OF THE CARNABYS, THE(1917); MIRROR, THE(1917); MOTHERHOOD(1917); FRIEND HUSBAND(1918); GINGER(1919); FROM NOW ON(1920)
Duke Everts
  PLAY MISTY FOR ME(1971)
Scott Every
  STRANGER IN HOLLYWOOD(1968)
Grenville Eves
  TWO-HEADED SPY, THE(1959, Brit.)
Ron Eveslage
  IT AIN'T EASY(1972), ph
H. P. Evetts
  HIDE IN PLAIN SIGHT(1980); CUTTER AND BONE(1981)
Nobel G. Evey
  GILDA(1946)
Greg Evigan
  SCORCHY(1976)
William Eville
Silents
  KNOW YOUR MEN(1921)
Brian Evis
  ODD ANGRY SHOT, THE(1979, Aus.)
Pat Evison
  CADDIE(1976, Aus.); EARTHLING, THE(1980); TIM(1981, Aus.); STARSTRUCK(1982, Aus.); CLINIC, THE(1983, Aus.)
1984
  SILENT ONE, THE(1984, New Zealand)
John Evitts
  SECOND BEST SECRET AGENT IN THE WHOLE WIDE WORLD, THE(1965, Brit.)
Hrvoje Evob
  APACHE GOLD(1965, Ger.)
David Evremond
Misc. Silents
  LA BELLE NIVERNAISE(1923, Fr.)
John Eward
Misc. Talkies
  ISLAND TRADER(1982)

Carolina Ewart
  WORLD'S GREATEST LOVER, THE(1977), cos
John Ewart
  RUGGED O'RIORDANS, THE(1949, Aus.); PETERSEN(1974, Aus.); LET THE BALLOON GO(1977, Aus.); NEWSFRONT(1979, Aus.); PICTURE SHOW MAN, THE(1980, Aus.); BUSH CHRISTMAS(1983, Aus.); KITTY AND THE BAGMAN(1983, Aus.)
1984
  RAZORBACK(1984, Aus.)
Stephen Ewart
  THREE MEN IN A BOAT(1933, Brit.)
Silents
  NATURE OF THE BEAST, THE(1919, Brit.); POSSESSION(1919, Brit.); TEMPORARY VAGABOND, A(1920, Brit.)
Stephen T. Ewart
Misc. Silents
  USURPER, THE(1919, Brit.)
Bruce Eweka
  LAST REBEL, THE(1971)
Tom Ewell
  THEY KNEW WHAT THEY WANTED(1940); DESERT BANDIT(1941); ADAM'S RIB(1949); AMERICAN GUERRILLA IN THE PHILIPPINES, AN(1950); LIFE OF HER OWN, A(1950); MR. MUSIC(1950); FINDERS KEEPERS(1951); UP FRONT(1951); BACK AT THE FRONT(1952); LOST IN ALASKA(1952); SEVEN YEAR ITCH, THE(1955); GIRL CAN'T HELP IT, THE(1956); GREAT AMERICAN PASTIME, THE(1956); LIEUTENANT WORE SKIRTS, THE(1956); NICE LITTLE BANK THAT SHOULD BE ROBBED, A(1958); TENDER IS THE NIGHT(1961); STATE FAIR(1962); SUPPOSE THEY GAVE A WAR AND NOBODY CAME?(1970); THEY ONLY KILL THEIR MASTERS(1972); TO FIND A MAN(1972); GREAT GATSBY, THE(1974); EASY MONEY(1983)
Gwenda Ewen
  DOCTOR'S DILEMMA, THE(1958, Brit.); TOWN LIKE ALICE, A(1958, Brit.); HAND, THE(1960, Brit.)
Linda Ewen
  CALIFORNIA SUITE(1978)
Bill Ewens
1984
  SECOND TIME LUCKY(1984, Aus./New Zealand)
James Ewens
  EMERGENCY CALL(1933), w
Silents
  FRUITS OF DESIRE, THE(1916)
Donald Ewer
  TIME LOCK(1959, Brit.)
Monica Ewer
  MONEY FOR SPEED(1933, Brit.), w; HE FOUND A STAR(1941, Brit.), w
Silents
  NOT FOR SALE(1924, Brit.), w
Arthur Ewers
Silents
  FOUR FEATHERS(1915)
H.H. Ewers
  ALRAUNE(1952, Ger.), w
Hanns Heinz Ewers
  DAUGHTER OF EVIL(1930, Ger.), w
Silents
  STUDENT OF PRAGUE, THE(1927, Ger.), w
H.J. Ewert
  SCHLAGER-PARADE(1953), p
Renate Ewert
  I SPIT ON YOUR GRAVE(1962, Fr.)
Lee Ewin
  FLYING FONTAINES, THE(1959), w
Leslie Ewin
  SCREAM AND SCREAM AGAIN(1970, Brit.)
Barbara Ewing
  DRACULA HAS RISEN FROM HIS GRAVE(1968, Brit.); TORTURE GARDEN(1968, Brit.); RECKONING, THE(1971, Brit.); EYE OF THE NEEDLE(1981)
Bill Ewing
  DEATHMASTER, THE(1972); HOAX, THE(1972); END, THE(1978)
Bob Ewing
  OTHER LOVE, THE(1947), makeup; LADY GAMBLES, THE(1949), makeup; NO MAN OF HER OWN(1950), makeup; TO PLEASE A LADY(1950), makeup
Cortez Ewing
  STARK FEAR(1963)
Diana Ewing
  WAY WE WERE, THE(1973); 80 STEPS TO JONAH(1969); PLAY IT AS IT LAYS(1972)
Geoffrey Ewing
1984
  HOME FREE ALL(1984)
Herbert Ewing
  GROUNDSTAR CONSPIRACY, THE(1972, Can.), spec eff
Iain Ewing
  OFFERING, THE(1966, Can.), w; WINTER KEPT US WARM(1968, Can.); STEREO(1969, Can.); ONLY THING YOU KNOW, THE(1971, Can.), a, m
John Christy Ewing
1984
  BREAKIN' 2: ELECTRIC BOOGALOO(1984)
John Ewing
  PARIS AFTER DARK(1943), art d; THEY CAME TO BLOW UP AMERICA(1943), art d; BIG NOISE, THE(1944), art d; IN THE MEANTIME, DARLING(1944), art d; LODGER, THE(1944), art d; SPELLBOUND(1945), art d; DUEL IN THE SUN(1946), art d; SO DEAR TO MY HEART(1949), art d
Loren Ewing
  LAST OF THE SECRET AGENTS?, THE(1966)
Lucille Ewing
1984
  MAKING THE GRADE(1984)

Montague Ewing
CHARMING DECEIVER, THE(1933, Brit.), m/l
Patricia Ann Ewing
WITHOUT HONOR(1949)
Patricia Ewing
FEELIN' GOOD(1966)
R. Ewing
FILE ON THELMA JORDAN, THE(1950), makeup
Rob Ewing
STEEL(1980), w
Robert Ewing
GREAT MAN'S LADY, THE(1942), makeup
Roger Ewing
NONE BUT THE BRAVE(1965, U.S./Jap.); SMITH(1969); PLAY IT AS IT LAYS(1972)
William R. Ewing
SLAYER, THE(1982), p, w
Jimmy Ewins
TREASURE AT THE MILL(1957, Brit.), ph
Exactly Sonnie Betsuie
SEARCHERS, THE(1956)
Christos Exarchos
ATLAS(1960)
T. Exarchos
ELECTRA(1962, Gr.)
C. Exbrayat
NAKED WOMAN, THE(1950, Fr.), w
Charles Exbrayat
RAVISHING IDIOT, A(1966, Ital./Fr.), w
Exit
PUTNEY SWOPE(1969)
Frederick Earl Exley
FAN'S NOTES, A(1972, Can.), w
Denise Exshaw
ALFIE DARLING(1975, Brit.), set d; WILBY CONSPIRACY, THE(1975, Brit.), set d; DANGEROUS DAVIES–THE LAST DETECTIVE(1981, Brit.), set d
Clive Exton
NIGHT MUST FALL(1964, Brit.), w; PLACE TO GO, A(1964, Brit.), w; THREE FACES OF A WOMAN(1965, Ital.), w; ISADORA(1968, Brit.), w; ENTERTAINING MR. SLOANE(1970, Brit.), w; 10 RILLINGTON PLACE(1971, Brit.), w; DOOMWATCH(1972, Brit.), w; RUNNING SCARED(1972, Brit.), w; AWAKENING, THE(1980), w
Lillian Exum
DRUMS O' VOODOO(1934)
Richard Eybner
MOZART STORY, THE(1948, Aust.); FOREVER MY LOVE(1962)
A. Eybozhenko
LAST GAME, THE(1964, USSR)
Lillian Ten Eyck
FLAME OF ARABY(1951); TATTERED DRESS, THE(1957)
Melissa Ten Eyck
GIRL CRAZY(1943)
Milissa Ten Eyck
HAPPY DAYS(1930)
Richard Eyer
IT HAPPENS EVERY THURSDAY(1953); MA AND PA KETTLE AT HOME(1954); DESPERATE HOURS, THE(1955); SINCERELY YOURS(1955); CANYON RIVER(1956); COME NEXT SPRING(1956); FRIENDLY PERSUASION(1956); KETTLES IN THE OZARKS, THE(1956); SLANDER(1956); BAILOUT AT 43,000(1957); INVISIBLE BOY, THE(1957); FORT DOBBS(1958); JOHNNY ROCCO(1958); SEVENTH VOYAGE OF SINBAD, THE(1958); HELL TO ETERNITY(1960)
Robert Eyer
DARK AT THE TOP OF THE STAIRS, THE(1960); BACK STREET(1961)
The Eyes of Blue
UP YOUR TEDDY BEAR(1970), m
Eyes of Blue & The Lady-birds
CONNECTING ROOMS(1971, Brit.)
Eveline Eyfel
BONJOUR TRISTESSE(1958)
Alice Eyland
MEET THE PEOPLE(1944); GEORGE WHITE'S SCANDALS(1945)
Frank A. Eyman
RIOT(1969)
Richard Eymann
GETTING STRAIGHT(1970)
Thea Eymasz
AMERICAN SOLDIER, THE(1970 Ger.), ed
Thea Eymes
BITTER TEARS OF PETRA VON KANT, THE(1972, Ger.), ed; EFFI BRIEST(1974, Ger.), ed; FEAR EATS THE SOUL(1974, Ger.), ed; MOTHER KUSTERS GOES TO HEAVEN(1976, Ger.), ed
Thea Eymesz
FOX AND HIS FRIENDS(1976, Ger.), ed; JAIL BAIT(1977, Ger.), ed
Florence Eymon
CEDDO(1978, Nigeria), ed
Eymont
OPEN ROAD, THE(1940, Fr.)
Louis Eymont
MARRIAGE OF FIGARO, THE(1963, Fr.)
Felix Eynas
WATERLOO(1970, Ital./USSR)
Howard Eynon
MAD MAX(1979, Aus.); MAN FROM SNOWY RIVER, THE(1983, Aus.)
Marc Eyraud
DIARY OF A CHAMBERMAID(1964, Fr./Ital.); BELLE DE JOUR(1968, Fr.); CONFESSION, THE(1970, Fr.); IT ONLY HAPPENS TO OTHERS(1971, Fr./Ital.); COUP DE GRACE(1978, Ger./Fr.)
Agnes Eyre [Ayres]
Misc. Silents
DAZZLING MISS DAVISON, THE(1917); DEBT, THE(1917); DEFEAT OF THE CITY, THE(1917)

David Eyre
CATTLE ANNIE AND LITTLE BRITCHES(1981), w; WOLFEN(1981), w
Laurence Eyre
Silents
VOLCANO(1926), w
Leonard Bucknall Eyre
JUNGLE OF CHANG(1951)
Mick Eyre
PALM BEACH(1979, Aus.)
Peter Eyre
HAVING A WILD WEEKEND(1965, Brit.); JULIUS CAESAR(1970, Brit.); PIED PIPER, THE(1972, Brit.); MAHLER(1974, Brit.); HEDDA(1975, Brit.); LUNA(1979, Ital.); DRAGONSLAYER(1981)
Richard Eyre
1984
LAUGHTER HOUSE(1984, Brit.), d; LOOSE CONNECTIONS(1984, Brit.), d; PLOUGHMAN'S LUNCH, THE(1984, Brit.), d
Jeff Eyrich
PERFECT COUPLE, A(1979); KING OF THE MOUNTAIN(1981)
Marc Eyruad
WISE GUYS(1969, Fr./Ital.)
D. Eysentals
WAR AND PEACE(1968, USSR)
Jacques Eyser
WOULD-BE GENTLEMAN, THE(1960, Fr.); SUCKER, THE(1966, Fr./Ital.)
William Eythe
OX-BOW INCIDENT, THE(1943); SONG OF BERNADETTE, THE(1943); EVE OF ST. MARK, THE(1944); WILSON(1944); WING AND A PRAYER(1944); COLONEL EFFINGHAM'S RAID(1945); HOUSE ON 92ND STREET, THE(1945); ROYAL SCANDAL, A(1945); CENTENNIAL SUMMER(1946); MEET ME AT DAWN(1947, Brit.); MR. RECKLESS(1948); SPECIAL AGENT(1949); CUSTOMS AGENT(1950)
Thomas Eytle
NAKED FURY(1959, Brit.); PLEASURE LOVERS, THE(1964, Brit.)
Tom Eytle
SUDDEN TERROR(1970, Brit.)
Tommy Eytle
CONCRETE JUNGLE, THE(1962, Brit.)
Alice Eyton
Silents
LITTLE COMRADE(1919), w; LOUISIANA(1919), w; LADY IN LOVE, A(1920), w; TILLIE(1922), w
Bessie Eyton
Silents
SPOILERS, THE(1914); CITY OF PURPLE DREAMS, THE(1918)
Misc. Silents
FIFTH MAN, THE(1914); CRISIS, THE(1915); JUNGLE LOVERS, THE(1915); CYCLE OF FATE, THE(1916); PRINCE CHAP, THE(1916); HEART OF TEXAS RYAN, THE(1917); LITTLE LOST SISTER(1917); BEWARE OF STRANGERS(1918); LEND ME YOUR NAME(1918); WHO SHALL TAKE MY LIFE?(1918); CHILDREN OF BANISHMENT(1919); MAN OF HONOR, A(1919); GIRL OF GOLD, THE(1925)
Frank Eyton
GIRL IN THE TAXI(1937, Brit.), m/l Arthur Wimperis; I THANK YOU(1941, Brit.), m
Kohei Ezaki
THRONE OF BLOOD(1961, Jap.), art d
Alec Ezard
JEDDA, THE UNCIVILIZED(1956, Aus.), ed
Alex Ezard
KING OF THE CORAL SEA(1956, Aus.), ed; WALK INTO HELL(1957, Aus.), ed
Leo Ezell
JUNGLE HEAT(1957); DIAMOND HEAD(1962)
V. Ezhov
MEXICO IN FLAMES(1982, USSR/Mex./Ital.), w
Hideaki Ezumi
GIRL I ABANDONED, THE(1970, Jap.)
Hassan Ezzat
INTRIGUE(1947)
Jackie Ezzell
HONEYSUCKLE ROSE(1980)

F

Fa'amgase
Misc. Silents
MOANA(1926)
Hella Faassen
1984
FOURTH MAN, THE(1984, Neth.)
Ae A Faaturia
LAST OF THE PAGANS(1936)
Margaret Fabares [Nanette Fabray]
PRIVATE LIVES OF ELIZABETH AND ESSEX, THE(1939)

Nanette Fabares [Fabray]
CHILD IS BORN, A(1940)
Shelley Fabares
GIRL RUSH, THE(1955); NEVER SAY GOODBYE(1956); ROCK, PRETTY BA-
BY(1956); MARJORIE MORNINGSTAR(1958); SUMMER LOVE(1958); RIDE THE
WILD SURF(1964); GIRL HAPPY(1965); HOLD ON(1966); SPINOUT(1966); CLAM-
BAKE(1967); TIME TO SING, A(1968)
Fabbri
GREATEST LOVE, THE(1954, Ital.), w
Bianca Maria Fabbri
RICE GIRL(1963, Fr./Ital.)

Diego Fabbri
HIS LAST TWELVE HOURS(1953, Ital.), w; CONJUGAL BED, THE(1963, Ital.), w;
YOUR SHADOW IS MINE(1963, Fr./Ital.), w; HOURS OF LOVE, THE(1965, Ital.), w;
MAGNIFICENT CUCKOLD, THE(1965, Fr./Ital.), w; SIX DAYS A WEEK(1966, Fr./
Ital./Span.), w; VOYAGE, THE(1974, Ital.), w
Jacques Fabbri
GRAND MANEUVER, THE(1956, Fr.); FRUIT IS RIPE, THE(1961, Fr./Ital.); LA
BELLE AMERICAINE(1961, Fr.); LOVE AND THE FRENCHWOMAN(1961, Fr.);
LADY IN THE CAR WITH GLASSES AND A GUN, THE(1970, U.S./Fr.); DIVA(1982,
Fr.)
Marisa Fabbri
SACCO AND VANZETTI(1971, Ital./Fr.); WEEKEND MURDERS, THE(1972, Ital.)
Ottavio Fabbri
1984
BURIED ALIVE(1984, Ital.), w
Roberto Fabbri
LOVE AND MARRIAGE(1966, Ital.)
Jacques Fabbrias
SEVEN DEADLY SINS, THE(1953, Fr./Ital.)
Enno Fabeni
UNDER THE SUN OF ROME(1949, Ital.)

Ann Faber
HAPPY TIME, THE(1952)
Barry Faber
HANGMAN'S WHARF(1950, Brit.); MISS PILGRIM'S PROGRESS(1950, Brit.)
Bob Faber
CRIMSON CANARY(1945), p
Charles H. Faber
HOUR BEFORE THE DAWN, THE(1944)
Henry Faber
WE'RE NOT MARRIED(1952)
Juliette Faber
STRANGERS IN THE HOUSE(1949, Fr.); PASSION FOR LIFE(1951, Fr.)
Leslie Faber
WHITE CARGO(1930, Brit.)
Silents
AFRAID OF LOVE(1925, Brit.); RINGER, THE(1928, Brit.)
Misc. Silents
CANDYTUFT, I MEAN VERONICA(1921, Brit.); WHITE HEN, THE(1921, Brit.);
THREE PASSIONS, THE(1928, Brit.); WHITE CARGO(1929, Brit.)
Max Faber
RADIO LOVER(1936, Brit.); SHOW FLAT(1936, Brit.)
Milos Faber
DEATH IS CALLED ENGELCHEN(1963, Czech.), w
Peter Faber
WARNING TO WANTONS, A(1949, Brit.); BRIDGE TOO FAR, A(1977, Brit.);
MYSTERIES(1979, Neth.); SOLDIER OF ORANGE(1979, Dutch)
Robert Faber
RIVERBOAT RHYTHM(1946), w; SNOW QUEEN, THE(1959, USSR), p
Ron Faber
ON THE YARD(1978); SOUP FOR ONE(1982)
Sherry Faber
DARKER THAN AMBER(1970)
Walter Faber
ISLE OF SIN(1963, Ger.)
Henri Fabert
BATTLE, THE(1934, Fr.)
Maxime Fabert
DOUBLE CRIME IN THE MAGINOT LINE(1939, Fr.)
Emilia Fabi
VIVA ITALIA(1978, Ital.)
Enid Fabia
GAY OLD DOG(1936, Brit.), w
Fabian
HOUND-DOG MAN(1959); HIGH TIME(1960); NORTH TO ALASKA(1960); LOVE IN
A GOLDFISH BOWL(1961); FIVE WEEKS IN A BALLOON(1962); LONGEST DAY,
THE(1962); MR. HOBBS TAKES A VACATION(1962); RIDE THE WILD SURF(1964);
DEAR BRIGETTE(1965); TEN LITTLE INDIANS(1965, Brit.); DR. GOLDFOOT AND
THE GIRL BOMBS(1966, Ital.); FIREBALL 590(1966); THUNDER ALLEY(1967);
MARYJANE(1968); WILD RACERS, THE(1968); DEVIL'S 8, THE(1969)
Misc. Talkies

Fabian the Dog
WHO DONE IT?(1956, Brit.)
Francois Fabian
BELLE DE JOUR(1968, Fr.)
Francoise Fabian
FERNANDEL THE DRESSMAKER(1957, Fr.); MICHAEL STROGOFF(1960, Fr./
Ital./Yugo.); THIEF OF PARIS, THE(1967, Fr./Ital.); DROP THEM OR I'LL
SHOOT(1969, Fr./Ger./Span.); MY NIGHT AT MAUD'S(1970, Fr.); CHLOE IN THE
AFTERNOON(1972, Fr.); DOWN THE ANCIENT STAIRCASE(1975, Ital.); BEN-
VENUTA(1983, Fr.)
John Fabian
PASSING STRANGER, THE(1954, Brit.); COCKLESHELL HEROES, THE(1955);
NIGHT MY NUMBER CAME UP, THE(1955, Brit.); ENEMY FROM SPACE(1957, Brit.);
SOLITARY CHILD, THE(1958, Brit.); TOWN LIKE ALICE, A(1958, Brit.); FIRST MAN
INTO SPACE(1959, Brit.); QUESTION OF ADULTERY, A(1959, Brit.); SAS-
QUATCH(1978), p, ph, ed
Max Fabian
Silents
DUST FLOWER, THE(1922), ph; STRANGER'S BANQUET(1922), ph; BARRIER,
THE(1926), ph
Maximilian Fabian
VOICE OF THE CITY(1929), ph
Silents
EXQUISITE SINNER, THE(1926), ph; IN OLD KENTUCKY(1927), ph; SHADOWS
OF THE NIGHT(1928), ph; HONEYMOON(1929), ph
Olga Fabian
MY PAL, WOLF(1944); VOICE IN THE WIND(1944); WATERFRONT(1944); HER
HIGHNESS AND THE BELLBOY(1945); WRONG MAN, THE(1956); JUDGMENT AT
NUREMBERG(1961); SHIP OF FOOLS(1965)
Paul Fabian
PROSTITUTION(1965, Fr.), ph; SLITHIS(1978), p
Robert Fabian
FABIAN OF THE YARD(1954, Brit.), w; ROOM 43(1959, Brit.)
Thomas Fabian
PLAYGIRLS AND THE BELLBOY, THE(1962, Ger.)
Warner Fabian
WILD PARTY, THE(1929), w; WHAT MEN WANT(1930), w; MEN IN HER LI-
FE(1931), w; WEEK-ENDS ONLY(1932), w
Silents
SUMMER BACHELORS(1926), w
Carlo Fabianelli
TAMING OF THE SHREW, THE(1967, U.S./Ital.), ed
Fabiani
STOLEN HOURS(1963), cos
Claudia Fabiani
FACTS OF MURDER, THE(1965, Ital.)
Joel Fabiani
LOOKING FOR MR. GOODBAR(1977); REUBEN, REUBEN(1983)
M. Fabiani
LA BALANCE(1983, Fr.), w
Vkasta Fabianova
KRAKATIT(1948, Czech.)
Vlasia Fabianova
BOHEMIAN RAPTURE(1948, Czech)
Anne Fabien
ENTRE NOUS(1983, Fr.)
Rachel Fabien
LA VIE CONTINUE(1982, Fr.), w
Farris Fabio
MASOCH(1980, Ital.)
Maya Fabio
FIVE GOLDEN HOURS(1961, Brit.)
Fabiola
STILL SMOKIN'(1983)
Luce Fabiole
BRIDE WORE BLACK, THE(1968, Fr./Ital.); TWO OF US, THE(1968, Fr.); LOVE AND
DEATH(1975)
Kazimierz Fabisiak
JOAN OF THE ANGELS(1962, Pol.)
Nanette Fabray
BAND WAGON, THE(1953); SUBTERRANEANS, THE(1960); HAPPY ENDING,
THE(1969); COCKEYED COWBOYS OF CALICO COUNTY, THE(1970); AMY(1981)
Nannette Fabray
HARPER VALLEY, P.T.A.(1978)
Alexandre Fabre
FRENCH CONNECTION 11(1975)
Dominique Fabre
SWORDSMAN OF SIENA, THE(1962, Fr./Ital.), w; MURDER AT 45 R.P.M.(1965,
Fr.), w; DAY THE HOTLINE GOT HOT, THE(1968, Fr./Span.), w
1984
LOUISIANE(1984, Fr./Can.), w
Emil Fabre
HONOR OF THE FAMILY(1931), w
Fabian Fabre
LISTEN, LET'S MAKE LOVE(1969, Fr./Ital.)
Fabienne Fabre
SUBVERSIVES, THE(1967, Ital.)
Fernand Fabre
MAN STOLEN(1934, Fr.); DOUBLE CRIME IN THE MAGINOT LINE(1939, Fr.);
MAN OF THE HOUR, THE(1940, Fr.); COLONEL CHABERT(1947, Fr.); LES JEUX
SONT FAITS(1947, Fr.); APRES L'AMOUR(1948, Fr.); SWORD AND THE ROSE,
THE(1953); DEADLY DECOYS, THE(1962, Fr.); MAXIME(1962, Fr.); RISE OF LOUIS
XIV, THE(1970, Fr.)
Fernard Fabre
MOULIN ROUGE(1952)
Jean Fabre
DUCHESS AND THE DIRTWATER FOX, THE(1976)

Jean-Jacques Fabre
LAST YEAR AT MARIENBAD(1962, Fr./Ital.), set d; LES CARABINIERS(1968, Fr./Ital.), art d; NUN, THE(1971, Fr.), art d
Maurice Fabre
BACKFIRE(1965, Fr.), w
Michel Fabre
BREATHLESS(1959, Fr.); VERY CURIOUS GIRL, A(1970, Fr.), w; BANZAI(1983, Fr.), w
Pierre Fabre
JULES AND JIM(1962, Fr.); WILD CHILD, THE(1970, Fr.); BED AND BOARD(1971, Fr.)
Saturnin Fabre
ROAD IS FINE, THE(1930, Fr.); PEPE LE MOKO(1937, Fr.); GENERALS WITHOUT BUTTONS(1938, Fr.); FRIEND WILL COME TONIGHT, A(1948, Fr.); DOCTEUR LAENNEC(1949, Fr.); GATES OF THE NIGHT(1950, Fr.); FRENCH WAY, THE(1952, Fr.); HOLIDAY FOR HENRIETTA(1955, Fr.); MOST WANTED MAN, THE(1962, Fr./Ital.)
Christine Fabrega
TWO MEN IN TOWN(1973, Fr.)
Manolo Fabregas
CAPTAIN SCARLETT(1953); CANDY MAN, THE(1969); TWO MULES FOR SISTER SARA(1970)
Fabienne Fabreges
Silents
PENNILESS MILLIONAIRE, THE(1921, Brit.)
Diego Fabri
GENERALE DELLA ROVERE(1960, Ital./Fr.), w; CONSTANTINE AND THE CROSS(1962, Ital.), w
Zoltan Fabri
BOYS OF PAUL STREET, THE(1969, Hung./US), d, w; WITNESS, THE(1982, Hung.)
Cecilia Fabricious
PACIFIC DESTINY(1956, Brit.)
Bent Fabricius-Bjerre
CASE OF THE 44'S, THE(1964 Brit./Den.), m; OPERATION LOVEBIRDS(1968, Den.), m
Hintz Fabricus
GLASS TOWER, THE(1959, Ger.)
Jean Fabricus
INSULT(1932, Brit.), w
Juliet Fabriga
NIGHT GAMES(1980)
Fabrizi
TEACHER AND THE MIRACLE, THE(1961, Ital./Span.), w
Aldo Fabrizi
OPEN CITY(1946, Ital.); TO LIVE IN PEACE(1947, Ital.), a, w; THREE STEPS NORTH(1951); ANTHONY OF PADUA(1952, Ital.); FATHER'S DILEMMA(1952, Ital.); TIMES GONE BY(1953, Ital.); CENTO ANNI D'AMORE(1954, Ital.); DONATELLA(1956, Ital.); ANGEL WORE RED, THE(1960); TEACHER AND THE MIRACLE, THE(1961, Ital./Span.), a, p&d; WONDERS OF ALADDIN, THE(1961, Fr./Ital.); THREE BITES OF THE APPLE(1967)
Franco Fabrizi
CALABUCH(1956, Span./Ital.); VITELLONI(1956, Ital./Fr.); WOMAN OF ROME(1956, Ital.); NIGHTS OF LUCRETIA BORGIA, THE(1960, Ital.); LE AMICHE(1962, Ital.); SWINDLE, THE(1962, Fr./Ital.); RUN WITH THE DEVIL(1963, Fr./Ital.); THREE FACES OF SIN(1963, Fr./Ital.); WASTREL, THE(1963, Ital.); DUEL OF CHAMPIONS(1964 Ital./Span.); LOVE ON THE RIVIERA(1964, Fr./Ital.); MORALIST, THE(1964, Ital.); DOLL THAT TOOK THE TOWN, THE(1965, Ital.); FACTS OF MURDER, THE(1965, Ital.); BIRDS, THE BEES AND THE ITALIANS, THE(1967); VISCOUNT, THE(1967, Fr./Span./Ital./Ger.); GIRL GAME(1968, Braz./Fr./Ital.); POSTMAN GOES TO WAR, THE(1968, Fr.); MADIGAN'S MILLIONS(1970, Span./Ital); DEATH IN VENICE(1971, Ital./Fr.); ITALIAN CONNECTION, THE(1973, U.S./Ital./Ger.); DON'T TOUCH WHITE WOMEN!(1974, Fr.); CLARETTA AND BEN(1983, Ital., Fr.)
Mario Fabrizi
CALL ME GENIUS(1961, Brit.); TWO-WAY STRETCH(1961, Brit.); ON THE BEAT(1962, Brit.); OPERATION SNATCH(1962, Brit.); RING-A-DING RHYTHM(1962, Brit. 73m Amicus/COL bw (G.B: IT'S TRAD, DAD!); VILLAGE OF DAUGHTERS(1962, Brit.); JUST FOR FUN(1963, Brit.); MOUSE ON THE MOON, THE(1963, Brit.); PUNCH AND JUDY MAN, THE(1963, Brit.)
Valeria Fabrizi
TORPEDO BAY(1964, Ital./Fr.); RINGO AND HIS GOLDEN PISTOL(1966, Ital.); WOMEN IN CELL BLOCK 7(1977, Ital./U.S.)
Arnaldo Fabrizio
GOLIATH AND THE SINS OF BABYLON(1964, Ital.); SEVEN SLAVES AGAINST THE WORLD(1965, Ital.)
Clara Fabry
CELESTE(1982, Ger.), ed
The Fabulous Freaks
CHRISTINA(1974, Can.)
Mark Fabus
AMERICAN GIGOLO(1980), set d
Adriana Facchetti
WONDERS OF ALADDIN, THE(1961, Fr./Ital.); TWO COLONELS, THE(1963, Ital.); PAYMENT IN BLOOD(1968, Ital.)
John Facenda
BURGLAR, THE(1956); MIDDLE AGE CRAZY(1980, Can.)
Gisela Fachelday
BITTER TEARS OF PETRA VON KANT, THE(1972, Ger.)
Marcesa Faciacani
CALL OF THE BLOOD(1948, Brit.)
Gisela Fackeldey
THEY WERE SO YOUNG(1955)
Donald Factor
THAT COLD DAY IN THE PARK(1969, U.S./Can.), p
Donald L. Factor
UNIVERSAL SOLDIER(1971, Brit.), p
Willy Factorouitch
LETTERS FROM MY WINDMILL(1955, Fr.), ph

Ghassan Fadallah
CIRCLE OF DECEIT(1982, Fr./Ger.)
Carlo Fadda
VENUS IN FURS(1970, Ital./Brit./Ger.), w; COUNT DRACULA(1971, Sp., Ital., Ger., Brit.), w
Thomas [Tom] Fadden
THAT NIGHT WITH YOU(1945)
Tom Fadden
DESTRY RIDES AGAIN(1939); I STOLE A MILLION(1939); CAPTAIN IS A LADY, THE(1940); CONGO MAISIE(1940); MAN FROM DAKOTA, THE(1940); ZANZIBAR(1940); COME LIVE WITH ME(1941); KISS THE BOYS GOODBYE(1941); SHEPHERD OF THE HILLS, THE(1941); GLASS KEY, THE(1942); LONE STAR RANGER(1942); MY FAVORITE BLONDE(1942); NIGHT BEFORE THE DIVORCE, THE(1942); PARDON MY SARONG(1942); REMARKABLE ANDREW, THE(1942); SUNDOWN JIM(1942); WINGS FOR THE EAGLE(1942); EDGE OF DARKNESS(1943); FRONTIER BADMEN(1943); GOOD FELLOWS, THE(1943); LADY TAKES A CHANCE, A(1943); NORTHERN PURSUIT(1943); HAIRY APE, THE(1944); HENRY ALDRICH'S LITTLE SECRET(1944); IN SOCIETY(1944); THIN MAN GOES HOME, THE(1944); THREE LITTLE SISTERS(1944); TOMORROW THE WORLD(1944); GREAT JOHN L. THE(1945); MEDAL FOR BENNY, A(1945); MURDER, HE SAYS(1945); NAUGHTY NINETIES(1945); STATE FAIR(1945); TRAIL TO VENGEANCE(1945); BIG SLEEP, THE(1946); CROSS MY HEART(1946); DRAGONWYCH(1946); STOLEN LIFE, A(1946); STRANGE LOVE OF MARTHA IVERS, THE(1946); WELL-GROOMED BRIDE, THE(1946); CHEYENNE(1947); DARK PASSAGE(1947); EASY COME, EASY GO(1947); PURSUED(1947); THAT HAGEN GIRL(1947); B. F.'S DAUGHTER(1948); DUDE GOES WEST, THE(1948); INSIDE STORY, THE(1948); MOONRISE(1948); ON OUR MERRY WAY(1948); STATE OF THE UNION(1948); DALLAS(1950); SINGING GUNS(1950); DRUMS IN THE DEEP SOUTH(1951); VENGEANCE VALLEY(1951); LAWLESS BREED, THE(1952); KANSAS PACIFIC(1953); THY NEIGHBOR'S WIFE(1953); PRINCE OF PLAYERS(1955); TALL MEN, THE(1955); INVASION OF THE BODY SNATCHERS(1956); BABY FACE NELSON(1957); EDGE OF ETERNITY(1959); TOBY TYLER(1960); POCKETFUL OF MIRACLES(1961); SECOND TIME AROUND, THE(1961); PARADISE ALLEY(1962); FLAREUP(1969); DIRTY DINGUS MAGEE(1970); DRAGNET(1974); EMPIRE OF THE ANTS(1977)
A. Fadeyev
WAR AND PEACE(1968, USSR)
Elena Fadeyeva
CHEREZ TERNII K SVEZDAM(1981 USSR)
Yelena Fadeyeva
SONS AND MOTHERS(1967, USSR)
William Fadiman
BAD FOR EACH OTHER(1954), p; LAST FRONTIER, THE(1955), p; JUBAL(1956), p; RAMPAGE(1963), p
Shekh Fadl
Misc. Silents
STAMPEDE(1930, Sudan)
Marion Faducha
Silents
PARTNERS OF THE TIDE(1921); SECOND HAND ROSE(1922)
George Faeder
JOE HILL(1971, Swed./U.S.)
Roberto Faenza
1984
CORRUPT(1984, Ital.), d, w
Misc. Talkies
COP KILLERS(1984), d
A. Faerber
NIGHT PEOPLE(1954)
Pearl Faessler
HOSTAGE, THE(1966)
Michael Faeth
MANITOU, THE(1978), cos
Michael R. Faeth
DAY OF THE ANIMALS(1977), cos
Giuseppe Faeti
PRINCE OF FOXES(1949)
Roger Fafal
INNOCENTS IN PARIS(1955, Brit.)
Tiger Fafara
GOOD MORNING, MISS DOVE(1955)
Alina Fafik
KNIGHTS OF THE TEUTONIC ORDER, THE(1962, Pol.), ed
Charlie Fag
Silents
AFTER MIDNIGHT(1921)
Gary Faga
STAR TREK: THE MOTION PICTURE(1979)
1984
STAR TREK III: THE SEARCH FOR SPOCK(1984)
Pete Faga
TWICE TOLD TALES(1963), spec eff
Bernard Fagan
SMILIN' THROUGH(1932), w
Charles Fagan
EARLY BIRD, THE(1936, Brit.); LUCK OF THE IRISH, THE(1937, Ireland); DEVIL'S ROCK(1938, Brit.); IRISH AND PROUD OF IT(1938, Ireland)
Fred M. Fagan
SAN FRANCISCO(1936)
Helene Fagan
WINTER KILLS(1979)
James B. Fagan
IMPROPER DUCHESS, THE(1936, Brit.), w
Silents
HAWTHORNE OF THE U.S.A.(1919), w
James Bernard Fagan
WHEEL OF LIFE, THE(1929), w; FORGOTTEN COMMANDMENTS(1932), w; BELLA DONNA(1934, Brit.), w; TEMPTATION(1946), w

Moyna Fagan
MAN BEHIND THE MASK, THE(1936, Brit.)
Myron Fagan
HOLY TERROR, A(1931), w
Myron C. Fagan
SMART WOMAN(1931), w
Patsy Fagan
SATURDAY NIGHT OUT(1964, Brit.)
Philip Fagan
ILLIAC PASSION, THE(1968)
Ronald J. Fagan
AMERICAN HOT WAX(1978), ed
Suzanna Fagan
Misc. Talkies
GRAD NIGHT(1980)
William Fagan
REMBRANDT(1936, Brit.)
Jimmie Fagas
ONCE YOU KISS A STRANGER(1969), m, md
Blanch Hays Fagen
REDS(1981)
Walter Fagerstrom
NIGHT GAMES(1980)
Hughette Faget
MURMUR OF THE HEART(1971, Fr./Ital./Ger.)
Huguette Faget
LAST STOP, THE(1949, Pol.); CHANEL SOLITAIRE(1981); LE BEAU MARIA-
GE(1982, Fr.)
Julien Faget
TARGET: HARRY(1980)
Paul Fagg
MATTER OF INNOCENCE, A(1968, Brit.)
Jack Faggard
SOMEWHERE IN TIME(1980), spec eff
Donald Fagin
YOU'VE GOT TO WALK IT LIKE YOU TALK IT OR YOU'LL LOSE THAT
BEAT(1971), m
Steve Fagin
ELECTRA GLIDE IN BLUE(1973)
Amedeco Fago
SWEET BODY OF DEBORAH, THE(1969, Ital./Fr.), art d
Amedeo Fago
LAST DAYS OF MUSSOLINI(1974, Ital.), art d; LEAP INTO THE VOID(1982,
Ital.), prod d
Daria Fago
LEAP INTO THE VOID(1982, Ital.)
Giovanni Fago
MAGNIFICENT BANDITS, THE(1969, Ital./Span.), d, w
Matteo Fago
LEAP INTO THE VOID(1982, Ital.)
Einar Fagstad
WHALERS, THE(1942, Swed.)
Brian Fahey
MAN IN THE DARK(1963, Brit.), m, md; CURSE OF THE VOODOO(1965, Brit.), m;
PLANK, THE(1967, Brit.), m
Michael Fahey
VON RICHTHOFEN AND BROWN(1970)
Myrna Fahey
I DIED A THOUSAND TIMES(1955); JEANNE EAGELS(1957); FACE OF A FUGI-
TIVE(1959); IMITATION OF LIFE(1959); STORY ON PAGE ONE, THE(1959); HOUSE
OF USHER(1960)
Varney Fahnbulleh
YOUNG GIANTS(1983)
Cimenli Fahrettin
MEETINGS WITH REMARKABLE MEN(1979, Brit.)
Anja Fahrmann
CHRONICLE OF ANNA MAGDALENA BACH(1968, Ital., Ger.)
Milton Fahrney
UNTAMED(1929)
Misc. Silents
NOT BUILT FOR RUNNIN'(1924); YANKEE SPEED(1924)
Douglas Fahy
WHAT A LIFE(1939)
Fai
FLASH GORDON(1980)
Zulma Faiad
NIGHT OF A THOUSAND CATS(1974, Mex.)
Stewart Faichney
DAY AFTER HALLOWEEN, THE(1981, Aus.); LAST OF THE KNUCKLEMEN,
THE(1981, Aus.)
Robert Faige
CAN'T HELP SINGING(1944)
Tusi Faiivae
OPERATION PETTICOAT(1959)
Sally Faile
NIGHT FLOWERS(1979), p
Anton Sammy Fain
FOOTLIGHT PARADE(1933), art d
Elmer Fain
ROUNDUP TIME IN TEXAS(1937)
John Fain
MUSCLE BEACH PARTY(1964); PAJAMA PARTY(1964); SURF PARTY(1964); HOW
TO STUFF A WILD BIKINI(1965); CALIFORNIA DREAMING(1979)
Jordana Fain
END OF INNOCENCE(1960, Arg.)
M.G. [Matty] Fain
JOHNNY ROCCO(1958)

Mattie Fain
FEDERAL BULLETS(1937)
Matty Fain
LET 'EM HAVE IT(1935); ONE HOUR LATE(1935); BORDER FLIGHT(1936); BULL-
DOG EDITION(1936); GREAT GUY(1936); LADY FROM NOWHERE(1936); LAW IN
HER HANDS, THE(1936); BOY OF THE STREETS(1937); HOUSE OF SECRETS,
THE(1937); LARCENY ON THE AIR(1937); LEFT-HANDED LAW(1937); MIDNIGHT
MADONNA(1937); SHADOWS OF THE ORIENT(1937); SHE'S DANGEROUS(1937);
THIRTEENTH MAN, THE(1937); BAREFOOT BOY(1938); MIDNIGHT IN-
TRUDER(1938); PERSONAL SECRETARY(1938); PORT OF MISSING GIRLS(1938);
WANTED BY THE POLICE(1938); ANOTHER THIN MAN(1939); NEWSBOY'S HO-
ME(1939); MERCY PLANE(1940); GET-AWAY, THE(1941); MONSTER AND THE
GIRL, THE(1941); ROAR OF THE PRESS(1941); FRISCO LILL(1942); STRANGE CASE
OF DR. RX, THE(1942); ALLOTMENT WIVES, INC.(1945); DEAD RECKONING(1947);
DOWN TO EARTH(1947); JOHNNY O'CLOCK(1947); I WOULDN'T BE IN YOUR
SHOES(1948); HOODLUM EMPIRE(1952); HELL'S ISLAND(1955); MAGNIFICENT
ROUGHNECKS(1956); TEN COMMANDMENTS, THE(1956); THIS COULD BE THE
NIGHT(1957)
Misc. Talkies
PORT OF MISSING GIRLS(1938)
Peter Fain
CYCLE SAVAGES(1969); RUN, ANGEL, RUN(1969), prod d; GAS-S-S-S!(1970); MEAN
STREETS(1973); NEW YORK, NEW YORK(1977); KING OF COMEDY, THE(1983)
Sammy Fain
DAMES(1934); GOIN' TO TOWN(1935), m; CALL ME MISTER(1951), m/l Rome;
MARDI GRAS(1958), m/l
Luigi Fainelli
GREAT WAR, THE(1961, Fr., Ital.)
Samson Fainsilber
END OF THE WORLD, THE(1930, Fr.); CLANDESTINE(1948, Fr.); ROYAL AFFAIRS
IN VERSAILLES(1957, Fr.); PROVIDENCE(1977, Fr.); CHARLES AND LUCIE(1982,
Fr.)
1984
LIFE IS A BED OF ROSES(1984, Fr.)
Jack Faint
SILVER DARLINGS, THE(1947, Brit.)
Adina Fair
DREAMER, THE(1970, Israel)
Bea Fair
DANGEROUS AGE, A(1960, Can.)
Eleanor Fair
NIGHT RIDER, THE(1932)
Misc. Talkies
FORTY-FIVE CALIBRE ECHO(1932)
Silents
END OF THE GAME, THE(1919)
Elinor Fair
SCARLET EMPRESS, THE(1934)
Silents
MIRACLE MAN, THE(1919); KISMET(1920); OCCASIONALLY YOURS(1920); IT
CAN BE DONE(1921); ABLEMINDED LADY, THE(1922); WHITE HANDS(1922);
EAGLE'S FEATHER, THE(1923); HAS THE WORLD GONE MAD!(1923); MYSTERI-
OUS WITNESS, THE(1923); ONE MILLION IN JEWELS(1923); LAW FORBIDS,
THE(1924); GOLD AND THE GIRL(1925); VOLGA BOATMAN, THE(1926); JIM THE
CONQUEROR(1927); YANKEE CLIPPER, THE(1927); LET 'ER GO GALLEGH-
ER(1928)
Misc. Silents
ROAD THROUGH THE DARK, THE(1918); BE A LITTLE SPORT(1919); LOST
PRINCESS, THE(1919); LOVE IS LOVE(1919); MARRIED IN HASTE(1919); VAGA-
BOND LUCK(1919); WORDS AND MUSIC BY...(1919); BROADWAY AND HO-
ME(1920); GIRL IN NUMBER 29, THE(1920); TIN PAN ALLEY(1920); BIG
STAKES(1922); DANGEROUS PASTIME(1922); FLYIN' THRU(1925); TIMBER
WOLF(1925); TRAPPED(1925); BACHELOR BRIDES(1926); MY FRIEND FROM
INDIA(1927); SIN TOWN(1929)
Florence Fair
FIREBIRD, THE(1934); DINKY(1935); FLORENTINE DAGGER, THE(1935); I AM A
THIEF(1935); I LIVE FOR LOVE(1935); IN CALIENTE(1935); MAN OF IRON(1935);
OIL FOR THE LAMPS OF CHINA(1935); SECRET BRIDE, THE(1935); STRAN-
DED(1935); FRESHMAN LOVE(1936); MURDER BY AN ARISTOCRAT(1936); SE-
COND WIFE(1936); UNDERCURRENT(1946)
Silents
SALLY OF THE SAWDUST(1925)
Jody Fair
BRAIN EATERS, THE(1958); HIGH SCHOOL CONFIDENTIAL(1958); HOT ROD
GANG(1958); GHOST OF DRAGSTRIP HOLLOW zero(1959); GIRLS' TOWN(1959); SEX
KITTENS GO TO COLLEGE(1960); YOUNG SAVAGES, THE(1961)
Joyce Fair
Misc. Silents
APPLE-TREE GIRL, THE(1917); VICTIM, THE(1917)
Julie Fair
UP THE MACGREGORS(1967, Ital./Span.); STATUE, THE(1971, Brit.)
Lenore Fair
Silents
RECKONING DAY, THE(1918)
Michael Fair
DRIFTER, THE(1966)
Ronald Fair
CORNBREAD, EARL AND ME(1975), w
Thomas Fair
BLOOD FEAST(1963)
Yvonne Fair
LADY SINGS THE BLUES(1972)
Antonio Faira
SECRET DOOR, THE(1964)
Bruce Fairbairn
VAMPIRE HOOKERS, THE(1979, Phil.)
Douglas Fairbairn
SHOOT(1976, Can.), w

Ken Fairbairn
FAKE'S PROGRESS(1950, Brit.), d, w; ALL AT SEA(1970, Brit.), d
Jay Fairbank
TALES THAT WITNESS MADNESS(1973, Brit.), w
Chris Fairbanks
AWAKENING, THE(1980)
Colonel Fairbanks
MATTER OF INNOCENCE, A(1968, Brit.)
Don Fairbanks
COUNT YOUR BULLETS(1972)
Douglas Fairbanks
IRON MASK, THE(1929); TAMING OF THE SHREW, THE(1929); REACHING FOR THE MOON(1931); MR. ROBINSON CRUSOE(1932), p; CRIME OVER LONDON(1936, Brit.), p; DESTINATION MILAN(1954, Brit.)
Silents
LAMB, THE(1915); AMERICAN ARISTOCRACY(1916); FLIRTING WITH FATE(1916); GOOD BAD MAN, THE(1916), a, w; HABIT OF HAPPINESS, THE(1916); MANHATTAN MADNESS(1916); MATRIMANIAC, THE(1916); REGGIE MIXES IN(1916); AMERICANO, THE(1917); DOWN TO EARTH(1917), a, w; IN AGAIN-OUT AGAIN(1917); MAN FROM PAINTED POST, THE(1917), a, w; MODERN MUSKETEER, A(1917); REACHING FOR THE MOON(1917); WILD AND WOOLLY(1917); ARIZONA(1918), a, d, w; HEADIN' SOUTH(1918); MR. FIX-IT(1918); SAY! YOUNG FELLOW(1918); HIS MAJESTY THE AMERICAN(1919), a, w; KNICKERBOCKER BUCKAROO, THE(1919), a, w; MARK OF ZORRO(1920), a, p; MOLLYCODDLE, THE(1920), w; WHEN THE CLOUDS ROLL BY(1920), a, w; NUT, THE(1921), a, p; THREE MUSKETEERS, THE(1921); ROBIN HOOD(1922), a, p; THIEF OF BAGDAD, THE(1924); DON Q, SON OF ZORRO(1925); BLACK PIRATE, THE(1926), a, w; GAUCHO, THE(1928), a, p, w; SHOW PEOPLE(1928)
Misc. Silents
DOUBLE TROUBLE(1915); HALF BREED, THE(1916); HIS PICTURE IN THE PAPERS(1916); BOUND IN MOROCCO(1918); HE COMES UP SMILING(1918)
Douglas Fairbanks, Jr.
BARKER, THE(1928); CARELESS AGE(1929); FAST LIFE(1929); FORWARD PASS, THE(1929); JAZZ AGE, THE(1929); OUR MODERN MAIDENS(1929); DAWN PATROL, THE(1930); LITTLE ACCIDENT(1930); LOOSE ANKLES(1930); ONE NIGHT AT SUSIE'S(1930); OUTWARD BOUND(1930); PARTY GIRL(1930); WAY OF ALL MEN, THE(1930); CHANCES(1931); I LIKE YOUR NERVE(1931); LITTLE CAESAR(1931); IT'S TOUGH TO BE FAMOUS(1932); LOVE IS A RACKET(1932); SCARLET DAWN(1932), a, w; UNION DEPOT(1932); CAPTURED!(1933); LIFE OF JIMMY DOLAN, THE(1933); MORNING GLORY(1933); NARROW CORNER, THE(1933); PARACHUTE JUMPER(1933); CATHERINE THE GREAT(1934, Brit.); SUCCESS AT ANY PRICE(1934); MAN OF THE MOMENT(1935, Brit.); MIMI(1935, Brit.); ACCUSED(1936, Brit.); AMATEUR GENTLEMAN(1936, Brit.); PRISONER OF ZENDA, THE(1937); WHEN THIEF MEETS THIEF(1937, Brit.), a, p; HAVING WONDERFUL TIME(1938); JOY OF LIVING(1938); RAGE OF PARIS, THE(1938); YOUNG IN HEART, THE(1938); GUNGA DIN(1939); RULERS OF THE SEA(1939); SUN NEVER SETS, THE(1939); ANGELS OVER BROADWAY(1940); GREEN HELL(1940); SAFARI(1940); CORSICAN BROTHERS, THE(1941); EXILE, THE(1947), a, p, w; SINBAD THE SAILOR(1947); THAT LADY IN ERMINE(1948); FIGHTING O'FLYNN, THE(1949), a, p, w; GREAT MANHUNT, THE(1951, Brit.); MR. DRAKE'S DUCK(1951, Brit.), a, p; ANOTHER MAN'S POISON(1952, Brit.), p; GENIE(1953, Brit.), a, p; THREE'S COMPANY(1953, Brit.), a, p; FOREVER MY HEART(1954, Brit.), a, p; LAST MOMENT, THE(1954, Brit.); RED DRESS, THE(1954, Brit.), p; SILKEN AFFAIR, THE(1957, Brit.), p; CHASE A CROOKED SHADOW(1958, Brit.), p; GHOST STORY(1981)
Silents
STEPHEN STEPS OUT(1923); AIR MAIL, THE(1925); STELLA DALLAS(1925); AMERICAN VENUS, THE(1926); BROKEN HEARTS OF HOLLYWOOD(1926); MAN BAIT(1926); IS ZAT SO?(1927); TEXAS STEER, A(1927); DEAD MAN'S CURVE(1928); POWER OF THE PRESS, THE(1928); TOILERS, THE(1928); WOMAN OF AFFAIRS, A(1928); OUR MODERN MAIDENS(1929)
Misc. Silents
WILD HORSE MESA(1925); BARKER, THE(1928); MODERN MOTHERS(1928)
Douglas Fairbanks, Sr.
MR. ROBINSON CRUSOE(1932); PRIVATE LIFE OF DON JUAN, THE(1934, Brit.)
Eleanor Fairbanks
Silents
TILLIE'S TOMATO SURPRISE(1915)
Flobelle Fairbanks
Silents
EYES RIGHT(1926); WHAT HAPPENED TO FATHER(1927)
Misc. Silents
CLIMBERS, THE(1927)
Gladys Fairbanks
Silents
POOR LITTLE RICH GIRL, A(1917); OUR LITTLE WIFE(1918)
Jay Fairbanks
SON OF DRACULA(1974, Brit.), w
Jerry Fairbanks
ROAD TO UTOPIA(1945), animation; BAMBOO SAUCER, THE(1968), p
Silents
ADVENTUROUS SOUL, THE(1927), ph
Lucile Fairbanks
STRAWBERRY BLONDE, THE(1941); MAN WHO RETURNED TO LIFE, THE(1942)
Lucille Fairbanks
CALLING ALL HUSBANDS(1940); FLIGHT ANGELS(1940); FUGITIVE FROM JUSTICE, A(1940); PASSAGE FROM HONG KONG(1941); KLONDIKE FURY(1942)
Madeline Fairbanks
Misc. Silents
FLYING TWINS, THE(1915); BIRD OF PREY, A(1916)
Marion Fairbanks
Misc. Silents
FLYING TWINS, THE(1915)
William Fairbanks
Silents
PEACEFUL PETERS(1922); WESTERN DEMON, A(1922); SPAWN OF THE DESERT(1923); BORDER WOMEN(1924); DOWN BY THE RIO GRANDE(1924); HER MAN(1924); MARRY IN HASTE(1924); OTHER KIND OF LOVE, THE(1924); RACING FOR LIFE(1924); FEARLESS LOVER, THE(1925); HANDSOME BRUTE, THE(1925); NEW CHAMPION(1925); SPEED MAD(1925); CATCH AS CATCH CAN(1927); DOWN GRADE, THE(1927); ONE CHANCE IN A MILLION(1927)

Misc. Silents
BROADWAY BUCKAROO(1921); GO GET HIM(1921); MONTANA BILL(1921); WESTERN ADVENTURER, A(1921); CLEAN UP, THE(1921); FIGHTING HEARTS(1922); HELL'S BORDER(1922); SHERIFF OF SUN-DOG, THE(1922); DEVIL'S DOORYARD, THE(1923); LAW RUSTLERS, THE(1923); SUN DOG TRAILS(1923); BATTLING FOOL, THE(1924); BEAUTIFUL SINNER, THE(1924); CALL OF THE MATE(1924); COWBOY AND THE FLAPPER, THE(1924); DO IT NOW(1924); FATAL MISTAKE, THE(1924); FIGHT FOR HONOR, A(1924); MAN FROM GOD'S COUNTRY(1924); MARTYR SEX, THE(1924); TAINTED MONEY(1924); THAT WILD WEST(1924); TORRENT, THE(1924); WOMEN FIRST(1924); FIGHT TO THE FINISH, A(1925); FIGHTING YOUTH(1925); GREAT SENSATION, THE(1925); FLYING HIGH(1926); MILE-A-MINUTE MAN, THE(1926); WINNING WALLOP, THE(1926); SPOILERS OF THE WEST(1927); THROUGH THICK AND THIN(1927); WHEN DANGER CALLS(1927); UNDER THE BLACK EAGLE(1928); WYOMING(1928)
Sidney Fairbrother
CHU CHIN CHOW(1934, Brit.)
Sydney Fairbrother
DOWN OUR STREET(1932, Brit.); INSULT(1932, Brit.); LUCKY LADIES(1932, Brit.); MURDER ON THE SECOND FLOOR(1932, Brit.); RETURN OF RAFFLES, THE(1932, Brit.); THIRD STRING, THE(1932, Brit.); EXCESS BAGGAGE(1933, Brit.); HOME, SWEET HOME(1933, Brit.); CRUCIFIX, THE(1934, Brit.); BREWSTER'S MILLIONS(1935, Brit.); PRIVATE SECRETARY, THE(1935, Brit.); ALL IN(1936, Brit.); FAME(1936, Brit.); GAY LOVE(1936, Brit.); LAST JOURNEY, THE(1936, Brit.); DREAMING LIPS(1937, Brit.); KING SOLOMON'S MINES(1937, Brit.); GAIETY GIRLS, THE(1938, Brit.); LITTLE DOLLY DAYDREAM(1938, Brit.); MAKE IT THREE(1938, Brit.); ROSE OF TRALEE(1938, Ireland)
Silents
IRON JUSTICE(1915, Brit.); AULD LANG SYNE(1917, Brit.); BACHELORS' CLUB, THE(1921, Brit.); DON QUIXOTE(1923, Brit.); HEARTSTRINGS(1923, Brit.); REST CURE, THE(1923, Brit.); NELL GWYNNE(1926, Brit.); MY LORD THE CHAUFFEUR(1927, Brit.)
Misc. Silents
ME AND M'PAL(1916, Brit.); TEMPTATION'S HOUR(1916, Brit.); IN BONDAGE(1919, Brit.); CHILDREN OF GIBEON, THE(1920, Brit.); LADDIE(1920, Brit.); GOLDEN DAWN, THE(1921, Brit.); ROTTERS, THE(1921, Brit.); BELOVED VAGABOND, THE(1923, Brit.); MAISIE'S MARRIAGE(1923, Brit.); SALLY BISHOP(1923, Brit.); REVEILLE(1924, Brit.); CONFETTI(1927, Brit.)
Victoria Fairbrother
SWEET WILLIAM(1980, Brit.)
Fairchild
NAUGHTY NINETIES, THE(1945), md
Dorothy Fairchild
Silents
SINS OF SOCIETY(1915); FRUITS OF DESIRE, THE(1916)
Edgar Fairchild
IN SOCIETY(1944), md; CRIMSON CANARY(1945), m; HER LUCKY NIGHT(1945), md; HERE COME THE CO-EDS(1945), md; HOUSE OF DRACULA(1945), m; I'LL REMEMBER APRIL(1945), md; PENTHOUSE RHYTHM(1945), md; PURSUIT TO ALGIERS(1945), m, md; SONG OF THE SARONG(1945), md; LITTLE GIANT(1946), m, md; SHE WROTE THE BOOK(1946), md
Edgar "Cookie" Fairchild
IF YOU KNEW SUSIE(1948), m
June Fairchild
UP IN SMOKE(1978); HEAD(1968); WHERE ANGELS GO...TROUBLE FOLLOWS(1968); DRIVE, HE SAID(1971); PRETTY MAIDS ALL IN A ROW(1971); SUMMERTREE(1971); TOP OF THE HEAP(1972); DETROIT 9000(1973); YOUR THREE MINUTES ARE UP(1973); THUNDERBOLT AND LIGHTFOOT(1974); STUDENT BODY, THE(1976)
Margaret Fairchild
RAIN PEOPLE, THE(1969); ULZANA'S RAID(1972); THIEF WHO CAME TO DINNER, THE(1973); EAT MY DUST!(1976); HEART BEAT(1979); MOMMIE DEAREST(1981)
Max Fairchild
TRUE STORY OF ESKIMO NELL, THE(1975, Aus.); GETTING OF WISDOM, THE(1977, Aus.); SUMMERFIELD(1977, Aus.); MONEY MOVERS(1978, Aus.); DIMBOOLA(1979, Aus.); MAD MAX(1979, Aus.)
Morgan Fairchild
SEDUCTION, THE(1982)
Patti Fairchild
DOUBLE STOP(1968)
W.E.C. Fairchild
OPERATION DISASTER(1951, Brit.), w
William Fairchild
COLONEL BOGEY(1948, Brit.), w; SONG FOR TOMORROW, A(1948, Brit.), w; BADGER'S GREEN(1949, Brit.), w; GLORY AT SEA(1952, Brit.), w; OUTCAST OF THE ISLANDS(1952, Brit.), w; PROJECT M7(1953, Brit.), w; FRONT PAGE STORY(1954, Brit.), w; MALTA STORY(1954, Brit.), w; LAND OF FURY(1955 Brit.), w; PASSAGE HOME(1955, Brit.), w; EXTRA DAY, THE(1956, Brit.), d&w; JOHN AND JULIE(1957, Brit.), d&w; SILENT ENEMY, THE(1959, Brit.), d&w; DO NOT DISTURB(1965), w; STAR!(1968), w; LAST SHOT YOU HEAR, THE(1969, Brit.), w; DARWIN ADVENTURE, THE(1972, Brit.), w; EMBASSY(1972, Brit.), w
William E.C. Fairchild
LONG DARK HALL, THE(1951, Brit.), w
Mitchell Faircloth
NEXT OF KIN(1983, Aus.)
Betty Faire
CROSS ROADS(1930, Brit.)
Silents
GAY CORINTHIAN, THE(1924); PRESUMPTION OF STANLEY HAY, MP, THE(1925, Brit.); ONLY WAY, THE(1926, Brit.); MAN WHO CHANGED HIS NAME, THE(1928, Brit.); BARNES MURDER CASE, THE(1930, Brit.)
Misc. Silents
DOOR THAT HAS NO KEY, THE(1921, Brit.); BENTLEY'S CONSCIENCE(1922, Brit.); LONELY LADY OF GROSVENOR, THE(1922, Brit.); ROMANCE OF THE MAYFAIR, A(1925, Brit.); CITY OF YOUTH, THE(1928, Brit.)
Robyn Faire
BAND OF ANGELS(1957)

Virginia Brown Faire
Silents
DEVIL'S MASTERPIECE, THE(1927)
Virginia Brown Faire
DONOVAN AFFAIR, THE(1929); HANDCUFFED(1929); LONESOME TRAIL, THE(1930); MURDER ON THE ROOF(1930); TRAILS OF DANGER(1930); SECRET MENACE(1931); LAST RIDE, THE(1932); LONE TRAIL, THE(1932); TEX TAKES A HOLIDAY(1932); WEST OF THE DIVIDE(1934)
Misc. Talkies
BREED OF THE WEST(1930); AFRICAN INCIDENT(1934); TRACY RIDES(1935)
Silents
AIR HAWK, THE(1924); PETER PAN(1924); ROMANCE RANCH(1924); WELCOME STRANGER(1924); RECOMPENSE(1925); BROADWAY BILLY(1926); RACING ROMANCE(1926); TEMPTRESS, THE(1926); WINGS OF THE STORM(1926); HAZARDOUS VALLEY(1927); WHITE FLANNELS(1927); DEVIL'S CHAPLAIN(1929)
Misc. Silents
FIGHTIN' MAD(1921); WITHOUT BENEFIT OF CLERGY(1921); OMAR THE TENTMAKER(1922); CRICKET ON THE HEARTH, THE(1923); SHADOWS OF THE NORTH(1923); THUNDERGATE(1923); LIGHTING RIDER, THE(1924); CALGARY STAMPEDE, THE(1925); FRIENDLY ENEMIES(1925); DESERT VALLEY(1926); MILE-A-MINUTE MAN, THE(1926); GUN GOSPEL(1927); PLEASURE BEFORE BUSINESS(1927); CANYON OF ADVENTURE, THE(1928); RACE FOR LIFE, A(1928); UNDRESSED(1928); BURNING THE WIND(1929)
Virginia Browne Faire
ALIAS THE BAD MAN(1931)
Misc. Talkies
HELL'S VALLEY(1931)
Silents
STORMSWEPT(1923); LOST WORLD, THE(1925)
Misc. Silents
UNDER NORTHERN LIGHTS(1920); VENGEANCE OF THE DEEP(1923); CHIP OF THE FLYING U(1926); FRENZIED FLAMES(1926); WOLF HUNTERS, THE(1926); TRACKED BY THE POLICE(1927); CHORUS KID, THE(1928); DANGER PATROL(1928); HOUSE OF SHAME, THE(1928); QUEEN OF THE CHORUS(1928); BODY PUNCH, THE(1929); UNTAMED JUSTICE(1929)
Tommy Gene Fairey
SAGEBRUSH TROUBADOR(1935)
Audrey Fairfax
GIDGET GOES TO ROME(1963)
Beatrice Fairfax
Silents
LOVELORN, THE(1927), w
Betty Fairfax
CLUNY BROWN(1946); DRAGONWYCH(1946); RENDEZVOUS 24(1946); MY OWN TRUE LOVE(1948); LORNA DOONE(1951); SON OF DR. JEKYLL, THE(1951); NOTORIOUS LANDLADY, THE(1962)
Deborah Fairfax
FRIGHTMARE(1974, Brit.)
Ferdinand Fairfax
NATE AND HAYES(1983, U.S./New Zealand), d
George Fairfax
LIBIDO(1973, Aus.)
James Fairfax
IF WINTER COMES(1947); IVY(1947); CHALLENGE, THE(1948); MRS. MIKE(1949); CUSTOMS AGENT(1950); FORTUNES OF CAPTAIN BLOOD(1950); TYRANT OF THE SEA(1950); AGAINST ALL FLAGS(1952); BATTLES OF CHIEF PONTIAC(1952); LAST TRAIN FROM BOMBAY(1952); MY COUSIN RACHEL(1952); DANGEROUS WHEN WET(1953); LOOSE IN LONDON(1953); WHITE GODDESS(1953)
Jimmy Fairfax
JULIA MISBEHAVES(1948); MIDNIGHT LACE(1960)
Lance Fairfax
BEGGAR STUDENT, THE(1931,Brit.); CARMEN(1931, Brit.)
Marian Fairfax
Silents
MAD MARRIAGE, THE(1921), w
Marion Fairfax
Silents
IMMIGRANT, THE(1915), w; ANTON THE TERRIBLE(1916), w; TENNESSEE'S PARDNER(1916), w; SECRET GAME, THE(1917), w; PUTTING IT OVER(1919), w; ROARING ROAD, THE(1919), w; DINTY(1920), w; BOB HAMPTON OF PLACER(1921), w; LYING TRUTH, THE(1922), d&w; SHERLOCK HOLMES(1922), w; PAINTED PEOPLE(1924), ed; TORMENT(1924), t; AS MAN DESIRES(1925), ed; CLOTHES MAKE THE PIRATE(1925), sup&w; IF I MARRY AGAIN(1925), ed; LOST WORLD, THE(1925), w; OLD LOVES AND NEW(1926), w
Thur Fairfax
Misc. Silents
GYPSY ROMANCE, THE(1926)
Virginia Fairfax
Misc. Silents
AMERICAN GENTLEMAN, AN(1915)
Chief Petty Officer Fairfield
ESCAPE FROM THE SEA(1968, Brit.)
William Fairfield
VALUE FOR MONEY(1957, Brit.), w
Fairfield Parlor
SUDDEN TERROR(1970, Brit.), m
Lyn Fairhurst
TOUCH OF DEATH(1962, Brit.), w; SING AND SWING(1964, Brit.), w; BE MY GUEST(1965, Brit.), w; DEVILS OF DARKNESS, THE(1965, Brit.), w
Fairlane
RIDER ON A DEAD HORSE(1962), m
Lynn Fairleigh
VOICES(1973, Brit.)
Norman Fairley
GOODBYE PORK PIE(1981, New Zealand); NATE AND HAYES(1983, U.S./New Zealand)
Victor Fairley
MY FRIEND THE KING(1931, Brit.); ILLEGAL(1932, Brit.); MR. QUINCEY OF MONTE CARLO(1933, Brit.); NAUGHTY CINDERELLA(1933, Brit.); POWER(1934, Brit.); KISS ME GOODBYE(1935, Brit.); TERROR ON TIPTOE(1936, Brit.); GYP-

SY(1937, Brit.); MAN WITH 100 FACES, THE(1938, Brit.); MR. SATAN(1938, Brit.); WE'RE GOING TO BE RICH(1938, Brit.); THREE COCKEYED SAILORS(1940, Brit.); NOW BARABBAS WAS A ROBBER(1949, Brit.); CAPTAIN'S PARADISE, THE(1953, Brit.); TWO-HEADED SPY, THE(1959, Brit.)
Gerald Fairlie
BULLDOG SEES IT THROUGH(1940, Brit.), w
Gerard Fairlie
SHOT IN THE DARK, A(1933, Brit.), w; OPEN ALL NIGHT(1934, Brit.), w; ACE OF SPADES, THE(1935, Brit.), w; ALIAS BULLDOG DRUMMOND(1935, Brit.), w; BORN FOR GLORY(1935, Brit.), w; CHARLIE CHAN IN SHANGHAI(1935), w; JACK AHOY!(1935, Brit.), w; LAD, THE(1935, Brit.), w; LAZYBONES(1935, Brit.), w; BIG NOISE, THE(1936, Brit.), w; CHICK(1936, Brit.), w; TROUBLED WATERS(1936, Brit.), w; BULLDOG DRUMMOND ESCAPES(1937), w; SCOTLAND YARD COMMANDS(1937, Brit.), w; CONSPIRATOR(1949, Brit.), w; CALLING BULLDOG DRUMMOND(1951, Brit.), w
Jean Fairlie
WHAT A CARVE UP!(1962, Brit.), cos; HORROR OF IT ALL, THE(1964, Brit.), cos; SPACEFLIGHT IC-1(1965, Brit.), cos
Victor Fairlie
HERE'S GEORGE(1932, Brit.)
Austin Fairman
ADVENTURES OF ROBIN HOOD, THE(1938); BULLDOG DRUMMOND'S PERIL(1938); BRITISH INTELLIGENCE(1940)
Blain Fairman
TRAP, THE(1967, Can./Brit.)
Charles Fairman
DISCIPLE OF DEATH(1972, Brit.), p
Churton Fairman
DISCIPLE OF DEATH(1972, Brit.), w
Huck Fairman
REFUGE(1981), p, d, w
Michael Fairman
ANDERSON TAPES, THE(1971); CHARLIE CHAN AND THE CURSE OF THE DRAGON QUEEN(1981)
Paul Fairman
INVASION OF THE SAUCER MEN(1957), w
Paul W. Fairman
TARGET EARTH(1954), w; EYE CREATURES, THE(1965), w
Ellen Faison
ROUND TRIP(1967); WHO KILLED MARY WHAT'SER NAME?(1971)
Frankie Faison
RAGTIME(1981); CAT PEOPLE(1982); HANKY-PANKY(1982); LITTLE SEX, A(1982); PERMANENT VACATION(1982)
1984
EXTERMINATOR 2(1984)
Frankie R. Faison
1984
C.H.U.D.(1984)
George Faison
1984
COTTON CLUB, THE(1984), ch
Matthew Faison
GETTING EVEN(1981); MOMMIE DEAREST(1981); TRUE CONFESSIONS(1981); STAR CHAMBER, THE(1983)
Sandra Faison
STERILE CUCKOO, THE(1969)
Sandy Faison
ALL THE RIGHT MOVES(1983)
A. Fait
Silents
BATTLESHIP POTEMKIN, THE(1925, USSR)
Andrei Fait
Misc. Silents
DEATH BAY(1926, USSR)
Arsen Fait
THIRTEEN, THE(1937, USSR)
Adam Faith
NEVER LET GO(1960, Brit.); WHAT A WHOPPER(1961, Brit.); MIX ME A PERSON(1962, Brit.); WHAT A CARVE UP!(1962, Brit.); STARDUST(1974, Brit.); YESTERDAY'S HERO(1979, Brit.); FOXES(1980); MC VICAR(1982, Brit.)
Dolores Faith
PHANTOM PLANET, THE(1961); V.D.(1961); WILD HARVEST(1962); SHELL SHOCK(1964); HUMAN DUPLICATORS, THE(1965); MUTINY IN OUTER SPACE(1965); ONE OF OUR SPIES IS MISSING(1966); THAT TENNESSEE BEAT(1966)
Gloria Faith
VAGABOND KING, THE(1930)
Percy Faith
LOVE ME OR LEAVE ME(1955), m; TAMMY, TELL ME TRUE(1961), m; I'D RATHER BE RICH(1964), m; THIRD DAY, THE(1965), m; OSCAR, THE(1966), m
Geoffrey Faithful
WEDDINGS ARE WONDERFUL(1938, Brit.), ph; HAPPIDROME(1943, Brit.), ph; DEVIL'S HARBOR(1954, Brit.), ph; ESCAPE BY NIGHT(1965, Brit.), ph
Marianne Faithful
MADE IN U.S.A.(1966, Fr.); ASSAULT ON AGATHON(1976, Brit./Gr.)
Yvonne Faithful
GENTLE TOUCH, THE(1956, Brit.)
Geoffrey Faithfull
LAST HOUR, THE(1930, Brit.), ph; WOULD YOU BELIEVE IT!(1930, Brit.), ph; YOU'D BE SURPRISED!(1930, Brit.), ph; 77 PARK LANE(1931, Brit.), ph; BORN LUCKY(1932, Brit.), ph; HIS LORDSHIP(1932, Brit.), ph; HOTEL SPLENDIDE(1932, Brit.), ph; MEN OF STEEL(1932, Brit.), ph; RETURN OF RAFFLES, THE(1932, Brit.), ph; SELF-MADE LADY(1932, Brit.), ph; I'M AN EXPLOSIVE(1933, Brit.), ph; PRINCE OF ARCADIA(1933, Brit.), ph; EASY MONEY(1934, Brit.), ph; FEATHERED SERPENT, THE(1934, Brit.), ph; NIGHT OF THE PARTY, THE(1934, Brit.), ph; HANDLE WITH CARE(1935, Brit.), ph; PHANTOM LIGHT, THE(1935, Brit.), ph; RIGHT AGE TO MARRY, THE(1935, Brit.), ph; SHADOW OF MIKE EMERALD, THE(1935, Brit.), ph; VANITY(1935), ph; 18 MINUTES(1935), ph; ALL THAT GLITTERS(1936, Brit.), ph; BUSMAN'S HOLIDAY(1936, Brit.), ph; HEIRLOOM MYSTERY, THE(1936, Brit.), ph; IF I WERE RICH(1936), ph; LUCK OF THE TURF(1936, Brit.), ph; NOT SO DUSTY(1936, Brit.), ph; NOTHING LIKE PUBLICITY(1936, Brit.),

ph; SUCH IS LIFE(1936, Brit.), ph; TERROR ON TIPTOE(1936, Brit.), ph; THEY DIDN'T KNOW(1936, Brit.), ph; TO CATCH A THIEF(1936, Brit.), ph; TOUCH OF THE MOON, A(1936, Brit.), ph; TROUBLE AHEAD(1936, Brit.), ph; TWICE BRANDED(1936, Brit.), ph; BORN THAT WAY(1937, Brit.), ph; FAREWELL TO CINDERELLA(1937, Brit.), ph; FATHER STEPS OUT(1937, Brit.), ph; FIFTY-SHILLING BOXER(1937, Brit.), ph; LITTLE MISS SOMEBODY(1937, Brit.), ph; PEARLS BRING TEARS(1937, Brit.), ph; PHANTOM SHIP(1937, Brit.), ph; RACING ROMANCE(1937, Brit.), ph; STRANGE ADVENTURES OF MR. SMITH, THE(1937, Brit.), ph; WHEN THE DEVIL WAS WELL(1937, Brit.), ph; WHY PICK ON ME?(1937, Brit.), ph; ALMOST A GENTLEMAN(1938, Brit.), ph; DARTS ARE TRUMPS(1938, Brit.), ph; EASY RICHES(1938, Brit.), ph; HIS LORDSHIP REGRETS(1938, Brit.), ph; IRISH AND PROUD OF IT(1938, Ireland), ph; LILY OF LAGUNA(1938, Brit.), ph; LITTLE DOLLY DAYDREAM(1938, Brit.), ph; MERELY MR. HAWKINS(1938, Brit.), ph; MIRACLES DO HAPPEN(1938, Brit.), ph; NIGHT JOURNEY(1938, Brit.), ph; PAID IN ERROR(1938, Brit.), ph; ROMANCE A LA CARTE(1938, Brit.), ph; YOU'RE THE DOCTOR(1938, Brit.), ph; ANYTHING TO DECLARE?(1939, Brit.), ph; BLIND FOLLY(1939, Brit.), ph; JAILBIRDS(1939, Brit.), ph; MUSIC HALL PARADE(1939, Brit.), ph; GARRISON FOLLIES(1940, Brit.), ph; PACK UP YOUR TROUBLES(1940, Brit.), ph; SOMEWHERE IN ENGLAND(1940, Brit.), ph; THREE SILENT MEN(1940, Brit.), ph; SOMEWHERE ON LEAVE(1942, Brit.), ph; HEADLINE(1943, Brit.), ph; I'LL WALK BESIDE YOU(1943, Brit.), ph; RHYTHM SERENADE(1943, Brit.), ph; SOMEWHERE IN CIVVIES(1943, Brit.), ph; KISS THE BRIDE GOODBYE(1944, Brit.), ph; MEET SEXTON BLAKE(1944, Brit.), ph; WORLD OWES ME A LIVING, THE(1944, Brit.), ph; FOR YOU ALONE(1945, Brit.), d; HOME SWEET HOME(1945, Brit.), ph; VARIETY JUBILEE(1945, Brit.), ph; HONEYMOON HOTEL(1946, Brit.), ph; I'LL TURN TO YOU(1946, Brit.), d; SEND FOR PAUL TEMPLE(1946, Brit.), ph; WHEN YOU COME HOME(1947, Brit.), ph; CUP-TIE HONEYMOON(1948, Brit.), ph; STORY OF SHIRLEY YORKE, THE(1948, Brit.), ph; GIRL WHO COULDN'T QUITE, THE(1949, Brit.), ph; HONEYMOON DEFERRED(1951, Brit.), ph; SCARLET THREAD(1951, Brit.), ph; DOWN AMONG THE Z MEN(1952, Brit.), ph; HAMMER THE TOFF(1952, Brit.), ph; HOLIDAY WEEK(1952, Brit.), ph; PAUL TEMPLE RETURNS(1952, Brit.), ph; SALUTE THE TOFF(1952, Brit.), ph; FLANNELFOOT(1953, Brit.), ph; FORCES' SWEETHEART(1953, Brit.), ph; LARGE ROPE, THE(1953, Brit.), ph; MARILYN(1953, Brit.), ph; BLACK RIDER, THE(1954, Brit.), ph; JOHNNY ON THE SPOT(1954, Brit.), ph; RADIO CAB MURDER(1954, Brit.), ph; RIVER BEAT(1954), ph; BLONDE BLACKMAILER(1955, Brit.), ph; SHADOW OF A MAN(1955, Brit.), ph; STOCK CAR(1955, Brit.), ph; BEHIND THE HEADLINES(1956, Brit.), ph; STRANGER IN TOWN(1957, Brit.), ph; THUNDER OVER TANGIER(1957, Brit.), ph; TIME IS MY ENEMY(1957, Brit.), ph; INBETWEEN AGE, THE(1958, Brit.), ph; KILL ME TOMORROW(1958, Brit.), ph; MARK OF THE PHOENIX(1958, Brit.), ph; SECRET MAN, THE(1958, Brit.), ph; STORMY CROSSING(1958, Brit.), ph; BOBBIKINS(1959, Brit.), ph; FIRST MAN INTO SPACE(1959, Brit.), ph; LIFE IN EMERGENCY WARD 10(1959, Brit.), ph; PRICE OF SILENCE, THE(1960, Brit.), ph; VILLAGE OF THE DAMNED(1960, Brit.), ph; GREEN HELMET, THE(1961, Brit.), ph; INVASION QUARTET(1961, Brit.), ph; MURDER SHE SAID(1961, Brit.), ph; OFFBEAT(1961, Brit.), ph; TWO-WAY STRETCH(1961, Brit.), ph; CORRIDORS OF BLOOD(1962, Brit.), ph; KILL OR CURE(1962, Brit.), ph; ON THE BEAT(1962, Brit.), ph; OPERATION SNATCH(1962, Brit.), ph; VILLAGE OF DAUGHTERS(1962, Brit.), ph; LADIES WHO DO(1964, Brit.), ph; MASTER SPY(1964, Brit.), ph; SPACEFLIGHT IC-1(1965, Brit.), ph; EXORCISM AT MIDNIGHT(1966, Brit. revised 1973, U.S.), ph; MURDER GAME, THE(1966, Brit.), ph; PANIC(1966, Brit.), ph; TERRORNAUTS, THE(1967, Brit.), ph

Geofrrey Faithfull
NAKED FURY(1959, Brit.), ph

Marianne Faithfull
I'LL NEVER FORGET WHAT'S 'IS NAME(1967, Brit.); GIRL ON A MOTORCYCLE, THE(1968, Fr./Brit.); HAMLET(1969, Brit.); GHOST STORY(1974, Brit.)

Erika Faivre
1984
SUNDAY IN THE COUNTRY, A(1984, Fr.)

Paul Faivre
ROOM UPSTAIRS, THE(1948, Fr.); NAKED WOMAN, THE(1950, Fr.); IT HAPPENED IN PARIS(1953, Fr.); AND GOD CREATED WOMAN(1957, Fr.); DEMONIAQUE(1958, Fr.); GATES OF PARIS(1958, Fr./Ital.); COUNTERFEITERS OF PARIS, THE(1962, Fr., Ital.); LONG ABSENCE, THE(1962, Fr./Ital.)

Edouardo Fajardo
LOS INVISIBLES(1961, Mex.)

Eduardo Fajardo
IMPORTANT MAN, THE(1961, Mex.); MACARIO(1961, Mex.); DJANGO(1966 Ital./Span.); MERCENARY, THE(1970, Ital./Span.); BAD MAN'S RIVER(1972, Span.); DON'T TURN THE OTHER CHEEK(1974, Ital./Ger./Span.); SONNY AND JED(1974, Ital.); HOUSE OF EXORCISM, THE(1976, Ital.)
1984
YELLOW HAIR AND THE FORTRESS OF GOLD(1984)

Edward Fajardo
CAULDRON OF DEATH, THE(1979, Ital.)

Joaquin Fajardo
WARKILL(1968, U.S./Phil.)

Eduardo Fajuardo
MAGNIFICENT BANDITS, THE(1969, Ital./Span.)

Scichiro Fakazawa
1984
BALLAD OF NARAYAMA, THE(1984, Jap.), d&w

Ladislaus Bus Fakete
FROM TOP TO BOTTOM(1933, Fr.), w

Magnia Fakhoury
CIRCLE OF DECEIT(1982, Fr./Ger.)

D. Fakiel
YIDDLE WITH HIS FIDDLE(1937, Pol.)

Dora Fakiel
WITHOUT A HOME(1939, Pol.)

Fala the Dog
PRINCESS O'ROURKE(1943)

John Falabella
NIGHTHAWKS(1981), cos

A.V. Falana
SHAFT IN AFRICA(1973)

Lola Falana
MAN CALLED ADAM, A(1966); LIBERATION OF L.B. JONES, THE(1970); KLANSMAN, THE(1974)
Misc. Talkies
LADY COCOA(1975)

Nino Falanga
SEVENTH VOYAGE OF SINBAD, THE(1958); LOVE AND MARRIAGE(1966, Ital.)

Vincenzo Falanga
INVESTIGATION OF A CITIZEN ABOVE SUSPICION(1970, Ital.)

Louis Falavigna
GIGOT(1962); FIVE MILES TO MIDNIGHT(1963, U.S./Fr./Ital.); TRAIN, THE(1965, Fr./Ital./U.S.); WHAT'S NEW, PUSSYCAT?(1965, U.S./Fr.); LES CREATURES(1969, Fr./Swed.)

Billy Falbo
LIVING VENUS(1961)
Misc. Talkies
ADVENTURES OF LUCKY PIERRE, THE(1961)

Paola Falchi
THEN THERE WERE THREE(1961)

Ake Falck
SWEDISH WEDDING NIGHT(1965, Swed.), a, d; TIME IN THE SUN, A(1970, Swed.), d, w

August Falck
Misc. Silents
MAN THERE WAS, A(1917, Swed.)

Ragnar Falck
CHILDREN, THE(1949, Swed.)

David Falcke
Silents
ARTISTIC TEMPERAMENT, THE(1919, Brit.), p; SINGLE MAN, THE(1919, Brit.), p; STARTING POINT, THE(1919, Brit.), p

Gina Falckenberg
BOCCACCIO(1936, Ger.)

Evaristo Falco
THIN RED LINE, THE(1964)

Louis Falco
FAME(1980), ch

Mike Falco
SILVER BEARS(1978); HOT STUFF(1979)

Andre Falcon
WITHOUT APPARENT MOTIVE(1972, Fr.); SERPENT, THE(1973, Fr./Ital./Ger.); STATE OF SIEGE(1973, Fr./U.S./Ital./Ger.); NADA GANG, THE(1974, Fr./Ital.); AND NOW MY LOVE(1975, Fr.); SORCERER(1977); NO TIME FOR BREAKFAST(1978, Fr.)

Andrew Falcon
STOLEN KISSES(1969, Fr.)

Bruno "Pop N' Taco" Falcon
1984
BREAKIN'(1984)

Gericho Falcon
WIRE SERVICE(1942), w

Peter Gonzales Falcon
HEARTBREAKER(1983)

Armando Falcone
SPIRIT AND THE FLESH, THE(1948, Ital.)

Stewart Falcone
BEYOND AND BACK(1978)

Alun Falconer
MAN UPSTAIRS, THE(1959, Brit.), w; CROSSROADS TO CRIME(1960, Brit.), w; NEVER LET GO(1960, Brit.), w; UNSTOPPABLE MAN, THE(1961, Brit.), w; CEREMONY, THE(1963, U.S./Span.), w; UNDERWORLD INFORMERS(1965, Brit.), w

John Falconer
PIED PIPER, THE(1972, Brit.)

Margaret Elizabeth Falconer
Silents
SONNY(1922)

Robert Falconer
KILL ME TOMORROW(1958, Brit.), w

Sheila Falconer
HALF A SIXPENCE(1967, Brit.)

Gerard Falconetti
CLAIRE'S KNEE(1971, Fr.); FRENCH LIEUTENANT'S WOMAN, THE(1981)

Armando Falconi
ROSSINI(1948, Ital.)

Dino Falconi
GRAN VARIETA(1955, Ital.), w

Dean Fales
COLLEGE HUMOR(1933), w

Enrico Fales
GANJA AND HESS(1973)

Joe Faletta
WHEN IN ROME(1952)

Irv Faling
BREAKHEART PASS(1976)

Camilla Falk
EDVARD MUNCH(1976, Norway/Swed.)

Erland Norden Falk
DEAR JOHN(1966, Swed.)

Gabriell Falk
ADDING MACHINE, THE(1969), cos

Gabriella Falk
TWO GENTLEMEN SHARING(1969, Brit.), cos; IN SEARCH OF GREGORY(1970, Brit./Ital.), cos; NIGHT DIGGER, THE(1971, Brit.), cos

Henri Falk
Silents
GOOD AND NAUGHTY(1926), w

Henry Falk
RENDEZ-VOUS(1932, Ger.), w

Lauritz Falk
GYPSY FURY(1950, Fr.); DEVIL, THE(1963); NIGHT GAMES(1966, Swed.)

Marianna Falk
FAREWELL, FRIEND(1968, Fr./Ital.)

Norbert Falk
TWO WORLD(1930, Brit.), w
Silents
ROSITA(1923), w

Norman Falk
CONGRESS DANCES(1932, Ger.), w

Peter Falk
WIND ACROSS THE EVERGLADES(1958); BLOODY BROOD, THE(1959, Can.); MURDER, INC.(1960); PRETTY BOY FLOYD(1960); SECRET OF THE PURPLE REEF, THE(1960); POCKETFUL OF MIRACLES(1961); PRESSURE POINT(1962); BALCONY, THE(1963); IT'S A MAD, MAD, MAD, MAD WORLD(1963); ROBIN AND THE SEVEN HOODS(1964); GREAT RACE, THE(1965); ITALIANO BRAVA GENTE(1965, Ital./USSR); PENELOPE(1966); LUV(1967); ANZIO(1968, Ital.); TOO MANY THIEVES(1968); CASTLE KEEP(1969); HUSBANDS(1970); MACHINE GUN McCAIN(1970, Ital.); WOMAN UNDER THE INFLUENCE, A(1974); MIKEY AND NICKY(1976); MURDER BY DEATH(1976); BRINK'S JOB, THE(1978); CHEAP DETECTIVE, THE(1978); IN-LAWS, THE(1979); ...ALL THE MARBLES(1981); GREAT MUPPET CAPER, THE(1981)
Misc. Talkies
OPERATION SNAFU(1970, Ital./Yugo.)

Robert Falk
COME TO THE STABLE(1949)

Ronald Falk
LONELY HEARTS(1983, Aus.)

Rossella Falk
8 ½(1963, Ital.); MODESTY BLAISE(1966, Brit.); MADE IN ITALY(1967, Fr./Ital.); LEGEND OF LYLAH CLARE, THE(1968); BLACK BELLY OF THE TARANTULA, THE(1972, Ital.)

Tom Falk
REBEL ANGEL(1962); M(1970); STONE KILLER, THE(1973); WESTWORLD(1973)

Vibeke Falk
GYPSY FURY(1950, Fr.)

Evelyn Falke
MAN FROM DOWN UNDER, THE(1943); EXPERIMENT PERILOUS(1944); THIS LOVE OF OURS(1945)

Jatta Falke
GENGHIS KHAN(U.S./Brit./Ger./Yugo)

C. Falkenberg
Silents
PLEASURE GARDEN, THE(1925, Brit./Ger.)

Eugenia [Jinx] Falkenberg
STRIKE ME PINK(1936)

Gina Falkenberg
CROSSROADS OF PASSION(1951, Fr.)

Jinx Falkenberg
SONG OF THE BUCKAROO(1939)

Kort Falkenberg
PORTLAND EXPOSE(1957); 36 HOURS(1965); IF HE HOLLERS, LET HIM GO(1968)

Margaret Falkenberg
SONG OF MEXICO(1945)

Paul Falkenberg
TRUNKS OF MR. O.F., THE(1932, Ger.), ed; M(1933, Ger.), w, ed; M(1951), w; GARDEN OF EDEN(1954), ed

Jinx Falkenburg
NOTHING SACRED(1937); SING FOR YOUR SUPPER(1941); TWO LATINS FROM MANHATTAN(1941); LUCKY LEGS(1942); SWEETHEART OF THE FLEET(1942); LAUGH YOUR BLUES AWAY(1943); SHE HAS WHAT IT TAKES(1943); TWO SENORITAS FROM CHICAGO(1943); COVER GIRL(1944); NINE GIRLS(1944); GAY SENORITA, THE(1945); TAHITI NIGHTS(1945); MEET ME ON BROADWAY(1946); TALK ABOUT A LADY(1946)

Kort Falkenburg
FATE IS THE HUNTER(1964)

Rudi Falkenhagen
SPETTERS(1983, Holland)

Patricia Falkenhain
END OF AUGUST, THE(1982)

Fritz Falkenstein
BREAKING THE ICE(1938), w

Julius Falkenstein
BEAUTIFUL ADVENTURE(1932, Ger.); CASE VAN GELDERN(1932, Ger.); TEMPEST(1932, Ger.); EMPRESS AND I, THE(1933, Ger.); HEART SONG(1933, Brit.)
Silents
SPIES(1929, Ger.)
Misc. Silents
OYSTER PRINCESS, THE(1919, Ger.)

James Falkland
TWIST OF SAND, A(1968, Brit.)

J. Meade Falkner
MOONFLEET(1955), w

Keith Falkner
MAYFAIR MELODY(1937, Brit.); SINGING COP, THE(1938, Brit.); THISTLEDOWN(1938, Brit.)

The Falkner Orchestra
JOHNNY DOUGHBOY(1943)

David Falkosky
PURSUIT OF D.B. COOPER, THE(1981)

Assane Fall
ROOTS OF HEAVEN, THE(1958); BROKEN ENGLISH(1981)

Richard Fall
LILIOM(1930), m; EAST LYNNE(1931), m

Tim Fall
1984
MAKING THE GRADE(1984)

Sir Raymond Falla
STORY OF ADELE H., THE(1975, Fr.)

Hans Fallada [Rudolf Ditzen]
LITTLE MAN, WHAT NOW?(1934), w

Gerard Fallec
DEADLIER THAN THE MALE(1957, Fr.)

Deborah Fallender
JABBERWOCKY(1977, Brit.)
1984
BEST DEFENSE(1984)

Susan Fallender
TRADING PLACES(1983)

Nina Fallenstein
EGON SCHIELE–EXCESS AND PUNISHMENT(1981, Ger.)

James Fallet
JOAN OF ARC(1948)

Rene Fallet
FANFAN THE TULIP(1952, Fr.), w; GATES OF PARIS(1958, Fr./Ital.), w; PARIS IN THE MONTH OF AUGUST(1968, Fr.), w

Joe Falletta
VARIETY LIGHTS(1965, Ital.)

E. Falletti
REVOLT OF THE MERCENARIES(1964, Ital./Span.), w

Amelia Falleur
EASY LIVING(1937); MAID OF SALEM(1937)

Mort Fallick
ACT ONE(1964), ed; LOVE AT FIRST BITE(1979), ed

Gil Fallman
GUNFIRE(1950)

Gilbert Fallman
FOR HEAVEN'S SAKE(1950); ONE TOO MANY(1950); MAN FROM PLANET X, THE(1951)

Bob Fallon
CHICAGO CALLING(1951)

Charles Fallon
STUDENT TOUR(1934); MAN WHO BROKE THE BANK AT MONTE CARLO, THE(1935); RUGGLES OF RED GAP(1935); GREAT ZIEGFELD, THE(1936); NEXT TIME WE LOVE(1936); PRINCESS COMES ACROSS, THE(1936); WIDOW FROM MONTE CARLO, THE(1936)

Gabriel Fallon
MEN OF IRELAND(1938, Ireland); YOU CAN'T FOOL AN IRISHMAN(1950, Ireland)

Gene Fallon
OPEN THE DOOR AND SEE ALL THE PEOPLE(1964)

John Fallon
FINAL EXAM(1981)

Joseph Fallon
TEXAS RANGERS, THE(1951)

Michaele Fallon
TWO-FACED WOMAN(1941)

Phillipa Fallon
GIRL IN THE KREMLIN, THE(1957); HIGH SCHOOL CONFIDENTIAL(1958); PRIVATE LIVES OF ADAM AND EVE, THE(1961)

Ronald Fallon
GREAT GUNDOWN, THE(1977), m

Terence Fallon
PRIMITIVES, THE(1962, Brit.)

Thomas F. Fallon
LAST WARNING, THE(1929), w; HOUSE OF FEAR, THE(1939), w
Silents
SACRED SILENCE(1919), w; WHILE NEW YORK SLEEPS(1920), w; JACQUELINE, OR BLAZING BARRIERS(1923), w

Tom Fallon
SECOND MATE, THE(1950, Brit.)

Charles Fallot
MAN STOLEN(1934, Fr.)

Jean Falloux
LAST ADVENTURE, THE(1968, Fr./Ital.), spec eff

Ruth Fallow
GLAMOUR FOR SALE(1940)

Ruth Fallows
ADVICE TO THE LOVELORN(1933); MADAME SPY(1934); NAVY BLUES(1937); SALESLADY(1938)

Glen Falls
SIX OF A KIND(1934)

Shirley Falls
MOTORCYCLE GANG(1957); YOUNG AND DANGEROUS(1957); MACHINE GUN KELLY(1958); SPIDER, THE(1958); THIS REBEL BREED(1960)

Thelma Falls-Hand
WHAT'S GOOD FOR THE GOOSE(1969, Brit.)

Gigliola Falluto
ANGELS OF DARKNESS(1956, Ital.), w

Elaine Falone
NIGHT THE LIGHTS WENT OUT IN GEORGIA, THE(1981); SHARKY'S MACHINE(1982)

George Falsey
Silents
SLIM SHOULDERS(1922), ph

Antonio Falsi
'TIS A PITY SHE'S A WHORE(1973, Ital.)

Eilen Falson
Misc. Talkies
DAWN OF THE MUMMY(1981)

Dennis Lee Falt
SLITHIS(1978)

Harold Faltermeier
1984
FLETCH(1984), m

Harold Faltermeyer
1984
BEVERLY HILLS COP(1984), m; THIEF OF HEARTS(1984), m
Arnost Faltynek
DO YOU KEEP A LION AT HOME?(1966, Czech.)
Bogdan Faluta
1984
FLIGHT TO BERLIN(1984, Ger./Brit.)
Georgie Fame
MINI-AFFAIR, THE(1968, Brit.); ENTERTAINING MR. SLOANE(1970, Brit.), m
Jacques Famery
GENDARME OF ST. TROPEZ, THE(1966, Fr./Ital.); LITTLE GIRL WHO LIVES DOWN THE LANE, THE(1977, Can.)
Moran Family
STARS OVER BROADWAY(1935)
Quillan Family
NOISY NEIGHBORS(1929)
Ho Fan
VERMILION DOOR(1969, Hong Kong)
Jason Fan
1984
BREAKIN' 2: ELECTRIC BOOGALOO(1984)
Jamaa Fanaka
EMMA MAE(1976), p,d&w; PENITENTIARY(1979), p,d&w; PENITENTIARY II(1982), p,d&w
Misc. Talkies
WELCOME HOME, BROTHER CHARLES(1975), d
Ugo Fancareggi
OPERATION ST. PETER'S(1968, Ital.)
B.C. Fancey
ROCK YOU SINNERS(1957, Brit.), p
E.J. Fancey
BALLOON GOES UP, THE(1942, Brit.), p; UP WITH THE LARK(1943, Brit.), p; SOHO CONSPIRACY(1951, Brit.), p; DOWN AMONG THE Z MEN(1952, Brit.), p; FLANNELFOOT(1953, Brit.), p; FORCES' SWEETHEART(1953, Brit.), p; JOHNNY ON THE SPOT(1954, Brit.), p; SHADOW OF A MAN(1955, Brit.), p; FLIGHT FROM VIENNA(1956, Brit.), p; ACCURSED, THE(1958, Brit.), p; ACTION STATIONS(1959, Brit.), p
Edwin J. Fancey
FIGHTING MAD(1957, Brit.), p
Malcolm Fancey
WORLD IS FULL OF MARRIED MEN, THE(1980, Brit.), p
Negus Fancey
MURDER ON THE CAMPUS(1963, Brit.), p
O. Negus Fancey
OLD MAC(1961, Brit.), p; SHOOT TO KILL(1961, Brit.), p
O'Negus Fancey
GIRLS OF LATIN QUARTER(1960, Brit.), p
Fanchan and Marco
INNOCENTS OF PARIS(1929), ch
Hampton Fancher
PARRISH(1961); ROME ADVENTURE(1962); OTHER SIDE OF THE MOUNTAIN, THE(1975); SURVIVAL(1976); BLADE RUNNER(1982), w
Fanchon
ALIBI(1929), ch; PADDY O'DAY(1935), ch; WHERE DO WE GO FROM HERE?(1945), ch; PLAINSMAN AND THE LADY(1946), ch; RENDEZVOUS WITH ANNIE(1946), ch; HIT PARADE OF 1947(1947), ch
Fanchon and Marco
HEARTS IN DIXIE(1929), ch
The Fanchonettes
THRILL OF A LIFETIME(1937); TURN OFF THE MOON(1937)
James Fanciscus
CAT O'NINE TAILS(1971, Ital./Ger./Fr.)
Dr. Arnold Fanck
S.O.S. ICEBERG(1933), w; NEW EARTH, THE(1937, Jap./Ger.), d, w
Fancon
SONG AND DANCE MAN, THE(1936), ch
Elena Fancora
WHITE NIGHTS(1961, Ital./Fr.)
Charles Fancourt
SUCH IS THE LAW(1930, Brit.)
Fandango
DEATHMASTER, THE(1972), cos
Alex Fane
UNDERWATER WARRIOR(1958)
Dorothy Fane
THREADS(1932, Brit.)
Silents
PICTURE OF DORIAN GRAY, THE(1916, Brit.); FLAG LIEUTENANT, THE(1919, Brit.); PRIDE OF THE FANCY, THE(1920, Brit.); LAUGHTER AND TEARS(1921, Brit.); CREATION(1922, Brit.); BULLDOG DRUMMOND(1923, Brit.); VORTEX, THE(1927, Brit.)
Misc. Silents
BARNABY(1919, Brit.); IN THE NIGHT(1920, Brit.); BLOOD MONEY(1921, Brit.); BONNIE BRIER BRUSH, THE(1921, Brit.); CORINTHIAN JACK(1921, Brit.); DANIEL DERONDA(1921, Brit.); LONELY LADY OF GROSVENOR, THE(1922, Brit.); LOST LEADER, A(1922, Brit.)
Ida Fane
Misc. Silents
BECAUSE(1921, Brit.)
Guy Fanelli
NIGHT OF LUST(1965, Fr.), w
Ottavio Fanfani
WAKE UP AND DIE(1967, Fr./Ital.)
Stephan Fanfara
HAPPY BIRTHDAY, GEMINI(1980), ed; LOVE(1982, Can.), ed
Vittorio Fanfoni
SERAFINO(1970, Fr./Ital.); RETURN OF SABATA(1972, Ital./Fr./Ger.)

Fanfulla
THIEF OF BAGHDAD, THE(1961, Ital./Fr.); SWORDSMAN OF SIENA, THE(1962, Fr./Ital.); LOVE AND LARCENY(1963, Fr./Ital.); FELLINI SATYRICON(1969, Fr./Ital.)
Fang
Silents
RANGE RIDERS, THE(1927)
Misc. Silents
SHERIFF'S GIRL(1926)
Charles Fang
MY SIN(1931)
Silents
HALDANE OF THE SECRET SERVICE(1923); JACQUELINE, OR BLAZING BARRIERS(1923); RAGGED EDGE, THE(1923)
Misc. Silents
JURY OF FATE, THE(1917); CYCLONE HIGGINS, D.D.(1918)
Charles A. Fang
Silents
GOD'S OUTLAW(1919)
Charlie Fang
Misc. Silents
PAGAN LOVE(1920)
David Fang
OUT OF THE TIGER'S MOUTH(1962)
Mei Fang
ONE NIGHT STAND(1976, Fr.)
Fang the Dog
Silents
WEST OF THE LAW(1926)
Ugo Fangareggi
TREASURE OF SAN GENNARO(1968, Fr./Ital./Ger.); LA NUIT DE VARENNES(1983, Fr./Ital.)
Juan Manuel Fangio
GRAND PRIX(1966)
Joe Fanham
Silents
SINGLE MAN, A(1929), t
Theo Fanidi
NAKED BRIGADE, THE(1965, U.S./Gr.), m
Sarah Fankboner
SUPERDAD(1974); SHAGGY D.A., THE(1976)
Al Fann
FRENCH CONNECTION, THE(1971); SUPER COPS, THE(1974); GOD TOLD ME TO(1976); LOVE IN A TAXI(1980); PARASITE(1982)
Frank Fanning
GUILTY?(1930); ST. LOUIS KID, THE(1934); LIVING ON VELVET(1935); UNDER YOUR SPELL(1936); SAN QUENTIN(1937); MR. MOTO'S GAMBLE(1938); DANCE HALL(1941); MEET JOHN DOE(1941); THUNDERING HOOFS(1941)
Silents
MASKED AVENGER, THE(1922), d
Frank C. Fanning
GREAT HOSPITAL MYSTERY, THE(1937)
Frank G. Fanning
CASE OF THE CURIOUS BRIDE, THE(1935); SHE COULDN'T TAKE IT(1935); SPECIAL AGENT(1935)
Paul Fanning
BRAIN THAT WOULDN'T DIE, THE(1959), art d
Rio Fanning
PRIMITIVES, THE(1962, Brit.)
George Fannon
O.S.S.(1946)
George J. Fannon
O.S.S.(1946)
Felicita Fanny
DEATH RIDES A HORSE(1969, Ital.)
Michel Fano
TRANS-EUROP-EXPRESS(1968, Fr.), m
Jiquel Fanol
Silents
FORBIDDEN WOMAN, THE(1920)
Michele Fansett
RECOMMENDATION FOR MERCY(1975, Can.)
Featherstone Fanshaw
CHICAGO 70(1970), ed
Carl-Henrik Fant
DEVIL'S WANTON, THE(1962, Swed.)
George Fant
INTERMEZZO(1937, Swed.); TIME OF DESIRE, THE(1957, Swed.); LOVE MATES(1967, Swed.)
Lou Fant
RESURRECTION(1980); AMY(1981)
Richard Fant
LAST TRAIN FROM BOMBAY(1952), ed
Roy Fant
DESIRE UNDER THE ELMS(1958); PRETTY BOY FLOYD(1960)
Andrea Fantacci
SEDUCED AND ABANDONED(1964, Fr./Ital.), set d; CLIMAX, THE(1967, Fr., Ital.), set d; HORNET'S NEST(1970), set d; SERAFINO(1970, Fr./Ital.), set d; ROMA(1972, Ital./Fr.), set d
G. Francesco Fantacci
DIRTY OUTLAWS, THE(1971, Ital.), set d
Andrea Fantasia
WAR AND PEACE(1956, Ital./U.S.); HERCULES(1959, Ital.); HERCULES UNCHAINED(1960, Ital./Fr.); CENTURION, THE(1962, Fr./Ital.); PRISONER OF THE IRON MASK(1962, Fr./Ital.); SON OF SAMSON(1962, Fr./Ital./Yugo.); FURY OF THE PAGANS(1963, Ital.); RAGE OF THE BUCCANEERS(1963, Ital.); SWORD OF EL CID, THE(1965, Span./Ital.)

Franco Fantasia

EL CID(1961, U.S./Ital.); PIRATE AND THE SLAVE GIRL, THE(1961, Fr./Ital.); QUEEN OF THE PIRATES(1961, Ital./Ger.); DAMON AND PYTHIAS(1962); SECRET MARK OF D'ARTAGNAN, THE(1963, Fr./Ital.); SON OF THE RED CORSAIR(1963, Ital.); HERCULES, SAMSON & ULYSSES(1964, Ital.); REVOLT OF THE MERCENARIES(1964, Ital./Span.); EL GRECO(1966, Ital., Fr.); ROVER, THE(1967, Ital.), a, fight director; NARCO MEN, THE(1969, Span./Ital.); BOUNTY HUNTERS, THE(1970, Ital.); LONG RIDE FROM HELL, A(1970, Ital.); WATERLOO(1970, Ital./USSR); ADIOS SABATA(1971, Ital./Span.); SLAVE OF THE CANNIBAL GOD(1979, Ital.); LION OF THE DESERT(1981, Libya/Brit.)

Frank Fantasia [Franco Fantasia]

DRUMS OF TABU, THE(1967, Ital./Span.)

Fantasy

MUSICAL MUTINY(1970)

John Fantauzzi

UP THE DOWN STAIRCASE(1967)

John Fante

DINKY(1935), w; EAST OF THE RIVER(1940), w; GOLDEN FLEECING, THE(1940), w; YOUTH RUNS WILD(1944), w; MY MAN AND I(1952), w; FULL OF LIFE(1956), w; JEANNE EAGELS(1957), w; RELUCTANT SAINT, THE(1962, U.S./Ital.), w; WALK ON THE WILD SIDE(1962), w; MY SIX LOVES(1963), w; MAYA(1966), w

Richard Fanti

TARGET HONG KONG(1952), ed

Dino Fantini

SINISTER URGE, THE(1961)

Dick Fantl

STRANGER'S RETURN(1933), ed; DARKEST AFRICA(1936), ed; NAVY BORN(1936), ed; CRIMINALS OF THE AIR(1937), ed; DODGE CITY TRAIL(1937), ed; FIGHT TO THE FINISH, A(1937), ed; MURDER IN GREENWICH VILLAGE(1937), ed; PAROLE RACKET(1937), ed; CATTLE RAIDERS(1938), ed; WOMEN IN PRISON(1938), ed

Richard Fantl

BEHIND PRISON GATES(1939), ed; BLAZING SIX SHOOTERS(1940), ed; LONE WOLF KEEPS A DATE, THE(1940), ed; NOBODY'S CHILDREN(1940), ed; RETURN OF WILD BILL, THE(1940), ed; BLONDE FROM SINGAPORE, THE(1941), ed; I WAS A PRISONER ON DEVIL'S ISLAND(1941), ed; OFFICER AND THE LADY, THE(1941), ed; SECRETS OF THE LONE WOLF(1941), ed; UNDER AGE(1941), ed; ALIAS BOSTON BLACKIE(1942), ed; BAD MEN OF THE HILLS(1942), ed; BOOGIE MAN WILL GET YOU, THE(1942), ed; MAN'S WORLD, A(1942), ed; SWEETHEART OF THE FLEET(1942), ed; AFTER MIDNIGHT WITH BOSTON BLACKIE(1943), ed; FOOTLIGHT GLAMOUR(1943), ed; GOOD LUCK, MR. YATES(1943), ed; LAUGH YOUR BLUES AWAY(1943), ed; MURDER IN TIMES SQUARE(1943), ed; THERE'S SOMETHING ABOUT A SOLDIER(1943), ed; BEAUTIFUL BUT BROKE(1944), ed; JAM SESSION(1944), ed; MR. WINKLE GOES TO WAR(1944), ed; STRANGE AFFAIR(1944), ed; BOSTON BLACKIE BOOKED ON SUSPICION(1945), ed; DANCING IN MANHATTAN(1945), ed; LET'S GO STEADY(1945), ed; ROUGH, TOUGH AND READY(1945), ed; BANDIT OF SHERWOOD FOREST, THE(1946), ed; DANGEROUS BUSINESS(1946), ed; NIGHT EDITOR(1946), ed; NOTORIOUS LONE WOLF, THE(1946), ed; ONE WAY TO LOVE(1946), ed; PERSONALITY KID(1946), ed; RETURN OF MONTE CRISTO, THE(1946), ed; FRAMED(1947), ed; LITTLE MISS BROADWAY(1947), ed; I SURRENDER DEAR(1948), ed; LADIES OF THE CHORUS(1948), ed; MANHATTAN ANGEL(1948), ed; MATING OF MILLIE, THE(1948), ed; PORT SAID(1948), ed; WOMAN FROM TANGIER, THE(1948), ed; BOSTON BLACKIE'S CHINESE VENTURE(1949), ed; DEVIL'S HENCHMEN, THE(1949), ed; KAZAN(1949), ed; MR. SOFT TOUCH(1949), ed; BEWARE OF BLONDIE(1950), ed; BEYOND THE PURPLE HILLS(1950), ed; HE'S A COCKEYED WONDER(1950), ed; MULE TRAIN(1950), ed; NEVADAN, THE(1950), ed; AL JENNINGS OF OKLAHOMA(1951), ed; CHINA CORSAIR(1951), ed; FURY OF THE CONGO(1951), ed; HURRICANE ISLAND(1951), ed; INDIAN UPRISING(1951), ed; MY TRUE STORY(1951), ed; WHEN THE REDSKINS RODE(1951), ed; CALIFORNIA CONQUEST(1952), ed; CRIPPLE CREEK(1952), ed; HAREM GIRL(1952), ed; RAINBOW 'ROUND MY SHOULDER(1952), ed; EL ALAMEIN(1954), ed

Robert Fantl

DURANGO KID, THE(1940), ed; FIVE LITTLE PEPPERS IN TROUBLE(1940), ed

Georges Fanto

OTHELLO(1955, U.S./Fr./Ital.), ph

Benedetta Fantoli

GUN, THE(1978, Ital.)

Barry Fantoni

JUST LIKE A WOMAN(1967, Brit.); STRANGE AFFAIR, THE(1968, Brit.); OTLEY(1969, Brit.)

Cesare Fantoni

HERCULES UNCHAINED(1960, Ital./Fr.); CARTHAGE IN FLAMES(1961, Fr./Ital.); CAESAR THE CONQUEROR(1963, Ital.)

Sergio Fantoni

ESTHER AND THE KING(1960, U.S./Ital.); GIANT OF MARATHON, THE(1960, Ital.); HERCULES UNCHAINED(1960, Ital./Fr.); ATOM AGE VAMPIRE(1961, Ital.); PRIZE, THE(1963); DO NOT DISTURB(1965); HIGH INFIDELITY(1965, Fr./Ital.); VON RYAN'S EXPRESS(1965); WHAT DID YOU DO IN THE WAR, DADDY?(1966); DIABOLICALLY YOURS(1968, Fr.); SENSO(1968, Ital.); HORNET'S NEST(1970); BAD MAN'S RIVER(1972, Span.)

Umberto Fantoni

FINE PAIR, A(1969, Ital.)

Maurice Labaye Fanykovy

EMBASSY(1972, Brit.), art d

Dan Fapp

GLAMOUR BOY(1941), ph; HENRY AND DIZZY(1942), ph

Daniel Fapp

HENRY ALDRICH GETS GLAMOUR(1942), ph; LADY BODYGUARD(1942), ph; MY HEART BELONGS TO DADDY(1942), ph; HENRY ALDRICH SWINGS IT(1943), ph; AND NOW TOMORROW(1944), ph; HENRY ALDRICH, BOY SCOUT(1944), ph; HENRY ALDRICH PLAYS CUPID(1944), ph; GIRLS OF PLEASURE ISLAND, THE(1953), ph; KNOCK ON WOOD(1954), ph; LIVING IT UP(1954), ph; RUN FOR COVER(1955), ph; HOLLYWOOD OR BUST(1956), ph; PARDNERS(1956), ph; DESIRE UNDER THE ELMS(1958), ph; ON THE BEACH(1959), ph; ALL THE YOUNG MEN(1960), ph; ONE, TWO, THREE(1961), ph; SEND ME NO FLOWERS(1964), ph; MAROONED(1969), ph; ONE-TRICK PONY(1980), ph

Daniel F. Fapp

BIRDS AND THE BEES, THE(1965), ph

Daniel L. Fapp

PRIORITIES ON PARADE(1942), ph; TRUE TO THE ARMY(1942), ph; HENRY ALDRICH HAUNTS A HOUSE(1943), ph; HENRY ALDRICH'S LITTLE SECRET(1944), ph; HOLD THAT BLONDE(1945), ph; KITTY(1945), ph; YOU CAME ALONG(1945), ph; TO EACH HIS OWN(1946), ph; DREAM GIRL(1947), ph; EASY COME, EASY GO(1947), ph; GOLDEN EARRINGS(1947), ph; SUDDENLY IT'S SPRING(1947), ph; HAZARD(1948), ph; BRIDE OF VENGEANCE(1949), ph; RED, HOT AND BLUE(1949), ph; SONG OF SURRENDER(1949), ph; SORROWFUL JONES(1949), ph; NO MAN OF HER OWN(1950), ph; REDHEAD AND THE COWBOY, THE(1950), ph; UNION STATION(1950), ph; DARLING, HOW COULD YOU!(1951), ph; LEMON DROP KID, THE(1951), ph; SAILOR BEWARE(1951), ph; ANYTHING CAN HAPPEN(1952), ph; JUMPING JACKS(1952), ph; STOOGE, THE(1952), ph; CADDY, THE(1953), ph; MONEY FROM HOME(1953), ph; ARTISTS AND MODELS(1955), ph; FAR HORIZONS, THE(1955), ph; YOU'RE NEVER TOO YOUNG(1955), ph; DEVIL'S HAIRPIN, THE(1957), ph; JOKER IS WILD, THE(1957), ph; KINGS GO FORTH(1958), ph; FIVE PENNIES, THE(1959), ph; LI'L ABNER(1959), ph; TRAP, THE(1959), ph; LET'S MAKE LOVE(1960), ph; WEST SIDE STORY(1961), ph; BACHELOR FLAT(1962), ph; PIGEON THAT TOOK ROME, THE(1962), ph; FUN IN ACAPULCO(1963), ph; GREAT ESCAPE, THE(1963), ph; MOVE OVER, DARLING(1963), ph; NEW KIND OF LOVE, A(1963), ph; PLEASURE SEEKERS, THE(1964), ph; UNSINKABLE MOLLY BROWN, THE(1964), ph; I'LL TAKE SWEDEN(1965), ph; LORD LOVE A DUCK(1966), ph; OUR MAN FLINT(1966), ph; SPINOUT(1966), ph; DOUBLE TROUBLE(1967), ph; FIVE CARD STUD(1968), ph; ICE STATION ZEBRA(1968), ph; SWEET NOVEMBER(1968), ph

James Farabee

SUPERFLY(1972), makeup

James Faracci

CHEECH AND CHONG'S NICE DREAMS(1981)

Stephanie Faracy

WHEN YOU COMIN' BACK, RED RYDER?(1979); HEAVEN CAN WAIT(1978); SCAVENGER HUNT(1979)

Alexander Farago

TOP HAT(1935), w

Dezso Farago

BLUE IDOL, THE(1931, Hung.), w

Joe Farago

I, THE JURY(1982); SILENT RAGE(1982)

1984

TERMINATOR, THE(1984)

Ladislas Farago

PATTON(1970), w; TORA! TORA! TORA!(1970, U.S./Jap.), w

Sandor Farago

MARRY THE BOSS' DAUGHTER(1941), w

Frances Edwards Faragoh

MY FRIEND FLICKA(1943), w

Francis Faragoh

BACK PAY(1930), w; LAST MAN(1932), d; UNDER-COVER MAN(1932), w; HAT, COAT AND GLOVE(1934), w; DANCING PIRATE(1936), w; LADY FROM LOUISIANA(1941), w

Francis E. Faragoh

RIGHT OF WAY, THE(1931), w; CHASING YESTERDAY(1935), w

Francis Edward Faragoh

HER PRIVATE AFFAIR(1930), w; IRON MAN, THE(1931), w; LITTLE CAESAR(1931), w; PRESTIGE(1932), w; BECKY SHARP(1935), w

Francis Edwards Faragoh

FRANKENSTEIN(1931), w; TOO YOUNG TO MARRY(1931), w; RETURN OF PETER GRIMM, THE(1935), w; MAD MARTINDALES, THE(1942), w; RENEGADES(1946), w; EASY COME, EASY GO(1947), w

Jameel Farah

BLACKBOARD JUNGLE, THE(1955); THREE VIOLENT PEOPLE(1956)

Soroya Farah

HOW DO I LOVE THEE?(1970)

Jameel Farah [Jamie Farr]

NO TIME FOR SERGEANTS(1958)

Daniel Faraldo

FIGHT FOR YOUR LIFE(1977); SLOW DANCING IN THE BIG CITY(1978); WALK PROUD(1979); RICH AND FAMOUS(1981); I, THE JURY(1982); LOVE AND MONEY(1982); LOSIN' IT(1983); SPRING BREAK(1983); TRENCHCOAT(1983)

1984

FEAR CITY(1984)

William Faralla

BALLAD OF CABLE HOGUE, THE(1970), p

Anthony Faramus

KING RAT(1965)

Mary Faranda

WEDDINGS AND BABIES(1960)

Farani

ABDICATION, THE(1974, Brit.), cos

Lucas Farara

SNIPER, THE(1952)

Sally Farb

TOUCH OF HER FLESH, THE(1967)

Buzz Farbar

BEYOND THE LAW(1968), a, p; WILD 90(1968)

Amy Farber

HOT TIMES(1974)

Arlene Farber

FRENCH CONNECTION, THE(1971)

Arlene Sue Farber

TEENAGE MOTHER(1967)

Bob Farber

DARK PASSAGE(1947)

Buzz Farber

MAIDSTONE(1970), a, p

Carol Farber

PUTNEY SWOPE(1969)

Hagit Farber
1984
SIGNAL 7(1984)
Harley Farber
ONCE IS NOT ENOUGH(1975)
Jerry Farber
MACBETH(1948)
Peter Farber
LUCKY STAR, THE(1980, Can.)
Robert Farber
ZOMBIES ON BROADWAY(1945), w
Steven Farber
1984
SIXTEEN CANDLES(1984)
Pamela Farbrother
CRY OF THE BANSHEE(1970, Brit.); DEVIL'S WIDOW, THE(1972, Brit.); FRIGHT-
MARE(1974, Brit.)
Max Farchild
ROAD WARRIOR, THE(1982, Aus.)
Bernard Farcy
MOON IN THE GUTTER, THE(1983, Fr./Ital.)
Fritz Fard
TOBRUK(1966)
Keahi Farden
BEYOND THE REEF(1981)
E. Fardon
NEXT OF KIN(1983, Aus.), makeup
Monique Fardoulis
WHO'S GOT THE BLACK BOX?(1970, Fr./Gr./Ital.), ed; ALICE, OR THE LAST
ESCAPADE(1977, Fr.), ed; HORSE OF PRIDE(1980, Fr.), ed; HATTER'S GHOST,
THE(1982, Fr.), ed
Pascal Fardoulis
IS PARIS BURNING?(1966, U.S./Fr.); MATTER OF DAYS, A(1969, Fr./Czech.);
MILKY WAY, THE(1969, Fr./Ital.)
Violet Farebrother
MURDER(1930, Brit.); MYSTERY AT THE VILLA ROSE(1930, Brit.); ENEMY OF
THE POLICE(1933, Brit.); THIS ACTING BUSINESS(1933, Brit.); NINE FORTY-
FIVE(1934, Brit.); IT'S A BET(1935, Brit.); MR. COHEN TAKES A WALK(1936, Brit.);
WHERE'S SALLY?(1936, Brit.); CHANGE FOR A SOVEREIGN(1937, Brit.); IT'S NOT
CRICKET(1937, Brit.); VOICE WITHIN, THE(1945, Brit.); CUP-TIE HONEY-
MOON(1948, Brit.); LOOK BEFORE YOU LOVE(1948, Brit.); MAN OF THE MO-
MENT(1955, Brit.); WOMAN FOR JOE, THE(1955, Brit.); SHE PLAYED WITH
FIRE(1957, Brit.); SOLITARY CHILD, THE(1958, Brit.)
Silents
EASY VIRTUE(1927, Brit.); WHEN BOYS LEAVE HOME(1928, Brit.)
Claude Farell
WOMAN'S ANGLE, THE(1954, Brit.)
Patrick Farelley
NESTING, THE(1981)
Alberto Farenese
WARRIOR EMPRESS, THE(1961, Ital./Fr.)
James Farentino
PAD, THE(AND HOW TO USE IT)* (1966, Brit.); ENSIGN PULVER(1964); PSYCHO-
MANIA(1964); WAR LORD, THE(1965); BANNING(1967); RIDE TO HANGMAN'S
TREE, THE(1967); ROSIE!(1967); ME, NATALIE(1969); STORY OF A WOMAN(1970,
U.S./Ital.); FINAL COUNTDOWN, THE(1980); DEAD AND BURIED(1981)
Paul Farentino
JUST TELL ME WHAT YOU WANT(1980); NIGHTHAWKS(1981)
1984
ONCE UPON A TIME IN AMERICA(1984)
Tony Farentino
SOMEBODY KILLED HER HUSBAND(1978); MIDSUMMER NIGHT'S SEX COME-
DY, A(1982)
Claude Farere
VITELLONI(1956, Ital./Fr.)
Abbas Fares
EGYPT BY THREE(1953)
Jude Farese
NEWMAN'S LAW(1974); KISS ME GOODBYE(1982); LOOKIN' TO GET OUT(1982);
SOME KIND OF HERO(1982)
1984
CITY HEAT(1984)
Misc. Talkies
HOLLYWOOD MAN, THE(1976)
Federico Farfan
MAN CALLED HORSE, A(1970), spec eff; WRATH OF GOD, THE(1972), spec eff
Frederico Farfan
DEVIL'S RAIN, THE(1975, U.S./Mex.), spec eff; RETURN OF A MAN CALLED
HORSE, THE(1976), spec eff
Robert Farfan
ALIAS THE DOCTOR(1932)
Antonio Fargas
PUTNEY SWOPE(1969); BELIEVE IN ME(1971); CISCO PIKE(1971); SHAFT(1971);
ACROSS 110TH STREET(1972); CLEOPATRA JONES(1973); CONRACK(1974); FOXY
BROWN(1974); GAMBLER, THE(1974); CORNBREAD, EARL AND ME(1975); CAR-
WASH(1976); NEXT STOP, GREENWICH VILLAGE(1976); PRETTY BABY(1978); UP
THE ACADEMY(1980)
Derek Farge
MY BROTHER JONATHAN(1949, Brit.)
Steven Fargnoli
1984
PURPLE RAIN(1984), p
Claudia Fargo
FOLIES DERGERE(1935)
George Fargo
KELLY'S HEROES(1970, U.S./Yugo.); DIRTY HARRY(1971); PLAY MISTY FOR
ME(1971); FARMER, THE(1977), w

James Fargo
ENFORCER, THE(1976), d; CARAVANS(1978, U.S./Iranian), d; EVERY WHICH
WAY BUT LOOSE(1978), d; GAME FOR VULTURES, A(1980, Brit.), d; FORCED
VENGEANCE(1982), d
Peter Fargo
ARIZONA KID, THE(1939)
Annie Fargue
LA GUERRE EST FINIE(1967, Fr./Swed.); LA PRISONNIERE(1969, Fr./Ital.); JE
T'AIME, JE T'AIME(1972, Fr./Swed.)
Gabriel Farguette
GLORY OF FAITH, THE(1938, Fr.)
Dick Farham
STUDENT TOUR(1934)
Suhaila Farhat
ADIOS AMIGO(1975)
Moris Farhi
PRIMITIVES, THE(1962, Brit.), w
Bette Faria
BYE-BYE BRASIL(1980, Braz.)
Celso Faria
KILLER FISH(1979, Ital./Braz.)
Reginaldo Faria
TRAIN ROBBERY CONFIDENTIAL(1965, Braz.)
Roberto Farias
TRAIN ROBBERY CONFIDENTIAL(1965, Braz.), p, d, w
Amir Farid
SIAVASH IN PERSEPOLIS(1966, Iran)
Dr. Farid
CONQUEST(1937)
Zaid Farid
FOUR FRIENDS(1981)
Farina
YOU SAID A MOUTHFUL(1932); LIFE OF JIMMY DOLAN, THE(1933); MAYOR OF
HELL, THE(1933)
Farina [Allen Hoskins]
RECKLESS(1935)
Aldo Farina
WHITE SISTER(1973, Ital./Span./Fr.)
Dennis Farina
THIEF(1981)
George Farina
TERROR IN THE WAX MUSEUM(1973)
Mimi Farina
FOOLS(1970)
1984
MASSIVE RETALIATION(1984)
Nino Farina
GRAND PRIX(1966)
Rafael Farina
SPANISH AFFAIR(1958, Span.)
Richard Farina
BEEN DOWN SO LONG IT LOOKS LIKE UP TO ME(1977), w
Sandy Farina
SGT. PEPPER'S LONELY HEARTS CLUB BAND(1978)
Evi Farinelli
MYTH, THE(1965, Ital.)
Massimo Farinelli
DEADLY TRAP, THE(1972, Fr./Ital.)
Gustaf Faringborg
EMIGRANTS, THE(1972, Swed.)
Ernest D. Farino
NIGHTBEAST(1982), spec eff; SPACEHUNTER: ADVENTURES IN THE FORBID-
DEN ZONE(1983), anim
Gabriella Farinon
ASSIGNMENT OUTER SPACE(1960, Ital.); BLOOD AND ROSES(1961, Fr./Ital.)
Faris
TAFFY AND THE JUNGLE HUNTER(1965), ed
Alexander Faris
QUARE FELLOW, THE(1962, Brit.), m; GEORGY GIRL(1966, Brit.), m; HE WHO
RIDES A TIGER(1966, Brit.), m, md
Jim Faris
PHANTOM TOLLBOOTH, THE(1970), ed
William Faris
MR. WASHINGTON GOES TO TOWN(1941), ed; KILLERS FROM SPACE(1954), ed;
TAFFY AND THE JUNGLE HUNTER(1965), p; GUN RIDERS, THE(1969), ed
William J. Faris
GANG BUSTERS(1955), p, ed; MA BARKER'S KILLER BROOD(1960), p
Minou Farjad
SIAVASH IN PERSEPOLIS(1966, Iran)
Joaquin Farjado
AMBUSH BAY(1966)
Herbert Farjean
PAINTED VEIL, THE(1934)
Silents
CAPTIVE GOD, THE(1916)
B. L. Farjeon
Silents
JUST DECEPTION, A(1917, Brit.), w
B.J. Farjeon
Silents
MIRIAM ROZELLA(1924, Brit.), w
Herbert Farjeon
EX-FLAME(1931), w; APRIL IN PARIS(1953)
J. Jefferson Farjeon
NUMBER SEVENTEEN(1928, Brit./Ger.), w; HOUSE OPPOSITE, THE(1931, Brit.),
w; MY FRIEND THE KING(1931, Brit.), w; GHOST CAMERA, THE(1933, Brit.), w;
PHANTOM LIGHT, THE(1935, Brit.), w; LAST JOURNEY, THE(1936, Brit.), w;
LIGHTNING CONDUCTOR(1938, Brit.), w

Jefferson Farjeon
NUMBER SEVENTEEN(1932, Brit.), w
Olivia Farjeon
SMASHING TIME(1967 Brit.)
Violetta Farjeon
SWORD OF LANCELOT(1963, Brit.)
Akos Farkas
TRAPEZE(1932, Ger.), ph; BOEFJE(1939, Ger.), ph
Emil Farkas
FORCE: FIVE(1981), w
Francois Farkas
I EAT YOUR SKIN(1971), ph
Karl Farkas
WONDER BAR(1934), w
Nicholas Farkas
DON QUIXOTE(1935, Fr.), ph
Nicolas Farkas
BATTLE, THE(1934, Fr.), d, w; SHOW GOES ON, THE(1938, Brit.), w
Nikolaus Farkas
MONEY ON THE STREET(1930, Aust.), ph; DANTON(1931, Ger.), ph
Zoltan Farkas
RED AND THE WHITE, THE(1969, Hung./USSR), ed; ROUND UP, THE(1969, Hung.), ed; WINTER WIND(1970, Fr./Hung.), ed
Akos Farkus
OPERATION MANHUNT(1954), ph
Warren Farlan
MRS. PARKINGTON(1944)
Lyn Farleigh
WATERSHIP DOWN(1978, Brit.)
Lynn Farleigh
THREE INTO TWO WON'T GO(1969, Brit.)
Albert Farley
KILL OR BE KILLED(1967, Ital.)
Bob Farley
BADGE 373(1973)
Brian Farley
SMILEY GETS A GUN(1959, Brit.)
Bryan Farley
JOY RIDE(1935, Brit.)
Dorothy Farley
LAW OF THE TONG(1931); ROAD TO RENO, THE(1938)
Dot Farley
THEY WON'T BELIEVE ME(1947); SHOULD A GIRL MARRY?(1929); WHY LEAVE HOME?(1929); HARMONY AT HOME(1930); LITTLE ACCIDENT(1930); ROAD TO PARADISE(1930); THIRD ALARM, THE(1930); DANCING DYNAMITE(1931); WHILE PARIS SLEEPS(1932); DOWN TO THEIR LAST YACHT(1934); LOVE PAST THIRTY(1934); DIAMOND JIM(1935); FALSE PRETENSES(1935); RING AROUND THE MOON(1936); LOVE IS NEWS(1937); TOO MANY WIVES(1937); LAWLESS VALLEY(1938); STRANGER FROM ARIZONA, THE(1938); I STOLE A MILLION(1939); WOMEN, THE(1939); $1,000 A TOUCHDOWN(1939); OBLIGING YOUNG LADY(1941); HAIL THE CONQUERING HERO(1944); SAN FERNANDO VALLEY(1944); FILE ON THELMA JORDAN, THE(1950); MAD WEDNESDAY(1950)
Misc. Talkies
DIVORCE MADE EASY(1929)
Silents
SMALL TOWN IDOL, A(1921); ACQUITTAL, THE(1923); BOY OF MINE(1923); ENEMY SEX, THE(1924); SIGNAL TOWER, THE(1924); SO BIG(1924); MY SON(1925); RUGGED WATER(1925); GRAND DUCHESS AND THE WAITER, THE(1926); LITTLE IRISH GIRL, THE(1926); MEMORY LANE(1926); ALL ABOARD(1927); KING OF KINGS, THE(1927); LOST LIMITED, THE(1927); NOBODY'S WIDOW(1927); HEAD MAN, THE(1928); LADY BE GOOD(1928)
Misc. Silents
LUST OF THE RED MAN, THE(1914); INHERITED PASSIONS(1916); FATAL MISTAKE, THE(1924); LURE OF THE TRACK(1925); TIRED BUSINESS MAN, THE(1927); YOURS TO COMMAND(1927)
Duke Farley
MISTY(1961)
Eddie Farley
MUSIC GOES ROUND, THE(1936)
Elizabeth Farley
DEATH PLAY(1976); AUDREY ROSE(1977); CHAPTER TWO(1979); BLACK MARBLE, THE(1980); SOME KIND OF HERO(1982)
Jackie Farley
MADWOMAN OF CHAILLOT, THE(1969); GAS-S-S-S!(1970)
James Farley
PERFECT CRIME, THE(1928); COURTIN' WILDCATS(1929); DANCE OF LIFE, THE(1929); GODLESS GIRL, THE(1929); VOICE OF THE CITY(1929); DANGER LIGHTS(1930); DYNAMITE(1930); FIGHTING CARAVANS(1931); THREE ROGUES(1931); DEADLINE, THE(1932); SCANDAL FOR SALE(1932); TEXAS CYCLONE(1932); HERE COMES THE GROOM(1934); JEALOUSY(1934); CAPTAIN JANUARY(1935); FRISCO KID(1935); FRONT PAGE WOMAN(1935); HOLD'EM YALE(1935); BRIDE WALKS OUT, THE(1936); DANCING PIRATE(1936); MILKY WAY, THE(1936); PETRIFIED FOREST, THE(1936); SONG OF THE SADDLE(1936); CALIFORNIA MAIL, THE(1937); CALIFORNIAN, THE(1937); GIRL WITH IDEAS, A(1937); ANGELS WITH DIRTY FACES(1938); GOLD IS WHERE YOU FIND IT(1938); PROFESSOR BEWARE(1938); QUICK MONEY(1938); SWEETHEARTS(1938); YOU CAN'T TAKE IT WITH YOU(1938); I STOLE A MILLION(1939); EAST SIDE KIDS(1940); HOUSE ACROSS THE BAY, THE(1940); SANTA FE TRAIL(1940); STRANGER ON THE THIRD FLOOR(1940); DEVIL AND DANIEL WEBSTER, THE(1941); I WANTED WINGS(1941); MY LIFE WITH CAROLINE(1941); RAWHIDE RANGERS(1941); RICHEST MAN IN TOWN(1941); QUIET PLEASE, MURDER(1942); SILVER BULLET, THE(1942); THIS GUN FOR HIRE(1942); FALLEN SPARROW, THE(1943); FRONTIER LAW(1943); NORTHERN PURSUIT(1943); SLEEPY LAGOON(1943); HEAVENLY DAYS(1944); MARSHAL OF GUNSMOKE(1944); IN OLD NEW MEXICO(1945); WONDER MAN(1945); MURDER IN THE MUSIC HALL(1946); POSTMAN ALWAYS RINGS TWICE, THE(1946); WORLD'S GREATEST SINNER, THE(1962)
Misc. Talkies
MIDNIGHT PHANTOM, THE(1935)

Silents
BRIDE'S SILENCE, THE(1917); NUGGET NELL(1919); ALIAS JIMMY VALENTINE(1920); BAR NOTHIN'(1921); GLEAM O'DAWN(1922); LITTLE WILDCAT(1922); TRAVELIN' ON(1922); LODGE IN THE WILDERNESS, THE(1926); KING OF KINGS, THE(1927)
Misc. Silents
SUE OF THE SOUTH(1919); CHALLENGE OF THE LAW, THE(1920); GIRL IN THE RAIN, THE(1920); ONE-MAN TRAIL, THE(1921); WHEN DANGER SMILES(1922); WILD BILL HICKOK(1923); LUCKY LARKIN(1930)
Jim Farley
SAN FRANCISCO(1936); WESTWARD HO(1936); SHE'S DANGEROUS(1937); SUBMARINE D-1(1937); UNION PACIFIC(1939); NOTHING BUT THE TRUTH(1941); GENTLE ANNIE(1944); ROGER TOUHY, GANGSTER!(1944); WHAT A MAN!(1944); THEY WERE EXPENDABLE(1945); LEAVE HER TO HEAVEN(1946)
Silents
GENERAL, THE(1927)
Misc. Silents
HIGHWAY OF HOPE, THE(1917)
Joe Farley
COURTIN' WILDCATS(1929)
Lesley Farley
SMART WOMAN(1948)
Leslie Farley
JIGGS AND MAGGIE IN SOCIETY(1948)
Linda Farley
Misc. Silents
PAY DAY(1918)
Morgan Farley
GREENE MURDER CASE, THE(1929); HALF-MARRIAGE(1929); LOVE DOCTOR, THE(1929); MIGHTY, THE(1929); DEVIL'S HOLIDAY, THE(1930); MAN FROM WYOMING, A(1930); MEN ARE LIKE THAT(1930); ONLY THE BRAVE(1930); SLIGHTLY SCARLET(1930); BELOVED(1934); GENTLEMAN'S AGREEMENT(1947); BEHIND LOCKED DOORS(1948); HOLLOW TRIUMPH(1948); MACBETH(1948); OPEN SECRET(1948); WALLS OF JERICHO(1948); WINNER'S CIRCLE, THE(1948); YOU WERE MEANT FOR ME(1948); ABBOTT AND COSTELLO MEET THE KILLER, BORIS KARLOFF(1949); SPECIAL AGENT(1949); THAT FORSYTE WOMAN(1949); TOP O' THE MORNING(1949); BARRICADE(1950); DOUBLE CROSSBONES(1950); GOODBYE, MY FANCY(1951); LADY FROM TEXAS, THE(1951); MAN WHO CHEATED HIMSELF, THE(1951); SEALED CARGO(1951); STRANGE DOOR, THE(1951); HIGH NOON(1952); MY WIFE'S BEST FRIEND(1952); WILD NORTH, THE(1952); ANGEL FACE(1953); JULIUS CAESAR(1953); REMAINS TO BE SEEN(1953); JIVARO(1954); BAREFOOT EXECUTIVE, THE(1971); SOYLENT GREEN(1973); LAST TYCOON, THE(1976); NICKELODEON(1976); HEAVEN CAN WAIT(1978); SGT. PEPPER'S LONELY HEARTS CLUB BAND(1978); DREAMER(1979)
Pat Farley
NAUGHTY MARIETTA(1935)
Patricia Farley
KING OF THE JUNGLE(1933); PICK-UP(1933); SUNSET PASS(1933); UNDER THE TONTO RIM(1933); GOOD DAME(1934); MERRY WIDOW, THE(1934); BARBARY COAST(1935)
Richard Farley
SUMMER HOLIDAY(1963, Brit.)
Tom Farley
MONEY MOVERS(1978, Aus.)
Walter Farley
BLACK STALLION, THE(1979), w; BLACK STALLION RETURNS, THE(1983), w
LaRue Farlow
AIR PATROL(1962); DON'T WORRY, WE'LL THINK OF A TITLE(1966)
Larve Farlow
I DIED A THOUSAND TIMES(1955)
Warren Farlow
FATHER IS A BACHELOR(1950); GUY WHO CAME BACK, THE(1951); TALK ABOUT A STRANGER(1952); SCANDAL AT SCOURIE(1953)
Wayne Farlow
FATHER IS A BACHELOR(1950); GUY WHO CAME BACK, THE(1951); TALK ABOUT A STRANGER(1952); SCANDAL AT SCOURIE(1953)
Georgiy Farmanyants
LITTLE HUMPBACKED HORSE, THE(1962, USSR)
Art Farmer
I WANT TO LIVE!(1958); SUBTERRANEANS, THE(1960)
Bill Farmer
SASQUATCH(1978), ph, ed
Buddy Farmer
1984
BEAR, THE(1984)
Eloise Farmer
PETTY GIRL, THE(1950)
Ernest Farmer
Misc. Talkies
WOMEN FOR SALE(1975), d
Frances Farmer
BORDER FLIGHT(1936); COME AND GET IT(1936); RHYTHM ON THE RANGE(1936); TOO MANY PARENTS(1936); EBB TIDE(1937); EXCLUSIVE(1937); TOAST OF NEW YORK, THE(1937); RIDE A CROOKED MILE(1938); FLOWING GOLD(1940); SOUTH OF PAGO PAGO(1940); AMONG THE LIVING(1941); BADLANDS OF DAKOTA(1941); WORLD PREMIERE(1941); SON OF FURY(1942); PARTY CRASHERS, THE(1958)
Frank Farmer
WATERMELON MAN(1970); SLUMBER PARTY '57(1977), w; BUDDY BUDDY(1981)
Gary Farmer
1984
POLICE ACADEMY(1984)
Geraldine Farmer
EAST SIDE, WEST SIDE(1949)
Jack Farmer
BRASS LEGEND, THE(1956)
Ken Farmer
SPLIT IMAGE(1982); UNCOMMON VALOR(1983)

Larry Farmer
FAST BREAK(1979)

Mark Farmer
MEMOIRS OF A SURVIVOR(1981, Brit.)

Marva Farmer
EMMA MAE(1976), cos
Misc. Talkies
CANDY TANGERINE MAN, THE(1975)

Michael Farmer
PERFECT UNDERSTANDING(1933, Brit.)

Michele Farmer
MONTE CARLO BABY(1953, Fr.)

Mimsy Farmer
SPENCER'S MOUNTAIN(1963); BUS RILEY'S BACK IN TOWN(1965); DEVIL'S ANGELS(1967); HOT RODS TO HELL(1967); RIOT ON SUNSET STRIP(1967); WILD RACERS, THE(1968); MORE(1969, Luxembourg); ROAD TO SALINA(1971, Fr./Ital.); FOUR FLIES ON GREY VELVET(1972, Ital.); TWO MEN IN TOWN(1973, Fr.); DEATH OF MARIO RICCI, THE(1983, Ital.); GIRL FROM TRIESTE, THE(1983, Ital.)
1984
BASILEUS QUARTET(1984, Ital.); BLACK CAT, THE(1984, Ital./Brit.)
Misc. Talkies
AUTOPSY(1980, Ital.)

Peter Farmer
SORCERESS(1983)

Reginald Farmer
CARWASH(1976)
1984
WILD LIFE, THE(1984)
Misc. Talkies
BABY NEEDS A NEW PAIR OF SHOES(1974)

Reginald H. Farmer
NATIONAL LAMPOON'S ANIMAL HOUSE(1978); WHERE THE BUFFALO ROAM(1980); FAST TIMES AT RIDGEMONT HIGH(1982)

Richard Farmer
GAL WHO TOOK THE WEST, THE(1949); HOLIDAY RHYTHM(1950); I SHOT BILLY THE KID(1950); LEAVE IT TO THE MARINES(1951)

Suzan Farmer
CRIMSON BLADE, THE(1964, Brit.); DEVIL-SHIP PIRATES, THE(1964, Brit.); SQUADRON 633(1964, U.S./Brit.); 633 SQUADRON(1964); DIE, MONSTER, DIE(1965, Brit.); DRACULA-PRINCE OF DARKNESS(1966, Brit.); RASPUTIN-THE MAD MONK(1966, Brit.); WHERE THE BULLETS FLY(1966, Brit.); CARNABY, M.D.(1967, Brit.); PERSECUTION(1974, Brit.)

Virginia Farmer
LUCKY JORDAN(1942); THIS GUN FOR HIRE(1942); HANGMEN ALSO DIE(1943); LADY IN THE DARK(1944); NONE BUT THE LONELY HEART(1944); UP IN ARMS(1944); FATAL WITNESS, THE(1945); STRANGLER OF THE SWAMP(1945); DEADLINE AT DAWN(1946); DECOY(1946); OUR HEARTS WERE GROWING UP(1946); TO EACH HIS OWN(1946); BRUTE FORCE(1947); BURY ME DEAD(1947); JOHNNY O'CLOCK(1947); THAT HAGEN GIRL(1947); ANOTHER PART OF THE FOREST(1948); LET'S LIVE A LITTLE(1948); SECRET BEYOND THE DOOR, THE(1948); FOLLOW ME QUIETLY(1949); GUN CRAZY(1949); SHOCKPROOF(1949); UNDERCOVER MAN, THE(1949); WOMAN'S SECRET, A(1949); BORN TO BE BAD(1950); CAPTAIN CAREY, U.S.A(1950); COMPANY SHE KEEPS, THE(1950); CYRANO DE BERGERAC(1950); MEN, THE(1950); SURRENDER(1950); DARLING, HOW COULD YOU!(1951); TALK ABOUT A STRANGER(1952)

Stavros Farnakis
ISLAND OF LOVE(1963)

Stephanie Farnay
DATE WITH DEATH, A(1959)

John Farndale
MAD MAX(1979, Aus.)

Tom Farndon
BRITANNIA OF BILLINGSGATE(1933, Brit.)

James Farnell
YUKON GOLD(1952)

Ellen Farner
UMBRELLAS OF CHERBOURG, THE(1964, Fr./Ger.)

Alberto Farnese
GOLD OF NAPLES(1957, Ital.); SIGN OF THE GLADIATOR(1959, Fr./Ger./Ital.); WONDERS OF ALADDIN, THE(1961, Fr./Ital.); SIEGE OF SYRACUSE(1962, Fr./Ital.); GLADIATOR OF ROME(1963, Ital.); SULEIMAN THE CONQUEROR(1963, Ital.); THREE FACES OF SIN(1963, Fr./Ital.); QUEEN OF THE NILE(1964, Ital.); LION OF ST. MARK(1967, Ital.)

Andrea Farnese
Misc. Talkies
BODY IS A SHELL, THE(1957)

Giuliano Farnese
EL GRECO(1966, Ital., Fr.)

Tatiana Farnese
SCHOOLGIRL DIARY(1947, Ital.)

Claude Farney
IMMORTAL STORY, THE(1969, Fr.), ed

Joe Farnham
BELLAMY TRIAL, THE(1929), w; MARIANNE(1929), w; SO THIS IS COLLEGE(1929), w; UNHOLY NIGHT, THE(1929), w; BIG HOUSE, THE(1930), w; FREE AND EASY(1930), w; LOVE IN THE ROUGH(1930), w; MONTANA MOON(1930), w; THIRTEENTH CHAIR, THE(1930), titles; WAR NURSE(1930), w; WAY OUT WEST(1930), w
Silents
SOUL MATES(1925), t; BEVERLY OF GRAUSTARK(1926), t; BROWN OF HARVARD(1926), t; EXIT SMILING(1926), t; EXQUISITE SINNER, THE(1926), t; ROAD TO MANDALAY, THE(1926), t; TELL IT TO THE MARINES(1926), t; WANING SEX, THE(1926), t; AFTER MIDNIGHT(1927), t; FAIR CO-ED, THE(1927), t; LONDON AFTER MIDNIGHT(1927), t; MOCKERY(1927), t; ON ZE BOULEVARD(1927), t; RED MILL, THE(1927), t; SLIDE, KELLY, SLIDE(1927), t; TWELVE MILES OUT(1927), t; UNKNOWN, THE(1927), t; ACROSS THE SINGAPORE(1928), t; ACTRESS, THE(1928), t; BIG CITY, THE(1928), t; CROWD, THE(1928), t; FOUR WALLS(1928), t; LATEST FROM PARIS, THE(1928), t; LAUGH, CLOWN, LAUGH(1928), t; TELLING THE WORLD(1928), t; WEST POINT(1928), t; DUKE STEPS OUT, THE(1929), t; FLYING FEET, THE(1929), t; MAN'S MAN, A(1929), t; THUNDER(1929), t; TRAIL OF '98, THE(1929), t; WHERE EAST IS EAST(1929), t

Joseph Farnham
Silents
DIANE OF STAR HOLLOW(1921), w; GREED(1925), t, ed; CAMERAMAN, THE(1928), t; WHILE THE CITY SLEEPS(1928), t

Joseph W. Farnham
Silents
LITTLE 'FRAID LADY, THE(1920), w; AMERICAN MANNERS(1924), t; RECKLESS ROMANCE(1924), t; BIG PARADE, THE(1925), t; BRIGHT LIGHTS(1925), t; HIS SECRETARY(1925), t

Matee Howe Farnham
WAYWARD(1932), w

Joe Farnharm
Silents
WEST OF ZANZIBAR(1928), t

Jeffery Farnol
Silents
MANHATTAN(1924), w

Jeffrey Farnol
AMATEUR GENTLEMAN(1936, Brit.), w
Silents
AMATEUR GENTLEMAN, THE(1920, Brit.), w; AMATEUR GENTLEMAN, THE(1926), w

Robert Farnon
JUST WILLIAM'S LUCK(1948, Brit.), m; ELIZABETH OF LADYMEAD(1949, Brit.), m; SPRING IN PARK LANE(1949, Brit.), m; CAPTAIN HORATIO HORNBLOWER(1951, Brit.), m; CIRCLE OF DANGER(1951, Brit.), m; MAYTIME IN MAYFAIR(1952, Brit.), m; GENTLEMEN MARRY BRUNETTES(1955, m, md); KING'S RHAPSODY(1955, Brit.), md; ALL FOR MARY(1956, Brit.), m; IT'S A WONDERFUL WORLD(1956, Brit.), m; LITTLE HUT, THE(1957), m; TRUE AS A TURTLE(1957, Brit.), m; SHERIFF OF FRACTURED JAW, THE(1958, Brit.), m; ROAD TO HONG KONG, THE(1962, U.S./Brit.), m, md; TRUTH ABOUT SPRING(1965, Brit.), m; SHALAKO(1968, Brit./Can.), m; DISAPPEARANCE, THE(1981, Brit./Can.), m

Shannon Farnon
LEO AND LOREE(1980)

Dick Farnsworth
COWBOYS, THE(1972); LIFE AND TIMES OF JUDGE ROY BEAN, THE(1972); DUCHESS AND THE DIRTWATER FOX, THE(1976)

Dick "Richard" Farnsworth
TEXAS ACROSS THE RIVER(1966); MONTE WALSH(1970); SOUL OF NIGGER CHARLEY, THE(1973)

Don Farnsworth
SQUIRM(1976), spec eff

Doug Farnsworth
RIDIN' DOWN THE TRAIL(1947)

Frank Farnsworth
WOMEN MUST DRESS(1935), w

Hill Farnsworth
PIRANHA(1978); SLAYER, THE(1982), stunts

Jane Farnsworth
10 VIOLENT WOMEN(1982)

Louise Farnsworth
Misc. Silents
MARVELOUS MACISTE, THE(1918, Ital.)

Michael Farnsworth
PERSECUTION AND ASSASSINATION OF JEAN-PAUL MARAT AS PERFORMED BY THE INMATES OF THE ASYLUM OF CHARENTON UNDER THE DIRECTION OF THE MARQUIS DE SADE, THE(1967, Brit.)

Richard Farnsworth
DUEL AT DIABLO(1966); POCKET MONEY(1972); ULZANA'S RAID(1972); ANOTHER MAN, ANOTHER CHANCE(1977 Fr/US); COMES A HORSEMAN(1978); RESURRECTION(1980); TOM HORN(1980); LEGEND OF THE LONE RANGER, THE(1981); RUCKUS(1981); GREY FOX, THE(1983, Can.); INDEPENDENCE DAY(1983)
1984
NATURAL, THE(1984); RHINESTONE(1984)

Richard "Dick" Farnsworth
WALTZ ACROSS TEXAS(1982)

Thomas Farnsworth
UP FROM THE BEACH(1965)

Dennis Farnum
ARRIVEDERCI, BABY!(1966, Brit.), m

Dorothy Farnum
PAGAN, THE(1929), w; UNHOLY NIGHT, THE(1929), w; CALL OF THE FLESH(1930), w; LADY'S MORALS, A(1930), w; REDEMPTION(1930), w; CONSTANT NYMPH, THE(1933, Brit.), w; EVENSONG(1934, Brit.), w; POWER(1934, Brit.), w; LORNA DOONE(1935, Brit.), w; FORBIDDEN TERRITORY(1938, Brit.), w
Silents
CUB, THE(1915); JIM THE PENMAN(1921), w; SALVATION NELL(1921), w; WIFE AGAINST WIFE(1921), w; SECRETS OF PARIS, THE(1922), w; DARLING OF THE RICH, THE(1923), w; JACQUELINE, OR BLAZING BARRIERS(1923), w; LOYAL LIVES(1923), w; MODERN MARRIAGE(1923), w; BABBITT(1924), w; BEAU BRUMMEL(1924), w; DARING YOUTH(1924), w; LOST LADY, A(1924), w; LOVER'S LANE(1924), w; TESS OF THE D'URBERVILLES(1924), w; OFF THE HIGHWAY(1925), w; RECOMPENSE(1925), w; ROSE OF THE WORLD(1925), w; TEMPTRESS(1926), w; TORRENT, THE(1926), w; DIVINE WOMAN, THE(1928), w

Dustin Farnum
BAR 20(1943)
Silents
LIGHTNING CONDUCTOR, THE(1914); SQUAW MAN, THE(1914); VIRGINIAN, THE(1914); CAPTAIN COURTESY(1915); PARSON OF PANAMINT, THE(1916); MAN IN THE OPEN, A(1919); OATH-BOUND(1922); TRAIL OF THE AXE, THE(1922); KENTUCKY DAYS(1923)
Misc. Silents
SOLDIERS OF FORTUNE(1914); CALL OF THE CUMBERLANDS, THE(1915); GENTLEMAN FROM INDIANA, A(1915); IRON STRAIN, THE(1915); BEN BLAIR(1916); DAVID GARRICK(1916); DAVY CROCKETT(1916); SON OF ERIN, A(1916); DURAND OF THE BAD LANDS(1917); NORTH OF FIFTY-THREE(1917); SCARLET PIMPERNEL, THE(1917); SPY, THE(1917); LIGHT OF WESTERN STARS, THE(1918); BIG HAPPINESS(1920); CORSICAN BROTHERS, THE(1920); DEVIL

WITHIN, THE(1921); PRIMAL LAW, THE(1921); IRON TO GOLD(1922); STRANGE IDOLS(1922); WHILE JUSTICE WAITS(1922); YOSEMITE TRAIL, THE(1922); BUCKING THE BARRIER(1923); BUSTER, THE(1923); GRAIL, THE(1923); MAN WHO WON, THE(1923); THREE WHO PAID(1923); MY MAN(1924); FLAMING FRONTIER, THE(1926)

Francis Farnum
CHARLIE CHAN AT THE CIRCUS(1936)

Franklin Farnum
HONOR OF THE RANGE(1934); HOPALONG CASSIDY(1935); IN EARLY ARIZONA(1938); HONEYMOON(1947); KNOCK ON ANY DOOR(1949); UNDERCOVER MAN, THE(1949)

Franklyn Farnum
BEYOND THE RIO GRANDE(1930); THIRD ALARM, THE(1930); LEFTOVER LADIES(1931); OKLAHOMA JIM(1931); THREE ROGUES(1931); 99 WOUNDS(1931); HONOR OF THE PRESS(1932); HUMAN TARGETS(1932); TEXAS BAD MAN(1932); ARIZONA CYCLONE(1934); DEATH OF THE DIAMOND(1934); FRONTIER DAYS(1934); COWBOY AND THE BANDIT, THE(1935); DESERT MESA(1935); FIGHTING CABALLERO(1935); GHOST RIDER, THE(1935); POWDERSMOKE RANGE(1935); FRONTIER JUSTICE(1936); THREE ON THE TRAIL(1936); PLAINSMAN, THE(1937); RANGER COURAGE(1937); PRISON TRAIN(1938); ROLLING CARAVANS(1938); ROMANCE OF THE ROCKIES(1938); STAGECOACH(1939); HOUSE ACROSS THE BAY, THE(1940); TIN PAN ALLEY(1940); LONE STAR LAW MEN(1942); SILVER QUEEN(1942); STARDUST ON THE SAGE(1942); CHEYENNE WILDCAT(1944); HAIL THE CONQUERING HERO(1944); DICK TRACY(1945); SARATOGA TRUNK(1945); STORK CLUB, THE(1945); WEEKEND AT THE WALDORF(1945); JOLSON STORY, THE(1946); SISTER KENNY(1946); FABULOUS TEXAN, THE(1947); MONSIEUR VERDOUX(1947); PERILS OF PAULINE, THE(1947); WELCOME STRANGER(1947); HOLLOW TRIUMPH(1948); I REMEMBER MAMA(1948); JOHNNY BELINDA(1948); MIRACLE OF THE BELLS, THE(1948); RACE STREET(1948); SILVER RIVER(1948); DEAR WIFE(1949); COLT .45(1950); DESTINATION MURDER(1950); MAD WEDNESDAY(1950); SUNSET BOULEVARD(1950); GROOM WORE SPURS, THE(1951); MATING SEASON, THE(1951); BOOTS MALONE(1952); CARRIE(1952); JUST FOR YOU(1952); MEET ME AT THE FAIR(1952); MONTANA BELLE(1952); MY PAL GUS(1952); SOMEBODY LOVES ME(1952); STRANGER WORE A GUN, THE(1953); GUYS AND DOLLS(1955); TEN WANTED MEN(1955); TEN COMMANDMENTS, THE(1956); OH, MEN! OH, WOMEN!(1957); PAL JOEY(1957); KING CREOLE(1958); ROCK-A-BYE BABY(1958)
Misc. Talkies
HELL'S VALLEY(1931); MARK OF THE SPUR(1932); BORDER GUNS(1934); LONE RIDER, THE(1934); WEST ON PARADE(1934); SILVER BULLET, THE(1935)
Silents
ANTHING ONCE(1917); ROUGH LOVER, THE(1918); LAST CHANCE, THE(1921); RAIDERS, THE(1921); STRUGGLE, THE(1921); SO THIS IS ARIZONA(1922); TRAIL'S END(1922); WHEN EAST COMES WEST(1922); BAFFLED(1924); WESTERN VENGEANCE(1924)
Misc. Silents
LOVE NEVER DIES(1916); STRANGER FROM SOMEWHERE, A(1916); BRINGING HOME FATHER(1917); CAR OF CHANCE, THE(1917); CLEAN-UP, THE(1917); CLOCK, THE(1917); DEVIL'S PAY DAY, THE(1917); MAN WHO TOOK A CHANCE, THE(1917); STORMY KNIGHT, A(1917); WINGED MYSTERY, THE(1917); EMPTY CAB, THE(1918); FAST COMPANY(1918); FIGHTING GRIN, THE(1918); IN JUDGEMENT OF(1918); SCARLET CAR, THE(1918); VANITY POOL, THE(1918); $5,000 REWARD(1918); GO GET 'EM GARRINGER(1919); VIRTUOUS MODEL, THE(1919); GALLOPING DEVILS(1920); FIGHTING STRANGER, THE(1921); HUNGER OF THE BLOOD, THE(1921); WHITE MASKS, THE(1921); ANGEL CITIZENS(1922); CROSS ROADS(1922); FIREBRAND, THE(1922); GOLD GRABBERS(1922); GUN SHY(1922); SMILING JIM(1922); TEXAS(1922); IT HAPPENED OUT WEST(1923); MAN GETTER, THE(1923); WOLVES OF THE BORDER(1923); CALIBRE 45(1924); COURAGE(1924); CROSSED TRAILS(1924); DESPERATE ADVENTURE, A(1924); TWO FISTED TENDERFOOT, A(1924); BANDIT TAMER, THE(1925); BORDER INTRIGUE(1925); DOUBLE-BARRELED JUSTICE(1925); DRUG STORE COWBOY(1925); GAMBLING FOOL, THE(1925); ROUGH GOING(1925); TWO GUN SAP(1925)

Geraldine Farnum
MAN FROM OKLAHOMA, THE(1945); SON OF PALEFACE(1952)

Joe Farnum
ALIAS JIMMY VALENTINE(1928), w
Silents
WAR PAINT(1926), t

Marshall Farnum
Silents
SPOILERS, THE(1914)
Misc. Silents
WORMWOOD(1915), d; DRIFTWOOD(1916), d; HOUSE OF MIRRORS, THE(1916), d; MY HUSBAND'S FRIEND(1918), d

Patricia Farnum
KID FROM SPAIN, THE(1932)

Patsy Farnum
42ND STREET(1933)

Peter Farnum
STACY'S KNIGHTS(1983)

William Farnum
DU BARRY, WOMAN OF PASSION(1930); SPOILERS, THE(1930), tech adv; CONNECTICUT YANKEE, A(1931); PAGAN LADY(1931); PAINTED DESERT, THE(1931); TEN NIGHTS IN A BARROOM(1931); DRIFTER, THE(1932); LAW OF THE SEA(1932); MR. ROBINSON CRUSOE(1932); ANOTHER LANGUAGE(1933); FLAMING GUNS(1933); SUPERNATURAL(1933); ARE WE CIVILIZED?(1934); CLEOPATRA(1934); COUNT OF MONTE CRISTO, THE(1934); GOOD DAME(1934); HAPPY LANDING(1934); MARRIAGE ON APPROVAL(1934); SCARLET LETTER, THE(1934); BETWEEN MEN(1935); CRUSADES, THE(1935); POWDERSMOKE RANGE(1935); SCHOOL FOR GIRLS(1935); SILVER STREAK, THE(1935); EAGLE'S BROOD, THE(1936); KID RANGER, THE(1936); GIT ALONG, LITTLE DOGIES(1937); MAID OF SALEM(1937); PUBLIC COWBOY NO. 1(1937); IF I WERE KING(1938); SANTA FE STAMPEDE(1938); SHINE ON, HARVEST MOON(1938); COLORADO SUNSET(1939); MEXICALI ROSE(1939); ROVIN' TUMBLEWEEDS(1939); SOUTH OF THE BORDER(1939); CONVICTED WOMAN(1940); HI-YO SILVER(1940); KIT CARSON(1940); VILLAIN STILL PURSUED HER, THE(1940); CHEERS FOR MISS BISHOP(1941); CORSICAN BROTHERS, THE(1941); GANGS OF SONORA(1941); LAST OF THE DUANES(1941); AMERICAN EMPIRE(1942); BOSS OF HANGTOWN MESA(1942); DEEP IN THE HEART OF TEXAS(1942); LONE STAR RANGER(1942); MEN OF TEXAS(1942); SILVER BULLET, THE(1942); SPOILERS, THE(1942); TISH(1942);

TODAY I HANG(1942); FRONTIER BADMEN(1943); HANGMEN ALSO DIE(1943); MUMMY'S CURSE, THE(1944); CAPTAIN KIDD(1945); WILDFIRE(1945); GOD'S COUNTRY(1946); PERILS OF PAULINE, THE(1947); BRIDE OF VENGEANCE(1949); DAUGHTER OF THE WEST(1949); SAMSON AND DELILAH(1949); TRAIL OF ROBIN HOOD(1950); HOLLYWOOD STORY(1951); JACK AND THE BEANSTALK(1952); LONE STAR(1952)
Misc. Talkies
IRISH GRINGO, THE(1935); LAST ASSIGNMENT, THE(1936)
Silents
SPOILERS, THE(1914); PLUNDERER, THE(1915); END OF THE TRAIL, THE(1916); FIRES OF CONSCIENCE(1916); AMERICAN METHODS(1917); TALE OF TWO CITIES, A(1917); LES MISERABLES(1918); ROUGH AND READY(1918); JUNGLE TRAIL, THE(1919); JOYOUS TROUBLEMAKERS, THE(1920); MOONSHINE VALLEY(1922); SHACKLES OF GOLD(1922)
Misc. Silents
BROKEN LAW, THE(1915); GILDED FOOL, THE(1915); NIGGER, THE(1915); SAMSON(1915); SOLDIER'S OATH, A(1915); WONDERFUL ADVENTURE, THE(1915); BATTLE OF HEARTS(1916); BONDMAN, THE(1916); MAN FROM BITTER ROOTS, THE(1916); MAN OF SORROW, A(1916); CONQUEROR, THE(1917); PRICE OF SILENCE, THE(1917); WHEN A MAN SEES RED(1917); HEART OF A LION, THE(1918); RAINBOW TRAIL, THE(1918); RIDERS OF THE PURPLE SAGE(1918); TRUE BLUE(1918); FOR FREEDOM(1919); LAST OF THE DUANES, THE(1919); LONE STAR RANGER, THE(1919); MAN HUNTER, THE(1919); WINGS OF THE MORNING, THE(1919); WOLVES OF THE NIGHT(1919); ADVENTURER, THE(1920); DRAG HARLAN(1920); HEART STRINGS(1920); IF I WERE KING(1920); ORPHAN, THE(1920); SCUTTLERS, THE(1920); HIS GREATEST SACRIFICE(1921); PERJURY(1921); STAGE ROMANCE, A(1922); WITHOUT COMPROMISE(1922); BRASS COMMANDMENTS(1923); GUNFIGHTER, THE(1923); MAN WHO FIGHTS ALONE, THE(1924)

Frank Faro
Misc. Talkies
MONEY IN MY POCKET(1962)

Lo Faro
LAST OF THE VIKINGS, THE(1962, Fr./Ital.), cos

Naida Faro
Silents
BREAKING POINT, THE(1924)

Nanette Faro
SUICIDE FLEET(1931)

Ninette Faro
ONCE A SINNER(1931)

Sean Faro
1984
STARMAN(1984)

Dorothy Farol
HONEYMOON OF HORROR(1964)

Marie-Ange Farot
1984
SUGAR CANE ALLEY(1984, Fr.)

Ahmed Faroughy
AMBUSH IN LEOPARD STREET(1962, Brit.), w

Olivar Farquat
MY THIRD WIFE GEORGE(1968)

Betty Farquhar
Silents
ONLY A MILL GIRL(1919, Brit.); ROGUE IN LOVE, A(1922, Brit.)
Misc. Silents
LADY AUDLEY'S SECRET(1920, Brit.); SILVER BRIDGE, THE(1920, Brit.); STELLA(1921)

Maisie Farquhar
MACBETH(1971, Brit.)

Malcolm Farquhar
ISLAND RESCUE(1952, Brit.)

Ralph Farquhar
YOUNGBLOOD(1978)

Robert Farquharson
MAN THEY COULDN'T ARREST, THE(1933, Brit.)

Audrey Farr
FLAME OF YOUTH(1949); NOT WANTED(1949)

Bobby Farr
LAND THAT TIME FORGOT, THE(1975, Brit.)

Carl Farr
GALLANT DEFENDER(1935); SONG OF THE SADDLE(1936); SOUTH OF ARIZONA(1938)

Charles Farr
SUTTER'S GOLD(1936)

Christopher Farr
WORLD ACCORDING TO GARP, The(1982)

Derek Farr
CLOUDS OVER EUROPE(1939, Brit.); OUTSIDER, THE(1940, Brit.); QUIET WEDDING(1941, Brit.); VOICE IN THE NIGHT, A(1941, Brit.); SPELL OF AMY NUGENT, THE(1945, Brit.); WANTED FOR MURDER(1946, Brit.); BOND STREET(1948, Brit.); CODE OF SCOTLAND YARD(1948); CONSPIRACY IN TEHERAN(1948, Brit.); QUIET WEEKEND(1948, Brit.); STORY OF SHIRLEY YORKE, THE(1948, Brit.); MAN ON THE RUN(1949, Brit.); SILENT DUST(1949, Brit.); SILK NOOSE, THE(1950, Brit.); MURDER WITHOUT CRIME(1951, Brit.); RELUCTANT HEROES(1951, Brit.); LITTLE BIG SHOT(1952, Brit.); DOUBLE CONFESSION(1953, Brit.); BANG! YOU'RE DEAD(1954, Brit.); EIGHT O'CLOCK WALK(1954, Brit.); FRONT PAGE STORY(1954, Brit.); YOUNG WIVES' TALE(1954, Brit.); DAM BUSTERS, THE(1955, Brit.); DOCTOR AT LARGE(1957, Brit.); MAN IN THE ROAD, THE(1957, Brit.); TOWN ON TRIAL(1957, Brit.); VALUE FOR MONEY(1957, Brit.); TRUTH ABOUT WOMEN(1958, Brit.); CIRCLE, THE(1959, Brit.); ATTEMPT TO KILL(1961, Brit.); PROJECTED MAN, THE(1967, Brit.); 30 IS A DANGEROUS AGE, CYNTHIA(1968, Brit.); POPE JOAN(1972, Brit.)

Felicia Farr
3:10 TO YUMA(1957); FIRST TEXAN, THE(1956); JUBAL(1956); LAST WAGON, THE(1956); REPRISAL(1956); TIMETABLE(1956); ONIONHEAD(1958); HELL BENT FOR LEATHER(1960); KISS ME, STUPID(1964); VENETIAN AFFAIR, THE(1967); KOTCH(1971); CHARLEY VARRICK(1973)

Misc. Talkies
ASYLUM FOR A SPY(1967)

Frankie Farr
NIGHT WORLD(1932)

Glen Farr
RIGHT STUFF, THE(1983), ed

Glenn Farr
FATSO(1980), ed; THIS IS ELVIS(1982), ed
1984
RUNAWAY(1984), ed

Hugh Farr
GALLANT DEFENDER(1935); OLD HOMESTEAD, THE(1935); MYSTERIOUS AVENGER, THE(1936); SONG OF THE SADDLE(1936); OLD WYOMING TRAIL, THE(1937); SOUTH OF ARIZONA(1938); RIO GRANDE(1950)

Jamie Farr
GREATEST STORY EVER TOLD, THE(1965); OUT OF SIGHT(1966); RIDE BEYOND VENGEANCE(1966); WHO'S MINDING THE MINT?(1967); WITH SIX YOU GET EGGROLL(1968); ARNOLD(1973); GONG SHOW MOVIE, THE(1980); CANNONBALL RUN, THE(1981)
1984
CANNONBALL RUN II(1984)

Judi Farr
JUST OUT OF REACH(1979, Aus.)

Karl Farr
MYSTERIOUS AVENGER, THE(1936); OLD WYOMING TRAIL, THE(1937); RIO GRANDE(1950)

Kevin Farr
DEADLY BLESSING(1981)

Kimberly Farr
MISSING(1982)

Lee Farr
TARAWA BEACHHEAD(1958); THUNDERING JETS(1958); TRUE STORY OF LYNN STUART, THE(1958); LONE TEXAN(1959); GUNFIGHTERS OF ABILE-NE(1960)

Lynn Farr
WEST OF SONORA(1948); WHIRLWIND RAIDERS(1948); RIDERS OF THE WHIS-TLING PINES(1949); RIM OF THE CANYON(1949); CALLAWAY WENT THATA-WAY(1951); RED BADGE OF COURAGE, THE(1951)

Michele Farr
MIRACLE WORKER, THE(1962)

Patricia Farr
SECRET CALL, THE(1931); HELLDORADO(1935); LADY IN SCARLET, THE(1935); ORCHIDS TO YOU(1935); LADY LUCK(1936); THREE OF A KIND(1936); ALL-AMERICAN SWEETHEART(1937); CRIMINALS OF THE AIR(1937); GIRLS CAN PLAY(1937); LADY BEHAVE(1937); SPEED TO SPARE(1937); TRADE WINDS(1938); MR. AND MRS. SMITH(1941); NEW WINE(1941); SKYLARK(1941); WEST POINT WIDOW(1941); THIS GUN FOR HIRE(1942); TO THE SHORES OF TRIPOLI(1942)

Pauline Farr
MAN WHO KNEW TOO MUCH, THE(1956)

Randy Farr
BIG HOUSE, U.S.A.(1955)

Tommy Farr
EXCUSE MY GLOVE(1936, Brit.); ALL FOR MARY(1956, Brit.)

Charles Farra
Misc. Silents
STRANGER OF THE HILLS, THE(1922)

Homer Farra
TEXAS RANGERS, THE(1936)

Mina Farragut
ONE NIGHT IN THE TROPICS(1940)

Jan Farrand
DETECTIVE, THE(1968)

Trevor Farrant
PIRATE MOVIE, THE(1982, Aus.), w

Anthony Farrar
SIN YOU SINNERS(1963), d; SWORD AND THE SORCERER, THE(1982)

David Farrar
ROYAL DIVORCE, A(1938, Brit.); SEXTON BLAKE AND THE HOODED TER-ROR(1938, Brit.); SILVER TOP(1938, Brit.); DANNY BOY(1941, Brit.); SHEEPDOG OF THE HILLS(1941, Brit.); DARK TOWER, THE(1943, Brit.); HEADLINE(1943, Brit.); HUNDRED POUND WINDOW, THE(1943, Brit.); NIGHT INVADER, THE(1943, Brit.); SUSPECTED PERSON(1943, Brit.); FOR THOSE IN PERIL(1944, Brit.); MEET SEX-TON BLAKE(1944, Brit.); WORLD OWES ME A LIVING, THE(1944, Brit.); 48 HOURS(1944, Brit.); ECHO MURDERS, THE(1945, Brit.); THEY MET IN THE DARK(1945, Brit.); LISBON STORY, THE(1946, Brit.); TROJAN BROTHERS, THE(1946); BLACK NARCISSUS(1947, Brit.); FRIEDA(1947, Brit.); MR. PERRIN AND MR. TRAILL(1948, Brit.); DIAMOND CITY(1949, Brit.); HOUR OF GLORY(1949, Brit.); CAGE OF GOLD(1950, Brit.); GOLDEN HORDE, THE(1951); OBSESSED(1951, Brit.); WILD HEART, THE(1952, Brit.); NIGHT WITHOUT STARS(1953, Brit.); BLACK SHIELD OF FALWORTH, THE(1954); DUEL IN THE JUNGLE(1954, Brit.); ESCAPE TO BURMA(1955); LET'S MAKE UP(1955, Brit.); PEARL OF THE SOUTH PACI-FIC(1955); SEA CHASE, THE(1955); PURSUIT OF THE GRAF SPEE(1957, Brit.); TEARS FOR SIMON(1957, Brit.); WOMAN AND THE HUNTER, THE(1957); I AC-CUSE(1958, Brit.); JOHN PAUL JONES(1959); SON OF ROBIN HOOD(1959, Brit.); WATUSI(1959); WEBSTER BOY, THE(1962, Brit.); 300 SPARTANS, THE(1962)

Geraldine Farrar
Silents
CARMEN(1915); TEMPTATION(1915); JOAN THE WOMAN(1916); RIDDLE: WOM-AN, THE(1920)
Misc. Silents
MARIA ROSA(1916); TEMPTATION(1916); DEVIL STONE, THE(1917); WOMAN GOD FORGOT, THE(1917); HELL CAT, THE(1918); TURN OF THE WHEEL, THE(1918); FLAME OF THE DESERT(1919); SHADOWS(1919); STRONGER VOW, THE(1919); WORLD AND ITS WOMAN, THE(1919); WOMAN AND THE PUPPET, THE(1920)

Gwen Farrar
SHE SHALL HAVE MUSIC(1935, Brit.); BELOVED IMPOSTER(1936, Brit.); TAKE A CHANCE(1937, Brit.)

James Farrar
COWBOY FROM SUNDOWN(1940); DREAM WIFE(1953)

Jane Farrar
PHANTOM OF THE OPERA(1943); CLIMAX, THE(1944); DOUBLE EX-POSURE(1944); SONG FOR MISS JULIE, A(1945)

Martha Farrar
1984
BOSTONIANS, THE(1984)

Robert Farrar
SCUM OF THE EARTH(1976), m; KEEP MY GRAVE OPEN(1980), m

Scott Farrar
FOES(1977), spec eff

Sonny Farrar
SHE SHALL HAVE MUSIC(1935, Brit.); HALF A SIXPENCE(1967, Brit.); CARRY ON LOVING(1970, Brit.)

Stanley Farrar
FEAR IN THE NIGHT(1947); FRENCH LINE, THE(1954); HOW TO BE VERY, VERY, POPULAR(1955); I'LL CRY TOMORROW(1955); FIRST TRAVELING SALESLADY, THE(1956); BADLANDS OF MONTANA(1957); PORTLAND EXPOSE(1957); FACE OF A FUGITIVE(1959)

Stewart Farrar
IT'S ALL OVER TOWN(1963, Brit.), w

Vince Farrar
SHANGHAI COBRA, THE(1945), ph

Vincent Farrar
BEHIND THAT CURTAIN(1929), ph; DON RICARDO RETURNS(1946), ph; RED DRAGON, THE(1946), ph; BLONDIE IN THE DOUGH(1947), ph; BLONDIE'S ANNI-VERSARY(1947), ph; BLONDIE'S HOLIDAY(1947), ph; CIGARETTE GIRL(1947), ph; FOR THE LOVE OF RUSTY(1947), ph; IT HAD TO BE YOU(1947), ph; 13TH HOUR, THE(1947), ph; BEST MAN WINS(1948), ph; BLONDIE'S REWARD(1948), ph; BLON-DIE'S SECRET(1948), ph; GENTLEMAN FROM NOWHERE, THE(1948), ph; I SUR-RENDER DEAR(1948), ph; MY DOG RUSTY(1948), ph; RUSTY LEADS THE WAY(1948), ph; SONG OF IDAHO(1948), ph; TRIPLE THREAT(1948), ph; BLONDIE HITS THE JACKPOT(1949), ph; BLONDIE'S BIG DEAL(1949), ph; BOSTON BLACK-IE'S CHINESE VENTURE(1949), ph; CRIME DOCTOR'S DIARY, THE(1949), ph; HOLIDAY IN HAVANA(1949), ph; MARY RYAN, DETECTIVE(1949), ph; BEAUTY ON PARADE(1950), ph; BEWARE OF BLONDIE(1950), ph; BLONDIE'S HERO(1950), ph; LAST OF THE BUCCANEERS(1950), ph; PALOMINO, THE(1950), ph; ROOKIE FIREMAN(1950), ph; WHEN YOU'RE SMILING(1950), ph

Vincent J. Farrar
DOWN MISSOURI WAY(1946), ph; QUEEN OF BURLESQUE(1946), ph; STORK BITES MAN(1947), ph

Walton Farrar
SWIFTY(1936), w

Walton T. Farrar
FEUD OF THE WEST(1936), w

Willie Farrar
JEDDA, THE UNCIVILIZED(1956, Aus.)

Bernard Farrel
PASSPORT TO PIMLICO(1949, Brit.); SAADIA(1953)

Brioni Farrel
MY TUTOR(1983)

Georges Farrel
SEA PIRATE, THE(1967, Fr./Span./Ital.), w

Jackie Farrel
MOONLIGHTING WIVES(1966)

John Farrel
BRINK'S JOB, THE(1978)

Paul Farrel
NATE AND HAYES(1983, U.S./New Zealand)

Alfred Farrell
WALLET, THE(1952, Brit.); JUNGLE STREET GIRLS(1963, Brit.)

Brian Farrell
POSTMAN ALWAYS RINGS TWICE, THE(1981)

Brioni Farrell
STUDENT NURSES, THE(1970)

Charles Farrell
RIVER, THE(1928); STREET ANGEL(1928); LUCKY STAR(1929); SUNNY SIDE UP(1929); CITY GIRL(1930); HAPPY DAYS(1930); HIGH SOCIETY BLUES(1930); LILIOM(1930); PRINCESS AND THE PLUMBER, THE(1930); SONG OF SOHO(1930, Brit.); BODY AND SOUL(1931); DELICIOUS(1931); FLYING FOOL, THE(1931, Brit.); GABLES MYSTERY, THE(1931); HEARTBREAK(1931); HOUSE OPPOSITE, THE(1931, Brit.); LIMPING MAN, THE(1931, Brit.); MAN WHO CAME BACK, THE(1931); MERELY MARY ANN(1931); AFTER TOMORROW(1932); FIRST YEAR, THE(1932); LUCKY LADIES(1932, Brit.); MONEY FOR NOTHING(1932, Brit.); TESS OF THE STORM COUNTRY(1932); TONIGHT'S THE NIGHT(1932, Brit.); WHY SAPS LEAVE HOME(1932); WILD GIRL(1932); AGGIE APPLEBY, MAKER OF MEN(1933); GIRL WITHOUT A ROOM(1933); NIGHT AND DAY(1933, Brit.); BIG SHAKEDOWN, THE(1934); CHANGE OF HEART(1934); FIGHTING YOUTH(1935); TWO HEARTS IN HARMONY(1935, Brit.); BOYS WILL BE BOYS(1936, Brit.); FLYING DOCTOR, THE(1936, Aus.); FORBIDDEN HEAVEN(1936); RED WAGON(1936); TROU-BLE AHEAD(1936, Brit.); UNDER PROOF(1936, Brit.); BOMBS OVER LONDON(1937, Brit.); ROMANCE AND RICHES(1937, Brit.); SCOTLAND YARD COMMANDS(1937, Brit.); FLIGHT TO FAME(1938); JUST AROUND THE CORNER(1938); MEET MR. PENNY(1938, Brit.); MOONLIGHT SONATA(1938, Brit.); NIGHT JOURNEY(1938, Brit.); JAILBIRDS(1939, Brit.); REBEL SON, THE ½(1939, Brit.); TAIL SPIN(1939); TREACHERY ON THE HIGH SEAS(1939, Brit.); CONVOY(1940); DEADLY GAME, THE(1941); BELL-BOTTOM GEORGE(1943, Brit.); MEET SEXTON BLAKE(1944, Brit.); DON CHICAGO(1945, Brit.); JOHNNY IN THE CLOUDS(1945, Brit.); THIS MAN IS MINE(1946 Brit.); I BECAME A CRIMINAL(1947); TURNERS OF PROSPECT ROAD, THE(1947, Brit.); NIGHT AND THE CITY(1950, Brit.); MADAME LOUISE(1951, Brit.); THERE WAS A YOUNG LADY(1953, Brit.); FINAL APPOINTMENT(1954, Brit.); HORNET'S NEST, THE(1955, Brit.); SEE HOW THEY RUN(1955, Brit.); STOLEN ASSIGNMENT(1955, Brit.); DEATH OVER MY SHOULDER(1958, Brit.); DIPLOMAT-IC CORPSE, THE(1958, Brit.); SHERIFF OF FRACTURED JAW, THE(1958, Brit.); STRANGE CASE OF DR. MANNING, THE(1958, Brit.); HIDDEN HOMICIDE(1959, Brit.); OPERATION CUPID(1960, Brit.); TOO YOUNG TO LOVE(1960, Brit.); GIRL HUNTERS, THE(1963, Brit.); CHIMES AT MIDNIGHT(1967, Span./Switz.); OH! WHAT A LOVELY WAR(1969, Brit.); VAMPIRE LOVERS, THE(1970, Brit.); COUNTESS DRACULA(1972, Brit.)

Silents
ROSITA(1923); FRESHMAN, THE(1925); OLD IRONSIDES(1926); SANDY(1926); RING, THE(1927, Brit.); ROUGH RIDERS, THE(1927); SEVENTH HEAVEN(1927)
Misc. Silents
CLASH OF THE WOLVES(1925); WINGS OF YOUTH(1925); FAZIL(1928); RED DANCE, THE(1928); STREET ANGEL(1928)

Cliff Farrell
OUTLAWED GUNS(1935), w

Colin Farrell
OH! WHAT A LOVELY WAR(1969, Brit.); LAND THAT TIME FORGOT, THE(1975, Brit.)

Eileen Farrell
INTERRUPTED MELODY(1955)

Eve Farrell
DYNAMITE DELANEY(1938)

Gillian Farrell
I OUGHT TO BE IN PICTURES(1982)

Glenda Farrell
LITTLE CAESAR(1931); I AM A FUGITIVE FROM A CHAIN GANG(1932); LIFE BEGINS(1932); MATCH KING, THE(1932); SCANDAL FOR SALE(1932); THREE ON A MATCH(1932); BUREAU OF MISSING PERSONS(1933); GAMBLING SHIP(1933); GIRL MISSING(1933); GRAND SLAM(1933); HAVANA WIDOWS(1933); KEYHOLE, THE(1933); LADY FOR A DAY(1933); MAN'S CASTLE, A(1933); MARY STEVENS, M.D.(1933); MYSTERY OF THE WAX MUSEUM, THE(1933); BIG SHAKEDOWN, THE(1934); DARK HAZARD(1934); HEAT LIGHTNING(1934); HI, NELLIE!(1934); I'VE GOT YOUR NUMBER(1934); KANSAS CITY PRINCESS(1934); MERRY WIVES OF RENO, THE(1934); PERSONALITY KID, THE(1934); GO INTO YOUR DANCE(1935); GOLD DIGGERS OF 1935(1935); IN CALIENTE(1935); LITTLE BIG SHOT(1935); MISS PACIFIC FLEET(1935); SECRET BRIDE, THE(1935); TRAVELING SALESLADY, THE(1935); WE'RE IN THE MONEY(1935); GOLD DIGGERS OF 1937(1936); HERE COMES CARTER(1936); HIGH TENSION(1936); LAW IN HER HANDS, THE(1936); NOBODY'S FOOL(1936); SNOWED UNDER(1936); ADVENTUROUS BLONDE(1937); BREAKFAST FOR TWO(1937); DANCE, CHARLIE, DANCE(1937); FLY-AWAY BABY(1937); HOLLYWOOD HOTEL(1937); SMART BLONDE(1937); YOU LIVE AND LEARN(1937, Brit.); BLONDES AT WORK(1938); EXPOSED(1938); PRISON BREAK(1938); ROAD TO RENO, THE(1938); STOLEN HEAVEN(1938); TORCHY BLANE IN CHINATOWN(1938); TORCHY GETS HER MAN(1938); TORCHY RUNS FOR MAYOR(1939); JOHNNY EAGER(1942); NIGHT FOR CRIME, A(1942); TALK OF THE TOWN(1942); TWIN BEDS(1942); CITY WITHOUT MEN(1943); EVER SINCE VENUS(1944); KLONDIKE KATE(1944); HEADING FOR HEAVEN(1947); I LOVE TROUBLE(1947); LULU BELLE(1948); MARY LOU(1948); APACHE WAR SMOKE(1952); GIRLS IN THE NIGHT(1953); SECRET OF THE INCAS(1954); SUSAN SLEPT HERE(1954); GIRL IN THE RED VELVET SWING, THE(1955); MIDDLE OF THE NIGHT(1959); DISORDERLY ORDERLY, THE(1964); KISSIN' COUSINS(1964); TIGER BY THE TAIL(1970)

Henry Farrell
WHATEVER HAPPENED TO BABY JANE?(1962), w; HUSH... HUSH, SWEET CHARLOTTE(1964), w; HOSTAGE, THE(1966), w; WHAT'S THE MATTER WITH HELEN?(1971), w; SUCH A GORGEOUS KID LIKE ME(1973, Fr.), w

Jack Farrell
Misc. Silents
POWDER(1916)

James Farrell
1984
PLAGUE DOGS, THE(1984, U.S./Brit.), ph

James T. Farrell
STUDS LONIGAN(1960), w

John Farrell
HONKY TONK(1941); OBLIGING YOUNG LADY(1941); CENTENNIAL SUMMER(1946); DESERT FURY(1947); GUILT OF JANET AMES, THE(1947); PORTRAIT OF JENNIE(1949); WHISTLE AT EATON FALLS(1951); WALK EAST ON BEACON(1952)

Jon Farrell
ACROSS THE BRIDGE(1957, Brit.)

Judy Farrell
J.W. COOP(1971); CHAPTER TWO(1979)

Ken Farrell
HEARTACHES(1947)

Kenneth Farrell
BORDER FEUD(1947); IT'S A JOKE, SON!(1947); PHILO VANCE'S SECRET MISSION(1947)

Leslie Farrell
TENDER IS THE NIGHT(1961); MOVE OVER, DARLING(1963)

Lynn Farrell
PROMISES IN THE DARK(1979); ROCK 'N' ROLL HIGH SCHOOL(1979)

M. Farrell
Silents
GOLD RUSH, THE(1925)

M.J. Farrell
SPRING MEETING(1941, Brit.), w; TREASURE HUNT(1952, Brit.), w

Margaret B. Farrell
MATING SEASON, THE(1951)

Margaret Farrell
THOSE ENDEARING YOUNG CHARMS(1945); GOLDEN EARRINGS(1947)

Marian Farrell
OREGON TRAIL, THE(1936)

Michael Farrell
1984
KILLPOINT(1984)

Mike Farrell
DOOMSDAY MACHINE(1967); PANIC IN THE CITY(1968); TARGETS(1968)

Nellie Farrell
WIFE TAKES A FLYER, THE(1942)

Neyneen Farrell
FROZEN JUSTICE(1929)
Silents
DOLLAR DEVILS(1923)

Nicholas Farrell
CHARRIOTS OF FIRE(1981, Brit.)
1984
GREYSTOKE: THE LEGEND OF TARZAN, LORD OF THE APES(1984)

Pat Farrell
PRINCESS AND THE PIRATE, THE(1944)

Paul Farrell
RIVER OF UNREST(1937, Brit.); MY BROTHER JONATHAN(1949, Brit.); CAPTAIN LIGHTFOOT(1955); RISING OF THE MOON, THE(1957, Ireland); SHAKE HANDS WITH THE DEVIL(1959, Ireland); THIS OTHER EDEN(1959, Brit.); POACHER'S DAUGHTER, THE(1960, Brit.); SIEGE OF SIDNEY STREET, THE(1960, Brit.); ALIVE AND KICKING(1962, Brit.); SHE DIDN'T SAY NO!(1962, Brit.); NEVER PUT IT IN WRITING(1964); DIE, MONSTER, DIE(1965, Brit.); GUNS IN THE HEATHER(1968, Brit.); HOT MILLIONS(1968, Brit.); MRS. BROWN, YOU'VE GOT A LOVELY DAUGHTER(1968, Brit.); SINFUL DAVEY(1969, Brit.); BROTHERLY LOVE(1970, Brit.); MAN WHO HAD POWER OVER WOMEN, THE(1970, Brit.); CLOCKWORK ORANGE, A(1971, Brit.)

Peggy Farrell
TAKING OFF(1971), cos; SENTINEL, THE(1977), cos; OLIVER'S STORY(1978), cos; NATURAL ENEMIES(1979), cos; GLORIA(1980), cos; NIGHT OF THE JUGGLER(1980), cos

Peter Farrell
MOON OVER THE ALLEY(1980, Brit.)

Richard Farrell
TENDER YEARS, THE(1947), ed; GREEN PROMISE, THE(1949), ed; TEXAS LADY(1955), ed; DESIRE IN THE DUST(1960), ed; HORIZONTAL LIEUTENANT, THE(1962), ed; LAST CHALLENGE, THE(1967), ed; SPEEDWAY(1968), ed; SOME KIND OF A NUT(1969), ed; DELTA FACTOR, THE(1970), ed; RABID(1976, Can.); IMPROPER CHANNELS(1981, Can.); SILENCE OF THE NORTH(1981, Can.)
Misc. Silents
BREAKING HOME TIES(1922)

Richard W. Farrell
BACHELOR IN PARADISE(1961), ed; JUMBO(1962), ed

Rusty Farrell
GEORGE WHITE'S SCANDALS(1945); JOHNNY ANGEL(1945)

Shanan Lee Farrell
1984
C.H.U.D.(1984)

Sharon Farrell
FORTY POUNDS OF TROUBLE(1962); SPY WITH MY FACE, THE(1966); LOVELY WAY TO DIE, A(1968); MARLOWE(1969); REIVERS, THE(1969); LOVE MACHINE, THE,(1971); IT'S ALIVE(1974); PREMONITION, THE(1976); FIFTH FLOOR, THE(1980); STUNT MAN, THE(1980); SEPARATE WAYS(1981); OUT OF THE BLUE(1982); LONE WOLF McQUADE(1983); SWEET SIXTEEN(1983)
1984
NIGHT OF THE COMET(1984)

Sondra Farrell
WHAT DID YOU DO IN THE WAR, DADDY?(1966)

Suzanne Farrell
MIDSUMMER NIGHT'S DREAM, A(1966); TURNING POINT, THE(1977)

Tim Farrell
JAIL BAIT(1954)

Timothy Farrell
GLEN OR GLENDA(1953); BLONDE PICKUP(1955)

Tod Farrell
OKLAHOMAN, THE(1957)

Tom Farrell
OUTLAWS OF TEXAS(1950); MARRYING KIND, THE(1952); NIGHT RAIDERS(1952)
1984
PARIS, TEXAS(1984, Ger./Fr.)

Tommy Farrell
AT WAR WITH THE ARMY(1950); DUCHESS OF IDAHO, THE(1950); GUNFIRE(1950); PYGMY ISLAND(1950); ABILENE TRAIL(1951); COLORADO AMBUSH(1951); STARLIFT(1951); STRANGERS ON A TRAIN(1951); STRIP, THE(1951); YANK IN KOREA, A(1951); FLESH AND FURY(1952); MEET DANNY WILSON(1952); YOU FOR ME(1952); FORTY-NINTH MAN, THE(1953); NORTH BY NORTHWEST(1959); WOMAN OBSESSED(1959); SAINTLY SINNERS(1962); SWINGIN' ALONG(1962); MY SIX LOVES(1963); KISSIN' COUSINS(1964); GUIDE FOR THE MARRIED MAN, A(1967)
Misc. Talkies
HIRED GUN(1952); WYOMING ROUNDUP(1952)

Tony Farrell
1984
PHILADELPHIA EXPERIMENT, THE(1984)

Tyra Farrell
SO FINE(1981)

Vessie Farrell
ESCAPADE(1935); HEALER, THE(1935)

William O Farrell
REPEAT PERFORMANCE(1947), w

Kai Farrelli
MY FAIR LADY(1964)

Patrick Farrelly
EXTERMINATOR, THE(1980)

Babs Farren
Misc. Silents
WHERE THE RAINBOW ENDS(1921, Brit.)

Jack Farren
FUZZ(1972), p

Robert Farren
CIAO MANHATTAN(1973), ed

Terry W. Farren
FINAL EXAM(1981)

William Farren
Silents
LA POUPEE(1920, Brit.)

Ann Farrer
AVENGERS, THE(1942, Brit.)
Ernie Farrer
LONG AND THE SHORT AND THE TALL, THE(1961, Brit.), cos; LITTLE ONES, THE(1965, Brit.), cos; RING OF BRIGHT WATER(1969, Brit.), cos
Greta Farrer
PSYCHOPATH, THE(1966, Brit.); DEADLY BEES,THE(1967, Brit.)
Claude Farrere
SACRIFICE OF HONOR(1938, Fr.), w
Cluade Farrere
BATTLE, THE(1934, Fr.), w
Donato Farretta
TANK COMMANDOS(1959)
Lisa Farringer
COFFY(1973); TRUCK TURNER(1974)
Misc. Talkies
KITTY CANT HELP IT(1975); CARHOPS(1980)
Adele Farrington
Silents
COUNTRY MOUSE, THE(1914); IT'S NO LAUGHING MATTER(1915); SCANDAL(1915); LOVE GIRL, THE(1916); PRICE MARK, THE(1917); PUTTING IT OVER(1919); IN OLD KENTUCKY(1920); MOLLYCODDLE, THE(1920); BLACK BEAUTY(1921); CHARM SCHOOL, THE(1921); CONNECTICUT YANKEE AT KING ARTHUR'S COURT, A(1921); HER MAD BARGAIN(1921); CRADLE, THE(1922); LITTLE WILDCAT(1922); ORDEAL, THE(1922); QUESTION OF HONOR, A(1922); GENTLEMAN OF LEISURE, A(1923); ONE STOLEN NIGHT(1923); SCARLET LILY, THE(1923); ALONG CAME RUTH(1924)
Misc. Silents
SUPREME TEST, THE(1915); DEVIL'S BOND WOMAN, THE(1916); HER BITTER CUP(1916); IF MY COUNTRY SHOULD CALL(1916); WHAT LOVE CAN DO(1916); HOUSE OF SILENCE, THE(1918); SCANDAL MONGERS(1918); FUGITIVE FROM MATRIMONY(1919); DON'T EVER MARRY(1920); GIRL IN THE WEB, THE(1920); TOO MUCH JOHNSON(1920); CHILD THOU GAVEST ME, THE(1921); BACHELOR DADDY, THE(1922); BOBBED HAIR(1922); TRAFFIC COP, THE(1926)
Betty Farrington
TRUE TO LIFE(1943); FALL OF EVE, THE(1929); ANYBODY'S WAR(1930); DOWN TO THEIR LAST YACHT(1934); I LIVE FOR LOVE(1935); ONE HOUR LATE(1935); MOON'S OUR HOME, THE(1936); SING ME A LOVE SONG(1936); THEODORA GOES WILD(1936); TRAIL OF THE LONESOME PINE, THE(1936); HOLLYWOOD HOTEL(1937); ACCIDENTS WILL HAPPEN(1938); YOU CAN'T TAKE IT WITH YOU(1938); LET US LIVE(1939); MADE FOR EACH OTHER(1939); OUR NEIGHBORS-THE CARTERS(1939); STRANGER ON THE THIRD FLOOR(1940); FOOTSTEPS IN THE DARK(1941); LADY EVE, THE(1941); SAINT IN PALM SPRINGS, THE(1941); TRIAL OF MARY DUGAN, THE(1941); WHISTLING IN THE DARK(1941); HENRY ALDRICH GETS GLAMOUR(1942); HOME IN WYOMIN'(1942); ICE-CAPADES REVUE(1942); MRS. WIGGS OF THE CABBAGE PATCH(1942); MY FAVORITE BLONDE(1942); MY HEART BELONGS TO DADDY(1942); STARDUST ON THE SAGE(1942); TAKE A LETTER, DARLING(1942); THANK YOUR LUCKY STARS(1943); YOUNG AND WILLING(1943); DOUBLE INDEMNITY(1944); HENRY ALDRICH PLAYS CUPID(1944); OUR HEARTS WERE YOUNG AND GAY(1944); UNINVITED, THE(1944); DUFFY'S TAVERN(1945); GEORGE WHITE'S SCANDALS(1945); NOCTURNE(1946); MY FAVORITE BRUNETTE(1947); SAMSON AND DELILAH(1949); FATHER OF THE BRIDE(1950); LAW AND THE LADY, THE(1951); TOO YOUNG TO KISS(1951); BAND WAGON, THE(1953)
Debbie Farrington
BLACK PANTHER, THE(1977, Brit.)
Frank Farrington
Silents
CLEAN UP, THE(1923); COURTSHIP OF MILES STANDISH, THE(1923)
Misc. Silents
THROUGH TURBULENT WATERS(1915)
Hugh Farrington
1984
TERMINATOR, THE(1984)
Kay Farrington
P.J.(1968)
Kaye Farrington
IN LIKE FLINT(1967)
Ken Farrington
ROBBERY(1967, Brit.)
Kenneth Farrington
KNACK ... AND HOW TO GET IT, THE(1965, Brit.); ONE WAY PENDULUM(1965, Brit.); SUMARINE X-1(1969, Brit.); PARTY PARTY(1983, Brit.)
Mark Farrington
PEACE FOR A GUNFIGHTER(1967)
Wendy Farrington
GRASSHOPPER, THE(1970)
Gianni Farrio
DEATH TOOK PLACE LAST NIGHT(1970, Ital./Ger.), m
Christopher Farris
NUTCRACKER(1982, Brit.)
Evelyn Farris
Silents
MASQUERADERS, THE(1915)
John Farris
BECAUSE THEY'RE YOUNG(1960), w; DEAR, DEAD DELILAH(1972), d&w; FURY, THE(1978), w
Mike Farris
9/30/55(1977)
William Farris
Silents
PENNINGTON'S CHOICE(1915)
Helen Farrish
CINDERELLA SWINGS IT(1942)
Vance Farroll
SCARLET WEEKEND, A(1932)
Julia Farron
ROMEO AND JULIET(1966, Brit.)

Anahita Farroschad
PARSIFAL(1983, Fr.)
Farrow
JOHN PAUL JONES(1959), w
John Charles Farrow
JOHN PAUL JONES(1959)
John Farrow
DANGEROUS WOMAN(1929), w; WHEEL OF LIFE, THE(1929), w; WOLF SONG(1929), w; BAD ONE, THE(1930), w; INSIDE THE LINES(1930), w; SEVEN DAYS LEAVE(1930), w; SHADOW OF THE LAW(1930), w; COMMON LAW, THE(1931), w; WOMAN OF EXPERIENCE, A(1931), w; WOMAN IN CHAINS(1932, Brit.), w; TARZAN ESCAPES(1936), w; MEN IN EXILE(1937), d; SHE LOVED A FIREMAN(1937), d; WEST OF SHANGHAI(1937), d; BROADWAY MUSKETEERS(1938), d; INVISIBLE MENACE, THE(1938), d; LITTLE MISS THOROUGHBRED(1938), d; MY BILL(1938), d; FIVE CAME BACK(1939), d; FULL CONFESSION(1939), d; RENO(1939), d; SAINT STRIKES BACK, THE(1939), d; SORORITY HOUSE(1939), d; WOMEN IN THE WIND(1939), d; BILL OF DIVORCEMENT(1940), d; MARRIED AND IN LOVE(1940), d; COMMANDOS STRIKE AT DAWN(1942), d; WAKE ISLAND(1942), d; CHINA(1943), d; HITLER GANG, THE(1944), d; YOU CAME ALONG(1945), d; CALIFORNIA(1946), d; TWO YEARS BEFORE THE MAST(1946), d; BLAZE OF NOON(1947), d; CALCUTTA(1947), d; EASY COME, EASY GO(1947), d; BEYOND GLORY(1948), d; BIG CLOCK, THE(1948), d; NIGHT HAS A THOUSAND EYES(1948), d; ALIAS NICK BEAL(1949), d; RED, HOT AND BLUE(1949), d, w; COPPER CANYON(1950), d; WHERE DANGER LIVES(1950), d; HIS KIND OF WOMAN(1951), d; SUBMARINE COMMAND(1951), d; BOTANY BAY(1953), d; HONDO(1953), d; KING OF THE KHYBER RIFLES(1953); PLUNDER OF THE SUN(1953), d; RIDE, VAQUERO!(1953), d; BULLET IS WAITING, A(1954), d; SEA CHASE, THE(1955), p&d; AROUND THE WORLD IN 80 DAYS(1956), w; BACK FROM ETERNITY(1956), p&d; UNHOLY WIFE, THE(1957), p&d; FORBIDDEN ISLAND(1959); JOHN PAUL JONES(1959), d
Silents
WHITE GOLD(1927), t; LADIES OF THE MOB(1928), w; FOUR FEATHERS(1929), t
John Villiers Farrow
LAST OF THE PAGANS(1936), w
Mia Farrow
GUNS AT BATASI(1964, Brit.); DANDY IN ASPIC, A(1968, Brit.); ROSEMARY'S BABY(1968); SECRET CEREMONY(1968, Brit.); JOHN AND MARY(1969); SEE NO EVIL(1971, Brit.); DOCTEUR POPAUL(1972, Fr.); PUBLIC EYE, THE(1972, Brit.); GREAT GATSBY, THE(1974); FULL CIRCLE(1977, Brit./Can.); AVALANCHE(1978); DEATH ON THE NILE(1978, Brit.); WEDDING, A(1978); HURRICANE(1979); HAUNTING OF JULIA, THE(1981, Brit./Can.); LAST UNICORN, THE(1982); MIDSUMMER NIGHT'S SEX COMEDY, A(1982); ZELIG(1983)
1984
BROADWAY DANNY ROSE(1984); SUPERGIRL(1984)
Misc. Talkies
SARAH AND THE SQUIRREL(1983)
Moira Farrow
PETERSEN(1974, Aus.)
Robbie Farrow
ABDUCTION(1975), m
Stephanie Farrow
EXPOSED(1983); ZELIG(1983)
Tisa Farrow
HOMER(1970); AND HOPE TO DIE(1972 Fr/US); SOME CALL IT LOVING(1973); ONLY GOD KNOWS(1974, Can.); STRANGE SHADOWS IN AN EMPTY ROOM(1977, Can./Ital.); FINGERS(1978); MANHATTAN(1979); WINTER KILLS(1979); ZOMBIE(1980, Ital.); GRIM REAPER, THE(1981, Ital.); SEARCH AND DESTROY(1981)
1984
LAST HUNTER, THE(1984, Ital.)
Misc. Talkies
BLAZING MAGNUM(1976); STRIKING BACK(1981)
Benny Farrugia
TRENCHCOAT(1983)
Ethel Farrugia
MAGUS, THE(1968, Brit.)
Juan Farsac
SAVAGE PAMPAS(1967, Span./Arg.), makeup
Daniel Farson
ANGRY SILENCE, THE(1960, Brit.)
Daniel Farston
MAD LITTLE ISLAND(1958, Brit.)
Hermione Farthingale
OH! WHAT A LOVELY WAR(1969, Brit.); SONG OF NORWAY(1970); GREAT WALTZ, THE(1972)
Frances Farwell
FRIENDLY PERSUASION(1956)
Leon Fary
Silents
GOLD RUSH, THE(1925)
Carla Faryll
Misc. Talkies
BODY IS A SHELL, THE(1957)
Sergio Fasanelli
WHITE SISTER(1973, Ital./Span./Fr.)
I. Fassant
SLASHER, THE(1975), w
Billy Fasbender
JE T'AIME, JE T'AIME(1972, Fr./Swed.)
Pasquale Fasciano
MAN COULD GET KILLED, A(1966)
Richard Fasciano
GREEK TYCOON, THE(1978)
Mike Fash
BRITTANIA HOSPITAL(1982, Brit.), ph; BETRAYAL(1983, Brit.), ph; RED MONARCH(1983, Brit.), ph
1984
SUCCESS IS THE BEST REVENGE(1984, Brit.), ph

Ruth Fasken
YOUTH WILL BE SERVED(1940), w
Anthony J. Faso
TERMS OF ENDEARMENT(1983), cos
Laurie Faso
HE KNOWS YOU'RE ALONE(1980)
Nina Faso
WILD PARTY, THE(1975)
Tony Faso
OLD BOYFRIENDS(1979), cos
George Fass
NIGHTMARE IN THE SUN(1964), w
Malcon Fassatt
Misc. Silents
HIS FATHER'S WIFE(1919)
Rainer Werner Fassbinder
AMERICAN SOLDIER, THE(1970 Ger.), a, d&w; BITTER TEARS OF PETRA VON KANT, THE(1972, Ger.), p,d&w; EFFI BRIEST(1974, Ger.), d&w; FEAR EATS THE SOUL(1974, Ger.), a, p,d&w; FOX AND HIS FRIENDS(1976, Ger.), a, d, w; MOTHER KUSTERS GOES TO HEAVEN(1976, Ger.), d, w; CHINESE ROULETTE(1977, Ger.), d&w, titles; JAIL BAIT(1977, Ger.), d&w; WHY DOES HERR R. RUN AMOK?(1977, Ger.), d, w, titles; DESPAIR(1978, Ger.), d; GERMANY IN AUTUMN(1978, Ger.), d; MARRIAGE OF MARIA BRAUN, THE(1979, Ger.), a, d, w; IN A YEAR OF THIRTEEN MOONS(1980, Ger.), d,w&ph, ed, art d; LILI MARLEEN(1981, Ger.), a, d; LOLA(1982, Ger.), d, w; VERONIKA VOSS(1982, Ger.), a, d, w; KAMIKAZE '89(1983, Ger.); QUERELLE(1983, Ger./Fr.), d&w
Kris Fasseas
TERROR IN THE JUNGLE(1968)
Jay Fassett
CHEAT, THE(1931); MY SIN(1931); YOUNG AND WILLING(1943)
Julia Fassett
ONE THIRD OF A NATION(1939)
Alvin Fast
BLACK SHAMPOO(1976), p, w; EATEN ALIVE(1976), w; ANGELS BRIGADE(1980), w
Alvin L. Fast
TOM(1973), w; SATAN'S CHEERLEADERS(1977), p, w
Howard Fast
RACHEL AND THE STRANGER(1948), w; SPARTACUS(1960), w; MAN IN THE MIDDLE(1964, U.S./Brit.), w; JIGSAW(1968), w
Russ Fast
HOT LEAD AND COLD FEET(1978)
lp: Russell Fast
Misc. Talkies
STARK RAVING MAD(1983)
Vladimir Fastenko
STAR INSPECTOR, THE(1980, USSR), ph
Boris Fastovich
Silents
NAPOLEON(1927, Fr.)
Oshannah Fastwolf
TRIAL OF BILLY JACK, THE(1974)
Chang Fat
TRAPPED IN A SUBMARINE(1931, Brit.)
Sorata Ra Fat
PASSPORT TO CHINA(1961, Brit.)
Wladimir Faters
LES CARABINIERS(1968, Fr./Ital.)
Natalya Fateyeva
MOSCOW-CASSIOPEIA(1974, USSR)
Jacques Fath
JENNY LAMOUR(1948, Fr.), cos
J. Fathke
FIRST SPACESHIP ON VENUS(1960, Ger./Pol.), w
Giuseppe Fatigati
LAUGH PAGLIACCI(1948, Ital.), d
Fatima
MOONLIGHTING WIVES(1966)
Alexandr Fatiushin
MOSCOW DOES NOT BELIEVE IN TEARS(1980, USSR)
Charles Fatone
Misc. Talkies
SCORING(1980)
Nick Fatool
PETE KELLY'S BLUES(1955)
Fatty George and His Orchestra
$100 A NIGHT(1968, Ger.)
Fatuma
WEST OF ZANZIBAR(1954, Brit.)
William Faucett
SEMINOLE UPRISING(1955)
Cory Faucher
ONE ON ONE(1977)
John Faucher
TAPS(1981)
L. G. Rigby Rene Fauchois
Silents
MONKEY TALKS, THE(1927), w
Rene Fauchois
CHRISTOPHER BEAN(1933), w; BOUDU SAVED FROM DROWNING(1967, Fr.), w
Dan Fauci
BLOODSUCKING FREAKS(1982)
Andrew Faulds
PASSPORT TO TREASON(1956, Brit.); BLOOD OF THE VAMPIRE(1958, Brit.); ONE THAT GOT AWAY, THE(1958, Brit.); PROFESSIONALS, THE(1960, Brit.); S.O.S. PACIFIC(1960, Brit.); MANIA(1961, Brit.); DESERT PATROL(1962, Brit.); MATTER OF WHO, A(1962, Brit.); PAYROLL(1962, Brit.); WHAT EVERY WOMAN WANTS(1962, Brit.); CLEOPATRA(1963); HELLFIRE CLUB, THE(1963, Brit.); JASON AND THE ARGONAUTS(1963, Brit.); CHIMES AT MIDNIGHT(1967, Span.,Switz.); ONE-EYED SOLDIERS(1967, U.S./Brit./Yugo.); CHARGE OF THE LIGHT BRIGADE, THE(1968,

Brit.); MUSIC LOVERS, THE(1971, Brit.); YOUNG WINSTON(1972, Brit.); MAHLER(1974, Brit.)
Jean Faulds
FRENCH LIEUTENANT'S WOMAN, THE(1981)
P.J. Faulener
PARISIAN, THE(1931, Fr.), ph
Wilbur Finley Fauley
Silents
JENNY BE GOOD(1920), w; QUEENIE(1921), w
John Henry Faulk
ALL THE WAY HOME(1963); BEST MAN, THE(1964); LOVIN' MOLLY(1974); LEADBELLY(1976)
Lauritz Faulk
FOREIGN INTRIGUE(1956)
Norman Faulk
CASEY'S SHADOW(1978)
Carl Faulker
LADY LUCK(1946)
Albert Faulkner
MALE ANIMAL, THE(1942)
Alta Faulkner
Silents
IS YOUR DAUGHTER SAFE?(1927)
Avery Faulkner
HILDUR AND THE MAGICIAN(1969)
Carl Faulkner
GREAT HOSPITAL MYSTERY, THE(1937); SAPS AT SEA(1940); FOR BEAUTY'S SAKE(1941); DICK TRACY(1945); CRACK-UP(1946); DEADLINE AT DAWN(1946); SUNSET PASS(1946); CROSSFIRE(1947); WOMAN ON THE BEACH, THE(1947); WINDOW, THE(1949)
David Faulkner
BELL JAR, THE(1979)
Ed Faulkner
MC LINTOCK!(1963); SOMETHING BIG(1971); RIDE IN A PINK CAR(1974, Can.)
Edward Faulkner
LITTLE SHEPHERD OF KINGDOM COME(1961); SERGEANT DEADHEAD(1965); SHENANDOAH(1965); TICKLE ME(1965); NAVY VS. THE NIGHT MONSTERS, THE(1966); GREEN BERETS, THE(1968); HELLFIGHTERS(1968); NOBODY'S PERFECT(1968); SHAKIEST GUN IN THE WEST, THE(1968); HANG YOUR HAT ON THE WIND(1969); UNDEFEATED, THE(1969); CHISUM(1970); RIO LOBO(1970); BAREFOOT EXECUTIVE, THE(1971); SCANDALOUS JOHN(1971); MAN, THE(1972)
Florence Ostern Faulkner
MACABRE(1958), w
Florette Faulkner
Silents
KID, THE(1921)
Gay Faulkner
WIZ, THE(1978)
Graham Faulkner
BROTHER SUN, SISTER MOON(1973, Brit./Ital.); PRIEST OF LOVE(1981, Brit.)
James Faulkner
GREAT WALTZ, THE(1972); ABDICATION, THE(1974, Brit.); CONDUCT UNBECOMING(1975, Brit.); GREAT EXPECTATIONS(1975, Brit.); NIGHT OF THE ASKARI(1978, Ger./South African); ZULU DAWN(1980, Brit.); PRIEST OF LOVE(1981, Brit.); EUREKA(1983, Brit.)
1984
REAL LIFE(1984, Brit.)
Misc. Talkies
ALBINO(1980)
John Faulkner
Misc. Silents
BLUE MOUNTAIN MYSTERY, THE(1922); QUEEN O' TURF(1922); KINGDOM OF TWILIGHT, THE(1929, Brit.)
Keith Faulkner
HAPPIEST DAYS OF YOUR LIFE(1950, Brit.); JOHNNY ON THE RUN(1953, Brit.); SCOTCH ON THE ROCKS(1954, Brit.); NAVY HEROES(1959, Brit.); LINDA(1960, Brit.); TUNES OF GLORY(1960, Brit.); MAN IN THE BACK SEAT, THE(1961, Brit.); PAYROLL(1962, Brit.); POT CARRIERS, THE(1962, Brit.); STRONGROOM(1962, Brit.); DREAM MAKER, THE(1963, Brit.); SINISTER MAN, THE(1965, Brit.)
Lee Faulkner
TOBRUK(1966)
Max Faulkner
HELL, HEAVEN OR HOBOKEN(1958, Brit.); THAT KIND OF GIRL(1963, Brit.); IPCRESS FILE, THE(1965, Brit.); SALT & PEPPER(1968, Brit.); PERFECT FRIDAY(1970, Brit.); SEE NO EVIL(1971, Brit.); DIRTY KNIGHT'S WORK(1976, Brit.)
Norbert Faulkner
LADY WITH RED HAIR(1940), w
Peter Faulkner
CHICAGO 70(1970)
R.A. Faulkner
Misc. Silents
WHY AMERICA WILL WIN(1918)
Ralph Faulkner
THREE MUSKETEERS, THE(1935); PRISONER OF ZENDA, THE(1937); STAR MAKER, THE(1939)
Silents
ANNE OF LITTLE SMOKY(1921); APRIL SHOWERS(1923)
Misc. Silents
GOD OF MANKIND(1928)
Sally Faulkner
HOT MILLIONS(1968, Brit.); BODY STEALERS, THE(1969); VAMPYRES, DAUGHTERS OF DRACULA(1977, Brit.); JAGUAR LIVES(1979)
Stephanie Faulkner
BUS IS COMING, THE(1971); J.D.'S REVENGE(1976); LAS VEGAS LADY(1976); VIRUS(1980, Jap.); HEARTBEEPS(1981); HIGH RISK(1981)
1984
PHILADELPHIA EXPERIMENT, THE(1984)
Misc. Talkies
DEATH JOURNEY(1976)

Tim Faulkner
RUNNERS(1983, Brit.)
Trader Faulkner
KILLER WALKS, A(1952, Brit.); MR. DENNING DRIVES NORTH(1953, Brit.);
QUESTION OF ADULTERY, A(1959, Brit.); SPANISH SWORD, THE(1962, Brit.); BAY
OF SAINT MICHEL, THE(1963, Brit.); MACBETH(1963); HIGH WIND IN JAMAICA,
A(1965); MURDER GAME, THE(1966, Brit.)
Virginia Faulkner
BRIDAL SUITE(1939), w
William Faulkner
STORY OF TEMPLE DRAKE, THE(1933), w; TODAY WE LIVE(1933), w; ROAD TO
GLORY, THE(1936), w; SLAVE SHIP(1937), w; GUNGA DIN(1939), w; TO HAVE AND
HAVE NOT(1944), w; SOUTHERNER, THE(1945), w; BIG SLEEP, THE(1946), w;
INTRUDER IN THE DUST(1949), w; LAND OF THE PHARAOHS(1955), w; TAR-
NISHED ANGELS, THE(1957), w; LONG, HOT SUMMER, THE(1958), w; SOUND
AND THE FURY, THE(1959), w; SANCTUARY(1961), w; REIVERS, THE(1969), w;
TOMORROW(1972), w
Andrew Fauls
CRAWLING EYE, THE(1958, Brit.)
Seagai Faumunina
DIAMOND HEAD(1962)
Kee Faun
OFFERING, THE(1966, Can.)
Richard Faun
TROIKA(1969)
Dian Fauntelle
DOCKS OF NEW ORLEANS(1948); QUEEN FOR A DAY(1951); MODERN MAR-
RIAGE, A(1962)
Diane Fauntelle
TWO BLONDES AND A REDHEAD(1947)
Gabriel Faure
1984
SUNDAY IN THE COUNTRY, A(1984, Fr.), m
John D. Faure
DUEL IN THE SUN(1946), ed; PAROLE, INC.(1949), ed
John Faure
PARADINE CASE, THE(1947), ed; STREET CORNER(1948), ed; INVISIBLE BOY,
THE(1957), ed; MONSTER THAT CHALLENGED THE WORLD, THE(1957), ed; BIG
COUNTRY, THE(1958), ed; LONELYHEARTS(1958), ed
Johnny Faure
VAMPIRE, THE(1957), ed
Licie Faure
TWIST, THE(1976, Fr.), w
Mrs. L. Faure
Silents
LOVE'S PENALTY(1921)
Rene Faure
RASPOUTINE(1954, Fr.)
Renee Faure
BELLMAN, THE(1947, Fr.); GREAT DAWN, THE(1947, Ital.); ANGELS OF THE
STREETS(1950, Fr.); ADORABLE CREATURES(1956, Fr.); JUDGE AND THE ASSAS-
SIN, THE(1979, Fr.)
Bob Faust
DANGEROUS VENTURE(1947)
Charles Faust
UNCOMMON VALOR(1983)
Ed Faust
Silents
ENEMY SEX, THE(1924); NEW LIVES FOR OLD(1925); GENTLEMEN PREFER
BLONDES(1928)
Hella Faust
RED-DRAGON(1967, Ital./Ger./US), ed
Irvin Faust
STEAGLE, THE(1971), w
Louis Faust
KING OF THE WILD HORSES(1947)
Louis R. Faust
PLUNDERERS, THE(1948); HELLFIRE(1949); LAST BANDIT, THE(1949)
Marte Faust
CAREERS(1929); LARCENY WITH MUSIC(1943)
Martin Faust
WHOOPEE(1930); HIGH SPEED(1932); HEIR TO TROUBLE(1936); NORTH STAR,
THE(1943)
Silents
STORK'S NEST, THE(1915); SILENT COMMAND, THE(1923); SPIDER WEBS(1927)
Misc. Silents
BLUE STREAK, THE(1917); I AM THE MAN(1924); HELLO CHEYENE(1928)
Martin J. Faust
Misc. Silents
JANE EYRE(1914), d
Marty Faust
HELL BOUND(1931); TERROR ABOARD(1933); SIX OF A KIND(1934); SOULS AT
SEA(1937); TRUE CONFESSION(1937); HERO FOR A DAY(1939); HOUSE OF THE
SEVEN GABLES, THE(1940); YOU'RE NOT SO TOUGH(1940); PARIS CALLING(1941);
INVISIBLE AGENT(1942); THEY DIED WITH THEIR BOOTS ON(1942); FALLEN
SPARROW, THE(1943)
Matty Faust
SADDLEMATES(1941)
Robert Faust
SELF-PORTRAIT(1973, U.S./Chile), p
Tom Faust
HARD BOILED MAHONEY(1947)
Victoria Faust
LADY OF BURLESQUE(1943); SCARLET CLUE, THE(1945); JOHNNY
O'CLOCK(1947)
Mario Faustinelli
MAGIC WORLD OF TOPO GIGIO, THE(1961, Ital.), w

David Faustino
I OUGHT TO BE IN PICTURES(1982); STAR CHAMBER, THE(1983)
Pedro Faustino
STEEL CLAW, THE(1961); SAMAR(1962)
Randy Faustino
1984
SAM'S SON(1984)
Hampe Faustman
CRIME AND PUNISHMENT(1948, Swed.), a, d; MATTER OF MORALS, A(1961,
U.S./Swed.)
Jacques Fauteux
NIKKI, WILD DOG OF THE NORTH(1961, U.S./Can.)
Ronald Fauteux
WHY ROCK THE BOAT?(1974, Can.), set d; ANGELA(1977, Can.), set d; LITTLE
GIRL WHO LIVES DOWN THE LANE, THE(1977, Can.), set d
Cleo Fauvel
ON VELVET(1938, Brit.)
Suzanne Fauvel
ETERNAL RETURN, THE(1943, Fr.), ed; SYMPHONIE PASTORALE(1948, Fr.), ed
Giuseppina Fava
UNDER THE SUN OF ROME(1949, Ital.)
Otello Fava
WITHOUT PITY(1949, Ital.); SEVEN HILLS OF ROME, THE(1958), makeup; LA
DOLCE VITA(1961, Ital./Fr.), makeup; RELUCTANT SAINT, THE(1962, U.S./Ital.),
makeup; WHITE SLAVE SHIP(1962, Fr./Ital.), makeup; BLACK SABBATH(1963,
Ital.), makeup; 8 ½(1963, Ital.), makeup; JULIET OF THE SPIRITS(1965, Fr./Ital./
W.Ger.), makeup; ROVER, THE(1967, Ital.), makeup; FRAULEIN DOKTOR(1969,
Ital./Yugo.), makeup; NUN AT THE CROSSROADS, A(1970, Ital./Span.), makeup
Suzanne Marie Fava
FAST TIMES AT RIDGEMONT HIGH(1982)
Max Favalelli
LA BELLE AMERICAINE(1961, Fr.); MOST WANTED MAN, THE(1962, Fr./Ital.), w
Robert Favart
GENTLEMEN MARRY BRUNETTES(1955); ROYAL AFFAIRS IN VERSAIL-
LES(1957, Fr.); EXTERMINATORS, THE(1965, Fr.); TRIPLE CROSS(1967, Fr./Brit.);
GODSON, THE(1972, Ital./Fr.); PAUL AND MICHELLE(1974, Fr./Brit.)
Alec Faversham
SHIPBUILDERS, THE(1943, Brit.); GAY INTRUDERS, THE(1946, Brit.); I KNOW
WHERE I'M GOING(1947, Brit.); LOVES OF JOANNA GODDEN, THE(1947, Brit.);
NIGHT COMES TOO SOON(1948, Brit.)
Phil Faversham
BRIGHT VICTORY(1951)
Philip Faversham
FOOTLIGHT PARADE(1933); HOUSE ON 56TH STREET, THE(1933); WORLD
CHANGES, THE(1933); BIG SHAKEDOWN, THE(1934); GAMBLING LADY(1934);
JIMMY THE GENT(1934); MASSACRE(1934); BUTTERFIELD 8(1960); MINX,
THE(1969)
Phillip Faversham
CAPTURED(1933)
William Faversham
LADY BY CHOICE(1934); BECKY SHARP(1935); MYSTERY WOMAN(1935); SE-
CRET OF THE CHATEAU(1935); ARIZONA DAYS(1937); SINGING BUCKAROO,
THE(1937)
Silents
ONE MILLION DOLLARS(1915); SIN THAT WAS HIS, THE(1920)
Misc. Silents
ONE MILLION DOLLARS(1915); RIGHT OF WAY, THE(1915); SILVER KING,
THE(1919); MAN WHO LOST HIMSELF, THE(1920); SIXTH COMMANDMENT,
THE(1924)
Otello Favia
PROMISE AT DAWN(1970, U.S./Fr.), makeup
Sophie Favier
1984
CHEECH AND CHONG'S THE CORSICAN BROTHERS(1984)
Guy Faviere
CHILDREN OF PARADISE(1945, Fr.)
M. Faviere
Silents
NAPOLEON(1927, Fr.)
Guy Favieres
IT HAPPENED AT THE INN(1945, Fr.); PANIQUE(1947, Fr.); EARRINGS OF
MADAME DE..., THE(1954, Fr.)
Gian Luca Favilla
ANOTHER TIME, ANOTHER PLACE(1983, Brit.)
1984
ANOTHER TIME, ANOTHER PLACE(1984, Brit.)
Leonardo Favio
HAND IN THE TRAP, THE(1963, Arg./Span.); TERRACE, THE(1964, Arg.); THE
EAVESDROPPER(1966, U.S./Arg.)
E. M. Favor
Silents
PECK'S BAD GIRL(1918)
Toni Favor
EVE OF ST. MARK, THE(1944)
George Fawcet
Silents
DESTINY'S ISLE(1922); ENEMY, THE(1927)
Bill Fawcett
TUMBLEWEED TRAIL(1946); BLACK HILLS(1948); CHECK YOUR GUNS(1948);
RIDE, RYDER, RIDE!(1949); RUN FOR THE HILLS(1953)
Misc. Talkies
MONTANA INCIDENT(1952)
Bill [William] Fawcett
STARS OVER TEXAS(1946); WILD COUNTRY(1947); TIOGA KID, THE(1948); TALL
MAN RIDING(1955)
Carolyn Fawcett
MY BODY HUNGERS(1967)

Charles Fawcett
ADVENTURES OF CAPTAIN FABIAN(1951); WHEN IN ROME(1952); EGYPT BY THREE(1953); DEVIL'S COMMANDMENT, THE(1956, Ital.); WAR AND PEACE(1956, Ital./U.S.); BOY ON A DOLPHIN(1957); HEAVEN ON EARTH(1960, Ital./U.S.); UNFAITHFULS, THE(1960, Ital.); COME SEPTEMBER(1961); LAST REBEL, THE(1961, Mex.); IT HAPPENED IN ATHENS(1962); LOVES OF SALAMMBO, THE(1962, Fr./Ital.); 300 SPARTANS, THE(1962); NO TIME TO KILL(1963, Brit./Swed./Ger.); WITCH'S CURSE, THE(1963, Ital.); DR. MABUSE'S RAYS OF DEATH(1964, Ger./Fr./Ital.); SAVAGE PAMPAS(1967, Span./Arg.); ONE STEP TO HELL(1969, U.S./Ital./Span.); UNCLE TOM'S CABIN(1969, Fr./Ital./Ger./Yugo.); DOWN THE ANCIENT STAIRCASE(1975, Ital.)

Daniel Fawcett
Misc. Talkies
TEENAGE TEASERS(1982)

Eric Fawcett
LIFE OF THE PARTY(1934, Brit.); THIRD CLUE, THE(1934, Brit.); PAY BOX ADVENTURE(1936, Brit.); LITTLE DOLLY DAYDREAM(1938, Brit.)

Farrah Fawcett
LOVE IS A FUNNY THING(1970, Fr./Ital.); SUNBURN(1979); SATURN 3(1980); CANNONBALL RUN, THE(1981)

Frances Fawcett
HUCKLEBERRY FINN(1974)

George Fawcett
LITTLE WILDCAT, THE(1928); FANCY BAGGAGE(1929); GAMBLERS, THE(1929); HEARTS IN EXILE(1929); HIS CAPTIVE WOMAN(1929); INNOCENTS OF PARIS(1929); LADY OF THE PAVEMENTS(1929); WONDER OF WOMEN(1929); BAD ONE, THE(1930); GREAT DIVIDE, THE(1930); HOT FOR PARIS(1930); LADIES OF LEISURE(1930); MEN ARE LIKE THAT(1930); ONCE A GENTLEMAN(1930); SWING HIGH(1930); WILD COMPANY(1930); DRUMS OF JEOPARDY(1931); PERSONAL MAID(1931); WOMAN OF EXPERIENCE, A(1931)
Silents
HABIT OF HAPPINESS, THE(1916); INTOLERANCE(1916); GREAT LOVE, THE(1918); HEARTS OF THE WORLD(1918); HUN WITHIN, THE(1918); GIRL WHO STAYED AT HOME, THE(1919); I'LL GET HIM YET(1919); OUT OF LUCK(1919); ROMANCE OF HAPPY VALLEY, A(1919); SCARLET DAYS(1919); BAB'S CANDIDATE(1920); BRANDED WOMAN, THE(1920); GREATEST QUESTION, THE(1920); LITTLE MISS REBELLION(1920), a, d; BURN 'EM UP BARNES(1921); HUSH MONEY(1921); LESSONS IN LOVE(1921); NOBODY(1921); SUCH A LITTLE QUEEN(1921), d; WAY OF A MAID, THE(1921); CURSE OF DRINK, THE(1922); EBB TIDE(1922); JOHN SMITH(1922); JAVA HEAD(1923); JUST LIKE A WOMAN(1923); MR. BILLINGS SPENDS HIS DIME(1923); ONLY 38(1923); SALOMY JANE(1923); BEDROOM WINDOW, THE(1924); BREAKING POINT, THE(1924); CODE OF THE SEA(1924); IN EVERY WOMAN'S LIFE(1924); LOST LADY, A(1924); TESS OF THE D'URBERVILLES(1924); FIGHTING CUB, THE(1925); JOANNA(1925); MERRY WIDOW, THE(1925); NINE AND THREE-FIFTHS SECONDS(1925); FLESH AND THE DEVIL(1926); SON OF THE SHEIK(1926); CAPTAIN SALVATION(1927); LOVE(1927); PAINTING THE TOWN(1927); TILLIE THE TOILER(1927); WEDDING MARCH, THE(1927); TEMPEST(1928); FOUR FEATHERS(1929)
Misc. Silents
FRAME-UP, THE(1915); MAJESTY OF THE LAW, THE(1915); CORNER, THE(1916); COUNTRY THAT GOD FORGOT, THE(1916); HEART OF TEXAS RYAN, THE(1917); PANTHEA(1917); SHIRLEY KAYE(1917); BELOVED TRAITOR, THE(1918); CINDERELLA MAN, THE(1918); HOPE CHEST, THE(1918); TALK OF THE TOWN(1918); RAILROADER, THE(1919); TURNING THE TABLES(1919); DANGEROUS BUSINESS(1920); DEADLINE AT ELEVEN(1920), d; IDOLS OF CLAY(1920); TWO WEEKS(1920); CHIVALROUS CHARLEY(1921); FOREVER(1921); LITTLE ITALY(1921); PAYING THE PIPER(1921); SENTIMENTAL TOMMY(1921); HIS WIFE'S HUSBAND(1922); ISLE OF DOUBT(1922); OLD HOMESTEAD, THE(1922); DRUMS OF FATE(1923); HIS CHILDREN'S CHILDREN(1923); WOMAN WITH FOUR FACES, THE(1923); HER LOVE STORY(1924); WEST OF THE WATER TOWER(1924); GO STRAIGHT(1925); HOME MAKER, THE(1925); PEACOCK FEATHERS(1925); SOME PUN'KINS(1925); SPORTING CHANCE, THE(1925); THERE YOU ARE!(1926); TWO CAN PLAY(1926); UNDER WESTERN SKIES(1926); LITTLE FIREBRAND, THE(1927); PRIVATE LIFE OF HELEN OF TROY, THE(1927); RIDING TO FAME(1927); SEE YOU IN JAIL(1927); SNOWBOUND(1927); SPRING FEVER(1927); VALLEY OF THE GIANTS, THE(1927); PROWLERS OF THE SEA(1928); PRINCE OF HEARTS, THE(1929); TIDE OF EMPIRE(1929)

Mrs. George Fawcett
INNOCENTS OF PARIS(1929); RIVER OF ROMANCE(1929)

George W. Fawcett
HELLO SISTER(1930)

James Fawcett
LIVING ON LOVE(1937)

L'Estrange Fawcett
HIGH TREASON(1929, Brit.), p, w; ALF'S BUTTON(1930, Brit.), p, w; BED AND BREAKFAST(1930, Brit.), p; GREAT GAME, THE(1930), p; LATIN LOVE(1930, Brit.), p; BRACELETS(1931, Brit.), p; DOWN RIVER(1931, Brit.), p; HAPPY ENDING, THE(1931, Brit.), p; NO LADY(1931, Brit.), p, w
Silents
SMASHING THROUGH(1928, Brit.), w

Tony Fawcett
MISSIONARY, THE(1982)

William Fawcett
DRIFTIN' RIVER(1946); GHOST TOWN RENEGADES(1947); GREEN DOLPHIN STREET(1947); HIGH WALL, THE(1947); PIONEER JUSTICE(1947); BARBARY PIRATE(1949); ROLL, THUNDER, ROLL(1949); CHAIN GANG(1950); STATE PENITENTIARY(1950); TYRANT OF THE SEA(1950); BIG CARNIVAL, THE(1951); CATTLE QUEEN(1951); COMIN' ROUND THE MOUNTAIN(1951); HILLS OF UTAH(1951); HONEYCHILE(1951); LONGHORN, THE(1951); MAGIC CARPET, THE(1951); MATING SEASON, THE(1951); STAGE TO BLUE RIVER(1951); VALLEY OF FIRE(1951); BARBED WIRE(1952); HAS ANYBODY SEEN MY GAL?(1952); JUNGLE JIM IN THE FORBIDDEN LAND(1952); KANSAS TERRITORY(1952); LION AND THE HORSE, THE(1952); OKLAHOMA ANNIE(1952); SPRINGFIELD RIFLE(1952); HOMESTEADERS, THE(1953); MARKSMAN, THE(1953); STAR OF TEXAS(1953); ALASKA SEAS(1954); LAW VS. BILLY THE KID, THE(1954); YELLOW MOUNTAIN, THE(1954); GANG BUSTERS(1955); LAY THAT RIFLE DOWN(1955); PIRATES OF TRIPOLI(1955); CANYON RIVER(1956); DAKOTA INCIDENT(1956); FIRST TRAVELING SALESLADY, THE(1956); PROUD ONES, THE(1956); BAND OF ANGELS(1957); GUN GLORY(1957); STORM RIDER, THE(1957); TIJUANA STORY, THE(1957); GOOD DAY FOR A HANGING(1958); NO TIME FOR SERGEANTS(1958); WALKING TAR-

GET, THE(1960); GYPSY(1962); MUSIC MAN, THE(1962); SAINTLY SINNERS(1962); WHEELER DEALERS, THE(1963); QUICK GUN, THE(1964); SEX AND THE SINGLE GIRL(1964); KING RAT(1965); JESSE JAMES MEETS FRANKENSTEIN'S DAUGHTER(1966); GNOME-MOBILE, THE(1967); HOSTILE GUNS(1967)

Farrah Fawcett-Majors
LOGAN'S RUN(1976); SOMEBODY KILLED HER HUSBAND(1978)

Michell Fawden
Misc. Talkies
CASS(1977)

Michelle Fawdon
CATHY'S CHILD(1979, Aus.)

White Fawn
Silents
HIS MASTER'S VOICE(1925)

Jesslyn Fax
REAR WINDOW(1954); HOW TO BE VERY, VERY, POPULAR(1955); KISS ME DEADLY(1955); AFFAIR TO REMEMBER, AN(1957); DESK SET(1957); SHOOT-OUT AT MEDICINE BEND(1957); MAN WHO DIED TWICE, THE(1958); NORTH BY NORTHWEST(1959); MUSIC MAN, THE(1962); PARADISE ALLEY(1962); FOUR FOR TEXAS(1963); FAMILY JEWELS, THE(1965); VERY SPECIAL FAVOR, A(1965); GHOST AND MR. CHICKEN, THE(1966); THREE ON A COUCH(1966); GNOME-MOBILE, THE(1967); ANGEL IN MY POCKET(1969); LOVE GOD?, THE(1969)

Peg Fax
WHAT!(1965, Fr./Brit./Ital.), cos

John Faxon
SENSATION HUNTERS(1945), w

Addalyn Fay
WHAT'S UP FRONT(1964)

Ann Fay
VANITY STREET(1932); SOMEWHERE IN SONORA(1933)

Bill Fay
GLADIATORS, THE(1970, Swed.)

Brendan Fay
HUSTLER, THE(1961); MAN ON A SWING(1974)

Frank Fay
MEET THE MAYOR(1938), w

Chris Fay
TREAD SOFTLY STRANGER(1959, Brit.)

Dorothy Fay
LAW OF THE TEXAN(1938); PRAIRIE JUSTICE(1938); STRANGER FROM ARIZONA, THE(1938); LONG SHOT, THE(1939); ROLLIN' WESTWARD(1939); SONG OF THE BUCKAROO(1939); SUNDOWN ON THE PRAIRIE(1939); GLAMOUR FOR SALE(1940); PHILADELPHIA STORY, THE(1940); RAINBOW OVER THE RANGE(1940); NORTH FROM LONE STAR(1941)

Frank Fay
MATRIMONIAL BED, THE(1930); UNDER A TEXAS MOON(1930); BRIGHT LIGHTS(1931); GOD'S GIFT TO WOMEN(1931); STARS OVER BROADWAY(1935); NOTHING SACRED(1937); MEET THE MAYOR(1938), a, p; I WANT A DIVORCE(1940); THEY KNEW WHAT THEY WANTED(1940); SPOTLIGHT SCANDALS(1943); LOVE NEST(1951)

Gaby Fay
I MARRIED A DOCTOR(1936); WHITE ANGEL, THE(1936)

Gaby Fay [Fay Holden]
GUNS OF THE PECOS(1937)

Herbie Fay
COME BLOW YOUR HORN(1963)

Hugh Fay
Silents
ALMOST MARRIED(1919); LITTLE ANNIE ROONEY(1925); SPUDS(1927)
Misc. Silents
FAVOR TO A FRIEND, A(1919)

Janet Fay
FATHER OF THE BRIDE(1950)

Janina Fay
NEVER TAKE CANDY FROM A STRANGER(1961, Brit.)

Jean Fay
HUCKLEBERRY FINN(1974)

Jimmy Fay
MILLION DOLLAR BABY(1935); PRINCESS O'HARA(1935)

Julia Fay
Silents
ADAM'S RIB(1923)

Marston Fay
BACK TO BATAAN(1945), ed; DESPERATE(1947), ed; ROUGHSHOD(1949), ed

Mary Fay
HOUSE DIVIDED, A(1932)

Mary Helen Fay
GIRL NEXT DOOR, THE(1953), w

Ned Fay
DOUBLE-BARRELLED DETECTIVE STORY, THE(1965)

Patricia Fay
GAMBLER, THE(1974)

Randall H. Fay
Silents
DON'T MARRY(1928), w; WOMAN WISE(1928), w

Vivian Fay
DANCE, GIRL, DANCE(1940); MA, HE'S MAKING EYES AT ME(1940); ONE NIGHT IN THE TROPICS(1940); SONG FOR MISS JULIE, A(1945)

Vivien Fay
DAY AT THE RACES, A(1937)

W. G. Fay
BLARNEY KISS(1933, Brit.); GENERAL JOHN REGAN(1933, Brit.); LAST CURTAIN, THE(1937, Brit.); STORM IN A TEACUP(1937, Brit.); SPRING MEETING(1941, Brit.); SPELL OF AMY NUGENT(1945, Brit.); ODD MAN OUT(1947, Brit.); PATIENT VANISHES, THE(1947, Brit.); TEMPTATION HARBOR(1949, Brit.); OLIVER TWIST(1951, Brit.); MY HEART GOES CRAZY(1953, Brit.)

William Fay
GUY WHO CAME BACK, THE(1951), w; CHAMP FOR A DAY(1953), w; KID GALAHAD(1962), w

Elliot Fayad
SPIDER BABY(1968), ed

Alice Faye
GEORGE WHITE'S SCANDALS(1934); NOW I'LL TELL(1934); SHE LEARNED ABOUT SAILORS(1934); 365 NIGHTS IN HOLLYWOOD(1934); EVERY NIGHT AT EIGHT(1935); GEORGE WHITE'S 1935 SCANDALS(1935); MUSIC IS MAGIC(1935); KING OF BURLESQUE(1936); POOR LITTLE RICH GIRL(1936); SING, BABY, SING(1936); STOWAWAY(1936); ON THE AVENUE(1937); WAKE UP AND LIVE(1937); YOU CAN'T HAVE EVERYTHING(1937); YOU'RE A SWEETHEART(1937); ALEXANDER'S RAGTIME BAND(1938); IN OLD CHICAGO(1938); SALLY, IRENE AND MARY(1938); BARRICADE(1939); HOLLYWOOD CAVALCADE(1939); ROSE OF WASHINGTON SQUARE(1939); TAIL SPIN(1939); LILLIAN RUSSELL(1940); LITTLE OLD NEW YORK(1940); TIN PAN ALLEY(1940); GREAT AMERICAN BROADCAST, THE(1941); THAT NIGHT IN RIO(1941); WEEKEND IN HAVANA(1941); GANG'S ALL HERE, THE(1943); HELLO, FRISCO, HELLO(1943); FOUR JILLS IN A JEEP(1944); FALLEN ANGEL(1945); STATE FAIR(1962); WON TON TON, THE DOG WHO SAVED HOLLYWOOD(1976); MAGIC OF LASSIE, THE(1978)

Anita Faye
CARNIVAL LADY(1933); SUCKER MONEY(1933)

Dorothy Faye
TRIGGER PALS(1939)

Eddie Faye
YETI(1977, Ital.)

Frances Faye
DOUBLE OR NOTHING(1937); PRETTY BABY(1978)

Georges Faye
ZAZIE(1961, Fr.)

Gwendolyn Faye
LIGHTNIN'(1930)

Herbie Faye
THOROUGHLY MODERN MILLIE(1967); TOP BANANA(1954); SHRIKE, THE(1955); HARDER THEY FALL, THE(1956); NEVER STEAL ANYTHING SMALL(1959); REQUIEM FOR A HEAVYWEIGHT(1962); THRILL OF IT ALL, THE(1963); DISORDERLY ORDERLY, THE(1964); PATSY, THE(1964); FAMILY JEWELS, THE(1965); FORTUNE COOKIE, THE(1966); ENTER LAUGHING(1967); NIGHT THEY RAIDED MINSKY'S, THE(1968); ANGEL IN MY POCKET(1969); LOVE GOD?, THE(1969); MELVIN AND HOWARD(1980)

Janina Faye
STORY OF ESTHER COSTELLO, THE(1957, Brit.); ADVENTURES OF HAL 5, THE(1958, Brit.); HORROR OF DRACULA, THE(1958, Brit.); DON'T TALK TO STRANGE MEN(1962, Brit.); DAY OF THE TRIFFIDS, THE(1963); DANCE OF DEATH, THE(1971, Brit.); SCHOOL FOR UNCLAIMED GIRLS(1973, Brit.)

Joey Faye
CLOSE-UP(1948); TOP BANANA(1954); TENDER TRAP, THE(1955); HEAR ME GOOD(1957); STREET OF SINNERS(1957); 10 NORTH FREDERICK(1958); THIRTY FOOT BRIDE OF CANDY ROCK, THE(1959); NORTH TO ALASKA(1960); THAT TOUCH OF MINK(1962); FOR LOVE OR MONEY(1963); DIARY OF A BACHELOR(1964); DEAD HEAT ON A MERRY-GO-ROUND(1966); NO WAY TO TREAT A LADY(1968); WHAT'S SO BAD ABOUT FEELING GOOD?(1968); GRISSOM GANG, THE(1971); WAR BETWEEN MEN AND WOMEN, THE(1972); FRONT, THE(1976); HOW TO SUCCEED IN BUSINESS WITHOUT REALLY TRYING(1976)
1984
DELIVERY BOYS(1984); ONCE UPON A TIME IN AMERICA(1984)

Juanina Faye
BEAUTY JUNGLE, THE(1966, Brit.)

Julia Faye
GODLESS GIRL, THE(1929); DYNAMITE(1930); NOT SO DUMB(1930); SQUAW MAN, THE(1931); ONLY YESTERDAY(1933); TILL WE MEET AGAIN(1936); YOU AND ME(1938); UNION PACIFIC(1939); NORTHWEST MOUNTED POLICE(1940); REMEMBER THE NIGHT(1940); REAP THE WILD WIND(1942); SO PROUDLY WE HAIL(1943); CASANOVA BROWN(1944); STORY OF DR. WASSELL, THE(1944); MASQUERADE IN MEXICO(1945); CALIFORNIA(1946); FEAR IN THE NIGHT(1947); PERILS OF PAULINE, THE(1947); UNCONQUERED(1947); WELCOME STRANGER(1947); JOAN OF ARC(1948); NIGHT HAS A THOUSAND EYES(1948); CHICAGO DEADLINE(1949); CONNECTICUT YANKEE IN KING ARTHUR'S COURT, A(1949); RED, HOT AND BLUE(1949); SAMSON AND DELILAH(1949); LAWLESS, THE(1950); SUNSET BOULEVARD(1950); WHERE DANGER LIVES(1950); GREATEST SHOW ON EARTH, THE(1952); TEN COMMANDMENTS, THE(1956)
Silents
OLD WIVES FOR NEW(1918); MALE AND FEMALE(1919); SOMETHING TO THINK ABOUT(1920); AFFAIRS OF ANATOL, THE(1921); NICE PEOPLE(1922); SATURDAY NIGHT(1922); NOBODY'S MONEY(1923); TEN COMMANDMENTS, THE(1923); CORPORAL KATE(1926); VOLGA BOATMAN, THE(1926); KING OF KINGS, THE(1927); YANKEE CLIPPER, THE(1927); CHICAGO(1928)
Misc. Silents
ROADSIDE IMPRESARIO, A(1917); STEPPING OUT(1919); VERY GOOD YOUNG MAN, A(1919); LIFE OF THE PARTY, THE(1920); CHANGING HUSBANDS(1924); HELL'S HIGHROAD(1925); MEET THE PRINCE(1926); HIS DOG(1927); MAIN EVENT, THE(1927); TURKISH DELIGHT(1927)

Julie Faye
COPPER CANYON(1950)

Moudoun Faye
MANDABI(1970, Fr./Senegal)

Patricia Faye
MUSIC HALL PARADE(1939, Brit.)

Randall Faye
HARMONY HEAVEN(1930, Brit.), w; SONG OF SOHO(1930, Brit.), w; BRANDED(1931), w; LASCA OF THE RIO GRANDE(1931), w; HIGH SOCIETY(1932, Brit.), w; LUCKY LADIES(1932, Brit.), w; MC KENNA OF THE MOUNTED(1932), w; TEXAS CYCLONE(1932), w; NAUGHTY CINDERELLA(1933, Brit.), w; FATHER AND SON(1934, Brit.), w; MURDER AT THE INN(1934, Brit.), w; HANDLE WITH CARE(1935, Brit.), p, w; LEND ME YOUR HUSBAND(1935, Brit.), p, w; MAN WITHOUT A FACE, THE(1935, Brit.), p, w; WINDFALL(1935, Brit.), p, w; GAY OLD DOG(1936, Brit.), p, w; IF I WERE RICH(1936, Brit.), p&d; LUCK OF THE TURF(1936, Brit.), p&d; MURDER IN THE OLD RED BARN(1936, Brit.), w; SUCH IS LIFE(1936, Brit.), d; THIS GREEN HELL(1936, Brit.), p,d&w; VANDERGILT DIAMOND MYSTERY, THE(1936, Brit.), p&d; BORN THAT WAY(1937, Brit.), p&d; MR. STRINGFELLOW SAYS NO(1937, Brit.), d, w; SCRUFFY(1938, Brit.), p&d; FACE AT THE WINDOW, THE(1939, Brit.), w; CHEYENNE WILDCAT(1944), w; FIREBRANDS OF ARIZONA(1944), w; RETURN OF THE VAMPIRE, THE(1944), w; GREAT STAGECOACH ROBBERY(1945), w; SCOTLAND YARD INVESTIGATOR(1945, Brit.), w; FABULOUS SUZANNE, THE(1946), w; GHOST GOES WILD, THE(1947), w

Randall H. Faye
SHE LEARNED ABOUT SAILORS(1934), w
Silents
STAGE MADNESS(1927), w; SHARP SHOOTERS(1928), w

Rita Faye
Misc. Talkies
GIRL FROM TOBACCO ROW, THE(1966)

Jacques Fayet
LOLA MONTES(1955, Fr./Ger.)

Adolf Faylauer
AND SO THEY WERE MARRIED(1936)

Adolph Faylauer
CROSSROADS(1942); IT HAPPENED ON 5TH AVENUE(1947)

Adolph Faylaver
FOLIES DERGERE(1935)

Frank Fayle
DUFFY'S TAVERN(1945)

Frank Faylen
BORDER FLIGHT(1936); BULLETS OR BALLOTS(1936); CHINA CLIPPER(1936); DOWN THE STRETCH(1936); GOLDEN ARROW, THE(1936); KING OF HOCKEY(1936); NIGHT WAITRESS(1936); CASE OF THE STUTTERING BISHOP, THE(1937); CHEROKEE STRIP(1937); DANCE, CHARLIE, DANCE(1937); EVER SINCE EVE(1937); KID GALAHAD(1937); MARKED WOMAN(1937); MR. DODD TAKES THE AIR(1937); PUBLIC WEDDING(1937); SAN QUENTIN(1937); SMART BLONDE(1937); TALENT SCOUT(1937); THAT CERTAIN WOMAN(1937); THEY WON'T FORGET(1937); INVISIBLE MENACE, THE(1938); TOO HOT TO HANDLE(1938); GONE WITH THE WIND(1939); IDIOT'S DELIGHT(1939); LUCKY NIGHT(1939); NICK CARTER, MASTER DETECTIVE(1939); NO PLACE TO GO(1939); RENO(1939); STAR MAKER, THE(1939); THUNDER AFLOAT(1939); WATERFRONT(1939); WOMEN IN THE WIND(1939); YOU CAN'T GET AWAY WITH MURDER(1939); CASTLE ON THE HUDSON(1940); CURTAIN CALL(1940); EDISON, THE MAN(1940); FIGHTING 69TH, THE(1940); GRAPES OF WRATH(1940); INVISIBLE STRIPES(1940); MARGIE(1940); MARRIED AND IN LOVE(1940); NO TIME FOR COMEDY(1940); THEY DRIVE BY NIGHT(1940); AFFECTIONATELY YOURS(1941); FOOTSTEPS IN THE DARK(1941); H.M. PULHAM, ESQ.(1941); INTERNATIONAL SQUADRON(1941); KNOCKOUT(1941); LET'S GO COLLEGIATE(1941); MODEL WIFE(1941); NO HANDS ON THE CLOCK(1941); RELUCTANT DRAGON, THE(1941); SERGEANT YORK(1941); TANKS A MILLION(1941); THIEVES FALL OUT(1941); TOP SERGEANT MULLIGAN(1941); UNHOLY PARTNERS(1941); ABOUT FACE(1942); ACROSS THE PACIFIC(1942); JOE SMITH, AMERICAN(1942); PALM BEACH STORY, THE(1942); PRIDE OF THE YANKEES, THE(1942); SOMEWHERE I'LL FIND YOU(1942); STAR SPANGLED RHYTHM(1942); TOUGH AS THEY COME(1942); WAKE ISLAND(1942); YANKEE DOODLE DANDY(1942); FALCON STRIKES BACK, THE(1943); FOLLOW THE BAND(1943); GANG'S ALL HERE, THE(1943); GET GOING(1943); GOOD MORNING, JUDGE(1943); GUY NAMED JOE, A(1943); MISSION TO MOSCOW(1943); MYSTERY OF THE 13TH GUEST, THE(1943); SALUTE FOR THREE(1943); SHE'S FOR ME(1943); SILVER SKATES(1943); SLIGHTLY DANGEROUS(1943); THANK YOUR LUCKY STARS(1943); THAT NAZTY NUISANCE(1943); THREE HEARTS FOR JULIA(1943); YANKS AHOY(1943); ADDRESS UNKNOWN(1944); AND THE ANGELS SING(1944); CANTERVILLE GHOST, THE(1944); SEE HERE, PRIVATE HARGROVE(1944); STANDING ROOM ONLY(1944); AFFAIRS OF SUSAN(1945); BRING ON THE GIRLS(1945); DUFFY'S TAVERN(1945); INCENDIARY BLONDE(1945); LOST WEEKEND, THE(1945); MASQUERADE IN MEXICO(1945); YOU CAME ALONG(1945); BLUE DAHLIA, THE(1946); BLUE SKIES(1946); CALIFORNIA(1946); CROSS MY HEART(1946); IT'S A WONDERFUL LIFE(1946); OUR HEARTS WERE GROWING UP(1946); TO EACH HIS OWN(1946); TWO YEARS BEFORE THE MAST(1946); WELL-GROOMED BRIDE, THE(1946); EASY COME, EASY GO(1947); PERILS OF PAULINE, THE(1947); ROAD TO RIO(1947); SUDDENLY IT'S SPRING(1947); TROUBLE WITH WOMEN, THE(1947); VARIETY GIRL(1947); WELCOME STRANGER(1947); BLOOD ON THE MOON(1948); HAZARD(1948); RACE STREET(1948); WHISPERING SMITH(1948); FRANCIS(1949); CONVICTED(1950); COPPER CANYON(1950); EAGLE AND THE HAWK, THE(1950); NEVADAN, THE(1950); DETECTIVE STORY(1951); FATHER'S LITTLE DIVIDEND(1951); FOURTEEN HOURS(1951); MY FAVORITE SPY(1951); PASSAGE WEST(1951); HANGMAN'S KNOT(1952); LUSTY MEN, THE(1952); SNIPER, THE(1952); 99 RIVER STREET(1953); LONE GUN, THE(1954); RED GARTERS(1954); RIOT IN CELL BLOCK 11(1954); LOOTERS, THE(1955); MC CONNELL STORY, THE(1955); AWAY ALL BOATS(1956); EVERYTHING BUT THE TRUTH(1956); SEVENTH CAVALRY(1956); TERROR AT MIDNIGHT(1956); DINO(1957); GUNFIGHT AT THE O.K. CORRAL(1957); THREE BRAVE MEN(1957); NORTH TO ALASKA(1960); FLUFFY(1965); MONKEY'S UNCLE, THE(1965); WHEN THE BOYS MEET THE GIRLS(1965); FUNNY GIRL(1968)
Misc. Talkies
CITY LIMITS(1941); FATHER STEPS OUT(1941)

Adolph Faylor
Silents
DREAM MELODY, THE(1929)

William Fayman
ESCAPE 2000(1983, Aus.), p

Dorothy Fayne
Misc. Silents
BIGAMIST, THE(1916)

Ida Fayne
Silents
OLD ARM CHAIR, THE(1920, Brit.)

Arthur Faynes
TIM(1981, Aus.)

Lise Fayolle
MEN PREFER FAT GIRLS(1981, Fr.), p; LA VIE CONTINUE(1982, Fr.), p; MOON IN THE GUTTER, THE(1983, Fr./Ital.), p
1984
HEAT OF DESIRE(1984, Fr.), p

Lise Fayolles
I SENT A LETTER TO MY LOVE(1981, Fr.), p

Eleanor Fayre
SONG OF THE FORGE(1937, Brit.)

A. Fayt
DAY THE WAR ENDED, THE(1961, USSR); PEACE TO HIM WHO ENTERS(1963, USSR)

Gloria Faythe
GOLD DIGGERS OF 1933(1933); DAMES(1934)

Edward Fayton
1984
PARIS, TEXAS(1984, Ger./Fr.)

Adrienne Fazan
DUCHESS OF IDAHO, THE(1950), ed

Adrienne Fazan
TWO WEEKS IN ANOTHER TOWN(1962), ed; DAY OF RECKONING(1933), ed; BRIDE WORE RED, THE(1937), ed; YOU'RE ONLY YOUNG ONCE(1938), ed; BARBARY COAST GENT(1944), ed; BETWEEN TWO WOMEN(1944), ed; ANCHORS AWEIGH(1945), ed; SHE WENT TO THE RACES(1945), ed; HOLIDAY IN MEXICO(1946), ed; SECRET HEART, THE(1946), ed; KISSING BANDIT, THE(1948), ed; THREE DARING DAUGHTERS(1948), ed; IN THE GOOD OLD SUMMERTIME(1949), ed; NANCY GOES TO RIO(1950), ed; PAGAN LOVE SONG(1950), ed; AMERICAN IN PARIS, AN(1951), ed; TEXAS CARNIVAL(1951), ed; EVERYTHING I HAVE IS YOURS(1952), ed; SINGIN' IN THE RAIN(1952), ed; GIVE A GIRL A BREAK(1953), ed; I LOVE MELVIN(1953), ed; DEEP IN MY HEART(1954), ed; IT'S ALWAYS FAIR WEATHER(1955), ed; KISMET(1955), ed; INVITATION TO THE DANCE(1956), ed; LUST FOR LIFE(1956), ed; DESIGNING WOMAN(1957), ed; GIGI(1958), ed; RELUCTANT DEBUTANTE, THE(1958), ed; BIG CIRCUS, THE(1959), ed; GAZEBO, THE(1959), ed; SOME CAME RUNNING(1959), ed; BELLS ARE RINGING(1960), ed; FOUR HORSEMEN OF THE APOCALYPSE, THE(1962), ed; COURTSHIP OF EDDY'S FATHER, THE(1963), ed; PRIZE, THE(1963), ed; LOOKING FOR LOVE(1964), ed; 36 HOURS(1965), ed; THIS PROPERTY IS CONDEMNED(1966), ed; WHO'S MINDING THE MINT?(1967), ed; WHERE ANGELS GO...TROUBLE FOLLOWS(1968), ed; WITH SIX YOU GET EGGROLL(1968), ed; COMIC, THE(1969), ed; CHEYENNE SOCIAL CLUB, THE(1970), ed; DON'T GO NEAR THE WATER(1975), ed

Eleanor Fazan
WILL ANY GENTLEMAN?(1955, Brit.); VALUE FOR MONEY(1957, Brit.); INADMISSIBLE EVIDENCE(1968, Brit.); OH! WHAT A LOVELY WAR(1969, Brit.), ch; LADY CAROLINE LAMB(1972, Brit./Ital.), ch; RULING CLASS, THE(1972, Brit.), ch; SAVAGE MESSIAH(1972, Brit.); O LUCKY MAN!(1973, Brit.); YANKS(1979), ch; HEAVEN'S GATE(1980), ch
1984
LASSITER(1984), a, ch

W. Fazan
BREAK THE NEWS(1938, Brit.)

William Fazan
MURDER(1930, Brit.); FLOOD TIDE(1935, Brit.); ONCE IN A NEW MOON(1935, Brit.); YOUNG AND INNOCENT(1938, Brit.); JAMAICA INN(1939, Brit.)

Imre Fazekas
Silents
LOVE ME AND THE WORLD IS MINE(1928), w

Lajos Fazekas
WINTER WIND(1970, Fr./Hung.)

Louise Fazenda
NOAH'S ARK(1928); TERROR, THE(1928); BROADWAY HOOFER, THE(1929); DESERT SONG, THE(1929); HARD TO GET(1929); HOT STUFF(1929); HOUSE OF HORROR(1929); ON WITH THE SHOW(1929); STARK MAD(1929); BRIDE OF THE REGIMENT(1930); HIGH SOCIETY BLUES(1930); LEATHERNECKING(1930); LOOSE ANKLES(1930); NO, NO NANETTE(1930); RAIN OR SHINE(1930); SPRING IS HERE(1930); VIENNESE NIGHTS(1930); WIDE OPEN(1930); CUBAN LOVE SONG, THE(1931); GUN SMOKE(1931); MAD PARADE, THE(1931); MISBEHAVING LADIES(1931); NEWLY RICH(1931); ONCE IN A LIFETIME(1932); RACING YOUTH(1932); UNWRITTEN LAW, THE(1932); ALICE IN WONDERLAND(1933); CARAVAN(1934); WONDER BAR(1934); BAD BOY(1935); BROADWAY GONDOLIER(1935); CASINO MURDER CASE, THE(1935); WINNING TICKET, THE(1935); COLLEEN(1936); DOUGHNUTS AND SOCIETY(1936); I MARRIED A DOCTOR(1936); WIDOW FROM MONTE CARLO, THE(1936); EVER SINCE EVE(1937); FIRST LADY(1937); MERRY-GO-ROUND OF 1938(1937); READY, WILLING AND ABLE(1937); ROAD BACK,THE(1937); DOWN ON THE FARM(1938); SWING YOUR LADY(1938); OLD MAID, THE(1939)
Silents
BULLIN' THE BULLSHEVIKI(1919); BEAUTIFUL AND DAMNED, THE(1922); FOG, THE(1923); GOLD DIGGERS, THE(1923); SPIDER AND THE ROSE, THE(1923); WANTERS, THE(1923); ABRAHAM LINCOLN(1924); LIGHTHOUSE BY THE SEA, THE(1924); COMPROMISE(1925); NIGHT CLUB, THE(1925); BAT, THE(1926); LADIES AT PLAY(1926); MISS NOBODY(1926); OLD SOAK, THE(1926); BABE COMES HOME(1927); GAY OLD BIRD, THE(1927); RED MILL, THE(1927); SAILOR'S SWEETHEART, A(1927); TEXAS STEER, A(1927); OUTCAST(1928); RILEY THE COP(1928); TILLIE'S PUNCTURED ROMANCE(1928); VAMPING VENUS(1928)
Misc. Silents
DOWN ON THE FARM(1920); MARRIED LIFE(1920); BEAUTY SHOP, THE(1922); BEING RESPECTABLE(1924); GALLOPING FISH(1924); LISTEN LESTER(1924); THIS WOMAN(1924); BOBBED HAIR(1925); BROADWAY BUTTERFLY, A(1925); GROUNDS FOR DIVORCE(1925); HOGAN'S ALLEY(1925); LOVE HOUR, THE(1925); PRICE OF PLEASURE, THE(1925); FOOTLOOSE WIDOWS(1926); LADY OF THE HAREM, THE(1926); MILLIONAIRES(1926); PASSIONATE QUEST(1926); CRADLE SNATCHERS, THE(1927); FINGER PRINTS(1927); SIMPLE SIS(1927); DOMESTIC TROUBLES(1928); FIVE AND TEN CENT ANNIE(1928); HEART TO HEART(1928); PAY AS YOU ENTER(1928)

Harry Fazer
RECKONING, THE(1932), w

Dino Fazio
BEN HUR(1959)

Giuseppe Fazio
DANGER: DIABOLIK(1968, Ital./Fr.)

Pippo Fazio
BEST OF ENEMIES, THE(1962)

Salvatore Fazio
SEDUCED AND ABANDONED(1964, Fr./Ital.)

Maurizio Lodi Fe
GIRL WITH A SUITCASE(1961, Fr./Ital.), p

Anna Maria Fea
KELLY'S HEROES(1970, U.S./Yugo.), cos

Hugh Feagin
IN THE YEAR 2889(1966); BULLET FOR PRETTY BOY, A(1970); DON'T LOOK IN THE BASEMENT(1973)

Margaret Fealey
SUMMER HOLIDAY(1948)

Margaret Fealy
LOVE PARADE, THE(1929); RETURN OF DR. FU MANCHU, THE(1930); CROSS-EXAMINATION(1932); ON PROBATION(1935); HOUSE OF THE SEVEN GABLES, THE(1940); MAD YOUTH(1940); WOLF MAN, THE(1941); THIS LAND IS MINE(1943); JAM SESSION(1944)

Maude Fealy
LAUGH AND GET RICH(1931); UNION PACIFIC(1939); UNFAITHFUL, THE(1947)
Silents
AMERICAN CONSUL, THE(1917)
Misc. Silents
MOTHS(1913); FROU FROU(1914); BONDWOMEN(1915); IMMORTAL FLAME, THE(1916); PAMELA'S PAST(1916)

Maue Fealy
DOUBLE LIFE, A(1947)

Kenneth Fearing
BIG CLOCK, THE(1948), w

Sheila Fearn
HAVING A WILD WEEKEND(1965, Brit.); LIKELY LADS, THE(1976, Brit.); GEORGE AND MILDRED(1980, Brit.); TIME BANDITS(1981, Brit.)

Cecil Fearnley
Misc. Silents
CELESTIAL CITY, THE(1929, Brit.)

Jane Fearnley
Silents
CHRISTIAN, THE(1914); LITTLE GRAY LADY, THE(1914); ETERNAL SIN, THE(1917)
Misc. Silents
MARBLE HEART, THE(1915)

Jane Fearnly
Silents
SCALES OF JUSTICE, THE(1914)

Peggy Fears
LOTTERY LOVER(1935)

Michael Feast
I START COUNTING(1970, Brit.); PRIVATE ROAD(1971, Brit.), a, m; BROTHER SUN, SISTER MOON(1973, Brit./Ital.); MC VICAR(1982, Brit.); DRAUGHTSMAN'S CONTRACT, THE(1983, Brit.)

Mickey Feast
MUSIC MACHINE, THE(1979, Brit.)

Feather Hat, Jr.
SEARCHERS, THE(1956)

Eddie Featherston
WORLDLY GOODS(1930); MY MAN GODFREY(1936); SHADOWS OF THE ORIENT(1937); THEY DRIVE BY NIGHT(1940)
Misc. Talkies
CROOKED ROAD(1932); CALLING ALL CARS(1935)

Ed Featherstone
IT'S A WONDERFUL LIFE(1946)

Eddie Featherstone
MARKED MEN(1940); PHANTOM THIEF, THE(1946)

Edward Featherstone
GIRL FROM CALGARY(1932)

Mark Featherstone-Witty
Misc. Talkies
DEADLY ENCOUNTER(1979)

Jean Featy
SPICE OF LIFE(1954, Fr.), ed

Christian Feazell
PSYCHO FROM TEXAS(1982)

Jim Feazell
HARD TRAIL(1969); FANDANGO(1970); PSYCHO FROM TEXAS(1982), p,d&w

Febe
CHILDREN OF CHANCE(1949, Brit.)

Kurt Fecher
BIG SHOW, THE(1961)

Ellen Fechner
FILM WITHOUT A NAME(1950, Ger.), w

Rick Feck
TRON(1982)

Marjorie Fectean
FOLLOW THE BOYS(1944)

Frank Feda
DIRTYMOUTH(1970)

Zhenya Fedchenko
VIOLIN AND ROLLER(1962, USSR)

Leander Fedden
SUMMER HOLIDAY(1963, Brit.)

Jan Fedder
DAS BOOT(1982)

Helga Feddersen
LOLA(1982, Ger.)

Sally Fedem
DARK SIDE OF TOMORROW, THE(1970)

I. Feder
Silents
SEVEN SISTERS, THE(1915)

Moishe Feder
Misc. Talkies
MIRELE EFROS(1939)

Sid Feder
MURDER, INC.(1960), w

Feder Sisters
CATSKILL HONEYMOON(1950)
Henry Federer
LOOKING GLASS WAR, THE(1970, Brit.), set d
Chuck Federico
Misc. Talkies
BACCHANALE(1970)
Tony Federico
EYES OF A STRANGER(1980)
V.F. Federov
HOUSE OF DEATH(1932, USSR), d
Reginald Federson
GREEN PASTURES(1936)
Birgitte Federspiel
ORDET(1957, Den.); STRANGER KNOCKS, A(1963, Den.); SUDDENLY, A WO-MAN!(1967, Den.); HAGBARD AND SIGNE(1968, Den./Iceland/Swed.); HUN-GER(1968, Den./Norway/Swed.); Z.P.G.(1972)
Egner Federspiel
COUNTERFEIT TRAITOR, THE(1962)
Ejner Federspiel
ORDET(1957, Den.)
K. Fedicheva
SLEEPING BEAUTY, THE(1966, USSR)
Tania Fedor
CROSSROADS(1938, Fr.); OPEN ROAD, THE(1940, Fr.); STRANGERS IN THE HOUSE(1949, Fr.); LUCRECE BORGIA(1953, Ital./Fr.); ROYAL AFFAIRS IN VER-SAILLES(1957, Fr.); TAKE IT ALL(1966, Can.)
Serge Fedoroff
1984
CHEECH AND CHONG'S THE CORSICAN BROTHERS(1984)
Irina Fedorova
NO GREATER LOVE(1944, USSR)
Z. Fedorova
GREAT CITIZEN, THE(1939, USSR)
Zoya Fedorova
MOSCOW DOES NOT BELIEVE IN TEARS(1980, USSR)
F. Fedorovskiy
HAMLET(1966, USSR)
J. Fedorowicz
WALKOVER(1969, Pol.)
Boris Fedotoff
FOLIES DERGERE(1935)
Dimitry Fedotoff
JOURNEY, THE(1959, U.S./Aust.)
D. Fedov
LULLABY(1961, USSR), m
Bertha Feducah
HEAVENLY DAYS(1944)
Berta Feducha
JULIA MISBEHAVES(1948)
Bertha Feducha
MRS. PARKINGTON(1944); STORY OF THREE LOVES, THE(1953)
Marion Feducha
Silents
KINGDOM WITHIN, THE(1922)
Misc. Silents
WHY WOMEN REMARRY(1923)
John Fee
SISTERS(1930)
Kathleen Fee
VISITING HOURS(1982, Can.)
Luk Won Fee
GOLDEN GATE GIRL(1941)
Melinda Fee
MOTHER GOOSE A GO-GO(1966); FADE TO BLACK(1980)
Vicki Fee
OUT OF SIGHT(1966)
Terence Feel
PERCY(1971, Brit.), w
Peter Feeley
1984
TAIL OF THE TIGER(1984, Aus.)
Terence Feely
QUEST FOR LOVE(1971, Brit.), w
Mona Feeman
GREATEST SHOW ON EARTH, THE(1952)
Francis Feeney
Silents
K-THE UNKNOWN(1924)
Misc. Silents
LITTLE MISS HAWKSHAW(1921), d
John Feeney
LIFE STUDY(1973)
Robert Feero
THX 1138(1971)
Katha Feffer
1984
UP THE CREEK(1984)
Jack Fegan
PICNIC AT HANGING ROCK(1975, Aus.)
John Fegan
OVERLANDERS, THE(1946, Brit./Aus.); MASSACRE HILL(1949, Brit.); KAN-GAROO(1952); SMILEY GETS A GUN(1959, Brit.)
Jorge Fegan
1984
ERENDIRA(1984, Mex./Fr./Ger.)
Ernest Fegte
BIRTH OF THE BLUES(1941), art d; ANGEL AND THE BADMAN(1947), art d; MODELS, INC.(1952), art d; STAGECOACH TO FURY(1956), art d; GOD IS MY PARTNER(1957), art d

Silents
WOMANHANDLED(1925), ed
Ernst Fegte
KISS AND MAKE UP(1934), art d; LADIES SHOULD LISTEN(1934), art d; WE'RE NOT DRESSING(1934), art d; ENTER MADAME(1935), art d; PARIS IN SPRING(1935), art d; SO RED THE ROSE(1935), art d; ANYTHING GOES(1936), art d; PRINCESS COMES ACROSS, THE(1936), art d; BIG BROADCAST OF 1938, THE(1937), art d; EASY LIVING(1937), art d; I MET HIM IN PARIS(1937), art d; SWING HIGH, SWING LOW(1937), art d; ARTISTS AND MODELS ABROAD(1938), art d; SING YOU SINNERS(1938), art d; YOU AND ME(1938), art d; CAFE SOCIE-TY(1939), art d; GREAT VICTOR HERBERT, THE(1939), art d; INVITATION TO HAPPINESS(1939), art d; NEVER SAY DIE(1939), art d; PARIS HONEYMOON(1939), art d; I WANT A DIVORCE(1940), art d; QUEEN OF THE MOB(1940), art d; RHYTHM ON THE RIVER(1940), art d; SAFARI(1940), art d; LADY EVE, THE(1941), art d; ONE NIGHT IN LISBON(1941), art d; VIRGINIA(1941), art d; I MARRIED A WITCH(1942), art d; LUCKY JORDAN(1942), art d; PALM BEACH STORY, THE(1942), art d; STAR SPANGLED RHYTHM(1942), art d; FIVE GRAVES TO CAIRO(1943), art d; RIDING HIGH(1943), art d; YOUNG AND WILLING(1943), art d; FRENCHMAN'S CREEK(1944), art d; GREAT MOMENT, THE(1944), art d; MIRACLE OF MORGAN'S CREEK, THE(1944), art d; PRINCESS AND THE PIRATE, THE(1944), art d; UNINVITED, THE(1944), art d; WONDER MAN(1945), art d; I'VE ALWAYS LOVED YOU(1946), prod d; MR. ACE(1946), prod d; CHRISTMAS EVE(1947), art d; ON OUR MERRY WAY(1948), art d; DESTINATION MOON(1950), prod d; QUE-BEC(1951), art d; MY HEART GOES CRAZY(1953, Brit.), art d; HELL SHIP MUTI-NY(1957), art d; QUIET GUN, THE(1957), art d; RESTLESS BREED, THE(1957), art d; ROCKABILLY BABY(1957), prod d; SIERRA STRANGER(1957), art d; YOUNG AND DANGEROUS(1957), art d; DESIRE IN THE DUST(1960), art d; B.S. I LOVE YOU(1971), art d
Silents
IN OLD KENTUCKY(1927), set d
Ernst Fegto
GENERAL DIED AT DAWN, THE(1936), art d
Frederick Feher
Misc. Silents
THAT MURDER IN BERLIN(1929, Ger.), d
Fredrick Feher
JIVE JUNCTION(1944)
Friedrich Feher
ROBBER SYMPHONY, THE(1937, Brit.), d, w, m
Silents
CABINET OF DR. CALIGARI, THE(1921, Ger.)
Gabor Feher
1984
REVOLT OF JOB, THE(1984, Hung./Ger.)
Hans Feher
ROBBER SYMPHONY, THE(1937, Brit.)
Tibor Feher
WITNESS, THE(1982, Hung.)
Gaby Fehling
GLASS TOWER, THE(1959, Ger.)
Eberhard Fehmers
GLADIATORS, THE(1970, Swed.)
Bekim Fehmiu
I EVEN MET HAPPY GYPSIES(1968, Yugo.); ADVENTURERS, THE(1970); DESERT-ER, THE(1971 Ital./Yugo.); CAGLIOSTRO(1975, Ital.); PERMISSION TO KILL(1975, U.S./Aust.); BLACK SUNDAY(1977)
Misc. Talkies
BATTLE OF THE EAGLES(1981)
Michele Fehr
WATCH ON THE RHINE(1943)
Phillis Fehr
INVISIBLE OPPONENT(1933, Ger.), ed
Rudi Fehr
MY LOVE CAME BACK(1940), ed; GREAT MR. NOBODY, THE(1941), ed; HONEY-MOON FOR THREE(1941), ed; MILLION DOLLAR BABY(1941), ed; NAVY BLUES(1941), ed; ALL THROUGH THE NIGHT(1942), ed; DESPERATE JOUR-NEY(1942), ed; WATCH ON THE RHINE(1943), ed; BETWEEN TWO WORLDS(1944), ed; CONSPIRATORS, THE(1944), ed; IN OUR TIME(1944), ed; DEVOTION(1946), ed; HUMORESQUE(1946), ed; NOBODY LIVES FOREVER(1946), ed; STOLEN LIFE, A(1946), ed; POSSESSED(1947), ed; VOICE OF THE TURTLE, THE(1947), ed; KEY LARGO(1948), ed; ROMANCE ON THE HIGH SEAS(1948), ed; BEYOND THE FOR-EST(1949), ed; GIRL FROM JONES BEACH, THE(1949), ed; INSPECTOR GENERAL, THE(1949), ed; DAMNED DON'T CRY, THE(1950), ed; ROCKY MOUNTAIN(1950), ed; GOODBYE, MY FANCY(1951), ed; DESERT SONG, THE(1953), p; HOUSE OF WAX(1953), ed; I CONFESS(1953), ed; DIAL M FOR MURDER(1954), ed; RIDING SHOTGUN(1954), ed; LAND OF THE PHARAOHS(1955), ed; ONE FROM THE HEART(1982), ed
Sandra Fehr
HOSTILE WITNESS(1968, Brit.)
Marianne Fehrenberg
PARSIFAL(1983, Fr.), ed
Gherdo Fehrer
ROMAN HOLIDAY(1953)
Honor Fehrson
IT HAPPENED HERE(1966, Brit.)
Kao Fei
DRAGON INN(1968, Chi.)
Lung Fei
EXIT THE DRAGON, ENTER THE TIGER(1977, Hong Kong)
Conrad Feia
TITANIC(1953); WOMAN'S WORLD(1954); D-DAY, THE SIXTH OF JUNE(1956)
Willie Feibel
FACE IN THE CROWD, A(1957)
Hal Feiberling
JOE PALOOKA IN THE SQUARED CIRCLE(1950)
Peter S. Feibleman
ENSIGN PULVER(1964), w

cos; DEAD RINGER(1964), cos; DEAR HEART(1964), cos; OUTRAGE, THE(1964), cos; ROBIN AND THE SEVEN HOODS(1964), cos; VIVA LAS VEGAS(1964), cos; JOY IN THE MORNING(1965), cos; HOMBRE(1967), cos

Eliot Feld
WEST SIDE STORY(1961)

Fritz Feld
BROADWAY(1929); ONE HYSTERICAL NIGHT(1930); EXPENSIVE HUS-BANDS(1937); HOLLYWOOD HOTEL(1937); I MET HIM IN PARIS(1937); LANCER SPY(1937); TOVARICH(1937); TRUE CONFESSION(1937); AFFAIRS OF AN-NABEL(1938); ARTISTS AND MODELS ABROAD(1938); BRINGING UP BABY(1938); CAMPUS CONFESSIONS(1938); GO CHASE YOURSELF(1938); GOLD DIGGERS IN PARIS(1938); I'LL GIVE A MILLION(1938); ROMANCE IN THE DARK(1938); AT THE CIRCUS(1939); EVERYTHING HAPPENS AT NIGHT(1939); IDIOT'S DELIGHT(1939); LITTLE ACCIDENT(1939); WHEN TOMORROW COMES(1939); I WAS AN ADVENTU-RESS(1940); IT'S A DATE(1940); LITTLE OLD NEW YORK(1940); MA, HE'S MAKING EYES AT ME(1940); MILLIONAIRE PLAYBOY(1940); SANDY IS A LADY(1940); VICTORY(1940); COME LIVE WITH ME(1941); FOUR JACKS AND A JILL(1941); MEXICAN SPITFIRE'S BABY(1941); SKYLARK(1941); THREE SONS O'GUNS(1941); WORLD PREMIERE(1941); YOU BELONG TO ME(1941); ICELAND(1942); MAISIE GETS HER MAN(1942); SHUT MY BIG MOUTH(1942); SLEEPYTIME GAL(1942); HENRY ALDRICH SWINGS IT(1943); HOLY MATRIMONY(1943); PHANTOM OF THE OPERA(1943); EVER SINCE VENUS(1944); KNICKERBOCKER HOLI-DAY(1944); PASSPORT TO DESTINY(1944); TAKE IT BIG(1944); CAPTAIN TUGBOAT ANNIE(1945); GEORGE WHITE'S SCANDALS(1945); GREAT JOHN L. THE(1945); HER SISTER'S SECRET(1946); I'VE ALWAYS LOVED YOU(1946); THE CATMAN OF PARIS(1946); WIFE OF MONTE CRISTO, THE(1946); CARNIVAL IN COSTA RI-CA(1947); SECRET LIFE OF WALTER MITTY, THE(1947); IF YOU KNEW SU-SIE(1948); JULIA MISBEHAVES(1948); MEXICAN HAYRIDE(1948); MY GIRL TISA(1948); NOOSE HANGS HIGH, THE(1948); TROUBLE MAKERS(1948); YOU GOTTA STAY HAPPY(1948); LOVABLE CHEAT, THE(1949); BELLE OF OLD MEX-ICO(1950); JACKPOT, THE(1950); JOURNEY INTO LIGHT(1951); KENTUCKY JU-BILEE(1951); LITTLE EGYPT(1951); MISSING WOMEN(1951); MY FAVORITE SPY(1951); RHYTHM INN(1951); AARON SLICK FROM PUNKIN CRICK(1952); HAS ANYBODY SEEN MY GAL?(1952); O. HENRY'S FULL HOUSE(1952); SKY HIGH(1952); CALL ME MADAM(1953); CRIME WAVE(1954); FRENCH LINE, THE(1954); LIVING IT UP(1954); PARIS PLAYBOYS(1954); RIDING SHOTGUN(1954); JAIL BUSTERS(1955); UP IN SMOKE(1957); IN THE MONEY(1958); JUKE BOX RHYTHM(1959); ERRAND BOY, THE(1961); POCKETFUL OF MIRACLES(1961); FOUR FOR TEXAS(1963); MIRACLE OF SANTA'S WHITE REINDEER, THE(1963); PROMISES, PROMISES(1963); WHO'S MINDING THE STORE?(1963); PATSY, THE(1964); THREE ON A COUCH(1966); BAREFOOT IN THE PARK(1967); WICKED DREAMS OF PAULA SCHULTZ, THE(1968); COMIC, THE(1969); HELLO, DOL-LY!(1969); COMPUTER WORE TENNIS SHOES, THE(1970); PHYNX, THE(1970); WHICH WAY TO THE FRONT?(1970); SUNSHINE BOYS, THE(1975); FREAKY FRIDAY(1976); SILENT MOVIE(1976); WON TON TON, THE DOG WHO SAVED HOLLYWOOD(1976); WORLD'S GREATEST LOVER, THE(1977); FUN ON A WEEK-END(1979); HERBIE GOES BANANAS(1980); HISTORY OF THE WORLD, PART 1(1981); HEIDI'S SONG(1982)
Silents
LAST COMMAND, THE(1928)

Gay Feld
MAN WITH TWO HEADS, THE(1972)

George Feld
SPRING SHOWER(1932, Hung.), ed; MACOMBER AFFAIR, THE(1947), ed

Harry Feld
Misc. Talkies
LIVING ORPHAN, THE(1939)

Milton Feld
BIG TOWN GIRL(1937), p; TIME OUT FOR ROMANCE(1937), p

Milton H. Feld
MIDNIGHT TAXI(1937), p; SING AND BE HAPPY(1937), p

Norman Feld
VIOLATORS, THE(1957)

Rudi Feld
SUMMER STORM(1944), art d; BACHELOR'S DAUGHTERS, THE(1946), art d; WHISTLE STOP(1946), art d; NEW ORLEANS(1947), art d; MY DEAR SE-CRETARY(1948), art d; VICIOUS CIRCLE, THE(1948), art d; PAROLE, INC.(1949), art d; GIRL ON THE BRIDGE, THE(1951), art d; STRANGE FASCINATION(1952), art d; ONE GIRL'S CONFESSION(1953), art d; OTHER WOMAN, THE(1954), art d; DEATH OF A SCOUNDREL(1956), art d; EDGE OF HELL(1956), art d; NAKED HILLS, THE(1956), art d; STORM FEAR(1956), prod d; WILD PARTY, THE(1956), art d; FIVE STEPS TO DANGER(1957), art d; FROM HELL IT CAME(1957), art d; HELLCATS OF THE NAVY(1957), art d; HIT AND RUN(1957), art d; LIZZIE(1957), art d; UNDER FIRE(1957), art d; ESCAPE FROM RED ROCK(1958), art d; TANK BATTALION(1958), art d; TWELVE TO THE MOON(1960), art d; OPERATION EICHMANN(1961), art d; GUN HAWK, THE(1963), art d; TERRIFIED!(1963), art d; BIG DADDY(1969), art d; FUN ON A WEEKEND(1979), art d

Rudy Feld
VOICE IN THE WIND(1944), art d

Eric Feldary
HOLD BACK THE DAWN(1941); FIRST COMES COURAGE(1943); FOR WHOM THE BELL TOLLS(1943); HOSTAGES(1943); MASTER RACE, THE(1944); U-BOAT PRISON-ER(1944); SALOME, WHERE SHE DANCED(1945); GOLDEN EARRINGS(1947); HIGH CONQUEST(1947); I, JANE DOE(1948); SIXTEEN FATHOMS DEEP(1948); SEALED CARGO(1951); IRON GLOVE, THE(1954); MAGNIFICENT ROUGHNECKS(1956); 27TH DAY, THE(1957); TENDER IS THE NIGHT(1961)

Mark Feldberg
GETTING EVEN(1981), d&w

Clarence Felder
MAN ON A SWING(1974); GOODBYE GIRL, THE(1977); SEDUCTION OF JOE TYNAN, THE(1979)
1984
SLAYGROUND(1984, Brit.)

Don Felder
1984
FLESHBURN(1984), m

Isabelle Felder
LES GAULOISES BLEUES(1969, Fr.)

Lou Felder
TIME AFTER TIME(1979, Brit.); FIRST FAMILY(1980); WHERE THE BUFFALO ROAM(1980)
1984
MICKI AND MAUDE(1984)

Michael Felder
LONG NIGHT, THE(1976), m

Robert Felder
STORMY WEATHER(1943)

Sarah Felder
WOLFEN(1981)

Wilton Felder
SANCTUARY(1961)

Jimmy Feldgate
CURSE OF THE VOODOO(1965, Brit.)

Sid Feldheim
NORMAN LOVES ROSE(1982, Aus.)

Fred Feldkamp
OPERATION MANHUNT(1954), p; SILKEN AFFAIR, THE(1957, Brit.), p

Andrea Feldman
Misc. Talkies
HEAT(1972)

Bert Feldman
REGAL CAVALCADE(1935, Brit.)

Charles K. Feldman
PITTSBURGH(1942), p; FOLLOW THE BOYS(1944), p; GLASS MENAGERIE, THE(1950), p; STREETCAR NAMED DESIRE, A(1951), p; SEVEN YEAR ITCH, THE(1955), p; WALK ON THE WILD SIDE(1962), p; SEVENTH DAWN, THE(1964), p; WHAT'S NEW, PUSSYCAT?(1965, U.S./Fr.), p; CASINO ROYALE(1967, Brit.), p; HONEY POT, THE(1967, Brit.), p

Corey Feldman
TIME AFTER TIME(1979, Brit.); FOX AND THE HOUND, THE(1981)
1984
FRIDAY THE 13TH–THE FINAL CHAPTER(1984); GREMLINS(1984)

D. Feldman
COSSACKS OF THE DON(1932, USSR), ph

Edward S. Feldman
OTHER SIDE OF THE MOUNTAIN, THE(1975), p; TWO-MINUTE WARNING(1976), p; OTHER SIDE OF THE MOUNTAIN–PART 2, THE(1978), p; LAST MARRIED COUPLE IN AMERICA, THE(1980), p; SENDER, THE(1982, Brit.), p
1984
HOT DOG...THE MOVIE(1984), p

Ellen Feldman
MOMMIE DEAREST(1981)

Ernie [Victor] Feldman
KING ARTHUR WAS A GENTLEMAN(1942, Brit.)

Gene Feldman
Misc. Talkies
DANNY(1979), d

Gladys Feldman
Silents
SHAMS OF SOCIETY(1921)

Jack Feldman
TRIBUTE(1980, Can.), m

Konstantin Feldman
Silents
BATTLESHIP POTEMKIN, THE(1925, USSR)

Marty Feldman
THINK DIRTY(1970, Brit.), a, w; MAGNIFICENT SEVEN DEADLY SINS, THE(1971, Brit.), w; YOUNG FRANKENSTEIN(1974); ADVENTURES OF SHER-LOCK HOLMES' SMARTER BROTHER, THE(1975, Brit.); SILENT MOVIE(1976); LAST REMAKE OF BEAU GESTE, THE(1977), a, d, w; IN GOD WE TRUST(1980), a, d, w; YELLOWBEARD(1983)
1984
SLAPSTICK OF ANOTHER KIND(1984)

Milton Feldman
BEWARE OF BLONDIE(1950), p; DAVID HARDING, COUNTERSPY(1950), p; ROOKIE FIREMAN(1950), p; GASOLINE ALLEY(1951), p; MY TRUE STORY(1951), p; SMUGGLER'S GOLD(1951), p

Mrs. Roy Feldman
SINCE YOU WENT AWAY(1944)

Phil Feldman
YOU'RE A BIG BOY NOW(1966), p; WILD BUNCH, THE(1969), p; BALLAD OF CABLE HOGUE, THE(1970), p; GODFATHER, THE, PART II(1974); TOY, THE(1982), p

Rachel Feldman
HOME MOVIES(1979), art d

Randolph Feldman
HELL NIGHT(1981), w

Ric O. Feldman
TELL ME THAT YOU LOVE ME, JUNIE MOON(1970)

Richard Feldman
TWO-MINUTE WARNING(1976)

Shari Feldman
SENDER, THE(1982, Brit.), cos
1984
HOT DOG...THE MOVIE(1984), cos; MASS APPEAL(1984), cos

Sherlock Feldman
GIRL RUSH, THE(1955)

Stan Feldman
MERRY WIVES OF TOBIAS ROUKE, THE(1972, Can.), p

Miriam Feldmann
PARSIFAL(1983, Fr.)

Emil Feldmar
PHANTOM OF SOHO, THE(1967, Ger.)

Sheldon Feldner
FRIENDS OF EDDIE COYLE, THE(1973); ESCAPE FROM ALCATRAZ(1979); SE-COND THOUGHTS(1983); STAR CHAMBER, THE(1983)

Ricardo Fellini
NIGHTS OF CABIRIA(1957, Ital.)
Riccardo Fellini
VITELLONI(1956, Ital./Fr.); CONJUGAL BED, THE(1963, Ital.)
Florence Fellman
STACY'S KNIGHTS(1983), art d, set d
1984
HEARTBREAKERS(1984), set d
Herman Fellner
BE MINE TONIGHT(1933, Brit.), p; WALTZ TIME(1933, Brit.), p; DISHONOR BRIGHT(1936, Brit.), p; PUBLIC NUISANCE NO. 1(1936, Brit.), p
Silents
GHOST TRAIN, THE(1927, Brit.), p
Tara Fellner
GREEN ICE(1981, Brit.); KING OF THE MOUNTAIN(1981)
Maurice Fellous
STOWAWAY IN THE SKY(1962, Fr.), ph; SECRET OF MAGIC ISLAND, THE(1964, Fr./Ital.), ph; SEVENTH JUROR, THE(1964, Fr.), ph; WOMEN AND WAR(1965, Fr.), ph; GALIA(1966, Fr./Ital.), ph; GREAT SPY CHASE, THE(1966, Fr.), ph; FEMMINA(1968 Fr./Ital./Ger.), ph; ROAD TO SALINA(1971, Fr./Ital.), ph
Roger Fellous
TONIGHT THE SKIRTS FLY(1956, Fr.), ph; NIGHTS OF SHAME(1961, Fr.), ph; VICE DOLLS(1961, Fr.), ph; DEVIL AND THE TEN COMMANDMENTS, THE(1962, Fr.), ph; TOMORROW IS MY TURN(1962, Fr./Ital./Ger.), ph; JULIE THE REDHEAD(1963, Fr.), ph; THREE PENNY OPERA(1963, Fr./Ger.), ph; DIARY OF A CHAMBERMAID(1964, Fr./Ital.), ph; STOP TRAIN 349(1964, Fr./Ital.), ph; TWO ARE GUILTY(1964, Fr.), ph; TIGHT SKIRTS, LOOSE PLEASURES(1966, Fr.), ph
Roger Felloux
ANATOMY OF A MARRIAGE(MY DAYS WITH JEAN-MARC AND MY NIGHTS WITH FRANCOISE)**1/2 (1964 Fr.), ph
Cliff Fellow
HUSTLER, THE(1961)
John D. Fellow
FIRE IN THE FLESH(1964, Fr.), w
Edith Fellowes
RIDER OF DEATH VALLEY(1932); JANE EYRE(1935); KEEPER OF THE BEES(1935)
Julian Fellowes
PRIEST OF LOVE(1981, Brit.)
Rockcliffe Fellowes
RENEGADES OF THE WEST(1932); PHANTOM BROADCAST, THE(1933)
Silents
IN SEARCH OF A SINNER(1920)
Misc. Silents
MAN'S WOMAN(1917); PANTHER WOMAN, THE(1919); CUP OF FURY, THE(1920); FLAPPER WIVES(1924); DECLASSE(1925); WITHOUT MERCY(1925); HONESTY-THE BEST POLICY(1926)
Rockliffe Fellowes
CHARLATAN, THE(1929); OUTSIDE THE LAW(1930); MONKEY BUSINESS(1931); VICE SQUAD, THE(1931); HOTEL CONTINENTAL(1932); LADIES OF THE BIG HOUSE(1932); LAWYER MAN(1933); RUSTY RIDES ALONE(1933)
Silents
MAN HUNT, THE(1918); STRANGER'S BANQUET(1922); PENROD AND SAM(1923); SIGNAL TOWER, THE(1924); EAST OF SUEZ(1925); ROSE OF THE WORLD(1925); SYNCOPATING SUE(1926); THIRD DEGREE, THE(1926); TAXI DANCER, THE(1926)
Misc. Silents
REGENERATION, THE(1915); WHERE LOVE LEADS(1916); BONDAGE OF FEAR, THE(1917); EASIEST WAY, THE(1917); WEB OF DESIRE, THE(1917); FRIEND HUSBAND(1918); WASP, THE(1918); PAGAN LOVE(1920); POINT OF VIEW, THE(1920); YES OR NO?(1920); BITS OF LIFE(1921); PRICE OF POSSESSION, THE(1921); ISLAND WIVES(1922); REMITTANCE WOMAN, THE(1923); TRIFLING WITH HONOR(1923); BORDER LEGION, THE(1924); BORROWED HUSBANDS(1924); CORNERED(1924); GARDEN OF WEEDS, THE(1924); COUNSEL FOR THE DEFENSE(1925); GOLDEN PRINCESS, THE(1925); ROAD TO GLORY, THE(1926); ROCKING MOON(1926); SILENCE(1926); SATIN WOMAN, THE(1927); UNDERSTANDING HEART, THE(1927)
Arthur Fellows
SINCE YOU WENT AWAY(1944), ed
Cynthia Hobard Fellows
HAVING WONDERFUL TIME(1938)
Don Fellows
DETECTIVE, THE(1968); PRETTY POISON(1968); TRICK BABY(1973); SPIKES GANG, THE(1974); INSIDE OUT(1975, Brit.); DEATH PLAY(1976); TWILIGHT'S LAST GLEAMING(1977, U.S./Ger.); VALENTINO(1977, Brit.); SUPERMAN II(1980); EYE OF THE NEEDLE(1981); RAIDERS OF THE LOST ARK(1981); FINAL OPTION, THE(1983, Brit.)
1984
ELECTRIC DREAMS(1984)
Edith Fellows
LAW AND LAWLESS(1932); DEVIL'S BROTHER, THE(1933); HIS GREATEST GAMBLE(1934); MRS. WIGGS OF THE CABBAGE PATCH(1934); DINKY(1935); ONE-WAY TICKET(1935); SHE MARRIED HER BOSS(1935); AND SO THEY WERE MARRIED(1936); PENNIES FROM HEAVEN(1936); LIFE BEGINS WITH LOVE(1937); CITY STREETS(1938); LITTLE ADVENTURESS, THE(1938); LITTLE MISS ROUGHNECK(1938); FIVE LITTLE PEPPERS AND HOW THEY GREW(1939); PRIDE OF THE BLUEGRASS(1939); FIVE LITTLE PEPPERS AT HOME(1940); FIVE LITTLE PEPPERS IN TROUBLE(1940); HER FIRST ROMANCE(1940); MUSIC IN MY HEART(1940); NOBODY'S CHILDREN(1940); OUT WEST WITH THE PEPPERS(1940); HER FIRST BEAU(1941); GIRLS' TOWN(1942); HEART OF THE RIO GRANDE(1942); STARDUST ON THE SAGE(1942); LILITH(1964)
Misc. Talkies
TUGBOAT PRINCESS(1936); CRIMINAL INVESTIGATOR(1942)
Edwina Fellows
STRANGE INVADERS(1983)
Judith Fellows
1984
SECRETS(1984, Brit.)

Owen Fellows
GIVE US THE MOON(1944, Brit.)
Robert Fellows
ANGEL FROM TEXAS, AN(1940), p; VIRGINIA CITY(1940), p; BOMBARDIER(1943), p; FALLEN SPARROW, THE(1943), p; IRON MAJOR, THE(1943), p; EXPERIMENT PERILOUS(1944), p; HEAVENLY DAYS(1944), p; MARINE RAIDERS(1944), p; STEP LIVELY(1944), p; TALL IN THE SADDLE(1944), p; BACK TO BATAAN(1945), p; HAVING WONDERFUL CRIME(1945), p; MAN ALIVE(1945), p; BLAZE OF NOON(1947), p; WILD HARVEST(1947), p; BEYOND GLORY(1948), p; SEALED VERDICT(1948), p; CHICAGO DEADLINE(1949), p; CONNECTICUT YANKEE IN KING ARTHUR'S COURT, A(1949), p; RED, HOT AND BLUE(1949), p; STREETS OF LAREDO(1949), p; LET'S DANCE(1950), p; APPOINTMENT WITH DANGER(1951), p; BIG JIM McLAIN(1952), p; HONDO(1953), p; ISLAND IN THE SKY(1953), p; PLUNDER OF THE SUN(1953), p; HIGH AND THE MIGHTY, THE(1954), p; TRACK OF THE CAT(1954), p; SCREAMING MIMI(1958), p; GIRL HUNTERS, THE(1963, Brit.), p, w
Robert M. Fellows
RING OF FEAR(1954), p
Rockliffe Fellows
HUDDLE(1932); 20,000 YEARS IN SING SING(1933)
Silents
BOY OF MINE(1923); CRYSTAL CUP, THE(1927)
Roger Fellows
GAME FOR SIX LOVERS, A(1962, Fr.), ph
Ruth Fellows
EMERGENCY CALL(1933)
W.T. Fellows
Misc. Silents
DANGEROUS MOMENT, THE(1921)
Hansjorg Felmy
ARENT WE WONDERFUL?(1959, Ger.); SHADOWS GROW LONGER, THE(1962, Switz./Ger.); RESTLESS NIGHT, THE(1964, Ger.); STATION SIX-SAHARA(1964, Brit./Ger.); MAD EXECUTIONERS, THE(1965, Ger.); TORN CURTAIN(1966); MONSTER OF LONDON CITY, THE(1967, Ger.); UNWILLING AGENT(1968, Ger.)
Jorg Felmy
THREE MOVES TO FREEDOM(1960, Ger.); BRAINWASHED(1961, Ger.)
Marc Felperlaan
LIFT, THE(1983, Neth.), ph
Joseph Sidney Felps
DESIRE IN THE DUST(1960)
Henry Gregor Felsen
ONCE UPON A HORSE(1958), w; FEVER HEAT(1968), w
Walter Felsenstein
FIDELIO(1961, Aust.), d, w
Laurelle Felsette
FATHER GOOSE(1964)
Nicole Felsette
FATHER GOOSE(1964)
Harry Feltcorn
RAMPARTS WE WATCH, THE(1940)
Kerry Feltham
CHICAGO 70(1970), p&d
Bostic Felton
COOL WORLD, THE(1963)
E. Felton
Silents
OLD CURIOSITY SHOP, THE(1913, Brit.)
Earl Felton
BENGAL TIGER(1936), w; FRESHMAN LOVE(1936), w; MAN HUNT(1936), w; BAD GUY(1937), w; CAPTAIN'S KID, THE(1937), w; EXTORTION(1938), w; NIGHT HAWK, THE(1938), w; PRISON NURSE(1938), w; CALLING ALL MARINES(1939), w; ORPHANS OF THE STREET(1939), w; SMUGGLED CARGO(1939), w; SOCIETY SMUGGLERS(1939), w; LONE WOLF TAKES A CHANCE, THE(1941), w; PITTSBURGH KID, THE(1941), w; SIERRA SUE(1941), w; WORLD PREMIERE(1941), w; HEART OF THE GOLDEN WEST(1942), w; SUNSET SERENADE(1942), w; MY BEST GAL(1944), w; PARDON MY PAST(1945), w; CRIMINAL COURT(1946), w; ANGEL ON THE AMAZON(1948), w; BEAUTIFUL BLONDE FROM BASHFUL BEND, THE(1949), w; TRAPPED(1949), w; ARMORED CAR ROBBERY(1950), w; HAPPY TIME, THE(1952), w; LAS VEGAS STORY, THE(1952), w; 20,000 LEAGUES UNDER THE SEA(1954), w; MARAUDERS, THE(1955), w; BANDIDO(1956), w; RAWHIDE YEARS, THE(1956), w; KILLERS OF KILIMANJARO(1960, Brit.), w
Felix Felton
NIGHT WAS OUR FRIEND(1951, Brit.); BEGGAR'S OPERA, THE(1953); DOCTOR IN THE HOUSE(1954, Brit.); ADVENTURES OF SADIE, THE(1955, Brit.); DOCTOR AT SEA(1955, Brit.); LADY GODIVA RIDES AGAIN(1955, Brit.); PACIFIC DESTINY(1956, Brit.); JUST MY LUCK(1957, Brit.); WEAPON, THE(1957, Brit.); ELECTRONIC MONSTER. THE(1960, Brit.); RING-A-DING RHYTHM(1962, Brit. 73m Amicus/COL bw (G.B: IT'S TRAD, DAD!); SECOND BEST SECRET AGENT IN THE WHOLE WIDE WORLD, THE(1965, Brit.); CHITTY CHITTY BANG BANG(1968, Brit.); UP IN THE AIR(1969, Brit.)
Greg Felton
RACE FOR YOUR LIFE, CHARLIE BROWN(1977)
Marlene Felton
KISS BEFORE DYING, A(1956); RAWHIDE YEARS, THE(1956); THREE BAD SISTERS(1956)
Verna Felton
IF I HAD MY WAY(1940); NORTHWEST PASSAGE(1940); DUMBO(1941); GIRLS OF THE BIG HOUSE(1945); SHE WROTE THE BOOK(1946); BUCCANEER'S GIRL(1950); CINDERELLA(1950); GUNFIGHTER, THE(1950); ALICE IN WONDERLAND(1951); LITTLE EGYPT(1951); NEW MEXICO(1951); BELLES ON THEIR TOES(1952); DON'T BOTHER TO KNOCK(1952); LADY AND THE TRAMP(1955); PICNIC(1955); OKLAHOMAN, THE(1957); TAMING SUTTON'S GAL(1957); SLEEPING BEAUTY(1959); GUNS OF THE TIMBERLAND(1960); MAN FROM BUTTON WILLOW, THE(1965); JUNGLE BOOK, THE(1967)
William Felton
Misc. Silents
MURDOCK TRIAL, THE(1914, Brit.); LANCASHIRE LASS, A(1915, Brit.); BOUNDARY HOUSE(1918, Brit.)

Kurt Feltz
DIE FLEDERMAUS(1964, Aust.), md
A.J. Fenady
STAKEOUT ON DOPE STREET(1958)
Andrew Fenady
TERROR IN THE WAX MUSEUM(1973), w
Andrew J. Fenady
STAKEOUT ON DOPE STREET(1958), p, w; YOUNG CAPTIVES, THE(1959), p, w; RIDE BEYOND VENGEANCE(1966), p, w; CHISUM(1970), p&w; ARNOLD(1973), p; TERROR IN THE WAX MUSEUM(1973), p; MAN WITH BOGART'S FACE, THE(1980), p, w
Georg Fenady
ARNOLD(1973), d; TERROR IN THE WAX MUSEUM(1973), d
Calvin Fenbry
VISITOR, THE(1980, Ital./U.S.)
Eric Fenby
JAMAICA INN(1939, Brit.), m
George Fencroft
99 WOUNDS(1931), w
Rosemarie Fendel
DREAM TOWN(1973, Ger.)
Freddie Fender
SHORT EYES(1977)
Freddy Fender
Misc. Talkies
SHE CAME TO THE VALLEY(1979)
Marjorie Fender
ONE GOOD TURN(1955, Brit.)
Reggie Fenderson
GANG WAR(1940)
Reginald Fenderson
REFORM SCHOOL(1939); AM I GUILTY?(1940); MAN, THE(1972)
Misc. Talkies
LIFE GOES ON(1938)
Lan Fendors
ONE FLEW OVER THE CUCKOO'S NEST(1975)
Edwige Fenech
NEXT!(1971, Ital./Span.); MEAN FRANK AND CRAZY TONY(1976, Ital.)
Hilda Fenemore
ISLAND OF DESIRE(1952, Brit.); WALLET, THE(1952, Brit.); ADVENTURE IN THE HOPFIELDS(1954, Brit.); END OF THE ROAD, THE(1954, Brit.); HANDS OF DESTINY(1954, Brit.); ROOM IN THE HOUSE(1955, Brit.); SOULS IN CONFLICT(1955, Brit.); ROCK AROUND THE WORLD(1957, Brit.); TREASURE AT THE MILL(1957, Brit.); INNOCENT SINNERS(1958, Brit.); SAFECRACKER, THE(1958, Brit.); YOUNG AND THE GUILTY, THE(1958, Brit.); FEET OF CLAY(1960, Brit.); WIND OF CHANGE, THE(1961, Brit.); STRONGROOM(1962, Brit.); THIS IS MY STREET(1964, Brit.); WITCHCRAFT(1964, Brit.); ESCAPE BY NIGHT(1965, Brit.); I WANT WHAT I WANT(1972, Brit.); BAWDY ADVENTURES OF TOM JONES, THE(1976, Brit.); STUD, THE(1979, Brit.)
Stephen Fenemore
YELLOW BALLOON, THE(1953, Brit.)
Chin Feng
FEMALE PRINCE, THE(1966, Hong Kong)
Heang Feng
DEEP THRUST-THE HAND OF DEATH(1973, Hong Kong), d
Hsu Feng
DRAGON INN(1968, Chi.)
Huang Feng
DEADLY CHINA DOLL(1973, Hong Kong), d
Julie Yeh Feng
SHEPHERD GIRL, THE(1965, Hong Kong)
Ku Feng
TRIPLE IRONS(1973, Hong Kong); SACRED KNIVES OF VENGEANCE, THE(1974, Hong Kong); GOLIATHON(1979, Hong Kong)
Lin Feng
SHEPHERD GIRL, THE(1965, Hong Kong)
Tien Feng
LAST WOMAN OF SHANG, THE(1964, Hong Kong); GRAND SUBSTITUTION, THE(1965, Hong Kong); VERMILION DOOR(1969, Hong Kong); FIVE FINGERS OF DEATH(1973, Hong Kong)
Yueh Feng
MADAME WHITE SNAKE(1963, Hong Kong), d; LAST WOMAN OF SHANG, THE(1964, Hong Kong), d; LADY GENERAL, THE(1965, Hong Kong), d
Amadeus Fengler
WHY DOES HERR R. RUN AMOK?(1977, Ger.)
Michael Fengler
WHY DOES HERR R. RUN AMOK?(1977, Ger.), d, w, titles; MARRIAGE OF MARIA BRAUN, THE(1979, Ger.), p
Jay Fenichel
FM(1978)
Lilly Fenichel
CIRCLE OF IRON(1979, Brit.), cos
A. Fenin
SECRET BRIGADE, THE(1951 USSR)
L. Fenin
MAGIC VOYAGE OF SINBAD, THE(1962, USSR)
L.A. Fenin
ALEXANDER NEVSKY(1939)
Kevin Fenlon
1984
KINGS AND DESPERATE MEN(1984, Brit.)
Margaret Fenly
HOUSE OF THE SEVEN GABLES, THE(1940)
Tanya Fenmore
TWILIGHT ZONE-THE MOVIE(1983)
Frederick Fenn
Silents
SUDS(1920), w

Jan Fenn
RIDE THE HIGH WIND(1967, South Africa)
Jean Fenn
SERENADE(1956)
Sherilyn Fenn
1984
WILD LIFE, THE(1984)
Suzanne Fenn
SATURDAY NIGHT AT THE BATHS(1975), ed; PRETTY BABY(1978), ed
Vincent M. Fenn
BOBBY WARE IS MISSING(1955), p
Sylvie Fennec
DROP THEM OR I'LL SHOOT(1969, Fr./Ger./Span.); FINO A FARTI MALE(1969, Fr./Ital.)
Albert Fennel
NEXT TO NO TIME(1960, Brit.), p; AND SOON THE DARKNESS(1970, Brit.), p
Albeit Fennell
GREEN SCARF, THE(1954, Brit.), p
Albert Fennell
ROOT OF ALL EVIL, THE(1947, Brit.), prod d; CURE FOR LOVE, THE(1950, Brit.), w; NORMAN CONQUEST(1953, Brit.), p; MARCH HARE, THE(1956, Brit.), p; BURN WITCH BURN(1962, Brit.), p; THERE WAS A CROOKED MAN(1962, Brit.), p; UNEARTHLY STRANGER, THE(1964, Brit.), p; DR. JEKYLL AND SISTER HYDE(1971, Brit.), p; LEGEND OF HELL HOUSE, THE(1973, Brit.), p; CAPTAIN KRONOS: VAMPIRE HUNTER(1974, Brit.), p
Elsa Fennell
PICKUP ALLEY(1957, Brit.), cos; MAN INSIDE, THE(1958, Brit.), cos; BANDIT OF ZHOBE, THE(1959), cos; KILLERS OF KILIMANJARO(1960, Brit.), cos; HEROES OF TELEMARK, THE(1965, Brit.), cos; HILL, THE(1965, Brit.), cos; ABOMINABLE DR. PHIBES, THE(1971, Brit.), cos; DIAMONDS ARE FOREVER(1971, Brit.), cos; RAILWAY CHILDREN, THE(1971, Brit.), cos; O LUCKY MAN!(1973, Brit.), cos; SEA WOLVES, THE(1981, Brit.), cos
Michael Fennell
CARWASH(1976)
Rufus Fennell
DARK SANDS(1938, Brit.)
Willie Fennell
LITTLE JUNGLE BOY(1969, Aus.); CATHY'S CHILD(1979, Aus.); EARTHLING, THE(1980)
Fennelly
VIGILANTE TERROR(1953), p
Parker Fennelly
LOST BOUNDARIES(1949); WHISTLE AT EATON FALLS(1951); TROUBLE WITH HARRY, THE(1955); KETTLES ON OLD MACDONALD'S FARM, THE(1957); IT HAPPENED TO JANE(1959); RUSSIANS ARE COMING, THE RUSSIANS ARE COMING, THE(1966); PRETTY POISON(1968); ANGEL IN MY POCKET(1969); HOW TO FRAME A FIGG(1971)
Vincent Fennelly
CHEROKEE UPPRISING(1950), p; BITTER CREEK(1954), p
Vincent M. Fennelly
ARIZONA TERRITORY(1950), p; OUTLAW GOLD(1950), p; OUTLAWS OF TEXAS(1950), p; SILVER RAIDERS(1950), p; ABILENE TRAIL(1951), p; CANYON RAIDERS(1951), p; COLORADO AMBUSH(1951), p; LONGHORN, THE(1951), p; MONTANA DESPERADO(1951), p; NEVADA BADMEN(1951), p; OKLAHOMA JUSTICE(1951), p; STAGE TO BLUE RIVER(1951), p; TEXAS LAWMEN(1951), p; WHISTLING HILLS(1951), p; CANYON AMBUSH(1952), p; DEAD MAN'S TRAIL(1952), p; FARGO(1952), p; KANSAS TERRITORY(1952), p; LAWLESS COWBOYS(1952), p; MAN FROM BLACK HILLS, THE(1952), p; MAVERICK, THE(1952), p; NIGHT RAIDERS(1952), p; TEXAS CITY(1952), p; WACO(1952), p; WAGONS WEST(1952), p; FIGHTING LAWMAN, THE(1953), p; HOMESTEADERS, THE(1953), p; MARKSMAN, THE(1953), p; REBEL CITY(1953), p; STAR OF TEXAS(1953), p; TEXAS BAD MAN(1953), p; TOPEKA(1953), p; DESPERADO, THE(1954), p; FORTYNINERS, THE(1954), p; TWO GUNS AND A BADGE(1954), p; AT GUNPOINT(1955), p; DIAL RED O(1955), p; SEVEN ANGRY MEN(1955), p; CRIME IN THE STREETS(1956), p; LAST OF THE BADMEN(1957), p; GUNS OF THE MAGNIFICENT SEVEN(1969), p; CANNON FOR CORDOBA(1970), p
George Fenneman
THING, THE(1951); MYSTERY LAKE(1953); ONCE YOU KISS A STRANGER(1969); HOW TO SUCCEED IN BUSINESS WITHOUT REALLY TRYING(1976)
John Fenner
FOR YOUR EYES ONLY(1981), art d; OCTOPUSSY(1983, Brit.), art d
1984
TOP SECRET!(1984), art d
Walter Fenner
SAP FROM SYRACUSE, THE(1930); SPEED DEVILS(1935); COVERED TRAILER, THE(1939); I AM NOT AFRAID(1939); JUAREZ(1939); MOUNTAIN RHYTHM(1939); PRIDE OF THE BLUEGRASS(1939); TORCHY RUNS FOR MAYOR(1939); WOMAN IS THE JUDGE, A(1939); YOU CAN'T FOOL YOUR WIFE(1940); HENRY ALDRICH, EDITOR(1942); HENRY ALDRICH GETS GLAMOUR(1942); GUADALCANAL DIARY(1943); IRON MAJOR, THE(1943); YOUTH ON PARADE(1943); HENRY ALDRICH PLAYS CUPID(1944); LOST ANGEL(1944); ONCE UPON A TIME(1944); SHANGHAI COBRA, THE(1945)
Perry Fennerman
LITTLEST HOBO, THE(1958), ph
Warren Fennerty
MURDER, INC.(1960)
Kevin Fennessy
TERROR EYES(1981)
Al Fenney
IT HAPPENED ON 5TH AVENUE(1947)
Heinz Fenschel
DOLLY GETS AHEAD(1931, Ger.), set d
Scott Fensome
LION OF THE DESERT(1981, Libya/Brit.)
Albert Fenton
Misc. Silents
OUR MUTUAL FRIEND(1921, Swed.)

Bernie Fenton
TOMORROW AT TEN(1964, Brit.), m, md; DEVILS OF DARKNESS, THE(1965, Brit.), m

Carol Fenton
WALKING ON AIR(1946, Brit.)

Donna J. Fenton
THIEF(1981)

Earl Fenton
LONE WOLF KEEPS A DATE, THE(1940), w; NIGHT PLANE FROM CHUNG-KING(1942), w; NARROW MARGIN, THE(1952), w

Ed Fenton
WAITRESS(1982)

Elizabeth Fenton
PAL JOEY(1957)

Felix Fenton
PICKWICK PAPERS, THE(1952, Brit.)

Frank E. Fenton
BEHIND JURY DOORS(1933, Brit.), w; REVENGE AT MONTE CARLO(1933), w

Frank Fenton
DINKY(1935), w; ANGEL'S HOLIDAY(1937), w; CHECKERS(1937), w; STEP LIVE-LY, JEEVES(1937), w; WILD AND WOOLLY(1937), w; WOMAN CHASES MAN(1937), w; DOWN ON THE FARM(1938), w; INTERNATIONAL SETTLEMENT(1938), w; KEEP SMILING(1938), w; WHILE NEW YORK SLEEPS(1938), w; SAINT IN LON-DON, THE(1939, Brit.), w; GOLDEN FLEECING, THE(1940), w; LITTLE ORVIE(1940), w; MILLIONAIRES IN PRISON(1940), w; SAINT TAKES OVER, THE(1940), w; DATE WITH THE FALCON, A(1941), w; GAY FALCON, THE(1941), w; FALCON TAKES OVER, THE(1942), w; HIGHWAYS BY NIGHT(1942), w; NAVY COMES THROUGH, THE(1942); CLAUDIA(1943); ISLE OF FORGOTTEN SINS(1943); LADY OF BURLESQUE(1943); MINESWEEPER(1943); SCREAM IN THE DARK, A(1943); SKY'S THE LIMIT, THE(1943), w; BIG NOISE, THE(1944); BUFFALO BILL(1944); DESTINY(1944); GOODNIGHT SWEETHEART(1944), w; HI, GOOD-LOOKIN'(1944); ROSIE THE RIVETER(1944); SECRET COMMAND(1944); GETTING GERTIE'S GAR-TER(1945); HOLD THAT BLONDE(1945); FRENCH KEY, THE(1946); IF I'M LUCK-Y(1946); LADY LUCK(1946), w; NOCTURNE(1946), w; SWAMP FIRE(1946); ADVENTURES OF DON COYOTE(1947); HIT PARADE OF 1947(1947); MAGIC TOWN(1947); NIGHT SONG(1947), w; OUT OF THE PAST(1947), w; PHILO VANCE'S SECRET MISSION(1947); BODYGUARD(1948); FOREIGN AFFAIR, A(1948); HAZ-ARD(1948); MEXICAN HAYRIDE(1948); RELENTLESS(1948); RENEGADES OF SONORA(1948); STATION WEST(1948), w; CLAY PIGEON, THE(1949); DOOLINS OF OKLAHOMA, THE(1949); GOLDEN STALLION, THE(1949); JOE PALOOKA IN THE BIG FIGHT(1949); RANGER OF CHEROKEE STRIP(1949); RUSTLERS(1949); LAW-LESS, THE(1950); MALAYA(1950), w; SIDESHOW(1950); STREETS OF GHOST TOWN(1950); TRIGGER, JR.(1950); TRIPOLI(1950); WALK SOFTLY, STRAN-GER(1950), w; WYOMING MAIL(1950); HIS KIND OF WOMAN(1951); MAN WITH A CLOAK, THE(1951), w; PRAIRIE ROUNDUP(1951); ROGUE RIVER(1951); SILVER CITY(1951); TEXANS NEVER CRY(1951); WILD NORTH, THE(1952), w; ESCAPE FROM FORT BRAVO(1953), w; ISLAND IN THE SKY(1953); RIDE, VAQUERO!(1953), w; VICKI(1953); GARDEN OF EVIL(1954), w; RIVER OF NO RETURN(1954), w; UNTAMED(1955), w; EMERGENCY HOSPITAL(1956); FURY AT GUNSIGHT PASS(1956); NAKED HILLS, THE(1956); THESE WILDER YEARS(1956), w; GUN THE MAN DOWN(1957); HELL BOUND(1957); WINGS OF EAGLES, THE(1957), w; JAYHAWKERS, THE(1959), w; MODERN MARRIAGE, A(1962)
Misc. Talkies
EYES OF THE JUNGLE(1953)

George Fenton
PRIVATE ROAD(1971, Brit.), m; GANDHI(1982), m; BLOODY KIDS(1983, Brit.), m; RUNNERS(1983, Brit.), m

James Fenton
GUILT(1930, Brit.); NO EXIT(1930, Brit.); SUCH IS THE LAW(1930, Brit.); WRITTEN LAW, THE(1931, Brit.)
Misc. Silents
RINGING THE CHANGES(1929, Brit.)

John Fenton
MISSING(1982)

Leonard Fenton
UP THE CREEK(1958, Brit.)
1984
GIVE MY REGARDS TO BROAD STREET(1984, Brit.)

Leslie Fenton
BROADWAY(1929); DANGEROUS WOMAN(1929); LAST PERFORMANCE, THE(1929); MAN I LOVE, THE(1929); OFFICE SCANDAL, THE(1929); PARIS BOUND(1929); WOMAN TRAP(1929); DYNAMITE(1930); GUILTY GENERATION, THE(1931); KICK IN(1931); MAN WHO CAME BACK, THE(1931); MURDER AT MIDNIGHT(1931); PAGAN LADY(1931); PUBLIC ENEMY, THE(1931); AIR MAIL(1932); FAMOUS FERGUSON CASE, THE(1932); HATCHET MAN, THE(1932); STRANGE LOVE OF MOLLY LOUVAIN, THE(1932); THUNDER BELOW(1932); F.P. 1(1933, Brit.); LADY KILLER(1933); NIGHT FLIGHT(1933); FUGITIVE ROAD(1934); I BELIEVED IN YOU(1934); MARIE GALANTE(1934); TAKE THE STAND(1934); CASINO MURDER CASE, THE(1935); CHINATOWN SQUAD(1935); EAST OF JA-VA(1935); MEN WITHOUT NAMES(1935); STAR OF MIDNIGHT(1935); STOLEN HARMONY(1935); STRANGE WIVES(1935); WHITE LIES(1935); LONGEST NIGHT, THE(1936); MURDER ON A BRIDLE PATH(1936); SWORN ENEMY(1936); TWO IN THE DARK(1936); CHINA PASSAGE(1937); HOUSE OF SECRETS, THE(1937); BOYS TOWN(1938); STRONGER THAN DESIRE(1939), d; TELL NO TALES(1939), d; GOLD-EN FLEECING, THE(1940), d; MAN FROM DAKOTA, THE(1940), d; SAINT'S VACA-TION, THE(1941, Brit.), d; TOMORROW THE WORLD(1944), d; PARDON MY PAST(1945), p&d; LULU BELLE(1948), d; ON OUR MERRY WAY(1948), d; SAI-GON(1948), d; WHISPERING SMITH(1948), d; STREETS OF LAREDO(1949), d; RED-HEAD AND THE COWBOY, THE(1950), d
Silents
ANCIENT MARINER, THE(1925); LAZYBONES(1925); SANDY(1926); WHAT PRICE GLORY(1926); DRAGNET, THE(1928); GATEWAY OF THE MOON, THE(1928); GIRLS GONE WILD(1929)
Misc. Silents
THUNDER MOUNTAIN(1925); BLACK PARADISE(1926); ROAD TO GLORY, THE(1926); SHAMROCK HANDICAP, THE(1926); FIRST KISS, THE(1928)

Lucille Fenton
CITIZEN SAINT(1947); I'D RATHER BE RICH(1964)

Mabel Fenton
Silents
HOW MOLLY MADE GOOD(1915)

Marc Fenton
Silents
AMERICAN MANNERS(1924)

Mark Fenton
Silents
CAMPBELLS ARE COMING, THE(1915); FLASHLIGHT, THE(1917); GIRL WHO WOULDN'T QUIT, THE(1918); KAISER, BEAST OF BERLIN, THE(1918); DEVIL TO PAY, THE(1920); PRINCE OF AVENUE A., THE(1920); CONQUERING POWER, THE(1921); FOUR HORSEMEN OF THE APOCALYPSE, THE(1921); LIFE'S DARN FUNNY(1921); UNKNOWN, THE(1921); WALLOP, THE(1921); LITTLE EVA AS-CENDS(1922); TOO MUCH BUSINESS(1922); YELLOW STAIN, THE(1922); ALIAS THE NIGHT WIND(1923); SPEED KING(1923)
Misc. Silents
CLOCK, THE(1917); FLIRTING WITH DEATH(1917); GATES OF DOOM, THE(1917); MAN WHO TOOK A CHANCE, THE(1917); PHANTOM'S SECRET, THE(1917); FIGHT FOR LOVE, A(1919); PASSING OF WOLF MACLEAN, THE(1924)

Robert Fentress
DEAD AND BURIED(1981), p

Phillip Fenty
SUPERFLY(1972), w

R. O. Fenuku
HAMILE(1965, Ghana), ph

Michael Fenway
SATAN'S BED(1965), a, ed

Jean Fenwich
DIVORCE(1945)

Adam Fenwick
1984
BREED APART, A(1984)

Andrew Gordon Fenwick
HIDE IN PLAIN SIGHT(1980)

Don Fenwick
SUBMARINE SEAHAWK(1959)

Ellen Fenwick
FAST TIMES AT RIDGEMONT HIGH(1982)

Gillie Fenwick
IMPROPER CHANNELS(1981, Can.)

Harry Fenwick
Misc. Silents
COME ON COWBOYS!(1924)

Irene Fenwick
Silents
SENTIMENTAL LADY, THE(1915); SPENDTHRIFT, THE(1915)
Misc. Silents
COMMUTORS, THE(1915); GREEN CLOAK, THE(1915); WOMAN NEXT DOOR, THE(1915); CHILD OF DESTINY, THE(1916); CONEY ISLAND PRINCESS, A(1916); GIRL LIKE THAT, A(1917); SIN WOMAN, THE(1917)

Jean Fenwick
THAT UNCERTAIN FEELING(1941); CRUSADES, THE(1935); DANTE'S INFER-NO(1935); ESCAPADE(1935); I'VE BEEN AROUND(1935); STRANGE WIVES(1935); MARY OF SCOTLAND(1936); CONQUEST(1937); FIRST 100 YEARS, THE(1938); IF I WERE KING(1938); MEN WITH WINGS(1938); SAY IT IN FRENCH(1938); ARREST BULLDOG DRUMMOND(1939, Brit.); TELL NO TALES(1939); TOWER OF LON-DON(1939); MONEY TO BURN(1940); NEW MOON(1940); NO, NO NANETTE(1940); THIRD FINGER, LEFT HAND(1940); ELLERY QUEEN AND THE MURDER RING(1941); WE WERE DANCING(1942); HAPPY GO LUCKY(1943); JANE EY-RE(1944); LAURA(1944); IVY(1947); FIGHTER SQUADRON(1948); MY OWN TRUE LOVE(1948); STREET CORNER(1948); EVERYTHING I HAVE IS YOURS(1952); LADY WANTS MINK, THE(1953); WITNESS TO MURDER(1954)

Jeanne Fenwick
CHANCES(1931)

Moya Fenwick
IT SEEMED LIKE A GOOD IDEA AT THE TIME(1975, Can.)

Peggy Fenwick
ALL THAT HEAVEN ALLOWS(1955), w

Perry Fenwick
PARTY PARTY(1983, Brit.)

Peter Fenyes
GOLDEN HEAD, THE(1965, Hung., U.S.), m

Eva Fenyessy
HIPPOLYT, THE LACKEY(1932, Hung.)

Leo Feodoroff
Silents
LAUGH, CLOWN, LAUGH(1928)

Nicolai Feokistov
SPACE SHIP, THE(1935, USSR)

Rahela Ferari
I EVEN MET HAPPY GYPSIES(1968, Yugo.)

Louis Feraud
COAST OF SKELETONS(1965, Brit.), cos

Albert Ferber
HANGMAN WAITS, THE(1947, Brit.), m; MARK OF CAIN, THE(1948, Brit.)

Carl Ferber
LOVE IS A SPLENDID ILLUSION(1970, Brit.)

Edna Ferber
MOTHER KNOWS BEST(1928), w; HARD TO GET(1929), w; SHOW BOAT(1929), w; ROYAL FAMILY OF BROADWAY, THE(1930), w; CIMARRON(1931), w; EXPERT, THE(1932), w; SO BIG(1932), w; DINNER AT EIGHT(1933), w; GLAMOUR(1934), w; COME AND GET IT(1936), w; SHOW BOAT(1936), w; STAGE DOOR(1937), w; NO PLACE TO GO(1939), w; SARATOGA TRUNK(1945), w; SHOW BOAT(1951), w; SO BIG(1953), w; GIANT(1956), w; CIMARRON(1960), w; ICE PALACE(1960), w
Silents
OUR MRS. McCHESNEY(1918), w; NO WOMAN KNOWS(1921), w; SO BIG(1924), w

Karl Ferber
SUNDAY BLOODY SUNDAY(1971, Brit.)

Nat Ferber
CIRCUMSTANTIAL EVIDENCE(1945), w

Hans Ferberg
FUGITIVE ROAD(1934)

Lionel Ferbos
1984
TIGHTROPE(1984)

Pam Ferdin
CHARLOTTE'S WEB(1973)

Pamelyn Ferdin
WHAT A WAY TO GO(1964); ONE AND ONLY GENUINE ORIGINAL FAMILY BAND, THE(1968); BOY NAMED CHARLIE BROWN, A(1969); BEGUILED, THE(1971); HAPPY BIRTHDAY, WANDA JUNE(1971); MEPHISTO WALTZ, THE(1971); WHAT'S THE MATTER WITH HELEN?(1971); TOOLBOX MURDERS, THE(1978); HEIDI'S SONG(1982)

Wendy Ferdin
ONE MAN'S WAY(1964)

John Ferdinand
GOODBYE PORK PIE(1981, New Zealand)

B. Ferdinandov
Misc. Silents
YOUR ACQUAINTANCE(1927, USSR)

Gaspar Ferdinandy
WINTER WIND(1970, Fr./Hung.)

Geza Ferdinandy
WINTER WIND(1970, Fr./Hung.)

Ilona Ference
STAR OF MY NIGHT(1954, Brit.); DIVIDED HEART, THE(1955, Brit.); TOO YOUNG TO LOVE(1960, Brit.)

Buddy Ferens
LAST GUNFIGHTER, THE(1961, Can.); CHANGE OF MIND(1969)

Rene Feret
LUMIERE(1976, Fr.)

Dante Feretti
SONS OF SATAN(1969, Ital./Fr./Ger.), set d

Christian Ferez
GERVAISE(1956, Fr.)

William Fergerson
Silents
BATTLE CRY OF PEACE, THE(1915)

Sioban Fergus
1984
FIRST TURN-ON!, THE(1984)

Tom Fergus
OVER THE EDGE(1979)

Al Ferguson
WAGON MASTER, THE(1929); NEAR THE RAINBOW'S END(1930); ONE WAY TRAIL, THE(1931); RED FORK RANGE(1931); LONE TRAIL, THE(1932); ARIZONA NIGHTS(1934); DESERT TRAIL(1935); GALLANT DEFENDER(1935); SHE COULDN'T TAKE IT(1935); FLASH GORDON(1936); SHOW BOAT(1936); NORTH OF THE RIO GRANDE(1937); ROUNDUP TIME IN TEXAS(1937); RUSTLER'S VALLEY(1937); IN EARLY ARIZONA(1938); COME ON RANGERS(1939); FRONTIERS OF '49(1939); TWO THOROUGHBREDS(1939); HOUSE ACROSS THE BAY, THE(1940); MY LITTLE CHICKADEE(1940); SADDLE MOUNTAIN ROUNDUP(1941); JACKASS MAIL(1942); JOURNEY FOR MARGARET(1942); REAP THE WILD WIND(1942); SHUT MY BIG MOUTH(1942); TALK OF THE TOWN(1942); TEXAS TO BATAAN(1942); VALLEY OF THE SUN(1942); GANGWAY FOR TOMORROW(1943); MADAME CURIE(1943); NORTH STAR, THE(1943); DEATH VALLEY RANGERS(1944); DEVIL RIDERS(1944); LAW OF THE SADDLE(1944); MAN IN HALF-MOON STREET, THE(1944); MRS. PARKINGTON(1944); OUTLAW TRAIL(1944); PEARL OF DEATH, THE(1944); RIDERS OF THE SANTA FE(1944); RUSTLER'S HIDEOUT(1944); SONORA STAGECOACH(1944); WESTWARD BOUND(1944); BEYOND THE PECOS(1945); HONEYMOON AHEAD(1945); LADY ON A TRAIN(1945); LIGHTNING RAIDERS(1945); NORTHWEST TRAIL(1945); ROAD TO UTOPIA(1945); SALOME, WHERE SHE DANCED(1945); SARATOGA TRUNK(1945); SENORITA FROM THE WEST(1945); SUDAN(1945); WILDFIRE(1945); GOD'S COUNTRY(1946); NIGHT IN PARADISE, A(1946); OVERLAND RIDERS(1946); WILD WEST(1946); BRUTE FORCE(1947); FABULOUS TEXAN, THE(1947); MOSS ROSE(1947); UNCONQUERED(1947); WHITE STALLION(1947); WILD HARVEST(1947); KISS THE BLOOD OFF MY HANDS(1948); PRAIRIE OUTLAWS(1948); FRANCIS(1949); JOHNNY STOOL PIGEON(1949); KNOCK ON ANY DOOR(1949); RED, HOT AND BLUE(1949); SAMSON AND DELILAH(1949); DALLAS(1950); MY FRIEND IRMA GOES WEST(1950); SUNSET BOULEVARD(1950); UNION STATION(1950); PLACE IN THE SUN, A(1951); VENGEANCE VALLEY(1951); CARRIE(1952); MILLION DOLLAR MERMAID(1952); SON OF PALEFACE(1952); BAND WAGON, THE(1953); FORBIDDEN(1953); SCANDAL AT SCOURIE(1953); WAR OF THE WORLDS, THE(1953); ROSE MARIE(1954)
Misc. Talkies
LARAMIE KID, THE(1935); ROAMIN' WILD(1936)
Silents
CAPTAIN'S COURAGE, A(1926); WEST OF THE LAW(1926); RANGE RIDERS, THE(1927); WESTERN COURAGE(1927); AVENGING RIDER, THE(1928); GRIT WINS(1929); HOOFBEATS OF VENGEANCE(1929); OUTLAWED(1929)
Misc. Silents
HIGH GEAR JEFFREY(1921); SMILING JIM(1922); FLAMES OF PASSION(1923); RANGE PATROL, THE(1923); WAY OF THE TRANSGRESSOR, THE(1923); DRIFTWOOD(1924); HARBOR PATROL(1924); SHACKLES OF FEAR(1924), a, d; TRAIL OF VENGEANCE, THE(1924), a, d; FIGHTING ROMEO, THE(1925), a, d; PHANTOM SHADOWS(1925), a, d; SCARLET AND GOLD(1925); BAITED TRAP(1926); OFFICER 444(1926); TENTACLES OF THE NORTH(1926); HEADIN' FOR DANGER(1928); TERROR(1928); TERROR MOUNTAIN(1928); MAN FROM NEVADA, THE(1929); SADDLE KING, THE(1929); SMILING TERROR, THE(1929); THUNDERING THOMPSON(1929); VAGABOND CUB, THE(1929); WOLVES OF THE CITY(1929)

Alfred Ferguson
Silents
FRAME UP, THE(1917)
Misc. Silents
LONE STAR(1916)

Alfred George Ferguson
FRENCHMAN'S CREEK(1944)

Allyn Ferguson
SOFI(1967), m; SUPPORT YOUR LOCAL GUNFIGHTER(1971), m; GET TO KNOW YOUR RABBIT(1972), m; COUNT OF MONTE CRISTO(1976, Brit.), m; AVALANCHE EXPRESS(1979), m

Anna Ferguson
WEE GEORDIE(1956, Brit.)

Anne Ferguson
HUMAN FACTOR, THE(1975)

Bianca Ferguson
1984
BUDDY SYSTEM, THE(1984)

Billy Ferguson
MELODY(1971, Brit.)

Casson Ferguson
Silents
ALIAS MARY BROWN(1918); JANE GOES A' WOOING(1919); JOHNNY GET YOUR GUN(1919); PUTTING IT OVER(1919); BUNTY PULLS THE STRINGS(1921); WHAT'S A WIFE WORTH?(1921); OVER THE BORDER(1922); GENTLEMAN OF LEISURE, A(1923); COBRA(1925); WEDDING SONG, THE(1925); KING OF KINGS, THE(1927)
Misc. Silents
GYPSY TRAIL, THE(1918); HOW COULD YOU, JEAN?(1918); ONLY ROAD, THE(1918); UNCLAIMED GOODS(1918); DRIFTERS, THE(1919); PARTNERS THREE(1919); MADAME X(1920); MERELY MARY ANN(1920); MUTINY OF THE ELSINORE, THE(1920); AT THE END OF THE WORLD(1921); UNKNOWN WIFE, THE(1921); LAW AND THE WOMAN, THE(1922); TRUTHFUL LIAR, THE(1922); GRUMPY(1923); HER REPUTATION(1923); FOR ALIMONY ONLY(1926); FORBIDDEN WATERS(1926)

Charles Ferguson
THEY WERE EXPENDABLE(1945); O.S.S.(1946)

Christopher Ferguson
WOMEN IN LOVE(1969, Brit.)

Dave Ferguson
Misc. Silents
SUMMER GIRL, THE(1916)

Don Ferguson
LONGEST YARD, THE(1974)

Donald Ferguson
OPERATION DIAMOND(1948, Brit.)

Elsie Ferguson
SCARLET PAGES(1930)
Silents
RISE OF JENNIE CUSHING, THE(1917); DANGER MARK, THE(1918); DOLL'S HOUSE, A(1918); ROSE OF THE WORLD(1918); AVALANCHE(1919); COUNTERFEIT(1919); MARRIAGE PRICE(1919); BROADWAY AFTER DARK(1924)
Misc. Silents
BARBARY SHEEP(1917); HEART OF THE WILDS(1918); LIE, THE(1918); SONG OF SONGS(1918); UNDER THE GREENWOOD TREE(1918); EYES OF THE SOUL(1919); HIS PARISIAN WIFE(1919); SOCIETY EXILE, A(1919); WITNESS FOR THE DEFENSE, THE(1919); LADY ROSE'S DAUGHTER(1920); FOOTLIGHTS(1921); FOREVER(1921); SACRED AND PROFANE LOVE(1921); OUTCAST(1922); UNKNOWN LOVER, THE(1925)

Frank Ferguson
THEY WON'T BELIEVE ME(1947); FATHER IS A PRINCE(1940); GAMBLING ON THE HIGH SEAS(1940); BODY DISAPPEARS, THE(1941); LIFE BEGINS FOR ANDY HARDY(1941); YOU'LL NEVER GET RICH(1941); BROADWAY(1942); CITY OF SILENT MEN(1942); MY GAL SAL(1942); REAP THE WILD WIND(1942); SPIRIT OF STANFORD, THE(1942); SPY SHIP(1942); TEN GENTLEMEN FROM WEST POINT(1942); THEY DIED WITH THEIR BOOTS ON(1942); THIS GUN FOR HIRE(1942); BOSS OF BIG TOWN(1943); MISSION TO MOSCOW(1943); PILOT NO. 5(1943); TRUCK BUSTERS(1943); DOLLY SISTERS, THE(1945); THRILL OF A ROMANCE(1945); BLONDE FOR A DAY(1946); CROSS MY HEART(1946); IF I'M LUCKY(1946); LADY CHASER(1946); LITTLE MISS BIG(1946); MAN I LOVE, THE(1946); NIGHT AND DAY(1946); O.S.S.(1946); PERFECT MARRIAGE, THE(1946); SEARCHING WIND, THE(1946); SECRETS OF A SORORITY GIRL(1946); SWELL GUY(1946); FABULOUS TEXAN, THE(1947); FARMER'S DAUGHTER, THE(1947); KILLER AT LARGE(1947); PERILS OF PAULINE, THE(1947); T-MEN(1947); TROUBLE WITH WOMEN, THE(1947); VARIETY GIRL(1947); WELCOME STRANGER(1947); ABBOTT AND COSTELLO MEET FRANKENSTEIN(1948); DYNAMITE(1948); FIGHTING FATHER DUNNE(1948); FORT APACHE(1948); HUNTED, THE(1948); INSIDE STORY, THE(1948); MIRACLE OF THE BELLS, THE(1948); RACHEL AND THE STRANGER(1948); THAT WONDERFUL URGE(1948); VICIOUS CIRCLE, THE(1948); WALK A CROOKED MILE(1948); WALLS OF JERICHO(1948); BARKLEYS OF BROADWAY, THE(1949); CAUGHT(1949); DANCING IN THE DARK(1949); FOLLOW ME QUIETLY(1949); FREE FOR ALL(1949); ROSEANNA McCOY(1949); SLIGHTLY FRENCH(1949); STATE DEPARTMENT–FILE 649(1949); THEY LIVE BY NIGHT(1949); FRENCHIE(1950); FURIES, THE(1950); GOOD HUMOR MAN, THE(1950); HE'S A COCKEYED WONDER(1950); KEY TO THE CITY(1950); LAWLESS, THE(1950); LOUISA(1950); RIGHT CROSS(1950); UNDER MEXICALI STARS(1950); WEST POINT STORY, THE(1950); BAREFOOT MAILMAN, THE(1951); ELOPEMENT(1951); MODEL AND THE MARRIAGE BROKER, THE(1951); ON DANGEROUS GROUND(1951); PEOPLE AGAINST O'HARA, THE(1951); SANTA FE(1951); THUNDER IN GOD'S COUNTRY(1951); WARPATH(1951); BEND OF THE RIVER(1952); BOOTS MALONE(1952); HAS ANYBODY SEEN MY GAL?(1952); IT GROWS ON TREES(1952); MA AND PA KETTLE AT THE FAIR(1952); MARRYING KIND, THE(1952); MILLION DOLLAR MERMAID(1952); MODELS, INC.(1952); OKLAHOMA ANNIE(1952); RANCHO NOTORIOUS(1952); RODEO(1952); ROOM FOR ONE MORE(1952); STARS AND STRIPES FOREVER(1952); WAGONS WEST(1952); WINNING TEAM, THE(1952); BEAST FROM 20,000 FATHOMS, THE(1953); BIG LEAGUER(1953); HANNAH LEE(1953); HOUSE OF WAX(1953); LONE HAND, THE(1953); MAIN STREET TO BROADWAY(1953); MARKSMAN, THE(1953); POWDER RIVER(1953); SO BIG(1953); STAR OF TEXAS(1953); TEXAS BAD MAN(1953); TROUBLE ALONG THE WAY(1953); WICKED WOMAN(1953); WOMAN THEY ALMOST LYNCHED, THE(1953); DRUM BEAT(1954); JOHNNY GUITAR(1954); OUTCAST, THE(1954); SHANGHAI STORY, THE(1954); STAR IS BORN, A(1954); AT GUNPOINT(1955); BATTLE FLAME(1955); CITY OF SHADOWS(1955); ETERNAL SEA, THE(1955); LAWLESS STREET, A(1955); MC CONNELL STORY, THE(1955); MOONFLEET(1955); NEW YORK CONFIDENTIAL(1955); TRIAL(1955); VIOLENT MEN, THE(1955); YOUNG AT HEART(1955);

GUN DUEL IN DURANGO(1957); IRON SHERIFF, THE(1957); LAWLESS EIGHTIES, THE(1957); PHANTOM STAGECOACH, THE(1957); THIS COULD BE THE NIGHT(1957); ANDY HARDY COMES HOME(1958); COLE YOUNGER, GUNFIGHTER(1958); LIGHT IN THE FOREST, THE(1958); MAN OF THE WEST(1958); TERROR IN A TEXAS TOWN(1958); BIG NIGHT, THE(1960); RAYMIE(1960); SUNRISE AT CAMPOBELLO(1960); POCKETFUL OF MIRACLES(1961); HUSH... HUSH, SWEET CHARLOTTE(1964); QUICK GUN, THE(1964); THOSE CALLOWAYS(1964); GREAT SIOUX MASSACRE, THE(1965)

George Ferguson
Silents
DAMAGED GOODS(1915)
Misc. Silents
BRUISER, THE(1916)

George-Ellen Ferguson
JANIE(1944)

Glenn Ferguson
THREE DAYS OF THE CONDOR(1975)

Graeme Ferguson
SAIL A CROOKED SHIP(1961); SEDUCERS, THE(1962), d; DOUBLE-BARRELLED DETECTIVE STORY, THE(1965), ph; VIRGIN PRESIDENT, THE(1968), p, d, w, ph

Harvey Ferguson
WOLF SONG(1929), w; HOT SATURDAY(1932), w; STAND UP AND FIGHT(1939), w

Helen Ferguson
IN OLD CALIFORNIA(1929); SCARLET PAGES(1930); KID MILLIONS(1934)
Silents
DESERT BLOSSOMS(1921); MAKING THE GRADE(1921); RIGHT WAY, THE(1921); ACCORDING TO HOYLE(1922); HUNGRY HEARTS(1922); NEVER SAY DIE(1924); ISLE OF HOPE, THE(1925); NINE AND THREE-FIFTHS SECONDS(1925); ROUGH SHOD(1925); SPOOK RANCH(1925); CHEATERS(1927); JAWS OF STEEL(1927)
Misc. Silents
FOOLS FOR LUCK(1917); SMALL TOWN GUY, THE(1917); GAMBLERS, THE(1919); LOST BATALLION, THE(1919); BURNING DAYLIGHT(1920); CHALLENGE OF THE LAW, THE(1920); GOING SOME(1920); JUST PALS(1920); MUTINY OF THE ELSINORE, THE(1920); ROMANCE PROMOTORS, THE(1920); SHOD WITH FIRE(1920); FREEZE OUT, THE(1921); MISS LULU BETT(1921); STRAIGHT FROM THE SHOULDER(1921); TO A FINISH(1921); CRUSADER, THE(1922); FLAMING HOUR, THE(1922); DOUBLE DEALING(1923); UNKNOWN PURPLE, THE(1923); RACING LUCK(1924); RIGHT OF THE STRONGEST, THE(1924); VALLEY OF HATE, THE(1924); CLOUD RIDER, THE(1925); MY NEIGHBOR'S WIFE(1925)

J. Don Ferguson
LINCOLN CONSPIRACY, THE(1977); NORMA RAE(1979); LITTLE DARLINGS(1980); LONG RIDERS, THE(1980); NIGHT THE LIGHTS WENT OUT IN GEORGIA, THE(1981); LOVELESS, THE(1982); SHARKY'S MACHINE(1982)
1984
TANK(1984)

Jane Ferguson
1984
MYSTERY MANSION(1984)

Janet Ferguson
TWO HUNDRED MOTELS(1971, Brit.)

Jay Ferguson
MODEL SHOP, THE(1969)

Jessie Lawrence Ferguson
1984
ADVENTURES OF BUCKAROO BANZAI: ACROSS THE 8TH DIMENSION, THE(1984)

Jim Ferguson
COPS AND ROBBERS(1973)

John Ferguson
PENNY SERENADE(1941)

Kate Ferguson
BREAK OF DAY(1977, Aus.); SPACED OUT(1981, Brit.); PIRATE MOVIE, THE(1982, Aus.)

Kathleen Ferguson
NIGHTMARE(1981)

Larry Ferguson
ST. HELENS(1981), w

Lester Ferguson
FATAL NIGHT, THE(1948, Brit.)

Margaret Ferguson
SIGN OF THE RAM, THE(1948), w

Mattie Ferguson
Silents
SPENDTHRIFT, THE(1915)

Michael Ferguson
LANDLORD, THE(1970)

Mildred Elsie Ferguson
Misc. Silents
HER OWN STORY(1922)

Morton Ferguson
Silents
GARRISON'S FINISH(1923), w

Myrtle Ferguson
WHEN THE LIGHTS GO ON AGAIN(1944); BLONDE FROM BROOKLYN(1945); EASY TO LOOK AT(1945); NIGHT IN PARADISE, A(1946); TWO GALS AND A GUY(1951)

Nellie Ferguson
IT ISN'T DONE(1937, Aus.)

Norm Ferguson
ALICE IN WONDERLAND(1951), anim d

Norman Ferguson
FANTASIA(1940), anim; PINOCCHIO(1940), d; DUMBO(1941), d; RELUCTANT DRAGON, THE(1941); THREE CABALLEROS, THE(1944), p, d; PETER PAN(1953), anim

Perry Ferguson
CHANCE AT HEAVEN(1933), art d; ANNIE OAKLEY(1935), art d; M'LISS(1936), art d; WOMAN REBELS, A(1936), art d; BRINGING UP BABY(1938), art d; HAVING WONDERFUL TIME(1938), art d; FIFTH AVENUE GIRL(1939), art d; GUNGA DIN(1939), art d; IN NAME ONLY(1939), art d; STORY OF VERNON AND IRENE

CASTLE, THE(1939), art d; BALL OF FIRE(1941), art d; CITIZEN KANE(1941), art d; PRIDE OF THE YANKEES, THE(1942), art d; NORTH STAR, THE(1943), art d; OUTLAW, THE(1943), art d; THEY GOT ME COVERED(1943), art d; CASANOVA BROWN(1944), art d; UP IN ARMS(1944), art d; BEST YEARS OF OUR LIVES, THE(1946), art d; KID FROM BOOKLYN, THE(1946), art d; SONG OF THE SOUTH(1946), art d; STRANGER THE(1946), art d; DESERT FURY(1947), art d; SECRET LIFE OF WALTER MITTY, THE(1947), art d; ROPE(1948), art d; SONG IS BORN, A(1948), art d; WITHOUT HONOR(1949), art d; SOUND OF FURY, THE(1950), art d; 711 OCEAN DRIVE(1950), prod d; GROOM WORE SPURS, THE(1951), art d; LADY SAYS NO, THE(1951), art d; BIG SKY, THE(1952), art d; MAIN STREET TO BROADWAY(1953), art d; DEAD RINGER(1964), art d; READY FOR THE PEOPLE(1964), art d; COFFY(1973), art d; SHAGGY D.A., THE(1976), art d; HERBIE GOES TO MONTE CARLO(1977), art d

Riki Ferguson
WORLD IS JUST A 'B' MOVIE, THE(1971)

Robert Ferguson
GO KART GO(1964, Brit.)

Ron Ferguson
HOT WATER(1937), w; BLIND ALIBI(1938), w; DOUBLE CROSS(1941), w

S.G. Ferguson
Misc. Talkies
SUPERSONIC SAUCER(1956, Brit.), d

Sally Ferguson
HER MAN(1930)

W. B. Ferguson
MAN WITH 100 FACES, THE(1938, Brit.), w

W. J. Ferguson
Silents
LITTLE MISS BROWN(1915); DREAM STREET(1921); JOHN SMITH(1922); KINDRED OF THE DUST(1922); PEACOCK ALLEY(1922); TO HAVE AND TO HOLD(1922); WORLD'S CHAMPION, THE(1922)
Misc. Silents
DEEP PURPLE, THE(1915); DEEP PURPLE, THE(1920)

William Ferguson
ONE PLUS ONE(1961, Can.)

Perry Ferguson II
LOVE AND THE MIDNIGHT AUTO SUPPLY(1978), art d

Guy Fergusson
GOLD EXPRESS, THE(1955, Brit.), d

Harvey Fergusson
IT HAPPENED IN HOLLYWOOD(1937), w

John Fergusson
WHITE ZOMBIE(1932)

Vittorio Feri
FURY OF THE PAGANS(1963, Ital.)

Luisa Ferida
ADVENTURE OF SALVATOR ROSA, AN(1940, Ital.); FEDORA(1946, Ital.)

Johannes Ferigo
FOREVER MY LOVE(1962)

Amouk Ferjac
JE T'AIME, JE T'AIME(1972, Fr./Swed.)

Anouck Ferjac
LIVE FOR LIFE(1967, Fr./Ital.)

Anouk Ferjac
LA GUERRE EST FINIE(1967, Fr./Swed.); THIS MAN MUST DIE(1970, Fr./Ital.); NO TIME FOR BREAKFAST(1978, Fr.); PEPPERMINT SODA(1979, Fr.); PIAF–THE EARLY YEARS(1982, U.S./Fr.)

Lone Ferk
BAD MAN'S RIVER(1972, Span.)

Betty Ferkauf
Silents
BROKEN HEARTS(1926)

Nancy Ferland
TAKING OFF(1971)

Francoise Ferley
PIAF–THE EARLY YEARS(1982, U.S./Fr.), w

Nicos Fermas
BAREFOOT BATTALION, THE(1954, Gr.)

Michel Fermaud
MAN WHO LOVED WOMEN, THE(1977, Fr.), w

Jeanette Fern
FLESH AND FANTASY(1943)

Johnny Fern
MEET JOHN DOE(1941)

Robert Fern
THE LADY DRACULA(1974), p, w

Vera Fern
TOO MANY GIRLS(1940)

Bruce Fernald
HOUSE ON 92ND STREET, THE(1945); DEADLINE FOR MURDER(1946)

C. B. Fernald
Silents
PURSUIT OF PAMELA, THE(1920, Brit.), w

John Fernald
DOMINANT SEX, THE(1937, Brit.), w; TERROR HOUSE(1942, Brit.); IT'S NEVER TOO LATE(1958, Brit.)

Margaret Fernald
CAESAR AND CLEOPATRA(1946, Brit.)

Fernandel
ANGELE(1934 Fr.); UN CARNET DE BAL(1938, Fr.); FRIC FRAC(1939, FR.); HARVEST(1939, Fr.); WELL-DIGGER'S DAUGHTER, THE(1946, Fr.); CARNIVAL(1953, Fr.); LITTLE WORLD OF DON CAMILLO, THE(1953, Fr./Ital.); ALI BABA(1954, Fr.); FRENCH TOUCH, THE(1954, Fr.); RED, INN, THE(1954, Fr.); AROUND THE WORLD IN 80 DAYS(1956); FERNANDEL THE DRESSMAKER(1957, Fr.); PARIS HOLIDAY(1958); FORBIDDEN FRUIT(1959, Fr.); LAW IS THE LAW, THE(1959, Fr.); BIG CHIEF, THE(1960, Fr.); COW AND I, THE(1961, Fr., Ital., Ger.); DYNAMITE JACK(1961, Fr.); DEVIL AND THE TEN COMMANDMENTS, THE(1962, Fr.); MOST WANTED MAN, THE(1962, Fr./Ital.); MY WIFE'S HUSBAND(1965, Fr./Ital.)

Emilio Fernandes
  NIGHT OF THE IGUANA, THE(1964)
Heitor Fernandes
  VOYAGE OF SILENCE(1968, Fr.)
Joao Fernandes
  DARKTOWN STRUTTERS(1975), ph; KIRLIAN WITNESS, THE(1978), ph; HUMAN
  EXPERIMENTS(1980), ph; LAND OF NO RETURN, THE(1981), ph; NESTING,
  THE(1981), ph; BIG SCORE, THE(1983), ph
  1984
  FRIDAY THE 13TH–THE FINAL CHAPTER(1984), ph; MISSING IN ACTION(1984),
  ph; ROSEBUD BEACH HOTEL(1984), ph
Miguel Fernandes
  RABID(1976, Can.); KIDNAPPING OF THE PRESIDENT, THE(1980, Can.); GHOST
  STORY(1981); AMATEUR, THE(1982); SPASMS(1983, Can.)
Nadyr Fernandes
  GENTLE RAIN, THE(1966, Braz.)
E. Fernandex
  Silents
  AUDREY(1916)
Abel Fernandez
  SECOND CHANCE(1953); ALASKA SEAS(1954); ROSE MARIE(1954); FORT YU-
  MA(1955); MANY RIVERS TO CROSS(1955); TARGET ZERO(1955); HARDER THEY
  FALL, THE(1956); LAST WAGON, THE(1956); PORK CHOP HILL(1959); SCARFACE
  MOB, THE(1962); APACHE UPRISING(1966); MADIGAN(1968)
Abel M. Fernandez
  DEVIL GODDESS(1955)
Agustin Fernandez
  FACE OF THE SCREAMING WEREWOLF(1959, Mex.)
Aida Fernandez
  NO EXIT(1962, U.S./Arg.), makeup
Angel Luis Fernandez
  1984
  SKYLINE(1984, Spain), ph
Anselmo Fernandez
  CARMEN(1949, Span.)
Anthony Fernandez
  SILKWOOD(1983)
Arturo Fernandez
  SOUND OF HORROR(1966, Span.)
  Misc. Talkies
  SOUNDS OF HORROR(1968)
Augustin Fernandez
  ENCHANTED ISLAND(1958)
Benjamin Fernandez
  CONAN THE BARBARIAN(1982), art d
  1984
  DUNE(1984), art d
Bijou Fernandez
  Silents
  JUST SUPPOSE(1926)
Buff Fernandez
  AMBUSH BAY(1966)
Carlos Fernandez
  BRAVE ONE, THE(1956)
E. Fernandez
  Misc. Silents
  FORTUNE TELLER, THE(1920)
E. L. Fernandez
  Silents
  EYE FOR EYE(1918); LOVE'S REDEMPTION(1921)
  Misc. Silents
  HEART OF THE SUNSET(1918)
Eddie Fernandez
  BLOOD DRINKERS, THE(1966, U.S./Phil.)
Emilio Fernandez
  LAND OF MISSING MEN, THE(1930); OKLAHOMA CYCLONE(1930); PASSION
  ISLAND(1943, Mex.), d&w; PORTRAIT OF MARIA(1946), d, w; PEARL,
  THE(1948, U.S./Mex.), d, w; TORCH, THE(1950), d, w; LA CUCARACHA(1961, Mex.);
  REWARD, THE(1965); APPALOOSA, THE(1966); COVENANT WITH DEATH, A(1966);
  RETURN OF THE SEVEN(1966, Span.); WAR WAGON, THE(1967); WILD BUNCH,
  THE(1969); PAT GARRETT AND BILLY THE KID(1973); BRING ME THE HEAD OF
  ALFREDO GARCIA(1974); BREAKOUT(1975); LUCKY LADY(1975); POLITICAL ASY-
  LUM(1975, Mex./Guatemalan)
  1984
  UNDER THE VOLCANO(1984)
Esperanza Fernandez
  1984
  BIZET'S CARMEN(1984, Fr./Ital.)
Esther Fernandez
  RANCHO GRANDE(1938, Mex.); TWO YEARS BEFORE THE MAST(1946); PANCHO
  VILLA RETURNS(1950, Mex.)
Felix Fernandez
  MAD QUEEN, THE(1950, Span.); COLOSSUS OF RHODES, THE(1961, Ital., Fr.,
  Span.); TEACHER AND THE MIRACLE, THE(1961, Ital./Span.); DEVIL MADE A
  WOMAN, THE(1962, Span.); SAVAGE GUNS, THE(1962, U.S./Span.); MISSION
  BLOODY MARY(1967, Fr./Ital./Span.)
Feliz Fernandez
  NOT ON YOUR LIFE(1965, Ital./Span.)
Fernando Fernandez
  FUGITIVE, THE(1947)
Freddy Fernandez
  DANIEL BOONE, TRAIL BLAZER(1957)
Gustavo Fernandez
  1984
  UNDER THE VOLCANO(1984)
Helio Fernandez
  BRASIL ANNO 2,000(1968, Braz.)

Honey Fernandez
  COUNTRYMAN(1982, Jamaica)
Jaime Fernandez
  ADVENTURES OF ROBINSON CRUSOE, THE(1954); REBELLION OF THE
  HANGED, THE(1954, Mex.); MASSACRE(1956); BULLET FOR THE GENERAL,
  A(1967, Ital.); GUNS FOR SAN SEBASTIAN(1968, U.S./Fr./Mex./Ital.)
Jesus Fernandez
  NAZARIN(1968, Mex.); TRISTANA(1970, Span./Ital./Fr.)
Joao Fernandez
  ABDUCTION(1975), ph
Jorge Fernandez
  SOFIA(1948), art d; FACE OF THE SCREAMING WEREWOLF(1959, Mex.), art d;
  REVENGERS, THE(1972, U.S./Mex.), art d
Jose Fernandez
  WHEN YOU'RE IN LOVE(1937); POSSESSION OF JOEL DELANEY, THE(1972)
Juan De Orduna Y Fernandez
  DON'T TURN THE OTHER CHEEK(1974, Ital./Ger./Span.), w
Juan Fernandez
  VALDEZ IS COMING(1971); UNCOMMON VALOR(1983)
  1984
  FEAR CITY(1984)
  Misc. Talkies
  AMAZING TRANSPLANT, THE(1970)
Juan Gomez Fernandez
  1984
  YELLOW HAIR AND THE FORTRESS OF GOLD(1984)
Capt. Manuel J. Fernandez, USAF
  MC CONNELL STORY, THE(1955), tech adv
Mara Fernandez
  SIX DAYS A WEEK(1966, Fr./Ital./Span.)
Margarita Fernandez
  RETURN OF THE JEDI(1983)
Miguel Fernandez
  ONE MAN(1979, Can.)
Paquito Fernandez
  TOM THUMB(1967, Mex.)
Peter Fernandez
  CITY ACROSS THE RIVER(1949); SISTERS, THE(1969, Gr.), titles; INFRA-
  MAN(1975, Hong Kong), w
Robert Fernandez
  Silents
  ALIAS JULIUS CAESAR(1922)
Roy Fernandez
  Silents
  SUCH A LITTLE QUEEN(1921)
Ruth Fernandez
  FIEND OF DOPE ISLAND(1961)
Sabatini Fernandez
  1984
  MISSING IN ACTION(1984)
Wilhelmenia Wiggins Fernandez
  DIVA(1982, Fr.)
Miguel Fernandez-Mila
  NEXT!(1971, Ital./Span.), ph
Fernando
  PLAINSMAN AND THE LADY(1946)
Dindo Fernando
  BLACK MAMA, WHITE MAMA(1973)
Tara Fernando
  YOUNG GIRLS OF ROCHEFORT, THE(1968, Fr.); OBLONG BOX, THE(1969, Brit.)
Rudolf Fernau
  CONFESS DR. CORDA(1960, Ger.); RETURN OF DR. MABUSE, THE(1961, Ger./Fr./
  Ital.); INVISIBLE DR. MABUSE, THE(1965, Ger.); MAD EXECUTIONERS, THE(1965,
  Ger.)
Ronald Fernee
  LORDS OF DISCIPLINE, THE(1983)
Hal Ferner
  Misc. Silents
  MILLIONAIRE ORPHAN, THE(1926)
Ernest Ferney
  STOLEN LIFE(1939, Brit.)
Georges Ferney
  SECOND BUREAU(1936, Fr.)
Larry Ferney
  HUCKLEBERRY FINN(1974)
Maxwell Fernie
  SOLO(1978, New Zealand/Aus.)
Dan Ferniel
  KISS TOMORROW GOODBYE(1950); CARIBBEAN(1952); ROBE, THE(1953)
Daniel Ferniel
  UNDERTOW(1949)
John Fernside
  UNCIVILISED(1937, Aus.); OVERLANDERS, THE(1946, Brit./Aus.); BUSH CHRIST-
  MAS(1947, Brit.); MASSACRE HILL(1949, Brit.); GLENROWAN AFFAIR, THE(1951,
  Aus.)
Ray Fernstrom
  LAST OF THE REDMEN(1947), ph; SWINGIN' SUMMER, A(1965), ph
Tiziano Feroldi
  GRAND PRIX(1966)
Pasquale Ferone
  LE BOUCHER(1971, Fr./Ital.)
Tanya Ferova
  GIRL FROM STARSHIP VENUS, THE(1975, Brit.)
Annette Ferra
  SANTA AND THE THREE BEARS(1970); WILD PARTY, THE(1975)
Margot Ferra
  SONG OF LIFE, THE(1931, Ger.)

Rachid Ferrache
ACE OF ACES(1982, Fr./Ger.)

Lisa Ferraday
SKY LINER(1949); CHINA CORSAIR(1951); I WAS AN AMERICAN SPY(1951); SHOW BOAT(1951); TOO YOUNG TO KISS(1951); BELLE OF NEW YORK, THE(1952); CALIFORNIA CONQUEST(1952); LAST TRAIN FROM BOMBAY(1952); MERRY WIDOW, THE(1952); RANCHO NOTORIOUS(1952); SNOWS OF KILIMANJARO, THE(1952); KENTUCKIAN, THE(1955); DEATH OF A SCOUNDREL(1956); FLAME OF STAMBOUL(1957)

Alain Ferral
STORY OF THE COUNT OF MONTE CRISTO, THE(1962, Fr./Ital.)

J. A. Ferral
UNDER FIRE(1983)

Giorgio Ferralonga
FOR A FEW DOLLARS MORE(1967, Ital./Ger./Span.), ed

Gloria Ferrandez
DARK RIVER(1956, Arg.)

Dean Ferrandini
BEYOND THE POSEIDON ADVENTURE(1979)
1984
ICE PIRATES, THE(1984)

Antonio Ferrandis
TRISTANA(1970, Span./Ital./Fr.); LEONOR(1977, Fr./Span./Ital.); TO BEGIN AGAIN(1982, Span.)

Giancarlo Ferrando
TORSO(1974, Ital.), ph; SCREAMERS(1978, Ital.), ph
1984
AFTER THE FALL OF NEW YORK(1984, Ital./Fr.), ph

Joe Ferrante
ESCAPE TO BURMA(1955); RARE BREED, THE(1966)

Traci Ferrante
I SPIT ON YOUR GRAVE(1983)

Giuseppe Ferranti
ZOMBIE CREEPING FLESH(1981, Ital./Span.), spec eff; NIGHT OF THE ZOMBIES(1983, Span./Ital.), makeup

Pino Ferranti
LOVE PROBLEMS(1970, Ital.), spec eff
1984
DON'T OPEN TILL CHRISTMAS(1984, Brit.), makeup

Henry Ferrantino
PRINCE OF THE CITY(1981)

Miguel Ferrar
HEARTBREAKER(1983)

Tony Ferrar
FIRECRACKER(1981)

Abel Ferrara
DRILLER KILLER(1979), d; MS. 45(1981), d
1984
FEAR CITY(1984), d

Al Ferrara
HITCH-HIKER, THE(1953); RIOT ON SUNSET STRIP(1967); MANSION OF THE DOOMED(1976)

Alberto Ferrara
HERO AT LARGE(1980)

Angelo Ferrara
WASTREL, THE(1963, Ital.), p; DUEL OF CHAMPIONS(1964 Ital./Span.), p

Cathy Ferrara
TOWARD THE UNKNOWN(1956)

Consuelo Ferrara
GIRL FROM TRIESTE, THE(1983, Ital.)

Franco Ferrara
INDISCRETION OF AN AMERICAN WIFE(1954, U.S./Ital.), md; MAMBO(1955, Ital.), md; ULYSSES(1955, Ital.), md; LA STRADA(1956, Ital.), md; FAREWELL TO ARMS, A(1957), md; THIS ANGRY AGE(1958, Ital./Fr.), md; VIKINGS, THE(1958), md; HANNIBAL(1960, Ital.), md; SCENT OF MYSTERY(1960), md; GREAT WAR, THE(1961, Fr., Ital.), md; LA DOLCE VITA(1961, Ital./Fr.), md; WHITE NIGHTS(1961, Ital./Fr.), md; DAMON AND PYTHIAS(1962), md; LA VIACCIA(1962, Fr./Ital.), md; SWORDSMAN OF SIENA, THE(1962, Fr./Ital.), md; LEOPARD, THE(1963, Ital.), md; RAILROAD MAN, THE(1965, Ital.), md; MONGOLS, THE(1966, Fr./Ital.), md; JOURNEY BENEATH THE DESERT(1967, Fr./Ital.), md; SENSO(1968, Ital.), md

Frank Ferrara
WARRIORS, THE(1979); HANKY-PANKY(1982)
1984
FIRSTBORN(1984)

Fred Ferrara
HAIR(1979)

James Ferreau
TOMBSTONE, THE TOWN TOO TOUGH TO DIE(1942)

Paul Ferrara
PARTY, THE(1968)

Pino Ferrara
SECRET OF SANTA VITTORIA, THE(1969); STATUE, THE(1971, Brit.)

Romano Ferrara
PLANETS AGAINST US, THE(1961, Ital./Fr.), d, w; SPY IN YOUR EYE(1966, Ital.), w

Tony Ferrara
ONCE IS NOT ENOUGH(1975)

Ashley Ferrare
REVENGE OF THE NINJA(1983)

Christina Ferrare
J.W. COOP(1971)

Cristina Ferrare
IMPOSSIBLE YEARS, THE(1968); MARY, MARY, BLOODY MARY(1975, U.S./Mex.)

Franco Ferrare
MAN FROM CAIRO, THE(1953), md

Antonio Ferrari
TREE OF WOODEN CLOGS, THE(1979, Ital.)

Ennio Ferrari
TRAGEDY OF A RIDICULOUS MAN, THE(1982, Ital.)

Fanny Ferrari
Silents
KISMET(1920)

Franco Ferrari
TEMPEST(1958, Ital./Yugo./Fr.), md

G. Ferrari
GREAT WHITE, THE(1982, Ital.), spec eff

Gaetano Ferrari
TRAGEDY OF A RIDICULOUS MAN, THE(1982, Ital.)

Giovanni Ferrari
ALLEGRO NON TROPPO(1977, Ital.), anim

Gustave Ferrari
MEN OF YESTERDAY(1936, Brit.)

Mario Ferrari
WHITE DEVIL, THE(1948, Ital.); QUEEN OF SHEBA(1953, Ital.); AVENGER, THE(1962, Fr./Ital.); MOSES(1976, Brit./Ital.)

Nick Ferrari
BABY, IT'S YOU(1983)

Otto Ferrari
HIDDEN HOMICIDE(1959, Brit.), m, md

Paolo Ferrari
FRIENDS FOR LIFE(1964, Ital.); WHITE VOICES(1965, Fr./Ital.); GIRL GAME(1968, Braz./Fr./Ital.)

William Ferrari
HEAVENLY BODY, THE(1943), art d; GASLIGHT(1944), art d; CLOCK, THE(1945), art d; ZIEGFELD FOLLIES(1945), ph; HARVEY GIRLS, THE(1946), art d; FIESTA(1947), art d; LIVING IN A BIG WAY(1947), art d; SLEEP, MY LOVE(1948), art d; ADAM'S RIB(1949), art d; DIAL 1119(1950), art d; REFORMER AND THE REDHEAD, THE(1950), art d; IT'S A BIG COUNTRY(1951), art d; KIND LADY(1951), art d; TEXAS CARNIVAL(1951), art d; THREE GUYS NAMED MIKE(1951), art d; ROGUE'S MARCH(1952), art d; JEOPARDY(1953), art d; SLIGHT CASE OF LARCENY, A(1953), art d; WITNESS TO MURDER(1954), art d; TERROR IN A TEXAS TOWN(1958), art d; TIME MACHINE, THE(1960; Brit./U.S.), art d; ATLANTIS, THE LOST CONTINENT(1961), art d; HOW THE WEST WAS WON(1962), art d

Enea Ferrario
EYES, THE MOUTH, THE(1982, Ital./Fr.), p

Anna Maria Ferraro
LOVE AND LARCENY(1963, Fr./Ital.)

John Ferraro
WOLFEN(1981); BABY, IT'S YOU(1983)

Joseph F. Ferraro
1984
PURPLE RAIN(1984)

Livio Ferraro
PLUCKED(1969, Fr./Ital.)

Luigi Ferraro
HELL RAIDERS OF THE DEEP(1954, Ital.)

Ralph Ferraro
SHE BEAST, THE(1966, Brit./Ital./Yugo.), m; KING'S PIRATE(1967), m

Giansiro Ferrata
LA NOTTE(1961, Fr./Ital.)

J. Ferrater-Mora
Misc. Talkies
HERO OF OUR TIME, A(1969), d

Sarah Ferrati
WITCH, THE(1969, Ital.)

Alessandro Ferrau
SWORD OF THE CONQUEROR(1962, Ital.), w; REBEL GLADIATORS, THE(1963, Ital.), w; HERCULES VS THE GIANT WARRIORS(1965 Fr./Ital.), w; MONGOLS, THE(1966, Fr./Ital.), w

Catherina Ferray
MR. H. C. ANDERSEN(1950, Brit.)

Catharina Ferraz
VIOLENT STRANGER(1957, Brit.)

Catherina Ferraz
CAPTAIN'S PARADISE, THE(1953, Brit.); FLAME AND THE FLESH(1954); THUNDERSTORM(1956); MAN ACCUSED(1959)

Catherine Ferraz
SNOWBOUND(1949, Brit.); WRONG NUMBER(1959, Brit.)

Cliff Ferre
ABOUT FACE(1952); SHE'S BACK ON BROADWAY(1953); THREE SAILORS AND A GIRL(1953); LUCKY ME(1954); THEM!(1954); YOUNG AT HEART(1955)

Leo Ferre
CAGE OF GOLD(1950, Brit.)

Michel Ferre
RISE OF LOUIS XIV, THE(1970, Fr.)

Janine Ferreau
SHANGHAI STORY, THE(1954)

Angel Ferreira
I'M DANCING AS FAST AS I CAN(1982)

Ari Ferreira
GIRL IN ROOM 13(1961, U.S./Braz.)

Bibi Ferreira
END OF THE RIVER, THE(1947, Brit.)

Roberto Ferreira
GIVEN WORD, THE(1964, Braz.)

Ken Ferrel
HEAVENLY DAYS(1944)

Pablo Ferrel
SURVIVE!(1977, Mex.)

Conchata Ferrell
NETWORK(1976); HEARTLAND(1980)
1984
NADIA(1984, U.S./Yugo.)

Larry D. Ferrell
1984
RIVER, THE(1984)

Patrick Ferrell
SUMMER RUN(1974), m
Phil Ferrell
DRIVE-IN(1976)
Ray Ferrell
HELL'S FIVE HOURS(1958); REMARKABLE MR. PENNYPACKER, THE(1959); PLUNDERERS, THE(1960); STRANGERS WHEN WE MEET(1960)
Raymond Ferrell
ZERO HOUR!(1957)
Rick Ferrell
BLACK GUNN(1972); TROUBLE MAN(1972)
Ron Ferrell
WARRIORS, THE(1979)
Tod Ferrell
GREAT AMERICAN PASTIME, THE(1956)
Todd Ferrell
TATTERED DRESS, THE(1957)
Tony Ferrell
GREAT FLAMARION, THE(1945)
Bran Ferren
ALTERED STATES(1980), spec eff; DEATHTRAP(1982), spec eff; TEMPEST(1982), spec eff
1984
PLACES IN THE HEART(1984), spec eff
Henry Ferrentino
SHAFT'S BIG SCORE!(1972)
Andrea Ferreol
LA GRANDE BOUFFE(1973, Fr.); 1★2?(1975, Fr.); DESPAIR(1978, Ger.); MYSTERIES(1979, Neth.); SOME LIKE IT COOL(1979, Ger./Aust./Ital./Fr.); TIN DRUM, THE(1979, Ger./Fr./Yugo./Pol.); INCORRIGIBLE(1980, Fr.); LAST METRO, THE(1981, Fr.); LOVERS AND LIARS(1981, Ital.); THREE BROTHERS(1982, Ital.); GIRL FROM TRIESTE, THE(1983, Ital.); LA NUIT DE VARENNES(1983, Fr./Ital.)
1984
LOUISIANE(1984, Fr./Can.)
Jean Francois Ferreol
HAMMETT(1982)
George Ferrer
ISLAND OF THE DOOMED(1968, Span./Ger.), p; LAST MERCENARY, THE(1969, Ital./Span./Ger.), p
Jose Ferrer
JOAN OF ARC(1948); WHIRLPOOL(1949); CRISIS(1950); CYRANO DE BERGERAC(1950); ANYTHING CAN HAPPEN(1952); MOULIN ROUGE(1952); MISS SADIE THOMPSON(1953); CAINE MUTINY, THE(1954); DEEP IN MY HEART(1954); COCKLESHELL HEROES, THE(1955), a, d; SHRIKE, THE(1955), a, d; GREAT MAN, THE(1957), a, d, w; HIGH COST OF LOVING, THE(1958), a, d; I ACCUSE(1958, Brit.), a, d; RETURN TO PEYTON PLACE(1961), d; LAWRENCE OF ARABIA(1962, Brit.); STATE FAIR(1962), d; NINE HOURS TO RAMA(1963, U.S./Brit.); STOP TRAIN 349(1964, Fr./Ital./Ger.); GREATEST STORY EVER TOLD, THE(1965); SHIP OF FOOLS(1965); ENTER LAUGHING(1967); YOUNG REBEL, THE(1969, Fr./Ital./Span.); BIG BUS, THE(1976); FOREVER YOUNG, FOREVER FREE(1976, South Afr.); VOYAGE OF THE DAMNED(1976, Brit.); BEHIND THE IRON MASK(1977); CRASH(1977); SENTINEL, THE(1977); DRACULA'S DOG(1978); FEDORA(1978, Ger./Fr.); PRIVATE FILES OF J. EDGAR HOOVER, THE(1978); SWARM, THE(1978); NATURAL ENEMIES(1979); BIG BRAWL, THE(1980); WHO HAS SEEN THE WIND(1980, Can.); BLOOD TIDE(1982); MIDSUMMER NIGHT'S SEX COMEDY, A(1982); BEING, THE(1983); TO BE OR NOT TO BE(1983)
1984
DUNE(1984); EVIL THAT MEN DO, THE(1984)
Misc. Talkies
ORDER TO KILL(1974); PACO(1976); BLOODY BIRTHDAY(1980)
Jose Luis R. Ferrer
FRANKENSTEIN'S BLOODY TERROR(1968, Span.), art d
Lupita Ferrer
CHILDREN OF SANCHEZ, THE(1978, U. S./Mex.)
Mel Ferrer
LOST BOUNDARIES(1949); BORN TO BE BAD(1950); SECRET FURY, THE(1950), d; VENDETTA(1950), d; BRAVE BULLS, THE(1951); RANCHO NOTORIOUS(1952); SCARAMOUCHE(1952); KNIGHTS OF THE ROUND TABLE(1953); LILI(1953); SAADIA(1953); OH ROSALINDA(1956, Brit.); WAR AND PEACE(1956, Ital./U.S.); PARIS DOES STRANGE THINGS(1957, Fr./Ital.); SUN ALSO RISES, THE(1957); VINTAGE, THE(1957); FRAULEIN(1958); GREEN MANSIONS(1959), d; WORLD, THE FLESH, AND THE DEVIL, THE(1959); BLOOD AND ROSES(1961, Fr./Ital.); DEVIL AND THE TEN COMMANDMENTS, THE(1962, Fr.); LONGEST DAY, THE(1962); FALL OF THE ROMAN EMPIRE, THE(1964); HANDS OF ORLAC, THE(1964, Brit./Fr.); PARIS WHEN IT SIZZLES(1964); SEX AND THE SINGLE GIRL(1964); EL GRECO(1966, Ital., Fr.), a, p; EVERY DAY IS A HOLIDAY(1966, Span.), d, w; WAIT UNTIL DARK(1967), p; NIGHT VISITOR, THE(1970, Swed./U.S.), p; TIME FOR LOVING, A(1971, Brit.), a, p; EMBASSY(1972, Brit.), p; W(1974), p; BRANNIGAN(1975, Brit.); EATEN ALIVE(1976); HI-RIDERS(1978); NORSEMAN, THE(1978); SCREAMERS(1978, Ital.); TEMPTER, THE(1978, Ital.); FIFTH FLOOR, THE(1980); GREAT ALLIGATOR(1980, Ital.); VISITOR, THE(1980, Ital./U.S.); LILI MARLEEN(1981, Ger.); CITY OF THE WALKING DEAD(1983, Span./Ital.)
Melchor Ferrer
FUGITIVE, THE(1947)
Melchor G. Ferrer
GIRL OF THE LIMBERLOST, THE(1945), d
Miguel Ferrer
1984
LOVELINES(1984); STAR TREK III: THE SEARCH FOR SPOCK(1984)
Miguell Ferrer
1984
FLASHPOINT(1984)
Patricia Ferrer
MADAME DEATH(1968, Mex.); VENGEANCE OF THE VAMPIRE WOMEN, THE(1969, Mex.)
Pilar Gomez Ferrer
WHITE SISTER(1973, Ital./Span./Fr.)

Sean Ferrer
THEY ALL LAUGHED(1981)
Tony Ferrer
VENGEANCE OF FU MANCHU, THE(1968, Brit./Ger./Hong Kong/Ireland)
Misc. Talkies
BLIND RAGE(1978); FORTRESS IN THE SUN(1978)
Anthony J. Ferrera
1984
NATURAL, THE(1984)
Bob Ferrera
HONKYTONK MAN(1982)
Franco Ferrera
WAR AND PEACE(1956, Ital./U.S.), md; SQUARE OF VIOLENCE(1963, U.S./Yugo.), md
Paolo Ferrera
UNFAITHFULS, THE(1960, Ital.)
Claude Ferrere
WOMAN FROM MONTE CARLO, THE(1932), w
Jacqueline Ferreri
TALES OF ORDINARY MADNESS(1983, Ital.), p
Marco Ferreri
CONJUGAL BED, THE(1963, Ital.), d, w; CASANOVA '70(1965, Ital.); MAN WITH THE BALLOONS, THE(1968, Ital./Fr.), d, w; DILLINGER IS DEAD(1969, Ital.), d, w; SEED OF MAN, THE(1970, Ital.), d, w; WIND FROM THE EAST(1970, Fr./Ital./Ger.); LA GRANDE BOUFFE(1973, Fr.), d, w; DON'T TOUCH WHITE WOMEN!(1974, Fr.), d, w; LIZA(1976, Fr./Ital.), d, w; BYE BYE MONKEY(1978, Ital/Fr.), d, w; TALES OF ORDINARY MADNESS(1983, Ital.), d, w
Anna Maria Ferrero
SKY IS RED, THE(1952, Ital.); LUXURY GIRLS(1953, Ital.); STRANGE DECEPTION(1953, Ital.); WAR AND PEACE(1956, Ital./U.S.); UNFAITHFULS, THE(1960, Ital.); DESERT WARRIOR(1961 Ital./Span.); LA NOTTE BRAVA(1962, Fr./Ital.); HUNCHBACK OF ROME, THE(1963, Ital.)
Danton Ferrero
SECRET SEVEN, THE(1940)
Fiorella Ferrero
WHITE SLAVE SHIP(1962, Fr./Ital.)
Maria Ferrero
AUSTERLITZ(1960, Fr./Ital./Yugo.)
Martin Ferrero
KNIGHTRIDERS(1981); I OUGHT TO BE IN PICTURES(1982)
Willi Ferrero
LA TERRA TREMA(1947, Ital.), md
Willy Ferrero
FUGITIVE LADY(1951), md; SKY IS RED, THE(1952, Ital.), md; OTHELLO(1955, U.S./Fr./Ital.), md
Marco Ferrerri
APE WOMAN, THE(1964, Ital.), d, w
Helen Ferrers
SALLY IN OUR ALLEY(1931, Brit.); BORN LUCKY(1932, Brit.); HELP YOURSELF(1932, Brit.); LOVE ON THE SPOT(1932, Brit.); RIVER HOUSE GHOST, THE(1932, Brit.); DICK TURPIN(1933, Brit.); GOING STRAIGHT(1933, Brit.); MAN WHO WON, THE(1933, Brit.); MEET MY SISTER(1933, Brit.); SUMMER LIGHTNING(1933, Brit.); GET YOUR MAN(1934, Brit.); GUEST OF HONOR(1934, Brit.); POWER(1934, Brit.); PRIMROSE PATH, THE(1934, Brit.); LOOK UP AND LAUGH(1935, Brit.); RED WAGON(1936)
Dante Ferreti
AND THE SHIP SAILS ON(1983, Ital./Fr.), art d
Dante Ferretti
MEDEA(1971, Ital./Fr./Ger.), art d; TILL MARRIAGE DO US PART(1979, Ital.), art d; ARABIAN NIGHTS(1980, Ital./Fr.), art d; CITY OF WOMEN(1980, Ital./Fr.), art d; LA NUIT DE VARENNES(1983, Fr./Ital.), art d; TALES OF ORDINARY MADNESS(1983, Ital.), prod d&art d
Robert Ferretti
ZAPPED!(1982), ed
Benoist Ferreux
FIVE DAYS ONE SUMMER(1982)
Benoit Ferreux
IT ONLY HAPPENS TO OTHERS(1971, Fr./Ital.); MURMUR OF THE HEART(1971, Fr./Ital./Ger.); VICTORY(1981)
1984
UNTIL SEPTEMBER(1984)
Fabien Ferreux
MURMUR OF THE HEART(1971, Fr./Ital./Ger.)
Constantino Ferri
BRIEF RAPTURE(1952, Ital.), md
Elda Ferri
1984
CORRUPT(1984, Ital.), p
Liani Ferri
LOVE SPECIALIST, THE(1959, Ital.), w
Mark Alan Ferri
Misc. Talkies
GETTING IT ON(1983)
Marsha Ferri
GOIN' SOUTH(1978)
Babette Ferrier
CHLOE IN THE AFTERNOON(1972, Fr.)
Granville Ferrier
COMMISSIONAIRE(1933, Brit.)
Jacques Ferrier
ROMAN HOLIDAY(1953)
Noel Ferrier
LITTLE JUNGLE BOY(1969, Aus.); DEMONSTRATOR(1971, Aus.); PRIVATE COLLECTION(1972, Aus.); ALVIN PURPLE(1974, Aus.); ALVIN RIDES AGAIN(1974, Aus.); SCOBIE MALONE(1975, Aus.); DEATHCHEATERS(1976, Aus.); ELIZA FRASER(1976, Aus.); YEAR OF LIVING DANGEROUSLY, THE(1982, Aus.); ESCAPE 2000(1983, Aus.); RETURN OF CAPTAIN INVINCIBLE, THE(1983, Aus./U.S.)

Pat Ferrier
DAMN YANKEES(1958), ch
Jacques Ferriere
SUCKER, THE(1966, Fr./Ital.)
Jean-Pierre Ferriere
WEB OF FEAR(1966, Fr./Span.), w
Martine Ferriere
SUNDAYS AND CYBELE(1962, Fr.); STOLEN KISSES(1969, Fr.); MISSISSIPPI MERMAID(1970, Fr./Ital.); SUCH A GORGEOUS KID LIKE ME(1973, Fr.)
Audrey Ferries
Misc. Silents
BEWARE OF MARRIED MEN(1928)
Lou Ferrigno
HERCULES(1983)
Kenneth Ferrill
NEW WINE(1941)
Frank Ferrin
HINDU, THE(1953, Brit.), p,d&w
Ralph Ferrin
HINDU, THE(1953, Brit.), art d
Carolyn Ferrini
HIDE IN PLAIN SIGHT(1980)
Francesco Ferrini
MAN OF LA MANCHA(1972)
Franco Ferrini
1984
ONCE UPON A TIME IN AMERICA(1984), w
Gianni Ferrio
FIANCES, THE(1964, Ital.), m; FEW BULLETS MORE, A(1968, Ital./Span.), m; GIRL GAME(1968, Braz./Fr./Ital.), m; DIRTY OUTLAWS, THE(1971, Ital.), m; MAN CALLED SLEDGE, A(1971, Ital.), m; MYSTERIOUS ISLAND OF CAPTAIN NEMO, THE(1973, Fr./Ital. 87m Span./Cameroon), m; DON'T TURN THE OTHER CHEEK(1974, Ital./Ger./Span.), m; NO WAY OUT(1975, Ital./Fr.), m
Caroline Ferriol
JACKSON COUNTY JAIL(1976), ed; STUNT MAN, THE(1980), ed; CUTTER AND BONE(1981), ed
Albert Ferris
LUCKY JORDAN(1942); SEARCHING WIND, THE(1946)
Audrey Ferris
JAZZ SINGER, THE(1927); LITTLE WILDCAT, THE(1928); WOMEN THEY TALK ABOUT(1928); FANCY BAGGAGE(1929); GLAD RAG DOLL, THE(1929); HONKY TONK(1929); UNDERTOW(1930); JUSTICE TAKES A HOLIDAY(1933)
Misc. Talkies
BEWARE OF BACHELORS(1928); MARRIAGE BARGAIN, THE(1935)
Silents
GINSBERG THE GREAT(1927); SAILOR IZZY MURPHY(1927); SILVER SLAVE, THE(1927); SLIGHTLY USED(1927); POWDER MY BACK(1928)
Misc. Silents
RINTY OF THE DESERT(1928)
Barbara Ferris
TOM THUMB(1958, Brit./U.S.); TERM OF TRIAL(1962, Brit.); BITTER HARVEST(1963, Brit.); CHILDREN OF THE DAMNED(1963, Brit.); PAIR OF BRIEFS, A(1963, Brit.); SPARROWS CAN'T SING(1963, Brit.); PLACE TO GO, A(1964, Brit.); HAVING A WILD WEEKEND(1965, Brit.); GIRL GETTERS, THE(1966, Brit.); INTERLUDE(1968, Brit.); NICE GIRL LIKE ME, A(1969, Brit.)
Beth Ferris
HEARTLAND(1980), p, w
Cheryl Ferris
STACY'S KNIGHTS(1983)
Fred Ferris
KIND OF LOVING, A(1962, Brit.); SOME PEOPLE(1964, Brit.)
Gamp Ferris
RING-A-DING RHYTHM(1962, Brit. 73m Amicus/COL bw (G.B: IT'S TRAD, DAD!), cos
Geoff Ferris
GREAT TRAIN ROBBERY, THE(1979, Brit.)
Irena Ferris
PATERNITY(1981)
1984
COVERGIRL(1984, Can.)
James Ferris
FRESH FROM PARIS(1955); PARIS FOLLIES OF 1956(1955)
Jane Ferris
ELECTRA GLIDE IN BLUE(1973)
John Ferris
SOMEONE AT THE DOOR(1950, Brit.), ed; CLOUDBURST(1952, Brit.), ed; NEVER LOOK BACK(1952, Brit.), ed; STRANGE CASE OF DR. MANNING, THE(1958, Brit.), ed; HIDDEN HOMICIDE(1959, Brit.), ed; HOME IS THE HERO(1959, Ireland), ed
Loraine Ferris
YOUNG CYCLE GIRLS, THE(1979)
Mark Ferris
INVASION OF THE STAR CREATURES(1962)
Melissa Ferris
SOMEBODY KILLED HER HUSBAND(1978)
Merle Ferris
Misc. Silents
STRONGER WILL, THE(1928)
Michael Ferris
TITANIC(1953); PAL JOEY(1957)
Miguel Ferris
REBELLION OF THE HANGED, THE(1954, Mex.)
Mike Ferris
KILLING OF A CHINESE BOOKIE, THE(1976), ph
Miriam Ferris
Silents
PICTURE OF DORIAN GRAY, THE(1916, Brit.)
Misc. Silents
IN THE GRIP OF THE SULTAN(1915, Brit.); MRS. CASSELL'S PROFESSION(1915, Brit.); BONNIE MARY(1918, Brit.); RIGHT ELEMENT, THE(1919, Brit.)

Paul Ferris
SORCERERS, THE(1967, Brit.), m, md; CONQUEROR WORM, THE(1968, Brit.), a, m; CREEPING FLESH,THE(1973, Brit.), m; PERSECUTION(1974, Brit.), m
Stan Ferris
TULIPS(1981, Can), d
Wally Ferris
ACROSS 110TH STREET(1972), w
Walter Ferris
UNDER TWO FLAGS(1936), w; DEATH TAKES A HOLIDAY(1934), w; LLOYDS OF LONDON(1936), w; HEIDI(1937), w; MAID OF SALEM(1937), w; FOUR MEN AND A PRAYER(1938), w; YANK AT OXFORD, A(1938), w; LITTLE PRINCESS, THE(1939), w; MAGNIFICENT FRAUD, THE(1939), w; SUSANNAH OF THE MOUNTIES(1939), w; SWISS FAMILY ROBINSON(1940), w; TOM BROWN'S SCHOOL DAYS(1940), w; MELODY FOR THREE(1941), w; GALLANT BLADE, THE(1948), w; AT SWORD'S POINT(1951), w
Harry Ferritt
MAGIC NIGHT(1932, Brit.), m
Miguel Angel Ferritz
PASSION ISLAND(1943, Mex.)
Miguel Angel Ferriz
LEGEND OF A BANDIT, THE(1945, Mex.)
Anthony Ferro
HAIR(1979)
Pablo Ferro
GREASER'S PALACE(1972)
Turi Ferro
MALICIOUS(1974, Ital.); BLOOD FEUD(1979, Ital.)
Talya Ferro
LET'S DO IT AGAIN(1975); SPARKLE(1976)
Turo Ferro
ERNESTO(1979, Ital.)
Robert C. Ferro, Jr.
FOOLS(1970)
Sharon Ferrol
ZELIG(1983)
Edda Ferronao
EASY LIFE, THE(1963, Ital.); LET'S TALK ABOUT WOMEN(1964, Fr./Ital.); ORGANIZER, THE(1964, Fr./Ital./Yugo.); CURSE OF THE BLOOD GHOULS(1969, Ital.)
Dan Ferrone
COME SPY WITH ME(1967); WELCOME TO HARD TIMES(1967); PLAZA SUITE(1971)
George Ferroni
BACCHANTES, THE(1963, Fr./Ital.), d
Giorgio Ferroni
TROJAN HORSE, THE(1962, Fr./Ital.), d; MILL OF THE STONE WOMEN(1963, Fr./Ital.), d, w; CONQUEST OF MYCENE(1965, Ital., Fr.), d, w
Rheya Ferrooh
SATAN'S MISTRESS(1982)
Franco Ferrrini
BINGO BONGO(1983, Ital.), w
Ferrule
WINGS OVER AFRICA(1939)
Ferrusquilla
LITTLEST OUTLAW, THE(1955); MASSACRE(1956); GUNS FOR SAN SEBASTIAN(1968, U.S./Fr./Mex./Ital.)
Jose Angel Espinosa Ferrusquilla
GIGANTES PLANETARIOS(1965, Mex.)
April Ferry
1984
MIKE'S MURDER(1984), a, cos
Christian Ferry
RAPTURE(1965), p; UP FROM THE BEACH(1965), p; BLUE MAX, THE(1966), p; GIVE HER THE MOON(1970, Fr./Ital.), p
David Ferry
HIGH-BALLIN'(1978); HOUNDS... OF NOTRE DAME, THE(1980, Can.); PARALLELS(1980, Can.)
1984
BAY BOY(1984, Can.)
Faith Ferry
SIERRA BARON(1958)
Frank Ferry
WING AND A PRAYER(1944)
Isidoro Martinez Ferry
FACE OF TERROR(1964, Span.), d
Jean Ferry
JENNY LAMOUR(1948, Fr.), w; MANON(1950, Fr.), w; DAUGHTERS OF DESTINY(1954, Fr./Ital.), w; NANA(1957, Fr./Ital.), w; NATHALIE(1958, Fr.), w; BABETTE GOES TO WAR(1960, Fr.), w; VERY PRIVATE AFFAIR, A(1962, Fr./Ital.), w; MADAME(1963, Fr./Ital./Span.), w; IMPOSSIBLE ON SATURDAY(1966, Fr./Israel), w; MAN FROM COCODY(1966, Fr/Ital.), w; MALPERTIUS(1972, Bel./Fr.), w
Mike Ferry
HOMER(1970)
Minna Ferry
Silents
GIRLS GONE WILD(1929)
Rafael Ferry
FROM HELL TO VICTORY(1979, Fr./Ital./Span.), set d
Stephen Ferry
SOUTH PACIFIC(1958); THIRTEEN FIGHTING MEN(1960); SPOOK WHO SAT BY THE DOOR, THE(1973); FAST CHARLIE... THE MOONBEAM RIDER(1979)
Steve Ferry
SAND PEBBLES, THE(1966)
Stephen Ferry II
SPOOK WHO SAT BY THE DOOR, THE(1973)
Gil Ferschtman
Misc. Talkies
AMERICAN GAME, THE(1979)

Christine Fersen
FRIENDS AND HUSBANDS(1983, Ger.)
Valerie Fersht
MEATBALLS(1979, Can.)
Alessandro Ferson
ULYSSES(1955, Ital.)
Erich Ferstl
NIGHT OF THE ASKARI(1978, Ger./South African), m
Rene Fert
Misc. Silents
6 ½ X 11(1927, Fr.)
Rene Ferte
TESTAMENT OF DR. MABUSE, THE(1943, Ger.)
Jean-Marie Fertey
THUNDER IN THE BLOOD(1962, Fr.); TIGHT SKIRTS, LOOSE PLEASURES(1966, Fr.)
Marcia Fertig
BUGS BUNNY'S THIRD MOVIE–1001 RABBIT TALES(1982), anim
Yannis Fertis
ELECTRA(1962, Gr.); HOT MONTH OF AUGUST, THE(1969, Gr.)
Pierre Ferval
LA MARSEILLAISE(1938, Fr.)
Christian Ferville
VISCOUNT, THE(1967, Fr./Span./Ital./Ger.)
Marcelle Fery
INNOCENTS IN PARIS(1955, Brit.)
Gabriel Ferzetti
RIPPED-OFF(1971, Ital.)
Gabriele Ferzetti
COUNTERFEITERS, THE(1953, Ital.); CENTO ANNI D'AMORE(1954, Ital.); DEFEND MY LOVE(1956, Ital.); DONATELLA(1956, Ital.); IT HAPPENED IN ROME(1959, Ital.); HANNIBAL(1960, Ital.); L'AVVENTURA(1960, Ital.); CRIME DOES NOT PAY(1962, Fr.); CROSS OF THE LIVING(1962,Fr.); JESSICA(1962, U.S./Ital./Fr.); LE AMICHE(1962, Ital.); LOVE ON THE RIVIERA(1964, Fr./Ital.); LOVE, THE ITALIAN WAY(1964, Ital.); RED LIPS(1964, Fr./Ital.); TORPEDO BAY(1964, Ital./Fr.); BIBLE...IN THE BEGINNING, THE(1966); WE STILL KILL THE OLD WAY(1967, Ital.); DEVIL IN LOVE, THE(1968, Ital.); BETTER A WIDOW(1969, Ital.); ON HER MAJESTY'S SECRET SERVICE(1969, Brit.); ONCE UPON A TIME IN THE WEST(1969, U.S./Ital.); THANK YOU, AUNT(1969, Ital.); CANNABIS(1970, Fr.); CONFESSION, THE(1970, Fr.); LOVE PROBLEMS(1970, Ital.); MACHINE GUN McCAIN(1970, Ital.); THAT SPLENDID NOVEMBER(1971, Ital./Fr.); HITLER: THE LAST TEN DAYS(1973, Brit./Ital.); NIGHT PORTER, THE(1974, Ital./U.S.); END OF THE GAME(1976, Ger./Ital.); MATTER OF TIME, A(1976, Ital./U.S.); MY FIRST LOVE(1978, Fr.); BURNING YEARS, THE(1979, Ital.); PSYCHIC, THE(1979, Ital.); INCHON(1981)
1984
BASILEUS QUARTET(1984, Ital.)
Misc. Talkies
BANDITS IN ROME(1967, Ital.)
Gabrielle Ferzetti
IMPERIAL VENUS(1963, Ital./Fr.)
Henri Fescourt
Misc. Silents
LA NUIT DU 13(1921, Fr.), d; LES GRANDS(1924, Fr.), d; UN FILS D'AMERIQUE(1925, Fr.), d; LA GLU(1927, Fr.), d; LA MAISON DU MALTAIS(1927, Fr.), d; L'OCCIDENT(1928, Fr.), d; MONTE-CRISTO(1929, Fr.), d
Richard Fescud
HITLER: THE LAST TEN DAYS(1973, Brit./Ital.)
Doris Fesette
EDGE OF FURY(1958); MADISON AVENUE(1962)
Michael Fessier
SOCIETY DOCTOR(1935), w; EXCLUSIVE STORY(1936), w; SPEED(1936), w; WOMEN ARE TROUBLE(1936), w; SONG OF THE CITY(1937), p, w; WOMEN MEN MARRY, THE(1937), p; VALLEY OF THE GIANTS(1938), w; ANGELS WASH THEIR FACES(1939), w; ESPIONAGE AGENT(1939), w; WINGS OF THE NAVY(1939), w; HE STAYED FOR BREAKFAST(1940), w; IT ALL CAME TRUE(1940), w; KNOCKOUT(1941), w; YOU'LL NEVER GET RICH(1941), w; YOU WERE NEVER LOVELIER(1942), w; FIRED WIFE(1943), w; GREENWICH VILLAGE(1944), w; HER PRIMITIVE MAN(1944), p, w; MERRY MONAHANS, THE(1944), p, w; SAN DIEGO, I LOVE YOU(1944), p, w; FRONTIER GAL(1945), p, w; THAT NIGHT WITH YOU(1945), p, w; THAT'S THE SPIRIT(1945), p, w; LOVER COME BACK(1946), p&w; SLAVE GIRL(1947), p, w; WOMAN THEY ALMOST LYNCHED, THE(1953), w; BOY FROM OKLAHOMA, THE(1954), w; RED GARTERS(1954), w
Ulli Fessl
SOPHIE'S CHOICE(1982)
Edward I. Fessler
BAYOU(1957), w, m
Michael Fessler
ALL-AMERICAN CHUMP(1936), p
Fred Festinger
WILD, WILD WINTER(1966)
Stepin Fetchet
Silents
NAMELESS MEN(1928)
Stepin Fetchit
BIG TIME(1929); FOX MOVIETONE FOLLIES(1929); GHOST TALKS, THE(1929); HEARTS IN DIXIE(1929); SALUTE(1929); SHOW BOAT(1929); THRU DIFFERENT EYES(1929); CAMEO KIRBY(1930); SWING HIGH(1930); NECK AND NECK(1931); WILD HORSE(1931); CAROLINA(1934); DAVID HARUM(1934); JUDGE PRIEST(1934); MARIE GALANTE(1934); STAND UP AND CHEER(1934 80m FOX bw); WORLD MOVES ON, THE(1934); BACHELOR OF ARTS(1935); CHARLIE CHAN IN EGYPT(1935); COUNTY CHAIRMAN, THE(1935); HELLDORADO(1935); ONE MORE SPRING(1935); STEAMBOAT ROUND THE BEND(1935); VIRGINIA JUDGE, THE(1935); DIMPLES(1936); THIRTY SIX HOURS TO KILL(1936); FIFTY ROADS TO TOWN(1937); LOVE IS NEWS(1937); ON THE AVENUE(1937); HIS EXCITING NIGHT(1938); ZENOBIA(1939); MIRACLE IN HARLEM(1948); BEND OF THE RIVER(1952); SUN SHINES BRIGHT, THE(1953); AMAZING GRACE(1974)
Misc. Talkies
BIG FIGHT, THE(1930); BIG TIMERS(1947)

Silents
IN OLD KENTUCKY(1927); TRAGEDY OF YOUTH, THE(1928); KID'S CLEVER, THE(1929)
Andre Fetet
ONCE IN PARIS(1978)
Ernest Fetge
AMAZING TRANSPARENT MAN, THE(1960), prod d
Jim Fetherolf
SAVAGE SAM(1963), spec eff; THREE LIVES OF THOMASINA, THE(1963, U.S./Brit.), spec eff
Ed Fetherston
I AM THE LAW(1938); TWO LATINS FROM MANHATTAN(1941)
Eddie Fetherston
TRUE TO THE NAVY(1930); MYSTERY TRAIN(1931); MOVIE CRAZY(1932); EVERY NIGHT AT EIGHT(1935); GOLDEN ARROW, THE(1936); LONE WOLF RETURNS, THE(1936); MILKY WAY, THE(1936); RETURN OF SOPHIE LANG, THE(1936); WEDDING PRESENT(1936); CRIMINALS OF THE AIR(1937); GAME THAT KILLS, THE(1937); MAN WHO CRIED WOLF, THE(1937); PAID TO DANCE(1937); SHADOW, THE(1937); SUBMARINE D-1(1937); WINGS OVER HONOLULU(1937); LONE WOLF IN PARIS, THE(1938); SQUADRON OF HONOR(1938); SWING, SISTER, SWING(1938); THERE'S ALWAYS A WOMAN(1938); WHO KILLED GAIL PRESTON?(1938); WOMEN IN PRISON(1938); YOU CAN'T TAKE IT WITH YOU(1938); GOLDEN BOY(1939); HERO FOR A DAY(1939); HOMICIDE BUREAU(1939); LONE WOLF SPY HUNT, THE(1939); MR. SMITH GOES TO WASHINGTON(1939); DANGER ON WHEELS(1940); HOLD THAT WOMAN(1940); MY SON IS GUILTY(1940); WOMEN WITHOUT NAMES(1940); MANPOWER(1941); MEET JOHN DOE(1941); PUBLIC ENEMIES(1941); UNSEEN ENEMY(1942); JOLSON STORY, THE(1946); SECOND CHANCE(1947); VARIETY GIRL(1947); MAN FROM COLORADO, THE(1948)
Misc. Talkies
RIDIN' FOOL, THE(1931)
Silents
OLD IRONSIDES(1926)
Edward [Eddie J] Fetherston
PECOS RIVER(1951)
R.C. Fetherston-Haugh
NORTHWEST MOUNTED POLICE(1940), w
Ed Fetherstone
BOSTON BLACKIE AND THE LAW(1946)
Eddie Fetherstone
FACE ON THE BARROOM FLOOR, THE(1932); TAXI!(1932); CAT'S PAW, THE(1934); HERE COMES THE NAVY(1934); ST. LOUIS KID, THE(1934); THEODORA GOES WILD(1936); KID GALAHAD(1937); CONFESSIONS OF BOSTON BLACKIE(1941); UNFINISHED BUSINESS(1941); LADY IN A JAM(1942); WHAT'S BUZZIN COUSIN?(1943)
Edward Fetherstone
HAPPY LANDING(1934)
Jan Fethke
THOUSAND EYES OF DR. MABUSE, THE(1960, Fr./Ital./Ger.), w
V. Fetisov
NINE DAYS OF ONE YEAR(1964, USSR), makeup
Buzz Fetshans
BIG WEDNESDAY(1978), p
Henry D. Fetter
PROMISES IN THE DARK(1979)
Peter Fetterman
NEITHER THE SEA NOR THE SAND(1974, Brit.), p; FULL CIRCLE(1977, Brit./Can.), p; HAUNTING OF JULIA, THE(1981, Brit./Can.), p; YES, GIORGIO(1982), p
Richard Fetterman
DANDY, THE ALL AMERICAN GIRL(1976), ed; TAKE DOWN(1979), ed
Curt Fetters
TERRIFIED!(1963), ph
Edmund Fetting
PORTRAIT OF LENIN(1967, Pol./USSR); SARAGOSSA MANUSCRIPT, THE(1972, Pol.)
Gary Fettis
OUTSIDERS, THE(1983), set d
Darrell Fetty
WIND AND THE LION, THE(1975); STUNTS(1977); BLOOD BEACH(1981)
Miriam Feuche
Misc. Silents
SHE(1917)
Walter Feuchtenberg
THREE PENNY OPERA(1963, Fr./Ger.); MADDEST CAR IN THE WORLD, THE(1974, Ger.)
Leon Feuchtwanger
POWER(1934, Brit.), w
Cy Feuer
DOWN IN ARKANSAW(1938), m; HIGGINS FAMILY, THE(1938), m; I STAND ACCUSED(1938), md; NIGHT HAWK, THE(1938), md; PALS OF THE SADDLE(1938), md; SHINE ON, HARVEST MOON(1938), md; ARIZONA KID, THE(1939), md; CALLING ALL MARINES(1939), m; COME ON RANGERS(1939), md; COVERED TRAILER, THE(1939), md; DAYS OF JESSE JAMES(1939), md; FIGHTING THOROUGHBREDS(1939), m; FLIGHT AT MIDNIGHT(1939), md; FORGED PASSPORT(1939), m; FRONTIER PONY EXPRESS(1939), md; FRONTIER VENGEANCE(1939), md; I WAS A CONVICT(1939), md; IN OLD CALIENTE(1939), md; JEEPERS CREEPERS(1939), md; MAIN STREET LAWYER(1939), md; MICKEY, THE KID(1939), m, md; MYSTERIOUS MISS X, THE(1939), md; PRIDE OF THE NAVY(1939), md; ROUGH RIDERS' ROUNDUP(1939), m; SABOTAGE(1939), md; SHE MARRIED A COP(1939), md; SHOULD HUSBANDS WORK?(1939), m; SMUGGLED CARGO(1939), md; S.O.S. TIDAL WAVE(1939), m, md; SOUTHWARD HO!(1939), md; STREET OF MISSING MEN(1939), md; WALL STREET COWBOY(1939), md; WOMAN DOCTOR(1939), md; ZERO HOUR, THE(1939), md; BARNYARD FOLLIES(1940), md; BORDER LEGION, THE(1940), md; BOWERY BOY(1940), m; COLORADO(1940), md; COVERED WAGON DAYS(1940), m; EARL OF PUDDLESTONE(1940), md; FORGOTTEN GIRLS(1940), md; FRIENDLY NEIGHBORS(1940), md; GANGS OF CHICAGO(1940), md; GHOST VALLEY RAIDERS(1940), md; GIRL FROM GOD'S COUNTRY(1940), md; GIRL FROM HAVANA(1940), md; GRAND OLE OPRY(1940), md; GRANDPA GOES TO TOWN(1940), md; HEROES OF THE SADDLE(1940), m; HIT PARADE OF 1941(1940), md; IN OLD MISSOURI(1940),

m; LONE STAR RAIDERS(1940), m; MELODY AND MOONLIGHT(1940), md; MONEY TO BURN(1940), md; ONE MAN'S LAW(1940), m; PIONEERS OF THE WEST(1940), m; RANGER AND THE LADY, THE(1940), m; ROCKY MOUNTAIN RANGERS(1940), m; SCATTERBRAIN(1940), md; SING, DANCE, PLENTY HOT(1940), md; TEXAS TERRORS(1940), m; TRAIL BLAZERS, THE(1940), m; UNDER TEXAS SKIES(1940), m; VILLAGE BARN DANCE(1940), m; WAGONS WESTWARD(1940), md; WHO KILLED AUNT MAGGIE?(1940), m&md; WOLF OF NEW YORK(1940), md; WOMEN IN WAR(1940), md; YOUNG BILL HICKOK(1940), md; YOUNG BUFFALO BILL(1940), md; APACHE KID, THE(1941), m; ARKANSAS JUDGE(1941), md; BAD MAN OF DEADWOOD(1941), m; BEHIND THE NEWS(1941), md; COUNTRY FAIR(1941), m; DEATH VALLEY OUTLAWS(1941), m; DESERT BANDIT(1941), m; DEVIL PAYS OFF, THE(1941), md; DOCTORS DON'T TELL(1941), md; GANGS OF SONORA(1941), m; GAY VAGABOND, THE(1941), m; GREAT TRAIN ROBBERY, THE(1941), m; ICE-CAPADES(1941), md; IN OLD CHEYENNE(1941), md; KANSAS CYCLONE(1941), m; LADY FOR A NIGHT(1941), md; LADY FROM LOUISIANA(1941), md; MAN BETRAYED, A(1941), md; MR. DISTRICT ATTORNEY(1941), m; NEVADA CITY(1941), m, md; OUTLAWS OF THE CHEROKEE TRAIL(1941), md; PETTICOAT POLITICS(1941), md; PHANTOM COWBOY, THE(1941), md; PITTSBURGH KID, THE(1941), md; PRAIRIE PIONEERS(1941), m; PUDDIN' HEAD(1941), md; RAGS TO RICHES(1941), m; RED RIVER VALLEY(1941), m; ROBIN HOOD OF THE PECOS(1941), md; ROOKIES ON PARADE(1941), md; SADDLEMATES(1941), m; SHERIFF OF TOMBSTONE(1941), md; SIS HOPKINS(1941), md; TUXEDO JUNCTION(1941), m; TWO GUN SHERIFF(1941), m, md; WYOMING WILDCAT(1941), md; GIRL FROM ALASKA(1942), md; HI, NEIGHBOR(1942), md; IN OLD CALIFORNIA(1942), md; JESSE JAMES, JR.(1942), m; JOAN OF OZARK(1942), md; MAN FROM CHEYENNE(1942), md; MOONLIGHT MASQUERADE(1942), md; OLD HOMESTEAD, THE(1942), md; PARDON MY STRIPES(1942), md; PHANTOM PLAINSMEN, THE(1942), md; RAIDERS OF THE RANGE(1942), m; REMEMBER PEARL HARBOR(1942), md; ROMANCE ON THE RANGE(1942), md; SHEPHERD OF THE OZARKS(1942), m, md; SLEEPYTIME GAL(1942), md; SOMBRERO KID, THE(1942), md; SONS OF THE PIONEERS(1942), md; SOUTH OF SANTA FE(1942), md; STAGECOACH EXPRESS(1942), md; SUNSET ON THE DESERT(1942), md; TRAGEDY AT MIDNIGHT, A(1942), m; YOKEL BOY(1942), md; DRUMS OF FU MANCHU(1943), m; YOUTH ON PARADE(1943), md; EARL CARROLL SKETCHBOOK(1946), md; PLAINSMAN AND THE LADY(1946), md; RENDEZVOUS WITH ANNIE(1946), md; THAT BRENNAN GIRL(1946), md; CALENDAR GIRL(1947), md; DRIFTWOOD(1947), md; HIT PARADE OF 1947(1947), md; WINTER WONDERLAND(1947), md; WYOMING(1947), md; FLAME, THE(1948), md; WHERE'S CHARLEY?(1952, Brit.), p; CABARET(1972), p; PIAF-THE EARLY YEARS(1982, U.S./Fr.), p

Debra Feuer
MOMENT BY MOMENT(1978)
Zachary Feuer
1984
RUNNING HOT(1984), p
Allan Feuerbach
PERSONAL BEST(1982)
Sol E. Feuerman
MIDDLETON FAMILY AT THE N.Y. WORLD'S FAIR(1939), ed
Emanuel Feuermann
Misc. Talkies
ADVENTURE IN MUSIC(1944)
Maya Feuiette
1984
THREE CROWNS OF THE SAILOR(1984, Fr.), p
Louis Feuillade
JUDEX(1966, Fr./Ital.), w
Misc. Silents
L'AVENTURE DES MILLIONS(1916, Fr.), d; LE MALHEUR QUI PASSE(1916, Fr.), d; NOTRA PAUVRE COEUR(1916, Fr.), d; UN MARIAGE DE RAISON(1916, Fr.), d; DESERTEUSE(1917, Fr.), d; HERR DOKTOR(1917, Fr.), d; LA FUGUE DE LILY(1917, Fr.), d; L'AUTRE(1917, Fr.), d; LE BANDEAU SUR LES YEUX(1917, Fr.), d; LE PASSE DE MONIQUE(1918, Fr.), d; LES PETITES MARIONETTES(1918, Fr.), d; LE NOCTURNE(1919, Fr.), d; L'ENGRENAGE(1919, Fr.), d; L'ENIGME(1919, Fr.), d; L'HOMME SAN VISAGE(1919, Fr.), d; VENDEMIAIRE(1919, Fr.), d; LA GOSSELINE(1923, Fr.), d; LE GAMIN DE PARIS(1923, Fr.), d; LA FILLE BIEN GARDEE(1924, Fr.), d; LUCETTE(1924, Fr.), d; PIERROT PIERRETTE(1924, Fr.), d
Serge Feuillard
1984
RAZOR'S EDGE, THE(1984)
Edwige Feuillere
GOLGOTHA(1937, Fr.); LUCREZIA BORGIA(1937, Fr.); COMPLIMENTS OF MR. FLOW(1941, Fr.); BLIND DESIRE(1948, Fr.); EAGLE WITH TWO HEADS(1948, Fr.); IDIOT, THE(1948, Fr.); WOMAN HATER(1949, Brit.); GAME OF LOVE, THE(1954, Fr.); ADORABLE CREATURES(1956, Fr.); LOVE IS MY PROFESSION(1959, Fr.); CRIME DOES NOT PAY(1962, Fr.); TASTE FOR WOMEN, A(1966, Fr./Ital.); LISTEN, LET'S MAKE LOVE(1969, Fr./Ital.)
Octave Feuillet
PARISIAN ROMANCE, A(1932), w
Edwige Feuilliere
TOPAZE(1935, Fr.)
Cy Feurer
MOUNTAIN MOONLIGHT(1941), md
Joseph Feury
JESUS TRIP, THE(1971), p
Peggy Feury
OUTSIDE IN(1972); LAST TYCOON, THE(1976); NEXT MAN, THE(1976); FRIDAY THE 13TH... THE ORPHAN(1979); HEARTACHES(1981, Can.)
1984
ALL OF ME(1984); CRIMES OF PASSION(1984)
Misc. Talkies
WITCH WHO CAME FROM THE SEA, THE(1976); ORPHAN, THE(1979)
Norman Feusier
DIAMOND TRAIL(1933)
Willy Feuter
ONE NIGHT WITH YOU(1948, Brit)
Werner Feuterrer
Misc. Silents
SURVIVAL(1930, Ger.)

Cy Fever
CYCLONE KID, THE(1942), m; ANGEL AND THE BADMAN(1947), md; THAT'S MY MAN(1947), md
Stephane Fey
GUNS(1980, Fr.)
Jean Feyday
DARK EYES(1938, Fr.), w
George Feydeau
HOTEL PARADISO(1966, U.S./Brit.), w
Georges Feydeau
GIRL FROM MAXIM'S, THE(1936, Brit.), w; FLEA IN HER EAR, A(1968, Fr.), w
J.P. Feydeau
SYMPHONIE FANTASTIQUE(1947, Fr.), w
Jean-Pierre Feydeau
DEVIL MADE A WOMAN, THE(1962, Span.), w
Jacques Feyder
DAYBREAK(1931), d; SON OF INDIA(1931), d; CARNIVAL IN FLANDERS(1936, Fr.), d; KNIGHT WITHOUT ARMOR(1937, Brit.), d; PORTRAIT OF A WOMAN(1946, Fr.), p,d&w; FLESH AND THE WOMAN(1954, Fr./Ital.), w; BACK STREETS OF PARIS(1962, Fr.), d
Silents
KISS, THE(1929), d
Misc. Silents
LE RAVIN SANS FOND(1917, Fr.), d; L'INSTINCT EST MAITRE(1917, Fr.), d; L'ATLANTIDE(1921, Fr.), d; CRAINQUEBILLE(1922, Fr.), d; GRIBICHE(1926, Fr.), d; L'IMAGE(1926, Fr.), d; VISAGE D'ENFANTS(1926, Fr.), d; CARMEN(1928, Fr.), d; THERESE RAQUIN(1928, Fr./Ger.), d
Paul Feyder
SECRET WORLD(1969, Fr.), d
L. Feyginova
MY NAME IS IVAN(1963, USSR), ed
Nigel Feyistan
CURSE OF THE VOODOO(1965, Brit.)
Jean Feyte
CONFESSIONS OF A ROGUE(1948, Fr.), ph; MONSIEUR VINCENT(1949, Fr.), ed; GATES OF THE NIGHT(1950, Fr.), ed; CAROLINE CHERIE(1951, Fr.), ed; CADET-ROUSSELLE(1954, Fr.), ed; CASINO DE PARIS(1957, Fr./Ger.), ed; SEVEN CAPITAL SINS(1962, Fr./Ital.), ed; LADIES OF THE PARK(1964, Fr.), ed; DIABOLICAL DR. Z, THE(1966 Span./Fr.), ed; FANTOMAS(1966, Fr./Ital.), ed; GENDARME OF ST. TROPEZ, THE(1966, Fr./Ital.), ed; OSS 117–MISSION FOR A KILLER(1966, Fr./Ital.), ed; SHADOW OF EVIL(1967, Fr./Ital.), ed
David Ffolkes
ALEXANDER THE GREAT(1956), cos; ISLAND IN THE SUN(1957), cos; JOURNEY TO THE CENTER OF THE EARTH(1959), cos; HEAVENS ABOVE!(1963, Brit.), cos; LONG SHIPS, THE(1964, Brit./Yugo.), cos; LIFE AT THE TOP(1965, Brit.), set d; FIGHTING PRINCE OF DONEGAL, THE(1966, Brit.), set d; KALEIDOSCOPE(1966, Brit.), set d; PROMISE HER ANYTHING(1966, Brit.), set d
Gladys Ffolliott
Silents
OLD BILL THROUGH THE AGES(1924, Brit.)
Gwen Ffrangcon-Davies
LADY JANE GREY(1936, Brit.); DEVIL'S OWN, THE(1967, Brit.); DEVIL'S BRIDE, THE(1968, Brit.)
Robert Fiacco
1984
LOVELINES(1984)
Eman Fiala
LEMONADE JOE(1966, Czech.)
George Fiala
SANTA CLAUS CONQUERS THE MARTIANS(1964), makeup
Karel Fiala
LEMONADE JOE(1966, Czech.)
Kveta Fialova
LEMONADE JOE(1966, Czech.); MURDER CZECH STYLE(1968, Czech.); ADELE HASN'T HAD HER SUPPER YET(1978, Czech.)
Clelia Fiamma
TIMES GONE BY(1953, Ital.)
Lewis Fiander
PASSWORD IS COURAGE, THE(1962, Brit.); I START COUNTING(1970, Brit.); DR. JEKYLL AND SISTER HYDE(1971, Brit.); DOCTOR PHIBES RISES AGAIN(1972, Brit.); ABDICATION, THE(1974, Brit.); ISLAND OF THE DAMNED(1976, Span.); SWEENEY 2(1978, Brit.)
Marcello Fianscanaro
MY WAY(1974, South Africa)
Gregorio Fiascanaro
MY WAY(1974, South Africa)
Giulio Fiaschi
RIGOLETTO(1949), p
Frank Fiasconaro
NEW ORLEANS AFTER DARK(1958)
Iaia Fiastri
WHITE SISTER(1973, Ital./Span./Fr.), w; BREAD AND CHOCOLATE(1978, Ital.), w
J. Fiastri
DROP DEAD, MY LOVE(1968, Italy), w
Jaja Fiastri
LOVE AND MARRIAGE(1966, Ital.), w
Carol Ficatier
TEMPEST(1982)
W.F. Fichelscher
DANCING HEART, THE(1959, Ger.), d&w
Al Fichlesfield
Misc. Silents
UP IN MARY'S ATTICK(1920)
Erwin Fichtner
Misc. Silents
HOUND OF THE BASKERVILLES, THE(1914, Ger.)
Mark Fickert
STREAMERS(1983)

Mary Fickett
KATHY O'(1958)

Enrica Fico
IDENTIFICATION OF A WOMAN(1983, Ital.)

Michel Fidanza
JONAH–WHO WILL BE 25 IN THE YEAR 2000(1976, Switz.)

Buster Fiddess
OUTBACK(1971, Aus.)

Shelby Fiddis
THINGS ARE TOUGH ALL OVER(1982)
1984
CHEECH AND CHONG'S THE CORSICAN BROTHERS(1984)

John Fiddy
I AM A GROUPIE(1970, Brit.), m; SWAPPERS, THE(1970, Brit.), m

Nick Fidenco
THOSE DIRTY DOGS(1974, U.S./Ital./Span.), m

Nico Fidenco
TEXICAN, THE(1966, U.S./Span.), m

Fides-Stella
LOVES OF SALAMMBO, THE(1962, Fr./Ital.), p

Jimmie Fidler
GARDEN OF THE MOON(1938)

Kathleen Fidler
FLASH THE SHEEPDOG(1967, Brit.), w

Hal Fieberling
JOE PALOOKA IN WINNER TAKE ALL(1948); CROOKED WAY, THE(1949); SET-UP, THE(1949); YES SIR, THAT'S MY BABY(1949); DIAL 1119(1950)

Hal Fieberling [Hal Baylor]
SANDS OF IWO JIMA(1949)

Felix Fiebich
SONG AND THE SILENCE, THE(1969)

Eva Fiebig
COUNTERFEIT TRAITOR, THE(1962)

Hans Fiebrandt
TINDER BOX, THE(1968, E. Ger.)

Bard Fiedel
DEADLY HERO(1976), m

Brad Fiedel
LOOKING UP(1977), m; JUST BEFORE DAWN(1980), m; NIGHT SCHOOL(1981), m; TERROR EYES(1981), m; HIT AND RUN(1982), m
1984
EYES OF FIRE(1984), m; TERMINATOR, THE(1984), m

Richard H. Fiedel
PEGGY(1950), art d

Jerry Fieding
BIG SLEEP, THE½(1978, Brit.), m

Eric Fiedler
1984
NIGHT SHADOWS(1984), makeup

Erich Fiedler
INTERMEZZO(1937, Ger.); JUDGE AND THE SINNER, THE(1964, Ger.)

John Fiedler
12 ANGRY MEN(1957); STAGE STRUCK(1958); RAISIN IN THE SUN, A(1961); THAT TOUCH OF MINK(1962); GUNS OF DIABLO(1964); KISS ME, STUPID(1964); WORLD OF HENRY ORIENT, THE(1964); GIRL HAPPY(1965); FINE MADNESS, A(1966); FITZWILLY(1967); BALLAD OF JOSIE(1968); ODD COUPLE, THE(1968); RASCAL(1969); TRUE GRIT(1969); SUPPOSE THEY GAVE A WAR AND NOBODY CAME?(1970); HONKY(1971); MAKING IT(1971); DEATHMASTER, THE(1972); SKYJACKED(1972); FORTUNE, THE(1975); SHAGGY D.A., THE(1976); RESCUERS, THE(1977); HARPER VALLEY, P.T.A.(1978); CANNONBALL RUN, THE(1981); FOX AND THE HOUND, THE(1981); SHARKY'S MACHINE(1982); SAVANNAH SMILES(1983)

Josef Fiedler
APRIL 1, 2000(1953, Aust.), m

Elfie Fiegert
TOXI(1952, Ger.)

Monty Fieguth
LAST WAVE, THE(1978, Aus.), spec eff

Erik Fiehn
STRANGER KNOCKS, A(1963, Den.), m

Alex Field
STOP PRESS GIRL(1949, Brit.)

Alexander Field
BEYOND THE CITIES(1930, Brit.); CALL OF THE SEA, THE(1930, Brit.); CROOKED BILLET, THE(1930, Brit.); LAST HOUR, THE(1930, Brit.); LORD RICHARD IN THE PANTRY(1930, Brit.); THIRD TIME LUCKY(1931, Brit.); CROOKED LADY, THE(1932, Brit.); DOWN OUR STREET(1932, Brit.); EBB TIDE(1932, Brit.); MEN OF STEEL(1932, Brit.); TIN GODS(1932, Brit.); WHEN LONDON SLEEPS(1932, Brit.); DICK TURPIN(1933, Brit.); F.P. 1(1933, Brit.); HEAD OF THE FAMILY(1933, Brit.); DOUBLE EVENT, THE(1934, Brit.); INVITATION TO THE WALTZ(1935, Brit.); NO MONKEY BUSINESS(1935, Brit.); BACKSTAGE(1937, Brit.); DON'T GET ME WRONG(1937, Brit.); MAKE IT THREE(1938, Brit.); RETURN OF THE FROG, THE(1938, Brit.); HUMAN MONSTER, THE(1940, Brit.); TORSO MURDER MYSTERY, THE(1940, Brit.); LET THE PEOPLE SING(1942, Brit.); NEXT OF KIN(1942, Brit.); WELCOME, MR. WASHINGTON(1944, Brit.); LOYAL HEART(1946, Brit.); DULCIMER STREET(1948, Brit.); POET'S PUB(1949, Brit.); WARNING TO WANTONS, A(1949, Brit.); SECRET VENTURE(1955, Brit.); THERE'S ALWAYS A THURSDAY(1957, Brit.); UNDERCOVER GIRL(1957, Brit.); NAKED FURY(1959, Brit.); WOMAN EATER, THE(1959, Brit.); PLEASURE LOVERS, THE(1964, Brit.)

Angela Field
1984
HOLLYWOOD HIGH PART II(1984)

Anne Field
MURDER CLINIC, THE(1967, Ital./Fr.)

Arthur J. Field
DANGEROUS PARTNERS(1945), p

Arthur L. Field
CANTERVILLE GHOST, THE(1944), p; TWICE BLESSED(1945), p

Ben Field
CASTE(1930, Brit.); ESCAPE(1930, Brit.); SALLY IN OUR ALLEY(1931, Brit.); MICHAEL AND MARY(1932, Brit.); MURDER ON THE SECOND FLOOR(1932, Brit.); RESERVED FOR LADIES(1932, Brit.); WHEN LONDON SLEEPS(1932, Brit.); GOOD COMPANIONS(1933, Brit.); LITTLE MISS NOBODY(1933, Brit.); MAN FROM TORONTO, THE(1933, Brit.); MRS. DANE'S DEFENCE(1933, Brit.); NIGHT AND DAY(1933, Brit.); LOYALTIES(1934, Brit.); MUSIC HALL(1934, Brit.); SAY IT WITH FLOWERS(1934, Brit.); SECRET OF THE LOCH, THE(1934, Brit.); SING AS WE GO(1934, Brit.); CLAIRVOYANT, THE(1935, Brit.); EVERYTHING OKAY(1936, Brit.); GIRL IN THE TAXI(1937, Brit.); I MARRIED A SPY(1938)
Silents
FACE AT THE WINDOW, THE(1920, Brit.); BACHELORS' CLUB, THE(1921, Brit.); MAN WHO CHANGED HIS NAME, THE(1928, Brit.)
Misc. Silents
LITTLE MISS NOBODY(1923, Brit.); VENETIAN LOVERS(1925, Brit.)

Betty Field
OF MICE AND MEN(1939); WHAT A LIFE(1939); SEVENTEEN(1940); VICTORY(1940); BLUES IN THE NIGHT(1941); SHEPHERD OF THE HILLS, THE(1941); ARE HUSBANDS NECESSARY?(1942); KING'S ROW(1942); FLESH AND FANTASY(1943); GREAT MOMENT, THE(1944); TOMORROW THE WORLD(1944); SOUTHERNER, THE(1945); GREAT GATSBY, THE(1949); PICNIC(1955); BUS STOP(1956); PEYTON PLACE(1957); HOUND-DOG MAN(1959); BUTTERFIELD 8(1960); BIRDMAN OF ALCATRAZ(1962); SEVEN WOMEN(1966); COOGAN'S BLUFF(1968)

Bob Field
ON VELVET(1938, Brit.)

Bradley Field
OFFENDERS, THE(1980)

C.C. Field
Misc. Silents
HUMAN ORCHID, THE(1916), d

Carole H. Field
I WANNA HOLD YOUR HAND(1978)

Charlotte Field
MYSTERIOUS RIDER, THE(1938); PRIDE OF THE WEST(1938)

Crystal Field
SPLENDOR IN THE GRASS(1961)
1984
BIRDY(1984)

Doris Field
Misc. Silents
WEB OF DESIRE, THE(1917)

Edward Salisbury Field
Silents
ZANDER THE GREAT(1925), w

Elinor Field
Silents
GIRLS DON'T GAMBLE(1921)
Misc. Silents
BLUE MOON, THE(1920); KENTUCKY COLONEL, THE(1920); HEARTS AND MASKS(1921); DON QUICKSHOT OF THE RIO GRANDE(1923); RED WARNING, THE(1923); SINGLE HANDED(1923)

Elvin Field
HAPPY LAND(1943); NONE SHALL ESCAPE(1944); CAPTAIN EDDIE(1945)
Misc. Talkies
SAGEBRUSH HEROES(1945)

Esther Field
MOTHERS OF TODAY(1939); ELI ELI(1940)

George Field
GOODBYE, MY LADY(1956), m
Silents
INSIDE THE LINES(1918); END OF THE GAME, THE(1919); DIAMONDS ADRIFT(1921); BLOOD AND SAND(1922); CRIMSON CHALLENGE, THE(1922); NORTH OF THE RIO GRANDE(1922); ADAM'S RIB(1923); MR. BILLINGS SPENDS HIS DIME(1923); STEPHEN STEPS OUT(1923); TIGER'S CLAW, THE(1923)
Misc. Silents
VOICE OF LOVE, THE(1916); WOMAN'S DARING, A(1916); DEUCE DUNCAN(1918); TESTING OF MILDRED VANE, THE(1918); TRICK OF FATE, A(1919); YOU NEVER KNOW(1922); TRIGGER FINGER(1924)

Grace Field
MY MAN GODFREY(1936); IT'S LOVE I'M AFTER(1937)
Silents
AVALANCHE, THE(1919)

Gustave Field
FLIGHT TO HONG KONG(1956), w

Harry Field
EBB TIDE(1937); ROOKIE FIREMAN(1950), w; LOVE IS A WOMAN(1967, Brit.), p; HAND OF NIGHT, THE(1968, Brit.), p; SYNDICATE, THE(1968, Brit.), p; CONNECTING ROOMS(1971, Brit.), p

Helen Field
Misc. Silents
DESPERATE TRAILS(1921)

Jackie Field
THRESHOLD(1983, Can.), art d

John Field
SECRET PEOPLE(1952, Brit.)

Jonathan Field
RACING ROMANCE(1937, Brit.); BEDTIME STORY(1938, Brit.); MERELY MR. HAWKINS(1938, Brit.); MURDER TOMORROW(1938, Brit.); PAID IN ERROR(1938, Brit.); HE FOUND A STAR(1941, Brit.); SALUTE JOHN CITIZEN(1942, Brit.); MILLIONS LIKE US(1943, Brit.); GIVE US THE MOON(1944, Brit.); I'LL BE YOUR SWEETHEART(1945, Brit.); HENRY V(1946, Brit.); I'LL TURN TO YOU(1946, Brit.); FOOLS RUSH IN(1949, Brit.); SHE SHALL HAVE MURDER(1950, Brit.); WORM'S EYE VIEW(1951, Brit.); FATHER'S DOING FINE(1952, Brit.); HIGH TERRACE(1957, Brit.)

Jonathon Field
IT'S IN THE BAG(1943, Brit.)

Josef Field
1984
POLICE ACADEMY(1984)
Juanita Field
TOP OF THE TOWN(1937)
Julian Field
SITTING ON THE MOON(1936), w
Julianna Field
GOLDENGIRL(1979)
Karin Field
CAVE OF THE LIVING DEAD(1966, Yugo./Ger.); FOUNTAIN OF LOVE, THE(1968, Aust.); WEB OF THE SPIDER(1972, Ital./Fr./Ger.); OFFICE GIRLS(1974)
Misc. Talkies
LEGEND OF HORROR(1972); MAD BUTCHER, THE(1972)
Logan Field
PIER 5, HAVANA(1959); THREE CAME TO KILL(1960); BLACULA(1972)
Lyle Field
GOOD GUYS AND THE BAD GUYS, THE(1969), cos
Margaret Field
WELCOME STRANGER(1947); BEYOND GLORY(1948); BIG CLOCK, THE(1948); NIGHT HAS A THOUSAND EYES(1948); PALEFACE, THE(1948); CHICAGO DEAD-LINE(1949); MY FRIEND IRMA(1949); SAMSON AND DELILAH(1949); IT'S A SMALL WORLD(1950); PAID IN FULL(1950); CHAIN OF CIRCUMSTANCE(1951); DAKOTA KID, THE(1951); MAN FROM PLANET X, THE(1951); YUKON MANHUNT(1951); CAPTIVE WOMEN(1952); CARRIE(1952); FOR MEN ONLY(1952); RAIDERS, THE(1952); STORY OF WILL ROGERS, THE(1952); SO THIS IS LOVE(1953); INSIDE DETROIT(1955); MODERN MARRIAGE, A(1962)
Margot Field
LOVERS, HAPPY LOVERS!(1955, Brit.)
Martin Field
MURDER IS MY BEAT(1955), w
Mary Field
CORPSE CAME C.O.D., THE(; BATTLE OF GALLIPOLI(1931, Brit.), ed; CALL IT A DAY(1937); PRINCE AND THE PAUPER, THE(1937); COWBOY FROM BROOK-LYN(1938); HIS EXCITING NIGHT(1938); THERE GOES MY HEART(1938); WHITE BANNERS(1938); DANCING CO-ED(1939); ETERNALLY YOURS(1939); FIGHTING GRINGO, THE(1939); GOOD GIRLS GO TO PARIS(1939); LITTLE ACCIDENT(1939); MADE FOR EACH OTHER(1939); SERGEANT MADDEN(1939); SOCIETY SMUG-GLERS(1939); STORY OF ALEXANDER GRAHAM BELL, THE(1939); STUNT PI-LOT(1939); WHEN TOMORROW COMES(1939); BANK DICK, THE(1940); CONVICTED WOMAN(1940); GIRLS OF THE ROAD(1940); HOWARDS OF VIR-GINIA, THE(1940); INVISIBLE MAN RETURNS, THE(1940); LEGION OF THE LAWLESS(1940); MA, HE'S MAKING EYES AT ME(1940); MY SON, MY SON!(1940); TRAIL BLAZERS, THE(1940); BALL OF FIRE(1941); DR. JEKYLL AND MR. HY-DE(1941); GIRL, A GUY AND A GOB, A(1941); GREAT MR. NOBODY, THE(1941); HOW GREEN WAS MY VALLEY(1941); ONE FOOT IN HEAVEN(1941); SHADOWS ON THE STAIRS(1941); WILD GEESE CALLING(1941); GAY SISTERS, THE(1942); GET HEP TO LOVE(1942); GORILLA MAN(1942); GREAT GILDERSLEEVE, THE(1942); I MARRIED A WITCH(1942); MAJOR AND THE MINOR, THE(1942); MEXICAN SPITFIRE AT SEA(1942); MISS ANNIE ROONEY(1942); MOKEY(1942); MRS. MINIVER(1942); NOW, VOYAGER(1942); THIS ABOVE ALL(1942); WAKE ISLAND(1942); YOU WERE NEVER LOVELIER(1942); HELLO, FRISCO, HEL-LO(1943); PRINCESS O'ROURKE(1943); SALUTE TO THE MARINES(1943); THREE HEARTS FOR JULIA(1943); FOUR JILLS IN A JEEP(1944); FRENCHMAN'S CREEK(1944); HENRY ALDRICH PLAYS CUPID(1944); JOHNNY DOESN'T LIVE HERE ANY MORE(1944); LADIES OF WASHINGTON(1944); MR. SKEFFING-TON(1944); ONCE UPON A TIME(1944); PORT OF 40 THIEVES(1944); AFFAIRS OF SUSAN(1945); LOVE LETTERS(1945); MINISTRY OF FEAR(1945); UNSEEN, THE(1945); WONDER MAN(1945); DARK CORNER, THE(1946); DON'T GAMBLE WITH STRANGERS(1946); HOUSE OF HORRORS(1946); LADY LUCK(1946); LITTLE GIANT(1946); MURDER IN THE MUSIC HALL(1946); ONE MORE TOMOR-ROW(1946); RENDEZVOUS WITH ANNIE(1946); SENTIMENTAL JOURNEY(1946); SONG OF THE SOUTH(1946); DARK PASSAGE(1947); LIFE WITH FATHER(1947); LOUISIANA(1947); MIRACLE ON 34TH STREET, THE(1947); OUT OF THE PAST(1947); SHOCKING MISS PILGRIM, THE(1947); TROUBLE WITH WOMEN, THE(1947); UNFAITHFUL, THE(1947); WELCOME STRANGER(1947); WHERE THERE'S LIFE(1947); CHICKEN EVERY SUNDAY(1948); IF YOU KNEW SU-SIE(1948); JOAN OF ARC(1948); MR. PEABODY AND THE MERMAID(1948); RO-MANCE ON THE HIGH SEAS(1948); SITTING PRETTY(1948); SONG IS BORN, A(1948); UP IN CENTRAL PARK(1948); CONNECTICUT YANKEE IN KING AR-THUR'S COURT, A(1949); DEAR WIFE(1949); HENRY, THE RAINMAKER(1949); TOP O' THE MORNING(1949); CHEAPER BY THE DOZEN(1950); EDGE OF DOOM(1950); FATHER MAKES GOOD(1950); LONE CLIMBER, THE(1950, Brit./Aust.), p; BARE-FOOT MAILMAN, THE(1951); PASSAGE WEST(1951); GREATEST SHOW ON EARTH, THE(1952); MONKEY BUSINESS(1952); SOMETHING TO LIVE FOR(1952); LADY WANTS MINK, THE(1953); FOUR GUNS TO THE BORDER(1954); LUCY GALLANT(1955); PRIVATE WAR OF MAJOR BENSON, THE(1955); TO HELL AND BACK(1955); PRICE OF FEAR, THE(1956); TOY TIGER(1956); MISSOURI TRAVEL-ER, THE(1958); RIDE A CROOKED TRAIL(1958); SEVEN WAYS FROM SUN-DOWN(1960)
Misc. Talkies
FATHER STEPS OUT(1941)
Medora Field
WHO KILLED AUNT MAGGIE?(1940), w; GIRL WHO DARED, THE(1944), w
Nicholas Field
LADY CAROLINE LAMB(1972, Brit./Ital.)
Norma Field
Misc. Talkies
GOSH(1974)
Norman Field
TREE GROWS IN BROOKLYN, A(1945); WHERE DO WE GO FROM HERE?(1945); DESTINATION BIG HOUSE(1950); MILKMAN, THE(1950); MISTER 880(1950); STORM WARNING(1950); CHICAGO CALLING(1951); STREET BANDITS(1951); GREATEST SHOW ON EARTH, THE(1952); INVITATION(1952); SOMETHING FOR THE BIRDS(1952); SOMETHING TO LIVE FOR(1952); CRAZYLEGS, ALL AMERI-CAN(1953); TWONKY, THE(1953); THEM!(1954); TOBOR THE GREAT(1954); MA AND PA KETTLE AT WAIKIKI(1955); UP THE SANDBOX(1972)
Misc. Talkies
ALICE GOODBODY(1974)

Pat Field
QUIET WEEKEND(1948, Brit.)
Patrick Field
GORKY PARK(1983)
Rachel Field
AND NOW TOMORROW(1944), w; TIME OUT OF MIND(1947), w
Rachel Lyman Field
ALL THIS AND HEAVEN TOO(1940), w
Robert Field
CROSS MY HEART(1937, Brit.); HOLIDAY'S END(1937, Brit.); TOO MANY HUS-BANDS(1938, Brit.); SONS OF THE SEA(1939, Brit.)
Ron Field
MARCO(1973), ch; ENTERTAINER, THE(1975), ch; NEW YORK, NEW YORK(1977), ch
Roy Field
SUPERMAN(1978), spec eff; SUPERMAN II(1980), spec eff; DARK CRYSTAL, THE(1982, Brit.), spec eff; SUPERMAN III(1983), spec eff
S. S. Field
PETE'S DRAGON(1977), w
S.S. Field
ON SUCH A NIGHT(1937), w
Salisbury Field
TWIN BEDS(1929), w; IN GAY MADRID(1930), w; NO LIMIT(1931), w; LADIES OF THE JURY(1932), w; SECRETS(1933), w; HIS GREATEST GAMBLE(1934), w; LIFE OF THE PARTY(1934, Brit.), w; WITCHING HOUR, THE(1934), w; TWIN BEDS(1942), w
Silents
TWIN BEDS(1920), w
Sally Field
WAY WEST, THE(1967); STAY HUNGRY(1976); HEROES(1977); SMOKEY AND THE BANDIT(1977); END, THE(1978); HOOPER(1978); BEYOND THE POSEIDON ADVENTURE(1979); NORMA RAE(1979); SMOKEY AND THE BANDIT II(1980); ABSENCE OF MALICE(1981); BACK ROADS(1981); KISS ME GOODBYE(1982)
1984
PLACES IN THE HEART(1984)
Shirley Ann Field
DRY ROT(1956, Brit.); IT'S A WONDERFUL WORLD(1956, Brit.); LOSER TAKES ALL(1956, Brit.); SIMON AND LAURA(1956, Brit.); FLESH IS WEAK, THE(1957, Brit.); GOOD COMPANIONS, THE(1957, Brit.); SILKEN AFFAIR, THE(1957, Brit.); IT'S NEVER TOO LATE(1958, Brit.); HORRORS OF THE BLACK MUSEUM(1959, U.S./Brit.); AND THE SAME TO YOU(1960, Brit.); ENTERTAINER, THE(1960, Brit.); ONCE MORE, WITH FEELING(1960); PEEPING TOM(1960, Brit.); MAN IN THE MOON(1961, Brit.); SATURDAY NIGHT AND SUNDAY MORNING(1961, Brit.); UPSTAIRS AND DOWNSTAIRS(1961, Brit.); WAR LOVER, THE(1962, U.S./Brit.); THESE ARE THE DAMNED(1965, Brit.); CARNABY, M.D.(1967, Brit.); HOUSE OF THE LIVING DEAD(1973, S. Afr.)
Shirley Anne Field
LUNCH HOUR(1962, Brit.); KINGS OF THE SUN(1963); ALFIE(1966, Brit.); HELL IS EMPTY(1967, Brit./Ital)
Shirley Anne "Ann" Field
TEARS FOR SIMON(1957, Brit.)
Shirley-Ann Field
TOUCH OF THE OTHER, A(1970, Brit.)
Sid Field
THAT'S THE TICKET(1940, Brit.); CARDBOARD CAVALIER, THE(1949, Brit.); MY HEART GOES CRAZY(1953, Brit.)
Susan Field
KITCHEN, THE(1961, Brit.); ADVENTURES OF SHERLOCK HOLMES' SMARTER BROTHER, THE(1975, Brit.)
Susi Field
CONQUEROR WORM, THE(1968, Brit.)
Sylvia Field
VOICE OF THE CITY(1929); TILLIE THE TOILER(1941); BLONDIE FOR VIC-TORY(1942); NOBODY'S DARLING(1943); GREAT MOMENT, THE(1944); HER PRIMITIVE MAN(1944); JUNIOR MISS(1945); SALOME, WHERE SHE DAN-CED(1945); ALL MINE TO GIVE(1957)
Silents
EXALTED FLAPPER, THE(1929)
Ted Field
1984
REVENGE OF THE NERDS(1984), p
Virginia Field
LADY IS WILLING, THE(1934, Brit.); PRIMROSE PATH, THE(1934, Brit.); CAREER WOMAN(1936); LADIES IN LOVE(1936); LLOYDS OF LONDON(1936); SING, BABY, SING(1936); THANK YOU, JEEVES(1936); ALI BABA GOES TO TOWN(1937); CHARL-IE CHAN AT MONTE CARLO(1937); LANCER SPY(1937); LONDON BY NIGHT(1937); THINK FAST, MR. MOTO(1937); MR. MOTO TAKES A VACATION(1938); BRIDAL SUITE(1939); CAPTAIN FURY(1939); CISCO KID AND THE LADY, THE(1939); ETERNALLY YOURS(1939); MR. MOTO'S LAST WARNING(1939); SUN NEVER SETS, THE(1939); DANCE, GIRL, DANCE(1940); HUDSON'S BAY(1940); WATERLOO BRIDGE(1940); KNOCKOUT(1941); SINGAPORE WOMAN(1941); ATLANTIC CON-VOY(1942); CRYSTAL BALL, THE(1943); STAGE DOOR CANTEEN(1943); PERFECT MARRIAGE, THE(1946); CHRISTMAS EVE(1947); DREAM GIRL(1947); IMPERFECT LADY, THE(1947); LADIES' MAN(1947); REPEAT PERFORMANCE(1947); VARIETY GIRL(1947); CONNECTICUT YANKEE IN KING ARTHUR'S COURT, A(1949); JOHN LOVES MARY(1949); DIAL 1119(1950); LADY PAYS OFF, THE(1951); WEEKEND WITH FATHER(1951); VEILS OF BAGDAD, THE(1953); ROCKABILLY BABY(1957); APPOINTMENT WITH A SHADOW(1958); EXPLOSIVE GENERATION, THE(1961); EARTH DIES SCREAMING, THE(1964, Brit.); FRIDAY THE 13TH(1980), art d; FRIDAY THE 13TH PART II(1981), prod d; STRANGER IS WATCHING, A(1982), art d; SPRING BREAK(1983), prod d
1984
EXTERMINATOR 2(1984), art d
Misc. Talkies
APPOINTMENT WITH A SHADOW(1957)
Marjorie Fieldding
YELLOW CANARY, THE(1944, Brit.)

Beatrix Fielden-Kaye
NO LIMIT(1935, Brit.); KEEP YOUR SEATS PLEASE(1936, Brit.); LOVE AT SEA(1936, Brit.); SHOW GOES ON, THE(1938, Brit.); TROUBLE BREWING(1939, Brit.)
Ann Fielder
DARK ANGEL, THE(1935)
David Fielder
SUPERMAN III(1983)
Harry Fielder
MC VICAR(1982, Brit.)
John Fielder
GREAT BANK ROBBERY, THE(1969); I AM THE CHEESE(1983)
Brig. Gen. Kendall J. Fielder
FROM HERE TO ETERNITY(1953), tech adv
Kitty Fielder
Silents
QUESTION OF TRUST, A(1920, Brit.)
Misc. Silents
YELLOW CLAW, THE(1920, Brit.)
Larry Fielder
EVERYBODY DOES IT(1949)
Pat Fielder
MONSTER THAT CHALLENGED THE WORLD, THE(1957), w; VAMPIRE, THE(1957), w; FLAME BARRIER, THE(1958), w; RETURN OF DRACULA, THE(1958), w; GERONIMO(1962), w
Richard Fielder
DISTANT TRUMPET, A(1964), w; THIS SAVAGE LAND(1969), w; ADAM'S WOMAN(1972, Austral.), w
Carnegie Fieldhouse
NOW AND FOREVER(1983, Aus.), p
Athene Fielding
GREEK TYCOON, THE(1978)
Daisy L. Fielding
MOUNTAINS O'MOURNE(1938, Brit.), w
Dorothy Fielding
PURSUIT OF D.B. COOPER, THE(1981); KISS ME GOODBYE(1982)
Ed Fielding
GUEST WIFE(1945)
Edward Fielding
ALL THIS AND HEAVEN TOO(1940); DOWN ARGENTINE WAY(1940); HOUSE ACROSS THE BAY, THE(1940); INVISIBLE MAN RETURNS, THE(1940); KITTY FOYLE(1940); MARYLAND(1940); REBECCA(1940); SOUTH OF SUEZ(1940); HOLD BACK THE DAWN(1941); I WANTED WINGS(1941); IN THE NAVY(1941); PARACHUTE BATTALION(1941); SCOTLAND YARD(1941); SKYLARK(1941); SO ENDS OUR NIGHT(1941); SUSPICION(1941); BEYOND THE BLUE HORIZON(1942); IN THIS OUR LIFE(1942); MAJOR AND THE MINOR, THE(1942); PACIFIC RENDEZVOUS(1942); PRIDE OF THE YANKEES, THE(1942); TEN GENTLEMEN FROM WEST POINT(1942); FLESH AND FANTASY(1943); HIGHER AND HIGHER(1943); MADAME CURIE(1943); MR. LUCKY(1943); PILOT NO. 5(1943); SHADOW OF A DOUBT(1943); SONG OF BERNADETTE, THE(1943); TENDER COMRADE(1943); WHAT A WOMAN!(1943); BELLE OF THE YUKON(1944); DEAD MAN'S EYES(1944); LADY IN THE DARK(1944); MAN IN HALF-MOON STREET, THE(1944); MR. SKEFFINGTON(1944); MRS. PARKINGTON(1944); MY PAL, WOLF(1944); SEE HERE, PRIVATE HARGROVE(1944); STORY OF DR. WASSELL, THE(1944); COLONEL EFFINGHAM'S RAID(1945); HAVING WONDERFUL CRIME(1945); MEDAL FOR BENNY, A(1945); MINISTRY OF FEAR(1945); SARATOGA TRUNK(1945); SPELLBOUND(1945); BEAUTIFUL CHEAT, THE(1946)
Silents
ETERNAL TEMPTRESS, THE(1917)
Misc. Silents
SHERLOCK HOLMES(1916); BEAUTIFUL ADVENTURE, THE(1917)
Fenella Fielding
FOLLOW A STAR(1959, Brit.); DOCTOR IN LOVE(1960, Brit.); FOXHOLE IN CAIRO(1960, Brit.); CARRY ON REGARDLESS(1961, Brit.); NO LOVE FOR JOHNNIE(1961, Brit.); DOCTOR IN DISTRESS(1963, Brit.); OLD DARK HOUSE, THE(1963, Brit.); IN THE DOGHOUSE(1964, Brit.); ARRIVEDERCI, BABY!(1966, Brit.); CARRY ON SCREAMING(1966, Brit.); LOCK UP YOUR DAUGHTERS(1969, Brit.)
Fennella Fielding
CARNABY, M.D.(1967, Brit.)
Gerald Fielding
I TAKE THIS WOMAN(1931); JUST A GIGOLO(1931); NIGHT CLUB LADY(1932); SCARLET EMPRESS, THE(1934); PRICE OF A SONG, THE(1935, Brit.); MAN BEHIND THE MASK, THE(1936, Brit.); CHUMP AT OXFORD, A(1940); NEW MOON(1940); IT HAD TO BE YOU(1947); LAST RITES(1980)
Guy Fielding
CANDLES AT NINE(1944, Brit.)
Henry Fielding
TOM JONES(1963, Brit.), w; LOCK UP YOUR DAUGHTERS(1969, Brit.), w; BAWDY ADVENTURES OF TOM JONES, THE(1976, Brit.), w; JOSEPH ANDREWS(1977, Brit.), w
Jan Fielding
KLUTE(1971)
Jerry Fielding
ADVISE AND CONSENT(1962), m; NUN AND THE SERGEANT, THE(1962), m; FOR THOSE WHO THINK YOUNG(1964), m, md; MC HALE'S NAVY(1964), m; MC HALE'S NAVY JOINS THE AIR FORCE(1965), m; WILD BUNCH, THE(1969), m; SUPPOSE THEY GAVE A WAR AND NOBODY CAME?(1970), m; JOHNNY GOT HIS GUN(1971), m; LAWMAN(1971), m; NIGHT COMERS, THE(1971, Brit.), m, md; STRAW DOGS(1971, Brit.), m; CHATO'S LAND(1972), m; JUNIOR BONNER(1972), m; MECHANIC, THE(1972), m, md; DEADLY TRACKERS(1973), m; OUTFIT, THE(1973), m; SCORPIO(1973), m; BRING ME THE HEAD OF ALFREDO GARCIA(1974), m; GAMBLER, THE(1974), m; SUPER COPS, THE(1974), m; BLACK BIRD, THE(1975), m; KILLER ELITE, THE(1975), m; BAD NEWS BEARS, THE(1976), m; ENFORCER, THE(1976), m; OUTLAW JOSEY WALES, THE(1976), m; DEMON SEED(1977), m; GAUNTLET, THE(1977), m; SEMI-TOUGH(1977), m; GRAY LADY DOWN(1978), m; BEYOND THE POSEIDON ADVENTURE(1979), m; BELOW THE BELT(1980), m; FUNERAL HOME(1982, Can.), m
Leo Fielding
ADVENTURES OF MARCO POLO, THE(1938)

Lisabeth Fielding
FOXFIRE(1955)
Lorraine Fielding
THIS TIME FOR KEEPS(1947), w
Majorie Fielding
PROJECT M7(1953, Brit.)
Margaret Fielding
ISLE OF LOST SHIPS(1929); PARIS(1929); MOON'S OUR HOME, THE(1936); TO MARY-WITH LOVE(1936); NANCY STEELE IS MISSING(1937); YOU CAN'T BUY LUCK(1937); YOU CAN'T HAVE EVERYTHING(1937)
Silents
MISCHIEF MAKER, THE(1916); EXILES, THE(1923); KENTUCKY DAYS(1923); NIGHT SHIP, THE(1925)
Misc. Silents
EVERY GIRL'S DREAM(1917)
Marjorie Fielding
CRIME OF PETER FRAME, THE(1938, Brit.); GIRL IN DISTRESS(1941, Brit.); QUIET WEDDING(1941, Brit.); ADVENTURE FOR TWO(1945, Brit.); FAME IS THE SPUR(1947, Brit.); EASY MONEY(1948, Brit.); QUIET WEEKEND(1948, Brit.); AMAZING MR. BEECHAM, THE(1949, Brit.); CONSPIRATOR(1949, Brit.); SPRING IN PARK LANE(1949, Brit.); MUDLARK, THE(1950, Brit.); TRIO(1950, Brit.); CIRCLE OF DANGER(1951, Brit.); LAVENDER HILL MOB, THE(1951, Brit.); PORTRAIT OF CLARE(1951, Brit.); CRASH OF SILENCE(1952, Brit.); FRANCHISE AFFAIR, THE(1952, Brit.); MAGIC BOX, THE(1952, Brit.); LAUGHING IN THE SUNSHINE(1953, Brit./Swed.); ROB ROY, THE HIGHLAND ROGUE(1954, Brit.); WOMAN'S ANGLE, THE(1954, Brit.)
Richard Fielding [Robert Maxwell]
SUPERMAN AND THE MOLE MEN(1951), w
Romaine Fielding
Silents
CRIMSON DOVE, THE(1917), d; WOMAN'S MAN(1920); MAN WORTH WHILE, THE(1921), a, d; NOOSE, THE(1928)
Misc. Silents
DESERT HONEYMOON, A(1915); EAGLE'S NEST(1915), a, d; VALLEY OF LOST HOPE, THE(1915), a, d; WESTERN GOVERNOR'S HUMANITY, A(1915), a, d; FOR THE FREEDOM OF THE WORLD(1917); MORAL COURAGE(1917), d; YOUTH(1917), d; RICH SLAVE, THE(1921), d; GUN GOSPEL(1927); TEN MODERN COMMANDMENTS(1927)
Sean Fielding
DESERT PATROL(1962, Brit.), w
Sol Baer Fielding
BRIGHT ROAD(1953), p; JEOPARDY(1953), p; TENNESSEE CHAMP(1954), p; TROOPER HOOK(1957), p
Tom Fielding
CHANGES(1969); MODEL SHOP, THE(1969); WALK IN THE SPRING RAIN, A(1970)
Misc. Talkies
MIDDLE PASSAGE(1978), d
A. Roland Fields
TIME OF YOUR LIFE, THE(1948), set d; BLOOD ON THE SUN(1945), set d; FRANCIS(1949), set d; STORY OF MOLLY X, THE(1949), set d; UNDERTOW(1949), set d; WINCHESTER '73(1950), art d
Al Fields
MAGNIFICENT AMBERSONS, THE(1942), set d; GOVERNMENT GIRL(1943), set d; I WALKED WITH A ZOMBIE(1943), set d; IRON MAJOR, THE(1943), set d; LEOPARD MAN, THE(1943), set d; TENDER COMRADE(1943), set d; THIS LAND IS MINE(1943), set d; MADEMOISELLE FIFI(1944), set d; ALL MY SONS(1948), set d; FAMILY HONEYMOON(1948), set d; ONE TOUCH OF VENUS(1948), set d; CALAMITY JANE AND SAM BASS(1949), set d; SWORD IN THE DESERT(1949), set d
Alex Fields
PRELUDE TO FAME(1950, Brit.)
Alexander Fields
RED WAGON(1936)
Arabella Fields
LOVE IN MOROCCO(1933, Fr.)
Benny Fields
BIG BROADCAST OF 1937, THE(1936); MINSTREL MAN(1944)
Betty Fields
OLD SPANISH CUSTOMERS(1932, Brit.); TONIGHT'S THE NIGHT(1932, Brit.); LOST IN THE LEGION(1934, Brit.); EVERYTHING OKAY(1936, Brit.); HOW TO SAVE A MARRIAGE-AND RUIN YOUR LIFE(1968)
Cal Fields
RED, WHITE AND BLACK, THE(1970)
Charlie Fields
BETSY, THE(1978); FISH HAWK(1981, Can.)
Chip Fields
BLUE COLLAR(1978)
Cliff Fields
DAY OF THE NIGHTMARE(1965)
Cornell Fields
BLACK RODEO(1972)
Darlene Fields
SNOW CREATURE, THE(1954); BETRAYED WOMEN(1955); GIRL RUSH, THE(1955); BETWEEN HEAVEN AND HELL(1956); MAN IS ARMED, THE(1956); GUNSIGHT RIDGE(1957); SPOOK CHASERS(1957)
David Fields
WORLD ACCORDING TO GARP, The(1982)
Don Fields
IT'S A BIG COUNTRY(1951)
Dorothy Fields
JOY OF LIVING(1938), w, m; FATHER TAKES A WIFE(1941), w; LET'S FACE IT(1943), w; STAGE DOOR CANTEEN(1943); SOMETHING FOR THE BOYS(1944), w; MEXICAN HAYRIDE(1948), w; SAXON CHARM, THE(1948), m/l; UP IN CENTRAL PARK(1948), w; ANNIE GET YOUR GUN(1950), w; LOVELY TO LOOK AT(1952), w; SWEET CHARITY(1969), w
Eddie Fields
SILENT PARTNER(1944); FABULOUS SUZANNE, THE(1946)
Eddy Fields
END OF THE ROAD(1944); ROAD TO THE BIG HOUSE(1947); GAMBLING HOUSE(1950); PRISONERS OF THE CASBAH(1953); SALOME(1953)

Edith Fields
QUEEN OF HEARTS(1936, Brit.); PROMISES IN THE DARK(1979); LOVING COUPLES(1980); FORCE: FIVE(1981); KISS ME GOODBYE(1982)
1984
MICKI AND MAUDE(1984)

Eleanor Fields
Silents
LITTLE EVA ASCENDS(1922)

Elinor Fields
JEALOUSY(1934)

Freddie Fields
LIPSTICK(1976), p; LOOKING FOR MR. GOODBAR(1977), p; WHOLLY MOSES(1980), p; VICTORY(1981), p

George Fields
CAMPUS SLEUTH(1948); SMART POLITICS(1948); I WAS AN AMERICAN SPY(1951)

Grace Fields
PREJUDICE(1949)

Gracie Fields
SALLY IN OUR ALLEY(1931, Brit.); LOOKING ON THE BRIGHT SIDE(1932, Brit.); THIS WEEK OF GRACE(1933, Brit.); LOVE, LIFE AND LAUGHTER(1934, Brit.); SING AS WE GO(1934, Brit.); LOOK UP AND LAUGH(1935, Brit.); QUEEN OF HEARTS(1936, Brit.); SHOW GOES ON, THE(1937, Brit.); SMILING ALONG(1938, Brit.); WE'RE GOING TO BE RICH(1938, Brit.); SHIPYARD SALLY(1940, Brit.), a, w; HOLY MATRIMONY(1943); STAGE DOOR CANTEEN(1943); MOLLY AND ME(1945); PARIS UNDERGROUND(1945)

Gwenn Fields
FATHER WAS A FULLBACK(1949)

Harry Fields
RETURN TO CAMPUS(1975), m

Herbert Fields
HIT THE DECK(1930), d&w; LEATHERNECKING(1930), w; FIFTY MILLION FRENCHMEN(1931), w; HOT HEIRESS(1931), w; DOWN TO THEIR LAST YACHT(1934), w; LET'S FALL IN LOVE(1934), w; ACCENT ON YOUTH(1935), w; HANDS ACROSS THE TABLE(1935), w; MISSISSIPPI(1935), w; PEOPLE WILL TALK(1935), w; SHIP CAFE(1935), w; SWEET SURRENDER(1935), w; LOVE BEFORE BREAKFAST(1936), w; LUCKIEST GIRL IN THE WORLD, THE(1936), w; FOOLS FOR SCANDAL(1938), w; JOY OF LIVING(1938), w; HONOLULU(1939), w; STRIKE UP THE BAND(1940), w; FATHER TAKES A WIFE(1941), w; PANAMA HATTIE(1942), w; DU BARRY WAS A LADY(1943), w; LET'S FACE IT(1943), w; SOMETHING FOR THE BOYS(1944), w; MEXICAN HAYRIDE(1948), w; UP IN CENTRAL PARK(1948), w; SLIGHTLY FRENCH(1949), w; ANNIE GET YOUR GUN(1950), w; HIT THE DECK(1955), w
Misc. Silents
PORCELAIN LAMP, THE(1921)

Issac Fields
RED, WHITE AND BLACK, THE(1970)

J. Don Fields
COUNTRY BOY(1966), art d

J. T. Fields
CURSE OF BIGFOOT, THE(1972), w

Jackie Fields
BIG CITY(1937)

Jeanne Fields
HUMAN HIGHWAY(1982), w

Jimmy Fields
SWEET CHARITY(1969)

Joe Fields
TAKING OF PELHAM ONE, TWO, THREE, THE(1974); PUTNEY SWOPE(1969); HI, MOM!(1970)

John Fields
CURSE OF BIGFOOT, THE(1972), d
Misc. Talkies
PINOCCHIO'S STORYBOOK ADVENTURES(1979)

John H. Fields
CAT PEOPLE(1982)

Joseph Fields
BIG SHOT, THE(1931), w; WATERFRONT LADY(1935), w; $1,000 A MINUTE(1935), w; GENTLEMAN FROM LOUISIANA(1936), w; PALM SPRINGS(1936), w; WALKING DEAD, THE(1936), w; REPORTED MISSING(1937), w; WHEN LOVE IS YOUNG(1937), w; FOOLS FOR SCANDAL(1938), w; TWO GIRLS ON BROADWAY(1940), w; LOUISIANA PURCHASE(1941), w; MY SISTER EILEEN(1942), w; JUNIOR MISS(1945), w; NIGHT IN CASABLANCA, A(1946), w; LOST HONEYMOON(1947), w; MAN FROM TEXAS, THE(1948), p; SMART WOMAN(1948); BRIDE FOR SALE(1949), w; FARMER TAKES A WIFE, THE(1953), w; GENTLEMEN PREFER BLONDES(1953), w; MY SISTER EILEEN(1955), w; TUNNEL OF LOVE, THE(1958), p, w; HAPPY ANNIVERSARY(1959), w; FLOWER DRUM SONG(1961), p, w

Joseph A. Fields
ANNIE OAKLEY(1935), w; LIGHTNING STRIKES TWICE(1935), w; GRAND JURY(1936), w; THAT GIRL FROM PARIS(1937), w; RICH MAN, POOR GIRL(1938), w; GIRL AND THE GAMBLER(1939), w; GIRL FROM MEXICO, THE(1939), w; MEXICAN SPITFIRE(1939), w; SPELLBINDER(1939), w; TWO THOROUGHBREDS(1939), w; DOUGHGIRLS, THE(1944), w

Josh Fields, M.D.
NOT AS A STRANGER(1955), tech adv

Juanita Fields
NEW FACES OF 1937(1937)

Juli Fields
1984
KARATE KID, THE(1984)

Karen Fields
SLEEPAWAY CAMP(1983)

Kathy Fields
HAPPY ENDING, THE(1969); JOHNNY GOT HIS GUN(1971)

Leigh Fields
MAN FROM TEXAS, THE(1948), w

Leonard Fields
COLLEGE LOVE(1929), w; MISSISSIPPI GAMBLER(1929), w; DEVIL'S MATE(1933), w; KING KELLY OF THE U.S.A(1934), d, w; MANHATTAN LOVE SONG(1934), d, w; SCARLET LETTER, THE(1934), w; UNKNOWN BLONDE(1934), w; STREAMLINE EXPRESS(1935), d, w; WOMAN WANTED(1935), w; ALL OVER TOWN(1937), p; IT COULD HAPPEN TO YOU(1937), p; MR. DISTRICT ATTORNEY(1941), p; I KILLED THAT MAN(1942), w; SECRETS OF THE UNDERGROUND(1943), p; CARTER CASE, THE(1947), p

Lew Fields
STORY OF VERNON AND IRENE CASTLE, THE(1939); LILLIAN RUSSELL(1940)
Misc. Silents
(; MAN WHO STOOD STILL, THE(1916); BARKER, THE(1917); FRIENDLY ENEMIES(1925)

Linda Fields
THAT'S THE WAY OF THE WORLD(1975)

Lois Fields
CRIME DOCTOR'S DIARY, THE(1949)

Lorraine Fields
1984
PROTOCOL(1984)

Lynn Fields
ANGEL IN MY POCKET(1969); SWEET CHARITY(1969)

Mary Fields
CRYSTAL BALL, THE(1943); LADY TAKES A CHANCE, A(1943); OTHER LOVE, THE(1947)

Maurie Fields
BREAK OF DAY(1977, Aus.); IN SEARCH OF ANNA(1978, Aus.); FIGHTING BACK(1983, Brit.)

Moses Fields
BLACK RODEO(1972)

Norman Fields
FARMER'S OTHER DAUGHTER, THE(1965); OCTAMAN(1971); SWEET JESUS, PREACHER MAN(1973)

P.K. Fields
SO FINE(1981)

Peppy Fields
HOT STUFF(1979)

Peter Allan Fields
SPY IN THE GREEN HAT, THE(1966), w

Poppy Fields
STOOLIE, THE(1972)

Ralph Fields
HAPPY ANNIVERSARY(1959), p

Randy Fields
SHELL SHOCK(1964), w

Richard Fields
Misc. Talkies
NIGHT OF THE DEMON(1980)

Rick Fields
VICE GIRLS, LTD.(1964)

Robert Fields
INCIDENT, THE(1967); THEY SHOOT HORSES, DON'T THEY?(1969); SPORTING CLUB, THE(1971); RHINOCEROS(1974); JETLAG(1981, U.S./Span.); STAR 80(1983)

Robert S. Fields
COVER ME BABE(1970)

Roland Fields
MILKMAN, THE(1950), set d

Salisbury Fields
SMART WOMAN(1931), w

Sam Fields
STAGE TO BLUE RIVER(1951), ed; DEAD MAN'S TRAIL(1952), ed; FARGO(1952), ed; MAN FROM BLACK HILLS, THE(1952), ed; MAVERICK, THE(1952), ed; NIGHT RAIDERS(1952), ed; TEXAS CITY(1952), ed; WACO(1952), ed; FIGHTING LAWMAN, THE(1953), ed; HOMESTEADERS, THE(1953), ed; MARKSMAN, THE(1953), ed; REBEL CITY(1953), ed; STAR OF TEXAS(1953), ed; TEXAS BAD MAN(1953), ed; TOPEKA(1953), ed; VIGILANTE TERROR(1953), ed; BITTER CREEK(1954), ed; DESPERADO, THE(1954), ed; FORTYNINERS, THE(1954), ed; JUNGLE GENTS(1954), ed

Sammy Fields
TEXAS LAWMEN(1951), ed; WHISTLING HILLS(1951), ed

Samuel Fields
LAWLESS COWBOYS(1952), ed; HUMAN JUNGLE, THE(1954), ed; TWO GUNS AND A BADGE(1954), ed

Samuel Fields [Mario Chiari]
GHOST, THE(1965, Ital.), art d

Shep Fields
CITIZENS BAND(1977), p

Sid Fields
IN SOCIETY(1944), w; MEXICAN HAYRIDE(1948); FOR HEAVEN'S SAKE(1950)

Sidney Fields
ALI BABA GOES TO TOWN(1937); LOVE IS NEWS(1937); NAUGHTY NINETIES, THE(1945); MY WILD IRISH ROSE(1947), w

Sidney H. Fields
STRIKE ME PINK(1936)

Stanley Fields
NEW YORK NIGHTS(1929); BORDER LEGION, THE(1930); HER MAN(1930); HOOK, LINE AND SINKER(1930); LADIES LOVE BRUTES(1930); MAMMY(1930); MANSLAUGHTER(1930); SEE AMERICA THIRST(1930); STREET OF CHANCE(1930); CITY STREETS(1931); CRACKED NUTS(1931); HOLY TERROR, A(1931); LITTLE CAESAR(1931); RIDERS OF THE PURPLE SAGE(1931); SKYLINE(1931); TRAVELING HUSBANDS(1931); DESTRY RIDES AGAIN(1932); GIRL CRAZY(1932); GIRL OF THE RIO(1932); HELL'S HIGHWAY(1932); KID FROM SPAIN, THE(1932); MOUTHPIECE, THE(1932); ONE WAY PASSAGE(1932); PAINTED WOMAN(1932); RACKETY RAX(1932); SHERLOCK HOLMES(1932); TWO KINDS OF WOMEN(1932); WAY BACK HOME(1932); DESTINATION UNKNOWN(1933); ISLAND OF LOST SOULS(1933); ROMAN SCANDALS(1933); TERROR ABOARD(1933); HE COULDN'T TAKE IT(1934); KID MILLIONS(1934); MANY HAPPY RETURNS(1934); NAME THE WOMAN(1934); PALOOKA(1934); ROCKY RHODES(1934); SING AND LIKE IT(1934); STRICTLY DYNAMITE(1934); CAPTAIN HURRICANE(1935); DARING YOUNG MAN, THE(1935); HELLDORADO(1935); MUTINY ON THE BOUNTY(1935); DEVIL IS A

SISSY, THE(1936); GAY DESPERADO, THE(1936); MINE WITH THE IRON DOOR, THE(1936); O'MALLEY OF THE MOUNTED(1936); SHOW BOAT(1936); TICKET TO PARADISE(1936); ALI BABA GOES TO TOWN(1937); ALL OVER TOWN(1937); COUNSEL FOR CRIME(1937); DANGER–LOVE AT WORK(1937); HIT PARADE, THE(1937); LAST TRAIN FROM MADRID, THE(1937); MAID OF SALEM(1937); MIDNIGHT COURT(1937); SHEIK STEPS OUT, THE(1937); SOULS AT SEA(1937); THREE LEGIONNAIRES, THE(1937); TOAST OF NEW YORK, THE(1937); WAY OUT WEST(1937); WELLS FARGO(1937); WIFE, DOCTOR AND NURSE(1937); ADVENTURES OF MARCO POLO, THE(1938); ALGIERS(1938); ARSENE LUPIN RETURNS(1938); FLIRTING WITH FATE(1938); OF HUMAN HEARTS(1938); PAINTED DESERT, THE(1938); PANAMINT'S BAD MAN(1938); ROLL ALONG, COWBOY(1938); SISTERS, THE(1938); STRAIGHT, PLACE AND SHOW(1938); WIDE OPEN FACES(1938); BLACKWELL'S ISLAND(1939); CHASING DANGER(1939); EXILE EXPRESS(1939); FUGITIVE AT LARGE(1939); HELL'S KITCHEN(1939); KID FROM KOKOMO, THE(1939); LIFE RETURNS(1939); OFF THE RECORD(1939); PACK UP YOUR TROUBLES(1939); GREAT PLANE ROBBERY, THE(1940); KING OF THE LUMBERJACKS(1940); NEW MOON(1940); SKI PATROL(1940); VIVA CISCO KID(1940); WYOMING(1940); I'LL SELL MY LIFE(1941); LADY FROM CHEYENNE(1941); WHERE DID YOU GET THAT GIRL?(1941)
Misc. Talkies
CONSTANT WOMAN, THE(1933)

Tara Fields
GANJA AND HESS(1973)

Tommy Fields
LOOK UP AND LAUGH(1935, Brit.); PENNY POOL, THE(1937, Brit.); SMILING ALONG(1938, Brit.)

Vanetta Fields
STAR IS BORN, A(1976)

Verna Fields
STUDS LONIGAN(1960), ed; CRY OF BATTLE(1963), ed; COUNTRY BOY(1966), ed; DEATHWATCH(1966), ed; TRACK OF THUNDER(1967), ed; WILD RACERS, THE(1968), ed; MEDIUM COOL(1969), ed; WHAT'S UP, DOC?(1972), ed; AMERICAN GRAFFITI(1973), ed; PAPER MOON(1973), ed; DAISY MILLER(1974), ed; MEMORY OF US(1974), ed; SUGARLAND EXPRESS, THE(1974), ed; JAWS(1975), ed

Virginia Fields
SUPER SPOOK(1975)

Vivian Fields
HONOR OF THE PRESS(1932)

W. C. Fields [Charles Bogle]
HER MAJESTY LOVE(1931); IF I HAD A MILLION(1932); MILLION DOLLAR LEGS(1932); ALICE IN WONDERLAND(1933); INTERNATIONAL HOUSE(1933); TILLIE AND GUS(1933); IT'S A GIFT(1934), w; MRS. WIGGS OF THE CABBAGE PATCH(1934); OLD-FASHIONED WAY, THE(1934); SIX OF A KIND(1934); YOU'RE TELLING ME(1934); DAVID COPPERFIELD(1935); MAN ON THE FLYING TRAPEZE, THE(1935), w; MISSISSIPPI(1935); POPPY(1936); BIG BROADCAST OF 1938, THE(1937); YOU CAN'T CHEAT AN HONEST MAN(1939); BANK DICK, THE(1940); MY LITTLE CHICKADEE(1940), a, w; NEVER GIVE A SUCKER AN EVEN BREAK(1941); FOLLOW THE BOYS(1944); SENSATIONS OF 1945(1944); SONG OF THE OPEN ROAD(1944); DOWN MEMORY LANE(1949)
Silents
JANICE MEREDITH(1924); "THAT ROYLE GIRL"(1925); SALLY OF THE SAWDUST(1925); IT'S THE OLD ARMY GAME(1926), w, t; SO'S YOUR OLD MAN(1926); POTTERS, THE(1927); TWO FLAMING YOUTHS(1927); TILLIE'S PUNCTURED ROMANCE(1928)
Misc. Silents
RUNNING WILD(1927); FOOLS FOR LUCK(1928)

Robert Fieldsteel
1984
LOVE STREAMS(1984)

Wilfred Fienburgh
NO LOVE FOR JOHNNIE(1961, Brit.), w

Jack Fier
FIVE LITTLE PEPPERS AND HOW THEY GREW(1939), p; SMASHING THE SPY RING(1939), p; DURANGO KID, THE(1940), p; BLONDE FROM SINGAPORE, THE(1941), p; MEDICO OF PAINTED SPRINGS, THE(1941), p; MYSTERY SHIP(1941), p; OUTLAWS OF THE PANHANDLE(1941), p; PINTO KID, THE(1941), p; RICHEST MAN IN TOWN(1941), p; SECRETS OF THE LONE WOLF(1941), p; STORK PAYS OFF, THE(1941), p; SWEETHEART OF THE CAMPUS(1941), p; BAD MEN OF THE HILLS(1942), p; DOWN RIO GRANDE WAY(1942), p; LAWLESS PLAINSMEN(1942), p; PARDON MY GUN(1942), p; RIDERS OF THE NORTHLAND(1942), p; SABOTAGE SQUAD(1942), p; SWEETHEART OF THE FLEET(1942), p; COWBOY IN THE CLOUDS(1943), p; DOUGHBOYS IN IRELAND(1943), p; FIGHTING BUCKAROO, THE(1943), p; HAIL TO THE RANGERS(1943), p; LAUGH YOUR BLUES AWAY(1943), p; LAW OF THE NORTHWEST(1943), p; ROBIN HOOD OF THE RANGE(1943), p; WHAT'S BUZZIN COUSIN?(1943), p; BLACK PARACHUTE, THE(1944), p; COWBOY CANTEEN(1944), p; COWBOY FROM LONESOME RIVER(1944), p; CYCLONE PRAIRIE RANGERS(1944), p; GHOST THAT WALKS ALONE, THE(1944), p; RIDING WEST(1944), p; SUNDOWN VALLEY(1944), p; SWING IN THE SADDLE(1944), p; THEY LIVE IN FEAR(1944), p; TWO-MAN SUBMARINE(1944), p; SERGEANT MIKE(1945), p

Steve Fierberg
FIRST TIME, THE(1983), ph

Steven Fierberg
FORTY DEUCE(1982), ph; VORTEX(1982), ph

Teven Fierberg
1984
MIXED BLOOD(1984), p

Enzo Fiermonte
MERCHANT OF SLAVES(1949, Ital.); BURIED ALIVE(1951, Ital.); NEVER TAKE NO FOR AN ANSWER(1952, Brit./Ital.); ROMEO AND JULIET(1954, Brit.); ANGELA(1955, Ital.); BEN HUR(1959); NAKED MAJA, THE(1959, Ital./U.S.); GODDESS OF LOVE, THE(1960, Ital./Fr.); PHAROAH'S WOMAN, THE(1961, Ital.); ROCCO AND HIS BROTHERS(1961, Fr./Ital.); AVENGER, THE(1962, Fr./Ital.); EVA(1962, Fr./Ital.); SODOM AND GOMORRAH(1962, U.S./Fr./Ital.); SLAVE, THE(1963, Ital.); SANDOKAN THE GREAT(1964, Fr./Ital./Span.); SECRET INVASION, THE(1964); HERCULES VS THE GIANT WARRIORS(1965 Fr./Ital.); GRAND PRIX(1966); WILD, WILD PLANET, THE(1967, Ital.); MINUTE TO PRAY, A SECOND TO DIE, A(1968, Ital.); BLACK VEIL FOR LISA, A(1969 Ital./Ger.); LONG RIDE FROM HELL, A(1970, Ital.); TRINITY IS STILL MY NAME(1971, Ital.); WAR BETWEEN THE PLANETS(1971, Ital.); MECHANIC, THE(1972)

Enzo Fiermonti
SNCW DEVILS, THE(1965, Ital.)

Paul Fiero
RED RIVER(1948)

Paul Fierra
INTRIGUE(1947)

Iole Fierro
ANGELO(1951, Ital.); MONSTER OF THE ISLAND(1953, Ital.)

Lee Fierro
JAWS(1975)

Paul Fierro
NEW YORK TOWN(1941); T-MEN(1947); CASBAH(1948); HE WALKED BY NIGHT(1948); LOVES OF CARMEN, THE(1948); RIVER LADY(1948); SECRET BEYOND THE DOOR, THE(1948); SORRY, WRONG NUMBER(1948); SCENE OF THE CRIME(1949); ABBOTT AND COSTELLO IN THE FOREIGN LEGION(1950); I WAS A SHOPLIFTER(1950); ONE WAY STREET(1950); CALLAWAY WENT THATAWAY(1951); HIS KIND OF WOMAN(1951); PASSAGE WEST(1951); YELLOW FIN(1951); FIGHTER, THE(1952); KANSAS CITY CONFIDENTIAL(1952); WACO(1952); FIGHTER ATTACK(1953); JEOPARDY(1953); PERILOUS JOURNEY, A(1953); RIDE, VAQUERO!(1953); SAN ANTONE(1953); WINGS OF THE HAWK(1953); ESCAPE TO BURMA(1955); CREATURE WALKS AMONG US, THE(1956); DIG THAT URANIUM(1956); RAW EDGE(1956); STAGECOACH TO FURY(1956); YAQUI DRUMS(1956); WAR DRUMS(1957); OREGON PASSAGE(1958); PIER 5, HAVANA(1959)

Valentina Fierro
OUT OF THE BLUE(1982)

Patrick Fierry
FRENCH POSTCARDS(1979)

Harvey Fierstein
1984
GARBO TALKS(1984)

Jacques Fieschi
1984
A NOS AMOURS(1984, Fr.)

Jean-Andre Fieschi
ALPHAVILLE, A STRANGE CASE OF LEMMY CAUTION(1965, Fr.)

Karl Fieseler
MY CHILDHOOD(1972, Brit.)

Fieve
LIQUID SKY(1982), makeup

Marcel Fieve
LIQUID SKY(1982)

Alan Fife
PAJAMA PARTY(1964); HOW TO STUFF A WILD BIKINI(1965); GHOST IN THE INVISIBLE BIKINI(1966)

Allen Fife
LOST, LONELY AND VICIOUS(1958)

Jack Fife
Silents
KING OF KINGS, THE(1927)

Maxine Fife
HAIL THE CONQUERING HERO(1944); ONE BODY TOO MANY(1944); OUR HEARTS WERE YOUNG AND GAY(1944); PRACTICALLY YOURS(1944); STORY OF DR. WASSELL, THE(1944); INCENDIARY BLONDE(1945); MEDAL FOR BENNY, A(1945); ROAD TO UTOPIA(1945)

Randy Fife
SILENT RAGE(1982), spec eff
1984
PLACES IN THE HEART(1984)

Shannon Fife
Silents
GOD'S HALF ACRE(1916), w; HABIT OF HAPPINESS, THE(1916), a, w; RAINBOW PRINCESS, THE(1916), w; JOHNNY-ON-THE-SPOT(1919), w; MAN AND HIS WOMAN(1920), w; LAVENDER BATH LADY, THE(1922), w; SECOND HAND LOVE(1923), w

Ada Fifford
Silents
FLORIDA ENCHANTMENT, A(1914)

Fifi
WHO'S MINDING THE STORE?(1963)

Steve Fifield
GREASED LIGHTNING(1977)

The Fifty Dancing Beauties
HIT THE ICE(1943)

Anton Fig
KING BLANK(1983), m

Stewart Figa
CLASS(1983)

Raul Figarola
SIXTEEN FATHOMS DEEP(1934)

Eddie Figge
ON THE SUNNYSIDE(1936, Swed.)

George Figgs
FEMALE TROUBLE(1975)

John Figlmiller
MARK OF THE WITCH(1970)

Max Figman
Silents
HOOSIER SCHOOLMASTER(1914); TRUTH WAGON, THE(1914), a, d; OLD HOME WEEK(1925)
Misc. Silents
MAN ON THE BOX, THE(1914); WHAT'S HIS NAME?(1914); JACK CHANTY(1915), a, d; MY BEST GIRL(1915)

Oscar Brimberton Figman
Silents
MANHATTAN(1924)

M. Figner
VIOLIN AND ROLLER(1962, USSR)

Ernst Figte
DEATH TAKES A HOLIDAY(1934), art d
Antonio Casas Figueroa
SWEET SUGAR(1972)
Carlos Figueroa
CRISIS(1950)
Gabrial Figueroa
MIRAGE(1972, Peru)
Gabriel Figueroa
PORTRAIT OF MARIA(1946, Mex.), ph; FUGITIVE, THE(1947), ph; PEARL, THE(1948, U.S./Mex.), ph; TARZAN AND THE MERMAIDS(1948), ph; LOS OL-VIDADOS(1950, Mex.), ph; TORCH, THE(1950), ph; REBELLION OF THE HANGED, THE(1954, Mex.), ph; EL(1955, Mex.), ph; IMPORTANT MAN, THE(1961, Mex.), ph; LA CUCARACHA(1961, Mex.), ph; LITTLE ANGEL(1961, Mex.), ph; MACARIO(1961, Mex.), ph; YOUNG ONE, THE(1961, Mex.), ph; EMPTY STAR, THE(1962, Mex.), ph; NIGHT OF THE IGUANA, THE(1964), ph; EXTERMINATING ANGEL, THE(1967, Mex.), ph; NAZARIN(1968, Mex.), ph; BIG CUBE, THE(1969), ph; KELLY'S HERO-ES(1970, U.S./Yugo.), ph; TWO MULES FOR SISTER SARA(1970), ph; INTER-VAL(1973, Mex./U.S.), ph; ONCE UPON A SCOUNDREL(1973), ph; CHILDREN OF SANCHEZ, THE(1978, U. S./Mex.), ph
1984
UNDER THE VOLCANO(1984), ph
Juan Ancona Figueroa
CAVEMAN(1981)
Laura Figueroa
CHANGE OF HABIT(1969); CROSS AND THE SWITCHBLADE, THE(1970); WHO SAYS I CAN'T RIDE A RAINBOW!(1971)
Lisa Figueroa
MAN, WOMAN AND CHILD(1983)
Reuben Figueroa
WHO SAYS I CAN'T RIDE A RAINBOW!(1971)
Ruben Figueroa
POPI(1969)
Debbie Figuley
1984
NIGHT PATROL(1984), makeup
Nikolai Figurovsky
WHEN THE TREES WERE TALL(1965, USSR), w
B. Fijewska
LAST STOP, THE(1949, Pol.)
T. Fijewski
BORDER STREET(1950, Pol.)
Tadeusz Fijewski
PORTRAIT OF LENIN(1967, Pol./USSR)
H. Fike
125 ROOMS OF COMFORT(1974, Can.), ph
Henri Fiks
CHICAGO 70(1970), ph; LOVE AT FIRST SIGHT(1977, Can.), ph
Henry Fiks
MOURNING SUIT, THE(1975, Can.), ph; THREE CARD MONTE(1978, Can.), ph; TITLE SHOT(1982, Can.), ph
Nicola Filacuridi
MADAME BUTTERFLY(1955 Ital./Jap.)
Anna Filamento
FRENCH QUARTER(1978)
Antonio Filauri
CASE OF THE CURIOUS BRIDE, THE(1935); COLLEEN(1936); LOVE IS NEWS(1937); NIGHT KEY(1937); THIS IS MY AFFAIR(1937); THREE BLIND MI-CE(1938); CODE OF THE SECRET SERVICE(1939); THEY KNEW WHAT THEY WANTED(1940); ROAD TO HAPPINESS(1942); TOUGH AS THEY COME(1942); SONG OF BERNADETTE, THE(1943); MASK OF DIMITRIOS, THE(1944); SECRETS OF SCOTLAND YARD(1944); WILSON(1944); NOB HILL(1945); MASK OF DIIJON, THE(1946); NOCTURNE(1946); THRILL OF BRAZIL, THE(1946); I WONDER WHO'S KISSING HER NOW(1947); MOTHER WORE TIGHTS(1947); NIGHT SONG(1947); CRY OF THE CITY(1948); KING OF THE BANDITS(1948); NIGHT HAS A THOUSAND EYES(1948); BIG SOMBRERO, THE(1949); GIRL FROM JONES BEACH, THE(1949); GREAT SINNER, THE(1949); SPY HUNT(1950); ON THE RIVERA(1951); TOO YOUNG TO KISS(1951); FIVE FINGERS(1952); THUNDER BAY(1953)
Frank Filban
STELLA DALLAS(1937)
Audrey Fildes
WHILE I LIVE(1947, Brit.); KIND HEARTS AND CORONETS(1949, Brit.)
William Fildew
Silents
FLIRTING WITH FATE(1916), ph; REGGIE MIXES IN(1916), ph; GOD'S OUT-LAW(1919), ph; IN FOR THIRTY DAYS(1919), ph; ISLAND OF INTRIGUE, THE(1919), ph; PETAL ON THE CURRENT, THE(1919), ph; BLAZING TRAIL, THE(1921), ph; NO WOMAN KNOWS(1921), ph; OUTSIDE THE LAW(1921), ph; PAID BACK(1922), ph; RECKLESS AGE, THE(1924), ph
William C. Fildew
Silents
ONE OF MANY(1917), ph
William E. Fildew
Silents
LAMB, THE(1915), ph; ALMOST MARRIED(1919), ph
Diane Filer
WHEN TOMORROW DIES(1966, Can.)
Frieda Filer
SPECTER OF THE ROSE(1946)
Tom Filer
BEAST WITH A MILLION EYES, THE(1956), w; SPACE CHILDREN, THE(1958), w; RIDE IN THE WHIRLWIND(1966)
Gary Files
THUNDERBIRD 6(1968, Brit.); MONEY MOVERS(1978, Aus.)
Arthur Costa Filho
DONA FLOR AND HER TWO HUSBANDS(1977, Braz.)
Dantas Filho
MARGIN, THE,(1969, Braz.)

Jardel Filho
EARTH ENTRANCED(1970, Braz.); PIXOTE(1981, Braz.)
Lauro Escorel Filho
BYE-BYE BRASIL(1980, Braz.), ph
Napoleao Lopes Filho
GIVEN WORD, THE(1964, Braz.)
Denise Filiatrault
FANTASTICA(1980, Can./Fr.)
Giovanni Filidoro
IT STARTED IN NAPLES(1960)
A. Filimonov
SPACE SHIP, THE(1935, USSR), w; SILVER DUST(1953, USSR), w
Gennady Filimonov
FAME(1980)
S. Filimonov
SKY CALLS, THE(1959, USSR)
V. Filina
SANDU FOLLOWS THE SUN(1965, USSR)
David Filinni
1984
MISSION, THE(1984)
Josef Filip
DO YOU KEEP A LION AT HOME?(1966, Czech.)
A. Filipashvili
FATHER OF A SOLDIER(1966, USSR), ph
Miroslawa Filipiak
BEADS OF ONE ROSARY, THE(1982, Pol.), ed
Andreas Filipidis
SUMMER LOVERS(1982)
Frantisek Filiposky
EMPEROR AND THE GOLEM, THE(1955, Czech.)
Frieda Filipovic
WITNESS OUT OF HELL(1967, Ger./Yugo.), w
Etelka Filipovski
I EVEN MET HAPPY GYPSIES(1968, Yugo.)
Frantisek Filipovsky
LOST FACE, THE(1965, Czech.); ON THE COMET(1970, Czech.); SIR, YOU ARE A WIDOWER(1971, Czech.); WISHING MACHINE(1971, Czech.); NINTH HEART, THE(1980, Czech.)
Alfredo Filippazzi
FIST IN HIS POCKET(1968, Ital.)
A. Filippenko
NIGHT BEFORE CHRISTMAS, A(1963, USSR), m
Mario Filippeschi
RIGOLETTO(1949)
Andreas Filippides
DREAM OF PASSION, A(1978, Gr.)
Andreas Filippidis
ISLAND OF LOVE(1963)
Angelo Filippini
DIRTY OUTLAWS, THE(1971, Ital.), ph; JOHNNY HAMLET(1972, Ital.), ph
Anna Filippini
WHITE NIGHTS(1961, Ital./Fr.)
Bruno Filippini
WITCHES, THE(1969, Fr./Ital.)
Gino Filippini
ANGELO IN THE CROWD(1952, Ital.), m; MELODY OF LOVE(1954, Ital.), m; DONATELLA(1956, Ital.), m
Rino Filippini
HEAVEN ON EARTH(1960, Ital./U.S.), ph; TROJAN HORSE, THE(1962, Fr./Ital.), ph
Jelo Filippo
CALL OF THE BLOOD(1948, Brit.)
Lou Filippo
ROCKY III(1982)
1984
CITY HEAT(1984)
Peiro Filippone
MADIGAN'S MILLIONS(1970, Span./Ital), art d
Piero Filippone
SEVEN HILLS OF ROME, THE(1958), set d; ANGEL WORE RED, THE(1960), art d; SAMSON AND THE SEVEN MIRACLES OF THE WORLD(1963, Fr./Ital.), art d; SON OF CAPTAIN BLOOD, THE(1964, U.S./Ital./Span.), art d; DAY IN COURT, A(1965, Ital.), art d; JOURNEY BENEATH THE DESERT(1967, Fr./Ital.), art d; DAY OF ANGER(1970, Ital./Ger.), art d; MERCENARY, THE(1970, Ital./Span.), art d
Pietro Filippone
DIARY OF A CLOISTERED NUN(1973, Ital./Fr./Ger.), art d; DON'T TURN THE OTHER CHEEK(1974, Ital./Ger./Span.), set d; SONNY AND JED(1974, Ital.), art d
Roberto Filippone
GERMANY, YEAR ZERO(1949, Ger.), set d
Piero Filipponi
NAKED MAJA, THE(1959, Ital./U.S.), art d
S. Filippov
TIGER GIRL(1955, USSR); TWELFTH NIGHT(1956, USSR); SONG OVER MOS-COW(1964, USSR)
V. Filippov
FORTY-NINE DAYS(1964, USSR)
Jan Filips
BY DESIGN(1982)
Ryszard Filipski
JOVITA(1970, Pol.)
Ya. Filipson
YOLANTA(1964, USSR)
Lena Filkovskaya
Misc. Silents
SCANDAL?(1929, USSR)
Dennis Fill
WHITE BUFFALO, THE(1977), cos

1984
ICE PIRATES, THE(1984), cos
Sylvette Fillacier
LA MATERNELLE(1933, Fr.)
Leo Filler
THEY WERE TEN(1961, Israel); SIMCHON FAMILY, THE(1969, Israel), w
Isabelle Filleul
1984
SUGAR CANE ALLEY(1984, Fr.), cos
Jonathan Filley
JAWS(1975)
Lou Fillipo
ROCKY(1976)
Clyde Fillmore
SHANGHAI GESTURE, THE(1941); UNHOLY PARTNERS(1941); MY SISTER EILEEN(1942); MYSTERY OF MARIE ROGET, THE(1942); TALK OF THE TOWN(1942); TWO YANKS IN TRINIDAD(1942); LAUGH YOUR BLUES AWAY(1943); MARGIN FOR ERROR(1943); MORE THE MERRIER, THE(1943); SWING FEVER(1943); WATCH ON THE RHINE(1943); WHEN JOHNNY COMES MARCHING HOME(1943); GYPSY WILDCAT(1944); LAURA(1944); ONCE UPON A TIME(1944); 3 IS A FAMILY(1944); COLONEL EFFINGHAM'S RAID(1945); LADY ON A TRAIN(1945); STRANGE VOYAGE(1945); BAD BASCOMB(1946)
Silents
CROOKED STREETS(1920); DEVIL'S PASSKEY, THE(1920); NURSE MARJORIE(1920); SOUL OF YOUTH, THE(1920); OUTSIDE WOMAN, THE(1921); SHAM(1921); STING OF THE LASH(1921); REAL ADVENTURE, THE(1922); ALIMONY(1924)
Misc. Silents
MILLIONAIRE PIRATE, THE(1919); SUNDOWN TRAIL, THE(1919); WHEN FATE DECIDES(1919); CITY SPARROW, THE(1920); MIDNIGHT GUEST, THE(1923)
James Fillmore
CRY BABY KILLER, THE(1958)
Nellie Fillmore
Silents
BABY MINE(1917)
Brent Barfod Film
JOURNEY TO THE SEVENTH PLANET(1962, U.S./Swed.), spec eff
Joy Filmer
HONEYMOON LIMITED(1936)
June Filmer
ROCKABYE(1932); LITTLE WOMEN(1933); ONE MAN'S JOURNEY(1933); HONEYMOON LIMITED(1936)
Robert Filmer
CARIBBEAN MYSTERY, THE(1945); THUNDERHEAD-SON OF FLICKA(1945); EL PASO KID, THE(1946); CHEYENNE(1947); WALLS OF JERICHO(1948); DESERT HAWK, THE(1950); VIVA ZAPATA!(1952); TREASURE OF THE GOLDEN CONDOR(1953)
Robert W. Filmer
PHANTOM VALLEY(1948)
Vic Filmer
OLD CURIOSITY SHOP, THE(1935, Brit.)
Patrick Filmer-Sankey
SUBWAY IN THE SKY(1959, Brit.), p; S.O.S. PACIFIC(1960, Brit.), p; HOT MONEY GIRL(1962, Brit./Ger.), p
Clyde Filmore
REMARKABLE ANDREW, THE(1942)
Misc. Silents
LADDER OF LIES, THE(1920)
Bowie Films
HIGH WIND IN JAMAICA, A(1965), spec eff; REPTILE, THE(1966, Brit.), spec eff; WHERE THE BULLETS FLY(1966, Brit.), spec eff; MUMMY'S SHROUD, THE(1967, Brit.), spec eff; THEY CAME FROM BEYOND SPACE(1967, Brit.), spec eff; SUMARINE X-1(1969, Brit.), spec eff; GUMSHOE(1972, Brit.), spec eff
Filo
LOVE IN THE AFTERNOON(1957)
Massimilano Filoni
MALICIOUS(1974, Ital.)
Massimiliano Filoni
WHITE SISTER(1973, Ital./Span./Fr.); MR. BILLION(1977); LUNA(1979, Ital.)
Elaine Filoon
UNCLE SCAM(1981)
Carmen Filpe
WILD GYPSIES(1969)
Carmen Filpi
WHICH WAY IS UP?(1977); ON THE NICKEL(1980); 10 TO MIDNIGHT(1983)
1984
ICE PIRATES, THE(1984)
Baron Fils
COURRIER SUD(1937, Fr.)
Numes Fils
INNOCENTS IN PARIS(1955, Brit.); FRENCH CANCAN(1956, Fr.)
Mrs. A. W. Filson
Silents
SQUAW MAN, THE(1914)
Al Filson
Silents
TRUTH WAGON, THE(1914); HAIRPINS(1920); TREASURE ISLAND(1920); CHICKENS(1921); MADE IN HEAVEN(1921); WATCH HIM STEP(1922)
Misc. Silents
HOMESPUN FOLKS(1920); GIRL FROM GOD'S COUNTRY, THE(1921)
Al W. Filson
Misc. Silents
AT PINEY RIDGE(1916); GARDEN OF ALLAH, THE(1916); UNTO THOSE WHO SIN(1916); LAD AND THE LION, THE(1917); MOUNTAIN DEW(1917); SCARLET CAR, THE(1918)
Sidney Filson
WORLD OF HANS CHRISTIAN ANDERSEN, THE(1971, Jap.)
1984
FEAR CITY(1984)

Sydney Filson
Misc. Talkies
FORCE FOUR(1975)
Hal Fimberg
WHO KILLED AUNT MAGGIE?(1940), w; BIG STORE, THE(1941), w; BOOGIE MAN WILL GET YOU, THE(1942), w; IN SOCIETY(1944), w; NATIONAL BARN DANCE(1944), w; WAVE, A WAC AND A MARINE, A(1944), w; YOU CAN'T RATION LOVE(1944), w; NAUGHTY NINETIES, THE(1945), w; OUR MAN FLINT(1966), w; IN LIKE FLINT(1967), w
Maria Fimiani
MAN ABOUT THE HOUSE, A(1947, Brit.)
Dennis Clark Fimple
SUMMERTREE(1971)
Dennis Fimple
CACTUS IN THE SNOW(1972); CULPEPPER CATTLE COMPANY, THE(1972); BOOTLEGGERS(1974); SPECTRE OF EDGAR ALLAN POE, THE(1974); TRUCK STOP WOMEN(1974); APPLE DUMPLING GANG, THE(1975); MACKINTOSH & T.J.(1975); CREATURE FROM BLACK LAKE, THE(1976); KING KONG(1976); STAY HUNGRY(1976); WINTERHAWK(1976); GOIN' SOUTH(1978); WISHBONE CUTTER(1978); EVICTORS, THE(1979)
1984
SWING SHIFT(1984)
Misc. Talkies
SMOKEY AND THE GOODTIME OUTLAWS(1978)
Jack Fina
IT'S GREAT TO BE YOUNG(1946); MELODY TIME(1948); DISC JOCKEY(1951)
Marianne Astrom-De Fina
NORTHERN LIGHTS(1978), prod d
Marina Finaly
ESCAPE 2000(1983, Aus.)
Donald P. Finamore
HERCULES IN NEW YORK(1970), ed
Joe Finan
JAMBOREE(1957)
Ernesto Finance
LOS AUTOMATAS DE LA MUERTE(1960, Mex.)
Colin Finbow
1984
DARK ENEMY(1984, Brit.), d, w
Sergio Fincato
CLIMAX, THE(1967, Fr., Ital.)
Charles Finch
I AM A GROUPIE(1970, Brit.)
Della Finch
GREAT MUPPET CAPER, THE(1981)
Flora Finch
HAUNTED HOUSE, THE(1928); COME ACROSS(1929); SWEET KITTY BELLAIRS(1930); SCARLET LETTER, THE(1934); POSTAL INSPECTOR(1936); SAN FRANCISCO(1936); SHOW BOAT(1936); WAY OUT WEST(1937); WOMEN, THE(1939)
Silents
NIGHT OUT, A(1916); GREAT ADVENTURE, THE(1918); OH, BOY!(1919); LESSONS IN LOVE(1921); ORPHANS OF THE STORM(1922); WHEN KNIGHTHOOD WAS IN FLOWER(1922); LUCK(1923); MONSIEUR BEAUCAIRE(1924); ROULETTE(1924); ADVENTUROUS SEX, THE(1925); EARLY BIRD, THE(1925); LOVER'S ISLAND(1925); KISS FOR CINDERELLA, A(1926); CAPTAIN SALVATION(1927); CAT AND THE CANARY, THE(1927); QUALITY STREET(1927)
Misc. Silents
PRUDENCE THE PIRATE(1916); MAN WANTED(1922); ORPHAN SALLY(1922); BROWN DERBY, THE(1926)
Harold E. Finch
NORMA RAE(1979)
Howard Finch
HELLFIGHTERS(1968)
Jack Finch
GANG WAR(1958); TWO LITTLE BEARS, THE(1961)
John Finch
BREAKING GLASS(1980, Brit.)
Jon Finch
VAMPIRE LOVERS, THE(1970, Brit.); MACBETH(1971, Brit.); SUNDAY BLOODY SUNDAY(1971, Brit.); FRENZY(1972, Brit.); LADY CAROLINE LAMB(1972, Brit./Ital.); DIAGNOSIS: MURDER(1974, Brit.); LAST DAYS OF MAN ON EARTH, THE(1975, Brit.); DEATH ON THE NILE(1978, Brit.); SABINA, THE(1979, Span./Swed.); GIRO CITY(1982, Brit.)
Matthew Finch
DENTIST IN THE CHAIR(1960, Brit.), w
Peter Finch
MR. CHEDWORTH STEPS OUT(1939, Aus.); MASSACRE HILL(1949, Brit.); MINIVER STORY, THE(1950, Brit./U.S.); RATS OF TOBRUK(1951, Aus.); WOODEN HORSE, THE(1951); STORY OF ROBIN HOOD, THE(1952, Brit.); TRAIN OF EVENTS(1952, Brit.); GREAT GILBERT AND SULLIVAN, THE(1953, Brit.); DETECTIVE, THE(1954, Qit.); ELEPHANT WALK(1954); HEART OF THE MATTER, THE(1954, Brit.); MAKE ME AN OFFER(1954, Brit.); JOSEPHINE AND MEN(1955, Brit.); PASSAGE HOME(1955, Brit.); WARRIORS, THE(1955); SIMON AND LAURA(1956, Brit.); PURSUIT OF THE GRAF SPEE(1957, Brit.); SHIRALEE, THE(1957, Brit.); ROBBERY UNDER ARMS(1958, Brit.); TOWN LIKE ALICE, A(1958, Brit.); WINDOM'S WAY(1958, Brit.); NUN'S STORY, THE(1959); KIDNAPPED(1960); MAN WITH THE GREEN CARNATION, THE(1960, Brit.); OPERATION AMSTERDAM(1960, Brit.); SINS OF RACHEL CADE, THE(1960); NO LOVE FOR JOHNNIE(1961, Brit.); I THANK A FOOL(1962, Brit.); IN THE COOL OF THE DAY(1963); GIRL WITH GREEN EYES(1964, Brit.); PUMPKIN EATER, THE(1964, Brit.); FLIGHT OF THE PHOENIX(1965); JUDITH(1965); 10:30 P.M. SUMMER(1966, U.S./Span.); FAR FROM THE MADDING CROWD(1967, Brit.); LEGEND OF LYLAH CLARE, THE(1968); RED TENT, THE(1971, Ital./USSR); SUNDAY BLOODY SUNDAY(1971, Brit.); SOMETHING TO HIDE(1972, Brit.); ENGLAND MADE ME(1973, Brit.); LOST HORIZON(1973); NELSON AFFAIR, THE(1973, Brit.); ABDICATION, THE(1974, Brit.); NETWORK(1976)
Scot Finch
FRENCH MISTRESS(1960, Brit.); KITCHEN, THE(1961, Brit.); MACBETH(1963; SQUADRON 633(1964, U.S./Brit.); 633 SQUADRON(1964); LIQUIDATOR, THE(1966, Brit.); CATLOW(1971, Span.), w; MAN CALLED NOON, THE(1973, Brit.), w; NIGHT

OF THE ASKARI(1978, Ger./South African), w; SEA WOLVES, THE(1981, Brit.)

Scott Finch
WHY BOTHER TO KNOCK(1964, Brit.); SPY WHO CAME IN FROM THE COLD, THE(1965, Brit.)

Stuart Finch
ON THE BEACH(1959)

Terry L. Finch
IN GOD WE TRUST(1980)

Frank Finch-Smiles
DOCTOR'S SECRET(1929)

David Fincher
TWICE UPON A TIME(1983), spec eff

Werner Finck
LOLA MONTES(1955, Fr./Ger.); AFFAIRS OF JULIE, THE(1958, Ger.); ROSES FOR THE PROSECUTOR(1961, Ger.); LOVE AT TWENTY(1963, Fr./Ital./Jap./Pol./Ger.)

Findeisen
GERMANY, YEAR ZERO(1949, Ger.), ed

Walter Finden
MEET JOHN DOE(1941)

John Findlater
WITH SIX YOU GET EGGROLL(1968); METEOR(1979)

Johnathan Findlater
1984
HARD TO HOLD(1984)

Maxwell Findlater
ACCIDENT(1967, Brit.)

David Findlay
Silents
PEACOCK FAN(1929)
Misc. Silents
SCARLET YOUTH(1928)

Diane Findlay
GAMERA THE INVINCIBLE(1966, Jap.)

Jim Findlay
BRITTANIA HOSPITAL(1982, Brit.)

John Findlay
LOVE TEST, THE(1935, Brit.), p; BIG NOISE, THE(1936, Brit.), p; END OF THE ROAD, THE(1936, Brit.), p; FIND THE LADY(1936, Brit.), p; HIGHLAND FLING(1936, Brit.), p; RHYTHM IN THE AIR(1936, Brit.), p; TROUBLED WATERS(1936, Brit.), p; UNDER PROOF(1936, Brit.), p; CATCH AS CATCH CAN(1937, Brit.), p; JENIFER HALE(1937, Brit.), p; MEMBER OF THE JURY(1937, Brit.), p; STRANGE EXPERIMENT(1937, Brit.), p; LAST BARRICADE, THE(1938, Brit.), p; VILLIERS DIAMOND, THE(1938, Brit.), p
Silents
DAWN OF A TOMORROW, THE(1915)

Linda Findlay
PAPERBACK HERO(1973, Can.)

Michael Findlay
SHRIEK OF THE MUTILATED(1974), d

Roberta Findlay
CHECKMATE(1973), ph

Roy Findlay
GAOL BREAK(1936, Brit.); LIGHTNING CONDUCTOR(1938, Brit.); WHO GOES NEXT?(1938, Brit.)

Ruth Findlay
LAST OF THE CLINTONS, THE(1935); GHOST TOWN(1937); HEROES OF THE ALAMO(1938); WOMEN, THE(1939)
Misc. Talkies
PECOS KID, THE(1935)
Silents
SALAMANDER, THE(1915)
Misc. Silents
MOONSTONE, THE(1915); FOOL'S REVENGE, THE(1916); SALAMANDER, THE(1916); WORLD AGAINST HIM, THE(1916)

Thomas Findlay
Silents
BURIED TREASURE(1921)

John Findletter
WHERE ANGELS GO...TROUBLE FOLLOWS(1968)

Ferguson Findley
MOB, THE(1951), w

John Findley
CONCERNING MR. MARTIN(1937, Brit.), p

Michael Findley [Julian Marsh]
SATAN'S BED(1965)

Roy Findley
DICK TURPIN(1933, Brit.)

Sylvia Findley
BLACK TUESDAY(1955); ROBBER'S ROOST(1955)

Timothy Findley
DON'T LET THE ANGELS FALL(1969, Can.), w

Tom Findley
Silents
LET'S GET MARRIED(1926)
Misc. Silents
LUCKY DEVIL(1925)

Eric Findon
Misc. Silents
CUPID IN CLOVER(1929, Brit.)

Avrum Fine
MOONRUNNERS(1975), ed

Billy Fine
CONCRETE JUNGLE, THE(1982), p; CHAINED HEAT(1983 U.S./Ger.), p

Bobby Fine
HOUSE ON SORORITY ROW, THE(1983), w

Bud Fine
OH, YEAH!(1929); RACKETEER, THE(1929); PACK UP YOUR TROUBLES(1932); IT'S A GIFT(1934); KID MILLIONS(1934); WE LIVE AGAIN(1934); ANYTHING GOES(1936); DRIFT FENCE(1936); MY DEAR MISS ALDRICH(1937); THUNDER AFLOAT(1939); RETURN OF FRANK JAMES, THE(1940); STRANGE CARGO(1940);

SECRET AGENT OF JAPAN(1942); WIFE WANTED(1946); SEA OF GRASS, THE(1947); FORCE OF EVIL(1948); SANTA FE(1951)

Budd Fine
BE YOURSELF(1930); PUTTIN' ON THE RITZ(1930); WHOOPEE(1930); TEXAS RANGER, THE(1931); RETURN OF SOPHIE LANG, THE(1936); ONLY ANGELS HAVE WINGS(1939); CONFESSIONS OF BOSTON BLACKIE(1941); PHANTOM SUBMARINE, THE(1941); CROSSROADS(1942); MR. LUCKY(1943); MIRACLE OF MORGAN'S CREEK, THE(1944); LADY IN THE LAKE(1947); MY FAVORITE BRUNETTE(1947); SUMMER HOLIDAY(1948); WINDOW, THE(1949); ON DANGEROUS GROUND(1951)
Silents
KING OF KINGS, THE(1927)

Buddy Fine
Silents
BATTLING BUTLER(1926)

Daniel Fine
1984
HIGHPOINT(1984, Can.), p

Douglas Fine
INCIDENT IN SHANGHAI(1937, Brit.)

Gerald Fine
WANDERLOVE(1970), p

Hank Fine
SHOWDOWN(1973), w

Harry Fine
WOMAN TO WOMAN(1946, Brit.); GHOSTS OF BERKELEY SQUARE(1947, Brit.); SILVER DARLINGS, THE(1947, Brit.); LAUGHING LADY, THE(1950, Brit.); TO HAVE AND TO HOLD(1951, Brit.); MAN WHO KNEW TOO MUCH, THE(1956); PLEASURE GIRLS, THE(1966, Brit.), p; PENTHOUSE, THE(1967, Brit.), p; LONG DAY'S DYING, THE(1968, Brit.), p; RISE AND RISE OF MICHAEL RIMMER, THE(1970); VAMPIRE LOVERS, THE(1970, Brit.), p, w; FRIGHT(1971, Brit.), p; LUST FOR A VAMPIRE(1971, Brit.), p; TWINS OF EVIL(1971, Brit.), p

Larry Fine
DANCING LADY(1933); MEET THE BARON(1933); FUGITIVE LOVERS(1934); HOLLYWOOD PARTY(1934); MYRT AND MARGE(1934); ROCKIN' IN THE ROCKIES(1945); GOLD RAIDERS, THE(1952); HAVE ROCRET, WILL TRAVEL(1959); THREE STOOGES IN ORBIT, THE(1962); THREE STOOGES MEET HERCULES, THE(1962); THREE STOOGES GO AROUND THE WORLD IN A DAZE, THE(1963); OUTLAWS IS COMING, THE(1965)

Laura Fine
ONE FROM THE HEART(1982)

Lesly Fine
NIGHT CREATURE(1979)

Mort Fine
NEXT MAN, THE(1976), w; GREEK TYCOON, THE(1978), w; CABOBLANCO(1981), w

Morton Fine
HANDLE WITH CARE(1958), p, w; FOOL KILLER, THE(1965), w; PAWNBROKER, THE(1965), w

Morton S. Fine
HOT SUMMER NIGHT(1957), p, w

Jay Fineberg
DIAMOND STUD(1970), p; HARD ROAD, THE(1970)

Doug Finell
BOOK OF NUMBERS(1973)

Redman Finely
Silents
KING OF KINGS, THE(1927)

William Finely
EATEN ALIVE(1976)

B.F. Fineman
SMASHING THE RACKETS(1938), p; APPOINTMENT IN BERLIN(1943), w

B.P. Fineman
THUNDERBOLT(1929), p; WITHOUT REGRET(1935), p; TARNISHED ANGEL(1938), p; BEAUTY FOR THE ASKING(1939), p; BLONDE INSPIRATION(1941), p; TARZAN'S SECRET TREASURE(1941), p; JOURNEY FOR MARGARET(1942), p; PILOT NO. 5(1943), p

Irving Fineman
ONCE UPON A TIME(1944), w; ROME ADVENTURE(1962), p,d&w

Joseph Fineman
DON'T ANSWER THE PHONE(1980), ed

Lorenzo Fineschi
MAN CALLED SLEDGE, A(1971, Ital.); STATUE, THE(1971, Brit.); DEAF SMITH AND JOHNNY EARS(1973, Ital.)

Stanley Finesmith
CROSS AND THE SWITCHBLADE, THE(1970)

David Finfar
YOU'VE GOT TO WALK IT LIKE YOU TALK IT OR YOU'LL LOSE THAT BEAT(1971), ed

David Finfer
REAL LIFE(1979), ed; DEFIANCE(1980), ed; MODERN ROMANCE(1981), ed

William Finger
SNOW DEVILS, THE(1965, Ital.), w; GREEN SLIME, THE(1969), w

Tom E. Finglass
YOU WILL REMEMBER(1941, Brit.); VARIETY JUBILEE(1945, Brit.)

Anthony Fingleton
BLOOD BATH(1976), p

Leonor Fini
ROMEO AND JULIET(1954, Brit.), cos; WALK WITH LOVE AND DEATH, A(1969), cos

Lt. Richard Finiels USAR
TOKYO FILE 212(1951)

Agnes Fink
SISTERS, OR THE BALANCE OF HAPPINESS(1982, Ger.)

Agustin J. Fink
PORTRAIT OF MARIA(1946, Mex.), p

Dale Fink
WYOMING(1947)

Edwin Fink
PRIVILEGE(1967, Brit.)
Harry Julian Fink
MAJOR DUNDEE(1965), w; ICE STATION ZEBRA(1968), w; BIG JAKE(1971), w; DIRTY HARRY(1971), w; CAHILL, UNITED STATES MARSHAL(1973), w; ENFORCER, THE(1976), w; SUDDEN IMPACT(1983), w
Henry Fink
KIBITZER, THE(1929); ON WITH THE SHOW(1929); GOLDIE GETS ALONG(1933)
Herbert Fink
TERROR IN THE JUNGLE(1968)
Hyman Fink
WINGS IN THE DARK(1935); HOLLYWOOD BOULEVARD(1936)
Irv Fink
LOOSE ENDS(1975)
Johanna Fink
PARSIFAL(1983, Fr.)
John Fink
LOVING(1970); CAREY TREATMENT, THE(1972); BATTLESTAR GALACTICA(1979)
Joseph Fink
DEVIL'S SISTERS, THE(1966), p; STING OF DEATH(1966), p; DEATH CURSE OF TARTU(1967), p
Margaret Fink
REMOVALISTS, THE(1975, Aus.), p; MY BRILLIANT CAREER(1980, Aus.), p
Martin Fink
PAYDAY(1972), p
Matt Fink
1984
PURPLE RAIN(1984)
Michael Fink
ONE FROM THE HEART(1982)
1984
ADVENTURES OF BUCKAROO BANZAI: ACROSS THE 8TH DIMENSION, THE(1984), spec eff
Misc. Talkies
FORCE FOUR(1975), d
Naomi Fink
SCREAM, BABY, SCREAM(1969)
R.M. Fink
BIG JAKE(1971), w; ENFORCER, THE(1976), w; SUDDEN IMPACT(1983), w
Richard S. Fink
STING OF DEATH(1966), p
Rita Fink
CAHILL, UNITED STATES MARSHAL(1973), w
Rita M. Fink
DIRTY HARRY(1971), w
Thomas Fink
PARSIFAL(1983, Fr.)
T.G. Finkbinder
REDEEMER, THE(1978)
Abem Finkel
DECEIVER, THE(1931), w; HI, NELLIE!(1934), w; BLACK FURY(1935), w; SPECIAL AGENT(1935), w; PUBLIC ENEMY'S WIFE(1936), w; ROAD GANG(1936), w; BLACK LEGION, THE(1937), w; MARKED WOMAN(1937), w; JEZEBEL(1938), w; WHITE BANNERS(1938), w; BIG SHOT, THE(1942), w; HUNDRED POUND WINDOW, THE(1943, Brit.), w; GOD IS MY CO-PILOT(1945), w; TONIGHT AND EVERY NIGHT(1945), w; TIME OUT OF MIND(1947), w
R. Finkel
FUGITIVE VALLEY(1941), d
Shimon Finkel
HANNAH K.(1983, Fr.)
1984
LITTLE DRUMMER GIRL, THE(1984)
Steve O.Z. Finkel
DEATH HUNT(1981)
Penney Finkelman
TERMS OF ENDEARMENT(1983), p
Wayne A. Finkelman
1984
GRANDVIEW, U.S.A.(1984), cos; PROTOCOL(1984), cos
Wayne Finkelman
PARTNERS(1982), cos
Anna Finkelstein
1984
DRIFTING(1984, Israel), ed
Heli Finkenzeller
BOCCACCIO(1936, Ger.); ROYAL WALTZ, THE(1936)
Robert Finkle
WRANGLER'S ROOST(1941), w
Fred Finklehoff
STOOGE, THE(1952), w
Fred Finklehoffe
BROTHER RAT AND A BABY(1940), w; STRIKE UP THE BAND(1940), w; BABES ON BROADWAY(1941), w; FOR ME AND MY GAL(1942), w; BEST FOOT FORWARD(1943), w; GIRL CRAZY(1943), w; MR. ACE(1946), w
Fred F. Finklehoffe
BROTHER RAT(1938), w; MEET ME IN ST. LOUIS(1944), w; EGG AND I, THE(1947), p; AT WAR WITH THE ARMY(1950), p, w; ABOUT FACE(1952), w; MY BOYS ARE GOOD BOYS(1978), w
Ken Finkleman
AIRPLANE II: THE SEQUEL(1982), d&w; GREASE 2(1982), w
I. Finklestein
MY FATHER'S HOUSE(1947, Palestine)
Levana Finklstein
MY MARGO(1969, Israel)
The Finks
BIG CUBE, THE(1969)

Bruce Finlavson
1984
SECOND TIME LUCKY(1984, Aus./New Zealand), cos
Cathy Finlay
RETURN OF THE SOLDIER, THE(1983, Brit.)
Donald Finlay
IT'S A GREAT DAY(1956, Brit.)
Frank Finlay
LONELINESS OF THE LONG DISTANCE RUNNER, THE(1962, Brit.); AGENT 8 3/4(1963, Brit.); DOCTOR IN DISTRESS(1963, Brit.); PRIVATE POTTER(1963, Brit.); COMEDY MAN, THE(1964); OTHELLO(1965, Brit.); UNDERWORLD INFORMERS(1965, Brit.); STUDY IN TERROR, A(1966, Brit./Ger.); WALK IN THE SHADOW(1966, Brit.); WILD AFFAIR, THE(1966, Brit.); DEADLY BEES,THE(1967, Brit.); I'LL NEVER FORGET WHAT'S 'IS NAME(1967, Brit.); JOKERS, THE(1967, Brit.); ROBBERY(1967, Brit.); INSPECTOR CLOUSEAU(1968, Brit.); SHOES OF THE FISHERMAN, THE(1968); TWISTED NERVE(1969, Brit.); CROMWELL(1970, Brit.); MOLLY MAGUIRES, THE(1970); ASSAULT(1971, Brit.); GUMSHOE(1972, Brit.); SITTING TARGET(1972, Brit.); SHAFT IN AFRICA(1973); NEITHER THE SEA NOR THE SAND(1974, Brit.); THREE MUSKETEERS, THE(1974, Panama); FOUR MUSKETEERS, THE(1975); WILD GEESE, THE(1978, Brit.); MURDER BY DECREE(1979, Brit.); ENIGMA(1983, Brit.); RETURN OF THE SOLDIER, THE(1983, Brit.)
1984
PLOUGHMAN'S LUNCH, THE(1984, Brit.); 1919(1984, Brit.)
George Finlay [Giorgio Stegani]
ADIOS GRINGO(1967, Ital./Fr./Span.), d, w
Jack Finlay
SEMINOLE(1953); DEMETRIUS AND THE GLADIATORS(1954)
James Thomas Finlay, Jr.
GEORGIA, GEORGIA(1972)
Jock Finlay
GHOST SHIP(1953, Brit.)
Peter Finlay
1984
ANOTHER TIME, ANOTHER PLACE(1984, Brit.)
Stephen Finlay
RETURN OF THE SOLDIER, THE(1983, Brit.)
Ursula Finlay
ROBBERY UNDER ARMS(1958, Brit.)
Alex Finlayson
OUR RELATIONS(1936); SOLDIER OF FORTUNE(1955); D-DAY, THE SIXTH OF JUNE(1956); JOURNEY TO THE CENTER OF THE EARTH(1959); NOTORIOUS LANDLADY, THE(1962); FATHER GOOSE(1964)
Bob Finlayson
OUR RELATIONS(1936)
Bruce Finlayson
CHANT OF JIMMIE BLACKSMITH, THE(1980, Aus.), cos; DEAD KIDS(1981 Aus./New Zealand), cos
1984
CAREFUL, HE MIGHT HEAR YOU(1984, Aus.), cos
James Finlayson
SHOW GIRL(1928); DAWN PATROL, THE(1930); FEET FIRST(1930); FOR THE DEFENSE(1930); YOUNG EAGLES(1930); PARDON US(1931); PACK UP YOUR TROUBLES(1932); THUNDER BELOW(1932); DEVIL'S BROTHER, THE(1933); DICK TURPIN(1933, Brit.); BIG BUSINESS(1934, Brit.); FATHER AND SON(1934, Brit.); NINE FORTY-FIVE(1934, Brit.); OH NO DOCTOR!(1934, Brit.); WHAT HAPPENED TO HARKNESS(1934, Brit.); BONNIE SCOTLAND(1935); HANDLE WITH CARE(1935, Brit.); WHO'S YOUR FATHER?(1935, Brit.); BOHEMIAN GIRL, THE(1936); OUR RELATIONS(1936); ALL OVER TOWN(1937); ANGEL(1937); PICK A STAR(1937); TOAST OF NEW YORK, THE(1937); WAY OUT WEST(1937); WISE GIRL(1937); BLOCKHEADS(1938); FLYING DEUCES, THE(1939); GREAT VICTOR HERBERT, THE(1939); HOLLYWOOD CAVALCADE(1939); RAFFLES(1939); FOREIGN CORRESPONDENT(1940); SAPS AT SEA(1940); ONE NIGHT IN LISBON(1941); TO BE OR NOT TO BE(1942); YANKS AHOY(1943); TILL THE CLOUDS ROLL BY(1946); PERILS OF PAULINE, THE(1947); GRAND CANYON TRAIL(1948); DOWN MEMORY LANE(1949); ROYAL WEDDING(1951)
Silents
SMALL TOWN IDOL, A(1921); LADY BE GOOD(1928)
Misc. Silents
HOME TALENT(1921); LADIES' NIGHT IN A TURKISH BATH(1928)
Jim Finlayson
JULIA MISBEHAVES(1948)
Jimmie Finlayson
HARD TO GET(1929); TWO WEEKS OFF(1929)
Jimmy Finlayson
WALL STREET(1929)
Silents
NO MAN'S LAW(1927); BACHELOR'S PARADISE(1928)
Jon Finlayson
ALVIN RIDES AGAIN(1974, Aus.); LONELY HEARTS(1983, Aus.)
1984
MELVIN, SON OF ALVIN(1984, Aus.)
Marion Finlayson
INCREDIBLE JOURNEY, THE(1963)
Betsee Finlee
HOMETOWN U.S.A.(1979)
Bill Finley
SISTERS(1973)
Evelyn Finley
ARIZONA FRONTIER(1940); DYNAMITE CANYON(1941); TRAIL RIDERS(1942); BLACK MARKET RUSTLERS(1943); JACK LONDON(1943); GHOST GUNS(1944); VALLEY OF VENGEANCE(1944); PRAIRIE RUSTLERS(1945); GUNNING FOR JUSTICE(1948); SUNDOWN RIDERS(1948); DIAMOND QUEEN, THE(1953)
Misc. Talkies
SHERIFF OF MEDICINE BOW, THE(1948)
Gene Finley
MORE AMERICAN GRAFFITI(1979), m
Greg Finley
FIRST NUDIE MUSICAL, THE(1976); PENNIES FROM HEAVEN(1981); SWORD AND THE SORCERER, THE(1982)

Jack Finley
MOB, THE(1951)
Kathy Finley
WHITE LIGHTNING(1973)
Larry Finley
BUSHWHACKERS, THE(1952), p; MAN WHO SHOT LIBERTY VALANCE, THE(1962); COWBOYS, THE(1972); CULPEPPER CATTLE COMPANY, THE(1972); MAN WHO LOVED CAT DANCING, THE(1973); POSSE(1975)
Muriel Finley
WHOOPEE(1930)
Murrel Finley
SIN TAKES A HOLIDAY(1930)
Ned Finley
Silents
KID, THE(1916)
Misc. Silents
MAKING OVER OF GEOFFREY MANNING, THE(1915); BOTTOM OF THE WELL(1917); BUCHANAN'S WIFE(1918); MENACE, THE(1918)
W. Franklin Finley
FIRST TIME, THE(1983), w
William Finley
MURDER A LA MOD(1968); WEDDING PARTY, THE(1969); PHANTOM OF THE PARADISE(1974); FURY, THE(1978); SIMON(1980); FUNHOUSE, THE(1981); SILENT RAGE(1982)
Arther Finn
SAY IT WITH DIAMONDS(1935, Brit.)
Arthur Finn
ANNIE, LEAVE THE ROOM(1935, Brit.); DREAMS COME TRUE(1936, Brit.); EXCUSE MY GLOVE(1936, Brit.); FAME(1936, Brit.); IMPROPER DUCHESS, THE(1936, Brit.); KING OF THE CASTLE(1936, Brit.); ONE GOOD TURN(1936, Brit.); BOMBS OVER LONDON(1937, Brit.); MERRY COMES TO STAY(1937, Brit.); YOU LIVE AND LEARN(1937, Brit.); HE LOVED AN ACTRESS(1938, Brit.); SHOW GOES ON, THE(1938, Brit.); WHAT WOULD YOU DO, CHUMS?(1939, Brit.)
Misc. Silents
UNDERWORLD OF LONDON, THE(1915, Brit.); WILD OATS(1915, Brit.)
Catharine Finn
SON OF A STRANGER(1957, Brit.)
Catherine Finn
FOLLY TO BE WISE(1953); TALE OF THREE WOMEN, A(1954, Brit.); DEADLY BEES,THE(1967, Brit.); TORTURE GARDEN(1968, Brit.); RECKONING, THE(1971, Brit.)
Misc. Talkies
THUNDERBIRDS 6(1968)
Cecily Finn
CROWNING TOUCH, THE(1959, Brit.), w
Christine Finn
NAUGHTY ARLETTE(1951, Brit.); LARGE ROPE, THE(1953, Brit.); THUNDERBIRD 6(1968, Brit.); THUNDERBIRDS ARE GO(1968, Brit.)
Cicely Finn
MAN WHO LIKED FUNERALS, THE(1959, Brit.), w
Earl Finn
RUN, ANGEL, RUN(1969); REBEL ROUSERS(1970); HISTORY OF THE WORLD, PART 1(1981)
Eddie Finn
Misc. Talkies
TOBO, THE HAPPY CLOWN(1965)
Edwin Finn
OLIVER!(1968, Brit.); JULIUS CAESAR(1970, Brit.); LOOT(1971, Brit.); TIME BANDITS(1981, Brit.)
Elsie Finn
I DREAM TOO MUCH(1935), w
Florence Finn
Misc. Silents
LITTLE WOMEN(1919)
George J. Finn
DOZENS, THE(1981)
James Hilary Finn
LAWYER'S SECRET, THE(1931), w
Jeffrey Finn
1984
HARRY AND SON(1984)
John Finn
1984
POPE OF GREENWICH VILLAGE, THE(1984)
Jonathan Finn
JAILBREAK(1936), w; ANGELS WASH THEIR FACES(1939), w; SMASHING THE MONEY RING(1939), w; YOU CAN'T GET AWAY WITH MURDER(1939), w; INVISIBLE STRIPES(1940), w; LADY FROM CHEYENNE(1941), w
Kate Finn
MYSTERY MAN, THE(1935), w
Lila Finn
SCARLET ANGEL(1952); INCIDENT IN AN ALLEY(1962); DRUM(1976)
Michael Finn
Misc. Talkies
MELON AFFAIR, THE(1979)
Michael J. Finn
Misc. Talkies
BLACK CONNECTION, THE(1974), d
Mickey Finn
MOTHER IS A FRESHMAN(1949); YOU'RE NEVER TOO YOUNG(1955); PARDNERS(1956); TIN STAR, THE(1957); EARTH VS. THE SPIDER(1958); GIRL IN THE WOODS(1958); SPIDER, THE(1958); BOY AND THE PIRATES, THE(1960); ONE-EYED JACKS(1961); MANCHURIAN CANDIDATE, THE(1962); SERGEANTS 3(1962); TARAS BULBA(1962); INCIDENT AT PHANTOM HILL(1966)
Pavel Finn
ARMED AND DANGEROUS(1977, USSR), w

Sam Finn
MANHATTAN MERRY-GO-ROUND(1937); HOUSE ACROSS THE BAY, THE(1940); DANGEROUS PARTNERS(1945); HOODLUM SAINT, THE(1946); OUR HEARTS WERE GROWING UP(1946); DEAD RECKONING(1947); HOLLOW TRIUMPH(1948); OH, YOU BEAUTIFUL DOLL(1949); SCENE OF THE CRIME(1949); SORROWFUL JONES(1949); FURIES, THE(1950); STRIP, THE(1951); WHEN WORLDS COLLIDE(1951); LAS VEGAS STORY, THE(1952)
Sammy Finn
MARY BURNS, FUGITIVE(1935); LAST GANGSTER, THE(1937); I STOLE A MILLION(1939); INVISIBLE STRIPES(1940); MY FAVORITE SPY(1942); MR. LUCKY(1943); MURDER, MY SWEET(1945); LETTER TO THREE WIVES, A(1948); DANCING IN THE DARK(1949); IMPACT(1949); PEOPLE AGAINST O'HARA, THE(1951); HERE COME THE MARINES(1952); JEANNE EAGELS(1957)
Sheila Finn
HALLELUJAH THE HILLS(1963)
Ted Finn
MAGIC SWORD, THE(1962)
Will Finn
SECRET OF NIMH, THE(1982), w, anim
Finnegan
TWO VOICES(1966)
Frank X. Finnegan
Silents
JULES OF THE STRONG HEART(1918), ph
Joe Finnegan
OPERATION BIKINI(1963); YOUNG FURY(1965); DUEL AT DIABLO(1966); DIRTY HARRY(1971); COAST TO COAST(1980); LEGEND OF THE LONE RANGER, THE(1981); RAGGEDY MAN(1981)
1984
ROMANCING THE STONE(1984)
John Finnegan
DIRTY HARRY(1971); PLAY IT AS IT LAYS(1972); WOMAN UNDER THE INFLUENCE, A(1974); KILLING OF A CHINESE BOOKIE, THE(1976); NICKELODEON(1976); OPENING NIGHT(1977); IN-LAWS, THE(1979)
1984
LOVE STREAMS(1984); NATURAL, THE(1984)
John P. Finnegan
HEROES(1977); LITTLE MISS MARKER(1980)
Katie Finnegan
FRATERNITY ROW(1977)
Mimi Finnegan
Silents
FINNEGAN'S BALL(1927)
Tom Finnegan
1984
REPO MAN(1984)
William Finnegan
SUPPORT YOUR LOCAL GUNFIGHTER(1971), p
Finnegan the Horse
IT AIN'T HAY(1943)
Eve Finnell
HOW TO MARRY A MILLIONAIRE(1953)
Michael Finnell
ROCK 'N' ROLL HIGH SCHOOL(1979), p; HOWLING, THE(1981), p
1984
GREMLINS(1984), p
Mike Finnell
CANNONBALL(1976, U.S./Hong Kong)
Mike Finneran
1984
JOHNNY DANGEROUSLY(1984)
William Finneran
CRY DR. CHICAGO(1971)
Gerald Finnerman
BUFFALO GUN(1961), ph; THEY CALL ME MISTER TIBBS(1970), ph
Gerald Perry Finnerman
BROTHER JOHN(1971), ph; SSSSSSSS(1973), ph; THAT MAN BOLT(1973), ph; TENDER FLESH(1976), ph; NIGHTMARES(1983), ph; SMORGASBORD(1983), ph
Jerry Finnerman
LOST MAN, THE(1969), ph; BARQUERO(1970), ph
Warren Finnerty
CONNECTION, THE(1962); ANDY(1965); PAWNBROKER, THE(1965); COOL HAND LUKE(1967); EASY RIDER(1969); FREE GRASS(1969); MARLOWE(1969); LAST MOVIE, THE(1971); PANIC IN NEEDLE PARK(1971); INJUN FENDER(1973); KID BLUE(1973); LAUGHING POLICEMAN, THE(1973)
Misc. Talkies
BRIG, THE(1965)
Alan Finney
ALVIN RIDES AGAIN(1974, Aus.), a, w; ELIZA FRASER(1976, Aus.)
Albert Finney
ENTERTAINER, THE(1960, Brit.); SATURDAY NIGHT AND SUNDAY MORNING(1961, Brit.); TOM JONES(1963, Brit.); VICTORS, THE(1963); NIGHT MUST FALL(1964, Brit.), a, p; TWO FOR THE ROAD(1967, Brit.); CHARLIE BUBBLES(1968, Brit.), a, d; SCROOGE(1970, Brit.); GUMSHOE(1972, Brit.); ALPHA BETA(1973, Brit.); MURDER ON THE ORIENT EXPRESS(1974, Brit.); DUELLISTS, THE(1977, Brit.); LOOKER(1981); LOOPHOLE(1981, Brit.); WOLFEN(1981); ANNIE(1982); SHOOT THE MOON(1982); DRESSER, THE(1983)
1984
UNDER THE VOLCANO(1984)
Bess Finney
SPOTS ON MY LEOPARD, THE(1974, S. Africa); FOREVER YOUNG, FOREVER FREE(1976, South Afr.)
Charles G. Finney
SEVEN FACES OF DR. LAO(1964), w
Ed Finney
TROUBLE IN TEXAS(1937), p; WESTBOUND STAGE(1940), p
Edward F. Finney
SONG OF THE GRINGO(1936), p; HEADIN' FOR THE RIO GRANDE(1937), p; RIDERS OF THE ROCKIES(1937), p; TEX RIDES WITH THE BOY SCOUTS(1937), p; STARLIGHT OVER TEXAS(1938), p

Edward Finney
ARIZONA DAYS(1937), p; HITTIN' THE TRAIL(1937), p; MYSTERY OF THE HOODED HORSEMEN, THE(1937), p; SING, COWBOY, SING(1937), p; FRONTIER TOWN(1938), p; ROLLIN' PLAINS(1938), p; UTAH TRAIL(1938), p; WHERE THE BUFFALO ROAM(1938), p; DOWN THE WYOMING TRAIL(1939), p; MAN FROM TEXAS, THE(1939), p; RIDERS OF THE FRONTIER(1939), p; ROLL, WAGONS, ROLL(1939), p; ROLLIN' WESTWARD(1939), p; SONG OF THE BUCKAROO(1939), p; SUNDOWN ON THE PRAIRIE(1939), p; ARIZONA FRONTIER(1940), p; COWBOY FROM SUNDOWN(1940), p; GOLDEN TRAIL, THE(1940), p; PALS OF THE SILVER SAGE(1940), p; RAINBOW OVER THE RANGE(1940), p; RHYTHM OF THE RIO GRANDE(1940), p; GENTLEMAN FROM DIXIE(1941), p; PIONEERS, THE(1941), p; RIDING THE CHEROKEE TRAIL(1941), p; RIOT SQUAD(1941), p&d; ROLLIN' HOME TO TEXAS(1941), p; SILVER STALLION(1941), p&d; KING OF THE STALLIONS(1942), p&d; CORREGIDOR(1943), p; STRANGE HOLIDAY(1945), p; PRAIRIE, THE(1948), p; BUFFALO BILL IN TOMAHAWK TERRITORY(1952), p

Evelyn Finney
COWBOY COMMANDOS(1943)

Jack Finney
FIVE AGAINST THE HOUSE(1955), w; INVASION OF THE BODY SNATCHERS(1956), w; HOUSE OF NUMBERS(1957), w; GOOD NEIGHBOR SAM(1964), w; ASSAULT ON A QUEEN(1966), w; INVASION OF THE BODY SNATCHERS(1978), w

Shirley Jo Finney
NEW GIRL IN TOWN(1977); HEY, GOOD LOOKIN'(1982)

Shirley Joe Finney
RIVER NIGER, THE(1976)

Joe Finnigan
PATSY, THE(1964)

Richard Finnochio
SAFE PLACE, A(1971)

Augusto Finocchi
DEAF SMITH AND JOHNNY EARS(1973, Ital.), w; ITALIAN CONNECTION, THE(1973, U.S./Ital./Ger.), w

Angelo Finocchiaro
RATATAPLAN(1979, Ital.)

August Finochi
COUNT DRACULA(1971, Sp., Ital., Ger., Brit.), w

Filopimin Finos
STEFANIA(1968, Gr.), p

Bernard Fins
NOOSE HANGS HIGH, THE(1948), w

Nat Finston
NEW ORLEANS(1947), md; BIG WHEEL, THE(1949), m

Nat W. Finston
PETER IBBETSON(1935), md; LAST OF THE PAGANS(1936), m; SECOND WOMAN, THE(1951), m

Nathanial W. Finston
BREAKFAST IN HOLLYWOOD(1946), m

Nathaniel Finston
LOVE ME TONIGHT(1932), md; DESIGN FOR LIVING(1933), m; SONG OF MY HEART(1947), p, md

Nathaniel W. Finston
INNOCENTS OF PARIS(1929), m; ONE HOUR WITH YOU(1932), md; SONG OF SONGS(1933), md; WAY TO LOVE, THE(1933), md

Alec Finter
WHAT HAPPENED THEN?(1934, Brit.); I'LL NEVER FORGET YOU(1951); STRANGER IN BETWEEN, THE(1952, Brit.); ISN'T LIFE WONDERFUL!(1953, Brit.); DUEL IN THE JUNGLE(1954, Brit.); GOLDEN MASK, THE(1954, Brit.); YOU CAN'T ESCAPE(1955, Brit.); VIOLENT STRANGER(1957, Brit.); MAN WITH A GUN(1958, Brit.)

Giulio Finzi
NINE MEN(1943, Brit.)

Gregory Fio Rito
OUTSIDER, THE(1962)

Carl Fior
TEAHOUSE OF THE AUGUST MOON, THE(1956)

Leonardo Fioravanti
AUGUSTINE OF HIPPO(1973, Ital.)

Bill Fiore
SWIMMER, THE(1968)

Bob Firks
CAN SHE BAKE A CHERRY PIE?(1983), ph

Carlo Fiore
GUNS, GIRLS AND GANGSTERS(1958); YOUNG CAPTIVES, THE(1959); DAVID AND GOLIATH(1961, Ital.), ph; MOVING FINGER, THE(1963), w

Domenico Fiore
GAS(1981, Can.)

Elena Fiore
LOVE AND ANARCHY(1974, Ital.); SEVEN BEAUTIES(1976, Ital.)

Frank Fiore
RIVALS(1972)

Gianni Fiore
NIGHTMARE(1981), ph

Maria Fiore
MELODY OF LOVE(1954, Ital.); GRAN VARIETA(1955, Ital.); NEOPOLITAN CAROUSEL(1961, Ital.); LET'S TALK ABOUT WOMEN(1964, Fr./Ital.)

Robert Fiore
THIRD WALKER, THE(1978, Can.), ph

William J. Fiore
HOUSE CALLS(1978)

Aldo Fiorelli
ANTHONY OF PADUA(1952, Ital.); HERCULES(1959, Ital.); WARRIOR EMPRESS, THE(1961, Ital./Fr.)

Nadia Fiorelli
DISHONORED(1950, Ital.)

Michael Fiorello
I, THE JURY(1982)

Thomas Fiorello
FORT APACHE, THE BRONX(1981)

Tom Fiorello
FORT APACHE, THE BRONX(1981), p

Tommy Fiorello
SOME OF MY BEST FRIENDS ARE...(1971)

Nada Fiorelly
GOLDEN COACH, THE(1953, Fr./Ital.)

Enrico Fiorentini
1984
PROTOCOL(1984), art d

Fiorenzo Fiorentini
TIGER AND THE PUSSYCAT, THE(1967, U.S., Ital.)

Mario Fioretti
BIG GAME, THE(1972), ph

Pia Fioretti
MANDRAGOLA(1966 Fr./Ital.)

Maurizio Fiori
MR. BILLION(1977)

Michael Fiorillo
HE KNOWS YOU'RE ALONE(1980); ROLLOVER(1981)

Guido Fiorina
PIRATES OF CAPRI, THE(1949), set d

Guido Fiorini
MIRACLE IN MILAN(1951, Ital.), art d; MILLER'S WIFE, THE(1957, Ital.), art d; CARTHAGE IN FLAMES(1961, Fr./Ital.), art d

Marc Fiorini
TENTACLES(1977, Ital.)

Silvana Fiorini
STRANGER RETURNS, THE(1968, U.S./Ital./Ger./Span.)

Giovanna Fiorino
SHAKE, RATTLE, AND ROCK!(1957)

Antonietta Fiorita
LISTEN, LET'S MAKE LOVE(1969, Fr./Ital.)

Ted Fiorito
OUT OF THIS WORLD(1945)

Ann Firbank
BEHIND THE MASK(1958, Brit.); CARRY ON NURSE(1959, Brit.); NOTHING BARRED(1961, Brit.); SERVANT, THE(1964, Brit.); DARLING(1965, Brit.); DEAD MAN'S CHEST(1965, Brit.); MAN COULD GET KILLED, A(1966); ACCIDENT(1967, Brit.); SEVERED HEAD, A(1971, Brit.); ASYLUM(1972, Brit.); STORIES FROM A FLYING TRUNK(1979, Brit.)

Anne Firbank
1984
PASSAGE TO INDIA, A(1984, Brit.)

Jane Fire
PERMANENT VACATION(1982)

Firehouse Five Plus Two
GROUNDS FOR MARRIAGE(1950); HIT PARADE OF 1951(1950)

Irving Fireman
BOY, A GIRL, AND A DOG, A(1946), w

Voices of the Firesign Theater
BELOW THE BELT(1980)

Eddie Firestone
JACKPOT, THE(1950); ONE MINUTE TO ZERO(1952); WE'RE NOT MARRIED(1952); WITH A SONG IN MY HEART(1952); BRASS LEGEND, THE(1956); GREAT LOCOMOTIVE CHASE, THE(1956); REVOLT OF MAMIE STOVER, THE(1956); BAILOUT AT 43,000(1957); JOE BUTTERFLY(1957); LAW AND JAKE WADE, THE(1958); MOUNTAIN ROAD, THE(1960); SCARFACE MOB, THE(1962); TWO FOR THE SEESAW(1962); DESTRUCTORS, THE(1968); PANIC IN THE CITY(1968); MAN CALLED GANNON, A(1969); SUPPOSE THEY GAVE A WAR AND NOBODY CAME?(1970); TODD KILLINGS, THE(1971); PICKUP ON 101(1972); PLAY IT AS IT LAYS(1972); STONE KILLER, THE(1973); W.C. FIELDS AND ME(1976)

Edward Firestone
GOOD MORNING, MISS DOVE(1955)

Elizabeth Firestone
ONCE MORE, MY DARLING(1949), m; THAT MAN FROM TANGIER(1953), m

Russell Firestone
SILHOUETTES(1982), w

Scott Firestone
BAD NEWS BEARS, THE(1976)

Sam Firks
BLOOD ON THE ARROW(1964), p

Lothar Firmans
MARRIAGE IN THE SHADOWS(1948, Ger.)

Trixie Firschke
BROADWAY MELODY OF 1940(1940)

D. Firsova
WAR AND PEACE(1968, USSR)

Javier First-Day-of-Light
WOLFEN(1981)

Sam Firstenberg
REVENGE OF THE NINJA(1983), d
1984
BREAKIN' 2: ELECTRIC BOOGALOO(1984), d; NINJA III–THE DOMINATION(1984), d

Anne Firth
GOOSE STEPS OUT, THE(1942, Brit.); BELL-BOTTOM GEORGE(1943, Brit.); SUSPECTED PERSON(1943, Brit.); DEMOBBED(1944, Brit.); VENGEANCE IS MINE(1948, Brit.); SCOTT OF THE ANTARCTIC(1949, Brit.)

Annie Firth
SPITFIRE(1943, Brit.)

Colin Firth
1984
ANOTHER COUNTRY(1984, Brit.); 1919(1984, Brit.)

Julian Firth
SCUM(1979, Brit.); RUNNERS(1983, Brit.)
1984
FOREVER YOUNG(1984, Brit.); LITTLE DRUMMER GIRL, THE(1984); OXFORD BLUES(1984)

Oskar Fischinger
Silents
WOMAN ON THE MOON, THE(1929, Ger.), ph, spec eff
Harry Fischler
TAXI DRIVER(1976)
Margie Fisco
ATOMIC BRAIN, THE(1964)
Martin Fiscoe
I WANNA HOLD YOUR HAND(1978); CHINA SYNDROME, THE(1979)
Libus Fiser
DAY THAT SHOOK THE WORLD, THE(1977, Yugo./Czech.), m
Lubos Fiser
ON THE COMET(1970, Czech.), m; ADELE HASN'T HAD HER SUPPER YET(1978, Czech.), m
Stanislav Fiser
LADY ON THE TRACKS, THE(1968, Czech.)
Lenka Fiserova
SKI FEVER(1969, U.S./Aust./Czech.)
Ruzena Fiserova
SEVENTH CONTINENT, THE(1968, Czech./Yugo.), w
Earle Fiset
IF YOU COULD SEE WHAT I HEAR(1982), set d
Doris Fisette
SERGEANT WAS A LADY, THE(1961)
Geraldine Fisette
STORY OF DR. WASSELL, THE(1944)
G. Fish
SKI BATTALION(1938, USSR), w
Hamilton Fish
REDS(1981)
J. Suzanne Fish
1984
FOOTLOOSE(1984)
Mark P. Fish
STERILE CUCKOO, THE(1969)
Mike Fish
MICKEY ONE(1965)
Nancy Fish
FUNNYMAN(1967); ME AND MY BROTHER(1969); STEELYARD BLUES(1973); EYE FOR AN EYE, AN(1981); SHOOT THE MOON(1982); SUDDEN IMPACT(1983)
1984
BIRDY(1984)
Nancy G. Fish
MORE AMERICAN GRAFFITI(1979)
Robert Fish
ASSASSINATION BUREAU, THE(1969, Brit.), w
Ted Fish
SUBMARINE SEAHAWK(1959); FOR LOVE OR MONEY(1963); SAND PEBBLES, THE(1966)
Tony Fish
MADMAN(1982)
Harry Fishbeck
ILLUSION(1929), ph; SATURDAY NIGHT KID, THE(1929), ph; EAGLE AND THE HAWK, THE(1933), ph; MILLIONS IN THE AIR(1935), ph; TWO FISTED(1935), ph; BORDER FLIGHT(1936), ph; TIMOTHY'S QUEST(1936), ph; BULLDOG DRUMMOND'S REVENGE(1937), ph; BULLDOG DRUMMOND'S PERIL(1938), ph; BULLDOG DRUMMOND'S BRIDE(1939), ph
Silents
WOMAN'S MAN(1920), ph; CURSE OF DRINK, THE(1922), ph; ALOMA OF THE SOUTH SEAS(1926), ph
Barnet Fishbein
JESUS(1979), w
Benjamin Fishbein
SINGING BLACKSMITH(1938); OVERTURE TO GLORY(1940); VILNA LEGEND, A(1949, U.S./Pol.)
James Fishburn
DEMONSTRATOR(1971, Aus.), p
Larry Fishburne
APOCALYPSE NOW(1979); RUMBLE FISH(1983)
1984
COTTON CLUB, THE(1984)
Larry Fishburne III
CORNBREAD, EARL AND ME(1975)
Laurence Fishburne III
FAST BREAK(1979); WILLIE AND PHIL(1980); DEATH WISH II(1982)
Doug Fishel, Jr.
BIRCH INTERVAL(1976)
David Fishelson
CITY NEWS(1983), a, p,d,w&ed
Mrs. Fisher
Misc. Silents
DUPLICITY OF HARGRAVES, THE(1917)
A.L. Fisher
FLYING FOOL, THE(1931, Brit.), ph
A.S. Fisher
PRINCE OF PEACE, THE(1951)
Adlai Zeph Fisher
PICNIC(1955)
Al Fisher
MISTER ROCK AND ROLL(1957); COUNTRY MUSIC HOLIDAY(1958)
Albert Fisher
DERANGED(1974, Can.), art d
Alex Fisher
WHO KILLED TEDDY BEAR?(1965); LADY LIBERTY(1972, Ital./Fr.)
Alfred Fisher
Silents
PRINCE AND THE PAUPER, THE(1915); RAILROADED(1923); FIGHTING AMERICAN, THE(1924); STORM DAUGHTER, THE(1924); ATTA BOY!(1926); DRIVEN FROM HOME(1927); MILLION FOR LOVE, A(1928)

Misc. Silents
Misc. Silents
BEAUTIFULLY TRIMMED(1920); BREATHLESS MOMENT, THE(1924); ROMANCE OF A ROGUE(1928)
Arem Fisher
Misc. Talkies
ALICE GOODBODY(1974); GOSH(1974)
Arthur Fisher
COUNT OF THE MONK'S BRIDGE, THE(1934, Swed.)
Audry Fisher
SECRET AGENT FIREBALL(1965, Fr./Ital.)
B. G. Fisher
48 HOURS(1982)
Misc. Talkies
CURSE OF THE HEADLESS HORSEMAN(1972)
Barbara Fisher
ROSE BOWL STORY, THE(1952)
Bill Fisher
CAPTAINS COURAGEOUS(1937); SHADOW OF THE THIN MAN(1941); WE WERE DANCING(1942)
Blanche Fisher
WORDS AND MUSIC(1929)
Bob Fisher
SNOW QUEEN, THE(1959, USSR), w; GLOBAL AFFAIR, A(1964), w; I'LL TAKE SWEDEN(1965), w; EIGHT ON THE LAM(1967), w; IMPOSSIBLE YEARS, THE(1968), w
Brandon Terence Fisher
DYNAMITERS, THE(1956, Brit.), d
Bruce M. Fisher
1984
CITY HEAT(1984)
Bud Fisher
Silents
ADVENTURE SHOP, THE(1918), w
Carrie Fisher
SHAMPOO(1975); STAR WARS(1977); BLUES BROTHERS, THE(1980); EMPIRE STRIKES BACK, THE(1980); UNDER THE RAINBOW(1981); RETURN OF THE JEDI(1983)
1984
GARBO TALKS(1984)
Cindy Fisher
HOMETOWN U.S.A.(1979); LIAR'S MOON(1982)
1984
STONE BOY, THE(1984)
Clay Fisher
SANTA FE PASSAGE(1955), w; TALL MEN, THE(1955), w; YELLOWSTONE KELLY(1959), w
Corey Fisher
M(1970)
Daisy Fisher
THINGS ARE LOOKING UP(1934, Brit.), w
Danny Fisher
CATTLE QUEEN OF MONTANA(1954); OUTLAW'S DAUGHTER, THE(1954)
Dave Fisher
PACK, THE(1977), d&w
David Fisher
FEARLESS FRANK(1967); LIAR'S MOON(1982), d&w
David A. Fisher
1984
TOY SOLDIERS(1984), d, w
David G. Fisher
Misc. Silents
LAW OF NATURE, THE(1919), a, d
Diane Fisher
SWANEE RIVER(1939); LILLIAN RUSSELL(1940); MAN I MARRIED, THE(1940); VILLAIN STILL PURSUED HER, THE(1940); YOUNG PEOPLE(1940)
Doug Fisher
STUD, THE(1979, Brit.)
Ed Fisher
IT CAME FROM BENEATH THE SEA(1955)
Eddie Fisher
ALL ABOUT EVE(1950); BUNDLE OF JOY(1956); BUTTERFIELD 8(1960); LAST PICTURE SHOW, THE(1971), m
1984
NOTHING LASTS FOREVER(1984)
Edward Fisher
THIEVES LIKE US(1974)
Edwin J. Fisher
FOR SINGLES ONLY(1968), spec eff
Elliot Fisher
LOVE TAKES FLIGHT(1937)
Elliott Fisher
MR. BOGGS STEPS OUT(1938); INVASION OF THE STAR CREATURES(1962), m
Ethel Fisher
Silents
MARY LATIMER, NUN(1920, Brit.)
Frances Fisher
CAN SHE BAKE A CHERRY PIE?(1983)
Fred Fisher
THEIR OWN DESIRE(1929), m; EASY TO WED(1946); DANCING IN THE DARK(1949); DAY AND THE HOUR, THE(1963, Fr./ Ital.); LADY IN THE CAR WITH GLASSES AND A GUN, THE(1970, U.S./Fr.)
Silents
HUSBAND HUNTERS(1927)
Freddie Fisher
THAT'S MY BABY(1944)
Gary Fisher
NED KELLY(1970, Brit.)

Gary D. Fisher
 SOLDIER, THE(1982)
George Fisher
 JOE PALOOKA IN THE BIG FIGHT(1949); CHAMPAGNE FOR CAESAR(1950); HARD, FAST, AND BEAUTIFUL(1951); SMALL TOWN STORY(1953, Brit.), w; DELAVINE AFFAIR, THE(1954, Brit.), w; CYBORG 2087(1966); MODESTY BLAISE(1966, Brit.); PSYCHO-CIRCUS(1967, Brit.); PRETTY POISON(1968); LADY LIBERTY(1972, Ital./Fr.); MELINDA(1972), a, stunts; MR. RICCO(1975), ch; HAWMPS!(1976), stunts; DOMINO PRINCIPLE, THE(1977); MOVIE MOVIE(1978); SWORD AND THE SORCERER, THE(1982); WHITE DOG(1982); MAN WITH TWO BRAINS, THE(1983); UNDER FIRE(1983)
1984
 CITY HEAT(1984); OH GOD! YOU DEVIL(1984); RED DAWN(1984)
Silents
 BATTLE OF GETTYSBURG(1914); CIVILIZATION(1916); CORNER IN COLLEENS, A(1916); HOME(1916); AND A STILL, SMALL VOICE(1918); LUCK AND PLUCK(1919); DEVIL TO PAY, THE(1920); PRINCE OF AVENUE A., THE(1920); TRAIL OF THE AXE, THE(1922); DIVORCE(1923); EXCITEMENT(1924); AFTER MARRIAGE(1925); JUSTICE OF THE FAR NORTH(1925)
Misc. Silents
 DARKENING TRAIL, THE(1915); SHELL FORTY-THREE(1916); THOROUGHBRED, THE(1916); ANNIE-FOR-SPITE(1917); ENVIRONMENT(1917); GENTLE INTRUDER, THE(1917); PERIWINKLE(1917); PRIDE AND THE MAN(1917); RAINBOW GIRL, THE(1917); THREE OF MANY(1917); WAX MODEL, THE(1917); FIRES OF YOUTH(1918); LITTLE SISTER OF EVERYBODY, A(1918); MRS. LEFFINGWELL'S BOOTS(1918); WITHIN THE CUP(1918); GATES OF BRASS(1919); HEARTS ASLEEP(1919); ROSE OF THE RIVER(1919); HEART OF A WOMAN, THE(1920); LAND OF JAZZ, THE(1920); WOMAN IN HIS HOUSE, THE(1920); BARE KNUCKLES(1921); COLORADO PLUCK(1921); HEARTS OF YOUTH(1921); MOONLIGHT FOLLIES(1921); BOWERY BISHOP, THE(1924); BLACK HILLS(1929)
George "Shug" Fisher
 HOOSIER HOLIDAY(1943); SWING YOUR PARTNER(1943); JAMBOREE(1944); LAST ROUND-UP, THE(1947); MAN WHO SHOT LIBERTY VALANCE, THE(1962); CAT, THE(1966)
Gerald Fisher
 SECRET CEREMONY(1968, Brit.), ph; MACHO CALLAHAN(1970), ph; WISE BLOOD(1979, U.S./Ger.), ph
Gerry Fisher
 ACCIDENT(1967, Brit.), ph; MIKADO, THE(1967, Brit.), ph; AMSTERDAM AFFAIR, THE(1968 Brit.), ph; INTERLUDE(1968, Brit.), ph; SEA GULL, THE(1968), ph; SEBASTIAN(1968, Brit.), ph; HAMLET(1969, Brit.), ph; NED KELLY(1970, Brit.), ph; GO-BETWEEN, THE(1971, Brit.), ph; MAN IN THE WILDERNESS(1971, U.S./Span.), ph; SEE NO EVIL(1971, Brit.), ph; MALPERTIUS(1972, Bel./Fr.), ph; ALL THE RIGHT NOISES(1973, Brit.), ph; AMAZING MR. BLUNDEN, THE(1973, Brit.), ph; DOLL'S HOUSE, A(1973, Brit.), ph; NELSON AFFAIR, THE(1973, Brit.), ph; OFFENSE, THE(1973, Brit.), ph; BUTLEY(1974, Brit.), ph; JUGGERNAUT(1974, Brit.), ph; S(1974), ph; ADVENTURES OF SHERLOCK HOLMES' SMARTER BROTHER, THE(1975, Brit.), ph; BRANNIGAN(1975, Brit.), ph; ROMANTIC ENGLISHWOMAN, THE(1975, Brit./Fr.), ph; MR. KLEIN(1976, Fr.), ph; ACES HIGH(1977, Brit.), ph; ISLAND OF DR. MOREAU, THE(1977), ph; LAST REMAKE OF BEAU GESTE, THE(1977), ph; FEDORA(1978, Ger./Fr.), ph; DON GIOVANNI(1979, Fr./Ital./Ger.), ph; NINTH CONFIGURATION, THE(1980), ph; VICTORY(1981), ph; WOLFEN(1981), ph; BETTER LATE THAN NEVER(1983), ph; LOVESICK(1983), ph; YELLOWBEARD(1983), ph
Gregor Fisher
 ANOTHER TIME, ANOTHER PLACE(1983, Brit.)
1984
 ANOTHER TIME, ANOTHER PLACE(1984, Brit.)
Gregory Fisher
1984
 1984(1984, Brit.)
Capt. H.G. Fisher, USAF
 OPERATION HAYLIFT(1950)
Ham Fisher
 PALOOKA(1934), w; JOE PALOOKA, CHAMP(1946), w; JOE PALOOKA IN WINNER TAKE ALL(1948), w; JOE PALOOKA IN THE BIG FIGHT(1949), w; JOE PALOOKA IN THE COUNTERPUNCH(1949), w; JOE PALOOKA IN THE SQUARED CIRCLE(1950), w; JOE PALOOKA MEETS HUMPHREY(1950), w; JOE PALOOKA IN TRIPLE CROSS(1951), w
Harry Fisher
Silents
 NO TRESPASSING(1922)
Misc. Silents
 SOMEWHERE IN GEORGIA(1916); POLLY OF THE FOLLIES(1922)
Harry A. Fisher
Silents
 BAB'S CANDIDATE(1920)
Harry Fisher, Jr.
Misc. Silents
 YANKEE GIRL, THE(1915)
Henry Fisher
 RIVER CHANGES, THE(1956)
Herbert Fisher
Misc. Talkies
 STOLEN PARADISE(1941)
Jack Fisher
 TOMORROW NEVER COMES(1978, Brit./Can.)
James B. Fisher
 WITHIN THESE WALLS(1945), w
Jay Fisher
1984
 ALLEY CAT(1984); POWER, THE(1984)
Jeanne Fisher
 TAPS(1981)
Jim Fisher
 CRACKING UP(1977)
Joan Fisher
 LET'S MAKE IT LEGAL(1951)

John Fisher
 WILDCAT(1942); JACK LONDON(1943)
Johnny Fisher
 DARK MOUNTAIN(1944)
Judith Fisher
 YOU CAN'T SEE 'ROUND CORNERS(1969, Aus.)
Kai Fisher
 HELLFIRE CLUB, THE(1963, Brit.)
Kym Fisher
 ZAPPED!(1982)
Larry Fisher
 GODLESS GIRL, THE(1929); KID MILLIONS(1934); LIFE BEGINS AT 40(1935); PADDY O'DAY(1935); CAPTAINS COURAGEOUS(1937); WHO KILLED GAIL PRESTON?(1938)
Silents
 LONG LIVE THE KING(1923); BREED OF THE SUNSETS(1928)
Lawrence Fisher
Misc. Silents
 FOR THE FREEDOM OF IRELAND(1920)
Lee Fisher
 WILD RIDERS(1971), art d
Leo Fisher
Silents
 PUPPET MAN, THE(1921, Brit.)
Leonard Fisher
 THEY WERE EXPENDABLE(1945)
Lola Fisher
 HARLOW(1965)
Maggie Fisher
Misc. Silents
 BACHELOR'S ROMANCE, THE(1915)
Maggie Halloway Fisher
Silents
 ASHES OF EMBERS(1916); MICE AND MEN(1916); OUT OF A CLEAR SKY(1918); JENNY BE GOOD(1920)
Misc. Silents
 LOST PRINCESS, THE(1919)
Margarita Fisher
Silents
 INFATUATION(1915); FAIR ENOUGH(1918); K–THE UNKNOWN(1924)
Misc. Silents
 CHARGE IT TO ME(1919); TIGER LILY, THE(1919); PAYMENT GUARANTEED(1921); UNCLE TOM'S CABIN(1927)
Mark Fisher
 AMERICAN WEREWOLF IN LONDON, AN(1981)
Marv Fisher
 SHARK'S TREASURE(1975)
Mary Ann Fisher
 ANDROID(1982), p; FORBIDDEN WORLD(1982), p
Mary Gale Fisher
 ONE MILLION B.C.(1940)
Max Fisher
 WHO'S THAT KNOCKING AT MY DOOR?(1968), ph
Maxine Fisher
 NUTCRACKER FANTASY(1979)
Mel Fisher
 INCREDIBLE PETRIFIED WORLD, THE(1959), ph
Michael Fisher
 PLACE TO GO, A(1964, Brit.), w; BUCKSKIN(1968), w; KILLERS THREE(1968), w; SAVAGE SEVEN, THE(1968), w; EARTHBOUND(1981), p, w; ON THE RUN(1983, Aus.), w
Millicent Fisher
Silents
 ALARM CLOCK ANDY(1920); BILLY JIM(1922)
Misc. Silents
 REGULAR FELLOW, A(1919); MAN OF COURAGE(1922)
Mollie Fisher
 PHANTOM FIEND, THE(1935, Brit.)
Molly Fisher
 ENEMY OF THE POLICE(1933, Brit.); I LIVED WITH YOU(1933, Brit.); FEATHERED SERPENT, THE(1934, Brit.); EXPERT'S OPINION(1935, Brit.); LITTLE BIT OF BLUFF, A(1935, Brit.); ONE GOOD TURN(1936, Brit.); SAM SMALL LEAVES TOWN(1937, Brit.)
Nancy Patricia Fisher
 PATSY, THE(1964)
Neil Fisher
 HUNGRY WIVES(1973)
Nelle Fisher
 UP IN CENTRAL PARK(1948)
Noel Fisher
Silents
 ONCE UPON A TIME(1918, Brit.)
Norman Fisher
 RICHARD III(1956, Brit.); MASQUERADE(1965, Brit.)
1984
 LAUGHTER HOUSE(1984, Brit.)
Pamela Fisher
 FLAMINGO AFFAIR, THE(1948, Brit.); TUNNEL OF LOVE, THE(1958), m/l
Ray Fisher
 SENTIMENTAL BLOKE(1932, Aus.); WHITE RAT(1972)
Richard Fisher
 YOU MUST GET MARRIED(1936, Brit.), w; BELL-BOTTOM GEORGE(1943, Brit.), w; SHOWTIME(1948, Brit.), w
Richard D. Fisher, Jr.
 TRADING PLACES(1983)
Robert Fisher
 CANCEL MY RESERVATION(1972), w
Silents
 DEVIL'S PLAYGROUND, THE(1918); AMERICAN WAY, THE(1919)

Robert C. Fisher
THEY RAID BY NIGHT(1942)
Ross Fisher
IT CAN BE DONE(1929), ph; FAIR WARNING(1931), ph; PHANTOM EXPRESS, THE(1932), ph
Silents
TWIN BEDS(1920), ph; DESERT BLOSSOMS(1921), ph; KEEPING UP WITH LIZZIE(1921), ph; LAVENDER AND OLD LACE(1921), ph; PRISONERS OF LOVE(1921), ph; DANGER POINT, THE(1922), ph; MAILMAN, THE(1923), ph; AFTER THE BALL(1924), ph; GALLOPING GALLAGHER(1924), ph; GEARED TO GO(1924), ph; LIGHTNING ROMANCE(1924), ph; NORTH OF NEVADA(1924), ph; RAINBOW RANGERS(1924), ph; EASY MONEY(1925), ph; RIDIN' THE WIND(1925), ph; HANDS ACROSS THE BORDER(1926), ph; REGULAR SCOUT, A(1926), ph; DON MIKE(1927), ph; SHIELD OF HONOR, THE(1927), ph; SUNSET DERBY, THE(1927), ph; HONEYMOON FLATS(1928), ph
Sallie Fisher
Misc. Silents
LITTLE SHEPHERD OF BARGIAN ROW, THE(1916)
Sgt. Fisher
THIS IS THE ARMY(1943)
Shug Fisher
STALLION CANYON(1949); RIO GRANDE(1950); MISTER ROBERTS(1955); GIANT GILA MONSTER, THE(1959); SERGEANT RUTLEDGE(1960); CHEYENNE AUTUMN(1964); GIT!(1965); SHENANDOAH(1965); REIVERS, THE(1969); GUNS OF A STRANGER(1973); CASTAWAY COWBOY, THE(1974); APPLE DUMPLING GANG RIDES AGAIN, THE(1979)
Misc. Talkies
RIDERS OF THE PONY EXPRESS(1949)
Sondra Fisher
MODERN MARRIAGE, A(1962)
Steve Fisher
NURSE FROM BROOKLYN(1938), w; NAVY SECRETS(1939), w; TYPHOON(1940), w; BERLIN CORRESPONDENT(1942), w; I WAKE UP SCREAMING(1942), w; TO THE SHORES OF TRIPOLI(1942), w; DESTINATION TOKYO(1944), w; JOHNNY ANGEL(1945), w; DEAD RECKONING(1947), w; LADY IN THE LAKE(1947), w; SONG OF THE THIN MAN(1947), w; THAT'S MY MAN(1947), w; HUNTED, THE(1948), w; I WOULDN'T BE IN YOUR SHOES(1948), w; TOKYO JOE(1949), w; ROADBLOCK(1951), w; BATTLE ZONE(1952), w; FLAT TOP(1952), w; WHISPERING SMITH VERSUS SCOTLAND YARD(1952, Brit.), w; BIG FRAME, THE(1953, Brit.), w; CITY THAT NEVER SLEEPS(1953), w; MAN FROM THE ALAMO, THE(1953), w; SAN ANTONE(1953), w; SEA OF LOST SHIPS(1953), w; TERROR STREET(1953), w; VICKI(1953), w; WOMAN THEY ALMOST LYNCHED(1953), w; HELL'S HALF ACRE(1954), w; SHANGHAI STORY, THE(1954), w; SUSAN SLEPT HERE(1954), w; BETRAYED WOMEN(1955), w; BIG TIP OFF, THE(1955), w; LAS VEGAS SHAKEDOWN(1955), w; NIGHT FREIGHT(1955), w; TOP GUN(1955), w; TOUGHEST MAN ALIVE(1955), w; COURAGE OF BLACK BEAUTY(1957), w; I, MOBSTER(1959), w; NOOSE FOR A GUNMAN(1960), w; SEPTEMBER STORM(1960), w; LAW OF THE LAWLESS(1964), w; QUICK GUN, THE(1964), w; BLACK SPURS(1965), w; YOUNG FURY(1965), w; JOHNNY RENO(1966), w; WACO(1966), w; FORT UTAH(1967), w; HOSTILE GUNS(1967), w; RED TOMAHAWK(1967), w; ARIZONA BUSHWHACKERS(1968), w; CLONES, THE(1973), w; GREAT GUNDOWN, THE(1977), w
Steven Fisher
RESTLESS BREED, THE(1957), w; CHEAP DETECTIVE, THE(1978); SUNSET COVE(1978)
Stewart Fisher
Silents
AMERICAN WAY, THE(1919)
Terence Fisher
WHERE THERE'S A WILL(1936, Brit), ed; WINDBAG THE SAILOR(1937, Brit.), ed; CANDLELIGHT IN ALGERIA(1944, Brit.), ed; THEY MET IN THE DARK(1945, Brit.), ed; WICKED LADY, THE(1946, Brit.), ed; MASTER OF BANKDAM, THE(1947, Brit.), ed; COLONEL BOGEY(1948, Brit.), d; GIRL IN THE PAINTING, THE(1948, Brit.), d; SONG FOR TOMORROW, A(1948, Brit.), d; MARRY ME!(1949, Brit.), d; ASTONISHED HEART, THE(1950, Brit.), d; HOME TO DANGER(1951, Brit.), d; SO LONG AT THE FAIR(1951, Brit.), d; DEAD ON COURSE(1952, Brit.), d; DISTANT TRUMPET(1952, Brit.), d; MAN BAIT(1952, Brit.), d; STOLEN FACE(1952, Brit.), d; BLOOD ORANGE(1953, Brit.), d; FOUR SIDED TRIANGLE(1953, Brit.), d, w; SPACEWAYS(1953, Brit.), d; THREE'S COMPANY(1953, Brit.), d; WOMAN IN HIDING(1953, Brit.), d, w; BLACK GLOVE(1954, Brit.), d; BLACKOUT(1954, Brit.), d; CHILDREN GALORE(1954, Brit.), d; FINAL APPOINTMENT(1954, Brit.), d; UNHOLY FOUR, THE(1954, Brit.), d; FLAW, THE(1955, Brit.), d; RACE FOR LIFE, A(1955, Brit.), d; STOLEN ASSIGNMENT(1955, Brit.), d; LAST MAN TO HANG, THE(1956, Brit.), d; CURSE OF FRANKENSTEIN, THE(1957, Brit.), d; HORROR OF DRACULA, THE(1958, Brit.), d; KILL ME TOMORROW(1958, Brit.), d; REVENGE OF FRANKENSTEIN, THE(1958, Brit.), d; HOUND OF THE BASKERVILLES, THE(1959, Brit.), d; MAN WHO COULD CHEAT DEATH, THE(1959, Brit.), d; MUMMY, THE(1959, Brit.), d; BRIDES OF DRACULA, THE(1960, Brit.), d; STRANGLERS OF BOMBAY, THE(1960, Brit.), d; CURSE OF THE WEREWOLF, THE(1961, Brit.), d; SWORD OF SHERWOOD FOREST(1961, Brit.), d; PHANTOM OF THE OPERA, THE(1962, Brit.), d; SHERLOCK HOLMES AND THE DEADLY NECKLACE(1962, Ger.), d; EARTH DIES SCREAMING, THE(1964, Brit.), d; GORGON, THE(1964, Brit.), d; HORROR OF IT ALL, THE(1964, Brit.), d; FRANKENSTEIN CREATED WOMAN(1965, Brit.), d; DRACULA-PRINCE OF DARKNESS(1966, Brit.), d; ISLAND OF TERROR(1967, Brit.), d; DEVIL'S BRIDE, THE(1968, Brit.), d; FRANKENSTEIN MUST BE DESTROYED!(1969, Brit.), d; ISLAND OF THE BURNING DAMNED(1971, Brit.), d; FRANKENSTEIN AND THE MONSTER FROM HELL(1974, Brit.), d
Terry Fisher
LOOKIN' TO GET OUT(1982)
Terry Louise Fisher
SECOND THOUGHTS(1983), w
Thomas Fisher
DEVIL'S RAIN, THE(1975, U.S./Mex.), spec eff
Tom Fisher
FOOD OF THE GODS, THE(1976), spec eff; DEMON SEED(1977), spec eff; QUINTET(1979), spec eff
Valeria Fisher
ROUGH, TOUGH WEST, THE(1952)

Vardis Fisher
JEREMIAH JOHNSON(1972), w
Victor Fisher
MAN BEAST(1956), ph; INCREDIBLE PETRIFIED WORLD, THE(1959), ph
W. D. Fisher
Silents
DAN(1914)
William S. Fisher
BORN TO WIN(1971), m
Emerson Fisher-Smith
MRS. MINIVER(1942); FIRST COMES COURAGE(1943)
H. L. Fisher-Smith
LOVE ON THE RUN(1936)
Duke Fishman
ROSEMARY'S BABY(1968)
Jack Fishman
STEPTOE AND SON(1972, Brit.), m
Jeff Fishman
1984
HOT MOVES(1984); KARATE KID, THE(1984)
Kenneth Harris Fishman
LAW AND DISORDER(1974), w
Melvin Fishman
STEPPENWOLF(1974), p
Bernard Fishwick
JOHNNY FRENCHMAN(1946, Brit.)
Doris Fishwick
MOON OVER THE ALLEY(1980, Brit.)
Misha Fishzon
Misc. Silents
HIS WIFE'S HUSBAND(1913, Pol.)
Enzo Fisichella
VIOLENT FOUR, THE(1968, Ital.)
Edria Fisk
Silents
JACQUELINE, OR BLAZING BARRIERS(1923)
Jack Fisk
ANGELS HARD AS THEY COME(1971), art d; COOL BREEZE(1972), art d; SLAMS, THE(1973), art d; TERMINAL ISLAND(1973), art d; BADLANDS(1974), art d; PHANTOM OF THE PARADISE(1974), prod d; DARKTOWN STRUTTERS(1975), set d; CARRIE(1976), art d; VIGILANTE FORCE(1976), art d; DAYS OF HEAVEN(1978), art d; ERASERHEAD(1978); MOVIE MOVIE(1978), art d; HEART BEAT(1979), prod d; RAGGEDY MAN(1981), d
Paul Fisk
EVICTORS, THE(1979), w
Peter Fisk
Misc. Talkies
BIJOU(1972)
Richard Fisk
BEHIND PRISON GATES(1939)
Warren Earl Fisk
SILVER CITY(1951)
Warren Fisk
COLT .45(1950)
Bert Fiske
FRISCO SAL(1945)
Bob Fiske
BLACK DRAGONS(1942); CYCLONE PRAIRIE RANGERS(1944)
George Fiske
MELODY OF THE PLAINS(1937)
Jack Fiske
DEAD PEOPLE(1974), art d
Richard Fiske
BLONDIE(1938); LITTLE ADVENTURESS, THE(1938); BLONDIE MEETS THE BOSS(1939); GOOD GIRLS GO TO PARIS(1939); HOMICIDE BUREAU(1939); KONGA, THE WILD STALLION(1939); MAN FROM SUNDOWN, THE(1939); PARENTS ON TRIAL(1939); TAMING OF THE WEST, THE(1939); FIVE LITTLE PEPPERS AT HOME(1940); ISLAND OF DOOMED MEN(1940); MAN FROM TUMBLEWEEDS, THE(1940); MEN WITHOUT SOULS(1940); MY SON IS GUILTY(1940); PIONEERS OF THE FRONTIER(1940); PRAIRIE SCHOONERS(1940); STRANGER FROM TEXAS, THE(1940); ACROSS THE SIERRAS(1941); DEVIL COMMANDS, THE(1941); LONE WOLF TAKES A CHANCE, THE(1941); MEDICO OF PAINTED SPRINGS, THE(1941); NORTH FROM LONE STAR(1941); OFFICER AND THE LADY, THE(1941); OUTLAWS OF THE PANHANDLE(1941); PHANTOM SUBMARINE, THE(1941); RICHEST MAN IN TOWN(1941); SON OF DAVY CROCKETT, THE(1941); MAJOR AND THE MINOR, THE(1942); VALLEY OF THE SUN(1942)
Robert Fiske
BATTLE OF GREED(1934); SKY PARADE(1936); SONG OF THE GRINGO(1936); CRIMINALS OF THE AIR(1937); DRUMS OF DESTINY(1937); RAW TIMBER(1937); ROARING SIX GUNS(1937); ADVENTURE IN SAHARA(1938); CASSIDY OF BAR 20(1938); COLORADO TRAIL(1938); FLIGHT INTO NOWHERE(1938); LAW COMMANDS, THE(1938); OLD LOUISIANA(1938); PURPLE VIGILANTES, THE(1938); SOUTH OF ARIZONA(1938); SUNSET TRAIL(1938); TEST PILOT(1938); WEST OF SANTA FE(1938); BURIED ALIVE(1939); I AM A CRIMINAL(1939); MAN FROM SUNDOWN, THE(1939); MYSTIC CIRCLE MURDER(1939); NORTH OF THE YUKON(1939); RACKETEERS OF THE RANGE(1939); TIMBER STAMPEDE(1939); BEFORE I HANG(1940); CAROLINA MOON(1940); EAST SIDE KIDS(1940); LAW AND ORDER(1940); PASSPORT TO ALCATRAZ(1940); TEXAS TERRORS(1940); ALONG THE RIO GRANDE(1941); APACHE KID, THE(1941); INTERNATIONAL LADY(1941); TODAY I HANG(1942); DEAD MAN'S GULCH(1943); TEXAS KID, THE(1944)
Misc. Talkies
VENGEANCE OF THE WEST(1942)
Warren Fiske
SON OF PALEFACE(1952)
Jeffrey Alan Fiskin
CUTTER AND BONE(1981), w; PURSUIT OF D.B. COOPER, THE(1981), w

Jeffrey Alladin Fiskin
ANGEL UNCHAINED(1970), w
Jeffrey Fiskin
1984
CRACKERS(1984), w
Geraldine Fissette
BALL OF FIRE(1941); GIRL, A GUY AND A GOB, A(1941)
Petros Fissoun
HOT MONTH OF AUGUST, THE(1969, Gr.); SISTERS, THE(1969, Gr.)
Fletcher Fist
NAKED KISS, THE(1964); WANDERLOVE(1970), a, p, d&w
Ben Fisz
1984
JIGSAW MAN, THE(1984, Brit.), p
S. Benjamin Fisz
SECRET, THE(1955, Brit.), p; CHILD IN THE HOUSE(1956, Brit.), p; HELL DRIV-ERS(1958, Brit.), p; SEA FURY(1959, Brit.), p; HEROES OF TELEMARK, THE(1965, Brit.), p; OPERATION SNAFU(1965, Brit.), p; BATTLE OF BRITAIN, THE(1969, Brit.), p, w; TOWN CALLED HELL, A(1971, Span./Brit.), p; ACES HIGH(1977, Brit.), p
Mordkhe Fiszelewicz
Misc. Silents
FATALNA KLATWA(1913, USSR)
Clyde Fitch
WISER SEX, THE(1932), w; BEAU BRUMMELL(1954), w
Silents
STRAIGHT ROAD, THE(1914), w; CLIMBERS, THE(1915), w; MOTH AND THE FLAME, THE(1915), w; SECOND IN COMMAND, THE(1915), w; CLIMBERS, THE(1919), w; TRUTH, THE(1920), w; BEAU BRUMMEL(1924), w; LOVER'S LA-NE(1924), w
Donald Fitch
Silents
DOWN BY THE RIO GRANDE(1924), w
George Fitch
THOSE WERE THE DAYS(1940), w
Guy Fitch
1984
RHINESTONE(1984)
John Fitch
RACERS, THE(1955), tech adv; WRONG BOX, THE(1966, Brit.)
Ken Fitch
1984
MOSCOW ON THE HUDSON(1984)
Louis Fitch
MECHANIC, THE(1972)
Louise Fitch
OPENING NIGHT(1977); TRUE CONFESSIONS(1981)
Misc. Talkies
STARBIRD AND SWEET WILLIAM(1975); ADVENTURES OF STAR BIRD(1978)
Robert Fitch
PENNIES FROM HEAVEN(1981)
Winnie Fitch
Misc. Silents
UNDERWORLD OF LONDON, THE(1915, Brit.)
John Fitchen
FIGHTING PIMPERNEL, THE(1950, Brit.)
Maj. Hugh Fite
PARACHUTE BATTALION(1941), w
Christian Fiter
RETURN OF MARTIN GUERRE, THE(1983, Fr.)
Jean-Marie Fitere
VIOLETTE(1978, Fr.), w
Jeff Fithian
WHAT A WAY TO GO(1964)
Fiti
PACIFIC DESTINY(1956, Brit.)
Laura Fitinghoff
CHILDREN, THE(1949, Swed.), w
Katie Fitroy
PLAYBOY OF THE WESTERN WORLD, THE(1963, Ireland)
Joe Fitt
ROLLERBALL(1975), spec eff
Terry Fitt
QUEST FOR FIRE(1982, Fr./Can.)
Carlo Fittanto
PORKY'S II: THE NEXT DAY(1983)
Margaret Fitts
SUN COMES UP, THE(1949), w; STARS IN MY CROWN(1950), w; TALK ABOUT A STRANGER(1952), w; CITY STORY(1954), w; MOONFLEET(1955), w; KING AND FOUR QUEENS, THE(1956), w
Erica Fitz
HERCULES IN NEW YORK(1970)
Veronika Fitz
SPESSART INN, THE(1961, Ger.)
Jason Fitz-Gerald
NIGHT SHIFT(1982)
Lewis Fitz-Gerald
FIGHTING BACK(1983, Brit.); WE OF THE NEVER NEVER(1983, Aus.)
Ute Fitz-Koska
KAMIKAZE '89(1983, Ger.)
Aubrey Fitz-maurice
Silents
ON LEAVE(1918, Brit.)
Arthur Fitz-Richard
RUBY GENTRY(1952), w
Arthur Fitz-Richards
SUN NEVER SETS, THE(1939), w

Foster Fitz-Simmons
BRIGHT LEAF(1950), w
Marsha Fitzalan
NELLY'S VERSION(1983, Brit.)
Paddy Fitzallen
ON THE BEACH(1959)
E. Fitzclarence
LAST WALTZ, THE(1936, Brit.)
Roy Fitzell
LOVES OF CARMEN, THE(1948); FIERCEST HEART, THE(1961), ch; SWEET CHARITY(1969)
Gwen Fitzer
WILD PARTY, THE(1956), cos
Aubrey Fitzgerald
HARMONY HEAVEN(1930, Brit.); GREAT GAY ROAD, THE(1931, Brit.); MAGIC NIGHT(1932, Brit.); DISCORD(1933, Brit.); LITTLE DAMOZEL, THE(1933, Brit.); CHICK(1936, Brit.); JURY'S EVIDENCE(1936, Brit.); PEG OF OLD DRURY(1936, Brit.); CROSS MY HEART(1937, Brit.); SONG OF THE FORGE(1937, Brit.); WHEN KNIGHTS WERE BOLD(1942, Brit.)
Silents
HUTCH STIRS 'EM UP(1923, Brit.); LAST WITNESS, THE(1925, Brit.); NELL GWYNNE(1926, Brit.)
Barry Fitzgerald
JUNO AND THE PAYCOCK(1930, Brit.); PLOUGH AND THE STARS, THE(1936); EBB TIDE(1937); BRINGING UP BABY(1938); DAWN PATROL, THE(1938); FOUR MEN AND A PRAYER(1938); MARIE ANTOINETTE(1938); FULL CONFES-SION(1939); PACIFIC LINER(1939); SAINT STRIKES BACK, THE(1939); LONG VOYAGE HOME, THE(1940); HOW GREEN WAS MY VALLEY(1941); SAN FRANCIS-CO DOCKS(1941); SEA WOLF, THE(1941); TARZAN'S SECRET TREASURE(1941); AMAZING MRS. HOLLIDAY(1943); CORVETTE K-225(1943); TWO TICKETS TO LONDON(1943); GOING MY WAY(1944); I LOVE A SOLDIER(1944); NONE BUT THE LONELY HEART(1944); AND THEN THERE WERE NONE(1945); DUFFY'S TAV-ERN(1945); INCENDIARY BLONDE(1945); STORK CLUB, THE(1945); CALIFOR-NIA(1946); TWO YEARS BEFORE THE MAST(1946); EASY COME, EASY GO(1947); VARIETY GIRL(1947); WELCOME STRANGER(1947); MISS TATLOCK'S MIL-LIONS(1948); NAKED CITY, THE(1948); SAINTED SISTERS, THE(1948); STORY OF SEABISCUIT, THE(1949); TOP O' THE MORNING(1949); UNION STATION(1950); SILVER CITY(1951); QUIET MAN, THE(1952); TONIGHT'S THE NIGHT(1954, Brit.); CATERED AFFAIR, THE(1956); ROONEY(1958, Brit.); BROTH OF A BOY(1959, Brit.)
Benedict Fitzgerald
WISE BLOOD(1979, U.S./Ger.), w
Bob Fitzgerald
GLOVE, THE(1980), ed
Brendan Fitzgerald
THEN THERE WERE THREE(1961); FANTASTIC VOYAGE(1966)
Cissie Fitzgerald
STRICTLY ILLEGAL(1935, Brit.)
Silents
KEEP MOVING(1915)
Cissy Fitzgerald
HIS LUCKY DAY(1929); PAINTED ANGEL, THE(1929); SEVEN FOOTPRINTS TO SATAN(1929); TRANSGRESSION(1931); ONLY YESTERDAY(1933); PATRICIA GETS HER MAN(1937, Brit.)
Silents
MAN BEHIND THE DOOR, THE(1914); FLOWING GOLD(1924); WOMAN WHO SINNED, A(1925); REDHEADS PREFERRED(1926); ARIZONA WILDCAT(1927); MA-TINEE LADIES(1927); TWO FLAMING YOUTHS(1927); LAUGH, CLOWN, LAUGH(1928); NO BABIES WANTED(1928)
Misc. Silents
WIN(K)SOME WIDOW, THE (1914); STEPPIN' OUT(1925); DANGER GIRL, THE(1926); LOVE THIEF, THE(1926); WOMEN LOVE DIAMONDS(1927)
Dallas Fitzgerald
Silents
BIG GAME(1921), d
Dallas M. Fitzgerald
Silents
INFAMOUS MISS REVELL, THE(1921), d; LIFE'S DARN FUNNY(1921), d; OFF-SHORE PIRATE, THE(1921), d; AFTER THE BALL(1924), d; PASSIONATE YOUTH(1925), d; OUT OF THE PAST(1927), d; WEB OF FATE(1927), d; JAZ-ZLAND(1928), d
Misc. Silents
OPEN DOOR, THE(1919), d; BLACKMAIL(1920), d; CHAINS OF EVIDENCE(1920), d; CINDERELLA'S TWIN(1920), d; PRICE OF REDEMPTION, THE(1920), d; MATCH-BREAKER, THE(1921), d; PLAYING WITH FIRE(1921), d; PUPPETS OF FATE(1921), d; GUTTERSNIPE, THE(1922), d; HER ACCIDENTAL HUSBAND(1923), d; MY LADY OF WHIMS(1925), d; TESSIE(1925), d; PRINCESS OF BROADWAY, THE(1927), d; ROSE OF KILDARE, THE(1927), d; WILFUL YOUTH(1927), d; WOM-AN'S LAW(1927), d; GIRL HE DIDN'T BUY, THE(1928), d; GOLDEN SHACK-LES(1928), d; LOOK OUT GIRL, THE(1928), d
Dan Fitzgerald
LINCOLN CONSPIRACY, THE(1977); PRIZE FIGHTER, THE(1979); EYES OF A STRANGER(1980); FINAL COUNTDOWN, THE(1980); NIGHT IN HEAVEN, A(1983)
1984
WHERE THE BOYS ARE '84(1984)
Misc. Talkies
KING FRAT(1979)
Daniel Fitzgerald
PORKY'S II: THE NEXT DAY(1983)
David Fitzgerald
WEDDING, A(1978)
Ed Fitzgerald
GO, JOHNNY, GO!(1959), ph; BRUSHFIRE(1962), ph; STAGECOACH TO DAN-CER'S PARK(1962), ph; CALIFORNIA(1963), ph; LASSIE'S GREAT ADVEN-TURE(1963), ph; RUNAWAY GIRL(1966), ph
Eddie Fitzgerald
OTHER WOMAN, THE(1954), ph; TENDER HEARTS(1955), ph; EDGE OF HELL(1956), ph; PARTY CRASHERS, THE(1958), ph

Edith Fitzgerald

PASSION FLOWER(1930), w; COMPROMISED(1931), w, w; FIVE AND TEN(1931), w; ILLICIT(1931), w; LAUGHING SINNERS(1931), w; MANY A SLIP(1931), w; BRIEF MOMENT(1933), w; EX-LADY(1933), w; TODAY WE LIVE(1933), w; PAINTED VEIL, THE(1934), w; WEDDING NIGHT, THE(1935), w; MY AMERICAN WIFE(1936), w; SMALL TOWN GIRL(1936), w; WITHIN THE LAW(1939), w

Edward Fitzgerald

LOS OLVIDADOS(1950, Mex.), set d; MY BROTHER, THE OUTLAW(1951), art d; ONE BIG AFFAIR(1952), art d; WICKED WOMAN(1953), ph; ADVENTURES OF ROBINSON CRUSOE, THE(1954), art d; GARDEN OF EVIL(1954), art d; EL(1955, Mex.), set d; NEW YORK CONFIDENTIAL(1955), ph; GREEN-EYED BLONDE, THE(1957), ph; LIVING IDOL, THE(1957), art d; MAGNIFICENT SEVEN, THE(1960), art d; GINA(1961, Fr./Mex.), art d; IMPORTANT MAN, THE(1961, Mex.), art d; LA CUCARACHA(1961, Mex.), art d; LITTLE RED RIDING HOOD(1963, Mex.), set d; MIGHTY JUNGLE, THE(1965, U.S./Mex.), art d; NAZARIN(1968, Mex.), art d; DAUGHTER OF DECEIT(1977, Mex.), set d; DEATH IN THE GARDEN(1977, Fr./Mex.), set d; ILLUSION TRAVELS BY STREETCAR, THE(1977, Mex.), art d

Silents

LOVER'S OATH, A(1925), w

Edward P. Fitzgerald

BAIT(1954), ph

Ella Fitzgerald

RIDE 'EM COWBOY(1942); PETE KELLY'S BLUES(1955); ST. LOUIS BLUES(1958); LET NO MAN WRITE MY EPITAPH(1960); UNCLE TOM'S CABIN(1969, Fr./Ital./Ger./Yugo.)

F. Scott Fitzgerald

MARIE ANTOINETTE(1938), w; THREE COMRADES(1938), w; YANK AT OXFORD, A(1938), w; GONE WITH THE WIND(1939), w; RAFFLES(1939), w; WINTER CARNIVAL(1939), w; GREAT GATSBY, THE(1949), w; LAST TIME I SAW PARIS, THE(1954), w; TENDER IS THE NIGHT(1961), w; GREAT GATSBY, THE(1974), w; LAST TYCOON, THE(1976), w

Silents

CHORUS GIRL'S ROMANCE, A(1920), w; OFF-SHORE PIRATE, THE(1921), w; BEAUTIFUL AND DAMNED, THE(1922), w; GRIT(1924), w; GREAT GATSBY, THE(1926), w

Fern Fitzgerald

BEACH GIRLS(1982)

Fred S. Fitzgerald

MORGAN'S MARAUDERS(1929), ph

Geraldine Fitzgerald

UNCLE HARRY(1945); BLIND JUSTICE(1934, Brit.); OPEN ALL NIGHT(1934, Brit.); ACE OF SPADES, THE(1935, Brit.); DEPARTMENT STORE(1935, Brit.); LAD, THE(1935, Brit.); LIEUTENANT DARING, RN(1935, Brit.); THREE WITNESSES(1935, Brit.); TURN OF THE TIDE(1935, Brit.); CAFE MASCOT(1936, Brit.); DEBT OF HONOR(1936, Brit.); DARK VICTORY(1939); MILL ON THE FLOSS(1939, Brit.); WUTHERING HEIGHTS(1939); CHILD IS BORN, A(1940); 'TIL WE MEET AGAIN(1940); FLIGHT FROM DESTINY(1941); SHINING VICTORY(1941); GAY SISTERS, THE(1942); WATCH ON THE RHINE(1943); LADIES COURAGEOUS(1944); WILSON(1944); NOBODY LIVES FOREVER(1946); O.S.S.(1946); THREE STRANGERS(1946); SO EVIL MY LOVE(1948, Brit.); OBSESSED(1951, Brit.); 10 NORTH FREDERICK(1958); FIERCEST HEART, THE(1961); PAWNBROKER, THE(1965); RACHEL, RACHEL(1968); LAST AMERICAN HERO, THE(1973); HARRY AND TONTO(1974); ECHOES OF A SUMMER(1976); BYE BYE MONKEY(1978, Ital/Fr.); ARTHUR(1981); MANGO TREE, THE(1981, Aus.); EASY MONEY(1983)

Gerry Fitzgerald

RADIO FOLLIES(1935, Brit.); SATURDAY NIGHT REVUE(1937, Brit.); STEPPING TOES(1938, Brit.); YOUNG AND INNOCENT(1938, Brit.); ME AND MY PAL(1939, Brit.)

J.A. Fitzgerald

Misc. Silents

IGNORANCE(1916), d; WIVES OF THE PROPHET, THE(1926), d

Jack Fitzgerald

FRANCES(1982)

James Fitzgerald

YOUNG CASSIDY(1965, U.S./Brit.)

Jay Fitzgerald

WHY RUSSIANS ARE REVOLTING(1970), ed

Jerry Fitzgerald

JOURNEY TOGETHER(1946, Brit.)

Joan Fitzgerald

JUKE GIRL(1942)

John Fitzgerald

JUVENILE COURT(1938); LITTLE TOUGH GUY(1938); GUNMAN HAS ESCAPED, A(1948, Brit.); FIGHTING PIMPERNEL, THE(1950, Brit.); FORCES' SWEETHEART(1953, Brit.); SCARLET WEB, THE(1954, Brit.); GOIN' SOUTH(1978), ed; ODD ANGRY SHOT, THE(1979, Aus.)

John D. Fitzgerald

GREAT BRAIN, THE(1978), w

Johnny Fitzgerald

BOY SLAVES(1938)

Johnny Lang Fitzgerald

RIDERS OF THE BLACK HILLS(1938)

Josephine Fitzgerald

SPRING IN PARK LANE(1949, Brit.); YOU CAN'T FOOL AN IRISHMAN(1950, Ireland); FOUR AGAINST FATE(1952, Brit.); JACQUELINE(1956, Brit.); BROTH OF A BOY(1959, Brit.); LADY IS A SQUARE, THE(1959, Brit.); TEENAGE BAD GIRL(1959, Brit.)

Kathy Fitzgerald

WISE BLOOD(1979, U.S./Ger.), p

Lewis Fitzgerald

BREAKER MORANT(1980, Aus.)

Lillian Fitzgerald

TEMPTATION(1936)

Margaret Fitzgerald

TWILIGHT ZONE–THE MOVIE(1983)

Mathew Fitzgerald

HAWAIIANS, THE(1970)

Maureen Fitzgerald

HEARTACHES(1981, Can.); LOVE(1982, Can.)

Michael Fitzgerald

WISE BLOOD(1979, U.S./Ger.), p

Mike Fitzgerald

FLAMING FRONTIER(1958, Can.)

Neil Fitzgerald

CHARLIE CHAN IN SHANGHAI(1935); INFORMER, THE(1935); MARY OF SCOTLAND(1936); PLOUGH AND THE STARS, THE(1936); LANCER SPY(1937); LONDON BY NIGHT(1937); LOST HORIZON(1937); PARNELL(1937); THIRTEENTH CHAIR, THE(1937); BULLDOG DRUMMOND IN AFRICA(1938); HOLIDAY(1938); MARIE ANTOINETTE(1938); ARREST BULLDOG DRUMMOND(1939, Brit.); BULLDOG DRUMMOND'S BRIDE(1939); RULERS OF THE SEA(1939); SERGEANT MADDEN(1939); NIAGARA(1953); MIRAGE(1965); SAVAGES(1972)

Nigel Fitzgerald

LARCENY STREET(1941, Brit.); CHANCE OF A LIFETIME(1950, Brit.); CAPTAIN LIGHTFOOT(1955); ROGUE'S YARN(1956, Brit.); GIDEON OF SCOTLAND YARD(1959, Brit.)

Nuala Fitzgerald

LAST ACT OF MARTIN WESTON, THE(1970, Can./Czech.); BROOD, THE(1979, Can.); SILENT PARTNER, THE(1979, Can.); CIRCLE OF TWO(1980, Can.)

Pat Fitzgerald

Silents

GAMBLE WITH HEARTS, A(1923, Brit.)

Richard Fitzgerald

MY SIX LOVES(1963); WOMEN IN LOVE(1969, Brit.)

Robert Fitzgerald

EMMA MAE(1976), ed; SCHIZOID(1980), ed

Sally Fitzgerald

WISE BLOOD(1979, U.S./Ger.), set d, cos

Sissy Fitzgerald

Silents

BABBITT(1924)

Teresa Fitzgerald [Maria Teresa Vianellol

HORRIBLE DR. HICHCOCK, THE(1964, Ital.)

Tim Fitzgerald

SCOTLAND YARD DRAGNET(1957, Brit.)

Timothy Fitzgerald

OPERATION MURDER(1957, Brit.)

Valerie Fitzgerald

JUD(1971)

Walter Fitzgerald

MURDER AT COVENT GARDEN(1932, Brit.); THIS ENGLAND(1941, Brit.); IN WHICH WE SERVE(1942, Brit.); SQUADRON LEADER X(1943, Brit.); GREAT DAY(1945, Brit.); STRAWBERRY ROAN(1945, Brit.); SAN DEMETRIO, LONDON(1947, Brit.); BLANCHE FURY(1948, Brit.); MINE OWN EXECUTIONER(1948, Brit.); EDWARD, MY SON(1949, U.S./Brit.); FALLEN IDOL, THE(1949, Brit.); HOUR OF GLORY(1949, Brit.); THIS WAS A WOMAN(1949, Brit.); TREASURE ISLAND(1950, Brit.); WINSLOW BOY, THE(1950); FLESH AND BLOOD(1951, Brit.); PICKWICK PAPERS, THE(1952, Brit.); APPOINTMENT IN LONDON(1953, Brit.); PROJECT M7(1953, Brit.); RINGER, THE(1953, Brit.); TWICE UPON A TIME(1953, Brit.); FRONT PAGE STORY(1954, Brit.); LEASE OF LIFE(1954, Brit.); PERSONAL AFFAIR(1954, Brit.); ADVENTURES OF SADIE, THE(1955, Brit.); BIRTHDAY PRESENT, THE(1957, Brit.); DECISION AGAINST TIME(1957, Brit.); SOMETHING OF VALUE(1957); DARBY O'GILL AND THE LITTLE PEOPLE(1959); THIRD MAN ON THE MOUNTAIN(1959); DAMN THE DEFIANT!(1962, Brit.); WE JOINED THE NAVY(1962, Brit.)

Wayne Fitzgerald

THUNDERBOLT AND LIGHTFOOT(1974), titles

William Fitzgerald

COCKLESHELL HEROES, THE(1955)

Anne Fitzgibbon

1984

FIRESTARTER(1984)

Basil Fitzgibbon

WHY ROCK THE BOAT?(1974, Can.); RABID(1976, Can.)

Colen Fitzgibbon

TRAP DOOR, THE(1980)

Maggie Fitzgibbon

SUNSTRUCK(1973, Aus.)

Patrick Fitzgibbon

FIXED BAYONETS(1951)

S.E. Fitzgibbon

DOWN OUR STREET(1932, Brit.), p; INSULT(1932, Brit.), p

Esme Fitzgibbons

Silents

RAT, THE(1925, Brit.)

Caroline Fitzharris

FILE ON THELMA JORDAN, THE(1950)

Victor Fitzherbert

UNCIVILISED(1937, Aus.)

Aubrey Fitzmaurice

Misc. Silents

TICKET-OF-LEAVE MAN, THE(1918, Brit.)

Eddie Fitzmaurice

HIS MAJESTY AND CO(1935, Brit.)

George Fitzmaurice

BARKER, THE(1928), d; HIS CAPTIVE WOMAN(1929), d; LOCKED DOOR, THE(1929), p&d; MAN AND THE MOMENT, THE(1929), d; BAD ONE, THE(1930), d; DEVIL TO PAY, THE(1930), d; ONE ROMANTIC NIGHT(1930), d; RAFFLES(1930), d; TIGER ROSE(1930), d; MATA HARI(1931), d; ONE HEAVENLY NIGHT(1931), d; STRANGERS MAY KISS(1931), d; UNHOLY GARDEN, THE(1931), d; AS YOU DESIRE ME(1932), d; ALL MEN ARE ENEMIES(1934), d; PETTICOAT FEVER(1936), d; SUZY(1936), d; EMPEROR'S CANDLESTICKS, THE(1937), d; LAST OF MRS. CHEYNEY, THE(1937), d; LIVE, LOVE AND LEARN(1937), d; ARSENE LUPIN RETURNS(1938), d; VACATION FROM LOVE(1938), d; ADVENTURE IN DIAMONDS(1940), d

Silents

WHEN ROME RULED(1914), w; ARMS AND THE WOMAN(1916), d; NEW YORK(1916), d; KICK IN(1917), d; INNOCENT(1918), d; NARROW PATH, THE(1918), d; NAULAHKA, THE(1918), d; AVALANCHE, THE(1919), a, d; COUNTER-

FEIT(1919), d; ON WITH THE DANCE(1920), d; KICK IN(1922), d; TO HAVE AND TO HOLD(1922), d; CYTHEREA(1924), d; DARK ANGEL, THE(1925), d; SON OF THE SHEIK(1926), d; NIGHT OF LOVE, THE(1927), d; TENDER HOUR, THE(1927), d; LILAC TIME(1928), d

Misc. Silents
QUEST OF THE SACRED GEM, THE(1914), d; AT BAY(1915), d; COMMUTORS, THE(1915), d; MELTING POT, THE(1915), d; STOP THIEF(1915), d; VIA WIRELESS(1915), d; BIG JIM GARRITY(1916), d; ROMANTIC JOURNEY, THE(1916), d; TEST, THE(1916), d; BLIND MAN'S LUCK(1917), d; HUNTING OF THE HAWK, THE(1917), d; IRON HEART, THE(1917), d; MARK OF CAIN, THE(1917), d; ON-THE-SQUARE GIRL, THE(1917), d; RECOIL, THE(1917), d; HILLCREST MYSTERY, THE(1918), d; JAPANESE NIGHTINGALE, A(1918), d; COMMON CLAY(1919), d; CRY OF THE WEAK, THE(1919), d; OUR BETTER SELVES(1919), d; PROFITEERS, THE(1919), d; SOCIETY EXILE, A(1919), d; WITNESS FOR THE DEFENSE, THE(1919), d; IDOLS OF CLAY(1920), d; RIGHT TO LOVE, THE(1920), d; EXPERIENCE(1921), d; FOREVER(1921), d; PAYING THE PIPER(1921), d; MAN FROM HOME, THE(1922), d; THREE LIVE GHOSTS(1922, Brit.), d; BELLA DONNA(1923), d; CHEAT, THE(1923), d; ETERNAL CITY, THE(1923), d; CYTHEREA(1924), d; TARNISH(1924), d; DARK ANGEL, THE(1925), d; HIS SUPREME MOMENT(1925), d; THIEF IN PARADISE, A(1925), d; LOVE MART, THE(1927), d; ROSE OF THE GOLDEN WEST(1927), d; BARKER, THE(1928), d

Kate Fitzmaurice
JEKYLL AND HYDE...TOGETHER AGAIN(1982)

Michael Fitzmaurice
HOUSE OF A THOUSAND CANDLES, THE(1936); PLOUGH AND THE STARS, THE(1936); GIRL WITH IDEAS, A(1937); REPORTED MISSING(1937); FOURTEEN HOURS(1951)

Amory Fitzpatrick
OPEN SEASON(1974, U.S./Span.)

Bettye Fitzpatrick
URBAN COWBOY(1980)

Brian Fitzpatrick
THREE COCKEYED SAILORS(1940, Brit.); FRONT LINE KIDS(1942, Brit.)

Charles Fitzpatrick
BADLANDS(1974)

Coleen Fitzpatrick
PLEASURE GIRLS, THE(1966, Brit.)

Colleen Fitzpatrick
Misc. Talkies
OUTBREAK OF HOSTILITIES(1979)

James Fitzpatrick
LAST ROSE OF SUMMER, THE(1937, Brit.), p&d

James A. Fitzpatrick
CAPTAIN'S TABLE, THE(1936, Brit.), p; DAVID LIVINGSTONE(1936, Brit.), p&d; AULD LANG SYNE(1937, Brit.), p&d; SONG OF MEXICO(1945), p,d&w
Silents
LADY OF THE LAKE, THE(1928, Brit.), d, w

Janet Fitzpatrick
MERRY COMES TO STAY(1937, Brit.)

Joan Fitzpatrick
BRIDAL PATH, THE(1959, Brit.)
Misc. Talkies
CAMERONS, THE(1974)

Kate Fitzpatrick
OFFICE PICNIC, THE(1974, Aus.); GREAT MACARTHY, THE(1975, Aus.); REMOVALISTS, THE(1975, Aus.); SUMMER OF SECRETS(1976, Aus.); RETURN OF CAPTAIN INVINCIBLE, THE(1983, Aus./U.S.)
1984
FANTASY MAN(1984, Aus.)
Misc. Talkies
NIGHT NURSE, THE(1977)

Katherine Fitzpatrick
DRACULA'S DOG(1978)

Ken Fitzpatrick
HOUSE OF DARK SHADOWS(1970), set d

Michael Fitzpatrick
LORDS OF DISCIPLINE, THE(1983)
1984
RAZOR'S EDGE, THE(1984); SCREAM FOR HELP(1984)

Pat Fitzpatrick
CALL ME MAME(1933, Brit.); SLEEPING CAR(1933, Brit.); GAOL BREAK(1936, Brit.); YOU LIVE AND LEARN(1937, Brit.); MOZART(1940, Brit.)

Robert Fitzpatrick
DEAR BRIGETTE(1965)

Ronald Fitzpatrick
WINNING TICKET, THE(1935)

Emily Fitzroy
BRIDGE OF SAN LUIS REY, THE(1929); SHOW BOAT(1929); FLIRTING WIDOW, THE(1930); MAN FROM BLANKLEY'S, THE(1930); NEW MOON(1930); SHE'S MY WEAKNESS(1930); SONG O' MY HEART(1930); IT'S A WISE CHILD(1931); MISBEHAVING LADIES(1931); UNFAITHFUL(1931); ARENT WE ALL?(1932, Brit.); HIGH SOCIETY(1932, Brit.); LUCKY LADIES(1932, Brit.); HER IMAGINARY LOVER(1933, Brit.); TIMBUCTOO(1933, Brit.); MAN WITH TWO FACES, THE(1934); TWO HEADS ON A PILLOW(1934); CHINA SEAS(1935); DON QUIXOTE(1935, Fr.); BOLD CABALLERO(1936); FRONTIERSMAN, THE(1938); VIGIL IN THE NIGHT(1940); FLAME OF NEW ORLEANS, THE(1941); TWO-FACED WOMAN(1941); FOREVER AND A DAY(1943); WHITE CLIFFS OF DOVER, THE(1944)
Silents
EAST LYNNE(1916); CLIMBERS, THE(1919); NEW YORK IDEA, THE(1920); WAY DOWN EAST(1920); JANE EYRE(1921); STRAIGHT IS THE WAY(1921); WIFE AGAINST WIFE(1921); NO TRESPASSING(1922); SPLENDID LIE, THE(1922); JEALOUS HUSBANDS(1923); STRANGERS OF THE NIGHT(1923); HIS HOUR(1924); LOVE'S WILDERNESS(1924); ARE PARENTS PEOPLE?(1925); LAZYBONES(1925); LEARNING TO LOVE(1925); NEVER THE TWAIN SHALL MEET(1925); OUTWITTED(1925); WINDING STAIR, THE(1925); ZANDER THE GREAT(1925); BAT, THE(1926); DON JUAN(1926); 'MARRIAGE LICENSE?'(1926); WHAT HAPPENED TO JONES(1926); FOREIGN DEVILS(1927); LOVE(1927); MARRIED ALIVE(1927); MOCKERY(1927); SEA TIGER, THE(1927); GENTLEMEN PREFER BLONDES(1928); LOVE ME AND THE WORLD IS MINE(1928); NO BABIES WANTED(1928); TRAIL OF '98, THE(1929)

Misc. Silents
OUT OF THE CHORUS(1921); FASCINATION(1922); DRIVEN(1923); GIRL OF THE LIMBERLOST, A(1924); UNTAMED YOUTH(1924); CHEERFUL FRAUD, THE(1927); ONCE AND FOREVER(1927); CASE OF LENA SMITH, THE(1929)

Louis Fitzroy
Silents
BLIND HUSBANDS(1919); FLAMES OF THE FLESH(1920); ON THE GO(1925)

Roy Fitzroy
COUNTY FAIR, THE(1932), w
Silents
STORMY WATERS(1928), sup

Anthony J. Fitzsimmons
STUCKEY'S LAST STAND(1980), ph, ed

Bronwyn Fitzsimmons
SPENCER'S MOUNTAIN(1963); RAVAGERS, THE(1965, U.S./Phil.)

Carolyn Fitzsimmons
FROGS(1972)

Charles FitzSimmons
QUIET MAN, THE(1952)

Cortland Fitzsimmons
70,000 WITNESSES(1932), w; DEATH OF THE DIAMOND(1934), w; LONGEST NIGHT, THE(1936), w; MANDARIN MYSTERY, THE(1937), w; DEATH OF A CHAMPION(1939), w; ALL-AMERICAN CO-ED(1941), w; DEVIL WITH HITLER, THE(1942), w; EARL CARROLL'S VANITIES(1945), w

Margot Fitzsimmons
I KNOW WHERE I'M GOING(1947, Brit.); CAPTIVE HEART, THE(1948, Brit.)

Maureen Fitzsimmons [Maureen O'Hara]
PLAYBOY, THE(1942, Brit.)

Peter Fitzsimmons
ONE IS A LONELY NUMBER(1972)

Ralph Fitzsimmons
STAMBOUL QUEST(1934); CHAMPAGNE WALTZ(1937)

Tom Fitzsimmons
SWASHBUCKLER(1976)

Charles Fitzsimons
LES MISERABLES(1952); WHAT PRICE GLORY?(1952); DESERT RATS, THE(1953); TITANIC(1953); CAPTAIN LIGHTFOOT(1955); LAST HURRAH, THE(1958); DEADLY COMPANIONS, THE(1961), p

John Fitzstephens
SPEED LOVERS(1968), ed

John J. Fitzstephens
JUST TELL ME WHAT YOU WANT(1980), ed; PRINCE OF THE CITY(1981), ed; DEATH VENGEANCE(1982), ed; DEATHTRAP(1982), ed

Neil Fitzwilliam
HALF A SIXPENCE(1967, Brit.)

Frank Fiumara
RHUBARB(1951)

Orietta Fiume
LA DOLCE VITA(1961, Ital./Fr.)

Allen Fiuzat
BENJI(1974); FOR THE LOVE OF BENJI(1977)

The Five Harmonica Rascals
HOME FROM HOME(1939, Brit.)

Five Lai Founs
DUMMY TALKS, THE(1943, Brit.)

Five Stars
ROCK BABY, ROCK IT(1957)

Robert S. Fiveson
CLONUS HORROR, THE(1979), p, d, w

Paul Fix
LUCKY STAR(1929); LADIES LOVE BRUTES(1930); AVENGER, THE(1931); FIGHTING SHERIFF, THE(1931); GOOD BAD GIRL, THE(1931); THREE GIRLS LOST(1931); DANCERS IN THE DARK(1932); LAST MILE, THE(1932); SCARFACE(1932); SOUTH OF THE RIO GRANDE(1932); BLOOD MONEY(1933); DEVIL'S MATE(1933); EMERGENCY CALL(1933); FARGO EXPRESS(1933); GUN LAW(1933); MAD GAME, THE(1933); RACING STRAIN(1933); SOMEWHERE IN SONORA(1933); SPHINX, THE(1933); ZOO IN BUDAPEST(1933); FLIRTATION WALK(1934); LITTLE MAN, WHAT NOW?(1934); ROCKY RHODES(1934); CRIMSON TRAIL, THE(1935); DESERT TRAIL(1935); DON'T BET ON BLONDES(1935); HIS FIGHTING BLOOD(1935); LET 'EM HAVE IT(1935); LIVING ON VELVET(1935); MEN WITHOUT NAMES(1935); MILLIONS IN THE AIR(1935); MISS PACIFIC FLEET(1935); MUTINY AHEAD(1935); RECKLESS(1935); THROWBACK, THE(1935); WORLD ACCUSES, THE(1935); AFTER THE THIN MAN(1936); BAR 20 RIDES AGAIN(1936); CHARLIE CHAN AT THE RACE TRACK(1936); EAGLE'S BROOD, THE(1936); EX-MRS. BRADFORD, THE(1936); NAVY BORN(1936); PHANTOM PATROL(1936); PLOT THICKENS, THE(1936); PRISONER OF SHARK ISLAND, THE(1936); ROAD TO GLORY, THE(1936); STRAIGHT FROM THE SHOULDER(1936); TWO IN A CROWD(1936); WINTERSET(1936); YELLOWSTONE(1936); ARMORED CAR(1937); BORDER CAFE(1937); DAUGHTER OF SHANGHAI(1937); GAME THAT KILLS, THE(1937); KING OF GAMBLERS(1937); MANNEQUIN(1937); ON SUCH A NIGHT(1937); PAID TO DANCE(1937); SOULS AT SEA(1937); WESTERN GOLD(1937); WOMAN IN DISTRESS(1937); CRIME RING(1938); CRIME TAKES A HOLIDAY(1938); GUN LAW(1938); KING OF ALCATRAZ(1938); MR. MOTO'S GAMBLE(1938); NIGHT HAWK, THE(1938); PENITENTIARY(1938); SAINT IN NEW YORK, THE(1938); SMASHING THE RACKETS(1938); WHEN G-MEN STEP IN(1938); BEHIND PRISON GATES(1939); CODE OF THE STREETS(1939); DISBARRED(1939); GIRL AND THE GAMBLER, THE(1939); HERITAGE OF THE DESERT(1939); MUTINY ON THE BLACKHAWK(1939); NEWS IS MADE AT NIGHT(1939); STAR REPORTER(1939); THOSE HIGH GREY WALLS(1939); TWO THOROUGHBREDS(1939); UNDERCOVER DOCTOR(1939); WALL STREET COWBOY(1939); BLACK DIAMONDS(1940); BLACK FRIDAY(1940); CROOKED ROAD, THE(1940); DR. CYCLOPS(1940); GHOST BREAKERS, THE(1940); GLAMOUR FOR SALE(1940); GREAT PLANE ROBBERY, THE(1940); OUTSIDE THE 3-MILE LIMIT(1940); QUEEN OF THE MOB(1940); STRANGE CARGO(1940); TRAIL OF THE VIGILANTES(1940); TRIPLE JUSTICE(1940); CITADEL OF CRIME(1941); DOWN MEXICO WAY(1941); FARGO KID, THE(1941); HOLD THAT GHOST(1941); MOB TOWN(1941); PUBLIC ENEMIES(1941); ROAR OF THE PRESS(1941); UNFINISHED BUSINESS(1941); ALIAS BOSTON BLACKIE(1942); DR. GILLESPIE'S NEW ASSISTANT(1942); ESCAPE FROM CRIME(1942); HIGHWAYS BY NIGHT(1942); HITLER--DEAD OR ALIVE(1942); JAIL HOUSE BLUES(1942); MISSOURI OUTLAW, A(1942); PITTSBURGH(1942); SHER-

LOCK HOLMES AND THE SECRET WEAPON(1942); SLEEPYTIME GAL(1942); SOUTH OF SANTA FE(1942); THAT OTHER WOMAN(1942); IN OLD OKLAHOMA(1943); MUG TOWN(1943); UNKNOWN GUEST, THE(1943); YOUTH ON PARADE(1943); FIGHTING SEABEES, THE(1944); TALL IN THE SADDLE(1944); BACK TO BATAAN(1945); DAKOTA(1945); FLAME OF THE BARBARY COAST(1945); GRISSLY'S MILLIONS(1945); TYCOON(1947); ANGEL IN EXILE(1948); PLUNDERERS, THE(1948); RED RIVER(1948); FIGHTING KENTUCKIAN, THE(1949); FIGHTING MAN OF THE PLAINS(1949); HELLFIRE(1949); SHE WORE A YELLOW RIBBON(1949); WAKE OF THE RED WITCH(1949); CALIFORNIA PASSAGE(1950); GREAT MISSOURI RAID, THE(1950); SURRENDER(1950); WARPATH(1951); DENVER AND RIO GRANDE(1952); RIDE THE MAN DOWN(1952); WHAT PRICE GLORY?(1952); DEVIL'S CANYON(1953); FAIR WIND TO JAVA(1953); HONDO(1953); ISLAND IN THE SKY(1953); STAR OF TEXAS(1953); HIGH AND THE MIGHTY, THE(1954); JOHNNY GUITAR(1954); RING OF FEAR(1954), w; BLOOD ALLEY(1955); SEA CHASE, THE(1955); TOP OF THE WORLD(1955); BAD SEED, THE(1956); GIANT(1956); MAN IN THE VAULT(1956); SANTIAGO(1956); STAGECOACH TO FURY(1956); STAR IN THE DUST(1956); TOWARD THE UNKNOWN(1956); DEVIL'S HAIRPIN, THE(1957); JET PILOT(1957); MAN IN THE SHADOW(1957); NIGHT PASSAGE(1957); GUNS, GIRLS AND GANGSTERS(1958); LAFAYETTE ESCADRILLE(1958); NOTORIOUS MR. MONKS, THE(1958); TO KILL A MOCKINGBIRD(1962); MAIL ORDER BRIDE(1964); OUTRAGE, THE(1964); BABY, THE RAIN MUST FALL(1965); SHENANDOAH(1965); SONS OF KATIE ELDER, THE(1965); EYE FOR AN EYE, AN(1966); INCIDENT AT PHANTOM HILL(1966); NEVADA SMITH(1966); RIDE BEYOND VENGEANCE(1966); EL DORADO(1967); WELCOME TO HARD TIMES(1967); BALLAD OF JOSIE(1968); DAY OF THE EVIL GUN(1968); UNDEFEATED, THE(1969); YOUNG BILLY YOUNG(1969); DIRTY DINGUS MAGEE(1970); ZABRISKIE POINT(1970); SHOOT OUT(1971); NIGHT OF THE LEPUS(1972); CAHILL, UNITED STATES MARSHAL(1973); PAT GARRETT AND BILLY THE KID(1973); GRAYEAGLE(1977); WANDA NEVADA(1979)
Misc. Talkies
VALLEY OF WANTED MEN(1935)
Paul P. Fix
TALL IN THE SADDLE(1944), w
Peter Paul Fixz
NOTORIOUS MR. MONKS, THE(1958), w
Umberto Fiz
PICKUP ALLEY(1957, Brit.); DAVID AND GOLIATH(1961, Ital.)
Lise Fjeldstad
HUNGER(1968, Den./Norway/Swed.)
Emil Fjellstrom
COUNT OF THE MONK'S BRIDGE, THE(1934, Swed.)
Olaf Fjord
Misc. Silents
LA MADONE DES SLEEPINGS(1928, Fr.); EROTIKON(1929, Czech.)
Mme. Fjorde
Silents
HOW MOLLY MADE GOOD(1915)
Julia Fjorsen
TOXI(1952, Ger.)
Karen Flack
HIGH WIND IN JAMAICA, A(1965)
Roberta Flack
RENALDO AND CLARA(1978); BUSTIN' LOOSE(1981), m
Niki Flacks
TRUMAN CAPOTE'S TRILOGY(1969); RAGGEDY ANN AND ANDY(1977); SEMI-TOUGH(1977)
Bob Flag
1984
1984(1984, Brit.)
Ezio Flagello
GODFATHER, THE, PART II(1974)
Florence Flager
Silents
JANE EYRE(1921)
Cash Flagg [Ray Dennis Steckler]
EEGAH!(1962); WILD GUITAR(1962); INCREDIBLY STRANGE CREATURES WHO STOPPED LIVING AND BECAME CRAZY MIXED-UP ZOMBIES, THE(1965); THRILL KILLERS, THE(1965); LEMON GROVE KIDS MEET THE MONSTERS, THE(1966)
Fannie Flagg
FIVE EASY PIECES(1970); SOME OF MY BEST FRIENDS ARE...(1971); STAY HUNGRY(1976); GREASE(1978); RABBIT TEST(1978)
James Montgomery Flagg
Silents
ADVENTURES OF KITTY COBB, THE(1914), w
Steve Flagg
HIT PARADE OF 1951(1950); FLYING LEATHERNECKS(1951); MILLION DOLLAR PURSUIT(1951); OPERATION PACIFIC(1951); LAS VEGAS STORY, THE(1952); ONE MINUTE TO ZERO(1952); PACE THAT THRILLS, THE(1952)
Steven Flagg
RACE STREET(1948); DANGEROUS PROFESSION, A(1949); EASY LIVING(1949)
Steven Flagg [Michael St. Angel]
VELVET TOUCH, THE(1948)
Ron Flagge
POSTMAN ALWAYS RINGS TWICE, THE(1981)
Kirsten Flagsted
BIG BROADCAST, THE(1932)
Richard Flagy
LOVE IN THE AFTERNOON(1957)
David Flaherty
Silents
TABU(1931), p
Frances Flaherty
LOUISIANA STORY(1948), w
Jack Flaherty
PAWNBROKER, THE(1965), set d
Joe Flaherty
HEAVY METAL(1981, Can.); GOING BERSERK(1983)

John Flaherty
SATAN'S MISTRESS(1982), art d
Joseph Flaherty
BY DESIGN(1982)
Joseph P. Flaherty
1941(1979); USED CARS(1980); STRIPES(1981)
Joseph X. Flaherty
ALEX AND THE GYPSY(1976); STRIPES(1981)
Mary Ellen Flaherty
HYSTERICAL(1983)
Michael Flaherty
OUTSIDER, THE(1980)
Pat Flaherty
COME ON, MARINES(1934); DEATH OF THE DIAMOND(1934); THIN MAN, THE(1934); CHINA SEAS(1935); CHINATOWN SQUAD(1935); G-MEN(1935); MUTINY ON THE BOUNTY(1935); FLYING HOSTESS(1936); HEARTS IN BONDAGE(1936); LOVE BEFORE BREAKFAST(1936); MY MAN GODFREY(1936); PIGSKIN PARADE(1936); PRINCESS COMES ACROSS, THE(1936); SONS O' GUNS(1936); TROUBLE FOR TWO(1936); DAY AT THE RACES, A(1937); FIGHT FOR YOUR LADY(1937); GIRL WITH IDEAS, A(1937); GO-GETTER, THE(1937); HOLD'EM NAVY!(1937); NAVY BLUE AND GOLD(1937); ON AGAIN-OFF AGAIN(1937); SHE LOVED A FIREMAN(1937); STAR IS BORN, A(1937); SUBMARINE D-1(1937); WOMAN-WISE(1937); ALWAYS IN TROUBLE(1938); HOLLYWOOD STADIUM MYSTERY(1938); JOY OF LIVING(1938); MAIN EVENT, THE(1938); SHE'S GOT EVERYTHING(1938); TELEPHONE OPERATOR(1938); THERE'S THAT WOMAN AGAIN(1938); CONVICT'S CODE(1939); KID NIGHTINGALE(1939); LEGION OF LOST FLYERS(1939); NEWSBOY'S HOME(1939); OFF THE RECORD(1939); ONLY ANGELS HAVE WINGS(1939); TELL NO TALES(1939); TORCHY PLAYS WITH DYNAMITE(1939); BLACK DIAMONDS(1940); CASTLE ON THE HUDSON(1940); FLIGHT COMMAND(1940); GRAPES OF WRATH(1940); HIS GIRL FRIDAY(1940); INVISIBLE STRIPES(1940); KNUTE ROCKNE-ALL AMERICAN(1940); MAN FROM MONTREAL, THE(1940); MIDNIGHT LIMITED(1940); MIRACLE ON MAIN STREET, A(1940); MY SON, MY SON!(1940); THEY DRIVE BY NIGHT(1940); AFFECTIONATELY YOURS(1941); BALL OF FIRE(1941); CITY, FOR CONQUEST(1941); HIGHWAY WEST(1941); MEET JOHN DOE(1941); SERGEANT YORK(1941); STRAWBERRY BLONDE, THE(1941); UNEXPECTED UNCLE(1941); CAPTAINS OF THE CLOUDS(1942); GENTLEMAN JIM(1942); IT HAPPENED IN FLATBUSH(1942); JUKE GIRL(1942); MY FAVORITE SPY(1942); PRIDE OF THE YANKEES, THE(1942); SABOTEUR(1942); WHO IS HOPE SCHUYLER?(1942); YANKEE DOODLE DANDY(1942); HIT THE ICE(1943); BEST YEARS OF OUR LIVES, THE(1946); DECOY(1946); HOME SWEET HOMICIDE(1946); IT SHOULDN'T HAPPEN TO A DOG(1946); NOCTURNE(1946); STEP BY STEP(1946); ANGEL AND THE BADMAN(1947); LONG NIGHT, THE(1947); RED HOUSE, THE(1947); WHERE THERE'S LIFE(1947); ALL MY SONS(1948); BABE RUTH STORY, THE(1948), a, tech. ad; COBRA STRIKES, THE(1948); GIVE MY REGARDS TO BROADWAY(1948); KEY LARGO(1948); NIGHT HAS A THOUSAND EYES(1948); NOOSE HANGS HIGH, THE(1948); TREASURE OF THE SIERRA MADRE, THE(1948); IT'S A GREAT FEELING(1949); ROSEANNA McCOY(1949); STRATTON STORY, THE(1949); BLONDIE'S HERO(1950); GOOD HUMOR MAN, THE(1950); HARVEY(1950); JACKIE ROBINSON STORY, THE(1950); PETTY GIRL, THE(1950); THREE LITTLE WORDS(1950); DETECTIVE STORY(1951); RACKET, THE(1951); BLACKBEARD THE PIRATE(1952); HOODLUM EMPIRE(1952); MEET DANNY WILSON(1952); MILLION DOLLAR MERMAID(1952); WINNING TEAM, THE(1952); BOWERY BOYS MEET THE MONSTERS, THE(1954); JUNGLE GENTS(1954); DESPERATE HOURS, THE(1955)
Robert Flaherty
ELEPHANT BOY(1937, Brit.), d
Silents
TABU(1931), p, w
Misc. Silents
MOANA(1926), d
Robert J. Flaherty
LOUISIANA STORY(1948), p&d, w
Vincent X. Flaherty
JIM THORPE-ALL AMERICAN(1951), w; PT 109(1963), w
William Flaherty
HELL BOUND(1957); MONOLITH MONSTERS, THE(1957)
William Barby Flaherty
GUNS FOR SAN SEBASTIAN(1968, U.S./Fr./Mex./Ital.), w
Flaiano
YOUNG HUSBANDS(1958, Ital./Fr.), w
Ennio Flaiano
LUXURY GIRLS(1953, Ital.), w; LUCKY TO BE A WOMAN(1955, Ital.), w; SIGN OF VENUS, THE(1955, Ital.), w; CALABUCH(1956, Span./Ital.), w; LA STRADA(1956, Ital.), w; VITELLONI(1956, Ital./Fr.), w; WHITE SHEIK, THE(1956, Ital.), w; NIGHTS OF CABIRIA(1957, Ital.), w; LA DOLCE VITA(1961, Ital./Fr.), w; BOCCACCIO '70(1962/Ital./Fr.), w; SWINDLE, THE(1962, Fr./Ital.), w; AMERICAN WIFE, AN(1965, Ital.), w; JULIET OF THE SPIRITS(1965, Fr./Ital./W.Ger.), w; NOT ON YOUR LIFE(1965, Ital./Span.), w; VARIETY LIGHTS(1965, Ital.), w; SWEET CHARITY(1969), w; RED(1970, Can.), w
Ernio Flaiano
LA NOTTE(1961, Fr./Ital.), w
Ennio Flainaoph
WOMAN OF ROME(1956, Ital.), w
Ennio Flaino
LIZA(1976, Fr./Ital.), w
Ennio Flajano
8 ½(1963, Ital.), w; LOVE ON THE RIVIERA(1964, Fr./Ital.), w; TENTH VICTIM, THE(1965, Fr./Ital.), w; RUN FOR YOUR WIFE(1966, Fr./Ital.), w; OLDEST PROFESSION, THE(1968, Fr./Ital./Ger.), w; TONIO KROGER(1968, Fr./Ger.), w
Robert Flake
BIG BOSS, THE(1941)
Marcos Flaksman
1984
BLAME IT ON RIO(1984), art d
Andree Flamand
LOVE IS A SPLENDID ILLUSION(1970, Brit.)

Didier Flamand
MAIS OU ET DONC ORNICAR(1979, Fr.)
Jacques Flamand
SOLO(1970, Fr.), art d
Thierry Flamand
1984
LE DERNIER COMBAT(1984, Fr.), set d
Fernand Flamant
LA MARSEILLAISE(1938, Fr.)
Georges Flamant
FOUR HUNDRED BLOWS, THE(1959)
Flame
FOR THE LOVE OF RUSTY(1947); MY DOG RUSTY(1948); NIGHT WIND(1948)
Flame the Dog
OUT OF THE BLUE(1947); MIRACULOUS JOURNEY(1948); NORTHWEST STAM-
PEDE(1948); RUSTY LEADS THE WAY(1948); RUSTY SAVES A LIFE(1949); RUSTY'S
BIRTHDAY(1949); SHEP COMES HOME(1949); YOUNG AND THE BRAVE,
THE(1963)
Flame the Movie Dog
Misc. Talkies
MY DOG SHEP(1948)
Goldie Flame
MALE AND FEMALE SINCE ADAM AND EVE(1961, Arg.)
Edouard Flament
LA MATERNELLE(1933, Fr.), m
Georges Flament
IT HAPPENED IN GIBRALTAR(1943, Fr.); MARKED GIRLS(1949, Fr.); LA
CHIENNE(1975, Fr.)
Ed Flamert
ARTHUR(1931, Fr.), m
The Flamingos
ROCK, ROCK, ROCK!(1956); GO, JOHNNY, GO!(1959)
Vincenzo Flamini
HE WHO SHOOTS FIRST(1966, Ital.), w; DIRTY HEROES(1971, Ital./Fr./Ger.), w
Luca Flamma
Silents
KING OF KINGS, THE(1927)
Camille Flammarion
END OF THE WORLD, THE(1930, Fr.), w
Nicky Flan
SCREWBALLS(1983)
Flanagan
Misc. Talkies
CYNTHIA'S SISTER(1975)
Agnes Flanagan
TWILIGHT OF HONOR(1963), makeup
Bud Flanagan
WILD BOY(1934, Brit.); FIRE HAS BEEN ARRANGED, A(1935, Brit.); OKAY FOR
SOUND(1937, Brit.), w; UNDERNEATH THE ARCHES(1937, Brit.); ALF'S BUTTON
AFLOAT(1938, Brit.); GASBAGS(1940, Brit.); WE'LL SMILE AGAIN(1942, Brit.), a, w;
THEATRE ROYAL(1943, Brit.), a, w; DREAMING(1944, Brit.), w; HERE COMES THE
SUN(1945, Brit.), a, w; JUDGMENT DEFERRED(1952, Brit.); LIFE IS A CIRCUS(1962,
Brit.); WILD AFFAIR, THE(1966, Brit.)
Buddy Flanagan
THEATRE ROYAL(1943, Brit.)
Candy Flanagan
GREASED LIGHTNING(1977), spec eff
Chris Flanagan
GODDESS, THE(1958)
Craig Flanagan
IRON MAJOR, THE(1943)
D. J. Flanagan
Silents
COMMON LAW, THE(1916)
Misc. Silents
CHIVALROUS CHARLEY(1921); BROAD ROAD, THE(1923)
E. J. Flanagan
KID COMES BACK, THE(1937), w
Edward Flanagan
Silents
DON'T CALL ME LITTLE GIRL(1921); HUNCH, THE(1921)
Edward "Bud" Flanagan [Dennis O'Keefe]
SARATOGA(1937)
Fionnuala Flanagan
ULYSSES(1967, U.S./Brit.); SINFUL DAVEY(1969, Brit.)
Fionnula Flanagan
MR. PATMAN(1980, Can.)
1984
REFLECTIONS(1984, Brit.)
Hubert E. Flanagan
DOWN TO THE SEA IN SHIPS(1949)
James Flanagan
Silents
KNIGHT OF THE EUCHARIST(1922)
Joanne Flanagan
DOGS OF WAR, THE(1980, Brit.)
John Flanagan
VON RICHTHOFEN AND BROWN(1970); MEDUSA TOUCH, THE(1978, Brit.);
SWEENEY 2(1978, Brit.)
Kellie Flanagan
WILD IN THE STREETS(1968)
Lynn Flanagan
Misc. Talkies
GIRLS OF 42ND STREET(1974)
Lynne Flanagan
PETERSEN(1974, Aus.)
Marc Flanagan
NIGHT SHIFT(1982)

Mark Flanagan
LORDS OF FLATBUSH, THE(1974)
Neil Flanagan
TORTURE DUNGEON(1970); GURU, THE MAD MONK(1971); MOMENT BY MO-
MENT(1978); S.O.B.(1981)
Ray Flanagan
FINNEGANS WAKE(1965)
Walter Flanagan
GANG THAT COULDN'T SHOOT STRAIGHT, THE(1971)
Flanagan & Allen
DREAMING(1944, Brit.)
Candy Flanagin
ELECTRA GLIDE IN BLUE(1973), spec eff; GREATEST, THE(1977, U.S./Brit.), spec
eff
W.H. "Candy" Flanagin
SOLDIER, THE(1982), spec eff
Rolland Flander
Silents
NEST, THE(1927)
Bruce Flanders
CHEAPER TO KEEP HER(1980); INDEPENDENCE DAY(1983)
Ed Flanders
GRASSHOPPER, THE(1970); TRIAL OF THE CATONSVILLE NINE, THE(1972);
MAC ARTHUR(1977); NINTH CONFIGURATION, THE(1980); PURSUIT OF D.B.
COOPER, THE(1981); TRUE CONFESSIONS(1981)
Ian Geer Flanders
SILENCE(1974)
Michael Flanders
DOCTOR IN DISTRESS(1963, Brit.); LONG AGO, TOMORROW(1971, Brit.)
Neil Flanders
GHASTLY ONES, THE(1968)
Ralph Flanders
LINCOLN CONSPIRACY, THE(1977)
Tommy Flanders
PSYCH-OUT(1968)
Robyn Flanery
STUDENT BODIES(1981)
Taylor Flaniken
HITCH-HIKER, THE(1953)
Craig Flannagan
GUY NAMED JOE, A(1943)
Roy Flannagan
READY FOR LOVE(1934), w
William Flannary
NIGHT PLANE FROM CHUNGKING(1942), art d
William Flanner
ABIE'S IRISH ROSE(1946), art d
Anne Flannery
SCARECROW, THE(1982, New Zealand)
1984
HEART OF THE STAG(1984, New Zealand)
Erin Flannery
CLASS OF 1984(1982, Can.); INCUBUS, THE(1982, Can.)
Jerrilyn Flannery
I WANT YOU(1951); MY PAL GUS(1952)
Jerrylyn Flannery
WAIT 'TIL THE SUN SHINES, NELLIE(1952)
Mary Flannery
THUNDERING HERD, THE(1934), w
Pat Flannery
WARRIORS, THE(1979)
Scamus Flannery
I'LL NEVER FORGET WHAT'S 'IS NAME(1967, Brit.), art d
Seamus Flannery
SMALL WORLD OF SAMMY LEE, THE(1963, Brit.), art d; REPULSION(1965,
Brit.), art d; SANDS OF THE KALAHARI(1965, Brit.), art d; HE WHO RIDES A
TIGER(1966, Brit.), art d; MAROC 7(1967, Brit.), art d; INADMISSIBLE EVIDEN-
CE(1968, Brit.), art d; YOU CAN'T WIN 'EM ALL(1970, Brit.), art d; UP THE
FRONT(1972, Brit.), art d; WICKER MAN, THE(1974, Brit.), art d; JACOB TWO-TWO
MEETS THE HOODED FANG(1979, Can.), art d; KLONDIKE FEVER(1980), prod d
1984
HIGHPOINT(1984, Can.), prod d
Sean Flannery
UP POMPEII(1971, Brit.), art d
Susan Flannery
GNOME-MOBILE, THE(1967); TOWERING INFERNO, THE(1974); GUMBALL RAL-
LY, THE(1976)
Walter Flannery
BY THE LIGHT OF THE SILVERY MOON(1953)
William E. Flannery
SISTER KENNY(1946), art d; NEVER WAVE AT A WAC(1952), art d; CRIMSON
KIMONO, THE(1959), art d
William Flannery
SONS OF THE LEGION(1938), art d; DISBARRED(1939), art d; $1,000 A TOUCH-
DOWN(1939), art d; GOLDEN GLOVES(1940), art d; UNTAMED(1940), art d; WOM-
EN WITHOUT NAMES(1940), art d; MRS. WIGGS OF THE CABBAGE
PATCH(1942), art d; TRUE TO THE ARMY(1942), art d; DIXIE(1943), art d; GOING
MY WAY(1944), art d; BELLS OF ST. MARY'S, THE(1945), art d; DUFFY'S TA-
VERN(1945), art d; INCENDIARY BLONDE(1945), art d; MURDER, HE SAYS(1945),
art d; VELVET TOUCH, THE(1948), prod d; SUN SETS AT DAWN, THE(1950), art d;
VALENTINO(1951), art d; MY SON, JOHN(1952), art d; SAVAGE, THE(1953), art d;
PHFFFT!(1954), art d; PICNIC(1955), art d; TARZAN'S HIDDEN JUNGLE(1955), art
d; FULL OF LIFE(1956), art d; HARDER THEY FALL, THE(1956), art d; THIRTY
FOOT BRIDE OF CANDY ROCK, THE(1959), art d
W. Flanney
PERSONS IN HIDING(1939), art d
D. J. Flannigan
Silents
FRUITS OF DESIRE, THE(1916)

Misc. Silents
ONE HOUR(1917); SLOTH(1917)
E. F. Flannigan
Silents
SPRINGTIME(1915)
J. Flannigan
Misc. Silents
EYES OF THE SOUL(1919)
Dan Flapp
WORLD PREMIERE(1941), ph
Flash
FLAMING SIGNAL(1933); CALL THE MESQUITEERS(1938); RANGE BEYOND THE BLUE(1947)
Silents
HIS MASTER'S VOICE(1925)
"Flash"
DICK BARTON STRIKES BACK(1949, Brit.)
Flash the Dog
FOR THE LOVE OF RUSTY(1947)
Silents
SHADOWS OF THE NIGHT(1928); HONEYMOON(1929)
"Flash" the Horse
DRIFTIN' RIVER(1946)
Gerry Flash
SAVAGE FRONTIER(1953)
Rod Flash [Rod Flash Ilush]
SEVEN TASKS OF ALI BABA, THE(1963, Ital.)
White Flash
WHERE THE BUFFALO ROAM(1938)
Flash Cadillac and the Continental Kids
AMERICAN GRAFFITI(1973)
Robert C. Flasher
WOMAN'S FACE(1941)
Elizabeth Flateau
KING ARTHUR WAS A GENTLEMAN(1942, Brit.)
Georges Flateau
ADVENTURES OF CAPTAIN FABIAN(1951)
Joel Flateau
FANNY(1961); VICTORS, THE(1963)
Michael Flatley
FOLLOW ME, BOYS!(1966)
Barry Flatman
DEAD ZONE, THE(1983); THRESHOLD(1983, Can.)
Richard Flato
HIGH CONQUEST(1947); THREE HUSBANDS(1950); TEXANS NEVER CRY(1951); RETURN OF THE FLY(1959); I'D RATHER BE RICH(1964)
Ernest Flatt
SINGIN' IN THE RAIN(1952); WHITE CHRISTMAS(1954)
Ernie Flatt
MAN WITH A CLOAK, THE(1951)
Gustave Flaubert
UNHOLY LOVE(1932), w; MADAME BOVARY(1949), w; LOVES OF SALAMMBO, THE(1962, Fr./Ital.), w
Erica Flaum
FINAL TERROR, THE(1983), ed
John Flaus
PALM BEACH(1979, Aus.)
Misc. Talkies
PLAINS OF HEAVEN, THE(1982)
Arthur Flaven
Misc. Silents
JUNGLE TRAIL OF THE SON OF TARZAN(1923), d
James Flavin
ALL-AMERICAN, THE(1932); MC KENNA OF THE MOUNTED(1932); OKAY AMERICA(1932); HELLO SISTER!(1933); KING KONG(1933); SHIP OF WANTED MEN(1933); BABY, TAKE A BOW(1934); BELOVED(1934); BIG RACE, THE(1934); CROSBY CASE, THE(1934); GIFT OF GAB(1934); CHINATOWN SQUAD(1935); G-MEN(1935); LITTLEST REBEL, THE(1935); MAN ON THE FLYING TRAPEZE, THE(1935); ONE-WAY TICKET(1935); PUBLIC HERO NO. 1(1935); REMEMBER LAST NIGHT(1935); RENDEZVOUS(1935); SECRETS OF CHINATOWN(1935); SHIPMATES FOREVER(1935); STRAIGHT FROM THE HEART(1935); MY MAN GODFREY(1936); TWO IN A CROWD(1936); ANGEL'S HOLIDAY(1937); CHARLIE CHAN ON BROADWAY(1937); GIRLS CAN PLAY(1937); I PROMISE TO PAY(1937); LEAGUE OF FRIGHTENED MEN(1937); LET'S GET MARRIED(1937); LIVE, LOVE AND LEARN(1937); MYSTERIOUS CROSSING(1937); THIS IS MY AFFAIR(1937); ALEXANDER'S RAGTIME BAND(1938); CHARLIE CHAN IN HONOLULU(1938); DUKE OF WEST POINT, THE(1938); I AM THE LAW(1938); PENITENTIARY(1938); RIDE A CROOKED MILE(1938); SHOPWORN ANGEL(1938); SWEETHEARTS(1938); SWING, SISTER, SWING(1938); TEST PILOT(1938); THANKS FOR EVERYTHING(1938); THREE LOVES HAS NANCY(1938); TOO HOT TO HANDLE(1938); WIVES UNDER SUSPICION(1938); YOU CAN'T TAKE IT WITH YOU(1938); CALLING ALL MARINES(1939); CISCO KID AND THE LADY, THE(1939); EACH DAWN I DIE(1939); HOUSEKEEPER'S DAUGHTER(1939); ICE FOLLIES OF 1939(1939); IRISH LUCK(1939); JESSE JAMES(1939); LADY'S FROM KENTUCKY, THE(1939); MICKEY, THE KID(1939); MR. WONG IN CHINATOWN(1939); ROSE OF WASHINGTON SQUARE(1939); SERGEANT MADDEN(1939); TELL NO TALES(1939); THEY SHALL HAVE MUSIC(1939); UNION PACIFIC(1939); WHEN TOMORROW COMES(1939); CASTLE ON THE HUDSON(1940); DEVIL'S PIPELINE, THE(1940); FIGHTING 69TH, THE(1940); FRAMED(1940); GHOST BREAKERS(1940); GIVE US WINGS(1940); GRAPES OF WRATH(1940); GREAT PROFILE, THE(1940); JOHNNY APOLLO(1940); KNUTE ROCKNE--ALL AMERICAN(1940); LONG VOYAGE HOME, THE(1940); MANHATTAN HEARTBEAT(1940); NORTHWEST MOUNTED POLICE(1940); QUEEN OF THE MOB(1940); REMEMBER THE NIGHT(1940); SAILOR'S LADY(1940); SOUTH OF PAGO PAGO(1940); TIN PAN ALLEY(1940); WOMEN WITHOUT NAMES(1940); YOUTH WILL BE SERVED(1940); AFFECTIONATELY YOURS(1941); BELLE STARR(1941); BUCK PRIVATES(1941); KATHLEEN(1941); LIFE BEGINS FOR ANDY HARDY(1941); MANPOWER(1941); MR. AND MRS. NORTH(1941); MR. AND MRS. SMITH(1941); NEW YORK TOWN(1941); NIGHT OF JANUARY 16TH(1941); POT O' GOLD(1941); REACHING FOR THE SUN(1941); SHADOW OF THE THIN MAN(1941); SKYLARK(1941); STRAWBERRY BLONDE, THE(1941); TEX-

AS(1941); WE GO FAST(1941); WESTERN UNION(1941); ZIEGFELD GIRL(1941); BROADWAY(1942); FINGERS AT THE WINDOW(1942); GENTLEMAN JIM(1942); I WAKE UP SCREAMING(1942); ICELAND(1942); JUKE BOX JENNY(1942); KID GLOVE KILLER(1942); LARCENY, INC.(1942); LIFE BEGINS AT 8:30(1942); REAP THE WILD WIND(1942); RIDE 'EM COWBOY(1942); SABOTEUR(1942); TEN GENTLEMEN FROM WEST POINT(1942); THRU DIFFERENT EYES(1942); TO THE SHORES OF TRIPOLI(1942); TOUGH AS THEY COME(1942); TREAT EM' ROUGH(1942); YANKEE DOODLE DANDY(1942); ACTION IN THE NORTH ATLANTIC(1943); AIR FORCE(1943); CORVETTE K-225(1943); FOOTLIGHT GLAMOUR(1943); HEAVEN CAN WAIT(1943); HELLO, FRISCO, HELLO(1943); IRON MAJOR, THE(1943); IT AIN'T HAY(1943); MISSION TO MOSCOW(1943); MURDER ON THE WATERFRONT(1943); RIDING HIGH(1943); SO PROUDLY WE HAIL(1943); THANK YOUR LUCKY STARS(1943); ABROAD WITH TWO YANKS(1944); FOUR JILLS IN A JEEP(1944); HERE COME THE WAVES(1944); HOLLYWOOD CANTEEN(1944); LAURA(1944); MR. WINKLE GOES TO WAR(1944); ONCE UPON A TIME(1944); PRINCESS AND THE PIRATE, THE(1944); TOGETHER AGAIN(1944); UNCERTAIN GLORY(1944); ANCHORS AWEIGH(1945); CONFLICT(1945); DON JUAN QUILLIGAN(1945); DUFFY'S TAVERN(1945); GOD IS MY CO-PILOT(1945); HOLD THAT BLONDE(1945); JOHNNY ANGEL(1945); MASQUERADE IN MEXICO(1945); MILDRED PIERCE(1945); MURDER, HE SAYS(1945); OVER 21(1945); SAN ANTONIO(1945); SHANGHAI COBRA, THE(1945); SPIDER, THE(1945); WITHIN THESE WALLS(1945); WITHOUT LOVE(1945); WONDER MAN(1945); ANGEL ON MY SHOULDER(1946); BIG SLEEP, THE(1946); CLOAK AND DAGGER(1946); COURAGE OF LASSIE(1946); EASY TO WED(1946); IT SHOULDN'T HAPPEN TO A DOG(1946); MIGHTY MCGURK, THE(1946); MISSING LADY, THE(1946); NOBODY LIVES FOREVER(1946); SENTIMENTAL JOURNEY(1946); STEP BY STEP(1946); STOLEN LIFE, A(1946); STRANGE LOVE OF MARTHA IVERS, THE(1946); TARS AND SPARS(1946); TWO YEARS BEFORE THE MAST(1946); YOUNG WIDOW(1946); DESERT FURY(1947); DISHONORED LADY(1947); EASY COME, EASY GO(1947); FABULOUS DORSEYS, THE(1947); IT HAPPENED ON 5TH AVENUE(1947); MY FAVORITE BRUNETTE(1947); NIGHTMARE ALLEY(1947); NORA PRENTISS(1947); ROBIN OF TEXAS(1947); SONG OF THE THIN MAN(1947); BUNGALOW 13(1948); FURY AT FURNACE CREEK(1948); NOOSE HANGS HIGH, THE(1948); ONE TOUCH OF VENUS(1948); PLUNDERERS, THE(1948); SECRET SERVICE INVESTIGATOR(1948); VELVET TOUCH, THE(1948); ABBOTT AND COSTELLO MEET THE KILLER, BORIS KARLOFF(1949); BLONDIE HITS THE JACKPOT(1949); DEVIL'S HENCHMEN, THE(1949); HOMICIDE(1949); MIGHTY JOE YOUNG(1949); MISSISSIPPI RHYTHM(1949); MY DREAM IS YOURS(1949); PRISON WARDEN(1949); ARMORED CAR ROBBERY(1950); DAKOTA LIL(1950); DESTINATION MURDER(1950); KEY TO THE CITY(1950); MY FRIEND IRMA GOES WEST(1950); SAVAGE HORDE, THE(1950); SOUTH SEA SINNER(1950); WHEN WILLIE COMES MARCHING HOME(1950); ACCORDING TO MRS. HOYLE(1951); COME FILL THE CUP(1951); FIGHTING COAST GUARD(1951); FLYING LEATHERNECKS(1951); FOLLOW THE SUN(1951); OH! SUSANNA(1951); SAILOR BEWARE(1951); CARRIE(1952); MILLION DOLLAR MERMAID(1952); MY PAL GUS(1952); O. HENRY'S FULL HOUSE(1952); ABBOTT AND COSTELLO GO TO MARS(1953); FIGHTER ATTACK(1953); HOT NEWS(1953); STAR OF TEXAS(1953); TROUBLE ALONG THE WAY(1953); MA AND PA KETTLE AT HOME(1954); MASSACRE CANYON(1954); UNTAMED HEIRESS(1954); APACHE AMBUSH(1955); MISTER ROBERTS(1955); NAKED STREET, THE(1955); FRANCIS IN THE HAUNTED HOUSE(1956); FOOTSTEPS IN THE NIGHT(1957); HOLD THAT HYPNOTIST(1957); NIGHT PASSAGE(1957); RESTLESS BREED, THE(1957); TOP SECRET AFFAIR(1957); UP IN SMOKE(1957); WILD IS THE WIND(1957); WINGS OF EAGLES, THE(1957); IN THE MONEY(1958); JOHNNY ROCCO(1958); LAST HURRAH, THE(1958); CHEYENNE AUTUMN(1964); GOOD TIMES(1967); IN COLD BLOOD(1967); BAREFOOT EXECUTIVE, THE(1971)
Misc. Talkies
RIOT SQUAD(1933); BRAND OF HATE(1934)
Martin Flavin
BIG HOUSE, THE(1930), w; PASSION FLOWER(1930), w; CRIMINAL CODE(1931), w; LAUGHING SINNERS(1931), w; THREE WHO LOVED(1931), w; TOO YOUNG TO MARRY(1931), w; AGE OF CONSENT(1932), w; LOVE BEGINS AT TWENTY(1936), w; PENITENTIARY(1938), w; CALLING ALL HUSBANDS(1940), w; CONVICTED(1950), w
Marvin Flavin
YOUR NUMBER'S UP(1931), m
Flavio
ATLAS AGAINST THE CYCLOPS(1963, Ital.)
Jessie Flaws
SWEDISH WEDDING NIGHT(1965, Swed.)
Lori Anne Flax
RAGING BULL(1980)
Harvey Flaxman
INTIMACY(1966), w; PREACHERMAN(1971), w; GRIZZLY(1976), p&w
John P. Flaxman
SOMETHING FOR EVERYONE(1970), p
Freddie Fleck
MAGNIFICENT AMBERSONS, THE(1942), d
Frederick Fleck
Misc. Silents
LITTLEST REBEL, THE(1914)
James Fleck
BUCKET OF BLOOD(1934, Brit.)
Jerry Fleck
LINCOLN CONSPIRACY, THE(1977)
Max Fleck
QUINTET(1979)
Fleecie the Lamb
LITTLEST HOBO, THE(1958)
Alicia Fleer
BORN AGAIN(1978)
Harry Fleer
UNEARTHLY, THE(1957); TORMENTED(1960); GUN HAWK, THE(1963); SHOCK CORRIDOR(1963); DEAR BRIGETTE(1965); WRECKING CREW, THE(1968)
Bill Fleet
1984
TANK(1984)

Jo Ann Fleet
TENANT, THE(1976, Fr.)
Preston M. Fleet
SHINBONE ALLEY(1971), p
Stanley Fleet
FIDDLER ON THE ROOF(1971)
Fleet the Dog
LOYAL HEART(1946, Brit.)
Fleeta
TORTILLA FLAT(1942)
John Fleeting
GONE TO THE DOGS(1939, Aus.); ANTS IN HIS PANTS(1940, Aus.); FORTY
THOUSAND HORSEMEN(1941, Aus.)
John Fleetwing
PACIFIC ADVENTURE(1947, Aus.)
Betty Fleetwood
THIS HAPPY BREED(1944, Brit.)
David Fleetwood
2001: A SPACE ODYSSEY(1968, U.S./Brit.)
Hugh Fleetwood
1984
CORRUPT(1984, Ital.), w
Susan Fleetwood
CLASH OF THE TITANS(1981); HEAT AND DUST(1983, Brit.)
Monte Fleguth
F.J. HOLDEN, THE(1977, Aus.), art d
Connie Fleischauer
MEDIUM COOL(1969)
Bruce Fleischer
R.P.M.(1970)
1984
CONAN THE DESTROYER(1984)
Charles Fleischer
DIE LAUGHING(1980); HAND, THE(1981)
1984
NIGHTMARE ON ELM STREET, A(1984)
Dave Fleischer
MR. BUG GOES TO TOWN(1941), d; TROCADERO(1944)
Leonora Fleischer
WITHOUT A HOME(1939, Pol.), titles
Max Fleischer
MR. BUG GOES TO TOWN(1941), p
P.F. Fleischer
JAZZ BABIES(1932), set d
Richard Fleischer
FOLLOW ME QUIETLY(1949), d; TRAPPED(1949), d; ARMORED CAR ROB-
BERY(1950), d; HAPPY TIME, THE(1952), d; NARROW MARGIN, THE(1952), d;
ARENA(1953), d; 20,000 LEAGUES UNDER THE SEA(1954), d; GIRL IN THE RED
VELVET SWING, THE(1955), d; VIOLENT SATURDAY(1955), d; BANDIDO(1956), d;
BETWEEN HEAVEN AND HELL(1956), d; VIKINGS, THE(1958), d; COMPUL-
SION(1959), d; THESE THOUSAND HILLS(1959), d; CRACK IN THE MIRROR(1960),
d; BIG GAMBLE, THE(1961), d; BARABBAS(1962, Ital.), d; FANTASTIC VOYA-
GE(1966), d; DOCTOR DOLITTLE(1967), d; THE BOSTON STRANGLER, THE(1968),
d; CHE!(1969), d; TORA! TORA! TORA!(1970, U.S./Jap.), d; LAST RUN, THE(1971), d;
SEE NO EVIL(1971, Brit.), d; 10 RILLINGTON PLACE(1971, Brit.), d; NEW CENTU-
RIONS, THE(1972), d; DON IS DEAD, THE(1973), d; SOYLENT GREEN(1973), d; MR.
MAJESTYK(1974), d; SPIKES GANG, THE(1974), d; MANDINGO(1975), d; INCREDI-
BLE SARAH, THE(1976, Brit.), d; CROSSED SWORDS(1978), d; ASHANTI(1979), d;
JAZZ SINGER, THE(1980), d; AMITYVILLE 3-D(1983), d
1984
CONAN THE DESTROYER(1984), d
Richard O. Fleischer
CHILD OF DIVORCE(1946), d; BANJO(1947), d; BODYGUARD(1948), d; SO THIS IS
NEW YORK(1948), d; CLAY PIGEON, THE(1949), d; TOUGH ENOUGH(1983), d
Stanley Fleischer
GREEN PASTURES(1936), art d; NURSE'S SECRET, THE(1941), art d; ESCAPE
FROM CRIME(1942), art d; GORILLA MAN(1942), art d; HIDDEN HAND, THE(1942),
art d; YOU CAN'T ESCAPE FOREVER(1942), art d; MURDER ON THE WATER-
FRONT(1943), art d; ENEMY OF WOMEN(1944), art d; MAKE YOUR OWN
BED(1944), art d; CHRISTMAS IN CONNECTICUT(1945), art d; DANGER SIG-
NAL(1945), art d; TOO YOUNG TO KNOW(1945), art d; BEAST WITH FIVE FIN-
GERS, THE(1946), art d; MAN I LOVE, THE(1946), art d; LOVE AND
LEARN(1947), art d; STALLION ROAD(1947), art d; THAT HAGEN GIRL(1947), art d;
SMART GIRLS DON'T TALK(1948), art d; WOMAN IN WHITE, THE(1948), art d;
GIRL FROM JONES BEACH, THE(1949), art d; IT'S A GREAT FEELING(1949), art d;
KISS IN THE DARK, A(1949), art d; GREAT JEWEL ROBBER, THE(1950), art d;
PERFECT STRANGERS(1950), art d; ROCKY MOUNTAIN(1950), art d; FORT
WORTH(1951), art d; GOODBYE, MY FANCY(1951), art d; SUGARFOOT(1951), art d;
LION AND THE HORSE, THE(1952), art d; MARA MARU(1952), Art d; DESERT
SONG, THE(1953), art d; HOUSE OF WAX(1953), art d; THUNDER OVER THE
PLAINS(1953), art d; CRIME WAVE(1954), art d; THEM!(1954), art d; ILLEGAL(1955),
art d; JUMP INTO HELL(1955), art d; LONE RANGER, THE(1955), art d; TALL MAN
RIDING(1955), set d; DAMN YANKEES(1958), art d; FORT DOBBS(1958), art d;
YELLOWSTONE KELLY(1959), art d; GOLD OF THE SEVEN SAINTS(1961), art d
Walter Fleischer
COUNTESS OF MONTE CRISTO, THE(1934), w
A. S. Fleischman
LAFAYETTE ESCADRILLE(1958), w; SPY IN THE SKY(1958), w; DEADLY COM-
PANIONS, THE(1961), w
Bunky Fleischman
KNUTE ROCKNE–ALL AMERICAN(1940)
Harry Fleischman
ONE MAN JUSTICE(1937); TRUE CONFESSION(1937); AMBUSH(1939); BARNA-
CLE BILL(1941); STAND BY FOR ACTION(1942)
Herbert Fleischman
RIO 70(1970, U.S./Ger./Span.)
Larry Fleischman
JOHNNY GOT HIS GUN(1971)

Sid Fleischman
GOODBYE, MY LADY(1956), w; ADVENTURES OF BULLWHIP GRIFFIN,
THE(1967), w; SCALAWAG(1973, Yugo.), w
A. S. Fleischmann
BLOOD ALLEY(1955), w
Ernest Fleischmann
INTERLUDE(1968, Brit.)
Harry Fleischmann
SHE ASKED FOR IT(1937); LET FREEDOM RING(1939); SOCIETY LAWYER(1939);
LOVE CRAZY(1941); CROSSROADS(1942); JACKASS MAIL(1942)
Mark Fleischmann
ARTHUR(1981)
Peter Fleischmann
DIE HAMBURGER KRANKHEIT(1979, Ger./Fr.), d, w
Charles Fleisher
NIGHT SHIFT(1982)
D. Fleisher
MR. BUG GOES TO TOWN(1941), w
Dave Fleisher
GULLIVER'S TRAVELS(1939), d
Max Fleisher
GULLIVER'S TRAVELS(1939), p
Stanley Fleisher
MURDER IN THE AIR(1940), art d; BRIGHT LEAF(1950), art d; GIRL HE LEFT
BEHIND, THE(1956), art d
Larry Fleishman
DEVIL'S EXPRESS(1975)
Harry Fleishmann
RANGERS OF FORTUNE(1940)
Joseph R. Fleisler
Silents
PANDORA'S BOX(1929, Ger.), ed
Dorothy Fleisman
FOLLOW THE FLEET(1936)
Charles Flekal
MAN CALLED FLINTSTONE, THE(1966), ph
Marietta Flematomas
300 SPARTANS, THE(1962)
Fleming
MAN WITH THE GOLDEN GUN, THE(1974, Brit.), w
Al Fleming
THEY CALL ME MISTER TIBBS(1970), makeup; GETAWAY, THE(1972), makeup
Alice Fleming
PLAYMATES(1941); WHO DONE IT?(1942); KEEP 'EM SLUGGING(1943); MAN-
TRAP, THE(1943); MOONLIGHT IN VERMONT(1943); MYSTERY BROAD-
CAST(1943); OVERLAND MAIL ROBBERY(1943); CHEYENNE WILDCAT(1944);
MARSHAL OF RENO(1944); RECKLESS AGE(1944); SAN ANTONIO KID, THE(1944);
SHERIFF OF LAS VEGAS(1944); STORM OVER LISBON(1944); TUCSON RAI-
DERS(1944); COLORADO PIONEERS(1945); GREAT STAGECOACH ROBBERY(1945);
LADY ON A TRAIN(1945); LONE TEXAS RANGER(1945); MARSHAL OF LARE-
DO(1945); MEDAL FOR BENNY, A(1945); PHANTOM OF THE PLAINS(1945);
SARATOGA TRUNK(1945); STATE FAIR(1945); CONQUEST OF CHEYENNE(1946);
DARK CORNER, THE(1946); DARK HORSE, THE(1946); QUEEN OF BURLES-
QUE(1946); SHERIFF OF REDWOOD VALLEY(1946); SUN VALLEY CYCLONE(1946);
SMASH-UP, THE STORY OF A WOMAN(1947); WAGON WHEELS WESTWARD(1956)
Misc. Talkies
CALIFORNIA GOLD RUSH(1946)
Misc. Silents
HIS GREATEST SACRIFICE(1921)
Alyce Fleming
IT'S A PLEASURE(1945)
Anne Fleming
SPOOK CHASERS(1957)
Art Fleming
MAC ARTHUR(1977); AIRPLANE II: THE SEQUEL(1982)
Athol Fleming
TRAPPED IN A SUBMARINE(1931, Brit.); TIN GODS(1932, Brit.); MIXED DOU-
BLES(1933, Brit.); YOU'RE IN THE ARMY NOW(1937, Brit.)
Atholl Fleming
LITTLE FRIEND(1934, Brit.); ALIAS BULLDOG DRUMMOND(1935, Brit.); SHAD-
OW OF MIKE EMERALD, THE(1935, Brit.); NON-STOP NEW YORK(1937, Brit.)
Barbara Fleming
SO'S YOUR UNCLE(1943)
Barry Fleming
COLONEL EFFINGHAM'S RAID(1945), w
Bob Fleming
LONE STAR RANGER, THE(1930); DESERT VENGEANCE(1931); TEXAS GUN
FIGHTER(1932)
Silents
NUGGET NELL(1919); AVENGING RIDER, THE(1928); BANTAM COWBOY,
THE(1928)
Misc. Silents
DAVY CROCKETT AT THE FALL OF THE ALAMO(1926); RIDING FOR LIFE(1926);
TRUMPIN' TROUBLE(1926); GUN GOSPEL(1927); MOJAVE KID, THE(1927); FIGH-
TIN' REDHEAD, THE(1928); RIDING RENEGADE, THE(1928)
Brandon Fleming
ELEVENTH COMMANDMENT(1933), w; FLAW, THE(1933, Brit.), w; GREAT
STUFF(1933, Brit.), w; MAYFAIR GIRL(1933, Brit.), w; WOMANHOOD(1934, Brit.),
w; ALL IN(1936, Brit.), w; IF I WERE RICH(1936), w; MELODY OF MY HEART(1936,
Brit.), p, w; SUCH IS LIFE(1936, Brit.), p, w; MR. STRINGFELLOW SAYS NO(1937,
Brit.), p, w; SOLUTION BY PHONE(1954, Brit.), p, w; FLAW, THE(1955, Brit.), p, w;
DYNAMITERS, THE(1956, Brit.), p, w; ALIVE ON SATURDAY(1957, Brit.), p, w;
THERE'S ALWAYS A THURSDAY(1957, Brit.), w; BANK RAIDERS, THE(1958,
Brit.), w; WOMAN EATER, THE(1959, Brit.), w; DANGEROUS AFTERNOON(1961,
Brit.), w
Silents
ELEVENTH COMMANDMENT, THE(1924, Brit.), w

Carol Fleming
MOVING FINGER, THE(1963)
Caryl S. Fleming
Silents
DEVIL'S PARTNER, THE(1923), d
Misc. Silents
CLOUDED NAME, THE(1919), d; VALLEY OF LOST SOULS, THE(1923), d
Charlotte Fleming
FROM THE LIFE OF THE MARIONETTES(1980, Ger.), cos
Claud Fleming
TOO MANY WIVES(1933, Brit.)
Claude Fleming
UNHOLY NIGHT, THE(1929); BRIDE OF THE REGIMENT(1930); CAPTAIN OF THE GUARD(1930); MAMBA(1930); ONE NIGHT AT SUSIE'S(1930); THIRTEENTH CANDLE, THE(1933, Brit.)
Misc. Silents
LIGHT THAT FAILED, THE(1916); TEST, THE(1916); SWORD OF DAMOCLES, THE(1920, Brit.)
Connie Fleming
END, THE(1978); STARTING OVER(1979)
Cynthia Fleming
INVASION OF THE BLOOD FARMERS(1972)
Ed Fleming
X-15(1961)
Edouard Fleming
NIGHT AFFAIR(1961, Fr.)
Edward Fleming
ENEMY GENERAL, THE(1960); OPERATION LOVEBIRDS(1968, Den.)
Edyie Fleming
FAN, THE(1981)
Elizabeth Fleming
MADIGAN(1968)
Eric Fleming
CONQUEST OF SPACE(1955); SPELL OF THE HYPNOTIST(1956); QUEEN OF OUTER SPACE(1958); CURSE OF THE UNDEAD(1959); GLASS BOTTOM BOAT, THE(1966)
Erin Fleming
LEGEND OF BLOOD MOUNTAIN, THE(1965); EVERYTHING YOU ALWAYS WANTED TO KNOW ABOUT SEX, BUT WE'RE AFRAID TO ASK(1972); SHEILA LEVINE IS DEAD AND LIVING IN NEW YORK(1975)
Misc. Talkies
LEGEND OF BLOOD MOUNTAIN, THE(1965)
Ethel Fleming
Misc. Silents
PUTTING THE BEE IN HERBERT(1917); PRETENDER, THE(1918); SILENT RIDER, THE(1918); UNTAMED(1918); MODERN HUSBANDS(1919); SMILES(1919)
Glen Fleming
TENDER MERCIES(1982)
Gus Fleming
SERPICO(1973); SEDUCTION OF JOE TYNAN, THE(1979)
Helen Fleming
PRAISE MARX AND PASS THE AMMUNITION(1970, Brit.)
Ian Fleming
DEVIL'S MAZE, THE(1929, Brit.); SCHOOL FOR SCANDAL, THE(1930, Brit.); SHERLOCK HOLMES' FATAL HOUR(1931, Brit.); LUCKY GIRL(1932, Brit.); MISSING REMBRANDT, THE(1932, Brit.); CALLED BACK(1933, Brit.); THIRD CLUE, THE(1934, Brit.); RIVERSIDE MURDER, THE(1935, Brit.); SCHOOL FOR STARS(1935, Brit.); SEXTON BLAKE AND THE MADEMOISELLE(1935, Brit.); TRIUMPH OF SHERLOCK HOLMES, THE(1935, Brit.); CROUCHING BEAST, THE(1936, U. S./Brit.); HEARTS OF HUMANITY(1936, Brit.); PRISON BREAKER(1936, Brit.); ROYAL EAGLE(1936, Brit.); DARBY AND JOAN(1937, Brit.); RACING ROMANCE(1937, Brit.); WHEN THIEF MEETS THIEF(1937, Brit.); ALMOST A HONEYMOON(1938, Brit.); CLAYDON TREASURE MYSTERY, THE(1938, Brit.); DOUBLE OR QUITS(1938, Brit.); IF I WERE BOSS(1938, Brit.); QUIET PLEASE(1938, Brit.); RETURN OF CAROL DEANE, THE(1938, Brit.); REVERSE BE MY LOT(1938, Brit.); DEAD MEN ARE DANGEROUS(1939, Brit.); ME AND MY PAL(1939, Brit.); MEN WITHOUT HONOUR(1939, Brit.); NURSEMAID WHO DISAPPEARED, THE(1939, Brit.); SHADOWED EYES(1939, Brit.); LION HAS WINGS, THE(1940, Brit.); NIGHT TRAIN(1940, Brit.); THREE SILENT MEN(1940, Brit.); TILLY OF BLOOMSBURY(1940, Brit.); GIRL IN DISTRESS(1941, Brit.); IT HAPPENED TO ONE MAN(1941, Brit.); MURDER AT THE BASKERVILLES(1941, Brit.); LET THE PEOPLE SING(1942, Brit.); SABOTAGE AT SEA(1942, Brit.); SALUTE JOHN CITIZEN(1942, Brit.); TALK ABOUT JACQUELINE(1942, Brit.); WINGS AND THE WOMAN(1942, Brit.); BUTLER'S DILEMMA, THE(1943, Brit.); ESCAPE TO DANGER(1943, Brit.); UP WITH THE LARK(1943, Brit.); HE SNOOPS TO CONQUER(1944, Brit.); YELLOW CANARY, THE(1944, Brit.); APPOINTMENT WITH CRIME(1945, Brit.); I DIDN'T DO IT(1945, Brit.); THEY KNEW MR. KNIGHT(1945, Brit.); THEY MET IN THE DARK(1945, Brit.); GEORGE IN CIVVY STREET(1946, Brit.); CAPTAIN BOYCOTT(1947, Brit.); TAWNY PIPIT(1947, Brit.); HATTER'S CASTLE(1948, Brit.); FOR THEM THAT TRESPASS(1949, Brit.); MATTER OF MURDER, A(1949, Brit.); QUARTET(1949, Brit.); FIVE ANGLES ON MURDER(1950, Brit.); SHADOW OF THE PAST(1950, Brit.); CHELSEA STORY(1951, Brit.); HAMMER THE TOFF(1952, Brit.); SALUTE THE TOFF(1952, Brit.); DEADLY NIGHTSHADE(1953, Brit.); IT'S A GRAND LIFE(1953, Brit.); MURDER WILL OUT(1953, Brit.); NORMAN CONQUEST(1953, Brit.); RECOIL(1953, Brit.); CIRCUMSTANIAL EVIDENCE(1954, Brit.); COMPANIONS IN CRIME(1954, Brit.); DELAYED ACTION(1954, Brit.); EMBEZZLER, THE(1954, Brit.); LAND OF FURY(1955 Brit.); POLICE DOG(1955, Brit.); HIGH FLIGHT(1957, Brit.); WOMAN POSSESSED, A(1958, Brit.); CRASH DRIVE(1959, Brit.); INNOCENT MEETING(1959, Brit.); MAN ACCUSED(1959); WEB OF SUSPICION(1959, Brit.); BLUEBEARD'S TEN HONEYMOONS(1960, Brit.); MAN WITH THE GREEN CARNATION, THE(1960, Brit.); TOO HOT TO HANDLE(1961, Brit.); DR. NO(1962, Brit.), w; LAMP IN ASSASSIN MEWS, THE(1962, Brit.); RETURN OF A STRANGER(1962, Brit.); WHAT EVERY WOMAN WANTS(1962, Brit.); FROM RUSSIA WITH LOVE(1963, Brit.), w; GOLDFINGER(1964, Brit.), w; NO, MY DARLING DAUGHTER(1964, Brit.), w; SEVENTY DEADLY PILLS(1964, Brit.); TAMAHINE(1964, Brit.); RETURN OF MR. MOTO(1965, Brit.); THUNDERBALL(1965, Brit.), w; YOUR MONEY OR YOUR WIFE(1965, Brit.); CASINO ROYALE(1967, Brit.), w; YOU ONLY LIVE TWICE(1967, Brit.), w; CHITTY CHITTY BANG BANG(1968, Brit.), w; ON HER MAJESTY'S SECRET SERVICE(1969, Brit.), w; DIAMONDS ARE FOREVER(1971, Brit.), w; LIVE AND LET DIE(1973, Brit.), w; SPY WHO LOVED ME, THE(1977, Brit.), w; MOONRAKER(1979, Brit.), w; FOR YOUR

EYES ONLY(1981), w; NEVER SAY NEVER AGAIN(1983), w; OCTOPUSSY(1983, Brit.), w
Misc. Silents
SECOND TO NONE(1926, Brit.); WARE CASE, THE(1928, Brit.)
James Louis Fleming
1984
PREPPIES(1984)
Jane Fleming [Silvia Sorente]
VISCOUNT, THE(1967, Fr./Span./Ital./Ger.)
Joan Fleming
RX MURDER(1958, Brit.), w
John B. Fleming
Silents
ARGYLE CASE, THE(1917)
John Fleming
LARCENY(1948), w
Johnny Fleming
JANIE(1944)
Juanita Fleming
VERDICT, THE(1982)
Julian Boone Fleming
HELL'S ANGELS(1930), art d
Silents
BEAU GESTE(1926), art d; DANCING MOTHERS(1926), art d; KISS FOR CINDERELLA, A(1926), art d
Lone Fleming
BLIND DEAD, THE(1972, Span.); DEMON WITCH CHILD(1974, Span.)
Misc. Talkies
TOMBS OF THE BLIND DEAD(1974)
Louis Fleming
HAPPY DEATHDAY(1969, Brit.), p
Marie Fleming
HARD PART BEGINS, THE(1973, Can.)
Mark Fleming
NIGHT OF BLOODY HORROR zero(1969)
Marvin Fleming
HEAVEN CAN WAIT(1978)
Michael Fleming
MAN WITH THE GOLDEN GUN, THE(1974, Brit.); CONDUCT UNBECOMING(1975, Brit.)
Neal Fleming
10 TO MIDNIGHT(1983)
Paul Fleming
JOYRIDE(1977)
Philip Fleming
NIGHT OF BLOODY HORROR zero(1969)
Rhonda Fleming
SINCE YOU WENT AWAY(1944); WHEN STRANGERS MARRY(1944); SPELLBOUND(1945); ABILENE TOWN(1946); SPIRAL STAIRCASE, THE(1946); ADVENTURE ISLAND(1947); OUT OF THE PAST(1947); CONNECTICUT YANKEE IN KING ARTHUR'S COURT, A(1949); GREAT LOVER, THE(1949); EAGLE AND THE HAWK, THE(1950); REDHEAD AND THE COWBOY, THE(1950); CROSSWINDS(1951); CRY DANGER(1951); HONG KONG(1951); LAST OUTPOST, THE(1951); LITTLE EGYPT(1951); GOLDEN HAWK, THE(1952); INFERNO(1953); PONY EXPRESS(1953); SERPENT OF THE NILE(1953); THOSE REDHEADS FROM SEATTLE(1953); TROPIC ZONE(1953); JIVARO(1954); YANKEE PASHA(1954); TENNESSEE'S PARTNER(1955); KILLER IS LOOSE, THE(1956); ODONGO(1956, Brit.); QUEEN OF BABYLON, THE(1956, Ital.); SLIGHTLY SCARLET(1956); WHILE THE CITY SLEEPS(1956); BUSTER KEATON STORY, THE(1957); GUN GLORY(1957); GUNFIGHT AT THE O.K. CORRAL(1957); BULLWHIP(1958); HOME BEFORE DARK(1958); ALIAS JESSE JAMES(1959); BIG CIRCUS, THE(1959); CROWDED SKY, THE(1960); REVOLT OF THE SLAVES, THE(1961, Ital./Span./Ger.); PATSY, THE(1964); AMERICAN WIFE, AN(1965, Ital.); RUN FOR YOUR WIFE(1966, Fr./Ital.); BACKTRACK(1969); WON TON TON, THE DOG WHO SAVED HOLLYWOOD(1976); NUDE BOMB, THE(1980)
Robbie Fleming
SIX PACK(1982)
Robert Fleming
DAWN TRAIL, THE(1931)
Silents
MAN FROM HOME, THE(1914)
Misc. Silents
LOVE MASK, THE(1916); BIFF BANG BUDDY(1924)
Ruby Fleming
JOKER IS WILD, THE(1957)
Susan Fleming
DANGEROUS AFFAIR, A(1931); LOVER COME BACK(1931); MEN ARE LIKE THAT(1931); RANGE FEUD, THE(1931); MILLION DOLLAR LEGS(1932); HE LEARNED ABOUT WOMEN(1933); HERITAGE OF THE DESERT(1933); I LOVE THAT MAN(1933); MY WEAKNESS(1933); CALL IT LUCK(1934); OLSEN'S BIG MOMENT(1934); SHE LEARNED ABOUT SAILORS(1934); BREAK OF HEARTS(1935); GOLD DIGGERS OF 1937(1936); GREAT ZIEGFELD, THE(1936); NAVY WIFE(1936); STAR FOR A NIGHT(1936); GOD'S COUNTRY AND THE WOMAN(1937)
Suzanne Fleming
LADIES OF THE JURY(1932)
Silents
ACE OF CADS, THE(1926)
Tom Fleming
KING LEAR(1971, Brit./Den.); MARY, QUEEN OF SCOTS(1971, Brit.); MEETINGS WITH REMARKABLE MEN(1979, Brit.)
Victor Fleming
ABIE'S IRISH ROSE(1928), d; VIRGINIAN, THE(1929), d; WOLF SONG(1929), p&d; COMMON CLAY(1930), d; RENEGADES(1930), d; RED DUST(1932), p&d; WET PARADE, THE(1932), d; BOMBSHELL(1933), d; WHITE SISTER, THE(1933), d; TREASURE ISLAND(1934), d; FARMER TAKES A WIFE, THE(1935), d; RECKLESS(1935), d, w; CAPTAINS COURAGEOUS(1937), d; TEST PILOT(1938), d; GONE WITH THE WIND(1939), d; WIZARD OF OZ, THE(1939), d; DR. JEKYLL AND MR. HYDE(1941), p&d; TORTILLA FLAT(1942), d; GUY NAMED JOE, A(1943), d; ADVENTURE(1945), d; JOAN OF ARC(1948), d

Silents
AMERICAN ARISTOCRACY(1916), ph; GOOD BAD MAN, THE(1916), ph; AMERICANO, THE(1917), ph; DOWN TO EARTH(1917), ph; IN AGAIN-OUT AGAIN(1917), ph; MAN FROM PAINTED POST, THE(1917), ph; MODERN MUSKETEER, A(1917), ph; REACHING FOR THE MOON(1917), ph; WILD AND WOOLLY(1917), ph; HIS MAJESTY THE AMERICAN(1919), ph; MOLLYCODDLE, THE(1920), d; WHEN THE CLOUDS ROLL BY(1920), d; WOMAN'S PLACE(1921), d; ANNA ASCENDS(1922), d; RED HOT ROMANCE(1922), d; LAW OF THE LAWLESS, THE(1923), d; TO THE LAST MAN(1923), d; CODE OF THE SEA(1924), d; EMPTY HANDS(1924), d; ADVENTURE(1925), d; DEVIL'S CARGO, THE(1925), d; LORD JIM(1925), d; BLIND GODDESS, THE(1926), d; ROUGH RIDERS, THE(1927), d; WAY OF ALL FLESH, THE(1927), d; AWAKENING, THE(1928), d
Misc. Silents
MAMA'S AFFAIR(1921), d; LANE THAT HAD NO TURNING, THE(1922), d; CALL OF THE CANYON, THE(1923), d; DARK SECRETS(1923), d; SON OF HIS FATHER, A(1925), d; MANTRAP(1926), d; HULA(1927), d

Walter Fleming
Misc. Talkies
VEILED ARISTOCRATS(1932)

G.T. Fleming-Roberts
FIND THE BLACKMAILER(1943), w; LADY CHASER(1946), w

Peter Flemingham
MAD MAX(1979, Aus.); DAY AFTER HALLOWEEN, THE(1981, Aus.)

Sara Flemington
YOUNG GIRLS OF ROCHEFORT, THE(1968, Fr.)

Alice Flemming
IN SOCIETY(1944); VIGILANTES OF DODGE CITY(1944)

Charlotte Flemming
DEVIL MAKES THREE, THE(1952); HIPPODROME(1961, Aust./Ger.), cos; GIRL AND THE LEGEND, THE(1966, Ger.), cos; CABARET(1972), cos; SERPENT'S EGG, THE(1977, Ger./U.S.), cos; FEDORA(1978, Ger./Fr.), cos

Edward Flemming
GREAT HOPE, THE(1954, Ital.)

Patrick Flemming
CHELSEA GIRLS, THE(1967)

Robert Flemying
OH! WHAT A LOVELY WAR(1969, Brit.)

Gordon Flemyng
FIVE TO ONE(1963, Brit.), d; JUST FOR FUN(1963, Brit.), d; DR. WHO AND THE DALEKS(1965, Brit.), d; DALEKS–INVASION EARTH 2155 A.D.(1966, Brit.), d; SOLO FOR SPARROW(1966, Brit.), d; GREAT CATHERINE(1968, Brit.), d; SPLIT, THE(1968), d; LAST GRENADE, THE(1970, Brit.), d

Robert Flemyng
HEAD OVER HEELS IN LOVE(1937, Brit.); BOND STREET(1948, Brit.); CONSPIRATOR(1949, Brit.); OUTSIDER, THE(1949, Brit.); BLACKMAILED(1951, Brit.); MAGIC BOX, THE(1952, Brit.); HOLLY AND THE IVY, THE(1954, Brit.); MAN WHO NEVER WAS, THE(1956, Brit.); FUNNY FACE(1957); LET'S BE HAPPY(1957, Brit.); CAST A DARK SHADOW(1958, Brit.); WINDOM'S WAY(1958, Brit.); CHANCE MEETING(1960, Brit.); TOUCH OF LARCENY, A(1960, Brit.); MYSTERY SUBMARINE(1963, Brit.); HORRIBLE DR. HICHCOCK, THE(1964, Ital.); QUILLER MEMORANDUM, THE(1966, Brit.); SPY WITH A COLD NOSE, THE(1966, Brit.); BLOOD BEAST TERROR, THE(1967, Brit.); DEADLY AFFAIR, THE(1967, Brit.); BATTLE OF BRITAIN, THE(1969, Brit.); BODY STEALERS, THE(1969); FIRECHASERS, THE(1970, Brit.); DARWIN ADVENTURE, THE(1972, Brit.); TRAVELS WITH MY AUNT(1972, Brit.); YOUNG WINSTON(1972, Brit.); MEDUSA TOUCH, THE(1978, Brit.); THIRTY NINE STEPS, THE(1978, Brit.)

Robtert Flemyng
BLUE LAMP, THE(1950, Brit.)

Harold Flender
PARIS BLUES(1961), w

The Flennoy Trio
MR. ACE(1946)

Paul Flessa
Misc. Talkies
TUCK EVERLASTING(1981)

Raymond Fleszar
1984
VAMPING(1984)

Miguel Fleta
SAIL INTO DANGER(1957, Brit.)

Barrie Fletcher
WOMEN IN LOVE(1969, Brit.)

Bill Fletcher
PEOPLE AGAINST O'HARA, THE(1951); CHIVATO(1961); REBELLION IN CUBA(1961); GROUP, THE(1966); HOUR OF THE GUN(1967); DEVIL'S BRIGADE, THE(1968); FIVE CARD STUD(1968)

Billy Fletcher
Silents
ROMANCE ROAD(1925)

Bramwell Fletcher
TO WHAT RED HELL(1929, Brit.); RAFFLES(1930); SO THIS IS LONDON(1930); DAUGHTER OF THE DRAGON(1931); MEN OF THE SKY(1931); MILLIONAIRE, THE(1931); ONCE A LADY(1931); SVENGALI(1931); FACE ON THE BARROOM FLOOR, THE(1932); MUMMY, THE(1932); SILENT WITNESS, THE(1932); MONKEY'S PAW, THE(1933); ONLY YESTERDAY(1933); RIGHT TO ROMANCE(1933); NANA(1934); LINE ENGAGED(1935, Brit.); SCARLET PIMPERNEL, THE(1935, Brit.); RANDOM HARVEST(1942); UNDYING MONSTER, THE(1942); WHITE CARGO(1942); IMMORTAL SERGEANT, THE(1943)
Misc. Silents
CHICK(1928, Brit.); S.O.S.(1928, Brit.)

Catherine Fletcher
HIGH AND DRY(1954, Brit.)

Cecil Fletcher
Silents
IRON JUSTICE(1915, Brit.); DANCER'S PERIL, THE(1917)
Misc. Silents
ESTHER REDEEMED(1915, Brit.); SONG OF SONGS, THE(1918)

Charlotte Fletcher
THREE HOURS TO KILL(1954); BIG FISHERMAN, THE(1959); SPEED CRAZY(1959); COME BLOW YOUR HORN(1963)

Christian Fletcher
1984
SUPERGIRL(1984)

Cyril Fletcher
YELLOW CANARY, THE(1944, Brit.); NICHOLAS NICKLEBY(1947, Brit.)

Dennis Fletcher
PINK FLOYD–THE WALL(1982, Brit.)

Dexter Fletcher
BUGSY MALONE(1976, Brit.); ELEPHANT MAN, THE(1980, Brit.)
1984
BOUNTY, THE(1984)

Diane Fletcher
MACBETH(1971, Brit.)

Dusty Fletcher
Misc. Talkies
BOARDING HOUSE BLUES(1948); KILLER DILLER(1948)

Dusty "Open the Door Richard" Fletcher
HI-DE-HO(1947)

Eileen Fletcher
HELL BOATS(1970, Brit.), makeup
1984
FOREVER YOUNG(1984, Brit.)

Ernest Fletcher
TERRORNAUTS, THE(1967, Brit.), spec eff

Freddie Fletcher
KES(1970, Brit.)

Gerry Fletcher
MASTER OF BANKDAM, THE(1947, Brit.), makeup; MARY HAD A LITTLE(1961, Brit.), makeup; SWORD OF SHERWOOD FOREST(1961, Brit.), makeup; HEAVENS ABOVE!(1963, Brit.), makeup; STATION SIX-SAHARA(1964, Brit./Ger.), makeup; STORK TALK(1964, Brit.), makeup; GIRL GETTERS, THE(1966, Brit.), makeup; TASTE THE BLOOD OF DRACULA(1970, Brit.), makeup

Graham Fletcher
PETER RABBIT AND TALES OF BEATRIX POTTER(1971, Brit.); STORIES FROM A FLYING TRUNK(1979, Brit.)

Guy Fletcher
THOSE WHO LOVE(1929, Brit.), w; FIFTY-SHILLING BOXER(1937, Brit.), w

H. David Fletcher
1984
BODY DOUBLE(1984)

Harold Fletcher
SPRING IN PARK LANE(1949, Brit.), makeup; ODETTE(1951, Brit.), makeup; MAGIC BOX, THE(1952, Brit.), makeup; INNOCENTS, THE(1961, U.S./Brit.), makeup; PORTRAIT OF A SINNER(1961, Brit.), makeup; I COULD GO ON SINGING(1963), makeup; NINE HOURS TO RAMA(1963, U.S./Brit.), makeup; EARTH DIES SCREAMING, THE(1964, Brit.), makeup; NIGHT TRAIN TO PARIS(1964, Brit.), makeup; PSYCHE 59(1964, Brit.), makeup; WITCHCRAFT(1964, Brit.), makeup; CURSE OF THE FLY(1965, Brit.), spec eff; RETURN OF MR. MOTO, THE(1965, Brit.), makeup; SPACEFLIGHT IC-1(1965, Brit.), makeup; LOST COMMAND, THE(1966), makeup; MURDER GAME, THE(1966, Brit.), makeup

Jack Fletcher
ANY WEDNESDAY(1966); TIGER MAKES OUT, THE(1967); RABBIT TEST(1978); PENNIES FROM HEAVEN(1981)

James Fletcher
MIGHTY MOUSE IN THE GREAT SPACE CHASE(1983), art d

Jay Fletcher
BORN TO WIN(1971); CALIFORNIA SPLIT(1974); LAW AND DISORDER(1974); MR. RICCO(1975); CUTTER AND BONE(1981)

Jerry Fletcher
SPECIAL AGENT(1935); MURDER WITH PICTURES(1936); ROSE BOWL(1936); EVER SINCE EVE(1937); HOLLYWOOD HOTEL(1937); SAN QUENTIN(1937); SUBMARINE D-1(1937); THEY WON'T FORGET(1937); INVITATION TO HAPPINESS(1939); FIGHTING 69TH, THE(1940); FREE, BLONDE AND 21(1940); TOO MANY HUSBANDS(1940)

Juanita Fletcher
MESQUITE BUCKAROO(1939)

Kent Fletcher
LORD OF THE FLIES(1963, Brit.)

Lawrence Fletcher
SEARCH FOR BRIDEY MURPHY, THE(1956)

Lester Fletcher
OPERATION EICHMANN(1961); HITLER(1962); HICKEY AND BOGGS(1972); YOUR THREE MINUTES ARE UP(1973)

Louise Fletcher
THIEVES LIKE US(1974); ONE FLEW OVER THE CUCKOO'S NEST(1975); RUSSIAN ROULETTE(1975); EXORCIST II: THE HERETIC(1977); CHEAP DETECTIVE, THE(1978); LADY IN RED, THE(1979); MAGICIAN OF LUBLIN, THE(1979, Israel/Ger.); NATURAL ENEMIES(1979); LUCKY STAR, THE(1980, Can.); MAMMA DRACULA(1980, Bel./Fr.); DEAD KIDS(1981 Aus./New Zealand); BRAINSTORM(1983); STRANGE INVADERS(1983)
1984
FIRESTARTER(1984)

Lucille Fletcher
SORRY, WRONG NUMBER(1948), w; BLINDFOLD(1966), w; NIGHT WATCH(1973, Brit.), w

Mari Fletcher
PLAY IT AGAIN, SAM(1972)

Marlene Fletcher
RAINBOW BOYS, THE(1973, Can.), ed

Neil Fletcher
BEYOND THE TIME BARRIER(1960); IN THE YEAR 2889(1966); MARS NEEDS WOMEN(1966); ZONTAR, THE THING FROM VENUS(1966); DEADLY BLESSING(1981)
Misc. Talkies
CREATURE OF DESTRUCTION(1967)

Nelson Fletcher
BROTHERS AND SISTERS(1980, Brit.)
Norman Fletcher
GOODBYE PORK PIE(1981, New Zealand)
Randy Arlyn Fletcher
HONEYSUCKLE ROSE(1980)
Robert Fletcher
BALLAD OF CABLE HOGUE, THE(1970), cos; STAR TREK: THE MOTION PIC-
TURE(1979), cos; CAVEMAN(1981), cos
1984
LAST STARFIGHTER, THE(1984), cos; STAR TREK III: THE SEARCH FOR
SPOCK(1984), cos
Robin Fletcher
M(1951); SLAUGHTER TRAIL(1951)
Ron Fletcher
TOP BANANA(1954), ch; SNOW WHITE AND THE THREE STOOGES(1961), ch;
SOLDIER BLUE(1970)
Roy Fletcher
INVISIBLE MAN, THE(1958, Mex.); SIERRA BARON(1958)
Scott Fletcher
THREE ON A SPREE(1961, Brit.), makeup
Stanley Fletcher
MAN WITH THE MAGNETIC EYES, THE(1945, Brit.), ph
Steve Fletcher
1984
BOUNTY, THE(1984)
Susan Fletcher
ONE PLUS ONE(1961, Can.)
Suzanne Fletcher
PERMANENT VACATION(1982)
1984
VARIETY(1984)
Tex Fletcher
SIX-GUN RHYTHM(1939)
Tommy Fletcher
HITCH IN TIME, A(1978, Brit.), ph
Wilfred Fletcher
HOUSE OF THE ARROW, THE(1930, Brit.); HORNET'S NEST, THE(1955, Brit.)
Wilifred Fletcher
CARDINAL, THE(1936, Brit.)
William Fletcher
RED SNOW(1952)
Misc. Silents
HER HONOR THE MAYOR(1920)
Graham Fletcher-Cook
LITTLE ROMANCE, A(1979, U.S./Fr.); FRENCH LIEUTENANT'S WOMAN,
THE(1981)
Rudolph C. Flethow
RETURN OF THE WHISTLER, THE(1948), p
Darlanne Fleugel
1984
ONCE UPON A TIME IN AMERICA(1984)
Francoise Fleury
1984
UNTIL SEPTEMBER(1984)
Jean Fleury
DEVIL IN THE FLESH, THE(1949, Fr.)
Jean-Claude Fleury
1984
PERILS OF GWENDOLINE, THE(1984, Fr.), p
Jeff Fleury
TEX(1982)
Laurette Fleury
ROAD IS FINE, THE(1930, Fr.)
Kathy Flewellen
Misc. Talkies
ASHES AND EMBERS(1982)
Anne Crawford Flexner
MRS. WIGGS OF THE CABBAGE PATCH(1934), w
Silents
ALL SOULS EVE(1921), w
Alain Flick
1984
AMERICAN DREAMER(1984)
Amanda Flick
TOURIST TRAP, THE(1979), set d
Pat C. Flick
SINGING KID, THE(1936), w; STAGE STRUCK(1936), w; BLACK LEGION,
THE(1937); MARRY THE GIRL(1937), w; NOBODY'S BABY(1937), w; LITTLE
TOUGH GUY(1938); MISSING GUEST, THE(1938); WIDE OPEN FACES(1938), w;
FOLLIES GIRL(1943)
Pat Flick
HIS EXCITING NIGHT(1938), w
Patsy Flick
MISS PACIFIC FLEET(1935), w; STARS OVER BROADWAY(1935), a, w
Vic Flick
HULLABALOO OVER GEORGIE AND BONNIE'S PICTURES(1979, Brit.), m
Elisabeth Flickenschildt
TOXI(1952, Ger.); MRS. WARREN'S PROFESSION(1960, Ger.); KING IN SHA-
DOW(1961, Ger.); DOG EAT DOG(1963, U.S./Ger./Ital.); FAUST(1963, Ger.); GIRL AND
THE LEGEND, THE(1966, Ger.); PHANTOM OF SOHO, THE(1967, Ger.)
Elizabeth Flickenschildt
AREN'T WE WONDERFUL?(1959, Ger.)
Ted Flicker
LEGEND OF THE LONE RANGER, THE(1981); SOGGY BOTTOM U.S.A.(1982), d
Theodore J. Flicker
TROUBLEMAKER, THE(1964), a, d, w; SPINOUT(1966), w; PRESIDENT'S ANA-
LYST, THE(1967), d&w; UP IN THE CELLAR(1970), d&w; JACOB TWO-TWO MEETS
THE HOODED FANG(1979, Can.), d&w

Charles Flickinger
NOBODY'S CHILDREN(1940); NIGHTMARE ALLEY(1947); YOU WERE MEANT
FOR ME(1948); ALIAS NICK BEAL(1949)
Serge Fliegers
MONTE CARLO STORY, THE(1957, Ital.)
Ed Fliegl
I STOLE A MILLION(1939)
Joseph R. Fliesler
Silents
PANDORA'S BOX(1929, Ger.), t
Edward Fligle
IN NAME ONLY(1939)
Ray Flin
MONSTER FROM THE GREEN HELL(1958), ph; THIS SAVAGE LAND(1969), ph
Hugo Flink
Misc. Silents
EARTHQUAKE MOTOR, THE(1917, Ger.)
John Flinn
ONE LITTLE INDIAN(1973)
Betty Flint
PRINCE OF PLAYERS(1955)
Christopher Flint
REDEEMER, THE(1978)
Derek Flint
DIFFERENT STORY, A(1978)
Eve K. Flint [Eva Finllestein]
RECKLESS LIVING(1931), w
Eva Kay Flint
SUBWAY EXPRESS(1931), w
Hazel Flint
Misc. Silents
BOOTLEGGERS, THE(1922)
Helen Flint
HANDY ANDY(1934); MANHATTAN LOVE SONG(1934); MIDNIGHT(1934); NINTH
GUEST, THE(1934); AH, WILDERNESS!(1935); DEVIL DOGS OF THE AIR(1935);
DOUBTING THOMAS(1935); WHILE THE PATIENT SLEPT(1935); EARLY TO
BED(1936); FURY(1936); GIVE ME YOUR HEART(1936); LITTLE LORD FAUNT-
LEROY(1936); RIFF-RAFF(1936); BLACK LEGION, THE(1937); BLONDE TROU-
BLE(1937); MARRIED BEFORE BREAKFAST(1937); SEA DEVILS(1937); STEP
LIVELY, JEEVES(1937); TIME TO KILL(1942)
John Flint
PRIEST OF LOVE(1981, Brit.)
Kelly Flint
CASANOVA BROWN(1944)
Maggie Flint
FUNNY MONEY(1983, Brit.)
1984
SCANDALOUS(1984)
Sam Flint
DEVIL'S MATE(1933); BELLE OF THE NINETIES(1934); CHAINED(1934); DEATH
OF THE DIAMOND(1934); EVELYN PRENTICE(1934); FUGITIVE LADY(1934); MRS.
WIGGS OF THE CABBAGE PATCH(1934); MURDER IN THE MUSEUM(1934);
OLD-FASHIONED WAY, THE(1934); STUDENT TOUR(1934); CRUSADES, THE(1935);
NEW FRONTIER, THE(1935); PEOPLE WILL TALK(1935); RECKLESS(1935); TALE
OF TWO CITIES, A(1935); WHOLE TOWN'S TALKING, THE(1935); WINGS IN THE
DARK(1935); ACCUSING FINGER, THE(1936); BIG BROWN EYES(1936); FACE IN
THE FOG, A(1936); FLORIDA SPECIAL(1936); LAWLESS NINETIES, THE(1936);
LONELY TRAIL, THE(1936); RED RIVER VALLEY(1936); WINDS OF THE WASTE-
LAND(1936); CRIMINALS OF THE AIR(1937); RED LIGHTS AHEAD(1937); ROAR-
ING SIX GUNS(1937); SARATOGA(1937); TWO MINUTES TO PLAY(1937);
WINDJAMMER(1937); LAST STAND, THE(1938); STATE POLICE(1938); I TAKE THIS
OATH(1940); DOUBLE DATE(1941); SINGING HILL, THE(1941); TUXEDO JUNC-
TION(1941); UNDER FIESTA STARS(1941); MOUNTAIN RHYTHM(1942); ROAD TO
HAPPINESS(1942); SOUTH OF SANTA FE(1942); CHATTERBOX(1943); CRIME DOC-
TOR'S STRANGEST CASE(1943); DEAD MEN WALK(1943); FALSE COLORS(1943);
KANSAN, THE(1943); OUTLAWS OF STAMPEDE PASS(1943); STRANGER FROM
PECOS, THE(1943); SWING YOUR PARTNER(1943); THUNDERING TRAILS(1943);
CHINESE CAT, THE(1944); CONTENDER, THE(1944); COVER GIRL(1944); GOIN' TO
TOWN(1944); LADY AND THE MONSTER, THE(1944); LIGHTS OF OLD SANTA
FE(1944); MAN FROM FRISCO(1944); MONSTER MAKER, THE(1944); MR. WINKLE
GOES TO WAR(1944); SILVER CITY KID(1944); STORY OF DR. WASSELL,
THE(1944); TOGETHER AGAIN(1944); ALONG THE NAVAJO TRAIL(1945); CAP-
TAIN TUGBOAT ANNIE(1945); I'LL TELL THE WORLD(1945); MAN FROM OK-
LAHOMA, THE(1945); NOB HILL(1945); SHADOW OF TERROR(1945); SHE GETS
HER MAN(1945); SWING OUT, SISTER(1945); ZIEGFELD FOLLIES(1945); GIL-
DA(1946); JUNIOR PROM(1946); LOCKET, THE(1946); MAGNIFICENT DOLL(1946);
MY PAL TRIGGER(1946); NIGHT AND DAY(1946); NOCTURNE(1946); SIOUX CITY
SUE(1946); SOMEWHERE IN THE NIGHT(1946); LIKELY STORY, A(1947); WILD
FRONTIER, THE(1947); FOUR FACES WEST(1948); PHANTOM VALLEY(1948);
SOUTHERN YANKEE, A(1948); STRAWBERRY ROAN, THE(1948); GAY AMIGO,
THE(1949); SMOKY MOUNTAIN MELODY(1949); CHEROKEE UPRISING(1950);
COUNTY FAIR(1950); FIREBALL, THE(1950); KANSAS RAIDERS(1950); RETURN
OF JESSE JAMES, THE(1950); ROCK ISLAND TRAIL(1950); TIMBER FURY(1950);
FORT SAVAGE RAIDERS(1951); LEAVE IT TO THE MARINES(1951); MILLIONAIRE
FOR CHRISTY, A(1951); SNAKE RIVER DESPERADOES(1951); STRANGERS ON A
TRAIN(1951); CARBINE WILLIAMS(1952); HAWK OF WILD RIVER, THE(1952);
LUSTY MEN, THE(1952); NORTHWEST TERRITORY(1952); ROAD AGENT(1952);
RUBY GENTRY(1952); SEA TIGER(1952); SKY HIGH(1952); STEEL TRAP, THE(1952);
YUKON GOLD(1952); COW COUNTRY(1953); MOONLIGHTER, THE(1953); VAN-
QUISHED, THE(1953); OUTLAW'S DAUGHTER(1954); RACING BLOOD(1954);
BIG TIP OFF, THE(1955); NIGHT FREIGHT(1955); NIGHT RUNNER, THE(1957);
SHOOT-OUT AT MEDICINE BEND(1957); I'LL GIVE MY LIFE(1959); PSYCHO(1960);
SNOW WHITE AND THE THREE STOOGES(1961); SOLDIER IN THE RAIN(1963)
Misc. Talkies
FIGHTING DEVIL DOGS(1938); BOSS OF BOOMTOWN(1944)
Alec Flinter
HUE AND CRY(1950, Brit.)

Rockey Flintermann
SENIORS, THE(1978); MORE AMERICAN GRAFFITI(1979)
Flip the dog
EDGE OF HELL(1956); NUDE IN HIS POCKET(1962, Fr.)
J.C. Flippen
OKLAHOMA(1955); SPIRIT IS WILLING, THE(1967)
Jay C. Flippen
MARIE GALANTE(1934); MILLION DOLLAR RANSOM(1934); BRUTE FOR-
CE(1947); INTRIGUE(1947); DOWN TO THE SEA IN SHIPS(1949); OH, YOU BEAUTI-
FUL DOLL(1949); THEY LIVE BY NIGHT(1949); WOMAN'S SECRET, A(1949);
BUCCANEER'S GIRL(1950); LOVE THAT BRUTE(1950); TWO FLAGS WEST(1950);
WINCHESTER '73(1950); YELLOW CAB MAN, THE(1950); FLYING LEATHER-
NECKS(1951); LADY FROM TEXAS, THE(1951); LEMON DROP KID, THE(1951);
MODEL AND THE MARRIAGE BROKER, THE(1951); PEOPLE AGAINST O'HARA,
THE(1951); BEND OF THE RIVER(1952); LAS VEGAS STORY, THE(1952); WOMAN
OF THE NORTH COUNTRY(1952); DEVIL'S CANYON(1953); EAST OF SUMA-
TRA(1953); THUNDER BAY(1953); WILD ONE, THE(1953); CARNIVAL STORY(1954);
FAR COUNTRY, THE(1955); IT'S ALWAYS FAIR WEATHER(1955); KISMET(1955);
MAN WITHOUT A STAR(1955); SIX BRIDGES TO CROSS(1955); STRATEGIC AIR
COMMAND(1955); KILLING, THE(1956); KING AND FOUR QUEENS, THE(1956);
SEVENTH CAVALRY(1956); DEERSLAYER, THE(1957); HALLIDAY BRAND,
THE(1957); HOT SUMMER NIGHT(1957); JET PILOT(1957); MIDNIGHT STORY,
THE(1957); NIGHT PASSAGE(1957); PUBLIC PIGEON NO. 1(1957); RESTLESS
BREED, THE(1957); RUN OF THE ARROW(1957); ESCAPE FROM RED ROCK(1958);
FROM HELL TO TEXAS(1958); PLUNDERERS, THE(1960); STUDS LONIGAN(1960);
WILD RIVER(1960); HOW THE WEST WAS WON(1962); LOOKING FOR LOVE(1964);
CAT BALLOU(1965); FIRECREEK(1968); HELLFIGHTERS(1968); SEVEN MINUTES,
THE(1971)
Ruth Brooks Flippen
THREE GUYS NAMED MIKE(1951), w; BECAUSE YOU'RE MINE(1952), w; LOVE
IS BETTER THAN EVER(1952), w; I LOVE MELVIN(1953), w; GIDGET GOES
HAWAIIAN(1961), w; SAIL A CROOKED SHIP(1961), w; GIDGET GOES TO RO-
ME(1963), w; TICKLISH AFFAIR, A(1963), w; LOOKING FOR LOVE(1964), w
Lucy Lee Flippin
FRONT, THE(1976); GOIN' SOUTH(1978); ONE AND ONLY, THE(1978); FLASH-
DANCE(1983)
John Flippou
ANNA OF RHODES(1950, Gr.), d
Ernie Flisher
LOVES OF JOANNA GODDEN, THE(1947, Brit.)
Sebastian Floch
HERBIE GOES TO MONTE CARLO(1977)
Sebastien Floche
QUARTET(1981, Brit./Fr.)
Mel Flock
WHEN THE LEGENDS DIE(1972)
David Flocker
GROUND ZERO(1973)
David P. Flocker
GROUND ZERO(1973), ph
James T. Flocker
GROUND ZERO(1973), p&d; LEGEND OF COUGAR CANYON(1974), p&d
Misc. Talkies
SECRET OF NAVAJO CAVE(1976), d; GHOSTS THAT STILL WALK(1977), d
Carol Sue Flockhart
SCALPS(1983)
Ove Flodin
PIMPERNEL SVENSSON(1953, Swed.)
Barbro Flodquist
NIGHT IS MY FUTURE(1962, Swed.)
Martin Floerchinger
WILD DUCK, THE(1977, Ger./Aust.)
Patrick Floersheim
DESTRUCTORS, THE(1974, Brit.); FRENCH CONNECTION 11(1975); DIVA(1982,
Fr.)
Scott Flohr
SQUAD CAR(1961), w
Virginia Flohri
ALIBI(1929)
David Flolkes
YOU ONLY LIVE TWICE(1967, Brit.), set d
Victor Floming
WORLD'S GREATEST SINNER, THE(1962)
Suzanne Flon
MOULIN ROUGE(1952); MONKEY IN WINTER, A(1962, Fr.); MR. ARKADIN(1962,
Brit./Fr./Span.); TRIAL, THE(1963, Fr./Ital./Ger.); NUTTY, NAUGHTY CHA-
TEAU(1964, Fr./Ital.); TRAIN, THE(1965, Fr./Ital./U.S.); ZITA(1968, Fr.); LEATHER
AND NYLON(1969, Fr./Ital.); MR. KLEIN(1976, Fr.); NO TIME FOR BREAK-
FAST(1978, Fr.); QUARTET(1981, Brit./Fr.)
1984
ONE DEADLY SUMMER(1984, Fr.)
Barbara Flood
SAFE PLACE, A(1971), a, cos
Dorothy Flood
RESURRECTION(1931)
Ellen Flood
CHANGE OF MIND(1969)
Gerald Flood
SMOKESCREEN(1964, Brit.); PATTON(1970); FRIGHTMARE(1974, Brit.)
James Flood
MARRIAGE BY CONTRACT(1928), d; MIDSTREAM(1929), d; MISTER ANTONI-
O(1929), d; WHISPERING WINDS(1929), d; SISTERS(1930), d; SWELLHEAD,
THE(1930), d; SHE-WOLF, THE(1931), d; LIFE BEGINS(1932), d; MOUTHPIECE,
THE(1932), d; UNDER-COVER MAN(1932), d; ALL OF ME(1934), d; SUCH WOMEN
ARE DANGEROUS(1934), d; SHANGHAI(1935), d; WINGS IN THE DARK(1935), d;
EVERYBODY'S OLD MAN(1936), d; WE'RE ONLY HUMAN(1936), d; MIDNIGHT
MADONNA(1937), d; SCOTLAND YARD COMMANDS(1937, Brit.), d, w; OFF THE
RECORD(1939), d; BIG FIX, THE(1947), d; STEPCHILD(1947), d

Silents
WHEN ODDS ARE EVEN(1923), d
Misc. Silents
TIMES HAVE CHANGED(1923), d; TENTH WOMAN, THE(1924), d; MAN WITH-
OUT A CONSCIENCE, THE(1925), d; SATAN IN SABLES(1925), d; WIFE WHO
WASN'T WANTED, THE(1925), d; HONEYMOON EXPRESS, THE(1926), d; WHY
GIRLS GO BACK HOME(1926), d; LADY IN ERMINE, THE(1927), d; THREE
HOURS(1927), d; COUNT OF TEN, THE(1928), d; DOMESTIC MEDDLERS(1928), d;
MARRIAGE BY CONRACT(1928), d
Joe Flood
STUDENT BODIES(1981)
John Flood
FIST OF FEAR, TOUCH OF DEATH(1980)
1984
FIRST TURN-ON!, THE(1984)
Kevin Flood
FRANKENSTEIN CREATED WOMAN(1965, Brit.)
Tone Floor
DOLL'S HOUSE, A(1973, Brit.)
M. Floquet
JE T'AIME, JE T'AIME(1972, Fr./Swed.)
Celia Flor
NO PLACE TO HIDE(1956)
Doug Flor
ROCKY II(1979)
Sheila Florance
CLAY(1964 Aus.); END PLAY(1975, Aus.); DEVIL'S PLAYGROUND, THE(1976, Aus.);
SUMMERFIELD(1977, Aus.)
Albert Florath
HIS MAJESTY, KING BALLYHOO(1931, Ger.); BERLIN ALEXANDERPLATZ(1933,
Ger.); BOCCACCIO(1936, Ger.)
Martin Florchinger
PINOCCHIO(1969, E. Ger.)
John Florea
PICKUP ON 101(1972), d
1984
INVISIBLE STRANGLER(1984), d
Misc. Talkies
WHERE'S WILLIE?(1978), d
Dann Florek
EDDIE MACON'S RUN(1983)
Florelle
THREEPENNY OPERA, THE(1931, Ger./U.S.); LILIOM(1935, Fr.); CRIME OF MON-
SIEUR LANGE, THE(1936, Fr.); GERVAISE(1956, Fr.)
Odette Florelle
MISTRESS OF ATLANTIS, THE(1932, Ger.); LES MISERABLES(1936, Fr.); AM-
PHYTRYON(1937, Ger.)
John Floren
JAWS 3-D(1983)
Davone Florence
BLUE COLLAR(1978)
Edwin Florence
MINI-AFFAIR, THE(1968, Brit.), art d
Fiona Florence
ROMA(1972, Ital./Fr.); VIVA ITALIA(1978, Ital.)
Norman Florence
LONG DUEL, THE(1967, Brit.)
Richie Florence
BALTIMORE BULLET, THE(1980)
Sheila Florence
PETERSEN(1974, Aus.); MAD MAX(1979, Aus.)
Florence and Alvarez
STUDENT TOUR(1934)
Louis Florencie
CHILDREN OF PARADISE(1945, Fr.); PANIQUE(1947, Fr.)
Jack Florency
MY LIFE TO LIVE(1963, Fr.)
Napoleon Florent
KISENGA, MAN OF AFRICA(1952, Brit.)
Diane Florentine
EGG AND I, THE(1947); WISTFUL WIDOW OF WAGON GAP, THE(1947); MA AND
PA KETTLE(1949); MA AND PA KETTLE GO TO TOWN(1950)
Florentine Gardens Revue
RHYTHM PARADE(1943)
Florenzo Florentini
ANTHONY OF PADUA(1952, Ital.), w
Louis Florentino
SECRET OF THE SACRED FOREST, THE(1970)
Nyall Florenz
SINGER NOT THE SONG, THE(1961, Brit.)
Alex Flores
SUPERBEAST(1972)
Azucena Flores
BLOOD WEDDING(1981, Sp.)
Bella Flores
W.I.A.(WOUNDED IN ACTION)*1/2 (1966)
1984
MISSING IN ACTION(1984)
Bill Flores
1984
IMPULSE(1984), cos
Enrique Flores
MIRAGE(1972, Peru)
Felipe Flores
OF LOVE AND DESIRE(1963)
Filipe Flores
MY BROTHER, THE OUTLAW(1951)

Henry Flores
MR. MOM(1983)
Iris Flores
TARZAN AND THE LEOPARD WOMAN(1946); RIDE THE PINK HORSE(1947); WOMEN IN THE NIGHT(1948)
Joseph Flores
Misc. Silents
FATHERHOOD(1915)
Mariela Flores
INCREDIBLE INVASION, THE(1971, Mex./U.S.)
Mariquita Flores
BLOOD AND SAND(1941)
Marissa Flores
TO THE SHORES OF TRIPOLI(1942)
Marta Flores
THAT MAN IN ISTANBUL(1966, Fr./Ital./Span.)
Maxine Flores
BABES ON BROADWAY(1941)
Miguel Angel Flores
MIRAGE(1972, Peru)
Pepa Flores
CARMEN(1983, Span.)
Polo Salazar Flores
HIGH RISK(1981)
Stefano Satta Flores
GIRL WITH A PISTOL, THE(1968, Ital.); GUN, THE(1978, Ital.); WHO IS KILLING THE GREAT CHEFS OF EUROPE?(1978, US/Ger.)
Tony Flores
ROLLIN' HOME TO TEXAS(1941)
Ursula Flores
1984
CAGED WOMEN(1984, Ital./Fr.)
Flores Brothers
THAT NIGHT IN RIO(1941)
Flores Brothers Trio
MEXICAN HAYRIDE(1948)
C. Ray Florhe
Misc. Silents
DEAD OR ALIVE(1921)
Agata Flori
OPERATION KID BROTHER(1967, Ital.)
Jean-Jacques Flori
SPERMULA(1976, Fr.), ph; TUSK(1980, Fr.), ph
Florian
LOVE AND DEATH(1975)
Barbara Florian
TIMES GONE BY(1953, Ital.); HEAVEN ON EARTH(1960, Ital./U.S.)
Tony Bill Florian
NEVER A DULL MOMENT(1968)
Werner Florian
GRAND ILLUSION(1938, Fr.)
Eugene Florimont
SLASHER, THE(1975), p
Florine
ETERNAL MELODIES(1948, Ital.), set d
Aldo Florio
FIVE GIANTS FROM TEXAS(1966, Ital./Span.), d
Angelo Florio
1984
ONCE UPON A TIME IN AMERICA(1984)
John Florio
COUNTRY GIRL, THE(1954)
Robert Florio
1984
BEAR, THE(1984), ed
Arthur Florman
TERROR FROM THE YEAR 5,000(1958), ph
Agatha Florry
Misc. Talkies
THEY CALL ME HALLELUJAH(1973)
Agatha Flory [Agata Flori]
UP THE MACGREGORS(1967, Ital./Span.); SEVEN GUNS FOR THE MACGREGORS(1968, Ital./Span.)
Med Flory
MAN'S FAVORITE SPORT(?) (1964); TROUBLE WITH GIRLS(AND HOW TO GET INTO IT), THE*1/2 (1969); GUN STREET(1962); MOVE OVER, DARLING(1963); SPENCER'S MOUNTAIN(1963); NIGHT OF THE GRIZZLY, THE(1966); DOCTOR, YOU'VE GOT TO BE KIDDING(1967); TEACHER, THE(1974); HUSTLE(1975); HEARSE, THE(1980); BOOGENS, THE(1982)
Misc. Talkies
LASSIE, THE VOYAGER(1966)
Ned Flory
NUTTY PROFESSOR, THE(1963)
Vera Flory
FEATHER, THE(1929, Brit.)
Misc. Silents
LES DEUX TIMIDES(1929, Fr.)
Jose Maria Flotats
ZITA(1968, Fr.)
Jose-Maria Flotats
LA GUERRE EST FINIE(1967, Fr./Swed.)
Rudloph C. Flothow
BOSTON BLACKIE'S CHINESE VENTURE(1949), p
Rudolph C. Flothow
CRIME DOCTOR'S STRANGEST CASE(1943), p; MARK OF THE WHISTLER, THE(1944), p; SHADOWS IN THE NIGHT(1944), p; WHISTLER, THE(1944), p; ADVENTURES OF RUSTY(1945), p; CRIME DOCTOR'S COURAGE, THE(1945), p; CRIME DOCTOR'S WARNING(1945), p; VOICE OF THE WHISTLER(1945), p; CRIME DOCTOR'S MAN HUNT(1946), p; JUST BEFORE DAWN(1946), p; SECRET OF THE WHISTLER(1946), p; CRIME DOCTOR'S GAMBLE(1947), p; KEY WITNESS(1947), p;

MILLERSON CASE, THE(1947), p; GENTLEMAN FROM NOWHERE, THE(1948), p; TRAPPED BY BOSTON BLACKIE(1948), p; CRIME DOCTOR'S DIARY, THE(1949), p; DEVIL'S HENCHMEN, THE(1949), p; LONE WOLF AND HIS LADY, THE(1949), p; MARY RYAN, DETECTIVE(1949), p; PRISON WARDEN(1949), p; SECRET OF ST. IVES, THE(1949), p; BODYHOLD(1950), p; CUSTOMS AGENT(1950), p; HE'S A COCKEYED WONDER(1950), p; AL JENNINGS OF OKLAHOMA(1951), p; CHINA CORSAIR(1951), p; CRIMINAL LAWYER(1951), p; PHANTOM OF THE JUNGLE(1955), p; THUNDER OVER SANGOLAND(1955), p
Rudolph Flothow
LUCKY BOY(1929), d; 13TH HOUR, THE(1947), p; WHITE GODDESS(1953), p
Mr. Flotsam
CRIMES OF STEPHEN HAWKE, THE(1936, Brit.)
Don Flourney
GIANT GILA MONSTER, THE(1959)
Elizabeth Flourney
BEDTIME FOR BONZO(1951); JET PILOT(1957)
Don Flournoy
BEYOND THE TIME BARRIER(1960)
Elizabeth Flournoy
ADAM'S RIB(1949); EMERGENCY WEDDING(1950); JACKPOT, THE(1950); LIFE OF HER OWN, A(1950); MRS. O'MALLEY AND MR. MALONE(1950); TEA FOR TWO(1950); UNDER MY SKIN(1950); WOMAN OF DISTINCTION, A(1950); CLOSE TO MY HEART(1951); COME FILL THE CUP(1951); FAMILY SECRET, THE(1951); I CAN GET IT FOR YOU WHOLESALE(1951); LULLABY OF BROADWAY, THE(1951); ON THE LOOSE(1951); STARLIFT(1951); HOODLUM EMPIRE(1952); OPERATION SECRET(1952); PLYMOUTH ADVENTURE(1952); SOMETHING FOR THE BIRDS(1952); MR. SCOUTMASTER(1953); THREE SAILORS AND A GIRL(1953); TITANIC(1953); GOOD MORNING, MISS DOVE(1955); EVERYTHING BUT THE TRUTH(1956); SERENADE(1956); THESE WILDER YEARS(1956); KELLY AND ME(1957)
Richard Flournoy
HERE COMES THE GROOM(1934), w; MISTER CINDERELLA(1936), w; FIT FOR A KING(1937), w; GENERAL SPANKY(1937), w; PICK A STAR(1937), w; RIDING ON AIR(1937), w; BLONDIE(1938), w; WIDE OPEN FACES(1938), w; BEWARE SPOOKS(1939), w; BLONDIE BRINGS UP BABY(1939), w, w; BLONDIE MEETS THE BOSS(1939), w; BLONDIE TAKES A VACATION(1939), w; BLONDIE HAS SERVANT TROUBLE(1940), w; BLONDIE ON A BUDGET(1940), w; BLONDIE PLAYS CUPID(1940), w; SO YOU WON'T TALK(1940), w; BLONDIE GOES LATIN(1941), w; GO WEST, YOUNG LADY(1941), w; BEDTIME STORY(1942), w; BLONDIE'S BLESSED EVENT(1942), w; NIGHT TO REMEMBER, A(1942), w; DANGEROUS BLONDES(1943), w; MORE THE MERRIER, THE(1943), w; AFFAIRS OF SUSAN(1945), w; ONE LAST FLING(1949), w; AFFAIR WITH A STRANGER(1953), w; SHE COULDN'T SAY NO(1954), w
Buck Flower
DRIVE-IN MASSACRE(1976), w
1984
STARMAN(1984)
Misc. Talkies
CANDY TANGERINE MAN, THE(1975)
David Flower
SLOW RUN(1968)
George Flower
ACROSS THE GREAT DIVIDE(1976)
George Buck Flower
FOG, THE(1980)
George "Buck" Flower
FURTHER ADVENTURES OF THE WILDERNESS FAMILY–PART TWO(1978); MOUNTAIN FAMILY ROBINSON(1979)
Misc. Talkies
DEVIL AND LEROY BASSETT, THE(1973); CAPTURE OF BIGFOOT, THE(1979); IN SEARCH OF GOLDEN SKY(1984)
Gilly Flower
NEW HOTEL, THE(1932, Brit.)
Joe Flower
DRIVE-IN(1976)
Newman Flower
Silents
ANSWER, THE(1916, Brit.), w
Verkema Flower
Misc. Talkies
MAG WHEELS(1978)
Verkina Flower
SUMMER CAMP(1979); TERROR ON TOUR(1980), art d & set d
A. D. Flowers
TAKE THE MONEY AND RUN(1969), spec eff; RIO LOBO(1970), spec eff; HAROLD AND MAUDE(1971), spec eff; SUPPORT YOUR LOCAL GUNFIGHTER(1971), spec eff; GODFATHER, THE(1972), spec eff; POSEIDON ADVENTURE, THE(1972), spec eff; SLEEPER(1973), spec eff; TOWERING INFERNO, THE(1974), spec eff; FURY, THE(1978), spec eff; 1941(1979), spec eff
Bess Flowers
GHOST TALKS, THE(1929); LIGHTNIN'(1930); MANSLAUGHTER(1930); BACHELOR APARTMENT(1931); FREE SOUL, A(1931); STRANGERS MAY KISS(1931); TEN CENTS A DANCE(1931); IF I HAD A MILLION(1932); ONE HOUR WITH YOU(1932); SINISTER HANDS(1932); SIN'S PAYDAY(1932); HARD TO HANDLE(1933); CHANGE OF HEART(1934); FUGITIVE LADY(1934); HOLLYWOOD PARTY(1934); IT HAPPENED ONE NIGHT(1934); I'VE GOT YOUR NUMBER(1934); PERSONALITY KID, THE(1934); STAND UP AND CHEER(1934 80m FOX bw); ESCAPADE(1935); GIRL FROM TENTH AVENUE, THE(1935); HANDS ACROSS THE TABLE(1935); I LIVE FOR LOVE(1935); IRISH IN US, THE(1935); OIL FOR THE LAMPS OF CHINA(1935); ONE EXCITING ADVENTURE(1935); SHE COULDN'T TAKE IT(1935); SHE MARRIED HER BOSS(1935); WHOLE TOWN'S TALKING, THE(1935); GOLDEN ARROW, THE(1936); MR. DEEDS GOES TO TOWN(1936); MY MAN GODFREY(1936); ONE IN A MILLION(1936); POLO JOE(1936); SWING TIME(1936); YOURS FOR THE ASKING(1936); AWFUL TRUTH, THE(1937); EVER SINCE EVE(1937); LAST TRAIN FROM MADRID, THE(1937); MARRY THE GIRL(1937); PAID TO DANCE(1937); SHADOW, THE(1937); WHEN YOU'RE IN LOVE(1937); WOMEN OF GLAMOUR(1937); 100 MEN AND A GIRL(1937); HOLIDAY(1938); I AM THE LAW(1938); LADY OBJECTS, THE(1938); LONE WOLF IN PARIS(1938); PENITENTIARY(1938); SHINING HOUR, THE(1938); THAT CERTAIN AGE(1938); WOMEN IN PRISON(1938); YOU CAN'T TAKE IT WITH YOU(1938); FIFTH AVENUE GIRL(1939); FORGOTTEN WOMAN, THE(1939); HOTEL FOR WOMEN(1939); LOVE AF-

Elinor Flynn
LADIES IN LOVE(1930); SHE-WOLF, THE(1931)

Emmett Flynn
VEILED WOMAN, THE(1929), d; THREE ROGUES(1931), w
Silents
NELLIE, THE BEAUTIFUL CLOAK MODEL(1924), d; YANKEE SENOR, THE(1926), d; YELLOW FINGERS(1926), d; MARRIED ALIVE(1927), d
Misc. Silents
IN THE PALACE OF THE KING(1923), d; MAN WHO CAME BACK, THE(1924), d; WINGS OF YOUTH(1925), d; PALACE OF PLEASURE, THE(1926), d

Emmett J. Flynn
HOLD YOUR MAN(1929), d; SHANNONS OF BROADWAY, THE(1929), d
Silents
CONNECTICUT YANKEE AT KING ARTHUR'S COURT, A(1921), d; LAST TRAIL(1921), d; SHAME(1921), d, w
Misc. Silents
MARRIED VIRGIN, THE(1918), d; BACHELOR'S WIFE, A(1919), d; BONDAGE OF BARBARA, THE(1919), d; EASTWARD HO!(1919), d; RACING STRAIN(1919), d; VIRTOUS SINNERS(1919), d; YVONNE FROM PARIS(1919), d; LEAVE IT TO ME(1920), d; LINCOLN HIGHWAYMAN, THE(1920), d; MAN WHO DARED, THE(1920), d; SHOD WITH FIRE(1920), d; UNTAMED, THE(1920), d; VALLEY OF TOMORROW, THE(1920), d; FOOL THERE WAS, A(1922), d; MONTE CRISTO(1922), d; WITHOUT COMPROMISE(1922), d; HELL'S HOLE(1923), d; GERALD CRANSTON'S LADY(1924), d; DANCERS, THE(1925), d; EAST LYNNE(1925), d

Eric Flynn
SILENT INVASION, THE(1962, Brit.); MR. BROWN COMES DOWN THE HILL(1966, Brit.); CHALLENGE FOR ROBIN HOOD, A(1968, Brit.); SAFARI 3000(1982)

Errol Flynn
IN THE WAKE OF THE BOUNTY(1933, Aus.); CAPTAIN BLOOD(1935); CASE OF THE CURIOUS BRIDE, THE(1935); DON'T BET ON BLONDES(1935); MURDER AT MONTE CARLO(1935, Brit.); CHARGE OF THE LIGHT BRIGADE, THE(1936); ANOTHER DAWN(1937); GREEN LIGHT(1937); PERFECT SPECIMEN, THE(1937); PRINCE AND THE PAUPER, THE(1937); ADVENTURES OF ROBIN HOOD, THE(1938); DAWN PATROL, THE(1938); FOUR'S A CROWD(1938); SISTERS, THE(1938); DODGE CITY(1939); PRIVATE LIVES OF ELIZABETH AND ESSEX, THE(1939); SANTA FE TRAIL(1940); SEA HAWK, THE(1940); VIRGINIA CITY(1940); DIVE BOMBER(1941); FOOTSTEPS IN THE DARK(1941); DESPERATE JOURNEY(1942); THEY DIED WITH THEIR BOOTS ON(1942); NORTHERN PURSUIT(1943); THANK YOUR LUCKY STARS(1943); UNCERTAIN GLORY(1944); OBJECTIVE, BURMA!(1945); SAN ANTONIO(1945); NEVER SAY GOODBYE(1946); CRY WOLF(1947); SILVER RIVER(1948); ADVENTURES OF DON JUAN(1949); IT'S A GREAT FEELING(1949); THAT FORSYTE WOMAN(1949); KIM(1950); MONTANA(1950); ROCKY MOUNTAIN(1950); ADVENTURES OF CAPTAIN FABIAN(1951), a, w; HELLO GOD(1951, U.S./Ital.); AGAINST ALL FLAGS(1952); MARA MARU(1952); MASTER OF BALLANTRAE, THE(1953, U.S./Brit.); CROSSED SWORDS(1954); KING'S RHAPSODY(1955, Brit.); LET'S MAKE UP(1955, Brit.); WARRIORS, THE(1955); BIG BOODLE, THE(1957); ISTANBUL(1957); SUN ALSO RISES, THE(1957); ROOTS OF HEAVEN, THE(1958); TOO MUCH, TOO SOON(1958); CUBAN REBEL GIRLS(1960), a, w

Erroll Flynn
GENTLEMAN JIM(1942); EDGE OF DARKNESS(1943); ESCAPE ME NEVER(1947); EXTRAORDINARY SEAMAN, THE(1969)

F. Pershing Flynn
1984
RAW COURAGE(1984), ph

Frederick Flynn
SLAYER, THE(1982)

Gerard Mannix Flynn
1984
CAL(1984, Ireland)

Gertrude Flynn
BAREFOOT CONTESSA, THE(1954); WAR AND PEACE(1956, Ital./U.S.); BOY ON A DOLPHIN(1957); I WANT TO LIVE!(1958); SUMMER PLACE, A(1959); PARRISH(1961); ROME ADVENTURE(1962); INVITATION TO A GUNFIGHTER(1964); VALLEY OF THE DOLLS(1967); FUNNY GIRL(1968)
1984
BAD MANNERS(1984)

Henry Flynn
EARL OF CHICAGO, THE(1940)

Howard F. Flynn
NIGHTMARES(1983)

J.M. Flynn
LEATHER AND NYLON(1969, Fr./Ital.), w

Joe Flynn
SEVEN LITTLE FOYS, THE(1955); BOSS, THE(1956); PANAMA SAL(1957); PORTLAND EXPOSE(1957); THIS HAPPY FEELING(1958); -30-(1959); CRY FOR HAPPY(1961); LAST TIME I SAW ARCHIE, THE(1961); LOVER COME BACK(1961); POLICE DOG STORY, THE(1961); SON OF FLUBBER(1963); MC HALE'S NAVY(1964); MC HALE'S NAVY JOINS THE AIR FORCE(1965); DIVORCE AMERICAN STYLE(1967); DID YOU HEAR THE ONE ABOUT THE TRAVELING SALESLADY?(1968); LOVE BUG, THE(1968); COMPUTER WORE TENNIS SHOES, THE(1970); BAREFOOT EXECUTIVE, THE(1971); HOW TO FRAME A FIGG(1971); $1,000,000 DUCK(1971); NOW YOU SEE HIM, NOW YOU DON'T(1972); SUPERDAD(1974); STRONGEST MAN IN THE WORLD, THE(1975); RESCUERS, THE(1977)
Misc. Talkies
CAMPER JOHN(1973)

John Flynn
SERGEANT, THE(1968), d; JERUSALEM FILE, THE(1972, U.S./Israel), d; OUTFIT, THE(1973), d&w; ROLLING THUNDER(1977), d; DEFIANCE(1980), d; TOUCHED(1983), d

John J. Flynn, Jr.
MAN WHO LOVED WOMEN, THE(1983)
1984
MICKI AND MAUDE(1984)

Joni Flynn
OCTOPUSSY(1983, Brit.)

Kelly Flynn
HUSH... HUSH, SWEET CHARLOTTE(1964); PATCH OF BLUE, A(1965)

Lefty Flynn
Silents
CHILDREN OF THE NIGHT(1921); NO-GUN MAN, THE(1924)
Misc. Silents
BREED OF THE BORDER, THE(1924); MILLIONAIRE COWBOY, THE(1924); O.U. WEST(1925); SPEED WILD(1925); COLLEGE BOOB, THE(1926); GLENISTER OF THE MOUNTED(1926); MULHALL'S GREAT CATCH(1926); SIR LUMBERJACK(1926); TRAFFIC COP, THE(1926)

Magnus Flynn
PROLOGUE(1970, Can.)

Mannix Flynn
EXCALIBUR(1981); LIGHT YEARS AWAY(1982, Fr./Switz.)

Margaret H. Flynn
TRADING PLACES(1983)

Marie Flynn
INTERMEZZO: A LOVE STORY(1939)

Mark Flynn
SUNSET COVE(1978)

Mary Flynn
MIDNIGHT LACE(1960)

Maurice B. Flynn
Silents
STOP THIEF(1920); JUST OUT OF COLLEGE(1921); LAST TRAIL(1921); OATHBOUND(1922); SMILES ARE TRUMPS(1922); WOMAN WHO WALKED ALONE, THE(1922); SALOMY JANE(1923); CODE OF THE SEA(1924); OPEN ALL NIGHT(1924); HEADS UP(1925); HIGH AND HANDSOME(1925); ROUGH SHOD(1925); SMILIN' AT TROUBLE(1925)
Misc. Silents
BUCKING THE LINE(1921); DANGEROUS CURVE AHEAD(1921); DRUMS OF FATE(1923); HELL'S HOLE(1923); SNOW BRIDE, THE(1923); UNINVITED GUEST, THE(1924)

Maurice Bennett "Lefty" Flynn
Silents
OH, BOY!(1919)

Michael Flynn
STRIPES(1981)

Miriam Flynn
NATIONAL LAMPOON'S CLASS REUNION(1982); MR. MOM(1983); NATIONAL LAMPOON'S VACATION(1983)

Pat Flynn
NOT OF THIS EARTH(1957)

Patrick Flynn
MAD DOG MORGAN(1976,Aus.), m

Pueblo Jim Flynn
BOWERY, THE(1933)

Ray Flynn
SAN QUENTIN(1937); CAUGHT IN THE DRAFT(1941); LADY EVE, THE(1941); LADY HAS PLANS, THE(1942); MR. LUCKY(1943); ILLEGAL ENTRY(1949)
Misc. Silents
BLOOD WILL TELL(1927), d

Rhonda Flynn
EYES OF A STRANGER(1980); SPRING BREAK(1983)

Richard Flynn
REBEL ANGEL(1962)

Rita Flynn
GIRL FROM WOOLWORTH'S, THE(1929); BE YOURSELF(1930); LORD BYRON OF BROADWAY(1930); SWEET MAMA(1930); TOP SPEED(1930); PUBLIC ENEMY, THE(1931)

Robert Flynn
EVIL OF FRANKENSTEIN, THE(1964, Brit.)

Robin Flynn
WHIP'S WOMEN(1968)

Ruth Ann Flynn
ROCKY II(1979)

Ruth Flynn
OCTOPUSSY(1983, Brit.)

Sean Flynn
WHERE THE BOYS ARE(1960); SON OF CAPTAIN BLOOD, THE(1964, U.S./Ital./Span.); STOP TRAIN 349(1964, Fr./Ital./Ger.); SINGAPORE, SINGAPORE(1969, Fr./Ital.)

Susann Flynn
FIVE WILD GIRLS(1966, Fr.)

Thomas T. Flynn
MAN FROM LARAMIE, THE(1955), w

Tony Flynn
WILD GUITAR(1962)

Dario Fo
IT HAPPENED IN ROME(1959, Ital.), w

Aldo Foa
JUDITH(1965)

Arnaldo Foa
VERGINITA(1953, Ital.)

Arnold Foa
SILENT ENEMY, THE(1959, Brit.); BARABBAS(1962, Ital.)

Arnoldo Foa
LUCRECE BORGIA(1953, Ital./Fr.); STRANGER ON THE PROWL(1953, Ital.); TIMES GONE BY(1953, Ital.); ANGELA(1955, Ital.); LOVE IN A HOT CLIMATE(1958, Fr./Span.); DESERT DESPERADOES(1959); ANGEL WORE RED, THE(1960); HEAVEN ON EARTH(1960, Ital./U.S.); NIGHTS OF LUCRETIA BORGIA, THE(1960, Ital.); DESERT WARRIOR(1961 Ital./Span.); DAMON AND PYTHIAS(1962); LOVES OF SALAMMBO, THE(1962, Fr./Ital.); RELUCTANT SAINT, THE(1962, U.S./Ital.); TARTARS, THE(1962, Ital./Yugo.); TRIAL, THE(1963, Fr./Ital./Ger.); LOVES OF SALAMMBO, THE(1962, Fr./Ital.); SHOES OF THE FISHERMAN, THE(1968); BORSALINO(1970, Fr.); TEMPTER, THE(1974, Ital./Brit.); DEVIL IS A WOMAN(1975, Brit./Ital.); MATTER OF TIME, A(1976, Ital./U.S.)

Betty Foa
COME SEPTEMBER(1961)

Marion Foale
KALEIDOSCOPE(1966, Brit.), cos
John Foan [Mario Bava]
CALTIKI, THE IMMORTAL MONSTER(1959, Ital.), ph
Joan Foantaine
WOMEN, THE(1939)
Piero Focaccia
BAMBOLE!(1965, Ital.)
Spiros Focas
ROCCO AND HIS BROTHERS(1961, Fr./Ital.); PSYCOSISSIMO(1962, Ital.); RUN WITH THE DEVIL(1963, Fr./Ital.); EIGHTEEN IN THE SUN(1964, Ital.); FEAR, THE(1967, Gr.); STEFANIA(1968, Gr.); LOVE CYCLES(1969, Gr.); SHAFT IN AFRICA(1973)
Nina Foch
CRY OF THE WEREWOLF(1944); NINE GIRLS(1944); RETURN OF THE VAMPIRE, THE(1944); SHADOWS IN THE NIGHT(1944); SHE'S A SOLDIER TOO(1944); SHE'S A SWEETHEART(1944); STRANGE AFFAIR(1944); BOSTON BLACKIE'S RENDEZVOUS(1945); ESCAPE IN THE FOG(1945); I LOVE A MYSTERY(1945); MY NAME IS JULIA ROSS(1945); PRISON SHIP(1945); SONG TO REMEMBER, A(1945); GUILT OF JANET AMES, THE(1947); JOHNNY O'CLOCK(1947); DARK PAST, THE(1948); JOHNNY ALLEGRO(1949); UNDERCOVER MAN, THE(1949); AMERICAN IN PARIS, AN(1951); ST. BENNY THE DIP(1951); SCARAMOUCHE(1952); YOUNG MAN WITH IDEAS(1952); FAST COMPANY(1953); SOMBRERO(1953); EXECUTIVE SUITE(1954); FOUR GUNS TO THE BORDER(1954); ILLEGAL(1955); YOU'RE NEVER TOO YOUNG(1955); TEN COMMANDMENTS, THE(1956); THREE BRAVE MEN(1957); CASH McCALL(1960); SPARTACUS(1960); SUCH GOOD FRIENDS(1971); MAHOGANY(1975); SALTY(1975); JENNIFER(1978); RICH AND FAMOUS(1981)
Karl Fode
FOREVER MY LOVE(1962); GOOD SOLDIER SCHWEIK, THE(1963, Ger.)
Bennet Fode
RIP-OFF(1971, Can.), p
Foden's Brass Band
SMALL MAN, THE(1935, Brit.)
Ladislas Foder
TOM THUMB(1958, Brit./U.S.), w; RETURN OF DR. MABUSE, THE(1961, Ger./Fr./Ital.), w
John Fodor
YOU'VE GOT TO WALK IT LIKE YOU TALK IT OR YOU'LL LOSE THAT BEAT(1971)
Ladislas Fodor
CHURCH MOUSE, THE(1934, Brit.), w; WHITE LILAC(1935, Brit.), w; VERY YOUNG LADY, A(1941), w; CAIRO(1942), w; GIRL TROUBLE(1942), w; ISLE OF MISSING MEN(1942), w; NIGHT BEFORE THE DIVORCE(1942), w; TALES OF MANHATTAN(1942), w; TAMPICO(1944), w; IMPERFECT LADY, THE(1947), w; OTHER LOVE, THE(1947), w; GREAT SINNER, THE(1949), w; SOUTH SEA SINNER(1950), w; MAN FROM CAIRO, THE(1953), w; SCOTLAND YARD HUNTS DR. MABUSE(1963, Ger.), w; DR. MABUSE'S RAYS OF DEATH(1964, Ger./Fr./Ital.), w; INVISIBLE DR. MABUSE, THE(1965, Ger.), w; CORRUPT ONES, THE(1967, Ger.), w; PHANTOM OF SOHO, THE(1967, Ger.), w; OLD SHATTERHAND(1968, Ger./Yugo./Fr./Ital.), w; FIGHT FOR ROME(1969, Ger./Rum.), w
Ladislaus Fodor
BEAUTY AND THE BOSS(1932), w; JEWEL ROBBERY(1932), w; KISS BEFORE THE MIRROR, THE(1933), w; THUNDER IN THE NIGHT(1935), w; GIRLS' DORMITORY(1936), w; UNGUARDED HOUR, THE(1936), w; WIVES UNDER SUSPICION(1938), w; CHARLIE CHAN IN THE CITY OF DARKNESS(1939), w; SEVEN SINNERS(1940), w; FOOTSTEPS IN THE DARK(1941), w; TERROR OF DR. MABUSE, THE(1965, Ger.), w
Laszlo Fodor
NORTH TO ALASKA(1960), w
Nicholas Fodor
WOMAN TO WOMAN(1929), w
Peter Fodor
WINTER WIND(1970, Fr./Hung.)
Henry Foehl
KING OF MARVIN GARDENS, THE(1972)
Franz F. Foehm
SEPTEMBER AFFAIR(1950)
Giorgio Foeldes
BARBER OF SEVILLE, THE(1947, Ital.), cos
Imre Foeldes
ALIAS THE DOCTOR(1932), w
Frank Foeldi
OTHER SIDE OF THE MOUNTAIN, THE(1975)
Dirk Foerster
FLOWERS FOR THE MAN IN THE MOON(1975, Ger.)
Saidu Fofana
HEART OF THE MATTER, THE(1954, Brit.)
Franco Fogagnolo
10,000 DOLLARS BLOOD MONEY(1966, Ital.), w
Brenda Fogarty
SUMMER CAMP(1979)
Misc. Talkies
TRIP WITH THE TEACHER(1975); FAIRY TALES(1979)
Mary Fogarty
1984
COLD FEET(1984)
Mary Lou Fogarty
TRAP DOOR, THE(1980)
Nils Fogeby
SHAME(1968, Swed.)
Jerry Fogel
TORA! TORA! TORA!(1970, U.S./Jap.); DAY OF THE LOCUST, THE(1975)
N. Fogel
WAR AND PEACE(1968, USSR)
Vladimir Fogel
Misc. Silents
DEATH RAY, THE(1925, USSR); BED AND SOFA(1926, USSR); BY THE LAW(1926, USSR); MISS MEND(1926, USSR); GIRL WITH THE HAT-BOX(1927, USSR); HOUSE ON TRUBNAYA SQUARE(1928, USSR)

Y. Fogelman
BALLAD OF COSSACK GLOOTA(1938, USSR), ph
Yuli Fogelman
DESERTER(1934, USSR), ph
Col. E.E. Fogelson
PEPE(1960)
Brenda Fogerty
Misc. Talkies
BEACH BUNNIES(1977)
Fay Fogg
I'D CLIMB THE HIGHEST MOUNTAIN(1951)
Kay Fogg
I'D CLIMB THE HIGHEST MOUNTAIN(1951)
Aleksander Fogiel
KNIGHTS OF THE TEUTONIC ORDER, THE(1962, Pol.); YELLOW SLIPPERS, THE(1965, Pol.); JOVITA(1970, Pol.); SARAGOSSA MANUSCRIPT, THE(1972, Pol.)
Alberto Fogliani
FLYING SAUCER, THE(1964, Ital.)
Mario Foglietti
FOUR FLIES ON GREY VELVET(1972, Ital.), w
Jacqueline Fogt
WHAT'S NEW, PUSSYCAT?(1965, U.S./Fr.); PAUL AND MICHELLE(1974, Fr./Brit.); LOVE AND DEATH(1975)
Jaqueline Fogt
FIENDISH PLOT OF DR. FU MANCHU, THE(1980)
Reginald Fogwell
CROSS ROADS(1930, Brit.), p&d, w; GUILT(1930, Brit.), p,d&w; SUCH IS THE LAW(1930, Brit.), w; MADAME GUILLOTINE(1931, Brit.), p, d, w; WRITTEN LAW, THE(1931, Brit.), p, d&w; BETRAYAL(1932, Brit.), d&w; WONDERFUL STORY, THE(1932, Brit.), p&d, w; PRINCE OF ARCADIA(1933, Brit.), p, w; TWO HEARTS IN WALTZ TIME(1934, Brit.), p, w; MURDER AT THE CABARET(1936, Brit.), p, d, w; TERROR ON TIPTOE(1936, Brit.), p
Misc. Silents
WARNING, THE(1928, Brit.), d
Roy Fogwell
MURDER AT THE CABARET(1936, Brit.), ph; SPECIAL EDITION(1938, Brit.), ph; TREACHERY ON THE HIGH SEAS(1939, Brit.), ph; BELL-BOTTOM GEORGE(1943, Brit.), ph; MILLIONS LIKE US(1943, Brit.), ph; HE SNOOPS TO CONQUER(1944, Brit.), ph; I DIDN'T DO IT(1945, Brit.), ph; FLY AWAY PETER(1948, Brit.), ph; LOVE IN WAITING(1948, Brit.), ph; TROUBLE IN THE AIR(1948, Brit.), ph; THOSE PEOPLE NEXT DOOR(1952, Brit.), ph
Pauline Fohnson
Misc. Silents
WOULD YOU BELIEVE IT!(1929, Brit.)
Sgt. Jack Foisie
STORY OF G.I. JOE, THE(1945)
Michel Fokine
TURNING POINT, THE(1977), ch
James Foland
NIGHT OF EVIL(1962)
Dennis Folbigge
ZULU(1964, Brit.)
Charlotte Folcher
MAN WITH THE BALLOONS, THE(1968, Ital./Fr.)
Amelia Folcini
LOVE HUNGER(1965, Arg.)
Robert Foldeak
FATHER(1967, Hung.)
Lawrence D. Foldes
MALIBU HIGH(1979), p; YOUNG WARRIORS(1983), d, w
Misc. Talkies
DON'T GO NEAR THE PARK(1981), d; GREAT SKYCOPTER RESCUE, THE(1982), d
Yolanda Foldes
GOLDEN EARRINGS(1947), w; MY OWN TRUE LOVE(1948), w
Erzebet Foldi
ALL THAT JAZZ(1979)
Leslie Foldvary
CONAN THE BARBARIAN(1982)
Peter Foldy
1984
HOT MOVES(1984), w
Peter Foleg
UNSEEN, THE(1981), d
Brian Foleman
RETURNING, THE(1983)
Barbara Foley
SOMETHING OF VALUE(1957); LORDS OF FLATBUSH, THE(1974)
Bill Foley
PROFESSOR TIM(1957, Ireland); BROTH OF A BOY(1959, Brit.); SIEGE OF SIDNEY STREET, THE(1960, Brit.); NEVER PUT IT IN WRITING(1964); YOUNG CASSIDY(1965, U.S./Brit.); PADDY(1970, Irish)
Brian Foley
VON RICHTHOFEN AND BROWN(1970); WELCOME TO THE CLUB(1971); ICE CASTLES(1978), ch
Clare Foley
JANIE(1944); JANIE GETS MARRIED(1946)
Dana Foley
LORDS OF FLATBUSH, THE(1974)
Daniel Foley
1984
MAJDHAR(1984, Brit.)
Daniel P. Foley
IRON ANGEL(1964), p; VELVET TRAP, THE(1966), p
Don Foley
LIGHT YEARS AWAY(1982, Fr./Switz.)
Dudley C. Foley, Jr.
DAMN CITIZEN(1958)

Elizabeth Foley
Silents
DOWN TO THE SEA IN SHIPS(1923); SILENT COMMAND, THE(1923)
Ellen Foley
HAIR(1979); TOOTSIE(1982); KING OF COMEDY, THE(1983)
Gene Foley
TEENAGE REBEL(1956)
George Foley
ANIMAL CRACKERS(1930), ph
Silents
ANSWER, THE(1916, Brit.); MUNITION GIRL'S ROMANCE, A(1917, Brit.); RAGGED MESSENGER, THE(1917, Brit.); WARE CASE, THE(1917, Brit.); ON LEAVE(1918, Brit.); SHEFFIELD BLADE, A(1918, Brit.); SNARE, THE(1918, Brit.); ODDS AGAINST HER, THE(1919, Brit.); TATTERLY(1919, Brit.); MARY LATIMER, NUN(1920, Brit.); PENNILESS MILLIONAIRE, THE(1921, Brit.); IN THE BLOOD(1923, Brit.)
Misc. Silents
BATTLE OF WATERLOO, THE(1913, Brit.); REVOLUTIONIST, THE(1914, Brit.); WHEN LONDON SLEEPS(1914, Brit.); LIFE OF AN ACTRESS, THE(1915, Brit.); LONDON FLAT MYSTERY, A(1915, Brit.); WOMAN WHO DID, THE(1915, Brit.); DRINK(1917, Brit.); GAMBLE FOR LOVE, A(1917, Brit.); BECAUSE(1918, Brit.); BETTA THE GYPSY(1918, Brit.); TICKET-OF-LEAVE MAN, THE(1918, Brit.); GRIP OF IRON, THE(1920, Brit.); LIGHTS OF HOME, THE(1920, Brit.); TRENT'S LAST CASE(1920, Brit.); LOWLAND CINDERELLA, A(1921, Brit.); VI OF SMITH'S ALLEY(1921, Brit.); COUPLE OF DOWN AND OUTS, A(1923, Brit.)
J.P. Foley
VERDICT, THE(1982)
Jack Foley
HINDU, THE(1953, Brit.), ed
Silents
GATE CRASHER, THE(1928), w; KID'S CLEVER, THE(1929), w
James Foley
1984
RECKLESS(1984), d
Jay Foley
MILESTONES(1975)
Joan Foley
METEOR(1979)
1984
FIRESTARTER(1984); LOVE STREAMS(1984); SWORDKILL(1984)
Joe Foley
WHISTLE AT EATON FALLS(1951)
John Foley
DISHONORED LADY(1947), ed
John M. Foley
LURED(1947), ed; FAREWELL TO ARMS, A(1957), ed
Kathy Foley
GNOME-MOBILE, THE(1967)
Louis B. Foley
Silents
ALADDIN'S OTHER LAMP(1917)
Louise Foley
HARPER VALLEY, P.T.A.(1978)
Pat Foley
MAN CALLED FLINTSTONE, THE(1966), ed; CHARLOTTE'S WEB(1973), ed
Red Foley
PIONEERS, THE(1941)
Richard Foley
Silents
GOLD RUSH, THE(1925)
Romey Foley
COLORADO PIONEERS(1945)
Sandra Foley
Misc. Talkies
ASSAULT WITH A DEADLY WEAPON(1983)
Elio Folgaresi
SWORD OF THE CONQUEROR(1962, Ital.)
Byron Folger
RUN FOR THE HILLS(1953)
Jeff Folger
1984
TANK(1984)
Miriam Folger
Misc. Silents
HER SECOND HUSBAND(1918)
Werner Folger
RESTLESS NIGHT, THE(1964, Ger.)
Manuel Folgoso
SARUMBA(1950)
Dan Foliart
ONLY WAY HOME, THE(1972), m
Joe Folino
HARD RIDE, THE(1971)
Linda Folk
1984
DUBEAT-E-O(1984), ed
Robert Folk
SAVAGE HARVEST(1981), m; SLAYER, THE(1982), m
1984
POLICE ACADEMY(1984), m; PURPLE HEARTS(1984), m
Sidney Folker
Misc. Silents
CORNER MAN, THE(1921, Brit.)
Sydney Folker
Silents
GIRL WHO LOVES A SOLDIER, THE(1916, Brit.); NOTORIOUS MRS. CARRICK, THE(1924, Brit.)
Misc. Silents
VI OF SMITH'S ALLEY(1921, Brit.)

Bob Folkerson
SHUT MY BIG MOUTH(1942); RUN FOR COVER(1955)
David Folkes
WHERE'S CHARLEY?(1952, Brit.), art d
Los Folkloristas
UNDER FIRE(1983)
The Folkloristas
1984
EL NORTE(1984), m
Casey Folks
QUEEN FOR A DAY(1951)
David Follander
1984
GOODBYE PEOPLE, THE(1984)
Julie Follansbee
DAY OF THE DOLPHIN, THE(1973)
Clay Follett
1984
MRS. SOFFEL(1984)
Ken Follett
EYE OF THE NEEDLE(1981), w
Stephen Follett
UNDERGROUND(1970, Brit.)
Follette and Lunard
MELODY PARADE(1943)
Joe Follino
HELL'S CHOSEN FEW(1968)
Stan Follis
HIDEOUS SUN DEMON, THE(1959), ph
Pat Follmer
VIXENS, THE(1969), ed
Pat Follner
MOONLIGHTING WIVES(1966), ed
Samantha Follows
1984
MRS. SOFFEL(1984)
Ted Follows
PAPERBACK HERO(1973, Can.)
Frants Folmer
SUNDOWNERS, THE(1960), set d
Jeff Folmsbee
LUGGAGE OF THE GODS(1983), p
Sandra Foloway
ROYAL SCANDAL, A(1945)
George Folren
CHEAT, THE(1931), ph
Lelise Folse
TERMS OF ENDEARMENT(1983)
Marisa Folse
CAT PEOPLE(1982)
George Folsey
APPLAUSE(1929), ph; BATTLE OF PARIS, THE(1929), ph; COCOANUTS, THE(1929), ph; GENTLEMEN OF THE PRESS(1929), ph; HOLE IN THE WALL(1929), ph; LETTER, THE(1929), ph; BIG POND, THE(1930), ph; DANGEROUS NAN McGREW(1930), ph; GLORIFYING THE AMERICAN GIRL(1930), ph; LAUGHTER(1930), ph; ROYAL FAMILY OF BROADWAY, THE(1930), ph; HONOR AMONG LOVERS(1931), ph; MY SIN(1931), ph; SECRETS OF A SECRETARY(1931), ph; SMILING LIEUTENANT, THE(1931), ph; STOLEN HEAVEN(1931), ph; ANIMAL KINGDOM, THE(1932), ph; BIG BROADCAST, THE(1932), ph; WISER SEX, THE(1932), ph; GOING HOLLYWOOD(1933), ph; MEN MUST FIGHT(1933), ph; REUNION IN VIENNA(1933), ph; STAGE MOTHER(1933), ph; STORM AT DAYBREAK(1933), ph; CHAINED(1934), ph; MEN IN WHITE(1934), ph; OPERATOR 13(1934), ph; FORSAKING ALL OTHERS(1935), ph; I LIVE MY LIFE(1935), ph; KIND LADY(1935), ph; PAGE MISS GLORY(1935), ph; GORGEOUS HUSSY, THE(1936), ph; GREAT ZIEGFELD, THE(1936), ph; HEARTS DIVIDED(1936), ph; BRIDE WORE RED, THE(1937), ph; LAST OF MRS. CHEYNEY, THE(1937), ph; MANNEQUIN(1937), ph; ARSENE LUPIN RETURNS(1938), ph; HOLD THAT KISS(1938), ph; SHINING HOUR, THE(1938), ph; FAST AND LOOSE(1939), ph; LADY OF THE TROPICS(1939), ph; REMEMBER?(1939), ph; SOCIETY LAWYER(1939), ph; THIRD FINGER, LEFT HAND(1940), ph; TWO GIRLS ON BROADWAY(1940), ph; COME LIVE WITH ME(1941), ph; DR. KILDARE'S WEDDING DAY(1941), ph; FREE AND EASY(1941), ph; LADY BE GOOD(1941), ph; MARRIED BACHELOR(1941), ph; TRIAL OF MARY DUGAN, THE(1941), ph; DR. GILLESPIE'S NEW ASSISTANT(1942), ph; GRAND CENTRAL MURDER(1942), ph; PANAMA HATTIE(1942), ph; RIO RITA(1942), ph; SEVEN SWEETHEARTS(1942), ph; GUY NAMED JOE, A(1943), ph; THOUSANDS CHEER(1943), ph; THREE HEARTS FOR JULIA(1943), ph; MEET ME IN ST. LOUIS(1944), ph; WHITE CLIFFS OF DOVER, THE(1944), ph; CLOCK, THE(1945), ph; ZIEGFELD FOLLIES(1945), ph; GREEN YEARS, THE(1946), ph; HARVEY GIRLS, THE(1946), ph; SECRET HEART, THE(1946), ph; GREEN DOLPHIN STREET(1947), ph; IF WINTER COMES(1947), ph; GREAT SINNER, THE(1949), ph; TAKE ME OUT TO THE BALL GAME(1949), ph; BIG HANGOVER, THE(1950), ph; LIFE OF HER OWN, A(1950), ph; MALAYA(1950), ph; ALL THE BROTHERS WERE VALIANT(1953), ph; DEEP IN MY HEART(1954), ph; EXECUTIVE SUITE(1954), ph; MEN OF THE FIGHTING LADY(1954), ph; SEVEN BRIDES FOR SEVEN BROTHERS(1954), ph; TENNESSEE CHAMP(1954), ph; COBWEB, THE(1955), ph; HIT THE DECK(1955), ph; FORBIDDEN PLANET(1956), ph; COUNT YOUR BLESSINGS(1959), ph; CASH McCALL(1960), ph; I PASSED FOR WHITE(1960), ph; BALCONY, THE(1963), ph
Silents
EDUCATION OF ELIZABETH, THE(1921), ph; ROAD TO LONDON, THE(1921, Brit.); NANCY FROM NOWHERE(1922), ph; ENCHANTED COTTAGE, THE(1924), ph; NECESSARY EVIL, THE(1925), ph; LADIES AT PLAY(1926), ph; AMERICAN BEAUTY(1927), ph; LADY BE GOOD(1928), ph
George Folsey, Jr.
GLASS HOUSES(1972), p, ed; HAMMER(1972), ed; BLACK CAESAR(1973), ed; SCHLOCK(1973), ed; TRADER HORN(1973), ed; J.D.'S REVENGE(1976), ed; NORMAN...IS THAT YOU?(1976), ed; CHICKEN CHRONICLES, THE(1977), ed; KENTUCKY FRIED MOVIE, THE(1977), ed; SOURDOUGH(1977), ed; TRACKS(1977), ed; NATIONAL LAMPOON'S ANIMAL HOUSE(1978), ed; BLUES BROTHERS, THE(1980), ed; AMERICAN WEREWOLF IN LONDON, AN(1981), p

George Folsey, Sr.
GLASS HOUSES(1972), ph

George J. Folsey
LAUGHING LADY, THE(1930), ph; TILL THE CLOUDS ROLL BY(1946), ph; STATE OF THE UNION(1948), ph; ADAM'S RIB(1949), ph; LAW AND THE LADY, THE(1951), ph; MAN WITH A CLOAK, THE(1951), ph; MR. IMPERIUM(1951), ph; NIGHT INTO MORNING(1951), ph; SHADOW IN THE SKY(1951), ph; VENGEANCE VALLEY(1951), ph; MILLION DOLLAR MERMAID(1952), ph; FASTEST GUN ALIVE(1956), ph; POWER AND THE PRIZE, THE(1956), ph; THESE WILDER YEARS(1956), ph; HOUSE OF NUMBERS(1957), ph; TIP ON A DEAD JOCKEY(1957), ph; HIGH COST OF LOVING, THE(1958), ph; IMITATION GENERAL(1958), ph; SADDLE THE WIND(1958), ph; TORPEDO RUN(1958), ph

Joe Folson
Misc. Talkies
IN THE RAPTURE(1976)

Megan Folson
HEARTLAND(1980)

Ray Folsum
RATTLERS(1976), animal t

Claudia Folts
DON'T GO IN THE HOUSE(1980)

Monica Folts
O.S.S.(1946)

Shawn Foltz
SPRING FEVER(1983, Can.)

Virginia Foltz
Misc. Silents
GLORIANA(1916)

Artye Folz
SHOW BOAT(1936)

Igor Fomchenko
VIOLIN AND ROLLER(1962, USSR)

Y. Fomichyov
HOUSE ON THE FRONT LINE, THE(1963, USSR)

Yu. Fomichyov
DAY THE WAR ENDED, THE(1961, USSR)

O. Fomichyova
THERE WAS AN OLD COUPLE(1967, USSR)

Amy Fonda
CHASE, THE(1966)

Gloria Fonda
Misc. Silents
COLLEGE ORPHAN, THE(1915); DRUGGED WATERS(1916)

Henry Fonda
FARMER TAKES A WIFE, THE(1935); I DREAM TOO MUCH(1935); WAY DOWN EAST(1935); MOON'S OUR HOME, THE(1936); SPENDTHRIFT(1936); TRAIL OF THE LONESOME PINE, THE(1936); SLIM(1937); THAT CERTAIN WOMAN(1937); WINGS OF THE MORNING(1937, Brit.); YOU ONLY LIVE ONCE(1937); BLOCKADE(1938); I MET MY LOVE AGAIN(1938); JEZEBEL(1938); MAD MISS MANTON, THE(1938); SPAWN OF THE NORTH(1938); DRUMS ALONG THE MOHAWK(1939); JESSE JAMES(1939); LET US LIVE(1939); STORY OF ALEXANDER GRAHAM BELL, THE(1939); YOUNG MR. LINCOLN(1939); CHAD HANNA(1940); GRAPES OF WRATH(1940); LILLIAN RUSSELL(1940); RETURN OF FRANK JAMES, THE(1940); LADY EVE, THE(1941); WILD GEESE CALLING(1941); YOU BELONG TO ME(1941); BIG STREET, THE(1942); MAGNIFICENT DOPE, THE(1942); MALE ANIMAL, THE(1942); RINGS ON HER FINGERS(1942); TALES OF MANHATTAN(1942); IMMORTAL SERGEANT, THE(1943); OX-BOW INCIDENT, THE(1943); MY DARLING CLEMENTINE(1946); DAISY KENYON(1947); FUGITIVE, THE(1947); LONG NIGHT, THE(1947); FORT APACHE(1948); ON OUR MERRY WAY(1948); JIGSAW(1949); MISTER ROBERTS(1955); WAR AND PEACE(1956, Ital./U.S.); WRONG MAN, THE(1956); TIN STAR, THE(1957); 12 ANGRY MEN(1957), a, p; STAGE STRUCK(1958); MAN WHO UNDERSTOOD WOMEN, THE(1959); WARLOCK(1959); ADVISE AND CONSENT(1962); HOW THE WEST WAS WON(1962); LONGEST DAY, THE(1962); SPENCER'S MOUNTAIN(1963); BEST MAN, THE(1964); FAIL SAFE(1964); SEX AND THE SINGLE GIRL(1964); BATTLE OF THE BULGE(1965); IN HARM'S WAY(1965); ROUNDERS, THE(1965); BIG HAND FOR THE LITTLE LADY, A(1966); THE DIRTY GAME(1966, Fr./Ital./Ger.); WELCOME TO HARD TIMES(1967); FIRECREEK(1968); MADIGAN(1968); THE BOSTON STRANGLER(1968); YOURS, MINE AND OURS(1968); ONCE UPON A TIME IN THE WEST(1969, U.S./Ital.); CHEYENNE SOCIAL CLUB, THE(1970); THERE WAS A CROOKED MAN(1970); TOO LATE THE HERO(1970); SOMETIMES A GREAT NOTION(1971); ASH WEDNESDAY(1973); SERPENT, THE(1973, Fr./Ital./Ger.); LAST DAYS OF MUSSOLINI(1974, Ital.); MY NAME IS NOBODY(1974, Ital./Fr./Ger.); MIDWAY(1976); ROLLERCOASTER(1977); TENTACLES(1977, Ital.); FEDORA(1978, Ger./Fr.); GREAT SMOKEY ROADBLOCK, THE(1978); SWARM, THE(1978); CITY ON FIRE(1979 Can.); METEOR(1979); WANDA NEVADA(1979)

Henry Fonda, Jr.
ON GOLDEN POND(1981)

Jane Fonda
TALL STORY(1960); CHAPMAN REPORT, THE(1962); PERIOD OF ADJUSTMENT(1962); WALK ON THE WILD SIDE(1962); IN THE COOL OF THE DAY(1963); SUNDAY IN NEW YORK(1963); JOY HOUSE(1964, Fr.); CAT BALLOU(1965); CIRCLE OF LOVE(1965, Fr.); ANY WEDNESDAY(1966); CHASE, THE(1966); BAREFOOT IN THE PARK(1967); GAME IS OVER, THE(1967, Fr.); HURRY SUNDOWN(1967); BARBARELLA(1968, Fr./Ital.); SPIRITS OF THE DEAD(1969, Fr./Ital.); THEY SHOOT HORSES, DON'T THEY?(1969); KLUTE(1971); DOLL'S HOUSE, A(1973, Brit.); STEELYARD BLUES(1973); TOUT VA BIEN(1973, Fr.); BLUE BIRD, THE(1976); FUN WITH DICK AND JANE(1977); JULIA(1977); CALIFORNIA SUITE(1978); COMES A HORSEMAN(1978); COMING HOME(1978); CHINA SYNDROME, THE(1979); ELECTRIC HORSEMAN, THE(1979); NINE TO FIVE(1980); ON GOLDEN POND(1981); ROLLOVER(1981)

Peter Fonda
TAMMY AND THE DOCTOR(1963); VICTORS, THE(1963); LILITH(1964); YOUNG LOVERS, THE(1964); WILD ANGELS, THE(1966); TRIP, THE(1967); EASY RIDER(1969), a, p, w; SPIRITS OF THE DEAD(1969, Fr./Ital.); HIRED HAND, THE(1971), a, d; LAST MOVIE, THE(1971); TWO PEOPLE(1973); DIRTY MARY, CRAZY LARRY(1974); OPEN SEASON(1974, U.S./Span.); IDAHO TRANSFER(1975), d; KILLER FORCE(1975, Switz./Ireland); RACE WITH THE DEVIL(1975); 92 IN THE SHADE(1975, U.S./Brit.); FIGHTING MAD(1976); FUTUREWORLD(1976); OUTLAW BLUES(1977); HIGH-BALLIN'(1978); WANDA NEVADA(1979), a, d; CANNONBALL

RUN, THE(1981); SPLIT IMAGE(1982); ALL RIGHT, MY FRIEND(1983, Japan); DANCE OF THE DWARFS(1983, U.S., Phil.); SPASMS(1983, Can.)

Phil Fondacaro
RETURN OF THE JEDI(1983)

Sal Fondacaro
RETURN OF THE JEDI(1983)

Marcel Fondat
BLOOD AND BLACK LACE(1965, Ital.), w

Marcello Fondato
EVERYBODY GO HOME!(1962, Fr./Ital.), w; BLACK SABBATH(1963, Ital.), w; BEBO'S GIRL(1964, Ital.), w; SIX DAYS A WEEK(1966, Fr./Ital./Span.), w; GRAND SLAM(1968, Ital., Span., Ger.), w; THREE NIGHTS OF LOVE(1969, Ital.), w; CERTAIN, VERY CERTAIN, AS A MATTER OF FACT... PROBABLE(1970, Ital,), d&w; MIDNIGHT PLEASURES(1975, Ital.), d, w; CHARLESTON(1978, Ital.), d, w; IMMORTAL BACHELOR, THE(1980, Ital.), d, w

Elena Fondra
JULIET OF THE SPIRITS(1965, Fr./Ital./W.Ger.)

Helen Fondra
ROMAN HOLIDAY(1953)

Stephanie Fondue
Misc. Talkies
CHEERLEADERS, THE(1973)

Jon Fondy
1984
REPO MAN(1984)

Tony Fones
UP THE CREEK(1958, Brit.), m

Peter Fonfield
MURDER BY DECREE(1979, Brit.)

Alice Fong
GOLDEN NEEDLES(1974)

Allen Fong [Fong Yuk-Ping]
1984
AH YING(1984, Hong Kong), d

Beal Fong
WE'VE NEVER BEEN LICKED(1943)

Benson Fong
CHARLIE CHAN AT THE OPERA(1936); BEHIND THE RISING SUN(1943); CHARLIE CHAN IN THE SECRET SERVICE(1944); CHINESE CAT, THE(1944); DESTINATION TOKYO(1944); DRAGON SEED(1944); KEYS OF THE KINGDOM, THE(1944); PURPLE HEART, THE(1944); THIRTY SECONDS OVER TOKYO(1944); UP IN ARMS(1944); BACK TO BATAAN(1945); CHINA SKY(1945); FIRST YANK INTO TOKYO(1945); NOB HILL(1945); SCARLET CLUE, THE(1945); SHANGHAI COBRA, THE(1945); DARK ALIBI(1946); DECEPTION(1946); RED DRAGON, THE(1946); CALCUTTA(1947); HAZARD(1948); WOMEN IN THE NIGHT(1948); BOSTON BLACKIE'S CHINESE VENTURE(1949); CHINATOWN AT MIDNIGHT(1949); THREE HUSBANDS(1950); KOREA PATROL(1951); PEKING EXPRESS(1951); BACK AT THE FRONT(1952); DRAGONFLY SQUADRON(1953); HIS MAJESTY O'KEEFE(1953); CONQUEST OF SPACE(1955); LEFT HAND OF GOD, THE(1955); SCARLET HOUR, THE(1956); FIVE GATES TO HELL(1959); WALK LIKE A DRAGON(1960); FLOWER DRUM SONG(1961); GIRLS! GIRLS! GIRLS!(1962); OUR MAN FLINT(1966); LOVE BUG, THE(1968); CHARLEY VARRICK(1973); STRONGEST MAN IN THE WORLD, THE(1975); OLIVER'S STORY(1978); S.O.B.(1981); JINXED!(1982)
Misc. Talkies
TIME FOR LOVE, A(1974); HE IS MY BROTHER(1976)

Bill Fong
HAWAIIANS, THE(1970)

Brian Fong
LOVE BUG, THE(1968)

Frances Fong
SOLDIER OF FORTUNE(1955); HELLFIGHTERS(1968); GOLDEN NEEDLES(1974); POWERFORCE(1983)

Harold Fong
UP IN SMOKE(1978); PURPLE HEART, THE(1944); FRANCIS(1949); I WAS AN AMERICAN SPY(1951); KOREA PATROL(1951); PEKING EXPRESS(1951); SAVAGE DRUMS(1951); STEEL HELMET, THE(1951); SUBMARINE COMMAND(1951); STORM OVER TIBET(1952); YANK IN INDO-CHINA, A(1952); FORBIDDEN(1953); NOT OF THIS EARTH(1957); PLEASURE OF HIS COMPANY, THE(1961); DIAMOND HEAD(1962); ONE WAY WAHINI(1965)

Harold G. Fong
SAIGON(1948)

Jon Fong
FLOWER DRUM SONG(1961); DONOVAN'S REEF(1963); MILLION EYES OF SU-MURU, THE(1967, Brit.); SERIAL(1980)

Jose Fong
NOBODY'S PERFEKT(1981)

Leo Fong
1984
KILLPOINT(1984), a, ch
Misc. Talkies
BLIND RAGE(1978); ENFORCER FROM DEATH ROW, THE(1978); LAST REUNION(1978)

Leslie Fong
TOKYO ROSE(1945); CALCUTTA(1947); DIRTY HARRY(1971)

Richard Fong
CONFESSIONS OF AN OPIUM EATER(1962)

Willie Fong
MY MOTHER(1933)

Wong Fong
GENERAL DIED AT DAWN, THE(1936)

O.W. Fonger
INVADERS, THE,(1941)

Paul Fonifas
CHAMPAGNE CHARLIE(1944, Brit.)

Luis Fonoll
NIGHT OF THE ZOMBIES(1983, Span./Ital.)

Angelino Fons
HUNT, THE(1967, Span.), w

Jorge Fons
JORY(1972), d
Carolyn Fonseca
DAMON AND PYTHIAS(1962)
Greg Fonseca
1984
EYES OF FIRE(1984), art d; HARDBODIES(1984), prod d; NIGHTMARE ON ELM STREET, A(1984), prod d; STRANGERS KISS(1984), set d
Olaf Fonss
Misc. Silents
ATLANTIS(1913, Ger./Den.)
Mia Fonssagrives
WHAT'S NEW, PUSSYCAT?(1965, U.S./Fr.), cos; CANDY(1968, Ital./Fr.), cos; ONLY GAME IN TOWN, THE(1970), cos; WALKING STICK, THE(1970, Brit.), cos
Francoise Fontages
HOUSE OF 1,000 DOLLS(1967, Ger./Span./Brit.)
Peter Fontain
THERE'S ALWAYS A THURSDAY(1957, Brit.)
Alisha Fontaine
GANG THAT COULDN'T SHOOT STRAIGHT, THE(1971); WHITE RAT(1972); SHAMUS(1973); GAMBLER, THE(1974); FRENCH QUARTER(1978); NATURAL ENE-MIES(1979)
Anne Fontaine
COUSINS IN LOVE(1982)
Corinne Fontaine
PLAYGIRLS AND THE VAMPIRE(1964, Ital.)
Dick Fontaine
HAPPY BIRTHDAY, DAVY(1970)
Eddie Fontaine
GIRL CAN'T HELP IT, THE(1956)
Evan-Burrows Fontaine
Silents
MADONNAS AND MEN(1920)
Frank Fontaine
HIT PARADE OF 1951(1950); NANCY GOES TO RIO(1950); STELLA(1950); CALL ME MISTER(1951); HERE COMES THE GROOM(1951); MODEL AND THE MARRIAGE BROKER, THE(1951); SCARED STIFF(1953)
Gyles Fontaine
BLOODSUCKING FREAKS(1982), ch
Jacqueline Fontaine
DALTON'S WOMEN, THE(1950); SKIPALONG ROSENBLOOM(1951); STRIP, THE(1951); OUTLAW WOMEN(1952); COUNTRY GIRL, THE(1954); LIEUTENANT WORE SKIRTS, THE(1956); BORN TO BE LOVED(1959); UNTAMED MIS-TRESS(1960); LADIES MAN, THE(1961); MURDERERS' ROW(1966)
Jean Fontaine
SINISTER URGE, THE(1961)
Joan Fontaine
UNTIL THEY SAIL(1957); DAMSEL IN DISTRESS, A(1937); MAN WHO FOUND HIMSELF, THE(1937); MUSIC FOR MADAME(1937); QUALITY STREET(1937); YOU CAN'T BEAT LOVE(1937); BLOND CHEAT(1938); DUKE OF WEST POINT, THE(1938); MAID'S NIGHT OUT(1938); MILLION TO ONE, A(1938); SKY GIANT(1938); GUNGA DIN(1939); MAN OF CONQUEST(1939); REBECCA(1940); SUSPICION(1941); THIS ABOVE ALL(1942); FRENCHMAN'S CREEK(1944); JANE EYRE(1944); AFFAIRS OF SUSAN(1945); FROM THIS DAY FORWARD(1946); IVY(1947); EMPEROR WALTZ, THE(1948); KISS THE BLOOD OFF MY HANDS(1948); LETTER FROM AN UNKNOWN WOMAN(1948); YOU GOTTA STAY HAPPY(1948); BORN TO BE BAD(1950); SEPTEMBER AFFAIR(1950); DARLING, HOW COULD YOU!(1951); IVANHOE(1952, Brit.); SOMETHING TO LIVE FOR(1952); BIGAMIST, THE(1953); DECAMERON NIGHTS(1953, Brit.); FLIGHT TO TANGIER(1953); CASANOVA'S BIG NIGHT(1954); OTHELLO(1955, U.S./Fr./Ital.); BEYOND A REA-SONABLE DOUBT(1956); SERENADE(1956); ISLAND IN THE SUN(1957); CERTAIN SMILE, A(1958); SOUTH PACIFIC(1958); TENDER IS THE NIGHT(1961); VOYAGE TO THE BOTTOM OF THE SEA(1961); DEVIL'S OWN, THE(1967, Brit.)
John Fontaine
YOU WERE MEANT FOR ME(1948); ARMY BOUND(1952); BATTLE ZONE(1952); FIGHTER ATTACK(1953); DRIVE A CROOKED ROAD(1954)
Laurie Fontaine
KISS ME, STUPID(1964)
Lilian Fontaine
LOST WEEKEND, THE(1945); IMPERFECT LADY, THE(1947); TIME OUT OF MIND(1947)
Lillian Fontaine
LOCKET, THE(1946); IVY(1947); SUDDENLY IT'S SPRING(1947); BIGA-MIST,THE(1953)
Lorne H. Fontaine
Silents
GILDED DREAM, THE(1920), w
Peter Fontaine
LOOK BEFORE YOU LOVE(1948, Brit.); DISTANT TRUMPET(1952, Brit.); DATE WITH DISASTER(1957, Brit.); STRANGE CASE OF DR. MANNING, THE(1958, Brit.); MIDNIGHT LACE(1960); CONFESSIONS OF A WINDOW CLEANER(1974, Brit.)
Richard Fontaine
HAPPY BIRTHDAY, DAVY(1970), p, d
Misc. Talkies
SINS OF RACHEL, THE(1975), d
Robert Fontaine
HAPPY TIME, THE(1952), w
William Fontaine
HALLELUJAH(1929)
William E. Fontaine
Misc. Silents
DECEIT(1923); VIRGIN OF SEMINOLE, THE(1923)
Gabrielle Fontan
DAYBREAK(1940, Fr.); APRES L'AMOUR(1948, Fr.); SYLVIA AND THE PHAN-TOM(1950, Fr.); TRAPEZE(1956); DEADLIER THAN THE MALE(1957, Fr.); GATES OF PARIS(1958, Fr./Ital.); JULIE THE REDHEAD(1963, Fr.)
Misc. Silents
GARDIENS DE PHARE(1929, Fr.)

Fontana
BAREFOOT CONTESSA, THE(1954), cos
Chris Fontana
HEART LIKE A WHEEL(1983)
Don Fontana
SPRING FEVER(1983, Can.)
Frank Fontana [Franco Fantasia]
RED-DRAGON(1967, Ital./Ger./US)
Franco Fontana
IL GRIDO(1962, U.S./Ital.), art d; LOVE, THE ITALIAN WAY(1964, Ital.), art d; MC GUIRE, GO HOME!(1966, Brit.), art d; OPERATION KID BROTHER(1967, Ital.), art d
Gilda Fontana
LAST TIME I SAW PARIS, THE(1954); SON OF SINBAD(1955); TALL MEN, THE(1955)
Jimmy Fontana
CRAZY DESIRE(1964, Ital.)
Paul Fontana
1984
HOT AND DEADLY(1984), m
Sorelle Fontana
GIDGET GOES TO ROME(1963), cos
Sorelle Fontana "Roma"
LE AMICHE(1962, Ital.), cos
Fontana Sisters
SUN ALSO RISES, THE(1957), cos
Manuel Fontanal
CASTLE OF PURITY(1974, Mex.), set d
Manuel Fontanals
TORCH, THE(1950), art d; INVASION OF THE VAMPIRES, THE(1961, Mex.), art d; MACARIO(1961, Mex.), art d; CURSE OF THE DOLL PEOPLE, THE(1968, Mex.), art d; SHARK(1970, U.S./Mex.), art d
Frederique Fontanarosa
BRIDE WORE BLACK, THE(1968, Fr./Ital.)
Renaud Fontanarosa
BRIDE WORE BLACK, THE(1968, Fr./Ital.)
Gabrielle Fontane
WAYS OF LOVE(1950, Ital./Fr.)
Theodor Fontane
EFFI BRIEST(1974, Ger.), w
Genevieve Fontanei
COCKTAIL MOLOTOV(1980, Fr.)
Genervievre Fontanel
MADAME ROSA(1977, Fr.)
Genevieve Fontanel
MONKEY IN WINTER, A(1962, Fr.); MAN WHO LOVED WOMEN, THE(1977, Fr.)
Deckard Fontanes
1984
DELIVERY BOYS(1984)
Lynn Fontanne
GUARDSMAN, THE(1931); STAGE DOOR CANTEEN(1943)
Lynne Fontanne
Silents
SECOND YOUTH(1924)
Eugenio Fontano
STRANGE DECEPTION(1953, Ital.), p
Jacqueline Fontel
PICNIC ON THE GRASS(1960, Fr.)
C.S. Fontelieu
WOMEN AND BLOODY TERROR(1970)
Stocker Fontelieu
MANDINGO(1975); OBSESSION(1976); FRENCH QUARTER(1978); TOY, THE(1982)
Catherine Fontenay
POIL DE CAROTTE(1932, Fr.); SYMPHONIE FANTASTIQUE(1947, Fr.); I SPIT ON YOUR GRAVE(1962, Fr.); LONG ABSENCE, THE(1962, Fr./Ital.)
Regis Fontenay
MY UNCLE(1958, Fr.)
Jacques Fonterary
FRENCH CONNECTION 11(1975), cos
Jacques Fonteray
RAPTURE(1965), cos; MARCO THE MAGNIFICENT(1966, Ital./Fr./Yugo./Egypt/ Afghanistan), cos; KING OF HEARTS(1967, Fr./Ital.), cos; UPPER HAND, THE(1967, Fr./Ital./Ger.), cos; SPIRITS OF THE DEAD(1969, Fr./Ital.), cos; DELUSIONS OF GRANDEUR(1971 Fr.), cos; BLUEBEARD(1972), cos; MOONRAKER(1979, Brit.), cos
Jacques Fonterey
BORSALINO(1970, Fr.), cos
Dame Margot Fonteyn
SWAN LAKE, THE(1967)
Margot Fonteyn
LITTLE BALLERINA, THE(1951, Brit.); ROMEO AND JULIET(1966, Brit.)
Jamie Fonti
MONKEY GRIP(1983, Aus.)
Cleto Fontini
INVINCIBLE GLADIATOR, THE(1963, c.u. Ital./Span.), p, w; GLADIATORS 7(1964, Span./Ital.), p; SECRET SEVEN, THE(1966, Ital./Span.), p; LIGHTNING BOLT(1967, Ital./Sp.), p
Lloyd Fonvielle
LORDS OF DISCIPLINE, THE(1983), w
Chee Foo
LIEUTENANT DARING, RN(1935, Brit.)
Lee Tong Foo
MR. WONG IN CHINATOWN(1939); MYSTERY OF MR. WONG, THE(1939); THE-RE'S A GIRL IN MY HEART(1949)
Lee Tung Foo
GENERAL DIED AT DAWN, THE(1936); SECRETS OF THE WASTELANDS(1941); ACROSS THE PACIFIC(1942); SOMEWHERE I'LL FIND YOU(1942); BEHIND THE RISING SUN(1943); MISSION TO MOSCOW(1943); DRAGON SEED(1944); THEY WERE EXPENDABLE(1945); IT SHOULDN'T HAPPEN TO A DOG(1946); CALCUT-TA(1947); CHINESE RING, THE(1947); CHECKERED COAT, THE(1948); LUXURY LINER(1948); MYSTERY OF THE GOLDEN EYE, THE(1948); SAIGON(1948); STRANGE GAMBLE(1948); STRATTON STORY, THE(1949); CARIBOO TRAIL,

THE(1950); SHORT GRASS(1950); THING, THE(1951); MACAO(1952); LOVE IS A MANY-SPLENDORED THING(1955); BADLANDS OF MONTANA(1957); MANCHURIAN CANDIDATE, THE(1962)

Lee Tung- Foo
THEY MET IN BOMBAY(1941)

Mah Foo
THE BEACHCOMBER(1938, Brit.)

Mei Lee Foo
BEHIND THE RISING SUN(1943); JACK LONDON(1943)

Tung Foo
CRISS CROSS(1949)

Wing Foo
DESTINATION TOKYO(1944); PURPLE HEART, THE(1944); PEKING EXPRESS(1951)

Wong Foo
Silents
PEACOCK FAN(1929)

Ralph Foody
MICKEY ONE(1965)

Richard Fools Bull
MAN CALLED HORSE, A(1970)

Frederick A. Foord
Silents
AMERICAN VENUS, THE(1926), art d

Kimberley Foorman
1984
POLICE ACADEMY(1984)

Teddy Brown Reginald Foort
DREAMING(1944, Brit.)

Annette Foosamer
WILD HARVEST(1962)

Annette Foosaner
LOVE CHILD(1982)

Alistair Foot
NO SEX PLEASE–WE'RE BRITISH(1979, Brit.), w

Geoff Foot
SUNBURN(1979), ed

Geoffrey Foot
GENGHIS KHAN(U.S./Brit./Ger./Yugo), ed; TAKE MY LIFE(1948, Brit.), ed; ONE WOMAN'S STORY(1949, Brit.), ed; MADELEINE(1950, Brit.), ed; GALLOPING MAJOR, THE(1951, Brit.), ed; BREAKING THE SOUND BARRIER(1952), ed; ROB ROY, THE HIGHLAND ROGUE(1954, Brit.), ed; INNOCENTS IN PARIS(1955, Brit.), ed; ONE GOOD TURN(1955, Brit.), ed; TROUBLE IN STORE(1955, Brit.), ed; SHE PLAYED WITH FIRE(1957, Brit.), ed; VALUE FOR MONEY(1957, Brit.), ed; ANOTHER TIME, ANOTHER PLACE(1958), ed; BLUE MURDER AT ST. TRINIAN'S(1958, Brit.), ed; BRIDAL PATH, THE(1959, Brit.), ed; LEFT, RIGHT AND CENTRE(1959), ed; IN THE NICK(1960, Brit.), ed; JAZZ BOAT(1960, Brit.), ed; KILLERS OF KILIMANJARO(1960, Brit.), ed; MAN WITH THE GREEN CARNATION, THE(1960, Brit.), ed; I LIKE MONEY(1962, Brit.), ed; MAIN ATTRACTION, THE(1962, Brit.), ed; POSTMAN'S KNOCK(1962, Brit.), ed; LONG SHIPS, THE(1964, Brit./Yugo.), ed; JOHNNY NOBODY(1965, Brit.), ed; GREAT ST. TRINIAN'S TRAIN ROBBERY, THE(1966, Brit.), ed; HAMMERHEAD(1968), ed; DESPERADOS, THE(1969), ed; RUN WILD, RUN FREE(1969, Brit.), ed; SUDDEN TERROR(1970, Brit.), ed; MAN IN THE WILDERNESS(1971, U.S./Span.), ed; DEATHLINE(1973, Brit.), ed; LEGEND OF HELL HOUSE, THE(1973, Brit.), ed; CONFESSIONS OF A POP PERFORMER(1975, Brit.), ed; CONFESSIONS FROM A HOLIDAY CAMP(1977, Brit.), ed; STAND UP VIRGIN SOLDIERS(1977, Brit.), ed; WATCHER IN THE WOODS, THE(1980, Brit.), ed

Michael Foot
MAD LITTLE ISLAND(1958, Brit.)

Moira Foot
ONE BRIEF SUMMER(1971, Brit.)

Bradbury Foote
BRIDE WORE RED, THE(1937), w; OF HUMAN HEARTS(1938), w; EDISON, THE MAN(1940), w; YOUNG TOM EDISON(1940), w; BILLY THE KID(1941), w; LADY, LET'S DANCE(1944), w; MADONNA'S SECRET, THE(1946), w; HIGH WALL, THE(1947), w; HOMICIDE FOR THREE(1948), w; KING OF THE GAMBLERS(1948), w; PRISONERS IN PETTICOATS(1950), w; MILLION DOLLAR PURSUIT(1951), w

Courtenay Foote
Silents
HOME SWEET HOME(1914); PURSUIT OF THE PHANTOM, THE(1914); CAPRICES OF KITTY, THE(1915); CAPTAIN COURTESY(1915); ASHES OF VENGEANCE(1923); TESS OF THE D'URBERVILLES(1924)
Misc. Silents
BUCKSHOT JOHN(1915); UP FROM THE DEPTHS(1915); CROSS CURRENTS(1916); LOVE'S CONQUEST(1918); LOVE'S LAW(1918); HIS PARISIAN WIFE(1919); TWO BRIDES, THE(1919); STAR ROVER, THE(1920); PASSION FLOWER, THE(1921); MADONNA OF THE STREETS(1924)

Courteney Foote
Silents
FALSE COLORS(1914)

Courtney Foote
Silents
BRONZE BELL, THE(1921)

Dick Foote
BAD MEN OF TOMBSTONE(1949); STREETS OF LAREDO(1949); BLUE GRASS OF KENTUCKY(1950); SADDLE LEGION(1951); CRASHING LAS VEGAS(1956)

Fred Foote
SILENT RAIDERS(1954)

Freddy Foote
JUNKET 89(1970, Brit.)

Frederick J. Foote
THEM!(1954)

Gene Foote
HEADIN' FOR BROADWAY(1980)

Hallie Foote
1984
C.H.U.D.(1984)

Horton Foote
STORM FEAR(1956), w; TO KILL A MOCKINGBIRD(1962), w; BABY, THE RAIN MUST FALL(1965), w; CHASE, THE(1966), w; HURRY SUNDOWN(1967), w; TOMORROW(1972), w; TENDER MERCIES(1982), p, w

Jennifer Foote
OH, HEAVENLY DOG!(1980)

John Tainter Foote
STORY OF SEABISCUIT, THE(1949), w

John Tainton Foote
MARK OF ZORRO, THE(1940), w

John Taintor Foote
KENTUCKY(1938), w; BROADWAY SERENADE(1939), w; SWANEE RIVER(1939), w; GREAT DAN PATCH, THE(1949), p&w
Silents
CONVOY(1927), w

Richard Foote
WILD HORSE MESA(1947); SIDESHOW(1950); YOUNG DANIEL BOONE(1950); DANGEROUS CHARTER(1962)

Sharon Foote
LITTLE SEX, A(1982)

Tex Foote
OUTBACK(1971, Aus.)

Hulbert Footner
Silents
SEALED VALLEY, THE(1915), w; MILLIONAIRE, THE(1921), w; YOUTH TO YOUTH(1922), w; HUNTRESS, THE(1923), w; RAMSHACKLE HOUSE(1924), w

Lois Foraker
DIRTY HARRY(1971)
1984
GREMLINS(1984)

Tom Foral
STRAWBERRY STATEMENT, THE(1970); BELIEVE IN ME(1971)

Arthur Foran, Jr.
KISS OF DEATH(1947)

Dick Foran
ACCENT ON YOUTH(1935); FARMER TAKES A WIFE, THE(1935); SHIPMATES FOREVER(1935); BIG NOISE, THE(1936); DANGEROUS(1936); EARTHWORM TRACTORS(1936); MOONLIGHT ON THE PRAIRIE(1936); PETRIFIED FOREST, THE(1936); PUBLIC ENEMY'S WIFE(1936); SONG OF THE SADDLE(1936); TRAILIN' WEST(1936); TREACHERY RIDES THE RANGE(1936); BLACK LEGION, THE(1937); BLAZING SIXES(1937); CALIFORNIA MAIL, THE(1937); CHEROKEE STRIP(1937); DEVIL'S SADDLE LEGION, THE(1937); EMPTY HOLSTERS(1937); GUNS OF THE PECOS(1937); LAND BEYOND THE LAW(1937); PERFECT SPECIMEN, THE(1937); PRAIRIE THUNDER(1937); SHE LOVED A FIREMAN(1937); BOY MEETS GIRL(1938); COWBOY FROM BROOKLYN(1938); FOUR DAUGHTERS(1938); HEART OF THE NORTH(1938); LOVE, HONOR AND BEHAVE(1938); OVER THE WALL(1938); SECRETS OF A NURSE(1938); SISTERS, THE(1938); DAUGHTERS COURAGEOUS(1939); FOUR WIVES(1939); HERO FOR A DAY(1939); I STOLE A MILLION(1939); INSIDE INFORMATION(1939); PRIVATE DETECTIVE(1939); FIGHTING 69TH, THE(1940); HOUSE OF THE SEVEN GABLES, THE(1940); MUMMY'S HAND, THE(1940); MY LITTLE CHICKADEE(1940); RANGERS OF FORTUNE(1940); FOUR MOTHERS(1941); HORROR ISLAND(1941); IN THE NAVY(1941); KEEP 'EM FLYING(1941); KID FROM KANSAS, THE(1941); MOB TOWN(1941); ROAD AGENT(1941); UNFINISHED BUSINESS(1941); BEHIND THE EIGHT BALL(1942); BUTCH MINDS THE BABY(1942); MUMMY'S TOMB, THE(1942); PRIVATE BUCKAROO(1942); RIDE 'EM COWBOY(1942); HE'S MY GUY(1943); HI, BUDDY(1943); EASY COME, EASY GO(1947); FORT APACHE(1948); DEPUTY MARSHAL(1949); EL PASO(1949); AL JENNINGS OF OKLAHOMA(1951); TREASURE OF RUBY HILLS(1955); PLEASE MURDER ME(1956); CHICAGO CONFIDENTIAL(1957); SIERRA STRANGER(1957); FEARMAKERS, THE(1958); THUNDERING JETS(1958); VIOLENT ROAD(1958); ATOMIC SUBMARINE, THE(1960); BIG NIGHT, THE(1960); STUDS LONIGAN(1960); DONOVAN'S REEF(1963); TAGGART(1964); BRIGHTY OF THE GRAND CANYON(1967)

James Foran
FORBIDDEN VALLEY(1938)

Mary Foran
SKIRTS AHOY!(1952); CLOWN, THE(1953); THE HYPNOTIC EYE(1960)

Mike Foran
EXPERIMENT IN TERROR(1962)

Nick [Dick] Foran
CHANGE OF HEART(1934); GENTLEMEN ARE BORN(1934); STAND UP AND CHEER(1934 80m FOX bw); IT'S A SMALL WORLD(1935); LADIES LOVE DANGER(1935); LOTTERY LOVER(1935); ONE MORE SPRING(1935)

Richard Foran
GUEST WIFE(1945)

June Foray
HINDU, THE(1953, Brit.); SNOW QUEEN, THE(1959, USSR); MAN CALLED FLINTSTONE, THE(1966); PHANTOM TOLLBOOTH, THE(1970)
Misc. Talkies
LOONEY, LOONEY, LOONEY BUGS BUNNY MOVIE, THE(1981)

June R. Foray
DAFFY DUCK'S MOVIE: FANTASTIC ISLAND(1983)

Katia Forbert
ALL-AROUND REDUCED PERSONALITY–OUTTAKES, THE(1978, Ger.), ph

Alan Forbes
ANOTHER SKY(1960 Brit.)

Alice Forbes
Silents
NOT GUILTY(1921)

Archibald Forbes
CHINA(1943), w

Brenda Forbes
PERFECT GENTLEMAN, THE(1935); VIGIL IN THE NIGHT(1940); MRS. MINIVER(1942); THIS ABOVE ALL(1942); WHITE CLIFFS OF DOVER, THE(1944)

Bryan Forbes
HELL, HEAVEN OR HOBOKEN(1958, Brit.), a, w; YESTERDAY'S ENEMY(1959, Brit.); ALL OVER THE TOWN(1949, Brit.); DEAR MR. PROHACK(1949, Brit.); HOUR OF GLORY(1949, Brit.); GREEN GROW THE RUSHES(1951, Brit.); WOODEN HORSE, THE(1951); FLESH AND FURY(1952); WORLD IN HIS ARMS, THE(1952); APPOINTMENT IN LONDON(1953, Brit.); SEA DEVILS(1953); WHEEL OF FATE(1953, Brit.);

INSPECTOR CALLS, AN(1954, Brit.); MAN WITH A MILLION(1954, Brit.); UP TO HIS NECK(1954, Brit.); COCKLESHELL HEROES, THE(1955), w; COLDITZ STORY, THE(1955, Brit.); PASSAGE HOME(1955, Brit.); BLACK TENT, THE(1956, Brit.), w; EXTRA DAY, THE(1956, Brit.); IT'S GREAT TO BE YOUNG(1956, Brit.); NOW AND FOREVER(1956, Brit.); SATELLITE IN THE SKY(1956); BABY AND THE BATTLESHIP, THE(1957, Brit.); ENEMY FROM SPACE(1957, Brit.); TRIPLE DECEPTION(1957, Brit.), w; KEY, THE(1958, Brit.); ANGRY SILENCE, THE(1960, Brit.), p, w; BREAKOUT(1960, Brit.), w; CAPTAIN'S TABLE, THE(1960, Brit.), w,John Whiting; GUNS OF NAVARONE, THE(1961); LEAGUE OF GENTLEMEN, THE(1961, Brit.), a, w; MAN IN THE MOON(1961, Brit.), w; WHISTLE DOWN THE WIND(1961, Brit.), d; L-SHAPED ROOM, THE(1962, Brit.), d&w; ONLY TWO CAN PLAY(1962, Brit.), w; OF HUMAN BONDAGE(1964, Brit.), a, d, w; SEANCE ON A WET AFTERNOON(1964 Brit.), p, d&w; STATION SIX-SAHARA(1964, Brit./Ger.), w; KING RAT(1965), d&w; MC GUIRE, GO HOME!(1966, Brit.), w; WRONG BOX, THE(1966, Brit.), p&d; WHISPERERS, THE(1967, Brit.), d&w; DEADFALL(1968, Brit.), d&w; MADWOMAN OF CHAILLOT, THE(1969), d; LONG AGO, TOMORROW(1971, Brit.), d&w; STEPFORD WIVES, THE(1975), d; SLIPPER AND THE ROSE, THE(1976, Brit.), a, d, w; INTERNATIONAL VELVET(1978, Brit.), p,d&w; HOPSCOTCH(1980), w; SUNDAY LOVERS(1980, Ital./Fr.), d; BETTER LATE THAN NEVER(1983), d&w
1984
  NAKED FACE, THE(1984), d, w
C. Scott Forbes
  PENTHOUSE, THE(1967, Brit.), w; PERFECT FRIDAY(1970, Brit.), w
Carole Forbes
  PIRATES OF PENZANCE, THE(1983)
Chris Forbes
  SLEEPER(1973); MOONRUNNERS(1975)
Christiana Forbes
  MARK OF CAIN, THE(1948, Brit.)
Christina Forbes
  2,000 WOMEN(1944, Brit.); SLEEPING CAR TO TRIESTE(1949, Brit.); PANDORA AND THE FLYING DUTCHMAN(1951, Brit.)
Christine Forbes
  MECHANIC, THE(1972)
Colin Forbes
  AVALANCHE EXPRESS(1979), w
Collette Forbes
Silents
  BLIND HEARTS(1921)
Don Forbes
  YESTERDAY'S HEROES(1940); SECRET AGENT OF JAPAN(1942); IN THIS CORNER(1948); LEFT HAND OF GOD, THE(1955)
Eileen Forbes
  MIRACLE IN SOHO(1957, Brit.)
Emma Forbes
  LONG AGO, TOMORROW(1971, Brit.)
Esther Forbes
  JOHNNY TREMAIN(1957), w
Francine Forbes
1984
  SPLATTER UNIVERSITY(1984)
Freddie Forbes
  MURDER AT THE CABARET(1936, Brit.); MUSIC HALL PARADE(1939, Brit.); OLD MOTHER RILEY AT HOME(1945, Brit.)
Gary Forbes
  HUMAN FACTOR, THE(1979, Brit.)
Gerald E. Forbes
  HAPPY MOTHER'S DAY... LOVE, GEORGE(1973)
Harry Forbes
  RED-HAIRED ALIBI, THE(1932), ph; DARING DAUGHTERS(1933), ph; IMPORTANT WITNESS, THE(1933), ph; REFORM GIRL(1933), ph; BIG TIME OR BUST(1934), ph; MARRYING WIDOWS(1934), ph; THUNDER OVER TEXAS(1934), ph; STORM OVER THE ANDES(1935), ph; WHAT PRICE CRIME?(1935), ph; DANGEROUS WATERS(1936), ph; FEDERAL AGENT(1936), ph; TOO MUCH BEEF(1936), ph; WHAT PRICE VENGEANCE?(1937), ph; CLIPPED WINGS(1938), w; WOMAN AGAINST THE WORLD(1938), ph; DEATH GOES NORTH(1939), ph; HEADLEYS AT HOME, THE(1939), ph
Hazel Forbes
  DOWN TO THEIR LAST YACHT(1934)
Henry Forbes
  FURY AND THE WOMAN(1937), ph
James Forbes
  INSPIRATION(1931), w; BACHELOR'S AFFAIRS(1932), w
James Grant Forbes
  THEIR OWN DESIRE(1929), w
John Forbes [John Carpenter]
  OUTLAW TREASURE(1955); I KILLED WILD BILL HICKOK(1956)
Kathryn Forbes
  I REMEMBER MAMA(1948), w
Kenneth Forbes
  AT WAR WITH THE ARMY(1950)
Lee Forbes
  NAKED WITCH, THE(1964)
Leonie Forbes
  CHILDREN OF BABYLON(1980, Jamaica)
Lou Forbes
  NIGHT KEY(1937), md; OH DOCTOR(1937), md; SHE'S DANGEROUS(1937), md; ADVENTURES OF TOM SAWYER, THE(1938), md; LITTLE ORPHAN ANNIE(1938), md; INTERMEZZO: A LOVE STORY(1939), md; MADE FOR EACH OTHER(1939), m, md; POT O' GOLD(1941), md; TOMORROW IS FOREVER(1946), md; JET OVER THE ATLANTIC(1960), m
Louis Forbes
  NOTHING SACRED(1937), md; GONE WITH THE WIND(1939), md; SINCE YOU WENT AWAY(1944), m; UP IN ARMS(1944), md; GETTING GERTIE'S GARTER(1945), md; STORY OF G.I. JOE, THE(1945), md; WONDER MAN(1945), md; FABULOUS DORSEYS, THE(1947), md; INTRIGUE(1947), m; PITFALL(1948), m; CROOKED WAY, THE(1949), m; MRS. MIKE(1949), md; JOHNNY ONE-EYE(1950), md; HOME TOWN STORY(1951), m; MAN WHO CHEATED HIMSELF, THE(1951), m; APPOINTMENT IN HONDURAS(1953), m; COUNT THE HOURS(1953), m; CATTLE

QUEEN OF MONTANA(1954), m; PASSION(1954), md; SILVER LODE(1954), m; ESCAPE TO BURMA(1955), m; PEARL OF THE SOUTH PACIFIC(1955), m; TENNESSEE'S PARTNER(1955), m; SLIGHTLY SCARLET(1956), m; RIVER'S EDGE, THE(1957), m; FROM THE EARTH TO THE MOON(1958), m; HONG KONG AFFAIR(1958), m; BAT, THE(1959), m; MOST DANGEROUS MAN ALIVE, THE(1961), m
Madeleine Forbes
  WILSON(1944)
Marcia Forbes
  TOYS ARE NOT FOR CHILDREN(1972)
Marion Forbes
  GOIN' HOME(1976)
Mary Elizabeth Forbes
  HOLIDAY(1930)
Misc. Silents
  CHILD IN JUDGEMENT, A(1915)
Mary Forbes
  HER PRIVATE LIFE(1929); SUNNY SIDE UP(1929); TRESPASSER, THE(1929); DEVIL TO PAY, THE(1930); EAST IS WEST(1930); SO THIS IS LONDON(1930); STRICTLY UNCONVENTIONAL(1930); THIRTEENTH CHAIR, THE(1930); BORN TO LOVE(1931); BRAT, THE(1931); CHANCES(1931); MAN WHO CAME BACK, THE(1931); WORKING GIRLS(1931); FAREWELL TO ARMS, A(1932); SILENT WITNESS, THE(1932); STEPPING SISTERS(1932); VANITY FAIR(1932); BOMBSHELL(1933); CAVALCADE(1933); BORN TO BE BAD(1934); BRITISH AGENT(1934); HAPPINESS AHEAD(1934); LOST LADY, A(1934); MOST PRECIOUS THING IN LIFE(1934); NOW I'LL TELL(1934); SADIE MCKEE(1934); SHOCK(1934); TWO HEADS ON A PILLOW(1934); WE LIVE AGAIN(1934); YOU CAN'T BUY EVERYTHING(1934); ANNA KARENINA(1935); CAPTAIN BLOOD(1935); LADDIE(1935); LES MISERABLES(1935); MC FADDEN'S FLATS(1935); PERFECT GENTLEMAN, THE(1935); ROBERTA(1935); STRANDED(1935); DIZZY DAMES(1936); SMALL TOWN GIRL(1936); THEODORA GOES WILD(1936); WIDOW FROM MONTE CARLO, THE(1936); ANOTHER DAWN(1937); AWFUL TRUTH, THE(1937); STAGE DOOR(1937); WEE WILLIE WINKIE(1937); WOMEN OF GLAMOUR(1937); 100 MEN AND A GIRL(1937); ALWAYS GOODBYE(1938); EVERYBODY SING(1938); OUTSIDE OF PARADISE(1938); YOU CAN'T TAKE IT WITH YOU(1938); ADVENTURES OF SHERLOCK HOLMES, THE(1939); HOLLYWOOD CAVALCADE(1939); ICE FOLLIES OF 1939(1939); NINOTCHKA(1939); OUTSIDE THESE WALLS(1939); RISKY BUSINESS(1939); SHOULD HUSBANDS WORK?(1939); SUN NEVER SETS, THE(1939); THESE GLAMOUR GIRLS(1939); YOU CAN'T CHEAT AN HONEST MAN(1939); ALL THIS AND HEAVEN TOO(1940); FLORIAN(1940); LADDIE(1940); PRIVATE AFFAIRS(1940); SOUTH OF SUEZ(1940); NOTHING BUT THE TRUTH(1941); PARIS CALLING(1941); WHEN LADIES MEET(1941); ALMOST MARRIED(1942); GREAT IMPERSONATION, THE(1942); KLONDIKE FURY(1942); THIS ABOVE ALL(1942); WE WERE DANCING(1942); DANGEROUS BLONDES(1943); FLESH AND FANTASY(1943); MR. LUCKY(1943); SHERLOCK HOLMES IN WASHINGTON(1943); TENDER COMRADE(1943); TWO TICKETS TO LONDON(1943); WHAT A WOMAN!(1943); WOMEN IN BONDAGE(1943); JANE EYRE(1944); EARL CARROLL'S VANITIES(1945); GUY, A GAL AND A PAL, A(1945); I'LL REMEMBER APRIL(1945); LADY ON A TRAIN(1945); PICTURE OF DORIAN GRAY, THE(1945); KID FROM BOOKLYN, THE(1946); STOLEN LIFE, A(1946); TERROR BY NIGHT(1946); CIGARETTE GIRL(1947); DOWN TO EARTH(1947); EXILE, THE(1947); IT HAD TO BE YOU(1947); IVY(1947); OTHER LOVE, THE(1947); SECRET LIFE OF WALTER MITTY, THE(1947); SONG OF LOVE(1947); YOU GOTTA STAY HAPPY(1948); LES MISERABLES(1952); HOUSEBOAT(1958)
Misc. Silents
  WOMEN WHO WIN(1919, Brit.); NANCE(1920, Brit.)
Meriel Forbes
  BORROW A MILLION(1934, Brit.); CASE FOR THE CROWN, THE(1934, Brit.); GIRLS PLEASE!(1934, Brit.); VINTAGE WINE(1935, Brit.); BELLES OF ST. CLEMENTS, THE(1936, Brit.); MR. COHEN TAKES A WALK(1936, Brit.); COME ON GEORGE(1939, Brit.); OVER THE MOON(1940, Brit.); BELLS GO DOWN, THE(1943, Brit.); GENTLE SEX, THE(1943, Brit.); YOUNG MAN'S FANCY(1943, Brit.); CAPTIVE HEART, THE(1948, Brit.); LONG DARK HALL, THE(1951, Brit.); MURDER ON MONDAY(1953, Brit.); OH! WHAT A LOVELY WAR(1969, Brit.)
Murray Forbes
  HOLLOW TRIUMPH(1948), w; BIG CATCH, THE(1968, Brit.)
Norman Forbes
Misc. Silents
  SECOND MRS. TANQUERAY, THE(1916, Brit.)
Phyllis Forbes
  ARABIAN NIGHTS(1942); WONDER MAN(1945)
Ralph Forbes
  GREEN GODDESS, THE(1930); HER WEDDING NIGHT(1930); INSIDE THE LINES(1930); LADY OF SCANDAL, THE(1930); LILIES OF THE FIELD(1930); MAMBA(1930); BACHELOR FATHER(1931); BEAU IDEAL(1931); SMILIN' THROUGH(1932); THUNDER BELOW(1932); AVENGER, THE(1933); CHRISTOPHER STRONG(1933); PHANTOM BROADCAST, THE(1933); PLEASURE CRUISE(1933); SOLITAIRE MAN, THE(1933); BARRETTS OF WIMPOLE STREET, THE(1934); BOMBAY MAIL(1934); FOUNTAIN, THE(1934); MYSTERY OF MR. X, THE(1934); OUTCAST LADY(1934); SHOCK(1934); TWENTIETH CENTURY(1934); AGE OF INDISCRETION(1935); ENCHANTED APRIL(1935); GOOSE AND THE GANDER, THE(1935); RESCUE SQUAD(1935); STRANGE WIVES(1935); STREAMLINE EXPRESS(1935); THREE MUSKETEERS(1935); DANIEL BOONE(1936); LOVE LETTERS OF A STAR(1936); MARY OF SCOTLAND(1936); PICCADILLY JIM(1936); ROMEO AND JULIET(1936); LAST OF MRS. CHEYNEY, THE(1937); LEGION OF MISSING MEN(1937); MAKE A WISH(1937); STAGE DOOR(1937); THIRTEENTH CHAIR, THE(1937); ANNABEL TAKES A TOUR(1938); CONVICTS AT LARGE(1938); IF I WERE KING(1938); KIDNAPPED(1938); WOMAN AGAINST THE WORLD(1938); WOMEN ARE LIKE THAT(1938); HOUND OF THE BASKERVILLES, THE(1939); MAGNIFICENT FRAUD, THE(1939); PRIVATE LIVES OF ELIZABETH AND ESSEX, THE(1939); TOWER OF LONDON(1939); CALLING PHILO VANCE(1940); CURTAIN CALL(1940); FRENCHMAN'S CREEK(1944)
Misc. Talkies
  I'LL NAME THE MURDERER(1936)
Silents
  OWD BOB(1924, Brit.); BEAU GESTE(1926); ENEMY, THE(1927); MR. WU(1927); ACTRESS, THE(1928); LATEST FROM PARIS, THE(1928); TRAIL OF '98, THE(1929)
Misc. Silents
  FIFTH FORM AT ST. DOMINIC'S, THE(1921, Brit.); LOWLAND CINDERELLA, A(1921, Brit.); COMIN' THRO' THE RYE(1923, Brit.); REVEILLE(1924, Brit.); RESTLESS YOUTH(1928); UNDER THE BLACK EAGLE(1928); WHIP, THE(1928)

Ralpi Forbes
ADVENTURE IN DIAMONDS(1940)
Sarah Forbes
WHISPERERS, THE(1967, Brit.); LONG AGO, TOMORROW(1971, Brit.)
Scott Forbes [Julian Dallas]
ROCKY MOUNTAIN(1950); DESERT FOX, THE(1951); HIGHWAYMAN, THE(1951); INSIDE THE WALLS OF FOLSOM PRISON(1951); OPERATION PACIFIC(1951); RATON PASS(1951); RELUCTANT WIDOW, THE(1951, Brit.); WHAT PRICE GLORY?(1952); CHARADE(1953); SUBTERFUGE(1969, US/Brit.); MIND OF MR. SOAMES, THE(1970, Brit.)
Sheila Forbes
PSYCHOMANIA(1964)
Sonny Forbes
CITY ON FIRE(1979 Can.)
Stanton Forbes
REFLECTION OF FEAR, A(1973), w
Violet Forbes
Silents
HUTCH STIRS 'EM UP(1923, Brit.)
William Forbes
UNEASY TERMS(1948, Brit.)
Michele Forbes-Fraser
SOMEWHERE IN FRANCE(1943, Brit.)
John Forbes-Robertson
KATHLEEN(1938, Ireland); SALUTE THE TOFF(1952, Brit.); BABY AND THE BATTLESHIP, THE(1957, Brit.); MODEL MURDER CASE, THE(1964, Brit.); BUNNY LAKE IS MISSING(1965); FIGHTING PRINCE OF DONEGAL, THE(1966, Brit.); PARTNER, THE(1966, Brit.); SPY WITH A COLD NOSE, THE(1966, Brit.); VAULT OF HORROR, THE(1973, Brit.); VENOM(1982, Brit.)
Johnston Forbes-Robertson
Silents
HAMLET(1913, Brit.)
Misc. Silents
PASSING OF THE THIRD FLOOR BACK, THE(1918, Brit.)
Peter Forbes-Robertson
CASE OF CHARLES PEACE, THE(1949, Brit.); THOSE PEOPLE NEXT DOOR(1952, Brit.); MODEL MURDER CASE, THE(1964, Brit.); ISLAND OF TERROR(1967, Brit.)
Sir Johnstone Forbes-Robertson
Misc. Silents
MASKS AND FACES(1917, Brit.)
Frank Forbes-Robinson
DANNY BOY(1934, Brit.)
Peter Forbes-Robinson
NIGHT AFTER NIGHT AFTER NIGHT(1970, Brit.)
Leo Forbstein
SALLY(1929), md; BLONDE CRAZY(1931), md; FIVE STAR FINAL(1931), md; LITTLE CAESAR(1931), md; HIGH PRESSURE(1932), md; TWO SECONDS(1932), md; WORLD CHANGES, THE(1933), m; FOG OVER FRISCO(1934), m; HEAT LIGHTNING(1934), md; TWENTY MILLION SWEETHEARTS(1934); COLLEEN(1936), md; DANGEROUS(1936), m; SING ME A LOVE SONG(1936), md; BOY MEETS GIRL(1938), md; EACH DAWN I DIE(1939), md; KING OF THE UNDERWORLD(1939), md; CASABLANCA(1942), md; CONSPIRATORS, THE(1944), md; DEVOTION(1946), md
Leo B. Forbstein
EVER SINCE EVE(1937), md; MALTESE FALCON, THE(1941), md; MANPOWER(1941), md
Leo F. Forbstein
BROADWAY BABIES(1929), md; SQUALL, THE(1929), m; DAWN PATROL, THE(1930), m; DOORWAY TO HELL(1930), m; SHOW GIRL IN HOLLYWOOD(1930), md; SINNER'S HOLIDAY(1930), md; SONG OF THE FLAME(1930), md; LOCAL BOY MAKES GOOD(1931), md; MILLIONAIRE, THE(1931), md; OTHER MEN'S WOMEN(1931), md; SMART MONEY(1931), md; TOO YOUNG TO MARRY(1931), md; BIG CITY BLUES(1932), md; CROWD ROARS, THE(1932), md; I AM A FUGITIVE FROM A CHAIN GANG(1932), m; STREET OF WOMEN(1932), md; TAXI!(1932), md; THREE ON A MATCH(1932), md; TIGER SHARK(1932), m; WINNER TAKE ALL(1932), md; FOOTLIGHT PARADE(1933), md; GOLD DIGGERS OF 1933(1933), md; HARD TO HANDLE(1933), md; KEYHOLE, THE(1933), md; LADIES THEY TALK ABOUT(1933), md; LADY KILLER(1933), md; LITTLE GIANT, THE(1933), md; MARY STEVENS, M.D.(1933), md; MAYOR OF HELL, THE(1933), md; PICTURE SNATCHER(1933), md; SOMEWHERE IN SONORA(1933), m; 20,000 YEARS IN SING SING(1933), md; 42ND STREET(1933), md; BABBITT(1934), m; BRITISH AGENT(1934), m; DAMES(1934), md; DOCTOR MONICA(1934), md; FASHIONS OF 1934(1934), md; FLIRTATION WALK(1934), md; HAROLD TEEN(1934), md; HE WAS HER MAN(1934), md; HERE COMES THE NAVY(1934), md; HOUSEWIFE(1934), md; SMARTY(1934), md; ST. LOUIS KID, THE(1934), md; TWENTY MILLION SWEETHEARTS(1934), md; UPPER WORLD(1934), md; WONDER BAR(1934), md; ALIBI IKE(1935), md; CASE OF THE LUCKY LEGS, THE(1935), md; CEILNG ZERO(1935), m; DEVIL DOGS OF THE AIR(1935), m; DON'T BET ON BLONDES(1935), md; DR. SOCRATES(1935), md; FRISCO KID(1935), md; FRONT PAGE WOMAN(1935), md; G-MEN(1935), md; GIRL FROM TENTH AVENUE, THE(1935), md; GOING HIGHBROW(1935), md; GOOSE AND THE GANDER, THE(1935), md; I FOUND STELLA PARISH(1935), md; IN CALIENTE(1935), md; IRISH IN US, THE(1935), md; LITTLE BIG SHOT(1935), m, md; LIVING ON VELVET(1935), md; MAN OF IRON(1935), md; MIDSUMMER'S NIGHT'S DREAM, A(1935), md; MISS PACIFIC FLEET(1935), md; OIL FOR THE LAMPS OF CHINA(1935), md; PAGE MISS GLORY(1935), md; PAYOFF, THE(1935), md; PERSONAL MAID'S SECRET(1935), md; SHIPMATES FOREVER(1935), md; SPECIAL AGENT(1935), md; STARS OVER BROADWAY(1935), md; STRANDED(1935), md; SWEET ADELINE(1935), md; TRAVELING SALESLADY, THE(1935), md; WE'RE IN THE MONEY(1935), md; ANTHONY ADVERSE(1936), md; CAIN AND MABEL(1936), md; FRESHMAN LOVE(1936), md; GIVE ME YOUR HEART(1936), md; GOLD DIGGERS OF 1937(1936), md; GOLDEN ARROW, THE(1936), md; I MARRIED A DOCTOR(1936), md; MOONLIGHT ON THE PRAIRIE(1936), md; MURDER OF DR. HARRIGAN, THE(1936), md; PETRIFIED FOREST, THE(1936), md; SATAN MET A LADY(1936), md; SINGING KID, THE(1936), md; SNOWED UNDER(1936), md; SONG OF THE SADDLE(1936), md; SONS O' GUNS(1936), md; STAGE STRUCK(1936), md; STORY OF LOUIS PASTEUR, THE(1936), md; THREE MEN ON A HORSE(1936), md; TREACHERY RIDES THE RANGE(1936), md; WHITE ANGEL, THE(1936), md; WIDOW FROM MONTE CARLO, THE(1936), md; BACK IN CIRCULATION(1937), m; CONFESSION(1937), md; FIRST LADY(1937), m; GO-GETTER, THE(1937), md; GREAT GARRICK, THE(1937), md;

HOLLYWOOD HOTEL(1937), md; IT'S LOVE I'M AFTER(1937), md; KID GALAHAD(1937), md; KING AND THE CHORUS GIRL, THE(1937), md; LIFE OF EMILE ZOLA, THE(1937), md; MARKED WOMAN(1937), md; MELODY FOR TWO(1937), md; MOUNTAIN JUSTICE(1937), md; MR. DODD TAKES THE AIR(1937), md; PERFECT SPECIMEN, THE(1937), md; PRINCE AND THE PAUPER, THE(1937), md; SLIM(1937), md; STOLEN HOLIDAY(1937), md; SUBMARINE D-1(1937), md; THAT CERTAIN WOMAN(1937), md; THEY WON'T FORGET(1937), md; TOVARICH(1937), md; BROTHER RAT(1938), m; COMET OVER BROADWAY(1938), md; COWBOY FROM BROOKLYN(1938), md; FOOLS FOR SCANDAL(1938), md; GARDEN OF THE MOON(1938), md; GOLD DIGGERS IN PARIS(1938), md; GOLD IS WHERE YOU FIND IT(1938), md; HARD TO GET(1938), md; JEZEBEL(1938), md; SECRETS OF AN ACTRESS(1938), md; SISTERS, THE(1938), md; SLIGHT CASE OF MURDER, A(1938), md; SWING YOUR LADY(1938), md; VALLEY OF THE GIANTS(1938), md; WHITE BANNERS(1938), md; WOMEN ARE LIKE THAT(1938), md; ANGELS WASH THEIR FACES(1939), md; BLACKWELL'S ISLAND(1939), md; DARK VICTORY(1939), md; FOUR WIVES(1939), md; GOING PLACES(1939), md; JUAREZ(1939), md; NAUGHTY BUT NICE(1939), md; OFF THE RECORD(1939), md; OLD MAID, THE(1939), md; ROARING TWENTIES, THE(1939), md; THEY MADE ME A CRIMINAL(1939), md; WINGS OF THE NAVY(1939), md; WOMEN IN THE WIND(1939), md; ALL THIS AND HEAVEN TOO(1940), md; CASTLE ON THE HUDSON(1940), m; DISPATCH FROM REUTERS, A(1940), md; FIGHTING 69TH, THE(1940), md; KNUTE ROCKNE–ALL AMERICAN(1940), md; LADY WITH RED HAIR(1940), md; LETTER, THE(1940), md; MY LOVE CAME BACK(1940), md; NO TIME FOR COMEDY(1940), m; SEA HAWK, THE(1940), md; SOUTH OF SUEZ(1940), md; 'TIL WE MEET AGAIN(1940), md; TORRID ZONE(1940), md; AFFECTIONATELY YOURS(1941), md; BRIDE CAME C.O.D., THE(1941), md; CITY, FOR CONQUEST(1941), md; DIVE BOMBER(1941), md; FLIGHT FROM DESTINY(1941), md; GREAT LIE, THE(1941), md; HIGH SIERRA(1941), md; MEET JOHN DOE(1941), md; OUT OF THE FOG(1941), md; UNDERGROUND(1941), md; GAY SISTERS, THE(1942), md; IN THIS OUR LIFE(1942), md; LARCENY, INC.(1942), md; MAN WHO CAME TO DINNER, THE(1942), md; NOW, VOYAGER(1942), md; THEY DIED WITH THEIR BOOTS ON(1942), md; WINGS FOR THE EAGLE(1942), md; YANKEE DOODLE DANDY(1942), md; AIR FORCE(1943), md; BACKGROUND TO DANGER(1943), md; CONSTANT NYMPH, THE(1943), md; NORTHERN PURSUIT(1943), md; OLD ACQUAINTANCE(1943), md; PRINCESS O'ROURKE(1943), md; THANK YOUR LUCKY STARS(1943), md; THIS IS THE ARMY(1943), md; DESTINATION TOKYO(1944), md; HOLLYWOOD CANTEEN(1944), md; IN OUR TIME(1944), md; JANIE(1944), md; MAKE YOUR OWN BED(1944), md; MASK OF DIMITRIOS, THE(1944), md; MR. SKEFFINGTON(1944), md; SHINE ON, HARVEST MOON(1944), md; TO HAVE AND HAVE NOT(1944), md; UNCERTAIN GLORY(1944), md; VERY THOUGHT OF YOU, THE(1944), md; CHRISTMAS IN CONNECTICUT(1945), md; CONFLICT(1945), md; DANGER SIGNAL(1945), md; ESCAPE IN THE DESERT(1945), md; GOD IS MY CO-PILOT(1945), md; HORN BLOWS AT MIDNIGHT, THE(1945), md; MILDRED PIERCE(1945), md; OBJECTIVE, BURMA!(1945), md; PILLOW TO POST(1945), md; PRIDE OF THE MARINES(1945), md; RHAPSODY IN BLUE(1945), md; ROUGHLY SPEAKING(1945), md; SAN ANTONIO(1945), md; SARATOGA TRUNK(1945), md; TOO YOUNG TO KNOW(1945), md; BIG SLEEP, THE(1946), md; CLOAK AND DAGGER(1946), md; DECEPTION(1946), md; HER KIND OF MAN(1946), md; HUMORESQUE(1946), md; JANIE GETS MARRIED(1946), md; MAN I LOVE, THE(1946), md; MY REPUTATION(1946), md; NEVER SAY GOODBYE(1946), md; NIGHT AND DAY(1946), md; NOBODY LIVES FOREVER(1946), md; OF HUMAN BONDAGE(1946), md; ONE MORE TOMORROW(1946), md; SHADOW OF A WOMAN(1946), md; STOLEN LIFE, A(1946), md; THREE STRANGERS(1946), md; DARK PASSAGE(1947), md; LIFE WITH FATHER(1947), md; LOVE AND LEARN(1947), md; MY WILD IRISH ROSE(1947), md; NORA PRENTISS(1947), md; POSSESSED(1947), md; PURSUED(1947), md; STALLION ROAD(1947), md; THAT HAGEN GIRL(1947), md; THAT WAY WITH WOMEN(1947), md; TWO MRS. CARROLLS, THE(1947), md; UNFAITHFUL, THE(1947), md; UNSUSPECTED, THE(1947), md; VOICE OF THE TURTLE, THE(1947), md; BIG PUNCH, THE(1948), md; DECISION OF CHRISTOPHER BLAKE, THE(1948), md; MY GIRL TISA(1948), md; ROMANCE ON THE HIGH SEAS(1948), md; ROPE(1948), m; TO THE VICTOR(1948), md; TREASURE OF THE SIERRA MADRE, THE(1948), md; TWO GUYS FROM TEXAS(1948), md; WALLFLOWER(1948), md; WHIPLASH(1948), md; WINTER MEETING(1948), md; WOMAN IN WHITE, THE(1948), md; NIGHT UNTO NIGHT(1949), md; ONE LAST FLING(1949), md
Charles Force
Silents
ATOM, THE(1918); SURGING SEAS(1924); GOLD RUSH, THE(1925)
Misc. Silents
HER HONOR THE MAYOR(1920); CUPID'S BRAND(1921); LONE RIDER, THE(1922); LOVE PIRATE, THE(1923)
Frank Force
1984
STAR TREK III: THE SEARCH FOR SPOCK(1984)
Jean Force
BORDER STREET(1950, Pol.), w
Ken Force
BINGO LONG TRAVELING ALL-STARS AND MOTOR KINGS, THE(1976)
Lewis Force
CLEGG(1969, Brit.), p
Lewis J. Force
NIGHT AFTER NIGHT AFTER NIGHT(1970, Brit.), d
Roy Force-Smith
ONLY GOD KNOWS(1974, Can.), art d
Ray Forchion
NOBODY'S PERFEKT(1981); SMOKEY AND THE BANDIT–PART 3(1983)
Raymond George Forchion
HOT STUFF(1979)
Carl Forcht
STALAG 17(1953)
Ada Ford
Misc. Silents
GOD'S PRODIGAL(1923, Brit.)
Alan Ford
SQUEEZE, THE(1977, Brit.); VENOM(1982, Brit.)
Aleksander Ford
BORDER STREET(1950, Pol.), d, w; KNIGHTS OF THE TEUTONIC ORDER, THE(1962, Pol.), d, w; MARTYR, THE(1976, Ger./Israel), d

Alexander Ford
EIGHTH DAY OF THE WEEK, THE(1959, Pol./Ger.), d, w

Amy Ford
DREAM ON(1981)

Anitra Ford
BIG BIRD CAGE, THE(1972); INVASION OF THE BEE GIRLS(1973); STACEY!(1973); DEAD PEOPLE(1974); LONGEST YARD, THE(1974)

Ann Ford
SON OF SINBAD(1955); LOVE MACHINE, THE,(1971); LOGAN'S RUN(1976)

Anna Ford
FINAL OPTION, THE(1983, Brit.)

Anne Ford
FRENCH LINE, THE(1954)

Anthony Ford
STRANGE SHADOWS IN AN EMPTY ROOM(1977, Can./Ital.), ph

Art Ford
COUNTRY MUSIC HOLIDAY(1958); SING, BOY, SING(1958)

Athol Ford
Silents
AS HE WAS BORN(1919, Brit.)

Audrey Ford
AIR HOSTESS(1949)

Barry Ford
VON RYAN'S EXPRESS(1965); WINNING(1969); LADIES AND GENTLEMEN, THE FABULOUS STAINS(1982)

Bert Ford
KEEPERS OF YOUTH(1931, Brit.), ph

Bette Ford
HONKYTONK MAN(1982); SUDDEN IMPACT(1983)

Bill Ford
DREAM OF KINGS, A(1969), set d

Billie Ford
Misc. Silents
FOUR FROM NOWHERE, THE(1925)

Bob Ford
GUADALCANAL DIARY(1943)

Brian D. Ford
OFFICER AND A GENTLEMAN, AN(1982)

Bryant Ford
STRANGERS IN THE NIGHT(1944), w

Brylo Ford
EXORCISM AT MIDNIGHT(1966, Brit. revised 1973, U.S.)

Carole Ann Ford
MIX ME A PERSON(1962, Brit.); DAY OF THE TRIFFIDS, THE(1963); GREAT ST. TRINIAN'S TRAIN ROBBERY, THE(1966, Brit.); MAN OUTSIDE, THE(1968, Brit.)

Cecil F. Ford
SQUADRON 633(1964, U.S./Brit.), p; 633 SQUADRON(1964), p

Cecil Ford
MEN OF IRELAND(1938, Ireland)

Celeste Ford
MIDNIGHT CLUB(1933)

Charles E. Ford
BILLY THE KID RETURNS(1938), p; MAN FROM MUSIC MOUNTAIN(1938), p; SHINE ON, HARVEST MOON(1938), p; COME ON RANGERS(1939), p

Charlotte Ford
LOVE STORY(1970)

Clebert Ford
TRICK BABY(1973); NIGHTHAWKS(1981)

Corey Ford
HER BODYGUARD(1933), w

Constance Ford
LAST HUNT, THE(1956); BAILOUT AT 43,000(1957); IRON SHERIFF, THE(1957); SUMMER PLACE, A(1959); HOME FROM THE HILL(1960); CLAUDELLE INGLISH(1961); ALL FALL DOWN(1962); CABINET OF CALIGARI, THE(1962); HOUSE OF WOMEN(1962); ROME ADVENTURE(1962); SHOOT OUT AT BIG SAG(1962); CARETAKERS, THE(1963); 99 AND 44/100% DEAD(1974)

Corey Ford
SOPHOMORE, THE(1929), w; HALF-NAKED TRUTH, THE(1932), w; SPORT PARADE, THE(1932), w; START CHEERING(1938), w; REMEMBER?(1939), w; TOPPER TAKES A TRIP(1939), w; WINTER CARNIVAL(1939), w; ZENOBIA(1939), w

Daisy Ford
DOUBLE CROSS(1941); REG'LAR FELLERS(1941)

Damon Ford
WEDDING PRESENT(1936)

Daniel Ford
GO TELL THE SPARTANS(1978), w

David Ford
MIDDLE OF THE NIGHT(1959); LOVING(1970); 1776(1972)

David L. Ford
WINDSPLITTER, THE(1971), p

Derek Ford
GUTTER GIRLS(1964, Brit.), w; SATURDAY NIGHT OUT(1964, Brit.), w; BLACK TORMENT, THE(1965, Brit.), w; STUDY IN TERROR, A(1966, Brit./Ger.), w; CORRUPTION(1968, Brit.), w; HELL BOATS(1970, Brit.), w; I AM A GROUPIE(1970, Brit.), d, w; SWAPPERS, THE(1970, Brit.), d, w; THIS, THAT AND THE OTHER(1970, Brit.), d, w; SUBURBAN WIVES(1973, Brit.), d&w; HOUSE THAT VANISHED, THE(1974, Brit.), w; GIRL FROM STARSHIP VENUS, THE(1975, Brit.), d&w
1984
DON'T OPEN TILL CHRISTMAS(1984, Brit.), w

Derrick Champ Ford
EDUCATION OF SONNY CARSON, THE(1974)

Donald Ford
GUTTER GIRLS(1964, Brit.), w; SATURDAY NIGHT OUT(1964, Brit.), w; STORK TALK(1964, Brit.), w; BLACK TORMENT, THE(1965, Brit.), w; STUDY IN TERROR, A(1966, Brit./Ger.), w; CORRUPTION(1968, Brit.), w; HELL BOATS(1970, Brit.), w; THIS, THAT AND THE OTHER(1970, Brit.), w

Dorothy Ford
LADY IN THE DARK(1944); HERE COME THE CO-EDS(1945); NOB HILL(1945); LOVE LAUGHS AT ANDY HARDY(1946); LOVER COME BACK(1946); ON OUR MERRY WAY(1948); ONE SUNDAY AFTERNOON(1948); THREE GODFATHERS,

THE(1948); SANDS OF IWO JIMA(1949); KEY TO THE CITY(1950); FLAME OF ARABY(1951); LET'S GO NAVY(1951); FEUDIN' FOOLS(1952); JACK AND THE BEANSTALK(1952); PERILOUS JOURNEY, A(1953); SEVEN YEAR ITCH, THE(1955); GUN BROTHERS(1956); PARDNERS(1956); WRONG BOX, THE(1966, Brit.); OCTOPUSSY(1983, Brit.), stunts

Eugene Ford
Misc. Silents
INNOCENCE OF LIZETTE, THE(1917); BIG DIAMOND ROBBERY, THE(1929), d

Eugenie Ford
Silents
MEMORY LANE(1926)

Evelyn Ford
FOUR GIRLS IN TOWN(1956); SOUTH PACIFIC(1958)

Frances Ford
FREE SOUL, A(1931)

Francis Ford
BLACK WATCH, THE(1929); ABRAHAM LINCOLN(1930); KATHLEEN MAVOURNEEN(1930); MOUNTED STRANGER, THE(1930); SONG OF THE CABELLERO(1930); SONS OF THE SADDLE(1930); FRANKENSTEIN(1931); SEAS BENEATH, THE(1931); AIR MAIL(1932); DESTRY RIDES AGAIN(1932); LAST RIDE, THE(1932); CHARLIE CHAN'S GREATEST CASE(1933); DR. BULL(1933); LIFE IN THE RAW(1933); MAN FROM MONTEREY, THE(1933); PILGRIMAGE(1933); ROMAN SCANDALS(1933); CHARLIE CHAN'S COURAGE(1934); GUN JUSTICE(1934); JUDGE PRIEST(1934); LOST PATROL, THE(1934); MURDER IN TRINIDAD(1934); WORLD MOVES ON, THE(1934); ARIZONIAN, THE(1935); GOIN' TO TOWN(1935); INFORMER, THE(1935); PADDY O'DAY(1935); STEAMBOAT ROUND THE BEND(1935); THIS IS THE LIFE(1935); WHOLE TOWN'S TALKING, THE(1935); CHARLIE CHAN AT THE CIRCUS(1936); CHARLIE CHAN'S SECRET(1936); EDUCATING FATHER(1936); GENTLE JULIA(1936); PLOUGH AND THE STARS, THE(1936); PRISONER OF SHARK ISLAND, THE(1936); SINS OF MAN(1936); CHECKERS(1937); LAST TRAIN FROM MADRID, THE(1937); PLAINSMAN, THE(1937); PRISONER OF ZENDA, THE(1937); ROAD BACK,THE(1937); SLAVE SHIP(1937); STAR IS BORN, A(1937); GIRL OF THE GOLDEN WEST, THE(1938); IN OLD CHICAGO(1938); KENTUCKY MOONSHINE(1938); TEXANS, THE(1938); BAD LANDS(1939); DRUMS ALONG THE MOHAWK(1939); GERONIMO(1939); STAGECOACH(1939); YOUNG MR. LINCOLN(1939); DIAMOND FRONTIER(1940); GRAPES OF WRATH(1940); LUCKY CISCO KID(1940); MAN FROM DAKOTA, THE(1940); SOUTH OF PAGO PAGO(1940); VIVA CISCO KID(1940); LAST OF THE DUANES(1941); TOBACCO ROAD(1941); WESTERN UNION(1941); LOVES OF EDGAR ALLAN POE, THE(1942); MAN WHO WOULDN'T DIE, THE(1942); OUTLAWS OF PINE RIDGE(1942); THEY DIED WITH THEIR BOOTS ON(1942); DESPERADOES, THE(1943); GIRLS IN CHAINS(1943); JITTERBUGS(1943); OX-BOW INCIDENT, THE(1943); BIG NOISE, THE(1944); BOWERY CHAMPS(1944); PRINCESS AND THE PIRATE, THE(1944); HANGOVER SQUARE(1945); INCENDIARY BLONDE(1945); MURDER, HE SAYS(1945); SAN ANTONIO(1945); STATE FAIR(1945); WILDFIRE(1945); ACCOMPLICE(1946); MY DARLING CLEMENTINE(1946); RENEGADES(1946); WAKE UP AND DREAM(1946); BANDITS OF DARK CANYON(1947); DRIFTWOOD(1947); HIGH TIDE(1947); UNCONQUERED(1947); EYES OF TEXAS(1948); FEUDIN', FUSSIN' AND A-FIGHTIN'(1948); FORT APACHE(1948); PLUNDERERS, THE(1948); THREE GODFATHERS, THE(1948); TIMBER TRAIL, THE(1948); FAR FRONTIER, THE(1949); FRONTIER INVESTIGATOR(1949); SAN ANTONE AMBUSH(1949); SHE WORE A YELLOW RIBBON(1949); FATHER MAKES GOOD(1950); WAGONMASTER(1950); LAWLESS BREED, THE(1952); QUIET MAN, THE(1952); TOUGHEST MAN IN ARIZONA(1952); IT HAPPENS EVERY THURSDAY(1953); MARSHAL'S DAUGHTER, THE(1953); SUN SHINES BRIGHT, THE(1953)
Silents
WASHINGTON AT VALLEY FORGE(1914), a, d&w; CAMPBELLS ARE COMING, THE(1915), a, d; AVENGING TRAIL, THE(1918), d; CRAVING, THE(1918), a, d&w; ANOTHER MAN'S BOOTS(1922); SO THIS IS ARIZONA(1922), a, d; TRAIL'S END(1922), d; HEARTS OF OAK(1924); LASH OF THE WHIP(1924), a, d&w; MEASURE OF A MAN, THE(1924); SPEED COP(1926); ONE GLORIOUS SCRAP(1927); LARIAT KID, THE(1929)
Misc. Silents
IN TREASON'S GRASP(1917), a, d; JOHN ERMINE OF THE YELLOWSTONE(1917), a, d; WHO WAS THE OTHER MAN?(1917), a, d; BERLIN VIA AMERICA(1918), a, d; ISLE OF INTRIGUE, THE(1918), a, d; CRIMSON SHOALS(1919), a, d; MAN FROM NOWHERE, A(1920), d; ACTION(1921); CYCLONE BLISS(1921), a, d; I AM THE WOMAN(1921), a, d; STAMPEDE, THE(1921), a, d; ANGEL CITIZENS(1922), a, d; BOSS OF CAMP 4, THE(1922); CROSS ROADS(1922), d; GOLD GRABBERS(1922), d; HEART OF LINCOLN, THE(1922), a, d; STORM GIRL(1922), a, d; THEY'RE OFF(1922), a, d; THUNDERING HOOFS(1922), a, d; COWBOY PRINCE, THE(1924), d; CUPID'S RUSTLER(1924), d; DIAMOND BANDIT, THE(1924), d; IN THE DAYS OF THE COVERED WAGON(1924), d; LASH OF PINTO PETE, THE(1924), d; MIDNIGHT SHADOWS(1924), d; RANGE BLOOD(1924), d; RODEO MIXUP, A(1924), a, d; WESTERN FEUDS(1924), d; WESTERN YESTERDAYS(1924), d; FOUR FROM NOWHERE, THE(1925), a, d; SIGN OF THE CACTUS, THE(1925); SOFT SHOES(1925); FALSE FRIENDS(1926), d; GHETTO SHAMROCK, THE(1926), d; HER OWN STORY(1926), d; MELODIES(1926), d; OFFICER 444(1926), d; DEVIL'S SADDLE, THE(1927); MEN OF DARING(1927); ONE GLORIOUS SCRAP(1927); WOLF'S TRAIL(1927), d; WOLVES OF THE AIR(1927), d; WRECK OF THE HESPERUS, THE(1927); BRANDED SOMBRERO, THE(1928); CALL OF THE HEART(1928), d

Franis Ford
Misc. Silents
RIDIN' THUNDER(1925)

Frank E. Ford
SPOOK WHO SAT BY THE DOOR, THE(1973)

Freddie Ford
FLAMINGO AFFAIR, THE(1948, Brit.), ph

Freddy Ford
PRIVATE ANGELO(1949, Brit.), spec eff

Frederick Ford
TURNERS OF PROSPECT ROAD, THE(1947, Brit.), ph; REVOLT AT FORT LARAMIE(1957); TOMAHAWK TRAIL(1957); FLAMING FRONTIER(1958, Can.), ph; WOLF DOG(1958, Can.), ph

Fritz Ford
MISTER ROBERTS(1955); BRIDGE AT REMAGEN, THE(1969); LAST MOVIE, THE(1971); MACK, THE(1973); CHALLENGE TO BE FREE(1976); DAMIEN–OMEN II(1978); NATIONAL LAMPOON'S VACATION(1983)

Garrett Ford
  RETURN OF SHERLOCK HOLMES(1936), w
George Ford
  I MARRIED AN ANGEL(1942); MAYOR OF 44TH STREET, THE(1942); GOVERN-MENT GIRL(1943); LOUISIANA HAYRIDE(1944); SAILOR'S HOLIDAY(1944); EVE KNEW HER APPLES(1945); DRAGONWYCH(1946); DICK BARTON-SPECIAL AGENT(1948, Brit.); DICK BARTON AT BAY(1950, Brit.); SHOW BOAT(1951); TURN-ING POINT, THE(1952); PAL JOEY(1957)
Glen Ford
  MR. SOFT TOUCH(1949)
Glenn Ford
  3:10 TO YUMA(1957; HEAVEN WITH A BARBED WIRE FENCE(1939); BABIES FOR SALE(1940); BLONDIE PLAYS CUPID(1940); CONVICTED WOMAN(1940); LADY IN QUESTION, THE(1940); MEN WITHOUT SOULS(1940); MY SON IS GUILTY(1940); GO WEST, YOUNG LADY(1941); SO ENDS OUR NIGHT(1941); TEXAS(1941); ADVEN-TURES OF MARTIN EDEN, THE(1942); FLIGHT LIEUTENANT(1942); DE-SPERADOES, THE(1943); DESTROYER(1943); GALLANT JOURNEY(1946); GILDA(1946); STOLEN LIFE, A(1946); FRAMED(1947); LOVES OF CARMEN, THE(1948); MAN FROM COLORADO, THE(1948); MATING OF MILLIE, THE(1948); RETURN OF OCTOBER, THE(1948); DOCTOR AND THE GIRL, THE(1949); LUST FOR GOLD(1949); UNDERCOVER MAN, THE(1949); CONVICTED(1950); FLYING MIS-SILE(1950); REDHEAD AND THE COWBOY, THE(1950); WHITE TOWER, THE(1950); FOLLOW THE SUN(1951); SECRET OF CONVICT LAKE, THE(1951); AFFAIR IN TRINIDAD(1952); GREEN GLOVE, THE(1952); YOUNG MAN WITH IDEAS(1952); APPOINTMENT IN HONDURAS(1953); BIG HEAT, THE(1953); MAN FROM THE ALAMO, THE(1953); PLUNDER OF THE SUN(1953); TERROR ON A TRAIN(1953); HUMAN DESIRE(1954); AMERICANO, THE(1955); BLACKBOARD JUNGLE, THE(1955); INTERRUPTED MELODY(1955); TRIAL(1955); VIOLENT MEN, THE(1955); FASTEST GUN ALIVE(1956); JUBAL(1956); RANSOM(1956); TEAHOUSE OF THE AUGUST MOON, THE(1956); COWBOY(1958); IMITATION GENERAL(1958); SHEEPMAN, THE(1958); TORPEDO RUN(1958); GAZEBO, THE(1959); IT STARTED WITH A KISS(1959); CIMARRON(1960); CRY FOR HAPPY(1961); POCKETFUL OF MIRACLES(1961); EXPERIMENT IN TERROR(1962); FOUR HORSEMEN OF THE APOCALYPSE, THE(1962); COURTSHIP OF EDDY'S FATHER, THE(1963); LOVE IS A BALL(1963); ADVANCE TO THE REAR(1964); DEAR HEART(1964); FATE IS THE HUNTER(1964); ROUNDERS, THE(1965); IS PARIS BURNING?(1966, U.S./Fr.); MONEY TRAP, THE(1966); RAGE(1966, U.S./Mex.); LAST CHALLENGE, THE(1967); TIME FOR KILLING, A(1967); DAY OF THE EVIL GUN(1968); HEAVEN WITH A GUN(1969); SMITH(1969); SANTEE(1973); DON'T GO NEAR THE WATER(1975); MIDWAY(1976); SUPERMAN(1978); VIRUS(1980, Jap.); VISITOR, THE(1980, Ital./U.S.); HAPPY BIRTHDAY TO ME(1981)
Gonzalee Ford
  DESPERATE CHARACTERS(1971)
Grace Ford
  DEVIL DOLL, THE(1936); BETWEEN TWO WOMEN(1937); BIG CITY(1937)
Greg Ford
  WINDSPLITTER, THE(1971)
Hal Ford
  Misc. Silents
  MAYBLOSSOM(1917)
Harriet Ford
  ARGYLE CASE, THE(1929), w; DUMMY, THE(1929), w; IN THE NEXT ROOM(1930), w; I MARRIED A DOCTOR(1936), w; CASE OF THE BLACK PARROT, THE(1941), w; MAKE YOUR OWN BED(1944), w
  Silents
  AUDREY(1916), w; ARGYLE CASE, THE(1917), w; LADY IN LOVE, A(1920), w
Harrison Ford
  DEAD HEAT ON A MERRY-GO-ROUND(1966); JOURNEY TO SHILOH(1968); GETTING STRAIGHT(1970); AMERICAN GRAFFITI(1973); CONVERSATION, THE(1974); HEROES(1977); STAR WARS(1977); FORCE 10 FROM NAVARONE(1978, Brit.); APOCALYPSE NOW(1979); FRISCO KID, THE(1979); HANOVER STREET(1979, Brit.); MORE AMERICAN GRAFFITI(1979); EMPIRE STRIKES BACK, THE(1980); RAIDERS OF THE LOST ARK(1981); BLADE RUNNER(1982); RETURN OF THE JEDI(1983)
  1984
  INDIANA JONES AND THE TEMPLE OF DOOM(1984)
Harrison Ford
  Misc. Talkies
  LOVE IN HIGH GEAR(1932)
  Silents
  ANTON THE TERRIBLE(1916); MOLLY ENTANGLED(1917); GOOD NIGHT, PAUL(1918); PAIR OF SILK STOCKINGS, A(1918); HAWTHORNE OF THE U.S.-A.(1919); ROMANCE AND ARABELLA(1919); EASY TO GET(1920); FOOD FOR SCANDAL(1920); LADY IN LOVE, A(1920); MISS HOBBS(1920); OH, LADY, LA-DY(1920); LOVE'S REDEMPTION(1921); HER GILDED CAGE(1922); SHA-DOWS(1922); AVERAGE WOMAN, THE(1924); JANICE MEREDITH(1924); PRICE OF A PARTY, THE(1924); "THAT ROYLE GIRL"(1925); PROUD FLESH(1925); ZANDER THE GREAT(1925); ALMOST A LADY(1926); NERVOUS WRECK, THE(1926); SAN-DY(1926); NIGHT BRIDE, THE(1927); NO CONTROL(1927); RUBBER TIRES(1927); RUSH HOUR, THE(1927); JUST MARRIED(1928); LET 'ER GO GALLEGHER(1928)
  Misc. Silents
  EXCUSE ME(1916); CRYSTAL GAZER, THE(1917); MYSTERIOUS MRS. M, THE(1917); ON THE LEVEL(1917); SUNSET TRAIL(1917); TIDES OF BARNEGAT, THE(1917); CRUISE OF THE MAKE-BELIEVES, THE(1918); LADY'S NAME, A(1918); MRS. LEFFINGWELL'S BOOTS(1918); PETTICOAT PILOT, A(1918); SAUCE FOR THE GOOSE(1918); SUCH A LITTLE PIRATE(1918); UNCLAIMED GOODS(1918); VI-VIETTE(1918); EXPERIMENTAL MARRIAGE(1919); GIRLS(1919); HAPPINESS A LA MODE(1919); LOTTERY MAN, THE(1919); THIRD KISS, THE(1919); VEILED ADVEN-TURE, THE(1919); WHO CARES?(1919); YOU NEVER SAID SUCH A GIRL(1919); HER BELOVED VILLIAN(1920); YOUNG MRS. WINTHROP(1920); HEART TO LET, A(1921); PASSION FLOWER, THE(1921); WEDDING BELLS(1921); WONDERFUL THING, THE(1921); FIND THE WOMAN(1922); PRIMITIVE LOVER, THE(1922); SMILIN' THROUGH(1922); WHEN LOVE COMES(1922); BRIGHT LIGHTS OF BROADWAY(1923); LITTLE OLD NEW YORK(1923); MAYTIME(1923); VANITY FAIR(1923); FOOL'S AWAKENING, A(1924); THREE MILES OUT(1924); LOVERS IN QUARANTINE(1925); MAD MARRIAGE, THE(1925); MARRIAGE WHIRL, THE(1925); WHEEL, THE(1925); HELL'S 400(1926); SONG AND DANCE MAN, THE(1926); UP IN MABEL'S ROOM(1926); GIRL IN THE PULLMAN, THE(1927); REJUVINATION OF AUNT MARY, THE(1927); BLONDE FOR A NIGHT, A(1928); GOLF WIDOWS(1928); THREE WEEK-ENDS(1928); WOMAN AGAINST THE

WORLD, A(1928)
Harrison J. Ford
  TIME FOR KILLING, A(1967)
Harry Ford
  Silents
  DIMPLES(1916)
Harry Chapman Ford
  Silents
  ANNA ASCENDS(1922), w
Helen Ford
  APARTMENT FOR PEGGY(1948); MODEL AND THE MARRIAGE BROKER, THE(1951); SECRET PEOPLE(1952, Brit.); SOUND OFF(1952); RAID, THE(1954)
Henry Ford
  EVERYTHING IN LIFE(1936, Brit.)
Hugh Ford
  Silents
  SUCH A LITTLE QUEEN(1914), d, w; ETERNAL CITY, THE(1915), d&w; PRINCE AND THE PAUPER, THE(1915), d&w; SOLD(1915), d, w; STILL WATERS(1915), w; DANGER MARK, THE(1918), d; CALL OF YOUTH, THE(1920, Brit.), d
  Misc. Silents
  CRUCIBLE, THE(1914), d; BELLA DONNA(1915), d; GRETNA GREEN(1915), d; JIM, THE PENMAN(1915), d; POOR SCHMALTZ(1915), d; WHEN WE WERE TWENTY-ONE(1915), d; LYDIA GILMORE(1916), d; WOMAN IN THE CASE, A(1916), d; SAPHO(1917), d; SEVEN KEYS TO BALDPATE(1917), d; SLAVE MARKET, THE(1917), d; SLEEPING FIRES(1917), d; MRS. DANE'S DEFENSE(1918), d; IN MIZZOURA(1919), d; MRS. WIGGS OF THE CABBAGE PATCH(1919), d; SECRET SERVICE(1919), d; WOMAN THOU GAVEST ME, THE(1919), d; CIVILIAN CLOTHES(1920), d; HIS HOUSE IN ORDER(1920), d; LADY ROSE'S DAUGHT-ER(1920), d; CALL OF YOUTH, THE(1921, Brit.), d; GREAT DAY, THE(1921, Brit.), d; PRICE OF POSSESSION, THE(1921), d
Hutchinson Ford
  BARNUM WAS RIGHT(1929), w
Ian Ford
  DREAM ON(1981)
J. Ford
  Misc. Talkies
  BLONDE GODDESS(1982)
Jack Ford
  LADY LUCK(1946); ESCAPE ME NEVER(1947)
  Silents
  CRAVING, THE(1918), d&w; OUTCASTS OF POKER FLAT, THE(1919), d; PRINCE OF AVENUE A., THE(1920), d; BIG PUNCH, THE(1921), d; WALLOP, THE(1921), d; LITTLE MISS SMILES(1922), d; NORTH OF HUDSON BAY(1923), d
Jack J. Ford
  HORN BLOWS AT MIDNIGHT, THE(1945); SHE WROTE THE BOOK(1946)
Jack [John] Ford
  Silents
  RIDERS OF VENGEANCE(1919), d, w; SILVER WINGS(1922), d
  Misc. Silents
  MARKED MAN, A(1917), d; SECRET MAN, THE(1917), d; STRAIGHT SHOO-TING(1917), d; BUCKING BROADWAY(1918), d; HELL BENT(1918), d; PHANTOM RIDERS, THE(1918), d; SCARLET DROP, THE(1918), d; THIEVES' GOLD(1918), d; THREE MOUNTED MEN(1918), d; WILD WOMEN(1918), d; WOMAN'S FOOL, A(1918), d; ACE OF THE SADDLE(1919), d; BARE FISTS(1919), d; FIGHT FOR LOVE, A(1919), d; GUN-FIGHTIN' GENTLEMAN, A(1919), d; RIDER OF THE LAW(1919), d; ROPED(1919), d; GIRL IN NUMBER 29, THE(1920), d; HITCHIN' POSTS(1920), d; JUST PALS(1920), d; MARKED MEN(1920), d; ACTION(1921), d; DESPERATE TRAILS(1921), d; FREEZE OUT, THE(1921), d; JACKIE(1921), d; SURE FIRE(1921), d; VILLAGE BLACKSMITH, THE(1922), d; FACE ON THE BARROOM FLOOR, THE(1923), d; THREE JUMPS AHEAD(1923), d
James Ford
  MAKING THE GRADE(1929); PRISONERS(1929); GREAT DIVIDE, THE(1930); WEDDING RINGS(1930); TEN CENTS A DANCE(1931); MOVIE CRAZY(1932); GREAT GUY(1936); MILKY WAY, THE(1936); MR. DODD TAKES THE AIR(1937); SLIGHTLY DANGEROUS(1943)
  Silents
  OUTCAST(1928)
  Misc. Silents
  WIZARD OF THE SADDLE(1928); CHILDREN OF THE RITZ(1929)
Jan Ford
  DEVIL ON WHEELS, THE(1947)
Jesse Hill Ford
  LIBERATION OF L.B. JONES, THE(1970), w
Jineane Ford
  1984
  CHATTANOOGA CHOO CHOO(1984)
Jo Ford
  NATE AND HAYES(1983, U.S./New Zealand), art d
John Ford
  BIG TIME(1929); BLACK WATCH, THE(1929), d; SALUTE(1929), d; BORN RECK-LESS(1930), d; MEN WITHOUT WOMEN(1930), d, w; UP THE RIVER(1930), d, w; ARROWSMITH(1931), d; BRAT, THE(1931), d; SEAS BENEATH, THE(1931), d; AIR MAIL(1932), d; FLESH(1932), d; DR. BULL(1933), d; PILGRIMAGE(1933), d; JUDGE PRIEST(1934), d; LOST PATROL, THE(1934), d; WORLD MOVES ON, THE(1934), d; INFORMER, THE(1935), d; STEAMBOAT ROUND THE BEND(1935), d; WHOLE TOWN'S TALKING, THE(1935), d; LAST OUTLAW, THE(1936), w; MARY OF SCOT-LAND(1936), d; PLOUGH AND THE STARS, THE(1936), d; PRISONER OF SHARK ISLAND, THE(1936), d; HURRICANE, THE(1937), d; MAN OF AFFAIRS(1937, Brit.); WEE WILLIE WINKIE(1937), d; FOUR MEN AND A PRAYER(1938), d; SUBMARINE PATROL(1938), d; DRUMS ALONG THE MOHAWK(1939), d; STAGECOACH(1939), d; YOUNG MR. LINCOLN(1939), d; GRAPES OF WRATH(1940), d; LONG VOYAGE HOME, THE(1940), d; HOW GREEN WAS MY VALLEY(1941), d; TOBACCO ROAD(1941), d; THEY WERE EXPENDABLE(1945), p, d; MY DARLING CLEMEN-TINE(1946), d; FUGITIVE, THE(1947), p, d; FORT APACHE(1948), p, d; THREE GODFATHERS, THE(1948), p, d; EVERYBODY DOES IT(1949); MIGHTY JOE YOUNG(1949); p; SHE WORE A YELLOW RIBBON(1949), p, d; RIO GRANDE(1950), p, d; WAGONMASTER(1950), p, d, w; WHEN WILLIE COMES MARCHING HO-ME(1950), d; TALES OF HOFFMANN, THE(1951, Brit.); QUIET MAN, THE(1952), p, d; WHAT PRICE GLORY?(1952), d; MOGAMBO(1953), d; SUN SHINES BRIGHT, THE(1953), p, d; LONG GRAY LINE, THE(1955), d; MISTER ROBERTS(1955), d;

SEARCHERS, THE(1956), d; RISING OF THE MOON, THE(1957, Ireland), d; WINGS OF EAGLES, THE(1957), d; LAST HURRAH, THE(1958), p&d; GIDEON OF SCOTLAND YARD(1959, Brit.), p, d; HORSE SOLDIERS, THE(1959), d; SERGEANT RUTLEDGE(1960), d; TWO RODE TOGETHER(1961), d; HOW THE WEST WAS WON(1962), d; MAN WHO SHOT LIBERTY VALANCE, THE(1962), d; DONOVAN'S REEF(1963), p&d; CHEYENNE AUTUMN(1964), d; YOUNG CASSIDY(1965, U.S./Brit.), d; SEVEN WOMEN(1966), d; 'TIS A PITY SHE'S A WHORE(1973, Ital.), w
Silents
HEARTS OF OAK(1924), d; IRON HORSE, THE(1924), d; FOUR SONS(1928), d; RILEY THE COP(1928), d; STRONG BOY(1929), d
Misc. Silents
CAMEO KIRBY(1923), d; HOODMAN BLIND(1923), d; FIGHTING HEART, THE(1925), d; KENTUCKY PRIDE(1925), d; LIGHTNIN'(1925), d; THANK YOU(1925), d; BLUE EAGLE, THE(1926), d; SHAMROCK HANDICAP, THE(1926), d; THREE BAD MEN(1926), d; UPSTREAM(1927), d; HANGMAN'S HOUSE(1928), d; MOTHER MACHREE(1928), d

Josephine Ford
WE OF THE NEVER NEVER(1983, Aus.), prod d

Judith Ford
BRINGING UP BABY(1938); CODE OF THE RANGERS(1938); GOLDWYN FOLLIES, THE(1938)

Judy Ford [Terry Moore]
MY GAL SAL(1942)

Julia Ford
TWO HEADS ON A PILLOW(1934)

Karen Ford
UNMARRIED WOMAN, AN(1978); WILLIE AND PHIL(1980)

Larkin Ford
Q(1982)

Lee Ford
IDOL OF THE CROWDS(1937); I STOLE A MILLION(1939)

Leicester Ford
Silents
GREAT K & A TRAIN ROBBERY, THE(1926), w

Lettie Ford
Silents
SPREADING DAWN, THE(1917)

Letty Ford
Misc. Silents
WEB OF DECEIT, THE(1920)

Lloyd Ford
GAME THAT KILLS, THE(1937); IDOL OF THE CROWDS(1937); HEAVENLY BODY, THE(1943)

Lonnie Ford
OVER-UNDER, SIDEWAYS-DOWN(1977)

Lottie Ford
Misc. Silents
HALF A ROGUE(1916)

Luci Ford
TRAIL TO SAN ANTONE(1947), w

Lucille Ford
I'VE GOT YOUR NUMBER(1934)

Marcia Ford
NO TIME TO KILL(1963, Brit./Swed./Ger.)

Mary Ford
QUEEN OF OUTER SPACE(1958); MISSILE TO THE MOON(1959); HELP!(1965, Brit.)
Silents
LOST CHORD, THE(1917, Brit.)

Mel Ford
MAGNIFICENT AMBERSONS, THE(1942)

Mercedes G. Ford
ROUSTABOUT(1964)

Michael Ford
VOYAGE TO THE BOTTOM OF THE SEA(1961); MADISON AVENUE(1962); DON'T WORRY, WE'LL THINK OF A TITLE(1966); MACHISMO–40 GRAVES FOR 40 GUNS(1970); LONGEST DAY, THE(1974); EMPIRE STRIKES BACK, THE(1980), set d; RAIDERS OF THE LOST ARK(1981), set d; RETURN OF THE JEDI(1983), set d

Michael C. Ford
SIMON, KING OF THE WITCHES(1971)

Mick Ford
SAILOR'S RETURN, THE(1978, Brit.); SCUM(1979, Brit.); LIGHT YEARS AWAY(1982, Fr./Switz.)

Mike Ford
KELLY'S HEROES(1970, U.S./Yugo.), set d

Montgomery Ford
LAST BLITZKRIEG, THE(1958)
Misc. Talkies
TODAY WE KILL...TOMORROW WE DIE(1971)

Montgomery Ford [Brett Halsey]
TODAY IT'S ME...TOMORROW YOU!(1968, Ital.)

Monty Ford
FALL GUY(1947)

Pam Ford
YELLOW SUBMARINE(1958, Brit.), animation

Patrick Ford
WAGONMASTER(1950), w; MISSOURI TRAVELER, THE(1958), p; YOUNG LAND, THE(1959), p; SERGEANT RUTLEDGE(1960), p

Paul Ford
HOUSE ON 92ND STREET, THE(1945); NAKED CITY, THE(1948); ALL THE KING'S MEN(1949); LUST FOR GOLD(1949); KID FROM TEXAS, THE(1950); PERFECT STRANGERS(1950); TEAHOUSE OF THE AUGUST MOON, THE(1956); MATCHMAKER, THE(1958); MISSOURI TRAVELER, THE(1958); ADVISE AND CONSENT(1962); MUSIC MAN, THE(1962); WHO'S GOT THE ACTION?(1962); IT'S A MAD, MAD, MAD, MAD WORLD(1963); NEVER TOO LATE(1965); BIG HAND FOR THE LITTLE LADY, A(1966); RUSSIANS ARE COMING, THE RUSSIANS ARE COMING, THE(1966); SPY WITH A COLD NOSE, THE(1966, Brit.); COMEDIANS, THE(1967); LOLA(1971, Brit./Ital.); RICHARD(1972); JOURNEY BACK TO OZ(1974)

Paul Leicester Ford
Silents
JANICE MEREDITH(1924), w

Peter Ford
ADVANCE TO THE REAR(1964); FATE IS THE HUNTER(1964); PROUD AND THE DAMNED, THE(1972); GALLIPOLI(1981, Aus.)

Phil Ford
INNER CIRCLE, THE(1946), d; SATURDAY NIGHT IN APPLE VALLEY(1965)
Silents
ACCORDING TO HOYLE(1922); PRIDE OF SUNSHINE ALLEY(1924)
Misc. Silents
STORM GIRL(1922); THUNDERING HOOFS(1922); FOUR FROM NOWHERE, THE(1925); OFFICER 444(1926)

Philip Ford
CRIME OF THE CENTURY(1946), d; INVISIBLE INFORMER(1946), d; LAST CROOKED MILE, THE(1946), d; MYSTERIOUS MR. VALENTINE, THE(1946), d; VALLEY OF THE ZOMBIES(1946), d; BANDITS OF DARK CANYON(1947), d; WEB OF DANGER, THE(1947), d; WILD FRONTIER, THE(1947), d; BOLD FRONTIERSMAN, THE(1948), d; DENVER KID, THE(1948), d; DESPERADOES OF DODGE CITY(1948), d; TIMBER TRAIL, THE(1948), d; TRAIN TO ALCATRAZ(1948), d; HIDEOUT(1949), d; LAW OF THE GOLDEN WEST(1949), d; OUTCASTS OF THE TRAIL(1949), d; POWDER RIVER RUSTLERS(1949), d; PRINCE OF THE PLAINS(1949), d; RANGER OF CHEROKEE STRIP(1949), d; SAN ANTONE AMBUSH(1949), d; SOUTH OF RIO(1949), d; WYOMING BANDIT, THE(1949), d; OLD FRONTIER, THE(1950), d; PIONEER MARSHAL(1950), d; PRISONERS IN PETTICOATS(1950), d; REDWOOD FOREST TRAIL(1950), d; TRIAL WITHOUT JURY(1950), d; VANISHING WESTERNER, THE(1950), d; DAKOTA KID, THE(1951), d; MISSING WOMEN(1951), d; PRIDE OF MARYLAND(1951), d; RODEO KING AND THE SENORITA(1951), d; UTAH WAGON TRAIN(1951), d; WELLS FARGO GUNMASTER(1951), d; BAL TABARIN(1952), d; DESPERADOES OUTPOST(1952), d

Phillip Ford
TIGER WOMAN, THE(1945), d; ANGEL IN EXILE(1948), d; CALIFORNIA FIREBRAND(1948), d; MARSHAL OF AMARILLO(1948), d; BUCKAROO SHERIFF OF TEXAS(1951), d

Rae Ford
Misc. Silents
AT THE OLD CROSSED ROADS(1914)

Ray Ford
WHEN DINOSAURS RULED THE EARTH(1971, Brit.)

Richard Ford
TERROR STREET(1953); PARATROOPER(1954, Brit.); LOVE MATCH, THE(1955, Brit.)

Robert Ford
MARGIE(1946); CLOWN, THE(1953); SECOND CHANCE(1953), ed; SPLIT SECOND(1953), ed; FRENCH LINE, THE(1954), ed; TOP OF THE WORLD(1955), ed; CONQUEROR, THE(1956), ed

Rosemarie Ford
NUTCRACKER(1982, Brit.)

Ross Ford
AIR FORCE(1943); MISSION TO MOSCOW(1943); MURDER ON THE WATERFRONT(1943); THIS IS THE ARMY(1943); LAST RIDE, THE(1944); CLOAK AND DAGGER(1946); DECEPTION(1946); DARK PASSAGE(1947); DEEP VALLEY(1947); MY WILD IRISH ROSE(1947); NORA PRENTISS(1947); UNFAITHFUL, THE(1947); UNSUSPECTED, THE(1947); VOICE OF THE TURTLE, THE(1947); BLONDIE'S REWARD(1948); FULLER BRUSH MAN(1948); GALLANT BLADE, THE(1948); JUNGLE PATROL(1948); MANHATTAN ANGEL(1948); SIGN OF THE RAM, THE(1948); SILVER RIVER(1948); AIR HOSTESS(1949); BARBARY PIRATE(1949); CHALLENGE TO LASSIE(1949); LAW OF THE BARBARY COAST(1949); NIGHT UNTO NIGHT(1949); FLYING MISSILE(1950); FRISCO TORNADO(1950); GIRLS' SCHOOL(1950); HE'S A COCKEYED WONDER(1950); FORCE OF ARMS(1951); ROUGH RIDERS OF DURANGO(1951); STREET BANDITS(1951); BLUE CANADIAN ROCKIES(1952); RAINBOW 'ROUND MY SHOULDER(1952); PROJECT MOONBASE(1953); REFORM SCHOOL GIRL(1957); OSCAR, THE(1966)

Roy Ford
ON HER MAJESTY'S SECRET SERVICE(1969, Brit.), ph; CALL HIM MR. SHATTER(1976, Hong Kong), ph; DRACULA AND THE SEVEN GOLDEN VAMPIRES(1978, Brit./Chi.), ph

Ruth Ford
SECRETS OF THE LONE WOLF(1941); ACROSS THE PACIFIC(1942); DEVIL'S TRAIL, THE(1942); ESCAPE FROM CRIME(1942); GORILLA MAN(1942); HIDDEN HAND, THE(1942); IN THIS OUR LIFE(1942); LADY GANGSTER(1942); LADY IS WILLING, THE(1942); MAN WHO RETURNED TO LIFE, THE(1942); MURDER IN THE BIG HOUSE(1942); SECRET ENEMIES(1942); ADVENTURES IN IRAQ(1943); AIR FORCE(1943); MURDER ON THE WATERFRONT(1943); PRINCESS O'ROURKE(1943); TRUCK BUSTERS(1943); KEYS OF THE KINGDOM, THE(1944); CIRCUMSTANTIAL EVIDENCE(1945); WOMAN WHO CAME BACK(1945); DRAGONWYCH(1946); STRANGE IMPERSONATION(1946); SANCTUARY(1961), w; ACT ONE(1964); TREE, THE(1969); 7254(1971); PLAY IT AS IT LAYS(1972); EYES OF THE AMARYLLIS, THE(1982)
Misc. Talkies
ROARING FRONTIERS(1941)

Seamus Ford
QUACKSER FORTUNE HAS A COUSIN IN THE BRONX(1970)
1984
CAL(1984, Ireland)

Colonel Starrett Ford
LONE COWBOY(1934); YOU CAN'T TAKE IT WITH YOU(1938); EARL OF CHICAGO, THE(1940)

Steven Ford
CATTLE ANNIE AND LITTLE BRITCHES(1981); YOUNG DOCTORS IN LOVE(1982)

Susan Ford
SECRET CAVE, THE(1953, Brit.)

Tennessee Ernie Ford
MAN IN THE SADDLE(1951)

Tom Ford
MARY BURNS, FUGITIVE(1935); EMPIRE OF THE ANTS(1977)

Vic Ford
SKIMPY IN THE NAVY(1949, Brit.)

Virginia Ann Ford
FUNNY GIRL(1968)
Wallace Ford
POSSESSED(1931); X MARKS THE SPOT(1931); ARE YOU LISTENING?(1932); BEAST OF THE CITY, THE(1932); CENTRAL PARK(1932); FREAKS(1932); SKYSCRAPER SOULS(1932); WET PARADE, THE(1932); EAST OF FIFTH AVE.(1933); EMPLOYEE'S ENTRANCE(1933); GOODBYE AGAIN(1933); HEADLINE SHOOTER(1933); HYPNOTIZED(1933); MY WOMAN(1933); NIGHT OF TERROR(1933); THREE-CORNERED MOON(1933); LOST PATROL, THE(1934); MEN IN WHITE(1934); MONEY MEANS NOTHING(1934); ANOTHER FACE(1935); GET THAT MAN(1935); IN SPITE OF DANGER(1935); INFORMER, THE(1935); MAN WHO RECLAIMED HIS HEAD, THE(1935); MARY BURNS, FUGITIVE(1935); MEN OF THE HOUR(1935); MYSTERIOUS MR. WONG(1935); NUT FARM, THE(1935); ONE FRIGHTENED NIGHT(1935); SHE COULDN'T TAKE IT(1935); SWELL-HEAD(1935); WHOLE TOWN'S TALKING, THE(1935); ABSOLUTE QUIET(1936); ROGUES' TAVERN, THE(1936); SON COMES HOME, A(1936); TWO IN THE DARK(1936); EXILED TO SHANGHAI(1937); SWING IT SAILOR(1937); YOU'RE IN THE ARMY NOW(1937, Brit.); DARK SANDS(1938, Brit.); HE LOVED AN ACTRESS(1938, Brit.); BACK DOOR TO HEAVEN(1939); GIVE US WINGS(1940); ISLE OF DESTINY(1940); LOVE, HONOR AND OH, BABY(1940); MUMMY'S HAND, THE(1940); SCATTERBRAIN(1940); TWO GIRLS ON BROADWAY(1940); MAN BETRAYED, A(1941); MURDER BY INVITATION(1941); ROAR OF THE PRESS(1941); ALL THROUGH THE NIGHT(1942); INSIDE THE LAW(1942); MUMMY'S TOMB, THE(1942); SCATTERGOOD SURVIVES A MURDER(1942); SEVEN DAYS LEAVE(1942); APE MAN, THE(1943); CROSS OF LORRAINE, THE(1943); MARINES COME THROUGH, THE(1943); SHADOW OF A DOUBT(1943); MACHINE GUN MAMA(1944); SECRET COMMAND(1944); BLOOD ON THE SUN(1945); GREAT JOHN L. THE(1945); ON STAGE EVERYBODY(1945); SPELLBOUND(1945); BLACK ANGEL(1946); CRACK-UP(1946); GREEN YEARS, THE(1946); GUY COULD CHANGE, A(1946); LOVER COME BACK(1946); RENDEZVOUS WITH ANNIE(1946); BELLE STARR'S DAUGHTER(1947); DEAD RECKONING(1947); MAGIC TOWN(1947); T-MEN(1947); CORONER CREEK(1948); EMBRACEABLE YOU(1948); SHED NO TEARS(1948); RED STALLION IN THE ROCKIES(1949); SET-UP, THE(1949); BREAKING POINT, THE(1950); DAKOTA LIL(1950); FURIES, THE(1950); HARVEY(1950); HE RAN ALL THE WAY(1951); PAINTING THE CLOUDS WITH SUNSHINE(1951); WARPATH(1951); FLESH AND FURY(1952); RODEO(1952); GREAT JESSE JAMES RAID, THE(1953); NEBRASKAN, THE(1953); BOY FROM OKLAHOMA, THE(1954); DESTRY(1954); SHE COULDN'T SAY NO(1954); THREE RING CIRCUS(1954); LAWLESS STREET, A(1955); LUCY GALLANT(1955); MAN FROM LARAMIE, THE(1955); SPOILERS, THE(1955); WICHITA(1955); FIRST TEXAN, THE(1956); JOHNNY CONCHO(1956); MAVERICK QUEEN, THE(1956); RAINMAKER, THE(1956); STAGECOACH TO FURY(1956); THUNDER OVER ARIZONA(1956); LAST HURRAH, THE(1958); MATCHMAKER, THE(1958); TWILIGHT FOR THE GODS(1958); WARLOCK(1959); TESS OF THE STORM COUNTRY(1961); PATCH OF BLUE, A(1965)
Misc. Talkies
I HATE WOMEN(1934); WOMAN'S MAN, A(1934)
Wally Ford
BLUES IN THE NIGHT(1941); MAN FROM TEXAS, THE(1948)
Weber Ford
QUICK AND THE DEAD, THE(1963), ed
Wesley Ford
HER FORGOTTEN PAST(1933), d; SECRET SINNERS(1933), p&d
Misc. Talkies
$20 A WEEK(1935), d
Whitey Ford
COUNTRY FAIR(1941); SAFE AT HOME(1962)
William Ford
COOL WORLD, THE(1963)
Ford, Harris and Jones
THANK YOUR LUCKY STARS(1943)
John Fordan
MISSION BLOODY MARY(1967, Fr./Ital./Span.)
Brinsley Forde
LEO THE LAST(1970, Brit.); DIAMONDS ARE FOREVER(1971, Brit.); BABYLON(1980, Brit.)
Culley Forde
SALOON BAR(1940, Brit.), p; THREE COCKEYED SAILORS(1940, Brit.), p; YOU CAN'T DO WITHOUT LOVE(1946, Brit.), p
Eugene Forde
SMOKY(1933), d; CHARLIE CHAN IN LONDON(1934), d; CHARLIE CHAN'S COURAGE(1934), d; GREAT HOTEL MURDER(1935), d; MYSTERY WOMAN(1935), d; YOUR UNCLE DUDLEY(1935), d; COUNTRY BEYOND, THE(1936), d; THIRTY SIX HOURS TO KILL(1936), d; CHARLIE CHAN AT MONTE CARLO(1937), d; CHARLIE CHAN ON BROADWAY(1937), d; LADY ESCAPES, THE(1937), d; MIDNIGHT TAXI(1937), d; STEP LIVELY, JEEVES(1937), d; INTERNATIONAL SETTLEMENT(1938), d; MEET THE GIRLS(1938), d; ONE WILD NIGHT(1938), d; HONEYMOON'S OVER, THE(1939), d; INSPECTOR HORNLEIGH(1939, Brit.), d; CHARLIE CHAN'S MURDER CRUISE(1940), d; CHARTER PILOT(1940), d; MICHAEL SHAYNE, PRIVATE DETECTIVE(1940), d; PIER 13(1940), d; BUY ME THAT TOWN(1941), d; DRESSED TO KILL(1941), d; MAN AT LARGE(1941), d; SLEEPERS WEST(1941), d; BERLIN CORRESPONDENT(1942), d; RIGHT TO THE HEART(1942), d; BACKLASH(1947), d; CRIMSON KEY, THE(1947), d; INVISIBLE WALL, THE(1947), d; JEWELS OF BRANDENBURG(1947), d
Silents
DAREDEVIL'S REWARD(1928), d; OUTLAWED(1929), d
Misc. Silents
PAINTED POST(1928), d; SON OF THE GOLDEN WEST(1928), d
Eugene J. Forde
CRIME DOCTOR'S STRANGEST CASE(1943), d; SHADOWS IN THE NIGHT(1944), d
Eugenia Forde
Misc. Silents
LYING LIPS(1916); WHITE ROSETTE, THE(1916)
Eugenie Forde
Silents
FAIR ENOUGH(1918); MAN WHO TURNED WHITE, THE(1919); THAT'S MY BABY(1926); CAPTAIN SALVATION(1927)
Misc. Silents
COURTESAN, THE(1916); LIGHT, THE(1916); UNDERTOW, THE(1916); ANNIE-FOR-SPITE(1917); CHARITY CASTLE(1917); CONSCIENCE(1917); GENTLE INTRUD-

ER, THE(1917); INNOCENCE OF LIZETTE, THE(1917); UPPER CRUST, THE(1917); VIRGIN OF STAMBOUL, THE(1920)
Eugne Forde
Misc. Silents
HELLO CHEYENE(1928), d
Florrie Forde
MY OLD DUTCH(1934, Brit.); SAY IT WITH FLOWERS(1934, Brit.); REGAL CAVALCADE(1935, Brit.)
Hal Forde
Misc. Silents
VANDERHOFF AFFAIR, THE(1915)
Leila Forde
PHANTOM OF THE OPERA, THE(1962, Brit.)
Seamus Forde
VON RICHTHOFEN AND BROWN(1970)
Tonie Forde
BOOTS! BOOTS!(1934, Brit.)
Victoria Forde
Misc. Silents
WESTERN BLOOD(1918)
Walter Forde
CHARLEY'S(BIG-HEARTED) AUNT*1/2 (1940), d; BED AND BREAKFAST(1930, Brit.), d; LAST HOUR, THE(1930, Brit.), d; LORD RICHARD IN THE PANTRY(1930, Brit.), d; WOULD YOU BELIEVE IT!(1930, Brit.), a, d, w; YOU'D BE SURPRISED!(1930, Brit.), a, d, w; SPLINTERS IN THE NAVY(1931, Brit.), d; THIRD TIME LUCKY(1931, Brit.), d; CONDEMNED TO DEATH(1932, Brit.), d; LORD BABS(1932, Brit.), d; RINGER, THE(1932, Brit.), d; GHOST TRAIN, THE(1933, Brit.), d; NIGHT AND DAY(1933, Brit.), d; ROME EXPRESS(1933, Brit.), p, d; CHU CHIN CHOW(1934, Brit.), d; ORDERS IS ORDERS(1934, Brit.), d; ALIAS BULLDOG DRUMMOND(1935, Brit.), d; BORN FOR GLORY(1935, Brit.), d; JACK AHOY!(1935, Brit.), d; FORBIDDEN MUSIC(1936, Brit.), d; KING OF THE DAMNED(1936, Brit.), d; CHEER BOYS CHEER(1939, Brit.), d; INSPECTOR HORNLEIGH ON HOLIDAY(1939, Brit.), d; LET'S BE FAMOUS(1939, Brit.), d; PHANTOM STRIKES, THE(1939, Brit.), d; SALOON BAR(1940, Brit.), d; SECRET FOUR, THE(1940, Brit.), d; THREE COCK-EYED SAILORS(1940, Brit.), d; GHOST TRAIN, THE(1941, Brit.), d; MAIL TRAIN(1941, Brit.), d; FLYING FORTRESS(1942, Brit.), d; PETERVILLE DIAMOND, THE(1942, Brit.), d; PLAYBOY, THE(1942, Brit.), d; IT'S THAT MAN AGAIN(1943, Brit.), d; TIME FLIES(1944, Brit.), d; YOU CAN'T DO WITHOUT LOVE(1946, Brit.), d; MASTER OF BANKDAM, THE(1947, Brit.), p, d; CARDBOARD CAVALIER, THE(1949, Brit.), p&d
Misc. Talkies
ALI BABA NIGHTS(1953), d
Silents
RED PEARLS(1930, Brit.), d
Misc. Silents
WAIT AND SEE(1928, Brit.), a, d; WHAT NEXT?(1928, Brit.), a, d; SILENT HOUSE, THE(1929, Brit.), d; WOULD YOU BELIEVE IT!(1929, Brit.), a, d
Whitty Vialva Forde
PRESSURE(1976, Brit.)
Frances Fordham
LINCOLN CONSPIRACY, THE(1977)
Peta Fordham
GREAT BRITISH TRAIN ROBBERY, THE(1967, Ger.), w
Alan Fordney
GRAND PRIX(1966); LOVE BUG, THE(1968)
Dorice Fordred
SILENT PASSENGER, THE(1935, Brit.); AS YOU LIKE IT(1936, Brit.); KNIGHT WITHOUT ARMOR(1937, Brit.); NURSEMAID WHO DISAPPEARED, THE(1939, Brit.); STOLEN LIFE(1939, Brit.)
John W. Fordson [Mario Costa]
BUFFALO BILL, HERO OF THE FAR WEST(1962, Ital.), d
Al Fordyce
Misc. Silents
COURTESAN, THE(1916)
John Fordyce
GATES TO PARADISE(1968, Brit./Ger.); HORNET'S NEST(1970)
Keith Fordyce
GET ON WITH IT(1963, Brit.)
Miss Fordyce
Silents
DIAMOND NECKLACE, THE(1921, Brit.)
Chester Fore
GIRL FROM AVENUE A(1940), art d
Ken Foree
DAWN OF THE DEAD(1979); WANDERERS, THE(1979); KNIGHTRIDERS(1981)
N. Foregger
Misc. Silents
DEVIL'S WHEEL, THE(1926, USSR)
Ronn Forella
LITTLE PRINCE, THE(1974, Brit.), ch; STRIPES(1981), ch
Giuseppe Forelli
INDISCRETION OF AN AMERICAN WIFE(1954, U.S./Ital.)
Bernard Foreman
SAFECRACKER, THE(1958, Brit.)
Building Foreman
SMUGGLERS' COVE(1948)
Carl Foreman
SPOOKS RUN WILD(1941), w; RHYTHM PARADE(1943), w; DAKOTA(1945), w; SO THIS IS NEW YORK(1948), w; CHAMPION(1949), w; CLAY PIGEON, THE(1949), w; HOME OF THE BRAVE(1949), w; MEN, THE(1950), w; YOUNG MAN WITH A HORN(1950), w; HIGH NOON(1952), w; SLEEPING TIGER, THE(1954, Brit.), w; KEY, THE(1958, Brit.), w; GUNS OF NAVARONE, THE(1961), p, w; VICTORS, THE(1963), p,d&w; MACKENNA'S GOLD(1969), p, w; YOUNG WINSTON(1972, Brit.), p, w; FORCE 10 FROM NAVARONE(1978, Brit.), p; WHEN TIME RAN OUT(1980), w
Carol Foreman
BROTHERS IN THE SADDLE(1949)
David Foreman
FRIDAY THE 13TH... THE ORPHAN(1979)

Debbie Lynn Foreman
I'M DANCING AS FAST AS I CAN(1982)
Deborah Foreman
STONE(1974, Aus.); VALLEY GIRL(1983)
Elaine Foreman
1984
LISTEN TO THE CITY(1984, Can.), ed
George Foreman
LET'S DO IT AGAIN(1975)
Grant Foreman
Misc. Silents
DO THE DEAD TALK?(1920)
Jamie Foreman
MC VICAR(1982, Brit.)
Jean Foreman
RHYTHM PARADE(1943)
John Foreman
BUTCH CASSIDY AND THE SUNDANCE KID(1969), p; WINNING(1969), p; PUZ-
ZLE OF A DOWNFALL CHILD(1970), p; WUSA(1970), p; THEY MIGHT BE
GIANTS(1971), p; LIFE AND TIMES OF JUDGE ROY BEAN, THE(1972), p; POCKET
MONEY(1972), p; MACKINTOSH MAN, THE(1973, Brit.), p; MAN WHO WOULD BE
KING, THE(1975, Brit.), p; GREAT TRAIN ROBBERY, THE(1979, Brit.), p
1984
ICE PIRATES, THE(1984), p
John C. Foreman
SOMETIMES A GREAT NOTION(1971), p
L. L. Foreman
SAVAGE, THE(1953), w; ARROW IN THE DUST(1954), w; LONE GUN, THE(1954),
w; STORM RIDER, THE(1957), w; GAMBLER WORE A GUN, THE(1961), w
Mahlon Foreman
WINDSPLITTER, THE(1971)
Phil Foreman
DEMON LOVER, THE(1977)
Plant Foreman
REACHING FOR THE SUN(1941)
Richard Foreman
Misc. Talkies
STRONG MEDICINE(1981), d
Ron Foreman
FEVER HEAT(1968); INSIDE AMY(1975), art d; HIGH RISK(1981), art d; LOVE
BUTCHER, THE(1982), art d
Ronald Kent Foreman
ROCKY III(1982), art d
1984
ICE PIRATES, THE(1984), art d
Ruth Foreman
SHARK RIVER(1953)
Stephen H. Foreman
JAZZ SINGER, THE(1980), w
Tom Foreman
RAWHIDE(1938)
John Fores
OUT OF THE CLOUDS(1957, Brit.), w
Maria Forescu
Silents
EMERALD OF THE EAST(1928, Brit.)
Fred Foresman
MOONSHINE COUNTY EXPRESS(1977)
Alan Forest
PHANTOM EXPRESS, THE(1932)
Allan Forest
Silents
NOISE IN NEWBORO, A(1923)
Anthony Forest
LIFE STUDY(1973); STRANGE SHADOWS IN AN EMPTY ROOM(1977, Can./Ital.)
Chet Forest
GOOD OLD SOAR, THE(1937), m/l Walter Donaldson
Daniel Forest
EYE FOR AN EYE, AN(1981)
Denis Forest
STRANGE BREW(1983)
Diana Forest
HOLD'EM NAVY!(1937)
Frank Forest
BIG BROADCAST OF 1937, THE(1936); CHAMPAGNE WALTZ(1937); I'LL TAKE
ROMANCE(1937); TAKE IT BIG(1944); FLESH EATERS, THE(1964), ed
Gaston Forest
SPRING FEVER(1983, Can.)
Jean Forest
Misc. Silents
CRAINQUEBILLE(1922, Fr.); GRIBICHE(1926, Fr.); VISAGE D'ENFANTS(1926, Fr.)
Jean-Claude Forest
BARBARELLA(1968, Fr./Ital.), w
John Forest
BLACK 13(1954, Brit.)
Mark Forest
GOLIATH AND THE DRAGON(1961, Ital./Fr.); SON OF SAMSON(1962, Fr./Ital./
Yugo.); GOLIATH AND THE SINS OF BABYLON(1964, Ital.); HERCULES AGAINST
THE SONS OF THE SUN(1964, Span./Ital.)
Michael Forest
SAGA OF THE VIKING WOMEN AND THEIR VOYAGE TO THE WATERS OF THE
GREAT SEA SERPENT, THE(1957); BEAST FROM THE HAUNTED CAVE(1960); SKI
TROOP ATTACK(1960); VALLEY OF THE REDWOODS(1960); HOUSE IS NOT A
HOME, A(1964); GLORY GUYS, THE(1965); DEATHWATCH(1966); MONEY JUNGLE,
THE(1968); SWEET RIDE, THE(1968); 100 RIFLES(1969); MY LOVER, MY SON(1970,
Brit.); DIRT GANG(1972); LOVES AND TIMES OF SCARAMOUCHE, THE(1976,
Ital.); MOHAMMAD, MESSENGER OF GOD(1976, Lebanon/Brit.); FINAL OPTION,
THE(1983, Brit.)

Mike Forest
ASSASSINATION OF TROTSKY, THE(1972 Fr./Ital.)
Peter Forest
CRY OF THE BANSHEE(1970, Brit.)
Sherwood Forest
PROLOGUE(1970, Can.), w
Carmine Foresta
GODFATHER, THE, PART II(1974); DOG DAY AFTERNOON(1975); PRINCE OF
THE CITY(1981)
Franco Foresta
FOR LOVE OF YOU(1933, Brit.)
Sean Forestal
NO BLADE OF GRASS(1970, Brit.), w
C. S. Forester
BORN FOR GLORY(1935, Brit.), w; COMMANDOS STRIKE AT DAWN, THE(1942),
w; EAGLE SQUADRON(1942), w; FOREVER AND A DAY(1943), w; AFRICAN
QUEEN, THE(1951, U.S./Brit.), w; CAPTAIN HORATIO HORNBLOWER(1951, Brit.),
w; SAILOR OF THE KING(1953, Brit.), w; PRIDE AND THE PASSION, THE(1957), w;
SINK THE BISMARCK!(1960, Brit.), w
Cay Forester
DAKOTA(1945); STRANGE IMPERSONATION(1946); QUEEN OF THE AMA-
ZONS(1947); CANON CITY(1948); HOLLOW TRIUMPH(1948); FIVE MINUTES TO
LIVE(1961); FUZZ(1972)
Gay Forester
VIOLENCE(1947)
M.K. Forester
FIVE MINUTES TO LIVE(1961), w
Sharon Forester
MOON OVER THE ALLEY(1980, Brit.)
William Forester
BADLANDS OF MONTANA(1957)
William A. Forester
PAJAMA GAME, THE(1957); CRY BABY KILLER, THE(1958)
Claire Forestier
KILLING GAME, THE(1968, Fr.), art d
Jean Forestier
SPIRITS OF THE DEAD(1969, Fr./Ital.), art d
Louis Forestier
ORDERS, THE(1977, Can.)
Louis Forestieri
1984
HOT MOVES(1984), m
Wenonah Forgay
Silents
LOVES OF RICARDO, THE(1926)
Huguette Forge
LANDRU(1963, Fr./Ital)
John Forgeham
PARTNER, THE(1966, Brit.); ITALIAN JOB, THE(1969, Brit.)
1984
SHEENA(1984)
Pierre Forget
TROUT, THE(1982, Fr.); L'ETOILE DU NORD(1983, Fr.)
Charles Forian
LITTLE DARLINGS(1980), set d
Allen Forienza
TWO GIRLS AND A SAILOR(1944)
Laura Forin
KREMLIN LETTER, THE(1970)
Emilio Foriscot
WEB OF VIOLENCE(1966, Ital./Span.), ph; BANDIDOS(1967, Ital.), ph; FRANKEN-
STEIN'S BLOODY TERROR(1968, Span.), ph; NEXT!(1971, Ital./Span.), ph
Giorgio Forlani
ALLEGRO NON TROPPO(1977, Ital.), anim
Remo Forlani
THREE FACES OF SIN(1963, Fr./Ital.), w; MADE IN U.S.A.(1966, Fr.)
Giuseppe Forli
MONTE CASSINO(1948, Ital.)
James Forlong
LIONHEART(1968, Brit.)
Michael Forlong
SUICIDE MISSION(1956, Brit.), p&d, w; GREEN HELMET, THE(1961, Brit.), d;
OVER THE ODDS(1961, Brit.), d; STORK TALK(1964, Brit.), d; LIONHEART(1968,
Brit.), p&d, w
Misc. Talkies
RAISING THE ROOF(1971, Brit.), d; HIJACK(1975, Brit.), d
Bill Forman
AT GUNPOINT(1955)
Carol Forman
FALCON'S ADVENTURE, THE(1946); NOCTURNE(1946); SAN QUENTIN(1946);
CODE OF THE WEST(1947); DESPERATE(1947); HONEYMOON(1947); UNDER THE
TONTO RIM(1947); DOCKS OF NEW ORLEANS(1948); FEATHERED SERPENT,
THE(1948); MOZART STORY, THE(1948, Aust.); BY THE LIGHT OF THE SILVERY
MOON(1953)
Misc. Talkies
GUNSMOKE(1947)
David Forman
GREASER'S PALACE(1972), set d
Eddie Forman
SKIPALONG ROSENBLOOM(1951), w
Henry James Forman
Silents
PONY EXPRESS, THE(1925), w
Joey Forman
ATOMIC KID, THE(1954); TWINKLE IN GOD'S EYE, THE(1955); HOT ROD
RUMBLE(1957); ANDY HARDY COMES HOME(1958); BIG OPERATOR, THE(1959);
ERRAND BOY, THE(1961); WHEELER DEALERS, THE(1963); CANDY(1968, Ital./
Fr.); WICKED DREAMS OF PAULA SCHULTZ, THE(1968); BOATNIKS, THE(1970);
NEW YORK, NEW YORK(1977); NUDE BOMB, THE(1980); EARTHBOUND(1981);
DOUBLE EXPOSURE(1982)

Lynn Forman
TRUMAN CAPOTE'S TRILOGY(1969)
Mary Forman
RESURRECTION(1931)
Milos Forman
LOVES OF A BLONDE(1966, Czech.), d, w; FIREMAN'S BALL, THE(1968, Czech.), d, w; TAKING OFF(1971), d, w; ONE FLEW OVER THE CUCKOO'S NEST(1975), d; HAIR(1979), d; RAGTIME(1981), d
1984
AMADEUS(1984), d
Tom Forman
CANYON OF MISSING MEN, THE(1930); CHEYENNE KID, THE(1930); SAGEBRUSH POLITICS(1930); MAN TRAILER, THE(1934); PALS OF THE RANGE(1935); FORBIDDEN TRAIL(1936); LAW FOR TOMBSTONE(1937)
Silents
CHIMMIE FADDEN(1915); CHIMMIE FADDEN OUT WEST(1915); KINDLING(1915); MARRIAGE OF KITTY, THE(1915); PUPPET CROWN, THE(1915); WILD GOOSE CHASE, THE(1915); WOMAN, THE(1915); AMERICAN CONSUL, THE(1917); KISS FOR SUSIE, A(1917); ON RECORD(1917); THOSE WITHOUT SIN(1917); ROUND UP, THE(1920), a, w; SINS OF ROZANNE(1920), d; CAPPY RICKS(1921), d; CITY OF SILENT MEN(1921), d; EASY ROAD, THE(1921), d; PRINCE THERE WAS, A(1921), d; WHITE AND UNMARRIED(1921), d; IF YOU BELIEVE IT, IT'S SO(1922), d; SHADOWS(1922), d; APRIL SHOWERS(1923), d; ARE YOU A FAILURE?(1923), d; MONEY! MONEY! MONEY!(1923), d; VIRGINIAN, THE(1923), d; FIGHTING AMERICAN, THE(1924), d; ROARING RAILS(1924), d; CRIMSON RUNNER, THE(1925), d; FLATTERY(1925), d; OFF THE HIGHWAY(1925), d
Misc. Silents
YOUNG ROMANCE(1915); PUBLIC OPINION(1916); SWEET KITTY BELLAIRS(1916); THOUSAND DOLLAR HUSBAND, THE(1916); TO HAVE AND TO HOLD(1916); UNPROTECTED(1916); YELLOW PAWN, THE(1916); COST OF HATRED, THE(1917); EVIL EYE, THE(1917); FORBIDDEN PATHS(1917); HASHIMURA TOGO(1917); HER STRANGE WEDDING(1917); TIDES OF BARNEGAT, THE(1917); FOR BETTER, FOR WORSE(1919); TOLD IN THE HILLS(1919); LADDER OF LIES, THE(1920), d; SEA WOLF, THE(1920); TREE OF KNOWLEDGE, THE(1920); WHITE SHOULDERS(1922), a, d; WOMAN CONQUERS, THE(1922), d; BROKEN WING, THE(1923), d; GIRL WHO CAME BACK, THE(1923), d; FLAMING FORTIES, THE(1924), d; FLATTERY(1925), d; MIDNIGHT FLYER, THE(1925), d; PEOPLE VS. NANCY PRESTON, THE(1925), d; DEVIL'S DICE(1926), a, d; KOSHER KITTY KELLY(1926); WHISPERING CANYON(1926), d; HEADIN' FOR DANGER(1928); CANYON OF MISSING MEN, THE(1930)
William Forman
PRIDE OF ST. LOUIS, THE(1952)
William R. Forman
KRAKATOA, EAST OF JAVA(1969), p
Win Forman
TRUMAN CAPOTE'S TRILOGY(1969); SUMMER WISHES, WINTER DREAMS(1973)
Domenico Formato
FOUR DAYS OF NAPLES, THE(1963, US/Ital.)
Beryl Formby
BOOTS! BOOTS!(1934, Brit.); OFF THE DOLE(1935, Brit.)
George Formby
BOOTS! BOOTS!(1934, Brit.), a, w; NO LIMIT(1935, Brit.); OFF THE DOLE(1935, Brit.), a, w; KEEP YOUR SEATS PLEASE(1936, Brit.); FEATHER YOUR NEST(1937, Brit.); KEEP FIT(1937, Brit.); I SEE ICE(1938); COME ON GEORGE(1939, Brit.); TROUBLE BREWING(1939, Brit.); IT'S IN THE AIR(1940, Brit.); LET GEORGE DO IT(1940, Brit.); SPARE A COPPER(1940, Brit.); SOUTH AMERICAN GEORGE(1941, Brit.); TURNED OUT NICE AGAIN(1941, Brit.); MUCH TOO SHY(1942, Brit.); WE'LL MEET AGAIN(1942, Brit.), p; BELL-BOTTOM GEORGE(1943, Brit.); GET CRACKING(1943, Brit.); RHYTHM SERENADE(1943, Brit.), p; HE SNOOPS TO CONQUER(1944, Brit.); I DIDN'T DO IT(1945, Brit.); GEORGE IN CIVVY STREET(1946, Brit.)
George Formby, Jr.
Misc. Silents
BY THE SHORTEST OF HEADS(1915, Brit.)
William Lopez Forment
CHOSEN SURVIVORS(1974 U.S.-Mex.), spec eff
Merrilisa Formento
ONE FROM THE HEART(1982)
Carl Formes
Silents
CONNECTICUT YANKEE AT KING ARTHUR'S COURT, A(1921)
Karl Formes
Silents
RED LANE, THE(1920); STRUGGLE, THE(1921)
Armando Formica
HELLO GOD(1951, U.S./Ital.)
Enrico Formichi
AIDA(1954, Ital.)
Fil Formicola
BUDDY BUDDY(1981)
1984
SPLASH(1984)
Aldo Formisano
FINE PAIR, A(1969, Ital.)
Roberta Formoso
BLACK MAMA, WHITE MAMA(1973), art d
Franco Fornari
DIARY OF A SCHIZOPHRENIC GIRL(1970, Ital.), ph
Giuseppe Fornari
SWEPT AWAY...BY AN UNUSUAL DESTINY IN THE BLUE SEA OF AUGUST(1975, Ital.), ph
Massimo Fornari
QUEENS, THE(1968, Ital./Fr.)
Pauline Forney
JAZZ HEAVEN(1929), w
Silents
GIRL FROM RIO, THE(1927), w, t

Sam Forney
PHANTOM OF THE PARADISE(1974)
Nino Fornicola
LE PETIT THEATRE DE JEAN RENOIR(1974, Fr.)
Eugene Fornier
NUTCRACKER FANTASY(1979), w
Richard Foronjy
SERPICO(1973); GAMBLER, THE(1974); FUN WITH DICK AND JANE(1977); ONE MAN JURY(1978); JERK, THE(1979); PRINCE OF THE CITY(1981); TRUE CONFESSIONS(1981)
1984
CITY HEAT(1984); ONCE UPON A TIME IN AMERICA(1984); REPO MAN(1984)
Konstantin Forostenko
1984
JAZZMAN(1984, USSR), art d
Jose Maria Forque
SONNY AND JED(1974, Ital.), w
Forquet
MATCHLESS(1967, Ital.), cos
Philippe Forquet
IN THE FRENCH STYLE(1963, U.S./Fr.); TAKE HER, SHE'S MINE(1963); YOUR SHADOW IS MINE(1963, Fr./Ital.); CAMILLE 2000(1969); WATERLOO(1970, Ital./USSR)
Phillippe Forquet
Misc. Talkies
TO DIE IN PARIS(1968)
Mr. Forrest
Silents
HARD TIMES(1915, Brit.)
A.J. Forrest
PICKUP ALLEY(1957, Brit.), w
Alan Forrest
Silents
EYES OF JULIA DEEP, THE(1918); AMAZING IMPOSTER, THE(1919)
Misc. Silents
SIGN OF THE SPADE, THE(1916); HER COUNTRY'S CALL(1917); MATE OF THE SALLY ANN, THE(1917); PEGGY LEADS THE WAY(1917); BIT OF JADE, A(1918); GHOST OF ROSY TAYLOR, THE(1918); POWERS THAT PREY(1918); SOCIAL BRIARS(1918)
Allan Forrest
Silents
AMERICAN METHODS(1917); PURPLE CIPHER, THE(1920); INVISIBLE FEAR, THE(1921); WHAT WOMEN WILL DO(1921); LIGHTS OF THE DESERT(1922); NEW TEACHER, THE(1922); SEEING'S BELIEVING(1922); TILLIE(1922); CRINOLINE AND ROMANCE(1923); HER FATAL MILLIONS(1923); LONG LIVE THE KING(1923); OLD CLOTHES(1925); ROSE OF THE WORLD(1925); CARNIVAL GIRL, THE(1926); PARTNERS AGAIN(1926); PRINCE OF PILSEN, THE(1926); SUMMER BACHELORS(1926); ANKLES PREFERRED(1927); LOVELORN, THE(1927); SALLY OF THE SCANDALS(1928)
Misc. Silents
SILENT COMMAND, THE(1915); AND THE LAW SAYS(1916); DULCIE'S ADVENTURE(1916); CHARITY CASTLE(1917); MELISSA OF THE HILLS(1917); BEAUTY AND THE ROGUE(1918); ROSEMARY CLIMBS THE HEIGHTS(1918); BACHELOR'S WIFE, A(1919); INTRUSION OF ISABEL, THE(1919); OVER THE GARDEN WALL(1919); YVONNE FROM PARIS(1919); GREAT AIR ROBBERY, THE(1920); CHEATED LOVE(1921); FORGOTTEN WOMAN(1921); HOLE IN THE WALL, THE(1921); MAN FROM LOST RIVER, THE(1921); THEY SHALL PAY(1921); HEART SPECIALIST, THE(1922); VERY TRULY YOURS(1922); MAN BETWEEN, THE(1923); DON'T DOUBT YOUR HUSBAND(1924); IN LOVE WITH LOVE(1924); SIREN OF SEVILLE, THE(1924); DRESSMAKER FROM PARIS, THE(1925); PAMPERED YOUTH(1925); FIFTH AVENUE(1926); PHANTOM BULLET, THE(1926); TWO CAN PLAY(1926); BLACK FEATHER(1928); DESERT BRIDE, THE(1928); WILD WEST SHOW, THE(1928); WINGED HORSEMAN, THE(1929)
Allen Forrest
DANGEROUS NAN McGREW(1930)
Ann Forrest
Silents
GRIM GAME, THE(1919); FAITH HEALER, THE(1921); WISE FOOL, A(1921); MAN WHO PLAYED GOD, THE(1922)
Misc. Silents
RAINBOW TRAIL, THE(1918); SPLENDID HAZARD, A(1920); GREAT IMPERSONATION, THE(1921); LOVE'S BOOMERANG(1922); MARRIAGE MORALS(1923); RIDIN' PRETTY(1925)
Anthony Forrest
NASTY HABITS(1976, Brit.); SPY WHO LOVED ME, THE(1977, Brit.)
Misc. Talkies
KILLER'S MOON(1978)
Arthur Forrest
CROWDED PARADISE(1956), w
Silents
WHEN KNIGHTHOOD WAS IN FLOWER(1922)
Bill Forrest
ADVENTURES OF KITTY O'DAY(1944)
Chester Forrest
DANCE, GIRL, DANCE(1940), m
Chet Forrest
GIRL DOWNSTAIRS, THE(1938), m; MARIE ANTOINETTE(1938), m/l; VACATION FROM LOVE(1938), m/l; DUDES ARE PRETTY PEOPLE(1942), m
Christina Forrest
NAUGHTY ARLETTE(1951, Brit.); WORM'S EYE VIEW(1951, Brit.); SCOTLAND YARD INSPECTOR(1952, Brit.); WOMAN IN HIDING(1953, Brit.); THREE CASES OF MURDER(1955, Brit.)
Christine Forrest
MARTIN(1979); KNIGHTRIDERS(1981); CREEPSHOW(1982)
Daniel Forrest
CHU CHU AND THE PHILLY FLASH(1981)
David Forrest
SING YOUR WAY HOME(1945); ONE OF OUR DINOSAURS IS MISSING(1975, Brit.), w

Deirdre Forrest
CLASS OF MISS MAC MICHAEL, THE(1978, Brit./U.S.)
Don Forrest
DESPERATE CARGO(1941); LONE RIDER IN GHOST TOWN, THE(1941)
Francis Forrest
FOUR FOR THE MORGUE(1962)
Frederic Forrest
WHEN THE LEGENDS DIE(1972); DON IS DEAD, THE(1973); GRAVY TRAIN, THE(1974); PERMISSION TO KILL(1975, U.S./Aust.); MISSOURI BREAKS, THE(1976); IT LIVES AGAIN(1978); APOCALYPSE NOW(1979); ROSE, THE(1979); HAMMETT(1982); ONE FROM THE HEART(1982)
1984
STONE BOY, THE(1984)
Frederick Forrest
CONVERSATION, THE(1974); VALLEY GIRL(1983)
George Forrest
SONG OF NORWAY(1970), w, m
Gladys Forrest
MAD WEDNESDAY(1950)
Hal Forrest
DANGER FLIGHT(1939), w; MYSTERY PLANE(1939), w; SKY PATROL(1939), w; STUNT PILOT(1939), w; ABBOTT AND COSTELLO GO TO MARS(1953)
Helen Forrest
BATHING BEAUTY(1944); TWO GIRLS AND A SAILOR(1944); YOU CAME ALONG(1945); IT STARTED IN PARADISE(1952, Brit.); SING ALONG WITH ME(1952, Brit.); FIRST MAN INTO SPACE(1959, Brit.); LOUISIANA HUSSY(1960); EMERGENCY(1962, Brit.)
Ingrid Forrest
SCHOOL FOR SECRETS(1946, Brit.)
Irene Forrest
THX 1138(1971); LIMIT, THE(1972); SITTING DUCKS(1979); HEARTBEEPS(1981)
Jack Forrest
WEREWOLF IN A GIRL'S DORMITORY(1961, Ital./Aust.), p
James Forrest
MR. SARDONICUS(1961); PIRATES OF TORTUGA(1961); NIGHTMARE IN WAX(1969); BODY AND SOUL(1981), ph
Jayne Forrest
SLIGHTLY TERRIFIC(1944)
John Forrest
COMING-OUT PARTY, A(; WE'VE NEVER BEEN LICKED(1943); DESTINATION TOKYO(1944); IMPOSTER, THE(1944); JANIE(1944); IDENTITY UNKNOWN(1945); GREAT EXPECTATIONS(1946, Brit.); BONNIE PRINCE CHARLIE(1948, Brit.); OUTSIDER, THE(1949, Brit.); ADAM AND EVELYNE(1950, Brit.); TOM BROWN'S SCHOOLDAYS(1951, Brit.); FRANCHISE AFFAIR, THE(1952, Brit.); GLORY AT SEA(1952, Brit.); NEARLY A NASTY ACCIDENT(1962, Brit.); BAWDY ADVENTURES OF TOM JONES, THE(1976, Brit.)
Johnny Forrest
SHE WENT TO THE RACES(1945)
Lottie Pickford Forrest
Silents
DON Q, SON OF ZORRO(1925)
Mabel Forrest
WINGS IN THE DARK(1935); HOLLYWOOD BOULEVARD(1936); TOO MANY PARENTS(1936); MR. SMITH GOES TO WASHINGTON(1939); SAN DIEGO, I LOVE YOU(1944); LADY ON A TRAIN(1945)
Misc. Silents
LOVE TRAP, THE(1923); MINE TO KEEP(1923); OTHER MEN'S DAUGHTERS(1923); SATIN GIRL, THE(1923)
Mable Forrest
HOLIDAY(1930)
Margaret Forrest
Silents
PURSUING VENGEANCE, THE(1916)
Martha Forrest
Misc. Silents
RICH SLAVE, THE(1921)
Michael Forrest
ATLAS(1960); THAT RIVIERA TOUCH(1968, Brit.); UNDER MILK WOOD(1973, Brit.)
Mike Forrest
LAST REBEL, THE(1971)
Milton Earl Forrest
HI, MOM!(1970); HOSPITAL, THE(1971)
Otto Forrest
WHISTLER, THE(1944); YOU WERE MEANT FOR ME(1948); MY PAL GUS(1952); SABRINA(1954)
Paul Forrest
RICHARD(1972)
Robert Forrest
KID FROM BOOKLYN, THE(1946); WE'RE NOT MARRIED(1952); ABBOTT AND COSTELLO GO TO MARS(1953); ABOVE AND BEYOND(1953); BIG HEAT, THE(1953); PUSHOVER(1954); SCARLET COAT, THE(1955); TRIAL(1955); BATTLE STATIONS(1956); RANSOM(1956); RAINTREE COUNTY(1957)
Sally Forrest
TILL THE CLOUDS ROLL BY(1946); BLAZE OF NOON(1947), ed; DANCING IN THE DARK(1949); NOT WANTED(1949); TAKE ME OUT TO THE BALL GAME(1949); MYSTERY STREET(1950); NEVER FEAR(1950); BANNERLINE(1951); EXCUSE MY DUST(1951); HARD, FAST, AND BEAUTIFUL(1951); STRANGE DOOR, THE(1951); STRIP, THE(1951); VENGEANCE VALLEY(1951); CODE TWO(1953); SON OF SINBAD(1955); RIDE THE HIGH IRON(1956); WHILE THE CITY SLEEPS(1956)
Steve Forrest
BAD AND THE BEAUTIFUL, THE(1952); BATTLE CIRCUS(1953); CLOWN, THE(1953); DREAM WIFE(1953); SO BIG(1953); TAKE THE HIGH GROUND(1953); PHANTOM OF THE RUE MORGUE(1954); PRISONER OF WAR(1954); ROGUE COP(1954); BEDEVILLED(1955); LIVING IDOL, THE(1957); IT HAPPENED TO JANE(1959); FIVE BRANDED WOMEN(1960); FLAMING STAR(1960); HELLER IN PINK TIGHTS(1960); SECOND TIME AROUND, THE(1961); YELLOW CANARY, THE(1963); RASCAL(1969); LATE LIZ, THE(1971); WILD COUNTRY, THE(1971); NORTH DALLAS FORTY(1979); MOMMIE DEAREST/(1981)

1984
SAHARA(1984)
Misc. Talkies
MAN IN A LOOKING GLASS, A(1965, Brit.); SAGITTARIUS MINE, THE(1972)
Steven Forrest
LONGEST DAY, THE(1962)
William Forrest
CORPSE CAME C.O.D., THE(; YOU CAN'T RUN AWAY FROM IT(1956); LONE WOLF MEETS A LADY, THE(1940); MAN WHO TALKED TOO MUCH, THE(1940); NOBODY'S CHILDREN(1940); SECRET SEVEN, THE(1940); BARNACLE BILL(1941); DIVE BOMBER(1941); DOWN IN SAN DIEGO(1941); FLIGHT FROM DESTINY(1941); HERE COMES MR. JORDAN(1941); HOLD THAT GHOST(1941); INTERNATIONAL LADY(1941); KEEP 'EM FLYING(1941); LIFE BEGINS FOR ANDY HARDY(1941); LONE WOLF TAKES A CHANCE, THE(1941); LUCKY DEVILS(1941); MEET JOHN DOE(1941); MILLION DOLLAR BABY(1941); PHANTOM SUBMARINE, THE(1941); SUN VALLEY SERENADE(1941); FLIGHT LIEUTENANT(1942); HITLER'S CHILDREN(1942); IN THIS OUR LIFE(1942); JOE SMITH, AMERICAN(1942); LUCKY JORDAN(1942); MY FAVORITE BLONDE(1942); MY FAVORITE SPY(1942); PRIORITIES ON PARADE(1942); SLEEPYTIME GAL(1942); SPY SHIP(1942); THEY DIED WITH THEIR BOOTS ON(1942); WAKE ISLAND(1942); YANKEE DOODLE DANDY(1942); AIR FORCE(1943); DU BARRY WAS A LADY(1943); FLIGHT FOR FREEDOM(1943); IRON MAJOR, THE(1943); IT AIN'T HAY(1943); MISSION TO MOSCOW(1943); MUG TOWN(1943); SO PROUDLY WE HAIL(1943); ABROAD WITH TWO YANKS(1944); FIGHTING SEABEES, THE(1944); FOLLOW THE BOYS(1944); HERE COME THE WAVES(1944); LAURA(1944); MARINE RAIDERS(1944); MR. SKEFFINGTON(1944); MR. WINKLE GOES TO WAR(1944); WILSON(1944); ANCHORS AWEIGH(1945); BEHIND CITY LIGHTS(1945); CARIBBEAN MYSTERY, THE(1945); GANGS OF THE WATERFRONT(1945); GIRLS OF THE BIG HOUSE(1945); GOD IS MY CO-PILOT(1945); ROAD TO ALCATRAZ(1945); ROUGH, TOUGH AND READY(1945); SALTY O'ROURKE(1945); WITHOUT LOVE(1945); YOUTH ON TRIAL(1945); DANGEROUS BUSINESS(1946); JOLSON STORY, THE(1946); KID FROM BOOKLYN, THE(1946); MEET ME ON BROADWAY(1946); NOBODY LIVES FOREVER(1946); TILL THE CLOUDS ROLL BY(1946); TILL THE END OF TIME(1946); WELL-GROOMED BRIDE, THE(1946); DEAD RECKONING(1947); DEVIL ON WHEELS, THE(1947); DEVIL SHIP(1947); GUILT OF JANET AMES, THE(1947); MIRACLE ON 34TH STREET, THE(1947); MOTHER WORE TIGHTS(1947); SARGE GOES TO COLLEGE(1947); SENATOR WAS INDISCREET, THE(1947); SPIRIT OF WEST POINT, THE(1947); ALIAS A GENTLEMAN(1948); FORT APACHE(1948); GENTLEMAN FROM NOWHERE, THE(1948); HOMECOMING(1948); RACE STREET(1948); THREE DARING DAUGHTERS(1948); TRAPPED BY BOSTON BLACKIE(1948); ANGELS IN DISGUISE(1949); ARSON, INC.(1949); DEVIL'S HENCHMEN, THE(1949); GIRL FROM JONES BEACH, THE(1949); STORY OF SEABISCUIT, THE(1949); TRAIL OF THE YUKON(1949); YOUNGER BROTHERS, THE(1949); EMERGENCY WEDDING(1950); SQUARE DANCE KATY(1950); FLIGHT TO MARS(1951); FOLLOW THE SUN(1951); FORT DODGE STAMPEDE(1951); GASOLINE ALLEY(1951); HARLEM GLOBETROTTERS, THE(1951); I WAS A COMMUNIST FOR THE F.B.I.(1951); I'LL SEE YOU IN MY DREAMS(1951); MISSING WOMEN(1951); SMUGGLER'S GOLD(1951); SPOILERS OF THE PLAINS(1951); DEADLINE–U.S.A.(1952); JET JOB(1952); NIGHT WITHOUT SLEEP(1952); ONE MINUTE TO ZERO(1952); ROSE BOWL STORY, THE(1952); STORY OF WILL ROGERS, THE(1952); BANDITS OF CORSICA, THE(1953); DESTINATION GOBI(1953); EDDIE CANTOR STORY, THE(1953); PRIVATE EYES(1953); WINNING OF THE WEST(1953); DEMETRIUS AND THE GLADIATORS(1954); FRENCH LINE, THE(1954); COURT-MARTIAL OF BILLY MITCHELL, THE(1955); FRANCIS IN THE NAVY(1955); GIRL IN THE RED VELVET SWING, THE(1955); MAN CALLED PETER, THE(1955); NEW YORK CONFIDENTIAL(1955); ONE DESIRE(1955); RAGE AT DAWN(1955); BEHIND THE HIGH WALL(1956); FIRST TRAVELING SALESLADY, THE(1956); PARDNERS(1956); THESE WILDER YEARS(1956); BAND OF ANGELS(1957); JAILHOUSE ROCK(1957); LOVING YOU(1957); LAST HURRAH, THE(1958); TOUGHEST GUN IN TOMBSTONE(1958); HORSE SOLDIERS, THE(1959); ONE-EYED JACKS(1961); PARADISE ALLEY(1962); SWEET BIRD OF YOUTH(1962); GOOD NEIGHBOR SAM(1964); BILLY THE KID VS. DRACULA(1966); MARRIAGE OF A YOUNG STOCKBROKER, THE(1971)
William Forrest, Jr.
THREE LITTLE GIRLS IN BLUE(1946)
Terry Forrestal
FLASH GORDON(1980)
1984
KILLING FIELDS, THE(1984, Brit.), stunts
Cay Forrester
BELOW THE DEADLINE(1946); PRETENDER, THE(1947); D.O.A.(1950); TO PLEASE A LADY(1950)
Misc. Talkies
SONG OF THE RANGE(1944)
Elizabeth Forrester
HOLIDAY(1930); AMERICAN TRAGEDY, AN(1931); BORN TO LOVE(1931)
Fay Forrester
BLONDE SAVAGE(1947)
Frederick Forrester
THESE THIRTY YEARS(1934)
Holgie Forrester
1984
CITY HEAT(1984); IMPULSE(1984)
Isola Forrester
Silents
ANTHING ONCE(1917), w
Izola Forrester
SHOP ANGEL(1932), w; SHE HAD TO CHOOSE(1934), w
Silents
EASY TO GET(1920), w; BLAZING TRAIL, THE(1921), w; YOUTH FOR SALE(1924), w
Kay Forrester
BLAZING GUNS(1943); SAN FERNANDO VALLEY(1944)
Larry Forrester
FATHOM(1967), w; TORA! TORA! TORA!(1970, U.S./Jap.), w
Lynne Forrester
SON OF SINBAD(1955)

Vivian Forrester
Silents
SOCIETY SNOBS(1921)
Forrester-Parant
CINDERELLA(1937, Fr.), p
Susan Forristal
ELECTRA GLIDE IN BLUE(1973); ONE-TRICK PONY(1980)
lp: Maria Forsa
Misc. Talkies
BIBI(1977)
Mimi Forsaythe
THREE RUSSIAN GIRLS(1943)
Edwin Forsberg
Silents
FORGIVEN, OR THE JACK O'DIAMONDS(1914)
Misc. Silents
ROMANCE OF THE UNDERWORLD, A(1918)
Tony Forsberg
FAUST(1964), ph; APOLLO GOES ON HOLIDAY(1968, Ger./Swed.), ph; VICTOR FRANKENSTEIN(1975, Swed./Ireland), ph; ADVENTURES OF PICASSO, THE(1980, Swed.), ph
Robert Forsch
FINAL CHORD, THE(1936, Ger.); MURDERERS AMONG US(1948, Ger.)
Keith Forsey
1984
NEVERENDING STORY, THE(1984, Ger.), m/l "The Neverending Story," Moroder
Norm Forsey
SCARECROW, THE(1982, New Zealand)
Harold Forshay
TO MARY–WITH LOVE(1936)
David Forshtay
FOREIGNER, THE(1978)
Bahman Forsi
CYCLE, THE(1979, Iran)
Bengst Forslund
HERE'S YOUR LIFE(1968, Swed.), w
Bengt Forslund
EMIGRANTS, THE(1972, Swed.), p, w; NEW LAND, THE(1973, Swed.), p, w
Connie Forslund
WAY WE WERE, THE(1973)
Constance Forslund
HAIL(1973); GREAT BANK HOAX, THE(1977); UNCOMMON VALOR(1983)
Erik Forslund
NIGHT IN JUNE, A(1940, Swed.)
Karl-Axel Forssberg
SHAME(1968, Swed.)
Lars Forssell
DOLL, THE(1964, Swed.), w
Louise Forsslund
CAPTAIN IS A LADY, THE(1940), w
E. Forst
Silents
SPLENDID SIN, THE(1919), w
Elmer Forst
Silents
OCCASIONALLY YOURS(1920), w
Emil Forst
Silents
PROWLERS OF THE NIGHT(1926), w
Willi Forst
ROYAL WALTZ, THE(1936); WHITE HORSE INN, THE(1959, Ger.), d
Misc. Silents
CAFE ELECTRIC(1927, Aust.); DANGERS OF THE ENGAGEMENT PERIOD(1929, Ger.)
Willy Forst
BURG THEATRE(1936, Ger.), d; OPERETTA(1949, Ger.), a, d, w; UNFINISHED SYMPHONY, THE(1953, Aust./Brit.), p, d
Mark Forstater
GREAT WALL OF CHINA, THE(1970, Brit.), p, ed; MONTY PYTHON AND THE HOLY GRAIL(1975, Brit.), p; GLITTERBALL, THE(1977, Brit), p; ODD JOB, THE(1978, Brit.), p; GRASS IS SINGING, THE(1982, Brit./Swed.), p; XTRO(1983, Brit.), p
1984
KILLING HEAT(1984), p; MARIGOLDS IN AUGUST(1984, S. Africa), p; NUMBER ONE(1984, Brit.), p
Leif Forstenberg
VIRGIN SPRING, THE(1960, Swed.); SILENCE, THE(1964, Swed.)
Forster
END OF THE WORLD, THE(1930, Fr.), ph
Alfred Forster
PUSS 'N' BOOTS(1967, Ger.), p
Allison Forster
GREGORY'S GIRL(1982, Brit.)
Ben Forster
FRENCH LIEUTENANT'S WOMAN, THE(1981)
Chris Forster
EDUCATION OF SONNY CARSON, THE(1974)
E.M. Forster
1984
PASSAGE TO INDIA, A(1984, Brit.), d&w
Irmgard Forster
TOWN WITHOUT PITY(1961, Ger./Switz./U.S.), makeup
Jack Forster
CRY FREEDOM(1961, Phil.)
Jaime Forster
ATTACK OF THE PUPPET PEOPLE(1958)
Jamie Forster
TO KILL A MOCKINGBIRD(1962)

Jane Forster
1984
FOREVER YOUNG(1984, Brit.)
Jill Forster
LIBIDO(1973, Aus.)
Jurgen Forster
MARRIAGE OF FIGARO, THE(1970, Ger.)
Laurence Forster
Silents
PRINCE AND THE BEGGARMAID, THE(1921, Brit.)
Margaret Forster
GEORGY GIRL(1966, Brit.), w
Nik Forster
BIG SLEEP, THE½(1978, Brit.)
1984
STRIKEBOUND(1984, Aus.)
Nora Forster
GENGHIS KHAN(U.S./Brit./Ger./Yugo)
Pat Forster
MANGO TREE, THE(1981, Aus.), cos; TIM(1981, Aus.), cos
Peter Forster
DANGEROUS CHARTER(1962); CLEOPATRA(1963); THREE STOOGES GO AROUND THE WORLD IN A DAZE, THE(1963); FATHER GOOSE(1964); ESCAPE FROM THE PLANET OF THE APES(1971); 1776(1972)
Ralph Forster
Silents
ADAM BEDE(1918, Brit.); PASSIONATE FRIENDS, THE(1922, Brit.)
Misc. Silents
DAUGHTER OF EVE, A(1919, Brit.); MISS CHARITY(1921, Brit.); HIS WIFE'S HUSBAND(1922, Brit.)
Robert Forster
REFLECTIONS IN A GOLDEN EYE(1967); JUSTINE(1969); MEDIUM COOL(1969); STALKING MOON, THE(1969); COVER ME BABE(1970); PIECES OF DREAMS(1970); JOURNEY THROUGH ROSEBUD(1972); DON IS DEAD, THE(1973); STUNTS(1977); AVALANCHE(1978); BLACK HOLE, THE(1979); ALLIGATOR(1980); VIGILAN-TE(1983)
Misc. Talkies
CRUNCH(1975,Brit.)
Roger Forster
RULES OF THE GAME, THE(1939, Fr.)
Rudolf Forster
ARIANE(1931, Ger.); THREEPENNY OPERA, THE(1931, Ger./U.S.); ISLAND OF LOST MEN(1939); WHITE HORSE INN, THE(1959, Ger.); REST IS SILENCE, THE(1960, Ger.); THREE MOVES TO FREEDOM(1960, Ger.); BRAINWASHED(1961, Ger.); RETURN OF DR. MABUSE, THE(1961, Ger./Fr./Ital.); GLASS OF WATER, A(1962, Cgr.); LULU(1962, Aus.); MAD EXECUTIONERS, THE(1965, Ger.); TONIO KROGER(1968, Fr./Ger.)
Rudolph Forster
CARDINAL, THE(1963)
Thilde Forster
WOMAN COMMANDS, A(1932), w
W. Forster
ROYAL WALTZ, THE(1936), w
Waltraud Forster
PUSS 'N' BOOTS(1967, Ger.)
Yvonne Forster
SONG FOR TOMORROW, A(1948, Brit.)
Glenna Forster-Jones
JOANNA(1968, Brit.); ONE PLUS ONE(1969, Brit.); HUMAN FACTOR, THE(1979, Brit.)
Frau Forster-Larringa
CRUISER EMDEN(1932, Ger.)
Richard Forstmann
WILD IS MY LOVE(1963)
Bill Forsyth
THAT SINKING FEELING(1979, Brit.), p,d&w; GREGORY'S GIRL(1982, Brit.), d&w; LOCAL HERO(1983, Brit.), d&w
1984
COMFORT AND JOY(1984, Brit.), d&w
Brigit Forsyth
NIGHT DIGGER, THE(1971, Brit.); LIKELY LADS, THE(1976, Brit.)
Bruce Forsyth
STAR!(1968); BEDKNOBS AND BROOMSTICKS(1971); MAGNIFICENT SEVEN DEADLY SINS, THE(1971, Brit.)
Charles Forsyth
EVERY NIGHT AT EIGHT(1935)
Ed Forsyth
THING WITH TWO HEADS, THE(1972), ed; SUPERCHICK(1973), d, ed; CHESTY ANDERSON, U.S. NAVY(1976), d
Edward Forsyth
LADY GODIVA RIDES AGAIN(1955, Brit.); YOU CAN'T ESCAPE(1955, Brit.)
Edward J. Forsyth
I'M GOING TO GET YOU ... ELLIOT BOY(1971, Can.), d, ed
Frank Forsyth
LAVENDER HILL MOB, THE(1951, Brit.); DOUBLE EXPOSURE(1954, Brit.); EMBEZZLER, THE(1954, Brit.); STOLEN ASSIGNMENT(1955, Brit.); SHADOW OF FEAR(1956, Brit.); MAN WITHOUT A BODY, THE(1957, Brit.); SURGEON'S KNIFE, THE(1957, Brit.); THUNDER OVER TANGIER(1957, Brit.); SOLITARY CHILD, THE(1958, Brit.); CARRY ON SERGEANT(1959, Brit.); INNOCENT MEETING(1959, Brit.); CIRCLE OF DECEPTON(1961, Brit.); ROOMMATES(1962, Brit.); YOUNG, WILLING AND EAGER(1962, Brit.); CARRY ON CABBIE(1963, Brit.); CARRY ON JACK(1963, Brit.); MAN IN THE DARK(1963, Brit.); CARRY ON SPYING(1964, Brit.); EVIL OF FRANKENSTEIN, THE(1964, Brit.); DR. TERROR'S HOUSE OF HOR-RORS(1965, Brit.); SKULL, THE(1965, Brit.); PSYCHOPATH, THE(1966, Brit.); TRAI-TOR'S GATE(1966, Brit./Ger.); DEADLY BEES,THE(1967, Brit.); TERRORNAUTS, THE(1967, Brit.); THEY CAME FROM BEYOND SPACE(1967, Brit.); OH! WHAT A LOVELY WAR(1969, Brit.); TALES FROM THE CRYPT(1972, Brit.); AND NOW THE SCREAMING STARTS(1973, Brit.); TALES THAT WITNESS MADNESS(1973, Brit.); VAULT OF HORROR, THE(1973, Brit.)

Frederick Forsyth
DAY OF THE JACKAL, THE(1973, Brit./Fr.), w; ODESSA FILE, THE(1974, Brit./Ger.), w; DOGS OF WAR, THE(1980, Brit.), w
James Forsyth
END OF THE ROAD, THE(1954, Brit.), w; FRANCIS OF ASSISI(1961), w
Myra Forsyth
WICKER MAN, THE(1974, Brit.)
Reginald Forsyth
CALLING THE TUNE(1936, Brit.)
Rosemary Forsyth
SHENANDOAH(1965); WAR LORD, THE(1965); TEXAS ACROSS THE RIVER(1966); SOME KIND OF A NUT(1969); WHAT EVER HAPPENED TO AUNT ALICE?(1969); WHERE IT'S AT(1969); HOW DO I LOVE THEE?(1970); BLACK EYE(1974); GRAY LADY DOWN(1978)
Stephen Forsyth
SEATED AT HIS RIGHT(1968, Ital.); HATCHET FOR A HONEYMOON(1969, Span./Ital.)
Steve Forsyth
LOVE AND MARRIAGE(1966, Ital.)
Vanessa Forsyth
ALL NEAT IN BLACK STOCKINGS(1969, Brit.)
William Forsyth
LOVE AND HISSES(1937), ed; LONG SHOT(1981, Brit.)
Forsythe
I THANK YOU(1941, Brit.)
Bill Forsythe
KING OF THE MOUNTAIN(1981); SMOKEY BITES THE DUST(1981); MAN WHO WASN'T THERE, THE(1983)
1984
CLOAK AND DAGGER(1984); ONCE UPON A TIME IN AMERICA(1984)
Blanche Forsythe
Silents
EAST LYNNE(1913, Brit.); IN THE HANDS OF THE LONDON CROOKS(1913, Brit.); JACK TAR(1915, Brit.); ROGUES OF LONDON, THE(1915, Brit.); TRAPPED BY THE LONDON SHARKS(1916, Brit.); JUST DECEPTION, A(1917, Brit.)
Misc. Silents
BRIGADIER GERARD(1915, Brit.); STRIFE ETERNAL, THE(1915, Brit.); MILL-OWNER'S DAUGHTER, THE(1916, Brit.); SHE(1916, Brit.)
Christine Forsythe
YOU CAN'T RATION LOVE(1944)
Drew Forsythe
CADDIE(1976, Aus.); DEATHCHEATERS(1976, Aus.); NEWSFRONT(1979, Aus.); DOT AND THE BUNNY(1983, Aus.)
Misc. Talkies
DOCTORS AND NURSES(1983)
Eleanor Forsythe
PROSTITUTE(1980, Brit.)
Eric Forsythe
RETURN OF THE SECAUCUS SEVEN(1980)
Frank Forsythe
BRAIN, THE(1965, Ger./Brit.)
Henderson Forsythe
DEATHDREAM(1972, Can.); GREEK TYCOON, THE(1978); INTERIORS(1978); SILKWOOD(1983)
Ida Forsythe
GREEN PASTURES(1936)
John Forsythe
NORTHERN PURSUIT(1943); DESTINATION TOKYO(1944); CAPTIVE CITY(1952); ESCAPE FROM FORT BRAVO(1953); GLASS WEB, THE(1953); IT HAPPENS EVERY THURSDAY(1953); TROUBLE WITH HARRY, THE(1955); AMBASSADOR'S DAUGHTER, THE(1956); EVERYTHING BUT THE TRUTH(1956); KITTEN WITH A WHIP(1964); MADAME X(1966); IN COLD BLOOD(1967); HAPPY ENDING, THE(1969); TOPAZ(1969, Brit.); MAHLER(1974, Brit.), md; ...AND JUSTICE FOR ALL(1979)
Mimi Forsythe
SENSATIONS OF 1945(1944)
Reginald Forsythe
STARS IN YOUR EYES(1956, Brit.)
Robert Forsythe
MAN, A WOMAN, AND A BANK, A(1979, Can.)
Wayne Forsythe
Misc. Talkies
VALLEY OF BLOOD(1973)
Elizabeth Forsythe-Hailey
RICH AND FAMOUS(1981)
Drew Forsyther
STONE(1974, Aus.)
Bill Fort
NO WAY TO TREAT A LADY(1968)
Garrett Elsden Fort
Silents
IN FAST COMPANY(1924), w; PORTS OF CALL(1925), w; BACHELOR'S BABY, THE(1927), w
Garrett Fort
APPLAUSE(1929), w; JEALOUSY(1929), w; LADY LIES, THE(1929), w; LETTER, THE(1929), w; BIG POND, THE(1930), w; DANGEROUS NAN McGREW(1930), w; OUTSIDE THE LAW(1930), w; ROADHOUSE NIGHTS(1930), w; SCOTLAND YARD(1930), w; DRACULA(1931), w; FRANKENSTEIN(1931), w; PANAMA FLO(1932), w; UNDER-COVER MAN(1932), w; YOUNG BRIDE(1932), w; 70,000 WITNESSES(1932), w; BEFORE DAWN(1933), w; LOST PATROL, THE,(1934), w; PRIVATE SCANDAL(1934), w; JALNA(1935), w; MILLS OF THE GODS(1935), w; DEVIL DOLL, THE(1936), w; DRACULA'S DAUGHTER(1936), w; STORM OVER BENGAL(1938), w; PANAMA LADY(1939), w; TWELVE CROWDED HOURS(1939), w; ZERO HOUR, THE(1939), w; MARK OF ZORRO, THE(1940), w; AMONG THE LIVING(1941), w; LADIES IN RETIREMENT(1941), w; LADY FOR A NIGHT(1941), w; STREET OF CHANCE(1942), w; MAN IN HALF-MOON STREET, THE(1944), w; BLOOD ON THE SUN(1945), w; INSIDE JOB(1946), w; MAD ROOM, THE(1969), w
Silents
ON TIME(1924), w; COMING OF AMOS, THE(1925), w; WHITE GOLD(1927), w; YANKEE CLIPPER, THE(1927), w; NAUGHTY BABY(1929), w

Mario Fort
LOST ON THE WESTERN FRONT(1940, Brit.), w
Sid Fort
COLOR ME DEAD(1969, Aus.), art d
Carol Forte
STONE COLD DEAD(1980, Can.)
Elena Forte
RED LIPS(1964, Fr./Ital.)
Fabian Forte
BULLET FOR PRETTY BOY, A(1970); LITTLE LAURA AND BIG JOHN(1973); GET CRAZY(1983)
Misc. Talkies
DAY THE LORD GOT BUSTED, THE(1976); KISS DADDY GOODBYE(1981)
Fabrizio Forte
PADRE PADRONE(1977, Ital.)
Joe Forte
WHEN YOU'RE IN LOVE(1937); OF HUMAN HEARTS(1938); CYCLOTRODE X(1946); MAGNIFICENT DOLL(1946); KILROY WAS HERE(1947); CALL NORTHSIDE 777(1948); WALLS OF JERICHO(1948); JUDGE, THE(1949); RIDERS IN THE SKY(1949); SLATTERY'S HURRICANE(1949); TASK FORCE(1949); COUNTY FAIR(1950); ROADBLOCK(1951); RODEO KING AND THE SENORITA(1951); ASSIGNMENT-PARIS(1952); SCARLET ANGEL(1952); THEM!(1954); CELL 2455, DEATH ROW(1955); YOUNG AT HEART(1955); FURY AT GUNSIGHT PASS(1956); HE LAUGHED LAST(1956); OUR MISS BROOKS(1956); BUSTER KEATON STORY, THE(1957); GUNFIGHT AT THE O.K. CORRAL(1957); LOVING YOU(1957); SHORT CUT TO HELL(1957); MATCHMAKER, THE(1958); RETURN TO WARBOW(1958); HOMICIDAL(1961); NUTTY PROFESSOR, THE(1963); LAW OF THE LAWLESS(1964); ROUSTABOUT(1964)
Josef Forte
REEFER MADNESS(1936); PALS OF THE SADDLE(1938); BEASTS OF BERLIN(1939); MY SON IS GUILTY(1940)
Joseph Forte
SECRET FURY, THE(1950)
Lou Forte
LET THEM LIVE(1937), md
Nick Apollo Forte
1984
BROADWAY DANNY ROSE(1984)
Russell Forte
KING OF THE MOUNTAIN(1981); NIGHT SHIFT(1982); ROCKY III(1982)
1984
JOHNNY DANGEROUSLY(1984)
Vincent Forte
OPERATION PACIFIC(1951); NIGHT OF THE WITCHES(1970), p; BARON BLOOD(1972, Ital.), w
Albert Fortell
FINAL OPTION, THE(1983, Brit.)
Bert Fortell
SALZBURG CONNECTION, THE(1972)
Kenneth Fortescue
BARRETTS OF WIMPOLE STREET, THE(1957); HIGH FLIGHT(1957, Brit.); HOW TO MURDER A RICH UNCLE(1957, Brit.); DESERT MICE(1960, Brit.); PETTICOAT PIRATES(1961, Brit.); BEST OF ENEMIES, THE(1962); GOLDEN RABBIT, THE(1962, Brit.); LAWRENCE OF ARABIA(1962, Brit.); WHY BOTHER TO KNOCK(1964, Brit.); BRIDES OF FU MANCHU, THE(1966, Brit.); CLUE OF THE TWISTED CANDLE(1968, Brit.); MAGIC CHRISTIAN, THE(1970, Brit.); WHO IS KILLING THE GREAT CHEFS OF EUROPE?(1978, US/Ger.); MIRROR CRACK'D, THE(1980, Brit.)
Kenneth Fortesque
TANK FORCE(1958, Brit.)
Chris Forth
PERSONALS, THE(1982)
George Forth
Silents
OUR LITTLE WIFE(1918)
Misc. Silents
HEART OF EZRA GREER, THE(1917); OH MARY BE CAREFUL(1921)
George J. Forth
Misc. Silents
SIXTEENTH WIFE, THE(1917)
Jane Forth
L'AMOUR(1973)
Carlo Forti
LA BOHEME(1965, Ital.)
Florella C. Forti
VOICE IN YOUR HEART, A(1952, Ital.)
Tony Fortich
SAMAR(1962)
Diane Fortier
CRIME WAVE(1954)
Herbert Fortier
SECOND HONEYMOON(1937)
Silents
NATION'S PERIL, THE(1915); BEYOND(1921); CHILDREN OF THE NIGHT(1921); CONNECTICUT YANKEE AT KING ARTHUR'S COURT, A(1921); SHARK MASTER, THE(1921); WHATEVER SHE WANTS(1921); LITTLE WILDCAT(1922); CLEAN UP, THE(1923); LEGALLY DEAD(1923); RAILROADED(1923); SLANDER THE WOMAN(1923); RIDGEWAY OF MONTANA(1924)
Misc. Silents
CIPHER KEY, THE(1915); MAN'S MAKING, THE(1915); PATH TO THE RAINBOW, THE(1915); RINGTAILED RHINOCEROS, THE(1915); CITY OF FAILING LIGHT, THE(1916); THOSE WHO TOIL(1916); GULF BETWEEN, THE(1918)
Rene Fortier
OUTRAGEOUS!(1977, Can.)
Robert Fortier
SHOW BOAT(1951); TEXAS CARNIVAL(1951); GIRL RUSH, THE(1955); FEARMAKERS, THE(1958); INCUBUS(1966); MC CABE AND MRS. MILLER(1971); THREE WOMEN(1977); HEAVEN CAN WAIT(1978); WEDDING, A(1978); POPEYE(1980)

Michel Fortin
JUDGE AND THE ASSASSIN, THE(1979, Fr.)
Robert Fortin
PHARAOH'S CURSE(1957)
Luciana Fortini
MINUTE TO PRAY, A SECOND TO DIE, A(1968, Ital.), cos
Romana Fortini
KILL BABY KILL(1966, Ital.), ed; DANGER: DIABOLIK(1968, Ital./Fr.), ed
Giuseppe Fortis
BLACK BELLY OF THE TARANTULA, THE(1972, Ital.)
Lee Fortner
CAPTURE THAT CAPSULE(1961)
Henry Fortson
Silents
PATSY(1921)
Ronald Fortt
ON THE BEACH(1959)
J.L. Fortuit
DESTRUCTORS, THE(1974, Brit.)
Jean-Louis Fortuit
COUSINS IN LOVE(1982)
Yvonne Fortuna
FRENCH CANCAN(1956, Fr.), makeup; PICNIC ON THE GRASS(1960, Fr.), makeup; MODIGLIANI OF MONTPARNASSE(1961, Fr./Ital.), makeup
Ugo Fortunati
LA NOTTE(1961, Fr./Ital.)
Pasquale Fortunato
CONFORMIST, THE(1971, Ital., Fr); THAT SPLENDID NOVEMBER(1971, Ital./Fr.)
Chris Fortune
SON OF SINBAD(1955)
Dick Fortune
COMBAT SQUAD(1953); HANNAH LEE(1953); MR. SCOUTMASTER(1953); WAR OF THE WORLDS, THE(1953)
Jan Fortune
VANISHING VIRGINIAN, THE(1941), w; MOKEY(1942), w
John Fortune
TAKE A GIRL LIKE YOU(1970, Brit,)
1984
BLOODBATH AT THE HOUSE OF DEATH(1984, Brit.)
Kim Fortune
OPERATION DAYBREAK(1976, U.S./Brit./Czech.); SPY WHO LOVED ME, THE(1977, Brit.); MOONRAKER(1979, Brit.); EDUCATING RITA(1983)
Matt Fortune
PLEASURE PLANTATION(1970)
Nadio Fortune
1984
ANOTHER TIME, ANOTHER PLACE(1984, Brit.)
Richard Fortune
SANTA FE(1951)
James Fortunes
DREAM OF KINGS, A(1969)
Juan Fortuny
LAS RATAS NO DUERMEN DE NOCHE(1974, Span./Fr.), d&w
Daniel Fortus
LADY LIBERTY(1972, Ital./Fr.)
Douglas Forward
LIMIT, THE(1972)
Robert Forward
TRACKDOWN(1976)
Anthony Forwood
MEET SIMON CHERRY(1949, Brit.); MAN IN BLACK, THE(1950, Brit.); BLACK WIDOW(1951, Brit.); TRAVELLER'S JOY(1951, Brit.); COLONEL MARCH INVESTIGATES(1952,Brit.); GAMBLER AND THE LADY, THE(1952, Brit.); STORY OF ROBIN HOOD, THE(1952, Brit.); KNIGHTS OF THE ROUND TABLE(1953); WOMAN IN HIDING(1953, Brit.); PAID TO KILL(1954, Brit.)
Andrea Forzano [Joseph Losey]
STRANGER ON THE PROWL(1953, Ital.), d
Gareth Forwood
BOFORS GUN, THE(1968, Brit.); PRIEST OF LOVE(1981, Brit.)
Giovanni Forzano
13 MEN AND A GUN(1938, Brit.), w
Rita Forzano
MORE THAN A MIRACLE(1967, Ital./Fr.)
Antonio Fos
VAMPIRE'S NIGHT ORGY, THE(1973, Span./Ital.), w
Victor Fosado
EL TOPO(1971, Mex.)
George Fosati
LOVE HUNGER(1965, Arg.)
Edwin Fosberg
Misc. Silents
MADAME X(1916)
Carla Foscari
DAVID AND GOLIATH(1961, Ital.); CURSE OF THE BLOOD GHOULS(1969, Ital.)
Massimo Foschi
INVESTIGATION OF A CITIZEN ABOVE SUSPICION(1970, Ital.); CHOSEN, THE(1978, Brit./Ital.)
Harold Foshay
Silents
KENNEDY SQUARE(1916); DESIRED WOMAN, THE(1918); YOUTH FOR SALE(1924)
Misc. Silents
SHADOW, THE(1921)
Howard Foshay
UNWRITTEN LAW, THE(1932)
Jane Fosher
Silents
KINGFISHER'S ROOST, THE(1922)

Robert Foshko
HIDE AND SEEK(1964, Brit.), w
George Fosley
BUCKTOWN(1975), ed
George J. Fosley
LOVELY TO LOOK AT(1952), ph
Alan Foss
THAT'LL BE THE DAY(1974, Brit.)
Allan Foss
WINTER'S TALE, THE(1968, Brit.)
Bjorn Foss
PRIZE, THE(1963)
Darrel Foss
Silents
PINCH HITTER, THE(1917); FROM THE GROUND UP(1921); HOMESPUN VAMP, A(1922)
Misc. Silents
EVEN BREAK, AN(1917); FIREFLY OF TOUGH LUCK, THE(1917); REGENERATES, THE(1917); CLOSIN' IN(1918); HER AMERICAN HUSBAND(1918); HER DECISION(1918); MAN WHO WOKE UP, THE(1918); RETURN OF MARY, THE(1918); SOUL IN TRUST, A(1918); TESTING OF MILDRED VANE, THE(1918); WITHOUT HONOR(1918); YOU CAN'T BELIEVE EVERYTHING(1918); JEANNE OF THE GUTTER(1919); PARISIAN TIGRESS, THE(1919); RED LANTERN, THE(1919); ROSE OF THE RIVER(1919); WALK-OFFS, THE(1920); LURING LIPS(1921); UNWILLING HERO, AN(1921); WOMAN HE MARRIED, THE(1922)
Darrell Foss
Silents
BRAT, THE(1919)
Darrell Foss
Misc. Silents
HELD IN TRUST(1920)
F. A. Foss [Lawrence]
1984
DADDY'S DEADLY DARLING(1984), w
Fanya Foss
GIRLS UNDER TWENTY-ONE(1940), w; AFFECTIONATELY YOURS(1941), w; RICHEST MAN IN TOWN(1941), w; STORK PAYS OFF, THE(1941), w
Jack Foss
FAST COMPANY(1938)
John Foss
1984
1984(1984, Brit.)
Kenelm Foss
MRS. DANE'S DEFENCE(1933, Brit.), w
Silents
LOVE IN A WOOD(1915, Brit.), a, w; ARSENE LUPIN(1916, Brit.), a, w; ASTHORE(1917, Brit.), w; AULD ROBIN GRAY(1917, Brit.), w; GRIT OF A JEW, THE(1917, Brit.), w; IF THOU WERT BLIND(1917, Brit.), w; LABOUR LEADER, THE(1917, Brit.), w; ADAM BEDE(1918, Brit.), w; ADMIRABLE CRICHTON, THE(1918, Brit.), w; ALL THE SAD WORLD NEEDS(1918, Brit.), w; MAN AND THE MOMENT, THE(1918, Brit.), a, w; ONCE UPON A TIME(1918, Brit.), a, w; PEEP BEHIND THE SCENES, A(1918, Brit.), d, w; DOUBLE LIFE OF MR. ALFRED BURTON, THE(1919, Brit.), d&w; FANCY DRESS(1919, Brit.), d&w; NOT GUILTY(1919, Brit.), a, w; UNDER SUSPICION(1919, Brit.), w; JOYOUS ADVENTURES OF ARISTIDE PUJOL, THE(1920, Brit.), a, p; ALL ROADS LEAD TO CALVARY(1921, Brit.), d&w; NO. 5 JOHN STREET(1921, Brit.), d&w
Misc. Silents
TOP DOG, THE(1918, Brit.); WAGES OF SIN, THE(1918, Brit.); LITTLE BIT OF FLUFF, A(1919, Brit.), d; WHOSOEVER SHALL OFFEND(1919, Brit.); BACHELOR HUSBAND, THE(1920 Brit.), d; BREED OF THE TRESHAMS, THE(1920, Brit.), d; GLAD EYE, THE(1920, Brit.), d; CHERRY RIPE(1921, Brit.), d; DOUBLE EVENT, THE(1921, Brit.), d; HEADMASTER, THE(1921, Brit.), d; WONDERFUL YEAR, THE(1921, Brit.), d; DICKY MONTEITH(1922, Brit.), d; HOUSE OF PERIL, THE(1922, Brit.), d; ROMANCE OF OLD BAGDAD, A(1922, Brit.), d; KEAN(1924, Fr.)
Wenke Foss
SONG OF NORWAY(1970)
Marc Fossard
LIFE AND LOVES OF BEETHOVEN, THE(1937, Fr.), ph; PEPE LE MOKO(1937, Fr.), ph; THEY WERE FIVE(1938, Fr.), ph; ENTENTE CORDIALE(1939, Fr.), ph; ESCAPE FROM YESTERDAY(1939, Fr.), ph; CHILDREN OF PARADISE(1945, Fr.), ph; PASSION FOR LIFE(1951, Fr.), ph; JUPITER(1952, Fr.), ph; MAIDEN, THE(1961, Fr.), ph; I SPIT ON YOUR GRAVE(1962, Fr.), ph; SWEET ECSTASY(1962, Fr.), ph; GENDARME OF ST. TROPEZ, THE(1966, Fr./Ital.), ph
Bob Fosse
GIVE A GIRL A BREAK(1953); KISS ME KATE(1953); MY SISTER EILEEN(1955), ch; PAJAMA GAME, THE(1957), ch; DAMN YANKEES(1958), a, ch; SWEET CHARITY(1969), d, ch; CABARET(1972), d, ch; LENNY(1974), d; LITTLE PRINCE, THE(1974, Brit.), a, ch; HOW TO SUCCEED IN BUSINESS WITHOUT REALLY TRYING(1976), ch; THIEVES(1977); ALL THAT JAZZ(1979), d, w, ch; STAR 80(1983), d&w
Bunty Fosse
TESHA(1929, Brit.)
Misc. Silents
LOVE'S BOOMERANG(1922)
Jill Fosse
DEAD AND BURIED(1981)
Robert "Bob" Fosse
MY SISTER EILEEN(1955)
William Fosser
ORDINARY PEOPLE(1980), set d; ON THE RIGHT TRACK(1981), art d
1984
NAKED FACE, THE(1984), prod d
William B. Fosser
T.R. BASKIN(1971), set d; COOLEY HIGH(1975), art d; DAMIEN–OMEN II(1978)
Shirley Fossett
OCTOPUSSY(1983, Brit.)
Vera Fossett
OCTOPUSSY(1983, Brit.)

Brigette Fossey
ENIGMA(1983)
Brigitte Fossey
FORBIDDEN GAMES(1953, Fr.); HAPPY ROAD, THE(1957); FAREWELL, FRIEND(1968, Fr./Ital.); WANDERER, THE(1969, Fr.); GOING PLACES(1974, Fr.); BLUE COUNTRY, THE(1977, Fr.); MAN WHO LOVED WOMEN, THE(1977, Fr.); MAIS OU ET DONC ORNICAR(1979, Fr.); QUINTET(1979); CHANEL SOLITAIRE(1981); LA BOUM(1983, Fr.)
S. Fostel
YIDDLE WITH HIS FIDDLE(1937, Pol.)
Foster
CRASHOUT(1955), w
Alan Foster
COME OUT FIGHTING(1945); BLACK MARKET BABIES(1946); VOICE OF THE TURTLE, THE(1947); MAN-EATER OF KUMAON(1948); STORY OF SEABISCUIT, THE(1949); ENFORCER, THE(1951); HAREM GIRL(1952); WINNING TEAM, THE(1952); MAN WITH BOGART'S FACE, THE(1980)
Misc. Talkies
SADDLE SERENADE(1945)
Alan Dean Foster
STAR TREK: THE MOTION PICTURE(1979), w
Andre D. Foster
NAKED CITY, THE(1948)
Art Foster
GENTLEMAN JIM(1942); GORILLA MAN(1942); ACTION IN THE NORTH ATLANTIC(1943); MYSTERIOUS DOCTOR, THE(1943); THANK YOUR LUCKY STARS(1943); ENTER ARSENE LUPIN(1944); FRENCHMAN'S CREEK(1944); IRISH EYES ARE SMILING(1944); CONFIDENTIAL AGENT(1945); GOD IS MY CO-PILOT(1945); ROAD TO UTOPIA(1945); SUDAN(1945); THEY WERE EXPENDABLE(1945); VERDICT, THE(1946); EXILE, THE(1947); IVY(1947); JOAN OF ARC(1948); JULIA MISBEHAVES(1948); KISS THE BLOOD OFF MY HANDS(1948); ROPE OF SAND(1949); SWORD IN THE DESERT(1949); WHITE HEAT(1949)
Arthur Foster
THIS IS THE ARMY(1943); BLONDE SAVAGE(1947)
Arthur Turner Foster
KLONDIKE ANNIE(1936); WHITE ANGEL, THE(1936)
Audrey Foster
MELODY AND ROMANCE(1937, Brit.)
Barry Foster
BATTLE HELL(1956, Brit.); HIGH FLIGHT(1957, Brit.); PURSUIT OF THE GRAF SPEE(1957, Brit.); DUNKIRK(1958, Brit.); SEA FURY(1959, Brit.); SURPRISE PACKAGE(1960); DESERT PATROL(1962, Brit.); PLAYBACK(1962, Brit.); KING AND COUNTRY(1964, Brit.); FAMILY WAY, THE(1966, Brit.); ROBBERY(1967, Brit.); INSPECTOR CLOUSEAU(1968, Brit.); BATTLE OF BRITAIN, THE(1969, Brit.); GURU, THE(1969, U.S./India); TWISTED NERVE(1969, Brit.); RYAN'S DAUGHTER(1970, Brit.); FRENZY(1972, Brit.); QUIET DAY IN BELFAST, A(1974, Can.); SWEENEY(1977, Brit.); WILD GEESE, THE(1978, Brit.); HEAT AND DUST(1983, Brit.)
Basil Foster
RADIO FOLLIES(1935, Brit.)
Silents
AUCTION MART, THE(1920, Brit.)
Bennett Foster
DESPERADOES ARE IN TOWN, THE(1956), w
Bill Foster
I DON'T CARE GIRL, THE(1952); NIAGARA(1953); BEST THINGS IN LIFE ARE FREE, THE(1956), ch; BERNARDINE(1957), ch; OKLAHOMAN, THE(1957); MARDI GRAS(1958), ch; ON THE DOUBLE(1961), ch; SMOKE IN THE WIND(1975)
Billy Foster
Silents
AMERICAN METHODS(1917), ph
Buddy Foster
ANGEL IN MY POCKET(1969); FOXES(1980)
Carey Foster
PAJAMA PARTY(1964); ROUSTABOUT(1964); WINTER A GO-GO(1965); POINT BLANK(1967)
Carole Tru Foster
OTHER SIDE OF THE MOUNTAIN–PART 2, THE(1978)
1984
HARD TO HOLD(1984)
Cherie Foster
WINTER A GO-GO(1965); VANISHING POINT(1971); WELCOME HOME, SOLDIER BOYS(1972)
Cheryl Foster
1984
INITIATION, THE(1984)
Clay Foster
KENNY AND CO.(1976)
Clayton Foster
HOUSE ON THE SAND(1967); NURSE SHERRI(1978)
Dan Foster
EVERY GIRL SHOULD BE MARRIED(1948); RETURN OF THE BADMEN(1948); VELVET TOUCH, THE(1948); SET-UP, THE(1949); THEY LIVE BY NIGHT(1949); WOMAN'S SECRET, A(1949); MAN WITH A CLOAK, THE(1951); PEOPLE AGAINST O'HARA, THE(1951); STRIP, THE(1951); TALL TARGET, THE(1951); THREE GUYS NAMED MIKE(1951); LOVE IS BETTER THAN EVER(1952); SCARAMOUCHE(1952); SINGIN' IN THE RAIN(1952)
Darby Foster
Silents
PADDY, THE NEXT BEST THING(1923, Brit.); THOU FOOL(1926, Brit.)
David Foster
MC CABE AND MRS. MILLER(1971), p; GETAWAY, THE(1972), p; DROWNING POOL, THE(1975), p; FIRST LOVE(1977), p; HEROES(1977), p; LEGACY, THE(1979, Brit.), p; CAVEMAN(1981), p; TIM(1981, Aus.); THING, THE(1982), p; SECOND THOUGHTS(1983), p
1984
MASS APPEAL(1984), p
David S. Foster
Silents
OVAL DIAMOND, THE(1916), w

David Skaats Foster
Silents
ROAD TO LONDON, THE(1921, Brit.), w
Dianne Foster
QUIET WOMAN, THE(1951, Brit.); BIG FRAME, THE(1953, Brit.); ISN'T LIFE WONDERFUL(1953, Brit.); STEEL KEY, THE(1953, Brit.); BAD FOR EACH OTHER(1954); DRIVE A CROOKED ROAD(1954); THREE HOURS TO KILL(1954); BAMBOO PRISON, THE(1955); KENTUCKIAN, THE(1955); VIOLENT MEN, THE(1955); BROTHERS RICO, THE(1957); MONKEY ON MY BACK(1957); NIGHT PASSAGE(1957); DEEP SIX, THE(1958); LAST HURRAH, THE(1958); GIDEON OF SCOTLAND YARD(1959, Brit.); KING OF THE ROARING TWENTIES–THE STORY OF ARNOLD ROTHSTEIN(1961); WHO'S BEEN SLEEPING IN MY BED?(1963)
Dick Foster
GYPSY(1962)
Don Foster
GREAT AMERICAN BUGS BUNNY-ROAD RUNNER CHASE(1979), anim
Donald Foster
HORSE SOLDIERS, THE(1959); PLEASE DON'T EAT THE DAISIES(1960); LORD LOVE A DUCK(1966)
Dorothy Foster
PAPER MOON(1973)
Dudley Foster
TWO-HEADED SPY, THE(1959, Brit.); TERM OF TRIAL(1962, Brit.); NEVER MENTION MURDER(1964, Brit.); LITTLE ONES, THE(1965, Brit.); RICOCHET(1966, Brit.); STUDY IN TERROR, A(1966, Brit./Ger.); WHERE'S JACK?(1969, Brit.); MOON ZERO TWO(1970, Brit.); RISE AND RISE OF MICHAEL RIMMER, THE(1970, Brit.); WUTHERING HEIGHTS(1970, Brit.); DULCIMA(1971, Brit.); PUBLIC EYE, THE(1972, Brit.)
Dwayne L. Foster
FRATERNITY ROW(1977)
Ed Foster
MUTINY IN THE BIG HOUSE(1939); SABOTEUR(1942); IT AIN'T HAY(1943); OPERATION SECRET(1952)
Eddie Foster
KID FROM SPAIN, THE(1932); GOLD DIGGERS OF 1933(1933); LADY BY CHOICE(1934); MEN OF THE NIGHT(1934); TWENTY MILLION SWEETHEARTS(1934); DANGEROUS(1936); KID GALAHAD(1937); LAST GANGSTER, THE(1937); MIDNIGHT COURT(1937); HIGHWAY PATROL(1938); I AM THE LAW(1938); ONLY ANGELS HAVE WINGS(1939); ANGELS OVER BROADWAY(1940); MUMMY'S HAND, THE(1940); STRANGE CARGO(1940); BALL OF FIRE(1941); FACE BEHIND THE MASK, THE(1941); GAMBLING DAUGHTERS(1941); ROAR OF THE PRESS(1941); LARCENY, INC.(1942); TRAMP, TRAMP, TRAMP(1942); GHOST AND THE GUEST(1943); SHOOT TO KILL(1947); SMART GIRLS DON'T TALK(1948); SCENE OF THE CRIME(1949); WHITE HEAT(1949); TRIPLE TROUBLE(1950); HOODLUM, THE(1951); HOODLUM EMPIRE(1952); KANSAS CITY CONFIDENTIAL(1952); KILLER APE(1953)
Edward Foster
HELD FOR RANSOM(1938); MARJORIE MORNINGSTAR(1958); PIER 5, HAVANA(1959); THREE STOOGES MEET HERCULES, THE(1962)
Eve Foster
HIGHLAND FLING(1936, Brit.)
Evelyn Foster
CHECKMATE(1935, Brit,); CROSS CURRENTS(1935, Brit.); MAD HATTERS, THE(1935, Brit.); BELLES OF ST. CLEMENTS, THE(1936, Brit.)
Fern Foster
Silents
MASTER CRACKSMAN, THE(1914)
Florence Foster
Misc. Silents
DAWN OF REVENGE(1922)
Frances Foster
TAKE A GIANT STEP(1959); WHO SAYS I CAN'T RIDE A RAINBOW!(1971); COPS AND ROBBERS(1973); PIECE OF THE ACTION, A(1977)
Frank Foster
RANDOLPH FAMILY, THE(1945, Brit.)
George Foster
BIRDS OF A FEATHER(1935, Brit.), w; PHYNX, THE(1970), p, w
Giles Foster
Misc. Talkies
AERODROME, THE(1983, Brit.), d
Glenn Foster
UGLY ONES, THE(1968, Ital./Span.)
Gloria Foster
COOL WORLD, THE(1963); NOTHING BUT A MAN(1964); COMEDIANS, THE(1967); ANGEL LEVINE, THE(1970); MAN AND BOY(1972)
Harry Foster
TWO SISTERS(1938), ed; LET'S ROCK(1958), p&d
Harve Foster
GLORY TRAIL, THE(1937); SONG OF THE SOUTH(1946), d
Misc. Talkies
FABULOUS JOE, THE(1946), d
Hebben Foster
Misc. Silents
BEETLE, THE(1919, Brit.)
Hebden Foster
Misc. Silents
LITTLE HOUR OF PETER WELLS, THE(1920, Brit.)
Helen Foster
GOLD DIGGERS OF BROADWAY(1929); PAINTED FACES(1929); SHOULD A GIRL MARRY?(1929); SO LONG LETTY(1929); BOILING POINT, THE(1932); GHOST CITY(1932); SADDLE BUSTER, THE(1932); SINISTER HANDS(1932); YOUNG BLOOD(1932); LUCKY LARRIGAN(1933); SCHOOL FOR GIRLS(1935); WESTERNER, THE(1940); PARACHUTE NURSE(1942); CALL NORTHSIDE 777(1948); NEVER WAVE AT A WAC(1952)
Silents
ON THE GO(1925); CALIFORNIA OR BUST(1927); NAUGHTY NANETTE(1927); OUTLAW DOG, THE(1927); SWEET SIXTEEN(1928); 13 WASHINGTON SQUARE(1928); HARVEST OF HATE, THE(1929); HOOFBEATS OF VENGEANCE(1929); LINDA(1929); SKY SKIDDER, THE(1929)

Misc. Silents
BANDIT'S BABY, THE(1925); RECKLESS COURAGE(1925); HANDS OFF(1927); WHEN A DOG LOVES(1927); HELLSHIP BRONSON(1928); ROAD TO RUIN, THE(1928); WON IN THE CLOUDS(1928); CIRCUMSTANTIAL EVIDENCE(1929)

Henry Foster
Silents
EUGENE ARAM(1914, Brit.)

Isabelle Foster
SCOUNDREL, THE(1935); SOAK THE RICH(1936)

Isobel Foster
Silents
PROFLIGATE, THE(1917, Brit.)

J. Byron Foster
CORPSE GRINDERS, THE(1972)

J. Morris Foster
Silents
HIGH SPEED(1917); ALL THE WORLD TO NOTHING(1919); SILENT VOW, THE(1922)
Misc. Silents
BELOVED JIM(1917); SECRET MAN, THE(1917); FIGHTING GRIN, THE(1918); MONEY ISN'T EVERYTHING(1918); WINNING GRANDMA(1918); PARISH PRIEST, THE(1921); GUNFIGHTER, THE(1923); MEN IN THE RAW(1923)

J.K. Foster
HONOR OF THE PRESS(1932), w

Jack Foster
NESTING, THE(1981), ed

Jack Danny Foster
1984
FLAMINGO KID, THE(1984)

James H. Foster
MY DOG, BUDDY(1960)

Jane Foster
1984
MRS. SOFFEL(1984)

Jeremy Foster
BLACK OAK CONSPIRACY(1977)

Jerry Foster
FRONTIER MARSHAL(1934)

Jill Foster
ALVIN PURPLE(1974, Aus.)

Jodie Foster
KANSAS CITY BOMBER(1972); NAPOLEON AND SAMANTHA(1972); ONE LITTLE INDIAN(1973); TOM SAWYER(1973); ALICE DOESN'T LIVE HERE ANYMORE(1975); BUGSY MALONE(1976, Brit.); ECHOES OF A SUMMER(1976); FREAKY FRIDAY(1976); TAXI DRIVER(1976); LITTLE GIRL WHO LIVES DOWN THE LANE, THE(1977, Can.); CANDLESHOE(1978); CARNY(1980); FOXES(1980); O'HARA'S WIFE(1983)
1984
HOTEL NEW HAMPSHIRE, THE(1984)

Joe Foster
HIGH SCHOOL CONFIDENTIAL(1958)

John Foster
WESTBOUND STAGE(1940), w; SHAFT'S BIG SCORE(1972)
1984
FEAR CITY(1984); VARIETY(1984), ph

Julia Foster
LONELINESS OF THE LONG DISTANCE RUNNER, THE(1962, Brit.); SMALL WORLD OF SAMMY LEE, THE(1963, Brit.); BARGEE, THE(1964, Brit.); ONE WAY PENDULUM(1965, Brit.); TWO LEFT FEET(1965, Brit.); ALFIE(1966, Brit.); GIRL GETTERS, THE(1966, Brit.); HALF A SIXPENCE(1967, Brit.); PERCY(1971, Brit.); GREAT MCGONAGALL, THE(1975, Brit.)
Misc. Talkies
ALL COPPERS ARE...(1972, Brit.)

Kylie Foster
KITTY AND THE BAGMAN(1983, Aus.)

Lawrence Foster
1984
CAL(1984, Ireland)

Lewis Foster
EIGHT GIRLS IN A BOAT(1934), w; LET'S TALK IT OVER(1934), w; STOLEN HARMONY(1935), w; ARMORED CAR(1937), w; ILLEGAL TRAFFIC(1938), w; SONS OF THE LEGION(1938), w; MILLION DOLLAR LEGS(1939), w; SUDDEN MONEY(1939), w; TOM SAWYER, DETECTIVE(1939), w

Lewis B. Foster
CHEATING BLONDES(1933), w

Lewis R. Foster
LOVE LETTERS OF A STAR(1936), d&w; MAGNIFICENT BRUTE, THE(1936), w; TWO IN A CROWD(1936), w; ARMORED CAR(1937), w; MAN WHO CRIED WOLF, THE(1937), d; SHE'S DANGEROUS(1937), d; MR. SMITH GOES TO WASHINGTON(1939), w; NIGHT WORK(1939), w; SOME LIKE IT HOT(1939), w; COMIN' ROUND THE MOUNTAIN(1940), w; FARMER'S DAUGHTER, THE(1940), w; GOLDEN GLOVES(1940), w; ADVENTURE IN WASHINGTON(1941), w; I LIVE ON DANGER(1942), w; MAYOR OF 44TH STREET, THE(1942), w; ALASKA HIGHWAY(1943), w; HERS TO HOLD(1943), w; MORE THE MERRIER, THE(1943), w; CAN'T HELP SINGING(1944), w; IT'S IN THE BAG(1945), w; NEVER SAY GOODBYE(1946), w; I WONDER WHO'S KISSING HER NOW(1947), w; CAPTAIN CHINA(1949), d, w; EL PASO(1949), d&w; LUCKY STIFF, THE(1949), w; MANHANDLED(1949), d, w; SPECIAL AGENT(1949), w; EAGLE AND THE HAWK, THE(1950), d, w; CROSSWINDS(1951), d, w; HONG KONG(1951), d, w; LAST OUTPOST, THE(1951), d; PASSAGE WEST(1951), w; BLAZING FOREST, THE(1952), w; JAMAICA RUN(1953), d, w; THOSE REDHEADS FROM SEATTLE(1953), d, w; TROPIC ZONE(1953), d&w; VANQUISHED, THE(1953), w; CRASHOUT(1955), d; TOP OF THE WORLD(1955), p, d; BOLD AND THE BRAVE, THE(1956), d; DAKOTA INCIDENT(1956), d; TONKA(1958), d, w; SIGN OF ZORRO, THE(1960), d

Linc Foster
KISS THEM FOR ME(1957); 10 NORTH FREDERICK(1958)

Linda Foster
JOHN GOLDFARB, PLEASE COME HOME(1964); ROUSTABOUT(1964); YOUNG FURY(1965); AMBUSHERS, THE(1967)

Lisa Foster
SPRING FEVER(1983, Can.)
Misc. Talkies
ATOR, THE INVINCIBLE(1984)

Louise Foster
Misc. Talkies
REUNION, THE(1977)

Maralee Foster
YOURS, MINE AND OURS(1968)

Margaret Foster
Silents
AT THE STAGE DOOR(1921)

Marion Foster
EMIL(1938, Brit.)

Marvin Foster
WARRIORS, THE(1979); ENDLESS LOVE(1981)

Maurice Foster
JOKERS, THE(1967, Brit.), p; PROJECTED MAN, THE(1967, Brit.), p; ASSIGNMENT K(1968, Brit.), p, w

Maximalian Foster
WHEN STRANGERS MARRY(1933), w

Maximilian Foster
Silents
SILENT PARTNER, THE(1923), w

Maxwell Foster
UNDERCOVER AGENT(1935, Brit.); NO HIGHWAY IN THE SKY(1951, Brit.); RELUCTANT WIDOW, THE(1951, Brit.); END OF THE LINE, THE(1959, Brit.); WOMAN EATER, THE(1959, Brit.)

May Foster
SCARLET EMPRESS, THE(1934)
Silents
KNIGHT OF THE WEST, A(1921); YELLOW FINGERS(1926)

Meg Foster
ADAM AT 6 A.M.(1970); TODD KILLINGS, THE(1971); THUMB TRIPPING(1972); TENDER FLESH(1976); DIFFERENT STORY, A(1978); CARNY(1980); TICKET TO HEAVEN(1981); OSTERMAN WEEKEND, THE(1983)

Michael Foster
GONE WITH THE WIND(1939), w; SONG FOR MISS JULIE, A(1945), w

Morris Foster
Silents
INNOCENT LIE, THE(1916); OVERLAND RED(1920)
Misc. Silents
CARDINAL RICHELIEU'S WARD(1914); NAIDRA, THE DREAM WOMAN(1914, Ger.); GOD'S WITNESS(1915); VOICE OF DESTINY, THE(1918); WHAT HAPPENED TO JONES(1920)

N. Foster
SIGN OF ZORRO, THE(1960), w

Norma Foster
CROOKS ANONYMOUS(1963, Brit.); MURDER AHOY(1964, Brit.); RING OF SPIES(1964, Brit.); SPY WITH A COLD NOSE, THE(1966, Brit.); STUDY IN TERROR, A(1966, Brit./Ger.); FOR SINGLES ONLY(1968); GREAT CATHERINE(1968, Brit.)

Norman Foster
GENTLEMEN OF THE PRESS(1929); LOVE AT FIRST SIGHT(1930); YOUNG MAN OF MANHATTAN(1930); CITY STREETS(1931); CONFESSIONS OF A CO-ED(1931); IT PAYS TO ADVERTISE(1931); MEN CALL IT LOVE(1931); NO LIMIT(1931); RECKLESS LIVING(1931); UP POPS THE DEVIL(1931); ALIAS THE DOCTOR(1932); COHENS, AND KELLYS IN HOLLYWOOD, THE(1932); GIRL OF THE RIO(1932); PLAY GIRL(1932); PROSPERITY(1932); SKYSCRAPER SOULS(1932); STEADY COMPANY(1932); STRANGE JUSTICE(1932); UNDER EIGHTEEN(1932); WEEK-END MARRIAGE(1932); BISHOP MISBEHAVES, THE(1933); PILGRIMAGE(1933); PROFESSIONAL SWEETHEART(1933); STATE FAIR(1933); WALLS OF GOLD(1933); ORIENT EXPRESS(1934); RAFTER ROMANCE(1934); STRICTLY DYNAMITE(1934); BEHIND GREEN LIGHTS(1935); BEHIND THE EVIDENCE(1935); ELINOR NORTON(1935); ESCAPE FROM DEVIL'S ISLAND(1935); FIRETRAP, THE(1935); HOOSIER SCHOOLMASTER(1935); LADIES CRAVE EXCITEMENT(1935); SUPERSPEED(1935); EVERYBODY'S OLD MAN(1936); FATAL LADY(1936); HIGH TENSION(1936); LEAVENWORTH CASE, THE(1936); FAIR WARNING(1937), d, w; THANK YOU, MR. MOTO(1937), d, w; THINK FAST, MR. MOTO(1937), d, w; I COVER CHINATOWN(1938), a, d; MR. MOTO TAKES A CHANCE(1938), d, w; MR. MOTO TAKES A VACATION(1938), d, w; MYSTERIOUS MR. MOTO(1938), d, w; WALKING DOWN BROADWAY(1938), d; CHARLIE CHAN AT TREASURE ISLAND(1939), d; CHARLIE CHAN IN RENO(1939), d; MR. MOTO'S LAST WARNING(1939), d; CHARLIE CHAN IN PANAMA(1940), d; VIVA CISCO KID(1940), d; RIDE, KELLY, RIDE(1941), d; SCOTLAND YARD(1941), d; JOURNEY INTO FEAR(1942), d; KISS THE BLOOD OFF MY HANDS(1948), d; RACHEL AND THE STRANGER(1948), d; TELL IT TO THE JUDGE(1949), d; FATHER IS A BACHELOR(1950), d; WOMAN ON THE RUN(1950), d, w; NAVAJO(1952), d&w; SKY FULL OF MOON(1952), d&w; SOMBRERO(1953), d, w; DAVY CROCKETT, KING OF THE WILD FRONTIER(1955), d; DAVY CROCKETT AND THE RIVER PIRATES(1956), d, w; SIGN OF ZORRO, THE(1960), d; INDIAN PAINT(1965), d&w; MERRY WIVES OF WINDSOR, THE(1966, Aust.), a, p, w; BRIGHTY OF THE GRAND CANYON(1967), d&w
Misc. Talkies
BLUEBEARD'S CASTLE(1969, Brit.)

Pam Foster
MACBETH(1971, Brit.)

Pamela Foster
CARNIVAL(1946, Brit.); DANCING YEARS, THE(1950, Brit.)

Peggy Foster
GETTING OVER(1981)

Phil Foster
CONQUEST OF SPACE(1955); PATSY, THE(1964); EVERY LITTLE CROOK AND NANNY(1972); BANG THE DRUM SLOWLY(1973); HAIL(1973); HAPPY HOOKER GOES TO WASHINGTON, THE(1977)

Phoebe Foster
TARNISHED LADY(1931); NIGHT ANGEL, THE(1931); DINNER AT EIGHT(1933); OUR BETTERS(1933); ANNA KARENINA(1935); GORGEOUS HUSSY, THE(1936); WHITE ANGEL, THE(1936)

Preston Foster
FOLLOW THE LEADER(1930); HIS WOMAN(1931); ALL-AMERICAN, THE(1932); DOCTOR X(1932); I AM A FUGITIVE FROM A CHAIN GANG(1932); LIFE BEGINS(1932); TWO SECONDS(1932); YOU SAID A MOUTHFUL(1932); CORRUPTION(1933); DEVIL'S MATE(1933); ELMER THE GREAT(1933); HOOPLA(1933); MAN WHO DARED, THE(1933); BAND PLAYS ON, THE(1934); HEAT LIGHTNING(1934); SENSATION HUNTERS(1934); SLEEPERS EAST(1934); WHARF ANGEL(1934); ANNIE OAKLEY(1935); ARIZONIAN, THE(1935); INFORMER, THE(1935); LAST DAYS OF POMPEII, THE(1935); PEOPLE'S ENEMY, THE(1935); STRANGERS ALL(1935); LOVE BEFORE BREAKFAST(1936); MUSS 'EM UP(1936); PLOUGH AND THE STARS, THE(1936); WE'RE ONLY HUMAN(1936); FIRST LADY(1937); OUTCASTS OF POKER FLAT, THE(1937); SEA DEVILS(1937); WE WHO ARE ABOUT TO DIE(1937); WESTLAND CASE, THE(1937); YOU CAN'T BEAT LOVE(1937); ARMY GIRL(1938); DOUBLE DANGER(1938); EVERYBODY'S DOING IT(1938); LADY IN THE MORGUE(1938); LAST WARNING, THE(1938); STORM, THE(1938); SUBMARINE PATROL(1938); UP THE RIVER(1938); CHASING DANGER(1939); GERONIMO(1939); MISSING EVIDENCE(1939); NEWS IS MADE AT NIGHT(1939); SOCIETY SMUGGLERS(1939); 20,000 MEN A YEAR(1939); CAFE HOSTESS(1940); MOON OVER BURMA(1940); NORTHWEST MOUNTED POLICE(1940); ROUNDUP, THE(1941); UNFINISHED BUSINESS(1941); AMERICAN EMPIRE(1942); GENTLEMAN AFTER DARK, A(1942); LITTLE TOKYO, U.S.A.(1942); NIGHT IN NEW ORLEANS, A(1942); SECRET AGENT OF JAPAN(1942); THUNDER BIRDS(1942); GUADALCANAL DIARY(1943); MY FRIEND FLICKA(1943); BERMUDA MYSTERY(1944); ROGER TOUHY, GANGSTER!(1944); ABBOTT AND COSTELLO IN HOLLYWOOD(1945); THUNDERHEAD-SON OF FLICKA(1945); TWICE BLESSED(1945); VALLEY OF DECISION, THE(1945); INSIDE JOB(1946); STRANGE TRIANGLE(1946); TANGIER(1946); KING OF THE WILD HORSES(1947); RAMROD(1947); HUNTED, THE(1948); THUNDERHOOF(1948); BIG CAT, THE(1949); I SHOT JESSE JAMES(1949); TOUGHER THEY COME, THE(1950); BIG GUSHER, THE(1951); BIG NIGHT, THE(1951); THREE DESPERATE MEN(1951); TOMAHAWK(1951); KANSAS CITY CONFIDENTIAL(1952); MONTANA TERRITORY(1952); I, THE JURY(1953); LAW AND ORDER(1953); MARSHAL'S DAUGHTER, THE(1953); DESTINATION 60,000(1957); ADVANCE TO THE REAR(1964); MAN FROM GALVESTON, THE(1964); TIME TRAVELERS, THE(1964); YOU'VE GOT TO BE SMART(1967); CHUBASCO(1968)

Preston S. Foster
LAST MILE, THE(1932); LADIES THEY TALK ABOUT(1933)

Ralph Foster
Silents
AUTOCRAT, THE(1919, Brit.); FATHER O'FLYNN(1919, Brit.); CALL OF YOUTH, THE(1920, Brit.)

Ray Foster
ROYAL BOX, THE(1930), ph; LIFE WITH FATHER(1947), spec eff; JUDGE, THE(1949), ph; LET'S MAKE LOVE(1960)

Raymond Foster
GREEN-EYED BLONDE, THE(1957); MY FAIR LADY(1964)

Richard Foster
RIVER, THE(1951)

Richard R. Foster
DAMN CITIZEN(1958)

Ron Foster
CAGE OF EVIL(1960); THREE CAME TO KILL(1960); OPERATION BOTTLENECK(1961); SECRET OF DEEP HARBOR(1961); HOUSE OF THE DAMNED(1963); PRIVATE LESSONS(1981)
1984
MUPPETS TAKE MANHATTAN, THE(1984); NINJA III-THE DOMINATION(1984)

Ronald Foster
ROCKABILLY BABY(1957); STORM RIDER, THE(1957); UNDER FIRE(1957); YOUNG AND DANGEROUS(1957); CATTLE EMPIRE(1958); DESERT HELL(1958); THUNDERING JETS(1958); DIARY OF A HIGH SCHOOL BRIDE(1959); MA BARKER'S KILLER BROOD(1960); MUSIC BOX KID, THE(1960); WALKING TARGET, THE(1960)

Royal Foster
BILL AND COO(1947), w

Ruth Foster
DIMENSION 5(1966)

Sheila Foster
DIRTY DINGUS MAGEE(1970)

Sherry Velvet Foster
NORMA RAE(1979)

Stan Foster
Misc. Talkies
MY NAME IS LEGEND(1975)

Steve Foster
CAYMAN TRIANGLE, THE(1977)

Stewart Foster
EVER SINCE VENUS(1944)

Stuart Foster
FABULOUS DORSEYS, THE(1947)

Susan Foster
BORN LOSERS(1967); BILLY JACK(1971); BOY WHO CRIED WEREWOLF, THE(1973)

Susanna Foster
GREAT VICTOR HERBERT, THE(1939); GLAMOUR BOY(1941); THERE'S MAGIC IN MUSIC(1941); STAR SPANGLED RHYTHM(1942); PHANTOM OF THE OPERA(1943); TOP MAN(1943); BOWERY TO BROADWAY(1944); CLIMAX, THE(1944); FOLLOW THE BOYS(1944); THIS IS THE LIFE(1944); FRISCO SAL(1945); THAT NIGHT WITH YOU(1945)

Terrea Foster
SCREWBALLS(1983)

Thaya Foster
FOLIES DERGERE(1935)

Vernon Foster
1984
SACRED GROUND(1984)

Vivian Foster
THIS WEEK OF GRACE(1933, Brit.)

W. Bert Foster
Silents
BULLDOG PLUCK(1927), w

Warren Foster
HEY THERE, IT'S YOGI BEAR(1964), w; MAN CALLED FLINTSTONE, THE(1966), w

Wayne Foster
MURDER IN MISSISSIPPI(1965)

William Foster
BLIND MAN'S BLUFF(1936, Brit.), w; PLUNDERERS OF PAINTED FLATS(1959); SHOOT OUT AT BIG SAG(1962); STAKEOUT!(1962); BIG DADDY(1969); GUNS OF A STRANGER(1973)
Misc. Talkies
OLE REX(1961)
Silents
MAN WHO TURNED WHITE, THE(1919), ph

William Foster, Jr.
SHEBA BABY(1975)

William C. Foster
Silents
TALE OF TWO CITIES, A(1917), ph; LES MISERABLES(1918), ph; OLIVER TWIST, JR.(1921), ph

Zenna Foster
CORPSE GRINDERS, THE(1972)

Frank Foster-Brown
STORM BOY(1976, Aus.)

William Foster-Davis
DR. NO(1962, Brit.)

Giovanni Fostini
ANGELA(1955, Ital.)

John Fostini
THRILL OF BRAZIL, THE(1946); BURNING CROSS, THE(1947); FUGITIVE LADY(1951); THREE STEPS NORTH(1951); ROMAN HOLIDAY(1953)

T.F. Fotherby
SHADOW OF FEAR(1963, Brit.), w

Blanche Fothergill
BONNIE PRINCE CHARLIE(1948, Brit.); MATTER OF MURDER, A(1949, Brit.)

A. C. Fotheringham-Lysons
Silents
AMATEUR GENTLEMAN, THE(1920, Brit.)

Rudolph C. Fothow
MYSTERIOUS INTRUDER(1946), p

Jacque Foti
TWO OF A KIND(1983)
1984
UNFAITHFULLY YOURS(1984)

Ricardo Foti
NEVER TAKE NO FOR AN ANSWER(1952, Brit./Ital.)

Fani Fotinou
PEDESTRIAN, THE(1974, Ger.)

Elli Fotiou
FEAR, THE(1967, Gr.); SISTERS, THE(1969, Gr.)

Dionysis Fotopoulos
DREAM OF PASSION, A(1978, Gr.), set d&cos

Mimi Fotopoulos
GIRL OF THE MOUNTAINS(1958, Gr.); FORTUNE TELLER, THE(1961, Gr.); GROUCH, THE(1961, Gr.)

Vassele Fotopoulos
ZORBA THE GREEK(1964, U.S./Gr.), art d; YOU'RE A BIG BOY NOW(1966), art d

Joan Fotre
NIGHTFALL(1956)

Vincent Fotre
MISSILE TO THE MOON(1959), w; NIGHT THEY KILLED RASPUTIN, THE(1962, Fr./Ital.), p; OPERATION CROSS EAGLES(1969, U.S./Yugo.), w

Pierre Foucard
OSS 117-MISSION FOR A KILLER(1966, Fr./Ital.), w; SHADOW OF EVIL(1967, Fr./Ital.), w

Pierre Foucasud
FANTOMAS(1966, Fr./Ital.), w

Francis Foucaud
WAR AND PEACE(1956, Ital./U.S.)

Pierre Foucaud
FANTOMAS STRIKES BACK(1965, Fr./Ital.), w

Andre Fouche
CESAR(1936, Fr.)

Miriam Fouche
Silents
PRIVATE PEAT(1918); GOING THE LIMIT(1925)
Misc. Silents
SOLDIERS OF CHANCE(1917)

Jean Fouchet
LA BONNE SOUPE(1964, Fr./Ital.), spec eff

Robert Fouik
REMAINS TO BE SEEN(1953)

Robert Fould
MOB, THE(1951); UNKNOWN MAN, THE(1951)

Angela Fouldes
SECRET PEOPLE(1952, Brit.)

Angela Foulds
MILLIONS LIKE US(1943, Brit.); HIDEOUT(1948, Brit.); LAST LOAD, THE(1948, Brit.)

Bryon Foulger
THEY WON'T BELIEVE ME(1947); SILVER SPURS(1943); CASANOVA BROWN(1944); MRS. PARKINGTON(1944); SNIPER, THE(1952)

Byran Foulger
CRIPPLE CREEK(1952)

Byron Foulger
YOU CAN'T RUN AWAY FROM IT(1956); AWFUL TRUTH, THE(1937); DUKE COMES BACK, THE(1937); LARCENY ON THE AIR(1937); LUCK OF ROARING CAMP, THE(1937); MAKE WAY FOR TOMORROW(1937); PRISONER OF ZENDA,

THE(1937); BORN TO BE WILD(1938); DELINQUENT PARENTS(1938); GANGSTER'S BOY(1938); KING OF THE NEWSBOYS(1938); SAY IT IN FRENCH(1938); TARNISHED ANGEL(1938); TEST PILOT(1938); YOU CAN'T TAKE IT WITH YOU(1938); ANDY HARDY GETS SPRING FEVER(1939); EXILE EXPRESS(1939); GIRL FROM RIO, THE(1939); I AM A CRIMINAL(1939); IN NAME ONLY(1939); LET US LIVE(1939); MAN THEY COULD NOT HANG, THE(1939); MILLION DOLLAR LEGS(1939); MR. SMITH GOES TO WASHINGTON(1939); MUTINY ON THE BLACKHAWK(1939); SECRET OF DR. KILDARE, THE(1939); SPELLBINDER, THE(1939); TELEVISION SPY(1939); UNION PACIFIC(1939); ARIZONA(1940); CHRISTMAS IN JULY(1940); DR. KILDARE'S CRISIS(1940); EDISON, THE MAN(1940); ELLERY QUEEN. MASTER DETECTIVE(1940); GREAT McGINTY, THE(1940); HEROES OF THE SADDLE(1940); I WANT A DIVORCE(1940); MAN WITH NINE LIVES, THE(1940); PAROLE FIXER(1940); SAINT'S DOUBLE TROUBLE, THE(1940); SKY MURDER(1940); UNTAMED(1940); DUDE COWBOY(1941); FOOLS OF DESIRE(1941); GAY VAGABOND, THE(1941); H.M. PULHAM, ESQ.(1941); MAN MADE MONSTER(1941); MEET BOSTON BLACKIE(1941); MYSTERY SHIP(1941); PENALTY, THE(1941); REMEMBER THE DAY(1941); RIDIN' ON A RAINBOW(1941); SHE KNEW ALL THE ANSWERS(1941); SIS HOPKINS(1941); SULLIVAN'S TRAVELS(1941); SWEETHEART OF THE CAMPUS(1941); YOU BELONG TO ME(1941); HARVARD, HERE I COME(1942); MAGNIFICENT DOPE, THE(1942); MAN FROM HEADQUARTERS(1942); MISS ANNIE ROONEY(1942); PACIFIC RENDEZVOUS(1942); PALM BEACH STORY, THE(1942); PANTHER'S CLAW, THE(1942); QUIET PLEASE, MURDER(1942); REAP THE WILD WIND(1942); ROAD TO HAPPINESS(1942); SABOTAGE SQUAD(1942); STAND BY FOR ACTION(1942); WRECKING CREW(1942); ADVENTURES OF A ROOKIE(1943); BLACK RAVEN, THE(1943); CONEY ISLAND(1943); DIXIE DUGAN(1943); FALCON STRIKES BACK, THE(1943); FIRST COMES COURAGE(1943); HANGMEN ALSO DIE(1943); HI DIDDLE DIDDLE(1943); HOPPY SERVES A WRIT(1943); HUMAN COMEDY, THE(1943); IN OLD OKLAHOMA(1943); KANSAN, THE(1943); MARGIN FOR ERROR(1943); SO PROUDLY WE HAIL(1943); SWEET ROSIE O'GRADY(1943); WHAT A WOMAN!(1943); ADVENTURES OF KITTY O'DAY(1944); BEAUTIFUL BUT BROKE(1944); DARK MOUNTAIN(1944); ENEMY OF WOMEN(1944); EVER SINCE VENUS(1944); GIRL RUSH(1944); HENRY ALDRICH'S LITTLE SECRET(1944); LADIES OF WASHINGTON(1944); MAISIE GOES TO RENO(1944); MARRIAGE IS A PRIVATE AFFAIR(1944); MIRACLE OF MORGAN'S CREEK, THE(1944); MUSIC IN MANHATTAN(1944); ROGER TOUHY, GANGSTER!(1944); SINCE YOU WENT AWAY(1944); SUMMER STORM(1944); SWING IN THE SADDLE(1944); THREE MEN IN WHITE(1944); WHISTLER, THE(1944); ADVENTURE(1945); ARSON SQUAD(1945); BLONDE FROM BROOKLYN(1945); BREWSTER'S MILLIONS(1945); CHEATERS, THE(1945); CIRCUMSTANTIAL EVIDENCE(1945); CORNERED(1945); DON JUAN QUILLIGAN(1945); GRISSLY'S MILLIONS(1945); HIDDEN EYE, THE(1945); LET'S GO STEADY(1945); LOST WEEKEND, THE(1945); MINISTRY OF FEAR(1945); NOB HILL(1945); SCARLET STREET(1945); SENSATION HUNTERS(1945); SNAFU(1945); WEEKEND AT THE WALDORF(1945); WONDER MAN(1945); COURAGE OF LASSIE(1946); DICK TRACY VS. CUEBALL(1946); FRENCH KEY, THE(1946); HOODLUM SAINT, THE(1946); HOUSE OF HORRORS(1946); MAGNIFICENT DOLL(1946); PLAINSMAN AND THE LADY(1946); POSTMAN ALWAYS RINGS TWICE, THE(1946); SENTIMENTAL JOURNEY(1946); SHOW-OFF, THE(1946); SUSPENSE(1946); TILL THE CLOUDS ROLL BY(1946); TWO SISTERS FROM BOSTON(1946); ADVENTURES OF DON COYOTE(1947); BELLS OF SAN FERNANDO(1947); CHINESE RING, THE(1947); DEAD RECKONING(1947); EASY COME, EASY GO(1947); HARD BOILED MAHONEY(1947); LINDA BE GOOD(1947); LONG NIGHT, THE(1947); MICHIGAN KID, THE(1947); SONG OF LOVE(1947); TOO MANY WINNERS(1947); TROUBLE WITH WOMEN, THE(1947); UNCONQUERED(1947); ARCH OF TRIUMPH(1948); HE WALKED BY NIGHT(1948); I SURRENDER DEAR(1948); KISSING BANDIT, THE(1948); LET'S LIVE A LITTLE(1948); OUT OF THE STORM(1948); RELENTLESS(1948); RETURN OF OCTOBER, THE(1948); SOUTHERN YANKEE, A(1948); THREE MUSKETEERS, THE(1948); ARSON, INC.(1949); DALTON GANG, THE(1949); DANCING IN THE DARK(1949); I SHOT JESSE JAMES(1949); INSPECTOR GENERAL, THE(1949); RED DESERT(1949); SAMSON AND DELILAH(1949); SATAN'S CRADLE(1949); STREETS OF LAREDO(1949); THEY LIVE BY NIGHT(1949); CHAMPAGNE FOR CAESAR(1950); DARK CITY(1950); EXPERIMENT ALCATRAZ(1950); GIRL FROM SAN LORENZO, THE(1950); KEY TO THE CITY(1950); RETURN OF JESSE JAMES, THE(1950); SALT LAKE RAIDERS(1950); TO PLEASE A LADY(1950); UNION STATION(1950); FBI GIRL(1951); GASOLINE ALLEY(1951); HOME TOWN STORY(1951); MILLIONAIRE FOR CHRISTY, A(1951); SEA HORNET, THE(1951); SUPERMAN AND THE MOLE MEN(1951); APACHE COUNTRY(1952); HOLD THAT LINE(1952); MY SIX CONVICTS(1952); SKIRTS AHOY!(1952); STEEL FIST, THE(1952); WE'RE NOT MARRIED(1952); BANDITS OF THE WEST(1953); BLADES OF THE MUSKETEERS(1953); CONFIDENTIAL CONNIE(1953); CRUISIN' DOWN THE RIVER(1953); MAGNETIC MONSTER, THE(1953); MOONLIGHTER, THE(1953); PARIS MODEL(1953); PERILOUS JOURNEY, A(1953); CATTLE QUEEN OF MONTANA(1954); SILVER LODE(1954); AT GUNPOINT(1955); SCARLET COAT, THE(1955); SPOILERS, THE(1955); DESPERADOES ARE IN TOWN, THE(1956); BUCKSKIN LADY, THE(1957); DINO(1957); GUN BATTLE AT MONTEREY(1957); RIVER'S EDGE, THE(1957); SIERRA STRANGER(1957); UP IN SMOKE(1957); DEVIL'S PARTNER, THE(1958); GOING STEADY(1958); IN THE MONEY(1958); LONG, HOT SUMMER, THE(1958); KING OF THE WILD STALLIONS(1959); MA BARKER'S KILLER BROOD(1960); TWELVE HOURS TO KILL(1960); POCKETFUL OF MIRACLES(1961); SON OF FLUBBER(1963); MARRIAGE ON THE ROCKS(1965); GNOME-MOBILE, THE(1967); COCK-EYED COWBOYS OF CALICO COUNTY, THE(1970); THERE WAS A CROOKED MAN(1970)

Misc. Talkies
IT'S ALL IN YOUR MIND(1938); ALIENS FROM ANOTHER PLANET(1967)

Byron K. Foulger
TENTH AVENUE KID(1938); GUNS OF DIABLO(1964)

Bob Foulk
WHITE HEAT(1949); CARRIE(1952); STRANGE LADY IN TOWN(1955)

Luther Foulk
LILITH(1964)

Robert Foulk
ROAD HOUSE(1948); THAT WONDERFUL URGE(1948); JOHNNY STOOL PIGEON(1949); WHIRLPOOL(1949); MYSTERY STREET(1950); WHERE THE SIDEWALK ENDS(1950); ELOPEMENT(1951); GUY WHO CAME BACK, THE(1951); SATURDAY'S HERO(1951); STRIP, THE(1951); WHIP HAND, THE(1951); CARBINE WILLIAMS(1952); DON'T BOTHER TO KNOCK(1952); MY PAL GUS(1952); SAN FRANCISCO STORY, THE(1952); SNIPER, THE(1952); WITHOUT WARNING(1952); GENTLEMEN PREFER BLONDES(1953); APACHE AMBUSH(1955); FAR COUNTRY, THE(1955); REBEL WITHOUT A CAUSE(1955); BACKLASH(1956); HOT BLOOD(1956); RAWHIDE YEARS, THE(1956); GREAT MAN, THE(1957); HOLD THAT

HYPNOTIST(1957); LAST OF THE BADMEN(1957); MY MAN GODFREY(1957); RAINTREE COUNTY(1957); SIERRA STRANGER(1957); TALL STRANGER, THE(1957); UNTAMED YOUTH(1957); DAY OF THE BAD MAN(1958); HELL'S FIVE HOURS(1958); LEFT-HANDED GUN, THE(1958); QUANTRILL'S RAIDERS(1958); STATE FAIR(1962); SWINGIN' ALONG(1962); WONDERFUL WORLD OF THE BROTHERS ERIMM, THE(1962); TAMMY AND THE DOCTOR(1963); TICKLISH AFFAIR, A(1963); ROBIN AND THE SEVEN HOODS(1964); HELL ON WHEELS(1967); LOVE BUG, THE(1968); SPLIT, THE(1968); BUNNY O'HARE(1971); SKIN GAME(1971); EMPEROR OF THE NORTH POLE(1973); PETE'S DRAGON(1977)

Robert C. Foulk
FORTY-NINTH MAN, THE(1953); VALLEY OF THE HEADHUNTERS(1953); BORN TO BE LOVED(1959)

Robert Foulke
CAST A LONG SHADOW(1959)

Ted Foulkes
THUNDERBOLT AND LIGHTFOOT(1974)

Thomas Foulkes
DON'T PANIC CHAPS!(1959, Brit.)

Jean-Louis Foulquier
1984
HERE COMES SANTA CLAUS(1984)

Fraser Foulsham
BREAKERS AHEAD(1935, Brit.), p; RIVER HOUSE MYSTERY, THE(1935, Brit.), d; HOWARD CASE, THE(1936, Brit.), p; SKY RAIDERS, THE(1938, Brit.), p,d&w

Raymond Foulton
YOU CAN'T WIN 'EM ALL(1970, Brit.), ed

George Foundas
SERENITY(1962); TAKE ME AWAY, MY LOVE(1962, Gr.); ZORBA THE GREEK(1964, U.S./Gr.); RED LANTERNS(1965, Gr.)

Georges Foundas
NEVER ON SUNDAY(1960, Gr.)

Clairette Founier
GENERALS WITHOUT BUTTONS(1938, Fr.)

Ed Fountain
SLEEPAWAY CAMP(1983), spec eff

Michael Fountain
SORCERESS(1983)

William E. Fountaine
Misc. Silents
DUNGEON, THE(1922); UNCLE JASPAR'S WILL(1922)

Germaine Fouquet
RASPOUTINE(1954, Fr.), ed

Marie-Claude Fouquet
YOUNG GIRLS OF ROCHEFORT, THE(1968, Fr.), cos

Four Aces
LET'S MAKE A NIGHT OF IT(1937, Brit.)

The Four Blackbirds
HARLEM ON THE PRAIRIE(1938)

Four Covans
ON WITH THE SHOW(1929)

The Four Emperors of Harmony
SHOW BOAT(1929)

The Four Esquires
TOP OF THE TOWN(1937)

Four Eton Boys
MOONLIGHT AND PRETZELS(1933)

Four Franks
LET'S MAKE A NIGHT OF IT(1937, Brit.)

Four Freshmen Quartet
RICH, YOUNG AND PRETTY(1951)

The Four Hot Shots
VOGUES OF 1938(1937)

Four Ink Spots
GREAT AMERICAN BROADCAST, THE(1941)

Four Mills Brothers
STRICTLY DYNAMITE(1934); SING AS YOU SWING(1937, Brit.)

The Four Mills Brothers
OPERATOR 13(1934); TWENTY MILLION SWEETHEARTS(1934)

Four Moroccans
HOLIDAY RHYTHM(1950)

The Four New Yorkers
SKY'S THE LIMIT, THE(1937, Brit.); SWEET DEVIL(1937, Brit.)

Four Playboys
NEW FACES OF 1937(1937)

The Four Playboys
YOU'RE A SWEETHEART(1937)

The Four Preps
GIDGET(1959)

The Four Singing Notables
WEST OF CARSON CITY(1940)

Four Singing Tramps
SWING IT, PROFESSOR(1937)

The Four Spirits of Rhythm
SWEETHEART OF THE CAMPUS(1941)

Four Squires
SWING IT, PROFESSOR(1937)

Four Step Brothers
GREENWICH VILLAGE(1944); THAT'S MY GAL(1947)

The Four Step Brothers
WHEN JOHNNY COMES MARCHING HOME(1943); CAROLINA BLUES(1944)

The Four Sweethearts
HI, BUDDY(1943)

The Four Teens
HIT THE ICE(1943); SEE MY LAWYER(1945)

The Four Tones
HARLEM ON THE PRAIRIE(1938)

The Four Toppers
SON OF INGAGI(1940)

The Four Tunes
HARLEM RIDES THE RANGE(1939)

The Four V's
I LOVE A BANDLEADER(1945)

The Four Williams Brothers
SOMETHING IN THE WIND(1947)

Four Yacht Club Boys
SINGING KID, THE(1936)

Roy Fouracre
SUBTERFUGE(1969, US/Brit.), art d

Christian Fourcade
LITTLE BOY LOST(1953)

Alain Fourez
SOLO(1970, Fr.)

Jean Jacques Fourgeaud
MAN WHO CAME FOR COFFEE, THE(1970, Ital.); FORTY DEUCE(1982), p

Annick Fourgerie
SUCH A GORGEOUS KID LIKE ME(1973, Fr.)

The Fourmost
FERRY ACROSS THE MERSEY(1964, Brit.)

Jean-Claude Fourneau
TRIAL OF JOAN OF ARC(1965, Fr.)

Marc Ernest Fourneau
1984
L'ARGENT(1984, Fr./Switz.)

Max Fournel
ONCE IN PARIS(1978)

Maria Fournery
1984
DEATHSTALKER, THE(1984)

Alain Fournier
WANDERER, THE(1969, Fr.), w

Charles Fournier
1984
HOTEL NEW HAMPSHIRE, THE(1984)

Claude Fournier
ALIEN THUNDER(1975, US/Can.), d, ph

Eugene A. Fournier
FRATERNITY ROW(1977), ed

Gerlaine Fournier
MONTE CARLO STORY, THE(1957, Ital.)

Marcel Fournier
RABID(1976, Can.)

Elizabeth Fournoy
TOO YOUNG TO KISS(1951)

Fourouzan
CYCLE, THE(1979, Iran)

The Foursome
GO WEST, YOUNG LADY(1941)

Athinodoros Fousalis
CANNON AND THE NIGHTINGALE, THE(1969, Gr.)

Christy Foushee
PASSION HOLIDAY(1963); HONEYMOON OF HORROR(1964)

Tom C. Fouts
EMIGRANTS, THE(1972, Swed.); NEW LAND, THE(1973, Swed.)

Anthony Foutz
TALES OF ORDINARY MADNESS(1983, Ital.), w

Ninon Fovieri
Misc. Silents
GOING STRAIGHT(1916)

Basil J. Fovos
POSTMAN ALWAYS RINGS TWICE, THE(1981)

Frank Fowell
Silents
GREATER NEED, THE(1916, Brit.), w; ENCHANTMENT(1920, Brit.), w; PENNILESS MILLIONAIRE, THE(1921, Brit.), w; MAN WITHOUT DESIRE, THE(1923, Brit.), w

Fred Fowell
VIOLENT PLAYGROUND(1958, Brit.)

Bob Fowke
WHITE HEAT(1949)

Conrad Fowkes
LOVIN' MOLLY(1974); PRINCE OF THE CITY(1981)

Derek Fowldes
HOTEL PARADISO(1966, U.S./Brit.)

Derek Fowlds
WE JOINED THE NAVY(1962, Brit.); DOCTOR IN DISTRESS(1963, Brit.); EAST OF SUDAN(1964, Brit.); TAMAHINE(1964, Brit.); FRANKENSTEIN CREATED WOMAN(1965, Brit.); SCHOOL FOR UNCLAIMED GIRLS(1973, Brit.); BEYOND THE FOG(1981, Brit.)

Chick Fowler
GIVEN WORD, THE(1964, Braz.), ph

H. E. Fowle
DEAR MR. PROHACK(1949, Brit.), ph; WOMAN IN THE HALL, THE(1949, Brit.), ph; MANIACS ON WHEELS(1951, Brit.), ph

H.E. Fowle
ESTHER WATERS(1948, Brit.), ph

Susannah Fowle
GETTING OF WISDOM, THE(1977, Aus.)

Alameda Fowler
FIFTEEN WIVES(1934)

Almeda Fowler
PARTY GIRL(1930); FALSE MADONNA(1932); CAROLINA(1934); DAMAGED LIVES(1937); HOTEL HAYWIRE(1937); YOU CAN'T TAKE IT WITH YOU(1938); RETURN OF FRANK JAMES, THE(1940); FACE BEHIND THE MASK, THE(1941); LADY EVE, THE(1941); EXPERIMENT PERILOUS(1944); MY BUDDY(1944); ONCE UPON A TIME(1944); STORM OVER LISBON(1944); EVE KNEW HER APPLES(1945); THEY WERE EXPENDABLE(1945); KID FROM BROOKLYN, THE(1946); NOTORIOUS(1946); TO EACH HIS OWN(1946); HUCKSTERS, THE(1947)

Art Fowler
TONTO BASIN OUTLAWS(1941); ARIZONA TRAIL(1943); BLACK MARKET RUSTLERS(1943); FRONTIER LAW(1943); WEST OF TEXAS(1943); LAND OF THE OUTLAWS(1944); LAW MEN(1944); OLD TEXAS TRAIL, THE(1944); RANGE LAW(1944)

Brenda Fowler
JUDGE PRIEST(1934); MIGHTY BARNUM, THE(1934); WORLD MOVES ON, THE(1934); RUGGLES OF RED GAP(1935); WAY DOWN EAST(1935); CASE AGAINST MRS. AMES, THE(1936); SECOND WIFE(1936); STORY OF LOUIS PASTEUR, THE(1936); SLIM(1937); GIRLS ON PROBATION(1938); OF HUMAN HEARTS(1938); STAGECOACH(1939); ALL THIS AND HEAVEN TOO(1940); COMIN' ROUND THE MOUNTAIN(1940); THEY DRIVE BY NIGHT(1940); UNTAMED(1940); MANPOWER(1941)
Silents
MONEY! MONEY! MONEY!(1923)
Misc. Silents
THIRTY A WEEK(1918)

Brendon Fowler
GINGER(1935)

Buck Fowler
SMALL TOWN IN TEXAS, A(1976)

Clement Fowler
HAMLET(1964); DINER(1982)

Donna Fowler
HANKY-PANKY(1982); STROKER ACE(1983)

Donna R. Fowler
LITTLE SEX, A(1982)

Dorothy Fowler
GOOD GIRLS GO TO PARIS(1939)

Edwin Fowler
SAINTED SISTERS, THE(1948); TASK FORCE(1949)

Frank Fowler
FAR HORIZONS, THE(1955); ATOMIC BRAIN, THE(1964)

Gene Fowler
ROADHOUSE MURDER, THE(1932), w; STATE'S ATTORNEY(1932), w; UNION DEPOT(1932), w; WHAT PRICE HOLLYWOOD?(1932), w; WAY TO LOVE, THE(1933), w; MIGHTY BARNUM, THE(1934), w; SHOOT THE WORKS(1934), w; CALL OF THE WILD(1935), w; CAREER WOMAN(1936), w; HALF ANGEL(1936), w; MESSAGE TO GARCIA, A(1936), w; PROFESSIONAL SOLDIER(1936), w; ALI BABA GOES TO TOWN(1937), w; LOVE UNDER FIRE(1937), w; NANCY STEELE IS MISSING(1937), w; SOME LIKE IT HOT(1939), w; EARL OF CHICAGO, THE(1940), w; BILLY THE KID(1941), w; BIG JACK(1949), w; BEAU JAMES(1957), w

Gene Fowler, Jr.
HANGMEN ALSO DIE(1943), ed; WOMAN IN THE WINDOW, THE(1945), ed; PHILO VANCE RETURNS(1947), ed; MY BROTHER, THE OUTLAW(1951), w; MAIN STREET TO BROADWAY(1953), ed; FRESH FROM PARIS(1955), ed; PARIS FOLLIES OF 1956(1955), ed; BEYOND A REASONABLE DOUBT(1956), ed; NAKED HILLS, THE(1956), ed; WHILE THE CITY SLEEPS(1956), ed; CHINA GATE(1957), ed; FORTY GUNS(1957), ed; I WAS A TEENAGE WEREWOLF(1957), d; RUN OF THE ARROW(1957), ed; GANG WAR(1958), d; I MARRIED A MONSTER FROM OUTER SPACE(1958), p&d; SHOWDOWN AT BOOT HILL(1958), d; HERE COME THE JETS(1959), d; OREGON TRAIL, THE(1959), d, w; REBEL SET, THE(1959), d; CHILD IS WAITING, A(1963), ed; IT'S A MAD, MAD, MAD, MAD WORLD(1963), ed; HANG'EM HIGH(1968), ed; MAN CALLED HORSE, A(1970), ed; MONTE WALSH(1970), ed; MOLLY AND LAWLESS JOHN(1972), ed; THUMB TRIPPING(1972), ed; SKATETOWN, U.S.A.(1979), ed; CAVEMAN(1981), ed; SMORGASBORD(1983), ed

Gene Fowler, Sr.
SENATOR WAS INDISCREET, THE(1947)

Gene N. Fowler
OREGON TRAIL, THE(1959)

George Fowler
FIRE MAIDENS FROM OUTER SPACE(1956, Brit.), p; HELLO LONDON(1958, Brit.), p, w; DR. BLOOD'S COFFIN(1961), p; MARY HAD A LITTLE(1961, Brit.), p; SNAKE WOMAN, THE(1961, Brit.), p; THREE ON A SPREE(1961, Brit.), p

George Fowler, Jr.
EASY RIDER(1969)

H. Waller Fowler, Jr.
PANIC IN THE STREETS(1950)

Harry Fowler
HELL, HEAVEN OR HOBOKEN(1958, Brit.); DARKENED SKIES(1930), ph; SALUTE JOHN CITIZEN(1942, Brit.); THOSE KIDS FROM TOWN(1942, Brit.); GET CRACKING(1943, Brit.); DON'T TAKE IT TO HEART(1944, Brit.); GIVE US THE MOON(1944, Brit.); 48 HOURS(1944, Brit.); GIRL ON THE CANAL, THE(1947, Brit.); TROUBLE IN THE AIR(1948, Brit.); FOR THEM THAT TRESPASS(1949, Brit.); NOW BARABBAS WAS A ROBBER(1949, Brit.); HUE AND CRY(1950, Brit.); SHE SHALL HAVE MURDER(1950, Brit.); TRIO(1950, Brit.); HIGH TREASON(1951, Brit.); MADAME LOUISE(1951, Brit.); SCARLET THREAD(1951, Brit.); MAN BAIT(1952, Brit.); ONCE A SINNER(1952, Brit.); PICKWICK PAPERS, THE(1952, Brit.); 13 EAST STREET(1952, Brit.); DAY TO REMEMBER, A(1953, Brit.); I BELIEVE IN YOU(1953, Brit.); TOP OF THE FORM(1953, Brit.); DON'T BLAME THE STORK(1954, Brit.); FUSS OVER FEATHERS(1954, Brit.); UP TO HIS NECK(1954, Brit.); STOCK CAR(1955, Brit.); BEHIND THE HEADLINES(1956, Brit.); FIRE MAIDENS FROM OUTER SPACE(1956, Brit.); HOME AND AWAY(1956, Brit.); BIRTHDAY PRESENT, THE(1957, Brit.); BOOBY TRAP(1957, Brit.); FIGHTING WILDCATS, THE(1957, Brit.); LUCKY JIM(1957, Brit.); TOWN ON TRIAL(1957, Brit.); DIPLOMATIC CORPSE, THE(1958, Brit.); SOAPBOX DERBY(1958, Brit.); SUPREME SECRET, THE(1958, Brit.); DON'T PANIC CHAPS!(1959, Brit.); HEART OF A MAN, THE(1959, Brit.); IDOL ON PARADE(1959, Brit.); NAVY HEROES(1959, Brit.); FLIGHT FROM SINGAPORE(1962, Brit.); CROOKS ANONYMOUS(1963, Brit.); JUST FOR FUN(1963, Brit.); LADIES WHO DO(1964, Brit.); TOMORROW AT TEN(1964, Brit.); ESCAPE BY NIGHT(1965, Brit.); LIFE AT THE TOP(1965, Brit.); NANNY, THE(1965, Brit.); SECRETS OF A WINDMILL GIRL(1966, Brit.); CARNABY, M.D.(1967, Brit.); START THE REVOLUTION WITHOUT ME(1970); SIR HENRY AT RAWLINSON END(1980, Brit.)
Silents
IF ONLY JIM(1921), ph; UNKNOWN, THE(1921), ph; WALLOP, THE(1921), ph; CUB REPORTER, THE(1922), ph; TAKING CHANCES(1922), ph; CROOKED ALLEY(1923), ph; TIPPED OFF(1923), ph

Harry M. Fowler
Silents
TARZAN OF THE APES(1918), ph
Helen Fowler
STRANGE INTRUDER(1956), w
Hugh Fowler
LES MISERABLES(1952), ed; PHONE CALL FROM A STRANGER(1952), ed; LIST OF ADRIAN MESSENGER, THE(1963), ed
Hugh S. Fowler
SOMETHING FOR THE BIRDS(1952), ed; GENTLEMEN PREFER BLONDES(1953), ed; TAXI(1953), ed; SEVEN CITIES OF GOLD(1955), ed; SEVEN YEAR ITCH, THE(1955), ed; LAST WAGON, THE(1956), ed; LOVE ME TENDER(1956), ed; ON THE THRESHOLD OF SPACE(1956), ed; PROUD ONES, THE(1956), ed; WAY TO THE GOLD, THE(1957), ed; WILL SUCCESS SPOIL ROCK HUNTER?(1957), ed; FIEND WHO WALKED THE WEST, THE(1958), ed; GIFT OF LOVE, THE(1958), ed; NICE LITTLE BANK THAT SHOULD BE ROBBED, A(1958), ed; SAY ONE FOR ME(1959), ed; STORY ON PAGE ONE(1959), ed; THESE THOUSAND HILLS(1959), ed; FLAMING STAR(1960), ed; LOST WORLD, THE(1960), ed; PIRATES OF TORTUGA(1961), ed; ADVENTURES OF A YOUNG MAN(1962), ed; BACHELOR FLAT(1962), ed; TWILIGHT OF HONOR(1963), ed; IN HARM'S WAY(1965), ed; WILD SEED(1965), ed; AND NOW MIGUEL(1966), ed; STAGECOACH(1966), ed; WAY...WAY OUT(1966), ed; IN LIKE FLINT(1967), ed; PLANET OF THE APES(1968), ed; PENDULUM(1969), ed; PATTON(1970), ed; CORKY(1972), ed; LIFE AND TIMES OF JUDGE ROY BEAN, THE(1972), ed
J. C. Fowler
MIDNIGHT PATROL, THE(1932); ARE WE CIVILIZED?(1934); CAROLINA(1934); CRACK-UP(1946)
Silents
GOLD RUSH, THE(1925); ONE PUNCH O'DAY(1926); WOLF'S CLOTHING(1927); CAMPUS KNIGHTS(1929)
Misc. Silents
RECKLESS COURAGE(1925)
J. C. "Jack" Fowler
TOAST OF NEW YORK, THE(1937)
J.O. Fowler
GOVERNMENT GIRL(1943); HEAVENLY DAYS(1944)
Jack Fowler
FIGHTING LEGION, THE(1930); GLASS KEY, THE(1942)
Silents
PASSIONATE YOUTH(1925); POWER OF THE WEAK, THE(1926); RANSON'S FOLLY(1926)
Jake Fowler
HORROR HIGH(1974), w
James Fowler
KISS THE BLOOD OFF MY HANDS(1948)
Jean Fowler
YOURS FOR THE ASKING(1936); UNDER WESTERN STARS(1938); RECESS(1967)
Joan Fowler
PHOBIA(1980, Can.)
John [Jack] Fowler
FIGHTING THRU(1931)
John Fowler
FROZEN RIVER(1929), w; HELL IS EMPTY(1967, Brit./Ital), w; DELIVERANCE(1972); SCUM(1979, Brit.)
Silents
PEACOCK FAN(1929)
Kim Fowler
PROMISES IN THE DARK(1979); MOTEL HELL(1980)
Marge Fowler
ELMER GANTRY(1960), ed
Marj Fowler
BRASS LEGEND, THE(1956), ed
Marjorie Fowler
MR. PEABODY AND THE MERMAID(1948), ed; MAN CRAZY(1953), ed; MAN IN THE ATTIC(1953), ed; CRIME OF PASSION(1957), ed; OH, MEN! OH, WOMEN!(1957), ed; STOPOVER TOKYO(1957), ed; THREE FACES OF EVE, THE(1957), ed; FRAULEIN(1958), ed; SEPARATE TABLES(1958), ed; MAN WHO UNDERSTOOD WOMEN, THE(1959), ed; LOVER COME BACK(1961), ed; FORTY POUNDS OF TROUBLE(1962), ed; MR. HOBBS TAKES A VACATION(1962), ed; OUTSIDER, THE(1962), ed; TAKE HER, SHE'S MINE(1963), ed; WHAT A WAY TO GO(1964), ed; DEAR BRIGETTE(1965), ed; DOCTOR DOLITTLE(1967), ed; ONCE YOU KISS A STRANGER(1969), ed; STRAWBERRY STATEMENT, THE(1970), ed; CONQUEST OF THE PLANET OF THE APES(1972), ed; IT'S MY TURN(1980), ed
Mary Fowler
Misc. Talkies
WEDDING ON THE VOLGA, THE(1929)
Maurice Fowler
FACES IN THE DARK(1960, Brit.), set d; KIND OF LOVING, A(1962, Brit.), set d; ROAD TO HONG KONG, THE(1962, U.S./Brit.), set d; VICTORS, THE(1963), set d; LAST SAFARI, THE(1967, Brit.), art d; GOODBYE MR. CHIPS(1969, U.S./Brit.), art d; BROTHERLY LOVE(1970, Brit.), art d; WELCOME TO THE CLUB(1971), art d; DIGBY, THE BIGGEST DOG IN THE WORLD(1974, Brit.), art d; MOHAMMAD, MESSENGER OF GOD(1976, Lebanon/Brit.), prod d; HEAVEN'S GATE(1980), art d; SUPERMAN II(1980), art d; EDUCATING RITA(1983), art d; HEAT AND DUST(1983, Brit.), art d
1984
SWORD OF THE VALIANT(1984, Brit.), prod d
Nelson Fowler
HONEYSUCKLE ROSE(1980)
Phil Fowler
HOLIDAY CAMP(1947, Brit.)
Phyllis Fowler
FORT TI(1953)
Richard Fowler
LET'S MAKE LOVE(1960)
Robert Fowler
BELOW THE BELT(1980), p&d, w

Susan Fowler
WEDDING PARTY, THE(1969)
Will Fowler
DOUGHGIRLS, THE(1944); THIS MAN'S NAVY(1945)
Will Fowler, Jr.
E.T. THE EXTRA-TERRESTRIAL(1982)
William Fowler
WITHOUT A TRACE(1983)
H. Fowler-Mears
PLAYBOY, THE(1942, Brit.), w
Glenys Fowles
FOUL PLAY(1978)
John Fowles
COLLECTOR, THE(1965), w; MAGUS, THE(1968, Brit.), w; FRENCH LIEUTENANT'S WOMAN, THE(1981), w
Doug Fowley
LIFE WITH BLONDIE(1946); ROSES ARE RED(1947); BEHIND LOCKED DOORS(1948); CAT WOMEN OF THE MOON(1953)
Douglas Fowley
GIFT OF GAB(1934); LET'S TALK IT OVER(1934); OPERATOR 13(1934); STUDENT TOUR(1934); THIN MAN, THE(1934); MISS PACIFIC FLEET(1935); NIGHT LIFE OF THE GODS(1935); OLD MAN RHYTHM(1935); STRAIGHT FROM THE HEART(1935); TRANSIENT LADY(1935); TWO FOR TONIGHT(1935); BIG BROWN EYES(1936); CRASH DONOVAN(1936); FIFTEEN MAIDEN LANE(1936); NAVY BORN(1936); RING AROUND THE MOON(1936); SING, BABY, SING(1936); SMALL TOWN GIRL(1936); THIRTY SIX HOURS TO KILL(1936); CHARLIE CHAN ON BROADWAY(1937); FIFTY ROADS TO TOWN(1937); LOVE AND HISSES(1937); ON THE AVENUE(1937); ONE MILE FROM HEAVEN(1937); SHE HAD TO EAT(1937); THIS IS MY AFFAIR(1937); TIME OUT FOR ROMANCE(1937); WAKE UP AND LIVE(1937); WILD AND WOOLLY(1937); WOMAN-WISE(1937); ALEXANDER'S RAGTIME BAND(1938); ARIZONA WILDCAT(1938); CITY GIRL(1938); KEEP SMILING(1938); MR. MOTO'S GAMBLE(1938); PASSPORT HUSBAND(1938); SUBMARINE PATROL(1938); TIME OUT FOR MURDER(1938); WALKING DOWN BROADWAY(1938); BOY FRIEND(1939); CHARLIE CHAN AT TREASURE ISLAND(1939); DODGE CITY(1939); HENRY GOES ARIZONA(1939); INSIDE STORY(1939); IT COULD HAPPEN TO YOU(1939); LUCKY NIGHT(1939); CAFE HOSTESS(1940); CHEROKEE STRIP(1940); EAST OF THE RIVER(1940); ELLERY QUEEN, MASTER DETECTIVE(1940); LEATHER-PUSHERS, THE(1940); PIER 13(1940); SLIGHTLY HONORABLE(1940); TWENTY MULE TEAM(1940); WAGONS WESTWARD(1940); DANGEROUS LADY(1941); DOCTORS DON'T TELL(1941); GREAT SWINDLE, THE(1941); PARSON OF PANAMINT, THE(1941); SECRETS OF THE WASTELANDS(1941); TANKS A MILLION(1941); DEVIL WITH HITLER, THE(1942); HAY FOOT(1942); I LIVE ON DANGER(1942); MAN IN THE TRUNK, THE(1942); MEET THE MOB(1942); MISSISSIPPI GAMBLER(1942); MR. WISE GUY(1942); PITTSBURGH(1942); SOMEWHERE I'LL FIND YOU(1942); STAND BY FOR ACTION(1942); SUNSET ON THE DESERT(1942); BAR 20(1943); CHANCE OF A LIFETIME, THE(1943); COLT COMRADES(1943); GILDERSLEEVE'S BAD DAY(1943); JITTERBUGS(1943); KANSAN, THE(1943); LOST CANYON(1943); MINESWEEPER(1943); RIDING HIGH(1943); SLEEPY LAGOON(1943); AND THE ANGELS SING(1944); DETECTIVE KITTY O'DAY(1944); JOHNNY DOESN'T LIVE HERE ANY MORE(1944); LADY IN THE DEATH HOUSE(1944); ONE BODY TOO MANY(1944); RACKET MAN, THE(1944); RATIONING(1944); SEE HERE, PRIVATE HARGROVE(1944); SHAKE HANDS WITH MURDER(1944); STORY OF DR. WASSELL, THE(1944); ALONG THE NAVAJO TRAIL(1945); DON'T FENCE ME IN(1945); DRIFTING ALONG(1946); FREDDIE STEPS OUT(1946); GLASS ALIBI, THE(1946); HIGH SCHOOL HERO(1946); IN FAST COMPANY(1946); LARCENY IN HER HEART(1946); RENDEZVOUS 24(1946); BACKLASH(1947); CARTER CASE, THE(1947); DESPERATE(1947); FALL GUY(1947); GAS HOUSE KIDS IN HOLLYWOOD(1947); HUCKSTERS, THE(1947); JUNGLE FLIGHT(1947); MERTON OF THE MOVIES(1947); RIDIN' DOWN THE TRAIL(1947); SCARED TO DEATH(1947); SEA OF GRASS, THE(1947); THREE ON A TICKET(1947); TRESPASSER, THE(1947); UNDERCOVER MAISIE(1947); WILD COUNTRY(1947); YANKEE FAKIR(1947); BLACK BART(1948); CORONER CREEK(1948); DENVER KID(1948); DOCKS OF NEW ORLEANS(1948); DUDE GOES WEST, THE(1948); GUN SMUGGLERS(1948); IF YOU KNEW SUSIE(1948); JOE PALOOKA IN WINNER TAKE ALL(1948); RENEGADES OF SONORA(1948); WATERFRONT AT MIDNIGHT(1948); ARSON, INC.(1949); BATTLEGROUND(1949); FLAXY MARTIN(1949); JOE PALOOKA IN THE COUNTERPUNCH(1949); MASSACRE RIVER(1949); MIGHTY JOE YOUNG(1949); RENEGADES OF THE SAGE(1949); SATAN'S CRADLE(1949); SEARCH FOR DANGER(1949); SUSANNA PASS(1949); TAKE ME OUT TO THE BALL GAME(1949); ARMORED CAR ROBBERY(1950); BEWARE OF BLONDIE(1950); BUNCO SQUAD(1950); EDGE OF DOOM(1950); HE'S A COCKEYED WONDER(1950); HOEDOWN(1950); KILLER SHARK(1950); MRS. O'MALLEY AND MR. MALONE(1950); RIDER FROM TUCSON(1950); RIO GRANDE PATROL(1950); STAGE TO TUCSON(1950); ACROSS THE WIDE MISSOURI(1951); CALLAWAY WENT THATAWAY(1951); CHAIN OF CIRCUMSTANCE(1951); CRIMINAL LAWYER(1951); FINDERS KEEPERS(1951); SOUTH OF CALIENTE(1951); TARZAN'S PERIL(1951); HORIZONS WEST(1952); JUST THIS ONCE(1952); MAN BEHIND THE GUN, THE(1952); ROOM FOR ONE MORE(1952); SINGIN' IN THE RAIN(1952); THIS WOMAN IS DANGEROUS(1952); CRUISIN' DOWN THE RIVER(1953); KANSAS PACIFIC(1953); NAKED JUNGLE, THE(1953); RED RIVER SHORE(1953); SLIGHT CASE OF LARCENY, A(1953); CASANOVA'S BIG NIGHT(1954); DEEP IN MY HEART(1954); HIGH AND THE MIGHTY, THE(1954); LONE GUN, THE(1954); THREE RING CIRCUS(1954); UNTAMED HEIRESS(1954); GIRL RUSH, THE(1955); LONESOME TRAIL, THE(1955); TEXAS LADY(1955); BANDIDO(1956); BROKEN STAR, THE(1956); MAN FROM DEL RIO(1956); ROCK, PRETTY BABY(1956); BADGE OF MARSHAL BRENNAN, THE(1957); BAYOU(1957); KELLY AND ME(1957); RAIDERS OF OLD CALIFORNIA(1957); THESE THOUSAND HILLS(1959); DESIRE IN THE DUST(1960); MACUMBA LOVE(1960), p&d; BUFFALO GUN(1961); BARABBAS(1962, Ital.); MIRACLE OF THE WHITE STALLIONS(1963); GUNS OF DIABLO(1964); NIGHTMARE IN THE SUN(1964); SEVEN FACES OF DR. LAO(1964); HOMEBODIES(1974); BLACK OAK CONSPIRACY(1977)
Misc. Talkies
GIFT FOR HEIDI, A(1958)
Douglas V. Fowley
GOOD GUYS AND THE BAD GUYS, THE(1969); WALKING TALL(1973); FROM NOON TO THREE(1976); WHITE BUFFALO, THE(1977); NORTH AVENUE IRREGULARS, THE(1979)

George Fowley
Silents
LIEUTENANT DARING RN AND THE WATER RATS(1924, Brit.)
Kim Fowley
CIAO MANHATTAN(1973), m
Eddie Fowlie
DOCTOR ZHIVAGO(1965), spec eff; HOW I WON THE WAR(1967, Brit.), spec eff; NICHOLAS AND ALEXANDRA(1971, Brit.), spec eff; ROBIN AND MARIAN(1976, Brit.), spec eff
Allan Fox
STREET SCENE(1931); YOUNG BRIDE(1932)
Allen Fox
FORGOTTEN COMMANDMENTS(1932); IT HAPPENED ONE NIGHT(1934); WINGS IN THE DARK(1935); WEDDING PRESENT(1936); GIRL WITH IDEAS, A(1937); HOLY TERROR, THE(1937); I AM THE LAW(1938); LETTER OF INTRODUCTION(1938); MIDNIGHT INTRUDER(1938); THERE'S THAT WOMAN AGAIN(1938); MILLION DOLLAR LEGS(1939); DR. CYCLOPS(1940); WOMEN WITHOUT NAMES(1940); JAM SESSION(1944); PRACTICALLY YOURS(1944); RAINBOW ISLAND(1944); CHRISTMAS IN CONNECTICUT(1945)
Angel Fox
AROUSERS, THE(1973)
Arthur Fox
THREE HOURS TO KILL(1954)
Bebe Fox
NEARLY EIGHTEEN(1943)
Bernard Fox
HOME AND AWAY(1956, Brit.); SPIN A DARK WEB(1956, Brit.); SAFECRACKER, THE(1958, Brit.); TWO-HEADED SPY, THE(1959, Brit.); LIST OF ADRIAN MESSENGER, THE(1963); HONEYMOON HOTEL(1964); QUICK, BEFORE IT MELTS(1964); STRANGE BEDFELLOWS(1965); HOLD ON(1966); MUNSTER, GO HOME(1966); ONE OF OUR SPIES IS MISSING(1966); BAMBOO SAUCER, THE(1968); STAR!(1968); $1,000,000 DUCK(1971); ARNOLD(1973); HERBIE GOES TO MONTE CARLO(1977); RESCUERS, THE(1977); PRIVATE EYES, THE(1980); YELLOWBEARD(1983)
Misc. Talkies
HOUSE OF THE DEAD(1980)
Beryl Fox
BY DESIGN(1982), p
Bobby Fox
INCIDENT IN AN ALLEY(1962)
Carey Fox
ROLLER BOOGIE(1979)
1984
DREAMSCAPE(1984); FIRESTARTER(1984)
Cary Fox
HELL NIGHT(1981)
Charles Fox
UNDERTAKER AND HIS PALS, THE(1966); INCIDENT, THE(1967), md; BARBARELLA(1968, Fr./Ital.), m; GOODBYE COLUMBUS(1969), m; PUFNSTUF(1970), m; MAKING IT(1971), m; STAR SPANGLED GIRL(1971), m; CORPSE GRINDERS, THE(1972); SEPARATE PEACE, A(1972), m; LAST AMERICAN HERO, THE(1973), m; LAUGHING POLICEMAN, THE(1973), m; BUG(1975), m; DROWNING POOL, THE(1975), m; OTHER SIDE OF THE MOUNTAIN, THE(1975), m; DUCHESS AND THE DIRTWATER FOX, THE(1976), m; TWO-MINUTE WARNING(1976), m; ONE ON ONE(1977), m; FOUL PLAY(1978), m; OUR WINNING SEASON(1978), m; LAST MARRIED COUPLE IN AMERICA, THE(1980), m; LITTLE DARLINGS(1980), m; NINE TO FIVE(1980), m; OH GOD! BOOK II(1980), m; WHY WOULD I LIE(1980), m; LOVE CHILD(1982), m; SIX PACK(1982), m; ZAPPED!(1982), m; STRANGE BREW(1983), m; TRENCHCOAT(1983), m
Charlie Fox
SSSSSSSS(1973)
Colin Fox
REINCARNATE, THE(1971, Can.); SILENCE OF THE NORTH(1981, Can.); CHRISTMAS STORY, A(1983)
1984
COVERGIRL(1984, Can.)
Misc. Talkies
MY PLEASURE IS MY BUSINESS(1974, Can.)
Craig Fox
PURPLE GANG, THE(1960)
Curly Fox
SECOND FIDDLE TO A STEEL GUITAR(1965)
David Fox
PARALLELS(1980, Can.); SILENCE OF THE NORTH(1981, Can.)
1984
MRS. SOFFEL(1984)
Dorothi Fox
GANG THAT COULDN'T SHOOT STRAIGHT, THE(1971); COME BACK CIHARLESTON BLUE(1972); THREE DAYS OF THE CONDOR(1975)
Dorothy Fox
WIZ, THE(1978); CENTENNIAL SUMMER(1946), ch; HAPPY HOOKER, THE(1975)
Misc. Talkies
HITTER, THE(1979)
Dorthi Fox
BANANAS(1971)
Earle Fox
SPIDER, THE(1931); TRANSATLANTIC(1931); SCARLET DAWN(1932); BEDTIME STORY, A(1933)
Misc. Silents
LAST MAN ON EARTH, THE(1924)
Edward Fox
MIND BENDERS, THE(1963, Brit.); FROZEN DEAD, THE(1967, Brit.); I'LL NEVER FORGET WHAT'S 'IS NAME(1967, Brit.); JOKERS, THE(1967, Brit.); LONG DUEL, THE(1967, Brit.); NAKED RUNNER, THE(1967, Brit.); JOURNEY INTO MIDNIGHT(1968, Brit.); BATTLE OF BRITAIN, THE(1969, Brit.); OH! WHAT A LOVELY WAR(1969, Brit.); SKULLDUGGERY(1970); GO-BETWEEN, THE(1971, Brit.); DAY OF THE JACKAL, THE(1973, Brit./Fr.); DOLL'S HOUSE, A(1973, Brit.); GALILEO(1975, Brit.); BRIDGE TOO FAR, A(1977, Brit.); DUELLISTS, THE(1977, Brit.); SQUEEZE, THE(1977, Brit.); BIG SLEEP, THE¼(1978, Brit.); FORCE 10 FROM NAVARONE(1978, Brit.); CAT AND THE CANARY, THE(1979, Brit.); SOLDIER OF ORANGE(1979, Dutch); MIRROR CRACK'D, THE(1980, Brit.); NIGHTHAWKS(1981); GANDHI(1982);

DRESSER, THE(1983); NEVER SAY NEVER AGAIN(1983)
1984
BOUNTY, THE(1984)
Elsa Fox
Misc. Silents
LAND JUST OVER YONDER, THE(1916)
Elsie Fox
LAST TRAIN FROM MADRID, THE(1937), w
Erika Fox
Misc. Talkies
HOOCH(1977)
Finis Fox
EVANGELINE(1929), w; RESURRECTION(1931), w
Silents
EASY TO MAKE MONEY(1919), w; FALSE EVIDENCE(1919), w; ALIAS JIMMY VALENTINE(1920), w; SHOULD A WOMAN TELL?(1920), w; ALIAS JIMMY GOD'S(1922), d&w; MERRY-GO-ROUND(1923), w; TIPPED OFF(1923), d; MY SON(1925), w; WOMAN WHO SINNED, A(1925), d&w; RAMONA(1928), w, t; EVANGELINE(1929), w&t
Misc. Silents
BAG AND BAGGAGE(1923), d; BISHOP OF THE OZARKS, THE(1923), d; MAN BETWEEN, THE(1923), d; DANGEROUS FRIENDS(1926), d
Frank Fox
CRIME OF PETER FRAME, THE(1938, Brit.); DOUBLE OR QUITS(1938, Brit.); LAST BARRICADE, THE(1938, Brit.); SAILING ALONG(1938, Brit.); CLOUDS OVER EUROPE(1939, Brit.); NORTH SEA PATROL(1939, Brit.)
Franklin Fox
HIGH TIDE AT NOON(1957, Brit.); FIRST MAN INTO SPACE(1959, Brit.)
Franklyn Fox
PAJAMA GAME, THE(1957)
Fred Fox
GOVERNMENT GIRL(1943); HEAVENLY DAYS(1944); BUFFALO BILL RIDES AGAIN(1947); KISS THE BLOOD OFF MY HANDS(1948); VICIOUS CIRCLE, THE(1948); LOVABLE CHEAT, THE(1949); WAKE OF THE RED WITCH(1949)
Fred S. Fox
OH GOD! BOOK II(1980), w
Frederic Louis Fox
OVERLAND PACIFIC(1954), w; HEADLINE HUNTERS(1955), w; DAKOTA INCIDENT(1956), w; WHEN GANGLAND STRIKES(1956), w; TAMING SUTTON'S GAL(1957), w; CHARRO(1969), w
Fredric Louis Fox
80 STEPS TO JONAH(1969), w
George Fox
EARTHQUAKE(1974), w
Misc. Silents
HOUSE WITHOUT CHILDREN, THE(1919); SUPREME PASSION, THE(1921)
Gerald Fox
FAME IS THE SPUR(1947, Brit.); HUE AND CRY(1950, Brit.)
Gladys Fox
Silents
BREAD(1918); PRIVATE SCANDAL, A(1921)
Grey Fox
LOVING COUPLES(1980), ed
Guy Fox
GUNS FOR SAN SEBASTIAN(1968, U.S./Fr./Mex./Ital.)
Haley Fox
RICH AND FAMOUS(1981)
Harry Fox
GO-GETTER, THE(1937); TALENT SCOUT(1937)
Huckleberry Fox
TERMS OF ENDEARMENT(1983)
1984
AMERICAN DREAMER(1984); MISUNDERSTOOD(1984)
J.R. Fox
HOSPITAL MASSACRE(1982), art d
J. Rae Fox
1984
HOSPITAL MASSACRE(1984), art d&set d; REPO MAN(1984), art d
James Fox
THOROUGHLY MODERN MILLIE(1967); SERVANT, THE(1964, Brit.); TAMAHINE(1964, Brit.); KING RAT(1965); THOSE MAGNIFICENT MEN IN THEIR FLYING MACHINES; OR HOW I FLEWFROM LONDON TO PARIS IN 25 HOURS AND 11 MINUTES(1965, Brit.); CHASE, THE(1966); DUFFY(1968, Brit.); ISADORA(1968, Brit.); ARABELLA(1969, U.S./Ital.); BLOODTHIRSTY BUTCHERS(1970), art d; TORTURE DUNGEON(1970), set d; GURU, THE MAD MONK(1971), set d; NO LONGER ALONE(1978); RUNNERS(1983, Brit.)
1984
GREYSTOKE: THE LEGEND OF TARZAN, LORD OF THE APES(1984); PASSAGE TO INDIA, A(1984, Brit.)
Misc. Talkies
PERFORMANCE(1970, Brit.)
Janet Fox
THEY KNEW WHAT THEY WANTED(1940)
Jimi Fox
GRAND THEFT AUTO(1977)
Jimmie Fox
DOUBLE CROSS(1941); WASHINGTON STORY(1952); CATERED AFFAIR, THE(1956)
Jimmy Fox
CHEYENNE RIDES AGAIN(1937); ACCIDENTS WILL HAPPEN(1938); COWBOY FROM BROOKLYN(1938); WAGONS ROLL AT NIGHT, THE(1941); STARDUST ON THE SAGE(1942)
John Fox
TRUNK, THE(1961, Brit.), m; GOLD GUITAR, THE(1966); RED, WHITE AND BLACK, THE(1970); SKATEBOARD(1978)
Silents
COVERED WAGON, THE(1923)
Misc. Silents
ONE GLORIOUS DAY(1922)

John Fox, Jr.
TRAIL OF THE LONESOME PINE, THE(1936), w; LITTLE SHEPHERD OF KINGDOM COME(1961), w
Silents
CUMBERLAND ROMANCE, A(1920), w; JACK O' CLUBS(1924); PONY EXPRESS, THE(1925); SPEED MAD(1925); MIDNIGHT MESSAGE, THE(1926); SILKS AND SADDLES(1929)
Misc. Silents
FRECKLES(1928)

John J. Fox
FRASIER, THE SENSUOUS LION(1973); ASSAULT ON PRECINCT 13(1976); EAT MY DUST!(1976)

John "Red" Fox
HARLOW(1965)

John William Fox
Silents
KENTUCKIANS, THE(1921), w

Johnny Fox
Silents
CALIFORNIA OR BUST(1927)
Misc. Silents
SPEEDING VENUS, THE(1926)

Jonathan Charles Fox
1984
RACING WITH THE MOON(1984)

Kathleen Fox
ROOM AT THE TOP(1959, Brit.)

Larry Fox
WESTLAND CASE, THE(1937), p

Lawrence W. Fox, Jr.
MAN WHO LOST HIMSELF, THE(1941), p

Lee Fox
DEVIL'S JEST, THE(1954, Brit.); CLOCKWORK ORANGE, A(1971, Brit.)

Linda Fox
Misc. Talkies
BIG BUST-OUT, THE(1973)

Lucy Fox
Silents
JUST FOR TONIGHT(1918); SONNY(1922); WHAT FOOLS MEN ARE(1922); ARIZONA ROMEO, THE(1925); BLUEBEARD'S SEVEN WIVES(1926)
Misc. Silents
WHY I WOULD NOT MARRY(1918); EMPIRE OF DIAMONDS, THE(1920); FLAMING CLUE, THE(1920); SOMETHING DIFFERENT(1920); WOMEN MEN FORGET(1920); MONEY MANIAC, THE(1921); TOILERS OF THE SEA(1923 US/Ital.); TEETH(1924); WISE VIRGIN, THE(1924); TRAIL RIDER, THE(1925)

Lyle Fox
DEMETRIUS AND THE GLADIATORS(1954)

Marcia Fox
DOCTOR IN TROUBLE(1970, Brit.); CREATURES THE WORLD FORGOT(1971, Brit.)

Marguerite Fox
Misc. Silents
BLADYS OF THE STEWPONY(1919, Brit.)

Marilyn Fox
OUTLAWS IS COMING, THE(1965); I WANNA HOLD YOUR HAND(1978)

Michael Fox
LAST TRAIN FROM BOMBAY(1952); VOODOO TIGER(1952); BEAST FROM 20,000 FATHOMS, THE(1953); GLASS WALL, THE(1953); MAGNETIC MONSTER, THE(1953); RUN FOR THE HILLS(1953); SERPENT OF THE NILE(1953); SIREN OF BAGDAD(1953); SKY COMMANDO(1953); GOG(1954); RIDERS TO THE STARS(1954); ROGUE COP(1954); BIG KNIFE, THE(1955); CONQUEST OF SPACE(1955); RUNNING WILD(1955); SCARLET COAT, THE(1955); GIRL IN THE KREMLIN, THE(1957); KISS THEM FOR ME(1957); PLUNDER ROAD(1957); TIJUANA STORY, THE(1957); TOP SECRET AFFAIR(1957); WAR OF THE SATELLITES(1958); INTERNS, THE(1962); WHATEVER HAPPENED TO BABY JANE?(1962); MISADVENTURES OF MERLIN JONES, THE(1964); NEW INTERNS, THE(1964); TIGER WALKS, A(1964); BILLIE(1965); LEGEND OF LYLAH CLARE, THE(1968); BLOODY MAMA(1970); YOUNG FRANKENSTEIN(1974); CLASS OF 1984(1982, Can.)
Misc. Talkies
SHOCK HILL(1966)

Michael J. Fox
MIDNIGHT MADNESS(1980)

Mickey Fox
BIG BAD MAMA(1974); CALIFORNIA SPLIT(1974); RENEGADE GIRLS(1974); CRAZY MAMA(1975); EAT MY DUST!(1976); BLOOD BEACH(1981); METALSTORM: THE DESTRUCTION OF JARED-SYN(1983)

Micky Fox
DR. HECKYL AND MR. HYPE(1980)

Mike Fox
MACHINE GUN KELLY(1958); DUNWICH HORROR, THE(1970)

Norman Fox
SOMETHING'S ROTTEN(1979, Can.), w

Norman A. Fox
GUNSMOKE(1953), w; TALL MAN RIDING(1955), w; RAWHIDE YEARS, THE(1956), w; NIGHT PASSAGE(1957), w

Paddy Fox
FRONTIER HELLCAT(1966, Fr./Ital./Ger./Yugo.); RAMPAGE AT APACHE WELLS(1966, Ger./Yugo.); FLAMING FRONTIER(1968, Ger./Yugo.)

Patricia Fox
TROJAN BROTHERS, THE(1946); BONNIE PRINCE CHARLIE(1948, Brit.)

Patrick Fox
NIGHTHAWKS(1981)

Paul Fox
LADIES MUST PLAY(1930), w; CRASH DIVE(1943), set d; CLUNY BROWN(1946), set d; LATE GEORGE APLEY, THE(1947), set d; CAN-CAN(1960), set d

Paul Hervey Fox
PRINCE OF DIAMONDS(1930), w; SOLDIERS AND WOMEN(1930), w; CUBAN LOVE SONG, THE(1931), w; DANGEROUSLY YOURS(1933), w; MANDALAY(1934), w; GRAND FINALE(1936, Brit.), w; HOUSE BROKEN(1936, Brit.), w; LAST TRAIN FROM MADRID, THE(1937), w; HIDEOUT IN THE ALPS(1938, Brit.), w; ROMANCE A LA CARTE(1938, Brit.), w; JUST LIKE A WOMAN(1939, Brit.), w; SAFARI(1940), w;

Paul S. Fox
HELLO, FRISCO, HELLO(1943), set d; HOLY MATRIMONY(1943), set d; LAURA(1944), prod d, set d; ROYAL SCANDAL, A(1945), set d; DARK CORNER, THE(1946), set d; DRAGONWYCH(1946), set d; RAZOR'S EDGE, THE(1946), set d; FOXES OF HARROW, THE(1947), set d; MOSS ROSE(1947), set d; LUCK OF THE IRISH(1948), set d; UNFAITHFULLY YOURS(1948), set d; WALLS OF JERICHO(1948), set d; DANCING IN THE DARK(1949), set d; FAN, THE(1949), set d; MOTHER IS A FRESHMAN(1949), set d; DAVID AND BATHSHEBA(1951), set d; HOUSE ON TELEGRAPH HILL(1951), set d; DON'T BOTHER TO KNOCK(1952), set d; MY PAL GUS(1952), set d; NIGHT WITHOUT SLEEP(1952), set d; KING OF THE KHYBER RIFLES(1953), set d; PRESIDENT'S LADY, THE(1953), set d; EGYPTIAN. THE(1954), set d; GOOD MORNING, MISS DOVE(1955), set d; RAINS OF RANCHIPUR, THE(1955), set d; VIEW FROM POMPEY'S HEAD, THE(1955), set d; KING AND I, THE(1956), set d; AFFAIR TO REMEMBER, AN(1957), set d; DESK SET(1957), set d; SUN ALSO RISES, THE(1957), set d; MAN WHO UNDERSTOOD WOMEN, THE(1959), set d; FROM THE TERRACE(1960), set d; SNOW WHITE AND THE THREE STOOGES(1961), set d; TENDER IS THE NIGHT(1961), set d; CLEOPATRA(1963), set d; MOVE OVER, DARLING(1963), set d; SHOCK TREATMENT(1964), set d

Paula Fox
DESPERATE CHARACTERS(1971), w

Peter Fox
FRATERNITY ROW(1977); FM(1978); YOUNG GIANTS(1983)
1984
NIGHT OF THE COMET(1984)

Reginald Fox
AMERICAN PRISONER, THE(1929 Brit.); COMPULSORY HUSBAND, THE(1930, Brit.)
Silents
AUTOCRAT, THE(1919, Brit.); FATHER O'FLYNN(1919, Brit.); NETS OF DESTINY(1924, Brit.); LIVINGSTONE(1925, Brit.); ROBINSON CRUSOE(1927, Brit.)
Misc. Silents
BRANDED SOUL, THE(1920, Brit.); FLAME, THE(1920, Brit.); DANIEL DERONDA(1921, Brit.); SHADOW OF EVIL(1921, Brit.); DIAMOND MAN, THE(1924, Brit.); PALAVER(1926, Brit.); TROUBLESOME WIVES(1928, Brit.)

Rica Fox
SVENGALI(1955, Brit.); RETURN FROM THE ASHES(1965, U.S./Brit.)

Robert P. Fox
RAILROADED(1947), set d; LET'S LIVE A LITTLE(1948), set d

Robin Fox
MODESTY BLAISE(1966, Brit.)

Roy Fox
Misc. Talkies
GLEN AND RANDA(1971)

Samantha Fox
1984
DELIVERY BOYS(1984)
Misc. Talkies
IN LOVE(1983); SIMPLY IRRESISTIBLE(1983)

Sidney Fox
BAD SISTER(1931); SIX CYLINDER LOVE(1931); STRICTLY DISHONORABLE(1931); AFRAID TO TALK(1932); MOUTHPIECE, THE(1932); MURDERS IN THE RUE MORGUE(1932); NICE WOMAN(1932); ONCE IN A LIFETIME(1932); DOWN TO THEIR LAST YACHT(1934); MIDNIGHT(1934); DON QUIXOTE(1935, Fr.); SCHOOL FOR GIRLS(1935)

Silas Fox
CLOWN AND THE KIDS, THE(1968, U.S./Bulgaria), p

Sonia Fox
NEVER TAKE CANDY FROM A STRANGER(1961, Brit.); DEAD MAN'S EVIDENCE(1962, Brit.)

Sonny Fox
CHRISMAS THAT ALMOST WASN'T. THE(1966, Ital.)

Spencer Fox
SHARK RIVER(1953)

Stephen Fox
Silents
ALL THE WORLD TO NOTHING(1919), w; THIS HERO STUFF(1919), w

Stephen Fox [Jules Furthman]
Silents
TREASURE ISLAND(1920), w

Sunny Fox
HARVEST MELODY(1943)

Suzanne Fox
ONE FROM THE HEART(1982)

Sydney Fox
FABULOUS WORLD OF JULES VERNE, THE(1961, Czech.), m

Ted Fox
TOILERS OF THE SEA(1936, Brit.), d

Templeton Fox
TONY ROME(1967); HOW DO I LOVE THEE?(1970)

Toby Fox
GALLANT ONE, THE(1964, U.S./Peru)

Virginia Fox
Silents
SUBMARINE PIRATE, A(1915)
Misc. Silents
ITCHING PALMS(1923)

Wallace Fox
NEAR THE TRAIL'S END(1931), d; PARTNERS OF THE TRAIL(1931), d; POWDERSMOKE RANGE(1935), d; RED MORNING(1935), d, w; YELLOW DUST(1936), d; RACING LADY(1937), d; GUN PACKER(1938), d; MEXICALI KID(1938), d; BOWERY BLITZKRIEG(1941), d; BOWERY AT MIDNIGHT(1942), d; CORPSE VANISHES(1942), d; LET'S GET TOUGH(1942), d; 'NEATH BROOKLYN BRIDGE(1942), d; SMART ALECKS(1942), d; GIRL FROM MONTEREY, THE(1943), d; KID DYNAMITE(1943), d; OUTLAWS OF STAMPEDE PASS(1943), d; BLOCK BUSTERS(1944), d; MILLION DOLLAR KID(1944), d; PRIDE OF THE PLAINS(1944), d; RIDERS OF THE SANTA FE(1944), d; BAD MEN OF THE BORDER(1945), p&d; CODE OF THE LAWLESS(1945), p&d; DOCKS OF NEW YORK(1945), d; MR. MUGGS RIDES AGAIN(1945), d; PILLOW OF DEATH(1945), d; GUNMAN'S CODE(1946),

p&d; RUSTLER'S ROUNDUP(1946), p&d; VALIANT HOMBRE, THE(1948), d; DARING CABALLERO, THE(1949), d; GAY AMIGO, THE(1949), d; WESTERN RENEGADES(1949), d; FENCE RIDERS(1950), p&d; GUNSLINGERS(1950), p&d; OVER THE BORDER(1950), p&d; WHITE GODDESS(1953), d

Misc. Talkies

BULLETS FOR BANDITS(1942), d; GHOST RIDER, THE(1943), d; SONG OF THE RANGE(1944), d; SIX GUN MESA(1950), d

Silents

AVENGING RIDER, THE(1928), d; MAN IN THE ROUGH(1928), d

Misc. Silents

COME AND GET IT(1929), d

Wallace F. Fox

Misc. Talkies

BLAZING BULLETS(1951), d

Wallace W Fox

CANNONBALL EXPRESS(1932), d

Wallace W. Fox

LONE STAR VIGILANTES, THE(1942), d; CAREER GIRL(1944), d; GREAT MIKE, THE(1944), d; MEN ON HER MIND(1944), d; TRAIL TO VENGEANCE(1945), p&d; GUN TOWN(1946), p&d; LAWLESS BREED, THE(1946), p&d; WILD BEAUTY(1946), p&d; ARIZONA TERRITORY(1950), d; OUTLAW GOLD(1950), d; SILVER RAIDERS(1950), d; WEST OF WYOMING(1950), d; MONTANA DESPERADO(1951), d

Misc. Talkies

DEVIL ON DECK(1932), d

Silents

BANDIT'S SON, THE(1927), d; BREED OF THE SUNSETS(1928), d; DRIFTIN' SANDS(1928), d; AMAZING VAGABOND(1929), d

Misc. Silents

RIDING RENEGADE, THE(1928), d; TRAIL OF COURAGE, THE(1928), d; LAUGHING AT DEATH(1929), d

Walter Fox

1984

TOY SOLDIERS(1984), w

William Fox

MOTHER KNOWS BEST(1928), p; BEHIND THAT CURTAIN(1929), p; LUCKY STAR(1929), p; SUNNY SIDE UP(1929), p; BIG PARTY, THE(1930), p; OH, FOR A MAN!(1930), p; RENEGADES(1930), p; SONG O' MY HEART(1930), p; UP THE RIVER(1930), p; DON'T BET ON WOMEN(1931), p; EAGLE AND THE HAWK, THE(1950), ed; NO PLACE FOR JENNIFER(1950, Brit.); SERENADE(1956); SHE ALWAYS GETS THEIR MAN(1962, Brit.); TERRORISTS, THE(1975, Brit.); FINAL CONFLICT, THE(1981)

Silents

WARRENS OF VIRGINIA, THE(1924); SEVENTH HEAVEN(1927), p

William [James] Fox

MAGNET, THE(1950, Brit.); MINIVER STORY, THE(1950, Brit./U.S.); LAVENDER HILL MOB, THE(1951, Brit.); ONE WILD OAT(1951, Brit.); SECRET PARTNER, THE(1961, Brit.); WHAT EVERY WOMAN WANTS(1962, Brit.)

William Price Fox, Jr.

COLD TURKEY(1971), w

Carl Fox-Duering

KING, QUEEN, KNAVE(1972, Ger./U.S.)

Les Foxcroft

WEEKEND OF SHADOWS(1978, Aus.); HOODWINK(1981, Aus.)

1984

BROTHERS(1984, Aus.)

Earl Foxe

Silents

ASHES OF EMBERS(1916)

Earl A. Foxe

CRACK-UP, THE(1937)

Earle Foxe

GHOST TALKS, THE(1929); THRU DIFFERENT EYES(1929); GOOD INTENTIONS(1930); DANCE, FOOLS, DANCE(1931); DESTRY RIDES AGAIN(1932); EXPERT, THE(1932); LADIES OF THE BIG HOUSE(1932); MIDNIGHT PATROL, THE(1932); PASSPORT TO HELL(1932); SO BIG(1932); STRANGERS IN LOVE(1932); THEY NEVER COME BACK(1932); THOSE WE LOVE(1932); UNION DEPOT(1932); ARIZONA TO BROADWAY(1933); BLONDIE JOHNSON(1933); MEN ARE SUCH FOOLS(1933); MIND READER, THE(1933); BIG SHAKEDOWN, THE(1934); LITTLE MAN, WHAT NOW?(1934); LOVE TIME(1934); MARY OF SCOTLAND(1936); DANGEROUSLY YOURS(1937); MURDER GOES TO COLLEGE(1937); WE'RE ON THE JURY(1937); MILITARY ACADEMY(1940); MY DARLING CLEMENTINE(1946)

Misc. Talkies

ST. LOUIS WOMAN(1935)

Silents

FLOOR ABOVE, THE(1914); HOME SWEET HOME(1914); ALIEN SOULS(1916); OUTWITTED(1917); PECK'S BAD GIRL(1918); INNOCENCE(1923); OH, YOU TONY!(1924); WAGES FOR WIVES(1925); LADIES MUST DRESS(1927); SLAVES OF BEAUTY(1927); FOUR SONS(1928); NEWS PARADE, THE(1928); NONE BUT THE BRAVE(1928); FUGITIVES(1929); NEW YEAR'S EVE(1929)

Misc. Silents

LOVE MASK, THE(1916); PUBLIC OPINION(1916); TRAIL OF THE LONESOME PINE, THE(1916); BLIND MAN'S LUCK(1917); HONEYMOON, THE(1917); PANTHEA(1917); FROM TWO TO SIX(1918); STUDIO GIRL, THE(1918); MAN SHE BROUGHT BACK, THE(1922); PRODIGAL JUDGE, THE(1922); FASHION ROW(1923); TRIP TO CHINATOWN, A(1926); UPSTREAM(1927); BLINDFOLD(1928); HANGMAN'S HOUSE(1928); SAILORS' WIVES(1928); BLACK MAGIC(1929)

lp: Fanne Foxe

Misc. Talkies

POSSE FROM HEAVEN(1975)

Jimmy Foxe

PUBLIC WEDDING(1937)

W. G. Foxley

BATTLE OF BRITAIN, THE(1969, Brit.)

Harry Foxwell

Silents

ONLY A MILL GIRL(1919, Brit.), a, p

Ivan Foxwell

GUILT IS MY SHADOW(1950, Brit.), p, w; NO ROOM AT THE INN(1950, Brit.), p, w; AFFAIR IN MONTE CARLO(1953, Brit.), p; COLDITZ STORY, THE(1955, Brit.), p, w; INTRUDER, THE(1955, Brit.), p; STOWAWAY GIRL(1957, Brit.), p, w; TOUCH OF

LARCENY, A(1960, Brit.), p, w; TIARA TAHITI(1962, Brit.), p, w; QUILLER MEMORANDUM, THE(1966, Brit.), p; DECLINE AND FALL... OF A BIRD WATCHER(1969, Brit.), p, w

Robert Foxworth

TREASURE OF MATECUMBE(1976); AIRPORT '77(1977); DAMIEN–OMEN II(1978); PROPHECY(1979); BLACK MARBLE, THE(1980)

1984

INVISIBLE STRANGLER(1984)

James Foxx

TIMBUKTU(1959)

John Foxx

IDENTIFICATION OF A WOMAN(1983, Ital.), m

Mickey Foxx

ROPE OF FLESH(1965)

Redd Foxx

COTTON COMES TO HARLEM(1970); NORMAN...IS THAT YOU?(1976)

Rhonda Foxx

Misc. Talkies

CHEERING SECTION(1977)

Bob Foy

RENDEZVOUS WITH ANNIE(1946)

Brian Foy

THAT'S GRATITUDE(1934), p; HIGH SCHOOL GIRL(1935), p; BROADWAY MUSKETEERS(1938), p; HELL'S KITCHEN(1939), p; CANON CITY(1948), p

Bryan Foy

HOME TOWNERS, THE(1928), d; LIGHTS OF NEW YORK(1928), d; QUEEN OF THE NIGHTCLUBS(1929), d; ROYAL BOX, THE(1930), d; GORILLA, THE(1931), d; DECEPTION(1933), p; MYRT AND MARGE(1934), p; I LIVE FOR LOVE(1935), p; MAN OF IRON(1935), p; PAYOFF, THE(1935), p; PERSONAL MAID'S SECRET(1935), p; SWELL-HEAD(1935), p; BRIDES ARE LIKE THAT(1936), p; CASE OF THE BLACK CAT, THE(1936), p; CASE OF THE VELVET CLAWS, THE(1936), p; DOWN THE STRETCH(1936), p; FRESHMAN LOVE(1936), p; HOT MONEY(1936), p; ISLE OF FURY(1936), p; JAILBREAK(1936), p; KING OF HOCKEY(1936), p; LAW IN HER HANDS, THE(1936), p; LOVE BEGINS AT TWENTY(1936), p; MAN HUNT(1936), p; MOONLIGHT ON THE PRAIRIE(1936), p; MURDER BY AN ARISTOCRAT(1936), p; MURDER OF DR. HARRIGAN, THE(1936), p; SONG OF THE SADDLE(1936), p; TIMES SQUARE PLAYBOY(1936), p; TRAILIN' WEST(1936), p; TREACHERY RIDES THE RANGE(1936), p; TWO AGAINST THE WORLD(1936), p; WIDOW FROM MONTE CARLO, THE(1936), p; ADVENTUROUS BLONDE(1937), p; CALIFORNIA MAIL, THE(1937), p; CASE OF THE STUTTERING BISHOP, THE(1937), p; DANCE, CHARLIE, DANCE(1937), p; DEVIL'S SADDLE LEGION, THE(1937), p; DRAEGERMAN COURAGE(1937), p; FOOTLOOSE HEIRESS, THE(1937), p; GUNS OF THE PECOS(1937), p; KID COMES BACK(1937), p; LAND BEYOND THE LAW(1937), p; LOVE IS ON THE AIR(1937), ed; MELODY FOR TWO(1937), p; MIDNIGHT COURT(1937), p; MISSING WITNESSES(1937), p; ONCE A DOCTOR(1937), p; OVER THE GOAL(1937), p; PENROD AND SAM(1937), p; PRAIRIE THUNDER(1937), p; PUBLIC WEDDING(1937), p; SH! THE OCTOPUS(1937), p; SHE LOVED A FIREMAN(1937), p; THAT MAN'S HERE AGAIN(1937), p; WEST OF SHANGHAI(1937), p; WHITE BONDAGE(1937), p; WINE, WOMEN AND HORSES(1937), p; ACCIDENTS WILL HAPPEN(1938), p; BELOVED BRAT(1938), p; DAREDEVIL DRIVERS(1938), p; GIRLS ON PROBATION(1938), p; HE COULDN'T SAY NO(1938), p; HEART OF THE NORTH(1938), p; INVISIBLE MENACE, THE(1938), p; LITTLE MISS THOROUGHBRED(1938), p; MR. CHUMP(1938), p; MY BILL(1938), p; MYSTERY HOUSE(1938), p; NANCY DREW–DETECTIVE(1938), p; OVER THE WALL(1938), p; PATIENT IN ROOM 18, THE(1938), p; PENROD AND HIS TWIN BROTHER(1938), p; PENROD'S DOUBLE TROUBLE(1938), p; SERGEANT MURPHY(1938), p; TORCHY BLANE IN CHINATOWN(1938), p; TORCHY BLANE IN PANAMA(1938), p; TORCHY GETS HER MAN(1938), p; WHEN WERE YOU BORN?(1938), p; CODE OF THE SECRET SERVICE(1939), p; DEAD END KIDS ON DRESS PARADE(1939), p; EVERYBODY'S HOBBY(1939), p; I AM NOT AFRAID(1939), p; KID NIGHTINGALE(1939), p; MAN WHO DARED, THE(1939), p; NANCY DREW–REPORTER(1939), p; NANCY DREW AND THE HIDDEN STAIRCASE(1939), p; NANCY DREW, TROUBLE SHOOTER(1939), p; NO PLACE TO GO(1939), p; ON TRIAL(1939), p; PRIDE OF THE BLUEGRASS(1939), p; PRIVATE DETECTIVE(1939), p; RETURN OF DR. X, THE(1939), p; SECRET SERVICE OF THE AIR(1939), p; SMASHING THE MONEY RING(1939), p; SWEEPSTAKES WINNER(1939), p; TORCHY PLAYS WITH DYNAMITE(1939), p; WATERFRONT(1939), p; CALLING PHILO VANCE(1940), p; DEVIL'S ISLAND(1940), p; FUGITIVE FROM JUSTICE, A(1940), p; GRANNY GET YOUR GUN(1940), p; MURDER IN THE AIR(1940), p; TEAR GAS SQUAD(1940), p; BODY DISAPPEARS, THE(1941), p; BERLIN CORRESPONDENT(1942), p; LITTLE TOKYO, U.S.A.(1942), p; LOVES OF EDGAR ALLAN POE, THE(1942), p; UNDYING MONSTER, THE(1942), p; DOLL FACE(1945), p; IF I'M LUCKY(1946), p; LOST HONEYMOON(1947), p; OUT OF THE BLUE(1947), p; TRAPPED(1949), p; BREAKTHROUGH(1950), p; GREAT JEWEL ROBBER, THE(1950), p; HIGHWAY 301(1950), p; I WAS A COMMUNIST FOR THE F.B.I.(1951), p; INSIDE THE WALLS OF FOLSOM PRISON(1951), p; TANKS ARE COMING, THE(1951), p; CATTLE TOWN(1952), p; LION AND THE HORSE, THE(1952), p; MIRACLE OF OUR LADY OF FATIMA, THE(1952), p; WINNING TEAM, THE(1952), p; HOUSE OF WAX(1953), p; CRIME WAVE(1954), p; MAD MAGICIAN, THE(1954), p; BAMBOO PRISON, THE(1955), p; WOMEN'S PRISON(1955), p; BATTLE STATIONS(1956), p; TRUE STORY OF LYNN STUART, THE(1958), p; BLUEPRINT FOR ROBBERY(1961), p; HOUSE OF WOMEN(1962), p; PT 109(1963), p

Misc. Talkies

ELYSIA(1933), d

Silents

COLLEGE(1927), w; FORTUNE HUNTER, THE(1927), w

Bryon Foy

EMPTY HOLSTERS(1937), p

Byron Foy

CHEROKEE STRIP(1937), p; GUADALCANAL DIARY(1943), p

Charles Foy

DOWN THE STRETCH(1936); HERE COMES CARTER(1936); POLO JOE(1936); DANCE, CHARLIE, DANCE(1937); EVER SINCE EVE(1937); FUGITIVE IN THE SKY(1937); MELODY FOR TWO(1937); MIDNIGHT COURT(1937); WINE, WOMEN AND HORSES(1937); HELL'S KITCHEN(1939); KING OF THE UNDERWORLD(1939); MUTINY IN THE BIG HOUSE(1939); EAST OF THE RIVER(1940); WAGONS ROLL AT NIGHT, THE(1941)

Charley Foy
HOT MONEY(1936); ADVENTUROUS BLONDE(1937); SARATOGA(1937); DAREDEVIL DRIVERS(1938); MIDNIGHT INTRUDER(1938); PENROD AND HIS TWIN BROTHER(1938); BLACKWELL'S ISLAND(1939); CONSPIRACY(1939); SWEEPSTAKES WINNER(1939); WOMAN OF THE TOWN, THE(1943); SEVEN LITTLE FOYS, THE(1955), tech adv

Eddie Foy
COLLEGE HOLIDAY(1936)

Eddie Foy, Jr.
QUEEN OF THE NIGHTCLUBS(1929); LEATHERNECKING(1930); MYRT AND MARGE(1934); CODE OF THE SECRET SERVICE(1939); COWBOY QUARTERBACK(1939); FRONTIER MARSHAL(1939); SECRET SERVICE OF THE AIR(1939); SMASHING THE MONEY RING(1939); WOMEN IN THE WIND(1939); FUGITIVE FROM JUSTICE, A(1940); LILLIAN RUSSELL(1940); MURDER IN THE AIR(1940); SCATTERBRAIN(1940); TEXAS RANGERS RIDE AGAIN(1940); CASE OF THE BLACK PARROT, THE(1941); COUNTRY FAIR(1941); FOUR JACKS AND A JILL(1941); PUDDIN' HEAD(1941); ROOKIES ON PARADE(1941); JOAN OF OZARK(1942); MOONLIGHT MASQUERADE(1942); POWDER TOWN(1942); YANKEE DOODLE DANDY(1942); YOKEL BOY(1942); DIXIE(1943); DIXIE DUGAN(1943); AND THE ANGELS SING(1944); WILSON(1944); HONEYCHILE(1951); FARMER TAKES A WIFE, THE(1953); LUCKY ME(1954); SEVEN LITTLE FOYS, THE(1955); PAJAMA GAME, THE(1957); BELLS ARE RINGING(1960); 30 IS A DANGEROUS AGE, CYNTHIA(1968, Brit.); WON TON TON, THE DOG WHO SAVED HOLLYWOOD(1976)

Eddy Foy, Jr.
GIDGET GOES HAWAIIAN(1961)

Freddie Foy
MIDNIGHT TAXI, THE(1928), w

Eddie Foy III
WOMEN'S PRISON(1955); BATTLE STATIONS(1956); OUTLAW'S SON(1957); RUN SILENT, RUN DEEP(1958); WHEN HELL BROKE LOOSE(1958)

Gloria Foy
DANCING LADY(1933)

Madeline Foy
BONNIE PARKER STORY, THE(1958); JET ATTACK(1958)

Mary Foy
STUDIO MURDER MYSTERY, THE(1929); DUMBBELLS IN ERMINE(1930); EMBARRASSING MOMENTS(1930); LADIES IN LOVE(1930); MAN FROM WYOMING, A(1930); WIDOW FROM CHICAGO, THE(1930); SCANDAL SHEET(1931); LADIES OF THE BIG HOUSE(1932); LOVE IS LIKE THAT(1933); SLIGHTLY MARRIED(1933); STRANGE PEOPLE(1933); CITY PARK(1934); HOUSE OF MYSTERY(1934); ONCE TO EVERY WOMAN(1934); TWO HEADS ON A PILLOW(1934); FRONT PAGE WOMAN(1935); LITTLE BIG SHOT(1935); LOVE IN BLOOM(1935); NAUGHTY MARIETTA(1935); NO RANSOM(1935); SCHOOL FOR GIRLS(1935); WHITE LIES(1935); FURY(1936); THUNDER TRAIL(1937); I STOLE A MILLION(1939); MAISIE(1939); ONE HOUR TO LIVE(1939)
Silents
STARDUST(1921); CRADLE BUSTER, THE(1922); SECOND FIDDLE(1923); WHITE ROSE, THE(1923); ICEBOUND(1924); IT'S THE OLD ARMY GAME(1926); ANKLES PREFERRED(1927); SLAVES OF BEAUTY(1927); LARIAT KID, THE(1929)
Misc. Silents
HEADLESS HORSEMAN, THE(1922); HOOSIER SCHOOLMASTER, THE(1924); POLLY OF THE MOVIES(1927)

Mary Lou Foy
QUEST FOR FIRE(1982, Fr./Can.)

Nancy Foy
FRANCES(1982)

Pat Foy
Misc. Silents
SALLY IN OUR ALLEY(1916)

Foy Williams & Riders Of The Purple Sage
GRAND CANYON TRAIL(1948)

Foy Willing and His Orchestra
TEXAS CARNIVAL(1951)

Foy Willing and Riders of Purple Sage
CALIFORNIA FIREBRAND(1948); NORTH OF THE GREAT DIVIDE(1950)

Foy Willing and Riders of the Purple Sage
TRIGGER, JR.(1950)

Foy Willing and the Riders of the Purple Sage
TWILIGHT ON THE PRAIRIE(1944); OUT CALIFORNIA WAY(1946); LAST FRONTIER UPRISING(1947); TIMBER TRAIL, THE(1948); DOWN DAKOTA WAY(1949); FAR FRONTIER, THE(1949); GOLDEN STALLION, THE(1949); SUSANNA PASS(1949); BELLS OF CORONADO(1950); SUNSET IN THE WEST(1950); TRAIL OF ROBIN HOOD(1950); TWILIGHT IN THE SIERRAS(1950); DISC JOCKEY(1951); HEART OF THE ROCKIES(1951); SPOILERS OF THE PLAINS(1951)

Eddie Foyer
BIG HOUSE, THE(1930)

Florence Foyer
MIDSTREAM(1929)

Gladys Foyle
Silents
KILTIES THREE(1918, Brit.)

Michael Foytenyi
WINTER KEPT US WARM(1968, Can.), ed

Gro Fraas
EDVARD MUNCH(1976, Norway/Swed.)

Mario Frabizi
POSTMAN'S KNOCK(1962, Brit.)

Clemente Fracassi
AIDA(1954, Ital.), d; SENSUALITA(1954, Ital.), d

Carla Fracci
NIJINSKY(1980, Brit.)

Maria Fracci
ROMEO AND JULIET(1968, Brit./Ital.)

Frank Fracht
HOUSEBOAT(1958), ed

Frack
LADY, LET'S DANCE(1944)

Jack Frack
HIT THE HAY(1945); NIGHT EDITOR(1946); SMOOTH AS SILK(1946)

Edward Fraction
BETRAYAL, THE(1948)

Jose Frade
NUN AT THE CROSSROADS, A(1970, Ital./Span.), w; DR. JEKYLL AND THE WOLFMAN(1971, Span.), p; VAMPIRE'S NIGHT ORGY, THE(1973, Span./Ital.), p; ERNESTO(1979, Ital.), p

Bernard Fradet
YOUNG GIRLS OF ROCHEFORT, THE(1968, Fr.)

Roger Fradet
IT HAPPENED IN ATHENS(1962); JUDEX(1966, Fr./Ital.); TIGHT SKIRTS, LOOSE PLEASURES(1966, Fr.); GODSON, THE(1972, Ital./Fr.)

Marcel Fradetal
JUDEX(1966, Fr./Ital.), ph

M. Fradkin
DAY THE WAR ENDED, THE(1961, USSR), m

Heinrich Fraenkel
WHEN LONDON SLEEPS(1934, Brit.), w; JUGGERNAUT(1937, Brit.), w

Helene Fraenkel
IT HAPPENED TOMORROW(1944), w

Wolfgang Fraenkel
TONIGHT WE SING(1953)

Yael Fraenkel
DREAM NO MORE(1950, Palestine)

Susanka Frey
OTHER SIDE OF THE UNDERNEATH, THE(1972, Brit.)

Pierre Frag
WISE GUYS(1969, Fr./Ital.); RISE OF LOUIS XIV, THE(1970, Fr.)
1984
MY NEW PARTNER(1984, Fr.)

Claudio Fragasso
ZOMBIE CREEPING FLESH(1981, Ital./Span.), w; NIGHT OF THE ZOMBIES(1983, Span./Ital.), w

Fragna
BALL AT THE CASTLE(1939, Ital.), m

Jerry Fragnol
SONG OF THE THIN MAN(1947)

Peter Frago
SAGA OF DEATH VALLEY(1939)

Hugo Fragonese
OLD SHATTERHAND(1968, Ger./Yugo./Fr./Ital.), d

Lotus Fragrance
INCIDENT IN SHANGHAI(1937, Brit.); WIFE OF GENERAL LING, THE(1938, Brit.)

Marvin Fragua
ULZANA'S RAID(1972)

Alfredo Fraile
SOFT SKIN ON BLACK SILK(1964, Fr./Span.), ph

Alfredo Fraille
SAVAGE GUNS, THE(1962, U.S./Span.), ph

Richard Fraink
ONE-EYED SOLDIERS(1967, U.S./Brit./Yugo.), w

Marc Fraiseau
RISE OF LOUIS XIV, THE(1970, Fr.)

Claire Fraisse
JOY(1983, Fr./Can.), cos; MOON IN THE GUTTER, THE(1983, Fr./Ital.), cos

Robert Fraisse
LADY CHATTERLEY'S LOVER(1981, Fr./Brit.), ph

Bill Fraker
FOX, THE(1967), ph

Billy Fraker
MONTE WALSH(1970)

Lois Fraker
CANDIDATE, THE(1972)

William Fraker
ONE FLEW OVER THE CUCKOO'S NEST(1975), ph

William A. Fraker
GAMES(1967), ph; PRESIDENT'S ANALYST, THE(1967), ph; BULLITT(1968), ph; ROSEMARY'S BABY(1968), ph; PAINT YOUR WAGON(1969), ph; MONTE WALSH(1970), d; DUSTY AND SWEETS McGEE(1971), a, ph; DAY OF THE DOLPHIN, THE(1973), ph; REFLECTION OF FEAR, A(1973), d; ALOHA, BOBBY AND ROSE(1975), ph; COONSKIN(1975), ph; RANCHO DELUXE(1975), ph; GATOR(1976), ph; KILLER INSIDE ME, THE(1976), ph; LIPSTICK(1976), ph; CLOSE ENCOUNTERS OF THE THIRD KIND(1977), ph; EXORCIST II: THE HERETIC(1977), ph; LOOKING FOR MR. GOODBAR(1977), ph; AMERICAN HOT WAX(1978), ph; HEAVEN CAN WAIT(1978), ph; OLD BOYFRIENDS(1979), ph; 1941(1979), ph; HOLLYWOOD KNIGHTS, THE(1980), ph; LEGEND OF THE LONE RANGER, THE(1981), d; BEST LITTLE WHOREHOUSE IN TEXAS, THE(1982), ph; SHARKY'S MACHINE(1982), ph; WARGAMES(1983), ph
1984
IRRECONCILABLE DIFFERENCES(1984), a, ph; PROTOCOL(1984), ph

Frakson
KING OF HEARTS(1936, Brit.)

Joseph Fraley
GOOD GUYS WEAR BLACK(1978), w; SILENT RAGE(1982), w

Oscar Fraley
SCARFACE MOB, THE(1962), w

Pat Fraley
NO HOLDS BARRED(1952)

Christina Framback
RAVEN'S END(1970, Swed.)

William Frambe
NOTHING BUT TROUBLE(1944)

William Frambes
DOUGHGIRLS, THE(1944); JANIE(1944); TWO GIRLS AND A SAILOR(1944); HOLD THAT BLONDE(1945); JUNIOR MISS(1945); LET'S GO STEADY(1945); STATE FAIR(1945); BRINGING UP FATHER(1946); CENTENNIAL SUMMER(1946); DO YOU LOVE ME?(1946); JANIE GETS MARRIED(1946); LIVE WIRES(1946); PRIDE OF ST. LOUIS, THE(1952)

Dawn Frame
CAT ATE THE PARAKEET, THE(1972); LAUGHING POLICEMAN, THE(1973)
Fred Frame
CROWD ROARS, THE(1932)
Grazina Frame
MURDER CAN BE DEADLY(1963, Brit.); WHAT A CRAZY WORLD(1963, Brit.); BARGEE, THE(1964, Brit.); SEASIDE SWINGERS(1965, Brit.); ALPHABET MURDERS, THE(1966)
Park Frame
Silents
MAN WHO TURNED WHITE, THE(1919), d
Misc. Silents
GRAY WOLF'S GHOST, THE(1919), d; MINTS OF HELL, THE(1919), d; PAGAN GOD, THE(1919), d; FORGOTTEN WOMAN(1921), d; LOOPED FOR LIFE(1924), d; DRUG STORE COWBOY(1925), d
Philip Frame
RETURN OF COUNT YORGA, THE(1971); LITTLE ARK, THE(1972)
Samuel Framer
Silents
GOD'S OUTLAW(1919)
Harry Frampton
SCOTT OF THE ANTARCTIC(1949, Brit.), makeup; MAN IN THE WHITE SUIT, THE(1952), makeup; SCAPEGOAT, THE(1959, Brit.), makeup; LEAGUE OF GENTLEMEN, THE(1961, Brit.), makeup; L-SHAPED ROOM, THE(1962, Brit.), makeup; THERE WAS A CROOKED MAN(1962, Brit.), makeup; MIND BENDERS, THE(1963, Brit.), makeup; THREE LIVES OF THOMASINA, THE(1963, U.S./Brit.), makeup; MOON-SPINNERS, THE(1964), makeup; MASQUERADE(1965, Brit.), makeup; GYPSY GIRL(1966, Brit.), makup; WALK IN THE SHADOW(1966, Brit.), makeup; SHUTTERED ROOM, THE(1968, Brit.), makeup; GOODBYE GEMINI(1970, Brit.), makeup; HOUSE THAT DRIPPED BLOOD, THE(1971, Brit.), makeup; SAY HELLO TO YESTERDAY(1971, Brit.), makeup; STRAW DOGS(1971, Brit.), makeup; RETURN OF THE PINK PANTHER, THE(1975, Brit.), makeup; PINK PANTHER STRIKES AGAIN, THE(1976, Brit.), makeup; LITTLEST HORSE THIEVES, THE(1977), makeup; REVENGE OF THE PINK PANTHER(1978), makeup
Harry G. Frampton
MAGIC CHRISTIAN, THE(1970, Brit.), makeup
Peter Frampton
DAVY(1958, Brit.); HOUSE THAT DRIPPED BLOOD, THE(1971, Brit.), makeup; SON OF DRACULA(1974, Brit.); SGT. PEPPER'S LONELY HEARTS CLUB BAND(1978)
Wayne Framson
ONLY WHEN I LAUGH(1981)
Charles Franc
THIS REBEL BREED(1960)
Jean Francais
IF PARIS WERE TOLD TO US(1956, Fr.), m
Jean Francaix
PEARLS OF THE CROWN(1938, Fr.), md; NAPOLEON(1955, Fr.), m; ROYAL AFFAIRS IN VERSAILLES(1957, Fr.), m; LADY L(1965, Fr./Ital.), m
Alexis France
LORNA DOONE(1935, Brit.); HEAD OFFICE(1936, Brit.); DULCIMER STREET(1948, Brit.); WOMAN IN THE HALL, THE(1949, Brit.); STOLEN FACE(1952, Brit.)
Anatole France
CHASING YESTERDAY(1935), w
Silents
THAIS(1914), w
Annie France
MOULIN ROUGE(1944, Fr.)
B. J. France
STROKER ACE(1983)
C. V. France
VICTORIA THE GREAT(1937, Brit.); LOVES OF ROBERT BURNS, THE(1930, Brit.); BLACK COFFEE(1931, Brit.); SKIN GAME, THE(1931, Brit.); THESE CHARMING PEOPLE(1931, Brit.); NIGHT LIKE THIS, A(1932, Brit.); LORD EDGEWARE DIES(1934, Brit.); REGAL CAVALCADE(1935, Brit.); SCROOGE(1935, Brit.); BROKEN BLOSSOMS(1936, Brit.); IF I WERE KING(1938); STRANGE BOARDERS(1938, Brit.); YANK AT OXFORD, A(1938); CHEER BOYS CHEER(1939, Brit.); WARE CASE, THE(1939, Brit.); NIGHT TRAIN(1940, Brit.); MISSING TEN DAYS(1941, Brit.); ADVENTURE IN BLACKMAIL(1943, Brit.); IT HAPPENED ONE SUNDAY(1944, Brit.); 48 HOURS(1944, Brit.); HALF-WAY HOUSE, THE(1945, Brit.)
Charles H. France
Misc. Silents
NATURAL LAW, THE(1917), d
Claude France
Misc. Silents
LE CARNIVAL DES VERITES(1920, Fr.); LE PRINCE CHARMANT(1925, Fr.); LA MADONE DES SLEEPINGS(1928, Fr.)
Dawson France
IT'S GREAT TO BE YOUNG(1956, Brit.); HEART WITHIN, THE(1957, Brit.); WINSTANLEY(1979, Brit.)
Floyd France
Misc. Silents
PRINCESS' NECKLACE, THE(1917), d; PUTTING THE BEE IN HERBERT(1917), d
Gilbert France
11 HARROWHOUSE(1974, Brit.)
Gloria France
LOVE IN THE AFTERNOON(1957); VERY PRIVATE AFFAIR, A(1962, Fr./Ital.)
Hermain France
Misc. Silents
DO THE DEAD TALK?(1920)
Ketty France
JUDEX(1966, Fr./Ital.)
Marie France
GOLDEN MASK, THE(1954, Brit.); WHAT A WHOPPER(1961, Brit.); LAST TOMAHAWK, THE(1965, Ger./Ital./Span.)
Maxine DeVille France
FANDANGO(1970)
Richard France
THERE'S ALWAYS VANILLA(1972); THE CRAZIES(1973); VORTEX(1982)

Rolla France
A NOUS LA LIBERTE(1931, Fr.)
Suzanne France
HALF A SIXPENCE(1967, Brit.)
Fernand Francell
CALL, THE(1938, Fr.)
Helen Francell
ONE TOUCH OF VENUS(1948)
Jacqueline Francell
CALL, THE(1938, Fr.); GLORY OF FAITH, THE(1938, Fr.)
Leno Jo Francen
NEW KIND OF LOVE, A(1963)
Victor Francen
END OF THE WORLD, THE(1930, Fr.); ARIANE, RUSSIAN MAID(1932, Fr.); SACRIFICE OF HONOR(1938, Fr.); DOUBLE CRIME IN THE MAGINOT LINE(1939, Fr.); END OF A DAY, THE(1939, Fr.); ENTENTE CORDIALE(1939, Fr.); J'ACCUSE(1939, Fr.); LIVING CORPSE, THE(1940, Fr.); OPEN ROAD(1940, Fr.); HOLD BACK THE DAWN(1941); TALES OF MANHATTAN(1942); TEN GENTLEMEN FROM WEST POINT(1942); TUTTLES OF TAHITI(1942); DESERT SONG, THE(1943); MADAME CURIE(1943); MISSION TO MOSCOW(1943); CONSPIRATORS, THE(1944); HOLLYWOOD CANTEEN(1944); IN OUR TIME(1944); MASK OF DIMITRIOS, THE(1944); PASSAGE TO MARSEILLE(1944); CONFIDENTIAL AGENT(1945); SAN ANTONIO(1945); BEAST WITH FIVE FINGERS, THE(1946); DEVOTION(1946); NIGHT AND DAY(1946); BEGINNING OR THE END, THE(1947); TO THE VICTOR(1948); ADVENTURES OF CAPTAIN FABIAN(1951); HELL AND HIGH WATER(1954); BEDEVILLED(1955); FAREWELL TO ARMS, A(1957); JOURNEY TO THE LOST CITY(1960, Ger./Fr./Ital.); FANNY(1961)
Deborah Frances
KIMBERLEY JIM(1965, South Africa)
Henri Frances
LES BICHES(1968, Fr.)
Jeanne Frances
KEEP YOUR POWDER DRY(1945)
Leopoldo Frances
AND GOD CREATED WOMAN(1957, Fr.); YELLOWBEARD(1983)
Madeline Frances
FALLGUY(1962)
Mary Frances
DRACULA VERSUS FRANKENSTEIN(1972, Span.)
Myra Frances
REMEMBRANCE(1982, Brit.)
Stephen Frances
AMERICAN SUCCESS COMPANY, THE(1980)
Tom Frances
MERRY WIDOW, THE(1934)
Vera Frances
KING ARTHUR WAS A GENTLEMAN(1942, Brit.); GET CRACKING(1943, Brit.); IT'S THAT MAN AGAIN(1943, Brit.); WATERLOO ROAD(1949, Brit.)
Antonia Franceschi
FAME(1980)
Gretillat Franceschi
DAVID GOLDER(1932, Fr.)
Paul Francesci
Silents
ARAB, THE(1924)
Francesco
LIPSTICK(1976)
Arcuri Francesco
SONNY AND JED(1974, Ital.)
Louis Francesco
CAVALCADE(1933), md
Franco Francese
JOAN AT THE STAKE(1954, Ital./Fr.), p
Micheline Francey
DEVIL IS AN EMPRESS, THE(1939, Fr.); CAGE OF NIGHTINGALES, A(1947, Fr.); RAVEN, THE(1948, Fr.); DANGER IS A WOMAN(1952, Fr.); HENRIETTE'S HOLIDAY(1953, Fr.); RASPOUTINE(1954, Fr.); HOLIDAY FOR HENRIETTA(1955, Fr.)
Aldo Franchetti
STRICTLY DISHONORABLE(1931); WONDER MAN(1945)
Donov Franchetti
THREE-WAY SPLIT(1970)
Rina Franchetti
LA DOLCE VITA(1961, Ital./Fr.); EYE OF THE NEEDLE, THE(1965, Ital./Fr.); BRUTE AND THE BEAST, THE(1968, Ital.)
Alfredo Franchi
CONDEMNED OF ALTONA, THE(1963)
Franco Franchi
TWELVE-HANDED MEN OF MARS, THE(1964, Ital./Span.); 00-2 MOST SECRET AGENTS(1965, Ital.); DR. GOLDFOOT AND THE GIRL BOMBS(1966, Ital.); PRIMITIVE LOVE(1966, Ital.); DOS COSMONAUTAS A LA FUERZA(1967, Span./*Ital.); WAR ITALIAN STYLE(1967, Ital.)
Sergio Franchi
SECRET OF SANTA VITTORIA, THE(1969)
Basilio Franchina
FATAL DESIRE(1953), w; WOMAN OF THE RIVER(1954, Fr./Ital.), p, w; FRENCH CONSPIRACY, THE(1973, Fr.), w
Busilio Franchina
FALL OF THE ROMAN EMPIRE, THE(1964), w
Sandro Franchina
GREATEST LOVE, THE(1954, Ital.)
Leonard Franchon
Misc. Silents
COTTON AND CATTLE(1921), d; COWBOY ACE, A(1921), d; FLOWING GOLD(1921), d; OUT OF THE CLOUDS(1921), d; RANGE PIRATE, THE(1921), d; RUSTLERS OF THE NIGHT(1921), d; TRAIL TO RED DOG, THE(1921), d
Richard Franchot
FOUR HORSEMEN OF THE APOCALYPSE, THE(1962)

Adolfo Franci
LITTLE MARTYR, THE(1947, Ital.), w; SHOE SHINE(1947, Ital.), w; MIRACLE IN MILAN(1951, Ital.), w

Carlo Franci
GLADIATOR OF ROME(1963, Ital.), m; INVINCIBLE GLADIATOR, THE(1963, c.u. Ital./Span.), m; WITCH'S CURSE, THE(1963, Ital.), m; HERCULES AGAINST THE MOON MEN(1965, Fr./Ital.), m; SECRET SEVEN, THE(1966, Ital./Span.), m; CHIMES AT MIDNIGHT(1967, Span.,Switz.), md

Diana Franci
SCHOOLGIRL DIARY(1947, Ital.)

Maria Grazia Franci
ANGELINA(1948, Ital.)

Aldo Francia
STATE OF SIEGE(1973, Fr./U.S./Ital./Ger.)

Luisa Francia
YOUNG MONK, THE(1978, Ger.); SISTERS, OR THE BALANCE OF HAPPINESS(1982, Ger.), w

Maria Grazia Francia
BITTER RICE(1950, Ital.)

Anne Francine
JULIET OF THE SPIRITS(1965, Fr./Ital./W.Ger.); SAVAGES(1972); STAND UP AND BE COUNTED(1972)

Bette Francine
DEADLINE-U.S.A.(1952)

Dolores Francine
REVOLT OF THE SLAVES, THE(1961, Ital./Span./Ger.)

Francis Francine
LONESOME COWBOYS(1968)

Mario Francini
HOUSE OF FREAKS(1973, Ital.), w

Michel Francini
PLAYTIME(1973, Fr.)

Paulo Francini
PIXOTE(1981, Braz.), p

Armando Francioli
WANDERING JEW, THE(1948, Ital.); WHITE DEVIL, THE(1948, Ital.); PHAROAH'S WOMAN, THE(1961, Ital.)

Germana Francioli
WHITE SLAVE SHIP(1962, Fr./Ital.)

G. Franciolini
SECRETS D'ALCOVE(1954, Fr./Ital.), d

Gianni Franciolini
HELLO, ELEPHANT(1954, Ital.), d; LOVE ON THE RIVIERA(1964, Fr./Ital.), d, w

Antonio Francioni
LA CAGE AUX FOLLES II(1981, Ital./Fr.)

Anthony Franciosa
FACE IN THE CROWD, A(1957); HATFUL OF RAIN, A(1957); THIS COULD BE THE NIGHT(1957); WILD IS THE WIND(1957); LONG, HOT SUMMER, THE(1958); CAREER(1959); NAKED MAJA, THE(1959, Ital./U.S.); STORY ON PAGE ONE, THE(1959); GO NAKED IN THE WORLD(1961); ACROSS 110TH STREET(1972); FIREPOWER(1979, Brit.); WORLD IS FULL OF MARRIED MEN, THE(1980, Brit.); DEATH WISH II(1982); JULIE DARLING(1982, Can./Ger.)
Misc. Talkies
GHOST IN THE NOONDAY SUN(1974)

Massimo Franciosa
YOUNG HUSBANDS(1958, Ital./Fr.), w; ASSASSIN, THE(1961, Ital./Fr.), w; ROCCO AND HIS BROTHERS(1961, Fr./Ital.), w; LA VIACCIA(1962, Fr./Ital.), w; CONJUGAL BED, THE(1963, Ital.), w; FOUR DAYS OF NAPLES, THE(1963, US/Ital.), w; LEOPARD, THE(1963, Ital.), w; WHITE VOICES(1965, Fr./Ital.), d, w; EL GRECO(1966, Ital., Fr.), w; GIRL AND THE GENERAL, THE(1967, Fr./Ital.), w; THREE NIGHTS OF LOVE(1969, Ital.), w; VOYAGE, THE(1974, Ital.), w; FRANKENSTEIN-ITALIAN STYLE(1977, Ital.), w

Nina Franciosa
1984
BLAME IT ON THE NIGHT(1984)

Tony Franciosa
PERIOD OF ADJUSTMENT(1962); PLEASURE SEEKERS, THE(1964); RIO CONCHOS(1964); ASSAULT ON A QUEEN(1966); MAN COULD GET KILLED, A(1966); SWINGER, THE(1966); FATHOM(1967); IN ENEMY COUNTRY(1968); SWEET RIDE, THE(1968); MAN CALLED GANNON, A(1969); WEB OF THE SPIDER(1972, Ital./Fr./Ger.); DROWNING POOL, THE(1975)
Misc. Talkies
KISS MY GRITS(1982)

David Franciosi
MAKE A FACE(1971)

Al Francis
TRAIN RIDE TO HOLLYWOOD(1975), ph

Aldwyn Francis
UNDER MILK WOOD(1973, Brit.)

Alec Francis
LION AND THE MOUSE, THE(1928); FEET FIRST(1930)
Silents
VOICE IN THE DARK(1921); WHAT'S A WIFE WORTH?(1921); MAN WHO SAW TOMORROW, THE(1922); ETERNAL THREE, THE(1923); GENTLEMAN OF LEISURE, A(1923); GOLD DIGGERS, THE(1923); LITTLE CHURCH AROUND THE CORNER(1923); SPIDER AND THE ROSE, THE(1923); CHAMPION OF LOST CAUSES(1925); MAN AND MAID(1925); OUTWITTED(1925); ROSE OF THE WORLD(1925); FOREVER AFTER(1926)
Misc. Silents
FOOL'S AWAKENING, A(1924); CIRCLE, THE(1925); COAST OF FOLLY, THE(1925); PALS FIRST(1926); LITTLE SNOB, THE(1928)

Alec B. Francis
TERROR, THE(1928); EVANGELINE(1929); EVIDENCE(1929); MISSISSIPPI GAMBLER(1929); SACRED FLAME, THE(1929); BISHOP MURDER CASE, THE(1930); CASE OF SERGEANT GRISCHA, THE(1930); MURDER WILL OUT(1930); OUTWARD BOUND(1930); ARROWSMITH(1931); CAPTAIN APPLEJACK(1931); MATA HARI(1931); ALIAS MARY SMITH(1932); LAST MAN(1932); LAST MILE, THE(1932); NO GREATER LOVE(1932); ALICE IN WONDERLAND(1933); HIS PRIVATE SECRETARY(1933); LOOKING FORWARD(1933); OLIVER TWIST(1933); CAT'S PAW, THE(1934); I'LL TELL THE WORLD(1934); MYSTERY OF MR. X, THE(1934); OUT-

CAST LADY(1934)
Silents
LOLA(1914); WHEN BROADWAY WAS A TRAIL(1914); WISHING RING, THE(1914); ARRIVAL OF PERPETUA, THE(1915); WOMAN AND WINE(1915); ALL MAN(1916); BALLET GIRL, THE(1916); FRUITS OF DESIRE, THE(1916); GILDED CAGE, THE(1916); AUCTION BLOCK, THE(1917); LEAP TO FAME(1918); PEST, THE(1919); COURAGE(1921); BEYOND THE ROCKS(1922); NORTH OF THE RIO GRANDE(1922); IS DIVORCE A FAILURE?(1923); THREE WISE FOOLS(1923); BEAU BRUMMEL(1924); RECKLESS SEX, THE(1925); RETURN OF PETER GRIMM, THE(1926); TRAMP, TRAMP, TRAMP(1926); YANKEE SENOR, THE(1926); CAMILLE(1927); SALLY IN OUR ALLEY(1927); TENDER HOUR, THE(1927); EVANGELINE(1929)
Misc. Silents
AFTER DARK(1915); ALIAS JIMMY VALENTINE(1915); PIT, THE(1915); HEART OF A HERO, THE(1916); HUMAN DRIFTWOOD(1916); PERILS OF DIVORCE(1916); WITHOUT A SOUL(1916); YELLOW PASSPORT, THE(1916); FAMILY HONOR, THE(1917); FORGET-ME-NOTS(1917); CINDERELLA MAN, THE(1918); FACE IN THE DARK, THE(1918); GLORIOUS ADVENTURE, THE(1918); HIDDEN FIRES(1918); THIRTY A WEEK(1918); VENUS MODEL, THE(1918); WANTED - A MOTHER(1918); DAY DREAMS(1919); FLAME OF THE DESERT(1919); HEARTSEASE(1919); PROBATION WIFE, THE(1919); GREAT MOMENT, THE(1921); VIRGINIA COURTSHIP, A(1921); FORGOTTEN LAW, THE(1922); SMILIN' THROUGH(1922); DRIVIN' FOOL, THE(1923); DO IT NOW(1924); HUMAN TERROR, THE(1924); BRIDGE OF SIGHS, THE(1925); CAPITAL PUNISHMENT(1925); THANK YOU(1925); THUNDER MOUNTAIN(1925); WAKING UP THE TOWN(1925); WANDERING FOOTSTEPS(1925); WHERE THE WORST BEGINS(1925); TRANSCONTINENTAL LIMITED(1926); MUSIC MASTER, THE(1927); BROADWAY DADDIES(1928); COMPANIONATE MARRIAGE, THE(1928); LIFE'S MOCKERY(1928); SHEPHERD OF THE HILL, THE(1928)

Alice B. Francis
Silents
SINS OF SOCIETY(1915)

Alma Francis
Misc. Silents
ISLE OF LOVE, THE(1922); LOVE LETTERS(1924); WOLF MAN, THE(1924)

Alun Francis
MOUSE AND THE WOMAN, THE(1981, Brit.), m; GIRO CITY(1982, Brit.), m

Anne Francis
THIS TIME FOR KEEPS(1947); SUMMER HOLIDAY(1948); PORTRAIT OF JENNIE(1949); SO YOUNG, SO BAD(1950); ELOPEMENT(1951); WHISTLE AT EATON FALLS(1951); DREAMBOAT(1952); LYDIA BAILEY(1952); LION IS IN THE STREETS, A(1953); ROCKET MAN, THE(1954); ROGUE COP(1954); SUSAN SLEPT HERE(1954); BAD DAY AT BLACK ROCK(1955); BATTLE FLAME(1955); BLACKBOARD JUNGLE, THE(1955); SCARLET COAT, THE(1955); FORBIDDEN PLANET(1956); GREAT AMERICAN PASTIME, THE(1956); RACK, THE(1956); HIRED GUN, THE(1957); CROWDED SKY, THE(1960); GIRL OF THE NIGHT(1960); SNOWBALL(1960, Brit.), w; BRAINSTORM(1965); SATAN BUG, THE(1965); FUNNY GIRL(1968); MORE DEAD THAN ALIVE(1968); HOOK, LINE AND SINKER(1969); IMPASSE(1969); LOVE GOD?, THE(1969); DON'T GO NEAR THE WATER(1975); PANCHO VILLA(1975, Span.); SURVIVAL(1976); BORN AGAIN(1978)

Arlene Francis
MURDERS IN THE RUE MORGUE(1932); STAGE DOOR CANTEEN(1943); ALL MY SONS(1948); ONE, TWO, THREE(1961); THRILL OF IT ALL, THE(1963)

Barbara Francis
BEAST OF YUCCA FLATS, THE(1961)

C. Francis
UNCIVILISED(1937, Aus.)

Captain Francis
MYSTERY OF MR. X, THE(1934)

Carl Olin Francis
RIDERS OF BLACK RIVER(1939)

Carole Francis
FINGERS(1978)

Cedric Francis
MANHUNT IN THE JUNGLE(1958), p

Charles Francis
STRANGE FACES(1938); HOWARDS OF VIRGINIA, THE(1940); BLACK SWAN, THE(1942); THANK YOUR LUCKY STARS(1943); PEARL OF DEATH, THE(1944)
Misc. Silents
BROKEN FETTERS(1916)

Charlotte Francis
SILENCE OF DEAN MAITLAND, THE(1934, Aus.)

Christine Francis
LOOKS AND SMILES(1982, Brit.)

Clive Francis
INSPECTOR CLOUSEAU(1968, Brit.); MAN WHO HAD POWER OVER WOMEN, THE(1970, Brit.); CLOCKWORK ORANGE, A(1971, Brit.); GIRL STROKE BOY(1971, Brit.); VILLAIN(1971, Brit.)

Coleman Francis
GIRL IN WHITE, THE(1952); SCARLET ANGEL(1952); SHE COULDN'T SAY NO(1954); THIS ISLAND EARTH(1955); SPRING AFFAIR(1960); BEAST OF YUCCA FLATS, THE(1961), d&w, ed; SKYDIVERS, THE(1963), d&w; MOTOR PSYCHO(1965); NIGHT TRAIN TO MUNDO FINE(1966), a, p, d&w
Misc. Talkies
RED ZONE CUBA(1972)

Colin Francis
MERRY CHRISTMAS MR. LAWRENCE(1983, Jap./Brit.)

Colman Francis
STAKEOUT ON DOPE STREET(1958)

Connie Francis
JAMBOREE(1957); SHERIFF OF FRACTURED JAW, THE(1958, Brit.); WHERE THE BOYS ARE(1960); FOLLOW THE BOYS(1963); LOOKING FOR LOVE(1964); WHEN THE BOYS MEET THE GIRLS(1965)

Cornelia Francis
Misc. Talkies
OUTBREAK OF HOSTILITIES(1979)

Dai Francis
DREAM MAKER, THE(1963, Brit.)

Danny Francis
HARLOW(1965); WHAT DID YOU DO IN THE WAR, DADDY?(1966)

Dena Francis
QUEST FOR FIRE(1982, Fr./Can.)
Derek Francis
BACKFIRE!(1961, Brit.); CONCRETE JUNGLE, THE(1962, Brit.); LISA(1962, Brit.);
NIGHT CREATURES(1962, Brit.); BITTER HARVEST(1963, Brit.); FAREWELL PER-
FORMANCE(1963, Brit.); HI-JACKERS(1963, Brit.); MASTER SPY(1964, Brit.);
RING OF SPIES(1964, Brit.); THIS IS MY STREET(1964, Brit.); TWO LIVING, ONE
DEAD(1964, Brit./Swed.); VERDICT, THE(1964, Brit.); LITTLE ONES, THE(1965, Brit.);
TOMB OF LIGEIA, THE(1965, Brit.); PRESS FOR TIME(1966, Brit.); RASPUTIN–THE
MAD MONK(1966, Brit.); NEVER BACK LOSERS(1967, Brit.); THOSE FANTASTIC
FLYING FOOLS(1967, Brit); CARRY ON DOCTOR(1968, Brit.); CROSSPLOT(1969,
Brit.); WHAT'S GOOD FOR THE GOOSE(1969, Brit.); CARRY ON HENRY VIII(1970,
Brit.); CARRY ON LOVING(1970, Brit.); MAN OF VIOLENCE(1970, Brit.); SCROO-
GE(1970, Brit.); SAY HELLO TO YESTERDAY(1971, Brit.); STATUE, THE(1971, Brit.);
TO THE DEVIL A DAUGHTER(1976, Brit./Ger.); JABBERWOCKY(1977, Brit.);
WICKED LADY, THE(1983, Brit.)
Diana Francis
GIRL IN THE WOODS(1958)
Dick Francis
POOR OLD BILL(1931, Brit.); HIS GRACE GIVES NOTICE(1933, Brit.); UMBRELLA,
THE(1933, Brit.); TANGLED EVIDENCE(1934, Brit.); REAL BLOKE, A(1935, Brit.);
ALL THAT GLITTERS(1936, Brit.); BROWN WALLET(1936, Brit.); HAPPY
FAMILY, THE(1936, Brit.); JURY'S EVIDENCE(1936, Brit.); MEN OF YESTER-
DAY(1936, Brit.); DANGEROUS MEDICINE(1938, Brit.); DREAMING(1944, Brit.);
HERE COMES THE SUN(1945, Brit.); MURDER IN REVERSE(1946, Brit.); WALTZ
TIME(1946, Brit.)
Dixie Francis
MY WEAKNESS(1933)
Enid Francis
Misc. Silents
PRICE OF HAPPINESS, THE(1916)
Eric Francis
HELL, HEAVEN OR HOBOKEN(1958, Brit.); MEN ARE CHILDREN TWICE(1953,
Brit.); DEVIL ON HORSEBACK(1954, Brit.); MAKE ME AN OFFER(1954, Brit.);
INDISCREET(1958); HAND IN HAND(1960, Brit.); AMOROUS MR. PRAWN,
THE(1965, Brit.); PRIVATE LIFE OF SHERLOCK HOLMES, THE(1970, Brit.);
THEATRE OF BLOOD(1973, Brit.); CONFESSIONS OF A POP PERFORMER(1975,
Brit.); SHILLINGBURY BLOWERS, THE(1980, Brit.)
Eugene Francis
THAT GANG OF MINE(1940); FLYING WILD(1941); PRIDE OF THE BOWERY(1941)
Eva Francis
Misc. Silents
CONEY ISLAND PRINCESS, A(1916)
Eve Francis
Misc. Silents
LE ROI DE LA MER(1917, Fr.); LA FETE ESPAGNOLE(1919, Fr.); ELDORADO(1921,
Fr.); FIEVRE(1921, Fr.); LE CHEMIN D'ERONA(1921, Fr.); LA FEMME DE NULLE
PART(1922, Fr.); L'INONDATION(1924, Fr.); ANTOINETTE SABRIER(1927, Fr.)
Fred Francis
MACOMBER AFFAIR, THE(1947), ph
Freddie Francis
GOLDEN SALAMANDER(1950, Brit.), ph; HELL IN KOREA(1956, Brit.), ph; TIME
WITHOUT PITY(1957, Brit.), ph; ROOM AT THE TOP(1959, Brit.), ph; STRANGE
AFFECTION(1959, Brit.), ph; BATTLE OF THE SEXES, THE(1960, Brit.), ph; NEXT
TO NO TIME(1960, Brit.), ph; SONS AND LOVERS(1960, Brit.), ph; VIRGIN IS-
LAND(1960, Brit.), ph; INNOCENTS, THE(1961, U.S./Brit.), ph; NEVER TAKE
CANDY FROM A STRANGER(1961, Brit.), ph; SATURDAY NIGHT AND SUNDAY
MORNING(1961, Brit.), ph; TWO AND TWO MAKE SIX(1962, Brit.), d; DAY OF THE
TRIFFIDS, THE(1963), d; NIGHTMARE(1963, Brit.), d; PARANOIAC(1963, Brit.), d;
EVIL OF FRANKENSTEIN, THE(1964, Brit.), d; NIGHT MUST FALL(1964, Brit.), ph;
BRAIN, THE(1965, Ger./Brit.), d; DR. TERROR'S HOUSE OF HORRORS(1965, Brit.),
d; HYSTERIA(1965, Brit.), d; SKULL, THE(1965, Brit.), d; PSYCHOPATH, THE(1966,
Brit.), d; TRAITOR'S GATE(1966, Brit./Ger.), d; DEADLY BEES, THE(1967, Brit.), d;
THEY CAME FROM BEYOND SPACE(1967, Brit.), d; DRACULA HAS RISEN FROM
HIS GRAVE(1968, Brit.), d; TORTURE GARDEN(1968, Brit.), d; MUMSY, NANNY,
SONNY, AND GIRLY(1970, Brit.), d; TROG(1970, Brit.), d; TALES FROM THE
CRYPT(1972, Brit.), d; TALES THAT WITNESS MADNESS(1973, Brit.), d; CRA-
ZE(1974, Brit.), d; SON OF DRACULA(1974, Brit.), d; GHOUL, THE(1975, Brit.), d;
ELEPHANT MAN, THE(1980, Brit.), ph; FRENCH LIEUTENANT'S WOMAN,
THE(1981), ph
1984
DUNE(1984), ph; JIGSAW MAN, THE(1984, Brit.), ph; MEMED MY HAWK(1984,
Brit.), ph
Misc. Talkies
LEGEND OF THE WEREWOLF(1974), d
Gina Francis
1984
ELECTRIC DREAMS(1984)
Glen Francis
RIDERS OF THE FRONTIER(1939)
Gordon Francis
UNDER A CLOUD(1937, Brit.), w
Holman Francis
Silents
CLOTHES MAKE THE PIRATE(1925), w
Ivor Francis
TIGER WALKS, A(1964); I LOVE MY WIFE(1970); PIECES OF DREAMS(1970);
HONKY(1971); LATE LIZ, THE(1971); STEAGLE, THE(1971); WORLD'S GREATEST
ATHLETE, THE(1973); SUPERDAD(1974); PRISONER OF SECOND AVENUE,
THE(1975); WACKIEST WAGON TRAIN IN THE WEST, THE(1976); NORTH AVE-
NUE IRREGULARS, THE(1979)
Misc. Talkies
ALIEN ZONE(1978); HOUSE OF THE DEAD(1980)
Jack Francis
MEN OF YESTERDAY(1936, Brit.), w; TALKING FEET(1937, Brit.), w; STEPPING
TOES(1938, Brit.), w; SECOND MATE, THE(1950, Brit.), w; MAKE MINE A MIL-
LION(1965, Brit.), w

Jan Francis
DRACULA(1979)
1984
CHAMPIONS(1984)
Misc. Talkies
CORVINI INHERITANCE(1984, Brit.)
Joan Francis
FAHRENHEIT 451(1966, Brit.)
John Francis
MANCHURIAN CANDIDATE, THE(1962); TOO YOUNG, TOO IMMORAL!(1962);
LAUGHING POLICEMAN, THE(1973); TO BE OR NOT TO BE(1983); YELLOW-
BEARD(1983)
Misc. Talkies
LEGACY OF SATAN(1973)
Misc. Silents
OUT OF THE RUINS(1928), d
Jon Francis
WILL PENNY(1968)
Julie Francis
Misc. Talkies
ROAD REBELS(1963)
June Francis
GIRL GRABBERS, THE(1968)
Karl Francis
MOUSE AND THE WOMAN, THE(1981, Brit.), p, d, w; GIRO CITY(1982, Brit.), d&w
1984
YR ALCOHOLIG LION(1984, Brit.), d&w
Kathee Francis
GNOME-MOBILE, THE(1967)
Katherine Francis
COCOANUTS, THE(1929)
Katherine [Kay] Francis
GENTLEMEN OF THE PRESS(1929)
Kathy Francis
SWINGIN' SUMMER, A(1965)
Kay Francis
DANGEROUS CURVES(1929); ILLUSION(1929); MARRIAGE PLAYGROUND,
THE(1929); BEHIND THE MAKEUP(1930); FOR THE DEFENSE(1930); LET'S GO
NATIVE(1930); NOTORIOUS AFFAIR, A(1930); PASSION FLOWER(1930); RAF-
FLES(1930); STREET OF CHANCE(1930); VIRTUOUS SIN, THE(1930); GIRLS ABOUT
TOWN(1931); GUILTY HANDS(1931); LADIES' MAN(1931); SCANDAL SHEET(1931);
TRANSGRESSION(1931); VICE SQUAD, THE(1931); 24 HOURS(1931); CYNA-
RA(1932); FALSE MADONNA(1932); JEWEL ROBBERY(1932); MAN WANTED(1932);
ONE WAY PASSAGE(1932); STRANGERS IN LOVE(1932); STREET OF WO-
MEN(1932); TROUBLE IN PARADISE(1932); HOUSE ON 56TH STREET, THE(1933);
I LOVED A WOMAN(1933); KEYHOLE, THE(1933); MARY STEVENS, M.D.(1933);
STORM AT DAYBREAK(1933); BRITISH AGENT(1934); DOCTOR MONICA(1934);
MANDALAY(1934); WONDER BAR(1934); GOOSE AND THE GANDER, THE(1935); I
FOUND STELLA PARISH(1935); LIVING ON VELVET(1935); STRANDED(1935);
GIVE ME YOUR HEART(1936); WHITE ANGEL, THE(1936); ANOTHER DAWN(1937);
CONFESSION(1937); FIRST LADY(1937); STOLEN HOLIDAY(1937); COMET OVER
BROADWAY(1938); MY BILL(1938); SECRETS OF AN ACTRESS(1938); WOMEN ARE
LIKE THAT(1938); IN NAME ONLY(1939); KING OF THE UNDERWORLD(1939);
WOMEN IN THE WIND(1939); IT'S A DATE(1940); LITTLE MEN(1940); PLAY
GIRL(1940); WHEN THE DALTONS RODE(1940); CHARLEY'S AUNT(1941); FEMI-
NINE TOUCH, THE(1941); MAN WHO LOST HIMSELF, THE(1941); ALWAYS IN MY
HEART(1942); BETWEEN US GIRLS(1942); FOUR JILLS IN A JEEP(1944); ALLOT-
MENT WIVES, INC.(1945), a, p; DIVORCE(1945), a, p; WIFE WANTED(1946), a, p
Kevin Francis
PERSECUTION(1974, Brit.), p; GHOUL, THE(1975, Brit.), p
Larry Francis
MURDER BY TELEVISION(1935)
Laura Francis
1984
OXFORD BLUES(1984)
Leslie Francis
SOULS AT SEA(1937); LIGHT THAT FAILED, THE(1939); WHEN LADIES
MEET(1941); MRS. MINIVER(1942)
Linda Francis
NAKED KISS, THE(1964)
Major Douglas Francis
JOURNEY FOR MARGARET(1942); MRS. PARKINGTON(1944); NATIONAL VELV-
ET(1944)
Margot Francis
1984
NOTHING LASTS FOREVER(1984), ed
Melvin Francis
STORY OF DR. WASSELL, THE(1944)
Michael Francis
SWAPPERS, THE(1970, Brit.), ph
Missy Francis
SCAVENGER HUNT(1979); MAN, WOMAN AND CHILD(1983)
Monica Francis
MAYTIME IN MAYFAIR(1952, Brit.)
Noel Francis
FOX MOVIETONE FOLLIES OF 1930(1930); ROUGH ROMANCE(1930); UP THE
RIVER(1930); BACHELOR APARTMENT(1931); BLONDE CRAZY(1931); SMART
MONEY(1931); SMART WOMAN(1931); EXPERT, THE(1932); FLAMES(1932); GUIL-
TY AS HELL(1932); I AM A FUGITIVE FROM A CHAIN GANG(1932); LADIES OF
THE BIG HOUSE(1932); MAN ABOUT TOWN(1932); MANHATTAN TOWER(1932);
MOUTHPIECE, THE(1932); MY PAL, THE KING(1932); NIGHT COURT(1932); SO
BIG(1932); UNDER-COVER MAN(1932); BUREAU OF MISSING PERSONS(1933);
HER RESALE VALUE(1933); HOLD ME TIGHT(1933); IMPORTANT WITNESS,
THE(1933); ONLY YESTERDAY(1933); FIFTEEN WIVES(1934); GOOD DAME(1934);
IMITATION OF LIFE(1934); LINEUP, THE(1934); LOUDSPEAKER, THE(1934);
WHAT'S YOUR RACKET?(1934); WHITE PARADE, THE(1934); MAN WHO RE-
CLAIMED HIS HEAD, THE(1935); MUTINY AHEAD(1935); STONE OF SILVER
CREEK(1935); WHITE COCKATOO(1935); LEFT-HANDED LAW(1937); SUDDEN
BILL DORN(1938)

Olin Francis
KISMET(1930); BATTLING BUCKAROO(1932); OUT OF SINGAPORE(1932); TEX TAKES A HOLIDAY(1932); PENAL CODE, THE(1933); LIGHTNING RANGE(1934); CIRCLE OF DEATH(1935); HARD ROCK HARRIGAN(1935); I CONQUER THE SEA(1936); O'MALLEY OF THE MOUNTED(1936); SWING TIME(1936); ROUGH RIDIN' RHYTHM(1937); BORN TO FIGHT(1938); OVERLAND STAGE RAIDERS(1938); PALS OF THE SADDLE(1938); RED RIVER RANGE(1938); TWO-GUN JUSTICE(1938); GUNGA DIN(1939); KNIGHT OF THE PLAINS(1939); NIGHT RIDERS, THE(1939); MAN FROM TUMBLEWEEDS, THE(1940); ROLLIN' HOME TO TEXAS(1941)
Misc. Talkies
FORTY-FIVE CALIBRE ECHO(1932); IRISH GRINGO, THE(1935); TAKE ME BACK TO OKLAHOMA(1940)
Silents
KNIGHT OF THE WEST, A(1921); WALLOPING WALLACE(1924); CROSS BREED(1927); KID BROTHER, THE(1927); FREE LIPS(1928); STORMY WATERS(1928)
Misc. Silents
FIGHTIN' DEVIL(1922); RARIN' TO GO(1924); LET'S GO GALLAGHER(1925)
Owen Francis
NO OTHER WOMAN(1933), w; MAGNIFICENT BRUTE, THE(1936), w; BILL CRACKS DOWN(1937), w; CRIMINALS OF THE AIR(1937), w; DANGEROUS ADVENTURE, A(1937), w; PACK UP YOUR TROUBLES(1939), w; 20,000 MEN A YEAR(1939), w; MAN FROM MONTREAL, THE(1940), w; SAILOR'S LADY(1940), w; SHOOTING HIGH(1940), w; THEY MADE ME A KILLER(1946), w
Silents
HARD WAY, THE(1916, Brit.)
Paul Francis
SKYDIVERS, THE(1963)
Ralph Francis, Jr.
LET FREEDOM RING(1939)
Raymond Francis
MR. DENNING DRIVES NORTH(1953, Brit.); COURT MARTIAL(1954, Brit.); STORM OVER THE NILE(1955, Brit.); DOUBLE CROSS(1956, Brit.); DECISION AGAINST TIME(1957, Brit.); STEEL BAYONET, THE(1958, Brit.); ALL THINGS BRIGHT AND BEAUTIFUL(1979, Brit.)
Richard Francis
WRONG DAMN FILM, THE zero(1975), ph; NEXT OF KIN(1983, Aus.), art d
Robert Francis
CAINE MUTINY, THE(1954); THEY RODE WEST(1954); BAMBOO PRISON, THE(1955); LONG GRAY LINE, THE(1955)
Samuel Francis
BABY MAKER, THE(1970)
Sandra Francis
BACHELOR OF HEARTS(1958, Brit.); SPY IN THE SKY(1958); TIME LOCK(1959, Brit.); TREAD SOFTLY STRANGER(1959, Brit.)
Sara Francis
Silents
LADY OF THE LAKE, THE(1928, Brit.)
Silvia Francis
NIGHT TRAIN FOR INVERNESS(1960, Brit.)
Stella Francis
EBB TIDE(1937)
Tom Francis
TRAVELING HUSBANDS(1931); LADIES OF THE JURY(1932)
Vera Francis
BACK ROOM BOY(1942, Brit.); GOOD TIME GIRL(1950, Brit.); PRESIDENT'S LADY, THE(1953); EMERGENCY HOSPITAL(1956)
Vera M. Francis
DEVIL GODDESS(1955)
William Francis
SOMETHING SHORT OF PARADISE(1979)
Wilma Francis
AND SUDDEN DEATH(1936); LADY BE CAREFUL(1936); BANK ALARM(1937); HIDEAWAY GIRL(1937); TRADE WINDS(1938); BORROWED HERO(1941); UNDER AGE(1941); MAN WITH TWO LIVES, THE(1942); GUEST WIFE(1945); SCARLET ANGEL(1952)
Misc. Talkies
STOLEN PARADISE(1941)
Yvonne Francis
UP THE ACADEMY(1980)
Francis Langford's Singing Scholars
FUN AT ST. FANNY'S(1956, Brit.)
The Francis Mangan Girls
MAN OF MAYFAIR(1931, Brit.)
Richard Francis-Bruce
1984
CAREFUL, HE MIGHT HEAR YOU(1984, Aus.), ed
Mario Francisci
QUEEN OF SHEBA(1953, Ital.), p
Pietro Francisci
ANTHONY OF PADUA(1952, Ital.), d, w; QUEEN OF SHEBA(1953, Ital.), d; ATTILA(1958, Ital.), d; HERCULES(1959, Ital.), d, w; HERCULES UNCHAINED(1960, Ital./Fr.), d, w; WARRIOR EMPRESS, THE(1961, Ital./Fr.), d, w; SIEGE OF SYRACUSE(1962, Fr./Ital.), d, w; HERCULES, SAMSON & ULYSSES(1964, Ital.), d&w, ed; STAR PILOT(1977, Ital.), d, w
Betty Francisco
BROADWAY(1929); SMILING IRISH EYES(1929); LOTUS LADY(1930); MADAME SATAN(1930); STREET OF CHANCE(1930); WIDOW FROM CHICAGO, THE(1930); CHARLIE CHAN CARRIES ON(1931); GOOD SPORT(1931); MYSTERY RANCH(1932); STOWAWAY(1932); WHOM THE GODS DESTROY(1934)
Silents
MIDSUMMER MADNESS(1920); RIDING WITH DEATH(1921); ACROSS THE CONTINENT(1922); ASHES OF VENGEANCE(1923); CRINOLINE AND ROMANCE(1923); NOISE IN NEWBORO, A(1923); POOR MEN'S WIVES(1923); EAST OF BROADWAY(1924); GAMBLING WIVES(1924); ON PROBATION(1924); FAIR PLAY(1925); JIMMIE'S MILLIONS(1925); WASTED LIVES(1925); MAN BAIT(1926); GAY RETREAT, THE(1927)

Misc. Silents
BROADWAY COWBOY, THE(1920); FURNANCE, THE(1920); GUILTY CONSCIENCE, A(1921); STRAIGHT FROM PARIS(1921); HER NIGHT OF NIGHTS(1922); DOUBLE DEALING(1923); BIG TIMBER(1924); PHANTOM OF THE FOREST, THE(1926); BOY OF THE STREETS, A(1927); QUEEN OF THE CHORUS(1928); YOU CAN'T BEAT THE LAW(1928); SPIRIT OF YOUTH, THE(1929)
Carole Francisco
1984
FIRESTARTER(1984)
Evelyn Francisco
GODLESS GIRL, THE(1929)
Silents
KING OF KINGS, THE(1927); KING OF THE HERD(1927)
Misc. Silents
O.U. WEST(1925)
Manuel Francisco
SPRING AFFAIR(1960), m; MARRIED TOO YOUNG(1962), m; DEADWOOD'76(1965), m
Margaret Francisco
Silents
KING OF KINGS, THE(1927)
Marguerite Francisco
BOY, A GIRL, AND A DOG, A(1946), ed
Rob Francisco
ONCE BEFORE I DIE(1967, U.S./Phil.)
Sanchez Francisco
BANG, BANG, YOU'RE DEAD(1966)
James Franciscus
FOUR BOYS AND A GUN(1957); MUGGER, THE(1958); I PASSED FOR WHITE(1960); OUTSIDER, THE(1962); MIRACLE OF THE WHITE STALLIONS(1963); YOUNGBLOOD HAWKE(1964); SNOW TREASURE(1968); MAROONED(1969); VALLEY OF GWANGI, THE(1969); BENEATH THE PLANET OF THE APES(1970); HELL BOATS(1970, Brit.); JONATHAN LIVINGSTON SEAGULL(1973); AMAZING DOBERMANS, THE(1976); GOOD GUYS WEAR BLACK(1978); GREEK TYCOON, THE(1978); CITY ON FIRE(1979 Can.); KILLER FISH(1979, Ital./Braz.); WHEN TIME RAN OUT(1980); BUTTERFLY(1982); GREAT WHITE, THE(1982, Ital.)
Alain Franck
MAN WITH THE TRANSPLANTED BRAIN, THE(1972, Fr./Ital./Ger.), w
Alexander Franck
Misc. Silents
LIAR, THE(1918)
Arnold Franck
TWO IN A SLEEPING BAG(1964, Ger.), w
Cesar Franck
DOUBLE INDEMNITY(1944), m; SANDRA(1966, Ital.), m; CELESTE(1982, Ger.), m
Helga Franck
IT'S HOT IN PARADISE(1962, Ger./Yugo.)
Sterling Franck
REBEL IN TOWN(1956)
Suzanne Franck
MY UNCLE(1958, Fr.)
Walter Franck
MASTER OF THE WORLD(1935, Ger.)
Caroline Francke
MISLEADING LADY, THE(1932), w; WISER SEX, THE(1932), w; BOMBSHELL(1933), w
Peter Francke
WATER FOR CANITOGA(1939, Ger.), w; TOXI(1952, Ger.), w; DEFECTOR, THE(1966, Ger./Fr.), w
R. Francke
VOICE WITHIN, THE(1945, Brit.), ph
Randy Francklan
NIGHTHAWKS(1981)
Don Francks
DRYLANDERS(1963, Can.); FINIAN'S RAINBOW(1968); MC CABE AND MRS. MILLER(1971); SUMMER'S CHILDREN(1979, Can.); FISH HAWK(1981, Can.); HEAVY METAL(1981, Can.); MY BLOODY VALENTINE(1981, Can.)
Misc. Talkies
FAST COMPANY(1979); TOMORROW MAN, THE(1979); ROCK 'N' RULE(1983)
Lili Francks
MC CABE AND MRS. MILLER(1971)
Franco
1984
WHITE ELEPHANT(1984, Brit.), m
Abel Franco
CAGE OF EVIL(1960); THIRD VOICE, THE(1960); ZOOT SUIT(1981)
1984
EL NORTE(1984)
Chuey Franco
MACHISMO—40 GRAVES FOR 40 GUNS(1970)
Chuy Franco
CISCO PIKE(1971)
Dominick Franco
HEAVEN ON EARTH(1960, Ital./U.S.), p
Fulvia Franco
TEMPEST(1958, Ital./Yugo./Fr.); LADY DOCTOR, THE(1963, Fr./Ital./Span.); HERCULES, SAMSON & ULYSSES(1964, Ital.); OF WAYWARD LOVE(1964, Ital./Ger.); HIGH INFIDELITY(1965, Fr./Ital.)
Gino Franco
FIGHTING MAD(1976)
Herminia Franco
DARK RIVER(1956, Arg.)
Jess Franco
VENUS IN FURS(1970, Ital./Brit./Ger.), d, w
Misc. Talkies
99 WOMEN(1969, Brit./Span./Ger./Ital.), d
Jess [Jesus] Franco
BLOOD OF FU MANCHU, THE(1968, Brit.), d; CASTLE OF FU MANCHU, THE(1968, Ger./Span./Ital./Brit.), d

Jesse Franco
ATTACK OF THE ROBOTS(1967, Fr./Span.), d; JUSTINE(1969, Ital./Span.), d
Jesus Franco
AWFUL DR. ORLOFF, THE(1964, Span./Fr.), d&w; DIABOLICAL DR. Z, THE(1966 Span./Fr.), d, w; RIO 70(1970, U.S./Ger./Span.), d; COUNT DRACULA(1971, Sp., Ital., Ger., Brit.), d, w; DRACULA VERSUS FRANKENSTEIN(1972, Span.), d&w
John Franco
NEVER FEAR(1950); PARTY GIRL(1958)
John Franco, Jr.
KING KONG(1976), set d; WORLD'S GREATEST LOVER, THE(1977), set d; END, THE(1978), set d; MAGIC(1978), set d
1984
COUNTRY(1984), set d
Larry Franco
ESCAPE FROM NEW YORK(1981), p; THING, THE(1982)
Larry J. Franco
1984
STARMAN(1984), p
Lidia Franco
IN THE WHITE CITY(1983, Switz./Portugal)
Pippo Franco
AVANTI!(1972)
Quico Franco
BLOOD WEDDING(1981, Sp.)
Ramon Franco
DEADLY FORCE(1983)
Tony Franco
Misc. Talkies
TAKE ONE(1977)
Michel Francoeur
QUEST FOR FIRE(1982, Fr./Can.)
Richard Francoeur
RULES OF THE GAME, THE(1939, Fr.); CAGE OF NIGHTINGALES, A(1947, Fr.); DEVIL IN THE FLESH, THE(1949, Fr.); GIGOT(1962)
Anne Francois
TROUT, THE(1982, Fr.)
Camille Francois
RULES OF THE GAME, THE(1939, Fr.), a, w, m
E. Francois
LAUGHING LADY, THE(1950, Brit.)
Helen Francois
TOUCH OF THE OTHER, A(1970, Brit.)
Jacques Francois
BARKLEYS OF BROADWAY, THE(1949); JUST A BIG, SIMPLE GIRL(1949, Fr.); ENCORE(1951, Brit.); EDWARD AND CAROLINE(1952, Fr.); GOLDEN MASK, THE(1954, Brit.); TO PARIS WITH LOVE(1955, Brit.); GRAND MANEUVER, THE(1956, Fr.); ROYAL AFFAIRS IN VERSAILLES(1957, Fr.); EGLANTINE(1972, Fr.); DAY OF THE JACKAL, THE(1973, Brit./Fr.); SORCERER(1977); LE GENDARME ET LES EXTRATERRESTRES(1978, Fr.); AFRICAN, THE(1983, Fr.); GIFT, THE(1983, Fr./Ital.); MAN, WOMAN AND CHILD(1983)
1984
UNTIL SEPTEMBER(1984)
Michel Francois
CAGE OF NIGHTINGALES, A(1947, Fr.); LES DERNIERES VACANCES(1947, Fr.); DEVIL IN THE FLESH, THE(1949, Fr.); LE CIEL EST A VOUS(1957, Fr.); SCARFACE(1983)
Nina Francoise
OUTLAND(1981)
Francomme
MY UNCLE(1958, Fr.)
Tiny Francone
CRY OF THE CITY(1948); IT'S A BIG COUNTRY(1951)
David Franden
FERRY ACROSS THE MERSEY(1964, Brit.), w
Lisbeth Frandsen
OPERATION LOVEBIRDS(1968, Den.)
Robert Frandsen
GREAT MOMENT, THE(1944)
Agnes Franey
QUEEN OF THE NIGHTCLUBS(1929); STOLEN KISSES(1929)
Bill Franey
EXCLUSIVE(1937); STORY OF VERNON AND IRENE CASTLE, THE(1939)
Silents
AFLAME IN THE SKY(1927)
Misc. Silents
MILE A MINUTE MORGAN(1924); ROYAL AMERICAN, THE(1927)
Billy Franey
BROADWAY HOOFER, THE(1929); FREIGHTERS OF DESTINY(1932); GHOST VALLEY(1932); PARTNERS(1932); RENEGADES OF THE WEST(1932); SOMEWHERE IN SONORA(1933); WAR OF THE RANGE(1933); STAGE TO CHINO(1940)
Silents
KNIGHT OF THE WEST, A(1921); WESTERN DEMON, A(1922); KING OF THE HERD(1927); LOST LIMITED, THE(1927); OUT ALL NIGHT(1927); SHE'S A SHEIK(1927); ANNE AGAINST THE WORLD(1929)
Misc. Silents
DANGEROUS DUDE, THE(1926)
William Franey
NO MORE WOMEN(1934); STAR PACKER, THE(1934); QUICK MONEY(1938)
Silents
TOWN SCANDAL, THE(1923); BORDER WOMEN(1924); KING OF THE TURF, THE(1926); HEROIC LOVER, THE(1929); ROYAL RIDER, THE(1929)
Misc. Silents
GREAT SENSATION, THE(1925); S.O.S. PERILS OF THE SEA(1925); RACING FOOL, THE(1927); CHEYENNE(1929)
Vassilios Frangadakis
BAREFOOT BATTALION, THE(1954, Gr.)
Ron Frangiapane
WORLD OF HANS CHRISTIAN ANDERSEN, THE(1971, Jap.), m

Guy Frangin
GENTLE CREATURE, A(1971, Fr.)
Ron Frangipane
ABDUCTION(1975), m
Ronald Frangipane
HOLY MOUNTAIN, THE(1973, U.S./Mex.), m
Takis Frangofinos
NIGHT AMBUSH(1958, Brit.)
Joe Franham
GOOD NEWS(1930), w
Freddie Franics
CREEPING FLESH,THE(1973, Brit.), d
Georges Franju
HORROR CHAMBER OF DR. FAUSTUS, THE(1962, Fr./Ital.), d, w; THERESE(1963, Fr.), d, w; JUDEX(1966, Fr./Ital.), d; SHADOWMAN(1974, Fr./Ital.), d, m
Frank
OH, HEAVENLY DOG!(1980), animal t
Adam Frank
1984
REVENGE OF THE NERDS(1984)
Alan Frank
NIGHT TO REMEMBER, A(1958, Brit.)
Alexander F. Frank
Misc. Silents
TRAIL OF THE CIGARETTE, THE(1920); WALL STREET MYSTERY, THE(1920)
Allan Frank
NEVER WAVE AT A WAC(1952); SIN OF MONA KENT, THE(1961)
Amy Frank
BROKEN JOURNEY(1948, Brit.); WHILE THE SUN SHINES(1950, Brit.)
Anne Frank
DIARY OF ANNE FRANK, THE(1959), w
Arnold Frank
Misc. Silents
PEAKS OF DESTINY(1927, Ger.), d
Astrid Frank
Misc. Talkies
AU PAIR GIRLS(1973)
Ben Frank
TERRIFIED!(1963); MURPH THE SURF(1974); JESSIE'S GIRLS(1976); DON'T ANSWER THE PHONE(1980); FOXES(1980); DEATH WISH II(1982)
1984
SLAPSTICK OF ANOTHER KIND(1984)
Bruno Frank
STORM IN A WATER GLASS(1931, Aust.), w; SUTTER'S GOLD(1936), w; HEART'S DESIRE(1937, Brit.), w; HUNCHBACK OF NOTRE DAME, THE(1939), w; ROYAL SCANDAL, A(1945), w; YOUNG REBEL, THE(1969, Fr./Ital./Span.), w
Carl Frank
LADY FROM SHANGHAI, THE(1948); SIX BRIDGES TO CROSS(1955)
Charles Frank
INHERITANCE, THE(1951, Brit.), d; OBSESSED(1951, Brit.), w; DISOBEDIENT(1953, Brit.), d&w; JOHNNY THE GIANT KILLER(1953, Fr.), d, w; TESTAMENT OF ORPHEUS, THE(1962, Fr.), titles; ONE AND ONLY, THE(1978); OTHER SIDE OF THE MOUNTAIN–PART 2, THE(1978); RIGHT STUFF, THE(1983)
Chris Frank
TOAST OF NEW YORK, THE(1937); ARSENE LUPIN RETURNS(1938); WIFE TAKES A FLYER, THE(1942); SOUTHERN YANKEE, A(1948)
Christian Frank
CAVALIER, THE(1928); HARD HOMBRE(1931); MY PAL, THE KING(1932); EMBARRASSING MOMENTS(1934); MAYTIME(1937); STRANGE CARGO(1940); DU BARRY WAS A LADY(1943)
Silents
RAGGED EDGE, THE(1923); BLACK CYCLONE(1925); ARIZONA BOUND(1927)
Misc. Silents
LOVE BANDIT, THE(1924)
Christian J. Frank
UNDER MONTANA SKIES(1930); VAGABOND KING, THE(1930); SUNSET PASS(1933); LADY BY CHOICE(1934); MERRY WIDOW, THE(1934); ESPIONAGE(1937); NEW MOON(1940); CROSSROADS(1942)
Silents
OUT OF THE SILENT NORTH(1922); WILD HONEY(1922); ANCIENT HIGHWAY, THE(1925); NEVADA(1927); CHICAGO AFTER MIDNIGHT(1928); EASY COME, EASY GO(1928); SECRET HOUR, THE(1928); SUNSET PASS(1929)
Misc. Silents
SUNSET PASS(1929)
Christopher Frank
FRENCH WAY, THE(1975, Fr.), w; MAIN THING IS TO LOVE, THE(1975, Ital./Fr.), w; ATTENTION, THE KIDS ARE WATCHING(1978, Fr.), w; THREE MEN TO DESTROY(1980, Fr.), w
Clarence E. Frank
MISTER ROBERTS(1955)
Constant Frank
HUDSON'S BAY(1940)
Consuelo Frank
LA NAVE DE LOS MONSTRUOS(1959, Mex.); MACARIO(1961, Mex.)
David Frank
WESTWORLD(1973); DIFFERENT STORY, A(1978), m
Eddie Frank
CHRISTINE JORGENSEN STORY, THE(1970)
Ellen Frank
GIRL FROM THE MARSH CROFT, THE(1935, Ger.); HANSEL AND GRETEL(1965, Ger.)
Ernst L. Frank
NAGANA(1933), d; ONE EXCITING ADVENTURE(1935), d
Evelyn Frank
SATAN'S SADISTS(1969)
Frederic M. Frank
UNCONQUERED(1947), w; SAMSON AND DELILAH(1949), w

Fredric Frank
ESCAPE TO GLORY(1940), w; HARMON OF MICHIGAN(1941), w

Fredric M. Frank
GREATEST SHOW ON EARTH, THE(1952), w; TEN COMMANDMENTS, THE(1956), w; EL CID(1961, U.S./Ital.), w

Geanne Frank
1984
BLACK ROOM, THE(1984)

Gerald Frank
GIRL IN BLACK STOCKINGS(1957); SEVEN GUNS TO MESA(1958)

Gerold Frank
I'LL CRY TOMORROW(1955), w; TOO MUCH, TOO SOON(1958), w; BELOVED INFIDEL(1959), w; THE BOSTON STRANGLER, THE(1968), w

Gunther Frank
WORLD IN MY POCKET, THE(1962, Fr./Ital./Ger.), makeup

Hal Frank
SOMEWHERE IN TIME(1980); THIEF(1981); CLASS(1983)

Harriet Frank
REIVERS, THE(1969), w

Milo Frank, Jr.
SILVER RIVER(1948), w; WHIPLASH(1948), w; RUN FOR COVER(1955), w; TEN WANTED MEN(1955), w; HIGH COST OF LOVING, THE(1958), p, w; LONG, HOT SUMMER, THE(1958), w; SOUND AND THE FURY, THE(1959), w; DARK AT THE TOP OF THE STAIRS, THE(1960), w; HOME FROM THE HILL(1960), w; HUD(1963), w; HOUSE OF CARDS(1969), w; CAREY TREATMENT, THE(1972), w; COWBOYS, THE(1972), w; CONRACK(1974), p, w; SPIKES GANG, THE(1974), w; NORMA RA-E(1979), w

Harry Frank
GREAT YEARNING, THE(1930, Ger.)
Misc. Silents
MOVING IMAGE, THE(1920, Ger.)

Herbert Frank
Silents
SOCIAL SECRETARY, THE(1916); IRON RING, THE(1917)
Misc. Silents
SECRET OF THE STORM COUNTRY, THE(1917)

Herbert J. Frank
Silents
ASHES OF EMBERS(1916)

Horst Frank
ROSEMARY(1960, Ger.); DEAD RUN(1961, Fr./Ital./Ger.); GIRL OF THE MOORS, THE(1961, Ger.); HEAD, THE(1961, Ger.); INDECENT(1962, Ger.); CORPSE OF BEVERLY HILLS, THE(1965, Ger.); I DEAL IN DANGER(1966); RED-DRAGON(1967, Ital./Ger./US); VENGEANCE OF FU MANCHU, THE(1968, Brit./Ger./Hong Kong/ Ireland); CAT O'NINE TAILS(1971, Ital./Ger./Fr.); DEAD ARE ALIVE, THE(1972, Yugo./Ger./Ital.); JOHNNY HAMLET(1972, Ital.); OPERATION GANYMED(1977, Ger.); NIGHT OF THE ASKARI(1978, Ger./South African)
Misc. Talkies
ALBINO(1980)

J. Herbert Frank
Silents
WISE HUSBANDS(; DESTRUCTION(1915); GOOD-BYE, BILL(1919); IDLE HANDS(1921); NOBODY(1921); SILVER LINING, THE(1921); JAZZMANIA(1923)
Misc. Silents
WHO KILLED JOE MERRION?(1915); CRUCIAL TEST, THE(1916); BRAND OF SATAN, THE(1917); DARKEST RUSSIA(1917); SCANDAL(1917); DODGING A MIL-LION(1918); TEMPERED STEEL(1918); EMPTY ARMS(1920); IDLE HANDS(1920); UP AND AT 'EM(1922)

Jacob Frank
MOTHER'S BOY(1929)
Misc. Talkies
HIS WIFE'S LOVER(1931)

Jeffrey Frank
ISLAND, THE(1980)

Jerome Frank
VOODOO ISLAND(1957)

Jerry Frank
HEROES OF THE HILLS(1938); NEWSBOY'S HOME(1939); WHO DONE IT?(1942); FLAMING TEEN-AGE, THE(1956); HELL BOUND(1957); JUNGLE HEAT(1957); FORT BOWIE(1958)

Jim Frank
DUCHESS AND THE DIRTWATER FOX, THE(1976)

Joanna Frank
AMERICA, AMERICA(1963); BORN WILD(1968); SAVAGE SEVEN, THE(1968)

Joanne Frank
JAM SESSION(1944); PHILO VANCE'S GAMBLE(1947); TWO TICKETS TO BROAD-WAY(1951)

John Frank
RODEO RHYTHM(1941); SUMMER AND SMOKE(1961)

Johnny B. Frank
1984
MIKE'S MURDER(1984)

Kerry Frank
BATTLE BEYOND THE STARS(1980)

Laurel Frank
DIMBOOLA(1979, Aus.)

Leonhard Frank
KARAMAZOV(1931, Ger.), w; HELL ON EARTH(1934, Ger.), w

Maroussia Frank
PERSECUTION AND ASSASSINATION OF JEAN-PAUL MARAT AS PERFORMED BY THE INMATES OF THE ASYLUM OF CHARENTON UNDER THE DIRECTION OF THE MARQUIS DE SADE, THE(1967, Brit.)

Melvin Frank
MY FAVORITE BLONDE(1942), w; STAR SPANGLED RHYTHM(1942), w; HAPPY GO LUCKY(1943), w; THANK YOUR LUCKY STARS(1943), w; AND THE ANGELS SING(1944), w; DUFFY'S TAVERN(1945), w; ROAD TO UTOPIA(1945), w; MON-SIEUR BEAUCAIRE(1946), w; OUR HEARTS WERE GROWING UP(1946), w; IT HAD TO BE YOU(1947), w; MR. BLANDINGS BUILDS HIS DREAM HOUSE(1948), p, w; RETURN OF OCTOBER, THE(1948), w; SOUTHERN YANKEE, A(1948), w; REFORM-ER AND THE REDHEAD, THE(1950), p,d&w; CALLAWAY WENT THATA-

WAY(1951), p,d&w; STRICTLY DISHONORABLE(1951), p,d&w; ABOVE AND BEYOND(1953), p&d; KNOCK ON WOOD(1954), p,d&w; WHITE CHRISTMAS(1954), w; COURT JESTER, THE(1956), p,d&w; THAT CERTAIN FEELING(1956), p&d, w; JAYHAWKERS, THE(1959), p, d, w; LI'L ABNER(1959), d, w; TRAP, THE(1959), p; FACTS OF LIFE, THE(1960), p, d, w; ROAD TO HONG KONG, THE(1962, U.S./Brit.), p, w; STRANGE BEDFELLOWS(1965), p&d, w; FUNNY THING HAPPENED ON THE WAY TO THE FORUM, A(1966), p, w; NOT WITH MY WIFE, YOU DON'T(1966), w; BUONA SERA, MRS. CAMPBELL(1968, Ital.), p&d, w; TOUCH OF CLASS, A(1973, Brit.), p&d, w; PRISONER OF SECOND AVENUE, THE(1975), p&d; DUCHESS AND THE DIRTWATER FOX, THE(1976), p&d, w; LOST AND FOUND(1979), p&d, w

Pat Frank
MAN'S FAVORITE SPORT(?)**1/2 (1964), w; HOLD BACK THE NIGHT(1956), w; WE SHALL RETURN(1963), w

Paul Frank
BEAUTY AND THE BOSS(1932), w; ADORABLE(1933), w; YES, MR. BROWN(1933, Brit.), w; CHURCH MOUSE, THE(1934, Brit.), w; JOSETTE(1938), w; INVISIBLE WALL, THE(1947), w; HOT SPUR(1968)

Penny Frank
FAME(1980)

Peter Frank
VERDICT, THE(1982), ed; DANIEL(1983), ed

"Piano" Frank
Misc. Talkies
DIRTY GERTY FROM HARLEM, USA(1946)

Ray Frank
Misc. Talkies
LEFT-HANDED(1972)

Richard Frank
1984
AMADEUS(1984)

Richard J. Frank
SHE MARRIED HER BOSS(1935)

Robert Frank
CHAPPAQUA(1967), ph; ME AND MY BROTHER(1969), d, ed

T. C. Frank [Tom Laughlin]
BORN LOSERS(1967), d; BILLY JACK(1971), d, w; BILLY JACK GOES TO WASH-INGTON(1977), d

Tony Frank
TENDER MERCIES(1982)
1984
RIVER RAT, THE(1984)

Vanya Frank
IMPROPER CHANNELS(1981, Can.)

W. R. Frank
BOY, A GIRL, AND A DOG, A(1946), p; CRY DANGER(1951), p

W.R. Frank
ENEMY OF WOMEN(1944), p; SITTING BULL(1954), p; WRESTLER, THE(1974), p

Will Frank
Silents
LAST EDITION, THE(1925)

Zoe Frank
HELL ON EARTH(1934, Ger.)

Frank & Imback
TREASURE OF MONTE CRISTO(1949), cos

Frank and Milt Britton Band
MOONLIGHT AND PRETZELS(1933)

Frank and Milt Britton Orchestra
SWEET MUSIC(1935)

Frank Boston and Betty
THOSE WERE THE DAYS(1934, Brit.)

Frank Lee's Tara Ceilidh Band
KATHLEEN(1938, Ireland)

Harriet Frank, Jr. Elmore Leonard
HOMBRE(1967), w

Frank's Fox Terriers
TONIGHT AT 8:30(1953, Brit.)

Franka
PERMISSION TO KILL(1975, U.S./Aust.), cos

Gilbert Frankau
CHRISTOPHER STRONG(1933), w
Silents
IF I MARRY AGAIN(1925), w

Joy Frankau
TILLY OF BLOOMSBURY(1940, Brit.); NOTORIOUS GENTLEMAN(1945, Brit.); TROJAN BROTHERS, THE(1946); TURNERS OF PROSPECT ROAD, THE(1947, Brit.)

Nicholas Frankau
RETURN OF THE SOLDIER, THE(1983, Brit.)

Pamela Frankau
GOLDEN CAGE, THE(1933, Brit.), w

Ronald Frankau
HER STRANGE DESIRE(1931, Brit.); SKIN GAME, THE(1931, Brit.); BRIDEGROOM FOR TWO(1932, Brit.); RADIO FOLLIES(1935, Brit.); HIS BROTHER'S KEEPER(1939, Brit.); MUCH TOO SHY(1942, Brit.), w; WHAT DO WE DO NOW?(1945, Brit.); DUAL ALIBI(1947, Brit.); GHOSTS OF BERKELEY SQUARE(1947, Brit.)

Blanche Franke
THAT FORSYTE WOMAN(1949)

Chris Franke
WINDS OF THE WASTELAND(1936); NO, NO NANETTE(1940)

Constant Franke
PARIS INTERLUDE(1934); RIP TIDE(1934); DESIRE(1936); SEVENTH HEA-VEN(1937); ARTISTS AND MODELS ABROAD(1938); NORTH STAR, THE(1943)
Silents
FOUR SONS(1928)

Dieter Franke
FLOWERS FOR THE MAN IN THE MOON(1975, Ger.)

Jerry Franke
REDHEAD FROM MANHATTAN(1954)

Tony Franke
MC HALE'S NAVY JOINS THE AIR FORCE(1965)

Ben Frankel
THEY MET IN THE DARK(1945, Brit.), m; SEVENTH VEIL, THE(1946, Brit.), m; DAYDREAK(1948, Brit.), m; PARIS EXPRESS, THE(1953, Brit.), m

Benjamin Frankel
DANCING WITH CRIME(1947, Brit.), m; DEAR MURDERER(1947, Brit.), m; DULCIMER STREET(1948, Brit.), m; MINE OWN EXECUTIONER(1948, Brit.), m; NIGHT BEAT(1948, Brit.), m; GAY LADY, THE(1949, Brit.), m; SALT TO THE DEVIL(1949, Brit.), m; SLEEPING CAR TO TRIESTE(1949, Brit.), m; HOTEL SAHARA(1951, Brit.), m; LONG DARK HALL, THE(1951, Brit.), m; SO LONG AT THE FAIR(1951, Brit.), m, md; IMPORTANCE OF BEING EARNEST, THE(1952, Brit.), m; ISLAND RESCUE(1952, Brit.), m; MAN IN THE WHITE SUIT, THE(1952), m; DOUBLE CONFESSION(1953, Brit.), m; FINAL TEST, THE(1953, Brit.), m; MR. DENNING DRIVES NORTH(1953, Brit.), m; PROJECT M7(1953, Brit.), m; ALWAYS A BRIDE(1954, Brit.), m; AUNT CLARA(1954, Brit.), m; FIRE OVER AFRICA(1954, Brit.), m; LOVE LOTTERY, THE(1954, Brit.), m; MAD ABOUT MEN(1954, Brit.), m; END OF THE AFFAIR, THE(1955, Brit.), m, md; FOOTSTEPS IN THE FOG(1955, Brit.), md; MAN WHO LOVED REDHEADS(1955, Brit.), m; PRISONER, THE(1955, Brit.), m, md; STORM OVER THE NILE(1955, Brit.), m, md; IRON PETTICOAT, THE(1956, Brit.), m, md; KID FOR TWO FARTHINGS, A(1956, Brit.), m; SIMON AND LAURA(1956, Brit.), m, md; BROTHERS IN LAW(1957, Brit.), m; TEARS FOR SIMON(1957, Brit.), m, md; HAPPY IS THE BRIDE(1958, Brit.), m&md; I ONLY ASKED!(1958, Brit.), m; ORDERS TO KILL(1958, Brit.), m; LIBEL(1959, Brit.), m; SURPRISE PACKAGE(1960), m; CURSE OF THE WEREWOLF, THE(1961), m; SEASON OF PASSION(1961, Aus./Brit.), m; GUNS OF DARKNESS(1962, Brit.), m&md; OLD DARK HOUSE, THE(1963, Brit.), m, md; NIGHT OF THE IGUANA, THE(1964), m, md; BATTLE OF THE BULGE(1965), m

Cyril Frankel
DEVIL ON HORSEBACK(1954, Brit.), d; MAKE ME AN OFFER(1954, Brit.), d; IT'S GREAT TO BE YOUNG(1956, Brit.), d; MAN OF AFRICA(1956, Brit.), d, w; NO TIME FOR TEARS(1957, Brit.), d; NEVER TAKE CANDY FROM A STRANGER(1961, Brit.), d; ALIVE AND KICKING(1962, Brit.), d; SHE DIDN'T SAY NO!(1962, Brit.), d; VERY EDGE, THE(1963, Brit.), d; WHY BOTHER TO KNOCK(1964, Brit.), d; OPERATION SNAFU(1965, Brit.), d; DEVIL'S OWN, THE(1967, Brit.), d; TRYGON FACTOR, THE(1969, Brit.), d; PERMISSION TO KILL(1975, U.S./Aust.), d
Misc. Talkies
SAINT AND THE BRAVE GOOSE, THE(1981, Brit.), d

Fanchon Frankel
Silents
JAKE THE PLUMBER(1927); SENSATION SEEKERS(1927)

Heinrich Frankel
YOUTHFUL FOLLY(1934, Brit.), w

Isidor Frankel
ELI ELI(1940), a, w

Al Franken
TUNNELVISION(1976); TRADING PLACES(1983)

Edgar Franken
HUSBANDS(1970)

Lies Franken
Misc. Talkies
ASSIGNMENT ABROAD(1955)

Rose Franken
ANOTHER LANGUAGE(1933), w; ALIAS MARY DOW(1935), w; ELINOR NORTON(1935), w; BELOVED ENEMY(1936), w; CLAUDIA(1943), w; CLAUDIA AND DAVID(1946), w; SECRET HEART, THE(1946), w

Steve Franken
AMERICANIZATION OF EMILY, THE(1964); TIME TRAVELERS, THE(1964); FOLLOW ME, BOYS!(1966); WILD, WILD WINTER(1966); PANIC IN THE CITY(1968); PARTY, THE(1968); ANGEL IN MY POCKET(1969); NUMBER ONE(1969); WHICH WAY TO THE FRONT?(1970); WESTWORLD(1973); MISSOURI BREAKS, THE(1976); AVALANCHE(1978); NORTH AVENUE IRREGULARS, THE(1979); FIENDISH PLOT OF DR. FU MANCHU, THE(1980); THERE GOES THE BRIDE(1980, Brit.); HARDLY WORKING(1981); CURSE OF THE PINK PANTHER(1983)

Julius Frankenberg
Misc. Silents
HUMANIZING MR. WINSBY(1916)

Julius Frankenburg
Misc. Silents
NINE-TENTHS OF THE LAW(1918)

John Frankenheimer
YOUNG STRANGER, THE(1957), d; YOUNG SAVAGES, THE(1961), d; ALL FALL DOWN(1962), d; BIRDMAN OF ALCATRAZ(1962), d; MANCHURIAN CANDIDATE, THE(1962), p, d, w; SEVEN DAYS IN MAY(1964), d; TRAIN, THE(1965, Fr./Ital./U.S.), d; GRAND PRIX(1966), d; SECONDS(1966), d; FIXER, THE(1968), d; EXTRAORDINARY SEAMAN, THE(1969), d; GYPSY MOTHS, THE(1969), d; I WALK THE LINE(1970), d; HORSEMEN, THE(1971), d; ICEMAN COMETH, THE(1973), d; IMPOSSIBLE OBJECT(1973), d; 99 AND 44/100% DEAD(1974), d; FRENCH CONNECTION 11(1975), d; BLACK SUNDAY(1977), d; PROPHECY(1979), d; CHALLENGE, THE(1982), d

Natanael Leon Frankenheimer
SANTO CONTRA LA INVASION DE LOS MARCIANOS(1966, Mex.)

Nathanael Leon Frankenstein
GIGANTES PLANETARIOS(1965, Mex.); CEREBROS DIABOLICOS(1966, Mex.); MADAME DEATH(1968, Mex.)

Paul Frankeur
CHILDREN OF PARADISE(1945, Fr.); MR. ORCHID(1948, Fr.); DEVIL'S DAUGHTER(1949, Fr.); JOUR DE FETE(1952, Fr.); NANA(1957, Fr./Ital.); COME DANCE WITH ME(1960, Fr.); NIGHT AFFAIR(1961, Fr.); LA VIACCIA(1962, Fr./Ital.); MAGNIFICENT TRAMP, THE(1962, Fr./Ital.); MONKEY IN WINTER, A(1962, Fr.); MILKY WAY, THE(1969, Fr./Ital.); DISCREET CHARM OF THE BOURGEOISIE, THE(1972, Fr.); PHANTOM OF LIBERTY, THE(1974, Fr.)

William Frankfather
FOUL PLAY(1978); PENNIES FROM HEAVEN(1981)

David Frankham
RETURN OF THE FLY(1959); TEN WHO DARED(1960); MASTER OF THE WORLD(1961); ONE HUNDRED AND ONE DALMATIANS(1961); SPIRAL ROAD, THE(1962); TALES OF TERROR(1962); KING RAT(1965); WRONG IS RIGHT(1982)

R. Frankie
WANTED FOR MURDER(1946, Brit.), ph

Frankie Bell and His Bellboys
ROCK AROUND THE CLOCK(1956)

Frankie Carle and His Orchestra
RIVERBOAT RHYTHM(1946); MARY LOU(1948)

Frankie Carle Orchestra
SWEETHEART OF SIGMA CHI(1946)

Frankie Lymon and The Teenagers
ROCK, ROCK, ROCK!(1956); MISTER ROCK AND ROLL(1957)

Brian Frankish
VICE SQUAD(1982), p

Betty Frankiss
PUBLIC LIFE OF HENRY THE NINTH, THE(1934, Brit.)

Rosemarie Frankland
HARD DAY'S NIGHT, A(1964, Brit.); I'LL TAKE SWEDEN(1965)

Chuck Frankle
NEST OF THE CUCKOO BIRDS, THE(1965)

Paula Frankle
YOU'VE GOT TO WALK IT LIKE YOU TALK IT OR YOU'LL LOSE THAT BEAT(1971)

Terrie Frankle
LUNCH WAGON(1981), w

Robert Franklia
SPOOK WHO SAT BY THE DOOR, THE(1973)

Aretha Franklin
BLUES BROTHERS, THE(1980)

Arthur Franklin
DUFFY'S TAVERN(1945), m

Barbara Franklin
OEDIPUS REX(1957, Can.)

Bob Franklin
MY BODY HUNGERS(1967); PUNISHMENT PARK(1971)

Bonnie Franklin
KETTLES IN THE OZARKS, THE(1956); WRONG MAN, THE(1956); SUMMER PLACE, A(1959)

Brian Franklin
TRACK THE MAN DOWN(1956, Brit.)

C. Lester Franklin
FOUR DEUCES, THE(1976), w

C. M. Franklin
Silents
LITTLE SCHOOL MA'AM, THE(1916), d; JACK AND THE BEANSTALK(1917), d; ALI BABA AND THE FORTY THIEVES(1918), d
Misc. Silents
LET KATHY DO IT(1916), d; ALADDIN AND THE WONDERFUL LAMP(1917), d; BABES IN THE WOODS(1917), d; TREASURE ISLAND(1917), d; GIRL WITH THE CHAMPAGNE EYES, THE(1918), d

C.M. & S.A. Franklin
Misc. Silents
SISTER OF SIX, A(1916), d; FAN FAN(1918), d

C. S. Franklin
BIG BLUFF, THE(1933), ed

Calvin Franklin
1984
SOLDIER'S STORY, A(1984)

Cherie Franklin
DIRTY LITTLE BILLY(1972)

Chester Franklin
YEARLING, THE(1946), spec eff
Silents
MARTHA'S VINDICATION(1916), d; ALL SOULS EVE(1921), d; SONG OF LOVE, THE(1923), d
Misc. Silents
CHILDREN IN THE HOUSE, THE(1916), d; GOING STRAIGHT(1916), d; WILD JUSTICE(1925), d; THIRTEENTH HOUR, THE(1927), d

Chester M. Franklin
FILE 113(1932), d; PARISIAN ROMANCE, A(1932), d; STOKER, THE(1932), d; VANITY FAIR(1932), d; IRON MASTER, THE(1933), d; SEQUOIA(1934), d; TOUGH GUY(1936), d; PAINTED HILLS, THE(1951), p
Silents
GRETCHEN, THE GREENHORN(1916), d; PRIVATE SCANDAL, A(1921), d; NANCY FROM NOWHERE(1922), d
Misc. Silents
YOU NEVER CAN TELL(1920), d; CASE OF BECKY, THE(1921), d; GAME CHICKEN, THE(1922), d; TOLL OF THE SEA, THE(1922), d; WHERE THE NORTH BEGINS(1923), d; BEHIND THE CURTAIN(1924), d; SILENT ACCUSER, THE(1924), d; DETECTIVES(1928), d

Clyde Franklin
DYNAMITE DELANEY(1938)

David Franklin
MY BRILLIANT CAREER(1980, Aus.)

Dean Franklin
CODE OF THE SECRET SERVICE(1939), w; FIGHTING 69TH, THE(1940), w

Diana Franklin
LAST AMERICAN VIRGIN, THE(1982)

Diane Franklin
AMITYVILLE II: THE POSSESSION(1982)
1984
SECOND TIME LUCKY(1984, Aus./New Zealand)

Don Franklin
SOMEWHERE IN TIME(1980)

Dwight Franklin
TREASURE ISLAND(1934), cos&tech adv; ANTHONY ADVERSE(1936), tech adv; PLAINSMAN, THE(1937), cos

Edgar Franklin
ANNE ONE HUNDRED(1933, Brit.), w; EASY MILLIONS(1933), w; WORKING MAN, THE(1933), w; EVERYBODY'S OLD MAN(1936), w; RICH MAN, POOR GIRL(1938), Jerome Chodorov

Silents
ALL NIGHT(1918), w; ANNEXING BILL(1918), w; MORE TROUBLE(1918), w; ONCE A PLUMBER(1920), w; SHOCKING NIGHT, A(1921), w; WHATEVER SHE WANTS(1921), w; NOISE IN NEWBORO, A(1923), w

Edna Franklin
TOY WIFE, THE(1938)

Elbert Franklin
VILLAIN STILL PURSUED HER, THE(1940), w

Eric Franklin
1984
L'ARGENT(1984, Fr./Switz.)

Gail Franklin
UNHOLY ROLLERS(1972)

Gary Franklin
ROLLERCOASTER(1977)

George Cory Franklin
PRAIRIE SCHOONERS(1940), w

George Franklin
INCUBUS, THE(1982, Can.), w

Gloria Franklin
LADY OF THE TROPICS(1939); MEET THE WILDCAT(1940); ROAD TO SINGAPORE(1940); GAY VAGABOND, THE(1941); DRUMS OF FU MANCHU(1943)

Gretchen Franklin
SHADOW OF FEAR(1956, Brit.); HIGH TERRACE(1957, Brit.); FLAME IN THE STREETS(1961, Brit.); DIE, MONSTER, DIE(1965, Brit.); MURDER GAME, THE(1966, Brit.); HOW I WON THE WAR(1967, Brit.); TWISTED NERVE(1969, Brit.); NIGHT VISITOR, THE(1970, Swed./U.S.)

Harold B. Franklin
GAMBLING(1934), p; VILLAIN STILL PURSUED HER, THE(1940), p

Harry Franklin
BRAVE ONE, THE(1956), w; TELL ME IN THE SUNLIGHT(1967)
Misc. Silents
ROGUE AND RICHES(1920), d

Harry Franklin, Sr.
SOUNDER, PART 2(1976)

Harry L. Franklin
Silents
KILDARE OF STORM(1918), d; JOHNNY-ON-THE-SPOT(1919), d; HER FIVE-FOOT HIGHNESS(1920), d
Misc. Silents
SUCCESSFUL ADVENTURE, THE(1918), d; SYLVIA ON A SPREE(1918), d; WINNING OF BEATRICE, THE(1918), d; AFTER HIS OWN HEART(1919), d; FOUR FLUSHER, THE(1919), d; FULL OF PEP(1919), d; IN HIS BROTHER'S PLACE(1919), d; THAT'S GOOD(1919), d; ALIAS MISS DODD(1920), d; ROUGE AND RICHES(1920), d; SECRET GIFT, THE(1920), d

Harry S. Franklin
RED SNOW(1952), d; GUN FEVER(1958), w

Hugh Franklin
CURSE OF THE LIVING CORPSE, THE(1964); WHAT'S SO BAD ABOUT FEELING GOOD?(1968)

Irene Franklin
CHANGE OF HEART(1934); DOWN TO THEIR LAST YACHT(1934); FINISHING SCHOOL(1934); LAZY RIVER(1934); PRESIDENT VANISHES, THE(1934); REGISTERED NURSE(1934); STRICTLY DYNAMITE(1934); VERY HONORABLE GUY, A(1934); WOMEN IN HIS LIFE, THE(1934); AFFAIR OF SUSAN(1935); DEATH FLIES EAST(1935); LADIES CRAVE EXCITEMENT(1935); FATAL LADY(1936); GARDEN OF ALLAH, THE(1936); SONG AND DANCE MAN, THE(1936); TIMOTHY'S QUEST(1936); WANTED: JANE TURNER(1936); WHIPSAW(1936); ALONG CAME LOVE(1937); BLAZING BARRIERS(1937); LAND BEYOND THE LAW(1937); MARRIED BEFORE BREAKFAST(1937); MIDNIGHT MADONNA(1937); SARATOGA(1937); FLIRTING WITH FATE(1938); REBELLIOUS DAUGHTERS(1938); FIXER DUGAN(1939)
Silents
WANTED FOR MURDER(1919)

Irving C. Franklin
PHANTOM EXPRESS, THE(1932), p

Irwin Franklin
MINSTREL MAN(1944), w

Irwin R. Franklin
HARLEM IS HEAVEN(1932), d&w; LADY CONFESSES, THE(1945), w

J.E. Franklin
BLACK GIRL(1972), w

Joe Franklin
COMEBACK TRAIL, THE(1982)
1984
BROADWAY DANNY ROSE(1984); GHOSTBUSTERS(1984)

John Franklin
SWORD OF SHERWOOD FOREST(1961, Brit.); YOUNG CASSIDY(1965, U.S./Brit.); WALK WITH LOVE AND DEATH, A(1969); AND SOON THE DARKNESS(1970, Brit.); LOOKING GLASS WAR, THE(1970, Brit.)
1984
CHILDREN OF THE CORN(1984)

Joyce Franklin
OH! WHAT A LOVELY WAR(1969, Brit.)

Judy Franklin
ROCK-A-BYE BABY(1958)

Leo Franklin
NOTHING BARRED(1961, Brit.)

Louise Franklin
EVERY GIRL SHOULD BE MARRIED(1948); LOOK OUT SISTER(1948); SKY DRAGON(1949); JUNGLE MAN-EATERS(1954); THUNDER OVER SANGOLAND(1955); HOT SPELL(1958)

Mark Franklin
SEMI-TOUGH(1977)

Martha Franklin
YOUNGER GENERATION(1929)
Silents
LITTLE MISS SMILES(1922); DON Q, SON OF ZORRO(1925); KEEP SMILING(1925); LOVE AND LEARN(1928); POINTS WEST(1929)

Misc. Silents
RACING LUCK(1924)

Maurice Franklin
UNKNOWN GUEST, THE(1943), w

Mildred Franklin
ON VELVET(1938, Brit.)

Miles Franklin
MY BRILLIANT CAREER(1980, Aus.), w

Miriam Franklin
COVER GIRL(1944); DOUBLE INDEMNITY(1944); HAIL THE CONQUERING HERO(1944); LADY IN THE DARK(1944); MASQUERADE IN MEXICO(1945)

Muriel Franklin
PIE IN THE SKY(1964); TRAMPLERS, THE(1966, Ital.)

Norman Franklin
EMPIRE OF THE ANTS(1977)

Pamela Franklin
INNOCENTS, THE(1961, U.S./Brit.); LION, THE(1962, Brit.); FLIPPER'S NEW ADVENTURE(1964); THIRD SECRET, THE(1964, Brit.); TIGER WALKS, A(1964); NANNY, THE(1965, Brit.); OUR MOTHER'S HOUSE(1967, Brit.); NIGHT OF THE FOLLOWING DAY, THE(1969, Brit.); PRIME OF MISS JEAN BRODIE, THE(1969, Brit.); SINFUL DAVEY(1969, Brit.); AND SOON THE DARKNESS(1970, Brit.); DAVID COPPERFIELD(1970, Brit.); NECROMANCY(1972); ACE ELI AND RODGER OF THE SKIES(1973); LEGEND OF HELL HOUSE, THE(1973, Brit.); FOOD OF THE GODS, THE(1976)
Misc. Talkies
WON'T WRITE HOME, MOM–I'M DEAD(1975, Brit.)

Patricia Franklin
CARRY ON LOVING(1970, Brit.); CARRY ON ENGLAND(1976, Brit.)

Paul Franklin
REEFER MADNESS(1936), w; HEADIN' EAST(1937), w; OUTLAWS OF THE ORIENT(1937), w; ROARING TIMBER(1937), w; SECRET VALLEY(1937), w; TROUBLE IN MOROCCO(1937), w; MAN HUNTERS OF THE CARIBBEAN(1938), w; RHYTHM OF THE SADDLE(1938), w; HOME ON THE PRAIRIE(1939), w; MAN FROM SUNDOWN, THE(1939), w; SPOILERS OF THE RANGE(1939), w; TIMBER STAMPEDE(1939), w; BLAZING SIX SHOOTERS(1940), w; DURANGO KID, THE(1940), w; STRANGER FROM TEXAS, THE(1940), w; THUNDERING FRONTIER(1940), w; WEST OF ABILENE(1940), w; ACROSS THE SIERRAS(1941), w; OUTLAWS OF THE PANHANDLE(1941), w; POWER DIVE(1941), w; RETURN OF DANIEL BOONE, THE(1941), w; SUNSET MURDER CASE(1941), w; THUNDERING HOOFS(1941), w; WHERE DID YOU GET THAT GIRL?(1941), w; DOWN RIO GRANDE WAY(1942), w; FIGHTING BILL FARGO(1942), w; RIDERS OF THE NORTHLAND(1942), w; DARK MOUNTAIN(1944), w; RIDE, RYDER, RIDE!(1949), w; ROLL, THUNDER, ROLL(1949), w; FIGHTING REDHEAD, THE(1950), w

Paul B. Franklin
SKYWAY(1933), w

Richard Franklin
TRUE STORY OF ESKIMO NELL, THE(1975, Aus.), p, d, w; FANTASM(1976, Aus.), d; PATRICK(1979, Aus.), p, d; ROAD GAMES(1981, Aus.), p, d; PSYCHO II(1983), d

Richard B. Franklin
1984
CLOAK AND DAGGER(1984), d

Rupert Franklin
Silents
KID, THE(1921); PRAIRIE WIFE, THE(1925)

Ruth Franklin
LOOKING UP(1977)

S. A. Franklin
Silents
LITTLE SCHOOL MA'AM, THE(1916), d; JACK AND THE BEANSTALK(1917), d; ALI BABA AND THE FORTY THIEVES(1918), d; BRIDE OF FEAR, THE(1918), d&w
Misc. Silents
LET KATHY DO IT(1916), d; ALADDIN AND THE WONDERFUL LAMP(1917), d; BABES IN THE WOODS(1917), d; TREASURE ISLAND(1917), d; CONFESSION(1918), d; SIX-SHOOTER ANDY(1918), d

Sandi Franklin
CLAUDINE(1974); LORD SHANGO(1975); FORT APACHE, THE BRONX(1981)

Shane Franklin
Misc. Talkies
MAN FROM NOWHERE, THE(1976, Brit.)

Sidney Franklin
DEVIL MAY CARE(1929), d; LAST OF MRS. CHEYNEY, THE(1929), d; LADY OF SCANDAL, THE(1930), d; LADY'S MORALS, A(1930), d; LUMMOX(1930); PUTTIN' ON THE RITZ(1930); GUARDSMAN, THE(1931), d; PRIVATE LIVES(1931), d; KID FROM SPAIN, THE(1932); SMILIN' THROUGH(1932), d; REUNION IN VIENNA(1933), d; BARRETTS OF WIMPOLE STREET, THE(1934), d; DARK ANGEL, THE(1935), d; GOOD EARTH, THE(1937), d; GONE WITH THE WIND(1939), d; GOODBYE MR. CHIPS(1939, Brit.), w; ON BORROWED TIME(1939), p; MORTAL STORM, THE(1940), p; WATERLOO BRIDGE(1940), p; MRS. MINIVER(1942), p; RANDOM HARVEST(1942), p; MADAME CURIE(1943), p; WHITE CLIFFS OF DOVER, THE(1944), p; YEARLING, THE(1946), p; COMMAND DECISION(1948), p; HOMECOMING(1948), p; MINIVER STORY, THE(1950, Brit./U.S.), p; STORY OF THREE LOVES, THE(1953), p; YOUNG BESS(1953), p; GYPSY COLT(1954), p; BARRETTS OF WIMPOLE STREET, THE(1957), d
Silents
MARTHA'S VINDICATION(1916), d; THREE MUSKETEERS, THE(1921); WELCOME CHILDREN(1921), d; EAST IS WEST(1922), d; IN HOLLYWOOD WITH POTASH AND PERLMUTTER(1924); ONE OF THE BRAVEST(1925); BEVERLY OF GRAUSTARK(1926), d; KING OF KINGS, THE(1927); QUALITY STREET(1927), d; WILD ORCHIDS(1929), d
Misc. Silents
CHILDREN IN THE HOUSE, THE(1916), d; GOING STRAIGHT(1916), d; SLEEPING LION, THE(1919); PRIMITIVE LOVER, THE(1922), d; VERMILION PENCIL, THE(1922); HER SISTER FROM PARIS(1925), d; DUCHESS OF BUFFALO, THE(1926), d; FIGHTING FAILURE, THE(1926); ROSE OF THE TENEMENTS(1926)

Sidney Franklin, Jr.
FEARLESS FAGAN(1952), w; SKY FULL OF MOON(1952), p; TORCH SONG(1953), p

Sidney A. Franklin, Jr.
GUN BATTLE AT MONTEREY(1957), d
Steve Franklin
HOTHEAD(1963)
Sydney Franklin
Silents
ACTRESS, THE(1928), d
Tommy Franklin
GRAND PRIX(1966)
Tom Franklin [Frank M. Thomas]
WEDNESDAY'S CHILD(1934)
Walter Franklin
Misc. Silents
WITH WINGS OUTSPREAD(1922)
Wendall James Franklin
BUS IS COMING, THE(1971), d
Wendell Phillips Franklin
Silents
FOUR SONS(1928)
William Franklin
TWIN HUSBANDS(1934)
Beth Franklyn
Silents
NOTHING BUT THE TRUTH(1920)
Fred Franklyn
FROM NOON TO THREE(1976); FOG, THE(1980)
Frederic Franklyn
HEARSE, THE(1980)
1984
UNFAITHFULLY YOURS(1984)
Frederick Franklyn
PUNISHMENT PARK(1971)
Fredric Franklyn
WILD PARTY, THE(1975)
Gretchen Franklyn
THREE MUSKETEERS, THE(1974, Panama)
Harold Franklyn
FROG, THE(1937, Brit.); CAESAR AND CLEOPATRA(1946, Brit.)
Hazel Franklyn
LADY POSSESSED(1952)
Herbert Franklyn
DOSS HOUSE(1933, Brit.)
Irwin Franklyn
WOMAN FROM TANGIER, THE(1948), w; DAUGHTER OF THE WEST(1949), w
Irwin R. Franklyn
WATERFRONT(1944), w
John Franklyn
SINFUL DAVEY(1969, Brit.)
Leo Franklyn
SPLENDID FELLOWS(1934, Aus.); TWO MINUTES' SILENCE(1934, Brit.); KEEP FIT(1937, Brit.); I'VE GOT A HORSE(1938, Brit.); AND THE SAME TO YOU(1960, Brit.); NIGHT WE GOT THE BIRD, THE(1961, Brit.); MAKE MINE A DOUBLE(1962, Brit.)
Milt Franklyn
GREAT AMERICAN BUGS BUNNY-ROAD RUNNER CHASE(1979), m; BUGS BUNNY'S THIRD MOVIE–1001 RABBIT TALES(1982), m
Murray Franklyn
1984
UNFAITHFULLY YOURS(1984)
Robert Franklyn
HILLS OF HOME(1948), m
Sidney A. Franklyn
Misc. Silents
HER ONLY WAY(1918), d
William Franklyn
LOVE MATCH, THE(1955, Brit.); ABOVE US THE WAVES(1956, Brit.); CITY AFTER MIDNIGHT(1957, Brit.); ENEMY FROM SPACE(1957, Brit.); FLESH IS WEAK, THE(1957, Brit.); OUT OF THE CLOUDS(1957, Brit.); TIME IS MY ENEMY(1957, Brit.); SNORKEL, THE(1958, Brit.); BIG DAY, THE(1960, Brit.); BREAKOUT(1960, Brit.); PIT OF DARKNESS(1961, Brit.); FURY AT SMUGGLERS BAY(1963, Brit.); SPY-LARKS(1965, Brit.); CUL-DE-SAC(1966, Brit.); GET CHARLIE TULLY(1976, Brit.); COUNT DRACULA AND HIS VAMPIRE BRIDE(1978, Brit.); NUTCRACKER(1982, Brit.)
Misc. Talkies
NUTCRACKER(1984)
John Franklyn-Robbins
ASYLUM(1972, Brit.); SWALLOWS AND AMAZONS(1977, Brit.); MEMOIRS OF A SURVIVOR(1981, Brit.)
1984
PLAGUE DOGS, THE(1984, U.S./Brit.)
Knut Frankman
OCEAN BREAKERS(1949, Swed.)
M. J. Frankovich
FUGITIVE LADY(1951), p; DECAMERON NIGHTS(1953, Brit.), p; FOOTSTEPS IN THE FOG(1955, Brit.), p; SPIN A DARK WEB(1956, Brit.), p; CACTUS FLOWER(1969), p; MAROONED(1969), p; THERE'S A GIRL IN MY SOUP(1970, Brit.), p; DOCTORS' WIVES(1971), p; LOVE MACHINE, THE(1971), p; BUTTERFLIES ARE FREE(1972), p; STAND UP AND BE COUNTED(1972), p; REPORT TO THE COMMISSIONER(1975), p; FROM NOON TO THREE(1976), p; SHOOTIST, THE(1976), p
M.J. "Mike" Frankovich
$(DOLLARS)**1/2 (1971), p
Mike Frankovich
GREAT AMERICAN BROADCAST, THE(1941); MEET JOHN DOE(1941); WEST POINT WIDOW(1941); JOE MACBETH(1955), p
M.J. Frankovitch
PORTRAIT IN SMOKE(1957, Brit.), p
M.J. Frankovitch [Montagu Marks]
FIRE OVER AFRICA(1954, Brit.), p

Mike Frankovitch
YESTERDAY'S HEROES(1940); BUCK PRIVATES(1941)
Billy Franks
MELODY(1971, Brit.)
Chloe Franks
TROG(1970, Brit.); HOUSE THAT DRIPPED BLOOD, THE(1971, Brit.); STRAW DOGS(1971, Brit.); WHO SLEW AUNTIE ROO?(1971, U.S./Brit.); TALES FROM THE CRYPT(1972, Brit.); ALL THE RIGHT NOISES(1973, Brit.); LITTLE NIGHT MUSIC, A(1977, Aust./U.S./Ger.); LITTLEST HORSE THIEVES, THE(1977); UNCANNY, THE(1977, Brit./Can.)
David Franks
STRANGE AFFECTION(1959, Brit.); BARBER OF STAMFORD HILL, THE(1963, Brit.)
Dennis Franks
RISING OF THE MOON, THE(1957, Ireland)
Frank E. Franks
MUSIC HALL PARADE(1939, Brit.)
James Franks
TOMORROW(1972)
Jennifer Franks
MONTY PYTHON'S THE MEANING OF LIFE(1983, Brit.)
Jerome Franks
DEADLINE AT DAWN(1946)
Jerome Franks, Jr.
CASANOVA IN BURLESQUE(1944)
Jerry Franks
STUDENT TOUR(1934); JOHNNY O'CLOCK(1947); BIG DOLL HOUSE, THE(1971)
Jerry Franks, Jr.
SUNBONNET SUE(1945)
L. Franks
THINGS HAPPEN AT NIGHT(1948, Brit.)
Michael Franks
ZANDY'S BRIDE(1974), m; BORN TO KILL(1975), m
Michelle Franks
DRIVE-IN(1976)
Una Franks
WOMEN IN BONDAGE(1943)
Peggy Frankston
PAUL AND MICHELLE(1974, Fr./Brit.); GUNS(1980, Fr.)
1984
UNTIL SEPTEMBER(1984)
Mary Frann
NASHVILLE REBEL(1966)
Misc. Talkies
WOMAN IN THE RAIN(1976)
Eric Franquelin
JOY(1983, Fr./Can.)
Fely Franquelli
CRY HAVOC(1943); FALLEN SPARROW, THE(1943); LEOPARD MAN, THE(1943); BACK TO BATAAN(1945)
Tom Fransden
MARRIED TOO YOUNG(1962)
Wayne Franson
1984
PREPPIES(1984)
Dalies Frantz
SWEETHEARTS(1938); BALALAIKA(1939); I TAKE THIS WOMAN(1940)
Jacques Frantz
1984
LES COMPERES(1984, Fr.)
William Franum
WOMAN'S FACE(1941)
Jean Franval
DIARY OF A CHAMBERMAID(1964, Fr./Ital.); BLACK JACK(1979, Brit.)
Arthur Franz
JUNGLE PATROL(1948); DOCTOR AND THE GIRL, THE(1949); RED LIGHT(1949); RED STALLION IN THE ROCKIES(1949); ROSEANNA McCOY(1949); SANDS OF IWO JIMA(1949); TARNISHED(1950); THREE SECRETS(1950); ABBOTT AND COSTELLO MEET THE INVISIBLE MAN(1951); FLIGHT TO MARS(1951); STRICTLY DISHONORABLE(1951); SUBMARINE COMMAND(1951); EIGHT IRON MEN(1952); MEMBER OF THE WEDDING, THE(1952); RAINBOW 'ROUND MY SHOULDER(1952); SNIPER, THE(1952); EDDIE CANTOR STORY, THE(1953); FLIGHT NURSE(1953); INVADERS FROM MARS(1953); BAD FOR EACH OTHER(1954); CAINE MUTINY, THE(1954); STEEL CAGE, THE(1954); BATTLE TAXI(1955); BOBBY WARE IS MISSING(1955); NEW ORLEANS UNCENSORED(1955); BEYOND A REASONABLE DOUBT(1956); RUNNING TARGET(1956); WILD PARTY, THE(1956); BACK FROM THE DEAD(1957); DEVIL'S HAIRPIN, THE(1957); HELLCATS OF THE NAVY(1957); UNHOLY WIFE, THE(1957); FLAME BARRIER, THE(1958); MONSTER ON THE CAMPUS(1958); YOUNG LIONS, THE(1958); WOMAN OBSESSED(1959); ATOMIC SUBMARINE, THE(1960); CARPETBAGGERS, THE(1964); ALVAREZ KELLY(1966); ANZIO(1968, Ital.); SWEET RIDE, THE(1968); SO LONG, BLUE BOY(1973); HUMAN FACTOR, THE(1975); THAT CHAMPIONSHIP SEASON(1982)
Misc. Talkies
SISTERS OF DEATH(1976)
Dennis Franz
FURY, THE(1978); REMEMBER MY NAME(1978); STONY ISLAND(1978); WEDDING, A(1978); PERFECT COUPLE, A(1979); DRESSED TO KILL(1980); POPEYE(1980); BLOW OUT(1981); PSYCHO II(1983)
1984
BODY DOUBLE(1984)
Eduard Franz
HOLLOW TRIUMPH(1948); IRON CURTAIN, THE(1948); FRANCIS(1949); MADAME BOVARY(1949); OH, YOU BEAUTIFUL DOLL(1949); OUTPOST IN MOROCCO(1949); WAKE OF THE RED WITCH(1949); WHIRLPOOL(1949); EMERGENCY WEDDING(1950); MAGNIFICENT YANKEE, THE(1950); VICIOUS YEARS, THE(1950); DESERT FOX, THE(1951); GREAT CARUSO, THE(1951); SHADOW IN THE SKY(1951); THING, THE(1951); UNKNOWN MAN, THE(1951); BECAUSE YOU'RE MINE(1952); EVERYTHING I HAVE IS YOURS(1952); ONE MINUTE TO ZERO(1952); DREAM WIFE(1953); JAZZ SINGER, THE(1953); LATIN LOVERS(1953); SINS OF JEZEBEL(1953); BEACHHEAD(1954); BROKEN LANCE(1954); SIGN OF

THE PAGAN(1954); INDIAN FIGHTER, THE(1955); LADY GODIVA(1955); LAST COMMAND, THE(1955); WHITE FEATHER(1955); BURNING HILLS, THE(1956); TEN COMMANDMENTS, THE(1956); THREE FOR JAMIE DAWN(1956); MAN AFRAID(1957); CERTAIN SMILE, A(1958); DAY OF THE BAD MAN(1958); LAST OF THE FAST GUNS, THE(1958); FOUR SKULLS OF JONATHAN DRAKE, THE(1959); STORY OF RUTH, THE(1960); FIERCEST HEART, THE(1961); FRANCIS OF ASSISI(1961); HATARI!(1962); BEAUTY AND THE BEAST(1963); CYBORG 2087(1966); PRESIDENT'S ANALYST, THE(1967); JOHNNY GOT HIS GUN(1971); TWILIGHT ZONE–THE MOVIE(1983)

Edward Franz
GOLDBERGS, THE(1950)

Elizabeth Franz
PILGRIM, FAREWELL(1980)

Helle Franz
TABLE FOR FIVE(1983)

J. J. Franz
Silents
END OF THE GAME, THE(1919)

Joel Franz
LONE STAR RANGER, THE(1930)

Joseph Franz
COLLEGE HOLIDAY(1936); INVITATION TO HAPPINESS(1939)
Silents
LOVE GAMBLER, THE(1922), d; NEW TEACHER, THE(1922), d; ALIAS THE NIGHT WIND(1923), d; PELL STREET MYSTERY, THE(1924), d
Misc. Silents
PRETENDER, THE(1918); PARISH PRIEST, THE(1921), d; SMILING JIM(1922), d; TRACKS(1922), d; YOUTH MUST HAVE LOVE(1922), d; HORSESHOE LUCK(1924), d; BLUE BLAZES(1926), d; DESPERATE GAME, THE(1926), d

Joseph J. Franz
GOOD DAME(1934)
Silents
STEPPING FAST(1923), d; EASY COME, EASY GO(1928)
Misc. Silents
BARE-FISTED GALLAGHER(1919), d; BLUE BANDANNA, THE(1919), d; DANGEROUS WATERS(1919), d; GRAY WOLF'S GHOST, THE(1919), d; SAGE BRUSH HAMLET, A(1919), d; BROADWAY COWBOY, THE(1920), d; CAVE GIRL, THE(1921), d; FIGHTIN' MAD(1921), d

Niklas Franz
DEGREE OF MURDER, A(1969, Ger.), w

Siegfried Franz
CANARIS(1955, Ger.), m; MRS. WARREN'S PROFESSION(1960, Ger.), m; GIRL OF THE MOORS, THE(1961, Ger.), m; DIE FASTNACHTSBEICHTE(1962, Ger.), m

Uta Franz
FOREVER MY LOVE(1962)

the Franz Althoff Circus of Austria
CIRCUS WORLD(1964)

Logan Franzee
SLAUGHTER'S BIG RIP-OFF(1973), spec eff

Bjorn Franzen
GLADIATORS, THE(1970, Swed.)

Charles Franzen
NIGHT THE LIGHTS WENT OUT IN GEORGIA, THE(1981)

Nell Franzen
Misc. Silents
COURTESAN, THE(1916); EMBERS(1916); LIFE'S BLIND ALLEY(1916)

Nellie Franzen
Misc. Silents
SAGEBRUSH GOSPEL(1924)

Harold Franzer-Simson
SOUTHERN MAID, A(1933, Brit.), m

Carlo Mario Franzero
CLEOPATRA(1963), w

Willy Franzl
FOREVER MY LOVE(1962), ch

Leon Frapie
LA MATERNELLE(1933, Fr.), w

Jean Jose Frappa
ACCUSED–STAND UP(1930, Fr.), w

Jill Frappier
IN PRAISE OF OLDER WOMEN(1978, Can.); STRANGE BREW(1983)

Paul Emile Frappier
IMPROPER CHANNELS(1981, Can.)

George Fras
PROUD RIDER, THE(1971, Can.), p

Jannakis Frasakis
SIGNS OF LIFE(1981, Ger.)

Paolo Frasca
ANGELINA(1948, Ital.), p

Bobby Frasco
BELLS OF ST. MARY'S, THE(1945)

Jimmy Frasco
SEPTEMBER AFFAIR(1950)

Michael Frasco
SEPTEMBER AFFAIR(1950)

Alec Fraser
LURE, THE(1933, Brit.); GREAT DEFENDER, THE(1934, Brit.); PHANTOM SHIP(1937, Brit.); MUTINY OF THE ELSINORE, THE(1939, Brit.)
Misc. Silents
GAMBLE IN LIVES, A(1920, Brit.); BONNIE BRIER BRUSH, THE(1921, Brit.); KNAVE OF DIAMONDS, THE(1921, Brit.); WILL, THE(1921, Brit.); WOMAN OF HIS DREAM, THE(1921, Brit.); WOMAN WITH THE FAN, THE(1921, Brit.); LITTLE BROTHER OF GOD(1922, Brit.)

Alex Fraser
GOOD COMPANIONS(1933, Brit.); BLONDE SAVAGE(1947); IF WINTER COMES(1947); ARGYLE SECRETS, THE(1948); SHAGGY(1948); SECRET OF ST. IVES, THE(1949); THREE CAME HOME(1950)

Alison Fraser
FOLLOW THAT HORSE!(1960, Brit.); THREE BITES OF THE APPLE(1967)

Anita Fraser
Silents
JUNE MADNESS(1922)

Bill Fraser
COMMON TOUCH, THE(1941, Brit.); SCOTLAND YARD INSPECTOR(1952, Brit.); CAPTAIN'S PARADISE, THE(1953, Brit.); MEET MR. LUCIFER(1953, Brit.); TERROR ON A TRAIN(1953); TONIGHT AT 8:30(1953, Brit.); BAREFOOT CONTESSA, THE(1954); DUEL IN THE JUNGLE(1954, Brit.); ALIAS JOHN PRESTON(1956); CHARLEY MOON(1956, Brit.); JUMPING FOR JOY(1956, Brit.); JUST MY LUCK(1957, Brit.); SECOND FIDDLE(1957, Brit.); ANOTHER TIME, ANOTHER PLACE(1958); MAN WHO LIKED FUNERALS, THE(1959, Brit.); ORDERS ARE ORDERS(1959, Brit.); FAST LADY, THE(1963, Brit.); WHAT A CRAZY WORLD(1963, Brit.); AMERICANIZATION OF EMILY, THE(1964); I'VE GOTTA HORSE(1965, Brit.); JOEY BOY(1965, Brit.); MASQUERADE(1965, Brit.); DIAMONDS FOR BREAKFAST(1968, Brit.); BEST HOUSE IN LONDON, THE(1969, Brit.); CAPTAIN NEMO AND THE UNDERWATER CITY(1969, Brit.); ALL THE WAY UP(1970, Brit.); UP POMPEII(1971, Brit.); UP THE CHASTITY BELT(1971, Brit.); UP THE FRONT(1972, Brit.); MOMENTS(1974, Brit.); EYE OF THE NEEDLE(1981); WAGNER(1983, Brit./Hung./Aust.)
Misc. Talkies
LOVE THY NEIGHBOUR(1973); THAT'S YOUR FUNERAL(1974, Brit.)

Bob Fraser
SIX-GUN RHYTHM(1939)

Bryant Fraser
PANIC IN NEEDLE PARK(1971); CHILD'S PLAY(1972); MARATHON MAN(1976)

Colin Fraser
SWITCH, THE(1963, Brit.), w

Constance Fraser
DISTANT TRUMPET(1952, Brit.); GENTLE TOUCH, THE(1956, Brit.); LADY MISLAID, A(1958, Brit.)

Dave Fraser
BEYOND REASONABLE DOUBT(1980, New Zeal.), m
1984
CONSTANCE(1984, New Zealand), m; WILD HORSES(1984, New Zealand), m

Dennis Fraser
TITANIC(1953)

Dick Fraser
ALASKA PATROL(1949)

Elisabeth Fraser
ONE FOOT IN HEAVEN(1941); BUSSES ROAR(1942); HIDDEN HAND, THE(1942); MAN WHO CAME TO DINNER, THE(1942); ALL MY SONS(1948); DEAR WIFE(1949); ROSEANNA McCOY(1949); CALLAWAY WENT THATAWAY(1951); SO BIG(1953); YOUNG AT HEART(1955); TUNNEL OF LOVE, THE(1958); TWO FOR THE SEESAW(1962); WHO'S BEEN SLEEPING IN MY BED?(1963); PATCH OF BLUE, A(1965); GLASS BOTTOM BOAT, THE(1966); SECONDS(1966); GRADUATE, THE(1967); WAY WEST, THE(1967); BALLAD OF JOSIE(1968)

Elizabeth Fraser
COMMANDOS STRIKE AT DAWN, THE(1942); HILLS OF OKLAHOMA(1950); WHEN I GROW UP(1951); DEATH OF A SALESMAN(1952); STEEL CAGE, THE(1954); TOP FLOOR GIRL(1959, Brit.); TONY ROME(1967)

Elizabeth [Liz] Fraser
WONDERFUL THINGS!(1958, Brit.)

Fil Fraser
HOUNDS... OF NOTRE DAME, THE(1980, Can.), p

Fiona Fraser
RIDE THE HIGH WIND(1967, South Africa); SWAPPERS, THE(1970, Brit.)

George Fraser
JOSETTE(1938), w; VOICE OF THE HURRICANE(1964), d

George MacDonald Fraser
THREE MUSKETEERS, THE(1974, Panama), w; FOUR MUSKETEERS, THE(1975), w; ROYAL FLASH(1975, Brit.), w; CROSSED SWORDS(1978), w; OCTOPUSSY(1983, Brit.), w

Harry Fraser
MONTANA KID, THE(1931), d, w; OKLAHOMA JIM(1931), d, w; BROADWAY TO CHEYENNE(1932), d, w; GHOST CITY(1932), d&w; HONOR OF THE MOUNTED(1932), d&w; LAND OF WANTED MEN(1932), d&w; LAW OF THE NORTH(1932), d&w; MASON OF THE MOUNTED(1932), d&w; TEXAS PIONEERS(1932), d, w; DIAMOND TRAIL(1933), d, w; RAINBOW RANCH(1933), d; 'NEATH THE ARIZONA SKIES(1934), d; RANDY RIDES ALONE(1934), d; FIGHTING PIONEERS(1935), d, w; LAST OF THE CLINTONS, THE(1935), d; RUSTLER'S PARADISE(1935), d; WAGON TRAIL(1935), d; WILD MUSTANG(1935), d; CAVALCADE OF THE WEST(1936), d; FEUD OF THE WEST(1936), d; RIDING AVENGER, THE(1936), d; ROMANCE RIDES THE RANGE(1936), d; ACES WILD(1937), d; DARK MANHATTAN(1937), d; GALLOPING DYNAMITE(1937), d; GHOST TOWN(1937), d; SPIRIT OF YOUTH(1937), d; FURY BELOW(1938), d; HEROES OF THE ALAMO(1938), d; SIX SHOOTIN' SHERIFF(1938), d; LURE OF THE WASTELAND(1939), d; LIGHTNING STRIKES WEST(1940), d; PHANTOM RANCHER(1940), d; OLD CHISHOLM TRAIL(1943), d&w; TENTING TONIGHT ON THE OLD CAMP GROUND(1943), w; DEAD OR ALIVE(1944), w; GUNSMOKE MESA(1944), d; WHISPERING SKULL, THE(1944), w; ENEMY OF THE LAW(1945), d&w; FLAMING BULLETS(1945), d&w; FRONTIER FUGITIVES(1945), d; I ACCUSE MY PARENTS(1945), w; THREE IN THE SADDLE(1945), d; AMBUSH TRAIL(1946), d; NAVAJO KID, THE(1946), d&w; SIX GUN MAN(1946), d&w; THUNDER TOWN(1946), d; STALLION CANYON(1949), d; ABILENE TRAIL(1951), w
Misc. Talkies
FROM BROADWAY TO CHEYENNE(1932), d; MAN FROM ARIZONA, THE(1932), d; VANISHING MEN(1932), d; FIGHTING THROUGH(1934), d; GUNFIRE(1935), d; RECKLESS BUCKAROO, THE(1935), d; SADDLE ACES(1935), d; TONTO KID, THE(1935), d; HAIR-TRIGGER CASEY(1936), d; WILDCAT SAUNDERS(1936), d; SONGS AND SADDLES(1938), d; OUTLAW ROUNDUP(1944), d
Silents
BURN 'EM UP BARNES(1921); LUCK(1923); WESTBOUND(1924)

Harry L. Fraser
WHITE GORILLA(1947), d; CHAINED FOR LIFE(1950), d
Misc. Silents
OIL AND ROMANCE(1925), d; QUEEN OF SPADES(1925), d; WEST OF THE MOJAVE(1925), d; GENERAL CUSTER AT LITTLE BIG HORN(1926), d; SHEEP TRAIL(1926), d

Harry S. Fraser
SAVAGE GIRL, THE(1932), d

Helen Fraser
BILLY LIAR(1963, Brit.); REPULSION(1965, Brit.); UNCLE, THE(1966, Brit.); BIRTH-DAY PARTY, THE(1968, Brit.); START THE REVOLUTION WITHOUT ME(1970); SOMETHING TO HIDE(1972, Brit.)

Henry Fraser
JUNGLE MAN(1941), d; BRAND OF THE DEVIL(1944), d

Hugh Fraser
FANTASIA(1940), anim; PINOCCHIO(1940), anim; DUMBO(1941), anim; MAKE MINE MUSIC(1946), anim; FUN AND FANCY FREE(1947), anim; CINDEREL-LA(1950), anim; ALICE IN WONDERLAND(1951), anim; PETER PAN(1953), anim; LADY AND THE TRAMP(1955), anim; MAN CALLED FLINTSTONE, THE(1966), anim; RITZ, THE(1976); HANOVER STREET(1979, Brit.); FIREFOX(1982); MISSION-ARY, THE(1982); CURSE OF THE PINK PANTHER(1983); DRAUGHTSMAN'S CON-TRACT, THE(1983, Brit.); NELLY'S VERSION(1983, Brit.)

Ian Fraser
SCROOGE(1970, Brit.), md; HOPSCOTCH(1980), m; FIRST MONDAY IN OC-TOBER(1981), m

James Fraser
FLOODTIDE(1949, Brit.)

Jean Fraser
Misc. Silents
DEVIL, THE SERVANT AND THE MAN, THE(1916)

Jeri Lynne Fraser
TWO TICKETS TO PARIS(1962)

Jill Fraser
PERSONAL BEST(1982), m

Jimmy Fraser
WILD PACK, THE(1972)

John Crawford Fraser
ACE OF SPADES, THE(1935, Brit.), w

John Fraser
GOOD BEGINNING, THE(1953, Brit.); MEN ARE CHILDREN TWICE(1953, Brit.); TITANIC(1953); DAM BUSTERS, THE(1955, Brit.); LIGHT TOUCH, THE(1955, Brit.); GOOD COMPANIONS, THE(1957, Brit.); WIND CANNOT READ, THE(1958, Brit.); MAN WITH THE GREEN CARNATION, THE(1960, Brit.); TUNES OF GLORY(1960, Brit.); EL CID(1961, U.S./Ital.); WALTZ OF THE TOREADORS(1962, Brit.); FURY AT SMUGGLERS BAY(1963, Brit.); TAMAHINE(1964, Brit.); OPERATION CROSS-BOW(1965, U.S./Ital.); REPULSION(1965, Brit.); STUDY IN TERROR, A(1966, Brit./Ger.); CARNABY, M.D.(1967, Brit.); ISADORA(1968, Brit.); MAN FROM HONG KONG(1975), p; SCHIZO(1977, Brit.)

Juliette May Fraser
MEMENTO MEI(1963)

Kevin Fraser
1984
RACING WITH THE MOON(1984)

Lee Fraser
WALK PROUD(1979); DEFIANCE(1980)

Liz Fraser
BULLDOG BREED, THE(1960, Brit.); DESERT MICE(1960, Brit.); DOCTOR IN LOVE(1960, Brit.); CALL ME GENIUS(1961, Brit.); CARRY ON REGARDLESS(1961, Brit.); DOUBLE BUNK(1961, Brit.); NIGHT WE GOT THE BIRD, THE(1961, Brit.); PURE HELL OF ST. TRINIAN'S, THE(1961, Brit.); TWO-WAY STRETCH(1961, Brit.); WATCH IT, SAILOR!(1961, Brit.); CARRY ON CRUISING(1962, Brit.); LIVE NOW-PAY LATER(1962, Brit.); MAKE MINE A DOUBLE(1962, Brit.); ROOMMATES(1962, Brit.); CARRY ON CABBIE(1963, Brit.); FURY AT SMUGGLERS BAY(1963, Brit.); MURDER CAN BE DEADLY(1963, Brit.); PAIR OF BRIEFS, A(1963, Brit.); AMERI-CANIZATION OF EMILY, THE(1964); AMOROUS MR. PRAWN, THE(1965, Brit.); SEASIDE SWINGERS(1965, Brit.); FAMILY WAY, THE(1966, Brit.); UP THE JUNC-TION(1968, Brit.); DAD'S ARMY(1971, Brit.)

Martine Fraser
TRAVELING EXECUTIONER, THE(1970)

Moira Fraser
MADELEINE(1950, Brit.)

Moyra Fraser
MAN WHO LOVED REDHEADS, THE(1955, Brit.); LEFT, RIGHT AND CEN-TRE(1959); V.I.P.s, THE(1963, Brit.); HERE WE GO ROUND THE MULBERRY BUSH(1968, Brit.); PRUDENCE AND THE PILL(1968, Brit.); BOY FRIEND, THE(1971, Brit.)

Natasha Fraser
LORDS OF DISCIPLINE, THE(1983)

Orlando Fraser
FRENCH LIEUTENANT'S WOMAN, THE(1981)

Paul Fraser
MISCHIEF(1969, Brit.)

Peter Fraser
BELL-BOTTOM GEORGE(1943, Brit.), w; I DIDN'T DO IT(1945, Brit.), w; GEORGE IN CIVVY STREET(1946, Brit.), w; YOU CAN'T DO WITHOUT LOVE(1946, Brit.), w; DANCING WITH CRIME(1947, Brit.), w; MODEL FOR MURDER(1960, Brit.), w; SORCERERS, THE(1967, Brit.); FRENCH LIEUTENANT'S WOMAN, THE(1981)

Phyllis Fraser
THIRTEEN WOMEN(1932); LUCKY DEVILS(1933); FIGHTING YOUTH(1935); LIT-TLE MEN(1935); EVERY SATURDAY NIGHT(1936); HARVESTER(1936); WINDS OF THE WASTELAND(1936); TOUGH TO HANDLE(1937); VIVACIOUS LADY(1938); FOR BEAUTY'S SAKE(1941)

Richard Fraser
HOW GREEN WAS MY VALLEY(1941); MAN HUNT(1941); YANK IN THE R.A.F., A(1941); BUSSES ROAR(1942); DESPERATE JOURNEY(1942); EAGLE SQUAD-RON(1942); GORILLA MAN(1942); JOAN OF PARIS(1942); EDGE OF DARK-NESS(1943); HOLY MATRIMONY(1943); THUMBS UP(1943); TRUCK BUSTERS(1943); LADIES COURAGEOUS(1944); FATAL WITNESS, THE(1945); PIC-TURE OF DORIAN GRAY, THE(1945); SCOTLAND YARD INVESTIGATOR(1945, Brit.); SHADOW OF TERROR(1945); TIGER WOMAN, THE(1945); WHITE PON-GO(1945); BEDLAM(1946); BLONDE FOR A DAY(1946); UNDERCOVER WOMAN, THE(1946); BLACKMAIL(1947); LONE WOLF IN LONDON(1947); PRIVATE AFFAIRS OF BEL AMI, THE(1947); COBRA STRIKES, THE(1948); RAW DEAL(1948); ROGUES' REGIMENT(1948); RED DANUBE, THE(1949)

Robert Fraser
LOVE PAST THIRTY(1934); SILVER SPURS(1936); ON THE GREAT WHITE TRAIL(1938); DAWN EXPRESS, THE(1942)
Misc. Talkies
TWO GUN CABALLERO(1931)

Robert W. Fraser
Silents
LIGHT AT DUSK, THE(1916)

Ron Fraser
GREAT MACARTHY, THE(1975, Aus.)

Ronald Fraser
BOBBIKINS(1959, Brit.); SUNDOWNERS, THE(1960); LONG AND THE SHORT AND THE TALL, THE(1961, Brit.); BEST OF ENEMIES, THE(1962); GIRL ON THE BOAT, THE(1962, Brit.); IN SEARCH OF THE CASTAWAYS(1962, Brit.); POT CARRIERS, THE(1962, Brit.); THERE WAS A CROOKED MAN(1962, Brit.); PRIVATE POT-TER(1963, Brit.); PUNCH AND JUDY MAN, THE(1963, Brit.); V.I.P.s, THE(1963, Brit.); CODE 7, VICTIM 5(1964, Brit.); CROOKS IN CLOISTERS(1964, Brit.); DAYLIGHT ROBBERY(1964, Brit.); MODEL MURDER CASE, THE(1964, Brit.); WHY BOTHER TO KNOCK(1964, Brit.); FLIGHT OF THE PHOENIX, THE(1965, Brit.); BEAUTY JUNGLE, THE(1966, Brit.); COUNTERFEIT CONSTABLE, THE(1966, Fr.); FATHOM(1967); WHISPERERS, THE(1967, Brit.); SEBASTIAN(1968, Brit.); BED SITTING ROOM, THE(1969, Brit.); SINFUL DAVEY(1969, Brit.); RISE AND RISE OF MICHAEL RIMMER, THE(1970, Brit.); TOO LATE THE HERO(1970); MAGNIFICENT SEVEN DEADLY SINS, THE(1971, Brit.); RENTADICK(1972, Brit.); PAPER TIGER(1975, Brit.); GET CHARLIE TULLY(1976, Brit.); SWALLOWS AND AMAZONS(1977, Brit.); WILD GEESE, THE(1978, Brit.); TRAIL OF THE PINK PANTHER, THE(1982)
Misc. Talkies
RISE AND RISE OF MICHAEL RIMMER, THE(1970, Brit.)

Ronnie Fraser
HELLIONS, THE(1962, Brit.)

Sally Fraser
BAR SINISTER, THE(1955); IT CONQUERED THE WORLD(1956); GIANT FROM THE UNKNOWN(1958); SPIDER, THE(1958); WAR OF THE COLOSSAL BEAST(1958); NORTH BY NORTHWEST(1959); ROADRACERS, THE(1959); ELMER GAN-TRY(1960); DANGEROUS CHARTER(1962)

Shelagh Fraser
YANK IN LONDON, A(1946, Brit.); MASTER OF BANKDAM, THE(1947, Brit.); ESTHER WATERS(1948, Brit.); HISTORY OF MR. POLLY, THE(1949, Brit.); EYE WITNESS(1950, Brit.); SALUTE THE TOFF(1952, Brit.); LAST MAN TO HANG, THE(1956, Brit.); RAISING A RIOT(1957, Brit.); SON OF ROBIN HOOD(1959, Brit.); DEVIL'S OWN, THE(1967, Brit.); ALF 'N' FAMILY(1968, Brit.); BODY STEALERS, THE(1969); STAIRCASE(1969 U.S./Brit./Fr.); THANK YOU ALL VERY MUCH(1969, Brit.); TWO GENTLEMEN SHARING(1969, Brit.); PERSECUTION(1974, Brit.); NOTH-ING BUT THE NIGHT(1975, Brit.); STAR WARS(1977)

Stanley Fraser
UNTIL THEY SAIL(1957); JULIA MISBEHAVES(1948); MAZE, THE(1953); WORLD WITHOUT END(1956); MY FAIR LADY(1964)

Teddie Fraser
PARDON MY SARONG(1942)

Tony Fraser
TRAVELING EXECUTIONER, THE(1970)
Silents
FLAMES OF PASSION(1922, Brit.)
Misc. Silents
BROKEN ROAD, THE(1921, Brit.)

W. Simpson Fraser
MURDER IN THE FAMILY(1938, Brit.)

Cecily Fraser-Smith
FOOTSTEPS IN THE NIGHT(1932, Brit.), w

Caroline Frasher
ANGELS OVER BROADWAY(1940); FLORIAN(1940)

Jim Frasher
MYSTERY STREET(1950); GENE AUTRY AND THE MOUNTIES(1951)

Jimmy Frasher
REDWOOD FOREST TRAIL(1950)

Harry L. Frasier
Silents
LITTLE BIG HORN(1927), d

Augusto Frassineti
THIEF OF BAGHDAD, THE(1961, Ital./Fr.), w; TORPEDO BAY(1964, Ital./Fr.), w; TIKO AND THE SHARK(1966, U.S./Ital./Fr.), w

Augusto Frassinetti
GIANT OF MARATHON, THE(1960, Ital.), w; GOLDEN ARROW, THE(1964, Ital.), w; ITALIANO BRAVA GENTE(1965, Ital./USSR), w

Antonio Fratalocchi
PAYMENT IN BLOOD(1968, Ital.), set d

Giovanni Fratalocchi
PSYCHOUT FOR MURDER(1971, Arg./Ital.), art d

Annie Fratellini
ZAZIE(1961, Fr.); CLOPORTES(1966, Fr., Ital.)

Rosanna Fratello
SACCO AND VANZETTI(1971, Ital./Fr.)

Cliff Frates
LITTLE LAURA AND BIG JOHN(1973)

Mervin W. Frates
PLAY MISTY FOR ME(1971)

Adrianao Fraticelli
FINE PAIR, A(1969, Ital.)

Franco Fraticelli
END OF THE WORLD(in Our Usual Bed In a Night Full of Rain), THE*1/2 (1978, Ital.), ed; DAVID AND GOLIATH(1961, Ital.), ed; HUNCHBACK OF ROME, THE(1963, Ital.), ed; SEVEN SEAS TO CALAIS(1963, Ital.), ed; VERONA TRIAL, THE(1963, Ital.), ed; GOLD FOR THE CAESARS(1964), ed; RED LIPS(1964, Fr./Ital.), ed; LOVE IN 4 DIMENSIONS(1965 Fr./Ital.), ed; MINNESOTA CLAY(1966, Ital./Fr./Span.), ed; HEAD OF THE FAMILY(1967, Ital./Fr.), ed; MATCHLESS(1967, Ital.), ed; WAKE UP AND DIE(1967, Fr./Ital.), ed; WEEKEND, ITALIAN STYLE(1967, Fr./Ital./Span.), ed; QUEENS, THE(1968, Ital./Fr.), ed; TREASURE OF SAN GENNARO(1968, Fr./Ital./Ger.), ed; VIOLENT FOUR, THE(1968, Ital.), ed; DAY OF ANGER(1970, Ital./Ger.), ed; MACHINE GUN McCAIN(1970, Ital.), ed; CAT O'NINE TAILS(1971, Ital./Ger./Fr.), ed; LOVE AND ANARCHY(1974, Ital.), ed; ALL SCREWED UP(1976,

Ital.), ed; SEVEN BEAUTIES(1976, Ital.), ed; SUSPIRIA(1977, Ital.), ed; BLOOD FEUD(1979, Ital.), ed; INFERNO(1980, Ital.), ed; COMIN' AT YA!(1981), e; TREASURE OF THE FOUR CROWNS(1983, Span./U.S.), ed

1984
JOKE OF DESTINY LYING IN WAIT AROUND THE CORNER LIKE A STREETBANDIT, A(1984, Ital.), ed

Gaio Fratini
TARTARS, THE(1962, Ital./Yugo.), w

Gina Fratini
STOP THE WORLD–I WANT TO GET OFF(1966, Brit.), cos

Paolo Fratini
SHOCK TROOPS(1968, Ital./Fr.)

Rodolfo Frattaioli
CHINA IS NEAR(1968, Ital.), art d

Benito Frattari
AMERICAN WIFE, AN(1965, Ital.), ph; RUN FOR YOUR WIFE(1966, Fr./Ital.), ph; RENT CONTROL(1981), ph

Franco Fratticelli
DEEP RED(1976, Ital.), ed

Gaio Frattini
HERCULES(1959, Ital.), w

Massimo Fratus
TREE OF WOODEN CLOGS, THE(1979, Ital.)

Maria Frau
MY SEVEN LITTLE SINS(1956, Fr./Ital.); GODDESS OF LOVE, THE(1960, Ital./Fr.)

Dietrich Frauboes
BATTLE OF BRITAIN, THE(1969, Brit.)

Ernestine Frauenberger
LONE CLIMBER, THE(1950, Brit./Aust.)

Bonaventura Fraulo
WEEKEND MURDERS, THE(1972, Ital.), set d

The Fraunfelder Family
SNOW WHITE AND THE SEVEN DWARFS(1937)

Fraunie Fraunholz
Silents
MILLION DOLLAR ROBBERY, THE(1914); WOMAN OF MYSTERY, THE(1914); SONG OF THE WAGE SLAVE, THE(1915)
Misc. Silents
ROGUES OF PARIS(1913); BENEATH THE CZAR(1914); BURGLAR AND THE LADY, THE(1914); DREAM WOMAN, THE(1914); BARBARA FRIETCHIE(1915); HER OWN WAY(1915); WHAT WILL PEOPLE SAY(1915); OCEAN WAIF, THE(1916); OTHER PEOPLE'S MONEY(1916); LITTLE BOY SCOUT, THE(1917)

Francis Fraunie
PERSONAL MAID(1931)

Antonio Frausto
MYSTERY IN MEXICO(1948)

Marcel Fravel
TRAFFIC(1972, Fr.)

Barbara Frawley
DOT AND THE BUNNY(1983, Aus.)

1984
CAMEL BOY, THE(1984, Aus.)

James Frawley
LADYBUG, LADYBUG(1963); TROUBLEMAKER, THE(1964); WILD, WILD WINTER(1966); CHRISTIAN LICORICE STORE, THE(1971), d; KID BLUE(1973), d; BIG BUS, THE(1976), d; MUPPET MOVIE, THE(1979), d

John Frawley
GREAT MACARTHY, THE(1975, Aus.); DEVIL'S PLAYGROUND, THE(1976, Aus.); ELIZA FRASER(1976, Aus.); TRESPASSERS, THE(1976, Aus.); BLUE FIN(1978, Aus.); LAST WAVE, THE(1978, Aus.); NIGHT OF THE PROWLER, THE(1979, Aus.)

Paul Frawley
LOVE IS NEWS(1937)

Tim Frawley
PLAY MISTY FOR ME(1971)

William Frawley
HELL AND HIGH WATER(1933); MOONLIGHT AND PRETZELS(1933); BOLERO(1934); CRIME DOCTOR, THE(1934); HERE IS MY HEART(1934); LEMON DROP KID, THE(1934); MISS FANE'S BABY IS STOLEN(1934); SHOOT THE WORKS(1934); WITCHING HOUR, THE(1934); ALIBI IKE(1935); CAR 99(1935); COLLEGE SCANDAL(1935); HARMONY LANE(1935); HOLD'EM YALE(1935); SHIP CAFE(1935); WELCOME HOME(1935); DESIRE(1936); F MAN(1936); GENERAL DIED AT DAWN, THE(1936); IT'S A GREAT LIFE(1936); PRINCESS COMES ACROSS, THE(1936); ROSE BOWL(1936); STRIKE ME PINK(1936); THREE CHEERS FOR LOVE(1936); THREE MARRIED MEN(1936); BLOSSOMS ON BROADWAY(1937); DOUBLE OR NOTHING(1937); HIGH, WIDE AND HANDSOME(1937); SOMETHING TO SING ABOUT(1937); MAD ABOUT MUSIC(1938); PROFESSOR BEWARE(1938); SONS OF THE LEGION(1938); TOUCHDOWN, ARMY(1938); AMBUSH(1939); EX-CHAMP(1939); GRAND JURY SECRETS(1939); HUCKLEBERRY FINN(1939); NIGHT WORK(1939); PERSONS IN HIDING(1939); ROSE OF WASHINGTON SQUARE(1939); ST. LOUIS BLUES(1939); STOP, LOOK, AND LOVE(1939); DANCING ON A DIME(1940); FARMER'S DAUGHTER, THE(1940); GOLDEN GLOVES(1940); ONE NIGHT IN THE TROPICS(1940); OPENED BY MISTAKE(1940); QUARTERBACK, THE(1940); RHYTHM ON THE RIVER(1940); SANDY GETS HER MAN(1940); UNTAMED(1940); BLONDIE IN SOCIETY(1941); BRIDE CAME C.O.D., THE(1941); CRACKED NUTS(1941); FOOTSTEPS IN THE DARK(1941); PUBLIC ENEMIES(1941); SIX LESSONS FROM MADAME LA ZONGA(1941); GENTLEMAN JIM(1942); GIVE OUT, SISTERS(1942); IT HAPPENED IN FLATBUSH(1942); MOONLIGHT IN HAVANA(1942); ROXIE HART(1942); TREAT EM' ROUGH(1942); WILDCAT(1942); LARCENY WITH MUSIC(1943); WE'VE NEVER BEEN LICKED(1943); WHISTLING IN BROOKLYN(1943); FIGHTING SEABEES, THE(1944); GOING MY WAY(1944); LAKE PLACID SERENADE(1944); FLAME OF THE BARBARY COAST(1945); HITCHHIKE TO HAPPINESS(1945); LADY ON A TRAIN(1945); ZIEGFELD FOLLIES(1945); CRIME DOCTOR'S MAN HUNT(1946); INNER CIRCLE, THE(1946); RENDEZVOUS WITH ANNIE(1946); VIRGINIAN, THE(1946); BLONDIE'S ANNIVERSARY(1947); DOWN TO EARTH(1947); HIT PARADE OF 1947(1947); I WONDER WHO'S KISSING HER NOW(1947); MIRACLE ON 34TH STREET, THE(1947); MONSIEUR VERDOUX(1947); MOTHER WORE TIGHTS(1947); MY WILD IRISH ROSE(1947); BABE RUTH STORY, THE(1948); CHICKEN EVERY SUNDAY(1948); GIRL FROM MANHATTAN(1948); GOOD SAM(1948); JOE PALOOKA IN WINNER TAKE ALL(1948); TEXAS, BROOKLYN AND HEAVEN(1948); EAST SIDE, WEST SIDE(1949); LADY TAKES A SAILOR,

THE(1949); LONE WOLF AND HIS LADY, THE(1949); BLONDIE'S HERO(1950); KILL THE UMPIRE(1950); KISS TOMORROW GOODBYE(1950); PRETTY BABY(1950); ABBOTT AND COSTELLO MEET THE INVISIBLE MAN(1951); LEMON DROP KID, THE(1951); RHUBARB(1951); RANCHO NOTORIOUS(1952); SAFE AT HOME(1962)

John Frayer
SWEET CHARITY(1969); HISTORY OF THE WORLD, PART 1(1981); TO BE OR NOT TO BE(1983)

Josephine Frayne
MARK, THE(1961, Brit.)

Stephen Frayne
Misc. Silents
CHILDREN OF COURAGE(1921, Brit.)

Viola Allen Frayne
Misc. Silents
JANE EYRE(1914)

Katy Fraysse
TARGET: HARRY(1980)

Robert Fraza
MYSTIC CIRCLE MURDER(1939)

Adrienne Frazan
BILLIE(1965), ed

Edmund Frazee
Misc. Silents
MRS. PLUM'S PUDDING(1915), d

Jane Frazee
MELODY AND MOONLIGHT(1940); ANGELS WITH BROKEN WINGS(1941); BUCK PRIVATES(1941); DON'T GET PERSONAL(1941); HELLZAPOPPIN'(1941); MOONLIGHT IN HAWAII(1941); SAN ANTONIO ROSE(1941); SING ANOTHER CHORUS(1941); ALMOST MARRIED(1942); GET HEP TO LOVE(1942); MOONLIGHT IN HAVANA(1942); MOONLIGHT MASQUERADE(1942); WHAT'S COOKIN'?(1942); HI'YA, CHUM(1943); KEEP 'EM SLUGGING(1943); RHYTHM OF THE ISLANDS(1943); WHEN JOHNNY COMES MARCHING HOME(1943); BEAUTIFUL BUT BROKE(1944); BIG BONANZA, THE(1944); COWBOY CANTEEN(1944); KANSAS CITY KITTY(1944); PRACTICALLY YOURS(1944); ROSIE THE RIVETER(1944); SHE'S A SWEETHEART(1944); SWING IN THE SADDLE(1944); SWINGIN' ON A RAINBOW(1945); TEN CENTS A DANCE(1945); GUY COULD CHANGE, A(1946); CALENDAR GIRL(1947); ON THE OLD SPANISH TRAIL(1947); SPRINGTIME IN THE SIERRAS(1947); GAY RANCHERO, THE(1948); GRAND CANYON TRAIL(1948); INCIDENT(1948); LAST OF THE WILD HORSES(1948); UNDER CALIFORNIA STARS(1948); RHYTHM INN(1951)

Logan Frazee
DEVIL'S BRIGADE, THE(1968), spec eff; LITTLE BIG MAN(1970), spec eff; SOMETHING BIG(1971), spec eff; PRIME CUT(1972), spec eff; TOWERING INFERNO, THE(1974), spec eff; FRENCH CONNECTION 11(1975), spec eff; FIRE SALE(1977), spec eff

Logan R. Frazee
WILLY WONKA AND THE CHOCOLATE FACTORY(1971), spec eff; TROUBLE MAN(1972), spec eff

Longan Frazee
CHINATOWN(1974), spec eff

Steve Frazee
MANY RIVERS TO CROSS(1955), w; RUNNING TARGET(1956), w; HIGH HELL(1958), w; WILD HERITAGE(1958), w; GOLD OF THE SEVEN SAINTS(1961), w

Stan Frazen
BLACK VEIL FOR LISA, A(1969 Ital./Ger.), ed

Stanley Frazen
APACHE CHIEF(1949), ed; OMOO OMOO, THE SHARK GOD(1949), ed; TREASURE OF MONTE CRISTO(1949), ed; MOTOR PATROL(1950), ed; GLASS WALL, THE(1953), ed; MAN-TRAP(1961), p; FRIDAY FOSTER(1975), ed; HYSTERICAL(1983), ed

Alex Frazer
BRUTE FORCE(1947); MOSS ROSE(1947); WEB, THE(1947); KIDNAPPED(1948); COWBOY AND THE INDIANS, THE(1949); BLONDE BANDIT, THE(1950); FANCY PANTS(1950); ROYAL WEDDING(1951); STRIP, THE(1951); LES MISERABLES(1952); GENTLEMEN PREFER BLONDES(1953); HANNAH LEE(1953); LOOSE IN LONDON(1953); SCANDAL AT SCOURIE(1953); WAR OF THE WORLDS, THE(1953); INTERRUPTED MELODY(1955); BIGGER THAN LIFE(1956); BOSS, THE(1956); MAN WHO KNEW TOO MUCH, THE(1956)

Bertrand Frazer
SANDERS OF THE RIVER(1935, Brit.)

Bob Frazer
NIGHT FOR CRIME, A(1942)

Connie Frazer
TOMCAT, THE(1968, Brit.)

Dan Frazer
LILIES OF THE FIELD(1963); LORD LOVE A DUCK(1966); COUNTERPOINT(1967); ...TICK...TICK...TICK...(1970); BANANAS(1971); FUZZ(1972); STOOLIE, THE(1972); CLEOPATRA JONES(1973); SUPER COPS, THE(1974)

Elizabeth Frazer
Silents
KENNEDY SQUARE(1916), w; KISS, THE(1916), w

Evelyn Frazer
FROZEN ALIVE(1966, Brit./Ger.), w

Harry Frazer
WINGS OF ADVENTURE(1930), w; FIGHTING PARSON, THE(1933), d

Harry L. Frazer
Misc. Silents
FIGHTING GOB, THE(1926), d; WILDCAT, THE(1926), d

Henrietta Frazer
SO THIS IS COLLEGE(1929), cos

Ian Frazer
ZORRO, THE GAY BLADE(1981), m&md

John Frazer
HONEYMOON LODGE(1943); WE'VE NEVER BEEN LICKED(1943)

June Frazer
GEORGE WHITE'S SCANDALS(1945); NIGHT IN PARADISE, A(1946)

Liz Frazer
I'M ALL RIGHT, JACK(1959, Brit.); CONFESSIONS FROM A HOLIDAY CAMP(1977, Brit.)

Moyra Frazer
DANCING YEARS, THE(1950, Brit.)

Nitra Frazer
Silents
MAN BEHIND THE DOOR, THE(1914)

Peter Frazer
ZEPPELIN(1971, Brit.)

Randy Frazer
1984
BROTHER FROM ANOTHER PLANET, THE(1984)

Robert Frazer
CAREERS(1929); DRAKE CASE, THE(1929); FROZEN JUSTICE(1929); TEN NIGHTS IN A BARROOM(1931); ARM OF THE LAW(1932); CROOKED CIRCLE(1932); DISCARDED LOVERS(1932); KING MURDER, THE(1932); RAINBOW TRAIL(1932); SADDLE BUSTER, THE(1932); WHITE ZOMBIE(1932); FIGHTING PARSON, THE(1933); JUSTICE TAKES A HOLIDAY(1933); VAMPIRE BAT, THE(1933); FIFTEEN WIVES(1934); FOUND ALIVE(1934); GREEN EYES(1934); GUILTY PARENTS(1934); MONTE CARLO NIGHTS(1934); NOTORIOUS BUT NICE(1934); TRAIL BEYOND, THE(1934); FIGHTING TROOPER, THE(1935); LADIES CRAVE EXCITEMENT(1935); MURDER MAN(1935); ONE IN A MILLION(1935); PUBLIC OPINION(1935); TRAILS OF THE WILD(1935); WORLD ACCUSES, THE(1935); BELOW THE DEADLINE(1936); DEATH FROM A DISTANCE(1936); GARDEN OF ALLAH, THE(1936); IT COULDN'T HAVE HAPPENED—BUT IT DID(1936); MURDER AT GLEN ATHOL(1936); LEFT-HANDED LAW(1937); VICE RACKET(1937); WE'RE IN THE LEGION NOW(1937); CIPHER BUREAU(1938); CRASHING THRU(1939); DAUGHTER OF THE TONG(1939); DISBARRED(1939); HOTEL IMPERIAL(1939); NAVY SECRETS(1939); RIDERS OF THE FRONTIER(1939); LOVE, HONOR AND OH, BABY(1940); MAD EMPRESS, THE(1940); ONE MAN'S LAW(1940); CRIMINALS WITHIN(1941); GANGS OF SONORA(1941); GUN MAN FROM BODIE, THE(1941); PALS OF THE PECOS(1941); ROAR OF THE PRESS(1941); BLACK DRAGONS(1942); CODE OF THE OUTLAW(1942); DAWN ON THE GREAT DIVIDE(1942); FLIGHT LIEUTENANT(1942); DEAD MAN'S GULCH(1943); STRANGER FROM PECOS, THE(1943); WAGON TRACKS WEST(1943); FORTY THIEVES(1944); LAW MEN(1944); PARTNERS OF THE TRAIL(1944)
Misc. Talkies
BEYOND THE LAW(1930); FIGHTING PILOT, THE(1935); NEVER TOO LATE(1935); GAMBLING WITH SOULS(1936)
Silents
BALLET GIRL, THE(1916); WITHOUT LIMIT(1921); AS A MAN LIVES(1923); JAZZMANIA(1923); AFTER THE BALL(1924); CHARMER, THE(1925); MISS BLUEBEARD(1925); SPLENDID ROAD, THE(1925); DAME CHANCE(1926); ISLE OF RETRIBUTION, THE(1926); ONE HOUR OF LOVE(1927); OUT OF THE PAST(1927); WANTED–A COWARD(1927); SCARLET DOVE, THE(1928); SIOUX BLOOD(1929)
Misc. Silents
LONE STAR RUSH, THE(1915); BOLSHEVISM ON TRIAL(1919); HER CODE OF HONOR(1919); LOVE, HATE AND A WOMAN(1921); FAITHLESS SEX, THE(1922); PARTNERS OF THE SUNSET(1922); WHEN THE DESERT CALLS(1922); LOVE PIKER, THE(1923); BREAD(1924); FOOLISH VIRGIN, THE(1924); MEN(1924); TRAFFIC IN HEARTS(1924); WHEN A MAN'S A MAN(1924); WOMEN WHO GIVE(1924); KEEPER OF THE BEES(1925); LOVE GAMBLE, THE(1925); OTHER WOMAN'S STORY, THE(1925); SCARLET WEST, THE(1925); WHITE DESERT, THE(1925); WHY WOMEN LOVE(1925); CITY, THE(1926); DESERT GOLD(1926); SECRET ORDERS(1926); SIN CARGO(1926); SPEEDING VENUS, THE(1926); BACK TO GOD'S COUNTRY(1927); SILENT HERO, THE(1927); BLACK BUTTERFLIES(1928); BURNING UP BROADWAY(1928); CITY OF PURPLE DREAMS(1928); OUT OF THE RUINS(1928); WOMAN I LOVE, THE(1929)

Robert W. Frazer
Misc. Silents
DAWN OF LOVE, THE(1916); DECOY, THE(1916)

Rupert Frazer
EYE OF THE NEEDLE(1981)

Ruth Frazer
FURY BELOW(1938)

Shelagh Frazer
WELCOME, MR. WASHINGTON(1944, Brit.); SECOND MRS. TANQUERAY, THE(1952, Brit.)

Walter Frazer
RIDERS OF THE WEST(1942)

William Frazer
SHERLOCK HOLMES' FATAL HOUR(1931, Brit.)

Cicely Frazer-Simpson
FATAL HOUR, THE(1937, Brit.), w

Frank Frazetta
FIRE AND ICE(1983), p, w

Holly Frazetta
FIRE AND ICE(1983)

Cliff Frazier
NORTH DALLAS FORTY(1979)
1984
CHATTANOOGA CHOO CHOO(1984)

clifford Frazier
VICE SQUAD(1982)

David O. Frazier
THOSE LIPS, THOSE EYES(1980)

Don Frazier
TAKE THE MONEY AND RUN(1969)

Dorothy Frazier
COAST TO COAST(1980)

Elvin Frazier
POLICE DOG STORY, THE(1961)

Gil Frazier
CROSS AND THE SWITCHBLADE, THE(1970)

Harry Frazier
MC CABE AND MRS. MILLER(1971); EAT MY DUST!(1976)

Joe Frazier
ROCKY(1976)

Kenny Frazier
HONEYSUCKLE ROSE(1980)

Loree Frazier
1984
TERMINATOR, THE(1984)

Robert Frazier
EASY MONEY(1936)
Misc. Silents
MR. POTTER OF TEXAS(1922); LIGHTING(1927); LITTLE SNOB, THE(1928)

Ron Frazier
HONKY TONK FREEWAY(1981); ROLLOVER(1981); WORLD ACCORDING TO GARP, The(1982)

Ronald C. Frazier
IT'S MY TURN(1980)

Sheila Frazier
SUPERFLY(1972); SUPERFLY T.N.T.(1973); THREE THE HARD WAY(1974); CALIFORNIA SUITE(1978); TWO OF A KIND(1983)
Misc. Talkies
HITTER, THE(1979)

Sheila E. Frazier
SUPER COPS, THE(1974)

Sterling Frazier
STARHOPS(1978)

Walt Frazier
AARON LOVES ANGELA(1975)

Gladys Frazin
RETURN OF THE RAT, THE(1929, Brit.); COMPULSORY HUSBAND, THE(1930, Brit.); KISS ME, SERGEANT(1930, Brit.); OTHER WOMAN, THE(1931, Brit.)
Misc. Talkies
BLUE PETER, THE(1928, Brit.); INSPIRATION(1928)

Sergio Frazzetto
MOUTH TO MOUTH(1978, Aus.)

Stephen Frears
GUMSHOE(1972, Brit.), d; LONG SHOT(1981, Brit.); BLOODY KIDS(1983, Brit.), d

Stan Freberg
CALLAWAY WENT THATAWAY(1951); GERALDINE(1953); LADY AND THE TRAMP(1955); TOM THUMB(1958, Brit./U.S.); IT'S A MAD, MAD, MAD, MAD WORLD(1963)
Misc. Talkies
LOONEY, LOONEY, LOONEY BUGS BUNNY MOVIE, THE(1981)

Gaston Freche
MURMUR OF THE HEART(1971, Fr./Ital./Ger.), m

Leila Frechet
CHANEL SOLITAIRE(1981); GIFT, THE(1983, Fr./Ital.)

Mark Frechette
ZABRISKIE POINT(1970)

Peter Frechette
GREASE 2(1982)
1984
NO SMALL AFFAIR(1984)

Nancy Frechtiling
HOMETOWN U.S.A.(1979), cos

Nancy Frechtling
VAN, THE(1977), makeup

Bernard Frechtman
GAME IS OVER, THE(1967, Fr.), w

Franklyn Fred
SECRET AGENT FIREBALL(1965, Fr./Ital.)

The Fred Keating Orchestra
TO BEAT THE BAND(1935)

Fred Parris and His Satins
SWEET BEAT(1962, Brit.)

Fred Waring and His Pennsylvanians
SYNCOPATION(1929); MELODY TIME(1948)

Fred Waring's Pennsylvanians
VARSITY SHOW(1937)

Bill Freda
FRIDAY THE 13TH(1980), ed; LOVE IN A TAXI(1980), ed

Fosca Freda
WANDERING JEW, THE(1948, Ital.)

Francesco Freda
TROJAN WOMEN, THE(1971), makeup

Franco Freda
NAKED MAJA, THE(1959, Ital./U.S.), makeup; RED DESERT(1965, Fr./Ital.), spec eff; NAVAJO JOE(1967, Ital./Span.), makeup; LISTEN, LET'S MAKE LOVE(1969, Fr./Ital.), makeup; PASSENGER, THE(1975, Ital.), makeup

Ricardo Freda
EXTERMINATORS, THE(1965 Fr.), d; ROMEO AND JULIET(1968, Ital./Span.), d&w

Riccardo Freda
RETURN OF THE BLACK EAGLE(1949, Ital.), d; DEVIL'S COMMANDMENT, THE(1956, Ital.), d; TRAPPED IN TANGIERS(1960, Ital./Span.), d, w; SAMSON AND THE SEVEN MIRACLES OF THE WORLD(1963, Fr./Ital.), d; WITCH'S CURSE, THE(1963, Ital.), d; MONGOLS, THE(1966, Fr./Ital.), d

William Freda
SPEED LOVERS(1968), ed

Lottie Freddie
NIGHT VISITOR, THE(1970, Swed./U.S.)

Freddie and The Dreamers
WHAT A CRAZY WORLD(1963, Brit.); CUCKOO PATROL(1965, Brit.); SEASIDE SWINGERS(1965, Brit.); OUT OF SIGHT(1966)

Freddie Bell and the Bell Boys
GET YOURSELF A COLLEGE GIRL(1964)

Freddie Fisher and His Schnickelfritz Band
JAMBOREE(1944)

Freddie Fisher Band
SEVEN DAYS ASHORE(1944)

Freddie Rich and Orchestra
WAVE, A WAC AND A MARINE, A(1944)

Freddie Slack and His Orchestra
REVEILLE WITH BEVERLY(1943); SKY'S THE LIMIT, THE(1943); HAT CHECK HONEY(1944)

Freddie Slack and Orchestra
SEVEN DAYS ASHORE(1944)
Freddie Slack Orchestra
HIGH SCHOOL HERO(1946)
The Freddie Slack Orchestra
BABES ON SWING STREET(1944)
Freddy Bell and his Bellboys
RUMBLE ON THE DOCKS(1956)
Freddy Fisher and His Orchestra
SULTAN'S DAUGHTER, THE(1943)
Freddy Martin & His Orchestra
SENIOR PROM(1958)
Freddy Martin and His Orchestra
SEVEN DAYS LEAVE(1942); STAGE DOOR CANTEEN(1943); MELODY TIME(1948)
Freddy Martin and His Orchestra
HIT PARADE OF 1943(1943)
The Freddy Martin Orchestra
MAYOR OF 44TH STREET, THE(1942)
Freddy Martin's Orchestra
WHAT'S BUZZIN COUSIN?(1943)
Serge Freddykarll
Silents
NAPOLEON(1927, Fr.)
Richard Frede
INTERNS, THE(1962), w; NEW INTERNS, THE(1964), w
Clifton Tip Fredell
DUSTY AND SWEETS McGEE(1971)
Claud Frederic
WARNING TO WANTONS, A(1949, Brit.)
Marc Frederic
FRANKENSTEIN'S DAUGHTER(1958), p; MISSILE TO THE MOON(1959), p; GIRL IN ROOM 13(1961, U.S./Braz.), p; TWO FOR THE ROAD(1967, Brit.), art d
Norman Frederic
GUN FEVER(1958); LONE RANGER AND THE LOST CITY OF GOLD, THE(1958)
Pauline Frederic
Silents
SPIDER, THE(1916)
Serge Frederic
TOMORROW IS MY TURN(1962, Fr./Ital./Ger.)
William Frederic
Silents
PURSUING VENGEANCE, THE(1916); PEACOCK ALLEY(1922)
Misc. Silents
RICHARD THE BRAZEN(1917); COINCIDENCE(1921)
Blanche Frederici
AWFUL TRUTH, THE(1929); JAZZ HEAVEN(1929); TRESPASSER, THE(1929); WONDER OF WOMEN(1929); BAD ONE, THE(1930); BILLY THE KID(1930); CAT CREEPS, THE(1930); KISMET(1930); LAST OF THE DUANES(1930); NUMBERED MEN(1930); OFFICE WIFE, THE(1930); PERSONALITY(1930); SOLDIERS AND WOMEN(1930); HONOR OF THE FAMILY(1931); MATA HARI(1931); MURDER BY THE CLOCK(1931); NIGHT NURSE(1931); TEN CENTS A DANCE(1931); WICKED(1931); WOMAN BETWEEN(1931); WOMAN HUNGRY(1931); FAREWELL TO ARMS, A(1932); HATCHET MAN, THE(1932); IF I HAD A MILLION(1932); LADY WITH A PAST(1932); LOVE ME TONIGHT(1932); MISS PINKERTON(1932); NIGHT CLUB LADY(1932); SO BIG(1932); THIRTEEN WOMEN(1932); THREE ON A MATCH(1932); YOUNG BRIDE(1932); ADORABLE(1933); ALIMONY MADNESS(1933); BARBARIAN, THE(1933); BEHIND JURY DOORS(1933, Brit.); FLYING DOWN TO RIO(1933); MAN OF THE FOREST(1933); SECRETS(1933); WAY TO LOVE, THE(1933); ALL OF ME(1934); IT HAPPENED ONE NIGHT(1934); THUNDERING HERD, THE(1934)
Silents
NO TRESPASSING(1922); GENTLEMEN PREFER BLONDES(1928); SADIE THOMPSON(1928)
Frederick
PRIVATE LIVES OF ADAM AND EVE, THE(1961), cos; EGLANTINE(1972, Fr.)
Ann Frederick
LUCK OF THE IRISH(1948)
Barbara Frederick
LOVER COME BACK(1961)
Brian Jay Frederick
YOUNG GIANTS(1983)
Cecil Frederick
HAPPIDROME(1943, Brit.)
Christopher Frederick
RAIDERS OF THE LOST ARK(1981)
Freddie Burke Frederick
EVIDENCE(1929); WALL STREET(1929); JAZZ CINDERELLA(1930); LADIES LOVE BRUTES(1930); SECOND WIFE(1930)
Misc. Talkies
SPY, THE(1931)
Silents
CROWD, THE(1928)
Freddie Frederick
IRON MASTER, THE(1933)
Silents
FANGS OF JUSTICE(1926); MARRY THE GIRL(1928); NEW YEAR'S EVE(1929)
Geoffrey Frederick
HELL IS A CITY(1960, Brit.); MAN AT THE CARLTON TOWER(1961, Brit.); SQUADRON 633(1964, U.S./Brit.); 633 SQUADRON(1964); BUNNY LAKE IS MISSING(1965); JIG SAW(1965, Brit.); HOT MILLIONS(1968, Brit.); NOTHING BUT THE NIGHT(1975, Brit.)
Hal Frederick
TWO GENTLEMEN SHARING(1969, Brit.)
Misc. Talkies
FOUR AGAINST THE DESERT(1979)
Harlow G. Frederick
YELLOWNECK(1955), p
Jane Frederick
PERSONAL BEST(1982)

Jerome Frederick
GHASTLY ONES, THE(1968), p
Jesse Frederick
1984
LAST HORROR FILM, THE(1984), m
John Frederick
CORVETTE K-225(1943); GUY NAMED JOE, A(1943); SHOES OF THE FISHERMAN, THE(1968); ONCE UPON A TIME IN THE WEST(1969, U.S./Ital.); ADVENTURERS, THE(1970); PUSSYCAT, PUSSYCAT, I LOVE YOU(1970); JENNIFER ON MY MIND(1971); STATUE, THE(1971, Brit.); DUCK, YOU SUCKER!(1972, Ital.)
Lee Frederick
THEY WON'T BELIEVE ME(1947); IT'S A WONDERFUL LIFE(1946); NOCTURNE(1946); DESPERATE(1947); WOMAN HUNT(1962)
Leon Frederick
ALEX IN WONDERLAND(1970)
Lynne Frederick
NICHOLAS AND ALEXANDRA(1971, Brit.); NO BLADE OF GRASS(1970, Brit.); HENRY VIII AND HIS SIX WIVES(1972, Brit.); VAMPIRE CIRCUS(1972, Brit.); AMAZING MR. BLUNDEN, THE(1973, Brit.); PHASE IV(1974); VOYAGE OF THE DAMNED(1976, Brit.); SCHIZO(1977, Brit.); PRISONER OF ZENDA, THE(1979)
Marc Frederick
CAREER GIRL(1960), p
Pauline Frederick
ON TRIAL(1928); EVIDENCE(1929); SACRED FLAME, THE(1929); THIS MODERN AGE(1931); PHANTOM OF CRESTWOOD, THE(1932); WAYWARD(1932); MY MOTHER(1933); SOCIAL REGISTER(1934); MY MARRIAGE(1936); RAMONA(1936); THANK YOU, MR. MOTO(1937)
Misc. Talkies
SELF DEFENSE(1933)
Silents
ETERNAL CITY, THE(1915); SOLD(1915); ASHES OF EMBERS(1916); AUDREY(1916); NANETTE OF THE WILDS(1916); OUT OF THE SHADOW(1919); MISTRESS OF SHENSTONE, THE(1921); SALVAGE(1921); STING OF THE LASH(1921); MARRIED FLIRTS(1924); JOSSELYN'S WIFE(1926); MUMSIE(1927, Brit.); NEST, THE(1927)
Misc. Silents
BELLA DONNA(1915); LYDIA GILMORE(1916); MOMENT BEFORE, THE(1916); WOMAN IN THE CASE, A(1916); WORLD'S GREAT SNARE, THE(1916); DOUBLE CROSSED(1917); HER BETTER SELF(1917); HUNGRY HEART, THE(1917); LOVE THAT LIVES, THE(1917); SAPHO(1917); SLAVE MARKET, THE(1917); SLEEPING FIRES(1917); DAUGHTER OF THE OLD SOUTH, A(1918); FEDORA(1918); HER FINAL RECKONING(1918); LA TOSCA(1918); MADAME JEALOUSY(1918); MRS. DANE'S DEFENSE(1918); RESURRECTION(1918); BONDS OF LOVE(1919); FEAR WOMAN, THE(1919); ONE WEEK OF LIFE(1919); PAID IN FULL(1919); PEACE OF ROARING RIVER, THE(1919); WOMAN ON THE INDEX, THE(1919); LOVES OF LETTY, THE(1920); MADAME X(1920); PALISER CASE, THE(1920); SLAVE OF VANITY, A(1920); WOMAN IN ROOM 13, THE(1920); LURE OF JADE, THE(1921); ROADS OF DESTINY(1921); GLORY OF CLEMENTINA, THE(1922); TWO KINDS OF WOMEN(1922); WOMAN BREED, THE(1922); LET NO MAN PUT ASUNDER(1924); THREE WOMEN(1924); SMOULDERING FIRES(1925); DEVIL'S ISLAND(1926); HER HONOR THE GOVERNOR(1926)
Scott Frederick
1984
CAL(1984, Ireland)
Vicki Frederick
COAST TO COAST(1980); ...ALL THE MARBLES(1981)
1984
BODY ROCK(1984)
William Frederick
Silents
PRINCE AND THE PAUPER, THE(1915); NEVER SAY QUIT(1919)
Misc. Silents
COMMON SENSE BRACKETT(1916)
Frederick's of Hollywood
WHAT'S UP FRONT(1964), cos
Adam Fredericks
1984
FIRST TURN-ON!, THE(1984), ed
Ann Fredericks
PLACE IN THE SUN, A(1951)
Arnold Fredericks
Silents
ONE MILLION DOLLARS(1915), w
Beverly Fredericks
FANDANGO(1970)
Brad Fredericks
SONG OF THE LOON(1970)
Carl Fredericks
MADMAN(1982)
Cecil Fredericks
HOME SWEET HOME(1945, Brit.)
Charles E. Fredericks
HOUSE IS NOT A HOME, A(1964)
Charles Fredericks
THUNDER PASS(1954); LAS VEGAS SHAKEDOWN(1955); NIGHT FREIGHT(1955); PORT OF HELL(1955); TARZAN'S HIDDEN JUNGLE(1955); TREASURE OF RUBY HILLS(1955); HELL CANYON OUTLAWS(1957); TENDER IS THE NIGHT(1961); ADVENTURES OF A YOUNG MAN(1962); CABINET OF CALIGARI, THE(1962); LAD: A DOG(1962); TO KILL A MOCKINGBIRD(1962); MY FAIR LADY(1964); GREAT RACE, THE(1965)
Dean Fredericks
PHANTOM PLANET, THE(1961); WILD HARVEST(1962); SAVAGE SAM(1963)
Eleanor Fredericks
LOCKED DOOR, THE(1929)
Ellsworth Fredericks
SO BIG(1953), ph; SEVEN ANGRY MEN(1955), ph; SHOTGUN(1955), ph; SUDDEN DANGER(1955), ph; FRIENDLY PERSUASION(1956), ph; INVASION OF THE BODY SNATCHERS(1956), ph; BUCKSKIN LADY, THE(1957), ph; TROOPER HOOK(1957), ph; LIGHT IN THE FOREST, THE(1958), ph; HIGH TIME(1960), ph; TALL STORY(1960), ph; LAST CHALLENGE, THE(1967), ph; WHERE WERE YOU WHEN THE

LIGHTS WENT OUT?(1968), ph; CHARRO(1969), ph
Harry Fredericks
Misc. Silents
WORLD OF TODAY, THE(1915)
Larry Fredericks
RACHEL, RACHEL(1968)
Lee Fredericks
SUN SETS AT DAWN, THE(1950)
Malcolm Fredericks
BURNING AN ILLUSION(1982, Brit.)
Marc Fredericks
SEEDS OF EVIL(1981), m
Peter Fredericks
THEY MIGHT BE GIANTS(1971)
Randy Fredericks
HALLS OF ANGER(1970)
Scott Fredericks
SEE NO EVIL(1971, Brit.); DEADLY FEMALES, THE(1976, Brit.)
William Fredericks
Silents
JOAN OF PLATTSBURG(1918)
Misc. Silents
SCRAP OF PAPER, THE(1920); WOMAN GOD SENT, THE(1920)
Gary Frederickson
GODFATHER, THE, PART II(1974), p
Gray Frederickson
1941(1979); ONE FROM THE HEART(1982), p; OUTSIDERS, THE(1983), p
Lynne Frederickson
GREEN SLIME, THE(1969)
Francoise Javet Frederix
1984
PAR OU T'ES RENTRE? ON T'A PAS VUE SORTIR(1984, Fr./Tunisia), ed
Marc Frederix
SERGEANT, THE(1968), art d; IF IT'S TUESDAY, THIS MUST BE BELGIUM(1969), art d; FRIENDS(1971, Brit.), art d; SOMEONE BEHIND THE DOOR(1971, Fr./Brit.), art d; CONDORMAN(1981), art d; ENIGMA(1983), art d
1984
AMERICAN DREAMER(1984), art d
Brigitte Fredersdorf
PUSS 'N' BOOTS(1967, Ger.)
Christian Fredersdorf
CARMEN, BABY(1967, Yugo./Ger.)
Herbert B. Fredersdorf
LONG IS THE ROAD(1948, Ger.), d; RUMPELSTILTSKIN(1965, Ger.), d; PUSS 'N' BOOTS(1967, Ger.), d
Donald P. Fredette
GUNS AND THE FURY, THE(1983), w
Paolo Frediani
CALIFORNIA SUITE(1978)
M. Fredkin
FAREWELL, DOVES(1962, USSR), m
Beatrice Fredman
FOUR FRIENDS(1981)
Norman Fredric
DISEMBODIED, THE(1957); ESCAPE FROM SAN QUENTIN(1957); UTAH BLAINE(1957); LIGHT IN THE FOREST, THE(1958)
Ann Fredrick
YOU WERE MEANT FOR ME(1948)
Geoffrey Fredrick
LISA(1962, Brit.)
Ellsworth Fredricks
PAD, THE(AND HOW TO USE IT)* (1966, Brit.), ph; BOB MATHIAS STORY, THE(1954), ph; AT GUNPOINT(1955), ph; DIAL RED O(1955), ph; CANYON RIVER(1956), ph; HOLD BACK THE NIGHT(1956), ph; WORLD WITHOUT END(1956), ph; YOUNG GUNS, THE(1956), ph; LAST OF THE BADMEN(1957), ph; SAYONARA(1957), ph; MARACAIBO(1958), ph; WILD RIVER(1960), ph; SANCTUARY(1961), ph; ESCAPE FROM ZAHRAIN(1962), ph; STRIPPER, THE(1963), ph; SEVEN DAYS IN MAY(1964), ph; YOUNG LOVERS, THE(1964), ph; JOY IN THE MORNING(1965), ph; MISTER BUDDWING(1966), ph; PICTURE MOMMY DEAD(1966), ph; POWER, THE(1968), ph; WITH SIX YOU GET EGGROLL(1968), ph; EYE OF THE CAT(1969), ph
Colin Fredricksen
SMASH PALACE(1982, New Zealand)
Olive Fredrickson
SILENCE OF THE NORTH(1981, Can.), w
Karen Fredrik
SUNSET COVE(1978)
Lars Fredriksen
GRAND THEFT AUTO(1977)
Marc Fredrix
THOSE DARING YOUNG MEN IN THEIR JAUNTY JALOPIES(1969, Fr./Brit./Ital.), art d
Bill Free
LAST DAYS OF BOOT HILL(1947); NIGHTMARE ALLEY(1947)
Stan Free
MOONLIGHTING WIVES(1966), m; MY BODY HUNGERS(1967), m
Colin Freear
ESCAPADE(1955, Brit.)
Ian Freebairn-Smith
VOICE OF THE HURRICANE(1964), m, md; STRAWBERRY STATEMENT, THE(1970), m; HAZING, THE(1978), m
Ian FreebairnSmith
DREAMS OF GLASS(1969), m
Freeborn
SUPERMAN III(1983), makeup
Denise Freeborn
SEARCH FOR BRIDEY MURPHY, THE(1956)

Graham Freeborn
SUPERMAN(1978), makeup; KEEP, THE(1983), makeup; RETURN OF THE JEDI(1983), makeup
Kay Freeborn
SUPERMAN(1978), makeup
Mark Freeborn
NOTHING PERSONAL(1980, Can.), set d; PORKY'S(1982), set d
Stewart Freeborn
KIDNAPPED(1960), makeup; DR. STRANGELOVE: OR HOW I LEARNED TO STOP WORRYING AND LOVE THE BOMB(1964), makeup
Stuart Freeborn
FOXHOLE IN CAIRO(1960, Brit.), makeup; I LIKE MONEY(1962, Brit.), makeup; TARZAN GOES TO INDIA(1962, U.S./Brit./Switz.), makeup; WALTZ OF THE TOREADORS(1962, Brit.), makeup; HEAVENS ABOVE!(1963, Brit.), makeup; SEANCE ON A WET AFTERNOON(1964 Brit.), makeup; THOSE MAGNIFICENT MEN IN THEIR FLYING MACHINES; OR HOW I FLEWFROM LONDON TO PARIS IN 25 HOURS AND 11 MINUTES(1965, Brit.), makeup; 2001: A SPACE ODYSSEY(1968, U.S./Brit.), makeup; OH! WHAT A LOVELY WAR(1969, Brit.), makeup; SEE NO EVIL(1971, Brit.), makeup; 10 RILLINGTON PLACE(1971, Brit.), makeup; YOUNG WINSTON(1972, Brit.), makeup; OMEN, THE(1976), makeup; STAR WARS(1977), makeup; SUPERMAN II(1980), makeup; RETURN OF THE JEDI(1983), spec eff
Alan Freed
DON'T KNOCK THE ROCK(1956); ROCK AROUND THE CLOCK(1956); ROCK, ROCK, ROCK!(1956); MISTER ROCK AND ROLL(1957); GO, JOHNNY, GO!(1959), a, p
Arnold Freed
WEREWOLF OF WASHINGTON(1973), m
Arthur Freed
PAGAN, THE(1929), m; THOSE THREE FRENCH GIRLS(1930), w; PRODIGAL, THE(1931), m; BABES IN ARMS(1939), p; LITTLE NELLIE KELLY(1940), p; STRIKE UP THE BAND(1940), p; BABES ON BROADWAY(1941), p; LADY BE GOOD(1941), p; FOR ME AND MY GAL(1942), p; PANAMA HATTIE(1942), p; BEST FOOT FORWARD(1943), p; CABIN IN THE SKY(1943), p; DU BARRY WAS A LADY(1943), p; GIRL CRAZY(1943), p; MEET ME IN ST. LOUIS(1944), p; CLOCK, THE(1945), p; YOLANDA AND THE THIEF(1945), p; ZIEGFELD FOLLIES(1945), p; HARVEY GIRLS, THE(1946), p; TILL THE CLOUDS ROLL BY(1946), p; GOOD NEWS(1947), p; EASTER PARADE(1948), p; PIRATE, THE(1948), p; SUMMER HOLIDAY(1948), p; ANY NUMBER CAN PLAY(1949), p; BARKLEYS OF BROADWAY, THE(1949), p; ON THE TOWN(1949), p; TAKE ME OUT TO THE BALL GAME(1949), p; ANNIE GET YOUR GUN(1950), p; CRISIS(1950), p; PAGAN LOVE SONG(1950), p; AMERICAN IN PARIS, AN(1951), p; ROYAL WEDDING(1951), p; SHOW BOAT(1951), p; BELLE OF NEW YORK, THE(1952), p; SINGIN' IN THE RAIN(1952), p; BAND WAGON, THE(1953), p; BRIGADOON(1954), p; IT'S ALWAYS FAIR WEATHER(1955), p; KISMET(1955), p; INVITATION TO THE DANCE(1956), p; SILK STOCKINGS(1957), p; GIGI(1958), p; BELLS ARE RINGING(1960), p; SUBTERRANEANS, THE(1960), p; LIGHT IN THE PIAZZA(1962), p
Bert Freed
BOOMERANG(1947); BLACK HAND, THE(1950); COMPANY SHE KEEPS, THE(1950); KEY TO THE CITY(1950); MA AND PA KETTLE GO TO TOWN(1950); NO WAY OUT(1950); WHERE THE SIDEWALK ENDS(1950); 711 OCEAN DRIVE(1950); DETECTIVE STORY(1951); HALLS OF MONTEZUMA(1951); RED MOUNTAIN(1951); ATOMIC CITY, THE(1952); SNOWS OF KILIMANJARO, THE(1952); TAKE THE HIGH GROUND(1953); TANGIER INCIDENT(1953); LONG, LONG TRAILER, THE(1954); MEN OF THE FIGHTING LADY(1954); COBWEB, THE(1955); DESPERATE HOURS, THE(1955); PATHS OF GLORY(1957); GODDESS, THE(1958); GAZEBO, THE(1959); SUBTERRANEANS, THE(1960); WHY MUST I DIE?(1960); WHATEVER HAPPENED TO BABY JANE?(1962); TWILIGHT OF HONOR(1963); FATE IS THE HUNTER(1964); INVITATION TO A GUNFIGHTER(1964); SHOCK TREATMENT(1964); NEVADA SMITH(1966); SWINGER, THE(1966); HANG'EM HIGH(1968); MADIGAN(1968); P.J.(1968); WILD IN THE STREETS(1968); THERE WAS A CROOKED MAN(1970); BILLY JACK(1971); EVEL KNIEVEL(1971); BARRACUDA(1978); LOVE AND THE MIDNIGHT AUTO SUPPLY(1978); TILL DEATH(1978); NORMA RAE(1979)
Bill Freed
THEY SAVED HITLER'S BRAIN(1964)
Donald Freed
ON THE THRESHOLD OF SPACE(1956); EXECUTIVE ACTION(1973), w
1984
SECRET HONOR(1984), w
Fred Freed
MY SEVEN LITTLE SINS(1956, Fr./Ital.), m
Gordon Freed
MACHISMO–40 GRAVES FOR 40 GUNS(1970), makeup
Herb Freed
HAUNTS(1977), p, d, w; BEYOND EVIL(1980), p, d, w; GRADUATION DAY(1981), p, d, w
Misc. Talkies
AWOL(1973), d
Josh Freed
TICKET TO HEAVEN(1981), a, w
Lazar Freed
ELI ELI(1940); OVERTURE TO GLORY(1940)
Misc. Talkies
LOVE AND SACRIFICE(1936); JEWISH MELODY, THE(1940)
Misc. Silents
SALOME OF THE TENEMENTS(1925)
Martin Freed
VIOLATORS, THE(1957)
Matt Freed
NO ESCAPE(1953), p
Ralph Freed
UNDER-PUP, THE(1939), m
Reuben Freed
TRIBUTE(1980, Can.), art d; BLOOD AND GUTS(1978, Can.), art d; CHANGELING, THE(1980, Can.), art d; PROM NIGHT(1980), art d; HIGH COUNTRY, THE(1981, Can.), art d; PORKY'S(1982), prod d
Sam Freed, Jr.
BABES ON SWING STREET(1944), m; MURDER IN THE BLUE ROOM(1944), md; RECKLESS AGE(1944), md; SINGING SHERIFF(1944), md; SOUTH OF DIXIE(1944), md

Stan Freed
MR. BUG GOES TO TOWN(1941)
George Freedland
HEART OF A NATION, THE(1943, Fr.), ed; MOONWOLF(1966, Fin./Ger.), d
Geprge Freedland
MOONWOLF(1966, Fin./Ger.), w
Thornton Freedland
SECRET WITNESS, THE(1931), d
Sam C. Freedle
GUN THE MAN DOWN(1957), w; GUN STREET(1962), w
Eugene Freedley
SUMMER STOCK(1950)
Vinton Freedley
STAGE DOOR CANTEEN(1943)
Ben Freedman
LAST OF THE RED HOT LOVERS(1972); SAVE THE TIGER(1973)
Benedict Freedman
MRS. MIKE(1949), w; ATOMIC KID, THE(1954), w; JAGUAR(1956), w; EVERY-THING'S DUCKY(1961), w
Danny Freedman
FORTUNE AND MEN'S EYES(1971, U.S./Can.); ONE MAN(1979, Can.)
David Freedman
PALMY DAYS(1931), w; HEART OF NEW YORK(1932), w; NEW FACES OF 1937(1937), w; ZIEGFELD FOLLIES(1945), w
Harry Freedman
BLOODY BROOD, THE(1959, Can.), m; ISABEL(1968, Can.), m; ACT OF THE HEART(1970, Can.), m; PYX, THE(1973, Can.), m
Herman Freedman
MOVIE STAR, AMERICAN STYLE, OR, LSD I HATE YOU!(1966), ed; ON HER BED OF ROSES(1966), ed; CATALINA CAPER, THE(1967), ed; CYCLE SAVAGES(1969), ed; DOBERMAN GANG, THE(1972), ed
Irving Freedman
HEARTACHES(1947), md
Jerrold Freedman
KANSAS CITY BOMBER(1972), d; BORDERLINE(1980), d, w
Milt Freedman
HISTORY OF THE WORLD, PART 1(1981)
Nancy Freedman
MRS. MIKE(1949), w
Paul Freedman
HESTER STREET(1975)
Ralph Freedman
JOHNNY O'CLOCK(1947)
Robert Freedman
Misc. Talkies
GOIN' ALL THE WAY(1982), d
Winifred Freedman
LAST AMERICAN VIRGIN, THE(1982)
Thornton Freeland
THREE LIVE GHOSTS(1929), d; BE YOURSELF(1930), d, w; WHOOPEE(1930), d; SIX CYLINDER LOVE(1931), d; LOVE AFFAIR(1932), d; THEY CALL IT SIN(1932), d; UNEXPECTED FATHER(1932), d; WEEK-END MARRIAGE(1932), d; FLYING DOWN TO RIO(1933), d; GEORGE WHITE'S SCANDALS(1934), d; BREWSTER'S MILLIONS(1935, Brit.), d; AMATEUR GENTLEMAN(1936, Brit.), d; SKY-LARKS(1936, Brit.), d; DARK SANDS(1938, Brit.), d; GAIETY GIRLS, THE(1938, Brit.), d; HOLD MY HAND(1938, Brit.), w; OVER THE MOON(1940, Brit.), d; SO THIS IS LONDON(1940, Brit.), d; TOO MANY BLONDES(1941), d; AMAZING MR. FOR-REST, THE(1943, Brit.), d; MEET ME AT DAWN(1947, Brit.), d; DEAR MR. PRO-HACK(1949, Brit.), d; LUCKY MASCOT, THE(1951, Brit.), d, w
Thorton Freeland
ACCUSED(1936, Brit.), d; MARRY THE BOSS' DAUGHTER(1941), d
I. Freeling
MY DREAM IS YOURS(1949), anim d
Nicolas Freeling
AMSTERDAM AFFAIR, THE(1968 Brit.), w
Aaron Freeman
THINGS ARE TOUGH ALL OVER(1982)
1984
TEACHERS(1984)
Adolph Freeman
SEARCHING WIND, THE(1946)
Al Freeman
FOREVER AND A DAY(1943), art d; CLOWN, THE(1953); THIS REBEL BREED(1960)
Al Freeman, Jr.
ENSIGN PULVER(1964); TROUBLEMAKER, THE(1964); DUTCHMAN(1966, Brit.); FOR PETE'S SAKE!(1966); DETECTIVE, THE(1968); FINIAN'S RAINBOW(1968); CASTLE KEEP(1969); LOST MAN, THE(1969); FABLE, A(1971), a, d; COUNTDOWN AT KUSINI(1976, Nigerian), w
Alan Freeman
RING-A-DING RHYTHM(1962, Brit. 73m Amicus/COL bw (G.B: IT'S TRAD, DAD!); JUST FOR FUN(1963, Brit.); DR. TERROR'S HOUSE OF HORRORS(1965, Brit.); SEBASTIAN(1968, Brit.)
Albert C. Freeman, Jr.
SNIPER'S RIDGE(1961)
Alvin Freeman
RIDING SHOTGUN(1954)
Anthony Freeman
STRANGER RETURNS, THE(1968, U.S./Ital./Ger./Span.)
Arny Freeman
PHFFFT!(1954); WHAT'S SO BAD ABOUT FEELING GOOD?(1968); POPI(1969); VALACHI PAPERS, THE(1972, Ital./Fr.); SUPER COPS, THE(1974)
Audrey Freeman
IS YOUR HONEYMOON REALLY NECESSARY?(1953, Brit.)
Barbara Freeman
STARK FEAR(1963)
Misc. Talkies
EVERYDAY(1976)

Bea Freeman
TEMPTATION(1936)
Bee Freeman
UNDERWORLD(1937)
Bill Freeman
BASKET CASE(1982)
Bob Freeman
TRADER HORNEE(1970), ed
C. Denis Freeman
GAY LADY, THE(1949, Brit.), w; HONEYMOON DEFERRED(1951, Brit.), w; LUCKY MASCOT, THE(1951, Brit.), w
Capt. Charles L. Freeman , Navy/ret.
OPERATION BIKINI(1963), tech adv
Charles D. Freeman
HONOLULU LU(1941)
Christine Freeman
JAWS II(1978)
Clair Freeman
NORTH STAR, THE(1943); FOLLOW THE BOYS(1944)
Damita Jo Freeman
PRIVATE BENJAMIN(1980)
Dave Freeman
PLANK, THE(1967, Brit.); THOSE FANTASTIC FLYING FOOLS(1967, Brit), w; MAGNIFICENT SEVEN DEADLY SINS, THE(1971, Brit.), w
David Freeman
FIRST LOVE(1977), w; BORDER, THE(1982), w
Davis Freeman [David Friedman]
SCUM OF THE EARTH(1963), p
Denis Freeman
STAR OF INDIA(1956, Brit.), w; ACROSS THE BRIDGE(1957, Brit.), w
Dennis Freeman
QUESTION OF ADULTERY, A(1959, Brit.), w; NATIONAL LAMPOON'S VACA-TION(1983)
Derek Freeman
Misc. Talkies
CARRINGTON SCHOOL MYSTERY, THE(1958, Brit.)
Devery Freeman
MAIN STREET LAWYER(1939), w; ZIEGFELD FOLLIES(1945), w; THRILL OF BRAZIL, THE(1946), w; GUILT OF JANET AMES(1947), w; FULLER BRUSH MAN(1948), w; KISS IN THE DARK, A(1949), w; MISS GRANT TAKES RICH-MOND(1949), w; TELL IT TO THE JUDGE(1949), w; BORDERLINE(1950), w; WATCH THE BIRDIE(1950), w; YELLOW CAB MAN, THE(1950), w; DEAR BRAT(1951), w; THREE SAILORS AND A GIRL(1953), w; FRANCIS JOINS THE WACS(1954), w; AIN'T MISBEHAVIN'(1955), w; FRANCIS IN THE NAVY(1955), w; DANCE WITH ME, HENRY(1956), w; FIRST TRAVELING SALESLADY, THE(1956), w; GIRL MOST LIKELY, THE(1957), w; PUBLIC PIGEON NO. 1(1957), w; TAPS(1981), w
Dink Freeman
SING FOR YOUR SUPPER(1941); MICKEY ONE(1965)
Douglas Freeman
AMERICAN GRAFFITI(1973), set d
Dusty Freeman
SEPIA CINDERELLA(1947)
Eric Freeman
GEORGE WHITE'S SCANDALS(1945); DO YOU LOVE ME?(1946)
Ernie Freeman
COOL ONES THE(1967), m; DOUBLE MAN, THE(1967), m; WHAT AM I BID?(1967), md; DUFFY(1968, Brit.), m; PINK JUNGLE, THE(1968), m
Everett Freeman
$1,000 A MINUTE(1935), w; MARRIED BEFORE BREAKFAST(1937), w; CHASER, THE(1938), w; YOU CAN'T CHEAT AN HONEST MAN(1939), w; GEORGE WASH-INGTON SLEPT HERE(1942), w; LARCENY, INC.(1942), w; THANK YOUR LUCKY STARS(1943), w; PRINCESS AND THE PIRATE, THE(1944), w; ZIEGFELD FOL-LIES(1945), w; IT HAPPENED ON 5TH AVENUE(1947), w; SECRET LIFE OF WALTER MITTY, THE(1947), w; LULU BELLE(1948), w; KISS IN THE DARK, A(1949), w; LADY TAKES A SAILOR, THE(1949), w; MISS GRANT TAKES RICH-MOND(1949), w; PRETTY BABY(1950), w; JIM THORPE–ALL AMERICAN(1951), w; TOO YOUNG TO KISS(1951), w; MILLION DOLLAR MERMAID(1952), w; DESTI-NATION GOBI(1953), w; KELLY AND ME(1957), w; MY MAN GODFREY(1957), w; MARJORIE MORNINGSTAR(1958), w; SUNDAY IN NEW YORK(1963), p; GLASS BOTTOM BOAT, THE(1966), p, w; WHERE WERE YOU WHEN THE LIGHTS WENT OUT?(1968), p, w; MALTESE BIPPY, THE(1969), p, w; HOW DO I LOVE THEE?(1970), p, w; ZIGZAG(1970), p
Frank Freeman, Jr.
WAR OF THE WORLDS, THE(1953); OMAR KHAYYAM(1957), p; HANGMAN, THE(1959), p
Fred Freeman
START THE REVOLUTION WITHOUT ME(1970), w; S(1974), w; BIG BUS, THE(1976), p&w
Gillian Freeman
LEATHER BOYS, THE(1965, Brit.), w; GIRL ON A MOTORCYCLE, THE(1968, Fr./Brit.), w; THAT COLD DAY IN THE PARK(1969, U.S./Can.), w; I WANT WHAT I WANT(1972, Brit.), w
Glen Freeman
CINDERELLA LIBERTY(1973)
Helen Freeman
ABRAHAM LINCOLN(1930); SYMPHONY OF SIX MILLION(1932); CHANCE AT HEAVEN(1933); DR. BULL(1933); HOLD YOUR MAN(1933); RIGHT TO ROMAN-CE(1933); SONG OF SONGS(1933); FASHIONS OF 1934(1934); FINISHING SCHOOL(1934); FOG(1934); NANA(1934); STAMBOUL QUEST(1934); AH, WILDER-NESS!(1935); DOUBTING THOMAS(1935); BULLDOG DRUMMOND COMES BACK(1937); SAFETY IN NUMBERS(1938); GHOST AND MRS. MUIR, THE(1942); HEAVENLY BODY, THE(1943); MADEMOISELLE FIFI(1944); MRS. PARKING-TON(1944); OUR HEARTS WERE YOUNG AND GAY(1944); DON JUAN QUIL-LIGAN(1945); SARATOGA TRUNK(1945); MONSIEUR BEAUCAIRE(1946); SO DARK THE NIGHT(1946); UNKNOWN, THE(1946); LATE GEORGE APLEY, THE(1947); PILGRIM LADY, THE(1947)
Silents
ARE YOU A MASON?(1915)

Howard Freeman
TIME OF YOUR LIFE, THE(1948); AIR RAID WARDENS(1943); GIRL CRAZY(1943); HITLER'S MADMAN(1943); HUMAN COMEDY, THE(1943); MADAME CURIE(1943); MARGIN FOR ERROR(1943); PILOT NO. 5(1943); SLIGHTLY DANGEROUS(1943); WHISTLING IN BROOKLYN(1943); CAROLINA BLUES(1944); LOST ANGEL(1944); MARK OF THE WHISTLER, THE(1944); MEET MISS BOBBY SOCKS(1944); MEET THE PEOPLE(1944); MR. WINKLE GOES TO WAR(1944); ONCE UPON A TIME(1944); RATIONING(1944); SECRET COMMAND(1944); UNWRITTEN CODE, THE(1944); DANCING IN MANHATTAN(1945); I'LL TELL THE WORLD(1945); MEXICANA(1945); SONG TO REMEMBER, A(1945); THAT NIGHT WITH YOU(1945); THIS LOVE OF OURS(1945); WHERE DO WE GO FROM HERE?(1945); YOU CAME ALONG(1945); ABILENE TOWN(1946); BLUE DAHLIA, THE(1946); CALIFORNIA(1946); CROSS MY HEART(1946); HOUSE OF HORRORS(1946); INSIDE JOB(1946); KILLERS, THE(1946); MONSIEUR BEAUCAIRE(1946); MY BROTHER TALKS TO HORSES(1946); NIGHT AND DAY(1946); PERFECT MARRIAGE, THE(1946); SO GOES MY LOVE(1946); SUSIE STEPS OUT(1946); SWELL GUY(1946); CASS TIMBERLANE(1947); CIGARETTE GIRL(1947); EASY COME, EASY GO(1947); LONG NIGHT, THE(1947); MAGIC TOWN(1947); THAT WAY WITH WOMEN(1947); ARTHUR TAKES OVER(1948); CRY OF THE CITY(1948); GIRL FROM MANHATTAN(1948); GIVE MY REGARDS TO BROADWAY(1948); IF YOU KNEW SUSIE(1948); LETTER FROM AN UNKNOWN WOMAN(1948); SNAKE PIT, THE(1948); SUMMER HOLIDAY(1948); UP IN CENTRAL PARK(1948); CHICAGO DEADLINE(1949); TAKE ONE FALSE STEP(1949); PERFECT STRANGERS(1950); DOUBLE DYNAMITE(1951); HERE COMES THE GROOM(1951); MILLION DOLLAR MERMAID(1952); SCARAMOUCHE(1952); TURNING POINT, THE(1952); RAIDERS OF THE SEVEN SEAS(1953); REMAINS TO BE SEEN(1953); DEAR BRIGETTE(1965)

J.E. Freeman
EYE FOR AN EYE, AN(1981)

Jack Freeman
ROMANOFF AND JULIET(1961), makeup; X-15(1961), ph; MANCHURIAN CANDIDATE, THE(1962), makeup; FOR LOVE OR MONEY(1963), makeup; TAMMY AND THE DOCTOR(1963), makeup; ISLAND OF THE BLUE DOLPHINS(1964), makeup; JOURNEY TO SHILOH(1968), makeup

Jamie Freeman
TAKING OFF(1971)

Jane Freeman
1984
SCRUBBERS(1984, Brit.)

Jeff Freeman
MAN ON THE PROWL(1957)

Jim Freeman
TOWERING INFERNO, THE(1974), ph; SKY RIDERS(1976, U.S./Gr.), ph

Joan Freeman
PISTOL HARVEST(1951); TEENAGE REBEL(1956); REMARKABLE MR. PENNYPACKER, THE(1959); COME SEPTEMBER(1961); PANIC IN YEAR ZERO!(1962); TOWER OF LONDON(1962); THREE STOOGES GO AROUND THE WORLD IN A DAZE, THE(1963); ROUSTABOUT(1964); ROUNDERS, THE(1965); FASTEST GUITAR ALIVE, THE(1967); RELUCTANT ASTRONAUT, THE(1967)
1984
FRIDAY THE 13TH–THE FINAL CHAPTER(1984)

Joel Freeman
SHAFT(1971), p; LOVE AT FIRST BITE(1979), p; OCTAGON, THE(1980), p

Joel D. Freeman
TROUBLE MAN(1972), p

John Freeman
LADY AND THE TRAMP(1955), anim; NATIONAL LAMPOON'S ANIMAL HOUSE(1978)
Misc. Talkies
LIFE AND LEGEND OF BUFFALO JONES, THE(1976); BUFFALO RIDER(1978)

Josh Freeman
MAN ON THE PROWL(1957)

Kathleen Freeman
CASBAH(1948); NAKED CITY, THE(1948); SAXON CHARM, THE(1948); MR. BELVEDERE GOES TO COLLEGE(1949); HOUSE BY THE RIVER(1950); LIFE OF HER OWN, A(1950); LONELY HEARTS BANDITS(1950); NO MAN OF HER OWN(1950); ONCE A THIEF(1950); REFORMER AND THE REDHEAD, THE(1950); CAUSE FOR ALARM(1951); LET'S MAKE IT LEGAL(1951); PLACE IN THE SUN, A(1951); BAD AND THE BEAUTIFUL, THE(1952); GREATEST SHOW ON EARTH, THE(1952); KID MONK BARONI(1952); LOVE IS BETTER THAN EVER(1952); MONKEY BUSINESS(1952); O. HENRY'S FULL HOUSE(1952); PRISONER OF ZENDA, THE(1952); SINGIN' IN THE RAIN(1952); TALK ABOUT A STRANGER(1952); WILD BLUE YONDER, THE(1952); AFFAIRS OF DOBIE GILLIS, THE(1953); DREAM WIFE(1953); GLASS WALL, THE(1953); GLASS WEB, THE(1953); HALF A HERO(1953); MAGNETIC MONSTER, THE(1953); PERILOUS JOURNEY, A(1953); SHE'S BACK ON BROADWAY(1953); ATHENA(1954); THREE RING CIRCUS(1954); ARTISTS AND MODELS(1955); FAR COUNTRY, THE(1955); KISS THEM FOR ME(1957); MIDNIGHT STORY, THE(1957); PAWNEE(1957); FLY, THE(1958); HOUSEBOAT(1958); MISSOURI TRAVELER, THE(1958); TOO MUCH, TOO SOON(1958); NORTH TO ALASKA(1960); ERRAND BOY, THE(1961); LADIES MAN, THE(1961); MADISON AVENUE(1962); WILD HARVEST(1962); NUTTY PROFESSOR, THE(1963); WHO'S MINDING THE STORE?(1963); DISORDERLY ORDERLY, THE(1964); MAIL ORDER BRIDE(1964); PATSY, THE(1964); MARRIAGE ON THE ROCKS(1965); ROUNDERS, THE(1965); THAT FUNNY FEELING(1965); THREE ON A COUCH(1966); POINT BLANK(1967); DEATH OF A GUNFIGHTER(1969); GOOD GUYS AND THE BAD GUYS, THE(1969); HOOK, LINE AND SINKER(1969); SUPPORT YOUR LOCAL SHERIFF(1969); BALLAD OF CABLE HOGUE, THE(1970); WHICH WAY TO THE FRONT?(1970); HEAD ON(1971); SUPPORT YOUR LOCAL GUNFIGHTER(1971); STAND UP AND BE COUNTED(1972); UNHOLY ROLLERS(1972); WHERE DOES IT HURT?(1972); YOUR THREE MINUTES ARE UP(1973); NORSEMAN, THE(1978); BLUES BROTHERS, THE(1980); HEARTBEEPS(1981)

Kay Freeman
SUMMERSPELL(1983)

Kenneth Freeman
MIRACLE IN HARLEM(1948)

Laurie Freeman
SEVENTH SURVIVOR, THE(1941, Brit.), ph

Lea David Freeman
LAZY RIVER(1934), w

Leonard Freeman
STEEL TOWN(1952), w; ALL-AMERICAN, THE(1953), w; CLAUDELLE INGLISH(1961), p, w; GOLD OF THE SEVEN SAINTS(1961), p, w; HANG'EM HIGH(1968), p, w

Lisa Freeman
MR. MOM(1983)
1984
BREAKIN'(1984); FRIDAY THE 13TH-THE FINAL CHAPTER(1984); SAVAGE STREETS(1984)

Lois Freeman
1984
ALPHABET CITY(1984), ed

Lyn Freeman
WITHOUT WARNING(1980), w

M. Freeman
FREUD(1962)

Maurice Freeman
STRANGERS ON A HONEYMOON(1937, Brit.)
Silents
STEPHEN STEPS OUT(1923)

Mervyn Freeman
BLONDE COMET(1941), ph; JUNGLE MAN(1941), ph

Michael Freeman
EIGHT ON THE LAM(1967); DIRTY HARRY(1971)

Mickey Freeman
SHAMUS(1973)

Mona Freeman
HERE COME THE WAVES(1944); 'TILL WE MEET AGAIN(1944); TOGETHER AGAIN(1944); DANGER SIGNAL(1945); JUNIOR MISS(1945); ROUGHLY SPEAKING(1945); BLACK BEAUTY(1946); OUR HEARTS WERE GROWING UP(1946); THAT BRENNAN GIRL(1946); DEAR RUTH(1947); MOTHER WORE TIGHTS(1947); VARIETY GIRL(1947); ISN'T IT ROMANTIC?(1948); DEAR WIFE(1949); HEIRESS, THE(1949); STREETS OF LAREDO(1949); COPPER CANYON(1950); I WAS A SHOPLIFTER(1950); BRANDED(1951); DARLING, HOW COULD YOU!(1951); DEAR BRAT(1951); LADY FROM TEXAS, THE(1951); FLESH AND FURY(1952); JUMPING JACKS(1952); THUNDERBIRDS(1952); ANGEL FACE(1953); BATTLE FLAME(1955); ROAD TO DENVER, THE(1955); HOLD BACK THE NIGHT(1956); HUK(1956); SHADOW OF FEAR(1956, Brit.); WAY OUT, THE(1956, Brit.); DRAGON WELLS MASSACRE(1957); WORLD WAS HIS JURY, THE(1958)

Monie Freeman
WAR DRUMS(1957)

Morgan Freeman
WHO SAYS I CAN'T RIDE A RAINBOW!(1971); BRUBAKER(1980); EYEWITNESS(1981)
1984
HARRY AND SON(1984); TEACHERS(1984)

Mort Freeman
1984
ONCE UPON A TIME IN AMERICA(1984); OVER THE BROOKLYN BRIDGE(1984)

Ned Freeman
RIDE THE MAN DOWN(1952), m

Paul Freeman
DOGS OF WAR, THE(1980, Brit.); RAIDERS OF THE LOST ARK(1981); LONG GOOD FRIDAY, THE(1982, Brit.); SENDER, THE(1982, Brit.); UNSUITABLE JOB FOR A WOMAN, AN(1982, Brit.); FINAL OPTION, THE(1983, Brit.)
1984
FLIGHT TO BERLIN(1984, Ger./Brit.)
Misc. Talkies
WHOSE CHILD AM I?(1976)

Pauline Freeman
DRUMS O' VOODOO(1934)

Raoul Freeman
DOWN TO EARTH(1947); JOHNNY O'CLOCK(1947); SECRET LIFE OF WALTER MITTY, THE(1947); EXECUTIVE SUITE(1954); LONG GRAY LINE, THE(1955)

Richard Freeman
Misc. Talkies
TOUCHABLES, THE(1968, Brit.), d

Robert Freeman
SECRET WORLD(1969, Fr.), d; BARE KNUCKLES(1978), ed; LOVE BUTCHER, THE(1982), ed

Russ Freeman
SUBTERRANEANS, THE(1960)

Russell E. Freeman
BREAKING AWAY(1979)

Ruth Freeman
Misc. Silents
GIANT OF HIS RACE, A(1921); SHOT IN THE NIGHT, A(1923)

Sari Freeman
TAKING OFF(1971)

Stella Freeman
HOUSE OF THE ARROW, THE(1930, Brit.)

Stevi Freeman
SIMON, KING OF THE WITCHES(1971)

Susan Freeman
SOMETHING TO LIVE FOR(1952)

Thomas Freeman
THIN RED LINE, THE(1964)

Warwick Freeman
DEMONSTRATOR(1971, Aus.), d

William Freeman
Silents
BIRTH OF A NATION, THE(1915)

Carl Freemanson
MEXICAN SPITFIRE OUT WEST(1940)

Sir Edmund Freemantle
Silents
NELSON(1918, Brit.)

Marion Freemont
Silents
TRUE HEART SUSIE(1919), w
W.J. Freemont
Silents
ACQUITTED(1916)
Howard Freen
DIRTY O'NEIL(1974), d, w
J. L. Freer-Hunt
KARMA(1933, Brit./India), d
Rick Freers
Misc. Talkies
SCORCHING FURY(1952), d
Paul Frees
FORCE OF EVIL(1948); RED LIGHT(1949); HUNT THE MAN DOWN(1950); TOAST OF NEW ORLEANS, THE(1950); HIS KIND OF WOMAN(1951); PLACE IN THE SUN, A(1951); THING, THE(1951); WHEN WORLDS COLLIDE(1951); BIG SKY, THE(1952); LAS VEGAS STORY, THE(1952); MILLION DOLLAR MERMAID(1952); UTOPIA(1952, Fr./Ital.); STAR, THE(1953); WAR OF THE WORLDS, THE(1953); RIOT IN CELL BLOCK 11(1954); SUDDENLY(1954); PRINCE OF PLAYERS(1955); FRANCIS IN THE HAUNTED HOUSE(1956); HARDER THEY FALL, THE(1956); JET PILOT(1957); MONOLITH MONSTERS, THE(1957); 27TH DAY, THE(1957); SPACE MASTER X-7(1958); SHAGGY DOG, THE(1959); SNOW QUEEN, THE(1959, USSR); BEATNIKS, THE(1960), d, w; TIME MACHINE, THE(1960; Brit./U.S.); GAY PURR-EE(1962); PUBLIC AFFAIR, A(1962); INCREDIBLE MR. LIMPET, THE(1964); MAN CALLED FLINTSTONE, THE(1966); ST. VALENTINE'S DAY MASSACRE, THE(1967); WILD IN THE STREETS(1968); MR. MAGOO'S HOLIDAY FESTIVAL(1970); LAST UNICORN, THE(1982); TWICE UPON A TIME(1983)
Misc. Talkies
CRICKET OF THE HEARTH, THE(1968); MILPITAS MONSTER, THE(1980)
Paul H. Frees
RAINS OF RANCHIPUR, THE(1955)
Wolf Frees
ODETTE(1951, Brit.); SO LITTLE TIME(1953, Brit.); GREEN BUDDHA, THE(1954, Brit.); MAN WHO NEVER WAS, THE(1956, Brit.); SAFECRACKER, THE(1958, Brit.); STEEL BAYONET, THE(1958, Brit.); DAY THEY ROBBED THE BANK OF ENGLAND, THE(1960, Brit.); DESERT PATROL(1962, Brit.); DOCTOR ZHIVAGO(1965); HEROES OF TELEMARK, THE(1965, Brit.); OPERATION CROSSBOW(1965, U.S./Ital.)
Ralph Freeto
LOUISIANA(1947)
The Freewheelers
ONCE UPON A COFFEE HOUSE(1965)
Lucien Fregis
MR. HULOT'S HOLIDAY(1954, Fr.); MY UNCLE(1958, Fr.); SUITOR, THE(1963, Fr.)
Roger Fregois
LE PETIT THEATRE DE JEAN RENOIR(1974, Fr.)
Fregolente
PRETTY BUT WICKED(1965, Braz.); LOLLIPOP(1966, Braz.)
A. Fregolente
TRAIN ROBBERY CONFIDENTIAL(1965, Braz.)
Hugo Fregonese
ONE WAY STREET(1950), d; SADDLE TRAMP(1950), d; APACHE DRUMS(1951), d; MARK OF THE RENEGADE(1951), d; MY SIX CONVICTS(1952), d; UNTAMED FRONTIER(1952), d; BLOWING WILD(1953), d; DECAMERON NIGHTS(1953, Brit.), d; MAN IN THE ATTIC(1953), d; RAID, THE(1954), d; BLACK TUESDAY(1955), d; HARRY BLACK AND THE TIGER(1958, Brit.), d; BEASTS OF MARSEILLES, THE(1959, Brit.), d; MARCO POLO(1962, Fr./Ital.), d; DR. MABUSE'S RAYS OF DEATH(1964, Ger./Fr./Ital.), d; SAVAGE PAMPAS(1967, Span./Arg.), d, w; ASSIGNMENT TERROR(1970, Ger./Span./Ital.), d
Albert G. Freguelli
Misc. Silents
BECAUSE(1921, Brit.), d
Elsie Freguson
Misc. Silents
HIS HOUSE IN ORDER(1920)
Helen Freguson
Misc. Silents
GIFT O' GAB(1917)
Frehel
PEPE LE MOKO(1937, Fr.); STORY OF A CHEAT, THE(1938, Fr.)
Charles Frehse
LUPE(1967)
Sally Frei
DR. GOLDFOOT AND THE BIKINI MACHINE(1965); UNDERTAKER AND HIS PALS, THE(1966)
James Freiberg
NIGHTMARE IN WAX(1969), set d
Fred Freiberger
SUSIE STEPS OUT(1946), w; BEAST FROM 20,000 FATHOMS, THE(1953), w; EGYPT BY THREE(1953), w; BIG CHASE, THE(1954), w; BLACK PIRATES, THE(1954, Mex.), w; GARDEN OF EVIL(1954), w; BIG BLUFF, THE(1955), w; MASSACRE(1956), w; BEGINNING OF THE END(1957), w; CRASH LANDING(1958), w; VIOLENT ONES, THE(1967), w
Manfred Freiberger
NIGHT PORTER, THE(1974, Ital./U.S.)
Fred Freiburger
STORK BITES MAN(1947), w
Jim Freiburger
10 TO MIDNIGHT(1983), art d
Catherine Freiburghaus
EVERY MAN FOR HIMSELF(1980, Fr.)
Hugo Freidhofer
HOME IN INDIANA(1944), m; QUEEN FOR A DAY(1951), m; YOUNG LIONS, THE(1958), m
Anna Freidman
SILENCE OF THE NORTH(1981, Can.)

John Freidrich
THANK GOD IT'S FRIDAY(1978)
Lloyd Freidus
FIGHT FOR YOUR LIFE(1977), ph
Jeff Freilich
CONQUEST OF THE EARTH(1980), p
Brian Freilino
FORCED ENTRY(1975)
Louis Freiman
CANTOR'S SON, THE(1937), w
B. Freindlich
TWELFTH NIGHT(1956, USSR)
Bruno Freindlich
FATHERS AND SONS(1960, USSR)
V. Freindlich
DON QUIXOTE(1961, USSR)
Elise Freinet
PASSION FOR LIFE(1951, Fr.), w
Fritz Freisler
Misc. Silents
OTHER SELF, THE(1918, Aust.), d
Peter Freistadt
1984
AMBASSADOR, THE(1984)
Robert Freitag
GREAT ESCAPE, THE(1963)
Eric Freiwald
RAIDERS OF TOMAHAWK CREEK(1950), w; LONE RANGER AND THE LOST CITY OF GOLD, THE(1958), w
Barbara Freking
PETTY GIRL, THE(1950); HIS KIND OF WOMAN(1951); TWO TICKETS TO BROADWAY(1951); LAS VEGAS STORY, THE(1952); CASANOVA'S BIG NIGHT(1954); JET PILOT(1957)
Friz Freleng
TWO GUYS FROM TEXAS(1948), anim; BUGS BUNNY, SUPERSTAR(1975); BUGS BUNNY'S THIRD MOVIE–1001 RABBIT TALES(1982), p, w; TRAIL OF THE PINK PANTHER, THE(1982), w; DAFFY DUCK'S MOVIE: FANTASTIC ISLAND(1983), p&d, w
Misc. Talkies
LOONEY, LOONEY, LOONEY BUGS BUNNY MOVIE, THE(1981), d
Anita Fremault [Anita Louise]
WONDER OF WOMEN(1929)
Mabel Fremier
Silents
FOOL THERE WAS, A(1915)
Fremin
NEST, THE(1982, Span.)
Anita Fremmault
FOUR DEVILS(1929)
Al Fremont
Silents
JOYOUS TROUBLEMAKERS, THE(1920); BIG PUNCH, THE(1921); QUEEN OF SHEBA, THE(1921); SHE'S A SHEIK(1927)
Misc. Silents
SQUARE SHOOTER, THE(1920); FIGHTING STREAK, THE(1922)
Alfred Fremont
Silents
WHEN A WOMAN SINS(1918); GIRL OF MY HEART(1920)
Misc. Silents
SIREN'S SONG, THE(1919)
June Fremont
Misc. Talkies
CYNTHIA'S SISTER(1975)
M.C. Fremont
AU HASARD, BALTHAZAR(1970, Fr.)
Adam French
1984
SUCCESS IS THE BEST REVENGE(1984, Brit.)
Arthur French
DIRTYMOUTH(1970); BLADE(1973); SUPER COPS, THE(1974); THREE DAYS OF THE CONDOR(1975); CARWASH(1976); HERO AIN'T NOTHIN' BUT A SANDWICH, A(1977); NIGHT OF THE JUGGLER(1980); HANKY-PANKY(1982)
Barbara French
WHERE THE BULLETS FLY(1966, Brit.)
Brian French
FAR SHORE, THE(1976, Can.), ed
Bruce French
MAN ON A SWING(1974); PIPE DREAMS(1976); ROLLERCOASTER(1977); BLOOD-BROTHERS(1978); MR. MOM(1983)
1984
FLETCH(1984)
Caroline French
Silents
FORGIVEN, OR THE JACK O'DIAMONDS(1914)
Misc. Silents
PAID IN FULL(1914)
Charles French
ARIZONA NIGHTS(1934); MAN FROM HELL, THE(1934); CRIMSON TRAIL, THE(1935); GUN PLAY(1936); COURAGE OF THE WEST(1937); HEADIN' FOR THE RIO GRANDE(1937); MR. SYCAMORE(1975), art d
Silents
BATTLE OF GETTYSBURG(1914); TYPHOON, THE(1914); CORNER IN COLLEENS, A(1916); PAWS OF THE BEAR(1917); KAISER'S SHADOW, THE(1918); MIDNIGHT PATROL, THE(1918); JUBILO(1919); BEYOND(1921); IF YOU BELIEVE IT, IT'S SO(1922); MIXED FACES(1922); WEST OF CHICAGO(1922); ABYSMAL BRUTE, THE(1923); LONELY ROAD, THE(1923); WOMAN OF PARIS, A(1923); ABRAHAM LINCOLN(1924); WAR PAINT(1926)
Misc. Silents
CLODHOPPER, THE(1917); LIFTED VEIL, THE(1917); FUSS AND FEATHERS(1918); HIRED MAN, THE(1918); HIS OWN HOME TOWN(1918); THREE X

GORDON(1918); VAMP, THE(1918); MINTS OF HELL, THE(1919); STRONGER THAN DEATH(1920); BEARCAT, THE(1922); HER OWN MONEY(1922); UNFOLDMENT, THE(1922); GOOD AS GOLD(1927)

Charles K. French
LAST WARNING, THE(1929); OVERLAND BOUND(1929); SPOILERS, THE(1930); CAUGHT(1931); DESTRY RIDES AGAIN(1932); HONOR OF THE PRESS(1932); SCARLET WEEKEND, A(1932); DESIGN FOR LIVING(1933); SATURDAY'S MILLIONS(1933); VIA PONY EXPRESS(1933); WAR OF THE RANGE(1933); PRESIDENT VANISHES, THE(1934); WHEN A MAN SEES RED(1934); MURDER BY TELEVISION(1935); NO MAN'S RANGE(1935); THROWBACK, THE(1935); TRAIL OF TERROR(1935); WESTERN COURAGE(1935); DESERT GUNS(1936); LAST OF THE WARRENS, THE(1936); MILKY WAY, THE(1936); PRISONER OF ZENDA, THE(1937); WHERE TRAILS DIVIDE(1937); ROVIN' TUMBLEWEEDS(1939); CHIP OF THE FLYING U(1940); SLIGHTLY HONORABLE(1940); MEET JOHN DOE(1941); GYPSY WILDCAT(1944)
Misc. Talkies
MAN OF ACTION(1933); TRACY RIDES(1935)
Silents
DESPOILER, THE(1915); ARYAN, THE(1916); CIVILIZATION(1916); PATRIOT, THE(1916); HATER OF MEN(1917); THIS HERO STUFF(1919); FLAMES OF THE FLESH(1920); LAST TRAIL(1921); NIGHT HORSEMAN, THE(1921); MORAN OF THE LADY LETTY(1922); ALIAS THE NIGHT WIND(1923); GENTLE JULIA(1923); OH, YOU TONY!(1924); PRIDE OF SUNSHINE ALLEY(1924); SAWDUST TRAIL(1924); LET 'ER BUCK(1925); SPEED MAD(1925); HANDS UP(1926); OH, WHAT A NIGHT!(1926); RAINMAKER, THE(1926); ADVENTUROUS SOUL, THE(1927); CROSS BREED(1927); DOWN GRADE, THE(1927); ONE CHANCE IN A MILLION(1927); KING OF THE RODEO(1929)
Misc. Silents
DISCIPLE, THE(1915); IRON STRAIN, THE(1915); GAMBLE IN SOULS, A(1916); NO-GOOD GUY, THE(1916); WEE LADY BETTY(1917); SIX FEET FOUR(1919); SPEED MANIAC, THE(1919); DAREDEVIL, THE(1920); PRAIRIE TRAILS(1920); SQUARE SHOOTER, THE(1920); TERROR, THE(1920); WHAT WOULD YOU DO?(1920); HANDS OFF(1921); ROAD DEMON, THE(1921); SMUDGE(1922); MAN'S SIZE(1923); TEXAS TRAIL, THE(1925); TOO MUCH YOUTH(1925); FRENZIED FLAMES(1926); HOLLYWOOD REPORTER, THE(1926); RUNAWAY EXPRESS, THE(1926); WINNING WALLOP, THE(1926); MEDDLIN' STRANGER, THE(1927); RIDE 'EM HIGH(1927); BIG HOP, THE(1928); COWBOY CAVALIER, THE(1928); RIDING FOR FAME(1928)

De French
1984
BOSTONIANS, THE(1984)

Dean French
1984
COUNTRY(1984)

Dennis French
WILD REBELS, THE(1967)

Dick French
FOG OVER FRISCO(1934); JIMMY THE GENT(1934); DEVIL DOGS OF THE AIR(1935); GILDED LILY, THE(1935); STRANDED(1935); GIVE ME YOUR HEART(1936); OUR RELATIONS(1936); POLO JOE(1936); HOLD'EM NAVY!(1937); LOVE IS NEWS(1937); SUBMARINE D-1(1937); TIME OUT FOR ROMANCE(1937); YOU CAN'T TAKE IT WITH YOU(1938); YOU'RE IN THE ARMY NOW(1941); ACROSS THE PACIFIC(1942); MAD MARTINDALES, THE(1942); THEY DIED WITH THEIR BOOTS ON(1942); DIXIE DUGAN(1943); MARGIN FOR ERROR(1943); PARIS AFTER DARK(1943); EASY TO LOOK AT(1945); GIRL ON THE SPOT(1946)

Ed French
GEEK MAGGOT BINGO(1983), spec eff
1984
ALPHABET CITY(1984), makeup; EXTERMINATOR 2(1984), makeup

Edward E. French
SMITHEREENS(1982)

Edward French
ONE JUMP AHEAD(1955, Brit.); NIGHTMARE(1981), makeup; SLEEPAWAY CAMP(1983), makeup

Edwige French
Misc. Talkies
NEXT VICTIM(1971)

Elsie French
LILIES OF THE FIELD(1934, Brit.)

Eugene French
Silents
TIMOTHY'S QUEST(1922), ph

F. French
Silents
LIFTING SHADOWS(1920)

George French
MAN ON THE FLYING TRAPEZE, THE(1935); SILVER SPURS(1936); FOREIGN CORRESPONDENT(1940); THANK YOUR LUCKY STARS(1943)
Silents
RECKLESS ROMANCE(1924); BASHFUL BUCCANEER(1925); LOST LIMITED, THE(1927); ONE GLORIOUS SCRAP(1927)
Misc. Silents
LION'S BREATH, THE(1916); HIS PAJAMA GIRL(1921); FLYIN' THRU(1925); SNOB BUSTER, THE(1925); WON IN THE CLOUDS(1928)

George B. French
WAY DOWN EAST(1935); TRUE CONFESSION(1937)
Silents
TARZAN OF THE APES(1918)

George K. French
Silents
LAZY LIGHTNING(1926); ARIZONA CYCLONE(1928)

Georgia French
HOLD'EM YALE(1935)
Silents
BLACK BEAUTY(1921)
Misc. Silents
TANGLED HEARTS(1916)

Gerald French
GROUND ZERO(1973)

Geroge French
Silents
ROMANCE OF TARZAN, THE(1918)

Harold French
EAST LYNNE ON THE WESTERN FRONT(1931, Brit.); JEALOUSY(1931, Brit.); OFFICER'S MESS, THE(1931, Brit.); CALLBOX MYSTERY, THE(1932, Brit.); WHEN LONDON SLEEPS(1932, Brit.); I ADORE YOU(1933, Brit.); MANNEQUIN(1933, Brit.); NIGHT OF THE GARTER(1933, Brit.); UMBRELLA, THE(1933, Brit.); DIPLOMATIC LOVER, THE(1934, Brit.); FACES(1934, Brit.); GIRL IN THE CROWD, THE(1934, Brit.); MURDER AT THE INN(1934, Brit.); GIRL HAS BEEN ARRANGED, A(1935, Brit.); CRIME OVER LONDON(1936, Brit.), w; TWO ON A DOORSTEP(1936, Brit.); CAVALIER OF THE STREETS, THE(1937, Brit.), d; WHEN THIEF MEETS THIEF(1937, Brit.), w; DEAD MEN ARE DANGEROUS(1939, Brit.), d; CASTLE OF CRIMES(1940, Brit.), d; GIRL IN DISTRESS(1941, Brit.), d; MAJOR BARBARA(1941, Brit.), d; AVENGERS, THE(1942, Brit.), d; TALK ABOUT JACQUELINE(1942, Brit.), d; UNPUBLISHED STORY(1942, Brit.), d; SECRET MISSION(1944, Brit.), d; MR. EMMANUEL(1945, Brit.), d; RANDOLPH FAMILY, THE(1945, Brit.), d; HIGH FURY(1947, Brit.), d, w; BLIND GODDESS, THE(1948, Brit.), d; QUIET WEEKEND(1948, Brit.), d; HER MAN GILBEY(1949, Brit.), d; MY BROTHER JONATHAN(1949, Brit.), d; ADAM AND EVELYNE(1950, Brit.), p&d; DANCING YEARS, THE(1950, Brit.), d; TRIO(1950, Brit.), d; ENCORE(1951, Brit.), d; HOUR OF THIRTEEN, THE(1952), d; ISN'T LIFE WONDERFUL!(1953, Brit.), d; PARIS EXPRESS, THE(1953, Brit.), d&w; FORBIDDEN CARGO(1954, Brit.), d; ROB ROY, THE HIGHLAND ROGUE(1954, Brit.), d; MAN WHO LOVED REDHEADS, THE(1955, Brit.), d

Hugh French
SIMPLY TERRIFIC(1938, Brit.); IF WINTER COMES(1947); WOMAN'S VENGEANCE, A(1947); COUNTESS OF MONTE CRISTO, THE(1948); MR. PEABODY AND THE MERMAID(1948); SWORD IN THE DESERT(1949); FANCY PANTS(1950); LUCKY NICK CAIN(1951); ROGUE'S MARCH(1952); SHADOW OF THE EAGLE(1955, Brit.); UNDER MILK WOOD(1973, Brit.), p

J. French
OUT OF TOWNERS, THE(1970)

Jacqueline French
MODEL AND THE MARRIAGE BROKER, THE(1951)

James French
1984
PURPLE RAIN(1984)

Jean French
KEEP YOUR POWDER DRY(1945)

Jimmy French
Silents
JUGGERNAUT, THE(1915), ph

John French
STORY OF ROBIN HOOD, THE(1952, Brit.); OFF THE WALL(1977)

L.A. French
OUR RELATIONS(1936), p

Leigh French
HOW SWEET IT IS(1968); NORWOOD(1970); WUSA(1970); ALL-AMERICAN BOY, THE(1973); LAUGHING POLICEMAN, THE(1973); ALOHA, BOBBY AND ROSE(1975); DROWNING POOL, THE(1975); WHITE LINE FEVER(1975, Can.); GREAT SMOKEY ROADBLOCK, THE(1978); HOLLYWOOD KNIGHTS, THE(1980); HALLOWEEN II(1981); HISTORY OF THE WORLD, PART 1(1981)

Leslie French
RADIO PIRATES(1935, Brit.); PEG OF OLD DRURY(1936, Brit.); THIS ENGLAND(1941, Brit.); WALLET, THE(1952, Brit.); ORDERS TO KILL(1958, Brit.); SCAPEGOAT, THE(1959, Brit.); SINGER NOT THE SONG, THE(1961, Brit.); LEOPARD, THE(1963, Ital.); RESCUE SQUAD, THE(1963, Brit.); MALPAS MYSTERY, THE(1967, Brit.); MORE THAN A MIRACLE(1967, Ital./Fr.); WITCHES, THE(1969, Fr./Ital.); DEATH IN VENICE(1971, Ital./Fr.)

Lloyd French
SNUFFY SMITH, YARD BIRD(1942), w

Marilyn French
WOMAN REBELS, A(1936)

Marinda French
QUADROON(1972)

Mary Jane French
GIRL CRAZY(1943); THEY WERE EXPENDABLE(1945); HOODLUM SAINT, THE(1946); TILL THE CLOUDS ROLL BY(1946); SHOW BOAT(1951)

Mary Jean French
HARVEY GIRLS, THE(1946)

Mary Meade French
IN LIKE FLINT(1967)

Michael French
HOW SWEET IT IS(1968)

Michaux French
Misc. Talkies
BRANDY IN THE WILDERNESS(1969)

Norma French
ASK ANY GIRL(1959); WHO SAYS I CAN'T RIDE A RAINBOW!(1971)

Norman French
HERITAGE(1935, Aus.); TYPHOON TREASURE(1939, Brit.)

Park French
BE YOURSELF(1930), set d; DU BARRY, WOMAN OF PASSION(1930), art d; LOTTERY BRIDE, THE(1930), prod d & art d; ONE ROMANTIC NIGHT(1930), set d; PUTTIN' ON THE RITZ(1930), art d; RAFFLES(1930), art d
Silents
LITTLE JOURNEY, A(1927), set d

Paul French
BAD ONE, THE(1930), art d

Pauline French
Silents
PAINTED FLAPPER, THE(1924)

Peg French
ON THE YARD(1978)

Phyl French
GOOD TIME GIRL(1950, Brit.)

Mrs. R. E. French
Silents
SILVER THREADS AMONG THE GOLD(1915)
Richard French
VALLEY OF HUNTED MEN(1942)
Rita French
KISS OF THE TARANTULA(1975)
Sadie French
BLACK CAT, THE(1966)
Susan French
IMPOSSIBLE YEARS, THE(1968); JAWS II(1978); SOMEWHERE IN TIME(1980)
Ted French
WEST OF THE ALAMO(1946); LAW OF THE LASH(1947); RANGE BEYOND THE
BLUE(1947); RIDIN' DOWN THE TRAIL(1947); WEST TO GLORY(1947); HAWK OF
POWDER RIVER, THE(1948); ALL THE KING'S MEN(1949); ROARING WEST-
WARD(1949); QUICK AND THE DEAD, THE(1963)
Tria French
STORY OF A THREE DAY PASS, THE(1968, Fr.)
Valerie French
CONSTANT HUSBAND, THE(1955, Brit.); JUBAL(1956); SECRET OF TREASURE
MOUNTAIN(1956); DECISION AT SUNDOWN(1957); GARMENT JUNGLE,
THE(1957); HARD MAN, THE(1957); 27TH DAY, THE(1957); FOUR SKULLS OF
JONATHAN DRAKE, THE(1959); STORY ON PAGE ONE, THE(1959); SHALA-
KO(1968, Brit.)
Victor French
CLOWN AND THE KID, THE(1961); QUICK AND THE DEAD, THE(1963); SPENC-
ER'S MOUNTAIN(1963); CHARRO(1969); DEATH OF A GUNFIGHTER(1969);
FLAP(1970); RIO LOBO(1970); THERE WAS A CROOKED MAN(1970); WILD ROV-
ERS(1971); CHATO'S LAND(1972); OTHER, THE(1972); HOUSE ON SKULL MOUN-
TAIN, THE(1974); NICKEL RIDE, THE(1974); OFFICER AND A GENTLEMAN,
AN(1982)
Misc. Talkies
CHOICES(1981)
French Can-Can Dancers
BAL TABARIN(1952)
Members of the French Resistance
SCHOOL FOR DANGER(1947, Brit.)
Edward Frency
TIME TO KILL, A(1955, Brit.)
Charles Frend
TRANSATLANTIC TUNNEL(1935, Brit.), ed; EAST MEETS WEST(1936, Brit.), ed;
SECRET AGENT, THE(1936, Brit.), ed; SABOTAGE(1937, Brit.), ed; SILENT BARRI-
ERS(1937, Brit.), ed; CITADEL, THE(1938), ed; YOUNG AND INNOCENT(1938, Brit.),
ed; GOODBYE MR. CHIPS(1939, Brit.), ed; CONQUEST OF THE AIR(1940), ed; LION
HAS WINGS, THE(1940, Brit.), ed; MAJOR BARBARA(1941, Brit.), ed; BIG BLOCK-
ADE, THE(1942, Brit.), d, w; SOMEWHERE IN FRANCE(1943, Brit.), d; JOHNNY
FRENCHMAN(1946, Brit.), d; LOVES OF JOANNA GODDEN, THE(1947, Brit.), d;
SAN DEMETRIO, LONDON(1947, Brit.), d, w; SCOTT OF THE ANTARCTIC(1949,
Brit.), d; MAGNET, THE(1950, Brit.), d; RUN FOR YOUR MONEY, A(1950, Brit.), d,
w; CRUEL SEA, THE(1953), d; LEASE OF LIFE(1954, Brit.), d; THIRD KEY,
THE(1957, Brit.), d; ALL AT SEA(1958, Brit.), d; TROUBLE IN THE SKY(1961,
Brit.), d; GIRL ON APPROVAL(1962, Brit.), d; TORPEDO BAY(1964, Ital./Fr.), d, w;
SKY BIKE, THE(1967, Brit.), d&w; GUNS IN THE HEATHER(1968, Brit.), w
A.G. Frenguelli
Misc. Silents
CRY FOR JUSTICE, THE(1919, Brit.), d
Alfonse Frenguelli
AWAKENING, THE(1938, Brit.), d
Anthony Frenguelli
Misc. Talkies
HOUSE OF DREAMS(1933), d
Tony Frenguelli
DR. SIN FANG(1937, Brit.), d; CHINATOWN NIGHTS(1938, Brit.), d
Mirella Freni
LA BOHEME(1965, Ital.)
Constantin Frenke
LONG VOYAGE HOME, THE(1940)
Eugen Frenke
LIFE RETURNS(1939), d, w; NUN AND THE SERGEANT, THE(1962), p
Eugene Frenke
TWO WHO DARED(1937, Brit.), d; EXILE EXPRESS(1939), p; LET'S LIVE A
LITTLE(1948), p; LADY IN THE IRON MASK(1952), p; MISS ROBIN CRUSOE(1954),
p&d; HEAVEN KNOWS, MR. ALLISON(1957), p; BARBARIAN AND THE GEISHA,
THE(1958), p; LAST SUNSET, THE(1961), p; ROYAL HUNT OF THE SUN, THE(1969,
Brit.), p
Mabel Frenyear
Misc. Silents
SOCIAL QUICKSANDS(1918)
Mario Frera
TWO WOMEN(1961, Ital./Fr.); EVERYBODY GO HOME!(1962, Fr./Ital.); LOVE AND
LARCENY(1963, Fr./Ital.)
Dorothy Frere
SNAKE WOMAN, THE(1961, Brit.); IT!(1967, Brit.); VAMPIRE CIRCUS(1972, Brit.)
Paul Frere
GRAND PRIX(1966)
Alain Frerot
TENANT, THE(1976, Fr.); RETURN OF MARTIN GUERRE, THE(1983, Fr.)
Bob Fresco
WINTER KEPT US WARM(1968, Can.), ph
Dave Fresco
SET-UP, THE(1949)
David Fresco
FRAMED(1947); KISS OF DEATH(1947); NORA PRENTISS(1947); FORCE OF
EVIL(1948); MALAYA(1950); RIGHT CROSS(1950); GIRL IN WHITE, THE(1952);
UNDERWORLD U.S.A.(1961); DON'T MAKE WAVES(1967); FUZZ(1972); AUDREY
ROSE(1977)
Jacques Fresco
PROJECT MOONBASE(1953), spec eff

Jimmy Fresco
NIGHT IN PARADISE, A(1946)
Mickey Fresco
NIGHT IN PARADISE, A(1946)
Robert Fresco
THIRD OF A MAN(1962); FIREBIRD 2015 AD(1981), ph
Robert M. Fresco
TARANTULA(1955), w; MONOLITH MONSTERS, THE(1957), w; PRIVATE NAVY
OF SGT. O'FARRELL, THE(1968), w
Marlies Frese
CELESTE(1982, Ger.), art d
Tina Frese
SHE DANCES ALONE(1981, Aust./U.S.), ed
Debbie Fresh
NEW CENTURIONS, THE(1972)
William Freshman
THOSE WHO LOVE(1929, Brit.); LATIN LOVE(1930, Brit.); BACHELOR'S BA-
BY(1932, Brit.); F.P. 1(1933, Brit.); LOVE'S OLD SWEET SONG(1933, Brit.); SCARLET
PIMPERNEL, THE(1935, Brit.); SENSATION(1936, Brit.), w; AREN'T MEN
BEASTS?(1937, Brit.), w; BACKSTAGE(1937, Brit.); GLAMOROUS NIGHT(1937, Brit.),
w; SPRING HANDICAP(1937, Brit.), w; HOLD MY HAND(1938, Brit.), w; JANE
STEPS OUT(1938, Brit.), w; YES, MADAM?(1938, Brit.), w; ANTS IN HIS PANTS(1940,
Aus.), d&w; POISON PEN(1941, Brit.), w; TERROR, THE(1941, Brit.), w; CONSPIRA-
CY IN TEHERAN(1948, Brit.), d
Silents
CREATION(1922, Brit.); BROKEN ROMANCE, A(1929, Brit.)
Misc. Silents
WAS SHE GUILTY?(1922, Brit.); GLORIOUS YOUTH(1928, Brit.); RISING GENERA-
TION, THE(1928, Brit.); WIDECOMBE FAIR(1928, Brit.)
Friedrich Freska
Silents
ONE ARABIAN NIGHT(1921, Ger.), w
Pierre Fresnay
MARIUS(1933, Fr.); KOENIGSMARK(1935, Fr.); MAN WHO KNEW TOO MUCH,
THE(1935, Brit.); CESAR(1936, Fr.); GRAND ILLUSION(1938, Fr.); CARNIVAL OF
SINNERS(1947, Fr.); MURDERER LIVES AT NUMBER 21, THE(1947, Fr.); FAN-
NY(1948, Fr.); RAVEN, THE(1948, Fr.); DEVIL'S DAUGHTER(1949, Fr.); MONSIEUR
VINCENT(1949, Fr.); STRANGERS IN THE HOUSE(1949, Fr.); AMAZING MONSIEUR
FABRE, THE(1952, Fr.); PERFECTIONIST, THE(1952, Fr.); VOYAGE TO AMERI-
CA(1952, Fr.)
Marie Fresnieres
KAMOURASKA(1973, Can./Fr.)
Maruchi Fresno
REDEEMER, THE(1965, Span.); DESPERATE ONES, THE(1968 U.S./Span.)
Maruschi Fresno
NIGHT HEAVEN FELL, THE(1958, Fr.)
E. Fress
LES GAULOISES BLEUES(1969, Fr.), art d
Bernard Fresson
HIROSHIMA, MON AMOUR(1959, Fr./Jap.); PLEASE, NOT NOW!(1963, Fr./Ital.);
SKY ABOVE HEAVEN(1964, Fr./Ital.); HOW NOT TO ROB A DEPARTMENT
STORE(1965, Fr./Ital.); IS PARIS BURNING?(1966, U.S./Fr.); LA GUERRE EST
FINIE(1967, Fr./Swed.); TRIPLE CROSS(1967, Fr./Brit.); BELLE DE JOUR(1968, Fr.);
FAREWELL, FRIEND(1968, Fr./Ital.); ZITA(1968, Fr.); LA PRISONNIERE(1969, Fr./
Ital.); Z(1969, Fr./Algeria); LADY IN THE CAR WITH GLASSES AND A GUN,
THE(1970, U.S./Fr.); JE T'AIME, JE T'AIME(1972, Fr./Swed.); FRENCH CONNEC-
TION 11(1975); 1★2?(1975, Fr.); TENANT, THE(1976, Fr.)
Ralph Freto
GANGSTER, THE(1947)
Joseph Fretwell
FRENCH CONNECTION, THE(1971), cos
Alvin W. Fretz
GHOST STORY(1981)
Clement Freud
MAKE MINE MINK(1960, Brit.); MURDER GAME, THE(1966, Brit.); MINI-AFFAIR,
THE(1968, Brit.); BEST HOUSE IN LONDON, THE(1969, Brit.)
Ralph Freud
MY WOMAN(1933); POLICE CALL(1933); DAY OF TRIUMPH(1954)
Stephen Freud
FREEWHEELIN'(1976), m
A. E. Freudeman
LOVE ME TONIGHT(1932), set d; ONE HOUR WITH YOU(1932), set d; SHE LOVES
ME NOT(1934), set d; ANYTHING GOES(1936), set d; KLONDIKE ANNIE(1936), set
d; MILKY WAY, THE(1936), set d; POPPY(1936), set d; THIRTEEN HOURS BY
AIR(1936), set d; HIGH, WIDE AND HANDSOME(1937), set d; MAID OF SA-
LEM(1937), set d; PLAINSMAN, THE(1937), set d; SOULS AT SEA(1937), set d;
SWING HIGH, SWING LOW(1937), set d; TRUE CONFESSION(1937), set d; IF I
WERE KING(1938), set d; SING YOU SINNERS(1938), set d; YOU AND ME(1938), set
d; LIGHT THAT FAILED, THE(1939), set d; NEVER SAY DIE(1939), set d; PARIS
HONEYMOON(1939), set d; STAR MAKER, THE(1939), set d; UNION PACIFIC(1939),
set d; GREAT McGINTY, THE(1940), set d; REMEMBER THE NIGHT(1940), set d
Henry R. Freuler
SAVAGE GIRL, THE(1932), p
John R. Freuler
TAKE THE HEIR(1930), p; RED FORK RANGE(1931), p; MURDER AT
DAWN(1932), p
Harry Freulich
AIR HAWKS(1935), ph; CHARGE OF THE LANCERS(1953), ph; JUNGLE MAN-
EATERS(1954), ph; TEEN-AGE CRIME WAVE(1955), ph
Henry Freulich
FOOTLIGHTS AND FOOLS(1929), ph; SMILING IRISH EYES(1929), ph; MEN OF
THE NIGHT(1934), ph; THAT'S GRATITUDE(1934), ph; BEHIND THE EVIDEN-
CE(1935), ph; GRAND EXIT(1935), ph; ONE-WAY TICKET(1935), ph; PUBLIC MEN-
ACE(1935), ph; UNKNOWN WOMAN(1935), ph; ADVENTURE IN
MANHATTAN(1936), ph; AND SO THEY WERE MARRIED(1936), ph; COME CLOS-
ER, FOLKS(1936), ph; DON'T GAMBLE WITH LOVE(1936), ph; HELL-SHIP MOR-
GAN(1936), ph; LADY FROM NOWHERE(1936), ph; LONE WOLF RETURNS,
THE(1936), ph; MEET NERO WOLFE(1936), ph; MORE THAN A SECRETARY(1936),
ph; SHAKEDOWN(1936), ph; COUNSEL FOR CRIME(1937), ph; IT'S ALL
YOURS(1937), ph; LEAGUE OF FRIGHTENED MEN(1937), ph; LET'S GET MAR-

RIED(1937), ph; MURDER IN GREENWICH VILLAGE(1937), ph; WOMEN OF GLA-
MOUR(1937), ph; BLONDIE(1938), ph; I AM THE LAW(1938), ph; LITTLE ADVEN-
TURESS, THE(1938), ph; THERE'S ALWAYS A WOMAN(1938), ph; WHEN G-MEN
STEP IN(1938), ph; WHO KILLED GAIL PRESTON?(1938), ph; BLONDIE BRINGS
UP BABY(1939), ph; BLONDIE MEETS THE BOSS(1939), ph; BLONDIE TAKES A
VACATION(1939), ph; FIRST OFFENDERS(1939), ph; FIVE LITTLE PEPPERS AND
HOW THEY GREW(1939), ph; GOOD GIRLS GO TO PARIS(1939), ph; MISSING
DAUGHTERS(1939), ph; BLONDIE HAS SERVANT TROUBLE(1940), ph; BLONDIE
ON A BUDGET(1940), ph; BLONDIE PLAYS CUPID(1940), ph; LONE WOLF MEETS
A LADY, THE(1940), ph; LONE WOLF STRIKES, THE(1940), ph; BLONDIE GOES
LATIN(1941), ph; BLONDIE IN SOCIETY(1941), ph; GO WEST, YOUNG LADY(1941),
ph; SHE KNEW ALL THE ANSWERS(1941), ph; TILLIE THE TOILER(1941), ph;
ATLANTIC CONVOY(1942), ph; BLONDIE FOR VICTORY(1942), ph; BLONDIE
GOES TO COLLEGE(1942), ph; BLONDIE'S BLESSED EVENT(1942), ph; BOOGIE
MAN WILL GET YOU, THE(1942), ph; BOSTON BLACKIE GETS HOL-
LYWOOD(1942), ph; MEET THE STEWARTS(1942), ph; SHUT MY BIG
MOUTH(1942), ph; DEVIL'S MASK, THE(1946), ph; IT'S GREAT TO BE
YOUNG(1946), ph; JUST BEFORE DAWN(1946), ph; PERSONALITY KID(1946), ph;
SHADOWED(1946), ph; TALK ABOUT A LADY(1946), ph; UNKNOWN, THE(1946),
ph; KEEPER OF THE BEES(1947), ph; LONE WOLF IN LONDON(1947), ph; SPORT
OF KINGS(1947), ph; TENDER YEARS, THE(1947), ph; WHEN A GIRL'S BEAUTI-
FUL(1947), ph; ADVENTURES IN SILVERADO(1948), ph; BLACK EAGLE(1948), ph;
LEATHER GLOVES(1948), ph; THUNDERHOOF(1948), ph; WOMAN FROM TANGI-
ER, THE(1948), ph; CHINATOWN AT MIDNIGHT(1949), ph; DEVIL'S HENCHMEN,
THE(1949), ph; KAZAN(1949), ph; LAW OF THE BARBARY COAST(1949), ph; MAKE
BELIEVE BALLROOM(1949), ph; NOT WANTED(1949), ph; PRISON WARD-
EN(1949), ph; RUSTY SAVES A LIFE(1949), ph; RUSTY'S BIRTHDAY(1949), ph;
SECRET OF ST. IVES, THE(1949), ph; SONG OF INDIA(1949), ph; BEWARE OF
BLONDIE(1950), ph; BUNCO SQUAD(1950), ph; GIRLS' SCHOOL(1950), ph; IRO-
QUOIS TRAIL, THE(1950), ph; VICIOUS YEARS, THE(1950), ph; BONANZA
TOWN(1951), ph; CORKY OF GASOLINE ALLEY(1951), ph; CYCLONE FURY(1951),
ph; FORT SAVAGE RAIDERS(1951), ph; HELLO GOD(1951, U.S./Ital.), ph; LADY
AND THE BANDIT, THE(1951), ph; MY TRUE STORY(1951), ph; SON OF DR.
JEKYLL, THE(1951), ph; UNDER THE GUN(1951), ph; UNKNOWN WORLD(1951),
ph; JUNCTION CITY(1952), ph; LAST TRAIN FROM BOMBAY(1952), ph; MONTANA
TERRITORY(1952), ph; OKINAWA(1952), ph; PATHFINDER, THE(1952), ph; TAR-
GET HONG KONG(1952), ph; CONQUEST OF COCHISE(1953), ph; FLAME OF
CALCUTTA(1953), ph; JACK MCCALL, DESPERADO(1953), ph; NEBRASKAN,
THE(1953), ph; PRINCE OF PIRATES(1953), ph; PRISONERS OF THE CAS-
BAH(1953), ph; SERPENT OF THE NILE(1953), ph; SIREN OF BAGDAD(1953), ph;
SLAVES OF BABYLON(1953), ph; BATTLE OF ROGUE RIVER(1954), ph; CANNI-
BAL ATTACK(1954), ph; EL ALAMEIN(1954), ph; IRON GLOVE, THE(1954), ph;
LAW VS. BILLY THE KID, THE(1954), ph; MASTERSON OF KANSAS(1954), ph;
MIAMI STORY, THE(1954), ph; SARACEN BLADE, THE(1954), ph; CHICAGO SYN-
DICATE(1955), ph; CROOKED WEB, THE(1955), ph; DUEL ON THE MISSISSIP-
PI(1955), ph; GUN THAT WON THE WEST, THE(1955), ph; INSIDE
DETROIT(1955), ph; IT CAME FROM BENEATH THE SEA(1955), ph; JUNGLE
MOON MEN(1955), ph; NEW ORLEANS UNCENSORED(1955), ph; PIRATES OF
TRIPOLI(1955), ph; SEMINOLE UPRISING(1955), ph; HE LAUGHED LAST(1956),
ph; HOUSTON STORY, THE(1956), ph; OVER-EXPOSED(1956), ph; REPRISAL(1956),
ph; WHITE SQUAW, THE(1956), ph; HARD MAN, THE(1957), ph; NO TIME TO BE
YOUNG(1957), ph; PHANTOM STAGECOACH, THE(1957), ph; 27TH DAY,
THE(1957), ph; GOOD DAY FOR A HANGING(1958), ph; RETURN TO WAR-
BOW(1958), ph; TARAWA BEACHHEAD(1958), ph

Carl Freund
SLEEPING PARTNERS(1930, Brit.), ph
Charles Freund
PAGAN LOVE SONG(1950)
Ellen Freund
1984
INITIATION, THE(1984), set d
Eric Freund
MR. EMMANUEL(1945, Brit.)
Erik Freund
SPITFIRE(1943, Brit.)
Jay Freund
PRISM(1971), p, ph, ed
1984
GO TELL IT ON THE MOUNTAIN(1984), ed
Misc. Talkies
AMERICAN GAME, THE(1979), d
Joshua Freund
LOOKING UP(1977)
Karl Freund
ALL QUIET ON THE WESTERN FRONT(1930), ph; BOUDOIR DIPLOMAT(1930),
ph; KNIGHT IN LONDON, A(1930, Brit./Ger.), ph; LOTTERY BRIDE, THE(1930), ph;
BAD SISTER(1931), ph; DRACULA(1931), ph; PERSONAL MAID(1931), ph; STRICT-
LY DISHONORABLE(1931), ph; UP FOR MURDER(1931), ph; AFRAID TO
TALK(1932), ph; AIR MAIL(1932), ph; BACK STREET(1932), ph; MUMMY,
THE(1932), d; MURDERS IN THE RUE MORGUE(1932), ph; SCANDAL FOR SA-
LE(1932), ph; KISS BEFORE THE MIRROR, THE(1933), ph; MOONLIGHT AND
PRETZELS(1933), d; COUNTESS OF MONTE CRISTO, THE(1934), d; GIFT OF
GAB(1934), d; I GIVE MY LOVE(1934), d; MADAME SPY(1934), d; UNCERTAIN
LADY(1934), d; MAD LOVE(1935), d; GREAT ZIEGFELD, THE(1936), ph; CON-
QUEST(1937), ph; GOOD EARTH, THE(1937), ph; PARNELL(1937), ph; LETTER OF
INTRODUCTION(1938), ph; MAN-PROOF(1938), ph; PORT OF SEVEN SEAS(1938),
ph; BALALAIKA(1939), ph; BARRICADE(1939), ph; GOLDEN BOY(1939), ph; ROSE
OF WASHINGTON SQUARE(1939), ph; TAIL SPIN(1939), ph; FLORIAN(1940), ph;
GREEN HELL(1940), ph; PRIDE AND PREJUDICE(1940), ph; WE WHO ARE
YOUNG(1940), ph; CHOCOLATE SOLDIER, THE(1941), ph; KEEPING COM-
PANY(1941), ph; TORTILLA FLAT(1942), ph; WAR AGAINST MRS. HADLEY,
THE(1942), ph; YANK AT ETON, A(1942), ph; CRY HAVOC(1943), ph; DU BARRY
WAS A LADY(1943), ph; GUY NAMED JOE, A(1943), ph; SEVENTH CROSS,
THE(1944), ph; THIN MAN GOES HOME, THE(1944), ph; DANGEROUS PART-
NERS(1945), ph; LETTER FOR EVIE, A(1945), ph; WITHOUT LOVE(1945), ph; TWO
SMART PEOPLE(1946), ph; UNDERCURRENT(1946), ph; THAT HAGEN GIRL(1947),
ph; THIS TIME FOR KEEPS(1947), ph; DECISION OF CHRISTOPHER BLAKE,
THE(1948), ph; KEY LARGO(1948), ph; WALLFLOWER(1948), ph; SOUTH OF ST.
LOUIS(1949), ph; BRIGHT LEAF(1950), ph; MONTANA(1950), ph

Silents
GOLEM: HOW HE CAME INTO THE WORLD, THE(1920, Ger.), ph; LAST LAUGH,
THE(1924, Ger.), ph; VARIETY(1925, Ger.), ph; METROPOLIS(1927, Ger.), ph; TAR-
TUFFE(1927, Ger.), ph
Karl W. Freund
BLOSSOMS IN THE DUST(1941), ph
Robert Freund
WILD REBELS, THE(1967)
H. Freuschtenicht
RIVER CHANGES, THE(1956)
Bill Freut
125 ROOMS OF COMFORT(1974, Can.), w
E. L. Frewen
Silents
ADVENTURES OF CAPTAIN KETTLE, THE(1922, Brit.)
Misc. Silents
MY LORD CONCEIT(1921, Brit.)
Matt Frewer
LORDS OF DISCIPLINE, THE(1983)
1984
SUPERGIRL(1984)
Frewer and Buckley
LIFE AND TIMES OF CHESTER-ANGUS RAMSGOOD, THE(1971, Can.), m
Albert Frey
FOR HEAVEN'S SAKE(1950)
Anny Frey
TRANSPORT FROM PARADISE(1967, Czech.)
Arno Frey
BEST OF ENEMIES(1933); HELL IN THE HEAVENS(1934); MYSTERY WO-
MAN(1935); RENDEZVOUS(1935); HUMAN CARGO(1936); LANCER SPY(1937); ES-
PIONAGE AGENT(1939); MIDNIGHT(1939); ARIZONA GANGBUSTERS(1940);
ESCAPE TO GLORY(1940); FIGHTING 69TH, THE(1940); MAN I MARRIED,
THE(1940); GREAT AMERICAN BROADCAST, THE(1941); H.M. PULHAM,
ESQ.(1941); MAN HUNT(1941); PARIS CALLING(1941); TWO-FACED WOMAN(1941);
UNDERGROUND(1941); DESPERATE JOURNEY(1942); GIRL TROUBLE(1942); JUN-
GLE SIREN(1942); MY FAVORITE BLONDE(1942); ONCE UPON A HONEY-
MOON(1942); PACIFIC RENDEZVOUS(1942); REUNION IN FRANCE(1942); TEXAS
MAN HUNT(1942); VALLEY OF HUNTED MEN(1942); WIFE TAKES A FLYER,
THE(1942); FIRST COMES COURAGE(1943); HANGMEN ALSO DIE(1943); NORTH-
ERN PURSUIT(1943); PARIS AFTER DARK(1943); THEY CAME TO BLOW UP
AMERICA(1943); TIGER FANGS(1943); TAMPICO(1944); U-BOAT PRISONER(1944);
ADVENTURES OF RUSTY(1945); ROYAL SCANDAL, A(1945); THRILL OF A RO-
MANCE(1945); WEEKEND AT THE WALDORF(1945); WHERE DO WE GO FROM
HERE?(1945); CLOAK AND DAGGER(1946); RENDEZVOUS 24(1946); 13 RUE MADE-
LEINE(1946); CASS TIMBERLANE(1947); GOLDEN EARRINGS(1947); NOOSE
HANGS HIGH, THE(1948); FOR HEAVEN'S SAKE(1950); IN A LONELY PLA-
CE(1950); DESERT RATS, THE(1953)
Barbara Frey
LOVE AT TWENTY(1963, Fr./Ital./Jap./Pol./Ger.)
Ellen Frey
Silents
METROPOLIS(1927, Ger.)
Eric Frey
MAGIC FACE, THE(1951, Aust.); ETERNAL WALTZ, THE(1959, Ger.); VIENNA
WALTZES(1961, Aust.); CARDINAL, THE(1963)
Erik Frey
LAST TEN DAYS, THE(1956, Ger.)
Erika Frey
GOOD SOLDIER SCHWEIK, THE(1963, Ger.)
Evelyn Frey
POWERS GIRL, THE(1942)
Jack Frey
EIGER SANCTION, THE(1975)
Katherine Frey
MIDSUMMER'S NIGHT'S DREAM, A(1935)
Leonard Frey
FINNEGANS WAKE(1965); BOYS IN THE BAND, THE(1970); MAGIC CHRISTIAN,
THE(1970, Brit.); TELL ME THAT YOU LOVE ME, JUNIE MOON(1970); FIDDLER ON
THE ROOF(1971); UP THE ACADEMY(1980); WHERE THE BUFFALO ROAM(1980);
TATTOO(1981)
Mary Frey
NIGHT OF TERROR(1933)
Nathaniel Frey
KISS THEM FOR ME(1957); DAMN YANKEES(1958); WHAT'S SO BAD ABOUT
FEELING GOOD?(1968)
Paul Frey
PARSIFAL(1983, Fr.)
Sami Frey
CLEO FROM 5 TO 7(1961, Fr.); TRUTH, THE(1961, Fr./Ital.); SEVEN CAPITAL
SINS(1962, Fr./Ital.); THERESE(1963, Fr.); DISORDER(1964, Fr./Ital.); BAND OF
OUTSIDERS(1966, Fr.); MANON 70(1968, Fr.); MISTER FREEDOM(1970, Fr.); CESAR
AND ROSALIE(1972, Fr.); POURQUOI PAS!(1979, Fr.)
1984
LITTLE DRUMMER GIRL, THE(1984)
Thomas Frey
POSSESSION(1981, Fr./Ger.)
Carl Freybe
MAN I MARRIED, THE(1940)
Bernard Freyd
LA BALANCE(1983, Fr.)
1984
AVE MARIA(1984, Fr.)
A. Freydin
RESURRECTION(1963, USSR), art d; GARNET BRACELET, THE(1966, USSR), art
d
Richard Freye
SNIPER, THE(1952)

Raymond Friedgen
KID FROM GOWER GULCH, THE(1949), p; HONG KONG AFFAIR(1958), w

Hugo Friedhofer
PAINTED WOMAN(1932), m; FACE IN THE SKY(1933), m; NOW I'LL TELL(1934), m; WORLD MOVES ON, THE(1934), m; CAPTAIN BLOOD(1935), m; ANOTHER DAWN(1937), md; TOPPER(1937), m; ADVENTURES OF MARCO POLO, THE(1938), m; RACKET BUSTERS(1938), md; PRIVATE LIVES OF ELIZABETH AND ESSEX, THE(1939), md; CITY, FOR CONQUEST(1941), md; CASABLANCA(1942), md; DESPERATE JOURNEY(1942), md; ALONG CAME JONES(1945), m; BANDIT OF SHERWOOD FOREST, THE(1946), m; BEST YEARS OF OUR LIVES, THE(1946), m; SO DARK THE NIGHT(1946), m; BISHOP'S WIFE, THE(1947), m; BODY AND SOUL(1947), m; SWORDSMAN, THE(1947), m; WILD HARVEST(1947), m; ADVENTURES OF CASANOVA(1948), m; ENCHANTMENT(1948), m; JOAN OF ARC(1948), m; SEALED VERDICT(1948), m; SONG IS BORN, A(1948), m; BRIDE OF VENGEANCE(1949), m; EDGE OF DOOM(1950), m; NO MAN OF HER OWN(1950), m; SOUND OF FURY, THE(1950), m; THREE CAME HOME(1950), m; TWO FLAGS WEST(1950), m; BIG CARNIVAL, THE(1951), m; FACE TO FACE(1952), m; LYDIA BAILEY(1952), m; MARRYING KIND, THE(1952), m; OUTCASTS OF POKER FLAT, THE(1952), m; ABOVE AND BEYOND(1953), m; HONDO(1953), m; THUNDER IN THE EAST(1953), m; VERA CRUZ(1954), m; RAINS OF RANCHIPUR, THE(1955), m; SEVEN CITIES OF GOLD(1955), m; SOLDIER OF FORTUNE(1955), m; VIOLENT SATURDAY(1955), m; WHITE FEATHER(1955), m; BETWEEN HEAVEN AND HELL(1956), m; HARDER THEY FALL, THE(1956), m; REVOLT OF MAMIE STOVER, THE(1956), m; AFFAIR TO REMEMBER, AN(1957), m; BOY ON A DOLPHIN(1957), m; SUN ALSO RISES, THE(1957), m; BARBARIAN AND THE GEISHA, THE(1958), m; IN LOVE AND WAR(1958), m; BLUE ANGEL, THE(1959), m; NEVER SO FEW(1959), m; THIS EARTH IS MINE(1959), m; WOMAN OBSESSED(1959), m; HOMICIDAL(1961), m; ONE-EYED JACKS(1961), m; GERONIMO(1962), m; SECRET INVASION, THE(1964), m; VON RICHTHOFEN AND BROWN(1970), m; PRIVATE PARTS(1972), m

Hugo W. Friedhofer
CHETNIKS(1943), m; PARIS AFTER DARK(1943), m; THEY CAME TO BLOW UP AMERICA(1943), m; LIFEBOAT(1944), m; LODGER, THE(1944), m; ROGER TOUHY, GANGSTER!(1944), m; WING AND A PRAYER(1944), m

Hugo Friedhoffer
CRIME SCHOOL(1938), md

David Friedkin
HOT SUMMER NIGHT(1957), d, w; HANDLE WITH CARE(1958), d, w; FOOL KILLER, THE(1965), p, w; PAWNBROKER, THE(1965), w

Gary Friedkin
UNDER THE RAINBOW(1981); YOUNG DOCTORS IN LOVE(1982)

Joel Friedkin
NOBODY'S CHILDREN(1940); WHO KILLED AUNT MAGGIE?(1940); FACE BEHIND THE MASK, THE(1941); OUTLAWS OF THE CHEROKEE TRAIL(1941); RICHEST MAN IN TOWN(1941); BAD MEN OF THE HILLS(1942); CYCLONE KID, THE(1942); DEVIL'S TRAIL, THE(1942); I MARRIED AN ANGEL(1942); PARDON MY GUN(1942); RAIDERS OF THE RANGE(1942); REUNION IN FRANCE(1942); SOMBRERO KID, THE(1942); LAUGH YOUR BLUES AWAY(1943); EXPERIMENT PERILOUS(1944); SUNDOWN VALLEY(1944); UNCERTAIN GLORY(1944); DON JUAN QUILLIGAN(1945); GOD IS MY CO-PILOT(1945); GREAT JOHN L. THE(1945); MURDER, HE SAYS(1945); EASY TO WED(1946); NOBODY LIVES FOREVER(1946); POSTMAN ALWAYS RINGS TWICE, THE(1946); UNEXPECTED GUEST(1946); HIGH WALL, THE(1947); JEWELS OF BRANDENBURG(1947); MAGIC TOWN(1947); SADDLE PALS(1947); SECRET LIFE OF WALTER MITTY, THE(1947); FALSE PARADISE(1948); FEUDIN', FUSSIN' AND A-FIGHTIN'(1948); HOLLOW TRIUMPH(1948); MONEY MADNESS(1948); PHANTOM VALLEY(1948); STRANGE GAMBLE(1948); IMPACT(1949); DAKOTA LIL(1950); HUMPHREY TAKES A CHANCE(1950); LIGHTNING GUNS(1950); BEDTIME FOR BONZO(1951); FURY OF THE CONGO(1951)

William Friedkin
GOOD TIMES(1967), d; BIRTHDAY PARTY, THE(1968, Brit.), d; NIGHT THEY RAIDED MINSKY'S, THE(1968), d; BOYS IN THE BAND, THE(1970), d; FRENCH CONNECTION, THE(1971), d; EXORCIST, THE(1973), d; SORCERER(1977), p&d; BRINK'S JOB, THE(1978), d; CRUISING(1980), d&w; DEAL OF THE CENTURY(1983), d

Franz R. Friedl
PILLARS OF SOCIETY(1936, Ger.), m

Jan Friedl
GETTING OF WISDOM, THE(1977, Aus.)

Alice Friedland
KILLING OF A CHINESE BOOKIE, THE(1976)

Alicia Friedland
Misc. Talkies
PLEASE DON'T EAT MY MOTHER(1972)

Dahlia Friedland
IMPOSSIBLE ON SATURDAY(1966, Fr./Israel)

Dalia Friedland
NEITHER BY DAY NOR BY NIGHT(1972, U.S./Israel)

Eddie Friedlander
ELI ELI(1940)

Howard Friedlander
GORDON'S WAR(1973), w; FAST CHARLIE... THE MOONBEAM RIDER(1979), w

Louis Friedlander [Lew Landers]
RAVEN, THE(1935), d; STORMY(1935), d; PAROLE(1936), d

Bert Friedlob
FIREBALL, THE(1950), p; BEYOND A REASONABLE DOUBT(1956), p

Helena Friedlova
MERRY WIVES, THE(1940, Czech.)

Gertrude Friedly
HAPPY DAYS(1930)

Alan Friedman
HARRIGAN'S KID(1943), w; LETTER FOR EVIE, A(1945), w; SHE WENT TO THE RACES(1945), w; KILLER DILL(1947), w; GIRLS ON THE LOOSE(1958), w

Andrew Friedman
SOUP FOR ONE(1982)

Anthony Friedman
BARTLEBY(1970, Brit.), p&w, d

Bernie Friedman
NEIGHBORS(1981)

Bruce Friedman
JEREMY(1973)

Bruce Jay Friedman
HEARTBREAK KID, THE(1972), w; STIR CRAZY(1980), w; DOCTOR DETROIT(1983), w
1984
LONELY GUY, THE(1984), w; SPLASH(1984), w

Budd Friedman
STAR 80(1983)

Danny Friedman
SLIPSTREAM(1974, Can.)

Dave Friedman
TRADER HORNEE(1970)

David Friedman
CONVICTS AT LARGE(1938), d

David F. Friedman
BLOOD FEAST(1963), p; TWO THOUSAND MANIACS!(1964), p, prod d; COLOR ME BLOOD RED(1965), p; SMELL OF HONEY, A SWALLOW OF BRINE! A(1966), p, w; SHE FREAK(1967), p, w; TRADER HORNEE(1970), p, w

Dov Friedman
CIRCLE OF IRON(1979, Brit.)
1984
SAHARA(1984)

Ed Friedman
1001 ARABIAN NIGHTS(1959), anim; MIGHTY MOUSE IN THE GREAT SPACE CHASE(1983), d

Eddie Friedman
WING AND A PRAYER(1944)

Eugene Friedman
PAPER LION(1968), ph

Gary W. Friedman
FULL MOON HIGH(1982), m

Gary William Friedman
SURVIVAL RUN(1980), m

Hanny Friedman
EYES OF LAURA MARS(1978)

Harry Friedman
WESTWARD HO(1936), w

Irving Friedman
BIG FIX, THE(1947), md; BORN TO SPEED(1947), md; DEVIL ON WHEELS, THE(1947), md; IT'S A JOKE, SON!(1947), md; LOST HONEYMOON(1947), md; LOVE FROM A STRANGER(1947), m; OUT OF THE BLUE(1947), md; PHILO VANCE RETURNS(1947), md; PHILO VANCE'S GAMBLE(1947), md; RAILROADED(1947), md; RED STALLION, THE(1947), md; REPEAT PERFORMANCE(1947), md; STEPCHILD(1947), md; T-MEN(1947), md; BEHIND LOCKED DOORS(1948), m; CANON CITY(1948), md; HE WALKED BY NIGHT(1948), md; HOLLOW TRIUMPH(1948), md; IN THIS CORNER(1948), md; LET'S LIVE A LITTLE(1948), md; MAN FROM TEXAS, THE(1948), md; MICKEY(1948), md; NOOSE HANGS HIGH, THE(1948), md; NORTHWEST STAMPEDE(1948), md; RAW DEAL(1948), md; SPIRITUALIST, THE(1948), md; BIG CAT, THE(1949), md; PORT OF NEW YORK(1949), md; RED STALLION IN THE ROCKIES(1949), md; TRAPPED(1949), md; TULSA(1949), md; PROWLER, THE(1951), md

Jeffrey Friedman
OUTLAW BLUES(1977)

Joann Friedman
KRAMER VS. KRAMER(1979)

Joe Friedman
EYES OF A STRANGER(1980); PORKY'S II: THE NEXT DAY(1983)

Joseph Friedman
LADY IS WILLING, THE(1934, Brit.), p; AFFAIRS OF A ROGUE, THE(1949, Brit.), p; ANGELO MY LOVE(1983), ph

Ken Friedman
WHITE LINE FEVER(1975, Can.), w; MR. BILLION(1977), p, w; HEART LIKE A WHEEL(1983), w
Misc. Talkies
DEATH BY INVITATION(1971), d

Kinky Friedman
RECORD CITY(1978)

Laurie Friedman
WAY WE LIVE, THE(1946, Brit.), ph; IT'S HARD TO BE GOOD(1950, Brit.), ph; EAST OF KILIMANJARO(1962, Brit./Ital.), ph; MIGHTY JUNGLE, THE(1965, U.S./Mex.), ph

Laving Friedman
FOR MEN ONLY(1952), m

Lewis Friedman
PRIVATE FILES OF J. EDGAR HOOVER, THE(1978), cos

Lisa Friedman
KING OF THE MOUNTAIN(1981)

Louis Friedman
IT LIVES AGAIN(1978), ed

Maria Friedman
MEDIUM COOL(1969)

Marley Friedman
SOUP FOR ONE(1982)

Marty Friedman
UNDERTAKER AND HIS PALS, THE(1966)

Max Friedman
ENCOUNTERS IN SALZBURG(1964, Ger.), d

Mike Friedman
THINGS ARE TOUGH ALL OVER(1982)

Monk Friedman
CRIME, INC.(1945)

Monroe Friedman
DR. CHRISTIAN MEETS THE WOMEN(1940), cos

Mort Friedman
PANIC BUTTON(1964), w

Nancy Friedman
STUDENT TEACHERS, THE(1973)

Norman Friedman
1984
TERMINATOR, THE(1984)
Peter Friedman
YOU BETTER WATCH OUT(1980); PRINCE OF THE CITY(1981); DANIEL(1983)
Phil Friedman
HOODLUM SAINT, THE(1946); HIGH BARBAREE(1947); CASBAH(1948)
Philip Friedman
LIKELY STORY, A(1947); RAGE(1972), w
Richard Friedman
YOUNG BILLY YOUNG(1969), set d; ROADIE(1980), set d
Richard Bruce Friedman
TRON(1982)
Ron Friedman
RECORD CITY(1978), w
Serge Friedman
MIDNIGHT FOLLY(1962, Fr.), w; DOUBLE DECEPTION(1963, Fr.), p
Seymour Friedman
TRAPPED BY BOSTON BLACKIE(1948), d; BOSTON BLACKIE'S CHINESE VENTURE(1949), d; CHINATOWN AT MIDNIGHT(1949), d; CRIME DOCTOR'S DIARY, THE(1949), d; DEVIL'S HENCHMEN, THE(1949), d; PRISON WARDEN(1949), d; RUSTY SAVES A LIFE(1949), d; RUSTY'S BIRTHDAY(1949), d; BODYHOLD(1950), d; COUNTERSPY MEETS SCOTLAND YARD(1950), d; CUSTOMS AGENT(1950), d; ROOKIE FIREMAN(1950), d; CRIMINAL LAWYER(1951), d; HER FIRST ROMANCE(1951), d; SON OF DR. JEKYLL, THE(1951), d; LOAN SHARK(1952), d; FLAME OF CALCUTTA(1953), d; I'LL GET YOU(1953, Brit.), d; KHYBER PATROL(1954), d; SAINT'S GIRL FRIDAY, THE(1954, Brit.), d; AFRICAN MANHUNT(1955), d; SECRET OF TREASURE MOUNTAIN(1956), d
Sharaga Friedman
SIMCHON FAMILY, THE(1969, Israel)
Sherwood Friedman
WACKIEST WAGON TRAIN IN THE WEST, THE(1976), w
Shraga Friedman
JUDITH(1965); SALLAH(1965, Israel)
Sonja Mays Friedman
WEEKEND(1968, Fr./Ital.), titles
Sonya Friedman
IT ONLY HAPPENS TO OTHERS(1971, Fr./Ital.), titles
Sonya Mays Friedman
LA PRISONNIERE(1969, Fr./Ital.), titles; INVESTIGATION OF A CITIZEN ABOVE SUSPICION(1970, Ital.), titles
Stephen Friedman
LOVIN' MOLLY(1974), p, w; SLAP SHOT(1977), p; BLOODBROTHERS(1978), p; FAST BREAK(1979), p; HERO AT LARGE(1980), p; EYE OF THE NEEDLE(1981), p
1984
ALL OF ME(1984), p
Stephen J. Friedman
LAST PICTURE SHOW, THE(1971), p; LITTLE DARLINGS(1980), p
Susan Friedman
APPRENTICESHIP OF DUDDY KRAVITZ, THE(1974, Can.)
Tom Friedman
TIME WALKER(1982), w
Tully Friedman
MEDIUM COOL(1969), p
Walter Friedman
SOME BLONDES ARE DANGEROUS(1937)
Jane Friedmann
TO LOVE(1964, Swed.)
James K. Friedrich
DAY OF TRIUMPH(1954), p
John Friedrich
BITTERSWEET LOVE(1976); ALMOST SUMMER(1978); WANDERERS, THE(1979); SMALL CIRCLE OF FRIENDS, A(1980); FAST-WALKING(1982); FINAL TERROR, THE(1983)
Misc. Talkies
CAMPSITE MASSACRE(1981)
Zbigniew Friedrich
HARD KNOCKS(1980, Aus.), ph&ed
Rainer Friedrichsen
1984
GERMANY PALE MOTHER(1984, Ger.)
Uwe Friedrichsen
FAUST(1963, Ger.); NO SURVIVORS, PLEASE(1963, Ger.); OPERATION GANYMED(1977, Ger.)
Hugo Friehofer
DANTE'S INFERNO(1935), m
Dick Friel
MC Q(1974)
Paula Friel
CHEAP DETECTIVE, THE(1978)
Richard M. Friel
Silents
EARLY BIRD, THE(1925), w
Tony Friel
RETURN OF THE JEDI(1983)
Colin Friels
BUDDIES(1983, Aus.); MONKEY GRIP(1983, Aus.)
Bente Friemel
1984
BIG MEAT EATER(1984, Can.)
Andrew W. Friend
CONCRETE JUNGLE, THE(1982), ph
Budd Friend
NEVER SAY GOODBYE(1946), set d; TWO MRS. CARROLLS, THE(1947), set d
Budd S. Friend
JOHNNY COOL(1963), set d; ADVANCE TO THE REAR(1964), set d; KISSIN' COUSINS(1964), set d; HOSTILE GUNS(1967), set d; WHO'S MINDING THE MINT?(1967), set d

Cliff Friend
FOX MOVIETONE FOLLIES OF 1930(1930), m
Helen Friend
LOVE PARADE, THE(1929)
J. B. Friend
NEIGHBORS(1981)
Joel Friend
HERE COME THE WAVES(1944); SWEETHEARTS OF THE U.S.A.(1944); VARIETY GIRL(1947); FRENCH LINE, THE(1954)
Rev. K.D. Friend
SWEET JESUS, PREACHER MAN(1973)
Philip Friend
INQUEST(1939, Brit.); MIDAS TOUCH, THE(1940, Brit.); SHEEPDOG OF THE HILLS(1941, Brit.); IN WHICH WE SERVE(1942, Brit.); NEXT OF KIN(1942, Brit.); PIMPERNEL SMITH(1942, Brit.); SUICIDE SQUADRON(1942, Brit.); BELLS GO DOWN, THE(1943, Brit.); FLEMISH FARM, THE(1943, Brit.); WE DIVE AT DAWN(1943, Brit.); GREAT DAY(1945, Brit.); ENCHANTMENT(1948); MY OWN TRUE LOVE(1948); SWORD IN THE DESERT(1949); SPY HUNT(1950); HIGHWAYMAN, THE(1951); SMUGGLER'S ISLAND(1951); THUNDER ON THE HILL(1951); BACKGROUND(1953, Brit.); DESPERATE MOMENT(1953, Brit.); DIAMOND WIZARD, THE(1954, Brit.); OPERATION CONSPIRACY(1957, Brit.); BETRAYAL, THE(1958, Brit.); SOLITARY CHILD, THE(1958, Brit.); SON OF ROBIN HOOD(1959, Brit.); WEB OF SUSPICION(1959, Brit.); FUR COLLAR, THE(1962, Brit.); STRANGLEHOLD(1962, Brit.); VULTURE, THE(1967, U.S./Brit./Can.)
Phillip Friend
BUCCANEER'S GIRL(1950)
Robert L. Friend
TARZAN'S DEADLY SILENCE(1970), d
William Friend
Silents
INVISIBLE POWER, THE(1921)
Alice Friendlich
STALKER(1982, USSR)
The Friends
DARK SIDE OF TOMORROW, THE(1970), m
Jack Frier
HOMICIDE BUREAU(1939), p
Michelangelo Frieri
SULEIMAN THE CONQUEROR(1963, Ital.), w
Aida Fries
LAST OF THE SECRET AGENTS?, THE(1966)
Charles Fries
CHOSEN SURVIVORS(1974 U.S.-Mex.), p; CAT PEOPLE(1982), p
Otto Fries
YOUNGER GENERATION(1929); MONKEY BUSINESS(1931); PARDON US(1931); MERRY WIDOW, THE(1934); MUSIC IN THE AIR(1934); MARY BURNS, FUGITIVE(1935); MYSTERY MAN, THE(1935); NIGHT AT THE OPERA, A(1935); NEXT TIME WE LOVE(1936); SMALL TOWN GIRL(1936); SONS O' GUNS(1936); TIMOTHY'S QUEST(1936); TRAIL OF THE LONESOME PINE, THE(1936); BULLDOG DRUMMOND COMES BACK(1937); EXPENSIVE HUSBANDS(1937); GIRL WITH IDEAS, A(1937); LOVE IN A BUNGALOW(1937); PICK A STAR(1937); PRESCRIPTION FOR ROMANCE(1937); PRISONER OF ZENDA, THE(1937); UNDER SUSPICION(1937); WHEN YOU'RE IN LOVE(1937); ALEXANDER'S RAGTIME BAND(1938); ARSENE LUPIN RETURNS(1938); BOY MEETS GIRL(1938); EVERY DAY'S A HOLIDAY(1938); MAD MISS MANTON, THE(1938); ROMANCE IN THE DARK(1938)
Silents
BRONCHO TWISTER(1927); RILEY THE COP(1928)
Otto A. Fries
HUMAN CARGO(1936)
Otto H. Fries
RIP TIDE(1934); STAMBOUL QUEST(1934); LOVE ON THE RUN(1936)
Ted Fries
REDWOOD FOREST TRAIL(1950)
Claude Fries-Greene
GREAT, MEADOW, THE(1931), ph
Hildegard Friese
GERMANY IN AUTUMN(1978, Ger.)
Kim Friese
GROUND ZERO(1973)
Otto Friese
HELL, HEAVEN OR HOBOKEN(1958, Brit.)
Claude Friese-Green
FIRES OF FATE(1932, Brit.), ph; HOUSE OF MYSTERY(1941, Brit.), ph
Claude Friese-Greene
ROMANCE OF SEVILLE, A(1929, Brit.), ph; LOOSE ENDS(1930, Brit.), ph; MIDDLE WATCH, THE(1930, Brit.), ph; SONG OF SOHO(1930, Brit.), ph; UNDER THE GREENWOOD TREE(1930, Brit.), ph; YELLOW MASK, THE(1930, Brit.), ph; FLYING FOOL, THE(1931, Brit.), ph; LOVE STORM, THE(1931, Brit.), ph; POOR OLD BILL(1931, Brit.), ph; UNEASY VIRTUE(1931, Brit.), ph; MAID OF THE MOUNTAINS, THE(1932, Brit.), ph; MY WIFE'S FAMILY(1932, Brit.), ph; SHADOW BETWEEN, THE(1932, Brit.), ph; FOR THE LOVE OF MIKE(1933, Brit.), ph; POLITICAL PARTY, A(1933, Brit.), ph; PRIDE OF THE FORCE, THE(1933, Brit.), ph; SOUTHERN MAID, A(1933, Brit.), ph; GIRLS WILL BE BOYS(1934, Brit.), ph; HAPPY(1934, Brit.), ph; SONG YOU GAVE ME, THE(1934, Brit.), ph; WHEN LONDON SLEEPS(1934, Brit.), ph; DRAKE THE PIRATE(1935, Brit.), ph; INVITATION TO THE WALTZ(1935, Brit.), ph; MUSIC HATH CHARMS(1935, Brit.), ph; NO MONKEY BUSINESS(1935, Brit.), ph; OLD CURIOSITY SHOP, THE(1935, Brit.), ph; GIVE HER A RING(1936, Brit.), ph; GYPSY MELODY(1936, Brit.), ph; PUBLIC NUISANCE NO. 1(1936, Brit.), ph; SCARAB MURDER CASE, THE(1936, Brit.), ph; YOU MUST GET MARRIED(1936, Brit.), ph; LET'S MAKE A NIGHT OF IT(1937, Brit.), ph; BLACK LIMELIGHT(1938, Brit.), ph; JANE STEPS OUT(1938, Brit.), ph; LOVES OF MADAME DUBARRY, THE(1938, Brit.), ph; JUST LIKE A WOMAN(1939, Brit.), ph; MIDDLE WATCH, THE(1939, Brit.), ph; SAINT IN LONDON, THE(1939, Brit.), ph; SHE COULDN'T SAY NO(1939, Brit.), ph; TORPEDOED!(1939), ph; BULLDOG SEES IT THROUGH(1940, Brit.), ph; FLYING SQUAD(1940, Brit.), ph; HIDDEN MENACE, THE(1940, Brit.), ph; MURDER IN THE NIGHT(1940, Brit.), ph; BANANA RIDGE(1941, Brit.), ph; FARMER'S WIFE, THE(1941, Brit.), ph; HARD STEEL(1941, Brit.), ph; STRANGLER, THE(1941, Brit.), ph; GREAT MR. HANDEL(1942, Brit.), ph; AMAZING MR. FORREST, THE(1943, Brit.), ph; ON APPROVAL(1944, Brit.), ph

John Friesen
WHY SHOOT THE TEACHER(1977, Can.)
Sandra Friesen
EUREKA(1983, Brit.)
Trixie Friganza
FREE AND EASY(1930); MYRT AND MARGE(1934); WANDERER OF THE WASTE-
LAND(1935); STAR IS BORN, A(1937); IF I HAD MY WAY(1940)
Silents
MIND OVER MOTOR(1923); BORROWED FINERY(1925); CHARMER, THE(1925);
COMING OF AMOS, THE(1925); PROUD FLESH(1925); ALMOST A LADY(1926);
RACING ROMEO(1927); GENTLEMEN PREFER BLONDES(1928); THANKS FOR
THE BUGGY RIDE(1928)
Misc. Silents
WHOLE TOWN'S TALKING, THE(1926)
Birgitte Frigast
Z.P.G.(1972)
Lorenza Frigeni
TREE OF WOODEN CLOGS, THE(1979, Ital.)
Enzo Frigerio
1900(1976, Ital.), art d
Ezio Frigerio
BEST OF ENEMIES, THE(1962), cos; CONDEMNED OF ALTONA, THE(1963), art d;
YESTERDAY, TODAY, AND TOMORROW(1964, Ital./Fr.), art d; GALILEO(1968,
Ital./Bul.), art d
Ione Frigerio
LITTLE MARTYR, THE(1947, Ital.)
Frightful the Falcon
MY SIDE OF THE MOUNTAIN(1969)
Miranda Frijda
1984
QUESTION OF SILENCE(1984, Neth.)
Nelly Frijda
1984
QUESTION OF SILENCE(1984, Neth.)
Anatol Frikin
PASSAGE TO MARSEILLE(1944)
Rude Frimel
NICKELODEON(1976)
Rudolf Friml
VAGABOND KING, THE(1930), w, m; ROSE MARIE(1936), w, m; FIREFLY,
THE(1937), m; NORTHWEST OUTPOST(1947), m; ROSE MARIE(1954), w, m
Rudolph Friml
LOTTERY BRIDE, THE(1930), m; VAGABOND KING, THE(1956), w
Rudolph Friml, Jr.
HOLLYWOOD CANTEEN(1944); UP IN ARMS(1944); WILD WEED(1949)
Rudy Friml
NIGHT AND DAY(1946); WHIPLASH(1948); JOHN LOVES MARY(1949); MY
DREAM IS YOURS(1949)
Rudy Friml, Jr.
NOBODY LIVES FOREVER(1946)
Peter Frinch
KISS ME AGAIN(1931), ed
Ketti Frings
HOLD BACK THE DAWN(1941), w; GUEST IN THE HOUSE(1944), w; LOOK
BEFORE YOU LOVE(1948), w; ACCUSED, THE(1949), w; COMPANY SHE
KEEPS, THE(1950), w; FILE ON THELMA JORDAN, THE(1950), w; BECAUSE OF
YOU(1952), w; COME BACK LITTLE SHEBA(1952), w; ABOUT MRS. LESLIE(1954),
w; FOXFIRE(1955), w; SHRIKE, THE(1955), w; MR. SYCAMORE(1975), w
Lola Frink
Silents
PRAISE AGENT, THE(1919)
Robert Frink
ME, NATALIE(1969)
Freddie Frinton
TROUBLE IN THE AIR(1948, Brit.); PENNY POINTS TO PARADISE(1951, Brit.);
FORCES' SWEETHEART(1953, Brit.); STARS IN YOUR EYES(1956, Brit.); MAKE
MINE MINK(1960, Brit.); WHAT A WHOPPER(1961, Brit.)
Jules Friquet
Misc. Silents
CAPTAIN OF HIS SOUL(1918)
Friquette
DON'T CRY WITH YOUR MOUTH FULL(1974, Fr.)
Maria Fris
DANCING HEART, THE(1959, Ger.)
Terence Frisby
THERE'S A GIRL IN MY SOUP(1970, Brit.), w
Larry Frisch
TEL AVIV TAXI(1957, Israel), p, d&w; PILLAR OF FIRE, THE(1963, Israel), p, d, w
Peter Frisch
BIG BUSINESS GIRL(1931), ed
Dan Frischman
GET CRAZY(1983)
David Frisco
QUEEN OF BURLESQUE(1946)
Joe Frisco
GORILLA, THE(1931); WESTERN JAMBOREE(1938); RIDE, TENDERFOOT, RI-
DE(1940); ATLANTIC CITY(1944); SHADY LADY(1945); THAT'S MY MAN(1947);
RIDING HIGH(1950); SWEET SMELL OF SUCCESS(1957)
Otto Frisco
MANDALAY(1934); STUDENT TOUR(1934)
Eric Frisdal
TEN DAYS' WONDER(1972, Fr.)
Brian Frishman
1941(1979); AMY(1981); BACK ROADS(1981)
Dan Frishman
RETURN OF THE JEDI(1983)
Daniel Frishman
LONE WOLF McQUADE(1983)

Paul Frison
FORGOTTEN WOMEN(1949); GUN CRAZY(1949)
Gianni Frisoni
LA CAGE AUX FOLLES II(1981, Ital./Fr.)
Varick Frissell
VIKING, THE(1931), p, w
Libero Frissi
ROMA(1972, Ital./Fr.)
Anne Fritch
FIEND(
H. T. Fritch
TRANSATLANTIC MERRY-GO-ROUND(1934), ed; SEA SPOILERS, THE(1936), ed
Hans Fritch
BANJO ON MY KNEE(1936), ed
Hansen Fritch
FIFTY ROADS TO TOWN(1937), ed; YOU CAN'T HAVE EVERYTHING(1937), ed
Hanson Fritch
PRESIDENT VANISHES, THE(1934), ed; CALL OF THE WILD(1935), ed; BORROW-
ING TROUBLE(1937), ed
Hanson T. Fritch
GOIN' TO TOWN(1944), ed
Peter Fritch
MOST IMMORAL LADY, A(1929), ed; SHOW GIRL IN HOLLYWOOD(1930), ed;
GOING WILD(1931), ed; LOOKING FOR TROUBLE(1934), ed
Richard Fritch
JOHNNY HOLIDAY(1949), ed
Robert Fritch
BOMBER'S MOON(1943), ed; MY FRIEND FLICKA(1943), ed; TAMPICO(1944), ed;
WAKE UP AND DREAM(1946), ed; UNFAITHFULLY YOURS(1948), ed; BEAUTI-
FUL BLONDE FROM BASHFUL BEND, THE(1949), ed; EVERYBODY DOES IT(1949),
ed; MISTER 880(1950), ed; ANNE OF THE INDIES(1951), ed; HALF ANGEL(1951),
ed; LET'S MAKE IT LEGAL(1951), ed; BELLES ON THEIR TOES(1952), ed; MY PAL
GUS(1952), ed; WAY OF A GAUCHO(1952), ed; DESTINATION GOBI(1953), ed;
DEMETRIUS AND THE GLADIATORS(1954), ed; GOD IS MY PARTNER(1957), ed;
LURE OF THE SWAMP(1957), ed; QUIET GUN, THE(1957), ed; FRONTIER
GUN(1958), ed; LONE TEXAN(1959), ed; ONE POTATO, TWO POTATO(1964), ed
Barbara Fritchie
LAST ROUND-UP, THE(1934); MURDER AT THE VANITIES(1934); MURDER ON
THE BLACKBOARD(1934); GAY DECEPTION, THE(1935); THUNDER MOUN-
TAIN(1935); WILD MUSTANG(1935)
Alfred Frith
WHITE DEATH(1936, Aus.)
Anne Frith
NIGHTBEAST(1982)
1984
ALIEN FACTOR, THE(1984)
Misc. Talkies
TERROR FROM THE UNKNOWN(1983)
J. Leslie Frith
MURDER IN THE OLD RED BARN(1936, Brit.)
Leslie Frith
DREYFUS CASE, THE(1931, Brit.)
Steve Frith
FIEND(
Berndt Fritiof
EMIGRANTS, THE(1972, Swed.), art d
Anne Lise Fritsch
DEATH OF MARIO RICCI, THE(1983, Ital.)
Gisela Fritsch
BEFORE WINTER COMES(1969, Brit.)
Guenther Fritsch
BODY AND SOUL(1947), art d
Gunther Fritsch
STOLEN IDENTITY(1953), d
Gunther V Fritsch
CURSE OF THE CAT PEOPLE, THE(1944), d; CIGARETTE GIRL(1947), d
Pete Fritsch
MARY BURNS, FUGITIVE(1935), ed
Peter Fritsch
I LIKE YOUR NERVE(1931), ed
Robert Fritsch
GIRL TROUBLE(1942), ed
Thomas Fritsch
AND SO TO BED(1965, Ger.); APOLLO GOES ON HOLIDAY(1968, Ger./Swed.);
UNCLE TOM'S CABIN(1969, Fr./Ital./Ger./Yugo.)
Willy Fritsch
LOVE WALTZ, THE(1930, Ger.); BOCCACCIO(1936, Ger.); FILM WITHOUT A
NAME(1950, Ger.); PLAYGIRLS AND THE BELLBOY, THE(1962,Ger.)
Silents
SPIES(1929, Ger.); WOMAN ON THE MOON, THE(1929, Ger.)
Misc. Silents
LAST WALTZ, THE(1927, Ger.)
Donnie Fritts
PAT GARRETT AND BILLY THE KID(1973)
1984
SONGWRITER(1984)
Axel Fritz
LOVING COUPLES(1966, Swed.)
Bobbi Fritz
SPRING BREAK(1983)
Joseph Fritz
HIGH-POWERED RIFLE, THE(1960), w; WALK TALL(1960), w
Ken Fritz
1984
EVIL THAT MEN DO, THE(1984); TERMINATOR, THE(1984)
Margie Fritz
FAST CHARLIE... THE MOONBEAM RIDER(1979), set d

Nils Fritz
JUST ONCE MORE(1963, Swed.)
Roger Fritz
CROSS OF IRON(1977, Brit., Ger.); DESPAIR(1978, Ger.); LILI MARLEEN(1981, Ger.); QUERELLE(1983, Ger./Fr.)
Shela Fritz
ROAD TO BALI(1952)
Fritz The Horse
Silents
TOLL GATE, THE(1920)
James Fritzell
GOOD NEIGHBOR SAM(1964), w; GHOST AND MR. CHICKEN, THE(1966), w
Jim Fritzell
RELUCTANT ASTRONAUT, THE(1967), w; DID YOU HEAR THE ONE ABOUT THE TRAVELING SALESLADY?(1968), w; SHAKIEST GUN IN THE WEST, THE(1968), w; ANGEL IN MY POCKET(1969), w
FritzFalkenstein
PERFECT SPECIMEN, THE(1937), w
Cornelius Frizell
LILITH(1964)
Lou Frizell
LAWMAN(1971)
David Frizzell
HONKYTONK MAN(1982)
Lefty Frizzell
SECOND FIDDLE TO A STEEL GUITAR(1965); LAST PICTURE SHOW, THE(1971), m
Lou Frizzell
REIVERS, THE(1969); STALKING MOON, THE(1969); TELL THEM WILLIE BOY IS HERE(1969); HALLS OF ANGER(1970); SUMMER OF '42(1971); HICKEY AND BOGGS(1972); OTHER, THE(1972); RAGE(1972); CRAZY WORLD OF JULIUS VROODER, THE(1974); FRONT PAGE, THE(1974); NICKEL RIDE, THE(1974)
Maurice Frizzell, Jr.
1984
BIRDY(1984)
Fabio Frizzi
PSYCHIC, THE(1979, Ital.), m; ZOMBIE(1980, Ital.), m; GATES OF HELL, THE(1983, U.S./Ital.), m
Fulvio Frizzi
PSYCHIC, THE(1979, Ital.), p
Gert Frobe
$(DOLLARS)**1/2 (1971); MAN ON A TIGHTROPE(1953); IT HAPPENED IN BROAD DAYLIGHT(1960, Ger./Switz.); ROSEMARY(1960, Ger.); THOUSAND EYES OF DR. MABUSE, THE(1960, Fr./Ital./Ger.); RETURN OF DR. MABUSE, THE(1961, Ger./Fr./Ital.); LONGEST DAY, THE(1962); THREE PENNY OPERA(1963, Fr./Ger.); GOLDFINGER(1964, Brit.); BACKFIRE(1965, Fr.); BANANA PEEL(1965, Fr.); GREED IN THE SUN(1965, Fr./ Ital.); HIGH WIND IN JAMAICA, A(1965); TERROR OF DR. MABUSE, THE(1965, Ger.); THOSE MAGNIFICENT MEN IN THEIR FLYING MACHINES; OR HOW I FLEWFROM LONDON TO PARIS IN 25 HOURS AND 11 MINUTES(1965, Brit.); ENOUGH ROPE(1966, Fr./Ital./Ger.); GIRL AND THE LEGEND, THE(1966, Ger.); IS PARIS BURNING?(1966, U.S./Fr.); THOSE FANTASTIC FLYING FOOLS(1967, Brit); TRIPLE CROSS(1967, Fr./Brit.); UPPER HAND, THE(1967, Fr./Ital./Ger.); CAROLINE CHERIE(1968, Fr.); CHITTY CHITTY BANG BANG(1968, Brit.); TONIO KROGER(1968, Fr./Ger.); THOSE DARING YOUNG MEN IN THEIR JAUNTY JALOPIES(1969, Fr./Brit./ Ital.); LUDWIG(1973, Ital./Ger./Fr.); SHADOWMAN(1974, Fr./Ital.); TEN LITTLE INDIANS(1975, Ital./Fr./Span./Ger.); SERPENT'S EGG, THE(1977, Ger./U.S.); BLOODLINE(1979)
Conny Froboess
ELUSIVE CORPORAL, THE(1963, Fr.)
Cornelia Froboess
VERONIKA VOSS(1982, Ger.)
Franz Frodl
BATTLE OF BRITAIN, THE(1969, Brit.), tech adv
Gert Froebe
SPECIAL DELIVERY(1955, Ger.); THEY WERE SO YOUNG(1955); ETERNAL WALTZ, THE(1959, Ger.); PRISONER OF THE VOLGA(1960, Fr./Ital.)
Carl Froehlich
NIGHT IS OURS(1930, Fr.), p; PRIVATE LIFE OF LOUIS XIV(1936, Ger.), p&d, w
Gustav Froehlich
BARCAROLE(1935, Ger.); HOUSE OF LIFE(1953, Ger.)
Pea Froehlich
LOLA(1982, Ger.), w
Carl Froelich
MAEDCHEN IN UNIFORM(1932, Ger.), p; DREAMER, THE(1936, Ger.), p; FOUR COMPANIONS, THE(1938, Ger.), d
Hugo Froelich
FOUR COMPANIONS, THE(1938, Ger.)
Oleg Froelich
Misc. Silents
DOUBLE, THE(1916, USSR); SPECTRE HAUNTS EUROPE, A(1923, USSR)
Anne Froelick
SHINING VICTORY(1941), w; MASTER RACE, THE(1944), w; MISS SUSIE SLAGLE'S(1945), w; EASY COME, EASY GO(1947), w; HARRIET CRAIG(1950), w
Ewa Froeling
FANNY AND ALEXANDER(1983, Swed./Fr./Ger.)
George Froeschel
MORTAL STORM, THE(1940), w; WATERLOO BRIDGE(1940), w; MRS. MINIVER(1942), w; RANDOM HARVEST(1942), w; WE WERE DANCING(1942), w; WHITE CLIFFS OF DOVER, THE(1944), w; COMMAND DECISION(1948), w; MINIVER STORY, THE(1950, Brit./U.S.), w; UNKNOWN MAN, THE(1951), w; SCARAMOUCHE(1952), w; NEVER LET ME GO(1953, U.S./Brit.), w; STORY OF THREE LOVES, THE(1953), w; BETRAYED(1954), w; ROSE MARIE(1954), w; QUENTIN DURWARD(1955), w; GABY(1956), w; ME AND THE COLONEL(1958), w; I AIM AT THE STARS(1960), w
Edgar Froese
KAMIKAZE '89(1983, Ger.), m
Louise Frogley
1984
ANOTHER TIME, ANOTHER PLACE(1984, Brit.), cos

Freddy Frogs
1984
FLAMINGO KID, THE(1984)
Alan Frohlich
HOW TO STUFF A WILD BIKINI(1965)
Elisabeth Frohlich
LANCER SPY(1937)
Gustav Frohlich
WHAT WOMEN DREAM(1933, Ger.)
Pia Frohlich
MARRIAGE OF MARIA BRAUN, THE(1979, Ger.), w
Roland Frohlich
HOPSCOTCH(1980)
Sid Frohlich
ONCE IS NOT ENOUGH(1975)
Sig Frohlich
STRIP, THE(1951); HARRY AND WALTER GO TO NEW YORK(1976); FIRST MONDAY IN OCTOBER(1981); TRUE CONFESSIONS(1981)
Sigmund Frohlich
LOOKIN' TO GET OUT(1982)
Bert Frohman
BACK DOOR TO HEAVEN(1939)
Charles Frohman
Silents
ROYAL FAMILY, A(1915), w
Clayton Frohman
UNDER FIRE(1983), w
Daniel Frohman
Silents
DAY OF DAYS, THE(1914), d
Mary Hubert Frohman
Misc. Silents
FAIRY AND THE WAIF, THE(1915), d
Mel Frohman
...ALL THE MARBLES(1981), w
Gustav Frolich
IMMORTAL VAGABOND(1931, Ger.)
Silents
METROPOLIS(1927, Ger.)
Josef Frolich
AMERICAN SUCCESS COMPANY, THE(1980)
Pea Frolich
VERONIKA VOSS(1982, Ger.), w
Rudy Frolich
MAN I MARRIED, THE(1940)
G. Frolov
DIMKA(1964, USSR)
K. Frolova
SUMMER TO REMEMBER, A(1961, USSR)
Soren Frolund
1984
ZAPPA(1984, Den.)
Max From
TRAIN, THE(1965, Fr./Ital./U.S.)
David Froman
HANKY-PANKY(1982)
Jane Froman
STARS OVER BROADWAY(1935); RADIO CITY REVELS(1938); WITH A SONG IN MY HEART(1952)
Lou Froman
SLIME PEOPLE, THE(1963), m
Margerita Froman
Misc. Silents
DEATH OF THE GODS(1917, USSR)
Richard L. Froman
DEMON SEED(1977), anim
Milton Frome
RIDE 'EM COWGIRL(1939); SMASHING THE MONEY RING(1939); SEVEN LITTLE FOYS, THE(1955); YOU'RE NEVER TOO YOUNG(1955); MAN WHO KNEW TOO MUCH, THE(1956); PARDNERS(1956); DELICATE DELINQUENT, THE(1957); FUZZY PINK NIGHTGOWN, THE(1957); HEAR ME GOOD(1957); LONELY MAN, THE(1957); PUBLIC PIGEON NO. 1(1957); SHORT CUT TO HELL(1957); YOUNG LIONS, THE(1958); GO, JOHNNY, GO!(1959); PLEASE DON'T EAT THE DAISIES(1960); ERRAND BOY, THE(1961); POLICE DOG STORY, THE(1961); IT'S ONLY MONEY(1962); BYE BYE BIRDIE(1963); NUTTY PROFESSOR, THE(1963); TICKLISH AFFAIR, A(1963); WHO'S MINDING THE STORE?(1963); DISORDERLY ORDERLY, THE(1964); I'D RATHER BE RICH(1964); JOHN GOLDFARB, PLEASE COME HOME(1964); WHAT A WAY TO GO(1964); BIRDS AND THE BEES, THE(1965); DR. GOLDFOOT AND THE BIKINI MACHINE(1965); FAMILY JEWELS, THE(1965); FLUFFY(1965); BATMAN(1966); SWINGER, THE(1966); WAY...WAY OUT(1966); ENTER LAUGHING(1967); ST. VALENTINE'S DAY MASSACRE, THE(1967); CHUBASCO(1968); WITH SIX YOU GET EGGROLL(1968); WHICH WAY TO THE FRONT?(1970); SHAGGY D.A., THE(1976)
Raymond Froment
TIME BOMB(1961, Fr./Ital.), p; LAST YEAR AT MARIENBAD(1962, Fr./Ital.), p; YOUNG WORLD, A(1966, Fr./Ital.), p; SHOCK TROOPS(1968, Ital./Fr.), p; SHADOWMAN(1974, Fr./Ital.), p
Airion Fromer
BOY...A GIRL, A(1969)
Ben Fromer
CARWASH(1976)
Fromet
Misc. Silents
GARDIENS DE PHARE(1929, Fr.)
Maria Fromet
ARIANE, RUSSIAN MAID(1932, Fr.)
Steven Fromewick
THEY ALL LAUGHED(1981)

V. Fromgoldt
  WAR AND PEACE(1968, USSR)
Steve Fromholtz
1984
  CLOAK AND DAGGER(1984); SONGWRITER(1984)
Steve Fromholz
  OUTLAW BLUES(1977)
Maxime Fromiot
  POIL DE CAROTTE(1932, Fr.)
Leon Fromkess
  PRISONER OF JAPAN(1942), p; SECRETS OF A CO-ED(1942), p; BLUE-
  BEARD(1944), p; GREAT MIKE, THE(1944), p; JIVE JUNCTION(1944), p; MIN-
  STREL MAN(1944), p; WHEN THE LIGHTS GO ON AGAIN(1944), p;
  DETOUR(1945), p; FOG ISLAND(1945), p; HOLLYWOOD AND VINE(1945), p; MAN
  WHO WALKED ALONE, THE(1945), p; MISSING CORPSE, THE(1945), p; STRANGE
  ILLUSION(1945), p; CLUB HAVANA(1946), p; WIFE OF MONTE CRISTO, THE(1946),
  p; BLOOD ON THE ARROW(1964), p; GREAT SIOUX MASSACRE, THE(1965), p;
  FLAREUP(1969), p
Ben Frommer
  CRAZY OVER HORSES(1951); BRIDE OF THE MONSTER(1955); HELL'S IS-
  LAND(1955); ARSON FOR HIRE(1959); C'MON, LET'S LIVE A LITTLE(1967); DR.
  HECKYL AND MR. HYPE(1980); AMERICAN POP(1981); DOCTOR DETROIT(1983);
  PSYCHO II(1983); SCARFACE(1983)
Edward R. Frommer
  SCARFACE(1983)
Pierre Fromont
  DIARY OF A BAD GIRL(1958, Fr.); THUNDER IN THE BLOOD(1962, Fr.)
Carolyn Fromson
  SEEMS LIKE OLD TIMES(1980)
Rosalie Fromson
  ROMAN SCANDALS(1933)
B. Fronczkowiak
  MAN OF MARBLE(1979, Pol.)
Pierre Frondale
  STAMBOUL(1931, Brit.), w
Signor Frondi
Silents
  LOVES OF RICARDO, THE(1926)
Barry Froner
  RUMBLE ON THE DOCKS(1956)
Dominic Frontiere
  MARRIAGE-GO-ROUND, THE(1960), m; ONE FOOT IN HELL(1960), m; SEVEN
  THIEVES(1960), m; RIGHT APPROACH, THE(1961), m; HERO'S ISLAND(1962), m;
  GLOBAL AFFAIR, A(1964), m; BILLIE(1965), m; INCUBUS(1966), m; HANG'EM
  HIGH(1968), m; NUMBER ONE(1969), m; POPI(1969), m; BARQUERO(1970), m; CHI-
  SUM(1970), m; NAME FOR EVIL, A(1970), m; CANCEL MY RESERVATION(1972),
  m; HAMMERSMITH IS OUT(1972), m; TRAIN ROBBERS, THE(1973), m; FREEBIE
  AND THE BEAN(1974), m; BRANNIGAN(1975, Brit.), m; CLEOPATRA JONES AND
  THE CASINO OF GOLD(1975 U. S. Hong Kong), m; GUMBALL RALLY, THE(1976), m;
  PIPE DREAMS(1976), m; STUNT MAN, THE(1980), m; MODERN PROBLEMS(1981),
  m; ROAR(1981), m
Rafael Frontura
  MAN AND THE BEAST, THE(1951, Arg.)
Dorothy Frooks
  REDS(1981)
Albert Froom
Misc. Silents
  DEEMSTER, THE(1917)
Sylvia Froos
  STAND UP AND CHEER(1934 80m FOX bw)
Milva [Deanna] Frosini
  SEED OF MAN, THE(1970, Ital.)
Alan Frost
  BRAIN EATERS, THE(1958)
Alice Frost
  PRIZE, THE(1963); I'LL TAKE SWEDEN(1965)
Ann Frost
  HALF A SIXPENCE(1967, Brit.)
Christopher Frost
  NO TIME FOR TEARS(1957, Brit.)
David Frost
  V.I.P.s, THE(1963, Brit.)
Don Frost
  TWILIGHT IN THE SIERRAS(1950); SKY HIGH(1952)
F. Harvey Frost
  SOMETHING'S ROTTEN(1979, Can.), d
George Frost
  MASTER OF BALLANTRAE, THE(1953, U.S./Brit.), makeup; QUIET AMERICAN,
  THE(1958), makeup; ROOTS OF HEAVEN, THE(1958), makeup; SUNDOWNERS,
  THE(1960), makeup; GUNS OF NAVARONE, THE(1961), makeup; LION, THE(1962,
  Brit.), makeup; SATAN NEVER SLEEPS(1962), makeup; TASTE OF HONEY, A(1962,
  Brit.), makeup; 300 SPARTANS, THE(1962), makeup; RUNNING MAN, THE(1963,
  Brit.), makeup; OF HUMAN BONDAGE(1964, Brit.), makeup; PUMPKIN EATER,
  THE(1964, Brit.), makeup; LIFE AT THE TOP(1965, Brit.), makeup; MISTER MO-
  SES(1965), makeup; SPY WHO CAME IN FROM THE COLD, THE(1965, Brit.),
  makeup; MAN FOR ALL SEASONS, A(1966, Brit.), makeup; OLIVER!(1968, Brit.),
  makeup; KREMLIN LETTER, THE(1970), makeup; ONE MORE TIME(1970, Brit.),
  makeup; SCROOGE(1970, Brit.), makeup; MARY, QUEEN OF SCOTS(1971, Brit.),
  makeup; MUSIC LOVERS, THE(1971, Brit.), makeup; LADY CAROLINE LAMB(1972,
  Brit./Ital.), makeup; NELSON AFFAIR, THE(1973, Brit.), makeup; NASTY HA-
  BITS(1976, Brit.), makeup; JULIA(1977), makeup; OCTOPUSSY(1983, Brit.), makeup
Gower Frost
1984
  SLAYGROUND(1984, Brit.), p
Irmgard Frost
  SWISS CONSPIRACY, THE(1976, U.S./Ger.)
Jack Frost
  HAPPY DAYS(1930); P.C. JOSSER(1931, Brit.); JOSSER IN THE ARMY(1932, Brit.);
  JOSSER JOINS THE NAVY(1932, Brit.); LOVE UP THE POLE(1936, Brit.)

Jackie Frost
  STRANGERS, THE(1955, Ital.)
Jacqueline Frost
  LOCKET, THE(1946)
Jean Sarah Frost
  GOODBYE, NORMA JEAN(1976); ANNIE HALL(1977)
Kelly Frost
Misc. Talkies
  PHANTOM KID, THE(1983)
Larry Frost
  STAKEOUT ON DOPE STREET(1958)
Lauren Frost
  HESTER STREET(1975); WHOLLY MOSES(1980)
Lee Frost
  CHROME AND HOT LEATHER(1971), d; THING WITH TWO HEADS, THE(1972), a,
  a, d, w; TOMB OF THE UNDEAD(1972); SWEET JESUS, PREACHER MAN(1973);
  POLICEWOMAN(1974), d, w; BLACK GESTAPO, THE(1975), a, d, w; RACE WITH
  THE DEVIL(1975), w; DIXIE DYNAMITE(1976), d, w
Misc. Talkies
  CHAIN GANG WOMEN(1972), d
Lelia Frost
Misc. Silents
  HEART OF EZRA GREER, THE(1917)
Lorraine Frost
Silents
  GOD'S HALF ACRE(1916)
Misc. Silents
  LIGHT OF HAPPINESS, THE(1916)
Margaret Frost
  STOP THE WORLD–I WANT TO GET OFF(1966, Brit.)
Maria Frost
  SECRETS OF SEX(1970, Brit.)
Michael Frost
  CRY DR. CHICAGO(1971); MORE AMERICAN GRAFFITI(1979); HOSPITAL MAS-
  SACRE(1982)
Philip Frost
  SCROOGE(1935, Brit.); MILL ON THE FLOSS(1939, Brit.)
Philip Sydney Frost
  WINGS OF THE MORNING(1937, Brit.)
Phillip Frost
  REMARKABLE MR. KIPPS(1942, Brit.)
R. L. Frost
  SURFTIDE 77(1962), d; NIGHT OF LUST(1965, Fr.), w; HOT SPUR(1968), d&w;
  SCAVENGERS, THE(1969), d
Rex Frost
  SMALL HOTEL(1957, Brit.), w
Ritchie Frost
  STAKEOUT ON DOPE STREET(1958)
Robert Frost
  SHED NO TEARS(1948), p; BLACK CAT, THE(1966)
Roger Frost
  TIME BANDITS(1981, Brit.)
Sadie Frost
Misc. Talkies
  HAY, HAY, HAY(1983, Brit.)
Terry Frost
  CYCLONE ON HORSEBACK(1941); LAW OF THE RANGE(1941); MOB TOWN(1941);
  GIRL FROM MONTEREY, THE(1943); CALIFORNIA JOE(1944); JAM SESSION(1944);
  MONSTER MAKER, THE(1944); MR. WINKLE GOES TO WAR(1944); RUSTLER'S
  HIDEOUT(1944); SWING HOSTESS(1944); TRAIL TO GUNSIGHT(1944); WATER-
  FRONT(1944); THERE GOES KELLY(1945); BLACK MARKET BABIES(1946); CARA-
  VAN TRAIL, THE(1946); DRIFTING ALONG(1946); FLYING SERPENT, THE(1946);
  GENTLEMAN FROM TEXAS(1946); WILD WEST(1946); APACHE ROSE(1947);
  GHOST TOWN RENEGADES(1947); PIONEER JUSTICE(1947); STAGE TO MESA
  CITY(1947); VACATION DAYS(1947); BLACK HILLS(1948); CHECK YOUR
  GUNS(1948); DEAD MAN'S GOLD(1948); HAWK OF POWDER RIVER, THE(1948);
  OKLAHOMA BADLANDS(1948); PRAIRIE OUTLAWS(1948); TIOGA KID, THE(1948);
  TORNADO RANGE(1948); LAWLESS CODE(1949); SON OF BILLY THE KID(1949);
  WEST OF EL DORADO(1949); WESTERN RENEGADES(1949); BARON OF ARIZONA,
  THE(1950); DALTON'S WOMEN, THE(1950); DESERT HAWK, THE(1950); LOUI-
  SA(1950); OUTLAWS OF TEXAS(1950); MAN WHO CHEATED HIMSELF, THE(1951);
  SILVER CANYON(1951); STAGE TO BLUE RIVER(1951); TEXAS LAWMEN(1951);
  VALLEY OF FIRE(1951); BARBED WIRE(1952); DEAD MAN'S TRAIL(1952); FAR-
  GO(1952); KANSAS TERRITORY(1952); MAN BEHIND THE GUN, THE(1952); MAVE-
  RICK, THE(1952); NIGHT RAIDERS(1952); WACO(1952); STRANGER WORE A GUN,
  THE(1953); WINNING OF THE WEST(1953); ONE DESIRE(1955); SPOILERS,
  THE(1955); TEN WANTED MEN(1955); CRASHING LAS VEGAS(1956); NIGHT THE
  WORLD EXPLODED, THE(1957); UTAH BLAINE(1957); WILD WESTERNERS,
  THE(1962)
Misc. Talkies
  MOON OVER MONTANA(1946); SILVER RANGE(1946); GUNMAN, THE(1952);
  TRAIL OF THE ARROW(1952)
Terry L. Frost
  TEXAS CITY(1952)
Toni Frost
  HIGHLY DANGEROUS(1950, Brit.); HOME TO DANGER(1951, Brit.); TO PARIS
  WITH LOVE(1955, Brit.)
Tony Frost
  WHISPERING SMITH VERSUS SCOTLAND YARD(1952, Brit.)
Warren Frost
  WAR OF THE COLOSSAL BEAST(1958)
Misc. Talkies
  JACKPOT(1982)
Wayne Frost
  FLASHDANCE(1983)
Janina Frostova
  LAKE PLACID SERENADE(1944)

J. L. Frothingham
Silents
TEN DOLLAR RAISE, THE(1921), p
Frou-Frou
MEET MY SISTER(1933, Brit.)
Jose Frowe
LAST SUNSET, THE(1961)
Lisa Fruchtman
HEAVEN'S GATE(1980), ed; STREET MUSIC(1982), ed; RIGHT STUFF, THE(1983), ed
George Fruechtenicht
NIGHT OF EVIL(1962)
A. E. Fruedeman
RHYTHM ON THE RANGE(1936), set d; WAIKIKI WEDDING(1937), set d
Jessica Frueh
SISTERS, OR THE BALANCE OF HAPPINESS(1982, Ger.)
Henry Fruelich
AMBUSH AT TOMAHAWK GAP(1953), ph
Patricia Fruen
Silents
WAY DOWN EAST(1920)
William Fruet
GOIN' DOWN THE ROAD(1970, Can.), w; RIP-OFF(1971, Can.), w; WEDDING IN WHITE(1972, Can.), d&w; SLIPSTREAM(1974, Can.), w; HOUSE BY THE LAKE, THE(1977, Can.), d&w; SEARCH AND DESTROY(1981), d; FUNERAL HOME(1982, Can.), p&d; SPASMS(1983, Can.), d
1984
BEDROOM EYES(1984, Can.), d
Misc. Talkies
STRIKING BACK(1981), d; TRAPPED(1982), d
William Fruete
DRYLANDERS(1963, Can.)
Thalie Fruges
MARRIAGE CAME TUMBLING DOWN, THE(1968, Fr.); MATTER OF DAYS, A(1969, Fr./Czech.); MAGNIFICENT ONE, THE(1974, Fr./Ital.)
Cesare Frugoni
SCREAMERS(1978, Ital.), w; NEST OF VIPERS(1979, Ital.), w
Kurt Fruh
VILLAGE, THE(1953, Brit./Switz.), w
Sharon Fruitin
DOC(1971)
Roy Frumkes
JAMAICA INN(1939, Brit.); COMEBACK TRAIL, THE(1982), w
Reynold Frutkin
SALLY'S HOUNDS(1968)
Ann Fry
RUN, ANGEL, RUN(1969)
Billy Fry
BIG BUSINESS(1930, Brit.)
Christopher Fry
BEGGAR'S OPERA, THE(1953), w; BARABBAS(1962, Ital.), w; BIBLE...IN THE BEGINNING, THE(1966), w
Clayton Fry
Misc. Silents
NOT FOR SALE(1924)
Gil Fry
TWIST ALL NIGHT(1961)
Howard Fry
ROYAL DEMAND, A(1933, Brit.)
John Fry
SCAVENGERS, THE(1969), art d
Michael Fry
DENTIST IN THE CHAIR(1960, Brit.)
Ron Fry
LEGEND OF HELL HOUSE, THE(1973, Brit.), prod d
Tom Fry
LORDS OF DISCIPLINE, THE(1983)
Virgil Fry
KLANSMAN, THE(1974)
Virginia Fry
Silents
NON-STOP FLIGHT, THE(1926)
Hal Fryar
OUTLAWS IS COMING, THE(1965)
Joseph Fryd
GOLD FOR THE CAESARS(1964), p; HERCULES, SAMSON & ULYSSES(1964, Ital.), p; SANDOKAN THE GREAT(1964, Fr./Ital./Span.), p; SNOW DEVILS, THE(1965, Ital.), p; MAN WHO LAUGHS, THE(1966, Ital.), p; RINGO AND HIS GOLDEN PISTOL(1966, Ital.), p; WAKE UP AND DIE(1967, Fr./Ital.), p; WILD, WILD PLANET, THE(1967, Ital.), p; WAR BETWEEN THE PLANETS(1971, Ital.), p
Helena Frydlova
SKELETON ON HORSEBACK(1940, Czech.)
Wera Frydtberg
AREN'T WE WONDERFUL?(1959, Ger.); PHONY AMERICAN, THE(1964, Ger.)
Andrea Frye
TOGETHER FOR DAYS(1972)
Buddy Frye
PRIME TIME, THE(1960), m
Chip Frye
Misc. Talkies
SECTOR 13(1982)
Clayton Frye
Silents
OLD HOME WEEK(1925)
Derek Frye [Harold Buchman
SLEEPING TIGER, THE(1954, Brit.), w
Dwight Frye
DOORWAY TO HELL(1930); BLACK CAMEL, THE(1931); DRACULA(1931); FRANKENSTEIN(1931); MALTESE FALCON, THE(1931); MAN TO MAN(1931); ATTORNEY FOR THE DEFENSE(1932); BY WHOSE HAND?(1932); STRANGE ADVEN-

TURE(1932); CIRCUS QUEEN MURDER, THE(1933); INVISIBLE MAN, THE(1933); VAMPIRE BAT, THE(1933); ATLANTIC ADVENTURE(1935); GREAT IMPERSONATION, THE(1935); ALIBI FOR MURDER(1936); CRIME OF DR. CRESPI, THE(1936); FLORIDA SPECIAL(1936); BEWARE OF LADIES(1937); MAN WHO FOUND HIMSELF, THE(1937); ROAD BACK, THE(1937); SHADOW, THE(1937); SOMETHING TO SING ABOUT(1937); ADVENTURE IN SAHARA(1938); FAST COMPANY(1938); INVISIBLE ENEMY(1938); NIGHT HAWK, THE(1938); WHO KILLED GAIL PRESTON?(1938); MAN IN THE IRON MASK, THE(1939); SON OF FRANKENSTEIN(1939); GANGS OF CHICAGO(1940); PHANTOM RAIDERS(1940); SKY BANDITS, THE(1940); MYSTERY SHIP(1941); PEOPLE VS. DR. KILDARE, THE(1941); GHOST OF FRANKENSTEIN, THE(1942); SLEEPYTIME GAL(1942); DEAD MEN WALK(1943); DRUMS OF FU MANCHU(1943); FRANKENSTEIN MEETS THE WOLF MAN(1943); SUBMARINE ALERT(1943)
Ellen Frye
CRAZY QUILT, THE(1966)
Gil Frye
MONSTER THAT CHALLENGED THE WORLD, THE(1957); BRIDE AND THE BEAST, THE(1958); MUSIC BOX KID, THE(1960)
Gilbert Frye
PRISONER OF JAPAN(1942); SONS OF ADVENTURE(1948); GREAT PLANE ROBBERY(1950); TIMBER FURY(1950); CLASH BY NIGHT(1952); CONFIDENCE GIRL(1952)
Joe Frye
GOIN' TO TOWN(1935)
John W. Frye
BOOTS MALONE(1952)
Katherine Frye
ROARIN' LEAD(1937); ONE MILLION B.C.(1940)
Kathryn Frye
MEXICALI ROSE(1939)
Kathy Frye
THREE RUSSIAN GIRLS(1943); CROSSED TRAILS(1948); WOMEN IN THE NIGHT(1948)
Kay Frye
HEART OF THE RIO GRANDE(1942); SHAMUS(1973)
Patricia A. Frye
1984
HARRY AND SON(1984)
Peter Frye
SEEDS OF FREEDOM(1943, USSR); HILL 24 DOESN'T ANSWER(1955, Israel), p, w; SELL OUT, THE(1976); JESUS(1979)
1984
1984(1984, Brit.)
Sean Frye
FUN WITH DICK AND JANE(1977); E.T. THE EXTRA-TERRESTRIAL(1982)
Stewart S. Frye
HIGH TIDE(1947), ed; PERILOUS WATERS(1948), ed
Stuart Frye
DAVY CROCKETT, INDIAN SCOUT(1950), ed; SOUTHSIDE 1-1000(1950), m
Theodore Frye
ROARIN' LEAD(1937)
Virgil Frye
QUEEN OF BLOOD(1966); JESUS TRIP, THE(1971); LIMIT, THE(1972); HOWZER(1973); BOBBIE JO AND THE OUTLAW(1976); MISSOURI BREAKS, THE(1976); UP FROM THE DEPTHS(1979, Phil.); DR. HECKYL AND MR. HYPE(1980); POSTMAN ALWAYS RINGS TWICE, THE(1981); TAKE THIS JOB AND SHOVE IT(1981); REVENGE OF THE NINJA(1983)
1984
HIGHWAY TO HELL(1984); HOT MOVES(1984); RUNNING HOT(1984)
William Frye
TROUBLE WITH ANGELS, THE(1966), p; WHERE ANGELS GO...TROUBLE FOLLOWS(1968), p; AIRPORT 1975(1974), p; AIRPORT '77(1977), p; RAISE THE TITANIC(1980, Brit.), p
Bryant Fryer
GUNGA DIN(1939)
Dick Fryer
STORMY(1935), ph; VOICE IN THE WIND(1944), ph
Richard Fryer
FLASH GORDON(1936), ph; SWING IT SAILOR(1937), ph
Silents
BOY OF MINE(1923), ph; CLEAN UP, THE(1923), ph; LEGALLY DEAD(1923), ph; BUCKING THE TRUTH(1926), ph
Robert Fryer
THE BOSTON STRANGLER, THE(1968), p; PRIME OF MISS JEAN BRODIE, THE(1969, Brit.), p; TRAVELS WITH MY AUNT(1972, Brit.), p; ABDICATION, THE(1974, Brit.), p; MAME(1974), p; GREAT EXPECTATIONS(1975, Brit.), p; VOYAGE OF THE DAMNED(1976, Brit.), p
Wally Fryer
DANCE HALL(1950, Brit.)
Alphonse Fryland
Misc. Silents
GOOD AND EVIL(1921)
James H. Frysinger
DARKER THAN AMBER(1970)
Tom Frysinger
WILD REBELS, THE(1967)
Jozef Fryzlewicz
CONDUCTOR, THE(1981, Pol.)
Mohamed Sghaier Ftouhi
1984
MISUNDERSTOOD(1984)
Ah Fu
TANGA-TIKA(1953)
Lee Tong Fu
MR. WONG, DETECTIVE(1938)
Wang Fu-ling
MADAME WHITE SNAKE(1963, Hong Kong), m; LAST WOMAN OF SHANG, THE(1964, Hong Kong), m; SHEPHERD GIRL, THE(1965, Hong Kong), m; MERMAID, THE(1966, Hong Kong), m

Thomas A. Fucci
1984
 NIGHTSONGS(1984), p
Thomas Anthony Fucci
 PURPLE HAZE(1982), p
Franz Fuchmann
 PRIVATE POOLEY(1962, Brit./E. Ger.), w
Bob Fuchs
1984
 ALPHABET CITY(1984)
Daniel Fuchs
 DAY THE BOOKIES WEPT, THE(1939), w; BIG SHOT, THE(1942), w; HARD WAY, THE(1942), w; BETWEEN TWO WORLDS(1944), w; GANGSTER, THE(1947), w; HOLLOW TRIUMPH(1948), w; CRISS CROSS(1949), w; PANIC IN THE STREETS(1950), w; STORM WARNING(1950), w; TAXI(1953), w; HUMAN JUNGLE, THE(1954), w; LOVE ME OR LEAVE ME(1955), w; INTERLUDE(1957), w
Daniels Fuchs
 JEANNE EAGELS(1957), w
Dick Fuchs
 NORTH AVENUE IRREGULARS, THE(1979)
Eddie Fuchs
 SKULLDUGGERY(1970)
Enzi Fuchs
 SOMETHING FOR EVERYONE(1970)
Gaby Fuchs
 MARK OF THE DEVIL(1970, Ger./Brit.); WEREWOLF VS. THE VAMPIRE WOMAN, THE(1970, Span./Ger.)
Gianni Fuchs
 GOLIATH AND THE DRAGON(1961, Ital./Fr.), p
Hannes Fuchs
 FIDELIO(1961, Aust.), ph; I LOVE YOU, I KILL YOU(1972, Ger.)
Herbert Fuchs
 HOUSE OF 1,000 DOLLS(1967, Ger./Span./Brit.); ASSIGNMENT K(1968, Brit.)
Herman Fuchs
 TATTOOED STRANGER, THE(1950), md
Hi Fuchs
 PROJECT X(1949), m
Kenneth Fuchs
 LILITH(1964)
Leo Fuchs
 STORY OF RUTH, THE(1960); FRENCH WAY, THE(1975, Fr.), p; FRISCO KID, THE(1979); SUNDAY LOVERS(1980, Ital./Fr.), p
Misc. Talkies
 AMERICAN MATCHMAKER(1940); I WANT TO BE A MOTHER(1937); MAZEL TOV, JEWS(1941)
Leo L. Fuchs
 GAMBIT(1966), p; FINE PAIR, A(1969, Ital.), p; CATHERINE & CO.(1976, Fr.), p, w
1984
 JUST THE WAY YOU ARE(1984), p
Manny Fuchs
 ONCE IN PARIS(1978), a, p
Mathias Fuchs
 CARDINAL, THE(1963); U-47 LT. COMMANDER PRIEN(1967, Ger.)
Matthias Fuchs
 LOLA(1982, Ger.)
1984
 WOMAN IN FLAMES, A(1984, Ger.)
Willy Sohm-Hannes Fuchs
 DON JUAN(1956, Aust.), ph
Joachim Fuchsberger
 DARK EYES OF LONDON(1961, Ger.); MYSTERY SUBMARINE(1963, Brit.); FACE OF FU MANCHU, THE(1965, Brit.); LAST TOMAHAWK, THE(1965, Ger./Ital./Span.); U-47 LT. COMMANDER PRIEN(1967, Ger.); HOW TO SEDUCE A PLAYBOY(1968, Aust./Fr./Ital.)
Salvatore Fucile
 BETTER A WIDOW(1969, Ital.)
Renato Fucini
 TIMES GONE BY(1953, Ital.), w
Fuddles
 WHERE'S POPPA?(1970)
Alan Fudge
 TWO PEOPLE(1973); BUG(1975); CAPRICORN ONE(1978); CHAPTER TWO(1979); BORDER, THE(1982); BRAINSTORM(1983)
1984
 NATURAL, THE(1984)
Kunio Fudimura
 JUNGLE HEAT(1957)
Ma Fue
Silents
 PURSUIT OF PAMELA, THE(1920, Brit.)
Beni Fuehrer
 BLUE LIGHT, THE(1932, Ger.)
Alma Fuentas
 LOS OLVIDADOS(1950, Mex.)
Amalia Fuentes
 BLOOD DRINKERS, THE(1966, U.S./Phil.); CURSE OF THE VAMPIRES(1970, Phil., U.S.)
Antonio Fuentes
 BOY WHO STOLE A MILLION, THE(1960, Brit.); HAPPY THIEVES, THE(1962); SAVAGE GUNS, THE(1962, U.S./Span.); GUNFIGHTERS OF CASA GRANDE(1965, U.S./Span.)
Carlos Fuentes
 WITCH, THE(1969, Ital.), w
Danny Fuentes
 UNHOLY ROLLERS(1972)
Ernie Fuentes
 UP IN SMOKE(1978); HERBIE GOES BANANAS(1980)

Larry Fuentes
 TIME AFTER TIME(1979, Brit.), spec eff
Miguel Angel Fuentes
 CAVEMAN(1981); GREEN ICE(1981, Brit.); FITZCARRALDO(1982); TRIUMPHS OF A MAN CALLED HORSE(1983, US/Mex.)
1984
 EVIL THAT MEN DO, THE(1984)
Misc. Talkies
 PUMA MAN, THE(1980)
Ruben Fuentes
 INTERVAL(1973, Mex./U.S.), m
Sonia Fuentes
 SANTO CONTRA LA HIJA DE FRANKENSTEIN(1971, Mex.)
Tito Fuentes
 SOLOMON KING(1974)
Arturo Fuento
 GOD FORGIVES–I DON'T!(1969, Ital./Span.)
Hans Fuerberg
 GENERAL DIED AT DAWN, THE(1936); HUMAN CARGO(1936); ARISE, MY LOVE(1940)
E.F. Fuerbringer
 MRS. WARREN'S PROFESSION(1960, Ger.)
De Garcia Fuerburg
Silents
 SCARAMOUCHE(1923)
Tamara Fuerst
 PERSECUTION AND ASSASSINATION OF JEAN-PAUL MARAT AS PERFORMED BY THE INMATES OF THE ASYLUM OF CHARENTON UNDER THE DIRECTION OF THE MARQUIS DE SADE, THE(1967, Brit.)
Ilse Fuerstenberg
 CAPTAIN FROM KOEPENICK(1933, Ger.); CANARIS(1955, Ger.); CAPTAIN FROM KOEPENICK, THE(1956, Ger.)
Robert Fuest
 JUST LIKE A WOMAN(1967, Brit.), d&w; AND SOON THE DARKNESS(1970, Brit.), d; WUTHERING HEIGHTS(1970, Brit.), d; ABOMINABLE DR. PHIBES, THE(1971, Brit.), d; DOCTOR PHIBES RISES AGAIN(1972, Brit.), d, w; DEVIL'S RAIN, THE(1975, U.S./Mex.), d
Willy Fueter
 HIGH FURY(1947, Brit.); SNOWBOUND(1949, Brit.)
Werner Fuetterer
 CRUISER EMDEN(1932, Ger.); DECISION BEFORE DAWN(1951); DEVIL'S GENERAL, THE(1957, Ger.); CITY OF SECRETS(1963, Ger.)
Misc. Silents
 THOU SHALT NOT STEAL(1929, Ger.)
Athol Fugard
 GUEST AT STEENKAMPSKRAAL, THE(1977, South Africa), a, w; MEETINGS WITH REMARKABLE MEN(1979, Brit.); MARIGOLDS IN AUGUST(1980, South Africa), a, w; GANDHI(1982)
1984
 GUEST, THE(1984, Brit.), a, w; KILLING FIELDS, THE(1984, Brit.); MARIGOLDS IN AUGUST(1984, S. Africa), a, w
Misc. Talkies
 BOESMAN AND LENA(1976)
Fugere
 YELLOW HAT, THE(1966, Brit.)
Frederik Fuglsang
 ELISABETH OF AUSTRIA(1931, Ger.), ph
The Fugs
 CHAPPAQUA(1967)
Fugsland and Holzki
 BECAUSE I LOVED YOU(1930, Ger.), ph
Charles Fuhr [Edward Ludwig]
 BOMBER'S MOON(1943), d
Ben Fuhrman
 HEROES(1977); 9/30/55(1977)
Richard Fuhrman
 NUNZIO(1978), art d; WINDOWS(1980), art d
E.O. Fuhrmann
 CASTLE, THE(1969, Ger.)
Robert Fuhrmann
1984
 HOT DOG...THE MOVIE(1984)
Yap Mook Fui
 SEVENTH DAWN, THE(1964)
Christian Fuin
 TRAIN, THE(1965, Fr./Ital./U.S.)
Fuji
 HOUSE OF BAMBOO(1955); KING AND I, THE(1956); CRIMSON KIMONO, THE(1959); WRECKING CREW, THE(1968); SLAUGHTER'S BIG RIP-OFF(1973); SUPERCHICK(1973)
Manami Fuji
 LOVE UNDER THE CRUCIFIX(1965, Jap.); WHISPERING JOE(1969, Jap.)
Tatsuya Fuji
 GAPPA THE TRIFIBIAN MONSTER(1967, Jap.); FRIENDLY KILLER, THE(1970, Jap.)
Yahiro Fuji
 SANSHO THE BAILIFF(1969, Jap.), w
Toge Fujihira
 MARK OF THE HAWK, THE(1958), ph
Hiroaki Fujii
 ODD OBSESSION(1961, Jap.), p, ed; FIRES ON THE PLAIN(1962, Jap.), ed
Kazafumi Fujii
 GAMERA VERSUS GAOS(1967, Jap.), spec eff; GAMERA VERSUS GUIRON(1969, Jap.), spec eff
Kozufumi Fujii
 GAMERA VERSUS ZIGRA(1971, Jap.), spec eff
Ryohei Fujii
 FRANKENSTEIN CONQUERS THE WORLD(1964, Jap./US), ed; GHIDRAH, THE THREE-HEADED MONSTER(1965, Jap.), ed; DESTROY ALL MONSTERS(1969, Jap.), ed; MONSTER ZERO(1970, Jap.), ed

Ippo Fujikawa
TROUT, THE(1982, Fr.)
J. Fujikawa
ANATAHAN(1953, Jap.)
Jerry Fujikawa
I WAS AN AMERICAN SPY(1951); JAPANESE WAR BRIDE(1952); JOURNEY, THE(1959, U.S./Aust.); NOBODY'S PERFECT(1968); EXTRAORDINARY SEAMAN, THE(1969); KING OF MARVIN GARDENS, THE(1972); CHINATOWN(1974); FAREWELL, MY LOVELY(1975); CAT FROM OUTER SPACE, THE(1978); END, THE(1978); SECOND THOUGHTS(1983)
Keisuke Fujikawa
SPACE CRUISER(1977 Jap.), w
Yu Fujiki
SAMURAI(PART II)** (1967, Jap.); NIGHT IN HONG KONG, A(1961, Jap.); LOWER DEPTHS, THE(1962, Jap.); STAR OF HONG KONG(1962, Jap.); KING KONG VERSUS GODZILLA(1963, Jap.); GODZILLA VS. THE THING(1964, Jap.); YEARNING(1964, Jap.); ATRAGON(1965, Jap.); WHITE ROSE OF HONG KONG(1965, Jap.); DAREDEVIL IN THE CASTLE(1969, Jap.); YOG-MONSTER FROM SPACE(1970, Jap.)
Masaya Fujima
TEAHOUSE OF THE AUGUST MOON, THE(1956), ch
Jun Fujimaki
MAJIN(1968, Jap.); FALCON FIGHTERS, THE(1970, Jap.); GATEWAY TO GLORY(1970, Jap.)
Fumiyo Fujimoto
MARINES, LET'S GO(1961)
Masumi Fujimoto
CHALLENGE TO LIVE(1964, Jap.), p; WHITE ROSE OF HONG KONG(1965, Jap.), p; DAPHNE, THE(1967), p; GOODBYE, MOSCOW(1968), p; MOMENT OF TERROR(1969, Jap.), p
Sanezumi Fujimoto
DIFFERENT SONS(1962, Jap.), p; EARLY AUTUMN(1962, Jap.), p; HAPPINESS OF US ALONE(1962, Jap.), p; WISER AGE(1962, Jap.), p; HONOLULU-TOKYO-HONG KONG(1963, Hong Kong/Jap.), p; LONELY LANE(1963, Jap.), p; SAGA OF THE VAGABONDS(1964, Jap.), p; YEARNING(1964, Jap.), p; IT STARTED IN THE ALPS(1966, Jap.), p; NIGHT IN BANGKOK(1966, Jap.), p; THREE DOLLS FROM HONG KONG(1966, Jap.), p; WE WILL REMEMBER(1966, Jap.), p; LET'S GO, YOUNG GUY!(1967, Jap.), p; SWORD OF DOOM, THE(1967, Jap.), p; THIN LINE, THE(1967, Jap.), p; TWO IN THE SHADOW(1968, Jap.), p; OUR SILENT LOVE(1969, Jap.), p; GLOWING AUTUMN(1981, Jap.), p
Tak Fujimoto
BADLANDS(1974), ph; BOOTLEGGERS(1974), ph; RENEGADE GIRLS(1974), ph; DEATH RACE 2000(1975), ph; CANNONBALL(1976, U.S./Hong Kong), ph; DR. BLACK AND MR. HYDE(1976), ph; REMEMBER MY NAME(1978), ph; STONY ISLAND(1978), ph; LAST EMBRACE(1979), ph; BORDERLINE(1980), ph; MELVIN AND HOWARD(1980), ph; WHERE THE BUFFALO ROAM(1980), ph; HEART LIKE A WHEEL(1983), ph
1984
SWING SHIFT(1984), ph
Arihiro Fujimura
TOPSY-TURVY JOURNEY(1970, Jap.)
Shiho Fujimura
ZATOICHI(1968, Jap.); FALCON FIGHTERS, THE(1970, Jap.)
Takako Fujino
PRODIGAL SON, THE(1964, Jap.)
Jerry Fujio
YOJIMBO(1961, Jap.)
Hiroshi Fujioka
PROPHECIES OF NOSTRADAMUS(1974, Jap.); TIDAL WAVE(1975, U.S./Jap.)
1984
SWORDKILL(1984)
John Fujioka
TIDAL WAVE(1975, U.S./Jap.); FUTUREWORLD(1976); MIDWAY(1976); MAC ARTHUR(1977); LAST FLIGHT OF NOAH'S ARK, THE(1980); OCTAGON, THE(1980); PRIVATE EYES, THE(1980); SOME KIND OF HERO(1982)
Takuya Fujioka
YOSAKOI JOURNEY(1970, Jap.)
Hiroyasu Fujishima
MECHANIC, THE(1972)
Noribumi Fujishima
FINAL WAR, THE(1960, Jap.)
Goro Fujita
GANGSTER VIP, THE(1968, Jap.), w
Midori Fujita
LAKE OF DRACULA(1973, Jap.)
Shigeya Fujita
LONGING FOR LOVE(1966, Jap.), w
Susumu Fujita
ESCAPADE IN JAPAN(1957); HIDDEN FORTRESS, THE(1959, Jap.); MYSTERIANS, THE(1959, Jap.); YOJIMBO(1961, Jap.); HIGH AND LOW(1963, Jap.); GODZILLA VS. THE THING(1964, Jap.); SAMURAI ASSASSIN(1965, Jap.); EMPEROR AND A GENERAL, THE(1968, Jap.); DAREDEVIL IN THE CASTLE(1969, Jap.); TORA! TORA! TORA!(1970, U.S./Jap.); WAR OF THE MONSTERS(1972, Jap.)
Toyo Fujita
OFFICER O'BRIEN(1930); RETURN OF DR. FU MANCHU, THE(1930)
Silents
WHERE LIGHTS ARE LOW(1921)
Misc. Silents
COURAGEOUS COWARD, THE(1919); DRAGON PAINTER, THE(1919); TONG MAN, THE(1919); TOKIO SIREN, A(1920)
Yumiko Fujita
MUDDY RIVER(1982, Jap.)
Kamatari Fujiwara
SEVEN SAMURAI, THE(1956, Jap.); HIDDEN FORTRESS, THE(1959, Jap.); IKIRU(1960, Jap.); YOJIMBO(1961, Jap.); DIFFERENT SONS(1962, Jap.); HAPPINESS OF US ALONE(1962, Jap.); LOWER DEPTHS, THE(1962, Jap.); SANJURO(1962, Jap.); MICKEY ONE(1965); RED BEARD(1966, Jap.); I LIVE IN FEAR(1967, Jap.); EYES, THE SEA AND A BALL(1968 Jap.); DAY THE SUN ROSE, THE(1969, Jap.); DOUBLE SUICIDE(1970, Jap.)

Kay Fujiwara
NEPTUNE FACTOR, THE(1973, Can.)
Naoki Fujiwara
SANSHO THE BAILIFF(1969, Jap.)
Reiko Fujiwara
BUDDHA(1965, Jap.); ZATOICHI(1968, Jap.)
Shinji Fujiwara
UNHOLY DESIRE(1964, Jap.), w; AFFAIR AT AKITSU(1980, Jap.), w
Tommy Fujiwara
GOIN' COCONUTS(1978)
Koji Fujiyama
GAMERA VERSUS BARUGON(1966, Jap./U.S.); GAMERA VERSUS ZIGRA(1971, Jap.)
Yoko Fujiyama
DIFFERENT SONS(1962, Jap.); DAGORA THE SPACE MONSTER(1964, Jap.); ATRAGON(1965, Jap.); WE WILL REMEMBER(1966, Jap.)
Yu Fujuki
DIFFERENT SONS(1962, Jap.); WAR OF THE GARGANTUAS, THE(1970, Jap.)
Shoki Fukae
FRIENDLY KILLER, THE(1970, Jap.)
Kuni Fukai
METAMORPHOSES(1978), prod d
Shiro Fukai
TRAITORS(1957, Jap.), m
Jun Fukamachi
HINOTORI(1980, Jap.), m
Mitsuaki Fukamizu
1984
BALLAD OF NARAYAMA, THE(1984, Jap.)
Eddie Fukano
FROM NASHVILLE WITH MUSIC(1969)
Kenta Fukasaku
CHALLENGE, THE(1982)
Kinji Fukasaku
GREEN SLIME, THE(1969), d; TORA! TORA! TORA!(1970, U.S./Jap.), d; MESSAGE FROM SPACE(1978, Jap.), d; VIRUS(1980, Jap.), d, w
Shichiro Fukazawa
BALLAD OF NARAYAMA(1961, Jap.), w
Derek Fuke
CHARGE OF THE LIGHT BRIGADE, THE(1968, Brit.)
Jun Fukuda
SECRET OF THE TELEGIAN, THE(1961, Jap.), d; WHITE ROSE OF HONG KONG(1965, Jap.), d; GODZILLA VERSUS THE SEA MONSTER(1966, Jap.), d; MAD ATLANTIC, THE(1967, Jap.), d; SON OF GODZILLA(1967, Jap.), d; YOUNG GUY GRADUATES(1969, Jap.), d; YOUNG GUY ON MT. COOK(1969, Jap.), d; WAR OF THE MONSTERS(1972, Jap.), d; GODZILLA VERSUS THE COSMIC MONSTER(1974, Jap.), d, w; GODZILLA VS. MEGALON(1976, Jap.), d, w; WAR OF THE PLANETS(1977, Jap.), d
Tadashi Fukuda
1984
WARRIORS OF THE WIND(1984, Jap.), anim
M. Fukuishima
TERROR BENEATH THE SEA(1966, Jap.), w
Akira Fukunaga
GO FOR BROKE(1951)
Sunshine Akira Fukunaga
BEACHHEAD(1954)
Takehiko Fukunaga
MOTHRA(1962, Jap.), w
Yasumichi Fukuzawa
THIN LINE, THE(1967, Jap.), ph; GOODBYE, MOSCOW(1968, Jap.), ph
Stedwell Fulcher
HORROR OF DRACULA, THE(1958, Brit.)
Enrico Fulchignoni
DIFFICULT YEARS(1950, Ital.), w
Felice Fulchignoni
JULIET OF THE SPIRITS(1965, Fr./Ital./W.Ger.)
Lucio Fulci
DAY IN COURT, A(1965, Ital.), w; 00-2 MOST SECRET AGENTS(1965, Ital.), d, w; DOS COSMONAUTAS A LA FUERZA(1967, Span./*Ital.), d; BRUTE AND THE BEAST, THE(1968, Ital.), d; OPERATION ST. PETER'S(1968, Ital.), d, w; PSYCHIC, THE(1979, Ital.), d, w; ZOMBIE(1980, Ital.), d; GATES OF HELL, THE(1983, U.S./Ital.), d, w
1984
BLACK CAT, THE(1984, Ital./Brit.), d, w; CONQUEST(1984, Ital./Span./Mex.), d; HOUSE BY THE CEMETERY, THE(1984, Ital.), d, w
Ludwig Fulda
TWO-FACED WOMAN(1941), w
Christopher Fulford
1984
PLOUGHMAN'S LUNCH, THE(1984, Brit.)
Wang Fuling
DRACULA AND THE SEVEN GOLDEN VAMPIRES(1978, Brit./Chi.), m
Sarah Jane Fulks [Jane Wyman]
KID FROM SPAIN, THE(1932); STOLEN HARMONY(1935); KING OF BURLESQUE(1936)
F. Fullbrook
Misc. Silents
BILLY'S SPANISH LOVE SPASM(1915, Brit.)
Donald Fullen
Misc. Silents
CUPID'S KNOCKOUT(1926)
Fran Fullenwider
MUTATIONS, THE(1974, Brit.); PINK PANTHER STRIKES AGAIN, THE(1976, Brit.); MONSTER CLUB, THE(1981, Brit.); NUTCRACKER(1982, Brit.)
Fuller
MONTE CARLO BABY(1953, Fr.), w

Albert C. Fuller
REMOTE CONTROL(1930), w
Barbara Fuller
ALIAS THE CHAMP(1949); FLAME OF YOUTH(1949); RED MENACE, THE(1949); HARBOR OF MISSING MEN(1950); LONELY HEARTS BANDITS(1950); ROCK ISLAND TRAIL(1950); SAVAGE HORDE, THE(1950); TARNISHED(1950); UN-MASKED(1950); CITY OF BAD MEN(1953); ROOMMATES, THE(1973)
Barbara E. Fuller
HOW SWEET IT IS(1968)
Barbra Fuller
TRIAL WITHOUT JURY(1950); WOMAN FROM HEADQUARTERS(1950)
Bill Fuller
PORKY'S(1982)
Brook Fuller
LEOPARD, THE(1963, Ital.); CHRISTMAS TREE, THE(1969, Fr.)
Charles Fuller
1984
SOLDIER'S STORY, A(1984), w
Misc. Silents
PATH OF DARKNESS, THE(1916)
Clem Fuller
TWILIGHT ON THE TRAIL(1941); SUNSET PASS(1946); GUN RUNNER(1949); SHADOWS OF THE WEST(1949); HIGH LONESOME(1950); SUNDOWNERS, THE(1950); CAVE OF OUTLAWS(1951); GREAT SIOUX UPRISING, THE(1953); GUNSMOKE(1953); RIDING SHOTGUN(1954); KETTLES ON OLD MACDONALD'S FARM, THE(1957); THIS HAPPY FEELING(1958)
Dale Fuller
GLAD RAG DOLL, THE(1929); HOUSE OF HORROR(1929); SACRED FLAME, THE(1929); MAN FROM BLANKLEY'S, THE(1930); OFFICE WIFE, THE(1930); EMMA(1932); TRIAL OF VIVIENNE WARE, THE(1932); HOUSE OF MYSTERY(1934); TWENTIETH CENTURY(1934); WE LIVE AGAIN(1934); TALE OF TWO CITIES, A(1935)
Silents
FOOLISH WIVES(1920); MERRY-GO-ROUND(1923); RENO(1923); SOULS FOR SALE(1923); BABBITT(1924); HIS HOUR(1924); HUSBANDS AND LOVERS(1924); MARRIAGE CIRCLE, THE(1924); BEN-HUR(1925); DEVIL'S CARGO, THE(1925); GREED(1925); LADY OF THE NIGHT(1925); MERRY WIDOW, THE(1925); UNCHAS-TENED WOMAN(1925); MEMORY LANE(1926); VOLCANO(1926); KING OF KINGS, THE(1927); WEDDING MARCH, THE(1927)
Misc. Silents
ONE WONDERFUL NIGHT(1922); SHADOW ON THE WALL, THE(1925); CANADI-AN, THE(1926); SPEEDING VENUS, THE(1926)
Delores Fuller
BRIDE OF THE MONSTER(1955)
Diane Fuller
JOURNEY AMONG WOMEN(1977, Aus.)
Dolores Fuller
GLEN OR GLENDA(1953); JAIL BAIT(1954)
Donald Fuller
Misc. Silents
FANATICS(1917)
Donna Fuller
1984
ANGEL(1984)
Ernest Fuller
WHAT A NIGHT!(1931, Brit.); LOST IN THE LEGION(1934, Brit.)
Frances Fuller
ONE SUNDAY AFTERNOON(1933); ELMER AND ELSIE(1934); GIRL IN THE RED VELVET SWING, THE(1955); THEY MIGHT BE GIANTS(1971); HOMEBODIES(1974)
Fred Fuller
MADE FOR EACH OTHER(1939)
George Fuller
SUNDOWN RIDERS(1948)
Gilber Fuller
300 YEAR WEEKEND(1971), m
Haidee Fuller
Silents
SQUAW MAN, THE(1914)
James Fuller
GREEN PASTURES(1936)
Janice Fuller
Misc. Talkies
HOW TO SCORE WITH GIRLS(1980)
Jean Fuller
FIRE IN THE STRAW(1943)
Jesse Fuller
Silents
THIEF OF BAGDAD, THE(1924); EAST OF SUEZ(1925)
Jimmy Fuller
SEPIA CINDERELLA(1947)
John C. Fuller
ARIZONA WHIRLWIND(1944), ed; LAND OF THE OUTLAWS(1944), ed; LAW MEN(1944), ed; MARKED TRAILS(1944), ed; OUTLAW TRAIL(1944), ed; RANGE LAW(1944), ed; SONORA STAGECOACH(1944), ed; WESTWARD BOUND(1944), ed; RIDIN' DOWN THE TRAIL(1947), ed; SILVER TRAILS(1948), ed; ACROSS THE RIO GRANDE(1949), ed; HIDDEN DANGER(1949), ed; RANGE LAND(1949), ed; SHAD-OWS OF THE WEST(1949), ed; TRAIL'S END(1949), ed; WEST OF EL DORADO(1949), ed; WESTERN RENEGADES(1949), ed; FENCE RIDERS(1950), ed; OVER THE BORDER(1950), ed; WEST OF WYOMING(1950), ed; COW COUNTRY(1953), ed; LOOSE IN LONDON(1953), ed; PARIS PLAYBOYS(1954), ed; RETURN FROM THE SEA(1954), ed; BOWERY TO BAGDAD(1955), ed; HIGH SOCIETY(1955), ed; SPY CHASERS(1956), ed; ZERO HOUR!(1957), ed
John Fuller
GUNNING FOR JUSTICE(1948), ed; RANGERS RIDE, THE(1948), ed; GUN LAW JUSTICE(1949), ed; GUN RUNNER(1949), ed; RANGE JUSTICE(1949), ed; MAZE, THE(1953), ed; GOLDEN IDOL, THE(1954), ed; LAWLESS RIDER, THE(1954), ed; PRIDE OF THE BLUE GRASS(1954), ed; SHOTGUN(1955), ed

Johnny Fuller
BACK TRAIL(1948), ed; PARTNERS OF THE SUNSET(1948), ed; RANGE RENE-GADES(1948), ed; LAW OF THE WEST(1949), ed
Kathryn Fuller
YES, GIORGIO(1982)
Lance Fuller
GLASS WEB, THE(1953); WAR ARROW(1953); CATTLE QUEEN OF MON-TANA(1954); MAGNIFICENT OBSESSION(1954); OTHER WOMAN, THE(1954); TAZA, SON OF COCHISE(1954); APACHE WOMAN(1955); PEARL OF THE SOUTH PACIFIC(1955); THIS ISLAND EARTH(1955); GIRLS IN PRISON(1956); KENTUCKY RIFLE(1956); SECRET OF TREASURE MOUNTAIN(1956); SHE-CREATURE, THE(1956); SLIGHTLY SCARLET(1956); RUNAWAY DAUGHTERS(1957); VOODOO WOMAN(1957); BRIDE AND THE BEAST, THE(1958); GOD'S LITTLE ACRE(1958); DAY OF THE OUTLAW(1959)
Misc. Talkies
FRONTIER WOMAN(1956)
Lee Fuller
CENTENNIAL SUMMER(1946), art d
Leland Fuller
GUADALCANAL DIARY(1943), art d; HEAVEN CAN WAIT(1943), art d; LADIES OF WASHINGTON(1944), art d; LAURA(1944), art d; SULLIVANS, THE(1944), art d; TAKE IT OR LEAVE IT(1944), art d; DOLLY SISTERS, THE(1945), art d; FALLEN ANGEL(1945), art d; WHERE DO WE GO FROM HERE?(1945), art d; DARK COR-NER, THE(1946), art d; HOMESTRETCH, THE(1947), art d; KISS OF DEATH(1947), art d; SITTING PRETTY(1948), art d; WHEN MY BABY SMILES AT ME(1948), art d; FAN, THE(1949), art d; WHIRLPOOL(1949), art d; YOU'RE MY EVERYTHING(1949), art d; THREE CAME HOME(1950), art d; FOURTEEN HOURS(1951), art d; ON THE RIVERA(1951), art d; VIVA ZAPATA!(1952), art d; WE'RE NOT MARRIED(1952), art d; DOWN AMONG THE SHELTERING PALMS(1953), art d; HOW TO MARRY A MILLIONAIRE(1953), art d; MAN IN THE ATTIC(1953), art d; PRESIDENT'S LADY, THE(1953), art d; DESIREE(1954), art d; HELL AND HIGH WATER(1954), art d; VIEW FROM POMPEY'S HEAD, THE(1955), art d; VIRGIN QUEEN, THE(1955), art d; GIRL CAN'T HELP IT, THE(1956), art d; LIEUTENANT WORE SKIRTS, THE(1956), art d; PROUD ONES, THE(1956), art d; HATFUL OF RAIN, A(1957), art d; WILL SUCCESS SPOIL ROCK HUNTER?(1957), art d; FRAULEIN(1958), art d; RALLY 'ROUND THE FLAG, BOYS!(1958), art d; SAY ONE FOR ME(1959), art d; ONE FOOT IN HELL(1960), art d; MADISON AVENUE(1962), art d
Leslie Fuller
KISS ME, SERGEANT(1930, Brit.); NOT SO QUIET ON THE WESTERN FRONT(1930, Brit.); WHY SAILORS LEAVE HOME(1930, Brit.); BILL'S LEGA-CY(1931, Brit.), a, w; OLD SOLDIERS NEVER DIE(1931, Brit.); POOR OLD BILL(1931, Brit.); WHAT A NIGHT!(1931, Brit.); LAST COUPON, THE(1932, Brit.); OLD SPANISH CUSTOMERS(1932, Brit.); TONIGHT'S THE NIGHT(1932, Brit.); HAWLEY'S OF HIGH STREET(1933, Brit.); POLITICAL PARTY, A(1933, Brit.); PRIDE OF THE FORCE, THE(1933, Brit.); DOCTOR'S ORDERS(1934, Brit.); LOST IN THE LEGION(1934, Brit.); OUTCAST, THE(1934, Brit.); CAPTAIN BILL(1935, Brit.); STOKER, THE(1935, Brit.); STRICTLY ILLEGAL(1935, Brit.); ONE GOOD TURN(1936, Brit.); BOYS WILL BE GIRLS(1937, Brit.); MIDDLE WATCH, THE(1939, Brit.); TWO SMART MEN(1940, Brit.); MY WIFE'S FAMILY(1941, Brit.); FRONT LINE KIDS(1942, Brit.); WHAT DO WE DO NOW?(1945, Brit.)
Lester Fuller
THEY ASKED FOR IT(1939), w; YOU CAN'T RATION LOVE(1944), d; THREE STEPS NORTH(1951), w; MONTE CARLO BABY(1953, Fr.), d
Louis Fuller
MOTOR PATROL(1950)
Misc. Talkies
SEVEN DOORS OF DEATH(1983), d
Marcus Fuller
STARK FEAR(1963), art d&set d
Margaret Fuller
LITTLE LAURA AND BIG JOHN(1973)
Mary Fuller
Misc. Silents
UNDER SOUTHERN SKIES(1915); HUNTRESS OF MEN, THE(1916); STRENGTH OF THE WEAK, THE(1916); THROWN TO THE LIONS(1916); LONG TRAIL, THE(1917); PUBLIC BE DAMNED(1917)
Maude Fuller
HIGH WIND IN JAMAICA, A(1965)
Michael W. Fuller
PEACE FOR A GUNFIGHTER(1967), w
Nancy Belle Fuller
HARD PART BEGINS, THE(1973, Can.)
Misc. Talkies
PINOCCHIO'S GREATEST ADVENTURE(1974)
Patricia Fuller
WHAT BECAME OF JACK AND JILL?(1972, Brit.)
Penny Fuller
ALL THE PRESIDENT'S MEN(1976)
Rhonda Fuller
STIGMA(1972)
Robert Fuller
TEENAGE THUNDER(1957); BRAIN FROM THE PLANET AROUS, THE(1958); INCIDENT AT PHANTOM HILL(1966); RETURN OF THE SEVEN(1966, Span.); SINAI COMMANDOS: THE STORY OF THE SIX DAY WAR(1968, Israel/Ger.); WHAT EVER HAPPENED TO AUNT ALICE?(1969); HARD RIDE, THE(1971); GATLING GUN, THE(1972); MUSTANG COUNTRY(1976); SEPARATE WAYS(1981); MEGAFOR-CE(1982)
Roger Fuller
ABOVE AND BEYOND(1953)
Rosalinde Fuller
CONTRABAND LOVE(1931, Brit.); COUNTY FAIR(1933, Brit.); PERFECT UNDER-STANDING(1933, Brit.); ESCAPE ME NEVER(1935, Brit.); IMMORTAL GENTLE-MAN(1935, Brit.)
Roy Fuller
SUBTERFUGE(1969, US/Brit.), ph
Sam Fuller
HATS OFF(1937), w; IT HAPPENED IN HOLLYWOOD(1937), w; GANGS OF NEW YORK(1938), w; FEDERAL MAN-HUNT(1939), w; BOWERY BOY(1940), w; POWER OF THE PRESS(1943), w; GANGS OF THE WATERFRONT(1945), w; LAST MOVIE, THE(1971); YOUNG NURSES, THE(1973); 1941(1979); STATE OF THINGS, THE(1983)

Samantha Fuller
WHITE DOG(1982)
Samuel Fuller
ADVENTURE IN SAHARA(1938), w; CONFIRM OR DENY(1941), w; I SHOT JESSE JAMES(1949), d&w; SHOCKPROOF(1949), w; BARON OF ARIZONA, THE(1950), d&w; FIXED BAYONETS(1951), d&w; STEEL HELMET, THE(1951), d&w; TANKS ARE COMING, THE(1951), w; PARK ROW(1952), p,d&w; SCANDAL SHEET(1952), w; PICKUP ON SOUTH STREET(1953), d&w; COMMAND, THE(1954), w; HELL AND HIGH WATER(1954), d, w; HOUSE OF BAMBOO(1955), a, d, w; CHINA GATE(1957), p,d&w; FORTY GUNS(1957), p,d&w; RUN OF THE ARROW(1957), p,d&w; CRIMSON KIMONO, THE(1959), p,d&w; VERBOTEN!(1959), p,d&w; UNDERWORLD U.S.-A.(1961), p,d&w; MERRILL'S MARAUDERS(1962), d, w; SHOCK CORRIDOR(1963), p,d&w; NAKED KISS, THE(1964), p,d&w; CAPETOWN AFFAIR(1967, U.S./South Afr.), w; PIERROT LE FOU(1968, Fr./Ital.); SHARK(1970, U.S./Mex.), d, w; DEAD PIGEON ON BEETHOVEN STREET(1972, Ger.), d&w; DEADLY TRACKERS(1973), w; KLANSMAN, THE(1974), w; AMERICAN FRIEND, THE(1977, Ger.); SCOTT JOPLIN(1977); BIG RED ONE, THE(1980), d&w; HAMMETT(1982); WHITE DOG(1982), a, d, w
1984
SLAPSTICK OF ANOTHER KIND(1984)
Sarita Fuller
THEIR OWN DESIRE(1929), w
Seymour Fuller
JAZZ BABIES(1932), art d
Suzanne Fuller
TELL-TALE HEART, THE(1962, Brit.)
Tex Fuller
NO BLADE OF GRASS(1970, Brit.)
Toria Fuller
THERE GOES THE BRIDE(1980, Brit.)
William Fuller
CHAMP, THE(1979); HOT STUFF(1979); PORKY'S II: THE NEXT DAY(1983)
Alexander Fullerton
LIONHEART(1968, Brit.), w
Carl Fullerton
WOLFEN(1981), makeup; SPASMS(1983, Can.), makeup
Fiona Fullerton
RUN WILD, RUN FREE(1969, Brit.); NICHOLAS AND ALEXANDRA(1971, Brit.); ALICE'S ADVENTURES IN WONDERLAND(1972, Brit.); HUMAN FACTOR, THE(1979, Brit.)
Melanie Fullerton
NIGHT OF THE LEPUS(1972)
Onofrio Fulli
QUIET PLACE IN THE COUNTRY, A(1970, Ital./Fr.)
S. Fullman
PRISONER OF CORBAL(1939, Brit.), w
Gene Fullmer
DEVIL'S BRIGADE, THE(1968)
George Fullwood
DEATHSPORT(1978), ch
Yemiko Fullwood
NAKED MAJA, THE(1959, Ital./U.S.)
Ray Fulmer
WILD IS MY LOVE(1963)
Ramona Fulmore
WILD HARVEST(1962)
Ilona Fulop
SPRING SHOWER(1932, Hung.), w
Tibor Fulop
FATHER(1967, Hung.)
Zsigmond Fulop
ROUND UP, THE(1969, Hung.)
Rene Fulop-Miller
GREAT MOMENT, THE(1944), w; GREAT SINNER, THE(1949), w
John Fultes
CORVETTE K-225(1943), spec eff
Doris Fulton
NEVER SAY GOODBYE(1946)
Eileen Fulton
GIRL OF THE NIGHT(1960)
Fitch Fulton
MIGHTY JOE YOUNG(1949), spec eff
Helen Fulton
Misc. Silents
VANITY FAIR(1915); UNPARDONABLE SIN, THE(1916)
Ian Fulton
DESIGN FOR MURDER(1940, Brit.); TOM BROWN'S SCHOOL DAYS(1940)
Irving Fulton
KNICKERBOCKER HOLIDAY(1944); MY BLUE HEAVEN(1950); COURT JESTER, THE(1956)
James F. Fulton
Silents
ETERNAL THREE, THE(1923); GREED(1925); AIR MAIL PILOT, THE(1928)
James Fulton
Misc. Silents
KILL-JOY, THE(1917)
Jeff Fulton
MY BLOODY VALENTINE(1981, Can.)
Jessie Lee Fulton
BULLET FOR PRETTY BOY, A(1970); LAST PICTURE SHOW, THE(1971); DON'T LOOK IN THE BASEMENT(1973); PAPER MOON(1973); SUGARLAND EXPRESS, THE(1974); DRIVE-IN(1976); FIVE DAYS FROM HOME(1978); RESURRECTION(1980); RAGGEDY MAN(1981)
Jimmy Fulton
Silents
ADVENTUROUS SOUL, THE(1927)
Misc. Silents
THRILL SEEKERS, THE(1927); GOD OF MANKIND(1928)

Joan Fulton
CUBAN PETE(1946); RUNAROUND, THE(1946); BUCK PRIVATES COME HOME(1947)
Joan [Shawlee] Fulton
IDEA GIRL(1946); INSIDE JOB(1946)
John Fulton
SHE GOES TO WAR(1929), ph; EYES OF THE WORLD, THE(1930), ph; HELL HARBOR(1930), ph; BRIDE OF FRANKENSTEIN, THE(1935), spec eff; ADVENTURE'S END(1937), spec eff; HELLZAPOPPIN'(1941), spec eff; KEEP 'EM FLYING(1941), spec eff; EAGLE SQUADRON(1942), spec eff; COBRA WOMAN(1944), spec eff; GYPSY WILDCAT(1944), spec eff; WONDER MAN(1945), spec eff; SECRET LIFE OF WALTER MITTY, THE(1947), spec eff; JOAN OF ARC(1948), spec eff; MY FOOLISH HEART(1949), spec eff; TULSA(1949), spec eff; MOUNTAIN, THE(1956), spec eff; VERTIGO(1958), spec eff; BAMBOO SAUCER, THE(1968), spec eff
John B. Fulton
FEAR STRIKES OUT(1957), spec eff
John P. Fulton
UNCLE HARRY(1945), spec eff; FRANKENSTEIN(1931), spec eff; AIR MAIL(1932), spec eff; MUMMY, THE(1932), spec eff; OLD DARK HOUSE, THE(1932), spec eff; INVISIBLE MAN, THE(1933), spec eff; GREAT IMPERSONATION, THE(1935), ph; MYSTERY OF EDWIN DROOD, THE(1935), spec eff; WEREWOLF OF LONDON, THE(1935), spec eff; DRACULA'S DAUGHTER(1936), spec eff; MAN I MARRY, THE(1936), ph; SEA SPOILERS, THE(1936), ph; SHOW BOAT(1936), spec eff; SUTTER'S GOLD(1936), ph; THE INVISIBLE RAY(1936), spec eff; TWO IN A CROWD(1936), spec eff; LADY FIGHTS BACK(1937), spec eff; NIGHT KEY(1937), spec eff; OH DOCTOR(1937), spec eff; ROAD BACK,THE(1937), spec eff; SHE'S DANGEROUS(1937), spec eff; WESTLAND CASE, THE(1937), spec eff; SON OF FRANKENSTEIN(1939), spec eff; INVISIBLE MAN RETURNS, THE(1940), spec eff; IN THE NAVY(1941), spec eff; INVISIBLE WOMAN, THE(1941), spec eff; MAN MADE MONSTER(1941), spec eff; THIS WOMAN IS MINE(1941), spec eff; GHOST OF FRANKENSTEIN, THE(1942), spec eff; INVISIBLE AGENT(1942), spec eff; PITTSBURGH(1942), spec eff; CALLING DR. DEATH(1943), ph, ed; CRAZY HOUSE(1943), spec eff; FRANKENSTEIN MEETS THE WOLF MAN(1943), spec eff; GUNG HO!(1943), spec eff; HIS BUTLER'S SISTER(1943), spec eff; ALI BABA AND THE FORTY THIEVES(1944), spec eff; CLIMAX, THE(1944), spec eff; FOLLOW THE BOYS(1944), spec eff; HOUSE OF FRANKENSTEIN(1944), spec eff; IMPOSTER, THE(1944), spec eff; IN SOCIETY(1944), spec eff; INVISIBLE MAN'S REVENGE(1944), spec eff; MERRY MONAHANS, THE(1944), ph; MURDER IN THE BLUE ROOM(1944), spec eff; SAN DIEGO, I LOVE YOU(1944), spec eff; SCARLET CLAW, THE(1944), spec eff; THIS IS THE LIFE(1944), spec eff; FRONTIER GAL(1945), spec eff; HERE COME THE CO-EDS(1945), spec eff; HOUSE OF DRACULA(1945), ph; LADY ON A TRAIN(1945), spec eff; PILLOW OF DEATH(1945), spec eff; SCARLET STREET(1945), spec eff; SUDAN(1945), spec eff; THAT NIGHT WITH YOU(1945), spec eff; THAT'S THE SPIRIT(1945), spec eff; WOMAN IN GREEN, THE(1945), spec eff; NIGHT IN PARADISE, A(1946), spec eff; SONG IS BORN, A(1948), spec eff; MAD WEDNESDAY(1950), spec eff; NAKED JUNGLE, THE(1953), spec eff; CASANOVA'S BIG NIGHT(1954), spec eff; COUNTRY GIRL, THE(1954), spec. eff; ELEPHANT WALK(1954), spec eff; REAR WINDOW(1954), spec eff; RED GARTERS(1954), spec eff; SABRINA(1954), spec eff; CONQUEST OF SPACE(1955), spec eff; DESPERATE HOURS, THE(1955), spec eff; RUN FOR COVER(1955), spec eff; STRATEGIC AIR COMMAND(1955), spec eff; TO CATCH A THIEF(1955), spec eff; TROUBLE WITH HARRY, THE(1955), spec eff; WE'RE NO ANGELS(1955), spec eff; MAN WHO KNEW TOO MUCH, THE(1956), spec eff; PROUD AND THE PROFANE, THE(1956), spec eff; RAINMAKER, THE(1956), spec eff; SEARCH FOR BRIDEY MURPHY, THE(1956), ph; TEN COMMANDMENTS, THE(1956), spec eff; THREE VIOLENT PEOPLE(1956), spec eff; VAGABOND KING, THE(1956), spec eff; DEVIL'S HAIRPIN, THE(1957), spec eff; FUNNY FACE(1957), spec eff; GUNFIGHT AT THE O.K. CORRAL(1957), spec eff; HEAR ME GOOD(1957), spec eff; JOKER IS WILD, THE(1957), spec eff; LONELY MAN, THE(1957), spec eff; LOVING YOU(1957), spec eff; OMAR KHAYYAM(1957), spec eff; SHORT CUT TO HELL(1957), spec eff; WILD IS THE WIND(1957), spec eff; HOT SPELL(1958), spec eff; HOUSEBOAT(1958), spec eff; I MARRIED A MONSTER FROM OUTER SPACE(1958), spec eff; KING CREOLE(1958), spec eff; MARACAIBO(1958), spec eff; SPACE CHILDREN, THE(1958), spec eff; ST. LOUIS BLUES(1958), spec eff; DON'T GIVE UP THE SHIP(1959), spec eff; FIVE PENNIES, THE(1959), spec eff; LI'L ABNER(1959), spec eff; RAT RACE, THE(1960), spec eff; VISIT TO A SMALL PLANET(1960), spec eff; LOVE IN A GOLDFISH BOWL(1961), spec eff; ON THE DOUBLE(1961), spec eff; ONE-EYED JACKS(1961), spec eff; PLEASURE OF HIS COMPANY, THE(1961), spec eff; SUMMER AND SMOKE(1961), spec eff; ESCAPE FROM ZAHRAIN(1962), spec eff; HATARI!(1962), spec eff; IT'S ONLY MONEY(1962), spec eff; PIGEON THAT TOOK ROME, THE(1962), spec eff; MY SIX LOVES(1963), spec eff; DISORDERLY ORDERLY, THE(1964), spec eff; HEROES OF TELEMARK, THE(1965, Brit.), spec eff; SEA PIRATE, THE(1967, Fr./Span./Ital.), spec eff
June Fulton
GAL WHO TOOK THE WEST, THE(1949); YES SIR, THAT'S MY BABY(1949)
Lou Fulton
ARIZONA GANGBUSTERS(1940); FRONTIER CRUSADER(1940); GUN CODE(1940); LADY IS WILLING, THE(1942)
Maude Fulton
NIX ON DAMES(1929), a, w; ONCE A GENTLEMAN(1930), w; SCARLET PAGES(1930), w; BRAT, THE(1931), w; CAPTAIN APPLEJACK(1931), w; COMMAND PERFORMANCE(1931), w; MALTESE FALCON, THE(1931), w; OTHER MEN'S WOMEN(1931), w; SAFE IN HELL(1931), w; PLAY GIRL(1932), w; UNDER EIGHTEEN(1932), w; BROADWAY BAD(1933), w; BROKEN DREAMS(1933), w; COHENS AND KELLYS IN TROUBLE, THE(1933); SONG AND DANCE MAN, THE(1936), w; GIRL FROM AVENUE A(1940), w
Silents
BRAT, THE(1919), w; HIS HOUR(1924), t; DON JUAN(1926), t; SALVATION JANE(1927), w; SILK LEGS(1927)
Patricia Fulton
Misc. Talkies
GUY FROM HARLEM, THE(1977)
Rad Fulton
COME NEXT SPRING(1956); TOWARD THE UNKNOWN(1956); WOMEN OF PITCAIRN ISLAND, THE(1957); JOY RIDE(1958); MARJORIE MORNINGSTAR(1958); NO TIME FOR SERGEANTS(1958); HELL BENT FOR LEATHER(1960); LAST SUNSET, THE(1961); NO, MY DARLING DAUGHTER(1964, Brit.); UNDERTAKER AND HIS PALS, THE(1966); JOURNEY BENEATH THE DESERT(1967, Fr./Ital.)

Rikki Fulton
SCOTCH ON THE ROCKS(1954, Brit.); GORKY PARK(1983); LOCAL HERO(1983, Brit.)
1984
COMFORT AND JOY(1984, Brit.)
Tyrone Fulton
MISTER BROWN(1972)
Wendy Fulton
FIRST TIME, THE(1983)
Larry W. Fultz
HOUSTON STORY, THE(1956)
Ronda Fultz
IN COLD BLOOD(1967); I DRINK YOUR BLOOD(1971)
Alberto Fumagalli
CAMMINA CAMMINA(1983, Ital.)
Franco Fumagalli
MARCO POLO(1962, Fr./Ital.), art d; ADVENTURERS, THE(1970), set d; STORY OF A WOMAN(1970, U.S./Ital.), set d; STATUE, THE(1971, Brit.), set d; OUTSIDER, THE(1980), art d
1984
MISUNDERSTOOD(1984), set d
Pietro Fumagalli
CITY OF WOMEN(1980, Ital./Fr.)
Rosa Fumeto
MOON IN THE GUTTER, THE(1983, Fr./Ital.)
Chiyoko Fumiya
IDIOT, THE(1963, Jap.)
Fun-Sen
ALIBI, THE(1939, Fr.)
Kazuo Funabashi
TOPSY-TURVY JOURNEY(1970, Jap.), w; YOSAKOI JOURNEY(1970, Jap.), w
Jun Funado
LOST WORLD OF SINBAD, THE(1965, Jap.)
Helen Funai
FUNNY THING HAPPENED ON THE WAY TO THE FORUM, A(1966); OUR MAN FLINT(1966)
Yoichi Funak
BUDDHA(1965, Jap.)
Kazuo Funaki
FAREWELL, MY BELOVED(1969, Jap.)
Yoichi Funaki
ENJO(1959, Jap.)
Eiji Funakoshi
GOLDEN DEMON(1956, Jap.); FIRES ON THE PLAIN(1962, Jap.); GAMERA THE INVINCIBLE(1966, Jap.); PASSION(1968, Jap.); GAMERA VERSUS GUIRON(1969, Jap.); THOUSAND CRANES(1969, Jap.)
Funambulists
MOONRAKER(1979, Brit.)
Toru Funamura
MAGIC BOY(1960, Jap.), md; OUR SILENT LOVE(1969, Jap.), m
Jun Funato
MAN FROM THE EAST, THE(1961, Jap.)
Rito Funay
WHIPLASH(1948)
Stephen Funchess
TENDER MERCIES(1982)
Mimi Funes
LILIOM(1935, Fr.)
Edsel Fung
EYE FOR AN EYE, AN(1981)
Gary Fung
KILL SQUAD(1982)
Patrica Fung
MISSION TO MOSCOW(1943)
Paul Fung
DANCE, GIRL, DANCE(1940); ACROSS THE PACIFIC(1942); CHINA GIRL(1942); JOAN OF OZARK(1942); REMEMBER PEARL HARBOR(1942); GUADALCANAL DIARY(1943); JACK LONDON(1943); PURPLE HEART, THE(1944); FIRST YANK INTO TOKYO(1945); GOD IS MY CO-PILOT(1945); SAMURAI(1945); LONE WOLF IN LONDON(1947)
Willie Fung
VIRGINIAN, THE(1929); DANGEROUS PARADISE(1930); SEA GOD, THE(1930); GUN SMOKE(1931); NIGHT NURSE(1931); WEST OF BROADWAY(1931); MASK OF FU MANCHU, THE(1932); MOUTHPIECE, THE(1932); ONE WAY PASSAGE(1932); RED DUST(1932); SHANGHAI EXPRESS(1932); BITTER TEA OF GENERAL YEN, THE(1933); NARROW CORNER, THE(1933); THRILL HUNTER, THE(1933); TUG-BOAT ANNIE(1933); CRIME DOCTOR, THE(1934); GAMBLING LADY(1934); GAY BRIDE, THE(1934); LOST LADY, A(1934); SEQUOIA(1934); CHINA SEAS(1935); HOPALONG CASSIDY(1935); OIL FOR THE LAMPS OF CHINA(1935); ONE-WAY TICKET(1935); RED MORNING(1935); ROCKY MOUNTAIN MYSTERY(1935); RUGGLES OF RED GAP(1935); SHANGHAI(1935); CALL OF THE PRAIRIE(1936); GENERAL DIED AT DAWN, THE(1936); SMALL TOWN GIRL(1936); STOWAWAY(1936); WHITE HUNTER(1936); COME ON, COWBOYS(1937); HAPPY-GO-LUCKY(1937); LOST HORIZON(1937); SECRET VALLEY(1937); TRIGGER TRIO, THE(1937); WE WHO ARE ABOUT TO DIE(1937); WEE WILLIE WINKIE(1937); WELLS FARGO(1937); BORDER WOLVES(1938); PRIDE OF THE WEST(1938); SINNERS IN PARADISE(1938); TOO HOT TO HANDLE(1938); BARRICADE(1939); HAWAIIAN NIGHTS(1939); HOLLYWOOD CAVALCADE(1939); HONOLULU(1939); MAISIE(1939); 6000 ENEMIES(1939); GREAT PROFILE, THE(1940); LETTER, THE(1940); SEVEN SINNERS(1940); GAY FALCON, THE(1941); PUBLIC ENEMIES(1941); SADDLE MOUNTAIN ROUNDUP(1941); BLACK SWAN, THE(1942); CAPTAINS OF THE CLOUDS(1942); DESTINATION UNKNOWN(1942); FLYING TIGERS(1942); HALF WAY TO SHANGHAI(1942); MEET THE STEWARTS(1942); NORTH TO THE KLONDIKE(1942); SEVEN DAYS LEAVE(1942); SPOILERS, THE(1942); TORTILLA FLAT(1942); THEY GOT ME COVERED(1943)
Silents
YELLOW BACK, THE(1926); FAR CALL, THE(1929)

Willy Fung
GIT ALONG, LITTLE DOGIES(1937); BURMA CONVOY(1941)
Annette Funicello
SHAGGY DOG, THE(1959); BABES IN TOYLAND(1961); BEACH PARTY(1963); BIKINI BEACH(1964); MISADVENTURES OF MERLIN JONES, THE(1964); MUSCLE BEACH PARTY(1964); PAJAMA PARTY(1964); BEACH BLANKET BINGO(1965); DR. GOLDFOOT AND THE BIKINI MACHINE(1965); HOW TO STUFF A WILD BIKINI(1965); SKI PARTY(1965); FIREBALL 590(1966); THUNDER ALLEY(1967); HEAD(1968)
Heinz Funk
GREAT BRITISH TRAIN ROBBERY, THE(1967, Ger.), m
Peter V. K. Funk
MY SIX LOVES(1963), w
Robert Funk
YOUR THREE MINUTES ARE UP(1973)
Terry Funk
PARADISE ALLEY(1978)
Georg Funkquist
AFFAIRS OF A MODEL(1952, Swed.); ILLICIT INTERLUDE(1954, Swed.); DEVIL'S EYE, THE(1960, Swed.); ALL THESE WOMEN(1964, Swed.)
George Funkquist
CRIME AND PUNISHMENT(1948, Swed.)
Georg Funquist
APPASSIONATA(1946, Swed.)
Lance Funston
1984
INITIATION, THE(1984)
Ada Fuoco
1984
HOTEL NEW HAMPSHIRE, THE(1984)
Charles Fuqua
PARDON MY SARONG(1942)
Jack Fuqua
Silents
PEACEFUL PETERS(1922), ph; KING OF THE HERD(1927), ph; FREE LIPS(1928), ph; SOULS AFLAME(1928), ph
Misc. Silents
ARCTIC ADVENTURE(1922)
Dorothy Furamura
NAVY WIFE(1956)
Douglas Furber
VAGABOND QUEEN, THE(1931, Brit.), w; HAPPY EVER AFTER(1932, Ger./Brit.), w; LOVE ON WHEELS(1932, Brit.), w; LUCKY GIRL(1932, Brit.), w; MAID OF THE MOUNTAINS, THE(1932, Brit.), w; MONEY MEANS NOTHING(1932, Brit.), w; FALLING FOR YOU(1933, Brit.), w; NIGHT AND DAY(1933, Brit.), w; THAT'S A GOOD GIRL(1933, Brit.), w; YES, MR. BROWN(1933, Brit.), w; WOMAN IN COMMAND, THE(1934 Brit.), w; BREWSTER'S MILLIONS(1935, Brit.), w; COME OUT OF THE PANTRY(1935, Brit.), w; QUEEN OF HEARTS(1936, Brit.), w; SKY'S THE LIMIT, THE(1937, Brit.), w; OH BOY!(1938, Brit.), w; LAMBETH WALK, THE(1940, Brit.), w; SO THIS IS LONDON(1940, Brit.), w; WHEN KNIGHTS WERE BOLD(1942, Brit.), w
Silents
BATTLING BUTLER(1926), w
Curt Furberg
BERLIN CORRESPONDENT(1942); BACKGROUND TO DANGER(1943); PARIS AFTER DARK(1943); SONG OF BERNADETTE, THE(1943); THREE HEARTS FOR JULIA(1943); JOAN OF ARC(1948); MISTER 880(1950)
Hans Furberg
SEAS BENEATH, THE(1931); AIR MAIL(1932); HEROES FOR SALE(1933); PARIS CALLING(1941); LADY HAS PLANS, THE(1942); ONCE UPON A HONEYMOON(1942); REUNION IN FRANCE(1942); 'TILL WE MEET AGAIN(1944)
Silents
FOUR SONS(1928)
Kurt Furberg
SEAS BENEATH, THE(1931); ONE NIGHT OF LOVE(1934)
Silents
KING OF KINGS, THE(1927)
Ernst Fritz Furbringer
MAN WHO WALKED THROUGH THE WALL, THE(1964, Ger.); CORPSE OF BEVERLY HILLS, THE(1965, Ger.); GIRL AND THE LEGEND, THE(1966, Ger.); IS PARIS BURNING?(1966, U.S./Fr.); HANNIBAL BROOKS(1969, Brit.)
Furcht
KAMIKAZE '89(1983, Ger.), set d
Beatrice Furdeaux
EDGE OF FURY(1958); TERROR FROM THE YEAR 5,000(1958)
Yves Furet
OSS 117–MISSION FOR A KILLER(1966, Fr./Ital.)
Barney Furey
NIGHT PARADE(1929, Brit.); PENAL CODE, THE(1933); WHEN A MAN RIDES ALONE(1933); FIGHTING CABALLERO(1935); POWDERSMOKE RANGE(1935); LAW RIDES, THE(1936); THUNDERBOLT(1936); DON'T TELL THE WIFE(1937)
Misc. Talkies
SILENT CODE, THE(1935)
Silents
SUNSHINE TRAIL, THE(1923); LOSER'S END, THE(1924); OUT OF THE WEST(1926); SONORA KID, THE(1927); SPLITTING THE BREEZE(1927); CAPTAIN CARELESS(1928); GUN LAW(1929); IDAHO RED(1929); OUTLAWED(1929)
Misc. Silents
FEET OF CLAY(1917); PHANTOM SHOTGUN, THE(1917); WESTERN BLOOD(1918); MAN TRACKERS, THE(1921); KING COWBOY(1928); LIGHTING SPEED(1928); DRIFTER, THE(1929)
Barney M. Furey
NEVADA(1936)
Fran Furey
OVER-UNDER, SIDEWAYS-DOWN(1977)
J. A. Furey
Silents
NEIGHBORS(1918)
Misc. Silents
AWAKENING OF HELENA RICHIE, THE(1916); SUNSHINE ALLEY(1917)

James A. Furey
Silents
GREATER THAN FAME(1920); ON WITH THE DANCE(1920)
Misc. Silents
PHIL-FOR-SHORT(1919); PLEASURE SEEKERS(1920)
James Furey
Silents
DESTRUCTION(1915)
Misc. Silents
DAWN(1919)
John Furey
FRIDAY THE 13TH PART II(1981)
1984
FRIDAY THE 13TH–THE FINAL CHAPTER(1984)
Lewis Furey
RUBBER GUN, THE(1977, Can.), m; JACOB TWO-TWO MEETS THE HOODED
FANG(1979, Can.), m; FANTASTICA(1980, Can./Fr.); AGENCY(1981, Can.), m
1984
AMERICAN DREAMER(1984), m
Peggy Furey
MAD DOG CALL(1961)
Howard Furgeson
SLUMBER PARTY MASSACRE, THE(1982)
Giacomo Furia
TOO BAD SHE'S BAD(1954, Ital.); GOLD OF NAPLES(1957, Ital.); BOCCACCIO
'70(1962/Ital./Fr.); VARIETY LIGHTS(1965, Ital.); MORE THAN A MIRACLE(1967,
Ital./Fr.); MY WIFE'S ENEMY(1967, Ital.); THAT MAN GEORGE!(1967, Fr./Ital./
Span.)
Giancamo Furia
TOTO IN THE MOON(1957, Ital./Span.)
Giuseppe Furia
NIGHT OF THE SHOOTING STARS, THE(1982, Ital.)
John Furia, Jr.
SINGING NUN, THE(1966), w
Lina Furia
TOO BAD SHE'S BAD(1954, Ital.)
Herve Furic
LES MISERABLES(1982, Fr.)
Daniel Furie
ENTITY, THE(1982)
Sidney Furie
BOYS IN COMPANY C, THE(1978, U.S./Hong Kong), d, w
Sidney J. Furie
DANGEROUS AGE, A(1960, Can.), p,d&w; DR. BLOOD'S COFFIN(1961), d; SNAKE
WOMAN, THE(1961, Brit.), d; THREE ON A SPREE(1961, Brit.), d; BOYS, THE(1962,
Brit.), p, d; DURING ONE NIGHT(1962, Brit.), p, d&w; WONDERFUL TO BE
YOUNG!(1962, Brit.), d; IPCRESS FILE, THE(1965, Brit.), d; LEATHER BOYS,
THE(1965, Brit.), d; SWINGER'S PARADISE(1965, Brit.), d; APPALOOSA, THE(1966),
d; NAKED RUNNER, THE(1967, Brit.), d; LAWYER, THE(1969), d, w; LITTLE
FAUSS AND BIG HALSY(1970), d; LADY SINGS THE BLUES(1972), d; HIT(1973), d;
SHEILA LEVINE IS DEAD AND LIVING IN NEW YORK(1975), d; GABLE AND
LOMBARD(1976), d; ENTITY, THE(1982), d
1984
PURPLE HEARTS(1984), p&d, w
Misc. Talkies
COOL SOUND FROM HELL, A(1959), d
Maks Furijan
SERGEANT JIM(1962, Yugo.)
Furio
PIZZA TRIANGLE, THE(1970, Ital./Span.), w
Alan Furlan
WAR AND PEACE(1956, Ital./U.S.); DESERT DESPERADOES(1959)
Rita Furlan
1984
RUSH(1984, Ital.)
Ferruccio Furlanetto
LA TRAVIATA(1982)
Eileen Furlong
PROFESSOR TIM(1957, Ireland)
John Furlong
ROPE OF FLESH(1965); FINDERS KEEPERS, LOVERS WEEPERS(1968); FRONT
PAGE, THE(1974); HUSTLE(1975); SWARM, THE(1978); POSTMAN ALWAYS RINGS
TWICE, THE(1981)
Kirby Furlong
MAME(1974)
Lynn Furlong
PRIZE OF ARMS, A(1962, Brit.)
"Tinker" Furlong
SONG OF LOVE(1947)
V.A. Furlong
RUN, ANGEL, RUN(1969), w
Barbara Joyce Furman
LOOKIN' TO GET OUT(1982)
Peter Furman
1984
ALLEY CAT(1984)
Roger Furman
COOL WORLD, THE(1963), set d; GEORGIA, GEORGIA(1972)
Rosa Furman
GUNS FOR SAN SEBASTIAN(1968, U.S./Fr./Mex./Ital.); TWO MULES FOR SISTER
SARA(1970)
Salvatore Furnari
LEGIONS OF THE NILE(1960, Ital.); HERCULES AND THE CAPTIVE WO-
MEN(1963, Fr./Ital.); SEVEN TASKS OF ALI BABA, THE(1963, Ital.); SEVEN
DWARFS TO THE RESCUE, THE(1965, Ital.)
Helmut Furnbacher
STEPPENWOLF(1974)

Yvonne Furneaux
AFFAIR IN MONTE CARLO(1953, Brit.); BEGGAR'S OPERA, THE(1953); GENIE,
THE(1953, Brit.); HOUSE OF THE ARROW, THE(1953, Brit.); MASTER OF BALLAN-
TRAE, THE(1953, U.S./Brit.); TONIGHT AT 8:30(1953, Brit.); CROSS CHANNEL(1955,
Brit.); WARRIORS, THE(1955); LISBON(1956); MUMMY, THE(1959, Brit.); LA DOLCE
VITA(1961, Ital./Fr.); LE AMICHE(1962, Ital.); STORY OF THE COUNT OF MONTE
CRISTO, THE(1962, Fr./Ital.); RUN WITH THE DEVIL(1963, Fr./Ital.); DR. MABUSE'S
RAYS OF DEATH(1964, Ger./Fr./Ital.); REPULSION(1965, Brit.); ENOUGH RO-
PE(1966, Fr./Ital./Ger.); CHAMPAGNE MURDERS, THE(1968, Fr.)
Misc. Talkies
SLAVE GIRL OF BABYLON(1962, Ital.); MAN IN A LOOKING GLASS, A(1965, Brit.)
Bill Furnell
TRUE CONFESSIONS(1981)
John Furnell
MAN WITH THE GREEN CARNATION, THE(1960, Brit.), w
Peter Furnell
REACH FOR GLORY(1963, Brit.)
Suzanne Furner
PICTURES(1982, New Zealand)
Betty Furness
RENEGADES OF THE WEST(1932); THIRTEEN WOMEN(1932); AGGIE APPLEBY,
MAKER OF MEN(1933); CHANCE AT HEAVEN(1933); CROSSFIRE(1933); EMER-
GENCY CALL(1933); FLYING DOWN TO RIO(1933); GREAT JASPER, THE(1933);
HEADLINE SHOOTER(1933); LUCKY DEVILS(1933); MIDSHIPMAN JACK(1933);
PROFESSIONAL SWEETHEART(1933); SCARLET RIVER(1933); BAND PLAYS ON,
THE(1934); BEGGARS IN ERMINE(1934); LET'S FALL IN LOVE(1934); LIFE OF
VERGIE WINTERS, THE(1934); WICKED WOMAN, A(1934); CALM YOUR-
SELF(1935); DANGEROUS CORNER(1935); GRIDIRON FLASH(1935); HERE COMES
COOKIE(1935); KEEPER OF THE BEES(1935); MAGNIFICENT OBSESSION(1935);
MC FADDEN'S FLATS(1935); SHADOW OF A DOUBT(1935); ALL-AMERICAN
CHUMP(1936); MISTER CINDERELLA(1936); PRESIDENT'S MYSTERY, THE(1936);
SWING TIME(1936); THREE WISE GUYS, THE(1936); FAIR WARNING(1937); GOOD
OLD SOAK, THE(1937); IT CAN'T LAST FOREVER(1937); MAMA STEPS OUT(1937);
THEY WANTED TO MARRY(1937); NORTH OF SHANGHAI(1939)
Edith Ellis Furness
MARY JANE'S PA(1935), w
Silents
SEVEN SISTERS, THE(1915), w
George Furness
LAST VOYAGE, THE(1960); MY GEISHA(1962)
Henry Furness
OVERLAND EXPRESS, THE(1938)
J.C. Furness
AND SUDDEN DEATH(1936), w
John Furness
EYE OF THE DEVIL(1967, Brit.), cos; LONG DUEL, THE(1967, Brit.), cos; VIKING
QUEEN, THE(1967, Brit.), cos; THOSE DARING YOUNG MEN IN THEIR JAUNTY
JALOPIES(1969, Fr./Ital./ Ital.), cos; VALLEY OF GWANGI, THE(1969), cos; KREM-
LIN LETTER, THE(1970), cos; DAISY MILLER(1974), cos; INTERNATIONAL VELV-
ET(1978, Brit.), cos
Lucille Furness
Misc. Silents
WILD CAT OF PARIS, THE(1919)
Marion Furness
MY GEISHA(1962)
Tammi Furness
SWORD AND THE SORCERER, THE(1982)
Grace Livingston Furniss
Silents
PRIDE OF JENNICO, THE(1914), w
John Furniss
GO-BETWEEN, THE(1971, Brit.), cos; CRY OF THE PENGUINS(1972, Brit.), cos;
SLEUTH(1972, Brit.), cos; DOLL'S HOUSE, A(1973, Brit.), cos; ENGLANO MADE
ME(1973, Brit.), cos; LITTLEST HORSE THIEVES, THE(1977), cos
Robert Furnival
JULIUS CAESAR(1970, Brit.), w
Georgia Furnstman
Silents
SEVEN SISTERS, THE(1915)
Odd Furoy
CHILDREN OF GOD'S EARTH(1983, Norwegian)
Art Furrer
BENJAMIN(1973, Ger.)
Ura B. Furrer
BIRCH INTERVAL(1976), ph
Urs Furrer
PLAYGROUND, THE(1965), ph; SIDELONG GLANCES OF A PIGEON KICKER,
THE(1970), ph; DESPERATE CHARACTERS(1971), ph; SHAFT(1971), ph; SHAFT'S
BIG SCORE(1972), ph; SEVEN UPS, THE(1973), ph; WHERE THE LILIES
BLOOM(1974), ph; BEEN DOWN SO LONG IT LOOKS LIKE UP TO ME(1977), ph
Urs B. Furrer
SOUNDER, PART 2(1976), ph
Barney Furrey
MEANEST GAL IN TOWN, THE(1934)
Elda Furry [Hedda Hopper]
Misc. Silents
BATTLE OF HEARTS(1916); SEVEN KEYS TO BALDPATE(1917)
Kevin Furry
SEMI-TOUGH(1977)
Jill Furse
GOODBYE MR. CHIPS(1939, Brit.); THERE AIN'T NO JUSTICE(1939, Brit.)
Judith Furse
GOODBYE MR. CHIPS(1939, Brit.); JOHNNY FRENCHMAN(1946, Brit.); BLACK
NARCISSUS(1947, Brit.); ONE NIGHT WITH YOU(1948, Brit); QUIET WEEK-
END(1948, Brit.); DEAR MR. PROHACK(1949, Brit.); HELTER SKELTER(1949, Brit.);
HER MAN GILBEY(1949, Brit.); MARRY ME!(1949, Brit.); WHILE THE SUN SHI-
NES(1950, Brit.); BROWNING VERSION, THE(1951, Brit.); NAUGHTY ARLET-
TE(1951, Brit.); MAN IN THE WHITE SUIT, THE(1952); I BELIEVE IN YOU(1953,
Brit.); HEART OF THE MATTER, THE(1954, Brit.); MAD ABOUT MEN(1954, Brit.);
COCKLESHELL HEROES, THE(1955); DOCTOR AT LARGE(1957, Brit.); BLUE

Margaret Furse *(cont.)*
MURDER AT ST. TRINIAN'S(1958, Brit.); FURTHER UP THE CREEK!(1958, Brit.); NOT A HOPE IN HELL(1960, Brit.); SANDS OF THE DESERT(1960, Brit.); SCENT OF MYSTERY(1960); WEEKEND WITH LULU, A(1961, Brit.); I THANK A FOOL(1962, Brit.); IMMORAL CHARGE(1962, Brit.); LIVE NOW–PAY LATER(1962, Brit.); CARRY ON CABBIE(1963, Brit.); MY SON, THE VAMPIRE(1963, Brit.); SWINGIN' MAIDEN, THE(1963, Brit.); CARRY ON SPYING(1964, Brit.); IN THE DOGHOUSE(1964, Brit.); AMOROUS ADVENTURES OF MOLL FLANDERS, THE(1965); GYPSY GIRL(1966, Brit.); SINFUL DAVEY(1969, Brit.); MAN IN THE WILDERNESS(1971, U.S./Span.)

Margaret Furse
ONE WOMAN'S STORY(1949, Brit.), cos; MADELEINE(1950, Brit.), cos; MUDLARK, THE(1950, Brit.), cos; NIGHT AND THE CITY(1950, Brit.), cos; I'LL NEVER FORGET YOU(1951), cos; OLIVER TWIST(1951, Brit.), cos; MASTER OF BALLANTRAE, THE(1953, U.S./Brit.), cos; MAN WITH A MILLION(1954, Brit.), cos; SPANISH GARDENER, THE(1957, Span.), cos; INN OF THE SIXTH HAPPINESS, THE(1958), cos; KIDNAPPED(1960), cos; SONS AND LOVERS(1960, Brit.), cos; IN SEARCH OF THE CASTAWAYS(1962, Brit.), cos; THREE LIVES OF THOMASINA, THE(1963, U.S./Brit.), cos; BECKET(1964, Brit.), cos; SHOT IN THE DARK, A(1964), cos; RETURN FROM THE ASHES(1965, U.S./Brit.), cos; YOUNG CASSIDY(1965, U.S./Brit.), cos; CAST A GIANT SHADOW(1966), cos; TRAP, THE(1967, Can./Brit.), cos; GREAT CATHERINE(1968, Brit.), cos; LION IN WINTER, THE(1968, Brit.), cos; ANNE OF THE THOUSAND DAYS(1969, Brit.), cos; SINFUL DAVEY(1969, Brit.), cos; SCROOGE(1970, Brit.), cos; MARY, QUEEN OF SCOTS(1971, Brit.), cos; DELICATE BALANCE, A(1973), cos; NELSON AFFAIR, THE(1973, Brit.), cos

Roger Furse
HENRY V(1946, Brit.), cos; ODD MAN OUT(1947, Brit.), prod d; HAMLET(1948, Brit.), prod d; UNDER CAPRICORN(1949), cos; IVANHOE(1952, Brit.), cos; HELEN OF TROY(1956, Ital), cos; RICHARD III(1956, Brit.), prod d; SAINT JOAN(1957), prod d; ROMAN SPRING OF MRS. STONE, THE(1961, U.S./Brit.), prod d; ROAD TO HONG KONG, THE(1962, U.S./Brit.), prod d

Anton Furst
LADY CHATTERLEY'S LOVER(1981, Fr./Brit.), prod d; UNSUITABLE JOB FOR A WOMAN, AN(1982, Brit.), prod d

Esther Furst
RING OF TERROR(1962)

Joseph Furst
EXODUS(1960); OFFBEAT(1961, Brit.); FREUD(1962); 55 DAYS AT PEKING(1963); ARRIVEDERCI, BABY!(1966, Brit.); BRIDES OF FU MANCHU, THE(1966, Brit.); MC GUIRE, GO HOME!(1966, Brit.); HAMMERHEAD(1968); GOODBYE GEMINI(1970, Brit.); SUDDEN TERROR(1970, Brit.); DIAMONDS ARE FOREVER(1971, Brit.); INN OF THE DAMNED(1974, Aus.)

Lopez Furst
THE EAVESDROPPER(1966, U.S./Arg.), m

Manfred Furst
VICIOUS CIRCLE, THE(1948); GREAT SINNER, THE(1949); QUESTION 7(1961, U.S./Ger.); LUDWIG(1973, Ital./Ger./Fr.)

Sigge Furst
SMILES OF A SUMMER NIGHT(1957, Swed.); LESSON IN LOVE, A(1960, Swed.); LOVE MATES(1967, Swed.); SHAME(1968, Swed.); PASSION OF ANNA, THE(1970, Swed.)

Stephen Furst
NATIONAL LAMPOON'S ANIMAL HOUSE(1978); SCAVENGER HUNT(1979); TAKE DOWN(1979); MIDNIGHT MADNESS(1980); UNSEEN, THE(1981); NATIONAL LAMPOON'S CLASS REUNION(1982); SILENT RAGE(1982)
1984
UP THE CREEK(1984)
Misc. Talkies
SWIM TEAM(1979); GETTING WASTED(1980)

Werner H. Furst
BLUEBEARD(1944), w

Ilse Furstenberg
BLUE ANGEL, THE(1930, Ger.); M(1933, Ger.); GOLDEN PLAGUE, THE(1963, Ger.)

Ira Furstenberg
HELLO–GOODBYE(1970); DEAF SMITH AND JOHNNY EARS(1973, Ital.)

George Furth
BEST MAN, THE(1964); NEW INTERNS, THE(1964); RAGE TO LIVE, A(1965); VERY SPECIAL FAVOR, A(1965); COOL ONES THE(1967); GAMES(1967); TAMMY AND THE MILLIONAIRE(1967); HOW TO SAVE A MARRIAGE–AND RUIN YOUR LIFE(1968); NOBODY'S PERFECT(1968); P.J.(1968); THE BOSTON STRANGLER, THE(1968); WHAT'S SO BAD ABOUT FEELING GOOD?(1968); BUTCH CASSIDY AND THE SUNDANCE KID(1969); BLAZING SADDLES(1974); SHAMPOO(1975); NORMAN...IS THAT YOU?(1976); AIRPORT '77(1977); OH, GOD!(1977); HOOPER(1978); CANNONBALL RUN, THE(1981); MEGAFORCE(1982); DOCTOR DETROIT(1983); MAN WITH TWO BRAINS, THE(1983)

Jaro Furth
BECAUSE I LOVED YOU(1930, Ger.); DIE MANNER UM LUCIE(1931)

Charles Furthman
BROADWAY(1929), w; THUNDERBOLT(1929), w; FOR THE DEFENSE(1930), w; HARD ROCK HARRIGAN(1935), w
Silents
LEGALLY DEAD(1923), w; CITY GONE WILD, THE(1927), w; UNDERWORLD(1927), w; DRAGNET, THE(1928), w

George Furthman
GIRL IN 419(1933), w

Jules Furthman
NEW YORK NIGHTS(1929), w; THUNDERBOLT(1929), w, w; COMMON CLAY(1930), w; MOROCCO(1930), w; RENEGADES(1930), w; BODY AND SOUL(1931), w; MERELY MARY ANN(1931), w; OVER THE HILL(1931), w; YELLOW TICKET, THE(1931), w; BLONDE VENUS(1932), w; SHANGHAI EXPRESS(1932), w; BOMBSHELL(1933), w; CHINA SEAS(1935), w; MUTINY ON THE BOUNTY(1935), w; COME AND GET IT(1936), w; SPAWN OF THE NORTH(1938), w; ONLY ANGELS HAVE WINGS(1939), w; WAY OF ALL FLESH, THE(1940), w; SHANGHAI GESTURE, THE(1941), w; OUTLAW, THE(1943), w; TO HAVE AND HAVE NOT(1944), w; BIG SLEEP, THE(1946), w; MOSS ROSE(1947), w; NIGHTMARE ALLEY(1947), w; PRETTY BABY(1950), w; PEKING EXPRESS(1951), w; JET PILOT(1957), p, w; RIO BRAVO(1959), w
Silents
FRAME UP, THE(1917), w; LAST TRAIL(1921), w; SINGING RIVER(1921), w; ARABIAN LOVE(1922), w; LOVE GAMBLER, THE(1922), w; PAWN TICKET 210(1922), w; RAGGED HEIRESS, THE(1922), w; YELLOW STAIN, THE(1922), w; ACQUITTAL, THE(1923), w; NORTH OF HUDSON BAY(1923), w; ANY WO-

MAN(1925), w; BIG PAL(1925), w; BARBED WIRE(1927), w; CASEY AT THE BAT(1927), w; CITY GONE WILD, THE(1927), w; WAY OF ALL FLESH, THE(1927), w; DRAGNET, THE(1928), w
Misc. Silents
LAND OF JAZZ, THE(1920), d

Jules G. Furthman
Silents
BIG PUNCH, THE(1921), w; BLUSHING BRIDE, THE(1921), d&w; CHEATER REFORMED, THE(1921), w; CALIFORNIA ROMANCE, A(1922), w; GLEAM O'DAWN(1922), w; ST. ELMO(1923), w
Misc. Silents
COLORADO PLUCK(1921), d

Hermann Furthmosek
ALMOST ANGELS(1962)

Dr. Wilhelm Furtwangler
DON GIOVANNI(1955, Brit.)

Yayoi Furusato
FINAL WAR, THE(1960, Jap.)

Hideo Furusawa
GULLIVER'S TRAVELS BEYOND THE MOON(1966, Jap.), anim d

Kengo Furusawa
TIGER FLIGHT(1965, Jap.), d; DON'T CALL ME A CON MAN(1966, Jap.), d; IT STARTED IN THE ALPS(1966, Jap.), d; SIEGE OF FORT BISMARK(1968, Jap.), d; COMPUTER FREE-FOR-ALL(1969, Jap.), d; DUEL AT EZO(1970, Jap.), d

Peter Furuta
DIFFERENT STORY, A(1978)

Osami Furuya
TORA! TORA! TORA!(1970, U.S./Jap.), ph

Billy Fury
PLAY IT COOL(1963, Brit.); I'VE GOTTA HORSE(1965, Brit.); THAT'LL BE THE DAY(1974, Brit.)

Ed Fury
FEMALE ON THE BEACH(1955); I DIED A THOUSAND TIMES(1955); RAW EDGE(1956); WILD WOMEN OF WONGO, THE(1959); MIGHTY URSUS(1962, Ital./Span.); SEVEN REVENGES, THE(1967, Ital.)
Misc. Talkies
COLOSSUS AND THE AMAZONS(1960)

Loretta Fury
MAN ON A SWING(1974)

Men Fury
KILL OR BE KILLED(1967, Ital.)

Judith Furze
ADVENTURES OF BARRY McKENZIE(1972, Austral.)

Lisa Fusaro
VIVA ZAPATA!(1952)

Angelo Fusco
IMPROPER CHANNELS(1981, Can.)

Anthony Fusco
SERIAL(1980)

Antonio Fusco
CLEOPATRA'S DAUGHTER(1963, Fr., Ital.), m

Giovanni Fusco
MYSTERY OF THE BLACK JUNGLE(1955), m; HIROSHIMA, MON AMOUR(1959, Fr./Jap.), m; COSSACKS, THE(1960, It.), m; L'AVVENTURA(1960, Ital.), m; PHAROAH'S WOMAN, THE(1961, Ital.), m; ECLIPSE(1962, Fr./Ital.), m; IL GRIDO(1962, U.S./Ital.), m; LE AMICHE(1962, Ital.), m; TROJAN HORSE, THE(1962, Fr./Ital.), m; RED SHEIK, THE(1963, Ital.), m; SANDOKAN THE GREAT(1964, Fr./Ital./Span.), m; INVASION 1700(1965, Fr./Ital./Yugo.), m; LIPSTICK(1965, Fr./Ital.), m; RED DESERT(1965, Fr./Ital.), m; TIME OF INDIFFERENCE(1965, Fr./Ital.), m; LA GUERRE EST FINIE(1967, Fr./Swed.), m; SUBVERSIVES, THE(1967, Ital.), m; DAY OF THE OWL(1968, Ital./Fr.), m; MAFIA(1969, Fr./Ital.), m; NUN AT THE CROSSROADS, A(1970, Ital./Span.), m; LADY WITHOUT CAMELLIAS, THE(1981, Ital.), m

Giuseppe Fusco
THREE NIGHTS OF LOVE(1969, Ital.), m

Jim Fusco
1984
JUST THE WAY YOU ARE(1984)

Maria Pia Fusco
BLUEBEARD(1972), w

Marie Pia Fusco
HITLER: THE LAST TEN DAYS(1973, Brit./Ital.), w

Tarcisio Fusco
THEN THERE WERE THREE(1961), m

Vera Fusek
ESCAPE IN THE SUN(1956, Brit.); FIVE BRANDED WOMEN(1960); GREAT VAN ROBBERY, THE(1963, Brit.)

Kazuko Fushimi
GOLDEN DEMON(1956, Jap.)

Alberto Fusi
OTHELLO(1955, U.S./Fr./Ital.), ph

Alverto Fusi
LADY IS FICKLE, THE(1948, Ital.), ph

Jeanne Fusier-Gil
RED CLOAK, THE(1961, Ital./Fr.)

Jeanne Fusier-Gir
FIRE IN THE STRAW(1943); RAVEN, THE(1948, Fr.); SIMPLE CASE OF MONEY, A(1952, Fr.); ROYAL AFFAIRS IN VERSAILLES(1957, Fr.)

Jeanne Fusler
CINDERELLA(1937, Fr.)

Harry Fuss
APRIL 1, 2000(1953, Aust.); INVISIBLE MAN, THE(1963, Ger.)

Claire Fussbach
RAMPAGE AT APACHE WELLS(1966, Ger./Yugo.), makeup

Sharon Fussey
CLASS OF MISS MAC MICHAEL, THE(1978, Brit./U.S.)

Fred Fuster
FIRST DEADLY SIN, THE(1980)

Brian Fustukian
 SILENCE OF THE NORTH(1981, Can.)
D. Fusu
 SANDU FOLLOWS THE SUN(1965, USSR)
Terumi Futagi
 ANGRY ISLAND(1960, Jap.)
Lori Futch
 GATOR(1976)
David Futcher
 INCIDENT AT MIDNIGHT(1966, Brit.)
Hugh Futcher
 CARRY ON SPYING(1964, Brit.); RATTLE OF A SIMPLE MAN(1964, Brit.); REPUL-
SION(1965, Brit.); FIVE MILLION YEARS TO EARTH(1968, Brit.); MRS. BROWN,
YOU'VE GOT A LOVELY DAUGHTER(1968, Brit.)
Jacques Futrelle
 MAN BEHIND THE MASK, THE(1936, Brit.), w
Silents
 ELUSIVE ISABEL(1916), w
Walter Futter
 HONG KONG NIGHTS(1935), p; CAVALCADE OF THE WEST(1936), p; FEUD OF
THE WEST(1936), p; FRONTIER JUSTICE(1936), p; LUCKY TERROR(1936), p; RID-
ING AVENGER, THE(1936), p; SWIFTY(1936), p; DARK SANDS(1938, Brit.), p, w;
AMAZING MONSIEUR FABRE, THE(1952, Fr.), p
Silents
 JANICE MEREDITH(1924), ed
The Futuras
 RAT FINK(1965)
Herbert Fux
 FUNERAL IN BERLIN(1966, Brit.); MARK OF THE DEVIL(1970, Ger./Brit.); LADY
FRANKENSTEIN(1971, Ital.); SONNY AND JED(1974, Ital.)
Misc. Talkies
 APE CREATURE(1968, Ger.)
Tatsumi Fuyamoto
 MONSTERS FROM THE UNKNOWN PLANET(1975, Jap.)
I. Fyedotova
 UNIVERSITY OF LIFE(1941, USSR)
Glen Fyfe
 OUT OF THE BLUE(1982)
Robert Fyfe
 XTRO(1983, Brit.)
Will Fyffe
 HAPPY(1934, Brit.); ROLLING HOME(1935, Brit.); ANNIE LAURIE(1936, Brit.);
DEBT OF HONOR(1936, Brit.); KING OF HEARTS(1936, Brit.); LOVE IN EXILE(1936,
Brit.); MEN OF YESTERDAY(1936, Brit.); WELL DONE, HENRY(1936, Brit.); COTTON
QUEEN(1937, Brit.); SPRING HANDICAP(1937, Brit.); SEZ O'REILLY TO MAC-
NAB(1938, Brit.); TO THE VICTOR(1938, Brit.); RULERS OF THE SEA(1939); FOR
FREEDOM(1940, Brit.); MISSING PEOPLE, THE(1940, Brit.); MYSTERIOUS MR.
REEDER, THE(1940, Brit.); THEY CAME BY NIGHT(1940, Brit.); NEUTRAL
PORT(1941, Brit.); PRIME MINISTER, THE(1941, Brit.); GIVE ME THE STARS(1944,
Brit.); HEAVEN IS ROUND THE CORNER(1944, Brit.); BROTHERS, THE(1948, Brit.)
Stephen Fyfield
 PIRATE MOVIE, THE(1982, Aus.)
Steven Fyfield
1984
 CAREFUL, HE MIGHT HEAR YOU(1984, Aus.)
Nicky Fylan
 STONE COLD DEAD(1980, Can.)
A. Fyodorinov
 THERE WAS AN OLD COUPLE(1967, USSR)
A. Fyodorova
 MUMU(1961, USSR)
I Fyodorova
 DUEL, THE(1964, USSR)
Victoria Fyodorova
 CRIME AND PUNISHMENT(1975, USSR)
Zoya Fyodorova
 GROWN-UP CHILDREN(1963, USSR)

The "G" Sisters
GOD'S GIFT TO WOMEN(1931)
The G-Men
DOUBLE TROUBLE(1967)
Franciska Gaal
BUCCANEER, THE(1938); GIRL DOWNSTAIRS, THE(1938); PARIS HONEY-MOON(1939)
Frances Gaar
FOOL KILLER, THE(1965)
Doron Gaash
JESUS CHRIST, SUPERSTAR(1973)
Marianne Gaba
MISSILE TO THE MOON(1959); PLEASE DON'T EAT THE DAISIES(1960); RAY-MIE(1960); CHOPPERS, THE(1961); LADIES MAN, THE(1961); ISLAND OF LO-VE(1963); PATSY, THE(1964); DR. GOLDFOOT AND THE BIKINI MACHINE(1965); HOW TO STUFF A WILD BIKINI(1965)
Scott Gaba
Misc. Talkies
CLOSE SHAVE(1981)
Gaston Gabaroche
FRENCH CANCAN(1956, Fr.)
Gennadiy Gabay
FORTY-NINE DAYS(1964, USSR), d
David Gabbai
GLORY BRIGADE, THE(1953)
Yehuda Gabbai
THEY WERE TEN(1961, Israel)
Till Gabbani
BENEATH THE 12-MILE REEF(1953), ph; 20,000 LEAGUES UNDER THE SEA(1954), ph
Naji Gabbay
RAINS OF RANCHIPUR, THE(1955); HELL WITH HEROES, THE(1968)
Kenneth Gabbert
FLASHDANCE(1983)
Otto Gabbo
GREAT GABBO, THE(1929)
Naji Gabby
SON OF SINBAD(1955)
Martin Gabel
LOST MOMENT, THE(1947), d; FOURTEEN HOURS(1951); M(1951); DEADLINE-U.S.A.(1952); THIEF, THE(1952); TIP ON A DEAD JOCKEY(1957); GOODBYE CHARL-IE(1964); MARNIE(1964); LORD LOVE A DUCK(1966); DIVORCE AMERICAN STY-LE(1967); LADY IN CEMENT(1968); THERE WAS A CROOKED MAN(1970); FRONT PAGE, THE(1974); FIRST DEADLY SIN, THE(1980)
Scilla Gabel
TARZAN'S GREATEST ADVENTURE(1959, Brit.); FRUIT IS RIPE, THE(1961, Fr./Ital.); QUEEN OF THE PIRATES(1961, Ital./Ger.); WHITE WARRIOR, THE(1961, Ital./Yugo.); SODOM AND GOMORRAH(1962, U.S./Fr./Ital.); VILLAGE OF DAUGH-TERS(1962, Brit.); MILL OF THE STONE WOMEN(1963, Fr./Ital.); THREE FACES OF SIN(1963, Fr./Ital.); TWO COLONELS, THE(1963, Ital.); REVENGE OF THE GLADIA-TORS(1965, Ital.); SEVEN SLAVES AGAINST THE WORLD(1965, Ital.); MODESTY BLAISE(1966, Brit.); HOW TO SEDUCE A PLAYBOY(1968, Aust./Fr./Ital.)
Gian Gabella
VERY HANDY MAN, A(1966, Fr./Ital.)
Luigi Gabellone
DAISY MILLER(1974)
Jean Gabin
FROM TOP TO BOTTOM(1933, Fr.); GOLGOTHA(1937, Fr.); LOWER DEPTHS, THE(1937, Fr.); PEPE LE MOKO(1937, Fr.); GRAND ILLUSION(1937, Fr.); LA BETE HUMAINE(1938, Fr.); PORT OF SHADOWS(1938, Fr.); THEY WERE FIVE(1938, Fr.); DAYBREAK(1940, Fr.); MOONTIDE(1942); IMPOSTER, THE(1944); STORMY WA-TERS(1946, Fr.); ROOM UPSTAIRS, THE(1948, Fr.); WALLS OF MALAPAGA, THE(1950, Fr./Ital.); LA MARIE DU PORT(1951, Fr.); HIS LAST TWELVE HOURS(1953, Ital.); LE PLAISIR(1954, Fr.); NAPOLEON(1955, Fr.); FRENCH CAN-CAN(1956, Fr.); DEADLIER THAN THE MALE(1957, Fr.); FOUR BAGS FULL(1957, Fr./Ital.); CASE OF DR. LAURENT(1958, Fr.); MAIGRET LAYS A TRAP(1958, Fr.); LOVE IS MY PROFESSION(1959, Fr.); NIGHT AFFAIR(1961, Fr.); COUNTERFEIT-ERS OF PARIS, THE(1962, Fr., Ital.); MAGNIFICENT TRAMP, THE(1962, Fr./Ital.); MONKEY IN WINTER, A(1962, Fr.); ANY NUMBER CAN WIN(1963 Fr.); MON-SIEUR(1964, Fr.); UPPER HAND, THE(1967, Fr./Ital./Ger.); LEATHER AND NY-LON(1965, Fr./Ital.); SICILIAN CLAN, THE(1970, Fr.); TWO MEN IN TOWN(1973, Fr.); CAT, THE(1975, Fr.); VERDICT(1975, Fr./Ital.)
Alain David Gabison
LITTLE ROMANCE, A(1979, U.S./Fr.)
David Gabison
CHANEL SOLITAIRE(1981)
1984
CHEECH AND CHONG'S THE CORSICAN BROTHERS(1984)
Christ Gable
WOMEN IN LOVE(1969, Brit.)
Christopher Gable
BOY FRIEND, THE(1971, Brit.), a, ch; MUSIC LOVERS, THE(1971, Brit.); SLIPPER AND THE ROSE, THE(1976, Brit.); WAGNER(1983, Brit./Hung./Aust.)
Clark Gable
DANCE, FOOLS, DANCE(1931); EASIEST WAY, THE(1931); FINGER POINTS, THE(1931); FREE SOUL, A(1931); LAUGHING SINNERS(1931); NIGHT NURSE(1931); PAINTED DESERT, THE(1931); POSSESSED(1931); SECRET SIX, THE(1931); SPORT-ING BLOOD(1931); SUSAN LENOX-HER FALL AND RISE(1931); HELL DI-VERS(1932); POLLY OF THE CIRCUS(1932); RED DUST(1932); STRANGE INTERLUDE(1932); DANCING LADY(1933); HOLD YOUR MAN(1933); NIGHT FLIGHT(1933); NO MAN OF HER OWN(1933); WHITE SISTER, THE(1933); CHAINED(1934); IT HAPPENED ONE NIGHT(1934); MANHATTAN MELO-DRAMA(1934); MEN IN WHITE(1934); AFTER OFFICE HOURS(1935); CALL OF THE WILD(1935); CHINA SEAS(1935); FORSAKING ALL OTHERS(1935); MUTINY ON

THE BOUNTY(1935); CAIN AND MABEL(1936); LOVE ON THE RUN(1936); SAN FRANCISCO(1936); WIFE VERSUS SECRETARY(1936); PARNELL(1937); SARATO-GA(1937); TEST PILOT(1938); TOO HOT TO HANDLE(1938); GONE WITH THE WIND(1939); IDIOT'S DELIGHT(1939); BOOM TOWN(1940); COMRADE X(1940); STRANGE CARGO(1940); HONKY TONK(1941); THEY MET IN BOMBAY(1941); SOMEWHERE I'LL FIND YOU(1942); ADVENTURE(1945); HUCKSTERS, THE(1947); COMMAND DECISION(1948); HOMECOMING(1948); ANY NUMBER CAN PLAY(1949); KEY TO THE CITY(1950); TO PLEASE A LADY(1950); ACROSS THE WIDE MISSOURI(1951); CALLAWAY WENT THATAWAY(1951); LONE STAR(1952); MOGAMBO(1953); NEVER LET ME GO(1953, U.S./Brit.); BETRAYED(1954); SOL-DIER OF FORTUNE(1955); TALL MEN, THE(1955); KING AND FOUR QUEENS, THE(1956); BAND OF ANGELS(1957); RUN SILENT, RUN DEEP(1958); TEACHER'S PET(1958); BUT NOT FOR ME(1959); IT STARTED IN NAPLES(1960); MISFITS, THE(1961)
Silents
FORBIDDEN PARADISE(1924); IRON HORSE, THE(1924)
Misc. Silents
WHITE MAN(1924)
Cynthia Gable
COAST TO COAST(1980)
Gilbert E. Gable
Silents
AS A MAN LIVES(1923), p
Heather Gable
Misc. Talkies
LONE STAR COUNTRY(1983)
Toni Gable
FRENCH WITHOUT TEARS(1939, Brit.); CAESAR AND CLEOPATRA(1946, Brit.)
Ernest Gabler
PLYMOUTH ADVENTURE(1952), w
Linda Gabler
1984
MRS. SOFFEL(1984)
Rudolph Gabler
PARSIFAL(1983, Fr.)
Sonia Gables
Misc. Talkies
MYRTE AND THE DEMONS(1948)
Louise Gabo
Misc. Talkies
MYSTERY RANCH(1934)
Anne-Lise Gabold
Z.P.G.(1972)
Annelise Gabold
KING LEAR(1971, Brit./Den.)
Eva Gabor
FORCED LANDING(1941); MIDNIGHT ANGEL(1941); PACIFIC BLACKOUT(1942); ROYAL SCANDAL, A(1945); WIFE OF MONTE CRISTO, THE(1946); SONG OF SURRENDER(1949); LOVE ISLAND(1952); PARIS MODEL(1953); CAPTAIN KIDD AND THE SLAVE GIRL(1954); LAST TIME I SAW PARIS, THE(1954); MAD MAGI-CIAN, THE(1954); ARTISTS AND MODELS(1955); MY MAN GODFREY(1957); GI-GI(1958); TRUTH ABOUT WOMEN, THE(1958, Brit.); IT STARTED WITH A KISS(1959); NEW KIND OF LOVE, A(1963); YOUNGBLOOD HAWKE(1964); ARIS-TOCATS, THE(1970); DON'T GO NEAR THE WATER(1975); RESCUERS, THE(1977); NUTCRACKER FANTASY(1979)
Ida Gabor
FOREVER MY LOVE(1962)
Lutz Gabor
WOMEN AND WAR(1965, Fr.)
Miklos Gabor
AGE OF ILLUSIONS(1967, Hung.); DIALOGUE(1967, Hung.); FATHER(1967, Hung.); WINDOWS OF TIME, THE(1969, Hung.)
Pal Gabor
ANGI VERA(1980, Hung.), d&w
1984
BRADY'S ESCAPE(1984, U.S./Hung.), d, w
Zsa Zsa Gabor
LOVELY TO LOOK AT(1952); MOULIN ROUGE(1952); WE'RE NOT MAR-RIED(1952); LILI(1953); STORY OF THREE LOVES, THE(1953); THREE RING CIRCUS(1954); DEATH OF A SCOUNDREL(1956); GIRL IN THE KREMLIN, THE(1957); COUNTRY MUSIC HOLIDAY(1958); LOVE IN A HOT CLIMATE(1958, Fr./Span.); MAN WHO WOULDN'T TALK, THE(1958, Brit.); QUEEN OF OUTER SPACE(1958); TOUCH OF EVIL(1958); FOR THE FIRST TIME(1959, U.S./Ger./Ital.); PEPE(1960); BOYS' NIGHT OUT(1962); ROAD TO HONG KONG, THE(1962, U.S./Brit.); ARRIVEDERCI, BABY!(1966, Brit.); PICTURE MOMMY DEAD(1966); JACK OF DIAMONDS(1967, U.S./Ger.); UP THE FRONT(1972, Brit.); WON TON TON, THE DOG WHO SAVED HOLLYWOOD(1976)
Zsa-Zsa Gabor
MOST WANTED MAN, THE(1962, Fr./Ital.)
Emile Gaboriau
FILE 113(1932), w
Fred Gabourie
HIGHWAY DRAGNET(1954); YUKON VENGEANCE(1954); SHACK OUT ON 101(1955); YAQUI DRUMS(1956)
Silents
OUR HOSPITALITY(1923), art d; THREE AGES, THE(1923), prod d; SHERLOCK, JR.(1924), art d; SEVEN CHANCES(1925), art d; GENERAL, THE(1927), prod d
Richard Gabourie
THREE CARD MONTE(1978, Can.), a, w; FINAL ASSIGNMENT(1980, Can.); TITLE SHOT(1982, Can.), a, w
Gabreillo
LOWER DEPTHS, THE(1937, Fr.)
Gabriel
WAYS OF LOVE(1950, Ital./Fr.)
Ben Gabriel
OFFICE PICNIC, THE(1974, Aus.); BREAK OF DAY(1977, Aus.); LET THE BALLOON GO(1977, Aus.); MANGO TREE, THE(1981, Aus.); FIGHTING BACK(1983, Brit.)

Bob Gabriel
DEAD DON'T DREAM, THE(1948)
David Gabriel
WOMAN FOR JOE, THE(1955, Brit.)
Ethel Gabriel
TWO MINUTES' SILENCE(1934, Brit.); SEASON OF PASSION(1961, Aus./Brit.)
Geoffrey Gabriel
DESIGN FOR MURDER(1940, Brit.)
Gilbert Gabriel
HOTEL IMPERIAL(1939), w; MAGNIFICENT FRAUD, THE(1939), w
Gilbert W. Gabriel
THIS WOMAN IS MINE(1941), w
Gloria Gabriel
DANGEROUS PROFESSION, A(1949)
Gudrun Gabriel
SISTERS, OR THE BALANCE OF HAPPINESS(1982, Ger.)
Guy Gabriel
I MARRIED AN ANGEL(1942)
Jean Gabriel
Misc. Silents
BETWEEN TWO HUSBANDS(1922); WAGES OF SIN, THE(1922)
John Gabriel
HIGHLY DANGEROUS(1950, Brit.); GLORY AT SEA(1952, Brit.); SECRET PEO-
PLE(1952, Brit.); MASTER PLAN, THE(1955, Brit.); HUNTERS, THE(1958); SOUTH
PACIFIC(1958); YOUNG LIONS, THE(1958); CAT GANG, THE(1959, Brit.); COM-
PELLED(1960, Brit.); IDENTITY UNKNOWN(1960, Brit.); STORY OF RUTH,
THE(1960); CURSE OF THE WEREWOLF, THE(1961); HIGHWAY TO BATTLE(1961,
Brit.); PURSUERS, THE(1961, Brit.); CORRIDORS OF BLOOD(1962, Brit.); GANG
WAR(1962, Brit.); OPERATION SNATCH(1962, Brit.); SIEGE OF THE SAXONS(1963,
Brit.); WINGS OF MYSTERY(1963, Brit.); RED LINE 7000(1965); SHARE OUT,
THE(1966, Brit.); STAGECOACH(1966); EL DORADO(1967); OH! WHAT A LOVELY
WAR(1969, Brit.); HELL'S BLOODY DEVILS(1970); DOOMSDAY VOYAGE(1972);
HIDING PLACE, THE(1975); IT'S MY TURN(1980); JUST TELL ME WHAT YOU
WANT(1980)
Silents
WON BY A HEAD(1920, Brit.), w
Larry Gabriel
TRUCK TURNER(1974); JIM, THE WORLD'S GREATEST(1976); TRACK-
DOWN(1976)
Lynn Gabriel
HEART OF THE WEST(1937); STAGE DOOR(1937)
Monique Gabriel
NIGHT SHIFT(1982)
Peter Gabriel
1984
BIRDY(1984), m
Phillip Jack Gabriel
1984
RENO AND THE DOC(1984, Can.)
Rajmund Gabriel
SKI FEVER(1969, U.S./Aust./Czech.)
Roman Gabriel
SKIDOO(1968); UNDEFEATED, THE(1969)
Gabrielle
NEW KIND OF LOVE, A(1963); LIVE A LITTLE, LOVE A LITTLE(1968)
Iris Gabrielle
WOMEN IN THE WIND(1939)
Monique Gabrielle
1984
HARD TO HOLD(1984); HOT MOVES(1984)
Nancy Gabrielle
PASSPORT TO PIMLICO(1949, Brit.); BLACK WINDMILL, THE(1974, Brit.)
Giacomo Gabrielli
SWINDLE, THE(1962, Fr./Ital.)
Yves Gabrielli
LIFE LOVE DEATH(1969, Fr./Ital.); TOUT VA BIEN(1973, Fr.)
Gabriello
SIMPLE CASE OF MONEY, A(1952, Fr.); DEVIL AND THE TEN COMMAND-
MENTS, THE(1962, Fr.)
Giacomo Gabriello
LA DOLCE VITA(1961, Ital./Fr.)

Charles Gabrielson
1984
BEAR, THE(1984)
Frank Gabrielson
SOMETHING FOR THE BOYS(1944), w; DON JUAN QUILLIGAN(1945), w; IT
SHOULDN'T HAPPEN TO A DOG(1946), w; FLIGHT OF THE DOVES(1971), w
Yevgeniy Gabrilovich
RESURRECTION(1963, USSR), w; PORTRAIT OF LENIN(1967, Pol./USSR), w
Gabriel Gabrio
LUCREZIA BORGIA(1937, Fr.); PEPE LE MOKO(1937, Fr.); HARVEST(1939, Fr.);
DEVIL'S ENVOYS, THE(1947, Fr.)
Silents
INSEPARABLES, THE(1929, Brit.)
Misc. Silents
ANTOINETTE SABRIER(1927, Fr.); LES MISERABLES(1927, Fr.)
Robert Gabriti
THE DIRTY GAME(1966, Fr./Ital./Ger.), art d
Raymond Gabutti
ROOTS OF HEAVEN, THE(1958), art d; SWEET AND SOUR(1964, Fr./Ital.), art d;
HOW NOT TO ROB A DEPARTMENT STORE(1965, Fr./Ital.), art d; YO YO(1967,
Fr.), art d
Alex Gaby
HOT RODS TO HELL(1967), w
Frank Gaby
MR. DYNAMITE(1941); SWEETHEART OF THE CAMPUS(1941)

Lili Gacel
END OF INNOCENCE(1960, Arg.)
Alice Gachet
MAN WHO WOULDN'T TALK, THE(1958, Brit.)
Dan Gachman
RETURN OF DRACULA, THE(1958)
Don Gachman
MONSTER THAT CHALLENGED THE WORLD, THE(1957)
Ratislava Gacic
FRAGRANCE OF WILD FLOWERS, THE(1979, Yugo.)
Dr. Dieter Gackstetter
LILI MARLEEN(1981, Ger.), ch
Renee Gad
DAVID COPPERFIELD(1935)
Donald Gadd
YOU'RE IN THE ARMY NOW(1937, Brit.)
Renee Gadd
AREN'T WE ALL?(1932, Brit.); HIS WIFE'S MOTHER(1932, Brit.); JOSSER JOINS
THE NAVY(1932, Brit.); MAID OF THE MOUNTAINS, THE(1932, Brit.); MONEY FOR
NOTHING(1932, Brit.); LETTING IN THE SUNSHINE(1933, Brit.); WHITE FACE(1933,
Brit.); HAPPY(1934, Brit.); LOVE CAPTIVE, THE(1934); UNCERTAIN LADY(1934);
CRIMSON CIRCLE, THE(1936, Brit.); MAN IN THE MIRROR, THE(1936, Brit.);
TOMORROW WE LIVE(1936, Brit.); WHERE'S SALLY?(1936, Brit.); BRIEF EC-
STASY(1937, Brit.); CLOTHES AND THE WOMAN(1937, Brit.); MAN WHO MADE
DIAMONDS, THE(1937, Brit.); UNDER A CLOUD(1937, Brit.); DANGEROUS SE-
CRETS(1938, Brit.); MEET MR. PENNY(1938, Brit.); MURDER IN THE NIGHT(1940,
Brit.); UNPUBLISHED STORY(1942, Brit.); THEY CAME TO A CITY(1944, Brit.);
DEAD OF NIGHT(1946, Brit.); FRIEDA(1947, Brit.); GOOD TIME GIRL(1950, Brit.)
Steve Gadd
ONE-TRICK PONY(1980)
Carlo Emilo Gadda
FACTS OF MURDER, THE(1965, Ital.), w
Betty Gadde
LADY LIES, THE(1929)
Carlo Gaddi
CONFORMIST, THE(1971, Ital., Fr); WHITE SISTER(1973, Ital./Span./Fr.)
Marshall Gaddis
1984
SLOW MOVES(1984)
Michael Gaddis
MEET THE CHUMP(1941); SLAVE GIRL(1947); SMART WOMAN(1948)
Mike Gaddis
GANGSTER, THE(1947)
Peggy Gaddis
Silents
PRETTY CLOTHES(1927), w; MILLION FOR LOVE, A(1928), w
Thomas E. Gaddis
BIRDMAN OF ALCATRAZ(1962), w
Amelia Gade
EXORCISM'S DAUGHTER zero(1974, Span.)
Analia Gade
GIRL FROM VALLADOLIO(1958, Span.)
Annalis Gade
MADAME(1963, Fr./Ital./Span.)
Svend Gade
Silents
ROSITA(1923), set d; WATCH YOUR WIFE(1926), d, w; JAZZ MAD(1928), w
Misc. Silents
HAMLET(1921, Ger.), d; FIFTH AVENUE MODELS(1925), d; PEACOCK FEATH-
ERS(1925), d; SIEGE(1925), d; BLONDE SAINT, THE(1926), d; INTO HER KING-
DOM(1926), d
William Gade
ROYAL BOX, THE(1930)
Alexander Gaden
Silents
AS A WOMAN SOWS(1916); DRIFTER, THE(1916); WHITE OAK(1921); NET,
THE(1923)
Misc. Silents
LEAH KLESCHNA(1913); UNBROKEN ROAD, THE(1915); I ACCUSE(1916); QUAL-
ITY OF FAITH, THE(1916); BANDBOX, THE(1919); CAPITOL, THE(1920); CYNTHIA-
OF-THE-MINUTE(1920)
Antonio Gades
PLEASURE SEEKERS, THE(1964), a, ch; BLOOD WEDDING(1981, Sp.); CAR-
MEN(1983, Span.), a, w, ch
1984
BIZET'S CARMEN(1984, Fr./Ital.), ch
Frederic Gadette
THIS IS NOT A TEST(1962), p, d, w
Gloria Gadhoke
WILD PARTY, THE(1975)
Steve Gadler
Z(1969, Fr./Algeria)
1984
UNTIL SEPTEMBER(1984)
Alan Gadney
MOONCHILD(1972), d&w
Daniel Gadouas
WAITING FOR CAROLINE(1969, Can.); YESTERDAY(1980, Can.)
Jon Gadsby
1984
BOUNTY, THE(1984); SECOND TIME LUCKY(1984, Aus./New Zealand)
Jacqueline Gadsden
Silents
SKID PROOF(1923); GOLDFISH, THE(1924); MAN AND MAID(1925); REGULAR
FELLOW, A(1925)
Lionel Gadsden
THREE WEIRD SISTERS, THE(1948, Brit.)

Jacquelin Gadsdon
Silents
NOT SO LONG AGO(1925); WEST OF ZANZIBAR(1928)
Misc. Silents
THIRTEENTH HOUR, THE(1927)
Jacqueline Gadsdon
Silents
MERRY WIDOW, THE(1925); RIDIN' THE WIND(1925); IT(1927); RED HAIR(1928)
Misc. Silents
FLAMING FORTIES, THE(1924); CITY OF PURPLE DREAMS(1928)
Jacqueline Gadsen
Misc. Silents
CHAPTER IN HER LIFE, A(1923)
Gad Gadugan
HAMILE(1965, Ghana)
Rudy Gaebell
DON'T TURN THE OTHER CHEEK(1974, Ital./Ger./Span.)
Anna Gael
HEAT OF MIDNIGHT(1966, Fr.); HELL IS EMPTY(1967, Brit./Ital); BEN-JAMIN(1968, Fr.); THERESE AND ISABELLE(1968, U.S./Ger.); BRIDGE AT REMA-GEN, THE(1969); EROTIQUE(1969, Fr.); TO COMMIT A MURDER(1970, Fr./Ital./Ger.); BLUE BLOOD(1973, Brit.); DRACULA AND SON(1976, Fr.); SWEENEY 2(1978, Brit.)
Misc. Talkies
HOUSE OF THE MISSING GIRLS(1974)
Josseline Gael
LES MISERABLES(1936, Fr.); CARNIVAL OF SINNERS(1947, Fr.)
Paul Gaer
GET TO KNOW YOUR RABBIT(1972), p; ELECTRIC HORSEMAN, THE(1979), w
Enrique Gaertner
SHADOWS GROW LONGER, THE(1962, Switz./Ger.), ph
Heinrich Gaertner
TALES OF THE UNCANNY(1932, Ger.), ph
Monika Gaertner
PARSIFAL(1983, Fr.)
Claus Theo Gaestner
OPERATION GANYMED(1977, Ger.)
Paulo Gaeta
MARGIN, THE,(1969, Braz.)
Marcelo Gaete
ALSINO AND THE CONDOR(1983, Nicaragua)
Phyllis Gaffeo
THREE DARING DAUGHTERS(1948)
Nestor R. Gaffet
HAND IN THE TRAP, THE(1963, Arg./Span.), p
John Gaffey
JAWS 3-D(1983)
Brian Gaffikin
NOTORIOUS LANDLADY, THE(1962)
Melanie Gaffin
ENTITY, THE(1982)
Yvonne Gaffin
VOTE FOR HUGGETT(1948, Brit.), cos
Arch A. Gaffney
NO MARRIAGE TIES(1933), w
Edwin Gaffney
OVERLAND STAGE RAIDERS(1938)
James Gaffney
FIEND OF DOPE ISLAND(1961), ed; LIGHT FANTASTIC(1964), ed
Liam Gaffney
MACUSHLA(1937, Brit.); IRISH AND PROUD OF IT(1938, Ireland); VILLIERS DIAMOND, THE(1938, Brit.); DR. O'DOWD(1940, Brit.); SECRET FOUR, THE(1940, Brit.); CAPTAIN BOYCOTT(1947, Brit.); BAD LORD BYRON, THE(1949, Brit.); LADY WITH A LAMP, THE(1951, Brit.); CURTAIN UP(1952, Brit.); SHADOW MAN(1953, Brit.); TWILIGHT WOMEN(1953, Brit.); WOMAN IN HIDING(1953, Brit.); JAZZ BOAT(1960, Brit.); MAN WITH THE GREEN CARNATION, THE(1960, Brit.); ISLAND OF TERROR(1967, Brit.)
Marjorey Gaffney
RAT, THE(1938, Brit.), w
Marjorie Gaffney
NIGHT OF THE GARTER(1933, Brit.), w; EVERGREEN(1934, Brit.), w; MY OLD DUTCH(1934, Brit.), w; FIRST A GIRL(1935, Brit.), w; ME AND MARL-BOROUGH(1935, Brit.), w; HEAD OVER HEELS IN LOVE(1937, Brit.), w; GANG, THE(1938, Brit.), w; MYSTERIOUS MR. REEDER, THE(1940, Brit.), w; SUICIDE LEGION(1940, Brit.), w
Maureen Gaffney
PARDON MY BRUSH(1964); BLACK KLANSMAN, THE(1966)
Maureene Gaffney
HARLOW(1965)
Robert Gaffney
LIGHT FANTASTIC(1964), p; TROUBLEMAKER, THE(1964), p; FRANKENSTEIN MEETS THE SPACE MONSTER(1965), d; SUPERFLY T.N.T.(1973), ph
Jimmy Gaffrey
STORK TALK(1964, Brit.)
Willy Gafni
MADRON(1970, U.S./Israel)
Rajah Gafsi
1984
MISUNDERSTOOD(1984)
B. Gage
1984
FLESHBURN(1984), w
Ben Gage
BIG OPERATOR, THE(1959)
Beth Gage
1984
FLESHBURN(1984), p

Danny Gage
SHAPE OF THINGS TO COME, THE(1979, Can.)
Edward Gage
INGAGI(1931), m
Elizabeth Gage
SKATEBOARD(1978), cos
Erford Gage
HITLER'S CHILDREN(1942); SEVEN MILES FROM ALCATRAZ(1942); ADVEN-TURES OF A ROOKIE(1943); FALCON IN DANGER, THE(1943); FALCON STRIKES BACK, THE(1943); FALLEN SPARROW, THE(1943); GANGWAY FOR TOMOR-ROW(1943); MR. LUCKY(1943); ROOKIES IN BURMA(1943); SEVENTH VICTIM, THE(1943); CURSE OF THE CAT PEOPLE, THE(1944); DAYS OF GLORY(1944)
G. Gage
1984
FLESHBURN(1984), w
Gary Gage
NIGHT OF EVIL(1962)
Geoff Gage
CAPTAIN MILKSHAKE(1970)
George Gage
SKATEBOARD(1978), d, w
1984
FLESHBURN(1984), d
Jack Gage
HOTEL BERLIN(1945), d
John Gage
VELVET TOUCH, THE(1948), d
Leona Gage
TALES OF TERROR(1962); HOUSE IS NOT A HOME, A(1964); SCREAM OF THE BUTTERFLY(1965)
Loren Gage
KAZAN(1949)
Loutz Gage
WINTER KILLS(1979)
Neva Gage
CAT PEOPLE(1982)
Nicholas Gage
CRAZY JOE(1974), w
Patricia Gage
WHY ROCK THE BOAT?(1974, Can.); RABID(1976, Can.)
Rodney Gage
MC CABE AND MRS. MILLER(1971)
1984
RUNAWAY(1984)
Russell Gage
THEM!(1954)
Sara Gage
NIGHT OF EVIL(1962)
Walter Gage
BUS RILEY'S BACK IN TOWN(1965), w
Eva Gagel
ALL-AROUND REDUCED PERSONALITY-OUTTAKES, THE(1978, Ger.)
Annie Gagen
WOLFEN(1981)
Ray Gaggett
Silents
QUEEN KELLY(1929)
Toni Gaggia
GIRL AND THE GENERAL, THE(1967, Fr./Ital.)
Oscar Gaghan
ROLLIN' PLAINS(1938)
Gagliano
OPERATION KID BROTHER(1967, Ital.), spec eff
Enzo Gagliardi
HOUSE CALLS(1978)
Vincenzo Gagliardi
MODERN PROBLEMS(1981)
Giovanna Gagliardo
ASSASSIN, THE(1961, Ital./Fr.); ROME WANTS ANOTHER CAESAR(1974, Ital.), w
Juan Luis Gagliardo
SEVEN GOLDEN MEN(1969, Fr./Ital./Span.)
Fryda Gagne
MAID OF SALEM(1937)
Hugette Gagne
HAPPY BIRTHDAY TO ME(1981), cos
Verne Gagne
WRESTLER, THE(1974)
Andre Gagnon
RUNNING(1979, Can.), m; PHOBIA(1980, Can.), m
Betty Gagnon
GAY RANCHERO, THE(1948)
Ginny Gagnon
HARRY AND WALTER GO TO NEW YORK(1976)
J. Leo Gagnon
WHY ROCK THE BOAT?(1974, Can.)
Jacques Gagnon
MY UNCLE ANTOINE(1971, Can.)
Lee Gagnon
SEIZURE(1974), m
Pfc. Rene A. Gagnon
SANDS OF IWO JIMA(1949)
Steve Gagnon
CHEAPER TO KEEP HER(1980)
Terry Gagnon
MANIAC(1980)
Jenny Gago
MAN WITH TWO BRAINS, THE(1983); UNDER FIRE(1983)
1984
IRRECONCILABLE DIFFERENCES(1984)

Pablo Gago
DRUMS OF TABU, THE(1967, Ital./Span.), set d
Philippe Gagon
ORDERS, THE(1977, Can.), m
Helen Gahagan
SHE(1935)
Oscar Gahan
CHEYENNE TORNADO(1935); TUMBLING TUMBLEWEEDS(1935); WESTERN FRONTIER(1935); FUGITIVE SHERIFF, THE(1936); LAWLESS RIDERS(1936); LIGHTNING BILL CARSON(1936); LONELY TRAIL, THE(1936); SINGING COWBOY, THE(1936); BAR Z BAD MEN(1937); GIT ALONG, LITTLE DOGIES(1937); GUNS IN THE DARK(1937); MOONLIGHT ON THE RANGE(1937); MYSTERY OF THE HOODED HORSEMEN, THE(1937); RIDERS OF THE DAWN(1937); ROAMING COWBOY, THE(1937); SILVER TRAIL, THE(1937); SING, COWBOY, SING(1937); SPRINGTIME IN THE ROCKIES(1937); TRUSTED OUTLAW, THE(1937); WHERE TRAILS DIVIDE(1937); YODELIN' KID FROM PINE RIDGE(1937); DANGER VALLEY(1938); GHOST TOWN RIDERS(1938); GUNSMOKE TRAIL(1938); HEROES OF THE ALAMO(1938); IN EARLY ARIZONA(1938); ROLLING CARAVANS(1938); WESTERN TRAILS(1938); MAN FROM SUNDOWN, THE(1939); NEW FRONTIER(1939); CARSON CITY KID(1940); BILLY THE KID TRAPPED(1942)
Oscar Gahen
COURAGE OF THE WEST(1937)
Berenice Gahm
CARDINAL, THE(1963)
Michael Gahr
GERMANY IN AUTUMN(1978, Ger.); WAR AND PEACE(1983, Ger.)
Roy Gahris
Misc. Silents
TROOPER 44(1917), d
Marie Gahva
CRY BLOOD, APACHE(1970)
Claude Gai
JACOB TWO-TWO MEETS THE HOODED FANG(1979, Can.)
G. Gai
GARNET BRACELET, THE(1966, USSR)
James Gaibbou
SACRED FLAME, THE(1929), ed
Corrado Gaida
CHINO(1976, Ital., Span., Fr.)
Vladimir Gaidaroff
Misc. Silents
RASPUTIN(1929, USSR)
V. Gaidarov
Misc. Silents
RUSSIA(1929, Ger.)
Vladamie Gaidarov
Misc. Silents
BLOOD NEED NOT BE SPILLED(1917, USSR)
Vladimir Gaidarov
Misc. Silents
MANON LESCAUT(1926, Ger.)
Nina Gaidarova
SUBWAY RIDERS(1981)
Gaidon
LOVE IN THE AFTERNOON(1957)
Vladimir Gaidrov
Misc. Silents
HER SACRIFICE(1917, USSR); FATHER SERGIUS(1918, USSR)
Vladimir Gaidrow
Misc. Silents
SCANDAL IN PARIS(1929, Ger.)
Giuseppe Gaieati
LAST CHANCE, THE(1945, Switz.)
Russel Gaige
UNDERGROUND AGENT(1942)
Russell Gaige
ONCE UPON A HONEYMOON(1942); GIRLS IN CHAINS(1943); WILSON(1944); SOMETHING FOR THE BIRDS(1952); FOREVER FEMALE(1953); SANGAREE(1953); VANQUISHED, THE(1953); TO CATCH A THIEF(1955); COURT JESTER, THE(1956)
Truman Gaige
1984
ULTIMATE SOLUTION OF GRACE QUIGLEY, THE(1984)
Albert Gail
FIVE WEEKS IN A BALLOON(1962), w
Bobby Gail
MAN WITH 100 FACES, THE(1938, Brit.)
Jane Gail
Silents
TRAFFIC IN SOULS(1913); PRISONER OF ZENDA, THE(1915, Brit.); RUPERT OF HENTZAU(1915, Brit.)
Misc. Silents
CALLED BACK(1914, Brit.); SHE STOOPS TO CONQUER(1914, Brit.); MIDDLEMAN, THE(1915, Brit.); 1914(1915, Brit.); GIRL WHO DIDN'T THINK, THE(1917); LIAR, THE(1918)
Jeanne Gail
WOMAN WHO CAME BACK(1945); TENDER YEARS, THE(1947); ARTHUR TAKES OVER(1948)
June Gail
Silents
20,000 LEAGUES UNDER THE SEA(1916)
Mary Gail
LADY OF BURLESQUE(1943)
Max Gail
D.C. CAB(1983)
1984
HEARTBREAKERS(1984)
Maxwell Gail
CARDIAC ARREST(1980)

Maxwell Gail, Jr.
DIRTY HARRY(1971); ORGANIZATION, THE(1971); NIGHT MOVES(1975)
Pam Gail
DINER(1982)
Pamela Gail
GNOME-MOBILE, THE(1967)
Philippa Gail
THIS IS MY STREET(1964, Brit.); RING OF BRIGHT WATER(1969, Brit.)
Misc. Talkies
SHE'LL FOLLOW YOU ANYWHERE(1971)
Zoe Gail
NO ORCHIDS FOR MISS BLANDISH(1948, Brit.)
Andre Gailhard
BATTLE, THE(1934, Fr.), m
Georges Gaili
YELLOW STOCKINGS(1930, Brit.)
Gretchen Gailing
JOAN OF ARC(1948)
Hans Gailing
CELESTE(1982, Ger.), art d
Gaillard
LA CHIENNE(1975, Fr.)
The Gaillard Brothers
HOME FROM HOME(1939, Brit.)
Bob Gaillard
Silents
ALL MAN(1918)
Jacques Gaillard
LE BEAU SERGE(1959, Fr.), ed; WEB OF PASSION(1961, Fr.), ed; SEVEN CAPITAL SINS(1962, Fr./Ital.), ed; LANDRU(1963, Fr./Ital), ed; THIRD LOVER, THE(1963, Fr./Ital.), ed; OPHELIA(1964, Fr.), ed; BEAUTIFUL SWINDLERS, THE(1967, Fr./Ital./Jap./Neth.), ed; CHAMPAGNE MURDERS, THE(1968, Fr.), ed; LES BICHES(1968, Fr.), ed; LA FEMME INFIDELE(1969, Fr./Ital.), ed; THIS MAN MUST DIE(1970, Fr./Ital.), ed; WHO'S GOT THE BLACK BOX?(1970, Fr./Gr./Ital.), ed; LE BOUCHER(1971, Fr./Ital.), ed; DOCTEUR POPAUL(1972, Fr.), ed; TEN DAYS' WONDER(1972, Fr.), ed; NADA GANG, THE(1974, Fr./Ital.), ed; JUST BEFORE NIGHTFALL(1975, Fr./Ital.), ed; DIRTY HANDS(1976, Fr/Ital./Ger.), ed
Marius Francois Gaillard
I BECAME A CRIMINAL(1947), m
Marius-Francois Gaillard
PORTRAIT OF INNOCENCE(1948, Fr.), m
Rene Gaillard
TWO ENGLISH GIRLS(1972, Fr.)
Robert Gaillard
MARIE OF THE ISLES(1960, Fr.), w
Silents
KID, THE(1916); TWO-EDGED SWORD, THE(1916); IN THE BALANCE(1917); ADVENTURE SHOP, THE(1918); JAMESTOWN(1923)
Misc. Silents
MAN WHO COULD'T BEAT GOD, THE(1915), a, d; WRITING ON THE WALL, THE(1916); SON OF THE HILLS, A(1917); STOLEN TREATY, THE(1917); CLUTCH OF CIRCUMSTANCE, THE(1918); HOARDED ASSETS(1918); SILENT STRENGTH(1919); BROADWAY BUBBLE, THE(1920)
Roger Gaillard
CAFE DE PARIS(1938, Fr.); LES ENFANTS TERRIBLES(1952, Fr.); ROYAL AFFAIRS IN VERSAILLES(1957, Fr.)
Slim Gaillard
GO, MAN, GO!(1954); CURIOUS FEMALE, THE(1969)
Barbara Gailling
OUR HITLER, A FILM FROM GERMANY(1980, Ger.), cos
Hans Gailling
JONATHAN(1973, Ger.), art d; OUR HITLER, A FILM FROM GERMANY(1980, Ger.), art d
Robert Gaillord
Silents
MR. BARNES OF NEW YORK(1914), a, d
Misc. Silents
CLEOPATRA(1913); IN HONOR'S WEB(1919)
Boyd Gaines
FAME(1980); PORKY'S(1982)
Bud Gaines
EASY TO LOVE(1953)
Charles Gaines
HUSBANDS(1970); THOMASINE AND BUSHROD(1974); STAY HUNGRY(1976), w
Courtney Gaines
1984
HARDBODIES(1984)
Ellen Gaines
HOT SPUR(1968)
Ernestine Gaines
Silents
ALOMA OF THE SOUTH SEAS(1926)
George Gaines
ONE IS A LONELY NUMBER(1972), set d; BOY WHO CRIED WEREWOLF, THE(1973); BANK SHOT(1974), set d; ZANDY'S BRIDE(1974), set d; FORTUNE, THE(1975), set d; ALL THE PRESIDENT'S MEN(1976), set d; SHAMPOO(1975), set d; MARATHON MAN(1976), set d; COMING HOME(1978), set d; HEAVEN CAN WAIT(1978), set d; PROPHECY(1979), set d; SKATETOWN, U.S.A.(1979), set d; HUNTER, THE(1980), set d; PARTNERS(1982), set d; BIG CHILL, THE(1983), set d; UNCOMMON VALOR(1983), set d
1984
CITY HEAT(1984), set d; COTTON CLUB, THE(1984), set d
James Gaines
ENTER THE NINJA(1982)
Misc. Talkies
ONE ARMED EXECUTIONER(1980); BLOOD DEBTS(1983)
Jimmy Gaines
THIRD OF A MAN(1962); ROUSTABOUT(1964)

Lenny Gaines
NEW YORK, NEW YORK(1977)

Leonard Gaines
BLUE COLLAR(1978); HARDCORE(1979); ROCKY II(1979); IDOLMAKER, THE(1980); WHERE THE BUFFALO ROAM(1980)
1984
ADVENTURES OF BUCKAROO BANZAI: ACROSS THE 8TH DIMENSION, THE(1984)

Marjorie Gaines
1941(1979)

Mel Gaines
FLESH AND THE SPUR(1957); MAN OR GUN(1958)

Otho Gaines
IMPOSTER, THE(1944)

Pearl Gaines
NAKED CITY, THE(1948)

Richard Gaines
HOWARDS OF VIRGINIA, THE(1940); NIGHT TO REMEMBER, A(1942); MORE THE MERRIER, THE(1943); TENDER COMRADE(1943); DOUBLE EXPOSURE(1944); DOUBLE INDEMNITY(1944); MR. WINKLE GOES TO WAR(1944); DON JUAN QUILLIGAN(1945); ENCHANTED COTTAGE, THE(1945); TWICE BLESSED(1945); BRIDE WORE BOOTS, THE(1946); DO YOU LOVE ME?(1946); HUMORESQUE(1946); NOBODY LIVES FOREVER(1946); SO GOES MY LOVE(1946); WHITE TIE AND TAILS(1946); BRUTE FORCE(1947); CASS TIMBERLANE(1947); DANGEROUS YEARS(1947); HUCKSTERS, THE(1947); INVISIBLE WALL, THE(1947); RIDE THE PINK HORSE(1947); UNCONQUERED(1947); EVERY GIRL SHOULD BE MARRIED(1948); THAT WONDERFUL URGE(1948); KISS FOR CORLISS, A(1949); LUCKY STIFF, THE(1949); STRANGE BARGAIN(1949); KEY TO THE CITY(1950); BIG CARNIVAL, THE(1951); FLIGHT TO MARS(1951); MARRY ME AGAIN(1953); DRUM BEAT(1954); LOVE ME OR LEAVE ME(1955); TRIAL(1955); FRANCIS IN THE HAUNTED HOUSE(1956); RANSOM(1956); FIVE STEPS TO DANGER(1957); JEANNE EAGELS(1957)

Robert Gaines
FRONT PAGE STORY(1954, Brit.), w

Walter Gaines
Misc. Talkies
ASSAULT WITH A DEADLY WEAPON(1983), d

Willaim Gaines
VAULT OF HORROR, THE(1973, Brit.), w

William Gaines
TALES FROM THE CRYPT(1972, Brit.), w

Carol Ann Gainey
STORY OF WILL ROGERS, THE(1952)

M.C. Gainey
1984
STARMAN(1984)

Michael Gainey
STORY OF WILL ROGERS, THE(1952); GOOD MORNING, MISS DOVE(1955); BLUE DENIM(1959)

Mike Gainey
TIME AFTER TIME(1979, Brit.)

Dede Gainor
DOWN THREE DARK STREETS(1954)

Courtney Gains
1984
CHILDREN OF THE CORN(1984)

Louise Gainsborough
BONNIE PRINCE CHARLIE(1948, Brit.); TRAPPED BY THE TERROR(1949, Brit.); SHADOW OF THE PAST(1950, Brit.)

Michael D. Gainsborough
MOMMIE DEAREST(1981)

Michael Gainsborough
SENSATION(1936, Brit.); SCRUFFY(1938, Brit.); SHIPBUILDERS, THE(1943, Brit.); I'LL TURN TO YOU(1946, Brit.); BLACK MARBLE, THE(1980); LOOKER(1981)

Serge Gainsbourg
COME DANCE WITH ME(1960, Fr.); FURY OF HERCULES, THE(1961, Ital.); REVOLT OF THE SLAVES, THE(1961, Ital./Span./Ger.); SAMSON(1961, Ital.); GAME FOR SIX LOVERS, A(1962, Fr.), m; SWEET SKIN(1965, Fr./Ital.), m; DEFECTOR, THE(1966, Ger./Fr.), m; OTHER ONE, THE(1967,Fr.), m; UNKNOWN MAN OF SHANDIGOR, THE(1967, Switz.); MARRIAGE CAME TUMBLING DOWN, THE(1968, Fr.), a, m; CANNABIS(1970, Fr.); MISTER FREEDOM(1970, Fr.), a, m; NAKED HEARTS(1970, Fr.), m; SLOGAN(1970, Fr.), a, m; ROMANCE OF A HORSE THIEF(1971); GOODBYE EMMANUELLE(1980, Fr.), m

Anne Gainsford
INADMISSIBLE EVIDENCE(1968, Brit.), cos

R. Gainter
POCKET MONEY(1972)

G. Leroy Gaintner
NIGHT OF THE LEPUS(1972)

Rene Gainville
ASSOCIATE, THE(1982 Fr./Ger.), d, w

Christina Gaioni
AND THE WILD, WILD WOMEN(1961, Ital.); PULP(1972, Brit.)

Cristina Gaioni
WOMEN IN CELL BLOCK 7(1977, Ital./U.S.)

Corrado Gaipa
PIZZA TRIANGLE, THE(1970, Ital./Span.); THAT SPLENDID NOVEMBER(1971, Ital./Fr.); GODFATHER, THE(1972); NO WAY OUT(1975, Ital./Fr.)

Gerald Gaiser
FUN WITH DICK AND JANE(1977, w

Pierre Dominique Gaisseau
ROUND TRIP(1967), d

Gant Gaither
MY SIX LOVES(1963), p

Grigori Gaj
RED TENT, THE(1971, Ital./USSR)

Ken Gajadhar
Misc. Talkies
DEATH MAY BE YOUR SANTA CLAUS(1969)

Vladimir Gajdarov
Misc. Silents
LOVE ONE ANOTHER(1922, Den.)

Cristina Gajoni
ASSASSIN, THE(1961, Ital./Fr.); MIGHTY URSUS(1962, Ital./Span.); LOVE AT TWENTY(1963, Fr./Ital./Jap./Pol./Ger.); RUN WITH THE DEVIL(1963, Fr./Ital.); STEPPE, THE(1963, Fr./Ital.); FACTS OF MURDER, THE(1965, Ital.)

Maria Cristina Gajoni
TEMPEST(1958, Ital./Yugo./Fr.)

Maria-Christina Gajoni
GUINGUETTE(1959, Fr.)

Cristina Gajonia
TWELVE-HANDED MEN OF MARS, THE(1964, Ital./Span.)

Janusz Gajos
CONDUCTOR, THE(1981, Pol.); MAN OF IRON(1981, Pol.); CONTRACT, THE(1982, Pol.)

Alex Gal
Misc. Talkies
FORBID THEM NOT(1961)

Shirley Galabow
HOT STUFF(1979)

Michel Galabru
GAME FOR SIX LOVERS, A(1962, Fr.); LAFAYETTE(1963, Fr.); WAR OF THE BUTTONS(1963 Fr.); MY WIFE'S HUSBAND(1965, Fr./Ital.), a, w; GENDARME OF ST. TROPEZ, THE(1966, Fr./Ital.); SUCKER, THE(1966, Fr./Ital.); LE GENDARME ET LES EXTRATERRESTRES(1978, Fr.); JUDGE AND THE ASSASSIN, THE(1979, Fr.); LA CAGE AUX FOLLES(1979, Fr./Ital.); LA CAGE AUX FOLLES II(1981, Ital./Fr.); CHOICE OF ARMS(1983, Fr.)
1984
ONE DEADLY SUMMER(1984, Fr.)

Eugenio Galadini
PRIMITIVE LOVE(1966, Ital.)

P. Galadzhev
WHEN THE TREES WERE TALL(1965, USSR), art d

Pyotr Galadzhev
Misc. Silents
BY THE LAW(1926, USSR)

Pytor Galadzhev
Misc. Silents
EXTRAORDINARY ADVENTURES OF MR. WEST IN THE LAND OF THE BOLSHEVIKS(1924, USSR)

Alberto Galan
PORTRAIT OF MARIA(1946, Mex.); TOAST TO LOVE(1951, Mex.)

Benny Galan
SANTO CONTRA LA INVASION DE LOS MARCIANOS(1966, Mex.)

Fred Galang
WALLS OF HELL, THE(1964, U.S./Phil.); BEACH RED(1967); ONCE BEFORE I DIE(1967, U.S./Phil.); MISSION BATANGAS(1968); IGOROTA, THE LEGEND OF THE TREE OF LIFE(1970, Phil.)
Misc. Talkies
FORTRESS IN THE SUN(1978)

Romeo N. Galang
BIONIC BOY, THE(1977, Hong Kong/Phil.), w

Ariathe Galani
1984
MELVIN, SON OF ALVIN(1984, Aus.)

Galanos
OH DAD, POOR DAD, MAMA'S HUNG YOU IN THE CLOSET AND I'M FEELIN' SO SAD(1967), cos
1984
PROTOCOL(1984), cos

Alekos Galanos
RED LANTERNS(1965, Gr.), w

L. Galanov
LAST GAME, THE(1964, USSR)

Ketty Galanta
Misc. Silents
FALL OF THE ROMANOFFS, THE(1917); EMPTY POCKETS(1918); PASSING OF THE THIRD FLOOR BACK, THE(1918, Brit.)

James Galante
DEATH WISH II(1982)

Jim Galante
DEATHSPORT(1978)

Alfredo Galaor
Silents
NERO(1922, U.S./Ital.)

The Galapagos Duck
REMOVALISTS, THE(1975, Aus.), m

Angelo Galassi
WAR AND PEACE(1956, Ital./U.S.); JESSICA(1962, U.S./Ital./Fr.)

Angiolo Galassi
FAREWELL TO ARMS, A(1957)

Livio Galassi
AUGUSTINE OF HIPPO(1973, Ital.)

Remo Galavotti
TWO WOMEN(1961, Ital./Fr.)

Rock Galbin
STRONGHOLD(1952, Mex.)

Christina Galbo
HOUSE THAT SCREAMED, THE(1970, Span.); DON'T OPEN THE WINDOW(1974, Ital.)

Archie Galbraith
DISCOVERIES(1939, Brit.)

Dorothy Galbraith
LADY IN DANGER(1934, Brit.)

Gary Galbraith
SECOND FIDDLE TO A STEEL GUITAR(1965), ph

John Kenneth Galbraith
  PROLOGUE(1970, Can.)
Maj. Charles S. Galbraith
  OBJECTIVE, BURMA!(1945), tech adv
Timothy Galbraith
  WINNING(1969)
Joe Galbreath
  BRAND OF FEAR(1949)
Richard Galbreath
  NIGHT OF EVIL(1962), p, d
A. Galdar
  BALLAD OF COSSACK GLOOTA(1938, USSR), w
P. Galdeburov
  ADMIRAL NAKHIMOV(1948, USSR)
Marcello Galdini
  GOSPEL ACCORDING TO ST. MATTHEW, THE(1966, Fr., Ital.)
Benito Perez Galdos
  NAZARIN(1968, Mex.), w; TRISTANA(1970, Span./Ital./Fr.), w
Alice Gale
Silents
  ROMEO AND JULIET(1916); DARLING OF PARIS, THE(1917); NEW YORK PEA-
COCK, THE(1917); TODAY(1917)
Misc. Silents
  CAMILLE(1917); BIRTH OF A RACE(1919)
Allan Gale
  HARVEST MELODY(1943), w
Allen Gale
  TROCADERO(1944), w
Angela Gale
Misc. Talkies
  SECRETARY, THE(1971)
Beresford Gale
  SANDERS OF THE RIVER(1935, Brit.)
Bert Gale
  PALM SPRINGS(1936)
Bob Gale
  I WANNA HOLD YOUR HAND(1978), w; 1941(1979), w; USED CARS(1980), p, w
Bobby Gale
  SUPER FUZZ(1981)
Charles Gale
1984
  MAKING THE GRADE(1984), w
Clita Gale
Silents
  RIDERS OF VENGEANCE(1919)
David Gale
  SAVAGE WEEKEND(1983)
Misc. Talkies
  GOLD DIGGERS, THE(1984, Brit.)
Deidre Gale
  LITTLE PRINCESS, THE(1939); GANG'S ALL HERE, THE(1943); HOUR BEFORE
THE DAWN, THE(1944)
Diedre Gale
  MOZART(1940, Brit.)
Eddra Gale
  8 ½(1963, Ital.); WHAT'S NEW, PUSSYCAT?(1965, U.S./Fr.); HOTEL PARADIS-
O(1966, U.S./Brit.); GAMES(1967); GRADUATE, THE(1967); I LOVE YOU, ALICE B.
TOKLAS!(1968); MALTESE BIPPY, THE(1969); MAN CALLED GANNON, A(1969);
STRAWBERRY STATEMENT, THE(1970); REVENGE OF THE CHEER-
LEADERS(1976); SOMEWHERE IN TIME(1980)
Edra Gale
  GIDGET GOES TO ROME(1963); THREE BITES OF THE APPLE(1967); FAREWELL,
MY LOVELY(1975)
Eric Gale
  EVENTS(1970), m; ONE-TRICK PONY(1980)
George Gale
  RIVER, THE(1951), ed; MONSOON(1953), ed; PHANTOM FROM SPACE(1953), ed
Gladys Gale
  SMART WOMAN(1931); DESIRABLE(1934); FUGITIVE LADY(1934); MEN OF THE
NIGHT(1934); SHE COULDN'T TAKE IT(1935); SHE MARRIED HER BOSS(1935);
KLONDIKE ANNIE(1936); NAVY BORN(1936); JOAN OF OZARK(1942); SO'S YOUR
UNCLE(1943); OUR HEARTS WERE GROWING UP(1946)
Jane Gale
  MELODY IN SPRING(1934)
Jean Gale
  KISS AND MAKE UP(1934); YOUNG AND BEAUTIFUL(1934); IT'S A WONDERFUL
LIFE(1946)
Joan Gale
  BLIND DATE(1934); MELODY IN SPRING(1934); NUT FARM, THE(1935); OUT-
LAWED GUNS(1935)
John Gale
  HELL, HEAVEN OR HOBOKEN(1958, Brit.); ACROSS THE BRIDGE(1957, Brit.);
BEHIND THE MASK(1958, Brit.); MAROC 7(1967, Brit.), p; DOCTOR PHIBES RISES
AGAIN(1972, Brit.), m
Johnnie Gale
  MYSTERY AT THE BURLESQUE(1950, Brit.)
June Gale
  MELODY IN SPRING(1934); FOLIES DERGERE(1935); RAINBOW'S END(1935);
HEROES OF THE RANGE(1936); ONE IN A MILLION(1936); RIDING AVENGER,
THE(1936); SWIFTY(1936); SING AND BE HAPPY(1937); THIN ICE(1937); THIS IS MY
AFFAIR(1937); YOU CAN'T HAVE EVERYTHING(1937); JOSETTE(1938); MY
LUCKY STAR(1938); TIME OUT FOR MURDER(1938); WHILE NEW YORK
SLEEPS(1938); CHARLIE CHAN AT TREASURE ISLAND(1939); ESCAPE, THE(1939);
HONEYMOON'S OVER, THE(1939); HOTEL FOR WOMEN(1939); INSIDE STO-
RY(1939); IT COULD HAPPEN TO YOU(1939); JONES FAMILY IN HOLLYWOOD,
THE(1939); PARDON OUR NERVE(1939); CITY OF CHANCE(1940)
Ken Gale
  WRONG IS RIGHT(1982)

1984
  IRRECONCILABLE DIFFERENCES(1984)
Lillian Gale
Silents
  WALLOPING WALLACE(1924)
Linda Gale
  TEENAGE GANG DEBS(1966)
Lorena Gale
1984
  HOTEL NEW HAMPSHIRE, THE(1984)
Lorraine Gale
  CASBAH(1948); LETTER FROM AN UNKNOWN WOMAN(1948)
Marguerite Gale
Silents
  HOW MOLLY MADE GOOD(1915); MAN HATER, THE(1917); JOAN OF THE
WOODS(1918)
Misc. Silents
  HAND INVISIBLE, THE(1919)
Marta Gale
  FOREVER AND A DAY(1943)
Melody Gale
  D.I., THE(1957)
Melvin Gale
  MESA OF LOST WOMEN, THE(1956), p
Michael Gale
  I WANTED WINGS(1941)
Nora Gale
  ARTISTS AND MODELS ABROAD(1938)
Norah Gale
  THRILL OF A LIFETIME(1937); WEEKEND MILLIONAIRE(1937, Brit.); COCOA-
NUT GROVE(1938); MEN WITH WINGS(1938); SAY IT IN FRENCH(1938); CAFE
SOCIETY(1939); HOTEL IMPERIAL(1939)
Peter Gale
  HAMLET(1969, Brit.)
Richard Gale
  MINIVER STORY, THE(1950, Brit./U.S.); MADAME LOUISE(1951, Brit.); MEET MR.
MALCOLM(1954, Brit.); WHO WAS MADDOX?(1964, Brit.); WINTER'S TALE,
THE(1968, Brit.)
Robert Gale
  TEXAS TORNADO(1934)
Roberta Gale
  ARE THESE OUR CHILDREN?(1931); GIRL OF THE RIO(1932); HER SPLENDID
FOLLY(1933); POLICE CALL(1933); HIDE-OUT(1934); ALIAS JOHN LAW(1935); NO
MAN'S RANGE(1935); CHEERS OF THE CROWD(1936)
Misc. Talkies
  MYSTERY RANCH(1934); TERROR OF THE PLAINS(1934); ST. LOUIS WO-
MAN(1935)
Sandra Gale
  FORT ALGIERS(1953)
Saundra Gale
  GLORY STOMPERS, THE(1967)
Scott Gale
  HOLLYWOOD HIGH(1977), a, m
Shirley Gale
  UNCLE VANYA(1958); RUNNING MAN, THE(1963, Brit.)
Vina Gale
  WORDS AND MUSIC(1929)
Walter Gale
  FAR FROM THE MADDING CROWD(1967, Brit.)
Wesley Gale
  SUNDOWN(1941); OCEAN'S ELEVEN(1960)
Zona Gale
  WHEN STRANGERS MEET(1934), w
Arturo Galea
  WHITE SHEIK, THE(1956, Ital.), ph
Bud Galea
  ENTER MADAME(1935)
Genevieve Galea
  LES CARABINIERS(1968, Fr./Ital.)
Henrik Galeen
  NOSFERATU, THE VAMPIRE(1979, Fr./Ger.), w
Silents
  GOLEM: HOW HE CAME INTO THE WORLD, THE(1920, Ger.), w; NOSFERATU,
THE VAMPIRE(1922, Ger.), w; STUDENT OF PRAGUE, THE(1927, Ger.), d&w;
AFTER THE VERDICT(1929, Brit.), d
Misc. Silents
  GOLEM, THE(1914, Ger.), a, d
Sytske Galema
  ROMAN HOLIDAY(1953)
Hetty Galen
  WORLD OF HANS CHRISTIAN ANDERSEN, THE(1971, Jap.); NIGHT THEY
ROBBED BIG BERTHA'S, THE(1975); RAGGEDY ANN AND ANDY(1977); SI-
MON(1980)
Janet Galen
Misc. Talkies
  STARK RAVING MAD(1983)
Mario Galento
  NATCHEZ TRACE(1960)
Misc. Talkies
  FRONTIER WOMAN(1956)
Tony Galento
  ON THE WATERFRONT(1954); BEST THINGS IN LIFE ARE FREE, THE(1956);
WIND ACROSS THE EVERGLADES(1958)
Carolyn Gales
  HIRED WIFE(1934)
V Galestian
  COLOR OF POMEGRANATES, THE(1980, Armenian)

Giovanna Galetti
BIG RED ONE, THE(1980)
Louis Emile Galey
PARIS IN THE MONTH OF AUGUST(1968, Fr.), p; 24 HOURS IN A WOMAN'S LIFE(1968, Fr./Ger.), p
Y. Galey
MAGIC WEAVER, THE(1965, USSR), art d
Timothy Galfas
MATILDA(1978), w; SUNNYSIDE(1979), d, w; SUMMER LOVERS(1982), ph
Misc. Talkies
BLACK STREETFIGHTER(1976), d; BLACK FIST(1977), d
Laszlo Galffi
WAGNER(1983, Brit./Hung./Aust.)
Lazlo Galffy
ANNA(1981, Fr./Hung.)
Harry Galfund
KING FOR A NIGHT(1933)
Laura J. Galgozy
SPRING BREAK(1983)
Geri Galian
CAMPUS SLEUTH(1948)
Fernando Galiana
CASTLE OF THE MONSTERS(1958, Mex.), w; SANTO EN EL MUSEO DE CE-RA(1963, Mex.), w; CURSE OF THE CRYING WOMAN, THE(1969, Mex.), w
Dino Galiano
SUPER FUZZ(1981), spec eff
Juan Luis Galiardo
ANTONY AND CLEOPATRA(1973, Brit.); WHITE SISTER(1973, Ital./Span./Fr.)
Misc. Talkies
ORDER TO KILL(1974)
Nilos Galiatsos
DREAM OF PASSION, A(1978, Gr.)
Alexandr Galich
HOUSE ON THE FRONT LINE, THE(1963, USSR), d
Steve Galich
ENDANGERED SPECIES(1982), spec eff
Jose Galicia
NEXT!(1971, Ital./Span.), art d
Jose Luis Galicia
KID RODELO(1966, U.S./Span.), art d; ONE STEP TO HELL(1969, U.S./Ital./Span.), art d; MURDERS IN THE RUE MORGUE(1971), prod d, art d
Denise Galick
DON'T ANSWER THE PHONE(1980)
Denise Galik
HAPPY HOOKER, THE(1975); CALIFORNIA SUITE(1978); HUMANOIDS FROM THE DEEP(1980); MELVIN AND HOWARD(1980); PARTNERS(1982); GET CRA-ZY(1983)
Hal Galili
GIRL HUNTERS, THE(1963, Brit.); MIRACLE OF THE WHITE STALLIONS(1963); DR. STRANGELOVE: OR HOW I LEARNED TO STOP WORRYING AND LOVE THE BOMB(1964); GOLDFINGER(1964, Brit.); PROMISE HER ANYTHING(1966, Brit.); ADDING MACHINE, THE(1969); LOOT(1971, Brit.); PINK PANTHER STRIKES AGAIN, THE(1976, Brit.); VALENTINO(1977, Brit.); WARLORDS OF ATLANTIS(1978, Brit.); ARABIAN ADVENTURE(1979, Brit.); SUPERMAN II(1980); OUTLAND(1981); RAGTIME(1981)
Hall Galilli
ISADORA(1968, Brit.)
Denise Galin
Misc. Talkies
DEADLY GAMES(1980)
Cesar Santos Galindo
LIVING COFFIN, THE(1965, Mex.), p
Eugenia Galindo
LIVING COFFIN, THE(1965, Mex.)
Jose Hector Galindo
SMOKY(1966)
Nacho Galindo
PERILOUS HOLIDAY(1946); FIESTA(1947); FRAMED(1947); TWILIGHT ON THE RIO GRANDE(1947); TYCOON(1947); RELENTLESS(1948); HOLIDAY IN HAVA-NA(1949); JOHNNY STOOL PIGEON(1949); SOUTH OF ST. LOUIS(1949); BELLE OF OLD MEXICO(1950); BORDERLINE(1950); DAKOTA LIL(1950); KILLER SHARK(1950); MONTANA(1950); SHOWDOWN, THE(1950); SURRENDER(1950); FLAMING FEATHER(1951); HAVANA ROSE(1951); LIGHTNING STRIKES TWI-CE(1951); YELLOW FIN(1951); LONE STAR(1952); MACAO(1952); HITCH-HIKER, THE(1953); WOMAN THEY ALMOST LYNCHED, THE(1953); BORDER RIVER(1954); BROKEN LANCE(1954); GYPSY COLT(1954); JUBILEE TRAIL(1954); OUTCAST, THE(1954); GREEN FIRE(1955); HEADLINE HUNTERS(1955); HELL'S IS-LAND(1955); JAGUAR(1956); THUNDER OVER ARIZONA(1956); GIRL MOST LIKE-LY, THE(1957); BUCHANAN RIDES ALONE(1958); SADDLE THE WIND(1958); BORN RECKLESS(1959); ONE-EYED JACKS(1961); MARRIAGE ON THE ROCKS(1965); EL DORADO(1967); PINK JUNGLE, THE(1968)
Misc. Talkies
GAY CAVALIER, THE(1946)
Pedro Galindo
LOS INVISIBLES(1961, Mex.), p
Pepito Galindo
PINK JUNGLE, THE(1968)
Sergio Galindo
MUSHROOM EATER, THE(1976, Mex.), w
Estera Galion
MARRY ME! MARRY ME!(1969, Fr.)
A. Galitti
SUNDAY LOVERS(1980, Ital./Fr.), ed
Natalie Galitzen
Silents
KING OF KINGS, THE(1927)
Andre Galitzine
CRIME AND PUNISHMENT(1935, Fr.), ed

Princess Galitzine
MAHOGANY(1975)
Michelle Galjour
CROSS AND THE SWITCHBLADE, THE(1970)
Noah Galkin
Misc. Silents
NEURASTHENIA(1929, USSR), d
Axelle Gall
LA TRAVIATA(1982)
Carl Gall
RECOMMENDATION FOR MERCY(1975, Can.)
Daniel Gall
YOUNG GIRLS OF ROCHEFORT, THE(1968, Fr.)
Jeff Gall
Misc. Talkies
BLUE MONEY(1975)
Robert Gall
SEZ O'REILLY TO MACNAB(1938, Brit.); HOOTS MON!(1939, Brit.)
David Gallacher
BIG CATCH, THE(1968, Brit.)
Frank Gallacher
HEATWAVE(1983, Aus.)
Ray Gallager
BORDER DEVILS(1932)
Robert Gallager
THRILL OF IT ALL, THE(1963)
Tom Gallaghan
BOILING POINT, THE(1932), ph
Bernadette Gallagher
BROTHERLY LOVE(1970, Brit.)
Carol Gallagher
GIRL CRAZY(1943)
Carole Gallagher
FALCON AND THE CO-EDS, THE(1943); GANGWAY FOR TOMORROW(1943); FALCON OUT WEST, THE(1944); DENVER KID, THE(1948)
Clara Gallagher
WEDDING PARTY, THE(1969)
Desmond Gallagher
NEWSBOY'S HOME(1939)
Don Gallagher
CODE OF THE FEARLESS(1939); OUTLAW'S PARADISE(1939)
Donald Gallagher
PLEASURE CRAZED(1929), d; THRU DIFFERENT EYES(1929); TEMPLE TO-WER(1930), d; COLLEGIATE(1936); LET THEM LIVE(1937), d; SH! THE OC-TOPUS(1937), w; JOHNNY HOLIDAY(1949)
Misc. Talkies
SIX-GUN TRAIL(1938)
Silents
EYE FOR EYE(1918)
Misc. Silents
LOVE'S OLD SWEET SONG(1923)
Frank Gallagher
Misc. Silents
RIDERS OF THE RANGE(1923)
Gerry Gallagher
CATHY'S CHILD(1979, Aus.)
Glen Gallagher
GIRL FROM JONES BEACH, THE(1949); CALLAWAY WENT THATAWAY(1951)
Glen B. Gallagher
FOOL'S GOLD(1946)
Glenn Gallagher
ADAM'S RIB(1949)
Helen Gallagher
STRANGERS WHEN WE MEET(1960); ROSELAND(1977)
Jack Gallagher
DEVIL BAT, THE(1941), p; SAND(1949)
Jeanne Gallagher
COOL AND THE CRAZY, THE(1958)
Jennifer Gallagher
TWICE UPON A TIME(1983), ed
Jim Gallagher
TRADING PLACES(1983)
John Gallagher
Misc. Talkies
BEACH HOUSE(1982), d
Kitty Gallagher
WEDDING PARTY, THE(1969)
Mel Gallagher
SANDPIPER, THE(1965); CHASE, THE(1966); WHEN THE LEGENDS DIE(1972)
Mike Gallagher
NORSEMAN, THE(1978)
Patti Gallagher
KING DINOSAUR(1955); TOP SECRET AFFAIR(1957)
Peter Gallagher
IDOLMAKER, THE(1980); SUMMER LOVERS(1982)
Ray Gallagher
SINNER'S HOLIDAY(1930); DESERT GUNS(1936); SONG OF THE TRAIL(1936)
Misc. Talkies
LONE BANDIT, THE(1934)
Silents
HALF A BRIDE(1928); TRAIL OF '98, THE(1929)
Misc. Silents
LION'S BREATH, THE(1916); PHANTOM MELODY, THE(1920)
Richard Gallagher
SNOW JOB(1972), w
Richard "Skeets" Gallagher
FAST COMPANY(1929); LET'S GO NATIVE(1930); POINTED HEELS(1930); SOCIAL LION, THE(1930); BIRD OF PARADISE(1932); MERRILY WE GO TO HELL(1932); TRIAL OF VIVIENNE WARE, THE(1932); PAST OF MARY HOLMES, THE(1933); CROSBY CASE, THE(1934); MAN I MARRY, THE(1936); POLO JOE(1936); YOURS

FOR THE ASKING(1936)
Silents
NEW YORK(1927); POTTERS, THE(1927); ALEX THE GREAT(1928); STOCKS AND BLONDES(1928)
Richard Z"Skeets" Gallagher
RIP TIDE(1934)
Ryhal Gallagher
CAYMAN TRIANGLE, THE(1977)
Sheila Gallagher
TOO YOUNG TO LOVE(1960, Brit.)
Skeets Gallagher
CLOSE HARMONY(1929); HER WEDDING NIGHT(1930); HONEY(1930); LOVE AMONG THE MILLIONAIRES(1930); IT PAYS TO ADVERTISE(1931); POSSESSED(1931); ROAD TO RENO(1931); CONQUERORS, THE(1932); NIGHT CLUB LADY(1932); PHANTOM OF CRESTWOOD, THE(1932); SPORT PARADE, THE(1932); UNWRITTEN LAW, THE(1932); ALICE IN WONDERLAND(1933); EASY MILLIONS(1933); REFORM GIRL(1933); TOO MUCH HARMONY(1933); BACHELOR BAIT(1934); IN THE MONEY(1934); MEANEST GAL IN TOWN, THE(1934); WOMAN UNAFRAID(1934); PERFECT CLUE, THE(1935); ESPIONAGE(1937); HATS OFF(1937); DANGER ON THE AIR(1938); MR. SATAN(1938, Brit.); IDIOT'S DELIGHT(1939); CITADEL OF CRIME(1941); ZIS BOOM BAH(1941); BROOKLYN ORCHID(1942); COLLEGE SWEETHEARTS(1942); DUKE OF CHICAGO(1949)
Silents
RACKET, THE(1928)
"Skeets" Gallagher
LIGHTNING STRIKES TWICE(1935)
Skeets [Richard] Gallagher
UP POPS THE DEVIL(1931)
Thomas Gallagher
DON'T SAY DIE(1950, Brit.); NIGHT AND THE CITY(1950, Brit.); THIRD MAN, THE(1950, Brit.); BABES IN BAGDAD(1952); GAMBLER AND THE LADY, THE(1952, Brit.); TIME GENTLEMEN PLEASE!(1953, Brit.); GOOD DIE YOUNG, THE(1954, Brit.); SAINT'S GIRL FRIDAY, THE(1954, Brit.); NO ROAD BACK(1957, Brit.); HOT MONEY GIRL(1962, Brit./Ger.); I LIKE MONEY(1962, Brit.); DAY OF THE TRIFFIDS, THE(1963); JUNGLE STREET GIRLS(1963, Brit.)
Tom Gallagher
CHEATERS(1934), ph
Toy Gallagher
Silents
ACTION GALORE(1925)
Don Gallaher
MYSTIC CIRCLE MURDER(1939), w; JIVE JUNCTION(1944), ch; MAN IN HALF-MOON STREET, THE(1944); ROAD TO UTOPIA(1945)
Donald Gallaher
MARRIED IN HOLLYWOOD(1929); NIX ON DAMES(1929), d; MAGNIFICENT FRAUD, THE(1939); KEEPER OF THE FLAME(1942); CRYSTAL BALL, THE(1943)
Silents
ETERNAL MAGDALENE, THE(1919)
Ed Gallaher
DISC JOCKEY(1951)
Thomas Gallaher
WRONG BOX, THE(1966, Brit.)
Nando Gallai
WAR AND PEACE(1956, Ital./U.S.)
Paul Gallan
7254(1971)
Adolf Galland
BATTLE OF BRITAIN, THE(1969, Brit.), tech adv
Jean Galland
HOUSE OF THE SPANIARD, THE(1936, Brit.); RECORD 413(1936, Fr.); SECOND BUREAU(1936, Fr.); ENTENTE CORDIALE(1939, Fr.); SAVAGE BRIGADE(1948, Fr.); EDWARD AND CAROLINE(1952, Fr.); EARRINGS OF MADAME DE..., THE(1954, Fr.); LE PLAISIR(1954, Fr.); FOREIGN INTRIGUE(1956); DOLL, THE(1962, Fr.); THANK HEAVEN FOR SMALL FAVORS(1965, Fr.)
Louise Gallandra
LEGACY OF BLOOD(1978)
John Gallant
FLASH GORDON(1980)
Kathleen Gallant
BRAVADOS, THE(1958)
Lorenzo Gallant
RAMPARTS WE WATCH, THE(1940)
Michael Gallant
1984
LOVE STREAMS(1984)
Gallant Bess the Horse
GALLANT BESS(1946)
Gallant Fox
WINNER'S CIRCLE, THE(1948)
Gallant Man the Horse
THAT'S MY MAN(1947)
Jean Gallard
LOLA MONTES(1955, Fr./Ger.)
Antonio Gallardo
DESPERATE MOMENT(1953, Brit.)
Aurelia Gallardo
1984
MIKE'S MURDER(1984)
Cesar Gallardo
Misc. Talkies
BAMBOO GODS AND IRON MEN(1974), d; HUSTLER SQUAD(1976), d
J. Gallardo
TEACHER AND THE MIRACLE, THE(1961, Ital./Span.), w
Lucy Gallardo
EXTERMINATING ANGEL, THE(1967, Mex.); SANTO CONTRA LA HIJA DE FRANKENSTEIN(1971, Mex.)
Manuel Gallardo
DRUMS OF TABU, THE(1967, Ital./Span.)

Miguel A. Gallardo
WHITE ORCHID, THE(1954)
Rosa Maria Gallardo
LOS INVISIBLES(1961, Mex.)
Silvana Gallardo
WINDWALKER(1980)
Keith Gallasch
STIR(1980, Aus.)
Alberta Gallatin
Silents
CHRISTIAN, THE(1914); MR. BARNES OF NEW YORK(1914)
John Gallaudet
ADVENTURE IN MANHATTAN(1936); ALIBI FOR MURDER(1936); COME CLOSER, FOLKS(1936); COUNTERFEIT(1936); FINAL HOUR, THE(1936); PENNIES FROM HEAVEN(1936); SHAKEDOWN(1936); CRIMINALS OF THE AIR(1937); DANGEROUS ADVENTURE, A(1937); DEVIL'S PLAYGROUND(1937); DOUBLE OR NOTHING(1937); GAME THAT KILLS, THE(1937); GIRLS CAN PLAY(1937); I PROMISE TO PAY(1937); I'LL TAKE ROMANCE(1937); PAID TO DANCE(1937); RACKETEERS IN EXILE(1937); SPEED TO SPARE(1937); DEVIL'S PARTY, THE(1938); LITTLE MISS ROUGHNECK(1938); MAIN EVENT, THE(1938); PENITENTIARY(1938); SING YOU SINNERS(1938); THERE'S ALWAYS A WOMAN(1938); WHO KILLED GAIL PRESTON?(1938); CODE OF THE SECRET SERVICE(1939); FEDERAL MAN-HUNT(1939); HERO FOR A DAY(1939); I AM NOT AFRAID(1939); MAN WHO DARED, THE(1939); MANHATTAN SHAKEDOWN(1939); MURDER IS NEWS(1939); ONE HOUR TO LIVE(1939); STAR MAKER, THE(1939); STREET OF MISSING MEN(1939); SUDDEN MONEY(1939); THEY ALL COME OUT(1939); TWELVE CROWDED HOURS(1939); WINGS OF THE NAVY(1939); FUGITIVE FROM JUSTICE, A(1940); GAMBLING ON THE HIGH SEAS(1940); GOLDEN GLOVES(1940); WAGONS WESTWARD(1940); FORCED LANDING(1941); GLAMOUR BOY(1941); NO GREATER SIN(1941); ROAD AGENT(1941); SHOT IN THE DARK, THE(1941); FLIGHT LIEUTENANT(1942); HOLIDAY INN(1942); SPIRIT OF STANFORD, THE(1942); STRANGE CASE OF DR. RX, THE(1942); TOUGH AS THEY COME(1942); SHADY LADY(1945); SHADOWS OVER CHINATOWN(1946); SO GOES MY LOVE(1946); WIFE WANTED(1946); FARMER'S DAUGHTER, THE(1947); LADY IN THE LAKE(1947); LONE WOLF IN MEXICO, THE(1947); LOUISIANA(1947); SPIRIT OF WEST POINT, THE(1947); APRIL SHOWERS(1948); DOCKS OF NEW ORLEANS(1948); FAMILY HONEYMOON(1948); STAGE STRUCK(1948); TEXAS, BROOKLYN AND HEAVEN(1948); OUTCASTS OF THE TRAIL(1949); TASK FORCE(1949); TENSION(1949); QUICKSAND(1950); RIGHT CROSS(1950); SIDE STREET(1950); TO PLEASE A LADY(1950); ANGELS IN THE OUTFIELD(1951); LITTLE EGYPT(1951); MISSING WOMEN(1951); TWO TICKETS TO BROADWAY(1951); CONFIDENCE GIRL(1952); EVERYTHING I HAVE IS YOURS(1952); CADDY, THE(1953); KID FROM LEFT FIELD, THE(1953); PICKUP ON SOUTH STREET(1953); NO MAN'S WOMAN(1955); JULIE(1956); TERROR AT MIDNIGHT(1956); WHEN GANGLAND STRIKES(1956); DECKS RAN RED, THE(1958); LONELYHEARTS(1958); GO NAKED IN THE WORLD(1961); PATSY, THE(1964); IN COLD BLOOD(1967)
Barbara Gallauner
HANSEL AND GRETEL(1965, Ger.)
Gayla Gallaway
ST. IVES(1976)
Layla Gallaway
RENEGADE GIRLS(1974)
Raymond Galle
GLORY OF FAITH, THE(1938, Fr.)
Arturo Gallea
MY WIDOW AND I(1950, Ital.), ph; BREAD, LOVE AND DREAMS(1953, Ital.), ph; VOLCANO(1953, Ital.), ph
Ely Galleani
REDNECK(1975, Ital./Span.)
Karlene Gallegly
HARRY AND WALTER GO TO NEW YORK(1976)
Gina Gallego
CHAMP, THE(1979); DEADLY FORCE(1983)
Jose Gallego
MASTER OF HORROR(1965, Arg.), ed
Dominique Gallegos
WINDWALKER(1980)
Jose Gallegos
SPLIT, THE(1968)
Joshua Gallegos
DEATH WISH II(1982)
Theo Gallehr
THERE IS STILL ROOM IN HELL(1963, Ger.), w
George Galleon
LANCASHIRE LUCK(1937, Brit.); MAN WHO MADE DIAMONDS, THE(1937, Brit.); MAYFAIR MELODY(1937, Brit.); WINDMILL, THE(1937, Brit.); YOU LIVE AND LEARN(1937, Brit.); IT'S IN THE BLOOD(1938, Brit.); SINGING COP, THE(1938, Brit.)
Suzie Galler
BUDDY BUDDY(1981)
Joe Gallerani
OCEAN'S ELEVEN(1960)
James Gallery
MR. MOM(1983)
Tom Gallery
Silents
CHORUS GIRL'S ROMANCE, A(1920); DINTY(1920); BOB HAMPTON OF PLACER(1921); HOME STUFF(1921); PATSY(1921); WALL FLOWER, THE(1922); ETERNAL THREE, THE(1923); DOG OF THE REGIMENT(1927); HOME STRUCK(1927); ONE-ROUND HOGAN(1927)
Misc. Silents
BRIGHT SKIES(1920); HEART OF TWENTY, THE(1920); SON OF WALLINGFORD, THE(1921); DAUGHTER OF LUXURY, A(1922); GRAND LARCENY(1922); ITCHING PALMS(1923); WRONGS RIGHTED(1924); LIMITED MAIL, THE(1925)
Lina Gallet
MOST WANTED MAN, THE(1962, Fr./Ital.), makeup; LA BONNE SOUPE(1964, Fr./Ital.), makeup
Carla Galletti
WHITE SISTER(1973, Ital./Span./Fr.)

Giovanna Galletti
OPEN CITY(1946, Ital.); ANGELO IN THE CROWD(1952, Ital.); NUN'S STORY, THE(1959); WONDERS OF ALADDIN, THE(1961, Fr./Ital.); SODOM AND GOMOR-RAH(1962, U.S./Fr./Ital.); BUONA SERA, MRS. CAMPBELL(1968, Ital.); LADY OF MONZA, THE(1970, Ital.); LOVE PROBLEMS(1970, Ital.)

George Galley
SECRET DOCUMENT – VIENNA(1954, Fr.)

Georges Galley
GORILLA(1964, Swed.)

Jean-Marie Galley
JUDGE AND THE ASSASSIN, THE(1979, Fr.)

Ariana Galli
MISTRESS FOR THE SUMMER, A(1964, Fr./Ital.)

Dina Galli
MY WIDOW AND I(1950, Ital.)

Eola Galli
CARNEGIE HALL(1947)

Georges Galli
Silents
BROKEN MELODY, THE(1929, Brit.)
Misc. Silents
YELLOW STOCKINGS(1928, Brit.)

Giulio Galli
TOO BAD SHE'S BAD(1954, Ital.)

Ida Galli
LA DOLCE VITA(1961, Ital./Fr.); FALL OF ROME, THE(1963, Ital.); LEOPARD, THE(1963, Ital.); HERCULES IN THE HAUNTED WORLD(1964, Ital.); WAR OF THE ZOMBIES, THE(1965 Ital.)

Rosina Galli
YELLOW JACK(1938); CONQUEST(1937); BLOCKADE(1938); INTERNATIONAL SETTLEMENT(1938); OF HUMAN HEARTS(1938); ESCAPE TO PARADISE(1939); FISHERMAN'S WHARF(1939); HOUSEKEEPER'S DAUGHTER(1939); OKLAHOMA KID, THE(1939); RAINS CAME, THE(1939); I TAKE THIS WOMAN(1940); MAN WHO TALKED TOO MUCH, THE(1940); THIS THING CALLED LOVE(1940); YOU CAN'T FOOL YOUR WIFE(1940); YOU'RE NOT SO TOUGH(1940); GAUCHOS OF EL DORADO(1941); MOB TOWN(1941); RAGS TO RICHES(1941); THEY MET IN BOM-BAY(1941); BUTCH MINDS THE BABY(1942); MAD DOCTOR OF MARKET STREET, THE(1942); MY GAL SAL(1942); PRIDE OF THE YANKEES, THE(1942); UNDER-GROUND AGENT(1942); FALLEN SPARROW, THE(1943); GOOD LUCK, MR. YA-TES(1943); PHANTOM OF THE OPERA(1943); PRINCESS O'ROURKE(1943); MAN FROM FRISCO(1944); WHERE DO WE GO FROM HERE?(1945); FUGITIVE LA-DY(1951); VOLCANO(1953, Ital.)

Ketti Gallian
MARIE GALANTE(1934); UNDER THE PAMPAS MOON(1935); ESPIONAGE(1937); SHALL WE DANCE(1937)

Cataldo Galliano
GOD FORGIVES–I DON'T!(1969, Ital./Span.), spec eff

Bob Gallico
GIRL HUNTERS, THE(1963, Brit.); SECRET DOOR, THE(1964)

Paul Gallico
MADISON SQUARE GARDEN(1932); WEDDING PRESENT(1936), w; WILD MONEY(1937), w; NO TIME TO MARRY(1938), w; JOE SMITH, AMERICAN(1942), w; PRIDE OF THE YANKEES, THE(1942), w; CLOCK, THE(1945), w; ASSIGNMENT-PARIS(1952), w; NEVER TAKE NO FOR AN ANSWER(1952, Brit./Ital.), w; LI-LI(1953), w; INDISCRETION OF AN AMERICAN WIFE(1954, U.S./Ital.), w; MERRY ANDREW(1958), w; BIG OPERATOR, THE(1959), w,Robert Smith; NEXT TO NO TIME(1960, Brit.), d&w; THREE LIVES OF THOMASINA, THE(1963, U.S./Brit.), w; POSEIDON ADVENTURE, THE(1972), w; MATILDA(1978), w; BEYOND THE POSEI-DON ADVENTURE(1979), w

Pauline Gallico
CLOCK, THE(1945), w; ASSIGNMENT-PARIS(1952), w; NEVER TAKE NO FOR AN ANSWER(1952, Brit./Ital.), w

Joe Gallien
1984
SONGWRITER(1984)

Alex Gallier
CURSE OF FRANKENSTEIN, THE(1957, Brit.); FIGHTING WILDCATS, THE(1957, Brit.); THUNDER OVER TANGIER(1957, Brit.); MAN INSIDE, THE(1958, Brit.); THREE CROOKED MEN(1958, Brit.); RUNAWAY, THE(1964, Brit.)

Gee Gee Galligan
HOUSE IS NOT A HOME, A(1964)

Tom Galligan
FILE 113(1932), ph; INTRUDER, THE(1932), ph; LOCAL BAD MAN(1932), ph; MAN'S LAND, A(1932), ph; PARISIAN ROMANCE, A(1932), ph; SPIRIT OF THE WEST(1932), ph; STOKER, THE(1932), ph; THIRTEENTH GUEST, THE(1932), ph; UNHOLY LOVE(1932), ph; VANITY FAIR(1932), ph; COWBOY COUNSELOR(1933), ph; DUDE BANDIT, THE(1933), ph; IRON MASTER, THE(1933), ph; LAUGHING AT LIFE(1933), ph; OFFICER 13(1933), ph; ONE YEAR LATER(1933), ph; SHRIEK IN THE NIGHT, A(1933), ph; PICTURE BRIDES(1934), ph; TAKE THE STAND(1934), ph; WHEN STRANGERS MEET(1934), ph; BOOTS OF DESTINY(1937), ph; KING OF THE SIERRAS(1938), ph

Zach Galligan
1984
GREMLINS(1984); NOTHING LASTS FOREVER(1984)

Fausto Gallii
OUTCRY(1949, Ital.), art d

Hal Gallili
RITZ, THE(1976)

Tim Gallin
WORLD ACCORDING TO GARP, The(1982)

Mario Gallina
LITTLE MARTYR, THE(1947, Ital.); ISLAND OF PROCIDA, THE(1952, Ital.)

Orlando Gallini
SUBWAY RIDERS(1981), ed

Randy Gallion
1984
BEVERLY HILLS COP(1984)

L. Gallis
DEVOTION(1955, USSR)

Leonid Gallis
TRAIN GOES EAST, THE(1949, USSR); FAREWELL, DOVES(1962, USSR); GARNET BRACELET, THE(1966, USSR); THREE SISTERS, THE(1969, USSR)

Joe Gallison
ALL THE YOUNG MEN(1960); LET NO MAN WRITE MY EPITAPH(1960); WACKI-EST SHIP IN THE ARMY, THE(1961)

Alberto Gallitti
WASTREL, THE(1963, Ital.), ed; GOLIATH AND THE SINS OF BABYLON(1964, Ital.), ed; REVENGE OF THE GLADIATORS(1965, Ital.), ed; SEVEN SLAVES AGAINST THE WORLD(1965, Ital.), ed; HELLBENDERS, THE(1967, U.S./Ital./Span.), ed; KISS THE GIRLS AND MAKE THEM DIE(1967, U.S./Ital.), ed; ANZIO(1968, Ital.), ed; MOTIVE WAS JEALOUSY, THE(1970 Ital./Span.), ed; PIZZA TRIANGLE, THE(1970, Ital./Span.), ed; THIS MAN CAN'T DIE(1970, Ital.), ed; PRIEST'S WIFE, THE(1971, Ital./Fr.), ed; MOSES(1976, Brit./Ital.), ed; SCENT OF A WOMAN(1976, Ital.), ed; VIVA ITALIA(1978, Ital.), ed

Robbie Gallivan
1984
BAY BOY(1984, Can.)

Denise Gallk
NEXT STOP, GREENWICH VILLAGE(1976)

Carmi Gallo
SPRING FEVER(1983, Can.), art d

Fred T. Gallo
GOING IN STYLE(1979), p; BODY HEAT(1981), p

Guy Gallo
1984
UNDER THE VOLCANO(1984), w

Inigo Gallo
SWISS CONSPIRACY, THE(1976, U.S./Ger.)

Jacques Gallo
LITTLE BOY LOST(1953); 27TH DAY, THE(1957); TENDER IS THE NIGHT(1961); MAGIC SWORD, THE(1962)

Joie Gallo
1984
BROADWAY DANNY ROSE(1984)

Lew Gallo
PT 109(1963); SOLDIER IN THE RAIN(1963); CHEAP DETECTIVE, THE(1978)
1984
HARD TO HOLD(1984)
Misc. Talkies
ALIENS FROM ANOTHER PLANET(1967)

Lou Gallo
ODDS AGAINST TOMORROW(1959); PORK CHOP HILL(1959)

Maria Rosa Gallo
HAND IN THE TRAP, THE(1963, Arg./Span.)

Marilyn Gallo
SECOND FIDDLE TO A STEEL GUITAR(1965)

Mario Gallo
TOO LATE BLUES(1962); CHILD IS WAITING, A(1963); LAUGHING POLICEMAN, THE(1973); WOMAN UNDER THE INFLUENCE, A(1974); CAPONE(1975); KING KONG(1976); BURNING YEARS, THE(1979, Ital.), w; RAGING BULL(1980); RE-VENGE OF THE NINJA(1983)

Nazareno Gallo
COUNTERFEITERS, THE(1953, Ital.), w

Phil Gallo
MOTHER'S DAY(1980), m

Gisele Gallois
FRUIT IS RIPE, THE(1961, Fr./Ital.); I SPIT ON YOUR GRAVE(1962, Fr.); SIN ON THE BEACH(1964, Fr.)

R. Gallois-Montbrun
OPERATION X(1951, Brit.), m; CRY, THE BELOVED COUNTRY(1952, Brit.), m

Marcel Gallon
SIX IN PARIS(1968, Fr.)

Pierre Gallon
1984
ONE DEADLY SUMMER(1984, Fr.)

Thomas Gallon
Silents
OFF THE HIGHWAY(1925), w

Tom Gallon
GREAT GAY ROAD, THE(1931, Brit.), w
Silents
PRINCESS OF HAPPY CHANCE, THE(1916, Brit.), w; HANGING JUDGE, THE(1918, Brit.), w; AS HE WAS BORN(1919, Brit.), w; TATTERLY(1919, Brit.), w; ROGUE IN LOVE, A(1922, Brit.), w

Carmen Gallone
DREAM OF BUTTERFLY, THE(1941, Ital.), d

Carmine Gallone
DRAGNET NIGHT(1931, Fr.), d; FAREWELL TO LOVE(1931, Brit.), d; FOR LOVE OF YOU(1933, Brit.), d; KING OF THE RITZ(1933, Brit.), p&d; TWO HEARTS IN WALTZ TIME(1934, Brit.), d; DIVINE SPARK, THE(1935, Brit./Ital.), d; KISS ME GOODBYE(1935, Brit.), d; MY HEART IS CALLING(1935, Brit.), d; DEFEAT OF HANNIBAL, THE(1937, Ital.), d, w, set d; ETERNAL MELODIES(1948, Ital.), d, w; RIGOLETTO(1949), d; MESSALINE(1952, Fr./Ital.), d&w; FATAL DESIRE(1953), d, w; SINGING TAXI DRIVER(1953, Ital.), p&d; AFFAIRS OF MESSALINA, THE(1954, Ital.), p,d&w; MATA HARI'S DAUGHTER(1954, Fr./Ital), d; MADAME BUTTER-FLY(1955 Ital./Jap.), d; MICHAEL STROGOFF(1960, Fr./Ital./Yugo.), d; CARTHAGE IN FLAMES(1961, Fr./Ital.), p, d, w
Misc. Silents
PAWNS OF PASSION(1929, Fr./USSR), d

Riccardo Gallone
HELL RAIDERS OF THE DEEP(1954, Ital.)

Umberto Gallone
RATATAPLAN(1979, Ital.)

Faye Gallos
LOOSE ENDS(1975)

Dada Gallotti
JOHNNY YUMA(1967, Ital.)
Jean-Claude Gallouin
GIFT, THE(1983, Fr./Ital.), set d
1984
ONE DEADLY SUMMER(1984, Fr.), art d
Janet Ann Gallow
GHOST OF FRANKENSTEIN, THE(1942); IT AIN'T HAY(1943); THAT NIGHT WITH YOU(1945)
Janet Gallow
'TILL WE MEET AGAIN(1944)
Phyllis Gallow
CANON CITY(1948)
Bob Galloway
KING KONG(1933)
Don Galloway
RARE BREED, THE(1966); GUNFIGHT IN ABILENE(1967); RIDE TO HANGMAN'S TREE, THE(1967); ROUGH NIGHT IN JERICHO(1967); SATAN'S MISTRESS(1982); BIG CHILL, THE(1983)
Grady Galloway
PONY SOLDIER(1952); RED SKIES OF MONTANA(1952)
James Galloway
RICHARD'S THINGS(1981, Brit.)
Leata Galloway
HAIR(1979)
Lindsay Galloway
FOUR DAYS(1951, Brit.), w; YOU'RE ONLY YOUNG TWICE(1952, Brit.), w; FLAT TWO(1962, Brit.), w; DOUBLE, THE(1963, Brit), w; SEVEN SEAS TO CALAIS(1963, Ital.), w; TWO LIVING, ONE DEAD(1964, Brit./Swed.), w
Michael Galloway
GORDON'S WAR(1973)
Morgan Galloway
HELLO TROUBLE(1932); LADIES OF THE JURY(1932); LENA RIVERS(1932)
Pamela Galloway
MEET MR. MALCOLM(1954, Brit.)
Samuel Gallu
THEATRE OF DEATH(1967, Brit.), d; MAN OUTSIDE, THE(1968, Brit.), d, w; LIMBO LINE, THE(1969, Brit.), d; GIVE'EM HELL, HARRY!(1975), w
John Galludet
PAROLE FIXER(1940); SECOND WOMAN, THE(1951)
Denise Gallup
1941(1979)
Dian Gallup
1941(1979)
Dave Galluzzo
TERROR ON TOUR(1980)
David B. Gally
Silents
OVERLAND RED(1920)
Lamberto Galm
DEATH TOOK PLACE LAST NIGHT(1970, Ital./Ger.), ph
Igor Galo
1984
MEMED MY HAWK(1984, Brit.)
A. Galperin
SPACE SHIP, THE(1935, USSR), ph
Alexander Galperson
MR. PERRIN AND MR. TRAILL(1948, Brit.), p; GOLDEN SALAMANDER(1950, Brit.), p
Lee Galpin
LORDS OF DISCIPLINE, THE(1983)
John Galsworthy
ESCAPE(1930, Brit.), w; OLD ENGLISH(1930), w; SKIN GAME, THE(1931, Brit.), w; LOYALTIES(1934, Brit.), w; ONE MORE RIVER(1934), w; TWENTY-ONE DAYS TOGETHER(1940, Brit.), w; ESCAPE(1948, Brit.), w; THAT FORSYTE WOMAN(1949), w
Silents
SCHOOL DAYS(1921); STRANGER, THE(1924), w
Marilyn Galsworthy
SPY WHO LOVED ME, THE(1977, Brit.)
Eddie Galt
SILENT RAGE(1982)
Galan Galt
SOULS AT SEA(1937); ANGELS WITH DIRTY FACES(1938); SPAWN OF THE NORTH(1938); OFF THE RECORD(1939); OUR LEADING CITIZEN(1939); REMEMBER THE NIGHT(1940)
John William Galt
HANGAR 18(1980)
Irene Galter
CENTO ANNI D'AMORE(1954, Ital.)
Sam Galter
DAY THE SKY EXPLODED, THE(1958, Fr./Ital.)
Ray Galton
CALL ME GENIUS(1961, Brit.), w; WRONG ARM OF THE LAW, THE(1963, Brit.), w; BARGEE, THE(1964, Brit.), w; SPY WITH A COLD NOSE, THE(1966, Brit.), w; LOOT(1971, Brit.), w; MAGNIFICENT SEVEN DEADLY SINS(1971, Brit.), w; UP THE CHASTITY BELT(1971, Brit.), w; STEPTOE AND SON(1972, Brit.), w
Roberto Galvadon
ADVENTURES OF CASANOVA(1948), d
Anne Galvan
HANGAR 18(1980)
Gilbert Galvan
BELLS OF SAN FERNANDO(1947)
Gilberto Galvan
JULIET OF THE SPIRITS(1965, Fr./Ital./W.Ger.)
Pablo Galvan
GARDEN OF EVIL(1954), set d; IMPORTANT MAN, THE(1961, Mex.), art d; TWO MULES FOR SISTER SARA(1970), set d

Pedro Galvan
SEVEN CITIES OF GOLD(1955); BLACK SCORPION, THE(1957); SIERRA BARON(1958); BIG CUBE, THE(1969); TWO MULES FOR SISTER SARA(1970)
Dino Galvani
ATLANTIC(1929 Brit.); FLYING SCOTSMAN, THE(1929, Brit.); THOSE WHO LOVE(1929, Brit.); PRICE OF THINGS, THE(1930, Brit.); BOAT FROM SHANGHAI(1931, Brit.); CHANCE OF A NIGHT-TIME, THE(1931, Brit); JEALOUSY(1931, Brit.); VAGABOND QUEEN, THE(1931, Brit.); MISSING REMBRANDT, THE(1932, Brit.); BROKEN ROSARY, THE(1934, Brit.); IN A MONASTERY GARDEN(1935); PRINCESS CHARMING(1935, Brit.); RUNAWAY QUEEN, THE(1935, Brit.); BALL AT SAVOY(1936, Brit.); DON'T RUSH ME(1936, Brit.); BOMBS OVER LONDON(1937, Brit.); CAFE COLETTE(1937, Brit.); MAN WHO MADE DIAMONDS, THE(1937, Brit.); DANCE OF DEATH, THE(1938, Brit.); LAST BARRICADE, THE(1938, Brit.); MR. SATAN(1938, Brit.); SPECIAL EDITION(1938, Brit.); VIPER, THE(1938, Brit.); PLAYBOY, THE(1942, Brit.); IT'S THAT MAN AGAIN(1943, Brit.); DETECTIVE, THE(1954, Qit.); LYONS IN PARIS, THE(1955, Brit.); FUN AT ST. FANNY'S(1956, Brit.); CHECKPOINT(1957, Brit.); SECOND FIDDLE(1957, Brit.); BLUEBEARD'S TEN HONEYMOONS(1960, Brit.)
Silents
HONEYMOON AHEAD(1927, Brit.); ADVENTUROUS YOUTH(1928, Brit.); PARADISE(1928, Brit.)
Misc. Silents
DIZZY LIMIT, THE(1930, Brit.)
Graziella Galvani
KAPO(1964, Ital./Fr./Yugo.); PIERROT LE FOU(1968, Fr./Ital.)
Milan Galvanic
Misc. Talkies
ROGUE, THE(1976)
Flavio Galvao
1984
GABRIELA(1984, Braz.)
Adrianna Galvez
GENTLEMAN FROM ARIZONA, THE(1940)
Fernando Galvez
HARD HOMBRE(1931)
Silents
EASY GOING GORDON(1925)
Jose Galvez
MACARIO(1961, Mex.); PEARL OF TLAYUCAN, THE(1964, Mex.); GIGANTES PLANETARIOS(1965, Mex.)
Venchito Galvez
1984
BONA(1984, Phil.)
Anne Galvin
1984
ON THE LINE(1984, Span.)
Don Galvin
FRIENDS OF EDDIE COYLE, THE(1973), set d
Fred Galvin
HELL SQUAD(1958)
Glen Galvin
ROSE BOWL(1936); LOOKING FOR LOVE(1964), spec eff
James Galvin
MAN ON A SWING(1974)
John Galvin
GOODBYE PORK PIE(1981, New Zealand)
Juan Carlos Galvin
SAVAGE PAMPAS(1967, Span./Arg.)
Kathy Galvin
LADY LIBERTY(1972, Ital./Fr.)
Ray Galvin
CHASE, THE(1966); SIMON, KING OF THE WITCHES(1971); WILD RIDERS(1971); UNHOLY ROLLERS(1972)
Dino Galvini
STRANGE BOARDERS(1938, Brit.)
Robyn Galwey
GALLIPOLI(1981, Aus.)
Rita Gam
THIEF, THE(1952); SAADIA(1953); NIGHT PEOPLE(1954); SIGN OF THE PAGAN(1954); MAGIC FIRE(1956); MOHAWK(1956); SIERRA BARON(1958); HANNIBAL(1960, Ital.); KING OF KINGS(1961); NO EXIT(1962, U.S./Arg.); KLUTE(1971); SHOOT OUT(1971); SUCH GOOD FRIENDS(1971); LAW AND DISORDER(1974); SEEDS OF EVIL(1981)
Fred Gamage
LIFE IN HER HANDS(1951, Brit.), ph
Samia Gamal
LITTLE MISS DEVIL(1951, Egypt); ALI BABA(1954, Fr.); VALLEY OF THE KINGS(1954)
Savia Gamal
DESERT WARRIOR(1961 Ital./Span.)
V. Gamaliya
SLEEPING BEAUTY, THE(1966, USSR), md
Tom Gaman
LORD OF THE FLIES(1963, Brit.)
Pierino Gamba
GREAT DAWN, THE(1947, Ital.)
Veronica Gamba
NIGHT IN HEAVEN, A(1983); SMOKEY AND THE BANDIT–PART 3(1983)
C. Gambarelli
CROSSED SWORDS(1954), makeup
Cesare Gambarelli
HOUSE OF CARDS(1969), makeup; STORY OF A WOMAN(1970, U.S./Ital.), makeup
Maria Gambarelli
HERE'S TO ROMANCE(1935), a, ch; HOORAY FOR LOVE(1935); LE AMICHE(1962, Ital.)

S. Gambashidze
THEY WANTED PEACE(1940, USSR); DRAGONFLY, THE(1955 USSR)
Cesare Gamberelli
SUMMERTIME(1955), makeup
Clara Gamberini
MONSTER OF THE ISLAND(1953, Ital.)
Claude Gambier
SEARCH, THE(1948)
Kenyon Gambier [Lorin Andrews Lathrop]
Silents
LOVE IN A HURRY(1919), w
Alain Gambin
CONFIDENTIALLY YOURS(1983, Fr.)
James Gambina
SATURDAY NIGHT FEVER(1977), tech adv
Jimmy Gambina
ROCKY(1976), a, tech adv
Ralph Gambina
MANCHURIAN CANDIDATE, THE(1962); CHAMP, THE(1979)
Donatella Gambini
AMARCORD(1974, Ital.)
James Gambino
PHANTOM OF THE PARADISE(1974)
Rafaello Gambino
IT HAPPENED IN ROME(1959, Ital.)
Bill Gamble
FOUL PLAY(1978)
Don Gamble
Silents
ABLEMINDED LADY, THE(1922), d&ph
Donald Gamble
THERE'S NO BUSINESS LIKE SHOW BUSINESS(1954); VIOLENT SATUR-
DAY(1955); UNDERWORLD U.S.A.(1961)
Duncan Gamble
BABY BLUE MARINE(1976)
Fred Gamble
Silents
GIRL FROM HIS TOWN, THE(1915); TUMBLEWEEDS(1925)
Misc. Silents
BULLET-PROOF(1920); FIREBRAND, THE(1922)
Frederick Gamble
Silents
BROADWAY SCANDAL(1918)
George Gamble
ON THE YARD(1978)
Jerry Gamble
DANTE'S INFERNO(1935)
Silents
13 WASHINGTON SQUARE(1928)
Jim Gamble
Misc. Silents
LONE FIGHTER(1923)
John Gamble
SCARFACE(1983)
Josh Gamble
Misc. Talkies
SECRETARY, THE(1971)
June Gamble
TNT JACKSON(1975)
Linda Gamble
SWEET RIDE, THE(1968)
Paul Gamble
1984
SECRETS(1984, Brit.)
Ralph Gamble
MR. SCOUTMASTER(1953); SUDDEN DANGER(1955); EDDY DUCHIN STORY,
THE(1956); IN THE MONEY(1958); UNWED MOTHER(1958)
Rollo Gamble
LOVE ON THE DOLE(1945, Brit.), w; SECRET PEOPLE(1952, Brit.); DARWIN
ADVENTURE, THE(1972, Brit.)
Sven-Eric Gamble
PORT OF CALL(1963, Swed.)
Tim Gamble
1984
GRANDVIEW, U.S.A.(1984)
Tom Gamble
SAILOR'S DON'T CARE(1940, Brit.)
Walburton Gamble
Silents
COST, THE(1920)
Warburton Gamble
TONIGHT OR NEVER(1931); AS YOU DESIRE ME(1932); FAST LIFE(1932); CHILD
OF MANHATTAN(1933); STUDY IN SCARLET, A(1933); TONIGHT IS OURS(1933); BY
CANDLELIGHT(1934); BLIND MAN'S BLUFF(1936, Brit.); SCOTLAND YARD COM-
MANDS(1937, Brit.); SPARE A COPPER(1940, Brit.)
Silents
FINE FEATHERS(1921)
Misc. Silents
AS A MAN THINKS(1919); LA BELLE RUSSE(1919); SOCIETY EXILE, A(1919); TWO
BRIDES, THE(1919); DANGEROUS LIES(1921, Brit.)
The Gamblers
I'VE GOTTA HORSE(1965, Brit.)
Don Federico Gamboa
SANTA(1932, Mex.), w
Elias Gamboa
TWO-GUN TROUBADOR(1939); DOWN MEXICO WAY(1941); UNDER FIESTA
STARS(1941)

Eliso Gamboa
LEOPARD MAN, THE(1943)
Jonee Gamboa
ENTER THE NINJA(1982)
Joonee Gamboa
WONDER WOMEN(1973, Phil.); YEAR OF LIVING DANGEROUSLY, THE(1982,
Aus.)
1984
MISSING IN ACTION(1984)
Julie Gambol
FACES(1968)
Fred Gambold
Silents
VIRGINIAN, THE(1923); RED MILL, THE(1927); LADDIE BE GOOD(1928)
Misc. Silents
BOY CRAZY(1922); BORN TO BATTLE(1926)
Michael Gambon
BEAST MUST DIE, THE(1974, Brit.); NOTHING BUT THE NIGHT(1975, Brit.)
Mike Gambon
OTHELLO(1965, Brit.)
G. Gamburg
WHEN THE TREES WERE TALL(1965, USSR), md
Gamby-Hale Girls
COCOANUTS, THE(1929)
Gamby-Hall Girls
HOLE IN THE WALL(1929)
Marion Game
LIKE A TURTLE ON ITS BACK(1981, Fr.)
Nadia Gamel
24 HOURS TO KILL(1966, Brit.)
Henry Gamer
PROLOGUE(1970, Can.); APPRENTICESHIP OF DUDDY KRAVITZ, THE(1974,
Can.); LIES MY FATHER TOLD ME(1975, Can.); LUCKY STAR, THE(1980, Can.)
Kenneth Gamet
CASE OF THE STUTTERING BISHOP, THE(1937), w; FLY-AWAY BABY(1937), w;
MIDNIGHT COURT(1937), w; MISSING WITNESSES(1937), w; SMART BLON-
DE(1937), w; BROADWAY MUSKETEERS(1938), w; NANCY DREW-DETEC-
TIVE(1938), w; EVERYBODY'S HOBBY(1939), w; NANCY
DREW-REPORTER(1939), w; NANCY DREW AND THE HIDDEN STAIRCASE(1939),
w; NANCY DREW, TROUBLE SHOOTER(1939), w; YOU CAN'T GET AWAY WITH
MURDER(1939), w; DEVIL'S ISLAND(1940), w; FLOWING GOLD(1940), w; GRAN-
NY GET YOUR GUN(1940), w; TEAR GAS SQUAD(1940), w; GREAT MR. NOBODY,
THE(1941), w; HIGHWAY WEST(1941), w; INTERNATIONAL SQUADRON(1941), w;
KISSES FOR BREAKFAST(1941), w; SMILING GHOST, THE(1941), w; STRANGE
ALIBI(1941), w; FLYING TIGERS(1942), w; JUKE GIRL(1942), w; PITTS-
BURGH(1942), w; BOMBER'S MOON(1943), w; TAMPICO(1944), w; BETRAYAL
FROM THE EAST(1945), w; ADVENTURES IN SILVERADO(1948), w; THUNDER-
HOOF(1948), w; BLONDE ICE(1949), w; CANADIAN PACIFIC(1949), w; DOOLINS
OF OKLAHOMA, THE(1949), w; WAKE OF THE RED WITCH(1949), w; SAVAGE
HORDE, THE(1950), w; FIGHTING COAST GUARD(1951), w; FLYING LEATHER-
NECKS(1951), w; INDIAN UPRISING(1951), w; MAN IN THE SADDLE(1951), w;
SANTA FE(1951), w; LAST OF THE COMANCHES(1952), w; THUNDERBIRDS(1952),
w; LAST POSSE, THE(1953), w; STRANGER WORE A GUN, THE(1953), w; HELL'S
OUTPOST(1955), w; LAWLESS STREET, A(1955), w; TEN WANTED MEN(1955), w;
MAVERICK QUEEN, THE(1956), w; DOMINO KID(1957), w; LAWLESS EIGHTIES,
THE(1957), w
Poupee Gamin
JOURNEY TO THE CENTER OF TIME(1967)
Douglas Gamley
ONE WISH TOO MANY(1956, Brit.), m; ADMIRABLE CRICHTON, THE(1957,
Brit.), m; ANOTHER TIME, ANOTHER PLACE(1958), m; TOM THUMB(1958, Brit./
U.S.), m; BEYOND THIS PLACE(1959, Brit.), m; GIDEON OF SCOTLAND
YARD(1959, Brit.), m; TARZAN'S GREATEST ADVENTURE(1959, Brit.), m; UGLY
DUCKLING, THE(1959, Brit.), m; FOXHOLE IN CAIRO(1960, Brit.), m; HORROR
HOTEL(1960, Brit.), m, md; LIGHT UP THE SKY(1960, Brit.), m; PORTRAIT OF A
SINNER(1961, Brit.), m; ROMAN SPRING OF MRS. STONE, THE(1961, U.S./Brit.),
md; WATCH IT, SAILOR!(1961, Brit.), m; HORROR OF IT ALL, THE(1964, Brit.), m;
RETURN OF MR. MOTO, THE(1965, Brit.), m; SPRING AND PORT WINE(1970,
Brit.), m; SUNDAY BLOODY SUNDAY(1971, Brit.), md; TALES FROM THE
CRYPT(1972, Brit.), m, md; VAULT OF HORROR(1973, Brit.), m; BEAST MUST
DIE, THE(1974, Brit.), m; FROM BEYOND THE GRAVE(1974, Brit.), m, md; MAD-
HOUSE(1974, Brit.), m; LAND THAT TIME FORGOT, THE(1975, Brit.), m; ENIG-
MA(1983), m
Lionel Gamlin
MAN IN THE MOON(1961, Brit.); SEANCE ON A WET AFTERNOON(1964 Brit.);
WRONG BOX, THE(1966, Brit.)
Robin Gammell
PYX, THE(1973, Can.); LIPSTICK(1976); FULL CIRCLE(1977, Brit./Can.); PROMISE,
THE(1979); CIRCLE OF TWO(1980, Can.); CREEPER, THE(1980, Can.); BELLS(1981,
Can.); HAUNTING OF JULIA, THE(1981, Brit./Can.); NIGHTMARES(1983); STAR
CHAMBER, THE(1983)
1984
HIGHPOINT(1984, Can.)
Herbert Gammersbach
NOT RECONCILED, OR "ONLY VIOLENCE HELPS WHERE IT RULES"(1969, Ger.)
Michele Gammino
CONFESSIONS OF A POLICE CAPTAIN(1971, Ital.)
James Gammon
COOL HAND LUKE(1967); JOURNEY TO SHILOH(1968); 1,000 PLANE RAID,
THE(1969); MACHO CALLAHAN(1970); MAN CALLED HORSE, A(1970); MACON
COUNTY LINE(1974); WILD McCULLOCHS, THE(1975); POM POM GIRLS,
THE(1976); BLACK OAK CONSPIRACY(1977); GREATEST, THE(1977, U.S./Brit.);
BELOW THE BELT(1980); ON THE NICKEL(1980); URBAN COWBOY(1980); BALLAD
OF GREGORIO CORTEZ, THE(1983)
Victor Gammon
MYSTERY OF MR. X, THE(1934); RIP TIDE(1934)
Roberto Gamonet
PUFNSTUF(1970)

Charles Gamora
SWISS MISS(1938)

Chris Gampel
WRONG MAN, THE(1956); DIRTYMOUTH(1970); DESPERATE CHARAC-TERS(1971); DEATH WISH(1974); ANNIE HALL(1977); FIREPOWER(1979, Brit.); CHANGELING, THE(1980, Can.)

Ken Gampu
DINGAKA(1965, South Africa); NAKED PREY, THE(1966, U.S./South Africa); SLAV-ERS(1977, Ger.); KING SOLOMON'S TREASURE(1978, Can.); WILD GEESE, THE(1978, Brit.); GAME FOR VULTURES, A(1980, Brit.); ZULU DAWN(1980, Brit.); KILL AND KILL AGAIN(1981)
1984
GODS MUST BE CRAZY, THE(1984, Botswana)
Misc. Talkies
BLACK TRASH(1978)

Morrison Gampu
NAKED PREY, THE(1966, U.S./South Africa)

Yvonne Gamy
LETTERS FROM MY WINDMILL(1955, Fr.)

Chester Gan
CHINA SEAS(1935); MYSTERIOUS MR. WONG(1935); STORMY(1935); DRIFT FENCE(1936); SAN FRANCISCO(1936); SEA SPOILERS, THE(1936); GOOD EARTH, THE(1937); SLAVE SHIP(1937); WEST OF SHANGHAI(1937); SHADOWS OVER SHANGHAI(1938); KING OF CHINATOWN(1939); MYSTERY OF MR. WONG, THE(1939); CARSON CITY KID(1940); MY LITTLE CHICKADEE(1940); 'TIL WE MEET AGAIN(1940); VICTORY(1940); WESTBOUND STAGE(1940); BURMA CON-VOY(1941); MAN MADE MONSTER(1941); PASSAGE FROM HONG KONG(1941); RAWHIDE RANGERS(1941); THEY MET IN BOMBAY(1941); ACROSS THE PACI-FIC(1942); BUSSES ROAR(1942); ESCAPE FROM HONG KONG(1942); FLYING TIGERS(1942); MOONTIDE(1942); TO THE SHORES OF TRIPOLI(1942); CHINA(1943); CRASH DIVE(1943); SALUTE TO THE MARINES(1943)

Eng Chee Gan
GLADIATORS, THE(1970, Swed.)

Ginny Gan
IN LIKE FLINT(1967)

Jennifer Gan
NAKED ANGELS(1969)

Paul Ganapoler
PEOPLE NEXT DOOR, THE(1970)

Abel Gance
END OF THE WORLD, THE(1930, Fr.), a, d, w; LIFE AND LOVES OF BEETHOV-EN, THE(1937, Fr.), p&d, w; LUCREZIA BORGIA(1937, Fr.), d; J'ACCUSE(1939, Fr.), p&d, w; LOUISE(1940, Fr.), d; AUSTERLITZ(1960, Fr./Ital./Yugo.), d&w
Silents
NAPOLEON(1927, Fr.), a, p,d&w
Misc. Silents
LA ZOME DE LA MORT(1917, Fr.), d; LE DROIT A LA VIE(1917, Fr.), d; MATER DOLOROSA(1917, Fr.), d; LA DIXIEME SYMPHONIE(1918, Fr.), d

Marguerite Gance
Silents
NAPOLEON(1927, Fr.)
Misc. Silents
FALL OF THE HOUSE OF USHER, THE(1928, Fr.)

George Ganchev
1984
RED DAWN(1984)

Mogens Gander
CHICAGO 70(1970), ph

Felix Gandera
DOUBLE CRIME IN THE MAGINOT LINE(1939, Fr.), p&d, w

Bob Gandett
PIGEON THAT TOOK ROME, THE(1962)

Alfred Gandolfi
VIKING, THE(1931), ph
Silents
SQUAW MAN, THE(1914), ph

Franco Gandolfi
VITELLONI(1956, Ital./Fr.)

Giorgio Gandos
SEVEN HILLS OF ROME, THE(1958)

Gandus
NO WAY OUT(1975, Ital./Fr.), w

Nolan Gane
Misc. Silents
LAST CONCERT, THE(1915)

Gustavo Ganem
ZORRO, THE GAY BLADE(1981)

G. Ganevskaya
MUMU(1961, USSR), cos; RESURRECTION(1963, USSR), cos

Mario Gang
ROYAL SCANDAL, A(1945); 13 RUE MADELEINE(1946)

Ruma Gangaly
RIVER, THE(1961, India)

Ray Gange
RUDE BOY(1980, Brit.), a, w

Ed Gangel
CAPTURE THAT CAPSULE(1961)

Paul Gangelin
JAZZ AGE, THE(1929), w; OFFICE SCANDAL, THE(1929), w; RACKETEER, THE(1929), w; WALL STREET(1929), w; HELL'S HOUSE(1932), w; BACHELOR MOTHER(1933), w; BELOVED(1934), w; KING OF PARIS, THE(1934, Brit.), w; BLACK MASK(1935, Brit.), w; BREWSTER'S MILLIONS(1935, Brit.), w; STREET SONG(1935, Brit.), w; DANGEROUS MEDICINE(1938, Brit.), w; RETURN OF CAROL DEANE, THE(1938, Brit.), w; NURSEMAID WHO DISAPPEARED, THE(1939, Brit.), w; TOO DANGEROUS TO LIVE(1939, Brit.), w; TARZAN'S SECRET TREASU-RE(1941), w; BOOGIE MAN WILL GET YOU, THE(1942), w; NAZI AGENT(1942), w; JUNIOR ARMY(1943), w; MAD GHOUL, THE(1943), w; MURDER IN TIMES SQUARE(1943), w; BIG BONANZA, THE(1944), w; BLACK PARACHUTE, THE(1944), w; COVER GIRL(1944), w; COWBOY CANTEEN(1944), w; SCARLET CLAW, THE(1944), w; STRANGERS IN THE NIGHT(1944), w; DALTONS RIDE AGAIN, THE(1945), w; SPORTING CHANCE, A(1945), w; MY PAL TRIGGER(1946), w; ROLL ON TEXAS MOON(1946), w; UNDER NEVADA SKIES(1946), w; SON OF GOD'S COUNTRY(1948), w; UNDER CALIFORNIA STARS(1948), w; SONS OF NEW MEX-ICO(1949), w; GIANT CLAW, THE(1957), w
Silents
NO-GUN MAN, THE(1924), w; FOREVER AFTER(1926), w; IS THAT NICE?(1926), w; ARIZONA BOUND(1927), w; SILKS AND SADDLES(1929), w

Victor Gangelin
TOYS IN THE ATTIC(1963), set d; STAGE DOOR CANTEEN(1943), set d; TARZAN'S DESERT MYSTERY(1943), set d; MAN ALIVE(1945), set d; NOT AS A STRAN-GER(1955), set d; SEARCHERS, THE(1956), set d; I WANT TO LIVE!(1958), set d; PROUD REBEL, THE(1958), set d; WEST SIDE STORY(1961), set d; SERGEANTS 3(1962), set d; DIARY OF A MADMAN(1963), set d; PROMISES, PROMISES(1963), set d; NAKED KISS, THE(1964), set d; DUEL AT DIABLO(1966), set d; TROUBLE WITH ANGELS, THE(1966), set d; WILD, WILD WINTER(1966), set d; HOUR OF THE GUN(1967), set d

Victor A. Gangelin
SALOME, WHERE SHE DANCED(1945), set d; CHASE, THE(1946), set d; MAD WEDNESDAY(1950), set d

Victory A. Gangelin
SINCE YOU WENT AWAY(1944), set d

Jack Ganghorn
Misc. Silents
HAWK OF THE HILLS(1929)

Rama Gangopadhaya
PATHER PANCHALI(1958, India)

The Gangsters
PROSTITUTE(1980, Brit.), m

Subodh Ganguly
APARAJITO(1959, India)

Sunil Ganguly
ADVERSARY, THE(1973, Ind.), d&w

Valentina Ganilaee Ganibalova
BLUE BIRD, THE(1976)

Tony Ganios
WANDERERS, THE(1979); BACK ROADS(1981); CONTINENTAL DIVIDE(1981); PORKY'S(1982); PORKY'S II: THE NEXT DAY(1983)
1984
BODY ROCK(1984)

Glenda Ganis
PIPE DREAMS(1976), cos

Ganjou Bros. and Juanita
VARIETY JUBILEE(1945, Brit.)

Gail Ganley
I'LL CRY TOMORROW(1955); DON'T KNOCK THE ROCK(1956); BLOOD OF DRACULA(1957); GIRL MOST LIKELY, THE(1957); NOT OF THIS EARTH(1957); MARJORIE MORNINGSTAR(1958)

Mary Ganley
GUY NAMED JOE, A(1943); MEET THE PEOPLE(1944)

Angela Gann
SWEET SUBSTITUTE(1964, Can.)
Misc. Talkies
CARESSED(1965)

Chester Gann
HIDEAWAY GIRL(1937); PALS OF THE SILVER SAGE(1940)

Earnest K. Gann
LAST FLIGHT OF NOAH'S ARK, THE(1980), w

Ernest K. Gann
BLAZE OF NOON(1947), w; RAGING TIDE, THE(1951), w; ISLAND IN THE SKY(1953), w; HIGH AND THE MIGHTY, THE(1954), w; SOLDIER OF FOR-TUNE(1955), w; TWILIGHT FOR THE GODS(1958), w; FATE IS THE HUNTER(1964), w

M.J. Gann
GIRL FROM POLTAVA(1937), d, w

Antoine Gannage
1984
MIXED BLOOD(1984), p

Al Gannaway
HIDDEN GUNS(1956), p, d, w

Albert C. Gannaway
BADGE OF MARSHAL BRENNAN, THE(1957), p&d; DANIEL BOONE, TRAIL BLAZER(1957), p, d; RAIDERS OF OLD CALIFORNIA(1957), p&d; MAN OR GUN(1958), d; NO PLACE TO LAND(1958), p&d; PLUNDERERS OF PAINTED FLATS(1959), p&d; BUFFALO GUN(1961), d; CHIVATO(1961), p&d; REBELLION IN CUBA(1961), p&d

Madeleine Ganne
CATHERINE & CO.(1976, Fr.)
1984
JUST THE WAY YOU ARE(1984)

Barbara Gannen
1941(1979)

Gayle Gannes
1984
PREY, THE(1984)

Lewis Gannet
DEFECTOR, THE(1966, Ger./Fr.), w

Chris Gannon
POOR COW(1968, Brit.)

James J. Gannon
REBEL ANGEL(1962), p; EVERY SPARROW MUST FALL(1964), p

John Gannon
SAN DIEGO, I LOVE YOU(1944)

Kim Gannon
SALUTE FOR THREE(1943), m

Maugene H. Gannon
ROUSTABOUT(1964)

Wilf Gannon
Misc. Silents
AUNTIE'S ANTICS(1929, Brit.), a, d

Glen Gano
SWING IN THE SADDLE(1944), ph; GUY, A GAL AND A PAL, A(1945), ph; UNTAMED WOMEN(1952), ph; INCREDIBLE TWO-HEADED TRANSPLANT, THE(1971), ph
Silents
SILENT CALL, THE(1921), ph
Glenn Gano
GOLD FEVER(1952), ph
Rina Ganor
CAST A GIANT SHADOW(1966); IMPOSSIBLE ON SATURDAY(1966, Fr./Israel); TWO KOUNEY LEMELS(1966, Israel); SIMCHON FAMILY, THE(1969, Israel); FLYING MATCHMAKER, THE(1970, Israel)
Gary Ganote
SCREAMS OF A WINTER NIGHT(1979), ed
Chester Gans
Misc. Talkies
FIGHTING THROUGH(1934)
Elisabeth Gans
LOVELESS, THE(1982)
Ron Gans
ST. VALENTINE'S DAY MASSACRE, THE(1967); TARZAN AND THE JUNGLE BOY(1968, US/Switz.); WILD RACERS, THE(1968); CURIOUS FEMALE, THE(1969); GAY DECEIVERS, THE(1969); STUDENT NURSES, THE(1970)
Ronald Gans
HELL NIGHT(1981)
Sharon Gans
SLAUGHTERHOUSE-FIVE(1972)
Clara Gansard
COUNTERFEITERS OF PARIS, THE(1962, Fr., Ital.); DAY AND THE HOUR, THE(1963, Fr./ Ital.); ENOUGH ROPE(1966, Fr./Ital./Ger.); IS PARIS BURNING?(1966, U.S./Fr.)
Gant
Misc. Talkies
GEORGIA ROSE(1930), d
Dan Lee Gant
MR. BILLION(1977)
David Gant
FIREFOX(1982); GANDHI(1982); MOONLIGHTING(1982, Brit.); VICTOR/VICTORIA(1982); DRAUGHTSMAN'S CONTRACT, THE(1983, Brit.); WICKED LADY, THE(1983, Brit.)
Harry Gant
STROKER ACE(1983)
1984
CANNONBALL RUN II(1984)
Harry A. Gant
Silents
ABSENT(1928), d&ph
Misc. Silents
SAGE-BRUSH LEAGUE, THE(1919), d
John Gant
RETURN OF THE PINK PANTHER, THE(1975, Brit.), spec eff
Kathryn Gant
1984
SHEENA(1984)
Richard Gant
NIGHT OF THE JUGGLER(1980)
Slim Gant
MY LITTLE CHICKADEE(1940)
Steven Gant
IN LOVE AND WAR(1958)
Richard Ganthony
Silents
MESSAGE FROM MARS, A(1913, Brit.), w
S. Gantillon
IT HAPPENED IN GIBRALTAR(1943, Fr.), w
Simon Gantillon
PERSONAL COLUMN(1939, Fr.), w; LURED(1947, w
Allen Gantley
ALL NIGHT LONG(1961, Brit.)
R. Gantman
MONSTER ISLAND(1981, Span./U.S.), w
Yuri Gantman
DERSU UZALA(1976, Jap./USSR), ph
Vallejo Gantner
CRUSADES, THE(1935); TILL WE MEET AGAIN(1936)
Julie Ganton
PARADISE(1982), cos
1984
BEDROOM EYES(1984, Can.), cos
Donald Gantry
SATURDAY NIGHT FEVER(1977); KRAMER VS. KRAMER(1979)
Gordon Gantry
CAESAR AND CLEOPATRA(1946, Brit.)
Marian Gants
WHY WOULD I LIE(1980)
Harry Gantt
WINDFLOWERS(1968)
Carl Gantvoort
Misc. Silents
CERTAIN RICH MAN, A(1921); LURE OF EGYPT, THE(1921); MAN OF THE FOREST, THE(1921); MYSTERIOUS RIDER(1921); GOLDEN DREAMS(1922); GRAY DAWN, THE(1922); HEART'S HAVEN(1922); WHEN ROMANCE RIDES(1922)
Armin Ganz
1984
BIRDY(1984), art d
Axel Ganz
RISE OF LOUIS XIV, THE(1970, Fr.)

Bruno Ganz
LUMIERE(1976, Fr.); AMERICAN FRIEND, THE(1977, Ger.); WILD DUCK, THE(1977, Ger./Aust.); BOYS FROM BRAZIL, THE(1978); NOSFERATU, THE VAMPIRE(1979, Fr./Ger.); LEFT-HANDED WOMAN, THE(1980, Ger.); CIRCLE OF DECEIT(1982, Fr./Ger.); GIRL FROM LORRAINE, A(1982, Fr./Switz.); IN THE WHITE CITY(1983, Switz./Portugal)
Lowell Ganz
NIGHT SHIFT(1982), w
1984
SPLASH(1984), a, w
Teresa Ganzel
TOY, THE(1982)
Misc. Talkies
C.O.D.(1983)
Alvin Ganzer
GIRLS OF PLEASURE ISLAND, THE(1953), d; LEATHER SAINT, THE(1956), d, w; COUNTRY MUSIC HOLIDAY(1958), d; WHEN THE BOYS MEET THE GIRLS(1965), d; THREE BITES OF THE APPLE(1967), p&d
Gerry Ganzer
LOVABLE CHEAT, THE(1949); POWDER RIVER RUSTLERS(1949); SUNSET BOULEVARD(1950); UNION STATION(1950); WHERE DANGER LIVES(1950); HIS KIND OF WOMAN(1951); CARRIE(1952)
R.J. Ganzert
ESCAPE FROM ALCATRAZ(1979); HONKYTONK MAN(1982)
Jack Ganzhorn
Silents
APACHE RAIDER, THE(1928)
Misc. Silents
THOROBRED(1922); FIGHTIN' ODDS(1925); VALLEY OF HUNTED MEN, THE(1928)
Yehoram Gaon
EVERY BASTARD A KING(1968, Israel); KAZABLAN(1974, Israel); OPERATION THUNDERBOLT(1978, ISRAEL)
Lola Gaos
VIRIDIANA(1962, Mex./Span.); NOT ON YOUR LIFE(1965, Ital./Span.); SOUND OF HORROR(1966, Span.); UGLY ONES, THE(1968, Ital./Span.); TRISTANA(1970, Span./Ital./Fr.)
Vassili Gaponenko
SPACE SHIP, THE(1935, USSR)
John Garabedian
ESCAPE FROM ALCATRAZ(1979)
Robert Garabedian
SATAN'S SATELLITES(1958)
Robert Garabedion
SALOME(1953)
Sergio Garafanolo
DEATH IN VENICE(1971, Ital./Fr.)
Peter Garafola
MADE FOR EACH OTHER(1971), makeup
Janos Garai
1984
BRADY'S ESCAPE(1984, U.S./Hung.)
Jean-Marc Garand
CORDELIA(1980, Fr., Can.), p
Suzanne Garand
MY UNCLE ANTOINE(1971, Can.), makeup
Valya Garanda
WITCHMAKER, THE(1969)
Serge Garant
TAKE IT ALL(1966, Can.), m
George Gararentz
HEIST, THE(1979, Ital.), m
Felix Garas
FINO A FARTI MALE(1969, Fr./Ital.), p
Kaz Garas
LAST SAFARI, THE(1967, Brit.); LOVE IS A FUNNY THING(1970, Fr./Ital.); BEN(1972)
Misc. Talkies
HALF A HOUSE(1979)
Henri Garat
AMPHYTRYON(1937, Ger.); GIRL IN THE TAXI(1937, Brit.)
Henry Garat
ADORABLE(1933); MAN STOLEN(1934, Fr.); COUNSEL FOR ROMANCE(1938, Fr.)
George Garate
NATIVE SON(1951, U.S., Arg.), ed
Jorge Garate
HAND IN THE TRAP, THE(1963, Arg./Span.), ed; GAMES MEN PLAY, THE(1968, Arg.), ed
Leo Garavaglia
SHOE SHINE(1947, Ital.)
George Garavarentz
1984
HAMBONE AND HILLIE(1984), m
Bill Garaway
ZABRISKIE POINT(1970)
Joaquim Garay
RED SKY AT MORNING(1971)
Joaquin Garay
THREE CABALLEROS, THE(1944); CRISIS(1950); SADDLE TRAMP(1950); FAST COMPANY(1953); LATIN LOVERS(1953)
Joaquin Garay III
HERBIE GOES BANANAS(1980)
Manuel Garay
VAMPIRES, THE(1969, Mex.)
Nestor Garay
SERAFINO(1970, Fr./Ital.); PSYCHOUT FOR MURDER(1971, Arg./Ital.); ALLEGRO NON TROPPO(1977, Ital.)

Paul Garay
GIRL MOST LIKELY, THE(1957)
Robin Garb
STAYING ALIVE(1983), md
Peter Garbarini
PAPER LION(1968), ph
Dave Garber
DESERT GOLD(1936), art d
David Garber
SITTING PRETTY(1933), art d
David H. Garber
MISSION GALACTICA: THE CYLON ATTACK(1979), spec eff
David M. Garber
CONQUEST OF THE EARTH(1980), spec eff
David S. Garber
Silents
BLAZING DAYS(1927), art d; HEY! HEY! COWBOY(1927), art d; ONE GLORIOUS
SCRAP(1927), art d; PAINTED PONIES(1927), art d; WESTERN ROVER, THE(1927),
art d; WESTERN WHIRLWIND, THE(1927), art d; ARIZONA CYCLONE(1928), art d;
CLEARING THE TRAIL(1928), art d; RAWHIDE KID, THE(1928), art d; KING OF
THE RODEO(1929), art d
Esther Garber
HOUDINI(1953)
Jan Garber
MAKE BELIEVE BALLROOM(1949)
John Garber
DIRTY HARRY(1971); WHOSE LIFE IS IT ANYWAY?(1981); PARTNERS(1982);
WARGAMES(1983)
Kathy Garber
KISS ME, STUPID(1964)
Matthew Garber
THREE LIVES OF THOMASINA, THE(1963, U.S./Brit.); MARY POPPINS(1964);
GNOME-MOBILE, THE(1967)
Terri Garber
1984
TOY SOLDIERS(1984)
Victor Garber
GODSPELL(1973)
Dean Garbett
FUNERAL HOME(1982, Can.)
Djolly Garbi
THANOS AND DESPINA(1970, Fr./Gr.)
Amato Garbine
STATUE, THE(1971, Brit.), makeup
Guilio Garbinetti
ROMEO AND JULIET(1954, Brit.)
Amato Garbini
300 SPARTANS, THE(1962), makeup; GOLIATH AND THE SINS OF BABY-
LON(1964, Ital.), makeup; REFLECTIONS IN A GOLDEN EYE(1967), makeup;
THREE BITES OF THE APPLE(1967), makeup; SHOES OF THE FISHERMAN,
THE(1968), makeup; THOSE DARING YOUNG MEN IN THEIR JAUNTY JALO-
PIES(1969, Fr./Brit./ Ital.), makeup; STATUE, THE(1971, Brit.); DUCK, YOU SUCK-
ER!(1972, Ital.), makeup
Greta Garbo
ANNA   CHRISTIE(1930);   ROMANCE(1930);   INSPIRATION(1931);   MATA
HARI(1931); SUSAN LENOX–HER FALL AND RISE(1931); AS YOU DESIRE
ME(1932); GRAND HOTEL(1932); QUEEN CHRISTINA(1933); PAINTED VEIL,
THE(1934); ANNA KARENINA(1935); CAMILLE(1937); CONQUEST(1937); NINOTC-
HKA(1939); TWO-FACED WOMAN(1941)
Silents
FLESH AND THE DEVIL(1926); TEMPTRESS, THE(1926); TORRENT, THE(1926);
LOVE(1927); DIVINE WOMAN, THE(1928); MYSTERIOUS LADY, THE(1928); WOM-
AN OF AFFAIRS, A(1928); KISS, THE(1929); MAN'S MAN, A(1929); SINGLE STAND-
ARD, THE(1929); WILD ORCHIDS(1929)
Misc. Silents
LEGEND OF GOSTA BERLING(1928, Swed.)
Ingrid Garbo
DRACULA'S GREAT LOVE(1972, Span.); TOUCH ME NOT(1974, Brit.)
James Garbo
SOUL OF NIGGER CHARLEY, THE(1973)
Jim Garbo
LAST REBEL, THE(1971)
Gerard Garbonaro
PATRIOT, THE(1928), m
Eugene Garbrilovich
IN THE NAME OF LIFE(1947, USSR), w
Mario Garbuglai
INNOCENT, THE(1979, Ital.), art d
Mario Garbuglia
FAREWELL TO ARMS, A(1957), art d; UNDER TEN FLAGS(1960, U.S./Ital.), art d;
DESERT WARRIOR(1961 Ital./Span.), art d; GREAT WAR, THE(1961, Fr., Ital.), art
d; ROCCO AND HIS BROTHERS(1961, Fr./Ital.), art d; LEOPARD, THE(1963, Ital.), art
d; DISORDER(1964, Fr./Ital.), art d; ORGANIZER, THE(1964, Fr./Ital./Yugo.), art d;
AFTER THE FOX(1966, U.S./Brit./Ital.), art d; SANDRA(1966, Ital.), art d; KISS THE
GIRLS AND MAKE THEM DIE(1967, U.S./Ital.), art d; STRANGER, THE(1967,
Algeria/Fr./Ital.), art d; WITCHES, THE(1969, Fr./Ital.), art d; WATERLOO(1970,
Ital./USSR), prod d; LADY LIBERTY(1972, Ital./Fr.), prod d; CHINO(1976, Ital., Span.,
Fr.), art d; CONVERSATION PIECE(1976, Ital., Fr.), art d; END OF THE GAME(1976,
Ger./Ital.), art d; ORCA(1977), prod d; LA CAGE AUX FOLLES(1979, Fr./Ital.), art d;
WIFEMISTRESS(1979, Ital.), art d; LION OF THE DESERT(1981, Libya/Brit.), prod d
Mario Garbuglio
CASANOVA '70(1965, Ital.), art d
Bernard Garbutt
SNOW WHITE AND THE SEVEN DWARFS(1937), anim
Frank E. Garbutt
Silents
LOUISIANA(1919), ph; HUCKLEBERRY FINN(1920), ph

James Garbutt
SUPERMAN(1978); THIRTY NINE STEPS, THE(1978, Brit.)
Dick Garce
LOST SQUADRON, THE(1932)
Suzanne Garceau
TI-CUL TOUGAS(1977, Can.)
Anthony Garcen
TO HELL AND BACK(1955)
Tony Garcen
TWINKLE IN GOD'S EYE, THE(1955)
Delia Garces
EL(1955, Mex.)
John Garces
ROBBY(1968)
Mauricio Garces
EMPTY STAR, THE(1962, Mex.); LIVING HEAD, THE(1969, Mex.)
Jose Luis Garci
TO BEGIN AGAIN(1982, Span.), p&d, w
Al Garcia
IN OLD MEXICO(1938); SEASON OF PASSION(1961, Aus./Brit.)
Misc. Silents
BAREE, SON OF KAZAN(1918); LAMB AND THE LION, THE(1919)
Alan Garcia
GAY DESPERADO, THE(1936)
Alejandro Alonso Garcia
1984
CONQUEST(1984, Ital./Span./Mex.), ph
Alfred Garcia
Misc. Silents
RESTITUTION(1918)
Allan Garcia
DECEIVER, THE(1931); SOUTH OF SANTA FE(1932); UNDER THE TONTO
RIM(1933); MODERN TIMES(1936); I'LL TAKE ROMANCE(1937)
Silents
GOLD RUSH, THE(1925); CIRCUS, THE(1928); MORGAN'S LAST RAID(1929); CITY
LIGHTS(1931)
Amadita Garcia
RIDE THE PINK HORSE(1947)
Andres Garcia
TINTORERA...BLOODY WATERS(1977, Brit./Mex.)
Andy Garcia
BLUE SKIES AGAIN(1983); NIGHT IN HEAVEN, A(1983)
Misc. Talkies
ENCOUNTERS OF THE DEEP(1984)
Bobby Garcia
Misc. Talkies
CYCLES SOUTH(1971)
Camillo Garcia
1984
ROMANCING THE STONE(1984)
Capt. Garcia
CRISIS(1950)
Carl Garcia
LOVE HUNGER(1965, Arg.)
Carlos Garcia
ZOOT SUIT(1981)
Ceferino Garcia
JOE PALOOKA, CHAMP(1946); WHIPLASH(1948)
Daniel Garcia
HIGH RISK(1981)
Darnell Garcia
Misc. Talkies
BLIND RAGE(1978); ENFORCER FROM DEATH ROW, THE(1978)
David Garcia
BLUE CANADIAN ROCKIES(1952); MONSTER FROM THE OCEAN FLOOR,
THE(1954); HELL'S ISLAND(1955); BEHIND THE HIGH WALL(1956); WAR-
LOCK(1959); SERPENTS OF THE PIRATE MOON, THE(1973), ph
Eddie Garcia
CURSE OF THE VAMPIRES(1970, Phil., U.S.); TWILIGHT PEOPLE(1972, Phil.);
BLACK MAMA, WHITE MAMA(1973); SAVAGE SISTERS(1974); WOMAN HUNT,
THE(1975, U.S./Phil.)
Misc. Talkies
BEAST OF THE YELLOW NIGHT(1971, U.S./Phil.); BAMBOO GODS AND IRON
MEN(1974)
Eduardo Garcia
CEREMONY, THE(1963, U.S./Span.)
Eliazar Garcia, Jr.
1984
UNDER THE VOLCANO(1984)
Ernest Garcia
Silents
AFTER FIVE(1915)
Misc. Silents
YOUNG ROMANCE(1915)
Esperanza Garcia
SAMAR(1962)
Eugenio Escudero Garcia
HUNTING PARTY, THE(1977, Brit.)
F. Garcia
POCKET MONEY(1972)
Capt. Fernando Garcia
FIREFLY, THE(1937); I MET HIM IN PARIS(1937)
Frank Garcia
SWEET SUGAR(1972)
Gino Garcia
1984
BODY ROCK(1984)

Hank Garcia
FUN WITH DICK AND JANE(1977)
Harry Garcia
RIDE THE PINK HORSE(1947); PALOMINO, THE(1950)
Misc. Talkies
BORDER FENCE(1951)
Henry Garcia
DUNGEONS OF HARROW(1964), w; NO MAN'S LAND(1964)
Misc. Talkies
RIO GRANDE(1949)
Honey Garcia
ZOOT SUIT(1981)
Irma Garcia
LOSIN' IT(1983)
Jessica Garcia
PURSUIT OF D.B. COOPER, THE(1981)
Joe Garcia
WHERE THE WEST BEGINS(1938); OVERLAND MAIL(1939); TALK OF THE
TOWN(1942); SAN ANTONIO KID, THE(1944); BLAZING FOREST, THE(1952)
John Garcia
GIANT(1956)
Jose Garcia
VALDEZ IS COMING(1971)
Joseph Garcia
CHINA SYNDROME, THE(1979)
Juan Garcia
PEARL, THE(1948, U.S./Mex.); BLOWING WILD(1953); VERA CRUZ(1954); TALL
MEN, THE(1955); RUN FOR THE SUN(1956); BRAVADOS, THE(1958); TEN DAYS TO
TULARA(1958); FACE OF THE SCREAMING WEREWOLF(1959, Mex.), w; UN-
DEFEATED, THE(1969); SOMETHING BIG(1971)
Ken Garcia
RAINBOW 'ROUND MY SHOULDER(1952)
Kenneth Garcia
CRISIS(1950)
Kenny Garcia
LIFE OF HER OWN, A(1950)
Larry Garcia
1984
KILLPOINT(1984)
Lea Garcia
BLACK ORPHEUS(1959 Fr./Ital./Braz.)
Leon Garcia
ADVENTURE IN THE HOPFIELDS(1954, Brit.); AND WOMEN SHALL WEEP(1960,
Brit.); YOUNG, WILLING AND EAGER(1962, Brit.); THESE ARE THE DAMNED(1965,
Brit.)
Louis Garcia
ANGELO MY LOVE(1983)
Lourdes Garcia
1984
BIZET'S CARMEN(1984, Fr./Ital.)
Marcia Garcia
WHAT'S THE MATTER WITH HELEN?(1971)
Margaret Garcia
HOW COME NOBODY'S ON OUR SIDE?(1975)
Margarita Garcia
SILVER STREAK(1976); LOSIN' IT(1983)
Mariano Garcia
LAST RUN, THE(1971), makeup
Maribel DeCirez Garcia
SHIP OF FOOLS(1965)
MariSol Garcia
1984
MIKE'S MURDER(1984)
May Garcia
Misc. Silents
CASEY AT THE BAT(1916)
Miki Garcia
STACEY!(1973)
Nicole Garcia
QUESTION, THE(1977, Fr.); BUTTERFLY ON THE SHOULDER, A(1978, Fr.); MON
ONCLE D'AMERIQUE(1980, Fr.); BEAU PERE(1981, Fr.); BOLERO(1982, Fr.)
1984
CORRUPT(1984, Ital.)
Patrick Garcia
PURSUIT OF D.B. COOPER, THE(1981)
Paul Garcia
FIREPOWER(1979, Brit.); TRADING PLACES(1983)
Priscilla Garcia
CHARLEY VARRICK(1973); ONCE UPON A SCOUNDREL(1973); HOW COME
NOBODY'S ON OUR SIDE?(1975)
R. Victor Garcia
INSIDE AMY(1975), ed
Rafael Escudero Garcia
HUNTING PARTY, THE(1977, Brit.)
Ramiro Gomez Garcia
REVOLT OF THE SLAVES, THE(1961, Ital./Span./Ger.), art d; MISSION BLOODY
MARY(1967, Fr./Ital./Span.), art d
Raul Garcia
UNDER FIRE(1983)
Rene Garcia
DEVIL IN THE FLESH, THE(1949, Fr.)
Rick Garcia
1984
FLETCH(1984)
Robert Garcia
KING OF THE GYPSIES(1978)
Ron Garcia
HAREM BUNCH; OR WAR AND PIECE, THE(1969), ph&set d; INSIDE AMY(1975),
p&d; YOUNG CYCLE GIRLS, THE(1979), ph

Misc. Talkies
TOY BOX, THE(1971), d
Ronald Garcia
HOT POTATO(1976), ph
Ronald V. Garcia
MACHISMO—40 GRAVES FOR 40 GUNS(1970), p, w, ph, ed; GREAT GUNDOWN,
THE(1977), ph; ONE FROM THE HEART(1982), ph
Rosa Garcia
TRISTANA(1970, Span./Ital./Fr.), cos
Rosita Garcia
LOVE IN MOROCCO(1933, Fr.); PRIVATE LIFE OF DON JUAN, THE(1934, Brit.);
THE BEACHCOMBER(1938, Brit.)
Russ Garcia
PAD, THE(AND HOW TO USE IT)* (1966, Brit.), m; THREE GUNS FOR TEX-
AS(1968), m
Russell Garcia
RADAR SECRET SERVICE(1950), m; TIME MACHINE, THE(1960; Brit./U.S.), m;
ATLANTIS, THE LOST CONTINENT(1961), m
Ruth Garcia
NIGHT PEOPLE(1954)
Sabrina Garcia
1984
BREAKIN' 2: ELECTRIC BOOGALOO(1984)
Sancho Garcia
GUNS OF THE MAGNIFICENT SEVEN(1969); RAIN FOR A DUSTY SUMMER(1971,
U.S./Span.); CALL OF THE WILD(1972, Ger./ Span./Ital./Fr.)
Santiago Garcia
VALDEZ IS COMING(1971)
Sara Garcia
LIVING IDOL, THE(1957)
Stella Garcia
PRIVATE LIVES OF ADAM AND EVE, THE(1961); LAST MOVIE, THE(1971); JOE
KIDD(1972)
Sutero Garcia, Jr.
MAN WHO LOVED CAT DANCING, THE(1973)
Tino Garcia
HARBOR LIGHTS(1963)
Tito Garcia
FINGER ON THE TRIGGER(1965, US/Span.); LIGHTNING BOLT(1967, Ital./Sp.); UP
THE MACGREGORS(1967, Ital./Span.); UGLY ONES, THE(1968, Ital./Span.); GOD
FORGIVES—I DON'T!(1969, Ital./Span.); MERCENARY, THE(1970, Ital./Span.); LIGHT
AT THE EDGE OF THE WORLD, THE(1971, U.S./Span./Lichtenstein); TOWN
CALLED HELL, A(1971, Span./Brit.); SUPERSONIC MAN(1979, Span.)
Vincent Garcia
FANCY PANTS(1950)
Violetta Garcia
HUNT, THE(1967, Span.)
Luce Garcia-Ville
LAST YEAR AT MARIENBAD(1962, Fr./Ital.); NATHALIE GRANGER(1972, Fr.)
The Garcias
NO LEAVE, NO LOVE(1946)
David Garcie
PARTY GIRL(1958)
Eddie Garcie
BEAST OF BLOOD(1970, U.S./Phil.)
Ginette Garcin
COUSIN, COUSINE(1976, Fr.); BLUE COUNTRY, THE(1977, Fr.); CHARLES AND
LUCIE(1982, Fr.)
1984
AMERICAN DREAMER(1984); EDITH AND MARCEL(1984, Fr.)
Henri Garcin
MATA HARI(1965, Fr./Ital.); LA VIE DE CHATEAU(1967, Fr.); DESTROY, SHE
SAID(1969, Fr.); LES GAULOISES BLEUES(1969, Fr.); SOMEONE BEHIND THE
DOOR(1971, Fr./Brit.); KILL! KILL! KILL!(1972, Fr./Ger./Ital./Span.); FRENCH WAY,
THE(1975, Fr.); VERDICT(1975, Fr./Ital.); CATHERINE & CO.(1976, Fr.); ALMOST
PERFECT AFFAIR, AN(1979); COCKTAIL MOLOTOV(1980, Fr.); WOMAN NEXT
DOOR, THE(1981, Fr.)
Patricia Garcin
LOVERS, THE(1959, Fr.)
Salvador Garcini
1984
ERENDIRA(1984, Mex./Fr./Ger.)
Joe Garcio
SINBAD THE SAILOR(1947); EL DORADO(1967)
Peter Garcy
CAPTAIN EDDIE(1945)
Dave Gard
TOP BANANA(1954)
Lamar Gard
SUPER VAN(1977), d
Vladimir Gardanov
IN THE NAME OF LIFE(1947, USSR), ph
Vyachesslav Gardanov
THUNDERSTORM(1934, USSR), ph
Angela C. Gardaphe
1984
REVENGE OF THE NERDS(1984)
Annie Birgit Garde
OPERATION CAMEL(1961, Den.); JOURNEY TO THE SEVENTH PLANET(1962,
U.S./Swed.); ERIC SOYA'S "17"(1967, Den.)
Betty Garde
QUEEN HIGH(1930); DAMAGED LOVE(1931); GIRL HABIT(1931); SECRETS OF A
SECRETARY(1931); CALL NORTHSIDE 777(1948); CRY OF THE CITY(1948); CA-
GED(1950); PRINCE WHO WAS A THIEF, THE(1951); ONE DESIRE(1955); WONDER-
FUL WORLD OF THE BROTHERS ERIMM, THE(1962)
Colin Garde
BANDIT OF ZHOBE, THE(1959), makeup; TERROR OF THE TONGS, THE(1961,
Brit.), makeup; MIKADO, THE(1967, Brit.), makeup; TWO GENTLEMEN SHA-
RING(1969, Brit.), makeup

James Garde
TWO WEEKS IN ANOTHER TOWN(1962)
Len Garde
DEAR MURDERER(1947, Brit.), makeup; WHEN THE BOUGH BREAKS(1947, Brit.), makeup; MIRANDA(1949, Brit.), makeup
Lester Garde
NO ORCHIDS FOR MISS BLANDISH(1948, Brit.), makeup
Bunny Gardel
MISFITS, THE(1961), makeup
Carlos Gardel
TANGO BAR(1935)
Nikos Gardelis
RED LANTERNS(1965, Gr.), ph; FEAR, THE(1967, Gr.), ph
Anthony Gardell
PRODUCERS, THE(1967)
Tess "Aunt Jemima" Gardella
SHOW BOAT(1929)
Theresa Gardella
STAND UP AND CHEER(1934 80m FOX bw)
Yvonne Gardelle
Silents
OCCASIONALLY YOURS(1920)
Eve Garden
Misc. Talkies
NAUGHTY NYMPHS(1974)
Helen Garden
MONTE CARLO(1930)
John Garden
DOUBLE CONFESSION(1953, Brit.), w; ODDS AGAINST TOMORROW(1959)
Mary Garden
Misc. Silents
THAIS(1917); SPLENDID SINNER, THE(1918)
Robert Garden
Misc. Talkies
GUNSMOKE(1947)
Garden Odyssey Enterprise
WEDDING NIGHT(1970, Ireland)
Maria Gardena
LITTLE MARTYR, THE(1947, Ital.)
Richard Gardener
CONFESSIONS OF AMANS, THE(1977)
Raleigh Gardenhire
SHOWDOWN(1973); THOMASINE AND BUSHROD(1974); SECOND THOUGHTS(1983); TIMERIDER(1983)
Vincent Gardenia
HOUSE ON 92ND STREET, THE(1945); COP HATER(1958); MURDER, INC.(1960); HUSTLER, THE(1961); MAD DOG COLL(1961); PARRISH(1961); VIEW FROM THE BRIDGE, A(1962, Fr./Ital.); THIRD DAY, THE(1965); JENNY(1969); WHERE'S POPPA?(1970); COLD TURKEY(1971); LITTLE MURDERS(1971); HICKEY AND BOGGS(1972); BANG THE DRUM SLOWLY(1973); DEATH WISH(1974); FRONT PAGE, THE(1974); RE: LUCKY LUCIANO(1974, Fr./Ital.); MANCHU EAGLE MURDER CAPER MYSTERY, THE(1975); FIRE SALE(1977); GREASED LIGHTNING(1977); HEAVEN CAN WAIT(1978); FIREPOWER(1979, Brit.); HOME MOVIES(1979); LAST FLIGHT OF NOAH'S ARK, THE(1980); DEATH WISH II(1982)
Raleigh Gardenshire
CATCH MY SOUL(1974)
Eduardo Gardere
AVENGERS, THE(1950)
Renee Gardes
UP FROM THE BEACH(1965)
Maurice Gardett
LA BELLE AMERICAINE(1961, Fr.)
Robert Gardett
SPELL OF THE HYPNOTIST(1956); CAST A GIANT SHADOW(1966)
Robert Gardette
CATTLE QUEEN(1951)
Gardin
ENEMIES OF PROGRESS(1934, USSR)
V. Gardin
LOSS OF FEELING(1935, USSR)
Vladimir Gardin
HOUSE OF GREED(1934, USSR)
Misc. Silents
ANNA KARENINA(1914, USSR), d; DAYS OF OUR LIFE(1914, USSR), d; GHOSTS(1915, USSR), d; NEST OF NOBLEMEN, A(1915, USSR), d; WAR AND PEACE(1915, USSR), d; THOUGHT(1916, USSR), d; SICKLE AND HAMMER(1921, USSR), d; LOCKSMITH AND CHANCELLOR(1923, USSR), d; SPECTRE HAUNTS EUROPE, A(1923, USSR), d; BEAR'S WEDDING, THE(1926, USSR), d; MARRIAGE OF THE BEAR, THE(1928, USSR), d
Becky Gardiner
TRIAL OF MARY DUGAN, THE(1929), w; WAR NURSE(1930), w; STINGAREE(1934), w
Silents
GREAT GATSBY, THE(1926), w; SEA HORSES(1926), w; NEW YORK(1927), w; SIN SISTER, THE(1929), w
Carol Gardiner
REMARKABLE MR. KIPPS(1942, Brit.)
Lt. Comdr. Charles H. Gardiner
WOMAN ON THE BEACH, THE(1947), tech adv
Cyril Gardiner
CROOKS TOUR(1940, Brit.)
David Gardiner
MAYTIME IN MAYFAIR(1952, Brit.)
Debbie Gardiner
THIS STUFF'LL KILL YA!(1971)
Douglas Gardiner
OUR TOWN(1940)

Faith Gardiner
ADULTEROUS AFFAIR(1966)
Howard Gardiner
FILE ON THELMA JORDAN, THE(1950); PONY EXPRESS(1953)
Jack Gardiner
JEDDA, THE UNCIVILIZED(1956, Aus.), ed
Joan Gardiner
GAY PURR-EE(1962)
John Gardiner
PASSWORD IS COURAGE, THE(1962, Brit.); TWO AND TWO MAKE SIX(1962, Brit.); NEVER PUT IT IN WRITING(1964)
Patrick Gardiner
VIKING QUEEN, THE(1967, Brit.); BROTHERLY LOVE(1970, Brit.)
Reginald Gardiner
PERFECT LADY, THE(1931, Brit.); JOSSER ON THE RIVER(1932, Brit.); BORROW A MILLION(1934, Brit.); DIPLOMATIC LOVER, THE(1934, Brit.); LEAVE IT TO SMITH(1934); VIRGINIA'S HUSBAND(1934, Brit.); LITTLE BIT OF BLUFF, A(1935, Brit.); REGAL CAVALCADE(1935, Brit.); BORN TO DANCE(1936); DAMSEL IN DISTRESS, A(1937); EVERYBODY SING(1938); GIRL DOWNSTAIRS, THE(1938); MARIE ANTOINETTE(1938); SWEETHEARTS(1938); FLYING DEUCES, THE(1939); NIGHT OF NIGHTS, THE(1939); DOCTOR TAKES A WIFE(1940); DULCY(1940); GREAT DICTATOR, THE(1940); MY LIFE WITH CAROLINE(1941); SUNDOWN(1941); YANK IN THE R.A.F., A(1941); CAPTAINS OF THE CLOUDS(1942); MAN WHO CAME TO DINNER, THE(1942); CLAUDIA(1943); FOREVER AND A DAY(1943); IMMORTAL SERGEANT, THE(1943); SWEET ROSIE O'GRADY(1943); CHRISTMAS IN CONNECTICUT(1945); DOLLY SISTERS, THE(1945); HORN BLOWS AT MIDNIGHT, THE(1945); MOLLY AND ME(1945); CLUNY BROWN(1946); DO YOU LOVE ME?(1946); ONE MORE TOMORROW(1946); I WONDER WHO'S KISSING HER NOW(1947); FURY AT FURNACE CREEK(1948); THAT LADY IN ERMINE(1948); THAT WONDERFUL URGE(1948); I'LL GET BY(1950); WABASH AVENUE(1950); ELOPEMENT(1951); HALLS OF MONTEZUMA(1951); ANDROCLES AND THE LION(1952); BLACK WIDOW(1954); AIN'T MISBEHAVIN'(1955); STORY OF MANKIND, THE(1957); ROCK-A-BYE BABY(1958); BACK STREET(1961); MR. HOBBS TAKES A VACATION(1962); WHAT A WAY TO GO(1964); BIRDS AND THE BEES, THE(1965); DO NOT DISTURB(1965); SERGEANT DEADHEAD(1965)
Robert Gardiner
MAIDSTONE(1970)
Paul Gardini
HUMPHREY TAKES A CHANCE(1950); VICIOUS YEARS, THE(1950)
Alice Gardner
MALE AND FEMALE SINCE ADAM AND EVE(1961, Arg.)
Anthony Gardner
HAVING A WILD WEEKEND(1965, Brit.); MISTER TEN PERCENT(1967, Brit.); ISADORA(1968, Brit.)
1984
SCANDALOUS(1984)
Arthur Gardner
HEART OF THE NORTH(1938); EACH DAWN I DIE(1939); MADE FOR EACH OTHER(1939); MYSTIC CIRCLE MURDER(1939); WATERFRONT(1939); HARD GUY(1941); I WANTED WINGS(1941); NAVY BLUES(1941); YOU'RE IN THE ARMY NOW(1941); WITHOUT WARNING(1952), p; VICE SQUAD(1953), p; DOWN THREE DARK STREETS(1954), p; MONSTER THAT CHALLENGED THE WORLD, THE(1957), p; VAMPIRE, THE(1957), a, p; FLAME BARRIER, THE(1958), p; RETURN OF DRACULA, THE(1958), p; GLORY GUYS, THE(1965), p; CLAMBAKE(1967), p; SCALPHUNTERS, THE(1968), p; SAM WHISKEY(1969), p; MC KENZIE BREAK, THE(1970), p; UNDERGROUND(1970, Brit.), p; HONKERS, THE(1972), p; WHITE LIGHTNING(1973), p; MC Q(1974), p; BRANNIGAN(1975, Brit.), p; GATOR(1976), p; SAFARI 3000(1982), p, w
Ava Gardner
H.M. PULHAM, ESQ.(1941); CALLING DR. GILLESPIE(1942); JOE SMITH, AMERICAN(1942); KID GLOVE KILLER(1942); REUNION IN FRANCE(1942); SUNDAY PUNCH(1942); THIS TIME FOR KEEPS(1942); WE WERE DANCING(1942); DU BARRY WAS A LADY(1943); GHOSTS ON THE LOOSE(1943); HITLER'S MADMAN(1943); PILOT NO. 5(1943); SWING FEVER(1943); YOUNG IDEAS(1943); LOST ANGEL(1944); MAISIE GOES TO RENO(1944); THREE MEN IN WHITE(1944); TWO GIRLS AND A SAILOR(1944); SHE WENT TO THE RACES(1945); KILLERS, THE(1946); WHISTLE STOP(1946); HUCKSTERS, THE(1947); SINGAPORE(1947); ONE TOUCH OF VENUS(1948); BRIBE, THE(1949); EAST SIDE, WEST SIDE(1949); GREAT SINNER, THE(1949); MY FORBIDDEN PAST(1951); PANDORA AND THE FLYING DUTCHMAN(1951, Brit.); SHOW BOAT(1951); LONE STAR(1952); SNOWS OF KILIMANJARO, THE(1952); BAND WAGON, THE(1953); KNIGHTS OF THE ROUND TABLE(1953); MOGAMBO(1953); RIDE, VAQUERO!(1953); BAREFOOT CONTESSA, THE(1954); AROUND THE WORLD IN 80 DAYS(1956); BHOWANI JUNCTION(1956); LITTLE HUT, THE(1957); SUN ALSO RISES, THE(1957); NAKED MAJA, THE(1959, Ital./U.S.); ON THE BEACH(1959); ANGEL WORE RED, THE(1960); 55 DAYS AT PEKING(1963); NIGHT OF THE IGUANA, THE(1964); SEVEN DAYS IN MAY(1964); BIBLE...IN THE BEGINNING, THE(1966); MAYERLING(1968, Brit./Fr.); DEVIL'S WIDOW, THE(1972, Brit.); LIFE AND TIMES OF JUDGE ROY BEAN, THE(1972); EARTHQUAKE(1974); PERMISSION TO KILL(1975, U.S./Aust.); BLUE BIRD, THE(1976); CASSANDRA CROSSING, THE(1977); SENTINEL, THE(1977); CITY ON FIRE(1979 Can.); KIDNAPPING OF THE PRESIDENT, THE(1980, Can.); PRIEST OF LOVE(1981, Brit.)
Bert Gardner
Silents
SPRINGTIME(1915)
Beverly Gardner
BLACK ANGELS, THE(1970)
Bob Gardner
Misc. Talkies
MAN ON A MISSION(1965), d
Buster Gardner
Silents
CIRCUS ACE, THE(1927); TUMBLING RIVER(1927)
Misc. Silents
EYES OF THE FOREST(1923); BEST BAD MAN, THE(1925); CRASHING THROUGH(1928)
Carol Gardner
BRIGAND OF KANDAHAR, THE(1965, Brit.)

Caron Gardner
EVIL OF FRANKENSTEIN, THE(1964, Brit.); GUTTER GIRLS(1964, Brit.); TRAITOR'S GATE(1966, Brit./Ger.); LOVE IS A WOMAN(1967, Brit.)
Charles Gardner
HONG KONG NIGHTS(1935), art d
Misc. Silents
UNEASY MONEY(1918)
Craig Gardner
DEMON, THE(1981, S. Africa); SAFARI 3000(1982)
Cyril Gardner
TRESPASSER, THE(1929), ed; GRUMPY(1930), d; ONLY SAPS WORK(1930), d; ROYAL FAMILY OF BROADWAY, THE(1930), d; RECKLESS LIVING(1931), p, w; DOOMED BATTALION, THE(1932), d; PERFECT UNDERSTANDING(1933, Brit.), d; BIG BUSINESS(1934, Brit.), d, w; DESIGNING WOMEN(1934, Brit.); WIDOW'S MIGHT(1934, Brit.), d; CHICK(1936, Brit.), w; ON THE BEACH(1959)
David Gardner
"EQUUS"(1977); PROM NIGHT(1980); WHO HAS SEEN THE WIND(1980, Can.); CLASS OF 1984(1982, Can.); IF YOU COULD SEE WHAT I HEAR(1982)
Misc. Talkies
BETHUNE(1977)
Dee Gardner
APRIL FOOLS, THE(1969)
Diane Gardner
GIGOT(1962)
Dick Gardner
DESK SET(1957)
Dolores Gardner
Misc. Silents
TRIPLE ACTION(1925); DESPERATE GAME, THE(1926)
Dorothy Gardner
UP IN ARMS(1944)
Ed Gardner
DUFFY'S TAVERN(1945), a, w
Edward F. Gardner
MAN WITH MY FACE, THE(1951), p
Erle Stanley Gardner
CASE OF THE HOWLING DOG, THE(1934), w; CASE OF THE CURIOUS BRIDE, THE(1935), w; CASE OF THE LUCKY LEGS, THE(1935), w; CASE OF THE BLACK CAT, THE(1936), w; CASE OF THE VELVET CLAWS, THE(1936), w; SPECIAL INVESTIGATOR(1936), w; CASE OF THE STUTTERING BISHOP, THE(1937), w; GRANNY GET YOUR GUN(1940), w
Frank Gardner
GUN HAWK, THE(1963); IT HAPPENED HERE(1966, Brit.)
Fred Gardner
ZABRISKIE POINT(1970), w
Gerald Gardner
WHICH WAY TO THE FRONT?(1970), w; WORLD'S GREATEST ATHLETE, THE(1973), w
Geraldine Gardner
NUTCRACKER(1982, Brit.)
Gladys Gardner
HEART OF THE RIO GRANDE(1942)
Gloria Gardner
HEART OF THE RIO GRANDE(1942)
Harvey Gardner
YOUNG DILLINGER(1965)
Helen Gardner
Silents
SYLVIA GRAY(1914)
Misc. Silents
CLEOPATRA(1913); PRINCESS OF BAGDAD(1913); DEVIL'S ANGEL, THE(1920)
Herb Gardner
THOUSAND CLOWNS, A(1965), w; WHO IS HARRY KELLERMAN AND WHY IS HE SAYING THOSE TERRIBLE THINGS ABOUT ME?(1971), p, w; THIEVES(1977), w
1984
GOODBYE PEOPLE, THE(1984), d&w
Hunter Gardner
GAMBLING(1934)
Hy Gardner
GIRL HUNTERS, THE(1963, Brit.)
Ivanetta Gardner
ISN'T IT ROMANTIC?(1948)
Jack Gardner
TRUE TO LIFE(1943); DR. SOCRATES(1935); SHE COULDN'T TAKE IT(1935); SHE MARRIED HER BOSS(1935); BULLETS OR BALLOTS(1936); GIRL WITH IDEAS, A(1937); SPEED TO SPARE(1937); STAGE DOOR(1937); COCOANUT GROVE(1938); GANGSTER'S BOY(1938); MIDNIGHT INTRUDER(1938); RECKLESS LIVING(1938); SWEETHEARTS(1938); YOU CAN'T TAKE IT WITH YOU(1938); FOR LOVE OR MONEY(1939); FORGOTTEN WOMAN, THE(1939); HELL'S KITCHEN(1939); HERO FOR A DAY(1939); I STOLE A MILLION(1939); LAUGH IT OFF(1939); MR. SMITH GOES TO WASHINGTON(1939); ONE HOUR TO LIVE(1939); PIRATES OF THE SKIES(1939); WINGS OF THE NAVY(1939); YOU CAN'T CHEAT AN HONEST MAN(1939); DANGER ON WHEELS(1940); MY SON IS GUILTY(1940); PRIMROSE PATH(1940); TWO GIRLS ON BROADWAY(1940); FACE BEHIND THE MASK, THE(1941); FOUR JACKS AND A JILL(1941); MEET JOHN DOE(1941); MEXICAN SPITFIRE'S BABY(1941); MR. AND MRS. SMITH(1941); YOU'RE IN THE ARMY NOW(1941); GLASS KEY, THE(1942); HITLER—DEAD OR ALIVE(1942); I MARRIED A WITCH(1942); JUKE GIRL(1942); LADY BODYGUARD(1942); LADY IN A JAM(1942); LUCKY LEGS(1942); MADAME SPY(1942); MAYOR OF 44TH STREET, THE(1942); SABOTAGE SQUAD(1942); SABOTEUR(1942); SEVEN DAYS LEAVE(1942); SPIRIT OF STANFORD, THE(1942); STRICTLY IN THE GROOVE(1942); TALK OF THE TOWN(1942); THERE'S ONE BORN EVERY MINUTE(1942); YOU'RE TELLING ME(1942); AIR RAID WARDENS(1943); FLESH AND FANTASY(1943); HENRY ALDRICH HAUNTS A HOUSE(1943); HONEYMOON LODGE(1943); LARCENY WITH MUSIC(1943); MISSION TO MOSCOW(1943); NO TIME FOR LOVE(1943); PILOT NO. 5(1943); SALUTE FOR THREE(1943); SHE HAS WHAT IT TAKES(1943); SO'S YOUR UNCLE(1943); THREE RUSSIAN GIRLS(1943); IT HAPPENED TOMORROW(1944); LOUISIANA HAYRIDE(1944); MAN FROM FRISCO(1944); MY BUDDY(1944); SINCE YOU WENT AWAY(1944); WHAT A MAN!(1944); MEDAL FOR

BENNY, A(1945); THOROUGHBREDS(1945); WOMAN IN THE WINDOW, THE(1945); REDHEAD FROM MANHATTAN(1954); MARK OF THE WITCH(1970)
Silents
NIGHT WORKERS, THE(1917); YOUTH TO YOUTH(1922); BLUFF(1924); SCARLET SEAS(1929), ed
Misc. Silents
GIFT O' GAB(1917); LAND OF LONG SHADOWS(1917); MEN OF THE DESERT(1917); OPEN PLACES(1917); RANGE BOSS, THE(1917)
Janet Gardner
1984
HARDBODIES(1984)
Jimmy Gardner
CURSE OF THE MUMMY'S TOMB, THE(1965, Brit.); HE WHO RIDES A TIGER(1966, Brit.); MURDER GAME, THE(1966, Brit.); COMMITTEE, THE(1968, Brit.); TAKE A GIRL LIKE YOU(1970, Brit.); SAY HELLO TO YESTERDAY(1971, Brit.); 10 RILLINGTON PLACE(1971, Brit.); 11 HARROWHOUSE(1974, Brit.); FLAME(1975, Brit.)
Joan Gardner
WEDDING REHEARSAL(1932, Brit.); MAN OUTSIDE, THE(1933, Brit.); CATHERINE THE GREAT(1934, Brit.); PRIVATE LIFE OF DON JUAN, THE(1934, Brit.); BARNACLE BILL(1935, Brit.); MEN OF TOMORROW(1935, Brit.); SCARLET PIMPERNEL, THE(1935, Brit.); DARK JOURNEY(1937, Brit.); FOREVER YOURS(1937, Brit.); MAN WHO COULD WORK MIRACLES, THE(1937, Brit.); GIRL THIEF, THE(1938); CHALLENGE, THE(1939, Brit.); REBEL SON, THE ½(1939, Brit.); WINGS OVER AFRICA(1939); BEACH GIRLS AND THE MONSTER, THE(1965), w; MR. MAGOO'S HOLIDAY FESTIVAL(1970)
John Gardner
LIQUIDATOR, THE(1966, Brit.), w; STONE KILLER, THE(1973), w; GRENDEL GRENDEL GRENDEL(1981, Aus.), d&w
Jon Gardner
CARBINE WILLIAMS(1952); MEET ME AT THE FAIR(1952); TALK ABOUT A STRANGER(1952); MA AND PA KETTLE ON VACATION(1953); MR. SCOUTMASTER(1953); MA AND PA KETTLE AT WAIKIKI(1955)
Karal Gardner
NEVER PUT IT IN WRITING(1964)
Kenny Gardner
MR. BUG GOES TO TOWN(1941)
Leonard Gardner
FAT CITY(1972), w
Lois Gardner
Misc. Silents
RESTITUTION(1918)
Louanna Gardner
BLACK SLEEP, THE(1956)
Luana Gardner
Misc. Talkies
ASSASSIN OF YOUTH(1937)
Marilyn Gardner
THRESHOLD(1983, Can.)
Marvin Gardner
RAGGEDY MAN(1981)
Marylin Gardner
AGENCY(1981, Can.)
Max Gardner
ROB ROY, THE HIGHLAND ROGUE(1954, Brit.)
Mitchel Gardner
NUTCRACKER FANTASY(1979)
Muriel Gardner
WORDS AND MUSIC(1929)
Nadine Gardner
1984
FINDERS KEEPERS(1984)
Nancy Gardner
DOCTORS' WIVES(1931)
Paul Gardner
TEN DAYS' WONDER(1972, Fr.), w; BUSTIN' LOOSE(1981)
Ralph Gardner
FOLLOW THE BOYS(1944); TWO GIRLS AND A SAILOR(1944)
Raymond Gardner
1984
GOODBYE PEOPLE, THE(1984)
Richard Gardner
YOUNG LIONS, THE(1958); HELL TO ETERNITY(1960); RISE AND FALL OF LEGS DIAMOND, THE(1960); SCANDALOUS JOHN(1971), w
Rita Gardner
ONE PLUS ONE(1961, Can.)
Robert Gardner
CLARENCE AND ANGEL(1981), p,d&w
Shayle Gardner
DISRAELI(1929); THREE LIVE GHOSTS(1929); RETURN OF DR. FU MANCHU, THE(1930); BLAME THE WOMAN(1932, Brit.); RIVER HOUSE GHOST, THE(1932, Brit.); WHEN LONDON SLEEPS(1934, Brit.); HER LAST AFFAIRE(1935, Brit.); LOVE TEST, THE(1935, Brit.); PHANTOM FIEND, THE(1935, Brit.); BROWN WALLET, THE(1936, Brit.); WOLF'S CLOTHING(1936, Brit.); UNDER THE RED ROBE(1937, Brit.); DISCOVERIES(1939, Brit.)
Silents
INDIAN LOVE LYRICS, THE(1923, Brit.); ST. ELMO(1923, Brit.); CHINESE BUNGALOW, THE(1926, Brit.); ALLEY CAT, THE(1929, Brit.)
Misc. Silents
COMIN' THRO' THE RYE(1923, Brit.); GUY FAWKES(1923, Brit.); CHINESE BUNGALOW, THE(1926, Brit.); THREE PASSIONS, THE(1928, Brit.); TOMMY ATKINS(1928, Brit.)
Stu Gardner
KLANSMAN, THE(1974), m
Tony Gardner
2000 YEARS LATER(1969); STATUE, THE(1971, Brit.)
Virginia Gardner
LADY OF BURLESQUE(1943); COVER GIRL(1944)

Luigi Gardneri
RIGHT HAND OF THE DEVIL, THE(1963)
Helen Gardom
WEDDING REHEARSAL(1932, Brit.), w
Lajos Gardonyi
HIPPOLYT, THE LACKEY(1932, Hung.)
Eva Gardos
1984
CITY GIRL, THE(1984), ed; JOY OF SEX(1984), ed
Pierre Gare
CONFIDENTIALLY YOURS(1983, Fr.)
S. Garel
RESURRECTION(1963, USSR)
Maurice Garell
BRIDE WORE BLACK, THE(1968, Fr./Ital.)
Peter Garell
PERMISSION TO KILL(1975, U.S./Aust.)
Leo Garen
MAIDSTONE(1970); HEX(1973), d, w
Curt Gareth
VERY NATURAL THING, A(1974)
Simi Garewal
SIDDHARTHA(1972)
James R. Garey
Silents
BATTLE OF LIFE, THE(1916), w
Peter Garey
SONG FOR MISS JULIE, A(1945); YOUNG WIDOW(1946)
Renee Garey
DOCTEUR LAENNEC(1949, Fr.), ed
Gene Garf
MAN OR GUN(1958), m
Alec Garfath
VILLAIN(1971, Brit.), makeup
Alex Garfath
WATCH YOUR STERN(1961, Brit.), makeup; WHAT A CARVE UP!(1962, Brit.), makeup; TOM JONES(1963, Brit.), makeup; SECRET CEREMONY(1968, Brit.), makeup; LEO THE LAST(1970, Brit.), makeup; X Y & ZEE(1972, Brit.), makeup
Jack Garfein
STRANGE ONE, THE(1957), d; SOMETHING WILD(1961), d, w
Juanita Garfias
STORM OVER THE ANDES(1935)
Alan Garfield
DEADHEAD MILES(1982)
Allan Garfield
Misc. Talkies
GOOD, THE BAD, AND THE BEAUTIFUL, THE(1975)
Allen Garfield
MARCH OF THE SPRING HARE(1969); HI, MOM!(1970); BANANAS(1971); BELIEVE IN ME(1971); ROOMMATES(1971); TAKING OFF(1971); CANDIDATE, THE(1972); SLITHER(1973); BUSTING(1974); CONVERSATION, THE(1974); FRONT PAGE, THE(1974); COMMITMENT, THE(1976)
1984
COTTON CLUB, THE(1984); TEACHERS(1984)
Misc. Talkies
CRY UNCLE(1973); PACO(1976); FYRE(1979)
Allen Garfield "Goorwitz"
PUTNEY SWOPE(1969); OWL AND THE PUSSYCAT, THE(1970); ORGANIZATION, THE(1971); YOU'VE GOT TO WALK IT LIKE YOU TALK IT OR YOU'LL LOSE THAT BEAT(1971); TOP OF THE HEAP(1972); NASHVILLE(1975); GABLE AND LOMBARD(1976); MOTHER, JUGS & SPEED(1976); SKATEBOARD(1978)
1984
IRRECONCILABLE DIFFERENCES(1984)
Brian Garfield
DEATH WISH(1974), w; LAST HARD MEN, THE(1976), w; HOPSCOTCH(1980), w; DEATH WISH II(1982), w
1984
FLESHBURN(1984), w
David Garfield
PROMISE, THE(1969, Brit.); HOT TOMORROWS(1978); ROSE, THE(1979); HERO AT LARGE(1980), ed; CHOSEN, THE(1982), ed; ALL THE RIGHT MOVES(1983), ed; STING II, THE(1983), ed
1984
FLASHPOINT(1984), ed
Frank Garfield
ZOMBIE CREEPING FLESH(1981, Ital./Span.); NIGHT OF THE ZOMBIES(1983, Span./Ital.)
Frank Garfield [Franco Giraldi]
SEVEN GUNS FOR THE MACGREGORS(1968, Ital./Span.), d
James Garfield
EVIL OF FRANKENSTEIN, THE(1964, Brit.)
John Garfield
FOOTLIGHT PARADE(1933); FOUR DAUGHTERS(1938); BLACKWELL'S ISLAND(1939); DAUGHTERS COURAGEOUS(1939); DUST BE MY DESTINY(1939); FOUR WIVES(1939); JUAREZ(1939); THEY MADE ME A CRIMINAL(1939); CASTLE ON THE HUDSON(1940); EAST OF THE RIVER(1940); FLOWING GOLD(1940); SATURDAY'S CHILDREN(1940); OUT OF THE FOG(1941); SEA WOLF, THE(1941); DANGEROUSLY THEY LIVE(1942); TORTILLA FLAT(1942); AIR FORCE(1943); FALLEN SPARROW, THE(1943); THANK YOUR LUCKY STARS(1943); BETWEEN TWO WORLDS(1944); DESTINATION TOKYO(1944); HOLLYWOOD CANTEEN(1944); PRIDE OF THE MARINES(1945); HUMORESQUE(1946); NOBODY LIVES FOREVER(1946); POSTMAN ALWAYS RINGS TWICE, THE(1946); BODY AND SOUL(1947); DAISY KENYON(1947); GENTLEMAN'S AGREEMENT(1947); FORCE OF EVIL(1948); JIGSAW(1949); WE WERE STRANGERS(1949); BREAKING POINT, THE(1950); DIFFICULT YEARS(1950, Ital.); UNDER MY SKIN(1950); HE RAN ALL THE WAY(1951)
John Garfield, Jr.
WARNING SHOT(1967); SWIMMER, THE(1968); MACKENNA'S GOLD(1969); THAT COLD DAY IN THE PARK(1969, U.S./Can.)

John D. Garfield
GOLDEN VOYAGE OF SINBAD, THE(1974, Brit.)
John David Garfield
OTHER SIDE OF THE MOUNTAIN, THE(1975); WHITE LINE FEVER(1975, Can.)
Johnny Garfield
CADDIE(1976, Aus.); ODD ANGRY SHOT, THE(1979, Aus.)
Julie Garfield
JOHN AND MARY(1969); LOVE STORY(1970); REVOLUTIONARY, THE(1970, Brit.); HOSPITAL, THE(1971); FRONT, THE(1976); KING OF THE GYPSIES(1978)
Leon Garfield
BLACK JACK(1979, Brit.), w
Michael Garfield
WARRIORS, THE(1979)
Warren Garfield
STRANGER IN TOWN, A(1968, U.S./Ital.), w
David Garfinkel
ESCAPE TO THE SUN(1972, Fr./Ger./Israel), ph
Gail Garfinkle
TULIPS(1981, Can)
Gayle Garfinkle
OH, HEAVENLY DOG!(1980); OF UNKNOWN ORIGIN(1983, Can.)
1984
HOTEL NEW HAMPSHIRE, THE(1984)
Louis Garfinkle
YOUNG GUNS, THE(1956), w; I BURY THE LIVING(1958), p, w; FACE OF FIRE(1959, U.S./Brit.), p, w; HELLBENDERS, THE(1967, U.S./Ital./Span.), w; MINUTE TO PRAY, A SECOND TO DIE, A(1968, Ital.), w; DOBERMAN GANG, THE(1972), w; LITTLE CIGARS(1973), w; DEER HUNTER, THE(1978), w
Art Garfunkel
CATCH-22(1970)
Arthur Garfunkel
CARNAL KNOWLEDGE(1971)
Beatrice Garga
Silents
METROPOLIS(1927, Ger.)
Danny Gargan
BLONDIE FOR VICTORY(1942)
Ed Gargan
TARNISHED LADY(1931); ADVENTURES OF GALLANT BESS(1948); GIRL HABIT(1931); MARY STEVENS, M.D.(1933); QUEEN CHRISTINA(1933); REGISTERED NURSE(1934); TWENTIETH CENTURY(1934); MAN ON THE FLYING TRAPEZE, THE(1935); DANGEROUS WATERS(1936); GREAT GUY(1936); NOBODY'S FOOL(1936); STAGE STRUCK(1936); TWO IN A CROWD(1936); GIRL WITH IDEAS, A(1937); GO-GETTER, THE(1937); WAKE UP AND LIVE(1937); CRIME SCHOOL(1938); DEVIL'S PARTY, THE(1938); STRAIGHT, PLACE AND SHOW(1938); THANKS FOR THE MEMORY(1938); PACK UP YOUR TROUBLES(1939); SPELLBINDER, THE(1939); CHARLIE CHAN IN PANAMA(1940); CHILD IS BORN, A(1940); GIRL FROM GOD'S COUNTRY(1940); JOHNNY APOLLO(1940); SPRING PARADE(1940); STREET OF MEMORIES(1940); THREE CHEERS FOR THE IRISH(1940); CITY, FOR CONQUEST(1941); DATE WITH THE FALCON, A(1941); MEET THE CHUMP(1941); MILLION DOLLAR BABY(1941); SAN FRANCISCO DOCKS(1941); TIGHT SHOES(1941); FALCON TAKES OVER, THE(1942); FALCON'S BROTHER, THE(1942); MY FAVORITE BLONDE(1942); OVER MY DEAD BODY(1942); FALCON AND THE CO-EDS, THE(1943); FALCON IN DANGER, THE(1943); FALCON STRIKES BACK, THE(1943); THANK YOUR LUCKY STARS(1943); FALCON OUT WEST, THE(1944); ONCE UPON A TIME(1944); THIN MAN GOES HOME, THE(1944); BULLFIGHTERS, THE(1945); FOLLOW THAT WOMAN(1945); HIGH POWERED(1945); NAUGHTY NINETIES, THE(1945); SHE WOULDN'T SAY YES(1945); SING YOUR WAY HOME(1945); CINDERELLA JONES(1946); CRACK-UP(1946); DEADLINE AT DAWN(1946); LITTLE GIANT(1946); IT HAPPENED ON 5TH AVENUE(1947); WEB OF DANGER, THE(1947); SOUTHERN YANKEE, A(1948); RED LIGHT(1949); FATHER OF THE BRIDE(1950); BEDTIME FOR BONZO(1951)
Edward Gargan
GAMBLING SHIP(1933); GIRL IN 419(1933); THREE-CORNERED MOON(1933); BELLE OF THE NINETIES(1934); GOOD DAME(1934); LEMON DROP KID, THE(1934); WE LIVE AGAIN(1934); WILD GOLD(1934); BEHIND GREEN LIGHTS(1935); BEHOLD MY WIFE(1935); CEILNG ZERO(1935); FALSE PRETENSES(1935); GILDED LILY, THE(1935); HANDS ACROSS THE TABLE(1935); HOLD'EM YALE(1935); IRISH IN US, THE(1935); PORT OF LOST DREAMS(1935); TWO FOR TONIGHT(1935); WE'RE IN THE MONEY(1935); ANYTHING GOES(1936); BRIDE COMES HOME(1936); GRAND JURY(1936); HEARTS IN BONDAGE(1936); MR. DEEDS GOES TO TOWN(1936); MY MAN GODFREY(1936); ROAMING LADY(1936); UNDER YOUR SPELL(1936); DANGER PATROL(1937); HIGH, WIDE AND HANDSOME(1937); JIM HANVEY, DETECTIVE(1937); MAN WHO FOUND HIMSELF, THE(1937); THAT'S MY STORY(1937); WE'RE ON THE JURY(1937); YOU CAN'T BUY LUCK(1937); AMAZING DR. CLITTERHOUSE, THE(1938); ANNABEL TAKES A TOUR(1938); BRINGING UP BABY(1938); TEXANS, THE(1938); UP THE RIVER(1938); WHILE NEW YORK SLEEPS(1938); ANOTHER THIN MAN(1939); CAFE SOCIETY(1939); FIXER DUGAN(1939); FOR LOVE OR MONEY(1939); HONOLULU(1939); LUCKY NIGHT(1939); NEWSBOY'S HOME(1939); NIGHT WORK(1939); SAINT STRIKES BACK, THE(1939); THEY ALL COME OUT(1939); YES, MY DARLING DAUGHTER(1939); $1,000 A TOUCHDOWN(1939); 20,000 MEN A YEAR(1939); ADVENTURE IN DIAMONDS(1940); BOWERY BOY(1940); BROTHER RAT AND A BABY(1940); DOCTOR TAKES A WIFE(1940); LONE WOLF KEEPS A DATE, THE(1940); NORTHWEST PASSAGE(1940); QUEEN OF THE MOB(1940); ROAD TO SINGAPORE(1940); SUSAN AND GOD(1940); WOLF OF NEW YORK(1940); AFFECTIONATELY YOURS(1941); DR. KILDARE'S VICTORY(1941); HERE COMES HAPPINESS(1941); LADY BE GOOD(1941); THIEVES FALL OUT(1941); TILLIE THE TOILER(1941); A-HAUNTING WE WILL GO(1942); FLY BY NIGHT(1942); FLYING WITH MUSIC(1942); MEET THE STEWARTS(1942); THEY ALL KISSED THE BRIDE(1942); HIT THE ICE(1943); IN OLD OKLAHOMA(1943); MY KINGDOM FOR A COOK(1943); PRINCESS O'ROURKE(1943); THEY GOT ME COVERED(1943); WEST SIDE KID(1943); DETECTIVE KITTY O'DAY(1944); SAN FERNANDO VALLEY(1944); DANGEROUS PARTNERS(1945); DIAMOND HORSESHOE(1945); EARL CARROLL'S VANITIES(1945); HER HIGHNESS AND THE BELLBOY(1945); SPORTING CHANCE, A(1945); WONDER MAN(1945); BEAUTIFUL CHEAT, THE(1946); BEHIND THE MASK(1946); DARK HORSE, THE(1946); GAY BLADES(1946); INNER CIRCLE, THE(1946); LIFE WITH BLONDIE(1946); BRASHER DOUBLOON, THE(1947); EXPOSED(1947); GHOST GOES WILD, THE(1947); LINDA BE GOOD(1947); SADDLE PALS(1947); THAT'S MY GAL(1947); TROUBLE WITH WOMEN, THE(1947); CAMPUS

HONEYMOON(1948); DAREDEVILS OF THE CLOUDS(1948); DUDE GOES WEST, THE(1948); SCUDDA-HOO! SCUDDA-HAY!(1948); SMART WOMAN(1948); STRIKE IT RICH(1948); YOU GOTTA STAY HAPPY(1948); HOLD THAT BABY!(1949); BELLE OF OLD MEXICO(1950); HIT PARADE OF 1951(1950); SQUARE DANCE KATY(1950); TRIPLE TROUBLE(1950); ABBOTT AND COSTELLO MEET THE INVISIBLE MAN(1951); CUBAN FIREBALL(1951)

Edward P. Gargan
LITTLE MISS BROADWAY(1947)

Edwin Gargan
SHE HAD TO CHOOSE(1934)

Jack Gargan
THEY WON'T BELIEVE ME(1947); STAGE DOOR(1937); CITY GIRL(1938); INVITATION TO HAPPINESS(1939); LADIES' DAY(1943); MR. LUCKY(1943); CASANOVA BROWN(1944); DICK TRACY(1945); WEST OF THE PECOS(1945); WOMAN IN THE WINDOW, THE(1945); BLUE DAHLIA, THE(1946); DARK MIRROR, THE(1946); FROM THIS DAY FORWARD(1946); KID FROM BOOKLYN, THE(1946); LIKELY STORY, A(1947); NIGHT SONG(1947); SECRET LIFE OF WALTER MITTY, THE(1947); WEB, THE(1947); EMPEROR WALTZ, THE(1948); GOOD SAM(1948); JOAN OF ARC(1948); LETTER FROM AN UNKNOWN WOMAN(1948); SONG IS BORN, A(1948); THAT WONDERFUL URGE(1948); WALLS OF JERICHO(1948); CHICAGO DEADLINE(1949); EAST SIDE, WEST SIDE(1949); GIRL FROM JONES BEACH, THE(1949); GREAT GATSBY, THE(1949); LOOK FOR THE SILVER LINING(1949); ONCE MORE, MY DARLING(1949); KISS TOMORROW GOODBYE(1950); MAGNIFICENT YANKEE, THE(1950); PEGGY(1950); SUMMER STOCK(1950); UNION STATION(1950); DOUBLE DYNAMITE(1951); RACKET, THE(1951); THREE GUYS NAMED MIKE(1951); TOO YOUNG TO KISS(1951); TWO TICKETS TO BROADWAY(1951); UNKNOWN MAN, THE(1951); CARRIE(1952); MEET ME AT THE FAIR(1952); SHE'S WORKING HER WAY THROUGH COLLEGE(1952); VICKI(1953); I'LL CRY TOMORROW(1955); MISTER CORY(1957); PARTY GIRL(1958)

William Gargan
FOLLOW THE LEADER(1930); ANIMAL KINGDOM, THE(1932); MISLEADING LADY, THE(1932); RAIN(1932); SPORT PARADE, THE(1932); AGGIE APPLEBY, MAKER OF MEN(1933); EMERGENCY CALL(1933); HEADLINE SHOOTER(1933); LUCKY DEVILS(1933); NIGHT FLIGHT(1933); STORY OF TEMPLE DRAKE, THE(1933); SWEEPINGS(1933); BRITISH AGENT(1934); FOUR FRIGHTENED PEOPLE(1934); LINEUP, THE(1934); STRICTLY DYNAMITE(1934); THINGS ARE LOOKING UP(1934, Brit.); BLACK FURY(1935); BRIGHT LIGHTS(1935); BROADWAY GONDOLIER(1935); DON'T BET ON BLONDES(1935); NIGHT AT THE RITZ, A(1935); TRAVELING SALESLADY, THE(1935); ALIBI FOR MURDER(1936); BLACKMAILER(1936); FLYING HOSTESS(1936); MAN HUNT(1936); MILKY WAY, THE(1936); NAVY BORN(1936); SKY PARADE(1936); BEHIND THE MIKE(1937); BREEZING HOME(1937); FURY AND THE WOMAN(1937); REPORTED MISSING(1937); SHE ASKED FOR IT(1937); SOME BLONDES ARE DANGEROUS(1937); WINGS OVER HONOLULU(1937); YOU ONLY LIVE ONCE(1937); YOU'RE A SWEETHEART(1937); CRIME OF DR. HALLET(1938); CROWD ROARS, THE(1938); DEVIL'S PARTY, THE(1938); PERSONAL SECRETARY(1938); ADVENTURES OF JANE ARDEN(1939); BROADWAY SERENADE(1939); HOUSE OF FEAR, THE(1939); HOUSEKEEPER'S DAUGHTER(1939); JOE AND ETHEL TURP CALL ON THE PRESIDENT(1939); THREE SONS(1939); WITHIN THE LAW(1939); WOMEN IN THE WIND(1939); DOUBLE ALIBI(1940); ISLE OF DESTINY(1940); SPORTING BLOOD(1940); STAR DUST(1940); THEY KNEW WHAT THEY WANTED(1940); TURNABOUT(1940); CHEERS FOR MISS BISHOP(1941); FLYING CADETS(1941); KEEP 'EM FLYING(1941); SEALED LIPS(1941); BOMBAY CLIPPER(1942); CLOSE CALL FOR ELLERY QUEEN, A(1942); DESPERATE CHANCE FOR ELLERY QUEEN, A(1942); DESTINATION UNKNOWN(1942); ENEMY AGENTS MEET ELLERY QUEEN(1942); I WAKE UP SCREAMING(1942); MAYOR OF 44TH STREET, THE(1942); MISS ANNIE ROONEY(1942); WHO DONE IT?(1942); HARRIGAN'S KID(1943); NO PLACE FOR A LADY(1943); SWING FEVER(1943); CANTERVILLE GHOST, THE(1944); BELLS OF ST. MARY'S, THE(1945); FOLLOW THAT WOMAN(1945); ONE EXCITING NIGHT(1945); SHE GETS HER MAN(1945); SONG OF THE SARONG(1945); BEHIND GREEN LIGHTS(1946); HOT CARGO(1946); MURDER IN THE MUSIC HALL(1946); NIGHT EDITOR(1946); RENDEZVOUS 24(1946); STRANGE IMPERSONATION(1946); SWELL GUY(1946); TILL THE END OF TIME(1946); ARGYLE SECRETS, THE(1948); DYNAMITE(1948); WATERFRONT AT MIDNIGHT(1948); MIRACLE IN THE RAIN(1956); RAWHIDE YEARS, THE(1956)

Omero Gargano
GIANT OF METROPOLIS, THE(1963, Ital.); SEVEN TASKS OF ALI BABA, THE(1963, Ital.)

Leon Garganoff
BATTLE, THE(1934, Fr.), p

Antonio Gargas
1984
FIRESTARTER(1984)

Bruno Gargin
MAGNIFICENT ONE, THE(1974, Fr./Ital.)

Giorgio Gargiullo
WILD EYE, THE(1968, Ital.); DAY OF ANGER(1970, Ital./Ger.)

A. Gargiulo
VORTEX(1982), makeup

Arnold Gargiulo
LUGGAGE OF THE GODS(1983), makeup

Jean Gargoet
I AM A CAMERA(1955, Brit.)

Jean Gargonne
1984
A NOS AMOURS(1984, Fr.), ed

Mario Gariazzo
TORMENTED, THE(1978, Ital.), d

Piero Antonio Gariazzo
Misc. Silents
AFTER SIX DAYS(1922), d

Antonio Garibaldi
SPECIAL DAY, A(1977, Ital./Can.)

Emilio Garibay
ADVENTURES OF ROBINSON CRUSOE, THE(1954)

Ricardo Garibay
LA CUCARACHA(1961, Mex.), w; LITTLE ANGEL(1961, Mex.), w; LITTLE RED RIDING HOOD(1963, Mex.), w

George Gariblan
ONCE THERE WAS A GIRL(1945, USSR), ph

Gregory Garibyan
SON OF THE REGIMENT(1948, USSR), ph

A. Garichev
GORDEYEV FAMILY, THE(1961, U.S.S.R.)

E. Garin
CZAR WANTS TO SLEEP(1934, U.S., USSR)

Erast Garin
OPTIMISTIC TRAGEDY, THE(1964, USSR)

Tamara Garina
LIFE IN THE BALANCE, A(1955); MAN CALLED HORSE, A(1970)

Enzo Garinei
TWELVE-HANDED MEN OF MARS, THE(1964, Ital./Span.)

Gerard Garino
1984
BIZET'S CARMEN(1984, Fr./Ital.)

Buddy Garion
ICE STATION ZEBRA(1968); MARLOWE(1969); SLAUGHTER(1972)

Roger Garis
NEVER TAKE CANDY FROM A STRANGER(1961, Brit.), w

Jack Gariss
TEN COMMANDMENTS, THE(1956), w

Paul Garkie
NIGHT AND DAY(1946)

Gianni Garko
AVENGER, THE(1962, Fr./Ital.); CRAZY DESIRE(1964, Ital.); EIGHTEEN IN THE SUN(1964, Ital.); KAPO(1964, Ital./Fr./Yugo.); MONGOLS, THE(1966, Fr./Ital.); PONTIUS PILATE(1967, Fr./Ital.); SAUL AND DAVID(1968, Ital./Span.); WATERLOO(1970, Ital./USSR); PSYCHIC, THE(1979, Ital.); HERCULES(1983)

John Garko
BAD MAN'S RIVER(1972, Span.)

Misc. Talkies
ENCOUNTERS OF THE DEEP(1984)

Johnny Garko
THOSE DIRTY DOGS(1974, U.S./Ital./Span.)

Beverly Garland
LIFE OF HER OWN, A(1950); GLASS WEB, THE(1953); NEANDERTHAL MAN, THE(1953); PROBLEM GIRLS(1953); BITTER CREEK(1954); DESPERADO, THE(1954); KILLER LEOPARD(1954); MIAMI STORY, THE(1954); ROCKET MAN, THE(1954); TWO GUNS AND A BADGE(1954); DESPERATE HOURS, THE(1955); NEW ORLEANS UNCENSORED(1955); SUDDEN DANGER(1955); CURUCU, BEAST OF THE AMAZON(1956); GUNSLINGER(1956); IT CONQUERED THE WORLD(1956); STEEL JUNGLE, THE(1956); SWAMP WOMEN(1956); BADLANDS OF MONTANA(1957); CHICAGO CONFIDENTIAL(1957); JOKER IS WILD, THE(1957); NAKED PARADISE(1957); NOT OF THIS EARTH(1957); SAGA OF HEMP BROWN, THE(1958); ALLIGATOR PEOPLE, THE(1959); STARK FEAR(1963); TWICE TOLD TALES(1963); PRETTY POISON(1968); MAD ROOM, THE(1969); AIRPORT 1975(1974); WHERE THE RED FERN GROWS(1974); SIXTH AND MAIN(1977); ROLLER BOOGIE(1979); IT'S MY TURN(1980)

Bunty Garland
SWAPPERS, THE(1970, Brit.)

Charles Garland
DESPERADO, THE(1954)

Geoff Garland
HAMLET(1964)

Grace Garland
GAY INTRUDERS, THE(1946, Brit.), ed; BONNIE PRINCE CHARLIE(1948, Brit.), ed; NIGHT BEAT(1948, Brit.), ed

Hamlin Garland
Silents
CAPTAIN OF THE GRAY HORSE TROOP, THE(1917), w; MONEY MAGIC(1917), w; RANGER OF THE BIG PINES(1925), w

Jane Garland
LADY IN A JAM(1942)

Janet Garland
ROSEMARY'S BABY(1968)

Joe Garland
1984
PHILADELPHIA EXPERIMENT, THE(1984), m/1

Judy Garland
PIGSKIN PARADE(1936); BROADWAY MELODY OF '38(1937); THOROUGHBREDS DON'T CRY(1937); EVERYBODY SING(1938); LISTEN, DARLING(1938); LOVE FINDS ANDY HARDY(1938); BABES IN ARMS(1939); WIZARD OF OZ, THE(1939); ANDY HARDY MEETS DEBUTANTE(1940); LITTLE NELLIE KELLY(1940); STRIKE UP THE BAND(1940); BABES ON BROADWAY(1941); LIFE BEGINS FOR ANDY HARDY(1941); ZIEGFELD GIRL(1941); FOR ME AND MY GAL(1942); GIRL CRAZY(1943); PRESENTING LILY MARS(1943); THOUSANDS CHEER(1943); MEET ME IN ST. LOUIS(1944); CLOCK, THE(1945); ZIEGFELD FOLLIES(1945); HARVEY GIRLS, THE(1946); TILL THE CLOUDS ROLL BY(1946); EASTER PARADE(1948); PIRATE, THE(1948); IN THE GOOD OLD SUMMERTIME(1949); SUMMER STOCK(1950); STAR IS BORN, A(1954); PEPE(1960); JUDGMENT AT NUREMBERG(1961); GAY PURR-EE(1962); CHILD IS WAITING, A(1963); I COULD GO ON SINGING(1963)

Melenie Garland
GO KART GO(1964, Brit.)

Michel Garland
GOODBYE AGAIN(1961); CANDIDE(1962, Fr.); CLOPORTES(1966, Fr., Ital.); TREASURE ISLAND(1972, Brit./Span./Fr./Ger.); PAUL AND MICHELLE(1974, Fr./Brit.)

Nicholas Garland
ADVENTURES OF BARRY McKENZIE(1972, Austral.), w

Patrick Garland
DOLL'S HOUSE, A(1973), d

Richard Garland
CIMARRON KID, THE(1951); BATTLE AT APACHE PASS, THE(1952); LAWLESS BREED(1952); RED BALL EXPRESS(1952); UNTAMED FRONTIER(1952); COLUMN SOUTH(1953); FOREVER FEMALE(1953); TORPEDO ALLEY(1953); VICKI(1953); DAWN AT SOCORRO(1954); JESSE JAMES VERSUS THE DALTONS(1954); MAN FROM BITTER RIDGE, THE(1955); RAGE AT DAWN(1955); FRIENDLY PERSUASION(1956); ATTACK OF THE CRAB MONSTERS(1957); MY GUN IS

QUICK(1957); UNDEAD, THE(1957); THIRTEEN FIGHTING MEN(1960); PANIC IN YEAR ZERO!(1962); MUTINY IN OUTER SPACE(1965)

Robert Garland
ELECTRIC HORSEMAN, THE(1979), w

Roger Garland
MY UNCLE ANTOINE(1971, Can.)

Rose Ann Garland
SLEEPING CAR TO TRIESTE(1949, Brit.)

Ruth Garland
SISTERS, THE(1938)

Thomas Garland
GOLDEN BOY(1939)

Timothy Garland
CATALINA CAPER, THE(1967); CHARLIE BUBBLES(1968, Brit.)

Tom Garland
GHOST DIVER(1957)

Tommy Garland
WHIPLASH(1948); HOUSE OF STRANGERS(1949)

Trish Garland
1941(1979)

Victor Garland
MAROONED(1933, Brit.); TIGER BAY(1933, Brit.)

William Garland
Misc. Silents
SOUL AND BODY(1921)

Gillian Garlick
MY WAY(1974, South Africa); FUNERAL FOR AN ASSASSIN(1977)

Stephen Garlick
HEADLINE HUNTERS(1968, Brit.); SCROOGE(1970, Brit.); DARK CRYSTAL, THE(1982, Brit.)

Miroslawa Garlicka
KNIGHTS OF THE TEUTONIC ORDER, THE(1962, Pol.), ed

Lee Garlington
PSYCHO II(1983)

Mary Garlington
POLYESTER(1981)

Mike Garlington
GAL YOUNG UN(1979)

Mickey Garlock
STOLEN HARMONY(1935)

Frank J. Garlotta
KELLY'S HEROES(1970, U.S./Yugo.)

Lee Garmes
BARKER, THE(1928), ph; DISRAELI(1929), ph; HIS CAPTIVE WOMAN(1929), ph; PRISONERS(1929), ph; SAY IT WITH SONGS(1929), ph; GREAT DIVIDE, THE(1930), ph; LILIES OF THE FIELD(1930), ph; MOROCCO(1930), ph; OTHER TOMORROW, THE(1930), ph; SONG OF THE FLAME(1930), ph; SPRING IS HERE(1930), ph; WHOOPEE(1930), ph; AMERICAN TRAGEDY, AN(1931), ph; BRIGHT LIGHTS(1931), ph; CITY STREETS(1931), ph; CONFESSIONS OF A CO-ED(1931), ph; DISHON-ORED(1931), ph; FIGHTING CARAVANS(1931), ph; KISS ME AGAIN(1931), ph; CALL HER SAVAGE(1932), ph; SCARFACE(1932), ph; SHANGHAI EXPRESS(1932), ph; SMILIN' THROUGH(1932), ph; STRANGE INTERLUDE(1932), ph; FACE IN THE SKY(1933), ph; MY LIPS BETRAY(1933), ph; SHANGHAI MADNESS(1933), ph; ZOO IN BUDAPEST(1933), ph; CRIME WITHOUT PASSION(1934), ph; GEORGE WHITE'S SCANDALS(1934), ph; SCOUNDREL, THE(1935), ph; ONCE IN A BLUE MOON(1936), ph; DREAMING LIPS(1937, Brit.), d; SKY'S THE LIMIT, THE(1937, Brit.), d, ph; GONE WITH THE WIND(1939), ph; ANGELS OVER BROADWAY(1940), d, ph; BEYOND TOMORROW(1940), p; LILAC DOMINO, THE(1940, Brit.), p; LYDIA(1941), ph; CHINA GIRL(1942), ph; FOOTLIGHT SERENADE(1942), ph; JUNGLE BOOK(1942), ph; FLIGHT FOR FREEDOM(1943), ph; FOREVER AND A DAY(1943), ph; GUEST IN THE HOUSE(1944), ph; NONE SHALL ESCAPE(1944), ph; SINCE YOU WENT AWAY(1944), ph; LOVE LETTERS(1945), ph; PARIS UNDERGROUND(1945), ph; DUEL IN THE SUN(1946), ph; SEARCHING WIND, THE(1946), ph; SPECTER OF THE ROSE(1946), ph; YOUNG WIDOW(1946), ph; NIGHTMARE ALLEY(1947), ph; PARADINE CASE, THE(1947), ph; SECRET LIFE OF WALTER MITTY, THE(1947), ph; CAUGHT(1949), ph; FIGHTING KENTUCKIAN, THE(1949), ph; MY FOOLISH HEART(1949), ph; ROSEANNA McCOY(1949), ph; MY FRIEND IRMA GOES WEST(1950), ph; OUR VERY OWN(1950), ph; DETECTIVE STORY(1951), ph; SATUR-DAY'S HERO(1951), ph; THAT'S MY BOY(1951), ph; ACTORS AND SIN(1952), ph; CAPTIVE CITY(1952), ph; LUSTY MEN, THE(1952), ph; HANNAH LEE(1953), p&d, ph; THUNDER IN THE EAST(1953), ph; DESPERATE HOURS, THE(1955), ph; LAND OF THE PHARAOHS(1955), ph; MAN WITH THE GUN(1955), ph; ABDULLAH'S HAREM(1956, Brit./Egypt.), ph; BOTTOM OF THE BOTTLE, THE(1956), ph; D-DAY, THE SIXTH OF JUNE(1956), ph; SHARKFIGHTERS, THE(1956), ph; BIG BOODLE, THE(1957), ph; ER LOVE A STRANGER(1958), ph; BIG FISHERMAN, THE(1959), ph; HAPPY ANNIVERSARY(1959), ph; MISTY(1961), ph; ADVENTURES OF A YOUNG MAN(1962), ph; LADY IN A CAGE(1964), ph; BIG HAND FOR THE LITTLE LADY, A(1966), ph; HOW TO SAVE A MARRIAGE–AND RUIN YOUR LIFE(1968), ph
Silents
I'LL GET HIM YET(1919), ph; GOAT GETTER(1925), ph; KEEP SMILING(1925), ph; CARNIVAL GIRL, THE(1926), ph; GRAND DUCHESS AND THE WAITER, THE(1926), ph; SOCIAL CELEBRITY, A(1926), ph

Harold Garmland
MY FATHER'S MISTRESS(1970, Swed.), art d

Francois Garnault
SLOGAN(1970, Fr.), ed

Francoise Garnault
IMMORTAL STORY, THE(1969, Fr.), ed

Alice Garner
MONKEY GRIP(1983, Aus.)

Anthony Garner
TAMING OF THE SHREW, THE(1967, U.S./Ital.)

Bill Garner
DIMBOOLA(1979, Aus.)

Cindy Garner
YOU CAME ALONG(1945); FLAME OF ARABY(1951); RED BALL EXPRESS(1952); MA AND PA KETTLE AT WAIKIKI(1955)

David Garner
TRAUMA(1962)

Dee Garner
ON DANGEROUS GROUND(1951)

Don Garner
CAPTAIN EDDIE(1945); MY DARLING CLEMENTINE(1946); THREE LITTLE GIRLS IN BLUE(1946); SONG OF SCHEHERAZADE(1947); THIS TIME FOR KEEPS(1947); LARCENY(1948); SUMMER HOLIDAY(1948); YOU GOTTA STAY HAPPY(1948); LADY WITHOUT PASSPORT, A(1950); TWO FLAGS WEST(1950); DANGER ZONE(1951); FBI GIRL(1951); SATURDAY'S HERO(1951); WILD BLUE YONDER, THE(1952); WILD STALLION(1952); LAW AND ORDER(1953)

Dorothy Garner
SHOW BUSINESS(1944); SINCE YOU WENT AWAY(1944)

Ed Garner
MUSCLE BEACH PARTY(1964); PAJAMA PARTY(1964); HOW TO STUFF A WILD BIKINI(1965); FIREBALL 590(1966); GHOST IN THE INVISIBLE BIKINI(1966); PICKUP ON 101(1972), p

Erroll Garner
NEW KIND OF LOVE, A(1963), m

Gene Garner
CAPTURE THAT CAPSULE(1961)

George Garner
KID FROM LEFT FIELD, THE(1953)

Glenn D. Garner
WHITE DOG(1982)

Granville Garner
BABYLON(1980, Brit.)

Helen Garner
PURE S(1976, Aus.); MONKEY GRIP(1983, Aus.), w

Hugh Garner
STONE COLD DEAD(1980, Can.), d&w

Jack Garner
WILD ROVERS(1971)

James Garner
JOAN OF ARC(1948); GIRL HE LEFT BEHIND, THE(1956); TOWARD THE UN-KNOWN(1956); SAYONARA(1957); SHOOT-OUT AT MEDICINE BEND(1957); DARBY'S RANGERS(1958); ALIAS JESSE JAMES(1959); UP PERISCOPE(1959); CASH McCALL(1960); CHILDREN'S HOUR, THE(1961); BOYS' NIGHT OUT(1962); GREAT ESCAPE, THE(1963); MOVE OVER, DARLING(1963); THRILL OF IT ALL, THE(1963); WHEELER DEALERS, THE(1963); AMERICANIZATION OF EMILY, THE(1964); ART OF LOVE, THE(1965); 36 HOURS(1965); DUEL AT DIABLO(1966); GRAND PRIX(1966); MAN COULD GET KILLED, A(1966); MISTER BUDD-WING(1966); HOUR OF THE GUN(1967); HOW SWEET IT IS(1968); PINK JUNGLE, THE(1968); MARLOWE(1969); SUPPORT YOUR LOCAL SHERIFF(1969); MAN CALLED SLEDGE, A(1971, Ital.); SKIN GAME(1971); SUPPORT YOUR LOCAL GUNFIGHTER(1971); THEY ONLY KILL THEIR MASTERS(1972); ONE LITTLE INDIAN(1973); CASTAWAY COWBOY, THE(1974); HEALTH(1980); FAN, THE(1981); VICTOR/VICTORIA(1982)
1984
TANK(1984)

Jay Garner
PENNIES FROM HEAVEN(1981); HANKY-PANKY(1982)

John Garner
THIS STUFF'LL KILL YA!(1971)

Kathy Garner
I'LL CRY TOMORROW(1955)

Martin Garner
BIG FIX, THE(1978); HEY, GOOD LOOKIN'(1982); TWILIGHT ZONE–THE MO-VIE(1983)
1984
OH GOD! YOU DEVIL(1984)

Mousey Garner
LAST OF THE RED HOT LOVERS(1972)

Mousie Garner
FOR THOSE WHO THINK YOUNG(1964)

Pat Garner
GAL YOUNG UN(1979)

Paul Garner
HIT PARADE, THE(1937)

Paul "Mousie" Garner
SATURDAY THE 14TH(1981)
1984
RHINESTONE(1984)

Paulyn Garner
IMITATION OF LIFE(1934)

Peggy Ann Garner
BLONDIE BRINGS UP BABY(1939); IN NAME ONLY(1939); EAGLE SQUAD-RON(1942); PIED PIPER, THE(1942); JANE EYRE(1944); KEYS OF THE KINGDOM, THE(1944); JUNIOR MISS(1945); NOB HILL(1945); TREE GROWS IN BROOKLYN, A(1945); HOME SWEET HOMICIDE(1946); DAISY KENYON(1947); SIGN OF THE RAM, THE(1948); BIG CAT, THE(1949); BOMBA THE JUNGLE BOY(1949); LOVABLE CHEAT, THE(1949); TERESA(1951); BLACK WIDOW(1954); CAT, THE(1966); WED-DING, A(1978)
Misc. Talkies
BLACK FOREST, THE(1954)

Rex Garner
MURDER AT 3 A.M.(1953, Brit.); PLANK, THE(1967, Brit.)

Ronnie Garner
ON DANGEROUS GROUND(1951)

Shay Garner
THUMBELINA(1970); HUMONGOUS(1982, Can.)

Shirley Garner
RAYMIE(1960)

Stewart Garner
CASANOVA BROWN(1944); PRINCESS AND THE PIRATE, THE(1944); ARSON SQUAD(1945)

Lisa Garneri
1984
FULL MOON IN PARIS(1984, Fr.)

Bob Garnet
SPIDER, THE(1958); WAR OF THE COLOSSAL BEAST(1958)
Amaryllis Garnett
GO-BETWEEN, THE(1971, Brit.)
Cara Garnett
FANNY HILL: MEMOIRS OF A WOMAN OF PLEASURE zero(1965); MOVIE STAR, AMERICAN STYLE, OR, LSD I HATE YOU!(1966)
Constance Garnett
UNCLE VANYA(1977, Brit.), w
David Garnett
SAILOR'S RETURN, THE(1978, Brit.), w
Gale Garnett
TRIBUTE(1980, Can.); MAD MONSTER PARTY(1967); HAPPY MOTHER'S DAY... LOVE, GEORGE(1973); CHILDREN, THE(1980)
Paul Garnett
Silents
RECKLESS ROMANCE(1924), ph
Phyllis Garnett
LADY GODIVA RIDES AGAIN(1955, Brit.)
Tay Garnett
OH, YEAH!(1929), d, w; SPIELER, THE(1929), d, w; HER MAN(1930), d, w; OFFICER O'BRIEN(1930), d; BAD COMPANY(1931), d, w; OKAY AMERICA(1932), d; ONE WAY PASSAGE(1932), d; PRESTIGE(1932), d, w; DESTINATION UNKNOWN(1933), d; S.O.S. ICEBERG(1933), d; CHINA SEAS(1935), d; SHE COULDN'T TAKE IT(1935), d; PROFESSIONAL SOLDIER(1936), d; LOVE IS NEWS(1937), d; SLAVE SHIP(1937), d; STAND-IN(1937), d; JOY OF LIVING(1938), d; TRADE WINDS(1938), d, w; ETERNALLY YOURS(1939), a, d; SEVEN SINNERS(1940), w; CAFE HOSTESS(1940), d; SLIGHTLY HONORABLE(1940), a, p&d; CHEERS FOR MISS BISHOP(1941), d; UNEXPECTED UNCLE(1941), p; WEEKEND FOR THREE(1941), p; MY FAVORITE SPY(1942), d; BATAAN(1943), d; CROSS OF LORRAINE, THE(1943), d; MRS. PARKINGTON(1944), d; SEE HERE, PRIVATE HARGROVE(1944), d; VALLEY OF DECISION, THE(1945), d; POSTMAN ALWAYS RINGS TWICE, THE(1946), d; WILD HARVEST(1947), d; CONNECTICUT YANKEE IN KING ARTHUR'S COURT, A(1949), d; FIREBALL, THE(1950), d, w; CAUSE FOR ALARM(1951), d; SOLDIERS THREE(1951), d; ONE MINUTE TO ZERO(1952), d; MAIN STREET TO BROADWAY(1953), d; BLACK KNIGHT, THE(1954), d; NIGHT FIGHTERS, THE(1960), d; DELTA FACTOR, THE(1970), p&d, w; CHALLENGE TO BE FREE(1976), a, d
Silents
NO CONTROL(1927), w; RUBBER TIRES(1927), w; WHITE GOLD(1927), w
Misc. Silents
CELEBRITY(1928), d
Taylor Garnett
FLYING FOOL(1929), d
Tony Garnett
BOYS, THE(1962, Brit.); RIVALS, THE(1963, Brit.); INCIDENT AT MIDNIGHT(1966, Brit.); KES(1970, Brit.), p, w; FAMILY LIFE(1971, Brit.), p; BLACK JACK(1979, Brit.), p; PROSTITUTE(1980, Brit.), p,d&w; DEEP IN THE HEART(1983), p
Lupe Garnica
TWO GALS AND A GUY(1951); TARZAN'S DEADLY SILENCE(1970)
Cameron Garnick
Misc. Talkies
CRY TO THE WIND(1979)
Bernard Garnier
DE L'AMOUR(1968, Fr./Ital.)
Daniele Garnier
MATTER OF DAYS, A(1969, Fr./Czech.)
Gerald Garnier
LOULOU(1980, Fr.)
Robert-Jules Garnier
ANTOINE ET ANTOINETTE(1947 Fr.), art d
Julian Garnsey
Silents
IDLE RICH, THE(1921), art d
Ettore Garofalo
MAMMA ROMA(1962, Ital.)
Joseph Garofalo
EVILSPEAK(1982), w
Franco Garofolo
HERCULES(1983)
Pauline Garon
GAMBLERS, THE(1929); IN THE HEADLINES(1929); THOROUGHBRED, THE(1930); BY APPOINTMENT ONLY(1933); EASY MILLIONS(1933); ONE YEAR LATER(1933); PHANTOM BROADCAST, THE(1933); WONDER BAR(1934); LOST IN THE STRATOSPHERE(1935); WHITE COCKATOO(1935); IT HAD TO HAPPEN(1936); HER HUSBAND'S SECRETARY(1937); SHALL WE DANCE(1937)
Silents
REPORTED MISSING(1922); SONNY(1922); ADAM'S RIB(1923); CRITICAL AGE, THE(1923); AVERAGE WOMAN, THE(1924); PAINTED FLAPPER, THE(1924); SPITFIRE, THE(1924); COMPROMISE(1925); FLAMING WATERS(1925); PASSIONATE YOUTH(1925); ROSE OF THE WORLD(1925); SPLENDID ROAD, THE(1925); DRIVEN FROM HOME(1927); EAGER LIPS(1927); LADIES AT EASE(1927)
Misc. Silents
CHILDREN OF DUST(1923); FORGIVE AND FORGET(1923); MARRIAGE MARKET, THE(1923); YOU CAN'T FOOL YOUR WIFE(1923); WHAT THE BUTLER SAW(1924, Brit.); FIGHTING YOUTH(1925); GREAT SENSATION, THE(1925); LOVE GAMBLE, THE(1925); SATAN IN SABLES(1925); SPEED(1925); WHERE WAS I?(1925); CHRISTINE OF THE BIG TOPS(1926); COLLEGE HERO, THE(1927); NAUGHTY(1927); PRINCESS OF BROADWAY, THE(1927); TEMPTATIONS OF A SHOP GIRL(1927); CANDY KID, THE(1928); DEVIL'S CAGE, THE(1928); DUGAN OF THE DUGOUTS(1928); GIRL HE DIDN'T BUY, THE(1928); HEART OF BROADWAY, THE(1928); MUST WE MARRY?(1928); RILEY OF THE RAINBOW DIVISION(1928)
Suzanne Garon
SPIRITS OF THE DEAD(1969, Fr./Ital.), ed
Martha Garotto
HERE COME THE CO-EDS(1945)
Cathy Garpershak
PORKY'S(1982)

Eddie Garr
OBEY THE LAW(1933); THAT'S MY STORY(1937)
Phyllis Garr
PIECES OF DREAMS(1970), cos; TELL ME THAT YOU LOVE ME, JUNIE MOON(1970), cos; BUNNY O'HARE(1971), cos; FROGS(1972), cos; WALKING TALL(1973), cos; SILVER STREAK(1976), cos; WORLD'S GREATEST LOVER, THE(1977), cos
Teri Garr
CONVERSATION, THE(1974); YOUNG FRANKENSTEIN(1974); WON TON TON, THE DOG WHO SAVED HOLLYWOOD(1976); CLOSE ENCOUNTERS OF THE THIRD KIND(1977); OH, GOD!(1977); BLACK STALLION, THE(1979); HONKY TONK FREEWAY(1981); ESCAPE ARTIST, THE(1982); ONE FROM THE HEART(1982); TOOTSIE(1982); BLACK STALLION RETURNS, THE(1983); MR. MOM(1983); STING II, THE(1983)
1984
FIRSTBORN(1984)
Misc. Talkies
WITCHES' BREW(1980)
Terri Garr
MARYJANE(1968)
Terry Garr
FOR PETE'S SAKE!(1966); HEAD(1968); CHANGES(1969); MOONSHINE WAR, THE(1970)
Martin Garralaga
GAY CABALLERO, THE(1932); LAWLESS BORDER(1935); SWEET ADELINE(1935); UNDER THE PAMPAS MOON(1935); CHARGE OF THE LIGHT BRIGADE, THE(1936); MESSAGE TO GARCIA, A(1936); SONG OF THE GRINGO(1936); ANOTHER DAWN(1937); BOOTS OF DESTINY(1937); LOVE UNDER FIRE(1937); RIDERS OF THE ROCKIES(1937); OUTLAW EXPRESS(1938); STARLIGHT OVER TEXAS(1938); ANOTHER THIN MAN(1939); CODE OF THE SECRET SERVICE(1939); FIGHTING GRINGO, THE(1939); JUAREZ(1939); LAW OF THE PAMPAS(1939); LEGION OF THE LAWLESS(1940); MAD EMPRESS, THE(1940); RANGERS OF FORTUNE(1940); RHYTHM OF THE RIO GRANDE(1940); STAGE TO CHINO(1940); INTERNATIONAL LADY(1941); LAW OF THE TROPICS(1941); SON OF DAVY CROCKETT, THE(1941); CASABLANCA(1942); IN OLD CALIFORNIA(1942); LADY HAS PLANS, THE(1942); UNDERCOVER MAN(1942); ADVENTURES IN IRAQ(1943); FOR WHOM THE BELL TOLLS(1943); OUTLAW, THE(1943); GOING MY WAY(1944); LARAMIE TRAIL, THE(1944); MAN FROM FRISCO(1944); PURPLE HEART, THE(1944); TAMPICO(1944); VOICE IN THE WIND(1944); ADVENTURE(1945); CISCO KID RETURNS, THE(1945); IN OLD NEW MEXICO(1945); MASQUERADE IN MEXICO(1945); SOUTH OF THE RIO GRANDE(1945); STRANGE VOYAGE(1945); WEST OF THE PECOS(1945); BEAUTY AND THE BANDIT(1946); PERILOUS HOLIDAY(1946); PERSONALITY KID(1946); PLAINSMAN AND THE LADY(1946); THRILL OF BRAZIL, THE(1946); VIRGINIAN, THE(1946); CARNIVAL IN COSTA RICA(1947); FRAMED(1947); LOST MOMENT, THE(1947); RIDE THE PINK HORSE(1947); SENATOR WAS INDISCREET, THE(1947); TWILIGHT ON THE RIO GRANDE(1947); TYCOON(1947); FEATHERED SERPENT, THE(1948); FOUR FACES WEST(1948); MADONNA OF THE DESERT(1948); PORT SAID(1948); ROGUES' REGIMENT(1948); SAXON CHARM, THE(1948); TREASURE OF THE SIERRA MADRE, THE(1948); UP IN CENTRAL PARK(1948); BIG SOMBRERO(1949); BRIBE, THE(1949); GREAT SINNER, THE(1949); HOLIDAY IN HAVANA(1949); JOE PALOOKA IN THE COUNTERPUNCH(1949); JOLSON SINGS AGAIN(1949); LAST BANDIT, THE(1949); SHEP COMES HOME(1949); STREETS OF SAN FRANCISCO(1949); SUSANNA PASS(1949); SWORD IN THE DESERT(1949); THERE'S A GIRL IN MY HEART(1949); BANDIT QUEEN(1950); CRISIS(1950); FORTUNES OF CAPTAIN BLOOD(1950); KID FROM TEXAS, THE(1950); LADY WITHOUT PASSPORT, A(1950); OUTRIDERS, THE(1950); BRANDED(1951); BRIDE OF THE GORILLA(1951); HAVANA ROSE(1951); AFRICAN TREASURE(1952); BELA LUGOSI MEETS A BROOKLYN GORILLA(1952); FABULOUS SENORITA, THE(1952); FIGHTER, THE(1952); FIVE FINGERS(1952); RING, THE(1952); SNOWS OF KILIMANJARO, THE(1952); TROPICAL HEAT WAVE(1952); WOMAN IN THE DARK(1952); HITCH-HIKER, THE(1953); LAW AND ORDER(1953); SAN ANTONE(1953); SECOND CHANCE(1953); JUBILEE TRAIL(1954); LAW VS. BILLY THE KID(1954); SECRET OF THE INCAS(1954); GREEN FIRE(1955); MAN ALONE, A(1955); BLACKJACK KETCHUM, DESPERADO(1956); SERENADE(1956); GUNSIGHT RIDGE(1957); MAN IN THE SHADOW(1957); UNKNOWN TERROR, THE(1957); LEFT-HANDED GUN, THE(1958); LONELY ARE THE BRAVE(1962); ISLAND OF THE BLUE DOLPHINS(1964); WHAT EVER HAPPENED TO AUNT ALICE?(1969)
Misc. Talkies
GAY CAVALIER, THE(1946); SOUTH OF MONTEREY(1946); RIDING THE CALIFORNIA TRAIL(1947)
Martin Garralagna
DON RICARDO RETURNS(1946)
Martin Garralga
ROSE OF THE RIO GRANDE(1938)
Ivo Garrani
DAY THE SKY EXPLODED, THE(1958, Fr./Ital.); HERCULES(1959, Ital.); GIANT OF MARATHON, THE(1960, Ital.); BLACK SUNDAY(1961, Ital.); CARTHAGE IN FLAMES(1961, Fr./Ital.); MORGAN THE PIRATE(1961, Fr./Ital.); COMMANDO(1962, Ital., Span., Bel., Ger.); NIGHT THEY KILLED RASPUTIN, THE(1962, Fr./Ital.); CAPTIVE CITY, THE(1963, Ital.); HERCULES AND THE CAPTIVE WOMEN(1963, Fr./Ital.); HUNCHBACK OF ROME, THE(1963, Ital.); LEOPARD, THE(1963, Ital.); SLAVE, THE(1963, Ital.); VERONA TRIAL, THE(1963, Ital.); LOVE A LA CARTE(1965, Ital.); CONQUERED CITY(1966, Ital.); ROVER, THE(1967, Ital.); CHASTITY BELT, THE(1968, Ital.); WATERLOO(1970, Ital./USSR); STREET PEOPLE(1976, U.S./Ital.)
Romo Garrara
RAIDERS OF THE LOST ARK(1981)
Don Garrard
FLAMING FRONTIER(1958, Can.); WOLF DOG(1958, Can.)
Paul Garrard
MUDLARK, THE(1950, Brit.)
Donna Garratt
DIAMONDS ARE FOREVER(1971, Brit.)
Evie Garratt
HAUNTING OF M, THE(1979)
Michael Garratt
WOMEN IN LOVE(1969, Brit.)

T.V. Garraway
JESSE JAMES' WOMEN(1954), p
Elaine Garreau
TWELVE CHAIRS, THE(1970); GREAT EXPECTATIONS(1975, Brit.)
Jean-Francois Garreaud
VIOLETTE(1978, Fr.)
Maurice Garrel
SUNDAYS AND CYBELE(1962, Fr.); DAY AND THE HOUR, THE(1963, Fr./ Ital.); SOFT SKIN, THE(1964, Fr.); TO COMMIT A MURDER(1970, Fr./Ital./Ger.); NADA GANG, THE(1974, Fr./Ital.)
1984
EDITH AND MARCEL(1984, Fr.)
Diane Garret
TURNING POINT, THE(1952)
Grant Garret
CLARENCE(1937), w
Richard Garret [Riccardo Garrone]
TERROR-CREATURES FROM THE GRAVE(1967, U.S./Ital.)
Shelia Garret
SARUMBA(1950)
Stephen Garret
HOUSE OF INTRIGUE, THE(1959, Ital.)
Darell L. Garretson
MIXED COMPANY(1974)
Oliver S. Garretson
THEY DRIVE BY NIGHT(1940), ed
Andi Garrett
I SAW WHAT YOU DID(1965)
Berkley Garrett
1984
CLOAK AND DAGGER(1984)
Berkley H. Garrett
BARBAROSA(1982); TENDER MERCIES(1982)
Betty Garrett
BIG CITY(1948); NEPTUNE'S DAUGHTER(1949); ON THE TOWN(1949); TAKE ME OUT TO THE BALL GAME(1949); MY SISTER EILEEN(1955); SHADOW ON THE WINDOW, THE(1957)
Bill Garrett
HANK WILLIAMS: THE SHOW HE NEVER GAVE(1982, Can.), md
Buck Garrett
FRONTIER PHANTOM, THE(1952)
Christopher Garrett
TIMERIDER(1983)
Diane Garrett
STOP THAT CAB(1951); PACE THAT THRILLS, THE(1952); RAINBOW 'ROUND MY SHOULDER(1952)
Don Garrett
FARMER TAKES A WIFE, THE(1953); SEMINOLE(1953); NAKED ALIBI(1954); RUMBLE ON THE DOCKS(1956); PLUNDER ROAD(1957); MURDER BY CONTRACT(1958); STUDS LONIGAN(1960)
Donna Garrett
WHAT'S UP, DOC?(1972); DRUM(1976)
1984
FOOTLOOSE(1984)
Dorothy Garrett
STORK CLUB, THE(1945)
Drum Garrett
1984
NEVERENDING STORY, THE(1984, Ger.)
Eddie Garrett
DIRTY HARRY(1971); ONCE IS NOT ENOUGH(1975); NEW YORK, NEW YORK(1977)
Eliza Garrett
SCHLOCK(1973); NATIONAL LAMPOON'S ANIMAL HOUSE(1978)
Ernie Garrett
ROLLOVER(1981)
Eveline Garrett
GORBALS STORY, THE(1950, Brit.)
Gary Garrett
CODE OF THE SADDLE(1947); FLASHING GUNS(1947); LAND OF THE LAWLESS(1947); PRAIRIE EXPRESS(1947); SONG OF THE WASTELAND(1947); HARPOON(1948)
George Garrett
YOUNG LOVERS, THE(1964), w; FRANKENSTEIN MEETS THE SPACE MONSTER(1965), w; PLAYGROUND, THE(1965), w
Grant Garrett
HOME ON THE RANGE(1935), w; RAINMAKERS, THE(1935), w; THIS WAY PLEASE(1937), w; THRILL OF A LIFETIME(1937), w; BEDTIME STORY(1942), w; HE'S MY GUY(1943), w; BARBARY COAST GENT(1944), w; RATIONING(1944), w; MIGHTY MCGURK, THE(1946), w
Guy Houston Garrett
HONEYSUCKLE ROSE(1980)
H.P. Garrett
SCANDAL SHEET(1931), w
Hank Garrett
RICHARD(1972); SERPICO(1973); DEATH WISH(1974); THREE DAYS OF THE CONDOR(1975); DEADLY HERO(1976); EXORCIST II: THE HERETIC(1977); SENTINEL, THE(1977); FIREPOWER(1979, Brit.); JAZZ SINGER, THE(1980); STING II, THE(1983)
1984
JOHNNY DANGEROUSLY(1984); ROSEBUD BEACH HOTEL(1984)
James Garrett
TIME AFTER TIME(1979, Brit.)
Jimmy Garrett
SECOND TIME AROUND, THE(1961)
John Garrett
DIARY OF A HIGH SCHOOL BRIDE(1959); THIRD VOICE, THE(1960); STAR CHAMBER, THE(1983)

Johnny Garrett
ISN'T IT ROMANTIC?(1948)
Joy Garrett
WHO?(1975, Brit./Ger.)
Kay Garrett
DEAD RECKONING(1947); HE WALKED BY NIGHT(1948); BIG BLUFF, THE(1955); HELL BOUND(1957)
Leif Garrett
WALKING TALL(1973); DEVIL TIMES FIVE(1974); MACON COUNTY LINE(1974); WALKING TALL, PART II(1975); FINAL CHAPTER–WALKING TALL zero(1977); GOD'S GUN(1977); KID VENGEANCE(1977); SGT. PEPPER'S LONELY HEARTS CLUB BAND(1978); SKATEBOARD(1978); OUTSIDERS, THE(1983)
Misc. Talkies
LONGSHOT(1982)
Lila Garrett
BAREFOOT EXECUTIVE, THE(1971), w
Lisa Garrett
DOLL SQUAD, THE(1973)
Martyn Garrett
BABY AND THE BATTLESHIP, THE(1957, Brit.); THREE MEN IN A BOAT(1958, Brit.)
Michael Garrett
WALK EAST ON BEACON(1952); BRASS LEGEND, THE(1956); SAVAGE MESSIAH(1972, Brit.), m
Oliver H. O. Garrett
Silents
DRAGNET, THE(1928), w
Oliver H. P Garrett
CITY STREETS(1931), w
Oliver H. P. Garrett
CHINATOWN NIGHTS(1929), w
Oliver H.P. Garrett
FOR THE DEFENSE(1930), w; STREET OF CHANCE(1930), w; TEXAN, THE(1930), w; THREE FACES EAST(1930), w; NIGHT NURSE(1931), w; VICE SQUAD, THE(1931), w; FAREWELL TO ARMS, A(1932), w; IF I HAD A MILLION(1932), w; MAN FROM YESTERDAY, THE(1932), w; WORLD AND THE FLESH, THE(1932), w; NIGHT FLIGHT(1933), w; STORY OF TEMPLE DRAKE, THE(1933), w; MANHATTAN MELODRAMA(1934), w; ONE-WAY TICKET(1935), w; SHE COULDN'T TAKE IT(1935), w; HER HUSBAND LIES(1937), w; HURRICANE, THE(1937), w; GONE WITH THE WIND(1939), w; ONE THIRD OF A NATION(1939), w; MAN I MARRIED, THE(1940), w; UNDERGROUND(1941), w; CAREFUL, SOFT SHOULDERS(1942), d&w; FLIGHT FOR FREEDOM(1943), w; DUEL IN THE SUN(1946), w; DEAD RECKONING(1947), w; SEALED CARGO(1951), w
Silents
LADIES OF THE MOB(1928), w
Otis Garrett
BEHIND THE MASK(1932), ed; CRUSADER, THE(1932), ed; UNWRITTEN LAW, THE(1932), ed; GIGOLETTES OF PARIS(1933), ed; VAMPIRE BAT, THE(1933), ed; WORLD GONE MAD, THE(1933), ed; UNKNOWN BLONDE(1934), ed; AGE OF INDISCRETION(1935), w; O'SHAUGHNESSY'S BOY(1935), w; NIGHT KEY(1937), ed; BLACK DOLL, THE(1938), d; DANGER ON THE AIR(1938), d; LADY IN THE MORGUE(1938), d; LAST EXPRESS, THE(1938), d; PERSONAL SECRETARY(1938), d; EXILE EXPRESS(1939), d; MYSTERY OF THE WHITE ROOM(1939), d; WITNESS VANISHES, THE(1939), d; MARGIE(1940), d; SANDY GETS HER MAN(1940), d; MEET THE CHUMP(1941), w
Otis M. Garrett
SIN OF NORA MORAN(1933), ed
Ottis Garrett
GUILTY GENERATION, THE(1931), ed
Patsy Garrett
TROUBLE WITH GIRLS(AND HOW TO GET INTO IT), THE*1/2 (1969); WICKED, WICKED(1973); BENJI(1974); FOR THE LOVE OF BENJI(1977)
Ralph Garrett
HOW TO BEAT THE HIGH COST OF LIVING(1980)
Robert Garrett
ROMANCE AND RICHES(1937, Brit.), p; TWO WHO DARED(1937, Brit.), p; CURTAIN UP(1952, Brit.), p; ALWAYS A BRIDE(1954, Brit.), p; PRIZE, THE(1963)
Roger Garrett
GRASSHOPPER, THE(1970); SAFE PLACE, A(1971); NIGHT OF THE COBRA WOMAN(1974, U.S./Phil.)
Roy Garrett
RANGE RENEGADES(1948)
Sam Garrett
Misc. Talkies
FLYING LARIATS(1931)
Scott Garrett
WATERMELON MAN(1970); BEN(1972); MAGIC(1978); FOXES(1980)
Sharon Garrett
BEACH PARTY(1963)
Snuff Garrett
ANY WHICH WAY YOU CAN(1980), md; BRONCO BILLY(1980), m; SMOKEY AND THE BANDIT II(1980), m; SHARKY'S MACHINE(1982), m
Stephen Garrett
WAR AND PEACE(1956, Ital./U.S.)
William Garrett
MAN IN THE MIRROR, THE(1936, Brit.), w
Silents
SECRET OF THE HILLS, THE(1921), w
Vera Garretto
MONTE CARLO STORY, THE(1957, Ital.)
Charles Garrey
DANGEROUS SEAS(1931, Brit.)
Joseph Garri
NIGHT OF EVIL(1962)
Ann Garrick
SIDE STREETS(1934), w
Beulah Garrick
PURSUIT OF HAPPINESS, THE(1971); DOG DAY AFTERNOON(1975)

Eve Garrick
THIS LOVE OF OURS(1945)
Gene Garrick
ROAD BACK,THE(1937); GREEN HELL(1940); PARIS CALLING(1941); DESPER-ATE JOURNEY(1942); SABOTEUR(1942); TEN GENTLEMEN FROM WEST POINT(1942); TOP SERGEANT(1942); SALOME, WHERE SHE DANCED(1945); THOROUGHBREDS(1945); NIGHT AND DAY(1946); O.S.S.(1946); GHOST GOES WILD, THE(1947); LUCK OF THE IRISH(1948); PERILOUS WATERS(1948)
Geraldine Garrick
SNAKE PIT, THE(1948)
John Garrick
MARRIED IN HOLLYWOOD(1929); SKY HAWK(1929); ARE YOU THERE?(1930); JUST IMAGINE(1930); LOTTERY BRIDE, THE(1930); SONG O' MY HEART(1930); ALWAYS GOODBYE(1931); CHARLIE CHAN CARRIES ON(1931); BAD COMPANY(1931); BRIDE OF THE LAKE(1934, Brit.); BROKEN MELODY, THE(1934, Brit.); CHU CHIN CHOW(1934, Brit.); TOO MANY MILLIONS(1934, Brit.); ANYTHING MIGHT HAPPEN(1935, Brit.); HIS MAJESTY AND CO(1935, Brit.); STREET SONG(1935, Brit.); TURN OF THE TIDE(1935, Brit.); LIVE AGAIN(1936, Brit.); ROYAL EAGLE(1936, Brit.); SHIPMATES O' MINE(1936, Brit.); TO CATCH A THIEF(1936, Brit.); TOUCH OF THE MOON, A(1936, Brit.); HIGH TREASON(1937, Brit.); KNIGHTS FOR A DAY(1937, Brit.); LAST ROSE OF SUMMER, THE(1937, Brit.); RIDING HIGH(1937, Brit.); TWO WHO DARED(1937, Brit.); SPECIAL EDITION(1938, Brit.); GREAT VICTOR HERBERT, THE(1939); CAPTAIN MOONLIGHT(1940, Brit.); SUI-CIDE LEGION(1940, Brit.)
Misc. Talkies
ALI BABA NIGHTS(1953)
Kathy Garrick
SCHIZOID(1980)
Pauline Garrick
RATS OF TOBRUK(1951, Aus.)
Rian Garrick
BATTLE OF THE CORAL SEA(1959); EDGE OF ETERNITY(1959); FLYING FON-TAINES, THE(1959)
Richard Garrick
BOOMERANG(1947); GREEN GRASS OF WYOMING(1948); STREETCAR NAMED DESIRE, A(1951); BONZO GOES TO COLLEGE(1952); DREAMBOAT(1952); O. HENRY'S FULL HOUSE(1952); SOMETHING FOR THE BIRDS(1952); STARS AND STRIPES FOREVER(1952); VIVA ZAPATA!(1952); CALL ME MADAM(1953); LAW AND ORDER(1953); POWDER RIVER(1953); SYSTEM, THE(1953); TROUBLE ALONG THE WAY(1953); DESIREE(1954); RIDING SHOTGUN(1954); MAN CALLED PETER, THE(1955); VIOLENT SATURDAY(1955); HIGH SOCIETY(1956); HILDA CRA-NE(1956); MOUNTAIN, THE(1956)
Silents
TESS OF THE STORM COUNTRY(1914); ACCORDING TO LAW(1916), d; DRIFTER, THE(1916), d; IDOL OF THE STAGE, THE(1916), a, d; RANK OUTSIDER(1920, Brit.), d
Misc. Silents
NEW ADAM AND EVE, THE(1915), d; QUALITY OF FAITH, THE(1916), d; TRENT'S LAST CASE(1920, Brit.), d
John Garrie
MORGAN!(1966, Brit.); IF ...(1968, Brit.); PRIVATE LIFE OF SHERLOCK HOLMES, THE(1970, Brit.); MADHOUSE(1974, Brit.)
Phillip Garrigan
SORCERESS(1983)
Rene Garriguenc
AVALANCHE(1946), m
John Garris
LOST WEEKEND, THE(1945)
Phil Garris
SHE WROTE THE BOOK(1946); TANGIER(1946); ONE TOUCH OF VENUS(1948); GLENN MILLER STORY, THE(1953); WALKING MY BABY BACK HOME(1953); FRANCIS IN THE NAVY(1955); DANCE WITH ME, HENRY(1956)
Philip Garris
SEX AND THE SINGLE GIRL(1964); WHAT DID YOU DO IN THE WAR, DAD-DY?(1966); IN THE HEAT OF THE NIGHT(1967)
Roger E. Garris
NARCOTICS STORY, THE(1958), w
David Garrison
MIDNIGHT MAN, THE(1974)
Elizabeth Garrison
Silents
OTHER MEN'S DAUGHTERS(1918); LOVE AUCTION, THE(1919); NOTHING BUT THE TRUTH(1920); MIXED FACES(1922)
Misc. Silents
PERFECT WOMAN, THE(1920); TRUTH ABOUT HUSBANDS, THE(1920)
Ellen Garrison
ZELIG(1983)
Greg Garrison
HEY, LET'S TWIST!(1961), d; TWO TICKETS TO PARIS(1962), d
Gregory Garrison
NORMA RAE(1979), set d; BACK ROADS(1981), set d
1984
AMERICAN DREAMER(1984), set d
Harold Garrison
REFORM SCHOOL(1939); GANG WAR(1940); TO HAVE AND HAVE NOT(1944)
Jan Garrison
BEACH RED(1967)
Jay Garrison
CROOKED ROAD, THE(, w
Joy Garrison
STRANGLEHOLD(1962, Brit.), w; BLAZE OF GLORY(1963, Brit.), w
Kathleen Garrison
DR. COPPELIUS(1968, U.S./Span.)
Michael Garrison
CROWDED SKY, THE(1960), p; DARK AT THE TOP OF THE STAIRS, THE(1960), p
Mike Garrison
GIRL IN GOLD BOOTS(1968); CORPSE GRINDERS, THE(1972); WORM EATERS, THE(1981)

Mrs. Garrison
Silents
OTHER MAN'S WIFE, THE(1919)
Pat Garrison
FLYING SAUCER, THE(1950)
Patricia Garrison
HARPOON(1948)
Richard Garrison
CRATER LAKE MONSTER, THE(1977)
Rita Garrison
JUNIOR BONNER(1972)
Rob Garrison
LOST AND FOUND(1979); PROM NIGHT(1980)
1984
KARATE KID, THE(1984)
Robert Garrison
WORM EATERS, THE(1981)
Misc. Silents
MICHAEL(1924, Ger.); CHAINED(1927, Ger.)
Sean Garrison
ONIONHEAD(1958); VIOLENT ROAD(1958); UP PERISCOPE(1959); BRIDGE TO THE SUN(1961); SPLENDOR IN THE GRASS(1961); MOMENT TO MOMENT(1966); BANNING(1967)
Sonny Garrison
LOST MAN, THE(1969)
Lisa Garritson
AIRPORT(1970)
Richard Garritt
BAD CHARLESTON CHARLIE(1973), ed
Paddy Garritty
MANGANINNIE(1982, Aus.)
Joe Garrity
TO ALL A GOODNIGHT(1980), prod d; FORBIDDEN WORLD(1982), art d; TIME WALKER(1982), art d
Joseph T. Garrity
1984
BREAKIN' 2: ELECTRIC BOOGALOO(1984), prod d; MAKING THE GRADE(1984), art d
Victor Garrivier
COUP DE TORCHON(1981, Fr.)
George Garro
GREATEST, THE(1977, U.S./Brit.)
Joseph Garro
UNDER CALIFORNIA STARS(1948)
Joseph A. Garro
TWILIGHT IN THE SIERRAS(1950)
Helene Garron
COVER GIRL(1944)
Luigi Garrone
BURIED ALIVE(1951, Ital.)
Riccardo Garrone
TWO NIGHTS WITH CLEOPATRA(1953, Ital.); GIRL WITH A SUITCASE(1961, Fr./Ital.); LA DOLCE VITA(1961, Ital./Fr.); WARRIOR EMPRESS, THE(1961, Ital./Fr.); COMMANDO(1962, Ital., Span., Bel., Ger.); EVA(1962, Fr./Ital.); LOVES OF SALAMM-BO, THE(1962, Fr./Ital.); SWORDSMAN OF SIENA, THE(1962, Fr./Ital.); FIASCO IN MILAN(1963, Fr./Ital.); YELLOW ROLLS-ROYCE, THE(1965, Brit.); MY WIFE'S ENEMY(1967, Ital.); PONTIUS PILATE(1967, Fr./Ital.); THREE BITES OF THE APPLE(1967); BANG BANG KID, THE(1968 U.S./Span./Ital.); NO ROOM TO DIE(1969, Ital.); MADIGAN'S MILLIONS(1970, Span./Ital); MAN CALLED SLEDGE, A(1971, Ital.)
Andrew Garroni
MANIAC(1980), p; VIGILANTE(1983), p
Romolo Garroni
CAESAR THE CONQUEROR(1963, Ital.), ph; LOVE NOW...PAY LATER(1966, Ital.), ph; LAST DAY OF THE WAR, THE(1969, U.S./Ital./Span.), ph; FLYING MATCHMAK-ER, THE(1970, Israel), ph
Sergio Garroni
STRANGER'S GUNDOWN, THE(1974, Ital.), d, w
William Garroni
STREET PEOPLE(1976, U.S./Ital.), ch; ROLLOVER(1981), ph
Dave Garroway
I SURRENDER DEAR(1948); IT HAPPENED TO JANE(1959)
Charles Garry
RAISE THE ROOF(1930); WATER GYPSIES, THE(1932, Brit.)
Misc. Silents
CUPID IN CLOVER(1929, Brit.)
Joe Garry
BACK DOOR TO HEAVEN(1939)
Tony Garsen
SOUTH SEA WOMAN(1953)
Ernest Garside
RIGHT TO LIVE, THE(1933, Brit.), p; THIRD CLUE, THE(1934, Brit.), p; LATE EXTRA(1935, Brit.), p; SMITH'S WIVES(1935, Brit.), p; WHITE LILAC(1935, Brit.), p
J.T. Garside
ILLEGAL(1932, Brit.), art d
John Garside
LYONS MAIL, THE(1931, Brit.); PASSING STRANGER, THE(1954, Brit.)
Anthony Garson
ARCTIC FLIGHT(1952)
Arline Garson
HOUSE OF DARK SHADOWS(1970), ed; PEOPLE NEXT DOOR, THE(1970), ed; SAM'S SONG(1971), ed; RIVALS(1972), ed; MAN WHO WOULD NOT DIE, THE(1975), ed; ALONE IN THE DARK(1982), ed
Greer Garson
GOODBYE MR. CHIPS(1939, Brit.); REMEMBER?(1939); PRIDE AND PREJUDI-CE(1940); BLOSSOMS IN THE DUST(1941); WHEN LADIES MEET(1941); MRS. MINIVER(1942); RANDOM HARVEST(1942); MADAME CURIE(1943); YOUNGEST PROFESSION, THE(1943); MRS. PARKINGTON(1944); ADVENTURE(1945); VALLEY OF DECISION, THE(1945); DESIRE ME(1947); JULIA MISBEHAVES(1948); THAT FORSYTE WOMAN(1949); MINIVER STORY, THE(1950, Brit./U.S.); LAW AND THE

LADY, THE(1951); JULIUS CAESAR(1953); SCANDAL AT SCOURIE(1953); HER TWELVE MEN(1954); STRANGE LADY IN TOWN(1955); PEPE(1960); SUNRISE AT CAMPOBELLO(1960); SINGING NUN, THE(1966); HAPPIEST MILLIONAIRE, THE(1967)

Harry Garson
Misc. Talkies
BEAST OF BORNEO(1935), d
Silents
FORBIDDEN WOMAN, THE(1920), d; CHARGE IT(1921), d; WHAT NO MAN KNOWS(1921), d; ENTER MADAME(1922), p; SIGN OF THE ROSE, THE(1922), d; NO-GUN MAN, THE(1924), d; HEADS UP(1925), d; HIGH AND HANDSOME(1925), d; SMILIN' AT TROUBLE(1925), d
Misc. Silents
FOR THE SOUL OF RAFAEL(1920), d; MIDCHANNEL(1920), d; WHISPERING DEVILS(1920), d; HUSH(1921), d; STRAIGHT FROM PARIS(1921), d; HANDS OF NARA, THE(1922), d; WORLDLY MADONNA, THE(1922), d; OLD SWEETHEART OF MINE, AN(1923), d; THUNDERING DAWN(1923), d; BREED OF THE BORDER, THE(1924), d; MILLIONAIRE COWBOY, THE(1924), d; O.U. WEST(1925), d; SPEED WILD(1925), d; COLLEGE BOOB, THE(1926), d; GLENISTER OF THE MOUNTED(1926), d; MULHALL'S GREAT CATCH(1926), d; SIR LUMBERJACK(1926), d; TRAFFIC COP, THE(1926), d

Henry Garson
RECKLESS MOMENTS, THE(1949), w; DON'T GIVE UP THE SHIP(1959), w; G.I. BLUES(1960), w; VISIT TO A SMALL PLANET(1960), w

Joe Garson
TO PLEASE A LADY(1950)

John Garson
PRIVATE ANGELO(1949, Brit.)

Mort Garson
BEWARE! THE BLOB(1972), m; BLACK EYE(1974), m

Natalie Garson
DANGEROUSLY YOURS(1937); FAST COMPANY(1938); TOY WIFE, THE(1938)

Pop Garson
FOLIES DERGERE(1935)

Crosbie Garstin
CHINA SEAS(1935), w

Edith Garten
SISTERS, OR THE BALANCE OF HAPPINESS(1982, Ger.)

James Garter
JOHNNY BANCO(1969, Fr./Ital./Ger.), w

Annabelle Garth
EYE OF THE CAT(1969)

Caswell Garth
OUT OF THE BLUE(1931, Brit.), w

Daniel Garth
BEHIND LOCKED DOORS(1976, S. Africa)
Misc. Talkies
ANY BODY...ANY WAY(1968)

David Garth
HIDEAWAY GIRL(1937), w; THERE GOES THE GROOM(1937), w; FOUR MEN AND A PRAYER(1938), w; FURY AT FURNACE CREEK(1948), w; MOULIN ROUGE(1952); STRANGER FROM VENUS, THE(1954, Brit.); JOHN OF THE FAIR(1962, Brit.); NEITHER THE SEA NOR THE SAND(1974, Brit.)

Michael Garth
PHANTOM FROM 10,000 LEAGUES, THE(1956); HELLCATS OF THE NAVY(1957); CASE AGAINST BROOKLYN, THE(1958); GOOD DAY FOR A HANGING(1958); PORK CHOP HILL(1959)

Mike Garth
TARAWA BEACHHEAD(1958)

Otis Garth
MR. SCOUTMASTER(1953); LAW VS. BILLY THE KID, THE(1954); THEM!(1954)

Borgar Gartharsson
HAGBARD AND SIGNE(1968, Den./Iceland/Swed.)

Christopher Gartin
1984
FIRSTBORN(1984)

Anne Gartlan
1984
GARBO TALKS(1984)

H. Gartner
BRIDEGROOM FOR TWO(1932, Brit.), ph

Heinrich Gartner
COPPER, THE(1930, Brit.), ph

Henry Gartner
FLAME OF LOVE, THE(1930, Brit.), ph; NIGHT BIRDS(1931, Brit.), ph; WOMAN DECIDES, THE(1932, Brit.), ph

Herbi Gartner
ERIC SOYA'S "17"(1967, Den.), art d

Lou Gartner
FALLGUY(1962)

Louis Gartner
STUNT MAN, THE(1980)

Sandra Gartner
Misc. Talkies
NAUGHTY SCHOOL GIRLS(1977)

Ernest Gartside
GARRISON FOLLIES(1940, Brit.), p; GORBALS STORY, THE(1950, Brit.), p; OBSESSED(1951, Brit.), p; THIRD VISITOR, THE(1951, Brit.), p; CASTLE IN THE AIR(1952, Brit.), p; GAY DOG, THE(1954, Brit.), p; COUNT FIVE AND DIE(1958, Brit.), p

Philip Gartside
CONTRABAND SPAIN(1955, Brit.), p

Rosetta Garuffi
LIFE STUDY(1973)

George Garvarentz
SOUTHERN STAR, THE(1969, Fr./Brit.), m; TRIUMPHS OF A MAN CALLED HORSE(1983, US/Mex.), m

Georges Garvarentz
DANIELLA BY NIGHT(1962, Fr/Ger.), m; DEVIL AND THE TEN COMMANDMENTS, THE(1962, Fr.), m; TALES OF PARIS(1962, Fr./Ital.), m; THREE FABLES OF LOVE(1963, Fr./Ital./Span.), m; DON'T TEMPT THE DEVIL(1964, Fr./Ital.), m; HOW NOT TO ROB A DEPARTMENT STORE(1965, Fr./Ital.), m; TAXI FOR TOBRUK(1965, Fr./Span./Ger.), m; FIVE WILD GIRLS(1966, Fr.), m; MARCO THE MAGNIFICENT(1966, Ital./Fr./Yugo./Egypt/Afghanistan), m; THAT MAN IN ISTANBUL(1966, Fr./Ital./Span.), m; CORRUPT ONES, THE(1967, Ger.), m; SEA PIRATE, THE(1967, Fr./Span./Ital.), m; TRIPLE CROSS(1967, Fr./Brit.), m; UPPER HAND, THE(1967, Fr./Ital./Ger.), m; VISCOUNT, THE(1967, Fr./Span./Ital./Ger.), m; PARIS IN THE MONTH OF AUGUST(1968, Fr.), m; POSTMAN GOES TO WAR, THE(1968, Fr.), m; THEY CAME TO ROB LAS VEGAS(1969, Fr./Ital./Span./Ger.), m; SOMEONE BEHIND THE DOOR(1971, Fr./Brit.), m; KILLER FORCE(1975, Switz./Ireland), m; GOLDEN LADY, THE(1979, Brit.), m

Andrew Garve
TOUCH OF LARCENY, A(1960, Brit.), w; TWO LETTER ALIBI(1962), w

George Garver
GLORY ALLEY(1952)

Kathy Garver
TEN COMMANDMENTS, THE(1956); MONKEY ON MY BACK(1957)

Peter Garves
REMARKABLE MR. KIPPS(1942, Brit.)

Jack Garvey
DELIRIUM(1979)

Nick Garvey
ACCEPTABLE LEVELS(1983, Brit.), m

Patricia Garvey
TORTURE DUNGEON(1970)

Robert Garvey
BLACK WHIP, THE(1956); PARDNERS(1956)

Stanley Garvey
EVERY NIGHT AT EIGHT(1935), w

Steve Garvey
GONG SHOW MOVIE, THE(1980)

Charles Garvice
MARIGOLD(1938, Brit.), w
Silents
JUST A GIRL(1916, Brit.), w

Edward Garvie
SOCIAL REGISTER(1934)

Parker Garvie
MURDER IS MY BUSINESS(1946); TANGIER(1946)

Anita Garvin
CHARLATAN, THE(1929); MODERN LOVE(1929); RED HOT RHYTHM(1930); SWISS MISS(1938)
Silents
BERTHA, THE SEWING MACHINE GIRL(1927); NIGHT WATCH, THE(1928); PLAY GIRL, THE(1928)
Misc. Silents
VALLEY OF HELL, THE(1927)

Bill Garvin
PAN-AMERICANA(1945)

Bob Garvin
MILKMAN, THE(1950)

Bobby V. Garvin
LANDLORD, THE(1970)

Gene Garvin
MODERN ROMANCE(1981)

Grace Garvin
FLOODTIDE(1949, Brit.)

Jean Garvin
SO BIG(1953)

John Garvin
PRAISE MARX AND PASS THE AMMUNITION(1970, Brit.)

Virginia Garvin
HI-DE-HO(1947)

James Garwood
SHAKEDOWN(1950)

John Garwood
HELL'S ANGELS ON WHEELS(1967); SAVAGE SEVEN, THE(1968); LOSERS, THE(1970); EVEL KNIEVEL(1971); SUPERBEAST(1972); CLEOPATRA JONES(1973); TASTE OF HELL, A(1973), a, p; FREEBIE AND THE BEAN(1974); HOW COME NOBODY'S ON OUR SIDE?(1975); STUNT MAN, THE(1980); 10 TO MIDNIGHT(1983)

Judith Garwood
ANGELS FROM HELL(1968)

Judy Garwood
NEW KIND OF LOVE, A(1963)

Kelton Garwood
MIRACLE OF THE HILLS, THE(1959); STORY OF RUTH, THE(1960); MOVE OVER, DARLING(1963); SANDPIPER, THE(1965); BIG DADDY(1969)

Norman Garwood
TIME BANDITS(1981, Brit.), art d; MISSIONARY, THE(1982), art d; RED MONARCH(1983, Brit.), prod d

William Garwood
Silents
LITTLE BROTHER, THE(1917)
Misc. Silents
ROBIN HOOD(1913); IMAR THE SERVITOR(1914); WOLF OF DEBT, THE(1915); BROKEN FETTERS(1916); MAGDALENE OF THE HILLS, A(1917); GUILTY MAN, THE(1918); HER MOMENT(1918); WIVES AND OTHER WIVES(1919)

Alberta Gary
THEY DIED WITH THEIR BOOTS ON(1942)

Ann Pearl Gary
FAN, THE(1981)

Ben Gary
STUDS LONIGAN(1960)

Bob Gary
NORTHERN PURSUIT(1943)

Eleanor Gary
LOVE IS A CAROUSEL(1970), a, m

Gene Gary
MISSION TO MOSCOW(1943); PARIS AFTER DARK(1943); NORTHWEST OUT-POST(1947); I, JANE DOE(1948); ROSE OF THE YUKON(1949); LUM AND ABNER ABROAD(1956)

Harold Gary
KISS OF DEATH(1947); UNDERCOVER GIRL(1950); LET'S ROCK(1958); MURDER, INC.(1960); SHANGRI-LA(1961); FRENCH CONNECTION, THE(1971)

Inez Gary
HIDDEN HAND, THE(1942)

Linda Gary
WOLFEN(1981)
Misc. Talkies
BABY DOLLS(1982)

Lorraine Gary
JAWS(1975); CARWASH(1976); I NEVER PROMISED YOU A ROSE GARDEN(1977); JAWS II(1978); JUST YOU AND ME, KID(1979); 1941(1979)

Lou Gary
LAST SUMMER(1969)

Micheline Gary
PICNIC ON THE GRASS(1960, Fr.)

Paul Gary
GUNFIGHT AT THE O.K. CORRAL(1957); JOKER IS WILD, THE(1957)

Romain Gary
ROOTS OF HEAVEN, THE(1958), w; MAN WHO UNDERSTOOD WOMEN, THE(1959), w; LONGEST DAY, THE(1962), w; LADY L(1965, Fr./Ital.), w; BIRDS COME TO DIE IN PERU(1968, Fr.), d&w; PROMISE AT DAWN(1970, U.S./Fr.), w; SKI BUM, THE(1971), w; KILL! KILL! KILL!(1972, Fr./Ger./Ital./Span.), d&w; WOMAN-LIGHT(1979, Fr./Ger./Ital.), d&w; CLAIR DE FEMME(1980,Fr.), w; WHITE DOG(1982), w

Sheila Gary
ILLIAC PASSION, THE(1968)

Gary Lewis and The Playboys
FAMILY JEWELS, THE(1965); SWINGIN' SUMMER, A(1965); OUT OF SIGHT(1966)

Jaime Garza
MISSING(1982)

Martha Garza
METEOR(1979)

Ed Garzero
FRENCH CONNECTION, THE(1971), set d

Luis Garzon
DANIEL(1983)

Miguel Garzon
MARY, MARY, BLOODY MARY(1975, U.S./Mex.), ph

Garzoni
CARNIVAL OF SINNERS(1947, Fr.)

Christian Gasc
LUMIERE(1976, Fr.), cos

Yves Gasc
BEAU PERE(1981, Fr.)

Brian Gascoigne
BLUE BLOOD(1973, Brit.), m; MALACHI'S COVE(1973, Brit.), m; UNDER MILK WOOD(1973, Brit.), m; PHASE IV(1974), m
1984
1919(1984, Brit.), m

Jill Gascoine
CONFESSIONS OF A POP PERFORMER(1975, Brit.)

Jean Gascon
MAN CALLED HORSE, A(1970); LUCKY STAR, THE(1980, Can.)

Gabriel Gascond
SERGEANT, THE(1968)

Jacqueline Gasden
Misc. Silents
MAN WHO WON, THE(1923)

Louis J. Gasiner
Misc. Silents
THAT MODEL FROM PARIS(1926), d

Jacek Gasiorowski
DANTON(1983), w

Waclaw Gasiorowski
CONQUEST(1937), w

Elizabeth Cleghorn Gaskell
Silents
HEARTSTRINGS(1923, Brit.), w

Jane Gaskell
ALL NEAT IN BLACK STOCKINGS(1969, Brit.), w

Marjorie Gaskell
LAZYBONES(1935, Brit.)

Mary Gaskell
I'LL STICK TO YOU(1933, Brit.); FACES(1934, Brit.); LUCKY LOSER(1934, Brit.)

Charles L. Gaskill
Silents
SYLVIA GRAY(1914), d&w; LIGHTS OF NEW YORK, THE(1916), w
Misc. Silents
CLEOPATRA(1913), d; PRINCESS OF BAGDAD(1913), d

Charles R. Gaskill
LIGHTS OF NEW YORK(1928), w

Ira Gaskill
NIGHT OF EVIL(1962)

Bill Gaskin
GYPSY(1962), cos

Jack Gaskins
THIN RED LINE, THE(1964); EVERY DAY IS A HOLIDAY(1966, Span.)

George Gaslini
SLASHER, THE(1975), ph

Giorgio Gaslini
LA NOTTE(1961, Fr./Ital.), m

Louis Gasnier
DARKENED ROOMS(1929), d; L'ENIGMATIQUE MONSIEUR PARKES(1930), d; SHADOW OF THE LAW(1930), d; SLIGHTLY SCARLET(1930), D; VIRTUOUS SIN, THE(1930), d; LAWYER'S SECRET, THE(1931), d; SILENCE(1931), d; CASE OF CLARA DEANE(1932), d; STRANGE CASE OF CLARA DEANE, THE(1932), d; GAMBLING SHIP(1933), d; LAST OUTPOST, THE(1935), d; TOPAZE(1935, Fr.), d; REEFER MADNESS(1936), d; BANK ALARM(1937), d; MURDER ON THE YUKON(1940), d; SUNSET MURDER CASE(1941), d; MARINES COME THROUGH, THE(1943), d
Misc. Talkies
STOLEN PARADISE(1941), d
Silents
KISMET(1920), d; WIFE'S AWAKENING, A(1921), d; MOTHERS-IN-LAW(1923), d; PLEASURES OF THE RICH(1926), d
Misc. Silents
DAUGHTERS OF THE RICH(1923), d; MAYTIME(1923), d; BREATH OF A SCAN-DAL, THE(1924), d; POISONED PARADISE: THE FORBIDDEN STORY OF MONTE CARLO(1924), d; TRIFLERS, THE(1924), d; WHITE MAN(1924), d; BOOMERANG, THE(1925), d; FAINT PERFUME(1925), d; PARASITE, THE(1925), d; PARISIAN LOVE(1925), d; STREETS OF SHANGHAI(1927), d

Louis J. Gasnier
GOLD RACKET, THE(1937), d
Silents
RICH MEN'S WIVES(1922), d; THORNS AND ORANGE BLOSSOMS(1922), d; HERO, THE(1923), d; POOR MEN'S WIVES(1923), d
Misc. Silents
GOOD WOMEN(1921), d; SILENT YEARS(1921), d; CALL OF HOME, THE(1922), d; WINE(1924), d; LOST AT SEA(1926), d; OUT OF THE STORM(1926), d; SIN CAR-GO(1926), d; BEAUTY SHOPPERS(1927), d; FASHION MADNESS(1928), d

Charles Gaspar
FOOLS' PARADE(1971), spec eff

Chuck Gaspar
HEAD(1968), spec eff; VALDEZ IS COMING(1971), spec eff; FAREWELL, MY LOVE-LY(1975), spec eff; MITCHELL(1975), spec eff; EXORCIST II: THE HERETIC(1977), spec eff; GAUNTLET, THE(1977), spec eff; NINE TO FIVE(1980), spec eff; BLUE THUNDER(1983), spec eff
1984
GHOSTBUSTERS(1984), spec eff

Dean Gaspar
GANDHI(1982)

Gesa Gaspar
GUESS WHO'S COMING TO DINNER(1967), spec eff

Geza Gaspar
LOVED ONE, THE(1965), spec eff; IN COLD BLOOD(1967), spec eff; LUV(1967), spec eff; HOW TO SAVE A MARRIAGE--AND RUIN YOUR LIFE(1968), spec eff; HAPPY ENDING, THE(1969), spec eff; R.P.M.(1970), spec eff

Ray Gaspard
SCREAMS OF A WINTER NIGHT(1979)

Pierre Gaspard-Huit
SCHEHERAZADE(1965, Fr./Ital./Span.), d, w

Nelson Gaspari
MARGIN, THE,(1969, Braz.)

Franco Gasparri
BLOOD, SWEAT AND FEAR(1975, Ital.)

Gianfranco Gasparri
GOLIATH AGAINST THE GIANTS(1963, Ital./Span.)

Chuck Gasper
STAR IS BORN, A(1976), spec eff

Elisabeth Gasper
EARTH ENTRANCED(1970, Braz.)

Gloria Gasper
TIGER AND THE FLAME, THE(1955, India)

Ivan Gasper
ARENA, THE(1973)

Luciano Gasper
EMBALMER, THE(1966, Ital.)

Luis Gasper
NARCO MEN, THE(1969, Span./Ital.)

Yvonne Gasperina
NIGHT AFFAIR(1961, Fr.), makeup

Bertram Gassby
Misc. Silents
CHEATING THE PUBLIC(1918)

Nathalie Gasse
NUDE ODYSSEY(1962, Fr./Ital.)

Sylvia Gassel
LILITH(1964)

Sylvia Gassell
CRUISING(1980)

Mary Lou Gassen
CUBA CROSSING(1980)

Ernest Gasser
NEARLY A NASTY ACCIDENT(1962, Brit.), makeup; TERM OF TRIAL(1962, Brit.), makeup; TIARA TAHITI(1962, Brit.), makeup; VICTORS, THE(1963), makeup; CHALK GARDEN, THE(1964, Brit.), makeup; YOUNG CASSIDY(1965, U.S./Brit.), makeup; CAPTAIN NEMO AND THE UNDERWATER CITY(1969, Brit.), makeup; DECLINE AND FALL... OF A BIRD WATCHER(1969, Brit.), makeup; PRIME OF MISS JEAN BRODIE, THE(1969, Brit.), makeup; LOOKING GLASS WAR, THE(1970, Brit.), makeup; PRIVATE LIFE OF SHERLOCK HOLMES, THE(1970, Brit.), makeup

Ernie Gasser
NIGHT DIGGER, THE(1971, Brit.), makeup

Yves Gasser
JONAH--WHO WILL BE 25 IN THE YEAR 2000(1976, Switz.), p; PROVIDENCE(1977, Fr.), p; NO TIME FOR BREAKFAST(1978, Fr.), p

Frank Gassman
WIND AND THE LION, THE(1975)

Vittorio Gassman
WANDERING JEW, THE(1948, Ital.); BITTER RICE(1950, Ital.); ANNA(1951, Ital.); VOICE IN YOUR HEART, A(1952, Ital.); CRY OF THE HUNTED(1953); GLASS WALL, THE(1953); SOMBRERO(1953); RHAPSODY(1954); DEFEND MY LOVE(1956, Ital.);

WAR AND PEACE(1956, Ital./U.S.); TEMPEST(1958, Ital./Yugo./Fr.); LOVE SPECIALIST, THE(1959, Ital.); MIRACLE, THE(1959); BIG DEAL ON MADONNA STREET, THE(1960); GREAT WAR, THE(1961, Fr., Ital.); BARABBAS(1962, Ital.); EASY LIFE, THE(1963, Ital.); FIASCO IN MILAN(1963, Fr./Ital.); LOVE AND LARCENY(1963, Fr./Ital.); AND SUDDENLY IT'S MURDER!(1964, Ital.); LET'S TALK ABOUT WOMEN(1964, Fr./Ital.); EYE OF THE NEEDLE, THE(1965, Ital./Fr.); ONE MILLION DOLLARS(1965, Ital.); THE DIRTY GAME(1966, Fr./Ital./Ger.); MAIDEN FOR A PRINCE, A(1967, Fr./Ital.); OPIATE '67(1967, Fr./Ital.); TIGER AND THE PUSSYCAT, THE(1967, U.S., Ital.); WOMAN TIMES SEVEN(1967, U.S./Fr./Ital.); CATCH AS CATCH CAN(1968, Ital.); DEVIL IN LOVE, THE(1968, Ital.); GHOSTS, ITALIAN STYLE(1969, Ital./Fr.); TWELVE PLUS ONE(1970, Fr./Ital.); MIDNIGHT PLEASURES(1975, Ital.); DESERT OF THE TARTARS, THE(1976 Fr./Ital./Iranian); SCENT OF A WOMAN(1976, Ital.); GOODNIGHT, LADIES AND GENTLEMEN(1977, Ital.); VIVA ITALIA(1978, Ital.); WEDDING, A(1978); QUINTET(1979); IMMORTAL BACHELOR, THE(1980, Ital.); NUDE BOMB, THE(1980); SHARKY'S MACHINE(1982); TEMPEST(1982); BENVENUTA(1983, Fr.)

1984

LIFE IS A BED OF ROSES(1984, Fr.)

Misc. Talkies

PROPHET, THE(1976)

Vittorio Gassmann

MAMBO(1955, Ital.)

Helmut Gassner

1984

LITTLE DRUMMER GIRL, THE(1984), art d

Hilary Gasson

SQUEEZE, THE(1977, Brit.)

Marcel Gassouk

DAY AND THE HOUR, THE(1963, Fr./ Ital.); JUST BEFORE NIGHTFALL(1975, Fr./Ital.); CHARLES AND LUCIE(1982, Fr.)

Michel Gast

I SPIT ON YOUR GRAVE(1962, Fr.), d

Helena Gastal

1984

BLAME IT ON RIO(1984), cos

Antonio Gastaldi

TWO WOMEN(1961, Ital./Fr.)

Ernesto Gastaldi

VAMPIRE AND THE BALLERINA, THE(1962, Ital.), w; ARIZONA COLT(1965, It./Fr./Span.), w; 10,000 DOLLARS BLOOD MONEY(1966, Ital.), w; SWEET BODY OF DEBORAH, THE(1969, Ital./Fr.), w; DAY OF ANGER(1970, Ital./Ger.), w; NEXT!(1971, Ital./Span.), w; MY NAME IS NOBODY(1974, Ital./Fr./Ger.), w; REASON TO LIVE, A REASON TO DIE, A(1974, Ital./Fr./Ger./Span.), w; TORSO(1974, Ital.), w; GENIUS, THE(1976, Ital./Fr./Ger.), w

Jany Gastaldi

1984

EDITH AND MARCEL(1984, Fr.)

Nick Gaster

XTRO(1983, Brit.), ed

Nicolas Gaster

1984

SLAYGROUND(1984, Brit.), ed

Leila Gastil

PERMANENT VACATION(1982)

George Gastine

MISTER 880(1950)

Andrew Gaston

FIRE IN THE STONE, THE(1983, Aus.)

Karen Gaston

FAREWELL, MY LOVELY(1975)

Mae Gaston

Silents

LOVE LIAR, THE(1916)

Misc. Silents

WASTED YEARS, THE(1916); JOHN ERMINE OF THE YELLOWSTONE(1917); PAINTED LIE, THE(1917); WHO WAS THE OTHER MAN?(1917); LOVE THAT DARES, THE(1919)

Mary Gaston

Misc. Silents

LONE STAR RUSH, THE(1915)

May Gaston

Silents

CRAVING, THE(1918)

Ralph Gaston

STALAG 17(1953)

Gaston & Andree

IT'S IN THE BAG(1936, Brit.)

Gaston and Andree

THOSE WERE THE DAYS(1934, Brit.)

Lisa Gastone

RUNAWAY BUS, THE(1954, Brit.)

Lisa Gastoni

DANCE LITTLE LADY(1954, Brit.); DOCTOR IN THE HOUSE(1954, Brit.); THEY WHO DARE(1954, Brit.); YOU KNOW WHAT SAILORS ARE(1954, Brit.); JOSEPHINE AND MEN(1955, Brit.); MAN OF THE MOMENT(1955, Brit.); BABY AND THE BATTLESHIP, THE(1957, Brit.); SECOND FIDDLE(1957, Brit.); THUNDER OVER TANGIER(1957, Brit.); BLUE MURDER AT ST. TRINIAN'S(1958, Brit.); CHAIN OF EVENTS(1958, Brit.); FEMALE FIENDS(1958, Brit.); HELLO LONDON(1958, Brit.); INTENT TO KILL(1958, Brit.); MENACE IN THE NIGHT(1958, Brit.); RX MURDER(1958, Brit.); THREE MEN IN A BOAT(1958, Brit.); TRUTH ABOUT WOMEN, THE(1958, Brit.); WRONG NUMBER(1959, Brit.); BREAKING POINT, THE(1961, Brit.); PASSPORT TO CHINA(1961, Brit.); EVA(1962, Fr./Ital.); GIDGET GOES TO ROME(1963); GREAT ARMORED CAR SWINDLE, THE(1964); MYTH, THE(1965, Ital.); MAN WHO LAUGHS, THE(1966, Ital.); WAKE UP AND DIE(1967, Fr./Ital.); WILD, WILD PLANET, THE(1967, Ital.); THANK YOU, AUNT(1969, Ital.); LAST DAYS OF MUSSOLINI(1974, Ital.)

Misc. Talkies

QUEEN OF THE SEAS(1960)

Phil Gastrock

PERFECT CRIME, THE(1928)

Silents

MASKED AVENGER, THE(1922)

Ed Gatchalian

STRYKER(1983, Phil.), m

Frank Gatcliff

ON THE BEACH(1959)

Melody Gate

BIG CAPER, THE(1957)

Robin Gatehouse

MOUSE THAT ROARED, THE(1959, Brit.)

Frederic Gately

I SAILED TO TAHITI WITH AN ALL GIRL CREW(1969), ph

Frederick Gately

HARPOON(1948), ph; NAKED HILLS, THE(1956), ph; BADLANDS OF MONTANA(1957), ph; I BURY THE LIVING(1958), ph; TANK BATTALION(1958), ph; WICKED, WICKED(1973), ph

Fredrick Gately

NAKED DAWN, THE(1955), ph

Lew Gater

WEST OF THE ROCKIES(1931), p

Andrew Gates

BIRCH INTERVAL(1976)

Betty Gates

Misc. Silents

SECRETS OF THE RANGE(1928)

Bob Gates

RETURN TO BOGGY CREEK(1977), p

Bud Gates

STALLION CANYON(1949)

David Gates

JOURNEY TO SHILOH(1968), m; BIRCH INTERVAL(1976)

Eleanor Gates

ONCE TO EVERY BACHELOR(1934), w; POOR LITTLE RICH GIRL(1936), w

Silents

POOR LITTLE RICH GIRL, A(1917), w

Fay Gates

HOLLYWOOD HIGH(1977), cos

H.L. Gates

HALF WAY TO HEAVEN(1929), d&w

Harvey Gates

MIDNIGHT TAXI, THE(1928), w; TERROR, THE(1928), w; DESERT SONG, THE(1929), w; FORWARD PASS, THE(1929), w; FROM HEADQUARTERS(1929), w; GLAD RAG DOLL, THE(1929), w; HEARTS IN EXILE(1929), w; REDEEMING SIN, THE(1929), w; SAY IT WITH SONGS(1929), w; STARK MAD(1929), w; IN THE NEXT ROOM(1930), w; SKY RAIDERS(1931), w; HELL DIVERS(1932), w; IF I HAD A MILLION(1932), w; MADAME RACKETEER(1932), w; MYSTERIOUS RIDER, THE(1933), w; BAND PLAYS ON, THE(1934), w; O'SHAUGHNESSY'S BOY(1935), w; WEREWOLF OF LONDON, THE(1935), w; FLYING HOSTESS(1936), w; VOICE OF BUGLE ANN(1936), w; LUCK OF ROARING CAMP, THE(1937), w; WHEN'S YOUR BIRTHDAY?(1937), w; FUGITIVE AT LARGE(1939), w; MEET DR. CHRISTIAN(1939), w; NAVY SECRETS(1939), w; MEN WITHOUT SOULS(1940), w; ZIS BOOM BAH(1941), w; BLACK DRAGONS(1942), w; COLLEGE SWEETHEARTS(1942), w; CORPSE VANISHES, THE(1942), w; LET'S GET TOUGH(1942), w; MR. WISE GUY(1942), w; CLANCY STREET BOYS(1943), w; DIVORCE(1945), w; DOCKS OF NEW YORK(1945), w; NORTHWEST TRAIL(1945), w; BELOW THE DEADLINE(1946), w; DON'T GAMBLE WITH STRANGERS(1946), w; LAST FRONTIER UPRISING(1947), w; RACING LUCK(1948), w

Silents

JUDGE NOT OR THE WOMAN OF MONA DIGGINGS(1915), w; MAN FROM MONTANA, THE(1917), w; BROADWAY SCANDAL(1918), w; FLAMES OF CHANCE, THE(1918), w; MADAME SPY(1918), w; STING OF THE LASH(1921), w; ENVIRONMENT(1922), w; CLEAN UP, THE(1923), w; DRUG TRAFFIC, THE(1923), w; LEGALLY DEAD(1923), w; MERRY-GO-ROUND(1923), w; SAWDUST(1923), w; SKID PROOF(1923), w; FIGHTING AMERICAN, THE(1924), w; CRIMSON RUNNER, THE(1925), w; BARRIER, THE(1926), w; BRUTE, THE(1927), w; SAILOR'S SWEETHEART, A(1927), w

Harvey H. Gates

WHAT A MAN(1930), w; 'NEATH BROOKLYN BRIDGE(1942), w; SMART ALECKS(1942), w; ALLOTMENT WIVES, INC.(1945), w; MR. MUGGS RIDES AGAIN(1945), w

Harvey Harris Gates

COUNTY FAIR, THE(1932), w

Henry Leyford Gates

Silents

JOANNA(1925), w

James C. Gates

TERROR IN THE JUNGLE(1968)

Joan Gates

GENTLE SEX, THE(1943, Brit.)

Joyce Gates

SUMMER STORM(1944)

Larry Gates

TOYS IN THE ATTIC(1963); GLORY ALLEY(1952); HAS ANYBODY SEEN MY GAL?(1952); ABOVE AND BEYOND(1953); FRANCIS COVERS THE BIG TOWN(1953); TAKE ME TO TOWN(1953); GIRL RUSH, THE(1955); INVASION OF THE BODY SNATCHERS(1956); BROTHERS RICO, THE(1957); JEANNE EAGELS(1957); STRANGE ONE, THE(1957); CAT ON A HOT TIN ROOF(1958); REMARKABLE MR. PENNYPACKER, THE(1959); SOME CAME RUNNING(1959); GREAT IMPOSTOR, THE(1960); ONE FOOT IN HELL(1960); ADA(1961); HOODLUM PRIEST, THE(1961); UNDERWORLD U.S.A.(1961); YOUNG SAVAGES, THE(1961); SPIRAL ROAD, THE(1962); CATTLE KING(1963); SAND PEBBLES, THE(1966); HOUR OF THE GUN(1967); IN THE HEAT OF THE NIGHT(1967); DEATH OF A GUNFIGHTER(1969); AIRPORT(1970); RE: LUCKY LUCIANO(1974, Fr./Ital.); FUNNY LADY(1975)

Leonard-John Gates

1984

CITY GIRL, THE(1984), w

Linda Lee Gates
MADAME CURIE(1943)

Marlyn Gates
IT'S MY TURN(1980)

Maxine Gates
HERE COME THE CO-EDS(1945); DARK HORSE, THE(1946); ALIAS NICK BEAL(1949); WHERE DANGER LIVES(1950); WOMAN OF DISTINCTION, A(1950); OKLAHOMA ANNIE(1952); EMERGENCY HOSPITAL(1956); GIANT(1956); UNHOLY ROLLERS(1972)

Nancy Gates
GREAT GILDERSLEEVE, THE(1942); HITLER'S CHILDREN(1942); MAGNIFICENT AMBERSONS, THE(1942); BEHIND THE RISING SUN(1943); GILDERSLEEVE'S BAD DAY(1943); THIS LAND IS MINE(1943); BRIDE BY MISTAKE(1944); MASTER RACE, THE(1944); NEVADA(1944); NIGHT OF ADVENTURE, A(1944); SPANISH MAIN, THE(1945); CHEYENNE TAKES OVER(1947); CHECK YOUR GUNS(1948); ROLL, THUNDER, ROLL(1949); AT SWORD'S POINT(1951); ATOMIC CITY, THE(1952); GREATEST SHOW ON EARTH, THE(1952); MEMBER OF THE WEDDING, THE(1952); TARGET HONG KONG(1952); TORCH SONG(1953); HELL'S HALF ACRE(1954); MASTERSON OF KANSAS(1954); SUDDENLY(1954); NO MAN'S WOMAN(1955); STRANGER ON HORSEBACK(1955); TOP OF THE WORLD(1955); BOTTOM OF THE BOTTLE, THE(1956); BRASS LEGEND, THE(1956); DEATH OF A SCOUNDREL(1956); MAGNIFICENT ROUGHNECKS(1956); SEARCH FOR BRIDEY MURPHY, THE(1956); WORLD WITHOUT END(1956); RAWHIDE TRAIL, THE(1958); GUNFIGHT AT DODGE CITY, THE(1959); SOME CAME RUNNING(1959); COMANCHE STATION(1960)
Misc. Talkies
RAWHIDE TRAIL, THE(1950); AGE OF PISCES(1972)

Neville Gates
TAKE A POWDER(1953, Brit.)

Pete Gates
SHADOW VALLEY(1947), m

Rich Gates
KENTUCKY FRIED MOVIE, THE(1977)

Richard Allen Gates
Silents
ARIZONA BOUND(1927), w; SHOOTIN' IRONS(1927), w

Rick Gates
HANG'EM HIGH(1968); WAR BETWEEN MEN AND WOMEN, THE(1972); SO LONG, BLUE BOY(1973)

Robert Gates
STATION WEST(1948)

Samantha Gates
FULL CIRCLE(1977, Brit./Can.); NO LONGER ALONE(1978); WATER BABIES, THE(1979, Brit.); HAUNTING OF JULIA, THE(1981, Brit./Can.)

Susan Gates
GNOME-MOBILE, THE(1967)

Tudor Gates
DATELINE DIAMONDS(1966, Brit.), w; BARBARELLA(1968, Fr./Ital.), w; DANGER: DIABOLIK(1968, Ital./Fr.), w; VAMPIRE LOVERS, THE(1970, Brit.), w; FRIGHT(1971, Brit.), w; LUST FOR A VAMPIRE(1971, Brit.), w; TWINS OF EVIL(1971, Brit.), w; OPTIMISTS, THE(1973, Brit.), w

William "Pop" Gates
HARLEM GLOBETROTTERS, THE(1951)

Marjorie Gateson
BELOVED BACHELOR, THE(1931); HUSBAND'S HOLIDAY(1931); FALSE MADONNA(1932); JAZZ BABIES(1932); OKAY AMERICA(1932); SILVER DOLLAR(1932); SOCIETY GIRL(1932); STREET OF WOMEN(1932); THIRTEEN WOMEN(1932); BLIND ADVENTURE(1933); BUREAU OF MISSING PERSONS(1933); COCKTAIL HOUR(1933); EMPLOYEE'S ENTRANCE(1933); KING'S VACATION, THE(1933); LADY KILLER(1933); LILLY TURNER(1933); MELODY CRUISE(1933); WALLS OF GOLD(1933); WORLD CHANGES, THE(1933); BIG HEARTED HERBERT(1934); CHAINED(1934); COMING OUT PARTY(1934); DOWN TO THEIR LAST YACHT(1934); FOG(1934); GENTLEMEN ARE BORN(1934); HAPPINESS AHEAD(1934); HI, NELLIE!(1934); LET'S FALL IN LOVE(1934); MILLION DOLLAR RANSOM(1934); OPERATOR 13(1934); SIDE STREETS(1934); GOIN' TO TOWN(1935); YOUR UNCLE DUDLEY(1935); ARIZONA MAHONEY(1936); BIG BROWN EYES(1936); FIRST BABY(1936); GENTLEMAN FROM LOUISIANA(1936); HIS FAMILY TREE(1936); MAN I MARRY, THE(1936); MILKY WAY, THE(1936); PRIVATE NUMBER(1936); THREE MARRIED MEN(1936); WIFE VERSUS SECRETARY(1936); FIRST LADY(1937); TURN OFF THE MOON(1937); VOGUES OF 1938(1937); WE HAVE OUR MOMENTS(1937); DUKE OF WEST POINT, THE(1938); GATEWAY(1938); MAKING THE HEADLINES(1938); NO TIME TO MARRY(1938); SPRING MADNESS(1938); STABLEMATES(1938); GERONIMO(1939); MY WIFE'S RELATIVES(1939); TOO BUSY TO WORK(1939); ESCAPE TO GLORY(1940); I'M NOBODY'S SWEETHEART NOW(1940); IN OLD MISSOURI(1940); PAROLE FIXER(1940); POP ALWAYS PAYS(1940); THIRD FINGER, LEFT HAND(1940); 'TIL WE MEET AGAIN(1940); BACK STREET(1941); HERE COMES HAPPINESS(1941); HONOLULU LU(1941); INTERNATIONAL LADY(1941); MOONLIGHT IN HAWAII(1941); OBLIGING YOUNG LADY(1941); PASSAGE FROM HONG KONG(1941); YOU'LL NEVER GET RICH(1941); DUDES ARE PRETTY PEOPLE(1942); JUKE BOX JENNY(1942); MEET THE STEWARTS(1942); RINGS ON HER FINGERS(1942); I DOOD IT(1943); NO TIME FOR LOVE(1943); RHYTHM OF THE ISLANDS(1943); SKY'S THE LIMIT, THE(1943); YOUNGEST PROFESSION, THE(1943); CASANOVA IN BURLESQUE(1944); EVER SINCE VENUS(1944); HI, GOOD-LOOKIN'(1944); SEVEN DAYS ASHORE(1944); ONE MORE TOMORROW(1946); CADDY, THE(1953)
Misc. Talkies
HOUSE OF MYSTERY, THE(1938)

The Gateway Trio
HOOTENANNY HOOT(1963)

Jimmy Gatherum
HEARSE, THE(1980)

Malu Gatica
LADY AND THE BANDIT, THE(1951); TARGET UNKNOWN(1951); CAPTAIN PIRATE(1952)

Frank Gatliff
PRIZE OF ARMS, A(1962, Brit.); IPCRESS FILE, THE(1965, Brit.); PROJECTED MAN, THE(1967, Brit.); OPERATION DAYBREAK(1976, U.S./Brit./Czech.)

Gerry Gatlin
TRIUMPHS OF A MAN CALLED HORSE(1983, US/Mex.)

Herb Gatlin
ACE ELI AND RODGER OF THE SKIES(1973)

Jerry Gatlin
HALLELUJAH TRAIL, THE(1965); SONS OF KATIE ELDER, THE(1965); EYE FOR AN EYE, AN(1966); FIVE CARD STUD(1968); BIG JAKE(1971); BUCK AND THE PREACHER(1972); COWBOYS, THE(1972); CULPEPPER CATTLE COMPANY, THE(1972); HONKERS, THE(1972), a, stunts; LEGEND OF NIGGER CHARLEY, THE(1972), a, stunts; ULZANA'S RAID(1972); TRAIN ROBBERS, THE(1973); BITE THE BULLET(1975); ROOSTER COGBURN(1975); DUCHESS AND THE DIRTWATER FOX, THE(1976); GREAT SCOUT AND CATHOUSE THURSDAY, THE(1976), stunts; COAST TO COAST(1980); CATTLE ANNIE AND LITTLE BRITCHES(1981)
1984
STARMAN(1984)

Mickey Gatlin
LENNY(1974)

John Gatrell
WALLET, THE(1952, Brit.); CARRY ON SERGEANT(1959, Brit.); PRIVATE LIFE OF SHERLOCK HOLMES, THE(1970, Brit.); GAMES THAT LOVERS PLAY(1971, Brit.)

Cesar Gattegno
PICKPOCKET(1963, Fr.)

E. Gatti
LILAC DOMINO, THE(1940, Brit.), w

Gabriella Gatti
ROSSINI(1948, Ital.)

John Gatti
LET'S MAKE LOVE(1960)

Marcello Gatti
FOUR DAYS OF NAPLES, THE(1963, US/Ital.), ph; AMERICAN WIFE, AN(1965, Ital.), ph; LA FUGA(1966, Ital.), ph; RUN FOR YOUR WIFE(1966, Fr./Ital.), ph; BATTLE OF ALGIERS, THE(1967, Ital./Alger.), ph; LOVE FACTORY(1969, Ital.), ph; BURN(1970), ph; ANONYMOUS VENETIAN, THE(1971), ph; BLACK BELLY OF THE TARANTULA(1972, Ital.), ph; CHE?(1973, Ital./Fr./Ger.), ph; MASSACRE IN ROME(1973, Ital.), ph; MOSES(1976, Brit./Ital.), ph; SALAMANDER, THE(1983, U.S./Ital./Brit.), ph

Albert Gattiker
RAMPARTS WE WATCH, THE(1940)

Giovanna Gattinoni
NIGHTS OF CABIRIA(1957, Ital.)

Alfonso Gatto
GOSPEL ACCORDING TO ST. MATTHEW, THE(1966, Fr., Ital.); TEOREMA(1969, Ital.)

Francesco Gatto
SEVEN DWARFS TO THE RESCUE, THE(1965, Ital.)

Lana Gatto
ITALIAN JOB, THE(1969, Brit.)

Peter Gatto
TOOTSIE(1982)

Roberto Gatto
LISTEN, LET'S MAKE LOVE(1969, Fr./Ital.)

John Gattrell
JOSSER ON THE FARM(1934, Brit.)

Andrew Gaty
RETURN OF CAPTAIN INVINCIBLE, THE(1983, Aus./U.S.), p, w

Nate Gatzert
STRAWBERRY ROAN(1933), w; FIDDLIN' BUCKAROO, THE(1934), w; HONOR OF THE RANGE(1934), w; SMOKING GUNS(1934), w; WHEELS OF DESTINY(1934), w; WESTERN COURAGE(1935), w; WESTERN FRONTIER(1935), w; AVENGING WATERS(1936), w; CATTLE THIEF, THE(1936), w; FUGITIVE SHERIFF, THE(1936), w; HEIR TO TROUBLE(1936), w; HEROES OF THE RANGE(1936), w; LAWLESS RIDERS(1936), w; UNKNOWN RANGER, THE(1936), w; LAW OF THE RANGER(1937), w; RANGER COURAGE(1937), w; RANGERS STEP IN, THE(1937), w; RECKLESS RANGER(1937), w; RIO GRANDE RANGER(1937), w; IN EARLY ARIZONA(1938), w; PHANTOM GOLD(1938), w; PIONEER TRAIL(1938), w; ROLLING CARAVANS(1938), w; STAGECOACH DAYS(1938), w; FRONTIERS OF '49(1939), w; LAW COMES TO TEXAS, THE(1939), w; LONE STAR PIONEERS(1939), w
Silents
ROYAL RIDER, THE(1929), w

Mathilde Gau
OLIVE TREES OF JUSTICE, THE(1967, Fr.)

Christian Gaubert
LIFE LOVE DEATH(1969, Fr./Ital.), md; MATTER OF DAYS, A(1969, Fr./Czech.), m; THREE INTO TWO WON'T GO(1969, Brit.), md; LITTLE GIRL WHO LIVES DOWN THE LANE, THE(1977, Can.), m

Daniele Gaubert
ENCOUNTERS IN SALZBURG(1964, Ger.); FLIGHT FROM ASHIYA(1964, U.S./Jap.); AND SO TO BED(1965, Ger.); CAMILLE 2000(1969); UNDERGROUND(1970, Brit.); SNOW JOB(1972)

Ginette Gaubert
CARNIVAL IN FLANDERS(1936, Fr.); ENTENTE CORDIALE(1939, Fr.); TESTAMENT OF DR. MABUSE, THE(1943, Ger.)

Gaucha
BEAR, THE(1963, Fr.)

Milton Gaucho
GIVEN WORD, THE(1964, Braz.)

The Gaucho Tango Orchestra
FIRST MRS. FRASER, THE(1932, Brit.)

Jennifer Gauci
PULP(1972, Brit.)

Phran Gauci
LIAR'S DICE(1980)

Yvonne Gaudeau
MARRIAGE OF FIGARO, THE(1963, Fr.)

Christian Gaudin
LOVE IN A HOT CLIMATE(1958, Fr./Span.), ed; MOST WANTED MAN, THE(1962, Fr./Ital.), ed; THREE FACES OF SIN(1963, Fr./Ital.), ed; YOUR TURN, DARLING(1963, Fr.), ed; SLEEPING CAR MURDER THE(1966, Fr.), ed; WEB OF FEAR(1966, Fr./Span.), ed; SHOCK TROOPS(1968, Ital./Fr.), ed

Jacqueline Gaudin
LETTERS FROM MY WINDMILL(1955, Fr.), ed
Pierre Gaudin
GORILLA GREETS YOU, THE(1958, Fr.), ed
Antonio Gaudio
Silents
HAUNTED PAJAMAS(1917), ph; AVENGING TRAIL, THE(1918), ph; EAST IS WEST(1922), ph; SONG OF LOVE, THE(1923), ph; HUSBANDS AND LOVERS(1924), ph; GAUCHO, THE(1928), ph
Misc. Silents
SEALED LIPS(1925), d
Eugene Gaudio
Silents
20,000 LEAGUES UNDER THE SEA(1916), ph; EYE FOR EYE(1918), ph; BRAT, THE(1919), ph
Gaetano Gaudio
HELL'S ANGELS(1930), ph; SKY DEVILS(1932), ph
Silents
TEMPTRESS, THE(1926), ph
Tonio Gaudio
Silents
NOTORIOUS LADY, THE(1927), ph
Tony Gaudio
GENERAL CRACK(1929), ph; ON WITH THE SHOW(1929), ph; SHE GOES TO WAR(1929), ph; TIGER ROSE(1930), ph; FRONT PAGE, THE(1931), ph; LADY WHO DARED, THE(1931), ph; LITTLE CAESAR(1931), ph; MASK OF FU MANCHU, THE(1932), ph; TIGER SHARK(1932), ph; BLONDIE JOHNSON(1933), ph; CAPTURED(1933), ph; EX-LADY(1933), ph; LADIES MUST LOVE(1933), ph; LADY KILLER(1933), ph; NARROW CORNER, THE(1933), ph; PRIVATE DETECTIVE 62(1933), ph; SILK EXPRESS, THE(1933), ph; VOLTAIRE(1933), ph; WORLD CHANGES, THE(1933), ph; DRAGON MURDER CASE, THE(1934), ph; HAPPINESS AHEAD(1934), ph; MAN WITH TWO FACES, THE(1934), ph; MANDALAY(1934), ph; UPPER WORLD(1934), ph; BORDERTOWN(1935), ph; CASE OF THE LUCKY LEGS, THE(1935), ph; DR. SOCRATES(1935), ph; FRONT PAGE WOMAN(1935), ph; GO INTO YOUR DANCE(1935), ph; LITTLE BIG SHOT(1935), ph; OIL FOR THE LAMPS OF CHINA(1935), ph; WHITE COCKATOO(1935), ph; ANTHONY ADVERSE(1936), ph; STORY OF LOUIS PASTEUR, THE(1936), ph; WHITE ANGEL, THE(1936), ph; ANOTHER DAWN(1937), ph; GOD'S COUNTRY AND THE WOMAN(1937), ph; KID GALAHAD(1937), ph; KING AND THE CHORUS GIRL, THE(1937), ph; LIFE OF EMILE ZOLA, THE(1937), ph; ADVENTURES OF ROBIN HOOD, THE(1938), ph; AMAZING DR. CLITTERHOUSE, THE(1938), ph; DAWN PATROL, THE(1938), ph; GARDEN OF THE MOON(1938), ph; SISTERS, THE(1938), ph; TORCHY BLANE IN PANAMA(1938), ph; JUAREZ(1939), ph; OLD MAID, THE(1939), ph; WE ARE NOT ALONE(1939), ph; BROTHER ORCHID(1940), ph; FIGHTING 69TH, THE(1940), ph; KNUTE ROCKNE–ALL AMERICAN(1940), ph; LETTER, THE(1940), ph; 'TIL WE MEET AGAIN(1940), ph; AFFECTIONATELY YOURS(1941), ph; GREAT LIE, THE(1941), ph; HIGH SIERRA(1941), ph; NAVY BLUES(1941), ph; LARCENY, INC.(1942), ph; MAN WHO CAME TO DINNER, THE(1942), ph; WINGS FOR THE EAGLE(1942), ph; YOU CAN'T ESCAPE FOREVER(1942), ph; BACKGROUND TO DANGER(1943), ph; CONSTANT NYMPH, THE(1943), ph; CORVETTE K-225(1943), ph; EXPERIMENT PERILOUS(1944), ph; I'LL BE SEEING YOU(1944), ph; SONG TO REMEMBER, A(1945), ph; BANDIT OF SHERWOOD FOREST, THE(1946), ph; I'VE ALWAYS LOVED YOU(1946), ph; SWELL GUY(1946), ph; LOVE FROM A STRANGER(1947), ph; THAT'S MY MAN(1947), ph; RED PONY, THE(1949), ph
Silents
BIG TREMAINE(1916), ph; PARADISE GARDEN(1917), ph; IN OLD KENTUCKY(1920), ph; INFERIOR SEX, THE(1920), ph; KISMET(1920), ph; SIN OF MARTHA QUEED, THE(1921), ph; TEN DOLLAR RAISE, THE(1921), ph; SHATTERED IDOLS(1922), ph; ADAM AND EVA(1923), ph; ASHES OF VENGEANCE(1923), ph; ONLY WOMAN, THE(1924), ph; AFFAIR OF THE FOLLIES, AN(1927), ph; RACKET, THE(1928), ph
Misc. Silents
PRICE OF SUCCESS, THE(1925), d
Gerardo Gaudioso
JOAN AT THE STAKE(1954, Ital./Fr.)
Jean Gaudray
Silents
NAPOLEON(1927, Fr.)
Tony Gaudro
FOG OVER FRISCO(1934), ph
Daniel Gaudry
GIFT, THE(1983, Fr./Ital.), ph
Yvonne Gaudry
GUESS WHAT HAPPENED TO COUNT DRACULA(1970)
The Gaudsmith Brothers
PIRATE, THE(1948)
Rol Gauffin
IS PARIS BURNING?(1966, U.S./Fr.)
Alexander Gauge
UNDERCOVER AGENT(1935, Brit.); INTERRUPTED JOURNEY, THE(1949, Brit.); FLESH AND BLOOD(1951, Brit.); MURDER IN THE CATHEDRAL(1952, Brit.); PICKWICK PAPERS, THE(1952, Brit.); GREAT GAME, THE(1953, Brit.); HOUSE OF BLACKMAIL(1953, Brit.); MARTIN LUTHER(1953); PENNY PRINCESS(1953, Brit.); DANCE LITTLE LADY(1954, Brit.); DOUBLE EXPOSURE(1954, Brit.); FAST AND LOOSE(1954, Brit.); GOLDEN LINK, THE(1954, Brit.); MYSTERY ON BIRD ISLAND(1954, Brit.); HANDCUFFS, LONDON(1955, Brit.); HORNET'S NEST, THE(1955, Brit.); PORT OF ESCAPE(1955, Brit.); SQUARE RING, THE(1955, Brit.); WILL ANY GENTLEMAN?(1955, Brit.); BREAKAWAY(1956, Brit.); IRON PETTICOAT, THE(1956, Brit.); SHADOW OF FEAR(1956, Brit.); NOVEL AFFAIR, A(1957, Brit.); TWO GROOMS FOR A BRIDE(1957); CROSS-UP(1958); NOTHING BARRED(1961, Brit.)
Homer Gaugh
GOLIATHON(1979, Hong Kong), d
Hans Gaugler
IT HAPPENED IN BROAD DAYLIGHT(1960, Ger./Switz.); SHADOWS GROW LONGER, THE(1962, Switz./Ger.)
Fabienne Gaugloff
TEN DAYS' WONDER(1972, Fr.)

Peter Gauhe
EFFI BRIEST(1974, Ger.); FEAR EATS THE SOUL(1974, Ger.)
M. Gaukhman-Sverdlov
SONG OVER MOSCOW(1964, USSR), art d
Patricia Gaul
1984
TEACHERS(1984)
Patti Gaul
BLOOD(1974, Brit.)
George Gaulden
LAST PICTURE SHOW, THE(1971)
Ray Gaulden
FIVE CARD STUD(1968), w
Gertrude Gault
KID FROM BOOKLYN, THE(1946)
John Gault
1984
AMERICAN NIGHTMARE(1984), w
Judith Gault
APPRENTICESHIP OF DUDDY KRAVITZ, THE(1974, Can.); PARTNERS(1976, Can.)
Judy Gault
MERRY WIVES OF TOBIAS ROUKE, THE(1972, Can.)
Pierre Gault
TONI(1968, Fr.), p
Slim Gault
SQUARE DANCE JUBILEE(1949)
Viola Gault
ON THIN ICE(1933, Brit.)
Dallas Gaultois
FOUR FAST GUNS(1959), w; WHEN THE CLOCK STRIKES(1961), w
Irving Gaumont
THIEVES FALL OUT(1941), w
Fred Gaunt
BROTHERS AND SISTERS(1980, Brit.)
Stacey Gaunt
Misc. Silents
BLEAK HOUSE(1922, Brit.)
Valerie Gaunt
CURSE OF FRANKENSTEIN, THE(1957, Brit.); HORROR OF DRACULA, THE(1958, Brit.)
William Gaunt
SINISTER MAN, THE(1965, Brit.)
Misc. Talkies
LEGEND OF CHAMPIONS(1983)
Gene Gaunthier
Silents
FROM THE MANGER TO THE CROSS(1913), a, w; CELEBRATED CASE, A(1914), w
Misc. Silents
WOLFE OR THE CONQUEST OF QUEBEC(1914)
Paul Gauntt
TRAVELING EXECUTIONER, THE(1970)
Gigi Gaus
STOOLIE, THE(1972)
Hal Gausman
SIGN OF ZORRO, THE(1960), set d; PARENT TRAP, THE(1961), set d; BON VOYAGE(1962), set d; SAVAGE SAM(1963), set d; SON OF FLUBBER(1963), set d; MARY POPPINS(1964), set d; MISADVENTURES OF MERLIN JONES, THE(1964), set d; THOSE CALLOWAYS(1964), set d; MONKEY'S UNCLE, THE(1965), set d; THAT DARN CAT(1965), set d; GNOME-MOBILE, THE(1967), set d; LOVE BUG, THE(1968), set d; ONE AND ONLY GENUINE ORIGINAL FAMILY BAND, THE(1968), set d; SMITH(1969), set d; COMPUTER WORE TENNIS SHOES, THE(1970), set d; WILD COUNTRY, THE(1971), set d; $1,000,000 DUCK(1971), set d; GREAT NORTHFIELD, MINNESOTA RAID, THE(1972), set d; WORLD'S GREATEST ATHLETE, THE(1973), set d; HERBIE RIDES AGAIN(1974), set d; ESCAPE TO WITCH MOUNTAIN(1975), set d; SWASHBUCKLER(1976), set d; MAC ARTHUR(1977), set d; NATIONAL LAMPOON'S ANIMAL HOUSE(1978), set d; SAME TIME, NEXT YEAR(1978), set d; LITTLE MISS MARKER(1980), set d
1984
CLOAK AND DAGGER(1984), set d; CRACKERS(1984), set d
Hal G. Gausman
GIRL FROM PETROVKA, THE(1974), set d
R.A. Gausman
YOU CAN'T CHEAT AN HONEST MAN(1939), set d; HIT THE ROAD(1941), set d; MOB TOWN(1941), set d; NEVER GIVE A SUCKER AN EVEN BREAK(1941), set d; ARABIAN NIGHTS(1942), set d; PHANTOM OF THE OPERA(1943), set d; SHADOW OF A DOUBT(1943), set d; WHITE SAVAGE(1943), set d; ALI BABA AND THE FORTY THIEVES(1944), set d
Russel A. Gausman
CRISS CROSS(1949), set d; FRANCIS(1949), set d
Russell Gausman
SON OF FRANKENSTEIN(1939), set d; TOWER OF LONDON(1939), set d; BLACK FRIDAY(1940), set d; HOUSE OF THE SEVEN GABLES, THE(1940), set d; FRONTIER BADMEN(1943), set d; PHANTOM LADY(1944), set d; I'LL BE YOURS(1947), set d; SMASH-UP, THE STORY OF A WOMAN(1947), set d; NAKED CITY, THE(1948), set d; SECRET BEYOND THE DOOR, THE(1948), set d; MILKMAN, THE(1950), set d
Russell A. Gausman
UNCLE HARRY(1945), set d; EAST SIDE OF HEAVEN(1939), set d; IF I HAD MY WAY(1940), set d; FLAME OF NEW ORLEANS, THE(1941), art d; SPOILERS, THE(1942), set d; FLESH AND FANTASY(1943), set d; CLIMAX, THE(1944), set d; HOUSE OF FRANKENSTEIN(1944), set d; BAD MEN OF THE BORDER(1945), set d; DALTONS RIDE AGAIN, THE(1945), set d; FRONTIER GAL(1945), set d; LADY ON A TRAIN(1945), set d; NAUGHTY NINETIES, THE(1945), set d; ON STAGE EVERYBODY(1945), set d; PILLOW OF DEATH(1945), set d; RENEGADES OF THE RIO GRANDE(1945), set d; SALOME, WHERE SHE DANCED(1945), set d; SCARLET STREET(1945), set d; SHADY LADY(1945), set d; SUDAN(1945), set d; THIS LOVE OF OURS(1945), set d; WOMAN IN GREEN, THE(1945), set d; WOMAN IN GREEN, THE(1945), set d; BLACK ANGEL(1946), set d; CANYON PASSAGE(1946), set d; KILLERS, THE(1946), set d; LOVER COME BACK(1946), set d; MAGNIFICENT DOLL(1946), set d; NIGHT IN PARADISE, A(1946), set d; SHE-WOLF OF LON-

DON(1946), set d; SMOOTH AS SILK(1946), set d; SPIDER WOMAN STRIKES BACK, THE(1946), set d; TANGIER(1946), set d; TERROR BY NIGHT(1946), set d; BRUTE FORCE(1947), set d; DOUBLE LIFE, A(1947), set d; IVY(1947), set d; PIRATES OF MONTEREY(1947), set d; RIDE THE PINK HORSE(1947), set d; SENATOR WAS INDISCREET, THE(1947), set d; SLAVE GIRL(1947), set d; VIGILANTES RETURN, THE(1947), set d; WEB, THE(1947), set d; WISTFUL WIDOW OF WAGON GAP, THE(1947), set d; WOMAN'S VENGEANCE, A(1947), set d; ALL MY SONS(1948), set d; FAMILY HONEYMOON(1948), set d; KISS THE BLOOD OFF MY HANDS(1948), set d; LETTER FROM AN UNKNOWN WOMAN(1948), set d; MEXICAN HAYRIDE(1948), set d; MR. PEABODY AND THE MERMAID(1948), set d; ONE TOUCH OF VENUS(1948), set d; SAXON CHARM, THE(1948), set d; TAP ROOTS(1948), set d; UP IN CENTRAL PARK(1948), set d; YOU GOTTA STAY HAPPY(1948), set d; ABANDONED(1949), set d; CALAMITY JANE AND SAM BASS(1949), set d; CITY ACROSS THE RIVER(1949), set d; ILLEGAL ENTRY(1949), set d; JOHNNY STOOL PIGEON(1949), set d; LADY GAMBLES, THE(1949), set d; MY DARLING(1949), set d; RED CANYON(1949), set d; STORY OF MOLLY X, THE(1949), set d; UNDERTOW(1949), set d; WOMAN IN HIDING(1949), set d; MYSTERY SUBMARINE(1950), set d; PEGGY(1950), set d; SHAKEDOWN(1950), set d; SPY HUNT(1950), set d; WINCHESTER '73(1950), art d; LADY PAYS OFF, THE(1951), set d; STRANGE DOOR, THE(1951), set d; THUNDER ON THE HILL(1951), set d; WEEKEND WITH FATHER(1951), set d; AGAINST ALL FLAGS(1952), set d; DUEL AT SILVER CREEK, THE(1952), set d; HAS ANYBODY SEEN MY GAL?(1952), set d; HORIZONS WEST(1952), set d; IT GROWS ON TREES(1952), set d; LAWLESS BREED, THE(1952), set d; LOST IN ALASKA(1952), set d; MEET DANNY WILSON(1952), set d; MEET ME AT THE FAIR(1952), set d; NO ROOM FOR THE GROOM(1952), set d; RAIDERS, THE(1952), set d; SON OF ALI BABA(1952), set d; UNTAMED FRONTIER(1952), set d; YANKEE BUCCANEER(1952), set d; ALL I DESIRE(1953), set d; MISSISSIPPI GAMBLER, THE(1953), set d; REDHEAD FROM WYOMING, THE(1953), set d; SEMINOLE(1953), set d; TAKE ME TO TOWN(1953), set d; WAR ARROW(1953), set d; ABBOTT AND COSTELLO MEET DR. JEKYLL AND MR. HYDE(1954), set d; MAGNIFICENT OBSESSION(1954), set d; SIGN OF THE PAGAN(1954), set d; TAZA, SON OF COCHISE(1954), set d; ALL THAT HEAVEN ALLOWS(1955), set d; CAPTAIN LIGHTFOOT(1955), set d; THIS ISLAND EARTH(1955), set d; WRITTEN ON THE WIND(1956), set d; BATTLE HYMN(1957), set d; INCREDIBLE SHRINKING MAN, THE(1957), set d; INTERLUDE(1957), set d; ISTANBUL(1957), set d; JOE DAKOTA(1957), set d; MAN IN THE SHADOW(1957), set d; NIGHT RUNNER, THE(1957), set d; TARNISHED ANGELS, THE(1957), set d; TATTERED DRESS, THE(1957), set d; LADY TAKES A FLYER, THE(1958), set d; PERFECT FURLOUGH, THE(1958), set d; RAW WIND IN EDEN(1958), set d; TIME TO LOVE AND A TIME TO DIE, A(1958), set d; TOUCH OF EVIL(1958), set d; TWILIGHT FOR THE GODS(1958), set d; IMITATION OF LIFE(1959), set d; NEVER STEAL ANYTHING SMALL(1959), set d; OPERATION PETTICOAT(1959), set d; PILLOW TALK(1959), set d; THIS EARTH IS MINE(1959), set d; SPARTACUS(1960), set d

Geoffrey Gaussen
DEVIL PROBABLY, THE(1977, FR.)

Norah Gaussen "Gorsen"
THOSE PEOPLE NEXT DOOR(1952, Brit.); PERSONAL AFFAIR(1954, Brit.)

Slim Gaut
SILVER CITY(1951); CARRIE(1952); SOMETHING TO LIVE FOR(1952); VAGABOND KING, THE(1956)

Pierre Gautard
ADOLESCENT, THE(1978, Fr./W.Ger.), ph

Gauthier
KING SOLOMON'S TREASURE(1978, Can.), art d

Baroness Teresa Gauthier
ROMAN HOLIDAY(1953)

Blanche Gauthier
THIRTEENTH LETTER, THE(1951)

Claude Gauthier
ORDERS, THE(1977, Can.)

Desiree Gauthier
PERSONAL BEST(1982)

Germain Gauthier
PICK-UP SUMMER(1981), m

Jack Gauthier
PLAYTIME(1973, Fr.)

Jacques Gauthier
LIGHT ACROSSS THE STREET, THE(1957, Fr.), a, p; LOVER'S NET(1957, Fr.), p

Jean Gauthier
Misc. Silents
HEART'S DESIRE(1917)

Jean-Michel Gauthier
BLONDE FROM PEKING, THE(1968, Fr.), ed

Paul Gauthier
RED(1970, Can.)

Vianney Gauthier
CORDELIA(1980, Fr., Can.), art d; SUZANNE(1980, Can.), art d

Vincent Gauthier
LE BEAU MARIAGE(1982, Fr.)

Blanche Gautier
FORBIDDEN JOURNEY(1950, Can.)

Dick Gautier
DIVORCE AMERICAN STYLE(1967); MARYJANE(1968); BLACK JACK(1973), a, p, w; MANCHU EAGLE MURDER CAPER MYSTERY, THE(1975); BILLY JACK GOES TO WASHINGTON(1977); FUN WITH DICK AND JANE(1977)

Henri Gautier
DEVIL IN THE FLESH, THE(1949, Fr.)

Jean Jacques Gautier
THREE FACES OF SIN(1963, Fr./Ital.), w

Jean-Michel Gautier
YOUR SHADOW IS MINE(1963, Fr./Ital.), ed; GENDARME OF ST. TROPEZ, THE(1966, Fr./Ital.), ed; SEA PIRATE, THE(1967, Fr./Span./Ital.), ed; SICILIAN CLAN, THE(1970, Fr.), ed

Richard Gautier
MARYJANE(1968), w

Jacqueline Gautler
LOUISE(1940, Fr.)

Jean Gautrat
GERVAISE(1956, Fr.)

David Gautreaux
STAR TREK: THE MOTION PICTURE(1979); HEARSE, THE(1980)

Sylvie Gautrelet
AFRICAN, THE(1983, Fr.), cos

Aldonna Gauvin
PAN-AMERICANA(1945)

Emile Gauvreau
SCANDAL FOR SALE(1932), w

Enrico Gauzzoni
Misc. Silents
MESSALINA(1924, Ital.), d

Cassandra Gava
NIGHT SHIFT(1982); HIGH ROAD TO CHINA(1983)

Roberto Gavaldon
LITTLEST OUTLAW, THE(1955), d; UNTOUCHED(1956), w; MACARIO(1961, Mex.), d, w; MUSHROOM EATER, THE(1976, Mex.), d, w

John Gavam
RETURN OF THE JEDI(1983)

Gavara
IMMORTAL VAGABOND(1931, Ger.)

Georges Gavarentz
PANIC BUTTON(1964), m; TIME OF THE WOLVES(1970, Fr.), m

Mauro Gavazzi
ROMEO AND JULIET(1968, Brit./Ital.), makeup; DEATH IN VENICE(1971, Ital./Fr.), makeup; THAT SPLENDID NOVEMBER(1971, Ital./Fr.), makeup

Gaveau
COMPLIMENTS OF MR. FLOW(1941, Fr.), ph

Charles Gaveau
DEVIL IS AN EMPRESS, THE(1939, Fr.), ph

Rene Gaveau
DEVIL IS AN EMPRESS, THE(1939, Fr.), ph

Suzanne Gaveau
OLIVE TREES OF JUSTICE, THE(1967, Fr.), ed

Pierre Gaveaux
FIDELIO(1961, Aust.), w; FIDELIO(1970, Ger.), w

Grace Gaven
LIFE IN HER HANDS(1951, Brit.); WHITE CORRIDORS(1952, Brit.)

Jean Gaven
OBSESSION(1954, Fr./Ital.); MAIDEN, THE(1961, Fr.); RIFF RAFF GIRLS(1962, Fr./Ital.); RIDER ON THE RAIN(1970, Fr./Ital.); AND HOPE TO DIE(1972 Fr/US); WHO IS KILLING THE GREAT CHEFS OF EUROPE?(1978, US/Ger.)
1984
ONE DEADLY SUMMER(1984, Fr.)
Misc. Talkies
OUR MEN IN BAGHDAD(1967, Ital.)

Raquel Gavia
1984
BLOOD SIMPLE(1984)

Bill Gavier
FOREIGN CORRESPONDENT(1940)

Rafael Gavilan
HANDS ACROSS THE TABLE(1935)

Amanda Gavin
BITTERSWEET LOVE(1976)

Bill Gavin
FUNNY MONEY(1983, Brit.)

Dara Gavin
NUN'S STORY, THE(1959)

Erica Gavin
RENEGADE GIRLS(1974)

Gerald Gavin
INTERNATIONAL SQUADRON(1941)

Grace Gavin
DISTANT TRUMPET(1952, Brit.); STOLEN FACE(1952, Brit.); SCOTCH ON THE ROCKS(1954, Brit.)

Jack Gavin
Silents
OUTLAW'S DAUGHTER, THE(1925)
Misc. Silents
WHITE SHEEP, THE(1924); BLACK CARGOES OF THE SOUTH SEAS(1929)

James Gavin
WEREWOLF, THE(1956); FACE OF A FUGITIVE(1959); COOGAN'S BLUFF(1968); NUDE BOMB, THE(1980); WHEN TIME RAN OUT(1980)

James W. Gavin
HEROES(1977)

Janie Gavin
EMPIRE OF THE ANTS(1977)

Jim Gavin
DOMINO PRINCIPLE, THE(1977)

Jimmy Gavin
1,000 SHAPES OF A FEMALE(1963); SQUARE ROOT OF ZERO, THE(1964)

John Gavin
THOROUGHLY MODERN MILLIE(1967); BEHIND THE HIGH WALL(1956); FOUR GIRLS IN TOWN(1956); QUANTEZ(1957); TIME TO LOVE AND A TIME TO DIE, A(1958); IMITATION OF LIFE(1959); BREATH OF SCANDAL, A(1960); MIDNIGHT LACE(1960); PSYCHO(1960); SPARTACUS(1960); BACK STREET(1961); ROMANOFF AND JULIET(1961); TAMMY, TELL ME TRUE(1961); NO ROSES FOR OSS 117(1968, Fr.); MADWOMAN OF CHAILLOT, THE(1969); PUSSYCAT, PUSSYCAT, I LOVE YOU(1970); JENNIFER(1978); HISTORY OF THE WORLD, PART 1(1981)
Misc. Talkies
HOUSE OF SHADOWS(1977, Arg.)

Mary Gavin
SUPERCHICK(1973); FANTASM(1976, Aus.)

Werton Gavin
TWILIGHT'S LAST GLEAMING(1977, U.S./Ger.)

Weston Gavin
SUPERMAN(1978); YANKS(1979); TRAIL OF THE PINK PANTHER, THE(1982)
Cassandra Gaviola
CONAN THE BARBARIAN(1982)
1984
BLACK ROOM, THE(1984)
Misc. Talkies
BLACK ROOM, THE(1983)
Sandi Gaviola
GRASSHOPPER, THE(1970)
Age Gavioli
COLOSSUS OF RHODES, THE(1961, Ital., Fr., Span.), w
Fred Gavlin
VICIOUS YEARS, THE(1950); TANK COMMANDOS(1959)
Gillis Gavois
QUERELLE(1983, Ger./Fr.)
Igors Gavon
NEIGHBORS(1981)
Costa Gavras
MADAME ROSA(1977, Fr.)
Aleksandar Gavric
DESPERADO TRAIL, THE(1965, Ger./Yugo.); FLAMING FRONTIER(1968, Ger./Yugo.)
Izabela Gavric
TWILIGHT TIME(1983, U.S./Yugo.)
Uri Gavriel
HANNAH K.(1983, Fr.)
1984
AMBASSADOR, THE(1984)
Vlastimir Gavrik
LONG SHIPS, THE(1964, Brit./Yugo.), art d
George Gavrilidis
POLICEMAN OF THE 16TH PRECINCT, THE(1963, Gr.)
M. Gavrilko
DIMKA(1964, USSR); WHEN THE TREES WERE TALL(1965, USSR)
Tatyana Gavrilova
UNCOMMON THIEF, AN(1967, USSR); KATERINA IZMAILOVA(1969, USSR)
Mark Gaweda
WEEKEND OF SHADOWS(1978, Aus.)
Irene Gawne
TALES FROM THE CRYPT(1972, Brit.)
Peter Gawthorn
HIS GLORIOUS NIGHT(1929)
Peter Gawthorne
BEHIND THAT CURTAIN(1929); SUNNY SIDE UP(1929); TEMPLE TOWER(1930); THOSE THREE FRENCH GIRLS(1930); CHARLIE CHAN CARRIES ON(1931); MAN WHO CAME BACK, THE(1931); C.O.D.(1932, Brit.); FLAG LIEUTENANT, THE(1932, Brit.); HIS LORDSHIP(1932, Brit.); HOUSE OF TRENT, THE(1933, Brit.); NIGHT AND DAY(1933, Brit.); PERFECT UNDERSTANDING(1933, Brit.); PRINCE OF ARCADIA(1933, Brit.); CAMELS ARE COMING, THE(1934, Brit.); DIRTY WORK(1934, Brit.); GIRLS PLEASE!(1934, Brit.); GRAND PRIX(1934, Brit.); LEAVE IT TO SMITH(1934); MONEY MAD(1934, Brit.); MY OLD DUTCH(1934, Brit.); SOMETHING ALWAYS HAPPENS(1934, Brit.); TWO HEARTS IN WALTZ TIME(1934, Brit.); CRIME UNLIMITED(1935, Brit.); IRON DUKE, THE(1935, Brit.); MAN OF THE MOMENT(1935, Brit.); ME AND MARLBOROUGH(1935, Brit.); MURDER AT MONTE CARLO(1935, Brit.); NO LIMIT(1935, Brit.); PHANTOM FIEND, THE(1935, Brit.); STORMY WEATHER(1935, Brit.); WHO'S YOUR FATHER?(1935, Brit.); CROUCHING BEAST, THE(1936, U. S./Brit.); EAST MEETS WEST(1936, Brit.); EVERYBODY DANCE(1936, Brit.); MAN BEHIND THE MASK, THE(1936, Brit.); POT LUCK(1936, Brit.); WOLF'S CLOTHING(1936, Brit.); BRIEF ECSTASY(1937, Brit.); FATHER STEPS OUT(1937, Brit.); GANGWAY(1937, Brit.); LAST ADVENTURERS, THE(1937, Brit); MR. STRINGFELLOW SAYS NO(1937, Brit.); RIDING HIGH(1937, Brit.); ROMANCE AND RICHES(1937, Brit.); TICKET OF LEAVE MAN, THE(1937, Brit.); TWO WHO DARED(1937, Brit.); UNDER A CLOUD(1937, Brit.); WHERE THERE'S A WILL(1937, Brit.); ALF'S BUTTON AFLOAT(1938, Brit.); CONVICT 99(1938, Brit.); EASY RICHES(1938, Brit.); HEY! HEY! U.S.A.(1938, Brit.); SCRUFFY(1938, Brit.); SWORD OF HONOUR(1938, Brit.); ASK A POLICEMAN(1939, Brit.); DEAD MEN ARE DANGEROUS(1939, Brit.); FLYING FIFTY-FIVE(1939, Brit.); HOME FROM HOME(1939, Brit.); WHAT WOULD YOU DO, CHUMS?(1939, Brit.); WHERE'S THAT FIRE?(1939, Brit.); AMONG HUMAN WOLVES(1940 Brit.); BAND WAGGON(1940, Brit.); CROOKS TOUR(1940, Brit.); GASBAGS(1940, Brit.); LAUGH IT OFF(1940, Brit.); THEY CAME BY NIGHT(1940, Brit.); THREE SILENT MEN(1940, Brit.); TORSO MURDER MYSTERY, THE(1940, Brit.); TWO FOR DANGER(1940, Brit.); I THANK YOU(1941, Brit.); MAIL TRAIN(1941, Brit.); OLD MOTHER RILEY'S GHOSTS(1941, Brit.); LET THE PEOPLE SING(1942, Brit.); MUCH TOO SHY(1942, Brit.); PIMPERNEL SMITH(1942, Brit.); WINGS AND THE WOMAN(1942, Brit.); WOMEN AREN'T ANGELS(1942, Brit.); BELL-BOTTOM GEORGE(1943, Brit.); HUNDRED POUND WINDOW, THE(1943, Brit.); LOVE ON THE DOLE(1945, Brit.); MURDER IN REVERSE(1946, Brit.); THIS MAN IS MINE(1946 Brit.); NOTHING VENTURE(1948, Brit.); CASE OF CHARLES PEACE, THE(1949, Brit.); HIGH JINKS IN SOCIETY(1949, Brit.); DEATH IS A NUMBER(1951, Brit.); SOHO CONSPIRACY(1951, Brit.); PAUL TEMPLE RETURNS(1952, Brit.); KNIGHTS OF THE ROUND TABLE(1953); PAID TO KILL(1954, Brit.); TALE OF THREE WOMEN, A(1954, Brit.)
Misc. Talkies
BOMBAY WATERFRONT(1952, Brit.)
Sue Gawthorne
THERE AIN'T NO JUSTICE(1939, Brit.)
William Gaxton
FIFTY MILLION FRENCHMEN(1931); THEIR BIG MOMENT(1934); BEST FOOT FORWARD(1943); HEAT'S ON, THE(1943); SOMETHING TO SHOUT ABOUT(1943); DIAMOND HORSESHOE(1945)
Silents
IT'S THE OLD ARMY GAME(1926); STEPPING ALONG(1926)
A. Gay
SHADOWS OF FORGOTTEN ANCESTORS(1967, USSR)
Arnetta Gay
ZOMBIE(1980, Ital.)

Barbara Gay
SLEEPING CAR TO TRIESTE(1949, Brit.)
Betsy Gay
MYSTERY PLANE(1939); WHAT'S BUZZIN COUSIN?(1943)
Dixie Gay
TWO WEEKS OFF(1929)
Silents
RED WINE(1928); WHY BE GOOD?(1929)
Dorothy Gay
CALL OF THE CIRCUS(1930)
Eula Gay
HIGH SCHOOL GIRL(1935)
Felice Testa Gay
HIRED KILLER, THE(1967, Fr./Ital.), p
Frank Gay
NIX ON DAMES(1929), w; NOT DAMAGED(1930), w; KING OF THE SIERRAS(1938), w; SILENCE OF THE NORTH(1981, Can.)
Silents
JOY STREET(1929), w
Git Gay
DREAMS(1960, Swed.)
Gregory Gay
THEY HAD TO SEE PARIS(1929); HOLLYWOOD BOULEVARD(1936); CASABLANCA(1942); CONSPIRATORS, THE(1944); BLOOD ON THE SUN(1945); CORNERED(1945); I LOVE A MYSTERY(1945); PURSUIT TO ALGIERS(1945); TIGER WOMAN, THE(1945); PASSKEY TO DANGER(1946); SO DARK THE NIGHT(1946); BLACKMAIL(1947); TRESPASSER, THE(1949); DANCING IN THE DARK(1949); CARGO TO CAPETOWN(1950); COUNTERSPY MEETS SCOTLAND YARD(1950); HARBOR OF MISSING MEN(1950); MASK OF THE AVENGER(1951); PEKING EXPRESS(1951); WHEN THE REDSKINS RODE(1951); BAL TABARIN(1952); LAST TRAIN FROM BOMBAY(1952); WORLD IN HIS ARMS, THE(1952); CHARGE OF THE LANCERS(1953); FLAME OF CALCUTTA(1953); REMAINS TO BE SEEN(1953); SAVAGE MUTINY(1953); SOUTH SEA WOMAN(1953); JUNGLE MAN-EATERS(1954); CREATURE WITH THE ATOM BRAIN(1955); BAILOUT AT 43,000(1957); KELLY AND ME(1957); OCEAN'S ELEVEN(1960); BLUE HAWAII(1961); HITLER(1962); METEOR(1979)
Inez Gay
FATHER'S SON(1941); MEET JOHN DOE(1941); MILLION DOLLAR BABY(1941); SHE COULDN'T SAY NO(1941)
Iva Gay
RADIO PIRATES(1935, Brit.)
Janice Gay
FOLLOW THE BOYS(1944)
Joan Gay
STRANDED(1935)
John Gay
THREEPENNY OPERA, THE(1931, Ger./U.S.), w; BEGGAR'S OPERA, THE(1953), w; RUN SILENT, RUN DEEP(1958), w; SEPARATE TABLES(1958), w; FOUR HORSEMEN OF THE APOCALYPSE, THE(1962), w; HAPPY THIEVES, THE(1962), w; MUTINY ON THE BOUNTY(1962), w; THREE PENNY OPERA(1963, Fr./Ger.), w; HALLELUJAH TRAIL, THE(1965), w; TEXAS ACROSS THE RIVER(1966), w; LAST SAFARI, THE(1967, Brit.), w; NO WAY TO TREAT A LADY(1968), w; POWER, THE(1968), w; ON HER MAJESTY'S SECRET SERVICE(1969, Brit.); SOLDIER BLUE(1970), w; SOMETIMES A GREAT NOTION(1971), w; POCKET MONEY(1972), w; HENNESSY(1975, Brit.), w; MATTER OF TIME, A(1976, Ital./U.S.), w; GOLDEN RENDEZVOUS(1977), w; MOON OVER THE ALLEY(1980, Brit.)
Maisie Gay
TO OBLIGE A LADY(1931, Brit.); OLD MAN, THE(1932, Brit.)
Marjorie Gay
Silents
VOLCANO(1926)
Misc. Silents
DANGEROUS FRIENDS(1926); FIGHTING MARINE, THE(1926)
Mary Gay
RATS OF TOBRUK(1951, Aus.)
Nancy Gay
MAN FROM THE RIO GRANDE, THE(1943); OVERLAND MAIL ROBBERY(1943); PRIDE OF THE PLAINS(1944)
Noel Gay
SLEEPLESS NIGHTS(1933, Brit.), m; NO FUNNY BUSINESS(1934, Brit.), m; TORPEDOED!(1939), m; LAMBETH WALK, THE(1940, Brit.), w; I THANK YOU(1941, Brit.), m
Norman Gay
YOUNG WINSTON(1972, Brit.); EXORCIST, THE(1973), ed; SHOCK WAVES(1977), ed; HONEYSUCKLE ROSE(1980), ed; SHINING, THE(1980)
1984
BRADY'S ESCAPE(1984, U.S./Hung.), ed, cos
Ramon Gay
AZTEC MUMMY, THE(1957, Mex.); EMPTY STAR, THE(1962, Mex.); YOUNG AND EVIL(1962, Mex.); CURSE OF THE AZTEC MUMMY, THE(1965, Mex.); ROBOT VS. THE AZTEC MUMMY, THE(1965, Mex.); CURSE OF THE DOLL PEOPLE, THE(1968, Mex.)
Robby Gay
SCHLAGER-PARADE(1953); JOURNEY TO THE LOST CITY(1960, Ger./Fr./Ital.), ch
Ronnie Gay
SMOKEY AND THE BANDIT(1977)
Gay Land and the Thunderbirds
MOONSHINE MOUNTAIN(1964)
Francoise Gayat
MOONRAKER(1979, Brit.)
Anne Gaybis
10 VIOLENT WOMEN(1982)
Annie Gaybis
FRIDAY THE 13TH PART III(1982)
Andree Gaydon
UNDER MILK WOOD(1973, Brit.)

Deborah Gaydos
SORCERESS(1983), animal d
Adrian Gaye
OPTIMISTS, THE(1973, Brit.), p
Albie Gaye
VAGABOND KING, THE(1956)
Frankie Gaye
PENITENTIARY(1979), m
George Gaye
CHARLIE CHAN AT THE OPERA(1936)
Gregory Gaye
HIGH SOCIETY BLUES(1930); RENEGADES(1930); WHAT A WIDOW(1930); YOUNG AS YOU FEEL(1931); ONCE IN A LIFETIME(1932); AFFAIRS OF A GENTLEMAN(1934); BRITISH AGENT(1934); HANDY ANDY(1934); DODSWORTH(1936); UNDER YOUR SPELL(1936); FIRST LADY(1937); LANCER SPY(1937); MAMA STEPS OUT(1937); PRESCRIPTION FOR ROMANCE(1937); THAT GIRL FROM PARIS(1937); TOVARICH(1937); WISE GIRL(1937); BULLDOG DRUMMOND'S PERIL(1938); LOVE, HONOR AND BEHAVE(1938); STRAIGHT, PLACE AND SHOW(1938); TEST PILOT(1938); THANKS FOR EVERYTHING(1938); TOO HOT TO HANDLE(1938); HOTEL FOR WOMEN(1939); NINOTCHKA(1939); PARIS HONEYMOON(1939); THREE MUSKETEERS, THE(1939); DOWN ARGENTINE WAY(1940); MAN FROM DAKOTA, THE(1940); FLIGHT LIEUTENANT(1942); I WAKE UP SCREAMING(1942); MY GAL SAL(1942); ONE DANGEROUS NIGHT(1943); PURPLE HEART, THE(1944); SEVEN DOORS TO DEATH(1944); PARIS UNDERGROUND(1945); SONG TO REMEMBER, A(1945); BACHELOR AND THE BOBBY-SOXER, THE(1947); UNFINISHED DANCE,THE(1947); MAGIC CARPET, THE(1951); EDDY DUCHIN STORY, THE(1956); PRIZE, THE(1963)
Misc. Talkies
COMMANDO CODY(1953)
Howard Gaye
Silents
HOME SWEET HOME(1914); BIRTH OF A NATION, THE(1915); DAPHNE AND THE PIRATE(1916); FLIRTING WITH FATE(1916); INTOLERANCE(1916); LITTLE SCHOOL MA'AM, THE(1916); ADVENTURE IN HEARTS, AN(1919); WHAT'S A WIFE WORTH?(1921); SCARAMOUCHE(1923); DANTE'S INFERNO(1924)
Misc. Silents
DIANA OF THE FOLLIES(1916); SPIRIT OF '76, THE(1917); SPY, THE(1917); RESTITUTION(1918), d; MY LADY'S LATCHKEY(1921); PRINCE OF LOVERS, A(1922, Brit.)
Lisa Gaye
GLENN MILLER STORY, THE(1953); DRUMS ACROSS THE RIVER(1954); MAGNIFICENT OBSESSION(1954); ROCK AROUND THE CLOCK(1956); SHAKE, RATTLE, AND ROCK!(1957); TEN THOUSAND BEDROOMS(1957); SIGN OF ZORRO, THE(1960); NIGHT OF EVIL(1962); FACE OF TERROR(1964, Span.); CASTLE OF EVIL(1967); VALLEY OF MYSTERY(1967); VIOLENT ONES, THE(1967)
Marvin Gaye
CHROME AND HOT LEATHER(1971); TROUBLE MAN(1972), m
Nora Gaye
1984
DUBEAT-E-O(1984)
Ronald Gaye
HEAVENLY DAYS(1944)
Vivian Gaye
FROG, THE(1937, Brit.)
Echlin Gayer
Silents
MAD DANCER(1925)
Misc. Silents
HER LOVE STORY(1924)
Richard Gayer
Misc. Talkies
ALTERNATIVE MISS WORLD, THE(1980), d
Emmanuel Gayet
LA VIE CONTINUE(1982, Fr.)
John Gayford
KILL HER GENTLY(1958, Brit.)
Barbara Gayle
ROCKABILLY BABY(1957)
Gay Gayle
THREE HUSBANDS(1950); MY FAVORITE SPY(1951)
Gretchen Gayle
FANTASM(1976, Aus.)
Jackie Gayle
SEVEN MINUTES, THE(1971); TEMPEST(1982)
1984
BROADWAY DANNY ROSE(1984)
Misc. Talkies
PEPPER AND HIS WACKY TAXI(1972)
Monica Gayle
HARD TRAIL(1969); HAREM BUNCH; OR WAR AND PIECE, THE(1969); WILD, FREE AND HUNGRY(1970); WORLD IS JUST A 'B' MOVIE, THE(1971); SWITCHBLADE SISTERS(1975); NEW GIRL IN TOWN(1977); LOVE AND THE MIDNIGHT AUTO SUPPLY(1978)
Patricia Gayle
NAKED KISS, THE(1964)
Peter Gayle
FORCE OF IMPULSE(1961), p
Rozelle Gayle
COAST TO COAST(1980); MAN WITH BOGART'S FACE, THE(1980); HONKYTONK MAN(1982)
Saundra Gayle
ANGELS FROM HELL(1968)
Anna Gaylor
BEASTS OF MARSEILLES, THE(1959, Brit.); LIFE UPSIDE DOWN(1965, Fr.); KILLING GAME, THE(1968, Fr.)
1984
AMERICAN DREAMER(1984); CHEECH AND CHONG'S THE CORSICAN BROTHERS(1984)

Brent Gaylor
JANIE(1944)
Gerry Gaylor
QUEEN OF OUTER SPACE(1958); FIVE GATES TO HELL(1959)
Cynthia Gaylord
SO DARK THE NIGHT(1946)
Harriet Gaylord
Silents
SCARAB RING, THE(1921), w
Joan Gaylord
HAPPY DAYS(1930)
John Gaylord
CLEOPATRA(1963)
Karen Gaylord
WONDER MAN(1945); GIRL FROM JONES BEACH, THE(1949)
Karen X. Gaylord
COVER GIRL(1944); KID FROM BOOKLYN, THE(1946); NIGHT IN PARADISE, A(1946); SECRET LIFE OF WALTER MITTY, THE(1947); SONG IS BORN, A(1948)
Martha Gaylord
SO FINE(1981)
Raymond Gaylord
FACE OF THE SCREAMING WEREWOLF(1959, Mex.)
George Gaynes
WAY WE WERE, THE(1973); JOY HOUSE(1964, Fr.); GROUP, THE(1966); MAROONED(1969); DOCTORS' WIVES(1971); HARRY AND WALTER GO TO NEW YORK(1976); NICKELODEON(1976); DEAD MEN DON'T WEAR PLAID(1982); TOOTSIE(1982); TO BE OR NOT TO BE(1983)
1984
MICKI AND MAUDE(1984); POLICE ACADEMY(1984)
Jessica Gaynes
1984
SWING SHIFT(1984)
Avril Gaynor
TOMCAT, THE(1968, Brit.)
Grace Gaynor
GUESS WHO'S COMING TO DINNER(1967)
1984
FLETCH(1984)
J.C. Gaynor
SATURDAY NIGHT AT THE BATHS(1975)
Janet Gaynor
STREET ANGEL(1928); CHRISTINA(1929); FOUR DEVILS(1929); LUCKY STAR(1929); SUNNY SIDE UP(1929); HAPPY DAYS(1930); HIGH SOCIETY BLUES(1930); DADDY LONG LEGS(1931); DELICIOUS(1931); MAN WHO CAME BACK, THE(1931); MERELY MARY ANN(1931); FIRST YEAR, THE(1932); TESS OF THE STORM COUNTRY(1932); ADORABLE(1933); PADDY, THE NEXT BEST THING(1933); STATE FAIR(1933); CAROLINA(1934); CHANGE OF HEART(1934); SERVANTS' ENTRANCE(1934); FARMER TAKES A WIFE, THE(1935); ONE MORE SPRING(1935); LADIES IN LOVE(1936); SMALL TOWN GIRL(1936); STAR IS BORN, A(1937); THREE LOVES HAS NANCY(1938); YOUNG IN HEART, THE(1938); BERNARDINE(1957)
Silents
JOHNSTOWN FLOOD, THE(1926); RETURN OF PETER GRIMM, THE(1926); SEVENTH HEAVEN(1927); SUNRISE–A SONG OF TWO HUMANS(1927)
Misc. Silents
BLUE EAGLE, THE(1926); MIDNIGHT KISS, THE(1926); SHAMROCK HANDICAP, THE(1926); 2 GIRLS WANTED(1927); STREET ANGEL(1928)
Jock Gaynor
Misc. Talkies
DEATHHEAD VIRGIN, THE(1974)
Mitzi Gaynor
MY BLUE HEAVEN(1950); GOLDEN GIRL(1951); TAKE CARE OF MY LITTLE GIRL(1951); BLOODHOUNDS OF BROADWAY(1952); I DON'T CARE GIRL, THE(1952); WE'RE NOT MARRIED(1952); DOWN AMONG THE SHELTERING PALMS(1953); THERE'S NO BUSINESS LIKE SHOW BUSINESS(1954); THREE YOUNG TEXANS(1954); ANYTHING GOES(1956); JOKER IS WILD, THE(1957); LES GIRLS(1957); SOUTH PACIFIC(1958); HAPPY ANNIVERSARY(1959); SURPRISE PACKAGE(1960); FOR LOVE OR MONEY(1963); BIRDS AND THE BEES, THE(1965)
Lamberto Gayou
VILLA!(1958)
Eunice Gayson
MELODY IN THE DARK(1948, Brit.); MY BROTHER JONATHAN(1949, Brit.); DANCE HALL(1950, Brit.); TO HAVE AND TO HOLD(1951, Brit.); MISS ROBIN HOOD(1952, Brit.); DANCE LITTLE LADY(1954, Brit.); COUNT OF TWELVE(1955, Brit.); ONE JUST MAN(1955, Brit.); LAST MAN TO HANG, THE(1956, Brit.); ZARAK(1956, Brit.); CARRY ON ADMIRAL(1957, Brit.); LIGHT FINGERS(1957, Brit.); OUT OF THE CLOUDS(1957, Brit.); HELLO LONDON(1958, Brit.); REVENGE OF FRANKENSTEIN, THE(1958, Brit.); DR. NO(1962, Brit.); FROM RUSSIA WITH LOVE(1963, Brit.)
Joe Gayton
UNCOMMON VALOR(1983), w
Joseph Gazal
PHYNX, THE(1970)
David Gazalet
OPERATION MANHUNT(1954), ed
Gilberto Gazcon
RAGE(1966, U.S./Mex.), p&d, w
Gyula Gazdag
CONFIDENCE(1980, Hung.)
Gwen Gaze
I COVER THE WAR(1937); BAR 20 JUSTICE(1938); PARTNERS OF THE PLAINS(1938); WEST OF PINTO BASIN(1940); DR. JEKYLL AND MR. HYDE(1941); UNDERGROUND RUSTLERS(1941); WRANGLER'S ROOST(1941); TWO FISTED JUSTICE(1943)
Heino Gaze
SCHLAGER-PARADE(1953), m
Larry Gaze
SMART WOMAN(1948)

Gazebo
LIMIT, THE(1972), cos

Clive Gazes
ASSASSINATION BUREAU, THE(1969, Brit.); CATCH ME A SPY(1971, Brit./Fr.); MUSIC LOVERS, THE(1971, Brit.)

Valeriu Gazhiu
SANDU FOLLOWS THE SUN(1965, USSR), w

Michael Gazlades
ANNA OF RHODES(1950, Gr.), d

Gwen Gazo
HOUSE OF ERRORS(1942)

Laurro Gazzalo
GOHA(1958, Tunisia)

Nic Gazzana
MAD MAX(1979, Aus.); PIRATE MOVIE, THE(1982, Aus.)

Don Gazzaniga
YOUR THREE MINUTES ARE UP(1973); THREE THE HARD WAY(1974); SPECIAL DELIVERY(1976), w

Ben Gazzara
STRANGE ONE, THE(1957); ANATOMY OF A MURDER(1959); YOUNG DOCTORS, THE(1961); CONVICTS FOUR(1962); CAPTIVE CITY, THE(1963, Ital.); PASSIONATE THIEF, THE(1963, Ital.); RAGE TO LIVE, A(1965); CONQUERED CITY(1966, Ital.); BRIDGE AT REMAGEN, THE(1969); IF IT'S TUESDAY, THIS MUST BE BELGIUM(1969); HUSBANDS(1970); NEPTUNE FACTOR, THE(1973, Can.); CAPONE(1975); KILLING OF A CHINESE BOOKIE, THE(1976); VOYAGE OF THE DAMNED(1976, Brit.); HIGH VELOCITY(1977); OPENING NIGHT(1977); SICILIAN CONNECTION, THE(1977); BLOODLINE(1979); SAINT JACK(1979); INCHON(1981); THEY ALL LAUGHED(1981); GIRL FROM TRIESTE, THE(1983, Ital.); TALES OF ORDINARY MADNESS(1983, Ital.)

The Gazzari Dancers
NIGHTMARE IN WAX(1969)

The Gazzarri Dancers
FLAREUP(1969)

Michael Gazzo
ALLIGATOR(1980); CUBA CROSSING(1980); BACK ROADS(1981)

Michael V. Gazzo
HATFUL OF RAIN, A(1957), w; MAN CALLED ADAM, A(1966); GANG THAT COULDN'T SHOOT STRAIGHT, THE(1971); GODFATHER, THE, PART II(1974); BLACK SUNDAY(1977); FINGERS(1978); KING OF THE GYPSIES(1978); FISH THAT SAVED PITTSBURGH, THE(1979); LOVE AND BULLETS(1979, Brit.)
1984
CANNONBALL RUN II(1984); FEAR CITY(1984)

Michael Vincente Gazzo
KING CREOLE(1958), w

Victor Gazzoli
LOVE IN THE AFTERNOON(1957)

Laura Gazzolo
FATHER'S DILEMMA(1952, Ital.)

Lauro Gazzolo
ETERNAL MELODIES(1948, Ital.); PEDDLIN' IN SOCIETY(1949, Ital.); SKY IS RED, THE(1952, Ital.); RING AROUND THE CLOCK(1953, Ital.)

Nando Gazzolo
HE WHO SHOOTS FIRST(1966, Ital.); SECRET SEVEN, THE(1966, Ital./Span.); HILLS RUN RED, THE(1967, Ital.)

Virgilio Gazzolo
DAY OF ANGER(1970, Ital./Ger.); AUGUSTINE OF HIPPO(1973, Ital.)

Virginio Gazzolo
AGE OF THE MEDICI, THE(1979, Ital.)

Alcide Gazzotto
EMBALMER, THE(1966, Ital.)

Jim Geallis
JUKE BOX RACKET(1960), p

Luella Gear
CAREFREE(1938); PERFECT MARRIAGE, THE(1946); JIGSAW(1949); PHFFFT!(1954)
Silents
ADAM AND EVA(1923)

Elfe Gearhart
DECISION BEFORE DAWN(1951)

Nigel Gearing
ASCENDANCY(1983, Brit.), w

Jean Gearon
BUTTERFLY ON THE SHOULDER, A(1978, Fr.), w

Valerie Gearon
NINE HOURS TO RAMA(1963, U.S./Brit.); INVASION(1965, Brit.); ANNE OF THE THOUSAND DAYS(1969, Brit.)

Douglas Gearrad
Misc. Silents
PLAYTHINGS(1918), d

Monica Gearson
BOYS FROM BRAZIL, THE(1978)

Alex Geary
ROCK-A-BYE BABY(1958)

Bud Geary
MEANEST GAL IN TOWN, THE(1934); WHOM THE GODS DESTROY(1934); DANTE'S INFERNO(1935); DARK ANGEL, THE(1935); LIVING ON VELVET(1935); GREAT GUY(1936); IT HAD TO HAPPEN(1936); PRISONER OF SHARK ISLAND, THE(1936); SAN FRANCISCO(1936); TRAIL OF THE LONESOME PINE, THE(1936); DEAD END(1937); HIGH FLYERS(1937); LANCER SPY(1937); WHEN YOU'RE IN LOVE(1937); PROFESSOR BEWARE(1938); THERE'S ALWAYS A WOMAN(1938); IDIOT'S DELIGHT(1939); NO, NO NANETTE(1940); NORTHWEST MOUNTED POLICE(1940); SAPS AT SEA(1940); GANGS OF SONORA(1941); OUTLAWS OF THE CHEROKEE TRAIL(1941); WEST OF CIMARRON(1941); ALIAS BOSTON BLACKIE(1942); BANDIT RANGER(1942); COWBOY SERENADE(1942); HOME IN WYOMIN'(1942); LIFE BEGINS AT 8:30(1942); MY FAVORITE SPY(1942); PHANTOM PLAINSMEN, THE(1942); PIRATES OF THE PRAIRIE(1942); QUIET PLEASE, MURDER(1942); RAIDERS OF THE RANGE(1942); SOMBRERO KID, THE(1942); SUNDOWN KID, THE(1942); TALK OF THE TOWN(1942); TRAMP, TRAMP, TRAMP(1942); TWO YANKS IN TRINIDAD(1942); UNDERGROUND AGENT(1942); BATAAN(1943); BORDERTOWN GUNFIGHTERS(1943); CALLING WILD BILL ELLIOTT(1943); CAN-

YON CITY(1943); CARSON CITY CYCLONE(1943); DEATH VALLEY MANHUNT(1943); DESTROYER(1943); FALLEN SPARROW, THE(1943); FIVE GRAVES TO CAIRO(1943); IMMORTAL SERGEANT, THE(1943); IRON MAJOR, THE(1943); LADIES' DAY(1943); MAN FROM THE RIO GRANDE, THE(1943); MAN FROM THUNDER RIVER, THE(1943); OVERLAND MAIL ROBBERY(1943); SANTA FE SCOUTS(1943); SEVENTH VICTIM, THE(1943); THUNDERING TRAILS(1943); BENEATH WESTERN SKIES(1944); CHEYENNE WILDCAT(1944); CODE OF THE PRAIRIE(1944); COWBOY FROM LONESOME RIVER(1944); FIREBRANDS OF ARIZONA(1944); HIDDEN VALLEY OUTLAWS(1944); LARAMIE TRAIL, THE(1944); MAN FROM FRISCO(1944); MARSHAL OF RENO(1944); MOJAVE FIREBRAND(1944); OUTLAWS OF SANTA FE(1944); PRIDE OF THE PLAINS(1944); SAN ANTONIO KID, THE(1944); SHERIFF OF LAS VEGAS(1944); SHERIFF OF SUNDOWN(1944); SILVER CITY KID(1944); STAGECOACH TO MONTEREY(1944); STORM OVER LISBON(1944); TUCSON RAIDERS(1944); VIGILANTES OF DODGE CITY(1944); BEHIND CITY LIGHTS(1945); CHEROKEE FLASH, THE(1945); COLORADO PIONEERS(1945); GREAT STAGECOACH ROBBERY(1945); LONE TEXAS RANGER(1945); MARSHAL OF LAREDO(1945); OREGON TRAIL(1945); PHANTOM OF THE PLAINS(1945); SANTA FE SADDLEMATES(1945); THREE'S A CROWD(1945); TOPEKA TERROR, THE(1945); TRAIL OF KIT CARSON(1945); CYCLOTRODE X(1946); LANDRUSH(1946); MAN FROM RAINBOW VALLEY, THE(1946); SHERIFF OF REDWOOD VALLEY(1946); SMOKY(1946); THUNDER TOWN(1946); UNDER ARIZONA SKIES(1946); FRISCO TORNADO(1950); WAGON WHEELS WESTWARD(1956)
Silents
EVERYMAN'S PRICE(1921)
Misc. Silents
FOUR HEARTS(1922)

Charles Geary
MEDIUM COOL(1969)

Dick Geary
PRISONER OF ZENDA, THE(1979)

Joan Geary
KITCHEN, THE(1961, Brit.); UP JUMPED A SWAGMAN(1965, Brit.); FRAULEIN DOKTOR(1969, Ital./Yugo.); MOON OVER THE ALLEY(1980, Brit.)

John Geary
WEBSTER BOY, THE(1962, Brit.)

Maine Geary
MADAME SATAN(1930)
Silents
ROBIN HOOD(1922); PAINTED FLAPPER, THE(1924); ARIZONA ROMEO, THE(1925)
Misc. Silents
THRU THE FLAMES(1923)

Pat Geary
STRAWBERRY ROAN(1945, Brit.); GAY INTRUDERS, THE(1946, Brit.)

Paul Geary
WILD, WILD WINTER(1966)

Richard Geary
GHOST DIVER(1957); RAWHIDE TRAIL, THE(1958); LOVE BUG, THE(1968); FRIDAY FOSTER(1975), stunts; HOPSCOTCH(1980)

Robert J. Geary
RIGHT STUFF, THE(1983)

Tony Geary
JOHNNY GOT HIS GUN(1971)

Winn Geary
WILD GYPSIES(1969)

Paul Geauff
VICE AND VIRTUE(1965, Fr./Ital.)

Olly Gebauer
CASE VAN GELDERN(1932, Ger.); MANULESCU(1933, Ger.)

Katren Gebelein
CITY OF WOMEN(1980, Ital./Fr.)

Gordon Gebert
COME TO THE STABLE(1949); HOLIDAY AFFAIR(1949); FLAME AND THE ARROW, THE(1950); SADDLE TRAMP(1950); CHICAGO CALLING(1951); FLYING LEATHERNECKS(1951); HOUSE ON TELEGRAPH HILL(1951); NIGHT INTO MORNING(1951); OPERATION PACIFIC(1951); NARROW MARGIN, THE(1952); TO HELL AND BACK(1955); SUMMER LOVE(1958)

M. A. Gebert
CLOSELY WATCHED TRAINS(1967, Czech.), titles

Allen Gebhardt
1984
WOMAN IN RED, THE(1984)

Fred Gebhardt
TWELVE TO THE MOON(1960), p, w; PHANTOM PLANET, THE(1961), p, w

George Gebhardt
Silents
THAIS(1914); PUPPET CROWN, THE(1915)
Misc. Silents
FIGHTING HOPE, THE(1915)

Charles Gebhart
Silents
OUTLAW REFORMS, THE(1914)

George Gebhart
Silents
DISHONORED MEDAL, THE(1914); ETERNAL LOVE(1917); MADAME SPY(1918)

Ernest Gebler
HOFFMAN(1970, Brit.), w

Otto Gebuehr
BARBERINA(1932, Ger.)

Otto Gebuhr
CITY OF TORMENT(1950, Ger.); DEVIL MAKES THREE, THE(1952); AFFAIRS OF DR. HOLL(1954, Ger.)
Silents
GOLEM: HOW HE CAME INTO THE WORLD, THE(1920, Ger.)

Vera Gebuhr
GERTRUD(1966, Den.)

Javon Gec
TEMPEST(1958, Ital./Yugo./Fr.)

Nicholas Gecks
WICKED LADY, THE(1983, Brit.)
1984
FOREVER YOUNG(1984, Brit.)
Salem Gedara
MOHAMMAD, MESSENGER OF GOD(1976, Lebanon/Brit.)
Bjorn Gedda
GRASS IS SINGING, THE(1982, Brit./Swed.)
1984
KILLING HEAT(1984)
Barbara Bel Geddes
CAUGHT(1949); SUMMERTREE(1971)
David Geddes
1984
MY KIND OF TOWN(1984, Can.), ph
Henry Geddes
TOTO AND THE POACHERS(1958, Brit.), p; LAST RHINO, THE(1961, Brit.), p,
d&w; EAGLE ROCK(1964, Brit.), p,d&w; RUNAWAY RAILWAY(1965, Brit.), w
Jack Geddes
TOUGH ASSIGNMENT(1949); I SHOT BILLY THE KID(1950); MARSHAL OF
HELDORADO(1950)
Neta Geddes
FREDDIE STEPS OUT(1946)
Peter Geddes
FINAL OPTION, THE(1983, Brit.)
Ralph Geddes
LAND OF NO RETURN, THE(1981), m
George Geddis
PASSING THROUGH(1977), ph
Peter Geddis
LITTLEST HORSE THIEVES, THE(1977)
Conroy Gedeon
1984
STAR TREK III: THE SEARCH FOR SPOCK(1984)
Freddie Gedeon
WILD PACK, THE(1972)
Lewis Gedge
SECRET CAVE, THE(1953, Brit.)
Jason Gedrick
1984
MASSIVE RETALIATION(1984)
Donald Gee
FERRY ACROSS THE MERSEY(1964, Brit.); BOFORS GUN, THE(1968, Brit.);
UNMAN, WITTERING AND ZIGO(1971, Brit.)
Dorothy Gee
PUBLIC ENEMY, THE(1931)
Edward Gee
TRAPPED IN A SUBMARINE(1931, Brit.)
Frederick Gee
GUN MAN FROM BODIE, THE(1941)
George Gee
BRIDEGROOM FOR TWO(1932, Brit.); CLEANING UP(1933, Brit.); LEAVE IT TO
ME(1933, Brit.); STRIKE IT RICH(1933, Brit.)
Silents
WEEKEND WIVES(1928, Brit.)
Hazel Gee
WHEN YOU COME HOME(1947, Brit.), ch; HANDS OF ORLAC, THE(1964, Brit./Fr.),
ch
Johnny Gee
FAMILY LIFE(1971, Brit.)
Parker Gee
DELINQUENT DAUGHTERS(1944); ROGUES GALLERY(1945); BLACK MARKET
BABIES(1946); SUSPENSE(1946); GANGSTER, THE(1947)
Paul Gee
1984
SHEENA(1984)
Prunella Gee
WILBY CONSPIRACY, THE(1975, Brit.); NEVER SAY NEVER AGAIN(1983)
Timothy Gee
LONG AGO, TOMORROW(1971, Brit.), ed; STEPFORD WIVES, THE(1975), ed;
SLIPPER AND THE ROSE, THE(1976, Brit.), ed; INTERNATIONAL VELVET(1978,
Brit.), ed; CLASH OF THE TITANS(1981), ed; SIGN OF FOUR, THE(1983, Brit.), ed
1984
ORDEAL BY INNOCENCE(1984, Brit.), m
Tony Gee
FOREST, THE(1983)
Z. Gee
UNCIVILISED(1937, Aus.)
Henry Geehl
JASSY(1948, Brit.), m
Andrew Geer
WILD BLUE YONDER, THE(1952), w; SEA CHASE, THE(1955), w
Ellen Geer
PETULIA(1968, U.S./Brit.); REIVERS, THE(1969); HAROLD AND MAUDE(1971);
KOTCH(1971); MEMORY OF US(1974), a, w; SILENCE(1974), a, w; OVER THE
EDGE(1979); ON THE NICKEL(1980); HEART LIKE A WHEEL(1983); SOMETHING
WICKED THIS WAY COMES(1983)
Misc. Talkies
BLOODY BIRTHDAY(1980)
Faith Geer
EXECUTIVE SUITE(1954)
Kevin Geer
FORCE OF ONE, A(1979)
Lennie Geer
GREAT LOCOMOTIVE CHASE, THE(1956); OKLAHOMAN, THE(1957); TALL
STRANGER, THE(1957); GANG WAR(1958); HIGH-POWERED RIFLE, THE(1960);
SHOOT OUT AT BIG SAG(1962); DESTRUCTORS, THE(1968); BIG DADDY(1969);
SWORD AND THE SORCERER, THE(1982)

Lenny Geer
HERO AT LARGE(1980)
Leonard Geer
MASTERSON OF KANSAS(1954); ROBBER'S ROOST(1955); ZOMBIES OF MORA
TAU(1957)
Leonard P. Geer
COAST TO COAST(1980)
1984
LOVE STREAMS(1984)
Mary Lou Geer
SOUND OFF(1952)
Raleigh Geer
SILENCE(1974)
Roman Geer
1984
AFTER THE FALL OF NEW YORK(1984, Ital./Fr.)
Tad Geer
SILENCE(1974)
Thad Geer
HUSTLE(1975)
1984
FRIDAY THE 13TH–THE FINAL CHAPTER(1984)
Will Geer
MISLEADING LADY, THE(1932); BECKY SHARP(1935); DEEP WATERS(1948);
ANNA LUCASTA(1949); INTRUDER IN THE DUST(1949); JOHNNY ALLEGRO(1949);
LUST FOR GOLD(1949); BROKEN ARROW(1950); COMMANCHE TERRITORY(1950);
CONVICTED(1950); DOUBLE CROSSBONES(1950); IT'S A SMALL WORLD(1950);
KID FROM TEXAS, THE(1950); TO PLEASE A LADY(1950); WINCHESTER '73(1950);
BAREFOOT MAILMAN, THE(1951); BRIGHT VICTORY(1951); TALL TARGET,
THE(1951); SALT OF THE EARTH(1954); MOBS INC(1956); ADVISE AND CON-
SENT(1962); SECONDS(1966); IN COLD BLOOD(1967); PRESIDENT'S ANALYST,
THE(1967); BANDOLERO!(1968); REIVERS, THE(1969); MOONSHINE WAR,
THE(1970); PIECES OF DREAMS(1970); BROTHER JOHN(1971); DEAR, DEAD
DELILAH(1972); JEREMIAH JOHNSON(1972); NAPOLEON AND SAMANTHA(1972);
EXECUTIVE ACTION(1973); ROWDYMAN, THE(1973, Can.); MEMORY OF US(1974);
SILENCE(1974); MANCHU EAGLE MURDER CAPER MYSTERY, THE(1975); BLUE
BIRD, THE(1976); MOVING VIOLATION(1976); BILLION DOLLAR HOBO,
THE(1977); MAFU CAGE, THE(1978)
Misc. Talkies
UNKNOWN POWERS(1979)
Gusa Geert
ATTILA(1958, Ital.), ch
Ron Geesin
SUNDAY BLOODY SUNDAY(1971, Brit.), m; GHOST STORY(1974, Brit.), m
1984
SWORD OF THE VALIANT(1984, Brit.), m
Judy Geeson
WINGS OF MYSTERY(1963, Brit.); BERSERK(1967); TO SIR, WITH LOVE(1967,
Brit.); HAMMERHEAD(1968); HERE WE GO ROUND THE MULBERRY BUSH(1968,
Brit.); PRUDENCE AND THE PILL(1968, Brit.); THREE INTO TWO WON'T GO(1969,
Brit.); TWO GENTLEMEN SHARING(1969, Brit.); EXECUTIONER, THE(1970, Brit.);
GOODBYE GEMINI(1970, Brit.); 10 RILLINGTON PLACE(1971, Brit.); DOOM-
WATCH(1972, Brit.); FEAR IN THE NIGHT(1972, Brit.); DIAGNOSIS: MURDER(1974,
Brit.); BRANNIGAN(1975, Brit.); CARRY ON ENGLAND(1976, Brit.); EAGLE HAS
LANDED, THE(1976, Brit.); DOMINIQUE(1978, Brit.); IT'S NOT THE SIZE THAT
COUNTS(1979, Brit.); HORROR PLANET(1982, Brit.)
1984
PLAGUE DOGS, THE(1984, U.S./Brit.)
Misc. Talkies
ONE OF THOSE THINGS(1974, Brit.); STAR MAIDENS(1976, Brit.); IN-
SEMINOID(1980)
Sally Geeson
OBLONG BOX, THE(1969, Brit.); WHAT'S GOOD FOR THE GOOSE(1969, Brit.); CRY
OF THE BANSHEE(1970, Brit.); CRY OF THE PENGUINS(1972, Brit.)
Misc. Talkies
BLESS THIS HOUSE(1972, Brit.)
Madeline Geffen
TAKING OFF(1971)
Moshe Geffen
EYEWITNESS(1981)
Rose Geffen
1984
HOME FREE ALL(1984)
Deborah Geffner
ALL THAT JAZZ(1979); STAR 80(1983)
1984
EXTERMINATOR 2(1984)
Jean-Pierre Geffroy
PORTRAIT OF INNOCENCE(1948, Fr.)
Yannick Geffroy
MONTE CARLO STORY, THE(1957, Ital.)
Elaine Gefner
HELL'S BELLES(1969)
Constantin Geftman
FRIEND WILL COME TONIGHT, A(1948, Fr.), p
Elisa Gegani
LUCKY TO BE A WOMAN(1955, Ital.)
Paul Gegauff
COUSINS, THE(1959, Fr.), w; PURPLE NOON(1961, Fr./Ital.), w; WEB OF PAS-
SION(1961, Fr.), w; OF FLESH AND BLOOD(1964, Fr./Ital.), w; OPHELIA(1964,
Fr.), w; CHAMPAGNE MURDERS, THE(1968, Fr.), w; DIABOLICALLY YOURS(1968,
Fr.), w; LES BICHES(1968, Fr.), w; WEEKEND(1968, Fr./Ital.); MORE(1969, Luxem-
bourg), w; THIS MAN MUST DIE(1970, Fr./Ital.), w; DOCTEUR POPAUL(1972,
Fr.), w; TEN DAYS' WONDER(1972, Fr.), w
1984
AVE MARIA(1984, Fr.), w
G. Gegechkori
DRAGONFLY, THE(1955 USSR)

Liz Geghardt
JULIUS CAESAR(1970, Brit.)
Jeanette Gegna
DELICIOUS(1931)
Maurice Gehaghty
DAKOTA LIL(1950), w
Fritz Gehlen
YOUNG TORLESS(1968, Fr./Ger.)
Martha Gehman
HONKY TONK FREEWAY(1981)
1984
FLAMINGO KID, THE(1984)
Richard Gehman
PATSY, THE(1964)
Rocky Gehr
1984
STAR TREK III: THE SEARCH FOR SPOCK(1984), spec eff
Terrence Gehr
CROSS CREEK(1983)
Joseph Gehrard
TWO OR THREE THINGS I KNOW ABOUT HER(1970, Fr.)
Jean Gehret
BOUDU SAVED FROM DROWNING(1967, Fr.), a, p; LA CHIENNE(1975, Fr.)
Lou Gehrig
RAWHIDE(1938)
Bo Gehring
DEMON SEED(1977), anim; NIGHTMARES(1983), spec eff
Jean Gehring
SIXTEEN FATHOMS DEEP(1934)
Ted Gehring
40 GUNS TO APACHE PASS(1967); THOMAS CROWN AFFAIR, THE(1968); YOUNG RUNAWAYS, THE(1968); VIVA MAX!(1969); MONTE WALSH(1970); THEY CALL ME MISTER TIBBS(1970); WILD ROVERS(1971); BAD COMPANY(1972); CULPEPPER CATTLE COMPANY, THE(1972); OKLAHOMA CRUDE(1973); WILLIE DYNAMITE(1973); PARALLAX VIEW, THE(1974); FAREWELL, MY LOVELY(1975); HINDENBURG, THE(1975); MACKINTOSH & T.J.(1975); NICKELODEON(1976); DOMINO PRINCIPLE, THE(1977); APPLE DUMPLING GANG RIDES AGAIN, THE(1979); ON THE AIR LINE WITH CAPTAIN MIDNIGHT(1979); WHEN TIME RAN OUT(1980); LEGEND OF THE LONE RANGER, THE(1981)
Lucy Gehrman
Misc. Talkies
GOD, MAN AND DEVIL(1949)
Fred Gehrmann
PRESCRIPTION FOR ROMANCE(1937)
Frederick Gehrmann
LANCER SPY(1937)
Lark Geib
WILD PARTY, THE(1975)
Lewis Geib
Silents
LITTLE CHURCH AROUND THE CORNER(1923), set d; LIGHTHOUSE BY THE SEA, THE(1924), art d
Jeremy Geidt
SO LITTLE TIME(1953, Brit.); PRIVATE POTTER(1963, Brit.)
Misc. Talkies
PRISM(1971)
Paul Geier
PRISM(1971)
Wendy Geier
JOE HILL(1971, Swed./U.S.)
Albert Geigel
MAN I MARRIED, THE(1940)
Eric Geiger
STARTING OVER(1979)
Franz Geiger
LOLA MONTES(1955, Fr./Ger.), w
Larry Geiger
SHADOW OF A WOMAN(1946)
Leonard Geiger
PRESSURE POINT(1962)
Miriam Geiger
WOMAN DOCTOR(1939), w
Myron Geiger
PHANTOM SUBMARINE, THE(1941); FOREST RANGERS, THE(1942)
Rod E. Geiger
PAISAN(1948, Ital.), p
Rod Geiger
SALT TO THE DEVIL(1949, Brit.), p
Steve Geiger
PLAINSONG(1982)
Mona Geijer-Falkner
SWEDENHIELMS(1935, Swed.); NIGHT IN JUNE, A(1940, Swed.)
Mona Geijer-Kalner
TWO LIVING, ONE DEAD(1964, Brit./Swed.)
Siegfried H. Geike
SKYJACKED(1972), makeup
Al Geil
UP POMPEII(1971, Brit.), ed
Corky Geil
JANIE(1944)
Joe Geil
YOU CAN'T TAKE IT WITH YOU(1938)
Joe "Corky" Geil
GET HEP TO LOVE(1942); MOONLIGHT IN HAVANA(1942); MOONLIGHT IN VERMONT(1943); PATRICK THE GREAT(1945)
Joseph Geil, Jr.
GIRL CRAZY(1943)

Voli Geiler
DESPAIR(1978, Ger.)
John Geilgud
GOOD COMPANIONS(1933, Brit.)
Alexander Geirot
Misc. Silents
SYMPHONY OF LOVE AND DEATH(1914, USSR); FLOWERS ARE LATE, THE(1917, USSR)
Rainer Geis
TWO IN A SLEEPING BAG(1964, Ger.), d
Sugar Geise
LADY TAKES A CHANCE, A(1943); MORE THE MERRIER, THE(1943); RHYTHM PARADE(1943); CASANOVA IN BURLESQUE(1944); ADVANCE TO THE REAR(1964)
John Geisel
Silents
EARLY BIRD, THE(1925), ph
John A. Geisel
RAMPARTS WE WATCH, THE(1940), ph
Ted Geisel [Dr. Seuss]
5,000 FINGERS OF DR. T. THE(1953), w
Linda Geiser
PAWNBROKER, THE(1965)
Barrie Geisinger
NIGHT THE LIGHTS WENT OUT IN GEORGIA, THE(1981)
Elaine Geisinger
LAST OF SHEILA, THE(1973)
Elliot Geisinger
PRINCE AND THE PAUPER, THE(1969), p, d, w; LAST OF SHEILA, THE(1973); AMITYVILLE HORROR, THE(1979), p; NIGHT THE LIGHTS WENT OUT IN GEORGIA, THE(1981), p
Alf Geisler
TORTURE ME KISS ME(1970)
Richard Geisman
STIGMA(1972)
Hans W. Geissendoerfer
WILD DUCK, THE(1977, Ger./Aust.), d&w
Hans W. Geissendorfer
JONATHAN(1973, Ger.), d&w
Dieter Geissler
ASSIGNMENT K(1968, Brit.); 48 HOURS TO ACAPULCO(1968, Ger.); EGON SCHIELE–EXCESS AND PUNISHMENT(1981, Ger.), p
1984
NEVERENDING STORY, THE(1984, Ger.), p
Francoise Geissler
NUN, THE(1971, Fr.), ed
Bill Geisslinger
1984
BEST DEFENSE(1984)
Kim Geist
1984
C.H.U.D.(1984)
Richard Geiwitz
FIEND(, a, ph; NIGHTBEAST(1982), ph
1984
ALIEN FACTOR, THE(1984)
Misc. Talkies
ALIEN FACTOR, THE(1978)
Ferenc Gejza
DESERTER AND THE NOMADS, THE(1969, Czech./Ital.)
Y. Gekebush
Misc. Silents
TWO DAYS(1929, USSR)
Zia Gelani
1984
INDIANA JONES AND THE TEMPLE OF DOOM(1984)
Ted Gelanza
Misc. Talkies
AROUSED(1968)
Arlene Gelb
LORDS OF FLATBUSH, THE(1974)
Ed Gelb
REVOLT IN THE BIG HOUSE(1958)
Jamie Gelb
LORDS OF FLATBUSH, THE(1974)
Stacy Gelb
LORDS OF FLATBUSH, THE(1974)
Susan Gelb
FIRST NUDIE MUSICAL, THE(1976)
Larry Gelbart
NOTORIOUS LANDLADY, THE(1962), w; THRILL OF IT ALL, THE(1963), w; FUNNY THING HAPPENED ON THE WAY TO THE FORUM, A(1966), w; NOT WITH MY WIFE, YOU DONT!(1966), w; WRONG BOX, THE(1966, Brit.), w; CHASTITY BELT, THE(1968, Ital.), w; FINE PAIR, A(1969, Ital.), w; OH, GOD!(1977), w; MOVIE MOVIE(1978), w; NEIGHBORS(1981), w; TOOTSIE(1982), w
1984
BLAME IT ON RIO(1984), w
Jack Gelber
CONNECTION, THE(1962), w
Leonard Gelber
OUT OF IT(1969)
Stasia Gelber
ECHOES OF SILENCE(1966)
Arnie Gelbert
MONTENEGRO(1981, Brit./Swed.), w
Larry Gelbmann
GANG WAR(1958)
Lawrence J. Gelbmann
YOUNG CAPTIVES, THE(1959)

Harry Geldard
WRECKING CREW, THE(1968)
C.H. Geldart
Silents
ROARING ROAD, THE(1919); LADY IN LOVE, A(1920); SINS OF ROZANNE(1920)
Misc. Silents
TOO MUCH JOHNSON(1920)
Clarence Geldart
Silents
JOHNNY GET YOUR GUN(1919); PUTTING IT OVER(1919); ALWAYS AUDA-CIOUS(1920)
Misc. Silents
WAY OF A MAN WITH A MAID, THE(1918); DAUGHTER OF THE WOLF, A(1919); SECRET GARDEN, THE(1919); VICKY VAN(1919)
Clarence H. Geldart
Silents
CROOKED STREETS(1920)
Ed Geldart
URBAN COWBOY(1980); RAGGEDY MAN(1981)
Leah Geldart
URBAN COWBOY(1980)
Clarence Gelder
STOKER, THE(1932)
Rainier Geldern
DECISION BEFORE DAWN(1951)
C.H. Geldert
Silents
THOSE WITHOUT SIN(1917)
Misc. Silents
HOSTAGE, THE(1917)
Charles H. Geldert
Misc. Silents
FAIR BARBARIAN, THE(1917); SPIRIT OF '17, THE(1918)
Clarence Geldert
SQUARE SHOULDERS(1929); UNHOLY NIGHT, THE(1929); BISHOP MURDER CASE, THE(1930); THIRTEENTH CHAIR, THE(1930); THIRTEEN WOMEN(1932); WHITE EAGLE(1932); DANCE MALL HOSTESS(1933); JUNGLE BRIDE(1933); LONE AVENGER, THE(1933); LUCKY DOG(1933); REVENGE AT MONTE CARLO(1933); RUSTY RIDES ALONE(1933); TELEGRAPH TRAIL, THE(1933); IN LOVE WITH LIFE(1934); MAN TRAILER, THE(1934); MARRIAGE ON APPROVAL(1934); TWEN-TIETH CENTURY(1934); MISSISSIPPI(1935)
Misc. Talkies
DARK ENDEAVOUR(1933); MAN TRAILER, THE(1934)
Silents
JOAN THE WOMAN(1916); BRAVEST WAY, THE(1918); ALL SOULS EVE(1921); WITCHING HOUR, THE(1921); ADAM'S RIB(1923); WOMAN OF PARIS, A(1923); FIGHTING AMERICAN, THE(1924); NORTH OF 36(1924); OH, DOCTOR(1924); HANDS ACROSS THE BORDER(1926); DRESS PARADE(1927); OVERLAND TELE-GRAPH, THE(1929); SIOUX BLOOD(1929)
Misc. Silents
WASTED LIVES(1923), d; MY NEIGHBOR'S WIFE(1925), d; RACING BLOOD(1926); ONE MAN GAME, A(1927)
Clarence H. Geldert
Silents
THOU ART THE MAN(1920)
Misc. Silents
GYPSY TRAIL, THE(1918)
Frank Geldert
Misc. Silents
HELL DIGGERS, THE(1921)
Ed Geldhart
SUGAR HILL(1974)
Bob Geldof
PINK FLOYD–THE WALL(1982, Brit.)
1984
NUMBER ONE(1984, Brit.)
Henry Geldzahler
1984
BIGGER SPLASH, A(1984)
Antonello Geleng
HERCULES(1983), prod d&art d
1984
AFTER THE FALL OF NEW YORK(1984, Ital./Fr.), art d
M.A. Geleng
GATES OF HELL, THE(1983, U.S./Ital.), art d
Massimo A. Geleng
SCREAMERS(1978, Ital.), prod d
Cecilie Gelers
TOWN WITHOUT PITY(1961, Ger./Switz./U.S.)
April Geleta
WHERE'S POPPA?(1970)
A. Geleva
GORDEYEV FAMILY, THE(1961, U.S.S.R.); TSAR'S BRIDE, THE(1966, USSR)
L. Geleya
TRAIN GOES EAST, THE(1949, USSR), ph
Samuel W. Gelfman
CANNONBALL(1976, U.S./Hong Kong), p; INCREDIBLE MELTING MAN, THE(1978), p
Donna Gelgur
NIGHT OF THE LEPUS(1972)
Daniel Gelin
FRIEND WILL COME TONIGHT, A(1948, Fr.); ROOM UPSTAIRS, THE(1948, Fr.); EDWARD AND CAROLINE(1952, Fr.); LA RONDE(1954, Fr.); LES MAINS SA-LES(1954, Fr.); NAPOLEON(1955, Fr.); ADORABLE CREATURES(1956, Fr.); MAN WHO KNEW TOO MUCH, THE(1956); WOMAN OF ROME(1956, Ital.); LOVER'S NET(1957, Fr.); PLEASE! MR. BALZAC(1957, Fr.); ROYAL AFFAIRS IN VER-SAILLES(1957, Fr.); LOVE IN A HOT CLIMATE(1958, Fr./Span.); PORT OF DESI-RE(1960, Fr.); CARTHAGE IN FLAMES(1961, Fr./Ital.); LONGEST DAY, THE(1962); TESTAMENT OF ORPHEUS, THE(1962, Fr.); JULIE THE REDHEAD(1963, Fr.); SEASON FOR LOVE, THE(1963, Fr.); LA BONNE SOUPE(1964, Fr./Ital.); IS PARIS

BURNING?(1966, U.S./Fr.); SLEEPING CAR MURDER THE(1966, Fr.); DESTROY, SHE SAID(1969, Fr.); SLOGAN(1970, Fr.); MURMUR OF THE HEART(1971, Fr./Ital./Ger.); FAR FROM DALLAS(1972, Fr.); LA NUIT DE VARENNES(1983, Fr./Ital.)
Danile Gelin
WITNESS OUT OF HELL(1967, Ger./Yugo.)
Manuel Gelin
JOY(1983, Fr./Can.)
1984
ONE DEADLY SUMMER(1984, Fr.)
Patricia Gelin
MONTENEGRO(1981, Brit./Swed.); FANNY AND ALEXANDER(1983, Swed./Fr./Ger.)
Xavier Gelin
DEVIL BY THE TAIL, THE(1969, Fr./Ital.); S(1974)
Gratien Gelinas
RED(1970, Can.)
Gelingk
M(1933, Ger.)
David Gell
SWAPPERS, THE(1970, Brit.)
William Gell
WEDDING OF LILLI MARLENE, THE(1953, Brit.), p; YANK IN ERMINE, A(1955, Brit.), p; CITY AFTER MIDNIGHT(1957, Brit.), p; AND THE SAME TO YOU(1960, Brit.), p; RATTLE OF A SIMPLE MAN(1964, Brit.), p; THEATRE OF DEATH(1967, Brit.), p; AMSTERDAM AFFAIR, THE(1968 Brit.), p; MAN OUTSIDE, THE(1968, Brit.), p; TASTE OF EXCITEMENT(1969, Brit.), p; VIOLENT ENEMY, THE(1969, Brit.), p
William J. Gell
LILLI MARLENE(1951, Brit.), p; HOLIDAY WEEK(1952, Brit.), p
Steve Gellar
WILD REBELS, THE(1967)
Berta Gellardi
Misc. Silents
BLEAK HOUSE(1920, Brit.)
Bruce Geller
SAIL A CROOKED SHIP(1961), w; CORKY(1972), p; HARRY IN YOUR POCK-ET(1973), p&d
E. Geller
DUEL, THE(1964, USSR)
Harold Geller
FURY AT SMUGGLERS BAY(1963, Brit.), m; JUNGLE STREET GIRLS(1963, Brit.), m, md
James J. Geller
LOVE FROM A STRANGER(1947), p
Joyce Geller
COOL ONES THE(1967), w
Robin Geller
BABY, IT'S YOU(1983)
Stephen Geller
PRETTY POISON(1968), w; SLAUGHTERHOUSE-FIVE(1972), w; VALACHI PA-PERS, THE(1972, Ital./Fr.), w; ASHANTI(1979), w
Baby Gellert
PLEASE DON'T EAT THE DAISIES(1960)
Hugo Gellert
REDS(1981)
Cesare Gelli
HAWKS AND THE SPARROWS, THE(1967, Ital.)
Danny Gellis
BIG FIX, THE(1978); CHAPTER TWO(1979)
Alexander Gellman
COWARDS(1970)
Judy Gellman
MEATBALLS(1979, Can.), cos
Sam Gellman
BORN TO KILL(1975), p
Stuart Gellman
DRY SUMMER(1967, Turkey), ed
Harold Gelman
INTERRUPTED MELODY(1955), md; SINGING NUN, THE(1966), md
Jacques Gelman
POR MIS PISTOLAS(1969, Mex.), p
Janice Gelman
INCREDIBLE TWO-HEADED TRANSPLANT, THE(1971)
Larry Gelman
BUSYBODY, THE(1967); CHRISTIAN LICORICE STORE, THE(1971); YOUR THREE MINUTES ARE UP(1973); SUPERDAD(1974); TUNNELVISION(1976); SLUMBER PARTY '57(1977); RABBIT TEST(1978)
1984
DREAMSCAPE(1984)
Misc. Talkies
CHATTERBOX(1977)
Milton Gelman
RIDE THE HIGH IRON(1956), w; CABOBLANCO(1981), w
Vittorio Gelmetti
RED DESERT(1965, Fr./Ital.), m
Pietro Gelmi
AND THERE CAME A MAN(1968, Ital.)
M. Gelovani
NEW HORIZONS(1939, USSR); THEY WANTED PEACE(1940, USSR)
Mikhail Gelovani
WINGS OF VICTORY(1941, USSR); VOW, THE(1947, USSR.)
David Gelpi
WOMEN AND BLOODY TERROR(1970)
Joan Gelpi
1984
ON THE LINE(1984, Span.), ph
Juan Gelpi
THAT MAN IN ISTANBUL(1966, Fr./Ital./Span.), ph; SEA PIRATE, THE(1967, Fr./Span./Ital.), ph; LAST MERCENARY, THE(1969, Ital./Span./Ger.), ph; THEY CAME TO ROB LAS VEGAS(1969, Fr./Ital./Span./Ger.), ph; SUMMERTIME KIL-

LER(1973), ph; CORRUPTION OF CHRIS MILLER, THE(1979, Span.), ph

Edwin Gelsey
SCARLET DAWN(1932), w

Envin Gelsey
CAMPUS CONFESSIONS(1938), w

Ernest Gelsey
GRAND SLAM(1933), w

Erwin Gelsey
JEWEL ROBBERY(1932), w; STRANGE LOVE OF MOLLY LOUVAIN, THE(1932), w; FLYING DOWN TO RIO(1933), w; GOLD DIGGERS OF 1933(1933), w; LIFE OF JIMMY DOLAN, THE(1933), w; PERSONALITY KID, THE(1934), w; BIG BROAD-CAST OF 1937, THE(1936), w; MUSS 'EM UP(1936), w; SWING TIME(1936), w; DOUBLE OR NOTHING(1937), w; HOLD'EM NAVY!(1937), w; TOUCHDOWN, ARMY(1938), w; SING YOUR WORRIES AWAY(1942), w; COVER GIRL(1944), w; THIS TIME FOR KEEPS(1947), w; TRESPASSER, THE(1947), w; GAMBLING HOUSE(1950), w

Erwin S. Gelsey
SWEET ADELINE(1935), w

Philipe Geluck
BENVENUTA(1983, Fr.)

Christine Gelvard
SLEEPING CAR TO TRIESTE(1949, Brit.)

Jay Gelzer
BROADWAY BABIES(1929), w; RICH PEOPLE(1929), w
Silents
COMPROMISE(1925), w

Ginger Gemell
TREASURE ISLAND(1972, Brit./Span./Fr./Ger.), ph

Enrico Gemelli
Silents
CABIRIA(1914, Ital.)

Firmin Gemier
Misc. Silents
MATER DOLOROSA(1917, Fr.); MAGICIAN, THE(1926)

Paul Gemignani
LITTLE NIGHT MUSIC, A(1977, Aust./U.S./Ger.), md

Rhoda Gemignani
DIE LAUGHING(1980)
1984
GHOSTBUSTERS(1984)

Marco Gemini
8 ½(1963, Ital.)

Leo Gemm
I ACCUSE(1958, Brit.)

Giuliano Gemma
LEOPARD, THE(1963, Ital.); MY SON, THE HERO(1963, Ital./Fr.); GOLIATH AND THE SINS OF BABYLON(1964, Ital.); HERCULES AGAINST THE SONS OF THE SUN(1964, Span./Ital.); ARIZONA COLT(1965, It./Fr./Span.); SCHEHERAZADE(1965, Fr./Ital./Span.); RETURN OF RINGO, THE(1966, Ital./Span.); PRICE OF POWER, THE(1969, Ital./Span.); SONS OF SATAN(1969, Ital./Fr./Ger.); DAY OF ANGER(1970, Ital./Ger.); WHEN WOMEN HAD TAILS(1970, Ital.); MASTER TOUCH, THE(1974, Ital./Ger.); DESERT OF THE TARTARS, THE(1976 Fr./Ital./Iranian)

Guilano Gemma
ADIOS GRINGO(1967, Ital./Fr./Span.)

Guiliano Gemma
BATTLE OF THE WORLDS(1961, Ital.)

Neil Gemmell
TIME GENTLEMEN PLEASE!(1953, Brit.)

Arturo Gemmiti
MONTE CASSINO(1948, Ital.), p&d, w

Charles Gemora
CIRCUS KID, THE(1928); INGAGI(1931); MURDERS IN THE RUE MORGUE(1932); SAVAGE GIRL, THE(1932); GILDERSLEEVE'S GHOST(1944); ROAD TO UTO-PIA(1945); WAR OF THE WORLDS, THE(1953); WHITE WITCH DOCTOR(1953); I MARRIED A MONSTER FROM OUTER SPACE(1958), makeup; JACK THE GIANT KILLER(1962), makeup

Charlie Gemora
MONSTER AND THE GIRL, THE(1941); ROAD TO ZANZIBAR(1941)

Michael Gempart
DOWNHILL RACER(1969); BLACK SPIDER, THE(1983, Swit.)

Jonathan Gems
1984
1984(1984, Brit.), w

Pam Gems
1984
1984(1984, Brit.)

Laura Gemser
TWO SUPER COPS(1978, Ital.); BUSHIDO BLADE, THE(1982 Brit./U.S.)
1984
CAGED WOMEN(1984, Ital./Fr.)
Misc. Talkies
ABSURD-ANTROPOPHAGOUS 2(1982); ATOR: THE FIGHTING EAGLE(1983)

Marcelle Genait
ROOM UPSTAIRS, THE(1948, Fr.)

Maria Genardi
MADONNA OF THE DESERT(1948)

Marie Genardi
BARNACLE BILL(1941)

Otto Genath
Silents
KRIEMHILD'S REVENGE(1924, Ger.), makeup; SIEGFRIED(1924, Ger.), makeup

Denise Gence
DEVIL AND THE TEN COMMANDMENTS, THE(1962, Fr.); MARRIAGE OF FIGARO, THE(1963, Fr.)

Jacques Gencel
HERE COMES THE GROOM(1951)

Valerie Genco
GEORGE(1973, U.S./Switz.), cos

Sari Gencsy
MEPHISTO(1981, Ger.)

Mike Gendel
1984
ONCE UPON A TIME IN AMERICA(1984)

Tuffy Genders
GREATEST SHOW ON EARTH, THE(1952)

Dana Gendian
POLTERGEIST(1982)

Jaimi Gendian
POLTERGEIST(1982)

Francois-Eric Gendron
VIOLETTE(1978, Fr.)

Jerry Gendron
Silents
NEAR LADY, THE(1923)

Leon Gendron
Silents
IF WOMEN ONLY KNEW(1921)

Leon Guerre Gendron
Misc. Silents
GIRL WITH A JAZZ HEART, THE(1920)

Leon P. Gendron
Misc. Silents
SCRAMBLED WIVES(1921)

Leon Pierre Gendron
Misc. Silents
GIRL WITH THE JAZZ HEART, THE(1920)

Pierre Gendron
SAL OF SINGAPORE(1929), w; BLUEBEARD(1944), w; MINSTREL MAN(1944), w; MONSTER MAKER, THE(1944), w; FOG ISLAND(1945), w
Silents
MAN WHO PLAYED GOD, THE(1922); OUTLAWS OF THE SEA(1923); JUST OFF BROADWAY(1924); ENCHANTED ISLAND, THE(1927)
Misc. Silents
LOVER OF CAMILLE, THE(1924); SCARLET HONEYMOON, THE(1925); WHAT PRICE BEAUTY(1928)

R. Gene
BEGGAR STUDENT, THE(1931,Brit.), w; BEGGAR STUDENT, THE(1958, Ger.), w

Gene Krupa and His Band
GEORGE WHITE'S SCANDALS(1945)

Gene Krupa and His Orchestra
BALL OF FIRE(1941)

Gene Krupa Orchestra
SMART POLITICS(1948)

Gene Vincent and His Blue Caps
GIRL CAN'T HELP IT, THE(1956)

Heide Genee
I LOVE YOU, I KILL YOU(1972, Ger.), ed; GERMANY IN AUTUMN(1978, Ger.), ed

Peter Genee
ALICE IN THE CITIES(1974, W. Ger.), p

Jan Geneen
1984
BLIND DATE(1984)

Sascha Geneen
SLEEPING PARTNERS(1930, Brit.), p

General Music Corp
NIGHT OF BLOODY HORROR zero(1969), m

Thanos Generalis
POLICEMAN OF THE 16TH PRECINCT, THE(1963, Gr.)

Henri Genes
NOUS IRONS A PARIS(1949, Fr.); COUNTERFEIT CONSTABLE, THE(1966, Fr.); SUCKER, THE(1966, Fr./Ital.)

A. Genesin
DREAM COME TRUE, A(1963, USSR)

Edmond Genest
HANKY-PANKY(1982)
Misc. Talkies
ALL THE YOUNG WIVES(1975)

Edmund Genest
WITHOUT A TRACE(1983)
Misc. Talkies
NAKED RIVER(1977)

Emile Genest
NIKKI, WILD DOG OF THE NORTH(1961, U.S./Can.); BIG RED(1962); INCREDIBLE JOURNEY, THE(1963); RAMPAGE(1963); CINCINNATI KID, THE(1965); KING'S PIRATE(1967); DON'T JUST STAND THERE(1968); HELL WITH HEROES, THE(1968); IN ENEMY COUNTRY(1968)
Misc. Talkies
SEPARATION(1977, Brit.)

Gudrun Genest
JUST A GIGOLO(1979, Ger.)

Veronique Genest
1984
BASILEUS QUARTET(1984, Ital.)

Jean Genet
BALCONY, THE(1963), w; DEATHWATCH(1966), w; MADEMOISELLE(1966, Fr./Brit.), w; PROLOGUE(1970, Can.); MAIDS, THE(1975, Brit.), w; QUERELLE(1983, Ger./Fr.), w

Adam Genette
THREE STEPS NORTH(1951)

Joseph Geneva
1984
NO SMALL AFFAIR(1984)

Andre Geneves
LE BOUCHER(1971, Fr./Ital.), p

Genevieve
SPY WITH A COLD NOSE, THE(1966, Brit.); BEAU PERE(1981, Fr.)

Silents
HOT WATER(1924)
Emile Genevois
LES MISERABLES(1936, Fr.); LA BETE HUMAINE(1938, Fr.); CASQUE D'OR(1956, Fr.); DIE GANS VON SEDAN(1962, Fr/Ger.)
Simone Genevois
Silents
NAPOLEON(1927, Fr.)
Emile Genevoix
PORTRAIT OF INNOCENCE(1948, Fr.)
Amerigo Gengarelli
TARTARS, THE(1962, Ital./Yugo.), ph; DUEL OF CHAMPIONS(1964 Ital./Span.), ph; SHE BEAST, THE(1966, Brit./Ital./Yugo.), ph
Paul Genge
FBI STORY, THE(1959); NORTH BY NORTHWEST(1959); BECAUSE THEY'RE YOUNG(1960); CROWDED SKY, THE(1960); SANDPIPER, THE(1965); HOT RODS TO HELL(1967); BULLITT(1968); OUTFIT, THE(1973)
S. Gengel
DIARY OF A NAZI(1943, USSR), w
Claude Genia
MANON 70(1968, Fr.)
Gilbert Geniat
ACT OF LOVE(1953)
Gilberte Geniat
LA BELLE AMERICAINE(1961, Fr.); DIARY OF A CHAMBERMAID(1964, Fr./Ital.); LA PRISONNIERE(1969, Fr./Ital.); LADY IN THE CAR WITH GLASSES AND A GUN, THE(1970, U.S./Fr.); VERY CURIOUS GIRL, A(1970, Fr.); SUCH A GORGEOUS KID LIKE ME(1973, Fr.)
1984
AMERICAN DREAMER(1984)
Marcelle Geniat
CRIME AND PUNISHMENT(1935, Fr.); CROSSROADS(1938, Fr.); THEY WERE FIVE(1938, Fr.); MAN OF THE HOUR, THE(1940, Fr.)
Andre Genin
HONEYMOON HOTEL(1946, Brit.)
Rene Genin
CRIME OF MONSIEUR LANGE, THE(1936, Fr.); LOWER DEPTHS, THE(1937, Fr.); PORT OF SHADOWS(1938, Fr.); DAYBREAK(1940, Fr.); IT HAPPENED AT THE INN(1945, Fr.); CAGE OF NIGHTINGALES, A(1947, Fr.); FORBIDDEN FRUIT(1959, Fr.); LAW IS THE LAW, THE(1959, Fr.); HORROR CHAMBER OF DR. FAUSTUS, THE(1962, Fr./Ital.); HOW NOT TO ROB A DEPARTMENT STORE(1965, Fr./Ital.); JUDEX(1966, Fr./Ital.)
Augusto Genina
KISS OF FIRE, THE(1940, Fr.), d; DEVOTION(1953, Ital.), d, w; FROU-FROU(1955, Fr.), d
Genius
JULIET OF THE SPIRITS(1965, Fr./Ital./W.Ger.)
Genius [Eugenio Mastropietro]
FELLINI SATYRICON(1969, Fr./Ital.)
Genji
GIRL IN GOLD BOOTS(1968)
Harvey Genkins
DON'T DRINK THE WATER(1969), ph; FIVE DAYS FROM HOME(1978), ph; H.O.T.S.(1979), ph
Marcelle Genlat
BLUE VEIL, THE(1947, Fr.)
Leo Genn
IMMORTAL GENTLEMAN(1935, Brit.); CAVALIER OF THE STREETS, THE(1937, Brit.); WHEN THIEF MEETS THIEF(1937, Brit.); DANGEROUS MEDICINE(1938, Brit.); KATE PLUS TEN(1938, Brit.); PYGMALION(1938, Brit.); RAT, THE(1938, Brit.); BLACKOUT(1940, Brit.); LAW AND DISORDER(1940, Brit.); MISSING TEN DAYS(1941, Brit.); YOUNG MR. PITT, THE(1942, Brit.); WAY AHEAD, THE(1945, Brit.); CAESAR AND CLEOPATRA(1946, Brit.); GREEN FOR DANGER(1946, Brit.); HENRY V(1946, Brit.); MOURNING BECOMES ELECTRA(1947); SNAKE PIT, THE(1948); VELVET TOUCH, THE(1948); MINIVER STORY, THE(1950, Brit./U.S.); NO PLACE FOR JENNIFER(1950, Brit.); QUO VADIS(1951); WOODEN HORSE, THE(1951); MAGIC BOX, THE(1952, Brit.); PLYMOUTH ADVENTURE(1952); AFFAIR IN MONTE CARLO(1953, Brit.); GIRLS OF PLEASURE ISLAND, THE(1953); GREEN SCARF, THE(1954, Brit.); PERSONAL AFFAIR(1954, Brit.); PARATROOPER(1954, Brit.); MOBY DICK(1956, Brit.); BEYOND MOMBASA(1957); STEEL BAYONET, THE(1958, Brit.); TANK FORCE(1958, Brit.); LADY CHATTERLEY'S LOVER(1959, Fr.); TOO HOT TO HANDLE(1961, Brit.); LONGEST DAY, THE(1962); 55 DAYS AT PEKING(1963); DR. MABUSE'S RAYS OF DEATH(1964, Ger./Fr./Ital.); TEN LITTLE INDIANS(1965, Brit.); KHARTOUM(1966, Brit.); PSYCHO-CIRCUS(1967, Brit.); DIE SCREAMING, MARIANNE(1970, Brit.); CONNECTING ROOMS(1971, Brit.); MACKINTOSH MAN, THE(1973, Brit.); FRIGHTMARE(1974, Brit.); MARTYR, THE(1976, Ger./Israel)
Misc. Talkies
UNDEFEATED, THE(1951, Brit.)
Irene Genna
VERGINITA(1953, Ital.)
Ren Gennard
Silents
LEECH, THE(1921)
Giorgio Gennari
DANGER: DIABOLIK(1968, Ital./Fr.)
Lina Gennari
UMBERTO D(1955, Ital.)
Gino Gennaro
FRONT, THE(1976)
Peter Gennaro
PAJAMA GAME, THE(1957); UNSINKABLE MOLLY BROWN, THE(1964), ch
Isabella Genoese
N. P.(1971, Ital.), art d
Arnaldo Genoino
HEROD THE GREAT(1960, Ital.), d
Andre Genoves
LES BICHES(1968, Fr.), p; LA FEMME INFIDELE(1969, Fr./Ital.), p; THIS MAN MUST DIE(1970, Fr./Ital.), p; WHO'S GOT THE BLACK BOX?(1970, Fr./Gr./Ital.), p; DOCTEUR POPAUL(1972, Fr.), p; TEN DAYS' WONDER(1972, Fr.), p; NADA GANG,

THE(1974, Fr./Ital.), p; JUST BEFORE NIGHTFALL(1975, Fr./Ital.), p; BAROCCO(1976, Fr.), p
Lea Genovese
MY FAIR LADY(1964)
Mike Genovese
ON THE RIGHT TRACK(1981); TAKE THIS JOB AND SHOVE IT(1981); THIEF(1981)
Peter Genovese
Q(1982)
Fritz Genschow
SLEEPING BEAUTY(1965, Ger.), a, p&d, w; GOOSE GIRL, THE(1967, Ger.), a, p&d, w
Kunibert Gensichen
JUDGE AND THE SINNER, THE(1964, Ger.)
Lewis Gensler
OLD MAN RHYTHM(1935), w, m; ARTISTS AND MODELS(1937), p; COLLEGE SWING(1938), p
Lewis E. Gensler
BIG BROADCAST OF 1937, THE(1936), p; YOURS FOR THE ASKING(1936), p
Peter Gent
NORTH DALLAS FORTY(1979), w
Queen Esther Gent
BOOK OF NUMBERS(1973)
Renzo Genta
DAY OF ANGER(1970, Ital./Ger.), w; JESSE AND LESTER, TWO BROTHERS IN A PLACE CALLED TRINITY(1972, Ital.), w
Helga Genth
TEXICAN, THE(1966, U.S./Span.)
Joanne Genthon
VERTIGO(1958)
Dennis Gentile
OUTBACK(1971, Aus.), art d
Fedele Gentile
PHAROAH'S WOMAN, THE(1961, Ital.); CAESAR THE CONQUEROR(1963, Ital.); GUILT IS NOT MINE(1968, Ital.)
Joe R. Gentile
STAKEOUT!(1962), p
Linda Gentile
TO ALL A GOODNIGHT(1980)
Marcella Gentile
GARDEN OF THE FINZI-CONTINIS, THE(1976, Ital./Ger.)
Robert Gentile
STRANGERS IN THE CITY(1962)
Vincent Gentile
ORCA(1977)
John Gentilella
HEY, GOOD LOOKIN'(1982), anim
Gentili
PISTOL FOR RINGO, A(1966, Ital./Span.), cos
Carlo Gentili
300 SPARTANS, THE(1962), set d; PISTOL FOR RINGO, A(1966, Ital./Span.), art d
Girorgio Gentili
MADIGAN'S MILLIONS(1970, Span./Ital), d
Giuseppe Gentili
MEDEA(1971, Ital./Fr./Ger.)
R. Gentili
GUILT IS NOT MINE(1968, Ital.), w
G. Gentill
HANNIBAL(1960, Ital.), set d
Giacomo Gentilomo
LAST OF THE VIKINGS, THE(1962, Fr./Ital.), d; GOLIATH AND THE VAMPIRES(1964, Ital.), d; HERCULES AGAINST THE MOON MEN(1965, Fr./Ital.), d, w
Alice Gentle
GOLDEN DAWN(1930); SONG OF THE FLAME(1930); FLYING DOWN TO RIO(1933)
Dennis Gentle
THEY'RE A WEIRD MOB(1966, Aus.), art d; AGE OF CONSENT(1969, Austral.), art d; SQUEEZE A FLOWER(1970, Aus.), art d
Lili Gentle
TEENAGE REBEL(1956); WILL SUCCESS SPOIL ROCK HUNTER?(1957); YOUNG AND DANGEROUS(1957); SING, BOY, SING(1958); MR. HOBBS TAKES A VACATION(1962)
Louis Gentle
OUT OF THE BLUE(1982)
Wally Gentleman
DRYLANDERS(1963, Can.), spec eff; REINCARNATE, THE(1971, Can.), spec eff; BEYOND THE DOOR(1975, Ital./U.S.), spec eff; SHAPE OF THINGS TO COME, THE(1979, Can.), spec eff
Avril Gentles
NIGHT MOVES(1975); OUTSIDER, THE(1980)
Norma Gentner
SONG IS BORN, A(1948)
Beau Gentry
HELL BENT FOR LEATHER(1960); AMERICAN GRAFFITI(1973)
Bill Gentry
RETURN FROM THE SEA(1954); FAREWELL, MY LOVELY(1975)
Bobbie Gentry
ODE TO BILLY JOE(1976), w
Capt. Gentry
CANON CITY(1948)
Chance Gentry
COME SPY WITH ME(1967); SPLIT, THE(1968)
Don Gentry
BREAKER! BREAKER!(1977)
Frank Gentry
FOURTEEN, THE(1973, Brit.)
Gene Gentry
TIME TO SING, A(1968)
George Gentry
RATS OF TOBRUK(1951, Aus.)

Jim Gentry
RAMRODDER, THE(1969); GOLDEN BOX, THE(1970)
John [Race] Gentry
THUNDER IN CAROLINA(1960)
Mike Gentry
PROJECTIONIST, THE(1970); I DRINK YOUR BLOOD(1971); COMEBACK TRAIL, THE(1982)
Minnie Gentry
COME BACK CIHARLESTON BLUE(1972); GEORGIA, GEORGIA(1972); BLACK CAESAR(1973); GREASED LIGHTNING(1977)
1984
BROTHER FROM ANOTHER PLANET, THE(1984)
Mrs. Gentry
NEW ADVENTURES OF TARZAN(1935)
Oak R. Gentry
MURPH THE SURF(1974)
Paul Gentry
CRATER LAKE MONSTER, THE(1977), ph; LASERBLAST(1978), spec eff & makeup
Paul W. Gentry
DAY TIME ENDED, THE(1980, Span.), p, spec eff
Race Gentry
LAWLESS BREED, THE(1952); BLACK HORSE CANYON(1954); BOLD AND THE BRAVE, THE(1956); THERE'S ALWAYS TOMORROW(1956); MEN IN WAR(1957)
Renee Gentry
GETTING OVER(1981)
Richard Gentry
KINFOLK(1970)
Robert Gentry
PLASTIC DOME OF NORMA JEAN, THE(1966); DEAR, DEAD DELILAH(1972)
Roger Gentry
WIZARD OF MARS(1964); DR. TERROR'S GALLERY OF HORRORS(1967); FANDANGO(1970); THING WITH TWO HEADS, THE(1972)
Tom Gentry
WORDS AND MUSIC(1929)
The Gentrys
IT'S A BIKINI WORLD(1967)
Rick Gentz
KILLER ELITE, THE(1975), set d
1984
TANK(1984), set d
Rick T. Gentz
DANDY, THE ALL AMERICAN GIRL(1976), set d; DEFIANCE(1980), set d; MOUNTAIN MEN, THE(1980), set d
Ludde Gentzel
DREAMS(1960, Swed.)
Gean Genung
Misc. Silents
MIRANDY SMILES(1918)
Gene Genung
Misc. Silents
SHOULD SHE OBEY?(1917)
Jochen Genzow
FEAR(1956, Ger.), p
Geo
1984
CHEECH AND CHONG'S THE CORSICAN BROTHERS(1984), m
Geo-Dorlys
LA MARSEILLAISE(1938, Fr.)
Atlas Geodesic
TURN ON TO LOVE(1969), w
Madeleine Geoffreoy
PERSONAL COLUMN(1939, Fr.)
Madeleine Geoffrey
CURTAIN RISES, THE(1939, Fr.)
Paul Geoffrey
EXCALIBUR(1981)
1984
GREYSTOKE: THE LEGEND OF TARZAN, LORD OF THE APES(1984)
Wallace Geoffrey
BROWN SUGAR(1931, Brit.); FLYING FOOL, THE(1931, Brit.); HOUSE OPPOSITE, THE(1931, Brit.); SECRET AGENT(1933, Brit.); BOOMERANG(1934, Brit.); OUTCAST, THE(1934, Brit.); RETURN OF BULLDOG DRUMMOND, THE(1934, Brit.); STOKER, THE(1935, Brit.), w; CHICK(1936, Brit.); LIVING DEAD, THE(1936, Brit.), w; SCARAB MURDER CASE, THE(1936, Brit.); ONE NIGHT IN PARIS(1940, Brit.); PERFECT WOMAN, THE(1950, Brit.), w
Wallace Geoffreys
LIFE GOES ON(1932, Brit.)
Robert Geoffrian
1984
SURROGATE, THE(1984, Can.), w
Robert Geoffrion
JOY(1983, Fr./Can.), w
Madeleine Geoffroy
SEVENTH JUROR, THE(1964, Fr.)
Odile Geoffroy
MY LIFE TO LIVE(1963, Fr.); LES CARABINIERS(1968, Fr./Ital.)
Konrad Georg
IS PARIS BURNING?(1966, U.S./Fr.)
George
HAPPIEST MILLIONAIRE, THE(1967)
A.E. George
Misc. Silents
BRIGADIER GERARD(1915, Brit.)
Abner George
TOMAHAWK(1951); BATTLES OF CHIEF PONTIAC(1952)
Alexander George
CATCH AS CATCH CAN(1937, Brit.), w

Amy Marie George
DEATH HUNT(1981)
Ann George
TOUCH OF THE SUN, A(1956, Brit.)
Annabelle George
NIGHTFALL(1956); NEW KIND OF LOVE, A(1963)
Anthony George
WHERE THE SIDEWALK ENDS(1950); YOU NEVER CAN TELL(1951); GUNFIRE AT INDIAN GAP(1957)
Arthur George
Misc. Silents
DIAMOND BANDIT, THE(1924)
Bennett George
UNDERCOVER MAN(1942)
Bill George
MASKED RAIDERS(1949)
Bonnie George
GREEK TYCOON, THE(1978)
Bud George
STUNTS(1977)
Burton George
Silents
HUMAN DESIRES(1924, Brit.), d, w
Misc. Silents
BLADE O' GRASS(1915), d; CELESTE OF THE AMBULANCE CORPS(1916), d; HERITAGE OF HATE, THE(1916), d; ISLE OF LIFE, THE(1916), d; LAW OF THE NORTH, THE(1917), d; EVE IN EXILE(1919), d; GINGER(1919), d; VALLEY OF DOUBT, THE(1920), d; CONCEIT(1921), d; DEVOTION(1921), d
Chief Dan George
ALIEN THUNDER(1975, US/Can.); AMERICATHON(1979)
Christopher George
GENTLE RAIN, THE(1966, Braz.); EL DORADO(1967); GAVILAN(1968); PROJECT X(1968); DEVIL'S 8, THE(1969); 1,000 PLANE RAID, THE(1969); CHISUM(1970); DELTA FACTOR, THE(1970); TIGER BY THE TAIL(1970); I ESCAPED FROM DEVIL'S ISLAND(1973); TRAIN ROBBERS, THE(1973); INBREAKER, THE(1974, Can.); DIXIE DYNAMITE(1976); GRIZZLY(1976); MIDWAY(1976); DAY OF THE ANIMALS(1977); FOES(1977), spec eff; EXTERMINATOR, THE(1980); GRADUATION DAY(1981); ENTER THE NINJA(1982); MORTUARY(1983); PIECES(1983, Span./ Puerto Rico)
Misc. Talkies
WHISKEY MOUNTAIN(1977); DAY SANTA CLAUS CRIED, THE(1980)
Crosby George
Silents
JUNE MADNESS(1922), w; EXCITEMENT(1924), w
Don George
CLIMAX, THE(1944), md; SAN DIEGO, I LOVE YOU(1944), md; SLIGHTLY TERRIFIC(1944), md; WEEKEND PASS(1944), md; PUTNEY SWOPE(1969)
Earl George
WRONG MAN, THE(1956); MISTER ROCK AND ROLL(1957)
Eliot George "Freeman"
LEATHER BOYS, THE(1965, Brit.), w
Ernest George
DOWN OUR STREET(1932, Brit.), d&w
Florence George
COLLEGE SWING(1938); TELL NO TALES(1939); ONE MORE TIME(1970, Brit.)
Frank George
DR. NO(1962, Brit.), spec eff; CITY UNDER THE SEA(1965, Brit.), spec eff; DRACULA HAS RISEN FROM HIS GRAVE(1968, Brit.), spec eff
George S. George
HEAT'S ON, THE(1943), w
George W. George
BODYGUARD(1948), w; EXPERIMENT ALCATRAZ(1950), w; MYSTERY SUBMARINE(1950), w; NEVADAN, THE(1950), w; PEGGY(1950), w; WOMAN ON PIER 13, THE(1950), w; RED MOUNTAIN(1951), w; WEEKEND WITH FATHER(1951), w; CITY OF BAD MEN(1953), w; THUNDER BAY(1953), w; ROCKET MAN, THE(1954), w; DESERT SANDS(1955), w; SMOKE SIGNAL(1955), w; URANIUM BOOM(1956), w; HALLIDAY BRAND, THE(1957), w; APACHE TERRITORY(1958), w; FORT DOBBS(1958), w; SON OF ROBIN HOOD(1959, Brit.), w; TWO LITTLE BEARS, THE(1961), p, w; MATTER OF INNOCENCE, A(1968, Brit.), p; TWISTED NERVE(1969, Brit.), p; NIGHT WATCH(1973, Brit.), p; RICH KIDS(1979), p; MY DINNER WITH ANDRE(1981), p
Gladys George
STRAIGHT IS THE WAY(1934); VALIANT IS THE WORD FOR CARRIE(1936); MADAME X(1937); THEY GAVE HIM A GUN(1937); LOVE IS A HEADACHE(1938); MARIE ANTOINETTE(1938); HERE I AM A STRANGER(1939); I'M FROM MISSOURI(1939); ROARING TWENTIES, THE(1939); CHILD IS BORN, A(1940); HOUSE ACROSS THE BAY, THE(1940); WAY OF ALL FLESH, THE(1940); HIT THE ROAD(1941); LADY FROM CHEYENNE(1941); MALTESE FALCON, THE(1941); HARD WAY, THE(1942); CRYSTAL BALL, THE(1943); NOBODY'S DARLING(1943); CHRISTMAS HOLIDAY(1944); MINSTREL MAN(1944); STEPPIN' IN SOCIETY(1945); BEST YEARS OF OUR LIVES, THE(1946); MILLIE'S DAUGHTER(1947); ALIAS A GENTLEMAN(1948); FLAMINGO ROAD(1949); BRIGHT LEAF(1950); UNDERCOVER GIRL(1950); DETECTIVE STORY(1951); HE RAN ALL THE WAY(1951); LULLABY OF BROADWAY, THE(1951); SILVER CITY(1951); IT HAPPENS EVERY THURSDAY(1953)
Silents
RED HOT DOLLARS(1920); CHICKENS(1921); EASY ROAD, THE(1921)
Misc. Silents
HOMESPUN FOLKS(1920); HOUSE THAT JAZZ BUILT, THE(1921)
Gorgeous George
ALIAS THE CHAMP(1949)
Gotz George
DIE FASTNACHTSBEICHTE(1962, Ger.); AMONG VULTURES(1964, Ger./Ital./Fr./ Yugo.); TREASURE OF SILVER LAKE(1965, Fr./Ger./Yugo.); FRONTIER HELLCAT(1966, Fr./Ital./Ger./Yugo.); HYPNOSIS(1966, Ger./Sp./Ital.); WIND FROM THE EAST(1970, Fr./Ital./Ger.)
Grace George
JOHNNY COME LATELY(1943)

Greg George
 RAINBOW BOYS, THE(1973, Can.)
H.V. George
 SUNDOWN RIDERS(1948), p
Heinrich George
 1914(1932, Ger.); BERLIN ALEXANDERPLATZ(1933, Ger.); PILLARS OF SOCIE-TY(1936, Ger.); DREYFUS CASE, THE(1940, Ger.); KOLBERG(1945, Ger.)
Silents
 METROPOLIS(1927, Ger.)
Misc. Silents
 MAN BY THE ROADSIDE, THE(1923, Ger.)
Henry George
Misc. Silents
 SHE(1925, Brit.)
Henry W. George
 DEPUTY DRUMMER, THE(1935, Brit.), d; TRUST THE NAVY(1935, Brit.), d; WHO'S YOUR FATHER?(1935, Brit.), d
Howard George
 JEKYLL AND HYDE...TOGETHER AGAIN(1982)
Isabel George
 DEATH IS A NUMBER(1951, Brit.); TAKE A POWDER(1953, Brit.); TWICE UPON A TIME(1953, Brit.); RIVER BEAT(1954); LOVE MATCH, THE(1955, Brit.)
Isobel George
 MOULIN ROUGE(1952); FOR BETTER FOR WORSE(1954, Brit.)
Ja George
 MAGNIFICENT DOLL(1946)
Jac George
 DODSWORTH(1936); DAMSEL IN DISTRESS, A(1937); MUSIC FOR MADA-ME(1937); JEZEBEL(1938); SWEETHEARTS(1938); LADY FOR A NIGHT(1941); HEAVENLY BODY, THE(1943); GYPSY WILDCAT(1944); MR. SKEFFINGTON(1944); STORM OVER LISBON(1944); MADAME BOVARY(1949); SINGIN' IN THE RAIN(1952); DESIREE(1954); LUCKY ME(1954)
Jack George
 EBB TIDE(1937); SHE'S DANGEROUS(1937); MARIE ANTOINETTE(1938); LOOK WHO'S LAUGHING(1941); SECRETS OF SCOTLAND YARD(1944); HONEYMOON AHEAD(1945); LADY CONFESSES, THE(1945); IT HAPPENED ON 5TH AVE-NUE(1947); LITTLE MISS BROADWAY(1947); QUEEN OF THE AMAZONS(1947); SONG OF MY HEART(1947); HARPOON(1948); JOAN OF ARC(1948); THAT LADY IN ERMINE(1948); LEAVE IT TO THE MARINES(1951); LITTLE EGYPT(1951); LOVE IS BETTER THAN EVER(1952); DREAM WIFE(1953); MURDER WITHOUT TEARS(1953)
James George
 DILLINGER(1973), cos
Jan George
 AMERICAN SOLDIER, THE(1970 Ger.)
Jean Craighead George
 MY SIDE OF THE MOUNTAIN(1969), w
Jimmy George
 OUR WINNING SEASON(1978), cos
Joe George
 PUZZLE OF A DOWNFALL CHILD(1970); SOME OF MY BEST FRIENDS ARE...(1971); ROLLERCOASTER(1977)
1984
 HIGHWAY TO HELL(1984); PROTOCOL(1984); RUNNING HOT(1984)
John George
 CONDEMNED(1929); OUTSIDE THE LAW(1930); WAY FOR A SAILOR(1930); SMART MONEY(1931); ISLAND OF LOST SOULS(1933); MONKEY'S PAW, THE(1933); TRICK FOR TRICK(1933); BABES IN TOYLAND(1934); CHARLIE CHAN IN EGYPT(1935); DANTE'S INFERNO(1935); MAN WHO BROKE THE BANK AT MONTE CARLO, THE(1935); JUNGLE PRINCESS, THE(1936); RIFF-RAFF(1936); ROSE MARIE(1936); TWO IN A CROWD(1936); IF I WERE KING(1938); SONG TO REMEMBER, A(1945); DEVIL'S PLAYGROUND, THE(1946); HOODLUM SAINT, THE(1946); SON OF PALEFACE(1952)
Silents
 SCARAMOUCHE(1923); DON JUAN(1926); ROAD TO MANDALAY, THE(1926); NIGHT OF LOVE, THE(1927); UNKNOWN, THE(1927); BIG CITY, THE(1928)
Jon George
 ESCAPE 2000(1983, Aus.), w; FINAL TERROR, THE(1983), w
Joseph George
 JENNIFER ON MY MIND(1971)
Judy George
 TWO LITTLE BEARS, THE(1961), w
Kathleen B. George
 GUN FURY(1953), w
Lance George
 THERE'S ALWAYS A THURSDAY(1957, Brit.)
Laszlo George
 RUNNING(1979, Can.), ph; NOTHING PERSONAL(1980, Can.), ph
1984
 BEAR, THE(1984), ph
Lazlo George
 HOMER(1970), ph; CIRCLE OF TWO(1980, Can.), ph
Len George
 LITTLE BIG MAN(1970)
Leonard George
 TURNING POINT, THE(1952); VIVA ZAPATA!(1952); SALOME(1953); DESI-REE(1954); STORY ON PAGE ONE, THE(1959); OCEAN'S ELEVEN(1960); RAINBOW BOYS, THE(1973, Can.)
Leslie George
Misc. Silents
 ROCK OF AGES(1918, Brit.)
Lynda Day George
 DAY OF THE ANIMALS(1977); RACQUET(1979); BEYOND EVIL(1980); JUNKMAN, THE(1982); MORTUARY(1983); PIECES(1983, Span./Puerto Rico); YOUNG WARRI-ORS(1983)
Misc. Talkies
 ALIENS FROM SPACESHIP EARTH(1977)

Mabelle George
 MISTER CINDERS(1934, Brit.)
Marie George
 MOTHER LODE(1982)
Mary George
 NATIVE LAND(1942); HALF ANGEL(1951); MOVE OVER, DARLING(1963)
Maud George
Silents
 EVEN AS YOU AND I(1917)
Misc. Silents
 BECKONING TRAIL, THE(1916)
Maude George
 VEILED WOMAN, THE(1929)
Silents
 TARGET, THE(1916); DEVIL'S PASSKEY, THE(1920); FOOLISH WIVES(1920); MERRY-GO-ROUND(1923); SIX DAYS(1923); TEMPORARY MARRIAGE(1923); TOR-MENT(1924); LOVE TOY, THE(1926); ALTARS OF DESIRE(1927); WEDDING MARCH, THE(1927); AFTER THE STORM(1928); ISLE OF LOST MEN(1928)
Misc. Silents
 BUSINESS IS BUSINESS(1915); FRAME-UP, THE(1915); GAY LORD WARING, THE(1916); IRON HAND, THE(1916); LANDON'S LEGACY(1916); POOL OF FLAME, THE(1916); SILENT BATTLE, THE(1916); SOCIAL BUCCANEER, THE(1916); HEART STRINGS(1917); PIPER'S PRICE, THE(1917); BLUE BLAZES RAWDEN(1918); MAR-RIAGE RING, THE(1918); MIDNIGHT STAGE, THE(1919); ROGUE'S ROMANCE, A(1919); POWER OF A LIE, THE(1922); GARDEN OF EDEN, THE(1928)
Muriel George
 HIS LORDSHIP(1932, Brit.); CLEANING UP(1933, Brit.); SOMETHING ALWAYS HAPPENS(1934, Brit.); KEY TO HARMONY(1935, Brit.); MY SONG FOR YOU(1935, Brit.); NELL GWYN(1935, Brit.); OLD FAITHFUL(1935, Brit.); BUSMAN'S HOLI-DAY(1936, Brit.); HAPPY FAMILY, THE(1936, Brit.); NOT SO DUSTY(1936, Brit.); BACKSTAGE(1937, Brit.); DOCTOR SYN(1937, Brit.); LANCASHIRE LUCK(1937, Brit.); MERRY COMES TO STAY(1937, Brit.); SONG OF THE ROAD(1937, Brit.); TALKING FEET(1937, Brit.); WHO'S YOUR LADY FRIEND?(1937, Brit.); DARTS ARE TRUMPS(1938, Brit.); MAN WITH 100 FACES, THE(1938, Brit.); SISTER TO ASSIST-ER, A(1938, Brit.); BRIGGS FAMILY, THE(1940, Brit.); MOZART(1940, Brit.); PACK UP YOUR TROUBLES(1940, Brit.); TWENTY-ONE DAYS TOGETHER(1940, Brit.); BOMB-SIGHT STOLEN(1941, Brit.); QUIET WEDDING(1941, Brit.); SOUTH AMERICAN GEORGE(1941, Brit.); VOICE IN THE NIGHT, A(1941, Brit.); YOU WILL REMEM-BER(1941, Brit.); UNPUBLISHED STORY(1942, Brit.); WINGS AND THE WO-MAN(1942, Brit.); YOUNG MR. PITT, THE(1942, Brit.); ALIBI, THE(1943, Brit.); BELLS GO DOWN, THE(1943, Brit.); KISS THE BRIDE GOODBYE(1944, Brit.); 48 HOURS(1944, Brit.); FOR YOU ALONE(1945, Brit.); I'LL BE YOUR SWEET-HEART(1945, Brit.); LOVE ON THE DOLE(1945, Brit.); RANDOLPH FAMILY, THE(1945, Brit.); VACATION FROM MARRIAGE(1945, Brit.); WHEN THE BOUGH BREAKS(1947, Brit.); YEARS BETWEEN, THE(1947, Brit.); SISTER TO ASSIST'ER, A(1948, Brit.); DANCING YEARS, THE(1950, Brit.); LAST HOLIDAY(1950, Brit.); SIMON AND LAURA(1956, Brit.)
Nathan George
 TAKING OF PELHAM ONE, TWO, THREE, THE(1974); KLUTE(1971); SER-PICO(1973); ONE FLEW OVER THE CUCKOO'S NEST(1975); SHORT EYES(1977); BRUBAKER(1980)
Ott George
 UNDER MY SKIN(1950)
Pat George
 T-BIRD GANG(1959)
Peter George
 SARABAND(1949, Brit.); DR. STRANGELOVE: OR HOW I LEARNED TO STOP WORRYING AND LOVE THE BOMB(1964), w
Ray George
 EASY LIVING(1949)
Richard George
 YOUNG AND INNOCENT(1938, Brit.); MURDER WILL OUT(1939, Brit.); INVAD-ERS, THE,(1941); LET THE PEOPLE SING(1942, Brit.); TOWER OF TERROR, THE(1942, Brit.); BELLS GO DOWN, THE(1943, Brit.); ESCAPE TO DANGER(1943, Brit.); FLEMISH FARM, THE(1943, Brit.); GENTLE SEX, THE(1943, Brit.); IT'S THAT MAN AGAIN(1943, Brit.); CANDLELIGHT IN ALGERIA(1944, Brit.); OLD MOTHER RILEY AT HOME(1945, Brit.); GREAT EXPECTATIONS(1946, Brit.); JOHNNY FRENCHMAN(1946, Brit.); QUIET WEEKEND(1948, Brit.); DICK BARTON AT BAY(1950, Brit.); FIGHTING PIMPERNEL, THE(1950, Brit.); NAKED HEART, THE(1955, Brit.); DEVIL'S PASS, THE(1957, Brit.); JOHN OF THE FAIR(1962, Brit.)
Rita George
 HOLLYWOOD BOULEVARD(1976)
Misc. Talkies
 COUNTRY BLUE(1975)
Rob George
 BLUE FIN(1978, Aus.)
Robert George
 ONE THIRD OF A NATION(1939); CONVICT STAGE(1965), spec eff
Roger George
 INVISIBLE INVADERS(1959), spec eff; AMAZING TRANSPARENT MAN, THE(1960), spec eff; YOUNG AND THE BRAVE, THE(1963), spec eff; PAJAMA PARTY(1964), spec eff; DR. GOLDFOOT AND THE BIKINI MACHINE(1965), spec eff; FORT COURAGEOUS(1965), spec eff; HUMAN DUPLICATORS, THE(1965), spec eff; MUTINY IN OUTER SPACE(1965), spec eff; DESTINATION INNER SPACE(1966), spec eff; GHOST IN THE INVISIBLE BIKINI(1966), spec eff; CASTLE OF EVIL(1967), spec eff; KILL A DRAGON(1967), spec eff; TRIP, THE(1967), spec eff; DESTRUCTORS, THE(1968), spec eff; DEVIL'S 8, THE(1969), spec eff; CHRISTINE JORGENSEN STORY, THE(1970), spec eff; DUNWICH HORROR, THE(1970), spec eff; LOSERS, THE(1970), sp eff; RETURN OF COUNT YORGA, THE(1971), spec eff; SIMON, KING OF THE WITCHES(1971), spec eff; HOLLYWOOD BOULEVARD(1976), spec eff; MASSACRE AT CENTRAL HIGH(1976), spec eff; SCORCHY(1976), spec eff; VIGI-LANTE FORCE(1976), spec eff; GRAND THEFT AUTO(1977), spec eff; TILL DEATH(1978), spec eff; STEEL(1980), spec eff; HOWLING, THE(1981), spec eff; MAUSOLEUM(1983), spec eff
1984
 INVISIBLE STRANGLER(1984), spec eff; REPO MAN(1984), spec eff; RUNNING HOT(1984), spec eff

Roland George
Misc. Talkies
ALIKI-MY LOVE(1963, U.S./Gr.)
S. C. George
OUTPOST IN MALAYA(1952, Brit.), w
Sue George
ROCK, PRETTY BABY(1956); DALTON GIRLS, THE(1957); RAINTREE COUNTY(1957); UNDERSEA GIRL(1957); GIDGET(1959)
Susan George
SONG IS BORN, A(1948); CUP FEVER(1965, Brit.); SORCERERS, THE(1967, Brit.); STRANGE AFFAIR, THE(1968, Brit.); UP THE JUNCTION(1968, Brit.); ALL NEAT IN BLACK STOCKINGS(1969, Brit.); DIE SCREAMING, MARIANNE(1970, Brit.); LOOKING GLASS WAR, THE(1970, Brit.); SPRING AND PORT WINE(1970, Brit.); SUDDEN TERROR(1970, Brit.); FRIGHT(1971, Brit.); LOLA(1971, Brit./Ital.); STRAW DOGS(1971, Brit.); DIRTY MARY, CRAZY LARRY(1974); SONNY AND JED(1974, Ital.); MANDINGO(1975); OUT OF SEASON(1975, Brit.); SMALL TOWN IN TEXAS, A(1976); TINTORERA...BLOODY WATERS(1977, Brit./Mex.); TOMORROW NEVER COMES(1978, Brit./Can.); ENTER THE NINJA(1982); HOUSE WHERE EVIL DWELLS, THE(1982); VENOM(1982, Brit.)
1984
JIGSAW MAN, THE(1984, Brit.)
Misc. Talkies
MISSION: MONTE CARLO(1981, Brit.); KISS MY GRITS(1982); CZECH MATE(1984, Brit.)
Thomas George
WACKY WORLD OF DR. MORGUS, THE(1962)
Tony George
TEN COMMANDMENTS, THE(1956); THREE BAD SISTERS(1956); CHICAGO CONFIDENTIAL(1957)
Tricia George
MISSIONARY, THE(1982)
Tudor George
EXPERIENCE PREFERRED... BUT NOT ESSENTIAL(1983, Brit.), cos
1984
FOREVER YOUNG(1984, Brit.), cos
Vicky George
MR. BILLION(1977)
Victoria George
EL DORADO(1967); LAST REBEL, THE(1971)
Vincent George
CHANGES(1969)
Virginia George
MARY BURNS, FUGITIVE(1935)
Will George
ROCKABILLY BABY(1957), w
William George
LURE OF THE SWAMP(1957), w; ONE FROM THE HEART(1982)
Zena George
SAFETY IN NUMBERS(1938), w
George Bean Group
PRIVILEGE(1967, Brit.)
George Lafaye Company
TO PARIS WITH LOVE(1955, Brit.)
George Melanchrino and His Orchestra
OLD MOTHER RILEY, HEADMISTRESS(1950, Brit.)
George Mitchell Show
DREAM MAKER, THE(1963, Brit.)
George Morgan and His Orchestra
WHOOPEE(1930)
George Ogle
Silents
WHEN KNIGHTHOOD WAS IN FLOWER(1922)
George Olsen and his Orchestra
HAPPY DAYS(1930)
"Georgeanne"
MOONSHINER'S WOMAN(1968)
Edith Georges
FOLIES BERGERE(1958, Fr.)
Georges and Jaina
BORN TO DANCE(1936)
Olga Georges-Picot
FAREWELL, FRIEND(1968, Fr./Ital.); MAN WHO HAUNTED HIMSELF, THE(1970, Brit.); CONNECTING ROOMS(1971, Brit.); JE T'AIME, JE T'AIME(1972, Fr./Swed.); DAY OF THE JACKAL, THE(1973, Brit./Fr.); PERSECUTION(1974, Brit.); CHILDREN OF RAGE(1975, Brit.-Israeli); LOVE AND DEATH(1975)
Georgette
FROM THE EARTH TO THE MOON(1958), cos
Wolfgang Georgi
STOP TRAIN 349(1964, Fr./Ital./Ger.)
The Georgia Crackers
DESERT VIGILANTE(1949)
Georgia State Senator Leroy Johnson
HOUSE ON SKULL MOUNTAIN, THE(1974)
Nicholas Georgiade
IT'S A MAD, MAD, MAD, MAD WORLD(1963); YOUNG RUNAWAYS, THE(1968); STACEY!(1973)
David Georgiades
WHITE HUNTER(1965)
Emile Georgiades
WHITE HUNTER(1965)
Vassilis Georgiades
RED LANTERNS(1965, Gr.), d
Elisa Georgiadis
GIRL FROM PETROVKA, THE(1974)
Nicholas Georgiadis
ROMEO AND JULIET(1966, Brit.), set d&cos; SWAN LAKE, THE(1967), set d&cos; TROJAN WOMEN, THE(1971), art d

Georgian Singers
LAUGH IT OFF(1940, Brit.)
The Georgian Singers
RIDING HIGH(1937, Brit.)
Andrew Georgias
Misc. Talkies
BIG TIME(1977), d
Wee Georgie
STEPPING TOES(1938, Brit.)
George Georgis
CANNON AND THE NIGHTINGALE, THE(1969, Gr.)
Phaedon Georgitsis
RED LANTERNS(1965, Gr.)
Phedon Georgitsis
DREAM OF PASSION, A(1978, Gr.)
G. Georgiu
CLEAR SKIES(1963, USSR); DUEL, THE(1964, USSR); SANDU FOLLOWS THE SUN(1965, USSR)
L. Georgiyeu
FAREWELL, DOVES(1962, USSR), art d
A. Georgiyevskaya
RESURRECTION(1963, USSR)
Christine Georgopulo
SPRING BREAK(1983)
Kimberly Georgoulis
1984
TIGHTROPE(1984)
Alice Georguli
POLICEMAN OF THE 16TH PRECINCT, THE(1963, Gr.)
Libuse Geprtova
LADY ON THE TRACKS, THE(1968, Czech.)
Ferdinando Gera
WHITE NIGHTS(1961, Ital./Fr.)
Folton Gera
VICTORY(1981)
Liliana Gerace
BEHIND CLOSED SHUTTERS(1952, Ital.); FIST IN HIS POCKET(1968, Ital.); L'ETOILE DU NORD(1983, Fr.)
Lillian Gerace
RICE GIRL(1963, Fr./Ital.)
Frank Geraci
PRISM(1971)
Roberto Geradi
LAST DAYS OF MUSSOLINI(1974, Ital.), ph
Zoraida Geradino
TERROR IN THE JUNGLE(1968), cos
Serge Geraert
THERESE AND ISABELLE(1968, U.S./Ger.)
Bob Geraghty
ANTS IN HIS PANTS(1940, Aus.)
Carmelita Geraghty
MISSISSIPPI GAMBLER(1929); PARIS BOUND(1929); THIS THING CALLED LOVE(1929); AFTER THE FOG(1930); MEN WITHOUT LAW(1930); ROGUE OF THE RIO GRANDE(1930); WHAT MEN WANT(1930); FIFTY MILLION FRENCHMEN(1931); FIGHTING THRU(1931); GRAFT(1931); MILLIE(1931); NIGHT LIFE IN RENO(1931); TEXAS RANGER, THE(1931); DEVIL PAYS, THE(1932); ESCAPADE(1932); FORGOTTEN WOMEN(1932); PRESTIGE(1932); FLAMING SIGNAL(1933); MALAY NIGHTS(1933); PHANTOM OF SANTA FE(1937)
Misc. Talkies
DARK ENDEAVOUR(1933)
Silents
JEALOUS HUSBANDS(1923); GEARED TO GO(1924); PASSIONATE YOUTH(1925); PLEASURE GARDEN, THE(1925, Brit./Ger.); GREAT GATSBY, THE(1926); JOSSELYN'S WIFE(1926); LAST TRAIL, THE(1927); MY BEST GIRL(1927); WHAT EVERY GIRL SHOULD KNOW(1927); GOOD-BYE KISS, THE(1928); OBJECT-ALIMONY(1929)
Misc. Silents
BAG AND BAGGAGE(1923); HIGH SPEED(1924); BRAND OF COWARDICE(1925); CYCLONE CAVALIER(1925); MY LADY OF WHIMS(1925); MYSTERIOUS STRANGER, THE(1925); FLYING MAIL, THE(1926); SLAVER, THE(1927); SOUTH OF PANAMA(1928)
Claudia Geraghty
REUBEN, REUBEN(1983)
Clive Geraghty
PADDY(1970, Irish); BLACK BEAUTY(1971, Brit./Ger./Span.)
Erin Geraghty
PETER RABBIT AND TALES OF BEATRIX POTTER(1971, Brit.); THAT'LL BE THE DAY(1974, Brit.)
Gerald Geraghty
STREET OF CHANCE(1930), titles; SUNSET PASS(1933), w; UNDER THE TONTO RIM(1933), w; SCOOP, THE(1934, Brit.), w; BAR 20 RIDES AGAIN(1936), w; JUNGLE PRINCESS, THE(1936), w; WELLS FARGO(1937), w; HER JUNGLE LOVE(1938), w; WESTERN JAMBOREE(1938), w; ARIZONA KID, THE(1939), w; BLUE MONTANA SKIES(1939), w; COME ON RANGERS(1939), w; IN OLD CALIENTE(1939), w; IN OLD MONTEREY(1939), w; MEXICALI ROSE(1939), w; MOUNTAIN RHYTHM(1939), w; SOUTH OF THE BORDER(1939), w; SOUTHWARD HO!(1939), w; WALL STREET COWBOY(1939), w; CARSON CITY KID(1940), w; HIDDEN GOLD(1940), w; PIONEERS OF THE WEST(1940), w; RANGER AND THE LADY, THE(1940), w; YOUNG BUFFALO BILL(1940), w; BADLANDS OF DAKOTA(1941), w; KING OF DODGE CITY(1941), w; SECRETS OF THE WASTELANDS(1941), w; SOUTH OF TAHITI(1941), w; SIN TOWN(1942), w; SUNSET ON THE DESERT(1942), w; FALCON AND THE CO-EDS, THE(1943), w; FALCON STRIKES BACK, THE(1943), w; FRONTIER BADMEN(1943), w; HAIL TO THE RANGERS(1943), w; HOPPY SERVES A WRIT(1943), w; FALCON IN HOLLYWOOD, THE(1944), w; FALCON IN MEXICO, THE(1944), w; ALONG THE NAVAJO TRAIL(1945), w; FRISCO SAL(1945), w; SHADY LADY(1945), w; CAT CREEPS, THE(1946), w; HELLDORADO(1946), w; HOME IN OKLAHOMA(1946), w; RAINBOW OVER TEXAS(1946), w; APACHE ROSE(1947), w; ON THE OLD SPANISH TRAIL(1947), w; WYOMING(1947), w; GRAND CANYON TRAIL(1948), w; PLUNDERERS, THE(1948), w; TRAIN TO ALCATRAZ(1948), w; RED MENACE, THE(1949), w; RIDERS IN THE SKY(1949), w; COW

TOWN(1950), w; MULE TRAIN(1950), w; SAVAGE HORDE, THE(1950), w; SUNSET IN THE WEST(1950), w; TRAIL OF ROBIN HOOD(1950), w; TRIGGER, JR.(1950), w; HILLS OF UTAH(1951), w; SILVER CANYON(1951), w; VALLEY OF FIRE(1951), w; BARBED WIRE(1952), w; BLUE CANADIAN ROCKIES(1952), w; OLD WEST, THE(1952), w; WAGON TEAM(1952), w; BANDITS OF THE WEST(1953), w; DOWN LAREDO WAY(1953), w; GOLDTOWN GHOST RIDERS(1953), w; IRON MOUNTAIN TRAIL(1953), w; ON TOP OF OLD SMOKY(1953), w; RED RIVER SHORE(1953), w; SAVAGE FRONTIER(1953), w; SHADOWS OF TOMBSTONE(1953), w; PHANTOM STALLION, THE(1954), w; WAGON WHEELS WESTWARD(1956), w
Silents
NAUGHTY BABY(1929), t

Maurice Geraghty
HILLS OF OLD WYOMING(1937), w; TROUBLE AT MIDNIGHT(1937), w; WEST-BOUND LIMITED(1937), w; LAW OF THE PLAINS(1938), w; MYSTERIOUS RIDER, THE(1938), w; SILVER ON THE SAGE(1939), w; APACHE TRAIL(1942), w; FAL-CON'S BROTHER, THE(1942), p; WEST OF TOMBSTONE(1942), w; FALCON AND THE CO-EDS, THE(1943), p; FALCON IN DANGER, THE(1943), p; FALCON STRIKES BACK, THE(1943), p; GOOD MORNING, JUDGE(1943), w; ACTION IN ARA-BIA(1944), p; FALCON IN HOLLYWOOD, THE(1944), p; FALCON IN MEXICO, THE(1944), p; CHINA SKY(1945), p; FALCON IN SAN FRANCISCO, THE(1945), p; WHIPLASH(1948), w; WHO KILLED "DOC" ROBBIN?(1948), w; CALAMITY JANE AND SAM BASS(1949), w; RED CANYON(1949), w; SWORD OF MONTE CRISTO, THE(1951), d&w; TOMAHAWK(1951), w; ROSE OF CIMARRON(1952), w; ROBBER'S ROOST(1955), w; LOVE ME TENDER(1956), w; MOHAWK(1956), w

Thomas Geraghty
Silents
AMERICAN CONSUL, THE(1917), w; THOSE WITHOUT SIN(1917), w; IN OLD KENTUCKY(1920), w

Thomas J. Geraghty
Silents
OLD HOME WEEK(1925), w; NEW KLONDIKE, THE(1926), w

Tom Geraghty
FOOTLIGHTS AND FOOLS(1929), w; TANNED LEGS(1929), w; MR. ROBINSON CRUSOE(1932), w; ELMER THE GREAT(1933), w; CHURCH MOUSE, THE(1934, Brit.), w; MR. WHAT'S-HIS-NAME(1935, Brit.), w; NO LIMIT(1935, Brit.), w; SO YOU WON'T TALK?(1935, Brit.), w; DEBT OF HONOR(1936, Brit.), w; KEEP YOUR SEATS PLEASE(1936, Brit.), w; SHE KNEW WHAT SHE WANTED(1936, Brit.), w; WINGS OF THE MORNING(1937, Brit.), w; TWO'S COMPANY(1939, Brit.), w; EVERYTHING IS RHYTHM(1940, Brit.), w; SHIPYARD SALLY(1940, Brit.), w; PLAYBOY, THE(1942, Brit.), w
Silents
ALWAYS AUDACIOUS(1920), w; WHEN THE CLOUDS ROLL BY(1920), w; FIRE-MAN, SAVE MY CHILD(1927), w; NAUGHTY BABY(1929), w, t
Misc. Silents
SPANISH JADE(1922, Brit.), d

Tom J. Geraghty
SMILING IRISH EYES(1929), w; WEARY RIVER(1929), w; SHARK WOMAN, THE(1941), ed
Silents
IN FOR THIRTY DAYS(1919), w; IT'S THE OLD ARMY GAME(1926), w; NOW WE'RE IN THE AIR(1927), w; BEAU SABREUR(1928), w; HAROLD TEEN(1928), w&t; WIFE SAVERS(1928), w

Alice Gerald
YOUNG GIRLS OF ROCHEFORT, THE(1968, Fr.)

Ara Gerald
ENLIGHTEN THY DAUGHTER(1934); WHITE ANGEL, THE(1936); FOOLS FOR SCANDAL(1938)

Eileen Gerald
TOO MANY HUSBANDS(1938, Brit.)

Harold Gerald
MY FAVORITE WIFE(1940)

Helen Gerald
DOUGHGIRLS, THE(1944); G.I. WAR BRIDES(1946); TARZAN AND THE LEOPARD WOMAN(1946); TOMORROW IS FOREVER(1946); TRAP, THE(1947)
Misc. Talkies
GAY CAVALIER, THE(1946)

Jim Gerald
NIGHT IS OURS(1930, Fr.); CONSTANT NYMPH, THE(1933, Brit.); BULLDOG DRUMMOND AT BAY(1937, Brit.); CLOTHES AND THE WOMAN(1937, Brit.); ROBBER SYMPHONY, THE(1937, Brit.); FRENCH WITHOUT TEARS(1939, Brit.); TESTAMENT OF DR. MABUSE, THE(1943, Ger.); ADVENTURES OF CAPTAIN FABIAN(1951); PARDON MY FRENCH(1951, U.S./Fr.); TAKE ME TO PARIS(1951, Brit.); MOULIN ROUGE(1952); BAREFOOT CONTESSA, THE(1954); DETECTIVE, THE(1954, Qit.); FOREIGN INTRIGUE(1956); PARIS DOES STRANGE THINGS(1957, Fr./Ital.); TIME BOMB(1961, Fr./Ital.)
Silents
ITALIAN STRAW HAT, AN(1927, Fr.)
Misc. Silents
LES DEUX TIMIDES(1929, Fr.)

Jimmy Gerald
MASK OF KOREA(1950, Fr.)

Luis Gerald
CHALLENGE, THE(1939, Brit.)

Mrs. Gerald
Silents
FRAILTY(1921, Brit.)

Pete Gerald
Misc. Silents
CRIMSON SHOALS(1919)

Peter Gerald
Silents
CRAVING, THE(1918)

Robert Gerald
MACHISMO—40 GRAVES FOR 40 GUNS(1970)

Vera Gerald
UNDER SUSPICION(1931); FLAW, THE(1933, Brit.); MELODY MAKER, THE(1933, Brit.)

Geraldine
MELODY AND ROMANCE(1937, Brit.); GIRL FEVER(1961)

Geraldo
SHOW GOES ON, THE(1938, Brit.), md; TORPEDOED!(1939), md; WE'LL MEET AGAIN(1942, Brit.)

Geraldo and His Band
ROAD HOUSE(1934, Brit.)

Geraldo and His Music
SCHOOL FOR STARS(1935, Brit.)

Geraldo and His Orchestra
FAME(1936, Brit.); NO PARKING(1938, Brit.); LAUGH IT OFF(1940, Brit.)

Geraldo and Orchestra
DANCE HALL(1950, Brit.)

Geraldo's Orchestra
WE'LL MEET AGAIN(1942, Brit.)

Paul Geraldy
Silents
NEST, THE(1927), w

Nisim Gerama
JESUS(1979)

Pierre Geran
TIGHT SKIRTS, LOOSE PLEASURES(1966, Fr.), ed

manny Gerard
EDUCATION OF SONNY CARSON, THE(1974), art d

Alain Gerard
GRAND PRIX(1966)

Alfredo Gerard
IT HAPPENED IN CANADA(1962, Can.)

Alice Gerard
Misc. Silents
BREAK THE NEWS TO MOTHER(1919)

Anne Gerard
LOVE CHILD(1982), w

Barney Gerard
LADY FROM NOWHERE(1931), w; LAWLESS WOMAN, THE(1931), w; BRINGING UP FATHER(1946), p, w, m; JIGGS AND MAGGIE IN SOCIETY(1948), p, w; JIGGS AND MAGGIE OUT WEST(1950), p, w; ACCORDING TO MRS. HOYLE(1951), p, w

Ben Gerard
TREE, THE(1969); HIDE IN PLAIN SIGHT(1980); BUSTIN' LOOSE(1981)

Bernard Gerard
FEMMINA(1968 Fr./Ital./Ger.), m; Z(1969, Fr./Algeria), md; ROAD TO SALI-NA(1971, Fr./Ital.), m, md; TRAFFIC(1972, Fr.), md

Carl Gerard
SECRET SERVICE(1931)
Silents
CRIME AND PUNISHMENT(1917); TOO MUCH BUSINESS(1922); YOUTH TO YOUTH(1922); SO THIS IS LOVE(1928)
Misc. Silents
LITTLE SAMARITAN, THE(1917); BODY AND SOUL(1920); UNCHARTED SEAS(1921); UNDER OATH(1922)

Charles Gerard
MEN WITHOUT WOMEN(1930); MIDNIGHT FOLLY(1962, Fr.), d; CROOK, THE(1971, Fr.); AND NOW MY LOVE(1975, Fr.); INCORRIGIBLE(1980, Fr.)
1984
EDITH AND MARCEL(1984, Fr.)
Silents
PLOW GIRL, THE(1916); HUN WITHIN, THE(1918); COUNTERFEIT(1919); ISLE OF CONQUEST(1919); NEW MOON, THE(1919); PEST, THE(1919); NEGLECTED WI-VES(1920); WHISPERS(1920); GILDED LILY, THE(1921); SURE FIRE FLINT(1922); DARLING OF THE RICH, THE(1923); OFF THE HIGHWAY(1925); WEDDING SONG, THE(1925); PLAY SAFE(1927)
Misc. Silents
HIS BROTHER'S WIFE(1916); LEGION OF DEATH, THE(1918); SOMETHING TO DO(1919); CONCEIT(1921); OUT OF THE CHORUS(1921); SHELTERED DAUGH-TERS(1921); FRENCH HEELS(1922); PAWNED(1922); CIRCE THE ENCHAN-TRESS(1924)

Christian Gerard
ANNE-MARIE(1936, Fr.)

Claire Gerard
CRIME AND PUNISHMENT(1935, Fr.); CRIME OF MONSIEUR LANGE, THE(1936, Fr.); LA BETE HUMAINE(1938, Fr.); RULES OF THE GAME, THE(1939, Fr.); PORTRAIT OF A WOMAN(1946, Fr.); HAPPY ROAD, THE(1957); PARIS DOES STRANGE THINGS(1957, Fr./Ital.)

Daniele Gerard
BED AND BOARD(1971, Fr.)

Douglas Gerard
MANHATTAN PARADE(1931)
Silents
ON TIME(1924)

Emanuel Gerard
SHAFT(1971), art d; SHAFT'S BIG SCORE(1972), art d

Geralynn Gerard
1984
DELIVERY BOYS(1984)

Gil Gerard
SOME OF MY BEST FRIENDS ARE...(1971); MAN ON A SWING(1974); AIRPORT '77(1977); BUCK ROGERS IN THE 25TH CENTURY(1979)
Misc. Talkies
HOOCH(1977)

Hal Gerard
SWISS MISS(1938); MORE THE MERRIER, THE(1943); JOE PALOOKA IN WINNER TAKE ALL(1948); SNOW DOG(1950); GHOST CHASERS(1951); LADY IN THE IRON MASK(1952); MURDER WITHOUT TEARS(1953); LEGION OF THE DOOMED(1958)

Harold [Hal] Gerard
SAN FRANCISCO DOCKS(1941)

Harry Gerard
MAN I LOVE, THE(1929), ph

Henriette Gerard
VAMPYR(1932, Fr./Ger.)
Henry Gerard
BLIND ADVENTURE(1933), ph
James W. Gerard
Silents
MY FOUR YEARS IN GERMANY(1918), w
Jay Gerard
OCEAN'S ELEVEN(1960)
Jim Gerard
Misc. Silents
LE VOYAGE IMAGINAIRE(1926, Fr.)
Jimmy Gerard
BELLBOY, THE(1960)
Joseph Gerard
OUTLAW DEPUTY, THE(1935)
Silents
KAISER, BEAST OF BERLIN, THE(1918)
Lise Kristen Gerard
STING II, THE(1983)
Malcolm Gerard
MATTER OF CHOICE, A(1963, Brit.)
Manny Gerard
INCIDENT, THE(1967), prod d; GOODBYE COLUMBUS(1969), art d; COTTON COMES TO HARLEM(1970), art d; SIDELONG GLANCES OF A PIGEON KICKER, THE(1970), art d
Margaret Gerard
DEATHCHEATERS(1976, Aus.); DAWN(1979, Aus.)
Marguerite Gerard
MR. HULOT'S HOLIDAY(1954, Fr.)
Menvin Gerard
CHECKERED COAT, THE(1948), w
Merwin Gerard
WINNING TEAM, THE(1952), w
Michael Gerard
THE DOUBLE McGUFFIN(1979)
Michel Gerard
1984
TO CATCH A COP(1984, Fr.), p, d, w
Monique Gerard
INNOCENTS IN PARIS(1955, Brit.)
Phillipe Gerard
FOLIES BERGERE(1958, Fr.), m
Pierre Gerard
1984
AMERICAN DREAMER(1984)
Rene Gerard
LEVIATHAN(1961, Fr.), w
Rolf Gerard
SILVER CHALICE, THE(1954), prod d, cos; INVITATION TO THE DANCE(1956), cos; HONEY POT, THE(1967, Brit.), cos
Rosemonde Gerard
Silents
GOOD LITTLE DEVIL, A(1914), w
Rupert Gerard
THEY WERE NOT DIVIDED(1951, Brit.)
Teddie Gerard
Silents
SEVENTH DAY, THE(1922)
Misc. Silents
CAVE GIRL, THE(1921)
Tilly Gerard
BELLBOY, THE(1960)
Tom Gerard
CONCRETE JUNGLE, THE(1962, Brit.)
Robert Gerardi
MADAME(1963, Fr./Ital./Span.), ph; END OF THE GAME(1976, Ger./Ital.), ph
Roberto Gerardi
GREAT WAR, THE(1961, Fr., Ital.), ph; CONDEMNED OF ALTONA, THE(1963), w; FIASCO IN MILAN(1963, Fr./Ital.), ph; RITA(1963, Fr./Ital.), ph; EMPTY CANVAS, THE(1964, Fr./Ital.), ph; MARRIAGE–ITALIAN STYLE(1964, Fr./Ital.), ph; MAIDEN FOR A PRINCE, A(1967, Fr./Ital.), ph; DROP DEAD, MY LOVE(1968, Italy), ph; THREE NIGHTS OF LOVE(1969, Ital.), ph; DETECTIVE BELLI(1970, Ital.), ph
Alfred Gerasch
ARIANE(1931, Ger.)
V. Gerasimchuk
KATERINA IZMAILOVA(1969, USSR)
A. Gerasimov
TRAIN GOES TO KIEV, THE(1961, USSR), ph
Aleksei Gerasimov
DREAM COME TRUE, A(1963, USSR), ph
S. Gerasimov
SEVEN BRAVE MEN(1936, USSR), d; CITY OF YOUTH(1938, USSR), d; NEW TEACHER, THE(1941, USSR), d&w
Sergei Gerasimov
AND QUIET FLOWS THE DON(1960 USSR), d&w
Misc. Silents
CLOAK, THE(1926, USSR); DEVIL'S WHEEL, THE(1926, USSR); CLUB OF THE BIG DEED, THE(1927, USSR)
Ye. Gerasimov
TRAIN GOES TO KIEV, THE(1961, USSR), ed
V. Gerasin
MARRIAGE OF BALZAMINOV, THE(1966, USSR)
Gergana Gerassimova
WITH LOVE AND TENDERNESS(1978, Bulgaria)
Linda Geray
MOTHER, JUGS & SPEED(1976)

Stephen Geray
NIGHT PLANE FROM CHUNGKING(1942)
Steve Geray
STUDENT'S ROMANCE, THE(1936, Brit.); LET'S MAKE A NIGHT OF IT(1937, Brit.); HIGH COMMAND(1938, Brit.); INSPECTOR HORNLEIGH(1939, Brit.); DARK STREETS OF CAIRO(1940); ONE NIGHT IN PARIS(1940, Brit.); BLUE, WHITE, AND PERFECT(1941); MAN AT LARGE(1941); CASTLE IN THE DESERT(1942); EYES IN THE NIGHT(1942); GENTLEMAN AT HEART, A(1942); MAD MARTINDALES, THE(1942); MOON AND SIXPENCE, THE(1942); SECRET AGENT OF JAPAN(1942); ABOVE SUSPICION(1943); BACKGROUND TO DANGER(1943); WHISTLING IN BROOKLYN(1943); MEET THE PEOPLE(1944); UNDER MY SKIN(1950); HOUSE ON TELEGRAPH HILL(1951); I CAN GET IT FOR YOU WHOLESALE(1951)
Steven Geray
DANCE BAND(1935, Brit.); STAR FELL FROM HEAVEN, A(1936, Brit.); LIGHTNING CONDUCTOR(1938, Brit.); WIFE TAKES A FLYER, THE(1942); APPOINTMENT IN BERLIN(1943); PHANTOM OF THE OPERA(1943); PILOT NO. 5(1943); CONSPIRATORS, THE(1944); IN SOCIETY(1944); MASK OF DIMITRIOS, THE(1944); SEVENTH CROSS, THE(1944); CORNERED(1945); CRIMSON CANARY(1945); HOTEL BERLIN(1945); MEXICANA(1945); SPELLBOUND(1945); TARZAN AND THE AMAZONS(1945); BLONDIE KNOWS BEST(1946); DEADLINE AT DAWN(1946); GILDA(1946); MR. DISTRICT ATTORNEY(1946); RETURN OF MONTE CRISTO, THE(1946); SO DARK THE NIGHT(1946); CRIME DOCTOR'S GAMBLE(1947); GUNFIGHTERS, THE(1947); I LOVE TROUBLE(1947); UNFAITHFUL, THE(1947); WHEN A GIRL'S BEAUTIFUL(1947); DARK PAST, THE(1948); LADIES OF THE CHORUS(1948); PORT SAID(1948); EL PASO(1949); HOLIDAY IN HAVANA(1949); LONE WOLF AND HIS LADY, THE(1949); ONCE MORE, MY DARLING(1949); SKY LINER(1949); TELL IT TO THE JUDGE(1949); ALL ABOUT EVE(1950); HARBOR OF MISSING MEN(1950); IN A LONELY PLACE(1950); LADY WITHOUT PASSPORT, A(1950); PYGMY ISLAND(1950); WOMAN ON THE RUN(1950); LITTLE EGYPT(1951); MY FAVORITE SPY(1951); SAVAGE DRUMS(1951); SECOND WOMAN, THE(1951); TARGET UNKNOWN(1951); AFFAIR IN TRINIDAD(1952); BAL TABARIN(1952); BIG SKY, THE(1952); LADY POSSESSED(1952); NIGHT WITHOUT SLEEP(1952); O. HENRY'S FULL HOUSE(1952); CALL ME MADAM(1953); GENTLEMEN PREFER BLONDES(1953); GOLDEN BLADE, THE(1953); GREAT DIAMOND ROBBERY(1953); ROYAL AFRICAN RIFLES, THE(1953); STORY OF THREE LOVES, THE(1953); TONIGHT WE SING(1953); FRENCH LINE, THE(1954); KNOCK ON WOOD(1954); PARIS PLAYBOYS(1954); TOBOR THE GREAT(1954); BULLET FOR JOEY, A(1955); DADDY LONG LEGS(1955); KISS OF FIRE(1955); NEW YORK CONFIDENTIAL(1955); TO CATCH A THIEF(1955); ATTACK!(1956); STAGECOACH TO FURY(1956); CERTAIN SMILE, A(1958); COUNT YOUR BLESSINGS(1959); VERBOTEN!(1959); DIME WITH A HALO(1963); EVIL OF FRANKENSTEIN, THE(1964, Brit.); WILD AND WONDERFUL(1964); SHIP OF FOOLS(1965); JESSE JAMES MEETS FRANKENSTEIN'S DAUGHTER(1966); SWINGER, THE(1966)
Misc. Talkies
BLIND SPOT(1947)
Alex Gerber
DEEP IN MY HEART(1954), lyrics
Anna Gerber
ACTION OF THE TIGER(1957)
David Gerber
PRAIRIE, THE(1948)
Emil Gerber
LAST CHANCE, THE(1945, Switz.)
Esther Gerber
WHERE IS MY CHILD?(1937)
Gale Gerber
GIRLS ON THE BEACH(1965)
Jay Gerber
DOG DAY AFTERNOON(1975)
Jerry Gerber
STALAG 17(1953)
Joan Gerber
SHINBONE ALLEY(1971); CHARLOTTE'S WEB(1973); MOUSE AND HIS CHILD, THE(1977); NUTCRACKER FANTASY(1979); HEIDI'S SONG(1982)
Ludwig H. Gerber
SHE-GODS OF SHARK REEF(1958), p
Neva Gerber
Silents
SPINDLE OF LIFE, THE(1917); IMPULSE(1922); SEVENTH SHERIFF, THE(1923); WESTERN FATE(1924); WEST OF THE LAW(1926); RANGE RIDERS, THE(1927); OLD CODE, THE(1928)
Misc. Silents
EYE FOR AN EYE, AN(1915); HIGH HAND, THE(1915); IMPERSONATION, THE(1916); LIKE WILDFIRE(1917); MR. OPP(1917); HELL BENT(1918); THREE MOUNTED MEN(1918); FIGHT FOR LOVE, A(1919); PITFALLS OF A BIG CITY(1919); ROPED(1919); WHEN A WOMAN STRIKES(1919); DANGEROUS PATHS(1921); YANKEE GO-GETTER, A(1921); PRICE OF YOUTH, THE(1922); IN THE WEST(1923); CALIFORNIA IN '49(1924); SAGEBRUSH GOSPEL(1924); TROUBLE TRAIL(1924); WHIRLWIND RANGER, THE(1924); DAUGHTER OF THE SIOUX, A(1925); TONIO, SON OF THE SIERRAS(1925); VIC DYSON PAYS(1925); WARRIOR GAP(1925); BAITED TRAP(1926); FORT FRAYNE(1926); OFFICER 444(1926); MYSTERY BRAND, THE(1927); RIDERS OF THE WEST(1927); YELLOW STREAK, A(1927); SADDLE KING, THE(1929); THUNDERING THOMPSON(1929)
M. Gerbidon
FRENCH TOUCH, THE(1954, Fr.), w
Gerbidon and Armat
Silents
HOTEL MOUSE, THE(1923, Brit.), w
Marcel Gerbidou
Silents
FRENCH DOLL, THE(1923), w
Gerdago
CONGRESS DANCES(1957, Ger.), cos; FOREVER MY LOVE(1962), cos; FOUNTAIN OF LOVE, THE(1968, Aust.), cos
Emily Gerdes
Silents
DYNAMITE DAN(1924); ELLA CINDERS(1926); AMAZING VAGABOND(1929)
Misc. Silents
DASHING THRU(1925)

George Gerdes
COME BACK BABY(1968)
Zinoviy Gerdt
NINE DAYS OF ONE YEAR(1964, USSR)
Don Gere
WEREWOLVES ON WHEELS(1971), m; SWEET SUGAR(1972), m
Richard Gere
REPORT TO THE COMMISSIONER(1975); BABY BLUE MARINE(1976); LOOKING FOR MR. GOODBAR(1977); BLOODBROTHERS(1978); DAYS OF HEAVEN(1978); YANKS(1979); AMERICAN GIGOLO(1980); OFFICER AND A GENTLEMAN, AN(1982); BEYOND THE LIMIT(1983); BREATHLESS(1983)
1984
COTTON CLUB, THE(1984)
Alexander Gerens
KOREA PATROL(1951), m; FAST AND THE FURIOUS, THE(1954), m
Georges Geret
DEAD RUN(1961, Fr./Ital./Ger.); DIARY OF A CHAMBERMAID(1964, Fr./Ital.); MATA HARI(1965, Fr./Ital.); CLOPORTES(1966, Fr., Ital.); IS PARIS BURNING?(1966, U.S./Fr.); POPPY IS ALSO A FLOWER, THE(1966); SLEEPING CAR MURDER THE(1966, Fr.); WEEKEND AT DUNKIRK(1966, Fr./Ital.); STRANGER, THE(1967, Algeria/Fr./Ital.); FEMMINA(1968 Fr./Ital./Ger.); SOUTHERN STAR, THE(1969, Fr./Brit.); THEY CAME TO ROB LAS VEGAS(1969, Fr./Ital./Span./Ger.); Z(1969, Fr./Algeria); MAN WITH CONNECTIONS, THE(1970, Fr.); QUIET PLACE IN THE COUNTRY, A(1970, Ital./Fr.); VERY CURIOUS GIRL, A(1970, Fr.); SPERMULA(1976, Fr.)
Anne Gerety
QUINTET(1979)
Peter Gerhard
APRIL 1, 2000(1953, Aust.); STORY OF VICKIE, THE(1958, Aust.)
Roberto Gerhard
SECRET PEOPLE(1952, Brit.), m; THIS SPORTING LIFE(1963, Brit.), m
Ute Gerhard
1984
WOMAN IN FLAMES, A(1984, Ger.)
Karl Gerhardt
IMMORTAL VAGABOND(1931, Ger.)
Ettore Geri
WOMAN ON FIRE, A(1970, Ital.); VOYAGE, THE(1974, Ital.); GARDEN OF THE FINZI-CONTINIS, THE(1976, Ital./Ger.)
Joan Gerians
MOTHER WORE TIGHTS(1947)
Eugene Gericke
I WAS A MALE WAR BRIDE(1949); LOVE THAT BRUTE(1950); FOLLOW THE SUN(1951)
Gene Gericko
MILLIONAIRE FOR CHRISTY, A(1951)
Ben Gerien
MADAME CURIE(1943); REDHEAD FROM MANHATTAN(1954)
Maile Gerima
Misc. Talkies
ASHES AND EMBERS(1982), d
Pierre Gerin
WOULD-BE GENTLEMAN, THE(1960, Fr.), p; MARRIAGE OF FIGARO, THE(1963, Fr.), p
Marion Gering
I TAKE THIS WOMAN(1931), d; 24 HOURS(1931), d; DEVIL AND THE DEEP(1932), d; LADIES OF THE BIG HOUSE(1932), d; MADAME BUTTERFLY(1932), d; JENNIE GERHARDT(1933), d; PICK-UP(1933), d; GOOD DAME(1934), d; READY FOR LOVE(1934), d; THIRTY-DAY PRINCESS(1934), d; RUMBA(1935), d; LADY OF SECRETS(1936), d; ROSE OF THE RANCHO(1936), d; THUNDER IN THE CITY(1937, Brit.), d; SHE MARRIED AN ARTIST(1938), d; SARUMBA(1950), p, d; VIOLATED PARADISE(1963, Ital./Jap.), p&d
Richard Gering
DIARY OF A HIGH SCHOOL BRIDE(1959); DATE BAIT(1960)
Giada Gerini
IDENTIFICATION OF A WOMAN(1983, Ital.)
Boris Geriup
HAMLET(1962, Ger.), ph
Virgil C. Gerlach
HELLBENDERS, THE(1967, U.S./Ital./Span.), w
Jordan Gerler
THIRTEEN WEST STREET(1962); ROLLING THUNDER(1977)
Jackie Gerlich
EAST SIDE OF HEAVEN(1939)
Piero Gerlini
BIGGEST BUNDLE OF THEM ALL, THE(1968); SERAFINO(1970, Fr./Ital.)
Pietro Gerlini
LION OF THE DESERT(1981, Libya/Brit.)
Andre Germain
CARNIVAL(1953, Fr.), ph; GOLDEN MISTRESS, THE(1954); DANIELLA BY NIGHT(1962, Fr/Ger.), ph
Anne Germain
YOUNG GIRLS OF ROCHEFORT, THE(1968, Fr.)
Gregory Germain
VIOLETTE(1978, Fr.)
Lud Germain
RED, INN, THE(1954, Fr.); I SPIT ON YOUR GRAVE(1962, Fr.); MAXIME(1962, Fr.); CHECKERBOARD(1969, Fr.)
Michael Germain
HYSTERICAL(1983), makeup
Stuart Germain
FAIL SAFE(1964); CATAMOUNT KILLING, THE(1975, Ger.)
Bob Germaine
T.A.G.: THE ASSASSINATION GAME(1982), makeup
Elizabeth Germaine
HELLFIGHTERS(1968)
Maeve Germaine
EDUCATING RITA(1983)

Mary Germaine
LAUGHTER IN PARADISE(1951, Brit.); CLOUDBURST(1952, Brit.); FATHER'S DOING FINE(1952, Brit.); NIGHT WON'T TALK, THE(1952, Brit.); WHERE'S CHARLEY?(1952, Brit.); FLANNELFOOT(1953, Brit.); FLOATING DUTCHMAN, THE(1953, Brit.); HOUSE OF BLACKMAIL(1953, Brit.); KNIGHTS OF THE ROUND TABLE(1953, Brit.); TWILIGHT WOMEN(1953, Brit.); DEVIL'S HARBOR(1954, Brit.); GREEN BUDDHA, THE(1954, Brit.)
Rudy Germaine
STRANGER WORE A GUN, THE(1953)
Roberto Germains
OCTOPUSSY(1983, Brit.)
Edward German
NELL GWYN(1935, Brit.), m
Rudy German
MEXICAN HAYRIDE(1948)
George Germanetti
MAN CALLED FLINTSTONE, THE(1966), anim
Gaia Germani
YOUR TURN, DARLING(1963, Fr.); TORPEDO BAY(1964, Ital./Fr.)
Gala Germani
CASTLE OF THE LIVING DEAD(1964, Ital./Fr.)
Andre Germann
THREE HOURS(1944, Fr.), ph
Don Germano
SWING OUT THE BLUES(1943)
Freddie Germanos
DREAM OF PASSION, A(1978, Gr.)
Maria Germanova
Misc. Silents
ANNA KARENINA(1914, USSR); YEKATERINA IVANOVNA(1915, USSR); CRIME AND PUNISHMENT(1929, Ger.)
Jeannine Germes-Vergne
TIME BOMB(1961, Fr./Ital.), cos; WEB OF PASSION(1961, Fr.), cos
Pietro Germi
BLACK 13(1954, Brit.), w; FOUR WAYS OUT(1954, Ital.), d; FIVE BRANDED WOMEN(1960); DIVORCE, ITALIAN STYLE(1962, Ital.), d, w; LA VIACCIA(1962, Fr./Ital.); SEDUCED AND ABANDONED(1964, Fr./Ital.), d, w; FACTS OF MURDER, THE(1965, Ital.), a, d, w; LIPSTICK(1965, Fr./Ital.); RAILROAD MAN, THE(1965, Ital.), a, d, w; BIRDS, THE BEES AND THE ITALIANS, THE(1967), p, d, w; CLIMAX, THE(1967, Fr., Ital.); SERAFINO(1970, Fr./Ital.), p&d, w; ALFREDO, ALFREDO(1973, Ital.), d, w
Nane Germon
BEAUTY AND THE BEAST(1947, Fr.); RED, INN, THE(1954, Fr.); LONG ABSENCE, THE(1962, Fr./Ital.); LIFE UPSIDE DOWN(1965, Fr.); THIEF OF PARIS, THE(1967, Fr./Ital.); LES BICHES(1968, Fr.); DIVA(1982, Fr.)
Louis Germonprez
Silents
GREED(1925), art d
Valery Germonprez
Silents
BLIND HUSBANDS(1919)
Peter Germyn
FINAL ASSIGNMENT(1980, Can.), m
Frank Gernardi
DINKY(1935)
Jan Gernat
STAR!(1968)
Carl Gernbach
DIE FLEDERMAUS(1964, Aust.)
Don Gerner
IROQUOIS TRAIL, THE(1950)
Bill Gernert
THAT TENNESSEE BEAT(1966), set d
George Gernon
Silents
POOR LITTLE RICH GIRL, A(1917)
Rudi Gernreich
EXODUS(1960), cos; SKIDOO(1968), cos; 2000 YEARS LATER(1969), a, cos
Frank Gero
FOUR BOYS AND A GUN(1957)
Jonathan Gero
BABY, IT'S YOU(1983)
Roger Geroge
HELL'S BELLES(1969), spec eff
Luis Gerold
REBEL, THE(1933, Ger.)
Raymond Gerome
GOODBYE AGAIN(1961); LOSS OF INNOCENCE(1961, Brit.); FRENCH GAME, THE(1963, Fr.); MURDER AT 45 R.P.M.(1965, Fr.); NIGHT OF THE GENERALS, THE(1967, Brit./Fr.); BRAIN, THE(1969, Fr./US); DEADLY TRAP, THE(1972, Fr./Ital.); TRAVELS WITH MY AUNT(1972, Brit.); DAY OF THE JACKAL, THE(1973, Brit./Fr.); MAGNIFICENT ONE, THE(1974, Fr./Ital.); DEAR DETECTIVE(1978, Fr.)
Clyde Geronimi
THREE CABALLEROS, THE(1944), d; MAKE MINE MUSIC(1946), d; MELODY TIME(1948), d; ADVENTURES OF ICHABOD AND MR. TOAD(1949), d; ALICE IN WONDERLAND(1951), d; PETER PAN(1953), d; LADY AND THE TRAMP(1955), d; SLEEPING BEAUTY(1959), d; ONE HUNDRED AND ONE DALMATIANS(1961), d
Jerome Geronimi
DIABOLIQUE(1955, Fr.), w; WAGES OF FEAR, THE(1955, Fr./Ital.), w; GRAND MANEUVER, THE(1956, Fr.), w; TRUTH, THE(1961, Fr./Ital.), w
Clyde Geronomi
CINDERELLA(1950), d
John Geroson
CANNIBALS IN THE STREETS(1982, Ital./Span.)
Massimo Gerotti
FABIOLA(1951, Ital.)
Katherine Fullerton Gerould
ROMANCE OF THE RIO GRANDE(1929), w; ROMANCE OF THE RIO GRANDE(1941), w

Silents
YANKEE SENOR, THE(1926), w

Leticia Gerrado
CUBA(1979)

Cande Gerrard
WILD WOMEN OF WONGO, THE(1959)

Carl Gerrard
LEATHERNECKING(1930); PUBLIC DEFENDER, THE(1931)

Silents
LADIES OF THE MOB(1928)

Misc. Silents
LOVE PIKER, THE(1923)

Charles Gerrard
CAUGHT IN THE FOG(1928); LIGHT FINGERS(1929); LONE WOLF'S DAUGHTER, THE(1929); ANYBODY'S WOMAN(1930); JOURNEY'S END(1930); DRACULA(1931); LION AND THE LAMB(1931); MENACE, THE(1932); FACING THE MUSIC(1933, Brit.); POLITICAL PARTY, A(1933, Brit.)

Silents
DOWN TO EARTH(1917); ANNA ASCENDS(1922); WHEN KNIGHTHOOD WAS IN FLOWER(1922); MAN ON THE BOX, THE(1925); BETTER 'OLE, THE(1926); NERVOUS WRECK, THE(1926); PAINTING THE TOWN(1927)

Misc. Silents
BEANS(1918); DEMON, THE(1918); PLAYTHINGS(1918); PETTIGREW'S GIRL(1919); BLACKBIRDS(1920); HEROES AND HUSBANDS(1922); DANGEROUS MAID, THE(1923); RICHARD, THE LION-HEARTED(1923); LOVING LIES(1924); ACCUSED(1925); CALIFORNIA STRAIGHT AHEAD(1925); FOR WIVES ONLY(1926); FRAMED(1927); HEART THIEF, THE(1927); ROMANCE OF A ROGUE(1928); CIRCUMSTANTIAL EVIDENCE(1929)

Douglas Gerrard
UNDER TWO FLAGS(1936); ARGYLE CASE, THE(1929); GENERAL CRACK(1929); GLAD RAG DOLL, THE(1929); HOTTENTOT, THE(1929); MADONNA OF AVENUE A(1929); LILIES OF THE FIELD(1930); SWEET KITTY BELLAIRS(1930); PUBLIC ENEMY, THE(1931); ROAD TO SINGAPORE(1931); ONE WAY PASSAGE(1932); TENDERFOOT, THE(1932); KING'S VACATION, THE(1933); BULLDOG DRUMMOND STRIKES BACK(1934); CLIVE OF INDIA(1935); MAN HUNT(1941); LODGER, THE(1944); LUCK OF THE IRISH(1948); ROAD HOUSE(1948); UNFAITHFULLY YOURS(1948)

Silents
COMMANDING OFFICER, THE(1915); DUMB GIRL OF PORTICI(1916); NAKED HEARTS(1916); ETERNAL LOVE(1917), a, d; MADAME SPY(1918), d; CABARET GIRL, THE(1919), d; IMPULSE(1922); TAILOR MADE MAN, A(1922); IN FAST COMPANY(1924); LIGHTHOUSE BY THE SEA, THE(1924); DOUBLING WITH DANGER(1926); PRIVATE IZZY MURPHY(1926); GINSBERG THE GREAT(1927); WOLF'S CLOTHING(1927)

Misc. Silents
MERCHANT OF VENICE, THE(1914); SHANNON OF THE SIXTH(1914); HIGH HAND, THE(1915); SOUL ENSLAVED, A(1916); UNDINE(1916); POLLY PUT THE KETTLE ON(1917), a, d; EMPTY CAB, THE(1918), d; MOTHER'S SECRET, A(1918), d; VELVET HAND, THE(1918), d; $5,000 REWARD(1918), d; HIS DIVORCED WIFE(1919), d; SEALED ENVELOPE, THE(1919), d; FORGED BRIDE, THE(1920), d; PHANTOM MELODY, THE(1920), d; COLLEGE WIDOW, THE(1927); DESIRED WOMAN, THE(1927); LADIES OF THE NIGHT CLUB(1928)

Douglass Gerrard
GHOST WALKS, THE(1935)

Frank Gerrard
Misc. Silents
DECEPTION(1918, Brit.)

Gene Gerrard
OUT OF THE BLUE(1931, Brit.), a, d; BRIDEGROOM FOR TWO(1932, Brit.); BROTHER ALFRED(1932, Brit.); LET ME EXPLAIN, DEAR(1932), a, d&w; LUCKY GIRL(1932, Brit.), a, d&w; MY WIFE'S FAMILY(1932, Brit.); LEAVE IT TO ME(1933, Brit.), a, w; LOVE NEST, THE(1933, Brit.), a, w; IT'S A BET(1935, Brit.); JOY RIDE(1935, Brit.); NO MONKEY BUSINESS(1935, Brit.); REGAL CAVALCADE(1935, Brit.); SCANDALS OF PARIS(1935, Brit.); FAITHFUL(1936, Brit.); MISTER HOBO(1936, Brit.); SUCH IS LIFE(1936, Brit.); WHERE'S SALLY?(1936, Brit.); WAKE UP FAMOUS(1937, Brit.), a, d; GLAMOUR GIRL(1938, Brit.); IT'S IN THE BLOOD(1938, Brit.), d

Harry Gerrard
WIVES BEWARE(1933, Brit.), ph

Henry Gerrard
BEGGARS OF LIFE(1928), ph; GREENE MURDER CASE, THE(1929), ph; THUNDERBOLT(1929), ph; WOMAN TRAP(1929), ph; FOLLOW THRU(1930), ph; HONEY(1930), ph; PLAYBOY OF PARIS(1930), ph; SAFETY IN NUMBERS(1930), ph; VAGABOND KING, THE(1930), ph; ALONG CAME YOUTH(1931), ph; DUDE RANCH(1931), ph; FIGHTING CARAVANS(1931), ph; MANY WATERS(1931, Brit.), ph; MOST DANGEROUS GAME, THE(1932), ph; PENGUIN POOL MURDER, THE(1932), ph; PHANTOM OF CRESTWOOD, THE(1932), ph; LITTLE WOMEN(1933), ph; LITTLE MINISTER, THE(1934), ph

Silents
SHOOTIN' IRONS(1927), ph; LADIES OF THE MOB(1928), ph; MAGNIFICENT FLIRT, THE(1928), ph

Henry W. Gerrard
FOUNTAIN, THE(1934), ph; MAN OF TWO WORLDS(1934), ph; OF HUMAN BONDAGE(1934), ph; SUCCESS AT ANY PRICE(1934), ph

Jack Gerrard
KENTUCKY MINSTRELS(1934, Brit.)

Mr. Gerrard
Silents
KIPPS(1921, Brit.)

Paul Gerrard
COUNT OF TWELVE(1955, Brit.), d

Pete Gerrard
TOAST OF NEW YORK, THE(1937)

Richard H. Gerrard
Silents
SWEET ADELINE(1926), w

Teddie Gerrard
Misc. Silents
BILLY'S SPANISH LOVE SPASM(1915, Brit.)

Tom Gerrard
TOO YOUNG TO LOVE(1960, Brit.); ZULU(1964, Brit.); SPY WHO LOVED ME, THE(1977, Brit.); YOU LIGHT UP MY LIFE(1977)

M. Gerri
RIOT(1969)

Robert Gerringer
WAY WE WERE, THE(1973); LOVELY WAY TO DIE, A(1968); GANG THAT COULDN'T SHOOT STRAIGHT, THE(1971); SENTINEL, THE(1977); KING OF THE GYPSIES(1978); HIDE IN PLAIN SIGHT(1980)

Flo Gerrish
SUPERCHICK(1973); DON'T ANSWER THE PHONE(1980); SCHIZOID(1980)

Paul Gerrits
FOUR HOURS TO KILL(1935); STOLEN HARMONY(1935); ON THE AVENUE(1937); LET'S MAKE IT LEGAL(1951)

Lisa Gerritsen
WAR BETWEEN MEN AND WOMEN, THE(1972); MIXED COMPANY(1974)

Dan Gerrity
1984
CRIMES OF PASSION(1984)

Patty Ann Gerrity
THREE BRAVE MEN(1957); CAT ON A HOT TIN ROOF(1958)

Patty Gerrity
TROUBLE WITH ANGELS, THE(1966)

William Gerrity
PSYCH-OUT(1968)

William C. Gerrity
BOYS IN THE BAND, THE(1970), set d

Daniel Gerroll
SIR HENRY AT RAWLINSON END(1980, Brit.); CHARRIOTS OF FIRE(1981, Brit.)

Curt Gerron
TRAPEZE(1932, Ger.)

Kurt Gerron
BLUE ANGEL, THE(1930, Ger.); BOMBARDMENT OF MONTE CARLO, THE(1931, Ger.); DOLLY GETS AHEAD(1931, Ger.); HIS MAJESTY, KING BALLYHOO(1931, Ger.); WHITE DEMON, THE(1932, Ger.), d

Misc. Silents
BERLIN AFTER DARK(1929, Ger.)

Al Gerrullo, Jr.
NIGHTHAWKS(1981)

Alex Gerry
PANHANDLE(1948); SAINTED SISTERS, THE(1948); I WAS A MALE WAR BRIDE(1949); TASK FORCE(1949); WHIRLPOOL(1949); COVERED WAGON RAID(1950); DAVID HARDING, COUNTERSPY(1950); KEY TO THE CITY(1950); MY BLUE HEAVEN(1950); PRISONERS IN PETTICOATS(1950); REFORMER AND THE REDHEAD, THE(1950); STORM WARNING(1950); TARNISHED(1950); THREE LITTLE WORDS(1950); TOAST OF NEW ORLEANS, THE(1950); WOMAN OF DISTINCTION, A(1950); YOUNG MAN WITH A HORN(1950); EXCUSE MY DUST(1951); DEADLINE-U.S.A.(1952); INVITATION(1952); JUMPING JACKS(1952); LOVE IS BETTER THAN EVER(1952); ROSE OF CIMARRON(1952); ANGEL FACE(1953); EDDIE CANTOR STORY, THE(1953); JAZZ SINGER, THE(1953); KID FROM LEFT FIELD, THE(1953); LILI(1953); THREE SAILORS AND A GIRL(1953); ALL THAT HEAVEN ALLOWS(1955); IT'S ALWAYS FAIR WEATHER(1955); COME ON, THE(1956); FUNNY FACE(1957); THIS HAPPY FEELING(1958); UNDERWATER WARRIOR(1958); PILLOW TALK(1959); BELLBOY, THE(1960); BACK STREET(1961); LADIES MAN, THE(1961); BON VOYAGE(1962); MY GEISHA(1962); TAMMY AND THE DOCTOR(1963); THRILL OF IT ALL, THE(1963); BRASS BOTTLE, THE(1964); HOUSE IS NOT A HOME, A(1964); I'D RATHER BE RICH(1964); HOW DO I LOVE THEE?(1970)

Alexander Gerry
CATCH-22(1970), tech adv; KELLY'S HEROES(1970, U.S./Yugo.), tech adv

Charles Gerry
Misc. Silents
WASP, THE(1918)

Lyn Gerry
ONE FROM THE HEART(1982)

Toni Gerry
BOOTS MALONE(1952); BLACK PIRATES, THE(1954, Mex.); DAY OF TRIUMPH(1954); BULLET FOR JOEY, A(1955); LUST FOR LIFE(1956); STORY OF MANKIND, THE(1957); OREGON PASSAGE(1958)

Vance Gerry
JUNGLE BOOK, THE(1967), w; ARISTOCATS, THE(1970), w; RESCUERS, THE(1977), w; FOX AND THE HOUND, THE(1981), w

Claude Gersene
HALLUCINATION GENERATION(1966)

Doneal G. Gersh
1984
TANK(1984)

Gary Gershaw
1984
RIVER, THE(1984)

Leonard Gershe
FUNNY FACE(1957), w, m; SILK STOCKINGS(1957), w; BUTTERFLIES ARE FREE(1972), w; FORTY CARATS(1973), w

Joseph Gershensen
FEMALE ANIMAL, THE(1958), md

Gershenson
JOE DAKOTA(1957), md

Joe Gershenson
LITTLE GIANT(1946), p; RUNAROUND, THE(1946), p; BLACK CASTLE, THE(1952), md

Joseph Gershenson
KANSAS RAIDERS(1950), m; MYSTERY SUBMARINE(1950), m; PEGGY(1950), md; SADDLE TRAMP(1950), m; SHAKEDOWN(1950), md; SPY HUNT(1950), md; UNDERCOVER GIRL(1950), md; WINCHESTER '73(1950), m; WYOMING MAIL(1950), md; ABBOTT AND COSTELLO MEET THE INVISIBLE MAN(1951), m; AIR CADET(1951), m; COMIN' ROUND THE MOUNTAIN(1951), md; FAT MAN, THE(1951), md; FLAME OF ARABY(1951), md; HOLLYWOOD STORY(1951), md; IRON MAN, THE(1951), md; LITTLE EGYPT(1951), md; MA AND PA KETTLE BACK ON THE FARM(1951), md; REUNION IN RENO(1951), md; SMUGGLER'S ISLAND(1951), md; STRANGE DOOR, THE(1951), md; TARGET UNKNOWN(1951), md; UNDER THE GUN(1951), m; UP FRONT(1951), m; FRANCIS GOES TO WEST

POINT(1952), md; HAS ANYBODY SEEN MY GAL?(1952), m, md; HERE COME THE NELSONS(1952), m; HORIZONS WEST(1952), md; JUST ACROSS THE STREET(1952), md; LAWLESS BREED, THE(1952), m; LOST IN ALASKA(1952), m, md; MA AND PA KETTLE AT THE FAIR(1952), md; MEET DANNY WILSON(1952), md; MEET ME AT THE FAIR(1952), md; RAIDERS, THE(1952), m; SAN FRANCISCO STORY, THE(1952), md; SON OF ALI BABA(1952), md; TREASURE OF LOST CANYON, THE(1952), md; YANKEE BUCCANEER(1952), md; ABBOTT AND COSTELLO GO TO MARS(1953), m; ALL I DESIRE(1953), m; FRANCIS COVERS THE BIG TOWN(1953), m; GIRLS IN THE NIGHT(1953), m; GLASS WEB, THE(1953), m; GLENN MILLER STORY, THE(1953), m; GOLDEN BLADE, THE(1953), m; IT CAME FROM OUTER SPACE(1953), m; LAW AND ORDER(1953), m; REDHEAD FROM WYOMING, THE(1953), md; SEMINOLE(1953), m; TAKE ME TO TOWN(1953), m; TUMBLEWEED(1953), md; VEILS OF BAGDAD, THE(1953), md; WALKING MY BABY BACK HOME(1953), md; WAR ARROW(1953), md; ABBOTT AND COSTELLO MEET DR. JEKYLL AND MR. HYDE(1954), md; BENGAL BRIGADE(1954), m; BLACK SHIELD OF FALWORTH, THE(1954), m; DAWN AT SOCORRO(1954), md; DESTRY(1954), md; FIREMAN SAVE MY CHILD(1954), m; JOHNNY DARK(1954), m; MA AND PA KETTLE AT HOME(1954), md; MAGNIFICENT OBSESSION(1954), md; RAILS INTO LARAMIE(1954), md; RICOCHET ROMANCE(1954), md; SASKAT-CHEWAN(1954), md; SIGN OF THE PAGAN(1954), md; SO THIS IS PARIS(1954), md; YELLOW MOUNTAIN, THE(1954), md; ABBOTT AND COSTELLO MEET THE KEYSTONE KOPS(1955), m; ABBOTT AND COSTELLO MEET THE MUMMY(1955), m; AIN'T MISBEHAVIN'(1955), md; ALL THAT HEAVEN ALLOWS(1955), m; CAPTAIN LIGHTFOOT(1955), m; CHIEF CRAZY HORSE(1955), md; FAR COUNTRY, THE(1955), m; FEMALE ON THE BEACH(1955), md; FOXFIRE(1955), md; FRANCIS IN THE NAVY(1955), md; KISS OF FIRE(1955), md; LADY GODIVA(1955), md; LOOTERS, THE(1955), md; MA AND PA KETTLE AT WAIKIKI(1955), md; MAN FROM BITTER RIDGE, THE(1955), md; MAN WITHOUT A STAR(1955), m, md; ONE DESIRE(1955), md; PRIVATE WAR OF MAJOR BENSON, THE(1955), md; PURPLE MASK, THE(1955), md; REVENGE OF THE CREATURE(1955), md; RUNNING WILD(1955), md; SECOND GREATEST SEX, THE(1955), md; SHRIKE, THE(1955), md; SIX BRIDGES TO CROSS(1955), md; SMOKE SIGNAL(1955), md; SPOILERS, THE(1955), md; SQUARE JUNGLE, THE(1955), md; TARANTULA(1955), md; THIS ISLAND EARTH(1955), md; TO HELL AND BACK(1955), md; BENNY GOODMAN STORY, THE(1956), m; CONGO CROSSING(1956), m; CREATURE WALKS AMONG US, THE(1956), m; DAY OF FURY, A(1956), md; FOUR GIRLS IN TOWN(1956), md; FRANCIS IN THE HAUNTED HOUSE(1956), md; I'VE LIVED BEFORE(1956), md; KETTLES IN THE OZARKS, THE(1956), md; MOLE PEOPLE, THE(1956), md; NEVER SAY GOODBYE(1956), md; PILLARS OF THE SKY(1956), md; PRICE OF FEAR, THE(1956), md; RAW EDGE(1956), md; RAWHIDE YEARS, THE(1956), md; ROCK, PRETTY BABY(1956), md; SHOWDOWN AT ABILENE(1956), md; STAR IN THE DUST(1956), md; THERE'S ALWAYS TOMORROW(1956), md; TOY TIGER(1956), md; UNGUARDED MOMENT, THE(1956), md; WALK THE PROUD LAND(1956), md; WORLD IN MY CORNER(1956), md; WRITTEN ON THE WIND(1956), md; DEADLY MANTIS, THE(1957), m; GIRL IN THE KREMLIN, THE(1957), m; GUN FOR A COWARD(1957), md; INCREDIBLE SHRINKING MAN, THE(1957), md; INTERLUDE(1957), m; ISTANBUL(1957), md; JOE BUTTERFLY(1957), md; JOE DAKOTA(1957), m; KELLY AND ME(1957), md; KETTLES ON OLD MACDONALD'S FARM, THE(1957), md; LAND UNKNOWN, THE(1957), m; LOVE SLAVES OF THE AMAZONS(1957), md; MAN IN THE SHADOW(1957), md; MAN OF A THOUSAND FACES(1957), md; MIDNIGHT STORY, THE(1957), m; MISTER CORY(1957), md; MONOLITH MONSTERS, THE(1957), m; MY MAN GODFREY(1957), md; NIGHT RUNNER, THE(1957), m; QUANTEZ(1957), md; SLAUGHTER ON TENTH AVENUE(1957), md; SLIM CARTER(1957), md; TARNISHED ANGELS, THE(1957), md; TATTERED DRESS, THE(1957), md; APPOINTMENT WITH A SHADOW(1958), m; BIG BEAT, THE(1958), m; DAMN CITIZEN(1958), md; KATHY O'(1958), md; LADY TAKES A FLYER, THE(1958), md; LIVE FAST, DIE YOUNG(1958), m, md; MONEY, WOMEN AND GUNS(1958), m; MONSTER ON THE CAMPUS(1958), p; ONCE UPON A HORSE(1958), md; PERFECT FURLOUGH, THE(1958), md; RAW WIND IN EDEN(1958), md; RESTLESS YEARS, THE(1958), m; RIDE A CROOKED TRAIL(1958), m, md; SAGA OF HEMP BROWN, THE(1958), m, md; STEP DOWN TO TERROR(1958), p; SUMMER LOVE(1958), md; THING THAT COULDN'T DIE, THE(1958), md; THIS HAPPY FEELING(1958), md; TOUCH OF EVIL(1958), md; VOICE IN THE MIRROR(1958), md; WILD HERITAGE(1958), m, md; CURSE OF THE UNDEAD(1959), p; IMITATION OF LIFE(1959), md; NEVER STEAL ANYTHING SMALL(1959), md; NO NAME ON THE BULLET(1959), md; PILLOW TALK(1959), md; SNOW QUEEN, THE(1959, USSR), md; STRANGER IN MY ARMS(1959), md; WILD AND THE INNOCENT, THE(1959), md; LEECH WOMAN, THE(1960), p; MIDNIGHT LACE(1960), md; PORTRAIT IN BLACK(1960), md; SPARTACUS(1960), md; LAST SUNSET, THE(1961), md; POSSE FROM HELL(1961), m; FREUD(1962), md; SIX BLACK HORSES(1962), md; FOR LOVE OR MONEY(1963), md; SHOWDOWN(1963), md; THRILL OF IT ALL, THE(1963), md; FATHER GOOSE(1964), md; I'D RATHER BE RICH(1964), md; ISLAND OF THE BLUE DOLPHINS(1964), md; LIVELY SET, THE(1964), md; NIGHT WALKER, THE(1964), md; SEND ME NO FLOWERS(1964), md; TAGGART(1964), md; LOVER AND KISSES(1965), md; SHENANDOAH(1965), md; GUNPOINT(1966), md; TEXAS ACROSS THE RIVER(1966), md; GAMES(1967), md; RELUCTANT ASTRONAUT, THE(1967), md; ROSIE!(1967), md; ROUGH NIGHT IN JERICHO(1967), md; IN ENEMY COUNTRY(1968), md; JOURNEY TO SHILOH(1968), md; SHAKIEST GUN IN THE WEST, THE(1968), md; SWEET CHARITY(1969), md

Joseph E. Gershenson
SCARLET ANGEL(1952), md

Ted J. Gershenson
BEHIND THE HIGH WALL(1956), m

Burton Gershfield
HEAD(1968), spec eff

Sandra Claire Gershman
1984
PURPLE RAIN(1984)

Gershom Parkington Quintet
DEATH AT A BROADCAST(1934, Brit.); MUSIC HALL(1934, Brit.)

Alfred Gershoni
DIAMONDS(1975, U.S./Israel), set d

Joseph Gershonson
CREATURE FROM THE BLACK LAGOON(1954), md

Theodore Gershuny
SILENT NIGHT, BLOODY NIGHT(1974), d, w

George Gershwin
SONG OF THE FLAME(1930), w; DELICIOUS(1931), m; GIRL CRAZY(1932), m; WORLD MOVES ON, THE(1934), m; SHALL WE DANCE(1937), m; GIRL CRAZY(1943), w; RHAPSODY IN BLUE(1945), m; FUNNY FACE(1957), m; PORGY AND BESS(1959), w, m; MANHATTAN(1979), m
Silents
LADY BE GOOD(1928), w

Ira Gershwin
GIRL CRAZY(1932), m; LADY IN THE DARK(1944), w; FUNNY FACE(1957), m; PORGY AND BESS(1959), w

Jerry Gershwin
HARPER(1966), p; KALEIDOSCOPE(1966, Brit.), p; BOBO, THE(1967, Brit.), p; SWEET NOVEMBER(1968), p; YOUR THREE MINUTES ARE UP(1973), p; BREAK-HEART PASS(1976), p

Frank Gersite
ABOVE AND BEYOND(1953)

Betty Lou Gerson
RED MENACE, THE(1949); UNDERCOVER GIRL(1950); ANNAPOLIS STORY, AN(1955); GREEN-EYED BLONDE, THE(1957); FLY, THE(1958); MIRACLE OF THE HILLS, THE(1959); ONE HUNDRED AND ONE DALMATIANS(1961)

Charles Gerson
Silents
PONY EXPRESS, THE(1925)

Eva Gerson
STREET OF SINNERS(1957)

Isaac Gerson
HOW WILLINGLY YOU SING(1975, Aus.)

Jeanne Gerson
BRIDE AND THE BEAST, THE(1958); SHE-GODS OF SHARK REEF(1958); PERILS OF PAULINE, THE(1967); VALLEY OF THE DOLLS(1967); TOUCH OF SATAN, THE(1971)
Misc. Talkies
TOUCH OF SATAN, THE(1974)

Ken Gerson
1984
STRANGERS KISS(1984)

Paul Gerson
BELLBOY, THE(1960)
Misc. Silents
CRICKET ON THE HEARTH, THE(1923)

Larry Gerson
VENGEANCE(1964)

Harry Gerstad
SPIRAL STAIRCASE, THE(1946), ed; TILL THE END OF TIME(1946), ed; CROSS-FIRE(1947), ed; SO WELL REMEMBERED(1947, Brit.), ed; UNKNOWN ISLAND(1948), ed; CHAMPION(1949), ed; GUN CRAZY(1949), ed; HOME OF THE BRAVE(1949), ed; TOUGH ASSIGNMENT(1949), ed; CYRANO DE BERGERAC(1950), ed; MEN, THE(1950), ed; ROCKETSHIP X-M(1950), ed; DEATH OF A SALESMAN(1952), ed; HIGH NOON(1952), ed; SNIPER, THE(1952), ed; COMBAT SQUAD(1953), ed; ALLIGATOR PEOPLE, THE(1959), ed; HERE COME THE JETS(1959), ed; ROOKIE, THE(1959), ed; FRECKLES(1960), ed; THIRTEEN FIGHTING MEN(1960), d; MAGIC SWORD, THE(1962), ed; OF LOVE AND DESIRE(1963), ed; BATMAN(1966), ed; WAR WAGON, THE(1967), ed; SECRET LIFE OF AN AMERICAN WIFE, THE(1968), ed; HARD CONTRACT(1969), ed; COVER ME BABE(1970), ed; BIG JAKE(1971), ed; WALKING TALL(1973), ed; FRAMED(1975), ed
Silents
JACK AND THE BEANSTALK(1917), ph; ALI BABA AND THE FORTY THIEVES(1918), ph

Henry Gerstad
BEN(1972), ed

John Gerstad
LOST BOUNDARIES(1949); COP HATER(1958); NO WAY TO TREAT A LADY(1968); SWIMMER, THE(1968); B.S. I LOVE YOU(1971); LADY LIBERTY(1972, Ital./Fr.)

M.B. Gerstad
BRIDGE OF SAN LUIS REY, THE(1929), ph

Meritt Gerstad
DARING YOUNG MAN, THE(1935), ph

Merrit Gerstad
TOM, DICK AND HARRY(1941), ph

Merritt Gerstad
NIGHT WORLD(1932), ph; PAYMENT DEFERRED(1932), ph; STRANGE JUSTICE(1932), ph; ONLY YESTERDAY(1933), ph; BELOVED(1934), ph; IMITATION OF LIFE(1934), ph; SOCIAL REGISTER(1934), ph; MAN WHO RECLAIMED HIS HEAD, THE(1935), ph; GIRLS' DORMITORY(1936), ph; LUCKIEST GIRL IN THE WORLD, THE(1936), ph; MAGNIFICENT BRUTE, THE(1936), ph; ONE RAINY AFTERNOON(1936), md; STRIKE ME PINK(1936), ph; AS GOOD AS MARRIED(1937), ph; SEVENTH HEAVEN(1937), ph; SHE MARRIED AN ARTIST(1938), ph; ETERNALLY YOURS(1939), ph; I'M FROM MISSOURI(1939), ph; WINTER CARNIVAL(1939), ph; HOUSE ACROSS THE BAY, THE(1940), ph; SLIGHTLY HONORABLE(1940), ph; NIGHT IN NEW ORLEANS, A(1942), ph; WATCH ON THE RHINE(1943), ph; CONFLICT(1945), ph
Silents
GALLOPING ACE, THE(1924), ph; MAN FROM WYOMING, THE(1924), ph; ICE FLOOD, THE(1926), ph; ROAD TO MANDALAY, THE(1926), ph

Merritt B. Gerstad
ALIAS JIMMY VALENTINE(1928), ph; DEVIL MAY CARE(1929), ph; WONDER OF WOMEN(1929), ph; LADY TO LOVE, A(1930), ph; NAVY BLUES(1930), ph; OUR BLUSHING BRIDES(1930), ph; THOSE THREE FRENCH GIRLS(1930), ph; DAYBREAK(1931), ph; FLYING HIGH(1931), ph; GENTLEMAN'S FATE(1931), ph; GREAT LOVER, THE(1931), ph; GUILTY HANDS(1931), ph; NEVER THE TWAIN SHALL MEET(1931), ph; WEST OF BROADWAY(1931), ph; FREAKS(1932), ph; SECRET OF MADAME BLANCHE, THE(1933), ph; NIGHT AT THE OPERA, A(1935), ph; ORCHIDS TO YOU(1935), ph; GREAT ZIEGFELD, THE(1936), ph
Silents
LONDON AFTER MIDNIGHT(1927), ph; MOCKERY(1927), ph; MAN'S MAN, A(1929), ph

Harry Gersted
Silents
GAMBLING IN SOULS(1919), ph; CHAIN LIGHTNING(1922), ph

Merritt Gersted
GOLDIE GETS ALONG(1933), ph; BULLDOG DRUMMOND'S SECRET POLICE(1939), ph
Merritt B. Gersted
THIRTEENTH CHAIR, THE(1930), ph
Ellen Gerstein
COAST TO COAST(1980); GOING APE!(1981)
1984
BODY ROCK(1984); JOY OF SEX(1984)
Bernard Gersten
ONE FROM THE HEART(1982), exec p
Berta Gersten
BENNY GOODMAN STORY, THE(1956)
Misc. Talkies
MIRELE EFROS(1939); GOD, MAN AND DEVIL(1949)
Frank Gerstle
SILENCERS, THE(; I WAS A COMMUNIST FOR THE F.B.I.(1951); UNKNOWN MAN, THE(1951); GLORY BRIGADE, THE(1953); LADY WANTS MINK, THE(1953); MAGNETIC MONSTER, THE(1953); VICKI(1953); KILLERS FROM SPACE(1954); LONG, LONG TRAILER, THE(1954); GANG BUSTERS(1955); I COVER THE UNDERWORLD(1955); TIGHT SPOT(1955); AUTUMN LEAVES(1956); BETWEEN HEAVEN AND HELL(1956); MAGNIFICENT ROUGHNECKS(1956); PROUD ONES, THE(1956); SLIGHTLY SCARLET(1956); STEEL JUNGLE, THE(1956); RIVER'S EDGE, THE(1957); TOP SECRET AFFAIR(1957); UNDER FIRE(1957); AMBUSH AT CIMARRON PASS(1958); FOUR SKULLS OF JONATHAN DRAKE, THE(1959); I, MOBSTER(1959); INSIDE THE MAFIA(1959); SUBMARINE SEAHAWK(1959); VICE RAID(1959); WASP WOMAN, THE(1959); THIRTEEN WEST STREET(1962); SHOCK CORRIDOR(1963); ATOMIC BRAIN, THE(1964); QUICK GUN, THE(1964); YOUNG DILLINGER(1965); WILD ANGELS, THE(1966); HELL ON WHEELS(1967); IF HE HOLLERS, LET HIM GO(1968)
Maury Gerstman
BACK TO GOD'S COUNTRY(1953), ph; I'VE LIVED BEFORE(1956), ph; BORN TO BE LOVED(1959), ph
Herman Gerstner
WONDERFUL WORLD OF THE BROTHERS ERIMM, THE(1962), w
Harry Gerstud
FIVE GATES TO HELL(1959), ed
Adolf Gerstung
HAMLET(1962, Ger.)
Gunther Gerszo
VAMPIRE'S COFFIN, THE(1958, Mex.), art d; LITTLE RED RIDING HOOD AND HER FRIENDS(1964, Mex.), set d; LIVING COFFIN, THE(1965, Mex.), art d; CHIQUITO PERO PICOSO(1967, Mex.), w; VAMPIRE, THE(1968, Mex.), art d
Valeska Gert
THREEPENNY OPERA, THE(1931, Ger./U.S.); COUP DE GRACE(1978, Ger./Fr.)
Misc. Silents
MIDSUMMER NIGHT'S DREAM, A(1928, Ger.); SUCH IS LIFE(1929, Czech)
Waleska Gert
JULIET OF THE SPIRITS(1965, Fr./Ital./W.Ger.)
Marion Gerth
NAUGHTY CINDERELLA(1933, Brit.); NURSEMAID WHO DISAPPEARED, THE(1939, Brit.); SAILOR'S DON'T CARE(1940, Brit.); FRONT LINE KIDS(1942, Brit.)
Sam Gertler
Misc. Talkies
JEWISH FATHER(1934)
Victor Gertler
TEMPEST(1932, Ger.), ed
Rudi Gertsch
DOWNHILL RACER(1969)
Maurice Gertsman
GUNMAN'S CODE(1946), ph
Maury Gertsman
RIDERS OF THE SANTA FE(1944), ph; TRAIL TO GUNSIGHT(1944), ph; WAVE, A WAC AND A MARINE, A(1944), ph; BAD MEN OF THE BORDER(1945), ph; BLONDE RANSOM(1945), ph; CODE OF THE LAWLESS(1945), ph; JUNGLE CAPTIVE(1945), ph; RENEGADES OF THE RIO GRANDE(1945), ph; SONG OF THE SARONG(1945), ph; STRANGE CONFESSION(1945), ph; TRAIL TO VENGEANCE(1945), ph; BLONDE ALIBI(1946), ph; BRUTE MAN, THE(1946), ph; CUBAN PETE(1946), ph; DANGER WOMAN(1946), ph; DRESSED TO KILL(1946), ph; GUN TOWN(1946), ph; INSIDE JOB(1946), ph; RUSTLER'S ROUNDUP(1946), ph; SHE-WOLF OF LONDON(1946), ph; TERROR BY NIGHT(1946), ph; WILD BEAUTY(1946), ph; SINGAPORE(1947), ph; TIME OUT OF MIND(1947), ph; ARE YOU WITH IT?(1948), ph; RACHEL AND THE STRANGER(1948), ph; ROGUES' REGIMENT(1948), ph; CITY ACROSS THE RIVER(1949), ph; JOHNNY STOOL PIGEON(1949), ph; MA AND PA KETTLE(1949), ph; COMMANCHE TERRITORY(1950), ph; DOUBLE CROSSBONES(1950), ph; FRENCHIE(1950), ph; LOUISA(1950), ph; ONE WAY STREET(1950), ph; SOUTH SEA SINNER(1950), ph; CATTLE DRIVE(1951), ph; REUNION IN RENO(1951), ph; SMUGGLER'S ISLAND(1951), ph; TARGET UNKNOWN(1951), ph; YOU NEVER CAN TELL(1951), ph; IT GROWS ON TREES(1952), ph; JUST ACROSS THE STREET(1952), ph; MA AND PA KETTLE AT THE FAIR(1952), ph; MEET DANNY WILSON(1952), ph; MEET ME AT THE FAIR(1952), ph; RED BALL EXPRESS(1952), ph; SON OF ALI BABA(1952), ph; ALL-AMERICAN, THE(1953), ph; GLASS WEB, THE(1953), ph; GOLDEN BLADE, THE(1953), ph; GREAT SIOUX UPRISING, THE(1953), ph; LONE HAND, THE(1953), ph; BENGAL BRIGADE(1954), ph; RAILS INTO LARAMIE(1954), ph; SO THIS IS PARIS(1954), ph; TANGANYIKA(1954), ph; ONE DESIRE(1955), ph; SPOILERS, THE(1955), ph; TO HELL AND BACK(1955), ph; BEHIND THE HIGH WALL(1956), ph; CREATURE WALKS AMONG US, THE(1956), ph; EVERYTHING BUT THE TRUTH(1956), ph; NEVER SAY GOODBYE(1956), ph; RAW EDGE(1956), ph; WORLD IN MY CORNER(1956), ph; GUN DUEL IN DURANGO(1957), ph; KELLY AND ME(1957), ph; MONKEY ON MY BACK(1957), ph; FOUR SKULLS OF JONATHAN DRAKE, THE(1959), ph; INSIDE THE MAFIA(1959), ph; INVISIBLE INVADERS(1959), ph; PIER 5, HAVANA(1959), ph; RIOT IN JUVENILE PRISON(1959), ph; TIMBUKTU(1959), ph; CAGE OF EVIL(1960), ph; GUNFIGHTERS OF ABILENE(1960), ph; MUSIC BOX KID, THE(1960), ph; THREE CAME TO KILL(1960), ph; FIVE GUNS TO TOMBSTONE(1961), ph; FRONTIER UPRISING(1961), ph; POLICE DOG STORY, THE(1961), ph; SIX BLACK HORSES(1962), ph; GUNFIGHT IN ABILENE(1967), ph

Maury Gertsnab
HOUSE OF HORRORS(1946), ph
Irving Gertz
COUNTERFEITERS, THE(1948), m; PREJUDICE(1949), m; DESTINATION MURDER(1950), m; EXPERIMENT ALCATRAZ(1950), m; TWO DOLLAR BETTOR(1951), m; BANDITS OF CORSICA, THE(1953), m; GUN BELT(1953), m; SHARK RIVER(1953), m; WHITE GODDESS(1953), m; KHYBER PATROL(1954), m; LONG WAIT, THE(1954), md; TOP GUN(1955), m, md; FIRST TRAVELING SALESLADY, THE(1956), m; GUN BROTHERS(1956), m&md; BADLANDS OF MONTANA(1957), m; HELL CANYON OUTLAWS(1957), m, md; HELL ON DEVIL'S ISLAND(1957), m, md; PLUNDER ROAD(1957), m, md; BADMAN'S COUNTRY(1958), m, md; FEARMAKERS, THE(1958), m; THUNDERING JETS(1958), m; ALLIGATOR PEOPLE, THE(1959), m; CURSE OF THE UNDEAD(1959), m; HELL BENT FOR LEATHER(1960), m; LEECH WOMAN, THE(1960), m; SEVEN WAYS FROM SUNDOWN(1960), m; THIRTEEN FIGHTING MEN(1960), m; WIZARD OF BAGHDAD, THE(1960), m; YOUNG JESSE JAMES(1960), m; FIERCEST HEART, THE(1961), m; MARINES, LET'S GO(1961), m; BRUSHFIRE(1962), m; FLUFFY(1965), m; NOBODY'S PERFECT(1968), m
Jami Gertz
ENDLESS LOVE(1981)
1984
ALPHABET CITY(1984); SIXTEEN CANDLES(1984)
Jamie Gertz
ON THE RIGHT TRACK(1981)
Jasper Gertzen
DECISION BEFORE DAWN(1951)
M. Gertzman
GIRL ON THE SPOT(1946), ph
Maury Gertzman
HOW TO MAKE A MONSTER(1958), ph
Raffaele Geruasco
NEOPOLITAN CAROUSEL(1961, Ital.), m
Pershing Gervais
DAMN CITIZEN(1958)
Carlo Gervasi
TAMING OF THE SHREW, THE(1967, U.S./Ital.), set d
Frank Gervasi
ROMMEL'S TREASURE(1962, Ital.), w
Burt Gervis
WIRE SERVICE(1942)
Jill Gervon
HOODLUM SAINT, THE(1946)
Sammy Gervon
IRON MAN, THE(1931)
George Gerwin
RED FORK RANGE(1931)
Joe Gerwin
1984
WHERE THE BOYS ARE '84(1984)
George Gerwing
TEX TAKES A HOLIDAY(1932); TOMBSTONE CANYON(1932)
Perry Gerwitz
PUTNEY SWOPE(1969); JOE(1970)
Misc. Talkies
FORBIDDEN UNDER THE CENSORSHIP OF THE KING(1973)
Camilla Gerzhofer
BURG THEATRE(1936, Ger.)
Bunther Gerzo
LIFE IN THE BALANCE, A(1955), art d
Gunter Gerzso
BRUTE, THE(1952, Mex.), set d
Gunther Gerzso
MYSTERY IN MEXICO(1948), art d
1984
UNDER THE VOLCANO(1984), prod d
Erwin Geschonneck
NAKED AMONG THE WOLVES(1967, Ger.)
Joe Geschwind
1984
PREPPIES(1984)
Christine Gess
GOING HIGHBROW(1935)
Adrienne Gessner
NO TIME FOR FLOWERS(1952); STOLEN IDENTITY(1953); BREATH OF SCANDAL, A(1960)
Elizabeth Gessner
JOHNNY BELINDA(1948), tech adv
Nicolas Gessner
BLONDE FROM PEKING, THE(1968, Fr.), d, w; TWELVE PLUS ONE(1970, Fr./Ital.), d, w; SOMEONE BEHIND THE DOOR(1971, Fr./Brit.), d, w; LITTLE GIRL WHO LIVES DOWN THE LANE, THE(1977, Can.), d
Peter Gessner
OVER-UNDER, SIDEWAYS-DOWN(1977), d, w
Robert Gessner
MASSACRE(1934), w
Sonia Gessner
BLOW TO THE HEART(1983, Ital.)
James Gesson
PRIME OF MISS JEAN BRODIE, THE(1969, Brit.), p
Inna Gest [Ina Guest]
BOYS OF THE CITY(1940); GUN CODE(1940); HARD GUY(1941); NORTH STAR, THE(1943); SIX GUN GOSPEL(1943); LADIES OF WASHINGTON(1944); UP IN ARMS(1944); NORTHWEST OUTPOST(1947); NO MINOR VICES(1948)
Merritt Gestard
Silents
UNKNOWN, THE(1927), ph
Stan Gester
INVASION OF THE ANIMAL PEOPLE(1962, U.S./Swed.)

Alvaro Gheri
LES CARABINIERS(1968, Fr./Ital.)
George Ghermanoff
ONE DANGEROUS NIGHT(1943)
Jacques Gheusi
ZAZIE(1961, Fr.); VERY PRIVATE AFFAIR, A(1962, Fr./Ital.); THIEF OF PARIS, THE(1967, Fr./Ital.)
Dana Ghia
BURN(1970); DIRTY OUTLAWS, THE(1971, Ital.); PRIEST'S WIFE, THE(1971, Ital./Fr.); TRINITY IS STILL MY NAME(1971, Ital.)
Fernando Ghia
LADY CAROLINE LAMB(1972, Brit./Ital.), p
Sandro Ghiani
PASSION OF LOVE(1982, Ital./Fr.)
Robert L. Ghiblieri
1984
BODY ROCK(1984)
Giuliana Ghidini
SWORD OF THE CONQUEROR(1962, Ital.), cos
Benedetto Ghiglia
SECRET AGENT SUPER DRAGON(1966, Fr./Ital./Ger./Monaco), m; SIX DAYS A WEEK(1966, Fr./Ital./Span.), m; ADIOS GRINGO(1967, Ital./Fr./Span.), m; STRANGER IN TOWN, A(1968, U.S./Ital.), m; PSYCHOUT FOR MURDER(1971, Arg./Ital.), m
Oscar Ghiglia
LA DOLCE VITA(1961, Ital./Fr.)
Umberto Ghignone
MYTH, THE(1965, Ital.), p
Ricardo Ghione
DUCK RINGS AT HALF PAST SEVEN, THE(1969, Ger./Ital.), w
Evans Ghiselli
SOMEWHERE IN TIME(1980)
Ghislaine "Gigi"
TWO GIRLS AND A SAILOR(1944)
Ali Ghito
EIGHT GIRLS IN A BOAT(1932, Ger.)
Robert Gho
GREEN TREE, THE(1965, Ital.)
Riyad Gholmieh
WHERE THE SPIES ARE(1965, Brit.)
Julie Gholson
WHERE THE LILIES BLOOM(1974)
Hany Ghorra
ONE MAN JURY(1978)
Smaran Ghosal
APARAJITO(1959, India)
Asit Ghosh
KISMET(1944)
Charu Ghosh
APARAJITO(1959, India)
Alice Ghostley
NEW FACES(1954); TO KILL A MOCKINGBIRD(1962); MY SIX LOVES(1963); FLIM-FLAM MAN, THE(1967); GRADUATE, THE(1967); WITH SIX YOU GET EGGROLL(1968); VIVA MAX!(1969); ACE ELI AND RODGER OF THE SKIES(1973); GATOR(1976); BLUE SUNSHINE(1978); GREASE(1978); RABBIT TEST(1978); RECORD CITY(1978)
1984
NOT FOR PUBLICATION(1984)
Maire Ni Ghrainne
FIGHTING PRINCE OF DONEGAL, THE(1966, Brit.); ULYSSES(1967, U.S./Brit.)
Roderick Ghyka
BATTLE OF LOVE'S RETURN, THE(1971)
Alberto Giacalone
FOREVER YOURS(1937, Brit.), p
Jim Giacama
GEEK MAGGOT BINGO(1983)
Norma Giacchero
ROMA(1972, Ital./Fr.)
Fosco Giachetti
DEFEAT OF HANNIBAL, THE(1937, Ital.); DREAM OF BUTTERFLY, THE(1941, Ital.); DAMNED, THE(1948, Fr.); CROSSROADS OF PASSION(1951, Fr.); COUNTERFEITERS, THE(1953, Ital.); LOVE AND LARCENY(1963, Fr./Ital.); WASTREL, THE(1963, Ital.); CONFORMIST, THE(1971, Ital., Fr)
Gianna Giachetti
LA VIACCIA(1962, Fr./Ital.)
Stacey Giachino
DORM THAT DRIPPED BLOOD, THE(1983), w
Franco Giacobini
ERIK THE CONQUEROR(1963, Fr./Ital.); CRAZY DESIRE(1964, Ital.); EIGHTEEN IN THE SUN(1964, Ital.); HERCULES IN THE HAUNTED WORLD(1964, Ital.); FASCIST, THE(1965, Ital.); EL GRECO(1966, Ital., Fr.); OPERATION KID BROTHER(1967, Ital.); MERCENARY, THE(1970, Ital./Span.); SONNY AND JED(1974, Ital.)
Giuseppe Giacosa
LA BOHEME(1965, Ital.), w
L. Giacosi
ISLAND OF PROCIDA, THE(1952, Ital.), w
Luigi Giacosi
FROM A ROMAN BALCONY(1961, Fr./Ital.); GUILT IS NOT MINE(1968, Ital.), w
Giandomenico Giagni
FRIENDS FOR LIFE(1964, Ital.), w
Giandomentico Giagni
ITALIANO BRAVA GENTE(1965, Ital./USSR), w
Piero Giagnoni
LAND OF THE PHARAOHS(1955); BOY ON A DOLPHIN(1957)
Nick Giakovief
ANNA OF RHODES(1950, Gr.), m
Stathis Giallelis
AMERICA, AMERICA(1963); CAST A GIANT SHADOW(1966); THE EAVESDROPPER(1966, U.S./Arg.); BLUE(1968); CHILDREN OF SANCHEZ, THE(1978, U. S./Mex.)

Louis Giambalvo
AIRPLANE II: THE SEQUEL(1982); NIGHTMARES(1983); SECOND THOUGHTS(1983)
Guido Giambartolomei
DAY THE SKY EXPLODED, THE(1958, Fr./Ital.), p; MONGOLS, THE(1966, Fr./Ital.), p
Joseph C. Giambelluca
ROCKY(1976)
Joey Giambra
HIDE IN PLAIN SIGHT(1980)
Nelide Giammarco
BREAD AND CHOCOLATE(1978, Ital.)
Patrizia Giammei
THREE(1969, Brit.)
Joey Gian
BLUE SKIES AGAIN(1983); NIGHT IN HEAVEN, A(1983)
Geretta Giancarlo
SMITHEREENS(1982)
Maria Pia Giancaro
RETURN OF SABATA(1972, Ital./Fr./Ger.)
Anna Giancinti
HORNET'S NEST(1970)
Luisa Giancinti
HORNET'S NEST(1970)
Ugo Giancomozzi
WHITE LINE, THE(1952, Ital.), md
Roberto Giandalla
FURY OF THE PAGANS(1963, Ital.), ed
Gina Gianelli
PSYCHOPATH, THE(1966, Brit.); DEADLY BEES,THE(1967, Brit.)
Alfredo Gianetti
RAILROAD MAN, THE(1965, Ital.), w
Gina Gianetti
Misc. Talkies
SIMPLY IRRESISTIBLE(1983)
Rosario Gianetti
GLADIATORS, THE(1970, Swed.)
Ronald Gianettino
HORROR OF PARTY BEACH, THE(1964), w
Glen Gianfrancisco
KING OF THE GYPSIES(1978)
Jennifer Dana Giangrasso
EASY MONEY(1983)
Giulio Gianini
SEVEN SEAS TO CALAIS(1963, Ital.), ph
Anthony I. Giannane
ESCAPE 2000(1983, Aus.), p
Raffaello Giannelli
LOVE SPECIALIST, THE(1959, Ital.), w
Dino Joseph Giannetta
SUMMER CAMP(1979), ch
Alfredo Giannetti
DIVORCE, ITALIAN STYLE(1962, Ital.), w; DOUBLE BED, THE(1965, Fr./Ital.), w; FACTS OF MURDER, THE(1965, Ital.), w; SWORD OF EL CID, THE(1965, Span./Ital.), w; ENGAGEMENT ITALIANO(1966, Fr./Ital.), d&w; CLIMAX, THE(1967, Fr., Ital.), w; SERAFINO(1970, Fr./Ital.), w
Branduani Gianni
MIRACLE IN MILAN(1951, Ital.)
Alex Giannini
HAMLET(1964)
Cheryl Giannini
WITHOUT A TRACE(1983)
Christian Giannini
1984
IMPULSE(1984)
Ettore Giannini
CROSSROADS OF PASSION(1951, Fr.), p; GREATEST LOVE, THE(1954, Ital.); NEOPOLITAN CAROUSEL(1961, Ital.), d, w
Giancarlo Giannini
END OF THE WORLD(in Our Usual Bed In a Night Full of Rain), THE*1/2 (1978, Ital.); ANZIO(1968, Ital.); ARABELLA(1969, U.S./Ital.); FRAULEIN DOKTOR(1969, Ital./Yugo.); SECRET OF SANTA VITTORIA, THE(1969); MOTIVE WAS JEALOUSY, THE(1970 Ital./Span.); PIZZA TRIANGLE, THE(1970, Ital./Span.); BLACK BELLY OF THE TARANTULA, THE(1972, Ital.); LOVE AND ANARCHY(1974, Ital.); DRAMA OF THE RICH(1975, Ital./Fr.); MIDNIGHT PLEASURES(1975, Ital.); SEVEN BEAUTIES(1976, Ital.), a, p; LA GRANDE BOURGEOISE(1977, Ital.); BLOOD FEUD(1979, Ital.); INNOCENT, THE(1979, Ital.); IMMORTAL BACHELOR, THE(1980, Ital.); LILI MARLEEN(1981, Ger.); LOVERS AND LIARS(1981, Ital.)
1984
AMERICAN DREAMER(1984)
Giancarlo Gianninni
SWEPT AWAY...BY AN UNUSUAL DESTINY IN THE BLUE SEA OF AUGUST(1975, Ital.)
Joe Giannone
MADMAN(1982), d&w
E. Giannopoulou
TAKE ME AWAY, MY LOVE(1962, Gr.), d
Claudia Giannotti
LOVE FACTORY(1969, Ital.)
Claudia Gianotti
WHITE, RED, YELLOW, PINK(1966, Ital.)
Cardiff Giant
SHADOW OF THE THIN MAN(1941)
Roberto Gianuiti
PSYCHIC, THE(1979, Ital.), w
Roberto Gianviti
PSYCOSISSIMO(1962, Ital.), w; SWORD OF THE CONQUEROR(1962, Ital.), w; LADY DOCTOR, THE(1963, Fr./Ital./Span.), w; GOLIATH AND THE SINS OF BABYLON(1964, Ital.), w; LOVE, THE ITALIAN WAY(1964, Ital.), w; HERCULES VS THE GIANT WARRIORS(1965 Fr./Ital.), w; SEVEN SLAVES AGAINST THE

WORLD(1965, Ital.), w; OPERATION ST. PETER'S(1968, Ital.), w

Mino Giarda
SUPERARGO VERSUS DIABOLICUS(1966, Ital./Span.), w

Giuseppe Giardina
NAKED MAJA, THE(1959, Ital./U.S.)

Mino Giardo
WEB OF VIOLENCE(1966, Ital./Span.), w

Robert Giarratano
1984
FEAR CITY(1984)

Tony Giarratano
Misc. Talkies
BED OF VIOLENCE(1967)

Ian Giatti
1984
OH GOD! YOU DEVIL(1984)

Angela Giavalisco
LA DOLCE VITA(1961, Ital./Fr.)

Barry Gibb
SGT. PEPPER'S LONELY HEARTS CLUB BAND(1978)

Charles Gibb
IT GROWS ON TREES(1952)

Donald Gibb
1984
MEATBALLS PART II(1984); REVENGE OF THE NERDS(1984)

Hunter Gibb
MAD MAX(1979, Aus.)

Ken Gibb
SUMMER CAMP(1979), ph

Kenneth Lloyd Gibb
DRIVE-IN MASSACRE(1976), ph

Maurice Gibb
SATURDAY NIGHT FEVER(1977), m; SGT. PEPPER'S LONELY HEARTS CLUB BAND(1978)
1984
BREED APART, A(1984), m

Max Gibb
ALWAYS ANOTHER DAWN(1948, Aus.)

Richard Gibb
RATTLERS(1976), ph; PURPLE HAZE(1982), ph

Robin Gibb
SGT. PEPPER'S LONELY HEARTS CLUB BAND(1978)

Wendy Gibb
RUGGED O'RIORDANS, THE(1949, Aus.)

Ken Gibbel
1984
PROTOCOL(1984); UP THE CREEK(1984)

Bessie Gibbens
Misc. Talkies
WAGES OF SIN, THE(1929)

Barry Gibberman
NEW YEAR'S EVIL(1980)

William Gibberson
CRY MURDER(1936); PROJECT X(1949); TATTOOED STRANGER, THE(1950)

Robyn Gibbes
1984
WILD HORSES(1984, New Zealand)

Cedric Gibbins
KISS ME KATE(1953), art d

Cedric Gibbon
BROADWAY MELODY, THE(1929), art d; TARZAN'S SECRET TREASURE(1941), art d; IF WINTER COMES(1947), art d; HIT THE DECK(1955), art d

Douglas Gibbon
HIGH FLIGHT(1957, Brit.)

James Gibbon
MAN WANTED(1932), ed; BUREAU OF MISSING PERSONS(1933), ed; BIG SHAKEDOWN, THE(1934), ed; HOUSEWIFE(1934), ed; MERRY FRINKS, THE(1934), ed; CASE OF THE LUCKY LEGS, THE(1935), ed; IRISH IN US, THE(1935), ed; MAYBE IT'S LOVE(1935), ed; CALL IT A DAY(1937), ed; CONFESSION(1937), ed; RACKET BUSTERS(1938), ed; ANGELS WASH THEIR FACES(1939), ed; YOU CAN'T GET AWAY WITH MURDER(1939), ed; FLIGHT ANGELS(1940), ed; FLOWING GOLD(1940), ed; INVISIBLE STRIPES(1940), ed; LADY WITH RED HAIR(1940), ed; BULLET SCARS(1942), ed; BUSSES ROAR(1942), ed; GORILLA MAN(1942), ed; SPY SHIP(1942), ed; MURDER ON THE WATERFRONT(1943), ed; SHERLOCK HOLMES AND THE SPIDER WOMAN(1944), ed

Jim Gibbon
EXPERT, THE(1932), ed

Joe Gibbon
FURTHER UP THE CREEK!(1958, Brit.)

P. Gibbon
MORE DEADLY THAN THE MALE(1961, Brit.), m

Ann Gibbons
SERVANTS' ENTRANCE(1934)

Ayllene Gibbons
HOUSE OF THE DAMNED(1963); MY FAIR LADY(1964); CAT BALLOU(1965); LOVED ONE, THE(1965); YOUNG DILLINGER(1965); CHAMBER OF HORRORS(1966); FINE MADNESS, A(1966); SAM WHISKEY(1969)

Carroll Gibbons
HELLO SWEETHEART(1935, Brit.); COMMON TOUCH, THE(1941, Brit.); NIGHT BOAT TO DUBLIN(1946, Brit.)

Cecric Gibbons
LITTLE NELLIE KELLY(1940), art d
Silents
SMART SET, THE(1928), set d

Cederic Gibbons
WAR NURSE(1930), art d; HILLS OF HOME(1948), art d

Cedric Gibbons
ALIAS JIMMY VALENTINE(1928), set d; LADY OF CHANCE, A(1928), art d; WIND, THE(1928), set d; BELLAMY TRIAL, THE(1929), set d; BRIDGE OF SAN LUIS REY, THE(1929), art d; HALLELUJAH(1929), art d; HIS GLORIOUS NIGHT(1929), art d;

LAST OF MRS. CHEYNEY, THE(1929), art d; MADAME X(1929), art d; MARIANNE(1929), art d; MYSTERIOUS ISLAND(1929), art d; OUR MODERN MAIDENS(1929), art d; PAGAN, THE(1929), art d; SO THIS IS COLLEGE(1929), art d; THEIR OWN DESIRE(1929), art d; TRIAL OF MARY DUGAN, THE(1929), art d; UNHOLY NIGHT, THE(1929), art d; UNTAMED(1929), art d; VOICE OF THE CITY(1929), art d; WONDER OF WOMEN(1929), art d; BIG HOUSE, THE(1930), art d; CHILDREN OF PLEASURE(1930), art d; DIVORCEE, THE(1930), art d; FREE AND EASY(1930), art d; IT'S A GREAT LIFE(1930), art d; LADY OF SCANDAL, THE(1930), art d; LADY'S MORALS, A(1930), art d; LET US BE GAY(1930), art d; MADAME SATAN(1930), art d; MEN OF THE NORTH(1930), art d; MIN AND BILL(1930), art d; MONTANA MOON(1930), art d; NAVY BLUES(1930), art d; NOT SO DUMB(1930), art d; OUR BLUSHING BRIDES(1930), art d; PAID(1930), art d; PASSION FLOWER(1930), art d; ROGUE SONG, THE(1930), art d; SEA BAT, THE(1930), art d; SHIP FROM SHANGHAI, THE(1930), art d; SINS OF THE CHILDREN(1930), art d; STRICTLY UNCONVENTIONAL(1930), art d; THEY LEARNED ABOUT WOMEN(1930), art d; THIS MAD WORLD(1930), art d; THOSE THREE FRENCH GIRLS(1930), art d; UNHOLY THREE, THE(1930), art d; WAY FOR A SAILOR(1930), art d; WAY OUT WEST(1930), art d; WISE GIRLS(1930), art d; WOMAN RACKET, THE(1930), art d; EASIEST WAY, THE(1931), art d; FREE SOUL, A(1931), art d; MAN IN POSSESSION, THE(1931), art d; NEW ADVENTURES OF GET-RICH-QUICK WALLINGFORD, THE(1931), art d; PRIVATE LIVES(1931), art d; SIN OF MADELON CLAUDET, THE(1931), art d; STRANGERS MAY KISS(1931), art d; TAILOR MADE MAN, A(1931), art d; BLONDIE OF THE FOLLIES(1932), art d; EMMA(1932), art d; GRAND HOTEL(1932), art d; KONGO(1932), art d; MASK OF FU MANCHU, THE(1932), art d; PROSPERITY(1932), art d; RASPUTIN AND THE EMPRESS(1932), art d; RED DUST(1932), art d; SMILIN' THROUGH(1932), art d; TARZAN, THE APE MAN(1932), art d; WET PARADE, THE(1932), art d & set d; DANCING LADY(1933), art d & set d; DINNER AT EIGHT(1933), art d; HOLD YOUR MAN(1933), art d; NIGHT FLIGHT(1933), art d; TODAY WE LIVE(1933), art d; WHITE SISTER, THE(1933), art d; BARRETTS OF WIMPOLE STREET, THE(1934), art d; CHAINED(1934), art d; EVELYN PRENTICE(1934), art d; GAY BRIDE, THE(1934), art d; MANHATTAN MELODRAMA(1934), art d; MEN IN WHITE(1934), art d; MERRY WIDOW, THE(1934), art d; OPERATOR 13(1934), art d; PAINTED VEIL, THE(1934), art d; PARIS INTERLUDE(1934), art d; STAMBOUL QUEST(1934), art d; STUDENT TOUR(1934), art d; TARZAN AND HIS MATE(1934), d; THIN MAN, THE(1934), art d; TREASURE ISLAND(1934), art d; AH, WILDERNESS!(1935), art d; BIOGRAPHY OF A BACHELOR GIRL(1935), art d; CHINA SEAS(1935), art d; DAVID COPPERFIELD(1935), art d; FORSAKING ALL OTHERS(1935), art d; MARK OF THE VAMPIRE(1935), art d; MURDER MAN(1935), art d; MUTINY ON THE BOUNTY(1935), art d; NAUGHTY MARIETTA(1935), art d; NIGHT AT THE OPERA, A(1935), art d; NO MORE LADIES(1935), art d; O'SHAUGHNESSY'S BOY(1935), art d; RECKLESS(1935), art d; SOCIETY DOCTOR(1935), art d; TALE OF TWO CITIES, A(1935), art d; WEST POINT OF THE AIR(1935), art d; AFTER THE THIN MAN(1936), art d; DEVIL DOLL, THE(1936), art d; DEVIL IS A SISSY, THE(1936), art d; FURY(1936), art d; GORGEOUS HUSSY, THE(1936), art d; GREAT ZIEGFELD, THE(1936), art d; HIS BROTHER'S WIFE(1936), art d; LIBELED LADY(1936), art d; LOVE ON THE RUN(1936), art d; MOONLIGHT MURDER(1936), art d; OLD HUTCH(1936), art d; RIFF-RAFF(1936), art d; ROMEO AND JULIET(1936), art d, set d; ROSE MARIE(1936), art d; SAN FRANCISCO(1936), art d; SMALL TOWN GIRL(1936), art d; SUZY(1936), art d; THREE WISE GUYS, THE(1936), art d; TROUBLE FOR TWO(1936), art d; UNGUARDED HOUR, THE(1936), art d; WHIPSAW(1936), art d; WIFE VERSUS SECRETARY(1936), art d; BIG CITY(1937), art d; BRIDE WORE RED, THE(1937), art d; CAPTAINS COURAGEOUS(1937), art d; DAY AT THE RACES, A(1937), art d; DOUBLE WEDDING(1937), art d; EMPEROR'S CANDLESTICKS, THE(1937), art d; FIREFLY, THE(1937), art d; GOOD EARTH, THE(1937), art d; LAST GANGSTER, THE(1937), art d; LAST OF MRS. CHEYNEY, THE(1937), art d; LONDON BY NIGHT(1937), art d; MADAME X(1937), art d; MANNEQUIN(1937), art d; MAYTIME(1937), art d; MY DEAR MISS ALDRICH(1937), art d; NAVY BLUE AND GOLD(1937), art d; NIGHT MUST FALL(1937), art d; PARNELL(1937), art d; PERSONAL PROPERTY(1937), art d; ROSALIE(1937), art d; SARATOGA(1937), art d; THEY GAVE HIM A GUN(1937), art d; THIRTEENTH CHAIR, THE(1937), art d; ARSENE LUPIN RETURNS(1938), art d; CHASER, THE(1938), art d; CHRISTMAS CAROL, A(1938), art d; DRAMATIC SCHOOL(1938), art d; FAST COMPANY(1938), art d; FIRST 100 YEARS, THE(1938), art d; GIRL OF THE GOLDEN WEST, THE(1938), art d; GREAT WALTZ, THE(1938), art d; HOLD THAT KISS(1938), art d; LISTEN, DARLING(1938), art d; LORD JEFF(1938), art d; LOVE FINDS ANDY HARDY(1938), art d; LOVE IS A HEADACHE(1938), art d; MARIE ANTOINETTE(1938), art d; OF HUMAN HEARTS(1938), art d; PARADISE FOR THREE(1938), art d; RICH MAN, POOR GIRL(1938), art d; SHINING HOUR, THE(1938), art d; SHOPWORN ANGEL(1938), art d; STABLEMATES(1938), art d; SWEETHEARTS(1938), art d; TEST PILOT(1938), art d; THREE COMRADES(1938), art d; TOY WIFE, THE(1938), art d; WOMAN AGAINST WOMAN(1938), art d; YOUNG DR. KILDARE(1938), art d; ANOTHER THIN MAN(1939), art d; BABES IN ARMS(1939), art d; DANCING CO-ED(1939), art d; FOUR GIRLS IN WHITE(1939), art d; ICE FOLLIES OF 1939(1939), art d; IDIOT'S DELIGHT(1939), art d; IT'S A WONDERFUL WORLD(1939), art d; JUDGE HARDY AND SON(1939), art d; LADY OF THE TROPICS(1939), art d; LET FREEDOM RING(1939), art d; MAISIE(1939), art d; MIRACLES FOR SALE(1939), art d; NINOTCHKA(1939), art d; REMEMBER?(1939), art d; SECRET OF DR. KILDARE, THE(1939), art d; SERGEANT MADDEN(1939), art d; SOCIETY LAWYER(1939), art d; STAND UP AND FIGHT(1939), art d; TELL NO TALES(1939), art d; THESE GLAMOUR GIRLS(1939), art d; THUNDER AFLOAT(1939), art d; WIZARD OF OZ, THE(1939), art d; WOMEN, THE(1939), art d; 6000 ENEMIES(1939), art d; BOOM TOWN(1940), art d; COMRADE X(1940), art d; CONGO MAISIE(1940), art d; DR. KILDARE'S CRISIS(1940), art d; DR. KILDARE'S STRANGE CASE(1940), art d; DULCY(1940), art d; EARL OF CHICAGO, THE(1940), art d; EDISON, THE MAN(1940), art d; ESCAPE(1940), art d; FLIGHT COMMAND(1940), art d; FLORIAN(1940), art d; FORTY LITTLE MOTHERS(1940), art d; GHOST COMES HOME, THE(1940), art d; GO WEST(1940), art d; I LOVE YOU AGAIN(1940), art d; I TAKE THIS WOMAN(1940), art d; MAN FROM DAKOTA, THE(1940), artd; MORTAL STORM, THE(1940), art d; NEW MOON(1940), art d; NORTHWEST PASSAGE(1940), art d; PHILADELPHIA STORY, THE(1940), art d; PRIDE AND PREJUDICE(1940), art d; SHOP AROUND THE CORNER, THE(1940), art d; SKY MURDER(1940), art d; SPORTING BLOOD(1940), art d; STRANGE CARGO(1940), art d; STRIKE UP THE BAND(1940), art d; SUSAN AND GOD(1940), art d; TWO GIRLS ON BROADWAY(1940), art d; WATERLOO BRIDGE(1940), art d; WE WHO ARE YOUNG(1940), art d; YOUNG TOM EDISON(1940), art d; BLOSSOMS IN THE DUST(1941), art d; CHOCOLATE SOLDIER, THE(1941), art d; COME LIVE WITH ME(1941), art d; DESIGN FOR SCANDAL(1941), art d; DOWN IN SAN DIEGO(1941), art; DR. JEKYLL AND MR. HYDE(1941), art d; DR. KILDARE'S WEDDING DAY(1941), art d; FEMININE TOUCH, THE(1941), art d; GET-AWAY,

THE(1941), art d; H.M. PULHAM, ESQ.(1941), art d; HONKY TONK(1941), art d; KATHLEEN(1941), art d; LADY BE GOOD(1941), art d; LIFE BEGINS FOR ANDY HARDY(1941), art d; LOVE CRAZY(1941), art d; MARRIED BACHELOR(1941), art d; MEN OF BOYS TOWN(1941), art d; SHADOW OF THE THIN MAN(1941), art d; SMILIN' THROUGH(1941), art d; THEY MET IN BOMBAY(1941), art d; TRIAL OF MARY DUGAN, THE(1941), art d; TWO-FACED WOMAN(1941), art d; UNHOLY PARTNERS(1941), art d; VANISHING VIRGINIAN, THE(1941), art d; WASHINGTON MELODRAMA(1941), art d; WHEN LADIES MEET(1941), art d; WHISTLING IN THE DARK(1941), art d; WILD MAN OF BORNEO, THE(1941), art d; ZIEGFELD GIRL(1941), art d; AFFAIRS OF MARTHA, THE(1942), art d; ANDY HARDY'S DOUBLE LIFE(1942), art d; CAIRO(1942), art d; CALLING DR. GILLESPIE(1942), art d; CROSSROADS(1942), art d; DR. GILLESPIE'S NEW ASSISTANT(1942), art d; EYES IN THE NIGHT(1942), art d; FINGERS AT THE WINDOW(1942), art d; FOR ME AND MY GAL(1942), art d; GRAND CENTRAL MURDER(1942), art d; HER CARDBOARD LOVER(1942), art d; I MARRIED AN ANGEL(1942), art d; JACKASS MAIL(1942), art d; JOE SMITH, AMERICAN(1942), art d; JOHNNY EAGER(1942), art d; JOURNEY FOR MARGARET(1942), art d; KEEPER OF THE FLAME(1942), art d; KID GLOVE KILLER(1942), art d; MAISIE GETS HER MAN(1942), art d; MRS. MINIVER(1942), art d; NORTHWEST RANGERS(1942), art d; OMAHA TRAIL, THE(1942), art d; PACIFIC RENDEZVOUS(1942), art d; PANAMA HATTIE(1942), art d; PIERRE OF THE PLAINS(1942), art d; RANDOM HARVEST(1942), art d; REUNION IN FRANCE(1942), art d; SEVEN SWEETHEARTS(1942), art d; SHIP AHOY(1942), art d; SOMEWHERE I'LL FIND YOU(1942), art d; STAND BY FOR ACTION(1942), art d; SUNDAY PUNCH(1942), art d; TARZAN'S NEW YORK ADVENTURE(1942), art d; TENNESSEE JOHNSON(1942), art d; TISH(1942), art d; TORTILLA FLAT(1942), art d; WAR AGAINST MRS. HADLEY, THE(1942), art d; WE WERE DANCING(1942), art d; WHISTLING IN DIXIE(1942), art d; WHITE CARGO(1942), art d; WOMAN OF THE YEAR(1942), art d; YANK AT ETON, A(1942), art d; AIR RAID WARDENS(1943), art d; BATAAN(1943), art d; CROSS OF LORRAINE, THE(1943), art d; CRY HAVOC(1943), art d; DR. GILLESPIE'S CRIMINAL CASE(1943), art d; DU BARRY WAS A LADY(1943), art d; GIRL CRAZY(1943), art d; GUY NAMED JOE, A(1943), art d; HARRIGAN'S KID(1943), art d; HEAVENLY BODY, THE(1943), art d; HUMAN COMEDY, THE(1943), art d; I DOOD IT(1943), art d; LASSIE, COME HOME(1943), art d; MADAME CURIE(1943), art d; MAN FROM DOWN UNDER, THE(1943), art d; PILOT NO. 5(1943), art d; PRESENTING LILY MARS(1943), art d; SALUTE TO THE MARINES(1943), art d; SLIGHTLY DANGEROUS(1943), art d; SONG OF RUSSIA(1943), art d; STRANGER IN TOWN, A(1943), art d; SWING FEVER(1943), art d; SWING SHIFT MAISIE(1943), art d; THOUSANDS CHEER(1943), art d; THREE HEARTS FOR JULIA(1943), art d; WHISTLING IN BROOKLYN(1943), art d; YOUNG IDEAS(1943), art d; YOUNGEST PROFESSION, THE(1943), art d; ANDY HARDY'S BLONDE TROUBLE(1944), art d; BETWEEN TWO WOMEN(1944), art d; DRAGON SEED(1944), art d; GASLIGHT(1944), art d; GENTLE ANNIE(1944), art d; KISMET(1944), art d; LOST ANGEL(1944), art d; LOST IN A HAREM(1944), art d; MAIN STREET AFTER DARK(1944), art d; MAISIE GOES TO RENO(1944), art d; MARRIAGE IS A PRIVATE AFFAIR(1944), art d; MEET ME IN ST. LOUIS(1944), art d; MEET THE PEOPLE(1944), art d; MRS. PARKINGTON(1944), art d; MUSIC FOR MILLIONS(1944), art d; NATIONAL VELVET(1944), art d; NOTHING BUT TROUBLE(1944), art d; RATIONING(1944), art d; SEE HERE, PRIVATE HARGROVE(1944), art d; SEVENTH CROSS, THE(1944), art d; THIN MAN GOES HOME, THE(1944), art d; THIRTY SECONDS OVER TOKYO(1944), art d; THREE MEN IN WHITE(1944), art d; TWO GIRLS AND A SAILOR(1944), art d; WHITE CLIFFS OF DOVER, THE(1944), art d; ADVENTURE(1945), art d; ANCHORS AWEIGH(1945), art d; CLOCK, THE(1945), art d; DANGEROUS PARTNERS(1945), art d; HER HIGHNESS AND THE BELLBOY(1945), art d; HIDDEN EYE, THE(1945), art d; KEEP YOUR POWDER DRY(1945), art d; LETTER FOR EVIE, A(1945), art d; OUR VINES HAVE TENDER GRAPES(1945), art d; PICTURE OF DORIAN GRAY, THE(1945), art d; SHE WENT TO THE RACES(1945), art d; SON OF LASSIE(1945), art d; THEY WERE EXPENDABLE(1945), art d; THIS MAN'S NAVY(1945), art d; THRILL OF A ROMANCE(1945), art d; TWICE BLESSED(1945), art d; VALLEY OF DECISION, THE(1945), art d; WEEKEND AT THE WALDORF(1945), art d; WHAT NEXT, CORPORAL HARGROVE?(1945), art d; WITHOUT LOVE(1945), art d; YOLANDA AND THE THIEF(1945), art d; ZIEGFELD FOLLIES(1945), art d; COURAGE OF LASSIE(1946), art d; EASY TO WED(1946), art d; FAITHFUL IN MY FASHION(1946), art d; GALLANT BESS(1946), art d; GREEN YEARS, THE(1946), art d; HARVEY GIRLS, THE(1946), art d; HOLIDAY IN MEXICO(1946), art d; HOODLUM SAINT, THE(1946), art d; LITTLE MISTER JIM(1946), art d; LOVE LAUGHS AT ANDY HARDY(1946), art d; MIGHTY MCGURK, THE(1946), art d; MY BROTHER TALKS TO HORSES(1946), art d; NO LEAVE, NO LOVE(1946), art d; POSTMAN ALWAYS RINGS TWICE, THE(1946), art d; SAILOR TAKES A WIFE, THE(1946), art d; SECRET HEART, THE(1946), art d; SHOW-OFF, THE(1946), art d; THREE WISE FOOLS(1946), art d; TILL THE CLOUDS ROLL BY(1946), art d; TWO SISTERS FROM BOSTON(1946), art d; TWO SMART PEOPLE(1946), art d; UNDERCURRENT(1946), art d; UP GOES MAISIE(1946), art d; YEARLING, THE(1946), art d; CASS TIMBERLANE(1947), art d; CYNTHIA(1947), art d; DARK DELUSION(1947), art d; DESIRE ME(1947), art d; FIESTA(1947), art d; GOOD NEWS(1947), art d; GREEN DOLPHIN STREET(1947), art d; HIGH BARBAREE(1947), art d; HIGH WALL, THE(1947), art d; HUCKSTERS, THE(1947), art d; IT HAPPENED IN BROOKLYN(1947), art d; KILLER McCOY(1947), art d; LADY IN THE LAKE(1947), art d; LIVING IN A BIG WAY(1947), art d; MERTON OF THE MOVIES(1947), art d; ROMANCE OF ROSY RIDGE, THE(1947), art d; SEA OF GRASS, THE(1947), art d; SONG OF LOVE(1947), art d; SONG OF THE THIN MAN(1947), art d; THIS TIME FOR KEEPS(1947), art d; UNDERCOVER MAISIE(1947), art d; UNFINISHED DANCE,THE(1947), art d; B. F.'S DAUGHTER(1948), art d; BRIDE GOES WILD, THE(1948), art d; COMMAND DECISION(1948), art d; DATE WITH JUDY, A(1948), art d; EASTER PARADE(1948), art d; HOMECOMING(1948), art d; JULIA MISBEHAVES(1948), art d; KISSING BANDIT, THE(1948), art d; LUXURY LINER(1948), art d; ON AN ISLAND WITH YOU(1948), art d; PIRATE, THE(1948), art d; SOUTHERN YANKEE, A(1948), art d; STATE OF THE UNION(1948), art d; SUMMER HOLIDAY(1948), art d; TENTH AVENUE ANGEL(1948), art d; THREE DARING DAUGHTERS(1948), art d; THREE MUSKETEERS, THE(1948), art d; ACT OF VIOLENCE(1949), art d; ADAM'S RIB(1949), art d; BARKLEYS OF BROADWAY, THE(1949), art d; BRIBE, THE(1949), art d; CHALLENGE TO LASSIE(1949), art d; DOCTOR AND THE GIRL, THE(1949), art d; EAST SIDE, WEST SIDE(1949), art d; GREAT SINNER, THE(1949), art d; IN THE GOOD OLD SUMMERTIME(1949), art d; INTRUDER IN THE DUST(1949), art d; LITTLE WOMEN(1949), art d; MADAME BOVARY(1949), art d; NEPTUNE'S DAUGHTER(1949), art d; ON THE TOWN(1949), art d; RED DANUBE, THE(1949), art d; SCENE OF THE CRIME(1949), art d; SECRET GARDEN, THE(1949), art d; STRATTON STORY, THE(1949), art d; SUN COMES UP, THE(1949), art d; TAKE ME OUT TO THE BALL GAME(1949), art d; TENSION(1949), art d; THAT FORSYTE WOMAN(1949), art d; THAT MIDNIGHT KISS(1949), art d; ANNIE GET YOUR GUN(1950), art d; ASPHALT JUNGLE, THE(1950), art d; BLACK HAND, THE(1950), art d; CRISIS(1950), art d; DEVIL'S DOORWAY(1950), art d; DIAL 1119(1950), art d; DUCHESS OF IDAHO, THE(1950), art d; FATHER OF THE BRIDE(1950), art d; GROUNDS FOR MARRIAGE(1950), art d; HAPPY YEARS, THE(1950), art d; KEY TO THE CITY(1950), art d; KIM(1950), art d; LADY WITHOUT PASSPORT, A(1950), art d; LIFE OF HER OWN, A(1950), art d; MAGNIFICENT YANKEE, THE(1950), art d; MALAYA(1950), art d; MRS. O'MALLEY AND MR. MALONE(1950), art d; MYSTERY STREET(1950), art d; NANCY GOES TO RIO(1950), art d; PAGAN LOVE SONG(1950), art d; PLEASE BELIEVE ME(1950), art d; REFORMER AND THE REDHEAD, THE(1950), art d; RIGHT CROSS(1950), art d; SHADOW ON THE WALL(1950), art d; SIDE STREET(1950), art d; SKIPPER SURPRISED HIS WIFE, THE(1950), art d; STARS IN MY CROWN(1950), art d; SUMMER STOCK(1950), art d; THREE LITTLE WORDS(1950), art d; TO PLEASE A LADY(1950), art d; TOAST OF NEW ORLEANS, THE(1950), art d; TWO WEEKS WITH LOVE(1950), art d; WATCH THE BIRDIE(1950), art d; YELLOW CAB MAN, THE(1950), art d; ACROSS THE WIDE MISSOURI(1951), art d; AMERICAN IN PARIS, AN(1951), art d; CALLAWAY WENT THATAWAY(1951), art d; CAUSE FOR ALARM(1951), art d; EXCUSE MY DUST(1951), art d; FATHER'S LITTLE DIVIDEND(1951), art d; GO FOR BROKE(1951), art d; GREAT CARUSO, THE(1951), art d; INSIDE STRAIGHT(1951), art d; IT'S A BIG COUNTRY(1951), art d; KIND LADY(1951), art d; LAW AND THE LADY, THE(1951), art d; LIGHT TOUCH, THE(1951), art d; MAN WITH A CLOAK, THE(1951), art d; MR. IMPERIUM(1951), art d; NIGHT INTO MORNING(1951), art d; NO QUESTIONS ASKED(1951), art d; PAINTED HILLS, THE(1951), art d; PEOPLE AGAINST O'HARA, THE(1951), art d; RED BADGE OF COURAGE, THE(1951), art d; RICH, YOUNG AND PRETTY(1951), art d; ROYAL WEDDING(1951), art d; SELLOUT, THE(1951), art d; SHADOW IN THE SKY(1951), art d; SHOW BOAT(1951), art d; SOLDIERS THREE(1951), art d; STRIP, THE(1951), art d; TALL TARGET, THE(1951), art d; TEXAS CARNIVAL(1951), art d; THREE GUYS NAMED MIKE(1951), art d; TOO YOUNG TO KISS(1951), art d; UNKNOWN MAN, THE(1951), art d; VENGEANCE VALLEY(1951), art d; WESTWARD THE WOMEN(1951), art d; BAD AND THE BEAUTIFUL, THE(1952), art d; BELLE OF NEW YORK, THE(1952), art d; CARBINE WILLIAMS(1952), art d; DESPERATE SEARCH(1952), art d; EVERYTHING I HAVE IS YOURS(1952), art d; GIRL IN WHITE, THE(1952), art d; GLORY ALLEY(1952), art d; HOLIDAY FOR SINNERS(1952), ait d; INVITATION(1952), art d; JUST THIS ONCE(1952), art d; LONE STAR(1952), art d; LOVE IS BETTER THAN EVER(1952), art d; LOVELY TO LOOK AT(1952), art d; MERRY WIDOW, THE(1952), art d; MILLION DOLLAR MERMAID(1952), art d; MY MAN AND I(1952), art d; PAT AND MIKE(1952), art d; PLYMOUTH ADVENTURE(1952), art d; PRISONER OF ZENDA, THE(1952), art d; ROGUE'S MARCH(1952), art d; SCARAMOUCHE(1952), art d; SINGIN' IN THE RAIN(1952), art d; SKIRTS AHOY!(1952), art d; SKY FULL OF MOON(1952), art d; TALK ABOUT A STRANGER(1952), art d; WASHINGTON STORY(1952), art d; WHEN IN ROME(1952), art d; WILD NORTH, THE(1952), art d; YOU FOR ME(1952), art d; YOUNG MAN WITH IDEAS(1952), art d; ABOVE AND BEYOND(1953), art d; ACTRESS, THE(1953), art d; CLOWN, THE(1953), art d; DREAM WIFE(1953), art d; EASY TO LOVE(1953), art d; ESCAPE FROM FORT BRAVO(1953), art d; FAST COMPANY(1953), art d; GIRL WHO HAD EVERYTHING, THE(1953), art d; GIVE A GIRL A BREAK(1953), art d; GREAT DIAMOND ROBBERY(1953), art d; I LOVE MELVIN(1953), art d; JEOPARDY(1953), art d; JULIUS CAESAR(1953), art d; LATIN LOVERS(1953), art d; LILI(1953), art d; NAKED SPUR, THE(1953), art d; REMAINS TO BE SEEN(1953), art d; RIDE, VAQUERO!(1953), art d; SCANDAL AT SCOURIE(1953), art d; SMALL TOWN GIRL(1953), art d; SOMBRERO(1953), art d; STORY OF THREE LOVES, THE(1953), art d; TAKE THE HIGH GROUND(1953), art d; TORCH SONG(1953), art d; YOUNG BESS(1953), art d; BRIGADOON(1954), art d; DEEP IN MY HEART(1954), art d; EXECUTIVE SUITE(1954), art d; LAST TIME I SAW PARIS, THE(1954), art d; LONG, LONG TRAILER, THE(1954), art d; MEN OF THE FIGHTING LADY(1954), art d; PRISONER OF WAR(1954), art d; RHAPSODY(1954), art d; ROGUE COP(1954), art d; ROSE MARIE(1954), art d; SEVEN BRIDES FOR SEVEN BROTHERS(1954), art d; BAD DAY AT BLACK ROCK(1955), art d; DIANE(1955), art d; GLASS SLIPPER, THE(1955), art d; GREEN FIRE(1955), art d; I'LL CRY TOMORROW(1955), art d; INTERRUPTED MELODY(1955), art d; IT'S ALWAYS FAIR WEATHER(1955), art d; KING'S THIEF, THE(1955), art d; KISMET(1955), art d; LOVE ME OR LEAVE ME(1955), art d; MANY RIVERS TO CROSS(1955), art d; MARAUDERS, THE(1955), art d; MOONFLEET(1955), art d; PRODIGAL, THE(1955), art d; SCARLET COAT, THE(1955), art d; TENDER TRAP, THE(1955), art d; TRIAL(1955), art d; CATERED AFFAIR, THE(1956), art d; FASTEST GUN ALIVE(1956), art d; FORBIDDEN PLANET(1956), art d; GABY(1956), art d; HIGH SOCIETY(1956), art d; INVITATION TO THE DANCE(1956), art d; LAST HUNT, THE(1956), art d; LUST FOR LIFE(1956), art d; MEET ME IN LAS VEGAS(1956), art d; OPPOSITE SEX, THE(1956), art d; RACK, THE(1956), art d; RANSOM(1956), art d; SOMEBODY UP THERE LIKES ME(1956), art d; SWAN, THE(1956), art d; THESE WILDER YEARS(1956), art d; TRIBUTE TO A BADMAN(1956), art d

Silents

BEATING THE GAME(1921), art d; INVISIBLE POWER, THE(1921), art d; MADE IN HEAVEN(1921), art d; COME ON OVER(1922), art d; GIMMIE(1923), art d; JAZZMANIA(1923), set d; HE WHO GETS SLAPPED(1924), set d; HIS HOUR(1924), art d; SNOB, THE(1924), set d; BEN-HUR(1925), set d; BIG PARADE, THE(1925), art d; BRIGHT LIGHTS(1925), set d; HIS SECRETARY(1925), set d; LADY OF THE NIGHT(1925), set d; MAN AND MAID(1925), art d; MERRY WIDOW, THE(1925), prod d; SOUL MATES(1925), set d; TOWER OF LIES, THE(1925), set d; UNHOLY THREE, THE(1925), set d; BEVERLY OF GRAUSTARK(1926), art d; BLACK BIRD, THE(1926), set d; BROWN OF HARVARD(1926), art d; EXIT SMILING(1926), set d; EXQUISITE SINNER, THE(1926), art d; FLESH AND THE DEVIL(1926), set d; LOVE'S BLINDNESS(1926), set d; MEMORY LANE(1926), set d; ROAD TO MANDALAY, THE(1926), art d; SCARLET LETTER, THE(1926), set d; TELL IT TO THE MARINES(1926), set d; TEMPTRESS, THE(1926), set d; TORRENT, THE(1926), set d; WANING SEX, THE(1926), set d; ADAM AND EVIL(1927), art d; AFTER MIDNIGHT(1927), set d; ALTARS OF DESIRE(1927), set d; ANNIE LAURIE(1927), set d; CALLAHANS AND THE MURPHYS, THE(1927), set d; CAPTAIN SALVATION(1927), set d; ENEMY, THE(1927), set d; FAIR CO-ED, THE(1927), art d; FOREIGN DEVILS(1927), art d; IN OLD KENTUCKY(1927), set d; LITTLE JOURNEY, A(1927), set d; LONDON AFTER MIDNIGHT(1927), set d; LOVE(1927), set d; LOVELORN, THE(1927), set d; MOCKERY(1927), set d; MR. WU(1927), set d; ON ZE BOULEVARD(1927), art d; QUALITY STREET(1927), set d; RED MILL, THE(1927), set d; SLIDE, KELLY, SLIDE(1927), set d; TAXI DANCER, THE(1927), set d; TEA FOR THREE(1927), set d; TILLIE THE TOILER(1927), art d; TWELVE MILES OUT(1927), set d; UNKNOWN, THE(1927), art d; ACROSS THE SINGAPORE(1928), set d; ACTRESS, THE(1928), set d; BABY MINE(1928), set d; BIG CITY, THE(1928), set d; CROWD, THE(1928), set d; DIVINE WOMAN, THE(1928), set d; EXCESS BAGGAGE(1928), set d; FOUR WALLS(1928), set d; LATEST FROM PARIS, THE(1928), set d; LAUGH, CLOWN, LAUGH(1928), set d;

MYSTERIOUS LADY, THE(1928), set d; OUR DANCING DAUGHTERS(1928), set d; SHOW PEOPLE(1928), set d; TELLING THE WORLD(1928), art d; WEST OF ZANZIBAR(1928), set d; WHILE THE CITY SLEEPS(1928), set d; WOMAN OF AFFAIRS, A(1928), art d; DUKE STEPS OUT, THE(1929), art d; FLYING FEET, THE(1929), art d; HONEYMOON(1929), art d; KISS, THE(1929), art d; MAN'S MAN, A(1929), art d; OUR MODERN MAIDENS(1929), art d; SINGLE MAN, A(1929), art d; SINGLE STANDARD, THE(1929), art d; SPITE MARRIAGE(1929), art d; TRAIL OF '98, THE(1929), art d; WHERE EAST IS EAST(1929), art d; WILD ORCHIDS(1929), art d

Cedrick Gibbons
KING SOLOMON'S MINES(1950), art d

Cedric Gibbons
STRICTLY DISHONORABLE(1951), art d; SLIGHT CASE OF LARCENY, A(1953), art d

Chris Gibbons
WILD GEESE, THE(1978, Brit.)

Edward Gibbons
COURT JESTER, THE(1956)

Edward Peter Gibbons
INVASION OF THE SAUCER MEN(1957)

Eliot Gibbons
STORM OVER THE ANDES(1935), w; FLIGHT AT MIDNIGHT(1939), w; GIVE US WINGS(1940), w; APACHE KID, THE(1941), w; DESERT BANDIT(1941), w; HONOLULU LU(1941), w; UNDER FIESTA STARS(1941), w; HIDDEN DANGER(1949), w

Elliot Gibbons
HONEYMOON DEFERRED(1940), w; FENCE RIDERS(1950), w

James Gibbons
SINNER'S HOLIDAY(1930), ed; GOD'S GIFT TO WOMEN(1931), ed; TAXI!(1932), ed; THEY CALL IT SIN(1932), ed; MIND READER, THE(1933), ed; SON OF A SAILOR(1933), ed; IN CALIENTE(1935), ed; FRESHMAN LOVE(1936), ed; GIVE ME YOUR HEART(1936), ed; SONS O' GUNS(1936), ed; GREAT O'MALLEY, THE(1937), spec eff; GREEN LIGHT(1937), ed; KID GALAHAD(1937), spec eff; MARKED WOMAN(1937), spec eff; PRINCE AND THE PAUPER, THE(1937), spec eff; SAN QUENTIN(1937), spec eff; COMET OVER BROADWAY(1938), ed; COWBOY FROM BROOKLYN(1938), ed; SERGEANT MURPHY(1938), ed; SLIGHT CASE OF MURDER, A(1938), ed; ON TRIAL(1939), ed; THEY DRIVE BY NIGHT(1940), spec eff; BULLETS FOR O'HARA(1941), ed

Jim Gibbons
SIDE SHOW(1931), ed; BLESSED EVENT(1932), ed; STREET OF WOMEN(1932), ed

Jimmy Gibbons
RECAPTURED LOVE(1930), ed; SIT TIGHT(1931), ed

Joe Gibbons
MAN WITH A GUN(1958, Brit.); TWO-WAY STRETCH(1961, Brit.); SHE KNOWS Y'KNOW(1962, Brit.); HELP!(1965, Brit.)

Mark Gibbons
SUPER VAN(1977), m

Pamela Gibbons
PUBERTY BLUES(1983, Aus.)

Paul Gibbons
WORDS AND MUSIC(1929); DANCERS IN THE DARK(1932)

Peter Gibbons
FRATERNITY ROW(1977), ph

Robert Gibbons
ONE SPY TOO MANY(1966); DOCTOR, YOU'VE GOT TO BE KIDDING(1967); VALLEY OF THE DOLLS(1967); SWEET NOVEMBER(1968)

Rodney Gibbons
MY BLOODY VALENTINE(1981, Can.), ph

Sanford Gibbons
PURSUIT OF D.B. COOPER, THE(1981)

A. Hamilton Gibbs
CHANCES(1931), w

Alan Gibbs
SAVAGE SEVEN, THE(1968); SOMETIMES A GREAT NOTION(1971); ELECTRA GLIDE IN BLUE(1973); SCORPIO(1973), stunts; MIDNIGHT MAN, THE(1974); CRAZY MAMA(1975), stunts; MITCHELL(1975); CANNONBALL(1976, U.S./Hong Kong), stunts; NICKELODEON(1976); SMOKEY AND THE BANDIT(1977), stunts

Alan R. Gibbs
MECHANIC, THE(1972), stunts
1984
CANNONBALL RUN II(1984); ICE PIRATES, THE(1984); RIVER, THE(1984), stunts

Allan Gibbs
JESUS TRIP, THE(1971); MECHANIC, THE(1972)

Angela Gibbs
CLEOPATRA JONES(1973); YOUNG NURSES, THE(1973); TOGETHER BROTHERS(1974)

Ann Gibbs
PRIVATE PARTS(1972)
1984
LIES(1984, Brit.)

Anthony Gibbs
FOR LOVE OR MONEY(1934, Brit.), w; MEN OF TOMORROW(1935, Brit.), w; ELDER BROTHER, THE(1937, Brit.), w; DR. BLOOD'S COFFIN(1961, Brit.), ed; OFFBEAT(1961, Brit.), ed; SNAKE WOMAN, THE(1961, Brit.), ed; UNSTOPPABLE MAN, THE(1961, Brit.), ed; LONELINESS OF THE LONG DISTANCE RUNNER, THE(1962, Brit.), ed; TASTE OF HONEY, A(1962, Brit.), ed; TIARA TAHITI(1962, Brit.), ed; GIRL WITH GREEN EYES(1964, Brit.), ed; LUCK OF GINGER COFFEY, THE(1964, U.S./Can.), ed; KNACK ... AND HOW TO GET IT, THE(1965, Brit.), ed; MADEMOISELLE(1966, Fr./Brit.), ed; SAILOR FROM GIBRALTAR, THE(1967, Brit.), ed; FIDDLER ON THE ROOF(1971), ed; JESUS CHRIST, SUPERSTAR(1973), ed; BLACK WINDMILL, THE(1974, Brit.), ed; ROLLERBALL(1975), ed; SAILOR WHO FELL FROM GRACE WITH THE SEA, THE(1976, Brit.), ed; BRIDGE TOO FAR, A(1977, Brit.), ed; BUTCH AND SUNDANCE: THE EARLY DAYS(1979, Brit.), ed; YESTERDAY'S HERO(1979, Brit.), ed

Antony Gibbs
DURING ONE NIGHT(1962, Brit.), ed; TOM JONES(1963, Brit.), ed; LOVED ONE, THE(1965), ed; PETULIA(1968, U.S./Brit.), ed; WALKABOUT(1971, Aus./U.S.), ed; ALL THE RIGHT NOISES(1973, Brit.), ed; RAGMAN'S DAUGHTER, THE(1974, Brit.), ed; DOGS OF WAR, THE(1980, Brit.), ed; RAGTIME(1981), ed; BAD BOYS(1983), ed

1984
DUNE(1984), ed

Archie Gibbs
U-BOAT PRISONER(1944), w

Charles Gibbs
COUNTERPLOT(1959)

David Gibbs
H.O.T.S.(1979)

Evelyn Gibbs
BUNNY LAKE IS MISSING(1965), cos; TORTURE GARDEN(1968, Brit.), cos; WUTHERING HEIGHTS(1970, Brit.), cos

Frank Gibbs
1984
HIGHPOINT(1984, Can.)

G. Gibbs
FAITHFUL CITY(1952, Israel), ph

Garrett Gibbs
FRATERNITY ROW(1977)

George Gibbs
VOLTAIRE(1933), W; WARLORDS OF ATLANTIS(1978, Brit.), spec eff; ARABIAN ADVENTURE(1979, Brit.), spec eff; FLASH GORDON(1980), spec eff
Silents
PARADISE GARDEN(1917), w; ENEMIES OF CHILDREN(1923), w

Gerald Gibbs
MEET MY SISTER(1933, Brit.), ph; SCHOONER GANG, THE(1937, Brit.), ph; SHADOWED EYES(1939, Brit.), ph; WORLD OWES ME A LIVING, THE(1944, Brit.), ph; DON CHICAGO(1945, Brit.), ph; LOYAL HEART(1946, Brit.), ph; NO ORCHIDS FOR MISS BLANDISH(1948, Brit.), ph; TIGHT LITTLE ISLAND(1949, Brit.), ph; EYE WITNESS(1950, Brit.), ph; PAPER GALLOWS(1950, Brit.), ph; PARDON MY FRENCH(1951, U.S./Fr.), ph; SECOND MRS. TANQUERAY, THE(1952, Brit.), ph; SING ALONG WITH ME(1952, Brit.), ph; BROKEN HORSESHOE, THE(1953, Brit.), ph; JOHNNY ON THE RUN(1953, Brit.), ph; OPERATION DIPLOMAT(1953, Brit.), ph; STEEL KEY, THE(1953, Brit.), ph; STRAW MAN, THE(1953, Brit.), ph; THERE WAS A YOUNG LADY(1953, Brit.), ph; BLACK 13(1954, Brit.), ph; DELAYED ACTION(1954, Brit.), ph; NIGHT OF THE FULL MOON, THE(1954, Brit.), ph; HILL 24 DOESN'T ANSWER(1955, Israel), ph; ROOM IN THE HOUSE(1955, Brit.), ph; FINGER OF GUILT(1956, Brit.), ph; AT THE STROKE OF NINE(1957, Brit.), ph; ENEMY FROM SPACE(1957, Brit.), ph; GREEN MAN, THE(1957, Brit.), ph; OPERATION CONSPIRACY(1957, Brit.), ph; SHE PLAYED WITH FIRE(1957, Brit.), ph; X THE UNKNOWN(1957, Brit.), ph; BLUE MURDER AT ST. TRINIAN'S(1958, Brit.), ph; SAFECRACKER, THE(1958, Brit.), ph; LEFT, RIGHT AND CENTRE(1959), ph; THIS OTHER EDEN(1959, Brit.), ph; TOO YOUNG TO LOVE(1960, Brit.), ph; PURE HELL OF ST. TRINIAN'S, THE(1961, Brit.), ph; BOYS, THE(1962, Brit.), ph; DEVIL'S AGENT, THE(1962, Brit.), ph; PRIZE OF ARMS, A(1962, Brit.), ph; DEVIL DOLL(1964, Brit.), ph; JOLLY BAD FELLOW, A(1964, Brit.), ph; STATION SIX-SAHARA(1964, Brit./Ger.), ph; CURSE OF THE VOODOO(1965, Brit.), ph; LEATHER BOYS, THE(1965, Brit.), ph; GREAT BRITISH TRAIN ROBBERY, THE(1967, Ger.), ph

Gerrard Gibbs
WEBSTER BOY, THE(1962, Brit.), ph

Gerry Gibbs
HOSTILE WITNESS(1968, Brit.), ph

Jill Gibbs
NO ROOM AT THE INN(1950, Brit.)

Justus Gibbs
IF HE HOLLERS, LET HIM GO(1968), spec eff; HOW TO COMMIT MARRIAGE(1969), spec eff; SOME KIND OF A NUT(1969), spec eff; 1,000 PLANE RAID, THE(1969), spec eff; THEY CALL ME MISTER TIBBS(1970), spec eff

Marla Gibbs
SWEET JESUS, PREACHER MAN(1973)

Matyelock Gibbs
VICTOR/VICTORIA(1982)
1984
SECRETS(1984, Brit.)

Michael Gibbs
EXPLOSIVE GENERATION, THE(1961)

Mike Gibbs
SECRETS(1971), m

Norman Alexander Gibbs
KISS ME GOODBYE(1982)

Philip Gibbs
DARKENED ROOMS(1929), w,Patrick Konesky

Phillip Gibbs
Silents
PARADISE(1928, Brit.), w

Phillip Hamilton Gibbs
Silents
RECKLESS LADY, THE(1926), w

Phyllis Gibbs
LORDS OF FLATBUSH, THE(1974)

R. Paton Gibbs
Silents
CONQUERED HEARTS(1918)

R. Payton Gibbs
Silents
JUNGLE, THE(1914)

R. Peyton Gibbs
Misc. Silents
HER SILENT SACRIFICE(1917)

Sir Philip Gibbs
CAPTURED(1933), w

Robert P. Gibbs
Misc. Silents
ROBINSON CRUSOE(1916)

Robert Paton Gibbs
Silents
AMAZING LOVERS(1921)

Sharyn Gibbs
STRANGERS WHEN WE MEET(1960)

Sheila Shand Gibbs
KILLER WALKS, A(1952, Brit.); GREAT GAME, THE(1953, Brit.); MR. DENNING DRIVES NORTH(1953, Brit.); HIGH AND DRY(1954, Brit.); LADY MISLAID, A(1958, Brit.); SEVEN-PER-CENT SOLUTION, THE(1977, Brit.)

Suzanne Gibbs
BLANCHE FURY(1948, Brit.); AFFAIRS OF ADELAIDE(1949, U. S./Brit); DRAGON OF PENDRAGON CASTLE, THE(1950, Brit.); MISS ROBIN HOOD(1952, Brit.); LOLITA(1962)

Tammy Gibbs
HITCHHIKERS, THE(1972)

Tony Gibbs
OSCAR WILDE(1960, Brit.), ed; BIRTHDAY PARTY, THE(1968, Brit.), ed; JUGGERNAUT(1974, Brit.), ed; F.I.S.T.(1978), ed

Jossiane Gibert
DRACULA VERSUS FRANKENSTEIN(1972, Span.)

Harry Gibey
Misc. Silents
GREAT POISON MYSTERY, THE(1914, Brit.)

Elaine Gibford
NIGHT TRAIN TO MUNDO FINE(1966)

John Gibham
1984
STUCK ON YOU(1984)

Belinda Giblin
PETERSEN(1974, Aus.); END PLAY(1975, Aus.)
Misc. Talkies
DEMOLITION(1977)

Charles Giblyn
MYSTERIOUS DR. FU MANCHU, THE(1929); WOMAN TRAP(1929); ONLY SAPS WORK(1930); PARTY GIRL(1930); PLAYBOY OF PARIS(1930); FIVE AND TEN(1931); MAID TO ORDER(1932); NIGHT WORLD(1932); PROSPERITY(1932); WHAT! NO BEER?(1933); THIS SIDE OF HEAVEN(1934)
Silents
BATTLE OF GETTYSBURG(1914), d; NOT MY SISTER(1916), d; PEGGY(1916), d; JUST FOR TONIGHT(1918), d; PECK'S BAD GIRL(1918), d; DARK MIRROR, THE(1920), d; KNOW YOUR MEN(1921), d; SINGING RIVER(1921), d; LOYAL LIVES(1923), d; PRICE OF A PARTY, THE(1924), d; ADVENTUROUS SEX, THE(1925), d; NOOSE, THE(1928)
Misc. Silents
CIVILIZATION'S CHILD(1916), d; HONOR THY NAME(1916), d; PHANTOM, THE(1916), d; SOMEWHERE IN FRANCE(1916), d; SORROWS OF LOVE, THE(1916), d; VAGABOND PRINCE, THE(1916), d; HONEYMOON, THE(1917), d; LESSON, THE(1917), d; PRICE SHE PAID, THE(1917), d; SCANDAL(1917), d; LET'S GET A DIVORCE(1918), d; PERFECT 36, A(1918), d; STUDIO GIRL, THE(1918), d; SUNSHINE NAN(1918), d; SPITE BRIDE, THE(1919), d; UPSTAIRS AND DOWN(1919), d; BLACK IS WHITE(1920), d; THIEF, THE(1920), d; TIGER'S CUB(1920), d; MOUNTAIN WOMAN, THE(1921), d; WOMAN'S WOMAN, A(1922), d; HYPOCRITES, THE(1923, Brit.), d; LEAVENWORTH CASE, THE(1923), d; LADIES BEWARE(1927), d

Gail Gibney
CITY NEWS(1983)

Sheridan Gibney
I AM A FUGITIVE FROM A CHAIN GANG(1932), w; TWO AGAINST THE WORLD(1932), w; WEEK-END MARRIAGE(1932), w; WORLD CHANGES, THE(1933), w; MASSACRE(1934), w; ANTHONY ADVERSE(1936), w; GREEN PASTURES(1936), w; STORY OF LOUIS PASTEUR, THE(1936), w; LETTER OF INTRODUCTION(1938), w; DISPUTED PASSAGE(1939), w; SOUTH OF SUEZ(1940), w; ONCE UPON A HONEYMOON(1942), w; OUR HEARTS WERE YOUNG AND GAY(1944), p, w; LOCKET, THE(1946), w

Catherine Giboyau
CHECKERBOARD(1969, Fr.), cos

Myriam Gibril
FEEDBACK(1979)

Alan Gibson
DURING ONE NIGHT(1962, Brit.); JOURNEY INTO MIDNIGHT(1968, Brit.), d; GOODBYE GEMINI(1970, Brit.), d; CRESCENDO(1972, Brit.), d; DRACULA A.D. 1972(1972, Brit.), d; CHECKERED FLAG OR CRASH(1978), d; COUNT DRACULA AND HIS VAMPIRE BRIDE(1978, Brit.), p, d
Misc. Talkies
TWO FACES OF EVIL, THE(1981, Brit.), d

Alex Gibson
1984
SUBURBIA(1984), m

Althea Gibson
HORSE SOLDIERS, THE(1959)

Amy Gibson
KING OF THE MOUNTAIN(1981)

Beau Gibson
STUNTS(1977)

Bernadette Gibson
NEXT OF KIN(1983, Aus.)

Billie Gibson
SHINING, THE(1980)

Blaine Gibson
ALICE IN WONDERLAND(1951), anim; PETER PAN(1953), anim; SLEEPING BEAUTY(1959), anim; ONE HUNDRED AND ONE DALMATIANS(1961), anim

Bob Gibson
FATTY FINN(1980, Aus.), ed

Brenda Gibson
MAFIA GIRLS, THE(1969)

Brian Gibson
BREAKING GLASS(1980, Brit.), d&w

Charles Gibson
Silents
SURE FIRE FLINT(1922), ph

Christine Gibson
OCTOPUSSY(1983, Brit.)

Colin Gibson
JOHN AND JULIE(1957, Brit.)

Curley Gibson
SINGING OUTLAW(1937); CODE OF THE SADDLE(1947)

Curly Gibson
PRAIRIE EXPRESS(1947)

Dana Gibson
SQUARE DANCE JUBILEE(1949)

Dave Gibson
1984
SILENT ONE, THE(1984, New Zealand), p

David Gibson
SCHLOCK(1973), m

Derek Gibson
JAGUAR LIVES(1979), p; DEATH SHIP(1980, Can.), p; TRIUMPHS OF A MAN CALLED HORSE(1983, US/Mex.), p
1984
BREED APART, A(1984), p

Diana Gibson
HIS NIGHT OUT(1935); DANGEROUS WATERS(1936); FLYING HOSTESS(1936); LOVE BEFORE BREAKFAST(1936); NOBODY'S FOOL(1936); TWO IN A CROWD(1936); YELLOWSTONE(1936); ADVENTURE'S END(1937); BEHIND THE HEADLINES(1937); MAN WHO FOUND HIMSELF, THE(1937); STAGE DOOR(1937); THEY WANTED TO MARRY(1937); GO CHASE YOURSELF(1938); WHEN TOMORROW COMES(1939)

Don Gibson
SATURDAY'S HERO(1951); ASSIGNMENT–PARIS(1952); OKINAWA(1952); ABOVE AND BEYOND(1953); LET'S DO IT AGAIN(1953); SEMINOLE(1953); CRIME WAVE(1954); BERMUDA AFFAIR(1956, Brit.); LOST LAGOON(1958); FROM NASHVILLE WITH MUSIC(1969)

Donna Gibson
WOMAN'S SECRET, A(1949); BEAUTY ON PARADE(1950)

E. B. Gibson
SON OF KONG(1933), spec eff

E.B. Gibson
KING KONG(1933), spec eff

Ed "Hoot" Gibson
Silents
GALLOPING KID, THE(1922)
Misc. Silents
LONE HAND, THE(1922); DEAD GAME(1923); GENTLEMAN FROM AMERICA, THE(1923)

Edmund Gibson
DARING GAME(1968), ph

Felicity Gibson
ONE BRIEF SUMMER(1971, Brit.); LADY CAROLINE LAMB(1972, Brit./Ital.)

Florence Gibson
Silents
GREED(1925); QUEEN KELLY(1929)
Misc. Silents
SAGE BRUSH HAMLET, A(1919)

Freda Gibson
HORROR HOTEL(1960, Brit.), cos

George Gibson
MAYBE IT'S LOVE(1930)

Gerrard Gibson
VIOLENT PLAYGROUND(1958, Brit.)

Gerry Gibson
SATURDAY NIGHT OUT(1964, Brit.)
1984
MICKI AND MAUDE(1984); PRODIGAL, THE(1984); RACING WITH THE MOON(1984)

Glenn Gibson
JOURNEY(1977, Can.), art d

Wing Cmdr. Guy Gibson
DAM BUSTERS, THE(1955, Brit.), w

Harriet Gibson
WHY WOULD I LIE(1980)

Harriett Gibson
HOAX, THE(1972)

Harry "The Hipster" Gibson
JUNIOR PROM(1946)

Heather Gibson
MELODY(1971, Brit.)

Helen Gibson
HUMAN TARGETS(1932); LAW AND LAWLESS(1932); KING OF THE ARENA(1933); WAY OF THE WEST, THE(1934); WHEELS OF DESTINY(1934); CYCLONE OF THE SADDLE(1935); STAGECOACH(1939); CROOKED RIVER(1950); FAST ON THE DRAW(1950); HOLLYWOOD STORY(1951); CITY THAT NEVER SLEEPS(1953); MA AND PA KETTLE AT HOME(1954); MAN WHO SHOT LIBERTY VALANCE, THE(1962)
Silents
NO MAN'S WOMAN(1921); WOLVERINE, THE(1921)
Misc. Silents
FIGHTING MAD(1917); NINE POINTS OF THE LAW(1922); THOROBRED(1922)

Henry Gibson
NUTTY PROFESSOR, THE(1963); KISS ME, STUPID(1964); OUTLAWS IS COMING, THE(1965); CHARLOTTE'S WEB(1973); LONG GOODBYE, THE(1973); NASHVILLE(1975); KENTUCKY FRIED MOVIE, THE(1977); LAST REMAKE OF BEAU GESTE, THE(1977); PERFECT COUPLE, A(1979); BLUES BROTHERS, THE(1980); HEALTH(1980); INCREDIBLE SHRINKING WOMAN, THE(1981); TULIPS(1981, Can)

Hoot Gibson
COURTIN' WILDCATS(1929), a, p; LONG, LONG TRAIL, THE(1929), a, p; CONCENTRATIN' KID, THE(1930), a, p; MOUNTED STRANGER, THE(1930), a, p; ROARING RANCH(1930), a, p; SPURS(1930), a, p; TRAILING TROUBLE(1930), a, p; TRIGGER TRICKS(1930), a, p; CLEARING THE RANGE(1931); HARD HOMBRE(1931); WILD HORSE(1931); BOILING POINT, THE(1932); GAY BUCKAROO, THE(1932); LOCAL BAD MAN(1932); MAN'S LAND, A(1932); SPIRIT OF THE WEST(1932); COWBOY COUNSELOR(1933); DUDE BANDIT, THE(1933); FIGHTING PARSON, THE(1933); POWDERSMOKE RANGE(1935); SUNSET RANGE(1935);

CAVALCADE OF THE WEST(1936); FEUD OF THE WEST(1936); FRONTIER JUSTICE(1936); LAST OUTLAW, THE(1936); LUCKY TERROR(1936); RIDING AVENGER, THE(1936); SWIFTY(1936); BLAZING GUNS(1943); LAW RIDES AGAIN, THE(1943); WILD HORSE STAMPEDE(1943); ARIZONA WHIRLWIND(1944); DEATH VALLEY RANGERS(1944); MARKED TRAILS(1944); OUTLAW TRAIL(1944); SONORA STAGECOACH(1944); WESTWARD BOUND(1944); FLIGHT TO NOWHERE(1946); MARSHAL'S DAUGHTER, THE(1953); HORSE SOLDIERS, THE(1959); OCEAN'S ELEVEN(1960)

Misc. Talkies
TRIGGER LAW(1944); UTAH KID, THE(1944)
Silents
KNIGHT OF THE RANGE, A(1916); HEADIN' SOUTH(1918); LOADED DOOR, THE(1922); RIDIN' WILD(1922); STEP ON IT!(1922); KINDLED COURAGE(1923); OUT OF LUCK(1923); SHOOTIN' FOR LOVE(1923); HOOK AND LADDER(1924); RIDE FOR YOUR LIFE(1924); SAWDUST TRAIL(1924); HURRICANE KID, THE(1925); LET 'ER BUCK(1925); SPOOK RANCH(1925); ARIZONA SWEEPSTAKES(1926); HEY! HEY! COWBOY(1927); PAINTED PONIES(1927); CLEARING THE TRAIL(1928); RAWHIDE KID, THE(1928); KING OF THE RODEO(1929), a, p; LARIAT KID, THE(1929); POINTS WEST(1929)
Misc. Silents
ACTION(1921); FIRE EATER, THE(1921); RED COURAGE(1921); SURE FIRE(1921); BEARCAT, THE(1922); HEADIN' WEST(1922); TRIMMED(1922); BLINKY(1923); DOUBLE DEALING(1923); RAMBLIN' KID, THE(1923); SINGLE HANDED(1923); THRILL CHASER, THE(1923); BROADWAY OR BUST(1924); HIT AND RUN(1924); RIDIN' KID FROM POWDER RIVER, THE(1924); 40-HORSE HAWKINS(1924); CALGARY STAMPEDE, THE(1925); SADDLE HAWK, THE(1925); TAMING OF THE WEST, THE(1925); BUCKAROO KID, THE(1926); CHIP OF THE FLYING U(1926); FLAMING FRONTIER, THE(1926); MAN IN THE SADDLE, THE(1926); PHANTOM BULLET, THE(1926); TEXAS STREAK, THE(1926); DENVER DUDE, THE(1927); GALLOPING FURY(1927); HERO ON HORSEBACK, A(1927); PRAIRIE KING, THE(1927); SILENT RIDER, THE(1927); DANGER RIDER, THE(1928); FLYIN' COWBOY, THE(1928); RIDING FOR FAME(1928); TRICK OF HEARTS, A(1928); WILD WEST SHOW, THE(1928); BURNING THE WIND(1929); SMILIN' GUNS(1929); WINGED HORSEMAN, THE(1929)

Hoot Gibson, Jr.
RAINBOW'S END(1935)
Jack Gibson
PRAIRIE EXPRESS(1947)
James Gibson
SOCIAL LION, THE(1930); MODERN HERO, A(1934), ed; KISSES FOR BREAKFAST(1941), ed; BATTLE OF THE SEXES, THE(1960, Brit.); RING OF BRIGHT WATER(1969, Brit.)
Silents
GREED(1925)
Jarriet Gibson
WORLD'S GREATEST LOVER, THE(1977)
Jim Gibson
ARIZONA KID, THE(1930)
John Gibson
RETURN OF THE LASH(1947); RUN SILENT, RUN DEEP(1958); SOMEBODY KILLED HER HUSBAND(1978); WARRIORS, THE(1979)
Judith Gibson
BOMBS OVER BURMA(1942); FLEET'S IN, THE(1942); HOLIDAY INN(1942); YOUNG AND WILLING(1943); DOUBLE INDEMNITY(1944); RETURN OF THE APE MAN(1944); STANDING ROOM ONLY(1944); SWEETHEARTS OF THE U.S.A.(1944)
Judy Gibson
JAZZ SINGER, THE(1980)
Julia Gibson
HI BEAUTIFUL(1944)
Julie Gibson
LET'S FACE IT(1943); AND THE ANGELS SING(1944); CONTENDER, THE(1944); GOING MY WAY(1944); HAIL THE CONQUERING HERO(1944); PRACTICALLY YOURS(1944); DUFFY'S TAVERN(1945); ARE YOU WITH IT?(1948); BLONDE ICE(1949); STREET OF DARKNESS(1958)
Misc. Talkies
STREET OF DARKNESS(1958)
Kathleen Gibson
HEIRLOOM MYSTERY, THE(1936, Brit.); BORN THAT WAY(1937, Brit.); CROSS MY HEART(1937, Brit.); LAST ROSE OF SUMMER, THE(1937, Brit.); MR. STRINGFELLOW SAYS NO(1937, Brit.); RIDING HIGH(1937, Brit.); HIGH COMMAND(1938, Brit.); GOOD OLD DAYS, THE(1939, Brit.)
Ken Gibson
ARTISTS AND MODELS ABROAD(1938); MAGNIFICENT DOPE, THE(1942)
Kenneth Gibson
IDLE RICH, THE(1929); WORDS AND MUSIC(1929); MADAME SATAN(1930); CLEOPATRA(1934); THIN MAN, THE(1934); DANTE'S INFERNO(1935); NEW MOON(1940); LADY EVE, THE(1941); HAIL THE CONQUERING HERO(1944); MIRACLE OF MORGAN'S CREEK, THE(1944); SAMSON AND DELILAH(1949); SUNSET BOULEVARD(1950); VICKI(1953); GARMENT JUNGLE, THE(1957); JEANNE EAGELS(1957)
Silents
BIG TOWN IDEAS(1921); ASHES OF VENGEANCE(1923)
Misc. Silents
BROAD DAYLIGHT(1922)
Kitty Gibson
1984
CAL(1984, Ireland)
Linda Gibson
TONIGHT FOR SURE(1962)
Lois Gibson
CRYPT OF THE LIVING DEAD zero(1973), w
Lorell Gibson
Silents
QUESTION, THE(1916)
Luke Gibson
JOURNEY(1977, Can.), a, m
Margaret Gibson
BONNIE PRINCE CHARLIE(1948, Brit.); NEVER A DULL MOMENT(1950); OUTRAGEOUS!(1977, Can.), w

Misc. Silents
COWARD, THE(1915); BAIT, THE(1916); HEART OF TARA, THE(1916); HIDDEN LAW, THE(1916); LEOPARD'S BRIDE, THE(1916); SOUL'S CYCLE, THE(1916)
Margaret Gibson [Patricia Palmer]
Misc. Silents
ISLAND OF DESIRE, THE(1917)
Marian Gibson
PRIVATE LESSONS(1981)
Martha Gibson
OUTRAGEOUS!(1977, Can.)
Mary Ann Gibson
SHAGGY D.A., THE(1976)
Mary Gibson
IT!(1967, Brit.), cos
Mel Gibson
MAD MAX(1979, Aus.); GALLIPOLI(1981, Aus.); TIM(1981, Aus.); ROAD WARRIOR, THE(1982, Aus.); YEAR OF LIVING DANGEROUSLY, THE(1982, Aus.)
1984
BOUNTY, THE(1984); MRS. SOFFEL(1984); RIVER, THE(1984)
Michael Gibson
ROADRACERS, THE(1959); ROSELAND(1977, m; SUMMERDOG(1977), m; COLD RIVER(1982), m
Mimi Gibson
I'LL SEE YOU IN MY DREAMS(1951); EVERYTHING I HAVE IS YOURS(1952); MY PAL GUS(1952); SLIGHT CASE OF LARCENY, A(1953); TORCH SONG(1953); EGYPTIAN, THE(1954); THERE'S NO BUSINESS LIKE SHOW BUSINESS(1954); AT GUNPOINT(1955); LAY THAT RIFLE DOWN(1955); REBEL IN TOWN(1956); STRANGE INTRUDER(1956); COURAGE OF BLACK BEAUTY(1957); DRANGO(1957); MONSTER THAT CHALLENGED THE WORLD, THE(1957); NO DOWN PAYMENT(1957); OKLAHOMAN, THE(1957); THREE FACES OF EVE, THE(1957); WINGS OF EAGLES, THE(1957); HOUSEBOAT(1958); I'LL GIVE MY LIFE(1959); REMARKABLE MR. PENNYPACKER, THE(1959); CHILDREN'S HOUR, THE(1961); ONE HUNDRED AND ONE DALMATIANS(1961); IF HE HOLLERS, LET HIM GO(1968)
Neil Gibson
DEVIL'S HARBOR(1954, Brit.)
Norman Gibson
COOLEY HIGH(1975)
Pat Gibson
OPERATION BULLSHINE(1963, Brit.)
Paulette Gibson
GETTING OVER(1981)
Misc. Talkies
REDNECK MILLER(1977)
Richard Gibson
GO-BETWEEN, THE(1971, Brit.)
Robert Gibson
OPERATION PETTICOAT(1959)
Ronnie Gibson
ON STAGE EVERYBODY(1945)
Sandy Gibson
1984
TEACHERS(1984), md
Sara Gibson
SCROOGE(1970, Brit.)
Sarah Gibson
JANE EYRE(1971, Brit.)
Sasha Gibson
Misc. Talkies
TANYA(1976)
Sonny Gibson
LOVE AND MONEY(1982)
Stephen Gibson
Misc. Talkies
BLACK LOLITA(1975), d
Sue Gibson
MOONLIGHTING WIVES(1966)
Tom Gibson
DANCE MALL HOSTESS(1933), w; CARYL OF THE MOUNTAINS(1936), w; ROMANCE RIDES THE RANGE(1936), w; SINGING COWBOY, THE(1936), w; SINGING BUCKAROO, THE(1937), d&w; CHEYENNE KID, THE(1940), w; COVERED WAGON TRAILS(1940), w; LAND OF THE SIX GUNS(1940), w; CYCLONE ON HORSEBACK(1941), w; SIX GUN GOLD(1941), w; MY FOOLISH HEART(1949); PAT AND MIKE(1952)
Silents
HIGH SPEED(1917), w; WEB OF THE LAW, THE(1923), d; PAYING THE LIMIT(1924), d&w; KID BOOTS(1926), w; LIGHTNING REPORTER(1926), w
Misc. Silents
GAME FIGHTER, A(1924), d; THREE DAYS TO LIVE(1924), d; WATERFRONT WOLVES(1924), d; MYSTERY OF THE LOST RANCH, THE(1925), d; RANGE BUZZARDS(1925), d; RECKLESS COURAGE(1925), d; STAMPEDE THUNDER(1925), d; TRIPLE ACTION(1925), d; WEST OF ARIZONA(1925), d; TEX(1926), d; BELLS OF ST. MARY'S, THE(1928, Brit.)
Tyler Gibson
JOAN OF OZARK(1942)
Victor Gibson
Silents
WEB OF THE LAW, THE(1923), w
Virginia Gibson
TEA FOR TWO(1950); GOODBYE, MY FANCY(1951); STARLIFT(1951); ABOUT FACE(1952); STOP, YOU'RE KILLING ME(1952); SHE'S BACK ON BROADWAY(1953); ATHENA(1954); SEVEN BRIDES FOR SEVEN BROTHERS(1954); I KILLED WILD BILL HICKOK(1956); FUNNY FACE(1957)
W.H. Gibson
Misc. Silents
VOLCANO, THE(1919)
Wayne Gibson
IT'S ALL OVER TOWN(1963, Brit.)

William Gibson
COBWEB, THE(1955), w; MIRACLE WORKER, THE(1962), w; TWO FOR THE SEESAW(1962), w

Wynn Gibson
HER BODYGUARD(1933)

Wynne Gibson
NOTHING BUT THE TRUTH(1929); CHILDREN OF PLEASURE(1930); FALL GUY, THE(1930); CITY STREETS(1931); GANG BUSTER, THE(1931); JUNE MOON(1931); KICK IN(1931); MAN OF THE WORLD(1931); ROAD TO RENO(1931); CASE OF CLARA DEANE, THE(1932); DEVIL IS DRIVING, THE(1932); IF I HAD A MILLION(1932); LADIES OF THE BIG HOUSE(1932); LADY AND GENT(1932); NIGHT AFTER NIGHT(1932); STRANGE CASE OF CLARA DEANE, THE(1932); TWO KINDS OF WOMEN(1932); AGGIE APPLEBY, MAKER OF MEN(1933); CRIME OF THE CENTURY, THE(1933); EMERGENCY CALL(1933); CAPTAIN HATES THE SEA, THE(1934); CROSBY CASE, THE(1934); GAMBLING(1934); I GIVE MY LOVE(1934); SLEEPERS EAST(1934); ADMIRALS ALL(1935, Brit.); ANY MAN'S WIFE(1936); COME CLOSER, FOLKS(1936); CROUCHING BEAST, THE(1936, U. S./Brit.); MICHAEL O'HALLORAN(1937); RACKETEERS IN EXILE(1937); TRAPPED BY G-MEN(1937); FLIRTING WITH FATE(1938); GANGS OF NEW YORK(1938); CAFE HOSTESS(1940); FORGOTTEN GIRLS(1940); MIRACLE ON MAIN STREET, A(1940); MY SON IS GUILTY(1940); DOUBLE CROSS(1941); MAN'S WORLD, A(1942); FALCON STRIKES BACK, THE(1943); MYSTERY BROADCAST(1943)

Ian Gibson-Smith
PASSING STRANGER, THE(1954, Brit.), p

Fulvio Gicca
SANDOKAN THE GREAT(1964, Fr./Ital./Span.), w

Judith Gick
SCHOOL FOR HUSBANDS(1939, Brit.)

Peggy Gick
PUSSYCAT ALLEY(1965, Brit.), art d; PARTY'S OVER, THE(1966, Brit.), art d; VENGEANCE OF FU MANCHU, THE(1968, Brit./Ger./Hong Kong/Ireland), art d

Darrell Giddens
WHICH WAY IS UP?(1977)

Nelson Gidding
I WANT TO LIVE!(1958), w; ONIONHEAD(1958), w; HELEN MORGAN STORY, THE(1959), w; ODDS AGAINST TOMORROW(1959), w; LISA(1962, Brit.), w; HAUNTING, THE(1963), w; NINE HOURS TO RAMA(1963, U.S./Brit.), w; LOST COMMAND, THE(1966), w; SKULLDUGGERY(1970), w; ANDROMEDA STRAIN, THE(1971), w; HINDENBURG, THE(1975), w; BEYOND THE POSEIDON ADVENTURE(1979), w

Al Giddings
SHARK'S TREASURE(1975), ph; DEEP, THE(1977), ph

Jack Giddings
Silents
OPEN ALL NIGHT(1924); NINE AND THREE-FIFTHS SECONDS(1925)
Misc. Silents
SKY'S THE LIMIT(1925)

Horton Giddy
LUCK OF A SAILOR, THE(1934, Brit.), w

Jack Giddy
GALLIPOLI(1981, Aus.)

Andre Gide
SYMPHONIE PASTORALE(1948, Fr.), w; LIFE BEGINS TOMORROW(1952, Fr.)

David Gideon
SIMON(1980)

Melville Gideon
HER FIRST AFFAIRE(1932, Brit.)

Ralph Gideon [Sheldon Reynolds]
PLACE CALLED GLORY, A(1966, Span./Ger.), d

Ray Gideon
ROCKY III(1982)

Raynold Gideon
MAN, A WOMAN, AND A BANK, A(1979, Can.), w
1984
STARMAN(1984), w

Cass Gidley
ISLAND IN THE SKY(1953)

Lela Gidley
Silents
AIN'T LOVE FUNNY?(1927), w

San Gie
WHIP'S WOMEN(1968)

Joe Gieb
MANITOU, THE(1978)

E. H. Giebler
Silents
CHASER, THE(1928), t

Robert Gieckler
RASCALS(1938)

Theresa Giehse
ANNA KARENINA(1948, Brit.); MARK OF CAIN, THE(1948, Brit.)

Therese Giehse
MAEDCHEN IN UNIFORM(1965, Ger./Fr.); BLACK MOON(1975, Fr.)

Ziggy Gieke
PUFNSTUF(1970), makeup

Michael Gielen
MOSES AND AARON(1975, Ger./Fr./Ital.), md

Gwen Bagni Gielgud
LAST WAGON, THE(1956), w

Irwin Gielgud
ABANDONED(1949), w; AMAZON QUEST(1949), w; I WAS A SHOPLIFTER(1950), w

John Gielgud
INSULT(1932, Brit.); SECRET AGENT, THE(1936, Brit.); PRIME MINISTER, THE(1941, Brit.); JULIUS CAESAR(1953); ROMEO AND JULIET(1954, Brit.); RICHARD III(1956, Brit.); BARRETTS OF WIMPOLE STREET, THE(1957); SAINT JOAN(1957); HAMLET(1964); LOVED ONE, THE(1965); CHIMES AT MIDNIGHT(1967, Span.,Switz.); ASSIGNMENT TO KILL(1968); CHARGE OF THE LIGHT BRIGADE, THE(1968, Brit.); SEBASTIAN(1968, Brit.); SHOES OF THE FISHERMAN, THE(1968); OH! WHAT A LOVELY WAR(1969, Brit.); JULIUS CAESAR(1970, Brit.); EAGLE IN A CAGE(1971, U.S./Yugo.); LOST HORIZON(1973); GOLD(1974, Brit.);

MURDER ON THE ORIENT EXPRESS(1974, Brit.); 11 HARROWHOUSE(1974, Brit.); GALILEO(1975, Brit.); ACES HIGH(1977, Brit.); JOSEPH ANDREWS(1977, Brit.); PROVIDENCE(1977, Fr.); HUMAN FACTOR, THE(1979, Brit.); ELEPHANT MAN, THE(1980, Brit.); FORMULA, THE(1980); ARTHUR(1981); CHARRIOTS OF FIRE(1981, Brit.); CONDUCTOR, THE(1981, Pol.); LION OF THE DESERT(1981, Libya/Brit.); GANDHI(1982); WAGNER(1983, Brit./Hung./Aust.); WICKED LADY, THE(1983, Brit.)
1984
SCANDALOUS(1984)
Misc. Silents
WHO IS THE MAN?(1924, Brit.)

Sir John Gielgud
HAMLET(1948, Brit.); AROUND THE WORLD IN 80 DAYS(1956); BECKET(1964, Brit.); MURDER BY DECREE(1979, Brit.); PORTRAIT OF THE ARTIST AS A YOUNG MAN, A(1979, Ireland); SPHINX(1981)

[Sir] John Gielgud
PRIEST OF LOVE(1981, Brit.)
Misc. Silents
CLUE OF THE NEW PIN, THE(1929, Brit.)

Val Gielgud
BLOCKADE(1928, Brit.); DEATH AT A BROADCAST(1934, Brit.); REGAL CAVALCADE(1935, Brit.), w; CAFE COLETTE(1937, Brit.), w; MEN ARE NOT GODS(1937, Brit.)

Val Gielgun
DEATH AT A BROADCAST(1934, Brit.), w

Stefan Gierasch
YOUNG DON'T CRY, THE(1957); HUSTLER, THE(1961); TRAVELING EXECUTIONER, THE(1970); JEREMIAH JOHNSON(1972); NEW CENTURIONS, THE(1972); WHAT'S UP, DOC?(1972); HIGH PLAINS DRIFTER(1973); CLAUDINE(1974); CORNBREAD, EARL AND ME(1975); GREAT TEXAS DYNAMITE CHASE, THE(1976); SILVER STREAK(1976); BLUE SUNSHINE(1978); CHAMP, THE(1979); BLOOD BEACH(1981)

Stefan Gierash
CARRIE(1976)

Christopher Francis Giercke
COCAINE COWBOYS(1979), p

Helene Giere
Silents
TIME TO LOVE(1927)

Fred Gierman
DEADLY GAME, THE(1941); CALLING DR. DEATH(1943); PARIS UNDERGROUND(1945); SEARCHING WIND, THE(1946)

Frederic Gierman
ONE IN A MILLION(1936)

Frederick Gierman
UNSEEN ENEMY(1942); U-BOAT PRISONER(1944); NIGHT IN CASABLANCA, A(1946)

Fred Giermann
UNDERGROUND(1941); GREAT IMPERSONATION, THE(1942); ONCE UPON A HONEYMOON(1942); EDGE OF DARKNESS(1943); HOSTAGES(1943); STRANGE DEATH OF ADOLF HITLER, THE(1943); CALCUTTA(1947); GOLDEN EARRINGS(1947)

Frederick Giermann
BEASTS OF BERLIN(1939); INTERNATIONAL SQUADRON(1941); HITLER-DEAD OR ALIVE(1942); LUCKY JORDAN(1942); CROSS OF LORRAINE, THE(1943); FIVE GRAVES TO CAIRO(1943); IMMORTAL SERGEANT, THE(1943); THEY CAME TO BLOW UP AMERICA(1943); SECRETS OF SCOTLAND YARD(1944); THEY LIVE IN FEAR(1944); UNWRITTEN CODE, THE(1944); COUNTER-ATTACK(1945)

Heinrich Gies
SHERLOCK HOLMES AND THE DEADLY NECKLACE(1962, Ger.); INVISIBLE DR. MABUSE, THE(1965, Ger.)

Sandra Gies
TICKET TO HEAVEN(1981)

Erich Giese
BERLIN ALEXANDERPLATZ(1933, Ger.), ph

J. H. Giesey
Silents
KAISER'S SHADOW, THE(1918), w

Therese Gieshe
LACOMBE, LUCIEN(1974)

Annie Giess
SERENADE FOR TWO SPIES(1966, Ital./Ger.)

J. U. Giesy
Silents
PINK TIGHTS(1920), w

James Giesy
Silents
MATRIMANIAC, THE(1916), w

C.M. Giffen
Misc. Silents
GOLDEN GODDESS, THE(1916)

F. L. Giffen
Silents
ONE-ROUND HOGAN(1927), w

Adam Gifford
FOREPLAY(1975), ph

Alan Gifford
KANGAROO KID, THE(1950, Aus./U.S.); IT STARTED IN PARADISE(1952, Brit.); LET'S MAKE UP(1955, Brit.); PRIZE OF GOLD, A(1955); IRON PETTICOAT, THE(1956, Brit.); MURDER ON APPROVAL(1956, Brit.); SATELLITE IN THE SKY(1956); HOUR OF DECISION(1957, Brit.); MAILBAG ROBBERY(1957, Brit.); CHAIN OF EVENTS(1958, Brit.); PARIS HOLIDAY(1958); SCREAMING MIMI(1958); TIME LOCK(1959, Brit.); ELECTRONIC MONSTER. THE(1960, Brit.); THREE MOVES TO FREEDOM(1960, Ger.); TOO YOUNG TO LOVE(1960, Brit.); BEWARE OF CHILDREN(1961, Brit.); BRAINWASHED(1961, Ger.); PASSPORT TO CHINA(1961, Brit.); TOWN WITHOUT PITY(1961, Ger./Switz./U.S.); ROAD TO HONG KONG, THE(1962, U.S./Brit.); WHERE THE SPIES ARE(1965, Brit.); ARRIVEDERCI, BABY!(1966, Brit.); CARRY ON COWBOY(1966, Brit.); DARK OF THE SUN(1968, Brit.); ISADORA(1968, Brit.); ONLY WHEN I LARF(1968, Brit.); 2001: A SPACE ODYSSEY(1968, U.S./Brit.); LEGEND OF NIGGER CHARLEY, THE(1972); PHASE IV(1974); RAGTIME(1981)

Allan Gifford
KING IN NEW YORK, A(1957, Brit.)
Camille Gifford
DIRTY TRICKS(1981, Can.), w
Frances Gifford
STAGE DOOR(1937); HAVING WONDERFUL TIME(1938); SKY GIANT(1938); MR. SMITH GOES TO WASHINGTON(1939); HOLD THAT WOMAN(1940); MERCY PLANE(1940); BORDER VIGILANTES(1941); LOUISIANA PURCHASE(1941); RELUCTANT DRAGON, THE(1941); WEST POINT WIDOW(1941); AMERICAN EMPIRE(1942); BEYOND THE BLUE HORIZON(1942); GLASS KEY, THE(1942); HENRY ALDRICH GETS GLAMOUR(1942); MY HEART BELONGS TO DADDY(1942); REMARKABLE ANDREW, THE(1942); STAR SPANGLED RHYTHM(1942); CRY HAVOC(1943); TARZAN TRIUMPHS(1943); MARRIAGE IS A PRIVATE AFFAIR(1944); OUR VINES HAVE TENDER GRAPES(1945); SHE WENT TO THE RACES(1945); THRILL OF A ROMANCE(1945); LITTLE MISTER JIM(1946); ARNELO AFFAIR, THE(1947); LUXURY LINER(1948); RIDING HIGH(1950); SKY COMMANDO(1953)
Frank Gifford
ALL-AMERICAN, THE(1953); UP PERISCOPE(1959); PAPER LION(1968); WORLD'S GREATEST ATHLETE, THE(1973); TWO-MINUTE WARNING(1976); VIVA KNIEVEL!(1977)
G. Adam Gifford
SLOW DANCING IN THE BIG CITY(1978)
Gloria E. Gifford
48 HOURS(1982)
Gloria Gifford
CALIFORNIA SUITE(1978); HALLOWEEN II(1981); D.C. CAB(1983); GOING BERSERK(1983)
1984
THIS IS SPINAL TAP(1984)
John Gifford
HELL AND HIGH WATER(1954)
Lillie Bea Gifford
ORDERS TO KILL(1958, Brit.)
Mary Gifford
PRIEST OF LOVE(1981, Brit.)
Mary Frances Gifford
NEW FACES OF 1937(1937)
Nick Gifford
MOUSE AND THE WOMAN, THE(1981, Brit.), ph
Ruth Gifford
MELODY RANCH(1940)
Thomas Gifford
DIRTY TRICKS(1981, Can.), w
Wendy Gifford
RECKONING, THE(1971, Brit.); MEDUSA TOUCH, THE(1978, Brit.)
1984
CHAMPIONS(1984)
Sally Gifft
DESPERATE CHARACTERS(1971), cos
Donn Gift
MAN ALIVE(1945); YEARLING, THE(1946); ENCHANTED VALLEY, THE(1948); FIGHTING FATHER DUNNE(1948); HAPPY YEARS, THE(1950)
Elaine Giftos
GAS-S-S-S!(1970); ON A CLEAR DAY YOU CAN SEE FOREVER(1970); STUDENT NURSES, THE(1970); EVERYTHING YOU ALWAYS WANTED TO KNOW ABOUT SEX, BUT WE'RE AFRAID TO ASK(1972); WRESTLER, THE(1974); PATERNITY(1981)
1984
ANGEL(1984)
Misc. Talkies
CRACKLE OF DEATH(1974)
Elio Gigante
FELLINI SATYRICON(1969, Fr./Ital.)
Marcello Gigante
EMBALMER, THE(1966, Ital.), m
Givi Gigauri
STEPCHILDREN(1962, USSR), art d
H.R. Giger
ALIEN(1979), cos
Jim Giggins
1984
MICKI AND MAUDE(1984)
Ann Giggs
DEAR, DEAD DELILAH(1972)
Benamino Gigli
NEOPOLITAN CAROUSEL(1961, Ital.)
Beniamino Gigli
FOREVER YOURS(1937, Brit.); BROKEN LOVE(1946, Ital.); LAUGH PAGLIACCI(1948, Ital.); SOHO CONSPIRACY(1951, Brit.); VOICE IN YOUR HEART, A(1952, Ital.); SINGING TAXI DRIVER(1953, Ital.)
Sabrina Gigli
JULIET OF THE SPIRITS(1965, Fr./Ital./W.Ger.)
Felix Giglio
SLEEPER(1973), md
Sandro Giglio
SATURDAY'S HERO(1951); STRICTLY DISHONORABLE(1951); WHEN WORLDS COLLIDE(1951); ASSIGNMENT-PARIS(1952); CAPTAIN PIRATE(1952); HOLIDAY FOR SINNERS(1952); SECOND CHANCE(1953); WAR OF THE WORLDS, THE(1953); HOUSE OF BAMBOO(1955); ROSE TATTOO, THE(1955); BIG BOODLE, THE(1957); FOR THE FIRST TIME(1959, U.S./Ger./Ital.); 300 SPARTANS, THE(1962)
Lupe Gigliotti
1984
BLAME IT ON RIO(1984)
Hubert Gignoux
COUSIN, COUSINE(1976, Fr.)
Regis Gignoux
BETWEEN US GIRLS(1942), w

B. Gigognini
FATHER'S DILEMMA(1952, Ital.), m
Alfonso Gil
Misc. Talkies
HERO OF OUR TIME, A(1969)
Basil Gil
MRS. DANE'S DEFENCE(1933, Brit.)
David Gil
GUESS WHAT WE LEARNED IN SCHOOL TODAY?(1970), p; JOE(1970), p; JOURNEY THROUGH ROSEBUD(1972), p
Gilbert Gil
PEPE LE MOKO(1937, Fr.); ABUSED CONFIDENCE(1938, Fr. ABUS DE CONFIANCE); HEART OF PARIS(1939, Fr.); SYMPHONIE FANTASTIQUE(1947, Fr.); FOOLISH HUSBANDS(1948, Fr.); PORTRAIT OF INNOCENCE(1948, Fr.); ROYAL AFFAIRS IN VERSAILLES(1957, Fr.); DON'T TEMPT THE DEVIL(1964, Fr./Ital.); TWO ARE GUILTY(1964, Fr.)
Jaime Camas Gil
GLASS SPHINX, THE(1968, Egypt/Ital./Span.), w
Joan Andre Gil
GUESS WHAT WE LEARNED IN SCHOOL TODAY?(1970), m
Jorge Gil
NOBODY'S PERFEKT(1981); SMOKEY AND THE BANDIT-PART 3(1983)
1984
WHERE THE BOYS ARE '84(1984)
Manolo Gil
UNSATISFIED, THE(1964, Span.)
Manuel Gil
NEXT!(1971, Ital./Span.)
Margarita Gil
BACKFIRE(1965, Fr.)
Rosemarie Gil
DEVIL WOMAN(1976, Phil.)
Vince Gil
MAD MAX(1979, Aus.)
Vincent Gil
STONE(1974, Aus.); SOLO(1978, New Zealand/Aus.); DAY AFTER HALLOWEEN, THE(1981, Aus.)
Adrian Gil-Spear
Silents
AUCTION BLOCK, THE(1917), w; POLLY OF THE CIRCUS(1917), w; LITTLE MISS HOOVER(1918), w
Nelly Gilad
FLYING MATCHMAKER, THE(1970, Israel), ed
Yvonne Gilan
AGATHA(1979, Brit.); CHARRIOTS OF FIRE(1981, Brit.); ANOTHER TIME, ANOTHER PLACE(1983, Brit.)
1984
ANOTHER TIME, ANOTHER PLACE(1984, Brit.)
Lesley Gilb
THE LADY DRACULA(1974)
Anna Gilbert
Silents
PARTNERS AGAIN(1926)
Anthony Gilbert
CANDLES AT NINE(1944, Brit.), w; MY NAME IS JULIA ROSS(1945), w; THEY MET IN THE DARK(1945, Brit.), w
1984
SILENT ONE, THE(1984, New Zealand)
Arlette Gilbert
YOUNG WORLD, A(1966, Fr./Ital.)
Ben Gilbert
1984
POWER, THE(1984)
Billy Gilbert
NOISY NEIGHBORS(1929); CHINATOWN AFTER DARK(1931); FIRST AID(1931); MILLION DOLLAR LEGS(1932); PACK UP YOUR TROUBLES(1932); SONS OF THE DESERT(1933); THIS DAY AND AGE(1933); COCKEYED CAVALIERS(1934); EVELYN PRENTICE(1934); MERRY WIDOW, THE(1934); ESCAPADE(1935); I DREAM TOO MUCH(1935); MAD LOVE(1935); MILLIONS IN THE AIR(1935); NIGHT AT THE OPERA, A(1935); BIG GAME, THE(1936); BRIDE WALKS OUT, THE(1936); DANGEROUS WATERS(1936); DEVIL DOLL, THE(1936); EARLY TO BED(1936); GRAND JURY(1936); KELLY THE SECOND(1936); LOVE ON A BET(1936); LOVE ON THE RUN(1936); NIGHT WAITRESS(1936); ONE RAINY AFTERNOON(1936); SUTTER'S GOLD(1936); THREE OF A KIND(1936); BROADWAY MELODY OF '38(1937); CAPTAINS COURAGEOUS(1937); CHINA PASSAGE(1937); FIGHT FOR YOUR LADY(1937); FIREFLY, THE(1937); LIFE OF THE PARTY, THE(1937); LIVE, LOVE AND LEARN(1937); MAN WHO FOUND HIMSELF, THE(1937); MAYTIME(1937); MUSIC FOR MADAME(1937); ON THE AVENUE(1937); OUTCASTS OF POKER FLAT, THE(1937); ROSALIE(1937); SEA DEVILS(1937); SNOW WHITE AND THE SEVEN DWARFS(1937); TOAST OF NEW YORK, THE(1937); WE'RE ON THE JURY(1937); WHEN YOU'RE IN LOVE(1937); 100 MEN AND A GIRL(1937); ARMY GIRL(1938); BLOCKHEADS(1938); BREAKING THE ICE(1938); GIRL DOWNSTAIRS, THE(1938); HAPPY LANDING(1938); JOY OF LIVING(1938); MAID'S NIGHT OUT(1938); MR. DOODLE KICKS OFF(1938); MY LUCKY STAR(1938); PECK'S BAD BOY WITH THE CIRCUS(1938); SHE'S GOT EVERYTHING(1938); DESTRY RIDES AGAIN(1939); FORGED PASSPORT(1939); MILLION DOLLAR LEGS(1939); RIO(1939); STAR MAKER, THE(1939); UNDER-PUP, THE(1939); CROSS COUNTRY ROMANCE(1940); GREAT DICTATOR, THE(1940); HIS GIRL FRIDAY(1940); LITTLE BIT OF HEAVEN, A(1940); LUCKY PARTNERS(1940); NIGHT AT EARL CARROLL'S, A(1940); NO, NO NANETTE(1940); QUEEN OF THE MOB(1940); SAFARI(1940); SANDY IS A LADY(1940); SCATTERBRAIN(1940); SEVEN SINNERS(1940); SING, DANCE, PLENTY HOT(1940); TIN PAN ALLEY(1940); VILLAIN STILL PURSUED HER, THE(1940); WOMEN IN WAR(1940); ANGELS WITH BROKEN WINGS(1941); MODEL WIFE(1941); NEW WINE(1941); ONE NIGHT IN LISBON(1941); REACHING FOR THE SUN(1941); WEEKEND IN HAVANA(1941); ARABIAN NIGHTS(1942); MR. WISE GUY(1942); SLEEPYTIME GAL(1942); SONG OF THE ISLANDS(1942); VALLEY OF THE SUN(1942); ALWAYS A BRIDESMAID(1943); CRAZY HOUSE(1943); SHANTYTOWN(1943); SPOTLIGHT SCANDALS(1943); STAGE DOOR CANTEEN(1943); CRAZY KNIGHTS(1944); EVER SINCE VENUS(1944); ANCHORS AWEIGH(1945); FUN AND FANCY FREE(1947); KISSING BANDIT, THE(1948); BRIDE OF VEN-

GEANCE(1949); DOWN AMONG THE SHELTERING PALMS(1953); FIVE WEEKS IN A BALLOON(1962); PARADISE ALLEY(1962)
Misc. Talkies
THREE OF A KIND(1944); TROUBLE CHASERS(1945)
Bob Gilbert
NEVER THE TWAIN SHALL MEET(1931); KID FROM GOWER GULCH, THE(1949); RED ROCK OUTLAW(1950); SILVER BANDIT, THE(1950); PARSON AND THE OUTLAW, THE(1957)
Bobby Gilbert
I WAS A COMMUNIST FOR THE F.B.I.(1951)
Boyd Gilbert
FIREFLY, THE(1937)
Bruce Gilbert
NINE TO FIVE(1980), p; ON GOLDEN POND(1981), p; ROLLOVER(1981), p
Buddy Gilbert
EDDIE MACON'S RUN(1983); TERMS OF ENDEARMENT(1983)
Carole Gilbert
SWAMP COUNTRY(1966)
Carolyn Gilbert
INCREDIBLE TWO-HEADED TRANSPLANT, THE(1971)
Charles Gilbert
HILLS OF DONEGAL, THE(1947, Brit.), art d; WHEN YOU COME HOME(1947, Brit.), art d; NO PLACE FOR JENNIFER(1950, Brit.), art d
Cindy Gilbert
PERSONAL BEST(1982)
Colin Gilbert
BIG RED ONE, THE(1980); LITTLE MISS MARKER(1980)
Connie Gilbert
1984
UTU(1984, New Zealand)
Dave Gilbert
PURSUIT OF D.B. COOPER, THE(1981)
David Gilbert
1984
BEAT STREET(1984), w
Denise Gilbert
CYCLE SAVAGES(1969)
Dennis Gilbert
CIRCUS BOY(1947, Brit.)
Dick Gilbert
PARDON US(1931); PACK UP YOUR TROUBLES(1932); DEVIL'S BROTHER, THE(1933); OUR RELATIONS(1936); DISC JOCKEY(1951)
Doris Gilbert
ATLANTIC CITY(1944), w; LADIES COURAGEOUS(1944), w; LAKE PLACID SERENADE(1944), w; STORM OVER LISBON(1944), w; LITTLE EGYPT(1951), w; GERALDINE(1953), w
Earle Gilbert
NAKED CITY, THE(1948)
Ed Gilbert
36 HOURS(1965)
Edmund Gilbert
JOHNNY GOT HIS GUN(1971); HOWZER(1973)
Edwin Gilbert
BLUES IN THE NIGHT(1941), w; ALL THROUGH THE NIGHT(1942), w; LARCENY, INC.(1942), w; MY WILD IRISH ROSE(1947), w
Elizabeth Gilbert
PAUL TEMPLE RETURNS(1952, Brit.)
Ella Gilbert
Misc. Silents
BIRDS' CHRISTMAS CAROL, THE(1917)
Ellen Gilbert
TARGET: HARRY(1980)
Eugenia Gilbert
COURTIN' WILDCATS(1929)
Silents
BACK TRAIL, THE(1924); HAIR TRIGGER BAXTER(1926); VALLEY OF BRAVERY, THE(1926); BY WHOSE HAND?(1927); MAN FROM HARDPAN, THE(1927); SWELLHEAD, THE(1927); AFTER THE STORM(1928); APACHE RAIDER, THE(1928)
Misc. Silents
WILDCAT JORDAN(1922); SOULS IN BONDAGE(1923); LADDIE(1926); TRANSCONTINENTAL LIMITED(1926); BORDER BLACKBIRDS(1927); DON DESPERADO(1927); LONG LOOP ON THE PECOS, THE(1927); DANGER RIDER, THE(1928); PHANTOM CITY, THE(1928)
Eugenie Gilbert
Misc. Silents
BEYOND THE ROCKIES(1926); MAN FROM THE WEST, THE(1926); TEST OF DONALD NORTON, THE(1926)
F. S. Gilbert
CANNABIS(1970, Fr.), w
Faith Gilbert
1,000 SHAPES OF A FEMALE(1963)
Fernando Gilbert
MADIGAN'S MILLIONS(1970, Span./Ital)
Florence Gilbert
Silents
HILLS OF MISSING MEN(1922); SPAWN OF THE DESERT(1923); LASH OF THE WHIP(1924); DESERT'S PRICE, THE(1926); JOHNSTOWN FLOOD, THE(1926); MAN FOUR-SQUARE, A(1926); RETURN OF PETER GRIMM, THE(1926); LOVE MAKES 'EM WILD(1927)
Misc. Silents
GUN SHY(1922); SHERIFF OF SUN-DOG, THE(1922); CUPID'S RUSTLER(1924); DIAMOND BANDIT, THE(1924); RODEO MIXUP, A(1924); WESTERN FEUDS(1924); WESTERN YESTERDAYS(1924)
Fran Gilbert
BUFFALO BILL RIDES AGAIN(1947), w
Franklin Gilbert
LIGHTHOUSE(1947), p

Fred Gilbert
TWO(1975)
George Gilbert
JULIUS CAESAR(1952)
Gerard Gilbert
COUNTERFEITERS, THE(1948)
Gloria Gilbert
VOGUES OF 1938(1937)
Helen Gilbert
ANDY HARDY GETS SPRING FEVER(1939); SECRET OF DR. KILDARE, THE(1939); FLORIAN(1940); BEYOND THE BLUE HORIZON(1942); FALCON TAKES OVER, THE(1942); ISLE OF MISSING MEN(1942); MEET ME IN ST. LOUIS(1944); MUSIC FOR MILLIONS(1944); DEATH VALLEY(1946); GOD'S COUNTRY(1946); GIRLS IN PRISON(1956)
Misc. Talkies
THREE OF A KIND(1944)
Henrietta Gilbert
Silents
ETERNAL SIN, THE(1917)
Henry Gilbert
LONG JOHN SILVER(1954, Aus.); LAND OF FURY(1955 Brit.); RETURN OF MR. MOTO, THE(1965, Brit.); REVOLUTIONARY, THE(1970, Brit.); SONG OF NORWAY(1970); GET CHARLIE TULLY(1976, Brit.)
Henry F. Gilbert
Silents
DOWN TO THE SEA IN SHIPS(1923), m
Herschel Gilbert
OPEN SECRET(1948), m, md; SHAMROCK HILL(1949), md
Herschel Burke Gilbert
THERE'S A GIRL IN MY HEART(1949), m; THREE HUSBANDS(1950), m; HIGHWAYMAN, THE(1951), m; MAGIC FACE, THE(1951, Aust.), m; SCARF, THE(1951), m; KID MONK BARONI(1952), m; MODELS, INC.(1952), md; NO TIME FOR FLOWERS(1952), m; RING, THE(1952), m; THIEF, THE(1952), m; WITHOUT WARNING(1952), m; MOON IS BLUE, THE(1953), m; PROJECT MOONBASE(1953), m; SABRE JET(1953), m; VICE SQUAD(1953), m, md; CARMEN JONES(1954), m; RIOT IN CELL BLOCK 11(1954), m; WITNESS TO MURDER(1954), m; NAKED DAWN, THE(1955), m, md; BEYOND A REASONABLE DOUBT(1956), m; BOLD AND THE BRAVE, THE(1956), m; COMANCHE(1956), m; NAKED HILLS, THE(1956), m&md; NIGHTMARE(1956), m; NO PLACE TO HIDE(1956), m, md; WHILE THE CITY SLEEPS(1956), m; CRIME AND PUNISHMENT, U.S.A.(1959), m; GERONIMO(1962), md; SAM WHISKEY(1969), m; SECRET OF THE SACRED FOREST, THE(1970), m; I DISMEMBER MAMA(1974), m
Herschel "Burke" Gilbert
MR. DISTRICT ATTORNEY(1946), m
Hylda Gilbert
SEVENTH DAWN, THE(1964), cos
Irene Gilbert
SHAKE HANDS WITH THE DEVIL(1959, Ireland), cos
J. Charles Gilbert
ONCE IN A BLUE MOON(1936)
J. Gilbert
LOVE BOUND(1932), w
Jack Gilbert
Silents
APOSTLE OF VENGEANCE, THE(1916); DARK ROAD, THE(1917); DEVIL DODGER, THE(1917); HATER OF MEN(1917); NANCY COMES HOME(1918); SHOULD A WOMAN TELL?(1920); LOVE'S PENALTY(1921), d&w
Misc. Silents
MOTHER INSTINCT, THE(1917); PRINCESS OF THE DARK, A(1917); UP OR DOWN(1917); DAWN OF UNDERSTANDING, THE(1918); SHACKLED(1918); BUSHER, THE(1919); MAN BENEATH, THE(1919); RED VIPER, THE(1919); DEEP WATERS(1920); WHITE CIRCLE, THE(1920); WHILE PARIS SLEEPS(1923)
Jack [John] Gilbert
Silents
EYE OF THE NIGHT, THE(1916)
Misc. Silents
SHELL FORTY-THREE(1916); CALVERT'S VALLEY(1922)
James Gilbert
FORBIDDEN CARGO(1954, Brit.); SCOTCH ON THE ROCKS(1954, Brit.); SUNSTRUCK(1973, Aus.), d
Jane Gilbert
INVISIBLE STRIPES(1940); 'TIL WE MEET AGAIN(1940)
Jean Gilbert
GIRL IN THE TAXI(1937, Brit.), m
Jimmy Gilbert
POLICE DOG(1955, Brit.)
Jo Gilbert
OVER 21(1945); HURRICANE ISLAND(1951); MAGIC CARPET, THE(1951); PEOPLE WILL TALK(1951); TOO YOUNG TO KISS(1951); GIRL IN WHITE, THE(1952); NEVER WAVE AT A WAC(1952); JULIUS CAESAR(1953); FRENCH LINE, THE(1954); GOOD MORNING, MISS DOVE(1955); PRODIGAL, THE(1955); ON THE THRESHOLD OF SPACE(1956); OPPOSITE SEX, THE(1956); BIG FISHERMAN, THE(1959)
Joanne Gilbert
HOUDINI(1953); RED GARTERS(1954); GREAT MAN, THE(1957); RIDE OUT FOR REVENGE(1957); HIGH COST OF LOVING, THE(1958)
Jody Gilbert
SERGEANT YORK(; CONFESSION(1937); CHASING DANGER(1939); EVERYTHING HAPPENS AT NIGHT(1939); NEW FRONTIER(1939); NINOTCHKA(1939); FLOWING GOLD(1940); HUDSON'S BAY(1940); LITTLE OLD NEW YORK(1940); STAR DUST(1940); HELLZAPOPPIN'(1941); NEVER GIVE A SUCKER AN EVEN BREAK(1941); REMEMBER THE DAY(1941); SHADOW OF THE THIN MAN(1941); WILD GEESE CALLING(1941); AFFAIRS OF MARTHA, THE(1942); HARD WAY, THE(1942); JOURNEY FOR MARGARET(1942); REUNION IN FRANCE(1942); RIDE 'EM COWBOY(1942); TUTTLES OF TAHITI(1942); HERS TO HOLD(1943); PRINCESS O'ROURKE(1943); LOST IN A HAREM(1944); MARRIAGE IS A PRIVATE AFFAIR(1944); TOGETHER AGAIN(1944); CHRISTMAS IN CONNECTICUT(1945); HOLD THAT BLONDE(1945); ROUGHLY SPEAKING(1945); CROSS MY HEART(1946); DEADLINE FOR MURDER(1946); DECOY(1946); SHOW-OFF, THE(1946); BLONDIE'S HOLIDAY(1947); ALBUQUERQUE(1948); ARE YOU WITH IT?(1948); BUNGALOW 13(1948); CASBAH(1948); MY DEAR SECRETARY(1948);

PALEFACE, THE(1948); SHAGGY(1948); TEXAS, BROOKLYN AND HEAVEN(1948); HELLFIRE(1949); KNOCK ON ANY DOOR(1949); LOVABLE CHEAT, THE(1949); ONE LAST FLING(1949); BLONDE BANDIT, THE(1950); BLONDE DYNAMITE(1950); HOUSE BY THE RIVER(1950); GENE AUTRY AND THE MOUNTIES(1951); ACTORS AND SIN(1952); SOMETHING TO LIVE FOR(1952); HOUDINI(1953); BUTCH CASSIDY AND THE SUNDANCE KID(1969); WILLARD(1971)

Jody S. Gilbert
SEVENTEEN(1940)

Joe Gilbert
NAZI AGENT(1942); JANIE(1944); DEAD RECKONING(1947); EVERYBODY DOES IT(1949); JOLSON SINGS AGAIN(1949); LAS VEGAS STORY, THE(1952); JAWS 3-D(1983)

John Gilbert
HIS GLORIOUS NIGHT(1929); REDEMPTION(1930); WAY FOR A SAILOR(1930); GENTLEMAN'S FATE(1931); PHANTOM OF PARIS, THE(1931); WEST OF BROADWAY(1931); DOWNSTAIRS(1932), a, w; FAST WORKERS(1933); QUEEN CHRISTINA(1933); CAPTAIN HATES THE SEA, THE(1934); MARCH HARE, THE(1956, Brit.); RABID(1976, Can.)
Silents
HELL'S HINGES(1916); MORE TROUBLE(1918); BAIT, THE(1921), w; SHAME(1921); ARABIAN LOVE(1922); CALIFORNIA ROMANCE, A(1922); GLEAM O'-DAWN(1922); LOVE GAMBLER, THE(1922); YELLOW STAIN, THE(1922); EXILES, THE(1923); MADNESS OF YOUTH(1923); ST. ELMO(1923); HE WHO GETS SLAPPED(1924); HIS HOUR(1924); JUST OFF BROADWAY(1924); MARRIED FLIRTS(1924); ROMANCE RANCH(1924); SNOB, THE(1924); BIG PARADE, THE(1925); MERRY WIDOW, THE(1925); FLESH AND THE DEVIL(1926); LOVE(1927); TWELVE MILES OUT(1927); FOUR WALLS(1928); SHOW PEOPLE(1928); WOMAN OF AFFAIRS, A(1928); MAN'S MAN, A(1929)
Misc. Silents
MASK, THE(1918); THREE X GORDON(1918); WEDLOCK(1918); HONOR FIRST(1922); MONTE CRISTO(1922); CAMEO KIRBY(1923); TRUXTON KING(1923); LONE CHANCE, THE(1924); MAN'S MATE, A(1924); WIFE OF THE CENTAUR(1924); WOLF MAN, THE(1924); BARDELYS THE MAGNIFICENT(1926); LA BOHEME(1926); MAN, WOMAN AND SIN(1927); SHOW, THE(1927); COSSACKS, THE(1928); MASKS OF THE DEVIL, THE(1928); DESERT NIGHTS(1929)

Johnny Gilbert
GIDGET GOES HAWAIIAN(1961)

Joseph Gilbert
TATTERED DRESS, THE(1957)

June Gilbert
10 TO MIDNIGHT(1983)

L.W. Gilbert
THIS DAY AND AGE(1933), m

L. Wolfe Gilbert
MARRIAGE BY CONTRACT(1928), m/l; LOVE, LIVE AND LAUGH(1929), m/l; TUCSON(1949), m/l "Nobody's Lost on the Lonesome Trail," "Ringin' the New Year In," I.B. Kornblum

Lauren Gilbert
CLOSE-UP(1948); FROM THE TERRACE(1960); GIRL OF THE NIGHT(1960); X-15(1961); UNSINKABLE MOLLY BROWN, THE(1964); FORTUNE COOKIE, THE(1966); WESTWORLD(1973)

Leatrice Gilbert
GUY NAMED JOE, A(1943)

Leatrice Joy Gilbert
OF HUMAN HEARTS(1938)

Lee Gilbert
GUN FEVER(1958), ed; NAVAJO RUN(1966), ed

Lewis Gilbert
DICK TURPIN(1933, Brit.); OVER THE MOON(1940, Brit.); MARRY ME!(1949, Brit.), w; LITTLE BALLERINA, THE(1951, Brit.), d, w; SCARLET THREAD(1951, Brit.), d; ONCE A SINNER(1952, Brit.), d; ALBERT, R.N.(1953, Brit.), d; HUNDRED HOUR HUNT(1953, Brit.), d, w; JOHNNY ON THE RUN(1953, Brit.), d; SLASHER, THE(1953, Brit.), d, w; TIME GENTLEMEN PLEASE!(1953, Brit.), d; GOOD DIE YOUNG, THE(1954, Brit.), d, w; SEA SHALL NOT HAVE THEM, THE(1955, Brit.), d, w; ADMIRABLE CRICHTON, THE(1957, Brit.), d; REACH FOR THE SKY(1957, Brit.), d, w; CARVE HER NAME WITH PRIDE(1958, Brit.), d, w; CAST A DARK SHADOW(1958, Brit.), d; CRY FROM THE STREET, A(1959, Brit.), d; FERRY TO HONG KONG(1959, Brit.), d&w; LIGHT UP THE SKY(1960, Brit.), p&d; SINK THE BISMARCK!(1960, Brit.), d; LOSS OF INNOCENCE(1961, Brit.), d; DAMN THE DEFIANT!(1962, Brit.), d; EMERGENCY(1962, Brit.), w; SEVENTH DAWN, THE(1964), d; ALFIE(1966, Brit.), p&d; YOU ONLY LIVE TWICE(1967, Brit.), d; ADVENTURERS, THE(1970), p&d, w; FRIENDS(1971, Brit.), p&d, w; PAUL AND MICHELLE(1974, Fr./Brit.), p&d, w; OPERATION DAYBREAK(1976, U.S./Brit./Czech.), d; SEVEN NIGHTS IN JAPAN(1976, Brit./Fr.), p&d; SPY WHO LOVED ME, THE(1977, Brit.), d; MOONRAKER(1979, Brit.), d; EDUCATING RITA(1983), p&d
Silents
MARCH HARE, THE(1919, Brit.); DEBT OF HONOR(1922, Brit.); WHEN GREEK MEETS GREEK(1922, Brit.); MONEY ISN'T EVERYTHING(1925, Brit.)
Misc. Silents
BOOTLE'S BABY(1914, Brit.); FOLLY OF DESIRE, THE OR THE SHULAMITE(1916); GWYNETH OF THE WELSH HILLS(1921, Brit.); HOUND OF THE BASKERVILLES, THE(1921, Brit.); WAS SHE JUSTIFIED?(1922, Brit.); CHAPPY - THAT'S ALL(1924, Brit.)

Loren Gilbert
HOOTENANNY HOOT(1963)

Lou Gilbert
VIVA ZAPATA!(1952); STREET OF SINNERS(1957); MIDDLE OF THE NIGHT(1959); REQUIEM FOR A HEAVYWEIGHT(1962); GOLDSTEIN(1964); ACROSS THE RIVER(1965); JULIET OF THE SPIRITS(1965, Fr./Ital./W.Ger.); FEARLESS FRANK(1967); PETULIA(1968, U.S./Brit.); GREAT WHITE HOPE, THE(1970); GOING HOME(1971); JENNIFER ON MY MIND(1971); MARATHON MAN(1976); LAST EMBRACE(1979); ON THE NICKEL(1980)

Maud Gilbert
Misc. Silents
SAMSON(1915)

Maude Gilbert
Misc. Silents
FOOL'S REVENGE, THE(1916)

Melissa Gilbert
NUTCRACKER FANTASY(1979)

Mercedes Gilbert
Misc. Silents
BODY AND SOUL(1925)

Michael Francis Gilbert
UNSTOPPABLE MAN, THE(1961, Brit.), w

Michael Gilbert
GUILTY?(1956, Brit.), w; BREAKOUT(1960, Brit.), w

Michel Gilbert
FORTUNE AND MEN'S EYES(1971, U.S./Can.)

Mickey Gilbert
SOMETIMES A GREAT NOTION(1971); POCKET MONEY(1972); ROOSTER COGBURN(1975); RETURN OF A MAN CALLED HORSE, THE(1976), stunts; SILVER STREAK(1976), stunts; FIRE SALE(1977), a, stunts; WORLD'S GREATEST LOVER, THE(1977), stunts; OUR WINNING SEASON(1978), stunts; APPLE DUMPLING GANG RIDES AGAIN, THE(1979); PRISONER OF ZENDA, THE(1979); PROMISE, THE(1979)

Neva Gilbert
COMBAT SQUAD(1953)

Nicholas Gilbert
1984
NEVERENDING STORY, THE(1984, Ger.)

Nina Gilbert
EVERY NIGHT AT EIGHT(1935); SERVICE DE LUXE(1938); DOUBLE LIFE, A(1947); NIGHTMARE ALLEY(1947)

O.P. Gilbert
HATRED(1941, Fr.), w

Olive Gilbert
DANCING YEARS, THE(1950, Brit.)

Oscar Paul Gilbert
SHANGHAI DRAMA, THE(1945, Fr.), w

Pat Gilbert
SING AND SWING(1964, Brit.)

Patti Gilbert
PHANTOM TOLLBOOTH, THE(1970)

Paul Gilbert
YOU CAN'T RUN AWAY FROM IT(1956); SO THIS IS PARIS(1954); SECOND GREATEST SEX, THE(1955); THREE NUTS IN SEARCH OF A BOLT(1964); CAT BALLOU(1965); SYLVIA(1965); WOMEN OF THE PREHISTORIC PLANET(1966)

Philip Gilbert
MAN OF THE MOMENT(1955, Brit.); SIMON AND LAURA(1956, Brit.); ACCOUNT RENDERED(1957, Brit.); CHECKPOINT(1957, Brit.); ROCK YOU SINNERS(1957, Brit.); BACHELOR OF HEARTS(1958, Brit.); DENTIST IN THE CHAIR(1960, Brit.); SINGER NOT THE SONG, THE(1961, Brit.); DIE, DIE, MY DARLING(1965, Brit.); FROZEN DEAD, THE(1967, Brit.); BLOOD AND LACE(1971), d; SUPERMAN III(1983)

Raye Gilbert
GEORGE WASHINGTON CARVER(1940)

Renee Gilbert
CAESAR AND CLEOPATRA(1946, Brit.)

Richard Gilbert
LOVE IN WAITING(1948, Brit.)

Robert Gilbert
WANDERING JEW, THE(1935, Brit.); MELODY OF MY HEART(1936, Brit.); PARIS AFTER DARK(1943); SONG OF THE SIERRAS(1946); INTRIGUE(1947); PARSON AND THE OUTLAW, THE(1957), p

Robert L. Gilbert
RAINBOW OVER THE ROCKIES(1947)

Ronnie Gilbert
DANGER WOMAN(1946); ISADORA(1968, Brit.); WINDFLOWERS(1968)

Ruth Gilbert
Misc. Talkies
ALICE IN WONDERLAND(1931)

Sky Gilbert
1984
LISTEN TO THE CITY(1984, Can.)

Stanley Gilbert
UP IN ARMS(1944)

Stephen Gilbert
WILLARD(1971), w

Steve Gilbert
PAUL AND MICHELLE(1974, Fr./Brit.)

Stuart Gilbert
PEARLS OF THE CROWN(1938, Fr.), titles

Sydney Gilbert
STEEL(1980), cos

Terry Gilbert
SUMMER HOLIDAY(1963, Brit.); WOMEN IN LOVE(1969, Brit.), ch; BOY FRIEND, THE(1971, Brit.), ch; MUSIC LOVERS, THE(1971, Brit.), ch; HENRY VIII AND HIS SIX WIVES(1972, Brit.), ch
1984
BOUNTY, THE(1984), ch

Victor Gilbert
Silents
SHAMS OF SOCIETY(1921)

W. S. Gilbert
MIKADO, THE(1939, Brit.), w; COOL MIKADO, THE(1963, Brit.), w

Walter Gilbert
SHE'S MY WEAKNESS(1930); GAMBLING(1934); BIRTH OF A BABY(1938); DYNAMITE DELANEY(1938)

William Gilbert
ESPIONAGE(1937)

William Schwenk Gilbert
MIKADO, THE(1967, Brit.), w

Sir William Gilbert
PIRATE MOVIE, THE(1982, Aus.), w; PIRATES OF PENZANCE, THE(1983), w

Willie Gilbert
HOW TO SUCCEED IN BUSINESS WITHOUT REALLY TRYING(1976), w

Yves Gilbert
BIQUEFARRE(1983, Fr.), m
Yvonne Gilbert
TWO THOUSAND MANIACS!(1964)
Anthony Gilberti
NUNZIO(1978)
Jennifer Gilberti
NUNZIO(1978)
Astrud Gilberto
GET YOURSELF A COLLEGE GIRL(1964)
Harry Gilbey
Silents
RAGGED MESSENGER, THE(1917, Brit.); ADVENTURES OF MR. PICKWICK, THE(1921, Brit.)
Misc. Silents
DEAD HEART, THE(1914, Brit.); AFTER DARK(1915, Brit.); PRODIGAL DAUGHTER, THE(1916, Brit.); BROKEN THREADS(1917, Brit.); MAN BEHIND "THE TIMES", THE(1917, Brit.); SYBIL(1921, Brit.)
James Gilbey
UNSUITABLE JOB FOR A WOMAN, AN(1982, Brit.)
Sheelagh Gilbey
HAUNTING OF M, THE(1979)
Iver Gilborn
PULP(1972, Brit.)
Steve Gilborn
1984
VAMPING(1984)
Ivan Gilborne
WILD, WILD PLANET, THE(1967, Ital.)
Bob Gilbreath
JET ATTACK(1958)
John Gilbreath
WITHOUT RESERVATIONS(1946); THERE GOES KELLY(1945); GOLDEN EARRINGS(1947)
Jon Gilbreath
THEY WERE EXPENDABLE(1945); O.S.S.(1946); RENDEZVOUS 24(1946); SEARCHING WIND, THE(1946)
Robert Gilbreath
OCEAN'S ELEVEN(1960)
Frank B. Gilbreth, Jr.
CHEAPER BY THE DOZEN(1950), w; BELLES ON THEIR TOES(1952), w
George Gilbreth
DEVIL'S HAIRPIN, THE(1957)
Jack Gilbreth
WIZARD OF GORE, THE(1970)
Phil Gilbreth
ZAPPED!(1982)
Jay Gilbuena
EAST OF JAVA(1935)
William Gilcher
BIQUEFARRE(1983, Fr.), p
Anne Gilchrist
SLEEPING CAR TO TRIESTE(1949, Brit.); WHAT A WHOPPER(1961, Brit.)
Bruce Gilchrist
DEMENTED(1980)
Connie Gilchrist
HULLABALOO(1940); BARNACLE BILL(1941); DOWN IN SAN DIEGO(1941); DR. KILDARE'S WEDDING DAY(1941); H.M. PULHAM, ESQ.(1941); MARRIED BACHELOR(1941); TWO-FACED WOMAN(1941); WILD MAN OF BORNEO, THE(1941); WOMAN'S FACE(1941); APACHE TRAIL(1942); GRAND CENTRAL MURDER(1942); JOHNNY EAGER(1942); SUNDAY PUNCH(1942); THIS TIME FOR KEEPS(1942); TORTILLA FLAT(1942); WAR AGAINST MRS. HADLEY, THE(1942); WE WERE DANCING(1942); WOMAN OF THE YEAR(1942); CRY HAVOC(1943); HEAVENLY BODY, THE(1943); HUMAN COMEDY, THE(1943); PRESENTING LILY MARS(1943); SWING SHIFT MAISIE(1943); THOUSANDS CHEER(1943); MUSIC FOR MILLIONS(1944); NOTHING BUT TROUBLE(1944); RATIONING(1944); SEE HERE, PRIVATE HARGROVE(1944); THIN MAN GOES HOME, THE(1944); JUNIOR MISS(1945); VALLEY OF DECISION, THE(1945); BAD BASCOMB(1946); FAITHFUL IN MY FASHION(1946); YOUNG WIDOW(1946); GOOD NEWS(1947); HUCKSTERS, THE(1947); SONG OF THE THIN MAN(1947); BIG CITY(1948); CHICKEN EVERY SUNDAY(1948); LETTER TO THREE WIVES, A(1948); LUXURY LINER(1948); TENTH AVENUE ANGEL(1948); ACT OF VIOLENCE(1949); LITTLE WOMEN(1949); STORY OF MOLLY X, THE(1949); BUCCANEER'S GIRL(1950); KILLER THAT STALKED NEW YORK, THE(1950); LOUISA(1950); PEGGY(1950); STARS IN MY CROWN(1950); TICKET TO TOMAHAWK(1950); TRIPOLI(1950); UNDERCOVER GIRL(1950); CHAIN OF CIRCUMSTANCE(1951); HERE COMES THE GROOM(1951); THUNDER ON THE HILL(1951); FLESH AND FURY(1952); HALF-BREED, THE(1952); ONE BIG AFFAIR(1952); GREAT DIAMOND ROBBERY(1953); HOUDINI(1953); IT SHOULD HAPPEN TO YOU(1954); LONG JOHN SILVER(1954, Aus.); FAR COUNTRY, THE(1955); MAN IN THE GREY FLANNEL SUIT, THE(1956); AUNTIE MAME(1958); MACHINE GUN KELLY(1958); SAY ONE FOR ME(1959); SOME CAME RUNNING(1959); INTERNS, THE(1962); SWINGIN' ALONG(1962); HOUSE IS NOT A HOME, A(1964); MISADVENTURES OF MERLIN JONES, THE(1964); TIGER WALKS, A(1964); FLUFFY(1965); MONKEY'S UNCLE, THE(1965); SYLVIA(1965); TICKLE ME(1965); TWO ON A GUILLOTINE(1965); SOME KIND OF A NUT(1969)
Gilly Gilchrist
1984
COMFORT AND JOY(1984, Brit.)
Anna Gilcrist
GET CHARLIE TULLY(1976, Brit.)
Fred Gildart
WHITE STALLION(1947)
Claude Gildas
BIRD WATCH, THE(1983, Fr.), p
Michael Gilden
RETURN OF THE JEDI(1983)

Richard Gilden
BLACK WHIP, THE(1956); RIDE A VIOLENT MILE(1957); UNKNOWN TERROR, THE(1957); BLOOD ARROW(1958); DESERT HELL(1958); LOST, LONELY AND VICIOUS(1958); BLACK KLANSMAN, THE(1966)
Linda Gildersleeve
Misc. Talkies
BEACH BUNNIES(1977)
Gildes
SECOND BUREAU(1936, Fr.); ENTENTE CORDIALE(1939, Fr.)
Anthony Gildes
Misc. Silents
LA ZOME DE LA MORT(1917, Fr.); MATER DOLOROSA(1917, Fr.)
Ken Gildin
HAIR(1979)
Berne Giler
LEGION OF THE LAWLESS(1940), w; TURNABOUT(1940), w; PIRATES OF THE PRAIRIE(1942), w; C-MAN(1949), w; NO QUESTIONS ASKED(1951), w; AFFAIR IN TRINIDAD(1952), w; TARZAN'S GREATEST ADVENTURE(1959, Brit.), w; WESTBOUND(1959), w; TARZAN THE MAGNIFICENT(1960, Brit.), w; TARZAN'S THREE CHALLENGES(1963), w; GUNS OF DIABLO(1964), w; GUNFIGHT IN ABILENE(1967), w; MIDAS RUN(1969), w
Bernie Giler
SHOWDOWN AT ABILENE(1956), w
David Giler
PARALLAX VIEW, THE(1974), w; BLACK BIRD, THE(1975), d&w; FUN WITH DICK AND JANE(1977), w; ALIEN(1979), p; SOUTHERN COMFORT(1981), p, w
Corliss Giles
Silents
IN SEARCH OF A SINNER(1920)
Misc. Silents
SHIRLEY KAYE(1917); HOUSE OF GLASS, THE(1918); MARIONETTES, THE(1918); LOVE, HONOR AND ?(1919); VOICES(1920); MOUNTAIN WOMAN, THE(1921)
David Giles
DANCE OF DEATH, THE(1971, Brit.), d; NICHOLAS AND ALEXANDRA(1971, Brit.)
Jim Giles
STAKEOUT ON DOPE STREET(1958)
Lem Giles
TRIGGER TRAIL(1944)
Len Giles
TRAIL TO GUNSIGHT(1944)
Michael Giles
1984
GHOST DANCE(1984, Brit.), m
Miranda Giles
MOUNTAIN MUSIC(1937)
Sandra Giles
LOST, LONELY AND VICIOUS(1958); MATCHMAKER, THE(1958); DADDY-O(1959); BLACK SPURS(1965); FLAREUP(1969); BLACK GUNN(1972)
Misc. Talkies
LUST TO KILL(1960); BORDER LUST(1967)
Pierre Gilette
BURGLARS, THE(1972, Fr./Ital.), ed
William Gilette
Misc. Silents
SHERLOCK HOLMES(1916)
Daniel Gilfether
Misc. Silents
MATRIMONIAL MARTYR, A(1916); SHADOWS AND SUNSHINE(1916); SULTANA, THE(1916); BRAND'S DAUGHTER(1917); CHECKMATE, THE(1917); GIRL ANGLE, THE(1917); HIS OLD-FASHIONED DAD(1917); SUNSHINE AND GOLD(1917); TOLD AT THE TWILIGHT(1917); TWIN KIDDIES(1917); WILDCAT, THE(1917); LOCKED HEART, THE(1918); WANTED - A BROTHER(1918)
C.B. Gilford
JOY RIDE(1958), w
Gwynn Gilford
FADE TO BLACK(1980)
Gwynne Gilford
BEWARE! THE BLOB(1972)
Jack Gilford
HEY, ROOKIE(1944); RECKLESS AGE(1944); DAYDREAMER, THE(1966); FUNNY THING HAPPENED ON THE WAY TO THE FORUM, A(1966); MISTER BUDDWING(1966); ENTER LAUGHING(1967); INCIDENT, THE(1967); WHO'S MINDING THE MINT?(1967); CATCH-22(1970); THEY MIGHT BE GIANTS(1971); SAVE THE TIGER(1973); HARRY AND WALTER GO TO NEW YORK(1976); CHEAPER TO KEEP HER(1980); WHOLLY MOSES(1980); CAVEMAN(1981)
Max M. Gilford
MUSTANG(1959)
Glenn Gilger
EIGHT ON THE LAM(1967); BOY NAMED CHARLIE BROWN, A(1969)
Jay Gilgore
CANYON RAIDERS(1951), w
John Gilgreen
36 HOURS(1965); STRAIGHT TIME(1978); PATERNITY(1981)
Jonathan Gili
OVERLORD(1975, Brit.), ed
Fatima Giliadova
Misc. Silents
CHILDREN OF THE NEW DAY(1930, USSR)
Al Gilkes
KISS ME AGAIN(1931), ph
Anthony Gilkison
BREAKERS AHEAD(1935, Brit.), d&w; MYSTERY ON BIRD ISLAND(1954, Brit.), p; SECRET OF THE FOREST, THE(1955, Brit.), p; SOAPBOX DERBY(1958, Brit.), p; WINGS OF MYSTERY(1963, Brit.), p
Al Gilks
SECRETS OF THE FRENCH POLICE(1932), ph; HELL AND HIGH WATER(1933), ph; NOTORIOUS SOPHIE LANG, THE(1934), ph; MAN ON THE FLYING TRAPEZE, THE(1935), ph; STRAIGHT FROM THE SHOULDER(1936), ph; RIDING ON AIR(1937), ph; VENDETTA(1950), ph

Silents
ENCHANTED HILL, THE(1926), ph
Alfred Gilks
HALF WAY TO HEAVEN(1929), ph; JEALOUSY(1929), ph; KIBITZER, THE(1929), ph; SWEETIE(1929), ph; TAILOR MADE MAN, A(1931), ph; MIDSHIPMAN JACK(1933), ph; LITTLE MISS MARKER(1934), ph; MISS FANE'S BABY IS STOLEN(1934), ph; YOU'RE TELLING ME(1934), ph; PEOPLE WILL TALK(1935), ph; RUGGLES OF RED GAP(1935), ph; AND SUDDEN DEATH(1936), ph; MILKY WAY, THE(1936), ph; CALLING DR. KILDARE(1939), ph; DANCING CO-ED(1939), ph; SECRET OF DR. KILDARE, THE(1939), ph; THESE GLAMOUR GIRLS(1939), ph; TWO WEEKS WITH LOVE(1950), ph; AMERICAN IN PARIS, AN(1951), ph; EXCUSE MY DUST(1951), ph; PAINTED HILLS, THE(1951), ph; BRIGHT ROAD(1953), ph
Silents
EXCUSE MY DUST(1920), ph; SINS OF ROZANNE(1920), ph; WHAT'S YOUR HURRY?(1920), ph; PECK'S BAD BOY(1921), ph; BEYOND THE ROCKS(1922), ph; HER GILDED CAGE(1922), ph; IMPOSSIBLE MRS. BELLEW, THE(1922), ph; MY AMERICAN WIFE(1923), ph; BLUFF(1924), ph; NORTH OF 36(1924), ph; AIR MAIL, THE(1925), ph; ANCIENT HIGHWAY, THE(1925), ph; RUGGED WATER(1925), ph; BLIND GODDESS, THE(1926), ph; OLD IRONSIDES(1926), ph; RED HAIR(1928), ph; WIFE SAVERS(1928), ph
Terry Gilkyson
SLAUGHTER TRAIL(1951); STAR IN THE DUST(1956)
Alexander Gill
Misc. Silents
VIRGIN LIPS(1928)
Basil Gill
HIGH TREASON(1929, Brit.); SCHOOL FOR SCANDAL, THE(1930, Brit.); GLAMOUR(1931, Brit.); SHOULD A DOCTOR TELL?(1931, Brit.); DIVINE SPARK, THE(1935, Brit./Ital.); IMMORTAL GENTLEMAN(1935, Brit.); REGAL CAVALCADE(1935, Brit.); WANDERING JEW, THE(1935, Brit.); CRIMSON CIRCLE, THE(1936, Brit.); GAOL BREAK(1936, Brit.); REMBRANDT(1936, Brit.); KNIGHT WITHOUT ARMOR(1937, Brit.); MAN OF AFFAIRS(1937, Brit.); CITADEL, THE(1938); DANGEROUS MEDICINE(1938, Brit.); SIDEWALKS OF LONDON(1940, Brit.)
Silents
ON THE BANKS OF ALLAN WATER(1916, Brit.); RAGGED MESSENGER, THE(1917, Brit.); ADMIRABLE CRICHTON, THE(1918, Brit.); MISSING THE TIDE(1918, Brit.); KEEPER OF THE DOOR(1919, Brit.); WORLDLINGS, THE(1920, Brit.)
Misc. Silents
CHAINS OF BONDAGE(1916, Brit.); SPINNER O' DREAMS(1918, Brit.); HOMEMAKER, THE(1919, Brit.); IRRESISTIBLE FLAPPER, THE(1919, Brit.); ROCKS OF VALPRE, THE(1919, Brit.); SOUL'S CRUCIFIXION, A(1919, Brit.); GOD'S GOOD MAN(1921, Brit.)
Beverly Gill
SCREAM BLACULA SCREAM(1973); SOYLENT GREEN(1973); SPOOK WHO SAT BY THE DOOR, THE(1973)
Brian Gill
QUEST FOR FIRE(1982, Fr./Can.)
Claes Gill
SHORT IS THE SUMMER(1968, Swed.)
Derek Gill
DOVE, THE(1974, Brit.), w; IF YOU COULD SEE WHAT I HEAR(1982), w
Florence Gill
EVERY NIGHT AT EIGHT(1935); WAY DOWN EAST(1935); EVER SINCE EVE(1937); LARCENY ON THE AIR(1937); MR. DODD TAKES THE AIR(1937); OBLIGING YOUNG LADY(1941); RELUCTANT DRAGON, THE(1941); I MARRIED A WITCH(1942)
Frank Gill, Jr.
WHO KILLED AUNT MAGGIE?(1940), w; CHATTERBOX(1943), w; HIT PARADE OF 1943(1943), w; SLEEPY LAGOON(1943), w; THUMBS UP(1943), w; ATLANTIC CITY(1944), w; BRAZIL(1944), w; CASANOVA IN BURLESQUE(1944), w; EARL CARROLL'S VANITIES(1945), w; MEXICANA(1945), w; EARL CARROLL SKETCHBOOK(1946), w; LADY PAYS OFF, THE(1951), w; EAST OF SUMATRA(1953), w; GERALDINE(1953), w; CAROLINA CANNONBALL(1955), w; MC HALE'S NAVY(1964), w
Geoffrey Gill
PEG O' MY HEART(1933)
Glaucio Gill
ROSE FOR EVERYONE, A(1967, Ital.), w
Gwenlian Gill
COME ON, MARINES(1934); IRISH AND PROUD OF IT(1938, Ireland)
Gwenlian Gill
MENACE(1934); MURDER AT THE VANITIES(1934); SHOCK(1934); BEHOLD MY WIFE(1935); FATHER BROWN, DETECTIVE(1935); FLAME IN THE HEATHER(1935, Brit.); WHITE LILAC(1935, Brit.); KING OF HEARTS(1936, Brit.); FALSE EVIDENCE(1937, Brit.); MURDER TOMORROW(1938, Brit.)
Helen Gill
AT THE EARTH'S CORE(1976, Brit.)
Misc. Silents
YOUTHFUL FOLLY(1920)
Inga Gill
SEVENTH SEAL, THE(1958, Swed.); BRINK OF LIFE(1960, Swed.)
Jack Gill
ROCK 'N' ROLL HIGH SCHOOL(1979)
John Gill
THIS SPORTING LIFE(1963, Brit.); NIGHT MUST FALL(1964, Brit.); PRIVILEGE(1967, Brit.); SOMETHING FOR EVERYONE(1970); GUNFIGHT, A(1971); ZEPPELIN(1971, Brit.); THOMASINE AND BUSHROD(1974)
John Richard Gill
SHOWDOWN(1973)
L. Gill
STRANGE BREW(1983), makeup
Linda Gill
1984
MRS. SOFFEL(1984), makeup
Maud Gill
GREENWOOD TREE, THE(1930, Brit.); SISTER TO ASSIST'ER, A(1930, Brit.); SUCH IS THE LAW(1930, Brit.); UNDER THE GREENWOOD TREE(1930, Brit.); MISCHIEF(1931, Brit.); CRIME AT BLOSSOMS, THE(1933, Brit.); EXCESS BAGGAGE(1933, Brit.); LILIES OF THE FIELD(1934, Brit.); LOOK UP AND LAUGH(1935, Brit.); KEEP YOUR SEATS PLEASE(1936, Brit.); LOVE AT SEA(1936, Brit.)

Silents
NOT FOR SALE(1924, Brit.); FARMER'S WIFE, THE(1928, Brit.)
Nancy Lou Gill
NOW THAT APRIL'S HERE(1958, Can.)
Paul Gill
MANY WATERS(1931, Brit.)
Penny Gill
ZAZA(1939)
Peter Gill
DAMN THE DEFIANT!(1962, Brit.); ZULU(1964, Brit.)
Phillipa Gill
PERFECT WOMAN, THE(1950, Brit.)
Renja Gill
SHADOWS GROW LONGER, THE(1962, Switz./Ger.)
Richard Gill
UNMAN, WITTERING AND ZIGO(1971, Brit.)
Robert Gill
MEN ARE CHILDREN TWICE(1953, Brit.), m; SO LITTLE TIME(1953, Brit.), m; GOLDEN MASK, THE(1954, Brit.), m; THEY WHO DARE(1954, Brit.), m; WOMAN'S ANGLE, THE(1954, Brit.), m
Thomas Gill
BORDER CAFE(1937), w
Tim Gill
TWO GROOMS FOR A BRIDE(1957)
Tom Gill
GAY CABALLERO, THE(1932), w; QUEEN OF HEARTS(1936, Brit.); HIGH COMMAND(1938, Brit.); MEET MR. PENNY(1938, Brit.); THIS MAN IS NEWS(1939, Brit.); DESIGN FOR MURDER(1940, Brit.); SOMETHING IN THE CITY(1950, Brit.); HOTEL SAHARA(1951, Brit.); I'LL NEVER FORGET YOU(1951); MEN OF THE SEA(1951, Brit.); MR. DRAKE'S DUCK(1951, Brit.); NO HIGHWAY IN THE SKY(1951, Brit.); MR. LORD SAYS NO(1952, Brit.); LIMPING MAN, THE(1953, Brit.); LOVE IN PAWN(1953, Brit.); TROPIC ZONE(1953), w; WEDDING OF LILLI MARLENE, THE(1953, Brit.); WEAK AND THE WICKED, THE(1954, Brit.); LADY GODIVA RIDES AGAIN(1955, Brit.); FUN AT ST. FANNY'S(1956, Brit.); JUMPING FOR JOY(1956, Brit.); SIMON AND LAURA(1956, Brit.); AFTER THE BALL(1957, Brit.); CARRY ON ADMIRAL(1957, Brit.); GOOD COMPANIONS, THE(1957, Brit.); PORTRAIT IN SMOKE(1957, Brit.); FURTHER UP THE CREEK!(1958, Brit.); UP THE CREEK(1958, Brit.); NAVY LARK, THE(1959, Brit.); DOUBLE BUNK(1961, Brit.); TERROR OF THE TONGS, THE(1961, Brit.); SWINGIN' MAIDEN, THE(1963, Brit.); YELLOW ROLLS-ROYCE, THE(1965, Brit.); SMASHING TIME(1967 Brit.); NICE GIRL LIKE ME, A(1969, Brit.)
William Gill
MIKEY AND NICKY(1976)
Jane Gill-Davis
LAMP STILL BURNS, THE(1943, Brit.); MAN IN GREY, THE(1943, Brit.); RANDOLPH FAMILY, THE(1945, Brit.)
Rebecca Gillaing
Misc. Talkies
CHOPPER SQUAD(1971)
Harry Gillam
MR. DRAKE'S DUCK(1951, Brit.), ph; TWO LEFT FEET(1965, Brit.), ph
Stu Gillam
BROTHERS(1977)
Hugh Gillan
BUTCH AND SUNDANCE: THE EARLY DAYS(1979)
Wilbur Gillan
LONGEST YARD, THE(1974)
Stuart Gillard
NEPTUNE FACTOR, THE(1973, Can.); ROWDYMAN, THE(1973, Can.); WHY ROCK THE BOAT?(1974, Can.); VIRUS(1980, Jap.); IF YOU COULD SEE WHAT I HEAR(1982), p, w; PARADISE(1982), d&w; SPRING FEVER(1983, Can.), w
Silvana Gillardo
DEATH WISH II(1982)
Andre Gille
STOWAWAY IN THE SKY(1962, Fr.)
Arlene Gillen
DERANGED(1974, Can.)
Ernest Gillen
Silents
ANY WOMAN(1925); HIS SECRETARY(1925); AUCTION BLOCK, THE(1926); BROWN OF HARVARD(1926)
Ernesto Gillen
Misc. Silents
SOUL OF MEXICO(1932, Mex.)
Jeff Gillen
SHE MAN, THE(1967), a, w; WILD REBELS, THE(1967); DARKER THAN AMBER(1970); DERANGED(1974, Can.), d; ABSENCE OF MALICE(1981); NOBODY'S PERFEKT(1981); CHRISTMAS STORY, A(1983); EASY MONEY(1983)
Jeffrey Gillen
CHILDREN SHOULDN'T PLAY WITH DEAD THINGS(1972)
Jim Gillen
THIN RED LINE, THE(1964); CRACK IN THE WORLD(1965); GUNFIGHTERS OF CASA GRANDE(1965, U.S./Span.)
Lee Gillen
RUN ACROSS THE RIVER(1961), w
David Giller
SKIN GAME(1971), w
Walter Giller
SCHLAGER-PARADE(1953); CAPTAIN FROM KOEPENICK, THE(1956, Ger.); HIPPODROME(1961, Aust./Ger.); ROSES FOR THE PROSECUTOR(1961, Ger.); HELDINNEN(1962, Ger.); CONJUGAL BED, THE(1963, Ital.); THREE PENNY OPERA(1963, Fr./Ger.); ENCOUNTERS IN SALZBURG(1964, Ger.); CORPSE OF BEVERLY HILLS, THE(1965, Ger.); FANNY HILL: MEMOIRS OF A WOMAN OF PLEASURE zero(1965); TONIO KROGER(1968, Fr./Ger.); FINE PAIR, A(1969, Ital.); JOHNNY BANCO(1969, Fr./Ital./Ger.); LEATHER AND NYLON(1969, Fr./Ital.); MADDEST CAR IN THE WORLD, THE(1974, Ger.)
Misc. Talkies
SUPER BUG(1975)

Grace Gillern
COVER GIRL(1944); ARSON SQUAD(1945); SHADOW OF TERROR(1945); UN-MASKED(1950)
Carol Gilles
NICE GIRL LIKE ME, A(1969, Brit.)
Genevieve Gilles
HELLO–GOODBYE(1970)
Gilbert Gilles
RETURN OF MARTIN GUERRE, THE(1983, Fr.)
Kirsten Gilles
THREE STOOGES VS. THE WONDER WOMEN(1975, Ital./Chi.)
Maurice Gilles
L'ATALANTE(1947, Fr.)
Max Gilles
TRESPASSERS, THE(1976, Aus.)
John Patrick Gillese
WINGS OF CHANCE(1961, Can.), w
A. Arnold Gillespie
MAN FROM DOWN UNDER, THE(1943), spec eff; KISMET(1944), spec eff; MRS. PARKINGTON(1944), spec eff; SEVENTH CROSS, THE(1944), spec eff; THIRTY SECONDS OVER TOKYO(1944), spec eff; CLOCK, THE(1945), spec eff; OUR VINES HAVE TENDER GRAPES(1945), spec eff; SON OF LASSIE(1945), spec eff; THEY WERE EXPENDABLE(1945), spec eff; THIS MAN'S NAVY(1945), spec eff; VALLEY OF DECISION, THE(1945), spec eff; WHAT NEXT, CORPORAL HARGROVE?(1945), spec eff; WITHOUT LOVE(1945), spec eff; YOLANDA AND THE THIEF(1945), spec eff; GREEN YEARS, THE(1946), spec eff; UP GOES MAISIE(1946), spec eff; CASS TIM-BERLANE(1947), spec eff; GREEN DOLPHIN STREET(1947), spec eff; HIGH BAR-BAREE(1947), spec eff; HIGH WALL, THE(1947), spec eff; HUCKSTERS, THE(1947), spec eff; LADY IN THE LAKE(1947), spec eff; THIS TIME FOR KEEPS(1947), spec eff; HOMECOMING(1948), spec eff; KISSING BANDIT, THE(1948), spec eff; STATE OF THE UNION(1948), spec eff; ADAM'S RIB(1949), spec eff; BRIBE, THE(1949), spec eff; EAST SIDE, WEST SIDE(1949), spec eff; STRATTON STORY, THE(1949), spec eff; CRISIS(1950), spec eff; KIM(1950), spec eff; MALAYA(1950), spec eff; PAGAN LOVE SONG(1950), spec eff; SIDE STREET(1950), spec eff; TO PLEASE A LADY(1950), spec eff; WATCH THE BIRDIE(1950), spec eff; PEOPLE AGAINST O'HARA, THE(1951), spec eff; STRIP, THE(1951), spec eff; TEXAS CARNIVAL(1951), spec eff; BAD AND THE BEAUTIFUL, THE(1952), spec eff; FEARLESS FAGAN(1952), spec eff; LOVELY TO LOOK AT(1952), spec eff; MERRY WIDOW, THE(1952), spec eff; PLYMOUTH ADVENTURE(1952), spec eff; SCARAMOUCHE(1952), spec eff; ABOVE AND BEYOND(1953), spec eff; ALL THE BROTHERS WERE VALIANT(1953), spec eff; DREAM WIFE(1953), spec eff; EXECUTIVE SUITE(1954), spec eff; LONG, LONG TRAILER, THE(1954), spec eff; RHAP-SODY(1954), spec eff; ROGUE COP(1954), spec eff; ROSE MARIE(1954), spec eff; DIANE(1955), spec eff; GREEN FIRE(1955), spec eff; PRODIGAL, THE(1955), spec eff; FORBIDDEN PLANET(1956), spec eff; GREAT AMERICAN PASTIME, THE(1956), spec eff; HIGH SOCIETY(1956), spec eff; OPPOSITE SEX, THE(1956), spec eff; JAIL-HOUSE ROCK(1957), spec eff; TORPEDO RUN(1958), spec eff; GREEN MAN-SIONS(1959), spec eff; NORTH BY NORTHWEST(1959), spec eff; WRECK OF THE MARY DEAR, THE(1959), spec eff; ADVENTURES OF HUCKLEBERRY FINN, THE(1960), spec eff; CIMARRON(1960), spec eff; ATLANTIS, THE LOST CONTI-NENT(1961), spec eff; FOUR HORSEMEN OF THE APOCALYPSE, THE(1962), spec eff; HOW THE WEST WAS WON(1962), spec eff; JUMBO(1962), spec eff; MUTINY ON THE BOUNTY(1962), spec eff; PRIZE, THE(1963), spec eff; UNSINKABLE MOLLY BROWN, THE(1964), spec eff; GREATEST STORY EVER TOLD, THE(1965), spec eff
Ann Gillespie
LOVESICK(1983)
Arnold Gillespie
NIGHT FLIGHT(1933), spec eff; EVELYN PRENTICE(1934), art d; OPERATOR 13(1934), art d; MUTINY ON THE BOUNTY(1935), art d; SAN FRANCISCO(1936), art d, spec eff; GOOD EARTH, THE(1937), art d; TEST PILOT(1938), spec eff; TOO HOT TO HANDLE(1938), spec eff; WIZARD OF OZ, THE(1939), spec eff; COMRADE X(1940), spec eff; FLIGHT COMMAND(1940), spec eff; BUGLE SOUNDS, THE(1941), spec eff; I MARRIED AN ANGEL(1942), spec eff; MRS. MINIVER(1942), spec eff; STAND BY FOR ACTION(1942), spec eff; TARZAN'S NEW YORK ADVENTURE(1942), spec eff; BATAAN(1943), spec eff; GUY NAMED JOE, A(1943), spec eff; HEAVENLY BODY, THE(1943), spec eff; PILOT NO. 5(1943), spec eff; SONG OF RUSSIA(1943), spec eff; WHITE CLIFFS OF DOVER, THE(1944), spec eff; SEA OF GRASS, THE(1947), spec eff; WINGS OF EAGLES, THE(1957), spec eff; RUN SILENT, RUN DEEP(1958), spec eff; BEN HUR(1959), spec eff
Silents
BLACK BIRD, THE(1926), set d; BROWN OF HARVARD(1926), art d; ROAD TO MANDALAY, THE(1926), art d; TELL IT TO THE MARINES(1926), set d; ALTARS OF DESIRE(1927), art d; FAIR CO-ED, THE(1927), art d; LONDON AFTER MID-NIGHT(1927), set d; CROWD, THE(1928), set d; DIVINE WOMAN, THE(1928), set d; LATEST FROM PARIS, THE(1928), set d
Beau Gillespie
HOT STUFF(1979)
Cass Gillespie
SUPER FUZZ(1981), spec eff
Cherry Gillespie
NUTCRACKER(1982, Brit.); OCTOPUSSY(1983, Brit.)
Dana Gillespie
SECRETS OF A WINDMILL GIRL(1966, Brit.); LOST CONTINENT, THE(1968, Brit.); MAHLER(1974, Brit.); PEOPLE THAT TIME FORGOT, THE(1977, Brit.); HOUND OF THE BASKERVILLES, THE(1980, Brit.)
1984
SCRUBBERS(1984, Brit.)
Debbie Gillespie
SWEET SIXTEEN(1983), makeup
Edward Gillespie
Silents
ALIEN, THE(1915)
Gina Gillespie
ANDY HARDY COMES HOME(1958); FACE OF A FUGITIVE(1959); IT HAPPENED TO JANE(1959); WHATEVER HAPPENED TO BABY JANE?(1962)
Harry Gillespie
THEY WON'T BELIEVE ME(1947)

Jim Gillespie
SWEET SIXTEEN(1983), makeup; WAVELENGTH(1983), makeup
John Gillespie
ISLAND OF DR. MOREAU, THE(1977)
1984
ICE PIRATES, THE(1984)
Kip Gillespie
RUBY(1977)
Linda Gillespie
ADULTEROUS AFFAIR(1966)
Robert Gillespie
SIEGE OF THE SAXONS(1963, Brit.); OTLEY(1969, Brit.); ATCH ME A SPY(1971, Brit./Fr.); SEVERED HEAD, A(1971, Brit.); NATIONAL HEALTH, OR NURSE NORTON'S AFFAIR, THE(1973, Brit.); AT THE EARTH'S CORE(1976, Brit.); THIRTY NINE STEPS, THE(1978, Brit.)
Tim Gillespie
MORTUARY(1983), makeup
William Gillespie
SONS OF THE DESERT(1933); RHAPSODY IN BLUE(1945)
Silents
DOCTOR JACK(1922); GRANDMA'S BOY(1922); WHY WORRY(1923); EXIT SMIL-ING(1926); VALLEY OF BRAVERY, THE(1926)
Misc. Silents
STOP, LOOK, AND LISTEN(1926)
Harvey T. Gillet
FOOL'S GOLD(1946), art d
Marie-Louise Gillet
LES ABYSSES(1964, Fr.), makeup
Barbara Gillett
HOT MONEY GIRL(1962, Brit./Ger.), cos
Fred L. Gillett
TWO TICKETS TO BROADWAY(1951)
Harvey Gillett
DOUBLE LIFE, A(1947), art d
Harvey D. Gillett
DEVIL'S PLAYGROUND, THE(1946), art d
Harvey T. Gillett
UNEXPECTED GUEST(1946), art d; DANGEROUS VENTURE(1947), art d; HOP-PY'S HOLIDAY(1947), art d
Roland Gillett
BORN LUCKY(1932, Brit.); FIND THE LADY(1936, Brit.), d, w; UNDER PROOF(1936, Brit.), d
Sidney J. Gillett
OUTSIDER, THE(1933, Brit.)
Barbara Gillette
ENTERTAINER, THE(1960, Brit.), cos
Betty Gillette
BIG CITY BLUES(1932) 65m WB bw; CROONER(1932); SCARLET DAWN(1932); FIRST YANK INTO TOKYO(1945); DEADLINE AT DAWN(1946); FALCON'S ALIBI, THE(1946); LADY LUCK(1946)
Charles Gillette
LUCKY DEVILS(1933)
Edwin Gillette
UNDERSEA GIRL(1957), ph
James Gillette
DESERT BANDIT(1941); RIDERS OF THE PURPLE SAGE(1941)
Joseph C. Gillette
BLOOD AND STEEL(1959), w
Larry R. Gillette
STRIPES(1981)
Penelope Gillette
NEWMAN'S LAW(1974)
Pierre Gillette
STOWAWAY IN THE SKY(1962, Fr.), ed; SUITOR, THE(1963, Fr.), ed; LA VIE DE CHATEAU(1967, Fr.), ed; SICILIAN CLAN, THE(1970, Fr.), ed; SERPENT, THE(1973, Fr./Ital./Ger.), ed
Robert Gillette
FLIGHT OF THE LOST BALLOON(1961)
Silents
STELLA DALLAS(1925)
Roland Gillette
BLAME THE WOMAN(1932, Brit.); CAPTAINS OF THE CLOUDS(1942), w
Ruth Gillette
FRONTIER MARSHAL(1934); WILD GOLD(1934); WOMAN IN THE DARK(1934); CONVENTION GIRL(1935); LIFE BEGINS AT 40(1935); SPANISH CAPE MYS-TERY(1935); BULLDOG EDITION(1936); GENTLEMAN FROM LOUISIANA(1936); GREAT ZIEGFELD, THE(1936); NAVY WIFE(1936); OFF TO THE RACES(1937); SARATOGA(1937); THIS IS MY AFFAIR(1937); CHASER, THE(1938); IN OLD CHICA-GO(1938); JOSETTE(1938); REBECCA OF SUNNYBROOK FARM(1938); SLANDER HOUSE(1938); LITTLE ACCIDENT(1939); MADE FOR EACH OTHER(1939); RETURN OF THE CISCO KID(1939); FOR BEAUTY'S SAKE(1941); MONSTER AND THE GIRL, THE(1941); SMALL TOWN DEB(1941); STREET OF CHANCE(1942); HELLO, FRISCO, HELLO(1943); EVERYBODY DOES IT(1949); IN A LONELY PLACE(1950); SHAGGY D.A., THE(1976); GOING APE!(1981)
Warrington Gillette
FRIDAY THE 13TH PART II(1981)
William Gillette
SECRET SERVICE(1931), w; SHERLOCK HOLMES' FATAL HOUR(1931, Brit.), w; SHERLOCK HOLMES(1932), w; ADVENTURES OF SHERLOCK HOLMES, THE(1939), w
Silents
SHERLOCK HOLMES(1922), w
Thomas Gillettei
Misc. Silents
INVISIBLE POWER, THE(1914), Cleo Ridgely
Mickey Gilley
URBAN COWBOY(1980); OFF THE WALL(1983)

Bill Gillham
1984
BREAKOUT(1984, Brit.), w
Ron Gillham
STRANGE INVADERS(1983)
Luciana Gilli
RED SHEIK, THE(1963, Ital.); SEVEN SEAS TO CALAIS(1963, Ital.)
Burton Gilliam
PAPER MOON(1973); THUNDERBOLT AND LIGHTFOOT(1974); AT LONG LAST LOVE(1975); FAREWELL, MY LOVELY(1975); HEARTS OF THE WEST(1975); GATOR(1976); ANOTHER MAN, ANOTHER CHANCE(1977 Fr/US); TELEFON(1977)
1984
FLETCH(1984)
David Gilliam
DIRTY HARRY(1971); FROGS(1972); SHARK'S TREASURE(1975); EAGLE HAS LANDED, THE(1976, Brit.)
Harry Gilliam
HER LAST AFFAIRE(1935, Brit.), ph; CRY FROM THE STREET, A(1959, Brit.), ph
Hugh Gilliam
1984
PURPLE HEARTS(1984)
Ralph Gilliam
TEST PILOT(1938); MAJOR AND THE MINOR, THE(1942)
Reg Gilliam
COLOR ME DEAD(1969, Aus.)
Reginald Gilliam
WITCH WITHOUT A BROOM, A(1967, U.S./Span.); CHRISTMAS KID, THE(1968, U.S., Span.)
Stu Gilliam
$1,000,000 DUCK(1971); MACK, THE(1973); FAREWELL, MY LOVELY(1975); DR. BLACK AND MR. HYDE(1976); APPLE DUMPLING GANG RIDES AGAIN, THE(1979); DEVIL AND MAX DEVLIN, THE(1981); OFF THE WALL(1983)
Terry Gilliam
AND NOW FOR SOMETHING COMPLETELY DIFFERENT(1972, Brit.), a, w, anim; MONTY PYTHON AND THE HOLY GRAIL(1975, Brit.), a, d, w; JABBERWOCKY(1977, Brit.), d, w; MONTY PYTHON'S LIFE OF BRIAN(1979, Brit.), a, w, anim d; TIME BANDITS(1981, Brit.), p&d; w; MONTY PYTHON'S THE MEANING OF LIFE(1983, Brit.), a, w, anim d
The Gillian Lynne Dancers
SEASIDE SWINGERS(1965, Brit.)
Luigi Gillianni
BOCCACCIO '70(1962/Ital./Fr.)
John Gilliar
WHERE'S POPPA?(1970)
Leslie Gilliat
ONLY TWO CAN PLAY(1962, Brit.), p; RING OF SPIES(1964, Brit.), p; AMOROUS MR. PRAWN, THE(1965, Brit.), p; JOEY BOY(1965, Brit.), p; TWO LEFT FEET(1965, Brit.), p; VIRGIN SOLDIERS, THE(1970, Brit.), p
Sidney Gilliat
YOU'D BE SURPRISED!(1930, Brit.); GENTLEMAN OF PARIS, A(1931), w; HAPPY ENDING, THE(1931, Brit.), w; LORD BABS(1932, Brit.), w; FACING THE MUSIC(1933, Brit.), w; FALLING FOR YOU(1933, Brit.), w; GHOST TRAIN, THE(1933, Brit.), w; ROME EXPRESS(1933, Brit.), d; CHU CHIN CHOW(1934, Brit.), w; FRIDAY THE 13TH(1934, Brit.), w; ORDERS IS ORDERS(1934, Brit.), w; ALIAS BULLDOG DRUMMOND(1935, Brit.), w; JACK AHOY!(1935, Brit.), w; MY HEART IS CALLING(1935, Brit.), w; KING OF THE DAMNED(1936, Brit.), w; MAN WHO LIVED AGAIN, THE(1936, Brit.), w; TWELVE GOOD MEN(1936, Brit.), w; WHERE THERE'S A WILL(1936, Brit.), w; STRANGERS ON A HONEYMOON(1937, Brit.), w; TAKE MY TIP(1937, Brit.), w; LADY VANISHES, THE(1938, Brit.), w; STRANGE BOARDERS(1938, Brit.), w; YANK AT OXFORD, A(1938), w; ASK A POLICEMAN(1939, Brit.), w; INSPECTOR HORNLEIGH ON HOLIDAY(1939, Brit.), w; JAMAICA INN(1939, Brit.), w; PHANTOM STRIKES, THE(1939, Brit.), w; THEY CAME BY NIGHT(1940, Brit.), w; GIRL IN THE NEWS, THE(1941, Brit.), w; REMARKABLE MR. KIPPS(1942, Brit.), w; YOUNG MR. PITT, THE(1942, Brit.), w; MILLIONS LIKE US(1943, Brit.), d&w; 2,000 WOMEN(1944, Brit.), w; NOTORIOUS GENTLEMAN(1945, Brit.), a, p, d, w; ADVENTURESS, THE(1946, Brit.), p, w; GREEN FOR DANGER(1946, Brit.), p, d, w; CAPTAIN BOYCOTT(1947, Brit.), p; DULCIMER STREET(1948, Brit.), p, d, w; BLUE LAGOON, THE(1949, Brit.), p; WATERLOO ROAD(1949, Brit.), d, w; HAPPIEST DAYS OF YOUR LIFE(1950, Brit.), p; GREAT MANHUNT, THE(1951, Brit.), p, d&w; GREAT GILBERT AND SULLIVAN, THE(1953, Brit.), p, d, w; BELLES OF ST. TRINIAN'S, THE(1954, Brit.), p; UP TO HIS NECK(1954, Brit.), w; LADY GODIVA RIDES AGAIN(1955, Brit.), w; WEE GEORDIE(1956, Brit.), p, w; GREEN MAN, THE(1957, Brit.), p, w; SHE PLAYED WITH FIRE(1957, Brit.), p, d, w; SMALLEST SHOW ON EARTH, THE(1957, Brit.), p; BLUE MURDER AT ST. TRINIAN'S(1958, Brit.), p, w; BRIDAL PATH, THE(1959, Brit.), p; LEFT, RIGHT AND CENTRE(1959), a, p, d, w; PURE HELL OF ST. TRINIAN'S, THE(1961, Brit.), p, w; ONLY TWO CAN PLAY(1962, Brit.), d; JOEY BOY(1965, Brit.), p; GREAT ST. TRINIAN'S TRAIN ROBBERY, THE(1966, Brit.), p&d
Sydney Gilliat
DOMMED CARGO(1936, Brit.), w; NIGHT TRAIN(1940, Brit.), w; CONSTANT HUSBAND, THE(1955, Brit.), p, d, w
Sidney Gilliate
ENDLESS NIGHT(1971, Brit.), d&w
Penelope Gilliatt
SUNDAY BLOODY SUNDAY(1971, Brit.), w
Sidney Gilliatt
FOLLY TO BE WISE(1953), p
Jean Gillibert
TRIAL OF JOAN OF ARC(1965, Fr.)
John Gillick
Misc. Talkies
I WAS A ZOMBIE FOR THE F.B.I.(1982)
Josephine Gillick
CALAMITY THE COW(1967, Brit.); CROMWELL(1970, Brit.)
Tom Gillick
MEN, THE(1950)
Jean Gillie
HIS MAJESTY AND CO(1935, Brit.); IT HAPPENED IN PARIS(1935, Brit.); SCHOOL FOR STARS(1935, Brit.); SMITH'S WIVES(1935, Brit.); WHILE PARENTS SLEEP(1935, Brit.); GIRL IN THE TAXI(1937, Brit.); LIVE WIRE, THE(1937, Brit.);

SWEET DEVIL(1937, Brit.); THIS'LL MAKE YOU WHISTLE(1938, Brit.); MIDDLE WATCH, THE(1939, Brit.); WHAT WOULD YOU DO, CHUMS?(1939, Brit.); SAILOR'S DON'T CARE(1940, Brit.); SPIDER, THE(1940, Brit.); TILLY OF BLOOMSBURY(1940, Brit.); GENTLE SEX, THE(1943, Brit.); SAINT MEETS THE TIGER, THE(1943, Brit.); FLIGHT FROM FOLLY(1945, Brit.); DECOY(1946); MACOMBER AFFAIR, THE(1947); TAWNY PIPIT(1947, Brit.)
Andrew Gillies
1984
BIG MEAT EATER(1984, Can.)
Carol Gillies
HIDING PLACE, THE(1975)
1984
SCRUBBERS(1984, Brit.); SECRETS(1984, Brit.)
Don Gillies
MASK, THE(1961, Can.), ch
Jacques Gillies
CASH ON DEMAND(1962, Brit.), w
Max Gillies
LIBIDO(1973, Aus.); CARS THAT ATE PARIS, THE(1974, Aus,); FIRM MAN, THE(1975, Aus.); GREAT MACARTHY, THE(1975, Aus.); TRUE STORY OF ESKIMO NELL, THE(1975, Aus.); PURE S(1976, Aus.); DIMBOOLA(1979, Aus.)
Edmund Gilligan
SEALED CARGO(1951), w
Mike Gilligan
SMILE ORANGE(1976, Jamaican), ed
Don Gilliland
ACROSS THE BRIDGE(1957, Brit.)
Helen Gilliland
STORM, THE(1938)
Larry Gilliland
OPERATION PETTICOAT(1959)
Richard Gilliland
BUG(1975); STAY HUNGRY(1976); WHITE BUFFALO, THE(1977)
Ron Gilliland
THEM NICE AMERICANS(1958, Brit.)
Hugh Gillin
PAPER MOON(1973); ROSE, THE(1979); FIRST MONDAY IN OCTOBER(1981); PSYCHO II(1983)
Misc. Talkies
HEROWORK(1977)
Hugh Gillin, Jr.
PRIME CUT(1972)
Jed Gillin
TRADING PLACES(1983)
Linda Gillin
MAGIC GARDEN OF STANLEY SWEETHART, THE(1970); TERROR HOUSE(1972); ALAMBRISTA!(1977); WINDOWS(1980); PATERNITY(1981)
Jane Gilling
STONE(1974, Aus.)
John Gilling
BLACK MEMORY(1947, Brit.), w; GREED OF WILLIAM HART, THE(1948, Brit.), w; GUNMAN HAS ESCAPED, A(1948, Brit.), w; HOUSE OF DARKNESS(1948, Brit.), w; MAN FROM YESTERDAY, THE(1949, Brit.), w; MATTER OF MURDER, A(1949, Brit.), d&w; ROOM TO LET(1949, Brit.), w; BLACKOUT(1950, Brit.), w; DARK INTERVAL(1950, Brit.), w; GUILT IS MY SHADOW(1950, Brit.), w; LADY CRAVED EXCITEMENT, THE(1950, Brit.), w; MAN IN BLACK, THE(1950, Brit.), w; NO TRACE(1950, Brit.), w; ROSSITER CASE, THE(1950, Brit.), w; CHELSEA STORY(1951, Brit.), w; QUIET WOMAN, THE(1951, Brit.), d&w; BLIND MAN'S BLUFF(1952, Brit.), w; DEAD ON COURSE(1952, Brit.), w; FRIGHTENED MAN, THE(1952, Brit.), d&w; KING OF THE UNDERWORLD(1952, Brit.), w; 13 EAST STREET(1952, Brit.), w; BIG FRAME, THE(1953, Brit.), w; DEADLY NIGHTSHADE(1953, Brit.), d; MURDER WILL OUT(1953, Brit.), d&w; RECOIL(1953), d&w; STEEL KEY, THE(1953, Brit.), w; WHITE FIRE(1953, Brit.), w; DESTINATION MILAN(1954, Brit.), w; DOUBLE EXPOSURE(1954, Brit.), d&w; EMBEZZLER, THE(1954, Brit.), d&w; ESCAPE BY NIGHT(1954, Brit.), d&w; GILDED CAGE, THE(1954, Brit.), d; PROFILE(1954, Brit.), w; WINDFALL(1954, Brit.), w; BOND OF FEAR(1956, Brit.), w; GAMMA PEOPLE, THE(1956), d, w; ODONGO(1956, Brit.), d&w; HIGH FLIGHT(1957, Brit.), d; PICKUP ALLEY(1957, Brit.), d; BLIND SPOT(1958, Brit.), w; CROSS-UP(1958), d, w; MAN INSIDE, THE(1958, Brit.), d, w; BANDIT OF ZHOBE, THE(1959), d&w; IDOL ON PARADE(1959, Brit.), d; IT TAKES A THIEF(1960, Brit.), d&w; KILLERS OF KILIMANJARO(1960, Brit.), w; MANIA(1961, Brit.), d, w; SHADOW OF THE CAT, THE(1961, Brit.), d; PIRATES OF BLOOD RIVER, THE(1962, Brit.), d, w; FURY AT SMUGGLERS BAY(1963, Brit.), p,d&w; MY SON, THE VAMPIRE(1963, Brit.), p&d; CRIMSON BLADE, THE(1964, Brit.), d&w; GORGON, THE(1964, Brit.), w; BLOOD BEAST FROM OUTER SPACE(1965, Brit.), d; BRIGAND OF KANDAHAR, THE(1965, Brit.), d&w; SECRET OF BLOOD ISLAND, THE(1965, Brit.), w; PANIC(1966, Brit.), d&w; PLAGUE OF THE ZOMBIES, THE(1966, Brit.), d; REPTILE, THE(1966, Brit.), d; WHERE THE BULLETS FLY(1966, Brit.), d; MUMMY'S SHROUD, THE(1967, Brit.), d&w; TROG(1970, Brit.), w
Rebecca Gilling
STONE(1974, Aus.); MAN FROM HONG KONG(1975)
Deborah Gillingham
PARTY PARTY(1983, Brit.), art d
Gary Gillingham
1984
HAMBONE AND HILLIE(1984), p
Joan Gillingham
GREAT GILBERT AND SULLIVAN, THE(1953, Brit.)
L. Gillingham
INGAGI(1931), ph
Mary Gillingham
FOUR AGAINST FATE(1952, Brit.)
Claude Gillingwater
WOMEN THEY TALK ABOUT(1928); GLAD RAG DOLL, THE(1929); SMILING IRISH EYES(1929); SO LONG LETTY(1929); STARK MAD(1929); STOLEN KISSES(1929); DUMBBELLS IN ERMINE(1930); FLIRTING WIDOW, THE(1930); GREAT DIVIDE, THE(1930); CONQUERING HORDE, THE(1931); GOLD DUST GERTIE(1931); ILLICIT(1931); KISS ME AGAIN(1931); TESS OF THE STORM COUNTRY(1932); ANN CARVER'S PROFESSION(1933); AVENGER, THE(1933); SKYWAY(1933); BEFORE MIDNIGHT(1934); CAPTAIN HATES THE SEA, THE(1934); CITY LIMITS(1934);

GREEN EYES(1934); IN LOVE WITH LIFE(1934); SHOW-OFF, THE(1934); UN-KNOWN BLONDE(1934); YOU CAN'T BUY EVERYTHING(1934); BABY FACE HARRINGTON(1935); CALM YOURSELF(1935); TALE OF TWO CITIES, A(1935); TOGETHER WE LIVE(1935); CAN THIS BE DIXIE?(1936); COUNTERFEIT(1936); FLORIDA SPECIAL(1936); POOR LITTLE RICH GIRL(1936); PRISONER OF SHARK ISLAND, THE(1936); TICKET TO PARADISE(1936); WIVES NEVER KNOW(1936); CONQUEST(1937); TOP OF THE TOWN(1937); THERE GOES MY HEART(1938); YANK AT OXFORD, A(1938); CAFE SOCIETY(1939)
Misc. Talkies
  BACK PAGE(1934)
Silents
  LITTLE LORD FAUNTLEROY(1921); DUST FLOWER, THE(1922); MY BOY(1922); STRANGER'S BANQUET(1922); ALICE ADAMS(1923); CRINOLINE AND RO-MANCE(1923); DULCY(1923); SOULS FOR SALE(1923); THREE WISE FOOLS(1923); WAGES FOR WIVES(1925); THAT'S MY BABY(1926); BARBED WIRE(1927); HUS-BANDS FOR RENT(1927); OH, KAY(1928)
Misc. Silents
  WILD PRIMROSE(1918); FOOLS FIRST(1922); REMEMBRANCE(1922); CHAPTER IN HER LIFE, A(1923); DADDIES(1924); HOW TO EDUCATE A WIFE(1924); IDLE TONGUES(1924); MADONNA OF THE STREETS(1924); THIEF IN PARADISE, A(1925); WE MODERNS(1925); INTO HER KINGDOM(1926); FAST AND FURI-OUS(1927); NAUGHTY BUT NICE(1927)
Claude Gillingwater, Jr.
  MEXICALI ROSE(1929); ACE OF ACES(1933); OLD MAN RHYTHM(1935)
Claude Gillingwater, Sr.
  DADDY LONG LEGS(1931); MISSISSIPPI(1935); STRANGE WIVES(1935); WOMAN IN RED, THE(1935); JUST AROUND THE CORNER(1938); LITTLE MISS BROAD-WAY(1938)
Ann Gillis
  GARDEN OF ALLAH, THE(1936); KING OF HOCKEY(1936); SINGING COWBOY, THE(1936); UNDER YOUR SPELL(1936); OFF TO THE RACES(1937); ADVENTURES OF TOM SAWYER, THE(1938); LITTLE ORPHAN ANNIE(1938); PECK'S BAD BOY WITH THE CIRCUS(1938); BEAU GESTE(1939); UNDER-PUP, THE(1939); ALL THIS AND HEAVEN TOO(1940); EDISON, THE MAN(1940); LITTLE MEN(1940); MY LOVE CAME BACK(1940); GLAMOUR BOY(1941); MR. DYNAMITE(1941); NICE GIRL?(1941); BAMBI(1942); MEET THE STEWARTS(1942); 'NEATH BROOKLYN BRIDGE(1942); TOUGH AS THEY COME(1942); MAN FROM MUSIC MOUN-TAIN(1943); IN SOCIETY(1944); JANIE(1944); SINCE YOU WENT AWAY(1944); WAVE, A WAC AND A MARINE, A(1944); JANIE GETS MARRIED(1946); 2001: A SPACE ODYSSEY(1968, U.S./Brit.)
Anne Gillis
  POSTAL INSPECTOR(1936); CHEATERS, THE(1945); GAY BLADES(1946); SWEET-HEART OF SIGMA CHI(1946); TIME OF THEIR LIVES, THE(1946); BIG TOWN AFTER DARK(1947)
Bill Gillis
  DUDE BANDIT, THE(1933); IT'S A SMALL WORLD(1935); TEXAS RANGERS, THE(1936)
Silents
  CONFLICT, THE(1921); RIDING WITH DEATH(1921)
Clarice Gillis
  CHANGES(1969)
Don Gillis
  MOURNING SUIT, THE(1975, Can.), m; RECOMMENDATION FOR MERCY(1975, Can.), m
Gwynn Gillis
  I, THE JURY(1982)
Jackson Gillis
  TARZAN'S JUNGLE REBELLION(1970), w
James Gillis
  BIG CHILL, THE(1983)
Jamie Gillis
  NIGHT OF THE ZOMBIES(1981); NIGHTHAWKS(1981)
Misc. Talkies
  DRACULA SUCKS(1979)
Joe Gillis
  WHY WOULD I LIE(1980)
Richard Gillis
  SCHLOCK(1973); BEES, THE(1978), m; DEMONOID(1981), m
Robert T. Gillis
  BOY NAMED CHARLIE BROWN, A(1969), ed; SNOOPY, COME HOME(1972), ed
Tom Gillis
  CRACKSMAN, THE(1963, Brit.)
William Gillis
  WESTERNER, THE(1940)
Silents
  LAST STRAW, THE(1920)
Alberto Gillitti
  MINUTE TO PRAY, A SECOND TO DIE, A(1968, Ital.), ed
Arita Gillman
Silents
  GOLD DIGGERS, THE(1923)
Karl Peter Gillman
  INTERMEZZO(1937, Ger.), w
Matt Gillman
  TREASURE ISLAND(1934)
Maurie Gillman
  DAD AND DAVE COME TO TOWN(1938, Aus.), m
Peter Gillman
  PILLARS OF SOCIETY(1936, Ger.), w
Rita Gillman
Silents
  ROBIN HOOD(1922)
Toni Gillman
  MOTEL HELL(1980)
Caroline Gillmer
  FIGHTING BACK(1983, Brit.)
Reuben Gillmer
Silents
  LOST CHORD, THE(1917, Brit.), w; LOVE'S OLD SWEET SONG(1917, Brit.), w; QUEEN OF MY HEART(1917, Brit.), w; KNAVE OF HEARTS, THE(1919, Brit.), w

Misc. Silents
  MEN WHO FORGET(1923), d
Noelle Gillmor
  EVE WANTS TO SLEEP(1961, Pol.), titles; WAR OF THE BUTTONS(1963 Fr.), titles; COUNTERFEIT CONSTABLE, THE(1966, Fr.), titles; TRANS-EUROP-EXPRESS(1968, Fr.), titles; SEVEN GOLDEN MEN(1969, Fr./Ital./Span.), w; VERY HAPPY ALEX-ANDER(1969, Fr.), titles
Helen Gillmore
Silents
  EAGLE'S MATE, THE(1914)
Margalo Gillmore
  WAYWARD(1932); HAPPY YEARS, THE(1950); PERFECT STRANGERS(1950); CAUSE FOR ALARM(1951); ELOPEMENT(1951); LAW AND THE LADY, THE(1951); SKIRTS AHOY!(1952); SCANDAL AT SCOURIE(1953); GABY(1956); HIGH SOCIE-TY(1956); UPSTAIRS AND DOWNSTAIRS(1961, Brit.); TROUBLE WITH ANGELS, THE(1966)
Marpalo Gillmore
  WOMAN'S WORLD(1954)
Rufus Gillmore
Silents
  ALSTER CASE, THE(1915), w
Stuart Gillmore
  NIGHT WORK(1939), ed
Noelle Gillmour
  MONDAY'S CHILD(1967, U.S., Arg.), w
Marion Gillon
  DARK END OF THE STREET, THE(1981), m
Mary Gillooly
  CAYMAN TRIANGLE, THE(1977)
Pascal Gillot
  JUST BEFORE NIGHTFALL(1975, Fr./Ital.)
Denis Gillson
  WAITING FOR CAROLINE(1969, Can.), ph
Arvid E. Gillstrom
Silents
  CLANCY'S KOSHER WEDDING(1927), d
Misc. Silents
  SWAT THE SPY(1918), d; TELL IT TO THE MARINES(1918), d; SMILES(1919), d; LEAVE IT TO GERRY(1924), d; LEGIONNAIRES IN PARIS(1927), d
Jan Gillum
  SOMEBODY UP THERE LIKES ME(1956)
Dinah Gilly
  INSULT(1932, Brit.)
Renee Gilly
  BARBER OF SEVILLE(1949, Fr.)
Ada Gilman
Silents
  IN AGAIN-OUT AGAIN(1917)
Don Gilman
  IF EVER I SEE YOU AGAIN(1978), art d
Dorothy Gilman
  MRS. POLLIFAX-SPY(1971), w
Fred Gilman
  COWBOY COUNSELOR(1933); DUDE BANDIT, THE(1933); RAINBOW'S END(1935); SUNSET RANGE(1935); MIGHTY MCGURK, THE(1946); SEA OF GRASS, THE(1947)
Silents
  CLEARING THE TRAIL(1928)
Horace Gilman
  NAKED PREY, THE(1966, U.S./South Africa)
Jack Gilman
  BLOCK BUSTERS(1944)
Keith Gilman
  ONE GOOD TURN(1955, Brit.)
Kenneth Gilman
  1984
  BEDROOM EYES(1984, Can.)
Larry Gilman
  H.O.T.S.(1979)
  1984
  WOMAN IN RED, THE(1984)
Lucy Gilman
  GANGSTER'S BOY(1938)
Matt Gilman
  SHADOW OF THE THIN MAN(1941)
Mildred Gilman
  SOB SISTER(1931), w
Peter Gilman
  DIAMOND HEAD(1962), w
Phyllis Gilman
  VOGUES OF 1938(1937)
Sam Gilman
  ROBE, THE(1953); DESIREE(1954); AWAY ALL BOATS(1956); FULL OF LIFE(1956); SHADOW ON THE WINDOW, THE(1957); YOUNG LIONS, THE(1958); ONE-EYED JACKS(1961); PT 109(1963); FLUFFY(1965); SOMETIMES A GREAT NOTION(1971); WILD ROVERS(1971); GATOR BAIT(1974); MACON COUNTY LINE(1974); MISSOURI BREAKS, THE(1976)
Helene Gilmer
  SCOTLAND YARD DRAGNET(1957, Brit.)
Reuben Gilmer
Silents
  ON THE BANKS OF ALLAN WATER(1916, Brit.), w; AVE MARIA(1918, Brit.), w; POWER OF RIGHT, THE(1919, Brit.), w
Andrew Gilmore
  MAD MAX(1979, Aus.)
Art Gilmore
  MISSION TO MOSCOW(1943); UNSUSPECTED, THE(1947); MY DREAM IS YOURS(1949); TEA FOR TWO(1950); WHEN WORLDS COLLIDE(1951); WIRETAP-PERS(1956); SUICIDE BATTALION(1958); GALLANT HOURS, THE(1960)

Arthur Gilmore
RENDEZVOUS 24(1946); IT SHOULD HAPPEN TO YOU(1954)
Arthur D. Gilmore
GANG WAR(1958)
Barney Gilmore
SMILING IRISH EYES(1929)
Silents
MAN WHO MADE GOOD, THE(1917); CONQUERED HEARTS(1918); MAN WORTH WHILE, THE(1921); BANDIT'S SON, THE(1927)
Misc. Silents
FIGHT FOR MILLIONS, THE(1913); GALLOPING COWBOY, THE(1926)
C. C. "Tex" Gilmore
FOREVER AMBER(1947)
Christopher Gilmore
WHAT'S GOOD FOR THE GOOSE(1969, Brit.), w
Denis Gilmore
THEM NICE AMERICANS(1958, Brit.); UNSTOPPABLE MAN, THE(1961, Brit.); THREE LIVES OF THOMASINA, THE(1963, U.S./Brit.); CUP FEVER(1965, Brit.); GOLDEN HEAD, THE(1965, Hung., U.S.); TOMB OF LIGEIA, THE(1965, Brit.); PSYCHOMANIA(1974, Brit.)
Dennis Gilmore
HAND IN HAND(1960, Brit.); FAHRENHEIT 451(1966, Brit.)
Doris Gilmore
ONE WAY OUT(1955, Brit.)
Dorothy Gilmore
CHOCOLATE SOLDIER, THE(1941); MADAME CURIE(1943); HARVEY GIRLS, THE(1946)
Douglas Gilmore
MARRIED IN HOLLYWOOD(1929); PLEASURE CRAZED(1929); SONG OF KENTUCKY(1929); CAMEO KIRBY(1930); HELL'S ANGELS(1930); DESERT VENGEANCE(1931); GIRL HABIT(1931); NAUGHTY FLIRT, THE(1931); UNFAITHFUL(1931)
Silents
LOVE'S BLINDNESS(1926); ROUGH HOUSE ROSIE(1927); TAXI DANCER, THE(1927); OBJECT–ALIMONY(1929)
Misc. Silents
DANCE MADNESS(1926); PARIS(1926); KISS IN A TAXI, A(1927)
Eleanore Gilmore
Silents
BIG PUNCH, THE(1921)
Frank Gilmore
Misc. Silents
LIFTED VEIL, THE(1917)
Gail Gilmore
BEACH BALL(1965); HARUM SCARUM(1965); VILLAGE OF THE GIANTS(1965)
Gale Gilmore
GIRL HAPPY(1965)
Helen Gilmore
Silents
EARL OF PAWTUCKET, THE(1915); HUCK AND TOM(1918); FICKLE WOMEN(1920); BLAZING TRAIL, THE(1921); IMPULSE(1922); TOO MUCH BUSINESS(1922); SAFETY LAST(1923); SENSATION SEEKERS(1927)
J.H. Gilmore
Silents
SCHOOL DAYS(1921)
Misc. Silents
DEMOCRACY(1920); LIFE(1920); WAKEFIELD CASE, THE(1921)
Jim Gilmore
ELECTRA GLIDE IN BLUE(1973)
John Gilmore
RAW EDGE(1956); HOUSE OF THE DAMNED(1963)
Jonathan Gilmore
VOYAGE TO THE BOTTOM OF THE SEA(1961)
Julia Gilmore
1984
MEMOIRS(1984, Can.), a, m
Lillian Gilmore
Misc. Talkies
RAWHIDE MAIL(1934); UNCONQUERED BANDIT(1935); WOLF RIDERS(1935)
Misc. Silents
MOJAVE KID, THE(1927); STRAIGHT SHOOTIN'(1927); PHANTOM FLYER, THE(1928)
Lowell Gilmore
DAYS OF GLORY(1944); JOHNNY ANGEL(1945); PICTURE OF DORIAN GRAY, THE(1945); STEP BY STEP(1946); STRANGE CONQUEST(1946); ARNELO AFFAIR, THE(1947); CALCUTTA(1947); DREAM GIRL(1947); BLACK ARROW(1948); PRINCE OF THIEVES, THE(1948); WALK A CROOKED MILE(1948); SECRET GARDEN, THE(1949); SWORD IN THE DESERT(1949); FORTUNES OF CAPTAIN BLOOD(1950); KING SOLOMON'S MINES(1950); ROGUES OF SHERWOOD FOREST(1950); TRIPOLI(1950); DARLING, HOW COULD YOU!(1951); HIGHWAYMAN, THE(1951); HONG KONG(1951); ROADBLOCK(1951); ANDROCLES AND THE LION(1952); LONE STAR(1952); PLYMOUTH ADVENTURE(1952); FRANCIS COVERS THE BIG TOWN(1953); DAY OF TRIUMPH(1954); SASKATCHEWAN(1954); MA AND PA KETTLE AT WAIKIKI(1955); SEA CHASE, THE(1955); COMANCHE(1956); JEANNE EAGELS(1957)
Margalo Gilmore
BEHAVE YOURSELF(1951)
Lt. Comdr. Morris D. Gilmore, U.S.N.
HELL BELOW(1933), tech adv
Paul Gilmore
Silents
PENITENTES, THE(1915)
Misc. Silents
ROSEMARY(1915); OTHER GIRL, THE(1916); SHRINE OF HAPPINESS, THE(1916)
Peter Gilmore
BOMB IN THE HIGH STREET(1961, Brit.); CARRY ON CABBIE(1963, Brit.); CARRY ON JACK(1963, Brit.); CARRY ON CLEO(1964, Brit.); MASTER SPY(1964, Brit.); I'VE GOTTA HORSE(1965, Brit.); SEASIDE SWINGERS(1965, Brit.); YOU MUST BE JOKING!(1965, Brit.); CARRY ON COWBOY(1966, Brit.); GREAT ST. TRINIAN'S TRAIN ROBBERY, THE(1966, Brit.); CARNABY, M.D.(1967, Brit.); DON'T LOSE

YOUR HEAD(1967, Brit.); FOLLOW THAT CAMEL(1967, Brit.); JOKERS, THE(1967, Brit.); CARRY ON DOCTOR(1968, Brit.); CARRY ON, UP THE KHYBER(1968, Brit.); OH! WHAT A LOVELY WAR(1969, Brit.); CARRY ON HENRY VIII(1970, Brit.); MY LOVER, MY SON(1970, Brit.); ABOMINABLE DR. PHIBES, THE(1971, Brit.); WARLORDS OF ATLANTIS(1978, Brit.)
Sally Gilmore
THEATRE OF BLOOD(1973, Brit.)
Stewart Gilmore
ARREST BULLDOG DRUMMOND(1939, Brit.), ed
Stuart Gilmore
MAN'S FAVORITE SPORT(?)**1/2 (1964), ed; TOYS IN THE ATTIC(1963), ed; THOROUGHLY MODERN MILLIE(1967), ed; WILD MONEY(1937), ed; CAMPUS CONFESSIONS(1938), ed; AMBUSH(1939), ed; MILLION DOLLAR LEGS(1939), ed; UNMARRIED(1939), ed; COMIN' ROUND THE MOUNTAIN(1940), ed; MOON OVER BURMA(1940), ed; UNTAMED(1940), ed; WAY OF ALL FLESH, THE(1940), ed; LADY EVE, THE(1941), ed; SULLIVAN'S TRAVELS(1941), ed; PALM BEACH STORY, THE(1942), ed; GREAT MOMENT, THE(1944), ed; HAIL THE CONQUERING HERO(1944), ed; HOUR BEFORE THE DAWN, THE(1944), ed; MIRACLE OF MORGAN'S CREEK, THE(1944), ed; OUT OF THIS WORLD(1945), ed; ROAD TO UTOPIA(1945), ed; VIRGINIAN, THE(1946), d; VENDETTA(1950), ed; HOT LEAD(1951), d; CAPTIVE WOMEN(1952), d; HALF-BREED, THE(1952), d; TARGET(1952), d; UNDERWATER!(1955), ed; CONQUEROR, THE(1956), ed sup; WAR AND PEACE(1956, Ital./U.S.), ed; ENEMY BELOW, THE(1957), ed; BARBARIAN AND THE GEISHA, THE(1958), ed; HUNTERS, THE(1958), ed, spec eff; STAGE STRUCK(1958), ed; HOLIDAY FOR LOVERS(1959), ed; JOURNEY TO THE CENTER OF THE EARTH(1959), ed; SOUND AND THE FURY, THE(1959), ed; ALAMO, THE(1960), ed; HATARI!(1962), ed; KID GALAHAD(1962), ed; TWO FOR THE SEESAW(1962), ed; WORLD OF HENRY ORIENT, THE(1964), ed; RAGE TO LIVE, A(1965), ed; RED LINE 7000(1965), ed; HAWAII(1966), ed; ROSIE!(1967), ed; YOURS, MINE AND OURS(1968), ed; SWEET CHARITY(1969), ed; AIRPORT(1970), ed; ANDROMEDA STRAIN, THE(1971), ed
Tex C.C. Gilmore
OBLIGING YOUNG LADY(1941)
Verna Gilmore
WOMAN FOR JOE, THE(1955, Brit.)
Virginia Gilmore
WINTER CARNIVAL(1939); LADDIE(1940); MANHATTAN HEARTBEAT(1940); JENNIE(1941); SWAMP WATER(1941); TALL, DARK AND HANDSOME(1941); WESTERN UNION(1941); BERLIN CORRESPONDENT(1942); LOVES OF EDGAR ALLAN POE, THE(1942); ORCHESTRA WIVES(1942); PRIDE OF THE YANKEES, THE(1942); SON OF FURY(1942); SUNDOWN JIM(1942); THAT OTHER WOMAN(1942); CHETNIKS(1943); WONDER MAN(1945); CARTER CASE, THE(1947); CLOSE-UP(1948); WALK EAST ON BEACON(1952)
Wendy Gilmore
SCHIZO(1977, Brit.)
William S. Gilmore
LAST REMAKE OF BEAU GESTE, THE(1977), p; TOUGH ENOUGH(1983), p
1984
AGAINST ALL ODDS(1984), p
William S. Gilmore, Jr.
DEFIANCE(1980), p
Arthur D. Gilmour
MOLE PEOPLE, THE(1956)
Catherine Gilmour
NIGHT SHIFT(1982)
Doris Gilmour
SELF-MADE LADY(1932, Brit.)
Geoff Gilmour
NED KELLY(1970, Brit.)
George Gilmour
APPLE, THE(1980 U.S./Ger.)
Ian Gilmour
MOUTH TO MOUTH(1978, Aus.); JUST OUT OF REACH(1979, Aus.); ODD ANGRY SHOT, THE(1979, Aus.)
J.H. Gilmour
Silents
KING LEAR(1916); NAULAHKA, THE(1918); IMPOSSIBLE CATHERINE(1919); KENTUCKIANS, THE(1921); SUCH A LITTLE QUEEN(1921)
Misc. Silents
VICTORY OF VIRTUE, THE(1915); OTHER PEOPLE'S MONEY(1916); CANDY GIRL, THE(1917); CROOKED ROMANCE, A(1917); MAN WITHOUT A COUNTRY, THE(1917); MARK OF CAIN, THE(1917); MARY LAWSON'S SECRET(1917); OVER THE HILL(1917); STREETS OF ILLUSION, THE(1917); CONVICT 993(1918); HILLCREST MYSTERY, THE(1918); KEY TO POWER, THE(1918); WAIFS(1918); WHIRLPOOL, THE(1918)
Victor Gilmour
DRIVER, THE(1978)
Joseph H. Gilmour
Misc. Silents
HER BELOVED ENEMY(1917)
Sally Gilmour
Misc. Talkies
ALL HALLOWE'EN(1952)
J.H. Gilmour [Gilmore]
Misc. Silents
FIRST LAW, THE(1918)
Yolande Gilot
GIFT, THE(1983, Fr./Ital.)
Guy Gilpatric
ACTION IN THE NORTH ATLANTIC(1943), w
April Gilpin
JAWS II(1978); EARTHBOUND(1981)
Charles Gilpin
Misc. Silents
TEN NIGHTS IN A BARROOM(1926)
Jay Gilpin
SOUTHERNER, THE(1945); ARCH OF TRIUMPH(1948)

Jean Gilpin
CATCH ME A SPY(1971, Brit./Fr.); WORLD IS FULL OF MARRIED MEN, THE(1980, Brit.)

John Gilpin
THEY WERE SISTERS(1945, Brit.); YEARS BETWEEN, THE(1947, Brit.); THEATRE OF BLOOD(1973, Brit.)

Marc Gilpin
JAWS II(1978); EARTHBOUND(1981); LEGEND OF THE LONE RANGER, THE(1981)
Misc. Talkies
WHERE'S WILLIE?(1978)

Sally Gilpin
HALF A SIXPENCE(1967, Brit.); MACBETH(1971, Brit.), ch; PUBLIC EYE, THE(1972, Brit.), ch; CROSSED SWORDS(1978), ch

Toni Gilpin
FAREWELL PERFORMANCE(1963, Brit.); GORGON, THE(1964, Brit.); SATURDAY NIGHT OUT(1964, Brit.); MUMMY'S SHROUD, THE(1967, Brit.)

Barbara Gilroy
Silents
OVAL DIAMOND, THE(1916)
Misc. Silents
COMMON SENSE BRACKETT(1916); DARK SILENCE, THE(1916); HER FATHER'S GOLD(1916)

Bert Gilroy
BORDER G-MAN(1938), p; GUN LAW(1938), p; LAWLESS VALLEY(1938), p; PAINTED DESERT, THE(1938), p; RENEGADE RANGER(1938), p; ARIZONA LEGION(1939), p; FIGHTING GRINGO, THE(1939), p; MARSHAL OF MESA CITY, THE(1939), p; RACKETEERS OF THE RANGE(1939), p; ROOKIE COP, THE(1939), p; TIMBER STAMPEDE(1939), p; TROUBLE IN SUNDOWN(1939), p; BULLET CODE(1940), p; LEGION OF THE LAWLESS(1940), p; POP ALWAYS PAYS(1940), p; PRAIRIE LAW(1940), p; STAGE TO CHINO(1940), p; TRIPLE JUSTICE(1940), p; WAGON TRAIN(1940), p; ALONG THE RIO GRANDE(1941), p; BANDIT TRAIL, THE(1941), p; CYCLONE ON HORSEBACK(1941), p; DUDE COWBOY(1941), p; FARGO KID, THE(1941), p; LAND OF THE OPEN RANGE(1941), p; ROBBERS OF THE RANGE(1941), p; SIX GUN GOLD(1941), p; THUNDERING HOOFS(1941), p; ARMY SURGEON(1942), p; BANDIT RANGER(1942), p; COME ON DANGER(1942), p; MEXICAN SPITFIRE'S ELEPHANT(1942), p; PIRATES OF THE PRAIRIE(1942), p; RIDING THE WIND(1942), p; ADVENTURES OF A ROOKIE(1943), p; AVENGING RIDER, THE(1943), p; FIGHTING FRONTIER(1943), p; LADIES' DAY(1943), p; MEXICAN SPITFIRE'S BLESSED EVENT(1943), p; PETTICOAT LARCENY(1943), p; RED RIVER ROBIN HOOD(1943), p; ROOKIES IN BURMA(1943), p; SAGEBRUSH LAW(1943), p

Charles Gilroy
1984
STRIKEBOUND(1984, Aus.)

Frank D. Gilroy
FASTEST GUN ALIVE(1956), w; GALLANT HOURS, THE(1960), w; SUBJECT WAS ROSES, THE(1968), w; ONLY GAME IN TOWN, THE(1970), w; DESPERATE CHARACTERS(1971), p&d; FROM NOON TO THREE(1976), d&w; ONCE IN PARIS(1978), p, d&w

Gabrielle Gilroy
Silents
ST. ELMO(1923, Brit.)

Ian Gilroy
STARSTRUCK(1982, Aus.)

David Gilruth
PLAYERS(1979)

Charles E. Gilson
RAMPARTS WE WATCH, THE(1940), ph
Silents
JOHNNY RING AND THE CAPTAIN'S SWORD(1921), ph; LUCK(1923), ph; EARLY BIRD, THE(1925), ph

Charles Gilson
Silents
NUMBER 17(1920), ph

Tom Gilson
RALLY 'ROUND THE FLAG, BOYS!(1958); YOUNG AND WILD(1958); CROWDED SKY, THE(1960); HOME FROM THE HILL(1960); THIS REBEL BREED(1960); THREAT, THE(1960); CONVICTS FOUR(1962)

Ethel Gilstrom
MEET JOHN DOE(1941)

Donal Giltinan
WE SHALL SEE(1964, Brit.), w

Donal Giltinian
CHANGE PARTNERS(1965, Brit.), w; DEAD MAN'S CHEST(1965, Brit.), w

H.W. Gim
MC LINTOCK!(1963); SEVEN WOMEN(1966); PAINT YOUR WAGON(1969); TRUE GRIT(1969)

Hom Wing Gim
HER HUSBAND'S AFFAIRS(1947); PEKING EXPRESS(1951)

Dick Gimble
HONEYSUCKLE ROSE(1980)

John Gimble
HONKYTONK MAN(1982)

Johnny Gimble
HONEYSUCKLE ROSE(1980)
1984
SONGWRITER(1984)

Jean-Marie Gimel
TIGHT SKIRTS, LOOSE PLEASURES(1966, Fr.), ed

Jean Gimello
CASTLE KEEP(1969)

Claudia Gimenez
1984
GABRIELA(1984, Braz.)

Juan Gimenez
HEAVY METAL(1981, Can.), anim

Raul Gimenez
LILI MARLEEN(1981, Ger.); LOLA(1982, Ger.)

Antonio Gimeno
PLANET OF THE VAMPIRES(1965, U.S./Ital./Span.), ed; HYPNOSIS(1966, Ger./Sp./Ital.), ed

John Giminez
WAY OUT(1966), a, w

Prudencio Giminez
DARK RIVER(1956, Arg.), md

The Gimma Boys
TRAPEZE(1956)

William Gimmi
NOW THAT APRIL'S HERE(1958, Can.), ph

Gena Gimmy
CURSE OF THE BLOOD GHOULS(1969, Ital.)

Barney Gimore
Silents
ALMOST A LADY(1926)

Jacob Gimpel
POSSESSED(1947); STRANGE FASCINATION(1952), m; STORY OF THREE LOVES, THE(1953)

Jakob Gimpel
GASLIGHT(1944)

Sandra Gimpel
GNOME-MOBILE, THE(1967)

Sandy Gimpel
SIXTH AND MAIN(1977), stunts

Teresa Gimpera
CRYPT OF THE LIVING DEAD zero(1973); EAGLE OVER LONDON(1973, Ital.); BRIEF VACATION, A(1975, Ital.); TEN LITTLE INDIANS(1975, Ital./Fr./Span./Ger.); SPIRIT OF THE BEEHIVE, THE(1976, Span.)

Theresa Gimpera
Misc. Talkies
HANNAH-QUEEN OF THE VAMPIRES(1972)

Allen Gin
PAL JOEY(1957)

Gina
FLASH GORDON(1980)

Betsy Gindele
WHERE ANGELS GO...TROUBLE FOLLOWS(1968)

Mark Gindes
LOVE AT FIRST BITE(1979), w

Bus Gindhart
MR. MAJESTYK(1974)

Mikhail Gindin
1812(1944, USSR), ph

Bryan Gindoff
LOSIN' IT(1983), p

Bryan Gindorff
HARD TIMES(1975), w

Jose Antonio Perez Giner
SAGA OF DRACULA, THE(1975, Span.), p

Magda Giner
SANTO CONTRA BLUE DEMON EN LA ATLANTIDA(1968, Mex.)

Carlos Gines
BYE-BYE BRASIL(1980, Braz.)

Rinaldo Gines
BYE-BYE BRASIL(1980, Braz.)

Jeanette Ginestet
CESAR(1936, Fr.), ed

Aveling Ginever
BARNACLE BILL(1935, Brit.), w; KNIGHTS FOR A DAY(1937, Brit.), p, d, w; WALKING ON AIR(1946, Brit.), d, w

Jack Ging
GHOST OF DRAGSTRIP HOLLOW(1959); DESIRE IN THE DUST(1960); SNIPER'S RIDGE(1961); TESS OF THE STORM COUNTRY(1961); INTIMACY(1966); HANG'EM HIGH(1968); PLAY MISTY FOR ME(1971); HIGH PLAINS DRIFTER(1973); SSSSSSSS(1973); THAT MAN BOLT(1973); WHERE THE RED FERN GROWS(1974)
Misc. Talkies
COMPANION, THE(1976); DIE SISTER, DIE(1978)

Jay Ginger
JETLAG(1981, U.S./Span.)

Johnny Ginger
OUTLAWS IS COMING, THE(1965)

Nancy Ginger
1984
BLOOD SIMPLE(1984)

Helene Gingold
Misc. Silents
HIDDEN HAND, THE(1916, Brit.)

Hermione Gingold
DANCE PRETTY LADY(1932, Brit.); SOMEONE AT THE DOOR(1936, Brit.); MERRY COMES TO STAY(1937, Brit.); MEET MR. PENNY(1938, Brit.); BUTLER'S DILEMMA, THE(1943, Brit.); PICKWICK PAPERS, THE(1952, Brit.); SLASHER, THE(1953, Brit.); ADVENTURES OF SADIE, THE(1955, Brit.); AROUND THE WORLD IN 80 DAYS(1956); BELL, BOOK AND CANDLE(1958); GIGI(1958); NAKED EDGE, THE(1961); GAY PURR-EE(1962); MUSIC MAN, THE(1962); I'D RATHER BE RICH(1964); HARVEY MIDDLEMAN, FIREMAN(1965); MUNSTER, GO HOME(1966); PROMISE HER ANYTHING(1966, Brit.); THOSE FANTASTIC FLYING FOOLS(1967, Brit); LITTLE NIGHT MUSIC, A(1977, Aust./U.S./Ger.)
1984
GARBO TALKS(1984)

Carmen Gingras
I CONFESS(1953)

Eden Ginn
FRATERNITY ROW(1977)

Hayward Ginn
Silents
ALIEN, THE(1915)

Jeff Ginn
REUBEN, REUBEN(1983), set d
Stewart Ginn
DEMONSTRATOR(1971, Aus.)
Robert Emmett Ginna
YOUNG CASSIDY(1965, U.S./Brit.), p; LAST CHALLENGE, THE(1967), w; BEFORE
WINTER COMES(1969, Brit.), p; BROTHERLY LOVE(1970, Brit.), p
Anthony I. Ginnane
FANTASM(1976, Aus.), p, w; PATRICK(1979, Aus.), p; SURVIVOR(1980, Aus.), p;
DAY AFTER HALLOWEEN, THE(1981, Aus.), p
1984
SECOND TIME LUCKY(1984, Aus./New Zealand), p; TREASURE OF THE YANKEE
ZEPHYR(1984), p
Antony L Ginnane
THIRST(1979, Aus.), p; DEAD KIDS(1981 Aus./New Zealand), p
Tony Ginnane
HARLEQUIN(1980, Aus.), p
Bob Ginnaven
ENCOUNTER WITH THE UNKNOWN(1973); So SAD ABOUT GLORIA(1973)
Misc. Talkies
DAY IT CAME TO EARTH, THE(1979)
Illa Ginnaven
TWO-LANE BLACKTOP(1971)
Robert Ginnaven
WHITE LIGHTNING(1973)
Abram S. Ginnes
GAILY, GAILY(1969), w
Randy Ginns
UP THE SANDBOX(1972)
Robert Ginns
GEORGE IN CIVVY STREET(1946, Brit.)
Allen Ginsberg
CHAPPAQUA(1967); ME AND MY BROTHER(1969); PROLOGUE(1970, Can.);
RENALDO AND CLARA(1978)
Arthur Ginsberg
1984
GIRLS NIGHT OUT(1984), ed
Claire Ginsberg
MICROWAVE MASSACRE(1983)
Donald Ginsberg
TURNERS OF PROSPECT ROAD, THE(1947, Brit.), ed; ARMCHAIR DETECTIVE,
THE(1952, Brit.), p; COLONEL MARCH INVESTIGATES(1952,Brit.), p; TREAD SOFT-
LY(1952, Brit.), p; LIMPING MAN, THE(1953, Brit.), p; NOBODY WAVED GOOD-
BYE(1965, Can.), ed; CHANGE OF MIND(1969), ed; FORTUNE AND MEN'S
EYES(1971, U.S./Can.), p; SEARCH AND DESTROY(1981), ed; LOVE(1982, Can.), ed
Henry Ginsberg
CONDEMNED(1929); GIANT(1956), p
Milton Moses Ginsberg
WEREWOLF OF WASHINGTON(1973), d,w&ed
Misc. Talkies
COMING APART(1969), d
A. Ginsburg
WINGS OF VICTORY(1941, USSR), ph
Don Ginsburg
I MISS YOU, HUGS AND KISSES(1978, Can.), ed
Norman Ginsburg
MR. EMMANUEL(1945, Brit.), w
Robin Ginsburg
DREAM ON(1981)
Norman Ginsbury
MAGIC BOW, THE(1947, Brit.), w; AFFAIRS OF A ROGUE, THE(1949, Brit.), w
Brad F. Ginter
FLESH FEAST(1970), p, d, w
Richie Ginther
GRAND PRIX(1966), a, tech adv
A. Gintsburg
SECRET BRIGADE, THE(1951 USSR), ph
Alexander Gintsburg
HYPERBOLOID OF ENGINEER GARIN, THE(1965, USSR), d, w
Robert Ginty
TWO-MINUTE WARNING(1976); COMING HOME(1978); EXTERMINATOR,
THE(1980); SCARAB(1982, U.S./Span.)
1984
ACT, THE(1984); EXTERMINATOR 2(1984)
Misc. Talkies
ALCHEMIST, THE(1981)
Three Ginx
DISCOVERIES(1939, Brit.)
Joey Ginza
Misc. Talkies
BLACK LOLITA(1975)
Natalia Ginzburg
GOSPEL ACCORDING TO ST. MATTHEW, THE(1966, Fr., Ital.)
Valeriy Ginzburg
WHEN THE TREES WERE TALL(1965, USSR), ph
Gio
RUMBLE FISH(1983)
Frank Gio
VALACHI PAPERS, THE(1972, Ital./Fr.); COPS AND ROBBERS(1973); SOR-
CERER(1977)
1984
ONCE UPON A TIME IN AMERICA(1984)
Gioacchino
DREAM OF BUTTERFLY, THE(1941, Ital.)
Vivi Gioi
RICE GIRL(1963, Fr./Ital.)
Eva Gioia
8 ½(1963, Ital.)

Paula Giokaris
WAR DRUMS(1957), cos; LONG ROPE, THE(1961), cos; PURPLE HILLS, THE(1961),
cos; TWO LITTLE BEARS, THE(1961), cos; I'LL TAKE SWEDEN(1965), cos; FOR-
TUNE COOKIE, THE(1966), cos; LORD LOVE A DUCK(1966), cos; WILD, WILD
WINTER(1966), cos
Vou Lee Giokaris
PROMISES, PROMISES(1963), cos; TERROR IN THE WAX MUSEUM(1973), cos
Voulee Giokaris
TROOPER HOOK(1957), cos; MAN WITH BOGART'S FACE, THE(1980), cos
Vivi Giol
EARTH CRIES OUT, THE(1949, Ital.); VERONA TRIAL, THE(1963, Ital.)
Marcello Giombini
GLADIATORS 7(1964, Span./Ital.), m; LOVE AND MARRIAGE(1966, Ital.), m;
KNIVES OF THE AVENGER(1967, Ital.), m; NARCO MEN, THE(1969, Span./Ital.), m;
RETURN OF SABATA(1972, Ital./Fr./Ger.), m
Marcelo Giombini
SABATA(1969, Ital.), m
Amadeo Giomini
DIARY OF A CLOISTERED NUN(1973, Ital./Fr./Ger.), ed
Amedeo Giomini
PSYCHOUT FOR MURDER(1971, Arg./Ital.), ed; ITALIAN CONNECTION,
THE(1973, U.S./Ital./Ger.), ed
Renato Giomini
TIGER OF THE SEVEN SEAS(1964, Fr./Ital.)
Romano Giomini
QUEEN OF THE NILE(1964, Ital.); MYSTERY OF THUG ISLAND, THE(1966,
Ital./Ger.)
Christian Gion
1984
HERE COMES SANTA CLAUS(1984), p&d, w
Joey Giondello
MOONRUNNERS(1975)
Gustavo Gionno
ROVER, THE(1967, Ital.)
Jean Giono
HARVEST(1939, Fr.), w; BAKER'S WIFE, THE(1940, Fr.), w; WAYS OF LOVE(1950,
Ital./Fr.), w; SOUTHERN STAR, THE(1969, Fr./Brit.), w
Marcello Giorda
DEFEAT OF HANNIBAL, THE(1937, Ital.); RIGOLETTO(1949); WHERE THE HOT
WIND BLOWS(1960, Fr., Ital.); GREAT WAR, THE(1961, Fr., Ital.)
Carlo Giordana
FELLINI SATYRICON(1969, Fr./Ital.)
Aldo Giordani
THREE STEPS NORTH(1951), ph; SINGING TAXI DRIVER(1953, Ital.), ph; TOO
BAD SHE'S BAD(1954, Ital.), ph; MINOTAUR, THE(1961, Ital.), ph; WHITE SLAVE
SHIP(1962, Fr./Ital.), ph; SEVEN DWARFS TO THE RESCUE, THE(1965, Ital.), ph;
MONGOLS, THE(1966, Fr./Ital.), ph; KILL OR BE KILLED(1967, Ital.), ph; THEY
CALL ME TRINITY(1971, Ital.), ph; TRINITY IS STILL MY NAME(1971, Ital.), ph;
MAN FROM THE EAST, A(1974, Ital./Fr.), ph
Pietro Paulo Giordani
PRIMITIVE LOVE(1966, Ital.), p
Robert Giordani
MR. PEEK-A-BOO(1951, Fr.), art d; MONTE CARLO BABY(1953, Fr.), art d; LET-
TERS FROM MY WINDMILL(1955, Fr.), art d; MOST WANTED MAN, THE(1962,
Fr./Ital.), art d; JUDEX(1966, Fr./Ital.), art d; SUCKER, THE(1966, Fr./Ital.), art d
Romolo Giordani
LA DOLCE VITA(1961, Ital./Fr.)
Aldo Giordano
ATOM AGE VAMPIRE(1961, Ital.), ph
Amodio Giordano
NIGHTBEAST(1982), makeup
1984
SPLATTER UNIVERSITY(1984), makeup
Arnold Giordano
OH! CALCUTTA!(1972), ph
Daniela Giordano
FIVE MAN ARMY, THE(1970, Ital.)
Domiziana Giordano
1984
NOSTALGHIA(1984, USSR/Ital.)
Mariangela Giordano
DESERT WARRIOR(1961 Ital./Span.); MIGHTY URSUS(1962, Ital./Span.); EYE OF
THE NEEDLE, THE(1965, Ital./Fr.); MAIDEN FOR A PRINCE, A(1967, Fr./Ital.)
Mariangella Giordano
NO ROOM TO DIE(1969, Ital.)
Umberto Giordano
FEDORA(1946, Ital.), m
Michael Giordano III
SUCH GOOD FRIENDS(1971)
A. Giordenngo
GREEN TREE, THE(1965, Ital.)
Gabriella Giorgelli
ORGANIZER, THE(1964, Fr./Ital./Yugo.); EL GRECO(1966, Ital., Fr.); THE DIRTY
GAME(1966, Fr./Ital./Ger.); BEAUTIFUL SWINDLERS, THE(1967, Fr./Ital./Jap./
Neth.); CHASTITY BELT, THE(1968, Ital.); IN SEARCH OF GREGORY(1970, Brit./
Ital.); CITY OF WOMEN(1980, Ital./Fr.)
Florence Giorgetti
LACEMAKER, THE(1977, Fr.)
Eleanora Giorgi
DIARY OF A CLOISTERED NUN(1973, Ital./Fr./Ger.)
Eleonora Giorgi
INFERNO(1980, Ital.)
Livio Giorgi
GODFATHER, THE, PART II(1974)
Piero Giorgi
MERCHANT OF SLAVES(1949, Ital.), m
Gabriella Giorgielli
ARTURO'S ISLAND(1963, Ital.); HERCULES(1983)

Joseph W. Girard
TERROR, THE(1928); STRICTLY DISHONORABLE(1931); FIGHTING TROOPER, THE(1935); KENTUCKY BLUE STREAK(1935); UNASHAMED(1938)
Silents
20,000 LEAGUES UNDER THE SEA(1916); IN HOLLYWOOD WITH POTASH AND PERLMUTTER(1924); NIGHT OWL, THE(1926); SPEED CRAZED(1926); BULLET MARK, THE(1928); PARTNERS IN CRIME(1928); STOP THAT MAN(1928); KING OF THE RODEO(1929)
Misc. Silents
HUNTRESS OF MEN, THE(1916); MAN FROM NOWHERE, THE(1916); DANGEROUS PATHS(1921); FLYING MAIL, THE(1926); MARLIE THE KILLER(1928); BACK FROM SHANGHAI(1929)
Maria Girard
DESPERATE WOMEN, THE(?)
Octavio Girard
FRONTIERS OF '49(1939)
Oliver Girard
TO COMMIT A MURDER(1970, Fr./Ital./Ger.), art d
Olivier Girard
LOVERS ON A TIGHTROPE(1962, Fr.), art d; LIFE UPSIDE DOWN(1965, Fr.), art d
Paulette Girard
VIOLATED PARADISE(1963, Ital./Jap.)
Roland Girard
THINGS OF LIFE, THE(1970, Fr./Ital./Switz.), p; MADAME ROSA(1977, Fr.), p
Wendy Girard
ANNIE HALL(1977)
Wesley Girard
HIGH GEAR(1933); DEAD END(1937)
William Girard
BERMUDA MYSTERY(1944), p; LADIES OF WASHINGTON(1944), p; BULLFIGHTERS, THE(1945), p; CARIBBEAN MYSTERY, THE(1945), p; CIRCUMSTANTIAL EVIDENCE(1945), p; IT SHOULDN'T HAPPEN TO A DOG(1946), p
Giuliano Girardi
SUNFLOWER(1970, Fr./Ital.)
Mirna Girardi
IL GRIDO(1962, U.S./Ital.)
Ray Girardin
MAX DUGAN RETURNS(1983)
Misc. Talkies
HOLLYWOOD MAN, THE(1976)
Etienne Girardo
CURLY TOP(1935)
Michele Girardon
GINA(1961, Fr./Mex.); HATARI!(1962); SEVEN CAPITAL SINS(1962, Fr./Ital.); WHITE SLAVE SHIP(1962, Fr./Ital.); MAGNIFICENT CUCKOLD, THE(1965, Fr./Ital.); TENDER SCOUNDREL(1967, Fr./Ital.); DEATH IN THE GARDEN(1977, Fr./Mex.)
Annie Girardot
MAIGRET LAYS A TRAP(1958, Fr.); LOVE AND THE FRENCHWOMAN(1961, Fr.); ROCCO AND HIS BROTHERS(1961, Fr./Ital.); CRIME DOES NOT PAY(1962, Fr.); LOVERS ON A TIGHTROPE(1962, Fr.); APE WOMAN, THE(1964, Ital.); LA BONNE SOUPE(1964, Fr./Ital./Yugo.); ORGANIZER, THE(1964, Fr./Ital.); MALE COMPANION(1965, Fr./Ital.); VICE AND VIRTUE(1965, Fr./Ital.); ENGAGEMENT ITALIANO(1966, Fr./Ital.); THE DIRTY GAME(1966, Fr./Ital./Ger.); LIVE FOR LIFE(1967, Fr./Ital.); DILLINGER IS DEAD(1969, Ital.); LES GAULOISES BLEUES(1969, Fr.); LIFE LOVE DEATH(1969, Fr./Ital.); WITCHES, THE(1969, Fr./Ital.); LOVE IS A FUNNY THING(1970, Fr./Ital.); SEED OF MAN, THE(1970, Ital.); STORY OF A WOMAN(1970, U.S./Ital.); SHOCK TREATMENT(1973, Fr.); DEAR DETECTIVE(1978, Fr.); NO TIME FOR BREAKFAST(1978, Fr.); ALL NIGHT LONG(1981); LA VIE CONTINUE(1982, Fr.)
Etienne Girardot
BISHOP MISBEHAVES, THE(1933); BLOOD MONEY(1933); KENNEL MURDER CASE, THE(1933); BORN TO BE BAD(1934); DRAGON MURDER CASE, THE(1934); FASHIONS OF 1934(1934); FIREBIRD, THE(1934); LITTLE MAN, WHAT NOW?(1934); MANDALAY(1934); RETURN OF THE TERROR(1934); TWENTIETH CENTURY(1934); CHASING YESTERDAY(1935); CLIVE OF INDIA(1935); GRAND OLD GIRL(1935); HOORAY FOR LOVE(1935); I LIVE MY LIFE(1935); IN OLD KENTUCKY(1935); METROPOLITAN(1935); WHOLE TOWN'S TALKING, THE(1935); COLLEGE HOLIDAY(1936); DEVIL IS A SISSY, THE(1936); GARDEN MURDER CASE, THE(1936); HALF ANGEL(1936); HEARTS DIVIDED(1936); LONGEST NIGHT, THE(1936); MUSIC GOES ROUND, THE(1936); BREAKFAST FOR TWO(1937); DANGER—LOVE AT WORK(1937); GREAT GARRICK, THE(1937); ROAD BACK, THE(1937); WAKE UP AND LIVE(1937); ARIZONA WILDCAT(1938); HAVING WONDERFUL TIME(1938); PORT OF SEVEN SEAS(1938); PROFESSOR BEWARE(1938); THERE GOES MY HEART(1938); EXILE EXPRESS(1939); FAST AND LOOSE(1939); FOR LOVE OR MONEY(1939); HUNCHBACK OF NOTRE DAME, THE(1939); LITTLE ACCIDENT(1939); STORY OF VERNON AND IRENE CASTLE, THE(1939); ISLE OF DESTINY(1940)
Silents
ARTIE, THE MILLIONAIRE KID(1916)
Hippolyte Girardot
1984
LE BON PLAISIR(1984, Fr.)
Hyppolite Girardot
1984
FIRST NAME: CARMEN(1984, Fr.)
Claude Giraud
CIRCLE OF LOVE(1965, Fr.); ADVENTURES OF RABBI JACOB, THE(1973, Fr.)
Daniel Giraud
RETURN OF MARTIN GUERRE, THE(1983, Fr.)
Joseph Giraud
FROM HEADQUARTERS(1929)
Octavia Giraud
DRIFTING WESTWARD(1939)
Octavio Giraud
OREGON TRAIL, THE(1936); CROSSROADS(1942)
Octavio J. Giraud
MESSAGE TO GARCIA, A(1936); CAFE METROPOLE(1937)

Renee Giraud
UNCANNY, THE(1977, Brit./Can.)
Wesley Giraud
ONE-MAN LAW(1932); WHISTLIN' DAN(1932); WAR OF THE RANGE(1933); NO GREATER GLORY(1934); TRUE CONFESSION(1937); SHOPWORN ANGEL(1938); DOCTOR TAKES A WIFE(1940)
Bernard Giraudeau
TWO MEN IN TOWN(1973, Fr.); PASSION OF LOVE(1982, Ital./Fr.); LA BOUM(1983, Fr.)
Jean Giraudoux
ANGELS OF THE STREETS(1950, Fr.), w; MADWOMAN OF CHAILLOT, THE(1969), w
Jean Girault
GENDARME OF ST. TROPEZ, THE(1966, Fr./Ital.), d, w; LE GENDARME ET LES EXTRATERRESTRES(1978, Fr.), d
G. Gircher-Cherikover
Misc. Silents
WANDERING STARS(1927, USSR), d
William Girdler
ABBY(1974), p, d; SHEBA BABY(1975), w, d; GRIZZLY(1976), d; PROJECT: KILL(1976), d; DAY OF THE ANIMALS(1977), d; MANITOU, THE(1978), p&d, w
Misc. Talkies
ASYLUM OF SATAN(1972), d; THREE ON A MEATHOOK(1973), d; ZEBRA KILLER, THE(1974), d
Margherita Girelli
DIVORCE, ITALIAN STYLE(1962, Ital.); CRAZY DESIRE(1964, Ital.)
Francoise Giret
TALES OF PARIS(1962, Fr./Ital.); SEVENTH JUROR, THE(1964, Fr.); MY BABY IS BLACK!(1965, Fr.)
Tian Giri
CAYMAN TRIANGLE, THE(1977)
Grete Girinec
FOUNTAIN OF LOVE, THE(1968, Aust.), ed
Gilbert Girion
1984
PHILADELPHIA EXPERIMENT, THE(1984)
Chorus Girl
NO TIME FOR LOVE(1943)
Cindy Girling
I MISS YOU, HUGS AND KISSES(1978, Can.); MEATBALLS(1979, Can.); KIDNAPPING OF THE PRESIDENT, THE(1980, Can.); DIRTY TRICKS(1981, Can.); TICKET TO HEAVEN(1981)
The Girls from Bahia
WILD PACK, THE(1972)
Francis Girod
LES GAULOISES BLEUES(1969, Fr.); WINTER WIND(1970, Fr./Hung.), w
1984
LE BON PLAISIR(1984, Fr.), d, w
Valerie Girodias
MADEMOISELLE(1966, Fr./Brit.)
Giulio Girola
LA DOLCE VITA(1961, Ital./Fr.)
Girolami
STAR PILOT(1977, Ital.), w
Bob Girolami
RABID(1976, Can.); ONE MAN(1979, Can.)
Enio Girolami
YOUNG HUSBANDS(1958, Ital./Fr.); LOVE ON THE RIVIERA(1964, Fr./Ital.); HELLBENDERS, THE(1967, U.S./Ital./Span.); PAYMENT IN BLOOD(1968, Ital.); JOHNNY HAMLET(1972, Ital.); 1990: THE BRONX WARRIORS(1983, Ital.)
Ennio Girolami
NIGHTS OF CABIRIA(1957, Ital.)
Lou Girolami
BANG THE DRUM SLOWLY(1973)
Robert Girolami
PROLOGUE(1970, Can.)
Stefani Girolami
1990: THE BRONX WARRIORS(1983, Ital.)
Adolfo Giron
SHE-DEVIL ISLAND(1936, Mex.)
Jacques Giron
AND GOD CREATED WOMAN(1957, Fr.)
Vince Gironda
JET PILOT(1957)
Vincent Gironda
FRENCHMAN'S CREEK(1944)
Vincent Girondo
STORM OVER LISBON(1944)
Marcello Girosi
FRISKY(1955, Ital.), w; SIGN OF VENUS, THE(1955, Ital.), p; MONTE CARLO STORY, THE(1957, Ital.), p, w; SCANDAL IN SORRENTO(1957, Ital./Fr.), p, w; BLACK ORCHID(1959), p; BREATH OF SCANDAL, A(1960), p; HELLER IN PINK TIGHTS(1960), p
Mario Girotti
FAST AND SEXY(1960, Fr./Ital.); HANNIBAL(1960, Ital.); CARTHAGE IN FLAMES(1961, Fr./Ital.); WONDERS OF ALADDIN, THE(1961, Fr./Ital.); SON OF SAMSON(1962, Fr./Ital./Yugo.); STORY OF JOSEPH AND HIS BRETHREN THE(1962, Ital.); LEOPARD, THE(1963, Ital.); SEVEN SEAS TO CALAIS(1963, Ital.); FRONTIER HELLCAT(1966, Fr./Ital./Ger./Yugo.); LAST OF THE RENEGADES(1966, Fr./Ital./Ger./Yugo.); RAMPAGE AT APACHE WELLS(1966, Ger./Yugo.); FLAMING FRONTIER(1968, Ger./Yugo.)
Massimo Girotti
DIFFICULT YEARS(1950, Ital.); BEHIND CLOSED SHUTTERS(1952, Ital.); DUEL WITHOUT HONOR(1953, Ital.); IT HAPPENED IN ROME(1959, Ital.); OSSESSIONE(1959, Ital.); COSSACKS, THE(1960, It.); GODDESS OF LOVE, THE(1960, Ital./Fr.); HEAD OF A TYRANT(1960, Fr./Ital.); HEROD THE GREAT(1960, Ital.); DUEL OF THE TITANS(1963, Ital.); IMPERIAL VENUS(1963, Ital./Fr.); RITA(1963, Fr./Ital.); GOLD FOR THE CAESARS(1964); MARCO THE MAGNIFICENT(1966, Ital./Fr./Yugo./Egypt/Afghanistan); SENSO(1968, Ital.); LISTEN, LET'S MAKE LOVE(1969, Fr./Ital.); TEOREMA(1969, Ital.); WITCHES, THE(1969, Fr./Ital.); ME-

Francoise Giroud
JULIETTA(1957, Fr.), w; WHERE THE HOT WIND BLOWS(1960, Fr., Ital.), w
1984
LE BON PLAISIR(1984, Fr.), w

Claude Giroux
THAT MAN GEORGE!(1967, Fr./Ital./Span.), p; SWEET HUNTERS(1969, Panama), p; TWELVE PLUS ONE(1970, Fr./Ital.), p

Fernande Giroux
RED(1970, Can.)

Francoise Giroux
ANTOINE ET ANTOINETTE(1947 Fr.), w

Jackelyn Giroux
TRICK OR TREATS(1982)
Misc. Talkies
TRICK OR TREATS(1983)

Jackie Giroux
CROSS AND THE SWITCHBLADE, THE(1970); SWEET SUGAR(1972); SLAUGHTER'S BIG RIP-OFF(1973); THIS IS A HIJACK(1973)

Lee Giroux
X-15(1961); SON OF FLUBBER(1963); RESURRECTION OF ZACHARY WHEELER, THE(1971)

Michael Girschek
DISORDER AND EARLY TORMENT(1977, Ger.), art d

Steven Girves
HORROR PLANET(1982, Brit.)

Henry Gisell
Silents
FINE FEATHERS(1915)

Alessandro Giselli
THANK YOU, AUNT(1969, Ital.), ed

Christine Gish
GENERAL MASSACRE(1973, U.S./Bel.)

Dorothy Gish
WOLVES(1930, Brit.); OUR HEARTS WERE YOUNG AND GAY(1944); CENTENNIAL SUMMER(1946); WHISTLE AT EATON FALLS(1951); CARDINAL, THE(1963)
Silents
FLOOR ABOVE, THE(1914); HOME SWEET HOME(1914); JUDITH OF BETHULIA(1914); MOUNTAIN RAT, THE(1914); JORDAN IS A HARD ROAD(1915); ATTA BOY'S LAST RACE(1916); GRETCHEN, THE GREENHORN(1916); LITTLE SCHOOL MA'AM, THE(1916); HEARTS OF THE WORLD(1918); HUN WITHIN, THE(1918); I'LL GET HIM YET(1919); NUGGET NELL(1919); OUT OF LUCK(1919); FLYING PAT(1920); LITTLE MISS REBELLION(1920); ORPHANS OF THE STORM(1922); CLOTHES MAKE THE PIRATE(1925); NIGHT LIFE OF NEW YORK(1925); ROMOLA(1925); LONDON(1926, Brit.); NELL GWYNNE(1926, Brit.); MADAME POMPADOUR(1927, Brit.)
Misc. Silents
BRED IN THE BONE(1915); OLD HEIDELBERG(1915); BETTY OF GRAYSTONE(1916); CHILDREN OF THE FEUD(1916); LITTLE MEENA'S ROMANCE(1916); SUSAN ROCKS THE BOAT(1916); HER OFFICAL FATHERS(1917); LITTLE YANK, THE(1917); STAGE STRUCK(1917); BATTLING JANE(1918); HOPE CHEST, THE(1918); BOOTS(1919); PEPPY POLLY(1919); TURNING THE TABLES(1919); MARY ELLEN COMES TO TOWN(1920); REMODELING HER HUSBAND(1920); GHOST IN THE GARRET, THE(1921); OH, JO!(1921); COUNTRY FLAPPER, THE(1922); BEAUTIFUL CITY, THE(1925); TIPTOES(1927, Brit.)

Lillian Gish
WIND, THE(1928); ONE ROMANTIC NIGHT(1930); HIS DOUBLE LIFE(1933); COMMANDOS STRIKE AT DAWN, THE(1942); TOP MAN(1943); MISS SUSIE SLAGLE'S(1945); DUEL IN THE SUN(1946); PORTRAIT OF JENNIE(1949); COBWEB, THE(1955); NIGHT OF THE HUNTER, THE(1955); ORDERS TO KILL(1958, Brit.); UNFORGIVEN, THE(1960); FOLLOW ME, BOYS!(1966); COMEDIANS, THE(1967); WARNING SHOT(1967); WEDDING, A(1978)
1984
HAMBONE AND HILLIE(1984)
Silents
BATTLE OF THE SEXES, THE(1914); ESCAPE, THE(1914); HOME SWEET HOME(1914); JUDITH OF BETHULIA(1914); BIRTH OF A NATION, THE(1915); LILY AND THE ROSE, THE(1915); DAPHNE AND THE PIRATE(1916); INNOCENT MAGDALENE, AN(1916); INTOLERANCE(1916); GREAT LOVE, THE(1918); GREATEST THING IN LIFE, THE(1918); HEARTS OF THE WORLD(1918); BROKEN BLOSSOMS(1919); ROMANCE OF HAPPY VALLEY, A(1919); TRUE HEART SUSIE(1919); GREATEST QUESTION, THE(1920); WAY DOWN EAST(1920); ORPHANS OF THE STORM(1922); WHITE SISTER, THE(1923); ROMOLA(1925); SCARLET LETTER, THE(1926); ANNIE LAURIE(1927); ENEMY, THE(1927)
Misc. Silents
LORD CHUMLEY(1914); CAPTAIN MACKLIN(1915); ENOCH ARDEN(1915); LOST HOUSE, THE(1915); SOULS TRIUMPHANT(1915); CHILDREN PAY, THE(1916); DIANA OF THE FOLLIES(1916); SOLD FOR MARRIAGE(1916); HOUSE BUILT UPON SAND, THE(1917); REMODELING HER HUSBAND(1920), d; LA BOHEME(1926)

Martin Gish
YOU LIGHT UP MY LIFE(1977)

Mrs. Mary Gish
Silents
HEARTS OF THE WORLD(1918)

Sheila Gish
RECKONING, THE(1971, Brit.); DAY IN THE DEATH OF JOE EGG, A(1972, Brit.); HITLER: THE LAST TEN DAYS(1973, Brit./Ital.); QUARTET(1981, Brit./Fr.)

Richard Gishler
I'M GOING TO GET YOU ... ELLIOT BOY(1971, Can.)

Lucy Wangiu Gishomo
1984
SHEENA(1984)

H.J. Giskes
HOUSE OF INTRIGUE, THE(1959, Ital.), w

Tomas Gislason
1984
ELEMENT OF CRIME, THE(1984, Den.), ed

Ewa Gislen
MONTENEGRO(1981, Brit./Swed.)

Toni Ann Gisondi
ANNIE(1982)

Robert Gist
MIRACLE ON 34TH STREET, THE(1947); DANGEROUS PROFESSION, A(1949); JIGSAW(1949); OH, YOU BEAUTIFUL DOLL(1949); SCENE OF THE CRIME(1949); STRATTON STORY, THE(1949); I WAS A SHOPLIFTER(1950); JACKPOT, THE(1950); STRANGERS ON A TRAIN(1951); ONE MINUTE TO ZERO(1952); ANGEL FACE(1953); BAND WAGON, THE(1953); D-DAY, THE SIXTH OF JUNE(1956); NAKED AND THE DEAD, THE(1958); WOLF LARSEN(1958); AL CAPONE(1959); FBI STORY, THE(1959); OPERATION PETTICOAT(1959); BLUEPRINT FOR ROBBERY(1961); JACK THE GIANT KILLER(1962); AMERICAN DREAM, AN(1966), d

Rod Gist
TUNNELVISION(1976); LADY IN RED, THE(1979); JAZZ SINGER, THE(1980); BUDDY BUDDY(1981); CUTTER AND BONE(1981)

Gary Gitchell
STUDENT BODY, THE(1976)

Ric Gitlin
MARRIAGE, A(1983)

Rick Gitlin
SQUEEZE PLAY(1981)

Ivry Gitlis
STORY OF ADELE H., THE(1975, Fr.)

Michael Gitomer
VAN, THE(1977)

June Gittelson
STUDENT TOUR(1934); WHITE PARADE, THE(1934); MARK OF THE VAMPIRE(1935); STORM OVER THE ANDES(1935); UNDER YOUR SPELL(1936); THERE'S THAT WOMAN AGAIN(1938); MR. SMITH GOES TO WASHINGTON(1939); NEW MOON(1940)

George Gittens
PRINCESS OF THE NILE(1954), ed; LIFE IN THE BALANCE, A(1955), ed; ROBBER'S ROOST(1955), ed; WHITE FEATHER(1955), ed; HOT CARS(1956), ed; KILLER IS LOOSE, THE(1956), ed; NIGHTMARE(1956), ed; BAILOUT AT 43,000(1957), ed; BIG CAPER, THE(1957), ed; I WAS A TEENAGE WEREWOLF(1957), ed; APPOINTMENT WITH A SHADOW(1958), ed; KATHY O'(1958), ed; VOICE IN THE MIRROR(1958), ed; CURSE OF THE UNDEAD(1959), ed; MONSTER OF PIEDRAS BLANCAS, THE(1959), ed; WILD AND THE INNOCENT, THE(1959), ed; TOWN TAMER(1965), ed

George A. Gittens
BLOODHOUNDS OF BROADWAY(1952), ed; DON'T BOTHER TO KNOCK(1952), ed; CITY OF BAD MEN(1953), ed; SILVER WHIP, THE(1953), ed; KISS BEFORE DYING, A(1956), ed; PHARAOH'S CURSE(1957), ed

Wyndham Gittens
LOST JUNGLE, THE(1934), w; GHOST PATROL(1936), w; FORBIDDEN VALLEY(1938), d&w; MEDICO OF PAINTED SPRINGS, THE(1941), w; PARDON MY GUN(1942), w
Silents
ALIMONY(1924), w; MEASURE OF A MAN, THE(1924), w; LODGE IN THE WILDERNESS, THE(1926), w; OUT OF THE WEST(1926), w; POWER OF THE WEAK, THE(1926), w; LORNA DOONE(1927), w; PRETTY CLOTHES(1927), t; STRANDED(1927), t; HEY RUBE!(1928), w; MARRY THE GIRL(1928), w
Misc. Silents
SHIP OF DOOM, THE(1917), d; ME UND GOTT(1918), d

Harry Gittes
DRIVE, HE SAID(1971), a, art d; HARRY AND WALTER GO TO NEW YORK(1976), p; GOIN' SOUTH(1978), p; TIMERIDER(1983), p

Lewis F. Gittier
EARTH CRIES OUT, THE(1949, Ital.), w

John Gittings
MERRY WIVES OF WINDSOR, THE(1966, Aust.)

Anthony Gittins
CASE FOR THE CROWN, THE(1934, Brit.), w; PRICE OF A SONG, THE(1935, Brit.), w

David Gittler
TAKING OFF(1971)

Robert Gittler
BUDDY HOLLY STORY, THE(1978), w

Anthony Gittleson
STUCK ON YOU(1983), w
1984
STUCK ON YOU(1984), w

Harry Gittleson
HAIR(1979)

Jane Gittleson
EARLY TO BED(1936)

June Gittleson
JAZZ CINDERELLA(1930); TWO SECONDS(1932); LOST IN THE STRATOSPHERE(1935); SWING YOUR LADY(1938); CONVICTED WOMAN(1940)

Jean Gitton
VICE AND VIRTUE(1965, Fr./Ital.), md

Alberto Giubilo
THREE FACES OF A WOMAN(1965, Ital.)

Joanne Giudici
1984
MEATBALLS PART II(1984)

Carlo Giuffere
MADAME(1963, Fr./Ital./Span.)

Aldo Giuffre
BEST OF ENEMIES, THE(1962); FOUR DAYS OF NAPLES, THE(1963, US/Ital.); HERCULES, SAMSON & ULYSSES(1964, Ital.); YESTERDAY, TODAY, AND TOMORROW(1964, Ital./Fr.); LOVE AND MARRIAGE(1966, Ital.); GOOD, THE BAD, AND THE UGLY, THE(1967, Ital./Span.); MADE IN ITALY(1967, Fr./Ital.); GHOSTS, ITALIAN STYLE(1969, Ital./Fr.); WHEN WOMEN HAD TAILS(1970, Ital.)

Carlo Giuffre
LOVE IN 4 DIMENSIONS(1965 Fr./Ital.); RAILROAD MAN, THE(1965, Ital.); GIRL WITH A PISTOL, THE(1968, Ital.); LOVE FACTORY(1969, Ital.)

(continued top of left column)
DEA(1971, Ital./Fr./Ger.); RED TENT, THE(1971, Ital./USSR); BARON BLOOD(1972, Ital.); CAGLIOSTRO(1975, Ital.); MR. KLEIN(1976, Fr.); STATELINE MOTEL(1976, Ital.); INNOCENT, THE(1979, Ital.); PASSION OF LOVE(1982, Ital./Fr.)

Giulio Cesare Giuffre
VOLCANO(1953, Ital.)
Luigi Giuliani
ARTURO'S ISLAND(1963, Ital.); EMPTY CANVAS, THE(1964, Fr./Ital.)
Massimo Giuliani
HIPPODROME(1961, Aust./Ger.); FACE IN THE RAIN, A(1963); VERY HANDY MAN, A(1966, Fr./Ital.)
Giampiero Giunti
THEY CALL ME TRINITY(1971, Ital.), ed
GiuseppePatroni-Griffi
GIRL WITH A SUITCASE(1961, Fr./Ital.), w
Angela Giussani
DANGER: DIABOLIK(1968, Ital./Fr.), w
Luciana Giussani
DANGER: DIABOLIK(1968, Ital./Fr.), w
Mario Giussani
CONJUGAL BED, THE(1963, Ital.)
Roberto Giussani
SEED OF MAN, THE(1970, Ital.), p
Arndt Giusti
HELL ON DEVIL'S ISLAND(1957), w
Ethel Giusti
HELL ON DEVIL'S ISLAND(1957), w
Grasiano Giusti
MOON IN THE GUTTER, THE(1983, Fr./Ital.)
Paolo Giusti
DIRTY HANDS(1976, Fr./Ital./Ger.)
Anacleto Giustini
MYSTERY OF THUG ISLAND, THE(1966, Ital./Ger.), makeup; SUPERARGO VERSUS DIABOLICUS(1966, Ital./Span.), makeup
Carlo Giustini
CHILDREN OF CHANCE(1950, Ital.); NAKED MAJA, THE(1959, Ital./U.S.); SAVAGE INNOCENTS, THE(1960, Brit.); EL CID(1961, U.S./Ital.); BARABBAS(1962, Ital.); STORY OF JOSEPH AND HIS BRETHREN THE(1962, Ital.); WORLD IN MY POCKET, THE(1962, Fr./Ital./Ger.); PONTIUS PILATE(1967, Fr./Ital.)
Carlo Giustini [Justini]
CHILDREN OF CHANCE(1949, Brit.)
Massimo Giustini
GUNS OF THE BLACK WITCH(1961, Fr./Ital.), makeup; MURDER CLINIC, THE(1967, Ital./Fr.), makeup
1984
LAST HUNTER, THE(1984, Ital.), makeup
Maurizio Giustini
QUEEN OF THE PIRATES(1961, Ital./Ger.), makeup; SEVEN SEAS TO CALAIS(1963, Ital.), makeup
Micaela Giustiniani
WAR AND PEACE(1956, Ital./U.S.)
Carlo Giustino
DAMON AND PYTHIAS(1962)
Eddy H. Given
WITCH'S CURSE, THE(1963, Ital.), w
Givenchy
BONJOUR TRISTESSE(1958), cos; CRACK IN THE MIRROR(1960), cos; ONCE MORE, WITH FEELING(1960), cos; CHARADE(1963), cos
Bernice Givens
GETTING OVER(1981)
Bob Givens
DAFFY DUCK'S MOVIE: FANTASTIC ISLAND(1983), prod d
Oliver Givens
TRADER HORN(1973)
Pierangelo Givera
CONFORMIST, THE(1971, Ital., Fr)
Oliver Givins
MR. RICCO(1975)
Katherine Givney
LOVER COME BACK(1931); KID FROM LEFT FIELD, THE(1953)
Kathryn Givney
FOLLOW THRU(1930); ISN'T IT ROMANTIC?(1948); MY FRIEND IRMA(1949); DOUBLE CROSSBONES(1950); MA AND PA KETTLE GO TO TOWN(1950); SIDE STREET(1950); LIGHTNING STRIKES TWICE(1951); LITTLE EGYPT(1951); OPERATION PACIFIC(1951); PLACE IN THE SUN, A(1951); TOO YOUNG TO KISS(1951); LET'S DO IT AGAIN(1953); THREE COINS IN THE FOUNTAIN(1954); COUNT THREE AND PRAY(1955); DADDY LONG LEGS(1955); GUYS AND DOLLS(1955); LADY GODIVA(1955); CONGO CROSSING(1956); WAYWARD BUS, THE(1957); CERTAIN SMILE, A(1958); MAN IN THE NET, THE(1959); FROM THE TERRACE(1960); FOUR HORSEMEN OF THE APOCALYPSE, THE(1962); THAT TOUCH OF MINK(1962); ONCE YOU KISS A STRANGER(1969)
George Givot
CHIEF, THE(1933); HOLLYWOOD PARTY(1934); PADDY O'DAY(1935); RIFF-RAFF(1936); BEG, BORROW OR STEAL(1937); HIT PARADE, THE(1937); STEP LIVELY, JEEVES(1937); THIN ICE(1937); WAKE UP AND LIVE(1937); 45 FATHERS(1937); HOLLYWOOD CAVALCADE(1939); YOUNG AS YOU FEEL(1940); FLYING WITH MUSIC(1942); ROAD TO MOROCCO(1942); BEHIND THE RISING SUN(1943); DU BARRY WAS A LADY(1943); FALCON AND THE CO-EDS, THE(1943); GOVERNMENT GIRL(1943); LEATHER BURNERS, THE(1943); RIFFRAFF(1947); APRIL IN PARIS(1953); THREE SAILORS AND A GIRL(1953); AIN'T MISBEHAVIN'(1955); LADY AND THE TRAMP(1955); RACERS, THE(1955); MIRACLE IN THE RAIN(1956); CHINA GATE(1957)
George Givut
CAPTAIN PIRATE(1952)
Richard Giza
1984
FALLING IN LOVE(1984)
Claudio Gizzi
CHE?(1973, Ital./Fr./Ger.), md
Giovanni Gizzi
Silents
QUO VADIS?(1913, Ital.)

Loris Gizzi
GREAT DAWN, THE(1947, Ital.); DIFFICULT YEARS(1950, Ital.); GUNS OF THE BLACK WITCH(1961, Fr./Ital.); NEOPOLITAN CAROUSEL(1961, Ital.); SAMSON AND THE SLAVE QUEEN(1963, Ital.); SULEIMAN THE CONQUEROR(1963, Ital.)
Debra Gjendem
STRANGE BREW(1983), art d
Steve Gjerde
PURPLE HAZE(1982)
Per Gjersoe
HUNGER(1968, Den./Norway/Swed.)
Lilianna Glabczynska
CONTRACT, THE(1982, Pol.)
Joy Glaccum
CHILDREN, THE(1980); PROWLER, THE(1981)
Bernadette Gladden
TRUCK TURNER(1974)
Lee Gladden
ON HER BED OF ROSES(1966)
Tholen Gladden
I REMEMBER MAMA(1948), ed; MY WORLD DIES SCREAMING(1958), ed
Roy Gladdish
PASSPORT TO PIMLICO(1949, Brit.)
Dorothea Glade
GIRL IN THE PAINTING, THE(1948, Brit.)
A. Gladkov
BALLAD OF A HUSSAR(1963, USSR), w
B. Gladkov
FORTY-NINE DAYS(1964, USSR)
Albert Glado
DEVIL'S DAUGHTER(1949, Fr.)
Jacqueline Gladson
Silents
HIS HOUR(1924)
Dana Gladstone
VAN NUYS BLVD.(1979); STAR CHAMBER, THE(1983)
Jacob Gladstone
OVERTURE TO GLORY(1940), w
Marilyn Gladstone
BORDER BADMEN(1945); PALEFACE, THE(1948); SHE COULDN'T SAY NO(1954)
Marlyn Gladstone
HAVING WONDERFUL CRIME(1945); FALL GUY(1947)
Steve Gladstone
HOT STUFF(1979)
Zeph Gladstone
OBLONG BOX, THE(1969, Brit.); OH! WHAT A LOVELY WAR(1969, Brit.)
David Gladwell
IF ...(1968, Brit.), ed; O LUCKY MAN!(1973, Brit.), ed; MEMOIRS OF A SURVIVOR(1981, Brit.), d, w
1984
1919(1984, Brit.), ed
Frances Gladwin
ZIEGFELD GIRL(1941); ARABIAN NIGHTS(1942); CATTLE STAMPEDE(1943); HARVEST MELODY(1943); WEST OF TEXAS(1943); WOLVES OF THE RANGE(1943); FRONTIER OUTLAWS(1944); LAURA(1944); THUNDERING GUN SLINGERS(1944); WINGED VICTORY(1944); STAGECOACH OUTLAWS(1945)
Joe Gladwin
KIND OF LOVING, A(1962, Brit.); NIGHT MUST FALL(1964, Brit.); CHARLIE BUBBLES(1968, Brit.); MIND OF MR. SOAMES, THE(1970, Brit.); RECKONING, THE(1971, Brit.); LITTLEST HORSE THIEVES, THE(1977)
Joe Gladwyn
WORK IS A FOUR LETTER WORD(1968, Brit.)
Timothy Glafas
1984
RHINESTONE(1984), ph
N. Glagoleva
OPTIMISTIC TRAGEDY, THE(1964, USSR), w
Glagolin
Misc. Silents
COWARD, THE(1914, USSR)
Boris Glagolin
Misc. Silents
COWARD, THE(1914, USSR), d; KIRA KIRALINA(1927, USSR), d
Gerald Glaister
SHARE OUT, THE(1966, Brit.), d
Gerard Glaister
CLUE OF THE SILVER KEY, THE(1961, Brit.), d; SET-UP, THE(1963, Brit.), d; PARTNER, THE(1966, Brit.), d
David Glaisyer
STRANGE AFFAIR, THE(1968, Brit.)
Natalia Glan
Misc. Silents
MISS MEND(1926, USSR)
Max Glandbard
HELL CANYON OUTLAWS(1957), w
Christine Glanville
THUNDERBIRDS ARE GO(1968, Brit.), puppeteer
Maxwell Glanville
OUT OF TOWNERS, THE(1970); COME BACK CIHARLESTON BLUE(1972)
1984
DESIREE(1984, Neth.)
Norbert Glanzberg
LIGHT ACROSSS THE STREET, THE(1957, Fr.), m; MICHAEL STROGOFF(1960, Fr./Ital./Yugo.), m; PRISONER OF THE VOLGA(1960, Fr./Ital.), m; LOVE AND THE FRENCHWOMAN(1961, Fr.), m
Ursula Glas
BLACK BEAUTY(1971, Brit./Ger./Span.)
Jimmy Glasberg
HU-MAN(1975, Fr.), ph

Lambart Glasby
Silents
RAT, THE(1925, Brit.)
Joan Glasco
ENDLESS LOVE(1981)
Gil Glascow
SCREAMS OF A WINTER NIGHT(1979)
A. Benjamin Glaser
ENTER MADAME(1935), p
Ariane Glaser
THIRTEEN FRIGHTENED GIRLS(1963)
Benjamin Glaser
BOLERO(1934), p; ARISE, MY LOVE(1940), w; TORTILLA FLAT(1942), w
Bunny Glaser
ORGY OF THE DEAD(1965)
Darel Glaser
BLESS THE BEASTS AND CHILDREN(1971)
Denise Glaser
LITTLE ROMANCE, A(1979, U.S./Fr.)
Lisa Glaser
HUMANOIDS FROM THE DEEP(1980)
Lulu Glaser
Silents
HOW MOLLY MADE GOOD(1915)
Misc. Silents
LOVE'S PILGRIMAGE TO AMERICA(1916)
Paul Michael Glaser
PHOBIA(1980, Can.)
[Paul] Michael Glaser
FIDDLER ON THE ROOF(1971)
Sabine Glaser
MAN WHO LOVED WOMEN, THE(1977, Fr.)
Vaughan Glaser
RULERS OF THE SEA(1939); WHAT A LIFE(1939); GIRL FROM AVENUE A(1940); THOSE WERE THE DAYS(1940); ADVENTURE IN WASHINGTON(1941); HENRY ALDRICH FOR PRESIDENT(1941); THIEVES FALL OUT(1941); HENRY ALDRICH GETS GLAMOUR(1942); HENRY AND DIZZY(1942); I MARRIED AN ANGEL(1942); MY FAVORITE SPY(1942); PRIDE OF THE YANKEES, THE(1942); SABOTEUR(1942); HENRY ALDRICH HAUNTS A HOUSE(1943); HENRY ALDRICH SWINGS IT(1943); ARSENIC AND OLD LACE(1944); ONCE UPON A TIME(1944)
Vaughn Glaser
MEET JOHN DOE(1941); HENRY ALDRICH, EDITOR(1942); SHADOW OF A DOUBT(1943); HENRY ALDRICH PLAYS CUPID(1944)
Bill Glasgow
INSIDE THE MAFIA(1959), art d; TIMBUKTU(1959), art d; VICE RAID(1959), art d; MUSIC BOX KID, THE(1960), art d; NOOSE FOR A GUNMAN(1960), art d
Ellen Glasgow
IN THIS OUR LIFE(1942), w
Len Glasgow
METEOR(1979)
William Glasgow
SHOOT TO KILL(1947), art d; PARIS MODEL(1953), art d; WORLD FOR RANSOM(1954), art d; BIG KNIFE, THE(1955), art d; KISS ME DEADLY(1955), art d; MAN FROM DEL RIO(1956), art d; RIDE BACK, THE(1957), art d; GUNS, GIRLS AND GANGSTERS(1958), art d; HONG KONG CONFIDENTIAL(1958), art d; IT! THE TERROR FROM BEYOND SPACE(1958), art d; TOUGHEST GUN IN TOMBSTONE(1958), art d; INVISIBLE INVADERS(1959), art d; PIER 5, HAVANA(1959), art d; RIOT IN JUVENILE PRISON(1959), art d; GUNFIGHTERS OF ABILENE(1960), art d; THREE CAME TO KILL(1960), art d; DONDI(1961), art d; HITLER(1962), art d; WHATEVER HAPPENED TO BABY JANE?(1962), art d; FOUR FOR TEXAS(1963), art d; HUSH... HUSH, SWEET CHARLOTTE(1964), art d; FLIGHT OF THE PHOENIX, THE(1965), art d; GUIDE FOR THE MARRIED MAN, A(1967), art d; LEGEND OF LYLAH CLARE, THE(1968), art d; WHAT EVER HAPPENED TO AUNT ALICE?(1969), art d; ...TICK...TICK...TICK...(1970), art d
Philip Glasier
SWORD AND THE ROSE, THE(1953)
Gus Glasmire
FUGITIVE FROM JUSTICE, A(1940)
Kubec Glasmon
BLONDE CRAZY(1931), w; PUBLIC ENEMY, THE(1931), w; SMART MONEY(1931), w; CROWD ROARS, THE(1932), w; FALSE FACES(1932), w; ROCKABYE(1932), w; TAXI!(1932), w; THREE ON A MATCH(1932), w; UNION DEPOT(1932), w; BOLERO(1934), w; JEALOUSY(1934), w; GLASS KEY, THE(1935), w; MEN WITHOUT NAMES(1935), w; SHOW THEM NO MERCY(1935), w; PAROLE(1936), w; MAN IN BLUE, THE(1937), p, w; SALESLADY(1938), w; CALLING DR. GILLESPIE(1942), w
Kate Glasner
HAIR(1979)
Kubec Glason
HANDY ANDY(1934), w
Susan Glaspell
RIGHT TO LOVE, THE(1931), w
Braham Glass
HOW WILLINGLY YOU SING(1975, Aus.)
Bridghid Glass
LENNY(1974)
Cecil Glass
LIFE AND TIMES OF CHESTER-ANGUS RAMSGOOD, THE(1971, Can.)
Dee Dee Glass
1984
SACRED HEARTS(1984, Brit.), p
Dick Glass
Misc. Talkies
HOLLYWOOD 90028(1973)
E.H. Glass
INFRA-MAN(1975, Hong Kong), ed&spec eff
Edward Glass
SPACED OUT(1981, Brit.), ed

Everett Glass
GIRL FROM MANHATTAN(1948); EASY LIVING(1949); GREAT SINNER, THE(1949); PINKY(1949); RECKLESS MOMENTS, THE(1949); UNDERCOVER MAN, THE(1949); COUNTERSPY MEETS SCOTLAND YARD(1950); FATHER MAKES GOOD(1950); MAGNIFICENT YANKEE, THE(1950); MOTHER DIDN'T TELL ME(1950); PETTY GIRL, THE(1950); TWO FLAGS WEST(1950); YOUNG MAN WITH A HORN(1950); JOURNEY INTO LIGHT(1951); MILLIONAIRE FOR CHRISTY, A(1951); MY FORBIDDEN PAST(1951); THING, THE(1951); TOO YOUNG TO KISS(1951); DEADLINE–U.S.A.(1952); DREAMBOAT(1952); GREATEST SHOW ON EARTH, THE(1952); MACAO(1952); INFERNO(1953); THREE SAILORS AND A GIRL(1953); DAY OF TRIUMPH(1954); DEMETRIUS AND THE GLADIATORS(1954); PURPLE MASK, THE(1955); TRIAL(1955); FRIENDLY PERSUASION(1956); HARDER THEY FALL, THE(1956); INVASION OF THE BODY SNATCHERS(1956); WORLD WITHOUT END(1956); PAL JOEY(1957); QUIET GUN, THE(1957); GUNMAN'S WALK(1958); SUMMER PLACE, A(1959); ELMER GANTRY(1960); MARRIAGE-GO-ROUND, THE(1960)
Everette Glass
JOAN OF ARC(1948)
Frankcina Glass
MARVIN AND TIGE(1983), w
Gaston Glass
UNDER TWO FLAGS(1936); GERALDINE(1929); GOT WHAT SHE WANTED(1930); JUST LIKE HEAVEN(1930); SHE GOT WHAT SHE WANTED(1930); TIGER ROSE(1930); RACETRACK(1933), w; MAN WHO BROKE THE BANK AT MONTE CARLO, THE(1935); DESIRE(1936); MARY OF SCOTLAND(1936); PRINCESS COMES ACROSS, THE(1936); SUTTER'S GOLD(1936); SYLVIA SCARLETT(1936); DEATH IN THE SKY(1937); ESPIONAGE(1937); KING AND THE CHORUS GIRL, THE(1937); VICE RACKET(1937); PARIS AFTER DARK(1943)
Misc. Talkies
CROOKED ROAD(1932); GAMBLING WITH SOULS(1936)
Silents
OPEN YOUR EYES(1919); BRANDED WOMAN, THE(1920); HER WINNING WAY(1921); KINGDOM WITHIN, THE(1922); LITTLE MISS SMILES(1922); RICH MEN'S WIVES(1922); SONG OF LIFE, THE(1922); GIMMIE(1923); HERO, THE(1923); MOTHERS-IN-LAW(1923); SPIDER AND THE ROSE, THE(1923); AFTER THE BALL(1924); FAIR PLAY(1925); JAZZ GIRL, THE(1926); SHOW GIRL, THE(1927); MY HOME TOWN(1928); NAME THE WOMAN(1928); OBEY YOUR HUSBAND(1928); RED MARK, THE(1928)
Misc. Silents
LET'S ELOPE(1919); LOST BATALLION, THE(1919); WOMAN OF LIES(1919); HUMORESQUE(1920); MOTHERS OF MEN(1920); WORLD AND HIS WIFE, THE(1920); GOD'S CRUCIBLE(1921); LOST BATTALION, THE(1921); THERE ARE NO VILLAINS(1921); GLASS HOUSES(1922); I AM THE LAW(1922); DAUGHTERS OF THE RICH(1923); GIRL WHO CAME BACK, THE(1923); I AM THE MAN(1924); TROUPING WITH ELLEN(1924); BAD LANDS, THE(1925); DANGER SIGNAL, THE(1925); FLYING FOOL(1925); PARISIAN NIGHTS(1925); PRICE OF SUCCESS, THE(1925); PURSUED(1925); THREE KEYS(1925); BROKEN HOMES(1926); CALL OF THE KLONDIKE, THE(1926); HER SACRIFICE(1926); MIDNIGHT LIMITED(1926); ROAD TO BROADWAY, THE(1926); ROMANCE OF A MILLION DOLLARS, THE(1926); TENTACLES OF THE NORTH(1926); WIVES AT AUCTION(1926); BETTER DAYS(1927); COMPASSION(1927); FALSE MORALS(1927); LOVE WAGER, THE(1927); SINEWS OF STEEL(1927); BROKEN BARRIERS(1928); GENTLEMAN PREFFERED, A(1928); INNOCENT LOVE(1928); WIFE'S RELATIONS, THE(1928); BEHIND CLOSED DOORS(1929); UNTAMED JUSTICE(1929)
George Glass
NAKED EDGE, THE(1961), p
Georges Glass
JULIE THE REDHEAD(1963, Fr.), p
Harry Glass
TOUCH OF FLESH, THE(1960), md
Jack Glass
MAGNETIC MONSTER, THE(1953), spec eff
Jack R. Glass
RIDERS TO THE STARS(1954), spec eff
Jackie Glass
SECRET WORLD(1969, Fr.), w
Joe Glass
ENCOUNTER WITH THE UNKNOWN(1973), p
Keith Glass
HANK WILLIAMS: THE SHOW HE NEVER GAVE(1982, Can.)
Max Glass
ENTENTE CORDIALE(1939, Fr.), p, w; RASPUTIN(1939, Fr.), p
Michael Glass
DEMON SEED(1977)
Montague Glass
Silents
HUNGRY HEARTS(1922), t; IN HOLLYWOOD WITH POTASH AND PERLMUTTER(1924), w, t; PARTNERS AGAIN(1926), w, t
Nanci Glass
THOSE LIPS, THOSE EYES(1980)
Nancy Glass
1984
MEATBALLS PART II(1984)
Ned Glass
PRAIRIE SCHOONERS(1940); KING OF DODGE CITY(1941); RICHEST MAN IN TOWN(1941); DAMNED DON'T CRY, THE(1950); HE'S A COCKEYED WONDER(1950); MYSTERY STREET(1950); PERFECT STRANGERS(1950); STORM WARNING(1950); CALLAWAY WENT THATAWAY(1951); IT'S A BIG COUNTRY(1951); PEOPLE AGAINST O'HARA, THE(1951); STOP, YOU'RE KILLING ME(1952); YOU FOR ME(1952); CLOWN, THE(1953); JENNIFER(1953); MR. SCOUTMASTER(1953); TROUBLE ALONG THE WAY(1953); WAR OF THE WORLDS, THE(1953); STEEL CAGE, THE(1954); YELLOW TOMAHAWK, THE(1954); SPELL OF THE HYPNOTIST(1956); BACK FROM THE DEAD(1957); HOT ROD RUMBLE(1957); JOKER IS WILD, THE(1957); NORTH BY NORTHWEST(1959); REBEL SET, THE(1959); WEST SIDE STORY(1961); EXPERIMENT IN TERROR(1962); KID GALAHAD(1962); WHO'S GOT THE ACTION?(1962); CHARADE(1963); PAPA'S DELICATE CONDITION(1963); BIG HAND FOR THE LITTLE LADY, A(1966); BLINDFOLD(1966); FORTUNE COOKIE, THE(1966); LOVE BUG, THE(1968); NEVER A DULL MOMENT(1968); LADY SINGS THE BLUES(1972); ALL-AMERICAN BOY, THE(1973); SAVE THE TIGER(1973); STREET MUSIC(1982)

Noel Glass
FOUR BOYS AND A GUN(1957)
Paul Glass
GIRL IN THE RED VELVET SWING, THE(1955); BEST THINGS IN LIFE ARE FREE, THE(1956); LIEUTENANT WORE SKIRTS, THE(1956); MAN IN THE GREY FLANNEL SUIT, THE(1956); ABDUCTORS, THE(1957), m; FEAR NO MORE(1961), m; LADY IN A CAGE(1964), m, md; NIGHTMARE IN THE SUN(1964), m, md; BUNNY LAKE IS MISSING(1965), m; GUESTS ARE COMING(1965, Pol.); CATCH MY SOUL(1974), md; OVERLORD(1975, Brit.), m; TO THE DEVIL A DAUGHTER(1976, Brit./Ger.), m
Randy Glass
WHERE THE BUFFALO ROAM(1980)
Ron Glass
CRAZY WORLD OF JULIUS VROODER, THE(1974)
Sandy Glass
LAST FLIGHT OF NOAH'S ARK, THE(1980), w
Seaman Glass
CHILDISH THINGS(1969)
Seamon Glass
SPARTACUS(1960); THIS IS NOT A TEST(1962); CAPTAIN NEWMAN, M.D.(1963); DELIVERANCE(1972); SLITHER(1973); BOOTLEGGERS(1974); HARRY AND WALTER GO TO NEW YORK(1976); WINTERHAWK(1976); DAMNATION ALLEY(1977); NORSEMAN, THE(1978); ROSE, THE(1979); PARTNERS(1982)
Sidney A. Glass
BLUE COLLAR(1978), w
William Glass
WHY RUSSIANS ARE REVOLTING(1970), ph
Irving Glassberg
WEB, THE(1947), ph; BLACK BART(1948), ph; CASBAH(1948), ph; FEUDIN', FUSSIN' AND A-FIGHTIN'(1948), ph; LARCENY(1948), ph; RIVER LADY(1948), ph; ARCTIC MANHUNT(1949), ph; CALAMITY JANE AND SAM BASS(1949), ph; RED CANYON(1949), ph; STORY OF MOLLY X, THE(1949), ph; SWORD IN THE DESERT(1949), ph; UNDERTOW(1949), ph; YES SIR, THAT'S MY BABY(1949), ph; I WAS A SHOPLIFTER(1950), ph; KANSAS RAIDERS(1950), ph; OUTSIDE THE WALL(1950), ph; SHAKEDOWN(1950), ph; SPY HUNT(1950), ph; CAVE OF OUTLAWS(1951), ph; FAT MAN, THE(1951), ph; FRANCIS GOES TO THE RACES(1951), ph; PRINCE WHO WAS A THIEF, THE(1951), ph; STRANGE DOOR, THE(1951), ph; BEND OF THE RIVER(1952), ph; BLACK CASTLE, THE(1952), ph; DUEL AT SILVER CREEK, THE(1952), ph; FLESH AND FURY(1952), ph; HERE COME THE NELSONS(1952), ph; LAWLESS BREED, THE(1952), ph; SALLY AND SAINT ANNE(1952), ph; MISSISSIPPI GAMBLER, THE(1953), ph; WALKING MY BABY BACK HOME(1953), ph; BLACK SHIELD OF FALWORTH, THE(1954), ph; BORDER RIVER(1954), ph; FRANCIS JOINS THE WACS(1954), ph; RIDE CLEAR OF DIABLO(1954), ph; CAPTAIN LIGHTFOOT(1955), ph; PURPLE MASK, THE(1955), ph; BACKLASH(1956), ph; FOUR GIRLS IN TOWN(1956), ph; OUTSIDE THE LAW(1956), ph; PRICE OF FEAR, THE(1956), ph; RAWHIDE YEARS, THE(1956), ph; SHOWDOWN AT ABILENE(1956), ph; JOE BUTTERFLY(1957), ph; TARNISHED ANGELS, THE(1957), ph; BIG BEAT, THE(1958), ph; DAY OF THE BAD MAN(1958), ph; LADY TAKES A FLYER, THE(1958), ph; TWILIGHT FOR THE GODS(1958), ph; CRY TOUGH(1959), ph; RABBIT TRAP, THE(1959), ph
Iving Glassberg
FRANCIS(1949), ph
Peter Glassberg
ROCKY(1976)
Michael Glassbourg
1984
LISTEN TO THE CITY(1984, Can.)
Maj. Robert Glassburn
Silents
DRESS PARADE(1927), w
Al Glasser
OMOO OMOO, THE SHARK GOD(1949), m; MURDER IS MY BEAT(1955), m; DESTINATION 60,000(1957), m
Albert Glasser
MONSTER MAKER, THE(1944), m; GAS HOUSE KIDS IN HOLLYWOOD(1947), m; PHILO VANCE RETURNS(1947), m; LAST OF THE WILD HORSES(1948), md; RETURN OF WILDFIRE, THE(1948), m, md; VALIANT HOMBRE, THE(1948), m; DARING CABALLERO, THE(1949), m; GAY AMIGO, THE(1949), m; GRAND CANYON(1949), m&md; I SHOT JESSE JAMES(1949), m; SATAN'S CRADLE(1949), m; TOUGH ASSIGNMENT(1949), m; TREASURE OF MONTE CRISTO(1949), m, md; EVERYBODY'S DANCIN'(1950), m; GIRL FROM SAN LORENZO, THE(1950), m; GUNFIRE(1950), md; RETURN OF JESSE JAMES, THE(1950), m; TRAIN TO TOMBSTONE(1950), m, md; WESTERN PACIFIC AGENT(1950), m; THREE DESPERATE MEN(1951), m, md; BUSHWHACKERS, THE(1952), m; GEISHA GIRL(1952), m; INVASION U.S.A.(1952), m; CAPTAIN JOHN SMITH AND POCAHONTAS(1953), m; MAN OF CONFLICT(1953), m; PARIS MODEL(1953), m, md; PORT SINISTER(1953), m; PROBLEM GIRLS(1953), m; DRAGON'S GOLD(1954), m; TOP BANANA(1954), md; TOP OF THE WORLD(1955), m, md; BOSS, THE(1956), m; HUK(1956), m; INDESTRUCTIBLE MAN, THE(1956), m, md; AMAZING COLOSSAL MAN, THE(1957), m; BAILOUT AT 43,000(1957), m; BIG CAPER, THE(1957), m; BUCKSKIN LADY, THE(1957), m; CYCLOPS(1957), m; FOUR BOYS AND A GUN(1957), m, md; HIRED GUN, THE(1957), m; MOTORCYCLE GANG(1957), m; SAGA OF THE VIKING WOMEN AND THEIR VOYAGE TO THE WATERS OF THE GREAT SEA SERPENT, THE(1957), m; STREET OF SINNERS(1957), m, md; VALERIE(1957), m; ATTACK OF THE PUPPET PEOPLE(1958), m; GIANT FROM THE UNKNOWN(1958), m; GIRL IN THE WOODS(1958), m&md; MUGGER, THE(1958), m; SNOWFIRE(1958), m; SPIDER, THE(1958), m; TEENAGE CAVEMAN(1958), m; WAR OF THE COLOSSAL BEAST(1958), m; WHEN HELL BROKE LOOSE(1958), m; NIGHT OF THE QUARTER MOON(1959), m, md; BOY AND THE PIRATES, THE(1960), m; OKLAHOMA TERRITORY(1960), m; TORMENTED(1960), m, md; 20,000 EYES(1961), m; AIR PATROL(1962), m, md; CONFESSIONS OF AN OPIUM EATER(1962), m; ZOTZ!(1962)
Bernard Glasser
GOLD RAIDERS, THE(1952), p; STORM RIDER, THE(1957), p; ESCAPE FROM RED ROCK(1958), p; SPACE MASTER X-7(1958), p; ALASKA PASSAGE(1959), p; RETURN OF THE FLY(1959), p; SERGEANT WAS A LADY, THE(1961), p,d&w; CRACK IN THE WORLD(1965), p; RUN LIKE A THIEF(1968, Span.), p&d
Isabel Glasser
MARRIAGE, A(1983)

Michael Glasser
BUTTERFLIES ARE FREE(1972)
Robert Glasser
TOKYO FILE 212(1951), m
Samuel Glasser
SAN FRANCISCO(1936)
Rick Glassey
ROAR(1981)
Gus Glassmire
SAY IT IN FRENCH(1938); CAFE SOCIETY(1939); IN NAME ONLY(1939); LADY'S FROM KENTUCKY, THE(1939); OUR LEADING CITIZEN(1939); UNION PACIFIC(1939); WOMAN DOCTOR(1939); MORTAL STORM, THE(1940); THEY MEET AGAIN(1941); TOM, DICK AND HARRY(1941); LIVING GHOST, THE(1942); MY GAL SAL(1942); HEAVENLY BODY, THE(1943); MAD GHOUL, THE(1943); STORY OF DR. WASSELL, THE(1944); WILSON(1944); BULLFIGHTERS, THE(1945); COLONEL EFFINGHAM'S RAID(1945); FALLEN ANGEL(1945); SCARLET STREET(1945)
Guss Glassmire
HOW'S ABOUT IT?(1943)
Erika Glassner
Misc. Silents
TRAGEDY OF LOVE(1923, Ger.)
Leopold Glasspoole
LET THE PEOPLE SING(1942, Brit.)
Frances Glaswin
PERFECT SNOB, THE(1941)
Ellsworth Glath
HOUSE ON 92ND STREET, THE(1945)
Bert Glatstein
1984
BREAKIN' 2: ELECTRIC BOOGALOO(1984), ed
Wolfgang Glattes
STAR 80(1983), p
Robin Glattley
SIERRA BARON(1958)
Gabby Glatzer
STARTING OVER(1979)
Gaby Glatzer
ROLLOVER(1981)
A. Glauberman
Silents
BATTLESHIP POTEMKIN, THE(1925, USSR)
Frank Glaubrecht
BRIDGE, THE(1961, Ger.)
Jean Glaude
KILL SQUAD(1982)
Bob Glaudini
LADY LIBERTY(1972, Ital./Fr.); CHAMELEON(1978), a, w
Robert Glaudini
PARASITE(1982); WAVELENGTH(1983)
Misc. Talkies
ALCHEMIST, THE(1981)
Louise Glaum
Silents
FORBIDDEN ADVENTURE, THE(1915); REWARD, THE(1915); ARYAN, THE(1916); HELL'S HINGES(1916); HOME(1916); ALIEN ENEMY, AN(1918); SAHARA(1919); SEX(1920)
Misc. Silents
MATRIMONY(1915); TOAST OF DEATH, THE(1915); D'ARTAGNAN(1916); HONOR THY NAME(1916); RETURN OF "DRAW" EGAN, THE(1916); SOMEWHERE IN FRANCE(1916); WOLF WOMAN, THE(1916); GOLDEN RULE KATE(1917); IDOLATORS(1917); LOVE OR JUSTICE(1917); STRANGE TRANSGRESSOR, A(1917); SWEETHEART OF THE DOOMED(1917); WEAKER SEX, THE(1917); GODDESS OF LOST LAKE, THE(1918); SHACKLED(1918); WEDLOCK(1918); FORBIDDEN FIRE(1919); LONE WOLF'S DAUGHTER, THE(1919); GREATER THAN LOVE(1920); LEOPARD WOMAN, THE(1920); LOVE(1920); LOVE MADNESS(1920); I AM GUILTY(1921); FIFTY-FIFTY(1925)
G. G. Glavany
HOURS OF LONELINESS(1930, Brit.), p,d&w
Guarino G. Glavany
Misc. Silents
DOWNSTREAM(1929, Brit.), d
Guarino Glavany
Silents
INSEPARABLES, THE(1929, Brit.), w
Ray Glavin
SWINGING BARMAIDS, THE(1976)
Erich Glavitza
LE MANS(1971)
Paul Glawion
THERE IS STILL ROOM IN HELL(1963, Ger.)
Paul Glawton
EMIL AND THE DETECTIVES(1964); I DEAL IN DANGER(1966)
Norbert Glazberg
PLAYMATES(1969, Fr./Ital.), m
Lois Glaze
Misc. Talkies
RACKETEER ROUND-UP(1934); GUNNERS AND GUNS(1935)
Peter Glaze
LIFE IS A CIRCUS(1962, Brit.); SING AND SWING(1964, Brit.)
Will H. Glaze
Silents
MARY LATIMER, NUN(1920, Brit.), w
Benjamin Glazer
BARKER, THE(1928), w; BEGGARS OF LIFE(1928), w; DANCE OF LIFE, THE(1929), w; STRANGE CARGO(1929), d, w; BOUDOIR DIPLOMAT(1930), w; DEVIL TO PAY, THE(1930), w; TOL'ABLE DAVID(1930), w; MATA HARI(1931), w; PAGAN LADY(1931), w; YOUR NUMBER'S UP(1931), p&w; FAREWELL TO ARMS, A(1932), w; TWO KINDS OF WOMEN(1932), w; BEDTIME STORY, A(1933), w; NO MAN OF HER OWN(1933), w; STORY OF TEMPLE DRAKE, THE(1933), p; WAY TO LOVE, THE(1933), p, w; SHE LOVES ME NOT(1934), p, w; WE'RE NOT DRESS-

ING(1934), p; BIG BROADCAST OF 1936, THE(1935), p; LOVE IN BLOOM(1935), p; PARIS IN SPRING(1935), p; ANYTHING GOES(1936), p; RHYTHM ON THE RANGE(1936), p; DOUBLE OR NOTHING(1937), p; EXCLUSIVE(1937), p; INTERNES CAN'T TAKE MONEY(1937), p; MOUNTAIN MUSIC(1937), p; PARIS CALLING(1941), p, w; SONG OF MY HEART(1947), d, w

Silents
MERRY WIDOW, THE(1925), w; MEMORY LANE(1926), w; SKYROCKET, THE(1926), w; WILD OATS LANE(1926), w; SEVENTH HEAVEN(1927), w; STREET OF SIN, THE(1928), w; TRAIL OF '98, THE(1929), w

Benjamin F. Glazer
CAROUSEL(1956), w
Silents
GREAT LOVE, THE(1925), w; FLESH AND THE DEVIL(1926), w

Caroline Glazer
CRAWLING EYE, THE(1958, Brit.)

David Glazer
1984
BAD MANNERS(1984), set d

Eugene Robert Glazer
1984
JOY OF SEX(1984)

Leslie Glazer
CRIMSON BLADE, THE(1964, Brit.)

Tom Glazer
FACE IN THE CROWD, A(1957), m

Menashe Glazier
TRUNK TO CAIRO(1966, Israel/Ger.)

Peter Glazier
GIRLS AT SEA(1958, Brit.), art d; LOOK BACK IN ANGER(1959), art d

Sidney Glazier
PRODUCERS, THE(1967), p; SEVENTH CONTINENT, THE(1968, Czech./Yugo.), p

James Glazman
YOU'LL LIKE MY MOTHER(1972)

Linda Glazman
LATITUDE ZERO(1969, U.S./Jap.), cos

A. Glazyrin
OPTIMISTIC TRAGEDY, THE(1964, USSR); WAR AND PEACE(1968, USSR)

Pat Gleasch
MIRACLE KID(1942)

Adda Gleason
COLLEGE COQUETTE, THE(1929); BITTER TEA OF GENERAL YEN, THE(1933); SHE MARRIED HER BOSS(1935); ONE MILLION B.C.(1940); SPIDER WOMAN STRIKES BACK, THE(1946); OUT OF THE PAST(1947); RHUBARB(1951)
Silents
RAMONA(1916); MAN BAIT(1926); OLD SOAK, THE(1926)
Misc. Silents
BOND WITHIN, THE(1916); FANATICS(1917); SHACKLES OF TRUTH(1917); SNAP JUDGEMENT(1917); SPIRIT OF '76, THE(1917); ONE WOMAN, THE(1918); THAT DEVIL, BATEESE(1918)

Jack C. [Jackie] Gleason
LARCENY, INC.(1942)

Jackie Gleason
NAVY BLUES(1941); ALL THROUGH THE NIGHT(1942); ORCHESTRA WIVES(1942); SPRINGTIME IN THE ROCKIES(1942); TRAMP, TRAMP, TRAMP(1942); DESERT HAWK, THE(1950); HUSTLER, THE(1961); GIGOT(1962), a, w, m; REQUIEM FOR A HEAVYWEIGHT(1962); PAPA'S DELICATE CONDITION(1963); SOLDIER IN THE RAIN(1963); SKIDOO(1968); DON'T DRINK THE WATER(1969); HOW TO COMMIT MARRIAGE(1969); HOW DO I LOVE THEE?(1970); MR. BILLION(1977); SMOKEY AND THE BANDIT(1977); SMOKEY AND THE BANDIT II(1980); TOY, THE(1982); SMOKEY AND THE BANDIT-PART 3(1983); STING II, THE(1983)

Jackie C. Gleason
ESCAPE FROM CRIME(1942); LADY GANGSTER(1942)

James Gleason
BROADWAY MELODY, THE(1929), w; FLYING FOOL(1929), w; HIGH VOLTAGE(1929), w; HIS FIRST COMMAND(1929), w; OH, YEAH!(1929), a, w; SHANNONS OF BROADWAY, THE(1929), a, w, titles; BIG MONEY(1930); DUMBBELLS IN ERMINE(1930), a, w; FALL GUY, THE(1930), w; HER MAN(1930); MAMMY(1930), w; MATRIMONIAL BED, THE(1930); PUTTIN' ON THE RITZ(1930); RAIN OR SHINE(1930), w; SWELLHEAD, THE(1930); WHAT A WIDOW(1930), w; BEYOND VICTORY(1931), a, w; BIG GAMBLE, THE(1931); FREE SOUL, A(1931); IT'S A WISE CHILD(1931); SUICIDE FLEET(1931); SWEEPSTAKES(1931); ALL-AMERICAN, THE(1932); BILLION DOLLAR SCANDAL(1932); BLONDIE OF THE FOLLIES(1932); CROOKED CIRCLE(1932); DEVIL IS DRIVING, THE(1932); FAST COMPANIONS(1932); LADY AND GENT(1932); PENGUIN POOL MURDER, THE(1932); BOWERY, THE(1933), w; CLEAR ALL WIRES(1933); HOOPLA(1933); CHANGE OF HEART(1934), w; MEANEST GAL IN TOWN, THE(1934); MURDER ON THE BLACKBOARD(1934); ORDERS IS ORDERS(1934, Brit.), a, w; SEARCH FOR BEAUTY(1934); HELLDORADO(1935); HOT TIP(1935), a, d; MURDER ON A HONEYMOON(1935); TWO FISTED(1935), w; WEST POINT OF THE AIR(1935); BIG GAME, THE(1936); DON'T TURN 'EM LOOSE(1936); EX-MRS. BRADFORD, THE(1936); MURDER ON A BRIDLE PATH(1936); PLOT THICKENS, THE(1936); WE'RE ONLY HUMAN(1936); YOURS FOR THE ASKING(1936); FORTY NAUGHTY GIRLS(1937); MANHATTAN MERRY-GO-ROUND(1937); ARMY GIRL(1938); GOODBYE BROADWAY(1938), w; HIGGINS FAMILY, THE(1938); COVERED TRAILER, THE(1939); MY WIFE'S RELATIVES(1939); SHOULD HUSBANDS WORK?(1939); EARL OF PUDDLESTONE(1940); GRANDPA GOES TO TOWN(1940); MONEY TO BURN(1940); AFFECTIONATELY YOURS(1941); BABES ON BROADWAY(1941); DATE WITH THE FALCON, A(1941); HERE COMES MR. JORDAN(1941); MEET JOHN DOE(1941); NINE LIVES ARE NOT ENOUGH(1941); TANKS A MILLION(1941); FALCON TAKES OVER, THE(1942); FOOTLIGHT SERENADE(1942); HAY FOOT(1942); MANILA CALLING(1942); MY GAL SAL(1942); TALES OF MANHATTAN(1942); CRASH DIVE(1943); GUY NAMED JOE, A(1943); ARSENIC AND OLD LACE(1944); KEYS OF THE KINGDOM, THE(1944); ONCE UPON A TIME(1944); CAPTAIN EDDIE(1945); CLOCK, THE(1945); THIS MAN'S NAVY(1945); TREE GROWS IN BROOKLYN, A(1945); HOME SWEET HOMICIDE(1946); HOODLUM SAINT, THE(1946); LADY LUCK(1946); WELL-GROOMED BRIDE, THE(1946); BISHOP'S WIFE, THE(1947); DOWN TO EARTH(1947); HOMESTRETCH, THE(1947); TYCOON(1947); DUDE GOES WEST, THE(1948); RETURN OF OCTOBER, THE(1948); SMART WOMAN(1948); WHEN MY BABY SMILES AT ME(1948); BAD BOY(1949); LIFE OF RILEY, THE(1949); MISS GRANT TAKES RICHMOND(1949); TAKE ONE FALSE STEP(1949); JACKPOT,

THE(1950); JOE PALOOKA IN THE SQUARED CIRCLE(1950); KEY TO THE CITY(1950); RIDING HIGH(1950); YELLOW CAB MAN, THE(1950); COME FILL THE CUP(1951); I'LL SEE YOU IN MY DREAMS(1951); JOE PALOOKA IN TRIPLE CROSS(1951); TWO GALS AND A GUY(1951); STORY OF WILL ROGERS, THE(1952); WE'RE NOT MARRIED(1952); WHAT PRICE GLORY?(1952); FOREVER FEMALE(1953); MOVIE STUNTMEN(1953); SUDDENLY(1954); GIRL RUSH, THE(1955); NIGHT OF THE HUNTER, THE(1955); STAR IN THE DUST(1956); LOVING YOU(1957); MAN IN THE SHADOW(1957); SPRING REUNION(1957); FEMALE ANIMAL, THE(1958); LAST HURRAH, THE(1958); MAN OR GUN(1958); MONEY, WOMEN AND GUNS(1958); ONCE UPON A HORSE(1958); ROCK-A-BYE BABY(1958); WORLD'S GREATEST LOVER, THE(1977)
Misc. Talkies
CAMPY KIDS FROM BOOT CAMP(1942); HOLLYWOOD THRILL-MAKERS(1954)
Silents
IS ZAT SO?(1927), w
Misc. Silents
COUNT OF TEN, THE(1928)

James Gleason, Sr.
ON YOUR TOES(1939)

Joseph Gleason
Silents
FORTUNE'S CHILD(1919), d; MISS DULCIE FROM DIXIE(1919), d
Misc. Silents
BELOVED IMPOSTER, THE(1918), d

June Gleason
HOUSE IS NOT A HOME, A(1964)

Keogh Gleason
TWO WEEKS IN ANOTHER TOWN(1962), set d; FOR ME AND MY GAL(1942), set d; WHAT NEXT, CORPORAL HARGROVE?(1945), set d; FATHER OF THE BRIDE(1950), set d; KING SOLOMON'S MINES(1950), set d; WATCH THE BIRDIE(1950), set d; AMERICAN IN PARIS, AN(1951), set d; FATHER'S LITTLE DIVIDEND(1951), set d; BAD AND THE BEAUTIFUL, THE(1952), set d; LONG, LONG TRAILER, THE(1954), set d; ROGUE COP(1954), set d; WINGS OF EAGLES, THE(1957), set d; COUNT YOUR BLESSINGS(1959), set d; TIME MACHINE, THE(1960, Brit./U.S.), set d; FOUR HORSEMEN OF THE APOCALYPSE, THE(1962), set d; HOOK, THE(1962), set d; COURTSHIP OF EDDY'S FATHER, THE(1963), set d; TICKLISH AFFAIR, A(1963), set d; WHEELER DEALERS, THE(1963), set d; GOODBYE CHARLIE(1964), set d; SANDPIPER, THE(1965), set d; WHEN THE BOYS MEET THE GIRLS(1965), set d; HOLD ON(1966), set d; MADE IN PARIS(1966), set d; PENELOPE(1966), set d; HOT RODS TO HELL(1967), set d; POINT BLANK(1967), set d; LEGEND OF LYLAH CLARE, THE(1968), set d; SPLIT, THE(1968), set d; YOUNG RUNAWAYS, THE(1968), set d; THERE WAS A CROOKED MAN(1970), set d; TRAVELING EXECUTIONER, THE(1970), set d

Keough Gleason
TWO SMART PEOPLE(1946), set d; TEXAS CARNIVAL(1951), set d

Lawrence Gleason, Jr.
PRIMROSE PATH(1940)

Lucile Gleason
LADIES MUST PLAY(1930), w; HIGGINS FAMILY, THE(1938); GRANDPA GOES TO TOWN(1940); LUCKY PARTNERS(1940); MONEY TO BURN(1940); STAGE DOOR CANTEEN(1943); TAKE IT BIG(1944); CLOCK, THE(1945)

Lucile Webster Gleason
GIRLS ABOUT TOWN(1931)

Lucille Gleason
PAGAN LADY(1931); GIRL OF THE RIO(1932); LOVE, HONOR, AND OH BABY!(1933); SOLITAIRE MAN, THE(1933); BELOVED(1934); I LIKE IT THAT WAY(1934); SUCCESSFUL FAILURE, A(1934); WOMAN UNAFRAID(1934); EX-MRS. BRADFORD, THE(1936); NAVY BLUES(1937); RED LIGHTS AHEAD(1937); BELOVED BRAT(1938); NURSE FROM BROOKLYN(1938); COVERED TRAILER, THE(1939); MY WIFE'S RELATIVES(1939); SHOULD HUSBANDS WORK?(1939); EARL OF PUDDLESTONE(1940); GAY FALCON, THE(1941); SHE'S IN THE ARMY(1942); DON'T FENCE ME IN(1945)

Lucille Webster Gleason
SHANNONS OF BROADWAY, THE(1929); NICE WOMAN(1932); DON'T BET ON LOVE(1933); KLONDIKE ANNIE(1936); RHYTHM ON THE RANGE(1936); FIRST LADY(1937)

Marilyn Gleason
TOY, THE(1982); SMOKEY AND THE BANDIT-PART 3(1983)

Mary Ellen Gleason
SECRET LIFE OF WALTER MITTY, THE(1947); MY FAVORITE SPY(1951); TWO TICKETS TO BROADWAY(1951); FRENCH LINE, THE(1954); SON OF SINBAD(1955)

Mary Pat Gleason
EASY MONEY(1983)

Michael Gleason
DEVIL'S ROCK(1938, Brit.); FAST CHARLIE... THE MOONBEAM RIDER(1979), w

Michi Gleason
BROKEN ENGLISH(1981), d, w

Moana Gleason
FROM HERE TO ETERNITY(1953)

Pat Gleason
BANK ALARM(1937); MAN BETRAYED, A(1937); SWING IT, PROFESSOR(1937); YOUNG DYNAMITE(1937); 23 ½ HOURS LEAVE(1937); CALL THE MESQUITEERS(1938); MARINES ARE HERE, THE(1938); SPY RING, THE(1938); SWEETHEARTS(1938); BROTHER ORCHID(1940); GANG'S ALL HERE(1941); IN THE NAVY(1941); LOVE CRAZY(1941); RAIDERS OF THE DESERT(1941); BROADWAY(1942); CITY OF SILENT MEN(1942); I KILLED THAT MAN(1942); JOAN OF OZARK(1942); POLICE BULLETS(1942); RUBBER RACKETEERS(1942); SLEEPYTIME GAL(1942); TOO MANY WOMEN(1942); DETECTIVE KITTY O'DAY(1944); JOHNNY DOESN'T LIVE HERE ANY MORE(1944); LAKE PLACID SERENADE(1944); COME OUT FIGHTING(1945); DETOUR(1945); EASY TO LOOK AT(1945); ON STAGE EVERYBODY(1945); ROGUES GALLERY(1945); THERE GOES KELLY(1945); CRIMINAL COURT(1946); LIVE WIRES(1946); NIGHT AND DAY(1946); DEADLINE(1948); INCIDENT(1948); FLAMINGO ROAD(1949); MUTINEERS, THE(1949); CALL OF THE KLONDIKE(1950); GHOST CHASERS(1951); LET'S GO NAVY(1951)
Misc. Talkies
SUNSET CARSON RIDES AGAIN(1948)

Paul Gleason
PRIVATE DUTY NURSES(1972); LITTLE LAURA AND BIG JOHN(1973); DOC SAVAGE... THE MAN OF BRONZE(1975); HE KNOWS YOU'RE ALONE(1980); ARTHUR(1981); FORT APACHE, THE BRONX(1981); PURSUIT OF D.B. COOPER, THE(1981); TENDER MERCIES(1982); TRADING PLACES(1983)

Paul X. Gleason
VIGILANTE FORCE(1976)

Redmond Gleason
CATTLE ANNIE AND LITTLE BRITCHES(1981)

Regina Gleason
OUTLAW'S DAUGHTER, THE(1954); DIAL RED O(1955); LAS VEGAS SHAKE-DOWN(1955); WALK THE DARK STREET(1956); TANK BATTALION(1958); SPEED CRAZY(1959); ON HER BED OF ROSES(1966); REVENGE OF THE CHEER-LEADERS(1976)

Russel Gleason
COVERED TRAILER, THE(1939)

Russell Gleason
FLYING FOOL(1929); SEVEN FACES(1929); SHADY LADY, THE(1929); SOPHOMORE, THE(1929); STRANGE CARGO(1929); ALL QUIET ON THE WESTERN FRONT(1930); OFFICER O'BRIEN(1930); SISTERS(1930); BEYOND VICTORY(1931); HOMICIDE SQUAD(1931); LAUGH AND GET RICH(1931); CASE OF CLARA DEANE, THE(1932); NICE WOMAN(1932); STRANGE CASE OF CLARA DEANE, THE(1932); PRIVATE JONES(1933); I CAN'T ESCAPE(1934); CONDEMNED TO LIVE(1935); HOT TIP(1935); HITCH HIKE TO HEAVEN(1936); BIG BUSINESS(1937); BORROWING TROUBLE(1937); HOT WATER(1937); OFF TO THE RACES(1937); TENDERFOOT GOES WEST, A(1937); DOWN ON THE FARM(1938); FURY BELOW(1938); HAVING WONDERFUL TIME(1938); HIGGINS FAMILY, THE(1938); LOVE ON A BUD-GET(1938); SAFETY IN NUMBERS(1938); TRIP TO PARIS, A(1938); EVERYBODY'S BABY(1939); HERE I AM A STRANGER(1939); MY WIFE'S RELATIVES(1939); NEWS IS MADE AT NIGHT(1939); SHOULD HUSBANDS WORK?(1939); UNDERCOVER AGENT(1939); EARL OF PUDDLESTONE(1940); GRANDPA GOES TO TOWN(1940); MONEY TO BURN(1940); YESTERDAY'S HEROES(1940); YOUNG AS YOU FEEL(1940); UNEXPECTED UNCLE(1941); DUDES ARE PRETTY PEOPLE(1942); FINGERS AT THE WINDOW(1942); SALUTE TO THE MARINES(1943); THREE HEARTS FOR JULIA(1943); LOST ANGEL(1944); MEET THE PEOPLE(1944)

William Gleason
THAT TOUCH OF MINK(1962); MINX, THE(1969)

Capt. Tome Gleave
BATTLE OF BRITAIN, THE(1969, Brit.), tech adv

Abraham Gleaves
GREEN PASTURES(1936)

George Glebeff
MISSION TO MOSCOW(1943)

George A. Gleboff
ROYAL SCANDAL, A(1945)

G. Glebov
SECRET BRIGADE, THE(1951 USSR)

Pyotor Glebov
YOLANTA(1964, USSR)

Pyotr Glebov
AND QUIET FLOWS THE DON(1960 USSR); TSAR'S BRIDE, THE(1966, USSR)

Valeriy Glebov
RED AND THE WHITE, THE(1969, Hung./USSR)

Gayle Glecker
LORDS OF FLATBUSH, THE(1974), w

Robert Glecker
FARMER TAKES A WIFE, THE(1935)

Robert Gleckler
MOTHER'S BOY(1929); SEA GOD, THE(1930); DEFENDERS OF THE LAW(1931); FINGER POINTS, THE(1931); TAKE A CHANCE(1933); DEFENSE RESTS, THE(1934); MILLION DOLLAR RANSOM(1934); NOW I'LL TELL(1934); PERSONALITY KID, THE(1934); STAMBOUL QUEST(1934); CASE OF THE CURIOUS BRIDE, THE(1935); DANTE'S INFERNO(1935); DARING YOUNG MAN, THE(1935); GLASS KEY, THE(1935); GREAT HOTEL MURDER(1935); HERE COMES THE BAND(1935); IT HAPPENED IN NEW YORK(1935); MR. DYNAMITE(1935); PERFECT CLUE, THE(1935); SHOW THEM NO MERCY(1935); TOO TOUGH TO KILL(1935); ABSO-LUTE QUIET(1936); FORGOTTEN FACES(1936); GIRL ON THE FRONT PAGE, THE(1936); GREAT GUY(1936); I'D GIVE MY LIFE(1936); LOVE BEGINS AT TWENTY(1936); SWORN ENEMY(1936); WHIPSAW(1936); YOURS FOR THE ASK-ING(1936); BULLDOG DRUMMOND'S REVENGE(1937); HOT WATER(1937); KING OF GAMBLERS(1937); MAN WHO CRIED WOLF, THE(1937); NORTH OF NO-ME(1937); PICK A STAR(1937); WINGS OVER HONOLULU(1937); ALEXANDER'S RAGTIME BAND(1938); GANGS OF NEW YORK(1938); GUN LAW(1938); LITTLE MISS BROADWAY(1938); RIDE A CROOKED MILE(1938); TARNISHED AN-GEL(1938); ORPHANS OF THE STREET(1939); STAND UP AND FIGHT(1939); THEY MADE ME A CRIMINAL(1939)

Nicholas Gledhill
1984
CAREFUL, HE MIGHT HEAR YOU(1984, Aus.)

James Gleeson
DAWN OVER IRELAND(1938, Irish)

Janet Gleeson
LITTLE AUSTRALIANS(1940, Aus.)

Nancy Gleeson
LITTLE AUSTRALIANS(1940, Aus.)

Patrick Gleeson
1984
PLAGUE DOGS, THE(1984, U.S./Brit.), m

Redmond Gleeson
PIPE DREAMS(1976)
1984
DREAMSCAPE(1984)

Tim Gleeson
DOING TIME(1979, Brit.), art d

Gregory Gleghorne
GLORIA(1980)

Therese Glehse
LAST CHANCE, THE(1945, Switz.)

Morris Gleitzman
1984
MELVIN, SON OF ALVIN(1984, Aus.), w

Maurice Gleize
Misc. Silents
LA MAIN QUI A TUE(1924, Fr.), d; LA NUIT ROUGE(1924, Fr.), d; LA JUS-TICIERE(1925, Fr.), d; LA FAUTE DE MONIQUE(1928, Fr.), d; LA MADONE DES SLEEPINGS(1928, Fr.), d; TU M'APPARTIENS(1929, Fr.), d

Michelle Gleizer
DEATH OF MARIO RICCI, THE(1983, Ital.)

R. Glemnitz
OFFICE GIRLS(1974)

Bernard Glemser
COME FLY WITH ME(1963), w

Archie Glen
MIDSHIPMAID GOB(1932, Brit.); VARIETY PARADE(1936, Brit.)

John Glen
KATHLEEN(1938, Ireland), w; BABY LOVE(1969, Brit.), ed; ON HER MAJESTY'S SECRET SERVICE(1969, Brit.), ed; CATLOW(1971, Span.), ed; MURPHY'S WAR(1971, Brit.), ed; SITTING TARGET(1972, Brit.), ed; DOLL'S HOUSE, A(1973), ed; GOLD(1974, Brit.), ed; CONDUCT UNBECOMING(1975, Brit.), ed; SEVEN NIGHTS IN JAPAN(1976, Brit./Fr.), ed; SPY WHO LOVED ME, THE(1977, Brit.), ed; WILD GEESE, THE(1978, Brit.), ed; MOONRAKER(1979, Brit.), ed; FOR YOUR EYES ONLY(1981), d; SEA WOLVES, THE(1981, Brit.), ed; OCTOPUSSY(1983, Brit.), d

Ron Glen
HAREM BUNCH; OR WAR AND PIECE, THE(1969)

Glen Gray and His Casa Loma Band
TIME OUT FOR RHYTHM(1941)

Glen Gray and his Casa Loma Orchestra
JAM SESSION(1944)

Gary Glendell
HEADIN' FOR BROADWAY(1980)

Ilone Glendening
CASE OF THE FRIGHTENED LADY, THE(1940. Brit.), ph

Candace Glendenning
NICHOLAS AND ALEXANDRA(1971, Brit.); SATAN'S SLAVE(1976, Brit.); BEYOND THE FOG(1981, Brit.)

Ernest Glendenning
Silents
WHEN KNIGHTHOOD WAS IN FLOWER(1922)

Hone Glendenning
JOHN WESLEY(1954, Brit.), ph

Raymond Glendenning
ASKING FOR TROUBLE(1942, Brit.); IT'S THAT MAN AGAIN(1943, Brit.); DREAM-ING(1944, Brit.); GALLOPING MAJOR, THE(1951, Brit.); FOUR AGAINST FATE(1952, Brit.); SMALL TOWN STORY(1953, Brit.); RAINBOW JACKET, THE(1954, Brit.); DRY ROT(1956, Brit.); SWINGIN' MAIDEN, THE(1963, Brit.); MAKE MINE A MIL-LION(1965, Brit.)

Hone Glending
SILK NOOSE, THE(1950, Brit.), ph

Hone Glendining
MIDNIGHT EPISODE(1951, Brit.), ph; SCARLET WEB, THE(1954, Brit.), ph

Ernest Glendinning
Misc. Silents
SEVENTH NOON, THE(1915)

Ethel Glendinning
END OF THE ROAD, THE(1936, Brit.); WRATH OF JEALOUSY(1936, Brit.)

Hone Glendinning
BYPASS TO HAPPINESS(1934, Brit.), ph; ROLLING HOME(1935, Brit.), ph; AULD LANG SYNE(1937, Brit.), ph; MERRY COMES TO STAY(1937, Brit.), ph; RIDING HIGH(1937, Brit.), ph; UNDER A CLOUD(1937, Brit.), ph; JOHN HALIFAX—GENTLE-MAN(1938, Brit.), ph; SEXTON BLAKE AND THE HOODED TERROR(1938, Brit.), ph; SILVER TOP(1938, Brit.), ph; FACE AT THE WINDOW, THE(1939, Brit.), ph; CHI-NESE DEN, THE(1940, Brit.), ph; CRIMES AT THE DARK HOUSE(1940, Brit.), ph; BUT NOT IN VAIN(1948, Brit.), ph; CODE OF SCOTLAND YARD(1948), ph; TRIAL OF MADAM X, THE(1948, Brit.), ph; FORBIDDEN(1949, Brit.), ph; SHADOW OF THE PAST(1950, Brit.), ph; NAUGHTY ARLETTE(1951, Brit.), ph; THREE STEPS IN THE DARK(1953, Brit.), ph; HARASSED HERO, THE(1954, Brit.), ph; MEET MR. MAL-COLM(1954, Brit.), ph; FLYING EYE, THE(1955, Brit.), ph

John Glendinning
LOST BOUNDARIES(1949)

Frank Glendon
CIRCLE OF DEATH(1935), d; FRONT PAGE WOMAN(1935)
Silents
CROSS BREED(1927)
Misc. Silents
DAWN OF UNDERSTANDING, THE(1918)

J. F. Glendon
Silents
SALAMANDER, THE(1915)

J. Frank Glendon
BORDER ROMANCE(1930); CHEYENNE CYCLONE, THE(1932); I AM A FUGITIVE FROM A CHAIN GANG(1932); LAW AND LAWLESS(1932); GUN LAW(1933); HER SPLENDID FOLLY(1933); RACING STRAIN, THE(1933); STRANGE PEOPLE(1933); TEXAS TORNADO(1934); CIRCLE OF DEATH(1935); JUSTICE OF THE RANGE(1935); SAGEBRUSH TROUBADOR(1935); BORDER CABALLERO(1936); KING OF THE PECOS(1936); LION'S DEN, THE(1936); TRAITOR, THE(1936)
Misc. Talkies
CROOKED ROAD(1932); RECKLESS RIDER, THE(1932)
Silents
BY THE WORLD FORGOT(1918); TALE OF TWO WORLDS, A(1921); WHAT DO MEN WANT?(1921); KISSED(1922); NIGHT LIFE IN HOLLYWOOD(1922); JUST LIKE A WOMAN(1923); RIP-TIDE, THE(1923); SOUTH SEA LOVE(1923)
Misc. Silents
TABLES TURNED(1915); HOUSE OF MIRRORS, THE(1916); DEFEAT OF THE CITY, THE(1917); DUPLICITY OF HARGRAVES, THE(1917); LIGHT IN DARK-NESS(1917); NIGHT IN NEW ARABIA, A(1917); RENAISSANCE AT CHARLEROI, THE(1917); CHANGING WOMAN, THE(1918); COVE OF MISSING MEN(1918); MY HUSBAND'S FRIEND(1918); WOOING OF PRINCESS PAT, THE(1918); WISHING RING MAN, THE(1919); FOR THE SOUL OF RAFAEL(1920); MIDCHANNEL(1920);

FORGOTTEN WOMAN(1921); HUSH(1921); BELLE OF ALASKA(1922); MORE TO BE PITIED THAN SCORNED(1922); YANKEE DOODLE, JR.(1922); SHATTERED FAITH(1923); TRICKS(1925); COMPASSION(1927)

The Reverend William Glenesk
FOR LOVE OF IVY(1968)

Agnes Glenn
RUSTLER'S VALLEY(1937)

Bob Glenn
PAL JOEY(1957)

Carrick Glenn
BURNING, THE(1981)

Charles Glenn
SALT & PEPPER(1968, Brit.), cos

Cynda Glenn
MODIGLIANI OF MONTPARNASSE(1961, Fr./Ital.)

Garrard Glenn
SEIZURE(1974), p

Glen Glenn
FIGHTING TEXAN(1937), ed; GUNSMOKE TRAIL(1938), ph

Grosvenor Glenn
JULIUS CAESAR(1952)

Jack Glenn
CRY MURDER(1936), d

Jackie Glenn
PLEASURE PLANTATION(1970)

Jacquelyn Glenn
PROJECTIONIST, THE(1970)

Jerry Glenn
BABES IN TOYLAND(1961)

John Glenn
BEN HUR(1959); PULP(1972, Brit.), ed

Leslie Glenn
PAY OR DIE(1960); RAYMIE(1960)

Libby Glenn
ISADORA(1968, Brit.); REVOLUTIONARY, THE(1970, Brit.)

Louise Glenn
FUNNY FACE(1957); WILD AND THE INNOCENT, THE(1959); IT'S A MAD, MAD, MAD, MAD WORLD(1963); BIG HAND FOR THE LITTLE LADY, A(1966)

Max Glenn
MOVING FINGER, THE(1963), ph

Montgomery Glenn
CASTLE OF BLOOD(1964, Fr./Ital.); HORRIBLE DR. HICHCOCK, THE(1964, Ital.)

Pierre Glenn
STATE OF SIEGE(1973, Fr./U.S./Ital./Ger.), ph; SUCH A GORGEOUS KID LIKE ME(1973, Fr.), ph; CLOCKMAKER, THE(1976, Fr.), ph; LET JOY REIGN SUPREME(1977, Fr.), ph; JUDGE AND THE ASSASSIN, THE(1979, Fr.); LITTLE ROMANCE, A(1979, U.S./Fr.), ph; LOULOU(1980, Fr.), ph; COUP DE TORCHON(1981, Fr.), ph

Pierre-William Glenn
DAY FOR NIGHT(1973, Fr.), ph; SMALL CHANGE(1976, Fr.), ph; AVALANCHE(1978), ph; DEATHWATCH(1980, Fr./Ger.), ph; CHOICE OF ARMS(1983, Fr.), ph; L'ETOILE DU NORD(1983, Fr.), ph

Raymond Glenn
Silents
LADIES AT EASE(1927)
Misc. Silents
RETURN OF BOSTON BLACKIE, THE(1927); TEMPTATIONS OF A SHOP GIRL(1927)

Robert Glenn
SILENCERS, THE(; HOTHEAD(1963); BULLET FOR PRETTY BOY, A(1970); LAST PICTURE SHOW, THE(1971)

Roy Glenn
CHICAGO CALLING(1951); AFFAIR IN TRINIDAD(1952); BOMBA AND THE JUNGLE GIRL(1952); ROYAL AFRICAN RIFLES, THE(1953); CARMEN JONES(1954); GOLDEN IDOL, THE(1954); KILLER LEOPARD(1954); RIOT IN CELL BLOCK 11(1954); MAN IN THE GREY FLANNEL SUIT, THE(1956); WRITTEN ON THE WIND(1956); GREEN-EYED BLONDE, THE(1957); TARZAN'S FIGHT FOR LIFE(1958); PORGY AND BESS(1959); SOUND AND THE FURY, THE(1959); RAISIN IN THE SUN, A(1961); SWEET BIRD OF YOUTH(1962); DEAD HEAT ON A MERRY-GO-ROUND(1966); MAN CALLED ADAM, A(1966); WAY WEST, THE(1967); FINIAN'S RAINBOW(1968); HANG'EM HIGH(1968); I LOVE YOU, ALICE B. TOKLAS(1968); SUPPORT YOUR LOCAL GUNFIGHTER(1971)

Roy Glenn, Jr.
MAN CALLED PETER, THE(1955)

Roy Glenn, Sr.
JUNGLE GENTS(1954)

Roy E. Glenn
LYDIA BAILEY(1952); TWILIGHT'S LAST GLEAMING(1977, U.S./Ger.)

Roy E. Glenn, Sr.
GUESS WHO'S COMING TO DINNER(1967); GREAT WHITE HOPE, THE(1970); ...TICK...TICK...TICK...(1970); ESCAPE FROM THE PLANET OF THE APES(1971)

Scott Glenn
BABY MAKER, THE(1970); ANGELS HARD AS THEY COME(1971); HEX(1973); NASHVILLE(1975); FIGHTING MAD(1976); APOCALYPSE NOW(1979); MORE AMERICAN GRAFFITI(1979); URBAN COWBOY(1980); CATTLE ANNIE AND LITTLE BRITCHES(1981); CHALLENGE, THE(1982); PERSONAL BEST(1982); KEEP, THE(1983); RIGHT STUFF, THE(1983)
1984
RIVER, THE(1984)
Misc. Talkies
SHE CAME TO THE VALLEY(1979)

Stanley Glenn
DESPERATE WOMEN, THE(?)

Glenn Miller Singers
CRAZY HOUSE(1943)

Beverly Glenn-Copeland
MONTREAL MAIN(1974, Can.), m

Daphne Glenne
Silents
ON LEAVE(1918, Brit.); HER LONELY SOLDIER(1919, Brit.)
Misc. Silents
TICKET-OF-LEAVE MAN, THE(1918, Brit.); LAMP OF DESTINY(1919, Brit.); LIFE OF A LONDON ACTRESS, THE(1919, Brit.)

Alison Glennie
ESCAPE FROM THE SEA(1968, Brit.)

Bert Glennon
GANG WAR(1928), d; PATRIOT, THE(1928), ph; PERFECT CRIME, THE(1928), d; SYNCOPATION(1929), d; GIRL OF THE PORT(1930), d; PARADISE ISLAND(1930), d; SECOND WIFE(1930), w; IN THE LINE OF DUTY(1931), d; BLONDE VENUS(1932), ph; HALF-NAKED TRUTH, THE(1932), ph; SOUTH OF SANTA FE(1932), d; ALICE IN WONDERLAND(1933), ph; CHRISTOPHER STRONG(1933), ph; GABRIEL OVER THE WHITE HOUSE(1933), ph; MELODY CRUISE(1933), ph; MORNING GLORY(1933), ph; GRAND CANARY(1934), ph; HELL IN THE HEAVENS(1934), ph; SCARLET EMPRESS, THE(1934), ph; SHE WAS A LADY(1934), ph; BAD BOY(1935), ph; GINGER(1935), ph; SHOW THEM NO MERCY(1935), ph; THUNDER IN THE NIGHT(1935), ph; CAN THIS BE DIXIE?(1936), ph; DIMPLES(1936), ph; HALF ANGEL(1936), ph; LITTLE MISS NOBODY(1936), ph; LLOYDS OF LONDON(1936), ph; PRISONER OF SHARK ISLAND, THE(1936), ph; HURRICANE, THE(1937), ph; DRUMS ALONG THE MOHAWK(1939), ph; STAGECOACH(1939), ph; SWANEE RIVER(1939), ph; HOWARDS OF VIRGINIA, THE(1940), ph; OUR TOWN(1940), ph; DIVE BOMBER(1941), ph; ONE NIGHT IN LISBON(1941), ph; RELUCTANT DRAGON, THE(1941), ph; VIRGINIA(1941), ph; DESPERATE JOURNEY(1942), ph; JUKE GIRL(1942), ph; THEY DIED WITH THEIR BOOTS ON(1942), ph; DESERT SONG, THE(1943), ph; MISSION TO MOSCOW(1943), ph; THIS IS THE ARMY(1943), ph; DESTINATION TOKYO(1944), ph; HOLLYWOOD CANTEEN(1944), ph; VERY THOUGHT OF YOU, THE(1944), ph; SAN ANTONIO(1945), ph; MR. DISTRICT ATTORNEY(1946), ph; ONE MORE TOMORROW(1946), ph; SHADOW OF A WOMAN(1946), ph; COPACABANA(1947), ph; RED HOUSE, THE(1947), ph; RUTHLESS(1948), ph; RED LIGHT(1949), ph; RIO GRANDE(1950), ph; WAGONMASTER(1950), ph; OPERATION PACIFIC(1951), ph; SEA HORNET, THE(1951), ph; ABOUT FACE(1952), ph; BIG TREES, THE(1952), ph; MAN BEHIND THE GUN, THE(1952), ph; HOUSE OF WAX(1953), ph; MOONLIGHTER, THE(1953), ph; THUNDER OVER THE PLAINS(1953), ph; CRIME WAVE(1954), ph; MAD MAGICIAN, THE(1954), ph; RIDING SHOTGUN(1954), ph; DAVY CROCKETT AND THE RIVER PIRATES(1956), ph; SERGEANT RUTLEDGE(1960), ph; LAD: A DOG(1962), ph; MAN FROM GALVESTON, THE(1964), ph
Misc. Talkies
AROUND THE CORNER(1930), d
Silents
RAMONA(1916), ph; NOBODY'S FOOL(1921), ph; TORRENT, THE(1921), ph; BURNING SANDS(1922), ph; EBB TIDE(1922), ph; WOMAN WHO WALKED ALONE, THE(1922), ph; JAVA HEAD(1923), ph; SALOMY JANE(1923), ph; TEN COMMANDMENTS, THE(1923), ph; OPEN ALL NIGHT(1924), ph; ARE PARENTS PEOPLE?(1925), ph; GOOD AND NAUGHTY(1926), ph; CITY GONE WILD, THE(1927), ph; UNDERWORLD(1927), ph; WE'RE ALL GAMBLERS(1927), ph; WOMAN ON TRIAL, THE(1927), ph; LAST COMMAND, THE(1928), ph; STREET OF SIN, THE(1928), ph; AIR LEGION, THE(1929), d

David Glennon
COMING HOME(1978)

Frank Glennon
ACES AND EIGHTS(1936)

Gordon Glennon
WICKED LADY, THE(1946, Brit.), w; KILLER WALKS, A(1952, Brit.), w; PRIVATE INFORMATION(1952, Brit.), w

Herbert Glennon
Silents
PATCHWORK GIRL OF OZ, THE(1914)

Ione Glennon
Silents
JACK AND THE BEANSTALK(1917)

James Glennon
1984
EL NORTE(1984), ph; UP THE CREEK(1984), ph; WILD LIFE, THE(1984), ph

Jim Glennon
RETURN OF THE JEDI(1983), ph

Dennis Glenny
KANGAROO(1952)

Peter Glenville
HIS BROTHER'S KEEPER(1939, Brit.); RETURN TO YESTERDAY(1940, Brit.); TWO FOR DANGER(1940, Brit.); HEAVEN IS ROUND THE CORNER(1944, Brit.); UNCENSORED(1944, Brit.); MADONNA OF THE SEVEN MOONS(1945, Brit.); GOOD TIME GIRL(1950, Brit.); PRISONER, THE(1955, Brit.), d; ME AND THE COLONEL(1958), d; SUMMER AND SMOKE(1961), d; TERM OF TRIAL(1962, Brit.), d&w; BECKET(1964, Brit.), d; HOTEL PARADISO(1966, U.S./Brit.), a, p&d; COMEDIANS, THE(1967), p&d

Shaun Glenville
JAILBIRDS(1939, Brit.); DR. O'DOWD(1940, Brit.)

Gordon Glenwright
DOVE, THE(1974, Brit.); INN OF THE DAMNED(1974, Aus.)

Barbara Glenz
KISMET(1944)

Viscount Glerawly
Silents
TEN COMMANDMENTS, THE(1923)

Max Glersberg
ALL THE KING'S HORSES(1935), w

Sharon Gless
STAR CHAMBER, THE(1983)

Molly Glessing
DANGEROUS WHEN WET(1953)

Nicola Glew
RUNNERS(1983, Brit.)

Vassilis Glezakos
TEMPEST(1982)

Evanthia Glezakou
TEMPEST(1982)
Frances Glick
PASSION HOLIDAY(1963)
Joe Glick
BOWERY, THE(1933)
Marc Glick
GAL YOUNG UN(1979)
Michael S. Glick
DEVIL'S RAIN, THE(1975, U.S./Mex.), p; BUSTIN' LOOSE(1981), p
Norman Glick
STARSHIP INVASIONS(1978, Can.), p
Phyllis Glick
BABY BLUE MARINE(1976)
James Glickenhaus
EXTERMINATOR, THE(1980), d&w; SOLDIER, THE(1982), p,d&w
Jim Glickenhaus
Misc. Talkies
ASTROLOGER, THE(1979), d
Paul Glicker
CANNONBALL(1976, U.S./Hong Kong)
Misc. Talkies
RUNNING SCARED(1980), d
Paul Glickler
Misc. Talkies
CHEERLEADERS, THE(1973), d
Ellis F. Glickman
Misc. Silents
LAST CONCERT, THE(1915)
I. Glickman
MORNING STAR(1962, USSR), w, ed
Joel Glickman
BROTHER JOHN(1971), p; BUCK AND THE PREACHER(1972), p
Marty Glickman
GO, MAN, GO!(1954); LOVELY WAY TO DIE, A(1968)
Mort Glickman
OUTLAWS OF PINE RIDGE(1942), m; SHADOWS ON THE SAGE(1942), m; SUN-DOWN KID, THE(1942), m; VALLEY OF HUNTED MEN(1942), m; BEYOND THE LAST FRONTIER(1943), m; DAYS OF OLD CHEYENNE(1943), m; DEAD MAN'S GULCH(1943), m; DEATH VALLEY MANHUNT(1943), m; FUGITIVE FROM SONO-RA(1943), m; MAN FROM THE RIO GRANDE, THE(1943), m; MAN FROM THUN-DER RIVER, THE(1943), m; OVERLAND MAIL ROBBERY(1943), m; RAIDERS OF SUNSET PASS(1943), m; SANTA FE SCOUTS(1943), m; THUNDERING TRAILS(1943), m; WAGON TRACKS WEST(1943), m; FORTY THIEVES(1944), m; GAMBLER'S CHOICE(1944), md; HIDDEN VALLEY OUTLAWS(1944), m; LARAMIE TRAIL, THE(1944), m; MACHINE GUN MAMA(1944), m, md; MOJAVE FIRE-BRAND(1944), m; OUTLAWS OF SANTA FE(1944), m; PRIDE OF THE PLAINS(1944), m; INNER CIRCLE, THE(1946), md; MAGNIFICENT ROGUE, THE(1946), md; MAN FROM RAINBOW VALLEY, THE(1946), md; MYSTERIOUS MR. VALENTINE, THE(1946), m; RED RIVER RENEGADES(1946), md; RIO GRANDE RAIDERS(1946), md; SANTA FE UPRISING(1946), md; STAGECOACH TO DENVER(1946), md; TRAF-FIC IN CRIME(1946), md; BLACKMAIL(1947), md; HOMESTEADERS OF PARADISE VALLEY(1947), md; LAST FRONTIER UPRISING(1947), m; MARSHAL OF CRIPPLE CREEK, THE(1947), md; OREGON TRAIL SCOUTS(1947), md; OTHER LOVE, THE(1947), md; RUSTLERS OF DEVIL'S CANYON(1947), md; SPOILERS OF THE NORTH(1947), md; TRESPASSER, THE(1947), md; UNDER COLORADO SKIES(1947), md; VIGILANTES OF BOOMTOWN(1947), md; WEB OF DANGER, THE(1947), md; WILD FRONTIER, THE(1947), md; LIGHTNIN' IN THE FO-REST(1948), m, md; MADONNA OF THE DESERT(1948), md; OKLAHOMA BAD-LANDS(1948), md; SECRET SERVICE INVESTIGATOR(1948), m, md; SLIPPY MCGEE(1948), md; TIMBER TRAIL, THE(1948), md
Paul Glickman
DAVID HOLZMAN'S DIARY(1968), ph; FEMALE BUNCH, THE(1969), ph; BLOOD OF FRANKENSTEIN(1970), ph; DREAMER, THE(1970, Israel), ph; SCARECROW IN A GARDEN OF CUCUMBERS(1972), ph; GOD TOLD ME TO(1976), ph; TRACKS(1977), ph; PRIVATE FILES OF J. EDGAR HOOVER, THE(1978), ph; SIT-TING DUCKS(1979), ph
1984
PERFECT STRANGERS(1984), ph; SPECIAL EFFECTS(1984), ph
Shirley Glickman
ROYAL WEDDING(1951)
Will Glickman
MRS. GIBBONS' BOYS(1962, Brit.), w
John Glidden
Silents
IN THE BLOOD(1923, Brit.)
Misc. Silents
BECAUSE(1921, Brit.)
John Gliddon
Silents
POWER OF RIGHT, THE(1919, Brit.); RANK OUTSIDER(1920, Brit.)
Misc. Silents
SANDS OF TIME, THE(1919, Brit.); DAWN OF THE TRUTH, THE(1920, Brit.); TEMPTRESS, THE(1920, Brit.); NIGHT HAWK, THE(1921, Brit.), d
K.B. Gliden
HURRY SUNDOWN(1967), w
Sandy Glieberman
RATTLERS(1976), ed
Rochus Gliese
FIDELIO(1961, Aust.), set d
Silents
SUNRISE–A SONG OF TWO HUMANS(1927), prod d
Hazen Glifford
RICHARD(1972)
Bratoljub Gligorijevic
INNOCENCE UNPROTECTED(1971, Yugo.)
I. Glikman
SONG OVER MOSCOW(1964, USSR), w

Arnold Glimcher
STILL OF THE NIGHT(1982)
Norman Glind
VICE GIRLS, LTD.(1964)
Ib Glindemann
JOURNEY TO THE SEVENTH PLANET(1962, U.S./Swed.), m, md; CRAZY PARA-DISE(1965, Den.), m
Ib Glinderman
OPERATION CAMEL(1961, Den.), m
Ib Glindermann
SUDDENLY, A WOMAN!(1967, Den.), m
T. Glinkina
SONG OVER MOSCOW(1964, USSR)
Wienczyslaw Glinski
KANAL(1961, Pol.); ECHO, THE(1964, Pol.)
Terry Glinwood
NATIONAL HEALTH, OR NURSE NORTON'S AFFAIR, THE(1973, Brit.), p
Erla Gliserman
RABID(1976, Can.), cos; HOUSE BY THE LAKE, THE(1977, Can.), cos
Judith Glizer
DESERTER(1934, USSR)
Misc. Silents
STRIKE(1925, USSR)
Helena Gloag
PRIME OF MISS JEAN BRODIE, THE(1969, Brit.); RING OF BRIGHT WATER(1969, Brit.); BROTHERLY LOVE(1970, Brit.); SCROOGE(1970, Brit.)
Julian Gloag
OUR MOTHER'S HOUSE(1967, Brit.), w
Brian Glober
ABSOLUTION(1981, Brit.)
Krzysztof Globisz
DANTON(1983)
Yoram Globous
MY MARGO(1969, Israel), p
Kenneth Globus
KID VENGEANCE(1977), w
Yoram Globus
FOUR DEUCES, THE(1976), p; GOD'S GUN(1977), p; OPERATION THUNDER-BOLT(1978, ISRAEL), p; MAGICIAN OF LUBLIN, THE(1979, Israel/Ger.), p; APPLE, THE(1980 U.S./Ger.), p; DR. HECKYL AND MR. HYPE(1980), p; HAPPY HOOKER GOES TO HOLLYWOOD, THE(1980), p; NEW YEAR'S EVIL(1980), p; SCHI-ZOID(1980), p; SEED OF INNOCENCE(1980), p; BODY AND SOUL(1981), p; DEATH WISH II(1982), p; ENTER THE NINJA(1982), p; HOSPITAL MASSACRE(1982), p; LAST AMERICAN VIRGIN, THE(1982), p; THAT CHAMPIONSHIP SEASON(1982), p; HERCULES(1983), p; NANA(1983, Ital.), p; REVENGE OF THE NINJA(1983), p; WICKED LADY, THE(1983, Brit.), p
1984
AMBASSADOR, THE(1984), p; BREAKIN' 2: ELECTRIC BOOGALOO(1984), p; HOS-PITAL MASSACRE(1984), p; LOVE STREAMS(1984), p; MISSING IN ACTION(1984), p; NAKED FACE, THE(1984), p; NINJA III–THE DOMINATION(1984), p; OVER THE BROOKLYN BRIDGE(1984), p; SAHARA(1984), p; SWORD OF THE VALIANT(1984, Brit.), p; ULTIMATE SOLUTION OF GRACE QUIGLEY, THE(1984), p
Dorothee Glocklen
IT'S HOT IN PARADISE(1962, Ger./Yugo.); SEVEN DARING GIRLS(1962, Ger.); ISLE OF SIN(1963, Ger.)
Pepi Glockner-Kramer
NO TIME FOR FLOWERS(1952)
Lawrence L. Glodman
THIRTY FOOT BRIDE OF CANDY ROCK, THE(1959), w
Arthur Glogau
MARRIAGE OF MARIA BRAUN, THE(1979, Ger.)
Nancy Glogow
FRATERNITY ROW(1977)
Anna Glomb
TALK ABOUT A STRANGER(1952)
George Glon
DEADLY TRAP, THE(1972, Fr./Ital.), set d
Georges Glon
LAST YEAR AT MARIENBAD(1962, Fr./Ital.), set d; WOMAN TIMES SEVEN(1967, U.S./Fr./Ital.), set d; FRENCH CONNECTION 11(1975), art d
Jean Glono
ANGELE(1934 Fr.), w
Charles Glore
MOONSHINE MOUNTAIN(1964), w
Anna Glori
ORGANIZER, THE(1964, Fr./Ital./Yugo.)
Enrico Glori
PEARLS OF THE CROWN(1938, Fr.); SPIRIT AND THE FLESH, THE(1948, Ital.); STRANGER ON THE PROWL(1953, Ital.); LOVES OF THREE QUEENS, THE(1954, Ital./Fr.); FROM A ROMAN BALCONY(1961, Fr./Ital.); LA DOLCE VITA(1961, Ital./Fr.); BARABBAS(1962, Ital.); DAMON AND PYTHIAS(1962); NIGHT THEY KILLED RASPUTIN, THE(1962, Fr./Ital.); DUEL OF THE TITANS(1963, Ital.); LOVE AND LARCENY(1963, Fr./Ital.); LADY WITHOUT CAMELLIAS, THE(1981, Ital.)
Gianni Glori
ANGELINA(1948, Ital.); DESERT DESPERADOES(1959)
Vittorio Glori
BELLISSIMA(1952, Ital.)
Vittorio Musy Glori
SIGN OF THE GLADIATOR(1959, Fr./Ger./Ital.)
Darlene Gloria
EARTH ENTRANCED(1970, Braz.); ALL NUDITY SHALL BE PUNISHED(1974, Brazil)
Leda Gloria
RING AROUND THE CLOCK(1953, Ital.); LAW IS THE LAW, THE(1959, Fr.)
Tina Gloriani
VIOLENT SUMMER(1961, Fr./Ital.); VAMPIRE AND THE BALLERINA, THE(1962, Ital.)

Gertrude Glorie
NAVAJO KID, THE(1946)
Vincent Glorioso
ATLANTIC CITY(1981, U.S./Can.)
Gloris the Dog
IN THE MONEY(1958)
June Glory
WITHOUT RESERVATIONS(1946); WORDS AND MUSIC(1929); GOLD DIGGERS OF 1933(1933); 42ND STREET(1933); DON'T GET PERSONAL(1936); PALEFACE, THE(1948); VICKI(1953)
Marie Glory
KING OF PARIS, THE(1934, Brit.); WITH A SMILE(1939, Fr.); ADORABLE CREATURES(1956, Fr.); AND GOD CREATED WOMAN(1957, Fr.)
Mercia Glossop
MIKADO, THE(1967, Brit.)
Rosemary Glosz
ONE NIGHT OF LOVE(1934); MARK OF THE VAMPIRE(1935); WAKE UP AND LIVE(1937)
Jan Glotzer
PERSONAL BEST(1982)
Ancil Gloudon
PIRANHA II: THE SPAWNING(1981, Neth.)
Dick Glouner
GAY DECEIVERS, THE(1969), ph
Donald C. Glouner
MAROONED(1969), spec eff
Richard Glouner
PAYDAY(1972), ph; CHRISTINA(1974, Can.), ph
Richard C. Glouner
DEVIL'S 8, THE(1969), ph; DUNWICH HORROR, THE(1970), ph; GLORY BOY(1971), ph; MAKING IT(1971), ph; SUMMERTREE(1971), ph; SOUL OF NIGGER CHARLEY, THE(1973), ph; GUMBALL RALLY, THE(1976), ph; GONG SHOW MOVIE, THE(1980), ph; MAN WITH BOGART'S FACE, THE(1980), ph
Edmund Glove
COURAGEOUS DR. CHRISTIAN, THE(1940)
Bill Glover
KING'S PIRATE(1967)
Brian Glover
KES(1970, Brit.); O LUCKY MAN!(1973, Brit.); BRANNIGAN(1975, Brit.); MR. QUILP(1975, Brit.); DIRTY KNIGHT'S WORK(1976, Brit.); JABBERWOCKY(1977, Brit.); SWEENEY(1977, Brit.); GREAT TRAIN ROBBERY, THE(1979, Brit.); AMERICAN WEREWOLF IN LONDON, AN(1981)
1984
LAUGHTER HOUSE(1984, Brit.), w; ORDEAL BY INNOCENCE(1984, Brit.)
Bruce Glover
WHO KILLED TEDDY BEAR?(1965); SWEET LOVE, BITTER(1967); C. C. AND COMPANY(1971); DIAMONDS ARE FOREVER(1971, Brit.); SCANDALOUS JOHN(1971); BLACK GUNN(1972); ONE LITTLE INDIAN(1973); WALKING TALL(1973); CHINATOWN(1974); HARD TIMES(1975); WALKING TALL, PART II(1975); FINAL CHAPTER–WALKING TALL zero(1977); STUNTS(1977); BIG SCORE, THE(1983)
C. Glover
ILLEGAL(1932, Brit.)
Charles Glover
MITCHELL(1975)
Crispin Glover
MY TUTOR(1983)
1984
FRIDAY THE 13TH–THE FINAL CHAPTER(1984); RACING WITH THE MOON(1984); TEACHERS(1984)
Cyd Glover
1984
BREAKIN' 2: ELECTRIC BOOGALOO(1984)
Danny Glover
ESCAPE FROM ALCATRAZ(1979); CHU CHU AND THE PHILLY FLASH(1981); OUT(1982)
1984
ICEMAN(1984); PLACES IN THE HEART(1984)
David Glover
DENTIST IN THE CHAIR(1960, Brit.); GET ON WITH IT(1963, Brit.); MYSTERY SUBMARINE(1963, Brit.); IPCRESS FILE, THE(1965, Brit.); FAHRENHEIT 451(1966, Brit.); FOLLOW THAT CAMEL(1967, Brit.); KES(1970, Brit.); PRIEST OF LOVE(1981, Brit.)
Ed Glover
SIDE STREET(1950)
Edmund Glover
FIGHTING 69TH, THE(1940); EAGLE SQUADRON(1942); MY FAVORITE SPY(1942); GHOST SHIP, THE(1943); FALCON OUT WEST, THE(1944); MADEMOISELLE FIFI(1944); MARINE RAIDERS(1944); MUSIC IN MANHATTAN(1944); NEVADA(1944); NIGHT OF ADVENTURE, A(1944); YOUTH RUNS WILD(1944); BACK TO BATAAN(1945); DICK TRACY(1945); FIRST YANK INTO TOKYO(1945); GEORGE WHITE'S SCANDALS(1945); THOSE ENDEARING YOUNG CHARMS(1945); TWO O'CLOCK COURAGE(1945); DEADLINE AT DAWN(1946); SHADOWS OF THE WEST(1949); IMPERSONATOR, THE(1962, Brit.); SEX AND THE SINGLE GIRL(1964)
Gertrude Glover
Misc. Silents
PHANTOM BUCCANEER, THE(1916)
Henry Glover
HEY, LET'S TWIST!(1961), m; TWO TICKETS TO PARIS(1962), m
John Glover
SHAMUS(1973); ANNIE HALL(1977); JULIA(1977); SOMEBODY KILLED HER HUSBAND(1978); LAST EMBRACE(1979); AMERICAN SUCCESS COMPANY, THE(1980); MELVIN AND HOWARD(1980); MOUNTAIN MEN, THE(1980); INCREDIBLE SHRINKING WOMAN, THE(1981); LITTLE SEX, A(1982)
1984
EVIL THAT MEN DO, THE(1984); FLASH OF GREEN, A(1984)
John R. Glover
BRUBAKER(1980)

Julian Glover
TOM JONES(1963, Brit.); GIRL WITH GREEN EYES(1964, Brit.); ALPHABET MURDERS, THE(1966); TIME LOST AND TIME REMEMBERED(1966, Brit.); THEATRE OF DEATH(1967, Brit.); FIVE MILLION YEARS TO EARTH(1968, Brit.); MAGUS, THE(1968, Brit.); ADDING MACHINE, THE(1969); ALFRED THE GREAT(1969, Brit.); LAST GRENADE, THE(1970, Brit.); RISE AND RISE OF MICHAEL RIMMER, THE(1970, Brit.); WUTHERING HEIGHTS(1970, Brit.); NICHOLAS AND ALEXANDRA(1971, Brit.); ANTONY AND CLEOPATRA(1973, Brit.); HITLER: THE LAST TEN DAYS(1973, Brit./Ital.); INTERNECINE PROJECT, THE(1974, Brit.); JUGGERNAUT(1974, Brit.); LUTHER(1974); GULLIVER'S TRAVELS(1977, Brit., Bel.); EMPIRE STRIKES BACK, THE(1980); FOR YOUR EYES ONLY(1981); HEAT AND DUST(1983, Brit.)
Rob Glover
SHOOT THE MOON(1982)
Rubeline Glover
DARK MANHATTAN(1937)
T.A. Glover
SONG OF FREEDOM(1938, Brit.), ph
William Glover
LOST IN THE STARS(1974); BIG FIX, THE(1978); TO BE OR NOT TO BE(1983)
Vadim Glowna
CROSS OF IRON(1977, Brit., Ger.); GERMANY IN AUTUMN(1978, Ger.)
Christoph Gluck
TESTAMENT OF ORPHEUS, THE(1962, Fr.), m
Christophe Willibald Gluck
ORPHEUS(1950, Fr.), m
Daniel Gluck
HISTORY OF THE WORLD, PART 1(1981), set d
Gisela Gluck
1984
FLIGHT TO BERLIN(1984, Ger./Brit.)
Joe Gluck
BORDER FEUD(1947), ed; CHEYENNE TAKES OVER(1947), ed; GHOST TOWN RENEGADES(1947), ed; SHADOW VALLEY(1947), ed; HAWK OF POWDER RIVER, THE(1948), ed; RIDE, RYDER, RIDE!(1949), ed
Joseph Gluck
CHECK YOUR GUNS(1948), ed; TORNADO RANGE(1948), ed; ALIMONY(1949), ed; SCARF, THE(1951), ed; DEMENTIA(1955), ed; RIDE THE HIGH IRON(1956), ed; OPERATION CIA(1965), ed
Joseph P. Gluck
FIGHTING REDHEAD, THE(1950), ed
Margel Gluck
RESCUE SQUAD(1935), w
Marvin Gluck
GREAT SIOUX MASSACRE, THE(1965), w
Sinclair Gluck
DARK HOUR, THE(1936), w
Wolfgang Gluck
5 SINNERS(1961, Ger.), d, w; $100 A NIGHT(1968, Ger.), d
E.M. Glucksman
HI-DE-HO(1947), p
Ernest D. Glucksman
ERRAND BOY, THE(1961), p; NUTTY PROFESSOR, THE(1963), p; PATSY, THE(1964), p
Alan Jay Glueckman
BUTCHER BAKER(NIGHTMARE MAKER)* (1982), w
A. Glushchenko
GORDEYEV FAMILY, THE(1961, U.S.S.R.)
John Gluskin
MIRACLE IN HARLEM(1948), m
Lud Gluskin
EVERYTHING'S ON ICE(1939), md; HOUSEKEEPER'S DAUGHTER(1939), md; MAN IN THE IRON MASK, THE(1939), md; DREAMING OUT LOUD(1940), md; INTERNATIONAL LADY(1941), md; THEY MET IN ARGENTINA(1941), md; BASHFUL BACHELOR, THE(1942), md; FRIENDLY ENEMIES(1942), md; SO THIS IS WASHINGTON(1943), md; TWO WEEKS TO LIVE(1943), md; ABROAD WITH TWO YANKS(1944), m; GOIN' TO TOWN(1944), md; STRANGE VOYAGE(1945), md; AVALANCHE(1946), md; PARTNERS IN TIME(1946), md; RETURN OF MONTE CRISTO, THE(1946), md; HIGH CONQUEST(1947), m; MICHAEL O'HALLORAN(1948), md; SIXTEEN FATHOMS DEEP(1948), md; MASSACRE RIVER(1949), md
V. Glyanko
SHADOWS OF FORGOTTEN ANCESTORS(1967, USSR)
John Glyder
COMPULSORY HUSBAND, THE(1930, Brit.), w; COMPULSORY WIFE, THE(1937, Brit.), w
Richard Glyer
SNIPER, THE(1952)
Celia Glyn
HOUSE OPPOSITE, THE(1931, Brit.)
Elinor Glyn
MAN AND THE MOMENT, THE(1929), w; KNOWING MEN(1930, Brit.), p&d, w; PRICE OF THINGS, THE(1930, Brit.), p&d, w; SUCH MEN ARE DANGEROUS(1930), w
Silents
ONE DAY(1916), w; MAN AND THE MOMENT, THE(1918, Brit.), w; AFFAIRS OF ANATOL, THE(1921), w; BEYOND THE ROCKS(1922), w; SIX DAYS(1923), w; HIS HOUR(1924), sup&w; MAN AND MAID(1925), w; SOUL MATES(1925), w; LOVE'S BLINDNESS(1926), w; IT(1927), a, w; RED HAIR(1928), w; SHOW PEOPLE(1928)
Pat Glyn
LAST DAYS OF DOLWYN, THE(1949, Brit.)
Patricia Glyn
ASTONISHED HEART, THE(1950, Brit.); INHERITANCE, THE(1951, Brit.); PROJECT M7(1953, Brit.)
Topsy Glyn
DRESSED TO KILL(1946)
Winifred Glyn
CAPTAIN EDDIE(1945)

David Glyn-Jones
MAN, A WOMAN, AND A BANK, A(1979, Can.)
John Glyn-Jones
VICE VERSA(1948, Brit.); LONG MEMORY, THE(1953, Brit.); COURT MAR-
TIAL(1954, Brit.); HEART OF THE MATTER, THE(1954, Brit.); LOVE LOTTERY,
THE(1954, Brit.); TRUTH ABOUT WOMEN, THE(1958, Brit.); BEYOND THIS PLA-
CE(1959, Brit.); I'M ALL RIGHT, JACK(1959, Brit.); MAN IN THE MOON(1961, Brit.);
TWO-WAY STRETCH(1961, Brit.); LOCKER 69(1962, Brit.); WALTZ OF THE TOREA-
DORS(1962, Brit.); SINISTER MAN, THE(1965, Brit.)
Anyavel Glynn
NATIONAL LAMPOON'S CLASS REUNION(1982)
Carlin Glynn
THREE DAYS OF THE CONDOR(1975); RESURRECTION(1980); CONTINENTAL
DIVIDE(1981); ESCAPE ARTIST, THE(1982)
1984
SIXTEEN CANDLES(1984)
Henry Glynn
ABOVE SUSPICION(1943)
Richard Glynn
KISS THE BLOOD OFF MY HANDS(1948)
Thomas Glynn
THREE STOOGES IN ORBIT, THE(1962)
Agnes Glynne
Misc. Silents
STUDY IN SCARLET, A(1914, Brit.); CINEMA GIRL'S ROMANCE, A(1915, Brit.);
VAGABOND'S REVENGE, A(1915, Brit.); LOVE TRAIL, THE(1916, Brit.)
Angela Glynne
BANK HOLIDAY(1938, Brit.); HARD STEEL(1941, Brit.); GERT AND DAISY CLEAN
UP(1942, Brit.); ROSE OF TRALEE(1942, Brit.); THOSE KIDS FROM TOWN(1942,
Brit.); DEMOBBED(1944, Brit.); GIVE ME THE STARS(1944, Brit.); FORTUNE LA-
NE(1947, Brit.); LAST LOAD, THE(1948, Brit.); HAPPIEST DAYS OF YOUR LIFE(1950,
Brit.); TERROR STREET(1953); HEATWAVE(1954, Brit.)
Ashley Glynne
MR. H. C. ANDERSEN(1950, Brit.)
Derek Glynne
Silents
WEAVERS OF FORTUNE(1922, Brit.)
Misc. Silents
TOO MUCH MONEY(1926)
Mary Glynne
INQUEST(1931, Brit.); GOOD COMPANIONS(1933, Brit.); OUTCAST, THE(1934,
Brit.); REGAL CAVALCADE(1935, Brit.); SCROOGE(1935, Brit.); GRAND FINA-
LE(1936, Brit.); HEIRLOOM MYSTERY, THE(1936, Brit.); LOST CHORD, THE(1937,
Brit.); WHO KILLED FEN MARKHAM?(1937, Brit.); EMIL(1938, Brit.)
Silents
CALL OF YOUTH, THE(1920, Brit.); APPEARANCES(1921)
Misc. Silents
CRY FOR JUSTICE, THE(1919, Brit.); HIS LAST DEFENCE(1919, Brit.); HUNDRETH
CHANCE, THE(1920, Brit.); UNMARRIED(1920, Brit.); BONNIE BRIER BRUSH,
THE(1921, Brit.); CALL OF YOUTH, THE(1921, Brit.); CANDYTUFT, I MEAN
VERONICA(1921, Brit.); DANGEROUS LIES(1921, Brit.); MYSTERY ROAD,
THE(1921, Brit.); PRINCESS OF NEW YORK, THE(1921 US/Brit.); WHITE HEN,
THE(1921, Brit.)
Maureen Glynne
ROYAL DIVORCE, A(1938, Brit.); GAY INTRUDERS, THE(1946, Brit.); TURNERS OF
PROSPECT ROAD, THE(1947, Brit.); OUTSIDER, THE(1949, Brit.); FRANCHISE
AFFAIR, THE(1952, Brit.)
Walter Glynne
SPLINTERS(1929, Brit.)
Yorgos Glynos
GIRL OF THE MOUNTAINS(1958, Gr.)
Friedrich Gnaas
RASPUTIN(1932, Ger.)
Friedrich Gnas
F.P. 1 DOESN'T ANSWER(1933, Ger.)
Frederick Gnass
DANTON(1931, Ger.)
Fritz Gnass
M(1933, Ger.)
Radames Gnattali
LOVE SLAVES OF THE AMAZONS(1957), m
Alberto Gnecco
PUT UP OR SHUT UP(1968, Arg.), m
Horst Gnekow
KING IN SHADOW(1961, Ger.)
G. Gnennaya
TRAIN GOES TO KIEV, THE(1961, USSR)
N. Gnepovskaya
MOTHER AND DAUGHTER(1965, USSR); SHADOWS OF FORGOTTEN ANCES-
TORS(1967, USSR)
G. Gnesin
Misc. Silents
BRAND(1915, USSR)
Anna Gneynner
FROM TOP TO BOTTOM(1933, Fr.), w
Walter Gnilka
DOWNHILL RACER(1969)
Diana Goad
SPRING FEVER(1983, Can.)
William Harrison Goadby
Silents
MORAL FIBRE(1921), w
Barbara Goalen
SLEEPING CAR TO TRIESTE(1949, Brit.); WONDERFUL THINGS!(1958, Brit.)
Jacques Goasguen
LOLA(1961, Fr./Ital.)
Marvin Goatcher
OFFICER AND A GENTLEMAN, AN(1982)

A.R. Gobbett
GABLES MYSTERY, THE(1931, Brit.), ed; GABLES MYSTERY, THE(1938, Brit.), ed
David W. Gobbett
Silents
AMATEUR GENTLEMAN, THE(1926), ph; RANSON'S FOLLY(1926), ph; WHITE
BLACK SHEEP, THE(1926), ph
A. Gobbi
AIDA(1954, Ital.), w
Bruno Marco Gobbi
HORNET'S NEST(1970)
Hilda Gobbi
DIALOGUE(1967, Hung.)
Jean-Francois Gobbi
ECHOES OF SILENCE(1966); Z(1969, Fr./Algeria); CONFESSION, THE(1970, Fr.)
Marco Gobbi
STATUE, THE(1971, Brit.)
Sergio Gobbi
TIME OF THE WOLVES(1970, Fr.), d, w
Tito Gobbi
BARBER OF SEVILLE, THE(1947, Ital.); THIS WINE OF LOVE(1948, Ital.); RIGO-
LETTO(1949, Ital.); GLASS MOUNTAIN, THE(1950, Brit); SOHO CONSPIRACY(1951, Brit.);
FATAL DESIRE(1953)
Hank Gobble
DEADLY COMPANIONS, THE(1961)
Pierre Gobeil
CORDELIA(1980, Fr., Can.)
Art Gobel
LOST SQUADRON, THE(1932)
Elisabeth Gobel
SHOEMAKER AND THE ELVES, THE(1967, Ger.)
George Gobel
I MARRIED A WOMAN(1958); BIRDS AND THE BEES, THE(1965); RABBIT
TEST(1978)
1984
ELLIE(1984)
Gunter Gobel
NOT RECONCILED, OR "ONLY VIOLENCE HELPS WHERE IT RULES"(1969, Ger.)
Heini Gobel
SNOW WHITE AND ROSE RED(1966, Ger.); SHOEMAKER AND THE ELVES,
THE(1967, Ger.)
Gary Gober
FRAMED(1975)
Mildred Gober
COWBOY AND THE KID,THE(1936)
Boy Gobert
REST IS SILENCE, THE(1960, Ger.); DIE FLEDERMAUS(1964, Aust.); LADY
HAMILTON(1969, Ger./Ital./Fr.); KAMIKAZE '89(1983, Ger.)
Sandrine Gobet
ANGEL, ANGEL, DOWN WE GO(1969)
Rene Harrison A. Gobett
SKIN GAME, THE(1931, Brit.), ed
Gabriel Gobin
TIME BOMB(1961, Fr./Ital.); COUNTERFEITERS OF PARIS, THE(1962, Fr., Ital.);
DIARY OF A CHAMBERMAID(1964, Fr./Ital.); UP FROM THE BEACH(1965);
MADEMOISELLE(1966, Fr./Brit.); THE DIRTY GAME(1966, Fr./Ital./Ger.); THIEF OF
PARIS, THE(1967, Fr./Ital.); MILKY WAY, THE(1969, Fr./Ital.)
Gebriel Gobin
DIVA(1982, Fr.)
Jean Gobin
CHEAT, THE(1950, Fr.)
Diane Goble
HERCULES IN NEW YORK(1970)
Goblin
NIGHT OF THE ZOMBIES(1983, Span./Ital.), m
Goblin and Buckboard
ST. HELENS(1981), m
The Goblins
1984
BURIED ALIVE(1984, Ital.), m
The Goblins
SUSPIRIA(1977, Ital.), m
Valerie Gobos
1984
WINDY CITY(1984)
Les Gobruegge
MUPPET MOVIE, THE(1979), art d
Gary Goch
CHILDREN SHOULDN'T PLAY WITH DEAD THINGS(1972), p
Constantine S. Gochis
REDEEMER, THE(1978), d
Len Gochman
IF EVER I SEE YOU AGAIN(1978)
Danielle Gochrach
TUNNELVISION(1976), makeup
Les Gock
PUBERTY BLUES(1983, Aus.), m, md
Angela Gockel
BELLA DONNA(1983, Ger.)
Alex Goda
VICE RAID(1959)
Alfonso Goda
MAIN STREET(1956, Span.)
Chantal Godaert
MATTER OF DAYS, A(1969, Fr./Czech.), makeup
Edward Godal
CHIPS(1938. Brit.), p&d
Silents
BLIND BOY, THE(1917, Brit.), p; NOBODY'S CHILD(1919, Brit.), p; QUEEN'S
EVIDENCE(1919, Brit.), p; 12-10(1919, Brit.), p; PUPPET MAN, THE(1921, Brit.), p;
AUDACIOUS MR. SQUIRE, THE(1923, Brit.), p; HEARTSTRINGS(1923, Brit.), p;

ADVENTUROUS YOUTH(1928, Brit.), p&d

Godfrey A. Godar
BOYS IN COMPANY C, THE(1978, U.S./Hong Kong), ph; GAME OF DEATH, THE(1979), ph

Claude Godard
MAIDEN, THE(1961, Fr.); PALACE OF NUDES(1961, Fr./Ital.)

Doris Godard
WEE GEORDIE(1956, Brit.)

Jean-Luc Godard
BREATHLESS(1959, Fr.), a, d&w; CLEO FROM 5 TO 7(1961, Fr.); WOMAN IS A WOMAN, A(1961, Fr./Ital.), d&w; PARIS BELONGS TO US(1962, Fr.); SEVEN CAPITAL SINS(1962, Fr./Ital.), d, w; CONTEMPT(1963, Fr./Ital.), a, d&w; MY LIFE TO LIVE(1963, Fr.), a, d&w; ALPHAVILLE, A STRANGE CASE OF LEMMY CAUTION(1965, Fr.), a, d&w; LE PETIT SOLDAT(1965, Fr.), a, d&w; MARRIED WOMAN, THE(1965, Fr.), a, d&w; BAND OF OUTSIDERS(1966, Fr.), d&w; DEFECTOR, THE(1966, Ger./Fr.); MADE IN U.S.A.(1966, Fr.), a, d, w; MASCULINE FEMININE(1966, Fr./Swed.), d&w; LA CHINOISE(1967, Fr.), d&w; LE GAI SAVOIR(1968, Fr.), d&w; LES CARABINIERS(1968, Fr./Ital.), d, w; OLDEST PROFESSION, THE(1968, Fr./Ital./Ger.), d, w; PIERROT LE FOU(1968, Fr./Ital.), d&w; SIX IN PARIS(1968, Fr.), w&d; WEEKEND(1968, Fr./Ital.), d&w; ONE PLUS ONE(1969, Brit.), d&w; TWO OR THREE THINGS I KNOW ABOUT HER(1970, Fr.), a, d&w; WIND FROM THE EAST(1970, Fr./Ital./Ger.), a, d, w, ed; TOUT VA BIEN(1973, Fr.), d&w; NUMBER TWO(1975, Fr.), d&w; EVERY MAN FOR HIMSELF(1980, Fr.), p, d, ed; BREATHLESS(1983), w; PASSION(1983, Fr./Switz.), d&w, ed
1984
FIRST NAME: CARMEN(1984, Fr.), a, d

John Godard
GUN FEVER(1958)

Irma Godau
GREAT YEARNING, THE(1930, Ger.)

Fred Goday
MESSAGE TO GARCIA, A(1936)

Rev. Thomas M. Godbold
THUNDER IN CAROLINA(1960)

Claude Godbout
CAT IN THE SACK, THE(1967, Can.)

Jacques Godbout
OF UNKNOWN ORIGIN(1983, Can.), spec eff

Alain Goddard
DRACULA AND SON(1976, Fr.), w

Alf Goddard
HIGH TREASON(1929, Brit.); LAST POST, THE(1929, Brit.); ALF'S BUTTON(1930, Brit.); BED AND BREAKFAST(1930, Brit.); BRAT, THE(1930, Brit.); EAST LYNNE ON THE WESTERN FRONT(1931, Brit.); HAPPY ENDING, THE(1931, Brit.); OLD SOLDIERS NEVER DIE(1931, Brit.); SPLINTERS IN THE NAVY(1931, Brit.); THIRD STRING, THE(1932, Brit.); ENEMY OF THE POLICE(1933, Brit.); PRIDE OF THE FORCE, THE(1933, Brit.); TOO MANY WIVES(1933, Brit.); LOST IN THE LEGION(1934, Brit.); IT'S A BET(1935, Brit.); NO LIMIT(1935, Brit.); STRICTLY ILLEGAL(1935, Brit.); KING SOLOMON'S MINES(1937, Brit.); NON-STOP NEW YORK(1937, Brit.); ROMANCE AND RICHES(1937, Brit.); BANK HOLIDAY(1938, Brit.); CONVICT 99(1938, Brit.); NIGHT JOURNEY(1938, Brit.); SONG OF FREEDOM(1938, Brit.); TO THE VICTOR(1938, Brit.); TROOPSHIP(1938, Brit.); LET'S BE FAMOUS(1939, Brit.); NORTH SEA PATROL(1939, Brit.); SPY FOR A DAY(1939, Brit.); WARE CASE, THE(1939, Brit.); MURDER IN THE NIGHT(1940, Brit.); RETURN TO YESTERDAY(1940, Brit.); SIDEWALKS OF LONDON(1940, Brit.); SOUTH AMERICAN GEORGE(1941, Brit.); LADY IN DISTRESS(1942, Brit.); YOUNG MR. PITT, THE(1942, Brit.); BUTLER'S DILEMMA, THE(1943, Brit.); SAINT MEETS THE TIGER, THE(1943, Brit.); I'LL BE YOUR SWEETHEART(1945, Brit.); JOHNNY IN THE CLOUDS(1945, Brit.); WAY AHEAD, THE(1945, Brit.); INNOCENTS IN PARIS(1955, Brit.)
Silents
SISTER TO ASSIST 'ER, A(1927, Brit.); SMASHING THROUGH(1928, Brit.)
Misc. Silents
REMEMBRANCE(1927, Brit.); SAILORS DON'T CARE(1928, Brit.); YOU KNOW WHAT SAILORS ARE(1928, Brit.); DOWN CHANNEL(1929, Brit.)

Alfred Goddard
Silents
WHEN BOYS LEAVE HOME(1928, Brit.)

Charles Goddard
GHOST BREAKERS, THE(1940), w

Charles W. Goddard
BROKEN WING, THE(1932), w; MISLEADING LADY, THE(1932), w; PERILS OF PAULINE, THE(1947), w; SCARED STIFF(1953), w; PERILS OF PAULINE, THE(1967), w

Dick Goddard
DEER HUNTER, THE(1978), set d; ONION FIELD, THE(1979), set d; INSIDE MOVES(1980), set d

Doris Goddard
IRON PETTICOAT, THE(1956, Brit.); ROBBERY UNDER ARMS(1958, Brit.); TIM(1981, Aus.)

Ed Goddard
MAYTIME(1937)

Frederick Goddard
Misc. Silents
(, d

Gary Goddard
TARZAN, THE APE MAN(1981), w

Grace Goddard
MANDARIN MYSTERY, THE(1937), ed

John Goddard
KID FROM LEFT FIELD, THE(1953); BATTLE TAXI(1955); STORM RIDER, THE(1957); SNIPER'S RIDGE(1961); WILD YOUTH(1961)

Keith Goddard
BLOCKHOUSE, THE(1974, Brit.), ph; EAST OF ELEPHANT ROCK(1976, Brit.), ph

Lindsay Goddard
JULIE DARLING(1982, Can./Ger.), art d

Lindsey Goddard
1984
BEDROOM EYES(1984, Can.), art d

Liza Goddard
I WANT WHAT I WANT(1972, Brit.); GET CHARLIE TULLY(1976, Brit.); WAGNER(1983, Brit./Hung./Aust.)

Malcolm Goddard
PERSECUTION AND ASSASSINATION OF JEAN-PAUL MARAT AS PERFORMED BY THE INMATES OF THE ASYLUM OF CHARENTON UNDER THE DIRECTION OF THE MARQUIS DE SADE, THE(1967, Brit.), ch; WHERE'S JACK?(1969, Brit.), ch

Mark Goddard
MONKEY'S UNCLE, THE(1965); RAGE TO LIVE, A(1965); LOVE-INS, THE(1967); BLUE SUNSHINE(1978); ROLLER BOOGIE(1979); STRANGE INVADERS(1983)

Nancy Goddard
MISTER BROWN(1972)

Patricia Goddard
UNEASY TERMS(1948, Brit.); LADY GODIVA RIDES AGAIN(1955, Brit.)

Paulette Goddard
GIRL HABIT(1931); KID FROM SPAIN, THE(1932); MOUTHPIECE, THE(1932); MODERN TIMES(1936); DRAMATIC SCHOOL(1938); YOUNG IN HEART, THE(1938); CAT AND THE CANARY, THE(1939); WOMEN, THE(1939); GHOST BREAKERS, THE(1940); GREAT DICTATOR, THE(1940); NORTHWEST MOUNTED POLICE(1940); SECOND CHORUS(1940); HOLD BACK THE DAWN(1941); NOTHING BUT THE TRUTH(1941); POT O' GOLD(1941); FOREST RANGERS, THE(1942); LADY HAS PLANS, THE(1942); REAP THE WILD WIND(1942); STAR SPANGLED RHYTHM(1942); CRYSTAL BALL, THE(1943); SO PROUDLY WE HAIL(1943); I LOVE A SOLDIER(1944); STANDING ROOM ONLY(1944); DUFFY'S TAVERN(1945); KITTY(1945); DIARY OF A CHAMBERMAID(1946); SUDDENLY IT'S SPRING(1947); UNCONQUERED(1947); VARIETY GIRL(1947); HAZARD(1948); IDEAL HUSBAND, AN(1948, Brit.); ON OUR MERRY WAY(1948); ANNA LUCASTA(1949); BRIDE OF VENGEANCE(1949); TORCH, THE(1950); BABES IN BAGDAD(1952); CHARGE OF THE LANCERS(1953); PARIS MODEL(1953); SINS OF JEZEBEL(1953); VICE SQUAD(1953); UNHOLY FOUR, THE(1954, Brit.); TIME OF INDIFFERENCE(1965, Fr./Ital.)

Peter Goddard
RUDE BOY(1980, Brit.), ed

Ralph Goddard
PURSUERS, THE(1961, Brit.), p; THREE SPARE WIVES(1962, Brit.), p

Renee Goddard
MURDER AT 3 A.M.(1953, Brit.)

Richard Goddard
JERK, THE(1979), set d; LONG RIDERS, THE(1980), set d; GOING APE!(1981), set d

Richard C. Goddard
48 HOURS(1982), set d
1984
STREETS OF FIRE(1984), set d

Roy Goddard
REGAL CAVALCADE(1935, Brit.), p; LAST MOMENT, THE(1954, Brit.), p

Air Marshal Sir Victor Goddard
NIGHT MY NUMBER CAME UP, THE(1955, Brit.), w

Willoughby Goddard
BAIT(1950, Brit.); TOUCH OF THE SUN, A(1956, Brit.); GREEN MAN, THE(1957, Brit.); HEART OF A CHILD(1958, Brit.); IN THE WAKE OF A STRANGER(1960, Brit.); INN FOR TROUBLE(1960, Brit.); MILLIONAIRESS, THE(1960, Brit.); DOUBLE BUNK(1961, Brit.); LONG SHADOW, THE(1961, Brit.); SECRET PARTNER, THE(1961, Brit.); GOLDEN RABBIT, THE(1962, Brit.); CHARGE OF THE LIGHT BRIGADE, THE(1968, Brit.); GAWAIN AND THE GREEN KNIGHT(1973, Brit.)

Willoughly Goddard
WRONG BOX, THE(1966, Brit.)

Bill Godden
BORN FREE(1966)

David Godden
FIGHTING BACK(1983, Brit.)

Jimmy Godden
BIG BUSINESS(1930, Brit.); HIS WIFE'S MOTHER(1932, Brit.); LAST COUPON, THE(1932, Brit.); MY WIFE'S FAMILY(1932, Brit.); CRIME ON THE HILL(1933, Brit.); FOR THE LOVE OF MIKE(1933, Brit.); HAWLEY'S OF HIGH STREET(1933, Brit.); MEET MY SISTER(1933, Brit.); MONEY TALKS(1933, Brit.); THEIR NIGHT OUT(1933, Brit.); GREAT DEFENDER, THE(1934, Brit.); HAPPY(1934, Brit.); LUCK OF A SAILOR, THE(1934, Brit.); MY SONG GOES ROUND THE WORLD(1934, Brit.); OUTCAST, THE(1934, Brit.); SOMETIMES GOOD(1934, Brit.); THOSE WERE THE DAYS(1934, Brit.); DANDY DICK(1935, Brit.); IT'S A BET(1935, Brit.); LEND ME YOUR WIFE(1935, Brit.); RADIO FOLLIES(1935, Brit.); REGAL CAVALCADE(1935, Brit.); GIVE HER A RING(1936, Brit.); KING OF THE CASTLE(1936, Brit.); LIVING DANGEROUSLY(1936, Brit.); SOMEONE AT THE DOOR(1936, Brit.); FEATHER YOUR NEST(1937, Brit.); SING AS YOU SWING(1937, Brit.); WEEKEND MILLIONAIRE(1937, Brit.); DANCE OF DEATH, THE(1938, Brit.); GLAMOUR GIRL(1938, Brit.); SPARE A COPPER(1940, Brit.); FARMER'S WIFE, THE(1941, Brit.)

John Godden
MAKE ME AN OFFER(1954, Brit.); BLUE FIN(1978, Aus.); ESCAPE 2000(1983, Aus.)

Rumer Godden
BLACK NARCISSUS(1947, Brit.), w; ENCHANTMENT(1948), w; RIVER, THE(1951), w; INNOCENT SINNERS(1958, Brit.), w; LOSS OF INNOCENCE(1961, Brit.), w; BATTLE OF THE VILLA FIORITA, THE(1965, Brit.), w

Albert Godderis
JOAN OF ARC(1948); PURPLE MASK, THE(1955); FUNNY FACE(1957); ME AND THE COLONEL(1958)

Marty Goddey
TALES FROM THE CRYPT(1972, Brit.)

Yvonne Godeau
MONSIEUR VINCENT(1949, Fr.)

Ann Godee
SECRET FURY, THE(1950)

Georges Godefroy
RED-DRAGON(1967, Ital./Ger./US), w

Max Goden
THEY ASKED FOR IT(1939), p

Albert Goderis
I CONFESS(1953)

Danielle Godet
FIGHTING PIMPERNEL, THE(1950, Brit.); SINGING TAXI DRIVER(1953, Ital.); JOY(1983, Fr./Can.)

Sylvain Godet
MADE IN U.S.A.(1966, Fr.)
Annette Godette
LOVE MERCHANT, THE(1966)
John Godey
TAKING OF PELHAM ONE, TWO, THREE, THE(1974), w; NEVER A DULL MOMENT(1968), w
Alexander Godfrey
1984
ONCE UPON A TIME IN AMERICA(1984)
Alma Godfrey
MIKADO, THE(1967, Brit.), ed
Arthur Godfrey
FOUR FOR TEXAS(1963); GLASS BOTTOM BOAT, THE(1966); WHERE ANGELS GO...TROUBLE FOLLOWS(1968); GREAT BANK HOAX, THE(1977); ANGELS BRIGADE(1980)
Bob Godfrey
HELP!(1965, Brit.)
Brian Godfrey
STAND UP VIRGIN SOLDIERS(1977, Brit.)
Dan Godfrey
Silents
AUNT RACHEL(1920, Brit.)
Derek Godfrey
GUNS OF DARKNESS(1962, Brit.); VENGEANCE OF SHE, THE(1968, Brit.); MIDSUMMER NIGHT'S DREAM, A(1969, Brit.); JULIUS CAESAR(1970, Brit.); ABOMINABLE DR. PHIBES, THE(1971, Brit.); HANDS OF THE RIPPER(1971, Brit.)
E. Godfrey
Misc. Silents
SONS OF THE SEA(1925, Brit.)
George Godfrey
SEA FURY(1929); BIG CITY(1937); RIDERS OF THE WHISTLING SKULL(1937)
Silents
OLD IRONSIDES(1926); ONE-ROUND HOGAN(1927), w; SAILOR'S SWEETHEART, A(1927), w
Isidore Godfrey
MIKADO, THE(1967, Brit.), md
John Godfrey
TIGER MAKES OUT, THE(1967), set d; NIGHT THEY RAIDED MINSKY'S, THE(1968), set d; SUBJECT WAS ROSES, THE(1968), set d; LANDLORD, THE(1970), set d; LOVING(1970), set d; VALACHI PAPERS, THE(1972, Ital./Fr.), set d; SEVEN UPS, THE(1973), set d; HARRY AND TONTO(1974), set d; ORCA(1977), set d; SATURDAY NIGHT FEVER(1977), set d; EYES OF LAURA MARS(1978), set d; KING OF THE GYPSIES(1978), set d; NIGHT OF THE JUGGLER(1980), set d; SIMON(1980), set d; EXPOSED(1983), set d
1984
GARBO TALKS(1984), set d
Louis Godfrey
HALF A SIXPENCE(1967, Brit.)
Mary Godfrey
Silents
HOUSE ON THE MARSH, THE(1920, Brit.)
Michael Godfrey
THEY CAN'T HANG ME(1955, Brit.); MEN OF SHERWOOD FOREST(1957, Brit.); SECOND BEST SECRET AGENT IN THE WHOLE WIDE WORLD, THE(1965, Brit.); MAGNIFICENT TWO, THE(1967, Brit.); HENRY VIII AND HIS SIX WIVES(1972, Brit.); MOHAMMAD, MESSENGER OF GOD(1976, Lebanon/Brit.)
Patrick Godfrey
HEAT AND DUST(1983, Brit.)
Peter Godfrey
DOWN RIVER(1931, Brit.), d; THIRD TIME LUCKY(1931, Brit.); CHARMING DECEIVER, THE(1933, Brit.); LEAVE IT TO ME(1933, Brit.); WHERE THERE'S A WILL(1937, Brit.); BLOCKADE(1938); LONE WOLF SPY HUNT, THE(1939), d; RAFFLES(1939); EARL OF CHICAGO, THE(1940); EDISON, THE MAN(1940); DR. JEKYLL AND MR. HYDE(1941); UNEXPECTED UNCLE(1941), d; HIGHWAYS BY NIGHT(1942), d; FOREVER AND A DAY(1943), a, w; MAKE YOUR OWN BED(1944), d; CHRISTMAS IN CONNECTICUT(1945), d; HOTEL BERLIN(1945), d; ONE MORE TOMORROW(1946), d; CRY WOLF(1947), d; ESCAPE ME NEVER(1947), d; THAT HAGEN GIRL(1947), d; TWO MRS. CARROLLS, THE(1947), a, d; DECISION OF CHRISTOPHER BLAKE, THE(1948), d; WOMAN IN WHITE, THE(1948), d; GIRL FROM JONES BEACH, THE(1949), d; ONE LAST FLING(1949), d; BARRICADE(1950), d; GREAT JEWEL ROBBER, THE(1950), d; HE'S A COCKEYED WONDER(1950), d; ONE BIG AFFAIR(1952), d; PLEASE MURDER ME(1956), d; GIRL IN BLACK STOCKINGS(1957), w
Philip Godfrey
DEADLOCK(1931, Brit.); EAST LYNNE ON THE WESTERN FRONT(1931, Brit.); LOVE WAGER, THE(1933, Brit.); HARD STEEL(1941, Brit.); SHEEPDOG OF THE HILLS(1941, Brit.); NIGHT INVADER, THE(1943, Brit); WE DIVE AT DAWN(1943, Brit.); IT HAPPENED ONE SUNDAY(1944, Brit.); MEET SEXTON BLAKE(1944, Brit.); UNCENSORED(1944, Brit.); LOVE ON THE DOLE(1945, Brit.)
Phillip Godfrey
BLACK ABBOT, THE(1934, Brit.), w; GIRL IN DISTRESS(1941, Brit.); AGITATOR, THE(1949)
Phyllis Godfrey
AND SO THEY WERE MARRIED(1936); GIVE ME YOUR HEART(1936); THANK YOUR LUCKY STARS(1943); LADY TAKES A SAILOR, THE(1949)
Rae Godfrey
Misc. Silents
MARKED CARDS(1918); MASK, THE(1918); TONY AMERICA(1918)
Renee Godfrey
UP IN ARMS(1944); BEDSIDE MANNER(1945); DOWN MISSOURI WAY(1946); TERROR BY NIGHT(1946); WINTER WONDERLAND(1947); FRENCH LEAVE(1948); INHERIT THE WIND(1960); TENDER IS THE NIGHT(1961); THOSE CALLOWAYS(1964)
Ruth Godfrey
TEN COMMANDMENTS, THE(1956), ch
Sam Godfrey
WASHINGTON MERRY-GO-ROUND(1932); AFTER TONIGHT(1933); BLONDIE JOHNSON(1933); EMPLOYEE'S ENTRANCE(1933); FRISCO JENNY(1933); I LOVED A WOMAN(1933); PAROLE GIRL(1933); SATURDAY'S MILLIONS(1933); THREE-

CORNERED MOON(1933); 20,000 YEARS IN SING SING(1933); LOST LADY, A(1934); LOVE CAPTIVE, THE(1934); MIGHTY BARNUM, THE(1934); VIVA VILLA!(1934); COLLEGE SCANDAL(1935); LOVE IN BLOOM(1935); PRIVATE WORLDS(1935)
Samuel Godfrey
HOUSE OF MYSTERY(1934); MEN WITHOUT NAMES(1935)
Samuel T. Godfrey
STRAIGHT FROM THE HEART(1935)
Tommy Godfrey
PASSPORT TO PIMLICO(1949, Brit.); MISSING NOTE, THE(1961, Brit.); HIDE AND SEEK(1964, Brit.); IF ...(1968, Brit.); WORK IS A FOUR LETTER WORD(1968, Brit.); RING OF BRIGHT WATER(1969, Brit.); GREAT MUPPET CAPER, THE(1981)
Vonne Godfrey
WALK THE DARK STREET(1956)
W. Godik
BORDER STREET(1950, Pol.)
Jacques Godin
LUCK OF GINGER COFFEY, THE(1964, U.S./Can.); PYX, THE(1973, Can.); ONE MAN(1979, Can.); YESTERDAY(1980, Can.); AMATEUR, THE(1982)
Karpo Acimovic Godina
EARLY WORKS(1970, Yugo.), ph, ed
Henrietta Godinet
RETURN TO PARADISE(1953); PACIFIC DESTINY(1956, Brit.)
Rebecca Godinez
JEANNE EAGELS(1957)
Salvador Godinez
FITZCARRALDO(1982)
Paul Godkin
HOW TO BE VERY, VERY, POPULAR(1955), ch; AROUND THE WORLD IN 80 DAYS(1956), ch; JOHN GOLDFARB, PLEASE COME HOME(1964), ch; PUFNSTUF(1970), ch
Anne Godley
RICOCHET(1966, Brit.)
Campbell Godley
ROB ROY, THE HIGHLAND ROGUE(1954, Brit.)
Michael Godley
REMEMBRANCE(1982, Brit.)
Jill Godmillow
PLEASANTVILLE(1976), ed
Jill Godmilow
1984
FAR FROM POLAND(1984), p&d
Dagmar Godowski
Silents
IN BORROWED PLUMES(1926)
Dagmar Godowsky
Silents
ALTAR STAIRS, THE(1922); STRANGER'S BANQUET(1922); TRAP, THE(1922); COMMON LAW, THE(1923); RED LIGHTS(1923); SOULS FOR SALE(1923); PLAYTHINGS OF DESIRE(1924); PRICE OF A PARTY, THE(1924); ROULETTE(1924); SAINTED DEVIL, A(1924)
Misc. Silents
BONDS OF HONOR(1919); FORGED BRIDE, THE(1920); HONOR BOUND(1920); PATH SHE CHOSE, THE(1920); MEDDLING WOMEN(1924); LOST CHORD, THE(1925)
Armando Robles Godoy
MIRAGE(1972, Peru), d&w
Arturo Godoy
GRANDPA GOES TO TOWN(1940)
Frank Godoy
SAFARI(1940)
Fred Godoy
GILDA(1946); THRILL OF BRAZIL, THE(1946); LONE WOLF IN MEXICO, THE(1947); HOLIDAY IN HAVANA(1949); WE WERE STRANGERS(1949)
Ledda Godoy
GRANDPA GOES TO TOWN(1940)
Mario Robles Godoy
MIRAGE(1972, Peru), ph
Miguel Godreau
ALTERED STATES(1980)
Constance Godridge
FIRST A GIRL(1935, Brit.); MURDER BY ROPE(1936, Brit.); BOYS WILL BE GIRLS(1937, Brit.); FACE BEHIND THE SCAR(1940, Brit.)
Peter Godsell
LOVE MATCH, THE(1955, Brit.); WEAPON, THE(1957, Brit.); ADVENTURES OF HAL 5, THE(1958, Brit.); GIDEON OF SCOTLAND YARD(1959, Brit.)
Vanda Godsell
FLANNELFOOT(1953, Brit.); LARGE ROPE, THE(1953, Brit.); BRAIN MACHINE, THE(1955, Brit.); HOUR OF DECISION(1957, Brit.); INNOCENT SINNERS(1958, Brit.); NO SAFETY AHEAD(1959, Brit.); HELL IS A CITY(1960, Brit.); IN THE WAKE OF A STRANGER(1960, Brit.); MAN WHO WAS NOBODY, THE(1960, Brit.); KONGA(1961, Brit.); SHADOW OF THE CAT, THE(1961, Brit.); SWORD OF SHERWOOD FOREST(1961, Brit.); NIGHT WITHOUT PITY(1962, Brit.); PAYROLL(1962, Brit.); POT CARRIERS, THE(1962, Brit.); TERM OF TRIAL(1962, Brit.); WALTZ OF THE TOREADORS(1962, Brit.); BITTER HARVEST(1963, Brit.); THIS SPORTING LIFE(1963, Brit.); VICTORS, THE(1963); WRONG ARM OF THE LAW, THE(1963, Brit.); 80,000 SUSPECTS(1963, Brit.); EARTH DIES SCREAMING, THE(1964, Brit.); SHOT IN THE DARK, A(1964); ESCAPE BY NIGHT(1965, Brit.); CANDIDATE FOR MURDER(1966, Brit.); DATELINE DIAMONDS(1966, Brit.); WHO KILLED THE CAT?(1966, Brit.); WRONG BOX, THE(1966, Brit.); PINK PANTHER STRIKES AGAIN, THE(1976, Brit.)
B. Godsey
TO ALL A GOODNIGHT(1980), ph
Bill Godsey
SUMMERDOG(1977), ph; COLD RIVER(1982), ph
F. J. Godsol
Silents
SHERLOCK HOLMES(1922), p
Phil Godstone
Silents
CUB REPORTER, THE(1922), p

Barry Godwin
YOU LIGHT UP MY LIFE(1977)
Christopher Godwin
DOING TIME(1979, Brit.)
Diane Godwin
CURTAINS(1983, Can.)
Frank Godwin
POSTMARK FOR DANGER(1956, Brit.), p; WOMEN IN A DRESSING GOWN(1957, Brit.), p; OPERATION BULLSHINE(1963, Brit.), p; SMALL WORLD OF SAMMY LEE, THE(1963, Brit.), p; NO TREE IN THE STREET(1964, Brit.), p; WHY BOTHER TO KNOCK(1964, Brit.), p; HEADLINE HUNTERS(1968, Brit.), p; DEMONS OF THE MIND(1972, Brit.), p, w
1984
BREAKOUT(1984, Brit.), p&d
Paul Godwin
1984
FOOTLOOSE(1984)
Ron Godwin
CYCLE SAVAGES(1969)
Godzina
HOLLYWOOD BOULEVARD(1976)
Art Goebel
Silents
AIR PATROL, THE(1928)
O.E. Goebel
Silents
ON THE STROKE OF THREE(1924), w
Misc. Silents
ETERNAL LIGHT, THE(1919), d; BLASPHEMER, THE(1921), d
Heinz Goedecke
EIGHT GIRLS IN A BOAT(1932, Ger.)
Carl Goefrey
Misc. Talkies
BEST, THE(1979)
Walter Goehr
GREAT EXPECTATIONS(1946, Brit.), m; I KNOW WHERE I'M GOING(1947, Brit.), md; STOP PRESS GIRL(1949, Brit.), m; LUCKY NICK CAIN(1951), m; BETRAYED(1954), m
Suzi Goei
YOUR THREE MINUTES ARE UP(1973)
Kermit Goell
ABILENE TOWN(1946), m/l Fred Spielman
Herman Goelliner
BENJAMIN(1973, Ger.)
Dave Goelz
MUPPET MOVIE, THE(1979); GREAT MUPPET CAPER, THE(1981); DARK CRYSTAL, THE(1982, Brit.)
1984
MUPPETS TAKE MANHATTAN, THE(1984)
Pieter Goemans
LAST BLITZKRIEG, THE(1958)
George Goepper
HEY THERE, IT'S YOGI BEAR(1964), anim; MAN CALLED FLINTSTONE, THE(1966), anim
Al Goering
STOLEN HARMONY(1935)
Alyce Goering
DEAD RECKONING(1947)
Gretchen Goertz
DIARY OF ANNE FRANK, THE(1959)
Albrecht Goes
RESTLESS NIGHT, THE(1964, Ger.), w
Peter-Paul Goest
NAKED AMONG THE WOLVES(1967, Ger.)
Stanley Goethals
Silents
OUTSIDE THE LAW(1921); ONE CLEAR CALL(1922); TRAP, THE(1922); LONELY ROAD, THE(1923)
Misc. Silents
LAST CARD, THE(1921)
Armour Goetten
TWIST ALL NIGHT(1961), set d
Elysabeth Goetten
CANON CITY(1948)
Bill Goettinger
SHE WORE A YELLOW RIBBON(1949)
Lislott Goettinger
GIRL WITH GREEN EYES(1964, Brit.)
Augustus Goetz
HEIRESS, THE(1949), w; CARRIE(1952), w; STAGE STRUCK(1958), w
Ben Goetz
Misc. Silents
INEVITABLE, THE(1917), d
Carl Goetz
Misc. Silents
THAT MURDER IN BERLIN(1929, Ger.)
Charles E. Goetz
GENTLEMAN FROM ARIZONA, THE(1940), p
Curt Goetz
TEMPORARY WIDOW, THE(1930, Ger./Brit.), w; PEOPLE WILL TALK(1951), w
E. Ray Goetz
PARIS(1929), w
Harry M. Goetz
LAST OF THE MOHICANS, THE(1936), p
Hayes Goetz
CALLING BULLDOG DRUMMOND(1951, Brit.), p; APACHE WAR SMOKE(1952), p; HOUR OF THIRTEEN, THE(1952), p; ARROW IN THE DUST(1954), p; HUMAN JUNGLE, THE(1954), p; PRIDE OF THE BLUE GRASS(1954), p; HOLD BACK THE NIGHT(1956), p; THREE FOR JAMIE DAWN(1956), p; SINGING NUN, THE(1966), p

Jindrich Goetz
DO YOU KEEP A LION AT HOME?(1966, Czech.), set d; END OF A PRIEST(1970, Czech.), art d; DIVINE EMMA, THE(1983, Czech,), art d
John Goetz
UNCLE VANYA(1958), d; WARM IN THE BUD(1970)
L.E. Goetz
TEN NIGHTS IN A BARROOM(1931), p
Peter Goetz
Misc. Talkies
JACKPOT(1982)
Peter Michael Goetz
PRINCE OF THE CITY(1981); WOLFEN(1981); WORLD ACCORDING TO GARP, The(1982)
1984
BEST DEFENSE(1984); C.H.U.D.(1984)
Ruth Goetz
HEIRESS, THE(1949), w; CARRIE(1952), w; RHAPSODY(1954), w; STAGE STRUCK(1958), w
Walter H. Goetz
PORT OF 40 THIEVES, THE(1944), p; GRISSLY'S MILLIONS(1945), p; TELL IT TO A STAR(1945), p; THREE'S A CROWD(1945), p; CRIME OF THE CENTURY(1946), p
William Goetz
ADVICE TO THE LOVELORN(1933), p; BOWERY, THE(1933), p; NO MARRIAGE TIES(1933), p; CARDINAL RICHELIEU(1935), p; CLIVE OF INDIA(1935), p; FOLIES DERGERE(1935), assoc p; JANE EYRE(1944), p; MAN FROM LARAMIE, THE(1955), p; AUTUMN LEAVES(1956), p; SAYONARA(1957), p; ME AND THE COLONEL(1958), p; THEY CAME TO CORDURA(1959), p; MOUNTAIN ROAD, THE(1960), p; SONG WITHOUT END(1960), p; CRY FOR HAPPY(1961), p; ASSAULT ON A QUEEN(1966), p
Mulle Goetz-Dickopp
GERMANY IN AUTUMN(1978, Ger.), ed
Heinz Goetze
MAD EXECUTIONERS, THE(1965, Ger.), prod d
Werner Goetze
JAMBOREE(1957)
Bernard Goetzke
Silents
FEAR O' GOD(1926, Brit./Ger.)
Misc. Silents
DESTINY(1921, Ger.); PETER THE GREAT(1923, Ger.); CITIES AND YEARS(1931, USSR)
Bernhard Goetzke
DAUGHTER OF EVIL(1930, Ger.); RASPUTIN(1932, Ger.); TRUNKS OF MR. O.F., THE(1932, Ger.)
Silents
PASSION(1920, Ger.); DECAMERON NIGHTS(1924, Brit.); KRIEMHILD'S REVENGE(1924, Ger.); SIEGFRIED(1924, Ger.)
Misc. Silents
FEAR O'GOD(1926, Brit.)
Gary Goetzman
DIVORCE AMERICAN STYLE(1967); YOURS, MINE AND OURS(1968); LAST EMBRACE(1979); MELVIN AND HOWARD(1980); BUSTIN' LOOSE(1981)
1984
SWING SHIFT(1984)
Richard Gofe
REMBRANDT(1936, Brit.); FOREVER YOURS(1937, Brit.)
Harper Goff
DETECTIVE STORY(1951); PETE KELLY'S BLUES(1955), a, prod d; VIKINGS, THE(1958), prod d; WILLY WONKA AND THE CHOCOLATE FACTORY(1971), art d
Ivan Goff
MY LOVE CAME BACK(1940), w; SUNSET IN WYOMING(1941), w; PREJUDICE(1949), w; WHITE HEAT(1949), w; BACKFIRE(1950), w; CAPTAIN HORATIO HORNBLOWER(1951, Brit.), w; COME FILL THE CUP(1951), w; GOODBYE, MY FANCY(1951), w; GLORY AT SEA(1952, Brit.), w; O. HENRY'S FULL HOUSE(1952), w; KING OF THE KHYBER RIFLES(1953), w; WHITE WITCH DOCTOR(1953), w; GREEN FIRE(1955), w; SERENADE(1956), w; BAND OF ANGELS(1957), w; MAN OF A THOUSAND FACES(1957), w; SHAKE HANDS WITH THE DEVIL(1959, Ireland), w; MIDNIGHT LACE(1960), w; PORTRAIT IN BLACK(1960), w; LEGEND OF THE LONE RANGER, THE(1981), w
John F. Goff
BUDDY HOLLY STORY, THE(1978); GETTING OVER(1981)
Misc. Talkies
DEVIL AND LEROY BASSETT, THE(1973)
John Goff
DRIVE-IN MASSACRE(1976), w; FOG, THE(1980); BUTTERFLY(1982), a, w; TIME TO DIE, A(1983), w
1984
HUNDRA(1984, Ital.), w
Misc. Talkies
ALPHA INCIDENT, THE(1976); CAPTURE OF BIGFOOT, THE(1979)
Silents
ALL DOLLED UP(1921)
Lloyd Goff
BODY AND SOUL(1947)
Max Goff
WOLFEN(1981)
Misc. Talkies
TEAM-MATES(1978)
Morris Goff
LUM AND ABNER ABROAD(1956)
Norris Goff
DREAMING OUT LOUD(1940); BASHFUL BACHELOR, THE(1942), a, w; SO THIS IS WASHINGTON(1943); TWO WEEKS TO LIVE(1943); GOIN' TO TOWN(1944); PARTNERS IN TIME(1946)
Peter Goff
HURRY SUNDOWN(1967)
Rusty Goff
HISTORY OF THE WORLD, PART 1(1981)

Rusty Goffe
FLASH GORDON(1980)
Sergio Goffi
HEIST, THE(1979, Ital.), d&w
Cora Goffin
Misc. Silents
DOWN UNDER DONOVAN(1922, Brit.)
P. Gofman
MEN OF THE SEA(1938, USSR)
Alan Goford
WILLIAM COMES TO TOWN(1948, Brit.)
E. Story Gofton
Silents
LAUGHTER AND TEARS(1921, Brit.)
Jack Goga
DOUBLE EXPOSURE(1982), m
Jan Gogdol
BEADS OF ONE ROSARY, THE(1982, Pol.)
Patrick Goggin
WHAT'S GOOD FOR THE GOOSE(1969, Brit.)
Michael Lee Gogin
UNDER THE RAINBOW(1981); WACKO(1983)
B. Goginava
FATHER OF A SOLDIER(1966, USSR)
Nicolai Gogol
REBEL SON, THE ½(1939, Brit.), w
Nikolai Gogol
INSPECTOR GENERAL, THE(1937, Czech.), w; INSPECTOR GENERAL, THE(1949), w; BLACK SUNDAY(1961, Ital.), w; TARAS BULBA(1962), w; GAMBLERS, THE(1969), d&w
Nikolai Vasilievich Gogol
OVERCOAT, THE(1965, USSR), w
Nikolay Gogol
NIGHT BEFORE CHRISTMAS, A(1963, USSR), w
Nikolay Vasilyevich Gogol
SOFI(1967), w
Ignacy Gogolewski
JOVITA(1970, Pol.)
David Goh
MARK OF THE HAWK, THE(1958)
Frank Goh
INN OF THE SIXTH HAPPINESS, THE(1958)
Walter Goher
I MARRIED A SPY(1938), m
Gerard Gohier
PRICE OF FLESH, THE(1962, Fr.), w
George Gohl
SAN FRANCISCO(1936)
Odette Goimbault
Silents
WAY OF AN EAGLE, THE(1918, Brit.); AS HE WAS BORN(1919, Brit.)
Misc. Silents
DOMBEY AND SON(1917, Brit.); SPINNER O' DREAMS(1918, Brit.); TOP DOG, THE(1918, Brit.); WAGES OF SIN, THE(1918, Brit.); LACKEY AND THE LADY, THE(1919, Brit.); WHOSOEVER SHALL OFFEND(1919, Brit.)
Ordette Goimbault
Silents
GREATEST WISH IN THE WORLD, THE(1918, Brit.)
Harry Goines
KELLY'S HEROES(1970, U.S./Yugo.)
Frederica Going
BIRTH OF A BABY(1938)
Jesse D. Goins
1984
UP THE CREEK(1984)
Jesse Goins
JEKYLL AND HYDE...TOGETHER AGAIN(1982); SECOND THOUGHTS(1983)
Jessie Goins
WARGAMES(1983)
Jesus Goiri
FITZCARRALDO(1982)
Alex E. Goitein
Misc. Talkies
CHERRY HILL HIGH(1977), d; CHEERLEADERS BEACH PARTY(1978), d
The Gojos
MOON ZERO TWO(1970, Brit.)
Mohan Gokhale
1984
MOHAN JOSHI HAAZIR HO(1984, India)
I. Gokleli
THEY WANTED PEACE(1940, USSR), m
Mona Golabek
PERFECT COUPLE, A(1979)
Menahem Golam
LEPKE(1975, U.S./Israel), p&d
Gila Golan
SHIP OF FOOLS(1965); OUR MAN FLINT(1966); THREE ON A COUCH(1966); CATCH AS CATCH CAN(1968, Ital.); VALLEY OF GWANGI, THE(1969)
Menachem Golan
GOD'S GUN(1977), p
Menaham Golan
MAGICIAN OF LUBLIN, THE(1979, Israel/Ger.), d, w; BODY AND SOUL(1981), p
Menahem Golan
SALLAH(1965, Israel), p; TRUNK TO CAIRO(1966, Israel/Ger.), p&d; MY MARGO(1969, Israel), d&w; WHAT'S GOOD FOR THE GOOSE(1969, Brit.), d, w; ESCAPE TO THE SUN(1972, Fr./Ger./Israel), p&d, w; KAZABLAN(1974, Israel), p&d, w; DIAMONDS(1975, U.S./Israel), p&d, w; KID VENGEANCE(1977), p; OPERATION THUNDERBOLT(1978, ISRAEL), p, d; MAGICIAN OF LUBLIN, THE(1979, Israel/Ger.), p; APPLE, THE(1980 U.S./Ger.), p, d&w; DR. HECKYL AND MR. HYPE(1980), p; HAPPY HOOKER GOES TO HOLLYWOOD, THE(1980), p; NEW YEAR'S EVIL(1980),

p; SCHIZOID(1980), p; DEATH WISH II(1982), p; ENTER THE NINJA(1982), d, w; HOSPITAL MASSACRE(1982), p; LAST AMERICAN VIRGIN, THE(1982), p; THAT CHAMPIONSHIP SEASON(1982), p; HERCULES(1983), p; HOUSE OF LONG SHADOWS, THE(1983, Brit.), p; NANA(1983, Ital.), p; REVENGE OF THE NINJA(1983), p; WICKED LADY, THE(1983, Brit.), p
1984
AMBASSADOR, THE(1984), p; BREAKIN' 2: ELECTRIC BOOGALOO(1984), p; HOSPITAL MASSACRE(1984), p; LOVE STREAMS(1984), p; MISSING IN ACTION(1984), p; NAKED FACE, THE(1984), p; NINJA III–THE DOMINATION(1984), p; OVER THE BROOKLYN BRIDGE(1984), p; SAHARA(1984), p; SWORD OF THE VALIANT(1984, Brit.), p; ULTIMATE SOLUTION OF GRACE QUIGLEY, THE(1984), p
Rachel Golan
YOUNG RACERS, THE(1963), makeup; SALLAH(1965, Israel), makeup; TRUNK TO CAIRO(1966, Israel/Ger.), makeup
Yoram Golan
1984
OVER THE BROOKLYN BRIDGE(1984), d; SAHARA(1984), w
Martin Golar
SPOOK WHO SAT BY THE DOOR, THE(1973)
Wieslaw Golas
LOTNA(1966, Pol.)
Joe Golbert
ONE DESIRE(1955)
Amber Rose Gold
SECOND-HAND HEARTS(1981)
Barbara Gold
SUMMER CAMP(1979)
Brandy Gold
1984
OH GOD! YOU DEVIL(1984)
David Gold
SWEET CHARITY(1969)
Debbie Gold
1984
WILD LIFE, THE(1984), md
Ernest Gold
GIRL OF THE LIMBERLOST, THE(1945), m; SMOOTH AS SILK(1946), m; EXPOSED(1947), m; LIGHTHOUSE(1947), m; WYOMING(1947), m; OLD LOS ANGELES(1948), m; UNKNOWN WORLD(1951), m; JENNIFER(1953), m; MAN CRAZY(1953), m; OTHER WOMAN, THE(1954), m; TENDER HEARTS(1955), m; EDGE OF HELL(1956), m, md; RUNNING TARGET(1956), m; MAN ON THE PROWL(1957), m; PRIDE AND THE PASSION, THE(1957), md; WITNESS FOR THE PROSECUTION(1957), md; YOUNG DON'T CRY, THE(1957), md; DEFIANT ONES, THE(1958), m; SCREAMING SKULL, THE(1958), m; TARZAN'S FIGHT FOR LIFE(1958), m; TOO MUCH, TOO SOON(1958), m; WINK OF AN EYE(1958), m; BATTLE OF THE CORAL SEA(1959), m; ON THE BEACH(1959), m; YOUNG PHILADELPHIANS, THE(1959), m; EXODUS(1960), m; INHERIT THE WIND(1960), m; FEVER IN THE BLOOD, A(1961), m; JUDGMENT AT NUREMBERG(1961), m; LAST SUNSET, THE(1961), m; PRESSURE POINT(1962), m; CHILD IS WAITING, A(1963), m; IT'S A MAD, MAD, MAD, MAD WORLD(1963), m; SHIP OF FOOLS(1965), m; SECRET OF SANTA VITTORIA, THE(1969), m; CROSS OF IRON(1977, Brit., Ger.), m; FUN WITH DICK AND JANE(1977), m; GOOD LUCK, MISS WYCKOFF(1979), m; THE RUNNER STUMBLES(1979), m; TOM HORN(1980), m; SAFARI 3000(1982), m
Harry Gold
WORLD'S GREATEST LOVER, THE(1977)
Harvey Gold
NICKEL RIDE, THE(1974)
1984
SAM'S SON(1984)
Heidi Gold
HERO AT LARGE(1980)
Jack Gold
BOFORS GUN, THE(1968, Brit.), d; RECKONING, THE(1971, Brit.), d; NATIONAL HEALTH, OR NURSE NORTON'S AFFAIR, THE(1973, Brit.), d; MAN FRIDAY(1975, Brit.), d; WHO?(1975, Brit./Ger.), d; ACES HIGH(1977, Brit.), p, d, w; MEDUSA TOUCH, THE(1978, Brit.), p, d; SAILOR'S RETURN, THE(1978, Brit.), d; PRAYING MANTIS(1982, Brit.), d; RED MONARCH(1983, Brit.), d
Jade Gold
RISKY BUSINESS(1983)
Jean Gold
CHILDREN OF PARADISE(1945, Fr.)
Jimmy Gold
HIGHLAND FLING(1936, Brit.); OKAY FOR SOUND(1937, Brit.), a, w; WISE GUYS(1937, Brit.); ALF'S BUTTON AFLOAT(1938, Brit.); GASBAGS(1940, Brit.); LIFE IS A CIRCUS(1962, Brit.)
Joel Gold
Misc. Talkies
JOE AND MAXI(1980), d
Kaethe Gold
SINS OF ROSE BERND, THE(1959, Ger.)
Laura Gold
1984
SPLATTER UNIVERSITY(1984)
Lee Gold
AFFAIRS OF MARTHA, THE(1942), w; GLAMOUR GIRL(1947), w; TAMANGO(1959, Fr.), w
Lisa Gold
HOMECOMING(1948)
Liz Gold
STOP THE WORLD–I WANT TO GET OFF(1966, Brit.)
Louis Gold
PIRATES OF PENZANCE, THE(1983)
Louise Gold
GREAT MUPPET CAPER, THE(1981); DARK CRYSTAL, THE(1982, Brit.)
Lynda Gold
RENEGADE GIRLS(1974)

Mel Gold
MAN WITH TWO BRAINS, THE(1983)
Mike Gold
ROAD TO LIFE(1932, USSR), titles
Milt Gold
PEACE KILLERS, THE(1971)
Myron J. Gold
RAGE, THE(1963, U.S./Mex.), d; RUN LIKE A THIEF(1968, Span.), w; MONITORS, THE(1969), w
Neal Gold
WARRIORS, THE(1979)
Peter Gold
BLOCKHOUSE, THE(1974, Brit.), ed
Ron Gold
RATTLERS(1976)
Misc. Talkies
RATTLERS(1976)
Sarah Gold
SATAN'S BED(1965)
Steve Gold
1984
HARDBODIES(1984)
Tracey Gold
SHOOT THE MOON(1982)
Travis Gold
RATTLERS(1976)
William Gold
MURDER CLINIC, THE(1967, Ital./Fr.)
Zachary Gold
TOP MAN(1943), w; HUMORESQUE(1946), w; SOUTH OF ST. LOUIS(1949), w
Ida Goldapple
KITCHEN, THE(1961, Brit.)
P. Goldbaum
ARMS AND THE MAN(1962, Ger.), p
Peter Goldbaum
WINTER WONDERLAND(1947), w
Willis Goldbeck
FREAKS(1932), w; PENGUIN POOL MURDER, THE(1932), w; ROADHOUSE MURDER, THE(1932), p; MURDER ON THE BLACKBOARD(1934), w; WEDNESDAY'S CHILD(1934), w; YOUNG DR. KILDARE(1938), w; CALLING DR. KILDARE(1939), w; SECRET OF DR. KILDARE, THE(1939), w; DR. KILDARE GOES HOME(1940), w; DR. KILDARE'S CRISIS(1940), w; DR. KILDARE'S STRANGE CASE(1940), w; DR. KILDARE'S VICTORY(1941), w; DR. KILDARE'S WEDDING DAY(1941), w; PEOPLE VS. DR. KILDARE, THE(1941), w; CALLING DR. GILLESPIE(1942), w; DR. GILLESPIE'S NEW ASSISTANT(1942), d, w; DR. GILLESPIE'S CRIMINAL CASE(1943), d; BETWEEN TWO WOMEN(1944), p&d; RATIONING(1944), d; THREE MEN IN WHITE(1944), d; SHE WENT TO THE RACES(1945), d; LOVE LAUGHS AT ANDY HARDY(1946), d; DARK DELUSION(1947), d; JOHNNY HOLIDAY(1949), d, w; TEN TALL MEN(1951), d, w; I DIED A THOUSAND TIMES(1955), p; LONE RANGER, THE(1955), p; COLOSSUS OF NEW YORK, THE(1958), w; SERGEANT RUTLEDGE(1960), p, w; MAN WHO SHOT LIBERTY VALANCE, THE(1962), p, w
Silents
SCARAMOUCHE(1923), w; ALASKAN, THE(1924), w; BLUFF(1924), w; OPEN ALL NIGHT(1924), w; PETER PAN(1924), w; SIDESHOW OF LIFE, THE(1924), w; KISS FOR CINDERELLA, A(1926), w; MARE NOSTRUM(1926), w; CONVOY(1927), w; ENEMY, THE(1927), w; LILAC TIME(1928), w; WILD ORCHIDS(1929), w
Andy Goldberg
GOODBYE GIRL, THE(1977); I'M DANCING AS FAST AS I CAN(1982)
Benny Goldberg
FIGHTING FOOLS(1949)
Dan Goldberg
MEATBALLS(1979, Can.), p, w; HEAVY METAL(1981, Can.), w; STRIPES(1981), p, w; SPACEHUNTER: ADVENTURES IN THE FORBIDDEN ZONE(1983), w
Daniel Goldberg
CANNIBAL GIRLS(1973), p, ed
Dave Goldberg
MARRIAGE BY CONTRACT(1928), m/l
David Goldberg
JESUS(1979)
Diana Goldberg
CATSKILL HONEYMOON(1950)
Heinz Goldberg
TALES OF THE UNCANNY(1932, Ger.), w; 1914(1932, Ger.), w
Ivan Goldberg
ROAD HOME, THE(1947, USSR), ph
Jack Goldberg
HARLEM IS HEAVEN(1932), p; BOY! WHAT A GIRL(1947), p; SEPIA CINDERELLA(1947), p; MIRACLE IN HARLEM(1948), p
Jakub Goldberg
KNIFE IN THE WATER(1963, Pol.), w
Jeff Goldberg
DEATH WISH(1974)
Jesse J. Goldberg
Silents
LIFE WITHOUT SOUL(1916), w; DUDE COWBOY, THE(1926), p
Joe Goldberg
THE EAVESDROPPER(1966, U.S./Arg.), w
Leonard Goldberg
BABY BLUE MARINE(1976), p; BAD NEWS BEARS IN BREAKING TRAINING, THE(1977), p; ALL NIGHT LONG(1981), p
Lou Goldberg
FRANKIE AND JOHNNY(1936), w; ON STAGE EVERYBODY(1945), p
Maxwell "Sonny" Goldberg
KING OF MARVIN GARDENS, THE(1972)
Mel Goldberg
LIVELY SET, THE(1964), w; HANG'EM HIGH(1968), w
Robert Goldberg
TO BE OR NOT TO BE(1983)

Robert B. Goldberg
HISTORY OF THE WORLD, PART 1(1981)
Rube Goldberg
SOUP TO NUTS(1930), w; ARTISTS AND MODELS(1937)
Silents
CAMPUS FLIRT, THE(1926), t
Tali Goldberg
DIAMONDS(1975, U.S./Israel)
William Goldberg
VICTIMS OF PERSECUTION(1933), p
W. Goldberger
FOR LOVE OF YOU(1933, Brit.), ph; KISS ME GOODBYE(1935, Brit.), ph
Willi Goldberger
REBEL, THE(1933, Ger.), ph
Willie Goldberger
BE MINE TONIGHT(1933, Brit.), ph
Willy Goldberger
HIS MAJESTY, KING BALLYHOO(1931, Ger.), ph; WHAT WOMEN DREAM(1933, Ger.), ph; AFFAIRS OF MAUPASSANT(1938, Aust.), ph
Charles Goldblatt
L'ATALANTE(1947, Fr.)
Hanan Goldblatt
FLYING MATCHMAKER, THE(1970, Israel)
Harold Goldblatt
CAPTAIN LIGHTFOOT(1955); JACQUELINE(1956, Brit.); RISING OF THE MOON, THE(1957, Ireland); NIGHT TO REMEMBER, A(1958, Brit.); ROONEY(1958, Brit.); SIEGE OF SIDNEY STREET, THE(1960, Brit.); BIG GAMBLE, THE(1961); FRANCIS OF ASSISI(1961); LISA(1962, Brit.); RELUCTANT SAINT, THE(1962, U.S./Ital.); CHILDREN OF THE DAMNED(1963, Brit.); MIND BENDERS, THE(1963, Brit.); NINE HOURS TO RAMA(1963, U.S./Brit.); RUNNING MAN, THE(1963, Brit.); CRIMSON BLADE, THE(1964, Brit.); YOUNG CASSIDY(1965, U.S./Brit.); REPTILE, THE(1966, Brit.); 25TH HOUR, THE(1967, Fr./Ital./Yugo.); SUNDAY BLOODY SUNDAY(1971, Brit.); SOMETHING TO HIDE(1972, Brit.); ABDICATION, THE(1974, Brit.)
Mark Goldblatt
PIRANHA(1978), ed; SPIRIT OF THE WIND(1979), ed; HUMANOIDS FROM THE DEEP(1980), ed; HALLOWEEN II(1981), ed; HOWLING, THE(1981), ed; ENTER THE NINJA(1982), ed; GET CRAZY(1983), ed; WAVELENGTH(1983), ed
1984
AMBASSADOR, THE(1984), ed; OVER THE BROOKLYN BRIDGE(1984), ed; TERMINATOR, THE(1984), ed
Stephen Goldblatt
OUTLAND(1981), ph; HUNGER, THE(1983), ph; RETURN OF THE SOLDIER, THE(1983, Brit.), ph
1984
COTTON CLUB, THE(1984), ph
Steven Goldblatt
BREAKING GLASS(1980, Brit.), ph
Jeff Goldblum
CALIFORNIA SPLIT(1974); NASHVILLE(1975); NEXT STOP, GREENWICH VILLAGE(1976); SPECIAL DELIVERY(1976); ST. IVES(1976); ANNIE HALL(1977); BETWEEN THE LINES(1977); SENTINEL, THE(1977); INVASION OF THE BODY SNATCHERS(1978); REMEMBER MY NAME(1978); THANK GOD IT'S FRIDAY(1978); BIG CHILL, THE(1983); RIGHT STUFF, THE(1983); THRESHOLD(1983, Can.)
1984
ADVENTURES OF BUCKAROO BANZAI: ACROSS THE 8TH DIMENSION, THE(1984)
Jesse J. Goldburg
Silents
FIGHTING SMILE, THE(1925), p; RIDERS OF MYSTERY(1925), sup; HAIR TRIGGER BAXTER(1926), p; VALLEY OF BRAVERY, THE(1926), p
Johnny Golde
1984
LAUGHTER HOUSE(1984, Brit.)
The Goldebriars
ONCE UPON A COFFEE HOUSE(1965)
Al Golden
BLOOD FEAST(1963)
Alfred Golden
ONE MILE FROM HEAVEN(1937), w
Annie Golden
HAIR(1979)
Bertina Golden
EAST SIDE SADIE(1929)
Bob Golden
CHINATOWN(1974); REPORT TO THE COMMISSIONER(1975)
David Golden
KRAMER VS. KRAMER(1979)
Eddie Golden
ADVENTURESS, THE(1946, Brit.); BROTH OF A BOY(1959, Brit.); HOME IS THE HERO(1959, Ireland); THIS OTHER EDEN(1959, Brit.); NIGHT FIGHTERS, THE(1960); POACHER'S DAUGHTER, THE(1960, Brit.); NEVER PUT IT IN WRITING(1964); YOUNG CASSIDY(1965, U.S./Brit.); ULYSSES(1967, U.S./Brit.); BLACK BEAUTY(1971, Brit./Ger./Span.)
Edward A. Golden
HITLER'S CHILDREN(1942), p
Edward Golden
NO GREATER SIN(1941), p; LIES MY FATHER TOLD ME(1960, Brit.)
Eleanor Golden
SPRING MADNESS(1938), w
Ella Golden
Silents
LOVE LIAR, THE(1916)
Eve Golden
MOON OVER HER SHOULDER(1941), w
Geoff Golden
BROTHERLY LOVE(1970, Brit.)

Geoffrey Golden
  PROFESSOR TIM(1957, Ireland); HOME IS THE HERO(1959, Ireland); THIS OTHER EDEN(1959, Brit.); BOYD'S SHOP(1960, Brit.); NIGHT FIGHTERS, THE(1960); POACHER'S DAUGHTER, THE(1960, Brit.); QUARE FELLOW, THE(1962, Brit.); NEVER PUT IT IN WRITING(1964); ULYSSES(1967, U.S./Brit.); SINFUL DAVEY(1969, Brit.)
Gladys Golden
  PUNISHMENT PARK(1971)
John Golden
  GIRL IN THE SHOW, THE(1929), w; LIGHTNIN'(1930), p; AFTER TOMORROW(1932), w; HER FIRST MATE(1933), w; STRANGE EXPERIMENT(1937, Brit.), w
John L. Golden
Silents
  SAPHEAD, THE(1921), p
Joseph Golden
Silents
  SENATOR, THE(1915), d
Misc. Silents
  COUNT OF MONTE CRISTO, THE(1913), d
Joseph A. Golden
Misc. Silents
  BETTER WOMAN, THE(1915), d; DIVORCED(1915), d; NOT GUILTY(1915), d; PRICE, THE(1915), d; LIBERTINE, THE(1916), d; LOVE'S CROSS ROADS(1916), d; PRIMA DONNA'S HUSBAND, THE(1916), d; LAW OF COMPENSATION, THE(1917), d; REDEMPTION(1917), d; FANGS OF THE WOLF(1924), d; LAW OF COMPENSATION(1927), d
Larry Golden
  WANDA NEVADA(1979)
1984
  HARD CHOICES(1984)
Max Golden
  BACK TO NATURE(1936), p; EDUCATING FATHER(1936), p; EVERY SATURDAY NIGHT(1936), p; BORROWING TROUBLE(1937), p; HOT WATER(1937), p; LAUGHING AT TROUBLE(1937), p; OFF TO THE RACES(1937), p; FOR LOVE OR MONEY(1939), p
Max H. Golden
  EXPOSED(1938), p; LITTLE TOUGH GUYS IN SOCIETY(1938), p; PERSONAL SECRETARY(1938), p; SWING THAT CHEER(1938), p; FAMILY NEXT DOOR, THE(1939), p; HAWAIIAN NIGHTS(1939), p
Michael Golden
  SEND FOR PAUL TEMPLE(1946, Brit.); HUNGRY HILL(1947, Brit.); ANOTHER SHORE(1948, Brit.); ESCAPE(1948, Brit.); SILK NOOSE, THE(1950, Brit.); POOL OF LONDON(1951, Brit.); CRY, THE BELOVED COUNTRY(1952, Brit.); GENTLE GUNMAN, THE(1952, Brit.); SALUTE THE TOFF(1952, Brit.); OPERATION DIPLOMAT(1953, Brit.); TERROR STREET(1953); BLACK RIDER, THE(1954, Brit.); BLACKOUT(1954, Brit.); GREEN SCARF, THE(1954, Brit.); CROSS CHANNEL(1955, Brit.); SQUARE RING, THE(1955, Brit.); TRACK THE MAN DOWN(1955, Brit.); WAY OUT, THE(1956, Brit.); DATE WITH DISASTER(1957, Brit.); MAN WITHOUT A BODY, THE(1957, Brit.); ROBBERY WITH VIOLENCE(1958, Brit.); TREAD SOFTLY STRANGER(1959, Brit.); DAY THEY ROBBED THE BANK OF ENGLAND, THE(1960, Brit.); MURDER SHE SAID(1961, Brit.); DURING ONE NIGHT(1962, Brit.)
Mickey Golden
  GOLDEN BOY(1939); FATHER OF THE BRIDE(1950); CLOWN, THE(1953); SERENADE(1956)
Mignonne Golden
Silents
  WALLOP, THE(1921)
Misc. Silents
  HEARTS UP!(1920)
Mildred Golden
  GREENE MURDER CASE, THE(1929); MOTHER AND SON(1931); RECKONING, THE(1932)
Miriam Golden
  SPECTER OF THE ROSE(1946)
Olive Golden
Silents
  JUST JIM(1915); KNIGHT OF THE RANGE, A(1916)
Olive Fuller Golden
Silents
  TESS OF THE STORM COUNTRY(1914)
Misc. Silents
  LOVE'S LARIAT(1916)
Pat Golden
  LIZZIE(1957)
Robert Golden
  ACROSS THE PLAINS(1939), ed; OKLAHOMA TERROR(1939), ed; OVERLAND MAIL(1939), ed; ARIZONA FRONTIER(1940), ed; CHEYENNE KID, THE(1940), ed; COVERED WAGON TRAILS(1940), ed; DOOMED TO DIE(1940), ed; GOLDEN TRAIL, THE(1940), ed; HIDDEN ENEMY(1940), ed; KID FROM SANTA FE, THE(1940), ed; LAND OF THE SIX GUNS(1940), ed; PALS OF THE SILVER SAGE(1940), ed; PIONEER DAYS(1940), ed; RIDERS FROM NOWHERE(1940), ed; BOWERY BLITZKRIEG(1941), ed; FLYING WILD(1941), ed; INVISIBLE GHOST, THE(1941), ed; NO GREATER SIN(1941), ed; PRIDE OF THE BOWERY(1941), ed; RIDING THE CHEROKEE TRAIL(1941), ed; SPOOKS RUN WILD(1941), ed; ZIS BOOM BAH(1941), ed; COLLEGE SWEETHEARTS(1942), ed; CORPSE VANISHES, THE(1942), ed; LET'S GET TOUGH(1942), ed; SMART ALECKS(1942), ed; MASTER RACE, THE(1944), p; GUILTY OF TREASON(1950), p; AT SWORD'S POINT(1951), ed; HOT LEAD(1951), ed; ROADBLOCK(1951), ed; WHIP HAND, THE(1951), ed; MACAO(1952), ed; RAID, THE(1954), ed; BENGAZI(1955), ed; BLACK TUESDAY(1955), ed; NIGHT OF THE HUNTER, THE(1955), ed; BANDIDO(1956), ed; DANCE WITH ME, HENRY(1956), ed; MAN FROM DEL RIO(1956), ed; FURY AT SHOWDOWN(1957), ed; GUN DUEL IN DURANGO(1957), ed; GUNSIGHT RIDGE(1957), ed; LASSIE'S GREAT ADVENTURE(1963), p; WILD ON THE BEACH(1965); WILLARD(1971); SUGARLAND EXPRESS, THE(1974)
Robert A. Golden
Silents
  HONEYMOON(1929), d

Robert S. Golden
  TEXAS, BROOKLYN AND HEAVEN(1948), p; LONE RANGER AND THE LOST CITY OF GOLD, THE(1958), ed
Ruth Fuller Golden
Silents
  HUMAN STUFF(1920)
Misc. Silents
  PEGEEN(1920)
Sally Anne Golden
  WANDERERS, THE(1979); FRIDAY THE 13TH(1980)
Sandra Golden
  SHEILA LEVINE IS DEAD AND LIVING IN NEW YORK(1975)
Sanford Golden
  PUNISHMENT PARK(1971)
Shelley Golden
  ROLLER BOOGIE(1979)
Sidney M. Golden
  EAST SIDE SADIE(1929), d&w
Golden Gate Quartet
  HIT PARADE OF 1943(1943); HOLLYWOOD CANTEEN(1944)
The Golden Gate Quartet
  SONG IS BORN, A(1948)
Golden Gate Quartette
  STAR SPANGLED RHYTHM(1942)
The Golden State Warriors
  INSIDE MOVES(1980)
The Golden Westerners
  GENTLEMAN FROM ARIZONA, THE(1940)
Billy Goldenberg
  CHANGE OF HABIT(1969), m; GRASSHOPPER, THE(1970), m; RED SKY AT MORNING(1971), m; PLAY IT AGAIN, SAM(1972), m; UP THE SANDBOX(1972), m; LAST OF SHEILA, THE(1973), m; BUSTING(1974), m; DOMINO PRINCIPLE, THE(1977), m; SCAVENGER HUNT(1979), m; REUBEN, REUBEN(1983), m
Devi Goldenberg
  HAPPY HOOKER GOES TO HOLLYWOOD, THE(1980), w
Devin Goldenberg
  GUESS WHAT WE LEARNED IN SCHOOL TODAY?(1970); SAVAGE WEEKEND(1983)
1984
  LAST HORROR FILM, THE(1984)
Harvey J. Goldenberg
  BANK SHOT(1974)
Heli Goldenberg
1984
  AMBASSADOR, THE(1984)
Mark Goldenberg
  SILENT RAGE(1982), m
R. Goldenberg
  FORBIDDEN TERRITORY(1938, Brit.), ph
Sam Goldenberg
  FALLEN SPARROW, THE(1943); MISSION TO MOSCOW(1943)
Samuel Goldenberg
Misc. Talkies
  SONG OF SONGS(1935)
Elliot Goldenthal
  COCAINE COWBOYS(1979), m
David Golder
  DAVID GOLDER(1932, Fr.)
Harry Golder
  WE'RE NOT MARRIED(1952)
Lew Golder
  SPIRIT OF YOUTH(1937), p; WOMAN AGAINST THE WORLD(1938), p
Abraham Goldfaden
  FLYING MATCHMAKER, THE(1970, Israel), w
Avraham Goldfaden
  TWO KOUNEY LEMELS(1966, Israel), w
Wolf Goldfaden
Misc. Talkies
  JOSEPH IN THE LAND OF EGYPT(1932); JEWISH FATHER(1934)
Silents
  BROKEN HEARTS(1926)
Lawrence G. Goldfarb
  STUCKEY'S LAST STAND(1980), p,d&w
Phil Goldfarb
  LAST SUMMER(1969), prod d
Michael Goldfinger
Misc. Talkies
  TEAM-MATES(1978)
Roy Goldfrey
  TORTURE GARDEN(1968, Brit.)
Marvin Goldhar
  OFFERING, THE(1966, Can.); RUNNING(1979, Can.)
Goldie
  KILLERS OF THE WILD(1940)
F. Wyndham Goldie
  UNDER THE RED ROBE(1937, Brit.)
Jack Goldie
  MY FAIR LADY(1964)
Michael Goldie
  DOCTOR IN DISTRESS(1963, Brit.); WHERE THE BULLETS FLY(1966, Brit.); PIED PIPER, THE(1972, Brit.)
Wyndham Goldie
  VICTORIA THE GREAT(1937, Brit.); BLACK MASK(1935, Brit.); CRIME UNLIMITED(1935, Brit.); LORNA DOONE(1935, Brit.); LAST CHANCE, THE(1937, Brit.); OLD BONES OF THE RIVER(1938, Brit.); RETURN OF CAROL DEANE, THE(1938, Brit.); SIXTY GLORIOUS YEARS(1938, Brit.); ARSENAL STADIUM MYSTERY, THE(1939, Brit.); INSPECTOR HORNLEIGH ON HOLIDAY(1939, Brit.); NIGHT TRAIN(1940, Brit.); GIRL IN THE NEWS, THE(1941, Brit.); SEVEN DAYS TO NOON(1950, Brit.); DOCTOR IN THE HOUSE(1954, Brit.); SECRET, THE(1955, Brit.); COSMIC MONSTERS(1958, Brit.)

Gayle Goldin
PRIVATE SCHOOL(1983)
Hubert Goldin
DAISY MILLER(1974)
Marilyn Goldin
BAROCCO(1976, Fr.), w; DANDY, THE ALL AMERICAN GIRL(1976), w
Nan Goldin
1984
VARIETY(1984)
Pat Goldin
BRINGING UP FATHER(1946); IT HAPPENED ON 5TH AVENUE(1947); KILROY WAS HERE(1947); SARGE GOES TO COLLEGE(1947); JIGGS AND MAGGIE IN SOCIETY(1948); KING OF THE BANDITS(1948); MASTER MINDS(1949); JIGGS AND MAGGIE OUT WEST(1950); GLORY ALLEY(1952); HOLD BACK TOMORROW(1955); TENDER HEARTS(1955); EDGE OF HELL(1956); KETTLES IN THE OZARKS, THE(1956); HIT AND RUN(1957); BORN TO BE LOVED(1959); HALF PINT, THE(1960)
Ricky Paull Goldin
1984
UNFAITHFULLY YOURS(1984)
Sidney Goldin
Misc. Talkies
HIS WIFE'S LOVER(1931), d; SHULAMIS(1931), d; UNCLE MOSES(1932), d
Sidney M. Goldin
Misc. Silents
LAST OF THE MAFFIA, THE(1915), d; FIGHTIN' COMEBACK, THE(1927)
Marian Goldina
FLAMING STAR(1960)
Miriam Goldina
LADIES OF THE BIG HOUSE(1932); ONE THIRD OF A NATION(1939); COP HATER(1958)
Bill Golding
UNDERGROUND(1970, Brit.)
Claire Golding
MAKE MINE MINK(1960, Brit.)
Jerry Golding
RATTLERS(1976), w
Joyce Golding
TROUBLE IN THE AIR(1948, Brit.)
Louis Golding
COTTON QUEEN(1937, Brit.), w; VOICE IN THE NIGHT, A(1941, Brit.), w; MR. EMMANUEL(1945, Brit.), w
Malcolm Golding
SIDDHARTHA(1972), art d
Pat Golding
FAST COMPANY(1953)
Paul Golding
1984
BEAT STREET(1984), w
Richard Golding
TALES OF HOFFMANN, THE(1951, Brit.); VIOLENT STRANGER(1957, Brit.); CRAWLING EYE, THE(1958, Brit.); MAN INSIDE, THE(1958, Brit.); GREAT ARMORED CAR SWINDLE, THE(1964); IT HAPPENED HERE(1966, Brit.)
Ronald Golding
NED KELLY(1970, Brit.)
Samuel R. Golding
BUCCANEER'S GIRL(1950), w
Sarah Golding
NICE GIRL LIKE ME, A(1969, Brit.)
William Golding
LORD OF THE FLIES(1963, Brit.), w
Bernard Goldman
STRICTLY FOR THE BIRDS(1963, Brit.)
Bo Goldman
ONE FLEW OVER THE CUCKOO'S NEST(1975), w; ROSE, THE(1979), w; MELVIN AND HOWARD(1980), w; SHOOT THE MOON(1982), w
Dan Goldman
WORLD ACCORDING TO GARP, The(1982)
Danny Goldman
M(1970); STRAWBERRY STATEMENT, THE(1970); TRIBES(1970); LONG GOODBYE, THE(1973); WORLD'S GREATEST ATHLETE, THE(1973); YOUNG FRANKENSTEIN(1974); MISSOURI BREAKS, THE(1976); SWAP MEET(1979); WHERE THE BUFFALO ROAM(1980)
David Goldman
WATCHED(1974), p
Derek Goldman
PRIVILEGED(1982, Brit.), ed
Edmund Goldman
SURRENDER—HELL!(1959), p; FIRST SPACESHIP ON VENUS(1960, Ger./Pol.), p
Erwin Goldman
SWEET SIXTEEN(1983), w
Gary Goldman
SECRET OF NIMH, THE(1982), p, w
Hal Goldman
OH GOD! BOOK II(1980), w
Harold Goldman
PETTICOAT FEVER(1936), w; EMPEROR'S CANDLESTICKS, THE(1937), w; GIRL DOWNSTAIRS, THE(1938), w; BUSMAN'S HONEYMOON(1940, Brit.), w; LITTLE BIT OF HEAVEN, A(1940), w; MY KINGDOM FOR A COOK(1943), w; KNICKERBOCKER HOLIDAY(1944), w; SHADOW OF SUSPICION(1944), w; MONEY JUNGLE, THE(1968), p
Hy Goldman
COME SPY WITH ME(1967), ed
James Goldman
LION IN WINTER, THE(1968, Brit.), w; NICHOLAS AND ALEXANDRA(1971, Brit.), w; THEY MIGHT BE GIANTS(1971), w; ROBIN AND MARIAN(1976, Brit.), w
John Goldman
MICHAEL AND MARY(1932, Brit.), ed

Larry Goldman
EXORCIST II: THE HERETIC(1977)
Lawrence Goldman
KILL OR BE KILLED(1950), w; TRIAL WITHOUT JURY(1950), w
Lawrence Louis Goldman
KRONOS(1957), w; WAR OF THE SATELLITES(1958), w
Les Goldman
PHANTOM TOLLBOOTH, THE(1970), p
Lorry Goldman
TUNNELVISION(1976); 10(1979); HOME FREE ALL(1983)
1984
BEST DEFENSE(1984); HOME FREE ALL(1984)
Louis Goldman
SAGA OF THE VIKING WOMEN AND THEIR VOYAGE TO THE WATERS OF THE GREAT SEA SERPENT, THE(1957), w
Marcy Goldman
KENTUCKY FRIED MOVIE, THE(1977)
Martin Goldman
LEGEND OF NIGGER CHARLEY, THE(1972), d, w
Misc. Talkies
DARK AUGUST(1975), d
Mia Goldman
1984
CHOOSE ME(1984), ed; 2010(1984), ed
Michael F. Goldman
JESSIE'S GIRLS(1976), p
Morris Goldman
TWENTY MILLION SWEETHEARTS(1934)
P. Goldman
MY FATHER'S HOUSE(1947, Palestine)
Peter Emanuel Goldman
WHEEL OF ASHES(1970, Fr.), d,w&ph
Peter Emmanuel Goldman
ECHOES OF SILENCE(1966), d,w,ph&ed
Philippe Goldman
SMALL CHANGE(1976, Fr.)
Rachael Goldman
DANIEL(1983)
Roy Goldman
TO BE OR NOT TO BE(1983)
Sharon Goldman
OVER-UNDER, SIDEWAYS-DOWN(1977); EYEWITNESS(1981)
Sharon Martin Goldman
SHEILA LEVINE IS DEAD AND LIVING IN NEW YORK(1975)
Steve Goldman
JIM, THE WORLD'S GREATEST(1976)
Wendy Goldman
NATIONAL LAMPOON'S CLASS REUNION(1982)
William Goldman
SOLDIER IN THE RAIN(1963), w; HARPER(1966), w; NO WAY TO TREAT A LADY(1968), w; BUTCH CASSIDY AND THE SUNDANCE KID(1969), w; HOT ROCK, THE(1972), w; GREAT WALDO PEPPER, THE(1975), w; STEPFORD WIVES, THE(1975), w; ALL THE PRESIDENT'S MEN(1976), w; MARATHON MAN(1976), w; BRIDGE TOO FAR, A(1977, Brit.), w; MAGIC(1978), w
John Goldmanan
NIGHT AND DAY(1933, Brit.), ed
Bo Goldmann
END OF THE GAME(1976, Ger./Ital.), w
Arnold Goldner
IT'S A DEAL(1930), m
Charles Goldner
ROOM FOR TWO(1940, Brit.); FLIGHT FROM FOLLY(1945, Brit.); MR. EMMANUEL(1945, Brit.); BRIGHTON ROCK(1947, Brit.); BOND STREET(1948, Brit.); BONNIE PRINCE CHARLIE(1948, Brit.); NO ORCHIDS FOR MISS BLANDISH(1948, Brit.); ONE NIGHT WITH YOU(1948, Brit); BLACK MAGIC(1949); DEAR MR. PROHACK(1949, Brit.); SALT TO THE DEVIL(1949, Brit.); LAUGHING LADY, THE(1950, Brit.); ROCKING HORSE WINNER, THE(1950, Brit.); THIRD TIME LUCKY(1950, Brit.); ENCORE(1951, Brit.); LUCKY NICK CAIN(1951); SECRET PEOPLE(1952, Brit.); CAPTAIN'S PARADISE, THE(1953, Brit.); MASTER OF BALLANTRAE, THE(1953, U.S./Brit.); MR. POTTS GOES TO MOSCOW(1953, Brit.); ALWAYS A BRIDE(1954, Brit.); DUEL IN THE JUNGLE(1954, Brit.); FLAME AND THE FLESH(1954); GOLDEN MASK, THE(1954, Brit.); END OF THE AFFAIR, THE(1955, Brit.); RACERS, THE(1955); SHADOW OF THE EAGLE(1955, Brit.)
Orville Goldner
KING KONG(1933), spec eff
Leila Goldoni
HYSTERIA(1965, Brit.)
Misc. Talkies
CHOICES(1981)
Lelia Goldoni
WE WERE STRANGERS(1949); SHADOWS(1960); THEATRE OF DEATH(1967, Brit.); ITALIAN JOB, THE(1969, Brit.); ALICE DOESN'T LIVE HERE ANYMORE(1975); DAY OF THE LOCUST, THE(1975); BABY BLUE MARINE(1976); BLOODBROTHERS(1978); INVASION OF THE BODY SNATCHERS(1978); UNSEEN, THE(1981)
Boris Goldovsky
DON JUAN(1956, Aust.), art d
Ray Goldrup
WINDWALKER(1980), w
Arnold Goldsborough
SEVENTH VEIL, THE(1946, Brit.)
Matthew Goldsby
STUDENT BODIES(1981)
Robert Goldsby
CANDIDATE, THE(1972)
Anthony Goldschmidt
SILENT MOVIE(1976), titles

Isadore Goldschmidt
LILAC DOMINO, THE(1940, Brit.), p
Isidore Goldschmidt
SOUTHERN ROSES(1936, Brit.), p; WHO IS GUILTY?(1940, Brit.), p
Per Goldschmidt
VENOM(1968, Den.)
Robert Goldschmidt
COLORADO PIONEERS(1945)
Sadore Goldschmidt
STARS LOOK DOWN, THE(1940, Brit.), p
Al Goldsmith
BROADWAY BIG SHOT(1942)
Charles Goldsmith
JOURNEY TO THE BEGINNING OF TIME(1966, Czech); NIGHT OF DARK SHADOWS(1971), ed
Clifford Goldsmith
WHAT A LIFE(1939), w; HENRY ALDRICH FOR PRESIDENT(1941), w; LIFE WITH HENRY(1941), w; HENRY ALDRICH, EDITOR(1942), w; HENRY AND DIZZY(1942), w; FATHER WAS A FULLBACK(1949), w
Clio Goldsmith
GIFT, THE(1983, Fr./Ital.)
1984
HEAT OF DESIRE(1984, Fr.)
Frank Goldsmith
CROOKED BILLET, THE(1930, Brit.); SUCH IS THE LAW(1930, Brit.)
Silents
AS IN A LOOKING GLASS(1916); NEW YORK PEACOCK, THE(1917); RISE OF JENNIE CUSHING, THE(1917); OTHER MEN'S DAUGHTERS(1918); OH, JOHNNY(1919); DEBT OF HONOR(1922, Brit.)
Misc. Silents
FATE'S BOOMERANG(1916); VELVET PAW, THE(1916); VERA, THE MEDIUM(1916); MAN'S WOMAN(1917); PAGE MYSTERY, THE(1917); REPUTATION(1917); DEBT OF HONOR, THE(1918); DIVINE SACRIFICE, THE(1918); HEART'S REVENGE, A(1918); PERILOUS VALLEY(1920)
George Goldsmith
JULIA MISBEHAVES(1948); FORCE: FIVE(1981), w
1984
CHILDREN OF THE CORN(1984), w
H. H. Goldsmith
WHAT'S GOOD FOR THE GOOSE(1969, Brit.)
I.G. Goldsmith
THREE HUSBANDS(1950), p; SCARF, THE(1951), d&w, p
Isadore Goldsmith
VOICE WITHIN, THE(1945, Brit.), p; BEDELIA(1946, Brit.), p; HATTER'S CASTLE(1948, Brit.), p
Isadore G. Goldsmith
OUT OF THE BLUE(1947), p
Jerald Goldsmith
FACE OF A FUGITIVE(1959), m
Jerry Goldsmith
BLACK PATCH(1957), m; CITY OF FEAR(1959), m; FREUD(1962), m; LONELY ARE THE BRAVE(1962), m; SPIRAL ROAD, THE(1962), m; GATHERING OF EAGLES, A(1963), m; LILIES OF THE FIELD(1963), m; LIST OF ADRIAN MESSENGER, THE(1963), m; PRIZE, THE(1963), m; STRIPPER, THE(1963), m; TAKE HER, SHE'S MINE(1963), m, md; FATE IS THE HUNTER(1964), m; RIO CONCHOS(1964), ph; SEVEN DAYS IN MAY(1964), m; SHOCK TREATMENT(1964), m; IN HARM'S WAY(1965), m; MORITURI(1965), m; PATCH OF BLUE, A(1965), m; SATAN BUG, THE(1965), m, md; VON RYAN'S EXPRESS(1965), m; BLUE MAX, THE(1966), m; ONE SPY TOO MANY(1966), m; OUR MAN FLINT(1966), m; SAND PEBBLES, THE(1966), m; SECONDS(1966), m; STAGECOACH(1966), m; TO TRAP A SPY(1966), m; TROUBLE WITH ANGELS, THE(1966), m; FLIM-FLAM MAN, THE(1967), m; HOUR OF THE GUN(1967), m; IN LIKE FLINT(1967), m; KARATE KILLERS, THE(1967), m; WARNING SHOT(1967), m; BANDOLERO!(1968), m; DETECTIVE, THE(1968), m; PLANET OF THE APES(1968), m; SEBASTIAN(1968, Brit.), m; CHAIRMAN, THE(1969), m; ILLUSTRATED MAN, THE(1969), m; JUSTINE(1969), m; 100 RIFLES(1969), m; BALLAD OF CABLE HOGUE, THE(1970), m; PATTON(1970), m; RIO LOBO(1970), m; TORA! TORA! TORA!(1970, U.S./Jap.), m; TRAVELING EXECUTIONER, THE(1970), m; ESCAPE FROM THE PLANET OF THE APES(1971), m; LAST RUN, THE(1971), m; MEPHISTO WALTZ, THE(1971), m; WILD ROVERS(1971), m; CULPEPPER CATTLE COMPANY, THE(1972), m; MAN, THE(1972), m; OTHER, THE(1972), m; ACE ELI AND RODGER OF THE SKIES(1973), m; DON IS DEAD, THE(1973), m; ONE LITTLE INDIAN(1973), m; PAPILLON(1973), m; SHAMUS(1973), m; CHINATOWN(1974), m; S(1974), m; BREAKOUT(1975), m; REINCARNATION OF PETER PROUD, THE(1975), m; TAKE A HARD RIDE(1975, U.S./Ital.), m; TERRORISTS, THE(1975, Brit.), m; WIND AND THE LION, THE(1975), m; BREAKHEART PASS(1976), m; LAST HARD MEN, THE(1976), m; LOGAN'S RUN(1976), m; OMEN, THE(1976), m; CASSANDRA CROSSING, THE(1977), m; DAMNATION ALLEY(1977), m; HIGH VELOCITY(1977), m; ISLANDS IN THE STREAM(1977), m; MAC ARTHUR(1977), m; TWILIGHT'S LAST GLEAMING(1977, U.S./Ger.), m; BOYS FROM BRAZIL, THE(1978), m; CAPRICORN ONE(1978), m; COMA(1978), m; DAMIEN—OMEN II(1978), m; MAGIC(1978), m; SWARM, THE(1978), m; ALIEN(1979), m; GREAT TRAIN ROBBERY, THE(1979, Brit.), m; PLAYERS(1979), m; STAR TREK: THE MOTION PICTURE(1979), m; CABOBLANCO(1981), m; FINAL CONFLICT, THE(1981), m; INCHON(1981), m; OUTLAND(1981), m; RAGGEDY MAN(1981), m; CHALLENGE, THE(1982), m; FIRST BLOOD(1982), m; NIGHT CROSSING(1982), m; POLTERGEIST(1982), m; SECRET OF NIMH, THE(1982), m; PSYCHO II(1983), m; SALAMANDER, THE(1983, U.S./Ital./Brit.), m; TWILIGHT ZONE–THE MOVIE(1983), m; UNDER FIRE(1983), m
1984
GREMLINS(1984), m; LONELY GUY, THE(1984), m; RUNAWAY(1984), m; SUPERGIRL(1984), m
Joel Goldsmith
LASERBLAST(1978), m; MAN WITH TWO BRAINS, THE(1983), m; TASTE OF SIN, A(1983), m
1984
HOLLYWOOD HOT TUBS(1984), m
Jonathan Goldsmith
GO TELL THE SPARTANS(1978); VISITING HOURS(1982, Can.), m

Ken Goldsmith
OUT OF SINGAPORE(1932), p; LITTLE MEN(1935), p; LEATHERNECKS HAVE LANDED, THE(1936), p; HOOSIER SCHOOLBOY(1937), p; HIS EXCITING NIGHT(1938), p; LITTLE TOUGH GUY(1938), p; SALESLADY(1938), p; SINNERS IN PARADISE(1938), p; STORM, THE(1938), p; BIG TOWN CZAR(1939), p; CALL A MESSENGER(1939), p; HERO FOR A DAY(1939), p; SOCIETY SMUGGLERS(1939), p; UNEXPECTED FATHER(1939), p; ARGENTINE NIGHTS(1940), p; GIVE US WINGS(1940), p; HONEYMOON DEFERRED(1940), p; I CAN'T GIVE YOU ANYTHING BUT LOVE, BABY(1940), p; INVISIBLE MAN RETURNS, THE(1940), p; LA CONGA NIGHTS(1940), p; OH JOHNNY, HOW YOU CAN LOVE!(1940), p; SLIGHTLY TEMPTED(1940), p, w; YOU'RE NOT SO TOUGH(1940), p; DON'T GET PERSONAL(1941), p; HELLO SUCKER(1941), p; HIT THE ROAD(1941), p; MEET THE CHUMP(1941), p; MELODY LANE(1941), p; MOB TOWN(1941), p; MOONLIGHT IN HAWAII(1941), p; SAN ANTONIO ROSE(1941), p; SING ANOTHER CHORUS(1941), p; ALMOST MARRIED(1942), p; JAIL HOUSE BLUES(1942), p; PRIVATE BUCKAROO(1942), p; THERE'S ONE BORN EVERY MINUTE(1942), p; TOUGH AS THEY COME(1942), p; WHAT'S COOKIN'?(1942), p; YOU'RE TELLING ME(1942), p; HOW'S ABOUT IT?(1943), p; IT COMES UP LOVE(1943), p; MR. BIG(1943), p; TOP MAN(1943), w
L. S. Goldsmith
MANHANDLED(1949), w
Lester Goldsmith
PASSAGE, THE(1979, Brit.), p
Lester M. Goldsmith
HAPPY BIRTHDAY, WANDA JUNE(1971), a, p
Martin Goldsmith
DETOUR(1945), w; LONE WOLF IN MEXICO, THE(1947), w; SHAKEDOWN(1950), w; NARROW MARGIN, THE(1952), w; OVERLAND PACIFIC(1954), w
Martin G. Goldsmith
CAST A LONG SHADOW(1959), w
Martin M. Goldsmith
DANGEROUS INTRUDER(1945), w; MISSION OVER KOREA(1953), w; HELL'S ISLAND(1955), w; GUNFIGHT AT DODGE CITY, THE(1959), w
Martin N. Goldsmith
FORT MASSACRE(1958), w
Merwin Goldsmith
PLAYGIRLS AND THE BELLBOY, THE(1962,Ger.); HERCULES IN NEW YORK(1970); SHAMUS(1973); BOARDWALK(1979); SO FINE(1981); SOUP FOR ONE(1982); LOVESICK(1983)
Michael Goldsmith
VOICE WITHIN, THE(1945, Brit.), w
Myron B. Goldsmith
I WAS AN AMERICAN SPY(1951), w
Paul Goldsmith
DAVID HOLZMAN'S DIARY(1968), ph; PLEASE STAND BY(1972), ph; JEREMY(1973), ph; RENALDO AND CLARA(1978), ph; HOMEWORK(1982), ph; WAVELENGTH(1983), ph
Silents
COLLEGE(1927)
Goldstein
M(1933, Ger.)
Abe Goldstein
FAT MAN, THE(1951)
Abe "Korky" Goldstein
TOBY TYLER(1960)
Allison Goldstein
LENNY(1974)
Bob Goldstein
DANCE WITH ME, HENRY(1956), p; SUNSHINE BOYS, THE(1975); HOUSE CALLS(1978); HAMMETT(1982), set d
Charlotte Goldstein
Misc. Talkies
POWER OF LIFE, THE(1938); THREE DAUGHTERS(1949)
Cleo Goldstein
THIS, THAT AND THE OTHER(1970, Brit.)
Frank Goldstein
STOOLIE, THE(1972)
Harold A. Goldstein
ONCE YOU KISS A STRANGER(1969), p
Herb Goldstein
EYES OF A STRANGER(1980); SUPER FUZZ(1981)
Jeff Goldstein
1984
AMERICAN DREAMER(1984), art d
Jennie Goldstein
TWO SISTERS(1938)
Jerry Goldstein
RIVER NIGER, THE(1976), m/l
Lenard Goldstein
FLAME OF ARABY(1951), p
Leonard Goldstein
BLACK BART(1948), p; FEUDIN', FUSSIN' AND A-FIGHTIN'(1948), p; LARCENY(1948), p; RIVER LADY(1948), p; ARCTIC MANHUNT(1949), p; CALAMITY JANE AND SAM BASS(1949), p; MA AND PA KETTLE(1949), p; RED CANYON(1949), p; YES SIR, THAT'S MY BABY(1949), p; COMMANCHE TERRITORY(1950), p; DESERT HAWK, THE(1950), p; DOUBLE CROSSBONES(1950), p; I WAS A SHOPLIFTER(1950), p; MA AND PA KETTLE GO TO TOWN(1950), p; ONE WAY STREET(1950), p; SADDLE TRAMP(1950), p; SLEEPING CITY, THE(1950), p; CAVE OF OUTLAWS(1951), p; FINDERS KEEPERS(1951), p; FRANCIS GOES TO THE RACES(1951), p; HOLLYWOOD STORY(1951), p; KATIE DID IT(1951), p; LADY FROM TEXAS, THE(1951), p; MA AND PA KETTLE BACK ON THE FARM(1951), p; PRINCE WHO WAS A THIEF, THE(1951), p; REUNION IN RENO(1951), p; TOMAHAWK(1951), p; UP FRONT(1951), p; YOU NEVER CAN TELL(1951), p; BACK AT THE FRONT(1952), p; BATTLE AT APACHE PASS(1952), p; DUEL AT SILVER CREEK, THE(1952), p; FLESH AND FURY(1952), p; FRANCIS GOES TO WEST POINT(1952), p; IT GROWS ON TREES(1952), p; JUST ACROSS THE STREET(1952), p; MA AND PA KETTLE AT THE FAIR(1952), p; MEET DANNY WILSON(1952), p; SALLY AND SAINT ANNE(1952), p; SCARLET ANGEL(1952), p; SON OF ALI BABA(1952), p; STEEL TOWN(1952), p; TREASURE OF LOST CANYON, THE(1952), p; UNTAMED FRONTIER(1952), p; CITY OF BAD MEN(1953), p; FRANCIS COVERS

THE BIG TOWN(1953), p; GOLDEN BLADE, THE(1953), p; IT HAPPENS EVERY THURSDAY(1953), p; KID FROM LEFT FIELD, THE(1953), p; MA AND PA KETTLE ON VACATION(1953), p; MR. SCOUTMASTER(1953), p; REDHEAD FROM WYOMING, THE(1953), p; TAKE ME TO TOWN(1953), p; VICKI(1953), p; GAMBLER FROM NATCHEZ, THE(1954), p; RAID(1954), p; ROCKET MAN, THE(1954), p; SIEGE AT RED RIVER, THE(1954), p; THREE YOUNG TEXANS(1954), p; BLACK TUESDAY(1955), p; LIFE IN THE BALANCE, A(1955), p; MA AND PA KETTLE AT WAIKIKI(1955), p; ROBBER'S ROOST(1955), p; DAY OF THE NIGHTMARE(1965), w

Leslie Goldstein
BELL JAR, THE(1979)

Louis Goldstein
MOTHERS OF TODAY(1939)

Marco Goldstein
LEPKE(1975, U.S./Israel)

Marek Goldstein
LONG IS THE ROAD(1948, Ger.), d

Michael Goldstein
GREEN FIELDS(1937); SINGING BLACKSMITH(1938)

Neal Goldstein
P.O.W., THE(1973), m

Ralph E. Goldstein
THEY ALL COME OUT(1939), ed

Robert Goldstein
BLACK TUESDAY(1955), p; ROBBER'S ROOST(1955), p; STRANGER ON HORSEBACK(1955), p; HISTORY OF THE WORLD, PART 1(1981), set d; SECOND THOUGHTS(1983), set d
Silents
BIRTH OF A NATION, THE(1915), cos

Ruby Goldstein
JOE LOUIS STORY, THE(1953)

William Goldstein
ABOMINABLE DR. PHIBES, THE(1971, Brit.), w; DOCTOR PHIBES RISES AGAIN(1972, Brit.), w; AMAZING DOBERMANS, THE(1976), w; BINGO LONG TRAVELING ALL-STARS AND MOTOR KINGS, THE(1976), m; NORMAN...IS THAT YOU?(1976), m; FORCE: FIVE(1981), m; FORCED VENGEANCE(1982), m
1984
UP THE CREEK(1984), m

Zina Goldstein
Misc. Talkies
PEOPLE THAT SHALL NOT DIE, A(1939)
Misc. Silents
HARSH FATHER, THE(1911, USSR)

William Goldstien
EYE FOR AN EYE, AN(1981), m

Phil Goldston
1984
ACT, THE(1984), m

Robert Goldston
UNCLE, THE(1966, Brit.), p; SEPARATE PEACE, A(1972), p; BELL JAR, THE(1979), p

Robert A. Goldston
GEORGY GIRL(1966, Brit.), p; BOFORS GUN, THE(1968, Brit.), p

Duke Goldstone
ON THE GREAT WHITE TRAIL(1938), ed; WOLVES OF THE SEA(1938), ed; DESTINATION MOON(1950), ed; GREAT RUPERT, THE(1950), ed

James Goldstone
JIGSAW(1968), d; MAN CALLED GANNON, A(1969), d; WINNING(1969), d; BROTHER JOHN(1971), d; GANG THAT COULDN'T SHOOT STRAIGHT, THE(1971), d; RED SKY AT MORNING(1971), d; THEY ONLY KILL THEIR MASTERS(1972), d; SWASHBUCKLER(1976), d; ROLLERCOASTER(1977), d; WHEN TIME RAN OUT(1980), d
Misc. Talkies
WHEN TIME RAN OUT(1980), d

John Goldstone
THREE SISTERS(1974, Brit.), p; LAST DAYS OF MAN ON EARTH, THE(1975, Brit.), p; ROCKY HORROR PICTURE SHOW, THE(1975, Brit.), p; MONTY PYTHON'S LIFE OF BRIAN(1979, Brit.), p; HOUND OF THE BASKERVILLES, THE(1980, Brit.), p; SHOCK TREATMENT(1981), p; MONTY PYTHON'S THE MEANING OF LIFE(1983, Brit.), p

Nat C. Goldstone
CASBAH(1948), p

Phil Goldstone
ALIAS THE BAD MAN(1931), p; FIGHTING THRU(1931), p; MORALS FOR WOMEN(1931), p; MURDER AT MIDNIGHT(1931), p; RANGE LAW(1931), p; TWO GUN MAN, THE(1931), p; HELL FIRE AUSTIN(1932), p; POCATELLO KID(1932), p; SUNSET TRAIL(1932), p; TEXAS GUN FIGHTER(1932), p; WHISTLIN' DAN(1932), p; SIN OF NORA MORAN(1933), d; SING SINNER, SING(1933), p; VAMPIRE BAT, THE(1933), p; DAMAGED GOODS(1937), p; SKY BANDITS, THE(1940), p
Silents
HER MAN(1924), p
Misc. Silents
MONTANA BILL(1921), d

Philip Goldstone
WORLD GONE MAD, THE(1933), p; AGE OF INDISCRETION(1935), p; O'SHAUGHNESSY'S BOY(1935), p; LAST OF THE PAGANS(1936), p

Richard Goldstone
HARMON OF MICHIGAN(1941), w; SET-UP, THE(1949), p; DIAL 1119(1950), p; OUTRIDERS, THE(1950), p; YELLOW CAB MAN, THE(1950), p; INSIDE STRAIGHT(1951), p; TALL TARGET, THE(1951), p; DEVIL MAKES THREE, THE(1952), p; TALK ABOUT A STRANGER(1952), p; TERROR ON A TRAIN(1953), p; TOBOR THE GREAT(1954), p, w; AFFAIR IN HAVANA(1957), p; EAST OF KILIMANJARO(1962, Brit./Ital.), p, w; NO MAN IS AN ISLAND(1962), p, d&w; SERGEANT, THE(1968), p

Lawrence Goldstraw
Misc. Talkies
BIM(1976)

J.H. Goldsworthy
Misc. Silents
YELLOW STREAK, A(1915); HER DEBT OF HONOR(1916)

John Goldsworthy
HANGOVER SQUARE(1945); DARK CORNER, THE(1946); NIGHT AND DAY(1946); LOVE FROM A STRANGER(1947); MOSS ROSE(1947); PARADINE CASE, THE(1947); EMPEROR WALTZ, THE(1948); LUCK OF THE IRISH(1948); THIRTEEN LEAD SOLDIERS(1948); EVERYBODY DOES IT(1949); WOMAN'S SECRET, A(1949); DESERT FOX, THE(1951); PRISONER OF ZENDA, THE(1952)
Silents
AMAZING LOVERS(1921); NOTORIETY(1922)
Misc. Silents
WIFE NUMBER TWO(1917); CAREER OF KATHERINE BUSH, THE(1919); MARRIAGE MORALS(1923)

John W. Goldsworthy
Silents
RED WIDOW, THE(1916)

Anne Goldthwaite
HIGHER AND HIGHER(1943); DEVOTION(1946)

M. Goldvani
Misc. Silents
POWER OF EVIL(1929, USSR/Armenian), d

Arthur Goldweit
STRIPES(1981), ch

1936 Goldwyn Girls
STRIKE ME PINK(1936)

Sam Goldwyn
STRIKE ME PINK(1936), P; REAL GLORY, THE(1939), p; SECRET LIFE OF WALTER MITTY, THE(1947), p; GUYS AND DOLLS(1955), p

Samuel Goldwyn
BULLDOG DRUMMOND(1929), p; CONDEMNED(1929), p; DEVIL TO PAY, THE(1930), p; RAFFLES(1930), p; WHOOPEE(1930), p; ARROWSMITH(1931), p; ONE HEAVENLY NIGHT(1931), p; PALMY DAYS(1931), p; STREET SCENE(1931), p; TONIGHT OR NEVER(1931), p; UNHOLY GARDEN, THE(1931), p; CYNARA(1932), p; GREEKS HAD A WORD FOR THEM(1932), p; KID FROM SPAIN, THE(1932), p; MASQUERADER, THE(1933), p; ROMAN SCANDALS(1933), p; KID MILLIONS(1934), p; NANA(1934), p; WE LIVE AGAIN(1934), p; BARBARY COAST(1935), p; DARK ANGEL, THE(1935), p; SPLENDOR(1935), p; WEDDING NIGHT, THE(1935), p; BELOVED ENEMY(1936), p; COME AND GET IT(1936), p; DODSWORTH(1936), p; THESE THREE(1936), p; DEAD END(1937), p; HURRICANE, THE(1937), p; STELLA DALLAS(1937), p; WOMAN CHASES MAN(1937), p; ADVENTURES OF MARCO POLO, THE(1938), p; COWBOY AND THE LADY, THE(1938), p; GOLDWYN FOLLIES, THE(1938), p; RAFFLES(1939), p; THEY SHALL HAVE MUSIC(1939), p; WUTHERING HEIGHTS(1939), p; WESTERNER, THE(1940), p; BALL OF FIRE(1941), p; PRIDE OF THE YANKEES, THE(1942), p; THEY GOT ME COVERED(1943), p; PRINCESS AND THE PIRATE, THE(1944), p; UP IN ARMS(1944), p; WONDER MAN(1945), p; BEST YEARS OF OUR LIVES, THE(1946), p; KID FROM BROOKLYN, THE(1946), p; BISHOP'S WIFE, THE(1947), p; ENCHANTMENT(1948), p; SONG IS BORN, A(1948), p; MY FOOLISH HEART(1949), p; ROSEANNA McCOY(1949), p; EDGE OF DOOM(1950), p; FIGHTING PIMPERNEL, THE(1950, Brit.), p; OUR VERY OWN(1950), p; I WANT YOU(1951), p; HANS CHRISTIAN ANDERSEN(1952), p; PORGY AND BESS(1959), p
Silents
CYTHEREA(1924), p; IN HOLLYWOOD WITH POTASH AND PERLMUTTER(1924), p; GREED(1925), p; AWAKENING, THE(1928), p

Samuel Goldwyn, Jr.
MAN WITH THE GUN(1955), p; SHARKFIGHTERS, THE(1956), p; PROUD REBEL, THE(1958), p; ADVENTURES OF HUCKLEBERRY FINN, THE(1960), p; YOUNG LOVERS, THE(1964), p&d; COTTON COMES TO HARLEM(1970), p; COME BACK CHARLESTON BLUE(1972), p; GOLDEN SEAL, THE(1983), p

A. Golebiowska
PASSENGER, THE(1970, Pol.)

Hildegarde Golez
JULIET OF THE SPIRITS(1965, Fr./Ital./W.Ger.)

Richard Golfier
SMALL CHANGE(1976, Fr.)

Susi Golgi
WARRIOR EMPRESS, THE(1961, Ital./Fr.)

David Golia
1984
HADLEY'S REBELLION(1984), ph

Rene Goliard
YOU ONLY LIVE ONCE(1969, Fr.)

John Golightly
HEROES OF TELEMARK, THE(1965, Brit.); ATTACK ON THE IRON COAST(1968, U.S./Brit.)
1984
1984(1984, Brit.)

Max Golightly
Misc. Talkies
KNOCKING AT HEAVEN'S DOOR(1980)

E. Golinchik
CITY OF YOUTH(1938, USSR)

Andre Golino
BATTLE OF LOVE'S RETURN, THE(1971), m

Valeria Golino
1984
JOKE OF DESTINY LYING IN WAIT AROUND THE CORNER LIKE A STREET-BANDIT, A(1984, Ital.)

Francesco Golisano
UNDER THE SUN OF ROME(1949, Ital.); MIRACLE IN MILAN(1951, Ital.)

Akexander Golitzen
LIST OF ADRIAN MESSENGER, THE(1963), art d

Alexander Golitzen
MAN'S FAVORITE SPORT(?)**1/2 (1964), art d; THAT UNCERTAIN FEELING(1941), art d; THOROUGHLY MODERN MILLIE(1967), art d; PAD, THE(AND HOW TO USE IT)* (1966, Brit.), art d; HURRICANE, THE(1937), art d; TRADE WINDS(1938), art d; ETERNALLY YOURS(1939), art d; FOREIGN CORRESPONDENT(1940), art d; HOUSE ACROSS THE BAY, THE(1940), art d; SLIGHTLY HONORABLE(1940), art d; SUNDOWN(1941), art d; ARABIAN NIGHTS(1942), prod d; EAGLE SQUADRON(1942), art d; GUNG HO!(1943), art d; PHANTOM OF THE OPERA(1943), art d; WE'VE NEVER BEEN LICKED(1943), art d; COBRA WOMAN(1944), art d; HI BEAUTIFUL(1944), art d; SAN DIEGO, I LOVE YOU(1944), art

d; SALOME, WHERE SHE DANCED(1945), p, art d; SCARLET STREET(1945), art d; MAGNIFICENT DOLL(1946), art d; NIGHT IN PARADISE, A(1946), art d; LOST MOMENT, THE(1947), art d; SMASH-UP, THE STORY OF A WOMAN(1947), art d; LETTER FROM AN UNKNOWN WOMAN(1948), art d; SAXON CHARM, THE(1948), art d; TAP ROOTS(1948), prod d; YOU GOTTA STAY HAPPY(1948), prod d; LADY GAMBLES, THE(1949), art d; SWORD IN THE DESERT(1949), art d; DOUBLE CROSSBONES(1950), art d; SPY HUNT(1950), art d; GOLDEN HORDE, THE(1951), art d; SMUGGLER'S ISLAND(1951), art d; UP FRONT(1951), art d; YOU NEVER CAN TELL(1951), art d; AGAINST ALL FLAGS(1952), art d; DUEL AT SILVER CREEK, THE(1952), art d; IT GROWS ON TREES(1952), art d; TREASURE OF LOST CANYON, THE(1952), art d; WORLD IN HIS ARMS, THE(1952), art d; ALL I DESIRE(1953), art d; DESERT LEGION(1953), art d; GIRLS IN THE NIGHT(1953), art d; GREAT SIOUX UPRISING, THE(1953), art d; GUNSMOKE(1953), art d; LAW AND ORDER(1953), art d; LONE HAND, THE(1953), art d; MAN FROM THE ALAMO, THE(1953), art d; MISSISSIPPI GAMBLER, THE(1953), art d; SEMINOLE(1953), art d; TAKE ME TO TOWN(1953), art d; THUNDER BAY(1953), art d; VEILS OF BAGDAD, THE(1953), art d; WAR ARROW(1953), art d; FRANCIS JOINS THE WACS(1954), art d; RICOCHET ROMANCE(1954), art d; SIGN OF THE PAGAN(1954), art d; SO THIS IS PARIS(1954), art d; ALL THAT HEAVEN ALLOWS(1955), art d; CAPTAIN LIGHTFOOT(1955), art d; CHIEF CRAZY HORSE(1955), art d; FAR COUNTRY, THE(1955), art d; FEMALE ON THE BEACH(1955), art d; FOXFIRE(1955), art d; FRANCIS IN THE NAVY(1955), art d; KISS OF FIRE(1955), art d; LADY GODIVA(1955), art d; LOOTERS, THE(1955), art d; MAN FROM BITTER RIDGE, THE(1955), art d; MAN WITHOUT A STAR(1955), art d; ONE DESIRE(1955), art d; PRIVATE WAR OF MAJOR BENSON, THE(1955), art d; PURPLE MASK, THE(1955), art d; REVENGE OF THE CREATURE(1955), art d; RUNNING WILD(1955), art d; SECOND GREATEST SEX, THE(1955), art d; SHRIKE, THE(1955), art d; SIX BRIDGES TO CROSS(1955), art d; SMOKE SIGNAL(1955), art d; SPOILERS, THE(1955), art d; SQUARE JUNGLE, THE(1955), art d; TARANTULA(1955), art d; THIS ISLAND EARTH(1955), art d; TO HELL AND BACK(1955), art d; CONGO CROSSING(1956), art d; DAY OF FURY, A(1956), art d; EVERYTHING BUT THE TRUTH(1956), art d; FOUR GIRLS IN TOWN(1956), art d; FRANCIS IN THE HAUNTED HOUSE(1956), art d; I'VE LIVED BEFORE(1956), art d; KETTLES IN THE OZARKS, THE(1956), art d; MOLE PEOPLE, THE(1956), art d; NEVER SAY GOODBYE(1956), art d; PILLARS OF THE SKY(1956), art d; PRICE OF FEAR, THE(1956), art d; RAW EDGE(1956), art d; RAWHIDE YEARS, THE(1956), art d; RED SUNDOWN(1956), art d; ROCK, PRETTY BABY(1956), art d; SHOWDOWN AT ABILENE(1956), art d; STAR IN THE DUST(1956), art d; THERE'S ALWAYS TOMORROW(1956), art d; TOY TIGER(1956), art d; UNGUARDED MOMENT, THE(1956), art d; WALK THE PROUD LAND(1956), art d; WORLD IN MY CORNER(1956), art d; WRITTEN ON THE WIND(1956), art d; BATTLE HYMN(1957), art d; DEADLY MANTIS, THE(1957), art d; GIRL IN THE KREMLIN, THE(1957), art d; GREAT MAN, THE(1957), art d; GUN FOR A COWARD(1957), art d; INCREDIBLE SHRINKING MAN, THE(1957), art d; INTERLUDE(1957), art d; ISTANBUL(1957), art d; JOE BUTTERFLY(1957), art d; JOE DAKOTA(1957), art d; KELLY AND ME(1957), art d; KETTLES ON OLD MACDONALD'S FARM, THE(1957), art d; LAND UNKNOWN, THE(1957), art d; MAN AFRAID(1957), art d; MAN IN THE SHADOW(1957), art d; MAN OF A THOUSAND FACES(1957), art d; MIDNIGHT STORY, THE(1957), art d; MISTER CORY(1957), art d; MONOLITH MONSTERS, THE(1957), art d; MY MAN GODFREY(1957), art d; NIGHT PASSAGE(1957), art d; NIGHT RUNNER, THE(1957), art d; QUANTEZ(1957), art d; SLAUGHTER ON TENTH AVENUE(1957), art d; SLIM CARTER(1957), art d; TARNISHED ANGELS, THE(1957), art d; TATTERED DRESS, THE(1957), art d; DAY OF THE BAD MAN(1958), art d; FEMALE ANIMAL, THE(1958), art d; KATHY O'(1958), art d; LADY TAKES A FLYER, THE(1958), art d; LAST OF THE FAST GUNS, THE(1958), art d; LIVE FAST, DIE YOUNG(1958), art d; MONEY, WOMEN AND GUNS(1958), art d; ONCE UPON A HORSE(1958), art d; PERFECT FURLOUGH, THE(1958), art d; RAW WIND IN EDEN(1958), art d; RESTLESS YEARS, THE(1958), art d; RIDE A CROOKED TRAIL(1958), art d; SAGA OF HEMP BROWN, THE(1958), art d; STEP DOWN TO TERROR(1958), art d; SUMMER LOVE(1958), art d; THING THAT COULDN'T DIE, THE(1958), art d; THIS HAPPY FEELING(1958), art d; TIME TO LOVE AND A TIME TO DIE, A(1958), art d; TOUCH OF EVIL(1958), art d; TWILIGHT FOR THE GODS(1958), art d; VOICE IN THE MIRROR(1958), art d; WILD HERITAGE(1958), art d; CURSE OF THE UNDEAD(1959), art d; IMITATION OF LIFE(1959), art d; NEVER STEAL ANYTHING SMALL(1959), art d; NO NAME ON THE BULLET(1959), art d; OPERATION PETTICOAT(1959), art d; PILLOW TALK(1959), art d; STRANGER IN MY ARMS(1959), art d; THIS EARTH IS MINE(1959), art d; WILD AND THE INNOCENT, THE(1959), art d; GREAT IMPOSTOR, THE(1960), art d; LEECH WOMAN, THE(1960), art d; MIDNIGHT LACE(1960), art d; SEVEN WAYS FROM SUNDOWN(1960), art d; SPARTACUS(1960), prod d; BACK STREET(1961), art d; FLOWER DRUM SONG(1961), art d; LAST SUNSET, THE(1961), art d; LOVER COME BACK(1961), art d; POSSE FROM HELL(1961), art d; PRIVATE LIVES OF ADAM AND EVE, THE(1961), art d; TAMMY, TELL ME TRUE(1961), art d; CAPE FEAR(1962), art d; FORTY POUNDS OF TROUBLE(1962), art d; IF A MAN ANSWERS(1962), art d; LONELY ARE THE BRAVE(1962), art d; OUTSIDER, THE(1962), art d; SIX BLACK HORSES(1962), art d; SPIRAL ROAD, THE(1962), art d; THAT TOUCH OF MINK(1962), art d; TO KILL A MOCKINGBIRD(1962), art d; CAPTAIN NEWMAN, M.D.(1963), art d; FOR LOVE OR MONEY(1963), art d; GATHERING OF EAGLES, A(1963), art d; SHOWDOWN(1963), art d; TAMMY AND THE DOCTOR(1963), art d; THRILL OF IT ALL, THE(1963), art d; UGLY AMERICAN, THE(1963), art d; BEDTIME STORY(1964), art d; FATHER GOOSE(1964), art d; I'D RATHER BE RICH(1964), art d; ISLAND OF THE BLUE DOLPHINS(1964), art d; KITTEN WITH A WHIP(1964), art d; LIVELY SET, THE(1964), art d; MC HALE'S NAVY(1964), art d; NIGHT WALKER, THE(1964), art d; SEND ME NO FLOWERS(1964), art d; TAGGART(1964), art d; WILD AND WONDERFUL(1964), art d; FLUFFY(1965), art d; I SAW WHAT YOU DID(1965), art d; LOVE AND KISSES(1965), art d; MC HALE'S NAVY JOINS THE AIR FORCE(1965), art d; MIRAGE(1965), art d; SHENANDOAH(1965), art d; STRANGE BEDFELLOWS(1965), art d; SWORD OF ALI BABA, THE(1965), art d; THAT FUNNY FEELING(1965), art d; VERY SPECIAL FAVOR, A(1965), art d; WAR LORD, THE(1965), art d; WILD SEED(1965), art d; APPALOOSA, THE(1966), art d; BEAU GESTE(1966), art d; GAMBIT(1966), art d; GHOST AND MR. CHICKEN, THE(1966), art d; GUNPOINT(1966), art d; INCIDENT AT PHANTOM HILL(1966), art d; LET'S KILL UNCLE(1966), art d; MADAME X(1966), art d; MOMENT TO MOMENT(1966), art d; MUNSTER, GO HOME(1966), art d; PLAINSMAN, THE(1966), art d; RARE BREED, THE(1966), art d; TEXAS ACROSS THE RIVER(1966), art d; TOBRUK(1966), art d; COUNTERPOINT(1967), art d; GAMES(1967), art d; GUNFIGHT IN ABILENE(1967), art d; KING'S PIRATE(1967), art d; PERILS OF PAULINE, THE(1967), art d; RELUCTANT ASTRONAUT, THE(1967), art d; RIDE TO HANGMAN'S TREE, THE(1967), art d; ROSIE!(1967), art d; ROUGH NIGHT IN JERICHO(1967), art d; YOUNG WARRIORS, THE(1967), art d; BALLAD OF JOSIE(1968), art d; COOGAN'S BLUFF(1968), art d; DID YOU HEAR THE ONE ABOUT

THE TRAVELING SALESLADY?(1968), art d; DON'T JUST STAND THERE(1968), art d; HELL WITH HEROES, THE(1968), art d; HELLFIGHTERS(1968), art d; IN ENEMY COUNTRY(1968), art d; JOURNEY TO SHILOH(1968), art d; LOVELY WAY TO DIE, A(1968), art d; MADIGAN(1968), art d; NOBODY'S PERFECT(1968), art d; PINK JUNGLE, THE(1968), art d; P.J.(1968), art d; SECRET WAR OF HARRY FRIGG, THE(1968), art d; SHAKIEST GUN IN THE WEST, THE(1968), art d; WHAT'S SO BAD ABOUT FEELING GOOD?(1968), art d; CHANGE OF HABIT(1969), art d; COLOSSUS: THE FORBIN PROJECT(1969), art d; DEATH OF A GUNFIGHTER(1969), art d; EYE OF THE CAT(1969), art d; HOUSE OF CARDS(1969), art d; LOST MAN, THE(1969), art d; LOVE GOD?, THE(1969), art d; MAN CALLED GANNON, A(1969), art d; SWEET CHARITY(1969), art d; TELL THEM WILLIE BOY IS HERE(1969), art d; WINNING(1969), art d; AIRPORT(1970), art d; COCKEYED COWBOYS OF CALICO COUNTY, THE(1970), art d; COMPANY OF KILLERS(1970), art d; I LOVE MY WIFE(1970), art d; PUFNSTUF(1970), art d; STORY OF A WOMAN(1970, U.S./Ital.), art d; HOW TO FRAME A FIGG(1971), art d; ONE MORE TRAIN TO ROB(1971), art d; PLAY MISTY FOR ME(1971), art d; RAID ON ROMMEL(1971), art d; RED SKY AT MORNING(1971), art d; SHOOT OUT(1971), art d; GREAT NORTHFIELD, MINNESOTA RAID, THE(1972), art d; JOE KIDD(1972), art d; SLAUGHTERHOUSE-FIVE(1972), art d; BREEZY(1973), art d; SHOWDOWN(1973), art d; THAT MAN BOLT(1973), art d; EARTHQUAKE(1974), prod d

Art Golitzen
FLOOD TIDE(1958), art d

George Golitzen
PARENT TRAP, THE(1961), p

Howard Golitzen
CLIMAX, THE(1944), art d

Gillian Goll
LOOKING UP(1977)

Linda Golla
ON THE RIGHT TRACK(1981)

Campbell Gollan
Misc. Silents
DUBARRY(1915)

Jo Golland
TRAP, THE(1967, Can./Brit.)

Joseph Golland
BEAR ISLAND(1980, Brit.-Can.)

Stuart Golland
LOOKS AND SMILES(1982, Brit.)

Jerome T. Gollard
JINX MONEY(1948), w

Jerome Todd Gollard
INNER SANCTUM(1948), w

Joseph Gollard
VISITOR, THE(1973, Can.)

Beatrice Gollenette
WINE, WOMEN, AND SONG(1934), ch

Alexander Golling
ODESSA FILE, THE(1974, Brit./Ger.)

Claudia Golling
AMERICAN SUCCESS COMPANY, THE(1980)

Franklin Gollings
CONNECTING ROOMS(1971, Brit.), d&w

Joseph Gollomb
MURDER AT THE VANITIES(1934), w

Natasa Gollova
EMPEROR AND THE GOLEM, THE(1955, Czech.)

Dr. Ernest Golm
MISSION TO MOSCOW(1943)

Ernest Golm
PHANTOM OF THE OPERA(1943); RHAPSODY IN BLUE(1945); NIGHT AND DAY(1946)

Lisa Golm
WITHOUT RESERVATIONS(1946); ESCAPE(1940); SO ENDS OUR NIGHT(1941); UNDERGROUND(1941); JOURNEY FOR MARGARET(1942); ABOVE SUSPICION(1943); BACKGROUND TO DANGER(1943); CALLING DR. DEATH(1943); MADAME CURIE(1943); MISSION TO MOSCOW(1943); THEY CAME TO BLOW UP AMERICA(1943); NIGHT AND DAY(1946); SHADOW OF A WOMAN(1946); CRY WOLF(1947); HIGH WALL, THE(1947); POSSESSED(1947); LETTER FROM AN UNKNOWN WOMAN(1948); ANNA LUCASTA(1949); DOCTOR AND THE GIRL, THE(1949); EAST SIDE, WEST SIDE(1949); GREAT SINNER, THE(1949); HOODLUM, THE(1951); PAYMENT ON DEMAND(1951); PLACE IN THE SUN, A(1951); INVITATION(1952); MY PAL GUS(1952); RIDE THE HIGH IRON(1956); MONKEY ON MY BACK(1957)

Liza Golm
COME BACK LITTLE SHEBA(1952)

Lia Golmar
OUTCRY(1949, Ital.)

Sheldon Golomb
RUSSIANS ARE COMING, THE RUSSIANS ARE COMING, THE(1966)

Arlene Golonka
LOVE WITH THE PROPER STRANGER(1963); DIARY OF A BACHELOR(1964); HARVEY MIDDLEMAN, FIREMAN(1965); PENELOPE(1966); BUSYBODY, THE(1967); WELCOME TO HARD TIMES(1967); HANG'EM HIGH(1968); AIRPORT '77(1977); IN-LAWS, THE(1979); LAST MARRIED COUPLE IN AMERICA, THE(1980); SEPARATE WAYS(1981); MY TUTOR(1983)

Len Golos
MAN MADE MONSTER(1941), w

N. Golosov
Misc. Silents
TSAR NIKOLAI II(1917, USSR)

N. Golovanov
BORIS GODUNOV(1959, USSR), w

S. Golovin
Misc. Silents
MISS PEASANT(1916, USSR)

Kira Golovko
WAR AND PEACE(1968, USSR)

V. Golovnenko
ITALIANO BRAVA GENTE(1965, Ital./USSR)
A. Golovnia
ADMIRAL NAKHIMOV(1948, USSR), ph
A. N. Golovnia
Silents
STORM OVER ASIA(1929, USSR), ph
A. Golovnya
GENERAL SUVOROV(1941, USSR), ph
Anatoli Golovnya
DESERTER(1934, USSR), ph
Kevin Golsby
MARCO POLO JUNIOR(1973, Aus.)
George Golsey
RECKLESS(1935), ph
Benny Golson
WHERE IT'S AT(1969), m
William Golstein
STOOLIE, THE(1972), m
Anna Goltz
M(1933, Ger.); TESTAMENT OF DR. MABUSE, THE(1943, Ger.)
Dennis Golub
LINE, THE(1982), ed
Mortie Golub
HIGH(1968, Can.)
Gregory Golubeff
WOMAN ACCUSED(1933); BOLERO(1934); MISSION TO MOSCOW(1943); MASK OF DIMITRIOS, THE(1944); NORTHWEST OUTPOST(1947); GIRL FROM JONES BEACH, THE(1949)
Larissa Golubkina
BALLAD OF A HUSSAR(1963, USSR)
Christine Goluding
MARVIN AND TIGE(1983), cos
Gregory Goluhoff
RHAPSODY IN BLUE(1945)
Gil Goluskin
GALLANT ONE, THE(1964, U.S./Peru)
Ray Goman
HAROLD AND MAUDE(1971)
Ray K. Goman
NIGHTMARE IN BLOOD(1978); ESCAPE FROM ALCATRAZ(1979)
Mikhail Gomarov
Misc. Silents
STRIKE(1925, USSR)
Ella Gombaszogi
MISS PRESIDENT(1935, Hung.)
Cristina Gombau
BLOOD WEDDING(1981, Sp.)
Anita Gombault
SECRET MISSION(1944, Brit.)
Ch. Gombault
CONFLICT(1939, Fr.), w
Minna Gombel
COMET OVER BROADWAY(1938); HERE COMES THE GROOM(1951)
Mina Gombell
WHITE COCKATOO(1935)
Minna Gombell
GREAT POWER, THE(1929); BAD GIRL(1931); GOOD SPORT(1931); SOB SISTER(1931); AFTER TOMORROW(1932); BACHELOR'S AFFAIRS(1932); CARELESS LADY(1932); DANCE TEAM(1932); FIRST YEAR, THE(1932); RAINBOW TRAIL(1932); STEPPING SISTERS(1932); WILD GIRL(1932); BIG BRAIN, THE(1933); HELLO SISTER!(1933); HOOPLA(1933); PLEASURE CRUISE(1933); WAY TO LOVE, THE(1933); WHAT PRICE INNOCENCE?(1933); WILD BOYS OF THE ROAD(1933); BABBITT(1934); CHEATING CHEATERS(1934); CROSS COUNTRY CRUISE(1934); HELL CAT, THE(1934); KEEP 'EM ROLLING(1934); LEMON DROP KID, THE(1934); MARRYING WIDOWS(1934); MERRY WIDOW, THE(1934); NO MORE WOMEN(1934); REGISTERED NURSE(1934); STRICTLY DYNAMITE(1934); THIN MAN, THE(1934); MISS PACIFIC FLEET(1935); TWO SINNERS(1935); WOMEN MUST DRESS(1935); BANJO ON MY KNEE(1936); CHAMPAGNE CHARLIE(1936); MAKE WAY FOR TOMORROW(1937); SLAVE SHIP(1937); WIFE, DOCTOR AND NURSE(1937); BLOCKHEADS(1938); GREAT WALTZ, THE(1938); GOING PLACES(1939); HUNCHBACK OF NOTRE DAME, THE(1939); SECOND FIDDLE(1939); STOP, LOOK, AND LOVE(1939); BOOM TOWN(1940); DOOMED CARAVAN(1941); HIGH SIERRA(1941); THIEVES FALL OUT(1941); MEXICAN SPITFIRE SEES A GHOST(1942); SALUTE FOR THREE(1943); CHIP OFF THE OLD BLOCK(1944); DESTINY(1944); JOHNNY DOESN'T LIVE HERE ANY MORE(1944); NIGHT CLUB GIRL(1944); MAN ALIVE(1945); PENTHOUSE RHYTHM(1945); SUNBONNET SUE(1945); SWINGIN' ON A RAINBOW(1945); TOWN WENT WILD, THE(1945); BEST YEARS OF OUR LIVES, THE(1946); PERILOUS HOLIDAY(1946); WYOMING(1947); MR. RECKLESS(1948); RETURN OF THE BADMEN(1948); SNAKE PIT, THE(1948); LAST BANDIT, THE(1949); PAGAN LOVE SONG(1950); I'LL SEE YOU IN MY DREAMS(1951)
Misc. Talkies
CADETS ON PARADE(1942)
Sy Gomberg
SUMMER STOCK(1950), w; TOAST OF NEW ORLEANS, THE(1950), w; WHEN WILLIE COMES MARCHING HOME(1950), w; BECAUSE YOU'RE MINE(1952), w; BLOODHOUNDS OF BROADWAY(1952), w; JOE BUTTERFLY(1957), w; KATHY O'(1958), p, w; WILD AND THE INNOCENT, THE(1959), p, w; THREE WARRIORS(1977), p, w
Gombo
SON OF MONGOLIA(1936, USSR)
Elias Gomboa
BANDIT QUEEN(1950)
Giorgio Gomelsky
LA COLLECTIONNEUSE(1971, Fr.), m
Joseph Gomersall
HOLIDAYS WITH PAY(1948, Brit.), art d

Alfredo Dias Gomes
GIVEN WORD, THE(1964, Braz.), w
Andre Gomes
1984
THREE CROWNS OF THE SAILOR(1984, Fr.)
Augie Gomes
ROLLIN' PLAINS(1938)
Eliezer Gomes
TRAIN ROBBERY CONFIDENTIAL(1965, Braz.)
Panchito Gomes
Misc. Talkies
PACO(1976)
Al Gomez
JOYSTICKS(1983), w
1984
CLOAK AND DAGGER(1984)
Alfonso Patino Gomez
CRIMINAL LIFE OF ARCHIBALDO DE LA CRUZ, THE(1962, Mex.), p
Angella Gomez
LOVES OF CARMEN, THE(1948)
Angie Gomez
KANSAS CYCLONE(1941)
Anna Maria Gomez
SEVEN CITIES OF GOLD(1955)
Antonio Gomez
BULLFIGHTER AND THE LADY(1951)
Arthur Gomez
PLAY UP THE BAND(1935, Brit.); MELODY CLUB(1949, Brit.); SILK NOOSE, THE(1950, Brit.); UP FOR THE CUP(1950, Brit.); MEN OF THE SEA(1951, Brit.); TALE OF FIVE WOMEN, A(1951, Brit.); OLD MOTHER RILEY(1952, Brit.); CAPTAIN'S PARADISE, THE(1953, Brit.); 23 PACES TO BAKER STREET(1956); STRANGER'S MEETING(1957, Brit.); LONG KNIFE, THE(1958, Brit.); DESPERATE MAN, THE(1959, Brit.); END OF THE LINE, THE(1959, Brit.)
Augie Gomez
FOURTH HORSEMAN, THE(1933); SINGING BUCKAROO, THE(1937); BLUE MONTANA SKIES(1939); ROUGH RIDERS' ROUNDUP(1939); SAGEBRUSH FAMILY TRAILS WEST, THE(1940); LONE RIDER IN GHOST TOWN, THE(1941); BILLY THE KID TRAPPED(1942); HAUNTED RANCH, THE(1943); GALLANT LEGION, THE(1948); OLD LOS ANGELES(1948)
Eddie Gomez
CRISIS(1950); SECOND CHANCE(1953); OCEAN'S ELEVEN(1960); MY BODYGUARD(1980)
Felipa Gomez
KEY LARGO(1948)
Fernando Fernan Gomez
SPIRIT OF THE BEEHIVE, THE(1976, Span.)
Frederico Gomez
MACHISMO–40 GRAVES FOR 40 GUNS(1970)
Henry Gomez
VIDEODROME(1983, Can.)
Ignacio Gomez
PROUD AND THE DAMNED, THE(1972)
Inez Gomez
WEST OF THE ROCKIES(1929); UNDER A TEXAS MOON(1930); DAWN TRAIL, THE(1931); JUNGLE PRINCESS, THE(1936)
Silents
GOLD RUSH, THE(1925); TEMPTRESS, THE(1926); KING OF KINGS, THE(1927)
Jerry Gomez
STARLIGHT OVER TEXAS(1938)
Jose Luis Gomez
1984
IT'S NEVER TOO LATE(1984, Span.)
Luis Gomez
CURSE OF THE DEVIL(1973, Span./Mex.), p
Maria Gomez
MAIN STREET(1956, Span.); PROFESSIONALS, THE(1966)
1984
BIZET'S CARMEN(1984, Fr./Ital.)
Marie Gomez
DARING GAME(1968); BARQUERO(1970)
Michel Gomez
ROSEMARY'S BABY(1968)
Mike Gomez
ZOOT SUIT(1981); BORDER, THE(1982)
1984
EL NORTE(1984)
Paloma Gomez
1984
YELLOW HAIR AND THE FORTRESS OF GOLD(1984)
Panchito Gomez
RUN FOR THE ROSES(1978); WALK PROUD(1979); BORDERLINE(1980); MAX DUGAN RETURNS(1983)
Phil Gomez
Misc. Talkies
IT HAPPENED IN HARLEM(1945)
Rafael Gomez
CRISIS(1950)
Ralph Gomez
ROAD TO RIO(1947); WHERE THERE'S LIFE(1947); HIS KIND OF WOMAN(1951)
Ramiro Gomez
HAPPY THIEVES, THE(1962), art d; GOLIATH AGAINST THE GIANTS(1963, Ital./Span.), art d; HYPNOSIS(1966, Ger./Sp./Ital.), art d; FAT ANGELS(1980, U.S./Span.), set d
Rita Gomez
SAVAGE SISTERS(1974); CALIFORNIA SUITE(1978)
Thomas Gomez
ARABIAN NIGHTS(1942); PITTSBURGH(1942); SHERLOCK HOLMES AND THE VOICE OF TERROR(1942); WHO DONE IT?(1942); CORVETTE K-225(1943); CRAZY HOUSE(1943); FRONTIER BADMEN(1943); WHITE SAVAGE(1943); BOWERY TO BROADWAY(1944); CAN'T HELP SINGING(1944); CLIMAX, THE(1944); DEAD

MAN'S EYES(1944); FOLLOW THE BOYS(1944); IN SOCIETY(1944); PHANTOM LADY(1944); DALTONS RIDE AGAIN, THE(1945); FRISCO SAL(1945); I'LL TELL THE WORLD(1945); PATRICK THE GREAT(1945); NIGHT IN PARADISE, A(1946); SWELL GUY(1946); CAPTAIN FROM CASTILE(1947); JOHNNY O'CLOCK(1947); RIDE THE PINK HORSE(1947); SINGAPORE(1947); ANGEL IN EXILE(1948); CASBAH(1948); FORCE OF EVIL(1948); KEY LARGO(1948); COME TO THE STABLE(1949); SORROW-FUL JONES(1949); THAT MIDNIGHT KISS(1949); EAGLE AND THE HAWK, THE(1950); FURIES, THE(1950); KIM(1950); WOMAN ON PIER 13, THE(1950); ANNE OF THE INDIES(1951); HARLEM GLOBETROTTERS, THE(1951); SELLOUT, THE(1951); MACAO(1952); MERRY WIDOW, THE(1952); PONY SOLDIER(1952); SOMBRERO(1953); ADVENTURES OF HAJJI BABA(1954); GAMBLER FROM NAT-CHEZ, THE(1954); LAS VEGAS SHAKEDOWN(1955); LOOTERS, THE(1955); MAG-NIFICENT MATADOR, THE(1955); NIGHT FREIGHT(1955); CONQUEROR, THE(1956); TRAPEZE(1956); BUT NOT FOR ME(1959); JOHN PAUL JONES(1959); SUMMER AND SMOKE(1961); STAY AWAY, JOE(1968); BENEATH THE PLANET OF THE APES(1970)

Vicente Gomez
BLOOD AND SAND(1941); FIGHTER, THE(1952), m; MOONFLEET(1955), m

Vincente Gomez
BLOOD AND SAND(1941), m; CAPTAIN FROM CASTILE(1947); KISSING BANDIT, THE(1948); CRISIS(1950); SNOWS OF KILIMANJARO, THE(1952)

Kosuke Gomi
SECRET SCROLLS(PART I)**1/2(1968, Jap.), w, w; HIKEN YABURI(1969, Jap.), w

Ryutaro Gomi
MAJIN(1968, Jap.)

Jumpei Gomigawa
ROAD TO ETERNITY(1962, Jap.), w

V. Gomolyaka
KIEV COMEDY, A(1963, USSR), m

Mikhail Gomorov
Silents
BATTLESHIP POTEMKIN, THE(1925, USSR)

A. Gomov
Misc. Silents
DEFENCE OF SEVASTOPOL(1911, USSR)

Bob Gompers
KID FROM BOOKLYN, THE(1946)

Theresa Gompers
THOSE DIRTY DOGS(1974, U.S./Ital./Span.)

Frank Gompert
G-MEN(1935), tech adv

John Gonatos
SIXTEEN FATHOMS DEEP(1948)

Enio Goncalves
BRASIL ANNO 2,000(1968, Braz.)

K. Goncalves
MAN COULD GET KILLED, A(1966)

Tina Goncalves
LOLLIPOP(1966, Braz.)

George Goncharoff
FEMALE BUNCH, THE(1969), ed

Sergei Goncharoff
WILD SCENE, THE(1970), ed

Vasili Goncharov
Misc. Silents
DEFENCE OF SEVASTOPOL(1911, USSR), d; 1812(1912, USSR), d; VOLGA AND SIBERIA(1914, USSR), d

Kiki Gonclaves
ADVENTURERS, THE(1970)

Eugene Goncz
DARK CORNER, THE(1946)

Greta Gonda
ROSSINI(1948, Ital.)

Janos Gonda
FATHER(1967, Hung.), m

Robert Gondek
QUEST FOR FIRE(1982, Fr./Can.)

Bonnie Gondel
HOT TIMES(1974)

Cleodon Gondin
BYE-BYE BRASIL(1980, Braz.)

Gene Gondo
TOKYO JOE(1949)

Toshihide Gondo
TWIN SISTERS OF KYOTO(1964, Jap.), w

Yukihiko Gondo
WE WILL REMEMBER(1966, Jap.)

Alfred Gondolfi
Silents
OAKDALE AFFAIR, THE(1919), ph

Jean-Francois Gondre
JUDGE AND THE ASSASSIN, THE(1979, Fr.)

Karina Gondy
LES GAULOISES BLEUES(1969, Fr.)

Quon Gong
GENERAL DIED AT DAWN, THE(1936); SAIGON(1948)

Pete Gonneau
TRAIN RIDE TO HOLLYWOOD(1975)

Pierre Gonneau
DOCTOR DEATH: SEEKER OF SOULS(1973)

Lou Gonsalves
DIAMOND HEAD(1962)

Mascha Gonska
AMERICAN SUCCESS COMPANY, THE(1980)

Rita Gonsouline
WOMEN AND BLOODY TERROR(1970)

Maria Gonta
ROAD TO LIFE(1932, USSR)

Maria Gonzaga
STATE OF THINGS, THE(1983), cos

Agustin Gonzales
THAT MAN IN ISTANBUL(1966, Fr./Ital./Span.)

Arling Gonzales
AMERICAN GUERRILLA IN THE PHILIPPINES, AN(1950)

Armando Gonzales
PAN-AMERICANA(1945)

Becky Gonzales
YOUNG DOCTORS IN LOVE(1982)

Carl Gonzales
LITTLE ONES, THE(1965, Brit.)

David Gonzales
SUDDEN IMPACT(1983)

Emilio Gonzales
HONEYSUCKLE ROSE(1980)

Enrique Gonzales
MANHUNT IN THE JUNGLE(1958)

Ernesto Gonzales
BANG THE DRUM SLOWLY(1973)

Federico Gonzales
DEADLY TRACKERS(1973)

Felix Gonzales
TEN DAYS TO TULARA(1958)

Fernando Gonzales
GOLDEN VOYAGE OF SINBAD, THE(1974, Brit.), art d; SINBAD AND THE EYE OF THE TIGER(1977, U.S./Brit.), art d

Fidel Gonzales
JOHNNY YUMA(1967, Ital.)

Frank Gonzales
SHINBONE ALLEY(1971), anim; ULZANA'S RAID(1972)

Fred Gonzales
AMERICAN GUERRILLA IN THE PHILIPPINES, AN(1950)

Gabriel Gonzales
KISMET(1944)

George Gonzales
BAD NEWS BEARS, THE(1976); BAD NEWS BEARS IN BREAKING TRAINING, THE(1977); BAD NEWS BEARS GO TO JAPAN, THE(1978)

Gilberto Gonzales
CAPTAIN FROM CASTILE(1947); LITTLEST OUTLAW, THE(1955)

Gonzales Gonzales
BENGAZI(1955); MAN IN THE VAULT(1956); THERE GOES THE BRIDE(1980, Brit.)

James Gonzales
JEANNE EAGELS(1957)

Jimmy Gonzales
I WAS A COMMUNIST FOR THE F.B.I.(1951)

Jose Gonzales
THREE OUTLAWS, THE(1956)

Jose G. Gonzales
HELL'S ISLAND(1955)

Jose Gonzales Gonzales
CHA-CHA-CHA BOOM(1956); PANAMA SAL(1957); FOR LOVE OR MONEY(1963)

Luci Aura Gonzales
MASSACRE(1956)

Marcos Gonzales
BLUE SKIES AGAIN(1983)

Maria Gonzales
FLIGHT(1960)

Mark Gonzales
Silents
ARGENTINE LOVE(1924)

Michel Gonzales
IS PARIS BURNING?(1966, U.S./Fr.)

Myrtle Gonzales
Misc. Silents
CAPTAIN ALVAREZ(1914); CHALICE OF COURAGE, THE(1915); END OF THE RAINBOW, THE(1916); GIRL OF LOST LAKE, THE(1916); IT HAPPENED IN HONOLULU(1916); ROMANCE OF BILLY GOAT HILL, A(1916); SECRET OF THE SWAMP, THE(1916); MUTINY(1917); SHOW-DOWN, THE(1917); SOUTHERN JUS-TICE(1917)

Pedro Gonzales,Jr.
MC LINTOCK!(1963)

Pedro Gonzales Gonzales
SHEEPMAN, THE(1958); HELLFIGHTERS(1968); CHISUM(1970)

Peter Gonzales
ROMA(1972, Ital./Fr.); END, THE(1978)

Poncho Gonzales
GOODBYE GIRL, THE(1977)

Ricardo Gonzales
LITTLEST OUTLAW, THE(1955)

Roberto Gonzales
Misc. Talkies
DEATH FORCE(1978)

Soledad Gonzales
FIREFLY, THE(1937); LONG VOYAGE HOME, THE(1940)

Steve Gonzales
LOSIN' IT(1983)

Vinnie Gonzales
KING OF COMEDY, THE(1983)

Gonzales-Gonzales
BOTTOM OF THE BOTTLE, THE(1956)

Jose Gonzales-Gonzales
KRONOS(1957); SHOWDOWN AT BOOT HILL(1958)

Pedre Gonzales-Gonzales
WON TON TON, THE DOG WHO SAVED HOLLYWOOD(1976)

Pedro Gonzales-Gonzales
WINGS OF THE HAWK(1953); RICOCHET ROMANCE(1954); RING OF FEAR(1954); STRANGE LADY IN TOWN(1955); SUPPORT YOUR LOCAL GUNFIGHTER(1971); SIX PACK ANNIE(1975)

Agustin Gonzalez
NEST, THE(1982, Span.); TO BEGIN AGAIN(1982, Span.)
1984
HOLY INNOCENTS, THE(1984, Span.)
Armando Gonzalez
CHEAP DETECTIVE, THE(1978)
Baby Gonzalez
FIEND OF DOPE ISLAND(1961)
Becky Gonzalez
NIGHT SHIFT(1982)
Canibal Gonzalez
CURIOUS DR. HUMPP(1967, Arg.), ph
Carmel Gonzalez
SPIRITISM(1965, Mex.)
Carmen Gonzalez
CASBAH(1948)
Cenon Gonzalez
MAD DOCTOR OF BLOOD ISLAND, THE(1969, Phil./U.S.); TWILIGHT PEO-PLE(1972, Phil.)
Charles Gonzalez
RANCHO NOTORIOUS(1952)
Clarence Gonzalez
BLACK RODEO(1972)
Dacia Gonzalez
RAGE(1966, U.S./Mex.)
Eddie Gonzalez
1984
DELIVERY BOYS(1984)
Ernesto Gonzalez
LAST SUMMER(1969); POSSESSION OF JOEL DELANEY, THE(1972)
Felix Gonzalez
SITTING BULL(1954); VILLA!(1958); OF LOVE AND DESIRE(1963); MISSING(1982)
Fernando Gonzalez
HARD CONTRACT(1969), set d; FIGURES IN A LANDSCAPE(1970, Brit.), art d; PEOPLE THAT TIME FORGOT, THE(1977, Brit.), art d; CLASH OF THE TI-TANS(1981), art d
Gilberto Gonzalez
PEARL, THE(1948, U.S./Mex.); STRONGHOLD(1952, Mex.)
James Gonzalez
MAN WITH A CLOAK, THE(1951); SPIRAL ROAD, THE(1962)
Jamie Gonzalez
WOMAN'S DEVOTION, A(1956)
Javier Jose Gonzalez
1984
MIKE'S MURDER(1984)
Joe Gonzalez
FAT ANGELS(1980, U.S./Span.), w
Jorge Gonzalez
1984
DELIVERY BOYS(1984)
Jose Gonzalez
I ESCAPED FROM DEVIL'S ISLAND(1973), set d; HERBIE GOES BANANAS(1980)
Jose Gonzalez Gonzalez
FROM NASHVILLE WITH MUSIC(1969)
Lupe Gonzalez
LOVES OF CARMEN, THE(1948)
Maggie Gonzalez
GETAWAY, THE(1972)
Margaret Millan Gonzalez
ANGELO MY LOVE(1983)
Mario Gonzalez
DEATH OF A BUREAUCRAT(1979, Cuba), ed; POURQUOI PAS!(1979, Fr.)
Myrtle Gonzalez
Silents
GREATER LAW, THE(1917)
Misc. Silents
GOD'S CRUCIBLE(1917)
Pancho Gonzalez
PLAYERS(1979)
Pedro Gonzalez Gonzalez
I DIED A THOUSAND TIMES(1955); YOUNG LAND, THE(1959); HOSTILE GUNS(1967); HOOK, LINE AND SINKER(1969); DREAMER(1979)
Rogelio A. Gonzalez
LA NAVE DE LOS MONSTRUOS(1959, Mex.), d
Roland Gonzalez
PUNISHMENT PARK(1971)
Servando Gonzalez
YANCO(1964, Mex.), d&w; FOOL KILLER, THE(1965), d
Willie Gonzalez
Misc. Talkies
ENTER THE DEVIL(1975)
Yolanda Gonzalez
MEXICAN HAYRIDE(1948)
Pedro Gonzalez-Gonzales
RIO BRAVO(1959)
Gonzalez-Gonzalez
HIGH AND THE MIGHTY, THE(1954)
Jose Gonzalez-Gonzalez
MERMAIDS OF TIBURON, THE(1962)
Pedro Gonzalez-Gonzalez
ADVENTURES OF BULLWHIP GRIFFIN, THE(1967); LOVE BUG, THE(1968)
James Gonzalles
WINTERTIME(1943), ch
Antonio Gonzalves
VOYAGE OF SILENCE(1968, Fr.)
Eiji Goo
FRIENDLY KILLER, THE(1970, Jap.)

Christopher Good
BRIDGE TOO FAR, A(1977, Brit.); VICTOR/VICTORIA(1982); BULLSHOT(1983)
Dick Good
WONDER BAR(1934)
Donald Good
WHAT THE BUTLER SAW(1950, Brit.), w
Frank Good
DANIEL BOONE(1936), ph; ISLE OF FURY(1936), ph
Silents
GRETCHEN, THE GREENHORN(1916), ph; LITTLE SCHOOL MA'AM, THE(1916), w; MARTHA'S VINDICATION(1916), ph; JACK AND THE BEANSTALK(1917), ph; ALI BABA AND THE FORTY THIEVES(1918), ph; LIGHTS OF THE DESERT(1922), ph; CIRCUS DAYS(1923), ph; RAG MAN, THE(1925), ph; WIZARD OF OZ, THE(1925), ph; GILDED BUTTERFLY, THE(1926), ph; JOHNNY GET YOUR HAIR CUT(1927), ph; LAWLESS LEGION, THE(1929), ph
Frank B. Good
DUDE RANGER, THE(1934), ph; PECK'S BAD BOY(1934), ph; COWBOY MIL-LIONAIRE(1935), ph; THUNDER MOUNTAIN(1935), ph; WHEN A MAN'S A MAN(1935), ph; WHISPERING SMITH SPEAKS(1935), ph; BORDER PATROLMAN, THE(1936), ph; MINE WITH THE IRON DOOR, THE(1936), ph; O'MALLEY OF THE MOUNTED(1936), ph; HOLLYWOOD COWBOY(1937), ph; PARK AVENUE LOG-GER(1937), ph; WINDJAMMER(1937), ph
Silents
CAROLYN OF THE CORNERS(1919), ph; CYCLONE, THE(1920), ph; BAR NO-THIN'(1921), ph; BIG PUNCH, THE(1921), ph; GET YOUR MAN(1921), ph; RIDING WITH DEATH(1921), ph; NEW TEACHER, THE(1922), ph; SMILES ARE TRUMPS(1922), ph; DADDY(1923), ph; LONG LIVE THE KING(1923), ph; ENEMY OF MEN, AN(1925), ph; OLD CLOTHES(1925), ph
Frank G. Good
HARD ROCK HARRIGAN(1935), ph
Jack Good
SWING TIME(1936); FATHER GOOSE(1964); CLAMBAKE(1967); CATCH MY SOUL(1974), p, w
Jerry Good
TWO HUNDRED MOTELS(1971, Brit.), p
John Good
SOMEONE TO REMEMBER(1943); MADEMOISELLE FIFI(1944); AVALAN-CHE(1946); GOLDEN EARRINGS(1947); HIGH CONQUEST(1947); PRIVATE AF-FAIRS OF BEL AMI, THE(1947); LETTER FROM AN UNKNOWN WOMAN(1948); RUTHLESS(1948)
Lana Good
Misc. Silents
KINGDOM OF HUMAN HEARTS, THE(1921)
Maurice Good
RISING OF THE MOON, THE(1957, Ireland); SIEGE OF SIDNEY STREET, THE(1960, Brit.); BOMB IN THE HIGH STREET(1961, Brit.); MURDER MOST FOUL(1964, Brit.); SKULL, THE(1965, Brit.); TRAITOR'S GATE(1966, Brit./Ger.); DEADLY BEES,THE(1967, Brit.); THEY CAME FROM BEYOND SPACE(1967, Brit.); FIVE MILLION YEARS TO EARTH(1968, Brit.); TROG(1970, Brit.)
Merle Good
HAPPY AS THE GRASS WAS GREEN(1973), d&w; HAZEL'S PEOPLE(1978), w
Peter B. Good
BROTHER RAT AND A BABY(1940); KNUTE ROCKNE–ALL AMERICAN(1940)
Phyllis Good
HAZEL'S PEOPLE(1978), cos
Richard Good
CITIZEN SAINT(1947)
Roger Good
WHAT THE BUTLER SAW(1950, Brit.), w; MAROC 7(1967, Brit.)
Stephen Good
MC KENZIE BREAK, THE(1970)
Elliot Goodale
Misc. Silents
BROADWAY GOLD(1923)
Grace Goodall
HANDY ANDY(1934); JUDGE PRIEST(1934); LEMON DROP KID, THE(1934); SHE COULDN'T TAKE IT(1935); SHE MARRIED HER BOSS(1935); SHOW THEM NO MERCY(1935); SINGING VAGABOND, THE(1935); STEAMBOAT ROUND THE BEND(1935); MAKE WAY FOR A LADY(1936); POPPY(1936); CALIFORNIA STRAIGHT AHEAD(1937); CITY STREETS(1938); MEN WITH WINGS(1938); PARA-DISE FOR THREE(1938); SAY IT IN FRENCH(1938); SHINING HOUR, THE(1938); WOMEN, THE(1939); YOU CAN'T CHEAT AN HONEST MAN(1939); $1,000 A TOUCHDOWN(1939)
Silents
BIG GAME(1921); EASY ROAD, THE(1921)
Misc. Silents
MOONLIGHT AND HONEYSUCKLE(1921); OPENING NIGHT, THE(1927)
Hedley Goodall
YELLOW CANARY, THE(1944, Brit.)
Jill Goodall
SPY WHO LOVED ME, THE(1977, Brit.)
Alf Goodard
DRUMS(1938, Brit.)
Silents
EVERY MOTHER'S SON(1926, Brit.)
Misc. Silents
CARRY ON!(1927, Brit.); JAWS OF HELL(1928, Brit.)
Joe Goodboy
Silents
PATRIOT, THE(1916); PRIMAL LURE, THE(1916)
George Goodchild
PUBLIC DEFENDER, THE(1931), w; CONDEMNED TO DEATH(1932, Brit.), w; NO ESCAPE(1936, Brit.), w
Tim Goodchild
LITTLE PRINCE, THE(1974, Brit.), cos
Ida Goodcuff
BATTLE OF LOVE'S RETURN, THE(1971)

Chesterfield "Billy" Goode
Misc. Silents
LAST CHALLENGE, THE(1916, Brit.)
Coleridge Goode
WALKING ON AIR(1946, Brit.)
Frederic Goode
FLOOD, THE(1963, Brit.), d; STOPOVER FOREVER(1964, Brit.), d; LOVE IS A
WOMAN(1967, Brit.), d; GREAT PONY RAID, THE(1968, Brit.), d; SYNDICATE,
THE(1968, Brit.), d
Misc. Talkies
AVALANCHE(1975, Brit.), d
Fredric Goode
HAND OF NIGHT, THE(1968, Brit.), d
Jack Goode
FLYING DOWN TO RIO(1933)
Laurie Goode
I WANT WHAT I WANT(1972, Brit.)
Lucy Goode
1984
SECRETS(1984, Brit.)
Reginald Butler Goode
Silents
SYNCOPATING SUE(1926), w
Richard Goode
GOING HOME(1971); HOSPITAL, THE(1971)
Ruth Goode
TONIGHT WE SING(1953), w
Gregory Goodell
HUMAN EXPERIMENTS(1980), p, d
John Goodell
Misc. Talkies
JACKPOT(1982), d
Arthur Henry Gooden
SMOKE TREE RANGE(1937), w
Robert Gooden
NIGHT OF THE LEPUS(1972)
Sam Gooden
THREE THE HARD WAY(1974)
Joan Goodfellow
LOLLY-MADONNA XXX(1973); SUNBURN(1979)
1984
FLASH OF GREEN, A(1984)
Misc. Talkies
BUSTER AND BILLIE(1974)
Jim Goodfriend
1984
MOSCOW ON THE HUDSON(1984)
Pliny Goodfriend
LOVE TRADER(1930), ph; FAST BULLETS(1936), ph; RIDING ON(1937), ph; SIL-
VER TRAIL, THE(1937), ph; SKULL AND CROWN(1938), ph
Silents
GAY AND DEVILISH(1922), ph
Misc. Silents
DIVORCEE, THE(1917)
Garry Goodgion
BONNIE AND CLYDE(1967); FIRST TO FIGHT(1967)
Philip Goodhand-Tait
UNIVERSAL SOLDIER(1971, Brit.), m
Goodhart
SUICIDE LEGION(1940, Brit.), m
Geoff Goodhart
THERE'S ALWAYS A THURSDAY(1957, Brit.)
Geoffrey Goodhart
CALLED BACK(1933, Brit.); SOLUTION BY PHONE(1954, Brit.), a, p; FLAW,
THE(1955, Brit.), p; DYNAMITERS, THE(1956, Brit.), p; ALIVE ON SATURDAY(1957,
Brit.), a, p; HOUSE IN THE WOODS, THE(1957, Brit.), a, p; BANK RAIDERS,
THE(1958, Brit.), p
William Goodhart
GENERATION(1969), w; EXORCIST II: THE HERETIC(1977), w; CLOUD DAN-
CER(1980), w
Geoffrey Goodheart
JEWEL, THE(1933, Brit.); ROMANCE IN RHYTHM(1934, Brit.); BUT NOT IN
VAIN(1948, Brit.), a, p; YOU CAN'T FOOL AN IRISHMAN(1950, Ireland); TOM
BROWN'S SCHOOLDAYS(1951, Brit.); TWILIGHT WOMEN(1953, Brit.); STOLEN
PLANS, THE(1962, Brit.)
Dean Goodhill
TIME FOR KILLING, A(1967)
Clarence Goodhue
LUCK OF GINGER COFFEY, THE(1964, U.S./Can.)
Clesson Goodhue
LITTLE GIRL WHO LIVES DOWN THE LANE, THE(1977, Can.)
William Maxwell Goodhue
SIN OF NORA MORAN(1933), w
Fred Goodich
FEAR NO EVIL(1981), ph
Harry Goodier
LITTLE ONES, THE(1965, Brit.)
Robert Goodier
MEET THE NAVY(1946, Brit.); OEDIPUS REX(1957, Can.); FORTUNE AND MEN'S
EYES(1971, U.S./Can.); APPRENTICESHIP OF DUDDY KRAVITZ, THE(1974, Can.);
LOST AND FOUND(1979); THRESHOLD(1983, Can.)
Daisy Goodill
SYLVIA SCARLETT(1936)
Peggy Goodin
MICKEY(1948), w; TAKE CARE OF MY LITTLE GIRL(1951), w
Anne Gooding
BRONCO BULLFROG(1972, Brit.)

Ben Gooding
SWEET CHARITY(1969)
Bruce Gooding
HAPPY BIRTHDAY TO ME(1981)
Tim Gooding
HEATWAVE(1983, Aus.), w
David Goodis
DARK PASSAGE(1947), w; UNFAITHFUL, THE(1947), w; BURGLAR, THE(1956),
w; NIGHTFALL(1956), w; SHOOT THE PIANO PLAYER(1962, Fr.), w; BURGLARS,
THE(1972, Fr./Ital.), w; MOON IN THE GUTTER, THE(1983, Fr./Ital.), w
Joel Goodkind
NIGHT IN PARADISE, A(1946)
Samuel A. Goodkind
GIANT CLAW, THE(1957), ed
Saul Goodkind
STORMY(1935), ed; SON OF DRACULA(1943), ed; HAT CHECK HONEY(1944), ed;
INVISIBLE MAN'S REVENGE(1944), ed; MUMMY'S GHOST, THE(1944), ed; OLD
TEXAS TRAIL, THE(1944), ed; HOUSE OF FEAR, THE(1945), ed; PURSUIT TO
ALGIERS(1945), ed; GIRL ON THE SPOT(1946), ed; FURY AT GUNSIGHT
PASS(1956), ed
Saul A. Goodkind
ENTER ARSENE LUPIN(1944), ed; CODE OF THE LAWLESS(1945), ed; EASY TO
LOOK AT(1945), ed; RIVER GANG(1945), ed; BLACK ANGEL(1946), ed; DRESSED
TO KILL(1946), ed; TERROR BY NIGHT(1946), ed; CREEPER, THE(1948), ed; THIR-
TEEN LEAD SOLDIERS(1948), ed; BLACKJACK KETCHUM, DESPERADO(1956),
ed; ROCK AROUND THE CLOCK(1956), ed; LIFE BEGINS AT 17(1958), ed; TRUE
STORY OF LYNN STUART, THE(1958), ed; FLYING FONTAINES, THE(1959), ed;
JUKE BOX RHYTHM(1959), ed; WIZARD OF BAGHDAD, THE(1960), ed
Saul H. Goodkind
ESCAPE FROM SAN QUENTIN(1957), ed
Sol Goodkind
RUSTLER'S ROUNDUP(1946), ed
Tracey Goodlad
LOOKS AND SMILES(1982, Brit.)
Ernee Goodleigh
Silents
LADY IN LOVE, A(1920)
Ken Goodlet
NED KELLY(1970, Brit.); DEMONSTRATOR(1971, Aus.); END PLAY(1975, Aus.)
Kenneth Goodlet
LET THE BALLOON GO(1977, Aus.)
Ken Goodlett
SCOBIE MALONE(1975, Aus.)
Michael Goodlife
CARVE HER NAME WITH PRIDE(1958, Brit.)
Michael Goodliffe
HOUR OF GLORY(1949, Brit.); STOP PRESS GIRL(1949, Brit.); CAPTAIN HORATIO
HORNBLOWER(1951, Brit.); WOODEN HORSE, THE(1951); CRY, THE BELOVED
COUNTRY(1952, Brit.); HOUR OF THIRTEEN, THE(1952); SEA DEVILS(1953);
FRONT PAGE STORY(1954, Brit.); ROB ROY, THE HIGHLAND ROGUE(1954, Brit.);
END OF THE AFFAIR, THE(1955, Brit.); QUENTIN DURWARD(1955); WAY OUT,
THE(1956, Brit.); PORTRAIT IN SMOKE(1957, Brit.); PURSUIT OF THE GRAF
SPEE(1957, Brit.); SHE PLAYED WITH FIRE(1957, Brit.); FURTHER UP THE
CREEK!(1958, Brit.); NIGHT TO REMEMBER, A(1958, Brit.); ONE THAT GOT AWAY,
THE(1958, Brit.); UP THE CREEK(1958, Brit.); WHITE TRAP, THE(1959, Brit.);
CONSPIRACY OF HEARTS(1960, Brit.); MAN WITH THE GREEN CARNATION,
THE(1960, Brit.); PEEPING TOM(1960, Brit.); SINK THE BISMARCK!(1960, Brit.);
THIRTY NINE STEPS, THE(1960, Brit.); DAY THE EARTH CAUGHT FIRE, THE(1961,
Brit.); NO LOVE FOR JOHNNIE(1961, Brit.); NUMBER SIX(1962, Brit.); TESTAMENT
OF ORPHEUS, THE(1962, Fr.); 80,000 SUSPECTS(1963, Brit.); GORGON, THE(1964,
Brit.); MAN IN THE MIDDLE(1964, U.S./Brit.); SEVENTH DAWN, THE(1964);
SQUADRON 633(1964, U.S./Brit.); WOMAN OF STRAW(1964, Brit.); 20,000 POUNDS
KISS, THE(1964, Brit.); 633 SQUADRON(1964); JIG SAW(1965, Brit.); VON RYAN'S
EXPRESS(1965); JOKERS, THE(1967, Brit.); NIGHT OF THE GENERALS, THE(1967,
Brit./Fr.); FIXER, THE(1968); CROMWELL(1970, Brit.); HENRY VIII AND HIS SIX
WIVES(1972, Brit.); HITLER: THE LAST TEN DAYS(1973, Brit./Ital.); TO THE DEVIL
A DAUGHTER(1976, Brit./Ger.)
Misc. Talkies
TROUBLED WATERS(1964, Brit.)
Charles Goodlin
DEVIL'S MESSENGER, THE(1962 U.S./Swed.)
A. Carter Goodloe
I LIVE MY LIFE(1935), w
A. Goodman
TASTE OF HONEY, A(1962, Brit.)
Adam Goodman
CAVALCADE OF THE WEST(1936)
Al Goodman
TALK OF HOLLYWOOD, THE(1929), md; QUEEN HIGH(1930), md; HELL'S HORI-
ZON(1955), art d; TWINKLE IN GOD'S EYE, THE(1955), art d; JAGUAR(1956), art d
Benny Goodman
SONG IS BORN, A(1948)
Coley Goodman
Misc. Silents
HARPER MYSTERY, THE(1913, Brit.)
Cousin Herald Goodman
SADDLE MOUNTAIN ROUNDUP(1941)
Daniel Carson Goodman
Silents
BATTLE OF THE SEXES, THE(1914), w; LOVE'S TOLL(1916), w; HAS THE WORLD
GONE MAD!(1923), w; BATTLE OF THE SEXES, THE(1928), w
Misc. Silents
THOUGHTLESS WOMEN(1920), d
Danny Goodman
Silents
APRIL SHOWERS(1923)
David Z. Goodman
STRANGLERS OF BOMBAY, THE(1960, Brit.), w; MONTE WALSH(1970), w;
DEATH VENGEANCE(1982), w; MAN, WOMAN AND CHILD(1983), w

David Zelag Goodman
LOVERS AND OTHER STRANGERS(1970), w; STRAW DOGS(1971, Brit.), w; MAN ON A SWING(1974), w; FAREWELL, MY LOVELY(1975), w; LOGAN'S RUN(1976), w; MARCH OR DIE(1977, Brit.), w; EYES OF LAURA MARS(1978), w

Debbie Goodman
NUTCRACKER(1982, Brit.)

Dody Goodman
BEDTIME STORY(1964); GREASE(1978); GREASE 2(1982); MAX DUGAN RETURNS(1983)
1984
SPLASH(1984)

Edward Goodman
MAN OF THE WORLD(1931), d; WOMEN LOVE ONCE(1931), d

George Goodman
NOCTURNE(1946); HE WALKED BY NIGHT(1948); RACE STREET(1948); UNCLE TOM'S CABIN(1969, Fr./Ital./Ger./Yugo.); HAPPINESS CAGE, THE(1972), p; SUPERBUG, SUPER AGENT(1976, Ger.)

George J. W. Goodman
WHEELER DEALERS, THE(1963), w

George W Goodman
COOL WORLD, THE(1963)

Georgie Goodman
WHIPLASH(1948)

Hal Goodman
INVITATION TO A GUNFIGHTER(1964), w

Harry Goodman
EYES THAT KILL(1947, Brit.), p; GUNMAN HAS ESCAPED, A(1948, Brit.), p

Harvey Goodman
RIVALS(1972), ph

Helen Goodman
GRASS EATER, THE(1961)

Isador Goodman
JEDDA, THE UNCIVILIZED(1956, Aus.), m, md

J. Kenneth Goodman
Misc. Silents
DUNGEON, THE(1922)

Jack Goodman
MEET THE MISSUS(1937), w; HOW'S ABOUT IT?(1943), w; GAY BLADES(1946), w; MICKEY ONE(1965)
Silents
JACK SPURLOCK, PRODIGAL(1918)

Jamie Goodman
Misc. Talkies
DYNAMITE(1972)

Joel Goodman
PROWLER, THE(1981), ed
1984
FRIDAY THE 13TH–THE FINAL CHAPTER(1984), ed; MISSING IN ACTION(1984), ed

John Goodman
UNCLE HARRY(1945), art d; OLD-FASHIONED WAY, THE(1934), art d; GIRL OF THE OZARKS(1936), art d; MURDER WITH PICTURES(1936), art d; HIGH, WIDE AND HANDSOME(1937), art d; MOUNTAIN MUSIC(1937), art d; WELLS FARGO(1937), art d; DANGEROUS TO KNOW(1938), art d; IF I WERE KING(1938), art d; ILLEGAL TRAFFIC(1938), art d; RULERS OF THE SEA(1939), art d; HOWARDS OF VIRGINIA, THE(1940), art d; PAROLE FIXER(1940), art d; TYPHOON(1940), art d; NIGHTMARE(1942), art d; FRANKENSTEIN MEETS THE WOLF MAN(1943), art d; GET GOING(1943), art d; HI' YA, SAILOR(1943), art d; HONEYMOON LODGE(1943), art d; HOW'S ABOUT IT?(1943), art d; LARCENY WITH MUSIC(1943), art d; LONE STAR TRAIL, THE(1943), art d; MAD GHOUL, THE(1943), art d; NEVER A DULL MOMENT(1943), art d; SING A JINGLE(1943), art d; SON OF DRACULA(1943), art d; TOP MAN(1943), art d; WHEN JOHNNY COMES MARCHING HOME(1943), art d; YOU'RE A LUCKY FELLOW, MR. SMITH(1943), art d; HAT CHECK HONEY(1944), art d; HI, GOOD-LOOKIN'(1944), art d; LADIES COURAGEOUS(1944), art d; GREAT MISSOURI RAID, THE(1950), art d; HIGH LONESOME(1950), art d; SUNDOWNERS, THE(1950), art d; FLAMING FEATHER(1951), art d; WARPATH(1951), art d; FLIGHT TO TANGIER(1953), art d; SEVEN LITTLE FOYS, THE(1955), art d; TROUBLE WITH HARRY, THE(1955), art d; MOUNTAIN, THE(1956), art d; SAD SACK, THE(1957), art d; HOUSEBOAT(1958), art d; HURRY SUNDOWN(1967), set d; EDDIE MACON'S RUN(1983); SURVIVORS, THE(1983)
1984
C.H.U.D.(1984); REVENGE OF THE NERDS(1984)

John B. Goodman
IT'S A GIFT(1934), art d; LEMON DROP KID, THE(1934), art d; THIRTEEN HOURS BY AIR(1936), art d; PITTSBURGH(1942), art d; SPOILERS, THE(1942), art d; FIRED WIFE(1943), art d; FLESH AND FANTASY(1943), art d; FOLLOW THE BAND(1943), art d; FRONTIER BADMEN(1943), art d; GOOD MORNING, JUDGE(1943), art d; GUNG HO!(1943), art d; HERS TO HOLD(1943), art d; HE'S MY GUY(1943), art d; HIT THE ICE(1943), art d; IT AIN'T HAY(1943), art d; KEEP 'EM SLUGGING(1943), art d; MOONLIGHT IN VERMONT(1943), art d; MR. BIG(1943), art d; PHANTOM OF THE OPERA(1943), art d; RHYTHM OF THE ISLANDS(1943), art d; SHADOW OF A DOUBT(1943), art d; SHERLOCK HOLMES FACES DEATH(1943), art d; SHE'S FOR ME(1943), art d; STRANGE DEATH OF ADOLF HITLER, THE(1943), art d; WE'VE NEVER BEEN LICKED(1943), art d; WHITE SAVAGE(1943), art d; ALI BABA AND THE FORTY THIEVES(1944), art d; CHRISTMAS HOLIDAY(1944), art d; CLIMAX, THE(1944), art d; COBRA WOMAN(1944), art d; DEAD MAN'S EYES(1944), art d; DESTINY(1944), art d; ENTER ARSENE LUPIN(1944), art d; FOLLOW THE BOYS(1944), art d; GHOST CATCHERS(1944), art d; GYPSY WILDCAT(1944), art d; HI BEAUTIFUL(1944), art d; HER PRIMITIVE MAN(1944), art d; HOUSE OF FRANKENSTEIN(1944), art d; IMPOSTER, THE(1944), art d; IN SOCIETY(1944), art d; JUNGLE WOMAN(1944), art d; MARSHAL OF GUNSMOKE(1944), art d; MERRY MONAHANS, THE(1944), art d; MOON OVER LAS VEGAS(1944), art d; MOONLIGHT AND CACTUS(1944), art d; MUMMY'S CURSE, THE(1944), art d; MUMMY'S GHOST, THE(1944), art d; MURDER IN THE BLUE ROOM(1944), art d; MY GAL LOVES MUSIC(1944), art d; NIGHT CLUB GIRL(1944), art d; OLD TEXAS TRAIL, THE(1944), art d; PARDON MY RHYTHM(1944), art d; PEARL OF DEATH, THE(1944), art d; PHANTOM LADY(1944), art d; RECKLESS AGE(1944), art d; RIDERS OF THE SANTA FE(1944), art d; SAN DIEGO, I LOVE YOU(1944), art d; SCARLET CLAW, THE(1944), art d; SHERLOCK HOLMES AND THE SPIDER WOMAN(1944), art d; SINGING SHERIFF, THE(1944), art d; SLIGHTLY TER-

RIFIC(1944), art d; SOUTH OF DIXIE(1944), art d; SWINGTIME JOHNNY(1944), art d; THIS IS THE LIFE(1944), art d; TRAIL TO GUNSIGHT(1944), art d; TRIGGER TRAIL(1944), art d; TWILIGHT ON THE PRAIRIE(1944), art d; WEEKEND PASS(1944), art d; WEIRD WOMAN(1944), art d; BAD MEN OF THE BORDER(1945), art d; DALTONS RIDE AGAIN, THE(1945), art d; EASY TO LOOK AT(1945), art d; FRISCO SAL(1945), art d; FROZEN GHOST, THE(1945), art d; HER LUCKY NIGHT(1945), art d; HERE COME THE CO-EDS(1945), art d; HONEYMOON AHEAD(1945), art d; HOUSE OF DRACULA(1945), art d; HOUSE OF FEAR, THE(1945), art d; I'LL REMEMBER APRIL(1945), art d; I'LL TELL THE WORLD(1945), art d; JUNGLE CAPTIVE(1945), art d; LADY ON A TRAIN(1945), art d; MEN IN HER DIARY(1945), art d; NAUGHTY NINETIES, THE(1945), art d; ON STAGE EVERYBODY(1945), art d; PATRICK THE GREAT(1945), art d; PENTHOUSE RHYTHM(1945), art d; PILLOW OF DEATH(1945), art d; PURSUIT TO ALGIERS(1945), art d; RENEGADES OF THE RIO GRANDE(1945), art d; RIVER GANG(1945), art d; SALOME, WHERE SHE DANCED(1945), art d; SCARLET STREET(1945), art d; SENORITA FROM THE WEST(1945), art d; SHADY LADY(1945), art d; SHE GETS HER MAN(1945), art d; SONG OF THE SARONG(1945), art d; STRANGE CONFESSION(1945), art d; SUDAN(1945), art d; SWING OUT, SISTER(1945), art d; THAT NIGHT WITH YOU(1945), art d; THAT'S THE SPIRIT(1945), art d; THIS LOVE OF OURS(1945), art d; TRAIL TO VENGEANCE(1945), art d; UNDER WESTERN SKIES(1945), art d; WOMAN IN GREEN, THE(1945), art d; CANYON PASSAGE(1946), art d; GUN TOWN(1946), art d; HOUSE OF HORRORS(1946), art d; LITTLE GIANT(1946), art d; NIGHT IN PARADISE, A(1946), art d; SPIDER WOMAN STRIKES BACK, THE(1946), art d; SWELL GUY(1946), art d; TANGIER(1946), art d; TERROR BY NIGHT(1946), art d; I'LL BE YOURS(1947), art d; GOOD SAM(1948), art d; HANG'EM HIGH(1968), art d

John S. Goodman
FRONTIER GAL(1945), art d

Joseph Goodman
HORRIBLE DR. HICHCOCK, THE(1964, Ital.), set d

Jules Eckert Goodman
MAN WHO CAME BACK, THE(1931), w; MAN WHO PLAYED GOD, THE(1932), w; SINCERELY YOURS(1955), w
Silents
MOTHER(1914), w; SILENT VOICE, THE(1915), w; ANTON THE TERRIBLE(1916), w; MAN WHO PLAYED GOD, THE(1922), w; IN HOLLYWOOD WITH POTASH AND PERLMUTTER(1924), w; PARTNERS AGAIN(1926), w

June Goodman
ULTIMATE THRILL, THE(1974)

Karen Goodman
MERMAIDS OF TIBURON, THE(1962)

Lee Goodman
IMITATION OF LIFE(1959)

Leonard Goodman
HAREM BUNCH; OR WAR AND PIECE, THE(1969); MACHISMO–40 GRAVES FOR 40 GUNS(1970)

Margaret Goodman
MAN ON THE RUN(1949, Brit.)

Michael Goodman
WHAT A CRAZY WORLD(1963, Brit.)

Michael H. Goodman
WALKING ON AIR(1946, Brit.), p

Miles Goodman
SLUMBER PARTY '57(1977), m; SKATETOWN, U.S.A.(1979), m; JINXED!(1982), m; MAN WHO WASN'T THERE, THE(1983), m; TABLE FOR FIVE(1983), m
1984
FOOTLOOSE(1984), m

P. Barney Goodman
MAD DOG COLL(1961)

Philip S. Goodman
WE SHALL RETURN(1963), d

Robert Goodman
EYES OF A STRANGER(1980); FINAL COUNTDOWN, THE(1980); NIGHT IN HEAVEN, A(1983)
1984
HARRY AND SON(1984); WHERE THE BOYS ARE '84(1984)

Ron Goodman
THOSE MAGNIFICENT MEN IN THEIR FLYING MACHINES; OR HOW I FLEW FROM LONDON TO PARIS IN 25 HOURS AND 11 MINUTES(1965, Brit.), md

Sandy Goodman
BLACK RODEO(1972)

Stuart Goodman
LILITH(1964)

Susan Goodman
MOLLY MAGUIRES, THE(1970)

Suzanne Goodman
INDIAN PAINT(1965)

Terence Goodman
ODE TO BILLY JOE(1976)

Terence O. Goodman
1984
NINJA III–THE DOMINATION(1984)

Terry Goodman
NEWS HOUNDS(1947); MONKEY BUSINESS(1952)

Williard W. Goodman
RIVALS(1972), p

Carol Goodner
THOSE WHO LOVE(1929, Brit.); FLYING SQUAD, THE(1932, Brit.); RINGER, THE(1932, Brit.); FIRE RAISERS, THE(1933, Brit.); STRANGE EVIDENCE(1933, Brit.); THERE GOES THE BRIDE(1933, Brit.); LEAVE IT TO SMITH(1934); STRIKE(1934, Brit.); MIMI(1935, Brit.); MUSIC HATH CHARMS(1935, Brit.); REGAL CAVALCADE(1935, Brit.); STUDENT'S ROMANCE, THE(1936, Brit.); DOMINANT SEX, THE(1937, Brit.); FROG, THE(1937, Brit.); ROYAL DIVORCE, A(1938, Brit.)

Rev. Donald Goodness
1984
FALLING IN LOVE(1984)

Irv Goodnoff
RATTLERS(1976), ph; BILLION DOLLAR HOBO, THE(1977), ph; FARMER, THE(1977), ph; NEW GIRL IN TOWN(1977), ph; SUPER VAN(1977), ph; JENNIFER(1978), ph; UNSEEN, THE(1981), ph; EVILSPEAK(1982), ph

Irvin Goodnoff
VAN, THE(1977), ph
1984
DADDY'S DEADLY DARLING(1984), ed
W. W. Goodpaster
MYSTERY LAKE(1953), ph
Arthur Goodrich
BUSINESS AND PLEASURE(1932), w; SO THIS IS LONDON(1940, Brit.), w
Arthur Frederick Goodrich
SO THIS IS LONDON(1930), w
Silents
FRONT PAGE STORY, A(1922), w; GLEAM O'DAWN(1922), w
Bert Goodrich
ROSEANNA McCOY(1949)
Edna Goodrich
Silents
ARMSTRONG'S WIFE(1915); AMERICAN MAID(1917)
Misc. Silents
HOUSE OF LIES, THE(1916); MAKING OF MADDALENA, THE(1916); DAUGHTER OF MARYLAND, A(1917); QUEEN X(1917); REPUTATION(1917); HER HUSBAND'S HONOR(1918); HER SECOND HUSBAND(1918); TREASON(1918); WHO LOVED HIM BEST?(1918)
Frances Goodrich
PENTHOUSE(1933), w; SECRET OF MADAME BLANCHE, THE(1933), w; FUGITIVE LOVERS(1934), w; HIDE-OUT(1934), w; THIN MAN, THE(1934), w; AH, WILDERNESS!(1935), w; NAUGHTY MARIETTA(1935), w; AFTER THE THIN MAN(1936), w; ROSE MARIE(1936), w; FIREFLY, THE(1937), w; THANKS FOR THE MEMORY(1938), w; ANOTHER THIN MAN(1939), w; SOCIETY LAWYER(1939), w; LADY IN THE DARK(1944), w; IT'S A WONDERFUL LIFE(1946), w; VIRGINIAN, THE(1946), w; EASTER PARADE(1948), w; PIRATE, THE(1948), w; SUMMER HOLIDAY(1948), w; TOO YOUNG TO KISS(1951), w; GIVE A GIRL A BREAK(1953), w; LONG, LONG TRAILER, THE(1954), w; SEVEN BRIDES FOR SEVEN BROTHERS(1954), w; GABY(1956), w; CERTAIN SMILE, A(1958), w; DIARY OF ANNE FRANK, THE(1959), w; FIVE FINGER EXERCISE(1962), w
Francis Goodrich
UP POPS THE DEVIL(1931), w; HITLER GANG, THE(1944), w; IN THE GOOD OLD SUMMERTIME(1949), w; FATHER OF THE BRIDE(1950), w; FATHER'S LITTLE DIVIDEND(1951), w
Jack Goodrich
BULLETS OR BALLOTS(1936); ANGELS WITH DIRTY FACES(1938); RACKET BUSTERS(1938); DARK VICTORY(1939); EACH DAWN I DIE(1939)
Silents
MAN WHO LAUGHS, THE(1927)
John Goodrich
SON-DAUGHTER, THE(1932), w; DELUGE(1933), w; FLAMING GOLD(1934), w; HEALER, THE(1935), w; CRACK-UP, THE(1937), w; BREACH OF PROMISE(1942, Brit.), w
Silents
SPECIAL DELIVERY(1927), w
John F. Goodrich
FAST LIFE(1929), w; LOVE RACKET, THE(1929), w; FLIRTING WIDOW, THE(1930), w, ed; LILIES OF THE FIELD(1930), w; RIDERS OF THE PURPLE SAGE(1931), w; LIFE RETURNS(1939), w
Silents
PUPPETS(1926), w; ROUGH RIDERS, THE(1927), w; LAST COMMAND, THE(1928), w
Louis Goodrich
BRAT, THE(1930, Brit.); FASCINATION(1931, Brit.); SHERLOCK HOLMES' FATAL HOUR(1931, Brit.); FLAG LIEUTENANT, THE(1932, Brit.); THIRTEENTH CANDLE, THE(1933, Brit.); GUEST OF HONOR(1934, Brit.); BROWN WALLET, THE(1936, Brit.); CAPTAIN'S TABLE, THE(1936, Brit.); FAIR EXCHANGE(1936, Brit.); MAYFAIR MELODY(1937, Brit.); FATHER O'FLYNN(1938, Irish)
Marcus Goodrich
NAVY BORN(1936), w; NIGHT WAITRESS(1936), w; MIGHTY TREVE, THE(1937), w
William Goodrich
Silents
SPECIAL DELIVERY(1927), d
William Goodrich [Fatty Arbuckle]
Silents
RED MILL, THE(1927), d
Bridget Goodricke
PETER RABBIT AND TALES OF BEATRIX POTTER(1971, Brit.)
Garry Goodron
CARDIAC ARREST(1980)
Garry Goodrow
CONNECTION, THE(1962); SUMMERTREE(1971); SLITHER(1973); STEELYARD BLUES(1973); FOUL PLAY(1978); ESCAPE FROM ALCATRAZ(1979); HERO AT LARGE(1980)
1984
HARD TO HOLD(1984); PREY, THE(1984)
Misc. Talkies
GLEN AND RANDA(1971)
Gary Goodrow
MOVING FINGER, THE(1963); KING OF MARVIN GARDENS, THE(1972); LOOSE SHOES(1980); BREATHLESS(1983); OFF THE WALL(1983)
Jason Goodrow
CANDIDATE, THE(1972)
Lizzie Goods
Silents
SEVEN SISTERS, THE(1915)
Alice Goodsell
HAPPY DAYS(1930)
Major Goodsell
SWEETHEART OF SIGMA CHI(1933)
Michael Goodsite
PURSUIT OF D.B. COOPER, THE(1981)

Barbara Goodson
MOTEL HELL(1980)
Bill Goodson
1984
BREAKIN' 2: ELECTRIC BOOGALOO(1984), ch
Gail Goodson
KID MILLIONS(1934); FOLIES DERGERE(1935); STRIKE ME PINK(1936); JOAN OF ARC(1948)
Gale Goodson
DANTE'S INFERNO(1935)
Muriel Goodspeed
FLASH GORDON(1936)
Alan Goodwin
MY BROTHER JONATHAN(1949, Brit.)
Alice Goodwin
RAINBOW OVER BROADWAY(1933)
Aline Goodwin
FIREBRAND JORDAN(1930)
Misc. Silents
RIDING FOR LIFE(1926)
Angela Goodwin
MAN WHO CAME FOR COFFEE, THE(1970, Ital.)
Misc. Talkies
AUTOPSY(1980, Ital.); LAST FEELINGS(1981)
Betty Goodwin
Misc. Silents
EMPTY SADDLE, THE(1925); ONE SHOT RANGER(1925); STAMPEDE THUNDER(1925); WEST OF ARIZONA(1925)
Bill Goodwin
LET'S MAKE MUSIC(1940); BLONDIE IN SOCIETY(1941); BLONDIE GOES TO COLLEGE(1942); HENRY ALDRICH GETS GLAMOUR(1942); WAKE ISLAND(1942); NO TIME FOR LOVE(1943); RIDING HIGH(1943); SO PROUDLY WE HAIL(1943); BATHING BEAUTY(1944); INCENDIARY BLONDE(1945); RIVER GANG(1945); SPELLBOUND(1945); STORK CLUB, THE(1945); EARL CARROLL SKETCHBOOK(1946); HOUSE OF HORRORS(1946); JOLSON STORY, THE(1946); TO EACH HIS OWN(1946); HEAVEN ONLY KNOWS(1947); HIT PARADE OF 1947(1947); MICKEY(1948); SO THIS IS NEW YORK(1948); IT'S A GREAT FEELING(1949); JOLSON SINGS AGAIN(1949); LIFE OF RILEY, THE(1949); TEA FOR TWO(1950); FIRST TIME, THE(1952); ATOMIC KID, THE(1954); LUCKY ME(1954); BUNDLE OF JOY(1956); OPPOSITE SEX, THE(1956); BIG BEAT, THE(1958); GOING STEADY(1958)
Connie Goodwin
FALL OF THE HOUSE OF USHER, THE(1952, Brit.)
Doug Goodwin
1984
HOLLYWOOD HIGH PART II(1984), m
Fred Goodwin
Silents
MR. FIX-IT(1918)
Garry Goodwin
CAPTIVE OF BILLY THE KID(1952)
Gary Goodwin
WHIRLWIND(1951); NIGHT STAGE TO GALVESTON(1952)
Gay Goodwin
WORLD WAS HIS JURY, THE(1958)
Gloria Goodwin
Silents
HER GREAT CHANCE(1918)
Gordon Goodwin
ATTACK OF THE KILLER TOMATOES(1978), m
Harold Goodwin
FLIGHT(1929); ALL QUIET ON THE WESTERN FRONT(1930); WIDOW FROM CHICAGO, THE(1930); DIRIGIBLE(1931); GRAFT(1931); LAWYER'S SECRET, THE(1931); HAT CHECK GIRL(1932); MOVIE CRAZY(1932); SKY BRIDE(1932); SYMPHONY OF SIX MILLION(1932); HALLELUJAH, I'M A BUM(1933); PLEASURE(1933); STRAWBERRY ROAN(1933); LONE COWBOY(1934); SHE WAS A LADY(1934); SMOKING GUNS(1934); WAGON WHEELS(1934); CRUSADES, THE(1935); ROMANCE IN MANHATTAN(1935); WESTERN FRONTIER(1935); DARK HOUR, THE(1936); THEODORA GOES WILD(1936); BREAKFAST FOR TWO(1937); FIGHT TO THE FINISH, A(1937); IT HAPPENED IN HOLLYWOOD(1937); ALEXANDER'S RAGTIME BAND(1938); CITY GIRL(1938); MY LUCKY STAR(1938); BOY FRIEND(1939); JESSE JAMES(1939); SECOND FIDDLE(1939); SUSANNAH OF THE MOUNTIES(1939); TOO BUSY TO WORK(1939); UNION PACIFIC(1939); WARE CASE, THE(1939, Brit.); YOUNG MR. LINCOLN(1939); CHARLIE CHAN AT THE WAX MUSEUM(1940); RAGTIME COWBOY JOE(1940); TEXAS RANGERS RIDE AGAIN(1940); VIVA CISCO KID(1940); FORCED LANDING(1941); INTERNATIONAL LADY(1941); TANKS A MILLION(1941); YOU'LL NEVER GET RICH(1941); ABOUT FACE(1942); HAY FOOT(1942); HE HIRED THE BOSS(1943); FRONTIER GAL(1945); SHE GETS HER MAN(1945); DON'T GAMBLE WITH STRANGERS(1946); LOVER COME BACK(1946); RIDE THE PINK HORSE(1947); SLAVE GIRL(1947); BOLD FRONTIERSMAN, THE(1948); CARSON CITY RAIDERS(1948); FAMILY HONEYMOON(1948); KISS THE BLOOD OFF MY HANDS(1948); RIVER LADY(1948); LADY GAMBLES, THE(1949); LAW OF THE GOLDEN WEST(1949); TOKYO JOE(1949); DANCE HALL(1950, Brit.); GREAT RUPERT, THE(1950); HAPPIEST DAYS OF YOUR LIFE(1950, Brit.); I WAS A SHOPLIFTER(1950); KID FROM TEXAS, THE(1950); MAGNET, THE(1950, Brit.); VANISHING WESTERNER(1950); ABBOTT AND COSTELLO MEET THE INVISIBLE MAN(1951); DOUBLE DYNAMITE(1951); GREEN GROW THE RUSHES(1951, Brit.); HERE COME THE NELSONS(1952); ISLAND RESCUE(1952, Brit.); JUDGMENT DEFERRED(1952, Brit.); MAN IN THE WHITE SUIT, THE(1952); PROMOTER, THE(1952, Brit.); ABBOTT AND COSTELLO GO TO MARS(1953); CRUEL SEA, THE(1953); MA AND PA KETTLE ON VACATION(1953); REDHEAD FROM WYOMING, THE(1953); ANGELS ONE FIVE(1954, Brit.); GAY DOG, THE(1954, Brit.); HARASSED HERO, THE(1954, Brit.); MAN WITH A MILLION(1954, Brit.); DAM BUSTERS, THE(1955, Brit.); MA AND PA KETTLE AT WAIKIKI(1955); ONE GOOD TURN(1955, Brit.); WICKED WIFE(1955, Brit.); YOU LUCKY PEOPLE(1955, Brit.); KID FOR TWO FARTHINGS, A(1956, Brit.); LADYKILLERS, THE(1956, Brit.); LAST MAN TO HANG, THE(1956, Brit.); NOW AND FOREVER(1956, Brit.); SHIP THAT DIED OF SHAME, THE(1956, Brit.); ZARAK(1956, Brit.); BRIDGE ON THE RIVER KWAI, THE(1957); JOE BUTTERFLY(1957); NIGHT PASSAGE(1957); SEA WIFE(1957, Brit.); THIRD KEY, THE(1957, Brit.); ALL AT SEA(1958, Brit.); GIRLS AT SEA(1958, Brit.); LAW AND DISORDER(1958, Brit.);

SQUARE PEG, THE(1958, Brit.); THREE MEN IN A BOAT(1958, Brit.); MUMMY, THE(1959, Brit.); UGLY DUCKLING, THE(1959, Brit.); WRONG NUMBER(1959, Brit.); OPERATION CUPID(1960, Brit.); PORTRAIT IN BLACK(1960); DESERT PATROL(1962, Brit.); HAIR OF THE DOG(1962, Brit.); NEARLY A NASTY ACCIDENT(1962, Brit.); NUMBER SIX(1962, Brit.); PHANTOM OF THE OPERA, THE(1962, Brit.); HIJACKERS, THE(1963, Brit.); MOVE OVER, DARLING(1963); TRAITORS, THE(1963, Brit.); FATE IS THE HUNTER(1964); CURSE OF THE MUMMY'S TOMB, THE(1965, Brit.); MORITURI(1965); OPERATION SNAFU(1965, Brit.); NEVER BACK LOSERS(1967, Brit.); DON'T RAISE THE BRIDGE, LOWER THE RIVER(1968, Brit.); FRANKENSTEIN MUST BE DESTROYED!(1969, Brit.); BUSHBABY, THE(1970, Brit.); BOY WHO CRIED WEREWOLF, THE(1973); JABBERWOCKY(1977, Brit.)
Silents
OVERLAND RED(1920); SUDS(1920); OLIVER TWIST, JR.(1921); FLIRT, THE(1922); KISSED(1922); MAN TO MAN(1922); SEEING'S BELIEVING(1922); TRACKED TO EARTH(1922); ALICE ADAMS(1923); GENTLE JULIA(1923); KINDLED COURAGE(1923); WANTERS, THE(1923); ARIZONA EXPRESS, THE(1924); RIDERS OF THE PURPLE SAGE(1925); BETTER 'OLE, THE(1926); COLLEGE(1927); CAMERAMAN, THE(1928)
Misc. Silents
LITTLE ORPHAN(1915); SAWDUST RING, THE(1917); SET FREE(1918); HEART O' THE HILLS(1919); PUPPY LOVE(1919); WINNING GIRL, THE(1919); SWEET LAVANDER(1920); HEARTS OF YOUTH(1921); BROADWAY GOLD(1923); BURNING WORDS(1923); RAMBLIN' KID, THE(1923); HIT AND RUN(1924); IN LOVE WITH LOVE(1924); THAT FRENCH LADY(1924); SECRET ORDERS(1926); TARZAN AND THE GOLDEN LION(1927); WHEN A DOG LOVES(1927); HER SUMMER HERO(1928)
Harold R. Goodwin
QUIET PLEASE, MURDER(1942)
Henrietta Goodwin
OLD ENGLISH(1930)
Herold Goodwin
BUCK PRIVATES(1941); COMIN' ROUND THE MOUNTAIN(1951); ABBOTT AND COSTELLO MEET THE KEYSTONE KOPS(1955); SPARTACUS(1960)
Howard Goodwin
WYOMING BANDIT, THE(1949); TO BE OR NOT TO BE(1983)
James Goodwin
YOUNG GUNS, THE(1956); ROCKABILLY BABY(1957); MORITURI(1965); EMPEROR OF THE NORTH POLE(1973)
Jim Goodwin
ICE STATION ZEBRA(1968); IN-LAWS, THE(1979)
Jimmy Goodwin
ATTACK!(1956); TEN SECONDS TO HELL(1959)
John Goodwin
AVENGER, THE(1933), w
Laurel Goodwin
GIRLS! GIRLS! GIRLS!(1962); PAPA'S DELICATE CONDITION(1963); STAGE TO THUNDER ROCK(1964); GLORY GUYS, THE(1965)
Nat C. Goodwin
Misc. Silents
OLIVER TWIST(1912); BUSINESS IS BUSINESS(1915); MARRIAGE BOND, THE(1916); WALL STREET TRAGEDY, A(1916)
Nigel Goodwin
TWO A PENNY(1968, Brit.)
Paul Goodwin
1984
PLACES IN THE HEART(1984)
Pauline Goodwin
MADAME LOUISE(1951, Brit.)
R.W. Goodwin
INSIDE MOVES(1980), p
Ralph Goodwin
REASON TO LIVE, A REASON TO DIE, A(1974, Ital./Fr./Ger./Span.)
Richard Goodwin
PETER RABBIT AND TALES OF BEATRIX POTTER(1971, Brit.), p, w; MURDER ON THE ORIENT EXPRESS(1974, Brit.), p; DEATH ON THE NILE(1978, Brit.), p; STORIES FROM A FLYING TRUNK(1979, Brit.), p; MIRROR CRACK'D, THE(1980, Brit.), p; EVIL UNDER THE SUN(1982, Brit.), p; BIDDY(1983, Brit.), p
1984
PASSAGE TO INDIA, A(1984, Brit.), p
Rick Goodwin
Misc. Talkies
11 X 14(1977)
Robert Goodwin
WATUSI(1959); LAST OF THE SECRET AGENTS?, THE(1966)
Robert L. Goodwin
Misc. Talkies
BLACK CHARIOT(1971), d
Robin Goodwin
SWAMP THING(1982), ph
Ron Goodwin
I'M ALL RIGHT, JACK(1959, Brit.), m; WHIRLPOOL(1959, Brit.), m; IN THE NICK(1960, Brit.), m; MAN WITH THE GREEN CARNATION, THE(1960, Brit.), m; VILLAGE OF THE DAMNED(1960, Brit.), m; INVASION QUARTET(1961, Brit.), m; MURDER SHE SAID(1961, Brit.), m, md; I THANK A FOOL(1962, Brit.), m, md; KILL OR CURE(1962, Brit.), m, md; POSTMAN'S KNOCK(1962, Brit.), m; VILLAGE OF DAUGHTERS(1962, Brit.), m; CRACKSMAN, THE(1963, Brit.), m; DAY OF THE TRIFFIDS, THE(1963), m; FOLLOW THE BOYS(1963), m; MURDER AT THE GALLOP(1963, Brit.), m; SWORD OF LANCELOT(1963, Brit.), m; LADIES WHO DO(1964, Brit.), m, md; MURDER AHOY(1964, Brit.), m, md; MURDER MOST FOUL(1964, Brit.), m, md; OF HUMAN BONDAGE(1964, Brit.), m; SQUADRON 633(1964, U.S./Brit.), m; 633 SQUADRON(1964), m; EARLY BIRD, THE(1965, Brit.), m; JOHNNY NOBODY(1965, Brit.), m; OPERATION CROSSBOW(1965, U.S./Ital.), m, md; THOSE MAGNIFICENT MEN IN THEIR FLYING MACHINES; OR HOW I FLEW FROM LONDON TO PARIS IN 25 HOURS AND 11 MINUTES(1965, Brit.), m; ALPHABET MURDERS, THE(1966), m; MAGNIFICENT TWO, THE(1967, Brit.), m; TRAP, THE(1967, Can./Brit.), m; MRS. BROWN, YOU'VE GOT A LOVELY DAUGHTER(1968, Brit.), m; THAT RIVIERA TOUCH(1968, Brit.), m; WHERE EAGLES DARE(1968, Brit.), m&md; BATTLE OF BRITAIN, THE(1969, Brit.), m; DECLINE AND FALL... OF A BIRD WATCHER(1969, Brit.), m; SUMARINE X-1(1969, Brit.), m; THOSE DARING YOUNG MEN IN THEIR JAUNTY JALOPIES(1969, Fr./Brit./ Ital.), m; EXECUTION-

ER, THE(1970, Brit.), m; FRENZY(1972, Brit.), m; GAWAIN AND THE GREEN KNIGHT(1973, Brit.), m; DEADLY STRANGERS(1974, Brit.), m; ONE OF OUR DINOSAURS IS MISSING(1975, Brit.), m; LITTLEST HORSE THIEVES, THE(1977, m, md); CANDLESHOE(1978), m; FORCE 10 FROM NAVARONE(1978, Brit.), m; UNIDENTIFIED FLYING ODDBALL, THE(1979, Brit.), m
Ruby Goodwin
VIEW FROM POMPEY'S HEAD, THE(1955); STRANGE INTRUDER(1956); ALLIGATOR PEOPLE, THE(1959); WILD IN THE COUNTRY(1961)
Sabine Goodwin
BIDDY(1983, Brit.)
Suki Goodwin
HELL NIGHT(1981)
Tod Goodwin
ROSE BOWL(1936)
Wayne Goodwin
GRAND THEFT AUTO(1977)
Fred Goodwine
Silents
DOWN TO EARTH(1917)
Aline Goodwins
FIRST YANK INTO TOKYO(1945)
Fred Goodwins
Silents
LOVE LIAR, THE(1916); AMARILLY OF CLOTHESLINE ALLEY(1918); ARTISTIC TEMPERAMENT, THE(1919, Brit.), d; HER WINNING WAY(1921)
Misc. Silents
FOR HUSBANDS ONLY(1918); MRS. LEFFINGWELL'S BOOTS(1918); WAY OF A MAN WITH A MAID, THE(1918); CHINESE PUZZLE, THE(1919, Brit.), d; COMMON CLAY(1919); FORBIDDEN(1919); BUILD THY HOUSE(1920, Brit.), d; COLONEL NEWCOME THE PERFECT GENTLEMAN(1920, Brit.), d; SCARLET KISS, THE(1920, Brit.), d; BLOOD MONEY(1921, Brit.), d
Lee Goodwins
YOUNG DYNAMITE(1937), d
Les Goodwins
ANYTHING FOR A THRILL(1937), d; HEADLINE CRASHER(1937), d; WITH LOVE AND KISSES(1937), d
Leslie Goodwins
RAINMAKERS, THE(1935), w; CRIME RING(1938), d; FUGITIVES FOR A NIGHT(1938), d; MR. DOODLE KICKS OFF(1938), d; TARNISHED ANGEL(1938), d; ALMOST A GENTLEMAN(1939), d; DAY THE BOOKIES WEPT, THE(1939), d; GIRL FROM MEXICO, THE(1939), d; MEXICAN SPITFIRE(1939), d; LET'S MAKE MUSIC(1940), d; MEN AGAINST THE SKY(1940), d; MEXICAN SPITFIRE OUT WEST(1940), d; MILLIONAIRE PLAYBOY(1940), d; POP ALWAYS PAYS(1940), d; SUED FOR LIBEL(1940), d; MEXICAN SPITFIRE'S BABY(1941), d; PARACHUTE BATTALION(1941), d; THEY MET IN ARGENTINA(1941), d; MEXICAN SPITFIRE AT SEA(1942), d; MEXICAN SPITFIRE SEES A GHOST(1942), d; MEXICAN SPITFIRE'S ELEPHANT(1942), d, w; ADVENTURES OF A ROOKIE(1943), d; GALS, INCORPORATED(1943), d; LADIES' DAY(1943), d; MEXICAN SPITFIRE'S BLESSED EVENT(1943), d; ROOKIES IN BURMA(1943), d; SILVER SKATES(1943), d; CASANOVA IN BURLESQUE(1944), d; GOIN' TO TOWN(1944), d; HI BEAUTIFUL(1944), d; MUMMY'S CURSE, THE(1944), d; MURDER IN THE BLUE ROOM(1944), d; SINGING SHERIFF, THE(1944), d; ANGEL COMES TO BROOKLYN, AN(1945), d; I'LL TELL THE WORLD(1945), d; RADIO STARS ON PARADE(1945), d; WHAT A BLONDE(1945), d; GENIUS AT WORK(1946), d; RIVERBOAT RHYTHM(1946), d; VACATION IN RENO(1946), p&d; LONE WOLF IN LONDON(1947), d; GOLD FEVER(1952), d; FIREMAN SAVE MY CHILD(1954), d; FRESH FROM PARIS(1955), d; PARIS FOLLIES OF 1956(1955), d; TAMMY AND THE MILLIONAIRE(1967), d; DRAGNET(1974), d
Norman Goodwins
COOL HAND LUKE(1967)
Robert Goody
FLASH GORDON(1980)
Richard Goolden
ONCE IN A NEW MOON(1935, Brit.); TELEVISION TALENT(1937, Brit.); MEET MR. PENNY(1938, Brit.); SCHOOL FOR HUSBANDS(1939, Brit.); MOZART(1940, Brit.); HEADLINE(1943, Brit.); VENGEANCE IS MINE(1948, Brit.); WEAPON, THE(1957, Brit.); HEIGHTS OF DANGER(1962, Brit.); DREAM MAKER, THE(1963, Brit.); IN THE DOGHOUSE(1964, Brit.); AMOROUS ADVENTURES OF MOLL FLANDERS, THE(1965); IT!(1967, Brit.); ONE MORE TIME(1970, Brit.)
George Goomishian
LORDS OF FLATBUSH, THE(1974)
Bill Goonz
SON OF THE RENEGADE(1953)
Howard Goorney
EVIL OF FRANKENSTEIN, THE(1964, Brit.); HILL, THE(1965, Brit.); BEDAZZLED(1967, Brit.); BERSERK(1967); WHERE'S JACK?(1969, Brit.); BLOOD ON SATAN'S CLAW, THE(1970, Brit.); MARRIAGE OF CONVENIENCE(1970, Brit.); TAKE A GIRL LIKE YOU(1970, Brit.); YOU CAN'T WIN 'EM ALL(1970, Brit.); CRUCIBLE OF HORROR(1971, Brit.); FIDDLER ON THE ROOF(1971); SAVAGE MESSIAH(1972, Brit.); INNOCENT BYSTANDERS(1973, Brit.); OFFENSE, THE(1973, Brit.); TO THE DEVIL A DAUGHTER(1976, Brit./Ger.)
Allen Goorwitz
BRINK'S JOB, THE(1978); STUNT MAN, THE(1980); CONTINENTAL DIVIDE(1981); BLACK STALLION RETURNS, THE(1983)
Misc. Talkies
SKETCHES OF A STRANGLER(?)
Allen Goorwitz [Garfield]
ONE-TRICK PONY(1980); ONE FROM THE HEART(1982); STATE OF THINGS, THE(1983)
A. Frederick Gooseen
STERILE CUCKOO, THE(1969)
Stephen Goosen
GALLANT BLADE, THE(1948), art d
Stephen Gooson
IT HAPPENED ONE NIGHT(1934), art d; BLACK ROOM, THE(1935), art d; CRIME AND PUNISHMENT(1935), set d; AWFUL TRUTH, THE(1937), art d; FRAMED(1947), art d; FULLER BRUSH MAN(1948), art d

Stephen Goossen
OVER 21(1945), art d
Ray Goossens
PINOCCHIO IN OUTER SPACE(1965, U.S./Bel.), d
Stephan Goosson
BANDIT OF SHERWOOD FOREST, THE(1946), art d
Stephen Goosson
CORPSE CAME C.O.D., THE(, art d; ARE YOU THERE?(1930), art d; FOX MOVIE-TONE FOLLIES OF 1930(1930), art d; JUST IMAGINE(1930), art d, set d; OH, FOR A MAN!(1930), art d; PRINCESS AND THE PLUMBER, THE(1930), set d; SUCH MEN ARE DANGEROUS(1930), art d; LADY FOR A DAY(1933), art d; ONE NIGHT OF LOVE(1934), art d; SHE COULDN'T TAKE IT(1935), art d; SHE MARRIED HER BOSS(1935), art d; KING STEPS OUT, THE(1936), art d & set d; MR. DEEDS GOES TO TOWN(1936), art d; PENNIES FROM HEAVEN(1936), art d; THEODORA GOES WILD(1936), art d; GIRLS CAN PLAY(1937), art d; I'LL TAKE ROMANCE(1937), art d; IT'S ALL YOURS(1937), art d; LOST HORIZON(1937), art d; PAID TO DANCE(1937), art d; SHADOW, THE(1937), art d; WHEN YOU'RE IN LOVE(1937), art d; GIRLS' SCHOOL(1938), art d; HOLIDAY(1938), art d; I AM THE LAW(1938), art d; JUVENILE COURT(1938), art d; SHE MARRIED AN ARTIST(1938), art d; THERE'S ALWAYS A WOMAN(1938), art d; WHO KILLED GAIL PRESTON?(1938), art d; YOU CAN'T TAKE IT WITH YOU(1938), art d; HOMICIDE BUREAU(1939), art d; LITTLE FOXES, THE(1941), art d; MEET JOHN DOE(1941), art d; CRY HAVOC(1943), art d; SWING FEVER(1943), art d; SEE HERE, PRIVATE HARGROVE(1944), art d; TOGETHER AGAIN(1944), art d; COUNTER-ATTACK(1945), art d; FIGHTING GUARDSMAN, THE(1945), art d; KISS AND TELL(1945), art d; SHE WOULDN'T SAY YES(1945), art d; SNAFU(1945), art d; THOUSAND AND ONE NIGHTS, A(1945), art d; TONIGHT AND EVERY NIGHT(1945), art d; GALLANT JOURNEY(1946), art d; GILDA(1946), art d; JOLSON STORY, THE(1946), art d; MEET ME ON BROAD-WAY(1946), art d; MR. DISTRICT ATTORNEY(1946), art d; ONE WAY TO LO-VE(1946), art d; PERILOUS HOLIDAY(1946), art d; RENEGADES(1946), art d; RETURN OF MONTE CRISTO, THE(1946), art d; TARS AND SPARS(1946), art d; THRILL OF BRAZIL, THE(1946), art d; WALLS CAME TUMBLING DOWN, THE(1946), art d; DEAD RECKONING(1947), art d; DOWN TO EARTH(1947), art d; HER HUSBAND'S AFFAIRS(1947), art d; I LOVE TROUBLE(1947), art d; IT HAD TO BE YOU(1947), art d; JOHNNY O'CLOCK(1947), art d; SWORDSMAN, THE(1947), art d; BLACK ARROW(1948), art d; LADY FROM SHANGHAI, THE(1948), art d; LOVES OF CARMEN, THE(1948), art d; MAN FROM COLORADO(1948), art d; MATING OF MILLIE, THE(1948), art d; RELENTLESS(1948), art d; RETURN OF OCTOBER, THE(1948), art d; SIGN OF THE RAM(1948), art d; TO THE ENDS OF THE EARTH(1948), art d
Silents
LOVE LIGHT, THE(1921), art d; EAST IS WEST(1922), art d; OLIVER TWIST(1922), art d; LET 'ER GO GALLEGHER(1928), art d; MAN-MADE WOMEN(1928), art d; MIDNIGHT MADNESS(1928), art d
Steven Goosson
GUILT OF JANET AMES, THE(1947), art d
Amy Gootenberg
1984
ALPHABET CITY(1984)
Barry Gootkind
LOOKIN' TO GET OUT(1982)
Gopa
LIVING FREE(1972, Brit.)
Ram Gopal
OUTPOST IN MALAYA(1952, Brit.); ELEPHANT WALK(1954), ch; PURPLE PLAIN, THE(1954, Brit.); NAVY HEROES(1959, Brit.)
Hal Goplerud
UP IN SMOKE(1978)
Claudio Gora
ISLAND OF PROCIDA, THE(1952, Ital.); SKY IS RED, THE(1952, Ital.), d, w; LUXURY GIRLS(1953, Ital.); TEMPEST(1958, Ital./Yugo./Fr.); GODDESS OF LOVE, THE(1960, Ital./Fr.); DOLL, THE(1962, Fr.); EVERYBODY GO HOME!(1962, Fr./Ital.); SWORDSMAN OF SIENA, THE(1962, Fr./Ital.); EASY LIFE, THE(1963, Ital.); GIDGET GOES TO ROME(1963); RUN WITH THE DEVIL(1963, Fr./Ital.); SLAVE, THE(1963, Ital.); VERONA TRIAL, THE(1963, Ital.); FACTS OF MURDER, THE(1965, Ital.); LOVE A LA CARTE(1965, Ital.); WHITE VOICES(1965, Fr./Ital.); TRAMPLERS, THE(1966, Ital.); HELLBENDERS, THE(1967, U.S./Ital./Span.); MADE IN ITALY(1967, Fr./Ital.); CATCH AS CATCH CAN(1968, Ital.); DANGER: DIABOLIK(1968, Ital./Fr.); UNCLE TOM'S CABIN(1969, Fr./Ital./Ger./Yugo.); FIVE MAN ARMY, THE(1970, Ital.); LOVE PROBLEMS(1970, Ital.); CONFESSIONS OF A POLICE CAPTAIN(1971, Ital.); LION OF THE DESERT(1981, Libya/Brit.)
Misc. Talkies
ANGEL FOR SATAN, AN(1966, Ital.)
Cogo Goragher
NUDE IN HIS POCKET(1962, Fr.), m
Alain Goraguer
I SPIT ON YOUR GRAVE(1962, Fr.), m; THAT MAN GEORGE!(1967, Fr./Ital./Span.), m; BEYOND FEAR(1977, Fr.), m
The Gorals
GUESTS ARE COMING(1965, Pol.)
Linda Goranson
TRAP, THE(1967, Can./Brit.)
Marie Goranzon
SHORT IS THE SUMMER(1968, Swed.)
Annie Gorassini
WARRIOR EMPRESS, THE(1961, Ital./Fr.); WASTREL, THE(1963, Ital.); 8 ½(1963, Ital.); STOP TRAIN 349(1964, Fr./Ital./Ger.); LITTLE NUNS, THE(1965, Ital.); MYTH, THE(1965, Ital.); 00-2 MOST SECRET AGENTS(1965, Ital.); DANGER: DIABOLIK(1968, Ital./Fr.)
B. Gorbachyov
DUEL, THE(1964, USSR), spec eff
Boris Gorbatov
TARAS FAMILY, THE(1946, USSR), w
Janos Gorbe
ROUND UP, THE(1969, Hung.)
Bernard Gorcey
ABIE'S IRISH ROSE(1928); GREAT DICTATOR, THE(1940); CLANCY STREET BOYS(1943); FOLLOW THE LEADER(1944); MILLION DOLLAR KID(1944); DOCKS OF NEW YORK(1945); MR. MUGGS RIDES AGAIN(1945); BOWERY BOMB-SHELL(1946); IN FAST COMPANY(1946); LIVE WIRES(1946); MR. HEX(1946);

SPOOK BUSTERS(1946); BOWERY BUCKAROOS(1947); HARD BOILED MAHO-NEY(1947); HIGH WALL, THE(1947); NEWS HOUNDS(1947); JINX MONEY(1948); NO MINOR VICES(1948); TROUBLE MAKERS(1948); ANGELS IN DISGUISE(1949); FIGHTING FOOLS(1949); HOLD THAT BABY!(1949); MASTER MINDS(1949); SET-UP, THE(1949); BLONDE DYNAMITE(1950); BLUES BUSTERS(1950); LUCKY LOS-ERS(1950); TRIPLE TROUBLE(1950); BOWERY BATTALION(1951); CRAZY OVER HORSES(1951); GHOST CHASERS(1951); JOURNEY INTO LIGHT(1951); LET'S GO NAVY(1951); PICKUP(1951); FEUDIN' FOOLS(1952); HERE COME THE MARI-NES(1952); HOLD THAT LINE(1952); NO HOLDS BARRED(1952); CLIPPED WINGS(1953); JALOPY(1953); LOOSE IN LONDON(1953); PRIVATE EYES(1953); BOWERY BOYS MEET THE MONSTERS, THE(1954); JUNGLE GENTS(1954); PARIS PLAYBOYS(1954); BOWERY TO BAGDAD(1955); HIGH SOCIETY(1955); JAIL BUST-ERS(1955); DIG THAT URANIUM(1956); SPY CHASERS(1956)
David Gorcey
JUVENILE COURT(1938); LITTLE TOUGH GUY(1938); LITTLE TOUGH GUYS IN SOCIETY(1938); PRAIRIE MOON(1938); CALL A MESSENGER(1939); CODE OF THE STREETS(1939); NEWSBOY'S HOME(1939); SERGEANT MADDEN(1939); THAT GANG OF MINE(1940); YOU'RE NOT SO TOUGH(1940); BOWERY BLITZ-KRIEG(1941); FLYING WILD(1941); PRIDE OF THE BOWERY(1941); SPOOKS RUN WILD(1941); LET'S GET TOUGH(1942); MR. WISE GUY(1942); SMART ALECKS(1942); BOWERY BOMBSHELL(1946); FRENCH KEY, THE(1946); IN FAST COMPANY(1946); MR. HEX(1946); SPOOK BUSTERS(1946); BOWERY BUCK-AROOS(1947); HARD BOILED MAHONEY(1947); NEWS HOUNDS(1947); ANGELS ALLEY(1948); JINX MONEY(1948); SMUGGLERS' COVE(1948); TROUBLE MA-KERS(1948); ANGELS IN DISGUISE(1949); FIGHTING FOOLS(1949); HOLD THAT BABY!(1949); MASTER MINDS(1949); WILD WEED(1949); ABBOTT AND COSTELLO IN THE FOREIGN LEGION(1950); BLONDE DYNAMITE(1950); BLUES BUS-TERS(1950); LUCKY LOSERS(1950); TRIPLE TROUBLE(1950); BOWERY BATTA-LION(1951); CRAZY OVER HORSES(1951); GHOST CHASERS(1951); LET'S GO NAVY(1951); FEUDIN' FOOLS(1952); HERE COME THE MARINES(1952); HOLD THAT LINE(1952); LOOSE IN LONDON(1953); BOWERY BOYS MEET THE MON-STERS, THE(1954); BOWERY TO BAGDAD(1955); DIG THAT URANIUM(1956); FIGHTING TROUBLE(1956); HOT SHOTS(1956); SPOOK CHASERS(1957); UP IN SMOKE(1957); IN THE MONEY(1958)
Elizabeth Gorcey
1984
FOOTLOOSE(1984); GRANDVIEW, U.S.A.(1984); KIDCO(1984)
Kay Marvis Gorcey
GHOSTS ON THE LOOSE(1943); MR. MUGGS STEPS OUT(1943)
Kay Marvis [Mrs. Leo] Gorcey
KID DYNAMITE(1943)
Leo Gorcey
MANNEQUIN(1937); PORTIA ON TRIAL(1937); ANGELS WITH DIRTY FA-CES(1938); CRIME SCHOOL(1938); ANGELS WASH THEIR FACES(1939); DEAD END KIDS ON DRESS PARADE(1939); HELL'S KITCHEN(1939); PRIVATE DETEC-TIVE(1939); THEY MADE ME A CRIMINAL(1939); BOYS OF THE CITY(1940); GALLANT SONS(1940); INVISIBLE STRIPES(1940); THAT GANG OF MINE(1940); ANGELS WITH BROKEN WINGS(1941); BOWERY BLITZKRIEG(1941); DOWN IN SAN DIEGO(1941); FLYING WILD(1941); OUT OF THE FOG(1941); PRIDE OF THE BOWERY(1941); ROAD TO ZANZIBAR(1941); SPOOKS RUN WILD(1941); BORN TO SING(1942); LET'S GET TOUGH(1942); MAISIE GETS HER MAN(1942); MR. WISE GUY(1942); 'NEATH BROOKLYN BRIDGE(1942); SMART ALECKS(1942); SUNDAY PUNCH(1942); CLANCY STREET BOYS(1943); DESTROYER(1943); GHOSTS ON THE LOOSE(1943); KID DYNAMITE(1943); MR. MUGGS STEPS OUT(1943); BLOCK BUSTERS(1944); BOWERY CHAMPS(1944); FOLLOW THE LEADER(1944); MILLION DOLLAR KID(1944); COME OUT FIGHTING(1945); DOCKS OF NEW YORK(1945); MR. MUGGS RIDES AGAIN(1945); ONE EXCITING NIGHT(1945); BOWERY BOMB-SHELL(1946); IN FAST COMPANY(1946); LIVE WIRES(1946); MR. HEX(1946); SPOOK BUSTERS(1946); BOWERY BUCKAROOS(1947); HARD BOILED MAHO-NEY(1947); NEWS HOUNDS(1947); ANGELS ALLEY(1948); JINX MONEY(1948); SMUGGLERS' COVE(1948); SO THIS IS NEW YORK(1948); TROUBLE MA-KERS(1948); ANGELS IN DISGUISE(1949); FIGHTING FOOLS(1949); HOLD THAT BABY!(1949); MASTER MINDS(1949); BLONDE DYNAMITE(1950); BLUES BUST-ERS(1950); LUCKY LOSERS(1950); TRIPLE TROUBLE(1950); BOWERY BATTA-LION(1951); CRAZY OVER HORSES(1951); GHOST CHASERS(1951); LET'S GO NAVY(1951); FEUDIN' FOOLS(1952); HERE COME THE MARINES(1952); HOLD THAT LINE(1952); NO HOLDS BARRED(1952); CLIPPED WINGS(1953); JALO-PY(1953); LOOSE IN LONDON(1953); PRIVATE EYES(1953); BOWERY BOYS MEET THE MONSTERS, THE(1954); JUNGLE GENTS(1954); PARIS PLAYBOYS(1954); BOWERY TO BAGDAD(1955); HIGH SOCIETY(1955); JAIL BUSTERS(1955); CRASH-ING LAS VEGAS(1956); DIG THAT URANIUM(1956); SPY CHASERS(1956); IT'S A MAD, MAD, MAD, MAD WORLD(1963); SECOND FIDDLE TO A STEEL GUI-TAR(1967); PHYNX, THE(1970)
Leo Gorcey, Jr.
ONE DARK NIGHT(1983)
Andrei Gorchilin
Misc. Silents
SICKLE AND HAMMER(1921, USSR)
Ken Gord
STARSHIP INVASIONS(1978, Can.), p; HIGH COUNTRY, THE(1981, Can.), p
Lisa Gord
ORIENT EXPRESS(1934)
Colin Gordan
MAN IN THE WHITE SUIT, THE(1952)
Jack Gordan
JAWS OF SATAN(1980)
Philip Gordan
1984
TERMINATOR, THE(1984)
William Gordean
SMOKEY AND THE BANDIT II(1980), ed; SHARKY'S MACHINE(1982), ed; STROKER ACE(1983), ed
1984
CANNONBALL RUN II(1984), ed
William D. Gordean
CANNONBALL RUN, THE(1981), ed
Larissa Gordeichik
DREAM COME TRUE, A(1963, USSR)

Fortune Gordein
ALL-AMERICAN, THE(1953)
James Gorden
SCAVENGERS, THE(1969)
Roy Gordeon
PERSONS IN HIDING(1939)
Emma Gordes
Silents
REBECCA OF SUNNYBROOK FARM(1917)
Jerry Gordet
WHO'S MINDING THE STORE?(1963)
Paul Gordeuax
CRIME DOES NOT PAY(1962, Fr.), w
Keith Gordey
1984
RUNAWAY(1984)
Lyudmila Gordeychik
HOUSE WITH AN ATTIC, THE(1964, USSR)
The Gordian Knot
YOUNG RUNAWAYS, THE(1968)
Anita Gordiana
VIVA VILLA!(1934)
Fortune Gordien
NORTH TO ALASKA(1960)
Nadine Gordimer
CITY LOVERS(1982, S. African), w
Jacob Gordin
WITHOUT A HOME(1939, Pol.), w
Michael Gordin
BOYS' NIGHT OUT(1962), d
Sacha Gordine
IDIOT, THE(1948, Fr.), p; DEDEE(1949, Fr.), p; LA MARIE DU PORT(1951, Fr.), p; BLACK ORPHEUS(1959 Fr./Ital./Braz.), p
Sasha Gordine
LA RONDE(1954, Fr.), p
Arthur Gordini
Silents
NET, THE(1923)
Abraham Gordon
KISS ME GOODBYE(1982)
Adrian Gordon
BALTIMORE BULLET, THE(1980), art d
Al Gordon
SYSTEM, THE(1953)
Alan Gordon
MUDLARK, THE(1950, Brit.); 13 EAST STREET(1952, Brit.); DEADLY NIGHT-SHADE(1953, Brit.); FOXY LADY(1971, Can.); CANNIBAL GIRLS(1973)
Albert Gordon
BLOODY PIT OF HORROR, THE(1965, Ital.)
Alex Gordon
JAIL BAIT(1954), w; LAWLESS RIDER, THE(1954), p; GIRLS IN PRISON(1956), p; SHE-CREATURE, THE(1956), p; DRAGSTRIP GIRL(1957), p; FLESH AND THE SPUR(1957), p; MOTORCYCLE GANG(1957), p; RUNAWAY DAUGHTERS(1957), p; VOODOO WOMAN(1957), p; JET ATTACK(1958), p; SUBMARINE SEAHAWK(1959), p; ATOMIC SUBMARINE, THE(1960), p; UNDERWATER CITY, THE(1962), w; BOUNTY KILLER, THE(1965), p; REQUIEM FOR A GUNFIGHTER(1965), p
Alice Gordon
JACKTOWN(1962)
Alvin J. Gordon
TENNESSEE CHAMP(1954)
Anita Gordon
FUN AND FANCY FREE(1947)
Ann Gordon
VARIETY PARADE(1936, Brit.)
Anthony Gordon
TIME AFTER TIME(1979, Brit.); UNDER THE RAINBOW(1981)
Arthur Gordon
REPRISAL(1956), w; ONE MAN'S WAY(1964), w
Asheton Gordon
ZACHARIAH(1971), prod d
Barbara Gordon
CHRISTINA(1974, Can.); PLAGUE(1978, Can.); IF YOU COULD SEE WHAT I HEAR(1982); I'M DANCING AS FAST AS I CAN(1982), w; THRESHOLD(1983, Can.)
Misc. Talkies
TRAPPED(1982)
Barry Gordon
GIRL CAN'T HELP IT, THE(1956); HANDS OF A STRANGER(1962); PRESSURE POINT(1962); THOUSAND CLOWNS, A(1965); SPIRIT IS WILLING, THE(1967); DOUBLE STOP(1968); OUT OF IT(1969); LOVE AT FIRST BITE(1979)
Barry Mark Gordon
SOMETHING WICKED THIS WAY COMES(1983), ed
Basil Gordon
WILLIAM COMES TO TOWN(1948, Brit.)
Ben Gordon
NOTHING PERSONAL(1980, Can.); LAST CHASE, THE(1981); UTILITIES(1983, Can.)
Benjamin Gordon
IMPROPER CHANNELS(1981, Can.)
Bernard Gordon
FLESH AND FURY(1952), w; LAWLESS BREED, THE(1952), w; CRIME WA-VE(1954), w; CRY OF BATTLE(1963), w; 55 DAYS AT PEKING(1963), w; THIN RED LINE, THE(1964), w; CUSTER OF THE WEST(1968, U.S., Span.), w; KRAKATOA, EAST OF JAVA(1969), w; BAD MAN'S RIVER(1972, Span.), p; HORROR EX-PRESS(1972, Span./Brit.), p; PANCHO VILLA(1975, Span.), p
Bert I. Gordon
SERPENT ISLAND(1954), p,d&w; KING DINOSAUR(1955), p, d, w; AMAZING COLOSSAL MAN, THE(1957), p&d, w, spec eff; BEGINNING OF THE END(1957), p&d; CYCLOPS(1957), p,d&w; ATTACK OF THE PUPPET PEOPLE(1958), p&d, w; EARTH VS. THE SPIDER(1958), p&d, w; SPIDER, THE(1958), p&d, w; WAR OF THE COLOSSAL BEAST(1958), p&d, w, spec eff; BOY AND THE PIRATES, THE(1960),

p&d; TORMENTED(1960), p, d, w; MAGIC SWORD, THE(1962), p&d, w; VILLAGE OF THE GIANTS(1965), p&d, spec eff; PICTURE MOMMY DEAD(1966), p&d; NE-CROMANCY(1972), p,d&w; MAD BOMBER, THE(1973), p,d&w, ph; FOOD OF THE GODS, THE(1976), p&d, w; EMPIRE OF THE ANTS(1977), p&d, w
Misc. Talkies
COMING, THE(1983), d
Bertie Gordon
Misc. Silents
CASTLES IN SPAIN(1920, Brit.); LORNA DOONE(1920, Brit.)
Bette Gordon
1984
VARIETY(1984), d, w
Betty Gordon
HAPPY DAYS(1930)
Bill Gordon
DISC JOCKEY(1951)
Bob Gordon
COACH(1978), ed; CHAMP, THE(1979)
Bobby Gordon
JAZZ SINGER, THE(1927); WIDE OPEN(1930); BIG BUSINESS GIRL(1931); COUN-SELLOR-AT-LAW(1933); STUDENT TOUR(1934); STRANGE WIVES(1935); TWO AGAINST THE WORLD(1936)
Silents
PENROD AND SAM(1923); MEASURE OF A MAN, THE(1924); LAZY LIGHT-NING(1926)
Misc. Silents
HIS PEOPLE(1925); MOUNTAINS OF MANHATTAN(1927); RACE FOR LIFE, A(1928)
Bruce Gordon
LADY FROM THE SEA, THE(1929, Brit.); GUEST OF HONOR(1934, Brit.); ELE-PHANT BOY(1937, Brit.); PHANTOM SHIP(1937, Brit.); SONG OF THE FORGE(1937, Brit.); NIGHT BOAT TO DUBLIN(1946, Brit.); LOVE HAPPY(1949); DOUBLE CROSS(1956, Brit.); BUCCANEER, THE(1958); CURSE OF THE UNDEAD(1959); KEY WITNESS(1960); RIDER ON A DEAD HORSE(1962); SCARFACE MOB, THE(1962); TOWER OF LONDON(1962); SLOW RUN(1968); HELLO DOWN THERE(1969); MA-CHISMO–40 GRAVES FOR 40 GUNS(1970); PIRANHA(1978); TIMERIDER(1983)
Silents
DEMOCRACY(1918, Brit.); AFTER MANY DAYS(1919, Brit.); ALL MEN ARE LIARS(1919, Brit.); FATE'S PLAYTHING(1920, Brit.); BRING HIM IN(1921); PRIVATE SCANDAL, A(1921); LOVE GAMBLER, THE(1922); KENTUCKY DAYS(1923); JUDG-MENT OF THE STORM(1924); WESTERN LUCK(1924); DON X(1925); GOLD AND THE GIRL(1925); AHEAD OF THE LAW(1926); BUCKING THE TRUTH(1926); DUDE COWBOY, THE(1926); UNKNOWN CAVALIER, THE(1926); BLAZING DAYS(1927); OUTLAW DOG, THE(1927); SONORA KID, THE(1927); PARTNERS IN CRIME(1928)
Misc. Silents
FIRST MEN IN THE MOON, THE(1919, Brit.); LITTLE CHILD SHALL LEAD THEM, A(1919, Brit.); FORBIDDEN VALLEY(1920); HOUSE OF THE TOLLING BELLS, THE(1920); ROBES OF SIN(1924); TAINTED MONEY(1924); 40TH DOOR, THE(1924); BRAND OF COWARDICE(1925); DANGER ZONE, THE(1925); MIDNIGHT MOL-LY(1925); NO MAN'S LAW(1925); SKY'S THE LIMIT(1925); SMOOTH AS SATIN(1925); STAMPEDIN' TROUBLE(1925); THREE WISE CROOKS(1925); BEYOND THE ROCK-IES(1926); DANGEROUS DUDE, THE(1926); ESCAPE, THE(1926); LAWLESS TRAILS(1926); MORAN OF THE MOUNTED(1926); SPEED LIMIT, THE(1926); STICK TO YOUR STORY(1926); DESERT DUST(1927); MYSTERY RIDER(1928); CLEAN-UP, THE(1929)
Bunny Gordon
WHITE CLIFFS OF DOVER, THE(1944)
C. Henry Gordon
UNDER TWO FLAGS(1936); YELLOW JACK(1938); RENEGADES(1930); BLACK CAMEL, THE(1931); CHARLIE CHAN CARRIES ON(1931); HUSH MONEY(1931); MATA HARI(1931); ONCE A SINNER(1931); WOMAN OF EXPERIENCE, A(1931); YOUNG AS YOU FEEL(1931); CROOKED CIRCLE(1932); DOOMED BATTALION, THE(1932); GAY CABALLERO, THE(1932); HELL'S HIGHWAY(1932); JEWEL ROB-BERY(1932); KONGO(1932); MISS PINKERTON(1932); RASPUTIN AND THE EM-PRESS(1932); ROAR OF THE DRAGON(1932); SCARFACE(1932); SCARLET DAWN(1932); STATE'S ATTORNEY(1932); STRANGE LOVE OF MOLLY LOUVAIN, THE(1932); THIRTEEN WOMEN(1932); WASHINGTON MASQUERADE(1932); AD-VICE TO THE LOVELORN(1933); BROADWAY THROUGH A KEYHOLE(1933); CHIEF, THE(1933); CLEAR ALL WIRES(1933); DEVIL'S IN LOVE, THE(1933); GABRIEL OVER THE WHITE HOUSE(1933); MADE ON BROADWAY(1933); NIGHT FLIGHT(1933); PENTHOUSE(1933); SECRET OF MADAME BLANCHE, THE(1933); STAGE MOTHER(1933); STORM AT DAYBREAK(1933); TURN BACK THE CLOCK(1933); WHISTLING IN THE DARK(1933); DEATH OF THE DIAMOND(1934); FUGITIVE LOVERS(1934); HIDE-OUT(1934); LAZY RIVER(1934); MEN IN WHI-TE(1934); STAMBOUL QUEST(1934); STRAIGHT IS THE WAY(1934); THIS SIDE OF HEAVEN(1934); WOMEN IN HIS LIFE, THE(1934); BIG BROADCAST OF 1936, THE(1935); CRUSADES, THE(1935); GREAT HOTEL MURDER(1935); PURSUIT(1935); BIG GAME, THE(1936); CHARGE OF THE LIGHT BRIGADE, THE(1936); HOLLY-WOOD BOULEVARD(1936); LOVE LETTERS OF A STAR(1936); PROFESSIONAL SOLDIER(1936); CHARLIE CHAN AT THE OLYMPICS(1937); CONQUEST(1937); SOPHIE LANG GOES WEST(1937); STAND-IN(1937); TRAPPED BY G-MEN(1937); TROUBLE IN MOROCCO(1937); ADVENTURE IN SAHARA(1938); INVISIBLE ENE-MY(1938); SHARPSHOOTERS(1938); TARZAN'S REVENGE(1938); CHARLIE CHAN IN THE CITY OF DARKNESS(1939); HERITAGE OF THE DESERT(1939); LONG SHOT, THE(1939); MAN OF CONQUEST(1939); RETURN OF THE CISCO KID(1939); TRAPPED IN THE SKY(1939); CHARLIE CHAN AT THE WAX MUSEUM(1940); KIT CARSON(1940); PASSPORT TO ALCATRAZ(1940)
Carl Gordon
GORDON'S WAR(1973); BINGO LONG TRAVELING ALL-STARS AND MOTOR KINGS, THE(1976)
1984
BROTHER FROM ANOTHER PLANET, THE(1984)
Silents
RAINBOW PRINCESS, THE(1916)
Charles Gordon
CAPTAIN TUGBOAT ANNIE(1945); ROAD TO ALCATRAZ(1945); THREE'S A CROWD(1945); VAMPIRE'S GHOST, THE(1945); SWAMP FIRE(1946)
Silents
CONNECTICUT YANKEE AT KING ARTHUR'S COURT, A(1921)

Cheryl Gordon
Misc. Silents
BONNIE MAY(1920)
Cheryl Gordon
Misc. Talkies
INCOMING FRESHMEN(1979)
Christine Gordon
I WALKED WITH A ZOMBIE(1943); MISSION TO MOSCOW(1943)
Claire Gordon
AND WOMEN SHALL WEEP(1960, Brit.); BULLDOG BREED, THE(1960, Brit.);
KONGA(1961, Brit.); TICKET TO PARADISE(1961, Brit.); SECOND BEST SECRET
AGENT IN THE WHOLE WIDE WORLD, THE(1965, Brit.); GREAT CATHERINE(1968,
Brit.); SUBURBAN WIVES(1973, Brit.)
Clarence Gordon
ONE HOUR TO LIVE(1939)
Clark Gordon
COLD WIND IN AUGUST(1961); GAILY, GAILY(1969)
Clarke Gordon
THREE CAME HOME(1950); WHEN WILLIE COMES MARCHING HOME(1950);
INVITATION TO A GUNFIGHTER(1964); ONE SPY TOO MANY(1966); WAY WEST,
THE(1967); JOURNEY TO SHILOH(1968); MORE DEAD THAN ALIVE(1968); IM-
PASSE(1969); GLASS HOUSES(1972); DIFFERENT STORY, A(1978); COAST TO
COAST(1980)
Cliff Gordon
MAN'S AFFAIR, A(1949, Brit.); MANIACS ON WHEELS(1951, Brit.), w; MEN ARE
CHILDREN TWICE(1953, Brit.), w
Colin Gordon
COMING-OUT PARTY, A(; EDWARD, MY SON(1949, U.S./Brit.); HELTER SKEL-
TER(1949, Brit.); CIRCLE OF DANGER(1951, Brit.); GREEN GROW THE RU-
SHES(1951, Brit.); LADY WITH A LAMP, THE(1951, Brit.); LAUGHTER IN
PARADISE(1951, Brit.); LONG DARK HALL, THE(1951, Brit.); THIRD VISITOR,
THE(1951, Brit.); TRAVELLER'S JOY(1951, Brit.); CRASH OF SILENCE(1952, Brit.);
HOUR OF THIRTEEN, THE(1952); FOLLY TO BE WISE(1953); GAY ADVENTURE,
THE(1953, Brit.); HEART OF THE MATTER, THE(1954, Brit.); UP TO HIS NECK(1954,
Brit.); CASE OF THE RED MONKEY(1955, Brit.); ESCAPADE(1955, Brit.); INNO-
CENTS IN PARIS(1955, Brit.); WICKED WIFE(1955, Brit.); EXTRA DAY, THE(1956,
Brit.); JUMPING FOR JOY(1956, Brit.); KEEP IT CLEAN(1956, Brit.); TOUCH OF THE
SUN, A(1956, Brit.); GREEN MAN, THE(1957, Brit.); JOHN AND JULIE(1957, Brit.);
KEY MAN, THE(1957, Brit.); UP IN THE WORLD(1957, Brit.); DOCTOR'S DILEMMA,
THE(1958, Brit.); ONE THAT GOT AWAY, THE(1958, Brit.); SAFECRACKER,
THE(1958, Brit.); BOBBIKINS(1959, Brit.); CROWNING TOUCH, THE(1959, Brit.);
MOUSE THAT ROARED, THE(1959, Brit.); BIG DAY, THE(1960, Brit.); DAY THEY
ROBBED THE BANK OF ENGLAND, THE(1960, Brit.); PLEASE TURN OVER(1960,
Brit.); VIRGIN ISLAND(1960, Brit.); HIS AND HERS(1961, Brit.); HOUSE OF MYS-
TERY(1961, Brit.); THREE ON A SPREE(1961, Brit.); ALIVE AND KICKING(1962,
Brit.); BOYS, THE(1962, Brit.); BURN WITCH BURN(1962); DEVIL'S AGENT,
THE(1962, Brit.); SEVEN KEYS(1962, Brit.); STRONGROOM(1962, Brit.); BITTER
HARVEST(1963, Brit.); CROOKS ANONYMOUS(1963, Brit.); HEAVENS ABOVE!(1963,
Brit.); RUNNING MAN, THE(1963, Brit.); IN THE DOGHOUSE(1964, Brit.); PINK
PANTHER, THE(1964); WHY BOTHER TO KNOCK(1964, Brit.); COUNTERFEIT
CONSTABLE, THE(1966, Fr.); FAMILY WAY, THE(1966, Brit.); GREAT ST. TRI-
NIAN'S TRAIN ROBBERY, THE(1966, Brit.); LIQUIDATOR, THE(1966, Brit.); PSY-
CHOPATH, THE(1966, Brit.); CASINO ROYALE(1967, Brit.); DON'T RAISE THE
BRIDGE, LOWER THE RIVER(1968, Brit.); MISCHIEF(1969, Brit.); SUBTER-
FUGE(1969, US/Brit.); TRYGON FACTOR, THE(1969, Brit.)
Misc. Talkies
BODY BENEATH, THE(1970)
Dan Gordon
GULLIVER'S TRAVELS(1939), w; MR. BUG GOES TO TOWN(1941), w; MUTI-
NEERS, THE(1949), w; SHOWDOWN, THE(1950), d&w; TRAIN RIDE TO HOLLY-
WOOD(1975), w; BEAST WITHIN, THE(1982)
1984
TANK(1984), w
Dane Gordon
HARD STEEL(1941, Brit.)
David Gordon
STRANGER'S MEETING(1957, Brit.), w
Debra Gordon
EFFECTS(1980); FLASHDANCE(1983)
Del Gordon
LAST OF THE CLINTONS, THE(1935); WILD MUSTANG(1935)
Denis Gordon
DAUGHTER OF DARKNESS(1948, Brit.)
Denise Gordon
FEEDBACK(1979)
Dick Gordon
WORDS AND MUSIC(1929); CHARLIE CHAN IN BLACK MAGIC(1944); ONCE
UPON A TIME(1944); WEEKEND AT THE WALDORF(1945); DEAD RECK-
ONING(1947); HER HUSBAND'S AFFAIRS(1947); FORCE OF EVIL(1948); ONE
TOUCH OF VENUS(1948); IMPACT(1949); DOUBLE DYNAMITE(1951); I WAS A
COMMUNIST FOR THE F.B.I.(1951); RACKET, THE(1951)
Silents
ROMANCE ROAD(1925)
Don Gordon
LET'S GO NAVY(1951); GIRLS IN THE NIGHT(1953); REVOLT AT FORT LARA-
MIE(1957); CRY TOUGH(1959); LOLLIPOP COVER, THE(1965), a, w; BULLITT(1968);
GAMBLERS, THE(1969); CANNON FOR CORDOBA(1970); WUSA(1970); LAST MOV-
IE, THE(1971); FUZZ(1972); SLAUGHTER(1972); Z.P.G.(1972); MACK, THE(1973);
PAPILLON(1973); EDUCATION OF SONNY CARSON, THE(1974); TOWERING IN-
FERNO, THE(1974); FINAL CONFLICT, THE(1981); ENTER THE NINJA(1982); OUT
OF THE BLUE(1982)
Misc. Talkies
ASYLUM FOR A SPY(1967)
Donald Gordon
WOMAN ON THE BEACH, THE(1947); ONCE MORE, MY DARLING(1949); RO-
SEANNA McCOY(1949); FORCE OF ARMS(1951); GUY WHO CAME BACK,
THE(1951); IT'S A BIG COUNTRY(1951); WHEN I GROW UP(1951); TALK ABOUT A
STRANGER(1952)

Donna Gordon
KILLING OF A CHINESE BOOKIE, THE(1976)
Dorothy Gordon
DUMMY TALKS, THE(1943, Brit.); SILVER FLEET, THE(1945, Brit.); LOVE IN
PAWN(1953, Brit.); TONIGHT AT 8:30(1953, Brit.); TWILIGHT WOMEN(1953, Brit.);
HOBSON'S CHOICE(1954, Brit.); GIRL RUSH, THE(1955); ALL FOR MARY(1956,
Brit.); LIEUTENANT WORE SKIRTS, THE(1956); REVOLT OF MAMIE STOVER,
THE(1956); TEARS FOR SIMON(1957, Brit.); HAUNTED STRANGLER, THE(1958,
Brit.); LIFE IN EMERGENCY WARD 10(1959, Brit.); SONS AND LOVERS(1960, Brit.);
SECRET PARTNER, THE(1961, Brit.); HOUSE OF WHIPCORD(1974, Brit.)
Silents
CHORUS GIRL'S ROMANCE, A(1920); PRICE OF SILENCE, THE(1920, Brit.)
Doug Gordon
IN NAME ONLY(1939)
Douglas Gordon
KEY, THE(1934); MYSTERY OF MR. X, THE(1934); DARK ANGEL, THE(1935);
DRACULA'S DAUGHTER(1936); LOVE ON THE RUN(1936); PERSONAL PROPER-
TY(1937); WOMEN OF GLAMOUR(1937); DAWN PATROL, THE(1938); RAF-
FLES(1939); WE ARE NOT ALONE(1939); FOREIGN CORRESPONDENT(1940); MRS.
MINIVER(1942)
Ed Gordon
SINGING COWGIRL, THE(1939); PUTNEY SWOPE(1969)
Eddie Gordon
SUNSET MURDER CASE(1941); LADY OF BURLESQUE(1943)
Edna Gordon
Silents
KING OF KINGS, THE(1927)
Edward Gordon
RIDE 'EM COWGIRL(1939)
Silents
ISLE OF HOPE, THE(1925); DUDE COWBOY, THE(1926)
Edward R. Gordon
Silents
REPENTANCE(1922, Brit.), d&w; LIEUTENANT DARING RN AND THE WATER
RATS(1924, Brit.), d
Misc. Silents
LOVE'S INFLUENCE(1922, Brit.), d; GUN-HAND GARRISON(1927), d; RIDIN'
LUCK(1927), d; WILD BORN(1927), d
Edwin Gordon
CHOSEN, THE(1982), w
Eileen Gordon
TOGETHER FOR DAYS(1972); THREE DAYS OF THE CONDOR(1975)
Elisabeth Gordon
NICE GIRL LIKE ME, A(1969, Brit.)
Eric Gordon
BOY WHO CRIED WEREWOLF, THE(1973)
Eva Gordon
Silents
LIFE'S DARN FUNNY(1921); LOST LADY, A(1924)
Misc. Silents
UNDER SUSPICION(1918); EVER SINCE EVE(1921); CHECHAHCOS, THE(1924)
Evan Gordon
HOMETOWN U.S.A.(1979)
Eve Gordon
WORLD ACCORDING TO GARP, The(1982)
Flash Gordon
RIDING HIGH(1943)
Flora Gordon
TORMENTED(1960), spec eff; VILLAGE OF THE GIANTS(1965), spec eff
Fortune Gordon
PRINCE VALIANT(1954)
Fred Gordon
SEPIA CINDERELLA(1947)
Fredi O. Gordon
PARADISE ALLEY(1978)
G. Swayne Gordon
FOLLIES GIRL(1943)
Gail Gordon
ROTTEN APPLE, THE(1963)
Gale Gordon
HERE WE GO AGAIN(1942); WOMAN OF DISTINCTION, A(1950); HERE COME
THE NELSONS(1952); FRANCIS COVERS THE BIG TOWN(1953); OUR MISS
BROOKS(1956); RALLY 'ROUND THE FLAG, BOYS!(1958); DON'T GIVE UP THE
SHIP(1959); THIRTY FOOT BRIDE OF CANDY ROCK, THE(1959); VISIT TO A
SMALL PLANET(1960); ALL HANDS ON DECK(1961); ALL IN A NIGHT'S
WORK(1961); DONDI(1961); SERGEANT DEADHEAD(1965); SPEEDWAY(1968)
Gavin Gordon
HIS FIRST COMMAND(1929); ROMANCE(1930); SILVER HORDE, THE(1930);
GREAT, MEADOW, THE(1931); SECRET SERVICE(1931); SHIPMATES(1931);
AMERICAN MADNESS(1932); MAN AGAINST WOMAN(1932); PHANTOM OF
CRESTWOOD(1932); TWO AGAINST THE WORLD(1932); BITTER TEA OF
GENERAL YEN, THE(1933); BLACK BEAUTY(1933); FEMALE(1933); HARD TO
HANDLE(1933); I ADORE YOU(1933, Brit.); MYSTERY OF THE WAX MUSEUM,
THE(1933); HAPPINESS AHEAD(1934); I WAS A SPY(1934, Brit.); LONE COW-
BOY(1934); SCARLET EMPRESS, THE(1934); WAKE UP AND DREAM(1934); BOR-
DERTOWN(1935); GRAND OLD GIRL(1935); LOVE ME FOREVER(1935); PAGE MISS
GLORY(1935); RED HOT TIRES(1935); STRANDED(1935); WOMEN MUST
DRESS(1935); LEAVENWORTH CASE, THE(1936); TICKET TO PARADISE(1936);
HIGH HAT(1937); THEY GAVE HIM A GUN(1937); TOAST OF NEW YORK,
THE(1937); WINDJAMMER(1937); I SEE ICE(1938); MURDER BY INVITATION(1941);
PAPER BULLETS(1941); SUSPICION(1941); I KILLED THAT MAN(1942); LONE
STAR VIGILANTES, THE(1942); MR. CELEBRITY(1942); CENTENNIAL SUM-
MER(1946); NOTORIOUS(1946); PHILO VANCE'S GAMBLE(1947); THREE ON A
TICKET(1947); KNOCK ON WOOD(1954); THERE'S NO BUSINESS LIKE SHOW
BUSINESS(1954); WHITE CHRISTMAS(1954); HIGH SOCIETY(1955); PARD-
NERS(1956); TEN COMMANDMENTS, THE(1956); VAGABOND KING, THE(1956);
CHICAGO CONFIDENTIAL(1957); JOHNNY TREMAIN(1957); MATCHMAKER,
THE(1958); BAT, THE(1959); POCKETFUL OF MIRACLES(1961); NUTTY PROFES-
SOR, THE(1963); PATSY, THE(1964)

Misc. Talkies
CHASING THROUGH EUROPE(1929)
Gay Gordon
ROOM FOR ONE MORE(1952)
Gerald Gordon
FORTY POUNDS OF TROUBLE(1962); ONE MAN'S WAY(1964); HELL UP IN HARLEM(1973); SO LONG, BLUE BOY(1973), d
Gerdina Gordon
5 SINNERS(1961, Ger.)
Gerti Gordon
BOYS FROM BRAZIL, THE(1978)
Gladys Gordon
MEN OF THE SEA(1951, Brit.)
Silents
WEB OF FATE(1927), w
Glen Gordon
YOU'RE IN THE NAVY NOW(1951)
Glen Charles Gordon
BRIGHT VICTORY(1951)
Glenn Gordon
CELL 2455, DEATH ROW(1955); FINGER MAN(1955)
Gloria Gordon
MY FRIEND IRMA(1949); THAT FORSYTE WOMAN(1949); O. HENRY'S FULL HOUSE(1952); BENEATH THE 12-MILE REEF(1953); NIAGARA(1953); TITANIC(1953); MAN CALLED PETER, THE(1955)
Misc. Silents
DANCING DAYS(1926); EXCLUSIVE RIGHTS(1926)
Gordon Gordon
MAKE HASTE TO LIVE(1954), w; EXPERIMENT IN TERROR(1962), w; THAT DARN CAT(1965), w
Grace Gordon
GODLESS GIRL, THE(1929)
Silents
MIND OVER MOTOR(1923)
Misc. Silents
AFFINITIES(1922)
Grant Gordon
SIX BRIDGES TO CROSS(1955); SUBJECT WAS ROSES, THE(1968)
Guy Gordon
PERSECUTION AND ASSASSINATION OF JEAN-PAUL MARAT AS PERFORMED BY THE INMATES OF THE ASYLUM OF CHARENTON UNDER THE DIRECTION OF THE MARQUIS DE SADE, THE(1967, Brit.)
Hal Gordon
LIMPING MAN, THE(1931, Brit.); OLD SOLDIERS NEVER DIE(1931, Brit.); OUT OF THE BLUE(1931, Brit.); POOR OLD BILL(1931, Brit.); UP FOR THE CUP(1931, Brit.); WINDJAMMER, THE(1931, Brit.); BROTHER ALFRED(1932, Brit.); HELP YOURSELF(1932, Brit.); HIS WIFE'S MOTHER(1932, Brit.); INDISCRETIONS OF EVE(1932, Brit.); INSULT(1932, Brit.); JOSSER IN THE ARMY(1932, Brit.); LAST COUPON, THE(1932, Brit.); LET ME EXPLAIN, DEAR(1932); LORD CAMBER'S LADIES(1932, Brit.); LUCKY GIRL(1932, Brit.); MONEY FOR NOTHING(1932, Brit.); NEW HOTEL, THE(1932, Brit.); OLD SPANISH CUSTOMERS(1932, Brit.); TONIGHT'S THE NIGHT(1932, Brit.); CRIME ON THE HILL(1933, Brit.); FACING THE MUSIC(1933, Brit.); FOR THE LOVE OF MIKE(1933, Brit.); HAWLEY'S OF HIGH STREET(1933, Brit.); MONEY TALKS(1933, Brit.); POLITICAL PARTY, A(1933, Brit.); PRIDE OF THE FORCE, THE(1933, Brit.); SLEEPLESS NIGHTS(1933, Brit.); SOUTHERN MAID, A(1933, Brit.); THEIR NIGHT OUT(1933, Brit.); GREAT DEFENDER, THE(1934, Brit.); HAPPY(1934, Brit.); LOST IN THE LEGION(1934, Brit.); MASTER AND MAN(1934, Brit.); MY SONG GOES ROUND THE WORLD(1934, Brit.); OUTCAST, THE(1934, Brit.); SOMETIMES GOOD(1934, Brit.); CAPTAIN BILL(1935, Brit.); DANCE BAND(1935, Brit.); DANDY DICK(1935, Brit.); DEPUTY DRUMMER, THE(1935, Brit.); INVITATION TO THE WALTZ(1935, Brit.); LEND ME YOUR WIFE(1935, Brit.); NO MONKEY BUSINESS(1935, Brit.); PLAY UP THE BAND(1935, Brit.); 18 MINUTES(1935, Brit.); IT'S IN THE BAG(1936, Brit.); KEEP YOUR SEATS PLEASE(1936, Brit.); MAN BEHIND THE MASK, THE(1936, Brit.); NO ESCAPE(1936, Brit.); ONE GOOD TURN(1936, Brit.); QUEEN OF HEARTS(1936, Brit.); SOUTHERN ROSES(1936, Brit.); KEEP FIT(1937, Brit.); ROMANCE AND RICHES(1937, Brit.); SABOTAGE(1937, Brit.); HIDEOUT IN THE ALPS(1938, Brit.); WE'RE GOING TO BE RICH(1938, Brit.); COME ON GEORGE(1939, Brit.); DEAD MEN TELL NO TALES(1939, Brit.); IT'S IN THE AIR(1940, Brit.); LET GEORGE DO IT(1940, Brit.); SPARE A COPPER(1940, Brit.); WE'LL SMILE AGAIN(1942, Brit.); OLD MOTHER RILEY, DETECTIVE(1943, Brit.); GIVE ME THE STARS(1944, Brit.); HEAVEN IS ROUND THE CORNER(1944, Brit.); IT HAPPENED ONE SUNDAY(1944, Brit.); KISS THE BRIDE GOODBYE(1944, Brit.); WELCOME, MR. WASHINGTON(1944, Brit.); I'LL TURN TO YOU(1946, Brit.)
Silents
HONEYMOON AHEAD(1927, Brit.)
Hal B. Gordon
SHARK RIVER(1953), ed
Hall Gordon
BREAK THE NEWS(1938, Brit.)
Hank Gordon
Misc. Talkies
INSTRUCTOR, THE(1983)
Hannah Gordon
SPRING AND PORT WINE(1970, Brit.); ALFIE DARLING(1975, Brit.); WATERSHIP DOWN(1978, Brit.); ELEPHANT MAN, THE(1980, Brit.)
Harold Gordon
IRON MISTRESS, THE(1952); VIVA ZAPATA!(1952); JAZZ SINGER, THE(1953); BENGAL BRIGADE(1954); EAST OF EDEN(1955); YELLOWNECK(1955); LOOK IN ANY WINDOW(1961), ed
Harold M. Gordon
MARA OF THE WILDERNESS(1966), ed
Harris Gordon
Silents
MILLION DOLLAR ROBBERY, THE(1914); OVAL DIAMOND, THE(1916); PRODIGAL WIFE, THE(1918); STOP THIEF(1920); BURNING SANDS(1922); OUT OF THE SILENT NORTH(1922); WOMAN WHO WALKED ALONE, THE(1922); WONDERFUL WIFE, A(1922); EASY GOING GORDON(1925)
Misc. Silents
GOD'S WITNESS(1915); MILL ON THE FLOSS, THE(1915); PRICE OF HER SILENCE, THE(1915); FIVE FAULTS OF FLO, THE(1916); HER FATHER'S GOLD(1916);

DOUBLE CROSSED(1917); IMAGE MAKER, THE(1917); BEYOND THE LAW(1918); WHY AMERICA WILL WIN(1918); SUSPENCE(1919); LIVE AND LET LIVE(1921); ROMANCE AND RUSTLERS(1925)
Harry Gordon
EL DIABLO RIDES(1939), w; TEENAGE MILLIONAIRE(1961), set d; HARLOW(1965), set d; SLITHER(1973), set d; ODE TO BILLY JOE(1976), set d
Hayes Gordon
RETURN OF CAPTAIN INVINCIBLE, THE(1983, Aus./U.S.)
Henry Gordon
HONOR OF THE FAMILY(1931)
Hilda Gordon
TRUTH ABOUT MURDER, THE(1946), w
Homer Gordon
GUN RANGER, THE(1937), w
Homer King Gordon
FIGHTING ROOKIE, THE(1934), w; KENTUCKY BLUE STREAK(1935), w; RIP ROARING RILEY(1935), w; IN OLD MONTANA(1939), w
Howard Gordon
IDOLMAKER, THE(1980)
Huntley Gordon
MARRIAGE PLAYGROUND, THE(1929); MELODY LANE(1929); SCANDAL(1929); FOX MOVIETONE FOLLIES OF 1930(1930); ALL-AMERICAN, THE(1932); BROADWAY TO CHEYENNE(1932); KING MURDER, THE(1932); MIDNIGHT WARNING, THE(1932); NIGHT WORLD(1932); PHANTOM EXPRESS, THE(1932); RED-HAIRED ALIBI, THE(1932); SALLY OF THE SUBWAY(1932); SPEED MADNESS(1932); CORRUPTION(1933); JUSTICE TAKES A HOLIDAY(1933); ONLY YESTERDAY(1933); RACETRACK(1933); SAILOR BE GOOD(1933); SECRETS(1933); WORLD GONE MAD, THE(1933); BOMBAY MAIL(1934); DANCING MAN(1934); EMBARRASSING MOMENTS(1934); FRONT PAGE WOMAN(1935); IRISH IN US, THE(1935); IT HAPPENED IN NEW YORK(1935); MURDER BY TELEVISION(1935); PAGE MISS GLORY(1935); SPANISH CAPE MYSTERY(1935); DANIEL BOONE(1936); FOLLOW THE FLEET(1936); KLONDIKE ANNIE(1936); YOURS FOR THE ASKING(1936); IDOL OF THE CROWDS(1937); PORTIA ON TRIAL(1937); STAGE DOOR(1937); GANGSTER'S BOY(1938); PROFESSOR BEWARE(1938); MR. WONG IN CHINATOWN(1939); LADY WITH RED HAIR(1940)
Misc. Talkies
FROM BROADWAY TO CHEYENNE(1932)
Silents
OUR MRS. McCHESNEY(1918); DARK MIRROR, THE(1920); OUT YONDER(1920); ENCHANTMENT(1921); SOCIETY SNOBS(1921); RECKLESS YOUTH(1922); WHAT FOOLS MEN ARE(1922); PLEASURE MAD(1923); SOCIAL CODE, THE(1923); WANTERS, THE(1923); ENEMY SEX, THE(1924); MARRIED FLIRTS(1924); NEVER THE TWAIN SHALL MEET(1925); GILDED BUTTERFLY, THE(1926); SENSATION SEEKERS(1927); GYPSY OF THE NORTH(1928); OUR DANCING DAUGHTERS(1928); OUTCAST(1928); SINNERS IN LOVE(1928)
Misc. Silents
CONFLICT, THE(1916); DESTROYERS, THE(1916); HIS WIFE'S GOOD NAME(1916); BELOVED IMPOSTER, THE(1918); COMMON CAUSE, THE(1918); MILLION DOLLAR DOLLIES, THE(1918); TOO MANY CROOKS(1919); UNKNOWN QUANTITY, THE(1919); ATONEMENT(1920); FRISKY MRS. JOHNSON, THE(1920); INVISIBLE BOND, THE(1920); GIRL FROM NOWHERE, THE(1921); TROPICAL LOVE(1921); HIS WIFE'S HUSBAND(1922); MAN WANTED(1922); WHAT'S WRONG WITH THE WOMEN?(1922); WHEN THE DESERT CALLS(1922); BLUEBEARD'S 8TH WIFE(1923); CHASTITY(1923); CORDELIA THE MAGNIFICENT(1923); MALE WANTED(1923); SHADOWS OF PARIS(1924); TRUE AS STEEL(1924); WINE(1924); LOVE HOUR, THE(1925); TRUTHFUL SEX, THE(1926); SALLY'S SHOULDERS(1928)
Huntly Gordon
ANYBODY'S WOMAN(1930); CHINA PASSAGE(1937)
Silents
AT THE STAGE DOOR(1921); HER FATAL MILLIONS(1923); NAME THE WOMAN(1928)
Misc. Silents
FAMOUS MRS. FAIR, THE(1923); YOUR FRIEND AND MINE(1923); DARING LOVE(1924); GREAT DIVIDE, THE(1925); MY WIFE AND I(1925); WIFE WHO WASN'T WANTED, THE(1925); GOLDEN COCOON, THE(1926); GOLDEN WEB, THE(1926); HER SECOND CHANCE(1926); LOST AT SEA(1926); OTHER WOMEN'S HUSBANDS(1926); SILKEN SHACKLES(1926); DON'T TELL THE WIFE(1927)
Inch Gordon
RUDE BOY(1980, Brit.)
Israel Gordon
1984
PURPLE RAIN(1984)
J. Huntley Gordon
THEIR BIG MOMENT(1934)
Jack Gordon
SAGEBRUSH POLITICS(1930); CRIME, INC.(1945); CLOSE CALL FOR BOSTON BLACKIE, A(1946); MR. SOFT TOUCH(1949); UNDERCOVER MAN, THE(1949); LAS VEGAS LADY(1976)
Jack H. Gordon
VISITOR, THE(1980, Ital./U.S.)
Jacques Gordon
BRUTE FORCE(1947), tech adv
Jacqui Gordon
DEAD MAN'S FLOAT(1980, Aus.); DAY AFTER HALLOWEEN, THE(1981, Aus.)
James B. Gordon
GUN THAT WON THE WEST, THE(1955), w; INSIDE DETROIT(1955), w; CHA-CHA-CHA BOOM(1956), w; DON'T KNOCK THE ROCK(1956), w; HOUSTON STORY, THE(1956), w; MIAMI EXPOSE(1956), w; ROCK AROUND THE CLOCK(1956), w; WEREWOLF, THE(1956), w; UTAH BLAINE(1957), w; JOURNEY TO THE CENTER OF THE EARTH(1959), spec eff; PIER 5, HAVANA(1959), w; FROM THE TERRACE(1960), spec eff; LOST WORLD, THE(1960), spec eff; NOOSE FOR A GUNMAN(1960), w; THREE CAME TO KILL(1960), w; TWIST AROUND THE CLOCK(1961), w; DON'T KNOCK THE TWIST(1962), w; TOWER OF LONDON(1962), w; HOOTENANNY HOOT(1963), w; HAWAII(1966), spec eff; HOLD ON(1966), w; FILE OF THE GOLDEN GOOSE, THE(1969, Brit.), w
James Gordon
BACHELOR FATHER(1931); FRONT PAGE, THE(1931); STOWAWAY(1932); NEIGHBORS' WIVES(1933); MASK, THE(1961, Can.), spec eff

Silents

MYSTERY OF THE POISON POOL, THE(1914); LAST OF THE MOHICANS, THE(1920); BAIT, THE(1921); OLD SWIMMIN' HOLE, THE(1921); LOVE GAMBLER, THE(1922); NANCY FROM NOWHERE(1922); ON THE HIGH SEAS(1922); HEARTS OF OAK(1924); IRON HORSE, THE(1924); TUMBLEWEEDS(1925); ICE FLOOD, THE(1926); MISS NOBODY(1926); SOCIAL HIGHWAYMAN, THE(1926); BABE COMES HOME(1927); WANTED–A COWARD(1927); WAR HORSE, THE(1927); ESCAPE, THE(1928); MASKED EMOTIONS(1929)

Misc. Silents

CAPRICE(1913); HOODMAN BLIND(1913), d; FINAL CLOSEUP, THE(1919); THUNDERBOLT, THE(1919); BEHIND THE DOOR(1920); MAN FROM LOST RIVER, THE(1921); SUNSET JONES(1921); TRAILIN'(1921); GAME CHICKEN, THE(1922); SELF-MADE MAN, A(1922); PUBLICITY MADNESS(1927)

Jill Gordon
1984

RHINESTONE(1984)

Joan Gordon
Silents

QUEEN OF SHEBA, THE(1921)

Joe Gordon

KID FROM CLEVELAND, THE(1949)

John Gordon

CIRCLE, THE(1959, Brit.); MACBETH(1971, Brit.)

John E. Gordon

BEWARE(1946), w; LOOK OUT SISTER(1948), w; LOVE ISLAND(1952), w

Jonathan Gordon

KING, MURRAY(1969), a, d

Joyce Gordon

IMPROPER CHANNELS(1981, Can.)
1984

JUST THE WAY YOU ARE(1984); POLICE ACADEMY(1984)

Julia Swayne Gordon

GIRL IN THE GLASS CAGE, THE(1929); IS EVERYBODY HAPPY?(1929); SCANDAL(1929); YOUNGER GENERATION(1929); DUDE WRANGLER, THE(1930); DUMB-BELLS IN ERMINE(1930); FOR THE LOVE O'LIL(1930); TODAY(1930); CAPTAIN APPLEJACK(1931); MISBEHAVING LADIES(1931); GOLDEN WEST, THE(1932); SECRETS OF THE FRENCH POLICE(1932); HELLO, EVERYBODY(1933)

Silents

BATTLE CRY OF PEACE, THE(1915); JUGGERNAUT, THE(1915); SINS OF THE MOTHERS(1915); ARSENE LUPIN(1917); IN THE BALANCE(1917); DESIRED WOMAN, THE(1918); CAPTAIN'S CAPTAIN, THE(1919); MISS DULCIE FROM DIXIE(1919); CHILD FOR SALE, A(1920); GREATER THAN FAME(1920); LIFTING SHADOWS(1920); BURN 'EM UP BARNES(1921); SHAMS OF SOCIETY(1921); SILVER LINING, THE(1921); DARLING OF THE RICH, THE(1923); SCARAMOUCHE(1923); TIE THAT BINDS, THE(1923); NOT SO LONG AGO(1925); BRIDE OF THE STORM(1926); EARLY TO WED(1926); FAR CRY, THE(1926); CHILDREN OF DIVORCE(1927); IT(1927); KING OF KINGS, THE(1927); WINGS(1927); ROAD HOUSE(1928); SCARLET DOVE, THE(1928); SMART SET, THE(1928); 13 WASHINGTON SQUARE(1928); ETERNAL WOMAN, THE(1929)

Misc. Silents

HAWK, THE(1917); MESSAGE OF THE MOUSE, THE(1917); SOLDIERS OF CHANCE(1917); SON OF THE HILLS, A(1917); SOUL MASTER, THE(1917); SOAP GIRL, THE(1918); BRAMBLE BUSH, THE(1919); MOONSHINE TRAIL, THE(1919); PAINTED WORLD, THE(1919); TWO WOMEN(1919); HELIOTROPE(1920); HAND-CUFFS OR KISSES(1921); PASSIONATE PILGRIM, THE(1921); WHY GIRLS LEAVE HOME(1921); HOW WOMEN LOVE(1922); MY OLD KENTUCKY HOME(1922); TILL WE MEET AGAIN(1922)

Julie Gordon

SUPER FUZZ(1981)

Julie Ann Gordon

IF EVER I SEE YOU AGAIN(1978)

Julie Swayne Gordon

GOLD DIGGERS OF BROADWAY(1929)

K. Gordon

THREE TALES OF CHEKHOV(1961, USSR), ed

Kay Gordon

HAPPY DAYS(1930); JUST IMAGINE(1930); MURDER WITH PICTURES(1936); COMET OVER BROADWAY(1938); HOUSE ACROSS THE BAY, THE(1940); JOAN OF OZARK(1942)

Kaye Gordon

TOP BANANA(1954)

Keith Gordon

JAWS II(1978); ALL THAT JAZZ(1979); HOME MOVIES(1979); DRESSED TO KILL(1980); CHRISTINE(1983)

Kelly Gordon

DADDY-O(1959)

Kid Gordon
Silents

PRIDE OF THE FANCY, THE(1920, Brit.)

Kilbourn Gordon

KONGO(1932), w

Kilbourne Gordon
Silents

BIG GAME(1921), w; WEST OF ZANZIBAR(1928), w

Kitty Gordon
Silents

AS IN A LOOKING GLASS(1916); ADELE(1919)

Misc. Silents

CRUCIAL TEST, THE(1916); HER MATERNAL RIGHT(1916); VERA, THE MEDIUM(1916); BELOVED ADVENTURESS, THE(1917); FORGET-ME-NOTS(1917); HER HOUR(1917); DIAMONDS AND PEARLS(1918); DIVINE SACRIFICE, THE(1918); INTERLOPER, THE(1918); MERELY PLAYERS(1918); PURPLE LILY, THE(1918); STOLEN ORDERS(1918); TINSEL(1918); WASP, THE(1918); MANDARIN'S GOLD(1919); SCAR, THE(1919); UNVEILING HAND, THE(1919)

L. MacArthur Gordon

SONG OF THE FORGE(1937, Brit.)

Lady Duff Gordon
Silents

WAY DOWN EAST(1920), cos

Lance Gordon

WOMEN AND BLOODY TERROR(1970); HILLS HAVE EYES, THE(1978); INDEPENDENCE DAY(1983)

Larry Gordon

DEVIL'S 8, THE(1969), w; RETURN OF THE SOLDIER, THE(1983, Brit.)

Lawrence Gordon

HARD TIMES(1975), p; DRIVER, THE(1978), p; END, THE(1978), p; WARRIORS, THE(1979), p; XANADU(1980), p; PATERNITY(1981), p; JEKYLL AND HYDE...TOGETHER AGAIN(1982), p; 48 HOURS(1982), p
1984

STREETS OF FIRE(1984), p

Lee Gordon

LOST MISSILE, THE(1958, U.S./Can.), p

Leo Gordon

ALL THE BROTHERS WERE VALIANT(1953); CHINA VENTURE(1953); GUN FURY(1953); HONDO(1953); RIOT IN CELL BLOCK 11(1954); SIGN OF THE PAGAN(1954); YELLOW MOUNTAIN, THE(1954); BAMBOO PRISON, THE(1955); MAN WITH THE GUN(1955); ROBBER'S ROOST(1955); SANTA FE PASSAGE(1955); SEVEN ANGRY MEN(1955); SOLDIER OF FORTUNE(1955); TEN WANTED MEN(1955); TENNESSEE'S PARTNER(1955); CONQUEROR, THE(1956); GREAT DAY IN THE MORNING(1956); JOHNNY CONCHO(1956); MAN WHO KNEW TOO MUCH, THE(1956); RED SUNDOWN(1956); SEVENTH CAVALRY(1956); STEEL JUNGLE, THE(1956); BABY FACE NELSON(1957); BLACK PATCH(1957), a, w; LURE OF THE SWAMP(1957); MAN IN THE SHADOW(1957); RESTLESS BREED, THE(1957); TALL STRANGER, THE(1957); APACHE TERRITORY(1958); CRY BABY KILLER, THE(1958), w; HOT CAR GIRL(1958), w; NOTORIOUS MR. MONKS, THE(1958); QUANTRILL'S RAIDERS(1958); RIDE A CROOKED TRAIL(1958); ATTACK OF THE GIANT LEECHES(1959); ESCORT WEST(1959), a, w; JAYHAWKERS, THE(1959); WASP WOMAN, THE(1959), w; NOOSE FOR A GUNMAN(1960); VALLEY OF THE REDWOODS(1960), w; CAT BURGLAR, THE(1961), w; INTRUDER, THE(1962); NUN AND THE SERGEANT, THE(1962); TARZAN GOES TO INDIA(1962, U.S./Brit./Switz.); HAUNTED PALACE, THE(1963); KINGS OF THE SUN(1963); MC LINTOCK!(1963); TERROR, THE(1963), w; KITTEN WITH A WHIP(1964); BOUNTY KILLER, THE(1965), w; GIRLS ON THE BEACH(1965); BEAU GESTE(1966); NIGHT OF THE GRIZZLY, THE(1966); TOBRUK(1966); DEVIL'S ANGELS(1967); HOSTILE GUNS(1967); ST. VALENTINE'S DAY MASSACRE, THE(1967); BUCKSKIN(1968); YOU CAN'T WIN 'EM ALL(1970, Brit.); MY NAME IS NOBODY(1974, Ital./Fr./Ger.); NEW GIRL IN TOWN(1977); FIRE AND ICE(1983)

Misc. Silents

THEN I'LL COME BACK TO YOU(1916); PARDNERS(1917)

Leo V. Gordon

CITY OF BAD MEN(1953); TOWER OF LONDON(1962), w; TOBRUK(1966), w; YOU CAN'T WIN 'EM ALL(1970, Brit.), w

Leon Gordon

WHITE CARGO(1930, Brit.), w; ANNABELLE'S AFFAIRS(1931), w; DON'T BET ON WOMEN(1931), w; HEARTBREAK(1931), w; SUSAN LENOX–HER FALL AND RISE(1931), w; FREAKS(1932), w; KONGO(1932), w; MAN ABOUT TOWN(1932), w; PAINTED WOMAN(1932), w; PASSPORT TO HELL(1932), w; SON-DAUGHTER, THE(1932), w; BISHOP MISBEHAVES, THE(1933), w; WHEN LADIES MEET(1933), w; TARZAN AND HIS MATE(1934), w; TRANSATLANTIC MERRY-GO-ROUND(1934), w; AGE OF INDISCRETION(1935), w; STOLEN HARMONY(1935), w; HIS BROTHER'S WIFE(1936), w; UNGUARDED HOUR, THE(1936), w; LAST OF MRS. CHEYNEY, THE(1937), w; YANK AT OXFORD, A(1938), w; BALALAIKA(1939), w; SOCIETY LAWYER(1939), w; BROADWAY MELODY OF 1940(1940), w; I LOVE YOU AGAIN(1940), w; THEY MET IN BOMBAY(1941), w; WHITE CARGO(1942), w; ABOVE SUSPICION(1943), p; MRS. PARKINGTON(1944), p; GREEN YEARS, THE(1946), p; THAT FORSYTE WOMAN(1949), p; KIM(1950), p, w; HOUR OF THIRTEEN, THE(1952), w; ROGUE'S MARCH(1952), p, w

Silents

ADAM AND EVA(1923)

Lesley Gordon

SUICIDE SQUADRON(1942, Brit.)

Leslie H. Gordon

LIVE WIRE, THE(1937, Brit.), w

Leslie Howard Gordon

DARK RED ROSES(1930, Brit.), w; LATIN LOVE(1930, Brit.), w; SUCH IS THE LAW(1930, Brit.), w; GREAT GAY ROAD, THE(1931, Brit.), w; HOUSE OF UNREST, THE(1931, Brit.), d&w; OTHER PEOPLE'S SINS(1931, Brit.), w; FIRST MRS. FRASER, THE(1932, Brit.), w; DOUBLE EVENT, THE(1934, Brit.), p; IT'S A BOY(1934, Brit.), w; MELODY AND ROMANCE(1937, Brit.), w

Silents

ALL THE WORLD'S A STAGE(1917, Brit.), a, w; FRAILTY(1921, Brit.), w; ELEVENTH HOUR, THE(1922, Brit.), w; HALF A TRUTH(1922, Brit.), w; PASSIONATE FRIENDS, THE(1922, Brit.), w

Lewis Gordon

WITCH WITHOUT A BROOM, A(1967, U.S./Span.); COMIN' AT YA!(1981); TREASURE OF THE FOUR CROWNS(1983, Span./U.S.)

Lewis H. Gordon [H.G. Lewis]

SCUM OF THE EARTH(1963), d

Lisa Gordon

STAR 80(1983)

Lita Gordon

NONE BUT THE LONELY HEART(1944)

Lloyd Gordon

FIRST NUDIE MUSICAL, THE(1976), a, ch; HOT TOMORROWS(1978), ch

Lyle Gordon

FARMER'S OTHER DAUGHTER, THE(1965)

Lynne Gordon

HOT ROCK, THE(1972)

M. Gordon

DOMMED CARGO(1936, Brit.), ed; MAN OF AFFAIRS(1937, Brit.), ed

MacArthur Gordon

WOMANHOOD(1934, Brit.); LAST WALTZ, THE(1936, Brit.); MELODY OF MY HEART(1936, Brit.); WELL DONE, HENRY(1936, Brit.)

Mack Gordon

BROADWAY THROUGH A KEYHOLE(1933), m; SITTING PRETTY(1933); COLLEGIATE(1936); JOHNNY APOLLO(1940), m; THREE LITTLE GIRLS IN BLUE(1946), p, m; YOU'RE MY EVERYTHING(1949); CALL ME MISTER(1951), m/l Rome

Marc Gordon
NEW LEAF, A(1971)
Margaret Gordon
STRANGLERS OF BOMBAY, THE(1960, Brit.); ANATOMIST, THE(1961, Brit.); DARLING(1965, Brit.)
Marianne Gordon
HOW TO STUFF A WILD BIKINI(1965); SULLIVAN'S EMPIRE(1967); ROSEMARY'S BABY(1968); LITTLE DARLINGS(1980)
Marjorie Gordon
DANGER TRAILS(1935); AFTER YOU, COMRADE(1967, S. Afr.)
Mark Gordon
DON'T DRINK THE WATER(1969); TAKE THE MONEY AND RUN(1969); NICKEL RIDE, THE(1974)
Martin Gordon
MAN WHO COULDN'T WALK, THE(1964, Brit.); MECHANIC, THE(1972)
Mary Gordon
SATURDAY NIGHT KID, THE(1929); DYNAMITE(1930); BLACK CAMEL, THE(1931); SUBWAY EXPRESS(1931); ALMOST MARRIED(1932); BLONDE VENUS(1932); DANCERS IN THE DARK(1932); PACK UP YOUR TROUBLES(1932); TEXAS CYCLONE(1932); TRIAL OF VIVIENNE WARE, THE(1932); WILD GIRL(1932); DESIGN FOR LIVING(1933); SHE DONE HIM WRONG(1933); BELOVED(1934); LITTLE MINISTER, THE(1934); MAN FROM HELL, THE(1934); BONNIE SCOTLAND(1935); IRISH IN US, THE(1935); MUTINY ON THE BOUNTY(1935); VANESSA, HER LOVE STORY(1935); WATERFRONT LADY(1935); WHOLE TOWN'S TALKING, THE(1935); AFTER THE THIN MAN(1936); FORGOTTEN FACES(1936); GREAT GUY(1936); LADY CONSENTS, THE(1936); LAUGHING IRISH EYES(1936); MARY OF SCOTLAND(1936); PLOUGH AND THE STARS, THE(1936); STAGE STRUCK(1936); YELLOWSTONE(1936); DAMSEL IN DISTRESS, A(1937); DOUBLE WEDDING(1937); GREAT O'MALLEY, THE(1937); LADY BEHAVE!(1937); MARRIED BEFORE BREAKFAST(1937); MEET THE BOY FRIEND(1937); ONE MAN JUSTICE(1937); PICK A STAR(1937); TOAST OF NEW YORK, THE(1937); WAY OUT WEST(1937); YOU CAN'T HAVE EVERYTHING(1937); ANGELS WITH DIRTY FACES(1938); CITY STREETS(1938); COWBOY FROM BROOKLYN(1938); KIDNAPPED(1938); ADVENTURES OF SHERLOCK HOLMES, THE(1939); CAPTAIN FURY(1939); DAY-TIME WIFE(1939); HOUND OF THE BASKERVILLES, THE(1939); JOE AND ETHEL TURP CALL ON THE PRESIDENT(1939); MARSHAL OF MESA CITY, THE(1939); MR. SMITH GOES TO WASHINGTON(1939); NIGHT OF NIGHTS, THE(1939); OFF THE RECORD(1939); PARENTS ON TRIAL(1939); RACKETEERS OF THE RANGE(1939); RULERS OF THE SEA(1939); SHE MARRIED A COP(1939); TAIL SPIN(1939); TELL NO TALES(1939); WINGS OF THE NAVY(1939); DOCTOR TAKES A WIFE(1940); I TAKE THIS OATH(1940); INVISIBLE MAN RETURNS, THE(1940); KITTY FOYLE(1940); MY SON IS GUILTY(1940); MY SON, MY SON!(1940); NO, NO NANETTE(1940); NOBODY'S CHILDREN(1940); PUBLIC DEB NO. 1(1940); QUEEN OF THE MOB(1940); SAPS AT SEA(1940); TEAR GAS SQUAD(1940); WHEN THE DALTONS RODE(1940); WOMEN WITHOUT NAMES(1940); APPOINTMENT FOR LOVE(1941); BORROWED HERO(1941); DOUBLE CROSS(1941); FLIGHT FROM DESTINY(1941); FOUR JACKS AND A JILL(1941); HOW GREEN WAS MY VALLEY(1941); INVISIBLE WOMAN, THE(1941); POT O' GOLD(1941); RIOT SQUAD(1941); SEALED LIPS(1941); UNEXPECTED UNCLE(1941); UNFINISHED BUSINESS(1941); BOMBAY CLIPPER(1942); DR. BROADWAY(1942); FLY BY NIGHT(1942); GENTLEMAN JIM(1942); HALF WAY TO SHANGHAI(1942); IT HAPPENED IN FLATBUSH(1942); MEET THE STEWARTS(1942); MUMMY'S TOMB, THE(1942); POWDER TOWN(1942); PRIDE OF THE YANKEES, THE(1942); SHERLOCK HOLMES AND THE SECRET WEAPON(1942); SHERLOCK HOLMES AND THE VOICE OF TERROR(1942); STRANGE CASE OF DR. RX, THE(1942); BOSS OF BIG TOWN(1943); FOREVER AND A DAY(1943); HERE COMES KELLY(1943); KEEP 'EM SLUGGING(1943); SARONG GIRL(1943); SHERLOCK HOLMES FACES DEATH(1943); SMART GUY(1943); SWEET ROSIE O'GRADY(1943); TWO TICKETS TO LONDON(1943); WHISPERING FOOTSTEPS(1943); YOU'RE A LUCKY FELLOW, MR. SMITH(1943); EVER SINCE VENUS(1944); FOLLOW THE LEADER(1944); HAT CHECK HONEY(1944); HOLLYWOOD CANTEEN(1944); HOUR BEFORE THE DAWN, THE(1944); IRISH EYES ARE SMILING(1944); LAST RIDE, THE(1944); MILLION DOLLAR KID(1944); PEARL OF DEATH, THE(1944); RACKET MAN, THE(1944); SECRETS OF SCOTLAND YARD(1944); SHERLOCK HOLMES AND THE SPIDER WOMAN(1944); CAPTAIN EDDIE(1945); DIVORCE(1945); KITTY(1945); SEE MY LAWYER(1945); STRANGE CONFESSION(1945); WOMAN IN GREEN, THE(1945); DARK HORSE, THE(1946); HOODLUM SAINT, THE(1946); IN FAST COMPANY(1946); LITTLE GIANT(1946); SENTIMENTAL JOURNEY(1946); SHADOWS OVER CHINATOWN(1946); SING WHILE YOU DANCE(1946); SINGIN' IN THE CORN(1946); EXPOSED(1947); INVISIBLE WALL, THE(1947); LONG NIGHT, THE(1947); STALLION ROAD(1947); ANGELS ALLEY(1948); FORT APACHE(1948); HIGHWAY 13(1948); STRANGE MRS. CRANE, THE(1948); DEPUTY MARSHAL(1949); SHAMROCK HILL(1949); FILE ON THELMA JORDAN, THE(1950); WEST OF WYOMING(1950)
Misc. Talkies
LAST ALARM, THE(1940)
Silents
CLANCY'S KOSHER WEDDING(1927); NAUGHTY NANETTE(1927); OLD CODE, THE(1928)
Mary Turner Gordon
Silents
BROADWAY ROSE(1922)
Maud Turner Gordon
Misc. Silents
MRS. DANE'S DEFENSE(1918)
Maude Turner Gordon
GLAD RAG DOLL, THE(1929); HOTTENTOT, THE(1929); ILLUSION(1929); KID GLOVES(1929); LAST OF MRS. CHEYNEY, THE(1929); MARRIAGE PLAYGROUND, THE(1929); SALLY(1929); FLORODORA GIRL, THE(1930); LAWFUL LARCENY(1930); HIGH STAKES(1931); LADIES' MAN(1931); BACK STREET(1932); CARELESS LADY(1932); SHOPWORN(1932); SINNERS IN THE SUN(1932); DESIRABLE(1934); FLIRTATION WALK(1934); MAN WITH TWO FACES, THE(1934); SHE LOVES ME NOT(1934); GOING HIGHBROW(1935); LIVING ON VELVET(1935); PERSONAL MAID'S SECRET(1935); AFTER THE THIN MAN(1936); EMPEROR'S CANDLESTICKS, THE(1937); WINGS OVER HONOLULU(1937); SWEETHEARTS(1938)
Silents
DANGER MARK, THE(1918); JUST FOR TONIGHT(1918); OAKDALE AFFAIR, THE(1919); AWAY GOES PRUDENCE(1920); BEYOND PRICE(1921); ENCHANTMENT(1921); BACK HOME AND BROKE(1922); EARLY BIRD, THE(1925); CHEAT-

ING CHEATERS(1927); HOT NEWS(1928); JUST MARRIED(1928); SPORTING GOODS(1928)
Misc. Silents
HER BETTER SELF(1917); HONEYMOON, THE(1917); SERVICE STAR, THE(1918); CIVILIAN CLOTHES(1920); HOME MADE(1927); NAUGHTY DUCHESS, THE(1928)
Maurice Gordon
SANTA CLAUS CONQUERS THE MARTIANS(1964), art d; DAYDREAMER, THE(1966), art d
Max Gordon
TRIP TO PARIS, A(1938), p; ABE LINCOLN IN ILLINOIS(1940), p; MY SISTER EILEEN(1942), p
Maxine Gordon
OFFENSE, THE(1973, Brit.)
McArthur Gordon
SUCH IS LIFE(1936, Brit.); SCRUFFY(1938, Brit.)
Michael Gordon
STRANGE BOARDERS(1938, Brit.), ed; BOSTON BLACKIE GOES HOLLYWOOD(1942), d; UNDERGROUND AGENT(1942), d; CRIME DOCTOR(1943), d; ONE DANGEROUS NIGHT(1943), d; WEB, THE(1947), d; ACT OF MURDER, AN(1948), d; ANOTHER PART OF THE FOREST(1948), d; ESTHER WATERS(1948, Brit.), w; ALL OVER THE TOWN(1949, Brit.), w; LADY GAMBLES, THE(1949), d; WOMAN IN HIDING(1949), d; CYRANO DE BERGERAC(1950), d; I CAN GET IT FOR YOU WHOLESALE(1951), d; SECRET OF CONVICT LAKE, THE(1951), d; MALTA STORY(1954, Brit.), ed; SIMBA(1955, Brit.), ed; SAFARI(1956), ed; RISING OF THE MOON, THE(1957, Ireland), ed; CURSE OF THE DEMON(1958), ed; PILLOW TALK(1959), d; PORTRAIT IN BLACK(1960), d; FOR LOVE OR MONEY(1963), d; MOVE OVER, DARLING(1963), d; VERY SPECIAL FAVOR, A(1965), d; IDOL, THE(1966, Brit.); TEXAS ACROSS THE RIVER(1966), d; IMPOSSIBLE YEARS, THE(1968), d; HOW DO I LOVE THEE?(1970), d
Misc. Talkies
ALL HALLOWE'EN(1952), d
Michael S. Gordon
WHEREVER SHE GOES(1953, Aus.), d&w
Mildred Gordon
MAKE HASTE TO LIVE(1954), w; EXPERIMENT IN TERROR(1962), w; THAT DARN CAT(1965), w
Mitchell Gordon
ATLAS AGAINST THE CYCLOPS(1963, Ital.)
Muriel Gordon
EMPLOYEE'S ENTRANCE(1933); GOLD DIGGERS OF 1933(1933); LONE AVENGER, THE(1933)
Neil Gordon
THIRD CLUE, THE(1934, Brit.), w; CLAYDON TREASURE MYSTERY, THE(1938, Brit.), w
Noele Gordon
LISBON STORY, THE(1946, Brit.); FACTS OF LOVE(1949, Brit.)
Nora Gordon
GREEN FINGERS(1947); JOURNEY AHEAD(1947, Brit.); FALLEN IDOL, THE(1949, Brit.); MY BROTHER JONATHAN(1949, Brit.); FIVE ANGLES ON MURDER(1950, Brit.); NIGHT WAS OUR FRIEND(1951, Brit.); MURDER AT 3 A.M.(1953, Brit.); TWICE UPON A TIME(1953, Brit.); WOMAN'S ANGLE, THE(1954, Brit.); CONSTANT HUSBAND, THE(1955, Brit.); POLICE DOG(1955, Brit.); WOMEN IN A DRESSING GOWN(1957, Brit.); HIGH JUMP(1959, Brit.); HORRORS OF THE BLACK MUSEUM(1959, U.S./Brit.); CARRY ON SPYING(1964, Brit.); NANNY, THE(1965, Brit.)
Norah Gordon
DANNY BOY(1941, Brit.); FACING THE MUSIC(1941, Brit.); OLD MOTHER RILEY'S CIRCUS(1941, Brit.); FRONT LINE KIDS(1942, Brit.); MARK OF CAIN, THE(1948, Brit.); FLOODTIDE(1949, Brit.); SING ALONG WITH ME(1952, Brit.); GLASS TOMB, THE(1955, Brit.); KID FOR TWO FARTHINGS, A(1956, Brit.); TOP FLOOR GIRL(1959, Brit.); SENTENCED FOR LIFE(1960, Brit.)
Oliver Gordon
EVERYTHING IN LIFE(1936, Brit.); INTIMATE RELATIONS(1937, Brit.); LITTLE MISS SOMEBODY(1937, Brit.)
Patrick Gordon
RETURN OF THE SOLDIER, THE(1983, Brit.)
Paul Gordon
IF I HAD MY WAY(1940); MEET ME AT THE FAIR(1952)
Silents
PRETENDERS, THE(1916)
Misc. Silents
WOMAN IN THE CASE, A(1916); GREAT WHITE TRAIL, THE(1917); VANITY(1917)
Paula Gordon
GUTTER GIRLS(1964, Brit.)
Peggy Gordon
MY FAVORITE SPY(1951)
Percy Gordon
TNT JACKSON(1975)
Pete Gordon
PACK UP YOUR TROUBLES(1932)
Misc. Silents
YOUTH AND ADVENTURE(1925)
Peter Gordon
BABES IN TOYLAND(1934); GUNMAN HAS ESCAPED, A(1948, Brit.); BLACK SLEEP, THE(1956); CITY NEWS(1983), m
Phil Gordon
LAST TIME I SAW ARCHIE, THE(1961); GOODBYE PORK PIE(1981, New Zealand)
Phillip Gordon
NATE AND HAYES(1983, U.S./New Zealand)
Phyllis Gordon
ANOTHER THIN MAN(1939)
R. Wells Gordon
HOWARDS OF VIRGINIA, THE(1940)
Ramon Gordon
PUTNEY SWOPE(1969)
Richard Gordon
BIRTH OF A BABY(1938); IN OLD NEW MEXICO(1945); 13 RUE MADELEINE(1946); SENATOR WAS INDISCREET, THE(1947); JOLSON SINGS AGAIN(1949); ST. BENNY THE DIP(1951); MARRYING KIND, THE(1952); PAULA(1952); DOCTOR IN THE HOUSE(1954, Brit.), w; PHFFFT!(1954); DOCTOR AT SEA(1955, Brit.), w; DOCTOR AT LARGE(1957, Brit.), w; CAPTAIN'S TABLE, THE(1960, Brit.), w,John Whiting; DOC-

TOR IN LOVE(1960, Brit.), w; DOCTOR IN DISTRESS(1963, Brit.), w; DEVIL DOLL(1964, Brit.), p; CARNABY, M.D.(1967, Brit.), w; DOCTOR IN TROUBLE(1970, Brit.), w; SECRETS OF SEX(1970, Brit.), p; HORROR HOSPITAL(1973, Brit.), p; CAT AND THE CANARY, THE(1979, Brit.), p; BEYOND THE FOG(1981, Brit.), p; HORROR PLANET(1982, Brit.), p

Richard H. Gordon
JOHNNY O'CLOCK(1947); SOMEBODY LOVES ME(1952)

Robert Gordon
GIRL FROM MONTEREY, THE(1943), w; KEEP 'EM SLUGGING(1943), w; SPORT OF KINGS(1947), d; BLACK EAGLE(1948), d; RECKLESS MOMENTS, THE(1949); JOE LOUIS STORY, THE(1953), d; IT CAME FROM BENEATH THE SEA(1955), d; DAMN CITIZEN(1958), d; RAWHIDE TRAIL, THE(1958), d; BLACK ZOO(1963), d; TARZAN AND THE JUNGLE BOY(1968, US/Switz.), d; GATLING GUN, THE(1972), d; BEST FRIENDS(1975), ed; LAS VEGAS LADY(1976), ed; MAKO: THE JAWS OF DEATH(1976); CLONUS HORROR, THE(1979), ed; MALIBU HIGH(1979); BLUE LAGOON, THE(1980), ed; LOVELESS, THE(1982), a, m; SUMMER LOVERS(1982), ed
1984
GRANDVIEW, U.S.A.(1984), ed
Misc. Talkies
BLIND SPOT(1947), d; RAWHIDE TRAIL, THE(1950), d
Silents
HUCK AND TOM(1918); PAIR OF SILK STOCKINGS, A(1918); IF WOMEN ONLY KNEW(1921); SUPER-SEX, THE(1922); MYSTERIOUS WITNESS, THE(1923); NIGHT SHIP, THE(1925)
Misc. Silents
HIRED MAN, THE(1918); MISSING(1918); CAPTAIN KIDD, JR.(1919); DAWN(1919); MOONSHINE TRAIL, THE(1919); MY HUSBAND'S OTHER WIFE(1919); YANKEE PRINCESS, A(1919); BLOOD BARRIER, THE(1920); DOLLARS AND THE WOMAN(1920); RESPECTABLE BY PROXY(1920); VICE OF FOOLS, THE(1920); ROSARY, THE(1922); GREATEST MENACE, THE(1923); MAIN STREET(1923); BORROWED HUSBANDS(1924); WILDCAT, THE(1924); ON THE THRESHOLD(1925); SHATTERED LIVES(1925); HEARTS AND SPANGLES(1926); KING OF THE PACK(1926)

Ronald Gordon
1984
MAKING THE GRADE(1984)

Rosco Gordon
ROCK BABY, ROCK IT(1957)

Rose Gordon
FIGHTING HERO(1934), w; COYOTE TRAILS(1935), w; FAST BULLETS(1936), w; SPEED REPORTER(1936), w; SANTA FE BOUND(1937), w

Ross Gordon
TENTACLES(1977, Ital.)

Roy Gordon
BOY SLAVES(1938); CAMPUS CONFESSIONS(1938); COCOANUT GROVE(1938); BLONDIE BRINGS UP BABY(1939); FIFTH AVENUE GIRL(1939); GREAT MAN VOTES, THE(1939); MILLION DOLLAR LEGS(1939); REAL GLORY, THE(1939); SPELLBINDER, THE(1939); BOOM TOWN(1940); FOREIGN CORRESPONDENT(1940); LONE WOLF STRIKES, THE(1940); MEN AGAINST THE SKY(1940); QUEEN OF THE MOB(1940); SUED FOR LIBEL(1940); WOLF OF NEW YORK(1940); LOVE CRAZY(1941); MARRIED BACHELOR(1941); NIGHT OF JANUARY 16TH(1941); STRAWBERRY BLONDE, THE(1941); TWO-FACED WOMAN(1941); LUCKY JORDAN(1942); MY FAVORITE SPY(1942); POWDER TOWN(1942); JACK LONDON(1943); SECRETS OF THE UNDERGROUND(1943); SO PROUDLY WE HAIL(1943); WHAT'S BUZZIN COUSIN?(1943); I LOVE A SOLDIER(1944); STANDING ROOM ONLY(1944); STORY OF DR. WASSELL, THE(1944); TAKE IT OR LEAVE IT(1944); CARIBBEAN MYSTERY, THE(1945); SHANGHAI COBRA, THE(1945); SPIDER, THE(1945); NEVER SAY GOODBYE(1946); NIGHT EDITOR(1946); CASS TIMBERLANE(1947); LAST ROUND-UP, THE(1947); NORA PRENTISS(1947); RAILROADED(1947); MICHAEL O'HALLORAN(1948); ANGELS IN DISGUISE(1949); APACHE CHIEF(1949); FOUNTAINHEAD, THE(1949); RIDERS IN THE SKY(1949); RIDERS OF THE WHISTLING PINES(1949); SONS OF NEW MEXICO(1949); BEYOND THE PURPLE HILLS(1950); BLONDE BANDIT, THE(1950); INDIAN TERRITORY(1950); MULE TRAIN(1950); MY FRIEND IRMA GOES WEST(1950); TWO FLAGS WEST(1950); RHUBARB(1951); TEXANS NEVER CRY(1951); LONE STAR(1952); ROAD TO BALI(1952); STARS AND STRIPES FOREVER(1952); FANGS OF THE ARCTIC(1953); ROBE, THE(1953); SANGAREE(1953); SO THIS IS LOVE(1953); TITANIC(1953); VANQUISHED, THE(1953); CATTLE QUEEN OF MONTANA(1954); SILVER LODE(1954); BIG COMBO, THE(1955); CROOKED WEB, THE(1955); GUN THAT WON THE WEST, THE(1955); MURDER IS MY BEAT(1955); SLIGHTLY SCARLET(1956); SPIRIT OF ST. LOUIS, THE(1957); UNEARTHLY, THE(1957); ZERO HOUR!(1957); ATTACK OF THE 50 FOOT WOMAN(1958); FEARMAKERS, THE(1958); WAR OF THE COLOSSAL BEAST(1958); PLUNDERERS OF PAINTED FLATS(1959); ALL IN A NIGHT'S WORK(1961); HAND OF DEATH(1962); SHOCK TREATMENT(1964); WHAT A WAY TO GO(1964)
Silents
SILVER WINGS(1922)

Russell Gordon
Misc. Silents
ROUNDING UP THE LAW(1922)

Ruth Gordon
ABE LINCOLN IN ILLINOIS(1940); DR. EHRLICH'S MAGIC BULLET(1940); TWO-FACED WOMAN(1941); ACTION IN THE NORTH ATLANTIC(1943); EDGE OF DARKNESS(1943); OVER 21(1945), w; DOUBLE LIFE, A(1947), w; ADAM'S RIB(1949), w; MARRYING KIND, THE(1952), w; PAT AND MIKE(1952), w; ACTRESS, THE(1953), w; INSIDE DAISY CLOVER(1965); LORD LOVE A DUCK(1966); ROSIE!(1967), w; ROSEMARY'S BABY(1968); WHAT EVER HAPPENED TO AUNT ALICE?(1969); WHERE'S POPPA?(1970); HAROLD AND MAUDE(1971); BIG BUS, THE(1976); EVERY WHICH WAY BUT LOOSE(1978); BOARDWALK(1979); SCAVENGER HUNT(1979); ANY WHICH WAY YOU CAN(1980); MY BODYGUARD(1980); JIMMY THE KID(1982)
Misc. Silents
WHIRL OF LIFE, THE(1915)

Sabina Gordon
MAYTIME IN MAYFAIR(1952, Brit.)

Sadie Gordon
Silents
BUNTY PULLS THE STRINGS(1921); KID, THE(1921); DON'T GET PERSONAL(1922); MERTON OF THE MOVIES(1924)

Shay Gordon
TIM DRISCOLL'S DONKEY(1955, Brit.)

Sid Gordon
ZIEGFELD FOLLIES(1945)

Sidney Gordon
BEHIND CLOSED SHUTTERS(1952, Ital.); ROMAN HOLIDAY(1953)

Stanley Gordon
CALL NORTHSIDE 777(1948)
Misc. Talkies
TODAY WE KILL...TOMORROW WE DIE(1971)

Steve Gordon
ONE AND ONLY, THE(1978), w; ARTHUR(1981), d&w; HEY, GOOD LOOKIN'(1982), anim

Stuart Gordon
LAST AFFAIR, THE(1976), ch

Susan Gordon
ATTACK OF THE PUPPET PEOPLE(1958); FIVE PENNIES, THE(1959); MAN IN THE NET, THE(1959); BOY AND THE PIRATES, THE(1960); TORMENTED(1960); PICTURE MOMMY DEAD(1966)

Taylor Gordon
EMPEROR JONES, THE(1933)

Vera Gordon
COHENS AND KELLYS IN ATLANTIC CITY, THE(1929); COHENS AND KELLYS IN AFRICA, THE(1930); COHENS AND KELLYS IN SCOTLAND, THE(1930); FIFTY MILLION FRENCHMEN(1931); WHEN STRANGERS MEET(1934); ANY MAN'S WIFE(1936); MICHAEL O'HALLORAN(1937); HAVING WONDERFUL TIME(1938); YOU AND ME(1938); BIG STREET, THE(1942); LIVING GHOST, THE(1942); STAGE DOOR CANTEEN(1943); ABIE'S IRISH ROSE(1946)
Silents
NORTH WIND'S MALICE, THE(1920); IN HOLLYWOOD WITH POTASH AND PERLMUTTER(1924); COHENS AND KELLYS, THE(1926); PRIVATE IZZY MURPHY(1926); COHENS AND THE KELLYS IN PARIS, THE(1928); FOUR WALLS(1928)
Misc. Silents
GREATEST LOVE, THE(1920); HUMORESQUE(1920); GOOD PROVIDER, THE(1922); YOUR BEST FRIEND(1922); POTASH AND PERLMUTTER(1923); KOSHER KITTY KELLY(1926); MILLIONAIRES(1926); SWEET DADDIES(1926)

Verna Gordon
MADAME SATAN(1930)

Vic Gordon
LONELY HEARTS(1983, Aus.); NEXT OF KIN(1983, Aus.)

Virginia Gordon
SURFTIDE 77(1962); TONIGHT FOR SURE(1962); HOT SPUR(1968)

Vivian Gordon
ZANDY'S BRIDE(1974)

Walter Gordon, Sr.
VISITOR, THE(1980, Ital./U.S.)

Warren Gordon
Silents
WOMAN'S MAN(1920), d

Wendy Gordon
1984
IRRECONCILABLE DIFFERENCES(1984)

William Gordon
TANGO BAR(1935); BACK TO BATAAN(1945), w; NOTORIOUS(1946)

William D. Gordon
SERGEANT RYKER(1968), w

the Gordon Gordons
DOWN THREE DARK STREETS(1954), w

The Gordon Ray Girls
TALKING FEET(1937, Brit.); NIGHT OF MAGIC, A(1944, Brit.)

Dennis Gordon-Orr
DEATHLINE(1973, Brit.), art d

Eva Gordos
VALLEY GIRL(1983), ed

Berry Gordy
MAHOGANY(1975), d

Denise Gordy
SCOTT JOPLIN(1977); D.C. CAB(1983)

John Gordy
PAPER LION(1968)

Robert L. Gordy
LADY SINGS THE BLUES(1972)

Altovise Gore
TENDER FLESH(1976)

Chester Gore
BIG BUSINESS(1937), art d; FIVE OF A KIND(1938), art d; ISLAND IN THE SKY(1938), art d; LOVE ON A BUDGET(1938), art d; SPEED TO BURN(1938), art d; UP THE RIVER(1938), art d; MR. MOTO IN DANGER ISLAND(1939), art d; LAST OF THE DUANES(1941), art d; JUST OFF BROADWAY(1942), art d; LONE STAR RANGER(1942), art d; THRU DIFFERENT EYES(1942), art d; TIME TO KILL(1942), art d; DANCING MASTERS, THE(1943), art d; JITTERBUGS(1943), art d; MY FRIEND FLICKA(1943), art d; HOME IN INDIANA(1944), art d; IT SHOULDN'T HAPPEN TO A DOG(1946), art d; JOHNNY COMES FLYING HOME(1946), art d; SMOKY(1946), art d; STREET WITH NO NAME, THE(1948), art d; FATHER WAS A FULLBACK(1949), art d; SAND(1949), art d; THIEVES' HIGHWAY(1949), art d; TWO FLAGS WEST(1950), art d; WHEN WILLIE COMES MARCHING HOME(1950), art d; GUY WHO CAME BACK, THE(1951), art d; O. HENRY'S FULL HOUSE(1952), art d; PONY SOLDIER(1952), art d; RED SKIES OF MONTANA(1952), art d; POWDER RIVER(1953), art d; SILVER WHIP, THE(1953), art d
Silents
COMING OF AMOS, THE(1925), art d

Christopher Gore
FAME(1980), w

Kenneth Gore
Silents
PEEP BEHIND THE SCENES, A(1918, Brit.)

Laura Gore
PEDDLIN' IN SOCIETY(1949, Ital.); CENTO ANNI D'AMORE(1954, Ital.)

Buddy Gorman
HEAVENLY BODY, THE(1943); HIGHER AND HIGHER(1943); AND THE ANGELS SING(1944); MEET ME IN ST. LOUIS(1944); SINCE YOU WENT AWAY(1944); 'TILL WE MEET AGAIN(1944); THOROUGHBREDS(1945); NIGHT AND DAY(1946); WIFE WANTED(1946); HER HUSBAND'S AFFAIRS(1947); NEWS HOUNDS(1947); ANGELS ALLEY(1948); SMUGGLERS' COVE(1948); TROUBLE MAKERS(1948); RECKLESS MOMENTS, THE(1949); WHITE HEAT(1949); BLUES BUSTERS(1950); LUCKY LOSERS(1950); TRIPLE TROUBLE(1950); BOWERY BATTALION(1951); GHOST CHASERS(1951); LET'S GO NAVY(1951); MODERN MARRIAGE, A(1962)

Charles Gorman
Silents
BRIDE OF FEAR, THE(1918); GAY RETREAT, THE(1927); FAR CALL, THE(1929)
Misc. Silents
CHILDREN OF THE FEUD(1916)

Chester Gorman
Misc. Talkies
APOCALYPSE 3:16(1964)

Cliff Gorman
JUSTINE(1969); BOYS IN THE BAND, THE(1970); COPS AND ROBBERS(1973); ROSEBUD(1975); UNMARRIED WOMAN, AN(1978); ALL THAT JAZZ(1979); NIGHT OF THE JUGGLER(1980)
1984
ANGEL(1984)

Em Gorman
Silents
ARE CHILDREN TO BLAME?(1922)
Misc. Silents
SOUL OF A CHILD, THE(1916)

Eric Gorman
SAINTS AND SINNERS(1949, Brit.); QUIET MAN, THE(1952); RISING OF THE MOON, THE(1957, Ireland)

Gayle Gorman
COPS AND ROBBERS(1973)

George Gorman
FUGITIVE LOVERS(1934)

Greg Gorman
TOOTSIE(1982)

Herbert Gorman
SUZY(1936), w

Jack Gorman
Misc. Silents
SOUL OF A CHILD, THE(1916), d; CORRUPTION(1917), d

John Gorman
MELODY(1971, Brit.); JABBERWOCKY(1977, Brit.)
Silents
PAINTED FLAPPER, THE(1924), d; WASTED LIVES(1925), d
Misc. Silents
LITTLE ORPHAN(1915), d; BUTTERFLY GIRL, THE(1921), d; WHY WOMEN REMARRY(1923), d; PRINCE OF BROADWAY, THE(1926), d; BLACK TEARS(1927), d

Lynne Gorman
NOBODY WAVED GOODBYE(1965, Can.); VIDEODROME(1983, Can.)

Mari Gorman
TAKING OF PELHAM ONE, TWO, THREE, THE(1974); GOODBYE COLUMBUS(1969); 10(1979); OH GOD! BOOK II(1980); MAX DUGAN RETURNS(1983)

Pat Gorman
ELEPHANT MAN, THE(1980, Brit.)

Patrick Gorman
THREE DAYS OF THE CONDOR(1975); NUDE BOMB, THE(1980)

Reg Gorman
IT TAKES ALL KINDS(1969, U.S./Aus.); NED KELLY(1970, Brit.); INN OF THE DAMNED(1974, Aus.)

Shay Gorman
CAPTAIN LIGHTFOOT(1955); KILL HER GENTLY(1958, Brit.); STEEL BAYONET, THE(1958, Brit.); CALCULATED RISK(1963, Brit.); EYES OF ANNIE JONES, THE(1963, Brit.); NINE HOURS TO RAMA(1963, U.S./Brit.); ISLAND OF TERROR(1967, Brit.); RUNNERS(1983, Brit.)

Tom Gorman
DETECTIVE, THE(1968)

William Gorman
Misc. Silents
FINDERS KEEPERS(1928)

Charles Gormley
BIG CATCH, THE(1968, Brit.), w. Laurence Henson; LONG SHOT(1981, Brit.)

Michael Gormley
ACCEPTABLE LEVELS(1983, Brit.)

Steve Gorn
THERE'S ALWAYS VANILLA(1972), m; HUNGRY WIVES(1973), m

Randy Gornel
HOLLYWOOD KNIGHTS, THE(1980)

Jay Gorney
JIMMY AND SALLY(1933), m; TAKE A CHANCE(1933), m; ROMANCE IN THE RAIN(1934), w; STAND UP AND CHEER(1934 80m FOX bw), m; REDHEADS ON PARADE(1935), w, m; COLLEGE HOLIDAY(1936), w; HEY, ROOKIE(1944), w; GAY SENORITA, THE(1945), p

Karen Gorney
DAVID AND LISA(1962)

Karen Lynn Gorney
SATURDAY NIGHT FEVER(1977)

Walt Gorney
FRIDAY THE 13TH(1980); ENDLESS LOVE(1981); FRIDAY THE 13TH PART II(1981); EASY MONEY(1983); TRADING PLACES(1983)
1984
FRIDAY THE 13TH–THE FINAL CHAPTER(1984)

Walter Gorney
COPS AND ROBBERS(1973); NUNZIO(1978)

Allan Gornick, Jr.
PERSONAL BEST(1982), ph

Michael Gornick
DAWN OF THE DEAD(1979), ph; MARTIN(1979), ph; KNIGHTRIDERS(1981), ph; CREEPSHOW(1982), ph

Laslo Gorog
TALES OF MANHATTAN(1942), w; SHE WOULDN'T SAY YES(1945), w; OF LOVE AND DESIRE(1963), w

Laszlo Gorog
MURDER IN THE MUSIC HALL(1946), w; MOLE PEOPLE, THE(1956), w; LAND UNKNOWN, THE(1957), w; SPIDER, THE(1958), w; TOO SOON TO LOVE(1960), w

Lazio Gorog
EARTH VS. THE SPIDER(1958), w

Monroe Gorog
AFFAIRS OF SUSAN(1945), w

Alain Goroguer
FANTASTIC PLANET(1973, Fr./Czech.), m

S. Gorokhova
SUN SHINES FOR ALL, THE(1961, USSR)

Mikhail Goronorov
SEEDS OF FREEDOM(1943, USSR)

Shirley Gorospe
IMPASSE(1969)

Rosa Gorostegui
TRISTANA(1970, Span./Ital./Fr.)

Marty Gorowitz
FAST BREAK(1979)

Romo Gorrara
HAMMERHEAD(1968)

Michael Gorrin
TAKING OF PELHAM ONE, TWO, THREE, THE(1974); DEAD TO THE WORLD(1961); ...AND JUSTICE FOR ALL(1979); HERO AT LARGE(1980); WINDOWS(1980)

Marleen Gorris
1984
QUESTION OF SILENCE(1984, Neth.), d&w

Sol Gorse
YOUNG DILLINGER(1965)

Norah Gorsen
WEE GEORDIE(1956, Brit.)

Frank Gorshin
BETWEEN HEAVEN AND HELL(1956); PROUD AND THE PROFANE, THE(1956); DRAGSTRIP GIRL(1957); INVASION OF THE SAUCER MEN(1957); PORTLAND EXPOSE(1957); TRUE STORY OF JESSE JAMES, THE(1957); TANK BATTALION(1958); WARLOCK(1959); BELLS ARE RINGING(1960); GREAT IMPOSTOR, THE(1960); STUDS LONIGAN(1960); WHERE THE BOYS ARE(1960); GEORGE RAFT STORY, THE(1961); RING OF FIRE(1961); SAIL A CROOKED SHIP(1961); THAT DARN CAT(1965); BATMAN(1966); RIDE BEYOND VENGEANCE(1966); SKIDOO(1968); RECORD CITY(1978)
Misc. Talkies
UNDERGROUND ACES(1981); UPPERCRUST, THE(1982)

Frank J. Gorshin
HOT ROD GIRL(1956); RUNAWAY DAUGHTERS(1957)

Alexandra Gorski
CATHERINE & CO.(1976, Fr.)

Peter Gorski
FAUST(1963, Ger.), d

Anthony Gorsline
ONE WAY TICKET TO HELL(1955)

William Gorsman
LOVE IN BLOOM(1935)

Charles Gorss
ACROSS THE RIVER(1965), m

Saul Gorss
SILENCERS, THE(; BULLETS OR BALLOTS(1936); LOVE BEGINS AT TWENTY(1936); SATAN MET A LADY(1936); GOD'S COUNTRY AND THE WOMAN(1937); READY, WILLING AND ABLE(1937); SAN QUENTIN(1937); MASK OF DIMITRIOS, THE(1944); MR. SKEFFINGTON(1944); THIN MAN GOES HOME, THE(1944); RAZOR'S EDGE, THE(1946); JOHNNY ALLEGRO(1949); KNOCK ON ANY DOOR(1949); TAKE ME OUT TO THE BALL GAME(1949); UNDERCOVER MAN, THE(1949); DAKOTA LIL(1950); HIS KIND OF WOMAN(1951); JEOPARDY(1953); UNCHAINED(1955); TEA AND SYMPATHY(1956); BULLWHIP(1958); LEGION OF THE DOOMED(1958); WARLOCK(1959); ICE PALACE(1960); SPARTACUS(1960); HOW THE WEST WAS WON(1962); RED TOMAHAWK(1967)

Sol Gorss
THEY WON'T BELIEVE ME(1947); SONS O' GUNS(1936); SUBMARINE D-1(1937); CODE OF THE SECRET SERVICE(1939); HELL'S KITCHEN(1939); PRIVATE DETECTIVE(1939); SECRET SERVICE OF THE AIR(1939); CASTLE ON THE HUDSON(1940); FIGHTING 69TH, THE(1940); THEY DRIVE BY NIGHT(1940); 'TIL WE MEET AGAIN(1940); DIVE BOMBER(1941); BULLET SCARS(1942); GEORGE WASHINGTON SLEPT HERE(1942); JUKE GIRL(1942); LADY GANGSTER(1942); THEY DIED WITH THEIR BOOTS ON(1942); AIR FORCE(1943); BABY FACE NELSON(1957)

Derek Gorst
LUCKY DAYS(1935, Brit.); ONCE A THIEF(1935, Brit.); FATAL HOUR, THE(1937, Brit.); INCIDENT IN SHANGHAI(1937, Brit.); LUCKY JADE(1937, Brit.); GABLES MYSTERY, THE(1938, Brit.); HIS LORDSHIP REGRETS(1938, Brit.); SINGING COP, THE(1938, Brit.); MYSTERIOUS MR. REEDER, THE(1940, Brit.)

Eldon Gorst
MILL ON THE FLOSS(1939, Brit.); RAGE IN HEAVEN(1941); EXILE, THE(1947)

Irene Gorst
CONFESSIONS OF A POP PERFORMER(1975, Brit.)

Harry Gorsuch
DELIRIUM(1979); ON THE RIGHT TRACK(1981)

Inge Gort
WANDERING JEW, THE(1948, Ital.)

Marjoe Gortner
WHEN YOU COMIN' BACK, RED RYDER?(1979), a, p; EARTHQUAKE(1974); BOBBIE JO AND THE OUTLAW(1976); FOOD OF THE GODS, THE(1976); SIDEWINDER ONE(1977); VIVA KNIEVEL!(1977); ACAPULCO GOLD(1978); STARCRASH(1979); MAUSOLEUM(1983)

1984
JUNGLE WARRIORS(1984, U.S./Ger./Mex.)

Adrian Gorton
ZORRO, THE GAY BLADE(1981), art d

Asheton Gorton
MAGIC CHRISTIAN, THE(1970, Brit.), prod d

Assheton Gorton
KNACK ... AND HOW TO GET IT, THE(1965, Brit.), art d; BLOW-UP(1966, Brit.), set d; WONDERWALL(1969, Brit.), art d; GET CARTER(1971, Brit.), prod d; PIED PIPER, THE(1972, Brit.), prod d; FRENCH LIEUTENANT'S WOMAN, THE(1981), prod d

John Gorton
DON'S PARTY(1976, Aus.)

Ron Gorton
PANIC BUTTON(1964, p, w; THAT'S THE WAY OF THE WORLD(1975)

Susan Gorton
MALIBU HIGH(1979)

Gloria Gorvin
TORN CURTAIN(1966)

A. Gorwin
Silents
DARLING OF THE RICH, THE(1923)

Jeremiah Gorwitz
COMMITMENT, THE(1976)

Mici Gory
PIED PIPER, THE(1942)

V. Goryunov
QUEEN OF SPADES(1961, USSR), makeup; MORNING STAR(1962, USSR), makeup

James Gosa
HIGH PLAINS DRIFTER(1973)

Tony Gosalves
CURSE OF THE VAMPIRES(1970, Phil., U.S.), spec eff

Tony Gosalvez
TWILIGHT PEOPLE(1972, Phil.)

Martin A. Gosch
ABBOTT AND COSTELLO IN HOLLYWOOD(1945), p

Rene Goscinny
LUCKY LUKE(1971, Fr./Bel.), p, d, w

Alfred Gosden
Silents
BRAZEN BEAUTY(1918), ph; SPITFIRE OF SEVILLE, THE(1919), ph; ALL DOLLED UP(1921), ph; MAD MARRIAGE, THE(1921), ph; SHOCKING NIGHT, A(1921), ph; GOING THE LIMIT(1925), ph

Freeman F. Gosden
AMOS 'N' ANDY(1930)

Maurice "Doberman" Gosfield
TEENAGE MILLIONAIRE(1961)

Maurice Gosfield
THRILL OF IT ALL, THE(1963)

Hideo Gosha
GOYOKIN(1969, Jap.), d, w; TENCHU!(1970, Jap.), d; ONIMASA(1983, Jap.), d, w

Robert Goshen
YOUNG AND THE BRAVE, THE(1963)

Russell Goslant
I AM THE CHEESE(1983)

Juergen Goslar
NIGHT OF THE ASKARI(1978, Ger./South African), d, w

Jurgen Goslar
ARENT WE WONDERFUL?(1959, Ger.); TERROR AFTER MIDNIGHT(1965, Ger.), d; SLAVERS(1977, Ger.), a, p&d; MANIAC MANSION(1978, Ital.), p&d
Misc. Talkies
ALBINO(1980), d

S. Goslavskaya
Misc. Silents
RUSLAN I LUDMILA(1915, USSR)

Nicholas Gosling
GLADIATORS, THE(1970, Swed.), w

Paolo Goslino
WEB OF THE SPIDER(1972, Ital./Fr./Ger.)

Rachel Goslins
NIGHTMARES(1983)

Evelyn Gosnell
Silents
DEVIL'S PASSKEY, THE(1920); UNDER THE RED ROBE(1923)

Raja Gosnell
1984
LONELY GUY, THE(1984), ed

Barry Gosney
CARRY ON JACK(1963, Brit.)

Marran Gosov
24-HOUR LOVER(1970, Ger.), d&w

Bick Goss
SWEET CHARITY(1969)

Bobby Goss
LEARNING TREE, THE(1969)

Helen Goss
HAIL AND FAREWELL(1936, Brit.); REVERSE BE MY LOT, THE(1938, Brit.); PLACE OF ONE'S OWN, A(1945, Brit.); RANDOLPH FAMILY, THE(1945, Brit.); THEY WERE SISTERS(1945, Brit.); WICKED LADY, THE(1946, Brit.); MAN OF EVIL(1948, Brit.); MARK OF CAIN, THE(1948, Brit.); MY SISTER AND I(1948, Brit.); WEAKER SEX, THE(1949, Brit.); FIVE ANGLES ON MURDER(1950, Brit.); PINK STRING AND SEALING WAX(1950, Brit.); STAGE FRIGHT(1950, Brit.); CHEER THE BRAVE(1951, Brit.); HONEYMOON DEFERRED(1951, Brit.); ISLAND RESCUE(1952, Brit.); OUTPOST IN MALAYA(1952, Brit.); PICKWICK PAPERS, THE(1952, Brit.); SOMETHING MONEY CAN'T BUY(1952, Brit.); SWORD AND THE ROSE, THE(1953); THREE CORNERED FATE(1954, Brit.); ACTION OF THE TIGER(1957); GIDEON OF SCOTLAND YARD(1959, Brit.); HOUND OF THE BASKERVILLES, THE(1959, Brit.); HOUSE OF FRIGHT(1961); MALAGA(1962, Brit.); HALF A SIXPENCE(1967, Brit.)

James Goss
SUBWAY EXPRESS(1931)

Joel Goss
PORKY'S II: THE NEXT DAY(1983)

Walter Goss
Silents
FINE MANNERS(1926); FIREMAN, SAVE MY CHILD(1927)
Misc. Silents
FASCINATING YOUTH(1926)

Harold Goss-Coyote
WINDWALKER(1980)

John Gossage
DREAMS COME TRUE(1936, Brit.), p; SKYLARKS(1936, Brit.), p; IT'S HARD TO BE GOOD(1950, Brit.), p; GREEN GROW THE RUSHES(1951, Brit.), p; ANGELS ONE FIVE(1954, Brit.), p; GAMMA PEOPLE, THE(1956), p, w; RX MURDER(1958, Brit.), p, w

John W. Gossage
LAST MAN TO HANG, THE(1956, Brit.), p

Andre Gosselain
NIGHT ENCOUNTER(1963, Fr./Ital.), m

Bernard Gosselin
TAKE IT ALL(1966, Can.), ph

Charles Gosselin
QUEST FOR FIRE(1982, Fr./Can.)

Sally Gosselin
TO SIR, WITH LOVE(1967, Brit.)

Suzanne Gossen
JUDEX(1966, Fr./Ital.)

Tommy Gosser
ON DANGEROUS GROUND(1951)

Charles Gosset
GREENWICH VILLAGE STORY(1963)

Dion Gossett
Misc. Talkies
TOUGH(1974)

Robert Gosset
1984
OVER THE BROOKLYN BRIDGE(1984)

Lou Gossett
LEO THE LAST(1970, Brit.); SKIN GAME(1971); TRAVELS WITH MY AUNT(1972, Brit.); LAUGHING POLICEMAN, THE(1973); WHITE DAWN, THE(1974); RIVER NIGER, THE(1976)

Lou Gossett, Jr.
J.D.'S REVENGE(1976)

Louis Gossett
RAISIN IN THE SUN, A(1961); LANDLORD, THE(1970); DEEP, THE(1977)

Louis Gossett, Jr.
BUSHBABY, THE(1970); CHOIRBOYS, THE(1977); OFFICER AND A GENTLEMAN, AN(1982); JAWS 3-D(1983)
1984
FINDERS KEEPERS(1984)

Ronald Gossop
COUNTRYMAN(1982, Jamaica)

Kari Gosswiller
PERSONAL BEST(1982)

Mario Gosta
BARBER OF SEVILLE, THE(1947, Ital.), d

Gordon Gostelow
IDOL, THE(1966, Brit.); IN SEARCH OF GREGORY(1970, Brit./Ital.); WUTHERING HEIGHTS(1970, Brit.); NICHOLAS AND ALEXANDRA(1971, Brit.)

Pierre Gostin [Gaston]
RAVAGER, THE(1970)

Thomas Goswell
CURSE OF THE WEREWOLF, THE(1961), art d; PASSPORT TO CHINA(1961, Brit.), art d; SCREAM OF FEAR(1961, Brit.), art d; TERROR OF THE TONGS, THE(1961, Brit.), art d

Tom Goswell
GAY ADVENTURE, THE(1953, Brit.), art d; INNOCENTS IN PARIS(1955, Brit.), art d

Archie Got
THUNDER BIRDS(1942); LADY FROM CHUNGKING(1943)

Roland Got
EXTORTION(1938); LETTER, THE(1940); STRIKE UP THE BAND(1940); SECRETS OF THE WASTELANDS(1941); THEY MET IN BOMBAY(1941); ACROSS THE PACIFIC(1942); DESTINATION TOKYO(1944); DRAGON SEED(1944)

Roland L. Got
NIGHT HAWK, THE(1938)

Mici Gota
VOODOO MAN(1944)

J. H. Gotch
Silents
WOODEN SHOES(1917)

Jan Gotch
OKAY FOR SOUND(1937, Brit.)

Lee Gotch
KANSAS CITY KITTY(1944)

Les Gotcher
SQUARE DANCE JUBILEE(1949)

Walter Gotell
NIGHT INVADER, THE(1943, Brit); 2,000 WOMEN(1944, Brit.); AFRICAN QUEEN, THE(1951, U.S./Brit.); LILLI MARLENE(1951, Brit.); WOODEN HORSE, THE(1951); ALBERT, R.N.(1953, Brit.); DESPERATE MOMENT(1953, Brit.); DUEL IN THE JUNGLE(1954, Brit.); PARATROOPER(1954, Brit.); MAN WHO KNEW TOO MUCH, THE(1956); DESERT ATTACK(1958, Brit.); MAN INSIDE, THE(1958, Brit.); BANDIT OF ZHOBE, THE(1959); NO SAFETY AHEAD(1959, Brit.); CIRCUS OF HORRORS(1960, Brit.); CIRCLE OF DECEPTON(1961, Brit.); DEVIL'S DAFFODIL, THE(1961, Brit./Ger.); GUNS OF NAVARONE, THE(1961); DEVIL'S AGENT, THE(1962, Brit.); HOT MONEY GIRL(1962, Brit./Ger.); ROAD TO HONG KONG, THE(1962, U.S./Brit.); FROM RUSSIA WITH LOVE(1963, Brit.); SWORD OF LANCELOT(1963, Brit.); 55 DAYS AT PEKING(1963); LORD JIM(1965, Brit.); SPY WHO CAME

IN FROM THE COLD, THE(1965, Brit.); THESE ARE THE DAMNED(1965, Brit.); ATTACK ON THE IRON COAST(1968, U.S./Brit.); FILE OF THE GOLDEN GOOSE, THE(1969, Brit.); OUR MISS FRED(1972, Brit.); BLACK SUNDAY(1977); MARCH OR DIE(1977, Brit.); SPY WHO LOVED ME, THE(1977, Brit.); BOYS FROM BRAZIL, THE(1978); CUBA(1979); MOONRAKER(1979, Brit.); STUD, THE(1979, Brit.); FOR YOUR EYES ONLY(1981); OCTOPUSSY(1983, Brit.)

1984

MEMED MY HAWK(1984, Brit.)

Frederic Gotfurt

TEMPTATION HARBOR(1949, Brit.), w; YOU CAN'T BEAT THE IRISH(1952, Brit.), w

Frederick Gotfurt

LADY MISLAID, A(1958, Brit.), w; WHY BOTHER TO KNOCK(1964, Brit.), w

Basil Goth

LITTLE FRIEND(1934, Brit.)

Ray Goth

SILVER STREAK(1976)

Sandor Goth

HIPPOLYT, THE LACKEY(1932, Hung.)

Stanley Gothals

Silents

INFAMOUS MISS REVELL, THE(1921)

Gotham Quartette

KISS ME, SERGEANT(1930, Brit.)

The Gotham Singers

UNDER THE GREENWOOD TREE(1930, Brit.)

Michael Gothard

HEROSTRATUS(1968, Brit.); UP THE JUNCTION(1968, Brit.); SCREAM AND SCREAM AGAIN(1970, Brit.); LAST VALLEY, THE(1971, Brit.); WHO SLEW AUNTIE ROO?(1971, U.S./Brit.); THREE MUSKETEERS, THE(1974, Panama); WARLORDS OF ATLANTIS(1978, Brit.); FOR YOUR EYES ONLY(1981)

Heinrich Gothe

Silents

WOMAN ON THE MOON, THE(1929, Ger.)

Robert Gothie

SANCTUARY(1961); PALM SPRINGS WEEKEND(1963)

Heinrich Gotho

M(1933, Ger.); TESTAMENT OF DR. MABUSE, THE(1943, Ger.)

Silents

METROPOLIS(1927, Ger.)

James T. Goto

BATTLE OF THE CORAL SEA(1959); GALLANT HOURS, THE(1960), a, tech adv

Shigeaki Goto

ANGRY ISLAND(1960, Jap.)

Toshio Goto

LIFE OF OHARU(1964, Jap.), ed

Dennis Gotobed

TOUCH, THE(1971, U.S./Swed.)

V. Gotovzev

1812(1944, USSR)

Wiktor Gotowicz

1984

SHIVERS(1984, Pol.)

Jurij Gotowtschikow

1984

MOSCOW ON THE HUDSON(1984)

Robert Gotschall

HONEYSUCKLE ROSE(1980)

Barbara Gott

HOUSE OF THE ARROW, THE(1930, Brit.); LORD RICHARD IN THE PANTRY(1930, Brit.); MYSTERY AT THE VILLA ROSE(1930, Brit.); SISTER TO ASSIST'ER, A(1930, Brit.); FLYING FOOL, THE(1931, Brit.); SALLY IN OUR ALLEY(1931, Brit.); SPORT OF KINGS, THE(1931, Brit.); BORN LUCKY(1932, Brit.); OFFICE GIRL, THE(1932, Brit.); WATER GYPSIES, THE(1932, Brit.); CLEANING UP(1933, Brit.); CRIME AT BLOSSOMS, THE(1933, Brit.); GOOD COMPANIONS(1933, Brit.); GREAT STUFF(1933, Brit.); SONG AT EVENTIDE(1934, Brit.); CHILDREN OF THE FOG(1935, Brit.); BELOVED VAGABOND, THE(1936, Brit.); PASTOR HALL(1940, Brit.)

Silents

NOT QUITE A LADY(1928, Brit.); PARADISE(1928, Brit.); WHEN BOYS LEAVE HOME(1928, Brit.)

Misc. Silents

LITTLE PEOPLE, THE(1926, Brit.); LILY OF KILLARNEY(1929, Brit.)

Barbare Gott

COMPROMISED!(1931, Brit.)

Karel Gott

LEMONADE JOE(1966, Czech.); MARTYRS OF LOVE(1968, Czech.)

Gino Gottarelli

VON RYAN'S EXPRESS(1965); RUSSIANS ARE COMING, THE RUSSIANS ARE COMING, THE(1966); STRIPES(1981)

Oscar Gottell

Silents

GREED(1925)

Otto Gottell

Silents

GREED(1925)

Walter Gottell

HELL, HEAVEN OR HOBOKEN(1958, Brit.)

Dov Gottesfeld

EYE FOR AN EYE, AN(1981); SWAMP THING(1982); EXPOSED(1983)

Polly Gottesman

WIND AND THE LION, THE(1975)

Howard Gottfried

HOSPITAL, THE(1971), p; NETWORK(1976), p; ALTERED STATES(1980), p

Fritz Gottfurcht

GIRL IN THE TAXI(1937, Brit.), w

Frederick Gottfurt

IT HAPPENED ONE SUNDAY(1944, Brit.), w

Jeremias Gotthelf

BLACK SPIDER, THE(1983, Swit.), w

Charles Gotthold

Misc. Silents

CHALLENGE, THE(1916); FATE'S BOOMERANG(1916)

Roland Gotti

VERTIGO(1958)

'Alex Gottlieb

FIRED WIFE(1943), p

Alex Gottleib

RIDE 'EM COWBOY(1942), p

Archie Gottler

FOX MOVIETONE FOLLIES(1929); SONG OF KENTUCKY(1929), w; THEY HAD TO SEE PARIS(1929), m

Jerome S. Gottler

HIGH SOCIETY(1955), w; SPY CHASERS(1956), w

Aaron Gottlieb

TORPEDO BOAT(1942), w

Alex Gottlieb

ARSON GANG BUSTERS(1938), w; I STAND ACCUSED(1938), w; INVISIBLE ENEMY(1938), w; EX-CHAMP(1939), w; GAMBLING SHIP(1939), w; INSIDE INFORMATION(1939), w; MYSTERY OF THE WHITE ROOM(1939), w; CONVICTED WOMAN(1940), w; DARK STREETS OF CAIRO(1940), w; FUGITIVE FROM JUSTICE, A(1940), w; MEET THE WILDCAT(1940), w; BUCK PRIVATES(1941), p; HOLD THAT GHOST(1941), p; HORROR ISLAND(1941), w; IN THE NAVY(1941), p; LUCKY DEVILS(1941), w; MEET THE CHUMP(1941), w; MYSTERY SHIP(1941), w; I LIVE ON DANGER(1942), w; PARDON MY SARONG(1942), p; WHO DONE IT?(1942), p; HIT THE ICE(1943), p; IT AIN'T HAY(1943), p; HOLLYWOOD CANTEEN(1944), p; JANIE(1944), p; MAKE YOUR OWN BED(1944), p; ESCAPE IN THE DESERT(1945), p; PILLOW TO POST(1945), p; CINDERELLA JONES(1946), p; HER KIND OF MAN(1946), p; JANIE GETS MARRIED(1946), p; MAN WHO DARED, THE(1946), w; TIME, THE PLACE AND THE GIRL, THE(1946), p; ALWAYS TOGETHER(1947), p; STALLION ROAD(1947), p; THAT HAGEN GIRL(1947), p; ROMANCE ON THE HIGH SEAS(1948), p; TWO GUYS FROM TEXAS(1948), p; WALLFLOWER(1948), p; GIRL FROM JONES BEACH, THE(1949), p; IT'S A GREAT FEELING(1949), p; ABBOTT AND COSTELLO MEET CAPTAIN KIDD(1952), p; FIGHTER, THE(1952), p; JACK AND THE BEANSTALK(1952), p; MACAO(1952), p; BLUE GARDENIA, THE(1953), p; MARRY ME AGAIN(1953), p, w; SUSAN SLEPT HERE(1954), w; THREE HOURS TO KILL(1954), w; ARIZONA RAIDERS(1965), w; FRANKIE AND JOHNNY(1966), w

Buck Gottlieb

KILLER AT LARGE(1947), p

Carl Gottlieb

MARYJANE(1968); M(1970); UP THE SANDBOX(1972); JAWS(1975), a, w; CANNONBALL(1976, U.S./Hong Kong); WHICH WAY IS UP?(1977), w; JAWS II(1978), w; JERK, THE(1979), a, w; CAVEMAN(1981), d, w; DOCTOR DETROIT(1983), w; JAWS 3-D(1983), w; STING II, THE(1983)

Carl A. Gottlieb

1984

JOHNNY DANGEROUSLY(1984)

David Gottlieb

CANNONBALL(1976, U.S./Hong Kong)

David Neil Gottlieb

Misc. Talkies

GAME SHOW MODELS(1977), d

Franz Josef Gottlieb

PHANTOM OF SOHO, THE(1967, Ger.), d

Gordon Gottlieb

VERY NATURAL THING, A(1974), m

Linda Gottlieb

LIMBO(1972), p

Louis Gottlieb

I LOVE YOU, ALICE B. TOKLAS!(1968)

Mark Gottlieb

Misc. Talkies

CALLIOPE(1971)

Morton Gottlieb

SLEUTH(1972, Brit.), p; SAME TIME, NEXT YEAR(1978), p; ROMANTIC COMEDY(1983), p

Paul Gottlieb

IN PRAISE OF OLDER WOMEN(1978, Can.), w; AGENCY(1981, Can.), w

Richard Gottlieb

RIDING HIGH(1943)

Stan Gottlieb

PUTNEY SWOPE(1969); OWL AND THE PUSSYCAT, THE(1970); ANDERSON TAPES, THE(1971); YOU'VE GOT TO WALK IT LIKE YOU TALK IT OR YOU'LL LOSE THAT BEAT(1971); GREASER'S PALACE(1972); SLAUGHTERHOUSE-FIVE(1972)

Stephen Gottlieb

IT AIN'T HAY(1943)

Theodore Gottlieb

SO DARK THE NIGHT(1946); FALL GUY(1947); LONE WOLF IN MEXICO, THE(1947)

John Gottowt

TALES OF THE UNCANNY(1932, Ger.)

Silents

NOSFERATU, THE VAMPIRE(1922, Ger.)

Misc. Silents

STUDENT OF PRAGUE, THE(1913, Ger.); ALGOL(1920, Ger.); WAXWORKS(1924, Ger.)

Ferdinand Gottschalk

TONIGHT OR NEVER(1931); DOOMED BATTALION, THE(1932); GRAND HOTEL(1932); MASK OF FU MANCHU, THE(1932); SIGN OF THE CROSS, THE(1932); BERKELEY SQUARE(1933); DANCING LADY(1933); EX-LADY(1933); FEMALE(1933); GIRL MISSING(1933); GOLD DIGGERS OF 1933(1933); GOODBYE AGAIN(1933); GRAND SLAM(1933); HORSEPLAY(1933); KEYHOLE, THE(1933); MIDNIGHT CLUB(1933); PAROLE GIRL(1933); REUNION IN VIENNA(1933); SHE HAD TO SAY YES(1933); WARRIOR'S HUSBAND, THE(1933); BOMBAY MAIL(1934); CLEOPATRA(1934); GAMBLING LADY(1934); I SELL ANYTHING(1934); KING KELLY OF THE U.S.A(1934); LONG LOST FATHER(1934); MADAME DU BARRY(1934); NANA(1934); NOTORIOUS SOPHIE LANG, THE(1934); RIP TIDE(1934); UPPER

WORLD(1934); WITCHING HOUR, THE(1934); BREAK OF HEARTS(1935); CLIVE OF INDIA(1935); FOLIES DERGERE(1935); GAY DECEPTION, THE(1935); I AM A THIEF(1935); I DREAM TOO MUCH(1935); LES MISERABLES(1935); MAN WHO BROKE THE BANK AT MONTE CARLO, THE(1935); MAN WHO RECLAIMED HIS HEAD, THE(1935); MELODY LINGERS ON, THE(1935); NIGHT LIFE OF THE GODS(1935); ONE EXCITING ADVENTURE(1935); RED SALUTE(1935); SECRET OF THE CHATEAU(1935); SING SING NIGHTS(1935); VAGABOND LADY(1935); BUNKER BEAN(1936); GARDEN OF ALLAH, THE(1936); MAN I MARRY, THE(1936); WHITE LEGION, THE(1936); ALI BABA GOES TO TOWN(1937); ALONG CAME LOVE(1937); CAFE METROPOLE(1937); CRIME NOBOBY SAW, THE(1937); I'LL TAKE ROMANCE(1937); THAT GIRL FROM PARIS(1937); ADVENTURES OF MARCO POLO, THE(1938); JOSETTE(1938); ROMANCE IN THE DARK(1938); STOLEN HEAVEN(1938)
Misc. Silents
ZAZA(1923)

Hans Gottschalk
HAMLET(1962, Ger.), p

Louis F. Gottschalk
Silents
BROKEN BLOSSOMS(1919), m; FOUR HORSEMEN OF THE APOCALYPSE, THE(1921), m; LITTLE LORD FAUNTLEROY(1921), m; THREE MUSKETEERS, THE(1921), m; ROSITA(1923), m

Norman Gottschalk
MICKEY ONE(1965); HOMEBODIES(1974)

Robert Gottschalk
DANGEROUS CHARTER(1962), p, d, w

Hugo Gottschlich
FOREVER MY LOVE(1962); GOOD SOLDIER SCHWEIK, THE(1963, Ger.)

Hugo Gottschlieh
WONDER BOY(1951, Brit./Aust.)

Fritz Gottwald
BOUDOIR DIPLOMAT(1930), w

Reginald Gottwaltz
SUCH IS LIFE(1936, Brit.), p

Reginald Gottwitz
MR. STRINGFELLOW SAYS NO(1937, Brit.), p

Mici Goty
IN OUR TIME(1944)

Carl Gotz
Silents
PANDORA'S BOX(1929, Ger.)

George Gotz
BLOOD OF FU MANCHU, THE(1968, Brit.)

Karl Gotz
Misc. Silents
CAGLIOSTRO(1920, Ger.); PAREMA, CRERATURE FROM THE STARWORLD(1922, Aust.)

Kurt Gotz
CORPSE OF BEVERLY HILLS, THE(1965, Ger.), w

Massimo Gotz
LITTLE ARK, THE(1972), art d

Heinz Gotze
INVISIBLE DR. MABUSE, THE(1965, Ger.), prod d

Hank Gotzenberg
MOTHER GOOSE A GO-GO(1966), ed

Bernhard Gotzke
Misc. Silents
MYSTERIES OF INDIA(1922, Ger.)

Georges Goubert
RISE OF LOUIS XIV, THE(1970, Fr.)

Jetta Goudal
LADY OF THE PAVEMENTS(1929); BUSINESS AND PLEASURE(1932)
Silents
OPEN ALL NIGHT(1924); COMING OF AMOS, THE(1925); WHITE GOLD(1927)
Misc. Silents
ROAD TO YESTERDAY, THE(1925); SALOME OF THE TENEMENTS(1925); SPANIARD, THE(1925); HER MAN O'WAR(1926); PARIS AT MIDNIGHT(1926); THREE FACES EAST(1926); FIGHTING LOVE(1927)

Alex Goudavich
JULIA MISBEHAVES(1948)

Ingrid Goude
TATTERED DRESS, THE(1957); BIG BEAT, THE(1958); ONCE UPON A HORSE(1958); WILD HERITAGE(1958); KILLER SHREWS, THE(1959); NEVER STEAL ANYTHING SMALL(1959)

Jane Goude
EAST SIDE OF HEAVEN(1939); THAT'S RIGHT–YOU'RE WRONG(1939); DOCTOR TAKES A WIFE(1940); THIRD FINGER, LEFT HAND(1940)

Elizabeth Goudge
GREEN DOLPHIN STREET(1947), w

Jean Goudier
BENVENUTA(1983, Fr.), ed

Robert Goudier
OPERATION MANHUNT(1954)

Alex Goudovitch
TEXAS CARNIVAL(1951)

Lex Goudsmith
LUCKY STAR, THE(1980, Can.)

Jetta Goufal
Misc. Silents
FORBIDDEN WOMAN, THE(1927)

Edwina Gough
SLITHER(1973)

Jim Gough
URBAN COWBOY(1980); EDDIE MACON'S RUN(1983)
1984
PLACES IN THE HEART(1984)

John Gough
TWO FOR TONIGHT(1935)

Silents
ANN'S FINISH(1918); GLEAM O'DAWN(1922); HIGH AND HANDSOME(1925); STREET OF SIN, THE(1928); AIR LEGION, THE(1929)
Misc. Silents
DREAM OR TWO AGO, A(1916); SANDS OF SACRIFICE(1917); BORDER JUSTICE(1925); THREE WISE CROOKS(1925); SECRET ORDERS(1926)

Johnnie Gough
HAUNTED HOUSE, THE(1928)

Johnny Gough
CIRCUS KID, THE(1928)
Silents
FLAMING WATERS(1925); AIN'T LOVE FUNNY?(1927); HOOK AND LADDER NO. 9(1927); JUDGMENT OF THE HILLS(1927)

Lloyd Gough
ALL MY SONS(1948); BABE RUTH STORY, THE(1948); BLACK BART(1948); RIVER LADY(1948); SOUTHERN YANKEE, A(1948); THAT WONDERFUL URGE(1948); ALWAYS LEAVE THEM LAUGHING(1949); ROSEANNA McCOY(1949); TENSION(1949); TULSA(1949); OUTSIDE THE WALL(1950); STORM WARNING(1950); SUNSET BOULEVARD(1950); SCARF, THE(1951); VALENTINO(1951); RANCHO NOTORIOUS(1952); TONY ROME(1967); MADIGAN(1968); SWEET RIDE, THE(1968); TELL THEM WILLIE BOY IS HERE(1969); GREAT WHITE HOPE, THE(1970); GLORY BOY(1971); EXECUTIVE ACTION(1973); EARTHQUAKE(1974); FRONT, THE(1976); HOUSE CALLS(1978); PRIVATE FILES OF J. EDGAR HOOVER, THE(1978)

Michael Gough
ANNA KARENINA(1948, Brit.); BLANCHE FURY(1948, Brit.); HOUR OF GLORY(1949, Brit.); SARABAND(1949, Brit.); HA' PENNY BREEZE(1950, Brit.); BLACKMAILED(1951, Brit.); NIGHT WAS OUR FRIEND(1951, Brit.); MAN IN THE WHITE SUIT, THE(1952); NO RESTING PLACE(1952, Brit.); SWORD AND THE ROSE, THE(1953, Brit.); TWICE UPON A TIME(1953, Brit.); ROB ROY, THE HIGHLAND ROGUE(1954, Brit.); RICHARD III(1956, Brit.); HOUSE IN THE WOODS, THE(1957, Brit.); REACH FOR THE SKY(1957, Brit.); HORROR OF DRACULA, THE(1958, Brit.); HORSE'S MOUTH, THE(1958, Brit.); NIGHT AMBUSH(1958, Brit.); HORRORS OF THE BLACK MUSEUM(1959, U.S./Brit.); MODEL FOR MURDER(1960, Brit.); KONGA(1961, Brit.); I LIKE MONEY(1962, Brit.); PHANTOM OF THE OPERA, THE(1962, Brit.); WHAT A CARVE UP!(1962, Brit.); BLACK ZOO(1963, Brit.); TAMAHINE(1964, Brit.); DR. TERROR'S HOUSE OF HORRORS(1965, Brit.); GAME FOR THREE LOSERS(1965, Brit.); SKULL, THE(1965, Brit.); CANDIDATE FOR MURDER(1966, Brit.); BERSERK(1967); THEY CAME FROM BEYOND SPACE(1967, Brit.); WALK WITH LOVE AND DEATH, A(1969); WOMEN IN LOVE(1969, Brit.); CRIMSON CULT, THE(1970, Brit.); JULIUS CAESAR(1970, Brit.); TROG(1970, Brit.); CRUCIBLE OF HORROR(1971, Brit.); GO-BETWEEN, THE(1971, Brit.); HENRY VIII AND HIS SIX WIVES(1972, Brit.); SAVAGE MESSIAH(1972, Brit.); HORROR HOSPITAL(1973, Brit.); LEGEND OF HELL HOUSE, THE(1973, Brit.); GALILEO(1975, Brit.); SATAN'S SLAVE(1976, Brit.); BOYS FROM BRAZIL, THE(1978); VENOM(1982, Brit.); DRESSER, THE(1983)
1984
MEMED MY HAWK(1984, Brit.); OXFORD BLUES(1984); TOP SECRET!(1984)

Sandra Gough
DRESSER, THE(1983)

Simon Gough
CRUCIBLE OF HORROR(1971, Brit.)

Terry Gough
WALKABOUT(1971, Aus./U.S.), art d

Trent Gough
COLD RIVER(1982)

Wilfred Gough
Silents
HIS HOUR(1924)

Abi Gouhad
ROLLERBALL(1975)

Roman Goul
KNIGHT WITHOUT ARMOR(1937, Brit.), tech adv

Jose R. Goula
HONEYMOON(1947)

Didier Goulard
BACKFIRE(1965, Fr.), w

Paulo Goulart
1984
GABRIELA(1984, Braz.)

Amy Kennedy Gould
WAY OF YOUTH, THE(1934, Brit.), w; CHECKMATE(1935, Brit,), w

Barbara Gould
KISS THEM FOR ME(1957); THREE BRAVE MEN(1957)

Berni Gould
SING FOR YOUR SUPPER(1941); TWIST ALL NIGHT(1961), w

Bill Gould
GUN JUSTICE(1934); FAST BULLETS(1936)
Misc. Talkies
TERROR OF THE PLAINS(1934)

Bob Gould
STAY HUNGRY(1976), set d; LATE SHOW, THE(1977), set d; MELVIN AND HOWARD(1980), set d; SERIAL(1980), set d
1984
JOY OF SEX(1984), set d

Bobby Gould
Silents
PATCHWORK GIRL OF OZ, THE(1914)

Bruce Gould
REUNION(1936), w

Charles S. Gould
JUNGLE MOON MEN(1955), d; BATTLE STATIONS(1956), w

Chester Gould
DICK TRACY(1945), w; DICK TRACY VS. CUEBALL(1946), w; DICK TRACY MEETS GRUESOME(1947), w; DICK TRACY'S DILEMMA(1947), w

Clifford Newton Gould
KRAKATOA, EAST OF JAVA(1969), w; MACHO CALLAHAN(1970), w

Dan Gould
REBELLION IN CUBA(1961)

Dave Gould
FLYING DOWN TO RIO(1933), ch; DOWN TO THEIR LAST YACHT(1934), ch; GAY DIVORCEE, THE(1934), ch; HIPS, HIPS, HOORAY(1934), ch; THREE ON A HONEY-MOON(1934), ch; BROADWAY MELODY OF 1936(1935), ch; FOLIES DER-GERE(1935), ch; BORN TO DANCE(1936), ch; BROADWAY MELODY OF '38(1937), ch; DAY AT THE RACES, A(1937), ch; BREAKING THE ICE(1938), ch; EVERYTHING'S ON ICE(1939), staging; BOYS FROM SYRACUSE(1940), ch; IT ALL CAME TRUE(1940), ch; SWEATER GIRL(1942), ch; GALS, INCORPORATED(1943), w; HANDS ACROSS THE BORDER(1943), ch; O, MY DARLING CLEMENTINE(1943), ch; RHYTHM PARADE(1943), d; CASANOVA IN BURLESQUE(1944), ch; LADY, LET'S DANCE(1944), ch; MY BEST GAL(1944), ch; ROSIE THE RIVETER(1944), ch

David Gould
HOLLYWOOD PARTY(1934), ch

Diana Gould
JENNY(1969), w

Don Gould
CHIVATO(1961)

Dorothy Gould
CHARLATAN, THE(1929); LADIES IN LOVE(1930)

Doug Gould
EARTHWORM TRACTORS(1936), ed; CALIFORNIA MAIL, THE(1937), ed; FLY-AWAY BABY(1937), ed; READY, WILLING AND ABLE(1937), ed; PENROD AND HIS TWIN BROTHER(1938), ed; WHEN WERE YOU BORN?(1938), ed; BLACKWELL'S ISLAND(1939), ed; COWBOY QUARTERBACK(1939), ed; NANCY DREW, TROUBLE SHOOTER(1939), ed; SECRET SERVICE OF THE AIR(1939), ed; KING OF THE LUMBERJACKS(1940), ed; KNOCKOUT(1941), ed; NINE LIVES ARE NOT ENOUGH(1941), ed; NURSE'S SECRET, THE(1941), ed; STEEL AGAINST THE SKY(1941), ed; ESCAPE FROM CRIME(1942), ed; CRIME BY NIGHT(1944), ed

Douglas Gould
DEAD END KIDS ON DRESS PARADE(1939), ed; SECRET ENEMIES(1942), ed

Eleanor Gould
HUSBANDS(1970)

Eleanor Cody Gould
DIRTYMOUTH(1970)

Elliot Gould
MOVE(1970); LADY VANISHES, THE(1980, Brit.)

Elliott Gould
QUICK, LET'S GET MARRIED(1965); NIGHT THEY RAIDED MINSKY'S, THE(1968); BOB AND CAROL AND TED AND ALICE(1969); GETTING STRAIGHT(1970); I LOVE MY WIFE(1970); M(1970); LITTLE MURDERS(1971), a, p; TOUCH, THE(1971, U.S./Swed.); LONG GOODBYE, THE(1973); BUSTING(1974); CALIFORNIA SPLIT(1974); S(1974); NASHVILLE(1975); WHIFFS(1975); WHO?(1975, Brit./Ger.); HARRY AND WALTER GO TO NEW YORK(1976); I WILL ...I WILL ...FOR NOW(1976); MEAN JOHNNY BARROWS(1976); BRIDGE TOO FAR, A(1977, Brit.); CAPRICORN ONE(1978); MATILDA(1978); ESCAPE TO ATHENA(1979, Brit.); MUP-PET MOVIE, THE(1979); SILENT PARTNER, THE(1979, Can.); FALLING IN LOVE AGAIN(1980); LAST FLIGHT OF NOAH'S ARK, THE(1980); DEVIL AND MAX DEVLIN, THE(1981); DIRTY TRICKS(1981, Can.)
1984
MUPPETS TAKE MANHATTAN, THE(1984); NAKED FACE, THE(1984); OVER THE BROOKLYN BRIDGE(1984)
Misc. Talkies
CONFESSION, THE(1964)

Eric Gould
ANNIE HALL(1977)

Glenn Gould
SLAUGHTERHOUSE-FIVE(1972), m

Gordon Gould
ZELIG(1983)

Graydon Gould
FLOODS OF FEAR(1958, Brit.); LINKS OF JUSTICE(1958); DURING ONE NIGHT(1962, Brit.); VICTORS, THE(1963)

Greta Gould
MIN AND BILL(1930)

Gretta Gould
JANE EYRE(1935); MAGNIFICENT OBSESSION(1935); SCHOOL FOR GIRLS(1935)

Hal Gould
TURN OFF THE MOON(1937)

Harold Gould
YELLOW CANARY, THE(1963); READY FOR THE PEOPLE(1964); INSIDE DAISY CLOVER(1965); SATAN BUG, THE(1965); AMERICAN DREAM, AN(1966); HAR-PER(1966); SPY WITH MY FACE, THE(1966); PROJECT X(1968); ARRANGEMENT, THE(1969); LAWYER, THE(1969); MRS. POLLIFAX-SPY(1971); WHERE DOES IT HURT?(1972); STING, THE(1973); FRONT PAGE, THE(1974); LOVE AND DEATH(1975); STRONGEST MAN IN THE WORLD, THE(1975); BIG BUS, THE(1976); GUS(1976); SILENT MOVIE(1976); ONE AND ONLY, THE(1978); SEEMS LIKE OLD TIMES(1980)

Harvey Gould
GUN SMOKE(1936), ph; MAD YOUTH(1940), ph; THAT GANG OF MINE(1940), ph

Heywood Gould
ROLLING THUNDER(1977), w; BOYS FROM BRAZIL, THE(1978), w; FORT AP-ACHE, THE BRONX(1981), w

Ina Gould
DAY OF THE LOCUST, THE(1975); ON THE NICKEL(1980); SILENT SCREAM(1980); SECOND THOUGHTS(1983)

John Gould
JOURNEY INTO DARKNESS(1968, Brit.), w; FIRST LOVE(1970, Ger./Switz.), w; ONLY WAY, THE(1970, Panama/Den./U.S.), w; BLOCKHOUSE, THE(1974, Brit.), w

John Gould [Jack Gold]
WHO?(1975, Brit./Ger.), w

Karsen Lee Gould
HEARTBEEPS(1981)
1984
ALMOST YOU(1984)

Lea Gould
CANNONBALL(1976, U.S./Hong Kong)

Lois Gould
SUCH GOOD FRIENDS(1971), w

Merle S. Gould
Misc. Talkies
BODY IS A SHELL, THE(1957), d

Michael Gould
PERSECUTION AND ASSASSINATION OF JEAN-PAUL MARAT AS PERFORMED BY THE INMATES OF THE ASYLUM OF CHARENTON UNDER THE DIRECTION OF THE MARQUIS DE SADE, THE(1967, Brit.)

Nancy Gould
GNOME-MOBILE, THE(1967); OUT OF THE BLUE(1982)

Nat Gould
Silents
DEAD CERTAINTY, A(1920, Brit.), w; RANK OUTSIDER(1920, Brit.), w

Randy Gould
NEW YEAR'S EVIL(1980)

Richard Gould
YANK IN KOREA, A(1951)

Rita Gould
FUGITIVE LADY(1934); KISS AND MAKE UP(1934); ROBERTA(1935); GIRLS' DORMITORY(1936); HE COULDN'T SAY NO(1938); WOMEN, THE(1939); FALLEN SPARROW, THE(1943); HIGHER AND HIGHER(1943); SO'S YOUR UNCLE(1943); SOUTH OF DIXIE(1944); STANDING ROOM ONLY(1944); HER LUCKY NIGHT(1945); I'LL TELL THE WORLD(1945); VICIOUS CIRCLE, THE(1948); BIG COMBO, THE(1955)
Misc. Silents
BLACK SHEEP, A(1915)

Robert Gould
CARRIE(1976), set d; DAYS OF HEAVEN(1978), set d; PLAYERS(1979), set d; POSTMAN ALWAYS RINGS TWICE, THE(1981), set d; SOUTHERN COMFORT(1981), set d
1984
CHOOSE ME(1984); SONGWRITER(1984); WILD LIFE, THE(1984), set d

Ross Gould
STALAG 17(1953); WE'RE NO ANGELS(1955)

Roy Gould
SALLY'S HOUNDS(1968), m

Sandra Gould
T-MEN(1947); JUNE BRIDE(1948); ROMANCE ON THE HIGH SEAS(1948); CITY ACROSS THE RIVER(1949); IT'S A GREAT FEELING(1949); MY DREAM IS YOURS(1949); STORY OF MOLLY X, THE(1949); TAKE ONE FALSE STEP(1949); CAGED(1950); JOE PALOOKA MEETS HUMPHREY(1950); NO HOLDS BAR-RED(1952); CLOWN, THE(1953); TEACHER'S PET(1958); IMITATION OF LIFE(1959); HONEYMOON HOTEL(1964); GHOST AND MR. CHICKEN, THE(1966); BAREFOOT EXECUTIVE, THE(1971); SKATETOWN, U.S.A.(1979)

Sara Jane Gould
NICKELODEON(1976); GOING BERSERK(1983)

Sid Gould
MAN FROM FRISCO(1944); TEENAGE MILLIONAIRE(1961); MOVE OVER, DAR-LING(1963); WHAT A WAY TO GO(1964); SUNSHINE BOYS, THE(1975); DUCHESS AND THE DIRTWATER FOX, THE(1976); HOT STUFF(1979); HISTORY OF THE WORLD, PART 1(1981)

Sondra Gould
EASY TO LOVE(1953)

Steve Gould
Misc. Talkies
DYNAMITE(1972)

Vi Gould
STRAWBERRY ROAN(1945, Brit.)

Violet Gould
WOLF'S CLOTHING(1936, Brit.); TWILIGHT HOUR(1944, Brit.); CHEER THE BRAVE(1951, Brit.); STOLEN ASSIGNMENT(1955, Brit.); KEEP IT CLEAN(1956, Brit.); TRIPLE DECEPTION(1957, Brit.)

Walter Gould
Silents
ONE LAW FOR BOTH(1917)

Will Gould
MOBS INC(1956), w

William Gould
PHANTOM THUNDERBOLT, THE(1933); RICHEST GIRL IN THE WORLD, THE(1934); SMOKING GUNS(1934); TRAIL DRIVE, THE(1934); WHEELS OF DESTI-NY(1934); HARD ROCK HARRIGAN(1935); MAN WHO RECLAIMED HIS HEAD, THE(1935); NIGHT AT THE OPERA, A(1935); WESTERN FRONTIER(1935); DESERT GUNS(1936); DESERT JUSTICE(1936); FUGITIVE SHERIFF, THE(1936); LOVE ON A BET(1936); SUTTER'S GOLD(1936); SWIFTY(1936); BREAKFAST FOR TWO(1937); HOOSIER SCHOOLBOY(1937); PINTO RUSTLERS(1937); PRESCRIPTION FOR RO-MANCE(1937); RANGER COURAGE(1937); RENFREW OF THE ROYAL MOUN-TED(1937); TOAST OF NEW YORK, THE(1937); GANGSTER'S BOY(1938); MR. MOTO TAKES A VACATION(1938); MR. WONG, DETECTIVE(1938); PURPLE VIGILANTES, THE(1938); WILD HORSE RODEO(1938); COWBOY QUARTERBACK(1939); DEAD END KIDS ON DRESS PARADE(1939); HOUSE OF FEAR, THE(1939); KING OF THE UNDERWORLD(1939); NANCY DREW AND THE HIDDEN STAIRCASE(1939); NAUGHTY BUT NICE(1939); NEWSBOY'S HOME(1939); OFF THE RECORD(1939); STREETS OF NEW YORK(1939); TORCHY PLAYS WITH DYNAMITE(1939); WOMEN IN THE WIND(1939); DR. CHRISTIAN MEETS THE WOMEN(1940); LIGHTNING STRIKES WEST(1940); MAN WHO TALKED TOO MUCH, THE(1940); MONEY AND THE WOMAN(1940); MURDER IN THE AIR(1940); NOBODY'S CHILDREN(1940); RAGTIME COWBOY JOE(1940); RIDERS OF PASCO BASIN(1940); TEAR GAS SQUAD(1940); THREE CHEERS FOR THE IRISH(1940); 'TIL WE MEET AGAIN(1940); WHEN THE DALTONS RODE(1940); BAD MEN OF MISSOURI(1941); FATHER TAKES A WIFE(1941); MAN FROM MONTANA(1941); MAN WHO LOST HIMSELF, THE(1941); MANPOWER(1941); MEET JOHN DOE(1941); NEVER GIVE A SUCKER AN EVEN BREAK(1941); NO GREATER SIN(1941); POT O' GOLD(1941); RICHEST MAN IN TOWN(1941); SEA WOLF, THE(1941); SEALED LIPS(1941); TANKS A MILLION(1941); TEXAS(1941); CITY OF SILENT MEN(1942); JUKE GIRL(1942); MADAME SPY(1942); MURDER IN THE BIG HOUSE(1942); PITTSBURGH(1942); SABOTEUR(1942); SPOILERS, THE(1942); STRANGE CASE OF DR. RX, THE(1942); TALK OF THE TOWN(1942); TRAMP, TRAMP, TRAMP(1942); FIGHTING FRON-TIER(1943); KEEP 'EM SLUGGING(1943); MISSION TO MOSCOW(1943); MUG TOWN(1943); ONCE UPON A TIME(1944); SAN ANTONIO(1945); BEAUTY AND THE BANDIT(1946); DEVIL THUMBS A RIDE, THE(1947); DICK TRACY MEETS GRUE-SOME(1947); DICK TRACY'S DILEMMA(1947); HER HUSBAND'S AFFAIRS(1947);

JEWELS OF BRANDENBURG(1947); LIKELY STORY, A(1947); MY WILD IRISH ROSE(1947); SMASH-UP, THE STORY OF A WOMAN(1947); VIOLENCE(1947); VOICE OF THE TURTLE, THE(1947); WILD HORSE MESA(1947); FOR THE LOVE OF MARY(1948); WINNER'S CIRCLE, THE(1948); YELLOW SKY(1948); I CHEATED THE LAW(1949); TASK FORCE(1949); MESSENGER OF PEACE(1950); OUTCAST OF BLACK MESA(1950); HEART OF THE ROCKIES(1951); MAN WHO CHEATED HIMSELF, THE(1951); MA AND PA KETTLE AT THE FAIR(1952); LAW AND ORDER(1953)
Misc. Talkies
LOSER'S END(1934); JUDGMENT BOOK, THE(1935); RIO RATTLER(1935); TRIGGER TOM(1935); UNCONQUERED BANDIT(1935); WOLF RIDERS(1935); WILDCAT SAUNDERS(1936)
Silents
PRIDE OF SUNSHINE ALLEY(1924)
Misc. Silents
SAVED BY RADIO(1922)
William H. Gould
WALLS OF JERICHO(1948)
William Howard Gould
MISSISSIPPI(1935); LONE WOLF RETURNS, THE(1936)
A.E. Gould-Porter
GIRLS OF PLEASURE ISLAND, THE(1953); DARLING LILI(1970)
Arthur Gould-Porter
NIGHTMARE(1942); NORTHERN PURSUIT(1943); JANE EYRE(1944); WHITE CLIFFS OF DOVER, THE(1944); DOUBLE LIFE, A(1947); KISS THE BLOOD OFF MY HANDS(1948); KIND LADY(1951); AGAINST ALL FLAGS(1952); ROGUE'S MARCH(1953); DANGEROUS WHEN WET(1953); ABBOTT AND COSTELLO MEET DR. JEKYLL AND MR. HYDE(1954); SO THIS IS PARIS(1954); LADY GODIVA(1955); VIRGIN QUEEN, THE(1955); THREE NUTS IN SEARCH OF A BOLT(1964); TORN CURTAIN(1966); KARATE KILLERS, THE(1967)
Arthur E. Gould-Porter
IRON CURTAIN, THE(1948); PIRATES OF TORTUGA(1961); ASSAULT ON A QUEEN(1966); BEDKNOBS AND BROOMSTICKS(1971)
Jetta Gouldal
Misc. Silents
CARDBOARD LOVER, THE(1928)
Stanley Goulder
SILENT PLAYGROUND, THE(1964, Brit.), d&w; GOLDEN HEAD, THE(1965, Hung., U.S.), w; EXORCISM AT MIDNIGHT(1966, Brit. revised 1973, U.S.), p,d&w
Misc. Talkies
TROUBLED WATERS(1964, Brit.), d
Goulding
HONEYMOON MERRY-GO-ROUND(1939, Brit.), w
Alf Goulding
ADVENTURES OF JANE, THE(1949, Brit.), d, w
Silents
LEARNING TO LOVE(1925); ATTA BOY!(1926), w
Misc. Silents
DON'T(1925), d; EXCUSE ME(1925), d; LADY, THE(1925); ALL AT SEA(1929), d
Alfred Goulding
ONE GOOD TURN(1936, Brit.), d; SAM SMALL LEAVES TOWN(1937, Brit.), d; SPLINTERS IN THE AIR(1937, Brit.), d; GANG, THE(1938, Brit.), d; HONEYMOON MERRY-GO-ROUND(1939, Brit.), d; CHUMP AT OXFORD, A(1940), d; EVERYTHING IS RHYTHM(1940, Brit.), d; DARK ROAD, THE(1948, Brit.), d; DICK BARTON-SPECIAL AGENT(1948, Brit.), d, w; DEVIL'S JEST, THE(1954, Brit.), d
Christine Goulding
PRIVATE EYES, THE(1980), cos
Dan Goulding
TIME OF THE HEATHEN(1962)
Edmond Goulding
WHITE BANNERS(1938), d
Edmund Goulding
BROADWAY MELODY, THE(1929), w; TRESPASSER, THE(1929), d&w; DEVIL'S HOLIDAY, THE(1930), d&w; GRAND PARADE, THE(1930), p&w; NIGHT ANGEL, THE(1931), d&w; REACHING FOR THE MOON(1931), d, w; BLONDIE OF THE FOLLIES(1932), d; FLESH(1932), d; GRAND HOTEL(1932), d; NO MAN OF HER OWN(1933), w; RIP TIDE(1934), d&w; DANTE'S INFERNO(1935), w; FLAME WITHIN, THE(1935), p,d&w; THAT CERTAIN WOMAN(1937), d&w; DAWN PATROL, THE(1938), d; DARK VICTORY(1939), d; OLD MAID, THE(1939), d; WE ARE NOT ALONE(1939), d; 'TIL WE MEET AGAIN(1940), d; TWO GIRLS ON BROADWAY(1940), w; GREAT LIE, THE(1941), d; CLAUDIA(1943), d; CONSTANT NYMPH, THE(1943), d; FOREVER AND A DAY(1943), p&d; FLIGHT FROM FOLLY(1945, Brit.), w; OF HUMAN BONDAGE(1946), d; RAZOR'S EDGE, THE(1946), d; NIGHTMARE ALLEY(1947), d; EVERYBODY DOES IT(1949), d; MISTER 880(1950), d; WE'RE NOT MARRIED(1952), d; DOWN AMONG THE SHELTERING PALMS(1953), d; TEENAGE REBEL(1956), d; MARDI GRAS(1958), d
Silents
QUEST OF LIFE, THE(1916), w; PERFECT LOVER, THE(1919), w; MADONNAS AND MEN(1920), w; SIN THAT WAS HIS, THE(1920), w; TOL'ABLE DAVID(1921), w; BROADWAY ROSE(1922), w; PEACOCK ALLEY(1922), w; SEVENTH DAY, THE(1922), w; JAZZMANIA(1923), w; DANTE'S INFERNO(1924), w; DANCING MOTHERS(1926), w; LOVE(1927), p&d
Misc. Silents
THREE LIVE GHOSTS(1922, Brit.); SALLY, IRENE AND MARY(1925), d; SUNUP(1925), d; PARIS(1926), d; WOMEN LOVE DIAMONDS(1927), d
Iris Goulding
PLYMOUTH ADVENTURE(1952)
Ivis Goulding
HOW TO MARRY A MILLIONAIRE(1953); SCANDAL AT SCOURIE(1953); TITANIC(1953); RAINS OF RANCHIPUR, THE(1955); SOLDIER OF FORTUNE(1955)
Louis Goulding
PROUD VALLEY, THE(1941, Brit.), w
Ray Goulding
THRILL OF A ROMANCE(1945); COLD TURKEY(1971); AUTHOR! AUTHOR!(1982)
Arthur Goulet
WANTED(1937, Brit.)
Robert Goulet
GAY PURR-EE(1962); HONEYMOON HOTEL(1964); I'D RATHER BE RICH(1964); I DEAL IN DANGER(1966); UNDERGROUND(1970, Brit.); ATLANTIC CITY(1981, U.S./Can.)

Teddy Burns Goulet
BIG RED(1962)
Violet Goulet
NIGHT HAS A THOUSAND EYES(1948)
Arthur Goulette
ILLEGAL(1932, Brit.)
Alfred Goulin
DEADLIER THAN THE MALE(1957, Fr.)
Arthur Goullet
DOWN RIVER(1931, Brit.); GENTLEMAN OF PARIS, A(1931); IT'S A KING(1933, Brit.); COLONEL BLOOD(1934, Brit.); CRIMSON CANDLE, THE(1934, Brit.); LADY JANE GREY(1936, Brit.); RED WAGON(1936); HEY! HEY! U.S.A.(1938, Brit.); STRANGE BOARDERS(1938, Brit.); FOR FREEDOM(1940, Brit.); MURDER AT THE BASKERVILLES(1941, Brit.); UNCENSORED(1944, Brit.); CARAVAN(1946, Brit.); END OF THE RIVER, THE(1947, Brit.); HA' PENNY BREEZE(1950, Brit.); KEEP IT CLEAN(1956, Brit.)
Arthur Goullett
KING SOLOMON'S MINES(1937, Brit.); NON-STOP NEW YORK(1937, Brit.)
Jerome Goulven
NIGHTS OF SHAME(1961, Fr.); THANK HEAVEN FOR SMALL FAVORS(1965, Fr.), p
Margarita Goumas
SERENITY(1962)
Pierre Goumy
HAIL MAFIA(1965, Fr./Ital.), m
James Gounaris
GODFATHER, THE, PART II(1974)
Charles Gounod
NOSFERATU, THE VAMPIRE(1979, Fr./Ger.), m
Augie Goupil
WAIKIKI WEDDING(1937)
Jeanne Goupil
PARADISE POUR TOUS(1982, Fr.)
Robert Goupil
MAN STOLEN(1934, Fr.)
Romain Goupil
EVERY MAN FOR HIMSELF(1980, Fr.), art d
Roger Goupillieres
DR. KNOCK(1936, Fr.), d
Harry A. Gourfain
BUY ME THAT TOWN(1941), w
Rosalind Gourgey
ONE WISH TOO MANY(1956, Brit.)
Victor Gourier
IN THE WAKE OF THE BOUNTY(1933, Aus.)
Victor Gouriet
TWO MINUTES' SILENCE(1934, Brit.); HERITAGE(1935, Aus.)
Jennine Marie Gourine
LITTLE SEX, A(1982)
Eileen Gourlay
WHAT A WHOPPER(1961, Brit.)
Meryl Gourley
ULYSSES(1967, U.S./Brit.)
Marcel Gourmet
IROQUOIS TRAIL, THE(1950)
The Gourmet's Delight
GAS-S-S-S!(1970)
Louise Gournay
JOHNNY FRENCHMAN(1946, Brit.)
Anne Goursand
ONE FROM THE HEART(1982), ed
Anne Goursaud
NIGHT THE LIGHTS WENT OUT IN GEORGIA, THE(1981), ed; OUTSIDERS, THE(1983), ed
Jeff Gourson
9/30/55(1977), ed; SOMEWHERE IN TIME(1980), ed; INCREDIBLE SHRINKING WOMAN, THE(1981), ed; TRON(1982), ed
1984
MIKE'S MURDER(1984), ed
Rolla Gourvitch
LIFE OF EMILE ZOLA, THE(1937); DEVIL'S ISLAND(1940)
Anne Gousaud
1984
AMERICAN DREAMER(1984), ed
Christine Gouse-Renal
VERY PRIVATE AFFAIR, A(1962, Fr./Ital.), p
Albert Gout
ADAM AND EVE(1958, Mex.), p&d
Alberto Gout
SHAME OF THE SABINE WOMEN, THE(1962, Mex.), p,d&w
Louis Gouthier
POIL DE CAROTTE(1932, Fr.)
Christopher Goutman
PROWLER, THE(1981)
Marvin Goux
TARAS BULBA(1962)
Christine Gouze-Renal
LIGHT ACROSSS THE STREET, THE(1957, Fr.); THIS SPECIAL FRIENDSHIP(1967, Fr.), p
Igor Gouzenko
IRON CURTAIN, THE(1948), w; OPERATION MANHUNT(1954)
Gidi Gov
WORLDS APART(1980, U.S., Israel)
Barbara Lee Govan
NO PLACE TO HIDE(1975)
Yvan Govar
CROSS OF THE LIVING(1963, Fr.), d

Marguerite Gove
Silents
LEND ME YOUR HUSBAND(1924), w
Jose Govea
SERENADE(1956)
Michael Gover
MAGNIFICENT TWO, THE(1967, Brit.); STRANGE AFFAIR, THE(1968, Brit.); FRANKENSTEIN MUST BE DESTROYED!(1969, Brit.); CLOCKWORK ORANGE, A(1971, Brit.); SUPERMAN(1978)
Mildred Gover
LITTLE MISS MARKER(1934); MRS. WIGGS OF THE CABBAGE PATCH(1934); HARMONY LANE(1935); HIGH SCHOOL GIRL(1935); PUBLIC OPINION(1935); RING AROUND THE MOON(1936); I'LL TAKE ROMANCE(1937); MIDNIGHT MADONNA(1937); PENROD AND SAM(1937); STELLA DALLAS(1937); WINGS OVER HONOLULU(1937); MY OLD KENTUCKY HOME(1938); SISTERS, THE(1938); WHO KILLED GAIL PRESTON?(1938); DAY-TIME WIFE(1939); DARK COMMAND, THE(1940); LADIES MUST LIVE(1940); MARYLAND(1940); SANTA FE TRAIL(1940); YOUTH WILL BE SERVED(1940); GREAT AMERICAN BROADCAST, THE(1941); RISE AND SHINE(1941); SING FOR YOUR SUPPER(1941); COLONEL EFFINGHAM'S RAID(1945)
Victor Gover
DERELICT, THE(1937, Brit.), p
Victor M. Gover
CURSE OF THE WRAYDONS, THE(1946, Brit.), d; KING OF THE UNDERWORLD(1952, Brit.), d
Misc. Talkies
MURDER AT SCOTLAND YARD(1952), d
Francesco Paolo Governale
ARABIAN NIGHTS(1980, Ital./Fr.)
Paul Governall
TRIPLE THREAT(1948)
Ian Govett
GALLIPOLI(1981, Aus.)
Marcella Govoni
RIGOLETTO(1949)
Tamara Govorkova
TAXI TO HEAVEN(1944, USSR)
Gloria Govrin
MIDSUMMER NIGHT'S DREAM, A(1966)
Frances Gow
RETURN TO PARADISE(1953)
James Gow
ONE NIGHT OF LOVE(1934), w; I DREAM TOO MUCH(1935), w; BUNKER BEAN(1936), w; MURDER ON A BRIDLE PATH(1936), w; MOONLIGHT IN HAWAII(1941), w; REPENT AT LEISURE(1941), w; TOMORROW THE WORLD(1944), w
John Gow
TROUBLE IN STORE(1955, Brit.), art d; THAT SINKING FEELING(1979, Brit.), ed; GREGORY'S GIRL(1982, Brit.), ed
Keith Gow
CARS THAT ATE PARIS, THE(1974, Aus,), w
Lee Gow
Misc. Silents
WAR OF THE TONGS, THE(1917)
Michael Gow
STIR(1980, Aus.)
Neil Gow
LILAC DOMINO, THE(1940, Brit.), w
Ronald Gow
SOUTHERN ROSES(1936, Brit.), w; LANCASHIRE LUCK(1937, Brit.), w; MR. SMITH CARRIES ON(1937, Brit.), w; LOVE ON THE DOLE(1945, Brit.), w
Dorothy Gowan
LOCKED DOOR, THE(1929)
Thomas Gowan
Misc. Talkies
FROZEN SCREAM(1980)
John Gowans
YOU LIGHT UP MY LIFE(1977)
John D. Gowans
STAR TREK: THE MOTION PICTURE(1979)
Curt Gowdy
HEAVEN CAN WAIT(1978)
Wilbert Gowdy
NEWMAN'S LAW(1974)
Frances Gowens
INTRUDER, THE(1955, Brit.)
Carlena Gower
TOWERING INFERNO, THE(1974)
Ruth Gower
SECRET VOICE, THE(1936, Brit.); FAMILY WAY, THE(1966, Brit.); OH! WHAT A LOVELY WAR(1969, Brit.)
Patrick Gowers
PERSECUTION AND ASSASSINATION OF JEAN-PAUL MARAT AS PERFORMED BY THE INMATES OF THE ASYLUM OF CHARENTON UNDER THE DIRECTION OF THE MARQUIS DE SADE, THE(1967, Brit.); HAMLET(1969, Brit.), m; VIRGIN AND THE GYPSY, THE(1970, Brit.), m, md; CHILDREN OF RAGE(1975, Brit.-Israeli), m; STEVIE(1978, Brit.), m
1984
BIGGER SPLASH, A(1984), m
Gene Gowing
HEADS UP(1930)
Misc. Silents
FACE VALUE(1927)
Sidney Gowing
Silents
DAUGHTER IN REVOLT, A(1927, Brit.), w
Ann Gowland
MOTHER WORE TIGHTS(1947); SEA OF GRASS, THE(1947)

C. H. Gowland
Silents
MOLLY ENTANGLED(1917)
Gibson Gowland
MYSTERIOUS ISLAND(1929); PHANTOM OF THE OPERA, THE(1929); HELL HARBOR(1930); SEA BAT, THE(1930); DOOMED BATTALION, THE(1932); LAND OF WANTED MEN(1932); WITHOUT HONORS(1932); S.O.S. ICEBERG(1933); PRIVATE LIFE OF DON JUAN, THE(1934, Brit.); SECRET OF THE LOCH, THE(1934, Brit.); STOKER, THE(1935, Brit.); HIGHLAND FLING(1936, Brit.); KING OF THE DAMNED(1936, Brit.); COTTON QUEEN(1937, Brit.); PHANTOM SHIP(1937, Brit.); HATE IN PARADISE(1938, Brit.); WIFE OF GENERAL LING, THE(1938, Brit.); RAFFLES(1939); NORTHWEST PASSAGE(1940); WOLF MAN, THE(1941); CROSSROADS(1942); GUY NAMED JOE, A(1943); HUMAN COMEDY, THE(1943); GOING MY WAY(1944); KITTY(1945); PICTURE OF DORIAN GRAY, THE(1945)
Silents
BLIND HUSBANDS(1919); HUTCH STIRS 'EM UP(1923, Brit.); GREED(1925); PHANTOM OF THE OPERA, THE(1925); PRAIRIE WIFE, THE(1925); COLLEGE DAYS(1926); DON JUAN(1926); OUTSIDER, THE(1926); ISLE OF FORGOTTEN WOMEN(1927); NIGHT OF LOVE, THE(1927)
Misc. Silents
SHIFTING SANDS(1922, Brit.); HARBOUR LIGHTS, THE(1923, Brit.); BORDER LEGION, THE(1924); TOPSY AND EVA(1927)
Gilson Gowland
WILSON(1944)
H. Gibson Gowland
Misc. Silents
RIGHT OF WAY, THE(1920)
Peter Gowland
13 RUE MADELEINE(1946)
T.H. Gibson Gowland
Misc. Silents
CLIMBER, THE(1917)
Gene Gowling
Misc. Talkies
DRIFTING SOULS(1932)
Milton Gowman
YOU WERE MEANT FOR ME(1948); WHERE THE SIDEWALK ENDS(1950)
Luba Goy
IMPROPER CHANNELS(1981, Can.)
Chantal Goya
MASCULINE FEMININE(1966, Fr./Swed.); SECRET WORLD(1969, Fr.)
Lydia Goya
MARACAIBO(1958); VIRGIN SACRIFICE(1959); HELLCATS, THE(1968); PARADISE ALLEY(1978)
Mona Goya
LADY FROM THE SEA, THE(1929, Brit.); FLAME OF LOVE, THE(1930, Brit.); NOT SO QUIET ON THE WESTERN FRONT(1930, Brit.); PRICE OF THINGS, THE(1930, Brit.); CLOTHES AND THE WOMAN(1937, Brit.); JUGGERNAUT(1937, Brit.); THIS MAN IN PARIS(1939, Brit.); WHIRLWIND OF PARIS(1946, Fr.)
Tito Goya
MARATHON MAN(1976); SHORT EYES(1977); GOING IN STYLE(1979); NIGHT OF THE JUGGLER(1980); FORT APACHE, THE BRONX(1981)
Manuel J. Goyanes
EVERY DAY IS A HOLIDAY(1966, Span.), p
Mara Goyanes
THAT HOUSE IN THE OUTSKIRTS(1980, Span.)
Michel Goyot
MY UNCLE(1958, Fr.)
Harry Goz
MARATHON MAN(1976); LOOKING UP(1977); MOMMIE DEAREST(1981)
Jutka Goz
NAKED WORLD OF HARRISON MARKS, THE(1967, Brit.)
Jack Gozdick
PUNISHMENT PARK(1971)
Yuskel Gozen
YOU CAN'T WIN 'EM ALL(1970, Brit.)
Bernie Gozier
GREEN DOLPHIN STREET(1947); ROAD TO BALI(1952); VIVA ZAPATA!(1952); DREAM WIFE(1953); NAKED JUNGLE, THE(1953); CREATURE FROM THE BLACK LAGOON(1954); KISS OF FIRE(1955); FLAME BARRIER, THE(1958)
Paolo Gozlino
SAUL AND DAVID(1968, Ital./Span.); VENGEANCE(1968, Ital./Ger.); WITCHES, THE(1969, Fr./Ital.); MAN OF LA MANCHA(1972)
Fyula Gozon
BLUE IDOL, THE(1931, Hung.)
Gyula Gozon
HIPPOLYT, THE LACKEY(1932, Hung.)
Julius Gozon
KIND STEPMOTHER(1936, Hung.)
Guido Gozzano
CENTO ANNI D'AMORE(1954, Ital.), w
Chantal Gozzi
GERVAISE(1956, Fr.)
Patricia Gozzi
SUNDAYS AND CYBELE(1962, Fr.); RAPTURE(1965)
Inez Graaf
VIBRATION(1969, Swed.)
Vera Graaf
WHITE CLIFFS OF DOVER, THE(1944)
Henri Graat
CONGRESS DANCES(1932, Ger.)
Fernand Graavey
BITTER SWEET(1933, Brit.); EARLY TO BED(1933, Brit./Ger.); RUNAWAY QUEEN, THE(1935, Brit.)
I. Grabbe
NINE DAYS OF ONE YEAR(1964, USSR)
N. Grabbe
GROWN-UP CHILDREN(1963, USSR); RESURRECTION(1963, USSR)

Pat Grabe
1984
SOLDIER'S STORY, A(1984)
Joseph Graber
KAZABLAN(1974, Israel); DIAMONDS(1975, U.S./Israel)
Fred Grabert
ZAPPED!(1982)
Betty Grable
HAPPY DAYS(1930); LET'S GO PLACES(1930); WHOOPEE(1930); KIKI(1931); PALMY DAYS(1931); GREEKS HAD A WORD FOR THEM(1932); HOLD 'EM JAIL(1932); KID FROM SPAIN, THE(1932); PROBATION(1932); CHILD OF MANHATTAN(1933); MELODY CRUISE(1933); SWEETHEART OF SIGMA CHI(1933); WHAT PRICE INNOCENCE?(1933); GAY DIVORCEE, THE(1934); STUDENT TOUR(1934); BY YOUR LEAVE(1935); NITWITS, THE(1935); OLD MAN RHYTHM(1935); COLLEGIATE(1936); DON'T TURN 'EM LOOSE(1936); FOLLOW THE FLEET(1936); PIGSKIN PARADE(1936); THIS WAY PLEASE(1937); THRILL OF A LIFETIME(1937); CAMPUS CONFESSIONS(1938); COLLEGE SWING(1938); GIVE ME A SAILOR(1938); DAY THE BOOKIES WEPT, THE(1939); MAN ABOUT TOWN(1939); MILLION DOLLAR LEGS(1939); DOWN ARGENTINE WAY(1940); TIN PAN ALLEY(1940); MOON OVER MIAMI(1941); YANK IN THE R.A.F., A(1941); FOOTLIGHT SERENADE(1942); I WAKE UP SCREAMING(1942); SONG OF THE ISLANDS(1942); SPRINGTIME IN THE ROCKIES(1942); CONEY ISLAND(1943); SWEET ROSIE O'GRADY(1943); FOUR JILLS IN A JEEP(1944); PIN UP GIRL(1944); DIAMOND HORSESHOE(1945); DOLLY SISTERS, THE(1945); DO YOU LOVE ME?(1946); MOTHER WORE TIGHTS(1947); SHOCKING MISS PILGRIM, THE(1947); THAT LADY IN ERMINE(1948); WHEN MY BABY SMILES AT ME(1948); BEAUTIFUL BLONDE FROM BASHFUL BEND, THE(1949); MY BLUE HEAVEN(1950); WABASH AVENUE(1950); CALL ME MISTER(1951); MEET ME AFTER THE SHOW(1951); FARMER TAKES A WIFE, THE(1953); HOW TO MARRY A MILLIONAIRE(1953); HOW TO BE VERY, VERY, POPULAR(1955); THREE FOR THE SHOW(1955)
Fred Grable
SHINBONE ALLEY(1971), anim
Mike Grabow
Misc. Talkies
KING FRAT(1979)
Grabowski
GIRLS' TOWN(1959)
Norm Grabowski
HOOPER(1978)
Norman Grabowski
COLLEGE CONFIDENTIAL(1960); HONEYMOON MACHINE, THE(1961); SON OF FLUBBER(1963); MISADVENTURES OF MERLIN JONES, THE(1964); ROUSTABOUT(1964); MONKEY'S UNCLE, THE(1965); SERGEANT DEADHEAD(1965); OUT OF SIGHT(1966); GNOME-MOBILE, THE(1967); HAPPIEST MILLIONAIRE, THE(1967); BLACKBEARD'S GHOST(1968); HORSE IN THE GRAY FLANNEL SUIT, THE(1968); NAKED APE, THE(1973); TOWERING INFERNO, THE(1974); CANNONBALL RUN, THE(1981)
Woo Woo Grabowski
SEX KITTENS GO TO COLLEGE(1960)
Adelaide Grace
Silents
ALL THE SAD WORLD NEEDS(1918, Brit.); ONCE UPON A TIME(1918, Brit.); GENERAL POST(1920, Brit.)
Misc. Silents
DUCHESS OF SEVEN DIALS, THE(1920); LITTLE WELSH GIRL, THE(1920, Brit.)
Carol Grace
GANGSTER STORY(1959); MIKEY AND NICKY(1976)
Dick Grace
LOST SQUADRON, THE(1932), w
Silents
WINGS(1927), a, stunts; LILAC TIME(1928)
Misc. Silents
FLYING FOOL(1925); WIDE OPEN(1927)
Edward Grace
DIRTYMOUTH(1970)
Misc. Silents
HOME-KEEPING HEARTS(1921)
Henry Grace
TWO WEEKS IN ANOTHER TOWN(1962), set d; TROUBLE WITH GIRLS(AND HOW TO GET INTO IT), THE*1/2 (1969), set d; DU BARRY WAS A LADY(1943), set d; ADAM'S RIB(1949), set d; MALAYA(1950), set d; DIANE(1955), set d; PRODIGAL, THE(1955), set d; SWAN, THE(1956), set d; CAT ON A HOT TIN ROOF(1958), set d; GIGI(1958), set d; HIGH COST OF LOVING, THE(1958), set d; HIGH SCHOOL CONFIDENTIAL(1958), set d; LAW AND JAKE WADE, THE(1958), set d; PARTY GIRL(1958), set d; SADDLE THE WIND(1958), set d; SHEEPMAN, THE(1958), set d; TUNNEL OF LOVE, THE(1958), set d; COUNT YOUR BLESSINGS(1959), set d; GREEN MANSIONS(1959), set d; NEVER SO FEW(1959), set d; NORTH BY NORTHWEST(1959), set d; SOME CAME RUNNING(1959), set d; WRECK OF THE MARY DEAR, THE(1959), set d; PLEASE DON'T EAT THE DAISIES(1960), set d; SUBTERRANEANS, THE(1960), set d; TIME MACHINE, THE(1960; Brit./U.S.), set d; GO NAKED IN THE WORLD(1961), set d; HONEYMOON MACHINE, THE(1961), set d; THUNDER OF DRUMS, A(1961), set d; TWO LOVES(1961), set d; ALL FALL DOWN(1962), set d; FOUR HORSEMEN OF THE APOCALYPSE, THE(1962), set d; HOOK, THE(1962), set d; HORIZONTAL LIEUTENANT, THE(1962), set d; HOW THE WEST WAS WON(1962), set d; JUMBO(1962), set d; LONGEST DAY, THE(1962); MUTINY ON THE BOUNTY(1962), set d; PERIOD OF ADJUSTMENT(1962), set d; RIDE THE HIGH COUNTRY(1962), set d; SWEET BIRD OF YOUTH(1962), set d; WONDERFUL WORLD OF THE BROTHERS GRIMM, THE(1962), set d; COURTSHIP OF EDDY'S FATHER, THE(1963), set d; DRUMS OF AFRICA(1963), set d; HOOTENANNY HOOT(1963), set d; IT HAPPENED AT THE WORLD'S FAIR(1963), set d; PRIZE, THE(1963), set d; SUNDAY IN NEW YORK(1963), set d; TICKLISH AFFAIR, A(1963), set d; TWILIGHT OF HONOR(1963), set d; WHEELER DEALERS, THE(1963), set d; ADVANCE TO THE REAR(1964), set d; GET YOURSELF A COLLEGE GIRL(1964), set d; GLOBAL AFFAIR, A(1964), set d; GUNS OF DIABLO(1964), set d; HONEYMOON HOTEL(1964), set d; KISSIN' COUSINS(1964), set d; LOOKING FOR LOVE(1964), set d; MAIL ORDER BRIDE(1964), set d; OUTRAGE, THE(1964), set d; QUICK, BEFORE IT MELTS(1964), set d; SEVEN FACES OF DR. LAO(1964), set d; SIGNPOST TO MURDER(1964), set d; UNSINKABLE MOLLY BROWN(1964), set d; VIVA LAS VEGAS(1964), set d; YOUR CHEATIN' HEART(1964), set d; CINCINNATI KID, THE(1965), set d; CLARENCE, THE CROSS-EYED LION(1965), set d;

GIRL HAPPY(1965), set d; HARUM SCARUM(1965), set d; JOY IN THE MORNING(1965), set d; ONCE A THIEF(1965), set d; PATCH OF BLUE, A(1965), set d; ROUNDERS, THE(1965), set d; SANDPIPER, THE(1965), set d; WHEN THE BOYS MEET THE GIRLS(1965), set d; ZEBRA IN THE KITCHEN(1965), set d; 36 HOURS(1965), set d; GLASS BOTTOM BOAT, THE(1966), set d; HOLD ON(1966), set d; MADE IN PARIS(1966), set d; MISTER BUDDWING(1966), set d; MONEY TRAP, THE(1966), set d; ONE OF OUR SPIES IS MISSING(1966), set d; PENELOPE(1966), set d; SEVEN WOMEN(1966), set d; SINGING NUN, THE(1966), set d; SPINOUT(1966), set d; SPY IN THE GREEN HAT, THE(1966), set d; SPY WITH MY FACE, THE(1966), set d; TO TRAP A SPY(1966), set d; DOCTOR, YOU'VE GOT TO BE KIDDING(1967), set d; DON'T MAKE WAVES(1967), set d; DOUBLE TROUBLE(1967), set d; FASTEST GUITAR ALIVE, THE(1967), set d; HOT RODS TO HELL(1967), set d; KARATE KILLERS, THE(1967), set d; LOVE-INS, THE(1967), set d; POINT BLANK(1967), set d; VENETIAN AFFAIR, THE(1967), set d; WELCOME TO HARD TIMES(1967), set d; FOR SINGLES ONLY(1968), set d; ICE STATION ZEBRA(1968), set d; IMPOSSIBLE YEARS, THE(1968), set d; LEGEND OF LYLAH CLARE, THE(1968), set d; LIVE A LITTLE, LOVE A LITTLE(1968), set d; POWER, THE(1968), set d; SOL MADRID(1968), set d; SPEEDWAY(1968), set d; SPLIT, THE(1968), set d; STAY AWAY, JOE(1968), set d; TIME TO SING, A(1968), set d; WHERE WERE YOU WHEN THE LIGHTS WENT OUT?(1968), set d; YOUNG RUNAWAYS, THE(1968), set d; EXTRAORDINARY SEAMAN, THE(1969), set d; GYPSY MOTHS, THE(1969), set d; HEAVEN WITH A GUN(1969), set d; MARLOWE(1969), set d; PHANTOM TOLLBOOTH, THE(1970), set d
Henry W. Grace
SECRET HEART, THE(1946), set d; THIS TIME FOR KEEPS(1947), set d; HOMECOMING(1948), set d; THREE MUSKETEERS, THE(1948), set d; ACT OF VIOLENCE(1949), set d; GREAT SINNER, THE(1949), set d; TAKE ME OUT TO THE BALL GAME(1949), set d; LIFE OF HER OWN, A(1950), set d
Jim Grace
STIGMA(1972)
Martin Grace
RAIDERS OF THE LOST ARK(1981); SEA WOLVES, THE(1981, Brit.); OCTOPUSSY(1983, Brit.), stunts
Martin Ryan Grace
INADMISSIBLE EVIDENCE(1968, Brit.)
Meyer Grace
COME OUT FIGHTING(1945); MR. HEX(1946); NEWS HOUNDS(1947); INCIDENT(1948); HOLD THAT BABY!(1949); JOE PALOOKA MEETS HUMPHREY(1950); NO HOLDS BARRED(1952)
Michael Grace
SATAN'S SLAVE(1976, Brit.)
Michael L. Grace
UNSEEN, THE(1981), w
Michele Grace
REAL LIFE(1979)
Nickolas Grace
HEAT AND DUST(1983, Brit.)
Richard V. Grace
DEVIL'S SQUADRON(1936), w
Roby Grace
Misc. Talkies
GUERILLAS IN PINK LACE(1964)
Sandy Grace
SCARFACE MOB, THE(1962), set d; DEATH OF A GUNFIGHTER(1969), set d
Suzanne Grace
OLD BOYFRIENDS(1979), cos
Valentine Grace
Silents
AYLWIN(1920, Brit.)
Wayne Grace
MC CABE AND MRS. MILLER(1971); LAUGHING POLICEMAN, THE(1973)
1984
FRIDAY THE 13TH–THE FINAL CHAPTER(1984)
William Grace
TOMB OF TORTURE(1966, Ital.), ph
Grace and Nicco
MOONLIGHT IN HAVANA(1942)
Bryan Gracey
INSIDE LOOKING OUT(1977, Aus.), ph
Yale Gracey
FANTASIA(1940), art d
V. Grachyov
SOUND OF LIFE, THE(1962, USSR)
Maria Gracia
LITTLE ANGEL(1961, Mex.); LITTLE RED RIDING HOOD(1963, Mex.); LITTLE RED RIDING HOOD AND HER FRIENDS(1964, Mex.); LITTLE RED RIDING HOOD AND THE MONSTERS(1965, Mex.)
Sancho Gracia
HOUSE OF 1,000 DOLLS(1967, Ger./Span./Brit.); SAVAGE PAMPAS(1967, Span./Arg.); RUN LIKE A THIEF(1968, Span.); LAST DAY OF THE WAR, THE(1969, U.S./Ital./Span.); ANTONY AND CLEOPATRA(1973, Brit.)
Misc. Talkies
ISLAND TRADER(1982)
Charlie Gracie
JAMBOREE(1957)
Sally Gracie
PATTERNS(1956); STAGE STRUCK(1958); FUGITIVE KIND, THE(1960); RAIN PEOPLE, THE(1969)
Paulo Gracindo
TARZAN AND THE GREAT RIVER(1967, U.S./Switz.); EARTH ENTRANCED(1970, Braz.)
Ed Graczyck
COME BACK TO THE 5 & DIME, JIMMY DEAN, JIMMY DEAN(1982), w
Genevieve Grad
CENTURION, THE(1962, Fr./Ital.); EMPIRE OF NIGHT, THE(1963, Fr.); HERO OF BABYLON(1963, Ital.); SANDOKAN THE GREAT(1964, Fr./Ital./Span.); GENDARME OF ST. TROPEZ, THE(1966, Fr./Ital.)

Peter Grad
OUT OF IT(1969)
Lew Grade
AUTUMN SONATA(1978, Swed.), p
Sir Lew Grade
CASSANDRA CROSSING, THE(1977), p
Lord Grade
FROM THE LIFE OF THE MARIONETTES(1980, Ger.), p
DonaldDa Gradi
DUMBO(1941), art d
Havelock Gradidge
CROWD INSIDE, THE(1971, Can.), ed
Vivian Gradin
WHERE ANGELS GO...TROUBLE FOLLOWS(1968)
Morris Gradman
HOW WILLINGLY YOU SING(1975, Aus.)
Antonio Gradoli
FACTS OF MURDER, THE(1965, Ital.); ROAD TO FORT ALAMO, THE(1966, Fr./Ital.); MISSION BLOODY MARY(1967, Fr./Ital./Span.); OPERATION KID BROTH-ER(1967, Ital.); ROMEO AND JULIET(1968, Ital./Span.); ADIOS SABATA(1971, Ital./Span.)
K. Gradopolov
Misc. Silents
LACE(1928, USSR)
V. Gradov
Misc. Silents
DEATH OF THE GODS(1917, USSR)
Charles Gradstreet
UNFINISHED DANCE,THE(1947)
The Graduates
CRACKING UP(1977)
Ben Gradus
CROWDED PARADISE(1956), p
Larry Gradus
FANTASTICA(1980, Can./Fr.), ch
Alex Gradussov
DARK OF THE SUN(1968, Brit.); SKULLDUGGERY(1970)
Anthony Gradwell [Antonio Gradoli]
SABATA(1969, Ital.)
Arthur Grady
REVOLT OF MAMIE STOVER, THE(1956)
Billy Grady, Jr.
RED BALL EXPRESS(1952), w
Blanche Grady
LOUISIANA PURCHASE(1941); YOUNG AND WILLING(1943)
Don Grady
MA BARKER'S KILLER BROOD(1960); WILD McCULLOCHS, THE(1975)
Ed Grady
LADY GREY(1980); REUBEN, REUBEN(1983)
Ed L. Grady
WOLFMAN(1979)
Misc. Talkies
LAST GAME, THE(1983)
James Grady
THREE DAYS OF THE CONDOR(1975), w
Kevin Grady
SEMI-TOUGH(1977)
Michael Grady
CARRY ON LOVING(1970, Brit.); SYMPTOMS(1976, Brit.)
Mike Grady
RETURN OF THE PINK PANTHER, THE(1975, Brit.); PIRATES OF PENZANCE, THE(1983)
Robert Grady
MARSHAL OF LAREDO(1945)
William Grady, Jr.
CODE TWO(1953), p; CRY OF THE HUNTED(1953), p; GYPSY COLT(1954), p; SUMMER LOVE(1958), p
Neola Graef
FANDANGO(1970)
Diane Graeff
EGG AND I, THE(1947)
Billy Graeff, Jr.
EVERYBODY DOES IT(1949)
Tom Graeff
TEENAGERS FROM OUTER SPACE(1959), p,d,w,ph,ed,md&spec eff
Vincent Graeff
BUFFALO BILL(1944); TREE GROWS IN BROOKLYN, A(1945); DARK CORNER, THE(1946); LITTLE MISS BIG(1946); YOU'RE MY EVERYTHING(1949); TWO TICK-ETS TO BROADWAY(1951)
William Graeff, Jr.
MONTE WALSH(1970); AARON LOVES ANGELA(1975)
Melissa Renee Graehl
1984
FOOTLOOSE(1984)
Bruce Graeme
HATE SHIP, THE(1930, Brit.), w; BLACK MASK(1935, Brit.), w; MISSING TEN DAYS(1941, Brit.), w; WAY OUT, THE(1956, Brit.), w; MENACE IN THE NIGHT(1958, Brit.), w
Joyce Graeme
HALF A SIXPENCE(1967, Brit.); THEATRE OF BLOOD(1973, Brit.)
Paul Graetz
VIENNA, CITY OF SONGS(1931, Ger.); POWER(1934, Brit.); ALIAS BULLDOG DRUMMOND(1935, Brit.); CAR OF DREAMS(1935, Brit.); MIMI(1935, Brit.); MURDER AT MONTE CARLO(1935, Brit.); 18 MINUTES(1935, Brit.); BENGAL TIGER(1936); HOT MONEY(1936); ISLE OF FURY(1936); LIVING DEAD, THE(1936, Brit.); MR. COHEN TAKES A WALK(1936, Brit.); PUBLIC ENEMY'S WIFE(1936); RED WA-GON(1936); APRIL BLOSSOMS(1937, Brit.); HEART'S DESIRE(1937, Brit.); HEART OF A NATION, THE(1943, Fr.); DEVIL IN THE FLESH(1949, Fr.), p; LOVERS, HAPPY LOVERS!(1955, Brit.), p; DOCTORS, THE(1956, Fr.), p; BITTER VIC-TORY(1958, Fr.), p; FROM A ROMAN BALCONY(1961, Fr./Ital.), p; VIEW FROM THE

BRIDGE, A(1962, Fr./Ital.), p; IS PARIS BURNING?(1966, U.S./Fr.), p
Silents
ONE ARABIAN NIGHT(1921, Ger.)
Misc. Silents
MONNA VANNA(1923, Ger.)
Gunter Graewert
MAN WHO WALKED THROUGH THE WALL, THE(1964, Ger.)
Allan Graf
LONG RIDERS, THE(1980); ROADIE(1980); SOUTHERN COMFORT(1981); I OUGHT TO BE IN PICTURES(1982); POLTERGEIST(1982)
1984
CITY HEAT(1984); IMPULSE(1984)
Allen Graf
DRIVER, THE(1978)
David Graf
FOUR FRIENDS(1981)
1984
IRRECONCILABLE DIFFERENCES(1984)
Fritz Graf
LOVE FEAST, THE(1966, Ger.), set d
Hella Graf
FINAL CHORD, THE(1936, Ger.)
Horst Graf
WHAT DID YOU DO IN THE WAR, DADDY?(1966)
Max Graf
Silents
WHITE HANDS(1922), p; FOG, THE(1923), p; FINNEGAN'S BALL(1927), sup&w
Otto Graf
DEVIL IN SILK(1968, Ger.); YOUNG LORD, THE(1970, Ger.)
Peter Graf
Misc. Talkies
BAR MITSVE(1935)
Robert Graf
ARENT WE WONDERFUL?(1959, Ger.); GREAT ESCAPE, THE(1963)
Suse Graf
PILLARS OF SOCIETY(1936, Ger.)
William N. Graf
SINFUL DAVEY(1969, Brit.), p
Billy Graff, Jr.
NEWSBOY'S HOME(1939)
David Graff
1984
POLICE ACADEMY(1984)
Fred Graff
CRY OF THE WEREWOLF(1944); LOUISIANA HAYRIDE(1944); U-BOAT PRISON-ER(1944); LEAVE IT TO BLONDIE(1945); ROUGH, TOUGH AND READY(1945); TONIGHT AND EVERY NIGHT(1945); BOSTON BLACKIE AND THE LAW(1946); FRAMED(1947); MAN FROM COLORADO, THE(1948); WALLS OF JERICHO(1948); UNION STATION(1950); PRINCE WHO WAS A THIEF, THE(1951)
Jo Graff
WILD SCENE, THE(1970)
Milton Graff
JUST BEFORE DAWN(1946)
Robert O. Graff
YOUNG CASSIDY(1965, U.S./Brit.), p
Wilton Graff
CORPSE CAME C.O.D., THE(; THEY WON'T BELIEVE ME(1947); EARL CARROLL'S VANITIES(1945); GANGS OF THE WATERFRONT(1945); PILLOW OF DEATH(1945); ROYAL SCANDAL, A(1945); STRANGE CONFESSION(1945); AVALANCHE(1946); PHANTOM THIEF, THE(1946); SHADOWED(1946); TRAFFIC IN CRIME(1946); UN-KNOWN, THE(1946); VALLEY OF THE ZOMBIES(1946); DEAD RECKONING(1947); DOUBLE LIFE, A(1947); GENTLEMAN'S AGREEMENT(1947); HIGH CON-QUEST(1947); KEY WITNESS(1947); WEB, THE(1947); ANOTHER PART OF THE FOREST(1948); DARK PAST, THE(1948); FAMILY HONEYMOON(1948); GALLANT BLADE, THE(1948); GENTLEMAN FROM NOWHERE, THE(1948); MOZART STORY, THE(1948, Aust.); RETURN OF THE WHISTLER, THE(1948); AND BABY MAKES THREE(1949); BLONDIE'S BIG DEAL(1949); CAUGHT(1949); ONCE MORE, MY DARLING(1949); TAKE ME OUT TO THE BALL GAME(1949); CONVICTED(1950); FORTUNES OF CAPTAIN BLOOD(1950); GIRLS' SCHOOL(1950); MOTHER DIDN'T TELL ME(1950); ROGUES OF SHERWOOD FOREST(1950); WEST POINT STORY, THE(1950); MASK OF THE AVENGER(1951); MR. IMPERIUM(1951); MY TRUE STORY(1951); FEARLESS FAGAN(1952); I DON'T CARE GIRL, THE(1952); MILLION DOLLAR MERMAID(1952); OPERATION SECRET(1952); SOMETHING FOR THE BIRDS(1952); SPRINGFIELD RIFLE(1952); YOUNG MAN WITH IDEAS(1952); LI-LI(1953); MISS SADIE THOMPSON(1953); SCANDAL AT SCOURIE(1953); KING RICHARD AND THE CRUSADERS(1954); STAR IS BORN, A(1954); SEA CHASE, THE(1955); BENNY GOODMAN STORY, THE(1956); LUST FOR LIFE(1956); BLOOD-LUST(1959); COMPULSION(1959); RETURN TO PEYTON PLACE(1961); SAIL A CROOKED SHIP(1961); LONNIE(1963)
Charles Graffeo
CHEECH AND CHONG'S NICE DREAMS(1981), set d
Charles M. Graffeo
STAR TREK II: THE WRATH OF KHAN(1982), set d
Phyllis Graffeo
EASY TO WED(1946); PEOPLE AGAINST O'HARA, THE(1951); STORY OF THREE LOVES, THE(1953); PRODIGAL, THE(1955); MAN IN THE GREY FLANNEL SUIT, THE(1956)
William H. Graffis
DICK TRACY MEETS GRUESOME(1947), w
Charles M. Graffo
1984
CANNONBALL RUN II(1984), set d
Frank Grafield [Franco Giraldi]
UP THE MACGREGORS(1967, Ital./Span.), d
Ion Grafini
POPE JOAN(1972, Brit.)
Fred Graft
SHADOWED(1946)

Edith Grafton
SYSTEM, THE(1953), w; HANDLE WITH CARE(1958), w
Gloria Grafton
CRY HAVOC(1943); LOST ANGEL(1944); UP GOES MAISIE(1946); JOAN OF ARC(1948)
James Grafton
SUNSTRUCK(1973, Aus.), p, w
Jimmy Grafton
DOWN AMONG THE Z MEN(1952, Brit.), w
Samuel Grafton
SYSTEM, THE(1953), w; HANDLE WITH CARE(1958), w
Sue Grafton
LOLLY-MADONNA XXX(1973), w
Terry Grafton
JANIE(1944)
Arturo Gragaglia
HEART AND SOUL(1950, Ital.)
Pierugo Gragnani
VAMPIRE AND THE BALLERINA, THE(1962, Ital.); LOVE AND LARCENY(1963, Fr./Ital.)
Ugo Gragnani
VAMPIRE AND THE BALLERINA, THE(1962, Ital.)
Francois Gragnon
FIRE WITHIN, THE(1964, Fr./Ital.)
Alec Graham
MEET MR. LUCIFER(1953, Brit.), w
Alex Graham
VENGEANCE IS MINE(1948, Brit.)
Angelo Graham
LITTLE BIG MAN(1970), art d; GETAWAY, THE(1972), art d; JUNIOR BONNER(1972), set d; WHEN THE LEGENDS DIE(1972), art d; DAY OF THE DOLPHIN, THE(1973), art d; GODFATHER, THE, PART II(1974), art d; FAREWELL, MY LOVELY(1975), art d; F.I.S.T.(1978), art d; OUR WINNING SEASON(1978), art d; APOCALYPSE NOW(1979), art d; ESCAPE ARTIST, THE(1982), art d; HAMMETT(1982), art d; ONE FROM THE HEART(1982), art d
1984
BEVERLY HILLS COP(1984), prod d; NATURAL, THE(1984), prod d
Angelo P. Graham
WARGAMES(1983), prod d
Anita Graham
LADY FROM THE SEA, THE(1929, Brit.); CONFESSIONS OF A WINDOW CLEANER(1974, Brit.); WHO IS KILLING THE GREAT CHEFS OF EUROPE?(1978, US/Ger.)
Ann Graham
GOLDWYN FOLLIES, THE(1938)
Anne Graham
THAT SINKING FEELING(1979, Brit.)
Arthur Graham
MAN ON THE RUN(1949, Brit.), ph; SECOND FIDDLE(1957, Brit.), ph; BLIND SPOT(1958, Brit.), ph; MENACE IN THE NIGHT(1958, Brit.), ph; DON'T PANIC CHAPS!(1959, Brit.), ph; LIFE IS A CIRCUS(1962, Brit.), ph
Barbara Graham
I WANT TO LIVE!(1958), w; COMMITMENT, THE(1976)
Barry Graham
HIGH COUNTRY, THE(1981, Can.)
Ben Graham
Silents
SENATOR, THE(1915)
Misc. Silents
BETTER WOMAN, THE(1915)
Betty Graham
PENROD AND SAM(1931); EL DORADO(1967)
Betty Jane Graham
NIGHT NURSE(1931); UP FOR MURDER(1931); HEARTS OF HUMANITY(1932); NO GREATER LOVE(1932); YOUNG AMERICA(1932); HUMANITY(1933); MUSIC IN THE AIR(1934); WICKED WOMAN, A(1934); ON PROBATION(1935); WINNING TICKET, THE(1935); GARDEN OF ALLAH, THE(1936); LOVE ON THE RUN(1936); FIVE LITTLE PEPPERS IN TROUBLE(1940); COVER GIRL(1944); LOUISIANA HAYRIDE(1944)
Misc. Talkies
ROUGH RIDIN' JUSTICE(1945)
Betty Jean Graham
BAND PLAYS ON, THE(1934)
Bill Graham
MUSCLE BEACH PARTY(1964); APOCALYPSE NOW(1979)
1984
COTTON CLUB, THE(1984)
Billy Graham
SOULS IN CONFLICT(1955, Brit.), a, p; RESTLESS ONES, THE(1965); FOR PETE'S SAKE!(1966); TWO A PENNY(1968, Brit.)
1984
PRODIGAL, THE(1984)
Misc. Talkies
TIME TO RUN(1974)
Blanche Graham
Silents
LIVINGSTONE(1925, Brit.)
Bob Graham
PEOPLE ARE FUNNY(1945); WEEKEND AT THE WALDORF(1945); I DON'T CARE GIRL, THE(1952); DUSTY AND SWEETS McGEE(1971); END OF AUGUST, THE(1982), d
Bobby Graham
GOLD FEVER(1952)
Cano Graham
ON THE NICKEL(1980)
Carroll Graham
SKY DEVILS(1932), w; BORDERTOWN(1935), w; GIRL LOVES BOY(1937), w; SWEETHEART OF THE NAVY(1937), w

Charles Graham
Silents
ONE MILLION DOLLARS(1915); AUCTION BLOCK, THE(1917); TIDES OF FATE(1917); UNTAMED LADY, THE(1926)
Misc. Silents
MODERN MAGDALEN, A(1915); HUMAN ORCHID, THE(1916); DAWN OF REVENGE(1922); LOVE NEST, THE(1922)
Charles C. Graham
Misc. Silents
AMERICAN GENTLEMAN, AN(1915)
Charles E. Graham
Silents
$5,000,000 COUNTERFEITING PLOT, THE(1914); CARDIGAN(1922)
Misc. Silents
MY OWN UNITED STATES(1918); SONG OF THE SOUL, THE(1920)
Clive Graham
HAMLET(1969, Brit.)
Connie Graham
PAL JOEY(1957)
David Graham
CROSSROADS TO CRIME(1960, Brit.); IN TROUBLE WITH EVE(1964, Brit.); SKIN GAME, THE(1965, Brit.); THUNDERBIRD 6(1968, Brit.); THUNDERBIRDS ARE GO(1968, Brit.)
1984
SUPERGIRL(1984); SWANN IN LOVE(1984, Fr.Ger.), m
David C. Graham
UNDERTAKER AND HIS PALS, THE(1966), p&d
Davy Graham
SERVANT, THE(1964, Brit.)
Denys Graham
MEN ARE CHILDREN TWICE(1953, Brit.); DUNKIRK(1958, Brit.); ZULU(1964, Brit.); MODESTY BLAISE(1966, Brit.)
Des Graham
HALF A SIXPENCE(1967, Brit.)
Dolores Graham
RAZOR'S EDGE, THE(1946)
Don Graham
RAZOR'S EDGE, THE(1946)
Dorthy Graham
Misc. Silents
EIGHT BELLS(1916)
Duke Graham
GIRL IN GOLD BOOTS(1968)
Ed Graham
DARK VICTORY(1939); MEET JOHN DOE(1941); MALE ANIMAL, THE(1942)
Eddie Graham
COWBOY FROM BROOKLYN(1938); ESPIONAGE AGENT(1939); WOMEN IN THE WIND(1939); MILLION DOLLAR BABY(1941); OUT OF THE FOG(1941)
Ernest A. Graham
Misc. Silents
CONVICT 99(1919, Brit.)
Erwin Graham
MAKE MINE MUSIC(1946), w
Frank A. Graham
CHALLENGE THE WILD(1954), p,d,w&ph
Frank Graham
SLEEPY LAGOON(1943); LADY AND THE MONSTER, THE(1944); THREE CABALLEROS, THE(1944)
Fred Graham
DEATH OF THE DIAMOND(1934); LIBELED LADY(1936); ROSE MARIE(1936); TROUBLE FOR TWO(1936); MAYTIME(1937); DODGE CITY(1939); EACH DAWN I DIE(1939); ROARING TWENTIES, THE(1939); NEW MOON(1940); SANTA FE MARSHAL(1940); AFFECTIONATELY YOURS(1941); KISSES FOR BREAKFAST(1941); MANPOWER(1941); SHADOW OF THE THIN MAN(1941); LADY BODYGUARD(1942); MY FAVORITE SPY(1942); PANAMA HATTIE(1942); REAP THE WILD WIND(1942); LONE STAR TRAIL, THE(1943); BUFFALO BILL(1944); MARSHAL OF RENO(1944); MOJAVE FIREBRAND(1944); OUTLAWS OF SANTA FE(1944); SILVER CITY KID(1944); STAGECOACH TO MONTEREY(1944); TUCSON RAIDERS(1944); BANDITS OF THE BADLANDS(1945); CHEROKEE FLASH, THE(1945); COLORADO PIONEERS(1945); DAKOTA(1945); PHANTOM OF THE PLAINS(1945); SANTA FE SADDLEMATES(1945); TOPEKA TERROR, THE(1945); WOMAN IN THE WINDOW, THE(1945); DO YOU LOVE ME?(1946); INNER CIRCLE, THE(1946); MY PAL TRIGGER(1946); OUT CALIFORNIA WAY(1946); PASSKEY TO DANGER(1946); BUFFALO BILL RIDES AGAIN(1947); ON THE OLD SPANISH TRAIL(1947); SEA OF GRASS, THE(1947); TRESPASSER, THE(1947); BOLD FRONTIERSMAN, THE(1948); FORT APACHE(1948); SON OF GOD'S COUNTRY(1948); STREET WITH NO NAME(1948); TIMBER TRAIL, THE(1948); FIGHTING KENTUCKIAN, THE(1949); PORT OF NEW YORK(1949); SAMSON AND DELILAH(1949); SHE WORE A YELLOW RIBBON(1949); THEY LIVE BY NIGHT(1949); TULSA(1949); WAKE OF THE RED WITCH(1949); CONVICTED(1950); DALLAS(1950); FULLER BRUSH GIRL, THE(1950); NO WAY OUT(1950); WHERE THE SIDEWALK ENDS(1950); WOMAN ON PIER 13, THE(1950); ANGELS IN THE OUTFIELD(1951); CLOSE TO MY HEART(1951); HEART OF THE ROCKIES(1951); LORNA DOONE(1951); OVERLAND TELEGRAPH(1951); STRIP, THE(1951); COLORADO SUNDOWN(1952); DREAMBOAT(1952); OLD OKLAHOMA PLAINS(1952); PRIDE OF ST. LOUIS, THE(1952); RANCHO NOTORIOUS(1952); SAN FRANCISCO STORY, THE(1952); SCARLET ANGEL(1952); CODE TWO(1953); ESCAPE FROM FORT BRAVO(1953); FARMER TAKES A WIFE, THE(1953); GOLDEN BLADE, THE(1953); PERILOUS JOURNEY, A(1953); WAR OF THE WORLDS, THE(1953), a, stunts; DEMETRIUS AND THE GLADIATORS(1954); REAR WINDOW(1954); WITNESS TO MURDER(1954); 20,000 LEAGUES UNDER THE SEA(1954); BACKLASH(1956); LAST HUNT, THE(1956); SEVEN MEN FROM NOW(1956); STEEL JUNGLE, THE(1956); WINGS OF EAGLES, THE(1957); VERTIGO(1958); GIANT GILA MONSTER, THE(1959); HORSE SOLDIERS, THE(1959); RIO BRAVO(1959); WOMAN OBSESSED(1959); NORTH TO ALASKA(1960); SEVEN WAYS FROM SUNDOWN(1960); ARIZONA RAIDERS(1965); POCKET MONEY(1972)
Freddie Graham
THEY WON'T BELIEVE ME(1947); WITHIN THESE WALLS(1945)

Frederick Graham
NIX ON DAMES(1929); PLEASURE CRAZED(1929); WALL STREET(1929)
Silents
SIN SISTER, THE(1929)
Garrett Graham
SKY DEVILS(1932), w; MAID HAPPY(1933, Brit.), w; GAMBLING(1934), w; SWEETHEART OF THE NAVY(1937), w
Silents
TEA FOR THREE(1927), t; TEXAS STEER, A(1927), t; ADORATION(1928), t; ES-CAPE, THE(1928), t; NOOSE, THE(1928), t; PIONEER SCOUT, THE(1928), t; RED WINE(1928), t; SUNSET LEGION, THE(1928), t
Gary Graham
HOLLYWOOD KNIGHTS, THE(1980)
Gary Rand Graham
HARDCORE(1979)
Genie Graham
BLACK 13(1954, Brit.)
Genine Graham
IDOL OF PARIS(1948, Brit.); HANGMAN'S WHARF(1950, Brit.); MYSTERY AT THE BURLESQUE(1950, Brit.); DANGEROUS CARGO(1954, Brit.); HELL BELOW ZE-RO(1954, Brit.); COUNT OF TWELVE(1955, Brit.); TIME TO REMEMBER(1962, Brit.)
George Graham
CHALLENGE THE WILD(1954); JOURNEY TO FREEDOM(1957); IT HAPPENED IN ATHENS(1962)
Gerrit Graham
HI, MOM!(1970); PHANTOM OF THE PARADISE(1974); BOBBIE JO AND THE OUTLAW(1976); CANNONBALL(1976, U.S./Hong Kong); SPECIAL DELIVERY(1976); TUNNELVISION(1976); DEMON SEED(1977); PRETTY BABY(1978); HOME MO-VIES(1979); USED CARS(1980); CREATURE WASN'T NICE,THE(1981); NATIONAL LAMPOON'S CLASS REUNION(1982); SOUP FOR ONE(1982)
Gerritt Graham
OLD BOYFRIENDS(1979)
Harry Graham
SOUTHERN MAID, A(1933, Brit.), w, cos; DIPLOMATIC LOVER, THE(1934, Brit.), w; GIRL FROM MAXIM'S, THE(1936, Brit.), w
Heather Graham
1984
MRS. SOFFEL(1984)
Henry Graham [Graham Greene]
DAY FOR NIGHT(1973, Fr.)
Herb Graham
FIRST NUDIE MUSICAL, THE(1976); HUMAN TORNADO, THE(1976); RICH AND FAMOUS(1981)
Herschel Graham
TILL THE CLOUDS ROLL BY(1946); JOAN OF ARC(1948); WE WERE STRAN-GERS(1949)
Hershel Graham
VICKI(1953)
Imogen Graham
REPULSION(1965, Brit.)
Irene Graham
VELVET TRAP, THE(1966)
James Graham
PREHISTORIC WOMEN(1950), ed; WRATH OF GOD, THE(1972), w
James P. Graham
HORROR HIGH(1974), p
Jane Graham
HEART OF THE RIO GRANDE(1942)
Janice Lee Graham
1984
UNTIL SEPTEMBER(1984), w
Jeanne Graham
CONFESSIONS OF AMANS, THE(1977)
Jo Graham
COUNTRY GENTLEMEN(1937), w; YOU CAN'T ESCAPE FOREVER(1942), d; GOOD FELLOWS, THE(1943), d
Joan Graham
LOVER COME BACK(1946)
Joe Graham
ALWAYS IN MY HEART(1942), d
John Graham
LOST WORLD, THE(1960); STUDS LONIGAN(1960); BARBER OF STAMFORD HILL, THE(1963, Brit.); PRIVATE POTTER(1963, Brit.); CHALLENGE FOR ROBIN HOOD, A(1968, Brit.); FIVE MILLION YEARS TO EARTH(1968, Brit.); HILDUR AND THE MAGICIAN(1969), a, w
John Michael Graham
HALLOWEEN(1978)
Julia Graham
LOVE IN BLOOM(1935)
Juliette Graham
SERPENTS OF THE PIRATE MOON, THE(1973)
K. Graham
STRANGE BREW(1983), makeup
Kenneth Graham
WHERE THE BULLETS FLY(1966, Brit.), m
Kenny Graham
SMALL WORLD OF SAMMY LEE, THE(1963, Brit.), m; NIGHT TRAIN TO PA-RIS(1964, Brit.), m
Kim Graham
RETURN TO MACON COUNTY(1975)
Laura Graham
MIDSUMMERS NIGHT'S DREAM, A(1961, Czech)
Laurie Graham
GUNFIGHT AT COMANCHE CREEK(1964)
Lee Graham
LET'S GO NAVY(1951); MAN IN THE GREY FLANNEL SUIT, THE(1956)
Lehmer "Lee" Graham
TITANIC(1953)

Lewis Graham
CRIME OF DR. CRESPI, THE(1936), w
Lyla Graham
RETURN OF JACK SLADE, THE(1955); KISS ME GOODBYE(1982); LAST AMERI-CAN VIRGIN, THE(1982); VICE SQUAD(1982)
Malcolm Graham
AULD LANG SYNE(1937, Brit.); LAST ROSE OF SUMMER, THE(1937, Brit.); SANDFLOW(1937); TOAST OF NEW YORK, THE(1937)
Margaret Graham
PREMONITION, THE(1976)
Margot Graham
CRIMSON PIRATE, THE(1952)
Marion Graham
NO, NO NANETTE(1940); COVER GIRL(1944)
Marvin Graham
HEART LIKE A WHEEL(1983)
Mary Graham
Silents
WOMAN'S MAN(1920)
Mary Jane Graham
SCANDAL FOR SALE(1932)
Michael Graham
CURSE OF THE FLY(1965, Brit.); PRIVILEGE(1967, Brit.); FIVE THE HARD WAY(1969)
Morland Graham
PRIVATE LIFE OF DON JUAN, THE(1934, Brit.); WHAT HAPPENED TO HARK-NESS(1934, Brit.); GET OFF MY FOOT(1935, Brit.); SCARLET PIMPERNEL, THE(1935, Brit.); FAIR EXCHANGE(1936, Brit.); I STAND CONDEMNED(1936, Brit.); TWELVE GOOD MEN(1936, Brit.); WHERE'S SALLY?(1936, Brit.); FULL SPEED AHEAD(1939, Brit.); JAMAICA INN(1939, Brit.); NIGHT TRAIN(1940, Brit.); OLD BILL AND SON(1940, Brit.); GHOST TRAIN, THE(1941, Brit.); THIS ENGLAND(1941, Brit.); VOICE IN THE NIGHT, A(1941, Brit.); BIG BLOCKADE, THE(1942, Brit.); SHIPS WITH WINGS(1942, Brit.); TOWER OF TERROR, THE(1942, Brit.); YOUNG MR. PITT, THE(1942, Brit.); SHIPBUILDERS, THE(1943, Brit.); GAY INTRUDERS, THE(1946, Brit.); HENRY V(1946, Brit.); UPTURNED GLASS, THE(1947, Brit.); BONNIE PRINCE CHARLIE(1948, Brit.); BROTHERS, THE(1948, Brit.); ESTHER WATERS(1948, Brit.); SHOWTIME(1948, Brit.); TIGHT LITTLE ISLAND(1949, Brit.)
Norman Graham
LOST, LONELY AND VICIOUS(1958), w; MACUMBA LOVE(1960), w
Paul Graham
PIRATE MOVIE, THE(1982, Aus.)
Peter Graham
BITTER HARVEST(1963, Brit.), d
Ranald Graham
SHANKS(1974), w; SWEENEY(1977, Brit.), w
1984
BREAKOUT(1984, Brit.), w
Randy Chance Graham
PRIVATE SCHOOL(1983)
Richard Graham
GUY NAMED JOE, A(1943); IN OLD OKLAHOMA(1943); GROUP, THE(1966)
1984
BOUNTY, THE(1984)
Rita Graham
NATIONAL LAMPOON'S CLASS REUNION(1982), ch
Robert Graham
LAST PARADE, THE(1931); EASY LIVING(1949); STRATTON STORY, THE(1949)
Robin Lee Graham
DOVE, THE(1974, Brit.), w
Rodney J. Graham
SUNDOWN RIDERS(1948), w
Ron Graham
CURIOUS FEMALE, THE(1969); GALLIPOLI(1981, Aus.)
Ronald Graham
OLD MAN RHYTHM(1935); TO BEAT THE BAND(1935); LADIES OF WASHING-TON(1944)
Ronnie Graham
HELLO LONDON(1958, Brit.); DIRTY LITTLE BILLY(1972)
Ronny Graham
NEW FACES(1954), a, w; WON TON TON, THE DOG WHO SAVED HOL-LYWOOD(1976); WORLD'S GREATEST LOVER, THE(1977); HISTORY OF THE WORLD, PART 1(1981); TO BE OR NOT TO BE(1983), a, w
1984
FINDERS KEEPERS(1984), w
S. Edwin Graham
Misc. Talkies
DEVIL MONSTER(1946, Brit.), d
Sheila Graham
CHALLENGE THE WILD(1954)
Sheilah Graham
THAT'S RIGHT–YOU'RE WRONG(1939); JIGGS AND MAGGIE IN SOCIETY(1948); IMPACT(1949); BELOVED INFIDEL(1959), w; GIRLS' TOWN(1959); COLLEGE CON-FIDENTIAL(1960)
Sonia Graham
CUP FEVER(1965, Brit.)
Stacey Graham
THIS EARTH IS MINE(1959)
Stacy Graham
PLUNDER ROAD(1957); HARVEY MIDDLEMAN, FIREMAN(1965)
Stephen Graham
GAS-S-S-S!(1970), a, set d
Steven Graham
SUMMER RUN(1974), p
Stretch Graham
Misc. Talkies
AMERICAN GAME, THE(1979)
Superstar Billy Graham
WRESTLER, THE(1974)

T. Max Graham
STING II, THE(1983)
Therese Graham
1984
COUNTRY(1984)
Tim Graham
HE WALKED BY NIGHT(1948); WHEN MY BABY SMILES AT ME(1948); FRANCIS(1949); SHAMROCK HILL(1949); PEGGY(1950); CAVE OF OUTLAWS(1951); HIGH NOON(1952); ABBOTT AND COSTELLO GO TO MARS(1953); NO ESCAPE(1953); TROUBLE ALONG THE WAY(1953); SEVEN BRIDES FOR SEVEN BROTHERS(1954); BRAIN FROM THE PLANET AROUS, THE(1958); BULLWHIP(1958); LAD: A DOG(1962); GUNFIGHT AT COMANCHE CREEK(1964)
Tommy Graham
DON'T TURN'EM LOOSE(1936); TOO MANY GIRLS(1940)
Violet Graham
LILY OF LAGUNA(1938, Brit.)
Silents
AULD LANG SYNE(1917, Brit.); BID FOR FORTUNE, A(1917, Brit.); MAN'S SHADOW, A(1920, Brit.)
Misc. Silents
WIRELESS(1915, Brit.); CHARLATAN, THE(1916, Brit.); DERELICTS(1917, Brit.)
Virginia Graham
1984
SLAPSTICK OF ANOTHER KIND(1984)
W. Stephen Graham
1984
MUPPETS TAKE MANHATTAN, THE(1984), art d
Wade Graham
ICE STATION ZEBRA(1968)
Wally Graham
JINXED!(1982), set d
Walter Graham
Misc. Talkies
DIVORCE MADE EASY(1929), d
William Graham
JUST WILLIAM'S LUCK(1948, Brit.); WILLIAM COMES TO TOWN(1948, Brit.); WATERHOLE NO. 3(1967), d; CHANGE OF HABIT(1969), d; SUMARINE X-1(1969, Brit.), d
Misc. Talkies
LAST GENERATION, THE(1971), d
William A. Graham
HONKY(1971), d; COUNT YOUR BULLETS(1972), d; TOGETHER BROTHERS(1974), d; WHERE THE LILIES BLOOM(1974), d; SOUNDER, PART 2(1976), d; HARRY TRACY-DESPERADO(1982, Can.), d
Willie Graham
SPORT OF KINGS, THE(1931, Brit.); THIRD TIME LUCKY(1931, Brit.)
Winifred Graham
Silents
TRAPPED BY THE MORMONS(1922, Brit.), w
Winston Graham
TAKE MY LIFE(1948, Brit.), w; NIGHT WITHOUT STARS(1953, Brit.), w; SHE PLAYED WITH FIRE(1957, Brit.), w; MARNIE(1964), w; WALKING STICK, THE(1970, Brit.), w
The Graham Bond Organization
GONKS GO BEAT(1965, Brit.)
Michael Graham-Cox
WATERSHIP DOWN(1978, Brit.)
Alec Grahame
FOR BETTER FOR WORSE(1954, Brit.), w; SQUARE RING, THE(1955, Brit.), w
Arthur Grahame
DIAMOND WIZARD, THE(1954, Brit.), ph
Bert Grahame
Misc. Silents
FAITH OF A CHILD, THE(1915, Brit.)
David Grahame
OCTOPUSSY(1983, Brit.)
Gloria Grahame
BLONDE FEVER(1944); WITHOUT LOVE(1945); IT'S A WONDERFUL LIFE(1946); CROSSFIRE(1947); IT HAPPENED IN BROOKLYN(1947); MERTON OF THE MOVIES(1947); SONG OF THE THIN MAN(1947); ROUGHSHOD(1949); WOMAN'S SECRET, A(1949); IN A LONELY PLACE(1950); BAD AND THE BEAUTIFUL, THE(1952); GREATEST SHOW ON EARTH, THE(1952); MACAO(1952); SUDDEN FEAR(1952); BIG HEAT, THE(1953); GLASS WALL(1953); MAN ON A TIGHTROPE(1953); PRISONERS OF THE CASBAH(1953); GOOD DIE YOUNG, THE(1954, Brit.); HUMAN DESIRE(1954); NAKED ALIBI(1954); COBWEB, THE(1955); NOT AS A STRANGER(1955); OKLAHOMA(1955); MAN WHO NEVER WAS, THE(1956, Brit.); RIDE OUT FOR REVENGE(1957); ODDS AGAINST TOMORROW(1959); RIDE BEYOND VENGEANCE(1966); BLOOD AND LACE(1971); CHANDLER(1971); TODD KILLINGS, THE(1971); LONERS, THE(1972); MANSION OF THE DOOMED(1976); MELVIN AND HOWARD(1980); NESTING, THE(1981); CHILLY SCENES OF WINTER(1982)
Misc. Talkies
NIGHTINGALE SANG IN BERKELEY SQUARE, A(1979)
Kenneth Grahame
ADVENTURES OF ICHABOD AND MR. TOAD(1949), w
Leonard Grahame
THEY CAME FROM BEYOND SPACE(1967, Brit.)
Margot Grahame
ONE EMBARRASSING NIGHT(1930, Brit.); COMPROMISED!(1931, Brit.); GLAMOUR(1931, Brit.); LIMPING MAN, THE(1931, Brit.); LOVE HABIT, THE(1931, Brit.); ROSARY, THE(1931, Brit.); STAMBOUL(1931, Brit.); UNEASY VIRTUE(1931, Brit.); ILLEGAL(1932, Brit.); WHY SAPS LEAVE HOME(1932, Brit.); I ADORE YOU(1933, Brit.); PRINCE OF ARCADIA(1933, Brit.); TIMBUCTOO(1933, Brit.); YES, MR. BROWN(1933, Brit.); BROKEN MELODY, THE(1934, Brit.); SORRELL AND SON(1934, Brit.); WITHOUT YOU(1934, Brit.); ARIZONIAN, THE(1935); INFORMER, THE(1935); THREE MUSKETEERS, THE(1935); COUNTERFEIT(1936); CRIME OVER LONDON(1936, Brit.); MAKE WAY FOR A LADY(1936); NIGHT WAITRESS(1936); TROUBLE AHEAD(1936, Brit.); TWO IN THE DARK(1936); CRIMINAL LAWYER(1937); FIGHT FOR YOUR LADY(1937); SOLDIER AND THE LADY, THE(1937); BUCCANEER, THE(1938); BROKEN JOURNEY(1948, Brit.); BLACK MAGIC(1949); LUCKY NICK CAIN(1951); NAUGHTY ARLETTE(1951, Brit.); ASSASSIN, THE(1953, Brit.);

BEGGAR'S OPERA, THE(1953); SAINT JOAN(1957); ORDERS ARE ORDERS(1959, Brit.)
Misc. Talkies
HOUSE OF DREAMS(1933); FABULOUS JOE, THE(1946)
Rona Grahame
THIRD MAN, THE(1950, Brit.)
Ronald Grahame
Silents
QUEEN OF THE WICKED(1916, Brit.), d&w
Tim Grahame
TWO LOST WORLDS(1950)
Lyla Grahm
1984
BREAKIN'(1984)
Barry Grail
TEN DAYS TO TULARA(1958)
A. Corney Grain
FIRE OVER ENGLAND(1937, Brit.)
Edmund Grainer
GIRL WITH IDEAS, A(1937), p
Ron Grainer
KIND OF LOVING, A(1962, Brit.), m, md; LIVE NOW–PAY LATER(1962, Brit.), m; TRIAL AND ERROR(1962, Brit.), m, md; GUEST, THE(1963, Brit.), m; MOUSE ON THE MOON, THE(1963, Brit.), m; MOON-SPINNERS, THE(1964), m, md; NIGHT MUST FALL(1964, Brit.), m, md; NOTHING BUT THE BEST(1964, Brit.), m, md; SOME PEOPLE(1964, Brit.), m; STATION SIX-SAHARA(1964, Brit./Ger.), m; TO SIR, WITH LOVE(1967, Brit.), m; ONLY WHEN I LARF(1968, Brit.), m; ASSASSINATION BUREAU, THE(1969, Brit.), m; BEFORE WINTER COMES(1969, Brit.), m; LOCK UP YOUR DAUGHTERS(1969, Brit.), m; HOFFMAN(1970, Brit.), m; IN SEARCH OF GREGORY(1970, Brit./Ital.), m; OMEGA MAN, THE(1971), m; STEPTOE AND SON(1972, Brit.), m; YELLOW DOG(1973, Brit.), m; BAWDY ADVENTURES OF TOM JONES, THE(1976, Brit.), m; DEVIL WITHIN HER, THE(1976, Brit.), m
M.C. Grainey
PENNIES FROM HEAVEN(1981)
Dorothy Grainger
LOVE, HONOR, AND OH BABY!(1933); MARRIAGE ON APPROVAL(1934); WOMAN OF THE TOWN, THE(1943); DEADLINE AT DAWN(1946); PALEFACE, THE(1948); DESPERADOES ARE IN TOWN, THE(1956)
Misc. Talkies
MANHATTAN BUTTERFLY(1935)
Edmund Grainger
HOLY TERROR, A(1931), p; GAY CABALLERO, THE(1932), p; DIAMOND JIM(1935), p; GREAT IMPERSONATION, THE(1935), p; IT HAPPENED IN NEW YORK(1935), p; MYSTERY OF EDWIN DROOD, THE(1935), p; LOVE BEFORE BREAKFAST(1936), p; SUTTER'S GOLD(1936), p; THE INVISIBLE RAY(1936), p; BREEZING HOME(1937), p; LADY FIGHTS BACK(1937), p; LET THEM LIVE(1937), p; OH DOCTOR(1937), p; PRESCRIPTION FOR ROMANCE(1937), p; WE HAVE OUR MOMENTS(1937), p; DEVIL'S PARTY, THE(1938), p; GOODBYE BROADWAY(1938), p; JURY'S SECRET, THE(1938), p; NURSE FROM BROOKLYN(1938), p; ROAD TO RENO, THE(1938), p; SERVICE DE LUXE(1938), p; WIVES UNDER SUSPICION(1938), p; FORGOTTEN WOMAN, THE(1939), p; HOUSE OF FEAR, THE(1939), p; FLIGHT ANGELS(1940), p; LADY WITH RED HAIR(1940), p; MAN WHO TALKED TOO MUCH, THE(1940), p; TUGBOAT ANNIE SAILS AGAIN(1940), p; FLIGHT FROM DESTINY(1941), p; HIGHWAY WEST(1941), p; INTERNATIONAL SQUADRON(1941), p; KNOCKOUT(1941), p; SMILING GHOST, THE(1941), p; STEEL AGAINST THE SKY(1941), p; THIEVES FALL OUT(1941), p; FLYING TIGERS(1942), p; WILD BILL HICKOK RIDES(1942), p; FABULOUS TEXAN, THE(1947), p; SANDS OF IWO JIMA(1949), p; WAKE OF THE RED WITCH(1949), p; FLYING LEATHERNECKS(1951), p; RACKET, THE(1951), p; BLACKBEARD THE PIRATE(1952), p; ONE MINUTE TO ZERO(1952), p; DEVIL'S CANYON(1953), p; SPLIT SECOND(1953), p; FRENCH LINE, THE(1954), p; TREASURE OF PANCHO VILLA, THE(1955), p; BUNDLE OF JOY(1956), p; GREAT DAY IN THE MORNING(1956), p; SHEEPMAN, THE(1958), p; TORPEDO RUN(1958), p; GREEN MANSIONS(1959), p; NEVER SO FEW(1959), p; HOME FROM THE HILL(1960), p
Gail Grainger
JAGUAR LIVES(1979)
Gawn Grainger
MASTERMIND(1977)
Gloria Grainger
DEVIL'S ROCK(1938, Brit.)
Gwen Grainger
1984
LITTLE DRUMMER GIRL, THE(1984)
J. Edmund Grainger
MATTER OF TIME, A(1976, Ital./U.S.), p
Jimmy Grainger, Jr.
Silents
JOY GIRL, THE(1927)
Meta Grainger
LUCK OF THE IRISH, THE(1937, Ireland)
Michael Grainger
TARZAN AND THE SHE-DEVIL(1953)
Mike Grainger
ANATOMY OF A PSYCHO(1961)
Porter Grainger
HARLEM IS HEAVEN(1932), m
Terence Grainger
EARLY BIRD, THE(1936, Brit.); DEVIL'S ROCK(1938, Brit.)
Michael Grais
DEATH HUNT(1981), w; POLTERGEIST(1982), w
Javier Grajeda
1984
BEST DEFENSE(1984)
Steve Grajeda
DANCERS IN THE DARK(1932)
Barbara Graley
NOVEL AFFAIR, A(1957, Brit.); EYE OF THE NEEDLE(1981)

Dina Gralla
Misc. Silents
PRINCE AND THE DANCER(1929, Ger.); THOU SHALT NOT STEAL(1929, Ger.)
Fulvio Gramaldi
INVESTIGATION OF A CITIZEN ABOVE SUSPICION(1970, Ital.)
Emma Gramatica
BROKEN LOVE(1946, Ital.); MIRACLE IN MILAN(1951, Ital.)
Hardie Gramatky
MELODY TIME(1948), w
Joseph Gramby
Silents
DIANE OF STAR HOLLOW(1921)
Valeria Gramignani
PIRATE AND THE SLAVE GIRL, THE(1961, Fr./Ital.)
Alan Gramley
ON THE YARD(1978)
Charles Gramlich
Misc. Silents
WHEN QUACKEL DID HYDE(1920), d
Yura Grammapykaty
MYSTERIOUS ISLAND(1941, USSR)
Emma Grammatica
DESTINY(1938)
Robin Grammell
CONCORDE, THE–AIRPORT '79(
Thanos Grammenas
RECONSTRUCTION OF A CRIME(1970, Ger.)
Thanos Grammenos
DAYS OF 36(1972, Gr.)
Albert Gran
MOTHER KNOWS BEST(1928); GERALDINE(1929); GOLD DIGGERS OF BROAD-WAY(1929); KIBITZER, THE(1929); OUR MODERN MAIDENS(1929); TANNED LEGS(1929); FOLLOW THRU(1930); LITTLE ACCIDENT(1930); MAN FROM BLANK-LEY'S, THE(1930); SWEETHEARTS AND WIVES(1930); BRAT, THE(1931); COMMAND PERFORMANCE(1931); KISS ME AGAIN(1931); MY PAST(1931); BEAUTY PARLOR(1932); FAST LIFE(1932); EMPLOYEE'S ENTRANCE(1933)
Silents
CAPRICE OF THE MOUNTAINS(1916); OUT OF THE DRIFTS(1916); AMERICAN BUDS(1918); BEVERLY OF GRAUSTARK(1926); EARLY TO WED(1926); CHILDREN OF DIVORCE(1927); LOVE MAKES 'EM WILD(1927); SEVENTH HEAVEN(1927); SOFT CUSHIONS(1927); FOUR SONS(1928); OUR MODERN MAIDENS(1929)
Misc. Silents
HER NIGHT OF ROMANCE(1924); TARNISH(1924); HONESTY-THE BEST POLICY(1926); MORE PAY - LESS WORK(1926)
Sverre Gran
PASSIONATE DEMONS, THE(1962, Norway), p
Vera Gran
WITHOUT A HOME(1939, Pol.)
Gran Teatro del Liceo Ballet
DR. COPPELIUS(1968, U.S./Span.)
Alexander Granach
DANTON(1931, Ger.); 1914(1932, Ger.); NINOTCHKA(1939); FOREIGN CORRESPONDENT(1940); MAN BETRAYED, A(1941); SO ENDS OUR NIGHT(1941); HALF WAY TO SHANGHAI(1942); JOAN OF OZARK(1942); JOAN OF PARIS(1942); WRECKING CREW(1942); FOR WHOM THE BELL TOLLS(1943); HANGMEN ALSO DIE(1943); MISSION TO MOSCOW(1943); THREE RUSSIAN GIRLS(1943); HITLER GANG, THE(1944); MY BUDDY(1944); SEVENTH CROSS, THE(1944); VOICE IN THE WIND(1944)
Silents
NOSFERATU, THE VAMPIRE(1922, Ger.)
Misc. Silents
MAN BY THE ROADSIDE, THE(1923, Ger.); WARNING SHADOWS(1924, Ger.)
Jose Rodrigues Granada
FOXTROT(1977, Mex./Swiss), set d
Jose Rodriguez Granada
SPIRITISM(1965, Mex.), art d; MACHO CALLAHAN(1970), art d; TARZAN'S DEADLY SILENCE(1970), art d; TWO MULES FOR SISTER SARA(1970), art d; DEVIL'S RAIN, THE(1975, U.S./Mex.), art d; CAVEMAN(1981), art d
1984
UNDER THE VOLCANO(1984), art d
Jose Rodriquez Granada
TARZAN AND THE VALLEY OF GOLD(1966 U.S./Switz.), art d
Maria Granada
SAVAGE GUNS, THE(1962, U.S./Span.); GUNFIGHTERS OF CASA GRANDE(1965, U.S./Span.); REQUIEM FOR A SECRET AGENT(1966, Ital.); SON OF A GUNFIGHT-ER(1966, U.S./Span.); BIG GUNDOWN, THE(1968, Ital.)
Ramon Rodriguez Granada
JET OVER THE ATLANTIC(1960), art d; LAST REBEL, THE(1961, Mex.), art d; RAGE(1966, U.S./Mex.), art d
Rosita Granada
QUANDO EL AMOR RIE(1933); BLOOD AND SAND(1941)
Victor Granadas
DAUGHTER OF THE WEST(1949), m
Lilly Granado
LA DOLCE VITA(1961, Ital./Fr.)
Manuel Granado
Misc. Silents
BANDOLERO, THE(1924)
Laura Granados
SAVAGE PAMPAS(1967, Span./Arg.)
Gerry Granahan
RACING FEVER(1964)
Gardy Granass
TROMBA, THE TIGER MAN(1952, Ger.)
Frank Granat
MATTER OF INNOCENCE, A(1968, Brit.), p; TWISTED NERVE(1969, Brit.), p
Charles Granata
GROUND ZERO(1973)

Dona Granata
1984
GOODBYE PEOPLE, THE(1984), cos
Graziella Granata
PIRATE AND THE SLAVE GIRL, THE(1961, Fr./Ital.); AMERICAN WIFE, AN(1965, Ital.); WHITE VOICES(1965, Fr./Ital.); RUN FOR YOUR WIFE(1966, Fr./Ital.); TASTE FOR WOMEN, A(1966, Fr./Ital.); VERY HANDY MAN, A(1966, Fr./Ital.); BEYOND THE LAW(1967, Ital.); CURSE OF THE BLOOD GHOULS(1969, Ital.); DUCK RINGS AT HALF PAST SEVEN, THE(1969, Ger./Ital.)
Andy Granatelli
LOVE BUG, THE(1968)
Johnny Granath
BLONDIE'S BIG MOMENT(1947)
A. Granberg
GARNET BRACELET, THE(1966, USSR), w
Don Granberry
GROUNDSTAR CONSPIRACY, THE(1972, Can.); SUPREME KID, THE(1976, Can.)
1984
MRS. SOFFEL(1984)
Don Granbery
HOUSE BY THE LAKE, THE(1977, Can.); STAR 80(1983)
Joe Granby
HER ADVENTUROUS NIGHT(1946); EVERY GIRL SHOULD BE MARRIED(1948); HIS KIND OF WOMAN(1951)
Joseph Granby
KISMET(1944); GREAT FLAMARION, THE(1945); DANNY BOY(1946); O.S.S.(1946); I'LL BE YOURS(1947); KISS THE BLOOD OFF HIS HANDS(1948); LADY FROM SHANGHAI, THE(1948); SIREN OF ATLANTIS(1948); SPECIAL AGENT(1949); REDWOOD FOREST TRAIL(1950); WHERE THE SIDEWALK ENDS(1950); VIVA ZAPA-TA!(1952); WRITTEN ON THE WIND(1956); TATTERED DRESS, THE(1957)
Silents
AWAKENING, THE(1917); PECK'S BAD GIRL(1918)
Misc. Silents
GREAT ROMANCE, THE(1919)
Chuy Granco
DOC SAVAGE... THE MAN OF BRONZE(1975)
Barbara Grand
COMMITMENT, THE(1976), w
Elizabeth Grand
TAKE DOWN(1979)
Gordon Grand
SPORT OF KINGS(1947), w
Murray Grand
TEMPEST(1982)
1984
MOSCOW ON THE HUDSON(1984)
Richard Grand
COMMITMENT, THE(1976), a, d, w
Misc. Talkies
FYRE(1979), d
Grand Ballett de Marquis de Cueras
NEOPOLITAN CAROUSEL(1961, Ital.)
Grand Magic Circus
EASY LIFE, THE(1971, Fr.)
Grand Master Melle Mel and the Furious Five
1984
BEAT STREET(1984)
Chabuca Granda
LAST MOVIE, THE(1971), m
Brian Grandbois
1984
RENO AND THE DOC(1984, Can.)
Joseph Grandby
JOAN OF ARC(1948)
Frank Grande
WORLD'S GREATEST SINNER, THE(1962), ph
George Grandee
DANCE, GIRL, DANCE(1933); MARRYING WIDOWS(1934); SWING IT, PROFES-SOR(1937), ch
Misc. Talkies
BEGGAR'S HOLIDAY(1934)
Georgie Grandee
Silents
MEDDLER, THE(1925)
Janine Grandel
SNOWS OF KILIMANJARO, THE(1952); SUNRISE AT CAMPOBELLO(1960); TAKE HER, SHE'S MINE(1963)
Connie Grandell
1984
PLACES IN THE HEART(1984)
Frankie Grandetta
Silents
WOMANPOWER(1926)
S.A. Grandi
ANYTHING FOR A SONG(1947, Ital.), p
Grandiere
SEA PIRATE, THE(1967, Fr./Span./Ital.), w
Elmer Grandin
HOUSE OF SECRETS(1929)
Silents
GETTING MARY MARRIED(1919)
Ethel Grandin
Silents
TRAFFIC IN SOULS(1913); HUNCH, THE(1921); TAILOR MADE MAN, A(1922)
Misc. Silents
GARMENTS OF YOUTH(1921)
Isabel Grandin
DOGS OF WAR, THE(1980, Brit.)

Robert Grandin
BROKEN LANCE(1954)
Victor Grandin
Silents
EARLY BIRD, THE(1925), w
Francesco Grandjacquet
OPEN CITY(1946, Ital.)
Carlos Grandjean
SOLDIER BLUE(1970), set d; REVENGERS, THE(1972, U.S./Mex.), set d; SLAUGH-
TER(1972), set d
G. Grandjean
FRENCH CANCAN(1956, Fr.), ch
Maurice Grandmaison
Misc. Talkies
CATACLYSM(1980)
F.J. Grandon
Misc. Silents
FIFTH MAN, THE(1914), d
Francis Grandon
Misc. Silents
CROSS CURRENTS(1916), d; DUMMY, THE(1917), d; GLORY(1917), d; NOBODY'S
GIRL(1920), d
Francis J. Grandon
Silents
CONQUERED HEARTS(1918), d; WILD HONEY(1919), d
Misc. Silents
LURE OF HEART'S DESIRE, THE(1916), d; NARROW PATH, THE(1916), d; PLAY-
ING WITH FIRE(1916), d; SOUL MARKET, THE(1916), d; HEART'S DESIRE(1917), d;
LITTLE BOY SCOUT, THE(1917), d; DAREDEVIL, THE(1918), d; LOVE'S LAW(1918),
d; LAMB AND THE LION, THE(1919), d; MODERN HUSBANDS(1919), d; MISS
NOBODY(1920), d
Frank Grandon
Misc. Silents
LOTUS BLOSSOM(1921), d; BARB WIRE(1922), d; SCARLET AND GOLD(1925), d
Gisele Grandre
MARTIAN IN PARIS, A(1961, Fr.)
Herve Grandsart
1984
FULL MOON IN PARIS(1984, Fr.)
Greta Grandstedt
CAUGHT SHORT(1930); MANHATTAN PARADE(1931); SECRET WITNESS,
THE(1931); STREET SCENE(1931); STRANGER ON THE THIRD FLOOR(1940);
THIRD FINGER, LEFT HAND(1940); SING ANOTHER CHORUS(1941); I ESCAPED
FROM THE GESTAPO(1943); ROUGHLY SPEAKING(1945); GANGSTER, THE(1947);
GREATEST SHOW ON EARTH, THE(1952)
Berthe Grandval
MIDNIGHT FOLLY(1962, Fr.); TALES OF PARIS(1962, Fr./Ital.); GERMINAL(1963,
Fr.); MONSIEUR(1964, Fr.); MOTHER AND THE WHORE, THE(1973, Fr.)
Charles Grandval
BOUDU SAVED FROM DROWNING(1967, Fr.)
Fred Grandy
LINCOLN CONSPIRACY, THE(1977)
Jan Grandys
EROICA(1966, Pol.), art d; PORTRAIT OF LENIN(1967, Pol./USSR), art d
Walter Granecki
DAY THE FISH CAME OUT, THE(1967. Brit./Gr.)
Mireille Granelli
FASCIST, THE(1965, Ital.)
Eddy Graneman
JAWS OF THE JUNGLE(1936), w
Eddie Granemann
THUNDER OVER TEXAS(1934), w
Gertrude Graner
GLASS MENAGERIE, THE(1950); LIFE OF HER OWN, A(1950); FAT MAN,
THE(1951); LAWLESS BREED, THE(1952); WITNESS TO MURDER(1954)
Robert Granere
MADIGAN(1968)
Bert Granet
GENTLEMAN FROM LOUISIANA(1936), w; LEGION OF TERROR(1936), w; BIG
SHOT, THE(1937), w; HIGH FLYERS(1937), w; MEET THE MISSUS(1937), w; SPEED
TO SPARE(1937), w; AFFAIRS OF ANNABEL(1938), w; ANNABEL TAKES A
TOUR(1938), w; GO CHASE YOURSELF(1938), w; LAW OF THE UNDER-
WORLD(1938), w; MAID'S NIGHT OUT(1938), w; MR. DOODLE KICKS OFF(1938), w;
QUICK MONEY(1938), w; CAREER(1939), w; DAY THE BOOKIES WEPT, THE(1939),
w; FIXER DUGAN(1939), w; CROSS COUNTRY ROMANCE(1940), w; LADDIE(1940),
w; MILLIONAIRE PLAYBOY(1940), w; FOOTLIGHT FEVER(1941), w; GIRL, A GUY
AND A GOB, A(1941), w; OBLIGING YOUNG LADY(1941), w; TIME OUT FOR
RHYTHM(1941), w; BRIDE BY MISTAKE(1944), w; SHOW BUSINESS(1944), w; SING
YOUR WAY HOME(1945), p; THOSE ENDEARING YOUNG CHARMS(1945), p; DO
YOU LOVE ME?(1946), w; LOCKET, THE(1946), p; BERLIN EXPRESS(1948), p;
TORCH, THE(1950), p; MARRYING KIND, THE(1952), p
Madeline Ann Graneto
O'HARA'S WIFE(1983), cos
Madeline Graneto
HEARTBEEPS(1981), cos
Douglas Grange
FURIES, THE(1950); SEPTEMBER AFFAIR(1950)
Harold "Red" Grange
Silents
RACING ROMEO(1927)
Maude Grange
Silents
EVEN AS YOU AND I(1917), w
Red Grange
Silents
ONE MINUTE TO PLAY(1926)
Todd Grange
WILD GYPSIES(1969)

Bert Granger
FOR WHOM THE BELL TOLLS(1943), set d; MINISTRY OF FEAR(1945), set d
Bertram Granger
FIVE GRAVES TO CAIRO(1943), set d; DOUBLE INDEMNITY(1944), set d; LOST
WEEKEND, THE(1945), set d; PALEFACE, THE(1948), set d; SAIGON(1948), set d;
SORRY, WRONG NUMBER(1948), set d; SORROWFUL JONES(1949), set d; STREETS
OF LAREDO(1949), set d; FILE ON THELMA JORDAN, THE(1950), set d; HURRI-
CANE SMITH(1952), set d; STOOGE, THE(1952), set d; DAVY CROCKETT AND THE
RIVER PIRATES(1956), set d; WESTWARD HO THE WAGONS!(1956), set d; PEYTON
PLACE(1957), set d; GANG WAR(1958), set d; ALIAS JESSE JAMES(1959), set d
Bertran Granger
FURIES, THE(1950), set d
Bertrand Granger
CONNECTICUT YANKEE IN KING ARTHUR'S COURT, A(1949), set d
Betty Granger
RUN OF THE ARROW(1957), set d
Dorothy Granger
TRUE TO LIFE(1943); TIP-OFF, THE(1931); FIGHTING FOOL, THE(1932); NIGHT
WORLD(1932); HE LEARNED ABOUT WOMEN(1933); KING FOR A NIGHT(1933); HE
COULDN'T TAKE IT(1934); I'LL TELL THE WORLD(1934); MERRY WIDOW,
THE(1934); AFFAIR OF SUSAN(1935); DIAMOND JIM(1935); I'VE BEEN
AROUND(1935); NITWITS, THE(1935); EX-MRS. BRADFORD, THE(1936); ROMEO
AND JULIET(1936); SHOW BOAT(1936); PRESCRIPTION FOR ROMANCE(1937);
ROAD BACK,THE(1937); DRAMATIC SCHOOL(1938); LETTER OF INTRODUC-
TION(1938); SHOPWORN ANGEL(1938); BLUE MONTANA SKIES(1939); WHEN
TOMORROW COMES(1939); NEW MOON(1940); WHEN THE DALTONS RODE(1940);
HONKY TONK(1941); LADY FROM CHEYENNE(1941); UNFINISHED BUSI-
NESS(1941); NORTH TO THE KLONDIKE(1942); PARDON MY STRIPES(1942); STAR
SPANGLED RHYTHM(1942); TAKE A LETTER, DARLING(1942); COWBOY IN
MANHATTAN(1943); SWEET ROSIE O'GRADY(1943); IN SOCIETY(1944); JOHNNY
DOESN'T LIVE HERE ANY MORE(1944); KNICKERBOCKER HOLIDAY(1944);
LADY IN THE DARK(1944); ONE BODY TOO MANY(1944); PRACTICALLY
YOURS(1944); ADVENTURE(1945); HERE COME THE CO-EDS(1945); JADE MASK,
THE(1945); MARSHAL OF LAREDO(1945); ON STAGE EVERYBODY(1945); SOUTH-
ERNER, THE(1945); SUNSET IN EL DORADO(1945); UNDER WESTERN
SKIES(1945); RUNAROUND, THE(1946); SHADOWS OVER CHINATOWN(1946);
KILLER DILL(1947); SECRET LIFE OF WALTER MITTY, THE(1947); MICHAEL
O'HALLORAN(1948); SEALED VERDICT(1948); STRANGE MRS. CRANE, THE(1948);
WALLS OF JERICHO(1948); MISS MINK OF 1949(1949); LONELY HEARTS BAN-
DITS(1950); ONE MINUTE TO ZERO(1952); SO BIG(1953); RAINTREE COUNTY(1957)
Edward Granger
CIMARRON(1960), p
Farley Granger
NORTH STAR, THE(1943); PURPLE HEART, THE(1944); ENCHANTMENT(1948);
ROPE(1948); ROSEANNA McCOY(1949); THEY LIVE BY NIGHT(1949); EDGE OF
DOOM(1950); OUR VERY OWN(1950); SIDE STREET(1950); BEHAVE YOUR-
SELF(1951); I WANT YOU(1951); STRANGERS ON A TRAIN(1951); HANS CHRIS-
TIAN ANDERSEN(1952); O. HENRY'S FULL HOUSE(1952); SMALL TOWN
GIRL(1953); STORY OF THREE LOVES, THE(1953); GIRL IN THE RED VELVET
SWING, THE(1955); NAKED STREET, THE(1955); SENSO(1968, Ital.); THEY CALL
ME TRINITY(1971, Ital.); ARNOLD(1973); MAN CALLED NOON, THE(1973, Brit.);
SERPENT, THE(1973, Fr./Ital./Ger.); SLASHER, THE(1975); MANIAC MAN-
SION(1978, Ital.); PROWLER, THE(1981)
Misc. Talkies
ROGUE'S GALLERY(1968); SOMETHING CREEPING IN THE DARK(1972, Ital.)
Gladys Granger
Silents
CAPPY RICKS(1921)
John Granger
ADVISE AND CONSENT(1962); TATTOO(1981)
Leeyan Granger
JESUS CHRIST, SUPERSTAR(1973); GOING BERSERK(1983); TO BE OR NOT TO
BE(1983)
1984
BLAME IT ON THE NIGHT(1984)
Libby Granger
WUTHERING HEIGHTS(1970, Brit.)
Louise Granger
RECOIL(1953)
Marc Granger
AMAZING MR. BLUNDEN, THE(1973, Brit.)
Michael Granger
HIAWATHA(1952); LES MISERABLES(1952); BIG HEAT, THE(1953); FORT VEN-
GEANCE(1953); MAGNETIC MONSTER, THE(1953); SALOME(1953); WHITE WITCH
DOCTOR(1953); BATTLE OF ROGUE RIVER(1954); EGYPTIAN. THE(1954); CREA-
TURE WITH THE ATOM BRAIN(1955); JUNGLE MOON MEN(1955); NEW ORLEANS
UNCENSORED(1955); MIAMI EXPOSE(1956); MOHAWK(1956); RUMBLE ON THE
DOCKS(1956); CALYPSO HEAT WAVE(1957); LOOKING FOR DANGER(1957); GUN-
MAN'S WALK(1958); MURDER BY CONTRACT(1958); PIER 5, HAVANA(1959)
Philip Granger
1984
BODY ROCK(1984)
Robert A. Granger
GUN FURY(1953), w
Shanton Granger
SATURDAY NIGHT IN APPLE VALLEY(1965)
Stewart Granger
CROOKED ROAD, THE(; OVER THE GARDEN WALL(1934, Brit.); GIVE HER A
RING(1936, Brit.); CONVOY(1940); SO THIS IS LONDON(1940, Brit.); LAMP STILL
BURNS, THE(1943, Brit.); MAN IN GREY, THE(1943, Brit.); THURSDAY'S
CHILD(1943, Brit.); UNDER SECRET ORDERS(1943, Brit.); SECRET MISSION(1944,
Brit.); MADONNA OF THE SEVEN MOONS(1945, Brit.); CAESAR AND CLEOPA-
TRA(1946, Brit.); CARAVAN(1946, Brit.); CAPTAIN BOYCOTT(1947, Brit.); LADY
SURRENDERS, A(1947, Brit.); MAGIC BOW, THE(1947, Brit.); BLANCHE FURY(1948,
Brit.); MAN OF EVIL(1948, Brit.); SARABAND(1949, Brit.); WATERLOO ROAD(1949,
Brit.); WOMAN HATER(1949, Brit.); ADAM AND EVELYNE(1950, Brit.); KING
SOLOMON'S MINES(1950); LIGHT TOUCH, THE(1951); SOLDIERS THREE(1951);
PRISONER OF ZENDA, THE(1952); SCARAMOUCHE(1952); WILD NORTH,
THE(1952); ALL THE BROTHERS WERE VALIANT(1953); SALOME(1953); YOUNG
BESS(1953); BEAU BRUMMELL(1954); FOOTSTEPS IN THE FOG(1955, Brit.); GREEN

FIRE(1955); MOONFLEET(1955); BHOWANI JUNCTION(1956); LAST HUNT, THE(1956); GUN GLORY(1957); LITTLE HUT, THE(1957); HARRY BLACK AND THE TIGER(1958, Brit.); WHOLE TRUTH, THE(1958, Brit.); NORTH TO ALASKA(1960); SECRET PARTNER, THE(1961, Brit.); COMMANDO(1962, Ital., Span., Bel., Ger.); SODOM AND GOMORRAH(1962, U.S./Fr./Ital.); SWORDSMAN OF SIENA, THE(1962, Fr./Ital.); AMONG VULTURES(1964, Ger./Ital./Fr./Yugo.); SECRET INVASION, THE(1964); FRONTIER HELLCAT(1966, Fr./Ital./Ger./Yugo.); RAMPAGE AT APACHE WELLS(1966, Ger./Yugo.); REQUIEM FOR A SECRET AGENT(1966, Ital.); LAST SAFARI, THE(1967, Brit.); RED-DRAGON(1967, Ital./Ger./US); FLAMING FRONTIER(1968, Ger./Yugo.); TRYGON FACTOR, THE(1969, Brit.); WILD GEESE, THE(1978, Brit.)
Misc. Talkies
KILLER'S CARNIVAL(1965)
William Granger
OTHER TOMORROW, THE(1930); FOOTLIGHT PARADE(1933); SIX-DAY BIKE RIDER(1934); WONDER BAR(1934)
Venancia Grangerard
GODFATHER, THE, PART II(1974)
Gilles Grangien
JUPITER(1952, Fr.), d
Gilles Grangier
NIGHT AFFAIR(1961, Fr.), d, w; COUNTERFEITERS OF PARIS, THE(1962, Fr., Ital.), d, w; MAGNIFICENT TRAMP, THE(1962, Fr./Ital.), d, w; MY WIFE'S HUSBAND(1965, Fr./Ital.), d
Lena Granhagen
HUGS AND KISSES(1968, Swed.)
Ewert Granholm
MY FATHER'S MISTRESS(1970, Swed.), p
Tina Grani
ERIK THE CONQUEROR(1963, Fr./Ital.), cos; WAR OF THE ZOMBIES, THE(1965 Ital.), cos
Trini Grani
BLACK SABBATH(1963, Ital.), cos
Grania
PUTNEY SWOPE(1969)
Bruno Granichstaedten
RUNAWAY QUEEN, THE(1935, Brit.), w
Lucienne Granier
ROYAL AFFAIRS IN VERSAILLES(1957, Fr.)
Monique Granier
1984
HERE COMES SANTA CLAUS(1984), makeup
Ron Granier
WE JOINED THE NAVY(1962, Brit.), m
Pierre Granier-Deferre
CLOPORTES(1966, Fr., Ital.), d; PARIS IN THE MONTH OF AUGUST(1968, Fr.), d, w; CAT, THE(1975, Fr.), d, w; LA CAGE(1975, Fr.), d, w; WOMAN AT HER WINDOW, A(1978, Fr./Ital./Ger.), d, w; L'ETOILE DU NORD(1983, Fr.), d, w
Jon Granik
TRAP, THE(1967, Can./Brit.); LAST ACT OF MARTIN WESTON, THE(1970, Can./Czech.); FORTUNE AND MEN'S EYES(1971, U.S./Can.); IN PRAISE OF OLDER WOMEN(1978, Can.); POWER PLAY(1978, Brit./Can.)
Carlos Granjean
GERONIMO(1962), set d; DEVIL'S RAIN, THE(1975, U.S./Mex.), set d
Arthur Grank
SHADOW OF THE CAT, THE(1961, Brit.), ph
George Granlich
SWISS MISS(1938)
Majlis Granlund
FANNY AND ALEXANDER(1983, Swed./Fr./Ger.)
Maria Granlund
FANNY AND ALEXANDER(1983, Swed./Fr./Ger.)
Nils T. Granlund
GOIN' TO TOWN(1944); TAKE IT BIG(1944)
Nils T. Granlund [N.T.G.]
RHYTHM PARADE(1943)
William Grannell
Misc. Talkies
GINGER(1972)
Karen Grannum
LOVE IN A TAXI(1980)
Budd Granoff
GONG SHOW MOVIE, THE(1980), p
Gertrude Granor
I NEVER PROMISED YOU A ROSE GARDEN(1977)
Alexei Granovsky
Misc. Silents
JEWISH LUCK(1925, USSR), d
Alexis Granowsky
SONG OF LIFE, THE(1931, Ger.), d; TRUNKS OF MR. O.F., THE(1932, Ger.), d, w; I STAND CONDEMNED(1936, Brit.), p; REBEL SON, THE ½(1939, Brit.), d
Brian Granrott
WE OF THE NEVER NEVER(1983, Aus.)
Greta Granstedt
CLOSE HARMONY(1929); EMBARRASSING MOMENTS(1930); SUNNY SKIES(1930); WHAT A MAN(1930); DECEIVER, THE(1931); AFTER TOMORROW(1932); HAT CHECK GIRL(1932); MC KENNA OF THE MOUNTED(1932); NIGHT CLUB LADY(1932); NIGHT WORLD(1932); THEY NEVER COME BACK(1932); CRIME WITHOUT PASSION(1934); ADVENTURES OF MARCO POLO, THE(1938); LAST EXPRESS, THE(1938); MARIE ANTOINETTE(1938); TELEPHONE OPERATOR(1938); THERE GOES MY HEART(1938); YOU AND ME(1938); BEASTS OF BERLIN(1939); WHEN TOMORROW COMES(1939); ROAD TO SINGAPORE(1940); DANGEROUS LADY(1941); LADY BODYGUARD(1942); FIRST COMES COURAGE(1943); HERE COME THE WAVES(1944); OUR VINES HAVE TENDER GRAPES(1945); NOCTURNE(1946); RAZOR'S EDGE, THE(1946); UNCONQUERED(1947); BLONDIE'S SECRET(1948); JOAN OF ARC(1948); CROOKED WAY, THE(1949); JOHNNY HOLIDAY(1949); SAMSON AND DELILAH(1949); DARK CITY(1950); ENFORCER, THE(1951); EDDIE CANTOR STORY, THE(1953); JUGGLER, THE(1953); RETURN OF DRACULA, THE(1958)

Silents
EXCESS BAGGAGE(1928)
Joseph Granston
CRAWLING HAND, THE(1963), w
A. Cameron Grant
IT'S A BIG COUNTRY(1951); GIRL IN WHITE, THE(1952); PAT AND MIKE(1952); GIRL WHO HAD EVERYTHING, THE(1953); DESIREE(1954); EXECUTIVE SUITE(1954); GOOD MORNING, MISS DOVE(1955); 23 PACES TO BAKER STREET(1956); BELOVED INFIDEL(1959)
Adam Grant
REAL LIFE(1979)
Al Grant
ONE HOUR TO LIVE(1939)
Albert Grant
GLAD RAG DOLL, THE(1929)
Alexander Grant
PETER RABBIT AND TALES OF BEATRIX POTTER(1971, Brit.)
Alfred Grant
GOLDEN BOY(1939); ONE DARK NIGHT(1939); REFORM SCHOOL(1939); AM I GUILTY?(1940); SON OF INGAGI(1940); WELL, THE(1951)
Allan Grant
THIRD OF A MAN(1962), d&w; BILLIE(1965)
Andrew Grant
GIRL FROM STARSHIP VENUS, THE(1975, Brit.)
Angie Grant
THIS, THAT AND THE OTHER(1970, Brit.); TALES FROM THE CRYPT(1972, Brit.)
Arthur Grant
YESTERDAY'S ENEMY(1959, Brit.), ph; OPERATOR 13(1934); WHEN WE ARE MARRIED(1943, Brit.), ph; CANDLES AT NINE(1944, Brit.), ph; HEAVEN IS ROUND THE CORNER(1944, Brit.), ph; GAY INTRUDERS, THE(1946, Brit.), ph; I'LL TURN TO YOU(1946, Brit.), ph; LOYAL HEART(1946, Brit.), ph; HILLS OF DONEGAL, THE(1947, Brit.), ph; MASTER OF BANKDAM, THE(1947, Brit.), ph; AGITATOR, THE(1949, Brit.), ph; DRAGON OF PENDRAGON CASTLE, THE(1950, Brit.), ph; GLASS MOUNTAIN, THE(1950, Brit.), ph; SECOND MATE, THE(1950, Brit.), ph; BRAVE DON'T CRY, THE(1952, Brit.), ph; JUDGMENT DEFERRED(1952, Brit.), ph; MISS ROBIN HOOD(1952, Brit.), ph; BACKGROUND(1953, Brit.), ph; WEDDING OF LILLI MARLENE, THE(1953, Brit.), ph; END OF THE ROAD, THE(1954, Brit.), ph; FUSS OVER FEATHERS(1954, Brit.), ph; SCOTCH ON THE ROCKS(1954, Brit.), ph; LOVE MATCH, THE(1955, Brit.), ph; YANK IN ERMINE, A(1955, Brit.), ph; ANGEL WHO PAWNED HER HARP, THE(1956, Brit.), ph; DRY ROT(1956, Brit.), ph; EXTRA DAY, THE(1956, Brit.), ph; RAMSBOTTOM RIDES AGAIN(1956, Brit.), ph; TOUCH OF THE SUN, A(1956, Brit.), ph; ABOMINABLE SNOWMAN OF THE HIMALAYAS, THE(1957, Brit.), ph; CARRY ON ADMIRAL(1957, Brit.), ph; JOHN AND JULIE(1957, Brit.), ph; NOT WANTED ON VOYAGE(1957, Brit.), ph; STRANGER'S MEETING(1957, Brit.), ph; COUNT FIVE AND DIE(1958, Brit.), ph; RX MURDER(1958, Brit.), ph; SPANIARD'S CURSE, THE(1958, Brit.), ph; UP THE CREEK(1958, Brit.), ph; NAVY HEROES(1959, Brit.), ph; ORDERS ARE ORDERS(1959, Brit.), ph; SON OF ROBIN HOOD(1959, Brit.), ph; BREAKOUT(1960, Brit.), ph; HELL IS A CITY(1960, Brit.), ph; STRANGLERS OF BOMBAY, THE(1960, Brit.), ph; CURSE OF THE WEREWOLF, THE(1961, Brit.), ph; PASSPORT TO CHINA(1961, Brit.), ph; TERROR OF THE TONGS, THE(1961, Brit.), ph; TROUBLE IN THE SKY(1961, Brit.), ph; UNSTOPPABLE MAN, THE(1961, Brit.), ph; WATCH IT, SAILOR!(1961, Brit.), ph; CASH ON DEMAND(1962, Brit.), ph; NIGHT CREATURES(1962, Brit.), ph; PHANTOM OF THE OPERA, THE(1962, Brit.), ph; PIRATES OF BLOOD RIVER, THE(1962, Brit.), ph; FRIENDS AND NEIGHBORS(1963, Brit.), ph; OLD DARK HOUSE, THE(1963, Brit.), ph; PARANOIAC(1963, Brit.), ph; 80,000 SUSPECTS(1963, Brit.), ph; FRANKENSTEIN CREATED WOMAN(1965, Brit.), ph; JIG SAW(1965, Brit.), ph; MAKE MINE A MILLION(1965, Brit.), ph; THESE ARE THE DAMNED(1965, Brit.), ph; TOMB OF LIGEIA, THE(1965, Brit.), ph; WHERE THE SPIES ARE(1965, Brit.), ph; BEAUTY JUNGLE, THE(1966, Brit.), ph; PLAGUE OF THE ZOMBIES, THE(1966, Brit.), ph; REPTILE, THE(1966, Brit.), ph; THEY'RE A WEIRD MOB(1966, Aus.), ph; DEVIL'S OWN, THE(1967, Brit.), ph; MUMMY'S SHROUD, THE(1967, Brit.), ph; CHALLENGE FOR ROBIN HOOD, A(1968, Brit.), ph; DEVIL'S BRIDE, THE(1968, Brit.), ph; DRACULA HAS RISEN FROM HIS GRAVE(1968, Brit.), ph; FIVE MILLION YEARS TO EARTH(1968, Brit.), ph; FRANKENSTEIN MUST BE DESTROYED!(1969, Brit.), ph; TASTE THE BLOOD OF DRACULA(1970, Brit.), ph; BLOOD FROM THE MUMMY'S TOMB(1972, Brit.), ph; DEMONS OF THE MIND(1972, Brit.), ph; FEAR IN THE NIGHT(1972, Brit.), ph
Barra Grant
DAUGHTERS OF SATAN(1972); IT AIN'T EASY(1972); MOTHER, JUGS & SPEED(1976); SLOW DANCING IN THE BIG CITY(1978), w
1984
MISUNDERSTOOD(1984), w
Bernard Grant
FLYING MATCHMAKER, THE(1970, Israel)
Beverly Grant
ILLIAC PASSION, THE(1968)
Bill Grant
LAST SAFARI, THE(1967, Brit.); EXORCIST II: THE HERETIC(1977)
Bob Grant
SPARROWS CAN'T SING(1963, Brit.); ALF 'N' FAMILY(1968, Brit.)
Bryan Grant
TEENAGERS FROM OUTER SPACE(1959)
Cameron Grant
POSTMAN ALWAYS RINGS TWICE, THE(1946); SCENE OF THE CRIME(1949); SUN COMES UP, THE(1949); SUMMER STOCK(1950); HE RAN ALL THE WAY(1951); MAN WITH A CLOAK, THE(1951); SILVER WHIP, THE(1953); SEA CHASE, THE(1955)
Camille Grant
MARLOWE(1969)
Campbell Grant
PINOCCHIO(1940), art d; ADVENTURES OF ICHABOD AND MR. TOAD(1949)
Cary Grant
WITHOUT RESERVATIONS(1946); BLONDE VENUS(1932); DEVIL AND THE DEEP(1932); HOT SATURDAY(1932); MADAME BUTTERFLY(1932); MERRILY WE GO TO HELL(1932); SINNERS IN THE SUN(1932); THIS IS THE NIGHT(1932); ALICE IN WONDERLAND(1933); EAGLE AND THE HAWK, THE(1933); GAMBLING SHIP(1933); I'M NO ANGEL(1933); SHE DONE HIM WRONG(1933); WOMAN ACCUSED(1933); BORN TO BE BAD(1934); KISS AND MAKE UP(1934); LADIES SHOULD LISTEN(1934); THIRTY-DAY PRINCESS(1934); ENTER MADAME(1935);

LAST OUTPOST, THE(1935); WINGS IN THE DARK(1935); BIG BROWN EYES(1936); SUZY(1936); SYLVIA SCARLETT(1936); WEDDING PRESENT(1936); AWFUL TRUTH, THE(1937); ROMANCE AND RICHES(1937, Brit.); TOAST OF NEW YORK, THE(1937); TOPPER(1937); WHEN YOU'RE IN LOVE(1937); BRINGING UP BABY(1938); HOLIDAY(1938); GUNGA DIN(1939); IN NAME ONLY(1939); ONLY ANGELS HAVE WINGS(1939); TOPPER TAKES A TRIP(1939); HIS GIRL FRIDAY(1940); HOWARDS OF VIRGINIA, THE(1940); MY FAVORITE WIFE(1940); PHILADELPHIA STORY, THE(1940); PENNY SERENADE(1941); SUSPICION(1941); ONCE UPON A HONEYMOON(1942); TALK OF THE TOWN(1942); MR. LUCKY(1943); ARSENIC AND OLD LACE(1944); DESTINATION TOKYO(1944); NONE BUT THE LONELY HEART(1944); ONCE UPON A TIME(1944); NIGHT AND DAY(1946); NOTORIOUS(1946); BACHELOR AND THE BOBBY-SOXER, THE(1947); BISHOP'S WIFE, THE(1947); EVERY GIRL SHOULD BE MARRIED(1948); MR. BLANDINGS BUILDS HIS DREAM HOUSE(1948); I WAS A MALE WAR BRIDE(1949); CRISIS(1950); PEOPLE WILL TALK(1951); MONKEY BUSINESS(1952); ROOM FOR ONE MORE(1952); DREAM WIFE(1953); TO CATCH A THIEF(1955); AFFAIR TO REMEMBER, AN(1957); KISS THEM FOR ME(1957); PRIDE AND THE PASSION, THE(1957); HOUSEBOAT(1958); INDISCREET(1958); NORTH BY NORTHWEST(1959); OPERATION PETTICOAT(1959); GRASS IS GREENER, THE(1960); THAT TOUCH OF MINK(1962); CHARADE(1963); FATHER GOOSE(1964); WALK, DON'T RUN(1966)

Charles Grant
1984
OXFORD BLUES(1984)

Chris Grant
TIME BANDITS(1981, Brit.)

Cindy Grant
MICROWAVE MASSACRE(1983)

Corenne Grant
Misc. Silents
LAW THAT DIVIDES, THE(1919)

Corinne Grant
Misc. Silents
LADY OF THE DUGOUT(1918)

Cy Grant
SAFARI(1956); SEA WIFE(1957, Brit.); CALYPSO(1959, Fr./It.); HONEY POT, THE(1967, Brit.); SHAFT IN AFRICA(1973); AT THE EARTH'S CORE(1976, Brit.)

David Grant
GREAT MCGONAGALL, THE(1975, Brit.), p

David Marshall Grant
FRENCH POSTCARDS(1979); HAPPY BIRTHDAY, GEMINI(1980); END OF AUGUST, THE(1982)

Deborah Grant
I WANT WHAT I WANT(1972, Brit.)

Diane Grant
CHICAGO 70(1970)

Dick Grant
STRANGE BREW(1983)

Don Grant
MILDRED PIERCE(1945)

Don Grant [Don Glut]
VON RYAN'S EXPRESS(1965)

Douglas Grant
PARIS CALLING(1941); LANDLORD, THE(1970)
Silents
SINGLE TRACK, THE(1921), w

Earl Grant
TENDER IS THE NIGHT(1961)

Edwin Grant
Silents
PRIVATE PEAT(1918)

Eldon Grant
BIG FELLA(1937, Brit.)

Frances Grant
DOUBTING THOMAS(1935); THUNDER MOUNTAIN(1935); CAVALRY(1936); RED RIVER VALLEY(1936); TRAITOR, THE(1936); OH, SUSANNA(1937); BORN TO FIGHT(1938)
Silents
SISTERS(1922); GENTLE JULIA(1923)

Frances E. Grant
Misc. Silents
SWORD OF FATE, THE(1921, Brit.), d

Frances M. Grant
Silents
IN WALKED MARY(1920)

Frances Meller Grant
Silents
BAB'S CANDIDATE(1920)

Frank Grant
Misc. Talkies
BROTHERHOOD OF DEATH(1976)

Gary Grant
PETER RABBIT AND TALES OF BEATRIX POTTER(1971, Brit.)

Gerald Grant
Misc. Talkies
SCORE(1973)

Gerrie Grant
WANDERLOVE(1970)

Gilly Grant
CLEGG(1969, Brit.); SCHOOL FOR SEX(1969, Brit.); BIG SWITCH, THE(1970, Brit.)

Gloria Grant
HOT ROD GANG(1958)

Gogi Grant
BIG BEAT, THE(1958)

Gordon Grant
JACKTOWN(1962)

Harry Grant
JAWS 3-D(1983)

Harvey Grant
IT HAPPENS EVERY THURSDAY(1953); TAKE ME TO TOWN(1953); MAGNIFICENT OBSESSION(1954); JUVENILE JUNGLE(1958); SONS OF KATIE ELDER, THE(1965)

Helen Grant
Silents
SHATTERED REPUTATIONS(1923)

Helena Grant
CHARLIE CHAN IN LONDON(1934); GIVE ME YOUR HEART(1936); QUALITY STREET(1937); SHALL WE DANCE(1937); VIVACIOUS LADY(1938); WUTHERING HEIGHTS(1939); NONE BUT THE LONELY HEART(1944); UNINVITED, THE(1944); LOVE LETTERS(1945); MINISTRY OF FEAR(1945); ANNA AND THE KING OF SIAM(1946); JUNGLE GODDESS(1948)

Hughie Grant
PRIVILEGED(1982, Brit.)

Jack Grant, Jr.
KNUTE ROCKNE–ALL AMERICAN(1940)

James Edward Grant
BIG BROWN EYES(1936), w; EX-MRS. BRADFORD, THE(1936), w; GREAT GUY(1936), w; MUSS 'EM UP(1936), w; WHIPSAW(1936), w; DANGER–LOVE AT WORK(1937), w; SHE HAD TO EAT(1937), w; SHE'S NO LADY(1937), w; JOSETTE(1938), w; THERE'S THAT WOMAN AGAIN(1938), w; WE'RE GOING TO BE RICH(1938, Brit.), w; MIRACLES FOR SALE(1939), w; BOOM TOWN(1940), w; I CAN'T GIVE YOU ANYTHING BUT LOVE, BABY(1940), w; MUSIC IN MY HEART(1940), w; THEY DARE NOT LOVE(1941), w; JOHNNY EAGER(1942), w; LADY IS WILLING, THE(1942), w; BELLE OF THE YUKON(1944), w; GAMBLER'S CHOICE(1944), w; GREAT JOHN L. THE(1945), p, w; ANGEL AND THE BADMAN(1947), d&w; PLUNDERERS, THE(1948), w; JOHNNY ALLEGRO(1949), w; SANDS OF IWO JIMA(1949), w; CALIFORNIA PASSAGE(1950), w; FATHER IS A BACHELOR(1950), w; ROCK ISLAND TRAIL(1950), w; SURRENDER(1950), w; BULLFIGHTER AND THE LADY(1951), w; FLYING LEATHERNECKS(1951), w; TWO OF A KIND(1951), w; BIG JIM McLAIN(1952), w; HONDO(1953), w; RING OF FEAR(1954), d, w; LAST WAGON, THE(1956), w; THREE VIOLENT PEOPLE(1956), w; PROUD REBEL, THE(1958), w; SHEEPMAN, THE(1958), w; ALAMO, THE(1960), w; COMANCHEROS, THE(1961), w; DONOVAN'S REEF(1963), w; MC LINTOCK!(1963), w; CIRCUS WORLD(1964), w; HOSTILE GUNS(1967), w; SUPPORT YOUR LOCAL GUNFIGHTER(1971), w

James Grant
GRAND JURY(1936), w

Jimmy Grant
BREAKING AWAY(1979)

Joe Grant
PINOCCHIO(1940), art d; DUMBO(1941), w; MAKE MINE MUSIC(1946), p

John Grant
BUCK PRIVATES(1941), w; HOLD THAT GHOST(1941), w; IN THE NAVY(1941), w; KEEP 'EM FLYING(1941), w; PARDON MY SARONG(1942), w; RIDE 'EM COWBOY(1942), w; RIO RITA(1942), w; WHO DONE IT?(1942), w; CORREGIDOR(1943); HIT THE ICE(1943), w; IT AIN'T HAY(1943), w; BOWERY TO BROADWAY(1944), p; IN SOCIETY(1944), w; LOST IN A HAREM(1944), w; HERE COME THE CO-EDS(1945), p, w; NAUGHTY NINETIES, THE(1945), p, w; TIME OF THEIR LIVES, THE(1946), w; BUCK PRIVATES COME HOME(1947), w; WISTFUL WIDOW OF WAGON GAP, THE(1947), w; ABBOTT AND COSTELLO MEET FRANKENSTEIN(1948), w; MEXICAN HAYRIDE(1948), w; NOOSE HANGS HIGH, THE(1948), w; ABBOTT AND COSTELLO MEET THE KILLER, BORIS KARLOFF(1949), w; ABBOTT AND COSTELLO IN THE FOREIGN LEGION(1950), w; ABBOTT AND COSTELLO MEET THE INVISIBLE MAN(1951), w; COMIN' ROUND THE MOUNTAIN(1951), w; MASK OF THE DRAGON(1951), w; ABBOTT AND COSTELLO MEET CAPTAIN KIDD(1952), w; MA AND PA KETTLE AT THE FAIR(1952), w; ABBOTT AND COSTELLO GO TO MARS(1953), w; ABBOTT AND COSTELLO MEET DR. JEKYLL AND MR. HYDE(1954), w; FIREMAN SAVE MY CHILD(1954), w; ABBOTT AND COSTELLO MEET THE KEYSTONE KOPS(1955), w; ABBOTT AND COSTELLO MEET THE MUMMY(1955), w; WOMAN EATER, THE(1959, Brit.); MALIBU HIGH(1979)

Johnny Grant
WHITE CHRISTMAS(1954); ROCK, PRETTY BABY(1956)

Jonathan Grant
MEAT CLEAVER MASSACRE(1977)

June Grant
RAMSBOTTOM RIDES AGAIN(1956, Brit.)

Katherine Grant
Misc. Silents
RIDIN' THUNDER(1925)

Kathryn Grant
FOREVER FEMALE(1953); CELL 2455, DEATH ROW(1955); PHENIX CITY STORY, THE(1955); TIGHT SPOT(1955); UNCHAINED(1955); REPRISAL(1956); STORM CENTER(1956); WILD PARTY, THE(1956); BROTHERS RICO, THE(1957); GUNS OF FORT PETTICOAT, THE(1957); MISTER CORY(1957); NIGHT THE WORLD EXPLODED, THE(1957); OPERATION MAD BALL(1957); GUNMAN'S WALK(1958); SEVENTH VOYAGE OF SINBAD, THE(1958); ANATOMY OF A MURDER(1959); BIG CIRCUS, THE(1959); 1001 ARABIAN NIGHTS(1959)

Kaydette Grant
BANG THE DRUM SLOWLY(1973)

Ken Grant
Misc. Talkies
ALTERNATIVE MISS WORLD, THE(1980)

Kenneth Grant
MAJOR AND THE MINOR, THE(1942)

Kim Grant
OH! WHAT A LOVELY WAR(1969, Brit.)

Kirby Grant
I DREAM TOO MUCH(1935); RED RIVER RANGE(1938); BLONDIE GOES LATIN(1941); DR. KILDARE'S VICTORY(1941); MY FAVORITE BLONDE(1942); HELLO, FRISCO, HELLO(1943); STRANGER FROM PECOS, THE(1943); BABES ON SWING STREET(1944); DESTINATION TOKYO(1944); GHOST CATCHERS(1944); HI, GOOD-LOOKIN'(1944); IN SOCIETY(1944); LAW MEN(1944); BAD MEN OF THE BORDER(1945); CODE OF THE LAWLESS(1945); EASY TO LOOK AT(1945); I'LL REMEMBER APRIL(1945); PENTHOUSE RHYTHM(1945); TRAIL TO VENGEANCE(1945); GUN TOWN(1946); GUNMAN'S CODE(1946); LAWLESS BREED, THE(1946); RUSTLER'S ROUNDUP(1946); SHE WROTE THE BOOK(1946); SPIDER WOMAN STRIKES BACK, THE(1946); SONG OF IDAHO(1948); BLACK MIDNIGHT(1949);

TRAIL OF THE YUKON(1949); WOLF HUNTERS, THE(1949); CALL OF THE KLONDIKE(1950); INDIAN TERRITORY(1950); SNOW DOG(1950); COMIN' ROUND THE MOUNTAIN(1951); RHYTHM INN(1951); YUKON MANHUNT(1951); NORTHWEST TERRITORY(1952); YUKON GOLD(1952); FANGS OF THE ARCTIC(1953); NORTHERN PATROL(1953); YUKON VENGEANCE(1954)
Misc. Talkies
SINGING SPURS(1948); FEUDIN' RHYTHM(1949)

Kirsty Grant
HARD KNOCKS(1980, Aus.)
1984
STRIKEBOUND(1984, Aus.)

Larry Grant
MAN OR GUN(1958)

Lawrence Grant
BULLDOG DRUMMOND(1929); CANARY MURDER CASE, THE(1929); IS EVERYBODY HAPPY?(1929); BOUDOIR DIPLOMAT(1930); CAT CREEPS, THE(1930); OH! SAILOR, BEHAVE!(1930); SAFETY IN NUMBERS(1930); COMMAND PERFORMANCE(1931); DAUGHTER OF THE DRAGON(1931); SQUAW MAN, THE(1931); UNHOLY GARDEN, THE(1931); DIVORCE IN THE FAMILY(1932); FAITHLESS(1932); JEWEL ROBBERY(1932); MAN ABOUT TOWN(1932); MASK OF FU MANCHU, THE(1932); SHANGHAI EXPRESS(1932); SPEAK EASILY(1932); CLEAR ALL WIRES(1933); LOOKING FORWARD(1933); QUEEN CHRISTINA(1933); BY CANDLELIGHT(1934); COUNT OF MONTE CRISTO, THE(1934); I'LL TELL THE WORLD(1934); NANA(1934); PAINTED VEIL, THE(1934); RIP TIDE(1934); DARK ANGEL, THE(1935); DEVIL IS A WOMAN, THE(1935); FEATHER IN HER HAT, A(1935); MAN WHO RECLAIMED HIS HEAD, THE(1935); TALE OF TWO CITIES, A(1935); THREE KIDS AND A QUEEN(1935); VANESSA, HER LOVE STORY(1935); WEREWOLF OF LONDON, THE(1935); HOUSE OF A THOUSAND CANDLES, THE(1936); KLONDIKE ANNIE(1936); LITTLE LORD FAUNTLEROY(1936); MARY OF SCOTLAND(1936); WHITE ANGEL, THE(1936); CONFESSION(1937); LOST HORIZON(1937); PRISONER OF ZENDA, THE(1937); UNDER THE RED ROBE(1937, Brit.); MARIE ANTOINETTE(1938); SERVICE DE LUXE(1938); YOUNG IN HEART, THE(1938); NINOTCHKA(1939); PRIDE OF THE BLUEGRASS(1939); RULERS OF THE SEA(1939); SON OF FRANKENSTEIN(1939); WIFE, HUSBAND AND FRIEND(1939); DISPATCH FROM REUTERS, A(1940); SON OF MONTE CRISTO(1940); WOMEN IN WAR(1940); DR. JEKYLL AND MR. HYDE(1941); RAGE IN HEAVEN(1941); GHOST OF FRANKENSTEIN, THE(1942); LIVING GHOST, THE(1942); CONFIDENTIAL AGENT(1945)
Misc. Talkies
THEIR MAD MOMENT(1931); S.O.S. COAST GUARD(1937)
Silents
KAISER, BEAST OF BERLIN, THE(1918); CHORUS GIRL'S ROMANCE, A(1920); ABRAHAM LINCOLN(1924); HIS HOUR(1924); GRAND DUCHESS AND THE WAITER, THE(1926); RED HAIR(1928); EXALTED FLAPPER, THE(1929)
Misc. Silents
TO HELL WITH THE KAISER(1918); SERENADE(1927); SERVICE FOR LADIES(1927); DOOMSDAY(1928)

Lee Grant
WHEN YOU COMIN' BACK, RED RYDER?(1979); DETECTIVE STORY(1951); STORM FEAR(1956); MIDDLE OF THE NIGHT(1959); BALCONY, THE(1963); AFFAIR OF THE SKIN, AN(1964); PIE IN THE SKY(1964); DIVORCE AMERICAN STYLE(1967); IN THE HEAT OF THE NIGHT(1967); VALLEY OF THE DOLLS(1967); BUONA SERA, MRS. CAMPBELL(1968, Ital.); BIG BOUNCE, THE(1969); MAROONED(1969); LANDLORD, THE(1970); THERE WAS A CROOKED MAN(1970); PLAZA SUITE(1971); PORTNOY'S COMPLAINT(1972); INTERNECINE PROJECT, THE(1974, Brit.); SHAMPOO(1975); VOYAGE OF THE DAMNED(1976, Brit.); AIRPORT '77(1977); DAMIEN—OMEN II(1978); MAFU CAGE, THE(1978); SWARM, THE(1978); LITTLE MISS MARKER(1980); TELL ME A RIDDLE(1980), d; CHARLIE CHAN AND THE CURSE OF THE DRAGON QUEEN(1981); VISITING HOURS(1982, Can.)
1984
CONSTANCE(1984, New Zealand); TEACHERS(1984)

Leon Grant
WANDERERS, THE(1979)

Leon W. Grant
1984
BEAT STREET(1984); BROTHER FROM ANOTHER PLANET, THE(1984)

Linda Grant
MECHANIC, THE(1972)

Lisa Grant
TRADER HORNEE(1970)

Louis Grant
NATIVE LAND(1942)

Louise Grant
JOE MACBETH(1955)

Mabel Grant
DRUMS O' VOODOO(1934)

Marhshall Grant
MADAME SPY(1942), p

Marian Grant
HUNTED MEN(1938), w; TRAMP, TRAMP, TRAMP(1942), w

Marshall Grant
DIAMOND FRONTIER(1940), p; SOUTH TO KARANGA(1940), p; BURMA CONVOY(1941), p; MR. DYNAMITE(1941), p; SAN FRANCISCO DOCKS(1941), p; BOMBAY CLIPPER(1942), p; DESTINATION UNKNOWN(1942), p; ESCAPE FROM HONG KONG(1942), p; TREAT 'EM ROUGH(1942), p; UNSEEN ENEMY(1942), p; LITTLE MISS BIG(1946), p; STRANGE CONQUEST(1946), p

Mary Grant
UP IN CENTRAL PARK(1948), cos; TECKMAN MYSTERY, THE(1955, Brit); WE'RE NO ANGELS(1955), cos; VAGABOND KING, THE(1956), cos; BACHELOR PARTY, THE(1957), cos; SEPARATE TABLES(1958), cos; DEVIL'S DISCIPLE, THE(1959), cos

Maxwell Grant
SHADOW STRIKES, THE(1937), w; INTERNATIONAL CRIME(1938), w

Michael Grant
HEAD ON(1981, Can.), p, d

Milt Grant
JAMBOREE(1957)

Moray Grant
MEET THE NAVY(1946, Brit.), ph; TROJAN BROTHERS, THE(1946), ph; GHOSTS OF BERKELEY SQUARE(1947, Brit.), ph; SPRINGTIME(1948, Brit.), ph; JACK OF DIAMONDS, THE(1949, Brit.), ph; NO ROOM AT THE INN(1950, Brit.), ph; NIGHT WAS OUR FRIEND(1951, Brit.), ph; UP THE CREEK(1958, Brit.), ph; HORROR OF FRANKENSTEIN, THE(1970, Brit.), ph; SCARS OF DRACULA, THE(1970, Brit.), ph; VAMPIRE LOVERS, THE(1970, Brit.), ph; I, MONSTER(1971, Brit.), ph; VAMPIRE CIRCUS(1972, Brit.), ph

Morlay Grant
THREE WEIRD SISTERS, THE(1948, Brit.), ph

Morton Grant
LOVE IS ON THE AIR(1937), w; SHE LOVED A FIREMAN(1937), w; HIS EXCITING NIGHT(1938), w; ROOKIE COP, THE(1939), w; TIMBER STAMPEDE(1939), w; STAGE TO CHINO(1940), w; TRIPLE JUSTICE(1940), w; WAGON TRAIN(1940), w; ALONG THE RIO GRANDE(1941), w; DUDE COWBOY(1941), w; FARGO KID, THE(1941), w; LAND OF THE OPEN RANGE(1941), w; MELODY LANE(1941), w; MOONLIGHT IN HAWAII(1941), w; ROBBERS OF THE RANGE(1941), w; BANDIT RANGER(1942), w; RIDING THE WIND(1942), w; VALLEY OF HUNTED MEN(1942), w; WESTWARD HO(1942), w; AVENGING RIDER, THE(1943), w; BAR 20(1943), w; BEYOND THE LAST FRONTIER(1943), w; SANTA FE SCOUTS(1943), w; SWING IN THE SADDLE(1944), w; TEN CENTS A DANCE(1945), w; SONG OF THE SOUTH(1946), w; GALLANT BLADE, THE(1948), w; BIG CAT, THE(1949), w; HOLIDAY IN HAVANA(1949), w; YOUNGER BROTHERS, THE(1949), w

Nat Grant
HOSPITAL, THE(1971); TAXI DRIVER(1976)

Neil Grant
MAN OF AFFAIRS(1937, Brit.), w; HIDEOUT IN THE ALPS(1938, Brit.), w

Nellie Grant
Silents
INNOCENCE OF RUTH, THE(1916); ALADDIN'S OTHER LAMP(1917); JUST A SONG AT TWILIGHT(1922)
Misc. Silents
CHILDREN OF EVE, THE(1915); SHADOWS FROM THE PAST(1915)

Norman Grant
MATTER OF INNOCENCE, A(1968, Brit.)

Paul Grant
RETURN OF THE JEDI(1983)

Pauline Grant
HAPPY GO LOVELY(1951, Brit.), ch; MELBA(1953, Brit.), ch; LET'S BE HAPPY(1957, Brit.), ch; AMOROUS ADVENTURES OF MOLL FLANDERS, THE(1965), ch

Philip Grant
I AM THE LAW(1938)

Phoenix Grant
YETI(1977, Ital.)

Richard Grant
PURPLE HEART DIARY(1951); FORBIDDEN PLANET(1956); ON THE THRESHOLD OF SPACE(1956); YOUNG GIANTS(1983)

Rita Grant
MUSIC HALL PARADE(1939, Brit.); GARRISON FOLLIES(1940, Brit.); FACING THE MUSIC(1941, Brit.); SOUTH AMERICAN GEORGE(1941, Brit.)

Robert Grant
MYSTERY SEA RAIDER(1940), w; SOFI(1967), ed

Roberta Grant
AGE OF CONSENT(1969, Austral.); IRISHMAN, THE(1978, Aus.)

Roy Grant
BLAZING GUNS(1943)

Sabrina Grant
HOSPITAL, THE(1971)

Sandra Grant
HOUSE IS NOT A HOME, A(1964)

Sarina C. Grant
CORNBREAD, EARL AND ME(1975); BINGO LONG TRAVELING ALL-STARS AND MOTOR KINGS, THE(1976); CARWASH(1976); COMA(1978)

Sheila Grant
PERSECUTION AND ASSASSINATION OF JEAN-PAUL MARAT AS PERFORMED BY THE INMATES OF THE ASYLUM OF CHARENTON UNDER THE DIRECTION OF THE MARQUIS DE SADE, THE(1967, Brit.)

Shelby Grant
JOHN GOLDFARB, PLEASE COME HOME(1964); PLEASURE SEEKERS, THE(1964); FANTASTIC VOYAGE(1966); OUR MAN FLINT(1966); WITCHMAKER, THE(1969)

Sidney Grant
Silents
POWER OF RIGHT, THE(1919, Brit.)

Stanely Grant
BIG NOISE, THE(1936, Brit.), ph

Stanley Grant
BLIND MAN'S BLUFF(1936, Brit.), ph; FIND THE LADY(1936, Brit.), ph; FULL SPEED AHEAD(1936, Brit.), ph; HIGHLAND FLING(1936, Brit.), ph; UNDER PROOF(1936, Brit.), ph; BEHIND YOUR BACK(1937, Brit.), ph; CATCH AS CATCH CAN(1937, Brit.), ph; CONCERNING MR. MARTIN(1937, Brit.), ph; FIVE POUND MAN, THE(1937, Brit.), ph; JENIFER HALE(1937, Brit.), ph; MACUSHLA(1937, Brit.), ph; MEMBER OF THE JURY(1937, Brit.), ph; PASSENGER TO LONDON(1937, Brit.), ph; THERE WAS A YOUNG MAN(1937, Brit.), ph; WISE GUYS(1937, Brit.), ph; BAD BOY(1938, Brit.), ph; LAST BARRICADE, THE(1938, Brit.), ph; VILLIERS DIAMOND, THE(1938, Brit.), ph; ODD MAN OUT(1947, Brit.), spec eff; OLIVER TWIST(1951, Brit.), spec eff; GHOST SHIP(1953, Brit.), ph; JOHN WESLEY(1954, Brit.), ph

Stephen Grant
ANGEL AND THE BADMAN(1947)

Stewart Grant
HERO(1982, Brit.)

Susan Lyall Grant
AS LONG AS THEY'RE HAPPY(1957, Brit.); SPANISH GARDENER, THE(1957, Span.)

Sydney Grant
Misc. Silents
JANE(1915)

Tom Grant
BREAKFAST IN BED(1978), m
Valentin Grant
Misc. Silents
MELTING POT, THE(1915)
Valentine Grant
Silents
INNOCENT LIE, THE(1916)
Misc. Talkies
BOLD EMMETT, IRELAND'S MARTYR(1915); NAN O' THE BACKWOODS(1915); DAUGHTER OF MACGREGOR, A(1916); BELGIAN, THE(1917)
Walter Grant
THIEF OF BAGHDAD, THE(1961, Ital./Fr.); HERCULES, SAMSON & ULYSSES(1964, Ital.)
Wyley Grant
DRIFTIN' RIVER(1946)
Wylie Grant
ACROSS THE PLAINS(1939); JESSE JAMES(1939); CARAVAN TRAIL, THE(1946)
Lucy Grantham
LAST HOUSE ON THE LEFT(1972)
Mark Grantham
MAN ACCUSED(1959), w; COMPELLED(1960, Brit.), w; DATE AT MIDNIGHT(1960, Brit.), w; ESCORT FOR HIRE(1960, Brit.), w; FEET OF CLAY(1960, Brit.), w; NIGHT TRAIN FOR INVERNESS(1960, Brit.), w; SENTENCED FOR LIFE(1960, Brit.), w; TASTE OF MONEY, A(1960, Brit.), w; SO EVIL SO YOUNG(1961, Brit.), w; DESIGN FOR LOVING(1962, Brit.), w; GANG WAR(1962, Brit.), w; SHE ALWAYS GETS THEIR MAN(1962, Brit.), w
Mary Lois Grantham
1984
PHILADELPHIA EXPERIMENT, THE(1984)
Robin Grantham
PEOPLE THAT TIME FORGOT, THE(1977, Brit.), makeup; XTRO(1983, Brit.), makeup
1984
SECRET PLACES(1984, Brit.), makeup
Sidney Grantham
SPLINTERS(1929, Brit.)
Ya. Grantinsh
WAR AND PEACE(1968, USSR)
Charles Granucci
WE WERE STRANGERS(1949)
Granval
END OF A DAY, THE(1939, Fr.)
Charles Granval
GOLGOTHA(1937, Fr.); PEPE LE MOKO(1937, Fr.); THEY WERE FIVE(1938, Fr.)
Jean-Pierre Granval
PICNIC ON THE GRASS(1960, Fr.)
Bernard "Bunny" Granville
DOORWAY TO HELL(1930)
Bonita Granville
SILVER DOLLAR(1932); WESTWARD PASSAGE(1932); CAVALCADE(1933); LIFE OF VERGIE WINTERS, THE(1934); GARDEN OF ALLAH, THE(1936); PLOUGH AND THE STARS, THE(1936); SONG OF THE SADDLE(1936); THESE THREE(1936); CALL IT A DAY(1937); IT'S LOVE I'M AFTER(1937); MAID OF SALEM(1937); QUALITY STREET(1937); BELOVED BRAT(1938); HARD TO GET(1938); MERRILY WE LIVE(1938); MY BILL(1938); NANCY DREW--DETECTIVE(1938); WHITE BANNERS(1938); ANGELS WASH THEIR FACES(1939); NANCY DREW--REPORTER(1939); NANCY DREW AND THE HIDDEN STAIRCASE(1939); NANCY DREW, TROUBLE SHOOTER(1939); ESCAPE(1940); FORTY LITTLE MOTHERS(1940); GALLANT SONS(1940); MORTAL STORM, THE(1940); THIRD FINGER, LEFT HAND(1940); THOSE WERE THE DAYS(1940); DOWN IN SAN DIEGO(1941); H.M. PULHAM, ESQ.(1941); PEOPLE VS. DR. KILDARE, THE(1941); WILD MAN OF BORNEO, THE(1941); GLASS KEY, THE(1942); HITLER'S CHILDREN(1942); NOW, VOYAGER(1942); SEVEN MILES FROM ALCATRAZ(1942); SYNCOPATION(1942); ANDY HARDY'S BLONDE TROUBLE(1944); SONG OF THE OPEN ROAD(1944); YOUTH RUNS WILD(1944); SENORITA FROM THE WEST(1945); BEAUTIFUL CHEAT, THE(1946); BREAKFAST IN HOLLYWOOD(1946); LOVE LAUGHS AT ANDY HARDY(1946); SUSPENSE(1946); TRUTH ABOUT MURDER, THE(1946); GUILTY, THE(1947); STRIKE IT RICH(1948); GUILTY OF TREASON(1950); LONE RANGER, THE(1955)
Charlotte Granville
JUST A GIGOLO(1931); 24 HOURS(1931); NOW AND FOREVER(1934); BEHOLD MY WIFE(1935); WEREWOLF OF LONDON, THE(1935); ROSE OF THE RANCHO(1936)
Silents
ANTICS OF ANN, THE(1917); IMPOSTER, THE(1918); DAMSEL IN DISTRESS, A(1919)
Misc. Silents
SQUARE DEAL, A(1917); GIRL AND THE JUDGE, THE(1918)
Frank Granville
Misc. Silents
SCARLET AND GOLD(1925)
Fred Leroy Granville
Silents
DIVORCE TRAP, THE(1919), ph; PRICE OF SILENCE, THE(1920, Brit.), d; SHARK MASTER, THE(1921), d, w; FORBIDDEN CARGOES(1925, Brit.), p&d
Misc. Silents
HONEYPOT, THE(1920, Brit.), d; FIGHTING LOVER, THE(1921), d; LOVE MAGGY(1921, Brit.), d; SMART SEX, THE(1921), d; SHIFTING SANDS(1922, Brit.), d; BELOVED VAGABOND, THE(1923, Brit.), d; SINS YE DO, THE(1924, Brit.), d
George Granville
BITE THE BULLET(1975), ed
Joan Granville
GARMENT JUNGLE, THE(1957); YOUNG CAPTIVES, THE(1959)
Renay Granville
Misc. Talkies
SWEET SAVIOR(1971)
Sydney Granville
MIKADO, THE(1939, Brit.)

Ursula Granville
THREE WEIRD SISTERS, THE(1948, Brit.)
Louis Grapes
NIGHT OF BLOODY HORROR zero(1969)
Marcus Grapes
SCOTT JOPLIN(1977)
Marcus J. Grapes
WOMEN AND BLOODY TERROR(1970)
Misc. Talkies
KEEP OFF! KEEP OFF!(1975)
Charles Grapewin
SHANNONS OF BROADWAY, THE(1929); ONLY SAPS WORK(1930); MILLIONAIRE, THE(1931); DISORDERLY CONDUCT(1932); LADY AND GENT(1932); WILD HORSE MESA(1932); BEAUTY FOR SALE(1933); DON'T BET ON LOVE(1933); HELLO, EVERYBODY(1933); HEROES FOR SALE(1933); KISS BEFORE THE MIRROR, THE(1933); MIDNIGHT MARY(1933); TORCH SINGER(1933); WILD BOYS OF THE ROAD(1933); CARAVAN(1934); LOUDSPEAKER, THE(1934); PRESIDENT VANISHES, THE(1934); QUITTERS, THE(1934); RETURN OF THE TERROR(1934); AH, WILDERNESS!(1935); ALICE ADAMS(1935); KING SOLOMON OF BROADWAY(1935); RENDEZVOUS(1935); SHANGHAI(1935); LISTEN, DARLING(1938); MAN WHO DARED, THE(1939); WIZARD OF OZ, THE(1939); THEY DIED WITH THEIR BOOTS ON(1942); FOLLOW THE BOYS(1944); WHEN I GROW UP(1951)
Charley Grapewin
HELL'S HOUSE(1932); NIGHT OF JUNE 13(1932); WOMAN IN ROOM 13, THE(1932); NO MAN OF HER OWN(1933); PILGRIMAGE(1933); ANNE OF GREEN GABLES(1934); JUDGE PRIEST(1934); SHE MADE HER BED(1934); TWO ALONE(1934); EIGHT BELLS(1935); ONE FRIGHTENED NIGHT(1935); PARTY WIRE(1935); SUPERSPEED(1935); LIBELED LADY(1936); PETRIFIED FOREST, THE(1936); SINNER TAKE ALL(1936); SMALL TOWN GIRL(1936); VOICE OF BUGLE ANN(1936); WITHOUT ORDERS(1936); BAD GUY(1937); BETWEEN TWO WOMEN(1937); BIG CITY(1937); BROADWAY MELODY OF '38(1937); CAPTAINS COURAGEOUS(1937); FAMILY AFFAIR, A(1937); GOOD EARTH, THE(1937); ARTISTS AND MODELS ABROAD(1938); BAD MAN OF BRIMSTONE(1938); GIRL OF THE GOLDEN WEST, THE(1938); OF HUMAN HEARTS(1938); SHOPWORN ANGEL(1938); THREE COMRADES(1938); THREE LOVES HAS NANCY(1938); BURN 'EM UP O'CONNER(1939); DUST BE MY DESTINY(1939); HERO FOR A DAY(1939); I AM NOT AFRAID(1939); SABOTAGE(1939); STAND UP AND FIGHT(1939); SUDDEN MONEY(1939); EARTHBOUND(1940); ELLERY QUEEN. MASTER DETECTIVE(1940); GRAPES OF WRATH(1940); JOHNNY APOLLO(1940); TEXAS RANGERS RIDE AGAIN(1940); ELLERY QUEEN AND THE MURDER RING(1941); ELLERY QUEEN AND THE PERFECT CRIME(1941); ELLERY QUEEN'S PENTHOUSE MYSTERY(1941); TOBACCO ROAD(1941); CLOSE CALL FOR ELLERY QUEEN, A(1942); DESPERATE CHANCE FOR ELLERY QUEEN, A(1942); ENEMY AGENTS MEET ELLERY QUEEN(1942); ATLANTIC CITY(1944); IMPATIENT YEARS, THE(1944); GUNFIGHTERS, THE(1947); ENCHANTED VALLEY, THE(1948); SAND(1949)
Charlie Grapewin
HELL AND HIGH WATER(1933); RHYTHM ON THE RIVER(1940)
Lorendana Grappasonni
MONSIGNOR(1982)
Stephane Grappelli
GOING PLACES(1974, Fr.), m; KING OF THE GYPSIES(1978)
Stephane Grappelly
TIME FLIES(1944, Brit.); LISBON STORY, THE(1946, Brit.)
Grant Garrett
MODEL WIFE(1941), w
Janette Gras
TO HAVE AND HAVE NOT(1944)
Jean Gras
DAY AND THE HOUR, THE(1963, Fr./ Ital.); MADEMOISELLE(1966, Fr./Brit.); THINGS OF LIFE, THE(1970, Fr./Ital./Switz.)
Mauri Grashin
TROUBLE WITH GIRLS(AND HOW TO GET INTO IT), THE*1/2 (1969), w; EXPOSED(1932), w; HIDE-OUT(1934), w; I'LL WAIT FOR YOU(1941), w; ICE-CAPADES REVUE(1942), w; PARDON MY STRIPES(1942), w; SLEEPYTIME GAL(1942), w; SONS OF THE PIONEERS(1942), w; WRECKING CREW(1942), w; X MARKS THE SPOT(1942), w; ROLL ON TEXAS MOON(1946), w; ARTHUR TAKES OVER(1948), w
Maurie Grashin
MOUNTAIN MOONLIGHT(1941), w
Christiane Graskoff
MEPHISTO(1981, Ger.)
Barbara Grass
YOUNG MONK, THE(1978, Ger.)
Gunter Grass
TIN DRUM, THE(1979, Ger./Fr./Yugo./Pol.), w
Clancy B. Grass III
VELVET VAMPIRE, THE(1971), m
The Grass Roots
WITH SIX YOU GET EGGROLL(1968)
Ken Grassano
1984
NATURAL, THE(1984)
Beretram Grassby
Misc. Silents
PARISIAN SCANDAL, A(1921)
Bertram Grassby
Silents
AMERICAN METHODS(1917); EVEN AS YOU AND I(1917); ROMANCE OF HAPPY VALLEY, A(1919); INFERIOR SEX, THE(1920); FIFTY CANDLES(1921); SLEEPWALKER, THE(1922); PRISONER, THE(1923); TIGER'S CLAW, THE(1923); GIRL ON THE STAIRS, THE(1924); HIS HOUR(1924); MIDNIGHT EXPRESS, THE(1924); ONE LAW FOR THE WOMAN(1924); BEAUTIFUL CHEAT, THE(1926); TAXI MYSTERY, THE(1926); BELOVED ROGUE, THE(1927)
Misc. Silents
GAY LORD WARING, THE(1916); LANDON'S LEGACY(1916); SON OF THE IMMORTALS, A(1916); WHIRLPOOL OF DESTINY, THE(1916); HER TEMPTATION(1917); SCARLET PIMPERNEL, THE(1917); SOUL OF SATAN, THE(1917); TO HONOR AND OBEY(1917); DEVIL'S WHEEL, THE(1918); FOR LIBERTY(1918); GRAY HORIZON, THE(1919); HOOP-LA(1919); LONE WOLF'S DAUGHTER, THE(1919); SALOME(1919); FOR THE SOUL OF RAFAEL(1920); MIDCHANNEL(1920); WEEKEND, THE(1920); WOMAN AND THE PUPPET, THE(1920); HER SOCIAL VA-

LUE(1921); HOLD YOUR HORSES(1921); STRAIGHT FROM PARIS(1921); BORDER-
LAND(1922); FOR THE DEFENSE(1922); SHATTERED DREAMS(1922); DANCER OF
THE NILE, THE(1923); PIONEER TRAILS(1923); FOOLS IN THE DARK(1924);
SHADOW OF THE EAST, THE(1924); SHE WOLVES(1925); MADE FOR LOVE(1926)

Jean-Pierre Grasset
TOMB OF TORTURE(1966, Ital.), ed

Pierre Grasset
RIFIFI(1956, Fr.)

Alex Grasshof
Misc. Talkies
PEPPER AND HIS WACKY TAXI(1972), d

Alex Grasshoff
JAILBREAKERS, THE(1960), p,d&w; MAGIC SPECTACLES(1961), ed
Misc. Talkies
CRACKLE OF DEATH(1974), d; SMOKEY AND THE GOODTIME OUTLAWS(1978),
d

Wolfgang Grasshoff
OPERATION GANYMED(1977, Ger.), ph

Jacques Grassi
MR. HULOT'S HOLIDAY(1954, Fr.), ed

Leonard Grassi
REG'LAR FELLERS(1941)

Raoul Grassilli
INVASION 1700(1965, Fr./Ital./Yugo.); MYTH, THE(1965, Ital.)

Marilee Grassini
KISS OF DEATH(1947)

Dolores Grassjan
1★2?(1975, Fr.), d&w

Karen Grassle
HARRY'S WAR(1981)

A. Grasso
GREEN TREE, THE(1965, Ital.), ph

Giovanni Grasso
GREAT DAWN, THE(1947, Ital.); MELODY OF LOVE(1954, Ital.)
Misc. Silents
LOST IN THE DARK(1914, Ital.)

Sal Grasso
SEVEN(1979), prod d

Lynn Grate
LOVE BUG, THE(1968)

The Grateful Dead
PETULIA(1968, U.S./Brit.)

Mr. Gratham
GREEN FINGERS(1947)

F. Dawson Gratrix
HONEYMOON MERRY-GO-ROUND(1939, Brit.), w

Xenia Gratsos
Misc. Talkies
HELL RIVER(1977)

Alejandro Grattan
ONLY ONCE IN A LIFETIME(1979), p, d&w

Alexander Grattan
NO RETURN ADDRESS(1961), p&d, w

Sidney Grattan
Misc. Silents
COMMON LEVEL, A(1920)

Stephen Grattan
Silents
ETERNAL SIN, THE(1917)
Misc. Silents
SHOULD A MOTHER TELL?(1915); RULING PASSION, THE(1916); SINS OF
MEN(1916); TORTURED HEART, A(1916); WINNING OF BEATRICE, THE(1918);
OTHER MEN'S SHOES(1920)

Bill Gratton
KNUTE ROCKNE–ALL AMERICAN(1940)

Billy Gratton
NEXT TIME WE LOVE(1936)

Patricia Gratton
RECKONING, THE(1971, Brit.)

Stephen Gratton
Misc. Silents
ROAD TO ARCADY, THE(1922)

Valeri Gratton
SING FOR YOUR SUPPER(1941)

Humphrey Gratz
BUFFALO BILL AND THE INDIANS, OR SITTING BULL'S HISTORY LES-
SON(1976)

Alan Gratzer
FM(1978)

Albin Grau
Silents
NOSFERATU, THE VAMPIRE(1922, Ger.), set d

Gil Grau
SOMETHING TO SHOUT ABOUT(1943), m; RAGE TO LIVE, A(1965), md

Harold Grau
STAGE STRUCK(1958)

Jorge Grau
FEMALE BUTCHER, THE(1972, Ital./Span.), d; DON'T OPEN THE WINDOW(1974,
Ital.), d, w; MONSTER ISLAND(1981, Span./U.S.), w

Marta Grau
DAY THE HOTLINE GOT HOT, THE(1968, Fr./Span.)

Judy Graubart
SIMON(1980); AUTHOR! AUTHOR!(1982)

Brigitte Graubner
GEORGE(1973, U.S./Switz.)

Paul Grauchet
WISE GUYS(1969, Fr./Ital.)

Janine Graudel
RETURN OF THE FLY(1959)

Ben Grauer
Silents
IDOL DANCER, THE(1920); ANNABEL LEE(1921)
Misc. Silents
MY FRIEND, THE DEVIL(1922)

Bunny Grauer
Misc. Silents
TOWN THAT FORGOT GOD, THE(1922)

Marshall Grauer
BLOOD WATERS OF DOCTOR Z(1982)

Sid Grauman
MAD ABOUT MUSIC(1938); STAR DUST(1940); DANCING IN THE DARK(1949)

Walter Grauman
DISEMBODIED, THE(1957), d; LADY IN A CAGE(1964), d; RAGE TO LIVE, A(1965),
d; I DEAL IN DANGER(1966), d; LAST ESCAPE, THE(1970, Brit.), d
Misc. Talkies
MANHUNT IN SPACE(1954), d

Walter E. Grauman
SQUADRON 633(1964, U.S./Brit.), d; 633 SQUADRON(1964), d

Bob Gravage
RARE BREED, THE(1966); UNDEFEATED, THE(1969); EARTHQUAKE(1974)

Robert Gravage
SOMETHING BIG(1971); GREAT NORTHFIELD, MINNESOTA RAID, THE(1972)

Cesare Gravain
Silents
ROSE OF PARIS, THE(1924)

Neville Grave
MIKADO, THE(1967, Brit.)

Serge Grave
GENERALS WITHOUT BUTTONS(1938, Fr.); STORY OF A CHEAT, THE(1938, Fr.)

V. Grave
OPTIMISTIC TRAGEDY, THE(1964, USSR)

Nick Gravenites
STEELYARD BLUES(1973), m

Chris Graver
TRICK OR TREATS(1982)

Christopher Graver
KISS ME GOODBYE(1982)

Gary Graver
KILL, THE(1968), d&w, ph; HARD TRAIL(1969), ph; SATAN'S SADISTS(1969), ph,
ed; BLOOD OF FRANKENSTEIN(1970), ph; DIAMOND STUD(1970), ph; HARD
ROAD, THE(1970), d,ph&ed; HELL'S BLOODY DEVILS(1970), ph; MACHISMO–40
GRAVES FOR 40 GUNS(1970), ph; WILD, FREE AND HUNGRY(1970), a, p; CLONES,
THE(1973), ph; INVASION OF THE BEE GIRLS(1973), ph; JESSIE'S GIRLS(1976),
ph; STUDENT BODY, THE(1976), ph; GRAND THEFT AUTO(1977), ph; MOONSHINE
COUNTY EXPRESS(1977), ph; DEATHSPORT(1978), ph; SUNSET COVE(1978), ph;
TOOLBOX MURDERS, THE(1978), ph; ATTIC, THE(1979), ph; SUNNYSIDE(1979),
ph; GLOVE, THE(1980), ph; SMOKEY BITES THE DUST(1981), ph; TEXAS LIGHT-
NING(1981), d&w; TRICK OR TREATS(1982), p,d,w,ph,ed; MORTUARY(1983), ph
1984
CHATTANOOGA CHOO CHOO(1984), ph; HOLLYWOOD HIGH PART II(1984), ph;
THEY'RE PLAYING WITH FIRE(1984), ph
Misc. Talkies
TRICK OR TREATS(1983), d

Jeff Graver
HARD ROAD, THE(1970)

Steve Gravers
HELL BENT FOR LEATHER(1960); OPERATION EICHMANN(1961); FORTY
POUNDS OF TROUBLE(1962); CAR, THE(1977); WIZARDS(1977)

Ann Graves
MAGIC SWORD, THE(1962)

Anne Graves
RUNAWAY GIRL(1966)

Bryan Graves
ISADORA(1968, Brit.), set d; THREE INTO TWO WON'T GO(1969, Brit.), set d;
MACBETH(1971, Brit.), set d; SAY HELLO TO YESTERDAY(1971, Brit.), set d;
DUELLISTS, THE(1977, Brit.), art d

Carolyn Graves
ROSE BOWL STORY, THE(1952)

Diana Graves
PRIVATE ANGELO(1949, Brit.); LADY POSSESSED(1952)

Ed Graves
OUR MAN FLINT(1966), art d; DOCTOR DOLITTLE(1967), art d; SECRET LIFE OF
AN AMERICAN WIFE, THE(1968), art d; HARD CONTRACT(1969), art d; BARE-
FOOT EXECUTIVE, THE(1971), art d; DOCTOR DEATH: SEEKER OF SOULS(1973),
art d

Ernest Graves
WALK EAST ON BEACON(1952); ONE PLUS ONE(1961, Can.); HERCULES IN NEW
YORK(1970); DOGS OF WAR, THE(1980, Brit.)

Frank Graves
CHIVATO(1961), w; REBELLION IN CUBA(1961), w; THOSE FANTASTIC FLYING
FOOLS(1967, Brit), set d

Gayla Graves
ROCK BABY, ROCK IT(1957); HOUSE OF WOMEN(1962)

George Graves
CROOKED LADY, THE(1932, Brit.); THOSE WERE THE DAYS(1934, Brit.); HO-
NOURS EASY(1935, Brit.); REGAL CAVALCADE(1935, Brit.); STAR FELL FROM
HEAVEN, A(1936, Brit.); WOLF'S CLOTHING(1936, Brit.); HEART'S DESIRE(1937,
Brit.); ROBBER SYMPHONY, THE(1937, Brit.); TENTH MAN, THE(1937, Brit.)

Janet Graves
TAKE A LETTER, DARLING(1942)

Jeffe Graves
SAFARI(1940)

Jesse Graves
WITHOUT RESERVATIONS(1946); EASY LIVING(1937); GOING PLACES(1939);
MARYLAND(1940); SON OF INGAGI(1940); LOVE CRAZY(1941); IS EVERYBODY
HAPPY?(1943); SOMEONE TO REMEMBER(1943); WILSON(1944); SHE WOULDN'T
SAY YES(1945); DO YOU LOVE ME?(1946); THREE LITTLE GIRLS IN BLUE(1946);

TOMORROW IS FOREVER(1946); DEAD RECKONING(1947); EGG AND I, THE(1947); JOHNNY O'CLOCK(1947)

Jesse A. Graves
JEZEBEL(1938)

Jessie Graves
YOU CAN'T TAKE IT WITH YOU(1938); SEA OF GRASS, THE(1947); SECRET BEYOND THE DOOR, THE(1948)

Joe Graves
Misc. Talkies
RETURN OF GILBERT AND SULLIVAN(1952)

John Graves
1984
WEEKEND PASS(1984)

Leonard Graves
JOKER IS WILD, THE(1957); THREE BRAVE MEN(1957); PORK CHOP HILL(1959)

Leslie Graves
PIRANHA II: THE SPAWNING(1981, Neth.); DEATH WISH II(1982)

Mark L. Graves
OFFICER AND A GENTLEMAN, AN(1982)

Peggy Graves
FIGHTING GENTLEMAN, THE(1932)

Peter Graves
LILY CHRISTINE(1932, Brit.); KING ARTHUR WAS A GENTLEMAN(1942, Brit.); MISS LONDON LTD.(1943, Brit.); BEES IN PARADISE(1944, Brit.); GIVE US THE MOON(1944, Brit.); I'LL BE YOUR SWEETHEART(1945, Brit.); WALTZ TIME(1946, Brit.); SHOWTIME(1948, Brit.); SPRINGTIME(1948, Brit.); SPRING IN PARK LANE(1949, Brit.); LAUGHING LADY, THE(1950, Brit.); MRS. FITZHERBERT(1950, Brit.); ENCORE(1951, Brit.); FORT DEFIANCE(1951); LADY WITH A LAMP, THE(1951, Brit.); ROGUE RIVER(1951); FOUR AGAINST FATE(1952, Brit.); MAYTIME IN MAYFAIR(1952, Brit.); RED PLANET MARS(1952); BENEATH THE 12-MILE REEF(1953); EAST OF SUMATRA(1953); STALAG 17(1953); WAR PAINT(1953); KILLERS FROM SPACE(1954); RAID, THE(1954); YELLOW TOMAHAWK, THE(1954); BLACK TUESDAY(1955); COURT-MARTIAL OF BILLY MITCHELL, THE(1955); FORT YUMA(1955); LET'S MAKE UP(1955, Brit.); LONG GRAY LINE, THE(1955); NAKED STREET, THE(1955); NIGHT OF THE HUNTER, THE(1955); ROBBER'S ROOST(1955); WICHITA(1955); CANYON RIVER(1956); HOLD BACK THE NIGHT(1956); IT CONQUERED THE WORLD(1956); ADMIRABLE CRICHTON, THE(1957, Brit.); BAYOU(1957); BEGINNING OF THE END(1957); DEATH IN SMALL DOSES(1957); WOLF LARSEN(1958); STRANGER IN MY ARMS(1959); RAGE TO LIVE, A(1965); TEXAS ACROSS THE RIVER(1966); WRONG BOX, THE(1966, Brit.); HOW I WON THE WAR(1967, Brit.); I'LL NEVER FORGET WHAT'S 'IS NAME(1967, Brit.); JOKERS, THE(1967, Brit.); VALLEY OF MYSTERY(1967); BALLAD OF JOSIE(1968); SERGEANT RYKER(1968); ADVENTURERS, THE(1970); FIVE MAN ARMY, THE(1970, Ital.); MAGIC CHRISTIAN, THE(1970, Brit.); PAUL AND MICHELLE(1974, Fr./Brit.); SIDECAR RACERS(1975, Aus.); SLIPPER AND THE ROSE, THE(1976, Brit.); CLONUS HORROR, THE(1979); AIRPLANE!(1980); SURVIVAL RUN(1980); AIRPLANE II: THE SEQUEL(1982); GUNS AND THE FURY, THE(1983); SAVANNAH SMILES(1983)
Misc. Talkies
CRUISE MISSILE(1978)

Phillip Graves
EVERY LITTLE CROOK AND NANNY(1972)

Ralph Graves
COLLEGE COQUETTE, THE(1929), w; FLIGHT(1929), a, w; GLAD RAG DOLL, THE(1929); SONG OF LOVE, THE(1929); HELL'S ISLAND(1930); LADIES OF LEISURE(1930), w; VENGEANCE(1930), w; DANGEROUS AFFAIR, A(1931); DIRIGIBLE(1931); SALVATION NELL(1931); WEST OF BROADWAY(1931), w; FELLER NEEDS A FRIEND(1932); HELL DIVERS(1932), w; HUDDLE(1932); SCANDAL FOR SALE(1932), w; WAR CORRESPONDENT(1932), w; BORN TO BE BAD(1934), w; TICKET TO CRIME(1934); OUTLAWS OF THE ORIENT(1937), w; ETERNALLY YOURS(1939); STREET OF MISSING MEN(1939); THREE TEXAS STEERS(1939); SPEED LIMITED(1940), a, w; DOUBLE EXPOSURE(1944), w; ALIMONY(1949); AMAZON QUEST(1949); JOE PALOOKA IN THE COUNTERPUNCH(1949)
Silents
I'LL GET HIM YET(1919); OUT OF LUCK(1919); SCARLET DAYS(1919); GREATEST QUESTION, THE(1920); LITTLE MISS REBELLION(1920); DREAM STREET(1921); COME ON OVER(1922); JILT, THE(1922); KINDRED OF THE DUST(1922); LONG CHANCE, THE(1922); EXTRA GIRL, THE(1923); JUST LIKE A WOMAN(1923); MIND OVER MOTOR(1923); DAUGHTERS OF TODAY(1924); WOMANPOWER(1926); KID SISTER, THE(1927), d; SWELL-HEAD, THE(1927), a, d; ALIAS THE DEACON(1928); BACHELOR'S PARADISE(1928); ETERNAL WOMAN, THE(1929); FLYING FEET, THE(1929)
Misc. Silents
MEN WHO HAVE MADE LOVE TO ME(1918); SPORTING LIFE(1918); YELLOW DOG, THE(1918); HOME TOWN GIRL, THE(1919); SCARLET SHADOW, THE(1919); WHAT AM I BID?(1919); WHITE HEATHER, THE(1919); MARY ELLEN COMES TO TOWN(1920); POLLY WITH A PAST(1920); GHOST PATROL, THE(1923); PRODIGAL DAUGHTERS(1923); BLARNEY(1926); COUNTRY BEYOND, THE(1926); RENO DIVORCE, A(1927), a, d; RICH MEN'S SONS(1927), a, d; BITTER SWEETS(1928); CHEER LEADER, THE(1928); SIDESHOW, THE(1928); SUBMARINE(1928); THAT CERTAIN THING(1928)

Robert Graves
JEALOUSY(1934); MADAME SPY(1934); MEN OF THE NIGHT(1934); SISTERS UNDER THE SKIN(1934); WONDER BAR(1934); DANTE'S INFERNO(1935); FOLIES DERGERE(1935); THIS IS THE LIFE(1935); EASY MONEY(1936); FATAL LADY(1936); WALKING ON AIR(1936); ESPIONAGE(1937); KING AND THE CHORUS GIRL, THE(1937); ARTISTS AND MODELS ABROAD(1938); SUEZ(1938); SHOUT, THE(1978, Brit.), w
Silents
RANGER OF THE BIG PINES(1925); SPUDS(1927)
Misc. Silents
CHRISTINE OF THE BIG TOPS(1926); TEST OF DONALD NORTON, THE(1926); SMILIN' GUNS(1929)

Robert Graves, Jr.
CODE OF HONOR(1930); MEN OF THE NORTH(1930); SHERLOCK HOLMES(1932)

Robert T. Graves
FORBIDDEN(1932)

Ron Graves
WHY WOULD I LIE(1980)

Taylor Graves
Silents
OLIVER TWIST(1922); MAILMAN, THE(1923); ONLY 38(1923); NORTH OF NEVADA(1924)

Teresa Graves
THAT MAN BOLT(1973); BLACK EYE(1974); OLD DRACULA(1975, Brit.)

Tommy Graves
FAT SPY(1966)

William Graves
OFFICER AND A GENTLEMAN, AN(1982)

Steve Gravesi
AL CAPONE(1959)

Fernand Gravet
KING AND THE CHORUS GIRL, THE(1937); FOOLS FOR SCANDAL(1938); GREAT WALTZ, THE(1938); COMPLIMENTS OF MR. FLOW(1941, Fr.); FOOLISH HUSBANDS(1948, Fr.)

Fernand Gravet [Gravey]
MADWOMAN OF CHAILLOT, THE(1969)

Fernand Gravey
LA RONDE(1954, Fr.); HOW TO STEAL A MILLION(1966); GUNS FOR SAN SEBASTIAN(1968, U.S./Fr./Mex./Ital.); GIVE HER THE MOON(1970, Fr./Ital.); PROMISE AT DAWN(1970, U.S./Fr.)

Fernand Gravey [Gravet]
ROYAL AFFAIRS IN VERSAILLES(1957, Fr.)

Claudia Gravi
1984
YELLOW HAIR AND THE FORTRESS OF GOLD(1984)

Carla Gravina
BIG DEAL ON MADONNA STREET, THE(1960); FIVE BRANDED WOMEN(1960); EVERYBODY GO HOME!(1962, Fr./Ital.); VIOLENT FOUR, THE(1968, Ital.); LADY OF MONZA, THE(1970, Ital.); WITHOUT APPARENT MOTIVE(1972, Fr.); ALFREDO, ALFREDO(1973, Ital.); AND NOW MY LOVE(1975, Fr.); NO WAY OUT(1975, Ital./Fr.); TEMPTER, THE(1978, Ital.)

Cesare Gravina
PHANTOM OF THE OPERA, THE(1929)
Silents
MADAME BUTTERFLY(1915); FOOLISH WIVES(1920); CIRCUS DAYS(1923); DADDY(1923); HUNCHBACK OF NOTRE DAME, THE(1923); MERRY-GO-ROUND(1923); FAMILY SECRET, THE(1924); CHARMER, THE(1925); GREED(1925); PHANTOM OF THE OPERA, THE(1925); CHEATING CHEATERS(1927); MAN WHO LAUGHS, THE(1927); WEDDING MARCH, THE(1927); DIVINE WOMAN, THE(1928); TRAIL OF '98, THE(1929)
Misc. Silents
MISS NOBODY(1917); MYSTERIOUS CLIENT, THE(1918); SCRATCH MY BACK(1920); GOD'S COUNTRY AND THE LAW(1921); HUMMING BIRD, THE(1924); CIRCUS CYCLONE, THE(1925); BURNING THE WIND(1929)

Mauro Gravina
HORNET'S NEST(1970)

Claudia Gravy
LAST DAY OF THE WAR, THE(1969, U.S./Ital./Span.); NUN AT THE CROSSROADS, A(1970, Ital./Span.)

Alan Gray
MR. PERRIN AND MR. TRAILL(1948, Brit.), m; AFRICAN QUEEN, THE(1951, U.S./Brit.), m; TWILIGHT WOMEN(1953, Brit.), m

Alec Gray
NEVER LOOK BACK(1952, Brit.), art d

Alexander Gray
SALLY(1929); NO, NO NANETTE(1930); SONG OF THE FLAME(1930); SPRING IS HERE(1930); VIENNESE NIGHTS(1930); MOONLIGHT AND PRETZELS(1933)

Allan Gray
F.P. 1 DOESN'T ANSWER(1933, Ger.), m; CHALLENGE, THE(1939, Brit.), m; PRISONER OF CORBAL(1939, Brit.), m; COLONEL BLIMP(1945, Brit.), m; SILVER FLEET, THE(1945, Brit.), m; STAIRWAY TO HEAVEN(1946, Brit.), m; I KNOW WHERE I'M GOING(1947, Brit.), m; MADNESS OF THE HEART(1949, Brit.), m; NO PLACE FOR JENNIFER(1950, Brit.), m; OBSESSED(1951, Brit.), m; RELUCTANT WIDOW, THE(1951, Brit.), m; OUTPOST IN MALAYA(1952, Brit.), m

Allen Gray
HER PANELLED DOOR(1951, Brit.), m

Anthony Gray
MOULIN ROUGE(1952)

Arlene Gray
STRANGE BARGAIN(1949)

Arnold Gray
MUMMY, THE(1932); PHANTOM BROADCAST, THE(1933); TAKE THE STAND(1934); NUT FARM, THE(1935); PRIVATE WORLDS(1935); SPANISH CAPE MYSTERY(1935); PAROLE(1936)
Misc. Silents
FLAME OF THE YUKON, THE(1926); WEST OF BROADWAY(1926); FANGS OF FATE(1928)

Barbara Gray
1984(1956, Brit.), cos; ISTANBUL(1957), w

Barry Gray
ERRAND BOY, THE(1961); DR. WHO AND THE DALEKS(1965, Brit.), m; ISLAND OF TERROR(1967, Brit.), spec eff; THUNDERBIRD 6(1968, Brit.), m; THUNDERBIRDS ARE GO(1968, Brit.), m; JOURNEY TO THE FAR SIDE OF THE SUN(1969, Brit.), m, md

Basil Gray
DINGAKA(1965, South Africa), m

Beatrice Gray
LAURA(1944); HOUSE OF DRACULA(1945); TRAIL TO VENGEANCE(1945); LITTLE GIANT(1946); LITTLE MISS BIG(1946); DOUBLE LIFE, A(1947); JOAN OF ARC(1948); ABBOTT AND COSTELLO MEET THE KILLER, BORIS KARLOFF(1949); LADY GAMBLES, THE(1949); FLESH AND FURY(1952); LATIN LOVERS(1953); I'VE LIVED BEFORE(1956)
Misc. Talkies
TRIGGER LAW(1944); UTAH KID, THE(1944); STRANGER FROM SANTA FE(1945)

Berkeley Gray
NORMAN CONQUEST(1953, Brit.), w
Betty Gray
Silents
HIS LAST DOLLAR(1914)
Bill Gray
LOVE AND BULLETS(1979, Brit.)
Misc. Talkies
CITIZEN SOLDIER(1984)
Billy Gray
UNCLE HARRY(1945); WITH LOVE AND KISSES(1937); MAN OF COURAGE(1943); CLUNY BROWN(1946); SPECTER OF THE ROSE(1946); TO EACH HIS OWN(1946); GANGSTER, THE(1947); FIGHTING FATHER DUNNE(1948); FATHER IS A BACHELOR(1950); IN A LONELY PLACE(1950); MISTER 880(1950); SINGING GUNS(1950); THREE LITTLE WORDS(1950); DAY THE EARTH STOOD STILL, THE(1951); GENE AUTRY AND THE MOUNTIES(1951); GUY WHO CAME BACK, THE(1951); JIM THORPE–ALL AMERICAN(1951); ON MOONLIGHT BAY(1951); TALK ABOUT A STRANGER(1952); ALL I DESIRE(1953); BY THE LIGHT OF THE SILVERY MOON(1953); GIRL NEXT DOOR, THE(1953); OUTLAW STALLION, THE(1954); SEVEN LITTLE FOYS, THE(1955); SCARLET HOUR, THE(1956); SOME LIKE IT HOT(1959); EXPLOSIVE GENERATION, THE(1961); TWO FOR THE SEESAW(1962); NAVY VS. THE NIGHT MONSTERS, THE(1966); DUSTY AND SWEETS McGEE(1971); WEREWOLVES ON WHEELS(1971)
Misc. Talkies
RETURN OF GILBERT AND SULLIVAN(1952)
Blanche Gray
Silents
SHAM(1921)
Misc. Silents
OLD LOVES FOR NEW(1918)
Bob Gray
Silents
DOLLY'S VACATION(1918)
Misc. Silents
DENNY FROM IRELAND(1918), d
Bonnie Gray
Misc. Talkies
FLYING LARIATS(1931)
Bruce Gray
ADULTEROUS AFFAIR(1966)
Campbell Gray
ODETTE(1951, Brit.)
Carole Gray
WONDERFUL TO BE YOUNG!(1962, Brit.); RATTLE OF A SIMPLE MAN(1964, Brit.); CURSE OF THE FLY(1965, Brit.); DEVILS OF DARKNESS, THE(1965, Brit.); BRIDES OF FU MANCHU, THE(1966, Brit.); ISLAND OF TERROR(1967, Brit.); OH! WHAT A LOVELY WAR(1969, Brit.)
Cary Gray
HENRY, THE RAINMAKER(1949)
Cecil Gray
LIVE AGAIN(1936, Brit.)
Chantal Gray
HUMAN FACTOR, THE(1979, Brit.)
Charles D. Gray
SECRET WAR OF HARRY FRIGG, THE(1968)
Charles Gray
TALES OF MANHATTAN(1942); ONE DESIRE(1955); BLACK WHIP, THE(1956); HOUSTON STORY, THE(1956); GOD IS MY PARTNER(1957); RIDE A VIOLENT MILE(1957); TROOPER HOOK(1957); UNKNOWN TERROR, THE(1957); CATTLE EMPIRE(1958); DESERT HELL(1958); I ACCUSE(1958, Brit.); DESPERATE MAN, THE(1959, Brit.); ENTERTAINER, THE(1960, Brit.); TOMMY THE TOREADOR(1960, Brit.); MAN IN THE MOON(1961, Brit.); MASQUERADE(1965, Brit.); NIGHT OF THE GENERALS, THE(1967, Brit./Fr.); YOU ONLY LIVE TWICE(1967, Brit.); DEVIL'S BRIDE, THE(1968, Brit.); MAN OUTSIDE, THE(1968, Brit.); FILE OF THE GOLDEN GOOSE, THE(1969, Brit.); CROMWELL(1970, Brit.); EXECUTIONER, THE(1970, Brit.); MOSQUITO SQUADRON(1970, Brit.); DIAMONDS ARE FOREVER(1971, Brit.); WILD ROVERS(1971); JUNIOR BONNER(1972); BEAST MUST DIE, THE(1974, Brit.); ROCKY HORROR PICTURE SHOW, THE(1975, Brit.); SEVEN NIGHTS IN JAPAN(1976, Brit./Fr.); SILVER BEARS(1978); LEGACY, THE(1979, Brit.); MIRROR CRACK'D, THE(1980, Brit.); SHOCK TREATMENT(1981)
1984
JIGSAW MAN, THE(1984, Brit.)
Charles H. Gray
CHARRO(1969); ORGANIZATION, THE(1971); NEW CENTURIONS, THE(1972); PROPHECY(1979)
Charlie Gray
TICKET TO HEAVEN(1981)
Claudia Gray
CAPTAIN'S PARADISE, THE(1953, Brit.)
Clifford B. Gray
Misc. Silents
CONEY ISLAND PRINCESS, A(1916)
Clifford Gray
Silents
RAINBOW PRINCESS, THE(1916)
Misc. Silents
THROWN TO THE LIONS(1916); INSPIRATIONS OF HARRY LARRABEE(1917); SOONER OR LATER(1920)
Clive Gray
UNMAN, WITTERING AND ZIGO(1971, Brit.)
Coleen Gray
STATE FAIR(1945); THREE LITTLE GIRLS IN BLUE(1946); KISS OF DEATH(1947); NIGHTMARE ALLEY(1947); FURY AT FURNACE CREEK(1948); RED RIVER(1948); SAND(1949); FATHER IS A BACHELOR(1950); RIDING HIGH(1950); SLEEPING CITY, THE(1950); APACHE DRUMS(1951); LUCKY NICK CAIN(1951); KANSAS CITY CONFIDENTIAL(1952); MODELS, INC.(1952); FAKE, THE(1953, Brit.); SABRE JET(1953); VANQUISHED, THE(1953); ARROW IN THE DUST(1954); LAS VEGAS SHAKEDOWN(1955); TENNESSEE'S PARTNER(1955); TWINKLE IN GOD'S EYE, THE(1955); BLACK WHIP, THE(1956); DEATH OF A SCOUNDREL(1956); FRONTIER GAMBLER(1956); KILLING, THE(1956); STAR IN THE DUST(1956); WILD DAKOTAS,

THE(1956); COPPER SKY(1957); DESTINATION 60,000(1957); VAMPIRE, THE(1957); HELL'S FIVE HOURS(1958); JOHNNY ROCCO(1958); LEECH WOMAN, THE(1960); PHANTOM PLANET, THE(1961); TOWN TAMER(1965); P.J.(1968); LATE LIZ, THE(1971)
Daniel J. Gray
Silents
PENROD(1922), ed; UNHOLY THREE, THE(1925), ed; EXIT SMILING(1926), ed; RED MILL, THE(1927), ed; TILLIE THE TOILER(1927), ed
David Gray
FAST AND LOOSE(1930), w; COAL MINER'S DAUGHTER(1980)
Davis Gray
ASPHYX, THE(1972, Brit.)
Dick Gray
Misc. Silents
MOLLY MAKE-BELIEVE(1916)
Dobie Gray
OUT OF SIGHT(1966); COMMITMENT, THE(1976), m
Dolly Gray
VALLEY OF THE DRAGONS(1961)
Dolores Gray
LADY FOR A NIGHT(1941); MR. SKEFFINGTON(1944); IT'S ALWAYS FAIR WEATHER(1955); KISMET(1955); OPPOSITE SEX, THE(1956); DESIGNING WOMAN(1957)
Don Gray
DEADLINE(1948)
Donald Gray
WELL DONE, HENRY(1936, Brit.); STRANGE EXPERIMENT(1937, Brit.); MURDER IN THE FAMILY(1938, Brit.); SWORD OF HONOUR(1938, Brit.); 13 MEN AND A GUN(1938, Brit.); FOUR FEATHERS, THE(1939, Brit.); WE'LL MEET AGAIN(1942, Brit.); IDOL OF PARIS(1948, Brit.); ISLAND OF DESIRE(1952, Brit.); BURNT EVIDENCE(1954, Brit.); DIAMOND WIZARD, THE(1954, Brit.); ATOMIC MAN, THE(1955, Brit.); FLIGHT FROM VIENNA(1956, Brit.); SATELLITE IN THE SKY(1956); SECRET TENT, THE(1956, Brit.); MURDER ON THE CAMPUS(1963, Brit.)
Misc. Talkies
SUPERSONIC SAUCER(1956, Brit.)
Dorian Gray
QUEEN OF SHEBA(1953, Ital.); NIGHTS OF CABIRIA(1957, Ital.); COMMANDO(1962, Ital., Span., Bel., Ger.); IL GRIDO(1962, U.S./Ital.); LOVE AND LARCENY(1963, Fr./Ital.); AND SUDDENLY IT'S MURDER!(1964, Ital.); LOVE ON THE RIVIERA(1964, Fr./Ital.)
Misc. Talkies
COLOSSUS AND THE AMAZONS(1960)
Dorothy Gray
PUBLIC ENEMY, THE(1931); GREAT JASPER, THE(1933); LITTLE WOMEN(1933); PRINCESS O'HARA(1935); ROSE MARIE(1936); SWEETHEARTS(1938); THREE RUSSIAN GIRLS(1943)
Duane Gray
UNKNOWN TERROR, THE(1957)
Dulcie Gray
2,000 WOMEN(1944, Brit.); MADONNA OF THE SEVEN MOONS(1945, Brit.); PLACE OF ONE'S OWN, A(1945, Brit.); THEY WERE SISTERS(1945, Brit.); WANTED FOR MURDER(1946, Brit.); MAN ABOUT THE HOUSE, A(1947, Brit.); YEARS BETWEEN, THE(1947, Brit.); MINE OWN EXECUTIONER(1948, Brit.); MY BROTHER JONATHAN(1949, Brit.); GLASS MOUNTAIN, THE(1950, Brit); FRANCHISE AFFAIR, THE(1952, Brit.); THERE WAS A YOUNG LADY(1953, Brit.); ANGELS ONE FIVE(1954, Brit.); MAN COULD GET KILLED, A(1966)
Eddie Gray
FIRST A GIRL(1935, Brit.); SKYLARKS(1936, Brit.); SMILING ALONG(1938, Brit.); DON CHICAGO(1945, Brit.); LIFE IS A CIRCUS(1962, Brit.); FAST LADY, THE(1963, Brit.)
Eden Gray
MAN WHO LOST HIMSELF, THE(1941); KING'S ROW(1942)
Misc. Silents
LOVERS IN QUARANTINE(1925)
Edna Gray
EIGHT GIRLS IN A BOAT(1932, Ger.)
Elisabetta Gray
JULIET OF THE SPIRITS(1965, Fr./Ital./W.Ger.)
Elspet Gray
FLY AWAY PETER(1948, Brit.); LOVE IN WAITING(1948, Brit.); GAY LADY, THE(1949, Brit.); RELUCTANT HEROES(1951, Brit.); JOHNNY ON THE SPOT(1954, Brit.); GOODBYE MR. CHIPS(1969, U.S./Brit.)
Elspeth Gray
BLIND GODDESS, THE(1948, Brit.); DEVIL'S HARBOR(1954, Brit.)
Eric Gray
Silents
SHOEBLACK OF PICCADILLY, THE(1920, Brit.)
Misc. Silents
WHERE THE RAINBOW ENDS(1921, Brit.)
Erin Gray
BUCK ROGERS IN THE 25TH CENTURY(1979); WINTER KILLS(1979); SIX PACK(1982)
Eve Gray
LOVES OF ROBERT BURNS, THE(1930, Brit.); WHY SAILORS LEAVE HOME(1930, Brit.); NIGHT BIRDS(1931, Brit.); WICKHAM MYSTERY, THE(1931, Brit.); BERMONDSEY KID, THE(1933, Brit.); FLAW, THE(1933, Brit.); SMITHY(1933, Brit.); BIG BUSINESS(1934, Brit.); CRIMSON CANDLE, THE(1934, Brit.); GUEST OF HONOR(1934, Brit.); WOMANHOOD(1934, Brit.); DEPARTMENT STORE(1935, Brit.); MURDER AT MONTE CARLO(1935, Brit.); THREE WITNESSES(1935, Brit.); HAPPY FAMILY, THE(1936, Brit.); JURY'S EVIDENCE(1936, Brit.); LAST JOURNEY, THE(1936, Brit.); MURDER ON THE SET(1936, Brit.); SUCH IS LIFE(1936, Brit.); THEY DIDN'T KNOW(1936, Brit.); TWICE BRANDED(1936, Brit.); FIFTY-SHILLING BOXER(1937, Brit.); PEARLS BRING TEARS(1937, Brit.); STRANGE ADVENTURES OF MR. SMITH, THE(1937, Brit.); VICAR OF BRAY, THE(1937, Brit.); WHEN THE DEVIL WAS WELL(1937, Brit.); WHO KILLED FEN MARKHAM?(1937, Brit.); AWAKENING, THE(1938, Brit.); HIS LORDSHIP REGRETS(1938, Brit.); MURDER AT THE BASKERVILLES(1941, Brit.)
Silents
ONE OF THE BEST(1927, Brit.); POPPIES OF FLANDERS(1927, Brit.); MOULIN ROUGE(1928, Brit.); SMASHING THROUGH(1928, Brit.)

Misc. Silents
SILVER LINING, THE(1927, Brit.)

F.M. Gray
FALCON TAKES OVER, THE(1942), art d

Feild Gray
POWDERSMOKE RANGE(1935), art d; DON'T TELL THE WIFE(1937), art d; LITTLE ORPHAN ANNIE(1938), art d; LADIES' DAY(1943), art d; LADY LUCK(1946), art d; LIKELY STORY, A(1947), art d; GUN SMUGGLERS(1948), art d; GUNS OF HATE(1948), art d; STATION WEST(1948), art d; JUDGE STEPS OUT, THE(1949), art d; MASKED RAIDERS(1949), art d; MYSTERIOUS DESPERADO, THE(1949), art d; RIDERS OF THE RANGE(1949), art d; RUSTLERS(1949), art d; STAGECOACH KID(1949), art d; LAW OF THE BADLANDS(1950), art d; STORM OVER WYOMING(1950), art d; GUNPLAY(1951), art d; HOT LEAD(1951), art d; PISTOL HARVEST(1951), art d; LAS VEGAS STORY, THE(1952), art d; LOAN SHARK(1952), art d; ROAD AGENT(1952), art d; TARGET(1952), art d; PETE KELLY'S BLUES(1955), art d; DAVY CROCKETT AND THE RIVER PIRATES(1956), art d; D.I., THE(1957), art d; JET PILOT(1957), art d; –30–(1959), art d; LAST TIME I SAW ARCHIE, THE(1961), art d

Feild M. Gray
EVERYBODY'S DOING IT(1938), art d; GO CHASE YOURSELF(1938), art d; MEXICAN SPITFIRE'S ELEPHANT(1942), art d; SEVEN MILES FROM ALCATRAZ(1942), art d; DOUBLE DYNAMITE(1951), art d

Fred Gray
HOT ICE(1952, Brit.); REVENGE OF THE CHEERLEADERS(1976)

Gary Gray
ADDRESS UNKNOWN(1944); I'LL BE SEEING YOU(1944); ONCE UPON A TIME(1944); ADVENTURES OF RUSTY(1945); RENDEZVOUS 24(1946); TO EACH HIS OWN(1946); BEST MAN WINS(1948); FIGHTING BACK(1948); GUN SMUGGLERS(1948); NIGHT WIND(1948); RACHEL AND THE STRANGER(1948); RETURN OF THE BADMEN(1948); WHISPERING SMITH(1948); GIRL FROM JONES BEACH, THE(1949); GREAT LOVER, THE(1949); LEAVE IT TO HENRY(1949); MASKED RAIDERS(1949); STREETS OF SAN FRANCISCO(1949); FATHER IS A BACHELOR(1950); FATHER MAKES GOOD(1950); FATHER'S WILD GAME(1950); TWO WEEKS WITH LOVE(1950); FATHER TAKES THE AIR(1951); PAINTED HILLS, THE(1951); RODEO(1952); EMERGENCY HOSPITAL(1956); TEENAGE REBEL(1956); PARTY CRASHERS, THE(1958); WILD HERITAGE(1958); TERROR AT BLACK FALLS(1962)
Misc. Talkies
COUNTRY TOWN(1971)

Geneva Gray
ANGELS ALLEY(1948); FIGHTING MAD(1948); GUN TALK(1948); MOTHER IS A FRESHMAN(1949); RIVER OF NO RETURN(1954)

George Gray
WELL-DIGGER'S DAUGHTER, THE(1946, Fr.)
Silents
ROAD TO RUIN, THE(1913, Brit.), a, d, w

Geraldine Gray
ISLE OF MISSING MEN(1942)

Gilda Gray
PICCADILLY(1932, Brit.); GREAT ZIEGFELD, THE(1936); ROSE MARIE(1936)
Silents
LAWFUL LARCENY(1923); ALOMA OF THE SOUTH SEAS(1926)
Misc. Silents
CABARET(1927); DEVIL DANCER, THE(1927)

Glenn E. Gray
INDEPENDENCE DAY(1983)

Gloria Gray
WESTERN PACIFIC AGENT(1950)
Misc. Silents
GHETTO SHAMROCK, THE(1926)

Glorian Gray
HOTEL VARIETY(1933)

Gordon Gray
Silents
ARSENE LUPIN(1917)
Misc. Silents
MONEY MILL, THE(1917)

Grania Gray
Silents
ON THE BANKS OF ALLAN WATER(1916, Brit.)

Greta Gray
LADY GODIVA RIDES AGAIN(1955, Brit.)

Harold Gray
LITTLE ORPHAN ANNIE(1932), w; LITTLE ORPHAN ANNIE(1938), w

Harriette Ann Gray
DOWN TO EARTH(1947)

Harry Gray
HALLELUJAH(1929); BLACK KING(1932); RED RIVER VALLEY(1936), m; JOIN THE MARINES(1937), md; COVERED WAGON DAYS(1940), p; RIDIN' DOWN THE CANYON(1942), p

Haskell Gray
ONLY GOD KNOWS(1974, Can.), w

Howard Gray
LOOKIN' TO GET OUT(1982)

Hugh Gray
FOREVER YOURS(1937, Brit.), w; DRUMS(1938, Brit.), w; CONQUEST OF THE AIR(1940), w; TWO FOR DANGER(1940, Brit.), w; KISS THE BLOOD OFF MY HANDS(1948), w; LOVES OF THREE QUEENS, THE(1954, Ital./Fr.), w; ULYSSES(1955, Ital.), w; HELEN OF TROY(1956, Ital), w

Ian Gray
JUST FOR FUN(1963, Brit.); STIR(1980, Aus.)

Jack Gray
LONE WOLF RETURNS, THE(1936); MEN AGAINST THE SKY(1940); QUIET DAY IN BELFAST, A(1974, Can.), w

Jamie Gray
Misc. Silents
MAN ALONE, THE(1923)

Jan Gray
LADY IN THE DEATH HOUSE(1944), m

Jane Gray
Silents
LITTLE GRAY LADY, THE(1914)

Janine Gray
AMERICANIZATION OF EMILY, THE(1964); PUMPKIN EATER, THE(1964, Brit.); QUICK, BEFORE IT MELTS(1964); THIRD DAY, THE(1965); PANIC(1966, Brit.)

Jeanne Gray
FOLLOW THE FLEET(1936)

Jeannie Gray
KID FROM SPAIN, THE(1932)

Jene Gray
SILVER BANDIT, THE(1950)

Jenifer Gray
COME ON, MARINES(1934); SWEETHEARTS(1938); THREE LOVES HAS NANCY(1938); NINOTCHKA(1939)

Jennifer Gray
WHEN TOMORROW COMES(1939); YOU CAN'T CHEAT AN HONEST MAN(1939)

Jenny Gray
FOLIES DERGERE(1935)

Jimmy Gray
FORBIDDEN(1953); LAW AND ORDER(1953)

Joan Gray
Misc. Silents
ROMANCE OF ANNIE LAURIE, THE(1920, Brit.)

Joe Gray
YOU AND ME(1938); GOLDEN BOY(1939); MIRACLE KID(1942); MR. HEX(1946); IT HAD TO BE YOU(1947); FIGHTING FOOLS(1949); FLESH AND FURY(1952); ROBIN AND THE SEVEN HOODS(1964)

Joey Gray
WHIPLASH(1948)

John Gray
LIGHTNING STRIKES TWICE(1935), w; FORTY NAUGHTY GIRLS(1937), w; SNUFFY SMITH, YARD BIRD(1942), w; ROCKIN' IN THE ROCKIES(1945), w; ABANDON SHIP(1957, Brit.); WINTER'S TALE, THE(1968, Brit.); NED KELLY(1970, Brit.); SACCO AND VANZETTI(1971, Ital./Fr.)
Silents
PURSUING VENGEANCE, THE(1916)

Judy Gray
ALIBI, THE(1943, Brit.)

Julie Gray
STRYKER(1983, Phil.)

Ken Gray
ELIZABETH OF LADYMEAD(1949, Brit.), ph

King Gray
WEST OF THE ROCKIES(1931), ph
Silents
RESCUE, THE(1917), ph; AMAZING WIFE, THE(1919), ph; FOOLS OF FORTUNE(1922), ph; TEMPTATION(1923), ph; FLATTERY(1925), ph

King D. Gray
Silents
FLASHLIGHT, THE(1917), ph

Larry Gray
VOYAGE TO THE BOTTOM OF THE SEA(1961)

Lawrence Gray
MARRIAGE BY CONTRACT(1928); MARIANNE(1929); CHILDREN OF PLEASURE(1930); FLORODORA GIRL, THE(1930); IT'S A GREAT LIFE(1930); SPRING IS HERE(1930); SUNNY(1930); GOING WILD(1931); MAN OF THE WORLD(1931); SHE-WOLF, THE(1931); GOLDEN HARVEST(1933); HERE COMES THE GROOM(1934); DANGER AHEAD(1935); OLD HOMESTEAD, THE(1935); DIZZY DAMES(1936); FACE IN THE FOG, A(1936); TIMBER WAR(1936)
Misc. Talkies
TEMPTATION(1930); IN PARIS, A.W.O.L.(1936)
Silents
ARE PARENTS PEOPLE?(1925); AMERICAN VENUS, THE(1926); KID BOOTS(1926); UNTAMED LADY, THE(1926); AFTER MIDNIGHT(1927); ANKLES PREFERRED(1927); CALLAHANS AND THE MURPHYS, THE(1927); CONVOY(1927); LADIES MUST DRESS(1927); PAJAMAS(1927); TELEPHONE GIRL, THE(1927); OH, KAY(1928); SHADOWS OF THE NIGHT(1928); SIN SISTER, THE(1929)
Misc. Silents
STAGE STRUCK(1925); EVERYBODY'S ACTING(1926); LOVE 'EM AND LEAVE 'EM(1926); PALM BEACH GIRL, THE(1926); DOMESTIC MEDDLERS(1928); LOVE HUNGRY(1928); MARRIAGE BY CONRACT(1928); RAINBOW, THE(1929)

Lenore Gray
Silents
DREAM MELODY, THE(1929), w

Leo Gray
NIGHTMARE ALLEY(1947)

Leo Z. Gray
WHITE TIE AND TAILS(1946)

Linda Gray
STAGE DOOR(1937); STELLA DALLAS(1937); SHADOWS OVER SHANGHAI(1938); NIGHT WAS OUR FRIEND(1951, Brit.); PICKWICK PAPERS, THE(1952, Brit.); INBETWEEN AGE, THE(1958, Brit.); DARK PLACES(1974, Brit.); THAT LUCKY TOUCH(1975, Brit.); DOGS(1976)

Lisa Gray
MILLION EYES OF SU-MURU, THE(1967, Brit.)
Silents
METROPOLIS(1927, Ger.)

Lorna Gray
ADVENTURE IN SAHARA(1938); MAN THEY COULD NOT HANG, THE(1939); MR. SMITH GOES TO WASHINGTON(1939); SMASHING THE SPY RING(1939); BULLETS FOR RUSTLERS(1940); CONVICTED WOMAN(1940); DRUMS OF THE DESERT(1940); TUXEDO JUNCTION(1941); RIDIN' DOWN THE CANYON(1942); O, MY DARLING CLEMENTINE(1943); SO PROUDLY WE HAIL(1943); GIRL WHO DARED, THE(1944); FASHION MODEL(1945)
Misc. Talkies
CITY LIMITS(1941); FATHER STEPS OUT(1941)

Lorna Gray [Adrian Booth]
RED RIVER RANGE(1938); STRANGER FROM TEXAS, THE(1940)
Louis Gray
LONE STAR RAIDERS(1940), p; GANGS OF SONORA(1941), p; OUTLAWS OF THE CHEROKEE TRAIL(1941), p; PALS OF THE PECOS(1941), p; PRAIRIE PIONEERS(1941), p; SADDLEMATES(1941), p; WEST OF CIMARRON(1941), p; CODE OF THE OUTLAW(1942), p; PHANTOM PLAINSMEN, THE(1942), p; RAIDERS OF THE RANGE(1942), p; SHADOWS ON THE SAGE(1942), p; VALLEY OF HUNTED MEN(1942), p; WESTWARD HO(1942), p; BEYOND THE LAST FRONTIER(1943), p; OVERLAND MAIL ROBBERY(1943), p; RAIDERS OF SUNSET PASS(1943), p; RIDERS OF THE RIO GRANDE(1943), p; SANTA FE SCOUTS(1943), p; THUNDERING TRAILS(1943), p; WAGON TRACKS WEST(1943), p; BENEATH WESTERN SKIES(1944), p; CHEYENNE WILDCAT(1944), p; FIREBRANDS OF ARIZONA(1944), p; HIDDEN VALLEY OUTLAWS(1944), p; LARAMIE TRAIL, THE(1944), p; MARSHAL OF RENO(1944), p; PRIDE OF THE PLAINS(1944), p; GREAT STAGECOACH ROBBERY(1945), p; LONE TEXAS RANGER(1945), p; MAN FROM OKLAHOMA, THE(1945), p; SUNSET IN EL DORADO(1945), p; HOME ON THE RANGE(1946), p; MAN FROM RAINBOW VALLEY, THE(1946), p; OUT CALIFORNIA WAY(1946), p; LAST FRONTIER UPRISING(1947), p; COURTIN' TROUBLE(1948), p; COWBOY CAVALIER(1948), p; CROSSED TRAILS(1948), p; OKLAHOMA BLUES(1948), p; OUTLAW BRAND(1948), p; PARTNERS OF THE SUNSET(1948), p; RANGE RENEGADES(1948), p; RANGERS RIDE, THE(1948), p; SILVER TRAILS(1948), p; SONG OF THE DRIFTER(1948), p; ACROSS THE RIO GRANDE(1949), p; BRAND OF FEAR(1949), p; GUN LAW JUSTICE(1949), p; GUN RUNNER(1949), p; LAWLESS CODE(1949), p; ROARING WESTWARD(1949), p
Lucille Gray
CURE FOR LOVE, THE(1950, Brit.)
Lynn Gray
SOUND OF FURY, THE(1950)
Mack Gray
CAR 99(1935); GLASS KEY, THE(1935); RUMBA(1935); SHE COULDN'T TAKE IT(1935); EXCLUSIVE(1937); NIGHT CLUB SCANDAL(1937); EACH DAWN I DIE(1939); I STOLE A MILLION(1939); INVITATION TO HAPPINESS(1939); SUDDEN MONEY(1939); HOUSE ACROSS THE BAY, THE(1940); INVISIBLE STRIPES(1940); THEY DRIVE BY NIGHT(1940); MEET JOHN DOE(1941); BROADWAY(1942); STAGE DOOR CANTEEN(1943); FOLLOW THE BOYS(1944); JOHNNY ANGEL(1945); NOCTURNE(1946); RACE STREET(1948); DANGEROUS PROFESSION, A(1949); TAKE ME OUT TO THE BALL GAME(1949); RHUBARB(1951); WHO'S GOT THE ACTION?(1962)
Madeline Gray
NOTHING BUT THE TRUTH(1929)
Maralou Gray
PIRATES OF TRIPOLI(1955); SECRET FILE: HOLLYWOOD(1962); DAY OF THE NIGHTMARE(1965)
Margaret Gray
Silents
ARIZONA CYCLONE(1928); BULLET MARK, THE(1928)
Margery Gray
RAGGEDY ANN AND ANDY(1977); HEIDI'S SONG(1982)
Marian Gray
CASANOVA BROWN(1944)
Marilyn Gray
VARIETY GIRL(1947); NIGHT HAS A THOUSAND EYES(1948)
Marion Gray
NIGHT AND DAY(1946); LET'S DANCE(1950); PLACE IN THE SUN, A(1951); SEARCH FOR BRIDEY MURPHY, THE(1956)
Martin Gray
OUT OF IT(1969)
Maxwell Gray
Silents
SEALED LIPS(1915), w
Michael Gray
OUR TIME(1974)
Mike Gray
CHINA SYNDROME, THE(1979), w; WAVELENGTH(1983), d&w
Minna Gray
Misc. Silents
DANGEROUS LIES(1921, Brit.)
Mora Gray
SEVEN MINUTES, THE(1971); MY TUTOR(1983)
Nadia Gray
CROOKED ROAD, THE(; MONSEIGNEUR(1950, Fr.); SPIDER AND THE FLY, THE(1952, Brit.); VALLEY OF EAGLES(1952, Brit.); MR. POTTS GOES TO MOSCOW(1953, Brit.); NIGHT WITHOUT STARS(1953, Brit.); CENTO ANNI D'AMORE(1954, Ital.); CROSSED SWORDS(1954); MELODY OF LOVE(1954, Ital.); FOLIES BERGERE(1958, Fr.); LA PARISIENNE(1958, Fr./Ital.); CAPTAIN'S TABLE, THE(1960, Brit.); GAME OF TRUTH, THE(1961, Fr.); LA DOLCE VITA(1961, Ital./Fr.); NEOPOLITAN CAROUSEL(1961, Ital.); VIOLENT SUMMER(1961, Fr./Ital.); CANDIDE(1962, Fr.); I LIKE MONEY(1962, Brit.); MANIAC(1963, Brit.); ENCOUNTERS IN SALZBURG(1964, Ger.); THUNDER AT THE BORDER(1966, Ger./Yugo.); NAKED RUNNER, THE(1967, Brit.); TWO FOR THE ROAD(1967, Brit.); OLDEST PROFESSION, THE(1968, Fr./Ital./Ger.)
Misc. Silents
SILVER KING, THE(1919)
Nan Gray
BABBITT(1934); FIREBIRD, THE(1934); MARY JANE'S PA(1935); CRASH DONOVAN(1936); DRACULA'S DAUGHTER(1936)
Nancy Gray
MORE THE MERRIER, THE(1943)
Noel Gray
THERE GOES THE BRIDE(1933, Brit.), w, m
Olga Gray
Silents
LITTLE LIAR, THE(1916)
Misc. Silents
FAILURE, THE(1915)
Paul Gray
AROUND THE WORLD UNDER THE SEA(1966)

Comdr. Paul N. Gray, USN
MEN OF THE FIGHTING LADY(1954), tech adv
Perry Gray
YES, GIORGIO(1982), set d
Peter Gray
DIANE(1955); HOUSE OF BAMBOO(1955); SCARLET HOUR, THE(1956); STEEL JUNGLE, THE(1956); SKIN GAME, THE(1965, Brit.)
Phil Gray
NEW YORK, NEW YORK(1977)
R. Henry Gray
Misc. Silents
MENTIONED IN CONFIDENCE(1917)
Randy Gray
TRUCK TURNER(1974)
Ray Gray
Misc. Silents
DOWN ON THE FARM(1920), d
Raymond Gray
IRON MAN, THE(1951)
Richard Gray
SING AS WE GO(1934, Brit.); WHAT HAPPENED THEN?(1934, Brit.); YOU'RE IN THE ARMY NOW(1937, Brit.)
Richard G. Gray
HIS FIGHTING BLOOD(1935), ed
Robert Gray
LITTLE AUSTRALIANS(1940, Aus.); LADY FROM SHANGHAI, THE(1948); TIME OF THE HEATHEN(1962), md; BORN AGAIN(1978)
1984
ADVENTURES OF BUCKAROO BANZAI: ACROSS THE 8TH DIMENSION, THE(1984)
Misc. Silents
RED VIRGIN, THE(1915); FLIGHT OF THE DUCHESS, THE(1916)
Roger Gray
HIT THE DECK(1930); FOOTLIGHT PARADE(1933); MERRY WIDOW, THE(1934); WE LIVE AGAIN(1934); BARBARY COAST(1935); NAUGHTY MARIETTA(1935); EVERYMAN'S LAW(1936); FURY(1936); LONE WOLF RETURNS, THE(1936); CAPTAINS COURAGEOUS(1937); DOUBLE WEDDING(1937); OH, SUSANNA(1937); PROFESSOR BEWARE(1938); REBELLION(1938); SWING YOUR LADY(1938); YOU AND ME(1938); DISPUTED PASSAGE(1939); LADY'S FROM KENTUCKY, THE(1939); ADVENTURE IN DIAMONDS(1940); ANGELS OVER BROADWAY(1940); MY SON IS GUILTY(1940); OUT WEST WITH THE PEPPERS(1940); ROAD TO SINGAPORE(1940); WESTERNER, THE(1940); PINTO KID, THE(1941); YOU BELONG TO ME(1941); PARDON MY GUN(1942); REDHEAD FROM MANHATTAN(1954)
Safly Gray
CAFE COLETTE(1937, Brit.)
Sally Gray
CHECKMATE(1935, Brit,); CROSS CURRENTS(1935, Brit.); LUCKY DAYS(1935, Brit.); CALLING THE TUNE(1936, Brit.); CHEER UP!(1936, Brit.); OVER SHE GOES(1937, Brit.); SATURDAY NIGHT REVUE(1937, Brit.); HOLD MY HAND(1938, Brit.); LIGHTNING CONDUCTOR(1938, Brit.); SWORD OF HONOUR(1938, Brit.); HONEYMOON MERRY-GO-ROUND(1939, Brit.); SAINT IN LONDON, THE(1939, Brit.); LAMBETH WALK, THE(1940, Brit.); MYSTERY OF ROOM 13(1941, Brit.); SAINT'S VACATION, THE(1941, Brit.); LADY IN DISTRESS(1942, Brit.); SUICIDE SQUADRON(1942, Brit.); CARNIVAL(1946, Brit.); GREEN FOR DANGER(1946, Brit.); I BECAME A CRIMINAL(1947); MARK OF CAIN, THE(1948, Brit.); HIDDEN ROOM, THE(1949, Brit.); SILENT DUST(1949, Brit.); I'LL GET YOU(1953, Brit.); KEEPER, THE(1976, Can.)
Sam Gray
SENTINEL, THE(1977); YOU BETTER WATCH OUT(1980); WOLFEN(1981); HANKY-PANKY(1982); LITTLE SEX, A(1982)
Sandra Gray
TO BE OR NOT TO BE(1983)
Shirley Gray
PHANTOM SHIP(1937, Brit.)
Simon Gray
BUTLEY(1974, Brit.), w
Spalding Gray
COWARDS(1970)
1984
ALMOST YOU(1984); HARD CHOICES(1984); KILLING FIELDS, THE(1984, Brit.); VARIETY(1984)
Stella Gray [Grace La Rue]
Misc. Silents
THAT'S GOOD(1919)
Stephen Gray
GARDEN OF EDEN(1954); HAPPY HOOKER GOES TO HOLLYWOOD, THE(1980), ph; FIGHTING BACK(1983, Brit.)
Silents
JOAN THE WOMAN(1916)
Stephen W. Gray
SAVANNAH SMILES(1983), ph
Tamu Gray
1984
PRODIGAL, THE(1984)
Thomas J. Gray
Silents
HOT WATER(1924), w
Tommy Gray
Silents
GIRL SHY(1924), w
Veleka Gray
I LOVE MY WIFE(1970)
Vernon Gray
DAY TO REMEMBER, A(1953, Brit.); GOLD EXPRESS, THE(1955, Brit.); TO PARIS WITH LOVE(1955, Brit.); NOW AND FOREVER(1956, Brit.); BARRETTS OF WIMPOLE STREET, THE(1957)
Vickie Gray
NAKED FURY(1959, Brit.)

Vivean Gray
LIBIDO(1973, Aus.); PICNIC AT HANGING ROCK(1975, Aus.); LAST WAVE, THE(1978, Aus.)

William Gray
UNTAMED(1929), ed; SPORTING BLOOD(1931), ed; DIVORCE IN THE FAMILY(1932), ed; CHIEF, THE(1933), ed; MEN MUST FIGHT(1933), ed; TOMB OF TORTURE(1966, Ital.); LAST MOVIE, THE(1971); HARD PART BEGINS, THE(1973, Can.), ed; HOWZER(1973); BLOOD AND GUTS(1978, Can.), w, ed; PROM NIGHT(1980), w; EYE FOR AN EYE, AN(1981), w; HUMONGOUS(1982, Can.), w; CROSS COUNTRY(1983, Can.), w
1984
PHILADELPHIA EXPERIMENT, THE(1984), w

William S. Gray
MADAME X(1929), ed; VOICE OF THE CITY(1929), ed; WAY OUT WEST(1930), ed; FLYING HIGH(1931), ed; GENTLEMAN'S FATE(1931), ed; POLITICS(1931), ed; FLESH(1932), ed; NEW MORALS FOR OLD(1932), ed; PASSIONATE PLUMBER(1932), ed; UNASHAMED(1932), ed; BROADWAY TO HOLLYWOOD(1933), ed; MADE ON BROADWAY(1933), ed; MIDNIGHT MARY(1933), ed; FUGITIVE LOVERS(1934), ed; MURDER IN THE PRIVATE CAR(1934), ed; SHOW-OFF, THE(1934), ed; STRAIGHT IS THE WAY(1934), ed; BABY FACE HARRINGTON(1935), ed; BIOGRAPHY OF A BACHELOR GIRL(1935), ed; IT'S IN THE AIR(1935), ed; GREAT ZIEGFELD, THE(1936), ed; PICCADILLY JIM(1936), ed; SINNER TAKE ALL(1936), ed; MAN OF THE PEOPLE(1937), ed; MARRIED BEFORE BREAKFAST(1937), ed; MY DEAR MISS ALDRICH(1937), ed; EVERYBODY SING(1938), ed

Willoughby Gray
MARK OF CAIN, THE(1948, Brit.); GUILT IS MY SHADOW(1950, Brit.); SHADOW OF THE PAST(1950, Brit.); HER PANELLED DOOR(1951, Brit.); MR. POTTS GOES TO MOSCOW(1953, Brit.); STRANGER FROM VENUS, THE(1954, Brit.); RICHARD III(1956, Brit.); MUMMY, THE(1959, Brit.); MAN OUTSIDE, THE(1968, Brit.); WATERLOO(1970, Ital./USSR), a, cons; YOUNG WINSTON(1972, Brit.); GAMEKEEPER, THE(1980, Brit.); ABSOLUTION(1981, Brit.)

Zella Gray
Silents
TAKING CHANCES(1922); TIPPED OFF(1923)

Rev. Duncan Gray, Jr.
HOME FROM THE HILL(1960)

Dan Grayam
LOOK IN ANY WINDOW(1961)

Paul Grayber
SHEBA BABY(1975)

Helen Grayco
CHA-CHA-CHA BOOM(1956)

Richard Grayden
WICKED WIFE(1955, Brit.)

Richard Graydon
STORY OF ROBIN HOOD, THE(1952, Brit.); ON HER MAJESTY'S SECRET SERVICE(1969, Brit.); LAST VALLEY, THE(1971, Brit.); INTERNATIONAL VELVET(1978, Brit.), stunts; FFOLKES(1980, Brit.); EYE OF THE NEEDLE(1981); OCTOPUSSY(1983, Brit.)

Diana Grayf
JOYRIDE(1977)

Peter Grayford
SINGAPORE, SINGAPORE(1969, Fr./Ital.)

Sydney Grayler
INVISIBLE KILLER, THE(1940)

Barbara Grayley
TIME IS MY ENEMY(1957, Brit.)

Richard Ford Grayling
EVEL KNIEVEL(1971); SIMON, KING OF THE WITCHES(1971)

Ernest Grayman
Silents
EYES RIGHT(1926), w

John Graysmark
WALKING STICK, THE(1970, Brit.), art d; DEVIL'S WIDOW, THE(1972, Brit.), art d; YOUNG WINSTON(1972, Brit.), art d; MAN WITH THE GOLDEN GUN, THE(1974, Brit.), art d; BIG SLEEP, THE½(1978, Brit.), art d; ESCAPE TO ATHENA(1979, Brit.), art d; FLASH GORDON(1980), art d; RAGTIME(1981), prod d; FIREFOX(1982), art d; LORDS OF DISCIPLINE, THE(1983), prod d
1984
BOUNTY, THE(1984), prod d

Ambrose Grayson
DICK BARTON STRIKES BACK(1949, Brit.), w; DR. MORELLE–THE CASE OF THE MISSING HEIRESS(1949, Brit.), w; DICK BARTON AT BAY(1950, Brit.), w

Charles Grayson
CRASH DONOVAN(1936), w; BREEZING HOME(1937), w; MAN WHO CRIED WOLF, THE(1937), w; MIGHTY TREVE, THE(1937), w; TOP OF THE TOWN(1937), w; WE HAVE OUR MOMENTS(1937), w; YOU'RE A SWEETHEART(1937), w; FRESHMAN YEAR(1938), w; PERSONAL SECRETARY(1938), w; RECKLESS LIVING(1938), w; STRANGE FACES(1938), w; SWING, SISTER, SWING(1938), w; SWING THAT CHEER(1938), w; YOUNG FUGITIVES(1938), w; FOR LOVE OR MONEY(1939), w; HAWAIIAN NIGHTS(1939), w; NEWSBOY'S HOME(1939), w; RISKY BUSINESS(1939), w; UNEXPECTED FATHER(1939), w; ALIAS THE DEACON(1940), w; BOYS FROM SYRACUSE(1940), w; DOUBLE ALIBI(1940), w; MA, HE'S MAKING EYES AT ME(1940), w; ONE NIGHT IN THE TROPICS(1940), w; PRIVATE AFFAIRS(1940), w; SANDY IS A LADY(1940), w; BAD MEN OF MISSOURI(1941), w; LAW OF THE TROPICS(1941), w; SHE COULDN'T SAY NO(1941), w; THIEVES FALL OUT(1941), w; UNDERGROUND(1941), w; WILD BILL HICKOK RIDES(1942), w; MUG TOWN(1943), w; OUTPOST IN MOROCCO(1949), w; WOMAN ON PIER 13, THE(1950), w; WILD BLUE YONDER, THE(1952), w; BATTLE HYMN(1957), w; BARBARIAN AND THE GEISHA, THE(1958), w

Dave Grayson
SMART WOMAN(1948), makeup; RED STALLION IN THE ROCKIES(1949), makeup; WALKING HILLS, THE(1949), makeup; WAR WAGON, THE(1967), makeup; GREEN BERETS, THE(1968), makeup; MITCHELL(1975), cos

David Grayson
HOOK, THE(1962), makeup; RIO LOBO(1970), makeup; TRAIN ROBBERS, THE(1973), makeup

Diane Grayson
PRIME OF MISS JEAN BRODIE, THE(1969, Brit.); SEE NO EVIL(1971, Brit.)

Donald Grayson
DODGE CITY TRAIL(1937); OLD WYOMING TRAIL, THE(1937); CALL OF THE ROCKIES(1938); CATTLE RAIDERS(1938); OUTLAWS OF THE PRAIRIE(1938)

Elizabeth Grayson
Misc. Silents
VENGEANCE OF NANA(1915, Brit.)

Eunice Grayson
DOWN AMONG THE Z MEN(1952, Brit.); BOTH SIDES OF THE LAW(1953, Brit.)

Garth Grayson
Silents
GIRL FROM DOWNING STREET, THE(1918, Brit.), w

Gayle Grayson
CHARRIOTS OF FIRE(1981, Brit.)

Genice Grayson
PRINCESS OF THE NILE(1954)

Geoffrey Grayson
WOMAN'S TEMPTATION, A(1959, Brit.), d

Godfrey Grayson
SHE COULDN'T SAY NO(1939, Brit.), d; ADVENTURES OF PC 49, THE(1949, Brit.), d; DICK BARTON STRIKES BACK(1949, Brit.), d; DR. MORELLE–THE CASE OF THE MISSING HEIRESS(1949, Brit.), d; MEET SIMON CHERRY(1949, Brit.), d, w; ROOM TO LET(1949, Brit.), d, w; DICK BARTON AT BAY(1950, Brit.), d; WHAT THE BUTLER SAW(1950, Brit.), d; TO HAVE AND TO HOLD(1951, Brit.), d; FAKE, THE(1953, Brit.), d; BLACK ICE, THE(1957, Brit.), d; HIGH JUMP(1959, Brit.), d; HONOURABLE MURDER, AN(1959, Brit.), d; INNOCENT MEETING(1959, Brit.), d; DATE AT MIDNIGHT(1960, Brit.), d; ESCORT FOR HIRE(1960, Brit.), d; SPIDER'S WEB, THE(1960, Brit.), d; PURSUERS, THE(1961, Brit.), d; SO EVIL SO YOUNG(1961, Brit.), d; BATTLEAXE, THE(1962, Brit.), d; DESIGN FOR LOVING(1962, Brit.), d; DURANT AFFAIR, THE(1962, Brit.), d; LAMP IN ASSASSIN MEWS, THE(1962, Brit.), d; SHE ALWAYS GETS THEIR MAN(1962, Brit.), d

Hal Grayson
NIGHT WORLD(1932), md

Jerry Grayson
WILD ON THE BEACH(1965)
1984
LONELY GUY, THE(1984)

Jessica Grayson
LITTLE FOXES, THE(1941)

Jessie Grayson
ONE DARK NIGHT(1939); SYNCOPATION(1942); CLAUDIA(1943); YOUNGEST PROFESSION, THE(1943); WILSON(1944); TOMORROW IS FOREVER(1946); CASS TIMBERLANE(1947); HOMECOMING(1948); OUR VERY OWN(1950)

John Grayson
TEAHOUSE OF THE AUGUST MOON, THE(1956)

Kathryn Grayson
ANDY HARDY'S PRIVATE SECRETARY(1941); VANISHING VIRGINIAN, THE(1941); RIO RITA(1942); SEVEN SWEETHEARTS(1942); THOUSANDS CHEER(1943); ANCHORS AWEIGH(1945); TILL THE CLOUDS ROLL BY(1946); TWO SISTERS FROM BOSTON(1946); IT HAPPENED IN BROOKLYN(1947); KISSING BANDIT, THE(1948); THAT MIDNIGHT KISS(1949); GROUNDS FOR MARRIAGE(1950); TOAST OF NEW ORLEANS, THE(1950); SHOW BOAT(1951); LOVELY TO LOOK AT(1952); DESERT SONG, THE(1953); KISS ME KATE(1953); SO THIS IS LOVE(1953); VAGABOND KING, THE(1956)

Kurt Grayson
MIDWAY(1976); FURTHER ADVENTURES OF THE WILDERNESS FAMILY–PART TWO(1978); OCTAGON, THE(1980)

Laura Grayson
PATERNITY(1981); LOVE AND MONEY(1982)

Madelon Grayson
GIRLS OF THE ROAD(1940); GLAMOUR FOR SALE(1940)

Mattie Grayson
1984
MAKING THE GRADE(1984)

Richard Grayson
CHAIN OF CIRCUMSTANCE(1951); EIGHT IRON MEN(1952); DOWN AMONG THE SHELTERING PALMS(1953); LILI(1953)

Shirley Grayson
RUN ACROSS THE RIVER(1961)

Victoria Grayson
ANOTHER SKY(1960 Brit.)

Wendy Grayson
Misc. Talkies
SECTOR 13(1982)

Brian Grazer
NIGHT SHIFT(1982), p
1984
SPLASH(1984), p, w

Bruce Graziano
CHRISTIAN LICORICE STORE, THE(1971)

Rocky Graziano
MISTER ROCK AND ROLL(1957); COUNTRY MUSIC HOLIDAY(1958); TEENAGE MILLIONAIRE(1961); TONY ROME(1967); NEW LIFE STYLE, THE(1970, Ger.)

Aldo Graziati
MIRACLE IN MILAN(1951, Ital.), ph

Aldo Graziati [G.R. Aldo]
UMBERTO D(1955, Ital.), ph; SENSO(1968, Ital.), ph

Enrico Grazioli
RATATAPLAN(1979, Ital.)

Franco Graziosi
DUCK, YOU SUCKER!(1972, Ital.); DEAF SMITH AND JOHNNY EARS(1973, Ital.)

Giorgio Graziosi
SIEGE OF SYRACUSE(1962, Fr./Ital.), w

Paolo Graziosi
CHINA IS NEAR(1968, Ital.); GALILEO(1968, Ital./Bul.)

Giorgio Grazlosi
ANTHONY OF PADUA(1952, Ital.), w

Mike Grazzo
BODY AND SOUL(1981)
Kresko Grcevic
RAT(1960, Yugo.), ph
Beatrice Greack
MORE THAN A MIRACLE(1967, Ital./Fr.)
Leon Greanin
TOAST TO LOVE(1951, Mex.)
Geraine Grear [Joan Barclay]
42ND STREET(1933)
Peter the Great
Misc. Silents
SIGN OF THE CLAW, THE(1926)
The Great Antonio
QUEST FOR FIRE(1982, Fr./Can.)
The Great John L
VENGEANCE(1964)
The Great John "L"
ISLAND OF DR. MOREAU, THE(1977)
the Great Velardi
EVERYBODY'S DANCIN'(1950)
the Greater Liberty Baptist Church Choir and Congregation
HARD TIMES(1975)
Wilfred Greatorex
HIGH COMMISSIONER, THE(1968, U.S./Brit.), w; BATTLE OF BRITAIN,
THE(1969, Brit.), w
Richard Greatrex
1984
ADERYN PAPUR(1984, Brit.), ph
Doc Greaves
DESERTER, THE(1971 Ital./Yugo.)
F.L. Greaves
STATUE, THE(1971, Brit.)
Fielding Greaves
RAGE(1972)
1984
RACING WITH THE MOON(1984)
Kristoffer Greaves
ROAD WARRIOR, THE(1982, Aus.)
Nigel Greaves
MEETINGS WITH REMARKABLE MEN(1979, Brit.)
William Greaves
MIRACLE IN HARLEM(1948); LOST BOUNDARIES(1949)
Misc. Talkies
FIGHT NEVER ENDS, THE(1947); SOULS OF SIN(1949)
Walter Greaza
13 RUE MADELEINE(1946); BOOMERANG(1947); CALL NORTHSIDE 777(1948);
LARCENY(1948); STREET WITH NO NAME, THE(1948); GREAT GATSBY,
THE(1949); NEW MEXICO(1951); IT HAPPENED TO JANE(1959)
Joe Greb
FIGHTING FOOLS(1949); HARDER THEY FALL, THE(1956)
Stevan Grebel
LOVERS OF TERUEL, THE(1962, Fr.)
Lewis Greber
TARZAN AND THE LEOPARD WOMAN(1946), art d
William J. Greber
ISLANDS IN THE STREAM(1977), prod d
N. Grebeshkova
DEVOTION(1955, USSR)
Nina Grebeshkova
MUMU(1961, USSR)
G. Grebner
LOSS OF FEELING(1935, USSR), w; GENERAL SUVOROV(1941, USSR), w
Georgi Grebner
ADVENTURE IN ODESSA(1954, USSR), w
Hilde Grebner
GREH(1962, Ger./Yugo.), ed
Jay Grecco
SHADOWS(1960)
German Grech
FINGER ON THE TRIGGER(1965, US/Span.); ROMEO AND JULIET(1968, Ital./
Span.)
A. Grechhany
BALLAD OF COSSACK GLOOTA(1938, USSR)
Aldo Greci
DEVIL'S MAN, THE(1967, Ital.), ph
Jose Greci
BEN HUR(1959); DUEL OF THE TITANS(1963, Ital.); REBEL GLADIATORS,
THE(1963, Ital.); GOLIATH AND THE SINS OF BABYLON(1964, Ital.)
Anthony Greco
NOTHING PERSONAL(1980, Can.), set d
1984
JUST THE WAY YOU ARE(1984), set d
Arthur Greco
FEVER HEAT(1968)
Betty Greco
ROAD DEMON(1938); WINNER TAKE ALL(1939); ONE MILLION B.C.(1940); TO-
MORROW IS FOREVER(1946); SPY HUNT(1950)
Buddy Greco
GIRL WHO KNEW TOO MUCH, THE(1969)
Corsetta Greco
FOUR WAYS OUT(1954, Ital.)
Cosetta Greco
NAPOLEON(1955, Fr.); DREAMS IN A DRAWER(1957, Fr./Ital.)
Debi Greco
1984
CANNONBALL RUN II(1984)

Ferdinando Greco
THREE BROTHERS(1982, Ital.)
Helen Greco
THAT CERTAIN AGE(1938)
Jena Greco
DANIEL(1983)
Joe Greco
PRIME TIME, THE(1960)
Jose Greco
MANOLETE(1950, Span.); SOMBRERO(1953), a, ch; AROUND THE WORLD IN 80
DAYS(1956); HOLIDAY FOR LOVERS(1959); SHIP OF FOOLS(1965); PROUD AND
THE DAMNED, THE(1972)
Misc. Talkies
REVENGE OF THE GLADIATORS(1962)
Juliette Greco
ORPHEUS(1950, Fr.); GREEN GLOVE, THE(1952); PARIS DOES STRANGE
THINGS(1957, Fr./Ital.); SUN ALSO RISES, THE(1957); BONJOUR TRISTESSE(1958);
NAKED EARTH, THE(1958, Brit.); ROOTS OF HEAVEN, THE(1958); WHIRL-
POOL(1959, Brit.); CRACK IN THE MIRROR(1960); BIG GAMBLE, THE(1961);
WHERE THE TRUTH LIES(1962, Fr.); NIGHT OF THE GENERALS, THE(1967,
Brit./Fr.); UNCLE TOM'S CABIN(1969, Fr./Ital./Ger./Yugo.)
Kristine Greco
COACH(1978)
Marcell Greco
SHEPHERD OF THE HILLS, THE(1964), ed
Mary Greco
GENERALE DELLA ROVERE(1960, Ital./Fr.)
Paul Greco
WARRIORS, THE(1979)
1984
BROADWAY DANNY ROSE(1984)
Suzanne Greco
THREES, MENAGE A TROIS(1968)
Alexandre Grecq
UP FROM THE BEACH(1965)
Torry Gredsted
LURE OF THE JUNGLE, THE(1970, Den.), w
Jean- Pierre Gredy
FORTY CARATS(1973), w
Geraine Greear
Silents
GAUCHO, THE(1928)
David Allen Greeene
COME BACK BABY(1968), m
Jessy Greek
SINGAPORE, SINGAPORE(1969, Fr./Ital.)
Evelyn Greeley
Silents
SECOND IN COMMAND, THE(1915); LOVE IN A HURRY(1919); OAKDALE AF-
FAIR, THE(1919); DIANE OF STAR HOLLOW(1921); JUST A SONG AT TWI-
LIGHT(1922); BULLDOG DRUMMOND(1923, Brit.)
Misc. Silents
(; TEMPEST AND SUNSHINE(1916); BURGLAR, THE(1917); GOOD FOR NOTHING,
THE(1917); PRICE OF PRIDE, THE(1917); BEAUTIFUL MRS. REYNOLDS, THE(1918);
BELOVED BLACKMAILER, THE(1918); BY HOOK OR CROOK(1918); HIS ROYAL
HIGHNESS(1918); HITTING THE TRAIL(1918); ROAD TO FRANCE, THE(1918);
BRINGING UP BETTY(1919); HIT OR MISS(1919); ME AND CAPTAIN KID(1919);
PHIL-FOR-SHORT(1919); THREE GREEN EYES(1919); HIS GREATEST SAC-
RIFICE(1921); PASTEBOARD CROWN, A(1922)
George Greeley
PEACEMAKER, THE(1956), m
Evelyn Greely
Silents
LEAP TO FAME(1918)
Philip Greem
TOUCH OF LARCENY, A(1960, Brit.), m
Green
JOHNNY TIGER(1966), md
Adolph Green
GOOD NEWS(1947), w; BARKLEYS OF BROADWAY, THE(1949), w; ON THE
TOWN(1949), w; SINGIN' IN THE RAIN(1952), w; BAND WAGON, THE(1953), w; IT'S
ALWAYS FAIR WEATHER(1955), w; AUNTIE MAME(1958), w; BELLS ARE RING-
ING(1960), w, m; WHAT A WAY TO GO(1964), w; SIMON(1980); MY FAVORITE
YEAR(1982)
1984
GARBO TALKS(1984)
Al Green
RESURRECTION(1931), ph; PRIDE OF ST. LOUIS, THE(1952); KID FROM LEFT
FIELD, THE(1953); PUTNEY SWOPE(1969)
Misc. Silents
LITTLE LOST SISTER(1917), d; PRINCESS OF PATCHES, THE(1917), d
Al M. Green
EVANGELINE(1929), ph
Silents
RAMONA(1928), ph; EVANGELINE(1929), ph
Alan Green
LOVE ON THE RUN(1936), w; LONG WAIT, THE(1954), w
Alex Green
CHRISTINA(1974, Can.)
Alfred Green
I LOVED A WOMAN(1933), d; FLOWING GOLD(1940), d
Silents
JUST OUT OF COLLEGE(1921), d
Misc. Silents
LAD AND THE LION, THE(1917), d; DOUBLE-DYED DECIEVER, A(1920), d; MAN
WHO HAD EVERYTHING, THE(1920), d; BACHELOR DADDY, THE(1922), d
Alfred D. Green
TARS AND SPARS(1946), d

Alfred E. Green
DISRAELI(1929), d; MAKING THE GRADE(1929), d; GREEN GODDESS, THE(1930), d; MAN FROM BLANKLEY'S, THE(1930), d; OLD ENGLISH(1930), d; SWEET KITTY BELLAIRS(1930), d; MEN OF THE SKY(1931), d; ROAD TO SINGAPORE(1931), d; SMART MONEY(1931), d; DARK HORSE, THE(1932), d; IT'S TOUGH TO BE FAMOUS(1932), d; RICH ARE ALWAYS WITH US, THE(1932), d; SILVER DOLLAR(1932), d; UNION DEPOT(1932), d; BABY FACE(1933), d; NARROW CORNER, THE(1933), d; PARACHUTE JUMPER(1933), d; AS THE EARTH TURNS(1934), d; DARK HAZARD(1934), d; GENTLEMEN ARE BORN(1934), d; HOUSEWIFE(1934), d; LOST LADY, A(1934), d; MERRY FRINKS, THE(1934), d; SIDE STREETS(1934), d; GIRL FROM TENTH AVENUE, THE(1935), d; GOOSE AND THE GANDER, THE(1935), d; HERE'S TO ROMANCE(1935), d; SWEET MUSIC(1935), d; COLLEEN(1936), d; DANGEROUS(1936), d; GOLDEN ARROW, THE(1936), d; MORE THAN A SECRETARY(1936), d; THEY MET IN A TAXI(1936), d, w; TWO IN A CROWD(1936), d; LEAGUE OF FRIGHTENED MEN(1937), d; LET'S GET MARRIED(1937), d; MR. DODD TAKES THE AIR(1937), d; THOROUGHBREDS DON'T CRY(1937), d; DUKE OF WEST POINT, THE(1938), d; RIDE A CROOKED MILE(1938), d; KING OF THE TURF(1939), d; 20,000 MEN A YEAR(1939), d; EAST OF THE RIVER(1940), d; SHOOTING HIGH(1940), d; SOUTH OF PAGO PAGO(1940), d; ADVENTURE IN WASHINGTON(1941), d; BADLANDS OF DAKOTA(1941), d; MAYOR OF 44TH STREET, THE(1942), d; MEET THE STEWARTS(1942), d; APPOINTMENT IN BERLIN(1943), d; THERE'S SOMETHING ABOUT A SOLDIER(1943), d; MR. WINKLE GOES TO WAR(1944), d; STRANGE AFFAIR(1944), d; THOUSAND AND ONE NIGHTS, A(1945), d; JOLSON STORY, THE(1946), d; COPACABANA(1947), d; FABULOUS DORSEYS, THE(1947), d; FOUR FACES WEST(1948), d; GIRL FROM MANHATTAN(1948), d; COVER-UP(1949), d; JACKIE ROBINSON STORY, THE(1950), d; SIERRA(1950), d; TWO GALS AND A GUY(1951), d; INVASION U.S.A.(1952), d; EDDIE CANTOR STORY, THE(1953), d; PARIS MODEL(1953), d; TOP BANANA(1954), d
Silents
IN OLD KENTUCKY(1920), d; LITTLE LORD FAUNTLEROY(1921), d; BACK HOME AND BROKE(1922), d; COME ON OVER(1922), d; MAN WHO SAW TOMORROW, THE(1922), d; OUR LEADING CITIZEN(1922), d; IN HOLLYWOOD WITH POTASH AND PERLMUTTER(1924), d; INEZ FROM HOLLYWOOD(1924), d; SALLY(1925), d; ELLA CINDERS(1926), a, d; IRENE(1926), d; IT MUST BE LOVE(1926), d; LADIES AT PLAY(1926), d; AUCTIONEER, THE(1927), d; IS ZAT SO?(1927), d
Misc. Silents
WEB OF CHANCE, THE(1919), d; SILK HUSBANDS AND CALICO WIVES(1920), d; THROUGH THE BACK DOOR(1921), d; GHOST BREAKER, THE(1922), d; NE'ER-DO-WELL, THE(1923), d; WOMAN-PROOF(1923), d; PIED PIPER MALONE(1924), d; MAN WHO FOUND HIMSELF, THE(1925), d; TALKER, THE(1925), d; GIRL FROM MONTMARTRE, THE(1926), d; COME TO MY HOUSE(1927), d; 2 GIRLS WANTED(1927), d; HONOR BOUND(1928), d

Alice Green
FRUIT IS RIPE, THE(1961, Fr./Ital.), ed

Allan Green
TOMORROW(1972), ph

Alma Green
Misc. Silents
HARD CASH(1921, Brit.)

Amy Green
INSPECTOR CALLS, AN(1954, Brit.)

Angela Green
HOLLYWOOD CANTEEN(1944); MILDRED PIERCE(1945); STALLION ROAD(1947)

Anna Katharine Green
LEAVENWORTH CASE, THE(1936), w

Anne Green
HER SISTER'S SECRET(1946), w

Anthony Green
GREAT GILBERT AND SULLIVAN, THE(1953, Brit.); TIM DRISCOLL'S DONKEY(1955, Brit.); SUPREME SECRET, THE(1958, Brit.); MAN WHO LIKED FUNERALS, THE(1959, Brit.)

Art Green
WAY OUT WEST(1937)

Austin Green
STORY OF MANKIND, THE(1957); OPERATION EICHMANN(1961); RING OF TERROR(1962); I'D RATHER BE RICH(1964); PRINCESS AND THE MAGIC FROG, THE(1965), p&d; JOURNEY TO THE CENTER OF TIME(1967); STERILE CUCKOO, THE(1969)

Babe Green
LOVE IS NEWS(1937); FALLEN SPARROW, THE(1943); GOVERNMENT GIRL(1943)

Belle Green
CRACK-UP(1946)

Bennett Green
TWO TICKETS TO BROADWAY(1951)

Bernard Green
EVERYTHING'S DUCKY(1961), m; ZOTZ!(1962), m; ALL THE WAY HOME(1963), m; BRASS BOTTLE, THE(1964), m; HARVEY MIDDLEMAN, FIREMAN(1965), md

Billy Green
FRISCO SAL(1945); NAUGHTY NINETIES, THE(1945); SHADY LADY(1945); SUNBONNET SUE(1945); VIOLENCE(1947); YES SIR, MR. BONES(1951); STONE(1974, Aus.), a, m

Billy M. Green
NEVER STEAL ANYTHING SMALL(1959)

Bonnie Green
PEPE(1960)

Burton Green
Silents
WANTED FOR MURDER(1919)

Cagle D. Green
GHOST STORY(1981)

Carolyn Green
1984
DELIVERY BOYS(1984)

Cecil Green
TO PLEASE A LADY(1950)

Charles Green
SOMEBODY UP THERE LIKES ME(1956)

Silents
EMPTY HANDS(1924)
Misc. Silents
BLUEBEARD'S 8TH WIFE(1923)

Charlie Green
KID FOR TWO FARTHINGS, A(1956, Brit.)

Chuck Green
PUTNEY SWOPE(1969)

Clarence Green
D.O.A.(1950), w; GUN RUNNERS, THE(1958), p

Clayton Green
Misc. Silents
LINKED BY FATE(1919, Brit.)

Cliff Green
PICNIC AT HANGING ROCK(1975, Aus.), w; BREAK OF DAY(1977, Aus.), w; LET THE BALLOON GO(1977, Aus.), w; SUMMERFIELD(1977, Aus.), w

Colin Green
O LUCKY MAN!(1973, Brit.)

Cora Green
Misc. Talkies
SWING(1938); MOON OVER HARLEM(1939)

Danford B. Green
OUTLAW BLUES(1977), ed; VOICES(1979), ed

Danny Green
ATLANTIC(1929 Brit.); CROOKED BILLET, THE(1930, Brit.); THINGS ARE LOOKING UP(1934, Brit.); CRIME OVER LONDON(1936, Brit.); BOMBS OVER LONDON(1937, Brit.); GANGWAY(1937, Brit.); NON-STOP NEW YORK(1937, Brit.); THREE COCKEYED SAILORS(1940, Brit.); FIDDLERS THREE(1944, Brit.); WELCOME, MR. WASHINGTON(1944, Brit.); ECHO MURDERS, THE(1945, Brit.); MADONNA OF THE SEVEN MOONS(1945, Brit.); NO ORCHIDS FOR MISS BLANDISH(1948, Brit.); SMUGGLERS, THE(1948, Brit.); GOOD TIME GIRL(1950, Brit.); LADY CRAVED EXCITEMENT, THE(1950, Brit.); SOMEONE AT THE DOOR(1950, Brit.); TAMING OF DOROTHY, THE(1950, Brit.); TALE OF FIVE WOMEN, A(1951, Brit.); LITTLE BIG SHOT(1952, Brit.); ONCE A SINNER(1952, Brit.); WHISPERING SMITH VERSUS SCOTLAND YARD(1952, Brit.); LAUGHING ANNE(1954, Brit./U.S.); JUMPING FOR JOY(1956, Brit.); KID FOR TWO FARTHINGS, A(1956, Brit.); LADYKILLERS, THE(1956, Brit.); ABANDON SHIP(1957, Brit.); PICKUP ALLEY(1957, Brit.); SEVENTH VOYAGE OF SINBAD, THE(1958); BEYOND THIS PLACE(1959, Brit.); HIDDEN HOMICIDE(1959, Brit.); GIRLS OF LATIN QUARTER(1960, Brit.); IN THE WAKE OF A STRANGER(1960, Brit.); MAN IN THE MOON(1961, Brit.); MILLION DOLLAR MANHUNT(1962, Brit.); FAST LADY, THE(1963, Brit.); OLD DARK HOUSE, THE(1963, Brit.); SMASHING TIME(1967 Brit.); STITCH IN TIME, A(1967, Brit.); FIXER, THE(1968)

David Green
ORDERS ARE ORDERS(1959, Brit.)

Dee Dee Green
CHOPPERS, THE(1961)

Dee Gee Green
COLD WIND IN AUGUST(1961)

Denis Green
WITNESS VANISHES, THE(1939); MEN AGAINST THE SKY(1940); NORTHWEST PASSAGE(1940); DR. JEKYLL AND MR. HYDE(1941); PARIS CALLING(1941); SCOTLAND YARD(1941); YANK IN THE R.A.F., A(1941); THIS ABOVE ALL(1942); FRENCHMAN'S CREEK(1944); LONE WOLF IN LONDON(1947); WOMAN FROM TANGIER, THE(1948); MIGHTY JOE YOUNG(1949)

Dennis Green
HOUND OF THE BASKERVILLES, THE(1939)

Doe Green
ENEMIES OF THE LAW(1931)

Donald Green
THUNDER BAY(1953)

Donald Green [Raffaele Masciocchi]
HORRIBLE DR. HICHCOCK, THE(1964, Ital.), ph; GHOST, THE(1965, Ital.), ph

Dorothy Green
POET'S PUB(1949, Brit.); BIG HEAT, THE(1953); BAD FOR EACH OTHER(1954); THEM!(1954); TRIAL(1955); NO TIME TO BE YOUNG(1957); RESTLESS YEARS, THE(1958); FACE OF A FUGITIVE(1959); HELEN MORGAN STORY, THE(1959); MAN-TRAP(1961); CRITIC'S CHOICE(1963); IT HAPPENED AT THE WORLD'S FAIR(1963); PALM SPRINGS WEEKEND(1963); ZEBRA IN THE KITCHEN(1965); TAMMY AND THE MILLIONAIRE(1967); SUPPOSE THEY GAVE A WAR AND NOBODY CAME?(1970)
Silents
WOMAN AND WINE(1915); AMERICAN WAY, THE(1919); PRAISE AGENT, THE(1919)
Misc. Silents
AFTER DARK(1915); COUNTRY BOY, THE(1915); HER MOTHER'S SECRET(1915); WONDERFUL ADVENTURE, THE(1915); DEVIL AT HIS ELBOW, THE(1916); PARISIAN ROMANCE, A(1916); ABC OF LOVE, THE(1919); DARK STAR, THE(1919); FOREST RIVALS(1919); GOOD-BAD WIFE, THE(1921)

Duke Green
CALL OF THE WILD(1935); SOMETHING TO SING ABOUT(1937); BEAU GESTE(1939); SECRET SERVICE OF THE AIR(1939); SANTA FE MARSHAL(1940); OUTLAWS OF PINE RIDGE(1942); THEY WERE EXPENDABLE(1945); KISS THE BLOOD OFF MY HANDS(1948); THREE FOR JAMIE DAWN(1956), ph; DONOVAN'S REEF(1963)

Earle Green
GUTTER GIRLS(1964, Brit.); PARTNER, THE(1966, Brit.)

Eddie Green
DUFFY'S TAVERN(1945)
Misc. Talkies
WHAT GOES UP(1939); COMES MIDNIGHT(1940)

Effie Green
TOMORROW(1972)

Elizabeth Green
FREAKS(1932)

Eve Green
DAY OF RECKONING(1933), w; TUGBOAT ANNIE(1933), w; YOU CAN'T BUY EVERYTHING(1934), w; YOURS FOR THE ASKING(1936), w; BORN TO KILL(1947), w

F.L. Green
ODD MAN OUT(1947, Brit.), w; LOST MAN, THE(1969), w

Faith Green
Silents
SKY PILOT, THE(1921), w

Frances Green
NEVER TAKE CANDY FROM A STRANGER(1961, Brit.)

Frances Nimmo Green
Silents
ONE CLEAR CALL(1922), w

Frank Green
TITFIELD THUNDERBOLT, THE(1953, Brit.); MONTE WALSH(1970)

Frank Sherwin Green
80,000 SUSPECTS(1963, Brit.), p

Frederick Laurence Green
FUGITIVE, THE(1940, Brit.), w

Garard Green
PROFILE(1954, Brit.); HIGH TERRACE(1957, Brit.); ZOO BABY(1957, Brit.); CRAWLING EYE, THE(1958, Brit.); STRANGE CASE OF DR. MANNING, THE(1958, Brit.); JACK THE RIPPER(1959, Brit.); NO SAFETY AHEAD(1959, Brit.); HAND, THE(1960, Brit.); SENTENCED FOR LIFE(1960, Brit.); EMERGENCY(1962, Brit.)

Garrard Green
COUNT OF TWELVE(1955, Brit.)

Gasted Green
ALONE AGAINST ROME(1963, Ital.), d; HORROR CASTLE(1965, Ital.), w

George Green
OH, YEAH!(1929), m; TOM BROWN OF CULVER(1932), w; SPIRIT OF CULVER, THE(1939), w; GIRL FROM MONTEREY, THE(1943), w; OMOO OMOO, THE SHARK GOD(1949), w; NATIVE SON(1951, U.S., Arg.)

George D. Green
APACHE CHIEF(1949), w

Gerald Green
HIS MAJESTY O'KEEFE(1953), w; LAST ANGRY MAN, THE(1959), w; FOXTROT(1977, Mex./Swiss), p; TINTORERA...BLOODY WATERS(1977, Brit./Mex.), p; SUNBURN(1979), p; HIGH RISK(1981), p

Gerard Green
HOUR OF DECISION(1957, Brit.); STEEL BAYONET, THE(1958, Brit.)

Gertie Green
EVERY NIGHT AT EIGHT(1935)

Gertrude Green
DEVIL'S SQUADRON(1936); GREAT GUY(1936); DOWN IN ARKANSAW(1938)

Gilbert Green
BY LOVE POSSESSED(1961); HOMICIDAL(1961); EXPERIMENT IN TERROR(1962); PRESSURE POINT(1962); DARK INTRUDER(1965); DON'T MAKE WAVES(1967); MAN, THE(1972); EXECUTIVE ACTION(1973); NORMA RAE(1979)

Grace Green
Silents
PENROD(1922)

Graham Green
SMUGGLERS, THE(1948, Brit.), w; LOOKS AND SMILES(1982, Brit.)

Griswold Green
FLAMING STAR(1960)

Guy Green
HI, GANG!(1941, Brit.), ph; ESCAPE TO DANGER(1943, Brit.), ph; SPELL OF AMY NUGENT, THE(1945, Brit.), ph; WAY AHEAD, THE(1945, Brit.), ph; CARNIVAL(1946, Brit.), w, ph; GREAT EXPECTATIONS(1946, Brit.), ph; BLANCHE FURY(1948, Brit.), ph; TAKE MY LIFE(1948, Brit.), ph; ONE WOMAN'S STORY(1949, Brit.), ph; ADAM AND EVELYNE(1950, Brit.), ph; MADELEINE(1950, Brit.), ph; CAPTAIN HORATIO HORNBLOWER(1951, Brit.), ph; OLIVER TWIST(1951, Brit.), ph; HOUR OF THIRTEEN, THE(1952), ph; STORY OF ROBIN HOOD, THE(1952, Brit.), ph; BEGGAR'S OPERA, THE(1953), ph; NIGHT WITHOUT STARS(1953, Brit.), ph; FOR BETTER FOR WORSE(1954, Brit.), ph; RIVER BEAT(1954), d; ROB ROY, THE HIGHLAND ROGUE(1954, Brit.), ph; I AM A CAMERA(1955, Brit.), ph; SOULS IN CONFLICT(1955, Brit.), ph; WARRIORS, THE(1955); POSTMARK FOR DANGER(1956, Brit.), d, w; TEARS FOR SIMON(1957, Brit.), d; TRIPLE DECEPTION(1957, Brit.), d; SNORKEL, THE(1958, Brit.), d; ANGRY SILENCE, THE(1960), d; S.O.S. PACIFIC(1960, Brit.), d; MARK, THE(1961, Brit.), d; DESERT PATROL(1962, Brit.), d; DIAMOND HEAD(1962), d; LIGHT IN THE PIAZZA(1962), d; PATCH OF BLUE, A(1965), d&w; MAGUS, THE(1968, Brit.), d; MATTER OF INNOCENCE, A(1968, Brit.), d; WALK IN THE SPRING RAIN, A(1970), d; LUTHER(1974), d; ONCE IS NOT ENOUGH(1975), d

H. F Green
CHESTY ANDERSON, U.S. NAVY(1976), w

Harlan Green
PUNISHMENT PARK(1971)

Harold Green
Misc. Talkies
CUTTING LOOSE(1980)

Harrison Green
MANHATTAN LOVE SONG(1934); SEA SPOILERS, THE(1936); SINGING COWBOY, THE(1936); BRIDE FOR HENRY, A(1937); MIDNIGHT COURT(1937); MR. BOGGS STEPS OUT(1938); YOU CAN'T FOOL YOUR WIFE(1940)

Harry Green
CLOSE HARMONY(1929); KIBITZER, THE(1929); MAN I LOVE, THE(1929); WHY BRING THAT UP?(1929); BE YOURSELF(1930); HONEY(1930); LIGHT OF WESTERN STARS, THE(1930); SEA LEGS(1930); SPOILERS, THE(1930); TRUE TO THE NAVY(1930); NO LIMIT(1931); MARRY ME(1932, Brit.); MR. SKITCH(1933); THIS DAY AND AGE(1933); TOO MUCH HARMONY(1933); BORN TO BE BAD(1934); BOTTOMS UP(1934); COMING OUT PARTY(1934); LOVE TIME(1934); SHE LEARNED ABOUT SAILORS(1934); WILD GOLD(1934); CISCO KID AND THE LADY, THE(1939); STAR DUST(1940); GLAD TIDINGS(1953, Brit.); JOE MACBETH(1955); KING IN NEW YORK, A(1957, Brit.); NEXT TO NO TIME(1960, Brit.)

Hilton Green
1984
SIXTEEN CANDLES(1984), p

Hilton A. Green
PSYCHO II(1983), p

Howard Green
BROADWAY SCANDALS(1929), w; DONOVAN AFFAIR, THE(1929), w; LONG, LONG TRAIL, THE(1929), w; SONG OF LOVE, THE(1929), w; PART TIME WIFE(1930), w; TRICK FOR TRICK(1933), w; GEORGE WHITE'S SCANDALS(1945), w; THERE'S ALWAYS A THURSDAY(1957, Brit.); MARK OF THE PHOENIX(1958, Brit.)
Silents
KID BROTHER, THE(1927), w; HEAD MAN, THE(1928), w

Howard J. Green
FLIGHT(1929), w; YOUNGER GENERATION(1929), w; CHEER UP AND SMILE(1930), w; MELODY MAN(1930), w; ON YOUR BACK(1930), w; PRINCESS AND THE PLUMBER, THE(1930), w; SOUP TO NUTS(1930), w; DANGEROUS AFFAIR, A(1931), w; MAKER OF MEN(1931), w; BLESSED EVENT(1932), w; COHENS, AND KELLYS IN HOLLYWOOD, THE(1932), w; I AM A FUGITIVE FROM A CHAIN GANG(1932), w; THEY CALL IT SIN(1932), w; MORNING GLORY(1933), w; LEMON DROP KID, THE(1934), w; MAN OF TWO WORLDS(1934), w; SHOOT THE WORKS(1934), w; SING AND LIKE IT(1934), p; SUCCESS AT ANY PRICE(1934), w; MEN WITHOUT NAMES(1935), w; RUMBA(1935), w; STAR OF MIDNIGHT(1935), w; DEVIL'S SQUADRON(1936), w; IF YOU COULD ONLY COOK(1936), w; MEET NERO WOLFE(1936), w; THEY MET IN A TAXI(1936), p; NEW FACES OF 1937(1937), w; THIS WAY PLEASE(1937), w; MAKING THE HEADLINES(1938), w; MEET THE GIRLS(1938), p; TIME OUT FOR MURDER(1938), p; INSIDE STORY(1939), w; CURTAIN CALL(1940), w; BIG BOSS, THE(1941), w; HARMON OF MICHIGAN(1941), w; MAD DOCTOR, THE(1941), w; TWO IN A TAXI(1941), w; SPIRIT OF STANFORD, THE(1942), w; AFTER MIDNIGHT WITH BOSTON BLACKIE(1943), w; DOUGHBOYS IN IRELAND(1943), w; HIGH EXPLOSIVE(1943), w; REVEILLE WITH BEVERLY(1943), w; RACKET MAN, THE(1944), w; TAKE IT BIG(1944), w; HAVING WONDERFUL CRIME(1945), w; SAN QUENTIN(1946), w; INVISIBLE WALL, THE(1947), w; WINNER'S CIRCLE, THE(1948), w; CHAIN GANG(1950), w; MILITARY ACADEMY WITH THAT TENTH AVENUE GANG(1950), w; STATE PENITENTIARY(1950), w; MY TRUE STORY(1951), w; HAWK OF WILD RIVER, THE(1952), w
Silents
WHITE PANTS WILLIE(1927), w; MARKED MONEY(1928), w; VAMPING VENUS(1928), w

Hugh Green
IF WINTER COMES(1947); HILLS OF HOME(1948)

Hughie Green
RADIO PIRATES(1935, Brit.); MELODY AND ROMANCE(1937, Brit.); DOWN OUR ALLEY(1939, Brit.); MUSIC HALL PARADE(1939, Brit.); TOM BROWN'S SCHOOL DAYS(1940); PAPER ORCHID(1949, Brit.); MEN OF THE SEA(1951, Brit.)

Ivan Green
1984
BEAR, THE(1984); RIVER, THE(1984)

Jack Green
GO CHASE YOURSELF(1938); TOO BUSY TO WORK(1939)

Jacky Green
MEN OF THE SEA(1951, Brit.)

James "Cannonball" Green
GOLDEN BOY(1939)

James D. Green
SERGEANT MURPHY(1938)

James Green
ONE HOUR TO LIVE(1939)

Jane Green
MARRIAGE IS A PRIVATE AFFAIR(1944); THIN MAN GOES HOME, THE(1944); YOLANDA AND THE THIEF(1945); BAD BASCOMB(1946); BLUE SIERRA(1946); COCKEYED MIRACLE, THE(1946); COURAGE OF LASSIE(1946); UNDERCURRENT(1946); YEARLING(1946); GENTLEMAN'S AGREEMENT(1947); GOOD NEWS(1947); MIRACLE ON 34TH STREET, THE(1947)

Janet Green
HANGMAN WAITS, THE(1947, Brit.), set d; CLOUDED YELLOW, THE(1950, Brit.), w; GOOD BEGINNING, THE(1953, Brit.), w; EYEWITNESS(1956, Brit.), w; AFFAIR IN HAVANA(1957), w; TEARS FOR SIMON(1957, Brit.), w; THIRD KEY, THE(1957, Brit.), w; CAST A DARK SHADOW(1958, Brit.), w; GYPSY AND THE GENTLEMAN, THE(1958, Brit.), w; SAPPHIRE(1959, Brit.), w; MIDNIGHT LACE(1960), w; VICTIM(1961, Brit.), w; SEVEN WOMEN(1966), w; WALK IN THE SHADOW(1966, Brit.), w

Janet-Laine Green
LOVE(1982, Can.)

Janice Green
1984
CITY GIRL, THE(1984)

Jeanette Green
HANGMAN WAITS, THE(1947, Brit.)

Jenny Green
Misc. Talkies
SUDDEN DEATH(1977)

Joanne Green
GREAT MUPPET CAPER, THE(1981), cos

Joe Green
LIKELY STORY, A(1947); ROLL, THUNDER, ROLL(1949); GIRL WHO KNEW TOO MUCH, THE(1969), m

Joey Green
EXORCIST II: THE HERETIC(1977)

John Green
LAW OF THE RANGE(1941), w; AMERICAN IN PARIS, AN(1951), md; BRIGADOON(1954), md; TWILIGHT OF HONOR(1963), m, md; ALVAREZ KELLY(1966), m; JOHNNY TIGER(1966), m; OLIVER!(1968, Brit.), md; THEY SHOOT HORSES, DON'T THEY?(1969), m, md; RUDE BOY(1980, Brit.); TERROR ON TOUR(1980)

John W. Green
FIRST BABY(1936), m

Johnny Green
HONOR AMONG LOVERS(1931), m; LITTLE TOUGH GUY(1938); BATHING BEAUTY(1944), m; LOST IN A HAREM(1944), m; WEEKEND AT THE WALDORF(1945), m, md; EASY TO WED(1946), m; SAILOR TAKES A WIFE, THE(1946), m; CYNTHIA(1947), md; FIESTA(1947), m; IT HAPPENED IN BROOKLYN(1947); SOMETHING IN THE WIND(1947), m; EASTER PARADE(1948), md; UP IN CENTRAL PARK(1948), md; INSPECTOR GENERAL, THE(1949), m, md; LIFE OF HER OWN, A(1950), md; SUMMER STOCK(1950), md; TOAST OF NEW ORLEANS, THE(1950), md; GREAT CARUSO, THE(1951), md; IT'S A BIG COUNTRY(1951), md; MR. IMPERIUM(1951), md; ROYAL WEDDING(1951), md; TOO YOUNG TO KISS(1951), md;

BECAUSE YOU'RE MINE(1952), m; RHAPSODY(1954), md; HIGH SOCIETY(1956), m, md; INVITATION TO THE DANCE(1956), md; RAINTREE COUNTY(1957), m; PEPE(1960), m; WEST SIDE STORY(1961), md; BYE BYE BIRDIE(1963), m

Jonathan Green
BABY MAKER, THE(1970)

Joseph Green [Giuseppi Vari]
WOLF LARSEN(1978, Ital.), d

Joseph J. Green
WILD MAN OF BORNEO, THE(1941)

Josh Green
AROUSERS, THE(1973)

Judd Green
HIGH TREASON(1929, Brit.); ESCAPED FROM DARTMOOR(1930, Brit.)
Silents
IF(1916, Brit.); KENT, THE FIGHTING MAN(1916, Brit.); ALL THE WORLD'S A STAGE(1917, Brit.); GREAT GAME, THE(1918, Brit.); NELSON(1918, Brit.); ON LEAVE(1918, Brit.); AMATEUR GENTLEMAN, THE(1920, Brit.); GENERAL JOHN REGAN(1921, Brit.); KIPPS(1921, Brit.); MASTER OF CRAFT, A(1922, Brit.); IN THE BLOOD(1923, Brit.); ALLEY OF GOLDEN HEARTS, THE(1924, Brit.); NETS OF DESTINY(1924, Brit.); NELL GWYNNE(1926, Brit.); ONLY WAY, THE(1926, Brit.); WOMAN TEMPTED, THE(1928, Brit.); POWER OVER MEN(1929, Brit.)
Misc. Silents
LAMP OF DESTINY(1919, Brit.); LIFE OF A LONDON ACTRESS, THE(1919, Brit.); CLASS AND NO CLASS(1921, Brit.); STIRRUP CUP SENSATION, THE(1924, Brit.); NAUGHTY HUSBANDS(1930, Brit.)

Julien Green
LEVIATHAN(1961, Fr.), w

Karen Green
LIZZIE(1957); ZEBRA IN THE KITCHEN(1965)

Karl Green
HOLD ON(1966); MRS. BROWN, YOU'VE GOT A LOVELY DAUGHTER(1968, Brit.)

Kathe Green
PARTY, THE(1968)

Keith Green
WORK IS A FOUR LETTER WORD(1968, Brit.), ed; EASY RIDER(1969)

Kenneth Green
HERO AIN'T NOTHIN' BUT A SANDWICH, A(1977)
Silents
PENROD(1922)

L. Green
UNDER YOUR HAT(1940, Brit.), w

Larry Green
FOUR BOYS AND A GUN(1957)

Lars Green
RETURN OF THE JEDI(1983)

Laurence Green
LIGHTNING CONDUCTOR(1938, Brit.), w

Lawrence Green
LAST BARRICADE, THE(1938, Brit.), w; WHO GOES NEXT?(1938, Brit.), w

Leif Green
GREASE 2(1982); JOYSTICKS(1983)

Leola Green
HARRY'S WAR(1981)

Leon Green
HUMAN FACTOR, THE(1979, Brit.)

Linda Green
WYOMING(1947); RETURN OF THE TEXAN(1952)

Little Mitzi Green
MARRIAGE PLAYGROUND, THE(1929)

Liz Green
NUTCRACKER(1982, Brit.)

Lois Green
GONE TO THE DOGS(1939, Aus.)

Lydia Green
RETURN OF THE JEDI(1983)

Lynda Mason Green
IMPROPER CHANNELS(1981, Can.)
1984
HIGHPOINT(1984, Can.)

Lynn Green
SHAPE OF THINGS TO COME, THE(1979, Can.)

Lynn Mason Green
SILENCE OF THE NORTH(1981, Can.)

Marie Green
WHARF ANGEL(1934); FLASH GORDON(1980)

Marika Green
CROSS OF THE LIVING(1963,Fr.); PICKPOCKET(1963, Fr.); SINGAPORE, SINGAPORE(1969, Fr./Ital.); RIDER ON THE RAIN(1970, Fr./Ital.)
1984
UNTIL SEPTEMBER(1984)

Martyn Green
MIKADO, THE(1939, Brit.); GREAT GILBERT AND SULLIVAN, THE(1953, Brit.); LOVELY WAY TO DIE, A(1968); ICEMAN COMETH, THE(1973)

Mary Green
CASE OF THE CURIOUS BRIDE, THE(1935); MISS PACIFIC FLEET(1935); PUBLIC ENEMY'S WIFE(1936); SHE WOULDN'T SAY YES(1945)

Mary-Pat Green
WILLIE AND PHIL(1980)

Matt Green
SAM'S SONG(1971)

Maury Green
CANDIDATE, THE(1972)

Max Green
HATTER'S CASTLE(1948, Brit.), ph

Max Green [Mutz Greenbaum]
YELLOW CANARY, THE(1944, Brit.), ph; MAN IN THE DINGHY, THE(1951, Brit.), ph

Melissa Green
ELECTRA GLIDE IN BLUE(1973)

Melvin Green, Jr.
SHAFT'S BIG SCORE(1972)

Melvyn Green
SLOW RUN(1968)

Michael Green
THAT LUCKY TOUCH(1975, Brit.); GREAT GUNDOWN, THE(1977); MELANIE(1982, Can.), w
Misc. Talkies
BIJOU(1972)

Michael W. Green
HALLOWEEN III: SEASON OF THE WITCH(1982)

Michelle Green
DARK END OF THE STREET, THE(1981); DOZENS, THE(1981)

Mick Green
SELL OUT, THE(1976), m

Millicent Green
THEY KNEW WHAT THEY WANTED(1940)

Mitzi Green
HONEY(1930); LOVE AMONG THE MILLIONAIRES(1930); SANTA FE TRAIL, THE(1930); TOM SAWYER(1930); DUDE RANCH(1931); FINN AND HATTIE(1931); HUCKLEBERRY FINN(1931); NEWLY RICH(1931); GIRL CRAZY(1932); LITTLE ORPHAN ANNIE(1932); TRANSATLANTIC MERRY-GO-ROUND(1934); BLOODHOUNDS OF BROADWAY(1952); LOST IN ALASKA(1952)

Mitzie Green
SKIPPY(1931)

Morris Lee Green
THIS REBEL BREED(1960), w

Nan Green
TEENAGE ZOMBIES(1960)

Nigel Green
MEET MR. MALCOLM(1954, Brit.); STRANGER FROM VENUS, THE(1954, Brit.); SEA SHALL NOT HAVE THEM, THE(1955, Brit.); FIND THE LADY(1956, Brit.); AS LONG AS THEY'RE HAPPY(1957, Brit.); REACH FOR THE SKY(1957, Brit.); BITTER VICTORY(1958, Fr.); GYPSY AND THE GENTLEMAN, THE(1958, Brit.); WITNESS IN THE DARK(1959, Brit.); MAN AT THE CARLTON TOWER(1961, Brit.); MYSTERIOUS ISLAND(1961, U.S./Brit.); PIT OF DARKNESS(1961, Brit.); SWORD OF SHERWOOD FOREST(1961, Brit.); CONCRETE JUNGLE, THE(1962, Brit.); CORRIDORS OF BLOOD(1962, Brit.); DURANT AFFAIR, THE(1962, Brit.); PLAYBACK(1962, Brit.); SPANISH SWORD, THE(1962, Brit.); JASON AND THE ARGONAUTS(1963, Brit.); MYSTERY SUBMARINE(1963, Brit.); MASQUE OF THE RED DEATH, THE(1964, U.S./Brit.); SATURDAY NIGHT OUT(1964, Brit.); ZULU(1964, Brit.); FACE OF FU MANCHU, THE(1965, Brit.); IPCRESS FILE, THE(1965, Brit.); SKULL, THE(1965, Brit.); KHARTOUM(1966, Brit.); LET'S KILL UNCLE(1966); TOBRUK(1966); AFRICA-TEXAS STYLE!(1967 U.S./Brit.); DEADLIER THAN THE MALE(1967, Brit.); MAN WHO FINALLY DIED, THE(1967, Brit.); PINK JUNGLE, THE(1968); WRECKING CREW, THE(1968); FRAULEIN DOKTOR(1969, Ital./Yugo.); PLAY DIRTY(1969, Brit.); KREMLIN LETTER, THE(1970); COUNTESS DRACULA(1972, Brit.); RULING CLASS, THE(1972, Brit.); GAWAIN AND THE GREEN KNIGHT(1973, Brit.)

Nisel Green
QUEEN'S GUARDS, THE(1963, Brit.)

Norman Green
KENTUCKY MINSTRELS(1934, Brit.)

Pamela Green
PEEPING TOM(1960, Brit.); NAKED WORLD OF HARRISON MARKS, THE(1967, Brit.)

Pat Green
DIE, MONSTER, DIE(1965, Brit.), p; LAST SHOT YOU HEAR, THE(1969, Brit.), prod d

Patrick Green
1984
RACING WITH THE MOON(1984), a, stunts

Patsy Green
NEXT TIME WE LOVE(1936)

Paul Green
CABIN IN THE COTTON(1932), w; DR. BULL(1933), w; STATE FAIR(1933), w; VOLTAIRE(1933), W; CAROLINA(1934), w; STATE FAIR(1945), w; STATE FAIR(1962), w; BRIMSTONE AND TREACLE(1982, Brit.), ed; MISSIONARY, THE(1982), ed

Peyton Green
1984
VARIETY(1984)

Phil Green
KNICKERBOCKER HOLIDAY(1944); UPSTAIRS AND DOWNSTAIRS(1961, Brit.), m; GIRL HUNTERS, THE(1963, Brit.), m; TWO LEFT FEET(1965, Brit.), m

Philip Green
MAN ABOUT THE HOUSE, A(1947, Brit.), md; TURNERS OF PROSPECT ROAD, THE(1947, Brit.), md; FOR THEM THAT TRESPASS(1949, Brit.), m; MAN ON THE RUN(1949, Brit.), m; SAINTS AND SINNERS(1949, Brit.), m; WHILE THE SUN SHINES(1950, Brit.), md; ISN'T LIFE WONDERFUL!(1953, Brit.), m; NORMAN CONQUEST(1953, Brit.), m; YELLOW BALLOON, THE(1953, Brit.), m; FUSS OVER FEATHERS(1954, Brit.), m; YOUNG WIVES' TALE(1954, Brit.), m; EXTRA DAY, THE(1956, Brit.), m; MARCH HARE, THE(1956, Brit.), m; WHO DONE IT?(1956, Brit.), m; CARRY ON ADMIRAL(1957, Brit.), m; JOHN AND JULIE(1957, Brit.), m, md; JUST MY LUCK(1957, Brit.), m; UP IN THE WORLD(1957, Brit.), m; WHITE HUNTRESS(1957, Brit.), m; INBETWEEN AGE, THE(1958, Brit.), m; INNOCENT SINNERS(1958, Brit.), m; ROONEY(1958, Brit.), m; SQUARE PEG, THE(1958, Brit.), m; BOBBIKINS(1959, Brit.), m; DON'T PANIC CHAPS!(1959, Brit.), m; FOLLOW A STAR(1959, Brit.), m; QUESTION OF ADULTERY, A(1959, Brit.), m; SAPPHIRE(1959, Brit.), m; SEA FURY(1959, Brit.), m; DESERT MICE(1960, Brit.), m; MAKE MINE MINK(1960, Brit.), m; OPERATION AMSTERDAM(1960, Brit.), m; PICCADILLY THIRD STOP(1960, Brit.), m; SHAKEDOWN, THE(1960, Brit.), m; FLAME IN THE STREETS(1961, Brit.), m, md; LEAGUE OF GENTLEMEN, THE(1961, Brit.), m, md; MAN IN THE MOON(1961, Brit.), m; SECRET PARTNER, THE(1961, Brit.), m; SINGER NOT THE SONG(1961, Brit.), m; VICTIM(1961, Brit.), m; ALIVE AND KICKING(1962, Brit.), m; DEVIL'S AGENT, THE(1962, Brit.), m; LIFE IS A CIRCUS(1962, Brit.), m; ON THE BEAT(1962, Brit.), m; STOLEN AIRLINER, THE(1962, Brit.), m; TIARA TAHITI(1962, Brit.), m; DREAM MAKER, THE(1963, Brit.), m, md; FRIENDS AND NEIGHBORS(1963, Brit.), m; MAID FOR MURDER(1963, Brit.), m,

Gerald Greenberg
TAKING OF PELHAM ONE, TWO, THREE, THE(1974), ed; BYE BYE BRAVER-MAN(1968), ed; THEY MIGHT BE GIANTS(1971), ed; STOOLIE, THE(1972), ed; HEAVEN'S GATE(1980), ed

Hank Greenberg
KID FROM CLEVELAND, THE(1949)

Harold Greenberg
DEATH SHIP(1980, Can.), p; TERROR TRAIN(1980, Can.), p

Henry Greenberg
AL CAPONE(1959), w

Henry F. Greenberg
CARETAKERS, THE(1963), w

Irving Greenberg
PARTY GIRL(1958)

Jeff Greenberg
FIRST NUDIE MUSICAL, THE(1976)

Jerry Greenberg
SUBJECT WAS ROSES, THE(1968), ed; BOYS IN THE BAND, THE(1970), ed; FRENCH CONNECTION, THE(1971), ed; ELECTRA GLIDE IN BLUE(1973), ed; SEVEN UPS, THE(1973), ed; HAPPY HOOKER, THE(1975), ed; MISSOURI BREAKS, THE(1976), ed; KRAMER VS. KRAMER(1979), ed; DRESSED TO KILL(1980), ed; STILL OF THE NIGHT(1982), ed; SCARFACE(1983), ed
1984
BODY DOUBLE(1984), ed

Joanne Greenberg
I NEVER PROMISED YOU A ROSE GARDEN(1977), w

Joseph Greenberg
Misc. Talkies
JEWISH DAUGHTER(1933)

Joseph Greenberg [Green]
Misc. Talkies
JOSEPH IN THE LAND OF EGYPT(1932)

Cpl. Max M. Greenberg, USA
BACK TO BATAAN(1945)

Richard Greenberg
XANADU(1980), spec eff

Robbie Greenberg
YOUNGBLOOD(1978), ph; TIME WALKER(1982), ph

Roberta Greenberg
LOOKIN' TO GET OUT(1982)

Stanley R. Greenberg
SKYJACKED(1972), w; SOYLENT GREEN(1973), w

Tina Greenberg
1984
DREAMSCAPE(1984)

Adam Greenburg
LAST AMERICAN VIRGIN, THE(1982), ph

Chris Greenburg
SUNDAY LOVERS(1980, Ital./Fr.), ed

Dan Greenburg
LIVE A LITTLE, LOVE A LITTLE(1968), w; DOC(1971); OH! CALCUTTA!(1972), w; I COULD NEVER HAVE SEX WITH ANY MAN WHO HAS SO LITTLE REGARD FOR MY HUSBAND(1973), a, w; PRIVATE LESSONS(1981), w; PRIVATE SCHOOL(1983), w

Ed Greenburg
THUMB TRIPPING(1972)

Gerald Greenburg
COME BACK CIHARLESTON BLUE(1972), ed

Chris Greenbury
WORLD'S GREATEST LOVER, THE(1977), ed; MUPPET MOVIE, THE(1979), ed; SURVIVAL RUN(1980), ed

Christopher Greenbury
WHERE THE BUFFALO ROAM(1980), ed; LIAR'S MOON(1982), ed; SOME KIND OF HERO(1982), ed; DOCTOR DETROIT(1983), ed; SMOKEY AND THE BANDIT-PART 3(1983), ed
1984
WOMAN IN RED, THE(1984), ed

Sidney Robin Greenbush
1984
HAMBONE AND HILLIE(1984)

Addison Greene
ONE DOWN TWO TO GO(1982)

Al M. Greene
Silents
JOANNA(1925), ph

Alexander Greene
RAT SAVIOUR, THE(1977, Yugo.), w

Alfred E. Greene
GRACIE ALLEN MURDER CASE(1939), d

Angela Greene
TOO YOUNG TO KNOW(1945); TIME, THE PLACE AND THE GIRL, THE(1946); ESCAPE ME NEVER(1947); LOVE AND LEARN(1947); KING OF THE BANDITS(1948); WALLFLOWER(1948); AT WAR WITH THE ARMY(1950); JUNGLE JIM IN THE FORBIDDEN LAND(1952); LADY WANTS MINK, THE(1953); LOOSE IN LONDON(1953); PERILOUS JOURNEY, A(1953); ROYAL AFRICAN RIFLES, THE(1953); SHOTGUN(1955); AFFAIR IN RENO(1957); SPOILERS OF THE FOREST(1957); NIGHT OF THE BLOOD BEAST(1958); COSMIC MAN, THE(1959); TICKLE ME(1965); DAY OF THE LOCUST, THE(1975); FUTUREWORLD(1976)

Barbara Greene
BLIND MAN'S BLUFF(1936, Brit.); WRATH OF JEALOUSY(1936, Brit.); MANY TANKS MR. ATKINS(1938, Brit.); MOONLIGHT SONATA(1938, Brit.); ANYTHING TO DECLARE?(1939, Brit.)

Barry Greene
1984
POLICE ACADEMY(1984)

Billy Greene
TANGIER(1946); MOTHER WORE TIGHTS(1947); MY WILD IRISH ROSE(1947); SHRIKE, THE(1955); THAT TOUCH OF MINK(1962)

Billy M. Greene
SLAUGHTER ON TENTH AVENUE(1957); SINGLE ROOM FURNISHED(1968)

Candy Greene
LOVE IN A FOUR LETTER WORLD(1970, Can.)

Charles Greene
TARGETS(1968), m

Clarence Greene
TOWN WENT WILD, THE(1945), p, w; GREAT PLANE ROBBERY(1950), w; WELL, THE(1951), p, W; THIEF, THE(1952), p, w; WICKED WOMAN(1953), p, w; NEW YORK CONFIDENTIAL(1955), p, w; FASTEST GUN ALIVE(1956), p; PILLOW TALK(1959), w; THUNDER IN THE SUN(1959), p; HOUSE IS NOT A HOME, A(1964), p, w; OSCAR, THE(1966), p, w; CAPER OF THE GOLDEN BULLS, THE(1967), p; COLOR ME DEAD(1969, Aus.), w

Claude Friese Greene
GREENWOOD TREE, THE(1930, Brit.), ph; MAN WHO WON, THE(1933, Brit.), ph; MAXWELL ARCHER, DETECTIVE(1942, Brit.), ph

Clay M. Greene
Silents
FORGIVEN, OR THE JACK O'DIAMONDS(1914), w; FORTUNE HUNTER, THE(1914), w; HOUSE NEXT DOOR, THE(1914), w; CLIMBERS, THE(1915), w; BROKEN CHAINS(1916), w; M'LISS(1918), w; PAWN TICKET 210(1922), w
Misc. Silents
OGRE AND THE GIRL, THE(1915), d; HER WAYWARD SISTER(1916), d

Clayton Greene
OUTSIDER, THE(1933, Brit.); MIDAS TOUCH, THE(1940, Brit.)

Danford Greene
CLAY PIGEON(1971), ed; BLAZING SADDLES(1974), ed; MASTER GUNFIGHTER, THE(1975), ed

Danford B. Greene
THAT COLD DAY IN THE PARK(1969, U.S./Can.), ed; M(1970), ed; ALOHA, BOBBY AND ROSE(1975), ed; KILLER INSIDE ME, THE(1976), ed; FUN WITH DICK AND JANE(1977), ed; WHICH WAY IS UP?(1977), ed; ROCKY II(1979), ed; HOLLYWOOD KNIGHTS, THE(1980), ed; PARTNERS(1982), ed
1984
SECRET DIARY OF SIGMUND FREUD, THE(1984), d

David Allen Greene
COME BACK BABY(1968), p,d,w,ph&ed

David Greene
DAUGHTER OF DARKNESS(1948, Brit.); HIDEOUT(1948, Brit.); GOLDEN MADONNA, THE(1949, Brit.); DARK LIGHT, THE(1951, Brit.); WOODEN HORSE, THE(1951); SEBASTIAN(1968, Brit.), d; SHUTTERED ROOM, THE(1968, Brit.), d; STRANGE AFFAIR, THE(1968, Brit.), d; I START COUNTING(1970, Brit.), p, d; PEOPLE NEXT DOOR, THE(1970), d; GODSPELL(1973), d, w; COUNT OF MONTE CRISTO(1976, Brit.), d; GRAY LADY DOWN(1978), d; HARD COUNTRY(1981), p, d; MARRIAGE, A(1983), p
1984
ACT, THE(1984), p

David Plunkett Greene
BUCKET OF BLOOD(1934, Brit.), w

Dee Greene
HONEYMOON AHEAD(1945)

Duke Greene
ROBIN OF TEXAS(1947)

Dunford Greene
BLUE SKIES AGAIN(1983), ed

Ellen Greene
NEXT STOP, GREENWICH VILLAGE(1976); I'M DANCING AS FAST AS I CAN(1982)

Eva Greene
STORM OVER THE ANDES(1935), w; STRANGE AFFAIR(1944), w

Eve Greene
PROSPERITY(1932), w; BEAUTY FOR SALE(1933), w; OPERATOR 13(1934), w; THIS SIDE OF HEAVEN(1934), w; GREAT IMPERSONATION, THE(1935), w; HER HUSBAND LIES(1937), w; WHEN LOVE IS YOUNG(1937), w; STOLEN HEAVEN(1938), w; LITTLE ACCIDENT(1939), w; MOONLIGHT IN HAWAII(1941), w; NIGHT OF JANUARY 16TH(1941), w; JOAN OF OZARK(1942), w; SWEATER GIRL(1942), w

Frances Nimmo Greene
Silents
DEVIL TO PAY, THE(1920), w

Frank Greene
FAST COMPANY(1929)

Frederick Dennis Greene
GREASED LIGHTNING(1977)

Gael Greene
LOVE(1982, Can.), w

Gilbert Greene
BOOK OF NUMBERS(1973)

Graham Greene
ORIENT EXPRESS(1934), w; TWENTY-ONE DAYS TOGETHER(1940, Brit.), w; THIS GUN FOR HIRE(1942), w; 48 HOURS(1944, Brit.), w; CONFIDENTIAL AGENT(1945), d; MINISTRY OF FEAR(1945), w; BRIGHTON ROCK(1947, Brit.), w; FUGITIVE, THE(1947), w; GREEN COCKATOO, THE(1947, Brit.), w; FALLEN IDOL, THE(1949, Brit.), w; THIRD MAN, THE(1950, Brit.), w; HEART OF THE MATTER, THE(1954, Brit.), w; END OF THE AFFAIR, THE(1955, Brit.), w; STRANGER'S HAND, THE(1955, Brit.), p, w; LOSER TAKES ALL(1956, Brit.), w; ACROSS THE BRIDGE(1957, Brit.), w; SAINT JOAN(1957), w; SHORT CUT TO HELL(1957), w; QUIET AMERICAN, THE(1958), w; OUR MAN IN HAVANA(1960, Brit.), w; COMEDIANS, THE(1967), w; TRAVELS WITH MY AUNT(1972), w; ENGLANO MADE ME(1973, Brit.), w; HUMAN FACTOR, THE(1979, Brit.), w; BEYOND THE LIMIT(1983), w; RUNNING BRAVE(1983, Can.)

Guy Greene
DECAMERON NIGHTS(1953, Brit.), ph

H. Richard Greene
I, THE JURY(1982)

Hal Greene
MURDER AT THE VANITIES(1934); SHE MARRIED HER BOSS(1935); EASY LIVING(1937)
Harold Greene
HOUSE OF THE SEVEN GABLES, THE(1940), w; MARKED MEN(1940), w; ON THE ISLE OF SAMOA(1950), w; BIG GUSHER, THE(1951), w; VICKI(1953), w; HIDE AND SEEK(1964, Brit.), w; TEXAS ACROSS THE RIVER(1966), w
Harold R. Greene
COUNTERSPY MEETS SCOTLAND YARD(1950), w; CHINA CORSAIR(1951), w; CRIMINAL LAWYER(1951), w; KANSAS CITY CONFIDENTIAL(1952), w
Harrison Greene
INTERNATIONAL HOUSE(1933); SATURDAY'S MILLIONS(1933); VAMPIRE BAT, THE(1933); KID MILLIONS(1934); MANHATTAN MELODRAMA(1934); MISS FANE'S BABY IS STOLEN(1934); MURDER ON THE CAMPUS(1934); MISS PACIFIC FLEET(1935); SHE COULDN'T TAKE IT(1935); SHE MARRIED HER BOSS(1935); STRANDED(1935); GENTLEMAN FROM LOUISIANA(1936); GUNS AND GUITARS(1936); TICKET TO PARADISE(1936); ANGEL'S HOLIDAY(1937); GO-GETTER, THE(1937); RANGE DEFENDERS(1937); SARATOGA(1937); TIME OUT FOR ROMANCE(1937); BORN TO BE WILD(1938); CAREER(1939); HONEYMOON'S OVER, THE(1939); ICE FOLLIES OF 1939(1939); LITTLE ACCIDENT(1939); NAUGHTY BUT NICE(1939); NEW FRONTIER(1939); HEROES OF THE SADDLE(1940); HOUSE ACROSS THE BAY, THE(1940); LADY IN QUESTION, THE(1940); ARKANSAS JUDGE(1941); KING OF DODGE CITY(1941); ROYAL MOUNTED PATROL, THE(1941); SON OF DAVY CROCKETT, THE(1941); STRAWBERRY BLONDE, THE(1941); THREE GIRLS ABOUT TOWN(1941); BLONDIE FOR VICTORY(1942); ICE-CAPADES REVUE(1942); JOHNNY EAGER(1942); MORE THE MERRIER, THE(1943); TWO SENORITAS FROM CHICAGO(1943); MAN FROM FRISCO(1944); ONCE UPON A TIME(1944); NOB HILL(1945); THOROUGHBREDS(1945); WHERE DO WE GO FROM HERE?(1945)
Misc. Talkies
RIOT SQUAD(1933)
Helen Greene
Silents
AMAZONS, THE(1917); BAB'S BURGLAR(1917); BAB'S DIARY(1917); IN AGAIN-OUT AGAIN(1917); ON THE QUIET(1918); EASY TO GET(1920)
Misc. Silents
HEARTACHES(1915); LASH OF DESTINY, THE(1916); BAB'S MATINEE IDOL(1917); DUMMY, THE(1917); WOMAN AND WIFE(1918); LET'S ELOPE(1919); HELP YOURSELF(1920)
Helene Greene
Silents
TRUTH, THE(1920)
Herbert Greene
COSMIC MAN, THE(1959), d
Misc. Talkies
OUTLAW QUEEN(1957), d
Howard Greene
TRAIL OF THE LONESOME PINE, THE(1936), ph; BIG CAT, THE(1949), ph; HORRORS OF THE BLACK MUSEUM(1959, U.S./Brit.); KITCHEN, THE(1961, Brit.); GIRL HUNTERS, THE(1963, Brit.); RIVALS, THE(1963, Brit.)
Howard J. Greene
HIGH SOCIETY BLUES(1930), w; DREAMING OUT LOUD(1940), w
Ira Greene
GEORGE WASHINGTON CARVER(1940), p; OVERTURE TO GLORY(1940), p
Jack Greene
ETERNALLY YOURS(1939); SAPS AT SEA(1940); SLIGHTLY HONORABLE(1940)
Jaclynne Greene
GIRLS IN THE NIGHT(1953); STAND AT APACHE RIVER, THE(1953); I COVER THE UNDERWORLD(1955); STRANGER ON HORSEBACK(1955); WINK OF AN EYE(1958); CRIMSON KIMONO, THE(1959)
James Greene
MAD DOG COLL(1961); TRAVELING EXECUTIONER, THE(1970); DOC(1971); BUG(1975); MISSOURI BREAKS, THE(1976); LINCOLN CONSPIRACY, THE(1977); GHOST STORY(1981); HANKY-PANKY(1982); LITTLE SEX, A(1982)
1984
BODY ROCK(1984)
Jerry Greene
OUTLAW BLUES(1977)
Jim Greene
SHEPHERD OF THE HILLS, THE(1964)
Joe Greene
WIFE WANTED(1946); WILD PARTY, THE(1956); THIRTY FOOT BRIDE OF CANDY ROCK, THE(1959); PUBLIC AFFAIR, A(1962), m; MOVIE STAR, AMERICAN STYLE, OR, LSD I HATE YOU!(1966), m; ON HER BED OF ROSES(1966), m; BOY...A GIRL, A(1969), m; CHILDISH THINGS(1969), m; TIGER BY THE TAIL(1970), m; BLACK SIX, THE(1974); TOGETHER BROTHERS(1974), w
John Greene
PLUNDERERS OF PAINTED FLATS(1959), w
John L. Greene
PRIVATE NAVY OF SGT. O'FARRELL, THE(1968), w
John T. Greene
LAST BLITZKRIEG, THE(1958)
Jon Greene
NEW YEAR'S EVIL(1980); SCHIZOID(1980); HOSPITAL MASSACRE(1982)
1984
ALLEY CAT(1984)
Joseph Greene
ARIZONA TRAIL(1943); ONCE UPON A TIME(1944); THIN MAN GOES HOME, THE(1944); SKIPALONG ROSENBLOOM(1951)
Joseph J. Greene
SULTAN'S DAUGHTER, THE(1943); OLD TEXAS TRAIL, THE(1944); WILSON(1944); BEHIND CITY LIGHTS(1945); CAPTAIN EDDIE(1945); NOB HILL(1945); TREE GROWS IN BROOKLYN, A(1945); DEVIL'S PLAYGROUND, THE(1946); SUSIE STEPS OUT(1946); MAN IN THE SHADOW(1957)
Kempton Greene
Silents
OUR LITTLE WIFE(1918); FORTUNE'S CHILD(1919)
Misc. Silents
CIPHER KEY, THE(1915); DESTINY'S SKEIN(1915); OGRE AND THE GIRL, THE(1915); REGENERATING LOVE, THE(1915); RACE SUICIDE(1916); BROWN IN

HARVARD(1917); FOREST RIVALS(1919); MY LITTLE SISTER(1919); DAUGHTER OF DEVIL DAN(1921); FAMILY CLOSET, THE(1921)
Laura Greene
FOR LOVE OF IVY(1968); PUTNEY SWOPE(1969)
Leon Greene
FUNNY THING HAPPENED ON THE WAY TO THE FORUM, A(1966); DON'T LOSE YOUR HEAD(1967, Brit.); ASSIGNMENT TO KILL(1968); CHALLENGE FOR ROBIN HOOD, A(1968, Brit.); DEVIL'S BRIDE, THE(1968, Brit.); 11 HARROWHOUSE(1974, Brit.); RITZ, THE(1976); SEVEN-PER-CENT SOLUTION, THE(1977, Brit.); FLASH GORDON(1980)
Loretta Greene
BLACK GIRL(1972); LEADBELLY(1976)
Lorne Greene
SILVER CHALICE, THE(1954); TIGHT SPOT(1955); AUTUMN LEAVES(1956); HARD MAN, THE(1957); PEYTON PLACE(1957); BUCCANEER, THE(1958); GIFT OF LOVE, THE(1958); LAST OF THE FAST GUNS, THE(1958); TRAP, THE(1959); ERRAND BOY, THE(1961); EARTHQUAKE(1974); TIDAL WAVE(1975, U.S./Jap.); BATTLESTAR GALACTICA(1979); MISSION GALACTICA: THE CYLON ATTACK(1979); CONQUEST OF THE EARTH(1980); KLONDIKE FEVER(1980); HEIDI'S SONG(1982)
Misc. Talkies
HIGH COUNTRY CALLING(1975)
Lt. George W. Greene, USNR
BACK TO BATAAN(1945)
Lynda Mason Greene
IF YOU COULD SEE WHAT I HEAR(1982)
Lynnie Greene
1984
OVER THE BROOKLYN BRIDGE(1984)
Margaret Greene
Silents
ONE LAW FOR BOTH(1917); ANNEXING BILL(1918)
Misc. Silents
NEDRA(1915); MARRIAGE BOND, THE(1916); ANGEL FACTORY, THE(1917)
Marie Greene
MA, HE'S MAKING EYES AT ME(1940)
Martin Greene
WHO IS HARRY KELLERMAN AND WHY IS HE SAYING THOSE TERRIBLE THINGS ABOUT ME?(1971)
Marty Greene
WINDOWS(1980); THEY ALL LAUGHED(1981)
Matt Greene
LEPKE(1975, U.S./Israel); RETURN TO MACON COUNTY(1975); WHIFFS(1975)
Misc. Talkies
SWEET SAVIOR(1971); I REMEMBER LOVE(1981)
Max Greene
HOTEL RESERVE(1946, Brit.), ph; MAN FROM MOROCCO, THE(1946, Brit.), d; COURTNEY AFFAIR, THE(1947, Brit.), ph; SO EVIL MY LOVE(1948, Brit.), ph; ELIZABETH OF LADYMEAD(1949, Brit.), ph; LAUGHING ANNE(1954, Brit./U.S.), ph; TROUBLE IN THE GLEN(1954, Brit.), ph; KING'S RHAPSODY(1955, Brit.), ph; LET'S MAKE UP(1955, Brit.), ph; BROTHERS IN LAW(1957, Brit.), ph; LUCKY JIM(1957, Brit.), ph&md; I'M ALL RIGHT, JACK(1959, Brit.), ph; FRENCH MISTRESS(1960, Brit.), ph; MAN IN A COCKED HAT(1960, Bri.), ph; RISK, THE(1961, Brit.), ph; SECRET WAYS, THE(1961), ph; HEAVENS ABOVE!(1963, Brit.), ph; SPARROWS CAN'T SING(1963, Brit.), ph
Max Greene [Mutz Greenbaum]
HOTEL RESERVE(1946, Brit.), d; WANTED FOR MURDER(1946, Brit.), ph; PICCADILLY INCIDENT(1948, Brit.), ph; SPRING IN PARK LANE(1949, Brit.), ph; NIGHT AND THE CITY(1950, Brit.), ph; LADY WITH A LAMP, THE(1951, Brit.), ph; ODETTE(1951, Brit.), ph; FOUR AGAINST FATE(1952, Brit.), ph; MAYTIME IN MAYFAIR(1952, Brit.), ph; TRENT'S LAST CASE(1953, Brit.), ph; MOONRAKER, THE(1958, Brit.), ph; TEENAGE BAD GIRL(1959, Brit.), ph
Maxine Greene
THEY SHOOT HORSES, DON'T THEY?(1969); UNCLE SCAM(1981)
Michael Greene
SPENCER'S MOUNTAIN(1963); NAKED ANGELS(1969); LAST MOVIE, THE(1971); PLAY IT AGAIN, SAM(1972); CLONES, THE(1973); HARRAD EXPERIMENT, THE(1973); HARRY AND WALTER GO TO NEW YORK(1976); MOUNTAIN MEN, THE(1980); AMERICANA(1981)
1984
MOSCOW ON THE HUDSON(1984)
Mike Greene
RED RUNS THE RIVER(1963); CALIFORNIA SPLIT(1974)
Mort Greene
LONE WOLF RETURNS, THE(1936)
Otis Greene
WHITE WITCH DOCTOR(1953); PRISONER OF WAR(1954); DISEMBODIED, THE(1957); VOODOO WOMAN(1957); SUNRISE AT CAMPOBELLO(1960); HANDLE WITH CARE(1964); PRETTY MAIDS ALL IN A ROW(1971)
Patricia Greene
KITCHEN, THE(1961, Brit.)
Radger Greene
PUNISHMENT PARK(1971)
Reuben Greene
BOYS IN THE BAND, THE(1970); MIKEY AND NICKY(1976)
Richard Greene
FOUR MEN AND A PRAYER(1938); KENTUCKY(1938); MY LUCKY STAR(1938); SUBMARINE PATROL(1938); HERE I AM A STRANGER(1939); HOUND OF THE BASKERVILLES, THE(1939); LITTLE PRINCESS, THE(1939); STANLEY AND LIVINGSTONE(1940); I WAS AN ADVENTURESS(1940); LITTLE OLD NEW YORK(1940); FLYING FORTRESS(1942, Brit.); UNPUBLISHED STORY(1942, Brit.); DON'T TAKE IT TO HEART(1944, Brit.); YELLOW CANARY, THE(1944, Brit.); FOREVER AMBER(1947); SHOWTIME(1948, Brit.); FAN, THE(1949); FIGHTING O'FLYNN, THE(1949); NOW BARABBAS WAS A ROBBER(1949, Brit.); DESERT HAWK, THE(1950); IF THIS BE SIN(1950, Brit.); LORNA DOONE(1951); OPERATION X(1951, Brit.); BLACK CASTLE, THE(1952); ROGUE'S MARCH(1952); BANDITS OF CORSICA, THE(1953); CAPTAIN SCARLETT(1953); CONTRABAND SPAIN(1955, Brit.); SHADOW OF THE EAGLE(1955, Brit.); BEYOND THE CURTAIN(1960, Brit.); SWORD OF SHERWOOD FOREST(1961, Brit.), a, p; FARMER'S OTHER DAUGHTER, THE(1965); BLOOD OF FU MANCHU, THE(1968, Brit.); CASTLE OF FU MANCHU, THE(1968,

Ger./Span./Ital./Brit.); RIVERRUN(1968), m; TALES FROM THE CRYPT(1972, Brit.); GETTING EVEN(1981), m
1984
  SPECIAL EFFECTS(1984)
Samya Greene
  LAST MOVIE, THE(1971)
Shecky Greene
  TONY ROME(1967); LOVE MACHINE, THE,(1971); WON TON TON, THE DOG WHO SAVED HOLLYWOOD(1976); HISTORY OF THE WORLD, PART 1(1981)
1984
  LOVELINES(1984); SPLASH(1984)
Sparky Greene
1984
  OASIS, THE(1984), p, d, w
Stanley Greene
  WIZ, THE(1978); NOTHING BUT A MAN(1964); FOR LOVE OF IVY(1968); LORD SHANGO(1975); JUST TELL ME WHAT YOU WANT(1980)
Steve Greene
1984
  HARDBODIES(1984), w
Victor Greene
  SAILOR'S HOLIDAY(1944), art d; PARIS UNDERGROUND(1945), art d; RED PONY, THE(1949), art d; HE'S A COCKEYED WONDER(1950), art d; ROOKIE FIREMAN(1950), art d; TOUGHER THEY COME, THE(1950), art d; NEVER TRUST A GAMBLER(1951), art d; SMUGGLER'S GOLD(1951), art d
Victor Hugo Greene
  HUMAN DESIRE(1954)
Victor M. Greene
  FLAME IN THE HEATHER(1935, Brit.), p; EARLY BIRD, THE(1936, Brit.), p; AGAINST THE TIDE(1937, Brit.), p, w; BEHIND YOUR BACK(1937, Brit.), p; FALSE EVIDENCE(1937, Brit.), p; FIRST NIGHT(1937, Brit.), p; LANDSLIDE(1937, Brit.), p; MACUSHLA(1937, Brit.), p; BEDTIME STORY(1938, Brit.), p; IRISH AND PROUD OF IT(1938, Ireland), p; MURDER TOMORROW(1938, Brit.), p; FLYING FIFTY-FIVE(1939, Brit.), p, w; SPIDER, THE(1940, Brit.), p, w
W. Howard Greene
  GARDEN OF ALLAH, THE(1936), ph; NOTHING SACRED(1937), ph; STAR IS BORN, A(1937), ph; MEN WITH WINGS(1938), ph; JESSE JAMES(1939), ph; UNTAMED(1940), ph; SHEPHERD OF THE HILLS, THE(1941), ph; PHANTOM OF THE OPERA(1943), ph; SALUTE TO THE MARINES(1943), ph; CAN'T HELP SINGING(1944), ph; CLIMAX, THE(1944), ph; COBRA WOMAN(1944), ph; GYPSY WILDCAT(1944), ph; IMPATIENT YEARS, THE(1944), ph; SALOME, WHERE SHE DANCED(1945), ph; NIGHT IN PARADISE, A(1946), ph; PIRATES OF MONTEREY(1947), ph; SLAVE GIRL(1947), ph; TYCOON(1947), ph; HIGH LONESOME(1950), ph; AL JENNINGS OF OKLAHOMA(1951), ph; WHEN WORLDS COLLIDE(1951), ph; BRIGAND, THE(1952), ph; GIRLS OF PLEASURE ISLAND, THE(1953), ph; GUN BELT(1953), ph; RAIDERS OF THE SEVEN SEAS(1953), ph; VIOLENT MEN, THE(1955), ph
Walter Greene
  PRIVATE AFFAIRS(1940), w; WHY GIRLS LEAVE HOME(1945), md; FIGHTING VIGILANTES, THE(1947), m; GHOST TOWN RENEGADES(1947), m; HOLLYWOOD BARN DANCE(1947), m; RANGE BEYOND THE BLUE(1947), md; RETURN OF THE LASH(1947), m; STAGE TO MESA CITY(1947), m; DEAD MAN'S GOLD(1948), m; FRONTIER REVENGE(1948), m; MARK OF THE LASH(1948), m; TORNADO RANGE(1948), m; WESTWARD TRAIL, THE(1948), m; DALTON GANG, THE(1949), m; OUTLAW COUNTRY(1949), md; RED DESERT(1949), m; RIMFIRE(1949), m; SHEP COMES HOME(1949), m, md; SON OF A BADMAN(1949), m; SON OF BILLY THE KID(1949), m; SQUARE DANCE JUBILEE(1949), m, md; CROOKED RIVER(1950), m; FAST ON THE DRAW(1950), md; HOSTILE COUNTRY(1950), m; MARSHAL OF HELDORADO(1950), md; WEST OF THE BRAZOS(1950), m, md; G.I. JANE(1951), m; KENTUCKY JUBILEE(1951), md; VANISHING OUTPOST, THE(1951), m; YES SIR, MR. BONES(1951), m; BLACK LASH, THE(1952), m; JESSE JAMES' WOMEN(1954), m; CARNIVAL ROCK(1957), m; TEENAGE DOLL(1957), m; TEENAGE THUNDER(1957), m; BRAIN FROM THE PLANET AROUS, THE(1958), m; TEENAGE MONSTER(1958), m; WAR OF THE SATELLITES(1958), m; I BOMBED PEARL HARBOR(1961, Jap.), m; TARZAN'S DEADLY SILENCE(1970), m, md
Silents
  JOHN SMITH(1922)
Walter D. Greene
Misc. Silents
  SALLY IN OUR ALLEY(1916)
Ward Greene
  THEY WON'T FORGET(1937), w; LADY AND THE TRAMP(1955), w
Wendy Greene
  WONDER WOMEN(1973, Phil.); LOVE LETTERS(1983), ed
William Greene
  ORDERS TO KILL(1958, Brit.); LIGHT IN THE PIAZZA(1962); LOLITA(1962)
Chris Greener
  ELEPHANT MAN, THE(1980, Brit.)
Christopher Greener
  MR. QUILP(1975, Brit.)
Dorothy Greener
  THEY MIGHT BE GIANTS(1971)
Josh Greenfeld
  OH GOD! BOOK II(1980), w
Calvin Greenfield
  YOUNG GIANTS(1983)
1984
  STRANGERS KISS(1984)
Darwin Greenfield
  PANIC IN THE STREETS(1950); HOUSE OF WAX(1953)
David Greenfield
  OFFICER AND A GENTLEMAN, AN(1982)
Debbie Greenfield
  PROM NIGHT(1980)
Josh Greenfield
  HARRY AND TONTO(1974), w
Larry Greenfield
  PUTNEY SWOPE(1969)

Ronald E. Greenfield
1984
  SOLDIER'S STORY, A(1984)
Rose Greenfield
  ELI ELI(1940)
Misc. Talkies
  LOVE AND SACRIFICE(1936); HER SECOND MOTHER(1940)
Jack Greenhaigh
  EVERYMAN'S LAW(1936), ph; RUSTLER'S HIDEOUT(1944), ph; ENEMY OF THE LAW(1945), ph; FBI GIRL(1951), ph
John Greenhaigh
  ADVENTURES OF CASANOVA(1948), ph
Dawn Greenhalgh
  ROWDYMAN, THE(1973, Can.)
Edward Greenhalgh
  THAT COLD DAY IN THE PARK(1969, U.S./Can.)
Jack Greenhalgh
  HIS FIGHTING BLOOD(1935), ph; TRAILS OF THE WILD(1935), ph; BORDER CABALLERO(1936), ph; LIGHTNING BILL CARSON(1936), ph; LION'S DEN, THE(1936), ph; REEFER MADNESS(1936), ph; ROARIN' GUNS(1936), ph; TIMBER WAR(1936), ph; TRAITOR, THE(1936), ph; ANYTHING FOR A THRILL(1937), ph; BORDER PHANTOM(1937), ph; FIGHTING TEXAN(1937), ph; GALLOPING DYNAMITE(1937), ph; HIGH HAT(1937), ph; LAWLESS LAND(1937), ph; ROARING SIX GUNS(1937), ph; ROGUE OF THE RANGE(1937), ph; ROUGH RIDIN' RHYTHM(1937), ph; SING WHILE YOU'RE ABLE(1937), ph; SWING IT, PROFESSOR(1937), ph; THANKS FOR LISTENING(1937), ph; TOUGH TO HANDLE(1937), ph; WHISTLING BULLETS(1937), ph; PHANTOM RANGER(1938), ph; RACING BLOOD(1938), ph; TWO-GUN JUSTICE(1938), ph; WEST OF RAINBOW'S END(1938), ph; WHERE THE WEST BEGINS(1938), ph; BAD BOY(1939), ph; BEASTS OF BERLIN(1939), ph; BURIED ALIVE(1939), ph; FIGHTING MAD(1939), ph; FRONTIER SCOUT(1939), ph; MYSTIC CIRCLE MURDER(1939), ph; TORTURE SHIP(1939), ph; ARIZONA GANGBUSTERS(1940), ph; BILLY THE KID IN TEXAS(1940), ph; FRONTIER CRUSADER(1940), ph; GUN CODE(1940), ph; HOLD THAT WOMAN(1940), ph; I TAKE THIS OATH(1940), ph; INVISIBLE KILLER, THE(1940), ph; MARKED MEN(1940), ph; MERCY PLANE(1940), ph; SECRETS OF A MODEL(1940), ph; BILLY THE KID WANTED(1941), ph; BILLY THE KID'S FIGHTING PALS(1941), ph; BILLY THE KID'S RANGE WAR(1941), ph; BILLY THE KID'S ROUNDUP(1941), ph; DANGEROUS LADY(1941), ph; DESPERATE CARGO(1941), ph; EMERGENCY LANDING(1941), ph; LONE RIDER AMBUSHED, THE(1941), ph; LONE RIDER CROSSES THE RIO, THE(1941), ph; LONE RIDER FIGHTS BACK, THE(1941), ph; LONE RIDER IN GHOST TOWN, THE(1941), ph; MR. WASHINGTON GOES TO TOWN(1941), ph; OUTLAWS OF THE RIO GRANDE(1941), ph; RIDERS OF BLACK MOUNTAIN(1941), ph; TEXAS MARSHAL, THE(1941), ph; BILLY THE KID TRAPPED(1942), ph; BROADWAY BIG SHOT(1942), ph; JUNGLE SIREN(1942), ph; LAW AND ORDER(1942), ph; LONE RIDER AND THE BANDIT, THE(1942), ph; MAD MONSTER, THE(1942), ph; MYSTERIOUS RIDER, THE(1942), ph; PRAIRIE PALS(1942), ph; PRISONER OF JAPAN(1942), ph; QUEEN OF BROADWAY(1942), ph; ROLLING DOWN THE GREAT DIVIDE(1942), ph; SHERIFF OF SAGE VALLEY(1942), ph; TEXAS MAN HUNT(1942), ph; TOMORROW WE LIVE(1942), ph; TOO MANY WOMEN(1942), ph; DEAD MEN WALK(1943), ph; FIGHTING FRONTIER(1943), ph; HITLER'S MADMAN(1943), ph; KID RIDES AGAIN, THE(1943), ph; MY SON, THE HERO(1943), ph; FUZZY SETTLES DOWN(1944), ph; SWING HOSTESS(1944), ph; VALLEY OF VENGEANCE(1944), ph; APOLOGY FOR MURDER(1945), ph; BIG SHOW-OFF, THE(1945), ph; BORDER BADMEN(1945), ph; FIGHTING BILL CARSON(1945), ph; HIS BROTHER'S GHOST(1945), ph; LADY CONFESSES, THE(1945), ph; LIGHTNING RAIDERS(1945), ph; PRAIRIE RUSTLERS(1945), ph; SHADOW OF TERROR(1945), ph; SHADOWS OF DEATH(1945), ph; STAGECOACH OUTLAWS(1945), ph; WHITE PONGO(1945), ph; YOUTH AFLAME(1945), ph; AMBUSH TRAIL(1946), ph; AVALANCHE(1946), ph; BLONDE FOR A DAY(1946), ph; DANNY BOY(1946), ph; FLYING SERPENT, THE(1946), ph; GAS HOUSE KIDS(1946), ph; GENTLEMEN WITH GUNS(1946), ph; LADY CHASER(1946), ph; LARCENY IN HER HEART(1946), ph; MASK OF DIIJON(1946), ph; MURDER IS MY BUSINESS(1946), ph; NAVAJO KID, THE(1946), ph; OUTLAW OF THE PLAINS(1946), ph; OVERLAND RIDERS(1946), ph; SIX GUN MAN(1946), ph; TERRORS ON HORSEBACK(1946), ph; ADVENTURE ISLAND(1947), ph; FEAR IN THE NIGHT(1947), ph; HEARTACHES(1947), ph; HIGH CONQUEST(1947), ph; HOLLYWOOD BARN DANCE(1947), ph; I COVER BIG TOWN(1947), ph; JUNGLE FLIGHT(1947), ph; SEVEN WERE SAVED(1947), ph; THREE ON A TICKET(1947), ph; TOO MANY WINNERS(1947), ph; LADY AT MIDNIGHT(1948), ph; MIRACULOUS JOURNEY(1948), ph; MONEY MADNESS(1948), ph; SIXTEEN FATHOMS DEEP(1948), ph; STRANGE MRS. CRANE, THE(1948), ph; SATAN'S CRADLE(1949), ph; STATE DEPARTMENT–FILE 649(1949), ph; WILD WEED(1949), ph; DAKOTA LIL(1950), ph; DANGER ZONE(1951), ph; FINGERPRINTS DON'T LIE(1951), ph; G.I. JANE(1951), ph; KENTUCKY JUBILEE(1951), ph; LEAVE IT TO THE MARINES(1951), ph; LOST CONTINENT(1951), ph; MASK OF THE DRAGON(1951), ph; NEW MEXICO(1951), ph; PIER 23(1951), ph; ROARING CITY(1951), ph; SAVAGE DRUMS(1951), ph; SLAUGHTER TRAIL(1951), ph; SWORD OF MONTE CRISTO, THE(1951), ph; THREE DESPERATE MEN(1951), ph; YES SIR, MR. BONES(1951), ph; SKY HIGH(1952), ph; ROBOT MONSTER(1953), ph
Jack Greenhalgh, Jr.
  KING OF THE SIERRAS(1938), ph
Jack H. Greenhalgh, Jr.
  STRANGE VOYAGE(1945), ph
John Greenhalgh
  GHOST PATROL(1936), ph
John H. Greenhalgh, Jr.
  ROGUE RIVER(1951), ph
Dorothy Greenhill
  COUNSEL'S OPINION(1933, Brit.), w; OVERNIGHT(1933, Brit.), w; FOR LOVE OR MONEY(1934, Brit.), w; ELDER BROTHER, THE(1937, Brit.), w; SILVER TOP(1938, Brit.), w
Geoffrey Greenhill
  RAGTIME(1981)
Mitch Greenhill
  LONG RIDERS, THE(1980)
Martha Greenhouse
  GROUP, THE(1966); WHERE'S POPPA?(1970); BANANAS(1971); STEPFORD WIVES, THE(1975); DANIEL(1983)

Andy Greenhut
SOME OF MY BEST FRIENDS ARE...(1971), cos
Robert Greenhut
STARDUST MEMORIES(1980), p; ARTHUR(1981), p; MIDSUMMER NIGHT'S SEX COMEDY, A(1982), p; ZELIG(1983), p
1984
BROADWAY DANNY ROSE(1984), p
Jack Greening
THREE STOOGES GO AROUND THE WORLD IN A DAZE, THE(1963); MY FAIR LADY(1964); WHAT A WAY TO GO(1964); WHERE LOVE HAS GONE(1964)
L. Stuart Greening
Silents
SHOEBLACK OF PICCADILLY, THE(1920, Brit.), d
Johnny Greenland
YOUNG GIRLS OF ROCHEFORT, THE(1968, Fr.)
Peter Greenlaw
L'AMOUR(1973)
Verina Greenlaw
HAUNTING, THE(1963); VERY EDGE, THE(1963, Brit.); FATHER GOOSE(1964); MASQUE OF THE RED DEATH, THE(1964, U.S./Brit.)
Charles Greenleaf
Misc. Silents
LITTLE GIRL NEXT DOOR, THE(1916)
Jim Greenleaf
NIGHT SHIFT(1982); JOYSTICKS(1983)
1984
TOY SOLDIERS(1984)
Ray [Raymond] Greenleaf
NAKED CITY, THE(1948)
Raymond Greenleaf
YOU CAN'T RUN AWAY FROM IT(1956); DEEP WATERS(1948); FOR THE LOVE OF MARY(1948); ALL THE KING'S MEN(1949); EAST SIDE, WEST SIDE(1949); KISS IN THE DARK, A(1949); PINKY(1949); PORT OF NEW YORK(1949); SLATTERY'S HURRICANE(1949); DAVID HARDING, COUNTERSPY(1950); HARRIET CRAIG(1950); NO SAD SONGS FOR ME(1950); ON THE ISLE OF SAMOA(1950); STORM WARNING(1950); TICKET TO TOMAHAWK(1950); AL JENNINGS OF OKLAHOMA(1951); FAMILY SECRET, THE(1951); FBI GIRL(1951); MILLIONAIRE FOR CHRISTY, A(1951); PIER 23(1951); SECRET OF CONVICT LAKE, THE(1951); TEN TALL MEN(1951); DEADLINE–U.S.A.(1952); HORIZONS WEST(1952); PAULA(1952); SHE'S WORKING HER WAY THROUGH COLLEGE(1952); WASHINGTON STORY(1952); ANGEL FACE(1953); BANDITS OF CORSICA, THE(1953); LAST POSSE, THE(1953); POWDER RIVER(1953); SOUTH SEA WOMAN(1953); THREE SAILORS AND A GIRL(1953); LIVING IT UP(1954); HEADLINE HUNTERS(1955); SON OF SINBAD(1955); TEXAS LADY(1955); VIOLENT MEN, THE(1955); VIOLENT SATURDAY(1955); NEVER SAY GOODBYE(1956); OVER-EXPOSED(1956); THREE VIOLENT PEOPLE(1956); WHEN GANGLAND STRIKES(1956); JEANNE EAGELS(1957); MONKEY ON MY BACK(1957); NIGHT THE WORLD EXPLODED, THE(1957); SPOILERS OF THE FOREST(1957); VAMPIRE, THE(1957); STORY ON PAGE ONE, THE(1959); FROM THE TERRACE(1960); WILD IN THE COUNTRY(1961)
Don Greenlee
SPOOK WHO SAT BY THE DOOR, THE(1973)
Sam Greenlee
SPOOK WHO SAT BY THE DOOR, THE(1973), p, w
Billy Greenlees
THAT SINKING FEELING(1979, Brit.)
William Greenlees
GREGORY'S GIRL(1982, Brit.)
Billy Greenless
1984
COMFORT AND JOY(1984, Brit.)
Alvin Greenman
MIRACLE ON 34TH STREET, THE(1947); MR. BELVEDERE GOES TO COLLEGE(1949); ONE MINUTE TO ZERO(1952); WE'RE NOT MARRIED(1952); BEAST FROM 20,000 FATHOMS, THE(1953); DOWN AMONG THE SHELTERING PALMS(1953)
Chip Greenman
TERROR ON TOUR(1980)
Joe Greenman
SORCERESS(1983), art d
Beatrice Greenough
MY FAIR LADY(1964)
George Greenough
CHAIN REACTION(1980, Aus.), ph
Rick Greenough
NATIONAL LAMPOON'S ANIMAL HOUSE(1978)
Terence Greenridge
RICHARD III(1956, Brit.)
Arthur Greenslade
JOANNA(1968, Brit.), md; PRIME OF MISS JEAN BRODIE, THE(1969, Brit.), md
Larry Greenspan
WINTER KEPT US WARM(1968, Can.)
Peter Greenspan
LIFE IN EMERGENCY WARD 10(1959, Brit.); FRENCH MISTRESS(1960, Brit.); DAMN THE DEFIANT!(1962, Brit.)
Janie Greenspun
BAWDY ADVENTURES OF TOM JONES, THE(1976, Brit.)
Pat Greenstein
1984
BEAR, THE(1984)
Sydney Greenstreet
MALTESE FALCON, THE(1941); ACROSS THE PACIFIC(1942); CASABLANCA(1942); IN THIS OUR LIFE(1942); THEY DIED WITH THEIR BOOTS ON(1942); BACKGROUND TO DANGER(1943); BETWEEN TWO WORLDS(1944); CONSPIRATORS, THE(1944); HOLLYWOOD CANTEEN(1944); MASK OF DIMITRIOS, THE(1944); PASSAGE TO MARSEILLE(1944); CHRISTMAS IN CONNECTICUT(1945); CONFLICT(1945); PILLOW TO POST(1945); DEVOTION(1946); THREE STRANGERS(1946); VERDICT, THE(1946); HUCKSTERS, THE(1947); THAT WAY WITH WOMEN(1947); RUTHLESS(1948); VELVET TOUCH, THE(1948); WOMAN IN WHITE, THE(1948); FLAMINGO ROAD(1949); IT'S A GREAT FEELING(1949); MALAYA(1950)

Diana Greentree
GETTING OF WISDOM, THE(1977, Aus.); LONELY HEARTS(1983, Aus.)
George Greenville
BIG BRAWL, THE(1980), ed
Dr. Harold Greenwald
GIRL OF THE NIGHT(1960), w
Kenneth Greenwald
ARGYLE SECRETS, THE(1948)
Robert Greenwald
XANADU(1980), d
Sanford E. Greenwald
SUNSET BOULEVARD(1950)
Stephen R. Greenwald
AMITYVILLE II: THE POSSESSION(1982), p
Ted Greenwald
REVENGE OF THE CHEERLEADERS(1976), w
Virginia Greenwald
HUNGRY WIVES(1973)
David Greenwalt
CLASS(1983), w; UTILITIES(1983, Can.), w; WACKO(1983), w
1984
AMERICAN DREAMER(1984), w
Al Greenway
HEART IS A LONELY HUNTER, THE(1968), makeup; GREAT BANK ROBBERY, THE(1969), makeup; WILD BUNCH, THE(1969), makeup
Albert S. Greenway
PARIS MODEL(1953), makeup
Ann Greenway
HALF-MARRIAGE(1929); NIGHT PARADE(1929, Brit.)
Arthur Greenway
TWO MINUTES' SILENCE(1934, Brit.)
Dan Greenway
SHOCK CORRIDOR(1963), makeup; WILD ON THE BEACH(1965), makeup; WINTER A GO-GO(1965), makeup; FRANKIE AND JOHNNY(1966), makeup; SAM WHISKEY(1969), makeup; PICKUP ON 101(1972), makeup
Lee Greenway
SIREN OF ATLANTIS(1948), makeup; THING, THE(1951), makeup; SHOOT OUT AT BIG SAG(1962), makeup
Tom Greenway
DEPUTY MARSHAL(1949); IMPACT(1949); BIG TIMBER(1950); DAKOTA LIL(1950); HARLEM GLOBETROTTERS, THE(1951); MOB, THE(1951); NEVER TRUST A GAMBLER(1951); HIGH NOON(1952); KANSAS CITY CONFIDENTIAL(1952); OUTCASTS OF POKER FLAT, THE(1952); WINNING TEAM, THE(1952); GLASS WEB, THE(1953); HOW TO MARRY A MILLIONAIRE(1953); MR. SCOUTMASTER(1953); RIDE, VAQUERO!(1953); MIAMI STORY, THE(1954); TIGHT SPOT(1955); GREEN-EYED BLONDE, THE(1957); LAST OF THE BADMEN(1957); PEYTON PLACE(1957); TRUE STORY OF JESSE JAMES, THE(1957); NICE LITTLE BANK THAT SHOULD BE ROBBED, A(1958); SHEEPMAN, THE(1958); SING, BOY, SING(1958); NORTH BY NORTHWEST(1959); STORY ON PAGE ONE, THE(1959); THESE THOUSAND HILLS(1959); SECOND TIME AROUND, THE(1961)
Gaul Greenwell
COOL AND THE CRAZY, THE(1958)
John Greenwell
SHARKY'S MACHINE(1982)
Patrick Greenwell
UP THE FRONT(1972, Brit.), m
Peter Greenwell
VIRGIN SOLDIERS, THE(1970, Brit.), m, md; OUR MISS FRED(1972, Brit.), m
Al Greenwood
ISLE OF THE DEAD(1945), set d; SUSIE STEPS OUT(1946), set d
Barrett Greenwood
Silents
KID SISTER, THE(1927)
Bobby Greenwood
DAUGHTERS OF SATAN(1972)
1984
CAGED FURY(1984, Phil.), w
Bruce Greenwood
BEAR ISLAND(1980, Brit.-Can.)
Charlotte Greenwood
SO LONG LETTY(1929); FLYING HIGH(1931); MAN IN POSSESSION, THE(1931); PALMY DAYS(1931); PARLOR, BEDROOM AND BATH(1931); CHEATERS AT PLAY(1932); ORDERS IS ORDERS(1934, Brit.); DOWN ARGENTINE WAY(1940); STAR DUST(1940); YOUNG PEOPLE(1940); MOON OVER MIAMI(1941); PERFECT SNOB, THE(1941); TALL, DARK AND HANDSOME(1941); SPRINGTIME IN THE ROCKIES(1942); DIXIE DUGAN(1943); GANG'S ALL HERE, THE(1943); HOME IN INDIANA(1944); UP IN MABEL'S ROOM(1944); WAKE UP AND DREAM(1946); DRIFTWOOD(1947); GREAT DAN PATCH, THE(1949); OH, YOU BEAUTIFUL DOLL(1949); PEGGY(1950); DANGEROUS WHEN WET(1953); GLORY(1955); OKLAHOMA(1955); OPPOSITE SEX, THE(1956)
Misc. Talkies
STEPPING OUT(1931)
Silents
BABY MINE(1928)
Misc. Silents
JANE(1915)
Don Greenwood
YELLOW CANARY, THE(1963), set d; RIOT ON SUNSET STRIP(1967), set d; SPIRIT IS WILLING, THE(1967), set d
Don Greenwood, Jr.
HOW THE WEST WAS WON(1962), set d; YOUR CHEATIN' HEART(1964), set d; HARUM SCARUM(1965), set d; KARATE KILLERS, THE(1967), set d; LIVE A LITTLE, LOVE A LITTLE(1968), set d; POWER, THE(1968), set d; SPEEDWAY(1968), set d; STAY AWAY, JOE(1968), set d; HEAVEN WITH A GUN(1969), set d; ...TICK...TICK...TICK...(1970), set d
Ed Greenwood
LEAP OF FAITH(1931, Brit.), d&w

Edwin Greenwood

TO WHAT RED HELL(1929, Brit.), d; GIRL IN THE NIGHT, THE(1931, Brit.), w; LOVE RACE, THE(1931, Brit.), w; LORD CAMBER'S LADIES(1932, Brit.), w; MAID OF THE MOUNTAINS, THE(1932, Brit.), w; MONEY TALKS(1933, Brit.), w; MAN WHO KNEW TOO MUCH, THE(1935, Brit.), w; WHILE PARENTS SLEEP(1935, Brit.), w; EAST MEETS WEST(1936, Brit.), w; OLD SPANISH CUSTOM, AN(1936, Brit.), w; MAN OF AFFAIRS(1937, Brit.), w; YOUNG AND INNOCENT(1938, Brit.), w; JAMAICA INN(1939, Brit.)

Silents

AUDACIOUS MR. SQUIRE, THE(1923, Brit.), d; HEARTSTRINGS(1923, Brit.), d; PHYSICIAN, THE(1928, Brit.), w

Misc. Silents

FAIR MAID OF PERTH, THE(1923, Brit.), d; WOMAN IN PAWN, A(1927, Brit.), d

Ethel Greenwood

GIANT(1956)

Harold Greenwood

PRINCE AND THE SHOWGIRL, THE(1957, Brit.)

Herbert Greenwood

Misc. Silents

WHITE DOVE, THE(1920)

Hugh Greenwood

MRS. MINIVER(1942)

Jack Greenwood

LONG KNIFE, THE(1958, Brit.), p; MAN WITH A GUN(1958, Brit.), p; DESPERATE MAN, THE(1959, Brit.), p; HORRORS OF THE BLACK MUSEUM(1959, U.S./Brit.), p; WITNESS, THE(1959, Brit.), p; WRONG NUMBER(1959, Brit.), p; MAN WHO WAS NOBODY, THE(1960, Brit.), p; URGE TO KILL(1960, Brit.), p; ATTEMPT TO KILL(1961, Brit.), p; BACKFIRE!(1961, Brit.), p; CLUE OF THE NEW PIN, THE(1961, Brit.), p; CLUE OF THE SILVER KEY, THE(1961, Brit.), p; FOURTH SQUARE, THE(1961, Brit.), p; MAN AT THE CARLTON TOWER(1961, Brit.), p; MAN DE-TAINED(1961, Brit.), p; CONCRETE JUNGLE, THE(1962, Brit.), p; DEATH TRAP(1962, Brit.), p; FLAT TWO(1962, Brit.), p; LOCKER 69(1962, Brit.), p; NUMBER SIX(1962, Brit.), p; PLAYBACK(1962, Brit.), p; TIME TO REMEMBER(1962, Brit.), p; ACCIDENTAL DEATH(1963, Brit.), p; DOUBLE, THE(1963, Brit), p; FIVE TO ONE(1963, Brit.), p; RETURN TO SENDER(1963, Brit.), p; RIVALS, THE(1963, Brit.), p; SET-UP, THE(1963, Brit.), p; TO HAVE AND TO HOLD(1963, Brit.), p; DOWN-FALL(1964, Brit.), p; FACE OF A STRANGER(1964, Brit.), p; NEVER MENTION MURDER(1964, Brit.), p; VERDICT, THE(1964, Brit.), p; WE SHALL SEE(1964, Brit.), p; WHO WAS MADDOX?(1964, Brit.), p; 20,000 POUNDS KISS, THE(1964, Brit.), p; ACT OF MURDER(1965, Brit.), p; CHANGE PARTNERS(1965, Brit.), p; DEAD MAN'S CHEST(1965, Brit.), p; GAME FOR THREE LOSERS(1965, Brit.), p; INVASION(1965, Brit.), p; SINISTER MAN, THE(1965, Brit.), p; CANDIDATE FOR MURDER(1966, Brit.), p; INCIDENT AT MIDNIGHT(1966, Brit.), p; MAIN CHANCE, THE(1966, Brit.), p; PARTNER, THE(1966, Brit.), p; RICOCHET(1966, Brit.), p; SHARE OUT, THE(1966, Brit.), p; SOLO FOR SPARROW(1966, Brit.), p; STRANGLER'S WEB(1966, Brit.), p; NEVER BACK LOSERS(1967, Brit.), p; ON THE RUN(1967, Brit.), p; CLUE OF THE TWISTED CANDLE(1968, Brit.), p; MARRIAGE OF CONVENIENCE(1970, Brit.), p

Jane Greenwood

HAMLET(1964), cos; CAN'T STOP THE MUSIC(1980), cos; ARTHUR(1981), cos; FOUR SEASONS, THE(1981), cos

Joan Greenwood

HE FOUND A STAR(1941, Brit.); MY WIFE'S FAMILY(1941, Brit.); GENTLE SEX, THE(1943, Brit.); THEY KNEW MR. KNIGHT(1945, Brit.); FRENZY(1946, Brit.); GIRL IN A MILLION, A(1946, Brit.); BAD SISTER(1947, Brit.); OCTOBER MAN, THE(1948, Brit.); SMUGGLERS, THE(1948, Brit.); BAD LORD BYRON, THE(1949, Brit.); KIND HEARTS AND CORONETS(1949, Brit.); SARABAND(1949, Brit.); TIGHT LITTLE ISLAND(1949, Brit.); FLESH AND BLOOD(1951, Brit.); MR. PEEK-A-BOO(1951, Fr.); IMPORTANCE OF BEING EARNEST, THE(1952, Brit.); MAN IN THE WHITE SUIT, THE(1952, Brit.); DETECTIVE, THE(1954, Qit.); YOUNG WIVES' TALE(1954, Brit.); LOV-ERS, HAPPY LOVERS!(1955, Brit.); MOONFLEET(1955); STAGE STRUCK(1958); MYSTERIOUS ISLAND(1961, U.S./Brit.); TOM JONES(1963, Brit.); MOON-SPIN-NERS, THE(1964); AMOROUS MR. PRAWN, THE(1965, Brit.); GIRL STROKE BOY(1971, Brit.); UNCANNY, THE(1977, Brit./Can.); WATER BABIES, THE(1979, Brit.); HOUND OF THE BASKERVILLES, THE(1980, Brit.); WAGNER(1983, Brit./Hung./Aust.)

Joey Greenwood

1984

KILLPOINT(1984)

John Greenwood

OLD SPANISH CUSTOM, AN(1936, Brit.), m; ELEPHANT BOY(1937, Brit.), m; DRUMS(1938, Brit.), m; PRISON WITHOUT BARS(1939, Brit.), m; TWENTY-ONE DAYS TOGETHER(1940, Brit.), m; NINE MEN(1943, Brit.), m; GIRL ON THE CANAL, THE(1947, Brit.), m; HUNGRY HILL(1947, Brit.), m; SAN DEMETRIO, LON-DON(1947, Brit.), m; SCHOOL FOR DANGER(1947, Brit.), m; LAST DAYS OF DOL-WYN, THE(1949, Brit.), m; MASSACRE HILL(1949, Brit.), m; QUARTET(1949, Brit.), m; LOST PEOPLE, THE(1950, Brit.), m; TRIO(1950, Brit.), m; GENTLE GUN-MAN, THE(1952, Brit.), m; WICKED WIFE(1955, Brit.), m; RICHARD III(1956, Brit.); HANKY-PANKY(1982)

Johnny Greenwood

SOUL OF NIGGER CHARLEY, THE(1973)

Noel Greenwood

Silents

MEG(1926, Brit.)

Paul Greenwood

FRIGHTMARE(1974, Brit.)

Reeva Greenwood

Silents

EMBARRASSMENT OF RICHES, THE(1918)

Robert Greenwood

SALUTE JOHN CITIZEN(1942, Brit.), w

Rosamond Greenwood

CURSE OF THE DEMON(1958)

Rosamund Greenwood

SCHOOL FOR STARS(1935, Brit.); MEN ARE NOT GODS(1937, Brit.); ROOM FOR TWO(1940, Brit.); PETERVILLE DIAMOND, THE(1942, Brit.); GIVE US THE MOON(1944, Brit.); HEAVEN IS ROUND THE CORNER(1944, Brit.); PRINCE AND THE SHOWGIRL, THE(1957, Brit.); IDOL ON PARADE(1959, Brit.); VILLAGE OF THE DAMNED(1960, Brit.); TERM OF TRIAL(1962, Brit.); MURDER GAME, THE(1966, Brit.); LOVING MEMORY(1970, Brit.); MISSIONARY, THE(1982)

1984

SECRET PLACES(1984, Brit.)

Rosamunde Greenwood

SEVERED HEAD, A(1971, Brit.)

Unity Greenwood

MAN IN THE DARK(1963, Brit.); WRONG BOX, THE(1966, Brit.)

Walter Greenwood

NO LIMIT(1935, Brit.), w; LOVE ON THE DOLE(1945, Brit.), w; MASSACRE HILL(1949, Brit.), w; CHANCE OF A LIFETIME(1950, Brit.), w; CURE FOR LOVE, THE(1950, Brit.), w

Winifred Greenwood

Silents

M'LISS(1918); DON'T CALL ME LITTLE GIRL(1921); FAITH HEALER, THE(1921); TO THE LAST MAN(1923); KING OF KINGS, THE(1927)

Misc. Silents

DOLLAR-A-YEAR MAN, THE(1921)

Winifred Greenwood

Silents

ADVENTURE IN HEARTS, AN(1919); PUTTING IT OVER(1919); ARE ALL MEN ALIKE?(1920)

Misc. Silents

DUST(1916); INNER STRUGGLE, THE(1916); LYING LIPS(1916); RECLAMATION, THE(1916); VOICE OF LOVE, THE(1916); WOMAN'S DARING, A(1916); CRYSTAL GAZER, THE(1917); INSPIRATIONS OF HARRY LARRABEE(1917); DANGER WITH-IN(1918); DECIDING KISS, THE(1918); MAGGIE PEPPER(1919); LIFE OF THE PARTY, THE(1920); SICK ABED(1920); YOUNG MRS. WINTHROP(1920)

Al Greer

TOAST OF NEW YORK, THE(1937)

Allan Greer

Misc. Talkies

DEFYING THE LAW(1935)

Allen Greer

DESERT MESA(1935); ROUGH RIDING RANGER(1935); RUSTLER'S PARADIS-E(1935); WAGON TRAIL(1935); FEUD OF THE WEST(1936); ROMANCE RIDES THE RANGE(1936); GALLOPING DYNAMITE(1937); GLORY TRAIL, THE(1937)

Arlynn Greer

WILD HARVEST(1962)

Belle Greer

CAPTAIN MILKSHAKE(1970)

Bettejane "Jane" Greer

GEORGE WHITE'S SCANDALS(1945); PAN-AMERICANA(1945); TWO O'CLOCK COURAGE(1945)

Bill Greer

Misc. Talkies

HELP ME...I'M POSSESSED(1976)

Dabbs Greer

DAMNED DON'T CRY, THE(1950); SOUND OF FURY, THE(1950); STORM WARN-ING(1950); CALL ME MISTER(1951); FATHER'S LITTLE DIVIDEND(1951); UN-KNOWN MAN, THE(1951); BAD AND THE BEAUTIFUL, THE(1952); DIPLOMATIC COURIER(1952); MONKEY BUSINESS(1952); ROOM FOR ONE MORE(1952); SCAR-LET ANGEL(1952); WE'RE NOT MARRIED(1952); ABOVE AND BEYOND(1953); AFFAIR WITH A STRANGER(1953); CHINA VENTURE(1953); DREAM WIFE(1953); HALF A HERO(1953); HOUSE OF WAX(1953); MR. SCOUTMASTER(1953); REMAINS TO BE SEEN(1953); TROUBLE ALONG THE WAY(1953); BITTER CREEK(1954); DESPERADO, THE(1954); LIVING IT UP(1954); PRIVATE HELL 36(1954); RIOT IN CELL BLOCK 11(1954); ROSE MARIE(1954); SHE COULDN'T SAY NO(1954); FOX-FIRE(1955); MC CONNELL STORY, THE(1955); SCARLET COAT, THE(1955); SEVEN ANGRY MEN(1955); SEVEN LITTLE FOYS, THE(1955); D-DAY, THE SIXTH OF JUNE(1956); HOT CARS(1956); HOT ROD GIRL(1956); INVASION OF THE BODY SNATCHERS(1956); BABY FACE NELSON(1957); CHAIN OF EVIDENCE(1957); MY MAN GODFREY(1957); PAWNEE(1957); SPIRIT OF ST. LOUIS, THE(1957); VAM-PIRE, THE(1957); YOUNG AND DANGEROUS(1957); I WANT TO LIVE!(1958); IT! THE TERROR FROM BEYOND SPACE(1958); DAY OF THE OUTLAW(1959); EDGE OF ETERNITY(1959); LAST TRAIN FROM GUN HILL(1959); LONE TEXAN(1959); SHOWDOWN(1963); ROUSTABOUT(1964); SHENANDOAH(1965); CHEYENNE SO-CIAL CLUB, THE(1970); RAGE(1972); WHITE LIGHTNING(1973); CHU CHU AND THE PHILLY FLASH(1981)

Misc. Talkies

GOD BLESS DR. SHAGETZ(1977)

Dabs Greer

CASH McCALL(1960)

Dan Greer

SEVEN ALONE(1975), ed; BAKER'S HAWK(1976), w; PONY EXPRESS RI-DER(1976), p, w; SEA GYPSIES, THE(1978), ed; MOUNTAIN FAMILY ROBIN-SON(1979), ed

Don Greer

Misc. Talkies

JEKYLL AND HYDE PORTFOLIO, THE(1972)

Donn Greer

JOYSTICKS(1983), art d

Ethel Loreen Greer

ROAD TO ZANZIBAR(1941)

Germaine Greer

RIDING ON(1937); UNIVERSAL SOLDIER(1971, Brit.)

Germaine Greer [Joan Barclay]

STRIKE ME PINK(1936)

Howard Greer

WONDER OF WOMEN(1929), cos; CHRISTOPHER STRONG(1933), cos; BRINGING UP BABY(1938), cos; CAREFREE(1938), cos; FIFTH AVENUE GIRL(1939), cos; MY FAVORITE WIFE(1940), cos; FOLLOW THE BOYS(1944), cos; PRACTICALLY YOURS(1944), cos; LADY ON A TRAIN(1945), cos; SPELLBOUND(1945), cos; HEART-BEAT(1946), cos; HIS KIND OF WOMAN(1951), cos; LAS VEGAS STORY, THE(1952), cos; FRENCH LINE, THE(1954), cos

Jane Greer

THEY WON'T BELIEVE ME(1947); DICK TRACY(1945); BAMBOO BLONDE, THE(1946); FALCON'S ALIBI, THE(1946); SUNSET PASS(1946); OUT OF THE PAST(1947); SINBAD THE SAILOR(1947); STATION WEST(1948); BIG STEAL, THE(1949); COMPANY SHE KEEPS, THE(1950); YOU'RE IN THE NAVY NOW(1951); DESPERATE SEARCH(1952); PRISONER OF ZENDA, THE(1952); YOU FOR ME(1952); CLOWN, THE(1953); DOWN AMONG THE SHELTERING PALMS(1953);

RUN FOR THE SUN(1956); MAN OF A THOUSAND FACES(1957); WHERE LOVE HAS GONE(1964); BILLIE(1965); OUTFIT, THE(1973)
1984
   AGAINST ALL ODDS(1984)
Karen Greer
   TWO GROOMS FOR A BRIDE(1957)
Linda Greer
   SCANDAL AT SCOURIE(1953)
Liza Greer
   ANGELS BRIGADE(1980)
Luanshiya Greer
   SMASHING TIME(1967 Brit.); THEY CAME FROM BEYOND SPACE(1967, Brit.)
Melody Greer
   SLENDER THREAD, THE(1965)
Michael Greer
   CURIOUS FEMALE, THE(1969); GAY DECEIVERS, THE(1969); DIAMOND STUD(1970); MAGIC GARDEN OF STANLEY SWEETHART, THE(1970); FORTUNE AND MEN'S EYES(1971, U.S./Can.); DEAD PEOPLE(1974); SUMMER SCHOOL TEACHERS(1977); ROSE, THE(1979)
1984
   LONELY GUY, THE(1984)
Misc. Talkies
   DIAMOND STUD(1970)
Rich Greer
   RAIN FOR A DUSTY SUMMER(1971, U.S./Span.), ed
Richard Greer
   CAPE CANAVERAL MONSTERS(1960), p; ROOMMATES, THE(1973), ed; WONDER WOMEN(1973, Phil.), ed
Robin Greer
   SATAN'S CHEERLEADERS(1977); ANGELS BRIGADE(1980)
Simon Greer
Silents
   FAIR PLAY(1925)
Claire Greet
   SIGN OF FOUR, THE(1932, Brit.); SIDEWALKS OF LONDON(1940, Brit.)
Clare Greet
   MURDER(1930, Brit.); ALIBI(1931, Brit.); MANY WATERS(1931, Brit.); THIRD TIME LUCKY(1931, Brit.); LORD BABS(1932, Brit.); LORD CAMBER'S LADIES(1932, Brit.); MRS. DANE'S DEFENCE(1933, Brit.); WHITE FACE(1933, Brit.); LITTLE FRIEND(1934, Brit.); POINTING FINGER, THE(1934, Brit.); MURDER IN THE OLD RED BARN(1936, Brit.); ROYAL EAGLE(1936, Brit.); SABOTAGE(1937, Brit.); EMIL(1938, Brit.); JAMAICA INN(1939, Brit.)
Silents
   LOVE AT THE WHEEL(1921, Brit.); RING, THE(1927, Brit.); MANXMAN, THE(1929, Brit.)
Dinah Greet
   HELP!(1965, Brit.), cos; THOSE MAGNIFICENT MEN IN THEIR FLYING MACHINES; OR HOW I FLEWFROM LONDON TO PARIS IN 25 HOURS AND 11 MINUTES(1965, Brit.), cos; HOW I WON THE WAR(1967, Brit.), cos; DIAMONDS FOR BREAKFAST(1968, Brit.), cos; INSPECTOR CLOUSEAU(1968, Brit.), cos; ITALIAN JOB, THE(1969, Brit.), cos; LOOKING GLASS WAR, THE(1970, Brit.), cos; YOU CAN'T WIN 'EM ALL(1970, Brit.), cos
Vernon Greeves
   HENRY V(1946, Brit.); PAPER ORCHID(1949, Brit.); WOMAN HATER(1949, Brit.); FINGER OF GUILT(1956, Brit.); LADY OF VENGEANCE(1957, Brit); LET'S BE HAPPY(1957, Brit.)
John Greewood
   PIMPERNEL SMITH(1942, Brit.), m; FRIEDA(1947, Brit.), m
Melanie Grefe
   PORKY'S II: THE NEXT DAY(1983)
William Grefe
   CHECKERED FLAG, THE(1963), d&w; RACING FEVER(1964), p,d&w; DEVIL'S SISTERS, THE(1966), d, w; STING OF DEATH(1966), d; DEATH CURSE OF TARTU(1967), d&w; WILD REBELS, THE(1967), d&w; HOOKED GENERATION, THE(1969), p&d, w; NAKED ZOO, THE(1970), p&d, w; STANLEY(1973), p&d, w; IMPULSE(1975), d; MAKO: THE JAWS OF DEATH(1976), p&d
Misc. Talkies
   WHISKEY MOUNTAIN(1977), d
Constantine Greftman
   CONFESSIONS OF A ROGUE(1948, Fr.), d
Max Greger
   PLAYGIRLS AND THE BELLBOY, THE(1962,Ger.)
Em Gregers
Misc. Silents
   HVEM ER HUN?(1914, Den.), a, d
Alan Gregg
   DEVIL'S SADDLE LEGION, THE(1937); RHYTHM OF THE SADDLE(1938)
Arnold Gregg
Silents
   WHITE YOUTH(1920); OLD SOAK, THE(1926); POWER OF THE WEAK, THE(1926); SKYROCKET, THE(1926)
Christian Gregg
   BREAK, THE(1962, Brit.)
Christina Gregg
   LIFE IN EMERGENCY WARD 10(1959, Brit.); COVER GIRL KILLER(1960, Brit.); TASTE OF MONEY, A(1960, Brit.); TWO WIVES AT ONE WEDDING(1961, Brit.); DON'T TALK TO STRANGE MEN(1962, Brit.); FATE TAKES A HAND(1962, Brit.); YOUNG, WILLING AND EAGER(1962, Brit.); YOUNG RACERS, THE(1963)
Colin Gregg
   REMEMBRANCE(1982, Brit.), p&d
Misc. Talkies
   BEGGING THE RING(1979, Brit.), d
Everley Gregg
   PRIVATE LIFE OF HENRY VIII, THE(1933); SCOUNDREL, THE(1935); GHOST GOES WEST, THE(1936); THUNDER IN THE CITY(1937, Brit.); BLONDES FOR DANGER(1938, Brit.); PYGMALION(1938, Brit.); SPIES OF THE AIR(1940, Brit.); IN WHICH WE SERVE(1942, Brit.); GENTLE SEX, THE(1943, Brit.); UNCENSORED(1944, Brit.); ADVENTURE FOR TWO(1945, Brit.); BRIEF ENCOUNTER(1945, Brit.); ADVENTURESS, THE(1946, Brit.); GREAT EXPECTATIONS(1946, Brit.); HUGGETTS ABROAD, THE(1949, Brit.); MARRY ME!(1949, Brit.); ASTONISHED HEART,

THE(1950, Brit.); FIVE ANGLES ON MURDER(1950, Brit.); STAGE FRIGHT(1950, Brit.); WORM'S EYE VIEW(1951, Brit.); FRANCHISE AFFAIR, THE(1952, Brit.); MOULIN ROUGE(1952); STOLEN FACE(1952, Brit.); DETECTIVE, THE(1954, Qit.); NIGHT OF THE FULL MOON, THE(1954, Brit.); CARRY ON ADMIRAL(1957, Brit.); TEARS FOR SIMON(1957, Brit.); ROOM AT THE TOP(1959, Brit.)
Everly Gregg
   WOMAN IN THE HALL, THE(1949, Brit.); MAGIC BOX, THE(1952, Brit.); MAN WHO NEVER WAS, THE(1956, Brit.); DEADLY RECORD(1959, Brit.)
Frances Gregg
   MARY BURNS, FUGITIVE(1935); WHIPSAW(1936)
Helen Gregg
Silents
   DOG LAW(1928), t; ORPHAN OF THE SAGE(1928), t; YOUNG WHIRLWIND(1928), t; AMAZING VAGABOND(1929), t; GUN LAW(1929), t; IDAHO RED(1929), t; ONE MAN DOG, THE(1929), t; OUTLAWED(1929), t; PALS OF THE PRAIRIE(1929), t
Hubert Gregg
   FLYING FORTRESS(1942, Brit.); IN WHICH WE SERVE(1942, Brit.); ROOT OF ALL EVIL, THE(1947, Brit.); VOTE FOR HUGGETT(1948, Brit.); FACTS OF LOVE(1949, Brit.); ONCE UPON A DREAM(1949, Brit.); THIRD VISITOR, THE(1951, Brit.); STORY OF ROBIN HOOD, THE(1952, Brit.); LANDFALL(1953, Brit.); FINAL APPOINTMENT(1954, Brit.); HIGH AND DRY(1954, Brit.); DOCTOR AT SEA(1955, Brit.); ROOM IN THE HOUSE(1955, Brit.); SVENGALI(1955, Brit.); SIMON AND LAURA(1956, Brit.); STARS IN YOUR EYES(1956, Brit.), a, w; THREE MEN IN A BOAT(1958, Brit.), w
John Gregg
   HEATWAVE(1983, Aus.)
Joyce Gregg
   WOMAN EATER, THE(1959, Brit.)
Julie Gregg
   GODFATHER, THE(1972); MAN OF LA MANCHA(1972)
Katherine Gregg
   LILITH(1964)
Olive Gregg
   PASSING STRANGER, THE(1954, Brit.); BEHIND THE HEADLINES(1956, Brit.); PSYCHOPATH, THE(1966, Brit.)
Reverend Gregg
   IMITATION OF LIFE(1934)
Sharon Gregg
1984
   REPO MAN(1984)
Virginia Gregg
   NOTORIOUS(1946); BODY AND SOUL(1947); GENTLEMAN'S AGREEMENT(1947); CASBAH(1948); GAY INTRUDERS, THE(1948); SPIRITUALIST, THE(1948); FLESH AND FURY(1952); DRAGNET(1954); I'LL CRY TOMORROW(1955); LOVE IS A MANY-SPLENDORED THING(1955); CRIME IN THE STREETS(1956); FASTEST GUN ALIVE(1956); TERROR AT MIDNIGHT(1956); D.I., THE(1957); PORTLAND EXPOSE(1957); TWILIGHT FOR THE GODS(1958); HANGING TREE, THE(1959); HOUND-DOG MAN(1959); OPERATION PETTICOAT(1959); ALL THE FINE YOUNG CANNIBALS(1960); PSYCHO(1960); MAN-TRAP(1961); HOUSE OF WOMEN(1962); SHOOT OUT AT BIG SAG(1962); SPENCER'S MOUNTAIN(1963); JOY IN THE MORNING(1965); TWO ON A GUILLOTINE(1965); BIG HAND FOR THE LITTLE LADY, A(1966); BUBBLE, THE(1967); MADIGAN(1968); HEAVEN WITH A GUN(1969); WALK IN THE SPRING RAIN, A(1970); NO WAY BACK(1976); S.O.B.(1981); HEIDI'S SONG(1982)
W. Hubert Gregg
   AFTER THE BALL(1957, Brit.), w
Walter Gregg
   HOUR OF THE GUN(1967); SINGLE ROOM FURNISHED(1968)
Pascal Greggory
   BRONTE SISTERS, THE(1979, Fr.); LE BEAU MARIAGE(1982, Fr.); PAULINE AT THE BEACH(1983, Fr.)
Helene Gregoire
   QUEST FOR FIRE(1982, Fr./Can.)
Arthur Gregor
   STRANGE CARGO(1929), d; WHAT PRICE DECENCY?(1933), d&w
Silents
   PHYLLIS OF THE FOLLIES(1928), w; SCARLET DOVE, THE(1928), d&w
Misc. Silents
   COUNT OF LUXEMBOURG, THE(1926), d; WOMEN'S WARES(1927), d
Manfred Gregor
   BRIDGE, THE(1961, Ger.), w; TOWN WITHOUT PITY(1961, Ger./Switz./U.S.), w
Martin Gregor
   TRANSPORT FROM PARADISE(1967, Czech.)
Nora Gregor
   BUT THE FLESH IS WEAK(1932); WHAT WOMEN DREAM(1933, Ger.); RULES OF THE GAME, THE(1939, Fr.)
Misc. Silents
   MICHAEL(1924, Ger.); CHAINED(1927, Ger.)
Mimosa Gregoretti
   CLIMAX, THE(1967, Fr., Ital.)
Ugo Gregoretti
   OMICRON(1963, Ital.), d&w; BEAUTIFUL SWINDLERS, THE(1967, Fr./Ital./Jap./Neth.), d
A. Gregoriades
   ELECTRA(1962, Gr.)
Rose Gregorio
   SWIMMER, THE(1968); DESPERATE CHARACTERS(1971); WHO IS HARRY KELLERMAN AND WHY IS HE SAYING THOSE TERRIBLE THINGS ABOUT ME?(1971); EYES OF LAURA MARS(1978); TRUE CONFESSIONS(1981)
Andre Gregory
   MY DINNER WITH ANDRE(1981), a, w; AUTHOR! AUTHOR!(1982)
1984
   PROTOCOL(1984)
Anne Gregory
Misc. Silents
   UNDER FALSE COLORS(1917)
B. Gregory
   "W" PLAN, THE(1931, Brit.)

Bob Gregory
KEEP FIT(1937, Brit.); RAT, THE(1938, Brit.); MOB TOWN(1941)
Bruce Gregory
PLEDGEMASTERS, THE(1971)
Carl Louis Gregory
Misc. Silents
LOVE'S FLAME(1920), d
Celia Gregory
AGATHA(1979, Brit.)
Count Gregory
GIRL FEVER(1961)
David Gregory
DANGEROUS YOUTH(1958, Brit.); AND WOMEN SHALL WEEP(1960, Brit.); GAOL-BREAK(1962, Brit.); YOUNG, WILLING AND EAGER(1962, Brit.); HI-JACKERS, THE(1963, Brit.); MARKED ONE, THE(1963, Brit.); THESE ARE THE DAMNED(1965, Brit.); WHERE THE BULLETS FLY(1966, Brit.)
Dick Gregory
WRONG BOX, THE(1966, Brit.); SWEET LOVE, BITTER(1967); PROLOGUE(1970, Can.)
Don Gregory
TRACK OF THUNDER(1967)
Dora Gregory
SKIN GAME, THE(1931, Brit.); DOMINANT SEX, THE(1937, Brit.); HIDDEN MEN-ACE, THE(1940, Brit.); IN WHICH WE SERVE(1942, Brit.)
Douglas Gregory
SIN YOU SINNERS(1963)
Ed Gregory
RAGING BULL(1980)
Edna Gregory
JAZZ SINGER, THE(1927)
Ena Gregory
LIVE, LOVE AND LEARN(1937)
Silents
PREPARED TO DIE(1923); DESERT FLOWER, THE(1925); DOUBLING WITH DANGER(1926); BLAZING DAYS(1927); DOWN THE STRETCH(1927); WESTERN ROVER, THE(1927)
Misc. Silents
SHORT SKIRTS(1921); DEFYING THE LAW(1922); DEVIL'S DOORYARD, THE(1923); LAW RUSTLERS, THE(1923); COLD NERVE(1925); BETTER MAN, THE(1926); ONE MAN TRAIL(1926); RED HOT LEATHER(1926); GRINNING GUNS(1927); MEN OF DARING(1927); ROMANTIC ROGUE(1927); ROUGH AND READY(1927)
Fabian Gregory
SAVAGE SEVEN, THE(1968)
Francis Gregory
BREAKERS AHEAD(1935, Brit.)
Frank Gregory
LIVING DANGEROUSLY(1936, Brit.), w; THEN THERE WERE THREE(1961), a, w; INVINCIBLE GLADIATOR, THE(1963, c.u. Ital./Span.), d; CASANOVA '70(1965, Ital.); AFTER YOU, COMRADE(1967, S. Afr.)
George Gregory
PUNISHMENT PARK(1971)
Gilliam Gregory
MAHLER(1974, Brit.), ch; THERE GOES THE BRIDE(1980, Brit.), ch
Gillian Gregory
BOY FRIEND, THE(1971, Brit.), ch; TOMMY(1975, Brit.), ch; BUGSY MALO-NE(1976, Brit.), ch; VALENTINO(1977, Brit.), ch; QUADROPHENIA(1979, Brit.), ch; SHOCK TREATMENT(1981), ch; RETURN OF THE JEDI(1983), ch
1984
PRIVATES ON PARADE(1984, Brit.), ch; TOP SECRET!(1984), ch
Grace Gregory
PERFECT MARRIAGE, THE(1946), set d; GOLDEN EARRINGS(1947), set d; SUD-DENLY IT'S SPRING(1947), set d; ACCUSED, THE(1949), set d; ROPE OF SAND(1949), set d; TURNING POINT, THE(1952), set d; COUNTRY GIRL, THE(1954), set d; ELEPHANT WALK(1954), set d; WHITE CHRISTMAS(1954), set d; DESPER-ATE HOURS, THE(1955), set d; WE'RE NO ANGELS(1955), set d; MOUNTAIN, THE(1956), set d; DEVIL'S HAIRPIN, THE(1957), set d; JOKER IS WILD, THE(1957), set d; HOUSEBOAT(1958), set d; MARACAIBO(1958), set d; LOVE WITH THE PROP-ER STRANGER(1963), set d; MY SIX LOVES(1963), set d
Iain Gregory
SWORD OF LANCELOT(1963, Brit.); GUTTER GIRLS(1964, Brit.); GONKS GO BEAT(1965, Brit.)
Iola Gregory
1984
ADERYN PAPUR(1984, Brit.)
Jackson Gregory
SUDDEN BILL DORN(1938), w; LARAMIE TRAIL, THE(1944), w
Silents
MAN FROM PAINTED POST, THE(1917), w; JOYOUS TROUBLEMAKERS, THE(1920), w; BILLY JIM(1922), w; MAN TO MAN(1922), w
James Gregory
SILENCERS, THE(; TWO WEEKS IN ANOTHER TOWN(1962); NAKED CITY, THE(1948); FROGMEN, THE(1951); NIGHTFALL(1956); SCARLET HOUR, THE(1956); BIG CAPER, THE(1957); GUN GLORY(1957); YOUNG STRANGER, THE(1957); ON-IONHEAD(1958); UNDERWATER WARRIOR(1958); AL CAPONE(1959); HEY BOY! HEY GIRL!(1959); X-15(1961); MANCHURIAN CANDIDATE, THE(1962); CAPTAIN NEWMAN, M.D.(1963); PT 109(1963); TWILIGHT OF HONOR(1963); DISTANT TRUM-PET, A(1964); QUICK, BEFORE IT MELTS(1964); RAGE TO LIVE, A(1965); SONS OF KATIE ELDER, THE(1965); MURDERERS' ROW(1966); AMBUSHERS, THE(1967); CLAMBAKE(1967); SECRET WAR OF HARRY FRIGG, THE(1968); LOVE GOD?, THE(1969); BENEATH THE PLANET OF THE APES(1970); HAWAIIANS, THE(1970); LATE LIZ, THE(1971); SHOOT OUT(1971); $1,000,000 DUCK(1971); STRONGEST MAN IN THE WORLD, THE(1975); OFF THE WALL(1977), p, ed; MAIN EVENT, THE(1979)
Jay Gregory
TAPS(1981)
Jennifer Gregory
Misc. Talkies
GOD'S BLOODY ACRE(1975)

John Gregory
SHOCK CORRIDOR(1963), ch; BLOOD BEAST FROM OUTER SPACE(1965, Brit.), m
1984
NUMBER ONE(1984, Brit.), ed
Johnny Gregory
STRONGROOM(1962, Brit.), m
Jon Gregory
KING'S RHAPSODY(1955, Brit.), a, ch; CONFESSIONS OF AN OPIUM EA-TER(1962), ch; JACK THE GIANT KILLER(1962), ch
Karen Gregory
PROUD RIDER, THE(1971, Can.)
Lady Gregory
RISING OF THE MOON, THE(1957, Ireland), w
Iain Gregory
GIRL GETTERS, THE(1966, Brit.)
Le Petit Gregory
SMALL CHANGE(1976, Fr.)
Lee Gregory
GODSEND, THE(1980, Can.)
Leonard Gregory
MC VICAR(1982, Brit.)
Lyndam Gregory
FUNNY MONEY(1983, Brit.)
Mark Gregory
1990: THE BRONX WARRIORS(1983, Ital.)
1984
WARRIORS OF THE WASTELAND(1984, Ital.)
Martin Gregory
SHOP ON MAIN STREET, THE(1966, Czech.)
Mary Ethel Gregory
1984
FOOTLOOSE(1984)
Mary Gregory
TROOPER HOOK(1957); ANGEL IN MY POCKET(1969); THEY SHOOT HORSES, DON'T THEY?(1969); SLEEPER(1973)
Michael Gregory
MR. RICCO(1975); TWO-MINUTE WARNING(1976)
1984
BEVERLY HILLS COP(1984)
Mildred Gregory
Silents
CLIMBERS, THE(1915); ACCORDING TO LAW(1916)
Misc. Silents
BONDWOMEN(1915)
Muriel Gregory
Silents
LIEUTENANT DARING RN AND THE WATER RATS(1924, Brit.); MONEY HABIT, THE(1924, Brit.)
Nigel Gregory
Misc. Talkies
KILLER'S MOON(1978)
Patricia Gregory
SHAKE, RATTLE, AND ROCK!(1957)
Paul Gregory
WHOOPEE(1930); CHILDREN OF DREAMS(1931); SIT TIGHT(1931); WINE, WOM-EN, AND SONG(1934); NIGHT OF THE HUNTER, THE(1955), p; NAKED AND THE DEAD, THE(1958), p
Robert Gregory
DEVIL'S MISTRESS, THE(1968)
Rowena Gregory
INTRUDER, THE(1955, Brit.); LADY GODIVA RIDES AGAIN(1955, Brit.); SILENT PLAYGROUND, THE(1964, Brit.)
Roxanne Gregory
WITHOUT A TRACE(1983)
Sebastian Gregory
FANDANGO(1970)
Misc. Talkies
HANG-UP, THE(1969); COME ONE, COME ALL(1970), d
Sharee Gregory
1984
JOY OF SEX(1984); MASS APPEAL(1984)
Sol K. Gregory
SEA GOD, THE(1930)
Stephen Gregory
HAIL THE CONQUERING HERO(1944)
Steve Gregory
STARLIFT(1951)
Teddy Gregory
DEVIL'S MISTRESS, THE(1968), ph
Thea Gregory
GOLDEN LINK, THE(1954, Brit.); PAID TO KILL(1954, Brit.); PROFILE(1954, Brit.); SOLUTION BY PHONE(1954, Brit.); WEAK AND THE WICKED, THE(1954, Brit.); SATELLITE IN THE SKY(1956)
Wallace Gregory
SWORN ENEMY(1936); TICKET TO PARADISE(1936)
Will Gregory
ROTTEN APPLE, THE(1963)
Silents
SENSATION SEEKERS(1927)
Florence Gregson
GOOD COMPANIONS(1933, Brit.); SING AS WE GO(1934, Brit.); NO LIMIT(1935, Brit.)
Jack Gregson
SUBMARINE COMMAND(1951)
James Gregson
VALUE FOR MONEY(1957, Brit.)
James R. Gregson
SING AS WE GO(1934, Brit.)

Jeannie Gregson
HAPPIDROME(1943, Brit.)
Jennie Gregson
TALKING FEET(1937, Brit.); OLD MOTHER RILEY'S CIRCUS(1941, Brit.)
Joan Gregson
NEPTUNE FACTOR, THE(1973, Can.)
John Gregson
DULCIMER STREET(1948, Brit.); SARABAND(1949, Brit.); SCOTT OF THE ANTARCTIC(1949, Brit.); TIGHT LITTLE ISLAND(1949, Brit.); CAIRO ROAD(1950, Brit.); TREASURE ISLAND(1950, Brit.); LAVENDER HILL MOB, THE(1951, Brit.); BRAVE DON'T CRY, THE(1952, Brit.); TRAIN OF EVENTS(1952, Brit.); ASSASSIN, THE(1953, Brit.); GENEVIEVE(1953, Brit.); TITFIELD THUNDERBOLT, THE(1953, Brit.); ANGELS ONE FIVE(1954, Brit.); CROWDED DAY, THE(1954, Brit.); FUSS OVER FEATHERS(1954, Brit.); HOLLY AND THE IVY, THE(1954, Brit.); WEAK AND THE WICKED, THE(1954, Brit.); THREE CASES OF MURDER(1955, Brit.); ABOVE US THE WAVES(1956, Brit.); CASH ON DELIVERY(1956, Brit.); JACQUELINE(1956, Brit.); MIRACLE IN SOHO(1957, Brit.); PURSUIT OF THE GRAF SPEE(1957, Brit.); TRUE AS A TURTLE(1957, Brit.); VALUE FOR MONEY(1957, Brit.); ROONEY(1958, Brit.); CAPTAIN'S TABLE, THE(1960, Brit.); FACES IN THE DARK(1960, Brit.); HAND IN HAND(1960, Brit.); S.O.S. PACIFIC(1960, Brit.); FRIGHTENED CITY, THE(1961, Brit.); SECRET OF MONTE CRISTO, THE(1961, Brit.); DESERT PATROL(1962, Brit.); LIVE NOW–PAY LATER(1962, Brit.); LONGEST DAY, THE(1962); TOMORROW AT TEN(1964, Brit.); NIGHT OF THE GENERALS, THE(1967, Brit./Fr.); FRIGHT(1971, Brit.)
Misc. Talkies
FLIGHT FROM TREASON(1960, Brit.); HANS BRINKER AND THE SILVER SKATES(1969)
Michael Gregson
EMBEZZLER, THE(1954, Brit.)
Richard Gregson
ANGRY SILENCE, THE(1960, Brit.), w; DOWNHILL RACER(1969), p
Stephen Gregson
UPSTAIRS AND DOWNSTAIRS(1961, Brit.)
Warwick Gregson
ENCHANTMENT(1948)
Thea Gregson [Thea Gregory]
MAGNET, THE(1950, Brit.)
Boris Gregurevitch
MICKEY ONE(1965)
George Greif
HARRY AND WALTER GO TO NEW YORK(1976)
Stephen Greif
NICHOLAS AND ALEXANDRA(1971, Brit.)
Misc. Talkies
GREAT RIVIERA BANK ROBBERY, THE(1979)
Lewis Greifer
CASH ON DEMAND(1962, Brit.), w; UP JUMPED A SWAGMAN(1965, Brit.), w; MAN WHO FINALLY DIED, THE(1967, Brit.), w
Samson X. Greiff
SMALL CIRCLE OF FRIENDS, A(1980)
Joe Greig
SPRING AND PORT WINE(1970, Brit.)
Margaret Greig
FLASH THE SHEEPDOG(1967, Brit.)
Richard Greig
ANIMAL CRACKERS(1930)
Robert Greig
BORN TO LOVE(1931); BEAUTY AND THE BOSS(1932); COHENS, AND KELLYS IN HOLLYWOOD, THE(1932); JEWEL ROBBERY(1932); LOVE ME TONIGHT(1932); MAN WANTED(1932); MERRILY WE GO TO HELL(1932); STEPPING SISTERS(1932); TENDERFOOT, THE(1932); TROUBLE IN PARADISE(1932); DANGEROUSLY YOURS(1933); IT'S GREAT TO BE ALIVE(1933); MIND READER, THE(1933); MORNING GLORY(1933); PLEASURE CRUISE(1933); ROBBERS' ROOST(1933); COCKEYED CAVALIERS(1934); EASY TO LOVE(1934); LOVE CAPTIVE, THE(1934); MADAME DU BARRY(1934); ONE MORE RIVER(1934); STINGAREE(1934); UPPER WORLD(1934); CLIVE OF INDIA(1935); GAY DECEPTION, THE(1935); MARK OF THE VAMPIRE(1935); ANY MAN'S WIFE(1936); DEVIL DOLL, THE(1936); EASY TO TAKE(1936); GREAT ZIEGFELD, THE(1936); LLOYDS OF LONDON(1936); ROSE MARIE(1936); SMALL TOWN GIRL(1936); STOWAWAY(1936); THEODORA GOES WILD(1936); TROUBLE FOR TWO(1936); UNGUARDED HOUR, THE(1936); EASY LIVING(1937); LADY BEHAVE(1937); MICHAEL O'HALLORAN(1937); MY DEAR MISS ALDRICH(1937); ALGIERS(1938); MIDNIGHT INTRUDER(1938); YOU CAN'T TAKE IT WITH YOU(1938); DRUMS ALONG THE MOHAWK(1939); HONEYMOON'S OVER, THE(1939); IT COULD HAPPEN TO YOU(1939); LITTLE ACCIDENT(1939); TOWER OF LONDON(1939); WAY DOWN SOUTH(1939); HUDSON'S BAY(1940); NO TIME FOR COMEDY(1940); LADY EVE, THE(1941); MOON OVER MIAMI(1941); SULLIVAN'S TRAVELS(1941); ARABIAN NIGHTS(1942); GIRL TROUBLE(1942); I MARRIED A WITCH(1942); MAD MARTINDALES, THE(1942); PALM BEACH STORY, THE(1942); LAUGH YOUR BLUES AWAY(1943); THREE HEARTS FOR JULIA(1943); GREAT MOMENT, THE(1944); MILLION DOLLAR KID(1944); MRS. PARKINGTON(1944); SUMMER STORM(1944); EARL CARROLL'S VANITIES(1945); HOLLYWOOD AND VINE(1945); LOVE, HONOR AND GOODBYE(1945); NOB HILL(1945); PICTURE OF DORIAN GRAY, THE(1945); FOREVER AMBER(1947); UNFAITHFULLY YOURS(1948)
Virginia Greig
1984
SUPERGIRL(1984)
Robert Greigs
CHEATERS, THE(1945)
Anita Greil
MAEDCHEN IN UNIFORM(1965, Ger./Fr.), makeup; GIRL AND THE LEGEND, THE(1966, Ger.), makeup
Paul Greimann
1984
FLASHPOINT(1984), prod d
Fritz Greiner
NUMBER SEVENTEEN(1928, Brit./Ger.); CRUISER EMDEN(1932, Ger.)
Misc. Silents
MANON LESCAUT(1926, Ger.)

Irving Greines
THIS LOVE OF OURS(1945)
Walter Greinhart
LEFT-HANDED WOMAN, THE(1980, Ger.)
Engelbert Greis
NOT RECONCILED, OR "ONLY VIOLENCE HELPS WHERE IT RULES"(1969, Ger.)
Elliot Greisinger
GREAT ADVENTURE, THE(1976, Span./Ital.), p
Alan Greisman
HEART BEAT(1979), p; MODERN PROBLEMS(1981), p
1984
FLETCH(1984), p; WINDY CITY(1984), p
M. Grekov
SANDU FOLLOWS THE SUN(1965, USSR)
Carol Grel
SO BIG(1953)
Michele Grellier
BERNADETTE OF LOURDES(1962, Fr.); MARRIAGE OF FIGARO, THE(1963, Fr.); IMMORAL MOMENT, THE(1967, Fr.)
Michelle Grellier
WOULD-BE GENTLEMAN, THE(1960, Fr.)
Brian Grellis
ONLY WHEN I LARF(1968, Brit.); SUMARINE X-1(1969, Brit.); MOSQUITO SQUADRON(1970, Brit.); TROG(1970, Brit.); FEAR IN THE NIGHT(1972, Brit.)
Ankie Grelson
1984
BLIND DATE(1984)
Henri Gremieux
CADET-ROUSSELLE(1954, Fr.)
Barry Gremillion
DRIVE-IN(1976)
Jean Gremillion
LUMIERE D'ETE(1943, Fr.), d
Jean Gremillon
STORMY WATERS(1946, Fr.), d; WOMAN WHO DARED(1949, Fr.), p&d; LE CIEL EST A VOUS(1957, Fr.), d
Misc. Silents
MALDONE(1928, Fr.), d; GARDIENS DE PHARE(1929, Fr.), d
W. Gremin
NO GREATER LOVE(1944, USSR)
Wolf Gremm
KAMIKAZE '89(1983, Ger.), d, w; QUERELLE(1983, Ger./Fr.)
Charles Gremora
PHANTOM OF THE RUE MORGUE(1954)
Carmen Grenada
WEST OF THE PECOS(1945)
Sylvia Grenade
END OF THE WORLD, THE(1930, Fr.)
Ole Grenberg
OCEAN BREAKERS(1949, Swed.)
Lillian Grencker
GURU, THE MAD MONK(1971), art d
Frederic Grendel
DIABOLIQUE(1955, Fr.), w; THREE FABLES OF LOVE(1963, Fr./Ital./Span.), w; VIOLETTE(1978, Fr.), w
Stephen Grendon
SWALLOWS AND AMAZONS(1977, Brit.)
Joyce Grenfell
LAMP STILL BURNS, THE(1943, Brit.); ADVENTURE FOR TWO(1945, Brit.); POET'S PUB(1949, Brit.); HAPPIEST DAYS OF YOUR LIFE(1950, Brit.); RUN FOR YOUR MONEY, A(1950, Brit.); STAGE FRIGHT(1950, Brit.); WHILE THE SUN SHINES(1950, Brit.); GALLOPING MAJOR, THE(1951, Brit.); LAUGHTER IN PARADISE(1951, Brit.); MAGIC BOX, THE(1952, Brit.); PICKWICK PAPERS, THE(1952, Brit.); GENEVIEVE(1953, Brit.); BELLES OF ST. TRINIAN'S, THE(1954, Brit.); FORBIDDEN CARGO(1954, Brit.); MAN WITH A MILLION(1954, Brit.); GOOD COMPANIONS, THE(1957, Brit.); BLUE MURDER AT ST. TRINIAN'S(1958, Brit.); HAPPY IS THE BRIDE(1958, Brit.); PURE HELL OF ST. TRINIAN'S, THE(1961, Brit.); OLD DARK HOUSE, THE(1963, Brit.); AMERICANIZATION OF EMILY, THE(1964); YELLOW ROLLS-ROYCE, THE(1965, Brit.)
Sir Wilfred Grenfell
VIKING, THE(1931)
Jack Grenhalgh
TRIGGER PALS(1939), ph
Cynthia Grenier
FINO A FARTI MALE(1969, Fr./Ital.)
Larry Grenier
OLD-FASHIONED WAY, THE(1934); REUNION IN FRANCE(1942)
Paul Grenier
1984
NIGHTMARE ON ELM STREET, A(1984)
Philippe Grenier
AND GOD CREATED WOMAN(1957, Fr.)
Henri Grenieux
HENRIETTE'S HOLIDAY(1953, Fr.)
Jered Edd Grenn
ROADIE(1980), cos
Aiden Grennell
CAPTAIN LIGHTFOOT(1955); SIEGE OF SIDNEY STREET, THE(1960, Brit.); ENTER INSPECTOR DUVAL(1961, Brit.); SWORD OF SHERWOOD FOREST(1961, Brit.); OUTSIDER, THE(1980)
Bert Grennon
LOTTERY LOVER(1935), ph
Joshua Grenrock
NIGHTMARES(1983)
Ashley Grenville
Misc. Talkies
PLUNGE INTO DARKNESS(1977)

Claire Grenville
WRONG IS RIGHT(1982)
Silents
RIGHT TO LIE, THE(1919)
Cynthia Grenville
1984
SECRETS(1984, Brit.)
George Grenville
$(DOLLARS)**1/2 (1971), ed; HAPPY ENDING, THE(1969), ed; EXECUTIVE ACTION(1973), ed; HAPPY MOTHER'S DAY... LOVE, GEORGE(1973), ed; TRIAL OF BILLY JACK, THE(1974), ed; LOOKING FOR MR. GOODBAR(1977), ed; LAST WORD, THE(1979), ed; TOM HORN(1980), ed; WRONG IS RIGHT(1982), ed
1984
PURPLE HEARTS(1984), ed
Pamela Grenville
SLEEPING CAR TO TRIESTE(1949, Brit.)
Pelham Grenville
Silents
GENTLEMAN OF LEISURE, A(1923), w
H. Grenville-Taylor
Silents
LASS O' THE LOOMS, A(1919, Brit.), p
Semion J. Grenvold
LIKELY STORY, A(1947)
Gres
LANCELOT OF THE LAKE(1975, Fr.), cos
Mme. Gres
ULYSSES(1955, Ital.), cos
Edith Gresham
BIRTH OF A BABY(1938)
Gloria Gresham
JUST TELL ME WHAT YOU WANT(1980), cos; ZORRO, THE GAY BLADE(1981), cos; AUTHOR! AUTHOR!(1982), cos; DINER(1982), cos; ESCAPE ARTIST, THE(1982), cos; WITHOUT A TRACE(1983), cos
1984
BODY DOUBLE(1984), cos; FLETCH(1984), cos; FOOTLOOSE(1984), cos; NATURAL, THE(1984), cos
Velma Gresham
PLAY GIRL(1932); WHITE ZOMBIE(1932); STRAIGHT FROM THE HEART(1935)
William Lindsay Gresham
NIGHTMARE ALLEY(1947), w
The Gresham Singers
SMALL MAN, THE(1935, Brit.)
Majorie Gresley
MR. PERRIN AND MR. TRAILL(1948, Brit.)
Marjorie Gresley
DEMOBBED(1944, Brit.); COLONEL BLIMP(1945, Brit.); MARK OF CAIN, THE(1948, Brit.); MUDLARK, THE(1950, Brit.); TONY DRAWS A HORSE(1951, Brit.); FLOATING DUTCHMAN, THE(1953, Brit.)
Googy Gress
1984
FIRST TURN-ON!, THE(1984); FLAMINGO KID, THE(1984)
Ronald Gress
ONE FROM THE HEART(1982)
Ulrich Gressieker
ALL-AROUND REDUCED PERSONALITY–OUTTAKES, THE(1978, Ger.)
Stephen Gressieux
1984
ANOTHER TIME, ANOTHER PLACE(1984, Brit.)
Tom Gressler
HOW TO BEAT THE HIGH COST OF LIVING(1980)
Dan Gressy
DUNKIRK(1958, Brit.)
Greta
MR. ACE(1946), cos; ON OUR MERRY WAY(1948), cos
Vera Gretch
INNOCENTS IN PARIS(1955, Brit.)
Sumner Gretchell
Silents
FLYING FEET, THE(1929)
Jacques Gretillat
CAFE DE PARIS(1938, Fr.); DEVIL IS AN EMPRESS, THE(1939, Fr.); ENTENTE CORDIALE(1939, Fr.); HEART OF PARIS(1939, Fr.)
Silents
NERO(1922, U.S./Ital.)
Heinrich Gretler
JAZZBAND FIVE, THE(1932, Ger.); M(1933, Ger.); TESTAMENT OF DR. MABUSE, THE(1943, Ger.); DEVIL MAKES THREE, THE(1952); HEIDI(1954, Switz.); HEIDI AND PETER(1955, Switz.); IT HAPPENED IN BROAD DAYLIGHT(1960, Ger./Switz.); COUNTERFEITERS OF PARIS, THE(1962, Fr., Ital.); TWO IN A SLEEPING BAG(1964, Ger.); GIRL AND THE LEGEND, THE(1966, Ger.)
Gretry
LA MARSEILLAISE(1938, Fr.), m
Fred Gretton
SMITH'S WIVES(1935, Brit.); LOVE UP THE POLE(1936, Brit.)
Lillian Greuze
Misc. Silents
RECOIL, THE(1917)
Gunther Greve
GREEN SLIME, THE(1969)
Klaus Detlef Grevenhorst
MAN ESCAPED, A(1957, Fr.)
Herbert Grevenius
ILLICIT INTERLUDE(1954, Swed.), w
Anna Grevier
LADY POSSESSED(1952)
Anthony Grevill-Bell
PERFECT FRIDAY(1970, Brit.), w

Edmond Greville
UNDER THE ROOFS OF PARIS(1930, Fr.); DANGEROUS SECRETS(1938, Brit.), d
Edmond T. Greville
GYPSY MELODY(1936, Brit.), d; BRIEF ECSTASY(1937, Brit.), d; WHAT A MAN!(1937, Brit.), d; I MARRIED A SPY(1938), w; UNDER SECRET ORDERS(1943, Brit.), d; BUT NOT IN VAIN(1948, Brit.), d; SILK NOOSE, THE(1950, Brit.), d; NAUGHTY ARLETTE(1951, Brit.), d; GUILTY?(1956, Brit.), d; TEMPTATION(1962, Fr.), p&d, w; HANDS OF ORLAC, THE(1964, Brit./Fr.), d, w; LIARS, THE(1964, Fr.), d; HORROR CASTLE(1965, Ital.), w
Vanda Greville
GENTLEMAN OF PARIS, A(1931); MILLION, THE(1931, Fr.); EBB TIDE(1932, Brit.)
Anthony Greville-Bell
STRANGE VENEGEANCE OF ROSALIE, THE(1972), w; THEATRE OF BLOOD(1973, Brit.), w
William A. Grew
SAP, THE(1929), w; NICE WOMAN(1932), w
Helmut Grewald
FIRST SPACESHIP ON VENUS(1960, Ger./Pol.), spec eff; FLOWERS FOR THE MAN IN THE MOON(1975, Ger.), ph
Leo Grex
INSPECTOR HORNLEIGH ON HOLIDAY(1939, Brit.), w
Grey
SABOTEUR(1942)
Albert L. Grey
Silents
HIS DARKER SELF(1924), p
Anne Grey
TAXI FOR TWO(1929, Brit.); BRAT, THE(1930, Brit.); CROSS ROADS(1930, Brit.); GUILT(1930, Brit.); SCHOOL FOR SCANDAL, THE(1930, Brit.); SQUEAKER, THE(1930, Brit.); CALENDAR, THE(1931, Brit.); GABLES MYSTERY, THE(1931, Brit.); HAPPY ENDING, THE(1931, Brit.); OTHER PEOPLE'S SINS(1931, Brit.); ARMS AND THE MAN(1932, Brit.); LEAP YEAR(1932, Brit.); LILY CHRISTINE(1932, Brit.); MURDER AT COVENT GARDEN(1932, Brit.); NUMBER SEVENTEEN(1932, Brit.); OLD MAN, THE(1932, Brit.); FAITHFUL HEART(1933, Brit.); BLARNEY KISS(1933, Brit.); FAITHFUL HEART(1933, Brit.); FIRE RAISERS, THE(1933, Brit.); GOLDEN CAGE, THE(1933, Brit.); HOUSE OF TRENT, THE(1933, Brit.); LURE, THE(1933, Brit.); ONE PRECIOUS YEAR(1933, Brit.); SHE WAS ONLY A VILLAGE MAIDEN(1933, Brit.); BORROWED CLOTHES(1934, Brit.); COLONEL BLOOD(1934, Brit.); LADY IN DANGER(1934, Brit.); LEAVE IT TO SMITH(1934); POISONED DIAMOND, THE(1934, Brit.); ROAD HOUSE(1934, Brit.); SCOOP, THE(1934, Brit.); BONNIE SCOTLAND(1935); BREAK OF HEARTS(1935); WANDERING JEW, THE(1935, Brit.); TOO MANY PARENTS(1936); DR. SIN FANG(1937, Brit.); LOST CHORD, THE(1937, Brit.); CHINATOWN NIGHTS(1938, Brit.)
Misc. Talkies
JUST MY LUCK(1936)
Misc. Silents
WARNING, THE(1928, Brit.)
Barbara Grey
NO HOLDS BARRED(1952)
Billy Grey
SUSPENSE(1946); SIERRA PASSAGE(1951)
Brad Grey
BURNING, THE(1981), w
Carolyn Grey
GLAMOUR GIRL(1947)
Charles Grey
SEVEN-PER-CENT SOLUTION, THE(1977, Brit.)
Christian Grey
NICKELODEON(1976)
Claire Grey
MAN OF COURAGE(1943)
Clifford Grey
LORD BABS(1932, Brit.), w; FACING THE MUSIC(1933, Brit.), w; FOR THE LOVE OF MIKE(1933, Brit.), w; KING OF THE RITZ(1933, Brit.), w; ROME EXPRESS(1933, Brit.), d; THIS IS THE LIFE(1933, Brit.), w; DOCTOR'S ORDERS(1934, Brit.), w; GIRLS WILL BE BOYS(1934, Brit.), w; LUCK OF A SAILOR, THE(1934, Brit.), w; MISTER CINDERS(1934, Brit.), w; MY SONG GOES ROUND THE WORLD(1934, Brit.), w; SONG YOU GAVE ME, THE(1934, Brit.), w; BREWSTER'S MILLIONS(1935, Brit.), w; CHARING CROSS ROAD(1935, Brit.), w; DRAKE THE PIRATE(1935, Brit.), w; INVITATION TO THE WALTZ(1935, Brit.), w; MIMI(1935, Brit.), w; GIVE HER A RING(1936, Brit.), w; QUEEN OF HEARTS(1936, Brit.), w; STUDENT'S ROMANCE, THE(1936, Brit.), w; BOYS WILL BE GIRLS(1937, Brit.), w; HEART'S DESIRE(1937, Brit.), w; PEARLS BRING TEARS(1937, Brit.), w; SING AS YOU SWING(1937, Brit.), w; HOLD MY HAND(1938, Brit.), w; YES, MADAM?(1938, Brit.), w; LUCKY TO ME(1939, Brit.), w; MIDDLE WATCH, THE(1939, Brit.), w; NORTH SEA PATROL(1939, Brit.), w; SHE COULDN'T SAY NO(1939, Brit.), w; LAMBETH WALK, THE(1940, Brit.), w; LILAC DOMINO, THE(1940, Brit.), m/l Charles Cuvillier; MY WIFE'S FAMILY(1941, Brit.), w; SLEEPING CAR TO TRIESTE(1949, Brit.), w
Silents
DAUGHTER OF THE SEA, A(1915); COST, THE(1920); SALLY(1925), w
Misc. Silents
CARNIVAL(1921, Brit.)
Corinne Grey
MARK OF THE PHOENIX(1958, Brit.)
Cynthia Grey
OLGA'S GIRLS(1964)
Denise Grey
DEVIL IN THE FLESH, THE(1949, Fr.); JULIETTA(1957, Fr.); CARVE HER NAME WITH PRIDE(1958, Brit.); SPUTNIK(1960, Fr.); LOVE AND THE FRENCH-WOMAN(1961, Fr.); LA BONNE SOUPE(1964, Fr./Ital.); HELLO–GOODBYE(1970); LA BOUM(1983, Fr.)
Dick Grey [Ottavio Scotti]
WHAT!(1965, Fr./Brit./Ital.), art d
Dorian Grey
APPOINTMENT FOR MURDER(1954, Ital.)
Doris Grey
Misc. Silents
HER BELOVED ENEMY(1917)

Duane Grey
CATTLE EMPIRE(1958); DESERT HELL(1958); BEAU GESTE(1966); SPLIT, THE(1968); CHARRO(1969); LONERS, THE(1972)

Earle Grey
ALIBI(1931, Brit.); LYONS MAIL, THE(1931, Brit.)

Ethel Grey
Misc. Silents
PEG O' MY HEART(1922)

Eve Grey
SCROOGE(1935, Brit.)

Frances Grey
UNASHAMED(1938)

Gloria Grey
LUCKY STAR(1929); MARRIED IN HOLLYWOOD(1929); HOLIDAY RHYTHM(1950); GANG WAR(1958)
Silents
SUPREME TEST, THE(1923); DANTE'S INFERNO(1924); HOUSE OF YOUTH, THE(1924); NO-GUN MAN, THE(1924); NIGHT WATCH, THE(1926); OFFICER JIM(1926)
Misc. Silents
BAG AND BAGGAGE(1923); GIRL OF THE LIMBERLOST, A(1924); MILLIONAIRE COWBOY, THE(1924); HEARTLESS HUSBANDS(1925); BOASTER, THE(1926); HIDDEN WAY, THE(1926); THRILLING YOUTH(1926); UNKNOWN DANGERS(1926); BRONCHO BUSTER, THE(1927); RANGE COURAGE(1927); THRILL SEEKERS, THE(1927); CLOUD DODGER, THE(1928); HOUND OF THE SILVER CREEK, THE(1928); PUT 'EM UP(1928)

Glorian Grey
BIG TOWN(1932)

Harry Grey
BOLD CABALLERO(1936), m; HEARTS IN BONDAGE(1936), md; SINGING COWBOY, THE(1936), m, md; THREE MESQUITEERS, THE(1936), m; TICKET TO PARADISE(1936), md; WINDS OF THE WASTELAND(1936), md; GHOST TOWN GOLD(1937), m; HAPPY-GO-LUCKY(1937), md; LARCENY ON THE AIR(1937), m; MANDARIN MYSTERY, THE(1937), m; NAVY BLUES(1937), m; OH, SUSANNA(1937), md; RIDERS OF THE WHISTLING SKULL(1937), md; LADIES IN DISTRESS(1938), p; PRAIRIE MOON(1938), p; RHYTHM OF THE SADDLE(1938), p; TENTH AVENUE KID(1938), p; WESTERN JAMBOREE(1938), p; BLUE MONTANA SKIES(1939), p; COWBOYS FROM TEXAS(1939), p; HOME ON THE PRAIRIE(1939), p; KANSAS TERRORS, THE(1939), p; MEXICALI ROSE(1939), p; MOUNTAIN RHYTHM(1939), p; HEROES OF THE SADDLE(1940), p; OKLAHOMA RENEGADES(1940), p; PIONEERS OF THE WEST(1940), p; ROCKY MOUNTAIN RANGERS(1940), p; TRAIL BLAZERS, THE(1940), p; UNDER TEXAS SKIES(1940), p; BACK IN THE SADDLE(1941), p; DOWN MEXICO WAY(1941), p; RIDIN' ON A RAINBOW(1941), p; SIERRA SUE(1941), p; SINGING HILL, THE(1941), p; SUNSET IN WYOMING(1941), p; UNDER FIESTA STARS(1941), p; BELLS OF CAPISTRANO(1942), p; CALL OF THE CANYON(1942), p; COWBOY SERENADE(1942), p; HEART OF THE RIO GRANDE(1942), p; HOME IN WYOMIN'(1942), p; STARDUST ON THE SAGE(1942), p; CALLING WILD BILL ELLIOTT(1943), p; HANDS ACROSS THE BORDER(1943), p; KING OF THE COWBOYS(1943), p; MAN FROM MUSIC MOUNTAIN(1943), p; MAN FROM THUNDER RIVER, THE(1943), p; NOBODY'S DARLING(1943), p; SHANTYTOWN(1943), p; SILVER SPURS(1943), p; SONG OF TEXAS(1943), p; COWBOY AND THE SENORITA(1944), p; LAKE PLACID SERENADE(1944), p; LIGHTS OF OLD SANTA FE(1944), p; MY BEST GAL(1944), p; SONG OF NEVADA(1944), p; THREE LITTLE SISTERS(1944), p; YELLOW ROSE OF TEXAS, THE(1944), p; LOVE, HONOR AND GOODBYE(1945), p; PORTRAIT OF A MOBSTER(1961), w
1984
ONCE UPON A TIME IN AMERICA(1984), w

Iris Grey
Silents
RAT, THE(1925, Brit.)

Rev. J.D. Grey
DAMN CITIZEN(1958)

Jack Grey
SO LONG LETTY(1929); HELL BOUND(1931); ALIAS MARY SMITH(1932); GAMBLING SHIP(1933); PICTURE SNATCHER(1933); MEXICAN SPITFIRE'S BABY(1941)
Misc. Silents
KINGDOM OF HUMAN HEARTS, THE(1921)

James Grey
POT LUCK(1936, Brit.)

Jane Grey
Silents
HER FIGHTING CHANCE(1917)
Misc. Silents
RIGHT OF WAY, THE(1915); FLOWER OF FAITH, THE(1916); LET KATHY DO IT(1916); MAN AND HIS ANGEL(1916); TEST, THE(1916); WAIFS, THE(1916); BIRTH OF A RACE(1919); WHEN MY SHIP COMES IN(1919); GOVERNOR'S LADY, THE(1923)

Jennifer Grey
1984
COTTON CLUB, THE(1984); RECKLESS(1984); RED DAWN(1984)

Jim Grey
TILL THE CLOUDS ROLL BY(1946)

Joe Grey
KNOCKOUT(1941)

Joel Grey
ABOUT FACE(1952); CALYPSO HEAT WAVE(1957); COME SEPTEMBER(1961); CABARET(1972); MAN ON A SWING(1974); BUFFALO BILL AND THE INDIANS, OR SITTING BULL'S HISTORY LESSON(1976); SEVEN-PER-CENT SOLUTION, THE(1977, Brit.)

John Grey
COQUETTE(1929), w; FEET FIRST(1930), w; WORLDLY GOODS(1930), w; MOVIE CRAZY(1932), w; FARMER IN THE DELL, THE(1936), w; MYSTERIOUS CROSSING(1937), w; TOO MANY WIVES(1937), w; I'M FROM THE CITY(1938), w; HAWAIIAN NIGHTS(1939), w; HOW'S ABOUT IT?(1943), w; SING A JINGLE(1943), w; SINGING SHERIFF, THE(1944), w; I LOVE A BANDLEADER(1945), w; SWINGIN' ON A RAINBOW(1945), w
Silents
MOLLY O'(1921), t; CAPTAIN JANUARY(1924), w; HOT WATER(1924), w; FRESHMAN, THE(1925), w; FOR HEAVEN'S SAKE(1926), w; KID BROTHER, THE(1927), w;

SPEEDY(1928), w

John W. Grey
Silents
LITTLE PATRIOT, A(1917), w; GRIM GAME, THE(1919), w

John Wesley Grey
Silents
GEARED TO GO(1924), w
Misc. Silents
WIDE OPEN(1927), d

June Grey
PICCADILLY NIGHTS(1930, Brit.)

King Grey
Silents
SPEED CRAZED(1926), ph

Kirby Grey
YOICKS!(1932, Brit.), p

Larry Grey
MR. CELEBRITY(1942); ALICE IN WONDERLAND(1951)

Lilian Grey
MELODY CLUB(1949, Brit.)

Linda Grey
LOVE IN WAITING(1948, Brit.); ROCKY II(1979)

Lionel Grey
Misc. Silents
FETTERED WOMAN, THE(1917)

Lorna Grey
UP IN THE AIR(1940); ADVENTURES OF KITTY O'DAY(1944)

Lorraine Grey
SEXTON BLAKE AND THE MADEMOISELLE(1935, Brit.)

Lynda Grey
LOUISIANA PURCHASE(1941); FLEET'S IN, THE(1942); MAJOR AND THE MINOR, THE(1942); STAR SPANGLED RHYTHM(1942); TAKE A LETTER, DARLING(1942); THIS GUN FOR HIRE(1942); CRYSTAL BALL, THE(1943); FOR WHOM THE BELL TOLLS(1943); SALUTE FOR THREE(1943); YOUNG AND WILLING(1943); LADY IN THE DARK(1944); UNINVITED, THE(1944)

Mack Grey
FLORIDA SPECIAL(1936)

Madeline Grey
IS EVERYBODY HAPPY?(1943); SOMEONE TO REMEMBER(1943); THAT'S MY BABY(1944)

Madelon Grey
ARTISTS AND MODELS(1937)

Manna Grey
Silents
ALL ROADS LEAD TO CALVARY(1921, Brit.)

Marion Grey
Silents
FAR FROM THE MADDING CROWD(1915, Brit.)

Martin Grey
1984
NATURAL, THE(1984)

Mary Grey
HIS MAJESTY AND CO(1935, Brit.)

Minna Grey
Silents
ALTAR CHAINS(1916, Brit.); JUST A GIRL(1916, Brit.); SOLDIER AND A MAN, A(1916, Brit.); IF THOU WERT BLIND(1917, Brit.); ONWARD CHRISTIAN SOLDIERS(1918, Brit.); EDGE O'BEYOND(1919, Brit.); MRS. THOMPSON(1919, Brit.); LAST ROSE OF SUMMER, THE(1920, Brit.); LIKENESS OF THE NIGHT, THE(1921, Brit.); IF FOUR WALLS TOLD(1922, Brit.); DAUGHTER OF LOVE, A(1925, Brit.)
Misc. Silents
MILESTONES(1916, Brit.); HAPPY WARRIOR, THE(1917, Brit.); LITTLE WOMEN(1917, Brit.); WANTED - A WIFE(1918, Brit.); WOMEN WHO WIN(1919, Brit.); HUSBAND HUNTER, THE(1920, Brit.); AFTERGLOW(1923, Brit.)

Miss Grey
Silents
IMPULSE(1922)

Monica Grey
UNDERCOVER GIRL(1957, Brit.); FEMALE FIENDS(1958, Brit.)

Nan Grey
ST. LOUIS KID, THE(1934); GREAT IMPERSONATION, THE(1935); HIS NIGHT OUT(1935); WOMAN IN RED, THE(1935); LOVE BEFORE BREAKFAST(1936); NEXT TIME WE LOVE(1936); SEA SPOILERS, THE(1936); SUTTER'S GOLD(1936); LET THEM LIVE(1937); LOVE IN A BUNGALOW(1937); MAN IN BLUE, THE(1937); SOME BLONDES ARE DANGEROUS(1937); THREE SMART GIRLS(1937); BLACK DOLL, THE(1938); DANGER ON THE AIR(1938); GIRLS' SCHOOL(1938); JURY'S SECRET, THE(1938); RECKLESS LIVING(1938); STORM, THE(1938); EX-CHAMP(1939); THREE SMART GIRLS GROW UP(1939); TOWER OF LONDON(1939); UNDER-PUP, THE(1939); HOUSE OF THE SEVEN GABLES, THE(1940); INVISIBLE MAN RETURNS, THE(1940); LITTLE BIT OF HEAVEN, A(1940); MARGIE(1940); SANDY IS A LADY(1940); YOU'RE NOT SO TOUGH(1940); UNDER AGE(1941)

Nevada Grey
Misc. Silents
BATTLING KING(1922)

Olga Grey
Silents
ABSENTEE-NRA, THE(1915); BIRTH OF A NATION, THE(1915); INTOLERANCE(1916)
Misc. Silents
DOUBLE TROUBLE(1915); GHOST HOUSE, THE(1917); GIRL AT HOME, THE(1917); JIM BLUDSO(1917); WHEN A MAN RIDES ALONE(1919)

Pamela Grey
SHELL SHOCK(1964)

R. Heaton Grey
Silents
DAWN(1917, Brit.)

R. Henry Grey
Silents
ALL OF A SUDDEN NORMA(1919)

Misc. Silents
BOOTS AND SADDLES(1916); BRAND'S DAUGHTER(1917); FEET OF CLAY(1917); GIRL WHO DOESN'T KNOW, THE(1917); PHANTOM SHOTGUN, THE(1917); NO CHILDREN WANTED(1918); PETTICOATS AND POLITICS(1918)

Ray Grey
Silents
GOLD RUSH, THE(1925)
Misc. Silents
GHOST IN THE GARRET, THE(1921)

Reatha Grey
Misc. Talkies
WELCOME HOME, BROTHER CHARLES(1975)

Richard Grey
MUSIC HATH CHARMS(1935, Brit.); SANDERS OF THE RIVER(1935, Brit.); GUNMAN HAS ESCAPED, A(1948, Brit.), p, d; GANGSTER STORY(1959), w; TWO-HEADED SPY, THE(1959, Brit.)

Richard M. Grey
EYES THAT KILL(1947, Brit.), d&w

Robert Grey
MAN'S CASTLE, A(1933)
Silents
SILENT PARTNER, THE(1923)
Misc. Silents
GAS, OIL AND WATER(1922)

Roger Grey
GEORGE WHITE'S SCANDALS(1934); LIGHTNING STRIKES TWICE(1935); BAREFOOT BOY(1938)

Romer Grey
MAVERICK QUEEN, THE(1956), w

Samantha Grey
HERE COME THE TIGERS(1978); NIGHT OF THE ZOMBIES(1981)

Schuyler Grey
SEARCH FOR BEAUTY(1934), w

Shirley Grey
PUBLIC DEFENDER, THE(1931); SECRET SERVICE(1931); AIR EAGLES(1932); BACK STREET(1932); CORNERED(1932); DRIFTING(1932); GET THAT GIRL(1932); ONE-MAN LAW(1932); RIDING TORNADO, THE(1932); TEXAS CYCLONE(1932); UPTOWN NEW YORK(1932); VIRTUE(1932); DON'T BET ON LOVE(1933); FROM HELL TO HEAVEN(1933); GIRL IN 419(1933); HOLD THE PRESS(1933); LIFE OF JIMMY DOLAN, THE(1933); LITTLE GIANT, THE(1933); OUT ALL NIGHT(1933); PRIVATE JONES(1933); TERROR ABOARD(1933); TOO MUCH HARMONY(1933); BEYOND THE LAW(1934); BOMBAY MAIL(1934); CRIME OF HELEN STANLEY(1934); DEFENSE HESTS, THE(1934); GIRL IN DANGER(1934); GREEN EYES(1934); HIS GREATEST GAMBLE(1934); I LIKE IT THAT WAY(1934); MURDER ON THE CAMPUS(1934); ONE IS GUILTY(1934); SISTERS UNDER THE SKIN(1934); TRANSATLANTIC MERRY-GO-ROUND(1934); TWIN HUSBANDS(1934); WEDNESDAY'S CHILD(1934); CIRCUMSTANTIAL EVIDENCE(1935); GIRL WHO CAME BACK, THE(1935); PEOPLE'S ENEMY, THE(1935); PUBLIC MENACE(1935); PUBLIC OPINION(1935); STRANDED(1935)
Misc. Talkies
DRIFTING SOULS(1932); TREASON(1933)

Sonny Grey
TWO ARE GUILTY(1964, Fr.)

Sydney D. Grey
Misc. Silents
CALL OF THE WILDERNESS, THE(1926)

Sylviane Grey
Misc. Silents
LE SECRET DE ROSETTE LAMBERT(1920, Fr.)

Terence Grey
DARK END OF THE STREET, THE(1981)

Thomas J. Grey
Silents
FRESHMAN, THE(1925), t

Tony Grey
NOW THAT APRIL'S HERE(1958, Can.); LILITH(1964)

Val Grey
MEDIUM COOL(1969)

Virfinia Grey
CAPTAIN IS A LADY, THE(1940)

Virginia Grey
MISBEHAVING LADIES(1931); SECRETS(1933); ST. LOUIS KID, THE(1934); SHE GETS HER MAN(1935); OLD HUTCH(1936); BAD GUY(1937); ROSALIE(1937); SECRET VALLEY(1937); DRAMATIC SCHOOL(1938); LADIES IN DISTRESS(1938); RICH MAN, POOR GIRL(1938); SHOPWORN ANGEL(1938); TEST PILOT(1938); YOUTH TAKES A FLING(1938); ANOTHER THIN MAN(1939); BROADWAY SERENADE(1939); HARDYS RIDE HIGH, THE(1939); IDIOT'S DELIGHT(1939); THUNDER AFLOAT(1939); WOMEN, THE(1939); GOLDEN FLEECING, THE(1940); HULLABALOO(1940); THREE CHEERS FOR THE IRISH(1940); BIG STORE, THE(1941); BLONDE INSPIRATION(1941); KEEPING COMPANY(1941); MR. AND MRS. NORTH(1941); WASHINGTON MELODRAMA(1941); WHISTLING IN THE DARK(1941); BELLS OF CAPISTRANO(1942); GRAND CENTRAL MURDER(1942); TARZAN'S NEW YORK ADVENTURE(1942); TISH(1942); IDAHO(1943); SECRETS OF THE UNDERGROUND(1943); STAGE DOOR CANTEEN(1943); SWEET ROSIE O'-GRADY(1943); STRANGERS IN THE NIGHT(1944); BLONDE RANSOM(1945); FLAME OF THE BARBARY COAST(1945); GRISSLY'S MILLIONS(1945); MEN IN HER DIARY(1945); HOUSE OF HORRORS(1946); SMOOTH AS SILK(1946); SWAMP FIRE(1946); GLAMOUR GIRL(1947); UNCONQUERED(1947); WYOMING(1947); JUNGLE JIM(1948); LEATHER GLOVES(1948); MEXICAN HAYRIDE(1948); MIRACULOUS JOURNEY(1948); SO THIS IS NEW YORK(1948); UNKNOWN ISLAND(1948); WHO KILLED "DOC" ROBBIN?(1948); THREAT, THE(1949); HIGHWAY 301(1950); BULLFIGHTER AND THE LADY(1951); SLAUGHTER TRAIL(1951); THREE DESPERATE MEN(1951); DESERT PURSUIT(1952); FIGHTING LAWMAN, THE(1953); PERILOUS JOURNEY, A(1953); FORTYNINERS, THE(1954); TARGET EARTH(1954); ALL THAT HEAVEN ALLOWS(1955); ETERNAL SEA, THE(1955); LAST COMMAND, THE(1955); ROSE TATTOO, THE(1955); ACCUSED OF MURDER(1956); CRIME OF PASSION(1957); JEANNE EAGELS(1957); RESTLESS YEARS, THE(1958); NO NAME ON THE BULLET(1959); PORTRAIT IN BLACK(1960); BACHELOR IN PARADISE(1961); BACK STREET(1961); FLOWER DRUM SONG(1961); TAMMY, TELL ME TRUE(1961); BLACK ZOO(1963); NAKED KISS, THE(1964); LOVE HAS MANY

FACES(1965); MADAME X(1966); ROSIE!(1967); AIRPORT(1970)
Silents
MICHIGAN KID, THE(1928)
Misc. Silents
UNCLE TOM'S CABIN(1927)

William Grey
CHANGELING, THE(1980, Can.), w

William S. Grey
IN GAY MADRID(1930), ed

Wilson Grey
TRAIN ROBBERY CONFIDENTIAL(1965, Braz.)
1984
MEMOIRS OF PRISON(1984, Braz.)

Yocasta Grey
GRAVEYARD OF HORROR(1971, Span.)

Zane Grey
BORDER LEGION, THE(1930), w; LAST OF THE DUANES(1930), w; LIGHT OF WESTERN STARS, THE(1930), w; LONE STAR RANGER, THE(1930), w; FIGHTING CARAVANS(1931), w; RIDERS OF THE PURPLE SAGE(1931), w; GOLDEN WEST, THE(1932), w; RAINBOW TRAIL(1932), w; WILD HORSE MESA(1932), w; HERITAGE OF THE DESERT(1933), w; LIFE IN THE RAW(1933), w; MAN OF THE FOREST(1933), w; MYSTERIOUS RIDER, THE(1933), w; ROBBERS' ROOST(1933), w; SUNSET PASS(1933), w; TO THE LAST MAN(1933), w; UNDER THE TONTO RIM(1933), w; WOMAN ACCUSED(1933), w; DUDE RANGER, THE(1934), w; LAST ROUND-UP, THE(1934), w; LAST TRAIL, THE(1934), w; THUNDERING HERD, THE(1934), w; WAGON WHEELS(1934), w; HOME ON THE RANGE(1935), w; ROCKY MOUNTAIN MYSTERY(1935), w; THUNDER MOUNTAIN(1935), w; WANDERER OF THE WASTELAND(1935), w; WEST OF THE PECOS(1935), w; ARIZONA MAHONEY(1936), w; ARIZONA RAIDERS, THE(1936), w; DESERT GOLD(1936), w; DRIFT FENCE(1936), w; END OF THE TRAIL(1936), w; KING OF THE ROYAL MOUNTED(1936), w; NEVADA(1936), w; WHITE DEATH(1936, Aus.); BORN TO THE WEST(1937), w; FORLORN RIVER(1937), w; THUNDER TRAIL(1937), w; MYSTERIOUS RIDER, THE(1938), w; ROLL ALONG, COWBOY(1938), w; HERITAGE OF THE DESERT(1939), w; RANGLE RIVER(1939, Aus.), w; BORDER LEGION, THE(1940), w; KNIGHTS OF THE RANGE(1940), w; LIGHT OF WESTERN STARS, THE(1940), w; LAST OF THE DUANES(1941), w; RIDERS OF THE PURPLE SAGE(1941), w; WESTERN UNION(1941), w; LONE STAR RANGER(1942), w; NEVADA(1944), w; WANDERER OF THE WASTELAND(1945), w; WEST OF THE PECOS(1945), w; SUNSET PASS(1946), w; CODE OF THE WEST(1947), w; GUNFIGHTERS, THE(1947), w; THUNDER MOUNTAIN(1947), w; UNDER THE TONTO RIM(1947), w; WILD HORSE MESA(1947), w; RED CANYON(1949), w; ROBBER'S ROOST(1955), w; VANISHING AMERICAN, THE(1955), w; MAVERICK QUEEN, THE(1956), w
Silents
RIDERS OF THE DAWN(1920), w; LAST TRAIL(1921), w; TO THE LAST MAN(1923), w; RAINBOW TRAIL, THE(1925), w; RIDERS OF THE PURPLE SAGE(1925), w; LAST TRAIL, THE(1927), w; NEVADA(1927), w; AVALANCHE(1928), w; STAIRS OF SAND(1929), w; SUNSET PASS(1929), w

Pete Grey Eyes
SEARCHERS, THE(1956)

Grey Shadow
SIGN OF THE WOLF(1941)

Grey Shadow the Dog
MY PAL, WOLF(1944)

Sydney Greylor
NEWSBOY'S HOME(1939)

Gus Greymountain
TRIAL OF BILLY JACK, THE(1974); POSSE(1975)

Clinton Greyn
ROBBERY(1967, Brit.); WOMAN TIMES SEVEN(1967, U.S./Fr./Ital.); GOODBYE MR. CHIPS(1969, U.S./Brit.); LOVE MACHINE, THE,(1971); RAID ON ROMMEL(1971)

Betty Greyson
GOODBYE COLUMBUS(1969)

Dave Greyson
NEW CENTURIONS, THE(1972), makeup

Cynthia Grezaffi
EASY RIDER(1969)

Sylvie Grezel
SMALL CHANGE(1976, Fr.)

Jim Grib
1984
SPLATTER UNIVERSITY(1984), ph

Henry Gribbin
COME BACK BABY(1968)

Robert Gribbin
Misc. Talkies
TRIP WITH THE TEACHER(1975); HITCHHIKE TO HELL(1978)

Bernard Gribble
ANOTHER SHORE(1948, Brit.), ed; BITTER SPRINGS(1950, Aus.), ed; MAGNET, THE(1950, Brit.), ed; MAN IN THE WHITE SUIT, THE(1952), ed; TRAIN OF EVENTS(1952, Brit.), ed; MEET MR. LUCIFER(1953, Brit.), ed; END OF THE ROAD, THE(1954, Brit.), ed; MAKE ME AN OFFER(1954, Brit.), ed; EXTRA DAY, THE(1956, Brit.), ed; GREEN MAN, THE(1957, Brit.), ed; JOHN AND JULIE(1957, Brit.), ed; STRANGE AFFECTION(1959, Brit.), ed; PICCADILLY THIRD STOP(1960, Brit.), ed; SHAKEDOWN, THE(1960, Brit.), ed; FRIGHTENED CITY, THE(1961, Brit.), ed; MARY HAD A LITTLE(1961, Brit.), ed; WHAT A WHOPPER(1961, Brit.), ed; ALIVE AND KICKING(1962, Brit.), ed; CAIRO(1963), ed; WEST 11(1963, Brit.), ed; YOU MUST BE JOKING!(1965, Brit.), ed; YOUR MONEY OR YOUR WIFE(1965, Brit.), ed; CANDIDATE FOR MURDER(1966, Brit.), ed; SHARE OUT, THE(1966, Brit.), ed; I'LL NEVER FORGET WHAT'S 'IS NAME(1967, Brit.), ed; JOKERS, THE(1967, Brit.), ed; CLUE OF THE TWISTED CANDLE(1968, Brit.), ed; HOSTILE WITNESS(1968, Brit.), ed; GAMES, THE(1970), ed; MARRIAGE OF CONVENIENCE(1970, Brit.), ed; CRY OF THE PENGUINS(1972, Brit.), ed; TALES THAT WITNESS MADNESS(1973, Brit.), ed; DEATH WISH(1974), ed; CRIME AND PASSION(1976, U.S., Ger.), ed; WON TON TON, THE DOG WHO SAVED HOLLYWOOD(1976), ed; SENTINEL, THE(1977), ed; SILVER BEARS(1978), ed; MOTEL HELL(1980), ed; WHITE DOG(1982), ed
1984
TOP SECRET!(1984), ed

Bill Gribble
LITTLE DARLINGS(1980); SIX PACK(1982)
1984
ROTWEILER: DOGS OF HELL(1984)
David Gribble
PRIVATE COLLECTION(1972, Aus.), ph; F.J. HOLDEN, THE(1977, Aus.), ph; MONKEY GRIP(1983, Aus.), ph
Donna Jo Gribble
YOU'RE NEVER TOO YOUNG(1955); SOMEBODY UP THERE LIKES ME(1956); REFORM SCHOOL GIRL(1957)
Harry Wagstaff Gribble
BILL OF DIVORCEMENT, A(1932), w; MADAME RACKETEER(1932), d; OUR BETTERS(1933), w; TRICK FOR TRICK(1933), w; NANA(1934), w; STELLA DALLAS(1937), w
Henry Wagstaff Gribble
HIS FAMILY TREE(1936), w
Leonard Gribble
ARSENAL STADIUM MYSTERY, THE(1939, Brit.), w
William Gribble
LINCOLN CONSPIRACY, THE(1977)
Eddie Gribbon
GANG WAR(1928); FANCY BAGGAGE(1929); FROM HEADQUARTERS(1929); TWIN BEDS(1929); TWO MEN AND A MAID(1929); TWO WEEKS OFF(1929); BORN RECKLESS(1930); DAMES AHOY(1930); GOOD INTENTIONS(1930); SONG OF THE WEST(1930); THEY LEARNED ABOUT WOMEN(1930); MR. LEMON OF ORANGE(1931); THREE ROGUES(1931); HIDDEN GOLD(1933); I CAN'T ESCAPE(1934); SEARCH FOR BEAUTY(1934); CYCLONE RANGER(1935); RIP ROARING RILEY(1935); SHE COULDN'T TAKE IT(1935); LOVE ON A BET(1936); MILLIONAIRE KID(1936); BIG SHOT, THE(1937); LIVE, LOVE AND LEARN(1937); YOU CAN'T BUY LUCK(1937); I COVER CHINATOWN(1938); MAID'S NIGHT OUT(1938); ON THE GREAT WHITE TRAIL(1938); SPY RING, THE(1938); IDIOT'S DELIGHT(1939); GREAT DICTATOR, THE(1940); LEATHER-PUSHERS, THE(1940); HONKY TONK(1941); CANYON CITY(1943); MR. MUGGS STEPS OUT(1943); SLEEPY LAGOON(1943); MR. HEX(1946); FIGHTING MAD(1948); JOE PALOOKA IN WINNER TAKE ALL(1948); SMART WOMAN(1948); SMUGGLERS' COVE(1948); STREET CORNER(1948); FIGHTING FOOLS(1949); JOE PALOOKA IN THE BIG FIGHT(1949); JOE PALOOKA IN THE COUNTERPUNCH(1949); HUMPHREY TAKES A CHANCE(1950); JOE PALOOKA IN THE SQUARED CIRCLE(1950); JOE PALOOKA MEETS HUMPHREY(1950); TRIPLE TROUBLE(1950); JOE PALOOKA IN TRIPLE CROSS(1951)
Misc. Talkies
RIO RATTLER(1935)
Silents
MOLLY O'(1921); SMALL TOWN IDOL, A(1921); ALIAS JULIUS CAESAR(1922); TAILOR MADE MAN, A(1922); AFTER THE BALL(1924); EAST OF BROADWAY(1924); JACK O' CLUBS(1924); BAT, THE(1926); MAN BAIT(1926); TELL IT TO THE MARINES(1926); CALLAHANS AND THE MURPHYS, THE(1927); CHEATING CHEATERS(1927); CONVOY(1927); NIGHT LIFE(1927); BACHELOR'S PARADISE(1928); NAMELESS MEN(1928); STOP THAT MAN(1928)
Misc. Silents
HOME TALENT(1921); PLAYING WITH FIRE(1921); DOUBLE DEALING(1923); FOURTH MUSKETEER, THE(1923); STREETS OF SHANGHAI(1927); UNITED STATES SMITH(1928)
Edward Gribbon
Misc. Silents
CAPTAIN FLY-BY-NIGHT(1922)
Harry Gribbon
MIDNIGHT DADDIES(1929); MYSTERIOUS ISLAND(1929); ON WITH THE SHOW(1929); SHAKEDOWN, THE(1929); SO LONG LETTY(1929); LOTTERY BRIDE, THE(1930); GORILLA, THE(1931); KID FROM SPAIN, THE(1932); RIDE HIM, COWBOY(1932); YOU SAID A MOUTHFUL(1932); BABY FACE(1933); LADIES THEY TALK ABOUT(1933)
Silents
EXTRA GIRL, THE(1923); KNOCKOUT REILLY(1927); CAMERAMAN, THE(1928); SHOW PEOPLE(1928); HONEYMOON(1929)
Misc. Silents
DOWN ON THE FARM(1920); UP IN MARY'S ATTICK(1920); CHINATOWN CHARLIE(1928)
James Gribbon
GREEN GODDESS, THE(1930), ed
A Gribov
VOW, THE(1947, USSR.)
A. Gribov
CONCENTRATION CAMP(1939, USSR)
Aleksey Gribov
SOUND OF LIFE, THE(1962, USSR); GROWN-UP CHILDREN(1963, USSR)
Alexei Gribov
MILITARY SECRET(1945, USSR)
A. Gribunina
Misc. Silents
CURSED MILLIONS(1917, USSR)
Grimes Grice
BEGUILED, THE(1971), w; POSSESSION OF JOEL DELANEY, THE(1972), w
Nigel Grice
OLIVER!(1968, Brit.)
Judy Gridley
MOONLIGHTING(1982, Brit.)
Lucas Gridoux
GOLGOTHA(1937, Fr.); LIFE AND LOVES OF BEETHOVEN, THE(1937, Fr.); PEPE LE MOKO(1937, Fr.); PANIQUE(1947, Fr.)
Sergio Grieco
NIGHTS OF LUCRETIA BORGIA, THE(1960, Ital.), d; PIRATE OF THE BLACK HAWK, THE(1961, Fr./Ital.), d, w; HUNS, THE(1962, Fr./Ital.), d; LOVES OF SALAMMBO, THE(1962, Fr./Ital.), d; COUNTERFEIT COMMANDOS(1981, Ital.), w
Grieg
DREAM OF BUTTERFLY, THE(1941, Ital.), m
Edvard Grieg
M(1933, Ger.), m; PEER GYNT(1965), m

Joe Grieg
PRAISE MARX AND PASS THE AMMUNITION(1970, Brit.)
Robert Grieg
NO LIMIT(1931); TONIGHT OR NEVER(1931); HORSE FEATHERS(1932); MEN MUST FIGHT(1933); PEG O' MY HEART(1933); THEY JUST HAD TO GET MARRIED(1933); FOLIES DERGERE(1935); THREE LIVE GHOSTS(1935); WOMAN WANTED(1935); ADVENTURES OF MARCO POLO, THE(1938); I MARRIED AN ANGEL(1942); MOON AND SIXPENCE, THE(1942); SON OF FURY(1942); TALES OF MANHATTAN(1942); MAD WEDNESDAY(1950)
Helmut Griem
GIRL FROM HONG KONG(1966, Ger.); MC KENZIE BREAK, THE(1970); CABARET(1972); LUDWIG(1973, Ital./Ger./Fr.); CHILDREN OF RAGE(1975, Brit.-Israeli); DESERT OF THE TARTARS, THE(1976 Fr./Ital./Iranian); VOYAGE OF THE DAMNED(1976, Brit.); BREAKTHROUGH(1978, Ger.); GERMANY IN AUTUMN(1978, Ger.); DIE HAMBURGER KRANKHEIT(1979, Ger./Fr.); LA PASSANTE(1983, Fr./Ger.); MALOU(1983)
David Alan Grier
STREAMERS(1983)
1984
SOLDIER'S STORY, A(1984)
Pam Grier
BIG DOLL HOUSE, THE(1971); BIG BIRD CAGE, THE(1972); TWILIGHT PEOPLE(1972, Phil.); ARENA, THE(1973); BLACK MAMA, WHITE MAMA(1973); COFFY(1973); SCREAM BLACULA SCREAM(1973); FOXY DROWN(1974); BUCKTOWN(1975); FRIDAY FOSTER(1975); SHEBA BABY(1975); GREASED LIGHTNING(1977); FORT APACHE, THE BRONX(1981); SOMETHING WICKED THIS WAY COMES(1983); TOUGH ENOUGH(1983)
Misc. Talkies
BIG DOLL HOUSE, THE(1971); WOMEN IN CAGES(1972)
Pamela Grier
HIT MAN(1972); DRUM(1976)
Roosevelt Grier
SKYJACKED(1972); RABBIT TEST(1978); GLOVE, THE(1980)
Rosey Grier
THING WITH TWO HEADS, THE(1972); TREASURE OF JAMAICA REEF, THE(1976)
Misc. Talkies
GLOVE, THE(1979)
Rosie Grier
Misc. Talkies
TIMBER TRAMPS(1975)
Rosy Grier
GONG SHOW MOVIE, THE(1980)
Edward Grierson
MY LOVER, MY SON(1970, Brit.), w
John Grierson
BRANDY FOR THE PARSON(1952, Brit.), p; BRAVE DON'T CRY, THE(1952, Brit.), p; JUDGMENT DEFERRED(1952, Brit.), p; MISS ROBIN HOOD(1952, Brit.), p; HORSE'S MOUTH, THE(1953, Brit.), p; TIME GENTLEMEN PLEASE!(1953, Brit.), p; SCOTCH ON THE ROCKS(1954, Brit.), p; MAN OF AFRICA(1956, Brit.), p
Johnathan Gries
MORE AMERICAN GRAFFITI(1979)
Jonathan Gries
SUNNYSIDE(1979); SWAP MEET(1979)
Sally Gries
GREATEST, THE(1977, U.S./Brit.)
Thomas Gries
BUSHWHACKERS, THE(1952), w
Tom Gries
DONOVAN'S BRAIN(1953), p; HELL'S HORIZON(1955), d&w; KING DINOSAUR(1955), w; GIRL IN THE WOODS(1958), d; MUSTANG(1959), w; WILL PENNY(1968), d&w; NUMBER ONE(1969), d; 100 RIFLES(1969), d, w; FOOLS(1970), d; HAWAIIANS, THE(1970), d; JOURNEY THROUGH ROSEBUD(1972), d; LADY ICE(1973), d; BREAKOUT(1975), d; BREAKHEART PASS(1976), d; GREATEST, THE(1977, U.S./Brit.), d
Ludolf Griesbach
CARNIVAL STORY(1954), ed
John Griesemer
1984
BROTHER FROM ANOTHER PLANET, THE(1984)
Herbert Griesner
GIRL FROM HONG KONG(1966, Ger.), makeup
Bill Grieve
KID FROM CLEVELAND, THE(1949)
Harold Grieve
Silents
WILD OATS LANE(1926), art d
Helen Grieve
OVERLANDERS, THE(1946, Brit./Aus.); BUSH CHRISTMAS(1947, Brit.)
John Grieve
THIRTY NINE STEPS, THE(1978, Brit.); EYE OF THE NEEDLE(1981)
Keith Grieve
HOT ICE(1952, Brit.)
Oriana Grieve
MIRROR CRACK'D, THE(1980, Brit.)
Russ Grieve
FUZZ(1972); DOGS(1976); HILLS HAVE EYES, THE(1978)
Joe Grifasi
DEER HUNTER, THE(1978); ON THE YARD(1978); SOMETHING SHORT OF PARADISE(1979); HIDE IN PLAIN SIGHT(1980); HONKY TONK FREEWAY(1981); STILL OF THE NIGHT(1982)
1984
FLAMINGO KID, THE(1984); POPE OF GREENWICH VILLAGE, THE(1984); SPLASH(1984)
Maurice Griffe
ANTOINE ET ANTOINETTE(1947 Fr.), w
Prudencia Griffel
LITTLE ANGEL(1961, Mex.); LITTLE RED RIDING HOOD(1963, Mex.); LITTLE RED RIDING HOOD AND HER FRIENDS(1964, Mex.)

C. Elliott Griffen
Silents
GIRL FROM HIS TOWN, THE(1915)
Chris Griffen
EXPERIENCE PREFERRED... BUT NOT ESSENTIAL(1983, Brit.), p
Eleanor Griffen
STREET OF MISSING MEN(1939), w
Gail Griffen
WORLD'S GREATEST SINNER, THE(1962)
Gary Griffen
ZACHARIAH(1971), ed; SNOW JOB(1972), ed; BLOOD BEACH(1981), ed
Walter Griffen
Silents
LOST LIMITED, THE(1927), ph; WHEEL OF DESTINY, THE(1927), ph
Simone Griffeth
LIKE A CROW ON A JUNE BUG(1972); DEATH RACE 2000(1975)
1984
HOUSE WHERE DEATH LIVES, THE(1984)
Giuseppe Patroni Griffi
MORE THAN A MIRACLE(1967, Ital./Fr.), w; WITCHES, THE(1969, Fr./Ital.), w; 'TIS A PITY SHE'S A WHORE(1973, Ital.), d; DRIVER'S SEAT, THE(1975, Ital.), d, w; DIVINE NYMPH, THE(1979, Ital.), d, w
Guiseppe Patroni Griffi
'TIS A PITY SHE'S A WHORE(1973, Ital.), w
Ethel Griffies
WATERLOO BRIDGE(1931); UNCLE HARRY(1945); OLD ENGLISH(1930); MANHATTAN PARADE(1931); MILLIONAIRE, THE(1931); ONCE A LADY(1931); ROAD TO SINGAPORE(1931); ARE YOU LISTENING?(1932); IMPATIENT MAIDEN(1932); LOVE ME TONIGHT(1932); WESTWARD PASSAGE(1932); HORSEPLAY(1933); LADY'S PROFESSION, A(1933); MIDNIGHT CLUB(1933); TONIGHT IS OURS(1933); TORCH SINGER(1933); WHITE WOMAN(1933); BULLDOG DRUMMOND STRIKES BACK(1934); HOUSE OF ROTHSCHILD, THE(1934); PAINTED VEIL, THE(1934); SADIE MCKEE(1934); WE LIVE AGAIN(1934); ANNA KARENINA(1935); HOLD'EM YALE(1935); JANE EYRE(1935); MYSTERY OF EDWIN DROOD, THE(1935); RETURN OF PETER GRIMM, THE(1935); VANESSA, HER LOVE STORY(1935); WEREWOLF OF LONDON, THE(1935); GUILTY MELODY(1936, Brit.); NOT SO DUSTY(1936, Brit.); TWICE BRANDED(1936, Brit.); KATHLEEN(1938, Ireland); MAN WITH 100 FACES, THE(1938, Brit.); I'M FROM MISSOURI(1939); STAR MAKER, THE(1939); WE ARE NOT ALONE(1939); IRENE(1940); STRANGER ON THE THIRD FLOOR(1940); VIGIL IN THE NIGHT(1940); WATERLOO BRIDGE(1940); BILLY THE KID(1941); GREAT GUNS(1941); HOW GREEN WAS MY VALLEY(1941); REMEMBER THE DAY(1941); YANK IN THE R.A.F., A(1941); BETWEEN US GIRLS(1942); CASTLE IN THE DESERT(1942); MRS. WIGGS OF THE CABBAGE PATCH(1942); POSTMAN DIDN'T RING, THE(1942); RIGHT TO THE HEART(1942); SON OF FURY(1942); TIME TO KILL(1942); FIRST COMES COURAGE(1943); FOREVER AND A DAY(1943); HOLY MATRIMONY(1943); JANE EYRE(1944); KEYS OF THE KINGDOM, THE(1944); MUSIC FOR MILLIONS(1944); PARDON MY RHYTHM(1944); WHITE CLIFFS OF DOVER, THE(1944); HORN BLOWS AT MIDNIGHT, THE(1945); MOLLY AND ME(1945); SARATOGA TRUNK(1945); THRILL OF A ROMANCE(1945); DEVOTION(1946); SING WHILE YOU DANCE(1946); HOMESTRETCH, THE(1947); MILLIE'S DAUGHTER(1947); BILLY LIAR(1963, Brit.); BIRDS, THE(1963); BUS RILEY'S BACK IN TOWN(1965)
Babette Griffin
CAESAR AND CLEOPATRA(1946, Brit.)
Bessie Griffin
TOGETHER BROTHERS(1974)
Bob Griffin
GREAT JESSE JAMES RAID, THE(1953); MACHINE GUN KELLY(1958)
C. Elliott Griffin
Silents
AT THE STAGE DOOR(1921); SHACKLES OF GOLD(1922)
Carleton E. Griffin
STAND UP AND CHEER(1934 80m FOX bw)
Carleton Griffin
STAR IS BORN, A(1937)
Carlton Elliott Griffin
Silents
GIRL FROM HIS TOWN, THE(1915)
Carlton Griffin
YOU CAN'T TAKE IT WITH YOU(1938); ANGELS OVER BROADWAY(1940); FIVE LITTLE PEPPERS IN TROUBLE(1940); LADY IN QUESTION, THE(1940)
Silents
GIRL SHY(1924); PAINTED FLAPPER, THE(1924); TRAMP, TRAMP, TRAMP(1926)
Misc. Silents
GREAT JEWEL ROBBERY, THE(1925); HER BIG ADVENTURE(1926)
Charles E. Griffin
LOVE IS NEWS(1937)
Charles Griffin
FAREWELL TO ARMS, A(1932), tech adv; HOUSE ACROSS THE BAY, THE(1940); HEAVENLY DAYS(1944); HOODLUM SAINT, THE(1946); TILL THE CLOUDS ROLL BY(1946); TOUGH ENOUGH(1983)
Chris Griffin
1984
FOREVER YOUNG(1984, Brit.), p; KIPPERBANG(1984, Brit.), p; SECRETS(1984, Brit.), p
Clare Griffin
RAW DEAL(1977, Aus.), cos; MAD MAX(1979, Aus.), cos
David Griffin
BLOOD BEAST TERROR, THE(1967, Brit.); IF ...(1968, Brit.); BATTLE OF BRITAIN, THE(1969, Brit.); TROG(1970, Brit.); WALKING STICK, THE(1970, Brit.); PRIVATES ON PARADE(1982)
1984
PRIVATES ON PARADE(1984, Brit.)
Dee Griffin
TWO OF A KIND(1983)
Dorlinda Griffin
1984
SUBURBIA(1984)

Eleanor Griffin
ONLY ANGELS HAVE WINGS(1939), w; I WANTED WINGS(1941), w; IN OLD OKLAHOMA(1943), w; Hl BEAUTIFUL(1944), w
Eleanore Griffin
LOVE IN A BUNGALOW(1937), w; THOROUGHBREDS DON'T CRY(1937), w; TIME OUT FOR ROMANCE(1937), w; WHEN LOVE IS YOUNG(1937), w; BOYS TOWN(1938), w; ST. LOUIS BLUES(1939), w; BLONDIE IN SOCIETY(1941), w; NOB HILL(1945), w; HARVEY GIRLS, THE(1946), w; TENTH AVENUE ANGEL(1948), w; GOOD MORNING, MISS DOVE(1955), w; MAN CALLED PETER, THE(1955), w; IMITATION OF LIFE(1959), w; THIRD MAN ON THE MOUNTAIN(1959), w; BACK STREET(1961), w; ONE MAN'S WAY(1964), w
Ellis Griffin
1984
BLESS THEIR LITTLE HEARTS(1984)
Eric Griffin
1984
VIGIL(1984, New Zealand)
Frank Griffin
LIGHTNING GUNS(1950); FORT SAVAGE RAIDERS(1951); DANGEROUS MISSION(1954); TEEN-AGE CRIME WAVE(1955); REVOLT OF MAMIE STOVER, THE(1956); BULLWHIP(1958); MAN CALLED HORSE, A(1970), makeup; HIRED HAND, THE(1971), makeup
1984
PROTOCOL(1984), makeup
Silents
ELLA CINDERS(1926), w; EASY PICKINGS(1927), p
Misc. Silents
CONDUCTOR 1492(1924), d
Frank C. Griffin
Misc. Silents
WHERE LOVE LEADS(1916), d; ROBERT'S ADVENTURE IN THE GREAT WAR(1920), d
Frank H. Griffin, Jr.
CINDERELLA LIBERTY(1973)
Maj. G.F. Griffin, RCMP
NORTHWEST MOUNTED POLICE(1940), tech adv
George Griffin
Silents
IN THE DAYS OF SAINT PATRICK(1920, Brit.)
Gerald Griffin
Silents
PAIR OF CUPIDS, A(1918)
Misc. Silents
FEATHERTOP(1916); SUNBEAM, THE(1916)
Gordon Griffin
ARABESQUE(1966)
Harold Griffin
LUCK OF THE IRISH, THE(1937, Ireland)
Jack Griffin
CHILDISH THINGS(1969); UNHOLY ROLLERS(1972); CHARLEY AND THE ANGEL(1973); WORLD'S GREATEST ATHLETE, THE(1973); HOUSE CALLS(1978); NORTH AVENUE IRREGULARS, THE(1979)
Jimmy Griffin
NONE BUT THE BRAVE(1965, U.S./Jap.)
John Howard Griffin
BLACK LIKE ME(1964), w
Jonathan Griffin
BIBLE...IN THE BEGINNING, THE(1966), w
Josephine Griffin
HOUSE OF THE ARROW, THE(1953, Brit.); CROWDED DAY, THE(1954, Brit.); PURPLE PLAIN, THE(1954, Brit.); WEAK AND THE WICKED, THE(1954, Brit.); ROOM IN THE HOUSE(1955, Brit.); EXTRA DAY, THE(1956, Brit.); MAN WHO NEVER WAS, THE(1956, Brit.); POSTMARK FOR DANGER(1956, Brit.); SPANISH GARDENER, THE(1957, Span.)
Joyce Griffin
HI, MOM!(1970)
Julann Griffin
1984
WOMAN IN RED, THE(1984)
Julia Griffin
LAWLESS RANGE(1935)
Kay Griffin
CURTAINS(1983, Can.)
Lyn Griffin
MR. PATMAN(1980, Can.)
Lynn Griffin
HIT MAN(1972), art d
Lynne Griffin
BLACK CHRISTMAS(1974, Can.); AMATEUR, THE(1982); CURTAINS(1983, Can.); STRANGE BREW(1983)
Margaret Griffin
TOO YOUNG TO LOVE(1960, Brit.)
Merv Griffin
CATTLE TOWN(1952); SO THIS IS LOVE(1953); THREE SAILORS AND A GIRL(1953); BOY FROM OKLAHOMA, THE(1954); PHANTOM OF THE RUE MORGUE(1954); HELLO DOWN THERE(1969); TWO-MINUTE WARNING(1976); SEDUCTION OF JOE TYNAN, THE(1979); MAN WITH TWO BRAINS, THE(1983)
1984
LONELY GUY, THE(1984); SLAPSTICK OF ANOTHER KIND(1984)
Michelle Griffin
SEMI-TOUGH(1977)
Myron Griffin
SUPERCHICK(1973)
Noni Griffin
IF YOU COULD SEE WHAT I HEAR(1982)
Pat Griffin
EXILE, THE(1947)

Patrick Griffin
MAN I LOVE, THE(1946); GAL WHO TOOK THE WEST, THE(1949)
Pete Griffin
1984
LISTEN TO THE CITY(1984, Can.)
Robert Griffin
BARRICADE(1950); BROKEN ARROW(1950); JOE PALOOKA IN THE SQUARED CIRCLE(1950); INDIAN UPRISING(1951); UNKNOWN MAN, THE(1951); MONTANA TERRITORY(1952); SERPENT OF THE NILE(1953); SLAVES OF BABYLON(1953); BLACK DAKOTAS, THE(1954); LAW VS. BILLY THE KID, THE(1954); BRASS LEGEND, THE(1956); PLEASE MURDER ME(1956); CRIME OF PASSION(1957); GUNSIGHT RIDGE(1957); I WAS A TEENAGE WEREWOLF(1957); BRAVADOS, THE(1958); SUMMER PLACE, A(1959); ICE PALACE(1960)
1984
SUBURBIA(1984)
Robert E. Griffin
MAGNIFICENT YANKEE, THE(1950); VENGEANCE VALLEY(1951); CONQUEST OF COCHISE(1953); INSIDE DETROIT(1955); SHOTGUN(1955); FURY AT SHOW-DOWN(1957); PAWNEE(1957); MONSTER FROM THE GREEN HELL(1958); NO PLACE TO LAND(1958)
Russell Griffin
Silents
JACQUELINE, OR BLAZING BARRIERS(1923); LAWFUL LARCENY(1923); AVER-AGE WOMAN, THE(1924)
Misc. Silents
MARRIAGE MORALS(1923); NEW SCHOOL TEACHER, THE(1924); PEARL OF LOVE, THE(1925)
Sean P. Griffin
HERE COME THE TIGERS(1978)
Stephanie Griffin
LAST WAGON, THE(1956)
Sunny Griffin
JOHN AND MARY(1969)
Ted Griffin
BOTTOM OF THE BOTTLE, THE(1956)
Tod Griffin
SHE DEVIL(1957); SHE DEMONS(1958)
Todd Griffin
DESPERADOES ARE IN TOWN, THE(1956)
Tom Griffin
EDGE, THE(1968); ICE(1970)
Victor Griffin
ANNIE(1982)
Walter Griffin
Silents
NOMADS OF THE NORTH(1920), ph; SILENT PARTNER, THE(1923), ph; BAF-FLED(1924), ph; WESTERN VENGEANCE(1924), ph; BARRIERS OF THE LAW(1925), ph; OUTWITTED(1925), ph; DAME CHANCE(1926), ph; JACK O'HEARTS(1926), ph; SWEET SIXTEEN(1928), ph
Wayne Griffin
LOVE(1982, Can.), ed
William Griffin
Misc. Silents
LAMB AND THE LION, THE(1919)
Z. Wayne Griffin
FAMILY HONEYMOON(1948), p; KEY TO THE CITY(1950), p; LONE STAR(1952), p
Lynn Griffis
CHEAP DETECTIVE, THE(1978)
S. R. Griffis
LOOSE ENDS(1975)
William Griffis
SIMON(1980)
Andy Griffith
FACE IN THE CROWD, A(1957); NO TIME FOR SERGEANTS(1958); ONION-HEAD(1958); SECOND TIME AROUND, THE(1961); ANGEL IN MY POCKET(1969); HEARTS OF THE WEST(1975)
Ann Griffith
FIGHTING TROUBLE(1956); FOOTSTEPS IN THE NIGHT(1957)
Bill Griffith
WHIRLWIND HORSEMAN(1938)
Billy Griffith
LET'S GO COLLEGIATE(1941); JIGGS AND MAGGIE OUT WEST(1950)
Catherine Griffith
NAUGHTY MARIETTA(1935)
Charles Griffith
ATTACK OF THE CRAB MONSTERS(1957), w; NOT OF THIS EARTH(1957), w; UNDEAD, THE(1957), w; ATLAS(1960), w; BEAST FROM THE HAUNTED CA-VE(1960), w; SKI TROOP ATTACK(1960), w; CREATURE FROM THE HAUNTED SEA(1961), w; WILD ANGELS, THE(1966), w; DEVIL'S ANGELS(1967), w; DEATH RACE 2000(1975), w
Charles B. Griffith
GUNSLINGER(1956), w; IT CONQUERED THE WORLD(1956); FLESH AND THE SPUR(1957), w; NAKED PARADISE(1957), w; ROCK ALL NIGHT(1957), w; TEEN-AGE DOLL(1957), w; GHOST OF THE CHINA SEA(1958), p, w; BUCKET OF BLOOD, A(1959), w; FORBIDDEN ISLAND(1959), p,d&w; LITTLE SHOP OF HORRORS(1961), w; EAT MY DUST!(1976), d&w; HOLLYWOOD BOULEVARD(1976); SWINGING BARMAIDS, THE(1976), w; UP FROM THE DEPTHS(1979, Phil.), d; DR. HECKYL AND MR. HYPE(1980), d&w; SMOKEY BITES THE DUST(1981), d
Cindi Griffith
SHADOW OF THE HAWK(1976, Can.)
Corinne Griffith
PRISONERS(1929); SATURDAY'S CHILDREN(1929); BACK PAY(1930); LILIES OF THE FIELD(1930); LILY CHRISTINE(1932, Brit.); PARADISE ALLEY(1962); PAPA'S DELICATE CONDITION(1963), w
Misc. Talkies
DIVINE LADY, THE(1929)
Silents
ADVENTURE SHOP, THE(1918); CLIMBERS, THE(1919); BAB'S CAN-DIDATE(1920); MORAL FIBRE(1921); SINGLE TRACK, THE(1921); COMMON LAW,

THE(1923); SIX DAYS(1923); LOVE'S WILDERNESS(1924); SYNCOPATING SUE(1926); OUTCAST(1928)
Misc. Silents
LAST MAN, THE(1916); I WILL REPAY(1917); LOVE DOCTOR, THE(1917); STOLEN TREATY, THE(1917); TRANSGRESSION(1917); WHO GOES THERE?(1917); CLUTCH OF CIRCUMSTANCE, THE(1918); GIRL OF TODAY, THE(1918); LOVE WATCH-ES(1918); MENACE, THE(1918); MISS AMBITION(1918); BRAMBLE BUSH, THE(1919); GIRL AT BAY, A(1919); GIRL PROBLEM, THE(1919); THIN ICE(1919); UNKNOWN QUANTITY, THE(1919); BROADWAY BUBBLE, THE(1920); DEADLINE AT ELEVEN(1920); GARTER GIRL, THE(1920); HUMAN COLLATERAL(1920); TOW-ER OF JEWELS, THE(1920); WHISPER MARKET, THE(1920); IT ISN'T BEING DONE THIS SEASON(1921); WHAT'S YOUR REPUTATION WORTH?(1921); DIVORCE COUPONS(1922); ISLAND WIVES(1922); RECEIVED PAYMENT(1922); VIRGIN'S SACRIFICE, A(1922); BLACK OXEN(1924); LILLIES OF THE FIELD(1924); SINGLE WIVES(1924); CLASSIFIED(1925); DECLASSE(1925); INFATUATION(1925); MAR-RIAGE WHIRL, THE(1925); INTO HER KINGDOM(1926); MADEMOISELLE MO-DISTE(1926); LADY IN ERMINE, THE(1927); THREE HOURS(1927); GARDEN OF EDEN, THE(1928)
D.W. Griffith
LADY OF THE PAVEMENTS(1929), d; ABRAHAM LINCOLN(1930), d; STRUGGLE, THE(1931), p&d, w; BROKEN BLOSSOMS(1936, Brit.), w; SAN FRANCISCO(1936), d; ONE MILLION B.C.(1940), d
Silents
AVENGING CONSCIENCE, THE(1914), d&w; BATTLE OF THE SEXES, THE(1914), d; CLASSMATES(1914), sup; DISHONORED MEDAL, THE(1914), sup; ESCAPE, THE(1914), d; HIS LAST DOLLAR(1914), d; HOME SWEET HOME(1914), d, w; JUDITH OF BETHULIA(1914), d&w; BIRTH OF A NATION, THE(1915), p&d, w, m; JORDAN IS A HARD ROAD(1915), sup; LAMB, THE(1915), sup; LILY AND THE ROSE, THE(1915), sup; MARTYRS OF THE ALAMO, THE(1915), sup; DAPHNE AND THE PIRATE(1916), w; HABIT OF HAPPINESS, THE(1916), w; INTOLERAN-CE(1916), d&w, m; GREAT LOVE, THE(1918), d; GREATEST THING IN LIFE, THE(1918), d; HEARTS OF THE WORLD(1918), d, m; BROKEN BLOSSOMS(1919), d&w, m; GIRL WHO STAYED AT HOME, THE(1919), d, w; ROMANCE OF HAPPY VALLEY, A(1919), d; SCARLET DAYS(1919), d; TRUE HEART SUSIE(1919), d; GREATEST QUESTION, THE(1920), d; IDOL DANCER, THE(1920), d; LOVE FLOW-ER, THE(1920), d&w; WAY DOWN EAST(1920), p&d, w; DREAM STREET(1921), d; ONE EXCITING NIGHT(1922), d&w; ORPHANS OF THE STORM(1922), p&d; WHITE ROSE, THE(1923), d; AMERICA(1924), p&d; ISN'T LIFE WONDERFUL(1924), p,d&w; "THAT ROYLE GIRL"(1925), p&d; SALLY OF THE SAWDUST(1925), d; SORROWS OF SATAN(1926), d; BATTLE OF THE SEXES, THE(1928), d
Misc. Silents
DRUMS OF LOVE(1928), d
David Griffith
MAN UPSTAIRS, THE(1959, Brit.)
Diane Griffith
COVER GIRL(1944)
Don Griffith
JUNGLE BOOK, THE(1967), art d; ARISTOCATS, THE(1970), anim; ROBIN HOOD(1973), art d; RESCUERS, THE(1977), art d; FOX AND THE HOUND, THE(1981), art d
E.H. Griffith
HOLIDAY(1930), d
Silents
DAWN OF THE EAST(1921), d; IF WOMEN ONLY KNEW(1921), d
Misc. Silents
FREE AIR(1922), d; GO-GETTER, THE(1923), d; UNSEEING EYES(1923), d; WEEK END HUSBANDS(1924), d; BAD COMPANY(1925), d; HEADLINES(1925), d; PRICE OF HONOR, THE(1927), d
Ed Griffith
EASY COME, EASY GO(1967); TREE, THE(1969)
Edith M. Griffith
AFFAIRS OF GERALDINE(1946)
Edward H. Griffith
PARIS BOUND(1929), d; RICH PEOPLE(1929), d; SHADY LADY, THE(1929), d, w; REBOUND(1931), d; ANIMAL KINGDOM, THE(1932), d; LADY WITH A PAST(1932), d; ANOTHER LANGUAGE(1933), d; BIOGRAPHY OF A BACHELOR GIRL(1935), d; NO MORE LADIES(1935), d; LADIES IN LOVE(1936), d; NEXT TIME WE LO-VE(1936), d; CAFE METROPOLE(1937), d; I'LL TAKE ROMANCE(1937), d; CAFE SOCIETY(1939), d; HONEYMOON IN BALI(1939), d; SAFARI(1940), d; BAHAMA PASSAGE(1941), p&d; ONE NIGHT IN LISBON(1941), p&d; VIRGINIA(1941), p&d, w; SKY'S THE LIMIT, THE(1943), d; YOUNG AND WILLING(1943), p&d; PERILOUS HOLIDAY(1946), d
Silents
BAB'S CANDIDATE(1920), d; ANOTHER SCANDAL(1924), d; ATTA BOY!(1926), d; AFRAID TO LOVE(1927), d; HOLD 'EM YALE!(1928), d
Misc. Silents
AWAKENING OF RUTH, THE(1917), d; BILLY AND THE BIG STICK(1917), d; ONE TOUCH OF NATURE(1917), d; YOUR OBEDIENT SERVANT(1917), d; GARTER GIRL, THE(1920), d; VICE OF FOOLS, THE(1920), d; LAND OF HOPE, THE(1921), d; SCRAMBLED WIVES(1921), d; WHITE MICE(1926), d; OPENING NIGHT, THE(1927), d; CAPTAIN SWAGGER(1928), d; LOVE OVER NIGHT(1928), d
Eleanor Griffith
ALIBI(1929)
Silents
CARDIGAN(1922)
Eva Griffith
RIDE A WILD PONY(1976, U.S./Aus.)
Fred Griffith
23 PACES TO BAKER STREET(1956)
Gary F. Griffith
1984
BODY DOUBLE(1984)
Geraldine Griffith
EXPERIENCE PREFERRED... BUT NOT ESSENTIAL(1983, Brit.)
Gordon Griffith
CRUSADES, THE(1935); DANGER AHEAD(1935); WHAT PRICE CRIME?(1935); BARS OF HATE(1936); GUN PLAY(1936); SPEED LIMITED(1940); ALL THE RIGHT NOISES(1973, Brit.)

Misc. Talkies
BLAZING JUSTICE(1936); OUTLAWS OF THE RANGE(1936)
Silents
TILLIE'S PUNCTURED ROMANCE(1914); NAKED HEARTS(1916); ROMANCE OF TARZAN, THE(1918); TARZAN OF THE APES(1918); HUCKLEBERRY FINN(1920); PENROD(1922); LITTLE ANNIE ROONEY(1925); CAT'S PAJAMAS, THE(1926)
Misc. Silents
CATCH MY SMOKE(1922); MORE TO BE PITIED THAN SCORNED(1922); JUNGLE TRAIL OF THE SON OF TARZAN(1923); STREET OF TEARS, THE(1924); BRANDED MAN(1928)

Gordon S. Griffith
WESTERN FRONTIER(1935)

H. L. Griffith
Silents
TESS OF THE STORM COUNTRY(1914)

Harriet Griffith
WORDS AND MUSIC(1929)

Harry Griffith
FOUND ALIVE(1934)
Silents
KINKAID, GAMBLER(1916); PENROD(1922)
Misc. Silents
SHOES(1916)

Honor Griffith
MOURNING SUIT, THE(1975, Can.), ed; JOURNEY(1977, Can.), ed

Hubert Griffith
BETRAYAL(1932, Brit.), d&w

Hugh Griffith
NEUTRAL PORT(1941, Brit.); SILVER DARLINGS, THE(1947, Brit.); DULCIMER STREET(1948, Brit.); SO EVIL MY LOVE(1948, Brit.); THREE WEIRD SISTERS, THE(1948, Brit.); AFFAIRS OF A ROGUE, THE(1949, Brit.); KIND HEARTS AND CORONETS(1949, Brit.); LAST DAYS OF DOLWYN, THE(1949, Brit.); RUN FOR YOUR MONEY, A(1950, Brit.); GALLOPING MAJOR, THE(1951, Brit.); LAUGHTER IN PARADISE(1951, Brit.); WILD HEART, THE(1952, Brit.); BEGGAR'S OPERA, THE(1953); TITFIELD THUNDERBOLT, THE(1953, Brit.); SLEEPING TIGER, THE(1954, Brit.); PASSAGE HOME(1955, Brit.); GOOD COMPANIONS, THE(1957, Brit.); LUCKY JIM(1957, Brit.); BEN HUR(1959); STORY ON PAGE ONE, THE(1959); DAY THEY ROBBED THE BANK OF ENGLAND, THE(1960, Brit.); EXODUS(1960); COUNTERFEIT TRAITOR, THE(1962); LISA(1962, Brit.); MUTINY ON THE BOUNTY(1962); TERM OF TRIAL(1962, Brit.); TOM JONES(1963, Brit.); BARGEE, THE(1964, Brit.); HIDE AND SEEK(1964, Brit.); AMOROUS ADVENTURES OF MOLL FLANDERS, THE(1965); HOW TO STEAL A MILLION(1966); POPPY IS ALSO A FLOWER, THE(1966); OH DAD, POOR DAD, MAMA'S HUNG YOU IN THE CLOSET AND I'M FEELIN' SO SAD(1967, Brit.); SAILOR FROM GIBRALTAR, THE(1967, Brit.); CHASTITY BELT, THE(1968, Ital.); DROP DEAD, MY LOVE(1968, Italy); FIXER, THE(1968); OLIVER!(1968, Brit.); CRY OF THE BANSHEE(1970, Brit.); START THE REVOLUTION WITHOUT ME(1970); WUTHERING HEIGHTS(1970, Brit.); ABOMINABLE DR. PHIBES, THE(1971, Brit.); WHO SLEW AUNTIE ROO?(1971, U.S./Brit.); DOCTOR PHIBES RISES AGAIN(1972, Brit.); CHE?(1973, Ital./Fr./Ger.); TAKE ME HIGH(1973, Brit.); CRAZE(1974, Brit.); LUTHER(1974); LAST DAYS OF MAN ON EARTH, THE(1975, Brit.); PASSOVER PLOT, THE(1976, Israel); JOSEPH ANDREWS(1977, Brit.); LAST REMAKE OF BEAU GESTE, THE(1977); SOME LIKE IT COOL(1979, Ger./Aust./Ital./Fr.); HOUND OF THE BASKERVILLES, THE(1980, Brit.)
Misc. Talkies
LEGEND OF THE WEREWOLF(1974); BRIDGES TO HEAVEN(1975)

J.J. Griffith
SHALAKO(1968, Brit.), w; CATLOW(1971, Span.), w

James Griffith
EVERY GIRL SHOULD BE MARRIED(1948); BLONDE ICE(1949); DAUGHTER OF THE WEST(1949); FIGHTING MAN OF THE PLAINS(1949); HOLIDAY AFFAIR(1949); OH, YOU BEAUTIFUL DOLL(1949); SEARCH FOR DANGER(1949); BREAKING POINT, THE(1950); CARIBOO TRAIL, THE(1950); DOUBLE DEAL(1950); GREAT MISSOURI RAID, THE(1950); INDIAN TERRITORY(1950); YOUNG MAN WITH A HORN(1950); AL JENNINGS OF OKLAHOMA(1951); APACHE DRUMS(1951); CHAIN OF CIRCUMSTANCE(1951); LADY PAYS OFF, THE(1951); EIGHT IRON MEN(1952); MA AND PA KETTLE AT THE FAIR(1952); RED SKIES OF MONTANA(1952); WAIT 'TIL THE SUN SHINES, NELLIE(1952); KANSAS PACIFIC(1953); KID FROM LEFT FIELD, THE(1953); LION IS IN THE STREETS, A(1953); NO ESCAPE(1953); BLACK DAKOTAS, THE(1954); BOY FROM OKLAHOMA, THE(1954); DAY OF TRIUMPH(1954); DRAGNET(1954); JESSE JAMES VERSUS THE DALTONS(1954); LAW VS. BILLY THE KID, THE(1954); MASTERSON OF KANSAS(1954); RAILS INTO LARAMIE(1954); SHANGHAI STORY, THE(1954); AT GUNPOINT(1955); COUNT THREE AND PRAY(1955); I COVER THE UNDERWORLD(1955); PHANTOM OF THE JUNGLE(1955); SON OF SINBAD(1955); ANYTHING GOES(1956); FIRST TEXAN, THE(1956); REBEL IN TOWN(1956); TRIBUTE TO A BADMAN(1956); DOMINO KID(1957); GUNS OF FORT PETTICOAT, THE(1957); OMAR KHAYYAM(1957); RAINTREE COUNTY(1957); VAMPIRE, THE(1957); BULLWHIP(1958); FRONTIER GUN(1958); MAN FROM GOD'S COUNTRY(1958); RETURN TO WARBOW(1958); SEVEN GUNS TO MESA(1958); BIG FISHERMAN, THE(1959); AMAZING TRANSPARENT MAN, THE(1960); NORTH TO ALASKA(1960); SPARTACUS(1960); HOW THE WEST WAS WON(1962); ADVANCE TO THE REAR(1964); MOTOR PSYCHO(1965), w; BIG HAND FOR THE LITTLE LADY, A(1966); DAY OF THE EVIL GUN(1968); HAIL, HERO!(1969); HEAVEN WITH A GUN(1969); SEVEN ALONE(1975); SPEEDTRAP(1978)
Misc. Talkies
NEW DAY AT SUNDOWN(1957)

James J. Griffith
RHUBARB(1951)
Misc. Talkies
NOT MY DAUGHTER(1975)

Jay Griffith
APPOINTMENT WITH MURDER(1948)

Jill Griffith
1984
CHATTANOOGA CHOO CHOO(1984), p

Jim Griffith
ALASKA PATROL(1949)

Jimmy Griffith
BRIGHT LEAF(1950)

John Griffith
WORDS AND MUSIC(1929)
Misc. Silents
HELL'S 400(1926), d

Julia Griffith
FORCED LANDING(1935); GIRL CRAZY(1943)
Misc. Silents
CLOUD DODGER, THE(1928)

Julie Griffith
PENAL CODE, THE(1933)

Katherine Griffith
Silents
BRAZEN BEAUTY(1918); HUCKLEBERRY FINN(1920); POLLYANNA(1920)
Misc. Silents
MOTHERS OF MEN(1917); FAST COMPANY(1918)

Kay Griffith
ALEXANDER'S RAGTIME BAND(1938); MY LUCKY STAR(1938); HOTEL FOR WOMEN(1939); WIFE, HUSBAND AND FRIEND(1939); COVERED WAGON DAYS(1940); STAR DUST(1940)

Kenneth Griffith
FARMER'S WIFE, THE(1941, Brit.); HARD STEEL(1941, Brit.); FOREST RANGERS, THE(1942); YOUNG AND WILLING(1943); LOVE ON THE DOLE(1945, Brit.); BOND STREET(1948, Brit.); CODE OF SCOTLAND YARD)(1948); BLUE SCAR(1949, Brit.); FORBIDDEN(1949, Brit.); HIGH TREASON(1951, Brit.); WATERFRONT WOMEN(1952, Brit.); TERROR STREET(1953); GREEN BUDDHA, THE(1954, Brit.); PRISONER, THE(1955, Brit.); PRIVATE'S PROGRESS(1956, Brit.); ROTTEN TO THE CORE(1956, Brit.); TIGER IN THE SMOKE(1956, Brit.); TRACK THE MAN DOWN(1956, Brit.); BROTHERS IN LAW(1957, Brit.); LUCKY JIM(1957, Brit.); CHAIN OF EVENTS(1958, Brit.); NIGHT TO REMEMBER, A(1958, Brit.); YOUR PAST IS SHOWING(1958, Brit.); EXPRESSO BONGO(1959, Brit.); I'M ALL RIGHT, JACK(1959, Brit.); LIBEL(1959, Brit.); MAN UPSTAIRS, THE(1959, Brit.); TIGER BAY(1959, Brit.); TWO-HEADED SPY, THE(1959, Brit.); CIRCUS OF HORRORS(1960, Brit.); FRENCH MISTRESS(1960, Brit.); SNOWBALL(1960, Brit.); FRIGHTENED CITY, THE(1961, Brit.); RISK, THE(1961, Brit.); ONLY TWO CAN PLAY(1962, Brit.); PAYROLL(1962, Brit.); WE JOINED THE NAVY(1962, Brit.); YOUNG, WILLING AND EAGER(1962, Brit.); HEAVENS ABOVE!(1963, Brit.); MURDER CAN BE DEADLY(1963, Brit.); BOBO, THE(1967, Brit.); WHISPERERS, THE(1967, Brit.); GREAT CATHERINE(1968, Brit.); LION IN WINTER(1968, Brit.); ASSASSINATION BUREAU, THE(1969, Brit.); DECLINE AND FALL... OF A BIRD WATCHER(1969, Brit.); GAMBLERS, THE(1969); JANE EYRE(1971, Brit.); TERROR FROM UNDER THE HOUSE(1971, Brit.); S(1974); SKY RIDERS(1976, U.S./Gr.); WILD GEESE, THE(1978, Brit.); SEA WOLVES, THE(1981, Brit.); REMEMBRANCE(1982, Brit.); FINAL OPTION, THE(1983, Brit.)

Kristin Griffith
INTERIORS(1978); EUROPEANS, THE(1979, Brit.)

Lillian Griffith
Silents
NUMBER 17(1920)

Linda A. Griffith
Silents
CHARITY?(1916), w

Linda A. Griffith [Linda Arvidson]
Silents
CHARITY?(1916)

Mark Griffith
LION IN WINTER, THE(1968, Brit.); HAMLET(1969, Brit.)

Master Gordon [Gordon Griffith]
Misc. Silents
LITTLE SUNSET(1915)

Melanie Griffith
DROWNING POOL, THE(1975); NIGHT MOVES(1975); SMILE(1975); JOYRIDE(1977); ONE ON ONE(1977); ROAR(1981)
1984
BODY DOUBLE(1984); FEAR CITY(1984)
Misc. Talkies
UNDERGROUND ACES(1981)

Mervyn E. Griffith
1984
BEAT STREET(1984)

Nona Griffith
UNSEEN, THE(1945); PERFECT MARRIAGE, THE(1946)

Olwen Griffith
UP THE JUNCTION(1968, Brit.)

Otis Griffith
PAJAMA GAME, THE(1957)

Peter Griffith
HALLOWEEN(1978)

Ray Griffith
CENTRAL PARK(1932), p; LIFE BEGINS(1932), p; TENDERFOOT, THE(1932), p; YOU SAID A MOUTHFUL(1932), p; BABY FACE(1933), p; ELMER THE GREAT(1933), p; HARD TO HANDLE(1933), p; LADIES THEY TALK ABOUT(1933), p; LITTLE GIANT, THE(1933), p; PICTURE SNATCHER(1933), p; VOLTAIRE(1933), p
Silents
FOLLIES GIRL, THE(1919)
Misc. Silents
RED-HAIRED CUPID, A(1918)

Raymond Griffith
BELOVED BACHELOR, THE(1931), w; BOUGHT(1931), w; EXPENSIVE WOMEN(1931), w; GIRLS ABOUT TOWN(1931), w; GOD'S GIFT TO WOMEN(1931), w; ADVICE TO THE LOVELORN(1933), p; BOWERY, THE(1933), p; FRISCO JENNY(1933), p; CARDINAL RICHELIEU(1935), p; CLIVE OF INDIA(1935), p; FOLIES DERGERE(1935), assoc p; GIRLS' DORMITORY(1936), p; PRIVATE NUMBER(1936), p; FIFTY ROADS TO TOWN(1937), p; HEIDI(1937), p; SECOND HONEYMOON(1937), p; SEVENTH HEAVEN(1937), p; THIN ICE(1937), p; WIFE, DOCTOR AND NURSE(1937), p; ALWAYS GOODBYE(1938), p; BARONESS AND THE BUTLER, THE(1938), p; REBECCA OF SUNNYBROOK FARM(1938), p; THREE BLIND MICE(1938), p; DRUMS ALONG THE MOHAWK(1939), p; THREE MUSKETEERS,

THE(1939), p; HE MARRIED HIS WIFE(1940), p; MAN I MARRIED, THE(1940), p; MARK OF ZORRO, THE(1940), p
Silents
ETERNAL THREE, THE(1923); RED LIGHTS(1923); SOULS FOR SALE(1923); NELLIE, THE BEAUTIFUL CLOAK MODEL(1924); NEVER SAY DIE(1924), w; OPEN ALL NIGHT(1924); FORTY WINKS(1925); MISS BLUEBEARD(1925); NIGHT CLUB, THE(1925); PATHS TO PARADISE(1925); REGULAR FELLOW, A(1925); HANDS UP(1926); SORROWS OF SATAN(1926); WET PAINT(1926); TIME TO LOVE(1927); WEDDING BILL$(1927)
Misc. Silents
FOOLS FIRST(1922); DAY OF FAITH, THE(1923); WHITE TIGER(1923); CHANGING HUSBANDS(1924); DAWN OF A TOMORROW, THE(1924); LILY OF THE DUST(1924); FINE CLOTHES(1925); WHEN WINTER WENT(1925); YOU'D BE SURPRISED(1926); TRENT'S LAST CASE(1929)
Richard Griffith
THEM NICE AMERICANS(1958, Brit.), p
Robert Griffith
FOR THOSE IN PERIL(1944, Brit.); GIVE ME THE STARS(1944, Brit.); NIGHT OF MAGIC, A(1944, Brit.); FOR YOU ALONE(1945, Brit.); GIRL ON THE CANAL, THE(1947, Brit.)
Rosemary Griffith
Misc. Talkies
BRIDGES TO HEAVEN(1975)
T. L. Griffith
Silents
MASTER MIND, THE(1920), ph; JIM THE PENMAN(1921), ph
Thomas Griffith
FOUND ALIVE(1934), animal d
Tom Griffith
FIEND(; NIGHTBEAST(1982)
1984
ALIEN FACTOR, THE(1984)
Misc. Talkies
ALIEN FACTOR, THE(1978)
Tracy Griffith
1984
FEAR CITY(1984)
William Griffith
GREAT ZIEGFELD, THE(1936); LARCENY ON THE AIR(1937); TIME OUT FOR ROMANCE(1937); EVERYBODY DOES IT(1949); PISTOL HARVEST(1951); JAWS II(1978)
William H. Griffith
OPERATOR 13(1934)
William M. Griffith
SING AND LIKE IT(1934); RANGE LAND(1949); DEVIL GODDESS(1955)
Albert Griffiths
HORROR CASTLE(1965, Ital.), set d
David Griffiths
GOLDEN LADY, THE(1979, Brit.), ph
Derek Griffiths
UP POMPEII(1971, Brit.); RISING DAMP(1980, Brit.)
Eira Griffiths
HAPPINESS OF THREE WOMEN, THE(1954, Brit.); UNDER MILK WOOD(1973, Brit.)
Eldon W. Griffiths
FEARLESS FAGAN(1952), w
Eva Griffiths
VOICES(1973, Brit.)
Fred Griffiths
IT ALWAYS RAINS ON SUNDAY(1949, Brit.); PASSPORT TO PIMLICO(1949, Brit.); STOP PRESS GIRL(1949, Brit.); LAVENDER HILL MOB, THE(1951, Brit.); JUDGMENT DEFERRED(1952, Brit.); CRUEL SEA, THE(1953); DOUBLE CONFESSION(1953, Brit.); I BELIEVE IN YOU(1953, Brit.); MEET MR. LUCIFER(1953, Brit.); COMPANIONS IN CRIME(1954, Brit.); HELL BELOW ZERO(1954, Brit.); SLEEPING TIGER, THE(1954, Brit.); WOMAN'S ANGLE, THE(1954, Brit.); SECRET VENTURE(1955, Brit.); SEE HOW THEY RUN(1955, Brit.); LADYKILLERS, THE(1956, Brit.); PANIC IN THE PARLOUR(1957, Brit.); RAISING A RIOT(1957, Brit.); TEARS FOR SIMON(1957, Brit.); YOU PAY YOUR MONEY(1957, Brit.); DUNKIRK(1958, Brit.); CARRY ON NURSE(1959, Brit.); CRY FROM THE STREET, A(1959, Brit.); I'M ALL RIGHT, JACK(1959, Brit.); LEFT, RIGHT AND CENTRE(1959); LIGHT UP THE SKY(1960, Brit.); NEXT TO NO TIME(1960, Brit.); OVER THE ODDS(1961, Brit.); THERE WAS A CROOKED MAN(1962, Brit.); JUNGLE STREET GIRLS(1963, Brit.); NO TREE IN THE STREET(1964, Brit.); TO SIR, WITH LOVE(1967, Brit.); CARRY ON LOVING(1970, Brit.); PERFECT FRIDAY(1970, Brit.)
Georgina Griffiths
MEMOIRS OF A SURVIVOR(1981, Brit.)
Graham Griffiths
Silents
WELCOME CHILDREN(1921)
Howard Griffiths
SECOND BEST SECRET AGENT IN THE WHOLE WIDE WORLD, THE(1965, Brit.), w
Jane Griffiths
DERELICT, THE(1937, Brit.); GAMBLER AND THE LADY, THE(1952, Brit.); DOUBLE CONFESSION(1953, Brit.); GREEN SCARF, THE(1954, Brit.); MAN WITH A MILLION(1954, Brit.); SHADOW OF A MAN(1955, Brit.); THREE SUNDAYS TO LIVE(1957, Brit.); ACCURSED, THE(1958, Brit.); TREAD SOFTLY STRANGER(1959, Brit.); THIRD ALIBI, THE(1961, Brit.); DEAD MAN'S EVIDENCE(1962, Brit.); DURANT AFFAIR, THE(1962, Brit.); IMPERSONATOR, THE(1962, Brit.); DOUBLE, THE(1963, Brit)
Joan Griffiths
LAST DAYS OF DOLWYN, THE(1949, Brit.)
Misc. Silents
DICK'S FAIRY(1921, Brit.); LITTLE MEG'S CHILDREN(1921, Brit.)
Keith Griffiths
BROTHERS AND SISTERS(1980, Brit.), p; RADIO ON(1980, Brit./Ger.), p
Kenneth Griffiths
1984(1956, Brit.)

Leon Griffiths
MANIA(1961, Brit.), w; SECRET OF MONTE CRISTO, THE(1961, Brit.), w; HELLFIRE CLUB, THE(1963, Brit.), w; GRISSOM GANG, THE(1971), w; SQUEEZE, THE(1977, Brit.), w
Linda Griffiths
LIANNA(1983)
1984
RENO AND THE DOC(1984, Can.)
Lt. C. Griffiths
IT CAME FROM BENEATH THE SEA(1955)
Lucy Griffiths
CHILDREN GALORE(1954, Brit.); WILL ANY GENTLEMAN?(1955, Brit.); LADYKILLERS, THE(1956, Brit.); TOUCH OF THE SUN, A(1956, Brit.); GREEN MAN, THE(1957, Brit.); GIDEON OF SCOTLAND YARD(1959, Brit.); PLEASE TURN OVER(1960, Brit.); MURDER SHE SAID(1961, Brit.); THIRD ALIBI, THE(1961, Brit.); MOUSE ON THE MOON, THE(1963, Brit.); MURDER AHOY(1964, Brit.); COP-OUT(1967, Brit.); CARRY ON AGAIN, DOCTOR(1969, Brit.); PUBLIC EYE, THE(1972, Brit.); UNDER MILK WOOD(1973, Brit.)
Mark Griffiths
1984
HARDBODIES(1984), d, w; HIGHWAY TO HELL(1984), d&w; RUNNING HOT(1984), d&w
Mary Griffiths
HERE WE GO ROUND THE MULBERRY BUSH(1968, Brit.); THREE SISTERS(1974, Brit.)
Mildred Griffiths
LASSIE, COME HOME(1943), set d; SLIGHTLY DANGEROUS(1943), set d; NATIONAL VELVET(1944), set d; VALLEY OF DECISION, THE(1945), set d; HARVEY GIRLS, THE(1946), set d; SEA OF GRASS, THE(1947), set d; TENTH AVENUE ANGEL(1948), set d
Olwen Griffiths
1984
SCRUBBERS(1984, Brit.)
Ray Griffiths
TIGER SHARK(1932), p
Reston Griffiths
SMASH PALACE(1982, New Zealand), art d
Richard Griffiths
ALL THINGS BRIGHT AND BEAUTIFUL(1979, Brit.); SUPERMAN II(1980); CHARRIOTS OF FIRE(1981, Brit.); FRENCH LIEUTENANT'S WOMAN, THE(1981); RAGTIME(1981); GANDHI(1982); GORKY PARK(1983)
1984
GREYSTOKE: THE LEGEND OF TARZAN, LORD OF THE APES(1984)
Robert Griffiths
FIGHTING PIMPERNEL, THE(1950, Brit.)
S.J. Griffiths
ANIMAL FARM(1955, Brit.), ph
Scott Griffiths
LET THE BALLOON GO(1977, Aus.)
Trevor Griffiths
REDS(1981), w
Yvonne Griffiths
IT'S A WONDERFUL DAY(1949, Brit.)
Griffiths-Moss
TALKING FEET(1937, Brit.)
S. Griffiths-Moss
PORTRAIT OF CLARE(1951, Brit.)
Ethel Griffles
FOUR FRIGHTENED PEOPLE(1934); ANNE OF WINDY POPLARS(1940); BILLY THE KID(1941)
D.G. Grigg
JEKYLL AND HYDE...TOGETHER AGAIN(1982), spec eff
Gene Grigg
SHEBA BABY(1975), spec eff; ST. IVES(1976), spec eff; AMSTERDAM KILL, THE(1978, Hong Kong), spec eff; CHANGELING, THE(1980, Can.), spec eff; NIGHT GAMES(1980), spec eff
Thelma Grigg
THAT CERTAIN SOMETHING(1941, Aus.); BUSH CHRISTMAS(1947, Brit.); LADY CRAVED EXCITEMENT, THE(1950, Brit.); TRAIN OF EVENTS(1952, Brit.)
Camila Griggs
FORCED VENGEANCE(1982)
Gene Griggs
ULTIMATE WARRIOR, THE(1975), spec eff; FUTUREWORLD(1976), spec eff
Loyal Griggs
CROSSWINDS(1951), ph; LAST OUTPOST, THE(1951), ph; PASSAGE WEST(1951), ph; SHANE(1953), ph; BRIDGES AT TOKO-RI, THE(1954), ph; ELEPHANT WALK(1954), ph; THREE RING CIRCUS(1954), ph; WHITE CHRISTMAS(1954), ph; WE'RE NO ANGELS(1955), ph; TEN COMMANDMENTS, THE(1956), ph; THAT CERTAIN FEELING(1956), ph; THREE VIOLENT PEOPLE(1956), ph; BUSTER KEATON STORY, THE(1957), ph; SAD SACK, THE(1957), ph; TIN STAR, THE(1957), ph; BUCCANEER, THE(1958), ph; HOT SPELL(1958), ph; TONKA(1958), ph; HANGMAN, THE(1959), ph; JAYHAWKERS, THE(1959), ph; G.I. BLUES(1960), ph; VISIT TO A SMALL PLANET(1960), ph; WALK LIKE A DRAGON(1960), ph; BLUEPRINT FOR ROBBERY(1961), ph; LOVE IN A GOLDFISH BOWL(1961), ph; MAN-TRAP(1961), ph; GIRLS! GIRLS! GIRLS!(1962), ph; PAPA'S DELICATE CONDITION(1963), ph; GREATEST STORY EVER TOLD, THE(1965), ph; IN HARM'S WAY(1965), ph; SLENDER THREAD, THE(1965), ph; TICKLE ME(1965), ph; NIGHT OF THE GRIZZLY, THE(1966), ph; BANNING(1967), ph; HURRY SUNDOWN(1967), ph; YOUNG WARRIORS, THE(1967), ph; IN ENEMY COUNTRY(1968), ph; P.J.(1968), ph; PAINT YOUR WAGON(1969), ph; ...TICK...TICK...TICK...(1970), ph; BUNNY O'HARE(1971), ph
Nancy Griggs
1984
FLASH OF GREEN, A(1984)
Peter Griggs
HONKYTONK MAN(1982)
B. Grigkov
TAXI TO HEAVEN(1944, USSR)

Marcel Grignon
TO THE VICTOR(1948), spec eff; ADVENTURES OF CAPTAIN FABIAN(1951), ph; PERFECTIONIST, THE(1952, Fr.), ph; SIMPLE CASE OF MONEY, A(1952, Fr.), ph; CADET-ROUSSELLE(1954, Fr.), ph; LA PARISIENNE(1958, Fr./Ital.), ph; LES LIAISONS DANGEREUSES(1961, Fr./Ital.), ph; WHERE THE TRUTH LIES(1962, Fr.), ph; GREED IN THE SUN(1965, Fr./ Ital.), ph; RAPTURE(1965), ph; TAXI FOR TOBRUK(1965, Fr./Span./Ger.), ph; VICE AND VIRTUE(1965, Fr./Ital.), ph; FANTOMAS(1966, Fr./Ital.), ph; IS PARIS BURNING?(1966, U.S./Fr.), ph; OSS 117-MISSION FOR A KILLER(1966, Fr./Ital.), ph; FIXER, THE(1968), ph; POSTMAN GOES TO WAR, THE(1968, Fr.), ph; MADRON(1970, U.S./Israel), ph; SHAFT IN AFRICA(1973), ph; BEAST, THE(1975, Fr.), ph; LE GENDARME ET LES EXTRATER-RESTRES(1978, Fr.), ph

Kurt Grigoleit
ALMOST ANGELS(1962), ph; I DEAL IN DANGER(1966), ph

Sasha Grigoriev
MOSCOW-CASSIOPEIA(1974, USSR); TEENAGERS IN SPACE(1975, USSR)

J. Grigorojew
THREE DAYS OF VIKTOR TSCHERNIKOFF(1968, USSR), w

Y. Grigoryev
NIGHT BEFORE CHRISTMAS, A(1963, USSR)

Yu. Grigoryev
WAR AND PEACE(1968, USSR)

M. Grigoryeva
SPRINGTIME ON THE VOLGA(1961, USSR)

S. Grigoryeva
DON QUIXOTE(1961, USSR)

Howard Grigsby
1984
SECOND TIME LUCKY(1984, Aus./New Zealand), w

Herb Grika
LAST BLITZKRIEG, THE(1958)

E. Grikurov
SON OF MONGOLIA(1936, USSR), m

Michael M. Grilikhes
DUEL AT DIABLO(1966), w

John Grillo
SCUM(1979, Brit.); FIREFOX(1982)

Nick Grillo
YOUNGBLOOD(1978), p

Robert Grillo
VERY NATURAL THING, A(1974)

Lara Grills
1984
FIRST TURN-ON!, THE(1984)

Lucky Grills
CADDIE(1976, Aus.); MONEY MOVERS(1978, Aus.)

Bobby Grim
WINNING(1969)

Grimaldi
GIGANTIS(1959, Jap./U.S.), ed

Alberto Grimaldi
FACE TO FACE(1967, Ital.), p; FOR A FEW DOLLARS MORE(1967, Ital./Ger./Span.), p; GOOD, THE BAD, AND THE UGLY, THE(1967, Ital./Span.), p; BIG GUNDOWN, THE(1968, Ital.), p; FELLINI SATYRICON(1969, Fr./Ital.), p; LISTEN, LET'S MAKE LOVE(1969, Fr./Ital.), p; SABATA(1969, Ital.), p; BOUNTY HUNTERS, THE(1970, Ital.), p; BURN(1970), p; COMPANEROS(1970 Ital./Span./Ger.), p; MERCENARY, THE(1970, Ital./Span.), p; QUIET PLACE IN THE COUNTRY, A(1970, Ital./Fr.), p; ADIOS SABATA(1971, Ital./Span.), p; RETURN OF SABATA(1972, Ital./Fr./Ger.), p; MAN FROM THE EAST, A(1974, Ital./Fr.), p; CASANOVA(1976, Ital.), p; 1900(1976, Ital.), p; ARABIAN NIGHTS(1980, Ital./Fr.), p; LOVERS AND LIARS(1981, Ital.), p

Augo Grimaldi
SINGLE ROOM FURNISHED(1968), ed

Dan Grimaldi
DON'T GO IN THE HOUSE(1980)

Frank Grimaldi
THREE TOUGH GUYS(1974, U.S./Ital.)

Fulvio Grimaldi
DEAF SMITH AND JOHNNY EARS(1973, Ital.)

Gabriella Grimaldi
QUIET PLACE IN THE COUNTRY, A(1970, Ital./Fr.); JOHNNY HAMLET(1972, Ital.)

Giovanni Grimaldi
SLAVE, THE(1963, Ital.), w; GLADIATORS 7(1964, Span./Ital.), w

Hugo Grimaldi
GIGANTIS(1959, Jap./U.S.), d; SNOW QUEEN, THE(1959, USSR), ed; SURRENDER-HELL!(1959), ed; ASSIGNMENT OUTER SPACE(1960, Ital.), p; I BOMBED PEARL HARBOR(1961, Jap.), p, w, ed; PHANTOM PLANET, THE(1961), ed; HERCULES AND THE CAPTIVE WOMEN(1963, Fr./Ital.), ed; HUMAN DUPLICATORS, THE(1965), p, d; MUTINY IN OUTER SPACE(1965), p, d, w; SINGLE ROOM FURNISHED(1968), p; CHASTITY(1969), ed; BIG FOOT(1973), ed; EXIT THE DRAGON, ENTER THE TIGER(1977, Hong Kong), w

Iliana Grimaldi
SWORD OF EL CID, THE(1965, Span./Ital.)

Louise Grimaldi
DON'T GO IN THE HOUSE(1980)

Marion Grimaldi
SEASIDE SWINGERS(1965, Brit.)

Ruggero Grimaldi
TWO COLONELS, THE(1963, Ital.), w

Sophie Grimaldi
CHRISTINE(1959, Fr.); HIGHWAY PICKUP(1965, Fr./Ital.)

Jean Grimaud
CASTLE OF BLOOD(1964, Fr./Ital.), w

Michel Grimaud
1984
SUNDAY IN THE COUNTRY, A(1984, Fr.), set d

Paul Grimault
CRIME OF MONSIEUR LANGE, THE(1936, Fr.)

Pierre Grimblat
EMPIRE OF NIGHT, THE(1963, Fr.), d, w; HOW NOT TO ROB A DEPARTMENT STORE(1965, Fr./Ital.), p&d, w; SLOGAN(1970, Fr.), d&w

Sir Arthur Grimble
PACIFIC DESTINY(1956, Brit.), w

Barbara Ann Grimes
NIGHT SHIFT(1982)

Barbara Grimes
MACBETH(1971, Brit.)

Bruce Grimes
CORRUPTION(1968, Brit.), prod d; EXPLOSION(1969, Can.), art d; SCHOOL FOR UNCLAIMED GIRLS(1973, Brit.), art d

Chester Grimes
ELECTRA GLIDE IN BLUE(1973)

Colin Grimes
MAN WHO HAD POWER OVER WOMEN, THE(1970, Brit.), art d; AND NOW FOR SOMETHING COMPLETELY DIFFERENT(1972, Brit.), art d; DOOMWATCH(1972, Brit.), art d; NOTHING BUT THE NIGHT(1975, Brit.), art d; LOVE AND BULLETS(1979, Brit.), art d; DRESSER, THE(1983), art d; KRULL(1983), art d

Frank Grimes
OUTSIDER, THE(1980); FUNHOUSE, THE(1981); BRITTANIA HOSPITAL(1982, Brit.)

Gary Grimes
SUMMER OF '42(1971); CULPEPPER CATTLE COMPANY, THE(1972); CAHILL, UNITED STATES MARSHAL(1973); CLASS OF '44(1973); SPIKES GANG, THE(1974); GUS(1976)

Jack Grimes
RIVER GANG(1945); PENDULUM(1969); COLD TURKEY(1971)

Karolyn Grimes
PARDON MY PAST(1945); BLUE SKIES(1946); IT'S A WONDERFUL LIFE(1946); BISHOP'S WIFE, THE(1947); MOTHER WORE TIGHTS(1947); PRIVATE AFFAIRS OF BEL AMI, THE(1947); RIO GRANDE(1950); HONEYCHILE(1951)

Rebecca Grimes
WINTER KILLS(1979)

Rosemary Grimes
ISLAND OF LOST SOULS(1933)

Stephen Grimes
WAY WE WERE, THE(1973), prod d; HEAVEN KNOWS, MR. ALLISON(1957), art d; ATTILA(1958, Ital.), spec eff; ROOTS OF HEAVEN, THE(1958), art d; UNFORGIVEN, THE(1960), art d; MISFITS, THE(1961), art d; LIST OF ADRIAN MESSENGER, THE(1963), art d; NIGHT OF THE IGUANA, THE(1964), art d; THIS PROPERTY IS CONDEMNED(1966), art d; REFLECTIONS IN A GOLDEN EYE(1967), prod d; SINFUL DAVEY(1969, Brit.), prod d; WALK WITH LOVE AND DEATH, A(1969), prod d; RYAN'S DAUGHTER(1970, Brit.), prod d; THREE DAYS OF THE CONDOR(1975), prod d; YAKUZA, THE(1975, U.S./Jap.), prod d; MURDER BY DEATH(1976), prod d; STRAIGHT TIME(1978), prod d; ELECTRIC HORSEMAN, THE(1979), prod d; URBAN COWBOY(1980), prod d; ON GOLDEN POND(1981), prod d; DRESSER, THE(1983), prod d; KRULL(1983), prod d; NEVER SAY NEVER AGAIN(1983), prod d

Stephen B. Grimes
FREUD(1962), art d

Stephen S. Grimes
TRUE CONFESSIONS(1981), prod d

Tammy Grimes
THREE BITES OF THE APPLE(1967); PLAY IT AS IT LAYS(1972); SOMEBODY KILLED HER HUSBAND(1978); THE RUNNER STUMBLES(1979); CAN'T STOP THE MUSIC(1980); LAST UNICORN, THE(1982)
Misc. Talkies
ARTHUR!! ARTHUR?(1970)

Tom Grimes
Misc. Silents
SECRET OF THE PUEBLO, THE(1923)

Tommy Grimes
Silents
HEADIN' SOUTH(1918)

Grimethorpe Colliery Band
LITTLEST HORSE THIEVES, THE(1977)

Jacob Grimm
SNOW WHITE AND THE SEVEN DWARFS(1937), w

Jakob Grimm
MAGIC FOUNTAIN, THE(1961), w; SNOW WHITE AND THE THREE STOOGES(1961), w; HANSEL AND GRETEL(1965, Ger.), w; RUMPELSTILTSKIN(1965, Ger.), w; SLEEPING BEAUTY(1965, Ger.), w; SNOW WHITE(1965, Ger.), w; GOLDEN GOOSE, THE(1966, E. Ger.), w; SNOW WHITE AND ROSE RED(1966, Ger.), w; GOOSE GIRL, THE(1967, Ger.), w; SHOEMAKER AND THE ELVES, THE(1967, Ger.), w; MR. MAGOO'S HOLIDAY FESTIVAL(1970), w

Maria Grimm
PROUD AND THE DAMNED, THE(1972); RECORD CITY(1978)

Michael Grimm
EIGER SANCTION, THE(1975)

Oliver Grimm
REACH FOR GLORY(1963, Brit.)

Wilhelm Grimm
SNOW WHITE AND THE SEVEN DWARFS(1937), w; MAGIC FOUNTAIN, THE(1961), w; SNOW WHITE AND THE THREE STOOGES(1961), w; HANSEL AND GRETEL(1965, Ger.), w; RUMPELSTILTSKIN(1965, Ger.), w; SLEEPING BEAUTY(1965, Ger.), w; SNOW WHITE(1965, Ger.), w; GOLDEN GOOSE, THE(1966, E. Ger.), w; SNOW WHITE AND ROSE RED(1966, Ger.), w; GOOSE GIRL, THE(1967, Ger.), w; SHOEMAKER AND THE ELVES, THE(1967, Ger.), w; MR. MAGOO'S HOLIDAY FESTIVAL(1970), w; PIED PIPER, THE(1972, Brit.), w

F. Grimmer
MOSCOW SHANGHAI(1936, Ger.)

Roger Grimsby
BANANAS(1971)
1984
GHOSTBUSTERS(1984)

Barry Grimshaw
HARRY IN YOUR POCKET(1973)
Jack Grimsley
MARCO POLO JUNIOR(1973, Aus.), m/1
Glyn Grimstead
RICHARD'S THINGS(1981, Brit.)
Borge Moller Grimstrup
REPTILICUS(1962, U.S./Den.)
Gordon Grimward
1984
BREAKOUT(1984, Brit.), ed
Burris Grimwood
SLEEP, MY LOVE(1948), makeup; WHO KILLED "DOC" ROBBIN?(1948), makeup
Herbert Grimwood
Silents
WHEN THE CLOUDS ROLL BY(1920); SONNY(1922); ROMOLA(1925); AMATEUR GENTLEMAN, THE(1926)
Adam Grinberg
TWO KOUNEY LEMELS(1966, Israel), ph
Nicholas Grinde
THIS MODERN AGE(1931), d; SHOPWORN(1932), d; VANITY STREET(1932), d
Nick Grinde
BISHOP MURDER CASE, THE(1930), d; DIVORCEE, THE(1930), w; GOOD NEWS(1930), d; REMOTE CONTROL(1930), d; BABES IN TOYLAND(1934), w; BORDER BRIGANDS(1935), d; LADIES CRAVE EXCITEMENT(1935), d; STONE OF SILVER CREEK(1935), d; JAILBREAK(1936), d; PUBLIC ENEMY'S WIFE(1936), d; CAPTAIN'S KID, THE(1937), d; EXILED TO SHANGHAI(1937), d; FUGITIVE IN THE SKY(1937), d; LOVE IS ON THE AIR(1937), d; PUBLIC WEDDING(1937), d; WHITE BONDAGE(1937), d; DELINQUENT PARENTS(1938), d; DOWN IN ARKANSAW(1938), d; FEDERAL MAN-HUNT(1939), d; KING OF CHINATOWN(1939), d; MAN THEY COULD NOT HANG, THE(1939), d; MILLION DOLLAR LEGS(1939), d; SUDDEN MONEY(1939), d; WOMAN IS THE JUDGE, A(1939), d; BEFORE I HANG(1940), d; CONVICTED WOMAN(1940), d; FRIENDLY NEIGHBORS(1940), d; GIRLS OF THE ROAD(1940), d; MAN WITH NINE LIVES, THE(1940), d; MEN WITHOUT SOULS(1940), d; SCANDAL SHEET(1940), d; MOUNTAIN MOONLIGHT(1941), d; GIRL FROM ALASKA(1942), d; HITLER–DEAD OR ALIVE(1942), d; WE'VE NEVER BEEN LICKED(1943), w; ROAD TO ALCATRAZ(1945), d
Silents
DESERT RIDER, THE(1929), d; MORGAN'S LAST RAID(1929), d
Misc. Silents
BEYOND THE SIERRAS(1928), d; RIDERS OF THE DARK(1928), d
Gerhard Grindel
CITY OF TORMENT(1950, Ger.), w
Organ Grinder
POOR LITTLE RICH GIRL(1936)
Murray Grindlay
SLEEPING DOGS(1977, New Zealand), m
Richard Grindle
IT'S A BIG COUNTRY(1951)
Judy Grindley
TWO HUNDRED MOTELS(1971, Brit.)
Phil Grindrod
BEES IN PARADISE(1944, Brit.), ph; GIVE US THE MOON(1944, Brit.), ph; I'LL BE YOUR SWEETHEART(1945, Brit.), ph; GEORGE IN CIVVY STREET(1946, Brit.), ph; THIS MAN IS MINE(1946 Brit.), ph; WATERLOO ROAD(1949, Brit.), ph; DEATH IS A NUMBER(1951, Brit.), ph; KILLER WALKS, A(1952, Brit.), ph; MY DEATH IS A MOCKERY(1952, Brit.), ph; GREAT GAME, THE(1953, Brit.), ph; HOUSE OF BLACKMAIL(1953, Brit.), ph; IS YOUR HONEYMOON REALLY NECESSARY?(1953, Brit.), ph; SHADOW MAN(1953, Brit.), ph; CROOKED SKY, THE(1957, Brit.), ph; SAIL INTO DANGER(1957, Brit.), ph; DIPLOMATIC CORPSE, THE(1958, Brit.), ph; VIOLENT MOMENT(1966, Brit.), ph
Philip Grindrod
INDISCRETIONS OF EVE(1932, Brit.), ph; SOUTHERN MAID, A(1933, Brit.), ph; RADIO FOLLIES(1935, Brit.), ph; REGAL CAVALCADE(1935, Brit.), ph; GIRL THIEF, THE(1938), ph; DEADLIEST SIN, THE(1956, Brit.), ph; WAY OUT, THE(1956, Brit.), ph; KEY MAN, THE(1957, Brit.), ph; SCOTLAND YARD DRAGNET(1957, Brit.), ph; VIOLENT STRANGER(1957, Brit.), ph; FEMALE FIENDS(1958, Brit.), ph
Phil Grindrof
HANDS OF DESTINY(1954, Brit.), ph
Alessandro Grinfan
ANONYMOUS VENETIAN, THE(1971)
Judy Gringer
CRAZY PARADISE(1965, Den.); VENOM(1968, Den.)
Marcel Gringon
DANGER IS A WOMAN(1952, Fr.), ph
Judy Grinham
OPERATION BULLSHINE(1963, Brit.)
N. Grinko
MY NAME IS IVAN(1963, USSR); PEACE TO HIM WHO ENTERS(1963, USSR); SHADOWS OF FORGOTTEN ANCESTORS(1967, USSR); WAR AND PEACE(1968, USSR)
Nikolai Grinko
SOLARIS(1972, USSR); ANDREI ROUBLOV(1973, USSR); STALKER(1982, USSR)
Amanda Grinling
AGENT 8 3/4(1963, Brit.); RETURN OF THE SOLDIER, THE(1983, Brit.)
1984
SECRET PLACES(1984, Brit.)
Jack Grinnage
LADY GODIVA(1955); REBEL WITHOUT A CAUSE(1955); CRASHING LAS VEGAS(1956); KING CREOLE(1958); WINK OF AN EYE(1958); WOLF LARSEN(1958); RIOT IN JUVENILE PRISON(1959); CAPTAIN NEWMAN, M.D.(1963); PRIVATE NAVY OF SGT. O'FARRELL, THE(1968); LIBERATION OF L.B. JONES, THE(1970); GLASS HOUSES(1972)
William Grinnell
Misc. Talkies
ABDUCTORS, THE(1972)
Philip Grinrod
PORT OF ESCAPE(1955, Brit.), ph

Durward Grinstead
MAID OF SALEM(1937), w
Jesse Edward Grinstead
Silents
TUMBLING RIVER(1927), w
J.E. Grinsted
SUNSET OF POWER(1936), w
Brad F. Grinter
SCREAM, BABY, SCREAM(1969)
Heather Grinter
THUMBELINA(1970)
Philip Grinwood
COUNTERFEIT PLAN, THE(1957, Brit.), ph
Maria Gripe
ELVIS! ELVIS!(1977, Swed.), w
Harry Gripp
Silents
KATHLEEN MAVOURNEEN(1919); SIBERIA(1926); TUMBLING RIVER(1927); FAR CALL, THE(1929)
Harry Grippe
Silents
ANOTHER SCANDAL(1924); GREAT K & A TRAIN ROBBERY, THE(1926); NO MAN'S GOLD(1926)
Jan Grippo
BOWERY BOMBSHELL(1946), p; IN FAST COMPANY(1946), p; LIVE WIRES(1946), p; MR. HEX(1946), p, w; SPOOK BUSTERS(1946), p; BOWERY BUCKAROOS(1947), p; HARD BOILED MAHONEY(1947), p; NEWS HOUNDS(1947), p; ANGELS ALLEY(1948), p; JINX MONEY(1948), p; SMUGGLERS' COVE(1948), p; TROUBLE MAKERS(1948), p; ANGELS IN DISGUISE(1949), p; FIGHTING FOOLS(1949), p; HOLD THAT BABY!(1949), p; MASTER MINDS(1949), p; BLONDE DYNAMITE(1950), p; BLUES BUSTERS(1950), p; LUCKY LOSERS(1950), p; TRIPLE TROUBLE(1950), p; BOWERY BATTALION(1951), p; CRAZY OVER HORSES(1951), p; GHOST CHASERS(1951), p; LET'S GO NAVY(1951), p
Joe Lo Grippo
GODFATHER, THE, PART II(1974)
Mme. Eva Grippon
CLEARING THE RANGE(1931)
V. Griqoryeva
SANDU FOLLOWS THE SUN(1965, USSR)
Angelo Grisante
WIZARDS(1977)
Andrea Grisanti
1984
NOSTALGHIA(1984, USSR/Ital.), prod d
Angelo Grisanti
WOMAN UNDER THE INFLUENCE, A(1974); OPENING NIGHT(1977); HEY, GOOD LOOKIN'(1982)
Christina Grisantii
WOMAN UNDER THE INFLUENCE, A(1974)
Louis Grisel
Silents
BROKEN CHAINS(1916); DANCER'S PERIL, THE(1917); LOVE IN A HURRY(1919); JANE EYRE(1921)
Louis R. Grisel
Silents
CRIMSON DOVE, THE(1917); POLLY OF THE CIRCUS(1917)
Thomas J. Griser
Silents
DOCTOR JACK(1922), w
David Grisman
BIG BAD MAMA(1974), m; CAPONE(1975), m; EAT MY DUST!(1976), m; KING OF THE GYPSIES(1978), m
Joseph R. Grismer
Silents
BROKEN CHAINS(1916), w; WAY DOWN EAST(1920), w
Michel Grisolia
CHOICE OF ARMS(1983, Fr.), w; L'ETOILE DU NORD(1983, Fr.), w
Michel Grisoni
CONFIDENTIALLY YOURS(1983, Fr.)
Wallace Grissell
JOHNNY DOUGHBOY(1943), ed; MARSHAL OF RENO(1944), d; VIGILANTES OF DODGE CITY(1944), d; WANDERER OF THE WASTELAND(1945), d
Wallace A. Grissell
CORPUS CHRISTI BANDITS(1945), d; WILD HORSE MESA(1947), d; WESTERN HERITAGE(1948), d; YANK IN INDO-CHINA, A(1952), d
Walter Grissell
OUTLAW, THE(1943), ed
John Grissmer
BRIDE, THE(1973), p, w; SCALPEL(1976), p, d&w
Jimmy Grisson
CAMPUS SLEUTH(1948)
Hal Grist
LOVE BUG, THE(1968)
Paul Grist
HIGH COMMISSIONER, THE(1968, U.S./Brit.); UNDER MILK WOOD(1973, Brit.)
Rosa Gristina
DEATH RIDES A HORSE(1969, Ital.), set d
Al Griswald
1984
SLAYGROUND(1984, Brit.), spec eff
Butch Griswald
WILD, FREE AND HUNGRY(1970)
James Griswald
Silents
GIRL OF THE GOLDEN WEST, THE(1915)
Al Griswold
WIZ, THE(1978), spec eff; RABID(1976, Can.), spec eff; HAIR(1979), spec eff
1984
BEAT STREET(1984), spec eff

Stephen Gross
BEGGARS IN ERMINE(1934); THANK YOU, JEEVES(1936), w
W.J. Gross
Silents
BAR SINISTER, THE(1917); ASHAMED OF PARENTS(1921)
Misc. Silents
PEGGY, THE WILL O' THE WISP(1917)
Walter Gross
MOSCOW SHANGHAI(1936, Ger.); TURKISH CUCUMBER, THE(1963, Ger.); PHONY AMERICAN, THE(1964, Ger.)
Willard Gross
CREATURE OF THE WALKING DEAD(1960, Mex.)
William Gross
Silents
PLUNDERER, THE(1915); OUT OF THE SHADOW(1919); RAINBOW(1921)
William J. Gross
Silents
PRUNELLA(1918)
Yoram Gross
LITTLE CONVICT, THE(1980, Aus.), p&d; DOT AND THE BUNNY(1983, Aus.), p&d, w
1984
CAMEL BOY, THE(1984, Aus.), p&d, w
Gib Grossac
PRICE OF FLESH, THE(1962, Fr.); DESTRUCTORS, THE(1974, Brit.)
Robert Grossbach
1984
BEST DEFENSE(1984), w
Jack Grossberg
BANANAS(1971), p; SLEEPER(1973), p
Arthur Grosse
REBEL, THE(1933, Ger.)
Herwart Grosse
PINOCCHIO(1969, E. Ger.)
Paul Grosse
THREE COMRADES(1938), art d
Art Grosser
GAS(1981, Can.)
Arthur Grosser
IN PRAISE OF OLDER WOMEN(1978, Can.)
1984
HOTEL NEW HAMPSHIRE, THE(1984)
Richard Grosser
MALATESTA'S CARNIVAL(1973), p
Frank Grossers
CIMARRON KID, THE(1951), ed
Peter Grosset
RIDER IN THE NIGHT, THE(1968, South Africa), ed
John Grossett
MISS SADIE THOMPSON(1953)
Antonio Grossi
EMBALMER, THE(1966, Ital.)
Fred Grossinger
WIND ACROSS THE EVERGLADES(1958)
Kurt Grosskurt
LUDWIG(1973, Ital./Ger./Fr.)
Kurt Grosskurth
MAGIC FIRE(1956); SKI FEVER(1969, U.S./Aust./Czech.)
Marjorie Grossland
DAY THE EARTH STOOD STILL, THE(1951)
T. Grosslichtova
INSPECTOR GENERAL, THE(1937, Czech.)
A. Grossman
CLOUDED CRYSTAL, THE(1948, Brit.), p
Abe Grossman
GIRL ON THE SPOT(1946), art d
Abraham Grossman
MOONLIGHT IN VERMONT(1943), art d; DESTINY(1944), art d; ENTER ARSENE LUPIN(1944), art d; JUNGLE WOMAN(1944), art d; MARSHAL OF GUNSMOKE(1944), art d; MOON OVER LAS VEGAS(1944), art d; MUMMY'S GHOST, THE(1944), art d; MY GAL LOVES MUSIC(1944), art d; RIDERS OF THE SANTA FE(1944), art d; SINGING SHERIFF, THE(1944), art d; TRAIL TO GUNSIGHT(1944), art d; TRIGGER TRAIL(1944), art d; TWILIGHT ON THE PRAIRIE(1944), art d; FROZEN GHOST, THE(1945), art d; HONEYMOON AHEAD(1945), art d; I'LL REMEMBER APRIL(1945), art d; I'LL TELL THE WORLD(1945), art d; PATRICK THE GREAT(1945), art d; PILLOW OF DEATH(1945), art d; RIVER GANG(1945), art d; SENORITA FROM THE WEST(1945), art d; STRANGE CONFESSION(1945), art d; TRAIL TO VENGEANCE(1945), art d; GUN TOWN(1946), art d; HOUSE OF HORRORS(1946), art d; INSIDE JOB(1946), art d; LITTLE MISS BIG(1946), art d; SHE-WOLF OF LONDON(1946), art d; SPIDER WOMAN STRIKES BACK, THE(1946), art d; TERROR BY NIGHT(1946), art d; WILD BEAUTY(1946), art d; MICHIGAN KID, THE(1947), art d; SLAVE GIRL(1947), art d
Albert Grossman
BAD MEN OF THE BORDER(1945), art d
Mrs. Alexander Grossman
Silents
WALLS OF PREJUDICE(1920, Brit.), w
Bernie Grossman
SENSATION HUNTERS(1934), m
Budd Grossman
GOING STEADY(1958), w; BACHELOR FLAT(1962), w
Doris Grossman
1984
JOHNNY DANGEROUSLY(1984)
Douglas Grossman
1984
UP THE CREEK(1984), w

F. Maury Grossman
FRESHMAN YEAR(1938), w; SWING THAT CHEER(1938), w
Harry Grossman
Misc. Silents
FACE TO FACE(1920), d; PERILOUS VALLEY(1920), d; WITS VS. WITS(1920), d
Helen Grossman
TEVYA(1939)
Hettie Grossman
Misc. Silents
SLAVE, THE(1918, Brit.)
Irving Grossman
CATSKILL HONEYMOON(1950)
Jack Grossman
MISCHIEF(1969, Brit.), p, w
Joe Grossman
FLYING SCOTSMAN, THE(1929, Brit.), w; LADY FROM THE SEA, THE(1929, Brit.), w
Karen Grossman
SLAYER, THE(1982), ph; MICROWAVE MASSACRE(1983), ph; RISKY BUSINESS(1983)
Kristine M. Grossman
1984
FLETCH(1984)
Ladislav Grossman
SHOP ON MAIN STREET, THE(1966, Czech.), w, w
Michael Grossman
ICE STATION ZEBRA(1968)
Miriam Grossman
Misc. Talkies
JEWISH KING LEAR(1935)
Oscar Grossman
SUCH GOOD FRIENDS(1971)
Sam Grossman
VAN, THE(1977), d
Stefan Grossman
JOE HILL(1971, Swed./U.S.), m
Ted Grossman
SSSSSSSS(1973); GIRL FROM PETROVKA, THE(1974); SUGARLAND EXPRESS, THE(1974); JAWS(1975); NIGHT MOVES(1975); JAWS II(1978), stunts; RAIDERS OF THE LOST ARK(1981); TWO OF A KIND(1983)
1984
BODY DOUBLE(1984); OH GOD! YOU DEVIL(1984); RACING WITH THE MOON(1984)
Ted M. Grossman
WHAT'S UP, DOC?(1972)
Wilbur Grossman
CACTUS IN THE SNOW(1972), ph
Ena Grossmith
TILLY OF BLOOMSBURY(1931, Brit.); COLONEL BLOOD(1934, Brit.); VIRGINIA'S HUSBAND(1934, Brit.); WIFE OR TWO, A(1935, Brit.); FAREWELL TO CINDERELLA(1937, Brit.)
Silents
VIRGINIA'S HUSBAND(1928, Brit.)
Misc. Silents
CANDYTUFT, I MEAN VERONICA(1921, Brit.)
George Grossmith
ARE YOU THERE?(1930); THOSE THREE FRENCH GIRLS(1930); WOMEN EVERYWHERE(1930), a, w; GOD IS MY WITNESS(1931); RESERVED FOR LADIES(1932, Brit.); WEDDING REHEARSAL(1932, Brit.), a, w; PRINCESS CHARMING(1935, Brit.); GIRL FROM MAXIM'S, THE(1936, Brit.)
Lawrence Grossmith
COUNSEL'S OPINION(1933, Brit.); TIGER BAY(1933, Brit.); FOR LOVE OR MONEY(1934, Brit.); LUCK OF A SAILOR, THE(1934, Brit.); PRIVATE LIFE OF DON JUAN, THE(1934, Brit.); ROLLING IN MONEY(1934, Brit.); SING AS WE GO(1934, Brit.); IT HAPPENED IN PARIS(1935, Brit.); EVERYTHING IN LIFE(1936, Brit.); GIRL IN THE TAXI(1937, Brit.); MAKE-UP(1937, Brit.); MEN ARE NOT GODS(1937, Brit.); SONG OF THE FORGE(1937, Brit.); ALL WOMEN HAVE SECRETS(1939); CAPTAIN FURY(1939); I'M FROM MISSOURI(1939); NO TIME FOR COMEDY(1940); OPENED BY MISTAKE(1940); LARCENY STREET(1941, Brit.); MURDER AT THE BASKERVILLES(1941, Brit.); GASLIGHT(1944)
Misc. Silents
BRASS BOTTLE, THE(1914, Brit.); COMMON CAUSE, THE(1918); HOUSE DIVIDED, A(1919)
Guy Grosso
LE GENDARME ET LES EXTRATERRESTRES(1978, Fr.); CHARLES AND LUCIE(1982, Fr.)
Sonny Grosso
FRENCH CONNECTION, THE(1971); SEVEN UPS, THE(1973), w; REPORT TO THE COMMISSIONER(1975); CRUISING(1980)
Florence Grosson
SOUTH RIDING(1938, Brit.)
Luise Grossova
SHOP ON MAIN STREET, THE(1966, Czech.)
Julia Grosthwaite
GET CHARLIE TULLY(1976, Brit.)
Beatrice Grosvenor
Silents
GOD IN THE GARDEN, THE(1921, Brit.)
Elizabeth Grosz
1984
CHEECH AND CHONG'S THE CORSICAN BROTHERS(1984)
Anthony Grot
SMILING IRISH EYES(1929), set d
Anton Grot
NOAH'S ARK(1928), art d; NOTORIOUS AFFAIR, A(1930), set d; SONG OF THE FLAME(1930), set d; TOP SPEED(1930), art d; BODY AND SOUL(1931), art d; LITTLE CAESAR(1931), art d; MAD GENIUS, THE(1931), set d; SURRENDER(1931), art d; ALIAS THE DOCTOR(1932), art d; BEAUTY AND THE BOSS(1932), art d; BIG CITY BLUES(1932) 65m WB bw, art d; DOCTOR X(1932), art d; SCARLET DAWN(1932), art d; TWO SECONDS(1932), art d; BABY FACE(1933), art d; EVER IN MY HEART(1933),

art d; FROM HEADQUARTERS(1933), art d; GOLD DIGGERS OF 1933(1933), art d; KEYHOLE, THE(1933), art d; MYSTERY OF THE WAX MUSEUM, THE(1933), art d; SON OF A SAILOR(1933), art d; 20,000 YEARS IN SING SING(1933), art d; BRITISH AGENT(1934), art d; DOCTOR MONICA(1934), art d; EASY TO LOVE(1934), art d; FIREBIRD, THE(1934), art d; GAMBLING LADY(1934), art d; HE WAS HER MAN(1934), art d; MANDALAY(1934), art d; SIDE STREETS(1934), art d; SIX-DAY BIKE RIDER(1934), art d; UPPER WORLD(1934), art d; CAPTAIN BLOOD(1935), art d; CASE OF THE CURIOUS BRIDE, THE(1935), art d; DR. SOCRATES(1935), art d; GOLD DIGGERS OF 1935(1935), art d; MIDSUMMER'S NIGHT'S DREAM, A(1935), art d; RED HOT TIRES(1935), art d; SECRET BRIDE, THE(1935), art d; STRANDED(1935), art d; TRAVELING SALESLADY, THE(1935), art d; ANTHONY ADVERSE(1936), art d; CONFESSION(1937), art d; GREAT GARRICK, THE(1937), art d; LIFE OF EMILE ZOLA, THE(1937), art d; STOLEN HOLIDAY(1937), art d; TOVARICH(1937), art d; FOOLS FOR SCANDAL(1938), art d; HARD TO GET(1938), art d; SECRETS OF AN ACTRESS(1938), art d; JUAREZ(1939), art d; PRIVATE LIVES OF ELIZABETH AND ESSEX, THE(1939), art d; THEY MADE ME A CRIMINAL(1939), art d; DISPATCH FROM REUTERS, A(1940), art d; SEA HAWK, THE(1940), art d; AFFECTIONATELY YOURS(1941), art d; SEA WOLF, THE(1941), art d; THANK YOUR LUCKY STARS(1943), art d; CONSPIRATORS, THE(1944), art d; MILDRED PIERCE(1945), art d; RHAPSODY IN BLUE(1945), art d; MY REPUTATION(1946), art d; NEVER SAY GOODBYE(1946), art d; ONE MORE TOMORROW(1946), art d; NORA PRENTISS(1947), art d; POSSESSED(1947), art d; TWO MRS. CARROLLS, THE(1947), art d; UNSUSPECTED, THE(1947), art d; JUNE BRIDE(1948), art d; ONE SUNDAY AFTERNOON(1948), art d; ROMANCE ON THE HIGH SEAS(1948), art d
Silents
VOLGA BOATMAN, THE(1926), art d; KING OF KINGS, THE(1927), art d; VANITY(1927), art d; WHITE GOLD(1927), art d; HOLD 'EM YALE!(1928), art d; STAND AND DELIVER(1928), art d; WALKING BACK(1928), art d
Vernon Grote
1984
PLACES IN THE HEART(1984)
William Grote
MAN WITHOUT A BODY, THE(1957, Brit.), w
Esther Grotes
KAZABLAN(1974, Israel)
Jan Groth
NOSFERATU, THE VAMPIRE(1979, Fr./Ger.)
Franz Grothe
ARENT WE WONDERFUL?(1959, Ger.), m; SPESSART INN, THE(1961, Ger.), m; TRAPP FAMILY, THE(1961, Ger.), m; ARMS AND THE MAN(1962, Ger.), m; HELDINNEN(1962, Ger.), m; MAN WHO WALKED THROUGH THE WALL, THE(1964, Ger.), m; TWO IN A SLEEPING BAG(1964, Ger.), m; HEIDI(1968, Aust.), m
Fritz Grothe
RENDEZ-VOUS(1932, Ger.), m
Manfred Grothe
MONSTER OF LONDON CITY, THE(1967, Ger.)
Sven Grothe
FLOWERS FOR THE MAN IN THE MOON(1975, Ger.)
Wilhelm Grothe
RUMPELSTILTSKIN(1965, Ger.); PUSS 'N' BOOTS(1967, Ger.)
Rosalba Grottesi
SHOOT LOUD, LOUDER... I DON'T UNDERSTAND(1966, Ital.)
Aldo Grotti
RED DESERT(1965, Fr./Ital.)
Arthur Groulx
THIRTEENTH LETTER, THE(1951)
Gilles Groulx
TAKE IT ALL(1966, Can.), ed; CAT IN THE SACK, THE(1967, Can.), d&w
Utah Ground
1984
NOT FOR PUBLICATION(1984), ch
Romulo Grounni
TWO KOUNEY LEMELS(1966, Israel), ph
Mitchell Group
IN-LAWS, THE(1979)
1984
OH GOD! YOU DEVIL(1984)
Spencer Davis Group
HERE WE GO ROUND THE MULBERRY BUSH(1968, Brit.), m
James Grout
RULING CLASS, THE(1972, Brit.); LOOPHOLE(1981, Brit.)
Rafael Perez Grovas
INVASION OF THE VAMPIRES, THE(1961, Mex.), p; BLUE DEMON VERSUS THE INFERNAL BRAINS(1967, Mex.), p
Charles Grove
GREAT MR. HANDEL, THE(1942, Brit.)
Danny Grove
RESCUE SQUAD, THE(1963, Brit.)
Elaine C. Grove
LIQUID SKY(1982)
Gerald Grove
Silents
MAN AND MAID(1925)
O. M. Grove
Silents
CIVILIZATION(1916), ph
R.L. Grove
DEATHMASTER, THE(1972), w
Sybil Grove
LET US BE GAY(1930); MAN FROM BLANKLEY'S, THE(1930); PRINCE OF DIAMONDS(1930); ALONG CAME YOUTH(1931); C.O.D.(1932, Brit.); HOTEL SPLENDIDE(1932, Brit.); OFFICE GIRL, THE(1932, Brit.); I'M AN EXPLOSIVE(1933, Brit.); MAID HAPPY(1933, Brit.); MAN FROM TORONTO, THE(1933, Brit.); MISTER CINDERS(1934, Brit.); STRAUSS' GREAT WALTZ(1934, Brit.); TOO MANY MILLIONS(1934, Brit.); FIGHTING STOCK(1935, Brit.); PRICE OF A SONG, THE(1935, Brit.); RADIO FOLLIES(1935, Brit.); GAY ADVENTURE, THE(1936, Brit.); KING OF HEARTS(1936, Brit.); LUCK OF THE TURF(1936, Brit.); RED WAGON(1936, Brit.); SENSATION(1936, Brit.); SHE KNEW WHAT SHE WANTED(1936, Brit.); THIS GREEN HELL(1936, Brit.); TROPICAL TROUBLE(1936, Brit.); MEN ARE NOT GODS(1937, Brit.); MERRY COMES TO STAY(1937, Brit.); RACING ROMANCE(1937, Brit.); SHOW

GOES ON, THE(1937, Brit.); WHAT A MAN!(1937, Brit.); WHY PICK ON ME?(1937, Brit.); MERELY MR. HAWKINS(1938, Brit.)
Silents
CAMPUS KNIGHTS(1929)
Venise Grove
BUSHWHACKERS, THE(1952)
The Grove Family
MAN OF THE MOMENT(1955, Brit.)
Ted Grove-Rogers
LONELY HEARTS(1983, Aus.)
Linda Grovenor
DIE LAUGHING(1980)
Robert Grovenor
STEELYARD BLUES(1973), ed
Barbara Grover
SKI BUM, THE(1971); PSYCHOPATH, THE(1973)
Misc. Talkies
EYE FOR AN EYE, AN(1975)
Cindy Grover
NETWORK(1976)
Cynthia Grover
JAWS II(1978)
Danny Grover
2001: A SPACE ODYSSEY(1968, U.S./Brit.)
Ed Grover
SERPICO(1973); DEATH WISH(1974); LAW AND DISORDER(1974); WHO?(1975, Brit./Ger.)
Edward Grover
REPORT TO THE COMMISSIONER(1975)
John Grover
FOR YOUR EYES ONLY(1981), ed; FINAL OPTION, THE(1983, Brit.), ed; OCTOPUSSY(1983, Brit.), ed
Mary Grover
LIVE A LITTLE, LOVE A LITTLE(1968); EVEL KNIEVEL(1971); SPECTRE OF EDGAR ALLAN POE, THE(1974)
Stanley Grover
NETWORK(1976); NORTH DALLAS FORTY(1979); ONION FIELD, THE(1979)
1984
GHOSTBUSTERS(1984)
Charles Groves
ROSARY, THE(1931, Brit.); FACE AT THE WINDOW, THE(1932, Brit.); EXCESS BAGGAGE(1933, Brit.); HIS GRACE GIVES NOTICE(1933, Brit.); IRON STAIR, THE(1933, Brit.); NIGHT JOURNEY(1938, Brit.); HARD STEEL(1941, Brit.); LOVE ON THE DOLE(1945, Brit.); WINSLOW BOY, THE(1950); ONE WILD OAT(1951, Brit.)
Misc. Silents
SANDS OF TIME, THE(1919, Brit.)
Clemence Groves
CONSTANT NYMPH, THE(1943)
Doris Groves
COME BACK PETER(1952, Brit.)
Florence Groves
WANTED BY SCOTLAND YARD(1939, Brit.); MYSTERY OF ROOM 13(1941, Brit.)
Frank Groves
CUP-TIE HONEYMOON(1948, Brit.)
Fred Groves
ESCAPE(1930, Brit.); SUSPENSE(1930, Brit.); OUT OF THE BLUE(1931, Brit.); SALLY IN OUR ALLEY(1931, Brit.); WORLD, THE FLESH, AND THE DEVIL, THE(1932, Brit.); GLIMPSE OF PARADISE, A(1934, Brit.); DANCE BAND(1935, Brit.); OLD CURIOSITY SHOP, THE(1935, Brit.); REGAL CAVALCADE(1935, Brit.); WOLVES OF THE UNDERWORLD(1935, Brit.); BELOVED IMPOSTER(1936, Brit.); ROYAL EAGLE(1936, Brit.); SECOND BUREAU(1937, Brit.); NO PARKING(1938, Brit.); STRANGE BOARDERS(1938, Brit.); THE BEACHCOMBER(1938, Brit.); VIPER, THE(1938, Brit.); CHALLENGE(1939, Brit.); TWENTY-ONE DAYS TOGETHER(1940, Brit.); IDEAL HUSBAND, AN(1948, Brit.); NIGHT BEAT(1948, Brit.); GIRL WHO COULDN'T QUITE, THE(1949, Brit.); MY BROTHER JONATHAN(1949, Brit.); MY BROTHER'S KEEPER(1949, Brit.); UP FOR THE CUP(1950, Brit.); OLD MOTHER RILEY(1952, Brit.)
Silents
FIRM OF GIRDLESTONE, THE(1915, Brit.); GRIT OF A JEW, THE(1917, Brit.); LABOUR LEADER, THE(1917, Brit.); JUDGE NOT(1920, Brit.); LONDON PRIDE(1920, Brit.); SQUIBS(1921, Brit.); CRIMSON CIRCLE, THE(1922, Brit.); MASTER OF CRAFT, A(1922, Brit.); SQUIBS WINS THE CALCUTTA SWEEP(1922, Brit.); SQUIBS, MP(1923, Brit.); SQUIBS' HONEYMOON(1926, Brit.)
Misc. Silents
IDOL OF PARIS, THE(1914, Brit.); LOSS OF THE BIRKENHEAD, THE(1914, Brit.); PRICE OF JUSTICE, THE(1914, Brit.); SUICIDE CLUB, THE(1914, Brit.); CHARITY ANN(1915, Brit.); FINE FEATHERS(1915, Brit.); FLORENCE NIGHTINGALE(1915, Brit.); FROM SHOPGIRL TO DUCHESS(1915, Brit.); GRIP(1915, Brit.); HER NAMLESS CHILD(1915, Brit.); HOME(1915, Brit.); MR. LYNDON AT LIBERTY(1915, Brit.); WILL OF HER OWN, A(1915, Brit.); WORLD'S DESIRE, THE(1915, Brit.); DESPERATION(1916, Brit.); MANXMAN, THE(1916, Brit.); MOTHERLOVE(1916, Brit.); DRINK(1917, Brit.); SMITH(1917, Brit.); CASTLE OF DREAMS(1919, Brit.); GARRYOWEN(1920, Brit.); MAYOR OF CASTERBRIDGE, THE(1921, Brit.); CRIMSON CIRCLE, THE(1922, Brit.); ROGUES OF THE TURF(1923, Brit.)
Gerardo Sei Groves
ANGEL ON THE AMAZON(1948)
Herman Groves
GUNS IN THE HEATHER(1968, Brit.), w; RIDE A NORTHBOUND HORSE(1969), w; STRONGEST MAN IN THE WORLD, THE(1975), w
Jerome Groves
SLAVE GIRL(1947)
Jerry Groves
ROAD TO BALI(1952); NAKED JUNGLE, THE(1953)
Jerry Seri Groves
SOUTH OF TAHITI(1941)
John Groves
GOLDEN SEAL, THE(1983), w

Lars Grundtman
LOVING COUPLES(1966, Swed.)
Lennart Grundtman
LOVING COUPLES(1966, Swed.)
Al Grundy
GENERAL MASSACRE(1973, U.S./Bel.)
Arthur Grundy
BEING THERE(1979)
Guy Grundy
FREEWHEELIN'(1976)
Ian Grundy
TRAPPED BY THE TERROR(1949, Brit.), w
Lloyd Grundy
1984
VIGIL(1984, New Zealand)
Mabel Barnes Grundy
Silents
MATING OF MARCUS, THE(1924, Brit.), w
Karl Grune
ABDUL THE DAMNED(1935, Brit.), d; CLOWN MUST LAUGH, A(1936, Brit.), d; PRISONER OF CORBAL(1939, Brit.), d; SILVER DARLINGS, THE(1947, Brit.), p
Misc. Silents
STREET, THE(1927, Ger.), d; AT THE EDGE OF THE WORLD(1929, Ger.), d; SPY OF MME. POMPADOUR(1929, Ger.), d
Marc Grunebaum
ADOPTION, THE(1978, Fr.), d, w
Jean-Jacques Grunenwald
DOCTEUR LAENNEC(1949, Fr.), m; MONSIEUR VINCENT(1949, Fr.), m; DIARY OF A COUNTRY PRIEST(1954, Fr.), m; LOVERS OF TOLEDO, THE(1954, Fr./Span./Ital.), m; LADIES OF THE PARK(1964, Fr.), m
Joachem Gruner
NOT RECONCILED, OR "ONLY VIOLENCE HELPS WHERE IT RULES"(1969, Ger.)
Mark Gruner
FANTASTIC PLANET(1973, Fr./Czech.); JAWS II(1978)
Allen Grunewald [Mario Caiano]
NIGHTMARE CASTLE(1966, Ital.), d
Berdine Grunewald
CRY, THE BELOVED COUNTRY(1952, Brit.)
Ingrid Grunewald
WEREWOLVES ON WHEELS(1971); THIS IS A HIJACK(1973), set d
Jean Jacques Grunewald
ANGELS OF THE STREETS(1950, Fr.), m
Jean-Jacques Grunewald
ANTOINE ET ANTOINETTE(1947 Fr.), m; EDWARD AND CAROLINE(1952, Fr.), m
Svea Grunfeld
BEAST OF BUDAPEST, THE(1958)
Moriz Grunhut
ECSTASY(1940, Czech.), p
Ilka Gruning
UNDERGROUND(1941); CASABLANCA(1942); DANGEROUSLY THEY LIVE(1942); DESPERATE JOURNEY(1942); FRIENDLY ENEMIES(1942); ICELAND(1942); KING'S ROW(1942); THIS IS THE ARMY(1943); MURDER IN THE MUSIC HALL(1946); RENDEZVOUS 24(1946); TEMPTATION(1946); DESPERATE(1947); REPEAT PERFORMANCE(1947); LETTER FROM AN UNKNOWN WOMAN(1948); CAPTAIN CHINA(1949); GREAT SINNER, THE(1949); CONVICTED(1950); PAYMENT ON DEMAND(1951)
Misc. Silents
BEYOND THE RIVER(1922, Ger.); SECRETS OF A SOUL(1925, Ger.)
James Grunn
TWO OF A KIND(1951), w
Alexandra Grunsberg
PARSIFAL(1983, Fr.)
Alicia Grunsky
AGENCY(1981, Can.), art d
George Gruntz
STEPPENWOLF(1974), m
Alfred Grunwald
JUST A GIGOLO(1931), w; BALL AT SAVOY(1936, Brit.), w
Cheryl Grunwald
CLOCKWORK ORANGE, A(1971, Brit.)
Morten Grunwald
EPILOGUE(1967, Den.); OPERATION LOVEBIRDS(1968, Den.)
Paul Grupp
PLAYGIRLS AND THE BELLBOY, THE(1962,Ger.), ph
Werner Grusch
1984
WHITE ELEPHANT(1984, Brit.), p&d, w
Michael Grushkoff
LUCKY LADY(1975), p
Dave Grusin
GRADUATE, THE(1967), m; WATERHOLE NO. 3(1967), m; CANDY(1968, Ital./Fr.), m; HEART IS A LONELY HUNTER, THE(1968), m; WHERE WERE YOU WHEN THE LIGHTS WENT OUT?(1968), m; GENERATION(1969), m; MAD ROOM, THE(1969), m; MAN CALLED GANNON, A(1969), m; TELL THEM WILLIE BOY IS HERE(1969), m; WINNING(1969), m; ADAM AT 6 A.M.(1970), m; HALLS OF ANGER(1970), m; GANG THAT COULDN'T SHOOT STRAIGHT, THE(1971), m; FUZZ(1972), m; GREAT NORTHFIELD, MINNESOTA RAID, THE(1972), m; FRIENDS OF EDDIE COYLE, THE(1973), m; MIDNIGHT MAN, THE(1974), m; NICKEL RIDE, THE(1974), m; THREE DAYS OF THE CONDOR(1975), m; YAKUZA, THE(1975, U.S./Jap.), m; FRONT, THE(1976), m; MURDER BY DEATH(1976), m; BOBBY DEERFIELD(1977), m; FIRE SALE(1977), m; MR. BILLION(1977), m; HEAVEN CAN WAIT(1978), m; ...AND JUSTICE FOR ALL(1979), m; CHAMP, THE(1979), m; ELECTRIC HORSEMAN, THE(1979), m; MY BODYGUARD(1980), m; ABSENCE OF MALICE(1981), m; ON GOLDEN POND(1981), m; REDS(1981), m; AUTHOR! AUTHOR!(1982), m; TOOTSIE(1982), m
1984
FALLING IN LOVE(1984), m; LITTLE DRUMMER GIRL, THE(1984), m; POPE OF GREENWICH VILLAGE, THE(1984), m; RACING WITH THE MOON(1984), m; SCANDALOUS(1984), m

David Grusin
DIVORCE AMERICAN STYLE(1967), ph; PURSUIT OF HAPPINESS, THE(1971), m; SHOOT OUT(1971), m; W. W. AND THE DIXIE DANCEKINGS(1975), m; GOODBYE GIRL, THE(1977), m
Larry Grusin
1984
GARBO TALKS(1984), w
Jerry Gruskin
TARZAN AND THE HUNTRESS(1947), w; TRESPASSER, THE(1947), w; CAMPUS HONEYMOON(1948), w; SLIPPY MCGEE(1948), w; LADY TAKES A SAILOR, THE(1949), w
Michael Gruskoff
SILENT RUNNING(1972), p; YOUNG FRANKENSTEIN(1974), p; RAFFERTY AND THE GOLD DUST TWINS(1975), p; MY FAVORITE YEAR(1982), p
1984
UNTIL SEPTEMBER(1984), p
Dorain Grusman
1984
REVENGE OF THE NERDS(1984), ch
Alexander Gruszynski
1984
ALMOST YOU(1984), ph; OASIS, THE(1984), ph
Alexander Gruter
FOR THE FIRST TIME(1959, U.S./Ger./Ital.), p; BIMBO THE GREAT(1961, Ger.), p; WORLD IN MY POCKET, THE(1962, Fr./Ital./Ger.), p
Johannes Grutzke
1984
WOMAN IN FLAMES, A(1984, Ger.)
Lothar Grutzner
GREAT BRITISH TRAIN ROBBERY, THE(1967, Ger.)
Bernard Gruver
BOY NAMED CHARLIE BROWN, A(1969), anim
Laura Gruver
OUT OF THIS WORLD(1945)
Jerzy Gruza
DEEP END(1970 Ger./U.S.), w
I. Gruzdev
CHILDHOOD OF MAXIM GORKY(1938, Russ.), w; UNIVERSITY OF LIFE(1941, USSR), w
A. Gruzinskiy
WAR AND PEACE(1968, USSR)
Stefan Gryff
GET CHARLIE TULLY(1976, Brit.); SWEENEY 2(1978, Brit.); REDS(1981)
Stephan Gryff
Misc. Talkies
CZECH MATE(1984, Brit.)
Stefan Gryft
JULIA(1977)
Lidia Grys
LOTNA(1966, Pol.), cos
Stefan Gryss
ISADORA(1968, Brit.)
Andrzej Grzybowski
YOUNG GIRLS OF WILKO, THE(1979, Pol./Fr.)
Denise Grzybowski
FIEND(
Manfred Gschneider
SOLDIER, THE(1982)
Tatjana Gsovsky
MAGIC FIRE(1956), ch
Tony Gu Gaudio
DAYS OF GLORY(1944), ph
Guacaran
MAYA(1982), m
Don Guadagno
TWELVE O'CLOCK HIGH(1949)
Guadalajara Trio
SLIGHTLY SCANDALOUS(1946); THAT'S MY GAL(1947)
The Guadalajara Trio
BOSS OF BULLION CITY(1941); MASKED RIDER, THE(1941); MASQUERADE IN MEXICO(1945); SOUTH OF THE RIO GRANDE(1945)
Nicole Guadauchon
LEGEND OF FRENCHIE KING, THE(1971, Fr./Ital./Span./Brit.), ed
Pamela Gual
CAVEMAN(1981)
Pina Gualandri
NIGHTS OF CABIRIA(1957, Ital.)
Massimo Gualdi
SHOOT FIRST, LAUGH LAST(1967, Ital./Ger./U.S.), p; STRANGER RETURNS, THE(1968, U.S./Ital./Ger./Span.), p
Michele Gualdi
Silents
WHITE SISTER, THE(1923)
Pierre Gualdi
VICE AND VIRTUE(1965, Fr./Ital.)
Michele Gualdieri
GRAN VARIETA(1955, Ital.), w
Riccardo Gualino
TARTARS, THE(1962, Ital./Yugo.), p
Carlo Gualtieri
COLOSSUS OF RHODES, THE(1961, Ital., Fr., Span.), w
Sal Guange
Misc. Talkies
TAKE ONE(1977)
Vince Guaraldi
BOY NAMED CHARLIE BROWN, A(1969), m
Alex Guard
UNSUITABLE JOB FOR A WOMAN, AN(1982, Brit.)

Christopher Guard
LITTLE NIGHT MUSIC, A(1977, Aust./U.S./Ger.); LOOPHOLE(1981, Brit.); MEMOIRS OF A SURVIVOR(1981, Brit.)
Domenic Guard
COUNT OF MONTE CRISTO(1976, Brit.)
Dominic Guard
GO-BETWEEN, THE(1971, Brit.); PICNIC AT HANGING ROCK(1975, Aus.); ABSOLUTION(1981, Brit.); UNSUITABLE JOB FOR A WOMAN, AN(1982, Brit.)
Dominic Guard, Jr.
NELSON AFFAIR, THE(1973, Brit.)
Kit Guard
SERGEANT YORK(; RACKETEER, THE(1929); NIGHT WORK(1930); DEFENDERS OF THE LAW(1931); SKY RAIDERS(1931); TWO-FISTED JUSTICE(1931); UNHOLY GARDEN, THE(1931); COUNTY FAIR, THE(1932); FLAMES(1932); LAST MAN(1932); THIRTEENTH GUEST, THE(1932); TOM BROWN OF CULVER(1932); BOWERY, THE(1933); CARNIVAL LADY(1933); FIGHTING CHAMP(1933); ONE YEAR LATER(1933); RACING STRAIN, THE(1933); CAT'S PAW, THE(1934); IT HAPPENED ONE NIGHT(1934); LADY BY CHOICE(1934); BARBARY COAST(1935); KID COURAGEOUS(1935); RECKLESS ROADS(1935); RIP ROARING RILEY(1935); STOLEN HARMONY(1935); SHADOWS OF THE ORIENT(1937); CODE OF THE RANGERS(1938); GUNSMOKE TRAIL(1938); HEROES OF THE HILLS(1938); IN EARLY ARIZONA(1938); PRISON TRAIN(1938); PROFESSOR BEWARE(1938); WHERE THE WEST BEGINS(1938); YOU AND ME(1938); YOU CAN'T TAKE IT WITH YOU(1938); EL DIABLO RIDES(1939); FLYING DEUCES, THE(1939); FRONTIER SCOUT(1939); FRONTIERS OF '49(1939); HOMICIDE BUREAU(1939); LONE STAR PIONEERS(1939); MAN FROM SUNDOWN, THE(1939); SIX-GUN RHYTHM(1939); CARSON CITY KID(1940); HOUSE ACROSS THE BAY, THE(1940); HONOLULU LU(1941); JESSE JAMES AT BAY(1941); MY FAVORITE SPY(1942); PARACHUTE NURSE(1942); IT AIN'T HAY(1943); LADY OF BURLESQUE(1943); HERE COME THE WAVES(1944); FRONTIER GAL(1945); SHE GETS HER MAN(1945); NIGHT IN PARADISE, A(1946); JOHNNY O'CLOCK(1947); TRAIL STREET(1947); WHEN MY BABY SMILES AT ME(1948); MASTER MINDS(1949); COPPER CANYON(1950); FORT DEFIANCE(1951); BUSHWHACKERS, THE(1952); CARRIE(1952); JOKER IS WILD, THE(1957)
Silents
ONE MINUTE TO PLAY(1926); DEAD MAN'S CURVE(1928); LINGERIE(1928)
Misc. Silents
HER FATHER SAID NO(1927); LEGIONNAIRES IN PARIS(1927)
Phillip Guard
ANGEL WHO PAWNED HER HARP, THE(1956, Brit.)
Pippa Guard
UNSUITABLE JOB FOR A WOMAN, AN(1982, Brit.)
Top Guard
SPLIT, THE(1968)
Colin Guarde
STAGE FRIGHT(1950, Brit.), makeup
Charles Guardino
LADY LIBERTY(1972, Ital./Fr.); IDOLMAKER, THE(1980)
Charlie Guardino
KILLER FISH(1979, Ital./Braz.)
Harry Guardino
PURPLE HEART DIARY(1951); SIROCCO(1951); FLESH AND FURY(1952); BIG TIP OFF, THE(1955); HOLD BACK TOMORROW(1955); HOUSEBOAT(1958); FIVE PENNIES, THE(1959); PORK CHOP HILL(1959); FIVE BRANDED WOMEN(1960); KING OF KINGS(1961); HELL IS FOR HEROES(1962); PIGEON THAT TOOK ROME, THE(1962); RHINO(1964); ADVENTURES OF BULLWHIP GRIFFIN, THE(1967); VALLEY OF MYSTERY(1967); HELL WITH HEROES, THE(1968); JIGSAW(1968); MADIGAN(1968); TREASURE OF SAN GENNARO(1968, Fr./Ital./Ger.); LOVERS AND OTHER STRANGERS(1970); DIRTY HARRY(1971); RED SKY AT MORNING(1971); THEY ONLY KILL THEIR MASTERS(1972); CAPONE(1975); WHIFFS(1975); ENFORCER, THE(1976); ST. IVES(1976); ROLLERCOASTER(1977); MATILDA(1978); GOLDENGIRL(1979); ANY WHICH WAY YOU CAN(1980)
Misc. Talkies
SLINGSHOT(1971)
Jerome Guardino
RED SKY AT MORNING(1971); BITTERSWEET LOVE(1976); CRASH(1977)
Jerry Guardino
OCTAMAN(1971)
Jose Guardiola
SPANISH AFFAIR(1958, Span.); TRAPPED IN TANGIERS(1960, Ital./Span.); DESERT WARRIOR(1961 Ital./Span.); CEREMONY, THE(1963, U.S./Span.); AVENGER, THE(1966, Ital.)
1984
HOLY INNOCENTS, THE(1984, Span.)
The Guardsman Quartet
RIDERS OF THE TIMBERLINE(1941)
The Guardsmen
PLAYMATES(1941); STAGECOACH BUCKAROO(1942)
Corrado Guarducci
COUSINS, THE(1959, Fr.); FIRST TASTE OF LOVE(1962, Fr.); LONG ABSENCE, THE(1962, Fr./Ital.)
Fabrizio Guarducci
SILHOUETTES(1982)
John Guare
TAKING OFF(1971), w; ATLANTIC CITY(1981, U.S./Can.), w
Frank Guarente
LAST ESCAPE, THE(1970, Brit.)
Giovanni Guareschi
LITTLE WORLD OF DON CAMILLO, THE(1953, Fr./Ital.), w
Alfredo Guarini
WALLS OF MALAPAGA, THE(1950, Fr./Ital.), p, w
Carlos Guarneros
VILLA!(1958)
Lupe Guarnica
GLORIA(1980)
Lu Guarnier
MOUSE AND HIS CHILD, THE(1977), anim

Ennio Guarniere
BROTHER SUN, SISTER MOON(1973, Brit./Ital.), ph
Anna Maria Guarnieri
YOUNG HUSBANDS(1958, Ital./Fr.); MAIDEN FOR A PRINCE, A(1967, Fr./Ital.)
Ennio Guarnieri
CONJUGAL BED, THE(1963, Ital.), ph; LUCIANO(1963, Ital.), ph; HIGH INFIDELITY(1965, Fr./Ital.), ph; WHITE VOICES(1965, Fr./Ital.), ph; GIRL AND THE GENERAL, THE(1967, Fr./Ital.), ph; MADE IN ITALY(1967, Fr./Ital.), ph; ANYONE CAN PLAY(1968, Ital.), ph; QUEENS, THE(1968, Ital./Fr.), ph; ARABELLA(1969, U.S./Ital.), ph; BETTER A WIDOW(1969, Ital.), ph; CAMILLE 2000(1969), ph; GIRL WHO COULDN'T SAY NO, THE(1969, Ital.), ph; SEVEN GOLDEN MEN(1969, Fr./Ital./Span.), ph; SHE AND HE(1969, Ital.), ph; MEDEA(1971, Ital./Fr./Ger.), ph; ASH WEDNESDAY(1973), ph; HITLER: THE LAST TEN DAYS(1973, Brit./Ital.), ph; VOYAGE, THE(1974, Ital.), ph; BRIEF VACATION, A(1975, Ital.), ph; DOWN THE ANCIENT STAIRCASE(1975, Ital.), ph; DRAMA OF THE RICH(1975, Ital./Fr.), ph; END OF THE GAME(1976, Ger./Ital.), ph; GARDEN OF THE FINZI-CONTINIS, THE(1976, Ital./Ger.), ph; CASSANDRA CROSSING, THE(1977), ph; INHERITANCE, THE(1978, Ital.), ph; WIFEMISTRESS(1979, Ital.), ph; VISITOR, THE(1980, Ital./U.S.), ph; LA TRAVIATA(1982), ph
Ennio Guarniier
LA GRANDE BOURGEOISE(1977, Ital.), ph
Umberto Guarracino
Misc. Silents
MACISTE IN HELL(1926, Ital.)
Sara Guash
SURVIVE!(1977, Mex.)
Russell A. Guasman
THERE'S ALWAYS TOMORROW(1956), set d
Dominic Guastaferro
ARTHUR(1981)
Vincent Guastaferro
KING OF THE MOUNTAIN(1981)
Charles Guasti
STAKEOUT ON DOPE STREET(1958)
Alexandre Guatalli
VIOLENT AND THE DAMNED, THE(1962, Braz.), m
Michele Guayini
ST. VALENTINE'S DAY MASSACRE, THE(1967)
Enrico Guazzoni
Silents
QUO VADIS?(1913, Ital.), d&w
Leonid Gubanov
THREE SISTERS, THE(1969, USSR)
Irina Gubanova
WAR AND PEACE(1968, USSR)
Tom Gubbins
CHINA SEAS(1935); WITHOUT REGRET(1935)
Ivo Gubel
SWEET LIGHT IN A DARK ROOM(1966, Czech.); FIFTH HORSEMAN IS FEAR, THE(1968, Czech.)
V. Gubenko
SONG OF THE FOREST(1963, USSR)
Peter Guber
DEEP, THE(1977), p; SIX WEEKS(1982), p
Reuben Guberman
HONEYMOON OF HORROR(1964); "IMP"PROBABLE MR. WEE GEE, THE(1966); SHANTY TRAMP(1967), w; SAVAGES FROM HELL(1968), w
S. Gubin
Misc. Silents
SCANDAL?(1929, USSR)
Steve Gucciardo
NUNZIO(1978)
Douglas Gudbye
DRIVE-IN MASSACRE(1976)
John Gude
GARDEN OF EDEN(1954)
Hans Gudegast
DAYTON'S DEVILS(1968)
Hans Gudegast [Eric Braeden]
OPERATION EICHMANN(1961); 100 RIFLES(1969)
Francis Gudemann
TREE, THE(1969), prod d
Paul Gerd Guderian
Silents
KRIEMHILD'S REVENGE(1924, Ger.), cos; SIEGFRIED(1924, Ger.), cos
Linda Guderman
MACABRE(1958)
William Gudgeon
Silents
NOTORIETY(1922)
Michel Gudin
IT ONLY HAPPENS TO OTHERS(1971, Fr./Ital.)
Yakov Gudkin
Misc. Silents
CHILDREN OF STORM(1926, USSR); KATKA'S REINETTE APPLES(1926, USSR); HOUSE IN THE SNOW-DRIFTS, THE(1928, USSR); PARISIAN COBBLER(1928, USSR); FRAGMENT OF AN EMPIRE(1930, USSR)
Rachel Gudmundson
TESTAMENT(1983)
Agust Gudmundsson
OUTLAW: THE SAGE OF GISLI(1982, Iceland), d&w
Ann Gudrun
TERROR STREET(1953); DIAMOND WIZARD, THE(1954, Brit.); DOCTOR IN THE HOUSE(1954, Brit.); MAN WITH A MILLION(1954, Brit.); TROUBLE IN THE GLEN(1954, Brit.); SEA SHALL NOT HAVE THEM, THE(1955, Brit.)
Mark Guebhard
DIVIDED HEART, THE(1955, Brit.)

Apu Guecia
FORT APACHE, THE BRONX(1981)
Lance Guecia
RUMBLE FISH(1983)
Lance William Guecia
FORT APACHE, THE BRONX(1981)
Jay Guedalia
TALK OF THE TOWN(1942)
Heidi Guedel
SECRET OF NIMH, THE(1982), anim
John Guedel
GENERAL SPANKY(1937), w; TORNADO(1943), m; PEOPLE ARE FUNNY(1945), w
Yvon Guedel
FRENCH CONSPIRACY, THE(1973, Fr.), p
Hilda Gueden
LIFE AND LOVES OF MOZART, THE(1959, Ger.)
Nicole Gueden
BRIDE IS MUCH TOO BEAUTIFUL, THE(1958, Fr.); LIFE UPSIDE DOWN(1965, Fr.)
Eduardo Guedes
PRAISE MARX AND PASS THE AMMUNITION(1970, Brit.), ed
Guillermo Alvarez Guedes
BIG BOODLE, THE(1957)
Joao Guedes
COUNTRY DOCTOR, THE(1963, Portuguese)
Luis Guedes
PRIDE AND THE PASSION, THE(1957); SEVENTH VOYAGE OF SINBAD, THE(1958)
Jay Guedillio
MEET JOHN DOE(1941)
C. T. Guedry
LOUISIANA STORY(1948)
Paul Guedry, Jr.
EASY RIDER(1969)
Annie Guegan
MADE IN U.S.A.(1966, Fr.); LA VIE DE CHATEAU(1967, Fr.)
Henri Guegan
DEAD RUN(1961, Fr./Ital./Ger.)
Pierre Gueguen
LOVERS ON A TIGHTROPE(1962, Fr.), ph
G. Gueguetchkori
COLOR OF POMEGRANATES, THE(1980, Armenian)
Maurizio Guelfi
LA DOLCE VITA(1961, Ital./Fr.)
Buster Guelich
LONE COWBOY(1934)
Jean Guelis
PURPLE NOON(1961, Fr./Ital.), ch; WHAT'S NEW, PUSSYCAT?(1965, U.S./Fr.), ch
Max Guelstorff
CAPTAIN FROM KOEPENICK(1933, Ger.)
Robert Guenette
DEFECTOR, THE(1966, Ger./Fr.), w; TREE, THE(1969), p,d&w
Carl Guenther
BURG THEATRE(1936, Ger.)
Felix Guenther
ELISABETH OF AUSTRIA(1931, Ger.), md
Ian Guenther
HARD PART BEGINS, THE(1973, Can.), m
Isa Guenther
HEIDI AND PETER(1955, Switz.)
William Gueralt
LE BOUCHER(1971, Fr./Ital.)
Behrooz Gueramian
CARAVANS(1978, U.S./Iranian)
Leo Guerard
YOUNG GIRLS OF ROCHEFORT, THE(1968, Fr.)
Camillo Guercio
SOMETHING FOR THE BIRDS(1952); KID FROM LEFT FIELD, THE(1953); TITANIC(1953); TREASURE OF THE GOLDEN CONDOR(1953)
Gary Guercio
ELECTRA GLIDE IN BLUE(1973)
James William Guercio
ELECTRA GLIDE IN BLUE(1973), p&d; SECOND-HAND HEARTS(1981), p
Lucy Angle Guercio
ELECTRA GLIDE IN BLUE(1973)
Anthony Guere [Antonio de la Guerra]
SECRET SEVEN, THE(1966, Ital./Span.), art d
Joe Guerena
MEMORY OF US(1974), art d; SILENCE(1974), prod d
Daniel Gueret
DOULOS–THE FINGER MAN(1964, Fr./Ital.), art d
Anastasia Guerguievaskia
THREE TALES OF CHEKHOV(1961, USSR)
Andrew Guerin
1984
PERILS OF GWENDOLINE, THE(1984, Fr.), art d
Bruce Guerin
Silents
KINDRED OF THE DUST(1922); COUNTRY KID, THE(1923); LOVER'S LANE(1924); REVELATION(1924); SALVATION HUNTERS, THE(1925)
Misc. Silents
LOVE IN THE DARK(1922)
Charles Guerin
VON RICHTHOFEN AND BROWN(1970), cos
Fort B. Guerin, Jr.
WAKAMBA!(1955), ph
Francois Guerin
JUPITER(1952, Fr.); DIARY OF A BAD GIRL(1958, Fr.); GIVE ME MY CHANCE(1958, Fr.); HORROR CHAMBER OF DR. FAUSTUS, THE(1962, Fr./Ital.); WEEKEND AT DUNKIRK(1966, Fr./Ital.)

Lenmana Guerin
FROM HELL IT CAME(1957)
M. Guerin
Misc. Talkies
BEST, THE(1979), d
Madeline Guerin
KAMOURASKA(1973, Can./Fr.), ed
Paul Guerin
Silents
MOLLY O'(1921), spec eff
Paul Andre Guerin
1984
COVERGIRL(1984, Can.), cos
Paul-Andre Guerin
OF UNKNOWN ORIGIN(1983, Can.), cos
Sean Patrick Guerin
ROMANTIC COMEDY(1983)
Raymond Guerin-Catelain
Misc. Silents
NANA(1926, Fr.)
Camille Guerini
HUNCHBACK OF NOTRE DAME, THE(1957, Fr.); GIGOT(1962); MONKEY IN WINTER, A(1962, Fr.); SEVENTH JUROR, THE(1964, Fr.); TWO ARE GUILTY(1964, Fr.)
Pierre Guerlais
CROISIERES SIDERALES(1941, Fr.), p, w
Enrique Guerner
MANOLETE(1950, Span.), ph; MAN WHO WAGGED HIS TAIL, THE(1961, Ital./Span.), ph
Claude Guerney
BROTHER ALFRED(1932, Brit.), w; GREEN FOR DANGER(1946, Brit.), w
Armando Guernieri
ISLAND OF PROCIDA, THE(1952, Ital.)
Otis L. Guernsey, Jr.
THIRTEEN FRIGHTENED GIRLS(1963), w
Antonino Guerra
MARRIAGE–ITALIAN STYLE(1964, Fr./Ital.), w
Blanca Guerra
1984
ERENDIRA(1984, Mex./Fr./Ger.)
Misc. Talkies
FALCON'S GOLD(1982)
Castulo Guerra
TWO OF A KIND(1983)
Luigi Antonio Guerra
DON'T TURN THE OTHER CHEEK(1974, Ital./Ger./Span.)
Mario Guerra
00-2 MOST SECRET AGENTS(1965, Ital.), w
Palmira Guerra
VIRIDIANA(1962, Mex./Span.)
Robert Guerra
ANNIE(1982), art d
Rogelio Guerra
GIGANTES PLANETARIOS(1965, Mex.)
Ruy Guerra
SWEET HUNTERS(1969, Panama), d, w; AGUIRRE, THE WRATH OF GOD(1977, W. Ger.)
1984
ERENDIRA(1984, Mex./Fr./Ger.), d
Tonino Guerra
L'AVVENTURA(1960, Ital.), w; ASSASSIN, THE(1961, Ital./Fr.), w; LA NOTTE(1961, Fr./Ital.), w; ECLIPSE(1962, Fr./Ital.), w; EMPTY CANVAS, THE(1964, Fr./Ital.), w; NAKED HOURS, THE(1964, Ital.), w; CASANOVA '70(1965, Ital.), w; RED DESERT(1965, Fr./Ital.), w; TENTH VICTIM, THE(1965, Fr./Ital.), w; BLOW-UP(1966, Brit.), w; SECRET SEVEN, THE(1966, Ital./Span.), w; MORE THAN A MIRACLE(1967, Ital./Fr.), w; CATCH AS CATCH CAN(1968, Ital.), w; QUEENS, THE(1968, Ital./Fr.), w; SAUL AND DAVID(1968, Ital./Span.), w; WILD EYE, THE(1968, Ital.), w; PLACE FOR LOVERS, A(1969, Ital./Fr.), w; IN SEARCH OF GREGORY(1970, Brit./Ital.), w; QUIET PLACE IN THE COUNTRY, A(1970, Ital./Fr.), w; SUNFLOWER(1970, Fr./Ital.), w; ZABRISKIE POINT(1970), w; WHITE SISTER(1973, Ital./Span./Fr.), w; AMARCORD(1974, Ital.), w; RE: LUCKY LUCIANO(1974, Fr./Ital.), w; BUTTERFLY ON THE SHOULDER, A(1978, Fr.), w; EBOLI(1980, Ital.), w; NIGHT OF THE SHOOTING STARS, THE(1982, Ital.), w; AND THE SHIP SAILS ON(1983, Ital./Fr.), w; IDENTIFICATION OF A WOMAN(1983, Ital.), w
1984
BIZET'S CARMEN(1984, Fr./Ital.), w; NOSTALGHIA(1984, USSR/Ital.), w
Ugo Guerra
COUNTERFEITERS, THE(1953, Ital.), w; GUNS OF THE BLACK WITCH(1961, Fr./Ital.), w; MAN WHO WAGGED HIS TAIL, THE(1961, Ital./Span.), w; ROMMEL'S TREASURE(1962, Ital.), w; RUN WITH THE DEVIL(1963, Fr./Ital.), w; FRIENDS FOR LIFE(1964, Ital.), w; MYTH, THE(1965, Ital.), w; MONGOLS, THE(1966, Fr./Ital.), w; VENGEANCE IS MINE(1969, Ital./Span.), p, w; DIRTY OUTLAWS, THE(1971, Ital.), p, w; JOHNNY HAMLET(1972, Ital.), p
John Guerrasio
JANE AUSTEN IN MANHATTAN(1980)
Carmen Guerrero
SHE-DEVIL ISLAND(1936, Mex.)
Chavo Guerrero
ONE AND ONLY, THE(1978)
Chito Guerrero
DYNAMITE JOHNSON(1978, Phil.)
Misc. Talkies
PAY OR DIE(1982)
Evelyn Guerrero
THINGS ARE TOUGH ALL OVER(1982); WILD WHEELS(1969); TRACKDOWN(1976); TOOLBOX MURDERS, THE(1978); CHEECH AND CHONG'S NEXT MOVIE(1980); CHEECH AND CHONG'S NICE DREAMS(1981)

Franco Guerrero
Misc. Talkies
ONE ARMED EXECUTIONER(1980)
Ross Guerrero
SIX PACK(1982)
Sergio Guerrero
QUEEN'S SWORDSMEN, THE(1963, Mex.), m; LITTLE RED RIDING HOOD AND HER FRIENDS(1964, Mex.), m; PEARL OF TLAYUCAN, THE(1964, Mex.), m; PUSS 'N' BOOTS(1964, Mex.), m
Tony Guerrero
NORTHWEST PASSAGE(1940)
Franco Guerri
HELL UP IN HARLEM(1973), ed
Francesco Guerrieri
BROTHER SUN, SISTER MOON(1973, Brit./Ital.)
Lorenza Guerrieri
NARCO MEN, THE(1969, Span./Ital.); FRANKENSTEIN-ITALIAN STYLE(1977, Ital.)
Romolo Guerrieri
10,000 DOLLARS BLOOD MONEY(1966, Ital.), d; JOHNNY YUMA(1967, Ital.), d, w; SWEET BODY OF DEBORAH, THE(1969, Ital./Fr.), d; DETECTIVE BELLI(1970, Ital.), d; COVERT ACTION(1980, Ital.), d
Vittorio Guerrieri
SPECIAL DAY, A(1977, Ital./Can.)
Vince Guerriero
MEATBALLS(1979, Can.)
Guerrini
CALABUCH(1956, Span./Ital.), w
Mino Guerrini
COMMANDO(1962, Ital., Span., Bel., Ger.), w; EVIL EYE(1964 Ital.), w; LOVE IN 4 DIMENSIONS(1965 Fr./Ital.), d&w; LOVE AND MARRIAGE(1966, Ital.), d, w
Orso Maria Guerrini
MATTER OF TIME, A(1976, Ital./U.S.)
Johnny Guerro
LEGEND OF COUGAR CANYON(1974)
Misc. Talkies
SECRET OF NAVAJO CAVE(1976)
Ugo Guerro
BULLET FOR SANDOVAL, A(1970, Ital./Span.), p, w
Paul Guers
TALE OF TWO CITIES, A(1958, Brit.); CRIME DOES NOT PAY(1962, Fr.); GAME FOR SIX LOVERS, A(1962, Fr.); GIRL WITH THE GOLDEN EYES, THE(1962, Fr.); I SPIT ON YOUR GRAVE(1962, Fr.); TALES OF PARIS(1962, Fr./Ital.); BAY OF ANGELS(1964, Fr.); MAGNIFICENT CUCKOLD, THE(1965, Fr./Ital.); FRUSTRATIONS(1967, Fr./Ital.)
Louba Guertchikoff
CHANEL SOLITAIRE(1981)
Paul Guertzman
WOLF OF WALL STREET, THE(1929)
Lucien Guervil
VICE AND VIRTUE(1965, Fr./Ital.)
Fausto Guerzoni
GREAT DAWN, THE(1947, Ital.); BICYCLE THIEF, THE(1949, Ital.); ISLAND OF PROCIDA, THE(1952, Ital.)
Christopher Guest
HOSPITAL, THE(1971); HOT ROCK, THE(1972); DEATH WISH(1974); FORTUNE, THE(1975); GIRLFRIENDS(1978); LAST WORD, THE(1979); LONG RIDERS, THE(1980); HEARTBEEPS(1981)
1984
THIS IS SPINAL TAP(1984), a, w, m, m/1
Don Guest
BLUE COLLAR(1978), p; HAMMETT(1982), p
1984
PARIS, TEXAS(1984, Ger./Fr.), p
Ina Guest
GOLDEN TRAIL, THE(1940)
James Guest
1984
DARK ENEMY(1984, Brit.)
Judith Guest
ORDINARY PEOPLE(1980), w
Lance Guest
HALLOWEEN II(1981); I OUGHT TO BE IN PICTURES(1982)
1984
JUST THE WAY YOU ARE(1984); LAST STARFIGHTER, THE(1984)
Maurice Guest
RHAPSODY(1954), w
Nicholas Guest
BELL JAR, THE(1979); LONG RIDERS, THE(1980); STAR TREK II: THE WRATH OF KHAN(1982); TRADING PLACES(1983)
Nicolas Guest
1984
CLOAK AND DAGGER(1984)
Susie Guest
GREAT MUPPET CAPER, THE(1981)
Tom Guest
JESUS CHRIST, SUPERSTAR(1973)
Val Guest
YESTERDAY'S ENEMY(1959, Brit.), d; CHARLEY'S(BIG-HEARTED) AUNT*1/2 (1940), w; WHY SAPS LEAVE HOME(1932, Brit.); NO MONKEY BUSINESS(1935, Brit.), w; ALL IN(1936, Brit.), w; PUBLIC NUISANCE NO. 1(1936, Brit.), w; STAR FELL FROM HEAVEN, A(1936, Brit.), w; OH, MR. PORTER!(1937, Brit.), w; OKAY FOR SOUND(1937, Brit.), w; WHERE THERE'S A WILL(1937, Brit.), w; WINDBAG THE SAILOR(1937, Brit.), w; ALF'S BUTTON AFLOAT(1938, Brit.), w; CONVICT 99(1938, Brit.), w; HEY! HEY! U.S.A.(1938, Brit.), w; OLD BONES OF THE RIVER(1938, Brit.), w; ASK A POLICEMAN(1939, Brit.), w; FROZEN LIMITS, THE(1939, Brit.), w; WHERE'S THAT FIRE?(1939, Brit.), w; BAND WAGGON(1940, Brit.), w; GASBAGS(1940, Brit.), w; GHOST TRAIN, THE(1941, Brit.), w; HI, GANG!(1941, Brit.), w; I THANK YOU(1941, Brit.), w; MAIL TRAIN(1941, Brit.), w; BACK ROOM BOY(1942, Brit.), w; KING ARTHUR WAS A GENTLEMAN(1942, Brit.), w; MISS

LONDON LTD.(1943, Brit.), d, w; BEES IN PARADISE(1944, Brit.), d, w; GIVE US THE MOON(1944, Brit.), d, w; I'LL BE YOUR SWEETHEART(1945, Brit.), d, w; WALKING ON AIR(1946, Brit.), w; JUST WILLIAM'S LUCK(1948, Brit.), d&w; WILLIAM COMES TO TOWN(1948, Brit.), d&w; PAPER ORCHID(1949, Brit.), w; BODY SAID NO!, THE(1950, Brit.), d&w; MISS PILGRIM'S PROGRESS(1950, Brit.), d, w; MYSTERY AT THE BURLESQUE(1950, Brit.), d&w; HAPPY GO LOVELY(1951, Brit.), w; MR. DRAKE'S DUCK(1951, Brit.), d&w; ANOTHER MAN'S POISON(1952, Brit.), w; MY HEART GOES CRAZY(1953, Brit.), w; PENNY PRINCESS(1953, Brit.), p,d&w; TIME GENTLEMEN PLEASE!(1953, Brit.), w; TOP OF THE FORM(1953, Brit.), w; DANCE LITTLE LADY(1954, Brit.), d&w, w; FAMILY AFFAIR(1954, Brit.), d, w; RUNAWAY BUS, THE(1954, Brit.), p; LYONS IN PARIS, THE(1955, Brit.), d&w; THEY CAN'T HANG ME(1955, Brit.), d, w; BLONDE BAIT(1956, U.S./Brit.), w; IT'S A WONDERFUL WORLD(1956, Brit.), d&w; THE CREEPING UNKNOWN(1956, Brit.), d, w; ABOMINABLE SNOWMAN OF THE HIMALAYAS, THE(1957, Brit.), d; BREAK IN THE CIRCLE, THE(1957, Brit.), d, w; CARRY ON ADMIRAL(1957, Brit.), d&w; ENEMY FROM SPACE(1957, Brit.), d, w; MEN OF SHERWOOD FOREST(1957, Brit.), d; WEAPON, THE(1957, Brit.), d; CAMP ON BLOOD ISLAND, THE(1958, Brit.), d, w; FURTHER UP THE CREEK!(1958, Brit.), d, w; UP THE CREEK(1958, Brit.), d, w; EXPRESSO BONGO(1959, Brit.), p, d; DENTIST IN THE CHAIR(1960, Brit.), w; HELL IS A CITY(1960, Brit.), d&w; DAY THE EARTH CAUGHT FIRE, THE(1961, Brit.), p&d, w; STOP ME BEFORE I KILL!(1961, Brit.), p&d, w; LIFE IS A CIRCUS(1962, Brit.), d, w; 80,000 SUSPECTS(1963, Brit.), p, d&w; JIG SAW(1965, Brit.), p,d&w; WHERE THE SPIES ARE(1965, Brit.), p, d, w; BEAUTY JUNGLE, THE(1966, Brit.), p&d, w; CASINO ROYALE(1967, Brit.), d; ASSIGNMENT K(1968, Brit.), d, w; TOOMORROW(1970, Brit.), d&w; WHEN DINOSAURS RULED THE EARTH(1971, Brit.), d&w; CONFESSIONS OF A WINDOW CLEANER(1974, Brit.), d, w; KILLER FORCE(1975, Switz./Ireland), d, w; SHILLINGBURY BLOWERS, THE(1980, Brit.), d; DANGEROUS DAVIES–THE LAST DETECTIVE(1981, Brit.), d, w
Misc. Talkies
AU PAIR GIRLS(1973), d; CHILD'S PLAY(1984, Brit.), d
Georges Guetary
AMERICAN IN PARIS, AN(1951)
Juergen Guett
BENJAMIN(1973, Ger.), w
Felisa L. Guevara
REVENGERS, THE(1972, U.S./Mex.), makeup
Ruben Guevara
UP IN SMOKE(1978)
Rubin Guevara
IT COMES UP LOVE(1943), m
Josephine Guevars
NEW LOVE(1968, Chile)
Paul Guevrement
QUEBEC(1951)
Paul Guevremont
THIRTEENTH LETTER, THE(1951); LUCK OF GINGER COFFEY, THE(1964, U.S./Can.); WAITING FOR CAROLINE(1969, Can.)
Mamadou Gueye
MANDABI(1970, Fr./Senegal)
Oumar Gueye
CEDDO(1978, Nigeria)
Yvon Guezel
TIME OUT FOR LOVE(1963, Ital./Fr.), p; ROAD TO SALINA(1971, Fr./Ital.), p
Bernet Guffey
CLOSE CALL FOR BOSTON BLACKIE, A(1946), ph
Burnett Guffey
SILENCERS, THE(, ph; KANSAS CITY KITTY(1944), ph; SAILOR'S HOLIDAY(1944), ph; SOUL OF A MONSTER, THE(1944), ph; U-BOAT PRISONER(1944), ph; UNWRITTEN CODE, THE(1944), ph; BLONDE FROM BROOKLYN(1945), ph; EADIE WAS A LADY(1945), ph; EVE KNEW HER APPLES(1945), ph; FIGHTING GUARDSMAN, THE(1945), ph; GAY SENORITA(1945), ph; GIRL OF THE LIMBERLOST, THE(1945), ph; I LOVE A MYSTERY(1945), ph; MY NAME IS JULIA ROSS(1945), ph; GALLANT JOURNEY(1946), ph; MEET ME ON BROADWAY(1946), ph; NIGHT EDITOR(1946), ph; NOTORIOUS LONE WOLF, THE(1946), ph; SO DARK THE NIGHT(1946), ph; FRAMED(1947), ph; JOHNNY O'CLOCK(1947), ph; GALLANT BLADE, THE(1948), ph; SIGN OF THE RAM, THE(1948), ph; TO THE ENDS OF THE EARTH(1948), ph; ALL THE KING'S MEN(1949), ph; AND BABY MAKES THREE(1949), ph; KNOCK ON ANY DOOR(1949), ph; RECKLESS MOMENTS, THE(1949), ph; UNDERCOVER MAN, THE(1949), ph; CONVICTED(1950), ph; EMERGENCY WEDDING(1950), ph; FATHER IS A BACHELOR(1950), ph; IN A LONELY PLACE(1950), ph; FAMILY SECRET, THE(1951), ph; SIROCCO(1951), ph; TWO OF A KIND(1951), ph; ASSIGNMENT-PARIS(1952), ph; SCANDAL SHEET(1952), ph; SNIPER, THE(1952), ph; FROM HERE TO ETERNITY(1953), ph; LAST POSSE, THE(1953), ph; HUMAN DESIRE(1954), ph; PRIVATE HELL 36(1954), ph; BAMBOO PRISON, THE(1955), ph; COUNT THREE AND PRAY(1955), ph; THREE STRIPES IN THE SUN(1955), ph; TIGHT SPOT(1955), ph; VIOLENT MEN, THE(1955), ph; BATTLE STATIONS(1956), ph; HARDER THEY FALL, THE(1956), ph; NIGHTFALL(1956), ph; STORM CENTER(1956), ph; BROTHERS RICO, THE(1957), ph; DECISION AT SUNDOWN(1957), ph; STRANGE ONE, THE(1957), ph; ME AND THE COLONEL(1958), ph; SCREAMING MIMI(1958), ph; TRUE STORY OF LYNN STUART, THE(1958), ph; EDGE OF ETERNITY(1959), ph; GIDGET(1959), ph; THEY CAME TO CORDURA(1959), ph; HELL TO ETERNITY(1960), ph; LET NO MAN WRITE MY EPITAPH(1960), ph; MOUNTAIN ROAD, THE(1960), ph; CRY FOR HAPPY(1961), ph; HOMICIDAL(1961), ph; MR. SARDONICUS(1961), ph; BIRDMAN OF ALCATRAZ(1962), ph; KID GALAHAD(1962), ph; FLIGHT FROM ASHIYA(1964, U.S./Jap.), ph; GOOD NEIGHBOR SAM(1964), ph; KING RAT(1965), ph; AMBUSHERS, THE(1967), ph; BONNIE AND CLYDE(1967), ph; SPLIT, THE(1968), ph; LEARNING TREE, THE(1969), ph; MADWOMAN OF CHAILLOT, THE(1969), ph; SOME KIND OF A NUT(1969), ph; WHERE IT'S AT(1969), ph; GREAT WHITE HOPE, THE(1970), ph; HALLS OF ANGER(1970), ph; SUPPOSE THEY GAVE A WAR AND NOBODY CAME?(1970), ph; STEAGLE, THE(1971), ph; HOW TO SUCCEED IN BUSINESS WITHOUT REALLY TRYING(1976), ph
Silents
IRON HORSE, THE(1924), ph
Cary Guffey
CLOSE ENCOUNTERS OF THE THIRD KIND(1977); STROKER ACE(1983)
1984
BEAR, THE(1984); NIGHT SHADOWS(1984)

Gary Guffey
CROSS CREEK(1983)
Pierre Guffrov
DEFECTOR, THE(1966, Ger./Fr.), art d
Pierre Guffroy
TESTAMENT OF ORPHEUS, THE(1962, Fr.), art d; IMMORAL MOMENT, THE(1967, Fr.), art d; BRIDE WORE BLACK, THE(1968, Fr./Ital.), art d; PIERROT LE FOU(1968, Fr./Ital.), art d; MILKY WAY, THE(1969, Fr./Ital.), art d; MOUCHETTE(1970, Fr./Ital.), art d; RIDER ON THE RAIN(1970, Fr./Ital.), art d; CESAR AND ROSALIE(1972, Fr.), art d; DISCREET CHARM OF THE BOURGEOISIE, THE(1972, Fr.), art d; PAUL AND MICHELLE(1974, Fr./Brit.), art d; TENANT, THE(1976, Fr.), prod d; THAT OBSCURE OBJECT OF DESIRE(1977, Fr./Span.), art d; TESS(1980, Fr./Brit.), prod d; HANNAH K.(1983, Fr.), art d
Madaleine Gug
LOVE IS MY PROFESSION(1959, Fr.), ed
Madelein Gug
ENOUGH ROPE(1966, Fr./Ital./Ger.), ed
Madeleine Gug
DEVIL IN THE FLESH, THE(1949, Fr.), ed; LOVE STORY(1949, Fr.), ed; SYLVIA AND THE PHANTOM(1950, Fr.), ed; JUPITER(1952, Fr.), ed; GAME OF LOVE, THE(1954, Fr.), ed; RED AND THE BLACK, THE(1954, Fr./Ital.), ed; RED, INN, THE(1954, Fr.), ed; DIABOLIQUE(1955, Fr./Ger.), ed; LOLA MONTES(1955, Fr./Ger.), ed; WAGES OF FEAR, THE(1955, Fr./Ital.), ed. Henri Rust; FOUR BAGS FULL(1957, Fr./Ital.), ed; GAMBLER, THE(1958, Fr.), ed; GREEN MARE, THE(1961, Fr./Ital.), ed; STORY OF THE COUNT OF MONTE CRISTO, THE(1962, Fr./Ital.), ed; MY WIFE'S HUSBAND(1965, Fr./Ital.), ed; TWO FOR THE ROAD(1967, Brit.), ed
Charles Guggenheim
GREAT ST. LOUIS BANK ROBBERY, THE(1959), p&d, d
Peggy Guggenheim
EVA(1962, Fr./Ital.)
Roslyn Gugino
FEAR NO EVIL(1981)
Vincent Gugleotti
1984
GOODBYE PEOPLE, THE(1984)
Marco Guglielmi
SAVAGE INNOCENTS, THE(1960, Brit.); LOST SOULS(1961, Ital.); PLANETS AGAINST US, THE(1961, Ital./Fr.); NIGHT THEY KILLED RASPUTIN, THE(1962, Fr./Ital.); STORY OF JOSEPH AND HIS BRETHREN THE(1962, Ital.); MILL OF THE STONE WOMEN(1963, Fr./Ital.); SEVEN SEAS TO CALAIS(1963, Ital.); VISIT, THE(1964, Ger./Fr./Ital./U.S.); SECRET AGENT SUPER DRAGON(1966, Fr./Ital./Ger./Monaco); SPY IN YOUR EYE(1966, Ital.); BANDIDOS(1967, Ital.); SHOOT FIRST, LAUGH LAST(1967, Ital./Ger./U.S.); ANYONE CAN PLAY(1968, Ital.); STRANGER RETURNS, THE(1968, U.S./Ital./Ger./Span.)
Riccardo Guglielmi
8 ½(1963, Ital.)
Geiogio Guglielmo
HEART AND SOUL(1950, Ital.)
Marco Gugliemi
ATTILA(1958, Ital.); ALWAYS VICTORIOUS(1960, Ital.)
John Gugolka
OUR MOTHER'S HOUSE(1967, Brit.); CHALLENGE FOR ROBIN HOOD, A(1968, Brit.); GOODBYE MR. CHIPS(1969, U.S./Brit.)
Jsepo Gugusha
CRY, THE BELOVED COUNTRY(1952, Brit.)
Bhupesh Guha
BWANA DEVIL(1953)
Bill Guhl
GRASS EATER, THE(1961); SHELL SHOCK(1964)
George Guhl
CASE OF THE CURIOUS BRIDE, THE(1935); FRONT PAGE WOMAN(1935); GOIN' TO TOWN(1935); MURDER MAN(1935); NIGHT AT THE OPERA, A(1935); NAVY BORN(1936); PETRIFIED FOREST, THE(1936); SING ME A LOVE SONG(1936); SWORN ENEMY(1936); TIMOTHY'S QUEST(1936); ADVENTUROUS BLONDE(1937); DOUBLE WEDDING(1937); FLY-AWAY BABY(1937); NIGHT CLUB SCANDAL(1937); PUBLIC WEDDING(1937); BLONDES AT WORK(1938); GOLD MINE IN THE SKY(1938); JEZEBEL(1938); TORCHY BLANE IN CHINATOWN(1938); TORCHY BLANE IN PANAMA(1938); TORCHY GETS HER MAN(1938); YOUNG FUGITIVES(1938); ANOTHER THIN MAN(1939); DODGE CITY(1939); GOOD GIRLS GO TO PARIS(1939); I AM NOT AFRAID(1939); NANCY DREW AND THE HIDDEN STAIRCASE(1939); ST. LOUIS BLUES(1939); STAR MAKER, THE(1939); STORY OF ALEXANDER GRAHAM BELL, THE(1939); TORCHY RUNS FOR MAYOR(1939); WHAT A LIFE(1939); BLONDIE ON A BUDGET(1940); CAPTAIN IS A LADY, THE(1940); REMEMBER THE NIGHT(1940); VIRGINIA CITY(1940); WHEN THE DALTONS RODE(1940); BARNACLE BILL(1941); GREAT TRAIN ROBBERY, THE(1941); LOVE CRAZY(1941); MURDER BY INVITATION(1941); RICHEST MAN IN TOWN(1941); SHE COULDN'T SAY NO(1941); WAGONS ROLL AT NIGHT, THE(1941); I MARRIED A WITCH(1942); SCATTERGOOD SURVIVES A MURDER(1942); BEHIND PRISON WALLS(1943); CRIME BY NIGHT(1944)
Jacques Guhl
DAISY MILLER(1974)
William Guhl
FARMER'S OTHER DAUGHTER, THE(1965); KINFOLK(1970)
Erich Guhne
GERMANY, YEAR ZERO(1949, Ger.)
Vittorio Gui
ROSSINI(1948, Ital.), m
Emilio Rodriques Guiar
HUNTING PARTY, THE(1977, Brit.)
Andre Guibert
DIARY OF A COUNTRY PRIEST(1954, Fr.)
Claire Guibert
TIME BOMB(1961, Fr./Ital.)
Jean-Paul Guibert
MAGNIFICENT TRAMP, THE(1962, Fr./Ital.), p
Etienne Guichard
1984
LE BAL(1984, Fr./Ital./Algeria)

Ernesto Guida
CONSTANTINE AND THE CROSS(1962, Ital.), w; REVENGE OF THE GLADIATORS(1965, Ital.), w
Gloria Guida
Misc. Talkies
TEASERS, THE(1977); BEST, THE(1979)
Raffaele Guida
JULIET OF THE SPIRITS(1965, Fr./Ital./W.Ger.)
Wandisa Guida
DEVIL'S COMMANDMENT, THE(1956, Ital.); REVOLT OF THE SLAVES, THE(1961, Ital./Span./Ger.); PRISONER OF THE IRON MASK(1962, Fr./Ital.); GLADIATOR OF ROME(1963, Ital.); SECRET AGENT FIREBALL(1965, Fr./Ital.)
Misc. Talkies
THREE SERGEANTS OF BENGAL(1965)
Antonella Guidelli
NIGHT OF THE SHOOTING STARS, THE(1982, Ital.)
Giovanni Guidelli
NIGHT OF THE SHOOTING STARS, THE(1982, Ital.)
Micol Guidelli
NIGHT OF THE SHOOTING STARS, THE(1982, Ital.)
Miriam Guidelli
NIGHT OF THE SHOOTING STARS, THE(1982, Ital.)
Mirio Guidelli
NIGHT OF THE SHOOTING STARS, THE(1982, Ital.)
Titta Guidelli
NIGHT OF THE SHOOTING STARS, THE(1982, Ital.)
James Guidera
1984
NO SMALL AFFAIR(1984)
Guidarino Guidi
FAREWELL TO ARMS, A(1957); WATERLOO(1970, Ital./USSR); AVANTI!(1972)
Paolo Guidi
ACCATTONE!(1961, Ital.)
Don Guidice
THREE DAYS OF THE CONDOR(1975), ed; YAKUZA, THE(1975, U.S./Jap.), ed; HARRY AND WALTER GO TO NEW YORK(1976), ed; TILT(1979), ed
Donald Guidice
NEW LEAF, A(1971), ed
King Guidice
Misc. Talkies
TIMBERESQUE(1937), d
Sonia Lo Guidice
JOURNEY TO LOVE(1953, Ital.)
Beatriz Guido
END OF INNOCENCE(1960, Arg.), w; SUMMERSKIN(1962, Arg.), w; HAND IN THE TRAP, THE(1963, Arg./Span.), w; TERRACE, THE(1964, Arg.), w; THE EAVESDROPPER(1966, U.S./Arg.), w; MONDAY'S CHILD(1967, U.S., Arg.), w; MAFIA, THE(1972, Arg.), w
Elizabeth Guido
ROAD TO SALINA(1971, Fr./Ital.), ed
Stewart Guidotti
WITNESS, THE(1959, Brit.); HELP!(1965, Brit.)
1984
SECRET PLACES(1984, Brit.)
Carlo Guiffre
SEVEN HILLS OF ROME, THE(1958); WHITE, RED, YELLOW, PINK(1966, Ital.)
Gus Guiffre
SILVER BEARS(1978)
Paul Guifoyle
SINBAD THE SAILOR(1947)
Frances Guihan
MIDSTREAM(1929), w; THROWBACK, THE(1935), w; BOSS RIDER OF GUN CREEK(1936), w; COWBOY AND THE KID,THE(1936), w; COWBOY STAR, THE(1936), w; BLACK ACES(1937), w; BOSS OF LONELY VALLEY(1937), w; EMPTY SADDLES(1937), w; LAW FOR TOMBSTONE(1937), w; LEFT-HANDED LAW(1937), w; SANDFLOW(1937), w; SMOKE TREE RANGE(1937), w; SUDDEN BILL DORN(1938), w; FRONTIER SCOUT(1939), w
Silents
PRETTY CLOTHES(1927), w; STRANDED(1927), w; THUMBS DOWN(1927), w; BACHELOR'S PARADISE(1928), w; MARRY THE GIRL(1928), w, t; MILLION FOR LOVE, A(1928), w, t
Francis Guihan
COCK O' THE WALK(1930), w; RIDE 'EM COWBOY(1936), w; WESTBOUND MAIL(1937), w
Raoul Guilad
MAGNIFICENT ONE, THE(1974, Fr./Ital.)
Sidney Guilaroff
YOUNG MAN WITH IDEAS(1952), spec eff
Sydney Guilaroff
ON THE TOWN(1949), hairstyles; LOVELY TO LOOK AT(1952), makeup; GOODBYE CHARLIE(1964); GRAND PRIX(1966), cos, makeup; IMPOSSIBLE YEARS, THE(1968), hairstyles; NEW YORK, NEW YORK(1977)
Sylvie Guilbault
QUEST FOR FIRE(1982, Fr./Can.)
Gib Guilbeau
BOXCAR BERTHA(1972), m
Nina Guilberg
WHAT PRICE CRIME?(1935)
Ann Morgan Guilbert
MAN FROM THE DINERS' CLUB, THE(1963); ONE MAN'S WAY(1964); GUIDE FOR THE MARRIED MAN, A(1967); HOW SWEET IT IS(1968); VIVA MAX!(1969)
Claire Guilbert
TAKE ME TO PARIS(1951, Brit.)
Francis Guilbert
HU-MAN(1975, Fr.), w
J. C. Guilbert
WEEKEND(1968, Fr./Ital.); MOUCHETTE(1970, Fr.)

Jean-Claude Guilbert
AU HASARD, BALTHAZAR(1970, Fr.)
Nina Guilbert
ONE YEAR LATER(1933); TRIGGER PALS(1939); SAGEBRUSH FAMILY TRAILS WEST, THE(1940); OUTLAWS OF THE DESERT(1941); WEST POINT WIDOW(1941); MAGNIFICENT AMBERSONS, THE(1942)
Yvette Guilbert
Silents
FAUST(1926, Ger.)
Luce Guilboult
ANGELA(1977, Can.)
Bruce Guilchard
1984
PURPLE HEARTS(1984)
Leo Guild
DEVIL'S MESSENGER, THE(1962 U.S./Swed.), w
Lynn Guild
GANG WAR(1958)
Nancy Guild
SOMEWHERE IN THE NIGHT(1946); BRASHER DOUBLOON, THE(1947); GIVE MY REGARDS TO BROADWAY(1948); BLACK MAGIC(1949); ABBOTT AND COSTELLO MEET THE INVISIBLE MAN(1951); LITTLE EGYPT(1951); FRANCIS COVERS THE BIG TOWN(1953); SUCH GOOD FRIENDS(1971)
Katherine Guildford
COME SEPTEMBER(1961)
Deryck Guiler
FERRY ACROSS THE MERSEY(1964, Brit.)
Willor Lee Guilford
Misc. Talkies
DAUGHTER OF THE CONGO, A(1930); EASY STREET(1930); TEN MINUTES TO LIVE(1932)
Ann Guilford-Grey
D.C. CAB(1983)
James Guilfoyle
SPEAKEASY(1929); CRIMINAL CODE(1931); SPECIAL AGENT K-7(1937); ALIMONY(1949); TWO LOST WORLDS(1950); MA AND PA KETTLE AT THE FAIR(1952)
Jimmy Guilfoyle
GET THAT GIRL(1932)
Paul Guilfoyle
SPECIAL AGENT(1935); CRIME OF DR. CRESPI, THE(1936); ROAMING LADY(1936); TWO-FISTED GENTLEMAN(1936); WANTED: JANE TURNER(1936); WINTERSET(1936); BEHIND THE HEADLINES(1937); CRASHING HOLLYWOOD(1937); DANGER PATROL(1937); FIGHT FOR YOUR LADY(1937); FLIGHT FROM GLORY(1937); HIDEAWAY(1937); SOLDIER AND THE LADY, THE(1937); SUPER SLEUTH(1937); WOMAN I LOVE, THE(1937); YOU CAN'T BEAT LOVE(1937); YOU CAN'T BUY LUCK(1937); BLIND ALIBI(1938); DOUBLE DANGER(1938); FUGITIVES FOR A NIGHT(1938); I'M FROM THE CITY(1938); LAW OF THE UNDERWORLD(1938); LAW WEST OF TOMBSTONE, THE(1938); MAD MISS MANTON, THE(1938); MAID'S NIGHT OUT(1938); QUICK MONEY(1938); SAINT IN NEW YORK, THE(1938); SHE'S GOT EVERYTHING(1938); SKY GIANT(1938); TARNISHED ANGEL(1938); THIS MARRIAGE BUSINESS(1938); HERITAGE OF THE DESERT(1939); NEWS IS MADE AT NIGHT(1939); ONE HOUR TO LIVE(1939); OUR LEADING CITIZEN(1939); PACIFIC LINER(1939); SABOTAGE(1939); SOCIETY LAWYER(1939); THOU SHALT NOT KILL(1939); UNEXPECTED FATHER(1939); BROTHER ORCHID(1940); EAST OF THE RIVER(1940); GRAPES OF WRATH(1940); MILLIONAIRES IN PRISON(1940); ONE CROWDED NIGHT(1940); REMEMBER THE NIGHT(1940); SAINT TAKES OVER, THE(1940); WILDCAT BUS(1940); SAINT IN PALM SPRINGS, THE(1941); MAN WHO RETURNED TO LIFE, THE(1942); TIME TO KILL(1942); WHO IS HOPE SCHUYLER?(1942); NORTH STAR, THE(1943); PETTICOAT LARCENY(1943); THREE RUSSIAN GIRLS(1943); WHITE SAVAGE(1943); IT HAPPENED TOMORROW(1944); MARK OF THE WHISTLER, THE(1944); MASTER RACE, THE(1944); SEVENTH CROSS, THE(1944); MISSING CORPSE, THE(1945); WHY GIRLS LEAVE HOME(1945); SWEETHEART OF SIGMA CHI(1946); VIRGINIAN, THE(1946); MILLERSON CASE, THE(1947); ROSES ARE RED(1947); SECOND CHANCE(1947); FOLLOW ME QUIETLY(1949); JUDGE, THE(1949); MIGHTY JOE YOUNG(1949); MISS MINK OF 1949(1949); THERE'S A GIRL IN MY HEART(1949); TROUBLE PREFERRED(1949); WHITE HEAT(1949); WOMAN'S SECRET, A(1949); BOMBA AND THE HIDDEN CITY(1950); DAVY CROCKETT, INDIAN SCOUT(1950); MESSENGER OF PEACE(1950); WOMAN ON PIER 13, THE(1950); JOURNEY INTO LIGHT(1951); WHEN I GROW UP(1951); ACTORS AND SIN(1952); CONFIDENCE GIRL(1952); JULIUS CAESAR(1953); TORCH SONG(1953); APACHE(1954); GOLDEN IDOL, THE(1954); CHIEF CRAZY HORSE(1955); TRIAL(1955); BOY AND THE PIRATES, THE(1960); TESS OF THE STORM COUNTRY(1961), d
Claude Guilhem
BANZAI(1983, Fr.), art d
Nina Guilherd
MOTH, THE(1934)
James Guilifoyle
RIDERS OF PASCO BASIN(1940)
Anne Guillard
PEPPERMINT SODA(1979, Fr.)
Jean-Bernard Guillard
1984
THREE CROWNS OF THE SAILOR(1984, Fr.)
Claude Guillaume
LE PETIT THEATRE DE JEAN RENOIR(1974, Fr.)
Patrick Guillaume
LA BALANCE(1983, Fr.)
Robert Guillaume
SUPERFLY T.N.T.(1973); SEEMS LIKE OLD TIMES(1980)
Alain Guille
BEAST, THE(1975, Fr.), art d
Frances V. Guille
STORY OF ADELE H., THE(1975, Fr.), w
Alain C. Guilleaume
DAUGHTERS OF DARKNESS(1971, Bel./ Fr./ Ger./ Ital.), p
M. Guillemaud
MILLION, THE(1931, Fr.), w

Marie-Helene Guillemin
WHY ROCK THE BOAT?(1974, Can.), ed
Agnes Guillemot
WOMAN IS A WOMAN, A(1961, Fr./Ital.), ed; CONTEMPT(1963, Fr./Ital.), ed; MY LIFE TO LIVE(1963, Fr.), ed; ALPHAVILLE, A STRANGE CASE OF LEMMY CAUTION(1965, Fr.), ed; LE PETIT SOLDAT(1965, Fr.), ed; MARRIED WOMAN, THE(1965, Fr.), ed; BAND OF OUTSIDERS(1966, Fr.), ed; MADE IN U.S.A.(1966, Fr.), ed; MASCULINE FEMININE(1966, Fr./Swed.), ed; LA CHINOISE(1967, Fr.), ed; DE L'AMOUR(1968, Fr./Ital.), ed; LES CARABINIERS(1968, Fr./Ital.), ed; OLDEST PROFESSION, THE(1968, Fr./Ital./Ger.), ed; WEEKEND(1968, Fr./Ital.), ed; LES GAULOISES BLEUES(1969, Fr.), ed; STOLEN KISSES(1969, Fr.), ed; MISSISSIPPI MERMAID(1970, Fr./Ital.), ed; COUSIN, COUSINE(1976, Fr.), ed; BLUE COUNTRY, THE(1977, Fr.), ed
Ernesto Guillen
SANTA(1932, Mex.)
John Guillerman
BRIDGE AT REMAGEN, THE(1969), d
John Guillermin
MELODY IN THE DARK(1948, Brit.), w; HIGH JINKS IN SOCIETY(1949, Brit.), p,d&w; PAPER GALLOWS(1950, Brit.), p, d&w; FOUR DAYS(1951, Brit.), d; SMART ALEC(1951, Brit.), d; MISS ROBIN HOOD(1952, Brit.), d; SCHOOL FOR BRIDES(1952, Brit.), d; BACHELOR IN PARIS(1953, Brit.), d; OPERATION DIPLOMAT(1953, Brit.), d, w; ADVENTURE IN THE HOPFIELDS(1954, Brit.), d; CROWDED DAY, THE(1954, Brit.), d; THUNDERSTORM(1956), d; TOWN ON TRIAL(1957, Brit.), d; WHOLE TRUTH, THE(1958, Brit.), d; TARZAN'S GREATEST ADVENTURE(1959, Brit.), d, w; DAY THEY ROBBED THE BANK OF ENGLAND, THE(1960, Brit.), d; NEVER LET GO(1960, Brit.), d, w; TARZAN GOES TO INDIA(1962, U.S./Brit./Switz.), d, w; WALTZ OF THE TOREADORS(1962, Brit.), d; GUNS AT BATASI(1964, Brit.), d; RAPTURE(1965), d; BLUE MAX, THE(1966), d; P.J.(1968), d; HOUSE OF CARDS(1969), d; EL CONDOR(1970), d; SKYJACKED(1972), d; SHAFT IN AFRICA(1973), d; TOWERING INFERNO, THE(1974), d; KING KONG(1976), d; DEATH ON THE NILE(1978, Brit.), d; MR. PATMAN(1980, Can.), d
1984
SHEENA(1984), d
John Guillesmin
HELL, HEAVEN OR HOBOKEN(1958, Brit.), d
Raoul Guillet
1984
THREE CROWNS OF THE SAILOR(1984, Fr.)
Marie-Noelle Guilliot
CONFIDENTIALLY YOURS(1983, Fr.)
Roger Guillo
RISE OF LOUIS XIV, THE(1970, Fr.)
Lucia Guillon
MIRACLE IN SOHO(1957, Brit.)
Alvaro Guillot
PHARAOH'S CURSE(1957)
Claudia Guillot
Misc. Silents
KING OF CRIME, THE(1914, Brit.)
Gilles Guillot
LET JOY REIGN SUPREME(1977, Fr.)
Maurice-Paul Guillot
SYMPHONIE FANTASTIQUE(1947, Fr.), md
Olga Guillot
YOUNG AND EVIL(1962, Mex.); HEROINA(1965)
Christian Guillouet
THANOS AND DESPINA(1970, Fr./Gr.), ph
Ofelia Guilmain
QUEEN'S SWORDSMEN, THE(1963, Mex.); LITTLE RED RIDING HOOD AND THE MONSTERS(1965, Mex.); MAN AND THE MONSTER, THE(1965, Mex.); EXTERMINATING ANGEL, THE(1967, Mex.); NAZARIN(1968, Mex.)
Julie Guilmette
FAST TIMES AT RIDGEMONT HIGH(1982)
Cecilia Guimaraes
IN THE WHITE CITY(1983, Switz./Portugal)
Paul Guimard
THINGS OF LIFE, THE(1970, Fr./Ital./Switz.), w, w
Julien Guimoar
BORSALINO(1970, Fr.)
Texas Guinan
QUEEN OF THE NIGHTCLUBS(1929); GLORIFYING THE AMERICAN GIRL(1930); BROADWAY THROUGH A KEYHOLE(1933)
Misc. Silents
FUEL OF LIFE(1917); GUN WOMAN, THE(1918); I AM THE WOMAN(1921); STAMPEDE, THE(1921)
Thomas Guinan
INCENDIARY BLONDE(1945), w
W.D. Guinan
INCENDIARY BLONDE(1945), w
Fabrice Guinard
JOY(1983, Fr./Can.)
Roque Guinart
ARTISTS AND MODELS ABROAD(1938)
Natacha Guinaudeau
1984
LES COMPERES(1984, Fr.)
Antonio Mas Guindal
DEVIL MADE A WOMAN, THE(1962, Span.), w
Christopher Guinee
NICE GIRL LIKE ME, A(1969, Brit.); CLASS OF MISS MAC MICHAEL, THE(1978, Brit./U.S.)
Jean Guinee [R. de Guichen]
L'ATALANTE(1947, Fr.), w
Alec Guiness
OUR MAN IN HAVANA(1960, Brit.)
Matthew Guiness
DUELLISTS, THE(1977, Brit.)

A.G. Guinle
SLEEPING CAR TO TRIESTE(1949, Brit.)
Amando Guinle
CAPTAIN'S PARADISE, THE(1953, Brit.)
Armand Guinle
TERROR SHIP(1954, Brit.); LOSER TAKES ALL(1956, Brit.)
Armande Guinle
ELECTRONIC MONSTER. THE(1960, Brit.)
Armando Guinle
STOWAWAY GIRL(1957, Brit.); SNORKEL, THE(1958, Brit.)
G.A. Guinle
SCHOOL FOR BRIDES(1952, Brit.)
H.G. Guinle
WOMAN TO WOMAN(1946, Brit.); DEVIL'S PLOT, THE(1948, Brit.)
Amando Guinlee
YOU PAY YOUR MONEY(1957, Brit.)
Ed Guinn
MONGREL(1982), m
Lew Guinn
SLIME PEOPLE, THE(1963), ed
Lewis J. Guinn
INVASION OF THE STAR CREATURES(1962), ed; RED, WHITE AND BLACK, THE(1970), ph, ed
Rick Guinn
Misc. Talkies
LIFE AND LEGEND OF BUFFALO JONES, THE(1976); MOUNTAIN CHARLIE(1982)
Alec Guinness
GREAT EXPECTATIONS(1946, Brit.); KIND HEARTS AND CORONETS(1949, Brit.); LAST HOLIDAY(1950, Brit.); MUDLARK, THE(1950, Brit.); RUN FOR YOUR MONEY, A(1950, Brit.); LAVENDER HILL MOB, THE(1951, Brit.); OLIVER TWIST(1951, Brit.); MAN IN THE WHITE SUIT, THE(1952); PROMOTER, THE(1952, Brit.); CAPTAIN'S PARADISE, THE(1953, Brit.); DETECTIVE, THE(1954, Qit.); MALTA STORY(1954, Brit.); PRISONER, THE(1955, Brit.); TO PARIS WITH LOVE(1955, Brit.); LADYKILLERS, THE(1956, Brit.); SWAN, THE(1956); BRIDGE ON THE RIVER KWAI, THE(1957); ALL AT SEA(1958, Brit.); HORSE'S MOUTH, THE(1958, Brit.), a, w; SCAPEGOAT, THE(1959, Brit.); TUNES OF GLORY(1960, Brit.); MAJORITY OF ONE, A(1961); DAMN THE DEFIANT!(1962, Brit.); LAWRENCE OF ARABIA(1962, Brit.); FALL OF THE ROMAN EMPIRE, THE(1964); DOCTOR ZHIVAGO(1965); SITUATION HOPELESS- BUT NOT SERIOUS(1965); HOTEL PARADISO(1966, U.S./Brit.); QUILLER MEMORANDUM, THE(1966, Brit.); COMEDIANS, THE(1967); CROMWELL(1970, Brit.); SCROOGE(1970, Brit.); BROTHER SUN, SISTER MOON(1973, Brit./Ital.); HITLER: THE LAST TEN DAYS(1973, Brit./Ital.); MURDER BY DEATH(1976); STAR WARS(1977); EMPIRE STRIKES BACK, THE(1980); RAISE THE TITANIC(1980, Brit.); LOVESICK(1983); RETURN OF THE JEDI(1983)
1984
PASSAGE TO INDIA, A(1984, Brit.)
Mathew Guinness
VIRGIN SOLDIERS, THE(1970, Brit.); ONE DAY IN THE LIFE OF IVAN DENISOVICH(1971, U.S./Brit./Norway)
Matthew Guinness
PROMOTER, THE(1952, Brit.)
Fred Guiol
WHAT'S YOUR RACKET?(1934), d; KENTUCKY KERNELS(1935), w; NITWITS, THE(1935), w; RAINMAKERS, THE(1935), d, w; MUMMY'S BOYS(1936), d; SILLY BILLIES(1936), d, w; GUNGA DIN(1939), w; VIGIL IN THE NIGHT(1940), w; TANKS A MILLION(1941), d; ABOUT FACE(1942), p; HAY FOOT(1942), p&d; YANKS AHOY(1943), p; HERE COMES TROUBLE(1948), d; GIANT(1956), w
Silents
SAILOR-MADE MAN, A(1921)
Misc. Silents
BATTLING ORIOLES, THE(1924), d
Fred L. Guiol
AS YOU WERE(1951), d; MR. WALKIE TALKIE(1952), d
Silents
SAFETY LAST(1923), ed, art d
Julian Guiomar
INCORRIGIBLE(1980, Fr.)
Julien Guiomar
KING OF HEARTS(1967, Fr./Ital.); THIEF OF PARIS, THE(1967, Fr./Ital.); MILKY WAY, THE(1969, Fr./Ital.); Z(1969, Fr./Algeria); VERY CURIOUS GIRL, A(1970, Fr.); BAROCCO(1976, Fr.)
1984
BIZET'S CARMEN(1984, Fr./Ital.); MY NEW PARTNER(1984, Fr.)
Fernand Guiot
THIEF OF PARIS, THE(1967, Fr./Ital.); BRAIN, THE(1969, Fr./US
1984
AMERICAN DREAMER(1984); UNTIL SEPTEMBER(1984)
Charles J. Guiotta
WRONG MAN, THE(1956)
Greg Guirard
SOUTHERN COMFORT(1981)
Raoul Guiraud
LA FEMME INFIDELE(1969, Fr./Ital.), set d
Lisa Guiraut
DAYS OF WINE AND ROSES(1962)
Janine Guise
SLIPPER EPISODE, THE(1938, Fr)
John Guise
1984
CHAMPIONS(1984)
Thomas Guise
Silents
CHICKEN CASEY(1917); LOVE IS AN AWFUL THING(1922); HELD TO ANSWER(1923); JAZZMANIA(1923); AFTER THE BALL(1924)
Misc. Silents
BUGLE CALL, THE(1916); SWEETHEART OF THE DOOMED(1917); VIVE LA FRANCE(1918); 23 ½ HOURS ON LEAVE(1919); WHEN A MAN LOVES(1920); BLACK OXEN(1924)

Thomas J. Guise
Silents
CRAB, THE(1917)
Thomas S. Guise
Silents
HOME(1916); TAR HEEL WARRIOR, THE(1917); WOODEN SHOES(1917)
Tom Guise
Silents
ALARM CLOCK ANDY(1920); SISTERS(1922); STRANGER'S BANQUET(1922); WOLF LAW(1922); GARRISON'S FINISH(1923)
Misc. Silents
WOMAN MICHAEL MARRIED, THE(1919); DON'T EVER MARRY(1920); PASSIONATE PILGRIM, THE(1921); CLAW, THE(1927)
Tom S. Guise
Silents
CROOKED ALLEY(1923); STEPPING FAST(1923); WEDDING BILL$(1927)
Misc. Silents
CROOKED ALLEY(1923); CROSSED WIRES(1923); SECRETS OF THE NIGHT(1925)
Windham Guise
Silents
FIRM OF GIRDLESTONE, THE(1915, Brit.); PURSUIT OF PAMELA, THE(1920, Brit.); GENERAL JOHN REGAN(1921, Brit.); GAME OF LIFE, THE(1922, Brit.); QUALIFIED ADVENTURER, THE(1925, Brit.); THOU FOOL(1926, Brit.); HIS HOUSE IN ORDER(1928, Brit.)
Misc. Silents
BLADYS OF THE STEWPONY(1919, Brit.); SWEETHEARTS(1919, Brit.)
Wyndam Guise
Misc. Silents
CONVICT 99(1919, Brit.)
Wyndham Guise
Silents
HOUSE OF TEMPERLEY, THE(1913, Brit.); DEMOCRACY(1918, Brit.); MRS. THOMPSON(1919, Brit.); PRIDE OF THE FANCY, THE(1920, Brit.); MR. NOBODY(1927, Brit.)
Misc. Silents
INCOMPARABLE MISTRESS BELLAIRS, THE(1914, Brit.); DIANA AND DESTINY(1916, Brit.)
Guido Guiseppone
BEAUTIFUL SWINDLERS, THE(1967, Fr./Ital./Jap./Neth.)
J. U. Guisey
Silents
CABARET, THE(1918), w
Robert Guisgand
JULIE THE REDHEAD(1963, Fr.), art d
Henri Guisoi
BALLERINA(1950, Fr.)
Guisol
BIZARRE BIZARRE(1939, Fr.)
Henri Guisol
CRIME OF MONSIEUR LANGE, THE(1936, Fr.); LOLA MONTES(1955, Fr./Ger.); STORY OF THE COUNT OF MONTE CRISTO, THE(1962, Fr./Ital.); MURDER AT 45 R.P.M.(1965, Fr.); LA CHIENNE(1975, Fr.)
Henry Guisol
DOUBLE CRIME IN THE MAGINOT LINE(1939, Fr.); PORTRAIT OF A WOMAN(1946, Fr.); MASK OF KOREA(1950, Fr.)
Rene Guissant
HATE SHIP, THE(1930, Brit.), ph
Rene Guissart
COMPULSORY HUSBAND, THE(1930, Brit.), ph; "W" PLAN, THE(1931, Brit.), ph; SWEET DEVIL(1937, Brit.), d
Silents
ADVENTURES OF CAROL, THE(1917), ph; FIGHTING ODDS(1917), ph; TREASURE ISLAND(1920), ph; BREAKING POINT, THE(1921), ph; LYING TRUTH, THE(1922), ph; PADDY, THE NEXT BEST THING(1923, Brit.), ph; RECOIL, THE(1924), ph; BEN-HUR(1925), ph
Rene Guissart, Jr.
LE MANS(1971), ph
Rene Guissatt
AMERICAN PRISONER, THE(1929 Brit.), ph
Fred Guisso
CROWD ROARS, THE(1932)
Cornelius Reese Arndt Guisti
STRANGE FACES(1938), w
Enrique Guitart
OPERATION DELILAH(1966, U.S./Span.)
Armando Guiterrez
PUSS 'N' BOOTS(1964, Mex.)
Manuel Guitian
DESERT WARRIOR(1961 Ital./Span.)
El Guito
BLOOD WEDDING(1981, Sp.)
Sacha Guitry
BONNE CHANCE(1935, Fr.), a, d&w; PASTEUR(1936, Fr.), a, d&w; PEARLS OF THE CROWN(1938, Fr.), a, d, w; STORY OF A CHEAT, THE(1938, Fr.), a, d&w; LUCKY PARTNERS(1940), w; NAPOLEON(1955, Fr.), a, d&w; IF PARIS WERE TOLD TO US(1956, Fr.), a, d&w; ROYAL AFFAIRS IN VERSAILLES(1957, Fr.), a, p,d&w
Sascha Guitry
SLEEPING PARTNERS(1930, Brit.), d&w
Laurence Guittard
LITTLE NIGHT MUSIC, A(1977, Aust./U.S./Ger.); SOMEBODY KILLED HER HUSBAND(1978)
Jean Guitton
ROTHSCHILD(1938, Fr.), w
Madelaine Guitty
Misc. Silents
MADAME SANS-GENE(1925)

John Guitz
ONE DOWN TWO TO GO(1982)
Lilia Guizar
SUN ALSO RISES, THE(1957)
Susana Guizar
LEGEND OF A BANDIT, THE(1945, Mex.)
Tito Guizar
UNDER THE PAMPAS MOON(1935); BIG BROADCAST OF 1938, THE(1937), m/l
Leo Robin; RANCHO GRANDE(1938, Mex.); TROPIC HOLIDAY(1938); ST. LOUIS
BLUES(1939); LLANO KID, THE(1940); BLONDIE GOES LATIN(1941); BRAZIL(1944);
MEXICANA(1945); THRILL OF BRAZIL, THE(1946); ON THE OLD SPANISH
TRAIL(1947); GAY RANCHERO, THE(1948); TIME AND THE TOUCH, THE(1962)
Misc. Talkies
PAPA SOLTERO(1939)
Frenchia Guizon
SLAMS, THE(1973); STONE KILLER, THE(1973)
Richard Guizon
GAMES(1967); HANG'EM HIGH(1968); EXTRAORDINARY SEAMAN, THE(1969);
PENDULUM(1969)
Mario Guizzardi
STATUE, THE(1971, Brit.)
Gukar
JAWS OF THE JUNGLE(1936)
Ayshe Gul
YOR, THE HUNTER FROM THE FUTURE(1983, Ital.)
Franco Gula
LEOPARD, THE(1963, Ital.)
Max Gulack
SOUP FOR ONE(1982)
Clu Gulager
KILLERS, THE(1964); AND NOW MIGUEL(1966); SULLIVAN'S EMPIRE(1967);
WINNING(1969); COMPANY OF KILLERS(1970); LAST PICTURE SHOW, THE(1971);
MOLLY AND LAWLESS JOHN(1972); MC Q(1974); OTHER SIDE OF MIDNIGHT,
THE(1977); FORCE OF ONE, A(1979)
1984
CHATTANOOGA CHOO CHOO(1984); INITIATION, THE(1984); LIES(1984, Brit.)
Misc. Talkies
LIES(1983)
Clu Gulagher
TOUCHED BY LOVE(1980)
Anthony Gulassa
Misc. Talkies
EVERYDAY(1976)
Inna Gulaya
WHEN THE TREES WERE TALL(1965, USSR)
Synove Gulbrandsen "Miss Norway"
YANKEE PASHA(1954)
Robert Gulbranson
OPERATION CIA(1965)
Wladyslaw Gulch
BEADS OF ONE ROSARY, THE(1982, Pol.)
Pierre Gulda
LE PETIT THEATRE DE JEAN RENOIR(1974, Fr.)
Peer Guldbrandsen
SCANDAL IN DENMARK(1970, Den.), p,d&w
Campbell Gulian
Misc. Silents
DAMAGED GOODS(1919, Brit.)
Bill Gulick
BEND OF THE RIVER(1952), w; HALLELUJAH TRAIL, THE(1965), w; SUPPORT
YOUR LOCAL GUNFIGHTER(1971), ed
William B. Gulick
WATUSI(1959), ed; ONE OF OUR SPIES IS MISSING(1966), ed; KARATE KILLERS,
THE(1967), ed; DIRTY DINGUS MAGEE(1970), ed
William Gulick
LAW AND THE LADY, THE(1951), ed; MR. IMPERIUM(1951), ed
Harry Gulkin
LIES MY FATHER TOLD ME(1975, Can.), p; JACOB TWO-TWO MEETS THE
HOODED FANG(1979, Can.), p; THRESHOLD(1983, Can.)
Jonathon Gulla
DEADLY BLESSING(1981)
Richard Gullage
GREATEST, THE(1977, U.S./Brit.)
Campbell Gullan
PLEASURE CRAZED(1929); SKY HAWK(1929), w; CASTE(1930, Brit.), d; IN-
QUEST(1931, Brit.); FLYING SQUAD, THE(1932, Brit.); POWER(1934, Brit.); STRI-
KE!(1934, Brit.); IRON DUKE, THE(1935, Brit.); PRICE OF A SONG(1935, Brit.);
EAST MEETS WEST(1936, Brit.); END OF THE ROAD, THE(1936, Brit.); WRATH OF
JEALOUSY(1936, Brit.), d; BLACK TULIP, THE(1937, Brit.); LAST CURTAIN,
THE(1937, Brit.); CLAYDON TREASURE MYSTERY, THE(1938, Brit.)
Silents
FAR FROM THE MADDING CROWD(1915, Brit.); GREAT ADVENTURE, THE(1915,
Brit.); WELSH SINGER, A(1915, Brit.); DOORSTEPS(1916, Brit.); PLACE IN THE SUN,
A(1916, Brit.); HER STORY(1920, Brit.); PRICE OF SILENCE, THE(1920, Brit.); GAME
OF LIFE, THE(1922, Brit.); IF FOUR WALLS TOLD(1922, Brit.); HOTEL MOUSE,
THE(1923, Brit.); LILY OF THE ALLEY(1923, Brit.)
Misc. Silents
COMIN' THRO' THE RYE(1916, Brit.); MILESTONES(1916, Brit.); CASTLE(1917,
Brit.); MEMBER OF THE TATTERSALL'S, A(1919, Brit.); RIGHT ELEMENT,
THE(1919, Brit.); SOME ARTIST(1919, Brit.); HONEYPOT, THE(1920, Brit.); LOVE IN
THE WILDERNESS(1920, Brit.); LOVE MAGGY(1921, Brit.); MR. PIM PASSES
BY(1921, Brit.); SINGLE LIFE(1921, Brit.); CASTLES IN THE AIR(1923, Brit.);
I'PAGLIACCI(1923, Brit.); RIGHT TO STRIKE, THE(1923, Brit.); STRANGLING
THREADS(1923, Brit.)
Alberta Gullatin
Silents
LITTLE MISS BROWN(1915)

Nina Gullbert
CAVALCADE OF THE WEST(1936)
Bill Gullick
ROAD TO DENVER, THE(1955), w
William B. Gullick
CHANDLER(1971), ed
Tom Gullikson
PLAYERS(1979)
Liesha Gullisson
LAST OF THE RED HOT LOVERS(1972)
Clifford Gulliver
LOVE UP THE POLE(1936, Brit.), d; MUSEUM MYSTERY(1937, Brit.), d
Dorothy Gulliver
COLLEGE LOVE(1929); NIGHT PARADE(1929, Brit.); PAINTED FACES(1929);
TROOPERS THREE(1930); UNDER MONTANA SKIES(1930); IN OLD CHEYEN-
NE(1931); FIGHTING MARSHAL, THE(1932); HONOR OF THE PRESS(1932); CHEAT-
ING BLONDES(1933); KING KONG(1933); OUTLAW JUSTICE(1933); REVENGE AT
MONTE CARLO(1933); STAND UP AND CHEER(1934 80m FOX bw); FIGHTING
CABALLERO(1935); IN EARLY ARIZONA(1938); LONE STAR PIONEERS(1939);
NORTH OF SHANGHAI(1939); FACES(1968); WON TON TON, THE DOG WHO
SAVED HOLLYWOOD(1976)
Misc. Talkies
PECOS DANDY, THE(1934)
Silents
DOG OF THE REGIMENT(1927); ONE GLORIOUS SCRAP(1927); SHIELD OF
HONOR, THE(1927); CLEARING THE TRAIL(1928); HONEYMOON FLATS(1928)
Misc. Silents
ONE GLORIOUS SCRAP(1927); RAMBLING RANGER, THE(1927); GOOD MORN-
ING JUDGE(1928); WILD WEST SHOW, THE(1928)
John Gulliver
JOANNA(1968, Brit.)
Tony Gulliver
RACING FEVER(1964); AROUND THE WORLD UNDER THE SEA(1966); STING OF
DEATH(1966)
Carmine Gullone
BEFORE HIM ALL ROME TREMBLED(1947, Ital.), d
Emilio Gulmaraes
COUNTRY DOCTOR, THE(1963, Portuguese)
Gulpilil
LAST WAVE, THE(1978, Aus.)
David Gulpilil
MAD DOG MORGAN(1976,Aus.); STORM BOY(1976, Aus.); RIGHT STUFF,
THE(1983)
Max Gulsdorff
Misc. Silents
HEADS UP, CHARLIE(1926, Ger.)
Janine Gulse
CAFE DE PARIS(1938, Fr.)
O. Gulstorff
PILLARS OF SOCIETY(1936, Ger.), set d
Lajos Gulyas
WITNESS, THE(1982, Hung.), p
Ye. Gulyayeva
SUMMER TO REMEMBER, A(1961, USSR)
Bryant Gumbel
HEAVEN CAN WAIT(1978)
Gilda Gumbo
1984
FIRST TURN-ON!, THE(1984)
Carlton Gumbs
CALYPSO(1959, Fr./It.)
Peter Gumeny
MURDER, INC.(1960); WHAT'S SO BAD ABOUT FEELING GOOD?(1968); HE
KNOWS YOU'RE ALONE(1980)
1984
FEAR CITY(1984); GARBO TALKS(1984)
Leonard Gumley
SANDS OF IWO JIMA(1949)
Christopher Gummer
NIGHTBEAST(1982)
1984
ALIEN FACTOR, THE(1984)
Betty Gumn
CURIOUS FEMALE, THE(1969)
Diane Gump
NEPTUNE'S DAUGHTER(1949); PRODIGAL, THE(1955); SERENADE(1956)
Eugene Gump
WRESTLER, THE(1974), w
H.S. Gump
BELLBOY, THE(1960)
Irving Gump
BULLFIGHTERS, THE(1945)
David Gumpilil
WALKABOUT(1971, Aus./U.S.)
K. Gun
LADY WITH THE DOG, THE(1962, USSR)
Natalia Gundareva
AUTUMN MARATHON(1982, USSR)
Gustel Gundelach
CODE 7, VICTIM 5(1964, Brit.)
Renee Gundelach
LEFT-HANDED WOMAN, THE(1980, Ger.), p
Per Gundemann
PEOPLE MEET AND SWEET MUSIC FILLS THE HEART(1969, Den./Swed.)
Jack Gundersen
PASSION HOLIDAY(1963)
Karen Gunderson
YOUNG SWINGERS, THE(1963)

Rick Gunderson
1984
  BODY DOUBLE(1984)
Roger Gunderson
  ROSE TATTOO, THE(1955)
Robert Gundlach
  RACHEL, RACHEL(1968), art d; DON'T DRINK THE WATER(1969), art d; PO-
  PI(1969), art d; LOVE STORY(1970), art d; BELIEVE IN ME(1971), art d; GANG THAT
  COULDN'T SHOOT STRAIGHT, THE(1971), art d; BAD COMPANY(1972), art d;
  COME BACK CIHARLESTON BLUE(1972), prod d; BANG THE DRUM SLOWL-
  Y(1973), prod d; CRAZY JOE(1974), art d; DEATH WISH(1974), prod d; KING
  KONG(1976), art d; THIEVES(1977), art d; EYES OF LAURA MARS(1978), art d;
  OLIVER'S STORY(1978), art d; DEATH VENGEANCE(1982), art d; I, THE JU-
  RY(1982), prod d
Per Gundmann
  WHILE THE ATTORNEY IS ASLEEP(1945, Den.)
Donald Gundrey
  PRINCESS AND THE MAGIC FROG, THE(1965), ph
Gareth Gundrey
  HOUND OF THE BASKERVILLES(1932, Brit.), w
Silents
  ARCADIANS, THE(1927, Brit.), p; SISTER TO ASSIST 'ER, A(1927, Brit.), p; PHYSI-
  CIAN, THE(1928, Brit.), p
V. Gareth Gundrey
  DEVIL'S MAZE, THE(1929, Brit.), p&d; JUST FOR A SONG(1930, Brit.), d&w;
  SYMPHONY IN TWO FLATS(1930, Brit.), d, w; STRONGER SEX, THE(1931, Brit.),
  d&w; HOUND OF THE BASKERVILLES(1932, Brit.), d
Silents
  ROSES OF PICARDY(1927, Brit.), w; PALAIS DE DANSE(1928, Brit.), p
V. Garuth Gundrey
Silents
  SMASHING THROUGH(1928, Brit.), p
Salih Guney
  YOU CAN'T WIN 'EM ALL(1970, Brit.)
Yilmaz Guney
  YOL(1982, Turkey), w, ed
Lea Gunghi
Silents
  QUO VADIS?(1913, Ital.)
V. Guniya
Misc. Silents
  CONQUEST OF THE CAUCASUS(1913, USSR)
Jiromasa Gunji
  SAMURAI ASSASSIN(1965, Jap.), w
Clint Gunkel
  YOUNG SINNER, THE(1965)
Adam Gunn
  HALLOWEEN II(1981)
Bill Gunn
  INTERNS, THE(1962); PENELOPE(1966); SPY WITH MY FACE, THE(1966); ANGEL
  LEVINE, THE(1970), w; GANJA AND HESS(1973), a, d&w
Misc. Talkies
  LOSING GROUND(1982)
Caryl Gunn
  IT HAPPENED IN ROME(1959, Ital.)
Charles Gunn
Silents
  CHICKEN CASEY(1917)
Misc. Silents
  EYE OF GOD, THE(1916); EVEN BREAK, AN(1917); FIREFLY OF TOUGH LUCK,
  THE(1917); LOVE OR JUSTICE(1917); MADCAP MADGE(1917); MOUNTAIN
  DEW(1917); PHANTOM HUSBAND, A(1917); SNARL, THE(1917); SWEETHEART OF
  THE DOOMED(1917); THREE OF MANY(1917); FRAMING FRAMERS(1918); WED-
  LOCK(1918); IT HAPPENED IN PARIS(1919); MIDNIGHT STAGE, THE(1919)
Earl Gunn
  MISSING WITNESSES(1937); ANGELS WITH DIRTY FACES(1938); ROMANCE OF
  THE REDWOODS(1939); DEVIL'S ISLAND(1940); ISLAND OF DOOMED MEN(1940);
  LADY IN QUESTION, THE(1940); MAD EMPRESS, THE(1940); BILLY THE
  KID(1941); GREAT COMMANDMENT, THE(1941); HONKY TONK(1941); SECRETS
  OF THE WASTELANDS(1941); SWAMP WOMAN(1941)
Misc. Talkies
  TEXAS RENEGADES(1940)
Frances Gunn
  CURTAINS(1983, Can.)
Fronzie Gunn
Silents
  LOVE AFLAME(1917); MADE IN HEAVEN(1921)
George W. Gunn
Silents
  POWER OF DECISION, THE(1917), w
Gilbert Gunn
  SAVE A LITTLE SUNSHINE(1938, Brit.), w; CHAMBER OF HORRORS(1941, Brit.),
  w; FARMER'S WIFE, THE(1941, Brit.); GOOD BEGINNING, THE(1953, Brit.), d, w;
  LANDFALL(1953, Brit.), w; MEN ARE CHILDREN TWICE(1953, Brit.), d; COSMIC
  MONSTERS(1958, Brit.), d; GIRLS AT SEA(1958, Brit.), p, d, w; MARK OF THE
  HAWK, THE(1958), d; WHAT A WHOPPER(1961, Brit.), d; MY WIFE'S FAMILY(1962,
  Brit.), d, w; OPERATION BULLSHINE(1963, Brit.), d, w; WINGS OF MYS-
  TERY(1963, Brit.), d&w
Misc. Talkies
  CRAWLING TERROR, THE(1958, Brit.), d; YOUNG DETECTIVE, THE(1964, Brit.), d
Herbert Gunn
  CHARLEY'S AUNT(1941); SUN VALLEY SERENADE(1941); ALWAYS IN MY
  HEART(1942); MAN WHO CAME TO DINNER, THE(1942); GUY NAMED JOE,
  A(1943); WE'VE NEVER BEEN LICKED(1943); DESTINATION TOKYO(1944)
James Gunn
  LADY OF BURLESQUE(1943), w; BORN TO KILL(1947), w; UNFAITHFUL,
  THE(1947), w; FLYING MISSILE(1950), w; HARRIET CRAIG(1950), w; BAREFOOT
  MAILMAN, THE(1951), w; AFFAIR IN TRINIDAD(1952), w; ALL I DESIRE(1953), w;
  OVER-EXPOSED(1956), w; YOUNG PHILADELPHIANS, THE(1959), w; BECAUSE
  THEY'RE YOUNG(1960), w

Jane Taylor Gunn
  WE OF THE NEVER NEVER(1983, Aus.), w
Jeanie Gunn
  RECKLESS(1935)
Judy Gunn
  ROOF, THE(1933, Brit.); LILIES OF THE FIELD(1934, Brit.); LOVE TEST, THE(1935,
  Brit.); PRIVATE SECRETARY, THE(1935, Brit.); RIVERSIDE MURDER, THE(1935,
  Brit.); VINTAGE WINE(1935, Brit.); WHITE LILAC(1935, Brit.); IN THE SOUP(1936,
  Brit.); LAST JOURNEY, THE(1936, Brit.); BEAUTY AND THE BARGE(1937, Brit.);
  FIVE POUND MAN, THE(1937, Brit.); MURDER AT THE BASKERVILLES(1941, Brit.)
Margaret Gunn
  GIRL IN THE CROWD, THE(1934, Brit.); LEAVE IT TO BLANCHE(1934, Brit.)
Moses Gunn
  NOTHING BUT A MAN(1964); WHAT'S SO BAD ABOUT FEELING GOOD?(1968);
  GREAT WHITE HOPE, THE(1970); WUSA(1970); EAGLE IN A CAGE(1971, U.S./
  Yugo.); SHAFT(1971); WILD ROVERS(1971); HOT ROCK, THE(1972); SHAFT'S BIG
  SCORE(1972); ICEMAN COMETH, THE(1973); AMAZING GRACE(1974); AARON
  LOVES ANGELA(1975); CORNBREAD, EARL AND ME(1975); ROLLERBALL(1975);
  REMEMBER MY NAME(1978); NINTH CONFIGURATION, THE(1980); RAG-
  TIME(1981); AMITYVILLE II: THE POSSESSION(1982)
1984
  FIRESTARTER(1984); NEVERENDING STORY, THE(1984, Ger.)
Neil M. Gunn
  SILVER DARLINGS, THE(1947, Brit.), w
Nicholas Gunn
  CHARLIE CHAN AND THE CURSE OF THE DRAGON QUEEN(1981)
Norman Gunn
  WIND OF CHANGE, THE(1961, Brit.)
Peter Gunn
  REDHEAD FROM MANHATTAN(1954)
Richard Gunn
  WE'VE NEVER BEEN LICKED(1943)
Robert Gunn
  I'LL FIX IT(1934)
Rocky Gunn
Misc. Talkies
  CHARLIE CHAN: HAPPINESS IS A WARM CLUE(1971)
Sheryl Gunn
  LEAP OF FAITH(1931, Brit.)
Ted Gunn
  HOMER(1970)
William Gunn
  SOUND AND THE FURY, THE(1959); LANDLORD, THE(1970), w
Fred Gunnarsson
  ELVIS! ELVIS!(1977, Swed.)
Frank Gunnell
  PICNIC AT HANGING ROCK(1975, Aus.)
Chester Gunnels
  SHINE ON, HARVEST MOON(1938); COME ON RANGERS(1939)
Robert Gunner
  JACKALS, THE(1967, South Africa); PLANET OF THE APES(1968)
Ann Gunning
  SPIDER AND THE FLY, THE(1952, Brit.); ROOM AT THE TOP(1959, Brit.)
Anne Gunning
  PORTRAIT OF CLARE(1951, Brit.)
Christopher Gunning
  GOODBYE GEMINI(1970, Brit.), m; HANDS OF THE RIPPER(1971, Brit.), m; IN
  CELEBRATION(1975, Brit.), m; GET CHARLIE TULLY(1976, Brit.), m
Paul Gunning
1984
  HOLLYWOOD HOT TUBS(1984)
Wid Gunning
  HOT STUFF(1929), p; SEVEN FOOTPRINTS TO SATAN(1929), p
Silents
  MISS NOBODY(1926), w; BABE COMES HOME(1927), p
Tinni Gunnlangsdottir
  OUTLAW: THE SAGE OF GISLI(1982, Iceland)
Lillian Gunns
  DEATH DRIVES THROUGH(1935, Brit.)
Milton Gunsberg
  TENNESSEE JOHNSON(1942), w
Roy S. Gunsburg
  DEATH VALLEY(1982)
Archibald Clavering Gunter
Silents
  FLORIDA ENCHANTMENT, A(1914), w; MAN BEHIND THE DOOR, THE(1914), w;
  MR. BARNES OF NEW YORK(1914), w
Gary Gunter
  LAST EMBRACE(1979)
George Gunter
  DEVIL'S BEDROOM, THE(1964), p, ph
Misc. Talkies
  YOUNG MAN'S BRIDE, THE(1968), d
Eugen Gunther
  STORM IN A WATER GLASS(1931, Aust.)
Hilda Gunther
  NIGHT PORTER, THE(1974, Ital./U.S.)
Isa Gunther
  HEIDI(1954, Switz.)
John Gunther
  THUNDER BIRDS(1942)
Ted Gunther
  COP HATER(1958); GREEN SLIME, THE(1969)
Wolfgang Gunther
  FROZEN ALIVE(1966, Brit./Ger.)
Bob Gunton
  ROLLOVER(1981)

Monty Gunty
WHAT'S SO BAD ABOUT FEELING GOOD?(1968)
Morty Gunty
1984
BROADWAY DANNY ROSE(1984)
Daro Gunzberg
CHANT OF JIMMIE BLACKSMITH, THE(1980, Aus.), cos
Milton Gunzberg
DEVIL COMMANDS, THE(1941), w
M.L. Gunzburg
BWANA DEVIL(1953), ph
Milton Gunzburg
SISTER KENNY(1946), w; SIERRA(1950), w
Roy Gunzburg
HAWMPS!(1976)
Anubhe Gupta
KANCHENJUNGHA(1966, India)
Banshi Chandra Gupta
PATHER PANCHALI(1958, India), art d; WORLD OF APU, THE(1960, India), art d
Dinen Gupta
RIVER, THE(1961, India), ph
Nina Gupta
GANDHI(1982)
Pinaki Sen Gupta
APARAJITO(1959, India); MUSIC ROOM, THE(1963, India)
Ramananda Sen Gupta
RIVER, THE(1951), ph
Ramani Sen Gupta
APARAJITO(1959, India)
Santi Gupta
APARAJITO(1959, India)
Sarada Gupta
Misc. Silents
THROW OF THE DICE(1930, Brit.)
Umas Das Gupta
PATHER PANCHALI(1958, India)
Shirley Sen Gupta
LONG DUEL, THE(1967, Brit.)
Alizia Gur
FROM RUSSIA WITH LOVE(1963, Brit.); NIGHT TRAIN TO PARIS(1964, Brit.); AGENT FOR H.A.R.M.(1966, Brit.); BEAUTY JUNGLE, THE(1966, Brit.); KILL A DRAGON(1967); HAND OF NIGHT, THE(1968, Brit.); TARZAN AND THE JUNGLE BOY(1968, US/Switz.)
Daliah Gur
RABBI AND THE SHIKSE, THE(1976, Israel)
Sascha Gura
Misc. Silents
HUNCHBACK AND THE DANCER, THE(1920, Ger.)
Ron Gural
1984
TIGHTROPE(1984)
Lyudmila Gurchenko
MARRIAGE OF BALZAMINOV, THE(1966, USSR)
G. I. Gurdjieff
MEETINGS WITH REMARKABLE MEN(1979, Brit.), w
Ronan Gure
LE BEAU MARIAGE(1982, Fr.), m
Nathalie Gureghian
1984
A NOS AMOURS(1984, Fr.)
Tatyana Guretskaya
HOME FOR TANYA, A(1961, USSR); LULLABY(1961, USSR)
Itamar Gurevich
RABBI AND THE SHIKSE, THE(1976, Israel)
David Gurfinkel
EVERY BASTARD A KING(1968, Israel), ph; NOT MINE TO LOVE(1969, Israel), w, ph; KAZABLAN(1974, Israel), ph; KID VENGEANCE(1977), ph; MAGICIAN OF LUBLIN, THE(1979, Israel/Ger.), ph; WORLDS APART(1980, U.S., Israel), ph; ENTER THE NINJA(1982), ph; REVENGE OF THE NINJA(1983), ph
1984
NAKED FACE, THE(1984), ph; SAHARA(1984), ph
David Gurfinkle
APPLE, THE(1980 U.S./Ger.), ph
Paul R. Gurian
CUTTER AND BONE(1981), p
Sigrid Gurie
ADVENTURES OF MARCO POLO, THE(1938); ALGIERS(1938); FORGOTTEN WOMAN, THE(1939); RIO(1939); DARK STREETS OF CAIRO(1940); THREE FACES WEST(1940); ENEMY OF WOMEN(1944); VOICE IN THE WIND(1944); SOFIA(1948); SWORD OF THE AVENGER(1948)
Ellen Gurin
WHO KILLED MARY WHAT'SER NAME?(1971)
Anna Gurit
EVERY BASTARD A KING(1968, Israel), ed
Valerij Gurjev
WATERLOO(1970, Ital./USSR)
T. Gurko
LAST GAME, THE(1964, USSR)
Burtram Gurleigh
Misc. Silents
JUST A MOTHER(1923)
Helen Gurley
SONGS AND BULLETS(1938), ed
Jim Gurley
HAPPIEST MILLIONAIRE, THE(1967)
Lisa Gurley
ENTITY, THE(1982)

Cindy Gurling
JULIE DARLING(1982, Can./Ger.)
Eugene Gurlitz
OH! CALCUTTA!(1972), art d
Gene Gurlitz
GREEK TYCOON, THE(1978), art d
Gordon Gurnee
FOLLOW THAT DREAM(1962), set d
Gordon Gurnell
IT'S A MAD, MAD, MAD, MAD WORLD(1963), art d
Barbara Gurney
Silents
SOUL OF YOUTH, THE(1920)
Beatrice Gurney
TERROR FROM THE YEAR 5,000(1958), art d
Dan Gurney
GRAND PRIX(1966); WINNING(1969)
Edmund Gurney
Silents
TOL'ABLE DAVID(1921)
Eric Gurney
MAKE MINE MUSIC(1946), w
Kate Gurney
Silents
AT THE VILLA ROSE(1920, Brit.); ALL ROADS LEAD TO CALVARY(1921, Brit.); CREATION(1922, Brit.); ROGUE IN LOVE, A(1922, Brit.); HEARTSTRINGS(1923, Brit.); MONEY HABIT, THE(1924, Brit.); PASSING OF MR. QUIN, THE(1928, Brit.)
Rachel Gurney
TOM BROWN'S SCHOOLDAYS(1951, Brit.); ROOM IN THE HOUSE(1955, Brit.); PORT AFRIQUE(1956, Brit.); TOUCH OF LARCENY, A(1960, Brit.); GAME FOR THREE LOSERS(1965, Brit.); FUNERAL IN BERLIN(1966, Brit.); I WANT WHAT I WANT(1972, Brit.)
Robert Gurney, Jr.
INVASION OF THE SAUCER MEN(1957), w; EDGE OF FURY(1958), d, w
Robert J. Gurney, Jr.
INVASION OF THE SAUCER MEN(1957), p; REFORM SCHOOL GIRL(1957), p; TERROR FROM THE YEAR 5,000(1958), p,d&w
Sharon Gurney
WOMEN IN LOVE(1969, Brit.); CRUCIBLE OF HORROR(1971, Brit.); DEATHLINE(1973, Brit.)
Val Gurney
Silents
ROAD TO RUIN, THE(1913, Brit.)
Barbara Gurnhill
WOMAN HATER(1949, Brit.)
John Gurnsey
NICE GIRL LIKE ME, A(1969, Brit.)
Holt Gurnstein
SHE MAN, THE(1967), ed
I. Gurov
GORDEYEV FAMILY, THE(1961, U.S.S.R.)
Juan Jose Gurrola
EL TOPO(1971, Mex.)
Rod Gurrucharri
TEXICAN, THE(1966, U.S./Span.), makeup
Eric Gurry
AUTHOR! AUTHOR!(1982); BAD BOYS(1983)
Peter Gurs
NORTHWEST OUTPOST(1947)
Bob Gurski
RAINBOW BOYS, THE(1973, Can.), set d
Alla Gursky
STALAG 17(1953)
K. Gurunanse
OUTCAST OF THE ISLANDS(1952, Brit.), ch
Louis Gurvich
NEW ORLEANS AFTER DARK(1958)
Anothany N. Gurvis
1984
GIRLS NIGHT OUT(1984), w
Anthony N. Gurvis
1984
GIRLS NIGHT OUT(1984), p
Adrian Gurvitz
SGT. PEPPER'S LONELY HEARTS CLUB BAND(1978)
Annabelle Gurwitch
1984
DELIVERY BOYS(1984)
I. Gubanova- Gurzo
QUEEN OF SPADES(1961, USSR)
I. Gurzo-Gubanova
SANDU FOLLOWS THE SUN(1965, USSR)
Gus Arnheim and His Cocoanut Grove Ambassador Band
STREET GIRL(1929)
Gus Arnheim and His Orchestra
FLYING HIGH(1931); GIFT OF GAB(1934); PALOOKA(1934)
The Gus Arnheim Orchestra
TROCADERO(1944)
Gus the Raccoon
MY SIDE OF THE MOUNTAIN(1969)
Bobbie Gusehoff
NAKED CITY, THE(1948)
V. Gusev
RESURRECTION(1963, USSR)
Victor Gusev
SIX P.M.(1946, USSR), w
Yuri Gusev
STAR INSPECTOR, THE(1980, USSR)

V. Gushtchinsky
DEFENSE OF VOLOTCHAYEVSK, THE(1938, USSR)
Wyndham Gusie
Misc. Silents
TOM JONES(1917, Brit.)
Simone Gusin
FINO A FARTI MALE(1969, Fr./Ital.)
Frank Guskie
FOURTH HORSEMAN, THE(1933)
Anna Guskin
Misc. Talkies
AMERICAN MATCHMAKER(1940)
Paul E. Guskin
JUST TELL ME WHAT YOU WANT(1980)
Erich Gusko
TINDER BOX, THE(1968, E. Ger.), ph
G. Guskov
MEET ME IN MOSCOW(1966, USSR)
Yevgeny Guslinsky
UNCLE VANYA(1972, USSR), ph
Chinto Gusman
APACHE DRUMS(1951)
Russell A. Gusman
SINGAPORE(1947), set d
Teri Gusman
Misc. Talkies
FIVE ANGRY WOMEN(1975)
Clay Guss
NAKED WITCH, THE(1964), w
Jack Guss
LADY IN CEMENT(1968), w
Lou Guss
LAUGHING POLICEMAN, THE(1973); HARRY AND TONTO(1974)
Louie Guss
NEW YORK, NEW YORK(1977)
Louis Guss
LOVE WITH THE PROPER STRANGER(1963); READY FOR THE PEOPLE(1964); CRAZY JOE(1974); LEPKE(1975, U.S./Israel); LUCKY LADY(1975); NICKELODEON(1976); FUN WITH DICK AND JANE(1977); H.O.T.S.(1979); WILLIE AND PHIL(1980); CHEECH AND CHONG'S NICE DREAMS(1981)
Lisa Gussack
BIMBO THE GREAT(1961, Ger.)
Larry Gust
WILD ON THE BEACH(1965)
Bosse Gustafson
OBSESSION(1968, Swed.), w
Carol Gustafson
TRUMAN CAPOTE'S TRILOGY(1969); GOING HOME(1971); THREE DAYS OF THE CONDOR(1975)
Dwight L. Gustafson
RED RUNS THE RIVER(1963), m, md
Steve Gustafson
HOMEWORK(1982)
Berit Gustafson
LOVING COUPLES(1966, Swed.)
Eric Gustafsson
ON THE SUNNYSIDE(1936, Swed.)
Gittan Gustafsson
WILD STRAWBERRIES(1959, Swed.), art d
Kersti Gustafsson
VICTOR FRANKENSTEIN(1975, Swed./Ireland), cos
Midget Gustav
Silents
BACHELOR'S BABY, THE(1927)
A. Gustavson
QUEEN OF SPADES(1961, USSR)
Gunold Gustavson
DEVIL, THE(1963)
Lanny Gustavson
TRACKDOWN(1976)
Kjell Gustavsson
SEA GULL, THE(1968), makeup
Paul Gustine
WITHOUT RESERVATIONS(1946); HILLS OF OLD WYOMING(1937); BLUE DAHLIA, THE(1946); NIGHT AND DAY(1946); PAINTING THE CLOUDS WITH SUNSHINE(1951)
Gutare
KING SOLOMON'S MINES(1950)
Beth Gutcheon
WITHOUT A TRACE(1983), w
Linda Gutemberg
ME(1970, Fr.)
Linda Gutenberg
COUSINS IN LOVE(1982), p
Steven Gutenberg
BOYS FROM BRAZIL, THE(1978)
Johannes Guter
Misc. Silents
LEAP INTO LIFE(1924, Ger.), d
Radmila Gutesa
WITNESS OUT OF HELL(1967, Ger./Yugo.)
Ray Guth
EMPEROR OF THE NORTH POLE(1973)
Raymond Guth
INSIDE THE MAFIA(1959); YOUNG CAPTIVES, THE(1959); OPERATION BIKINI(1963); HOSTAGE, THE(1966); FLIM-FLAM MAN, THE(1967); REIVERS, THE(1969); MONTE WALSH(1970); GRISSOM GANG, THE(1971); BAD COMPANY(1972); CULPEPPER CATTLE COMPANY, THE(1972); FUNNY LADY(1975); BIG BUS, THE(1976); SOME KIND OF HERO(1982)

John Guthbridge
MAN IN THE MOON(1961, Brit.), ed
Fred Guthe
CURTAINS(1983, Can.), ph
Martin Gutheridge
PINK FLOYD-THE WALL(1982, Brit.), spec eff
Carl Gutherie
EMBRACEABLE YOU(1948), ph
Hertha Guthmar
ARIANE(1931, Ger.)
J.D. Guthridge
FAITHFUL CITY(1952, Israel), ed
John Guthridge
MY SISTER AND I(1948, Brit.), ed; SALT TO THE DEVIL(1949, Brit.), ed; DESPERATE MOMENT(1953, Brit.), ed; HELL BELOW ZERO(1954, Brit.), ed; LAND OF FURY(1955 Brit.), ed; AS LONG AS THEY'RE HAPPY(1957, Brit.), ed; INNOCENT SINNERS(1958, Brit.), ed; MAD LITTLE ISLAND(1958, Brit.), ed; SAPPHIRE(1959, Brit.), ed; ALL NIGHT LONG(1961, Brit.), ed; VICTIM(1961, Brit.), ed; LITTLE PRINCE, THE(1974, Brit.), ed; MOSES(1976, Brit./Ital.), ed
John D. Guthridge
LOOK BEFORE YOU LOVE(1948, Brit.), ed; VICE VERSA(1948, Brit.), ed; ADAM AND EVELYNE(1950, Brit.), ed; FIVE ANGLES ON MURDER(1950, Brit.), ed; BROWNING VERSION, THE(1951, Brit.), ed; IMPORTANCE OF BEING EARNEST, THE(1952, Brit.), ed; MADE IN HEAVEN(1952, Brit.), ed; JACQUELINE(1956, Brit.), ed; JUMPING FOR JOY(1956, Brit.), ed; TIGER IN THE SMOKE(1956, Brit.), ed; ALLIGATOR NAMED DAISY, AN(1957, Brit.), ed; HELL DRIVERS(1958, Brit.), ed; DOUBLE BUNK(1961, Brit.), ed; LEAGUE OF GENTLEMEN, THE(1961, Brit.), ed; MIND BENDERS, THE(1963, Brit.), ed; PLACE TO GO, A(1964, Brit.), ed; WOMAN OF STRAW(1964, Brit.), ed; MASQUERADE(1965, Brit.), ed; WALK IN THE SHADOW(1966, Brit.), ed
A.B. Guthrie
BIG SKY, THE(1952), w
A.B. Guthrie, Jr.
SHANE(1953), w; KENTUCKIAN, THE(1955), w; THESE THOUSAND HILLS(1959), w
Alfred Bertram Guthrie, Jr.
WAY WEST, THE(1967), w
Arlo Guthrie
ALICE'S RESTAURANT(1969), a, w, m; RENALDO AND CLARA(1978)
Carl E. Guthrie
FINDERS KEEPERS(1951), ph; BOP GIRL GOES CALYPSO(1957), ph; DALTON GIRLS, THE(1957), ph; HELL BOUND(1957), ph; QUANTEZ(1957), ph; TATTERED DRESS, THE(1957), ph; FORT BOWIE(1958), ph; FRANKENSTEIN 1970(1958), ph; HOUSE ON HAUNTED HILL(1958), ph; MACABRE(1958), ph
Carl Guthrie
BETWEEN TWO WORLDS(1944), ph; IN OUR TIME(1944), ph; JANIE(1944), ph; CHRISTMAS IN CONNECTICUT(1945), ph; HOTEL BERLIN(1945), ph; TOO YOUNG TO KNOW(1945), ph; HER KIND OF MAN(1946), ph; JANIE GETS MARRIED(1946), ph; ALWAYS TOGETHER(1947), ph; CRY WOLF(1947), ph; APRIL SHOWERS(1948), ph; BIG PUNCH, THE(1948), ph; WOMAN IN WHITE, THE(1948), ph; FLAXY MARTIN(1949), ph; GIRL FROM JONES BEACH, THE(1949), ph; ONE LAST FLING(1949), ph; BACKFIRE(1950), ph; BARRICADE(1950), ph; CAGED(1950), ph; HIGHWAY 301(1950), ph; STORM WARNING(1950), ph; THIS SIDE OF THE LAW(1950), ph; UNDERCOVER GIRL(1950), ph; BEDTIME FOR BONZO(1951), ph; HOLLYWOOD STORY(1951), ph; IRON MAN, THE(1951), ph; BONZO GOES TO COLLEGE(1952), ph; FRANCIS GOES TO WEST POINT(1952), ph; RAIDERS, THE(1952), ph; ALL I DESIRE(1953), ph; FRANCIS COVERS THE BIG TOWN(1953), ph; GIRLS IN THE NIGHT(1953), ph; HOT NEWS(1953), ph; JAZZ SINGER, THE(1953), ph; PRIVATE EYES(1953), ph; THREE SAILORS AND A GIRL(1953), ph; DAWN AT SOCORRO(1954), ph; JOHNNY DARK(1954), ph; LONG JOHN SILVER(1954, Aus.), ph; MA AND PA KETTLE AT HOME(1954), ph; PLAYGIRL(1954), ph; YANKEE PASHA(1954), ph; FRANCIS IN THE NAVY(1955), ph; JAIL BUSTERS(1955), ph; KISS OF FIRE(1955), ph; LADY GODIVA(1955), ph; DEATH IN SMALL DOSES(1957), ph; GIRL IN THE KREMLIN, THE(1957), ph; OKLAHOMAN, THE(1957), ph; SHOOT-OUT AT MEDICINE BEND(1957), ph; UNTAMED YOUTH(1957), ph; BEAST OF BUDAPEST, THE(1958), ph; FORT MASSACRE(1958), ph; JOY RIDE(1958), ph; TOO MUCH, TOO SOON(1958), ph; VIOLENT ROAD(1958), ph; BATTLE CRY(1959), ph; GUNFIGHT AT DODGE CITY, THE(1959), ph; KING OF THE WILD STALLIONS(1959), ph; UP PERISCOPE(1959), ph; YELLOWSTONE KELLY(1959), ph; DONDI(1961), ph; EVERYTHING'S DUCKY(1961), ph; FIVE MINUTES TO LIVE(1961), ph; GEORGE RAFT STORY, THE(1961), ph; KING OF THE ROARING TWENTIES-THE STORY OF ARNOLD ROTHSTEIN(1961), ph; TWENTY PLUS TWO(1961), ph; X-15(1961), ph; LIVELY SET, THE(1964), ph; READY FOR THE PEOPLE(1964), ph
Caroline Guthrie
GREGORY'S GIRL(1982, Brit.); LOCAL HERO(1983, Brit.)
1984
COMFORT AND JOY(1984, Brit.)
Gigi Guthrie
1984
LISTEN TO THE CITY(1984, Can.)
Jack Guthrie
HOLLYWOOD BARN DANCE(1947)
John Guthrie
LAND OF FURY(1955 Brit.), w
Keith Guthrie
WEREWOLVES ON WHEELS(1971)
Kenneth Guthrie
CHILDREN OF THE FOG(1935, Brit.)
Lester D. Guthrie
AMAZING TRANSPARENT MAN, THE(1960), p
Lynne Guthrie
WORKING GIRLS, THE(1973); TEARS OF HAPPINESS(1974)
Tani Guthrie
THIRSTY DEAD, THE(1975); POSTMAN ALWAYS RINGS TWICE, THE(1981)
Tani Phelps Guthrie
DAUGHTERS OF SATAN(1972)

Terry Guthrie
PORKY'S(1982)
Tyrone Guthrie
THE BEACHCOMBER(1938, Brit.); SIDEWALKS OF LONDON(1940, Brit.);
OEDIPUS REX(1957, Can.), d
Walt Guthrie
RETURN TO MACON COUNTY(1975)
Walter Guthrie
NIGHT THEY ROBBED BIG BERTHA'S, THE zero(1975)
Woody Guthrie
THEY LIVE BY NIGHT(1949), m; BOUND FOR GLORY(1976), w
Carl E. Guthriel
SUMMER LOVE(1958), ph
Miguel Gutierez
SALOME(1953)
Alberto Gutierrez
VILLA!(1958)
Alfredo Gutierrez
UNDER FIRE(1983)
1984
EVIL THAT MEN DO, THE(1984)
Amador Gutierrez
ARABIAN NIGHTS(1942)
Antonio Gutierrez
VIRGIN SACRIFICE(1959); MIGHTY JUNGLE, THE(1965, U.S./Mex.)
Armando Gutierrez
BEAST OF HOLLOW MOUNTAIN, THE(1956); LITTLE RED RIDING HOOD AND
THE MONSTERS(1965, Mex.)
Eduardo Gutierrez
SILENCE, THE(1964, Swed.)
Ernie Gutierrez
MR. HOBBS TAKES A VACATION(1962)
Fernando E. Gutierrez
EDDIE MACON'S RUN(1983)
Gary Gutierrez
RIGHT STUFF, THE(1983), spec eff
Javier A. Gutierrez
EDDIE MACON'S RUN(1983)
Jose Maria Gutierrez
MAFIA, THE(1972, Arg.)
Joseph Gutierrez
SCANDALOUS JOHN(1971)
Olga Gutierrez
SEVEN CITIES OF GOLD(1955)
Quentin Gutierrez
1984
REPO MAN(1984)
Tonio Gutierrez
JAGUAR(1980, Phil.)
Vincente Gutierrez
HEARTBREAKER(1983), w
Zaide Silvia Gutierrez
1984
EL NORTE(1984)
Robert Gutin
RETURN TO CAMPUS(1975)
Alicia Gutirrez
PROSTITUTION(1965, Fr.); RAGE(1966, U.S./Mex.)
Robert Gutknecht
THING, THE(1951)
Georg Gutlich
CONFESS DR. CORDA(1960, Ger.); DIE GANS VON SEDAN(1962, Fr/Ger.)
Arthur Gutman
GREAT WALTZ, THE(1938), md
D. Gutman
CAPTAIN GRANT'S CHILDREN(1939, USSR), a, d
Misc. Silents
NEW BABYLON, THE(1929, USSR)
David Gutman
Misc. Silents
TRAITOR(1926, USSR)
James C. Gutman
SOMETHING SHORT OF PARADISE(1979), p
Karl Gutman
Silents
WOMAN OF PARIS, A(1923)
Walter Gutman
UNSTRAP ME(1968), a, d&w; MARCH ON PARIS 1914–OF GENERALOBERST
ALEXANDER VON KLUCK–AND HIS MEMORY OF JESSIE HOLLADAY(1977), a,
p,d&w, ph, ed
Gene Gutowski
REPULSION(1965, Brit.), p; CUL-DE-SAC(1966, Brit.), p; FEARLESS VAMPIRE
KILLERS, OR PARDON ME BUT YOUR TEETH ARE IN MY NECK, THE(1967), p;
ADVENTURES OF GERARD, THE(1970, Brit.), p, w; DAY AT THE BEACH, A(1970),
p; ROMANCE OF A HORSE THIEF(1971), p
Helo Gutschwager
COUNTERFEIT TRAITOR, THE(1962)
Bertha Guttenberg
CANTOR'S SON, THE(1937)
Steve Guttenberg
CHICKEN CHRONICLES, THE(1977); CAN'T STOP THE MUSIC(1980); DI-
NER(1982); MAN WHO WASN'T THERE, THE(1983)
1984
POLICE ACADEMY(1984)
Steven Guttenberg
PLAYERS(1979)
Lucy Gutteridge
GREEK TYCOON, THE(1978)

1984
TOP SECRET!(1984)
Martin Gutteridge
HANOVER STREET(1979, Brit.), spec eff; GREEN ICE(1981, Brit.), spec eff; SUPER-
MAN III(1983), spec eff
Leon Gutterman
SMART WOMAN(1948), w
Amos Guttman
1984
DRIFTING(1984, Israel), d, w
Arthur Guttman
TRAPEZE(1932, Ger.), m; DREAM OF SCHONBRUNN(1933, Aus.), m; I TAKE THIS
WOMAN(1940), m; HANGMEN ALSO DIE(1943), md; ENEMY OF WOMEN(1944), m
Henry Guttman
DEVIL AND THE DEEP(1932); GREAT IMPERSONATION, THE(1942); INVISIBLE
AGENT(1942); JOURNEY FOR MARGARET(1942); ONCE UPON A HONEY-
MOON(1942); PIED PIPER, THE(1942); IMMORTAL SERGEANT, THE(1943); MIS-
SION TO MOSCOW(1943); THEY GOT ME COVERED(1943); WINGS OVER THE
PACIFIC(1943); O.S.S.(1946); GOLDEN EARRINGS(1947); NIGHT HAS A THOUSAND
EYES(1948); RED, HOT AND BLUE(1949)
Richard A. Guttman
BACK DOOR TO HELL(1964), w
1984
HIGHPOINT(1984, Can.), w
Ronald Guttman
DANTON(1983); HANNAH K.(1983, Fr.)
Arthur Guttmann
DANTON(1931, Ger.), m; NEW WINE(1941), md
Artur Guttmann
HIS MAJESTY, KING BALLYHOO(1931, Ger.), m, md
Henry Guttmann
THEY CAME TO BLOW UP AMERICA(1943)
Anita Gutwell
FREUD(1962)
Mary Gutzi
1984
OVER THE BROOKLYN BRIDGE(1984)
Bertil Guve
FANNY AND ALEXANDER(1983, Swed./Fr./Ger.)
1984
AFTER THE REHEARSAL(1984, Swed.)
Alice Guy
Misc. Silents
GIRL WITH THE GREEN EYES, THE(1916), d
Claude Guy
LITTLE BOY LOST(1953)
Edmonde Guy
DEVIL IS AN EMPRESS, THE(1939, Fr.)
Misc. Silents
LA PRINCESSE MANDANE(1928, Fr.)
Elizabeth Guy
WANDERER, THE(1969, Fr.)
Eula Guy
OVER THE HILL(1931); REBECCA OF SUNNYBROOK FARM(1932); RICH ARE
ALWAYS WITH US, THE(1932); HOUSEWIFE(1934); JIMMY THE GENT(1934);
MADAME DU BARRY(1934); EXPENSIVE HUSBANDS(1937); MARRY THE BOSS'
DAUGHTER(1941); MOON OVER HER SHOULDER(1941); TWO-FACED WO-
MAN(1941); THEY CAME TO BLOW UP AMERICA(1943); WOMAN OF THE TOWN,
THE(1943); MARRIAGE IS A PRIVATE AFFAIR(1944); ONCE UPON A TIME(1944);
STORM OVER LISBON(1944); GLASS ALIBI, THE(1946); SPIDER WOMAN STRIKES
BACK, THE(1946); UNDERCURRENT(1946); HIGH WALL, THE(1947); PRETENDER,
THE(1947); YANKEE FAKIR(1947); DATE WITH JUDY, A(1948); JOAN OF
ARC(1948); MIRACLE OF THE BELLS, THE(1948); SAINTED SISTERS, THE(1948);
SAXON CHARM, THE(1948); THAT WONDERFUL URGE(1948); YELLOW SKY(1948);
BRIDE FOR SALE(1949); THEY LIVE BY NIGHT(1949); HARVEY(1950); MY BLUE
HEAVEN(1950); MYSTERY STREET(1950); SIDE STREET(1950); ENFORCER,
THE(1951); PAULA(1952)
Felicia Guy
NAKED ANGELS(1969)
Jack Guy
Misc. Talkies
THAT GIRL IS A TRAMP(1974), d
Jennifer Guy
PERSECUTION(1974, Brit.)
Lizette Guy
SO THIS IS PARIS(1954)
Mr. Guy
LIMIT, THE(1972), cos
R. Henry Guy
Silents
NOBODY'S FOOL(1921)
Rory Guy
AROUSERS, THE(1973); JIM, THE WORLD'S GREATEST(1976)
Tim Guy
SEMI-TOUGH(1977)
Tony Guy
WATERSHIP DOWN(1978, Brit.), anim
1984
PLAGUE DOGS, THE(1984, U.S./Brit.), anim
Guy Jones and His Band
LITTLE DOLLY DAYDREAM(1938, Brit.)
Guy Lombardo and His Orchestra
STAGE DOOR CANTEEN(1943); NO LEAVE, NO LOVE(1946)
Alice Guy-Blache
Silents
GREAT ADVENTURE, THE(1918), d
Kit Guyatt
MATCHLESS(1974, Aus.), ed; OFFICE PICNIC, THE(1974, Aus.), ed

Victor Guyay
PROSTITUTION(1965, Fr.)
Henry Guybert
ADVENTURES OF RABBI JACOB, THE(1973, Fr.)
Henri Guybet
GIFT, THE(1983, Fr./Ital.)
1984
DOG DAY(1984, Fr.)
Lionel Guyett
FLASH GORDON(1980)
Raoul Guylad
TRANS-EUROP-EXPRESS(1968, Fr.); TENANT, THE(1976, Fr.)
Van Guylder
RAMRODDER, THE(1969), d&w
Derek Guyler
FAST LADY, THE(1963, Brit.)
Deryck Guyler
MAD ABOUT MEN(1954, Brit.); RAMSBOTTOM RIDES AGAIN(1956, Brit.); RING-A-DING RHYTHM(1962, Brit. 73m Amicus/COL bw (G.B: IT'S TRAD, DAD!); HARD DAY'S NIGHT, A(1964, Brit.); NURSE ON WHEELS(1964, Brit.); SMOKESCREEN(1964, Brit.); BIG JOB, THE(1965, Brit.); PLEASE SIR(1971, Brit.); ONE OF OUR DINOSAURS IS MISSING(1975, Brit.); NO SEX PLEASE–WE'RE BRITISH(1979, Brit.)
Katie Guymon
WHOSE LIFE IS IT ANYWAY?(1981)
Fabienne Guyon
1984
LIFE IS A BED OF ROSES(1984, Fr.)
Jean Guyon
JULIE THE REDHEAD(1963, Fr.)
Jacqueline Guyot
LAFAYETTE(1963, Fr.), cos; LADY L(1965, Fr./Ital.), cos; YO YO(1967, Fr.), cos; MILKY WAY, THE(1969, Fr./Ital.), cos; STORY OF ADELE H., THE(1975, Fr.), cos
Raymonde Guyot
ASSOCIATE, THE(1982 Fr./Ger.), ed
Sheila Guyse
SEPIA CINDERELLA(1947); MIRACLE IN HARLEM(1948)
Shelia Guyse
BOY! WHAT A GIRL(1947)
George Guyton
Silents
MIND OVER MOTOR(1923)
Misc. Silents
GOOD MEN AND BAD(1923)
Robert Guza, Jr.
PROM NIGHT(1980), w; MELANIE(1982, Can.), w; CURTAINS(1983, Can.), w
Augustine Guzman
MESSAGE TO GARCIA, A(1936)
Avianka Guzman
1984
MICKI AND MAUDE(1984)
Claudio Guzman
CARETAKERS, THE(1963), art d; TOUCHED BY LOVE(1980), art d
Misc. Talkies
LINDA LOVELACE FOR PRESIDENT(1975), d
Enrique Guzman
INCREDIBLE INVASION, THE(1971, Mex./U.S.)
Eugenio Guzman
STATE OF SIEGE(1973, Fr./U.S./Ital./Ger.)
Jesus Guzman
EVERY DAY IS A HOLIDAY(1966, Span.); UP THE MACGREGORS(1967, Ital./Span.); MAGNIFICENT BANDITS, THE(1969, Ital./Span.)
Luis Guzman
1984
VARIETY(1984)
Pato Guzman
PRESIDENT'S ANALYST, THE(1967), prod d; I LOVE YOU, ALICE B. TOKLAS!(1968), prod d; LAWYER, THE(1969), art d; ALEX IN WONDERLAND(1970), prod d; MARRIAGE OF A YOUNG STOCKBROKER, THE(1971), prod d; PLAY IT AS IT LAYS(1972), prod d; BLUME IN LOVE(1973), prod d; UNMARRIED WOMAN, AN(1978), prod d; IN-LAWS, THE(1979), prod d; HIDE IN PLAIN SIGHT(1980), prod d; WILLIE AND PHIL(1980), prod d; TEMPEST(1982), prod d
1984
MOSCOW ON THE HUDSON(1984), prod d
Robert E. Guzman
DESERT SONG, THE(1929)
Teri Guzman
PETS(1974)
Margherita Guzzinati
WITCH, THE(1969, Ital.); MACHINE GUN McCAIN(1970, Ital.)
Dominic Guzzo
GROUND ZERO(1973)
Ragnar Gvale
FOUR SONS(1940)
Francis Gwaltney
BETWEEN HEAVEN AND HELL(1956), w
Brian Gwaspari
SWEENEY 2(1978, Brit.)
Ann-Marie Gwatkin
1984
SACRED HEARTS(1984, Brit.); SECRET PLACES(1984, Brit.)
Edmund Gween
FRIDAY THE 13TH(1934, Brit.)
Edmund Gwen
YANK AT ETON, A(1942)
Edmund Gwenn
HINDLE WAKES(1931, Brit.); SKIN GAME, THE(1931, Brit.); CONDEMNED TO DEATH(1932, Brit.); FRAIL WOMEN(1932, Brit.); LOVE ON WHEELS(1932, Brit.); MONEY FOR NOTHING(1932, Brit.); BE MINE TONIGHT(1933, Brit.); BISHOP MISBEHAVES, THE(1933, Brit.); EARLY TO BED(1933, Brit./Ger.); GOOD COMPANIONS(1933, Brit.); MAROONED(1933, Brit.); SMITHY(1933, Brit.); ADMIRAL'S SE-CRET, THE(1934, Brit.); CHANNEL CROSSING(1934, Brit.); FATHER AND SON(1934, Brit.); FOR LOVE OR MONEY(1934, Brit.); I WAS A SPY(1934, Brit.); PASSING SHADOWS(1934, Brit.); SPRING IN THE AIR(1934, Brit.); STRAUSS' GREAT WALTZ(1934, Brit.); WARN LONDON!(1934, Brit.); JAVA HEAD(1935, Brit.); ALL-AMERICAN CHUMP(1936); ANTHONY ADVERSE(1936); LABURNUM GROVE(1936, Brit.); MAD HOLIDAY(1936); SYLVIA SCARLETT(1936); WALKING DEAD, THE(1936); PARNELL(1937); PENNY PARADISE(1938, Brit.); SOUTH RIDING(1938, Brit.); YANK AT OXFORD, A(1938); CHEER BOYS CHEER(1939, Brit.); DOCTOR TAKES A WIFE(1940); EARL OF CHICAGO, THE(1940); FOREIGN CORRESPONDENT(1940); MAD MEN OF EUROPE(1940, Brit.); PRIDE AND PREJUDICE(1940); CHARLEY'S AUNT(1941); CHEERS FOR MISS BISHOP(1941); DEVIL AND MISS JONES, THE(1941); ONE NIGHT IN LISBON(1941); SCOTLAND YARD(1941); RANDOM HARVEST(1942); FOREVER AND A DAY(1943); LASSIE, COME HOME(1943); MEANEST MAN IN THE WORLD, THE(1943); BETWEEN TWO WORLDS(1944); KEYS OF THE KINGDOM, THE(1944); BEWITCHED(1945); DANGEROUS PARTNERS(1945); SHE WENT TO THE RACES(1945); OF HUMAN BONDAGE(1946); UNDERCURRENT(1946); GREEN DOLPHIN STREET(1947); LIFE WITH FATHER(1947); MIRACLE ON 34TH STREET, THE(1947); APARTMENT FOR PEGGY(1948); HILLS OF HOME(1948); CHALLENGE TO LASSIE(1949); FOR HEAVEN'S SAKE(1950); LOUISA(1950); MISTER 880(1950); PRETTY BABY(1950); WOMAN OF DISTINCTION, A(1950); PEKING EXPRESS(1951); BONZO GOES TO COLLEGE(1952); LES MISERABLES(1952); SALLY AND SAINT ANNE(1952); SOMETHING FOR THE BIRDS(1952); BIGAMIST,THE(1953); MR. SCOUTMASTER(1953); STUDENT PRINCE, THE(1954); THEM!(1954); BAR SINISTER, THE(1955); TROUBLE WITH HARRY, THE(1955); CALABUCH(1956, Span./Ital.)
Misc. Silents
SKIN GAME, THE(1920, Brit.); UNMARRIED(1920, Brit.)
Tadeusz Gwiazdowski
KANAL(1961, Pol.)
Jack Gwillan
SINK THE BISMARCK!(1960, Brit.)
David Gwillim
ISLAND AT THE TOP OF THE WORLD, THE(1974)
Jack Gwillim
PURSUIT OF THE GRAF SPEE(1957, Brit.); ONE THAT GOT AWAY, THE(1958, Brit.); CIRCUS OF HORRORS(1960, Brit.); FLAME OVER INDIA(1960, Brit.); SENTENCED FOR LIFE(1960, Brit.); MIDSUMMERS NIGHT'S DREAM, A(1961, Czech); SWORD OF SHERWOOD FOREST(1961, Brit.); IN SEARCH OF THE CASTAWAYS(1962, Brit.); LAWRENCE OF ARABIA(1962, Brit.); LISA(1962, Brit.); JASON AND THE ARGONAUTS(1963, Brit.); RIVALS, THE(1963, Brit.); BOY TEN FEET TALL, A(1965, Brit.); CURSE OF THE MUMMY'S TOMB, THE(1965, Brit.); PUSSYCAT ALLEY(1965, Brit.); MAN FOR ALL SEASONS, A(1966, Brit.); KISS THE GIRLS AND MAKE THEM DIE(1967, U.S./Ital.); BATTLE OF BRITAIN, THE(1969, Brit.); BUSHBABY, THE(1970); CROMWELL(1970, Brit.); PATTON(1970); CLASH OF THE TITANS(1981)
Ifor Ab Gwilym
1984
YR ALCOHOLIG LION(1984, Brit.), m
Mike Gwilym
HOPSCOTCH(1980); PRIEST OF LOVE(1981, Brit.); VENOM(1982, Brit.)
Robert Gwilym
EXPERIENCE PREFERRED... BUT NOT ESSENTIAL(1983, Brit.)
Edith Gwinn
HOT TOMORROWS(1978)
Maggie Gwinn
1984
MASS APPEAL(1984)
Alfred Gwyn
DEVIL'S MESSENGER, THE(1962 U.S./Swed.), m
Michael Gwynn
DOCTOR'S DILEMMA, THE(1958, Brit.); DUNKIRK(1958, Brit.); REVENGE OF FRANKENSTEIN, THE(1958, Brit.); SECRET PLACE, THE(1958, Brit.); NEVER TAKE CANDY FROM A STRANGER(1961, Brit.); QUESTION 7(1961, U.S./Ger.); BARABBAS(1962, Ital.); WHAT A CARVE UP!(1962, Brit.); CLEOPATRA(1963); JASON AND THE ARGONAUTS(1963, Brit.); FALL OF THE ROMAN EMPIRE, THE(1964); SOME PEOPLE(1964, Brit.); HAVING A WILD WEEKEND(1965, Brit.); CROWNING GIFT, THE(1967, Brit.); DEADLY BEES,THE(1967, Brit.); SCARS OF DRACULA, THE(1970, Brit.); VIRGIN SOLDIERS, THE(1970, Brit.)
Anne Gwynne
LITTLE ACCIDENT(1939); OKLAHOMA FRONTIER(1939); UNEXPECTED FATHER(1939); BAD MAN FROM RED BUTTE(1940); BLACK FRIDAY(1940); FRAMED(1940); GIVE US WINGS(1940); HONEYMOON DEFERRED(1940); MAN FROM MONTREAL, THE(1940); SANDY IS A LADY(1940); SPRING PARADE(1940); BLACK CAT, THE(1941); DON'T GET PERSONAL(1941); MELODY LANE(1941); MOB TOWN(1941); NICE GIRL?(1941); ROAD AGENT(1941); TIGHT SHOES(1941); WASHINGTON MELODRAMA(1941); BROADWAY(1942); JAIL HOUSE BLUES(1942); MEN OF TEXAS(1942); RIDE 'EM COWBOY(1942); SIN TOWN(1942); STRANGE CASE OF DR. RX, THE(1942); YOU'RE TELLING ME(1942); FRONTIER BADMEN(1943); TOP MAN(1943); WE'VE NEVER BEEN LICKED(1943); BABES ON SWING STREET(1944); HOUSE OF FRANKENSTEIN(1944); LADIES COURAGEOUS(1944); MOON OVER LAS VEGAS(1944); MURDER IN THE BLUE ROOM(1944); SOUTH OF DIXIE(1944); WEIRD WOMAN(1944); FEAR(1946); GLASS ALIBI, THE(1946); I RING DOORBELLS(1946); DICK TRACY MEETS GRUESOME(1947); GHOST GOES WILD, THE(1947); KILLER DILL(1947); ENCHANTED VALLEY, THE(1948); PANHANDLE(1948); ARSON, INC.(1949); BLAZING SUN, THE(1950); CALL OF THE KLONDIKE(1950); KING OF THE BULLWHIP(1950); BREAKDOWN(1953); PHANTOM OF THE JUNGLE(1955); TEENAGE MONSTER(1958); ADAM AT 6 A.M.(1970)
Dorothy Gwynne
Misc. Silents
YELLOW STREAK, A(1915)
Fred Gwynne
ON THE WATERFRONT(1954); MUNSTER, GO HOME(1966); LUNA(1979, Ital.); SIMON(1980); SO FINE(1981)
1984
COTTON CLUB, THE(1984)
Misc. Talkies
MYSTERIOUS STRANGER(1982)

Jack Gwynne
MODEL WIFE(1941)
Mary Gwynne
STRIKE ME PINK(1936)
Michael Gwynne
RUNAWAY BUS, THE(1954, Brit.); VILLAGE OF THE DAMNED(1960, Brit.)
Michael C. Gwynne
PAYDAY(1972); HARRY IN YOUR POCKET(1973); TERMINAL MAN, THE(1974); SPECIAL DELIVERY(1976); BUTCH AND SUNDANCE: THE EARLY DAYS(1979); RAISE THE TITANIC(1980, Brit.); HARRY TRACY–DESPERADO(1982, Can.); THRESHOLD(1983, Can.)
Olga Gwynne
MEET MR. LUCIFER(1953, Brit.)
Peter Gwynne
DOVE, THE(1974, Brit.); SIDECAR RACERS(1975, Aus.); RIDE A WILD PONY(1976, U.S./Aus.); TIM(1981, Aus.)
Rori Gwynne
HOW SWEET IT IS(1968)
Tarna Gwynne
GENTLE TOUCH, THE(1956, Brit.)
Geoffrey Gwyther
Misc. Silents
RED ACES(1929, Brit.)
Guy Gy-Mas
MAN OF EVIL(1948, Brit.)
Laszlo Gyarfas
Misc. Silents
PAUL STREET BOYS(1929)
Thelma Gyath
WITHOUT RESERVATIONS(1946)
Agi Gyenes
JUST FOR THE HELL OF IT(1968)
Misc. Talkies
JUST FOR THE HELL OF IT(1968)
Magda Gyenes
1984
UNFAITHFULLY YOURS(1984)
Arpad Gyenge
DIALOGUE(1967, Hung.)
Sven Gyldmark
REPTILICUS(1962, U.S./Den.), m, md; SCANDAL IN DENMARK(1970, Den.), m
Ann-Marie Gyllen
MAKE WAY FOR LILA(1962, Swed./Ger.)
Marianne Gyllenhammar
NIGHT IS MY FUTURE(1962, Swed.)
Ann-Marie Gyllenspetz
BRINK OF LIFE(1960, Swed.)
Christer Gynge
GLADIATORS, THE(1970, Swed.)
Denise Gyngell
DARWIN ADVENTURE, THE(1972, Brit.)
Misc. Talkies
ZOO ROBBERY(1973, Brit.)
Michael Gyngell
DARWIN ADVENTURE, THE(1972, Brit.)
Paul Gyngell
DARWIN ADVENTURE, THE(1972, Brit.)
Misc. Talkies
ZOO ROBBERY(1973, Brit.)
Ketty Gyni
BAREFOOT BATTALION, THE(1954, Gr.)
Emmy Gynt
Misc. Silents
L'INVITATION AU VOYAGE(1927, Fr.)
Greta Gynt
LAST CURTAIN, THE(1937, Brit.); SECOND BEST BED(1937, Brit.); LAST BARRICADE, THE(1938, Brit.); SEXTON BLAKE AND THE HOODED TERROR(1938, Brit.); ARSENAL STADIUM MYSTERY, THE(1939, Brit.); MIDDLE WATCH, THE(1939, Brit.); SHE COULDN'T SAY NO(1939, Brit.); TOO DANGEROUS TO LIVE(1939, Brit.); BULLDOG SEES IT THROUGH(1940, Brit.); CROOKS TOUR(1940, Brit.); HUMAN MONSTER, THE(1940, Brit.); ROOM FOR TWO(1940, Brit.); TWO FOR DANGER(1940, Brit.); COMMON TOUCH, THE(1941, Brit.); AT DAWN WE DIE(1943, Brit.); IT'S THAT MAN AGAIN(1943, Brit.); MR. EMMANUEL(1945, Brit.); DEAR MURDERER(1947, Brit.); CALENDAR, THE(1948, Brit.); EASY MONEY(1948, Brit.); MR. PERRIN AND MR. TRAILL(1948, Brit.); TAKE MY LIFE(1948, Brit.); LUCKY NICK CAIN(1951); SOLDIERS THREE(1951); I'M A STRANGER(1952, Brit.); WHISPERING SMITH VERSUS SCOTLAND YARD(1952, Brit.); MY HEART GOES CRAZY(1953, Brit.); RINGER, THE(1953, Brit.); THREE STEPS IN THE DARK(1953, Brit.); DESTINATION MILAN(1954, Brit.); DEVIL'S HARBOR(1954, Brit.); FORBIDDEN CARGO(1954, Brit.); LAST MOMENT, THE(1954, Brit.); SEE HOW THEY RUN(1955, Brit.); SHADOW OF THE EAGLE(1955, Brit.); SHE PLAYED WITH FIRE(1957, Brit.); STRANGE CASE OF DR. MANNING, THE(1958, Brit.); CROWNING TOUCH, THE(1959, Brit.); NAVY HEROES(1959, Brit.); WITNESS, THE(1959, Brit.); BLUEBEARD'S TEN HONEYMOONS(1960, Brit.); MY WIFE'S FAMILY(1962, Brit.); RUNAWAY, THE(1964, Brit.)
Misc. Talkies
BORN FOR TROUBLE(1955)
Greta Gynte
ROAD BACK,THE(1937)
Gyorgy Gyoffy
DIALOGUE(1967, Hung.)
Imre Gyongyossy
ADRIFT(1971, Czech.), w
1984
REVOLT OF JOB, THE(1984, Hung./Ger.), d, w
Gabriel E. Gyorffy
1984
UNFAITHFULLY YOURS(1984)

Laszlo Gyorgy
DIALOGUE(1967, Hung.); ROUND UP, THE(1969, Hung.)
Andras Gyorky
ANGI VERA(1980, Hung.), art d
Anna Gyory
TAKING OFF(1971)
Gypsy Band Gyula Howath
UNFINISHED SYMPHONY, THE(1953, Aust./Brit.)
Robert Gys
CRIME OF MONSIEUR LANGE, THE(1936, Fr.), set d; GYPSY FURY(1950, Fr.), set d; LOVE AND THE FRENCHWOMAN(1961, Fr.), art d
Adreevan Gysegham
CROMWELL(1970, Brit.)
Ladislav Gzela
LEMONADE JOE(1966, Czech.); SWEET LIGHT IN A DARK ROOM(1966, Czech.)
Olga Gzovskaya
Misc. Silents
WOMAN WITH A DAGGER(1916, USSR)
Olga Gzovskaya
Misc. Silents
BLOOD NEED NOT BE SPILLED(1917, USSR); HER SACRIFICE(1917, USSR)

H

Xuan Ha
HOA-BINH(1971, Fr.)

Minnie Ha Ha
Silents
MICKEY(1919)

Kaethe Haack
DAUGHTER OF EVIL(1930, Ger.); EMIL AND THE DETECTIVE(1931, Ger.); BEAUTIFUL ADVENTURE(1932, Ger.); CAPTAIN FROM KOEPENICK(1933, Ger.); ETERNAL LOVE(1960, Ger.)

Kate Haack
PEDESTRIAN, THE(1974, Ger.)

Kathe Haack
DAY AFTER THE DIVORCE, THE(1940, Ger.); DANIELLA BY NIGHT(1962, Fr/Ger.); INDECENT(1962, Ger.)
Misc. Silents
ALGOL(1920, Ger.)

Mortan Haack
COME SEPTEMBER(1961), cos; PLANET OF THE APES(1968), cos

Morton Haack
WILD HERITAGE(1958), cos; PLEASE DON'T EAT THE DAISIES(1960), cos; JUMBO(1962), cos; UNSINKABLE MOLLY BROWN, THE(1964), cos; WALK, DON'T RUN(1966), cos; WHAT'S THE MATTER WITH HELEN?(1971), cos

Bill Haade
CAGED(1950)

Bill "William" Haade
TIMBER QUEEN(1944)

William [L.] Haade
WELL-GROOMED BRIDE, THE(1946)

William Haade
SERGEANT YORK(; KID GALAHAD(1937); MISSING WITNESSES(1937); AMAZING DR. CLITTERHOUSE, THE(1938); DOWN ON THE FARM(1938); HE COULDN'T SAY NO(1938); HOLLYWOOD STADIUM MYSTERY(1938); IF I WERE KING(1938); INVISIBLE MENACE, THE(1938); SHADOWS OVER SHANGHAI(1938); SING YOU SINNERS(1938); TELEPHONE OPERATOR(1938); TEXANS, THE(1938); THREE COMRADES(1938); FULL CONFESSION(1939); GERONIMO(1939); ISLAND OF LOST MEN(1939); KID NIGHTINGALE(1939); NIGHT WORK(1939); RENO(1939); TOM SAWYER, DETECTIVE(1939); UNION PACIFIC(1939); UNMARRIED(1939); $1,000 A TOUCHDOWN(1939); BULLET CODE(1940); CHEROKEE STRIP(1940); EARL OF CHICAGO, THE(1940); GRAPES OF WRATH(1940); INVISIBLE STRIPES(1940); JOHNNY APOLLO(1940); KNUTE ROCKNE–ALL AMERICAN(1940); LILLIAN RUSSELL(1940); MAN FROM DAKOTA, THE(1940); NORTHWEST MOUNTED POLICE(1940); ONE CROWDED NIGHT(1940); SAINT'S DOUBLE TROUBLE, THE(1940); STAGE TO CHINO(1940); THEY DRIVE BY NIGHT(1940); WHO KILLED AUNT MAGGIE?(1940); AFFECTIONATELY YOURS(1941); CITADEL OF CRIME(1941); DANCE HALL(1941); DESERT BANDIT(1941); HONKY TONK(1941); IN OLD CHEYENNE(1941); KANSAS CYCLONE(1941); MAN HUNT(1941); PENALTY, THE(1941); PIRATES ON HORSEBACK(1941); RISE AND SHINE(1941); ROBIN HOOD OF THE PECOS(1941); ROUNDUP, THE(1941); SAILORS ON LEAVE(1941); SHEPHERD OF THE HILLS, THE(1941); UNFINISHED BUSINESS(1941); YOU'RE IN THE ARMY NOW(1941); DR. BROADWAY(1942); GENTLEMAN AFTER DARK, A(1942); HEART OF THE GOLDEN WEST(1942); HEART OF THE RIO GRANDE(1942); I MARRIED A WITCH(1942); ICELAND(1942); JACKASS MAIL(1942); JUKE GIRL(1942); JUST OFF BROADWAY(1942); MAN FROM CHEYENNE(1942); PITTSBURGH(1942); REAP THE WILD WIND(1942); RIGHT TO THE HEART(1942); SHEPHERD OF THE OZARKS(1942); SPOILERS, THE(1942); STAR SPANGLED RHYTHM(1942); TO THE SHORES OF TRIPOLI(1942); TORPEDO BOAT(1942); YOU'RE TELLING ME(1942); DANCING MASTERS, THE(1943); DAYS OF OLD CHEYENNE(1943); HANGMEN ALSO DIE(1943); SCREAM IN THE DARK, A(1943); SHE HAS WHAT IT TAKES(1943); SING A JINGLE(1943); SONG OF TEXAS(1943); THANK YOUR LUCKY STARS(1943); YOU'RE A LUCKY FELLOW, MR. SMITH(1943); BUFFALO BILL(1944); HERE COME THE WAVES(1944); MAN FROM FRISCO(1944); ROGER TOUHY, GANGSTER!(1944); SEVEN DAYS ASHORE(1944); SHERIFF OF LAS VEGAS(1944); YELLOW ROSE OF TEXAS, THE(1944); DAKOTA(1945); FALLEN ANGEL(1945); HONEYMOON AHEAD(1945); I'LL TELL THE WORLD(1945); NOB HILL(1945); PHANTOM OF THE PLAINS(1945); AFFAIRS OF GERALDINE(1946); GUY COULD CHANGE, A(1946); IN OLD SACRAMENTO(1946); LADY CHASER(1946); MY PAL TRIGGER(1946); SENTIMENTAL JOURNEY(1946); VALLEY OF THE ZOMBIES(1946); BIG TOWN AFTER DARK(1947); BUCK PRIVATES COME HOME(1947); DEEP VALLEY(1947); DOWN TO EARTH(1947); EXPOSED(1947); IT HAPPENED IN BROOKLYN(1947); MAGIC TOWN(1947); PILGRIM LADY, THE(1947); SECRET LIFE OF WALTER MITTY, THE(1947); TROUBLE WITH WOMEN, THE(1947); UNCONQUERED(1947); UNDER COLORADO SKIES(1947); WEB, THE(1947); WHERE THERE'S LIFE(1947); GOOD SAM(1948); INSIDE STORY, THE(1948); KEY LARGO(1948); LAST OF THE WILD HORSES(1948); LULU BELLE(1948); MICHAEL O'HALLORAN(1948); NIGHT HAS A THOUSAND EYES(1948); SHAGGY(1948); SONG IS BORN, A(1948); STRIKE IT RICH(1948); TAP ROOTS(1948); ALASKA PATROL(1949); FOUNTAINHEAD, THE(1949); GAL WHO TOOK THE WEST, THE(1949); NIGHT UNTO NIGHT(1949); SCENE OF THE CRIME(1949); WYOMING BANDIT, THE(1949); FATHER OF THE BRIDE(1950); JOE PALOOKA IN THE SQUARED CIRCLE(1950); NO MAN OF HER OWN(1950); OLD FRONTIER, THE(1950); OUTCAST OF BLACK MESA(1950); TRIAL WITHOUT JURY(1950); WOMAN ON PIER 13, THE(1950); BUCKAROO SHERIFF OF TEXAS(1951); LEAVE IT TO THE MARINES(1951); OH! SUSANNA(1951); RAWHIDE(1951); SANTA FE(1951); SEA HORNET, THE(1951); STOP THAT CAB(1951); THREE DESPERATE MEN(1951); YANK IN KOREA, A(1951); CARSON CITY(1952); HERE COME THE NELSONS(1952); KANSAS CITY CONFIDENTIAL(1952); RANCHO NOTORIOUS(1952); SKIRTS AHOY!(1952); RED RIVER SHORE(1953); JUBILEE TRAIL(1954); SILVER LODE(1954); UNTAMED HEIRESS(1954); ABBOTT AND COSTELLO MEET THE KEYSTONE KOPS(1955); SPOILERS OF THE FOREST(1957)

Romy Haag
DIE HAMBURGER KRANKHEIT(1979, Ger./Fr.)

Walter Haag
KING IN SHADOW(1961, Ger.), art d; ROSES FOR THE PROSECUTOR(1961, Ger.), art d

Haaga/Jacobsen
BUS IS COMING, THE(1971), art d

Margarethe Haagen
HELP I'M INVISIBLE(1952, Ger.)

Renee Haal
KITTY FOYLE(1940); HURRY, CHARLIE, HURRY(1941); HIGHWAYS BY NIGHT(1942)

Renee Haal "Godfrey"
UNEXPECTED UNCLE(1941)

Rolv Haan
CHILDREN OF GOD'S EARTH(1983, Norwegian), ph

Charles F. Haas
HER ADVENTUROUS NIGHT(1946), p

Charles Haas
I MET HIM IN PARIS(1937); MOONRISE(1948), p, w; SCREAMING EAGLES(1956), d; SHOWDOWN AT ABILENE(1956), d; STAR IN THE DUST(1956), d; SUMMER LOVE(1958), d; WILD HERITAGE(1958), d; BEAT GENERATION, THE(1959), d; BIG OPERATOR, THE(1959), d; GIRLS' TOWN(1959), d; PLATINUM HIGH SCHOOL(1960), d

Charlie Haas
TEX(1982), a, w

Deanna Haas
DEVONSVILLE TERROR, THE(1983)

Dolly Haas
DOLLY GETS AHEAD(1931, Ger.); TREMENDOUSLY RICH MAN, A(1932, Ger.); GIRLS WILL BE BOYS(1934, Brit.); BROKEN BLOSSOMS(1936, Brit.); SPY OF NAPOLEON(1939, Brit.); I CONFESS(1953)

Dorothy Haas
UNFINISHED BUSINESS(1941)

Ed Haas
DISORDERLY ORDERLY, THE(1964), w

Elizabeth Haas
1984
VAMPING(1984), cos
Silents
FLAMES OF CHANCE, THE(1918), w

Florence Haas
Silents
SILVER WINGS(1922)

Gene Haas
ROLLIN' HOME TO TEXAS(1941)

Hans Haas
ROMMEL'S TREASURE(1962, Ital.), ph

Horst A. Haas
SINAI COMMANDOS: THE STORY OF THE SIX DAY WAR(1968, Israel/Ger.), m

Hugh Haas
PRINCESS AND THE PIRATE, THE(1944); PRIVATE AFFAIRS OF BEL AMI, THE(1947)

Hugo Haas
SKELETON ON HORSEBACK(1940, Czech.), a, w, p&d; DAYS OF GLORY(1944); STRANGE AFFAIR(1944); SUMMER STORM(1944); BELL FOR ADANO, A(1945); DAKOTA(1945); JEALOUSY(1945); WHAT NEXT, CORPORAL HARGROVE?(1945); HOLIDAY IN MEXICO(1946); TWO SMART PEOPLE(1946); FIESTA(1947); FOXES OF HARROW, THE(1947); MERTON OF THE MOVIES(1947); NORTHWEST OUTPOST(1947); CASBAH(1948); MY GIRL TISA(1948); FIGHTING KENTUCKIAN, THE(1949); KING SOLOMON'S MINES(1950); VENDETTA(1950); GIRL ON THE BRIDGE, THE(1951), a, p&d, w; PICKUP(1951), a, p&d, w; STRANGE FASCINATION(1952), a, p,d&w; ONE GIRL'S CONFESSION(1953), a, p,d&w; THY NEIGHBOR'S WIFE(1953), a, p,d&w; BAIT(1954), a, p&d; OTHER WOMAN, THE(1954), a, p,d&w; HOLD BACK TOMORROW(1955), p,d&w; TENDER HEARTS(1955), a, p,d&w; EDGE OF HELL(1956), a, p,d,&w; HIT AND RUN(1957), a, p,d&w; LIZZIE(1957), a, d; BORN TO BE LOVED(1959), a, p,d&w; NIGHT OF THE QUARTER MOON(1959), d; PARADISE ALLEY(1962), a, p,d&w

Ingrid Haas
MONSTER OF LONDON CITY, THE(1967, Ger.), makeup

Ivan Haas
OTHER WOMAN, THE(1954)

Joanne Haas
REIVERS, THE(1969), cos; OTHER, THE(1972), cos; EMPIRE OF THE ANTS(1977), cos

Leonard Haas
1984
PREPPIES(1984)

Lukas Haas
TESTAMENT(1983)

Robert H. Haas
STORY OF LOUIS PASTEUR, THE(1936), art d

Robert Haas
CROONER(1932), art d; SILVER DOLLAR(1932), art d; THREE ON A MATCH(1932), art d; WINNER TAKE ALL(1932), art d; BUREAU OF MISSING PERSONS(1933), art d; FRISCO JENNY(1933), art d; HARD TO HANDLE(1933), art d; LADY KILLER(1933), art d; LITTLE GIANT, THE(1933), art d; PICTURE SNATCHER(1933), art d; WORLD CHANGES, THE(1933), art d; DAMES(1934), art d; DARK HAZARD(1934), art d; FRIENDS OF MR. SWEENEY(1934), art d; GENTLEMEN ARE BORN(1934), art d; HI, NELLIE!(1934), art d; HOUSEWIFE(1934), art d; KEY, THE(1934), art d; MODERN HERO, A(1934), art d; REGISTERED NURSE(1934), art d; SWEET ADELINE(1935), art d; SWEET MUSIC(1935), art d; SNOWED UNDER(1936), art d; THREE MEN ON A HORSE(1936), art d; BLACK LEGION, THE(1937), art d; EVER SINCE EVE(1937), art d; HOLLYWOOD HOTEL(1937), art d; KING AND THE CHORUS GIRL, THE(1937), art d; MR. DODD TAKES THE AIR(1937), art d; PERFECT SPECIMEN, THE(1937), art d; PRINCE AND THE PAUPER, THE(1937), art d; THEY WON'T FORGET(1937), art d; ANGELS WITH DIRTY FACES(1938), art d; GOLD DIGGERS IN PARIS(1938), art d; JEZEBEL(1938), art d; DARK VICTORY(1939), art d; OLD MAID, THE(1939), art d; KNUTE ROCKNE–ALL AMERICAN(1940), art d; CITY, FOR CONQUEST(1941), art d; DIVE BOMBER(1941), art d;

MALTESE FALCON, THE(1941), art d; STRAWBERRY BLONDE, THE(1941), art d; ACROSS THE PACIFIC(1942), art d; GAY SISTERS, THE(1942), art d; IN THIS OUR LIFE(1942), art d; JUKE GIRL(1942), art d; MAN WHO CAME TO DINNER, THE(1942), art d; NOW, VOYAGER(1942), art d; EDGE OF DARKNESS(1943), art d; JANIE(1944), art d; MR. SKEFFINGTON(1944), art d; UNCERTAIN GLORY(1944), art d; ROUGHLY SPEAKING(1945), art d; STOLEN LIFE, A(1946), art d; VOICE OF THE TURTLE, THE(1947), art d; JOHNNY BELINDA(1948), art d; MY GIRL TISA(1948), art d; INSPECTOR GENERAL, THE(1949), art d; JOHN LOVES MARY(1949), art d; MY DREAM IS YOURS(1949), art d; DAMNED DON'T CRY, THE(1950), art d; GLASS MENAGERIE, THE(1950), art d

Silents

WHITE SISTER, THE(1923), art d

Robert M. Haas

SHE GOES TO WAR(1929), art d; HELL HARBOR(1930), art d; GOOSE AND THE GANDER, THE(1935), art d; I FOUND STELLA PARISH(1935), art d; LIVING ON VELVET(1935), art d; OIL FOR THE LAMPS OF CHINA(1935), art d; PAGE MISS GLORY(1935), art d; SHIPMATES FOREVER(1935), art d; MURDER OF DR. HARRIGAN, THE(1936), art d; DEVOTION(1946), art d

Walter Haas

Silents

MANHATTAN KNIGHTS(1928), ph

Waltraut Haas

APRIL 1, 2000(1953, Aust.); BEGGAR STUDENT, THE(1958, Ger.)

Charles Haase

HALF-WAY HOUSE, THE(1945, Brit.), ed

Gunter Haase

ESCAPE TO BERLIN(1962, U.S./Switz./Ger.), ph

Henjo Haase

DAY THAT SHOOK THE WORLD, THE(1977, Yugo./Czech.)

John Haase

DEAR BRIGETTE(1965), w; PETULIA(1968, U.S./Brit.), w

Louis Haase

MAN HUNT(1936), ed

Rod Haase

HERO AT LARGE(1980); HISTORY OF THE WORLD, PART 1(1981)

O.L. Haavik

SLENDER THREAD, THE(1965)

Bohumil Haba

EMPEROR AND THE GOLEM, THE(1955, Czech.), ph

Mohammed Habachi

LAWRENCE OF ARABIA(1962, Brit.)

Habanera Sextette

HELL HARBOR(1930)

Rose Habart

WHO IS HOPE SCHUYLER?(1942)

Cox Habbema

1984

QUESTION OF SILENCE(1984, Neth.)

Eddy Habbema

SOLDIER OF ORANGE(1979, Dutch)

Mary Habberfield

BELLS GO DOWN, THE(1943, Brit.), ed

John Habberton

Silents

HELEN'S BABIES(1924), w

Hans Habe

CROSS OF LORRAINE, THE(1943), w; DEVIL'S AGENT, THE(1962, Brit.), w

Roswitha Habedank

EMIL AND THE DETECTIVES(1964)

Joseph Habelton

Misc. Silents

WASTED YEARS, THE(1916)

Alessandro Haber

CHINA IS NEAR(1968, Ital.)

1984

BASILEUS QUARTET(1984, Ital.)

David Haber

CORNBREAD, EARL AND ME(1975), art d; DRIVER, THE(1978), art d; ONLY WHEN I LAUGH(1981), art d; MAX DUGAN RETURNS(1983), art d

David M. Haber

UP THE SANDBOX(1972), set d; CAPRICORN ONE(1978), art d; LEGEND OF THE LONE RANGER, THE(1981), art d; BEAST WITHIN, THE(1982), prod d

1984

ICE PIRATES, THE(1984), art d

Holly Haber

HARD COUNTRY(1981)

Joyce Haber

CONQUEST OF THE PLANET OF THE APES(1972)

Karen Haber

1984

WILD LIFE, THE(1984)

Leonard Haber

HOT STUFF(1979)

Mark Haber

SOMEBODY KILLED HER HUSBAND(1978)

Martin Haber

LUGGAGE OF THE GODS(1983)

Nicholas S. Haber

Misc. Silents

SYRIAN IMMIGRANT, THE(1921)

Paul Haber

FEAR NO EVIL(1981)

Sandy Haber

MASK, THE(1961, Can.), w

Sheldon Haber

RAGING BULL(1980), art d

Abe Haberman

MAN WHO CHEATED HIMSELF, THE(1951), makeup; LONELYHEARTS(1958), makeup; MUNSTER, GO HOME(1966), makeup

Linda Haberman

FAN, THE(1981)

Emil Habib

HOT MONTH OF AUGUST, THE(1969, Gr.), ed

Nat Habib

HANKY-PANKY(1982)

Ralph Habib

SECRETS D'ALCOVE(1954, Fr./Ital.), d; DOCTORS, THE(1956, Fr.), d

Habiba

$100 A NIGHT(1968, Ger.)

1984

MISUNDERSTOOD(1984)

Habibi

PASSION HOLIDAY(1963)

Matthias Habich

COUP DE GRACE(1978, Ger./Fr.)

Hans Habietinek

MIRACLE OF THE WHITE STALLIONS(1963)

Jim Habif

MEAT CLEAVER MASSACRE(1977)

Joe Hachey

OVER THE HILL(1931); AMATEUR DADDY(1932)

Cristina Hachuel

SCARAB(1982, U.S./Span.)

Herman Hack

ONE WAY TRAIL, THE(1931); WHEN A MAN RIDES ALONE(1933); RANDY RIDES ALONE(1934); LAWLESS FRONTIER, THE(1935); PARADISE CANYON(1935); RAINBOW VALLEY(1935); TOMBSTONE TERROR(1935); WESTERN FRONTIER(1935); TOLL OF THE DESERT(1936); GUN LORDS OF STIRRUP BASIN(1937); IDAHO KID, THE(1937); RANGERS STEP IN, THE(1937); SING, COWBOY, SING(1937); SINGING OUTLAW(1937); SUNDOWN SAUNDERS(1937); GUN LAW(1938); PHANTOM RANGER(1938); WESTERN TRAILS(1938); NEW FRONTIER(1939); SILVER ON THE SAGE(1939); WESTERN CARAVANS(1939); MELODY RANCH(1940); PHANTOM RANCHER(1940); PIONEERS OF THE WEST(1940); RANGER AND THE LADY, THE(1940); RIDERS FROM NOWHERE(1940); SHERIFF OF TOMBSTONE(1941); SINGING HILL, THE(1941); SUNSET IN WYOMING(1941); WRANGLER'S ROOST(1941); BILLY THE KID TRAPPED(1942); MISSOURI OUTLAW, A(1942); PHANTOM PLAINSMEN, THE(1942); CALLING WILD BILL ELLIOTT(1943); LOST CANYON(1943); RIDERS OF THE DEADLINE(1943); WESTERN CYCLONE(1943); DEVIL RIDERS(1944); SAN ANTONIO KID, THE(1944); SHERIFF OF SUNDOWN(1944); CHEROKEE FLASH, THE(1945); PRAIRIE RUSTLERS(1945); TRAIL OF KIT CARSON(1945); HOMESTEADERS OF PARADISE VALLEY(1947); MARAUDERS, THE(1947); UNDER THE TONTO RIM(1947); SON OF GOD'S COUNTRY(1948); VALIANT HOMBRE, THE(1948); GUN LAW JUSTICE(1949); POWDER RIVER RUSTLERS(1949); COW TOWN(1950); OVER THE BORDER(1950); DESERT OF LOST MEN(1951); LONGHORN, THE(1951); PACK TRAIN(1953)

Peter Hack

GOOSE GIRL, THE(1967, Ger.)

Shelley Hack

ANNIE HALL(1977); IF EVER I SEE YOU AGAIN(1978); TIME AFTER TIME(1979, Brit.); KING OF COMEDY, THE(1983)

Hal Hackady

LET'S ROCK(1958), w; SENIOR PROM(1958), w; HEY, LET'S TWIST!(1961), w; TWO TICKETS TO PARIS(1962), w

Jerry Hackady

LET'S ROCK(1958)

George Hackathorne

SQUALL, THE(1929); CAPTAIN OF THE GUARD(1930); HIDE-OUT, THE(1930); LONESOME TRAIL, THE(1930); FLAMING GUNS(1933); MY MOTHER(1933); MAGNIFICENT OBSESSION(1935); STRANGE WIVES(1935); SHOW BOAT(1936); I COVER CHINATOWN(1938); GONE WITH THE WIND(1939)

Silents

AMARILLY OF CLOTHESLINE ALLEY(1918); HUCK AND TOM(1918); SPLENDID SIN, THE(1919); LAST OF THE MOHICANS, THE(1920); HIGH HEELS(1921); SIN OF MARTHA QUEED, THE(1921); WHAT DO MEN WANT?(1921); NOTORIETY(1922); MERRY-GO-ROUND(1923); JUDGMENT OF THE STORM(1924); SURGING SEAS(1924); HIS MASTER'S VOICE(1925); NIGHT LIFE OF NEW YORK(1925); CHEATERS(1927)

Misc. Silents

TOM SAWYER(1917); SUE OF THE SOUTH(1919); TO PLEASE ONE WOMAN(1920); LIGHT IN THE CLEARING, THE(1921); LITTLE MINISTER, THE(1921); GRAY DAWN, THE(1922); HUMAN HEARTS(1922); WORLDLY MADONNA, THE(1922); HUMAN WRECKAGE(1923); TURMOIL, THE(1924); CAPITAL PUNISHMENT(1925); WANDERING FIRES(1925); HIGHBINDERS, THE(1926); SEA URCHIN, THE(1926, Brit.); PAYING THE PRICE(1927); SALLY'S SHOULDERS(1928); TIP-OFF, THE(1929)

A.W. Hackel

DEMON FOR TROUBLE, A(1934), p; ALIAS JOHN LAW(1935), p; BETWEEN MEN(1935), p; BRANDED A COWARD(1935), p; COURAGEOUS AVENGER, THE(1935), p; KID COURAGEOUS(1935), p; NO MAN'S MAN(1935), p; RIDER OF THE LAW, THE(1935), p; SMOKEY SMITH(1935), p; TOMBSTONE TERROR(1935), p; TRAIL OF TERROR(1935), p; WESTERN JUSTICE(1935), p; CAVALRY(1936), p; CROOKED TRAIL, THE(1936), p; EVERYMAN'S LAW(1936), p; KID RANGER, THE(1936), p; LAST OF THE WARRENS, THE(1936), p; LAW RIDES, THE(1936), p; UNDERCOVER MAN(1936), p; ARIZONA GUNFIGHTER(1937), p; BAR Z BAD MEN(1937), p; BOOTHILL BRIGADE(1937), p; BORDER PHANTOM(1937), p; DESERT PHANTOM(1937), p; DOOMED AT SUNDOWN(1937), p; GAMBLING TERROR, THE(1937), p; GUN LORDS OF STIRRUP BASIN(1937), p; GUN RANGER, THE(1937), p; GUNS IN THE DARK(1937), p; LAWLESS LAND(1937), p; LAWMAN IS BORN, A(1937), p; LIGHTNIN' CRANDALL(1937), p; RED ROPE, THE(1937), p; RIDIN' THE LONE TRAIL(1937), p; ROGUE OF THE RANGE(1937), p; SUNDOWN SAUNDERS(1937), p; TRAIL OF VENGEANCE(1937), p; TRUSTED OUTLAW, THE(1937), p; COLORADO KID(1938), p; DESERT PATROL(1938), p; DURANGO VALLEY RAIDERS(1938), p; FEUD MAKER(1938), p; PAROLED–TO DIE(1938), p; THUNDER IN THE DESERT(1938), p; AM I GUILTY?(1940), p; BORROWED HERO(1941), p; MURDER BY INVITATION(1941), p; LIVING GHOST, THE(1942), p; MAN WITH TWO LIVES, THE(1942), p; ONE THRILLING NIGHT(1942), p; PHANTOM KILLER(1942), p; GENTLE GANGSTER, A(1943), p; SHADOW OF SUSPICION(1944), p; STRANGE HOLIDAY(1945), p

R.W. Hackel
VALLEY OF THE LAWLESS(1936), p
Siegrid Hackenberg
CONFESS DR. CORDA(1960, Ger.)
David Hacker
IT AIN'T HAY(1943)
Joseph Hacker
MR. RICCO(1975)
Michael Hacker
ONE FROM THE HEART(1982)
Slim Hacker
SIX-GUN RHYTHM(1939)
Hacker Duo
HI' YA, SAILOR(1943)
Hans Hackermann
CIRCLE OF DECEIT(1982, Fr./Ger.)
Walter Hacket
HYDE PARK CORNER(1935, Brit.), w
Joachim Hackethal
TIN DRUM, THE(1979, Ger./Fr./Yugo./Pol.)
John Hacketl
TALES OF TERROR(1962)
Albert Hackett
WHOOPEE(1930); UP POPS THE DEVIL(1931), w; PENTHOUSE(1933), w; SECRET OF MADAME BLANCHE, THE(1933), w; FUGITIVE LOVERS(1934), w; HIDE-OUT(1934), w; THIN MAN, THE(1934), w; AH, WILDERNESS!(1935), w; NAUGHTY MARIETTA(1935), w; AFTER THE THIN MAN(1936), w; ROSE MARIE(1936), w; FIREFLY, THE(1937), w; THANKS FOR THE MEMORY(1938), w; ANOTHER THIN MAN(1939), w; SOCIETY LAWYER(1939), w; HITLER GANG, THE(1944), w; LADY IN THE DARK(1944), w; IT'S A WONDERFUL LIFE(1946), w; VIRGINIAN, THE(1946), w; EASTER PARADE(1948), w; PIRATE, THE(1948), w; SUMMER HOLI-DAY(1948), w; IN THE GOOD OLD SUMMERTIME(1949), w; FATHER OF THE BRIDE(1950), w; FATHER'S LITTLE DIVIDEND(1951), w; TOO YOUNG TO KISS(1951), w; GIVE A GIRL A BREAK(1953), w; LONG, LONG TRAILER, THE(1954), w; SEVEN BRIDES FOR SEVEN BROTHERS(1954), w; GABY(1956), w; CERTAIN SMILE, A(1958), w; DIARY OF ANNE FRANK, THE(1959), w; FIVE FINGER EXER-CISE(1962), w
Silents
ANNE OF GREEN GABLES(1919); AWAY GOES PRUDENCE(1920); MOLLY O'(1921); DARLING OF THE RICH, THE(1923)
Arleen Hackett
Misc. Silents
IN THE PALACE OF THE KING(1915)
Buddy Hackett
WALKING MY BABY BACK HOME(1953); FIREMAN SAVE MY CHILD(1954); GOD'S LITTLE ACRE(1958); ALL HANDS ON DECK(1961); EVERYTHING'S DUCK-Y(1961); MUSIC MAN, THE(1962); WONDERFUL WORLD OF THE BROTHERS ERIMM, THE(1962); IT'S A MAD, MAD, MAD, MAD WORLD(1963); MUSCLE BEACH PARTY(1964); GOLDEN HEAD, THE(1965, Hung., U.S.); LOVE BUG, THE(1968); GOOD GUYS AND THE BAD GUYS, THE(1969); LOOSE SHOES(1980)
1984
HEY BABE!(1984, Can.)
Dotti Hackett
HOLLYWOOD BARN DANCE(1947)
Earl Hackett
ROARIN' GUNS(1936)
Florence Hackett
HOUSE OF WOMEN(1962), cos; LOOKING FOR LOVE(1964), cos; MARLOWE(1969), cos; SUPPORT YOUR LOCAL SHERIFF(1969), cos; ZIGZAG(1970), cos
Silents
CLIMBERS, THE(1915); EVIDENCE(1915)
Gillian Hackett
1984
ANNE DEVLIN(1984, Ireland)
Hal Hackett
LOVE LAUGHS AT ANDY HARDY(1946); CAMPUS HONEYMOON(1948); SUM-MER HOLIDAY(1948)
James K. Hackett
Silents
PRIDE OF JENNICO, THE(1914), w
Misc. Silents
WALLS OF JERICHO, THE(1914), d; GREATER SINNER, THE(1919)
Jay Hackett
PUBERTY BLUES(1983, Aus.)
Joan Hackett
GROUP, THE(1966); ASSIGNMENT TO KILL(1968); WILL PENNY(1968); SUPPORT YOUR LOCAL SHERIFF(1969); RIVALS(1972); LAST OF SHEILA, THE(1973); TERMI-NAL MAN, THE(1974); MACKINTOSH & T.J.(1975); TREASURE OF MATECUM-BE(1976); ONE-TRICK PONY(1980); ONLY WHEN I LAUGH(1981); ESCAPE ARTIST, THE(1982)
John Hackett
BACK DOOR TO HELL(1964), a, w; FLIGHT TO FURY(1966, U.S./Phil.); RIDE IN THE WHIRLWIND(1966); HARRY AND WALTER GO TO NEW YORK(1976)
Misc. Talkies
FORTRESS OF THE DEAD(1965)
Jonathan Hackett
LADY VANISHES, THE(1980, Brit.)
Karl Hackett
FRISCO KID(1935); CAVALRY(1936); DOWN TO THE SEA(1936); LIGHTNING BILL CARSON(1936); LION'S DEN, THE(1936); STORMY TRAILS(1936); TRAITOR, THE(1936); ARIZONA GUNFIGHTER(1937); BORDER PHANTOM(1937); DESERT PHANTOM(1937); FIREFLY, THE(1937); GOLD RACKET, THE(1937); GUN LORDS OF STIRRUP BASIN(1937); HAPPY-GO-LUCKY(1937); LAW AND LEAD(1937); RED ROPE, THE(1937); ROOTIN' TOOTIN' RHYTHM(1937); SING, COWBOY, SING(1937); TEX RIDES WITH THE BOY SCOUTS(1937); TEXAS TRAIL(1937); TRAIL OF VENGEANCE(1937); WHISTLING BULLETS(1937); COLORADO KID(1938); DOWN IN ARKANSAW(1938); DURANGO VALLEY RAIDERS(1938); FEUD MAKER(1938); FRONTIER TOWN(1938); PAROLED–TO DIE(1938); PHANTOM RANGER(1938); RANGER'S ROUNDUP, THE(1938); ROLLIN' PLAINS(1938); SONGS AND BUL-LETS(1938); STARLIGHT OVER TEXAS(1938); UTAH TRAIL(1938); WHERE THE

BUFFALO ROAM(1938); LURE OF THE WASTELAND(1939); SUNDOWN ON THE PRAIRIE(1939); CHIP OF THE FLYING U(1940); FRONTIER CRUSADER(1940); MAN FROM MONTREAL, THE(1940); MURDER ON THE YUKON(1940); RANGE BUST-ERS, THE(1940); YUKON FLIGHT(1940); BILLY THE KID IN SANTA FE(1941); BILLY THE KID'S RANGE WAR(1941); BOSS OF BULLION CITY(1941); DEATH VALLEY OUTLAWS(1941); JESSE JAMES AT BAY(1941); LONE RIDER IN GHOST TOWN, THE(1941); MAN FROM MONTANA(1941); OUTLAWS OF THE CHEROKEE TRAIL(1941); OUTLAWS OF THE RIO GRANDE(1941); PIONEERS, THE(1941); TEXAS MARSHAL, THE(1941); COME ON DANGER(1942); IN OLD CALIFOR-NIA(1942); JESSE JAMES, JR.(1942); LONE RIDER IN CHEYENNE, THE(1942); MISSOURI OUTLAW, A(1942); PHANTOM KILLER(1942); PIRATES OF THE PRAI-RIE(1942); PRAIRIE PALS(1942); RIDING THE WIND(1942); ROLLING DOWN THE GREAT DIVIDE(1942); SONS OF THE PIONEERS(1942); TEXAS MAN HUNT(1942); WESTERN MAIL(1942); AVENGING RIDER, THE(1943); BORDERTOWN GUN-FIGHTERS(1943); KID RIDES AGAIN, THE(1943); LOST CANYON(1943); SAGE-BRUSH LAW(1943); THUNDERING TRAILS(1943); WESTERN CYCLONE(1943); WILD HORSE RUSTLERS(1943); WOLVES OF THE RANGE(1943); ARIZONA WHIRLWIND(1944); BRAND OF THE DEVIL(1944); CALIFORNIA JOE(1944); CODE OF THE PRAIRIE(1944); DEATH RIDES THE PLAINS(1944); DEATH VALLEY RANGERS(1944); MOJAVE FIREBRAND(1944); PINTO BANDIT, THE(1944); SONO-RA STAGECOACH(1944); THUNDERING GUN SLINGERS(1944); TUCSON RAID-ERS(1944); WESTWARD BOUND(1944); ENEMY OF THE LAW(1945); FRONTIER FUGITIVES(1945); HIS BROTHER'S GHOST(1945); LIGHTNING RAIDERS(1945); PRAIRIE RUSTLERS(1945); SHADOWS OF DEATH(1945); CANYON PASSAGE(1946); GENTLEMEN WITH GUNS(1946); GHOST OF HIDDEN VALLEY(1946); GUNMAN'S CODE(1946); LAWLESS BREED, THE(1946); OUTLAW OF THE PLAINS(1946); TER-RORS ON HORSEBACK(1946); FABULOUS TEXAN, THE(1947); MICHIGAN KID, THE(1947)
Misc. Talkies
BULLDOG COURAGE(1935); SIX-GUN TRAIL(1938); TAKE ME BACK TO OK-LAHOMA(1940); LONE RIDER IN FRONTIER FURY, THE(1941); RENEGADE, THE(1943); CODE OF THE PLAINS(1947); FRONTIER FIGHTERS(1947)
Lillian Hackett
Silents
ONCE A PLUMBER(1920); IN HOLLYWOOD WITH POTASH AND PERLMUT-TER(1924); LADIES AT EASE(1927)
Misc. Silents
DANGER(1923)
Norman Hackett
Silents
CRIMSON DOVE, THE(1917)
Raymond Hackett
FOOTLIGHTS AND FOOLS(1929); GIRL IN THE SHOW, THE(1929); MADAME X(1929); TRIAL OF MARY DUGAN, THE(1929); BLUSHING BRIDES(1930); CAT CREEPS, THE(1930); LET US BE GAY(1930); NOT SO DUMB(1930); NUMBERED MEN(1930); ON YOUR BACK(1930); OUR BLUSHING BRIDES(1930); SEA WOLF, THE(1930); SEED(1931)
Misc. Silents
GINGER(1919); FAITHLESS LOVER(1928)
Sandy Hackett
1984
CANNONBALL RUN II(1984); HOT DOG...THE MOVIE(1984)
Shelah Hackett
HALF-BREED, THE(1952); NOT WITH MY WIFE, YOU DON'T!(1966), ch
Walter C. Hackett
FREEDOM OF THE SEAS(1934, Brit.), w
Walter Hackett
SWEETHEARTS AND WIVES(1930), w; CAPTAIN APPLEJACK(1931), w; IT PAYS TO ADVERTISE(1931), w; 77 PARK LANE(1931, Brit.), w; BARTON MYSTERY, THE(1932, Brit.), w; LIFE GOES ON(1932, Brit.), w; WHITE SISTER, THE(1933), w; ROAD HOUSE(1934, Brit.), w; THEIR BIG MOMENT(1934), w; ONE NEW YORK NIGHT(1935), w; GAY ADVENTURE, THE(1936, Brit.), w; ESPIONAGE(1937), w; LOVE UNDER FIRE(1937), w; TAKE A CHANCE(1937, Brit.), w; THUNDER IN THE CITY(1937, Brit.), w
Silents
STRANGERS OF THE NIGHT(1923), w
Wayne Hackett
VICE SQUAD(1982)
William Hackett
Silents
GOLD RUSH, THE(1925)
Misc. Silents
PERILS OF THE WEST(1922)
Taylor Hackford
IDOLMAKER, THE(1980), d; OFFICER AND A GENTLEMAN, AN(1982), d
1984
AGAINST ALL ODDS(1984), p, d
Norman Hackforth
TWENTY QUESTIONS MURDER MYSTERY, THE(1950, Brit.)
Cmdr. Hackforth-Jones
CLUE OF THE MISSING APE, THE(1953, Brit.), w
Penne Hackforth-Jones
ALVIN PURPLE(1974, Aus.)
Penny Hackforth-Jones
Misc. Talkies
IMAGE OF DEATH(1977, Brit.)
Eugeniusz Hackiewicz
MOONLIGHTING(1982, Brit.)
Dennis Hackin
WANDA NEVADA(1979), p, w; BRONCO BILLY(1980), p, w
H. Samuel Hackin
WANDA NEVADA(1979)
Karlheinz Hackl
SOPHIE'S CHOICE(1982)
Bob Hackman
DAMNATION ALLEY(1977); MAGIC(1978)
Gene Hackman
MAD DOG COLL(1961); LILITH(1964); COVENANT WITH DEATH, A(1966); HA-WAII(1966); BANNING(1967); BONNIE AND CLYDE(1967); FIRST TO FIGHT(1967); SPLIT, THE(1968); DOWNHILL RACER(1969); GYPSY MOTHS, THE(1969); MA-

ROONED(1969); RIOT(1969); I NEVER SANG FOR MY FATHER(1970); CISCO PIKE(1971); DOCTORS' WIVES(1971); FRENCH CONNECTION, THE(1971); POSEIDON ADVENTURE, THE(1972); PRIME CUT(1972); SCARECROW(1973); CONVERSATION, THE(1974); YOUNG FRANKENSTEIN(1974); ZANDY'S BRIDE(1974); BITE THE BULLET(1975); FRENCH CONNECTION 11(1975); LUCKY LADY(1975); NIGHT MOVES(1975); BRIDGE TOO FAR, A(1977, Brit.); DOMINO PRINCIPLE, THE(1977); HUNTING PARTY, THE(1977, Brit.); MARCH OR DIE(1977, Brit.); SUPERMAN(1978); SUPERMAN II(1980); ALL NIGHT LONG(1981); REDS(1981); EUREKA(1983, Brit.); UNCOMMON VALOR(1983); UNDER FIRE(1983)
1984
MISUNDERSTOOD(1984)
Richard Hackman
SCARECROW(1973); NIGHT MOVES(1975)
Robert Hackman
FALLING IN LOVE AGAIN(1980)
1984
SLAPSTICK OF ANOTHER KIND(1984)
Alan Hackney
PRIVATE'S PROGRESS(1956, Brit.), w; I'M ALL RIGHT, JACK(1959, Brit.), w; SWORD OF SHERWOOD FOREST(1961, Brit.), w; TWO-WAY STRETCH(1961, Brit.), w; WATCH YOUR STERN(1961, Brit.), w; OPERATION SNATCH(1962, Brit.), w; YOU MUST BE JOKING!(1965, Brit.), w; DECLINE AND FALL... OF A BIRD WATCHER(1969, Brit.), w
Doris Hackney
MIDNIGHT(1983)
John Hackney
MONTY PYTHON AND THE HOLY GRAIL(1975, Brit.), ed
M.L. Hackney
SCHOONER GANG, THE(1937, Brit.), w
Pearl Hackney
COOL IT, CAROL!(1970, Brit.); SCHIZO(1977, Brit.); YANKS(1979)
1984
PLOUGHMAN'S LUNCH, THE(1984, Brit.)
W. Devenport Hackney
SCHOONER GANG, THE(1937, Brit.), p&d, w
Lark Hackshaw
1984
BAD MANNERS(1984)
Don Hackstaff
STACY'S KNIGHTS(1983)
Gilbert Hackworth
BABY AND THE BATTLESHIP, THE(1957, Brit.), w
Mike Hackworth
TOWN THAT DREADED SUNDOWN, THE(1977)
Frank R. Hacobson
JONI(1980), p
Alex Hacohen
KID VENGEANCE(1977), p
Hadank
M(1933, Ger.)
Gunther Hadank
KING IN SHADOW(1961, Ger.)
Moshe Hadar
CLOUDS OVER ISRAEL(1966, Israel), w
Eli Hadash
WILD GYPSIES(1969)
Aaron Haddad
JUSTINE(1969), tech adv
John Haddad
WHITE HUNTER(1965)
Suhiel Haddad
1984
LITTLE DRUMMER GIRL, THE(1984)
Connie Lynn Hadden
PIRANHA II: THE SPAWNING(1981, Neth.)
George Hadden
CHARLIE CHAN'S COURAGE(1934), d
Pauline Hadden
ARIZONA GANGBUSTERS(1940); RIDERS OF BLACK MOUNTAIN(1941)
Peter Hadden
PUBLIC NUISANCE NO. 1(1936, Brit.)
Robert Hadden
COOL AND THE CRAZY, THE(1958)
Victor Haddick
LUCK OF THE IRISH, THE(1937, Ireland), w
Jack Haddock
CASE OF PATTY SMITH, THE(1962)
Julie Anne Haddock
GREAT SANTINI, THE(1979); SCAVENGER HUNT(1979)
William Haddock
SUNRISE AT CAMPOBELLO(1960)
Misc. Silents
BANKER'S DAUGHTER, THE(1914), d; GIRL WHO DIDN'T THINK, THE(1917), d
William F. Haddock
MIRACLE WORKER, THE(1962)
Silents
AS A WOMAN SOWS(1916), d; TIMOTHY'S QUEST(1922); MAD DANCER(1925)
Misc. Silents
I ACCUSE(1916), d
Dayle Haddon
PAPERBACK HERO(1973, Can.); WORLD'S GREATEST ATHLETE, THE(1973); SPERMULA(1976, Fr.); NORTH DALLAS FORTY(1979)
1984
BEDROOM EYES(1984, Can.)
Harriette Haddon
THRILL OF A LIFETIME(1937); SAY IT IN FRENCH(1938); YOU AND ME(1938); CAFE SOCIETY(1939); ZAZA(1939); THANK YOUR LUCKY STARS(1943)

Larry Haddon
HANDS OF A STRANGER(1962)
Pauline Haddon
SOULS AT SEA(1937); FORGOTTEN WOMAN, THE(1939); COWBOY FROM SUNDOWN(1940); MARGIE(1940); UNTAMED(1940)
Peter Haddon
LATIN LOVE(1930, Brit.); DEATH AT A BROADCAST(1934, Brit.); NO MONKEY BUSINESS(1935, Brit.); SILENT PASSENGER, THE(1935, Brit.); WHO'S YOUR FATHER?(1935, Brit.); BELOVED VAGABOND, THE(1936, Brit.); DON'T RUSH ME(1936, Brit.); HOUSE OF THE SPANIARD, THE(1936, Brit.); SECRET OF STAMBOUL, THE(1936, Brit.); OVER THE MOON(1940, Brit.); HELTER SKELTER(1949, Brit.); MOULIN ROUGE(1952); SECOND MRS. TANQUERAY, THE(1952, Brit.)
Ron Haddrick
DAWN(1979, Aus.); DOT AND THE BUNNY(1983, Aus.)
1984
CAMEL BOY, THE(1984, Aus.)
Ronn Haddrick
SHIRLEY THOMPSON VERSUS THE ALIENS(1968, Aus.)
Roy Haddrick
RIDE A WILD PONY(1976, U.S./Aus.)
Anne Haddy
THEY'RE A WEIRD MOB(1966, Aus.); DOT AND THE BUNNY(1983, Aus.); FIGHTING BACK(1983, Brit.)
Dorothy Hadel
Silents
FLIRTING WITH FATE(1916)
Hajo Hadeler
WHEN TOMORROW DIES(1966, Can.), ed
Charles Haden
SYNANON(1965)
Nancy Haden
FRATERNITY ROW(1977)
Sara Haden
AFFAIRS OF A GENTLEMAN(1934); ANNE OF GREEN GABLES(1934); FINISHING SCHOOL(1934); FOUNTAIN, THE(1934); HAT, COAT AND GLOVE(1934); LIFE OF VERGIE WINTERS, THE(1934); MUSIC IN THE AIR(1934); SPITFIRE(1934); WHITE PARADE, THE(1934); BLACK FURY(1935); CAPTAIN JANUARY(1935); MAD LOVE(1935); MAGNIFICENT OBSESSION(1935); O'SHAUGHNESSY'S BOY(1935); WAY DOWN EAST(1935); CAN THIS BE DIXIE?(1936); CRIME OF DR. FORBES(1936); EVERYBODY'S OLD MAN(1936); HALF ANGEL(1936); LITTLE MISS NOBODY(1936); POOR LITTLE RICH GIRL(1936); REUNION(1936); BARRIER, THE(1937); FAMILY AFFAIR, A(1937); FIRST LADY(1937); LAST OF MRS. CHEYNEY, THE(1937); LAUGHING AT TROUBLE(1937); UNDER COVER OF NIGHT(1937); OUT WEST WITH THE HARDYS(1938); YOU'RE ONLY YOUNG ONCE(1938); ANDY HARDY GETS SPRING FEVER(1939); FOUR GIRLS IN WHITE(1939); HARDYS RIDE HIGH, THE(1939); JUDGE HARDY AND SON(1939); REMEMBER?(1939); SECRET OF DR. KILDARE, THE(1939); TELL NO TALES(1939); ANDY HARDY MEETS DEBUTANTE(1940); BOOM TOWN(1940); HULLABALOO(1940); SHOP AROUND THE CORNER, THE(1940); BARNACLE BILL(1941); H.M. PULHAM, ESQ.(1941); KEEPING COMPANY(1941); LIFE BEGINS FOR ANDY HARDY(1941); LOVE CRAZY(1941); TRIAL OF MARY DUGAN, THE(1941); WASHINGTON MELODRAMA(1941); AFFAIRS OF MARTHA, THE(1942); ANDY HARDY'S DOUBLE LIFE(1942); COURTSHIP OF ANDY HARDY, THE(1942); SOMEWHERE I'LL FIND YOU(1942); WOMAN OF THE YEAR(1942); ABOVE SUSPICION(1943); BEST FOOT FORWARD(1943); PILOT NO. 5(1943); THOUSANDS CHEER(1943); YOUNGEST PROFESSION, THE(1943); ANDY HARDY'S BLONDE TROUBLE(1944); LOST ANGEL(1944); OUR VINES HAVE TENDER GRAPES(1945); SHE WOULDN'T SAY YES(1945); BAD BASCOMB(1946); LOVE LAUGHS AT ANDY HARDY(1946); MR. ACE(1946); OUR HEARTS WERE GROWING UP(1946); SHE-WOLF OF LONDON(1946); SO GOES MY LOVE(1946); BISHOP'S WIFE, THE(1947); RACHEL AND THE STRANGER(1948); BIG CAT, THE(1949); ROUGHSHOD(1949); GREAT RUPERT, THE(1950); LIFE OF HER OWN, A(1950); RODEO(1952); WAGONS WEST(1952); LION IS IN THE STREETS, A(1953); OUTLAW'S DAUGHTER, THE(1954); BETRAYED WOMEN(1955); ANDY HARDY COMES HOME(1958)
Abby Hadfield
MIKADO, THE(1967, Brit.)
Harry Hadfield
Silents
CHIMMIE FADDEN OUT WEST(1915)
Misc. Silents
LOVE AND AMBITION(1917)
Penny Hadfield
MY BLOODY VALENTINE(1981, Can.), art d
Michael Hadge
MISTER BUDDWING(1966)
Jita Hadi
TROUBLE MAN(1972)
Shifi Hadi
SHADOWS(1960), m
Brahim Hadjadj
STRANGER, THE(1967, Algeria/Fr./Ital.)
Marc Hadjadj
1984
UNTIL SEPTEMBER(1984)
Kostas Hadjichristos
LISA, TOSCA OF ATHENS(1961, Gr.); POLICEMAN OF THE 16TH PRECINCT, THE(1963, Gr.)
Manos Hadjidakis
NEVER ON SUNDAY(1960, Gr.), m; IT HAPPENED IN ATHENS(1962), m; 300 SPARTANS, THE(1962), m; AMERICA, AMERICA(1963), m; NINE MILES TO NOON(1963), m&md; WE HAVE ONLY ONE LIFE(1963, Gr.), m; TOPKAPI(1964), m; MADALENA(1965, Gr.), m; DRY SUMMER(1967, Turkey), m; BLUE(1968), m; INVINCIBLE SIX, THE(1970, U.S./Iran), m; PEDESTRIAN, THE(1974, Ger.), m
1984
MEMED MY HAWK(1984, Brit.), m
Tomas Hadl
FIFTH HORSEMAN IS FEAR, THE(1968, Czech.)

Janet Hadland
STUNTS(1977)
Walter Hadler
PLEASE STAND BY(1972)
Bert Hadley
Silents
LITTLE PAL(1915); NINA, THE FLOWER GIRL(1917); PARTNERS OF THE TI-
DE(1921); VIRGINIAN, THE(1923); KING OF KINGS, THE(1927)
Misc. Silents
HER MOMENT(1918); BEGGAR PRINCE, THE(1920); THREE GOLD COINS(1920);
FLYING U RANCH, THE(1927)
Don Hadley
LEGEND OF BLOOD MOUNTAIN, THE(1965), p, w
Florence Hadley
TWO(1975)
Fred Hadley
NEVER GIVE A SUCKER AN EVEN BREAK(1941)
Silents
PRICE OF A PARTY, THE(1924)
Mary Hadley
WHO'S GOT THE ACTION?(1962), makeup
Nancy Hadley
FRONTIER UPRISING(1961); LATE LIZ, THE(1971)
Priscilla Hadley
1,000 SHAPES OF A FEMALE(1963)
Raymond C. Hadley
Misc. Silents
BROADWAY BILL(1918)
Reed Hadley
FEMALE FUGITIVE(1938); HOLLYWOOD STADIUM MYSTERY(1938); CALLING
DR. KILDARE(1939); ORPHANS OF THE STREET(1939); SERGEANT MAD-
DEN(1939); STRONGER THAN DESIRE(1939); BANK DICK, THE(1940); FLIGHT
COMMAND(1940); I TAKE THIS WOMAN(1940); MAN FROM MONTREAL,
THE(1940); MEET THE WILDCAT(1940); SKI PATROL(1940); FLAME OF NEW
ORLEANS, THE(1941); I'LL WAIT FOR YOU(1941); ROAD AGENT(1941); SUNSET
MURDER CASE(1941); UNFINISHED BUSINESS(1941); WHISTLING IN THE
DARK(1941); ZIEGFELD GIRL(1941); ARIZONA TERRORS(1942); I MARRIED A
WITCH(1942); JAIL HOUSE BLUES(1942); JUKE BOX JENNY(1942); LADY IN A
JAM(1942); MYSTERY OF MARIE ROGET, THE(1942); NOW, VOYAGER(1942);
GUADALCANAL DIARY(1943); EVE OF ST. MARK, THE(1944); IN THE MEANTIME,
DARLING(1944); RAINBOW ISLAND(1944); ROGER TOUHY, GANGSTER!(1944);
WILSON(1944); WING AND A PRAYER(1944); BELL FOR ADANO, A(1945); CARIB-
BEAN MYSTERY, THE(1945); CIRCUMSTANTIAL EVIDENCE(1945); DIAMOND
HORSESHOE(1945); DOLL FACE(1945); HOUSE ON 92ND STREET, THE(1945);
DARK CORNER, THE(1946); IF I'M LUCKY(1946); IT SHOULDN'T HAPPEN TO A
DOG(1946); LEAVE HER TO HEAVEN(1946); SHOCK(1946); 13 RUE MADELEI-
NE(1946); BRASHER DOUBLOON, THE(1947); CAPTAIN FROM CASTILE(1947);
FABULOUS TEXAN, THE(1947); T-MEN(1947); CANON CITY(1948); HE WALKED BY
NIGHT(1948); IRON CURTAIN, THE(1948); LAST OF THE WILD HORSES(1948);
MAN FROM TEXAS, THE(1948); PANHANDLE(1948); RETURN OF WILDFIRE,
THE(1948); SOUTHERN YANKEE, A(1948); WALK A CROOKED MILE(1948); GRAND
CANYON(1949); I SHOT JESSE JAMES(1949); RIDERS OF THE RANGE(1949);
RIMFIRE(1949); WYOMING BANDIT, THE(1949); BARON OF ARIZONA, THE(1950);
DALLAS(1950); MOTOR PATROL(1950); RETURN OF JESSE JAMES, THE(1950);
INSURANCE INVESTIGATOR(1951); LITTLE BIG HORN(1951); HALF-BREED,
THE(1952); WILD BLUE YONDER, THE(1952); KANSAS PACIFIC(1953); WOMAN
THEY ALMOST LYNCHED(1953); HIGHWAY DRAGNET(1954); BIG HOUSE,
U.S.A.(1955); MOBS INC(1956); MORO WITCH DOCTOR(1964, U.S./Phil.); YOUNG
DILLINGER(1965); ST. VALENTINE'S DAY MASSACRE, THE(1967); BRAIN OF
BLOOD(1971, Phil.)
Mark Hadlow
SCARECROW, THE(1982, New Zealand); NATE AND HAYES(1983, U.S./New Zea-
land)
1984
CONSTANCE(1984, New Zealand)
Michael Hadlow
TITANIC(1953); ABBOTT AND COSTELLO MEET DR. JEKYLL AND MR. HY-
DE(1954); TO CATCH A THIEF(1955)
Zdena Hadrbolcova
DEATH OF TARZAN, THE(1968, Czech)
Hadrian
M(1933, Ger.)
Ted Hadworth
ESCAPE FROM EAST BERLIN(1962), art d
Laoura Hadzivageli
FOR YOUR EYES ONLY(1981)
Horatius Haeberle
LAST WORD, THE(1979), w
Horst Haechler
LAST BRIDGE, THE(1957, Aust.); AS THE SEA RAGES(1960 Ger.), d
Marcel Haedrich
CRACK IN THE MIRROR(1960), w
Rolf Haedrich
STOP TRAIN 349(1964, Fr./Ital./Ger.), d
Charles Haefeli
LES MISERABLES(1935)
Silents
AFRAID TO FIGHT(1922); WOLF'S CLOTHING(1927)
Mark Hall Haefeli
CHILD'S PLAY(1972)
Charles Haefell
JAM SESSION(1944)
Jockey Haefley
RAINBOW RANCH(1933)
Dorothy Haefling
COOL AND THE CRAZY, THE(1958)
Julius Haemann
NO MONKEY BUSINESS(1935, Brit.), p

Gunther Haenel
MIRACLE OF THE WHITE STALLIONS(1963)
Mary Ann Haenel
DEER HUNTER, THE(1978)
Gitte Haenning
HAGBARD AND SIGNE(1968, Den./Iceland/Swed.)
George Haentzchel
CONFESS DR. CORDA(1960, Ger.), m
Georg Haentzschel
GIRL AND THE LEGEND, THE(1966, Ger.), m
Karin Zetlitz Haerem
1984
KAMILLA(1984, Norway)
Gerhard Haerter
SECRET AGENT SUPER DRAGON(1966, Fr./Ital./Ger./Monaco)
Keshav Haeseler
NOBODY'S PERFEKT(1981)
Blandine Hafela
ROCK, ROCK, ROCK!(1956), ed
Oswald Hafenrichter
HAPPIEST DAYS OF YOUR LIFE(1950, Brit.), ed; THIRD MAN, THE(1950, Brit.),
ed; SMALLEST SHOW ON EARTH, THE(1957, Brit.), ed; LAW AND DISORDER(1958,
Brit.), ed; FACES IN THE DARK(1960, Brit.), ed; FOXHOLE IN CAIRO(1960, Brit.),
ed; JET STORM(1961, Brit.), ed; HAPPY THIEVES, THE(1962), ed; SPARROWS
CAN'T SING(1963, Brit.), ed; HANDS OF ORLAC, THE(1964, Brit./Fr.), ed; LADIES
WHO DO(1964, Brit.), ed; BRAIN, THE(1965, Ger./Brit.), ed; DR. WHO AND THE
DALEKS(1965, Brit.), ed; SKULL, THE(1965, Brit.), ed; PSYCHOPATH, THE(1966,
Brit.), ed; TRAITOR'S GATE(1966, Brit./Ger.), ed; DEADLY BEES,THE(1967, Brit.),
ed; GREAT BRITISH TRAIN ROBBERY, THE(1967, Ger.), ed; DANGER ROUTE(1968,
Brit.), ed; FILE OF THE GOLDEN GOOSE, THE(1969, Brit.), ed; TRYGON FACTOR,
THE(1969, Brit.), ed; CRY OF THE BANSHEE(1970, Brit.), ed; TROG(1970, Brit.), ed;
CREEPING FLESH,THE(1973, Brit.), ed; VAULT OF HORROR, THE(1973, Brit.), ed
Johanna Hafer
TOXI(1952, Ger.)
Clair Haffaker
CHINO(1976, Ital., Span., Fr.), w
Elizabeth Haffenden
WRATH OF JEALOUSY(1936, Brit.), cos; JASSY(1948, Brit.), cos; MAN OF
EVIL(1948, Brit.), cos; SMUGGLERS, THE(1948, Brit.), cos; OBSESSED(1951, Brit.),
cos; SO LONG AT THE FAIR(1951, Brit.), cos; BEAU BRUMMELL(1954), cos; FOOT-
STEPS IN THE FOG(1955, Brit.), cos; QUENTIN DURWARD(1955), cos; WARRIORS,
THE(1955), cos; BHOWANI JUNCTION(1956), cos; INVITATION TO THE DAN-
CE(1956), cos; MOBY DICK(1956, Brit.), cos; BARRETTS OF WIMPOLE STREET,
THE(1957), cos; HEAVEN KNOWS, MR. ALLISON(1957), cos; I ACCUSE(1958, Brit.),
cos; BEN HUR(1959), cos; SUNDOWNERS, THE(1960), cos; I THANK A FOOL(1962,
Brit.), cos; KILL OR CURE(1962, Brit.), cos; VILLAGE OF DAUGHTERS(1962, Brit.),
cos; AMOROUS ADVENTURES OF MOLL FLANDERS, THE(1965), cos; AR-
RIVEDERCI, BABY!(1966, Brit.), cos; LIQUIDATOR, THE(1966, Brit.), cos; MAN FOR
ALL SEASONS, A(1966, Brit.), cos; HALF A SIXPENCE(1967, Brit.), cos; CHITTY
CHITTY BANG BANG(1968, Brit.), cos; PRIME OF MISS JEAN BRODIE, THE(1969,
Brit.), cos; FIDDLER ON THE ROOF(1971), cos; POPE JOAN(1972, Brit.), cos; DAY OF
THE JACKAL, THE(1973, Brit./Fr.), cos; HOMECOMING, THE(1973), cos; LU-
THER(1974), cos; CONDUCT UNBECOMING(1975, Brit.), cos
Elizabeth Haffenden
MAN IN GREY, THE(1943, Brit.), cos
Oswald Haffenrichter
IDEAL HUSBAND, AN(1948, Brit.), ed; FALLEN IDOL, THE(1949, Brit.), ed
Jack Hafferkamp
LAST AFFAIR, THE(1976)
E. Haffner
NIGHT PEOPLE(1954)
Erna Haffner
THREE PENNY OPERA(1963, Fr./Ger.)
Jack Haffner
MAN BEAST(1956); INCREDIBLE PETRIFIED WORLD, THE(1959); INVASION OF
THE ANIMAL PEOPLE(1962, U.S./Swed.)
Robin Haffner
NUTCRACKER FANTASY(1979)
Achmed Hafiz
SIGNS OF LIFE(1981, Ger.)
Max Hafler
RUNNERS(1983, Brit.)
Lou Hafley
PIRATES OF TORTUGA(1961), set d; STATE FAIR(1962), set d; SWINGIN'
ALONG(1962), set d
Lucien Hafley
RIO CONCHOS(1964), set d; FLIGHT OF THE PHOENIX, THE(1965), set d; RE-
WARD, THE(1965), set d; I DEAL IN DANGER(1966), set d
Lucien M. Hafley
PETE'S DRAGON(1977), set d
Dudley Hafner
Misc. Talkies
MISSION TO DEATH(1966)
Ingrid Hafner
BLUEBEARD'S TEN HONEYMOONS(1960, Brit.); FIVE TO ONE(1963, Brit.); AMOR-
OUS ADVENTURES OF MOLL FLANDERS, THE(1965)
Robert Hafner
EXILES, THE(1966), m
David Haft]
HANNIE CALDER(1971, Brit.), w
Kensuke Haga
GOODBYE GIRL, THE(1977)
The Hagadash Trio
EVERY BASTARD A KING(1968, Israel)
Suey Hagadorn
MILESTONES(1975)
Charlotte Hagaler
WORDS AND MUSIC(1929)

Al Hagan
Misc. Silents
MODERN JEAN VAL JEAN; OR A FRAME UP, A(1930)
Anna Hagan
SHADOW OF THE HAWK(1976, Can.)
Chris Hagan
TAPS(1981)
Dorothy Hagan
Silents
NANCY FROM NOWHERE(1922)
Edna Hagan
STRUGGLE, THE(1931)
Garrick Hagan
ANTONY AND CLEOPATRA(1973, Brit.)
Howard Hagan
LOST COMMAND, THE(1966); TOWN CALLED HELL, A(1971, Span./Brit.); WIND AND THE LION, THE(1975)
James Hagan
ONE SUNDAY AFTERNOON(1933), w; ONE SUNDAY AFTERNOON(1948), w
Ken Hagan
DR. FRANKENSTEIN ON CAMPUS(1970, Can.)
Pat Hagan
LIEUTENANT DARING, RN(1935, Brit.)
Vic Hagan
DEAR MURDERER(1947, Brit.); SAINTS AND SINNERS(1949, Brit.)
Victor Hagan
LIEUTENANT DARING, RN(1935, Brit.)
Clyde Hagar
STRIKE ME PINK(1936)
Dorothy Hagar
Misc. Silents
HELL'S END(1918)
Dot Hagar
Misc. Silents
WILD LIFE(1918)
Freddy Hagar
SNOW DEVILS, THE(1965, Ital.)
Ivan Hagar
Misc. Talkies
ANY BODY...ANY WAY(1968)
Karol Hagar
WHERE HAS POOR MICKEY GONE?(1964, Brit.); LION IN WINTER, THE(1968, Brit.)
Chieko Hagashiyama
LIFE OF OHARU(1964, Jap.)
Patsy Hagate
THERE AIN'T NO JUSTICE(1939, Brit.); GOOD DIE YOUNG, THE(1954, Brit.)
Douglas Hage
NIGHT IN JUNE, A(1940, Swed.); ILLICIT INTERLUDE(1954, Swed.); NIGHT IS MY FUTURE(1962, Swed.)
Thomas J. Hageboeck
1984
BEVERLY HILLS COP(1984)
Charles H. Hagedon
RAINTREE COUNTY(1957), tech adv
Charles K. Hagedon
LOVE-INS, THE(1967), art d; PHANTOM TOLLBOOTH, THE(1970), art d
Hermann Hagedorn
Silents
ROUGH RIDERS, THE(1927), w
Anne Hagegard
FACE TO FACE(1976, Swed.), prod d
Richard Hageman
IF I WERE KING(1938), m; RULERS OF THE SEA(1939), m; STAGECOACH(1939), m; HOWARDS OF VIRGINIA, THE(1940), m; LONG VOYAGE HOME, THE(1940), m; PARIS CALLING(1941), m; SHANGHAI GESTURE, THE(1941), m; THERE'S MAGIC IN MUSIC(1941); HI DIDDLE DIDDLE(1943); SENSATIONS OF 1945(1944); BACHELOR'S DAUGHTERS, THE(1946); ANGEL AND THE BADMAN(1947), m; FUGITIVE, THE(1947), m, md; MOURNING BECOMES ELECTRA(1947), m; NEW ORLEANS(1947); FORT APACHE(1948), m; THREE GODFATHERS, THE(1948), a, m; SHE WORE A YELLOW RIBBON(1949), m; GROUNDS FOR MARRIAGE(1950); TOAST OF NEW ORLEANS, THE(1950); WAGONMASTER(1950), m; GREAT CARUSO, THE(1951); STOLEN IDENTITY(1953), m; RHAPSODY(1954); FUN ON A WEEK-END(1979)
Hans Hagemeyer
LAST BLITZKRIEG, THE(1958)
Anna Hagen
LYDIA(1964, Can.); GROUNDSTAR CONSPIRACY, THE(1972, Can.)
Camille Hagen
1984
UNFAITHFULLY YOURS(1984)
Carla Hagen
GIRL FROM HONG KONG(1966, Ger.)
Charles Hagen
FOLIES DERGERE(1935)
Claire Hagen
WONDER WOMEN(1973, Phil.)
Donnell Hagen
STONY ISLAND(1978)
Earle Hagen
WITH A SONG IN MY HEART(1952), art d; MAN ON A TIGHTROPE(1953), md; SPRING REUNION(1957), m; MAN WHO UNDERSTOOD WOMEN, THE(1959), md; NEW INTERNS, THE(1964), m
Edna Hagen
Silents
KISS FOR CINDERELLA, A(1926)
Erica Hagen
LAST AMERICAN HERO, THE(1973); SOYLENT GREEN(1973); THUNDERBOLT AND LIGHTFOOT(1974); MOTHER, JUGS & SPEED(1976); SILENT MOVIE(1976)

G. Hagen
SUMMERSPELL(1983)
George Hagen
WAY TO LOVE, THE(1933)
Holger Hagen
IDEAL LODGER, THE(1957, Ger.); MAN ON A STRING(1960); COUNTERFEIT TRAITOR, THE(1962); PHONY AMERICAN, THE(1964, Ger.)
Howard Hagen
THIN RED LINE, THE(1964)
Hubs Hagen
48 HOURS TO ACAPULCO(1968, Ger.), ph; 24-HOUR LOVER(1970, Ger.), ph
Ira Hagen
FUNERAL IN BERLIN(1966, Brit.)
Jack Hagen
JOHNNY HOLIDAY(1949)
Jean Hagen
ADAM'S RIB(1949); AMBUSH(1950); ASPHALT JUNGLE, THE(1950); LIFE OF HER OWN, A(1950); SIDE STREET(1950); NIGHT INTO MORNING(1951); NO QUESTIONS ASKED(1951); SHADOW IN THE SKY(1951); CARBINE WILLIAMS(1952); SINGIN' IN THE RAIN(1952); ARENA(1953); HALF A HERO(1953); LATIN LOVERS(1953); BIG KNIFE, THE(1955); SPRING REUNION(1957); SHAGGY DOG, THE(1959); SUNRISE AT CAMPOBELLO(1960); PANIC IN YEAR ZERO!(1962); DEAD RINGER(1964)
Julius Hagen
FEATHER, THE(1929, Brit.), p; TO WHAT RED HELL(1929, Brit.), p; CALL OF THE SEA, THE(1930, Brit.), p; HOUSE OF THE ARROW, THE(1930, Brit.), p; LORD RICHARD IN THE PANTRY(1930, Brit.), p; MYSTERY AT THE VILLA ROSE(1930, Brit.), p; ALIBI(1931, Brit.), p; BILL'S LEGACY(1931, Brit.), p; BLACK COFFEE(1931, Brit.), p; BOAT FROM SHANGHAI(1931, Brit.), p; BROWN SUGAR(1931, Brit.), p; LYONS MAIL, THE(1931, Brit.), p; ROSARY, THE(1931, Brit.), p; SHERLOCK HOLMES' FATAL HOUR(1931, Brit.), p; SPLINTERS IN THE NAVY(1931, Brit.), p; CHINESE PUZZLE, THE(1932, Brit.), p; CONDEMNED TO DEATH(1932, Brit.), p; CROOKED LADY, THE(1932, Brit.), p; FACE AT THE WINDOW, THE(1932, Brit.), p; FRAIL WOMEN(1932, Brit.), p; MARRIAGE BOND, THE(1932, Brit.), p; MISSING REMBRANDT, THE(1932, Brit.), p; MURDER AT COVENT GARDEN(1932, Brit.), p; WHEN LONDON SLEEPS(1932, Brit.), p; WORLD, THE FLESH, AND THE DEVIL, THE(1932, Brit.), p; EXCESS BAGGAGE(1933, Brit.), p; GHOST CAMERA, THE(1933, Brit.), p; HIS GRACE GIVES NOTICE(1933, Brit.), p; HOME, SWEET HOME(1933, Brit.), p; I LIVED WITH YOU(1933, Brit.), p; IRON STAIR, THE(1933, Brit.), p; MAN OUTSIDE, THE(1933, Brit.), p; MANNEQUIN(1933, Brit.), p; MEDICINE MAN, THE(1933, Brit.), p; ROOF, THE(1933, Brit.), p; SHOT IN THE DARK, A(1933, Brit.), p; THIS WEEK OF GRACE(1933, Brit.), p; UMBRELLA, THE(1933, Brit.), p; ADMIRAL'S SECRET, THE(1934, Brit.), p; ARE YOU A MASON?(1934, Brit.), p; BLACK ABBOT, THE(1934, Brit.), p; BLIND JUSTICE(1934, Brit.), p; BRIDE OF THE LAKE(1934, Brit.), p; BROKEN MELODY, THE(1934, Brit.), p; FOUR MASKED MEN(1934, Brit.), p; KENTUCKY MINSTRELS(1934, Brit.), p; LASH, THE(1934, Brit.), p; LORD EDGE-WARE DIES(1934, Brit.), p; MAN WHO CHANGED HIS NAME, THE(1934, Brit.), p; MUSIC HALL(1934, Brit.), p; NIGHT CLUB QUEEN(1934, Brit.), p; OPEN ALL NIGHT(1934, Brit.), p; POINTING FINGER, THE(1934, Brit.), p; RIVER WOLVES, THE(1934, Brit.), p; SAY IT WITH FLOWERS(1934, Brit.), p; TANGLED EVIDENCE(1934, Brit.), p; WHISPERING TONGUES(1934, Brit.), p; ACE OF SPADES, THE(1935, Brit.), p; ANNIE, LEAVE THE ROOM(1935, Brit.), p; ANYTHING MIGHT HAPPEN(1935, Brit.), p; DEPARTMENT STORE(1935, Brit.), p; FIRE HAS BEEN ARRANGED, A(1935, Brit.), p; FLOOD TIDE(1935, Brit.), p; IN A MONASTERY GARDEN(1935), p; INSIDE THE ROOM(1935, Brit.), p; LAD, THE(1935, Brit.), p; LAZYBONES(1935, Brit.), p; PHANTOM FIEND, THE(1935, Brit.), p; PRIVATE SECRETARY, THE(1935, Brit.), p; SCROOGE(1935, Brit.), p; SHE SHALL HAVE MUSIC(1935, Brit.), p; SQUIBS(1935, Brit.), p; STREET SONG(1935, Brit.), p; THAT'S MY UNCLE(1935, Brit.), p; THREE WITNESSES(1935, Brit.), p; TRIUMPH OF SHER-LOCK HOLMES, THE(1935, Brit.), p; VINTAGE WINE(1935, Brit.), p; WANDERING JEW, THE(1935, Brit.), p; WOLVES OF THE UNDERWORLD(1935, Brit.), p; BROKEN BLOSSOMS(1936, Brit.), p; ELIZA COMES TO STAY(1936, Brit.), p; IN THE SOUP(1936, Brit.), p; LAST JOURNEY, THE(1936, Brit.), p; MAN IN THE MIRROR, THE(1936, Brit.), p; MORALS OF MARCUS, THE(1936, Brit.), p; MURDER ON THE SET(1936, Brit.), p; SHADOW, THE(1936, Brit.), p; BEAUTY AND THE BARGE(1937, Brit.), p; CLOTHES AND THE WOMAN(1937, Brit.), p; DEATH CROONS THE BLUES(1937, Brit.), p; HIGH TREASON(1937, Brit.), p; JUGGERNAUT(1937, Brit.), p; LOST CHORD, THE(1937, Brit.), p; UNDERNEATH THE ARCHES(1937, Brit.), p; VICAR OF BRAY, THE(1937, Brit.), p; WHO KILLED FEN MARKHAM?(1937, Brit.), p; HIDEOUT IN THE ALPS(1938, Brit.), p; MAKE IT THREE(1938, Brit.), p; SPY OF NAPOLEON(1939, Brit.), p; CAPTAIN MOONLIGHT(1940, Brit.), p; MURDER AT THE BASKERVILLES(1941, Brit.), p
Silents
ALL THE WORLD'S A STAGE(1917, Brit.), p; FAKE, THE(1927, Brit.), p; FURTHER ADVENTURES OF THE FLAG LIEUTENANT(1927, Brit.), p; PASSING OF MR. QUIN, THE(1928, Brit.), p
Kevin Hagen
GUNSMOKE IN TUCSON(1958); PORK CHOP HILL(1959); RIDER ON A DEAD HORSE(1962); MAN FROM GALVESTON, THE(1964); RIO CONCHOS(1964); SHE-NANDOAH(1965); LAST CHALLENGE, THE(1967); LEARNING TREE, THE(1969); SOUL OF NIGGER CHARLEY, THE(1973); HUNTER, THE(1980)
Laurie Hagen
GLASS HOUSES(1972); CHEAP DETECTIVE, THE(1978)
Lilo Hagen
TOWN WITHOUT PITY(1961, Ger./Switz./U.S.), cos
Paul Hagen
OPERATION CAMEL(1961, Den.); CRAZY PARADISE(1965, Den.); EPILOGUE(1967, Den.); MY FATHER'S MISTRESS(1970, Swed.); SCANDAL IN DENMARK(1970, Den.)
Ross Hagen
HELLCATS, THE(1968); MINI-SKIRT MOB(1968); SPEEDWAY(1968); DEVIL'S 8, THE(1969); FIVE THE HARD WAY(1969), a, p; ORGANIZATION, THE(1971); MELINDA(1972); BAD CHARLESTON CHARLIE(1973), a, p, w; WONDER WO-MEN(1973, Phil.), a, p; NIGHT CREATURE(1979), a, p; GLOVE, THE(1980), d
1984
ANGEL(1984)
Misc. Talkies
MARK OF THE GUN(1969); PUSHING UP DAISIES(1971); ANGELS' WILD WOM-EN(1972); DEADLY AND THE BEAUTIFUL(1974); SUPERCOCK(1975); GLOVE, THE(1979), d

Uta Hagen
OTHER, THE(1972); BOYS FROM BRAZIL, THE(1978)
Vic Hagen
HERE COMES THE SUN(1945, Brit.)
Victor Hagen
FULL SPEED AHEAD(1936, Brit.); PASSENGER TO LONDON(1937, Brit.); TWIN FACES(1937, Brit.)
Walter Hagen
Misc. Silents
GREEN GRASS WIDOWS(1928)
The Hagenbeck-Wallace Circus Wild Animals
LOST JUNGLE, THE(1934)
William Hagens
CRIME OF THE CENTURY(1946), w; PASSKEY TO DANGER(1946), w
Al Hager
FRAMED(1975)
Betty Hager
ONE MAN JURY(1978)
Ivan Hager
BEHIND LOCKED DOORS(1976, S. Africa)
Peter Hager
SKIN GAME, THE(1965, Brit.); BATTLE OF BRITAIN, THE(1969, Brit.)
Reggie Hager
CAPTAIN MILKSHAKE(1970), spec eff
Steven Hager
1984
BEAT STREET(1984), w
Ann Hagerman
MIGHTY MOUSE IN THE GREAT SPACE CHASE(1983), ed
Helge Hagerman
CHILDREN, THE(1949, Swed.); LESSON IN LOVE, A(1960, Swed.)
James Hagerman
DIARY OF A MAD HOUSEWIFE(1970), cos
Ron Hagerthy
FORCE OF ARMS(1951); I WAS A COMMUNIST FOR THE F.B.I.(1951); STARLIFT(1951); CHARGE AT FEATHER RIVER, THE(1953); CITY THAT NEVER SLEEPS(1953); MAKE HASTE TO LIVE(1954); EIGHTEEN AND ANXIOUS(1957); HORSE SOLDIERS, THE(1959); SAINTLY SINNERS(1962); GUNS OF DIABLO(1964); HOSTAGE, THE(1966); RUNAWAY GIRL(1966)
Ronald F. Hagerthy
TITANIC(1953)
Don Hagerty
MOBS INC(1956)
H.B. Hagerty
STUNTS(1977)
Julie Hagerty
AIRPLANE!(1980); AIRPLANE II: THE SEQUEL(1982); MIDSUMMER NIGHT'S SEX COMEDY, A(1982)
Michael Hagerty
DOCTOR DETROIT(1983)
Klaus Hagerup
1984
KAMILLA(1984, Norway)
Taryn Hagey
1984
AGAINST ALL ODDS(1984)
Russell Hagg
GIRL ON A MOTORCYCLE, THE(1968, Fr./Brit.), art d; CLOCKWORK ORANGE, A(1971, Brit.), art d; RAW DEAL(1977, Aus.), p, d; BMX BANDITS(1983), w
Jenny Haggar
Misc. Silents
MAID OF CEFN YDFA, THE(1914, Brit.)
William Haggar, Jr.
Misc. Silents
MAID OF CEFN YDFA, THE(1914, Brit.), a, d
H. Rider Haggard
SHE(1935), w; KING SOLOMON'S MINES(1937, Brit.), w; WATUSI(1959), w; SHE(1965, Brit.), w; VENGEANCE OF SHE, THE(1968, Brit.), w; KING SOLOMON'S TREASURE(1978, Can.), w
Silents
DAWN(1917, Brit.), w
Sir Henry Rider Haggard
KING SOLOMON'S MINES(1950), w
Mark Haggard
BLACK EYE(1974), w; FIRST NUDIE MUSICAL, THE(1976), d; CREATURE WASN'T NICE,THE(1981), p
Merle Haggard
HILLBILLYS IN A HAUNTED HOUSE(1967); KILLERS THREE(1968); FROM NASHVILLE WITH MUSIC(1969)
Piers Haggard
BLOOD ON SATAN'S CLAW, THE(1970, Brit.), d; WEDDING NIGHT(1970, Ireland), d, w; FIENDISH PLOT OF DR. FU MANCHU, THE(1980), d; QUATERMASS CONCLUSION(1980, Brit.), d; VENOM(1982, Brit.), d
Roy Haggard, Sr.
NATCHEZ TRACE(1960)
Stephen Haggard
JAMAICA INN(1939, Brit.); MOZART(1940, Brit.); YOUNG MR. PITT, THE(1942, Brit.)
David Haggart
SINFUL DAVEY(1969, Brit.), w
Don Haggarty
Misc. Talkies
ADVENTURES OF STAR BIRD(1978)
John Haggarty
CAUGHT IN THE NET(1960, Brit.), d; MURDER IN EDEN(1962, Brit.), w
Captain Haggerty
HOME MOVIES(1979)

Arthur Haggerty
ONE DOWN TWO TO GO(1982)
Capt. Arthur Haggerty
SHAMUS(1973)
Ben Haggerty
MALAYA(1950)
Benjamin Haggerty
Silents
LITTLE EVA ASCENDS(1922)
Misc. Silents
KAZAN(1921)
Dan Haggerty
TENDER WARRIOR, THE(1971); BURY ME AN ANGEL(1972); HEX(1973); LIFE AND TIMES OF GRIZZLY ADAMS, THE(1974); ADVENTURES OF FRONTIER FREMONT, THE(1976); KING OF THE MOUNTAIN(1981)
Misc. Talkies
LEGEND OF THE WILD(1981)
Diane Haggerty
GOOD TIMES(1967)
Don Haggerty
AIR STRIKE(1955); GANGSTER, THE(1947); DEAD DON'T DREAM, THE(1948); FALSE PARADISE(1948); FIGHTING FATHER DUNNE(1948); GENTLEMAN FROM NOWHERE, THE(1948); GUN SMUGGLERS(1948); SILENT CONFLICT(1948); SINISTER JOURNEY(1948); THAT LADY IN ERMINE(1948); TRAIN TO ALCATRAZ(1948); CANADIAN PACIFIC(1949); RUSTLERS(1949); SANDS OF IWO JIMA(1949); SCENE OF THE CRIME(1949); SOUTH OF RIO(1949); ARMORED CAR ROBBERY(1950); ASPHALT JUNGLE, THE(1950); COWBOY AND THE PRIZEFIGHTER(1950); DYNAMITE PASS(1950); GAMBLING HOUSE(1950); KID FROM TEXAS, THE(1950); SIDE STREET(1950); STORM OVER WYOMING(1950); SUNDOWNERS, THE(1950); VANISHING WESTERNER, THE(1950); VIGILANTE HIDEOUT(1950); ANGELS IN THE OUTFIELD(1951); CALLAWAY WENT THATAWAY(1951); CAUSE FOR ALARM(1951); GO FOR BROKE(1951); MR. IMPERIUM(1951); QUEBEC(1951); SPOILERS OF THE PLAINS(1951); STRIP, THE(1951); BRONCO BUSTER(1952); DENVER AND RIO GRANDE(1952); HOODLUM EMPIRE(1952); NARROW MARGIN, THE(1952); WILD STALLION(1952); CITY OF BAD MEN(1953); COMBAT SQUAD(1953); HANNAH LEE(1953); ROAR OF THE CROWD(1953); CRY VENGEANCE(1954); JUBILEE TRAIL(1954); LOOPHOLE(1954); NAKED ALIBI(1954); PHANTOM STALLION, THE(1954); RETURN FROM THE SEA(1954); ROCKET MAN, THE(1954); ANNAPOLIS STORY, AN(1955); DESPERATE HOURS, THE(1955); STRATEGIC AIR COMMAND(1955); TEXAS LADY(1955); CALLING HOMICIDE(1956); CRASHING LAS VEGAS(1956); BACK FROM THE DEAD(1957); CHAIN OF EVIDENCE(1957); FOOTSTEPS IN THE NIGHT(1957); JET PILOT(1957); SAD SACK, THE(1957); SPOILERS OF THE FOREST(1957); SPRING REUNION(1957); BLOOD ARROW(1958); CATTLE EMPIRE(1958); CROOKED CIRCLE, THE(1958); DAY OF THE BAD MAN(1958); MAN WHO DIED TWICE, THE(1958); GUNFIGHT AT DODGE CITY, THE(1959); SOME CAME RUNNING(1959); PURPLE GANG, THE(1960); SEVEN WAYS FROM SUNDOWN(1960); HELL IS FOR HEROES(1962); KILLERS, THE(1964); MUSCLE BEACH PARTY(1964); GREAT SIOUX MASSACRE, THE(1965); LOVED ONE, THE(1965); THAT FUNNY FEELING(1965); NIGHT OF THE GRIZZLY, THE(1966); P.J.(1968); DIRTY HARRY(1971); RESURRECTION OF ZACHARY WHEELER, THE(1971); SKIN GAME(1971)
Misc. Talkies
WHEN THE NORTH WIND BLOWS(1974); STARBIRD AND SWEET WILLIAM(1975)
Donald Haggerty
PRIVATE WAR OF MAJOR BENSON, THE(1955)
Fred Haggerty
CIRCUS OF HORRORS(1960, Brit.); THERE WAS A CROOKED MAN(1962, Brit.); FROM RUSSIA WITH LOVE(1963, Brit.); PINK PANTHER STRIKES AGAIN, THE(1976, Brit.)
H.B. Haggerty
DREAM OF KINGS, A(1969); PAINT YOUR WAGON(1969); EARTHQUAKE(1974); FRAMED(1975); FOUR DEUCES, THE(1976); FINAL CHAPTER–WALKING TALL(1977); DEATHSPORT(1978); ONE AND ONLY, THE(1978); BUCK ROGERS IN THE 25TH CENTURY(1979); BIG BRAWL, THE(1980)
1984
MICKI AND MAUDE(1984)
Hard-boiled Haggerty
SHADOW OF THE THIN MAN(1941)
Hardboiled Haggerty
WRESTLER, THE(1974)
John Haggerty
MYSTERY ON BIRD ISLAND(1954, Brit.), d, w
Little Billie Haggerty
EX-FLAME(1931)
Nord Haggerty
1984
ALPHABET CITY(1984), prod d
Brahim Haggiag
BATTLE OF ALGIERS, THE(1967, Ital./Alger.)
Ever Haggiag
DILLINGER IS DEAD(1969, Ital.), p
Robert Haggiag
THIEF OF VENICE, THE(1952), p; BIRDS, THE BEES AND THE ITALIANS, THE(1967), p; CANDY(1968, Ital./Fr.), p
John Haggott
SHADOWED(1946), p; FOR THE LOVE OF RUSTY(1947), p; KEEPER OF THE BEES(1947), p
Jim Hagimori
THREE CAME HOME(1950)
John B. Hagin
Misc. Silents
HONEYMOON RANCH(1920)
John Hagin
Misc. Silents
WEST OF THE RIO GRANDE(1921)
Taski Hagio
BIG CITY(1937)

Kenichi Hagiwara
KAGEMUSHA(1980, Jap.)
Kenji Hagiwara
NO GREATER LOVE THAN THIS(1969, Jap.), ph
Tessho Hagiwara
LAS VEGAS FREE-FOR-ALL(1968, Jap.), m
Roy David Hagle
JACKSON COUNTY JAIL(1976)
Nik Hagler
EDDIE MACON'S RUN(1983)
Lewis J. Hagleton
CLEGG(1969, Brit.), w
Britt Hagman
INTERMEZZO(1937, Swed.)
Harriet Hagman
THIRTEEN WOMEN(1932)
Larry Hagman
ENSIGN PULVER(1964); FAIL SAFE(1964); CAVERN, THE(1965, Ital./Ger.); IN HARM'S WAY(1965); GROUP, THE(1966); UP IN THE CELLAR(1970); BEWARE! THE BLOB(1972), d; HARRY AND TONTO(1974); STARDUST(1974, Brit.); BIG BUS, THE(1976); EAGLE HAS LANDED, THE(1976, Brit.); MOTHER, JUGS & SPEED(1976); CHECKERED FLAG OR CRASH(1978); SUPERMAN(1978); S.O.B.(1981)
Pecka Hagman
WALPURGIS NIGHT(1941, Swed.)
Stuart Hagmann
STRAWBERRY STATEMENT, THE(1970), d; BELIEVE IN ME(1971), d
Frank Hagney
SILENCERS, THE(; OH, YEAH!)1929); FIGHTING CARAVANS(1931); NO LIMIT(1931); RECKLESS LIVING(1931); SIT TIGHT(1931); SQUAW MAN, THE(1931); HOUSE DIVIDED, A(1932); IF I HAD A MILLION(1932); RIDE HIM, COWBOY(1932); TOM BROWN OF CULVER(1932); WHITE EAGLE(1932); YOU SAID A MOUTHFUL(1932); DANCING LADY(1933); HOLD YOUR MAN(1933); ROMAN SCANDALS(1933); SITTING PRETTY(1933); TERROR ABOARD(1933); TILLIE AND GUS(1933); GREEN EYES(1934); HONOR OF THE RANGE(1934); TREASURE ISLAND(1934); NAUGHTY MARIETTA(1935); WESTERN FRONTIER(1935); HERE COMES TROUBLE(1936); HEROES OF THE RANGE(1936); PLOUGH AND THE STARS, THE(1936); THUNDERBOLT(1936); VALLEY OF THE LAWLESS(1936); WILDCAT TROOPER(1936); CONFLICT(1937); GHOST TOWN GOLD(1937); HOLLYWOOD COWBOY(1937); NIGHT KEY(1937); RIDERS OF THE DAWN(1937); WILD HORSE ROUND-UP(1937); WINDJAMMER(1937); ANGELS WITH DIRTY FACES(1938); PROFESSOR BEWARE(1938); STABLEMATES(1938); KID FROM KOKOMO, THE(1939); TIMBER STAMPEDE(1939); DARK COMMAND, THE(1940); INVISIBLE MAN RETURNS, THE(1940); MAN FROM DAKOTA, THE(1940); NORTHWEST PASSAGE(1940); RANGERS OF FORTUNE(1940); SOUTH OF SUEZ(1940); LONE RIDER AMBUSHED, THE(1941); LONE RIDER CROSSES THE RIO, THE(1941); LONE RIDER FIGHTS BACK, THE(1941); LONE RIDER IN GHOST TOWN, THE(1941); MISBEHAVING HUSBANDS(1941); SWAMP WOMAN(1941); BROADWAY BIG SHOT(1942); GENTLEMAN JIM(1942); GLASS KEY, THE(1942); IN OLD CALIFORNIA(1942); MEN OF TEXAS(1942); MR. CELEBRITY(1942); MY FAVORITE SPY(1942); SIN TOWN(1942); TEXAS MAN HUNT(1942); THIS TIME FOR KEEPS(1942); CALLING WILD BILL ELLIOTT(1943); CORREGIDOR(1943); SHE HAS WHAT IT TAKES(1943); BLAZING FRONTIER(1944); DESTINY(1944); FRENCHMAN'S CREEK(1944); LAW OF THE SADDLE(1944); LOUISIANA HAYRIDE(1944); MAN IN HALF-MOON STREET, THE(1944); ONCE UPON A TIME(1944); SHINE ON, HARVEST MOON(1944); ALONG CAME JONES(1945); SARATOGA TRUNK(1945); SENORITA FROM THE WEST(1945); EASY TO WED(1946); GIRL ON THE SPOT(1946); IT'S A WONDERFUL LIFE(1946); NIGHT IN PARADISE, A(1946); ROAD TO RIO(1947); SEA OF GRASS, THE(1947); TOO MANY WINNERS(1947); UNCONQUERED(1947); WILD HARVEST(1947); WISTFUL WIDOW OF WAGON GAP, THE(1947); HARPOON(1948); JOAN OF ARC(1948); KISS THE BLOOD OFF MY HANDS(1948); NIGHT HAS A THOUSAND EYES(1948); PALEFACE, THE(1948); RIVER LADY(1948); SOUTHERN YANKEE, A(1948); THREE MUSKETEERS, THE(1948); GRAND CANYON(1949); KNOCK ON ANY DOOR(1949); ON THE TOWN(1949); MAN IN THE SADDLE(1951); MY FAVORITE SPY(1951); SANTA FE(1951); SON OF DR. JEKYLL, THE(1951); HANGMAN'S KNOT(1952); SAN FRANCISCO STORY, THE(1952); PERILOUS JOURNEY, A(1953); STRANGER WORE A GUN, THE(1953); RIOT IN CELL BLOCK 11(1954); SILVER CHALICE, THE(1954); THREE HOURS TO KILL(1954); LAWLESS STREET, A(1955); LUCY GALLANT(1955); MAN ALONE, A(1955); CRASHING LAS VEGAS(1956); FRIENDLY PERSUASION(1956); HARDER THEY FALL, THE(1956); GUNFIGHT AT THE O.K. CORRAL(1957); KETTLES ON OLD MACDONALD'S FARM, THE(1957); ZOMBIES OF MORA TAU(1957); LAST TRAIN FROM GUN HILL(1959); MC LINTOCK!(1963)
Silents
ANNE OF LITTLE SMOKY(1921); GALLOPING GALLAGHER(1924); LIGHTNING ROMANCE(1924); POISON(1924); ROARING RAILS(1924); NEW CHAMPION(1925); FANGS OF JUSTICE(1926); ICE FLOOD, THE(1926); SEA BEAST, THE(1926); ALL ABOARD(1927); LAST TRAIL, THE(1927); ONE-ROUND HOGAN(1927); FREE LIPS(1928); MIDNIGHT MADNESS(1928); RAWHIDE KID, THE(1928); CAPTAIN LASH(1929); MASKED EMOTIONS(1929)
Misc. Silents
GAUNTLET, THE(1920); DANGEROUS COWARD, THE(1924); WILD JUSTICE(1925); LONE HAND SAUNDERS(1926); ON YOUR TOES(1927); GLORIOUS TRAIL, THE(1928)
Frank S. Hagney
PACK UP YOUR TROUBLES(1932); MYSTERIOUS MR. MOTO(1938); TOMORROW WE LIVE(1942)
Shlomit Hagoel
1984
LITTLE DRUMMER GIRL, THE(1984)
Garrick Hagon
LAST GUNFIGHTER, THE(1961, Can.); ONE PLUS ONE(1961, Can.); MOHAMMAD, MESSENGER OF GOD(1976, Lebanon/Brit.); SPY WHO LOVED ME, THE(1977, Brit.); STAR WARS(1977); TWILIGHT'S LAST GLEAMING(1977, U.S./Ger.)
Rex Hagon
REINCARNATE, THE(1971, Can.)
Rich Hagood
SUGAR HILL(1974)

Berj Hagopian
CODE OF SILENCE(1960), p; INVASION OF THE STAR CREATURES(1962), p
Edward Hagopian
TRAPEZE(1956)
Lars Hagstrom
GLADIATORS, THE(1970, Swed.), ed
Albert Hague
FAME(1980); NIGHTMARES(1983)
Andre Haguet
SECRET DOCUMENT – VIENNA(1954, Fr.), d; THUNDER IN THE BLOOD(1962, Fr.), d, w
William Haguet
LA MARSEILLAISE(1938, Fr.)
George Hagy
SUGARLAND EXPRESS, THE(1974)
Patte Wheat Hahan
DOCTOR, YOU'VE GOT TO BE KIDDING(1967), w
Dennis Hahat
TURNING POINT, THE(1977)
Alfred Hahm
HAPPY(1934, Brit.), w
Archie Hahn
PHANTOM OF THE PARADISE(1974); SUNSHINE BOYS, THE(1975); CANNONBALL(1976, U.S./Hong Kong)
1984
MEATBALLS PART II(1984); PROTOCOL(1984); THIS IS SPINAL TAP(1984)
Birgitta Hahn
LOVING COUPLES(1966, Swed.), cos
Edwin C. Hahn
ONLY ANGELS HAVE WINGS(1939), spec eff
Gisela Hahn
THEY CALL ME TRINITY(1971, Ital.); CESAR AND ROSALIE(1972, Fr.); DON'T TURN THE OTHER CHEEK(1974, Ital./Ger./Span.); ALIEN CONTAMINATION(1982, Ital.)
Misc. Talkies
MISTER SCARFACE(1977)
Jess Hahn
HAPPY ROAD, THE(1957); NATHALIE(1958, Fr.); FEMALE, THE(1960, Fr.); BIG GAMBLE, THE(1961); TIME BOMB(1961, Fr./Ital.); CARTOUCHE(1962, Fr./Ital.); TRIAL, THE(1963, Fr./Ital./Ger.); STOP TRAIN 349(1964, Fr./Ital./Ger.); TOPKAPI(1964); WHAT'S NEW, PUSSYCAT?(1965, U.S./Fr.); GREAT SPY CHASE, THE(1966, Fr.); SECRET AGENT SUPER DRAGON(1966, Fr./Ital./Ger./Monaco); UP TO HIS EARS(1966, Fr./Ital.); TRIPLE CROSS(1967, Fr./Brit.); POSTMAN GOES TO WAR, THE(1968, Fr.); NIGHT OF THE FOLLOWING DAY, THE(1969, Brit.); WISE GUYS(1969, Fr./Ital.); BAD MAN'S RIVER(1972, Span.); MYSTERIOUS ISLAND OF CAPTAIN NEMO, THE(1973, Fr./Ital. 87m Span./Cameroon); THREE TOUGH GUYS(1974, U.S./Ital.); MEAN FRANK AND CRAZY TONY(1976, Ital.); SICILIAN CONNECTION, THE(1977); MAMMA DRACULA(1980, Bel./Fr.)
Misc. Talkies
FULLER REPORT, THE(1966)
Jordon Hahn
SAFE PLACE, A(1971)
Lisa Hahn
Misc. Talkies
ALIEN CONTAMINATION(1981)
Louis Hahn
Misc. Silents
DOLLY DOES HER BIT(1918)
Manon Hahn
JUDGE AND THE SINNER, THE(1964, Ger.), cos; MAEDCHEN IN UNIFORM(1965, Ger./Fr.), cos
Otto Hahn
LETTER, THE(1940); TWO GIRLS ON BROADWAY(1940)
Paul Hahn
DESPERATE WOMEN, THE(?); AMAZING COLOSSAL MAN, THE(1957); ANGRY RED PLANET, THE(1959)
Pauline Hahn
TOO YOUNG TO LOVE(1960, Brit.)
Philip Hahn
Silents
NIGHTINGALE, THE(1914); SENATOR, THE(1915); CLARION, THE(1916)
Misc. Silents
GARDEN OF LIES, THE(1915); SCARLET OATH, THE(1916)
Ross Hahn
SHELL SHOCK(1964), spec eff; WAR IS HELL(1964), p
Susan Hahn
STILL SMOKIN'(1983)
Unjin Hahn
MONSTER WANGMAGWI(1967, S. K.)
Peter Hahne
DEAD RUN(1961, Fr./Ital./Ger.), p
Charles Haid
CHOIRBOYS, THE(1977); OLIVER'S STORY(1978); WHO'LL STOP THE RAIN?(1978); ALTERED STATES(1980)
1984
HOUSE OF GOD, THE(1984)
Misc. Talkies
HOUSE OF GOD, THE(1979)
Liane Haid
DIE MANNER UM LUCIE(1931); IMMORTAL VAGABOND(1931, Ger.); MOZART(1940, Brit.)
Silents
WOMAN'S SECRET, A(1924, Brit.)
Katsu kaika Haida
TOKYO FILE 212(1951)
Katsuhiko Haida
ESCAPADE IN JAPAN(1957)

Dina Haidar
CIRCLE OF DECEIT(1982, Fr./Ger.)
Sara Haidez
Misc. Silents
GREATER WOMAN, THE(1917)
Caroline Haig
HALF A SIXPENCE(1967, Brit.)
David Haig
1984
DARK ENEMY(1984, Brit.)
Don Haig
125 ROOMS OF COMFORT(1974, Can.), p; SUMMER'S CHILDREN(1979, Can.), p
Douglas Haig
SINS OF THE FATHERS(1928); WELCOME DANGER(1929); CAUGHT SHORT(1930); CISCO KID(1931); ATTORNEY FOR THE DEFENSE(1932); THAT'S MY BOY(1932); HIGH GEAR(1933)
Misc. Talkies
MAN'S BEST FRIEND(1935)
Gloria Haig
SEE HOW THEY RUN(1955, Brit.)
Jack Haig
EMILY(1976, Brit.)
Michael Haig
1984
WILD HORSES(1984, New Zealand)
Noel Haig
WACKY WORLD OF DR. MORGUS, THE(1962), w
Peter Haig
ORDERS ARE ORDERS(1959, Brit.)
Maj. Raoul Haig
WINDJAMMER(1937), w
Roul Haig
OKEFENOKEE(1960), d; WACKY WORLD OF DR. MORGUS, THE(1962), d, w
Sid Haig
FIREBRAND, THE(1962); IT'S A BIKINI WORLD(1967); POINT BLANK(1967); HELICOPTER SPIES, THE(1968); HELL WITH HEROES, THE(1968); SPIDER BABY(1968); CHE!(1969); PIT STOP(1969); BIG DOLL HOUSE, THE(1971); C. C. AND COMPANY(1971); DIAMONDS ARE FOREVER(1971, Brit.); THX 1138(1971); BIG BIRD CAGE, THE(1972); BLACK MAMA, WHITE MAMA(1973); COFFY(1973); DON IS DEAD, THE(1973); EMPEROR OF THE NORTH POLE(1973); WONDER WOMEN(1973, Phil.); FOXY DROWN(1974); SAVAGE SISTERS(1974); WOMAN HUNT, THE(1975, U.S./Phil.); SWASHBUCKLER(1976); CHU CHU AND THE PHILLY FLASH(1981); GALAXY OF TERROR(1981)
Misc. Talkies
BIG DOLL HOUSE, THE(1971); AFTERMATH, THE(1980)
Sidney Haig
BEYOND ATLANTIS(1973, Phil.)
Terry Haig
PYX, THE(1973, Can.); CITY ON FIRE(1979 Can.); ONE MAN(1979, Can.); GAS(1981, Can.); HAPPY BIRTHDAY TO ME(1981)
Tony Haig
HARD RIDE, THE(1971); SWARM, THE(1978)
Caroline Haigh
ELEPHANT MAN, THE(1980, Brit.)
Charles Haigh
VILLAIN, THE(1979); PURSUIT OF D.B. COOPER, THE(1981)
Colin Haigh
BUTLEY(1974, Brit.)
Kenneth Haigh
COMPANIONS IN CRIME(1954, Brit.); HIGH FLIGHT(1957, Brit.); SAINT JOAN(1957); TEENAGE BAD GIRL(1959, Brit.); CLEOPATRA(1963); HARD DAY'S NIGHT, A(1964, Brit.); WEEKEND AT DUNKIRK(1966, Fr./Ital.); DEADLY AFFAIR, THE(1967, Brit.); LOVELY WAY TO DIE, A(1968); EAGLE IN A CAGE(1971, U.S./Yugo.); MAN AT THE TOP(1973, Brit.); ROBIN AND MARIAN(1976, Brit.)
Misc. Talkies
BITCH, THE(1979)
Peter Haigh
SIMON AND LAURA(1956, Brit.); BAND OF THIEVES(1962, Brit.); SING AND SWING(1964, Brit.); CONQUEROR WORM, THE(1968, Brit.)
Daniel Haight
ON OUR MERRY WAY(1948); SO DEAR TO MY HEART(1949)
George Haight
GOODBYE AGAIN(1933), w; GOLD DIGGERS OF 1937(1936), w; IN NAME ONLY(1939), p; STORY OF VERNON AND IRENE CASTLE, THE(1939), p; LUCKY PARTNERS(1940), p; HONEYMOON FOR THREE(1941), w; KATHLEEN(1941), p; WHISTLING IN THE DARK(1941), p; WHISTLING IN DIXIE(1942), p; SWING SHIFT MAISIE(1943), p; WHISTLING IN BROOKLYN(1943), p; LOST IN A HAREM(1944), p; MAISIE GOES TO RENO(1944), p; SEE HERE, PRIVATE HARGROVE(1944), p; KEEP YOUR POWDER DRY(1945), p; WHAT NEXT, CORPORAL HARGROVE?(1945), p; UP GOES MAISIE(1946), p; LADY IN THE LAKE(1947), p; UNDERCOVER MAISIE(1947), p
Gordon Haight
HONKY TONK FREEWAY(1981)
Jack Haigis
LUGGAGE OF THE GODS(1983), ed
Bradley Hail
MAJOR AND THE MINOR, THE(1942)
Susan Hail
ELECTRA GLIDE IN BLUE(1973)
Henri Haile
PARADISIO(1962, Brit.), w
Arthur Hailey
CONCORDE, THE–AIRPORT '79(, w; ZERO HOUR!(1957), w; TIME LOCK(1959, Brit.), w; YOUNG DOCTORS, THE(1961), w; HOTEL(1967), w; AIRPORT(1970), w
Bert Hailey
DAD AND DAVE COME TO TOWN(1938, Aus.), w
Marian Hailey
JENNY(1969); LOVERS AND OTHER STRANGERS(1970); SURVIVORS, THE(1983)

Oliver Hailey
JUST YOU AND ME, KID(1979), w; RICH AND FAMOUS(1981)
Marian Hailey-Moss
SEDUCTION OF JOE TYNAN, THE(1979)
Nelson Hailparn
VOICES(1979)
Corey Haim
1984
FIRSTBORN(1984)
Paul Ben Haim
HILL 24 DOESN'T ANSWER(1955, Israel), m
Victor Haim
1984
BLAME IT ON RIO(1984)
Julius Haimann
WHAT WOMEN DREAM(1933, Ger.), p; GIRL THIEF, THE(1938), p
Connie Haimes
WAVE, A WAC AND A MARINE, A(1944)
Eric Haims
WHY WOULD I LIE(1980)
Eric Jeffrey Haims
Misc. Talkies
JEKYLL AND HYDE PORTFOLIO, THE(1972), d
Abrasha Haimson
STOP THAT CAB(1951), p
Horace Hain
Silents
KIDNAPPED(1917)
Mary Hain
WAIT 'TIL THE SUN SHINES, NELLIE(1952)
Harriet Haindl
MURPH THE SURF(1974)
Horace Haine
Silents
TRUTH, THE(1920)
Robert Haine
GIRL IN THE GLASS CAGE, THE(1929)
Alan Haines
MILLIONS LIKE US(1943, Brit.); MADONNA OF THE SEVEN MOONS(1945, Brit.); MINE OWN EXECUTIONER(1948, Brit.), cos; EYES OF ANNIE JONES, THE(1963, Brit.)
Bert Haines
Silents
GO WEST(1925), ph; BATTLING BUTLER(1926), ph; COLLEGE(1927), ph; GENERAL, THE(1927), ph; STEAMBOAT BILL, JR.(1928), ph
Bob Haines
EBB TIDE(1937)
Brian Haines
MOMENT OF INDISCRETION(1958, Brit.); INNOCENT MEETING(1959, Brit.); NEVER MENTION MURDER(1964, Brit.); PARTNER, THE(1966, Brit.); IT!(1967, Brit.); ON THE RUN(1967, Brit.)
Connie Haines
MOON OVER LAS VEGAS(1944); TWILIGHT ON THE PRAIRIE(1944); DUCHESS OF IDAHO, THE(1950)
Daniel Haines
THE INVISIBLE RAY(1936)
David Haines
SKIPPY(1931); WOMAN TRAP(1936)
Donald Haines
LITTLE MAN, WHAT NOW?(1934); NO GREATER GLORY(1934); NOW I'LL TELL(1934); STRAIGHT FROM THE HEART(1935); TALE OF TWO CITIES, A(1935); LITTLE MISS NOBODY(1936); LOVE AND HISSES(1937); KIDNAPPED(1938); THREE COMRADES(1938); NEVER SAY DIE(1939); SERGEANT MADDEN(1939); BOYS OF THE CITY(1940); EAST SIDE KIDS(1940); FUGITIVE FROM A PRISON CAMP(1940); RETURN OF WILD BILL, THE(1940); SEVENTEEN(1940); THAT GANG OF MINE(1940); BOWERY BLITZKRIEG(1941); FLYING WILD(1941); PRIDE OF THE BOWERY(1941); SPOOKS RUN WILD(1941)
Fred Haines
ULYSSES(1967, U.S./Brit.), w; STEPPENWOLF(1974), d&w
Jim Haines
LONG SHOT(1981, Brit.)
Larry Haines
ODD COUPLE, THE(1968); SEVEN UPS, THE(1973)
Lloyd Haines
ICE STATION ZEBRA(1968); MADIGAN(1968)
Louis Haines
Silents
BEYOND PRICE(1921)
Minna Gale Haines
Silents
PORT OF MISSING MEN(1914)
Patricia Haines
OPERATION CONSPIRACY(1957, Brit.); BLOOD BEAST FROM OUTER SPACE(1965, Brit.); LAST SHOT YOU HEAR, THE(1969, Brit.); WALK A CROOKED PATH(1969, Brit.); VIRGIN WITCH, THE(1973, Brit.)
Reah Haines
Silents
MAN FROM PAINTED POST, THE(1917)
Rhea Haines
Silents
COUNTRY MOUSE, THE(1914); ODYSSEY OF A NORTH, AN(1914); NINA, THE FLOWER GIRL(1917); SCARLET DAYS(1919); ALWAYS AUDACIOUS(1920); MASTER STROKE, A(1920); GIRLS DON'T GAMBLE(1921)
Richard Haines
STUCK ON YOU(1983), ed
1984
FIRST TURN-ON!, THE(1984), ed; STUCK ON YOU(1984), ed

Richard W. Haines
1984
SPLATTER UNIVERSITY(1984), a, p, d, w, ed
Rob Haines
MICHAEL O'HALLORAN(1948)
Robert Haines
GUILTY?(1930); UNDERCOVER MAN, THE(1949)
Robert T. Haines
SHANNONS OF BROADWAY, THE(1929); DYNAMITE(1930); THESE THIRTY YEARS(1934); GIGOLETTE(1935)
Silents
NOOSE, THE(1928)
Misc. Silents
HEART OF NEW YORK, THE(1916); VICTIM, THE(1917); CAPITOL, THE(1920); DOES IT PAY?(1923); GOVERNOR'S LADY, THE(1923)
Ron Haines
Misc. Talkies
LEGEND OF ALFRED PACKER, THE(1979)
Ronald Haines
DEADLOCK(1943, Brit.), p&d; MAN WITH THE MAGNETIC EYES, THE(1945, Brit.), p,d&w; MR. H. C. ANDERSEN(1950, Brit.), p&d, w
Ronnie Haines
RUN FOR YOUR MONEY, A(1950, Brit.)
Sol Haines
SONG OF SCHEHERAZADE(1947)
Thomas Haines
Misc. Silents
BEAUTY SHOPPERS(1927)
Victor Haines
PAISAN(1948, Ital.), w
William Haines
ALIAS JIMMY VALENTINE(1928); FREE AND EASY(1930); GIRL SAID NO, THE(1930); NAVY BLUES(1930); REMOTE CONTROL(1930); WAY OUT WEST(1930); JUST A GIGOLO(1931), a, art d; NEW ADVENTURES OF GET-RICH-QUICK WALLINGFORD, THE(1931); TAILOR MADE MAN, A(1931); ARE YOU LISTENING?(1932); FAST LIFE(1932); YOUNG AND BEAUTIFUL(1934); MARINES ARE COMING, THE(1935)
Silents
SOULS FOR SALE(1923); THREE WISE FOOLS(1923); MIDNIGHT EXPRESS, THE(1924); LITTLE ANNIE ROONEY(1925); TOWER OF LIES, THE(1925); BROWN OF HARVARD(1926); MEMORY LANE(1926); MIKE(1926); TELL IT TO THE MARINES(1926); LITTLE JOURNEY, A(1927); SLIDE, KELLY, SLIDE(1927); EXCESS BAGGAGE(1928); SHOW PEOPLE(1928); SMART SET, THE(1928); TELLING THE WORLD(1928); WEST POINT(1928); DUKE STEPS OUT, THE(1929); MAN'S MAN, A(1929)
Misc. Silents
GAIETY GIRL, THE(1924); DENIAL, THE(1925); FIGHTING THE FLAMES(1925); FOOL AND HIS MONEY, A(1925); SALLY, IRENE AND MARY(1925); SLAVE OF FASHION, A(1925); WHO CARES(1925); LOVEY MARY(1926); THRILL HUNTER, THE(1926); SPRING FEVER(1927); SPEEDWAY(1929)
William Wister Haines
MAN OF IRON(1935), w; BLACK LEGION, THE(1937), w; MR. DODD TAKES THE AIR(1937), w; SLIM(1937), w; TEXANS, THE(1938), w; BEYOND GLORY(1948), w; COMMAND DECISION(1948), w; RACKET, THE(1951), w; ONE MINUTE TO ZERO(1952), w; ETERNAL SEA, THE(1955), w; WINGS OF EAGLES, THE(1957), w; TORPEDO RUN(1958), w
Zachary Haines
GUESS WHAT WE LEARNED IN SCHOOL TODAY?(1970)
James Hainesworth
SHAFT(1971)
Betty Jean Hainey
DIMPLES(1936); LITTLE MISS NOBODY(1936); POSTMAN DIDN'T RING, THE(1942)
Daniel Hainey
1984
AMERICAN NIGHTMARE(1984), ph; CITY GIRL, THE(1984), ph
Marcella Hainia
BOUDU SAVED FROM DROWNING(1967, Fr.)
Marcelle Hainia
IT HAPPENED AT THE INN(1945, Fr.)
Leopold Hainisch
LAST TEN DAYS, THE(1956, Ger.); HIPPODROME(1961, Aust./Ger.); DIE HAMBURGER KRANKHEIT(1979, Ger./Fr.)
Otto Hainisch
SIGNALS-AN ADVENTURE IN SPACE(1970, E. Ger./Pol.), ph, spec eff
Zachary Hains
1984
PERFECT STRANGERS(1984)
Edward Haire
DID YOU HEAR THE ONE ABOUT THE TRAVELING SALESLADY?(1968), ed
Jester Hairston
SUNDOWN(1941); GYPSY COLT(1954); TARZAN'S HIDDEN JUNGLE(1955); ALAMO, THE(1960); RAYMIE(1960); SUMMER AND SMOKE(1961); TO KILL A MOCKINGBIRD(1962); IN THE HEAT OF THE NIGHT(1967); FINIAN'S RAINBOW(1968); LADY SINGS THE BLUES(1972)
Margaret Hairston
PORGY AND BESS(1959)
William Hairston
TAKE THE HIGH GROUND(1953)
Dr. Harry J. Haiseld
Misc. Silents
BLACK STORK, THE(1917)
Bill Haislip
Misc. Talkies
BARBARA(1970)
Capt. Harvey Haislip, U.S.N.
STAND BY FOR ACTION(1942), w

Cdr. Harvey Haislip
THUNDER AFLOAT(1939), w; FLIGHT COMMAND(1940), w
Lt. Cmdr. Harvey Haislip, U.S.N.
FOLLOW THE FLEET(1936), tech adv
Harvey S. Haislip
FLYING MISSILE(1950), w
Irene Haisman
TIME, THE PLACE AND THE GIRL, THE(1929)
Silents
ABYSMAL BRUTE, THE(1923); SLANDER THE WOMAN(1923)
Mervyn Haisman
CRIMSON CULT, THE(1970, Brit.), w
Bernard Haitink
MAHLER(1974, Brit.), m
Jacques Haitkin
HOT TOMORROWS(1978), ph; THEY WENT THAT-A-WAY AND THAT-A-WAY(1978), ph; PRIZE FIGHTER, THE(1979), ph; PRIVATE EYES, THE(1980), ph; GALAXY OF TERROR(1981), ph; PROTECTORS, BOOK 1, THE(1981), ph; ST. HELENS(1981), ph; HOUSE WHERE EVIL DWELLS, THE(1982), ph
1984
MAKING THE GRADE(1984), ph; NIGHTMARE ON ELM STREET, A(1984), ph
Heimo Haitto
THERE'S MAGIC IN MUSIC(1941)
Izet Hajdarhodzic
KAYA, I'LL KILL YOU(1969, Yugo./Fr.)
Bernard Hajdenberg
EVENTS(1970), ed
A. Hajdu
LYDIA(1964, Can.), m
Andre Hajdu
LIFT, THE(1965, Brit./Can.), m
Paul K. Haje
THX 1138(1971)
Miroslav Hajek
DO YOU KEEP A LION AT HOME?(1966, Czech.), ed; LEMONADE JOE(1966, Czech.), ed; LOVES OF A BLONDE(1966, Czech.), ed; SWEET LIGHT IN A DARK ROOM(1966, Czech.), ed; DAISIES(1967, Czech.), ed; END OF AUGUST AT THE HOTEL OZONE, THE(1967, Czech.), ed; TRANSPORT FROM PARADISE(1967, Czech.), ed; DIAMONDS OF THE NIGHT(1968, Czech.), ed; FIFTH HORSEMAN IS FEAR, THE(1968, Czech.), ed; FIREMAN'S BALL, THE(1968, Czech.), ed; MARTYRS OF LOVE(1968, Czech.), ed; MURDER CZECH STYLE(1968, Czech.), ed; REPORT ON THE PARTY AND THE GUESTS, A(1968, Czech.), ed; SIGN OF THE VIRGIN(1969, Czech.), ed; DIVINE EMMA, THE(1983, Czech,), ed
Mirslav Hajek
MARKETA LAZAROVA(1968, Czech.), ed
Ron Hajek
Misc. Talkies
SWINGING CHEERLEADERS, THE(1974)
Grethe Hajer
EDVARD MUNCH(1976, Norway/Swed.), art d
Haji
MOTOR PSYCHO(1965); GOOD MORNING... AND GOODBYE(1967); KILLING OF A CHINESE BOOKIE, THE(1976)
Misc. Talkies
UP YOUR ALLEY(1975); MELON AFFAIR, THE(1979)
Dilys Hajlett
WHAT CHANGED CHARLEY FARTHING?(1976, Brit.)
Stephen Hajnal
BRAIN THAT WOULDN'T DIE, THE(1959), ph
Joe Hajos
DANGER IS A WOMAN(1952, Fr.), m; ACT OF LOVE(1953), m; LE PLAISIR(1954, Fr.), m
Joseph Hajos
TALE OF FIVE WOMEN, A(1951, Brit.), m
Karl Hajos
MOROCCO(1930), m; DISHONORED(1931), m; FIGHTING CARAVANS(1931), m; SONG OF SONGS(1933), m; FOUR FRIGHTENED PEOPLE(1934), m; MANHATTAN MOON(1935), m; RIDERS OF THE WHISTLING SKULL(1937), m; HITLER'S MADMAN(1943), m; SULTAN'S DAUGHTER, THE(1943), m, md; CHARLIE CHAN IN THE SECRET SERVICE(1944), md; SUMMER STORM(1944), m, md; DANGEROUS INTRUDER(1945), m; MAN WHO WALKED ALONE, THE(1945), m; MISSING CORPSE, THE(1945), m; PHANTOM OF 42ND STREET, THE(1945), m; SHADOW OF TERROR(1945), m; DOWN MISSOURI WAY(1946), m; DRIFTIN' RIVER(1946), md; QUEEN OF BURLESQUE(1946), md; SECRETS OF A SORORITY GIRL(1946), md; STARS OVER TEXAS(1946), md; WILD WEST(1946), md; APPOINTMENT WITH MURDER(1948), m; DEVIL'S CARGO, THE(1948), m; LOVABLE CHEAT, THE(1949), m; SEARCH FOR DANGER(1949), m; IT'S A SMALL WORLD(1950), m; KILL OR BE KILLED(1950), m
Dean Hajum
STAR 80(1983)
Fikret Hakan
THERE IS STILL ROOM IN HELL(1963, Ger.); YOU CAN'T WIN 'EM ALL(1970, Brit.); TARGET: HARRY(1980)
Ardell Hake
SCARED TO DEATH(1981), m
Janet Hake
PERSONAL BEST(1982)
Abdul Hakeim
PUTNEY SWOPE(1969)
Andre Hakim
MR. BELVEDERE RINGS THE BELL(1951), p; O. HENRY'S FULL HOUSE(1952), p; POWDER RIVER(1953), p; MAN WHO NEVER WAS, THE(1956, Brit.), p; SEA WIFE(1957, Brit.), p; LA BONNE SOUPE(1964, Fr./Ital.), p; FRIEND OF THE FAMILY(1965, Fr./Ital.), p; HELLO-GOODBYE(1970), p
Eric Hakim
BLAME THE WOMAN(1932, Brit.), p; OUTSIDER, THE(1933, Brit.), p; WIVES BEWARE(1933, Brit.), p

Gaston Hakim
IT'S HOT IN PARADISE(1962, Ger./Yugo.), p
Raphael Hakim
HER HUSBAND'S AFFAIRS(1947), p; BELL' ANTONIO(1962, Ital.), p
Raymond Hakim
PEPE LE MOKO(1937, Fr.), p; LA BETE HUMAINE(1938, Fr.), p; HEART-BEAT(1946), p; LONG NIGHT, THE(1947), p; WITHOUT HONOR(1949), p; HUNCH-BACK OF NOTRE DAME, THE(1957, Fr.), p; PURPLE NOON(1961, Fr./Ital.), p; WEB OF PASSION(1961, Fr.), p; ECLIPSE(1962, Fr./Ital.), p; EVA(1962, Fr./Ital.), p; CIR-CLE OF LOVE(1965, Fr.), p; HIGHWAY PICKUP(1965, Fr./Ital.), p; WEEKEND AT DUNKIRK(1966, Fr./Ital.), p; BELLE DE JOUR(1968, Fr.), p; ISADORA(1968, Brit.), p
Robert Hakim
PEPE LE MOKO(1937, Fr.), p; LA BETE HUMAINE(1938, Fr.), p; SOUTHERNER, THE(1945), p; HEARTBEAT(1946), p; WITHOUT HONOR(1949), p; HUNCHBACK OF NOTRE DAME, THE(1957, Fr.), p; PURPLE NOON(1961, Fr./Ital.), p; WEB OF PASSION(1961, Fr.), p; ECLIPSE(1962, Fr./Ital.), p; EVA(1962, Fr./Ital.), p; CIRCLE OF LOVE(1965, Fr.), p; HIGHWAY PICKUP(1965, Fr./Ital.), p; WEEKEND AT DUN-KIRK(1966, Fr./Ital.), p; BELLE DE JOUR(1968, Fr.), p; ISADORA(1968, Brit.), p
Richard Hakins
HIT PARADE, THE(1937)
Fritz Hakl
TIN DRUM, THE(1979, Ger./Fr./Yugo./Pol.)
Alex Hakobian
ONE MAN JURY(1978)
Hakki Haktan
DRY SUMMER(1967, Turkey)
Truong Minh Hal
DON'T CRY, IT'S ONLY THUNDER(1982)
Hal Grayson's Recording Orchestra
NIGHT WORLD(1932)
Hal Kemp and his Orchestra
RADIO CITY REVELS(1938)
Hal McIntyre and his Orchestra
EADIE WAS A LADY(1945)
Hal Wright and his Circus
CALLING ALL CROOKS(1938, Brit.)
Vlastimil Hala
LEMONADE JOE(1966, Czech.), m; HAPPY END(1968, Czech.), m
Jean Halain
SIMPLE CASE OF MONEY, A(1952, Fr.), w; CADET-ROUSSELLE(1954, Fr.), w; CASINO DE PARIS(1957, Fr./Ger.), w; STORY OF THE COUNT OF MONTE CRISTO, THE(1962, Fr./Ital.), w; FANTOMAS STRIKES BACK(1965, Fr./Ital.), w; FAN-TOMAS(1966, Fr./Ital.), w; OSS 117–MISSION FOR A KILLER(1966, Fr./Ital.), w; MADMAN OF LAB 4, THE(1967, Fr.), w
Loda Halama
GAMBLING HOUSE(1950)
Halamar & Konarski
FLIGHT FROM FOLLY(1945, Brit.); LISBON STORY, THE(1946, Brit.)
John Halas
ANIMAL FARM(1955, Brit.), p&d, w; MONSTER OF HIGHGATE PONDS, THE(1961, Brit.), p
George Halasz
LINDA BE GOOD(1947), w
Judit Halasz
AGE OF ILLUSIONS(1967, Hung.); FATHER(1967, Hung.)
Laszlo Halasz
ANGI VERA(1980, Hung.)
Garry Halberg
KING KONG(1976)
Ilona Halberstadt
JOURNEYS FROM BERLIN–1971(1980)
Hugo Halbig
MERRY WIVES OF WINDSOR, THE(1966, Aust.), art d
Herbert Halbik
THIRD MAN, THE(1950, Brit.)
Anna Halcewicz-Pleskaczewska
JOVITA(1970, Pol.)
Bert Haldane
Silents
EAST LYNNE(1913, Brit.), d; ROAD TO RUIN, THE(1913, Brit.), d; LURE OF LONDON, THE(1914, Brit.), d; DARKEST LONDON(1915, Brit.), d; JACK TAR(1915, Brit.), d; ROGUES OF LONDON, THE(1915, Brit.), d; MARY LATIMER, NUN(1920, Brit.), d
Misc. Silents
LIGHTS O' LONDON, THE(1914, Brit.), d; BRIGADIER GERARD(1915, Brit.), d; BY THE SHORTEST OF HEADS(1915, Brit.), d; DO UNTO OTHERS(1915, Brit.), d; FIVE NIGHTS(1915, Brit.), d; STRIFE ETERNAL, THE(1915, Brit.), d; TICKET-OF-LEAVE MAN, THE(1918, Brit.), d; ROMANCE OF LADY HAMILTON, THE(1919, Brit.), d; GRIP OF IRON, THE(1920, Brit.), d; WINDING ROAD, THE(1920), d
Don Haldane
REINCARNATE, THE(1971, Can.), d
Donald Haldane
NIKKI, WILD DOG OF THE NORTH(1961, U.S./Can.), d; DRYLANDERS(1963, Can.), d
Georges Haldas
DEATH OF MARIO RICCI, THE(1983, Ital.), w
Edward Haldeman
LADY BODYGUARD(1942), w; SWEET AND LOWDOWN(1944), w
Tim Haldeman
GOOD MORNING, MISS DOVE(1955); BOY WHO CRIED WEREWOLF, THE(1973); NIGHT MOVES(1975); CHANGE OF SEASONS, A(1980); MOUNTAIN MEN, THE(1980); PRIVATE BENJAMIN(1980)
Hans Halden
COURT CONCERT, THE(1936, Ger.)
Bert Haldene
Misc. Silents
TRUTH AND JUSTICE(1916, Brit.), d

Frances Haldern
GOT WHAT SHE WANTED(1930); FIRST YANK INTO TOKYO(1945)
Alan Hale
LEATHERNECK, THE(1929); SAILORS' HOLIDAY(1929); SAL OF SIN-GAPORE(1929); SAP, THE(1929); SPIELER, THE(1929); RED HOT RHYTHM(1930); SHE GOT WHAT SHE WANTED(1930); ALOHA(1931); NIGHT ANGEL, THE(1931); SEA GHOST, THE(1931); SIN OF MADELON CLAUDET, THE(1931); SUSAN LENOX-HER FALL AND RISE(1931); MATCH KING, THE(1932); REBECCA OF SUNNY-BROOK FARM(1932); SO BIG(1932); UNION DEPOT(1932); DESTINATION UN-KNOWN(1933); ELEVENTH COMMANDMENT(1933); WHAT PRICE DECENCY?(1933); BABBITT(1934); FOG OVER FRISCO(1934); GREAT EXPECTA-TIONS(1934); IMITATION OF LIFE(1934); IT HAPPENED ONE NIGHT(1934); LITTLE MAN, WHAT NOW?(1934); LITTLE MINISTER, THE(1934); LOST PATROL, THE,(1934); MISS FANE'S BABY IS STOLEN(1934); OF HUMAN BONDAGE(1934); PICTURE BRIDES(1934); SCARLET LETTER, THE(1934); ANOTHER FACE(1935); CRUSADES, THE(1935); GOOD FAIRY, THE(1935); GRAND OLD GIRL(1935); LAST DAYS OF POMPEII, THE(1935); COUNTRY BEYOND, THE(1936); MESSAGE TO GARCIA, A(1936); PAROLE(1936); TWO IN THE DARK(1936); YELLOWSTONE(1936); GOD'S COUNTRY AND THE WOMAN(1937); HIGH, WIDE AND HANDSOME(1937); MUSIC FOR MADAME(1937); PRINCE AND THE PAUPER, THE(1937); STELLA DALLAS(1937); THIN ICE(1937); WHEN THIEF MEETS THIEF(1937, Brit.); ADVEN-TURES OF MARCO POLO, THE(1938); ADVENTURES OF ROBIN HOOD, THE(1938); ALGIERS(1938); FOUR MEN AND A PRAYER(1938); LISTEN, DARLING(1938); SISTERS, THE(1938); VALLEY OF THE GIANTS(1938); DODGE CITY(1939); DUST BE MY DESTINY(1939); MAN IN THE IRON MASK, THE(1939); ON YOUR TOES(1939); PACIFIC LINER(1939); PRIVATE LIVES OF ELIZABETH AND ESSEX, THE(1939); FIGHTING 69TH, THE(1940); GREEN HELL(1940); SANTA FE TRAIL(1940); SEA HAWK, THE(1940); THEY DRIVE BY NIGHT(1940); THREE CHEERS FOR THE IRISH(1940); TUGBOAT ANNIE SAILS AGAIN(1940); VIRGINIA CITY(1940); FOOT-STEPS IN THE DARK(1941); GREAT MR. NOBODY, THE(1941); MANPOWER(1941); SMILING GHOST, THE(1941); STRAWBERRY BLONDE, THE(1941); THIEVES FALL OUT(1941); CAPTAINS OF THE CLOUDS(1942); DESPERATE JOURNEY(1942); GEN-TLEMAN JIM(1942); JUKE GIRL(1942); ACTION IN THE NORTH ATLANTIC(1943); THANK YOUR LUCKY STARS(1943); THIS IS THE ARMY(1943); ADVENTURES OF MARK TWAIN, THE(1944); DESTINATION TOKYO(1944); JANIE(1944); MAKE YOUR OWN BED(1944); ESCAPE IN THE DESERT(1945); GOD IS MY CO-PI-LOT(1945); ROUGHLY SPEAKING(1945); MAN I LOVE, THE(1946); NIGHT AND DAY(1946); PERILOUS HOLIDAY(1946); TIME, THE PLACE AND THE GIRL, THE(1946); CHEYENNE(1947); MY WILD IRISH ROSE(1947); PURSUED(1947); THAT WAY WITH WOMEN(1947); MY GIRL TISA(1948); ADVENTURES OF DON JUAN(1949); ALWAYS LEAVE THEM LAUGHING(1949); HOUSE ACROSS THE STREET, THE(1949); INSPECTOR GENERAL, THE(1949); SOUTH OF ST. LOUIS(1949); YOUNGER BROTHERS, THE(1949); COLT .45(1950); ROGUES OF SHERWOOD FOREST(1950); STARS IN MY CROWN(1950)
Silents
ETERNAL TEMPTRESS, THE(1917); LIFE'S WHIRLPOOL(1917); FOUR HORSE-MEN OF THE APOCALYPSE, THE(1921); VOICE IN THE DARK(1921); WISE FOOL, A(1921); DICTATOR, THE(1922); ROBIN HOOD(1922); SHIRLEY OF THE CIR-CUS(1922); TRAP, THE(1922); COVERED WAGON, THE(1923); ELEVENTH HOUR, THE(1923); LONG LIVE THE KING(1923); CRIMSON RUNNER, THE(1925); DICK TURPIN(1925); FLATTERY(1925); WEDDING SONG, THE(1925), d; HEARTS AND FISTS(1926); RUBBER TIRES(1927), d; VANITY(1927); LEOPARD LADY, THE(1928); OH, KAY(1928)
Misc. Silents
POWER OF THE PRESS, THE(1914); WOMAN IN BLACK, THE(1914); BEAST, THE(1916); LOVE THIEF, THE(1916); PUDD'NHEAD WILSON(1916); PURPLE LADY, THE(1916); ROLLING STONES(1916); WOMAN IN THE CASE, A(1916); ONE HOUR(1917); PRICE SHE PAID, THE(1917); OVER THE WIRE(1921); DOLL'S HOUSE, A(1922); ONE GLORIOUS DAY(1922); CAMEO KIRBY(1923); QUICKSANDS(1923); CODE OF THE WILDERNESS(1924); GIRLS MEN FORGET(1924); ONE NIGHT IN ROME(1924); TROUBLES OF A BRIDE(1924); BRAVEHEART(1925), d; FLAT-TERY(1925); SCARLET HONEYMOON, THE(1925), d; FORBIDDEN WATERS(1926), d; RISKY BUSINESS(1926), d; SPORTING LOVER, THE(1926), d; COP, THE(1928), d; POWER(1928); SKYSCRAPER(1928)
Alan Hale, Jr.
ALL-AMERICAN CO-ED(1941); DIVE BOMBER(1941); I WANTED WINGS(1941); EAGLE SQUADRON(1942); RUBBER RACKETEERS(1942); TO THE SHORES OF TRIPOLI(1942); TOP SERGEANT(1942); WAKE ISLAND(1942); NO TIME FOR LO-VE(1943); WATCH ON THE RHINE(1943); MONSIEUR BEAUCAIRE(1946); SWEET-HEART OF SIGMA CHI(1946); IT HAPPENED ON 5TH AVENUE(1947); SARGE GOES TO COLLEGE(1947); SPIRIT OF WEST POINT, THE(1947); HOMECOMING(1948); MUSIC MAN(1948); ONE SUNDAY AFTERNOON(1948); IT HAPPENS EVERY SPRING(1949); RIDERS IN THE SKY(1949); RIM OF THE CANYON(1949); BLAZING SUN, THE(1950); FOUR DAYS LEAVE(1950, Switz.); GUNFIGHTER, THE(1950); KILL THE UMPIRE(1950); SHORT GRASS(1950); WEST POINT STORY, THE(1950); WHIPPED, THE(1950); AT SWORD'S POINT(1951); HOME TOWN STORY(1951); HONEYCHILE(1951); SIERRA PASSAGE(1951); ARCTIC FLIGHT(1952); BIG TREES, THE(1952); LADY IN THE IRON MASK(1952); MAN BEHIND THE GUN, THE(1952); MR. WALKIE TALKIE(1952); SPRINGFIELD RIFLE(1952); WAIT 'TIL THE SUN SHINES, NELLIE(1952); CAPTAIN JOHN SMITH AND POCAHONTAS(1953); CAP-TAIN KIDD AND THE SLAVE GIRL(1954); DESTRY(1954); IRON GLOVE, THE(1954); LAW VS. BILLY THE KID, THE(1954); ROGUE COP(1954); SILVER LODE(1954); INDIAN FIGHTER, THE(1955); MAN ALONE, A(1955); MANY RIVERS TO CROSS(1955); SEA CHASE, THE(1955); YOUNG AT HEART(1955); CANYON RI-VER(1956); CRUEL TOWER, THE(1956); KILLER IS LOOSE, THE(1956); THREE OUTLAWS, THE(1956); AFFAIR IN RENO(1957); ALL MINE TO GIVE(1957); BATTLE HYMN(1957); TRUE STORY OF JESSE JAMES, THE(1957); LADY TAKES A FLYER, THE(1958); UP PERISCOPE(1959); THUNDER IN CAROLINA(1960); LONG ROPE, THE(1961); CRAWLING HAND, THE(1963); SWINGIN' MAIDEN, THE(1963, Brit.); ADVANCE TO THE REAR(1964); BULLET FOR A BADMAN(1964); HANG'EM HIGH(1968); THERE WAS A CROOKED MAN(1970); TIGER BY THE TAIL(1970); GIANT SPIDER INVASION(1971); BEHIND THE IRON MASK(1977); NORTH AVE-NUE IRREGULARS, THE(1979)
1984
JOHNNY DANGEROUSLY(1984)
Misc. Talkies
YELLOW HAIRED KID, THE(1952); TRAIL BLAZERS(1953); EVIDENCE OF POW-ER(1979); GREAT MONKEY RIP-OFF, THE(1979)

Alan Hale, Sr.
OUR RELATIONS(1936); HOLLYWOOD CANTEEN(1944); HOTEL BERLIN(1945); WHIPLASH(1948)
Misc. Talkies
NEIGHBORHOOD HOUSE(1936), d
Allene Hale
Misc. Silents
LOVE HUNGER, THE(1919)
Barbara Hale
AROUND THE WORLD(1943); GILDERSLEEVE'S BAD DAY(1943); GOVERNMENT GIRL(1943); HIGHER AND HIGHER(1943); IRON MAJOR, THE(1943); MEXICAN SPITFIRE'S BLESSED EVENT(1943); SEVENTH VICTIM, THE(1943); FALCON IN HOLLYWOOD, THE(1944); FALCON OUT WEST(1944); GOIN' TO TOWN(1944); HEAVENLY DAYS(1944); FIRST YANK INTO TOKYO(1945); WEST OF THE PECOS(1945); LADY LUCK(1946); LIKELY STORY, A(1947); AND BABY MAKES THREE(1949); BOY WITH THE GREEN HAIR, THE(1949); CLAY PIGEON, THE(1949); JOLSON SINGS AGAIN(1949); WINDOW, THE(1949); EMERGENCY WEDDING(1950); JACKPOT, THE(1950); LORNA DOONE(1951); FIRST TIME, THE(1952); LAST OF THE COMANCHES(1952); LION IS IN THE STREETS, A(1953); LONE HAND, THE(1953); SEMINOLE(1953); FAR HORIZONS, THE(1955); UNCHAINED(1955); HOUSTON STORY, THE(1956); SEVENTH CAVALRY(1956); OKLAHOMAN, THE(1957); SLIM CARTER(1957); DESERT HELL(1958); BUCKSKIN(1968); AIRPORT(1970); RED, WHITE AND BLACK, THE(1970); GIANT SPIDER INVASION, THE(1975); BIG WEDNESDAY(1978)
Barnaby Hale
ADVANCE TO THE REAR(1964); VIVA LAS VEGAS(1964)
Bernadette Hale
FLIGHT THAT DISAPPEARED, THE(1961)
Bill Hale
COURTIN' TROUBLE(1948); FRONTIER AGENT(1948); GUN TALK(1948); HIDDEN DANGER(1949); RANGE JUSTICE(1949); RAIDERS OF TOMAHAWK CREEK(1950); LORNA DOONE(1951); SILVER CANYON(1951); WE'RE NOT MARRIED(1952); HANNAH LEE(1953); BATTLE OF ROGUE RIVER(1954); HIGHWAY DRAGNET(1954); MASSACRE CANYON(1954); APACHE AMBUSH(1955); FIRST TRAVELING SALESLADY, THE(1956); GIANT(1956); CATTLE EMPIRE(1958); SNOWFIRE(1958); AIRBORNE(1962); STAKEOUT!(1962)
Binnie Hale
THIS IS THE LIFE(1933, Brit.); HYDE PARK CORNER(1935, Brit.); PHANTOM LIGHT, THE(1935, Brit.); LOVE FROM A STRANGER(1937, Brit.); TAKE A CHANCE(1937, Brit.)
Birdie Hale
ONLY WHEN I LAUGH(1981)
Bobbie Hale
MAN HUNT(1941); YANK IN THE R.A.F., A(1941); NIGHTMARE(1942); KNICKERBOCKER HOLIDAY(1944)
Bobby Hale
DISPATCH FROM REUTERS, A(1940); SUSAN AND GOD(1940); RAGE IN HEAVEN(1941); INVISIBLE AGENT(1942); MRS. MINIVER(1942); THANK YOUR LUCKY STARS(1943); GASLIGHT(1944); MAN IN HALF-MOON STREET, THE(1944); TEMPTATION(1946); MILLION DOLLAR MERMAID(1952)
Bruce Hale
LUCKY PARTNERS(1940)
Chanin Hale
SYNANON(1965); GUIDE FOR THE MARRIED MAN, A(1967); GUNN(1967); NIGHT THEY RAIDED MINSKY'S, THE(1968); WICKED DREAMS OF PAULA SCHULTZ, THE(1968); WILL PENNY(1968)
Chester Hale
PAINTED VEIL, THE(1934), ch; STUDENT TOUR(1934), ch; ANNA KARENINA(1935), ch; NIGHT AT THE OPERA, A(1935), ch; RECKLESS(1935), ch; ROSE MARIE(1936), ch
Creighton Hale
SERGEANT YORK(; SEVEN FOOTPRINTS TO SATAN(1929); GREAT DIVIDE, THE(1930); HOLIDAY(1930); GRIEF STREET(1931); SHOP ANGEL(1932); MASQUERADER, THE(1933); BULLDOG DRUMMOND STRIKES BACK(1934); GEORGE WHITE'S SCANDALS(1934); SENSATION HUNTERS(1934); THIN MAN, THE(1934); LIFE BEGINS AT 40(1935); MEN WITHOUT NAMES(1935); DEATH FROM A DISTANCE(1936); HOLLYWOOD BOULEVARD(1936); MILLIONAIRE KID(1936); PRINCESS COMES ACROSS, THE(1936); UNDER YOUR SPELL(1936); CHARLIE CHAN ON BROADWAY(1937); INTERNATIONAL SETTLEMENT(1938); INDIANAPOLIS SPEEDWAY(1939); KID NIGHTINGALE(1939); NANCY DREW AND THE HIDDEN STAIRCASE(1939); PRIVATE DETECTIVE(1939); RETURN OF DR. X, THE(1939); ROARING TWENTIES, THE(1939); TORCHY PLAYS WITH DYNAMITE(1939); ALL THIS AND HEAVEN TOO(1940); CALLING PHILO VANCE(1940); CHILD IS BORN, A(1940); FIGHTING 69TH, THE(1940); FLIGHT ANGELS(1940); KNUTE ROCKNE-ALL AMERICAN(1940); LADY WITH RED HAIR(1940); MAN WHO TALKED TOO MUCH, THE(1940); MONEY AND THE WOMAN(1940); MY LOVE CAME BACK(1940); ONE MILLION B.C.(1940); SANTA FE TRAIL(1940); TUGBOAT ANNIE SAILS AGAIN(1940); BRIDE CAME C.O.D., THE(1941); DIVE BOMBER(1941); FOOTSTEPS IN THE DARK(1941); KNOCKOUT(1941); LAW OF THE TROPICS(1941); MALTESE FALCON, THE(1941); NINE LIVES ARE NOT ENOUGH(1941); SHE COULDN'T SAY NO(1941); STRAWBERRY BLONDE, THE(1941); BULLET SCARS(1942); CASABLANCA(1942); GAY SISTERS, THE(1942); GORILLA MAN(1942); HIDDEN HAND, THE(1942); LARCENY, INC.(1942); MALE ANIMAL, THE(1942); MAN WHO CAME TO DINNER, THE(1942); MURDER IN THE BIG HOUSE(1942); YANKEE DOODLE DANDY(1942); ACTION IN THE NORTH ATLANTIC(1943); MYSTERIOUS DOCTOR, THE(1943); OLD ACQUAINTANCE(1943); THANK YOUR LUCKY STARS(1943); WATCH ON THE RHINE(1943); CRIME BY NIGHT(1944); MEET THE PEOPLE(1944); MR. SKEFFINGTON(1944); UNCERTAIN GLORY(1944); HUMORESQUE(1946); NIGHT AND DAY(1946); STOLEN LIFE, A(1946); CRY WOLF(1947); LIFE WITH FATHER(1947); NORA PRENTISS(1947); PERILS OF PAULINE, THE(1947); POSSESSED(1947); STALLION ROAD(1947); THAT WAY WITH WOMEN(1947); TWO MRS. CARROLLS, THE(1947); JOHNNY BELINDA(1948); SMART GIRLS DON'T TALK(1948); FOUNTAINHEAD, THE(1949); GIRL FROM JONES BEACH, THE(1949); JOHN LOVES MARY(1949); KISS IN THE DARK, A(1949); NIGHT UNTO NIGHT(1949); STORY OF SEABISCUIT, THE(1949); MONTANA(1950); PERFECT STRANGERS(1950); SUNSET BOULEVARD(1950); ENFORCER, THE(1951); GOODBYE, MY FANCY(1951); ON MOONLIGHT BAY(1951); MILLION DOLLAR MERMAID(1952); SCARLET ANGEL(1952); SERENADE(1956); WESTBOUND(1959)

Silents
CHARITY?(1916); ANNEXING BILL(1918); MRS. SLACKER(1918); DAMSEL IN DISTRESS, A(1919); OH, BOY!(1919); CHILD FOR SALE, A(1920); IDOL DANCER, THE(1920); WAY DOWN EAST(1920); ORPHANS OF THE STORM(1922); THREE WISE FOOLS(1923); MARRIAGE CIRCLE, THE(1924); WAGES FOR WIVES(1925); BEVERLY OF GRAUSTARK(1926); MIDNIGHT MESSAGE, THE(1926); ANNIE LAURIE(1927); CAT AND THE CANARY, THE(1927); THUMBS DOWN(1927)
Misc. Silents
THREE OF US, THE(1915); OLD HOMESTEAD, THE(1916); SNOW WHITE(1917); FOR SALE(1918); GREAT VICTORY, WILSON OR THE KAISER?, THE(1918); HIS BONDED WIFE(1918); WAIFS(1918); WOMAN THE GERMANS SHOT(1918); BLACK CIRCLE, THE(1919); LOVE CHEAT, THE(1919); THIRTEENTH CHAIR, THE(1919); WHY GERMANY MUST PAY(1919); FORBIDDEN LOVE(1921); FASCINATION(1922); HER MAJESTY(1922); TEA-WITH A KICK(1923); TRILBY(1923); NAME THE MAN(1924); RIDERS UP(1924); WINE OF YOUTH(1924); BRIDGE OF SIGHS, THE(1925); EXCHANGE OF WIVES(1925); SEVEN DAYS(1925); SHADOW ON THE WALL, THE(1925); OH, BABY!(1926); POOR GIRL'S ROMANCE, A(1926); SPEEDING THROUGH(1926); HOUSE OF SHAME, THE(1928); RILEY OF THE RAINBOW DIVISION(1928); ROSE-MARIE(1928); SISTERS OF EVE(1928); SEVEN FOOTPRINTS TO SATAN(1929)
Diana Hale
GOOD FELLOWS, THE(1943); MY FRIEND FLICKA(1943); THUNDERHEAD-SON OF FLICKA(1945); IT'S ALIVE(1974)
Donna Hale
Misc. Silents
FIGHTIN' THRU(1924)
Dorothy Hale
CATHERINE THE GREAT(1934, Brit.)
Doug Hale
NIGHT THEY ROBBED BIG BERTHA'S, THE(1975)
Misc. Talkies
BRASS RING, THE(1975); MANHUNTER(1983)
Elvi Hale
TRUE AS A TURTLE(1957, Brit.); HAPPY IS THE BRIDE(1958, Brit.); NAVY LARK, THE(1959, Brit.); MAN DETAINED(1961, Brit.); HEROES OF TELEMARK, THE(1965, Brit.)
Fiona Hale
INTERRUPTED MELODY(1955); SHOTGUN(1955)
Florence Hale
Silents
OLIVER TWIST(1922)
Frank Hale
Silents
KID, THE(1921)
Frank J. Hale
DR. COPPELIUS(1968, U.S./Span.), p
Frona Hale
Silents
BABBITT(1924); SKINNER'S DRESS SUIT(1926)
Misc. Silents
BLACK SHEEP(1921); FIGHTING JACK(1926)
George Hale
HOLLYWOOD PARTY(1934), ch; CRAZY HOUSE(1943), ch; FOLLOW THE BOYS(1944), ch
Georgia Hale
Silents
GOLD RUSH, THE(1925); SALVATION HUNTERS, THE(1925); GREAT GATSBY, THE(1926); RAINMAKER, THE(1926); WHEEL OF DESTINY, THE(1927); FLOATING COLLEGE, THE(1928); GYPSY OF THE NORTH(1928); RAWHIDE KID, THE(1928)
Misc. Silents
MAN OF THE FOREST(1926); HILLS OF PERIL(1927); TRICK OF HEARTS, A(1928); WOMAN AGAINST THE WORLD, A(1928)
Georgie Hale
HEADS UP(1930), ch
Georgina Hale
BOY FRIEND, THE(1971, Brit.); EAGLE IN A CAGE(1971, U.S./Yugo.); BUTLEY(1974, Brit.); MAHLER(1974, Brit.); SWEENEY 2(1978, Brit.); WATCHER IN THE WOODS, THE(1980, Brit.); WORLD IS FULL OF MARRIED MEN, THE(1980, Brit.); MC VICAR(1982, Brit.)
Grace Hale
GLAMOUR(1934); GOODBYE LOVE(1934); HARVESTER, THE(1936); TICKET TO PARADISE(1936)
Gretchen Hale
TURNING POINT, THE(1952)
Henry Hale
MAGNIFICENT OBSESSION(1935); HE STAYED FOR BREAKFAST(1940)
Jane Hale
TOMORROW WE LIVE(1942); ABBOTT AND COSTELLO IN HOLLYWOOD(1945)
Jean Hale
PSYCHOMANIA(1964); TAGGART(1964); MC HALE'S NAVY JOINS THE AIR FORCE(1965); OSCAR, THE(1966); IN LIKE FLINT(1967); ST. VALENTINE'S DAY MASSACRE, THE(1967)
Joe Hale
PETE'S DRAGON(1977), anim
John Hale
HOUSEWIFE(1934); LOST LADY, A(1934); SINGING KID, THE(1936); INSIDE DAISY CLOVER(1965); ANNE OF THE THOUSAND DAYS(1969, Brit.), w; BIG DADDY(1969); MIND OF MR. SOAMES, THE(1970, Brit.), w; MARY, QUEEN OF SCOTS(1971, Brit.), w
Johnathan Hale
LIGHTNING STRIKES TWICE(1935); CHARLIE CHAN AT THE RACE TRACK(1936); EDUCATING FATHER(1936); JACK LONDON(1943)
Jonathan Hale
YELLOW JACK(1938); ALICE ADAMS(1935); G-MEN(1935); NIGHT AT THE OPERA, A(1935); PAGE MISS GLORY(1935); PUBLIC HERO NO. 1(1935); THREE LIVE GHOSTS(1935); CASE AGAINST MRS. AMES, THE(1936); CHARLIE CHAN'S SECRET(1936); DEVIL IS A SISSY, THE(1936); FLYING HOSTESS(1936); FURY(1936); NAVY WIFE(1936); SPENDTHRIFT(1936); THIRTY SIX HOURS TO KILL(1936); TOO MANY PARENTS(1936); VOICE OF BUGLE ANN(1936); CARNIVAL QUEEN(1937); CHARLIE CHAN AT THE OLYMPICS(1937); DANGER-LOVE AT WORK(1937);

EXILED TO SHANGHAI(1937); HAPPY-GO-LUCKY(1937); JOHN MEADE'S WOMAN(1937); LEAGUE OF FRIGHTENED MEN(1937); MADAME X(1937); MAN OF THE PEOPLE(1937); MAN WHO FOUND HIMSELF, THE(1937); MIDNIGHT MADONNA(1937); MYSTERIOUS CROSSING(1937); OUTCAST(1937); RACKETEERS IN EXILE(1937); SARATOGA(1937); SHE'S DANGEROUS(1937); STAR IS BORN, A(1937); THIS IS MY AFFAIR(1937); WINGS OVER HONOLULU(1937); YOU ONLY LIVE ONCE(1937); ARSENE LUPIN RETURNS(1938); BLONDIE(1938); BOYS TOWN(1938); BREAKING THE ICE(1938); DUKE OF WEST POINT, THE(1938); FIRST 100 YEARS, THE(1938); FUGITIVES FOR A NIGHT(1938); GANGS OF NEW YORK(1938); HER JUNGLE LOVE(1938); LETTER OF INTRODUCTION(1938); MEN WITH WINGS(1938); OVER THE WALL(1938); ROAD DEMON(1938); SAINT IN NEW YORK, THE(1938); TARNISHED ANGEL(1938); THERE'S THAT WOMAN AGAIN(1938); WIVES UNDER SUSPICION(1938); AMAZING MR. WILLIAMS(1939); BARRICADE(1939); BIG GUY, THE(1939); BLONDIE BRINGS UP BABY(1939); BLONDIE MEETS THE BOSS(1939); FUGITIVE AT LARGE(1939); IN NAME ONLY(1939); IN OLD MONTEREY(1939); SAINT STRIKES BACK, THE(1939); STAND UP AND FIGHT(1939); STORY OF ALEXANDER GRAHAM BELL, THE(1939); THUNDER AFLOAT(1939); WINGS OF THE NAVY(1939); BLONDIE HAS SERVANT TROUBLE(1940); BLONDIE PLAYS CUPID(1940); DULCY(1940); JOHNNY APOLLO(1940); MELODY AND MOONLIGHT(1940); PRIVATE AFFAIRS(1940); SAINT TAKES OVER, THE(1940); SAINT'S DOUBLE TROUBLE, THE(1940); WE WHO ARE YOUNG(1940); BLONDIE GOES LATIN(1941); BLONDIE IN SOCIETY(1941); BUGLE SOUNDS, THE(1941); FLIGHT FROM DESTINY(1941); GREAT SWINDLE, THE(1941); HER FIRST BEAU(1941); PITTSBURGH KID, THE(1941); RINGSIDE MAISIE(1941); SAINT IN PALM SPRINGS, THE(1941); STRANGE ALIBI(1941); BLONDIE FOR VICTORY(1942); BLONDIE GOES TO COLLEGE(1942); BLONDIE'S BLESSED EVENT(1942); CALLING DR. GILLESPIE(1942); FLIGHT LIEUTENANT(1942); JOE SMITH, AMERICAN(1942); LONE STAR RANGER(1942); MISS ANNIE ROONEY(1942); AMAZING MRS. HOLLIDAY(1943); FOOTLIGHT GLAMOUR(1943); HANGMEN ALSO DIE(1943); IT'S A GREAT LIFE(1943); NOBODY'S DARLING(1943); SWEET ROSIE O'GRADY(1943); THERE'S SOMETHING ABOUT A SOLDIER(1943); AND NOW TOMORROW(1944); BLACK PARACHUTE, THE(1944); DEAD MAN'S EYES(1944); END OF THE ROAD(1944); HOLLYWOOD CANTEEN(1944); MY BUDDY(1944); SINCE YOU WENT AWAY(1944); THIS IS THE LIFE(1944); ALLOTMENT WIVES, INC.(1945); DAKOTA(1945); DIVORCE(1945); G.I. HONEYMOON(1945); LEAVE IT TO BLONDIE(1945); MAN ALIVE(1945); PHANTOM SPEAKS, THE(1945); STRANGE MR. GREGORY, THE(1945); ANGEL ON MY SHOULDER(1946); BLONDIE KNOWS BEST(1946); BLONDIE'S LUCKY DAY(1946); CAT CREEPS, THE(1946); EASY TO WED(1946); GAY BLADES(1946); LIFE WITH BLONDIE(1946); RIVERBOAT RHYTHM(1946); WALLS CAME TUMBLING DOWN, THE(1946); WIFE WANTED(1946); BEGINNING OR THE END, THE(1947); GHOST GOES WILD, THE(1947); HER HUSBAND'S AFFAIRS(1947); HIGH WALL, THE(1947); VIGILANTES RETURN, THE(1947); CALL NORTHSIDE 777(1948); DISASTER(1948); JOHNNY BELINDA(1948); KING OF THE GAMBLERS(1948); MICHAEL O'HALLORAN(1948); ROCKY(1948); SILVER RIVER(1948); TAP ROOTS(1948); DANGEROUS PROFESSION, A(1949); FOUNTAINHEAD, THE(1949); JUDGE, THE(1949); ROSE OF THE YUKON(1949); STAMPEDE(1949); STATE DEPARTMENT–FILE 649(1949); FEDERAL AGENT AT LARGE(1950); SHORT GRASS(1950); THREE HUSBANDS(1950); TRIPLE TROUBLE(1950); INSURANCE INVESTIGATOR(1951); LET'S GO NAVY(1951); RODEO KING AND THE SENORITA(1951); STRANGERS ON A TRAIN(1951); SUNNY SIDE OF THE STREET(1951); MY PAL GUS(1952); SCANDAL SHEET(1952); SON OF PALEFACE(1952); STEEL TRAP, THE(1952); BLUEPRINT FOR MURDER, A(1953); GLORY BRIGADE, THE(1953); KANSAS PACIFIC(1953); TAXI(1953); DUFFY OF SAN QUENTIN(1954); MEN OF THE FIGHTING LADY(1954); RIOT IN CELL BLOCK 11(1954); SHE COULDN'T SAY NO(1954); ILLEGAL(1955); NIGHT HOLDS TERROR, THE(1955); JAGUAR(1956); OPPOSITE SEX, THE(1956); THREE OUTLAWS, THE(1956); KISS THEM FOR ME(1957); TOP SECRET AFFAIR(1957); WAY TO THE GOLD, THE(1957); FOUR FOR TEXAS(1963)
Misc. Talkies
BEHIND SOUTHERN LINES(1952)

Karen Hale
I WAS A COMMUNIST FOR THE F.B.I.(1951); ONE MINUTE TO ZERO(1952); ROOM FOR ONE MORE(1952); THIS WOMAN IS DANGEROUS(1952)
1984
SUPERGIRL(1984)

Lionel Hale
MONEY FOR SPEED(1933, Brit.), w

Louise Closser Hale
HOLE IN THE WALL(1929); PARIS(1929); BIG BOY(1930); DANGEROUS NAN McGREW(1930); PRINCESS AND THE PLUMBER, THE(1930); BORN TO LOVE(1931); CAPTAIN APPLEJACK(1931); DADDY LONG LEGS(1931); DEVOTION(1931); PLATINUM BLONDE(1931); REBOUND(1931); FAITHLESS(1932); LETTY LYNTON(1932); MAN WHO PLAYED GOD, THE(1932); MOVIE CRAZY(1932); NEW MORALS FOR OLD(1932); REBECCA OF SUNNYBROOK FARM(1932); SHANGHAI EXPRESS(1932); SKY BRIDE(1932); SON-DAUGHTER, THE(1932); ANOTHER LANGUAGE(1933); BARBARIAN, THE(1933); DINNER AT EIGHT(1933); NO MORE ORCHIDS(1933); STORM AT DAYBREAK(1933); TODAY WE LIVE(1933); WHITE SISTER, THE(1933)

Martin Hale
CAPRICE(1967), w

Mary Hale
CALLING DR. DEATH(1943)

May Hale
WOMEN, THE(1939)

Michael Hale
DEVIL BAT'S DAUGHTER, THE(1946); KILLERS, THE(1946)

Mildred Hale
KISS THE BLOOD OFF MY HANDS(1948)

Monte Hale
BIG BONANZA, THE(1944); BANDITS OF THE BADLANDS(1945); COLORADO PIONEERS(1945); OREGON TRAIL(1945); ROUGH RIDERS OF CHEYENNE(1945); TOPEKA TERROR, THE(1945); HOME ON THE RANGE(1946); MAN FROM RAINBOW VALLEY, THE(1946); OUT CALIFORNIA WAY(1946); SUN VALLEY CYCLONE(1946); ALONG THE OREGON TRAIL(1947); LAST FRONTIER UPRISING(1947); UNDER COLORADO SKIES(1947); CALIFORNIA FIREBRAND(1948); SON OF GOD'S COUNTRY(1948); TIMBER TRAIL, THE(1948); LAW OF THE GOLDEN WEST(1949); OUTCASTS OF THE TRAIL(1949); PRINCE OF THE PLAINS(1949); RANGER OF CHEROKEE STRIP(1949); SAN ANTONE AMBUSH(1949); SOUTH OF RIO(1949); MISSOURIANS, THE(1950); OLD FRONTIER, THE(1950); PIONEER MARSHAL(1950); TRAIL OF ROBIN HOOD(1950); VANISHING WESTERNER, THE(1950); YUKON VENGEANCE(1954); GIANT(1956); CHASE,

THE(1966)

Nancy Hale
JUST FOR YOU(1952); MY SON, JOHN(1952); WAR OF THE WORLDS, THE(1953); LORD OF THE JUNGLE(1955); WHITE SQUAW, THE(1956); FLIGHT THAT DISAPPEARED, THE(1961)

Patty Hale
ALWAYS IN MY HEART(1942); I WAS FRAMED(1942)

Rex Hale
RACING BLOOD(1938), d

Richard Hale
GIRL IN THE CASE(1944); KNICKERBOCKER HOLIDAY(1944); NONE SHALL ESCAPE(1944); COUNTER-ATTACK(1945); THOUSAND AND ONE NIGHTS, A(1945); ABILENE TOWN(1946); BADMAN'S TERRITORY(1946); DEVIL'S MASK, THE(1946); MAN WHO DARED, THE(1946); OTHER LOVE, THE(1947); PORT SAID(1948); ALL THE KING'S MEN(1949); BEAUTIFUL BLONDE FROM BASHFUL BEND, THE(1949); CONVICTED(1950); DESERT HAWK, THE(1950); KIM(1950); FLAME OF ARABY(1951); INSIDE STRAIGHT(1951); LAW AND THE LADY, THE(1951); MAN WITH A CLOAK, THE(1951); SOLDIERS THREE(1951); UNKNOWN MAN, THE(1951); MIRACLE OF OUR LADY OF FATIMA, THE(1952); ROGUE'S MARCH(1952); SCARAMOUCHE(1952); SPRINGFIELD RIFLE(1952); DIAMOND QUEEN, THE(1953); JULIUS CAESAR(1953); SAN ANTONE(1953); SEA OF LOST SHIPS(1953); PASSION(1954); RED GARTERS(1954); CANYON CROSSROADS(1955); JUPITER'S DARLING(1955); MOONFLEET(1955); FRIENDLY PERSUASION(1956); PILLARS OF THE SKY(1956); SHORT CUT TO HELL(1957); VOICE IN THE MIRROR(1958); BEN HUR(1959); SERGEANTS 3(1962); TO KILL A MOCKINGBIRD(1962); TOWER OF LONDON(1962); SCANDALOUS JOHN(1971); LIMIT, THE(1972); RAFFERTY AND THE GOLD DUST TWINS(1975)
Silents
CAPRICE OF THE MOUNTAINS(1916)

Robert Hale
WHERE IS THIS LADY?(1932, Brit.); STRAUSS' GREAT WALTZ(1934, Brit.); WHAT HAPPENED TO HARKNESS(1934, Brit.); DARK ANGEL, THE(1935); REGAL CAVALCADE(1935, Brit.); IT'S LOVE AGAIN(1936, Brit.); SYLVIA SCARLETT(1936); COMPULSORY WIFE, THE(1937, Brit.); STORM IN A TEACUP(1937, Brit.); SPOT OF BOTHER, A(1938, Brit.); PRINCESS AND THE PIRATE, THE(1944); HANGOVER SQUARE(1945); KISS THE BLOOD OFF MY HANDS(1948)
Silents
EYES RIGHT(1926)

Roland Hale
ME, NATALIE(1969)

Ron Hale
ALL THE PRESIDENT'S MEN(1976)

Ruth Hale
KID FROM SPAIN, THE(1932)

Sally Hale
ISN'T IT ROMANTIC?(1948)

Scott Hale
GIRL ON THE RUN(1961); KILLERS, THE(1964); MADIGAN(1968); DIRTY HARRY(1971); CHARLEY VARRICK(1973); SHOOTIST, THE(1976), w

Shanon Hale
PARADISE, HAWAIIAN STYLE(1966)

Sonnie Hale
HAPPY EVER AFTER(1932, Ger./Brit.); BE MINE TONIGHT(1933, Brit.); EARLY TO BED(1933, Brit./Ger.); ARE YOU A MASON?(1934, Brit.); EVERGREEN(1934, Brit.); FRIDAY THE 13TH(1934, Brit.); WILD BOY(1934, Brit.); FIRST A GIRL(1935, Brit.); MARRY THE GIRL(1935, Brit.); MY HEART IS CALLING(1935, Brit.); MY SONG FOR YOU(1935, Brit.); IT'S LOVE AGAIN(1936, Brit.); GANGWAY(1937, Brit.), d, w; HEAD OVER HEELS IN LOVE(1937, Brit.), d; SAILING ALONG(1938, Brit.), d, w; LET'S BE FAMOUS(1939, Brit.); PHANTOM STRIKES, THE(1939, Brit.); FIDDLERS THREE(1944, Brit.); MY HEART GOES CRAZY(1953, Brit.)

Spencer Hale
IT'S A GREAT DAY(1956, Brit.)

Tony Hale
PEOPLE THAT TIME FORGOT, THE(1977, Brit.)

Victoria Hale
THAT TENDER TOUCH(1969); ONE DOWN TWO TO GO(1982)

Walter Hale
Silents
LIGHTNING CONDUCTOR, THE(1914), a, d

William Hale
LONNIE(1963), d; GUNFIGHT IN ABILENE(1967), d; JOURNEY TO SHILOH(1968), d
Silents
GREATEST QUESTION, THE(1920), w

Jiri Halek
MOST BEAUTIFUL AGE, THE(1970, Czech.)

Richard Haler
CORRUPT ONES, THE(1967, Ger.)

A. G. Hales
Silents
SHEFFIELD BLADE, A(1918, Brit.), w

Donn Hales
EX-FLAME(1931), ed

Eric Hales
ANNE ONE HUNDRED(1933, Brit.); CHELSEA LIFE(1933, Brit.); THIRTEENTH CANDLE, THE(1933, Brit.); PERFECT FLAW, THE(1934, Brit.); SECRET OF THE LOCH, THE(1934, Brit.); BLUE SMOKE(1935, Brit.); LUCKY DAYS(1935, Brit.); MR. WHAT'S-HIS-NAME(1935, Brit.); WEDNESDAY'S LUCK(1936, Brit.); CROSS MY HEART(1937, Brit.); LAST CURTAIN, THE(1937, Brit.); STRANGE EXPERIMENT(1937, Brit.); THERE WAS A YOUNG MAN(1937, Brit.); UNDER THE RED ROBE(1937, Brit.)
Misc. Silents
HUMAN CARGO(1929, Brit.); SECOND MATE, THE(1929, Brit.); SCRAGS(1930, Brit.)

Gordon Hales
SEVENTH VEIL, THE(1946, Brit.), ed; DEAR MURDERER(1947, Brit.), ed; WHEN THE BOUGH BREAKS(1947, Brit.), ed; BLIND GODDESS, THE(1948, Brit.), ed; HERE COME THE HUGGETTS(1948, Brit.), ed; MIRANDA(1949, Brit.), ed; CLOUDED YELLOW, THE(1950, Brit.), ed; LOST PEOPLE, THE(1950, Brit.), ed; PARDON MY FRENCH(1951, U.S./Fr.), ed; SO LONG AT THE FAIR(1951, Brit.), ed; ANOTHER MAN'S POISON(1952, Brit.), ed; LONG MEMORY, THE(1953, Brit.), ed; VILLAGE,

THE(1953, Brit./Switz.), ed; DETECTIVE, THE(1954, Qit.), ed; DOCTOR'S DILEMMA, THE(1958, Brit.), ed; ORDERS TO KILL(1958, Brit.), ed; VILLAGE OF THE DAMNED(1960, Brit.), ed; SEASON OF PASSION(1961, Aus./Brit.), ed; WAR LOVER, THE(1962, U.S./Brit.), ed; RETURN TO SENDER(1963, Brit.), d; 20,000 POUNDS KISS, THE(1964, Brit.), ed; GYPSY GIRL(1966, Brit.), ed; COUNTESS FROM HONG KONG, A(1967, Brit.), ed; FRANKENSTEIN MUST BE DESTROYED!(1969, Brit.), ed

Jonathan Hales
MIRROR CRACK'D, THE(1980, Brit.), w; LOOPHOLE(1981, Brit.), w

Julian Halevy
CIRCUS WORLD(1964), w; PSYCHE 59(1964, Brit.), w; YOUNG LOVERS, THE(1964), w; CRACK IN THE WORLD(1965), w; CUSTER OF THE WEST(1968, U.S., Span.), w; PLACE FOR LOVERS, A(1969, Ital./Fr.), w; PANCHO VILLA(1975, Span.), w

Ludovic Halevy
Silents
SO THIS IS PARIS(1926), w

Aileen Haley
I MARRIED AN ANGEL(1942); GIRL CRAZY(1943); GUY NAMED JOE, A(1943); THOUSANDS CHEER(1943); ZIEGFELD FOLLIES(1945); HOODLUM SAINT, THE(1946)

Alex Haley
SUPERFLY T.N.T.(1973), w

Averil Haley
OUT OF THE BLUE(1931, Brit.)

Bill Haley
DON'T KNOCK THE ROCK(1956)

Earl Haley
KING OF THE WILD HORSES, THE(1934), d, w; GENTLEMAN FROM ARIZONA, THE(1940), d, w

J.A. Haley
KNUTE ROCKNE–ALL AMERICAN(1940), tech adv

Jack Haley
FOLLOW THRU(1930); SITTING PRETTY(1933); HERE COMES THE GROOM(1934); CORONADO(1935); GIRL FRIEND, THE(1935); REDHEADS ON PARADE(1935); SPRING TONIC(1935); F MAN(1936); MISTER CINDERELLA(1936); PIGSKIN PARADE(1936); POOR LITTLE RICH GIRL(1936); DANGER–LOVE AT WORK(1937); PICK A STAR(1937); SHE HAD TO EAT(1937); WAKE UP AND LIVE(1937); ALEXANDER'S RAGTIME BAND(1938); HOLD THAT CO-ED(1938); REBECCA OF SUNNYBROOK FARM(1938); THANKS FOR EVERYTHING(1938); WIZARD OF OZ, THE(1939); MOON OVER MIAMI(1941); NAVY BLUES(1941); BEYOND THE BLUE HORIZON(1942); HIGHER AND HIGHER(1943); ONE BODY TOO MANY(1944); TAKE IT BIG(1944); GEORGE WHITE'S SCANDALS(1945); PEOPLE ARE FUNNY(1945); SCARED STIFF(1945); SING YOUR WAY HOME(1945); VACATION IN RENO(1946)

Jack Haley, Jr.
NORWOOD(1970), d; LOVE MACHINE, THE,(1971), d; BETTER LATE THAN NEVER(1983), p

Jack Haley, Sr.
NORWOOD(1970)

Jackie Earle Haley
BAD NEWS BEARS, THE(1976); BAD NEWS BEARS IN BREAKING TRAINING, THE(1977); DAMNATION ALLEY(1977); BAD NEWS BEARS GO TO JAPAN, THE(1978); BREAKING AWAY(1979); LOSIN' IT(1983)

Jackie Haley
OUTSIDE MAN, THE(1973, U.S./FR.); DAY OF THE LOCUST, THE(1975)

Jeff Haley
THANK GOD IT'S FRIDAY(1978), set d; GREAT SANTINI, THE(1979), set d; PROMISE, THE(1979), set d
1984
BEVERLY HILLS COP(1984), set d; SWING SHIFT(1984), set d

Jonathan Nicholas Haley
EYE OF THE NEEDLE(1981)

Michael Haley
LADY LIBERTY(1972, Ital./Fr.)

Mike Haley
HONEYMOON KILLERS, THE(1969)

Patsy Haley
Silents
REFEREE, THE(1922)

Paul Haley
EXPERIENCE PREFERRED... BUT NOT ESSENTIAL(1983, Brit.)

Tess Haley
ONE FROM THE HEART(1982)

Veronica Haley
NO ROOM AT THE INN(1950, Brit.)

Cristobal Halffter
GIRL FROM VALLADOLIO(1958, Span.), m; HAND IN THE TRAP, THE(1963, Arg./Span.), m; 10:30 P.M. SUMMER(1966, U.S./Span.), m; DESPERATE ONES, THE(1968 U.S./Span.), m

Rodolfo Halffter
LOS OLVIDADOS(1950, Mex.), m; NAZARIN(1968, Mex.), m

Rudolfo Halffter
LIVING IDOL, THE(1957), m

Samy Halfon
HIROSHIMA, MON AMOUR(1959, Fr./Jap.), p; TRANS-EUROP-EXPRESS(1968, Fr.), a, p

Marc Halford
FIRST TASTE OF LOVE(1962, Fr.)

Anthony Halfpenny
GAY LADY, THE(1949, Brit.)

Tony Halfpenny
YOUNG WOODLEY(1930, Brit.); EYES OF FATE(1933, Brit.)

H.B. Halicki
GONE IN 60 SECONDS(1974), a, p,d&w; JUNKMAN, THE(1982), a, p,d&w, prod d

Ronald Halicki
GONE IN 60 SECONDS(1974), a, m

Bryant Haliday
BEYOND THE FOG(1981, Brit.)

John Haliday
THREE CABALLEROS, THE(1944), ed

Roger Haliday
MY SON IS GUILTY(1940); LUCKY DEVILS(1941)

Edwin Halietz
DOCTOR OF ST. PAUL, THE(1969, Ger.), m

Henia Halil
YOU CAN'T WIN 'EM ALL(1970, Brit.)

Jacques Halk
AZAIS(1931, Fr.), p

Elen Halkova
MERRY WIVES, THE(1940, Czech.)

Elena Halkova
DEATH OF TARZAN, THE(1968, Czech)

Adalyn Hall
FUGITIVE LADY(1934)

Adam Hall [Elleston Trevor]
QUILLER MEMORANDUM, THE(1966, Brit.), w

Adelaide Hall
THIEF OF BAGHDAD, THE(1940, Brit.)

Adrian Hall
CHITTY CHITTY BANG BANG(1968, Brit.); KADOYNG(1974, Brit.)

Al Hall
SMILING IRISH EYES(1929), ed; KISMET(1930), ed; SONG OF THE FLAME(1930), ed; BROADMINDED(1931), ed; LAST FLIGHT, THE(1931), ed; WOMAN HUNGRY(1931), ed; OKAY AMERICA(1932)
Silents
FAR CRY, THE(1926), ed; MISS NOBODY(1926), ed; LILAC TIME(1928), ed

Al K. Hall
COME AND GET IT(1936); WOMAN CHASES MAN(1937); WEST OF CARSON CITY(1940)

Alan Hall
GLITTERBALL, THE(1977, Brit), ph

Albert Hall
WILLIE DYNAMITE(1973); APOCALYPSE NOW(1979)

Albert P. Hall
LEADBELLY(1976)

Alex Hall
Silents
DOING THEIR BIT(1918); LEECH, THE(1921)

Alexander Hall
JAZZ BABIES(1932), d; MADAME RACKETEER(1932), d; SINNERS IN THE SUN(1932), d; GIRL IN 419(1933), d; MIDNIGHT CLUB(1933), d; SHE DONE HIM WRONG(1933), ed; TORCH SINGER(1933), d; LIMEHOUSE BLUES(1934), d; LITTLE MISS MARKER(1934), d; MISS FANE'S BABY IS STOLEN(1934), d; PURSUIT OF HAPPINESS, THE(1934), d; ANNAPOLIS FAREWELL(1935), d; GOIN' TO TOWN(1935), d; GIVE US THIS NIGHT(1936), d; YOURS FOR THE ASKING(1936), d; EXCLUSIVE(1937), d; I AM THE LAW(1938), d; THERE'S ALWAYS A WOMAN(1938), d; THERE'S THAT WOMAN AGAIN(1938), d; AMAZING MR. WILLIAMS(1939), d; GOOD GIRLS GO TO PARIS(1939), d; LADY'S FROM KENTUCKY, THE(1939), d; DOCTOR TAKES A WIFE(1940), d; HE STAYED FOR BREAKFAST(1940), d; THIS THING CALLED LOVE(1940), d; HERE COMES MR. JORDAN(1941), d; BEDTIME STORY(1942), d; MY SISTER EILEEN(1942), d; THEY ALL KISSED THE BRIDE(1942), d; HEAVENLY BODY, THE(1943), d; ONCE UPON A TIME(1944), d; SHE WOULDN'T SAY YES(1945), d; DOWN TO EARTH(1947), d; GREAT LOVER, THE(1949), d; LOUISA(1950), d; LOVE THAT BRUTE(1950), d; UP FRONT(1951), d; BECAUSE YOU'RE MINE(1952), d; LET'S DO IT AGAIN(1953), d; FOREVER DARLING(1956), d

Alfred Hall
DOUBLE TROUBLE(1941); GAMBLING DAUGHTERS(1941); LADY EVE, THE(1941); MEET JOHN DOE(1941); BROADWAY BIG SHOT(1942); MR. CELEBRITY(1942); MY HEART BELONGS TO DADDY(1942); SCATTERGOOD SURVIVES A MURDER(1942); SUNDAY PUNCH(1942); WE WERE DANCING(1942); HEAVEN CAN WAIT(1943); YOUTH ON PARADE(1943)

Allan Hall
DESERT JUSTICE(1936), w

Allen Hall
TOLL OF THE DESERT(1936), w; NIGHT SHIFT(1982), spec eff; MAN WITH TWO BRAINS, THE(1983), spec eff

Amelia Hall
1984
ICEMAN(1984)

Angus Hall
UP IN THE CELLAR(1970), d&w; MADHOUSE(1974, Brit.), w

Anthony Hall
ATLANTIS, THE LOST CONTINENT(1961)

Anthony Michael Hall
SIX PACK(1982); NATIONAL LAMPOON'S VACATION(1983)
1984
SIXTEEN CANDLES(1984)

Arch Hall
MYSTERIOUS RIDER, THE(1938); CORPSE GRINDERS, THE(1972), w

Archie Hall
OVERLAND STAGE RAIDERS(1938); RHYTHM OF THE SADDLE(1938); SAGEBRUSH FAMILY TRAILS WEST, THE(1940); LONE RIDER IN GHOST TOWN, THE(1941); TWO GUN SHERIFF(1941); APOLOGY FOR MURDER(1945); BORDER BADMEN(1945); HIS BROTHER'S GHOST(1945); DEATH VALLEY(1946), set d

Arch Hall, Jr.
CHOPPERS, THE(1961); WILD GUITAR(1962); SADIST, THE(1963); NASTY RABBIT, THE(1964); DEADWOOD'76(1965), a, w

Arch Hall, Sr.
CHOPPERS, THE(1961), p, w; MAGIC SPECTACLES(1961), p, w; NASTY RABBIT, THE(1964), w; WHAT'S UP FRONT(1964), w

Arch W. Hall, Jr.
EEGAH!(1962)

Arthur Stuart Hall
CHAMPAGNE WALTZ(1937)

Ashley Woodman Hall
1984
NO SMALL AFFAIR(1984)
Audrey Hall
FOLIES DERGERE(1935)
Barbara Hall
ONCE MORE, WITH FEELING(1960)
Ben Hall
GIRL FROM WOOLWORTH'S, THE(1929); HOT STUFF(1929); IN THE HEAD-LINES(1929); SOUTH SEA ROSE(1929); WALL STREET(1929); MAN FROM WYOM-ING, A(1930); MILLIONAIRE, THE(1931); SEAS BENEATH, THE(1931); ALIAS MARY SMITH(1932); GORILLA SHIP, THE(1932); STRICTLY PERSONAL(1933); LOVE PAST THIRTY(1934); SEQUOIA(1934); 365 NIGHTS IN HOLLYWOOD(1934); MEN WITH-OUT NAMES(1935); NAUGHTY MARIETTA(1935); RACING LUCK(1935); RED SA-LUTE(1935); STEAMBOAT ROUND THE BEND(1935); AFTER THE THIN MAN(1936); FURY(1936); GIRL OF THE OZARKS(1936); PIGSKIN PARADE(1936); PLOUGH AND THE STARS, THE(1936); MUSIC FOR MADAME(1937); SMOKE TREE RANGE(1937); TOAST OF NEW YORK, THE(1937); YOU ONLY LIVE ONCE(1937); ALGIERS(1938); MARIE ANTOINETTE(1938); MILLION TO ONE, A(1938); RIDERS OF THE BLACK HILLS(1938); SERVICE DE LUXE(1938); STRANGE FACES(1938); GRAPES OF WRATH(1940); MY LITTLE CHICKADEE(1940); ONE MILLION B.C.(1940); SECOND CHORUS(1940); RIDIN' ON A RAINBOW(1941); I MARRIED AN ANGEL(1942); MY DARLING CLEMENTINE(1946); NOOSE HANGS HIGH, THE(1948)
Silents
SKYROCKET, THE(1926); DOWN THE STRETCH(1927); HAROLD TEEN(1928); HOT NEWS(1928)
Misc. Silents
FOR LADIES ONLY(1927)
Benny Hall
NIX ON DAMES(1929)
Bert Hall
Silents
ROMANCE OF THE AIR, A(1919)
Misc. Silents
BORDER SCOUTS, THE(1922), d
Lt. Bert Hall
Silents
ROMANCE OF THE AIR, A(1919), w
Berta Hall
PORT OF CALL(1963, Swed.)
Betty Hall
LADY IN THE DARK(1944); KNOCK ON ANY DOOR(1949)
Silents
LASS O' THE LOOMS, A(1919, Brit.); STING OF THE LASH(1921)
Misc. Silents
FOOLISH MONTE CARLO(1922)
Bill Hall
DESTINY(1944); HARVEY GIRLS, THE(1946)
Blair Hall
Silents
ALIAS MRS. JESSOP(1917), w; EASY ROAD, THE(1921), w
Bob Hall
COOL AND THE CRAZY, THE(1958); SHALAKO(1968, Brit.)
Bobbie Hall
MY FAVORITE SPY(1951)
Bobby Hall
RUN LIKE A THIEF(1968, Span.); HELL'S ANGELS '69(1969); ANIMALS, THE(1971); HONKERS, THE(1972); KID BLUE(1973)
Bradley Hall
WAGONS ROLL AT NIGHT, THE(1941)
Brian Hall
CONFESSIONS OF A WINDOW CLEANER(1974, Brit.); LAND THAT TIME FOR-GOT, THE(1975, Brit.); DIRTY KNIGHT'S WORK(1976, Brit.); SWEENEY 2(1978, Brit.); LONG GOOD FRIDAY, THE(1982, Brit.); MC VICAR(1982, Brit.)
Bruce Edward Hall
1984
MUPPETS TAKE MANHATTAN, THE(1984)
Bruce Hall
SWEET JESUS, PREACHER MAN(1973); FM(1978)
C. Daniel Hall
OUTCASTS OF THE CITY(1958), art d
Cameron Hall
ADVENTURE'S END(1937); YES, MADAM?(1938, Brit.); LILAC DOMINO, THE(1940, Brit.); THREE SILENT MEN(1940, Brit.); HARD STEEL(1941, Brit.); I THANK YOU(1941, Brit.); NEUTRAL PORT(1941, Brit.); SOUTH AMERICAN GEORGE(1941, Brit.); STRANGLER, THE(1941, Brit.); KING ARTHUR WAS A GENTLEMAN(1942, Brit.); SPELL OF AMY NUGENT, THE(1945, Brit.); I'LL TURN TO YOU(1946, Brit.); LOYAL HEART(1946, Brit.); MAN ON THE RUN(1949, Brit.); MY BROTHER JONA-THAN(1949, Brit.); MADELEINE(1950, Brit.); MR. LORD SAYS NO(1952, Brit.); SLASHER, THE(1953, Brit.); PASSING STRANGER, THE(1954, Brit.); FOOTSTEPS IN THE FOG(1955, Brit.); IMPULSE(1955, Brit.); PORT OF ESCAPE(1955, Brit.); ROTTEN TO THE CORE(1956, Brit.); ANOTHER TIME, ANOTHER PLACE(1958); BLOOD OF THE VAMPIRE(1958, Brit.); STORMY CROSSING(1958, Brit.); SATURDAY NIGHT AND SUNDAY MORNING(1961, Brit.); REACH FOR GLORY(1963, Brit.)
Carl Hall
HAIR(1979)
Cecelia Hall
PETEY WHEATSTRAW(1978), ed
Charles D. Hall
WATERLOO BRIDGE(1931), art d; BROADWAY(1929), art d; ALL QUIET ON THE WESTERN FRONT(1930), art d; DRACULA(1931), art d; FRANKENSTEIN(1931), art d; OLD DARK HOUSE, THE(1932), art d; DON'T BET ON LOVE(1933), art d; INVISIBLE MAN, THE(1933), art d; BLACK CAT, THE(1934), art d; BRIDE OF FRANKENSTEIN, THE(1935), art d; MODERN TIMES(1936), art d; MY MAN GOD-FREY(1936), art d; NEXT TIME WE LOVE(1936), art d; SHOW BOAT(1936), art d; ROAD BACK,THE(1937), art d; MERRILY WE LIVE(1938), art d; SWISS MISS(1938), art d; THERE GOES MY HEART(1938), art d; HOUSEKEEPER'S DAUGHTER(1939), art d; TOPPER TAKES A TRIP(1939), art d; ZENOBIA(1939), art d; CAPTAIN CAUTION(1940), art d. Nicolai Remisoff; ONE MILLION B.C.(1940), art d; SAPS AT SEA(1940), art d; ROAD SHOW(1941), art d; TANKS A MILLION(1941), art d; DUDES

ARE PRETTY PEOPLE(1942), art d; THAT NAZTY NUISANCE(1943), art d; NOT WANTED(1949), art d; RED PLANET MARS(1952), prod d, art d; SHIELD FOR MURDER(1954), prod d
Silents
GOLD RUSH, THE(1925), art d; PHANTOM OF THE OPERA, THE(1925), art d; COHENS AND KELLYS, THE(1926), art d; CAT AND THE CANARY, THE(1927), set d; MAN WHO LAUGHS, THE(1927), art d; CIRCUS, THE(1928), art d; KID'S CLEVER, THE(1929), art d; CITY LIGHTS(1931), art d
Charles Hall
WITHOUT RESERVATIONS(1946); PHANTOM OF THE OPERA, THE(1929), prod d; WHY BRING THAT UP?(1929); MILLION DOLLAR LEGS(1932); GAY DIVORCEE, THE(1934); KID MILLIONS(1934); TOP HAT(1935); SWING TIME(1936); CHUMP AT OXFORD, A(1940); MEXICAN SPITFIRE OUT WEST(1940); TOP SERGEANT MULLI-GAN(1941); HAY FOOT(1942), art d; MAN FROM HEADQUARTERS(1942); SEVEN DAYS LEAVE(1942); FOREVER AND A DAY(1943); HONEYMOON LODGE(1943); SO'S YOUR UNCLE(1943); LODGER, THE(1944); HER LUCKY NIGHT(1945); ON STAGE EVERYBODY(1945); SHE GETS HER MAN(1945); MILKMAN, THE(1950)
1984
PHILADELPHIA EXPERIMENT, THE(1984)
Misc. Talkies
CITY LIMITS(1941)
Charlie Hall
LET'S GO NATIVE(1930); PARDON US(1931); PACK UP YOUR TROUBLES(1932); SONS OF THE DESERT(1933); OUR RELATIONS(1936); PICK A STAR(1937); ONE NIGHT IN THE TROPICS(1940); YOU CAN'T FOOL YOUR WIFE(1940); FALCON TAKES OVER, THE(1942)
Cheryl Hall
VILLAIN(1971, Brit.); FOURTEEN, THE(1973, Brit.); NO SEX PLEASE–WE'RE BRITISH(1979, Brit.)
Christy Hall
SECRET LIFE OF AN AMERICAN WIFE, THE(1968)
Chuck Hall
ALICE, SWEET ALICE(1978), ph
Misc. Talkies
STEVIE, SAMSON AND DELILAH(1975)
Claude Hall
STATE FAIR(1962); DEVIL'S BEDROOM, THE(1964), a, w; CINCINNATI KID, THE(1965)
Claudia Hall
SIX BRIDGES TO CROSS(1955)
Clayton Hall
NAKED MAJA, THE(1959, Ital./U.S.)
Cliff Hall
FOLLIES GIRL(1943)
Conrad Hall
RUNNING TARGET(1956), w; EDGE OF FURY(1958), ph; MORITURI(1965), ph; WILD SEED(1965), ph; HARPER(1966), ph; INCUBUS(1966), ph; PROFESSIONALS, THE(1966), ph; COOL HAND LUKE(1967), ph; DIVORCE AMERICAN STYLE(1967), ph; IN COLD BLOOD(1967), ph; HELL IN THE PACIFIC(1968), ph; BUTCH CASSIDY AND THE SUNDANCE KID(1969), ph; HAPPY ENDING, THE(1969), ph; TELL THEM WILLIE BOY IS HERE(1969), ph; TRUMAN CAPOTE'S TRILOGY(1969), ph; FAT CITY(1972), ph; ELECTRA GLIDE IN BLUE(1973), ph; CATCH MY SOUL(1974), ph; DAY OF THE LOCUST, THE(1975), ph; SMILE(1975), ph; MARATHON MAN(1976), ph
Cyndy Hall
URBAN COWBOY(1980)
Cynthia Hall
HIGH YELLOW(1965)
Dan Hall
RUBY GENTRY(1952), art d; MOONLIGHTER, THE(1953), art d; UNEARTHLY, THE(1957), art d
Daniel Hall
VAMPIRE BAT, THE(1933), art d; WORLD GONE MAD, THE(1933), art d; EAST OF JAVA(1935), ph; RED SNOW(1952), art d; BLUE GARDENIA, THE(1953), art d; MARRY ME AGAIN(1953), art d
Danny Hall
MRS. PARKINGTON(1944), spec eff; SEVENTH CROSS, THE(1944), spec eff; OUR VINES HAVE TENDER GRAPES(1945), spec eff; SON OF LASSIE(1945), spec eff; WITHOUT LOVE(1945), spec eff; SHAMROCK HILL(1949), art d; THERE'S A GIRL IN MY HEART(1949), art d; JAPANESE WAR BRIDE(1952), art d; DESERT SANDS(1955), art d
David Hall
HOT FOR PARIS(1930), art d; WOMEN OF ALL NATIONS(1931), art d; SECOND HONEYMOON(1937), art d; WIFE, DOCTOR AND NURSE(1937), art d; I'LL GIVE A MILLION(1938), art d; JOSETTE(1938), art d; STORY OF G.I. JOE, THE(1945), art d; GREATEST STORY EVER TOLD, THE(1965), art d, set d; HIT(1973); 99 AND 44/100% DEAD(1974)
Deanna Jean Hall
WEST POINT WIDOW(1941)
Debbie Hall
ON THE RIGHT TRACK(1981)
Deirdre Hall
SPECIAL DELIVERY(1976)
Delores Hall
Silents
NIGHT LIFE IN HOLLYWOOD(1922)
Denny Hall
TWO LOST WORLDS(1950), art d
Denver Hall
JOHNNY FRENCHMAN(1946, Brit.); CIRCUS BOY(1947, Brit.)
Devon Hall
DUTCHMAN(1966, Brit.)
Diane Hall
TEN COMMANDMENTS, THE(1956)
Dickie Hall
SHADOW OF THE THIN MAN(1941); MEET THE PEOPLE(1944)
Dolores Hall
DARLING, HOW COULD YOU!(1951); PLACE IN THE SUN, A(1951); GREATEST SHOW ON EARTH, THE(1952)

Donald Hall
YOUNGER GENERATION(1929); OH, FOR A MAN!(1930); SAN FRANCISCO(1936); MEET JOHN DOE(1941); GOVERNMENT GIRL(1943)
Silents
CHRISTIAN, THE(1914); MR. BARNES OF NEW YORK(1914); ALIAS MRS. JESSOP(1917); GREAT ADVENTURE, THE(1918); GREAT SHADOW, THE(1920); WOMAN'S BUSINESS, A(1920)
Misc. Silents
HEARTS AND THE HIGHWAY(1915); MORTMAIN(1915); PLAYING DEAD(1915); HESPER OF THE MOUNTAINS(1916); LAW DECIDES, THE(1916); SALVATION JOAN(1916); SEX LURE, THE(1916); ON-THE-SQUARE GIRL, THE(1917); RAGGEDY QUEEN, THE(1917); LOVE AND THE WOMAN(1919); BROKEN MELODY, THE(1920); GREATEST LOVE, THE(1920)

Doncho Hall
SNUFFY SMITH, YARD BIRD(1942), w

Donna Hall
HAWK OF WILD RIVER, THE(1952); SON OF SINBAD(1955); CHEYENNE AUTUMN(1964)

Dorothy Hall
NOTHING BUT THE TRUTH(1929); LAUGHING LADY, THE(1930); WORKING GIRLS(1931); NOTHING BUT A MAN(1964)
Misc. Silents
BROADWAY DRIFTER, THE(1927); WINNING OAR, THE(1927)

Ed Hall
SHADOWS OF DEATH(1945)

Eddie Hall
CORREGIDOR(1943); I LOVE A SOLDIER(1944); I'LL BE SEEING YOU(1944); JAM SESSION(1944); ONCE UPON A TIME(1944); PRACTICALLY YOURS(1944); SINCE YOU WENT AWAY(1944); DUFFY'S TAVERN(1945); GANGS OF THE WATERFRONT(1945); THOROUGHBREDS(1945); CALCUTTA(1947)

Edith Hall
Misc. Silents
CRASHING COURAGE(1923)

Edna Hall
IN THE NAVY(1941)
Misc. Silents
DOUBLE ACTION DANIELS(1925)

Elena Hall
DEATH RIDES A HORSE(1969, Ital.)

Elizabeth Hall
DEMONSTRATOR(1971, Aus.)

Ella Hall
MADAME SATAN(1930); BITTER TEA OF GENERAL YEN, THE(1933)
Silents
LOVE GIRL, THE(1916); SECRET LOVE(1916); NEW LOVE FOR OLD(1918); THIRD ALARM, THE(1922)
Misc. Silents
HERITAGE(1915); JEWEL(1915); SILENT COMMAND, THE(1915); BUGLER OF ALGIERS, THE(1916); CRIPPLED HAND, THE(1916); LITTLE EVE EDGARTON(1916); CHARMER, THE(1917); HER SOUL'S INSPIRATION(1917); JEWEL IN PAWN, A(1917); LITTLE ORPHAN, THE(1917); MY LITTLE BOY(1917); POLLY REDHEAD(1917); SPOTTED LILY, THE(1917); BEAUTY IN CHAINS(1918); HEART OF RACHAEL, THE(1918); MOTHER'S SECRET, A(1918); WHICH WOMAN?(1918); UNDER THE TOP(1919); HEART OF LINCOLN, THE(1922); FLYING DUTCHMAN, THE(1923); WESTBOUND LIMITED, THE(1923)

Ellen Hall
OUTLAWS OF STAMPEDE PASS(1943); BRAND OF THE DEVIL(1944); LUMBERJACK(1944); RAIDERS OF THE BORDER(1944); RANGE LAW(1944); UP IN ARMS(1944); VOODOO MAN(1944); HAVING WONDERFUL CRIME(1945); WONDER MAN(1945); THUNDER TOWN(1946); LAWLESS CODE(1949)
Misc. Talkies
CALL OF THE ROCKIES(1944)

Emmanuel Hall
TOGETHER FOR DAYS(1972)

Emmett Campbell Hall
Silents
POLLY OF THE CIRCUS(1917), w

Ernest Hall
SHE-WOLF, THE(1931), ph

Evelyn Hall
MARRIED IN HOLLYWOOD(1929); SHE GOES TO WAR(1929); CAPTAIN OF THE GUARD(1930); HELL'S ANGELS(1930); OH, FOR A MAN!(1930); RETURN OF DR. FU MANCHU, THE(1930); ALEXANDER HAMILTON(1931); ALONG CAME YOUTH(1931); LOVERS COURAGEOUS(1932); RANDOLPH FAMILY, THE(1945, Brit.); THREE CASES OF MURDER(1955, Brit.)
Silents
MY BEST GIRL(1927); OUR DANCING DAUGHTERS(1928)

Evelyn Walsh Hall
FIVE STAR FINAL(1931)
Silents
SIX DAYS(1923); PACE THAT THRILLS, THE(1925)

F. Paul Hall
MA BARKER'S KILLER BROOD(1960), w; RAIDERS FROM BENEATH THE SEA(1964), w

Fern Hall
WOMAN THEY ALMOST LYNCHED, THE(1953); CITY OF SHADOWS(1955); NO MAN'S WOMAN(1955)

Foxy Hall
OUR RELATIONS(1936)

Frank E. Hall
LOST ANGEL(1944), ed

Frank Hall
BURGLAR, THE(1956); ASTOUNDING SHE-MONSTER, THE(1958), w

Franklin Hall
Misc. Silents
MISTER 44(1916)

Gene Hall
I MET MY LOVE AGAIN(1938)

Genee Hall
SANTA FE STAMPEDE(1938)

George Edward Hall
Silents
JUDGE HER NOT(1921), d&w
Misc. Silents
PRAIRIE MYSTERY, THE(1922), d

George Edwardes Hall
Silents
BABBLING TONGUES(1917), w; NOBODY'S CHILD(1919, Brit.), d, w; QUEEN'S EVIDENCE(1919, Brit.), w; 12-10(1919, Brit.), w
Misc. Silents
TEMPTRESS, THE(1920, Brit.), d

George Hall
BARBER OF STAMFORD HILL, THE(1963, Brit.), m; PRIVATE POTTER(1963, Brit.), m

Georgine Hall
BEING THERE(1979)

Geraldine Hall
MORE THAN A SECRETARY(1936); BRINGING UP BABY(1938); BIG CARNIVAL, THE(1951); CAPTIVE CITY(1952); PHFFFT!(1954); SECRET OF THE INCAS(1954); OVER-EXPOSED(1956); PROUD AND THE PROFANE, THE(1956)

Gertrude Hall
Silents
LAST CHANCE, THE(1921)

Gita Hall
GUN RUNNERS, THE(1958); WOLF LARSEN(1958)

Gordon Hall
RAMPARTS WE WATCH, THE(1940)

Grayson Hall
SATAN IN HIGH HEELS(1962); NIGHT OF THE IGUANA, THE(1964); THAT DARN CAT(1965); ADAM AT 6 A.M.(1970); HOUSE OF DARK SHADOWS(1970); NIGHT OF DARK SHADOWS(1971)

Hallene Hall
THIS LAND IS MINE(1943)

Harvey Hall
BAY OF SAINT MICHEL, THE(1963, Brit.); MOUSE ON THE MOON, THE(1963, Brit.); MASQUE OF THE RED DEATH, THE(1964, U.S./Brit.); ZULU(1964, Brit.); I'LL NEVER FORGET WHAT'S 'IS NAME(1967, Brit.); GAMES, THE(1970); VAMPIRE LOVERS, THE(1970, Brit.); LUST FOR A VAMPIRE(1971, Brit.); TWINS OF EVIL(1971, Brit.)

Henry Hall
FEET FIRST(1930); RENO(1930); FREE SOUL, A(1931); IN THE LINE OF DUTY(1931); MIDNIGHT WARNING, THE(1932); PACK UP YOUR TROUBLES(1932); SECRETS OF WU SIN(1932); TANGLED DESTINIES(1932); THIRTEENTH GUEST, THE(1932); BACHELOR MOTHER(1933); DEVIL'S MATE(1933); LAWYER MAN(1933); PENAL CODE, THE(1933); RAINBOW RANCH(1933); SITTING PRETTY(1933); STORY OF TEMPLE DRAKE, THE(1933); DUDE RANGER, THE(1934); INSIDE INFORMATION(1934); OUR DAILY BREAD(1934); SAGEBRUSH TRAIL(1934); CIRCLE OF DEATH(1935); DESERT TRAIL(1935); G-MEN(1935); MARY BURNS, FUGITIVE(1935); MURDER BY TELEVISION(1935); MUSIC HATH CHARMS(1935, Brit.); ON PROBATION(1935); SPLENDOR(1935); DEATH FROM A DISTANCE(1936); GUN SMOKE(1936); JAILBREAK(1936); COUNTY FAIR(1937); DEATH IN THE SKY(1937); HEADLINE CRASHER(1937); MOUNTAIN JUSTICE(1937); RIO GRANDE RANGER(1937); ROOTIN' TOOTIN' RHYTHM(1937); THEY WON'T FORGET(1937); YODELIN' KID FROM PINE RIDGE(1937); APE, THE(1940); BLAZING SIX SHOOTERS(1940); CHIP OF THE FLYING U(1940); HAUNTED HOUSE, THE(1940); PRAIRIE LAW(1940); SANTA FE TRAIL(1940); PIRATES ON HORSEBACK(1941); RELUCTANT DRAGON, THE(1941); STICK TO YOUR GUNS(1941); BOSS OF HANGTOWN MESA(1942); MAD MONSTER, THE(1942); MURDER IN THE BIG HOUSE(1942); QUEEN OF BROADWAY(1942); STAGECOACH BUCKAROO(1942); APE MAN, THE(1943); GIRLS IN CHAINS(1943); HARVEST MELODY(1943); JOHNNY COME LATELY(1943); KID DYNAMITE(1943); LADIES' DAY(1943); NORTH STAR, THE(1943); RAIDERS OF SAN JOAQUIN(1943); RETURN OF THE RANGERS, THE(1943); RIDERS OF THE RIO GRANDE(1943); WEST OF TEXAS(1943); WE'VE NEVER BEEN LICKED(1943); DEAD OR ALIVE(1944); HEAVENLY DAYS(1944); SONORA STAGECOACH(1944); VOODOO MAN(1944); WHISPERING SKULL, THE(1944); APOLOGY FOR MURDER(1945); DALTONS RIDE AGAIN, THE(1945); ENEMY OF THE LAW(1945); JADE MASK, THE(1945); LIGHTNING RAIDERS(1945); MARKED FOR MURDER(1945); PHANTOM OF THE PLAINS(1945); SAN ANTONIO(1945); FLYING SERPENT, THE(1946); LARCENY IN HER HEART(1946); NAVAJO KID, THE(1946); TERRORS ON HORSEBACK(1946); GHOST TOWN RENEGADES(1947); HIGH WALL, THE(1947); NIGHTMARE ALLEY(1947); PIONEER JUSTICE(1947); SONG OF THE WASTELAND(1947); WILD COUNTRY(1947); CANON CITY(1948); CROSSED TRAILS(1948); PANHANDLE(1948); SOUTHERN YANKEE, A(1948); CHALLENGE OF THE RANGE(1949); COVER-UP(1949); PETTY GIRL, THE(1950); BANK RAIDERS, THE(1958, Brit.), ph
Misc. Talkies
GUNSMOKE ON THE GUADALUPE(1935); DEATH IN THE AIR(1937)

Herschel Hall
Silents
CHICKENS(1921), w

Hilton Hall
WIRE SERVICE(1942), ph

Holly Hall
FOLLOW THE LEADER(1930)

Holworthy Hall
VALIANT, THE(1929), w; MAN WHO WOULDN'T TALK, THE(1940), w

Howard Hall
Silents
ACCORDING TO LAW(1916); CLARION, THE(1916); ALIAS MRS. JESSOP(1917)
Misc. Silents
CROWN PRINCE'S DOUBLE, THE(1916); HUMAN ORCHID, THE(1916); HUNGRY HEART, THE(1917); LOVE AND AMBITION(1917); NATURAL LAW, THE(1917); WEAVERS OF LIFE(1917); FLOWER OF THE DUSK(1918); TREASON(1918); GOLD CURE, THE(1919); SUNSHINE HARBOR(1922)

Huntz Hall

DEAD END(1937); ANGELS WITH DIRTY FACES(1938); CRIME SCHOOL(1938); LITTLE TOUGH GUY(1938); ANGELS WASH THEIR FACES(1939); CALL A MESSENGER(1939); DEAD END KIDS ON DRESS PARADE(1939); HELL'S KITCHEN(1939); RETURN OF DR. X, THE(1939); THEY MADE ME A CRIMINAL(1939); GIVE US WINGS(1940); YOU'RE NOT SO TOUGH(1940); BOWERY BLITZKRIEG(1941); HIT THE ROAD(1941); MOB TOWN(1941); SPOOKS RUN WILD(1941); ZIS BOOM BAH(1941); COLLEGE SWEETHEARTS(1942); LET'S GET TOUGH(1942); MR. WISE GUY(1942); 'NEATH BROOKLYN BRIDGE(1942); PRIVATE BUCKAROO(1942); SMART ALECKS(1942); TOUGH AS THEY COME(1942); CLANCY STREET BOYS(1943); GHOSTS ON THE LOOSE(1943); JUNIOR ARMY(1943); KEEP 'EM SLUGGING(1943); KID DYNAMITE(1943); MR. MUGGS STEPS OUT(1943); MUG TOWN(1943); BLOCK BUSTERS(1944); BOWERY CHAMPS(1944); FOLLOW THE LEADER(1944); MILLION DOLLAR KID(1944); BRING ON THE GIRLS(1945); COME OUT FIGHTING(1945); MR. MUGGS RIDES AGAIN(1945); WALK IN THE SUN, A(1945); WONDER MAN(1945); BOWERY BOMBSHELL(1946); IN FAST COMPANY(1946); LIVE WIRES(1946); MR. HEX(1946); SPOOK BUSTERS(1946); BOWERY BUCKAROOS(1947); HARD BOILED MAHONEY(1947); NEWS HOUNDS(1947); ANGELS ALLEY(1948); JINX MONEY(1948); SMUGGLERS' COVE(1948); TROUBLE MAKERS(1948); ANGELS IN DISGUISE(1949); FIGHTING FOOLS(1949); HOLD THAT BABY!(1949); MASTER MINDS(1949); BLONDE DYNAMITE(1950); BLUES BUSTERS(1950); LUCKY LOSERS(1950); TRIPLE TROUBLE(1950); BOWERY BATTALION(1951); CRAZY OVER HORSES(1951); GHOST CHASERS(1951); LET'S GO NAVY(1951); FEUDIN' FOOLS(1952); HERE COME THE MARINES(1952); HOLD THAT LINE(1952); NO HOLDS BARRED(1952); CLIPPED WINGS(1953); JALOPY(1953); LOOSE IN LONDON(1953); PRIVATE EYES(1953); BOWERY BOYS MEET THE MONSTERS, THE(1954); JUNGLE GENTS(1954); PARIS PLAYBOYS(1954); BOWERY TO BAGDAD(1955); HIGH SOCIETY(1955); JAIL BUSTERS(1955); CRASHING LAS VEGAS(1956); DIG THAT URANIUM(1956); FIGHTING TROUBLE(1956); HOT SHOTS(1956); SPY CHASERS(1956); HOLD THAT HYPNOTIST(1957); LOOKING FOR DANGER(1957); SPOOK CHASERS(1957); UP IN SMOKE(1957); IN THE MONEY(1958); SECOND FIDDLE TO A STEEL GUITAR(1965); GENTLE GIANT(1967); PHYNX, THE(1970); HERBIE RIDES AGAIN(1974); MANCHU EAGLE MURDER CAPER MYSTERY, THE(1975); WON TON TON, THE DOG WHO SAVED HOLLYWOOD(1976); VALENTINO(1977, Brit.); ESCAPE ARTIST, THE(1982)
Misc. Talkies
GAS PUMP GIRLS(1979)

Iris Hall
Misc. Silents
SYMBOL OF THE UNCONQUERED(1921)

Irlin Hall
HER PANELLED DOOR(1951, Brit.)

Irlyn Hall
PRIVATE'S PROGRESS(1956, Brit.)

Irma Hall
BOOK OF NUMBERS(1973); SPLIT IMAGE(1982)

Ivan Hall
FUNERAL FOR AN ASSASSIN(1977), p, d; KILL OR BE KILLED(1980), d; KILL AND KILL AGAIN(1981), d

J. A. Hall
Silents
ETERNAL GRIND, THE(1916)

J. Albert Hall
Silents
ETERNAL CITY, THE(1915); SALAMANDER, THE(1915)

James Hall
CANARY MURDER CASE, THE(1929); SATURDAY NIGHT KID, THE(1929); SMILING IRISH EYES(1929); THIS IS HEAVEN(1929); DANGEROUS NAN McGREW(1930); HELL'S ANGELS(1930); LET'S GO NATIVE(1930); MAYBE IT'S LOVE(1930); THIRD ALARM, THE(1930); DIVORCE AMONG FRIENDS(1931); GOOD BAD GIRL, THE(1931); LIGHTNING FLYER(1931); MAN TO MAN(1931); MILLIE(1931); SHE-WOLF, THE(1931); SPORTING CHANCE(1931); MANHATTAN TOWER(1932); AND NOW MIGUEL(1966); WHO IS HARRY KELLERMAN AND WHY IS HE SAYING THOSE TERRIBLE THINGS ABOUT ME?(1971); CHINA SYNDROME, THE(1979); FORCE OF ONE, A(1979)
Silents
RANSOM, THE(1916); CAMPUS FLIRT, THE(1926); ROLLED STOCKINGS(1927); SILK LEGS(1927); FIFTY-FIFTY GIRL, THE(1928); FOUR SONS(1928); JUST MARRIED(1928)
Misc. Silents
STRANDED IN PARIS(1926); HOTEL IMPERIAL(1927); LOVE'S GREATEST MISTAKE(1927); RITZY(1927); SENORITA(1927); SWIM, GIRL, SWIM(1927); FLEET'S IN, THE(1928); CASE OF LENA SMITH, THE(1929)

James Norman Hall
MUTINY ON THE BOUNTY(1935), w; HURRICANE, THE(1937), w; TUTTLES OF TAHITI(1942), w; PASSAGE TO MARSEILLE(1944), w; HIGH BARBAREE(1947), w; BOTANY BAY(1953), w; MUTINY ON THE BOUNTY(1962), w; HURRICANE(1979), w

Jane Hall
THESE GLAMOUR GIRLS(1939), w; IT'S A DATE(1940), w; PATRICK THE GREAT(1945), w; HARVEY GIRLS, THE(1946), w; NANCY GOES TO RIO(1950), w; ONLY WAY HOME, THE(1972)
Silents
MADAME BUTTERFLY(1915)

Jeff Hall
RACE FOR YOUR LIFE, CHARLIE BROWN(1977), anim

Jenni Hall
GOODBYE GEMINI(1970, Brit.), w

Jennie Hall
MY LOVER, MY SON(1970, Brit.), w

Jerry Hall
MAN IN THE GREY FLANNEL SUIT, THE(1956); URBAN COWBOY(1980); WILLIE AND PHIL(1980)

Jim Hall
DESPERATE CHARACTERS(1971), m

Joanna Hall
FUTUREWORLD(1976)

Jody Hall
FIDDLER ON THE ROOF(1971)

John Hall
FURTHER UP THE CREEK!(1958, Brit.); MIDNIGHT(1983)

Jon Hall
HURRICANE, THE(1937); KIT CARSON(1940); SAILOR'S LADY(1940); SOUTH OF PAGO PAGO(1940); ALOMA OF THE SOUTH SEAS(1941); ARABIAN NIGHTS(1942); EAGLE SQUADRON(1942); INVISIBLE AGENT(1942); TUTTLES OF TAHITI(1942); WHITE SAVAGE(1943); ALI BABA AND THE FORTY THIEVES(1944); COBRA WOMAN(1944); GYPSY WILDCAT(1944); INVISIBLE MAN'S REVENGE(1944); LADY IN THE DARK(1944); SAN DIEGO, I LOVE YOU(1944); MEN IN HER DIARY(1945); SUDAN(1945); LAST OF THE REDMEN(1947); MICHIGAN KID, THE(1947); VIGILANTES RETURN, THE(1947); PRINCE OF THIEVES, THE(1948); DEPUTY MARSHAL(1949); MUTINEERS, THE(1949); ZAMBA(1949); ON THE ISLE OF SAMOA(1950); CHINA CORSAIR(1951); HURRICANE ISLAND(1951); WHEN THE REDSKINS RODE(1951); BRAVE WARRIOR(1952); LAST TRAIN FROM BOMBAY(1952); WHITE GODDESS(1953); PHANTOM OF THE JUNGLE(1955); THUNDER OVER SANGOLAND(1955); HELL SHIP MUTINY(1957); FORBIDDEN ISLAND(1959); BEACH GIRLS AND THE MONSTER, THE(1965), a, d; FIVE THE HARD WAY(1969), p, ph
Misc. Talkies
LION MAN, THE(1936); EYES OF THE JUNGLE(1953)

Josephine Hall
LOVE PARADE, THE(1929)

Juanita Hall
SOUTH PACIFIC(1958); FLOWER DRUM SONG(1961)
Misc. Talkies
PARADISE IN HARLEM(1939)

Justin Hall
1984
C.H.U.D.(1984)

Kate Hall
ELECTRA GLIDE IN BLUE(1973)

Katherine Hall
RENDEZVOUS AT MIDNIGHT(1935)

Kay Hall
SOMEONE(1968); HOFFMAN(1970, Brit.)

Ken G. Hall
SQUATTER'S DAUGHTER(1933, Aus.), p&d; SILENCE OF DEAN MAITLAND, THE(1934, Aus.), d; GRANDAD RUDD(1935, Aus.), d; THOROUGHBRED(1936, Aus.), d; IT ISN'T DONE(1937, Aus.), d; TALL TIMBERS(1937, Aus.), d; WILD INNOCENCE(1937, Aus.), p&d; BROKEN MELODY(1938, Aus.), d; DAD AND DAVE COME TO TOWN(1938, Aus.), d; LOVERS AND LUGGERS(1938, Aus.), d; GONE TO THE DOGS(1939, Aus.), d; MR. CHEDWORTH STEPS OUT(1939, Aus.), d; VENGEANCE OF THE DEEP(1940, Aus.), p&d; SMITHY(1946, Aus.), d; PACIFIC ADVENTURE(1947, Aus.), d, w
Misc. Talkies
LET GEORGE DO IT(1938, Aus.), d; TIMBERLAND TERROR(1940, Aus.), d

Ken Hall
ON OUR SELECTION(1930, Aus.), d; ORPHAN OF THE WILDERNESS(1937, Aus.), d, animal

Kevin Hall
1984
WILD LIFE, THE(1984)

Kevin Peter Hall
ONE DARK NIGHT(1983)

Kirby Hall
FANTASM(1976, Aus.)

Larue Hall
MISS JESSICA IS PREGNANT(1970)

Laura Nelson Hall
Misc. Silents
STUBBORNESS OF GERALDINE, THE(1915)

Laurence Hall
Misc. Talkies
I WAS A ZOMBIE FOR THE F.B.I.(1982)

PFC Lawrence C. Hall, USA
BACK TO BATAAN(1945)

Leslie Hall
JOURNEY TO SHILOH(1968), cos

Lillian Hall
Silents
WANTED FOR MURDER(1919); ABABIAN KNIGHT, AN(1920); FICKLE WOMEN(1920); LAST OF THE MOHICANS, THE(1920); OLIVER TWIST, JR.(1921); SECRET OF THE HILLS, THE(1921); SHOCKING NIGHT, A(1921)
Misc. Silents
LITTLE WOMEN(1919); MY LITTLE SISTER(1919); TAXI(1919); GOING SOME(1920); SHERRY(1920); HEARTS OF YOUTH(1921)

Linda Hall
PASSION HOLIDAY(1963); HOW TO BEAT THE HIGH COST OF LIVING(1980)

Lindsay Hall
Misc. Silents
DORIAN'S DIVORCE(1916); SUBMARINE EYE, THE(1917)

Lindsay J. Hall
Silents
WHEN BROADWAY WAS A TRAIL(1914)
Misc. Silents
TOGETHER(1918)

Lisa Hall
SHARKY'S MACHINE(1982)

Liz Hall
CRY DR. CHICAGO(1971)

Lois Hall
EVERY GIRL SHOULD BE MARRIED(1948); FAMILY HONEYMOON(1948); DAUGHTER OF THE JUNGLE(1949); DUKE OF CHICAGO(1949); ROARING WESTWARD(1949); CHEROKEE UPPRISING(1950); FRONTIER OUTPOST(1950); HORSEMEN OF THE SIERRAS(1950); JOE PALOOKA IN THE SQUARED CIRCLE(1950); MY BLUE HEAVEN(1950); PETTY GIRL, THE(1950); TEXAS DYNAMO(1950); WOMAN OF DISTINCTION, A(1950); CLOSE TO MY HEART(1951); COLORADO AMBUSH(1951); SECRETS OF MONTE CARLO(1951); SLAUGHTER TRAIL(1951); CAR-

RIE(1952); NIGHT RAIDERS(1952); TEXAS CITY(1952); SEVEN BRIDES FOR SEVEN BROTHERS(1954)
Misc. Talkies
BLAZING BULLETS(1951)
Lorraine Hall
ONE MORE TIME(1970, Brit.)
Louis Hall
HERE COME THE GIRLS(1953)
Manly P. Hall
WHEN WERE YOU BORN?(1938), w
Margaret Hall
BELL JAR, THE(1979); SO FINE(1981)
Margie Hall
FAREWELL, MY LOVELY(1975)
Marian Hall
GORILLA MAN(1942); HIDDEN HAND, THE(1942); SECRET ENEMIES(1942)
Marianne Hall
TRIAL OF BILLY JACK, THE(1974)
Marion Hall
HENRY ALDRICH SWINGS IT(1943)
Mark Hall
ACROSS THE GREAT DIVIDE(1976); LIFEGUARD(1976)
Martha Hall
Silents
KID, THE(1921)
Mary Hall
Silents
ANNE OF GREEN GABLES(1919)
Misc. Silents
REDEMPTION(1917); SHARK, THE(1920)
May Hall
Misc. Silents
BATTLING JANE(1918)
Mayre Hall
Misc. Silents
BATTLE OF BALLOTS, THE(1915); SMART SEX, THE(1921)
Mel Hall
SENSATIONS OF 1945(1944)
Michael Grant Hall
WILD PARTY, THE(1975)
Michael Hall
BEST YEARS OF OUR LIVES, THE(1946); BLACK HILLS AMBUSH(1952); LAST MUSKETEER, THE(1952); BLOOD OF DRACULA(1957)
Mike Hall
WORLD IS JUST A 'B' MOVIE, THE(1971)
Mildred Hall
Silents
GOLD RUSH, THE(1925)
Milton Hall
REFORM SCHOOL(1939)
Natalie Hall
TROPICAL TROUBLE(1936, Brit.)
Newton Hall
Silents
DINTY(1920); PENROD(1922); PENROD AND SAM(1923); ABRAHAM LINCOLN(1924); STELLA DALLAS(1925)
Norman Hall
FRONTIER PONY EXPRESS(1939), w; WALL STREET COWBOY(1939), w; BLACK HILLS EXPRESS(1943), w; BUCKAROO FROM POWDER RIVER(1948), w
Norman S. Hall
FLIRTING WITH DANGER(1935), w; BORDER CABALLERO(1936), w; LEGION OF MISSING MEN(1937), w; BOY'S REFORMATORY(1939), w; OUTLAWS OF PINE RIDGE(1942), w; SOMBRERO KID, THE(1942), w; SUNDOWN KID, THE(1942), w; BORDERTOWN GUNFIGHTERS(1943), w; CARSON CITY CYCLONE(1943), w; DAYS OF OLD CHEYENNE(1943), w; DEAD MAN'S GULCH(1943), w; DEATH VALLEY MANHUNT(1943), w; FUGITIVE FROM SONORA(1943), w; MAN FROM THE RIO GRANDE, THE(1943), w; THUNDERING TRAILS(1943), w; CALIFORNIA JOE(1944), w; MOJAVE FIREBRAND(1944), w; OUTLAWS OF SANTA FE(1944), w; SAN ANTONIO KID, THE(1944), w; SHERIFF OF LAS VEGAS(1944), w; SHERIFF OF SUNDOWN(1944), w; STAGECOACH TO MONTEREY(1944), w; VIGILANTES OF DODGE CITY(1944), w; CORPUS CHRISTI BANDITS(1945), w; TOPEKA TERROR, THE(1945), w; RED RIVER RENEGADES(1946), w; RIO GRANDE RAIDERS(1946), w; LAST DAYS OF BOOT HILL(1947), w; DAREDEVILS OF THE CLOUDS(1948), w; SLIPPY MCGEE(1948), w; SUNDOWN IN SANTA FE(1948), w; WHIRLWIND RAIDERS(1948), w; BRIMSTONE(1949), w; LAW OF THE GOLDEN WEST(1949), w; ROSE OF THE YUKON(1949), w; SAN ANTONE AMBUSH(1949), w; SOUTH OF RIO(1949), w; BEYOND THE PURPLE HILLS(1950), w; INDIAN TERRITORY(1950), w; UNMASKED(1950), w; GENE AUTRY AND THE MOUNTIES(1951), w; TEXANS NEVER CRY(1951), w; WHIRLWIND(1951), w; APACHE COUNTRY(1952), w; MONTANA BELLE(1952), w; PACK TRAIN(1953), w; WINNING OF THE WEST(1953), w
Norman Shannon Hall
MISSOURI TRAVELER, THE(1958), w; YOUNG LAND, THE(1959), w
Oakley Hall
WARLOCK(1959), w; DOWNHILL RACER(1969), w
Parnell Hall
1984
C.H.U.D.(1984), a, w
Pat Hall
EVERY GIRL SHOULD BE MARRIED(1948); HOLIDAY AFFAIR(1949); TWO TICKETS TO BROADWAY(1951)
Patricia Hall
ABBOTT AND COSTELLO MEET THE KILLER, BORIS KARLOFF(1949); GAL WHO TOOK THE WEST, THE(1949)
Patrick Hall
RECKONING, THE(1971, Brit.), w
Cpt. Paul R. Hall
Silents
MAN THE ARMY MADE, A(1917, Brit.)

Pauline Hall
Silents
GOVERNOR'S BOSS, THE(1915)
Peter Hall
DOCTOR FAUSTUS(1967, Brit.), cos; WORK IS A FOUR LETTER WORD(1968, Brit.), d; MIDSUMMER NIGHT'S DREAM, A(1969, Brit.), d; THREE INTO TWO WON'T GO(1969, Brit.), d; PERFECT FRIDAY(1970, Brit.), d; HOMECOMING, THE(1973), d; PEDESTRIAN, THE(1974, Ger.)
Peter J. Hall
ABDICATION, THE(1974, Brit.), cos
Philip B. Hall
COWARDS(1970)
Philip Baker Hall
MAN WITH BOGART'S FACE, THE(1980)
1984
SECRET HONOR(1984), a, cos
Phillip Baker Hall
DREAM ON(1981)
Porter Hall
SECRETS OF A SECRETARY(1931); MURDER IN THE PRIVATE CAR(1934); THIN MAN, THE(1934); CASE OF THE LUCKY LEGS, THE(1935); AND SUDDEN DEATH(1936); GENERAL DIED AT DAWN, THE(1936); PETRIFIED FOREST, THE(1936); PRINCESS COMES ACROSS, THE(1936); SATAN MET A LADY(1936); SNOWED UNDER(1936); STORY OF LOUIS PASTEUR, THE(1936); TOO MANY PARENTS(1936); BULLDOG DRUMMOND ESCAPES(1937); HOTEL HAYWIRE(1937); KING OF GAMBLERS(1937); LET'S MAKE A MILLION(1937); MAKE WAY FOR TOMORROW(1937); PLAINSMAN, THE(1937); SOULS AT SEA(1937); THIS WAY PLEASE(1937); TRUE CONFESSION(1937); WELLS FARGO(1937); WILD MONEY(1937); ARKANSAS TRAVELER, THE(1938); BULLDOG DRUMMOND'S PERIL(1938); DANGEROUS TO KNOW(1938); KING OF ALCATRAZ(1938); MEN WITH WINGS(1938); PRISON FARM(1938); SCANDAL STREET(1938); STOLEN HEAVEN(1938); GRAND JURY SECRETS(1939); HENRY GOES ARIZONA(1939); MR. SMITH GOES TO WASHINGTON(1939); THEY SHALL HAVE MUSIC(1939); TOM SAWYER, DETECTIVE(1939); ARIZONA(1940); DARK COMMAND, THE(1940); HIS GIRL FRIDAY(1940); TRAIL OF THE VIGILANTES(1940); MR. AND MRS. NORTH(1941); PARSON OF PANAMINT, THE(1941); SULLIVAN'S TRAVELS(1941); BUTCH MINDS THE BABY(1942); REMARKABLE ANDREW, THE(1942); TENNESSEE JOHNSON(1942); DESPERADOES, THE(1943); STRANGER IN TOWN, A(1943); WOMAN OF THE TOWN, THE(1943); DOUBLE INDEMNITY(1944); GOING MY WAY(1944); GREAT MOMENT, THE(1944); MARK OF THE WHISTLER, THE(1944); MIRACLE OF MORGAN'S CREEK, THE(1944); STANDING ROOM ONLY(1944); BLOOD ON THE SUN(1945); BRING ON THE GIRLS(1945); KISS AND TELL(1945); MURDER, HE SAYS(1945); WEEKEND AT THE WALDORF(1945); MIRACLE ON 34TH STREET, THE(1947); SINGAPORE(1947); UNCONQUERED(1947); CHICKEN EVERY SUNDAY(1948); THAT WONDERFUL URGE(1948); YOU GOTTA STAY HAPPY(1948); BEAUTIFUL BLONDE FROM BASHFUL BEND, THE(1949); INTRUDER IN THE DUST(1949); BIG CARNIVAL, THE(1951); CARBINE WILLIAMS(1952); HALF-BREED, THE(1952); HOLIDAY FOR SINNERS(1952); PONY EXPRESS(1953); VICE SQUAD(1953); RETURN TO TREASURE ISLAND(1954)
Rachel Hall
1984
NATURAL, THE(1984)
Ralph James Hall
MIXED COMPANY(1974), ed
Raymond Hall
WOLFPEN PRINCIPLE, THE(1974, Can.), ed; ROCKERS(1980)
Rene Hall
FIRST NUDIE MUSICAL, THE(1976)
Richard Hall
BORN TO SING(1942); RATIONING(1944); ROCKERS(1980)
Robert Hall
NIGHT BOAT TO DUBLIN(1946, Brit.), w; FRANCHISE AFFAIR, THE(1952, Brit.), p, w; GOOD BEGINNING, THE(1953, Brit.), p, w; DESTINATION MILAN(1954, Brit.), w; YOU CAN'T ESCAPE(1955, Brit.), p, w; SMALL HOTEL(1957, Brit.), p; LADY MISLAID, A(1958, Brit.), p; MOONRAKER, THE(1958, Brit.), w; SANDS OF THE DESERT(1960, Brit.), w; BARABBAS(1962, Ital.); CUSTER OF THE WEST(1968, U.S., Span.); KRAKATOA, EAST OF JAVA(1969); DIAMOND STUD(1970); CLOSE ENCOUNTERS OF THE THIRD KIND(1977), ph
Misc. Talkies
DIAMOND STUD(1970)
Robin Hall
MAN FROM SNOWY RIVER, THE(1983, Aus.), cos
Roger Hall
MIDDLE AGE SPREAD(1979, New Zealand), w; CHARRIOTS OF FIRE(1981, Brit.), art d
Russ Hall
KLONDIKE ANNIE(1936)
Russell Hall
MY LITTLE CHICKADEE(1940)
Ruth Hall
DOORWAY TO HELL(1930); DRUMS OF JEOPARDY(1931); HER MAJESTY LOVE(1931); LOCAL BOY MAKES GOOD(1931); MONKEY BUSINESS(1931); BETWEEN FIGHTING MEN(1932); DYNAMITE RANCH(1932); GAMBLING SEX(1932); HEART OF NEW YORK(1932); KID FROM SPAIN, THE(1932); MISS PINKERTON(1932); ONE WAY PASSAGE(1932); RICH ARE ALWAYS WITH US, THE(1932); RIDE HIM, COWBOY(1932); UNION DEPOT(1932); FLAMING GUNS(1933); LAUGHING AT LIFE(1933); MAN FROM MONTEREY, THE(1933); RETURN OF CASEY JONES(1933); STRAWBERRY ROAN(1933); BADGE OF HONOR(1934); BELOVED(1934); MURDER ON THE CAMPUS(1934); MEET THE MAYOR(1938); GEORGE WHITE'S SCANDALS(1945); JULIA MISBEHAVES(1948); I DON'T CARE GIRL, THE(1952); FARMER TAKES A WIFE, THE(1953); HOW TO MARRY A MILLIONAIRE(1953)
Sam Hall
HOUSE OF DARK SHADOWS(1970), w; NIGHT OF DARK SHADOWS(1971), w
Sands Hall
KING OF THE GYPSIES(1978); SOMEBODY KILLED HER HUSBAND(1978)
Sarah Hall
RUDE BOY(1980, Brit.)

Scott H. Hall
BLOOD FEAST(1963); COLOR ME BLOOD RED(1965)
Shannah Hall
BOOGEYMAN II(1983)
Shari Hall
1984
THIS IS SPINAL TAP(1984)
Sharon Hall
VANISHING OUTPOST, THE(1951)
Shashawnee Hall
STACY'S KNIGHTS(1983)
1984
BODY ROCK(1984); NIGHTMARE ON ELM STREET, A(1984)
Shelly Chee Chee Hall
TRADING PLACES(1983)
Sheridan Hall
Silents
STEADFAST HEART, THE(1923), d
Sherry Hall
DANCE, FOOLS, DANCE(1931); HAT CHECK GIRL(1932); ANOTHER LAN-
GUAGE(1933); ABOVE THE CLOUDS(1934); EVELYN PRENTICE(1934); I SELL
ANYTHING(1934); IT HAPPENED ONE NIGHT(1934); JEALOUSY(1934); MANHAT-
TAN MELODRAMA(1934); OPERATOR 13(1934); STUDENT TOUR(1934); THIN MAN,
THE(1934); TWENTIETH CENTURY(1934); GOING HIGHBROW(1935); MAGNIFI-
CENT OBSESSION(1935); NO MORE LADIES(1935); RENDEZVOUS(1935); FU-
RY(1936); HIS BROTHER'S WIFE(1936); LIBELED LADY(1936); RIFF-RAFF(1936);
SAN FRANCISCO(1936); THEODORA GOES WILD(1936); UNDER YOUR
SPELL(1936); AFFAIRS OF CAPPY RICKS(1937); GIRL WITH IDEAS, A(1937); HIGH,
WIDE AND HANDSOME(1937); LET'S GET MARRIED(1937); LOVE IN A BUNGA-
LOW(1937); LOVE IS NEWS(1937); MAN WHO CRIED WOLF, THE(1937); WINGS
OVER HONOLULU(1937); MEN WITH WINGS(1938); MEXICALI ROSE(1939); TOO
BUSY TO WORK(1939); ARISE, MY LOVE(1940); GENTLEMAN FROM ARIZONA,
THE(1940); RETURN OF FRANK JAMES, THE(1940); AROUND THE WORLD(1943);
DANCING MASTERS, THE(1943); GIRL RUSH(1944); GREENWICH VILLAGE(1944);
MUSIC IN MANHATTAN(1944); ISLE OF THE DEAD(1945); ON STAGE EVERY-
BODY(1945); SCARLET STREET(1945); THEY WERE EXPENDABLE(1945); ACCOM-
PLICE(1946); MONSIEUR BEAUCAIRE(1946); SHADOW RETURNS, THE(1946);
LADY IN THE LAKE(1947); FORCE OF EVIL(1948); DANCING IN THE DARK(1949);
LADY GAMBLES, THE(1949); WHITE HEAT(1949); FATHER OF THE BRIDE(1950);
GAMBLING HOUSE(1950); MAGNIFICENT YANKEE, THE(1950); MISTER 880(1950);
MYSTERY STREET(1950); THREE LITTLE WORDS(1950); IT'S A BIG COUN-
TRY(1951); PROWLER, THE(1951); STRIP, THE(1951); WELL, THE(1951); CAR-
RIE(1952)
Sherry Hall, Jr.
CAPTAINS COURAGEOUS(1937)
Siana Lee Hall
ROCK 'N' ROLL HIGH SCHOOL(1979), ch
Sidney Hall
HOUSE OF SECRETS(1929), w
Stanley Hall
PRINCE OF PLAYERS(1955)
Steve Hall
Silents
GIRLS WHO DARE(1929)
Stewart Hall
LAKE PLACID SERENADE(1944)
Stuart Hall
HARMONY HEAVEN(1930, Brit.); FIRST AID(1931); CAVALCADE(1933); WITHOUT
REGRET(1935); DAWN PATROL, THE(1938); RAGE IN HEAVEN(1941); FOREVER
AND A DAY(1943); LATE GEORGE APLEY, THE(1947); SOLDIERS THREE(1951);
FIVE FINGERS(1952)
Susan Hall
CHILDRENS GAMES(1969), p, w; MY BLOODY VALENTINE(1981, Can.), cos
Terrence Hall
Misc. Talkies
CONVOY BUDDIES(1977)
Terri Hall
Misc. Talkies
GUMS(1976)
Terry Hall
OTHER SIDE OF THE MOUNTAIN, THE(1975)
Tex Hall
WEREWOLVES ON WHEELS(1971)
Thurston Hall
WITHOUT RESERVATIONS(1946); AFTER THE DANCE(1935); BLACK ROOM,
THE(1935); CASE OF THE MISSING MAN, THE(1935); CRIME AND PUNISH-
MENT(1935); FEATHER IN HER HAT, A(1935); GIRL FRIEND, THE(1935); GUARD
THAT GIRL(1935); HOORAY FOR LOVE(1935); LOVE ME FOREVER(1935); MET-
ROPOLITAN(1935); ONE-WAY TICKET(1935); PUBLIC MENACE(1935); TOO TOUGH
TO KILL(1935); DEVIL'S SQUADRON(1936); DON'T GAMBLE WITH LOVE(1936);
KILLER AT LARGE(1936); KING STEPS OUT, THE(1936); LADY FROM NO-
WHERE(1936); LONE WOLF RETURNS, THE(1936); MAN WHO LIVED TWICE(1936);
PRIDE OF THE MARINES(1936); ROAMING LADY(1936); SHAKEDOWN(1936);
THEODORA GOES WILD(1936); THREE WISE GUYS, THE(1936); TRAPPED BY
TELEVISION(1936); TWO-FISTED GENTLEMAN(1936); COUNSEL FOR
CRIME(1937); DON'T TELL THE WIFE(1937); I PROMISE TO PAY(1937); IT CAN'T
LAST FOREVER(1937); MURDER IN GREENWICH VILLAGE(1937); OH DOC-
TOR(1937); PAID TO DANCE(1937); PAROLE RACKET(1937); VENUS MAKES TROU-
BLE(1937); WE HAVE OUR MOMENTS(1937); WOMEN OF GLAMOUR(1937);
AFFAIRS OF ANNABEL(1938); AMAZING DR. CLITTERHOUSE, THE(1938); CAM-
PUS CONFESSIONS(1938); EXTORTION(1938); FAST COMPANY(1938); LITTLE
MISS ROUGHNECK(1938); MAIN EVENT, THE(1938); NO TIME TO MARRY(1938);
OUT WEST WITH THE HARDYS(1938); PENITENTIARY(1938); PROFESSOR
BEWARE(1938); SQUADRON OF HONOR(1938); THERE'S ALWAYS A WO-
MAN(1938); WOMEN ARE LIKE THAT(1938); DANCING CO-ED(1939); DAY THE
BOOKIES WEPT, THE(1939); DODGE CITY(1939); EACH DAWN I DIE(1939); EX-
CHAMP(1939); FIRST LOVE(1939); GOING PLACES(1939); HAWAIIAN
NIGHTS(1939); JEEPERS CREEPERS(1939); MILLION DOLLAR LEGS(1939); MUTI-
NY ON THE BLACKHAWK(1939); STAR MAKER, THE(1939); YOU CAN'T CHEAT
AN HONEST MAN(1939); ALIAS THE DEACON(1940); BLONDIE ON A BUD-
GET(1940); BLUE BIRD, THE(1940); FRIENDLY NEIGHBORS(1940); GOLDEN FLE-
ECING, THE(1940); GREAT McGINTY, THE(1940); IN OLD MISSOURI(1940); LONE
WOLF KEEPS A DATE, THE(1940); LONE WOLF MEETS A LADY, THE(1940);
MILLIONAIRES IN PRISON(1940); MONEY TO BURN(1940); SUED FOR LI-
BEL(1940); VIRGINIA CITY(1940); ACCENT ON LOVE(1941); CITY, FOR CON-
QUEST(1941); DESIGN FOR SCANDAL(1941); FLIGHT FROM DESTINY(1941);
GREAT LIE, THE(1941); HOLD THAT GHOST(1941); IN THE NAVY(1941); INVISI-
BLE WOMAN, THE(1941); LIFE WITH HENRY(1941); LONE WOLF TAKES A
CHANCE, THE(1941); MIDNIGHT ANGEL(1941); NINE LIVES ARE NOT
ENOUGH(1941); REMEMBER THE DAY(1941); REPENT AT LEISURE(1941); SE-
CRETS OF THE LONE WOLF(1941); SHE KNEW ALL THE ANSWERS(1941); SWING
IT SOLDIER(1941); TUXEDO JUNCTION(1941); UNEXPECTED UNCLE(1941);
WASHINGTON MELODRAMA(1941); WHERE DID YOU GET THAT GIRL?(1941);
CALL OF THE CANYON(1942); COUNTER-ESPIONAGE(1942); GREAT GILDER-
SLEEVE, THE(1942); GREAT MAN'S LADY, THE(1942); HARD WAY, THE(1942);
HELLO ANNAPOLIS(1942); NIGHT BEFORE THE DIVORCE, THE(1942); PACIFIC
BLACKOUT(1942); RINGS ON HER FINGERS(1942); SHEPHERD OF THE
OZARKS(1942); SLEEPYTIME GAL(1942); TWIN BEDS(1942); WE WERE DAN-
CING(1942); CRASH DIVE(1943); FOOTLIGHT GLAMOUR(1943); HE HIRED THE
BOSS(1943); HERE COMES ELMER(1943); HOOSIER HOLIDAY(1943); I DOOD
IT(1943); ONE DANGEROUS NIGHT(1943); SHERLOCK HOLMES IN WASHING-
TON(1943); THIS LAND IS MINE(1943); YOUNGEST PROFESSION, THE(1943);
COVER GIRL(1944); EVER SINCE VENUS(1944); FOLLOW THE BOYS(1944); GOOD-
NIGHT SWEETHEART(1944); GREAT MOMENT, THE(1944); IN SOCIETY(1944);
SOMETHING FOR THE BOYS(1944); SONG OF NEVADA(1944); WILSON(1944);
BLONDE FROM BROOKLYN(1945); BREWSTER'S MILLIONS(1945); BRING ON THE
GIRLS(1945); COLONEL EFFINGHAM'S RAID(1945); DON JUAN QUILLIGAN(1945);
GAY SENORITA, THE(1945); LADY ON A TRAIN(1945); SARATOGA TRUNK(1945);
THRILL OF A ROMANCE(1945); WEST OF THE PECOS(1945); DANGEROUS BUSI-
NESS(1946); ONE MORE TOMORROW(1946); SHE WROTE THE BOOK(1946); THREE
LITTLE GIRLS IN BLUE(1946); TWO SISTERS FROM BOSTON(1946); BLACK
GOLD(1947); FARMER'S DAUGHTER, THE(1947); IT HAD TO BE YOU(1947);
MOURNING BECOMES ELECTRA(1947); SECRET LIFE OF WALTER MITTY,
THE(1947); UNFINISHED DANCE,THE(1947); WELCOME STRANGER(1947); BLON-
DIE'S SECRET(1948); KING OF THE GAMBLERS(1948); MANHATTAN AN-
GEL(1948); MIRACULOUS JOURNEY(1948); THREE DARING DAUGHTERS(1948);
UP IN CENTRAL PARK(1948); BRIDE FOR SALE(1949); FOUNTAINHEAD,
THE(1949); RIM OF THE CANYON(1949); RUSTY SAVES A LIFE(1949); SQUARE
DANCE JUBILEE(1949); STAGECOACH KID(1949); TELL IT TO THE JUDGE(1949);
BANDIT QUEEN(1950); BELLE OF OLD MEXICO(1950); BRIGHT LEAF(1950);
CHAIN GANG(1950); FEDERAL AGENT AT LARGE(1950); GIRLS' SCHOOL(1950);
ONE TOO MANY(1950); BELLE LE GRAND(1951); TEXAS CARNIVAL(1951); WHIRL-
WIND(1951); CARSON CITY(1952); IT GROWS ON TREES(1952); NIGHT STAGE TO
GALVESTON(1952); ONE BIG AFFAIR(1952); SKIRTS AHOY!(1952); WAC FROM
WALLA WALLA, THE(1952); BAND WAGON, THE(1953); AFFAIR IN RENO(1957)
Misc. Talkies
SON OF RUSTY, THE(1947); SWING THE WESTERN WAY(1947); WHIRL-
WIND(1951)
Silents
PRICE MARK, THE(1917); ALIEN ENEMY, AN(1918); BRAZEN BEAUTY(1918);
KAISER'S SHADOW, THE(1918); MIDNIGHT PATROL, THE(1918); SPITFIRE OF
SEVILLE, THE(1919); IDLE HANDS(1921); ROYAL OAK, THE(1923, Brit.)
Misc. Silents
CLEOPATRA(1917); LOVE LETTERS(1917); FLARE-UP SAL(1918); MATING OF
MARCELLA, THE(1918); TYRANT FEAR(1918); EXQUISIT THIEF, THE(1919); UN-
PAINTED WOMAN, THE(1919); WHO WILL MARRY ME?(1919); EMPTY
ARMS(1920); IDLE HANDS(1920); VALLEY OF DOUBT, THE(1920); IRON TRAIL,
THE(1921); MOTHER ETERNAL(1921); FAIR LADY(1922); NEGLECTED WO-
MEN(1924, Brit.)
Tom Hall
PAPERBACK HERO(1973, Can.), art d
Tom T. Hall
HARPER VALLEY, P.T.A.(1978), w; DEADHEAD MILES(1982), m
Tommy Hall
NORTH STAR, THE(1943)
Tony Hall
ROCK YOU SINNERS(1957, Brit.); RECOMMENDATION FOR MERCY(1975, Can.),
art d; LOVE AT FIRST SIGHT(1977, Can.), art d; WELCOME TO BLOOD CITY(1977,
Brit./Can.), art d
Valerie Hall
PAN-AMERICANA(1945)
Vincent Hall
THAT LUCKY TOUCH(1975, Brit.)
Virginia Hall
EIGHT GIRLS IN A BOAT(1934); SOMEBODY LOVES ME(1952); OLD OVERLAND
TRAIL(1953); SMALL TOWN GIRL(1953); WAR OF THE WORLDS, THE(1953)
Walter Hall
RING OF BRIGHT WATER(1969, Brit.); LITTLEST HORSE THIEVES, THE(1977)
Walter Richard Hall
Silents
MY DAD(1922), w
Misc. Silents
HATE(1917), d
Willard Lee Hall
Silents
CONQUERING POWER, THE(1921); SCARAMOUCHE(1923)
William Hall
UNCLE HARRY(1945); FLYING HOSTESS(1936); MAGNIFICENT BRUTE,
THE(1936); POSTAL INSPECTOR(1936); ESCAPE BY NIGHT(1937); OH DOC-
TOR(1937); WINDJAMMER(1937); SPY RING, THE(1938); IN OLD MONTEREY(1939);
HOLD THAT WOMAN(1940); HARMON OF MICHIGAN(1941); OFFICER AND THE
LADY, THE(1941); TIMBER(1942); WILDCAT(1942); WRECKING CREW(1942); MUG
TOWN(1943); SCARLET STREET(1945); SHADY LADY(1945); SHE GETS HER
MAN(1945); WEEKEND AT THE WALDORF(1945); CALIFORNIA(1946); TIME OF
THEIR LIVES, THE(1946); BACHELOR AND THE BOBBY-SOXER, THE(1947);
SUDDENLY IT'S SPRING(1947); WEB OF DANGER, THE(1947); LETTER FROM AN
UNKNOWN WOMAN(1948); GREATEST SHOW ON EARTH, THE(1952)

Willie Hall
BLUES BROTHERS, THE(1980)

Willis Hall
LONG AND THE SHORT AND THE TALL, THE(1961, Brit.), w; WHISTLE DOWN THE WIND(1961, Brit.), w; KIND OF LOVING, A(1962, Brit.), w; VALIANT, THE(1962, Brit./Ital.), w; BILLY LIAR(1963, Brit.), w; WEST 11(1963, Brit.), w; MAN IN THE MIDDLE(1964, U.S./Brit.), w; MATTER OF INNOCENCE, A(1968, Brit.), w; LOCK UP YOUR DAUGHTERS(1969, Brit.), w

Winter Hall
HIGH SEAS(1929, Brit.); KITTY(1929, Brit.); LOVE PARADE, THE(1929); RACKETEER, THE(1929); WOMAN TO WOMAN(1929); LOST ZEPPELIN(1930); PASSION FLOWER(1930); ROAD TO PARADISE(1930); CONFESSIONS OF A CO-ED(1931); GIRLS DEMAND EXCITEMENT(1931); TOMORROW AND TOMORROW(1932); MONKEY'S PAW, THE(1933); BARRETTS OF WIMPOLE STREET, THE(1934); BRITISH AGENT(1934); JUDGE PRIEST(1934); MERRY WIDOW, THE(1934); PURSUIT OF HAPPINESS, THE(1934); CRUSADES, THE(1935); MUTINY ON THE BOUNTY(1935); RENDEZVOUS(1935); TALE OF TWO CITIES, A(1935); LLOYDS OF LONDON(1936); THE INVISIBLE RAY(1936); TWO IN A CROWD(1936); SLAVE SHIP(1937); TOAST OF NEW YORK, THE(1937); FOUR MEN AND A PRAYER(1938)
Silents
ROMANCE OF THE REDWOODS, A(1917); SPINDLE OF LIFE, THE(1917); BRAVEST WAY, THE(1918); KAISER, BEAST OF BERLIN, THE(1918); NEW LOVE FOR OLD(1918); ALIAS MIKE MORAN(1919); MONEY CORRAL, THE(1919); ALIAS JIMMY VALENTINE(1920); FAITH(1920); FORBIDDEN WOMAN, THE(1920); AFFAIRS OF ANATOL, THE(1921); BREAKING POINT, THE(1921); CHEATED HEARTS(1921); LITTLE CLOWN, THE(1921); WHAT EVERY WOMAN KNOWS(1921); WITCHING HOUR, THE(1921); BURNING SANDS(1922); EAST IS WEST(1922); ON THE HIGH SEAS(1922); SATURDAY NIGHT(1922); ASHES OF VENGEANCE(1923); LITTLE CHURCH AROUND THE CORNER(1923); HUSBANDS AND LOVERS(1924); ONLY WOMAN, THE(1924); BEN-HUR(1925); COMPROMISE(1925); GIRL WHO WOULDN'T WORK, THE(1925); RAFFLES, THE AMATEUR CRACKSMAN(1925); PARADISE(1928, Brit.); AFTER THE VERDICT(1929, Brit.)
Misc. Silents
PRIMROSE RING, THE(1917); SACRIFICE(1917); SILENT LADY, THE(1917); BEAUTY IN CHAINS(1918); HITTING THE HIGH SPOTS(1918); HOUSE OF SILENCE, THE(1918); MISSING(1918); TURN IN THE ROAD, THE(1919); WHY SMITH LEFT HOME(1919); BEHOLD MY WIFE!(1920); DEADLIER SEX, THE(1920); HEARTS ARE TRUMPS(1920); HUSHED HOUR, THE(1920); CHILD THOU GAVEST ME, THE(1921); GREAT IMPERSONATION, THE(1921); THUNDERING DAWN(1923); VOICE FROM THE MINARET, THE(1923); WASTED LIVES(1923); FORGER, THE(1928, Brit.); WRECKER, THE(1928, Brit.)

Zooey Hall
BORN WILD(1968); LEARNING TREE, THE(1969); FORTUNE AND MEN'S EYES(1971, U.S./Can.); I DISMEMBER MAMA(1974)

The Hall Johnson Choir
BANJO ON MY KNEE(1936); DIMPLES(1936); FOLLOW YOUR HEART(1936); GREEN PASTURES(1936); HEARTS DIVIDED(1936); RAINBOW ON THE RIVER(1936); LOST HORIZON(1937); MY OLD KENTUCKY HOME(1938); SWANEE RIVER(1939); WAY DOWN SOUTH(1939); ZENOBIA(1939); IN OLD MISSOURI(1940); LADY FOR A NIGHT(1941); MEET JOHN DOE(1941); HEART OF THE GOLDEN WEST(1942); SYNCOPATION(1942); TALES OF MANHATTAN(1942); CABIN IN THE SKY(1943)

Lilian Hall-Davies
Misc. Silents
BROWN SUGAR(1922, Brit.); CASTLES IN THE AIR(1923, Brit.)

Lillian Hall-Davies
Silents
FARMER'S WIFE, THE(1928, Brit.)

Lilian Hall-Davis
HER REPUTATION(1931, Brit.); MANY WATERS(1931, Brit.)
Silents
UNWANTED, THE(1924, Brit.); IF YOUTH BUT KNEW(1926, Brit.); RING, THE(1927, Brit.); ROSES OF PICARDY(1927, Brit.)
Misc. Silents
AFTERGLOW(1923, Brit.); I'PAGLIACCI(1923, Brit.); BOADICEA(1926, Brit.)

Peggy Hallack
NO TIME FOR SERGEANTS(1958)

Steve Halladay
KING OF THE MOUNTAIN(1981)

Charles Hallahan
GOING IN STYLE(1979); NIGHTWING(1979); HIDE IN PLAIN SIGHT(1980); THING, THE(1982); SILKWOOD(1983); TWILIGHT ZONE–THE MOVIE(1983)
1984
KIDCO(1984)

Robert Hallak
PIPPI IN THE SOUTH SEAS(1974, Swed./Ger.); CAN SHE BAKE A CHERRY PIE?(1983)

Hallam
NIGHTHAWKS(1978, Brit.), w

Eleanor Hallam
MELODY OF MY HEART(1936, Brit.); ASKING FOR TROUBLE(1942, Brit.); LOYAL HEART(1946, Brit.); NO ROOM AT THE INN(1950, Brit.); WHAT THE BUTLER SAW(1950, Brit.)

Francis Hallam
SCARLET PIMPERNEL, THE(1935, Brit.), set d

H.B. Hallam
DIVORCE OF LADY X. THE(1938, Brit.); SEXTON BLAKE AND THE HOODED TERROR(1938, Brit.)

Harold B. Hallam
OLD MOTHER RILEY IN PARIS(1938, Brit.)

Henry Hallam
Silents
AUDREY(1916); GIRL WITHOUT A SOUL, THE(1917); JUST FOR TONIGHT(1918); CLIMBERS, THE(1919); KATHLEEN MAVOURNEEN(1919); NEVER SAY QUIT(1919); HEART OF MARYLAND, THE(1921); TOL'ABLE DAVID(1921)
Misc. Silents
COQUETTE, THE(1915); PRETENDERS, THE(1915); VANDERHOFF AFFAIR, THE(1915); BLACK CROOK, THE(1916); GOD'S LAW AND MAN'S(1917); BONNIE ANNIE LAURIE(1918); HOW COULD YOU, CAROLINE?(1918); HELP! HELP! POLICE!(1919); LION AND THE MOUSE, THE(1919); PREY, THE(1920)

John Hallam
CHARGE OF THE LIGHT BRIGADE, THE(1968, Brit.); WALK WITH LOVE AND DEATH, A(1969); WHERE'S JACK?(1969, Brit.); NICHOLAS AND ALEXANDRA(1971, Brit.); LAST VALLEY, THE(1971, Brit.); MURPHY'S WAR(1971, Brit.); VILLAIN(1971, Brit.); ANTONY AND CLEOPATRA(1973, Brit.); OFFENSE, THE(1973, Brit.); WICKER MAN, THE(1974, Brit.); HENNESSY(1975, Brit.); DIRTY KNIGHT'S WORK(1976, Brit.); PEOPLE THAT TIME FORGOT, THE(1977, Brit.); FLASH GORDON(1980); DRAGONSLAYER(1981)

Paul Hallam
NIGHTHAWKS(1978, Brit.), p

Hanita Hallan
THEY WERE SO YOUNG(1955)

Comdr. Herman E. Halland, USN
THIS MAN'S NAVY(1945), w

Ute Hallant
U-47 LT. COMMANDER PRIEN(1967, Ger.)

Susan Hallaran
MARRYING KIND, THE(1952)

C.M. Hallard
ALMOST A HONEYMOON(1930, Brit.); KNOWING MEN(1930, Brit.); TWO WORLD(1930, Brit.); "W" PLAN, THE(1931, Brit.); BATTLE OF GALLIPOLI(1931, Brit.); COMPROMISED!(1931, Brit.); CHINESE PUZZLE, THE(1932, Brit.); WOMAN DECIDES, THE(1932, Brit.); SECRET AGENT(1933, Brit.); ROLLING IN MONEY(1934, Brit.); THIRD CLUE, THE(1934, Brit.); NIGHT MAIL(1935, Brit.); REGAL CAVALCADE(1935, Brit.); I STAND CONDEMNED(1936, Brit.); KING OF THE DAMNED(1936, Brit.); LIVE WIRE, THE(1937, Brit.); SKY'S THE LIMIT, THE(1937, Brit.); TWO OF US, THE(1938, Brit.)
Silents
BRIDAL CHAIR, THE(1919, Brit.); EDGE O'BEYOND(1919, Brit.); MRS. THOMPSON(1919, Brit.); HER STORY(1920, Brit.)
Misc. Silents
WANTED - A WIFE(1918, Brit.); GAMBLERS ALL(1919, Brit.); IN BONDAGE(1919, Brit.); HUSBAND HUNTER, THE(1920, Brit.); IN THE NIGHT(1920, Brit.); LOVE IN THE WILDERNESS(1920, Brit.); PAUPER MILLIONAIRE, THE(1922, Brit.); DOLORES(1928, Brit.)

Jane Hallaren
HERO AT LARGE(1980); BODY HEAT(1981); MODERN ROMANCE(1981); LIANNA(1983)
1984
UNFAITHFULLY YOURS(1984)

Henry Hallat
DOMMED CARGO(1936, Brit.); YOU'RE IN THE ARMY NOW(1937, Brit.)

Henry Hallatt
VICTORIA THE GREAT(1937, Brit.); POWER(1934, Brit.); GANGWAY(1937, Brit.); SIXTY GLORIOUS YEARS(1938, Brit.)

Judy Hallatt
EVERYTHING IN LIFE(1936, Brit.)

May Hallatt
EYES OF FATE(1933, Brit.); VIRGINIA'S HUSBAND(1934, Brit.); TALKING FEET(1937, Brit.); HUMAN MONSTER, THE(1940, Brit.); LAMBETH WALK, THE(1940, Brit.); BLACK NARCISSUS(1947, Brit.); GIRL ON THE CANAL, THE(1947, Brit.); NAUGHTY ARLETTE(1951, Brit.); PICKWICK PAPERS, THE(1952, Brit.); SPIDER AND THE FLY, THE(1952, Brit.); ROB ROY, THE HIGHLAND ROGUE(1954, Brit.); GOLD EXPRESS, THE(1955, Brit.); WICKED WIFE(1955, Brit.); SEPARATE TABLES(1958); ROOM AT THE TOP(1959, Brit.); MAKE MINE MINK(1960, Brit.); DANGEROUS AFTERNOON(1961, Brit.); FOLLOW THAT MAN(1961, Brit.); BITTER HARVEST(1963, Brit.)

Neil Hallatt
STRICTLY CONFIDENTIAL(1959, Brit.); TRANSATLANTIC(1961, Brit.)

Nils Hallberg
TIME OF DESIRE, THE(1957, Swed.); PORT OF CALL(1963, Swed.)

Orville Hallberg
MOTOR PSYCHO(1965), spec eff

William Hallberg
ODE TO BILLY JOE(1976)

Carol Halleck
Misc. Talkies
RED ROSES OF PASSION(1967)

Dan Halleck
CACTUS IN THE SNOW(1972)

Jean-Pierre Hallee
ONE MAN(1979, Can.)

E. Darrell Hallenbeck
ONE OF OUR SPIES IS MISSING(1966), d
1984
TOY SOLDIERS(1984), p

Harry Hallenberg
PIRATES OF MONTEREY(1947), ph

Barry Hallenberger
RIDING HIGH(1943), ph

Harry Hallenberger
FORLORN RIVER(1937), ph; NIGHT WORK(1939), ph; LOUISIANA PURCHASE(1941), ph; VIRGINIAN, THE(1946), ph
Silents
PECK'S BAD BOY(1921), ph; IN HOLLYWOOD WITH POTASH AND PERLMUTTER(1924), ph

Henry Hallenberger
Silents
SPECIAL DELIVERY(1927), ph

Ines Hallendal
"IMP"PROBABLE MR. WEE GEE, THE(1966)

Barbara Haller
IT HAPPENED IN BROAD DAYLIGHT(1960, Ger./Switz.)

Bernard Haller
EASY LIFE, THE(1971, Fr.); ASSOCIATE, THE(1982 Fr./Ger.)

Dan Haller
HOT CAR GIRL(1958), art d; NIGHT OF THE BLOOD BEAST(1958), art d; NO PLACE TO LAND(1958), art d; WAR OF THE SATELLITES(1958), art d; BUCKET OF BLOOD, A(1959), art d; DIARY OF A HIGH SCHOOL BRIDE(1959), art d; GHOST OF DRAGSTRIP HOLLOW(1959), art d; PLUNDERERS OF PAINTED FLATS(1959), art

Daniel Haller
d; TANK COMMANDOS(1959), art d

Daniel Haller
DEVIL'S PARTNER, THE(1958), art d; MACHINE GUN KELLY(1958), art d; I, MOBSTER(1959), art d; WASP WOMAN, THE(1959), prod d&art d; HOUSE OF USHER(1960), prod d; VALLEY OF THE REDWOODS(1960), art d; CAT BURGLAR, THE(1961), art d; LITTLE SHOP OF HORRORS(1961), art d; MASTER OF THE WORLD(1961), prod d, art d; PIT AND THE PENDULUM, THE(1961), prod d&art d; PANIC IN YEAR ZERO!(1962), art d& set d; PREMATURE BURIAL, THE(1962), art d; TALES OF TERROR(1962), art d; TOWER OF LONDON(1962), art d; "X"–THE MAN WITH THE X-RAY EYES(1963), art d; DIARY OF A MADMAN(1963), art d; HAUNTED PALACE, THE(1963), art d; OPERATION BIKINI(1963), art d; RAVEN, THE(1963), art d; TERROR, THE(1963), art d; BIKINI BEACH(1964), art d; COMEDY OF TERRORS, THE(1964), art d; MASQUE OF THE RED DEATH, THE(1964, U.S./Brit.), prod d; PAJAMA PARTY(1964), art d; CITY UNDER THE SEA(1965, Brit.), p; DIE, MONSTER, DIE(1965, Brit.), d; DR. GOLDFOOT AND THE BIKINI MACHINE(1965), art d; FIREBALL 590(1966), art d; GHOST IN THE INVISIBLE BIKINI(1966), art d; DEVIL'S ANGELS(1967), d; THUNDER ALLEY(1967), art d; WILD RACERS, THE(1968), d; DUNWICH HORROR, THE(1970), d; PADDY(1970, Irish), d; PIECES OF DREAMS(1970), d; BUCK ROGERS IN THE 25TH CENTURY(1979), d

Ernest Haller
DARK STREETS(1929), ph; DRAG(1929), ph; WEARY RIVER(1929), ph; YOUNG NOWHERES(1929), ph; DAWN PATROL, THE(1930), ph; LASH, THE(1930), ph; NOTORIOUS AFFAIR, A(1930), ph; ONE NIGHT AT SUSIE'S(1930), ph; SON OF THE GODS(1930), ph; SUNNY(1930), ph; WEDDING RINGS(1930), ph; CHANCES(1931), ph; FINGER POINTS, THE(1931), ph; GIRLS ABOUT TOWN(1931), ph; HONOR OF THE FAMILY(1931), ph; I LIKE YOUR NERVE(1931), ph; MILLIE(1931), ph; TEN CENTS A DANCE(1931), ph; 24 HOURS(1931), ph; NIGHT AFTER NIGHT(1932), ph; RICH ARE ALWAYS WITH US, THE(1932), ph; SCARLET DAWN(1932), ph; STREET OF WOMEN(1932), ph; THE CRASH(1932), ph; WOMAN FROM MONTE CARLO, THE(1932), ph; EMPEROR JONES, THE(1933), ph; HOUSE ON 56TH STREET, THE(1933), ph; INTERNATIONAL HOUSE(1933), ph; KING OF THE JUNGLE(1933), ph; MURDERS IN THE ZOO(1933), ph; BRITISH AGENT(1934), ph; DESIRABLE(1934), ph; EASY TO LOVE(1934), ph; FIREBIRD, THE(1934), ph; JOURNAL OF A CRIME(1934), ph; KEY, THE(1934), ph; MERRY WIVES OF RENO, THE(1934), ph; AGE OF INDISCRETION(1935), ph; CAPTAIN BLOOD(1935), ph; ESCAPADE(1935), ph; MARY JANE'S PA(1935), ph; SECRET BRIDE, THE(1935), ph; DANGEROUS(1936), ph; PETTICOAT FEVER(1936), ph; PUBLIC ENEMY'S WIFE(1936), ph; VOICE OF BUGLE ANN(1936), ph; CALL IT A DAY(1937), ph; CAPTAIN'S KID, THE(1937), ph; GREAT GARRICK, THE(1937), ph; GREAT O'MALLEY, THE(1937), ph; MOUNTAIN JUSTICE(1937), ph; THAT CERTAIN WOMAN(1937), ph; BROTHER RAT(1938), ph; FOUR DAUGHTERS(1938), ph; FOUR'S A CROWD(1938), ph; JEZEBEL(1938), ph; DARK VICTORY(1939), ph; GONE WITH THE WIND(1939), ph; ROARING TWENTIES, THE(1939), ph; ALL THIS AND HEAVEN TOO(1940), ph; INVISIBLE STRIPES(1940), ph; IT ALL CAME TRUE(1940), ph; NO TIME FOR COMEDY(1940), ph; BRIDE CAME C.O.D., THE(1941), ph; FOOTSTEPS IN THE DARK(1941), ph; HONEYMOON FOR THREE(1941), ph; MANPOWER(1941), ph; OUTLAWS OF THE CHEROKEE TRAIL(1941), ph; GEORGE WASHINGTON SLEPT HERE(1942), ph; IN THIS OUR LIFE(1942), ph; PRINCESS O'ROURKE(1943), ph; DOUGHGIRLS, THE(1944), ph, spec eff; MR. SKEFFINGTON(1944), ph; MILDRED PIERCE(1945), ph; SARATOGA TRUNK(1945), ph; DECEPTION(1946), ph; DEVOTION(1946), ph; HUMORESQUE(1946), ph; STOLEN LIFE, A(1946), ph; VERDICT, THE(1946), ph; UNFAITHFUL, THE(1947), ph; MY GIRL TISA(1948), ph; WINTER MEETING(1948), ph; ALWAYS LEAVE THEM LAUGHING(1949), ph; MY DREAM IS YOURS(1949), ph; CHAIN LIGHTNING(1950), ph; DALLAS(1950), ph; FLAME AND THE ARROW, THE(1950), ph; JIM THORPE–ALL AMERICAN(1951), ph; ON MOONLIGHT BAY(1951), ph; MONSOON(1953), ph; CARNIVAL STORY(1954), ph; REBEL WITHOUT A CAUSE(1955), ph; TIGER AND THE FLAME, THE(1955, India), ph; COME ON, THE(1956), ph; CRUEL TOWER, THE(1956), ph; DAKOTA INCIDENT(1956), ph; MAGIC FIRE(1956), ph; STRANGE INTRUDER(1956), ph; BACK FROM THE DEAD(1957), ph; HELL ON DEVIL'S ISLAND(1957), ph; MEN IN WAR(1957), ph; PLUNDER ROAD(1957), ph; YOUNG DON'T CRY, THE(1957), ph; GOD'S LITTLE ACRE(1958), ph; HELL'S FIVE HOURS(1958), ph; MAN OF THE WEST(1958), ph; MIRACLE, THE(1959), ph; SPEED CRAZY(1959), ph; BOY AND THE PIRATES, THE(1960), ph; THIRD VOICE, THE(1960), ph; ARMORED COMMAND(1961), ph; CHIVATO(1961), ph; FEAR NO MORE(1961), ph; THREE BLONDES IN HIS LIFE(1961), ph; MARRIED TOO YOUNG(1962), ph; PRESSURE POINT(1962), ph; WHATEVER HAPPENED TO BABY JANE?(1962), ph; LILIES OF THE FIELD(1963), ph; DEAD RINGER(1964), ph; RESTLESS ONES, THE(1965), ph
Silents
NEGLECTED WIVES(1920), ph; GILDED LILY, THE(1921), ph; SALVATION NELL(1921), ph; SUCH A LITTLE QUEEN(1921), ph; WIFE AGAINST WIFE(1921), ph; NEW COMMANDMENT, THE(1925), ph; HAIR TRIGGER BAXTER(1926), ph; RECKLESS LADY, THE(1926), ph; WILDERNESS WOMAN, THE(1926), ph; CONVOY(1927), ph; FRENCH DRESSING(1927), ph; HAROLD TEEN(1928), ph; NAUGHTY BABY(1929), ph

Ernie Haller
BLUES IN THE NIGHT(1941), ph

Gisela Haller
24-HOUR LOVER(1970, Ger.), ed

Hans Haller
THAT TENDER TOUCH(1969), m

Herman Haller
LAST CHANCE, THE(1945, Switz.), ed; HEIDI AND PETER(1955, Switz.), ed; GOOD SOLDIER SCHWEIK, THE(1963, Ger.), ed

Hermann Haller
SEARCH, THE(1948), ed; FOUR IN A JEEP(1951, Switz.), m; RETURN OF DR. MABUSE, THE(1961, Ger./Fr./Ital.), ed; TOWN WITHOUT PITY(1961, Ger./Switz./U.S.), ed; SHADOWS GROW LONGER, THE(1962, Switz./Ger.), ed; JUDGE AND THE SINNER, THE(1964, Ger.), ed; INVISIBLE DR. MABUSE, THE(1965, Ger.), ed; TREASURE OF SILVER LAKE(1965, Fr./Ger./Yugo.), ed; FRONTIER HELLCAT(1966, Fr./Ital./Ger./Yugo.), ed; LAST OF THE RENEGADES(1966, Fr./Ital./Ger./Yugo.), ed; RAMPAGE AT APACHE WELLS(1966, Ger./Yugo.), ed; BLOOD DEMON(1967, Ger.), ed; FLAMING FRONTIER(1968, Ger./Yugo.), ed

Michael Haller
MARA OF THE WILDERNESS(1966), art d; SOFI(1967), art d; HEIDI(1968, Aust.), w; 2000 YEARS LATER(1969), art d; HAROLD AND MAUDE(1971), prod d, art d; THX 1138(1971), art d; LAST DETAIL, THE(1973), prod d; RANCHO DELUXE(1975), art d

Mike Haller
WHERE DOES IT HURT?(1972), art d; COMING HOME(1978), prod d

Ray Haller
HIDDEN VALLEY(1932)
Silents
INEZ FROM HOLLYWOOD(1924)

Robert Haller
Silents
BLUEBEARD'S SEVEN WIVES(1926), ph

Ty Haller
DR. FRANKENSTEIN ON CAMPUS(1970, Can.); GROUNDSTAR CONSPIRACY, THE(1972, Can.); DESERTERS(1983, Can.)

Jane Halleran
PUZZLE OF A DOWNFALL CHILD(1970)

Staffan Hallerstram
TOUCH, THE(1971, U.S./Swed.)

Knud Hallest
REPTILICUS(1962, U.S./Den.); CHRISTINE KEELER AFFAIR, THE(1964, Brit.)

Al Hallet
PACK UP YOUR TROUBLES(1932)

Helen Hallet
THREE LIVE GHOSTS(1929), w

Henry Hallet
DEPARTMENT STORE(1935, Brit.)

James Hallet
SEA FURY(1929)

Neil Hallet
ROTTEN TO THE CORE(1956, Brit.); TWO-HEADED SPY, THE(1959, Brit.)

Al Hallett
Silents
HAUNTED RANGE, THE(1926)
Misc. Silents
PASSING OF WOLF MACLEAN, THE(1924)

David Hallett
Silents
ALL ROADS LEAD TO CALVARY(1921, Brit.)

George Hallett
WOMAN AGAINST THE WORLD(1938)

H. C. Hallett
Silents
LIGHTNING ROMANCE(1924)

Henry Hallett
HOUND OF THE BASKERVILLES(1932, Brit.); RINGER, THE(1932, Brit.); LET'S BE FAMOUS(1939, Brit.); SALUTE JOHN CITIZEN(1942, Brit.)
Misc. Silents
FOUL PLAY(1920, Brit.)

Jack Hallett
1984
SPLASH(1984)

Neal Hallett
VIRGIN WITCH, THE(1973, Brit.)

Neil Hallett
THREE STEPS IN THE DARK(1953, Brit.); BRAIN MACHINE, THE(1955, Brit.); X THE UNKNOWN(1957, Brit.); TOP FLOOR GIRL(1959, Brit.); WOMAN'S TEMPTATION, A(1959, Brit.); MODEL FOR MURDER(1960, Brit.); OPERATION CUPID(1960, Brit.); I AM A GROUPIE(1970, Brit.); MELODY(1971, Brit.); 1,000 CONVICTS AND A WOMAN(1971, Brit.); GAME FOR VULTURES, A(1980, Brit.)

Erwin Halletz
FANNY HILL: MEMOIRS OF A WOMAN OF PLEASURE zero(1965), m; PRIEST OF ST. PAULI, THE(1970, Ger.), m

Beryl Halley
Misc. Silents
BROADWAY BOOB, THE(1926)

Ina Halley
OUR DAILY BREAD(1950, Ger.); MERRY WIVES OF WINDSOR, THE(1952, Ger.)

Tom Halley
YELLOW SUBMARINE(1958, Brit.), animation

Heino Hallhuber
SERPENT'S EGG, THE(1977, Ger./U.S.), ch

Tom Hallick
MRS. POLLIFAX-SPY(1971); HANGAR 18(1980); SATAN'S MISTRESS(1982)
1984
RARE BREED(1984)

Barry Halliday
BREATH OF LIFE(1962, Brit.); ISLAND OF THE BURNING DAMNED(1971, Brit.)

Brett Halliday
MICHAEL SHAYNE, PRIVATE DETECTIVE(1940), w; BLUE, WHITE, AND PERFECT(1941), w; DRESSED TO KILL(1941), w; SLEEPERS WEST(1941), w; MAN WHO WOULDN'T DIE, THE(1942), w; TIME TO KILL(1942), w; BLONDE FOR A DAY(1946), w; LARCENY IN HER HEART(1946), w; MURDER IS MY BUSINESS(1946), w; TOO MANY WINNERS(1947), w; THREE CASES OF MURDER(1955, Brit.), w

Brett Halliday [Davis Dresser]
THREE ON A TICKET(1947), w

Bryant Halliday
DEVIL DOLL(1964, Brit.); CURSE OF THE VOODOO(1965, Brit.); PROJECTED MAN, THE(1967, Brit.)

Clive Halliday
NOTORIOUS LANDLADY, THE(1962); MY FAIR LADY(1964)

Clive L. Halliday
FROM THE TERRACE(1960); PREMATURE BURIAL, THE(1962); MARY POPPINS(1964); PRINCESS AND THE MAGIC FROG, THE(1965)

Don Halliday
LADY AND THE TRAMP(1955), ed

Donald Halliday
MELODY TIME(1948), ed; SLEEPING BEAUTY(1959), ed; ONE HUNDRED AND ONE DALMATIANS(1961), ed; SWORD IN THE STONE, THE(1963), ed

Elizabeth Halliday
TWILIGHT'S LAST GLEAMING(1977, U.S./Ger.)
Frank Halliday
DECEIVER, THE(1931)
Frederick Halliday
JOURNEY TO THE CENTER OF THE EARTH(1959)
Hugh Halliday
BREATH OF LIFE(1962, Brit.); PERFECT FRIDAY(1970, Brit.)
Jack Halliday
Misc. Silents
DEVIL'S TOY, THE(1916)
Jackson Halliday
STRUGGLE, THE(1931); NOTORIOUS LANDLADY, THE(1962)
Jeni Halliday
GUEST AT STEENKAMPSKRAAL, THE(1977, South Africa), prod d
1984
GUEST, THE(1984, Brit.), prod d
Joan Halliday
MRS. PYM OF SCOTLAND YARD(1939, Brit.)
John Halliday
EAST SIDE SADIE(1929); RECAPTURED LOVE(1930); SCARLET PAGES(1930); CAPTAIN APPLEJACK(1931); CONSOLATION MARRIAGE(1931); FATHER'S SON(1931); FIFTY MILLION FRENCHMEN(1931); MILLIE(1931); ONCE A SINNER(1931); RULING VOICE, THE(1931); SMART WOMAN(1931); TRANSATLANTIC(1931); AGE OF CONSENT(1932); BIRD OF PARADISE(1932); IMPATIENT MAIDEN(1932); MAN CALLED BACK, THE(1932); MEN OF CHANCE(1932); WEEKENDS ONLY(1932); BED OF ROSES(1933); HOUSE ON 56TH STREET, THE(1933); PERFECT UNDERSTANDING(1933, Brit.); TERROR ABOARD(1933); WOMAN ACCUSED(1933); DESIRABLE(1934); FINISHING SCHOOL(1934); HAPPINESS AHEAD(1934); HOUSEWIFE(1934); REGISTERED NURSE(1934); RETURN OF THE TERROR(1934); WITCHING HOUR, THE(1934); DARK ANGEL, THE(1935); MELODY LINGERS ON, THE(1935); MYSTERY WOMAN(1935); PETER IBBETSON(1935); DESIRE(1936); FATAL LADY(1936); HOLLYWOOD BOULEVARD(1936); THREE CHEERS FOR LOVE(1936); ARSENE LUPIN RETURNS(1938); BLOCKADE(1938); THAT CERTAIN AGE(1938); HOTEL FOR WOMEN(1939); INTERMEZZO: A LOVE STORY(1939); ESCAPE TO GLORY(1940); PHILADELPHIA STORY, THE(1940); LYDIA(1941)
Misc. Talkies
SPY, THE(1931)
Misc. Silents
LOVE EXPERT, THE(1920); WOMAN GIVES, THE(1920)
Lena Halliday
INQUEST(1931, Brit.); GIRLS PLEASE!(1934, Brit.)
Silents
HONEYMOON AHEAD(1927, Brit.)
Marjorie Halliday
DREAMBOAT(1952); MONKEY BUSINESS(1952)
Michael Halliday
CAT AND MOUSE(1958, Brit), w
Peter Halliday
DUNKIRK(1958, Brit.); NIGHT CREATURES(1962, Brit.); SUNDAY BLOODY SUNDAY(1971, Brit.); MADHOUSE(1974, Brit.); GIRO CITY(1982, Brit.)
Misc. Talkies
FAST KILL(1973)
Stephen Halliday
LOVE IS A WOMAN(1967, Brit.), ph; TWIST OF SAND, A(1968, Brit.), ph
Lori Hallier
MY BLOODY VALENTINE(1981, Can.)
Bill Halligan
ONE WAY PASSAGE(1932); MURDER AMONG FRIENDS(1941); DIXIE(1943); HE'S MY GUY(1943); JIVE JUNCTION(1944)
Derek Halligan
ACCEPTABLE LEVELS(1983, Brit.)
Dick Halligan
GO TELL THE SPARTANS(1978), m; FORCE OF ONE, A(1979), m; CHEAPER TO KEEP HER(1980), m; OCTAGON, THE(1980), m
1984
FEAR CITY(1984), m
Erin Halligan
I'M DANCING AS FAST AS I CAN(1982)
George Halligan
HELD FOR RANSOM(1938), ed; MYSTIC CIRCLE MURDER(1939), ed; RODEO RHYTHM(1941), ed
Misc. Silents
THOROBRED(1922), d
Liam Halligan
1984
PIGS(1984, Ireland)
Maureen Halligan
SWORD OF SHERWOOD FOREST(1961, Brit.); DEAD MAN'S EVIDENCE(1962, Brit.); SHE DIDN'T SAY NO!(1962, Brit.)
Richard Halligan
OWL AND THE PUSSYCAT, THE(1970), m
Tom Halligan
TRAIL DUST(1936)
Tom J. Halligan
GLASS HOUSES(1972)
William Halligan
FOLLOW THE LEADER(1930); PUBLIC DEFENDER, THE(1931); BLESSED EVENT(1932); BY WHOSE HAND?(1932); CROONER(1932); DANCERS IN THE DARK(1932); LADY AND GENT(1932); EARL OF PUDDLESTONE(1940); HIRED WIFE(1940); HOUSE ACROSS THE BAY, THE(1940); THIRD FINGER, LEFT HAND(1940); 'TIL WE MEET AGAIN(1940); YOU CAN'T FOOL YOUR WIFE(1940); BLONDE COMET(1941); COWBOY AND THE BLONDE, THE(1941); DOUBLE CROSS(1941); EMERGENCY LANDING(1941); GREAT AMERICAN BROADCAST, THE(1941); PAPER BULLETS(1941); PLAYMATES(1941); REMEMBER THE DAY(1941); TOM, DICK AND HARRY(1941); BROADWAY BIG SHOT(1942); FOREIGN AGENT(1942); GENTLEMAN AT HEART, A(1942); LIFE BEGINS AT 8:-30(1942); LUCKY JORDAN(1942); MOONTIDE(1942); MR. CELEBRITY(1942); TALES OF MANHATTAN(1942); BLACK HILLS EXPRESS(1943); LEOPARD MAN,

THE(1943); PILOT NO. 5(1943); RIDERS OF THE DEADLINE(1943); SEVENTH VICTIM, THE(1943); GREAT MIKE, THE(1944); HAIRY APE, THE(1944); DICK TRACY(1945); HER HIGHNESS AND THE BELLBOY(1945); SPIDER, THE(1945); WEEKEND AT THE WALDORF(1945); WITHIN THESE WALLS(1945); DARK MIRROR, THE(1946); IF I'M LUCKY(1946); POSTMAN ALWAYS RINGS TWICE, THE(1946); TILL THE CLOUDS ROLL BY(1946)
Richard Hallinan
PORTRAIT OF THE ARTIST AS A YOUNG MAN, A(1979, Ireland), p
Susan Hallinan
ENTER INSPECTOR DUVAL(1961, Brit.); GREAT TRAIN ROBBERY, THE(1979, Brit.)
Alison Halliwell
WINSTANLEY(1979, Brit.)
David Halliwell
LITTLE MALCOLM(1974, Brit.), w
Miles Halliwell
IT HAPPENED HERE(1966, Brit.); WINSTANLEY(1979, Brit.)
Henry Hallman
Silents
CHARITY?(1916); ALADDIN'S OTHER LAMP(1917)
Daniel Hallo
TOWN ON TRIAL(1957, Brit.), art d
William Hallop
AIR STRIKE(1955)
Edith Hallor
MAID OF SALEM(1937)
Silents
THOU SHALT NOT(1914); MAN AND THE WOMAN, A(1917)
Misc. Silents
WRATH(1917); BLUE PEARL, THE(1920); CHILDREN OF DESTINY(1920); INSIDE OF THE CUP, THE(1921); JUST OUTSIDE THE DOOR(1921)
Ernest Hallor
Silents
ANY WOMAN(1925), ph; HIGH AND HANDSOME(1925), ph; WHIP WOMAN, THE(1928), ph
Ethel Hallor
Silents
CUB REPORTER, THE(1922)
Misc. Silents
STOLEN HONOR(1918); WOMAN(1919)
Ray Hallor
FAST LIFE(1929); IN OLD CALIFORNIA(1929); NOISY NEIGHBORS(1929); TRUTH ABOUT YOUTH, THE(1930)
Silents
KIDNAPPED(1917); LAST EDITION, THE(1925); LEARNING TO LOVE(1925); SALLY(1925); IT MUST BE LOVE(1926); RED DICE(1926); DRIVEN FROM HOME(1927); MAN CRAZY(1927); AVENGING SHADOW, THE(1928); MANHATTAN KNIGHTS(1928); NAMELESS MEN(1928)
Misc. Silents
CIRCUS COWBOY, THE(1924); STORM BREAKER, THE(1925); HIGH FLYER, THE(1926); HAUNTED SHIP, THE(1927); QUARANTINED RIVALS(1927); TONGUES OF SCANDAL(1927); BLACK PEARL, THE(1928); TROPICAL NIGHTS(1928)
Jack Halloran
BLOOD ON THE SUN(1945)
John Halloran
BADMAN'S TERRITORY(1946); ANGEL AND THE BADMAN(1947); LAST ROUND-UP, THE(1947); ALBUQUERQUE(1948); FIGHTING MAN OF THE PLAINS(1949); LADY TAKES A SAILOR, THE(1949); STATE DEPARTMENT–FILE 649(1949); KISS TOMORROW GOODBYE(1950); HOODLUM EMPIRE(1952); WILD STALLION(1952); FAIR WIND TO JAVA(1953); JACK SLADE(1953); VANQUISHED, THE(1953); JUBILEE TRAIL(1954); CULT OF THE COBRA(1955); FAR COUNTRY, THE(1955); VIOLENT MEN, THE(1955); REVOLT OF MAMIE STOVER, THE(1956); TRIBUTE TO A BADMAN(1956); DEERSLAYER, THE(1957); HALLIDAY BRAND, THE(1957); KRONOS(1957); SHORT CUT TO HELL(1957); BONNIE PARKER STORY, THE(1958); NEVER STEAL ANYTHING SMALL(1959); ROSEMARY'S BABY(1968)
John Hallow
1984
HOME FREE ALL(1984)
Carol Halloway
MAID OF SALEM(1937); OH DOCTOR(1937); THUNDER TRAIL(1937)
Silents
IF ONLY JIM(1921); RAINBOW TRAIL, THE(1925); JAKE THE PLUMBER(1927)
Misc. Silents
CORDELIA THE MAGNIFICENT(1923)
Jack Halloway
Silents
OVERALLS(1916), d
Misc. Silents
MAN FROM MANHATTAN, THE(1916), d
Jean Halloway
SUMMER HOLIDAY(1948), w
Maggie Halloway
Misc. Silents
SHERRY(1920)
Lynn Hallowell
ANY WHICH WAY YOU CAN(1980); BODY HEAT(1981); GOING BERSERK(1983)
Todd Hallowell
1984
CLOAK AND DAGGER(1984), art d; FLETCH(1984), art d
Maria Hallowi
HAND OF NIGHT, THE(1968, Brit.)
Ethel Halls
EASY TO LOOK AT(1945)
Ethel May Halls
MILKY WAY, THE(1936); PRISON FARM(1938); HONEYMOON IN BALI(1939); OUR LEADING CITIZEN(1939); THOU SHALT NOT KILL(1939); HEROES OF THE SADDLE(1940); STANDING ROOM ONLY(1944); LADY ON A TRAIN(1945); LOVE LETTERS(1945); CROSS MY HEART(1946)

Ethyl Halls
MICHAEL O'HALLORAN(1948)
Ethyl May Halls
ISLAND OF LOST MEN(1939); DARK HORSE, THE(1946); DOUBLE LIFE, A(1947); TAKE ONE FALSE STEP(1949); KATIE DID IT(1951); NIGHT RUNNER, THE(1957)
Don Hallstrom
SATIN MUSHROOM, THE(1969), a, ed
Otto Hallstrom
LURE OF THE JUNGLE, THE(1970, Den.)
Hans P. Hallwachs
DEGREE OF MURDER, A(1969, Ger.)
Joy Hallward
KNOCK ON ANY DOOR(1949); BORN TO BE BAD(1950); IN A LONELY PLACE(1950); SHE COULDN'T SAY NO(1954); WITNESS TO MURDER(1954)
Joyce Hallward
MAGNIFICENT OBSESSION(1954)
Ebba Hally
GOLD DIGGERS OF 1933(1933)
Johnny Hallyday
TALES OF PARIS(1962, Fr./Ital.); DROP THEM OR I'LL SHOOT(1969, Fr./Ger./Span.)
Alfred Halm
DOLLY GETS AHEAD(1931, Ger.), w; CRUISER EMDEN(1932, Ger.), w
Harry Halm
WHITE HORSE INN, THE(1959, Ger.), w
Martin Halm
ERNESTO(1979, Ital.)
Denise Halma
PRIVATE BENJAMIN(1980)
Halma and Konarski
NO ORCHIDS FOR MISS BLANDISH(1948, Brit.)
Sandor Halmagyi
1984
BRADY'S ESCAPE(1984, U.S./Hung.)
Kurt Halme
WOZZECK(1962, E. Ger.), p
Gunter Maria Halmer
GANDHI(1982)
Gunther Maria Halmer
SOPHIE'S CHOICE(1982)
Robert Halmi
VISIT TO A CHIEF'S SON(1974), p, w; HUGO THE HIPPO(1976, Hung./U.S.), p
Robert Halmi, Jr.
1984
BRADY'S ESCAPE(1984, U.S./Hung.), p
Roziska Halmos
ROMANTIC COMEDY(1983)
Rozsika Halmos
IN-LAWS, THE(1979)
1984
BEST DEFENSE(1984)
Rolf Halmquist
MAGICIAN, THE(1959, Swed.), ph; VIRGIN SPRING, THE(1960, Swed.), ph
Grace Halo
WHOLE TOWN'S TALKING, THE(1935)
Billy Halop
DEAD END(1937); ANGELS WITH DIRTY FACES(1938); CRIME SCHOOL(1938); LITTLE TOUGH GUY(1938); ANGELS WASH THEIR FACES(1939); CALL A MESSENGER(1939); DEAD END KIDS ON DRESS PARADE(1939); DUST BE MY DESTINY(1939); HELL'S KITCHEN(1939); THEY MADE ME A CRIMINAL(1939); YOU CAN'T GET AWAY WITH MURDER(1939); GIVE US WINGS(1940); TOM BROWN'S SCHOOL DAYS(1940); YOU'RE NOT SO TOUGH(1940); HIT THE ROAD(1941); MOB TOWN(1941); TOUGH AS THEY COME(1942); JUNIOR ARMY(1943); MUG TOWN(1943); GAS HOUSE KIDS(1946); FOR LOVE OR MONEY(1963); MOVE OVER, DARLING(1963); GLOBAL AFFAIR, A(1964); MISTER BUDDWING(1966); FITZWILLY(1967)
Florence Halop
NANCY DREW–REPORTER(1939)
William Halop
DANGEROUS YEARS(1947); CHALLENGE OF THE RANGE(1949); TOO LATE FOR TEARS(1949)
Augustyn Halotta
BEADS OF ONE ROSARY, THE(1982, Pol.)
Robert Halper
CRY DR. CHICAGO(1971), p
Art Halperin
BABY, IT'S YOU(1983)
Edward Halperin
SHE GOES TO WAR(1929), p; PARTY GIRL(1930), p; WHITE ZOMBIE(1932), p; SUPERNATURAL(1933), p; BACHELOR BAIT(1934), w; REVOLT OF THE ZOMBIES(1936), p; NATION AFLAME(1937), p; CODE OF THE CACTUS(1939), w; DANGER AHEAD(1940), w; SKY BANDITS, THE(1940), w; YUKON FLIGHT(1940), w
Edward R. Halperin
Silents
CONVOY(1927), p
Sol Halperin
MARRIED IN HOLLYWOOD(1929), ph; DOUBLE CROSS ROADS(1930), ph
V. Halperin
PARTY GIRL(1930), w; REVOLT OF THE ZOMBIES(1936), w
Victor Halperin
SHE GOES TO WAR(1929), p; PARTY GIRL(1930), d; EX-FLAME(1931), d; WHITE ZOMBIE(1932), d; SUPERNATURAL(1933), p, d; BACHELOR BAIT(1934), w; I CONQUER THE SEA(1936), p&d; REVOLT OF THE ZOMBIES(1936), d; NATION AFLAME(1937), p, d; BURIED ALIVE(1939), d; TORTURE SHIP(1939), d; GIRLS' TOWN(1942), d; LONE STAR TRAIL, THE(1943), w
Misc. Silents
DANCE MAGIC(1927), d

Victor Hugo Halperin
Silents
DANGER POINT, THE(1922), w; IN BORROWED PLUMES(1926), d; CONVOY(1927), p
Misc. Silents
GREATER THAN MARRIAGE(1924), d; WHEN A GIRL LOVES(1924), d; SCHOOL FOR WIVES(1925), d; UNKNOWN LOVER, THE(1925), d
Dan Halperine
1984
SCARRED(1984), p
A. Halpern
TAXI TO HEAVEN(1944, USSR), ph
Barbara Halpern
GNOME-MOBILE, THE(1967)
Dina Halpern
DYBBUK THE(1938, Pol.)
Edmond Halpern
TEL AVIV TAXI(1957, Israel), m
Riesa Halpern
SINGING BLACKSMITH(1938)
Sigmund Halperon
RED DANUBE, THE(1949)
Lillian Halpert
TAKING OFF(1971)
Michael Halphie
AWAKENING, THE(1980); OCTOPUSSY(1983, Brit.)
Ellen Halpin
SWEET CHARITY(1969)
George Halpin
Silents
LUCK AND PLUCK(1919)
Luke Halpin
FLIPPER(1963); FLIPPER'S NEW ADVENTURE(1964); IF IT'S TUESDAY, THIS MUST BE BELGIUM(1969); MAKO: THE JAWS OF DEATH(1976); SHOCK WAVES(1977); HOT STUFF(1979); EYES OF A STRANGER(1980); ISLAND CLAWS(1981); NOBODY'S PERFEKT(1981)
Sandy Halpin
TOWING(1978)
Daria Halprin
ZABRISKIE POINT(1970); JERUSALEM FILE, THE(1972, U.S./Israel)
Johan Halsborg
EDVARD MUNCH(1976, Norway/Swed.)
Betty Halsey
HAPPY DAYS(1930)
Brent Halsey
SPEED CRAZY(1959)
Brett Halsey
GLASS WEB, THE(1953); JOHNNY DARK(1954); MA AND PA KETTLE AT HOME(1954); TO HELL AND BACK(1955); THREE BAD SISTERS(1956); HOT ROD RUMBLE(1957); CRY BABY KILLER, THE(1958); HIGH SCHOOL HELLCATS(1958); LAFAYETTE ESCADRILLE(1958); BEST OF EVERYTHING, THE(1959); BLOOD AND STEEL(1959); FOUR FAST GUNS(1959); RETURN OF THE FLY(1959); SUBMARINE SEAHAWK(1959); ATOMIC SUBMARINE, THE(1960); DESIRE IN THE DUST(1960); GIRL IN LOVER'S LANE, THE(1960); JET OVER THE ATLANTIC(1960); RETURN TO PEYTON PLACE(1961); TWICE TOLD TALES(1963); MAGNIFICENT CUCKOLD, THE(1965, Fr./Ital.); SPY IN YOUR EYE(1966, Ital.); WEB OF VIOLENCE(1966, Ital./Span.); ANYONE CAN PLAY(1968, Ital.); WHERE DOES IT HURT?(1972)
Misc. Talkies
AVENGER OF VENICE(1965)
Forest Halsey
SWEETHEARTS AND WIVES(1930), w
Forrest Halsey
CAREERS(1929), w; HER PRIVATE LIFE(1929), w; MOST IMMORAL LADY, A(1929), w; PAINTED ANGEL, THE(1929), w; PRISONERS(1929), w; SATURDAY'S CHILDREN(1929), w; FURIES, THE(1930), w; ONE NIGHT AT SUSIE'S(1930), w; KEPT HUSBANDS(1931), w; LADY WHO DARED, THE(1931), w; ALIAS MARY DOW(1935), w; SILVER QUEEN(1942), w
Silents
SALOMY JANE(1914); STAIN, THE(1914), w; ASHES OF EMBERS(1916), w; DUST OF DESIRE(1919), w; FLAMES OF THE FLESH(1920), w; WHITE YOUTH(1920), w; MAN WHO PLAYED GOD, THE(1922), w; RULING PASSION, THE(1922), w; RAGGED EDGE, THE(1923), w; MONSIEUR BEAUCAIRE(1924), w; SAINTED DEVIL, A(1924), w; SOCIETY SCANDAL, A(1924), w; SALLY OF THE SAWDUST(1925), w; ACE OF CADS(1926), w; DANCING MOTHERS(1926), w; SORROWS OF SATAN(1926), w; NEW YORK(1927), w; OUTCAST(1928), t; WHIP WOMAN, THE(1928), w; MAN'S MAN, A(1929), w
Genitha Halsey
ANGEL WHO PAWNED HER HARP, THE(1956, Brit.)
Jim Halsey
HANGUP(1974), art d
Mary Halsey
FALCON'S BROTHER, THE(1942); FALCON AND THE CO-EDS, THE(1943); FALLEN SPARROW, THE(1943); GOVERNMENT GIRL(1943); LADIES' DAY(1943); MEXICAN SPITFIRE'S BLESSED EVENT(1943); SEVENTH VICTIM, THE(1943); FALCON OUT WEST, THE(1944); MUSIC IN MANHATTAN(1944); NEVADA(1944); PAN-AMERICANA(1945)
Mary Jane Halsey
42ND STREET(1933); MERRY WIDOW, THE(1934)
Richard Halsey
TRIBUTE(1980, Can.), ed; UP IN THE CELLAR(1970), ed; NO DRUMS, NO BUGLES(1971), ed; PAYDAY(1972), ed; PAT GARRETT AND BILLY THE KID(1973), ed; HARRY AND TONTO(1974), ed; W. W. AND THE DIXIE DANCEKINGS(1975), ed; NEXT STOP, GREENWICH VILLAGE(1976), ed; ROCKY(1976), ed; FIRE SALE(1977), ed; THANK GOD IT'S FRIDAY(1978), ed; BOULEVARD NIGHTS(1979), ed; AMERICAN GIGOLO(1980), ed; AMATEUR, THE(1982), ed; THAT CHAMPIONSHIP SEASON(1982), ed; LOSIN' IT(1983), ed
1984
BODY ROCK(1984), ed; DREAMSCAPE(1984), ed; MOSCOW ON THE HUDSON(1984), ed

Margaret Halstan
MIDDLE WATCH, THE(1930, Brit.); BEGGAR STUDENT, THE(1931,Brit.); DRAKE THE PIRATE(1935, Brit.); OLD MOTHER RILEY IN SOCIETY(1940, Brit.); BLOOD ORANGE(1953, Brit.); HOLLY AND THE IVY, THE(1954, Brit.); LIGHT TOUCH, THE(1955, Brit.); GENTLE TOUCH, THE(1956, Brit.)
Silents
PROFIT AND THE LOSS(1917, Brit.); WORLDLINGS, THE(1920, Brit.)
Harry Halstead
MRS. GIBBONS' BOYS(1962, Brit.), p
Henry Halstead
DARK ROAD, THE(1948, Brit.), p; DICK BARTON–SPECIAL AGENT(1948, Brit.), p; DICK BARTON AT BAY(1950, Brit.), p; UP FOR THE CUP(1950, Brit.), p; RELUCTANT HEROES(1951, Brit.), p; TAKE ME TO PARIS(1951, Brit.), p; WORM'S EYE VIEW(1951, Brit.), p; LITTLE BIG SHOT(1952, Brit.), p; UP THE CREEK(1958, Brit.), p
John Halstead
POOR COW(1968, Brit.)
Henry Halsted
NOT WANTED ON VOYAGE(1957, Brit.), p; FURTHER UP THE CREEK!(1958, Brit.), p
Halston
PIECES OF DREAMS(1970), cos; TELL ME THAT YOU LOVE ME, JUNIE MOON(1970), cos; PLAY IT AS IT LAYS(1972), cos
Margaret Halston
QUIET WEDDING(1941, Brit.); WINGS AND THE WOMAN(1942, Brit.)
Rondo Halten
HOUSE OF HORRORS(1946)
Fred Haltiner
HANNIBAL BROOKS(1969, Brit.); LE MANS(1971)
Charles Halton
HONOR AMONG LOVERS(1931); STORM AT DAYBREAK(1933); TWENTY MILLION SWEETHEARTS(1934); COME AND GET IT(1936); DODSWORTH(1936); GOLD DIGGERS OF 1937(1936); MORE THAN A SECRETARY(1936); SING ME A LOVE SONG(1936); BLACK LEGION, THE(1937); BLOSSOMS ON BROADWAY(1937); DEAD END(1937); PARTNERS IN CRIME(1937); PENROD AND SAM(1937); PICK A STAR(1937); PRISONER OF ZENDA, THE(1937); READY, WILLING AND ABLE(1937); ROAD BACK,THE(1937); STOLEN HOLIDAY(1937); TALENT SCOUT(1937); TROUBLE AT MIDNIGHT(1937); WOMAN CHASES MAN(1937); BLUEBEARD'S EIGHTH WIFE(1938); GOLD IS WHERE YOU FIND IT(1938); I AM THE LAW(1938); I'LL GIVE A MILLION(1938); MAD MISS MANTON, THE(1938); MAN TO REMEMBER, A(1938); PENITENTIARY(1938); PENROD AND HIS TWIN BROTHER(1938); PENROD'S DOUBLE TROUBLE(1938); ROOM SERVICE(1938); SAINT IN NEW YORK, THE(1938); STOLEN HEAVEN(1938); YOUNG IN HEART, THE(1938); CHARLIE CHAN AT TREASURE ISLAND(1939); DODGE CITY(1939); EX-CHAMP(1939); FEDERAL MAN-HUNT(1939); GOLDEN BOY(1939); INDIANAPOLIS SPEEDWAY(1939); JESSE JAMES(1939); JUAREZ(1939); NANCY DREW–REPORTER(1939); NEWS IS MADE AT NIGHT(1939); NO PLACE TO GO(1939); RENO(1939); SUDDEN MONEY(1939); SWANEE RIVER(1939); THEY ASKED FOR IT(1939); THEY MADE HER A SPY(1939); YOUNG MR. LINCOLN(1939); BRIGHAM YOUNG–FRONTIERSMAN(1940); CALLING ALL HUSBANDS(1940); DOCTOR TAKES A WIFE(1940); DR. CYCLOPS(1940); DR. EHRLICH'S MAGIC BULLET(1940); FOREIGN CORRESPONDENT(1940); GANGS OF CHICAGO(1940); LILLIAN RUSSELL(1940); SHOP AROUND THE CORNER, THE(1940); STRANGER ON THE THIRD FLOOR(1940); THEY DRIVE BY NIGHT(1940); TUGBOAT ANNIE SAILS AGAIN(1940); TWENTY MULE TEAM(1940); VIRGINIA CITY(1940); WESTERNER, THE(1940); YOUNG PEOPLE(1940); BEHIND THE NEWS(1941); BODY DISAPPEARS, THE(1941); DANCE HALL(1941); H.M. PULHAM, ESQ.(1941); I WAS A PRISONER ON DEVIL'S ISLAND(1941); LADY SCARFACE(1941); LOOK WHO'S LAUGHING(1941); MEET THE CHUMP(1941); MR. AND MRS. SMITH(1941); MR. DISTRICT ATTORNEY(1941); ONE FOOT IN HEAVEN(1941); SMILING GHOST, THE(1941); THREE SONS O'GUNS(1941); TOBACCO ROAD(1941); UNHOLY PARTNERS(1941); VERY YOUNG LADY, A(1941); ACROSS THE PACIFIC(1942); CAPTAINS OF THE CLOUDS(1942); HENRY ALDRICH, EDITOR(1942); IN OLD CALIFORNIA(1942); JUKE BOX JENNY(1942); LADY BODYGUARD(1942); LADY IS WILLING, THE(1942); PRIORITIES ON PARADE(1942); SABOTEUR(1942); SPOILERS, THE(1942); THAT OTHER WOMAN(1942); THERE'S ONE BORN EVERY MINUTE(1942); THEY ALL KISSED THE BRIDE(1942); TO BE OR NOT TO BE(1942); TOMBSTONE, THE TOWN TOO TOUGH TO DIE(1942); WHISPERING GHOSTS(1942); YOU CAN'T ESCAPE FOREVER(1942); FLESH AND FANTASY(1943); GOVERNMENT GIRL(1943); HEAVEN CAN WAIT(1943); JITTERBUGS(1943); MY KINGDOM FOR A COOK(1943); WHISPERING FOOTSTEPS(1943); ADDRESS UNKNOWN(1944); ENEMY OF WOMEN(1944); RATIONING(1944); SHADOWS IN THE NIGHT(1944); THIN MAN GOES HOME, THE(1944); UP IN ARMS(1944); WILSON(1944); FIGHTING GUARDSMAN, THE(1945); MAMA LOVES PAPA(1945); ONE EXCITING NIGHT(1945); RHAPSODY IN BLUE(1945); SHE WENT TO THE RACES(1945); TOWN WENT WILD, THE(1945); TREE GROWS IN BROOKLYN, A(1945); BECAUSE OF HIM(1946); BEST YEARS OF OUR LIVES, THE(1946); IT'S A WONDERFUL LIFE(1946); SINGIN' IN THE CORN(1946); SISTER KENNY(1946); THREE LITTLE GIRLS IN BLUE(1946); GHOST GOES WILD, THE(1947); IF YOU KNEW SUSIE(1948); MY DEAR SECRETARY(1948); THREE GODFATHERS, THE(1948); DARING CABALLERO, THE(1949); HIDEOUT(1949); JOE PALOOKA IN THE SQUARED CIRCLE(1950); STELLA(1950); TRAVELING SALESWOMAN(1950); WHEN WILLIE COMES MARCHING HOME(1950); GASOLINE ALLEY(1951); HERE COMES THE GROOM(1951); CARRIE(1952); MOONLIGHTER, THE(1953); SLIGHT CASE OF LARCENY, A(1953); STAR IS BORN, A(1954); FRIENDLY PERSUASION(1956)
Silents
CLIMBERS, THE(1919)
Misc. Silents
ADVENTURER, THE(1917)
Percy Halton
Misc. Silents
FAIRY AND THE WAIF, THE(1915)
Jim Halty
NATIONAL LAMPOON'S ANIMAL HOUSE(1978)
1984
STAR TREK III: THE SEARCH FOR SPOCK(1984)
Jimmy Halty
CASEY'S SHADOW(1978)

Jose Halufi
PLAY DIRTY(1969, Brit.)
O. Clement Halverson
SHOCK(1946), set d
Marie Halvey
CASE OF SERGEANT GRISCHA, THE(1930), ed; LAWFUL LARCENY(1930), ed; LUMMOX(1930), ed
Silents
LAUGH, CLOWN, LAUGH(1928), ed; RESCUE, THE(1929), ed
Jean Halvez
Silents
SEVEN CHANCES(1925), w
Chkristine Halward
SON OF ROBIN HOOD(1959, Brit.)
Chris Halward
HA' PENNY BREEZE(1950, Brit.); JOHNNY, YOU'RE WANTED(1956, Brit.)
Al Ham
HARLOW(1965), m; STOP THE WORLD–I WANT TO GET OFF(1966, Brit.), w, md; GIVE'EM HELL, HARRY!(1975), p
Changyong Ham
MONSTER WANGMAGWI(1967, S. K.), ph
Donald Ham
STINGRAY(1978), p
Harry Ham
Silents
MADCAP BETTY(1915); NEARLY A LADY(1915); ANTICS OF ANN, THE(1917)
Misc. Silents
FATHER AND THE BOYS(1915); WEB OF CHANCE, THE(1919); BROKEN ROAD, THE(1921, Brit.); FOUR FEATHERS, THE(1921, Brit.)
Lucita Ham
VERY YOUNG LADY, A(1941)
Otto Ham
COWBOY SERENADE(1942)
Mic Hama
NIGHT OF THE SEAGULL, THE(1970, Jap.)
Mie Hama
NIGHT IN HONG KONG, A(1961, Jap.); DIFFERENT SONS(1962, Jap.); KING KONG VERSUS GODZILLA(1963, Jap.); YOUTH AND HIS AMULET, THE(1963, Jap.); YEARNING(1964, Jap.); WHAT'S UP, TIGER LILY?(1966); MAD ATLANTIC, THE(1967, Jap.); YOU ONLY LIVE TWICE(1967, Brit.); KING KONG ESCAPES(1968, Jap.); LAS VEGAS FREE-FOR-ALL(1968, Jap.); SIEGE OF FORT BISMARK(1968, Jap.)
Miye Hama
LOST WORLD OF SINBAD, THE(1965, Jap.)
Nie Hama
BEAUTIFUL SWINDLERS, THE(1967, Fr./Ital./Jap./Neth.)
Hans W. Hamacher
THREE PENNY OPERA(1963, Fr./Ger.); PHANTOM OF SOHO, THE(1967, Ger.)
Akira Hamada
PLEASURES OF THE FLESH, THE(1965)
Harry Hamada
FROGMEN, THE(1951); GO FOR BROKE(1951); I WAS AN AMERICAN SPY(1951)
Mitsuo Hamada
GANGSTER VIP, THE(1968, Jap.)
Pearl Hamada
GEISHA GIRL(1952)
Tatsuo Hamada
OHAYO(1962, Jap.), art d; SCANDAL(1964, Jap.), art d; PORTRAIT OF CHIEKO(1968, Jap.), art d; TOKYO STORY(1972, Jap.), prod d, art d; LATE AUTUMN(1973, Jap.), art d; AFFAIR AT AKITSU(1980, Jap.), art d
Torahiko Hamada
GIRARA(1967, Jap.)
Yuko Hamada
GAMERA VERSUS GUIRON(1969, Jap.)
Yuriko Hamada
LIFE OF OHARU(1964, Jap.)
Ron Hamady
FADE TO BLACK(1980), p
1984
SURF II(1984), p
Yoshihiro Hamaguchi
FIRES ON THE PLAIN(1962, Jap.)
Jun Hamamura
NAKED YOUTH(1961, Jap.); ODD OBSESSION(1961, Jap.); TEMPTRESS AND THE MONK, THE(1963, Jap.); GAMERA THE INVINCIBLE(1966, Jap.); NO GREATER LOVE THAN THIS(1969, Jap.); KURAGEJIMA–LEGENDS FROM A SOUTHERN ISLAND(1970, Jap.)
Yoshiyasu Hamamura
TOKYO STORY(1972, Jap.), ed
Richard Haman
FAST-WALKING(1982), art d
Richard Y. Haman
MEPHISTO WALTZ, THE(1971), art d
L'nelle Hamanaka
VIRGIN PRESIDENT, THE(1968)
Alan Hamane
ROLLERBALL(1975)
Kazumi Hamazaki
HARBOR LIGHT YOKOHAMA(1970, Jap.), ph
Art Hamberger
DOUBLE TROUBLE(1941)
Paul Hambides
CITY LOVERS(1982, S. African), ph
Phyllis Hambledon
NO PLACE FOR JENNIFER(1950, Brit.), w
Stuart Hamblen
ARIZONA KID, THE(1939); IN OLD MONTEREY(1939); SOMBRERO KID, THE(1942); CARSON CITY CYCLONE(1943); KING OF THE COWBOYS(1943); PLAINSMAN AND THE LADY(1946); SAVAGE HORDE, THE(1950)

Duffy Hambleton
MITCHELL(1975); JACKSON COUNTY JAIL(1976)
Harry Hambleton
LONG JOHN SILVER(1954, Aus.)
Florence Hamblin
WHERE DANGER LIVES(1950)
Arthur Hambling
"W" PLAN, THE(1931, Brit.); NIGHT IN MONTMARTE, A(1931, Brit.); OTHER PEOPLE'S SINS(1931, Brit.); SCOOP, THE(1934, Brit.); LOOK UP AND LAUGH(1935, Brit.); LORNA DOONE(1935, Brit.); SCARLET PIMPERNEL, THE(1935, Brit.); FRENCH LEAVE(1937, Brit.); LAST CHANCE, THE(1937, Brit.); ALMOST A HONEYMOON(1938, Brit.); LIGHTNING CONDUCTOR(1938, Brit.); MANY TANKS MR. ATKINS(1938, Brit.); SOUTH RIDING(1938, Brit.); ANYTHING TO DECLARE?(1939, Brit.); PHANTOM STRIKES, THE(1939, Brit.); BULLDOG SEES IT THROUGH(1940, Brit.); LOST ON THE WESTERN FRONT(1940, Brit.); SECRET FOUR, THE(1940, Brit.); THREE SILENT MEN(1940, Brit.); HARD STEEL(1941, Brit.); HOUSE OF MYSTERY(1941, Brit.); PIMPERNEL SMITH(1942, Brit.); WINGS AND THE WOMAN(1942, Brit.); HAPPIDROME(1943, Brit.); SAINT MEETS THE TIGER, THE(1943, Brit.); DEMOBBED(1944, Brit.); HE SNOOPS TO CONQUER(1944, Brit.); IT HAPPENED ONE SUNDAY(1944, Brit.); VARIETY JUBILEE(1945, Brit.); HENRY V(1946, Brit.); JOHNNY FRENCHMAN(1946, Brit.); ODD MAN OUT(1947, Brit.); DAUGHTER OF DARKNESS(1948, Brit.); DON'T EVER LEAVE ME(1949, Brit.); IT ALWAYS RAINS ON SUNDAY(1949, Brit.); IT'S NOT CRICKET(1949, Brit.); MY BROTHER'S KEEPER(1949, Brit.); LAVENDER HILL MOB, THE(1951, Brit.); MEN OF THE SEA(1951, Brit.); FOUR AGAINST FATE(1952, Brit.); MR. LORD SAYS NO(1952, Brit.); TRAIN OF EVENTS(1952, Brit.); TERROR ON A TRAIN(1953)
Garry Hambling
PRESS FOR TIME(1966, Brit.), ed
Gerald Hambling
MAGNIFICENT TWO, THE(1967, Brit.), ed
Gerry Hambling
WHOLE TRUTH, THE(1958, Brit.), ed; BULLDOG BREED, THE(1960, Brit.), ed; KITCHEN, THE(1961, Brit.), ed; MAID FOR MURDER(1963, Brit.), ed; EARLY BIRD, THE(1965, Brit.), ed; SPYLARKS(1965, Brit.), ed; STITCH IN TIME, A(1967, Brit.), ed; THAT RIVIERA TOUCH(1968, Brit.), ed; ADDING MACHINE, THE(1969), ed; BUGSY MALONE(1976, Brit.), ed; MOSES(1976, Brit./Ital.), ed; MIDNIGHT EXPRESS(1978, Brit.), ed; FAME(1980), ed; HEARTACHES(1981, Can.); PINK FLOYD–THE WALL(1982, Brit.), ed; SHOOT THE MOON(1982), ed
1984
ANOTHER COUNTRY(1984, Brit.), ed; BIRDY(1984), ed
Mark Hambourg
TALKING FEET(1937, Brit.); COMMON TOUCH, THE(1941, Brit.)
John Hambrick
TELEFON(1977)
Danchell E. Hambro
TEMPORARY WIDOW, THE(1930, Ger./Brit.)
Lenny Hambro
DIRTYMOUTH(1970), m
Dorothy Hamburg
ZAZA(1939)
William H. Hamby
Silents
CHALLENGE OF CHANCE, THE(1919), w
William Henry Hamby
Silents
GALLOPING KID, THE(1922), w
Sinaia Hamdan
CLOUDS OVER ISRAEL(1966, Israel)
Emad Hamdy
GLASS SPHINX, THE(1968, Egypt/Ital./Span.)
Hans Hameau
CONFESSION(1937), w
Willy Hameister
Silents
CABINET OF DR. CALIGARI, THE(1921, Ger.), ph
Bill Hamel
DESERT HELL(1958)
Peter Hamel
FILM WITHOUT A NAME(1950, Ger.)
Tania Hamel
1984
SUGAR CANE ALLEY(1984, Fr.)
Veronica Hamel
CANNONBALL(1976, U.S./Hong Kong); BEYOND THE POSEIDON ADVENTURE(1979); WHEN TIME RAN OUT(1980)
William Hamel
STREETS OF LAREDO(1949); FILE ON THELMA JORDAN, THE(1950); HELLGATE(1952); DREAM WIFE(1953); PONY EXPRESS(1953); UNKNOWN TERROR, THE(1957)
William R. Hamel
BLACK WHIP, THE(1956); COPPER SKY(1957)
Lucien Hamelin
TROUBLE-FETE(1964, Can.)
Lynn Hamelton
SHADOWS(1960)
Chris Hameon
PERMANENT VACATION(1982)
Frank Hamer, Jr.
OTHER SIDE OF BONNIE AND CLYDE, THE(1968)
Mrs. Frank Hamer
OTHER SIDE OF BONNIE AND CLYDE, THE(1968)
Fred Hamer
Silents
BROKEN BLOSSOMS(1919)
Gerald Hamer
THREE WITNESSES(1935, Brit.); SWING TIME(1936); ANGEL(1937); BLOND CHEAT(1938); SWEETHEARTS(1938); BULLDOG DRUMMOND'S BRIDE(1939); FOREVER AND A DAY(1943); SHERLOCK HOLMES FACES DEATH(1943); SHERLOCK HOLMES IN WASHINGTON(1943); ENTER ARSENE LUPIN(1944); HI BEAUTIFUL(1944); LODGER, THE(1944); SCARLET CLAW, THE(1944); PURSUIT TO

ALGIERS(1945); TERROR BY NIGHT(1946); IVY(1947); SIGN OF THE RAM, THE(1948); LORNA DOONE(1951)
Gladys Hamer
ALF'S CARPET(1929, Brit.); KISSING CUP'S RACE(1930, Brit.); LORD RICHARD IN THE PANTRY(1930, Brit.); TO OBLIGE A LADY(1931, Brit.); OFFICE GIRL, THE(1932, Brit.); GREAT STUFF(1933, Brit.); EASY MONEY(1934, Brit.); GREAT DEFENDER, THE(1934, Brit.); THAT'S MY UNCLE(1935, Brit.); THREE WITNESSES(1935, Brit.)
Silents
MONTY WORKS THE WIRES(1921, Brit.); REST CURE, THE(1923, Brit.); NOT FOR SALE(1924, Brit.); MONEY ISN'T EVERYTHING(1925, Brit.); MY LORD THE CHAUFFEUR(1927, Brit.); PASSION ISLAND(1927, Brit.); SMASHING THROUGH(1928, Brit.)
Misc. Silents
GOLD CURE, THE(1925)
Joseph Hamer
PATERNITY(1981)
Pat Hamer
SATAN IN HIGH HEELS(1962)
Robert Hamer
THE BEACHCOMBER(1938, Brit.), ed; JAMAICA INN(1939, Brit.), ed; SIDEWALKS OF LONDON(1940, Brit.), ed; TURNED OUT NICE AGAIN(1941, Brit.), ed; SHIPS WITH WINGS(1942, Brit.), ed; MY LEARNED FRIEND(1943, Brit.), p; SOMEWHERE IN FRANCE(1943, Brit.), p; FIDDLERS THREE(1944, Brit.), p; SAN DEMETRIO, LONDON(1947, Brit.), p, w; IT ALWAYS RAINS ON SUNDAY(1949, Brit.), d, w; KIND HEARTS AND CORONETS(1949, Brit.), d, w; PINK STRING AND SEALING WAX(1950, Brit.), d, w; HIS EXCELLENCY(1952, Brit.), d, w; SPIDER AND THE FLY, THE(1952, Brit.), d; LONG MEMORY, THE(1953, Brit.), d, w; DETECTIVE, THE(1954, Qit.), d, w; TO PARIS WITH LOVE(1955, Brit.), d; SCAPEGOAT, THE(1959, Brit.), d, w; SCHOOL FOR SCOUNDRELS(1960, Brit.), d; 55 DAYS AT PEKING(1963), w; JOLLY BAD FELLOW, A(1964, Brit.), w
Rusty Hamer
DANCE WITH ME, HENRY(1956)
Mark Hamil
WIZARDS(1977)
Murray Hamilkton
GRADUATE, THE(1967)
Brian Hamill
EXPOSED(1983)
Bryan Hamill
WILD 90(1968)
Charlotte Hamill
HAPPY DAYS(1930)
Elaine Hamill
GRANDAD RUDD(1935, Aus.); LOVERS AND LUGGERS(1938, Aus.); OUTSIDER, THE(1940, Brit.); VENGEANCE OF THE DEEP(1940, Aus.)
Eva Hamill
MEN ON HER MIND(1944)
John Hamill
NO BLADE OF GRASS(1970, Brit.); TROG(1970, Brit.); BEAST IN THE CELLAR, THE(1971, Brit.); TRAVELS WITH MY AUNT(1972, Brit.); NATIONAL HEALTH, OR NURSE NORTON'S AFFAIR, THE(1973, Brit.); BEYOND THE FOG(1981, Brit.)
Mark Hamill
STAR WARS(1977); CORVETTE SUMMER(1978); BIG RED ONE, THE(1980); EMPIRE STRIKES BACK, THE(1980); NIGHT THE LIGHTS WENT OUT IN GEORGIA, THE(1981); BRITTANIA HOSPITAL(1982, Brit.); RETURN OF THE JEDI(1983)
Pete Hamill
DOC(1971), w; BADGE 373(1973), a, w
Vincent Hamill
PUTNEY SWOPE(1969)
Aileen Hamilton
SAP FROM SYRACUSE, THE(1930), cos; SLIGHTLY DANGEROUS(1943), w; CHRISTMAS IN CONNECTICUT(1945), w
Alana Hamilton
RAVAGERS, THE(1979)
Alex Hamilton
BLUE LAGOON, THE(1980)
Alma Hamilton
Misc. Silents
LIBERTINE, THE(1916)
Andrew Hamilton
HERE WE GO ROUND THE MULBERRY BUSH(1968, Brit.)
Anne Hamilton
Misc. Silents
VALLEY OF LOST SOULS, THE(1923)
Archie Hamilton
FIRE AND ICE(1983)
Arthur Hamilton
PETE KELLY'S BLUES(1955), m
Barbara Hamilton
SONG IS BORN, A(1948); COME DANCE WITH ME(1950, Brit.); LADY CRAVED EXCITEMENT, THE(1950, Brit.); DANGEROUS AGE, A(1960, Can.); ONE PLUS ONE(1961, Can.); LOST AND FOUND(1979)
Barry Hamilton
FUZZ(1972)
Bernard Hamilton
BRIGHT VICTORY(1951); JUNGLE MAN-EATERS(1954); CONGO CROSSING(1956)
Bernie Hamilton
JACKIE ROBINSON STORY, THE(1950); LET NO MAN WRITE MY EPITAPH(1960); DEVIL AT FOUR O'CLOCK, THE(1961); UNDERWORLD U.S.A.(1961); YOUNG ONE, THE(1961, Mex.); THIRTEEN WEST STREET(1962); CAPTAIN SINDBAD(1963); ONE POTATO, TWO POTATO(1964); SYNANON(1965); SULLIVAN'S EMPIRE(1967); SWIMMER, THE(1968); LOST MAN, THE(1969); LOSERS, THE(1970); WALK THE WALK(1970); ORGANIZATION, THE(1971); HAMMER(1972); SCREAM BLACULA SCREAM(1973); BUCKTOWN(1975)
Bert Hamilton
SLIGHT CASE OF MURDER, A(1938); SHADOWS OF THE WEST(1949)
Betty Hamilton
VICTIMS OF PERSECUTION(1933); PRIVATE LIFE OF DON JUAN, THE(1934, Brit.)

Big John Hamilton
TWO RODE TOGETHER(1961); BANDOLERO!(1968); HELLFIGHTERS(1968); UN-DEFEATED, THE(1969); RIDE IN A PINK CAR(1974, Can.); SUGARLAND EXPRESS, THE(1974); TOUGH ENOUGH(1983)

"Big" John Hamilton
MC LINTOCK!(1963)

Bill Hamilton
WEST OF THE ALAMO(1946); FINAL OPTION, THE(1983, Brit.)

Bret Hamilton
MISS GRANT TAKES RICHMOND(1949); HOT ROD(1950); MAGNIFICENT YAN-KEE, THE(1950); I WAS AN AMERICAN SPY(1951); RACKET, THE(1951); MODERN MARRIAGE, A(1962)

Bruce Hamilton
WHIRLPOOL(1949)

Carey Hamilton
MAGNIFICENT DOLL(1946)

Charles Hamilton
STRANGE CARGO(1929); I AM THE LAW(1938); JUVENILE COURT(1938); MEN WITH WINGS(1938); WHO KILLED GAIL PRESTON?(1938); YOU CAN'T TAKE IT WITH YOU(1938); MEDICO OF PAINTED SPRINGS, THE(1941); WIFE TAKES A FLYER, THE(1942); PRACTICALLY YOURS(1944); VALLEY OF THE ZOMBIES(1946); HER HUSBAND'S AFFAIRS(1947); THAT WONDERFUL URGE(1948); JOHNNY ALLEGRO(1949); FULLER BRUSH GIRL, THE(1950); PONY EXPRESS(1953)

Charles "Chuck" Hamilton
ISLAND OF DOOMED MEN(1940); MISS GRANT TAKES RICHMOND(1949)

Chico Hamilton
REPULSION(1965, Brit.), m, md; CONFESSOR(1973), m; COONSKIN(1975), m; MR. RICCO(1975), m; BY DESIGN(1982), m

Chuck Hamilton
TRIAL OF VIVIENNE WARE, THE(1932); HERE COMES THE NAVY(1934); WED-DING PRESENT(1936); WHEN YOU'RE IN LOVE(1937); PROFESSOR BEWA-RE(1938); EACH DAWN I DIE(1939); TEXAS RANGERS RIDE AGAIN(1940); FACE BEHIND THE MASK, THE(1941); SON OF DAVY CROCKETT, THE(1941); IRON MAJOR, THE(1943); ONE DANGEROUS NIGHT(1943); WEIRD WOMAN(1944); OVER 21(1945); SCARLET STREET(1945); SHADY LADY(1945); SPANISH MAIN, THE(1945); DANGER WOMAN(1946); BUCK PRIVATES COME HOME(1947); DEAD RECKON-ING(1947); LAST ROUND-UP, THE(1947); SINBAD THE SAILOR(1947); UNCON-QUERED(1947); FORCE OF EVIL(1948); I, JANE DOE(1948); JOAN OF ARC(1948); KNOCK ON ANY DOOR(1949); ROSEANNA McCOY(1949); ABBOTT AND COSTELLO IN THE FOREIGN LEGION(1950); CONVICTED(1950); ENFORCER, THE(1951); FLAME OF ARABY(1951); MASK OF THE AVENGER(1951); SANTA FE(1951); KETTLES ON OLD MACDONALD'S FARM, THE(1957)

Cindy Hamilton
CANNIBALS IN THE STREETS(1982, Ital./Span.)

Clare Hamilton [Flory Fitzsimmons]
HOTEL RESERVE(1946, Brit.)

Clayton Hamilton
GIRL HABIT(1931), w
Silents
THIRTY DAYS(1922), w

Colin Hamilton
HARRY AND WALTER GO TO NEW YORK(1976); TWO-MINUTE WARNING(1976); TRUE CONFESSIONS(1981); FLASHDANCE(1983)

Cosmo Hamilton
PERFECT GENTLEMAN, THE(1935), w; EXILE, THE(1947), w
Silents
MIDSUMMER MADNESS(1920), w; WEALTH(1921), w; RECKLESS YOUTH(1922), w; ANOTHER SCANDAL(1924), w; PARADISE(1926), w

Curtis Hamilton
BAND OF ANGELS(1957)

Dan Hamilton
HERCULES IN NEW YORK(1970); BELL JAR, THE(1979)

David Hamilton
CONFESSIONS OF A POP PERFORMER(1975, Brit.); COUSINS IN LOVE(1982), d

Dick Hamilton
MAIL ORDER BRIDE(1964), makeup; VELVET TRAP, THE(1966)

David Hamilton [Ubaldo Terzano]
WHAT!(1965, Fr./Brit./Ital.), ph

Dolly Hamilton
HIGH FURY(1947, Brit.), makeup

Don Hamilton
80 STEPS TO JONAH(1969)

Donald Hamilton
SILENCERS, THE(, w; VIOLENT MEN, THE(1955), w; FIVE STEPS TO DAN-GER(1957), w; BIG COUNTRY, THE(1958), w; MURDERERS' ROW(1966), w; AM-BUSHERS, THE(1967), w; WRECKING CREW, THE(1968), w

Donna Hamilton
KID FROM BOOKLYN, THE(1946); GUNMEN OF ABILENE(1950); WHEN YOU'RE SMILING(1950)

Dore Hamilton
TERRORNAUTS, THE(1967, Brit.), makeup; UP THE JUNCTION(1968, Brit.), make-up

Dorothy Hamilton
MURDER BY ROPE(1936, Brit.)

Dorrie Hamilton
IDEAL HUSBAND, AN(1948, Brit.), makeup; FALLEN IDOL, THE(1949, Brit.), makeup

Dran Hamilton
DIRTY LITTLE BILLY(1972); ULZANA'S RAID(1972)

Duffy Hamilton
THX 1138(1971), stunts

Fenton Hamilton
EASY TO LOVE(1953); LIMIT, THE(1972), ph; BLACK CAESAR(1973), ph; HELL UP IN HARLEM(1973), ph; IT'S ALIVE(1974), ph; IT LIVES AGAIN(1978), ph

Florence Hamilton
Misc. Silents
ACCOMPLICE, THE(1917); CIGARETTE GIRL, THE(1917); MORAL CODE, THE(1917)

Floyd Hamilton
OTHER SIDE OF BONNIE AND CLYDE, THE(1968)

Frances Hamilton
RIDE BEYOND VENGEANCE(1966), cos
Silents
NAUGHTY BABY(1929)

Frank Hamilton
SUBTERRANEANS, THE(1960); SIDELONG GLANCES OF A PIGEON KICKER, THE(1970); LADY LIBERTY(1972, Ital./Fr.); PATERNITY(1981); STRANGER IS WATCHING, A(1982)

Fred Hamilton
BROTHER RAT(1938); WINGS OF THE NAVY(1939)

G.P. Hamilton
Silents
SAMSON(1914), d
Misc. Silents
LUST OF THE RED MAN, THE(1914), d; ALOHA OE(1915), d; INHERITED PAS-SIONS(1916), d; MATERNAL SPARK, THE(1917), d; CAPTAIN OF HIS SOUL(1918), d

Gay Hamilton
CHALLENGE FOR ROBIN HOOD, A(1968, Brit.); BARRY LYNDON(1975, Brit.); DUELLISTS, THE(1977, Brit.)
Misc. Talkies
DAY SANTA CLAUS CRIED, THE(1980)

George Hamilton
TWO WEEKS IN ANOTHER TOWN(1962); TAP ROOTS(1948); WELL, THE(1951); LONE STAR(1952); SCARLET ANGEL(1952); MISSISSIPPI GAMBLER, THE(1953); PRESIDENT'S LADY, THE(1953); CRIME AND PUNISHMENT, U.S.A.(1959); ALL THE FINE YOUNG CANNIBALS(1960); HOME FROM THE HILL(1960); WHERE THE BOYS ARE(1960); ANGEL BABY(1961); BY LOVE POSSESSED(1961); THUNDER OF DRUMS, A(1961); LIGHT IN THE PIAZZA(1962); VICTORS, THE(1963); ACT ONE(1964); LOOKING FOR LOVE(1964); YOUR CHEATIN' HEART(1964); VIVA MARIA(1965, Fr./Ital.); DOCTOR, YOU'VE GOT TO BE KIDDING(1967); JACK OF DIAMONDS(1967, U.S./Ger.); THAT MAN GEORGE!(1967, Fr./Ital./Span.); TIME FOR KILLING, A(1967); POWER, THE(1968); EVEL KNIEVEL(1971), a, p; MAN WHO LOVED CAT DANCING, THE(1973); ONCE IS NOT ENOUGH(1975); HAPPY HOOKER GOES TO WASHINGTON, THE(1977); SEXTETTE(1978); FROM HELL TO VIC-TORY(1979, Fr./Ital./Span.); LOVE AT FIRST BITE(1979); ZORRO, THE GAY BLA-DE(1981), a, p
Misc. Talkies
TOGETHERNESS(1970); SCORPIO SCARAB, THE(1972)

George Hamilton IV
HOOTENANNY HOOT(1963); SECOND FIDDLE TO A STEEL GUITAR(1965)

Gilbert Hamilton
Misc. Silents
WOMAN OF LIES(1919), d

Gilbert P. Hamilton
Silents
OPEN YOUR EYES(1919), d
Misc. Silents
EVERYWOMAN'S HUSBAND(1918), d; FALSE AMBITION(1918), d; GOLDEN FLEECE, THE(1918), d; HIGH TIDE(1918), d; LAST REBEL, THE(1918), d; SOUL IN TRUST, A(1918), d; VORTEX, THE(1918), d; COAX ME(1919), d

Graeme Hamilton
TROUBLE IN THE AIR(1948, Brit.), ed

Gustave Hamilton
CHILDREN OF PARADISE(1945, Fr.)

Guy Hamilton
RINGER, THE(1953, Brit.), d; DRAGNET(1954); INSPECTOR CALLS, AN(1954, Brit.), d; COLDITZ STORY, THE(1955, Brit.), d, w; INTRUDER, THE(1955, Brit.), d; CHARLEY MOON(1956, Brit.), d; STOWAWAY GIRL(1957, Brit.), d, w; DEVIL'S DISCIPLE, THE(1959), d; TOUCH OF LARCENY, A(1960, Brit.), d, w; BEST OF ENEMIES, THE(1962), d; GOLDFINGER(1964, Brit.), d; MAN IN THE MIDDLE(1964, U.S./Brit.), d; FUNERAL IN BERLIN(1966, Brit.), d; PARTY'S OVER, THE(1966, Brit.), d; BATTLE OF BRITAIN, THE(1969, Brit.), d; LIVE AND LET DIE(1973, Brit.), d; MAN WITH THE GOLDEN GUN, THE(1974, Brit.), d; FORCE 10 FROM NAVARONE(1978, Brit.), d; MIRROR CRACK'D, THE(1980, Brit.), d; EVIL UNDER THE SUN(1982, Brit.), d

Hal Hamilton
LE MANS(1971)

Hale Hamilton
COMMON CLAY(1930); GOOD INTENTIONS(1930); PAID(1930); BEAU IDEAL(1931); CHAMP, THE(1931); CUBAN LOVE SONG,THE(1931); DANCE, FOOLS, DANCE(1931); DRUMS OF JEOPARDY(1931); GREAT LOVER, THE(1931); MURDER AT MIDNIGHT(1931); NEVER THE TWAIN SHALL MEET(1931); NEW ADVEN-TURES OF GET-RICH-QUICK WALLINGFORD, THE(1931); REBOUND(1931); STRANGERS MAY KISS(1931); SUSAN LENOX–HER FALL AND RISE(1931); TAIL-OR MADE MAN, A(1931); CALL HER SAVAGE(1932); I AM A FUGITIVE FROM A CHAIN GANG(1932); LIFE BEGINS(1932); LOVE AFFAIR(1932); MANHATTAN TOWER(1932); MOST DANGEROUS GAME, THE(1932); SUCCESSFUL CALAMITY, A(1932); THOSE WE LOVE(1932); THREE ON A MATCH(1932); TWO AGAINST THE WORLD(1932); BLACK BEAUTY(1933); EMPLOYEE'S ENTRANCE(1933); ONE MAN'S JOURNEY(1933); PAROLE GIRL(1933); REFORM GIRL(1933); SITTING PRETTY(1933); STRANGE PEOPLE(1933); BIG HEARTED HERBERT(1934); CITY PARK(1934); CURTAIN AT EIGHT(1934); DOCTOR MONICA(1934); GIRL FROM MISSOURI, THE(1934); QUITTERS, THE(1934); TWIN HUSBANDS(1934); WHEN STRANGERS MEET(1934); AFTER OFFICE HOURS(1935); CALM YOURSELF(1935); DANTE'S INFERNO(1935); GRAND OLD GIRL(1935); HOLD'EM YALE(1935); I LIVE MY LIFE(1935); LET 'EM HAVE IT(1935); MARINES ARE COMING, THE(1935); NITWITS, THE(1935); THREE KIDS AND A QUEEN(1935); WOMAN IN RED, THE(1935); ADVENTURES OF MARCO POLO, THE(1938); MEET THE MAYOR(1938)
Silents
JOHNNY-ON-THE-SPOT(1919); GREAT GATSBY, THE(1926); SUMMER BACHE-LORS(1926); TIN GODS(1926); TELEPHONE GIRL, THE(1927)
Misc. Silents
FIVE THOUSAND AN HOUR(1918); OPPORTUNITY(1918); WINNING OF BEA-TRICE, THE(1918); AFTER HIS OWN HEART(1919); FOUR FLUSHER, THE(1919); FULL OF PEP(1919); IN HIS BROTHER'S PLACE(1919); THAT'S GOOD(1919); MANICURE GIRL, THE(1925); GIRL IN THE RAIN(1927)

Hank Hamilton
MECHANIC, THE(1972); KILLER ELITE, THE(1975); CAR, THE(1977)
Harry Hamilton
BANJO ON MY KNEE(1936), w; I COVER CHINATOWN(1938), w; MAIN STREET LAWYER(1939), w; SKY FULL OF MOON(1952), m/l
Henry Hamilton
Silents
SINS OF SOCIETY(1915), w; ROYAL OAK, THE(1923, Brit.), w
Ian Hamilton
ROMEO AND JULIET(1966, Brit.); SHARE OUT, THE(1966, Brit.); LAST SHOT YOU HEAR, THE(1969, Brit.); KILLER FORCE(1975, Switz./Ireland); SAFARI 3000(1982)
J. Frank Hamilton
MEN OF TEXAS(1942); AMAZING MRS. HOLLIDAY(1943); HEADIN' FOR GOD'S COUNTRY(1943); SHANTYTOWN(1943)
Jaeme Hamilton
STRANGE HOLIDAY(1969, Aus.)
James Hamilton
GIVE'EM HELL, HARRY!(1975), set d
Silents
ANKLES PREFERRED(1927), w
Capt. James E. Hamilton
DRAGNET(1954), tech adv
James Shelley Hamilton
Silents
NORTH OF 36(1924), w; AIR MAIL, THE(1925), w; ANCIENT HIGHWAY, THE(1925), w; RUGGED WATER(1925), w; ENCHANTED HILL, THE(1926), w; SEA HORSES(1926), w; TIN GODS(1926), w
James Shelly Hamilton
Silents
SUMMER BACHELORS(1926), w
Jane Hamilton
ROMAN SCANDALS(1933); KID MILLIONS(1934); OLD MAN RHYTHM(1935); ROBERTA(1935); FOLLOW THE FLEET(1936); PAID TO DANCE(1937); GOLDWYN FOLLIES, THE(1938); WHO KILLED GAIL PRESTON?(1938); THAT HAGEN GIRL(1947); EVERYBODY DOES IT(1949)
Jean Hamilton
ON STAGE EVERYBODY(1945)
Jeff Hamilton
SPOOK WHO SAT BY THE DOOR, THE(1973)
Jill Hamilton
MILLION EYES OF SU-MURU, THE(1967, Brit.)
Jim Hamilton
HELL SQUAD(1958)
Joe Hamilton
STRANGE LADY IN TOWN(1955); SOLID GOLD CADILLAC, THE(1956); JET ATTACK(1958); CAGE OF EVIL(1960)
John F. Hamilton
ALLEGHENY UPRISING(1939); GOLD RUSH MAISIE(1940); SAINT'S DOUBLE TROUBLE, THE(1940); UNDERCOVER MAN, THE(1949)
John H. Hamilton
GUY WHO CAME BACK, THE(1951)
John Hamilton
TO WHAT RED HELL(1929, Brit.); DANGEROUS NAN McGREW(1930); HEADS UP(1930); MYSTERY AT THE VILLA ROSE(1930, Brit.); WHITE CARGO(1930, Brit.); LEGION OF TERROR(1936); LOVE LETTERS OF A STAR(1936); TWO IN A CROWD(1936); BAD GUY(1937); CRIMINALS OF THE AIR(1937); FIFTY ROADS TO TOWN(1937); IT COULD HAPPEN TO YOU(1937); MAN BETRAYED, A(1937); MAN WHO CRIED WOLF, THE(1937); NIGHT CLUB SCANDAL(1937); SEVENTH HEAVEN(1937); SINGING MARINE, THE(1937); THAT CERTAIN WOMAN(1937); THREE SMART GIRLS(1937); TWO WISE MAIDS(1937); 100 MEN AND A GIRL(1937); ANGELS WITH DIRTY FACES(1938); DR. RHYTHM(1938); HUNTED MEN(1938); I STAND ACCUSED(1938); MR. MOTO'S GAMBLE(1938); MR. WONG, DETECTIVE(1938); OVER THE WALL(1938); YOU CAN'T TAKE IT WITH YOU(1938); ESPIONAGE AGENT(1939); FIRST OFFENDERS(1939); FORGED PASSPORT(1939); FORGOTTEN WOMAN, THE(1939); I STOLE A MILLION(1939); MURDER IS NEWS(1939); ROARING TWENTIES, THE(1939); ROSE OF WASHINGTON SQUARE(1939); SECRET SERVICE OF THE AIR(1939); SMASHING THE MONEY RING(1939); SPIRIT OF CULVER, THE(1939); STRONGER THAN DESIRE(1939); THEY SHALL HAVE MUSIC(1939); DEVIL'S ISLAND(1940); DR. EHRLICH'S MAGIC BULLET(1940); FATAL HOUR, THE(1940); FLIGHT COMMAND(1940); GREAT PLANE ROBBERY, THE(1940); INVISIBLE STRIPES(1940); LADY WITH RED HAIR(1940); MURDER IN THE AIR(1940); OH JOHNNY, HOW YOU CAN LOVE!(1940); TEAR GAS SQUAD(1940); TUGBOAT ANNIE SAILS AGAIN(1940); BODY DISAPPEARS, THE(1941); BORROWED HERO(1941); CHEERS FOR MISS BISHOP(1941); MALTESE FALCON, THE(1941); MEET JOHN DOE(1941); NINE LIVES ARE NOT ENOUGH(1941); ACROSS THE PACIFIC(1942); ALWAYS IN MY HEART(1942); BIG SHOT, THE(1942); ENEMY AGENTS MEET ELLERY QUEEN(1942); ESCAPE FROM CRIME(1942); GREAT MAN'S LADY, THE(1942); I KILLED THAT MAN(1942); IN THIS OUR LIFE(1942); LUCKY JORDAN(1942); OVER MY DEAD BODY(1942); PHANTOM KILLER(1942); THEY DIED WITH THEIR BOOTS ON(1942); TO THE SHORES OF TRIPOLI(1942); ADVENTURES OF A ROOKIE(1943); ALLERGIC TO LOVE(1943); GOVERNMENT GIRL(1943); LARCENY WITH MUSIC(1943); MISSION TO MOSCOW(1943); SO'S YOUR UNCLE(1943); SPY TRAIN(1943); ACTION IN ARABIA(1944); CRAZY KNIGHTS(1944); DOUGHGIRLS, THE(1944); GIRL WHO DARED, THE(1944); HI BEAUTIFUL(1944); HI, GOOD-LOOKIN'(1944); I'M FROM ARKANSAS(1944); LAKE PLACID SERENADE(1944); MAN FROM FRISCO(1944); MEET MISS BOBBY SOCKS(1944); MUSIC IN MANHATTAN(1944); MY GAL LOVES MUSIC(1944); PORT OF 40 THIEVES, THE(1944); SHERIFF OF LAS VEGAS(1944); STANDING ROOM ONLY(1944); SWINGTIME JOHNNY(1944); UP IN ARMS(1944); CIRCUMSTANTIAL EVIDENCE(1945); FIRST YANK INTO TOKYO(1945); I'LL TELL THE WORLD(1945); JOHNNY ANGEL(1945); NAUGHTY NINETIES, THE(1945); NORTHWEST TRAIL(1945); ON STAGE EVERYBODY(1945); STRANGE ILLUSION(1945); BADMAN'S TERRITORY(1946); GIRL ON THE SPOT(1946); HOME ON THE RANGE(1946); JOHNNY COMES FLYING HOME(1946); MADONNA'S SECRET(1946); MAGNIFICENT DOLL(1946); SHADOWS OVER CHINATOWN(1946); STEP BY STEP(1946); WIFE WANTED(1946); BANDITS OF DARK CANYON(1947); BEGINNING OR THE END, THE(1947); FABULOUS TEXAN, THE(1947); I'LL BE YOURS(1947); IT HAPPENED ON 5TH AVENUE(1947); NEWS HOUNDS(1947); RAIDERS OF THE SOUTH(1947); SEA OF GRASS, THE(1947); SECRET LIFE OF WALTER MITTY, THE(1947); SONG OF MY

HEART(1947); THAT'S MY GAL(1947); TOO MANY WINNERS(1947); TROUBLE WITH WOMEN, THE(1947); VIOLENCE(1947); DESPERADOES OF DODGE CITY(1948); GALLANT LEGION, THE(1948); RETURN OF THE BADMEN(1948); WALK A CROOKED MILE(1948); ALIAS THE CHAMP(1949); BANDIT KING OF TEXAS(1949); CANADIAN PACIFIC(1949); FIGHTING MAN OF THE PLAINS(1949); JUDGE, THE(1949); LAW OF THE GOLDEN WEST(1949); SHERIFF OF WICHITA(1949); WYOMING BANDIT, THE(1949); BELLS OF CORONADO(1950); DAVY CROCKETT, INDIAN SCOUT(1950); MISSOURIANS, THE(1950); PIONEER MARSHAL(1950); MILLION DOLLAR PURSUIT(1951); SUGARFOOT(1951); PACE THAT THRILLS, THE(1952); TARGET(1952); DONOVAN'S BRAIN(1953); EL PASO STAMPEDE(1953); IRON MOUNTAIN TRAIL(1953); JACK McCALL, DESPERADO(1953); MAN OF CONFLICT(1953); MARSHAL OF CEDAR ROCK(1953); RUN FOR THE HILLS(1953); ON THE WATERFRONT(1954); SITTING BULL(1954); CHICAGO CONFIDENTIAL(1957); OUTCASTS OF THE CITY(1958); DEADLY COMPANIONS, THE(1961); MALENKA, THE VAMPIRE(1972, Span./Ital.); RED SUN(1972, Fr./Ital./Span.)
Silents
PASSIONATE ADVENTURE, THE(1924, Brit.); SHADOW OF EGYPT, THE(1924, Brit.); LAST WITNESS, THE(1925, Brit.); MONEY ISN'T EVERYTHING(1925, Brit.); FEAR O' GOD(1926, Brit./Ger.); RINGER, THE(1928, Brit.)
Misc. Silents
FEAR O'GOD(1926, Brit.); SILVER LINING, THE(1927, Brit.); BURGOMASTER OF STILEMONDE, THE(1928, Brit.); HELLCAT, THE(1928, Brit.); WINDOW IN PICCADILLY, A(1928, Brit.); THIRD EYE, THE(1929, Brit.); THREE KINGS, THE(1929, Brit.); WHITE CARGO(1929, Brit.)
John R. Hamilton
GREAT FLAMARION, THE(1945); HIGH WALL, THE(1947); CHECKERED COAT, THE(1948); PRISON WARDEN(1949); BODYHOLD(1950); MAGNIFICENT YANKEE, THE(1950); MILITARY ACADEMY WITH THAT TENTH AVENUE GANG(1950)
Joseph Hamilton
TIGHT SPOT(1955); TEENAGE CAVEMAN(1958); PLUNDERERS, THE(1960); HOODLUM PRIEST, THE(1961); ONE MAN'S WAY(1964); CAT BALLOU(1965); GIT!(1965)
Josh Hamilton
1984
FIRSTBORN(1984)
Joshua Hamilton
GOOD DISSONANCE LIKE A MAN, A(1977)
Judd Hamilton
STARCRASH(1979)
1984
LAST HORROR FILM, THE(1984), a, p, w
Judge Hamilton
Silents
BRANDED A BANDIT(1924)
Julian Hamilton
PICCADILLY NIGHTS(1930, Brit.)
Julie Hamilton
QUACKSER FORTUNE HAS A COUSIN IN THE BRONX(1970)
June Hamilton
ADVENTURES OF BARRY McKENZIE(1972, Austral.), cos
Keith Hamilton
CLEOPATRA JONES(1973); MIXED COMPANY(1974)
Kenneth Eric Hamilton
HONEYSUCKLE ROSE(1980)
Kim Hamilton
SOMETHING OF VALUE(1957); ODDS AGAINST TOMORROW(1959); LEECH WOMAN, THE(1960); WIZARD OF BAGHDAD, THE(1960); TO KILL A MOCKINGBIRD(1962); WILD ANGELS, THE(1966); BODY AND SOUL(1981)
Kipp Hamilton
GOOD MORNING, MISS DOVE(1955); BIGGER THAN LIFE(1956); NEVER SO FEW(1959); UNFORGIVEN, THE(1960); HARLOW(1965); WAR OF THE GARGANTUAS, THE(1970, Jap.)
Kit Hamilton
1984
HARDBODIES(1984)
Larry Hamilton
ESCAPE FROM THE SEA(1968, Brit.)
Laura Hamilton
WHY LEAVE HOME?(1929)
Lauren Hamilton
1984
ALPHABET CITY(1984)
Leigh Hamilton
MAN, A WOMAN, AND A BANK, A(1979, Can.); FORCED VENGEANCE(1982)
Lilian Hamilton
OUTRAGE(1950)
Lillian Hamilton
ON THE LOOSE(1951)
Linda Hamilton
T.A.G.: THE ASSASSINATION GAME(1982)
1984
CHILDREN OF THE CORN(1984); STONE BOY, THE(1984); TERMINATOR, THE(1984)
Lloyd Hamilton
BLACK WATERS(1929); TANNED LEGS(1929); ARE YOU THERE?(1930)
Silents
OCCASIONALLY YOURS(1920); HIS DARKER SELF(1924)
Misc. Silents
SELF-MADE FAILURE, A(1924)
Louise Hamilton
Misc. Silents
SOULS TRIUMPHANT(1915)
Lynn Hamilton
BROTHER JOHN(1971); SEVEN MINUTES, THE(1971); BUCK AND THE PREACHER(1972); LADY SINGS THE BLUES(1972); HANGUP(1974); LEADBELLY(1976)
Mahlon Hamilton
HONKY TONK(1929); RICH PEOPLE(1929); CODE OF HONOR(1930); SPORTING CHANCE(1931); STRANGERS OF THE EVENING(1932); WESTERN LIMITED(1932); ESCAPADE(1935); HIGH SCHOOL GIRL(1935); MISSISSIPPI(1935); BOSS RIDER OF

GUN CREEK(1936); HIGH BARBAREE(1947); HUCKSTERS, THE(1947)
Silents
LAW OF THE LAND, THE(1917); DANGER MARK, THE(1918); ADELE(1919); DADDY LONG LEGS(1919); IN OLD KENTUCKY(1920); PAID BACK(1922); HEART RAIDER, THE(1923); PLAYTHINGS OF DESIRE(1924); RECOIL, THE(1924); ENEMIES OF YOUTH(1925); WINDING STAIR, THE(1925); SINGLE STANDARD, THE(1929)
Misc. Silents
FINAL JUDGEMENT, THE(1915); BLACK BUTTERFLY, THE(1916); ETERNAL QUESTION, THE(1916); EXTRAVAGANCE(1916); MOLLY MAKE-BELIEVE(1916); BRIDGES BURNED(1917); EXILE(1917); MORE TRUTH THAN POETRY(1917); RED WOMAN, THE(1917); SILENCE SELLERS, THE(1917); SOUL OF MAGDALEN, THE(1917); TO THE DEATH(1917); UNDYING FLAME, THE(1917); WAITING SOUL, THE(1917); DEATH DANCE, THE(1918); HER KINGDOM OF DREAMS(1919); DEADLIER SEX, THE(1920); EARTHBOUND(1920); GREATER THAN LOVE(1920); HALF A CHANCE(1920); THIRD GENERATION, THE(1920); I AM GUILTY(1921); LADIES MUST LIVE(1921); THAT GIRL MONTANA(1921); TRUANT HUSBAND, THE(1921); UNDER THE LASH(1921); GREEN TEMPTATION, THE(1922); LANE THAT HAD NO TURNING, THE(1922); PEG O' MY HEART(1922); UNDER OATH(1922); MIDNIGHT GUEST, THE(1923); WHEEL, THE(1925); MORGANSON'S FINISH(1926); HER INDISCRETIONS(1927); WHAT PRICE LOVE(1927); LIFE'S CROSSROADS(1928); WHITE FLAME(1928)

Marc Hamilton
GREAT LOCOMOTIVE CHASE, THE(1956); MAN FROM DEL RIO(1956); MOLE PEOPLE, THE(1956)

Margaret Hamilton
ANOTHER LANGUAGE(1933); BROADWAY BILL(1934); HAT, COAT AND GLOVE(1934); BY YOUR LEAVE(1935); FARMER TAKES A WIFE, THE(1935); WAY DOWN EAST(1935); CHATTERBOX(1936); MOON'S OUR HOME, THE(1936); THESE THREE(1936); WITNESS CHAIR, THE(1936); GOOD OLD SOAK, THE(1937); I'LL TAKE ROMANCE(1937); LAUGHING AT TROUBLE(1937); MOUNTAIN JUSTICE(1937); NOTHING SACRED(1937); SARATOGA(1937); WHEN'S YOUR BIRTHDAY?(1937); YOU ONLY LIVE ONCE(1937); ADVENTURES OF TOM SAWYER, THE(1938); BREAKING THE ICE(1938); FOUR'S A CROWD(1938); MOTHER CAREY'S CHICKENS(1938); SLIGHT CASE OF MURDER, A(1938); STABLEMATES(1938); ANGELS WASH THEIR FACES(1939); BABES IN ARMS(1939); MAIN STREET LAWYER(1939); WIZARD OF OZ, THE(1939); I'M NOBODY'S SWEETHEART NOW(1940); MY LITTLE CHICKADEE(1940); PLAY GIRL(1940); VILLAIN STILL PURSUED HER, THE(1940); GAY VAGABOND, THE(1941); INVISIBLE WOMAN, THE(1941); AFFAIRS OF MARTHA, THE(1942); MEET THE STEWARTS(1942); TWIN BEDS(1942); CITY WITHOUT MEN(1943); JOHNNY COME LATELY(1943); OX-BOW INCIDENT, THE(1943); GUEST IN THE HOUSE(1944); GEORGE WHITE'S SCANDALS(1945); FAITHFUL IN MY FASHION(1946); JANIE GETS MARRIED(1946); DISHONORED LADY(1947); DRIFTWOOD(1947); BUNGALOW 13(1948); STATE OF THE UNION(1948); TEXAS, BROOKLYN AND HEAVEN(1948); BEAUTIFUL BLONDE FROM BASHFUL BEND, THE(1949); RED PONY, THE(1949); SUN COMES UP, THE(1949); GREAT PLANE ROBBERY(1950); MAD WEDNESDAY(1950); RIDING HIGH(1950); WABASH AVENUE(1950); COMIN' ROUND THE MOUNTAIN(1951); PEOPLE WILL TALK(1951); THIRTEEN GHOSTS(1960); PARADISE ALLEY(1962); DAYDREAMER, THE(1966); ROSIE!(1967); ANGEL IN MY POCKET(1969); BREWSTER McCLOUD(1970); ANDERSON TAPES, THE(1971); JOURNEY BACK TO OZ(1974)

Mark Hamilton
THIS ISLAND EARTH(1955); GIANT(1956)
Silents
RAINBOW TRAIL, THE(1925); SPARROWS(1926); AFLAME IN THE SKY(1927); SONORA KID, THE(1927); HEART TROUBLE(1928); SMOKE BELLEW(1929)
Misc. Silents
MAN FROM RED GULCH, THE(1925)

Mary Hamilton
WOMEN WHO PLAY(1932, Brit.)

Maxwell Hamilton
MIRACLE OF THE BELLS, THE(1948)

Melody Hamilton
9/30/55(1977)

Michael Hamilton [Elio Scardamaglia]
MURDER CLINIC, THE(1967, Ital./Fr.), p&d

Mickie Hamilton
TI-CUL TOUGAS(1977, Can.), cos

Murray Hamilton
WAY WE WERE, THE(1973); BRIGHT VICTORY(1951); WHISTLE AT EATON FALLS(1951); GIRL HE LEFT BEHIND, THE(1956); TOWARD THE UNKNOWN(1956); JEANNE EAGELS(1957); SPIRIT OF ST. LOUIS, THE(1957); DARBY'S RANGERS(1958); HOUSEBOAT(1958); NO TIME FOR SERGEANTS(1958); TOO MUCH, TOO SOON(1958); ANATOMY OF A MURDER(1959); FBI STORY, THE(1959); TALL STORY(1960); HUSTLER, THE(1961); CARDINAL, THE(1963); PAPA'S DELICATE CONDITION(1963); THIRTEEN FRIGHTENED GIRLS(1963); AMERICAN DREAM, AN(1966); SECONDS(1966); BROTHERHOOD, THE(1968); NO WAY TO TREAT A LADY(1968); SERGEANT RYKER(1968); THE BOSTON STRANGLER, THE(1968); IF IT'S TUESDAY, THIS MUST BE BELGIUM(1969); DROWNING POOL, THE(1975); JAWS(1975); CASEY'S SHADOW(1978); JAWS II(1978); AMITYVILLE HORROR, THE(1979); 1941(1979); BRUBAKER(1980); HYSTERICAL(1983)

Nancy Hamilton
FOOLS FOR SCANDAL(1938), w; DU BARRY WAS A LADY(1943), w

Neal Hamilton
SILK EXPRESS, THE(1933)

Neil Hamilton
PATRIOT, THE(1928); DANGEROUS WOMAN(1929); DARKENED ROOMS(1929); KIBITZER, THE(1929); LOVE TRAP, THE(1929); MYSTERIOUS DR. FU MANCHU, THE(1929); STUDIO MURDER MYSTERY, THE(1929); ANYBODY'S WAR(1930); CAT CREEPS, THE(1930); DAWN PATROL, THE(1930); LADIES MUST PLAY(1930); RETURN OF DR. FU MANCHU, THE(1930); WIDOW FROM CHICAGO, THE(1930); COMMAND PERFORMANCE(1931); EX-FLAME(1931); GREAT LOVER, THE(1931); LAUGHING SINNERS(1931); SIN OF MADELON CLAUDET, THE(1931); STRANGERS MAY KISS(1931); THIS MODERN AGE(1931); ANIMAL KINGDOM, THE(1932); ARE YOU LISTENING?(1932); PAYMENT DEFERRED(1932); TARZAN, THE APE MAN(1932); TWO AGAINST THE WORLD(1932); WET PARADE, THE(1932); WHAT PRICE HOLLYWOOD?(1932); WOMAN IN ROOM 13, THE(1932); AS THE DEVIL COMMANDS(1933); LADIES MUST LOVE(1933); ONE SUNDAY AFTERNOON(1933); TERROR ABOARD(1933); WORLD GONE MAD, THE(1933); BLIND DATE(1934);

FUGITIVE LADY(1934); HERE COMES THE GROOM(1934); ONCE TO EVERY BACHELOR(1934); TARZAN AND HIS MATE(1934); TWO HEADS ON A PILLOW(1934); BY YOUR LEAVE(1935); DARING YOUNG MAN, THE(1935); KEEPER OF THE BEES(1935); MUTINY AHEAD(1935); ONE EXCITING ADVENTURE(1935); EVERYTHING IN LIFE(1936, Brit.); HONEYMOON LIMITED(1936); SOUTHERN ROSES(1936, Brit.); YOU MUST GET MARRIED(1936, Brit.); LADY BEHAVE(1937); MR. STRINGFELLOW SAYS NO(1937, Brit.); PORTIA ON TRIAL(1937); ARMY GIRL(1938); HOLLYWOOD STADIUM MYSTERY(1938); I MARRIED A SPY(1938); SAINT STRIKES BACK, THE(1939); QUEEN OF THE MOB(1940); DANGEROUS LADY(1941); FATHER TAKES A WIFE(1941); FEDERAL FUGITIVES(1941); LOOK WHO'S LAUGHING(1941); THEY MEET AGAIN(1941); LADY IS WILLING, THE(1942); TOO MANY WOMEN(1942); X MARKS THE SPOT(1942); ALL BY MYSELF(1943); BOMBARDIER(1943); SECRETS OF THE UNDERGROUND(1943); SKY'S THE LIMIT, THE(1943); WHEN STRANGERS MARRY(1944); BREWSTER'S MILLIONS(1945); DEVIL'S HAND, THE(1961); LITTLE SHEPHERD OF KINGDOM COME(1961); GOOD NEIGHBOR SAM(1964); PATSY, THE(1964); FAMILY JEWELS, THE(1965); BATMAN(1966); MADAME X(1966); STRATEGY OF TERROR(1969); WHICH WAY TO THE FRONT?(1970)
Misc. Talkies
ANYBODY'S WAR(1930); SPY, THE(1931)
Silents
WHITE ROSE, THE(1923); AMERICA(1924); ISN'T LIFE WONDERFUL(1924); SIDESHOW OF LIFE, THE(1924); NEW BROOMS(1925); BEAU GESTE(1926); GREAT GATSBY, THE(1926); JOY GIRL, THE(1927); SHIELD OF HONOR, THE(1927); DON'T MARRY(1928); HOT NEWS(1928); TAKE ME HOME(1928); WHAT A NIGHT!(1928); WHY BE GOOD?(1929)
Misc. Silents
GOLDEN PRINCESS, THE(1925); LITTLE FRENCH GIRL, THE(1925); MEN AND WOMEN(1925); STREET OF FORGOTTEN MEN, THE(1925); DESERT GOLD(1926); DIPLOMACY(1926); SPLENDID CRIME, THE(1926); MUSIC MASTER, THE(1927); SPOTLIGHT, THE(1927); TEN MODERN COMMANDMENTS(1927); GRIP OF THE YUKON, THE(1928); MOTHER MACHREE(1928); SHOWDOWN, THE(1928); SOMETHING ALWAYS HAPPENS(1928); THREE WEEK-ENDS(1928)

Dr. Nikola Hamilton
Misc. Silents
FIENDS OF HELL(1914, Brit.)

Pat Hamilton
LAST DETAIL, THE(1973)

Patricia Hamilton
BITTER HARVEST(1963, Brit.), w; WHY ROCK THE BOAT?(1974, Can.); MIDDLE AGE CRAZY(1980, Can.); WHO HAS SEEN THE WIND(1980, Can.); MY BLOODY VALENTINE(1981, Can.)

Patrick Hamilton
GASLIGHT(1940), w; GASLIGHT(1944), w; HANGOVER SQUARE(1945), w; ROPE(1948), w

Paula Hamilton
1984
FOUR DAYS IN JULY(1984)

Peter Hamilton
SMALL TOWN STORY(1953, Brit.), ph

Phillips Hamilton
YOUNG DON'T CRY, THE(1957)

Phyllis Hamilton
MAN WHO TALKED TOO MUCH, THE(1940); THEY DRIVE BY NIGHT(1940)

Raye Hamilton
Silents
ACTION GALORE(1925)

Reed Hamilton
Misc. Silents
LOVE'S LAW(1918)

Reid Hamilton
CREATION OF THE HUMANOIDS(1962)

Richard Hamilton
LADYBUG, LADYBUG(1963); TRUMAN CAPOTE'S TRILOGY(1969); RESURRECTION(1980); ARTHUR(1981); I'M DANCING AS FAST AS I CAN(1982); SILKWOOD(1983)
1984
PROTOCOL(1984)

Rita Hamilton
OUR VERY OWN(1950)

Robert "Bones" Hamilton
BIG GAME, THE(1936)

Roy Hamilton
WHIP HAND, THE(1951), w; BLADES OF THE MUSKETEERS(1953), w; CAT WOMEN OF THE MOON(1953), w; LET'S ROCK(1958)

Russ Hamilton
6.5 SPECIAL(1958, Brit.)

Scott Hamilton
TARGETS(1968), makeup; WILD GYPSIES(1969), makeup

Shorty Hamilton
Silents
TRAIL'S END(1922)
Misc. Silents
DAUGHTER OF THE DON, THE(1918); DENNY FROM IRELAND(1918); NUGGET IN THE ROUGH, A(1918); PEN VULTURES(1918); PRISONER OF WAR, THE(1918); RANGER, THE(1918); SNAIL, THE(1918); WHEN ARIZONA WON(1919); WHITE MASKS, THE(1921); CROSS ROADS(1922); GOLD GRABBERS(1922)

"Shorty" Hamilton
Silents
SO THIS IS ARIZONA(1922)
Misc. Silents
ANGEL CITIZENS(1922)

Stella Hamilton
TROUBLE IN THE AIR(1948, Brit.); GOOD DIE YOUNG, THE(1954, Brit.)

Steven Hamilton
HERO(1982, Brit.)

Sue Hamilton
DR. GOLDFOOT AND THE BIKINI MACHINE(1965); SERGEANT DEADHEAD(1965); FIREBALL 590(1966); GHOST IN THE INVISIBLE BIKINI(1966)

Suzanna Hamilton
BRIMSTONE AND TREACLE(1982, Brit.)
1984
1984(1984, Brit.)
Tai Hamilton
NOTORIOUS CLEOPATRA, THE(1970)
Tammas J. Hamilton
TIMES SQUARE(1980)
Ted Hamilton
PIRATE MOVIE, THE(1982, Aus.)
Toni Hamilton
WARM IN THE BUD(1970)
Tony Hamilton
NOCTURNA(1979)
Vonn Hamilton
GEORGE WHITE'S SCANDALS(1945)
Ward Hamilton
NIGHT UNTO NIGHT(1949), makeup
Warren Hamilton, Jr.
SWEET JESUS, PREACHER MAN(1973), ed; BLACK SAMSON(1974), w; KISS OF
THE TARANTULA(1975), w
Wendy Hamilton
MAN WHO HAD POWER OVER WOMEN, THE(1970, Brit.); SCARS OF DRACULA,
THE(1970, Brit.)
William Hamilton
LONE WOLF'S DAUGHTER, THE(1929), ed; RIO RITA(1929), ed; CIMAR-
RON(1931), ed; WOMAN BETWEEN(1931), ed; CONQUERORS, THE(1932), ed;
HELL'S HIGHWAY(1932), ed; LOST SQUADRON, THE(1932), ed; ROAR OF THE
DRAGON(1932), ed; STATE'S ATTORNEY(1932), ed; AFTER TONIGHT(1933), ed;
BEFORE DAWN(1933), ed; DIPLOMANIACS(1933), ed; EMERGENCY CALL(1933),
ed; NO OTHER WOMAN(1933), ed; TOPAZE(1933), ed; CRIME DOCTOR, THE(1934),
ed; GAY DIVORCEE, THE(1934), ed; HIS GREATEST GAMBLE(1934), ed; KEEP 'EM
ROLLING(1934), ed; LITTLE MINISTER, THE(1934), ed; THEIR BIG MO-
MENT(1934), ed; BREAK OF HEARTS(1935), ed; FRECKLES(1935), ed; ROBER-
TA(1935), ed; SEVEN KEYS TO BALDPATE(1935), ed; TOP HAT(1935), ed; BUNKER
BEAN(1936), d; MURDER ON A BRIDLE PATH(1936), d; WINTERSET(1936), ed;
SHALL WE DANCE(1937), ed; STAGE DOOR(1937), ed; SUPER SLEUTH(1937), ed;
CAREFREE(1938), ed; HAVING WONDERFUL TIME(1938), ed; FIFTH AVENUE
GIRL(1939), ed; HUNCHBACK OF NOTRE DAME, THE(1939), ed; IN NAME ON-
LY(1939), ed; STORY OF VERNON AND IRENE CASTLE, THE(1939), ed; PRIMROSE
PATH(1940), ed; TOM BROWN'S SCHOOL DAYS(1940), ed; TOO MANY GIRLS(1940),
ed; MR. AND MRS. SMITH(1941), ed; SUSPICION(1941), ed; UNEXPECTED UN-
CLE(1941), ed; BIG STREET, THE(1942), ed; CALL OUT THE MARINES(1942), d&w
Silents
CLASSMATES(1924), ed; ENCHANTED COTTAGE, THE(1924), ed; SHORE LEA-
VE(1925), ed; ANNIE LAURIE(1927), ed; CAPTAIN SALVATION(1927), ed; OUR
DANCING DAUGHTERS(1928), ed
William S. Hamilton
UNCOMMON VALOR(1983)
Wm. Hamilton
WINTERSET(1936), ed
Zanna Hamilton
SWALLOWS AND AMAZONS(1977, Brit.)
Virginia Hamilton-Kearse
JOANNA(1968, Brit.), cos
Mohamed Lekhdar Hamina
HASSAN, TERRORIST(1968, Algerian), d
Shabani Hamisi
TOTO AND THE POACHERS(1958, Brit.); LAST RHINO, THE(1961, Brit.)
Dilys Hamlett
MIX ME A PERSON(1962, Brit.); ASSAULT(1971, Brit.); DIAGNOSIS: MUR-
DER(1974, Brit.)
Molly Hamley-Clifford
WHAT A NIGHT!(1931, Brit.); TEMPTATION(1935, Brit.); TICKET OF LEAVE(1936,
Brit.); EASY RICHES(1938, Brit.); MIRACLES DO HAPPEN(1938, Brit.); MURDER
TOMORROW(1938, Brit.); PAID IN ERROR(1938, Brit.); DEADLOCK(1943, Brit.);
DARK SECRET(1949, Brit.); MAGNET, THE(1950, Brit.); MEET MR. LUCIFER(1953,
Brit.)
Arline Hamlin
HALLS OF ANGER(1970)
Catherine Hamlin
UP THE MACGREGORS(1967, Ital./Span.)
Edith Hamlin
LADYBUG, LADYBUG(1963), ed
George Hamlin
ZELIG(1983)
Harry Hamlin
MOVIE MOVIE(1978); CLASH OF THE TITANS(1981); KING OF THE MOUN-
TAIN(1981); MAKING LOVE(1982); BLUE SKIES AGAIN(1983)
Jeff Hamlin
ONE FROM THE HEART(1982)
Joanne Hamlin
1984
MUPPETS TAKE MANHATTAN, THE(1984)
Joe Hamlin
UP THE MACGREGORS(1967, Ital./Span.)
John Harold Hamlin
Silents
MAN OF NERVE, A(1925), w; PAINTED PONIES(1927), w
Judge Walter B. Hamlin
NEW ORLEANS UNCENSORED(1955)
Marilyn Hamlin
SHAFT'S BIG SCORE(1972); SAVAGE WEEKEND(1983)
Mary Hamlin
ALEXANDER HAMILTON(1931), w
Walter Hamlin
STREET OF DARKNESS(1958)

Marvin Hamlisch
WAY WE WERE, THE(1973), m; VALLEY OF THE DOLLS(1967); SWIMMER,
THE(1968), m; APRIL FOOLS, THE(1969), m; TAKE THE MONEY AND RUN(1969),
m; FLAP(1970), m; MOVE(1970), m; BANANAS(1971), m; KOTCH(1971), m; SOME-
THING BIG(1971), m; WAR BETWEEN MEN AND WOMEN, THE(1972), m; SAVE
THE TIGER(1973), m, md; WORLD'S GREATEST ATHLETE, THE(1973), m; ENTER-
TAINER, THE(1975), p, m; PRISONER OF SECOND AVENUE, THE(1975), m; SPY
WHO LOVED ME, THE(1977, Brit.), m; ICE CASTLES(1978), m; SAME TIME, NEXT
YEAR(1978), m; CHAPTER TWO(1979), m; STARTING OVER(1979), m; SEEMS LIKE
OLD TIMES(1980), m; PENNIES FROM HEAVEN(1981), m; I OUGHT TO BE IN
PICTURES(1982), m; SOPHIE'S CHOICE(1982), m; ROMANTIC COMEDY(1983), m
Marvin Hamlish
FAT CITY(1972), m
Dan Hamlon
Silents
20,000 LEAGUES UNDER THE SEA(1916)
Brenda Hamlyn
WOMAN TO WOMAN(1946, Brit.)
A. R. Hamm
Silents
DON'T TELL EVERYTHING(1921), ph
Al Hamm
BEWARE! THE BLOB(1972), ph
Peter Hamm
WHY DOES HERR R. RUN AMOK?(1977, Ger.)
Robert Hamm
ACE ELI AND RODGER OF THE SKIES(1973)
Sam Hamm
NEVER CRY WOLF(1983), w
Robert Hammack
STARLIFT(1951)
Warren Hammack
EYE CREATURES, THE(1965); HIGH YELLOW(1965); MARS NEEDS WO-
MEN(1966); ZONTAR, THE THING FROM VENUS(1966); HELLCATS, THE(1968);
FIVE THE HARD WAY(1969); JOHNNY VIK(1973)
Richard Hammat
OUTLAND(1981)
Edna Hammel
Silents
EMBARRASSMENT OF RICHES, THE(1918)
John Hammel
1984
GIVE MY REGARDS TO BROAD STREET(1984, Brit.)
Rex Hammel
Silents
ANGEL OF CROOKED STREET, THE(1922); NINETY AND NINE, THE(1922)
Al Hammer
WALK IN THE SUN, A(1945); FABULOUS SUZANNE, THE(1946)
Alvin Hammer
DOLL FACE(1945); CRACK-UP(1946); LADY LUCK(1946); DEAD RECK-
ONING(1947); MIRACLE ON 34TH STREET, THE(1947); MOTHER WORE
TIGHTS(1947); WINTER WONDERLAND(1947); ARCH OF TRIUMPH(1948); ARGYLE
SECRETS, THE(1948); CANON CITY(1948); HOLLOW TRIUMPH(1948); JOAN OF
ARC(1948); LADY FROM SHANGHAI, THE(1948); NOOSE HANGS HIGH, THE(1948);
TEXAS, BROOKLYN AND HEAVEN(1948); MA AND PA KETTLE(1949); RED PONY,
THE(1949); DAKOTA LIL(1950); THREE HUSBANDS(1950); LOVE NEST(1951); GRIS-
SOM GANG, THE(1971); SAM'S SONG(1971); UNHOLY ROLLERS(1972); HUST-
LE(1975); LITTLE MISS MARKER(1980)
Ben Hammer
JOHNNY GOT HIS GUN(1971); INVASION OF THE BEE GIRLS(1973);
HAUNTS(1977); COMPETITION, THE(1980)
1984
HIGHWAY TO HELL(1984); RUNNING HOT(1984)
Charles Hammer
BLACK DIAMONDS(1932, Brit.), p,d&w
Don Hammer
DRIVE, HE SAID(1971); NEWMAN'S LAW(1974)
1984
RHINESTONE(1984)
Earl Hammer, Jr.
SPENCER'S MOUNTAIN(1963), w
E.N. "Dick" Hammer
STALLION CANYON(1949)
Ina Hammer
Silents
KING LEAR(1916)
Misc. Silents
HOUSE OF FEAR, THE(1915)
James Hammer
Silents
GOLD RUSH, THE(1925)
Jan Hammer
NIGHT IN HEAVEN, A(1983), m
1984
GIMME AN 'F'(1984), m
Jerry Hammer
WHO SAYS I CAN'T RIDE A RAINBOW!(1971), p
Len Hammer
DIARY OF A BACHELOR(1964)
Mark Hammer
RAISE THE TITANIC(1980, Brit.)
Mike Hammer
CATSKILL HONEYMOON(1950)
Robert Hammer
THIRTEEN FIGHTING MEN(1960), w; DON'T ANSWER THE PHONE(1980), p&d,
w
Rudolph Hammer
VOYAGE TO THE END OF THE UNIVERSE(1963, Czech.), makeup

Ten Hammer
BEASTMASTER, THE(1982)
Theodore S. Hammer
GETTING TOGETHER(1976), prod d
Todd Hammer
WHO SAYS I CAN'T RIDE A RAINBOW!(1971)
Will Hammer
PUBLIC LIFE OF HENRY THE NINTH, THE(1934, Brit.), p; BANK MESSENGER
MYSTERY, THE(1936, Brit.), p; SONG OF FREEDOM(1938, Brit.)
William Hammer
JESSIE'S GIRLS(1976)
Ralph Hammeras
JUST IMAGINE(1930), art d, set d; BODY AND SOUL(1931), spec eff; IN OLD
CHICAGO(1938), spec eff; 20,000 LEAGUES UNDER THE SEA(1954), ph; GIANT
GILA MONSTER, THE(1959), spec eff; MY DOG, BUDDY(1960), ph
Gosta Hammerback
BRINK OF LIFE(1960, Swed.), p
Gordon Hammersley
CHARRIOTS OF FIRE(1981, Brit.)
Arthur Hammerstein
LOTTERY BRIDE, THE(1930), p
Elaine Hammerstein
Silents
ARGYLE CASE, THE(1917); WANTED FOR MURDER(1919); DAUGHTER PAYS,
THE(1920); GREATER THAN FAME(1920); WHISPERS(1920); WAY OF A MAID,
THE(1921); ONE WEEK OF LOVE(1922); RECKLESS YOUTH(1922); RUPERT OF
HENTZAU(1923); SOULS FOR SALE(1923); MIDNIGHT EXPRESS, THE(1924); AFT-
ER BUSINESS HOURS(1925); EVERY MAN'S WIFE(1925)
Misc. Silents
MOONSTONE, THE(1915); CO-RESPONDENT, THE(1917); MODERN OTHELLO,
A(1917); ACCIDENTAL HONEYMOON, THE(1918); HER MAN(1918); WOMAN ETER-
NAL, THE(1918); COUNTRY COUSIN, THE(1919); LOVE OR FAME(1919); PLEASURE
SEEKERS(1920); POINT OF VIEW, THE(1920); SHADOW OF ROSALIE BYRNES,
THE(1920); WOMAN GAME, THE(1920); GIRL FROM NOWHERE, THE(1921); HAND-
CUFFS OR KISSES(1921); MIRACLE OF MANHATTAN, THE(1921); POOR, DEAR
MARGARET KIRBY(1921); REMORSELESS LOVE(1921); EVIDENCE(1922); UNDER
OATH(1922); WHY ANNOUNCE YOUR MARRIAGE?(1922); BROADWAY
GOLD(1923); DRUMS OF JEOPARDY, THE(1923); DARING LOVE(1924); FOOLISH
VIRGIN, THE(1924); ONE GLORIOUS NIGHT(1924); PAINT AND POWDER(1925);
PARISIAN NIGHTS(1925); S.O.S. PERILS OF THE SEA(1925); UNWRITTEN LAW,
THE(1925); CHECKERED FLAG, THE(1926); LADIES OF LEISURE(1926)
June Hammerstein
TENDER HEARTS(1955); EDGE OF HELL(1956)
Oscar Hammerstein
STORY OF VERNON AND IRENE CASTLE, THE(1939), w
Oscar Hammerstein II
DESERT SONG, THE(1929), w; GOLDEN DAWN(1930), w; NEW MOON(1930), w;
SONG OF THE FLAME(1930), w, m; SONG OF THE WEST(1930), w; SUNNY(1930),
w, m; VIENNESE NIGHTS(1930), w; CHILDREN OF DREAMS(1931), w; MUSIC IN
THE AIR(1934), w; SWEET ADELINE(1935), w; ROSE MARIE(1936), w; SHOW
BOAT(1936), w; HIGH, WIDE AND HANDSOME(1937), w; SWING HIGH, SWING
LOW(1937), w; LADY OBJECTS, THE(1938), m; NEW MOON(1940), w; SUNNY(1941),
w; DESERT SONG, THE(1943), w; BROADWAY RHYTHM(1944), w; STATE
FAIR(1945), w; SHOW BOAT(1951), w; DESERT SONG, THE(1953), w; MAIN
STREET TO BROADWAY(1953); CARMEN JONES(1954), w; DEEP IN MY
HEART(1954), lyrics; ROSE MARIE(1954), w; OKLAHOMA!(1955), m; CAROU-
SEL(1956), w; KING AND I, THE(1956), w; SOUTH PACIFIC(1958), w; STATE
FAIR(1962), w; SOUND OF MUSIC, THE(1965), w
Barbara Hammes
1984
SLOW MOVES(1984)
Dashiell Hammett
CITY STREETS(1931), w; MALTESE FALCON, THE(1931), w; THIN MAN,
THE(1934), w; WOMAN IN THE DARK(1934), w; GLASS KEY, THE(1935), w; MR.
DYNAMITE(1935), w; AFTER THE THIN MAN(1936), w; SATAN MET A LADY(1936),
w; ANOTHER THIN MAN(1939), w; MALTESE FALCON, THE(1941), w; SHADOW
OF THE THIN MAN(1941), w; GLASS KEY, THE(1942), w; WATCH ON THE RHI-
NE(1943), w; THIN MAN GOES HOME, THE(1944), w; SONG OF THE THIN
MAN(1947), w
Mike Hammett
FROM THE MIXED-UP FILES OF MRS. BASIL E. FRANKWEILER(1973)
Jackie Hammette
NEPTUNE'S DAUGHTER(1949)
Alexander Hammid
MEDIUM, THE(1951), ed
David Hammil
1984
GARBO TALKS(1984)
Lucille Hammil
Silents
BATTLE CRY OF PEACE, THE(1915)
Ellen Hammill
DON'T GO IN THE HOUSE(1980), p, w
Edna Hammon
Silents
SEVEN CHANCES(1925)
Kay Hammon
ALMOST A DIVORCE(1931, Brit.)
A. C. Hammond
LOVE STORM, THE(1931, Brit.), ed; MY WIFE'S FAMILY(1932, Brit.), ed; NUMBER
SEVENTEEN(1932, Brit.), ed
Alicia Hammond
NO RETURN ADDRESS(1961)
Bennett Hammond
PILGRIMAGE(1972)
Beryl Hammond
RED LINE 7000(1965)

Bill Hammond
NORTHWEST TRAIL(1945); RIDERS OF THE DAWN(1945); RANGE BEYOND THE
BLUE(1947); RADAR SECRET SERVICE(1950); ON DANGEROUS GROUND(1951)
Billy Hammond
WEST TO GLORY(1947); RIDE, RYDER, RIDE!(1949); SHADOWS OF THE
WEST(1949); STALLION CANYON(1949); FIGHTING REDHEAD, THE(1950)
C. Norman Hammond
Silents
HOP, THE DEVIL'S BREW(1916); BRONZE BELL, THE(1921); DOCTOR JACK(1922);
SMILES ARE TRUMPS(1922)
Misc. Silents
WOLVES OF THE RAIL(1918); MIDLANDERS, THE(1920)
C.N. Hammond
Misc. Silents
WHAT LOVE CAN DO(1916)
Brian Hammond
INNOCENT SINNERS(1958, Brit.); TIGER BAY(1959, Brit.); LONELINESS OF THE
LONG DISTANCE RUNNER, THE(1962, Brit.)
Charles C. Hammond
Silents
ALIEN ENEMY, AN(1918)
Charles Hammond
Silents
MANON LESCAUT(1914); SPREADING DAWN, THE(1917); SALLY OF THE SAW-
DUST(1925)
Misc. Silents
WOMEN MEN MARRY(1922)
Coral Hammond
SCANDAL AT SCOURIE(1953); MA AND PA KETTLE AT HOME(1954)
David Hammond
WALLS OF JERICHO(1948); SIMON, KING OF THE WITCHES(1971), p; RAISE THE
TITANIC(1980, Brit.)
Diana Hammond
INTENT TO KILL(1958, Brit.)
Dorothy Hammond
JUBILEE WINDOW(1935, Brit.); MR. WHAT'S-HIS-NAME(1935, Brit.); IT'S YOU I
WANT(1936, Brit.); NOTHING LIKE PUBLICITY(1936, Brit.)
Earl Hammond
SATAN IN HIGH HEELS(1962); HIRED KILLER, THE(1967, Fr./Ital.); WORLD OF
HANS CHRISTIAN ANDERSEN, THE(1971, Jap.)
Edward Hammond
GHOST TALKS, THE(1929), w
Frank Hammond
PERSONALITY(1930); CASE AGAINST MRS. AMES, THE(1936); FATAL LA-
DY(1936); MR. DEEDS GOES TO TOWN(1936); HOTEL HAYWIRE(1937); PUBLIC
WEDDING(1937); TOAST OF NEW YORK, THE(1937); CAPTAIN IS A LADY,
THE(1940); STRANGER ON THE THIRD FLOOR(1940)
Frank B. Hammond
OH DOCTOR(1937)
Frank E. Hammond
MAID OF SALEM(1937)
Frank H. Hammond
SPLENDOR(1935)
Gilmore Hammond
Silents
GILDED SPIDER, THE(1916)
Misc. Silents
BLACK SHEEP OF THE FAMILY, THE(1916); MARK OF CAIN, THE(1916)
Hally Hammond
PISTOL FOR RINGO, A(1966, Ital./Span.); RETURN OF RINGO, THE(1966, Ital./
Span.)
Harriet Hammond
Silents
GOLDEN GIFT, THE(1922); MAN AND MAID(1925)
Misc. Silents
LIVE AND LET LIVE(1921); CONFIDENCE(1922); MAN FROM RED GULCH,
THE(1925); MIDSHIPMAN, THE(1925); SEVENTH BANDIT, THE(1926)
J. Michael Hammond
1984
LAST NIGHT AT THE ALAMO(1984)
Jack Hammond
NO RETURN ADDRESS(1961)
John Hammond
LITTLE BIG MAN(1970), m; CROSS CREEK(1983)
1984
PRODIGAL, THE(1984)
John Paul Hammond
LOOSE ENDS(1975), m
Johnny Hammond
Misc. Talkies
ENFORCER FROM DEATH ROW, THE(1978)
Kathleen Hammond
Silents
WITHOUT HOPE(1914)
Kay Hammond
TRESPASSER, THE(1929); ABRAHAM LINCOLN(1930); CHILDREN OF CHAN-
CE(1930, Brit.); HER PRIVATE AFFAIR(1930); CARNIVAL(1931, Brit.); FASCINA-
TION(1931, Brit.); NIGHT IN MONTMARTE, A(1931, Brit.); OUT OF THE BLUE(1931,
Brit.); MONEY MEANS NOTHING(1932, Brit.); NIGHT LIKE THIS, A(1932, Brit.);
NINE TILL SIX(1932, Brit.); SALLY BISHOP(1932, Brit.); THIRD STRING, THE(1932,
Brit.); BRITANNIA OF BILLINGSGATE(1933, Brit.); DOUBLE HARNESS(1933);
RACETRACK(1933); SLEEPING CAR(1933, Brit.); UMBRELLA, THE(1933, Brit.);
BYPASS TO HAPPINESS(1934, Brit.); EIGHT GIRLS IN A BOAT(1934); WAY DOWN
EAST(1935); TWO ON A DOORSTEP(1936, Brit.); GIRL IN DISTRESS(1941, Brit.);
BLITHE SPIRIT(1945, Brit.); CALL OF THE BLOOD(1948, Brit.); GIRL IN THE RED
VELVET SWING, THE(1955); FIVE GOLDEN HOURS(1961, Brit.)
Len Hammond
TOO HOT TO HANDLE(1938), w; CONFIRM OR DENY(1941), p

Lloyd Hammond
Misc. Silents
FIRST WOMAN, THE(1922)
Lynn Hammond
Silents
SILVER WINGS(1922)
Marcus Hammond
PLAGUE OF THE ZOMBIES, THE(1966, Brit.); WHERE THE BULLETS FLY(1966, Brit.)
Marie Lynn Hammond
TICKET TO HEAVEN(1981)
Michael Hammond
NEVER TAKE CANDY FROM A STRANGER(1961, Brit.); BLOOD ON THE AR-ROW(1964)
Nicholas Hammond
LORD OF THE FLIES(1963, Brit.); SOUND OF MUSIC, THE(1965); SKYJACK-ED(1972); SUPERDAD(1974)
Norah Hammond
HOUSE IN THE WOODS, THE(1957, Brit.)
Patricia Lee Hammond
LAST RITES(1980)
Patti Hammond
NUTCRACKER(1982, Brit.)
Peter Hammond
THEY KNEW MR. KNIGHT(1945, Brit.); HOLIDAY CAMP(1947, Brit.); FLY AWAY PETER(1948, Brit.); HERE COME THE HUGGETTS(1948, Brit.); VOTE FOR HUG-GETT(1948, Brit.); FOOLS RUSH IN(1949, Brit.); HELTER SKELTER(1949, Brit.); HUGGETTS ABROAD, THE(1949, Brit.); ADVENTURERS, THE(1951, Brit.); OPERA-TION DISASTER(1951, Brit.); RELUCTANT WIDOW, THE(1951, Brit.); COME BACK PETER(1952, Brit.); FATHER'S DOING FINE(1952, Brit.); ALF'S BABY(1953, Brit.); DEADLIEST SIN, THE(1956, Brit.); SECRET TENT, THE(1956, Brit.); SPIN A DARK WEB(1956, Brit.); X THE UNKNOWN(1957, Brit.); IT'S NEVER TOO LATE(1958, Brit.); JACK THE RIPPER(1959, Brit.), w; MODEL FOR MURDER(1960, Brit.); SPRING AND PORT WINE(1970, Brit.), d
Misc. Talkies
PHANTOM KID, THE(1983), d
Reid Hammond
SCANDAL INCORPORATED(1956)
Richard Hammond
FOREIGN CORRESPONDENT(1940)
Roger Hammond
GAME FOR THREE LOSERS(1965, Brit.); LOCK UP YOUR DAUGHTERS(1969, Brit.); THANK YOU ALL VERY MUCH(1969, Brit.); PIED PIPER, THE(1972, Brit.)
Ronald Hammond
Silents
QUEEN MOTHER, THE(1916, Brit.)
Sheila Hammond
UGLY DUCKLING, THE(1959, Brit.)
Victor Hammond
ADVENTURES OF KITTY O'DAY(1944), w; DETECTIVE KITTY O'DAY(1944), w; MARKED TRAILS(1944), w; FASHION MODEL(1945), w; SOUTH OF THE RIO GRANDE(1945), w; BOWERY BOMBSHELL(1946), w; IN FAST COMPANY(1946), w
Vikki Hammond
BLUE MURDER AT ST. TRINIAN'S(1958, Brit.)
Virginia Hammond
ANYBODY'S WOMAN(1930); LADY SURRENDERS, A(1930); NEWLY RICH(1931); CHANDU THE MAGICIAN(1932); NO ONE MAN(1932); RICH ARE ALWAYS WITH US, THE(1932); ROCKABYE(1932); THE CRASH(1932); CHANCE AT HEAVEN(1933); EAGLE AND THE HAWK, THE(1933); TORCH SINGER(1933); CHARLIE CHAN'S COURAGE(1934); COME ON, MARINES(1934); DESIRABLE(1934); DOCTOR MONI-CA(1934); GREAT EXPECTATIONS(1934); LOST LADY, A(1934); SEARCH FOR BEAUTY(1934); GOIN' TO TOWN(1935); GREAT IMPERSONATION, THE(1935); LADY TUBBS(1935); RUMBA(1935); STRAIGHT FROM THE HEART(1935); VIR-GINIA JUDGE, THE(1935); ROMEO AND JULIET(1936)
Silents
KISS, THE(1916); MISS CRUSOE(1919)
Misc. Silents
DISCARD, THE(1916); BATTLER, THE(1919); CROOK OF DREAMS(1919); HAND INVISIBLE, THE(1919); WORLD TO LIVE IN, THE(1919); MANHATTAN KNIGHT, A(1920)
Walter Hammond
CAPTAIN NEWMAN, M.D.(1963), spec eff; MADAME X(1966), spec eff
William C. Hammond
FOOL AND THE PRINCESS, THE(1948, Brit.), d&w; LONE CLIMBER, THE(1950, Brit./Aust.), d; FLYING EYE, THE(1955, Brit.), d, w; ROCKETS IN THE DUNES(1960, Brit.), d
William Hammond
Misc. Talkies
CARRINGTON SCHOOL MYSTERY, THE(1958, Brit.), d
Kay Hammonf
TEN COMMANDMENTS, THE(1956)
E. W. Hammons
LAST MILE, THE(1932), p
Imad Hammoud
CIRCLE OF DECEIT(1982, Fr./Ger.)
Earl Hamner, Jr.
PALM SPRINGS WEEKEND(1963), w; CHARLOTTE'S WEB(1973), w; WHERE THE LILIES BLOOM(1974), w
Robert Hamner
LONG ROPE, THE(1961), w
Olivia Hamnett
LAST WAVE, THE(1978, Aus.); EARTHLING, THE(1980)
Misc. Talkies
PLUNGE INTO DARKNESS(1977)
Clara Smith Hamon
Misc. Silents
FATE(1921)

Jean Hamon
YOUNG GIRLS OF ROCHEFORT, THE(1968, Fr.), ed
Lucienne Hamon
HO(1968, Fr.), w; ZITA(1968, Fr.), w
Cynthia Hamowy
CARWASH(1976)
Howard Hampden
Misc. Silents
IN THE SPIDER'S WEB(1924)
Walter Hampden
HUNCHBACK OF NOTRE DAME, THE(1939); ALL THIS AND HEAVEN TOO(1940); NORTHWEST MOUNTED POLICE(1940); REAP THE WILD WIND(1942); THEY DIED WITH THEIR BOOTS ON(1942); ADVENTURES OF MARK TWAIN, THE(1944); DOUBLE LIFE, A(1947), tech adv; ALL ABOUT EVE(1950); FIRST LEGION, THE(1951); FIVE FINGERS(1952); SOMBRERO(1953); TREASURE OF THE GOLDEN CONDOR(1953); SABRINA(1954); SILVER CHALICE, THE(1954); PRODIGAL, THE(1955); STRANGE LADY IN TOWN(1955); VAGABOND KING, THE(1956)
Misc. Silents
WARFARE OF THE FLESH, THE(1917)
Irena Hampel
SOPHIE'S CHOICE(1982)
Genevieve Hamper
Silents
UNDER THE RED ROBE(1923)
Misc. Silents
BLINDNESS OF DEVOTION(1915); GREEN-EYED MONSTER, THE(1916); SPIDER AND THE FLY, THE(1916); TANGLED LIVES(1917)
Genvieve Hamper
Misc. Silents
UNFAITHFUL WIFE, THE(1915)
Barbara Hampshire
CARRY ON ENGLAND(1976, Brit.)
David Hampshire
PIRATES OF PENZANCE, THE(1983)
Melanie Hampshire
BLOW-UP(1966, Brit.)
Susan Hampshire
WOMAN IN THE HALL, THE(1949, Brit.); EXPRESSO BONGO(1959, Brit.); LONG SHADOW, THE(1961, Brit.); UPSTAIRS AND DOWNSTAIRS(1961, Brit.); DURING ONE NIGHT(1962, Brit.); THREE LIVES OF THOMASINA, THE(1963, U.S./Brit.); NIGHT MUST FALL(1964, Brit.); SWINGER'S PARADISE(1965, Brit.); FIGHTING PRINCE OF DONEGAL, THE(1966, Brit.); PARIS IN THE MONTH OF AUGUST(1968, Fr.); THOSE DARING YOUNG MEN IN THEIR JAUNTY JALOPIES(1969, Fr./Brit./Ital.); TRYGON FACTOR, THE(1969, Brit.); VIOLENT ENEMY, THE(1969, Brit.); DAVID COPPERFIELD(1970, Brit.); LIVING FREE(1972, Brit.); MALPERTIUS(1972, Bel./Fr.); NEITHER THE SEA NOR THE SAND(1974, Brit.)
Stephany Hampson
IT SHOULD HAPPEN TO YOU(1954)
Adrienne Hampton
INDEPENDENCE DAY(1983); PORKY'S II: THE NEXT DAY(1983)
1984
RHINESTONE(1984)
Benjamin B. Hampton
Misc. Silents
MYSTERIOUS RIDER(1921), d; GOLDEN DREAMS(1922), d; HEART'S HA-VEN(1922), d
Bill Hampton
HIDEOUS SUN DEMON, THE(1959)
Bruce Hampton
SAILOR'S LADY(1940)
Christopher Hampton
DOLL'S HOUSE, A(1973), w; BEYOND THE LIMIT(1983), w
Deborra Hampton
TWO OF A KIND(1983)
Edith Hampton
Misc. Silents
WOMAN OF FLESH, A(1927)
Gladys Hampton
Misc. Silents
TANGLED TRAILS(1921)
Grace Hampton
WITHOUT RESERVATIONS(1946); ALMOST MARRIED(1932); UNEXPECTED FA-THER(1932); GIGOLETTE(1935); PICCADILLY JIM(1936); LADY LUCK(1946); DOWN TO EARTH(1947); CAGED(1950); HARVEY(1950)
Silents
PURSUING VENGEANCE, THE(1916)
Grayce Hampton
BAT WHISPERS, THE(1930); BROADMINDED(1931); EX-BAD BOY(1931); SHANG-HAI GESTURE, THE(1941); STANDING ROOM ONLY(1944); HER HIGHNESS AND THE BELLBOY(1945); HOLD THAT BLONDE(1945); MINISTRY OF FEAR(1945); JOHNNY COMES FLYING HOME(1946); EXILE, THE(1947); SILVER RIVER(1948); SITTING PRETTY(1948); SNAKE PIT, THE(1948); GIRL FROM JONES BEACH, THE(1949); KISS IN THE DARK, A(1949); LOVE THAT BRUTE(1950); MATING SEASON, THE(1951); FOREVER FEMALE(1953)
Hope Hampton
ROAD TO RENO, THE(1938); HEY, LET'S TWIST!(1961)
Silents
MODERN SALOME, A(1920); BAIT, THE(1921); LOVE'S PENALTY(1921); STAR-DUST(1921); LIGHT IN THE DARK, THE(1922); GOLD DIGGERS, THE(1923); LAW-FUL LARCENY(1923); PRICE OF A PARTY, THE(1924); LOVER'S ISLAND(1925)
Misc. Silents
DOES IT PAY?(1923); TRUTH ABOUT WOMEN, THE(1924); FIFTY-FIFTY(1925); UNFAIR SEX, THE(1926)
Howard Hampton
SUBMARINE SEAHAWK(1959)
James Hampton
SOLDIER BLUE(1970); HUSTLE(1975); MACKINTOSH & T.J.(1975); W. W. AND THE DIXIE DANCEKINGS(1975); HAWMPS!(1976); CAT FROM OUTER SPACE, THE(1978); CHINA SYNDROME, THE(1979); HANGAR 18(1980); CONDORMAN(1981)

Misc. Talkies
FADE-IN(1968)
Jane Hampton
ONE TOO MANY(1950)
Janice Hampton
ROCKY II(1979), ed; WINDWALKER(1980), ed
Jesse D. Hampton
Silents
END OF THE GAME, THE(1919), d
Misc. Silents
DRIFTERS, THE(1919), d; WHAT EVERY WOMAN WANTS(1919), d
Jim Hampton
LONGEST YARD, THE(1974)
Jimmy R. Hampton
HUSTLE(1975)
Julie Hampton
1984
PROTOCOL(1984)
Kimberley Hampton
DOLL'S HOUSE, A(1973)
Larry Hampton
DUEL AT DIABLO(1966), spec eff; PAINT YOUR WAGON(1969), spec eff; SUPPOSE THEY GAVE A WAR AND NOBODY CAME?(1970), spec eff
Lawrence A. Hampton
SOLDIER IN THE RAIN(1963), spec eff
Lionel Hampton
PENNIES FROM HEAVEN(1936); BENNY GOODMAN STORY, THE(1956); FORCE OF IMPULSE(1961), a, md
Louis Hampton
DANGEROUS CARGO(1939, Brit.)
Louise Hampton
NINE TILL SIX(1932, Brit.); GOODBYE MR. CHIPS(1939, Brit.); HIS LORDSHIP GOES TO PRESS(1939, Brit.); MIDDLE WATCH, THE(1939, Brit.); BUSMAN'S HONEYMOON(1940, Brit.); CASTLE OF CRIMES(1940, Brit.); SAINT MEETS THE TIGER, THE(1943, Brit.); BEDELIA(1946, Brit.); CHRISTMAS CAROL, A(1951, Brit.); FILES FROM SCOTLAND YARD(1951, Brit.); STORY OF ROBIN HOOD, THE(1952, Brit.); BACKGROUND(1953, Brit.); HORSE'S MOUTH, THE(1953, Brit.)
Silents
ELEVENTH COMMANDMENT, THE(1924, Brit.)
Margaret Hampton
Misc. Silents
ARIZONA WHIRLWIND, THE(1927)
Mary Hampton
ULTIMATE THRILL, THE(1974)
Melvin C. Hampton
REVENGE OF THE NINJA(1983)
Myra Hampton
TRIAL OF MARY DUGAN, THE(1929); ONCE A SINNER(1931)
Orville H. Hampton
EXPERIMENT ALCATRAZ(1950), w; RED SNOW(1952), w; SCOTLAND YARD INSPECTOR(1952, Brit.), w; CALYPSO HEAT WAVE(1957), w; BADMAN'S COUNTRY(1958), w; HONG KONG CONFIDENTIAL(1958), w; JET ATTACK(1958), w; ALLIGATOR PEOPLE, THE(1959), w; FOUR SKULLS OF JONATHAN DRAKE, THE(1959), w; INSIDE THE MAFIA(1959), w; RIOT IN JUVENILE PRISON(1959), w; ATOMIC SUBMARINE, THE(1960), w; CAGE OF EVIL(1960), w; DOG'S BEST FRIEND, A(1960), w; GUNFIGHTERS OF ABILENE(1960), w; OKLAHOMA TERRITORY(1960), w; THREE CAME TO KILL(1960), w; YOUNG JESSE JAMES(1960), w; OPERATION BOTTLENECK(1961), w; POLICE DOG STORY, THE(1961), w; SNAKE WOMAN, THE(1961, Brit.), w; YOU HAVE TO RUN FAST(1961), w; JACK THE GIANT KILLER(1962), w; BEAUTY AND THE BEAST(1963), w; ONE POTATO, TWO POTATO(1964), w; RIOT ON SUNSET STRIP(1967), w; TIME TO SING, A(1968), w; YOUNG RUNAWAYS, THE(1968), w
Orville Hampton
HI-JACKED(1950), w; I SHOT BILLY THE KID(1950), w; MOTOR PATROL(1950), w; TRAIN TO TOMBSTONE(1950), w; FINGERPRINTS DON'T LIE(1951), w; LEAVE IT TO THE MARINES(1951), w; MASK OF THE DRAGON(1951), w; THREE DESPERATE MEN(1951), w; JUNGLE, THE(1952), w; OUTLAW WOMEN(1952), w; SKY HIGH(1952), w; FANGS OF THE WILD(1954), w; NEW ORLEANS UNCENSORED(1955), w; BLACK WHIP, THE(1956), w; FRONTIER GAMBLER(1956), w; LAST OF THE DESPERADOES(1956), w; THREE OUTLAWS, THE(1956), w; TOUGHEST GUN IN TOMBSTONE(1958), w; DETROIT 9000(1973), w; FRIDAY FOSTER(1975), w
Paul Hampton
SENIOR PROM(1958); WILD IS MY LOVE(1963); MORE DEAD THAN ALIVE(1968); WUSA(1970); LADY SINGS THE BLUES(1972); PRIVATE DUTY NURSES(1972); HIT(1973); THEY CAME FROM WITHIN(1976, Can.); DIMBOOLA(1979, Aus.); BUTTERFLY(1982)
Raye Hampton
Silents
RAINBOW RANGERS(1924); NORTHERN CODE(1925); ON THE GO(1925); QUICKER'N LIGHTNIN'(1925); GALLOPING GOBS, THE(1927)
Misc. Silents
WESTERN GRIT(1924); CYCLONE COWBOY, THE(1927)
Richard Hampton
OTHELLO(1965, Brit.), m; TERRORISTS, THE(1975, Brit.)
Robert Hampton [Riccardo Freda]
CALTIKI, THE IMMORTAL MONSTER(1959, Ital.), d; HORRIBLE DR. HICHCOCK, THE(1964, Ital.), d; GHOST, THE(1965, Ital.), d
Roger Hampton
NICKELODEON(1976); HALLOWEEN II(1981)
Ruth Hampton
GLENN MILLER STORY, THE(1953); LAW AND ORDER(1953); TAKE ME TO TOWN(1953); JOHNNY DARK(1954); RICOCHET ROMANCE(1954)
Sandra Hampton
MOUSE ON THE MOON, THE(1963, Brit.)
Susie Hampton
Misc. Talkies
FAST KILL(1973)

William J. Hampton
Misc. Talkies
METAMORPHOSIS(1951), d
V. Hamr
MATTER OF DAYS, A(1969, Fr./Czech.), makeup
Burwell Hamrick
Misc. Silents
JOHN ERMINE OF THE YELLOWSTONE(1917); BRUTE BREAKER, THE(1919); THROUGH A GLASS WINDOW(1922)
Abdellatif Hamrouni
1984
MISUNDERSTOOD(1984)
Harry Hamsel
FANTASIA(1940), anim
Max Hamsen
VIENNA, CITY OF SONGS(1931, Ger.)
Renita Hamsher
WOMEN AND BLOODY TERROR(1970)
Keith Hamshere
IN SEARCH OF THE CASTAWAYS(1962, Brit.); PLAY IT COOL(1963, Brit.)
Knut Hamsun
HUNGER(1968, Den./Norway/Swed.), w; SHORT IS THE SUMMER(1968, Swed.), w; MYSTERIES(1979, Neth.), w
Jasmina Hamzavi
ALL NEAT IN BLACK STOCKINGS(1969, Brit.)
Bong Soo Han
TRIAL OF BILLY JACK, THE(1974); FORCE: FIVE(1981)
Master Bong Soo Han
KENTUCKY FRIED MOVIE, THE(1977); LITTLE DRAGONS, THE(1980)
Misc. Talkies
KILL THE GOLDEN GOOSE(1979)
Chin Han
LADY GENERAL, THE(1965, Hong Kong); FEMALE PRINCE, THE(1966, Hong Kong); SACRED KNIVES OF VENGEANCE, THE(1974, Hong Kong)
Chinag Han
CALL HIM MR. SHATTER(1976, Hong Kong)
Hsieh Han
DRAGON INN(1968, Chi.)
Iris Han
PENNY SERENADE(1941)
Joseph Han
DRUMS OF TABU, THE(1967, Ital./Span.)
Otto Han
DAY-TIME WIFE(1939); PENNY SERENADE(1941); TOKYO JOE(1949)
S. Y. Han
MATTER OF INNOCENCE, A(1968, Brit.)
Shirley Han
REVENGE OF THE SHOGUN WOMEN(1982, Taiwan)
Young Hwa Han
BRUBAKER(1980)
Li Han-hsiang
LOVE ETERNE, THE(1964, Hong Kong), d&w; MAGNIFICENT CONCUBINE, THE(1964, Hong Kong), d; EMPRESS WU(1965, Hong Kong), d; ENCHANTING SHADOW, THE(1965, Hong Kong), d
Hajime Hana
ALONE ON THE PACIFIC(1964, Jap.); DON'T CALL ME A CON MAN(1966, Jap.); LAS VEGAS FREE-FOR-ALL(1968, Jap.); COMPUTER FREE-FOR-ALL(1969, Jap.); HOTSPRINGS HOLIDAY(1970, Jap.)
Moki Hana
DEVIL AT FOUR O'CLOCK, THE(1961)
Sonja Hana
OUTPOST IN MALAYA(1952, Brit.)
Sonya Hana
COLONEL MARCH INVESTIGATES(1952,Brit.)
Elko Hanabusa
HOUSE OF BAMBOO(1955)
Sigrid Hanack
INSIDE OUT(1975, Brit.)
Lou Hanagan
HAPPY BIRTHDAY, DAVY(1970), m
Masaaki Hanai
GALAXY EXPRESS(1982, Jap.), ed
Ralph Hanalei
CASTAWAY COWBOY, THE(1974)
Ralph Hanalie
BLUE HAWAII(1961)
Blanche Hanalis
WEDDINGS AND BABIES(1960), w; TROUBLE WITH ANGELS, THE(1966), w; WHERE ANGELS GO...TROUBLE FOLLOWS(1968), w; FROM THE MIXED-UP FILES OF MRS. BASIL E. FRANKWEILER(1973), w; FISH HAWK(1981, Can.), w
Stephen Hanan
PIRATES OF PENZANCE, THE(1983)
Charles Hanawalt
HARD RIDE, THE(1971), p
Joseph Hanaway
Misc. Silents
DEAD LINE, THE(1920)
Yoshiaki Hanayagi
SANSHO THE BAILIFF(1969, Jap.)
Tokue Hanazawa
RED LION(1971, Jap.)
Jack Hanbury
FLAME IN THE STREETS(1961, Brit.), p; LIVE NOW–PAY LATER(1962, Brit.), p; THIS IS MY STREET(1964, Brit.), p; THREE HATS FOR LISA(1965, Brit.), p; GYPSY GIRL(1966, Brit.), p
Maie Hanbury
Misc. Silents
SINS YE DO, THE(1924, Brit.)

Victor Hanbury
BEGGAR STUDENT, THE(1931,Brit.), d; WHERE IS THIS LADY?(1932, Brit.), d; DICK TURPIN(1933, Brit.), d; NO FUNNY BUSINESS(1934, Brit.), d, w; SPRING IN THE AIR(1934, Brit.), d&w; ADMIRALS ALL(1935, Brit.), d; AVENGING HAND, THE(1936, Brit.), d; BALL AT SAVOY(1936, Brit.), d; BELOVED IMPOSTER(1936, Brit.), d; SECOND BUREAU(1937, Brit.), d; IT HAPPENED TO ONE MAN(1941, Brit.), p; ESCAPE TO DANGER(1943, Brit.), d; SQUADRON LEADER X(1943, Brit.), p; GREAT DAY(1945, Brit.), p; HOTEL RESERVE(1946, Brit.), p, d; DAUGHTER OF DARKNESS(1948, Brit.), p; DEATM GOES TO SCHOOL(1953, Brit.), p; GLAD TIDINGS(1953, Brit.), p; LARGE ROPE, THE(1953, Brit.), p; NOOSE FOR A LADY(1953, Brit.), p; RIVER BEAT(1954), p

Victor Hanbury [Joseph Losey]
SLEEPING TIGER, THE(1954, Brit.), p&d

W. Victor Hanbury
SCANDALS OF PARIS(1935, Brit.), p,d&w; FACE BEHIND THE SCAR(1940, Brit.), d

Diana Hance
TROPICAL TROUBLE(1936, Brit.)

Edith Hancke
COURT MARTIAL(1962, Ger.)

Barbara Hancock
FINIAN'S RAINBOW(1968); NIGHT GOD SCREAMED, THE(1975)

David Hancock
PUNISHMENT PARK(1971), art d

Eleanor Hancock
Silents
KISS FOR SUSIE, A(1917); LITTLE COMRADE(1919); JILT, THE(1922)
Misc. Silents
CAVE GIRL, THE(1921); TIGER TRUE(1921)

Elinor Hancock
Silents
MIDNIGHT ROMANCE, A(1919); SPLENDID SIN, THE(1919); OUT OF THE STORM(1920); NOT GUILTY(1921); RAGE OF PARIS, THE(1921); ROOKIE'S RETURN, THE(1921); COME ON OVER(1922); OUT OF LUCK(1923)
Misc. Silents
SPIRIT OF ROMANCE, THE(1917); BARBARIAN, THE(1921); FIGHTING LOVER, THE(1921)

Mrs. H. R. Hancock
Silents
MR. FIX-IT(1918)

Herbert Hancock
Silents
LEECH, THE(1921), d

Herbie Hancock
BLOW-UP(1966, Brit.), m; SPOOK WHO SAT BY THE DOOR, THE(1973), m; DEATH WISH(1974), m
1984
SOLDIER'S STORY, A(1984), m

Hunter Hancock
ROCK AROUND THE WORLD(1957, Brit.)

John Hancock
BROTHER JOHN(1971); LET'S SCARE JESSICA TO DEATH(1971), d; BANG THE DRUM SLOWLY(1973), d; BABY BLUE MARINE(1976), d; FOUL PLAY(1978); CALIFORNIA DREAMING(1979), d; IN-LAWS, THE(1979); 10(1979); BLACK MARBLE, THE(1980); FIRST FAMILY(1980); ...ALL THE MARBLES(1981); AIRPLANE II: THE SEQUEL(1982); STING II, THE(1983)
1984
CITY HEAT(1984); SOLDIER'S STORY, A(1984); TANK(1984)

Lou Hancock
EDDIE MACON'S RUN(1983)
1984
PLACES IN THE HEART(1984)

Lynn Hancock
EVILSPEAK(1982)

Michael Hancock
DELIVERANCE(1972), makeup

Mike Hancock
SEPARATE PEACE, A(1972), makeup; SCOTT JOPLIN(1977), makeup

Peter Hancock
TERROR ABOARD(1933); CAR 99(1935); WINGS IN THE DARK(1935)

Prentis Hancock
THIRTY NINE STEPS, THE(1978, Brit.)

Sheila Hancock
BULLDOG BREED, THE(1960, Brit.); LIGHT UP THE SKY(1960, Brit.); GIRL ON THE BOAT, THE(1962, Brit.); TWICE AROUND THE DAFFODILS(1962, Brit.); CARRY ON CLEO(1964, Brit.); MOON-SPINNERS, THE(1964); NIGHT MUST FALL(1964, Brit.); HOW I WON THE WAR(1967, Brit.); ANNIVERSARY, THE(1968, Brit.); TAKE A GIRL LIKE YOU(1970, Brit,); WILDCATS OF ST. TRINIAN'S, THE(1980, Brit.)

Tony Hancock
ORDERS ARE ORDERS(1959, Brit.); CALL ME GENIUS(1961, Brit.), a, w; PUNCH AND JUDY MAN, THE(1963, Brit.), a, w; THOSE MAGNIFICENT MEN IN THEIR FLYING MACHINES; OR HOW I FLEWFROM LONDON TO PARIS IN 25 HOURS AND 11 MINUTES(1965, Brit.); WRONG BOX, THE(1966, Brit.)

Wladyslaw Hancza
GUESTS ARE COMING(1965, Pol.)

Charles Hand
ALL I DESIRE(1953)

Chip Hand
WILD McCULLOCHS, THE(1975)
1984
LOVELINES(1984), w

Danelle Hand
CAT PEOPLE(1982)

David D. Hand
BAMBI(1942), p

David Hand
SNOW WHITE AND THE SEVEN DWARFS(1937), d

Frederic W. Hand
KRAMER VS. KRAMER(1979)

Frederick Hand
Misc. Silents
MILLIONAIRE BABY, THE(1915)

Herman Hand
FIGHTING CARAVANS(1931), m; FAREWELL TO ARMS, A(1932), m

Irene Hand
YOU MUST BE JOKING!(1965, Brit.)

W. Victor Handbury
CROUCHING BEAST, THE(1936, U. S./Brit.), d

George Frederick Handel
FINAL CHORD, THE(1936, Ger.), m
1984
WHITE ELEPHANT(1984, Brit.), m

George Frederik Handel
TESTAMENT OF ORPHEUS, THE(1962, Fr.), m

Leo A. Handel
CASE OF PATTY SMITH, THE(1962), p,d&w

Wolfram Handel
NAKED AMONG THE WOLVES(1967, Ger.)

Linda Handelman
MEDIUM COOL(1969)

Stanley Myron Handelman
HARVEY MIDDLEMAN, FIREMAN(1965)

Leslie Handford
MY BROTHER'S KEEPER(1949, Brit.)

Peter Handford
KEY, THE(1958, Brit.), makeup

Gordon Handforth
ESCAPE FROM ALCATRAZ(1979)

Lucy Handforth
Silents
MIND OVER MOTOR(1923)

Ruth Handforth
Silents
INTOLERANCE(1916); LITTLE LIAR, THE(1916); LONG LIVE THE KING(1923)
Misc. Silents
SIREN'S SONG, THE(1919)

Peter Handke
LEFT-HANDED WOMAN, THE(1980, Ger.), d&w

Irene Handl
MISSING, BELIEVED MARRIED(1937, Brit.); STRANGE BOARDERS(1938, Brit.); MRS. PYM OF SCOTLAND YARD(1939, Brit.); DR. O'DOWD(1940, Brit.); FUGITIVE, THE(1940, Brit.); GASBAGS(1940, Brit.); GEORGE AND MARGARET(1940, Brit.); NIGHT TRAIN(1940, Brit.); GIRL IN THE NEWS, THE(1941, Brit.); FLEMISH FARM, THE(1943, Brit.); GET CRACKING(1943, Brit.); I'LL WALK BESIDE YOU(1943, Brit.); IT'S IN THE BAG(1943, Brit.); MILLIONS LIKE US(1943, Brit.); RHYTHM SERENADE(1943, Brit.); GIVE US THE MOON(1944, Brit.); KISS THE BRIDE GOODBYE(1944, Brit.); UNCENSORED(1944, Brit.); WELCOME, MR. WASHINGTON(1944, Brit.); BRIEF ENCOUNTER(1945, Brit.); FOR YOU ALONE(1945, Brit.); GREAT DAY(1945, Brit.); MR. EMMANUEL(1945, Brit.); RANDOLPH FAMILY, THE(1945, Brit.); SPELL OF AMY NUGENT, THE(1945, Brit.); GAY INTRUDERS, THE(1946, Brit.); I'LL TURN TO YOU(1946, Brit.); HILLS OF DONEGAL, THE(1947, Brit.); CODE OF SCOTLAND YARD)(1948, Brit.); FOOL AND THE PRINCESS, THE(1948, Brit.); CARDBOARD CAVALIER, THE(1949, Brit.); DARK SECRET(1949, Brit.); FOR THEM THAT TRESPASS(1949, Brit.); HER MAN GILBEY(1949, Brit.); HISTORY OF MR. POLLY, THE(1949, Brit.); SILENT DUST(1949, Brit.); TEMPTATION HARBOR(1949, Brit.); ADAM AND EVELYNE(1950, Brit.); PERFECT WOMAN, THE(1950, Brit.); STAGE FRIGHT(1950, Brit.); ONE WILD OAT(1951, Brit.); TREASURE HUNT(1952, Brit.); MEET MR. LUCIFER(1953, Brit.); MR. POTTS GOES TO MOSCOW(1953, Brit.); WEDDING OF LILLI MARLENE, THE(1953, Brit.); BURNT EVIDENCE(1954, Brit.); DUEL IN THE JUNGLE(1954, Brit.); MAD ABOUT MEN(1954, Brit.); WEAK AND THE WICKED, THE(1954, Brit.); YOUNG WIVES' TALE(1954, Brit.); KID FOR TWO FARTHINGS, A(1956, Brit.); WHO DONE IT?(1956, Brit.); BROTHERS IN LAW(1957, Brit.); SILKEN AFFAIR, THE(1957, Brit.); SMALL HOTEL(1957, Brit.); HAPPY IS THE BRIDE(1958, Brit.); IT'S NEVER TOO LATE(1958, Brit.); KEY, THE(1958, Brit.); LAW AND DISORDER(1958, Brit.); CROWNING TOUCH, THE(1959, Brit.); I'M ALL RIGHT, JACK(1959, Brit.); LEFT, RIGHT AND CENTRE(1959); CARRY ON CONSTABLE(1960, Brit.); DESERT MICE(1960, Brit.); DOCTOR IN LOVE(1960, Brit.); FRENCH MISTRESS(1960, Brit.); INN FOR TROUBLE(1960, Brit.); MAKE MINE MINK(1960, Brit.); MAN IN A COCKED HAT(1960, Bri.); NEXT TO NO TIME(1960, Brit.); SCHOOL FOR SCOUNDRELS(1960, Brit.); BEWARE OF CHILDREN(1961, Brit.); CALL ME GENIUS(1961, Brit.); DOUBLE BUNK(1961, Brit.); NIGHT WE GOT THE BIRD, THE(1961, Brit.); NOTHING BARRED(1961, Brit.); PURE HELL OF ST. TRINIAN'S, THE(1961, Brit.); TWO-WAY STRETCH(1961, Brit.); UPSTAIRS AND DOWNSTAIRS(1961, Brit.); WATCH IT, SAILOR!(1961, Brit.); WEEKEND WITH LULU, A(1961, Brit.); MAKE MINE A DOUBLE(1962, Brit.); HEAVENS ABOVE!(1963, Brit.); JUST FOR FUN(1963, Brit.); MORGAN!(1966, Brit.); WRONG BOX, THE(1966, Brit.); SMASHING TIME(1967 Brit.); LIONHEART(1968, Brit.); MINI-AFFAIR, THE(1968, Brit.); ITALIAN JOB, THE(1969, Brit.); WONDERWALL(1969, Brit.); DOCTOR IN TROUBLE(1970, Brit.); ON A CLEAR DAY YOU CAN SEE FOREVER(1970); PRIVATE LIFE OF SHERLOCK HOLMES, THE(1970, Brit.); LAST REMAKE OF BEAU GESTE, THE(1977); STAND UP VIRGIN SOLDIERS(1977, Brit.); HOUND OF THE BASKERVILLES, THE(1980, Brit.)

Edward Handler
KEEP 'EM SLUGGING(1943), w

Evan Handler
TAPS(1981); DEAR MR. WONDERFUL(1983, Ger.)

Ken Handler
1984
DELIVERY BOYS(1984), d&w
Misc. Talkies
PLACE WITHOUT PARENTS, A(1974), d; TRUCKIN'(1975), d

Dorthy Curnow Handley
ROSIE THE RIVETER(1944), w

Jim Handley
FANTASIA(1940), d; RELUCTANT DRAGON, THE(1941), cartoon d

Thomas Handley
ON THE WATERFRONT(1954)

Tom Handley
UNKNOWN WORLD(1951)
Tommy Handley
IT'S THAT MAN AGAIN(1943, Brit.); TIME FLIES(1944, Brit.)
W.H. Handley
DEVIL'S BEDROOM, THE(1964)
Toby Handman
NOCTURNA(1979)
Wanda Handrix
STAGE TO THUNDER ROCK(1964)
Dita Hands
INNOCENTS IN PARIS(1955, Brit.)
Richard Handwerk
QUESTION 7(1961, U.S./Ger.)
Harry Handworth
Silents
TOLL OF MAMON(1914), d&w; ARTIE, THE MILLIONAIRE KID(1916), d; QUESTION, THE(1916), d
Misc. Silents
WHEN FATE LEADS TRUMP(1914), d; IN THE SHADOW(1915), a, d
Octavia Handworth
Silents
TOLL OF MAMON(1914)
Misc. Silents
PATH FORBIDDEN, THE(1914); WHEN FATE LEADS TRUMP(1914); GREAT RUBY, THE(1915); IN THE SHADOW(1915); CITY OF FAILING LIGHT, THE(1916); RACE SUICIDE(1916); FOOTLIGHTS(1921)
Bill Handy
WINDOWS(1980)
James Handy
TAPS(1981); VERDICT, THE(1982)
W. C. Handy
ST. LOUIS BLUES(1958), w
Clarence Handyside
Silents
JUNGLE, THE(1914); ONE OF OUR GIRLS(1914)
Clarence Handysides
Silents
MICE AND MEN(1916); ROSE OF THE WORLD(1918)
Misc. Silents
HIS PICTURE IN THE PAPERS(1916); SAINTS AND SINNERS(1916); SALESLADY, THE(1916); SILKS AND SATINS(1916)
Jan Handzlik
AUNTIE MAME(1958)
Yukiyoshi Hane
1984
WARRIORS OF THE WIND(1984, Jap.), anim
Kentaro Haneda
NUTCRACKER FANTASY(1979), m; TIME SLIP(1981, Jap.), m
H.W. Hanemann
ACE OF ACES(1933), w; FLYING DOWN TO RIO(1933), w; NO MARRIAGE TIES(1933), w; SWEEPINGS(1933), w; MEANEST GAL IN TOWN, THE(1934), w; RAFTER ROMANCE(1934), w; OLD MAN RHYTHM(1935), w; SILVER STREAK, THE(1935), w; SPRING TONIC(1935), w; HOUSE OF A THOUSAND CANDLES, THE(1936), w; RIFF-RAFF(1936), w; CADET GIRL(1941), w; TAHITI HONEY(1943), w
Allison Hanes
Misc. Talkies
LONE STAR COUNTRY(1983)
Anne Haney
HOPSCOTCH(1980); NIGHT THE LIGHTS WENT OUT IN GEORGIA, THE(1981); FRANCES(1982); SOME KIND OF HERO(1982); INDEPENDENCE DAY(1983); OSTERMAN WEEKEND, THE(1983)
1984
IMPULSE(1984)
Bette Jean Haney
DINKY(1935)
Betty Jean Haney
MARY JANE'S PA(1935)
Beverly Haney
SUSPENSE(1946)
Carol Haney
WONDER MAN(1945); ON THE TOWN(1949); SUMMER STOCK(1950); KISS ME KATE(1953); PAJAMA GAME, THE(1957)
Darel Haney
SIEGE(1983, Can.)
David Haney
SENIORS, THE(1978); RESURRECTION(1980); HARD COUNTRY(1981); UNDER THE RAINBOW(1981)
Dorothy Haney
TERROR OF THE BLOODHUNTERS(1962)
John Haney
THAT'S THE WAY OF THE WORLD(1975)
Kevin Haney
BASKET CASE(1982), spec eff
Paul Haney
CURSE OF THE LIVING CORPSE, THE(1964); CROSS AND THE SWITCHBLADE, THE(1970)
Sonja Haney
WALK, DON'T RUN(1966); DOCTOR DETROIT(1983)
Joan Hanfling
SAVAGES(1972), cos
Alec Hanford
Hl BEAUTIFUL(1944)
Ray Hanford
ROSE BOWL(1936); THUNDER TRAIL(1937)
Misc. Silents
HELL'S CRATER(1918); WOLF BLOOD(1925)

Ruth Hanforth
Silents
ATOM, THE(1918)
Helen Hanft
NEXT STOP, GREENWICH VILLAGE(1976); MANHATTAN(1979); STARDUST MEMORIES(1980); WILLIE AND PHIL(1980); ARTHUR(1981); HONKY TONK FREEWAY(1981)
Jules Hanft
Silents
KID, THE(1921); ABRAHAM LINCOLN(1924)
Karl Hanft
SPESSART INN, THE(1961, Ger.)
Tham Thuy Hang
S.T.A.B.(1976, Hong Kong/Thailand)
Johann Hange
WHALERS, THE(1942, Swed.)
Ian Hanham
GREAT MUPPET CAPER, THE(1981)
Nellie Hanham
LONG AGO, TOMORROW(1971, Brit.)
Nelly Hanham
GIRL HUNTERS, THE(1963, Brit.)
Joene Hanhardt
THIEF(1981)
Susumu Hani
SHE AND HE(1967, Jap.), d, w
Frank Hanilton
TRUE STORY OF ESKIMO NELL, THE(1975, Aus.)
Don Hanin
IN A LONELY PLACE(1950)
Israel Hanin
FAITHFUL CITY(1952, Israel)
Pierre Hanin
PIERROT LE FOU(1968, Fr./Ital.)
Roger Hanin
BREATHLESS(1959, Fr.); CAT, THE(1959, Fr.); TAMANGO(1959, Fr.); NIGHT AFFAIR(1961, Fr.); ROCCO AND HIS BROTHERS(1961, Fr./Ital.); DEADLY DECOYS, THE(1962, Fr.), w; RIFF RAFF GIRLS(1962, Fr./Ital.); THEY CAME TO ROB LAS VEGAS(1969, Fr./Ital./Span./Ger.); REVENGERS, THE(1972, U.S./Mex.); NO WAY OUT(1975, Ital./Fr.)
Misc. Talkies
OUR MEN IN BAGHDAD(1967, Ital.)
Gary Hanisch
NORTHERN LIGHTS(1978)
Betty Hanisee
PEER GYNT(1965)
Hank Caldwell and his Saddle Kings
LAWLESS RIDER, THE(1954)
Kunu Hank
TOM SAWYER(1973)
Hank the Dog
Silents
SHIELD OF HONOR, THE(1927)
Charles Hankel
TODAY I HANG(1942), ed
Charles Hankel, Jr.
RETURN OF THE RANGERS, THE(1943), ed
Barry Hankerson
PIPE DREAMS(1976)
Tom Hankerson
Misc. Talkies
CANDY TANGERINE MAN, THE(1975)
Hall Hankett
SECRET HEART, THE(1946)
Anthony Hankey
MATINEE IDOL(1933, Brit.); GET OFF MY FOOT(1935, Brit.); MY HEART IS CALLING(1935, Brit.); TEMPTATION(1935, Brit.); SHOW FLAT(1936, Brit.); TWO ON A DOORSTEP(1936, Brit.); MAN WHO MADE DIAMONDS, THE(1937, Brit.), w; QUIET PLEASE(1938, Brit.), w; SIMPLY TERRIFIC(1938, Brit.), w; TOO DANGEROUS TO LIVE(1939, Brit.), d
Harry Hankin
LOVE AND DEATH(1975)
Kathryne Hankin
WORDS AND MUSIC(1929)
Larry Hankin
FUNNYMAN(1967); HOW SWEET IT IS(1968); VIVA MAX!(1969); PHYNX, THE(1970); THUMB TRIPPING(1972); STEELYARD BLUES(1973); ESCAPE FROM ALCATRAZ(1979); DIE LAUGHING(1980); ANNIE(1982); STAR CHAMBER, THE(1983); STING II, THE(1983)
Misc. Talkies
LUCIFER'S WOMEN(1978)
St. John Hankin
Silents
NOT QUITE A LADY(1928, Brit.), w
Brian Hankins
CIRCLE OF DECEPTON(1961, Brit.); DR. TERROR'S HOUSE OF HORRORS(1965, Brit.)
Peter Hankins
SAVAGE(1962)
Hank Hankinson
KID GALAHAD(1937)
Michael Hankinson
CRIME ON THE HILL(1933, Brit.), w; BROKEN MELODY, THE(1934, Brit.), w; GIRLS PLEASE!(1934, Brit.), w; TEN MINUTE ALIBI(1935, Brit.), w; CHICK(1936, Brit.), d; HOUSE BROKEN(1936, Brit.), d; SCARAB MURDER CASE, THE(1936, Brit.), d; TICKET OF LEAVE(1936, Brit.), d, w; COMMAND PERFORMANCE(1937, Brit.), w; HIDEOUT IN THE ALPS(1938, Brit.), w

Hank Hankison
INVITATION TO HAPPINESS(1939)
Howard Hanks
INDIANAPOLIS SPEEDWAY(1939), w
Michael Hanks
1984
NIGHT OF THE COMET(1984)
Steve Hanks
ISLAND CLAWS(1981)
Tom Hanks
HE KNOWS YOU'RE ALONE(1980)
1984
SPLASH(1984)
Wade Hanks
1984
EYES OF FIRE(1984), ph
Ted Hanlan
1984
POLICE ACADEMY(1984)
Bill Hanley
GRAND PRIX(1966), w
Brendon Hanley
SECRET PLACE, THE(1958, Brit.)
Bridget Hanley
1984
CHATTANOOGA CHOO CHOO(1984)
Clifford Hanley
WHY BOTHER TO KNOCK(1964, Brit.), w
Daniel P. Hanley
NIGHT SHIFT(1982), ed
1984
SPLASH(1984), ed
David Hanley
FLASH THE SHEEPDOG(1967, Brit.)
Dell Hanley
TOP BANANA(1954)
Eddie Hanley
PORTRAIT OF A MOBSTER(1961)
Frank Hanley
BIG TIP OFF, THE(1955); LAS VEGAS SHAKEDOWN(1955)
Gerald Hanley
BLUE MAX, THE(1966), w; LAST SAFARI, THE(1967, Brit.), w
Jack Hanley
ROOGIE'S BUMP(1954), w; MISSILE FROM HELL(1960, Brit.), w
James Hanley
FOX MOVIETONE FOLLIES OF 1930(1930), m
James F. Hanley
BLAZE O' GLORY(1930), m
Silents
SECOND HAND ROSE(1922), w
Jennie Hanley
DEVIL'S WIDOW, THE(1972, Brit.)
Jenny Hanley
JOANNA(1968, Brit.); ON HER MAJESTY'S SECRET SERVICE(1969, Brit.); SCARS OF DRACULA, THE(1970, Brit.); FLESH AND BLOOD SHOW, THE(1974, Brit.); ALFIE DARLING(1975, Brit.); UNDERCOVERS HERO(1975, Brit.)
Jimmy Hanley
LITTLE FRIEND(1934, Brit.); THOSE WERE THE DAYS(1934, Brit.); BORN FOR GLORY(1935, Brit.); REGAL CAVALCADE(1935, Brit.); TRANSATLANTIC TUNNEL(1935, Brit.); BOYS WILL BE BOYS(1936, Brit.); RED WAGON(1936); COTTON QUEEN(1937, Brit.); LANDSLIDE(1937, Brit.); NIGHT RIDE(1937, Brit.); COMING OF AGE(1938, Brit.); HOUSEMASTER(1938, Brit.); THERE AIN'T NO JUSTICE(1939, Brit.); GASLIGHT(1940); SALUTE JOHN CITIZEN(1942, Brit.); GENTLE SEX, THE(1943, Brit.); KISS THE BRIDE GOODBYE(1944, Brit.); FOR YOU ALONE(1945, Brit.); QUERY(1945, Brit.); WAY AHEAD, THE(1945, Brit.); HENRY V(1946, Brit.); MURDER IN REVERSE(1946, Brit.); HOLIDAY CAMP(1947, Brit.); MASTER OF BANKDAM, THE(1947, Brit.); CAPTIVE HEART, THE(1948, Brit.); HERE COME THE HUGGETTS(1948, Brit.); BOYS IN BROWN(1949, Brit.); DON'T EVER LEAVE ME(1949, Brit.); FACTS OF LOVE(1949, Brit.); HUGGETTS ABROAD, THE(1949, Brit.); IT ALWAYS RAINS ON SUNDAY(1949, Brit.); ROOM TO LET(1949, Brit.); BLUE LAMP, THE(1950, Brit.); IT'S HARD TO BE GOOD(1950, Brit.); GALLOPING MAJOR, THE(1951, Brit.); BLACK RIDER, THE(1954, Brit.); RADIO CAB MURDER(1954, Brit.); DEEP BLUE SEA, THE(1955, Brit.); SATELLITE IN THE SKY(1956); LOST CONTINENT, THE(1968, Brit.)
Katie Hanley
GODSPELL(1973); XANADU(1980)
Leo Hanley
HAPPY DAYS(1930)
Robert Hanley
PRIVATE BENJAMIN(1980)
William Hanley
GYPSY MOTHS, THE(1969), w
Maurice Hanline
LOTTERY LOVER(1935), w; ONE RAINY AFTERNOON(1936), w; IT'S LOVE I'M AFTER(1937), w; FOUR WIVES(1939), w; STEEL AGAINST THE SKY(1941), w
Alma Hanlon
Silents
KEEP MOVING(1915); FINAL CURTAIN, THE(1916)
Misc. Silents
DEVIL'S PRAYER-BOOK, THE(1916); FADED FLOWER, THE(1916); GOLD AND THE WOMAN(1916); WILD OATS(1916); GOD OF LITTLE CHILDREN(1917); GOLDEN GOD, THE(1917); GREAT BRADLEY MYSTERY, THE(1917); LAW THAT FAILED, THE(1917); MYSTIC HOUR, THE(1917); PUBLIC DEFENDER(1917); WHIP, THE(1917); SINS OF THE CHILDREN(1918); WHEN YOU AND I WERE YOUNG(1918); PROFITEER, THE(1919)
Bert Hanlon
CITY STREETS(1931); SURRENDER(1931); FAMOUS FERGUSON CASE, THE(1932); GOLDEN WEST, THE(1932); ME AND MY GAL(1932); SOCIETY GIRL(1932); TOO BUSY TO WORK(1932); TRIAL OF VIVIENNE WARE, THE(1932); MY WEAKNESS(1933), w; SAILOR'S LUCK(1933), w; EVERY NIGHT AT EIGHT(1935), w; FARMER TAKES A WIFE, THE(1935); MARY BURNS, FUGITIVE(1935); TWO FOR TONIGHT(1935); WINGS IN THE DARK(1935); BIG BROWN EYES(1936), w; GREAT ZIEGFELD, THE(1936); SPENDTHRIFT(1936), w; STRAIGHT FROM THE SHOULDER(1936); DOUBLE OR NOTHING(1937); PARK AVENUE LOGGER(1937); AMAZING DR. CLITTERHOUSE, THE(1938); BOY MEETS GIRL(1938); NAUGHTY BUT NICE(1939); ROARING TWENTIES, THE(1939); SWEEPSTAKES WINNER(1939); INVISIBLE STRIPES(1940); LADY OF BURLESQUE(1943); HIGH WALL, THE(1947); DECISION OF CHRISTOPHER BLAKE, THE(1948); FORCE OF EVIL(1948); FIGHTING FOOLS(1949); GREAT SINNER, THE(1949)
Brooke Hanlon
Silents
IT MUST BE LOVE(1926), w
Dan Hanlon
Misc. Silents
GREAT PROBLEM, THE(1916)
Jack Hanlon
SHAKEDOWN, THE(1929); WAGON MASTER, THE(1929)
Jackie Hanlon
HIDE-OUT, THE(1930); PARADE OF THE WEST(1930)
Roy Hanlon
VULTURE, THE(1967, U.S./Brit./Can.)
Thomas Hanlon
GIFT OF GAB(1934)
Tom Hanlon
MAYBE IT'S LOVE(1930); NIGHT ALARM(1935); MILKY WAY, THE(1936); NAVY BLUE AND GOLD(1937); KENTUCKY MOONSHINE(1938); LADY'S FROM KENTUCKY, THE(1939); HEROES OF THE SADDLE(1940); CRACKED NUTS(1941); HARMON OF MICHIGAN(1941); HERE COMES MR. JORDAN(1941); HOME IN WYOMIN'(1942); RIDE 'EM COWBOY(1942); IT AIN'T HAY(1943); FOLLOW THE BOYS(1944); EVE KNEW HER APPLES(1945); IT'S A PLEASURE(1945); WOMAN IN THE WINDOW, THE(1945); DOWN TO EARTH(1947); FATHER WAS A FULLBACK(1949); IT HAPPENS EVERY SPRING(1949); UNDERCOVER MAN, THE(1949); I'LL GET BY(1950); RIGHT CROSS(1950); TO PLEASE A LADY(1950); GUY WHO CAME BACK, THE(1951); HOLD THAT LINE(1952); LOVE IS BETTER THAN EVER(1952); PRIDE OF ST. LOUIS, THE(1952); JALOPY(1953); WHITE LIGHTNING(1953)
Don Hanmer
SPECIAL DELIVERY(1955, Ger.); COUNTERFEIT KILLER, THE(1968); PAPILLON(1973); ST. IVES(1976)
Ronald Hanmer
MADE IN HEAVEN(1952, Brit.), m
Ryo Hanmura
TIME SLIP(1981, Jap.), w
Gisela Hann
ERNESTO(1979, Ital.)
Gordon Hann
ACCEPTABLE LEVELS(1983, Brit.), w
Joseph Hann
KRAKATOA, EAST OF JAVA(1969)
Hanna
ANCHORS AWEIGH(1945)
Betty Hanna
MAN'S FAVORITE SPORT(?) (1964); CATTLE QUEEN OF MONTANA(1954); HOW COME NOBODY'S ON OUR SIDE?(1975)
Billy Hanna
LIAR'S MOON(1982), w
Emil Hanna
TRIPOLI(1950)
Franklin Hanna
Silents
KIDNAPPED(1917); AMERICAN WAY, THE(1919)
Franklyn Hanna
Silents
MY LADY INCOG(1916); DOING THEIR BIT(1918); JUST SYLVIA(1918)
Misc. Silents
UPHEAVAL, THE(1916); RICHARD THE BRAZEN(1917); WEB OF DECEIT, THE(1920)
Henry Hanna
CAPTAINS COURAGEOUS(1937); LOVE IS ON THE AIR(1937)
Mark Hanna
BORDER SADDLEMATES(1952); FLIGHT TO TANGIER(1953); KING RICHARD AND THE CRUSADERS(1954); CHICAGO SYNDICATE(1955); FIVE AGAINST THE HOUSE(1955); MAN WITHOUT A STAR(1955); PIRATES OF TRIPOLI(1955); GUNSLINGER(1956), w; AMAZING COLOSSAL MAN, THE(1957), w; FLESH AND THE SPUR(1957), w; NAKED PARADISE(1957), w; NOT OF THIS EARTH(1957), w; UNDEAD, THE(1957), w; ATTACK OF THE 50 FOOT WOMAN(1958), w; JET ATTACK(1958), w; RAYMIE(1960), w; CHIVATO(1961), w; REBELLION IN CUBA(1961), w; GATLING GUN, THE(1972), w; SLAUGHTER(1972), w
Mary Hanna
SOUTHWEST PASSAGE(1954)
Phil Hanna
THRILL OF A ROMANCE(1945)
Sam Hanna
ROPE OF FLESH(1965)
William Hanna
DANGEROUS WHEN WET(1953), anim; INVITATION TO THE DANCE(1956), anim.; HEY THERE, IT'S YOGI BEAR(1964), p&d, w; MAN CALLED FLINTSTONE, THE(1966), p&d, w; PROJECT X(1968), p; CHARLOTTE'S WEB(1973), p; HEIDI'S SONG(1982), p
Dan P. Hannafin
SHAFT'S BIG SCORE(1972)
Daniel P. Hannafin
1984
LONELY GUY, THE(1984)
David Hannaford
LAST LOAD, THE(1948, Brit.); NOW BARABBAS WAS A ROBBER(1949, Brit.); DRAGON OF PENDRAGON CASTLE, THE(1950, Brit.); SECOND MATE, THE(1950, Brit.); CASTLE IN THE AIR(1952, Brit.); PICKWICK PAPERS, THE(1952, Brit.); I BELIEVE IN YOU(1953, Brit.); EIGHT O'CLOCK WALK(1954, Brit.); END OF THE ROAD, THE(1954, Brit.); FLYING EYE, THE(1955, Brit.); ONE JUMP AHEAD(1955,

Brit.); EXTRA DAY, THE(1956, Brit.); JUMPING FOR JOY(1956, Brit.); MY SON, THE VAMPIRE(1963, Brit.)

Pinkie Hannaford
WILLIAM COMES TO TOWN(1948, Brit.)

Bob E. Hannah
NORMA RAE(1979)

Bob Hannah
CARNY(1980); COAL MINER'S DAUGHTER(1980); JAWS OF SATAN(1980); LOVE-LESS, THE(1982); SIX PACK(1982); THRESHOLD(1983, Can.)
1984
TANK(1984)

Daryl Hannah
HARD COUNTRY(1981); BLADE RUNNER(1982); SUMMER LOVERS(1982); FINAL TERROR, THE(1983)
1984
POPE OF GREENWICH VILLAGE, THE(1984); RECKLESS(1984); SPLASH(1984)
Misc. Talkies
CAMPSITE MASSACRE(1981)

Don Hannah
1984
NIGHTMARE ON ELM STREET, A(1984)

Dorothy Hannah
BRASHER DOUBLOON, THE(1947), w

Duncan Hannah
FOREIGNER, THE(1978)

James Hannah, Jr.
DARK PLACES(1974, Brit.), p

Jo-Anne Hannah
CURTAINS(1983, Can.)

Linde Hannah
ALL BY MYSELF(1943), w

Page Hannah
ON THE RIGHT TRACK(1981)
1984
RACING WITH THE MOON(1984)

Richard Hannah
STAR CHAMBER, THE(1983), ph

Robert Hannah
HOUSE BY THE LAKE, THE(1977, Can.), stunts; RUNNING(1979, Can.)

Truck Hannah
FAST COMPANY(1929)
Silents
WARMING UP(1928)

John Hannahan
COOL AND THE CRAZY, THE(1958)

Ken Hannam
SUNDAY TOO FAR AWAY(1975, Aus.), d; BREAK OF DAY(1977, Aus.), d; SUM-MERFIELD(1977, Aus.), d; DAWN(1979, Aus.), d

Brian Hannan
DEAD MAN'S FLOAT(1980, Aus.)

Chester W. Hannan
SHANE(1953)

Nicolas Hannan
PRIME MINISTER, THE(1941, Brit.)

Peter Hannan
FULL CIRCLE(1977, Brit./Can.), ph; STUD, THE(1979, Brit.), ph; MOON OVER THE ALLEY(1980, Brit.), ph; BRIMSTONE AND TREACLE(1982, Brit.), ph; MISSIONARY, THE(1982), ph; MONTY PYTHON'S THE MEANING OF LIFE(1983, Brit.), ph
1984
RAZOR'S EDGE, THE(1984), ph

Brian Hannat
THREE TO GO(1971,Aus.), d&w; ROAD WARRIOR, THE(1982, Aus.), w

Charles Hannawalt
DEMENTIA 13(1963), p, ph

David Hannay
SOLO(1978, New Zealand/Aus.), p

Pat Hanne
HAPPY DAYS(1930)

Peggy Hanneasey
RETURN OF THE FROG, THE(1938, Brit.), ed

Grace Hanneford
NORTHWEST TRAIL(1945); RED PONY, THE(1949)

Poodles Hanneford
CIRCUS KID, THE(1928); CIRCUS CLOWN(1934); OUR LITTLE GIRL(1935); NORTH-WEST TRAIL(1945); SAN ANTONIO(1945); RED PONY, THE(1949); GOLDEN HORDE, THE(1951); WHEN I GROW UP(1951); SPRINGFIELD RIFLE(1952)

The Hannefords
JUMBO(1962)

Dietrich V. Hanneken
EMBRACEABLE YOU(1948), w

Elsie Hanneman
Misc. Silents
IN THE WATER(1923)

Walter Hanneman
GUEST IN THE HOUSE(1944), ed; BLOOD ON THE SUN(1945), ed; GETTING GERTIE'S GARTER(1945), ed; ROYAL AFRICAN RIFLES, THE(1953), ed; BOB MATHIAS STORY, THE(1954), ed; CANNON FOR CORDOBA(1970), ed; BEST LIT-TLE WHOREHOUSE IN TEXAS, THE(1982), ed

H.W. Hannemann
WHERE SINNERS MEET(1934), w

Karl Hannemann
HIS MAJESTY, KING BALLYHOO(1931, Ger.)

Walt Hannemann
ONLY THE VALIANT(1951), ed; LOST IN THE STARS(1974), ed; CHARLIE CHAN AND THE CURSE OF THE DRAGON QUEEN(1981), ed

Walter A. Hannemann
HELL'S FIVE HOURS(1958), ed; MAURIE(1973), ed

Walter Hannemann
TIME OF YOUR LIFE, THE(1948), ed; TEXAS MASQUERADE(1944), ed; KISS TOMORROW GOODBYE(1950), ed; HIAWATHA(1952), ed; JET JOB(1952), ed; ROSE BOWL STORY, THE(1952), ed; WAGONS WEST(1952), ed; DRAGONFLY SQUA-DRON(1953), ed; FORT VENGEANCE(1953), ed; KANSAS PACIFIC(1953), ed; SAFA-RI DRUMS(1953), ed; AL CAPONE(1959), ed; GO, JOHNNY, GO!(1959), ed; PAY OR DIE(1960), ed; ARMORED COMMAND(1961), ed; WINGS OF CHANCE(1961, Can.), ed; HITLER(1962), ed; DREAM OF KINGS, A(1969), ed; GUNS OF THE MAGNIFI-CENT SEVEN(1969), ed; KRAKATOA, EAST OF JAVA(1969), ed; EL CONDOR(1970), ed; REVENGERS, THE(1972, U.S./Mex.), ed; TWO-MINUTE WARNING(1976), ed; SMOKEY AND THE BANDIT(1977), ed; OTHER SIDE OF THE MOUNTAIN–PART 2, THE(1978), ed; VILLAIN, THE(1979), ed; NUDE BOMB, THE(1980), ed

Chick Hannen
ROLL, WAGONS, ROLL(1939)

Hermione Hannen
LEAVE IT TO BLANCHE(1934, Brit.); LIFE OF THE PARTY(1934, Brit.)

Nicholas Hannen
F.P. 1(1933, Brit.); MAN THEY COULDN'T ARREST, THE(1933, Brit.); MURDER AT THE INN(1934, Brit.); DICTATOR, THE(1935, Brit./Ger.); HAIL AND FARE-WELL(1936, Brit.); WHO KILLED JOHN SAVAGE?(1937, Brit.); MARIGOLD(1938, Brit.); SPY FOR A DAY(1939, Brit.); HENRY V(1946, Brit.); WINSLOW BOY, THE(1950); HELL IS SOLD OUT(1951, Brit.); QUO VADIS(1951); THREE STEPS IN THE DARK(1953, Brit.); QUENTIN DURWARD(1955); RICHARD III(1956, Brit.); SEA WIFE(1957, Brit.); DUNKIRK(1958, Brit.); RX MURDER(1958, Brit.); FRANCIS OF ASSISI(1961); TERM OF TRIAL(1962, Brit.)

Peter Hannen
FOOTSTEPS IN THE NIGHT(1932, Brit.); WATER GYPSIES, THE(1932, Brit.); FLAME(1975, Brit.), ph

Nephi Hannermann
CASTAWAY COWBOY, THE(1974)

Richard Hanners
CHILD, THE(1977)

Art Hannes
TAXI(1953)

James Hanney
NATIVE LAND(1942)

Marc Hannibal
FOOLS(1970); GRASSHOPPER, THE(1970)

Mark Hannibal
MAN FROM O.R.G.Y., THE(1970); THREE STOOGES VS. THE WONDER WO-MEN(1975, Ital./Chi.)

Terry Hannigan
PALM BEACH(1979, Aus.), m

William Hanning
GULLIVER'S TRAVELS(1939), anim d

Janet Hannington
DAYLIGHT ROBBERY(1964, Brit.)

Will Morris Hannis
LAST PICTURE SHOW, THE(1971)

Eva Von Hanno
AUTUMN SONATA(1978, Swed.)

Betty Hannon
LEAVE HER TO HEAVEN(1946); NIGHT HAS A THOUSAND EYES(1948); PALE-FACE, THE(1948); SUMMER STOCK(1950); WHERE DANGER LIVES(1950); ROYAL WEDDING(1951)

Chick Hannon
FIGHTING DEPUTY, THE(1937); GUNS IN THE DARK(1937); MYSTERY OF THE HOODED HORSEMEN, THE(1937); RECKLESS RANGER(1937); RIDERS OF THE DAWN(1937); SING, COWBOY, SING(1937); SINGING OUTLAW(1937); STARS OVER ARIZONA(1937); TROUBLE IN TEXAS(1937); TRUSTED OUTLAW, THE(1937); DAN-GER VALLEY(1938); STARLIGHT OVER TEXAS(1938); COME ON RANGERS(1939); MAN FROM TEXAS, THE(1939); ARIZONA FRONTIER(1940); CARSON CITY KID(1940); COWBOY FROM SUNDOWN(1940); LIGHTNING STRIKES WEST(1940); MELODY RANCH(1940); RANGER AND THE LADY, THE(1940); RHYTHM OF THE RIO GRANDE(1940); WESTBOUND STAGE(1940); PIONEERS, THE(1941); ROBIN HOOD OF THE PECOS(1941); TUMBLEDOWN RANCH IN ARIZONA(1941); WRAN-GLER'S ROOST(1941); MAN FROM CHEYENNE(1942); SOMBRERO KID, THE(1942); WILD HORSE STAMPEDE(1943); LAND OF THE OUTLAWS(1944); CHEROKEE FLASH, THE(1945); CODE OF THE SADDLE(1947); SIX GUN SERENADE(1947); NAVAJO TRAIL RAIDERS(1949); VIGILANTE HIDEOUT(1950)

Judge James Hannon
ALICE'S RESTAURANT(1969)

Susan Hannon
TICKET TO HEAVEN(1981)

Tim Hannon
1984
NIGHT OF THE COMET(1984)

Alberta Hannum
ROSEANNA McCOY(1949), w

Marilyn Hanold
SOLID GOLD CADILLAC, THE(1956); GARMENT JUNGLE, THE(1957); SUBMA-RINE SEAHAWK(1959); FRANKENSTEIN MEETS THE SPACE MONSTER(1965); IN LIKE FLINT(1967)

Luis Hanore
FOLIES DERGERE(1935)

Anna Hanoszek
SEVEN DARING GIRLS(1962, Ger.), cos

Dick Hanover
YEAR OF THE HORSE, THE(1966)

Bill Hanrahan
RAGING BULL(1980)

Lynn Hanratty
JOHNNY GOT HIS GUN(1971)

Laurence Hanray
MY LEARNED FRIEND(1943, Brit.); NICHOLAS NICKLEBY(1947, Brit.)

Lawrence Hanray
BEYOND THE CITIES(1930, Brit.); HER REPUTATION(1931, Brit.); LEAP YEAR(1932, Brit.); LOVE ON WHEELS(1932, Brit.); WEDDING REHEARSAL(1932, Brit.); FAITHFUL HEART(1933, Brit.); GOOD COMPANIONS(1933, Brit.); HIS GRACE GIVES NOTICE(1933, Brit.); MAN FROM TORONTO, THE(1933, Brit.); OVER-

NIGHT(1933, Brit.); PRIVATE LIFE OF HENRY VIII, THE(1933); THERE GOES THE BRIDE(1933, Brit.); THIS WEEK OF GRACE(1933, Brit.); ADVENTURE LIMITED(1934, Brit.); CATHERINE THE GREAT(1934, Brit.); CHU CHIN CHOW(1934, Brit.); EASY MONEY(1934, Brit.); GREAT DEFENDER, THE(1934, Brit.); LOYALTIES(1934, Brit.); THOSE WERE THE DAYS(1934, Brit.); WHAT HAPPENED THEN?(1934, Brit.); BREWSTER'S MILLIONS(1935, Brit.); EXPERT'S OPINION(1935, Brit.); LORNA DOONE(1935, Brit.); MIMI(1935, Brit.); MURDER AT MONTE CARLO(1935, Brit.); SCARLET PIMPERNEL, THE(1935, Brit.); STREET SONG(1935, Brit.); BELOVED IMPOSTER(1936, Brit.); REMBRANDT(1936, Brit.); SOMEONE AT THE DOOR(1936, Brit.); ACTION FOR SLANDER(1937, Brit.); BOMBS OVER LONDON(1937, Brit.); DARK JOURNEY(1937, Brit.); FIRE OVER ENGLAND(1937, Brit.); GIRL IN THE TAXI(1937, Brit.); IT'S NEVER TOO LATE TO MEND(1937, Brit.); KNIGHT WITHOUT ARMOR(1937, Brit.); KNIGHTS FOR A DAY(1937, Brit.); LAST CHANCE, THE(1937, Brit.); MAN WHO COULD WORK MIRACLES, THE(1937, Brit.); SCOTLAND YARD COMMANDS(1937, Brit.); SHOW GOES ON, THE(1937, Brit.); MOONLIGHT SONATA(1938, Brit.); ROYAL DIVORCE, A(1938, Brit.); SHOW GOES ON, THE(1938, Brit.); MISSING PEOPLE, THE(1940, Brit.); MOZART(1940, Brit.); TWENTY-ONE DAYS TOGETHER(1940, Brit.); LARCENY STREET(1941, Brit.); OLD MOTHER RILEY'S CIRCUS(1941, Brit.); QUIET WEDDING(1941, Brit.); ON APPROVAL(1944, Brit.); HOTEL RESERVE(1946, Brit.); LADY SURRENDERS, A(1947, Brit.); HATTER'S CASTLE(1948, Brit.); MINE OWN EXECUTIONER(1948, Brit.)
Silents
PIPES OF PAN, THE(1923, Brit.)

Regis Hanrion
DEVIL PROBABLY, THE(1977, FR.)

Crystal Hans
SHE MAN, THE(1967)

Dorothy Hans
I MARRIED AN ANGEL(1942)

Marie-Francoise Hans
JOY(1983, Fr./Can.), w

Kali Hansa
Misc. Talkies
NIGHT OF THE SORCERORS(1970)

Helen Hansard
FALLEN ANGEL(1945), set d; ON THE OLD SPANISH TRAIL(1947), set d; TRESPASSER, THE(1947), set d; UNDER COLORADO SKIES(1947), set d; SATAN'S CRADLE(1949), set d

Paul Hansard
ONE THAT GOT AWAY, THE(1958, Brit.); HEROES OF TELEMARK, THE(1965, Brit.); OH! WHAT A LOVELY WAR(1969, Brit.); SUMARINE X-1(1969, Brit.); PRIVATE LIFE OF SHERLOCK HOLMES, THE(1970, Brit.); TROG(1970, Brit.); GOLD(1974, Brit.)

Lorraine Hansberry
RAISIN IN THE SUN, A(1961), w

Anna Maria Hanschke
LUDWIG(1973, Ital./Ger./Fr.)

Arthur Hansel
DR. TARR'S TORTURE DUNGEON(1972, Mex.); MARY, MARY, BLOODY MARY(1975, U.S./Mex.); 10 TO MIDNIGHT(1983)

Howard Hansel
Misc. Silents
LONG TRAIL, THE(1917), d

Howell Hansel
Silents
TILLIE'S TOMATO SURPRISE(1915), d
Misc. Silents
DEEMSTER, THE(1917), d

Ray Hansel
RED RUNS THE RIVER(1963)

Arthur Hansell
CAST A GIANT SHADOW(1966)

Al Hansen
HEARSE, THE(1980)
1984
HARD TO HOLD(1984)

Alan Hansen
Misc. Talkies
TWO CATCH TWO(1979)

Aleth "Speed" Hansen
MY DARLING CLEMENTINE(1946)

Andy Hansen
JAWS 3-D(1983)

Arne Hansen
1984
ZAPPA(1984, Den.)

Art Hansen
ROLLOVER(1981)

Bibbe Hansen
TASTE OF SIN, A(1983)

Bibi Hansen
PHANTOM OF THE PARADISE(1974)

"Boots" Hansen
HELLFIGHTERS(1968), tech adv

Carl Hansen
CRACK-UP(1946)

Catherine Hansen
MAGIC FOUNTAIN, THE(1961)

Cecil Dan Hansen
SECOND TIME AROUND, THE(1961), w

Charles Hansen
SOAK THE RICH(1936), ph

Dale Hansen
LEGACY OF BLOOD(1978)

Danna Hansen
RANCHO DELUXE(1975); SIX PACK ANNIE(1975); BEING THERE(1979)

Dirk Hansen
COUNTERFEIT TRAITOR, THE(1962); NO SURVIVORS, PLEASE(1963, Ger.)

E.H. Hansen
RAINS CAME, THE(1939), spec eff

Earl Hansen
I'VE LIVED BEFORE(1956)

Earle Hansen
SILENT RAIDERS(1954)

Einar Hansen
Misc. Silents
HER BIG NIGHT(1926); LADY IN ERMINE, THE(1927); MASKED WOMAN, THE(1927)

Eleanor Hansen
LETTER OF INTRODUCTION(1938); MAD MISS MANTON, THE(1938); RECKLESS LIVING(1938)

Elenor Hansen
CRIME OF DR. HALLET(1938)

Florence Hansen
IRON MAJOR, THE(1943)

Gail Hansen
WONDER WOMEN(1973, Phil.)

Gale Hansen
ZELIG(1983)

Gary Hansen
INN OF THE DAMNED(1974, Aus.), prod d; CATHY'S CHILD(1979, Aus.), ph; BATTLETRUCK(1982), prod d; MANGANINNIE(1982, Aus.), ph; NEXT OF KIN(1983, Aus.), ph
1984
HEART OF THE STAG(1984, New Zealand), prod d

Greger Hansen
1984
CLASS ENEMY(1984, Ger.)

Greta Hansen
BLUE SQUADRON, THE(1934, Brit.)

Grete Hansen
POWER(1934, Brit.)

Grethe Hansen
BRITANNIA OF BILLINGSGATE(1933, Brit.)

Gunnar Hansen
TEXAS CHAIN SAW MASSACRE, THE(1974); DEMON LOVER, THE(1977)

Gunnar Robert Hansen
WHILE THE ATTORNEY IS ASLEEP(1945, Den.), w

H.C. Hansen
PASSIONATE DEMONS, THE(1962, Norway), art d

Hans Hansen
SOCIAL REGISTER(1934); HOUSE ON 92ND STREET, THE(1945)

Heide Hansen
FANNY HILL: MEMOIRS OF A WOMAN OF PLEASURE zero(1965)

Heidi Hansen
SUPERBUG, SUPER AGENT(1976, Ger.)

Helen Hansen
CLASH BY NIGHT(1952)

Helge Hansen
JOURNEY TO THE SEVENTH PLANET(1962, U.S./Swed.), set d; REPTILICUS(1962, U.S./Den.), set d

Janis Hansen
OH DAD, POOR DAD, MAMA'S HUNG YOU IN THE CLOSET AND I'M FEELIN' SO SAD(1967); AIRPORT(1970); CANNON FOR CORDOBA(1970)

Jo Hansen
ONE WAY WAHINI(1965), m; MADMAN(1982), spec eff, makeup

Joachim Hansen
MAKE WAY FOR LILA(1962, Swed./Ger.); INVISIBLE MAN, THE(1963, Ger.); ORDERED TO LOVE(1963, Ger.); CAVERN, THE(1965, Ital./Ger.); FROZEN ALIVE(1966, Brit./Ger.); IS PARIS BURNING?(1966, U.S./Fr.); ASSIGNMENT K(1968, Brit.); MISSION STARDUST(1968, Ital./Span./Ger.); BRIDGE AT REMAGEN, THE(1969); UNDERGROUND(1970, Brit.); EAGLE HAS LANDED, THE(1976, Brit.); BOYS FROM BRAZIL, THE(1978); BREAKTHROUGH(1978, Ger.)

John Hansen
CHRISTINE JORGENSEN STORY, THE(1970); IN SEARCH OF HISTORIC JESUS(1980); EARTHBOUND(1981)

Joshua Hansen
DIFFERENT STORY, A(1978)

Juanita Hansen
SENSATION HUNTERS(1934)
Silents
MARTYRS OF THE ALAMO, THE(1915); MEDIATOR, THE(1916); RISKY ROAD, THE(1918); ROUGH LOVER, THE(1918); POPPY GIRL'S HUSBAND, THE(1919); GIRL FROM THE WEST(1923)
Misc. Silents
MAGIC CLOAK OF OZ, THE(1914); GLORY(1917); BROADWAY LOVE(1918); FAST COMPANY(1918); MATING OF MARCELLA(1918); SEA FLOWER, THE(1918); BREEZY JIM(1919); LOMBARDI, LTD.(1919); ROUGH RIDING ROMANCE(1919); JUNGLE PRINCESS, THE(1923)

Kai Hansen
Misc. Silents
1812(1912, USSR), d

Karen Hansen
Misc. Talkies
FUGITIVE KILLER(1975)
Silents
TELEPHONE GIRL, THE(1927)

Karl Bendix Hansen
CLINIC, THE(1983, Aus.)

Lars Hansen
INFORMER, THE(1929, Brit.)

Linda Hansen
SEVENTY DEADLY PILLS(1964, Brit.)

Lorna Hansen
FANGS OF THE ARCTIC(1953)

Lory Hansen
POINT OF TERROR(1971)
Margo Hansen
Misc. Talkies
CLOSET CASANOVA, THE(1979)
Martin Hansen
OPERATION LOVEBIRDS(1968, Den.)
Michael Hansen
TIMBER FURY(1950), w
Monika Hansen
I LOVE YOU, I KILL YOU(1972, Ger.)
Myrna Hansen
MAGNIFICENT OBSESSION(1954); PLAYGIRL(1954); SO THIS IS PARIS(1954); YANKEE PASHA(1954); CULT OF THE COBRA(1955); FRANCIS IN THE NAVY(1955); MAN WITHOUT A STAR(1955); PURPLE MASK, THE(1955); THERE'S ALWAYS TOMORROW(1956); RAINTREE COUNTY(1957); PARTY GIRL(1958); ASK ANY GIRL(1959); GOODBYE CHARLIE(1964); BLACK CAESAR(1973)
Nina Hansen
NORTHWEST OUTPOST(1947); SONG OF MY HEART(1947); VICIOUS CIRCLE, THE(1948); STAGE STRUCK(1958); INCIDENT, THE(1967); SATURDAY NIGHT FEVER(1977)
Owen Hansen
ROSE BOWL(1936)
Patti Hansen
RICH KIDS(1979); THEY ALL LAUGHED(1981)
1984
HARD TO HOLD(1984)
Paul Hansen
COUNT YORGA, VAMPIRE(1970); RETURN OF COUNT YORGA, THE(1971)
Peter Hansen
BRANDED(1951); DRUM BEAT(1954); PRISONER OF WAR(1954); TOP OF THE WORLD(1955); PROUD AND THE PROFANE, THE(1956); TEN COMMANDMENTS, THE(1956); THREE VIOLENT PEOPLE(1956); FIVE STEPS TO DANGER(1957); DEEP SIX, THE(1958); HARLOW(1965); SNOW TREASURE(1968), w
Preston Hansen
Misc. Talkies
LOCH NESS HORROR, THE(1983)
Rolf Hansen
DEVIL IN SILK(1968, Ger.), d
Rudy Hansen
GOODBYE CHARLIE(1964)
Speed Hansen
UNDER THE BIG TOP(1938)
Sverre Hansen
HUNGER(1968, Den./Norway/Swed.); ONE DAY IN THE LIFE OF IVAN DENISOVICH(1971, U.S./Brit./Norway)
Tom Hansen
SKIDOO(1968), ch
Valda Hansen
NIGHT OF THE GHOULS(1959)
Velda J. Hansen
GREAT NORTHFIELD, MINNESOTA RAID, THE(1972)
William Hansen
PINKY(1949); SIDE STREET(1950); MEMBER OF THE WEDDING, THE(1952); BRAMBLE BUSH, THE(1960); YOUNG DOCTORS, THE(1961); FAIL SAFE(1964); ARRANGEMENT, THE(1969); WILLARD(1971); 1776(1972); LAUGHING POLICEMAN, THE(1973); SAVE THE TIGER(1973); HOMEBODIES(1974); TERMINAL MAN, THE(1974)
Willy Berg Hansen
CRAZY PARADISE(1965, Den.), prod d
Aguste Hansen-Kleinmichel
DECISION BEFORE DAWN(1951)
Therese Hanses
1984
THEY'RE PLAYING WITH FIRE(1984)
Ray Hansford
COLLEGE HOLIDAY(1936)
Pamela Hansford-Johnson
TROJAN BROTHERS, THE(1946), w
Hansi
MAN ON A TIGHTROPE(1953)
Ann Hanslip
GREAT GILBERT AND SULLIVAN, THE(1953, Brit.); KNIGHTS OF THE ROUND TABLE(1953); BLACK GLOVE(1954, Brit.); FABIAN OF THE YARD(1954, Brit.); LADY GODIVA RIDES AGAIN(1955, Brit.); THREE CASES OF MURDER(1955, Brit.); WHERE THERE'S A WILL(1955, Brit.)
Ernst Hansman
DISPATCH FROM REUTERS, A(1940)
Rhonda Hansome
GETTING TOGETHER(1976)
Misc. Talkies
FEELIN' UP(1983)
Aleth "Speed" Hanson
TRUMPET BLOWS, THE(1934)
Arthur Hanson
ZERO HOUR!(1957); THEY CAME TO CORDURA(1959)
Barry Hanson
LONG GOOD FRIDAY, THE(1982, Brit.), p; BLOODY KIDS(1983, Brit.), p; RUNNERS(1983, Brit.), p
Beverly Hanson
PAT AND MIKE(1952)
Blanche Hanson
Misc. Silents
VALLEY OF DECISION, THE(1916)
Carl Eric Hanson
ACE OF ACES(1933)
Carl Hanson
DICK TRACY(1945); LIKELY STORY, A(1947); FORCE OF EVIL(1948)

Charles S. Hanson
1984
RIVER, THE(1984)
Connie Hanson
URBAN COWBOY(1980)
Curtis Hanson
AROUSERS, THE(1973), d&w; SILENT PARTNER, THE(1979, Can.), w; LITTLE DRAGONS, THE(1980), p, d; WHITE DOG(1982), w; LOSIN' IT(1983), d; NEVER CRY WOLF(1983), w
Curtis Lee Hanson
DUNWICH HORROR, THE(1970), w
David Hanson
SLAP SHOT(1977)
Dorothy Hanson
Silents
ELUSIVE PIMPERNEL, THE(1919, Brit.)
Duane Hanson
I, MAUREEN(1978, Can.), p
Edith Hanson
IT STARTED IN THE ALPS(1966, Jap.)
Einar Hanson
Silents
BARBED WIRE(1927); CHILDREN OF DIVORCE(1927); WOMAN ON TRIAL, THE(1927)
Misc. Silents
GUNNAR HEDE'S SAGA(1922, Swed.); INTO HER KINGDOM(1926); FASHIONS FOR WOMEN(1927)
Eleanor Hanson
LITTLE TOUGH GUY(1938)
Eric Hanson
UP THE ACADEMY(1980)
Erick Hanson
ISLE OF THE DEAD(1945)
Frank Hanson
HANGOVER SQUARE(1945)
Fred Hanson
BATTLE FLAME(1955)
Gladys Hanson
Silents
STRAIGHT ROAD, THE(1914); CLIMBERS, THE(1915)
Misc. Silents
EVANGELIST, THE(1915); PRIMROSE PATH, THE(1915); HAVOC, THE(1916)
Gordon Hanson
AGAINST A CROOKED SKY(1975)
Helen Hanson
AGAINST THE WIND(1948, Brit.)
Jack Hanson
BOY...A GIRL, A(1969), p; DIRTY HARRY(1971)
Jamiel Hanson
ROAD TO MOROCCO(1942)
John Hanson
SECRETS(1971), p; NORTHERN LIGHTS(1978), p,d&w, ed
Jonathon Hanson
MAROC 7(1967, Brit.)
Judy Hanson
SUGAR HILL(1974)
Kristina Hanson
DINOSAURUS(1960)
Lara Hanson
WIND, THE(1928)
Lars Hanson
ON THE SUNNYSIDE(1936, Swed.); WALPURGIS NIGHT(1941, Swed.)
Silents
FLESH AND THE DEVIL(1926); SCARLET LETTER, THE(1926); CAPTAIN SALVATION(1927); DIVINE WOMAN, THE(1928)
Misc. Silents
SAGA OF GOSTA BERLING, THE(1924, Fr.); BUTTONS(1927); LEGEND OF GOSTA BERLING(1928, Swed.)
Lawrence Hanson, Jr.
PUBLIC AFFAIR, A(1962), p
Lorna Hanson
MR. SARDONICUS(1961)
Marcy Hanson
10(1979)
Maria Hanson
PORT AFRIQUE(1956, Brit.)
Paul Hanson
LOST PATROL, THE,(1934); ROSE OF TRALEE(1938, Ireland)
Peter Hanson
GOLDBERGS, THE(1950); DARLING, HOW COULD YOU!(1951); LAST OUTPOST, THE(1951); PASSAGE WEST(1951); WHEN WORLDS COLLIDE(1951); SOMETHING TO LIVE FOR(1952); SAVAGE, THE(1953); BULLET FOR JOEY, A(1955); VIOLENT MEN, THE(1955); CRY IN THE NIGHT, A(1956); HELL ON FRISCO BAY(1956); SMASH PALACE(1982, New Zealand), w
Preston Hanson
JULIUS CAESAR(1953); OPERATION PETTICOAT(1959); CAGE OF EVIL(1960); GOODBYE, NORMA JEAN(1976)
Ray Hanson
WEDDING PRESENT(1936); CONFLICT(1945)
Raymond Hanson
THREE IN ONE(1956, Aus.), ed
Speed Hanson
WESTERNER, THE(1940)
Steve Hanson
RAIDERS OF THE LOST ARK(1981)
Susan Hanson
HAVING A WILD WEEKEND(1965, Brit.)

Tom Hanson
NIGHT TRAIN TO MUNDO FINE(1966); HELLCATS, THE(1968)
Valerie Hanson
BLACK RIDER, THE(1954, Brit.)
Wahnetta Hanson
Misc. Silents
FAILURE, THE(1915)
Arvid Hanssen
CHILDREN OF GOD'S EARTH(1983, Norwegian), w
Erling Hansson
Misc. Silents
LEAVES FROM SATAN'S BOOK(1921, Den.)
Knut Hansson
TERRORISTS, THE(1975, Brit.)
Lena Hansson
SWEDISH WEDDING NIGHT(1965, Swed.)
Maud Hansson
SEVENTH SEAL, THE(1958, Swed.); WILD STRAWBERRIES(1959, Swed.)
Siv Hansson
CHILDREN, THE(1949, Swed.)
Robert Hantz
SUPER COPS, THE(1974)
Emmerich Hanus
Misc. Silents
OTHER, THE(1912, Ger.)
Josef Hanus
DEATH OF TARZAN, THE(1968, Czech), ph; LADY ON THE TRACKS, THE(1968, Czech.), ph
Ladislav Hanus
SHOP ON MAIN STREET, THE(1966, Czech.), p
Vaclav Hanus
KRAKATIT(1948, Czech.), ph; SWEET LIGHT IN A DARK ROOM(1966, Czech.), ph; SIR, YOU ARE A WIDOWER(1971, Czech.), ph
Hana Hanusova
FIREMAN'S BALL, THE(1968, Czech.)
Hanwell Silver Band
VALUE FOR MONEY(1957, Brit.)
Joe Hanworth
MY WIFE'S BEST FRIEND(1952)
Joseph C. Hanwright
UNCLE JOE SHANNON(1978), d
Jiri Hanzl
LEMONADE JOE(1966, Czech.)
Josef Hanzlik
NINTH HEART, THE(1980, Czech.), d&w
Li Hao
SACRED KNIVES OF VENGEANCE, THE(1974, Hong Kong)
Petr Hapka
NINTH HEART, THE(1980, Czech.), m
Ken Hapner
HANGAR 18(1980)
Thomas Happer
1984
NEW YORK NIGHTS(1984)
Clifford Happy
MOVIE MOVIE(1978); NATIONAL LAMPOON'S ANIMAL HOUSE(1978)
Don Happy
WESTBOUND(1959)
Marguerite Happy
WARGAMES(1983), stunts
Mary Happy
HUMPHREY TAKES A CHANCE(1950)
The Happy Wanderers
WHAT A CRAZY WORLD(1963, Brit.)
Aki Hara
THAT FUNNY FEELING(1965)
Chisako Hara
DIPLOMAT'S MANSION, THE(1961, Jap.); DIFFERENT SONS(1962, Jap.)
Ioru Hara
LAST UNICORN, THE(1982), anim
Izumi Hara
HAPPINESS OF US ALONE(1962, Jap.); OUR SILENT LOVE(1969, Jap.)
Kazutami Hara
CREATURE CALLED MAN, THE(1970, Jap.), ph
Setsuko Hara
NEW EARTH, THE(1937, Jap./Ger.); WOMEN IN PRISON(1957, Jap.); LIFE OF A COUNTRY DOCTOR(1961, Jap.); EARLY AUTUMN(1962, Jap.); WAYSIDE PEBBLE, THE(1962, Jap.); CHUSHINGURA(1963, Jap.); IDIOT, THE(1963, Jap.); TOKYO STORY(1972, Jap.); LATE AUTUMN(1973, Jap.)
Harada
YAKUZA, THE(1975, U.S./Jap.)
Ernest Harada
I, THE JURY(1982)
1984
DREAMSCAPE(1984); WOMAN IN RED, THE(1984)
Ernest Kazuyoshi Harada
ROSEMARY'S BABY(1968)
Itoko Harada
GIRARA(1967, Jap.)
Yoshio Harada
BANISHED(1978, Jap.)
J. D. Haragan
Silents
LAW OF THE LAND, THE(1917)
Buddy Harak
EXILE EXPRESS(1939), ch
James Harakas
BENEATH THE 12-MILE REEF(1953)

Jim Harakas
Misc. Talkies
OUTLAW QUEEN(1957)
Phil Haran
ST. VALENTINE'S DAY MASSACRE, THE(1967)
Ronnie Haran
COME SEPTEMBER(1961)
Shifra Haran
JOURNEY INTO FEAR(1942)
Vlastimil Harapes
MARKETA LAZAROVA(1968, Czech.)
Haya Harareet
HILL 24 DOESN'T ANSWER(1955, Israel); BEN HUR(1959); SECRET PARTNER, THE(1961, Brit.); INTERNS, THE(1962); DOLL THAT TOOK THE TOWN, THE(1965, Ital.); JOURNEY BENEATH THE DESERT(1967, Fr./Ital.); OUR MOTHER'S HOUSE(1967, Brit.), w
Harari
DEMONIAQUE(1958, Fr.)
Clement Harari
ME AND THE COLONEL(1958); TAMANGO(1959, Fr.); LONG ABSENCE, THE(1962, Fr./Ital.); FIVE MILES TO MIDNIGHT(1963, U.S./Fr./Ital.); NIGHT ENCOUNTER(1963, Fr./Ital.); SECRET AGENT FIREBALL(1965, Fr./Ital.); SLEEPING CAR MURDER THE(1966, Fr.); MONKEYS, GO HOME!(1967); SELLERS OF GIRLS(1967, Fr.); TRIPLE CROSS(1967, Fr./Brit.); SHADOWMAN(1974, Fr./Ital.); ONCE IN PARIS(1978); FIENDISH PLOT OF DR. FU MANCHU, THE(1980); FLIGHT OF THE EAGLE(1983, Swed.)
Robert Harari
HITTING A NEW HIGH(1937), w; MUSIC FOR MADAME(1937), w; DAY-TIME WIFE(1939), w; ICE-CAPADES(1941), w; SUN VALLEY SERENADE(1941), w; JOAN OF OZARK(1942), w; LARCENY WITH MUSIC(1943), w; FOREIGN AFFAIR, A(1948), w; MILLIONAIRE FOR CHRISTY, A(1951), w; THREE STEPS NORTH(1951), w
Mici Haraszthy
HIPPOLYT, THE LACKEY(1932, Hung.)
Laszlo Haraszti
FATHER(1967, Hung.)
Laszlone Haraszti
FATHER(1967, Hung.)
Bill Harbach
GOOD NEWS(1947); SONG OF THE THIN MAN(1947); B. F.'S DAUGHTER(1948)
Ernest Harbach
SUNNY(1930), m
Otto A. Harbach
ROSE MARIE(1936), w; ROSE MARIE(1954), w
Otto Harbach
DESERT SONG, THE(1929), w; GOLDEN DAWN(1930), w; NO, NO NANETTE(1930), w; SONG OF THE FLAME(1930), w; SUNNY(1930), w; MEN OF THE SKY(1931), a, w; CAT AND THE FIDDLE(1934), w; ROBERTA(1935), w; FIREFLY, THE(1937), w; NO, NO NANETTE(1940), w; SUNNY(1941), w; DESERT SONG, THE(1943), w; UP IN MABEL'S ROOM(1944), w; TEA FOR TWO(1950), w; LOVELY TO LOOK AT(1952), w; DESERT SONG, THE(1953), w; DEEP IN MY HEART(1954), lyrics
Silents
KID BOOTS(1926), w
Karl Harbacher
Misc. Silents
NEW YEAR'S EVE(1923, Ger.)
Carl Harbaugh
DEVIL'S BROTHER, THE(1933); THREE LEGIONNAIRES, THE(1937), w; PRISON FARM(1938); TEXANS, THE(1938); ST. LOUIS BLUES(1939); THEY DRIVE BY NIGHT(1940); HIGH SIERRA(1941); MANPOWER(1941); STRAWBERRY BLONDE, THE(1941); GENTLEMAN JIM(1942); THEY DIED WITH THEIR BOOTS ON(1942); NORTHERN PURSUIT(1943); UNCERTAIN GLORY(1944); FIGHTER SQUADRON(1948); DISTANT DRUMS(1951); WORLD IN HIS ARMS, THE(1952); FAR COUNTRY, THE(1955); TALL MEN, THE(1955); BAND OF ANGELS(1957)
Silents
SERPENT, THE(1916); BRAVE AND BOLD(1918), d&w; JACK SPURLOCK, PRODIGAL(1918), d; OTHER MEN'S DAUGHTERS(1918), d; OTHER MAN'S WIFE, THE(1919), d; NORTH WIND'S MALICE, THE(1920), d; BIG TOWN IDEAS(1921), d; JAZZMANIA(1923); SILENT COMMAND, THE(1923); COLLEGE(1927), a, w; GOODBYE KISS, THE(1928), w, t; STEAMBOAT BILL, JR.(1928), w&t
Misc. Silents
CARMEN(1915); BIG JIM GARRITY(1916); IRON WOMAN, THE(1916), d; TEST, THE(1916); ALL FOR A HUSBAND(1917), d; BROADWAY SPORT, THE(1917), d; DERELICT, THE(1917), d; RICH MAN'S PLAYTHING, A(1917), d; SCARLET LETTER, THE(1917), d; WHEN FALSE TONGUES SPEAK(1917), a, d; MARRIAGES ARE MADE(1918), d; POPPY TRAIL, THE(1920), d; BUCKING THE LINE(1921), d; HICKVILLE TO BROADWAY(1921), d; TOMBOY, THE(1921), d
Elizabeth "Libby" Harben
VOGUES OF 1938(1937)
Hubert Harben
VICTORIA THE GREAT(1937, Brit.); BATTLE OF GALLIPOLI(1931, Brit.); UNEASY VIRTUE(1931, Brit.); FIRES OF FATE(1932, Brit.); SHADOW BETWEEN, THE(1932, Brit.); TIMBUCTOO(1933, Brit.); LADY IN DANGER(1934, Brit.); LILIES OF THE FIELD(1934, Brit.); SECRET OF THE LOCH, THE(1934, Brit.); CITY OF BEAUTIFUL NONSENSE, THE(1935, Brit.); FIGHTING STOCK(1935, Brit.); SCROOGE(1935, Brit.); DISHONOR BRIGHT(1936, Brit.); LIVING DANGEROUSLY(1936, Brit.); FOR VALOR(1937, Brit.); OLD IRON(1938, Brit.); ROYAL DIVORCE, A(1938, Brit.); MOZART(1940, Brit.); SUICIDE LEGION(1940, Brit.)
Silents
GREAT ADVENTURE, THE(1915, Brit.); EVERY MOTHER'S SON(1926, Brit.)
Joan Harben
KEY TO HARMONY(1935, Brit.); ENCORE(1951, Brit.); MAN IN THE WHITE SUIT, THE(1952)
Philip Harben
MEET MR. LUCIFER(1953, Brit.)
Phillip Harben
MAN OF THE MOMENT(1955, Brit.)
Will N. Harben
Silents
DESIRED WOMAN, THE(1918), w

Harry Harber
KIDNAPPERS, THE(1964, U.S./Phil.), w
Harry Paul Harber
TERROR IS A MAN(1959, U.S./Phil.), w
Paul Harber
MAN FROM DEL RIO(1956); PLUNDER ROAD(1957); KIDNAPPERS, THE(1964, U.S./Phil.)
Marvin Harbert
INCREDIBLE PETRIFIED WORLD, THE(1959), art d
Slim Harbert
LOUISIANA(1947)
Milo Harbich
FINAL CHORD, THE(1936, Ger.), ed; LIFE BEGINS ANEW(1938, Ger.), ed
Robert Harbin
LIMPING MAN, THE(1953, Brit.)
Sizette Harbin
LYDIA BAILEY(1952)
Suzette Harbin
TO HAVE AND HAVE NOT(1944); FOXES OF HARROW, THE(1947); LOOK OUT SISTER(1948); SKY DRAGON(1949); DESTINATION MURDER(1950); BOMBA AND THE JUNGLE GIRL(1952); SKIRTS AHOY!(1952)
Richard Harbinger
T-BIRD GANG(1959), d
David Harbonn
1984
JUST THE WAY YOU ARE(1984), set d
Gayle Harbor
1984
FIRSTBORN(1984)
Carl Harbord
AMERICAN PRISONER, THE(1929 Brit.); INFORMER, THE(1929, Brit.); HATE SHIP, THE(1930, Brit.); HOURS OF LONELINESS(1930, Brit.); SUCH IS THE LAW(1930, Brit.); BATTLE OF GALLIPOLI(1931, Brit.); FASCINATION(1931, Brit.); DANCE PRETTY LADY(1932, Brit.); SHE WAS ONLY A VILLAGE MAIDEN(1933, Brit.); SCARLET PIMPERNEL, THE(1935, Brit.); 18 MINUTES(1935, Brit.); LOVE AT SEA(1936, Brit.); CAVALIER OF THE STREETS, THE(1937, Brit.); HEART'S DESIRE(1937, Brit.); CAPTAINS OF THE CLOUDS(1942); EAGLE SQUADRON(1942); LONDON BLACKOUT MURDERS(1942); SAHARA(1943); DRESSED TO KILL(1946); CHRISTMAS EVE(1947); MACOMBER AFFAIR, THE(1947); WOMAN'S VENGEANCE, A(1947); ROPE OF SAND(1949)
Silents
BOLIBAR(1928, Brit.)
Gordon Harbord
EIGHT O'CLOCK WALK(1954, Brit.), w
William Harbord
Silents
LURE OF LONDON, THE(1914, Brit.)
Christine Harbort
MEPHISTO(1981, Ger.)
Sandy Harbott
COLOR ME DEAD(1969, Aus.)
Pearl Harbour
KING OF COMEDY, THE(1983)
Mason Harbringer
Silents
DEVIL'S MASTERPIECE, THE(1927), w
Carl Harbrough
WHITE HEAT(1949)
E. W. Harburg
FINIAN'S RAINBOW(1968), w
E. Y. Harburg
BROADWAY GONDOLIER(1935), w; MEET THE PEOPLE(1944), p
Sandy Harbutt
SQUEEZE A FLOWER(1970, Aus.); STONE(1974, Aus.), a, p&d, w
Cyril Harcourt
THEY JUST HAD TO GET MARRIED(1933), w
Silents
PLACE IN THE SUN, A(1916, Brit.), w; PAIR OF SILK STOCKINGS, A(1918), w
David Harcourt
BROKEN JOURNEY(1948, Brit.), ph; EASY MONEY(1948, Brit.), ph; BAD LORD BYRON, THE(1949, Brit.), ph; CHRISTOPHER COLUMBUS(1949, Brit.), ph; DIAMOND CITY(1949, Brit.), ph; MARRY ME!(1949, Brit.), ph; HIGHLY DANGEROUS(1950, Brit.), ph; HOTEL SAHARA(1951, Brit.), ph; BILLION DOLLAR BRAIN(1967, Brit.), ph
George Harcourt
Misc. Silents
CONTINENTAL GIRL, A(1915)
James Harcourt
HOBSON'S CHOICE(1931, Brit.); COUNTY FAIR(1933, Brit.); PARIS PLANE(1933, Brit.); ALL AT SEA(1935, Brit.); OLD CURIOSITY SHOP, THE(1935, Brit.); AVENGING HAND, THE(1936, Brit.); DOMMED CARGO(1936, Brit.); LABURNUM GROVE(1936, Brit.); MEN ARE NOT GODS(1937, Brit.); FOLLOW YOUR STAR(1938, Brit.); KATE PLUS TEN(1938, Brit.); PENNY PARADISE(1938, Brit.); YOU'RE THE DOCTOR(1938, Brit.); I MET A MURDERER(1939, Brit.); WINGS OVER AFRICA(1939); CASTLE OF CRIMES(1940, Brit.); FACE BEHIND THE SCAR(1940, Brit.); NIGHT TRAIN(1940, Brit.); COURAGEOUS MR. PENN, THE(1941, Brit.); FARMER'S WIFE, THE(1941, Brit.); HARD STEEL(1941, Brit.); THIS ENGLAND(1941, Brit.); YOUNG MR. PITT, THE(1942, Brit.); HE SNOOPS TO CONQUER(1944, Brit.); LOVE ON THE DOLE(1945, Brit.); ADVENTURESS, THE(1946, Brit.); GRAND ESCAPADE, THE(1946, Brit.); JOHNNY FRENCHMAN(1946, Brit.); MEET ME AT DAWN(1947, Brit.); HIDDEN ROOM, THE(1949, Brit.)
Jessica Harcourt
Misc. Silents
BLACK CARGOES OF THE SOUTH SEAS(1929)
Kate Harcourt
NATE AND HAYES(1983, U.S./New Zealand)
Leslie Harcourt
VILLIERS DIAMOND, THE(1938, Brit.); GOOSE STEPS OUT, THE(1942, Brit.); YOUNG MR. PITT, THE(1942, Brit.); BELLS GO DOWN, THE(1943, Brit.); MY LEARNED FRIEND(1943, Brit.); JOHNNY FRENCHMAN(1946, Brit.)

William Harcourt
Misc. Silents
IT MIGHT HAPPEN TO YOU(1920)
Simon Harcourt-Smith
QUEEN'S GUARDS, THE(1963, Brit.), w
The Hard Corps
SALLY'S HOUNDS(1968)
Harry Harde
Silents
MODERN SALOME, A(1920), ph
LaCrisia Hardee
CONRACK(1974)
Ernest Harden
Misc. Talkies
CAMPSITE MASSACRE(1981)
Ernest Harden, Jr.
THREE DAYS OF THE CONDOR(1975); FINAL TERROR, THE(1983)
Jack Harden
BUSHWHACKERS, THE(1952); MAVERICK QUEEN, THE(1956); SATAN'S SATELLITES(1958)
Jacques Harden
GERVAISE(1956, Fr.); LOLA(1961, Fr./Ital.); LONG ABSENCE, THE(1962, Fr./Ital.)
Ray Harden
DESERT RATS, THE(1953)
Sasha Harden
CHINA GATE(1957); ENEMY BELOW, THE(1957); VERBOTEN!(1959)
Uva Harden
SOME OF MY BEST FRIENDS ARE...(1971)
Sarah Hardenberg
SUMMER HOLIDAY(1963, Brit.)
Sarah Hardenburg
STOP THE WORLD–I WANT TO GET OFF(1966, Brit.); HALF A SIXPENCE(1967, Brit.)
James Harder
PATERNITY(1981)
Jane Harders
SHIRLEY THOMPSON VERSUS THE ALIENS(1968, Aus.); CHANT OF JIMMIE BLACKSMITH, THE(1980, Aus.); EARTHLING, THE(1980)
Robert Harders
HOME MOVIES(1979), w
Crofton Hardester
ANDROID(1982)
Charlene Hardey
LIFE OF HER OWN, A(1950); TAKE CARE OF MY LITTLE GIRL(1951)
Jeanne Hardeyn
SHAMELESS OLD LADY, THE(1966, Fr.)
James Hardie
1984
GHOSTBUSTERS(1984)
Kate Hardie
RUNNERS(1983, Brit.)
1984
NUMBER ONE(1984, Brit.)
Neil Hardie
Misc. Silents
YELLOW BULLET, THE(1917)
Russell Hardie
BROADWAY TO HOLLYWOOD(1933); CHRISTOPHER BEAN(1933); STAGE MOTHER(1933); BAND PLAYS ON, THE(1934); MEN IN WHITE(1934); MURDER IN THE PRIVATE CAR(1934); OPERATOR 13(1934); PURSUED(1934); SEQUOIA(1934); IN OLD KENTUCKY(1935); SPEED DEVILS(1935); WEST POINT OF THE AIR(1935); DOWN TO THE SEA(1936); HARVESTER, THE(1936); KILLER AT LARGE(1936); MEET NERO WOLFE(1936); CAMILLE(1937); FROGMEN, THE(1951); WHISTLE AT EATON FALLS(1951); COP HATER(1958); FAIL SAFE(1964); GROUP, THE(1966)
Bradley Hardiman
1984
SCRUBBERS(1984, Brit.)
Hilary Hardiman
INADMISSIBLE EVIDENCE(1968, Brit.)
James Hardiman
HOUSE WHERE EVIL DWELLS, THE(1982), w
Terence Hardiman
LOOPHOLE(1981, Brit.)
Terrence Hardiman
POPE JOAN(1972, Brit.); GANDHI(1982)
1984
SAHARA(1984)
Danny Hardin
ENEMIES OF THE LAW(1931)
Eileen Hardin
WESTWARD TRAIL, THE(1948)
Jerry Hardin
THUNDER ROAD(1958); OUR TIME(1974); MITCHELL(1975); FOES(1977); 1941(1979); HEARTLAND(1980); HONKY TONK FREEWAY(1981); REDS(1981); CHILLY SCENES OF WINTER(1982); HONKYTONK MAN(1982); MISSING(1982); TEMPEST(1982); CUJO(1983)
1984
HEARTBREAKERS(1984); MASS APPEAL(1984)
Josh Hardin
WILSON(1944)
Melora Hardin
NORTH AVENUE IRREGULARS, THE(1979)
Neal Hardin
Silents
JOHNNY-ON-THE-SPOT(1919)
Neil Hardin
Misc. Silents
SUNSHINE AND GOLD(1917); UNDERSTUDY, THE(1917); LITTLE MISS GROWN-UP(1918); MIDNIGHT BURGLAR, THE(1918); MODERN HUSBANDS(1919)

Reg Hardin
ON HER MAJESTY'S SECRET SERVICE(1969, Brit.)
Rellie Hardin
BRONZE BUCKAROO, THE(1939)
Rink Hardin
THAT TENNESSEE BEAT(1966)
Sherry Hardin
HOLLYWOOD HIGH(1977)
Misc. Talkies
HOLLYWOOD HIGH(1976)
Ty Hardin
LAST TRAIN FROM GUN HILL(1959); CHAPMAN REPORT, THE(1962); MERRILL'S MARAUDERS(1962); PALM SPRINGS WEEKEND(1963); PT 109(1963); WALL OF NOISE(1963); BATTLE OF THE BULGE(1965); BERSERK(1967); SAVAGE PAMPAS(1967, Span./Arg.); CUSTER OF THE WEST(1968, U.S., Span.); ONE STEP TO HELL(1969, U.S./Ital./Span.); LAST REBEL, THE(1971); DRUMMER OF VENGEANCE(1974, Brit.)
Alfred Harding
Misc. Silents
BOYS OF THE OTTER PATROL(1918, Brit.)
Ann Harding
CONDEMNED(1929); PARIS BOUND(1929); GIRL OF THE GOLDEN WEST(1930); HER PRIVATE AFFAIR(1930); HOLIDAY(1930); DEVOTION(1931); EAST LYNNE(1931); ANIMAL KINGDOM, THE(1932); CONQUERORS, THE(1932); PRESTIGE(1932); WESTWARD PASSAGE(1932); DOUBLE HARNESS(1933); RIGHT TO ROMANCE(1933); WHEN LADIES MEET(1933); FOUNTAIN, THE(1934); GALLANT LADY(1934); LIFE OF VERGIE WINTERS, THE(1934); BIOGRAPHY OF A BACHELOR GIRL(1935); ENCHANTED APRIL(1935); FLAME WITHIN, THE(1935); PETER IBBETSON(1935); LADY CONSENTS, THE(1936); WITNESS CHAIR, THE(1936); LOVE FROM A STRANGER(1937, Brit.); EYES IN THE NIGHT(1942); MISSION TO MOSCOW(1943); NORTH STAR, THE(1943); JANIE(1944); NINE GIRLS(1944); THOSE ENDEARING YOUNG CHARMS(1945); JANIE GETS MARRIED(1946); CHRISTMAS EVE(1947); IT HAPPENED ON 5TH AVENUE(1947); MAGNIFICENT YANKEE, THE(1950); TWO WEEKS WITH LOVE(1950); UNKNOWN MAN, THE(1951); I'VE LIVED BEFORE(1956); MAN IN THE GREY FLANNEL SUIT, THE(1956); STRANGE INTRUDER(1956)
Bertita Harding
JUAREZ(1939), w; MAGIC FIRE(1956), w
Bill Harding
FAMILY AFFAIR(1954, Brit.), w; LYONS IN PARIS, THE(1955, Brit.), w
Brian Harding
FUSS OVER FEATHERS(1954, Brit.)
Brooks B. Harding
Silents
FRESHMAN, THE(1925), w
C. F. Harding
Silents
FATE'S PLAYTHING(1920, Brit.), w
Catherine Harding
MOONLIGHTING(1982, Brit.)
Elizabeth Harding
HAMMER(1972); YOUR THREE MINUTES ARE UP(1973); CHINATOWN(1974)
Ellerine Harding
EDUCATION OF SONNY CARSON, THE(1974)
Evelyn Harding
Silents
NOT GUILTY(1919, Brit.)
Misc. Silents
TOP DOG, THE(1918, Brit.); SPLENDID FOLLY(1919, Brit.)
Frank Harding
STAKEOUT ON DOPE STREET(1958); GET OUTTA TOWN(1960); MARRIED TOO YOUNG(1962)
George Harding
RIDE THE HIGH WIND(1967, South Africa), w
Gilbert Harding
GENTLE GUNMAN, THE(1952, Brit.); HORSE'S MOUTH, THE(1953, Brit.); MEET MR. LUCIFER(1953, Brit.); TALE OF THREE WOMEN, A(1954, Brit.); AS LONG AS THEY'RE HAPPY(1957, Brit.); EXPRESSO BONGO(1959, Brit.); LEFT, RIGHT AND CENTRE(1959); MY WIFE'S FAMILY(1962, Brit.)
Misc. Talkies
BEHIND THE HEADLINES(1953)
Gina Harding
FOR LOVE OF IVY(1968)
Harry Harding
Silents
HUTCH STIRS 'EM UP(1923, Brit.), w
Ian Harding
Misc. Silents
THIRD EYE, THE(1929, Brit.)
Jack Harding
Silents
JACK, SAM AND PETE(1919, Brit.)
Jacki Harding
LADY VANISHES, THE(1980, Brit.)
Jackie Lou Harding
FOLLOW THE BOYS(1944); HI, GOOD-LOOKIN'(1944); WEIRD WOMAN(1944)
Jeff Harding
1984
RAZOR'S EDGE, THE(1984); SCREAM FOR HELP(1984)
Joan Harding
JEANNE EAGELS(1957)
John Briard Harding
KISSING BANDIT, THE(1948), w; MY WIFE'S BEST FRIEND(1952), w
John F. Harding
HE LOVED AN ACTRESS(1938, Brit.), w
John Harding
77 PARK LANE(1931, Brit.), p; FAME(1936, Brit.), w; LOVE ME OR LEAVE ME(1955); MEET ME IN LAS VEGAS(1956); JOKER IS WILD(1957); THIS COULD BE THE NIGHT(1957); GUN RUNNERS, THE(1958); OUTCASTS OF THE CITY(1958); 10 NORTH FREDERICK(1958); CRIME AND PUNISHMENT,

U.S.A.(1959); FROM THE TERRACE(1960); PLEASE DON'T EAT THE DAISIES(1960); FEAR NO MORE(1961); VERY SPECIAL FAVOR, A(1965); HAWAII(1966); THIS PROPERTY IS CONDEMNED(1966); IMPOSSIBLE YEARS, THE(1968)
1984
GIVE MY REGARDS TO BROAD STREET(1984, Brit.)
June Harding
TROUBLE WITH ANGELS, THE(1966)
Kay Harding
MUMMY'S CURSE, THE(1944); SCARLET CLAW, THE(1944); WEIRD WOMAN(1944)
Lilly Harding
TRENCHCOAT(1983)
Lorraine Harding
Silents
ANNABEL LEE(1921)
Lyn Harding
SLEEPING PARTNERS(1930, Brit.); SPECKLED BAND, THE(1931, Brit.); BARTON MYSTERY, THE(1932, Brit.); CONSTANT NYMPH, THE(1933, Brit.); LASH, THE(1934, Brit.); MAN WHO CHANGED HIS NAME, THE(1934, Brit.); WILD BOY(1934, Brit.); ESCAPE ME NEVER(1935, Brit.); TRIUMPH OF SHERLOCK HOLMES, THE(1935, Brit.); MAN WHO LIVED AGAIN, THE(1936, Brit.); OLD SPANISH CUSTOM, AN(1936, Brit.); FIRE OVER ENGLAND(1937, Brit.); KNIGHT WITHOUT ARMOR(1937, Brit.); PLEASE TEACHER(1937, Brit.); UNDERNEATH THE ARCHES(1937, Brit.); PEARLS OF THE CROWN(1938, Fr.); GOODBYE MR. CHIPS(1939, Brit.); MUTINY OF THE ELSINORE, THE(1939, Brit.); SPY OF NAPOLEON(1939, Brit.); MISSING PEOPLE, THE(1940, Brit.); MURDER AT THE BASKERVILLES(1941, Brit.); PRIME MINISTER, THE(1941, Brit.)
Silents
WHEN KNIGHTHOOD WAS IN FLOWER(1922); FURTHER ADVENTURES OF THE FLAG LIEUTENANT(1927, Brit.); LAND OF HOPE AND GLORY(1927, Brit.)
Misc. Silents
BACHELOR HUSBAND, THE(1920 Brit.); BARTON MYSTERY, THE(1920, Brit.); YOLANDA(1924)
Marion Harding
Misc. Silents
TAME CAT, THE(1921)
Mitchell Harding
PUNISHMENT PARK(1971)
Nathan Harding
HUSTLE(1975)
Pat Harding
LONG GRAY LINE, THE(1955)
Paul Harding
PORKY'S(1982), set d
Reg Harding
SEE NO EVIL(1971, Brit.); LEGACY, THE(1979, Brit.); RAIDERS OF THE LOST ARK(1981)
Stewart Harding
SPACEHUNTER: ADVENTURES IN THE FORBIDDEN ZONE(1983), w
Tex Harding
OUTLAWS OF THE ROCKIES(1945); ROUGH, TOUGH AND READY(1945); LAWLESS EMPIRE(1946); DESERT VIGILANTE(1949)
Misc. Talkies
BLAZING THE WESTERN TRAIL(1945); BOTH BARRELS BLAZING(1945); RETURN OF THE DURANGO KID(1945); RUSTLERS OF THE BADLANDS(1945); TEXAS PANHANDLE(1945); FRONTIER GUNLAW(1946)
Vince Harding
GROUP, THE(1966)
Vincent Harding
MARY HAD A LITTLE(1961, Brit.); 20,000 POUNDS KISS, THE(1964, Brit.); KNACK ... AND HOW TO GET IT, THE(1965, Brit.); ONE WAY PENDULUM(1965, Brit.); FAR FROM THE MADDING CROWD(1967, Brit.); CAPTAIN NEMO AND THE UNDERWATER CITY(1969, Brit.)
C. M. Hardinge
CARNIVAL(1931, Brit.), w
Rex Hardinge
SEXTON BLAKE AND THE BEARDED DOCTOR(1935, Brit.), w
Alexander Hardini
LONG IS THE ROAD(1948, Ger.)
Linda Hardisty
GREEN SLIME, THE(1969)
Cedrick Hardman
CANDIDATE, THE(1972); STIR CRAZY(1980)
Frank Hardman
MOON ZERO TWO(1970, Brit.), w
Holly Hardman
TERROR EYES(1981)
Karl Hardman
NIGHT OF THE LIVING DEAD(1968), a, p, makeup
Nate Hardman
1984
BLESS THEIR LITTLE HEARTS(1984)
Ric Hardman
RARE BREED, THE(1966), w
Rich Hardman
BIG NIGHT, THE(1960), w
Rick Hardman
GUNMAN'S WALK(1958), w
Paul Hardmuth
I WAS A MALE WAR BRIDE(1949); ODONGO(1956, Brit.); HOUSE OF THE SEVEN HAWKS, THE(1959)
Charley Hardnett
VISITOR, THE(1980, Ital./U.S.)
Kadeem Hardson
1984
BEAT STREET(1984)
Michael Hardstark
ALICE, SWEET ALICE(1978)

Bill Hardsway
NIGHT AND DAY(1946)
Eloise Hardt
YOU BELONG TO ME(1941); ARABIAN NIGHTS(1942); CASANOVA BROWN(1944);
DARK CORNER, THE(1946); HOMECOMING(1948); GREAT SINNER, THE(1949);
LITTLE WOMEN(1949); ESCAPE FROM FORT BRAVO(1953); NIGHT OF THE
IGUANA, THE(1964); INCUBUS(1966); GAMES(1967); GAY DECEIVERS, THE(1969);
LATE LIZ, THE(1971); SAVE THE TIGER(1973); PROMISES IN THE DARK(1979);
WINTER KILLS(1979); LOOKER(1981)
1984
IRRECONCILABLE DIFFERENCES(1984)
Harry Hardt
COPPER, THE(1930, Brit.); ECHO OF A DREAM(1930, Ger.); CASE VAN GEL-
DERN(1932, Ger.); ETERNAL WALTZ, THE(1959, Ger.); MARK OF THE DEVIL
II(1975, Ger./Brit.)
Karin Hardt
EIGHT GIRLS IN A BOAT(1932, Ger.); TOWN WITHOUT PITY(1961, Ger./Switz./
U.S.); SLEEPING BEAUTY(1965, Ger.); JUST A GIGOLO(1979, Ger.)
Ludwig Hardt
ARIZONA(1940); UNDERGROUND(1941); DESPERATE JOURNEY(1942); KING'S
ROW(1942)
W. Hardt
STRANGE WORLD(1952)
Hans Hardt-Hardtloff
NAKED AMONG THE WOLVES(1967, Ger.); PINOCCHIO(1969, E. Ger.)
Bruno Hardt-Warden
MARRIED IN HOLLYWOOD(1929), w
Paul Hardtmuth
HIGHLY DANGEROUS(1950, Brit.); LOST PEOPLE, THE(1950, Brit.); THIRD MAN,
THE(1950, Brit.); WONDER BOY(1951, Brit./Aust.); DESPERATE MOMENT(1953,
Brit.); SHADOW MAN(1953, Brit.); DIAMOND WIZARD, THE(1954, Brit.); ALL FOR
MARY(1956, Brit.); GAMMA PEOPLE, THE(1956); CURSE OF FRANKENSTEIN,
THE(1957, Brit.); DR. BLOOD'S COFFIN(1961)
Cedric Hardwick
ROME EXPRESS(1933, Brit.)
Mark Hardwick
1984
BROADWAY DANNY ROSE(1984)
Thelma Hardwick
CHANCE AT HEAVEN(1933); RIGHT TO ROMANCE(1933)
Tony Hardwick
PALM BEACH(1979, Aus.)
Sir Cedric Hardwicke
DREYFUS CASE, THE(1931, Brit.); BELLA DONNA(1934, Brit.); GHOUL, THE(1934,
Brit.); KING OF PARIS, THE(1934, Brit.); LADY IS WILLING, THE(1934, Brit.);
ORDERS IS ORDERS(1934, Brit.); POWER(1934, Brit.); BECKY SHARP(1935); LES
MISERABLES(1935); NELL GWYN(1935, Brit.); CALLING THE TUNE(1936, Brit.);
LABURNUM GROVE(1936, Brit.); LADY JANE GREY(1936, Brit.); PEG OF OLD
DRURY(1936, Brit.); THINGS TO COME(1936, Brit.); GREEN LIGHT(1937); KING
SOLOMON'S MINES(1937, Brit.); HUNCHBACK OF NOTRE DAME, THE(1939); ON
BORROWED TIME(1939); STANLEY AND LIVINGSTONE(1939); HOWARDS OF
VIRGINIA, THE(1940); INVISIBLE MAN RETURNS, THE(1940); TOM BROWN'S
SCHOOL DAYS(1940); VICTORY(1940); SUNDOWN(1941); SUSPICION(1941); COM-
MANDOS STRIKE AT DAWN, THE(1942); GHOST OF FRANKENSTEIN, THE(1942);
INVISIBLE AGENT(1942); VALLEY OF THE SUN(1942); CROSS OF LORRAINE,
THE(1943); FOREVER AND A DAY(1943), a, p&d; MOON IS DOWN, THE(1943);
KEYS OF THE KINGDOM, THE(1944); LODGER, THE(1944); WILSON(1944); WING
AND A PRAYER(1944); PICTURE OF DORIAN GRAY, THE(1945); BEWARE OF
PITY(1946, Brit.); SENTIMENTAL JOURNEY(1946); IMPERFECT LADY, THE(1947);
IVY(1947); LURED(1947); NICHOLAS NICKLEBY(1947, Brit.); SONG OF MY
HEART(1947); TYCOON(1947); WOMAN'S VENGEANCE, A(1947); I REMEMBER
MAMA(1948); ROPE(1948); CONNECTICUT YANKEE IN KING ARTHUR'S COURT,
A(1949); NOW BARABBAS WAS A ROBBER(1949, Brit.); WHITE TOWER, THE(1950);
WINSLOW BOY, THE(1950); DESERT FOX, THE(1951); MR. IMPERIUM(1951);
CARIBBEAN(1952); GREEN GLOVE, THE(1952); BOTANY BAY(1953); SALO-
ME(1953); WAR OF THE WORLDS, THE(1953); BAIT(1954); DIANE(1955); AROUND
THE WORLD IN 80 DAYS(1956); GABY(1956); HELEN OF TROY(1956, Ital); POWER
AND THE PRIZE, THE(1956); RICHARD III(1956, Brit.); TEN COMMANDMENTS,
THE(1956); VAGABOND KING, THE(1956); BABY FACE NELSON(1957); PRINCE
AND THE SHOWGIRL, THE(1957, Brit.); STORY OF MANKIND, THE(1957); MAGIC
FOUNTAIN, THE(1961); FIVE WEEKS IN A BALLOON(1962); PUMPKIN EATER,
THE(1964, Brit.); MAN FOR ALL SEASONS, A(1966, Brit.); DEADLY AFFAIR,
THE(1967, Brit.); LONG DUEL, THE(1967, Brit.); ROMEO AND JULIET(1968, Brit./
Ital.); JULIUS CAESAR(1970, Brit.); OCTOPUSSY(1983, Brit.)
Silents
NELSON(1926, Brit.)
Clarke Hardwicke
DARK DELUSION(1947); HIGH BARBAREE(1947); SONG OF THE THIN MAN(1947)
Derek Hardwicke
JULIUS CAESAR(1970, Brit.)
Edward Hardwicke
GUY NAMED JOE, A(1943); HELL BELOW ZERO(1954, Brit.); MEN OF SHERWOOD
FOREST(1957, Brit.); OTHELLO(1965, Brit.); FLEA IN HER EAR, A(1968, Fr.);
OTLEY(1969, Brit.); RECKONING, THE(1971, Brit.); BLACK WINDMILL, THE(1974,
Brit.); ODD JOB, THE(1978, Brit.); VENOM(1982, Brit.)
Jean Hardwicke
OPERATION DIPLOMAT(1953, Brit.)
Ames Hardy
LEAP OF FAITH(1931, Brit.)
Martin Hardy [Sergio Martino]
MURDER CLINIC, THE(1967, Ital./Fr.), w
Beryl Hardy
PLEASE TURN OVER(1960, Brit.)
Betty Hardy
DEVIL ON HORSEBACK(1954, Brit.)
Brian Hardy
BUGSY MALONE(1976, Brit.)

Charlete Hardy
TWO TICKETS TO BROADWAY(1951)
Cherry Hardy
WRONG MAN, THE(1956)
Elizabeth Hardy
AMAZING MONSIEUR FABRE, THE(1952, Fr.)
Francoise Hardy
NUTTY, NAUGHTY CHATEAU(1964, Fr./Ital.); WHAT'S NEW, PUSSYCAT?(1965,
U.S./Fr.); GRAND PRIX(1966); MASCULINE FEMININE(1966, Fr./Swed.); SOLO(1970,
Fr.), art d; DAUGHTERS OF DARKNESS(1971, Bel./ Fr./ Ger./ Ital.), art d
Frank Hardy
LOUISIANA STORY(1948); THREE IN ONE(1956, Aus.), w
Silents
MANON LESCAUT(1914)
Gari Hardy
JOHN GOLDFARB, PLEASE COME HOME(1964); SPEEDWAY(1968)
Gerard Hardy
DANTON(1983)
Glenn Hardy
DAY THE EARTH STOOD STILL, THE(1951); TAXI(1953)
Hagood Hardy
SECOND WIND(1976, Can.), m; I, MAUREEN(1978, Can.), m; KLONDIKE FE-
VER(1980), m; DIRTY TRICKS(1981, Can.), m
Henry Hardy
OH, HEAVENLY DOG!(1980)
Imre Hardy
Misc. Silents
STRAUSS, THE WALTZ KING(1929, Ger.)
J.L. Hardy
KEY, THE(1934), w
Jocelyn Hardy
EVERYTHING IS THUNDER(1936, Brit.), w
Joe Hardy
TELL ME IN THE SUNLIGHT(1967)
John Hardy
BOTANY BAY(1953); JULIUS CAESAR(1953)
Misc. Talkies
FIGHTER PILOTS(1977)
Jonathan Hardy
ADVENTURES OF BARRY McKENZIE(1972, Austral.); BREAKER MORANT(1980,
Aus.), w; SCARECROW, THE(1982, New Zealand); LONELY HEARTS(1983, Aus.)
1984
CONSTANCE(1984, New Zealand), w
Jonathon Hardy
DEVIL'S PLAYGROUND, THE(1976, Aus.); MAD MAX(1979, Aus.)
Joseph Hardy
HUSBANDS(1970); GREAT EXPECTATIONS(1975, Brit.), d; FOR PETE'S SA-
KE(1977)
Laurel and Hardy
DANCING MASTERS, THE(1943)
Laurence Hardy
CRUEL SEA, THE(1953); LOVE IS A BALL(1963); WOMAN OF STRAW(1964, Brit.);
GOODBYE GEMINI(1970, Brit.); MAN WHO HAUNTED HIMSELF, THE(1970, Brit.)
Lindsay Hardy
WORLD FOR RANSOM(1954), w; LOVE IS A BALL(1963), w
Marianne Hardy
VICE AND VIRTUE(1965, Fr./Ital.)
Mark Hardy
MARY HAD A LITTLE(1961, Brit.)
Martin Hardy [Luciano Martino]
WHAT!(1965, Fr./Brit./Ital.), w
Michele Hardy
HALF A SIXPENCE(1967, Brit.); SONG OF NORWAY(1970)
Mildred Hardy
THIS LAND IS MINE(1943)
Oliver Hardy
ROGUE SONG, THE(1930); PARDON US(1931); PACK UP YOUR TROUBLES(1932);
DEVIL'S BROTHER, THE(1933); SONS OF THE DESERT(1933); BABES IN TOY-
LAND(1934); HOLLYWOOD PARTY(1934); BONNIE SCOTLAND(1935); BOHEMIAN
GIRL, THE(1936); OUR RELATIONS(1936); PICK A STAR(1937); WAY OUT
WEST(1937); BLOCKHEADS(1938); SWISS MISS(1938); FLYING DEUCES, THE(1939);
ZENOBIA(1939); CHUMP AT OXFORD, A(1940); SAPS AT SEA(1940); GREAT
GUNS(1941); A-HAUNTING WE WILL GO(1942); AIR RAID WARDENS(1943); JIT-
TERBUGS(1943); BIG NOISE, THE(1944); NOTHING BUT TROUBLE(1944); FIGHT-
ING KENTUCKIAN, THE(1949); RIDING HIGH(1950); UTOPIA(1952, Fr./Ital.)
Silents
LITTLE WILDCAT(1922); ONE STOLEN NIGHT(1923); THREE AGES, THE(1923);
WIZARD OF OZ, THE(1925); NO MAN'S LAW(1927)
Patricia Hardy
GIRLS IN THE NIGHT(1953); DON'T KNOCK THE ROCK(1956)
Peter Hardy
HORROR CASTLE(1965, Ital.)
Rene Hardy
BITTER VICTORY(1958, Fr.), w; TRIPLE CROSS(1967, Fr./Brit.), w; POSTMAN
GOES TO WAR, THE(1968, Fr.), w
Robert Hardy
TORPEDO RUN(1958); SPY WHO CAME IN FROM THE COLD, THE(1965, Brit.);
BERSERK(1967); HOW I WON THE WAR(1967, Brit.); 10 RILLINGTON PLACE(1971,
Brit.); DEMONS OF THE MIND(1972, Brit.); NIGHT OF THE LEPUS(1972); YOUNG
WINSTON(1972, Brit.); GAWAIN AND THE GREEN KNIGHT(1973, Brit.); YELLOW
DOG(1973, Brit.); DARK PLACES(1974, Brit.); PSYCHOMANIA(1974, Brit.)
Robin Hardy
WICKER MAN, THE(1974, Brit.), d
Rod Hardy
THIRST(1979, Aus.), d
Sam B. Hardy
Misc. Silents
OVER NIGHT(1915); HIS FATHER'S WIFE(1919)

Sam Hardy

ACQUITTED(1929); BIG NEWS(1929); FAST COMPANY(1929); GIVE AND TA-RE(1929); MEXICALI ROSE(1929); ON WITH THE SHOW(1929); RAINBOW MAN(1929); BORROWED WIVES(1930); BURNING UP(1930); FLORODORA GIRL, THE(1930); RENO(1930); SONG OF THE WEST(1930); TRUE TO THE NAVY(1930); ANNABELLE'S AFFAIRS(1931); JUNE MOON(1931); MAGNIFICENT LIE(1931); MILLIONAIRE, THE(1931); MIRACLE WOMAN, THE(1931); PEACH O' RENO(1931); DARK HORSE, THE(1932); MAKE ME A STAR(1932); PHANTOM OF CRESTWOOD, THE(1932); ANN VICKERS(1933); BIG BRAIN, THE(1933); FACE IN THE SKY(1933); GOLDIE GETS ALONG(1933); KING KONG(1933); ONE SUNDAY AFTER-NOON(1933); THREE-CORNERED MOON(1933); ALONG CAME SALLY(1934, Brit.); CURTAIN AT EIGHT(1934); GAY BRIDE, THE(1934); I GIVE MY LOVE(1934); LITTLE MISS MARKER(1934); TRANSATLANTIC MERRY-GO-ROUND(1934); BREAK OF HEARTS(1935); HOORAY FOR LOVE(1935); MAN ON THE FLYING TRAPEZE, THE(1935), w; NIGHT ALARM(1935); POWDERSMOKE RANGE(1935)
Misc. Talkies
ALONG CAME SALLY(1933)
Silents
BLUEBEARD'S SEVEN WIVES(1926); TEXAS STEER, A(1927); OUTCAST(1928); MAN'S MAN, A(1929)
Misc. Silents
WOMAN'S EXPERIENCE, A(1918); GET-RICH-QUICK WALLINGFORD(1921); MIGHTY LAK' A ROSE(1923); WHEN LOVE GROWS COLD(1925); GREAT DECEP-TION, THE(1926); BROADWAY NIGHTS(1927); HIGH HAT(1927); ORCHIDS AND ERMINE(1927); BIG NOISE, THE(1928); BURNING UP BROADWAY(1928); BUTTER AND EGG MAN, THE(1928); NIGHT BIRD, THE(1928); TURN BACK THE HOURS(1928); RAINBOW, THE(1929)

Sam T. Hardy
Misc. Silents
AT FIRST SIGHT(1917)

Samuel B. Hardy
Silents
JUDY FORGOT(1915)

Sophie Hardy
DESPERADO TRAIL, THE(1965, Ger./Yugo.); THREE HATS FOR LISA(1965, Brit.); ATTACK OF THE ROBOTS(1967, Fr./Span.); TASTE OF EXCITEMENT(1969, Brit.); TRYGON FACTOR, THE(1969, Brit.); ROAD TO SALINA(1971, Fr./Ital.)

Stuart Hardy
FORBIDDEN VALLEY(1938), w; SIERRA(1950), w

Ted Hardy
YOU CAN'T CHEAT AN HONEST MAN(1939)

Thomas Hardy
GREENWOOD TREE, THE(1930, Brit.), w; UNDER THE GREENWOOD TREE(1930, Brit.), w; SECRET CAVE, THE(1953, Brit.), w; FAR FROM THE MADDING CROWD(1967, Brit.), w; TESS(1980, Fr./Brit.), w
Silents
FAR FROM THE MADDING CROWD(1915, Brit.), w; TESS OF THE D'URBER-VILLES(1924), w

Timothy Hardy
PERSECUTION AND ASSASSINATION OF JEAN-PAUL MARAT AS PERFORMED BY THE INMATES OF THE ASYLUM OF CHARENTON UNDER THE DIRECTION OF THE MARQUIS DE SADE, THE(1967, Brit.)

William Hardy
HELLFIGHTERS(1968)
1984
PREPPIES(1984)
Silents
QUEEN OF SHEBA, THE(1921)

Nabuko Hardychuck
BY DESIGN(1982)

Betty Hare
TREAD SOFTLY(1952, Brit.)

Bill Hare
FINNEY(1969), p,d,w,&ed

Bobby Hare
YOU CAN'T CHEAT AN HONEST MAN(1939)

Donovan Hare
ONE MAN(1979, Can.)

Doris Hare
JUBILEE WINDOW(1935, Brit.); NIGHT MAIL(1935, Brit.); DISCOVERIES(1939, Brit.); NORTH SEA PATROL(1939, Brit.); SHE COULDN'T SAY NO(1939, Brit.); HISTORY OF MR. POLLY, THE(1949, Brit.); STRANGER'S MEETING(1957, Brit.); ANOTHER TIME, ANOTHER PLACE(1958); LEAGUE OF GENTLEMEN, THE(1961, Brit.); PLACE TO GO, A(1964, Brit.); ON THE BUSES(1972, Brit.); CONFESSIONS OF A POP PERFORMER(1975, Brit.); CONFESSIONS FROM A HOLIDAY CAMP(1977, Brit.)
Misc. Talkies
HOLIDAY ON THE BUSES(1974, Brit.)

Ellin Hare
ACCEPTABLE LEVELS(1983, Brit.), w, ed

Ernest Hare
HENRY V(1946, Brit.)

Harry Hare
GEISHA BOY, THE(1958)

J. Robertson Hare
ONE EMBARRASSING NIGHT(1930, Brit.); CAR OF DREAMS(1935, Brit.); FIGHT-ING STOCK(1935, Brit.); TWO OF US, THE(1938, Brit.)

Julia Hare
MR. BILLION(1977)

Ken Hare
I'M ALL RIGHT, JACK(1959, Brit.), m; CREATURES THE WORLD FORGOT(1971, Brit.)

Kevin Hare
ONE MAN(1979, Can.)

Lumsden Hare
UNDER TWO FLAGS(1936); BLACK WATCH, THE(1929); MASQUERADE(1929), a, d; SALUTE(1929); SKY HAWK(1929); CRAZY THAT WAY(1930); SCOTLAND YARD(1930); SO THIS IS LONDON(1930); ALWAYS GOODBYE(1931); ARROWS-MITH(1931); CHARLIE CHAN CARRIES ON(1931); ROAD TO SINGAPORE(1931); SVENGALI(1931); UNDER SUSPICION(1931); SILENT WITNESS, THE(1932); HIS

DOUBLE LIFE(1933); INTERNATIONAL HOUSE(1933); BLACK MOON(1934); HOUSE OF ROTHSCHILD, THE(1934); LITTLE MINISTER, THE(1934); MAN OF TWO WORLDS(1934); OUTCAST LADY(1934); WORLD MOVES ON, THE(1934); CLIVE OF INDIA(1935); CRUSADES, THE(1935); FOLIES DERGERE(1935); FRECKLES(1935); GREAT IMPERSONATION, THE(1935); LADY TUBBS(1935); LIVES OF A BENGAL LANCER(1935); SHE(1935); THREE MUSKETEERS, THE(1935); CHARGE OF THE LIGHT BRIGADE, THE(1936); LAST OF THE MOHICANS, THE(1936); LLOYDS OF LONDON(1936); PRINCESS COMES ACROSS, THE(1936); PROFESSIONAL SOL-DIER(1936); LAST OF MRS. CHEYNEY, THE(1937); LIFE BEGINS WITH LOVE(1937); LIFE OF EMILE ZOLA, THE(1937); CAPTAIN FURY(1939); GUNGA DIN(1939); DISPATCH FROM REUTERS, A(1940); HUDSON'S BAY(1940); NORTHWEST PAS-SAGE(1940); REBECCA(1940); BLONDE FROM SINGAPORE, THE(1941); CONFIRM OR DENY(1941); DR. JEKYLL AND MR. HYDE(1941); ONE NIGHT IN LISBON(1941); PASSAGE FROM HONG KONG(1941); SHADOWS ON THE STAIRS(1941); SUSPI-CION(1941); GORILLA MAN(1942); LONDON BLACKOUT MURDERS(1942); RAN-DOM HARVEST(1942); THIS ABOVE ALL(1942); FOREVER AND A DAY(1943); HOLY MATRIMONY(1943); JACK LONDON(1943); MADAME CURIE(1943); MISSION TO MOSCOW(1943); CANTERVILLE GHOST, THE(1944); KEYS OF THE KINGDOM, THE(1944); LODGER, THE(1944); PASSPORT TO DESTINY(1944); WHITE CLIFFS OF DOVER, THE(1944); LOVE LETTERS(1945); VALLEY OF DECISION, THE(1945); SISTER KENNY(1946); EXILE, THE(1947); GREEN DOLPHIN STREET(1947); IMPER-FECT LADY, THE(1947); IT HAPPENED IN BROOKLYN(1947); IVY(1947); PRIVATE AFFAIRS OF BEL AMI, THE(1947); SECRET LIFE OF WALTER MITTY, THE(1947); SWORDSMAN, THE(1947); HILLS OF HOME(1948); MR. PEABODY AND THE MERMAID(1948); CHALLENGE TO LASSIE(1949); FIGHTING O'FLYNN, THE(1949); THAT FORSYTE WOMAN(1949); FORTUNES OF CAPTAIN BLOOD(1950); DAVID AND BATHSHEBA(1951); DESERT FOX, THE(1951); LADY AND THE BANDIT, THE(1951); DIPLOMATIC COURIER(1952); FIVE FINGERS(1952); MY COUSIN RACHEL(1952); JULIUS CAESAR(1953); YOUNG BESS(1953); KING RICHARD AND THE CRUSADERS(1954); ROSE MARIE(1954); JOHNNY TREMAIN(1957); COUNT YOUR BLESSINGS(1959); FOUR SKULLS OF JONATHAN DRAKE, THE(1959); OREGON TRAIL, THE(1959)
Misc. Talkies
AND NOW TOMORROW(1952)
Silents
ARMS AND THE WOMAN(1916); AS IN A LOOKING GLASS(1916); ENVY(1917); AVALANCHE, THE(1919); EDUCATION OF ELIZABETH, THE(1921); SHERLOCK HOLMES(1922); ON THE BANKS OF THE WABASH(1923); SECOND YOUTH(1924); FUGITIVES(1929); GIRLS GONE WILD(1929)
Misc. Silents
LOVE'S CRUCIBLE(1916); TEST, THE(1916); BARBARY SHEEP(1917); LIGHT WITHIN, THE(1918); COUNTRY COUSIN, THE(1919); BLUE PEARL, THE(1920); CHILDREN NOT WANTED(1920); FRISKY MRS. JOHNSON, THE(1920); MOTHERS OF MEN(1920); THOUGHTLESS WOMEN(1920)

Marguerite Hare
Misc. Silents
RIGHT TO LIVE, THE(1921, Brit.)

Marilyn Hare
ANGELS WITH BROKEN WINGS(1941); LADY FOR A NIGHT(1941); HI, NEIGH-BOR(1942); ICE-CAPADES REVUE(1942); SHEPHERD OF THE OZARKS(1942); YO-KEL BOY(1942); WEST OF TEXAS(1943); SINCE YOU WENT AWAY(1944)

Philippa Hare
SERVANT, THE(1964, Brit.); IDOL, THE(1966, Brit.)

Robertson Hare
ON APPROVAL(1930, Brit.); PLUNDER(1931, Brit.); TONS OF MONEY(1931, Brit.); NIGHT LIKE THIS, A(1932, Brit.); THARK(1932, Brit.); CUCKOO IN THE NEST, THE(1933, Brit.); JUST MY LUCK(1933, Brit.); TURKEY TIME(1933, Brit.); ARE YOU A MASON?(1934, Brit.); CUP OF KINDNESS, A(1934, Brit.); DIRTY WORK(1934, Brit.); FRIDAY THE 13TH(1934, Brit.); IT'S A BOY(1934, Brit.); FOREIGN AFFAIRES(1935, Brit.); OH DADDY!(1935, Brit.); STORMY WEATHER(1935, Brit.); POT LUCK(1936, Brit.); YOU MUST GET MARRIED(1936, Brit.); AREN'T MEN BEASTS?(1937, Brit.); YOU'RE IN THE ARMY NOW(1937, Brit.); SPOT OF BOTHER, A(1938, Brit.); SO THIS IS LONDON(1940, Brit.); BANANA RIDGE(1941, Brit.); WOMEN AREN'T AN-GELS(1942, Brit.); HE SNOOPS TO CONQUER(1944, Brit.); THINGS HAPPEN AT NIGHT(1948, Brit.); ONE WILD OAT(1951, Brit.); MAGIC BOX, THE(1952, Brit.); ADVENTURES OF SADIE, THE(1955, Brit.); THREE MEN IN A BOAT(1958, Brit.); NIGHT WE GOT THE BIRD, THE(1961, Brit.); MY WIFE'S FAMILY(1962, Brit.); SEVEN KEYS(1962, Brit.); WONDERFUL TO BE YOUNG!(1962, Brit.); CROOKS ANONYMOUS(1963, Brit.); MURDER ON THE CAMPUS(1963, Brit.); HOTEL PARADISO(1966, U.S./Brit.); SALT & PEPPER(1968, Brit.)
Misc. Talkies
RAISING THE ROOF(1971, Brit.)

Sir John Hare
Misc. Silents
PAIR OF SPECTACLES, A(1916, Brit.); VICAR OF WAKEFIELD, THE(1916, Brit.); CASTLE(1917, Brit.)

Sybil Hare
Misc. Silents
LOVES AND ADVENTURES IN THE LIFE OF SHAKESPEARE(1914, Brit.)

Walter Benjamin Hare
AARON SLICK FROM PUNKIN CRICK(1952), d&w

Will Hare
WRONG MAN, THE(1956); EFFECT OF GAMMA RAYS ON MAN-IN-THE-MOON MARIGOLDS, THE(1972); BLACK OAK CONSPIRACY(1977); HEAVEN CAN WAIT(1978); BUTCH AND SUNDANCE: THE EARLY DAYS(1979); ELECTRIC HORSEMAN, THE(1979); ROSE, THE(1979); PENNIES FROM HEAVEN(1981); EN-TER THE NINJA(1982)
1984
SILENT NIGHT, DEADLY NIGHT(1984)

Harta Hareiter
AS THE SEA RAGES(1960 Ger.), art d

Herta Hareiter
TURKISH CUCUMBER, THE(1963, Ger.), art d; HOW TO SEDUCE A PLAY-BOY(1968, Aust./Fr./Ital.), art d

Herta Hareiter-Pischinger
SALZBURG CONNECTION, THE(1972), art d

Ava Harela
YELLOWBEARD(1983)

Marte Harell
CONGRESS DANCES(1957, Ger.); ENCOUNTERS IN SALZBURG(1964, Ger.)
Marthe Harell
VIENNA WALTZES(1961, Aust.); ASSIGNMENT K(1968, Brit.)
Chuck Haren
JUMBO(1962)
Dean Harens
SUSPECT, THE(1944); CRACK-UP(1946); ROSIE!(1967)
John Haretakis
GLORY BRIGADE, THE(1953)
Dorian Harewood
SPARKLE(1976); GRAY LADY DOWN(1978); LOOKER(1981)
1984
AGAINST ALL ODDS(1984); TANK(1984)
Leigh Harfine
CAREFUL, SOFT SHOULDERS(1942), m
Alec Harford
DOSS HOUSE(1933, Brit.); SYLVIA SCARLETT(1936); MEN IN EXILE(1937); ON AGAIN–OFF AGAIN(1937); SERGEANT MURPHY(1938); EARL OF CHICAGO, THE(1940); SOUTH OF SUEZ(1940); LODGER, THE(1944); NATIONAL VELVET(1944); NONE BUT THE LONELY HEART(1944); KISS THE BLOOD OFF MY HANDS(1948); THREE MUSKETEERS, THE(1948); SON OF DR. JEKYLL, THE(1951); FACE TO FACE(1952); BOTANY BAY(1953); LADY GODIVA(1955)
Alex Harford
FOUR JILLS IN A JEEP(1944); MOSS ROSE(1947); JOAN OF ARC(1948); HOUDINI(1953)
Betty Harford
WILD AND THE INNOCENT, THE(1959); INSIDE DAISY CLOVER(1965); 9/30/55(1977); CHINA SYNDROME, THE(1979)
Frank Harford
YODELIN' KID FROM PINE RIDGE(1937), m/l
Carlheinz Hargesheimer
NOT RECONCILED, OR "ONLY VIOLENCE HELPS WHERE IT RULES"(1969, Ger.)
Heinrich Hargesheimer
NOT RECONCILED, OR "ONLY VIOLENCE HELPS WHERE IT RULES"(1969, Ger.)
Mickey Hargitay
SLAUGHTER ON TENTH AVENUE(1957); WILL SUCCESS SPOIL ROCK HUNTER?(1957); LOVES OF HERCULES, THE(1960); PROMISES, PROMISES(1963); BLOODY PIT OF HORROR, THE(1965, Ital.); PRIMITIVE LOVE(1966, Ital.); LADY FRANKENSTEIN(1971, Ital.)
Misc. Talkies
REVENGE OF THE GLADIATORS(1962)
Norman Hargood
INTRUDER, THE(1955, Brit.)
Clarence Hargrave
NARROW MARGIN, THE(1952)
Doris Hargrave
WHOLE SHOOTIN' MATCH, THE(1979); WHERE THE BUFFALO ROAM(1980)
1984
CLOAK AND DAGGER(1984); LAST NIGHT AT THE ALAMO(1984)
Ron Hargrave
FORCE OF ARMS(1951); FLESH AND FURY(1952); RED SKIES OF MONTANA(1952); JACK SLADE(1953); KID FROM LEFT FIELD, THE(1953); VICKI(1953); DANCE WITH ME, HENRY(1956); UNWED MOTHER(1958); WAKE ME WHEN IT'S OVER(1960)
T.J. Hargrave
SUCH GOOD FRIENDS(1971)
William Hargraves
HAPPY DAYS(1930)
Christine Hargreaves
RECKONING, THE(1971, Brit.); HIRELING, THE(1973, Brit.); ALL THINGS BRIGHT AND BEAUTIFUL(1979, Brit.); PINK FLOYD–THE WALL(1982, Brit.)
1984
1984(1984, Brit.)
David Hargreaves
OTHELLO(1965, Brit.); AGATHA(1979, Brit.)
Fred Hargreaves
Misc. Talkies
SHERIFF'S SECRET, THE(1931)
Henry Hargreaves
Misc. Silents
SHADOWS(1915, Brit.)
Janet Hargreaves
DEADLY AFFAIR, THE(1967, Brit.); FRANKENSTEIN AND THE MONSTER FROM HELL(1974, Brit.)
John Hargreaves
DON QUIXOTE(1973, Aus.), p; REMOVALISTS, THE(1975, Aus.); DEATHCHEATERS(1976, Aus.); DON'S PARTY(1976, Aus.); MAD DOG MORGAN(1976,Aus.); LONG WEEKEND(1978, Aus.); ODD ANGRY SHOT, THE(1979, Aus.); BEYOND REASONABLE DOUBT(1980, New Zeal.); HOODWINK(1981, Aus.); KILLING OF ANGEL STREET, THE(1983, Aus.)
1984
CAREFUL, HE MIGHT HEAR YOU(1984, Aus.)
Lance Z. Hargreaves
CROOKED SKY, THE(1957, Brit.), w; FIGHTING WILDCATS, THE(1957, Brit.), w; FIRST MAN INTO SPACE(1959, Brit.), w; DEVIL DOLL(1964, Brit.), w; BATTLE BENEATH THE EARTH(1968, Brit.), w
Reginald Hargreaves
REUNION(1932, Brit.), w
Robert Hargreaves
CHARMING DECEIVER, THE(1933, Brit.), m/l; HERO(1982, Brit.), ed
1984
GHOST DANCE(1984, Brit.), ed
Sir Gerald Hargreaves
ATLANTIS, THE LOST CONTINENT(1961), w
William Hargreaves
FAME(1936, Brit.), w

Dean Hargrove
ONE SPY TOO MANY(1966), w; HELICOPTER SPIES, THE(1968), w; MANCHU EAGLE MURDER CAPER MYSTERY, THE(1975), d, w
Marion Hargrove
MILLIONS IN THE AIR(1935); SEE HERE, PRIVATE HARGROVE(1944), w; WHAT NEXT, CORPORAL HARGROVE?(1945), w; GIRL HE LEFT BEHIND, THE(1956), w; JOE BUTTERFLY(1957), w; CASH McCALL(1960), w; BOYS' NIGHT OUT(1962), w; FORTY POUNDS OF TROUBLE(1962), w; MUSIC MAN, THE(1962), w
Wayne Harht
NORSEMAN, THE(1978)
Sumi Hari
KRAKATOA, EAST OF JAVA(1969)
Tatsuhiko Hari
SANJURO(1962, Jap.)
Wilfred Hari
AFFAIRS OF A GENTLEMAN(1934); MELODY IN SPRING(1934); ENTER MADAME(1935); THEODORA GOES WILD(1936); DR. EHRLICH'S MAGIC BULLET(1940); SECRET AGENT OF JAPAN(1942)
Winifred Hari
COWBOY STAR, THE(1936)
Zaharira Harifai
SALLAH(1965, Israel)
Ron Harimann
CHANGE OF MIND(1969)
Joy Harington
CALCUTTA(1947); SLEEPING CAR TO TRIESTE(1949, Brit.)
Theo Harisch
PERMISSION TO KILL(1975, U.S./Aust.), art d; BEHIND THE IRON MASK(1977), art d
Richard B. Harison
Misc. Talkies
EASY STREET(1930)
Dominique Harispuru
MEN PREFER FAT GIRLS(1981, Fr.), p; LES MISERABLES(1982, Fr.), p
Michael Hark
TWO LEFT FEET(1965, Brit.), ed
Allen Harker
MARIGOLD(1938, Brit.), w
Charmienne Harker
CHINESE RING, THE(1947); UNCONQUERED(1947); EVERY GIRL SHOULD BE MARRIED(1948); PALEFACE, THE(1948); RACE STREET(1948); DANGEROUS PROFESSION, A(1949); ABBOTT AND COSTELLO IN THE FOREIGN LEGION(1950); MILKMAN, THE(1950); SECRET FURY, THE(1950); UNION STATION(1950); WHEN WORLDS COLLIDE(1951); GREATEST SHOW ON EARTH, THE(1952); SON OF PALEFACE(1952); FRENCH LINE, THE(1954)
Chermienne Harker
FOXFIRE(1955)
Ed Harker
DREAM ON(1981), d,w&ph
Gordon Harker
RETURN OF THE RAT, THE(1929, Brit.); TAXI FOR TWO(1929, Brit.); CROOKED BILLET, THE(1930, Brit.); ESCAPE(1930, Brit.); SQUEAKER, THE(1930, Brit.); "W" PLAN, THE(1931, Brit.); CALENDAR, THE(1931, Brit.); SHADOWS(1931, Brit.); SPORT OF KINGS, THE(1931, Brit.); STRONGER SEX, THE(1931, Brit.); THIRD TIME LUCKY(1931, Brit.); CONDEMNED TO DEATH(1932, Brit.); CRIMINAL AT LARGE(1932, Brit.); LOVE ON WHEELS(1932, Brit.); RINGER, THE(1932, Brit.); BRITANNIA OF BILLINGSGATE(1933, Brit.); LUCKY NUMBER, THE(1933, Brit.); MAN THEY COULDN'T ARREST, THE(1933, Brit.); ROME EXPRESS(1933, Brit.); THIS IS THE LIFE(1933, Brit.); WHITE FACE(1933, Brit.); DIRTY WORK(1934, Brit.); FRIDAY THE 13TH(1934, Brit.); MY OLD DUTCH(1934, Brit.); ROAD HOUSE(1934, Brit.); ADMIRALS ALL(1935, Brit.); HYDE PARK CORNER(1935, Brit.); LAD, THE(1935, Brit.); PHANTOM LIGHT, THE(1935, Brit.); SQUIBS(1935, Brit.); AMATEUR GENTLEMAN(1936, Brit.); BOYS WILL BE BOYS(1936, Brit.); MILLIONS(1936, Brit.); WOLF'S CLOTHING(1936, Brit.); BEAUTY AND THE BARGE(1937, Brit.); FROG, THE(1937, Brit.); BLONDES FOR DANGER(1938, Brit.); LIGHTNING CONDUCTOR(1938, Brit.); NO PARKING(1938, Brit.); RETURN OF THE FROG, THE(1938, Brit.); INSPECTOR HORNLEIGH(1939, Brit.); INSPECTOR HORNLEIGH ON HOLIDAY(1939, Brit.); TWO'S COMPANY(1939, Brit.); SALOON BAR(1940, Brit.); MAIL TRAIN(1941, Brit.); ONCE A CROOK(1941, Brit.); WARN THAT MAN(1943, Brit.); THINGS HAPPEN AT NIGHT(1948, Brit.); FACTS OF LOVE(1949, Brit.); SECOND MATE, THE(1950, Brit.); TAMING OF DOROTHY, THE(1950, Brit.); FOUR AGAINST FATE(1952, Brit.); BANG! YOU'RE DEAD(1954, Brit.); TOUCH OF THE SUN, A(1956, Brit.); OUT OF THE CLOUDS(1957, Brit.); SMALL HOTEL(1957, Brit.); LEFT, RIGHT AND CENTRE(1959)
Silents
RING, THE(1927, Brit.); CHAMPAGNE(1928, Brit.); FARMER'S WIFE, THE(1928, Brit.)
Jane Harker
DECEPTION(1946); NIGHT AND DAY(1946); LOVE AND LEARN(1947); POSSESSED(1947); THAT WAY WITH WOMEN(1947); UNFAITHFUL, THE(1947)
Sylvia Harker
FOOL AND THE PRINCESS, THE(1948, Brit.)
Wiley Harker
FIRST MONDAY IN OCTOBER(1981); LOOKIN' TO GET OUT(1982)
1984
CITY HEAT(1984); MICKI AND MAUDE(1984)
Mary S. Harkey
NEW GIRL IN TOWN(1977)
Dennis Harkin
BRIEF ENCOUNTER(1945, Brit.); HOLIDAY CAMP(1947, Brit.); EASY MONEY(1948, Brit.); JASSY(1948, Brit.); WATERLOO ROAD(1949, Brit.); SILK NOOSE, THE(1950, Brit.); TRIO(1950, Brit.); HOME TO DANGER(1951, Brit.)
Kate Harkin
COP HATER(1958)
Kathryn Harkin
RHINOCEROS(1974)
Jim Harkins
LOVE AT FIRST SIGHT(1930)

John Harkins
TIGER MAKES OUT, THE(1967); POPI(1969); THREE SISTERS, THE(1977); ACAPULCO GOLD(1978); ABSENCE OF MALICE(1981); SIX WEEKS(1982); AMITYVILLE 3-D(1983)
1984
BIRDY(1984)
Philip Harkins
SURRENDER–HELL!(1959), w
Percy Harkness
GOLDEN APPLES OF THE SUN(1971, Can.)
Carter Harkness
Misc. Silents
CY WHITTAKER'S WARD(1917)
Richard Harkness
1984
SIGNAL 7(1984), ed
Sam Harkness
AMERICAN HOT WAX(1978)
Tom Harkness
SEX AND THE SINGLE GIRL(1964)
John Harkrider
WHOOPEE(1930), cos; ROMAN SCANDALS(1933), cos; SWING TIME(1936), cos; LOVE IN A BUNGALOW(1937), art d; THREE SMART GIRLS(1937), art d&cos
John W. Harkrider
NANA(1934), cos
Bob Harks
FLASHDANCE(1983)
Macey Harlam
Silents
HABIT OF HAPPINESS, THE(1916); MANHATTAN MADNESS(1916); SHAMS OF SOCIETY(1921); ALWAYS THE WOMAN(1922); WHEN KNIGHTHOOD WAS IN FLOWER(1922); WITHOUT FEAR(1922)
Misc. Silents
PERILS OF DIVORCE(1916); ROMANTIC JOURNEY, THE(1916); BARBARY SHEEP(1917); MONEY MAD(1918); L' APACHE(1919); TOBY'S BOW(1919); PLAYTHING OF BROADWAY, THE(1921); YOU FIND IT EVERYWHERE(1921)
Macy Harlam
Silents
AFTER MIDNIGHT(1921)
Jane Harlan
TWO LOST WORLDS(1950)
Jeff Harlan
BOOGENS, THE(1982)
Kenneth Harlan
PARADISE ISLAND(1930); UNDER MONTANA SKIES(1930); AIR POLICE(1931); WOMEN MEN MARRY(1931); WIDOW IN SCARLET(1932); CAPPY RICKS RETURNS(1935); WANDERER OF THE WASTELAND(1935); CASE OF THE VELVET CLAWS, THE(1936); CHINA CLIPPER(1936); FLYING HOSTESS(1936); MAN HUNT(1936); PUBLIC ENEMY'S WIFE(1936); SAN FRANCISCO(1936); SONG OF THE SADDLE(1936); THEY MET IN A TAXI(1936); TRAIL DUST(1936); WALKING DEAD, THE(1936); BLAZING SIXES(1937); GUNSMOKE RANCH(1937); HIDEAWAY GIRL(1937); MARKED WOMAN(1937); PARADISE ISLE(1937); PENROD AND SAM(1937); RENFREW OF THE ROYAL MOUNTED(1937); SHADOW STRIKES, THE(1937); SOMETHING TO SING ABOUT(1937); WINE, WOMEN AND HORSES(1937); ACCIDENTS WILL HAPPEN(1938); BLONDES AT WORK(1938); DUKE OF WEST POINT, THE(1938); HELD FOR RANSOM(1938); LAW OF THE TEXAN(1938); LITTLE ADVENTURESS, THE(1938); MILLION TO ONE, A(1938); PRIDE OF THE WEST(1938); SALESLADY(1938); SUNSET TRAIL(1938); UNDER WESTERN STARS(1938); WHIRLWIND HORSEMAN(1938); HEADLEYS AT HOME, THE(1939); I AM NOT AFRAID(1939); ON TRIAL(1939); PORT OF HATE(1939); RANGE WAR(1939); HOUSE ACROSS THE BAY, THE(1940); LITTLE BIT OF HEAVEN, A(1940); MURDER IN THE AIR(1940); PRAIRIE SCHOONERS(1940); SANTA FE MARSHAL(1940); BULLETS FOR O'HARA(1940); DANGEROUS LADY(1941); DESPERATE CARGO(1941); KING OF DODGE CITY(1941); MEET JOHN DOE(1941); MILLION DOLLAR BABY(1941); PAPER BULLETS(1941); PRIDE OF THE BOWERY(1941); SECRET EVIDENCE(1941); WIDE OPEN TOWN(1941); BANDIT RANGER(1942); BLACK DRAGONS(1942); CORPSE VANISHES, THE(1942); DAWN EXPRESS, THE(1942); DEEP IN THE HEART OF TEXAS(1942); FIGHTING BILL FARGO(1942); FOREIGN AGENT(1942); HITLER–DEAD OR ALIVE(1942); JUKE GIRL(1942); KLONDIKE FURY(1942); PHANTOM KILLER(1942); SUNDOWN KID, THE(1942); LAW RIDES AGAIN, THE(1943); MELODY PARADE(1943); UNDERDOG, THE(1943); WILD HORSE STAMPEDE(1943); DEATH VALLEY RANGERS(1944)
Misc. Talkies
WIDOW IN SCARLET(1932)
Silents
BREAD(1918); HOODLUM THE(1919); DOLLARS AND SENSE(1920); LOVE, HONOR AND OBEY(1920); PENALTY, THE(1920); DAWN OF THE EAST(1921); LESSONS IN LOVE(1921); NOBODY(1921); WOMAN'S PLACE(1921); BEAUTIFUL AND DAMNED, THE(1922); THORNS AND ORANGE BLOSSOMS(1922); APRIL SHOWERS(1923); EAST SIDE–WEST SIDE(1923); LITTLE CHURCH AROUND THE CORNER(1923); TEMPORARY MARRIAGE(1923); VIRGINIAN, THE(1923); ON THE STROKE OF THREE(1924); RANGER OF THE BIG PINES(1925); FIGHTING EDGE(1926); ICE FLOOD, THE(1926); KING OF THE TURF, THE(1926); TWINKLETOES(1926); CHEATING CHEATERS(1927); EASY PICKINGS(1927); STAGE KISSES(1927)
Misc. Silents
BETSY'S BURGLAR(1917); CHEERFUL GIVERS(1917); FLAME OF THE YUKON, THE(1917); LASH OF POWER, THE(1917); MAN'S MAN, A(1917); HER BODY IN BOND(1918); MARRIAGE LIE, THE(1918); MIDNIGHT MADNESS(1918); MODEL'S CONFESSION, THE(1918); MY UNMARRIED WIFE(1918); PRICE OF A GOOD TIME, THE(1918); WIFE HE BOUGHT, THE(1918); WINE GIRL, THE(1918); LAW THAT DIVIDES, THE(1919); MICROBE, THE(1919); TREMBLING HOUR, THE(1919); DANGEROUS BUSINESS(1920); BARRICADE, THE(1921); I AM THE LAW(1922); MARRIED FLAPPER, THE(1922); PRIMITIVE LOVER, THE(1922); RECEIVED PAYMENT(1922); TOLL OF THE SEA, THE(1922); WORLD'S A STAGE, THE(1922); BROKEN WING, THE(1923); GIRL WHO CAME BACK, THE(1923); BUTTERFLY(1924); FOR ANOTHER WOMAN(1924); MAN WITHOUT A HEART, THE(1924); POISONED PARADISE: THE FORBIDDEN STORY OF MONTE CARLO(1924); SOILED(1924); TWO SHALL BE BORN(1924); VIRGIN, THE(1924); WHITE MAN(1924); BOBBED HAIR(1925); CROWED HOUR, THE(1925); DRUSILLA WITH A

MILLION(1925); GOLDEN STRAIN, THE(1925); MARRIAGE WHIRL, THE(1925); RE-CREATION OF BRIAN KENT, THE(1925); FIGHTING EDGE, THE(1926); SAP, THE(1926); STREETS OF SHANGHAI(1927); WILFUL YOUTH(1927); CODE OF THE AIR(1928); MIDNIGHT ROSE(1928); UNITED STATES SMITH(1928)
Macey Harlan
Silents
ETERNAL CITY, THE(1915)
Marion Harlan
Silents
INNOCENCE(1923); KISS BARRIER, THE(1925); SEVEN CHANCES(1925); MAN FOUR-SQUARE, A(1926); TONY RUNS WILD(1926)
Misc. Silents
HIT AND RUN(1924); ROUGH GOING(1925)
Otis Harlan
BARNUM WAS RIGHT(1929); BROADWAY(1929); CLEAR THE DECKS(1929); GIRL OVERBOARD(1929); HIS LUCKY DAY(1929); MISSISSIPPI GAMBLER(1929); SHOW BOAT(1929); CAPTAIN OF THE GUARD(1930); DAMES AHOY(1930); EMBARRASSING MOMENTS(1930); LOOSE ANKLES(1930); MOUNTAIN JUSTICE(1930); PARADE OF THE WEST(1930); TAKE THE HEIR(1930); ALOHA(1931); BIG SHOT, THE(1931); MAN TO MAN(1931); MILLIE(1931); AIR EAGLES(1932); NO LIVING WITNESS(1932); PARTNERS(1932); RACING YOUTH(1932); RIDE HIM, COWBOY(1932); RIDER OF DEATH VALLEY(1932); THAT'S MY BOY(1932); SIN OF NORA MORAN(1933); TELEGRAPH TRAIL, THE(1933); WOMEN WON'T TELL(1933); I CAN'T ESCAPE(1934); KING KELLY OF THE U.S.A(1934); LET'S TALK IT OVER(1934); MARRIAGE ON APPROVAL(1934); MUSIC IN THE AIR(1934); OLD-FASHIONED WAY, THE(1934); CHINATOWN SQUAD(1935); DIAMOND JIM(1935); DR. SOCRATES(1935); HOOSIER SCHOOLMASTER(1935); MIDSUMMER'S NIGHT'S DREAM, A(1935); WESTERN FRONTIER(1935); CAN THIS BE DIXIE?(1936); HITCH HIKE LADY(1936); SNOW WHITE AND THE SEVEN DWARFS(1937); WESTERN GOLD(1937); MR. BOGGS STEPS OUT(1938); OUTLAWS OF SONORA(1938); TEXANS, THE(1938); LIFE RETURNS(1939)
Misc. Talkies
EVIL EYE OF KALINOR, THE(1934)
Silents
DIAMONDS ADRIFT(1921); KEEPING UP WITH LIZZIE(1921); GAY AND DEVILISH(1922); RIGHT THAT FAILED, THE(1922); NEAR LADY, THE(1923); SPIDER AND THE ROSE, THE(1923); ABRAHAM LINCOLN(1924); LULLABY, THE(1924); OH, DOCTOR(1924); ONE LAW FOR THE WOMAN(1924); WELCOME STRANGER(1924); NINE AND THREE-FIFTHS SECONDS(1925); REDEEMING SIN, THE(1925); MIDNIGHT MESSAGE, THE(1926); PRINCE OF PILSEN, THE(1926); UNKNOWN CAVALIER, THE(1926); WHAT HAPPENED TO JONES(1926); DOWN THE STRETCH(1927); SILKS AND SADDLES(1929)
Misc. Silents
BLACK SHEEP, A(1915); ROMANCE PROMOTORS, THE(1920); FOOLISH AGE, THE(1921); UNDERSTUDY, THE(1922); UP AND AT 'EM(1922); WORLD'S A STAGE, THE(1922); PIONEER TRAILS(1923); VICTOR, THE(1923); CLEAN HEART, THE(1924); WHOLE TOWN'S TALKING, THE(1926); CHEERFUL FRAUD, THE(1927); DON'T TELL THE WIFE(1927); GALLOPING FURY(1927); SILENT RIDER, THE(1927); SILK STOCKINGS(1927); GOOD MORNING JUDGE(1928); GRIP OF THE YUKON, THE(1928); CLEAR THE DECKS(1929); TAKE THE HEIR(1930)
Richard Harlan
MERCY PLANE(1940), d
Misc. Talkies
PAPA SOLTERO(1939), d
Silents
CLASSMATES(1924)
Rita Harlan
Silents
ANGEL CHILD(1918)
Rosita Harlan
MESSAGE TO GARCIA, A(1936); ARIZONA WILDCAT(1938)
Russ Harlan
TARZAN'S DESERT MYSTERY(1943), ph
Russell Harlan
MAN'S FAVORITE SPORT [?](; HOPALONG RIDES AGAIN(1937), ph; NORTH OF THE RIO GRANDE(1937), ph; RUSTLER'S VALLEY(1937), ph; TEXAS TRAIL(1937), ph; BAR 20 JUSTICE(1938), ph; CASSIDY OF BAR 20(1938), ph; FRONTIERSMAN, THE(1938), ph; HEART OF ARIZONA(1938), ph; IN OLD MEXICO(1938), ph; MYSTERIOUS RIDER, THE(1938), ph; PARTNERS OF THE PLAINS(1938), ph; PRIDE OF THE WEST(1938), ph; SUNSET TRAIL(1938), ph; HERITAGE OF THE DESERT(1939), ph; LAW OF THE PAMPAS(1939), ph; RANGE WAR(1939), ph; RENEGADE TRAIL(1939), ph; SILVER ON THE SAGE(1939), ph; CHEROKEE STRIP(1940), ph; HIDDEN GOLD(1940), ph; KNIGHTS OF THE RANGE(1940), ph; LIGHT OF WESTERN STARS, THE(1940), ph; LLANO KID, THE(1940), ph; SANTA FE MARSHAL(1940), ph; SHOWDOWN, THE(1940), ph; STAGECOACH WAR(1940), ph; THREE MEN FROM TEXAS(1940), ph; BORDER VIGILANTES(1941), ph; DOOMED CARAVAN(1941), ph; IN OLD COLORADO(1941), ph; OUTLAWS OF THE DESERT(1941), ph; PARSON OF PANAMINT, THE(1941), ph; PIRATES ON HORSEBACK(1941), ph; ROUNDUP, THE(1941), ph; SECRETS OF THE WASTELANDS(1941), ph; STICK TO YOUR GUNS(1941), ph; TWILIGHT ON THE TRAIL(1941), ph; AMERICAN EMPIRE(1942), ph; SILVER QUEEN(1942), ph; TOMBSTONE, THE TOWN TOO TOUGH TO DIE(1942), ph; UNDERCOVER MAN(1942), ph; BAR 20(1943), ph; BORDER PATROL(1943), ph; COLT COMRADES(1943), ph; FALSE COLORS(1943), ph; HOPPY SERVES A WRIT(1943), ph; KANSAN, THE(1943), ph; LEATHER BURNERS, THE(1943), ph; LOST CANYON(1943), ph; RIDERS OF THE DEADLINE(1943), ph; WOMAN OF THE TOWN, THE(1943), ph; FORTY THIEVES(1944), ph; LUMBERJACK(1944), ph; MYSTERY MAN(1944), ph; TEXAS MASQUERADE(1944), ph; WALK IN THE SUN, A(1945), ph; RAMROD(1947), ph; FOUR FACES WEST(1948), ph; RED RIVER(1948), ph; BAD MEN OF TOMBSTONE(1949), ph; GUN CRAZY(1949), ph; KANGAROO KID, THE(1950, Aus./U.S.), ph; SOUTHSIDE 1-1000(1950), ph; TARZAN AND THE SLAVE GIRL(1950), ph; MAN WHO CHEATED HIMSELF, THE(1951), ph; THING, THE(1951), ph; BIG SKY, THE(1952), ph; RING, THE(1952), ph; RUBY GENTRY(1952), ph; RIOT IN CELL BLOCK 11(1954), ph; BLACKBOARD JUNGLE, THE(1955), ph; LAND OF THE PHARAOHS(1955), ph; LAST HUNT, THE(1956), ph; LUST FOR LIFE(1956), ph; SOMETHING OF VALUE(1957), ph; THIS COULD BE THE NIGHT(1957), ph; WITNESS FOR THE PROSECUTION(1957), ph; KING CREOLE(1958), ph; DAY OF THE OUTLAW(1959), ph; OPERATION PETTICOAT(1959), ph; RIO BRAVO(1959), ph; POLLYANNA(1960), ph; SUNRISE AT CAMPOBELLO(1960), ph; HATARI!(1962), ph; SPIRAL ROAD, THE(1962), ph; TO KILL A MOCKINGBIRD(1962), ph; GATHERING OF EAGLES,

Raffles Harman
ELEPHANT CALLED SLOWLY, AN(1970, Brit.)
Sylvia Harman
TWO(1975)
Dolly Harmer
THE BLACK HAND GANG(1930, Brit.)
Frances Harmer
Silents
ONE WILD WEEK(1921), w
Juliet Harmer
JUST LIKE A WOMAN(1967, Brit.); QUEST FOR LOVE(1971, Brit.)
Lillian Harmer
HUCKLEBERRY FINN(1931); SHE-WOLF, THE(1931); SMART WOMAN(1931); GUILTY AS HELL(1932); NEW MORALS FOR OLD(1932); ALICE IN WONDERLAND(1933); BOWERY, THE(1933); JENNIE GERHARDT(1933); NO MAN OF HER OWN(1933); SHRIEK IN THE NIGHT, A(1933); CHANGE OF HEART(1934); KANSAS CITY PRINCESS(1934); LADY BY CHOICE(1934); LONE COWBOY(1934); MANDALAY(1934); PUBLIC HERO NO. 1(1935); ROMANCE IN MANHATTAN(1935); STRANDED(1935); THREE KIDS AND A QUEEN(1935); DANCING FEET(1936); DON'T GET PERSONAL(1936); LITTLE MISS NOBODY(1936); RAINBOW ON THE RIVER(1936); RIFF-RAFF(1936); SWORN ENEMY(1936); FIRST LADY(1937); FUGITIVE IN THE SKY(1937); GREAT O'MALLEY, THE(1937); INTERNES CAN'T TAKE MONEY(1937); MAKE A WISH(1937); PRISONER OF ZENDA, THE(1937)
Shirley Harmer
HANGMAN, THE(1959)
Harald Harmland
DOLL, THE(1964, Swed.), art d
Bill Harmon
NO. 96(1974, Aus.), p
David P. Harmon
JOHNNY CONCHO(1956), w; REPRISAL(1956), w; ROCK ALL NIGHT(1957), w; SHADOW ON THE WINDOW, THE(1957), w; BIG BEAT, THE(1958), w; LAST OF THE FAST GUNS, THE(1958), w; WONDERFUL WORLD OF THE BROTHERS ERIMM, THE(1962), w
Deborah Harmon
USED CARS(1980)
Fred Harmon
ROLL, THUNDER, ROLL(1949), w
Gred Harmon
STAGECOACH TO DENVER(1946), w
Helen Harmon
WHERE THE LILIES BLOOM(1974)
Henry Harmon
Silents
LOVE, HONOR AND OBEY(1920)
Misc. Silents
OUT OF THE FOG(1919); OLD LADY 31(1920); QUEEN OF THE MOULIN ROUGE(1922)
Jack Harmon
STAR IS BORN, A(1954); PAPER MOON(1973), spec eff
Jim Harmon
LEMON GROVE KIDS MEET THE MONSTERS, THE(1966), w
John Harmon
ADVENTURES OF GALLANT BESS(1948); RENDEZVOUS(1935); KING OF ALCATRAZ(1938); MISSING GUEST, THE(1938); SLIGHT CASE OF MURDER, A(1938); GAMBLING SHIP(1939); GOLDEN BOY(1939); I WAS A CONVICT(1939); INSIDE INFORMATION(1939); KING OF THE UNDERWORLD(1939); PIRATES OF THE SKIES(1939); RETURN OF DR. X, THE(1939); DEVIL'S ISLAND(1940); FUGITIVE FROM JUSTICE, A(1940); GANGS OF CHICAGO(1940); NIGHT AT EARL CARROLL'S, A(1940); QUEEN OF THE MOB(1940); WAY OF ALL FLESH, THE(1940); WOMEN WITHOUT NAMES(1940); BUY ME THAT TOWN(1941); DEADLY GAME, THE(1941); HIT THE ROAD(1941); HONOLULU LU(1941); LIFE BEGINS FOR ANDY HARDY(1941); MANPOWER(1941); PITTSBURGH KID, THE(1941); RAIDERS OF THE DESERT(1941); SECRETS OF THE LONE WOLF(1941); SHEPHERD OF THE HILLS, THE(1941); TWO IN A TAXI(1941); BROADWAY(1942); CALL OF THE CANYON(1942); DANGEROUSLY THEY LIVE(1942); I WAS FRAMED(1942); LUCKY JORDAN(1942); TRAMP, TRAMP, TRAMP(1942); AFTER MIDNIGHT WITH BOSTON BLACKIE(1943); FIND THE BLACKMAILER(1943); TRUCK BUSTERS(1943); WHITE SAVAGE(1943); ROGER TOUHY, GANGSTER!(1944); SILENT PARTNER(1944); CONFLICT(1945); BELOW THE DEADLINE(1946); DANGEROUS MONEY(1946); O.S.S.(1946); THEY MADE ME A KILLER(1946); BRUTE FORCE(1947); FALL GUY(1947); FEAR IN THE NIGHT(1947); LOUISIANA(1947); MONSIEUR VERDOUX(1947); MOONRISE(1948); WHIPLASH(1948); ALIAS THE CHAMP(1949); CROOKED WAY, THE(1949); HOMICIDE(1949); LADY GAMBLES, THE(1949); ONCE MORE, MY DARLING(1949); STREETS OF SAN FRANCISCO(1949); BLONDE DYNAMITE(1950); DESTINATION BIG HOUSE(1950); JOE PALOOKA IN THE SQUARED CIRCLE(1950); TALES OF ROBIN HOOD(1951); HORIZONS WEST(1952); JACK SLADE(1953); MAN IN THE DARK(1953); RUN FOR THE HILLS(1953); TANGIER INCIDENT(1953); BITTER CREEK(1954); JUNGLE GENTS(1954); THREE YOUNG TEXANS(1954); JAIL BUSTERS(1955); MAN FROM BITTER RIDGE, THE(1955); SPOILERS, THE(1955); CANYON RIVER(1956); THREE VIOLENT PEOPLE(1956); GOD IS MY PARTNER(1957); LOOKING FOR DANGER(1957); MONSTER OF PIEDRAS BLANCAS, THE(1959); 7TH COMMANDMENT, THE(1961); FOR LOVE OR MONEY(1963); MOVE OVER, DARLING(1963); ONE MAN'S WAY(1964); LAS VEGAS HILLBILLYS(1966); STREET IS MY BEAT, THE(1966); TEXAS ACROSS THE RIVER(1966); FUNNY GIRL(1968); HONKERS, THE(1972); UNHOLY ROLLERS(1972); MALIBU HIGH(1979)
Misc. Talkies
HITCHHIKE TO HELL(1978)
Joy Harmon
MAD DOG COLL(1961); ONE WAY WAHINI(1965); VILLAGE OF THE GIANTS(1965); COOL HAND LUKE(1967); ANGEL IN MY POCKET(1969)
Julian Harmon
UNKNOWN, THE(1946), w; SEVEN WERE SAVED(1947), w; DANGER ZONE(1951), w; PIER 23(1951), w; ROARING CITY(1951), w; GIRLS ON THE LOOSE(1958), w
Kelly Harmon
JONATHAN LIVINGSTON SEAGULL(1973); CALIFORNIA SUITE(1978)

Larry Harmon
TOO YOUNG TO KISS(1951)
Lee Harmon
STAR SPANGLED GIRL(1971), makeup; CHINATOWN(1974), makeup; HEAVEN CAN WAIT(1978), makeup
Manny Harmon
WALKING ON AIR(1936)
Marie Harmon
HERS TO HOLD(1943); HAT CHECK HONEY(1944); HI, GOOD-LOOKIN'(1944); LADIES COURAGEOUS(1944); RECKLESS AGE(1944); SOUTH OF DIXIE(1944); HER LUCKY NIGHT(1945); BEHIND THE MASK(1946); EL PASO KID, THE(1946); GIRL ON THE SPOT(1946); LARCENY IN HER HEART(1946); SECRETS OF A SORORITY GIRL(1946); SHE WROTE THE BOOK(1946); NIGHT TIME IN NEVADA(1948); SECRET BEYOND THE DOOR, THE(1948); NOT WANTED(1949)
Misc. Talkies
SPRINGTIME IN TEXAS(1945); GUNSMOKE(1947)
Mark Harmon
COMES A HORSEMAN(1978); BEYOND THE POSEIDON ADVENTURE(1979)
Marlene Harmon
PERSONAL BEST(1982)
Pat Harmon
DARK STREETS(1929); SAL OF SINGAPORE(1929); LET'S GO NATIVE(1930); GANG BUSTER, THE(1931); SECRET MENACE(1931); TEN CENTS A DANCE(1931); PACK UP YOUR TROUBLES(1932); BOWERY, THE(1933); FOURTH HORSEMAN, THE(1933); NIGHT OF TERROR(1933); SONS OF THE DESERT(1933); PORT OF LOST DREAMS(1935); MAD WEDNESDAY(1950)
Misc. Talkies
TWO GUN CABALLERO(1931); SILENT CODE, THE(1935)
Silents
KENTUCKY DERBY, THE(1922); ETERNAL STRUGGLE, THE(1923); AMERICAN MANNERS(1924); BACK TRAIL, THE(1924); HOT WATER(1924); MIDNIGHT EXPRESS, THE(1924); RIDGEWAY OF MONTANA(1924); SAWDUST TRAIL(1924); SURGING SEAS(1924); FRESHMAN, THE(1925); LURE OF THE WILD, THE(1925); BARRIER, THE(1926); COLLEGE DAYS(1926); DIXIE FLYER, THE(1926); FIGHTING EDGE(1926); JOSSELYN'S WIFE(1926); UNKNOWN CAVALIER, THE(1926); BACHELOR'S BABY, THE(1927); HAZARDOUS VALLEY(1927); WARNING, THE(1927); HOMESICK(1928); SUNSET PASS(1929)
Misc. Silents
FIREBRAND, THE(1922); MIDNIGHT GUEST, THE(1923); FIGHT TO THE FINISH, A(1925); S.O.S. PERILS OF THE SEA(1925); BREED OF THE SEA(1926); PHANTOM BULLET, THE(1926); WINNING THE FUTURITY(1926); COURT-MARTIAL(1928)
Patsy Harmon
NIGHT AND DAY(1946)
Patty Joy Harmon
UNDER THE YUM-YUM TREE(1963); YOUNG DILLINGER(1965)
Rena Harmon
VAN NUYS BLVD.(1979)
Renee Harmon
1984
EXECUTIONER PART II, THE(1984), a, p
Misc. Talkies
FROZEN SCREAM(1980)
Robert Harmon
1984
BLACK ROOM, THE(1984), ph
Sidney Harmon
TALK OF THE TOWN(1942), w; DRUMS IN THE DEEP SOUTH(1951), w; MARA MARU(1952), w; MUTINY(1952), w; MAN CRAZY(1953), p; BIG COMBO, THE(1955), p; WILD PARTY, THE(1956), p; MEN IN WAR(1957), p; ANNA LUCASTA(1958), p; GOD'S LITTLE ACRE(1958), p; DAY OF THE OUTLAW(1959), p; HAND IN HAND(1960, Brit.), w; THIN RED LINE, THE(1964), p
Steve Harmon
ONE AND ONLY GENUINE ORIGINAL FAMILY BAND, THE(1968)
Tom Harmon
HARMON OF MICHIGAN(1941); SWEETHEART OF SIGMA CHI(1946); SPIRIT OF WEST POINT, THE(1947); TRIPLE THREAT(1948); THAT'S MY BOY(1951); PAT AND MIKE(1952); ROSE BOWL STORY, THE(1952); ALL-AMERICAN, THE(1953); CADDY, THE(1953); OFF LIMITS(1953); ANNAPOLIS STORY, AN(1955); RETURN TO CAMPUS(1975)
Harmonaires
ONE TOO MANY(1950)
The Harmonettes
SECRET SINNERS(1933)
The Harmonica Band
SUNSHINE AHEAD(1936, Brit.)
The Harmonious Miners
BLACK DIAMONDS(1932, Brit.)
Harmony Quartet
ON WITH THE SHOW(1929)
Julie Harmount
JINXED!(1982), set d
Henning Harmssen
NOT RECONCILED, OR "ONLY VIOLENCE HELPS WHERE IT RULES"(1969, Ger.)
Raimund Harmstorf
CALL OF THE WILD(1972, Ger./ Span./Ital./Fr.)
Raymund Harmstorf
COUNTERFEIT COMMANDOS(1981, Ital.)
Falk Harnack
DAS LETZTE GEHEIMNIS(1959, Ger.), d; RESTLESS NIGHT, THE(1964, Ger.), d
Faten Harnama
CAIRO(1963)
Sunny Harnett
FUNNY FACE(1957)
Sheldon Harnick
RAGGEDY ANN AND ANDY(1977)
Wolf Harnisch
TIME TO LOVE AND A TIME TO DIE, A(1958); 5 SINNERS(1961, Ger.)

Wolf Harnish
BATTLE OF BRITAIN, THE(1969, Brit.)

Nicholaus Harnoncourt
CHRONICLE OF ANNA MAGDALENA BACH(1968, Ital., Ger.)

Scott Harold
HOT NEWS(1936, Brit.); PATRICIA GETS HER MAN(1937, Brit.); DOUBLE OR QUITS(1938, Brit.); LILY OF LAGUNA(1938, Brit.); ROSE OF TRALEE(1938, Ireland); 13 MEN AND A GUN(1938, Brit.); NURSEMAID WHO DISAPPEARED, THE(1939, Brit.); TAWNY PIPIT(1947, Brit.); AFFAIRS OF ADELAIDE(1949, U.S./Brit.); BROWNING VERSION, THE(1951, Brit.); MAN IN THE WHITE SUIT, THE(1952); PASSAGE HOME(1955, Brit.)

Harold and Lola
PAN-AMERICANA(1945)

Ralf Harolde
AMOS 'N' ANDY(1930); DIXIANA(1930); FRAMED(1930); HOOK, LINE AND SINKER(1930); OFFICER O'BRIEN(1930); YOUNG DESIRE(1930); ALEXANDER HAMILTON(1931); ARE THESE OUR CHILDREN?(1931); NIGHT NURSE(1931); SAFE IN HELL(1931); SECRET WITNESS, THE(1931); SMART MONEY(1931); TIP-OFF, THE(1931); EXPERT, THE(1932); HOLLYWOOD SPEAKS(1932); WINNER TAKE ALL(1932); CHEATING BLONDES(1933); DELUGE(1933); HER RESALE VALUE(1933); I'M NO ANGEL(1933); NIGHT FLIGHT(1933); PICTURE SNATCHER(1933); BABY, TAKE A BOW(1934); FIFTEEN WIVES(1934); HE WAS HER MAN(1934); JIMMY THE GENT(1934); ONCE TO EVERY BACHELOR(1934); SHE LOVES ME NOT(1934); WITCHING HOUR, THE(1934); FORCED LANDING(1935); GREAT GOD GOLD(1935); MILLION DOLLAR BABY(1935); PERFECT CLUE, THE(1935); SILK HAT KID(1935); STOLEN HARMONY(1935); TALE OF TWO CITIES, A(1935); ACCUSING FINGER, THE(1936); FIFTEEN MAIDEN LANE(1936); HUMAN CARGO(1936); IF YOU COULD ONLY COOK(1936); LITTLE RED SCHOOLHOUSE(1936); MY MARRIAGE(1936); OUR RELATIONS(1936); SONG AND DANCE MAN, THE(1936); HER HUSBAND LIES(1937); LAST TRAIN FROM MADRID, THE(1937); MAN BETRAYED, A(1937); ONE MILE FROM HEAVEN(1937); THIS IS MY AFFAIR(1937); ROOKIE COP, THE(1939); UNDERCOVER AGENT(1939); BAD MAN OF DEADWOOD(1941); LUCKY DEVILS(1941); NO GREATER SIN(1941); RAGS TO RICHES(1941); RAIDERS OF THE DESERT(1941); RIDIN' ON A RAINBOW(1941); SAN FRANCISCO DOCKS(1941); SEA WOLF, THE(1941); SEALED LIPS(1941); BABY FACE MORGAN(1942); BROADWAY(1942); I KILLED THAT MAN(1942); SIN TOWN(1942); ROGER TOUHY, GANGSTER!(1944); MURDER, MY SWEET(1945); PHANTOM SPEAKS, THE(1945); CRIMSON KEY, THE(1947); DESPERATE(1947); JEWELS OF BRANDENBURG(1947); ASSIGNED TO DANGER(1948); BEHIND LOCKED DOORS(1948); HAZARD(1948); ALASKA PATROL(1949); KILLER SHARK(1950); NEW KIND OF LOVE, A(1963)
Misc. Silents
SUNSHINE HARBOR(1922)

Ralph Harolde
CONQUEST(1937); HORROR ISLAND(1941); BARN OF THE NAKED DEAD(1976), w

Kasha Haroldi
MADAME SATAN(1930)

Ralf Harolds
STORK PAYS OFF, THE(1941)

Eghiche Harout
FIVE FINGERS(1952); MY SON, JOHN(1952)

Eghishe Harout
KING OF THE KHYBER RIFLES(1953)

Eglfshe Harout
EGYPTIAN. THE(1954)

Bill Harp
1984
GRANDVIEW, U.S.A.(1984), set d

Helen Harp
Misc. Talkies
TOMBS OF THE BLIND DEAD(1974)

Kenneth Harp
FEAR AND DESIRE(1953)

Ray Harp
BEN(1972), cos

Shraga Harpaz
WORLDS APART(1980, U.S., Israel)

Udi Harpaz
1984
NINJA III—THE DOMINATION(1984), m

Ann Harper
RENDEZVOUS 24(1946)

Barbara Harper
PORT OF ESCAPE(1955, Brit.), w

Barbara S. Harper
ACCOUNT RENDERED(1957, Brit.), w; NIGHT CREATURES(1962, Brit.), w

Betty Harper
JIGSAW(1949); SILKWOOD(1983)

Bruce Harper
GUILT OF JANET AMES, THE(1947)

Dave Harper
PARDON MY GUN(1942); TALK OF THE TOWN(1942); TWO YANKS IN TRINIDAD(1942)

David Harper
SKYJACKED(1972), w
1984
FLETCH(1984)

Dianne Harper
STAR TREK II: THE WRATH OF KHAN(1982)

Donn Harper
MONKEY HUSTLE, THE(1976)

Ed Harper
CHRISTMAS TREE, THE(1966, Brit.), p, w; TWO GENTLEMEN SHARING(1969, Brit.), prod d

Edward Harper
TRADER HORN(1973), w

Gerald Harper
EXTRA DAY, THE(1956, Brit.); STARS IN YOUR EYES(1956, Brit.); TIGER IN THE SMOKE(1956, Brit.); ADMIRABLE CRICHTON, THE(1957, Brit.); NIGHT TO REMEMBER, A(1958, Brit.); TUNES OF GLORY(1960, Brit.); LEAGUE OF GENTLEMEN, THE(1961, Brit.); WONDERFUL TO BE YOUNG!(1962, Brit.); PUNCH AND JUDY MAN, THE(1963, Brit.); SWINGER'S PARADISE(1965, Brit.); STRANGLER'S WEB(1966, Brit.); SHOES OF THE FISHERMAN, THE(1968); LADY VANISHES, THE(1980, Brit.)

Gus Harper [Gustave D'Arpe]
JOHNNY YUMA(1967, Ital.)

Harriet Harper
RETURN FROM THE ASHES(1965, U.S./Brit.); FAR FROM THE MADDING CROWD(1967, Brit.); VIRGIN AND THE GYPSY, THE(1970, Brit.)

Harry Harper
1984
ELEMENT OF CRIME, THE(1984, Den.)

Henry Harper
SCAVENGER HUNT(1979), w

Hubert Harper
HEART IS A LONELY HUNTER, THE(1968)

Hugh Harper
MOONLIGHTING(1982, Brit.)

Vice Admiral J.E.T. Harper
FOR FREEDOM(1940, Brit.)

Jack C. Harper
GOING HOME(1971)

James Harper
1984
FIRSTBORN(1984)

Jessica Harper
PHANTOM OF THE PARADISE(1974); LOVE AND DEATH(1975); SUSPIRIA(1977, Ital.); EVICTORS, THE(1979); STARDUST MEMORIES(1980); PENNIES FROM HEAVEN(1981); SHOCK TREATMENT(1981); MY FAVORITE YEAR(1982)

Kamie Harper
1984
BREAKIN' 2: ELECTRIC BOOGALOO(1984)

Kathleen Harper
DIRTY HARRY(1971); PICKUP ON 101(1972)

Kenneth Harper
FOR BETTER FOR WORSE(1954, Brit.), p; BLONDE SINNER(1956, Brit.), p; ACTION OF THE TIGER(1957), p; PASSIONATE SUMMER(1959, Brit.), p; GO TO BLAZES(1962, Brit.), p; WONDERFUL TO BE YOUNG!(1962, Brit.), p; SUMMER HOLIDAY(1963, Brit.), p; FRENCH DRESSING(1964, Brit.), p; SWINGER'S PARADISE(1965, Brit.), p; TWO WEEKS IN SEPTEMBER(1967, Fr./Brit.), p; PRUDENCE AND THE PILL(1968, Brit.), bp; VIRGIN AND THE GYPSY, THE(1970, Brit.), p; TAKE ME HIGH(1973, Brit.), p

Kyra Harper
PARALLELS(1980, Can.)

Leni Harper
PIRATES OF PENZANCE, THE(1983)

Lynn Harper
CHRISTINE JORGENSEN STORY, THE(1970)

Marjorie Harper
LIFE AND TIMES OF GRIZZLY ADAMS, THE(1974)

Marlon Harper
PRECIOUS JEWELS(1969)

Mary Harper
1984
RIVER RAT, THE(1984)

Pat Harper
KID FROM SPAIN, THE(1932); WESTERN JAMBOREE(1938), w

Patricia Harper
DAMES(1934); PRAIRIE PALS(1942), w; BLACK MARKET RUSTLERS(1943), w; RAIDERS OF SAN JOAQUIN(1943), w; WESTERN CYCLONE(1943), w; BLAZING FRONTIER(1944), w; DEATH RIDES THE PLAINS(1944), w; DRIFTER, THE(1944), w; MY GAL LOVES MUSIC(1944), w; TRAIL TO GUNSIGHT(1944), w; CODE OF THE LAWLESS(1945), w; TOPEKA TERROR, THE(1945), w; BORDER FEUD(1947), w; GHOST TOWN RENEGADES(1947), w; RANGE BEYOND THE BLUE(1947), w

Paul Harper
RUN, ANGEL, RUN(1969); WILD BUNCH, THE(1969); FANDANGO(1970); J.W. COOP(1971); CULPEPPER CATTLE COMPANY, THE(1972)

Rand Harper
FOREVER FEMALE(1953); REAR WINDOW(1954); SABRINA(1954); FEAR STRIKES OUT(1957); JOHNNY TROUBLE(1957)

Ray Harper
TRAPPED BY BOSTON BLACKIE(1948)

Redd Harper
STRAWBERRY ROAN, THE(1948)

Robert Harper
PREMONITION, THE(1976); MOMMIE DEAREST(1981); CREEPSHOW(1982); END OF AUGUST, THE(1982)
1984
ONCE UPON A TIME IN AMERICA(1984)

Ron Harper
SOLDIER, THE(1982)

Roy Harper
MADE(1972, Brit.)

Sally Harper
YOUNG AMERICA(1942); CRASH DIVE(1943)

Samantha Harper
OH! CALCUTTA!(1972); I NEVER PROMISED YOU A ROSE GARDEN(1977); I OUGHT TO BE IN PICTURES(1982); LOOKIN' TO GET OUT(1982)

Shari Belafonte Harper
IF YOU COULD SEE WHAT I HEAR(1982)

Susan Harper
PHANTASM(1979)

Terri Harper
LOVE GOD?, THE(1969)

Tess Harper
TENDER MERCIES(1982); AMITYVILLE 3-D(1983); SILKWOOD(1983)
1984
FLASHPOINT(1984)
Thomas Harper
Misc. Silents
CALL OF THE SEA, THE(1915)
Toni Harper
MANHATTAN ANGEL(1948); MAKE BELIEVE BALLROOM(1949); HOW TO STUFF A WILD BIKINI(1965)
Tracy Harper
SENDER, THE(1982, Brit.)
Valerie Harper
FREEBIE AND THE BEAN(1974); CHAPTER TWO(1979); LAST MARRIED COUPLE IN AMERICA, THE(1980)
1984
BLAME IT ON RIO(1984)
Virgil Harper
TIN MAN(1983), ph
Harper's Bazaar Models
BACK STREET(1961)
Fred Harpman
TAKE THE MONEY AND RUN(1969), art d; DELIVERANCE(1972), art d; TERMINAL MAN, THE(1974), art d; DOC SAVAGE... THE MAN OF BRONZE(1975), art d; DAMIEN–OMEN II(1978), prod d; CHEECH AND CHONG'S NEXT MOVIE(1980), prod d; RICH AND FAMOUS(1981), art d
Howard Harpster
MAYBE IT'S LOVE(1930)
Michael Harpster
STUNTS(1977), w
Joan Harpur
1984
PIGS(1984, Ireland)
Keith J. Harr
OFFICER AND A GENTLEMAN, AN(1982)
Silver Harr
CYCLONE KID(1931); KID MILLIONS(1934); WILD HORSE RUSTLERS(1943); GHOST OF HIDDEN VALLEY(1946); WILD FRONTIER, THE(1947)
Johnny Harra
THIS IS ELVIS(1982)
Archibald Harradine
JAMAICA INN(1939, Brit.)
Archie Harradine
MR. PERRIN AND MR. TRAILL(1948, Brit.)
Don Harral
TEX(1982)
James N. Harrel
OUTLAW BLUES(1977)
Scotty Harrel
OLD CHISHOLM TRAIL(1943)
Cindy Harrell
FINAL TERROR, THE(1983)
Claudette Harrell
RESURRECTION(1980)
Dean Harrell
Silents
WAY OF ALL FLESH, THE(1927)
Georgia Harrell
1984
FIRST TURN-ON!, THE(1984), a, w
James Harrell
BULLET FOR PRETTY BOY, A(1970); GREAT WALDO PEPPER, THE(1975); WHOLE SHOOTIN' MATCH, THE(1979)
1984
COUNTRY(1984)
James N. Harrell
RACE WITH THE DEVIL(1975); RESURRECTION(1980); URBAN COWBOY(1980); RAGGEDY MAN(1981)
Jim Harrell
PAPER MOON(1973); SUGARLAND EXPRESS, THE(1974); MACKINTOSH & T.J.(1975)
Jordan Cae Harrell
WARRIORS, THE(1979)
Michele Harrell
EXTERMINATOR, THE(1980)
Peter Harrell
VICE SQUAD(1982)
Peter Harrell III
SUGAR HILL(1974)
Bud Harrelson
ODD COUPLE, THE(1968)
Cathi Harrer
CARNY(1980)
Michael Harreschou
SAFARI 3000(1982), w
Lincoln Harrice
GROOVE TUBE, THE(1974)
David Harries
UNDER MILK WOOD(1973, Brit.)
Davyd Harries
OVERLORD(1975, Brit.)
Ivor Harries
WOLFPEN PRINCIPLE, THE(1974, Can.)
Ronnie Harries
GOOD BEGINNING, THE(1953, Brit.); MEN ARE CHILDREN TWICE(1953, Brit.)
Judy Harriet
SAY ONE FOR ME(1959)

Hank Harrigan
SOD SISTERS(1969)
Hedda Harrigan
LAUGHING LADY, THE(1930)
Mary Harrigan
WILD IS MY LOVE(1963)
Michael Harrigan
SUPERMAN(1978)
Nedda Harrigan
I'LL FIX IT(1934); CASE OF THE BLACK CAT, THE(1936); CHARLIE CHAN AT THE OPERA(1936); FUGITIVE IN THE SKY(1937); THANK YOU, MR. MOTO(1937); MEN ARE SUCH FOOLS(1938); TRIP TO PARIS, A(1938); HONEYMOON'S OVER, THE(1939); ON TRIAL(1939); CASTLE ON THE HUDSON(1940); DEVIL'S ISLAND(1940); SCANDAL SHEET(1940)
Robert Harrigan
CARDINAL RICHELIEU(1935)
William Harrigan
NIX ON DAMES(1929); BORN RECKLESS(1930); ON THE LEVEL(1930); MEN ON CALL(1931); DISGRACED(1933); GIRL IN 419(1933); INVISIBLE MAN, THE(1933); PICK-UP(1933); G-MEN(1935); MELODY LINGERS ON, THE(1935); SILK HAT KID(1935); STRANDED(1935); FRANKIE AND JOHNNY(1936); HIS FAMILY TREE(1936); WHIPSAW(1936); EXILED TO SHANGHAI(1937); FEDERAL BULLETS(1937); OVER THE GOAL(1937); HAWAII CALLS(1938); BACK DOOR TO HEAVEN(1939); FOLLIES GIRL(1943); CITIZEN SAINT(1947); DESERT FURY(1947); FARMER'S DAUGHTER, THE(1947); FLYING LEATHERNECKS(1951); STEEL TOWN(1952); FRANCIS COVERS THE BIG TOWN(1953); ROOGIE'S BUMP(1954); STREET OF SINNERS(1957)
Misc. Silents
AFFAIR OF THREE NATIONS, AN(1915)
John Harrington
Misc. Silents
STREET OF FORGOTTEN MEN, THE(1925)
Ann Harriman
SHARE OUT, THE(1966, Brit.)
Carley Harriman
SONG FOR MISS JULIE, A(1945), p
Fawne Harriman
T.R. BASKIN(1971)
Richard Harriman
Misc. Talkies
INCOMING FRESHMEN(1979)
Bill Harrington
SINK THE BISMARCK!(1960, Brit.), spec eff
Buck Harrington
SHAKE HANDS WITH MURDER(1944); DUFFY'S TAVERN(1945); CALL NORTHSIDE 777(1948); JUST FOR YOU(1952); VERTIGO(1958)
Cicely Harrington
Silents
LADY NOGGS-PEERESS(1929, Brit.), w
Cleo Harrington
DRACULA'S DOG(1978)
Curtis Harrington
MARDI GRAS(1958), w; NIGHT TIDE(1963), d&w; GAMES(1967), d, w; WHAT'S THE MATTER WITH HELEN?(1971), d; WHO SLEW AUNTIE ROO?(1971, U.S./Brit.), d; KILLING KIND, THE(1973), d; RUBY(1977), d
Delphi Harrington
NIGHT OF THE JUGGLER(1980); LITTLE SEX, A(1982)
Doreen Harrington
UP THE JUNCTION(1968, Brit.)
Fred Harrington
Misc. Silents
MUTINY(1917)
George Harrington
Silents
ALL MEN ARE LIARS(1919, Brit.); KEEPER OF THE DOOR(1919, Brit.); UNREST(1920, Brit.); RUNNING WATER(1922, Brit.)
Hamtree Harrington
HIS WOMAN(1931); POCOMANIA(1939)
J.F. Harrington
SHIPS OF HATE(1931), ed
J.S. Harrington
SHOULD A GIRL MARRY?(1929), ed; DUGAN OF THE BAD LANDS(1931), ed
Silents
MAN FROM HEADQUARTERS(1928), ed; SWEET SIXTEEN(1928), ed; ANNE AGAINST THE WORLD(1929), ed; DEVIL'S CHAPLAIN(1929), ed
James Harrington
RED MENACE, THE(1949)
Jean Harrington
DEADLY FEMALES, THE(1976, Brit.)
Joe Harrington
Silents
LAUGHING AT DANGER(1924)
Misc. Silents
BROADWAY GALLANT, THE(1926); GOLD FROM WEEPAH(1927)
John Harrington
LOCAL BOY MAKES GOOD(1931); MUTINY ON THE BOUNTY(1935); BIG GAME, THE(1936); SWING TIME(1936); WOMEN ARE TROUBLE(1936); CHECKERS(1937); COUNTERFEIT LADY(1937); DANGEROUSLY YOURS(1937); STEP LIVELY, JEEVES(1937)
Silents
TIN GODS(1926)
John S. Harrington
HANDCUFFED(1929), ed
Silents
ISLE OF LOST MEN(1928), ed
Joseph Harrington
DR. KILDARE'S VICTORY(1941), w
Silents
IDLE RICH, THE(1921); FRESHMAN, THE(1925); DOUBLING WITH DANGER(1926)

Misc. Silents
MERRY CAVALIER, THE(1926)
Joy Harrington
FOREVER AND A DAY(1943); GASLIGHT(1944); OUR HEARTS WERE YOUNG AND GAY(1944); MY NAME IS JULIA ROSS(1945); TONIGHT AND EVERY NIGHT(1945); VALLEY OF DECISION, THE(1945); MADNESS OF THE HEART(1949, Brit.)
Kate Harrington
COME ON DANGER(1942); RIDING THE WIND(1942); WINTERTIME(1943); MADIGAN(1968); RACHEL, RACHEL(1968); HOSPITAL, THE(1971); CHILD'S PLAY(1972); SENTINEL, THE(1977)
Keith Harrington
SHE COULDN'T SAY NO(1954)
Laura Harrington
DARK END OF THE STREET, THE(1981)
1984
ADVENTURES OF BUCKAROO BANZAI: ACROSS THE 8TH DIMENSION, THE(1984); CITY GIRL, THE(1984); JOY OF SEX(1984)
Laurence Harrington
JULIUS CAESAR(1970, Brit.)
Luba Harrington
MAIDSTONE(1970)
Lucy Harrington
RISKY BUSINESS(1983)
Mary Lou Harrington
MY FAVORITE WIFE(1940); IT COMES UP LOVE(1943)
Misc. Talkies
BOY FROM STALINGRAD, THE(1943)
Michael Harrington
1984
BEVERLY HILLS COP(1984)
Mike Harrington
INCREDIBLY STRANGE CREATURES WHO STOPPED LIVING AND BECAME CRAZY MIXED-UP ZOMBIES, THE(1965), art d
Mildred Harrington
TURN OFF THE MOON(1937), w
Pamela Harrington
SECRET PEOPLE(1952, Brit.)
Pat Harrington
52ND STREET(1937); STAGE STRUCK(1958); EASY COME, EASY GO(1967); PRESIDENT'S ANALYST, THE(1967); 2000 YEARS LATER(1969); COMPUTER WORE TENNIS SHOES, THE(1970); EVERY LITTLE CROOK AND NANNY(1972)
Misc. Talkies
TWO THOUSAND YEARS LATER(1969)
Pat Harrington, Jr.
MOVE OVER, DARLING(1963); WHEELER DEALERS, THE(1963); CANDIDATE, THE(1972)
Misc. Talkies
NINE LIVES OF FRITZ THE CAT, THE(1974)
Prudence Harrington
MARRY ME! MARRY ME!(1969, Fr.)
Ramsey Harrington
Misc. Talkies
FOR MEMBERS ONLY(1960), d
Rudy Harrington
KILLING, THE(1956), cos; SEVEN MEN FROM NOW(1956), cos
Jim Harriott
WARGAMES(1983)
A. A. Harris
HERE COMES THE SUN(1945, Brit.)
Adele Harris
Silents
AS MEN LOVE(1917), w
Al Harris
TEVYA(1939)
Alan Harris
HOLIDAY RHYTHM(1950); PROWLER, THE(1951); YOU FOR ME(1952); JOE MACBETH(1955), art d; LAST MAN TO HANG, THE(1956, Brit.), art d; SATAN'S MISTRESS(1982)
Alan M. Harris
DEVIL'S WEDDING NIGHT, THE(1973, Ital.), w
Alan N. Harris
THERE IS NO 13(1977), p
Albert Harris
SHOWDOWN AT BOOT HILL(1958), m, md; STATE FAIR(1962)
Alexander Harris
ALL AT SEA(1958, Brit.)
Alfred Harris
GREAT MR. HANDEL, THE(1942, Brit.); MEET SEXTON BLAKE(1944, Brit.); TWILIGHT HOUR(1944, Brit.); MURDER IN REVERSE(1946, Brit.); WHAT THE BUTLER SAW(1950, Brit.)
Alfred A. Harris
NOTHING VENTURE(1948, Brit.)
Allan Harris
SMALLEST SHOW ON EARTH, THE(1957, Brit.), art d; INTENT TO KILL(1958, Brit.), art d; LAW AND DISORDER(1958, Brit.), art d; HOME IS THE HERO(1959, Ireland), art d; SECRET OF MONTE CRISTO, THE(1961, Brit.), art d; IMMORAL CHARGE(1962, Brit.), art d
Allen Harris
ON THE LOOSE(1951)
Andrew Harris
FAREWELL, MY LOVELY(1975); MAKING LOVE(1982)
Andy Harris
1984
COMFORT AND JOY(1984, Brit.), art d
Anita Harris
FOLLOW THAT CAMEL(1967, Brit.); LOVE IS A WOMAN(1967, Brit.); CARRY ON DOCTOR(1968, Brit.)

Ann Harris
WITHOUT EACH OTHER(1962); HONEYMOON KILLERS, THE(1969)
Anthony Harris
BEWARE! THE BLOB(1972), p, w; COACH(1978), m
Arlene Harris
HERE COMES ELMER(1943); HITCHHIKE TO HAPPINESS(1945); ONE EXCITING WEEK(1946); MAIN STREET KID, THE(1947); HOLD BACK TOMORROW(1955); NORTH TO ALASKA(1960)
Arline Harris
HI BEAUTIFUL(1944)
Art Harris
MAN WHO WOULD NOT DIE, THE(1975), m
Ashley Harris
ROCKERS(1980)
Augustus Harris
Silents
ROYAL OAK, THE(1923, Brit.), w
Misc. Silents
DERBY WINNER, THE(1915, Brit.)
Averell Harris
MY SIN(1931); SECRETS OF A SECRETARY(1931); TOO MANY GIRLS(1940)
Averill Harris
HIS WOMAN(1931)
Barbara Harris
THOUSAND CLOWNS, A(1965); OH DAD, POOR DAD, MAMA'S HUNG YOU IN THE CLOSET AND I'M FEELIN' SO SAD(1967); PLAZA SUITE(1971); WHO IS HARRY KELLERMAN AND WHY IS HE SAYING THOSE TERRIBLE THINGS ABOUT ME?(1971); WAR BETWEEN MEN AND WOMEN, THE(1972); MIXED COMPANY(1974); MANCHU EAGLE MURDER CAPER MYSTERY, THE(1975); NASHVILLE(1975); FAMILY PLOT(1976); FREAKY FRIDAY(1976); MOVIE MOVIE(1978); NORTH AVENUE IRREGULARS, THE(1979); SEDUCTION OF JOE TYNAN, THE(1979); SECOND-HAND HEARTS(1981)
Baxter Harris
...AND JUSTICE FOR ALL(1979)
1984
ONCE UPON A TIME IN AMERICA(1984)
Ben Harris
DAKOTA LIL(1950); LAS VEGAS STORY, THE(1952); MISS SADIE THOMPSON(1953)
Berkeley Harris
BULLET FOR A BADMAN(1964); MC HALE'S NAVY JOINS THE AIR FORCE(1965); SHENANDOAH(1965); GROOVE TUBE, THE(1974)
Beth Harris
MARY, QUEEN OF SCOTS(1971, Brit.)
Blake Harris
CHANGE OF SEASONS, A(1980)
Bob Harris
JACK OF DIAMONDS(1967, U.S./Ger.), m; ANGELS FROM HELL(1968); LOVE BUG, THE(1968); SPEEDWAY(1968); HELL'S ANGELS '69(1969); DIRTY HARRY(1971); EVEL KNIEVEL(1971); HIT MAN(1972); MADE(1972, Brit.); WHAT'S UP, DOC?(1972); DILLINGER(1973); STUDENT TEACHERS, THE(1973); TRUCK TURNER(1974); HERBIE GOES TO MONTE CARLO(1977)
1984
FLASH OF GREEN, A(1984)
Brad Harris
MONKEY ON MY BACK(1957); SPARTACUS(1960); THIRTEEN FIGHTING MEN(1960); FURY OF HERCULES, THE(1961, Ital.); SAMSON(1961, Ital.); IT HAPPENED IN ATHENS(1962); GOLIATH AGAINST THE GIANTS(1963, Ital./Span.); FANTASTIC THREE, THE(1967, Ital./Ger./Fr./Yugo.); MUTATIONS, THE(1974, Brit.); HERCULES(1983)
Misc. Talkies
OUR MAN IN JAMAICA(1965); TEN MILLION DOLLAR GRAB(1966, Ital.); SPY TODAY, DIE TOMORROW(1967); MAD BUTCHER, THE(1972)
Bud Harris
ONE HOUR TO LIVE(1939); MY LITTLE CHICKADEE(1940); BUCK PRIVATES(1941)
Misc. Talkies
MOON OVER HARLEM(1939)
Buddy Harris
UNMASKED(1929), ph
Burt Harris
YEAR OF THE HORSE, THE(1966); STOOLIE, THE(1972)
Misc. Talkies
SECRET OF THE CHINESE CARNATION, THE(1965); ISLAND OF LOST GIRLS(1975)
Burtt Harris
ODDS AGAINST TOMORROW(1959); NIGHT OF EVIL(1962); WANDERERS, THE(1979); PRINCE OF THE CITY(1981), p; DEATHTRAP(1982), p; VERDICT, THE(1982); DANIEL(1983), a, p
1984
GARBO TALKS(1984), a, p
Caroline Harris
Silents
MADAME BUTTERFLY(1915); ETERNAL SAPHO, THE(1916); ONE OF MANY(1917)
Misc. Silents
HONOR OF MARY BLAKE, THE(1916); BOY GIRL, THE(1917)
Cassandra Harris
GREEK TYCOON, THE(1978); ROUGH CUT(1980, Brit.); FOR YOUR EYES ONLY(1981)
Charles Harris
SINGLE SIN(1931), ed; SCARLET LETTER, THE(1934), ed; SHE HAD TO CHOOSE(1934), ph; SMOKING GUNS(1934), ed; WHEELS OF DESTINY(1934), ed
Charles K. Harris
EXTRAVAGANCE(1930), ed
Silents
ASHAMED OF PARENTS(1921), w; SLIM SHOULDERS(1922), w; AFTER THE BALL(1924), w; CHICAGO AFTER MIDNIGHT(1928), w

Charles P. Harris
SMOKEY AND THE BANDIT–PART 3(1983)
Cheire Harris
1984
SLAPSTICK OF ANOTHER KIND(1984)
Chris Harris
RITZ, THE(1976)
Christopher Harris
LORD OF THE FLIES(1963, Brit.)
Clare Harris
JEWEL, THE(1933, Brit.); WHAT HAPPENED TO HARKNESS(1934, Brit.)
Clarence Harris
SKULLDUGGERY(1970)
Clarence J. Harris
Silents
CAPRICE OF THE MOUNTAINS(1916), w
Misc. Silents
BARBARA FRIETCHIE(1915), d
Claude Harris
Silents
SANCTUARY(1916, Brit.), p&d
Clifford Harris
Misc. Silents
HEARTS OF THE WOODS(1921)
Connie Harris
HARLEM ON THE PRAIRIE(1938)
Corra Harris
I'D CLIMB THE HIGHEST MOUNTAIN(1951), w
Craig Harris
BLOODEATERS(1980), makeup
Crampton Harris
PROFESSOR BEWARE(1938), w; PROFESSIONALS, THE(1966), w
Curtis Harris
OUTLAW BLUES(1977)
Cynthia Harris
ISADORA(1968, Brit.); UP THE SANDBOX(1972); I COULD NEVER HAVE SEX WITH ANY MAN WHO HAS SO LITTLE REGARD FOR MY HUSBAND(1973); TEMPEST(1982); REUBEN, REUBEN(1983)
Damian Harris
OTLEY(1969, Brit.)
Dane Harris
I'LL BE SEEING YOU(1944)
Daniel Harris
1984
STUCK ON YOU(1984)
Darren Harris
1984
SIXTEEN CANDLES(1984)
David Harris
SLENDER THREAD, THE(1965); SHE-DEVILS ON WHEELS(1968); WARRIORS, THE(1979)
1984
PURPLE HEARTS(1984); SOLDIER'S STORY, A(1984)
David D. Harris
BRUBAKER(1980)
Dean Harris
CRAZE(1974, Brit.)
Del Harris
DISEMBODIED, THE(1957), ed
Dennis Harris
ALAMBRISTA!(1977)
Denny Harris
SILENT SCREAM(1980), d
Derek Harris
SINCE YOU WENT AWAY(1944)
Dina Harris
HORROR OF PARTY BEACH, THE(1964)
Dixie Harris
WHEN YOU COMIN' BACK, RED RYDER?(1979)
Donald Harris
SWAP MEET(1979), art d
Doris Harris
RED RUNS THE RIVER(1963)
Dorothy Harris
WHITE WITCH DOCTOR(1953)
Doug Harris
CLARENCE AND ANGEL(1981), ph
Douglas Harris
STATE OF SIEGE(1973, Fr./U.S./Ital./Ger.)
E.W. Harris
Misc. Silents
LAW UNTO HIMSELF, A(1916)
Earle Tex Harris
WAKE ISLAND(1942)
Ed Harris
BORDERLINE(1980); DREAM ON(1981); KNIGHTRIDERS(1981); CREEP-SHOW(1982); RIGHT STUFF, THE(1983); UNDER FIRE(1983)
1984
FLASH OF GREEN, A(1984); PLACES IN THE HEART(1984); SWING SHIFT(1984)
Eddie Harris
SGT. PEPPER'S LONELY HEARTS CLUB BAND(1978)
Silents
DYNAMITE DAN(1924); ISLE OF FORGOTTEN WOMEN(1927); JAKE THE PLUMBER(1927); KING OF THE HERD(1927)
Edna Harris
GARDEN OF ALLAH, THE(1936); NIGHT FOR CRIME, A(1942); X MARKS THE SPOT(1942); SO'S YOUR UNCLE(1943); NIGHT AND DAY(1946); FALL GUY(1947); SMART GIRLS DON'T TALK(1948); TAKE ME OUT TO THE BALL GAME(1949)

Edna M. Harris
GREEN PASTURES(1936)
Edna Mae Harris
FURY(1936); SPIRIT OF YOUTH(1937)
Misc. Talkies
LYING LIPS(1939); PARADISE IN HARLEM(1939); SUNDAY SINNERS(1941)
Eleanor Harris
KIDNAPPED(1938), w; EVERY GIRL SHOULD BE MARRIED(1948), w
Elizabeth Harris
FRIC FRAC(1939, FR.), ed
Elmer Harris
FATHER AND SON(1929), w; SO LONG LETTY(1929), w; YOUNG SINNERS(1931), w; SKYSCRAPER SOULS(1932), w; SOCIETY GIRL(1932), w; BARBARIAN, THE(1933), w; CROSS COUNTRY CRUISE(1934), w; LOOKING FOR TROUBLE(1934), w; LET 'EM HAVE IT(1935), w; THREE WISE GUYS, THE(1936), w; JOHNNY BELINDA(1948), w
Silents
PRETTY MRS. SMITH(1915), w; ADVENTURE IN HEARTS, AN(1919), w; MISS HOBBS(1920), w; AFFAIRS OF ANATOL, THE(1921), w; ALL SOULS EVE(1921), w; DUCKS AND DRAKES(1921), sup&w; EDUCATION OF ELIZABETH, THE(1921), w; SHAM(1921), w; SPEED GIRL, THE(1921), w; HER GILDED CAGE(1922), w; TESS OF THE STORM COUNTRY(1922), w; GARRISON'S FINISH(1923), sup&w; GIRL ON THE STAIRS, THE(1924), sup & w; NO MORE WOMEN(1924), p, w; AWFUL TRUTH, THE(1925), w; COMING OF AMOS, THE(1925), ed; MATINEE IDOL, THE(1928), w; NAME THE WOMAN(1928), d&w; RANSOM(1928), w; SO THIS IS LOVE(1928), w; OBJECT-ALIMONY(1929), w
Emmylou Harris
HONEYSUCKLE ROSE(1980)
Estelle Harris
LOOKING UP(1977); SUMMERDOG(1977)
1984
ONCE UPON A TIME IN AMERICA(1984)
Fox Harris
FORBIDDEN WORLD(1982); HAMMETT(1982); LOOKIN' TO GET OUT(1982)
1984
REPO MAN(1984)
Frank Harris
COWBOY(1958), w
1984
KILLPOINT(1984), p, d,w&ph, ed
Silents
DAWN(1917, Brit.)
Sen. Fred Harris
CANDIDATE, THE(1972)
Fred Harris II
NO MAN IS AN ISLAND(1962)
George Harris
CAPTAIN BILL(1935, Brit.), w; STOKER, THE(1935, Brit.), a, w; HAPPY DAYS ARE HERE AGAIN(1936, Brit.); GLADIATORS, THE(1970, Swed.); YANKS(1979); FLASH GORDON(1980); RAGTIME(1981); RAIDERS OF THE LOST ARK(1981)
Misc. Talkies
WHAT DO I TELL THE BOYS AT THE STATION(1972)
Silents
JOHNSTOWN FLOOD, THE(1926)
George Harris II
COPS AND ROBBERS(1973); SUPERMAN(1978)
George W. Harris
DOGS OF WAR, THE(1980, Brit.)
Georgie Harris
DON'T BE A DUMMY(1932, Brit.); COMMISSIONAIRE(1933, Brit.); I ADORE YOU(1933, Brit.); DOCTOR'S ORDERS(1934, Brit.); WITHOUT YOU(1934, Brit.); CAPTAIN BILL(1935, Brit.); RADIO FOLLIES(1935, Brit.); STRICTLY ILLEGAL(1935, Brit.), a, w; ONE GOOD TURN(1936, Brit.), a, w; BOYS WILL BE GIRLS(1937, Brit.); RHYTHM RACKETEER(1937, Brit.); SATURDAY NIGHT REVUE(1937, Brit.); REVERSE BE MY LOT, THE(1938, Brit.)
Silents
FLOATING COLLEGE, THE(1928)
Geraldine Harris
YOU'RE MY EVERYTHING(1949)
Gordon Harris
HELL, HEAVEN OR HOBOKEN(1958, Brit.); SCOTLAND YARD DRAGNET(1957, Brit.); GIDEON OF SCOTLAND YARD(1959, Brit.); NAVY LARK, THE(1959, Brit.); TOUCH OF LARCENY, A(1960, Brit.); MURDER SHE SAID(1961, Brit.); MURDER AT THE GALLOP(1963, Brit.)
Grace Harris
STALKING MOON, THE(1969), cos; OUT OF TOWNERS, THE(1970), cos
Graham Harris
BEAST IN THE CELLAR, THE(1971, Brit.), p; NIGHT HAIR CHILD(1971, Brit.), p
Greg Harris
JAWS II(1978)
Harold Harris
SPOOK WHO SAT BY THE DOOR, THE(1973)
Harriett Harris
Misc. Silents
MODERN CAIN, A(1925)
Harry B. Harris
Silents
LIGHT OF VICTORY(1919), ph; IN FOLLY'S TRAIL(1920), ph
Misc. Silents
RISKY BUSINESS(1920), d; DESPERATE YOUTH(1921), d; MAN TAMER, THE(1921), d; RICH GIRL, POOR GIRL(1921), d; SHORT SKIRTS(1921), d; TROUPER, THE(1922), d
Heath Harris
JOURNEY AMONG WOMEN(1977, Aus.), stunts; BREAKER MORANT(1980, Aus.), stunts; GALLIPOLI(1981, Aus.)
Helen Harris
Silents
NOBODY'S FOOL(1921)

Henry Harris
ALMOST A DIVORCE(1931, Brit.), ph; CHELSEA LIFE(1933, Brit.), ph; LORD OF THE MANOR(1933, Brit.), ph; PURSE STRINGS(1933, Brit.), ph; SECRET OF STAMBOUL, THE(1936, Brit.), ph; BRIEF ECSTASY(1937, Brit.), ph; SKY'S THE LIMIT, THE(1937, Brit.), ph; STREET SINGER, THE(1937, Brit.), ph; THIS MAN IN PARIS(1939, Brit.), ph; THIS MAN IS NEWS(1939, Brit.), ph; BAND WAGGON(1940, Brit.), ph; STARS LOOK DOWN, THE(1940, Brit.), ph; LARCENY STREET(1941, Brit.), ph; YOU WILL REMEMBER(1941, Brit.), ph; STAIRWAY TO HEAVEN(1946, Brit.), spec eff; HAMLET(1948, Brit.), spec eff; ONE NIGHT WITH YOU(1948, Brit), spec eff; VICE VERSA(1948, Brit.), spec eff; UP FOR THE CUP(1950, Brit.), ph; MR. PEEK-A-BOO(1951, Fr.), spec eff
Misc. Silents
FOOLISH LIVES(1922)

Holly Harris
THE HYPNOTIC EYE(1960); WHY MUST I DIE?(1960); DOGS(1976)

Howard Harris
HIGHER AND HIGHER(1943), w; COPACABANA(1947), w; LINDA BE GOOD(1947), w; NOOSE HANGS HIGH, THE(1948), w

Ivy Harris
Silents
POTTERS, THE(1927); JUST MARRIED(1928); THREE SINNERS(1928)
Misc. Silents
FASCINATING YOUTH(1926); GENTLEMAN OF PARIS, A(1927)

Jack Harris
SHERLOCK HOLMES' FATAL HOUR(1931, Brit.), ed; MISSING REMBRANDT, THE(1932, Brit.), ed; MORALS OF MARCUS, THE(1936, Brit.), ed; SHADOW, THE(1936, Brit.), ed; SON OF FRANKENSTEIN(1939); PASTOR HALL(1940, Brit.), ed; THIS HAPPY BREED(1944, Brit.), ed; ADVENTURE FOR TWO(1945, Brit.), ed; BLITHE SPIRIT(1945, Brit.), ed; BRIEF ENCOUNTER(1945, Brit.), ed; GREAT EXPECTATIONS(1946, Brit.), ed; BLANCHE FURY(1948, Brit.), ed; TAKE MY LIFE(1948, Brit.), ed; GOLDEN SALAMANDER(1950, Brit.), ed; CAPTAIN HORATIO HORNBLOWER(1951, Brit.), ed; MANIACS ON WHEELS(1951, Brit.), ed; OLIVER TWIST(1951, Brit.), ed; CRIMSON PIRATE, THE(1952, Brit.), ed; IVORY HUNTER(1952, Brit.), ed; FARMER TAKES A WIFE, THE(1953); MASTER OF BALLANTRAE, THE(1953, U.S./Brit.), ed; RAINBOW JACKET, THE(1954, Brit.), ed; LADYKILLERS, THE(1956, Brit.), ed; OUT OF THE CLOUDS(1957, Brit.), ed; PRINCE AND THE SHOWGIRL, THE(1957, Brit.), ed; ALL AT SEA(1958, Brit.), ed; INDISCREET(1958), ed; SCAPEGOAT, THE(1959, Brit.), ed; ONCE MORE, WITH FEELING(1960), ed; SUNDOWNERS, THE(1960), ed; SQUAD CAR(1961); BILLY BUDD(1962), ed; STAKEOUT!(1962); CHALK GARDEN, THE(1964, Brit.), ed; BOY TEN FEET TALL, A(1965, Brit.), ed; HE WHO RIDES A TIGER(1966, Brit.), ed; MIDSUMMER NIGHT'S DREAM, A(1969, Brit.), ed; TAKE A GIRL LIKE YOU(1970, Brit,), ed; SCHLOCK(1973); THREE SISTERS(1974, Brit.), ed
Silents
SISTER TO ASSIST 'ER, A(1927, Brit.)
Misc. Silents
BIG DRIVE, THE(1928)

Jack H. Harris
BLOB, THE(1958), p; 4D MAN(1959), p; DINOSAURUS(1960), p, w; MOTHER GOOSE A GO-GO(1966), p, d&w; EQUINOX(1970), p

James Harris
Silents
RANSON'S FOLLY(1915)
Misc. Silents
FAITH AND FORTUNE(1915); BARKER, THE(1917)

James B. Harris
KILLING, THE(1956), p; PATHS OF GLORY(1957), p; LOLITA(1962), p; BEDFORD INCIDENT, THE(1965, Brit.), p&d; SOME CALL IT LOVING(1973), p,d&w; TELEFON(1977), p; FAST-WALKING(1982), p&d, w

James W. Harris
NORMA RAE(1979)

Jane Harris
RIVER, THE(1951)

Jed Harris
BROADWAY(1929), w; LIGHT TOUCH, THE(1951), w; NIGHT PEOPLE(1954), w; OPERATION MAD BALL(1957), p, w

Jeff Harris
1984
JOHNNY DANGEROUSLY(1984), w

Jennifer Harris
RIVER, THE(1951)

Jerry Harris
MALE SERVICE(1966)

Jet Harris
JUST FOR FUN(1963, Brit.)

Jim Harris
SQUEEZE PLAY(1981); WAITRESS(1982)

Jo Ann Harris
MARYJANE(1968); GAY DECEIVERS, THE(1969); BEGUILED, THE(1971); SPORTING CLUB, THE(1971)
Misc. Talkies
TEENAGE TEASE(1983)

Joan Harris
RED SHOES, THE(1948, Brit.)
1984
KILLING FIELDS, THE(1984, Brit.)

JoAnn Harris
ACT OF VENGEANCE(1974)
Misc. Talkies
ELIMINATOR, THE(1982)

Joanne Harris
PARALLAX VIEW, THE(1974)

Joe Harris
THEY SHOOT HORSES, DON'T THEY?(1969)
Silents
HUMAN STUFF(1920); OVERLAND RED(1920); WALLOP, THE(1921); PARDON MY NERVE!(1922)
Misc. Silents
THREE MOUNTED MEN(1918); ACE OF THE SADDLE(1919); BARE FISTS(1919); FIGHT FOR LOVE, A(1919); RIDER OF THE LAW(1919); HITCHIN' POSTS(1920);

MARKED MEN(1920); FREEZE OUT, THE(1921); BEARCAT, THE(1922)

Joel Chandler Harris
SONG OF THE SOUTH(1946), w

John Harris
SEA SHALL NOT HAVE THEM, THE(1955, Brit.), w; RARE BREED, THE(1966); CHILDISH THINGS(1969), art d; TALES FROM THE CRYPT(1972, Brit.), ph

Johnny Harris
BLOOMFIELD(1971, Brit./Israel), m; FRAGMENT OF FEAR(1971, Brit.), m; MAN IN THE WILDERNESS(1971, U.S./Span.), m; I WANT WHAT I WANT(1972, Brit.), m&md; EVIL, THE(1978), m

Jon Harris
TELL ME A RIDDLE(1980)

Jon Harris III
STRYKER(1983, Phil.)

Jonathan Harris
BOTANY BAY(1953); BIG FISHERMAN, THE(1959)
Misc. Talkies
CATCH ME IF YOU CAN(1959)

Joseph Harris
Silents
GIRL FROM HIS TOWN, THE(1915); OUTCASTS OF POKER FLAT, THE(1919); RIDERS OF VENGEANCE(1919); LOADED DOOR, THE(1922); CRASHIN' THRU(1923)
Misc. Silents
DRAGON, THE(1916); PEARL OF PARADISE, THE(1916); BUTTERFLY GIRL, THE(1917); CANYON OF THE FOOLS(1923)

Joseph B. Harris
Silents
GAUCHO, THE(1928), t

Judy Harris
WILD RIVER(1960)

Julie Harris
GOODBYE MR. CHIPS(1939, Brit.), cos; MY BROTHER'S KEEPER(1949, Brit.), cos; ONCE UPON A DREAM(1949, Brit.), cos; HOTEL SAHARA(1951, Brit.), cos; MR. DRAKE'S DUCK(1951, Brit.), cos; TRAVELLER'S JOY(1951, Brit.), cos; MEMBER OF THE WEDDING, THE(1952); DESPERATE MOMENT(1953, Brit.), cos; NIGHT WITHOUT STARS(1953, Brit.), cos; SO LITTLE TIME(1953, Brit.), cos; YOU KNOW WHAT SAILORS ARE(1954, Brit.), cos; EAST OF EDEN(1955); I AM A CAMERA(1955, Brit.); LAND OF FURY(1955 Brit.), cos; PRISONER, THE(1955, Brit.), cos; MIRACLE IN SOHO(1957, Brit.), cos; GYPSY AND THE GENTLEMAN, THE(1958, Brit.), cos; SHERIFF OF FRACTURED JAW, THE(1958, Brit.), cos; TRUTH ABOUT WOMEN, THE(1958, Brit.); POACHER'S DAUGHTER, THE(1960, Brit.); SWISS FAMILY ROBINSON(1960), cos; LOSS OF INNOCENCE(1961, Brit.), cos; NAKED EDGE, THE(1961), cos; PORTRAIT OF A SINNER(1961, Brit.), cos; REQUIEM FOR A HEAVYWEIGHT(1962); WAR LOVER, THE(1962, U.S./Brit.), cos; WE JOINED THE NAVY(1962, Brit.), cos; HAUNTING, THE(1963); CHALK GARDEN, THE(1964, Brit.), cos; HARD DAY'S NIGHT, A(1964, Brit.), cos; PSYCHE 59(1964, Brit.), cos; TAMAHINE(1964, Brit.), cos; DARLING(1965, Brit.), cos; HELP!(1965, Brit.), cos; HARPER(1966); WRONG BOX, THE(1966, Brit.), cos; YOU'RE A BIG BOY NOW(1966); EYE OF THE DEVIL(1967, Brit.), cos; REFLECTIONS IN A GOLDEN EYE(1967); DEADFALL(1968, Brit.), cos; JOURNEY INTO MIDNIGHT(1968, Brit.); PRUDENCE AND THE PILL(1968, Brit.), cos; SPLIT, THE(1968); DECLINE AND FALL... OF A BIRD WATCHER(1969, Brit.), cos; GOODBYE MR. CHIPS(1969, U.S./Brit.), cos; PEOPLE NEXT DOOR, THE(1970); PRIVATE LIFE OF SHERLOCK HOLMES, THE(1970, Brit.), cos; PUBLIC EYE, THE(1972, Brit.), cos; LIVE AND LET DIE(1973, Brit.), cos; HIDING PLACE, THE(1975); ROLLERBALL(1975), cos; SLIPPER AND THE ROSE, THE(1976, Brit.), cos; VOYAGE OF THE DAMNED(1976, Brit.); CANDLESHOE(1978), cos; BELL JAR, THE(1979); DRACULA(1979), cos; LOST AND FOUND(1979), cos; GREAT MUPPET CAPER, THE(1981), cos; HOUND OF THE BASKERVILLES, THE(1983, Brit.), cos; SIGN OF FOUR, THE(1983, Brit.), cos

Julius Harris
TAKING OF PELHAM ONE, TWO, THREE, THE(1974); NOTHING BUT A MAN(1964); SLAVES(1969); LET'S DO IT AGAIN(1975); KING KONG(1976); ALAMBRISTA!(1977); ISLANDS IN THE STREAM(1977); LOOKING FOR MR. GOODBAR(1977); FIRST FAMILY(1980); GORP(1980); GOING BERSERK(1983)

Julius W. Harris
SHAFT'S BIG SCORE(1972); SUPERFLY(1972); TROUBLE MAN(1972); BLACK CAESAR(1973); HELL UP IN HARLEM(1973); LIVE AND LET DIE(1973, Brit.); SALTY(1975)

June Harris
UP IN ARMS(1944); OUT OF THIS WORLD(1945); UNCONQUERED(1947); JOAN OF ARC(1948)

Katherine Harris
Silents
LOST BRIDEGROOM, THE(1916); NEARLY A KING(1916)

Kay Harris
TILLIE THE TOILER(1941); LUCKY LEGS(1942); PARACHUTE NURSE(1942); SABOTAGE SQUAD(1942); SPIRIT OF STANFORD, THE(1942); FIGHTING BUCKAROO, THE(1943); ROBIN HOOD OF THE RANGE(1943)

Ken Harris
GAY PURR-EE(1962), anim; HEY THERE, IT'S YOGI BEAR(1964), anim

Kenneth Harris
Silents
IDLE RICH, THE(1921), w

Kenny Harris
TOO YOUNG, TOO IMMORAL!(1962), m

Kimberly Harris
1,000 SHAPES OF A FEMALE(1963)

Larry Harris
DEAD END(1937); COCOANUT GROVE(1938); ETERNALLY YOURS(1939); PUBLIC ENEMIES(1941)

Lawrence Harris
Misc. Talkies
THURSDAY MORNING MURDERS, THE(1976)

Lawson Harris
Misc. Silents
LAW OR LOYALTY(1926), d

Lee Anne Harris
I, THE JURY(1982)
Lee Harris
EXPLOSIVE GENERATION, THE(1961)
Leigh Harris
SORCERESS(1983)
Misc. Talkies
SORCERESS(1983)
Leland Harris
ALL ABOUT EVE(1950)
Len Harris
ONCE UPON A DREAM(1949, Brit.), ph; MY WIFE'S LODGER(1952, Brit.), ph; ONCE A SINNER(1952, Brit.), ph; BACHELOR IN PARIS(1953, Brit.), ph; FURTHER UP THE CREEK!(1958, Brit.), ph; NAKED WORLD OF HARRISON MARKS, THE(1967, Brit.), ph
Lenore Harris
Silents
FRIDAY THE 13TH(1916)
Leon Harris
ON THE YARD(1978), art d; STAR TREK: THE MOTION PICTURE(1979), art d; DINER(1982), art d
Leon R. Harris
DEVIL AND MAX DEVLIN, THE(1981), art d
Leonard Harris
TAXI DRIVER(1976); HERO AT LARGE(1980)
Leonore Harris
Silents
TODAY(1917)
Misc. Silents
DECOY, THE(1916); HUMAN DRIFTWOOD(1916); FAITHLESS SEX, THE(1922)
Lewis Harris
SHORT EYES(1977), p
Lionel Harris
TALES OF HOFFMANN, THE(1951, Brit.); BRANDY FOR THE PARSON(1952, Brit.); IVANHOE(1952, Brit.); SCOTLAND YARD INSPECTOR(1952, Brit.); SECRET PEOPLE(1952, Brit.); SCOTCH ON THE ROCKS(1954, Brit.); DOUBLE, THE(1963, Brit.), d
Lorenzo Jodie Harris
YOU BETTER WATCH OUT(1980), prod d
Lucretia Harris
Silents
KENTUCKY CINDERELLA, A(1917); NOBODY'S FOOL(1921)
Misc. Silents
INTRUSION OF ISABEL, THE(1919)
Lynette Harris
I, THE JURY(1982); SORCERESS(1983)
Misc. Talkies
SORCERESS(1983)
Lynn Harris
MONKEY HUSTLE, THE(1976)
Misc. Talkies
COCKTAIL HOSTESSES, THE(1976)
Mai Harris
GERVAISE(1956, Fr.), titles; QUEENS, THE(1968, Ital./Fr.), titles
Mamie Harris
STATE FAIR(1962)
Marcia Harris
SATURDAY'S CHILDREN(1929); BIG TRAIL, THE(1930); ALOHA(1931); YOUNG AS YOU FEEL(1931); THREE WISE GIRLS(1932)
Silents
GREAT EXPECTATIONS(1917); POOR LITTLE RICH GIRL, A(1917); PRUNELLA(1918); ANNE OF GREEN GABLES(1919); KATHLEEN MAVOURNEEN(1919); BRIDE FOR A NIGHT, A(1923); ON THE BANKS OF THE WABASH(1923); ISN'T LIFE WONDERFUL(1924); SINNERS IN HEAVEN(1924); RECKLESS LADY, THE(1926); SORROWS OF SATAN(1926); SO'S YOUR OLD MAN(1926); BACKSTAGE(1927); TAKE ME HOME(1928)
Misc. Silents
LITTLE BOY SCOUT, THE(1917); HEART TO LET, A(1921)
Marie T. Harris
LOVED ONE, THE(1965), cos
Marilyn Harris
FRANKENSTEIN(1931); OVER THE HILL(1931); WILD GIRL(1932); WICKED WOMAN, A(1934); SHOW BOAT(1936)
Marilynn Harris
HENRY ALDRICH GETS GLAMOUR(1942); STANDING ROOM ONLY(1944)
Marion Harris
DEVIL MAY CARE(1929); TROUBLE AHEAD(1936, Brit.)
Mark Harris
DEVIL'S SISTERS, THE(1966); LAST OF THE SECRET AGENTS?, THE(1966); BANG THE DRUM SLOWLY(1973), w; STANLEY(1973); LENNY(1974); LINCOLN CONSPIRACY, THE(1977); ABSENCE OF MALICE(1981)
1984
MICKI AND MAUDE(1984)
Martin Harris
REMOVALISTS, THE(1975, Aus.); ELIZA FRASER(1976, Aus.); MAD DOG MORGAN(1976,Aus.)
Mary Ann Harris
CARNIVAL OF SOULS(1962)
Mary Lou Harris
1984
MUPPETS TAKE MANHATTAN, THE(1984)
Misc. Talkies
FLICKER UP(1946)
Maurice Harris
DUNGEONS OF HARROW(1964)
Max Harris
BABY LOVE(1969, Brit.), m; ON THE BUSES(1972, Brit.), m; ONE OF OUR DINOSAURS IS MISSING(1975, Brit.)

Mercer Harris
DEATH OF A GUNFIGHTER(1969); HAIL, HERO!(1969); COMPANY OF KILLERS(1970)
Michael Harris
FLESH AND THE SPUR(1957); 27TH DAY, THE(1957); SHRIEK OF THE MUTILATED(1974); MAKING LOVE(1982)
lp: Michelle Harris
Misc. Talkies
MATTER OF LOVE, A(1979)
Mickey Harris
THIN MAN GOES HOME, THE(1944)
Mildred Harris
MELODY OF LOVE, THE(1928); SEA FURY(1929); SIDE STREET(1929); MELODY MAN(1930); NO, NO NANETTE(1930); LADY TUBBS(1935); GREAT GUY(1936); REAP THE WILD WIND(1942); HAIL THE CONQUERING HERO(1944)
Misc. Talkies
NEVER TOO LATE(1935)
Silents
WARRENS OF VIRGINIA, THE(1915); INTOLERANCE(1916); OLD FOLKS AT HOME, THE(1916); AMERICANO, THE(1917); CUPID BY PROXY(1918); PRINCE THERE WAS, A(1921); FOG, THE(1923); IN FAST COMPANY(1924); ONE LAW FOR THE WOMAN(1924); EASY MONEY(1925); FIGHTING CUB, THE(1925); IRON MAN, THE(1925); ISLE OF RETRIBUTION, THE(1926); ADVENTUROUS SOUL, THE(1927); GIRL FROM RIO, THE(1927); HUSBAND HUNTERS(1927); ONE HOUR OF LOVE(1927); OUT OF THE PAST(1927); SHOW GIRL, THE(1927); SWELL-HEAD, THE(1927); WANDERING GIRLS(1927); HEART OF A FOLLIES GIRL, THE(1928); LINGERIE(1928); POWER OF THE PRESS, THE(1928)
Misc. Silents
MAGIC CLOAK OF OZ, THE(1914); ENOCH ARDEN(1915); BAD BOYS(1917); COLD DECK, THE(1917); GOLDEN RULE KATE(1917); BORROWED CLOTHES(1918); DOCTOR AND THE WOMAN, THE(1918); FOR HUSBANDS ONLY(1918); PRICE OF A GOOD TIME, THE(1918); FORBIDDEN(1919); HOME(1919); WHEN A GIRL LOVES(1919); FOOL'S PARADISE(1921); DARING YEARS, THE(1923); BY DIVINE RIGHT(1924); DESERT HAWK, THE(1924); SHADOW OF THE EAST, THE(1924); SOILED(1924); STEPPING LIVELY(1924); TRAFFIC IN HEARTS(1924); UNMARRIED WIVES(1924); BEYOND THE BORDER(1925); DRESSMAKER FROM PARIS, THE(1925); PRIVATE AFFAIRS(1925); SUPER SPEED(1925); UNKNOWN LOVER, THE(1925); CRUISE OF THE JASPER B, THE(1926); DANGEROUS TRAFFIC(1926); MYSTERY CLUB, THE(1926); SELF STARTER, THE(1926); WOLF HUNTERS, THE(1926); ROSE OF THE BOWERY(1927); WOLVES OF THE AIR(1927); HEARTS OF MEN(1928); LAST LAP(1928); SPEED CLASSIC, THE(1928)
Mitchell Harris
SEA WOLF, THE(1930); CONNECTICUT YANKEE, A(1931); FAIR WARNING(1931); PEACH O' RENO(1931); FREIGHTERS OF DESTINY(1932); GHOST VALLEY(1932); SCANDAL FOR SALE(1932); THIRTEEN WOMEN(1932); HYPNOTIZED(1933); VICTIMS OF PERSECUTION(1933); AWFUL TRUTH, THE(1937); HOLIDAY(1938)
Mona Harris
POET'S PUB(1949, Brit.)
Mosetta Harris
1984
WHAT YOU TAKE FOR GRANTED(1984)
Muriel G. Harris
MOTHER GOOSE A GO-GO(1966), p, prod d
Nancy Harris
DIRT GANG, THE(1972); ONLY WAY HOME, THE(1972)
Norris Harris
NOCTURNA(1979)
Owen Harris
SUBMARINE SEAHAWK(1959), w; FLIGHT THAT DISAPPEARED, THE(1961), w; FRONTIER UPRISING(1961), w; GAMBLER WORE A GUN, THE(1961), w; SECRET OF DEEP HARBOR(1961), w; DEADLY DUO(1962), w; INCIDENT IN AN ALLEY(1962), w; UNDERWATER CITY, THE(1962), w
Pamela Harris
TIN PAN ALLEY(1940), w; I'LL GET BY(1950), w
Paul Harris
ALL NIGHT LONG(1961, Brit.); FOR LOVE OF IVY(1968); MACK, THE(1973); TRUCK TURNER(1974)
Misc. Talkies
BABY NEEDS A NEW PAIR OF SHOES(1974); JIVE TURKEY(1976)
Paul E. Harris
SLAMS, THE(1973); LET'S DO IT AGAIN(1975)
Phil Harris
MELODY CRUISE(1933); MAN ABOUT TOWN(1939); BUCK BENNY RIDES AGAIN(1940); DREAMING OUT LOUD(1940); I LOVE A BANDLEADER(1945); WABASH AVENUE(1950); HERE COMES THE GROOM(1951); STARLIFT(1951); WILD BLUE YONDER, THE(1952); HIGH AND THE MIGHTY, THE(1954); ANYTHING GOES(1956); GOODBYE, MY LADY(1956); WHEELER DEALERS, THE(1963); PATSY, THE(1964); COOL ONES THE(1967); JUNGLE BOOK, THE(1967); ARISTOCATS, THE(1970); LAST PICTURE SHOW, THE(1971), m; GATLING GUN, THE(1972); ROBIN HOOD(1973)
Philippa Harris
OUTSIDE MAN, THE(1973, U.S./FR.)
R.R. Harris
STONE OF SILVER CREEK(1935), w
Ray Harris
SAILORS' HOLIDAY(1929), w; BRIDE OF THE REGIMENT(1930), w; STRICTLY MODERN(1930), w, titles; WEDDING RINGS(1930), w; FALSE MADONNA(1932), w; HE LEARNED ABOUT WOMEN(1933), w; THREE-CORNERED MOON(1933), w; MANY HAPPY RETURNS(1934), w; WE'RE RICH AGAIN(1934), w; ENCHANTED APRIL(1935), w; HOORAY FOR LOVE(1935), w; LADDIE(1935), w; MAN ON THE FLYING TRAPEZE, THE(1935), w; DANCING PIRATE(1936), w; TICKET TO PARADISE(1936), w; STORY OF ALEXANDER GRAHAM BELL, THE(1939), w; MOUNTAIN RHYTHM(1942), w
Silents
QUARTERBACK, THE(1926), w; POTTERS, THE(1927), w; SPORTING GOODS(1928), w; WARMING UP(1928), w; SUNSET PASS(1929), w, t
Ray S. Harris
HILLBILLY BLITZKRIEG(1942), w

Raymond S. Harris
Silents
AVERAGE WOMAN, THE(1924), w; IS LOVE EVERYTHING?(1924), w; LEND ME YOUR HUSBAND(1924), w; SPITFIRE, THE(1924), w; YOUTH FOR SALE(1924), w, t

Renee Harris
HOMEWORK(1982)

Rhina Harris
Misc. Talkies
THAT MAN OF MINE(1947)

Richard Harris
SHAKE HANDS WITH THE DEVIL(1959, Ireland); WRECK OF THE MARY DEAR, THE(1959); NIGHT FIGHTERS, THE(1960); ATTEMPT TO KILL(1961, Brit.), w; GUNS OF NAVARONE, THE(1961); LONG AND THE SHORT AND THE TALL, THE(1961, Brit.); MAN DETAINED(1961, Brit.), w; ALIVE AND KICKING(1962, Brit.); LOCKER 69(1962, Brit.), w; MUTINY ON THE BOUNTY(1962); STRONGROOM(1962, Brit.), w; THIS SPORTING LIFE(1963, Brit.); HEROES OF TELEMARK, THE(1965, Brit.); MAJOR DUNDEE(1965); RED DESERT(1965, Fr./Ital.); THREE FACES OF A WOMAN(1965, Ital.); BIBLE...IN THE BEGINNING, THE(1966); HAWAII(1966); MAIN CHANCE, THE(1966, Brit.), w; CAMELOT(1967); CAPRICE(1967); ON THE RUN(1967, Brit.), w; BAMBOO SAUCER, THE(1968), ed; CROMWELL(1970, Brit.); I START COUNTING(1970, Brit.), w; LADY IN THE CAR WITH GLASSES AND A GUN, THE(1970, U.S./Fr.), w; MAN CALLED HORSE, A(1970); MOLLY MAGUIRES, THE(1970); BLOOMFIELD(1971, Brit./Israel), a, d, w; CHANDLER(1971), ed; CHRISTIAN LICORICE STORE, THE(1971), ed; MAN IN THE WILDERNESS(1971, U.S./Span.); CANDIDATE, THE(1972), ed; DEADLY TRACKERS(1973); CATCH MY SOUL(1974), ed; JUGGERNAUT(1974, Brit.); 99 AND 44/100% DEAD(1974); SMILE(1975), ed; ECHOES OF A SUMMER(1976); RETURN OF A MAN CALLED HORSE, THE(1976); ROBIN AND MARIAN(1976, Brit.); CASSANDRA CROSSING, THE(1977); GOLDEN RENDEZVOUS(1977); GULLIVER'S TRAVELS(1977, Brit., Bel.); ORCA(1977); WILD GEESE, THE(1978, Brit.); ALMOST PERFECT AFFAIR, AN(1979), ed; LAST WORD, THE(1979); RAVAGERS, THE(1979); GAME FOR VULTURES, A(1980, Brit.); TARZAN, THE APE MAN(1981); TOY, THE(1982), ed; TRIUMPHS OF A MAN CALLED HORSE(1983, US/Mex.)
1984
HIGHPOINT(1984, Can.)

Richard A. Harris
DUSTY AND SWEETS McGEE(1971), ed; BAD NEWS BEARS, THE(1976), ed; SEMI-TOUGH(1977), ed; BAD NEWS BEARS GO TO JAPAN, THE(1978), ed; ISLAND, THE(1980), ed; SURVIVORS, THE(1983), ed
1984
FLETCH(1984), ed

Robert Harris
"W" PLAN, THE(1931, Brit.); MANHATTAN MOON(1935), w; WEREWOLF OF LONDON, THE(1935), w; WHEN'S YOUR BIRTHDAY?(1937), p; UNDERGROUND GUERRILLAS(1944, Brit.); COLONEL BLIMP(1945, Brit.); NAKED CITY, THE(1948); FOR THEM THAT TRESPASS(1949, Brit.); LAUGHING ANNE(1954, Brit./U.S.); THAT LADY(1955, Brit.); BIG CAPER, THE(1957); OSCAR WILDE(1960, Brit.); CONVICTS FOUR(1962); MODEL MURDER CASE, THE(1964, Brit.); SECRET OF MY SUCCESS, THE(1965, Brit.); DECLINE AND FALL... OF A BIRD WATCHER(1969, Brit.); LADY CAROLINE LAMB(1972, Brit./Ital.); YOUNG WINSTON(1972, Brit.); MASSACRE IN ROME(1973, Ital.); TERRORISTS, THE(1975, Brit.); ON THE YARD(1978), cos

Robert H. Harris
BUNDLE OF JOY(1956); FUZZY PINK NIGHTGOWN, THE(1957); INVISIBLE BOY, THE(1957); NO DOWN PAYMENT(1957); PEYTON PLACE(1957); HOW TO MAKE A MONSTER(1958); GEORGE RAFT STORY, THE(1961); OPERATION EICHMANN(1961); TWENTY PLUS TWO(1961); AMERICA, AMERICA(1963); MIRAGE(1965); APACHE UPRISING(1966); VALLEY OF THE DOLLS(1967); GREAT NORTHFIELD, MINNESOTA RAID, THE(1972); MAN IN THE GLASS BOOTH, THE(1975)

Robin Harris
ONE MILE FROM HEAVEN(1937), w; CITY GIRL(1938), w

Roland "Bob" Harris
SLAMS, THE(1973)

Rolf Harris
YOU LUCKY PEOPLE(1955, Brit.); CRASH DRIVE(1959, Brit.); WEB OF SUSPICION(1959, Brit.); LITTLE CONVICT, THE(1980, Aus.)

Ronald Harris
REBECCA OF SUNNYBROOK FARM(1932); JANE EYRE(1944)

Ronnie Harris
HAPPINESS OF THREE WOMEN, THE(1954, Brit.)

Ronny Harris
CONRACK(1974)

Rosalind Harris
FIDDLER ON THE ROOF(1971)
1984
COTTON CLUB, THE(1984)

Rosemary Harris
BEAU BRUMMELL(1954); SHIRALEE, THE(1957, Brit.); FLEA IN HER EAR, A(1968, Fr.); UNCLE VANYA(1977, Brit.); BOYS FROM BRAZIL, THE(1978)
1984
PLOUGHMAN'S LUNCH, THE(1984, Brit.)

Ross Harris
SCREAM, BABY, SCREAM(1969); TESTAMENT(1983)

Rossie Harris
ANOTHER MAN, ANOTHER CHANCE(1977 Fr/US)

Roy Harris
FLYING CADETS(1941); LAW OF THE RANGE(1941); MOB TOWN(1941); RAWHIDE RANGERS(1941); SAN ANTONIO ROSE(1941); NORTH TO THE KLONDIKE(1942); TOP SERGEANT(1942)
Misc. Talkies
TEXAS TROUBLE SHOOTERS(1942)

Roy Harris [Riley Hill]
FIREFLY, THE(1937); OKLAHOMA FRONTIER(1939); MEN OF THE TIMBERLAND(1941)

Sam Harris
CARNIVAL BOAT(1932); NOW AND FOREVER(1934); SUSAN AND GOD(1940); MR. AND MRS. SMITH(1941); LURED(1947); SOUTH SEA WOMAN(1953); VANQUISHED, THE(1953)

Major Sam Harris
DR. JEKYLL AND MR. HYDE(1932); LOVE ME TONIGHT(1932); QUEEN CHRISTINA(1933); TUGBOAT ANNIE(1933); THIRTY-DAY PRINCESS(1934); DARK ANGEL, THE(1935); FEATHER IN HER HAT, A(1935); LIVES OF A BENGAL LANCER(1935); OLD MAN RHYTHM(1935); CHARGE OF THE LIGHT BRIGADE, THE(1936), tech adv; ROSE MARIE(1936); ANGEL(1937); ANOTHER DAWN(1937); DAMSEL IN DISTRESS, A(1937); FIGHT FOR YOUR LADY(1937); I COVER THE WAR(1937); LANCER SPY(1937); ANNABEL TAKES A TOUR(1938); SAY IT IN FRENCH(1938); IN NAME ONLY(1939); LIGHT THAT FAILED, THE(1939); RAINS CAME, THE(1939); ROARING TWENTIES, THE(1939); WUTHERING HEIGHTS(1939); YOU CAN'T CHEAT AN HONEST MAN(1939); ADVENTURE IN DIAMONDS(1940); IRENE(1940); SAFARI(1940); SAN ANTONIO ROSE(1941); WEEK-END IN HAVANA(1941); KEEPER OF THE FLAME(1942); RANDOM HARVEST(1942); GOVERNMENT GIRL(1943); MR. LUCKY(1943); OLD ACQUAINTANCE(1943); MEET ME IN ST. LOUIS(1944); SECRETS OF SCOTLAND YARD(1944); WILSON(1944); PICTURE OF DORIAN GRAY, THE(1945); SARATOGA TRUNK(1945); JOLSON STORY, THE(1946); LADY LUCK(1946); IF WINTER COMES(1947); IMPERFECT LADY, THE(1947); MOSS ROSE(1947); STALLION ROAD(1947); B. F.'S DAUGHTER(1948); CASBAH(1948); NIGHT HAS A THOUSAND EYES(1948); UNFAITHFULLY YOURS(1948); OH, YOU BEAUTIFUL DOLL(1949); FANCY PANTS(1950); LET'S DANCE(1950); LIFE OF HER OWN, A(1950); WHEN WILLIE COMES MARCHING HOME(1950); PLACE IN THE SUN, A(1951); PAULA(1952); QUIET MAN, THE(1952); LET'S DO IT AGAIN(1953); MA AND PA KETTLE ON VACATION(1953); STORY OF THREE LOVES, THE(1953); YOUNG BESS(1953); DIAL M FOR MURDER(1954); GIRL IN THE RED VELVET SWING, THE(1955); GUYS AND DOLLS(1955); STORY OF MANKIND, THE(1957); WINGS OF EAGLES, THE(1957); TWO RODE TOGETHER(1961); HATARI!(1962); MAN WHO SHOT LIBERTY VALANCE, THE(1962); DONOVAN'S REEF(1963); ISLAND OF LOVE(1963); CHEYENNE AUTUMN(1964); MARY POPPINS(1964); MY FAIR LADY(1964)

Sarah Harris
ELECTRIC HORSEMAN, THE(1979)

Shannon Harris
RAW WEEKEND(1964)

Sherman A. Harris
LONE RANGER AND THE LOST CITY OF GOLD, THE(1958), p

Sibyl Harris
BUNKER BEAN(1936); MOUNTAIN JUSTICE(1937); MR. DODD TAKES THE AIR(1937); ANGELS WASH THEIR FACES(1939); OFF THE RECORD(1939); ALL THIS AND HEAVEN TOO(1940); CHILD IS BORN, A(1940); MY SON, MY SON!(1940); UNTAMED(1940)

Sid Harris
STORMY CROSSING(1958, Brit.), w; VARAN THE UNBELIEVABLE(1962, U.S./Jap.), w; WILD HARVEST(1962), w

Slim Harris
DIAMOND CITY(1949, Brit.); SIMBA(1955, Brit.); SAFARI(1956)

Sophia Harris
GREAT EXPECTATIONS(1946, Brit.), cos

Sophie Harris
LONELINESS OF THE LONG DISTANCE RUNNER, THE(1962, Brit.), cos; TASTE OF HONEY, A(1962, Brit.), cos

Souter Harris
RAGMAN'S DAUGHTER, THE(1974, Brit.), p

Stacy B. Harris
CAST A LONG SHADOW(1959)

Stacy Harris
APPOINTMENT WITH DANGER(1951); HIS KIND OF WOMAN(1951); GREAT SIOUX UPRISING, THE(1953); REDHEAD FROM WYOMING, THE(1953); DRAGNET(1954); NEW ORLEANS UNCENSORED(1955); BRASS LEGEND, THE(1956); COMANCHE(1956); MOUNTAIN, THE(1956); RAINTREE COUNTY(1957); GOOD DAY FOR A HANGING(1958); HUNTERS, THE(1958); NEW ORLEANS AFTER DARK(1958); FOUR FOR THE MORGUE(1962); BRAINSTORM(1965); GREAT SIOUX MASSACRE, THE(1965); AMERICAN DREAM, AN(1966); MONEY TRAP, THE(1966); BLOODY MAMA(1970); SWAPPERS, THE(1970, Brit.)

Steve Harris
ICE PALACE(1960); RIGHT APPROACH, THE(1961); YELLOW CANARY, THE(1963); CHAFED ELBOWS(1967)

Stevie Harris
NAKED CITY, THE(1948)

Sybil Harris
THEY WON'T FORGET(1937); CRIME SCHOOL(1938); DELINQUENT PARENTS(1938); FEDERAL MAN-HUNT(1939)

Sydney Harris
MY UNCLE ANTOINE(1971, Can.)

Ted Harris
BLACULA(1972); MISTER BROWN(1972)

Teresa Harris
BANJO ON MY KNEE(1936); I WALKED WITH A ZOMBIE(1943)

Tex Harris
NO TIME FOR LOVE(1943)

Theodosia Harris
Silents
MARTYRS OF THE ALAMO, THE(1915), w

Theresa Harris
MOROCCO(1930); MERRILY WE GO TO HELL(1932); BABY FACE(1933); GOLD DIGGERS OF 1933(1933); HOLD YOUR MAN(1933); MORNING GLORY(1933); PRIVATE DETECTIVE 62(1933); PROFESSIONAL SWEETHEART(1933); DESIRABLE(1934); DRUMS O' VOODOO(1934); JEZEBEL(1938); TOY WIFE, THE(1938); ONE HOUR TO LIVE(1939); TELL NO TALES(1939); WOMEN, THE(1939); BUCK BENNY RIDES AGAIN(1940); LOVE THY NEIGHBOR(1940); SANTA FE TRAIL(1940); BLOSSOMS IN THE DUST(1941); FLAME OF NEW ORLEANS, THE(1941); OUR WIFE(1941); TOUGH AS THEY COME(1942); WHAT'S BUZZIN' COUSIN?(1943); SMOOTH AS SILK(1946); THREE LITTLE GIRLS IN BLUE(1946); MIRACLE ON 34TH STREET, THE(1947); OUT OF THE PAST(1947); BIG CLOCK, THE(1948); VELVET TOUCH, THE(1948); NEPTUNE'S DAUGHTER(1949); FILE ON THELMA JORDAN, THE(1950); GROUNDS FOR MARRIAGE(1950); AL JENNINGS OF OKLAHOMA(1951); FRENCH LINE, THE(1954); SPOILERS OF THE FOREST(1957)
Misc. Talkies
BARGAIN WITH BULLETS(1937)

Timothy Harris
CHEAPER TO KEEP HER(1980), w; TRADING PLACES(1983), w
Todd Harris
GIRL, THE BODY, AND THE PILL, THE(1967)
Tom Harris
WESTERN FRONTIER(1935); MANCHURIAN CANDIDATE, THE(1962); XTRO(1983, Brit.), spec eff
Tracy Harris
LONG GOODBYE, THE(1973)
Vernon Harris
JOY RIDE(1935, Brit.), a, w; IMPROPER DUCHESS, THE(1936, Brit.), w; SHOW FLAT(1936, Brit.); TROPICAL TROUBLE(1936, Brit.), a, w; CLAYDON TREASURE MYSTERY, THE(1938, Brit.); GABLES MYSTERY, THE(1938, Brit.); LAST BARRICADE, THE(1938, Brit.); TROOPSHIP(1938, Brit.); ADVENTURES OF PC 49, THE(1949, Brit.), w; CASE FOR PC 49, A(1951, Brit.), w; ALBERT, R.N.(1953, Brit.), w; HUNDRED HOUR HUNT(1953, Brit.), w; JOHNNY ON THE RUN(1953, Brit.), d; SLASHER, THE(1953, Brit.), w; THERE WAS A YOUNG LADY(1953, Brit.), w; GOOD DIE YOUNG, THE(1954, Brit.), w; SEA SHALL NOT HAVE THEM, THE(1955, Brit.), w; ADMIRABLE CRICHTON, THE(1957, Brit.), w; REACH FOR THE SKY(1957, Brit.), w; CARVE HER NAME WITH PRIDE(1958, Brit.), w; THREE MEN IN A BOAT(1958, Brit.), w; CRY FROM THE STREET, A(1959, Brit.), w; FERRY TO HONG KONG(1959, Brit.), w; LIGHT UP THE SKY(1960, Brit.), w; ALMOST ANGELS(1962), w; EMERGENCY(1962, Brit.), w; OLIVER!(1968, Brit.), w; FRIENDS(1971, Brit.), w; PAUL AND MICHELLE(1974, Fr./Brit.), w
Viola Harris
HIGH SCHOOL HELLCATS(1958); DON'T KNOCK THE TWIST(1962); SLENDER THREAD, THE(1965); FIRE SALE(1977)
Virginia Harris
Misc. Silents
PRISONER OF WAR, THE(1918); WHEN ARIZONA WON(1919)
Wadsworth Harris
ONE NIGHT OF LOVE(1934); PLAINSMAN, THE(1937)
Silents
SCARLET SIN, THE(1915); LOVE GIRL, THE(1916); ALL NIGHT(1918); KAISER, BEAST OF BERLIN, THE(1918); MADAME SPY(1918)
Misc. Silents
GIFT GIRL, THE(1917); HERO OF THE HOUR, THE(1917); KIDDER & KO.(1918); IRON RIDER, THE(1920)
Wendworth Harris
Silents
DUMB GIRL OF PORTICI(1916)
William Harris
MOONSHINE MOUNTAIN(1964); COLOR ME BLOOD RED(1965)
Willie Harris
DIRTY HARRY(1971); WORLD IS JUST A 'B' MOVIE, THE(1971); TOP OF THE HEAP(1972); TRADER HORN(1973)
Winifred Harris
LOVE DOCTOR, THE(1929); RACKETEER, THE(1929); FAST AND LOOSE(1930); OUANGA(1936, Brit.); LIFE OF THE PARTY, THE(1937); LIVE, LOVE AND LEARN(1937); NIGHT MUST FALL(1937); STELLA DALLAS(1937); AMAZING DR. CLITTERHOUSE, THE(1938); ESPIONAGE AGENT(1939); KID FROM KOKOMO, THE(1939); KID NIGHTINGALE(1939); ROSE OF WASHINGTON SQUARE(1939); WOMEN, THE(1939); BRITISH INTELLIGENCE(1940); CHILD IS BORN, A(1940); I LOVE YOU AGAIN(1940); MONEY TO BURN(1940); NEW MOON(1940); DOWN IN SAN DIEGO(1941); FOOTSTEPS IN THE DARK(1941); LIFE WITH HENRY(1941); CAPTAINS OF THE CLOUDS(1942); WOMAN OF THE YEAR(1942); CLAUDIA(1943); FOUR JILLS IN A JEEP(1944); STANDING ROOM ONLY(1944); LOVE LETTERS(1945); CENTENNIAL SUMMER(1946); DOWN TO EARTH(1947); IMPERFECT LADY, THE(1947); LONE WOLF IN MEXICO, THE(1947); MY WILD IRISH ROSE(1947); SONG OF LOVE(1947); THAT HAGEN GIRL(1947); JULIA MISBEHAVES(1948); MR. PEABODY AND THE MERMAID(1948); FAN, THE(1949); KNOCK ON WOOD(1954)
Misc. Silents
CRUCIBLE OF LIFE, THE(1918)
Andrew Harrison
LITTLEST HORSE THIEVES, THE(1977)
Anne Harrison
FARMER'S DAUGHTER, THE(1940)
Beatrice Harrison
ADVENTURE FOR TWO(1945, Brit.)
Bertram Harrison
Silents
$5,000,000 COUNTERFEITING PLOT, THE(1914), d
Beryl Harrison
I LIVED WITH YOU(1933, Brit.)
Bill Harrison
SWEET CHARITY(1969)
Misc. Talkies
BIJOU(1972)
Brian Harrison
SALT & PEPPER(1968, Brit.); MONEY MOVERS(1978, Aus.); PUBERTY BLUES(1983, Aus.)
Bud Harrison
ROAD TO UTOPIA(1945); POSTMAN ALWAYS RINGS TWICE, THE(1946)
C. William Harrison
GUNS OF FORT PETTICOAT, THE(1957), w
Carey Harrison
MARRIED IN HOLLYWOOD(1929); LAST OUTPOST, THE(1935); PEPPER(1936); MAGNIFICENT DOPE, THE(1942); GUY NAMED JOE, A(1943); FOLLOW THE BOYS(1944); SECRETS OF SCOTLAND YARD(1944); CODE OF THE LAWLESS(1945); DON JUAN QUILLIGAN(1945); HOUSE OF DRACULA(1945); ON STAGE EVERYBODY(1945); SENORITA FROM THE WEST(1945); GIRL ON THE SPOT(1946); CASBAH(1948)
Silents
WEDDING MARCH, THE(1927)
Carole Harrison
ELEPHANT MAN, THE(1980, Brit.)
1984
LOOSE CONNECTIONS(1984, Brit.)

Carroll Harrison
INTERNS, THE(1962)
Cary Harrison
UNFAITHFUL, THE(1947); GIRL FROM JONES BEACH, THE(1949)
Cathryn Harrison
IMAGES(1972, Ireland); PIED PIPER, THE(1972, Brit.); BLACK MOON(1975, Fr.); DRESSER, THE(1983)
Charles Harrison
WE'RE GOING TO BE RICH(1938, Brit.)
Dan Harrison
SWEET SMELL OF LOVE(1966, Ital./Ger.)
Misc. Talkies
NO DIAMONDS FOR URSULA(1967)
David Harrison
REMARKABLE MR. PENNYPACKER, THE(1959); DARLING(1965, Brit.)
Dean Harrison
TENSION AT TABLE ROCK(1956), ed; GIRL MOST LIKELY, THE(1957), ed
Dennis Harrison
GUILTY BYSTANDER(1950)
Diane Harrison
CRYSTAL BALL, THE(1943), ed
Doane Harrison
SHOW FOLKS(1928), ed; BIG NEWS(1929), ed; HIGH VOLTAGE(1929), ed; HIS FIRST COMMAND(1929), ed; LEATHERNECK, THE(1929), ed; OFFICE SCANDAL, THE(1929), ed; RACKETEER, THE(1929), ed; SHADY LADY, THE(1929), ed; SOPHOMORE, THE(1929), ed; SPIELER, THE(1929), ed; THIS THING CALLED LOVE(1929), ed; HER MAN(1930), ed; ANNAPOLIS FAREWELL(1935), ed; THIRTEEN HOURS BY AIR(1936), ed; EASY LIVING(1937), ed; INTERNES CAN'T TAKE MONEY(1937), ed; THRILL OF A LIFETIME(1937), ed; ARTISTS AND MODELS ABROAD(1938), ed; STOLEN HEAVEN(1938), ed; MIDNIGHT(1939), ed; NIGHT OF NIGHTS, THE(1939), ed; ARISE, MY LOVE(1940), ed; DANCING ON A DIME(1940), ed; REMEMBER THE NIGHT(1940), ed; HOLD BACK THE DAWN(1941), ed; NEW YORK TOWN(1941), ed; BEYOND THE BLUE HORIZON(1942), ed; MAJOR AND THE MINOR, THE(1942), ed; TAKE A LETTER, DARLING(1942), ed; FIVE GRAVES TO CAIRO(1943), ed; DOUBLE INDEMNITY(1944), ed; PRACTICALLY YOURS(1944), ed; UNINVITED, THE(1944), ed; LOST WEEKEND, THE(1945), ed; UNSEEN, THE(1945), ed; OUR HEARTS WERE GROWING UP(1946), ed; EMPEROR WALTZ, THE(1948), ed; FOREIGN AFFAIR, A(1948), ed; MR. MUSIC(1950), ed; SUNSET BOULEVARD(1950), ed; JUST FOR YOU(1952), ed; FOREVER FEMALE(1953), ed; STALAG 17(1953), ed
Silents
JIMMIE'S MILLIONS(1925), ed; BLUE STREAK, THE(1926), ed; DOUBLING WITH DANGER(1926), d; NIGHT PATROL, THE(1926), ed; MAN-MADE WOMEN(1928), ed
Doanne Harrison
GOLDEN GLOVES(1940), ed
Donald Harrison
REMARKABLE MR. PENNYPACKER, THE(1959)
Dorothy Harrison
BARNYARD FOLLIES(1940)
Edgar Harrison
HAVING A WILD WEEKEND(1965, Brit.)
Eric Harrison
Silents
WORLDLINGS, THE(1920, Brit.), d&w
Misc. Silents
KEY OF THE WORLD, THE(1918, Brit.); SOME ARTIST(1919, Brit.); WESTWARD HO!(1919, Brit.)
Estelle Harrison
Silents
KNIGHT OF THE WEST, A(1921)
George Harrison
HARD DAY'S NIGHT, A(1964, Brit.); HELP!(1965, Brit.); WONDERWALL(1969, Brit.), m; LITTLE MALCOLM(1974, Brit.), p; MONTY PYTHON'S LIFE OF BRIAN(1979, Brit.)
Gilbert Harrison
MAKE MINE A DOUBLE(1962, Brit.)
Gillian Harrison
LET'S MAKE UP(1955, Brit.); EYEWITNESS(1956, Brit.); BLOW YOUR OWN TRUMPET(1958, Brit.)
Misc. Talkies
SUPERSONIC SAUCER(1956, Brit.)
Gordon Harrison
1984
PLAGUE DOGS, THE(1984, U.S./Brit.), prod d
Gracie Harrison
WITHOUT A TRACE(1983)
Gregory Harrison
JIM, THE WORLD'S GREATEST(1976); FRATERNITY ROW(1977)
1984
RAZORBACK(1984, Aus.)
Hal Harrison, Jr.
BAKER'S HAWK(1976), w; PONY EXPRESS RIDER(1976), p, d, w; SOGGY BOTTOM U.S.A.(1982), w
Harriet Harrison
YANKS(1979)
Harry Harrison
SOYLENT GREEN(1973), w
Harvey Harrison
BURNING, THE(1981), ph; AMIN-THE RISE AND FALL(1982, Kenya), ph; STILL SMOKIN'(1983), ph
1984
CHEECH AND CHONG'S THE CORSICAN BROTHERS(1984), ph
Harvey Harrison, Jr.
MAGNIFICENT SEVEN DEADLY SINS, THE(1971, Brit.), ph
Hermann Harrison
SWEET KITTY BELLAIRS(1930), w
Howard Harrison
STRANGE AFFAIR, THE(1968, Brit.), p

Hugh Harrison
NEXT TIME WE LOVE(1936)

Irma Harrison
ALIBI(1929)

Silents
LOVE'S PENALTY(1921); ONE EXCITING NIGHT(1922)

Misc. Silents
RED VIPER, THE(1919); FIGHTING KENTUCKIANS, THE(1920); DAUGHTER OF DEVIL DAN(1921); FOR WOMAN'S FAVOR(1924); YELLOWBACK, THE(1929)

Irma A. Harrison
VENGEANCE(1930)

J. Harrison
Misc. Silents
VERA, THE MEDIUM(1916)

James H. Harrison
SILVER RIVER(1948); WESTERN RENEGADES(1949); ANNIE GET YOUR GUN(1950)

James Harrison
HANDCUFFED(1929); SAINT IN PALM SPRINGS, THE(1941); UP IN ARMS(1944); WOMAN IN THE WINDOW, THE(1945); PANHANDLE(1948); SILENT CONFLICT(1948); FIGHTING MAN OF THE PLAINS(1949); LAW OF THE WEST(1949); STAMPEDE(1949); KEY TO THE CITY(1950); CALLAWAY WENT THATAWAY(1951); TALL TARGET, THE(1951); VENGEANCE VALLEY(1951); CARBINE WILLIAMS(1952)

1984
SUBURBIA(1984)

Silents
LESSONS IN LOVE(1921); CRITICAL AGE, THE(1923); COLLEGE DAYS(1926)

Jan Harrison
FORT BOWIE(1958)

Jean Harrison
GANGSTER, THE(1947); ROYAL WEDDING(1951)

Jenilee Harrison
1984
TANK(1984)

Jennifer Harrison
1984
DARK ENEMY(1984, Brit.)

Jester Harrison
IN THIS OUR LIFE(1942)

Jimmie Harrison
LAWLESS NINETIES, THE(1936)

Jimmy Harrison
SHE COULDN'T TAKE IT(1935); MEET JOHN DOE(1941); MEXICAN SPITFIRE'S BABY(1941)

Silents
BACKSTAGE(1927); HUSBAND HUNTERS(1927)

Misc. Silents
IN SEARCH OF A HERO(1926)

Joan Harrison
UNCLE HARRY(1945), p; THEY WON'T BELIEVE ME(1947), p; JAMAICA INN(1939, Brit.), w; FOREIGN CORRESPONDENT(1940), w; SUSPICION(1941), w; SABOTEUR(1942), w; DARK WATERS(1944), w; PHANTOM LADY(1944), p; NOCTURNE(1946), p; RIDE THE PINK HORSE(1947), p; ONCE MORE, MY DARLING(1949), p; EYE WITNESS(1950, Brit.), p; CIRCLE OF DANGER(1951, Brit.), p; JOURNEY INTO DARKNESS(1968, Brit.), p; JOURNEY INTO MIDNIGHT(1968, Brit.), p

John D. Harrison
FOUR HOURS TO KILL(1935), ed

John Harrison
SAFARI(1956); MAN WHO COULD CHEAT DEATH, THE(1959, Brit.); MUMMY, THE(1959, Brit.); PASSIONATE SUMMER(1959, Brit.); TARZAN THE MAGNIFICENT(1960, Brit.); LOLITA(1962); TASTE OF HONEY, A(1962, Brit.); SHAME, SHAME, EVERYBODY KNOWS HER NAME(1969); SHOCK WAVES(1977), w; EFFECTS(1980), a, p; KNIGHTRIDERS(1981); CREEPSHOW(1982), m

John Kent Harrison
BELLS(1981, Can.), w

Joseph Harrison
LAST STAGECOACH WEST, THE(1957), ed; LAWLESS EIGHTIES, THE(1957), ed; PANAMA SAL(1957), ed; JUVENILE JUNGLE(1958), ed; YOUNG AND WILD(1958), ed

Joshua Harrison
LUGGAGE OF THE GODS(1983), art d

June Harrison
BRINGING UP FATHER(1946); CITIZEN SAINT(1947); LAND OF THE LAWLESS(1947); JIGGS AND MAGGIE IN SOCIETY(1948); JIGGS AND MAGGIE OUT WEST(1950)

Misc. Talkies
JIGGS AND MAGGIE IN COURT(1948)

Karyn Harrison
BEST LITTLE WHOREHOUSE IN TEXAS, THE(1982)

1984
LONELY GUY, THE(1984)

Kathleen Harrison
HOBSON'S CHOICE(1931, Brit.); MAN FROM TORONTO, THE(1933, Brit.); GHOUL, THE(1934, Brit.); GREAT DEFENDER, THE(1934, Brit.); WHAT HAPPENED THEN?(1934, Brit.); LINE ENGAGED(1935, Brit.); BROKEN BLOSSOMS(1936, Brit.); EVERYBODY DANCE(1936, Brit.); AREN'T MEN BEASTS?(1937, Brit.); NIGHT MUST FALL(1937); TENTH MAN, THE(1937, Brit.); WANTED(1937, Brit.); ALMOST A GENTLEMAN(1938, Brit.); BANK HOLIDAY(1938, Brit.); CONVICT 99(1938, Brit.); I'VE GOT A HORSE(1938, Brit.); DISCOVERIES(1939, Brit.); HOME FROM HOME(1939, Brit.); FLYING SQUAD, THE(1940, Brit.); OUTSIDER, THE(1940, Brit.); THEY CAME BY NIGHT(1940, Brit.); TILLY OF BLOOMSBURY(1940, Brit.); WHO IS GUILTY?(1940, Brit.); GHOST TRAIN, THE(1941, Brit.); GIRL IN THE NEWS, THE(1941, Brit.); GIRL MUST LIVE, A(1941, Brit.); I THANK YOU(1941, Brit.); MAJOR BARBARA(1941, Brit.); ONCE A CROOK(1941, Brit.); IN WHICH WE SERVE(1942, Brit.); MUCH TOO SHY(1942, Brit.); REMARKABLE MR. KIPPS(1942, Brit.); IT HAPPENED ONE SUNDAY(1944, Brit.); MEET SEXTON BLAKE(1944, Brit.); GREAT DAY(1945, Brit.); RANDOLPH FAMILY, THE(1945, Brit.); ADVENTURESS, THE(1946, Brit.); WANTED FOR MURDER(1946, Brit.); HOLIDAY CAMP(1947, Brit.); BOND

STREET(1948, Brit.); CODE OF SCOTLAND YARD)(1948); HERE COME THE HUGGETTS(1948, Brit.); VOTE FOR HUGGETT(1948, Brit.); HUGGETTS ABROAD, THE(1949, Brit.); NOW BARABBAS WAS A ROBBER(1949, Brit.); TEMPTATION HARBOR(1949, Brit.); TRIO(1950, Brit.); WINSLOW BOY, THE(1950); CHRISTMAS CAROL, A(1951, Brit.); OLIVER TWIST(1951, Brit.); MAGIC BOX, THE(1952, Brit.); MR. LORD SAYS NO(1952, Brit.); PICKWICK PAPERS, THE(1952, Brit.); WATERFRONT WOMEN(1952, Brit.); DOUBLE CONFESSION(1953, Brit.); GAY ADVENTURE, THE(1953, Brit.); LANDFALL(1953, Brit.); TURN THE KEY SOFTLY(1954, Brit.); LET'S MAKE UP(1955, Brit.); WHERE THERE'S A WILL(1955, Brit.); ALL FOR MARY(1956, Brit.); HOME AND AWAY(1956, Brit.); IT'S A WONDERFUL WORLD(1956, Brit.); CAST A DARK SHADOW(1958, Brit.); BEASTS OF MARSEILLES, THE(1959, Brit.); CRY FROM THE STREET, A(1959, Brit.); ALIVE AND KICKING(1962, Brit.); BIG MONEY, THE(1962, Brit.); DOG AND THE DIAMONDS, THE(1962, Brit.); MRS. GIBBONS' BOYS(1962, Brit.); FAST LADY, THE(1963, Brit.); WEST 11(1963, Brit.); OPERATION SNAFU(1965, Brit.); LOCK UP YOUR DAUGHTERS(1969, Brit.)

Ken Harrison
MARK OF THE WITCH(1970), ed

1984
MEATBALLS PART II(1984), m

Kirsten Harrison
OCTOPUSSY(1983, Brit.)

Linda Harrison
FAT SPY(1966); WAY...WAY OUT(1966); GUIDE FOR THE MARRIED MAN, A(1967); PLANET OF THE APES(1968); BENEATH THE PLANET OF THE APES(1970)

Lottie Harrison
MR. MUGGS STEPS OUT(1943); SPOTLIGHT SCANDALS(1943); LOST IN A HAREM(1944); DRIFTIN' RIVER(1946); LOVER COME BACK(1946); ROMANCE OF THE WEST(1946)

Louis Reeves Harrison
Silents
GREYHOUND, THE(1914), w

Lyman Harrison
NO MAN'S LAND(1964)

Lynda Lee Harrison
WILD HARVEST(1962)

Lynette Harrison
10 TO MIDNIGHT(1983)

Lynn Harrison
LILAC DOMINO, THE(1940, Brit.), ed; LITTLE IODINE(1946), ed; SUSIE STEPS OUT(1946), ed; ADVENTURES OF DON COYOTE(1947), ed; STORK BITES MAN(1947), ed; SLEEP, MY LOVE(1948), ed

Marc Harrison
DIRTY KNIGHT'S WORK(1976, Brit.)

Marcus Harrison
Misc. Silents
WOMAN, WAKE UP!(1922), d

Margaret Harrison
MURDER WITH PICTURES(1936); SMALL TOWN STORY(1953, Brit.); WAY OUT, THE(1956, Brit.)

Mark Harrison
CIRCLE CANYON(1934)

Maurice Harrison
FINAL APPOINTMENT(1954, Brit.), w; STOLEN ASSIGNMENT(1955, Brit.), w; YOU LUCKY PEOPLE(1955, Brit.), w; DIPLOMATIC CORPSE, THE(1958, Brit.), w; DEAD LUCKY(1960, Brit.), w

Max Harrison
SOMEWHERE IN POLITICS(1949, Brit.); SOHO CONSPIRACY(1951, Brit.); SANDWICH MAN, THE(1966, Brit.)

Michael Harrison
NOCTURNA(1979)

Michael Harrison [Sunset Carson]
STAGE DOOR CANTEEN(1943)

Mickey Harrison
TRAIL RIDERS(1942)

Mildred Harrison
CURIOUS FEMALE, THE(1969)

Mona K. Harrison
Misc. Silents
LIGHT(1915, Brit.); DERELICTS(1917, Brit.)

Nell Harrison
PRODUCERS, THE(1967)

Nicole Harrison
1984
AMERICAN TABOO(1984)

Nicolle Harrison
1984
AMERICAN TABOO(1984), w

Nigel Harrison
ROADIE(1980)

Noel Harrison
BEST OF ENEMIES, THE(1962); AGENT 8 3/4(1963, Brit.); AMOROUS ADVENTURES OF MOLL FLANDERS, THE(1965); WHERE THE SPIES ARE(1965, Brit.); TAKE A GIRL LIKE YOU(1970, Brit,)

Norman Harrison
LOCKER 69(1962, Brit.), d; CALCULATED RISK(1963, Brit.), d; INCIDENT AT MIDNIGHT(1966, Brit.), d

P.S. Harrison
DEERSLAYER(1943), p, w

Paul Carter Harrison
LORD SHANGO(1975), w; YOUNGBLOOD(1978), w

Paul Harrison
HOUSE OF SEVEN CORPSES, THE(1974), p,d&w

Peter Harrison
DEADLY AFFAIR, THE(1967, Brit.)

Peter Scott Harrison
1984
FOREVER YOUNG(1984, Brit.); SECRETS(1984, Brit.)

Philip Harrison
MORGAN!(1966, Brit.), art d; HOW I WON THE WAR(1967, Brit.), art d; DUF-FY(1968, Brit.), art d;WORK IS A FOUR LETTER WORD(1968,Brit.), art d;WUTHER-ING HEIGHTS(1970, Brit.), art d; COUNTESS DRACULA(1972, Brit.), art d; MADE(1972, Brit.), prod d; LAST DAYS OF MAN ON EARTH, THE(1975, Brit.), art d; LISZTOMANIA(1975, Brit.), art d; OLD DRACULA(1975, Brit.), art d; VALEN-TINO(1977, Brit.), art d; HANOVER STREET(1979, Brit.), prod d; OUTLAND(1981), prod d; NEVER SAY NEVER AGAIN(1983), prod d
1984
RAZOR'S EDGE, THE(1984), prod d

Phillip Harrison
RITZ, THE(1976), prod d; PIRATES OF PENZANCE, THE(1983)

Rene Harrison
MURDER(1930, Brit.), ed

Rex Harrison
GREAT GAME, THE(1930); SCHOOL FOR SCANDAL, THE(1930, Brit.); GET YOUR MAN(1934, Brit.); LEAVE IT TO BLANCHE(1934, Brit.); ALL AT SEA(1935, Brit.); MEN ARE NOT GODS(1937, Brit.);STORM IN A TEACUP(1937, Brit.); CITADEL, THE(1938); CONTINENTAL EXPRESS(1939, Brit.); SCHOOL FOR HUSBANDS(1939, Brit.); NIGHT TRAIN(1940, Brit.); OVER THE MOON(1940, Brit.); SIDEWALKS OF LON-DON(1940, Brit.); MAJOR BARBARA(1941, Brit.); MISSING TEN DAYS(1941, Brit.); GHOST AND MRS. MUIR, THE(1942); BLITHE SPIRIT(1945, Brit.); NOTORIOUS GENTLEMAN(1945, Brit.); ANNA AND THE KING OF SIAM(1946); JOURNEY TOGETHER(1946, Brit.); YANK IN LONDON, A(1946, Brit.); FOXES OF HARROW, THE(1947); ESCAPE(1948, Brit.); UNFAITHFULLY YOURS(1948); LONG DARK HALL, THE(1951, Brit.); FOUR POSTER, THE(1952); MAIN STREET TO BROAD-WAY(1953); KING RICHARD AND THE CRUSADERS(1954); CONSTANT HUSBAND, THE(1955, Brit.); RELUCTANT DEBUTANTE, THE(1958); MIDNIGHT LACE(1960); HAPPY THIEVES, THE(1962); CLEOPATRA(1963); MY FAIR LADY(1964); AGONY AND THE ECSTASY, THE(1965); YELLOW ROLLS-ROYCE, THE(1965, Brit.); DOC-TOR DOLITTLE(1967); HONEY POT, THE(1967, Brit.); FLEA IN HER EAR, A(1968, Fr.); STAIRCASE(1969 U.S./Brit./Fr.); BEHIND THE IRON MASK(1977); CROSSED SWORDS(1978); ASHANTI(1979); TIME TO DIE, A(1983)
Misc. Talkies
SHALIMAR(1978, India); KINGFISHER, THE(1982)

Rhoisin Harrison
DON'S PARTY(1976, Aus.), art d

Rich Harrison
MOUSE AND HIS CHILD, THE(1977), ed

Richard Harrison
CHAMPAGNE CHARLIE(1944, Brit.); HE SNOOPS TO CONQUER(1944, Brit.); JEANNE EAGELS(1957); KRONOS(1957); BATTLE CRY(1959); MASTER OF THE WORLD(1961); GRINGO(1963, Span./Ital.); INVINCIBLE GLADIATOR, THE(1963, c.u. Ital./Span.); GLADIATORS 7(1964, Span./Ital.); SECRET AGENT FIREBALL(1965, Fr./Ital.); HE WHO RIDES A TIGER(1966, Brit.), art d; DOCTOR FAUSTUS(1967, Brit.); VENGEANCE(1968, Ital./Ger.); PUSSYCAT, PUSSYCAT, I LOVE YOU(1970); TWO HUNDRED MOTELS(1971, Brit.), ed; JESSE AND LESTER, TWO BROTHERS IN A PLACE CALLED TRINITY(1972, Ital.), a, p
1984
BAY BOY(1984, Can.), art d
Misc. Talkies
AVENGER OF THE SEVEN SEAS(1960); THREE SERGEANTS OF BENGAL(1965); KILLING GROUND, THE(1972); PLACE CALLED TRINITY, A(1975); TRINITY(1975); BLOOD DEBTS(1983)

Ricky Harrison
HUMAN FACTOR, THE(1975)

Robert Harrison
1984
HOTEL NEW HAMPSHIRE, THE(1984)

Robert Harrison, Jr.
NIGHT THE LIGHTS WENT OUT IN GEORGIA, THE(1981)

Roger Harrison
CAT AND THE CANARY, THE(1979, Brit.), ed

Sally Harrison
AND NOW THE SCREAMING STARTS(1973, Brit.); CONFESSIONS OF A POP PERFORMER(1975, Brit.)

Sam Harrison
FRENCH LEAVE(1931, Brit.), p

Sandra Harrison
BLOOD OF DRACULA(1957)

Sarah Harrison
WRONG BOX, THE(1966, Brit.)

Saul Harrison
Misc. Silents
CUSTOMARY TWO WEEKS, THE(1917), d; SALT OF THE EARTH(1917), d

Sid Harrison
SANDWICH MAN, THE(1966, Brit.)

Simon Harrison
WIND AND THE LION, THE(1975); SKY RIDERS(1976, U.S./Gr.); YANKS(1979)

Sonya Harrison
WALK, DON'T RUN(1966)

Stephen Harrison
OVERNIGHT(1933, Brit.), ed; PRIVATE LIFE OF HENRY VIII, THE(1933), ed; STRANGE EVIDENCE(1933, Brit.), ed; CATHERINE THE GREAT(1934, Brit.), ed; FOR LOVE OR MONEY(1934, Brit.), ed; PRIVATE LIFE OF DON JUAN, THE(1934, Brit.), ed; BARON OF ARIZONA, THE(1950); NAVY BOUND(1951)

Stephen S. Harrison
BLUE GRASS OF KENTUCKY(1950); YOUNG DANIEL BOONE(1950)

Steven Harrison
VIXENS, THE(1969)

Susan Harrison
SWEET SMELL OF SUCCESS(1957); KEY WITNESS(1960)

Syd Harrison
SOMEWHERE IN POLITICS(1949, Brit.); SOHO CONSPIRACY(1951, Brit.)

Tony Harrison
NO SAFETY AHEAD(1959, Brit.)

Vangie Harrison
DE SADE(1969), cos; MAGIC CHRISTIAN, THE(1970, Brit.), cos; THERE'S A GIRL IN MY SOUP(1970, Brit.), cos; GET CARTER(1971, Brit.), cos; OFFENSE, THE(1973, Brit.), cos; OLD DRACULA(1975, Brit.), cos; RITZ, THE(1976), cos; SUPERMAN

III(1983), cos

Vangy Harrison
PIED PIPER, THE(1972, Brit.), cos

W.H. Harrison
TWO-LANE BLACKTOP(1971)

Walter Harrison
JULIET OF THE SPIRITS(1965, Fr./Ital./W.Ger.)

William Harrison
ROLLERBALL(1975), w

Yvonne Harrison
PAPER MOON(1973)

Marcia Harriss
GREENE MURDER CASE, THE(1929)

Rory Harrity
FROM THE TERRACE(1960); WHERE THE BOYS ARE(1960)

Holger Harrivirta
DAY THE EARTH FROZE, THE(1959, Fin./USSR), d

Chuck Harrod
RAT FINK(1965); SWEET CHARITY(1969)

Rafaelle Harrod
NASTY RABBIT, THE(1964), makeup

Kathryn Harrold
NIGHTWING(1979); HUNTER, THE(1980); MODERN ROMANCE(1981); PURSUIT OF D.B. COOPER, THE(1981); SENDER, THE(1982, Brit.); YES, GIORGIO(1982)
1984
HEARTBREAKERS(1984)

Scott Harrold
THIS'LL MAKE YOU WHISTLE(1938, Brit.); MIDAS TOUCH, THE(1940, Brit.); THREE SILENT MEN(1940, Brit.); PORTRAIT OF CLARE(1951, Brit.); CRY, THE BELOVED COUNTRY(1952, Brit.)

Donald Harron
BEST OF EVERYTHING, THE(1959); I DEAL IN DANGER(1966); SPY WITH MY FACE, THE(1966); HOSPITAL, THE(1971)

Jessie Harron
Silents
HEARTS OF THE WORLD(1918)

John Harron
STREET GIRL(1929); BIG BOY(1930); CZAR OF BRODWAY, THE(1930); LAUGH AND GET RICH(1931); LAW OF THE TONG(1931); BEAUTY PARLOR(1932); CROWD ROARS, THE(1932); MIDNIGHT WARNING, THE(1932); WHITE ZOMBIE(1932); MURDER IN THE MUSEUM(1934); SYMPHONY OF LIVING(1935); SMALL TOWN GIRL(1936); LOVE IS ON THE AIR(1937); MARKED WOMAN(1937); MISSING WITNESSES(1937); PRAIRIE THUNDER(1937); SLIM(1937); TALENT SCOUT(1937); ACCIDENTS WILL HAPPEN(1938); ANGELS WITH DIRTY FACES(1938); BOY MEETS GIRL(1938); COWBOY FROM BROOKLYN(1938); DAREDEVIL DRI-VERS(1938); GOLD IS WHERE YOU FIND IT(1938); INVISIBLE MENACE, THE(1938); JEZEBEL(1938); MYSTERY HOUSE(1938); TORCHY BLANE IN PANA-MA(1938); TORCHY GETS HER MAN(1938); ANGELS WASH THEIR FACES(1939); CODE OF THE SECRET SERVICE(1939); COWBOY QUARTERBACK(1939); DARK VICTORY(1939); EACH DAWN I DIE(1939); ESPIONAGE AGENT(1939); GOING PLACES(1939); INDIANAPOLIS SPEEDWAY(1939); KID FROM KOKOMO, THE(1939); KING OF THE UNDERWORLD(1939); NANCY DREW, TROUBLE SHOOTER(1939); NAUGHTY BUT NICE(1939); OKLAHOMA KID, THE(1939); ON TRIAL(1939); ROARING TWENTIES, THE(1939); SECRET SERVICE OF THE AIR(1939); SWEEPSTAKES WINNER(1939); TORCHY PLAYS WITH DYNAMI-TE(1939); TORCHY RUNS FOR MAYOR(1939); WOMEN IN THE WIND(1939); FIGHTING 69TH, THE(1940)
Misc. Talkies
SISTER TO JUDAS(1933)
Silents
PENROD(1922); RAGGED HEIRESS, THE(1922); PAINTED FLAPPER, THE(1924); BELOW THE LINE(1925); BRIDE OF THE STORM(1926); GILDED HIGHWAY, THE(1926); LITTLE IRISH GIRL, THE(1926); NIGHT CRY, THE(1926); MAN IN HOBBLES, THE(1928)
Misc. Silents
FIVE DOLLAR BABY, THE(1922); WHAT SHALL I DO?(1924); MY WIFE AND I(1925); SATAN IN SABLES(1925); WIFE WHO WASN'T WANTED, THE(1925); BOY FRIEND, THE(1926); FALSE ALARM, THE(1926); HELL-BENT FOR HEAVEN(1926); ONCE AND FOREVER(1927); SILK STOCKINGS(1927); FINDERS KEEPERS(1928); GREEN GRASS WIDOWS(1928); THEIR HOUR(1928)

Johnny Harron
EASIEST WAY, THE(1931); CITY PARK(1934); STOLEN SWEETS(1934)
Silents
HEARTS OF THE WORLD(1918); DULCY(1923); GOLD DIGGERS, THE(1923); SUPREME TEST, THE(1923); LEARNING TO LOVE(1925); LOVE MAKES 'EM WILD(1927); NIGHT LIFE(1927); OLD SHOES(1927)
Misc. Silents
WESTBOUND LIMITED, THE(1923); BEHIND THE CURTAIN(1924); ROSE OF THE TENEMENTS(1926); CLOSED GATES(1927); NAUGHTY(1927)

Mrs. Harron
Silents
HEARTS OF THE WORLD(1918)

Phil Harron
MACAO(1952)

Robert Harron
Silents
AVENGING CONSCIENCE, THE(1914); BATTLE OF THE SEXES, THE(1914); ESCAPE, THE(1914); GREAT LEAP, THE(1914); HOME SWEET HOME(1914); JUDITH OF BETHULIA(1914); BIRTH OF A NATION, THE(1915); INTOLERAN-CE(1916); LITTLE LIAR, THE(1916); GREAT LOVE, THE(1918); GREATEST THING IN LIFE, THE(1918); HEARTS OF THE WORLD(1918); GIRL WHO STAYED AT HOME, THE(1919); ROMANCE OF HAPPY VALLEY, A(1919); TRUE HEART SU-SIE(1919); GREATEST QUESTION, THE(1920)
Misc. Silents
VICTIM, THE(1914); HER SHATTERED IDOL(1915); OUTCAST, THE(1915); CHILD OF THE PARIS STREETS, A(1916); HOODOO ANN(1916); MARRIAGE OF MOLLY-O, THE(1916); WHARF RAT, THE(1916); WILD GIRL OF THE SIERRAS, A(1916); BAD BOYS(1917); OLD FASHIONED YOUNG MAN, AN(1917); SUNSHINE ALLEY(1917); COINCIDENCE(1921)

Chris Harrop
LEOPARD IN THE SNOW(1979, Brit./Can.), p
Harrose
STREET IS MY BEAT, THE(1966), m
Kathryn Harrow
HELL'S ANGELS ON WHEELS(1967)
Lisa Harrow
TEMPTER, THE(1974, Ital./Brit.); ALL CREATURES GREAT AND SMALL(1975, Brit.); DEVIL IS A WOMAN, THE(1975, Brit./Ital.); ALL THINGS BRIGHT AND BEAUTIFUL(1979, Brit.); FINAL CONFLICT, THE(1981)
Richard Harrow
GANJA AND HESS(1973)
Misc. Talkies
BLOOD COUPLE(1974)
Robert Harrow
WILD HARVEST(1962)
Charly Harroway
1984
NINJA III–THE DOMINATION(1984)
Elizabeth Harrowe
I PASSED FOR WHITE(1960)
Elizabeth Harrower
PLYMOUTH ADVENTURE(1952); THUNDER PASS(1954); MARJORIE MORNING-STAR(1958); TEACHER'S PET(1958); DON'T KNOCK THE TWIST(1962); WILD WESTERNERS, THE(1962); STERILE CUCKOO, THE(1969); TRUE GRIT(1969)
Deborah Harry
FOREIGNER, THE(1978); ROADIE(1980); UNION CITY(1980); VIDEODROME(1983, Can.)
Geo Harry
MISTRESS FOR THE SUMMER, A(1964, Fr./Ital.)
Student Harry
TOOMORROW(1970, Brit.)
Harry Acres and His Band
LET'S MAKE A NIGHT OF IT(1937, Brit.)
Harry Hudson and his Band
BOOTS! BOOTS!(1934, Brit.)
Harry James and His Music Makers
PRIVATE BUCKAROO(1942); BEST FOOT FORWARD(1943)
Harry James and his Orchestra
SPRINGTIME IN THE ROCKIES(1942); BATHING BEAUTY(1944)
Harry James Music Makers
DO YOU LOVE ME?(1946)
Harry James Orchestra
TWO GIRLS AND A SAILOR(1944)
Harry James' Music Makers
IF I'M LUCKY(1946)
Harry Owens and His Royal Hawaiian Orchestra
COCOANUT GROVE(1938)
Harry Owens and His Royal Hawaiians
IT'S A DATE(1940); SONG OF THE ISLANDS(1942); HAT CHECK HONEY(1944); LAKE PLACID SERENADE(1944)
Harry Parry's Swing Band
WHAT DO WE DO NOW?(1945, Brit.)
Harry Roy's Band
RHYTHM RACKETEER(1937, Brit.); EVERYTHING IS RHYTHM(1940, Brit.)
Harry S. Pepper and His White Coons
KENTUCKY MINSTRELS(1934, Brit.)
Harry-Krimer
Silents
NAPOLEON(1927, Fr.)
Harry-Max
STOLEN KISSES(1969, Fr.)
Harryhausen
GOLDEN VOYAGE OF SINBAD, THE(1974, Brit.), spec eff
Ray Harryhausen
MIGHTY JOE YOUNG(1949), spec eff; IT CAME FROM BENEATH THE SEA(1955), spec eff; EARTH VS. THE FLYING SAUCERS(1956), spec eff; 20 MILLION MILES TO EARTH(1957), a, w, spec eff; SEVENTH VOYAGE OF SINBAD, THE(1958), spec eff; THREE WORLDS OF GULLIVER, THE(1960, Brit.), spec eff; MYSTERIOUS IS-LAND(1961, U.S./Brit.), spec eff; JASON AND THE ARGONAUTS(1963, Brit.), spec eff; FIRST MEN IN THE MOON(1964, Brit.), spec eff; ONE MILLION YEARS B.C.(1967, Brit./U.S.), spec eff; VALLEY OF GWANGI, THE(1969), spec eff; TROG(1970, Brit.), spec eff; GOLDEN VOYAGE OF SINBAD, THE(1974, Brit.), p; SINBAD AND THE EYE OF THE TIGER(1977, U.S./Brit.), p, w, spec eff; CLASH OF THE TITANS(1981), p, spec eff
Walter Harsburgh
ADVENTURERS, THE(1951, Brit.)
Caren Harsh
NIGHT AND DAY(1946)
David S. Harsley
MAGNIFICENT OBSESSION(1954), spec eff
Al Harsten
CONVICT'S CODE(1930), ph
Adriana Hart
SEVEN HILLS OF ROME, THE(1958)
Al Hart
YOU'RE TELLING ME(1934)
Silents
MAN HUNT, THE(1918); NEGLECTED WIVES(1920); DIANE OF STAR HOL-LOW(1921); DOUBLING FOR ROMEO(1921); SO THIS IS ARIZONA(1922); TRAIL'S END(1922); SPAWN OF THE DESERT(1923); PONY EXPRESS, THE(1925)
Misc. Silents
COTTON AND CATTLE(1921); COWBOY ACE, A(1921); FLOWING GOLD(1921); OUT OF THE CLOUDS(1921); RANGE PIRATE, THE(1921); RUSTLERS OF THE NIGHT(1921); TRAIL TO RED DOG, THE(1921); WHITE MASKS, THE(1921); ANGEL CITIZENS(1922); CROSS ROADS(1922); GOLD GRABBERS(1922); RIDIN' ROWDY, THE(1927); .45 CALIBRE WAR(1929)

Albert Hart
MAKING THE GRADE(1929); AMERICAN TRAGEDY, AN(1931); I TAKE THIS WOMAN(1931); HOME ON THE RANGE(1935)
Silents
JOAN OF THE WOODS(1918); CHALLENGE OF CHANCE, THE(1919); LOVE IN A HURRY(1919); MISS CRUSOE(1919); OAKDALE AFFAIR, THE(1919); CROOKED ALLEY(1923); KINDLED COURAGE(1923); SUNSHINE TRAIL, THE(1923); EXCITE-MENT(1924); MAN FROM HARDPAN, THE(1927)
Misc. Silents
SLAVE MARKET, THE(1917); QUICKENING FLAME, THE(1919); OUTLAW EX-PRESS, THE(1926); DEVIL'S TWIN, THE(1927); LONG LOOP ON THE PECOS, THE(1927); BALLYHOO BUSTER, THE(1928); BOSS OF RUSTLER'S ROOST, THE(1928)
Alex Hart
Misc. Silents
GALLOPING COWBOY, THE(1926)
Anne Hart
COP-OUT(1967, Brit.)
Babe Hart
TONY ROME(1967)
Barry Hart
AGATHA(1979, Brit.)
Ben Hart
HOLIDAYS WITH PAY(1948, Brit.), ph; SOMEWHERE IN POLITICS(1949, Brit.), ph; GIRL IS MINE, THE(1950, Brit.), ph
Silents
GOLD RUSH, THE(1925)
Ben R. Hart
BIRDS OF A FEATHER(1931, Brit.), d; DANGEROUS ASSIGNMENT(1950, Brit.), d&ph
Misc. Silents
FROZEN FATE(1929, Brit.), d
Bertha Hart
Misc. Talkies
POWER OF LIFE, THE(1938)
Beverly Hart
HOSPITAL MASSACRE(1982)
Bill Hart
HERO'S ISLAND(1962); DUEL AT DIABLO(1966); HURRY SUNDOWN(1967); GETA-WAY, THE(1972); APPLE DUMPLING GANG RIDES AGAIN, THE(1979); LEGEND OF THE LONE RANGER, THE(1981)
1984
CITY HEAT(1984)
Bob Hart
Silents
JOANNA(1925)
Bobby Hart
UNHOLY ROLLERS(1972), m
Bret Hart
Silents
M'LISS(1918), w
Brian Hart
PUNISHMENT PARK(1971)
Buddy Hart
OUTLAW'S SON(1957); LITTLEST HOBO, THE(1958); ICE STATION ZEBRA(1968); CHANGES(1969); SWEET CHARITY(1969)
Caitlin Hart
CLASS(1983)
Charles Hart
JUVENILE COURT(1938); MY LITTLE CHICKADEE(1940); GREEN GRASS OF WYOMING(1948)
Christa Hart
WOMEN AND BLOODY TERROR(1970)
Christina Hart
RED SKY AT MORNING(1971); CHARLEY VARRICK(1973); MAD BOMBER, THE(1973); ROOMMATES, THE(1973); MEAN DOG BLUES(1978)
Chuck Hart
1984
HARDBODIES(1984)
Daniel Hart
SMALL HOURS, THE(1962), m; CARMEN, BABY(1967, Yugo./Ger.), m
David Hart
BELOVED ENEMY(1936), w; LONG IS THE ROAD(1948, Ger.); GYPSY AND THE GENTLEMAN, THE(1958, Brit.)
1984
RIVER, THE(1984)
Diana Hart
HAPPY GO LOVELY(1951, Brit.); GAMES THAT LOVERS PLAY(1971, Brit.)
Misc. Silents
LE BLED(1929, Fr.)
Diane Hart
AFFAIRS OF ADELAIDE(1949, U. S./Brit); I'LL NEVER FORGET YOU(1951); FATHER'S DOING FINE(1952, Brit.); PICKWICK PAPERS, THE(1952, Brit.); SOME-THING MONEY CAN'T BUY(1952, Brit.); YOU'RE ONLY YOUNG TWICE(1952, Brit.); ONE JUMP AHEAD(1955, Brit.); KEEP IT CLEAN(1956, Brit.); CROWNING TOUCH, THE(1959, Brit.); ENTER INSPECTOR DUVAL(1961, Brit.); MY WIFE'S FAMILY(1962, Brit.)
Diane Lee Hart
CANNONBALL(1976, U.S./Hong Kong); POM POM GIRLS, THE(1976)
Dianne Lee Hart
GIANT SPIDER INVASION, THE(1975)
Dolores Hart
LOVING YOU(1957); WILD IS THE WIND(1957); KING CREOLE(1958); LONELY-HEARTS(1958); PLUNDERERS, THE(1960); WHERE THE BOYS ARE(1960); FRAN-CIS OF ASSISI(1961); SAIL A CROOKED SHIP(1961); LISA(1962, Brit.); COME FLY WITH ME(1963)
Dorothy Hart
GUNFIGHTERS, THE(1947); COUNTESS OF MONTE CRISTO, THE(1948); LARCE-NY(1948); NAKED CITY, THE(1948); CALAMITY JANE AND SAM BASS(1949); STORY OF MOLLY X, THE(1949); TAKE ONE FALSE STEP(1949); UNDERTOW(1949);

OUTSIDE THE WALL(1950); I WAS A COMMUNIST FOR THE F.B.I.(1951); INSIDE THE WALLS OF FOLSOM PRISON(1951); RATON PASS(1951); LOAN SHARK(1952); TARZAN'S SAVAGE FURY(1952)

Ed Hart
NO MORE LADIES(1935); SPECIAL AGENT(1935); GOLDEN ARROW, THE(1936); PUBLIC ENEMY'S WIFE(1936); SWORN ENEMY(1936); THEODORA GOES WILD(1936); NORA PRENTISS(1947)

Eddie Hart
MANHATTAN MELODRAMA(1934); STUDENT TOUR(1934); MEN OF THE HOUR(1935); PICK A STAR(1935); SHE LOVED A FIREMAN(1937); TOAST OF NEW YORK, THE(1937); CALL THE MESQUITEERS(1938); CITY GIRL(1938); RHYTHM OF THE SADDLE(1938); FOUR JACKS AND A JILL(1941); I'LL WAIT FOR YOU(1941); LOVE CRAZY(1941); JACKASS MAIL(1942); MAYOR OF 44TH STREET, THE(1942); IRON MAJOR, THE(1943); ADVENTURE(1945); I'LL TELL THE WORLD(1945); JOHNNY ANGEL(1945); NOB HILL(1945); SPIDER, THE(1945); SWING OUT, SISTER(1945); THOSE ENDEARING YOUNG CHARMS(1945); WITHIN THESE WALLS(1945); DEADLINE AT DAWN(1946); KID FROM BROOKLYN, THE(1946); POSSESSED(1947); IF YOU KNEW SUSIE(1948)

Edward Hart
HELL'S HIGHWAY(1932); NAVY BLUE AND GOLD(1937)

Eloise Hart
POWERS GIRL, THE(1942); COVER GIRL(1944); UP IN ARMS(1944)

Eric Hart
1984
SILENT NIGHT, DEADLY NIGHT(1984)

Everett Hart
FAT MAN, THE(1951)

F. Kende Hart
VICE GIRLS, LTD.(1964)

F. William Hart
DEAD TO THE WORLD(1961), p

Ferdinand Hart
BEAUTIFUL ADVENTURE(1932, Ger.); 1914(1932, Ger.); GOLEM, THE(1937, Czech./ Fr.); DREYFUS CASE, THE(1940, Ger.)

Florence Hart
Silents
IT CAN BE DONE(1921)

Fran Hart
1984
WHAT YOU TAKE FOR GRANTED(1984)

Frances Noyes Hart
BELLAMY TRIAL, THE(1929), w

Fred Hart
IN OLD CALIFORNIA(1929), w

Glen Hart
TARZANA, THE WILD GIRL(1973), p

Gordon Hart
CASE OF THE BLACK CAT, THE(1936); CHARGE OF THE LIGHT BRIGADE, THE(1936); DOWN THE STRETCH(1936); DRACULA'S DAUGHTER(1936); GOLD DIGGERS OF 1937(1936); ISLE OF FURY(1936); KING OF HOCKEY(1936); SING ME A LOVE SONG(1936); BLAZING SIXES(1937); CASE OF THE STUTTERING BISHOP, THE(1937); CHEROKEE STRIP(1937); DEVIL'S SADDLE LEGION, THE(1937); EMPTY HOLSTERS(1937); FLY-AWAY BABY(1937); FUGITIVE IN THE SKY(1937); GREAT O'MALLEY, THE(1937); GUNS OF THE PECOS(1937); HER HUSBAND'S SECRETARY(1937); LAND BEYOND THE LAW(1937); MELODY FOR TWO(1937); MIDNIGHT COURT(1937); ONCE A DOCTOR(1937); WEST OF SHANGHAI(1937); WHITE BONDAGE(1937); WRONG ROAD, THE(1937); CASSIDY OF BAR 20(1938); LADY IN THE MORGUE(1938); MAN FROM MUSIC MOUNTAIN(1938); OVERLAND STAGE RAIDERS(1938); HOME ON THE PRAIRIE(1939); ON TRIAL(1939); ROVIN' TUMBLEWEEDS(1939); SHOULD A GIRL MARRY?(1939); WOMEN IN THE WIND(1939); RIDERS OF PASCO BASIN(1940); SCATTERGOOD PULLS THE STRINGS(1941); SECRETS OF THE WASTELANDS(1941)

Gypsy Hart
Silents
GOLD RUSH, THE(1925)
Misc. Silents
FLOWER OF DOOM, THE(1917); PULSE OF LIFE, THE(1917)

H. Tom Hart
SILENT CALL, THE(1961)

H. Tommy Hart
WORLD IN MY CORNER(1956)

Hal Hart
RENEGADES OF THE RIO GRANDE(1945)

Harold Tommy Hart
MISS SADIE THOMPSON(1953); NIGHT PASSAGE(1957)

Harry Hart
SECRETS(1971), ph

Harvey Hart
BUS RILEY'S BACK IN TOWN(1965), d; DARK INTRUDER(1965), d; SULLIVAN'S EMPIRE(1967), d; SWEET RIDE, THE(1968), d; FORTUNE AND MEN'S EYES(1971, U.S./Can.), d; PYX, THE(1973, Can.), d; SHOOT(1976, Can.), d; HIGH COUNTRY, THE(1981, Can.), d; UTILITIES(1983, Can.), d

Hazel Hart
Silents
WESTERN HEARTS(1921)

Helena Hart
SHOOT(1976, Can.)

Henry Hart
D.O.A.(1950); SLEEPING CITY, THE(1950)

Jack Hart
VENGEANCE IS MINE(1948, Brit.)

James V. Hart
MANIAC!(1977), p

Janan Hart
REVOLT OF MAMIE STOVER, THE(1956)

Jean Hart
MERRY WIDOW, THE(1934); ROSE TATTOO, THE(1955)

Jeanne Hart
FOLIES DERGERE(1935); ROMEO AND JULIET(1936); GLAMOUR FOR SALE(1940)

Jeremy Hart
I'M GOING TO GET YOU ... ELLIOT BOY(1971, Can.)

Jim Hart
1984
GIMME AN 'F'(1984), w

John Fredric Hart
GREAT BRAIN, THE(1978)

John Hart
DAUGHTER OF SHANGHAI(1937); DANGEROUS TO KNOW(1938); HUNTED MEN(1938); ILLEGAL TRAFFIC(1938); KING OF ALCATRAZ(1938); PRISON FARM(1938); TIP-OFF GIRLS(1938); DISBARRED(1939); MILLION DOLLAR LEGS(1939); PERSONS IN HIDING(1939); $1,000 A TOUCHDOWN(1939); NORTHWEST MOUNTED POLICE(1940); VACATION DAYS(1947); VIGILANTES RETURN, THE(1947); JOE PALOOKA IN THE COUNTERPUNCH(1949); CHAMPAGNE FOR CAESAR(1950); COWBOY AND THE PRIZEFIGHTER(1950); FIGHTING REDHEAD, THE(1950); STATE PENITENTIARY(1950); FURY OF THE CONGO(1951); LONGHORN, THE(1951); STAGE TO BLUE RIVER(1951); TEXAS LAWMEN(1951); WARPATH(1951); CARIBBEAN(1952); KANSAS TERRITORY(1952); TEXAS CITY(1952); WILD BLUE YONDER, THE(1952); CROOKED WEB, THE(1955); MAN WHO LOVED REDHEADS, THE(1955, Brit.); TEN COMMANDMENTS, THE(1956); DIARY OF A HIGH SCHOOL BRIDE(1959); INSIDE THE MAFIA(1959); SHAGGY DOG, THE(1959); VICE RAID(1959); NOOSE FOR A GUNMAN(1960); ATOM AGE VAMPIRE(1961, Ital.); JUMBO(1962); CAPTAIN NEWMAN, M.D.(1963); CINCINNATI KID, THE(1965); DAY OF THE NIGHTMARE(1965); SANDPIPER, THE(1965); 36 HOURS(1965); DON'T WORRY, WE'LL THINK OF A TITLE(1966), w; HOLD ON(1966); KILL BABY KILL(1966, Ital.), w; FLAME OVER VIETNAM(1967, Span./Ger.), w; RIOT ON SUNSET STRIP(1967); MR. MAGOO'S HOLIDAY FESTIVAL(1970); PHYNX, THE(1970); SIMON, KING OF THE WITCHES(1971); BLACKENSTEIN(1973); SANTEE(1973); LEGEND OF THE LONE RANGER, THE(1981)
1984
INVISIBLE STRANGLER(1984)
Misc. Talkies
STAGECOACH DRIVER(1951)

Josef Hart
INTIMATE LIGHTING(1969, Czech.), m

Joy Hart
FORTY THOUSAND HORSEMEN(1941, Aus.)

Judith Hart
FLIGHT THAT DISAPPEARED, THE(1961), w

June Hart
DANCE BAND(1935, Brit.); LADY GODIVA RIDES AGAIN(1955, Brit.)

Kathryn Hart
"X"-THE MAN WITH THE X-RAY EYES(1963); ADVANCE TO THE REAR(1964); SEDUCTION, THE(1982)

Larry Hart
EVERGREEN(1934, Brit.), m

Laura Frances Hart
MOONLIGHTING(1982, Brit.)

Leslie Hart
FLOOD, THE(1963, Brit.)

Lionel Hart
IN THE WAKE OF THE BOUNTY(1933, Aus.), md

Lorenz Hart
HEADS UP(1930), w; LEATHERNECKING(1930), w; MELODY MAN(1930), w; SPRING IS HERE(1930), w; HOT HEIRESS(1931), w; TEN CENTS A DANCE(1931), w; HALLELUJAH, I'M A BUM(1933); BABES IN ARMS(1939), w; ON YOUR TOES(1939), w; BOYS FROM SYRACUSE(1940), w; TOO MANY GIRLS(1940), w, m; THEY MET IN ARGENTINA(1941), m; I MARRIED AN ANGEL(1942), w; PAL JOEY(1957), w

Louis G. Hart
SCARLET ANGEL(1952)

Louis Hart
GUADALCANAL DIARY(1943); GUY NAMED JOE, A(1943); TAMPICO(1944); BIG DADDY(1969)

Loyd David Hart
EDDIE MACON'S RUN(1983)

Ludwig Hart
RAGE IN HEAVEN(1941)

Mabel Hart
OVER THE WALL(1938); ISN'T IT ROMANTIC?(1948)

Malcolm Hart
VANISHING POINT(1971), w

Margie Hart
LURE OF THE ISLANDS(1942)

Maria Hart
BORDER OUTLAWS(1950); FIGHTING STALLION, THE(1950); CATTLE QUEEN(1951); LUSTY MEN, THE(1952); OUTLAW WOMEN(1952)

Marion Hart
CONNECTING ROOMS(1971, Brit.), d&w

Mary Hart
LOVE IS ON THE AIR(1937); COME ON RANGERS(1939); EVERYTHING'S ON ICE(1939); MY WIFE'S RELATIVES(1939); MYSTERIOUS MISS X, THE(1939); SHOULD HUSBANDS WORK?(1939); PAROLE FIXER(1940)

Mary Hart [Lynne Roberts]
SHINE ON, HARVEST MOON(1938); FRONTIER PONY EXPRESS(1939); IN OLD CALIENTE(1939); ROUGH RIDERS' ROUNDUP(1939); SOUTHWARD HO!(1939)

Maurice Hart
DISC JOCKEY(1951); JOKER IS WILD, THE(1957)

Melissa Hart
1984
RIVER RAT, THE(1984)

Michele Hart
MORGAN'S MARAUDERS(1929)

Morgan Hart
MAN WHO WASN'T THERE, THE(1983)
Misc. Talkies
MADHOUSE(1982)

Moss Hart
FLESH(1932), w; ONCE IN A LIFETIME(1932), w; MASQUERADER, THE(1933), w; BROADWAY MELODY OF 1936(1935), w; FRANKIE AND JOHNNY(1936), w; YOU CAN'T TAKE IT WITH YOU(1938), w; GEORGE WASHINGTON SLEPT HERE(1942), w; MAN WHO CAME TO DINNER, THE(1942), w; LADY IN THE DARK(1944), w; WINGED VICTORY(1944), w; GENTLEMAN'S AGREEMENT(1947), w; DECISION OF CHRISTOPHER BLAKE, THE(1948), w; HANS CHRISTIAN ANDERSEN(1952), w; STAR IS BORN, A(1954), w; PRINCE OF PLAYERS(1955), w; ACT ONE(1964), p,d&w; THAT LUCKY TOUCH(1975, Brit.), w

Neal Hart
TRIGGER TRICKS(1930); WILD HORSE(1931); LAW AND ORDER(1932); DUDE BANDIT, THE(1933); TEXAS RANGERS, THE(1936); RENEGADE RANGER(1938); STORY OF VERNON AND IRENE CASTLE, THE(1939); CORPUS CHRISTI BANDITS(1945); STATE FAIR(1945); SADDLE PALS(1947); STAMPEDE(1949)
Misc. Talkies
GUNS FOR HIRE(1932); RECKLESS RIDER, THE(1932)
Silents
MAN FROM MONTANA, THE(1917); DANGER VALLEY(1921); KINGFISHER'S ROOST, THE(1922); LURE OF GOLD(1922), a, d&w; SOUTH OF NORTHERN LIGHTS(1922), a, d&w
Misc. Silents
LOVE'S LARIAT(1916); SMASHING THROUGH(1918); WHEN THE DESERT SMILES(1919), a, d; HELL'S OASIS(1920), a, d; BLACK SHEEP(1921); GOD'S GOLD(1921); TANGLED TRAILS(1921); BUTTERFLY RANGE(1922), a, d; HEART OF A TEXAN, THE(1922); RANGELAND(1922), a, d; TABLE TOP RANCH(1922); WEST OF THE PECOS(1922), a, d; BELOW THE RIO GRANDE(1923), a, d; DEVIL'S BOWL, THE(1923), d; FIGHTING STRAIN, THE(1923), a, d; FORBIDDEN RANGE, THE(1923), a, d; SALTY SAUNDERS(1923), a, d; SECRET OF THE PUEBLO, THE(1923), a, d; BRANDED A THIEF(1924), a, d; LAWLESS MEN(1924), a, d; LEFT HAND BRAND, THE(1924), a, d; SAFE GUARDED(1924); TRUCKER'S TOP HAND(1924), a, d; VALLEY OF VANISHING MEN, THE(1924), a, d; VERDICT OF THE DESERT, THE(1925), a, d

Neila Hart
SINCE YOU WENT AWAY(1944)

Nina Hart
TAKING OFF(1971)

Pamela Hart
SUMMER HOLIDAY(1963, Brit.); STOP THE WORLD–I WANT TO GET OFF(1966, Brit.); YOUNG GIRLS OF ROCHEFORT, THE(1968, Fr.)

Peter Hart
MAN IN THE DARK(1963, Brit.), m

Ralph Hart
FLIGHT THAT DISAPPEARED, THE(1961), w

Richard Hart
DESIRE ME(1947); GREEN DOLPHIN STREET(1947); B. F.'S DAUGHTER(1948); BLACK BOOK, THE(1949); OUTSIDER, THE(1949, Brit.); I BELIEVE IN YOU(1953, Brit.); LOVERS, HAPPY LOVERS!(1955, Brit.); OPERATION SNAFU(1965, Brit.)

Rick Hart
MONEY MOVERS(1978, Aus.)

Robert Hart
COURT JESTER, THE(1956)

Rod Hart
JUNIOR BONNER(1972)

Roxanne Hart
BELL JAR, THE(1979); VERDICT, THE(1982)
1984
OH GOD! YOU DEVIL(1984); OLD ENOUGH(1984)

Ruth Hart
THIN ICE(1937); ARSENE LUPIN RETURNS(1938)

Shelly Hart
SUMMER CAMP(1979)

Stan Warnow Hart
HURRY UP OR I'LL BE 30(1973), ed

Stanley Hart
MOVE(1970), w

Stephan Hart
WILLIE AND PHIL(1980)

Stephen Hart
MAGIC(1978)

Stuart Hart
SEVEN HILLS OF ROME, THE(1958)

Sunshine Hart
Silents
SYNCOPATING SUE(1926); MY BEST GIRL(1927); RED MILL, THE(1927); MAN IN HOBBLES, THE(1928)

Susan Hart
SLIME PEOPLE, THE(1963); FOR THOSE WHO THINK YOUNG(1964); PAJAMA PARTY(1964); RIDE THE WILD SURF(1964); CITY UNDER THE SEA(1965, Brit.); DR. GOLDFOOT AND THE BIKINI MACHINE(1965); GHOST IN THE INVISIBLE BIKINI(1966)

Teddy Hart
MILLION DOLLAR LEGS(1932); DIPLOMANIACS(1933); AFTER THE THIN MAN(1936); THREE MEN ON A HORSE(1936); FOOTLOOSE HEIRESS, THE(1937); HOTEL HAYWIRE(1937); MARRY THE GIRL(1937); READY, WILLING AND ABLE(1937); TALENT SCOUT(1937); THAT MAN'S HERE AGAIN(1937); YOU'RE THE ONE(1941); MY FAVORITE SPY(1942); LADY LUCK(1946); MA AND PA KETTLE GO TO TOWN(1950); FAT MAN, THE(1951); MA AND PA KETTLE BACK ON THE FARM(1951); GIRL IN EVERY PORT, A(1952); MA AND PA KETTLE ON VACATION(1953); MA AND PA KETTLE AT WAIKIKI(1955); MICKEY ONE(1965)

Terry Hart
SATIN MUSHROOM, THE(1969)

Tommy Hart
MAN WITH THE GOLDEN ARM, THE(1955); TO HELL AND BACK(1955)

Uke Hart
ONLY WAY HOME, THE(1972), m

Veronica Hart
1984
DELIVERY BOYS(1984)

Misc. Talkies
R.S.V.P.(1984)

Vivian Hart
GIRL SAID NO, THE(1937)

Walter Hart
PRIMROSE PATH(1940), w; GOLDBERGS, THE(1950), d

William S. Hart
O'MALLEY OF THE MOUNTED(1936), w
Silents
APOSTLE OF VENGEANCE, THE(1916), a, d; ARYAN, THE(1916), a, d; CAPTIVE GOD, THE(1916); HELL'S HINGES(1916), a, d; PATRIOT, THE(1916), a, d; PRIMAL LURE, THE(1916), a, d; TRUTHFUL TULLIVER(1917), a, d; BRANDING BROADWAY(1918); BREED OF MEN(1919), a, d; MONEY CORRAL, THE(1919), a, d&w; POPPY GIRL'S HUSBAND, THE(1919), a, d; SAND(1920), a, w; TESTING BLOCK, THE(1920), a, w; TOLL GATE, THE(1920), a, w; O'MALLEY OF THE MOUNTED(1921), a, w; WHITE OAK(1921), a, w; TRAVELIN' ON(1922), a, w; SINGER JIM MCKEE(1924), a, w; TUMBLEWEEDS(1925), a, d; SHOW PEOPLE(1928)
Misc. Silents
BARGAIN, THE(1914); DARKENING TRAIL, THE(1915), a, d; DISCIPLE, THE(1915), a, d; ON THE NIGHT STAGE(1915); BETWEEN MEN(1916), a, d; DAWN MAKER, THE(1916), a, d; DEVIL'S DOUBLE, THE(1916), a, d; RETURN OF "DRAW" EGAN, THE(1916), a, d; COLD DECK, THE(1917), a, d; DESERT MAN, THE(1917), d; GUNFIGHTER, THE(1917), a, d; NARROW TRAIL, THE(1917), a, d; SILENT MAN, THE(1917), a, d; SQUARE DEAL MAN, THE(1917), a, d; TRUTHFUL TULLIVER(1917), a, d; WOLF LOWRY(1917), a, d; BLUE BLAZES RAWDEN(1918), a, d; BORDER WIRELESS, THE(1918), a, d; RIDDLE GAWNE(1918), a, d; SELFISH YATES(1918), a, d; SHARK MONROE(1918), a, d; TIGER MAN, THE(1918), a, d; WOLVES OF THE RAIL(1918), a, d; JOHN PETTICOATS(1919); SQUARE DEAL SANDERSON(1919), a, d; WAGON TRACKS(1919); CRADLE OF COURAGE, THE(1920); TOLL GATE, THE(1920); THREE WORD BRAND(1921); WHISTLE, THE(1921); WILD BILL HICKOK(1923), a, d

Robert Hart-Davis
Misc. Talkies
BEWARE MY BRETHREN(1972, Brit.), d

Ludwig Hartau
Misc. Silents
FOUR AROUND THE WOMAN(1921, Ger.)

Robert Hartberg
1914(1932, Ger.); M(1933, Ger.)

Betty Harte
Silents
MYSTERY OF THE POISON POOL, THE(1914); PRIDE OF JENNICO, THE(1914)
Misc. Silents
WOMAN'S TRIUMPH, A(1914); BAIT, THE(1916); MAN FROM BITTER ROOTS, THE(1916); ETERNAL PEACE(1922)

Bret Harte
WILD GIRL(1932), w; M'LISS(1936), w; LUCK OF ROARING CAMP, THE(1937), w; OUTCASTS OF POKER FLAT, THE(1937), w; OUTCASTS OF POKER FLAT, THE(1952), w; TENNESSEE'S PARTNER(1955), w
Silents
SALOMY JANE(1914), w; TENNESSEE'S PARDNER(1916), w; OUTCASTS OF POKER FLAT, THE(1919), w; SALOMY JANE(1923), w

Jerry Harte
EMPIRE STRIKES BACK, THE(1980); LOOPHOLE(1981, Brit.); SENDER, THE(1982, Brit.)

Kathryn Harte
LONG ROPE, THE(1961)

Maria Harte
DEVIL MADE A WOMAN, THE(1962, Span.)

Michael Harte
SILVER STREAK(1976), cos; MAGIC(1978)

Michael J. Harte
OH, GOD!(1977), cos

Jean Hartelle
THUNDER BAY(1953)

Charles Harter
NIGHT TRAIN TO MUNDO FINE(1966)

Lloyd Harter
SING, BOY, SING(1958)

Robert Harter
DAYDREAMER, THE(1966)

Jack Hartfield
LUCKY LEGS(1942), w; FOREVER AND A DAY(1943), w; GIRL ON THE SPOT(1946), w

Katheleen Hartfield
I WALKED WITH A ZOMBIE(1943)

Alec Hartford
HEART OF THE NORTH(1938)

David Hartford
ROUGH ROMANCE(1930); OVER THE HILL(1931)
Silents
TESS OF THE STORM COUNTRY(1914); CIVILIZATION(1916), d; DAME CHANCE(1926); JACK O'HEARTS(1926), p&d
Misc. Silents
IT HAPPENED IN PARIS(1919), d; MAN IN THE SHADOW, THE(1926), d; THEN CAME THE WOMAN(1926), d

David M. Hartford
Silents
BRIDE OF HATE, THE(1917); INSIDE THE LINES(1918), d; NOMADS OF THE NORTH(1920), d, w
Misc. Silents
SIN YE DO, THE(1916); BLOOD WILL TELL(1917); MAN OF BRONZE, THE(1918), d; ROSE O' PARADISE(1918); TURN OF THE CARD, THE(1918); BACK TO GOD'S COUNTRY(1919 US/Can.), d; GOLDEN SNARE, THE(1921), d; GOD'S GREAT WILDERNESS(1927), d

Dee Hartford
GIRL IN EVERY PORT, A(1952); RED LINE 7000(1965); SURVIVAL(1976)

Eden Hartford
STORY OF MANKIND, THE(1957); INVISIBLE INVADERS(1959); FLIGHT THAT DISAPPEARED, THE(1961); GAMBLER WORE A GUN, THE(1961); WHEN THE CLOCK STRIKES(1961)

Huntington Hartford
FACE TO FACE(1952), p

James Hartford
DR. GOLDFOOT AND THE BIKINI MACHINE(1965), w; DR. GOLDFOOT AND THE GIRL BOMBS(1966, Ital.), w

Karen Hartford
SPECTRE OF EDGAR ALLAN POE, THE(1974)

Ken Hartford
MONSTER(1979), p

Kenneth Hartford
SPECTRE OF EDGAR ALLAN POE, THE(1974), w
Misc. Talkies
LUCIFER COMPLEX, THE(1978), d

Stephan Hartford
HAUNTING OF M, THE(1979)

Robert Hartford-Davis
CROSSTRAP(1962, Brit.), d; THAT KIND OF GIRL(1963, Brit.), p; GUTTER GIRLS(1964, Brit.), p&d; SATURDAY NIGHT OUT(1964, Brit.), p&d; BLACK TORMENT, THE(1965, Brit.), p, d; GONKS GO BEAT(1965, Brit.), p, d; PRESS FOR TIME(1966, Brit.), p; SANDWICH MAN, THE(1966, Brit.), d, w; CORRUPTION(1968, Brit.), d; EXPLOSION(1969, Can.), w; INCENSE FOR THE DAMNED(1970, Brit.), d; BLACK GUNN(1972), d; SCHOOL FOR UNCLAIMED GIRLS(1973, Brit.), d; TAKE, THE(1974), d
Misc. Talkies
FIEND, THE(1971, Brit.), d; HELL HOUSE GIRLS(1975, Brit.), d

Christel Harthaus
KAMIKAZE '89(1983, Ger.)

Ben Hartigan
PSYCHO II(1983)

P.C. Hartigan
Misc. Silents
SWAT THE SPY(1918)

Pat Hartigan
MIDNIGHT TAXI, THE(1928); STATE STREET SADIE(1928); TENDERLOIN(1928); FROM HEADQUARTERS(1929); IN OLD ARIZONA(1929); MAN HUNTER, THE(1930); OTHER MEN'S WOMEN(1931); HANDLE WITH CARE(1932); JUDGE PRIEST(1934); HUMAN CARGO(1936); THAT GIRL FROM PARIS(1937); LITTLE OLD NEW YORK(1940)
Silents
DOWN TO THE SEA IN SHIPS(1923); ABRAHAM LINCOLN(1924); KING OF THE WILD HORSES, THE(1924); WELCOME STRANGER(1924); WESTERN LUCK(1924); BELOW THE LINE(1925); FIGHTING EDGE(1926); RANSON'S FOLLY(1926); BOWERY CINDERELLA(1927); ENCHANTED ISLAND, THE(1927); JOHNNY GET YOUR HAIR CUT(1927); FAR CALL, THE(1929)
Misc. Silents
FURY(1922); DARLING OF NEW YORK, THE(1923); WHERE THE NORTH BEGINS(1923)

William Hartigan
Misc. Silents
OUT OF THE SHOWS(1920)

Karl Hartl
TEMPORARY WIDOW, THE(1930, Ger./Brit.), w; IMMORTAL VAGABOND(1931, Ger.), w; F.P. 1(1933, Brit.), d; F.P. 1 DOESN'T ANSWER(1933, Ger.), d; GOLD(1934, Ger.), d; MAN WHO WAS SHERLOCK HOLMES, THE(1937, Ger.), d, w; MOZART STORY, THE(1948, Aust.), d; ANGEL WITH THE TRUMPET, THE(1950, Brit.), p, w; WONDER BOY(1951, Brit./Aust.), p&d, w; HOUSE OF LIFE(1953, Ger.), d&w; LIFE AND LOVES OF MOZART, THE(1959, Ger.), d&w

Carl Hartle
DOOMED BATTALION, THE(1932), w

Dale Hartleben
INSIDE STRAIGHT(1951); HER TWELVE MEN(1954)

Jerry Hartleben
3:10 TO YUMA(1957); INSIDE STRAIGHT(1951); BUCCANEER, THE(1958); KING OF THE WILD STALLIONS(1959)

Betty Hartley
LUCKY NUMBER, THE(1933, Brit.)

Bill Hartley
SWEET SUBSTITUTE(1964, Can.)

Bunny Hartley
THAT NIGHT IN RIO(1941)

Charles Hartley
Silents
NEIGHBORS(1918); PRUNELLA(1918); OH, BOY!(1919)
Misc. Silents
SUBMARINE EYE, THE(1917)

Esdras Hartley
TAXI!(1932), art d; TENDERFOOT, THE(1932), art d; CONVENTION CITY(1933), art d; HAVANA WIDOWS(1933), art d; HOUSE ON 56TH STREET, THE(1933), art d; LADIES THEY TALK ABOUT(1933), art d; MAYOR OF HELL, THE(1933), art d; WILD BOYS OF THE ROAD(1933), art d; HERE COMES THE NAVY(1934), art d; I'VE GOT YOUR NUMBER(1934), art d; JIMMY THE GENT(1934), art d; TWENTY MILLION SWEETHEARTS(1934), art d; ALIBI IKE(1935), art d; DON'T BET ON BLONDES(1935), art d; GOING HIGHBROW(1935), art d; I LIVE FOR LOVE(1935), art d; IRISH IN US, THE(1935), art d; MARY JANE'S PA(1935), art d; MISS PACIFIC FLEET(1935), art d; RIGHT TO LIVE, THE(1935), art d; SPECIAL AGENT(1935), art d; WHILE THE PATIENT SLEPT(1935), art d; WOMAN IN RED, THE(1935), art d; CASE OF THE VELVET CLAWS, THE(1936), art d; FRESHMAN LOVE(1936), art d; HOT MONEY(1936), art d; ISLE OF FURY(1936), art d; MAN HUNT(1936), art d; MOONLIGHT ON THE PRAIRIE(1936), art d; SONG OF THE SADDLE(1936), art d; TWO AGAINST THE WORLD(1936), art d; SAN QUENTIN(1937), art d; WINE, WOMEN AND HORSES(1937), art d; BOY MEETS GIRL(1938), art d; COWBOY FROM BROOKLYN(1938), art d; RACKET BUSTERS(1938), art d; SWING YOUR LADY(1938), art d; OKLAHOMA KID, THE(1939), art d; RETURN OF DR. X, THE(1939), art d; KING OF THE LUMBERJACKS(1940), art d; FLIGHT FROM DESTINY(1941), art d

Silents
LIGHTHOUSE BY THE SEA, THE(1924), art d

Gabrielle Hartley
DAWN(1979, Aus.); CLINIC, THE(1983, Aus.)

H. "Doc" Hartley
RODEO RHYTHM(1941)

Irving Hartley
Silents
NO MOTHER TO GUIDE HER(1923); MAN AND MAID(1925)

Jack Hartley
STREET OF SINNERS(1957)

Jane Hartley
LOST LAGOON(1958)

Jean Hartley
POLICE CALL(1933), w

Jennie Hartley
THEY DRIVE BY NIGHT(1938, Brit.)

John Hartley
BOY TROUBLE(1939); GRAND JURY SECRETS(1939); MILLION DOLLAR LEGS(1939); NIGHT WORK(1939); PERSONS IN HIDING(1939); UNMARRIED(1939); $1,000 A TOUCHDOWN(1939); FARMER'S DAUGHTER, THE(1940); FRIENDLY NEIGHBORS(1940); GRAND OLE OPRY(1940); THOSE WERE THE DAYS(1940); WAY OF ALL FLESH, THE(1940); LADY EVE, THE(1941); YANK IN THE R.A.F., A(1941); TEN GENTLEMEN FROM WEST POINT(1942); LITTLEST HORSE THIEVES, THE(1977)

L.P. Hartley
GO-BETWEEN, THE(1971, Brit.), w; HIRELING, THE(1973, Brit.), w

Linda Hartley
FIRE IN THE STONE, THE(1983, Aus.)

Mariette Hartley
RIDE THE HIGH COUNTRY(1962); DRUMS OF AFRICA(1963); MARNIE(1964); MAROONED(1969); BARQUERO(1970); RETURN OF COUNT YORGA, THE(1971); MAGNIFICENT SEVEN RIDE, THE(1972); SKYJACKED(1972); IMPROPER CHANNELS(1981, Can.); O'HARA'S WIFE(1983)

Mehan Hartley
NORAH O'NEALE(1934, Brit.)

Neil Hartley
SAILOR FROM GIBRALTAR, THE(1967, Brit.), p; CHARGE OF THE LIGHT BRIGADE, THE(1968, Brit.), p; HAMLET(1969, Brit.), p; NED KELLY(1970, Brit.), p; JOSEPH ANDREWS(1977, Brit.), p
1984
HOTEL NEW HAMPSHIRE, THE(1984), p

Nellie Hartley
Misc. Silents
MYSTERY OF NO. 47, THE(1917)

Paul Hartley
TWO HEARTS IN HARMONY(1935, Brit.)

Ray Hartley
THEY'RE A WEIRD MOB(1966, Aus.)

Richard Hartley
GALILEO(1975, Brit.), m; ROCKY HORROR PICTURE SHOW, THE(1975, Brit.), md; ROMANTIC ENGLISHWOMAN, THE(1975, Brit./Fr.), m; ACES HIGH(1977, Brit.), m; LADY VANISHES, THE(1980, Brit.), m; SHOCK TREATMENT(1981), m; TROUT, THE(1982, Fr.), m
1984
SHEENA(1984), m

Richard Hartley [Alberto Gallitti]
MURDER CLINIC, THE(1967, Ital./Fr.), ed

Robert Hartley
MARRYING KIND, THE(1952)

Steve Hartley
DREAM ON(1981)

Steven Hartley
TIMERIDER(1983)

Tamara Hartley
1984
RIVER RAT, THE(1984)

Ted Hartley
MURDERERS' ROW(1966); WALK, DON'T RUN(1966); BAREFOOT IN THE PARK(1967); ICE STATION ZEBRA(1968); MAN, THE(1972); HIGH PLAINS DRIFTER(1973)

William B. Hartley
CRUEL TOWER, THE(1956), w

Gene Hartline
GRAND THEFT AUTO(1977); DEATHSPORT(1978); HOMETOWN U.S.A.(1979); TIME AFTER TIME(1979, Brit.); SEPARATE WAYS(1981), stunts; SMOKEY BITES THE DUST(1981), stunts
1984
GRANDVIEW, U.S.A.(1984)

Lore Hartling
CONFESS DR. CORDA(1960, Ger.)

Beth Hartman
SOULS AT SEA(1937); REMEMBER THE NIGHT(1940); MATING SEASON, THE(1951)

Bill Hartman
FAST CHARLIE... THE MOONBEAM RIDER(1979)

Broes Hartman
HIDING PLACE, THE(1975)

David Hartman
GANG WAR(1928); BALLAD OF JOSIE(1968); DID YOU HEAR THE ONE ABOUT THE TRAVELING SALESLADY?(1968); NOBODY'S PERFECT(1968); ISLAND AT THE TOP OF THE WORLD, THE(1974)

Don Hartman
TRUE TO LIFE(1943), w; CORONADO(1935), w; GAY DECEPTION, THE(1935), w; HERE COMES COOKIE(1935), w; OLD MAN RHYTHM(1935), w; REDHEADS ON PARADE(1935), w; ROMANCE IN MANHATTAN(1935), w; PRINCESS COMES ACROSS, THE(1936), w; CHAMPAGNE WALTZ(1937), w; WAIKIKI WEDDING(1937), w; TROPIC HOLIDAY(1938), w; NEVER SAY DIE(1939), w; PARIS HONEYMOON(1939), w; STAR MAKER, THE(1939), w; ROAD TO SINGAPORE(1940), w; THOSE WERE THE DAYS(1940), w; LIFE WITH HENRY(1941),

w; NOTHING BUT THE TRUTH(1941), w; ROAD TO ZANZIBAR(1941), w; MY FAVORITE BLONDE(1942), w; ROAD TO MOROCCO(1942), w; PRINCESS AND THE PIRATE, THE(1944), w; UP IN ARMS(1944), w; WONDER MAN(1945), w; KID FROM BOOKLYN, THE(1946), w; DOWN TO EARTH(1947), p, w; IT HAD TO BE YOU(1947), p, d, w; EVERY GIRL SHOULD BE MARRIED(1948), p&d; HOLIDAY AFFAIR(1949), p&d; IT'S A BIG COUNTRY(1951), d; MR. IMPERIUM(1951), d, w; DESIRE UNDER THE ELMS(1958), p; MATCHMAKER, THE(1958), p

Eddie Hartman
SHIP AHOY(1942)

Edmund Hartman
FACE OF MARBLE, THE(1946), w; PALEFACE, THE(1948), w; FANCY PANTS(1950), w; CADDY, THE(1953), w

Edmund I. Hartman
BEHIND THE HEADLINES(1937), w

Edmund L. Hartman
ENEMY AGENT(1940), w; SAN FRANCISCO DOCKS(1941), w

Edward Hartman
BIG NOISE, THE(1936), w

Elizabeth Hartman
EBB TIDE(1937); PATCH OF BLUE, A(1965); GROUP, THE(1966); YOU'RE A BIG BOY NOW(1966); FIXER, THE(1968); BEGUILED, THE(1971); WALKING TALL(1973); FULL MOON HIGH(1982); SECRET OF NIMH, THE(1982)

Ema Hartman
OUR MAN FLINT(1966)

Ena Hartman
GAMES(1967); AIRPORT(1970); TERMINAL ISLAND(1973)

F.G. Hartman
Misc. Silents
FOREST KING, THE(1922), d

Ferris Hartman
Misc. Silents
PHANTOM HUSBAND, A(1917), d; FRAMING FRAMERS(1918), d

Fred Hartman
SNIPER, THE(1952)
Silents
KING SPRUCE(1920), ph

George Hartman
MIDAS RUN(1969)

Grace Hartman
SUNNY(1941); HIGHER AND HIGHER(1943)

Greta Hartman
Silents
LES MISERABLES(1918)

Gretchen Hartman
COLLEGE COQUETTE, THE(1929); SHE GOES TO WAR(1929); TIME, THE PLACE AND THE GIRL, THE(1929); ROOM FOR ONE MORE(1952)
Silents
LITTLE 'FRAID LADY, THE(1920); DO AND DARE(1922)
Misc. Silents
BEAST, THE(1916); LOVE THIEF, THE(1916); MARRIED IN NAME ONLY(1917); HOUSE WITHOUT CHILDREN, THE(1919)

Jan Hartman
NIGHT CHILD(1975, Brit./Ital.), w

Joe Hartman
I MARRIED AN ANGEL(1942)

Jonathan Hartman
SHAPE OF THINGS TO COME, THE(1979, Can.)

Lauren Hartman
1984
IRRECONCILABLE DIFFERENCES(1984)

Lee Hartman
THERE'S ALWAYS VANILLA(1972)

Lisa Hartman
DEADLY BLESSING(1981)
1984
WHERE THE BOYS ARE '84(1984)
Misc. Talkies
JUST TELL ME YOU LOVE ME(1979)

Margot Hartman
CURSE OF THE LIVING CORPSE, THE(1964); PSYCHOMANIA(1964)

Paul Hartman
SUNNY(1941); HIGHER AND HIGHER(1943); MAN ON A TIGHTROPE(1953); INHERIT THE WIND(1960); SOLDIER IN THE RAIN(1963); THRILL OF IT ALL, THE(1963); THOSE CALLOWAYS(1964); INSIDE DAISY CLOVER(1965); LUV(1967); RELUCTANT ASTRONAUT, THE(1967); HOW TO SUCCEED IN BUSINESS WITHOUT REALLY TRYING(1976)
Misc. Silents
CINDERELLA(1926, Ger.)

Peter Hartman
SERENITY(1962), m

Phil Hartman
MY WIFE'S BEST FRIEND(1952)
1984
WEEKEND PASS(1984)

Ras Daniel Hartman
HARDER THEY COME, THE(1973, Jamaica)

Ruth Hartman
Silents
MAN WHO COULD NOT LOSE, THE(1914); LAST CHAPTER, THE(1915)

Tom Hartman
GUNS OF A STRANGER(1973)

Victoria Hartman
MOTEL HELL(1980)

Warren Hartman
OFFERING, THE(1966, Can.), cos

William Hartman
Misc. Silents
GOD OF LITTLE CHILDREN(1917)

William S. Hartman
Misc. Silents
DESERT MAN, THE(1917)

Angela Hartmann
TURKISH CUCUMBER, THE(1963, Ger.)

Carl von Hartmann
Silents
AWAKENING, THE(1928)

Edmund Hartmann
DON'T GET PERSONAL(1936), w; SWEETHEART OF THE CAMPUS(1941), w; LADY BODYGUARD(1942), w; TRUE TO THE ARMY(1942), w; VARIETY GIRL(1947), w; LET'S LIVE A LITTLE(1948), w; SORROWFUL JONES(1949), w; LEMON DROP KID, THE(1951), w; MY FAVORITE SPY(1951), w; HERE COME THE GIRLS(1953), w; CASANOVA'S BIG NIGHT(1954), w; SWORD OF ALI BABA, THE(1965), w; SHAKIEST GUN IN THE WEST, THE(1968), w

Edmund L. Hartmann
WANTED: JANE TURNER(1936), w; WITHOUT ORDERS(1936), w; CHINA PASSAGE(1937), w; HIDEAWAY(1937), w; MAN WHO FOUND HIMSELF, THE(1937), w; LAST EXPRESS, THE(1938), w; LAST WARNING, THE(1938), w; LAW OF THE UNDERWORLD(1938), w; BIG TOWN CZAR(1939), w; EX-CHAMP(1939), w; TWO BRIGHT BOYS(1939), w; DIAMOND FRONTIER(1940), w; MA, HE'S MAKING EYES AT ME(1940), w; SOUTH TO KARANGA(1940), w; FEMININE TOUCH, THE(1941), w; KEEP 'EM FLYING(1941), w; TIME OUT FOR RHYTHM(1941), w; RIDE 'EM COWBOY(1942), w; SHERLOCK HOLMES AND THE SECRET WEAPON(1942), w; HI'YA, CHUM(1943), w; ALI BABA AND THE FORTY THIEVES(1944), w; GHOST CATCHERS(1944), p, w; IN SOCIETY(1944), p, w; SCARLET CLAW, THE(1944), w; DANGEROUS PARTNERS(1945), w; HERE COME THE CO-EDS(1945), w; NAUGHTY NINETIES, THE(1945), p, w; SEE MY LAWYER(1945), p, w; SUDAN(1945), w

Georg Hartmann
CABARET(1972); SERPENT'S EGG, THE(1977, Ger./U.S.)

Michael Hartmann
GAME FOR VULTURES, A(1980, Brit.), w

Paul Hartmann
F.P. 1 DOESN'T ANSWER(1933, Ger.); INVISIBLE OPPONENT(1933, Ger.); INHERITANCE IN PRETORIA(1936, Ger.); BIMBO THE GREAT(1961, Ger.); ROSES FOR THE PROSECUTOR(1961, Ger.); LONGEST DAY, THE(1962)
Misc. Silents
HAUNTED CASTLE, THE(1921, Ger.); VANINA(1922, Ger.); CHRONICLES OF THE GRAY HOUSE, THE(1923, Ger.)

Phil Hartmann
PANDEMONIUM(1982)

Ron Hartmann
REINCARNATE, THE(1971, Can.)

Ronald Hartmann
BLOODY BROOD, THE(1959, Can.)

Sadakichi Hartmann
Silents
THIEF OF BAGDAD, THE(1924)

Siegfried Hartmann
TINDER BOX, THE(1968, E. Ger.), d, w

Susan Hartmann
RAZOR'S EDGE, THE(1946)

The Hartmans
45 FATHERS(1937)

Kathleen Hartnagel
SCANDAL AT SCOURIE(1953)

Billy [William] Hartnell
SAY IT WITH MUSIC(1932, Brit.); I'M AN EXPLOSIVE(1933, Brit.); LURE, THE(1933, Brit.); SEEING IS BELIEVING(1934, Brit.); SWINGING THE LEAD(1934, Brit.); WHILE PARENTS SLEEP(1935, Brit.); MIDNIGHT AT THE WAX MUSEUM(1936, Brit.); NOTHING LIKE PUBLICITY(1936, Brit.); THEY DRIVE BY NIGHT(1938, Brit.); MURDER WILL OUT(1939, Brit.); TOO DANGEROUS TO LIVE(1939, Brit.); FLYING FORTRESS(1942, Brit.); PETERVILLE DIAMOND, THE(1942, Brit.); SABOTAGE AT SEA(1942, Brit.); WINGS AND THE WOMAN(1942, Brit.); BELLS GO DOWN, THE(1943, Brit.); DARK TOWER, THE(1943, Brit.); HEADLINE(1943, Brit.); SUSPECTED PERSON(1943, Brit.); QUERY(1945, Brit.); STRAWBERRY ROAN(1945, Brit.); WAY AHEAD, THE(1945, Brit.)

Max Hartnell
NO BLADE OF GRASS(1970, Brit.)

Norman Hartnell
SOUTHERN MAID, A(1933, Brit.), cos; THAT'S A GOOD GIRL(1933, Brit.), cos; RETURN OF BULLDOG DRUMMOND, THE(1934, Brit.), cos; WEEKEND MILLIONAIRE(1937, Brit.), cos; SAILING ALONG(1938, Brit.), cos; NOVEL AFFAIR, A(1957, Brit.), cos; SUDDENLY, LAST SUMMER(1959, Brit.), cos; NEVER PUT IT IN WRITING(1964), cos

William Hartnell
PERFECT FLAW, THE(1934, Brit.); APPOINTMENT WITH CRIME(1945, Brit.); MURDER IN REVERSE(1946, Brit.); BRIGHTON ROCK(1947, Brit.); ODD MAN OUT(1947, Brit.); ESCAPE(1948, Brit.); AGITATOR, THE(1949); NOW BARABBAS WAS A ROBBER(1949, Brit.); TEMPTATION HARBOR(1949, Brit.); LOST PEOPLE, THE(1950, Brit.); DARK MAN, THE(1951, Brit.); MAGIC BOX, THE(1952, Brit.); PICKWICK PAPERS, THE(1952, Brit.); DOUBLE CONFESSION(1953, Brit.); RINGER, THE(1953, Brit.); HOLLY AND THE IVY, THE(1954, Brit.); FOOTSTEPS IN THE FOG(1955, Brit.); JOSEPHINE AND MEN(1955, Brit.); WILL ANY GENTLEMAN?(1955, Brit.); BATTLE HELL(1956, Brit.); DOUBLE CROSS(1956, Brit.); PRIVATE'S PROGRESS(1956, Brit.); TONS OF TROUBLE(1956, Brit.); DATE WITH DISASTER(1957, Brit.); SCOTLAND YARD DRAGNET(1957, Brit.); HELL DRIVERS(1958, Brit.); ON THE RUN(1958, Brit.); CARRY ON SERGEANT(1959, Brit.); DESPERATE MAN, THE(1959, Brit.); MOUSE THAT ROARED, THE(1959, Brit.); SHAKE HANDS WITH THE DEVIL(1959, Ireland); STRICTLY CONFIDENTIAL(1959, Brit.); AND THE SAME TO YOU(1960, Brit.); JACKPOT(1960, Brit.); PICCADILLY THIRD STOP(1960, Brit.); MAKE MINE A DOUBLE(1962, Brit.); HEAVENS ABOVE!(1963, Brit.); THIS SPORTING LIFE(1963, Brit.); TO HAVE AND TO HOLD(1963, Brit.); TOMORROW AT TEN(1964, Brit.); PUSSYCAT ALLEY(1965, Brit.)

Barbara Hartnett
E.T. THE EXTRA-TERRESTRIAL(1982)

Ned Hartnett
LINCOLN CONSPIRACY, THE(1977)

Lynn Hartoch
MURDERERS' ROW(1966)
Constantine Hartofolis
GOING IN STYLE(1979)
Michael Harton
BATTLETRUCK(1982), ed
Wally Harton
HELL IS FOR HEROES(1962), cos
Nico Hartos
INCIDENT, THE(1967)
Samuel Hartridge
FROM HEADQUARTERS(1929), w
Kenneth Harts
DAUGHTER OF THE SUN GOD(1962), d&w
Harold Hartsell
Silents
SEATS OF THE MIGHTY, THE(1914)
Ann Hartsfield
INTRUDER IN THE DUST(1949)
Fred Hartsook
ESCORT WEST(1959), w
Fred K. Hartsook
SONG OF SCHEHERAZADE(1947)
Christopher Hartstone
CAPTAIN NEMO AND THE UNDERWATER CITY(1969, Brit.)
Cathryn Hartt
PINK MOTEL(1983)
Hugo Hartung
ARENT WE WONDERFUL?(1959, Ger.), w
Richard Hartunian
HOT ROD RUMBLE(1957)
Norman Hartweg
FARMER'S OTHER DAUGHTER, THE(1965)
John Hartwell
FAN, THE(1981), w
Oliver Hartwell
LARCENY(1948); WALLS OF JERICHO(1948); LAS VEGAS STORY, THE(1952); MAN CALLED PETER, THE(1955)
Knut Hartwig
JUDGE AND THE SINNER, THE(1964, Ger.)
Wolf C. Hartwig
LADY HAMILTON(1969, Ger./Ital./Fr.), p; OFFICE GIRLS(1974), p; CROSS OF IRON(1977, Brit., Ger.), p
Wolfgang Hartwig
HEAD, THE(1961, Ger.), p; PLAYGIRLS AND THE BELLBOY, THE(1962,Ger.), p; SEVEN DARING GIRLS(1962, Ger.), p; ISLE OF SIN(1963, Ger.), p
Patricia Harty
HARVEY MIDDLEMAN, FIREMAN(1965)
Seamus Harty
YOU CAN'T FOOL AN IRISHMAN(1950, Ireland)
Veola Harty
Misc. Silents
LASCA(1919)
David Hartz
STRONGER THAN DESIRE(1939), w
Harry Hartz
CROWD ROARS, THE(1932)
Ruddy Hartz
NOBODY'S CHILDREN(1940)
Maurice Hartzband
THAT NIGHT(1957), ph; STAGE STRUCK(1958), ph
Morris Hartzband
ROCK, ROCK, ROCK!(1956), ph; MISTER ROCK AND ROLL(1957), ph; VIOLATORS, THE(1957), ph; I NEVER SANG FOR MY FATHER(1970), ph
Morris "Moe" Hartzband
LOVELY WAY TO DIE, A(1968), ph
Morris Hartzbrand
PAPER LION(1968), ph
Duane Hartzell
BLACK SAMSON(1974), ed; JENNIFER(1978), ed; JONI(1980), ed; GETTING EVEN(1981), ed
Robert Hartzell
MAN WHO WALKED ALONE, THE(1945)
Sumi Haru
M(1970)
Masumi Harukawa
INSECT WOMAN, THE(1964, Jap.); UNHOLY DESIRE(1964, Jap.); HOTSPRINGS HOLIDAY(1970, Jap.)
Slade Harulbert
TEXAS BUDDIES(1932)
Avind Harum
SONG OF NORWAY(1970)
Eivand Harum
WILLIE AND PHIL(1980)
Eivind Harum
NIGHTHAWKS(1981); SOLDIER, THE(1982)
Haruosato
PORTRAIT OF CHIEKO(1968, Jap.), w
Dafydd Harvard
BEAST IN THE CELLAR, THE(1971, Brit.)
Emile A. Harvard
Misc. Talkies
FUGITIVE KILLER(1975), d
Rene Harvard
GIGOT(1962)
Holt Harvel
SOUTHERN MAID, A(1933, Brit.), cos

John Harvel
BEGGAR STUDENT, THE(1931,Brit.), p, d; CAPTIVATION(1931, Brit), p&d
Rich Harvel
KENTUCKY FRIED MOVIE, THE(1977), art d
Rainbow Harvest
1984
OLD ENOUGH(1984)
Alex Harvey
1984
COUNTRY(1984)
Allen Harvey
MANGANINNIE(1982, Aus.)
Ann Harvey
MAKING LOVE(1982)
Anne Harvey
NED KELLY(1970, Brit.)
Anthony Harvey
CAESAR AND CLEOPATRA(1946, Brit.); PRIVATE'S PROGRESS(1956, Brit.), ed; BROTHERS IN LAW(1957, Brit.), ed; HAPPY IS THE BRIDE(1958, Brit.), ed; I'M ALL RIGHT, JACK(1959, Brit.), ed; ANGRY SILENCE, THE(1960, Brit.), ed; MAN IN A COCKED HAT(1960, Bri.), ed; MILLIONAIRESS, THE(1960, Brit.), ed; L-SHAPED ROOM, THE(1962, Brit.), ed; LOLITA(1962), ed; DR. STRANGELOVE: OR HOW I LEARNED TO STOP WORRYING AND LOVE THE BOMB(1964), ed; SPY WHO CAME IN FROM THE COLD, THE(1965, Brit.), ed; DUTCHMAN(1966, Brit.), d, ed; WHISPERERS, THE(1967, Brit.), ed; LION IN WINTER, THE(1968, Brit.), d; THEY MIGHT BE GIANTS(1971), d; ABDICATION, THE(1974, Brit.), d; EAGLE'S WING(1979, Brit.), d; PLAYERS(1979), d; RICHARD'S THINGS(1981, Brit.), d
1984
ULTIMATE SOLUTION OF GRACE QUIGLEY, THE(1984), d
Ashley Harvey
RUNNERS(1983, Brit.)
Barry Harvey
HOW THE WEST WAS WON(1962)
Bert Harvey
Silents
SPIDER WEBS(1927)
Bill Harvey
HALF A SIXPENCE(1967, Brit.)
Bob Harvey
PAJAMA PARTY(1964); PATSY, THE(1964); HOW TO STUFF A WILD BIKINI(1965); SERGEANT DEADHEAD(1965); GHOST IN THE INVISIBLE BIKINI(1966); SKIN DEEP(1978, New Zealand)
Brenda Harvey
CRUCIFIX, THE(1934, Brit.); QUIET PLEASE(1938, Brit.)
Byron Harvey, Jr.
HARVEY GIRLS, THE(1946)
Charles Harvey
SABRINA(1954)
Cheryl Harvey
WHICH WAY IS UP?(1977); JONI(1980)
Clarence Harvey
TOAST OF NEW YORK, THE(1937); ST. LOUIS BLUES(1939); ZAZA(1939)
Silents
FRIDAY THE 13TH(1916)
Misc. Silents
CHIMES, THE(1914)
Clem Harvey
JOHNNY GUITAR(1954); OCEAN'S ELEVEN(1960); ARMORED COMMAND(1961); ONE-EYED JACKS(1961); THUNDER OF DRUMS, A(1961); STATE FAIR(1962)
Cody Harvey
1984
STONE BOY, THE(1984)
Danny Harvey
1984
WHERE THE BOYS ARE '84(1984)
Dave Harvey
SECRET OF THE SACRED FOREST, THE(1970)
David Harvey
HANK WILLIAMS: THE SHOW HE NEVER GAVE(1982, Can.)
Dennis Harvey
Silents
OLD CURIOSITY SHOP, THE(1921, Brit.)
Dirk Harvey
HARUM SCARUM(1965)
Don Harvey
FOR YOU I DIE(1947); COUNTERFEITERS, THE(1948); ANGELS IN DISGUISE(1949); RIMFIRE(1949); SON OF A BADMAN(1949); WILD WEED(1949); CHAIN GANG(1950); DYNAMITE PASS(1950); FIGHTING STALLION, THE(1950); FORBIDDEN JUNGLE(1950); GIRL FROM SAN LORENZO, THE(1950); GUNMEN OF ABILENE(1950); HOEDOWN(1950); LOST VOLCANO, THE(1950); TYRANT OF THE SEA(1950); ACCORDING TO MRS. HOYLE(1951); HURRICANE ISLAND(1951); JOE PALOOKA IN TRIPLE CROSS(1951); NIGHT RIDERS OF MONTANA(1951); PRAIRIE ROUNDUP(1951); TEXANS NEVER CRY(1951); MARA MARU(1952); NORTHWEST TERRITORY(1952); OLD WEST, THE(1952); OPERATION SECRET(1952); YANK IN INDO-CHINA, A(1952); PRINCE OF PIRATES(1953); GOLDEN IDOL, THE(1954); PUSHOVER(1954); DIG THAT URANIUM(1956); TOWARD THE UNKNOWN(1956); WILD WESTERNERS, THE(1962); IT'S A MAD, MAD, MAD, MAD WORLD(1963); DRAGNET(1974)
Misc. Talkies
TRAIL OF THE RUSTLERS(1950)
Don C. Harvey
MUTINEERS, THE(1949); APACHE AMBUSH(1955); CREATURE WITH THE ATOM BRAIN(1955); FAR COUNTRY, THE(1955); GANG BUSTERS(1955); PICNIC(1955); SCARLET COAT, THE(1955); VIOLENT MEN, THE(1955); WOMEN'S PRISON(1955); WYOMING RENEGADES(1955); BLACKJACK KETCHUM, DESPERADO(1956); JUBAL(1956); WEREWOLF, THE(1956); WRITTEN ON THE WIND(1956); BEGINNING OF THE END(1957); DINO(1957); NO TIME TO BE YOUNG(1957); BUCHANAN RIDES ALONE(1958); GUNMEN FROM LAREDO(1959)

Donald Harvey
VICIOUS CIRCLE, THE(1948)

Ed Harvey
MR. RICCO(1975), w

Edward Harvey
O.S.S.(1946); DOWN TO EARTH(1947); IT HAD TO BE YOU(1947); UNSTOPPABLE MAN, THE(1961, Brit.); SPY WHO CAME IN FROM THE COLD, THE(1965, Brit.); THESE ARE THE DAMNED(1965, Brit.)

Edwin Harvey
Misc. Silents
JACK CHANTY(1915)

Eileen Harvey
BEGGAR'S OPERA, THE(1953)

Fletcher Harvey
Misc. Silents
MELTING POT, THE(1915)

Forrester Harvey
DEVOTION(1931); GUILTY HANDS(1931); MAN IN POSSESSION, THE(1931); TAILOR MADE MAN, A(1931); BUT THE FLESH IS WEAK(1932); KONGO(1932); MYSTERY RANCH(1932); RED DUST(1932); SHANGHAI EXPRESS(1932); SKY DEVILS(1932); SMILIN' THROUGH(1932); TARZAN, THE APE MAN(1932); THOSE WE LOVE(1932); WET PARADE, THE(1932); DESTINATION UNKNOWN(1933); EAGLE AND THE HAWK, THE(1933); INVISIBLE MAN, THE(1933); MIDNIGHT CLUB(1933); GREAT EXPECTATIONS(1934); LIMEHOUSE BLUES(1934); MAN OF TWO WORLDS(1934); MENACE(1934); MYSTERY OF MR. X, THE(1934); PAINTED VEIL, THE(1934); TARZAN AND HIS MATE(1934); BEST MAN WINS, THE(1935); CAPTAIN BLOOD(1935); CAPTAIN HURRICANE(1935); CHINA SEAS(1935); GILDED LILY, THE(1935); JALNA(1935); MYSTERY OF EDWIN DROOD, THE(1935); PERFECT GENTLEMAN, THE(1935); RIGHT TO LIVE, THE(1935); TALE OF TWO CITIES, A(1935); VAGABOND LADY(1935); WITHOUT REGRET(1935); LLOYDS OF LONDON(1936); LOVE BEFORE BREAKFAST(1936); PETTICOAT FEVER(1936); RETURN OF SOPHIE LANG, THE(1936); SUZY(1936); WHITE HUNTER(1936); BULLDOG DRUMMOND COMES BACK(1937); FIGHT FOR YOUR LADY(1937); MAN WHO CRIED WOLF, THE(1937); PERSONAL PROPERTY(1937); PRINCE AND THE PAUPER, THE(1937); SOULS AT SEA(1937); THOROUGHBREDS DON'T CRY(1937); BULLDOG DRUMMOND IN AFRICA(1938); KIDNAPPED(1938); MYSTERIOUS MR. MOTO(1938); SWEETHEARTS(1938); BULLDOG DRUMMOND'S SECRET POLICE(1939); LADY'S FROM KENTUCKY, THE(1939); PRIVATE LIVES OF ELIZABETH AND ESSEX, THE(1939); RAFFLES(1939); WITNESS VANISHES, THE(1939); CHUMP AT OXFORD, A(1940); EARL OF PUDDLESTONE(1940); INVISIBLE MAN RETURNS, THE(1940); LITTLE NELLIE KELLY(1940); ON THEIR OWN(1940); REBECCA(1940); TOM BROWN'S SCHOOL DAYS(1940); DR. JEKYLL AND MR. HYDE(1941); FREE AND EASY(1941); MEET JOHN DOE(1941); MERCY ISLAND(1941); SCOTLAND YARD(1941); WOLF MAN, THE(1941); YANK IN THE R.A.F., A(1941); MRS. MINIVER(1942); THIS ABOVE ALL(1942); MYSTERIOUS DOCTOR, THE(1943); LODGER, THE(1944); MAN IN HALF-MOON STREET, THE(1944); NONE BUT THE LONELY HEART(1944); SECRETS OF SCOTLAND YARD(1944); SCOTLAND YARD INVESTIGATOR(1945, Brit.); DEVOTION(1946)
Silents
FLAG LIEUTENANT, THE(1926, Brit.); IF YOUTH BUT KNEW(1926, Brit.); NELL GWYNNE(1926, Brit.); RING, THE(1927, Brit.)
Misc. Silents
SOMEBODY'S DARLING(1925, Brit.); SPANGLES(1928, Brit.)

Frank Harvey
LOVE STORM, THE(1931, Brit.), a, w; LOVE CONTRACT, THE(1932, Brit.); MAYOR'S NEST, THE(1932, Brit.); UP FOR THE DERBY(1933, Brit.); HERITAGE(1935, Aus.); WHITE DEATH(1936, Aus.), w; IT ISN'T DONE(1937, Aus.), a, w; TALL TIMBERS(1937, Aus.); BROKEN MELODY(1938, Aus.), a, w; DAD AND DAVE COME TO TOWN(1938, Aus.), w; LOVERS AND LUGGERS(1938, Aus.), w; MURDER TOMORROW(1938, Brit.), w; GONE TO THE DOGS(1939, Aus.), w; MR. CHEDWORTH STEPS OUT(1939, Aus.), w; VENGEANCE OF THE DEEP(1940, Aus.), a, w; IT HAPPENED ONE SUNDAY(1944, Brit.), w; THINGS HAPPEN AT NIGHT(1948, Brit.), w; ELIZABETH OF LADYMEAD(1949, Brit.), w; SEVEN DAYS TO NOON(1950, Brit.), w; HIGH TREASON(1951, Brit.), a, w; LONG MEMORY, THE(1953, Brit.), w; CREST OF THE WAVE(1954, Brit.), w; JOSEPHINE AND MEN(1955, Brit.), w; PRIVATE'S PROGRESS(1956, Brit.), w; BROTHERS IN LAW(1957, Brit.), w; I'M ALL RIGHT, JACK(1959, Brit.), w; BREAKOUT(1960, Brit.), w; THIRTY NINE STEPS, THE(1960, Brit.), w; UPSTAIRS AND DOWNSTAIRS(1961, Brit.), w; WORLD IN MY POCKET, THE(1962, Fr./Ital./Ger.), w; HEAVENS ABOVE!(1963, Brit.), w; NO, MY DARLING DAUGHTER(1964, Brit.), w
Misc. Talkies
TIMBERLAND TERROR(1940, Aus.)

Frank Harvey, Jr.
SALOON BAR(1940, Brit.), w; GIRL IN THE PAINTING, THE(1948, Brit.), w; MY BROTHER'S KEEPER(1949, Brit.), w

Fred Harvey
FIREBRAND JORDAN(1930)

George Y. Harvey
CANARY MURDER CASE, THE(1929); PIGSKIN PARADE(1936)
Silents
WIFE SAVERS(1928)

Georgette Harvey
SOCIAL REGISTER(1934); BACK DOOR TO HEAVEN(1939); MIDDLETON FAMILY AT THE N.Y. WORLD'S FAIR(1939)

Georgia Harvey
Silents
ALL FOR A GIRL(1915)

Gladys Harvey
Silents
NELSON(1926, Brit.)

Graham Harvey
1984
CONSTANCE(1984, New Zealand)

Griselda Harvey
GIDEON OF SCOTLAND YARD(1959, Brit.)

Grizelda Harvey
INFORMER, THE(1935)

Harry Harvey
THEY WON'T BELIEVE ME(1947); DR. SOCRATES(1935); ONE MORE SPRING(1935); HITCH HIKE TO HEAVEN(1936); LONE WOLF RETURNS, THE(1936); MOON'S OUR HOME, THE(1936); OREGON TRAIL, THE(1936); PUBLIC ENEMY'S WIFE(1936); THEODORA GOES WILD(1936); TICKET TO PARADISE(1936); UNDER YOUR SPELL(1936); COUNTRY GENTLEMEN(1937); GHOST TOWN GOLD(1937); HEADLINE CRASHER(1937); HERE'S FLASH CASEY(1937); HIGH HAT(1937); KID GALAHAD(1937); SPECIAL AGENT K-7(1937); BORN TO FIGHT(1938); GANGSTER'S BOY(1938); HELD FOR RANSOM(1938); MAN FROM MUSIC MOUNTAIN(1938); MAN'S COUNTRY(1938); PAINTED TRAIL, THE(1938); ROMANCE OF THE LIMBERLOST(1938); SIX SHOOTIN' SHERIFF(1938); SPY RING, THE(1938); UNDER THE BIG TOP(1938); CODE OF THE FEARLESS(1939); DAUGHTER OF THE TONG(1939); IN OLD MONTANA(1939); LONE STAR PIONEERS(1939); PIRATES OF THE SKIES(1939); ROLLIN' WESTWARD(1939); STANLEY AND LIVINGSTONE(1939); TWO-GUN TROUBADOR(1939); HOUSE ACROSS THE BAY, THE(1940); MEN AGAINST THE SKY(1940); MERCY PLANE(1940); PALS OF THE SILVER SAGE(1940); PHANTOM RANCHER(1940); STRIKE UP THE BAND(1940); DOUBLE CROSS(1941); FARGO KID, THE(1941); OBLIGING YOUNG LADY(1941); ROBBERS OF THE RANGE(1941); ROLLIN' HOME TO TEXAS(1941); SIX GUN GOLD(1941); MEXICAN SPITFIRE'S ELEPHANT(1942); NIGHT PLANE FROM CHUNGKING(1942), w; PRIDE OF THE YANKEES, THE(1942); RANGERS TAKE OVER, THE(1942); STRANGE CASE OF DR. RX, THE(1942); HEAT'S ON, THE(1943); IT AIN'T HAY(1943); RETURN OF THE RANGERS, THE(1943); SO'S YOUR UNCLE(1943); GANGSTERS OF THE FRONTIER(1944); I'M FROM ARKANSAS(1944); LADY, LET'S DANCE(1944); SPOOK TOWN(1944); YOUTH RUNS WILD(1944); PATRICK THE GREAT(1945); CRACK-UP(1946); CROSS MY HEART(1946); FALCON'S ADVENTURE, THE(1946); FALCON'S ALIBI, THE(1946); GENIUS AT WORK(1946); LADY LUCK(1946); NOCTURNE(1946); STEP BY STEP(1946); SUNSET PASS(1946); BEAT THE BAND(1947); CODE OF THE WEST(1947); CROSSFIRE(1947); DICK TRACY MEETS GRUESOME(1947); DICK TRACY'S DILEMMA(1947); NIGHT SONG(1947); SECRET LIFE OF WALTER MITTY, THE(1947); SINBAD THE SAILOR(1947); THUNDER MOUNTAIN(1947); UNDER THE TONTO RIM(1947); WOMAN ON THE BEACH, THE(1947); ALL MY SONS(1948); ARIZONA RANGER, THE(1948); IF YOU KNEW SUSIE(1948); MY DOG RUSTY(1948); PALEFACE, THE(1948); TRAIN TO ALCATRAZ(1948); ARCTIC MANHUNT(1949); DEAR WIFE(1949); DEATH VALLEY GUNFIGHTER(1949); FRANCIS(1949); I CHEATED THE LAW(1949); LEAVE IT TO HENRY(1949); MISS GRANT TAKES RICHMOND(1949); RECKLESS MOMENTS, THE(1949); RUSTY SAVES A LIFE(1949); STAGECOACH KID(1949); THEY LIVE BY NIGHT(1949); BEYOND THE PURPLE HILLS(1950); CONVICTED(1950); COW TOWN(1950); EMERGENCY WEDDING(1950); HOEDOWN(1950); IT'S A SMALL WORLD(1950); RIO GRANDE PATROL(1950); STORM WARNING(1950); TEA FOR TWO(1950); UNMASKED(1950); ARIZONA MANHUNT(1951); BIG CARNIVAL, THE(1951); DAY THE EARTH STOOD STILL, THE(1951); GUY WHO CAME BACK, THE(1951); HILLS OF UTAH(1951); HOME TOWN STORY(1951); RODEO KING AND THE SENORITA(1951); SILVER CITY BONANZA(1951); TAKE CARE OF MY LITTLE GIRL(1951); WHIRLWIND(1951); HIGH NOON(1952); MA AND PA KETTLE AT THE FAIR(1952); NARROW MARGIN, THE(1952); SCARLET ANGEL(1952); SNIPER, THE(1952); TARGET(1952); WAGON TEAM(1952); WE'RE NOT MARRIED(1952); BANDITS OF THE WEST(1953); LAW AND ORDER(1953); MARSHAL'S DAUGHTER, THE(1953); OLD OVERLAND TRAIL(1953); TUMBLEWEED(1953); HIGHWAY DRAGNET(1954); OUTLAW STALLION, THE(1954); 20,000 LEAGUES UNDER THE SEA(1954); NAKED STREET, THE(1955); WYOMING RENEGADES(1955); SHEEPMAN, THE(1958); POLLYANNA(1960)
Misc. Talkies
IN OLD MONTANA(1939); RIDIN' THE TRAIL(1940); TEXAS RENEGADES(1940)
Misc. Silents
TWIN TRIANGLE, THE(1916), d; BRAND'S DAUGHTER(1917), d; CLEAN GUN, THE(1917), d; DEVIL'S BAIT, THE(1917), d; FEET OF CLAY(1917), d; PHANTOM SHOTGUN, THE(1917), d; STOLEN PLAY, THE(1917), d; YELLOW BULLET, THE(1917), d

Harry Harvey, Jr.
RANGERS STEP IN, THE(1937); KING OF THE SIERRAS(1938); DANGER FLIGHT(1939); TWO-GUN TROUBADOR(1939); MANPOWER(1941); REMEMBER THE DAY(1941); WAGONS ROLL AT NIGHT, THE(1941); MOONLIGHT IN VERMONT(1943); SHOW BUSINESS(1944); ROUGHLY SPEAKING(1945); TREE GROWS IN BROOKLYN, A(1945); DANGEROUS YEARS(1947); DARK PAST, THE(1948); WOMAN OF DISTINCTION, A(1950); SHOTGUN(1955); FORBIDDEN PLANET(1956); TEA AND SYMPATHY(1956); TEAHOUSE OF THE AUGUST MOON, THE(1956); OPERATION PETTICOAT(1959); SPARTACUS(1960)

Harry Harvey, Sr.
KING OF THE SIERRAS(1938); NOB HILL(1945); KEY TO THE CITY(1950); OUTCASTS OF POKER FLAT, THE(1952); GLENN MILLER STORY, THE(1953); SHOWDOWN AT ABILENE(1956); MAN IN THE SHADOW(1957); SHOOT-OUT AT MEDICINE BEND(1957); RETURN OF DRACULA, THE(1958); CAT BALLOU(1965); RIDE BEYOND VENGEANCE(1966); TROUBLE WITH ANGELS, THE(1966)

Helen Harvey
HIGH TREASON(1951, Brit.); WHITE CORRIDORS(1952, Brit.)

Henry A. Harvey, Sr.
MURDER IS MY BEAT(1955)

Herk Harvey
CARNIVAL OF SOULS(1962), a, p&d

Hermione Harvey
VALUE FOR MONEY(1957, Brit.)

Hester Harvey
DOLLAR(1938, Swed.)

Jack Harvey
HEADIN' FOR TROUBLE(1931); RIDERS OF THE GOLDEN GULCH(1932); STRICTLY DYNAMITE(1934), w; COUNTRY GENTLEMEN(1937), w; PHANTOM OF 42ND STREET, THE(1945), w; LAST OF THE WILD HORSES(1948), w; LET'S LIVE A LITTLE(1948), w; UNKNOWN ISLAND(1948), w; GRAND CANYON(1949), w; CITY BENEATH THE SEA(1953), w; CHAFED ELBOWS(1967)
Misc. Silents
WOLF OF DEBT, THE(1915), d; LORDS OF HIGH DECISION, THE(1916), d

Jacqueline Harvey
DOCTOR FAUSTUS(1967, Brit.), a, ch

James Harvey
TO HAVE AND TO HOLD(1951, Brit.), ph; UNHOLY FOUR, THE(1954, Brit.), ph; STOLEN ASSIGNMENT(1955, Brit.), ph; STRANGE CASE OF DR. MANNING, THE(1958, Brit.), ph; HAND, THE(1960, Brit.), ph; JUNGLE STREET GIRLS(1963, Brit.), ph; IN TROUBLE WITH EVE(1964, Brit.), ph; MAN WHO COULDN'T WALK,

THE(1964, Brit.), ph; PLEASURE LOVERS, THE(1964, Brit.), ph

Jean G. Harvey
SOLID GOLD CADILLAC, THE(1956); BAND OF ANGELS(1957)

Jean Harvey
CHICAGO CALLING(1951); WEREWOLF, THE(1956); CIRCLE OF DECEPTON(1961, Brit.); AMBUSH IN LEOPARD STREET(1962, Brit.); DREAM MAKER, THE(1963, Brit.)

Jim Harvey
SPY IN THE SKY(1958), ph

Jimmy Harvey
TREACHERY ON THE HIGH SEAS(1939, Brit.), ph; ROSSITER CASE, THE(1950, Brit.), ph; CLOUDBURST(1952, Brit.), ph; SCOTLAND YARD INSPECTOR(1952, Brit.), ph; BLOOD ORANGE(1953, Brit.), ph; NOOSE FOR A LADY(1953, Brit.), ph; TERROR STREET(1953), ph; BLACK GLOVE(1954, Brit.), ph; HEATWAVE(1954, Brit.), ph; PAID TO KILL(1954, Brit.), ph; DEADLY GAME, THE(1955, Brit.), ph; LYONS IN PARIS, THE(1955, Brit.), ph; RACE FOR LIFE, A(1955, Brit.), ph; BLACK ICE, THE(1957, Brit.), ph; FIGHTING WILDCATS, THE(1957, Brit.), ph; LIGHT FINGERS(1957, Brit.), ph; MEN OF SHERWOOD FOREST(1957, Brit.), ph; UNDERCOVER GIRL(1957, Brit.), ph; YOU PAY YOUR MONEY(1957, Brit.), ph; DEATH OVER MY SHOULDER(1958, Brit.), ph; RUNAWAY, THE(1964, Brit.), ph

Jimmy W. Harvey
STRICTLY CONFIDENTIAL(1959, Brit.), ph; OPERATION CUPID(1960, Brit.), ph

Joan Harvey
PRETTY BOY FLOYD(1960); HANDS OF A STRANGER(1962)

John Harvey
FOUR JILLS IN A JEEP(1944); PIN UP GIRL(1944); SPIDER, THE(1945); GUNMAN HAS ESCAPED, A(1948, Brit.); DICK BARTON STRIKES BACK(1949, Brit.); PRIVATE ANGELO(1949, Brit.); CHANCE OF A LIFETIME(1950, Brit.); SILK NOOSE, THE(1950, Brit.); BLACK WIDOW(1951, Brit.); DARK LIGHT, THE(1951, Brit.); FILES FROM SCOTLAND YARD(1951, Brit.); FOUR DAYS(1951, Brit.); MAN WITH MY FACE, THE(1951); SMART ALEC(1951, Brit.); CASTLE IN THE AIR(1952, Brit.); LADY GODIVA RIDES AGAIN(1955, Brit.); LONG HAUL, THE(1957, Brit.); TRUE AS A TURTLE(1957, Brit.); X THE UNKNOWN(1957, Brit.); EDGE OF FURY(1958); MAN WHO WOULDN'T TALK, THE(1958, Brit.); UGLY DUCKLING, THE(1959, Brit.); STRANGLERS OF BOMBAY, THE(1960, Brit.); DOUBLE BUNK(1961, Brit.); TWO-WAY STRETCH(1961, Brit.); PHANTOM OF THE OPERA, THE(1962, Brit.); HEAVENS ABOVE!(1963, Brit.); KISS OF EVIL(1963, Brit.); WRONG ARM OF THE LAW, THE(1963, Brit.); CRIMSON BLADE, THE(1964, Brit.); JOEY BOY(1965, Brit.); PSYCHOPATH, THE(1966, Brit.); DEADLY BEES, THE(1967, Brit.); THEY CAME FROM BEYOND SPACE(1967, Brit.); CHALLENGE FOR ROBIN HOOD, A(1968, Brit.); SACCO AND VANZETTI(1971, Ital./Fr.); BLACK WINDMILL, THE(1974, Brit.)
Silents
NO BABIES WANTED(1928), d
Misc. Silents
WOMAN WHO BELIEVED, THE(1922), d; RIGHT MAN, THE(1925), d; KEEP GOING(1926), d

John Joseph Harvey
Silents
KAISER'S FINISH, THE(1918), d

John Martin Harvey
LYONS MAIL, THE(1931, Brit.)
Silents
ONLY WAY, THE(1926, Brit.)
Misc. Silents
BURGOMASTER OF STILEMONDE, THE(1928, Brit.)

Jolly Lee Harvey
MAYTIME(1937)

Ken Harvey
UNDERCOVER MAN, THE(1949); BRIGHT VICTORY(1951); YOU'RE IN THE NAVY NOW(1951); FLYING MATCHMAKER, THE(1970, Israel)

Kenneth Harvey
KISS THE BLOOD OFF MY HANDS(1948); FOURTEEN HOURS(1951); MOB, THE(1951)

Laurance Harvey
WALK ON THE WILD SIDE(1962)

Laurence Harvey
HOUSE OF DARKNESS(1948, Brit.); MAN FROM YESTERDAY, THE(1949, Brit.); MAN ON THE RUN(1949, Brit.); BLACK ROSE, THE(1950, Brit.); CAIRO ROAD(1950, Brit.); SCARLET THREAD(1951, Brit.); KILLER WALKS, A(1952, Brit.); I BELIEVE IN YOU(1953, Brit.); LANDFALL(1953, Brit.); TWILIGHT WOMEN(1953, Brit.); GOOD DIE YOUNG, THE(1954, Brit.); KING RICHARD AND THE CRUSADERS(1954); ROMEO AND JULIET(1954, Brit.); I AM A CAMERA(1955, Brit.); INNOCENTS IN PARIS(1955, Brit.); STORM OVER THE NILE(1955, Brit.); AFTER THE BALL(1957, Brit.); THREE MEN IN A BOAT(1958, Brit.); TRUTH ABOUT WOMEN, THE(1958, Brit.); EXPRESSO BONGO(1959, Brit.); ROOM AT THE TOP(1959, Brit.); SILENT ENEMY, THE(1959, Brit.); ALAMO, THE(1960); BUTTERFIELD 8(1960); LONG AND THE SHORT AND THE TALL, THE(1961, Brit.); SUMMER AND SMOKE(1961); TWO LOVES(1961); GIRL NAMED TAMIRO, A(1962); MANCHURIAN CANDIDATE, THE(1962); WONDERFUL WORLD OF THE BROTHERS ERIMM, THE(1962); CEREMONY, THE(1963, U.S./Span.), a, p&d, w; RUNNING MAN, THE(1963, Brit.); OF HUMAN BONDAGE(1964, Brit.); OUTRAGE, THE(1964); DARLING(1965, Brit.); LIFE AT THE TOP(1965, Brit.); SPY WITH A COLD NOSE, THE(1966, Brit.); DANDY IN ASPIC, A(1968, Brit.); WINTER'S TALE, THE(1968, Brit.); FIGHT FOR ROME(1969, Ger./Rum.); SHE AND HE(1969, Ital.), a, p; MAGIC CHRISTIAN, THE(1970, Brit.); WUSA(1970); ESCAPE TO THE SUN(1972, Fr./Ger./Israel); NIGHT WATCH(1973, Brit.); TENDER FLESH(1976), a, d
Misc. Talkies
REBUS(1969, Ger./Ital./Span./Arg.)

Lee Harvey
GORGEOUS HUSSY, THE(1936)

Len Harvey
BERMONDSEY KID, THE(1933, Brit.); EXCUSE MY GLOVE(1936, Brit.)

Lew Harvey
ARGYLE CASE, THE(1929); GREYHOUND LIMITED, THE(1929); BIG BOY(1930); HOLD EVERYTHING(1930); MAN TROUBLE(1930); SWEET MAMA(1930); BRITISH AGENT(1934); GAY BRIDE, THE(1934); MANHATTAN MELODRAMA(1934); FRISCO KID(1935); I FOUND STELLA PARISH(1935); NO MORE LADIES(1935); FIREFLY, THE(1937); HOLY TERROR, THE(1937); BLACKMAIL(1939); OKLAHOMA KID, THE(1939); ROARING TWENTIES, THE(1939); DANCE, GIRL, DANCE(1940); INVISI-

BLE STRIPES(1940); HONKY TONK(1941); IRON MAJOR, THE(1943); GILDA(1946); DESERT FURY(1947); TRAIL STREET(1947); RETURN OF THE BADMEN(1948); FILE ON THELMA JORDAN, THE(1950)
Silents
BROADWAY AFTER DARK(1924); EVE'S LOVER(1925); LADY OF THE NIGHT(1925); PRETTY LADIES(1925); RANGER OF THE BIG PINES(1925); FIGHTING EDGE(1926); WOLF'S CLOTHING(1927)

Lilian Harvey
KNIGHT IN LONDON, A(1930, Brit./Ger.); LOVE WALTZ, THE(1930, Ger.); TEMPORARY WIDOW, THE(1930, Ger./Brit.); LEAP OF FAITH(1931, Brit.); HAPPY EVER AFTER(1932, Ger./Brit.); EMPRESS AND I, THE(1933, Ger.); HEART SONG(1933, Brit.); INVITATION TO THE WALTZ(1935, Brit.); BLACK ROSES(1936, Ger.)

Lillian Harvey
CONGRESS DANCES(1932, Ger.); MY LIPS BETRAY(1933); MY WEAKNESS(1933); I AM SUZANNE(1934); LET'S LIVE TONIGHT(1935)

Lola Harvey
KISS ME, SERGEANT(1930, Brit.), a, w; NOT SO QUIET ON THE WESTERN FRONT(1930, Brit.), w; WHY SAILORS LEAVE HOME(1930, Brit.), a, w; OLD SOLDIERS NEVER DIE(1931, Brit.), w; POOR OLD BILL(1931, Brit.), w; WHAT A NIGHT!(1931, Brit.), a, w; OLD SPANISH CUSTOMERS(1932, Brit.), a, w; TO-NIGHT'S THE NIGHT(1932, Brit.), a, w; POLITICAL PARTY, A(1933, Brit.), w; PRIDE OF THE FORCE, THE(1933, Brit.), a, w; DOCTOR'S ORDERS(1934, Brit.), w; LOST IN THE LEGION(1934, Brit.), a, w; OUTCAST, THE(1934, Brit.), w

Lou Harvey
STORY OF SEABISCUIT, THE(1949)

Lyn Harvey
TICKET TO HEAVEN(1981)

M. B. Harvey
Silents
NOTORIOUS MRS. SANDS, THE(1920), w

Margaret Harvey
CAESAR AND CLEOPATRA(1946, Brit.)

Marilyn Harvey
ASTOUNDING SHE-MONSTER, THE(1958); ROSEMARY'S BABY(1968)

Marshall Harvey
LUNCH WAGON(1981), w; SWORD AND THE SORCERER, THE(1982), ed

Martin Harvey
DARK JOURNEY(1937, Brit.)
Misc. Silents
BROKEN MELODY, THE(1916, Brit.); BREED OF THE TRESHAMS, THE(1920, Brit.)

Michael Harvey
KNUTE ROCKNE–ALL AMERICAN(1940); SEA HAWK, THE(1940); THEY DRIVE BY NIGHT(1940); FEAR IN THE NIGHT(1947); TYCOON(1947); BERLIN EXPRESS(1948); RETURN OF THE BADMEN(1948); DUCK, YOU SUCKER!(1972, Ital.); DON'T LOOK IN THE BASEMENT(1973)

Michael Martin Harvey
ROBBER SYMPHONY, THE(1937, Brit.); CAESAR AND CLEOPATRA(1946, Brit.); MONKEY'S PAW, THE(1948, Brit.); CASE OF CHARLES PEACE, THE(1949, Brit.)
Silents
ONLY WAY, THE(1926, Brit.)

Mike Harvey
VELVET TRAP, THE(1966); STATUE, THE(1971, Brit.)

Morris Harvey
MAN FROM CHICAGO, THE(1931, Brit.); DOWN OUR STREET(1932, Brit.); OFFICE GIRL, THE(1932, Brit.); FACING THE MUSIC(1933, Brit.); SOUTHERN MAID, A(1933, Brit.); FOR LOVE OR MONEY(1934, Brit.); SING AS WE GO(1934, Brit.); HELLO SWEETHEART(1935, Brit.); LOOK UP AND LAUGH(1935, Brit.); LOVE TEST, THE(1935, Brit.); SCROOGE(1935, Brit.); SQUIBS(1935, Brit.); CROWN VS STEVENS(1936); DREAMS COME TRUE(1936, Brit.); IN THE SOUP(1936, Brit.); MYSTERIOUS MR. DAVIS, THE(1936, Brit.); TROPICAL TROUBLE(1936, Brit.); SKY'S THE LIMIT, THE(1937, Brit.); CAPTAIN MOONLIGHT(1940, Brit.); CROOKS TOUR(1940, Brit.); LILAC DOMINO, THE(1940, Brit.); OLD MOTHER RILEY IN BUSINESS(1940, Brit.); TWENTY-ONE DAYS TOGETHER(1940, Brit.); GREAT MR. HANDEL, THE(1942, Brit.); LET THE PEOPLE SING(1942, Brit.); ROSE OF TRALEE(1942, Brit.); OLD MOTHER RILEY OVERSEAS(1943, Brit.)

Muriel Martin Harvey
Silents
HARD WAY, THE(1916, Brit.)

Nita Harvey
SWINGING THE LEAD(1934, Brit.); VANITY(1935); WHO'S YOUR FATHER?(1935, Brit.); SKY RAIDERS, THE(1938, Brit.)

Orwin Harvey
PRISONER OF ZENDA, THE(1979); FINAL COUNTDOWN, THE(1980); TOY, THE(1982)
1984
FIRESTARTER(1984)

Paul Harvey
AWFUL TRUTH, THE(1929); WISER SEX, THE(1932); ADVICE TO THE LOVE-LORN(1933); AFFAIRS OF CELLINI, THE(1934); BORN TO BE BAD(1934); CHARLIE CHAN'S COURAGE(1934); HANDY ANDY(1934); HOUSE OF ROTHSCHILD, THE(1934); KID MILLIONS(1934); LOOKING FOR TROUBLE(1934); PRESIDENT VANISHES, THE(1934); SHE WAS A LADY(1934); WICKED WOMAN, A(1934); ALIBI IKE(1935); BROADWAY MELODY OF 1936(1935); FOUR HOURS TO KILL(1935); GOIN' TO TOWN(1935); I'LL LOVE YOU ALWAYS(1935); THANKS A MILLION(1935); WHOLE TOWN'S TALKING, THE(1935); AUGUST WEEK-END(1936, Brit.); GENERAL DIED AT DAWN, THE(1936); PETRIFIED FOREST, THE(1936); POSTAL INSPECTOR(1936); PRIVATE NUMBER(1936); RETURN OF SOPHIE LANG, THE(1936); ROSE OF THE RANCHO(1936); THREE MEN ON A HORSE(1936); WALKING DEAD, THE(1936); WITNESS CHAIR, THE(1936); YELLOWSTONE(1936); BIG CITY(1937); BLACK LEGION, THE(1937); DEVIL IS DRIVING, THE(1937); HIGH FLYERS(1937); MIND YOUR OWN BUSINESS(1937); MY DEAR MISS ALDRICH(1937); ON AGAIN-OFF AGAIN(1937); PLAINSMAN, THE(1937); SOLDIER AND THE LADY, THE(1937); 23 ½ HOURS LEAVE(1937); ALGIERS(1938); CHARLIE CHAN IN HONOLULU(1938); HIGGINS FAMILY, THE(1938); IF I WERE KING(1938); I'LL GIVE A MILLION(1938); LOVE ON A BUDGET(1938); REBECCA OF SUNNYBROOK FARM(1938); SISTERS, THE(1938); SLIGHT CASE OF MURDER, A(1938); THERE'S THAT WOMAN AGAIN(1938); FORGOTTEN WOMAN, THE(1939); GORILLA, THE(1939); MEET DR. CHRISTIAN(1939); MR. MOTO IN DANGER ISLAND(1939); NEVER SAY DIE(1939); NEWS IS MADE AT NIGHT(1939); STANLEY AND LIVINGSTONE(1939); THEY SHALL HAVE MUSIC(1939); ARIZONA(1940); BROTHER RAT AND A BABY(1940);

DR. EHRLICH'S MAGIC BULLET(1940); HIGH SCHOOL(1940); MANHATTAN HEARTBEAT(1940); MARINES FLY HIGH, THE(1940); MARYLAND(1940); SAILOR'S LADY(1940); TYPHOON(1940); BEHIND THE NEWS(1941); GREAT GUNS(1941); HIGH SIERRA(1941); LAW OF THE TROPICS(1941); OUT OF THE FOG(1941); PUDDIN' HEAD(1941); REMEMBER THE DAY(1941); RIDE ON VAQUERO(1941); RISE AND SHINE(1941); THREE GIRLS ABOUT TOWN(1941); YOU BELONG TO ME(1941); YOU'RE IN THE ARMY NOW(1941); BLONDIE'S BLESSED EVENT(1942); HEART OF THE GOLDEN WEST(1942); MAN WHO WOULDN'T DIE, THE(1942); MOONLIGHT MASQUERADE(1942); TRAGEDY AT MIDNIGHT, A(1942); YOU CAN'T ESCAPE FOREVER(1942); MAN FROM MUSIC MOUNTAIN(1943); MYSTERY BROADCAST(1943); THANK YOUR LUCKY STARS(1943); FOUR JILLS IN A JEEP(1944); HENRY ALDRICH PLAYS CUPID(1944); IN THE MEANTIME, DARLING(1944); JAMBOREE(1944); CHICAGO KID, THE(1945); DON'T FENCE ME IN(1945); HORN BLOWS AT MIDNIGHT, THE(1945); MAMA LOVES PAPA(1945); PILLOW TO POST(1945); SOUTHERNER, THE(1945); SPELLBOUND(1945); STATE FAIR(1945); SWINGIN' ON A RAINBOW(1945); THOROUGHBREDS(1945); BAMBOO BLONDE, THE(1946); BLONDIE'S LUCKY DAY(1946); EASY TO WED(1946); GAY BLADES(1946); HELLDORADO(1946); IN FAST COMPANY(1946); THEY MADE ME A KILLER(1946); UP GOES MAISIE(1946); CARTER CASE, THE(1947); DANGER STREET(1947); HIGH BARBAREE(1947); LATE GEORGE APLEY, THE(1947); OUT OF THE BLUE(1947); WHEN A GIRL'S BEAUTIFUL(1947); WYOMING(1947); BLONDIE'S REWARD(1948); CALL NORTHSIDE 777(1948); FAMILY HONEYMOON(1948); GIVE MY REGARDS TO BROADWAY(1948); LIGHTNIN' IN THE FOREST(1948); SMUGGLERS' COVE(1948); SOUTHERN YANKEE, A(1948); SPEED TO SPARE(1948); WATERFRONT AT MIDNIGHT(1948); DOWN TO THE SEA IN SHIPS(1949); DUKE OF CHICAGO(1949); FOUNTAINHEAD, THE(1949); GIRL FROM JONES BEACH, THE(1949); JOHN LOVES MARY(1949); MAKE BELIEVE BALLROOM(1949); MR. BELVEDERE GOES TO COLLEGE(1949); TAKE ONE FALSE STEP(1949); FATHER OF THE BRIDE(1950); FLYING MISSILE(1950); LAWLESS, THE(1950); MILKMAN, THE(1950); RIDING HIGH(1950); SIDE STREET(1950); SKIPPER SURPRISED HIS WIFE, THE(1950); STELLA(1950); THREE LITTLE WORDS(1950); TICKET TO TOMAHAWK(1950); UNMASKED(1950); WHEN WILLIE COMES MARCHING HOME(1950); YELLOW CAB MAN, THE(1950); EXCUSE MY DUST(1951); FATHER'S LITTLE DIVIDEND(1951); LET'S GO NAVY(1951); THUNDER IN GOD'S COUNTRY(1951); UP FRONT(1951); DREAMBOAT(1952); FIRST TIME, THE(1952); HAS ANYBODY SEEN MY GAL?(1952); HERE COME THE NELSONS(1952); SKIRTS AHOY!(1952); APRIL IN PARIS(1953); CALAMITY JANE(1953); GIRL WHO HAD EVERYTHING, THE(1953); REMAINS TO BE SEEN(1953); SABRINA(1954); HIGH SOCIETY(1955); THREE FOR THE SHOW(1955)

Peter Harvey
PRIVATE ENTERPRISE, A(1975, Brit.), art d
1984
CHINESE BOXES(1984, Ger./Brit.), ph; GHOST DANCE(1984, Brit.), ph

Phil Harvey
FOUR GIRLS IN TOWN(1956); I'VE LIVED BEFORE(1956); WRITTEN ON THE WIND(1956); DEADLY MANTIS, THE(1957); LAND UNKNOWN, THE(1957); MONOLITH MONSTERS, THE(1957); TARNISHED ANGELS, THE(1957); BIG BEAT, THE(1958); MONSTER ON THE CAMPUS(1958); PERFECT FURLOUGH(1958); TOUCH OF EVIL(1958); VOICE IN THE MIRROR(1958); WILD HERITAGE(1958); WHY MUST I DIE?(1960)

R. Paul Harvey
Misc. Silents
MEN WHO HAVE MADE LOVE TO ME(1918)

Raymond Harvey
GOIN' COCONUTS(1978), w

Capt. Raymond Harvey
FIXED BAYONETS(1951), tech adv

Richard Harvey
BEYOND THE LIMIT(1983), m; HOUSE OF LONG SHADOWS, THE(1983, Brit.), m
1984
WINTER FLIGHT(1984, Brit.), m

Robert Harvey
1984
TIGHTROPE(1984)

Robin Harvey
TRAP DOOR, THE(1980)

Rodney Harvey
1984
DELIVERY BOYS(1984); MIXED BLOOD(1984)

Ron Harvey
FIST OF FEAR, TOUCH OF DEATH(1980), a, w

Russ Harvey
DUNGEONS OF HARROW(1964); NO MAN'S LAND(1964), a, p,d&w

Sharon Harvey
SWEET CHARITY(1969); AIRPORT(1970)

Susan Harvey
LAND RAIDERS(1969); ONE BRIEF SUMMER(1971, Brit.)

Tom Harvey
LUCK OF GINGER COFFEY, THE(1964, U.S./Can.); LAWYER, THE(1969); MY SIDE OF THE MOUNTAIN(1969); HOMER(1970); DEALING: OR THE BERKELEY-TO-BOSTON FORTY-BRICK LOST-BAG BLUES(1971); FORTUNE AND MEN'S EYES(1971, U.S./Can.); SECOND WIND(1976, Can.); SILENCE OF THE NORTH(1981, Can.); STRANGE BREW(1983)
1984
MRS. SOFFEL(1984)
Misc. Talkies
ONLY WAY OUT IS DEAD, THE(1970)

Tony Harvey
TAKING OFF(1971)

Tracey Harvey
CLINIC, THE(1983, Aus.)

Verna Harvey
NIGHT COMERS, THE(1971, Brit.); CHATO'S LAND(1972); THAT'LL BE THE DAY(1974, Brit.)

W. Harvey
FLYING SQUAD, THE(1940, Brit.), ph

W.J. Harvey
DARK SECRET(1949, Brit.), ph

Walter Harvey
DREYFUS CASE, THE(1931, Brit.), ph; HOBSON'S CHOICE(1931, Brit.), ph; LOVE LIES(1931, Brit.), ph; MAN FROM CHICAGO, THE(1931, Brit.), ph; BROTHER ALFRED(1932, Brit.), ph; FACING THE MUSIC(1933, Brit.), ph; MONEY TALKS(1933, Brit.), ph; THEIR NIGHT OUT(1933, Brit.), ph; SENSATION(1936, Brit.), ph; BULLDOG DRUMMOND AT BAY(1937, Brit.), ph; DOMINANT SEX, THE(1937, Brit.), ph; RIVER OF UNREST(1937, Brit.), ph; TENTH MAN, THE(1937, Brit.), ph; YELLOW SANDS(1938, Brit.), ph; YES, MADAM?(1938, Brit.), ph; JUST WILLIAM(1939, Brit.), ph; NORTH SEA PATROL(1939, Brit.), ph; CASTLE OF CRIMES(1940, Brit.), ph; IT HAPPENED TO ONE MAN(1941, Brit.), ph; MY WIFE'S FAMILY(1941, Brit.), ph; SPRING MEETING(1941, Brit.), ph; TERROR, THE(1941, Brit.), ph; SPELL OF AMY NUGENT, THE(1945, Brit.), ph; SONG FOR TOMORROW, A(1948, Brit.), ph; BADGER'S GREEN(1949, Brit.), ph; LADY CRAVED EXCITEMENT, THE(1950, Brit.), ph; SOMEONE AT THE DOOR(1950, Brit.), ph; WHAT THE BUTLER SAW(1950, Brit.), ph; BLACK WIDOW(1951, Brit.), ph; CASE FOR PC 49, A(1951, Brit.), ph; DARK LIGHT, THE(1951, Brit.), ph; DEAD ON COURSE(1952, Brit.), ph; DEATH OF AN ANGEL(1952, Brit.), ph; GAMBLER AND THE LADY, THE(1952, Brit.), ph; MAN BAIT(1952, Brit.), ph; STOLEN FACE(1952, Brit.), ph; WHISPERING SMITH VERSUS SCOTLAND YARD(1952, Brit.), ph; BAD BLONDE(1953, Brit.), ph; FAMILY AFFAIR(1954, Brit.), ph; SAINT'S GIRL FRIDAY, THE(1954, Brit.), ph; GLASS TOMB, THE(1955, Brit.), ph; STOLEN FACE(1952, Brit.), ph; ONE WAY OUT(1955, Brit.), ph; BLONDE BAIT(1956, U.S./Brit.), ph; THE CREEPING UNKNOWN(1956, Brit.), ph; BREAK IN THE CIRCLE, THE(1957, Brit.), ph

Walter J. Harvey
BIG CHANCE, THE(1957, Brit.), ph; KILL HER GENTLY(1958, Brit.), ph; BROTH OF A BOY(1959, Brit.), ph; END OF THE LINE, THE(1959, Brit.), ph; MURDER IN EDEN(1962, Brit.), ph; SHADOW OF FEAR(1963, Brit.), ph

Walter James Harvey
MEIN KAMPF-MY CRIMES(1940, Brit.), ph

William Fryer Harvey
BEAST WITH FIVE FINGERS, THE(1946), w

Wilma Harvey
YOUR NUMBER'S UP(1931)

Dixon R. Harvin
CORREGIDOR(1943), p

Ronn Harvin
NORTH STAR, THE(1943)

Kaarina Harvistola
MONTENEGRO(1981, Brit./Swed.)

Dixon R. Harwin
DEADLY GAME, THE(1941), p; DOUBLE TROUBLE(1941), p; CITY OF SILENT MEN(1942), p; INSIDE THE LAW(1942), p; THEY RAID BY NIGHT(1942), p

Anthony Harwood
ADDING MACHINE, THE(1969)

Bill Harwood
MISSISSIPPI(1935)

Bo Harwood
MINNIE AND MOSKOWITZ(1971), md; WOMAN UNDER THE INFLUENCE, A(1974), m; KILLING OF A CHINESE BOOKIE, THE(1976), m; OPENING NIGHT(1977), m; HAPPY BIRTHDAY TO ME(1981), m
1984
LOVE STREAMS(1984), m

Charles Harwood
DIE LAUGHING(1980)

Florence Harwood
WOMAN IN CHAINS(1932, Brit.); SHOW GOES ON, THE(1937, Brit.)

H.M. Harwood
MAN IN POSSESSION, THE(1931), w; CYNARA(1932), w; LOOKING FORWARD(1933), w; QUEEN CHRISTINA(1933), w; PERSONAL PROPERTY(1937), w

Harold Marsh Harwood
Silents
'MARRIAGE LICENSE?'(1926), w

Johanna Harwood
DR. NO(1962, Brit.), w; CALL ME BWANA(1963, Brit.), w; FROM RUSSIA WITH LOVE(1963, Brit.), w; DON'T PLAY WITH MARTIANS(1967, Fr.), w

John Harwood
TENTH MAN, THE(1937, Brit.); WEEKEND MILLIONAIRE(1937, Brit.); PERSECUTION AND ASSASSINATION OF JEAN-PAUL MARAT AS PERFORMED BY THE INMATES OF THE ASYLUM OF CHARENTON UNDER THE DIRECTION OF THE MARQUIS DE SADE, THE(1967, Brit.)

Natasha Harwood
GIRL WITH A PISTOL, THE(1968, Ital.)

Ronald Harwood
BARBER OF STAMFORD HILL, THE(1963, Brit.), w; PRIVATE POTTER(1963, Brit.), w; HIGH WIND IN JAMAICA, A(1965), w; ARRIVEDERCI, BABY!(1966, Brit.), p,d&w; DIAMONDS FOR BREAKFAST(1968, Brit.), w; GIRL WITH A PISTOL, THE(1968, Ital.), w; CROMWELL(1970, Brit.), w; SUDDEN TERROR(1970, Brit.), w; ONE DAY IN THE LIFE OF IVAN DENISOVICH(1971, U.S./Brit./Norway), w; OPERATION DAYBREAK(1976, U.S./Brit./Czech.), w; DRESSER, THE(1983), w

Shuna Harwood
FULL CIRCLE(1977, Brit./Can.), cos; ODD JOB, THE(1978, Brit.), cos; MISSIONARY, THE(1982), cos
1984
SWORD OF THE VALIANT(1984, Brit.), cos

Stewart Harwood
ODD JOB, THE(1978, Brit.); BLOODY KIDS(1983, Brit.)

Stuart Harwood
SQUEEZE, THE(1977, Brit.); EYE OF THE NEEDLE(1981)

Edward S. Harworth
MUTINY(1952), art d

Claude Harz
HAMLET(1964); HOMER(1970), w; GET BACK(1973, Can.), w

Bernard Harzbrun
FAR COUNTRY, THE(1955), art d

Wojciech J. Has
PARTINGS(1962, Pol.), d, w; SARAGOSSA MANUSCRIPT, THE(1972, Pol.), d

Ali Mohammad Hasan
JERUSALEM FILE, THE(1972, U.S./Israel)

Olive Hasbrouck
CLEAR THE DECKS(1929)
Silents
RIDGEWAY OF MONTANA(1924); COHENS AND KELLYS, THE(1926); REGULAR SCOUT, A(1926); RUSTLER'S RANCH(1926); WOMAN WHO DID NOT CARE, THE(1927); ROYAL RIDER, THE(1929)
Misc. Silents
BIG TIMBER(1924); CALL OF COURAGE, THE(1925); HIDDEN LOOT(1925); BORDER SHERIFF, THE(1926); RIDIN' RASCAL, THE(1926); SIX SHOOTIN' ROMANCE, A(1926); FIGHTING THREE, THE(1927); INTERFERIN' GENT, THE(1927); OBLIGIN' BUCKAROO, THE(1927); RIDE 'EM HIGH(1927); RIDIN' ROWDY, THE(1927); SET FREE(1927); SHAMROCK AND THE ROSE, THE(1927); TEARIN' INTO TROUBLE(1927); WHITE PEBBLES(1927); COWBOY CAVALIER, THE(1928); DESPERATE COURAGE(1928); FLYIN' COWBOY, THE(1928); CLEAR THE DECKS(1929)

Josie Hascall
TOUCH OF FLESH, THE(1960)

Lon Haschal
HIS WOMAN(1931)

Paul S. Haschke
SYNCOPATION(1929), w

Annemarie Hase
CITY OF TORMENT(1950, Ger.)

Keiji Hasebe
ENJO(1959, Jap.), w; ODD OBSESSION(1961, Jap.), w; INSECT WOMAN, THE(1964, Jap.), w; UNHOLY DESIRE(1964, Jap.), w; KURAGEJIMA-LEGENDS FROM A SOUTHERN ISLAND(1970, Jap.), w; BANISHED(1978, Jap.), w

Toshiro Hasebe
HOTSPRINGS HOLIDAY(1970, Jap.), w

Martijn Hasebos
1984
QUESTION OF SILENCE(1984, Neth.), m

Akio Hasegawa
SHE AND HE(1967, Jap.); FALCON FIGHTERS, THE(1970, Jap.)

Hideo Hasegawa
1984
BALLAD OF NARAYAMA, THE(1984, Jap.)

Kazuhiko Hasegawa
MAN WHO STOLE THE SUN, THE(1980, Jap.), d, w

Kazuo Hasegawa
GATE OF HELL(1954, Jap.); ACTOR'S REVENGE, AN(1963, Jap.); GREAT WALL, THE(1965, Jap.)

Kiyoshi Hasegawa
SUN ABOVE, DEATH BELOW(1969, Jap.), ph; WAR OF THE MONSTERS(1972, Jap.), ph; HINOTORI(1980, Jap.), ph

Machiko Hasegawa
SECRETS OF A WOMAN'S TEMPLE(1969, Jap.)

Uhei Hasegawa
SCOUNDREL, THE(1935)

Jaroslav Hasek
SCHWEIK'S NEW ADVENTURES(1943, Brit.), w

Jaroslaw Hasek
GOOD SOLDIER SCHWEIK, THE(1963, Ger.), w

Vlastimil Hasek
DEVIL'S TRAP, THE(1964, Czech.); DEATH OF TARZAN, THE(1968, Czech)

Irwin Hasen
DONDI(1961), w

Walter Hasenclever
RENDEZ-VOUS(1932, Ger.), w

Joyce Hash
HORROR HIGH(1974)

Joye Hash
LAST PICTURE SHOW, THE(1971)

Hash the Dog
Silents
ROMANCE ROAD(1925)

Robert C. Hasha
BEAUTY ON PARADE(1950)

Joe Hasham
NO. 96(1974, Aus.)

Mark Hashfield
UNDERCOVER GIRL(1957, Brit.); THREE MEN IN A BOAT(1958, Brit.)

Ed Hashim
GHOST TOWN(1956); QUINCANNON, FRONTIER SCOUT(1956)

Edmund Hashim
OUTSIDER, THE(1962); AND NOW MIGUEL(1966); HELLFIGHTERS(1968); SHAFT(1971)

Isao Hashimoto
LIVE YOUR OWN WAY(1970, Jap.)

Kiyoshi Hashimoto
PANDA AND THE MAGIC SERPENT(1961, Jap.), art d

Ko Hashimoto
KILL(1968, Jap.)

Shinobu Hashimoto
RASHOMON(1951, Jap.), w; SEVEN SAMURAI, THE(1956, Jap.), w; HIDDEN FORTRESS, THE(1959, Jap.), w; IKIRU(1960, Jap.), w; I BOMBED PEARL HARBOR(1961, Jap.), w; THRONE OF BLOOD(1961, Jap.), w; LOWER DEPTHS, THE(1962, Jap.), w; HAHAKIRI(1963, Jap.), w; PRESSURE OF GUILT(1964, Jap.), w; PRODIGAL SON, THE(1964, Jap.), w; SAMURAI ASSASSIN(1965, Jap.), w; WHITE ROSE OF HONG KONG(1965, Jap.), w; I LIVE IN FEAR(1967, Jap.), w; REBELLION(1967, Jap.), w; SWORD OF DOOM, THE(1967, Jap.), w; EMPEROR AND A GENERAL, THE(1968, Jap.), w; UNDER THE BANNER OF SAMURAI(1969, Jap.), w; DODESKA-DEN(1970, Jap.), w; TENCHU!(1970, Jap.), w; YELLOW DOG(1973, Brit.), w; PROPHECIES OF NOSTRADAMUS(1974, Jap.), w; TIDAL WAVE(1975, U.S./Jap.), w

Nick Hasir
POSTMAN ALWAYS RINGS TWICE, THE(1981)

Sophia Haskas
CATHY'S CHILD(1979, Aus.)

Al Haskel
I DREAM TOO MUCH(1935); SILVER LODE(1954)

Leonhard Haskel
Misc. Silents
STREET, THE(1927, Ger.)

Al Haskell
DESPERATE TRAILS(1939); KANSAS TERRORS, THE(1939); MAN FROM SUNDOWN, THE(1939); MEXICALI ROSE(1939); ROUGH RIDERS' ROUNDUP(1939); TEXAS TERRORS(1940); DOWN MEXICO WAY(1941); MASKED RIDER, THE(1941); SHERIFF OF TOMBSTONE(1941); WRANGLER'S ROOST(1941); WYOMING WILDCAT(1941); LONE STAR VIGILANTES, THE(1942); WESTERN CYCLONE(1943); MASQUERADE IN MEXICO(1945); SPANISH MAIN, THE(1945); ROARING WESTWARD(1949); CRISIS(1950); STRANGER WORE A GUN, THE(1953); VIGILANTE TERROR(1953)

Ara Haskell
HUMAN SIDE, THE(1934)

David Haskell
GODSPELL(1973); DEAL OF THE CENTURY(1983)
1984
BODY DOUBLE(1984)

Helen Haskell
Silents
PAIR OF SILK STOCKINGS, A(1918)

Jack Haskell
BRIDE OF THE REGIMENT(1930), ch; SHOW GIRL IN HOLLYWOOD(1930), ch; SONG OF THE FLAME(1930), ch; VIENNESE NIGHTS(1930), ch; MYRT AND MARGE(1934), ch; POOR LITTLE RICH GIRL(1936), ch; HOLY TERROR, THE(1937), ch; THIS IS MY AFFAIR(1937), ch; WAKE UP AND LIVE(1937), ch

Jean Haskell
Silents
SOULS FOR SALE(1923)

Jimmie Haskell
LOVE IN A GOLDFISH BOWL(1961), m, md; GUN HAWK, THE(1963), m&md; SURF PARTY(1964), m; BLACK SPURS(1965), m; I'LL TAKE SWEDEN(1965), m; LOVE AND KISSES(1965), m; TOWN TAMER(1965), m; WILD ON THE BEACH(1965), m; APACHE UPRISING(1966), m; JOHNNY RENO(1966), m; WACO(1966), m; FORT UTAH(1967), m; HOSTILE GUNS(1967), m; RED TOMAHAWK(1967), m; ARIZONA BUSHWHACKERS(1968), m; BUCKSKIN(1968), m; WICKED DREAMS OF PAULA SCHULTZ, THE(1968), m; 1,000 PLANE RAID, THE(1969), m, md; ZACHARIAH(1971), m; HONKERS, THE(1972), m; NIGHT OF THE LEPUS(1972), m; DIRTY MARY, CRAZY LARRY(1974), m; LIPSTICK(1976), m; DEATH GAME(1977), m; JOYRIDE(1977), m; HARD COUNTRY(1981), m

Peter Haskell
FINNEGANS WAKE(1965); CHRISTINA(1974, Can.)
Misc. Talkies
LEGEND OF EARL DURAND, THE(1974)

Byron Hasken
'TIL WE MEET AGAIN(1940), spec eff

Trevor Hasketh
KES(1970, Brit.)

Byron Haskin
CAUGHT IN THE FOG(1928), ph; SINGING FOOL, THE(1928), ph; GLAD RAG DOLL, THE(1929), ph; MADONNA OF AVENUE A(1929), ph; REDEEMING SIN, THE(1929), ph; ONE EMBARRASSING NIGHT(1930, Brit.), d; GUILTY GENERATION, THE(1931), ph; IT'S TOUGH TO BE FAMOUS(1932), ph; SIDE STREETS(1934), ph; BLACK FURY(1935), ph; MIDSUMMER'S NIGHT'S DREAM, A(1935), spec eff; PERSONAL MAID'S SECRET(1935), ph; COLLEEN(1936), ed; I MARRIED A DOCTOR(1936), ph; STAGE STRUCK(1936), ph; GREEN LIGHT(1937), ph; PERFECT SPECIMEN, THE(1937), spec eff; SLIM(1937), spec eff; SUBMARINE D-1(1937), spec eff; GOLD IS WHERE YOU FIND IT(1938), spec eff; DODGE CITY(1939), spec eff; PRIVATE LIVES OF ELIZABETH AND ESSEX, THE(1939), spec eff; ROARING TWENTIES, THE(1939), spec eff; WE ARE NOT ALONE(1939), spec eff; BROTHER ORCHID(1940), spec eff; DISPATCH FROM REUTERS, A(1940), spec eff; FIGHTING 69TH, THE(1940), spec eff; FLOWING GOLD(1940), spec eff; INVISIBLE STRIPES(1940), spec eff; IT ALL CAME TRUE(1940), spec eff; KNUTE ROCKNE-ALL AMERICAN(1940), spec eff; SANTA FE TRAIL(1940), spec eff; SEA HAWK, THE(1940), spec eff; THEY DRIVE BY NIGHT(1940), spec eff; TORRID ZONE(1940), spec eff; VIRGINIA CITY(1940), spec eff; CITY, FOR CONQUEST(1941), spec eff; DIVE BOMBER(1941), spec eff; GREAT LIE, THE(1941), spec eff; HIGH SIERRA(1941), spec eff; MANPOWER(1941), spec eff; SEA WOLF, THE(1941), spec eff; WAGONS ROLL AT NIGHT, THE(1941), spec eff; ACROSS THE PACIFIC(1942), spec eff; IN THIS OUR LIFE(1942), spec eff; WILD BILL HICKOK RIDES(1942), spec eff; WINGS FOR THE EAGLE(1942), spec eff; TRUCK BUSTERS(1943), spec eff; ARSENIC AND OLD LACE(1944), spec eff; PASSAGE TO MARSEILLE(1944), spec eff; MAN-EATER OF KUMAON(1948), d; TOO LATE FOR TEARS(1949), d; TREASURE ISLAND(1950, Brit.), d; SILVER CITY(1951), d; TARZAN'S PERIL(1951), d; WARPATH(1951), d; DENVER AND RIO GRANDE(1952), d; HIS MAJESTY O'KEEFE(1953), d; NAKED JUNGLE, THE(1953), d; WAR OF THE WORLDS, THE(1953), d; LONG JOHN SILVER(1954, Aus.), d; CONQUEST OF SPACE(1955), d; BOSS, THE(1956), d; FIRST TEXAN, THE(1956), d; FROM THE EARTH TO THE MOON(1958), d; LITTLE SAVAGE, THE(1959), d; JET OVER THE ATLANTIC(1960), d; SEPTEMBER STORM(1960), d; ARMORED COMMAND(1961), d; CAPTAIN SINDBAD(1963), d; ROBINSON CRUSOE ON MARS(1964), d; POWER, THE(1968), d
Silents
SLANDER THE WOMAN(1923), ph; GINSBERG THE GREAT(1927), d; IRISH HEARTS(1927), d; MATINEE LADIES(1927), d
Misc. Silents
SIREN, THE(1927), d

Paul Haskin
BLOODEATERS(1980)

Byron Haskins
ON TRIAL(1928), ph; DEADLINE, THE(1932), ph; AS THE EARTH TURNS(1934), ph; I WALK ALONE(1948), d
Silents
ON THIN ICE(1925), ph; ACROSS THE PACIFIC(1926), ph; DON JUAN(1926), ph; SEA BEAST, THE(1926), ph; WOLF'S CLOTHING(1927), ph

Edith Haskins
HOUSE ACROSS THE BAY, THE(1940)

Grace S. Haskins
Silents
  JUST LIKE A WOMAN(1923), w
James Haskins
1984
  COTTON CLUB, THE(1984), w
Jamie Haskins
  HE KNOWS YOU'RE ALONE(1980)
Susan Haskins
  BETWEEN THE LINES(1977)
Courtney Haslam
  TIME OF YOUR LIFE, THE(1948), cos
George Haslam
  GHOST SHIP(1953, Brit.), art d; JOHN OF THE FAIR(1962, Brit.), art d
Heorge Haslam
  HOUSE OF DARKNESS(1948, Brit.), art d
Berit Rytter Hasle
  EDVARD MUNCH(1976, Norway/Swed.)
William Haslem
  CRIMES OF THE FUTURE(1969, Can.)
Emil Hasler
  BLUE ANGEL, THE(1930, Ger.), set d; M(1933, Ger.), prod d, art d; WHAT WOMEN DREAM(1933, Ger.), art d; DIE FASTNACHTSBEICHTE(1962, Ger.), art d; MAEDCHEN IN UNIFORM(1965, Ger./Fr.), set d
Silents
  WOMAN ON THE MOON, THE(1929, Ger.), art d
Emile Hasler
  TESTAMENT OF DR. MABUSE, THE(1943, Ger.), prod d, art d
Joachim Hasler
  FIRST SPACESHIP ON VENUS(1960, Ger./Pol.), ph
John Hasler
1984
  BREAKOUT(1984, Brit.)
Jessie Haslett
Silents
  SEVENTH HEAVEN(1927)
Charles Hasley
  MUSCLE BEACH PARTY(1964)
William Hasley
  DRIVER, THE(1978)
Veslemoy Haslund
  HUNGER(1968, Den./Norway/Swed.)
Tatsuo Hasoya
  ROAD TO ETERNITY(1962, Jap.), p
Hussain Hasri
  LIVES OF A BENGAL LANCER(1935)
Charlie Hass
  OVER THE EDGE(1979), w
Hugo Hass
  FOR THE LOVE OF MARY(1948)
John G. Hass
Silents
  GREAT ADVENTURE, THE(1918), ph
Robert Hass
  ANOTHER DAWN(1937), art d; LIFE WITH FATHER(1947), art d
Robert M. Hass
  JANIE GETS MARRIED(1946), art d
Silents
  GILDED LILY, THE(1921), art d; NEW COMMANDMENT, THE(1925), art d; ROMOLA(1925), art d; BLUEBEARD'S SEVEN WIVES(1926), art d; RECKLESS LADY, THE(1926), art d; WILDERNESS WOMAN, THE(1926), art d
Walter Hass
Silents
  DREAM MELODY, THE(1929), ph; ONE SPLENDID HOUR(1929), ph
Christopher Hassall
  KING'S RHAPSODY(1955, Brit.), w
Imogen Hassall
  EARLY BIRD, THE(1965, Brit.); LONG DUEL, THE(1967, Brit.); CARRY ON LOVING(1970, Brit.); EL CONDOR(1970); INCENSE FOR THE DAMNED(1970, Brit.); MUMSY, NANNY, SONNY, AND GIRLY(1970, Brit.); TAKE A GIRL LIKE YOU(1970, Brit,); TOOMORROW(1970, Brit.); VIRGIN AND THE GYPSY, THE(1970, Brit.); WHEN DINOSAURS RULED THE EARTH(1971, Brit.); CHARLEY-ONE-EYE(1973, Brit.)
Abdul Hassan
  LIVES OF A BENGAL LANCER(1935)
Al Hassan
  LAST REBEL, THE(1971); SOUL OF NIGGER CHARLEY, THE(1973)
Ibrahim Bin Hassan
  SPIRAL ROAD, THE(1962)
Ismet Hassan
  PRIVATE LIFE OF SHERLOCK HOLMES, THE(1970, Brit.)
Jamiel Hassan
  CHANGE OF HEART(1934)
Hassan Hassani
  Z(1969, Fr./Algeria)
The Hassani Troupe
  OCTOPUSSY(1983, Brit.)
Peggy Hassard
  ISLAND OF DESIRE(1952, Brit.)
Charles Hasse
  MY LEARNED FRIEND(1943, Brit.), ed; DEAD OF NIGHT(1946, Brit.), ed; MY BROTHER JONATHAN(1949, Brit.), ed; PRIVATE ANGELO(1949, Brit.), ed; HUE AND CRY(1950, Brit.), ed; MRS. FITZHERBERT(1950, Brit.), ed; NO ROOM AT THE INN(1950, Brit.), ed; MIDNIGHT EPISODE(1951, Brit.), ed; FAKE, THE(1953, Brit.), ed; HUNDRED HOUR HUNT(1953, Brit.), ed; SLASHER, THE(1953, Brit.), ed; CHILD IN THE HOUSE(1956, Brit.), ed; SHE DIDN'T SAY NO!(1962, Brit.), ed
Kurt Hasse
  AS THE SEA RAGES(1960 Ger.), ph; BOOMERANG(1960, Ger.), ph; TOWN WITHOUT PITY(1961, Ger./Switz./U.S.), ph; VOR SONNENUNTERGANG(1961, Ger), ph; YOUNG GO WILD, THE(1962, Ger.), ph; SITUATION HOPELESS–BUT NOT SERIOUS(1965), ph

Laura Hasse
Silents
  CAPTAIN LASH(1929), w
Louis Hasse
  MURDER BY AN ARISTOCRAT(1936), ed
O.E. Hasse
  BIG LIFT, THE(1950); DECISION BEFORE DAWN(1951); I CONFESS(1953); BETRAYED(1954); CANARIS(1955, Ger.); ABOVE US THE WAVES(1956, Brit.); ADVENTURES OF ARSENE LUPIN(1956, Fr./Ital.); GLASS TOWER, THE(1959, Ger.); MRS. WARREN'S PROFESSION(1960, Ger.); LULU(1962, Aus.); ELUSIVE CORPORAL, THE(1963, Fr.); DR. MABUSE'S RAYS OF DEATH(1964, Ger./Fr./Ital.); STATE OF SIEGE(1973, Fr./U.S./Ital./Ger.)
Otto Edward [O.E.] Hasse
  VICE AND VIRTUE(1965, Fr./Ital.)
George Hassel
  FLAME WITHIN, THE(1935)
David Hasselhoff
  REVENGE OF THE CHEERLEADERS(1976); STARCRASH(1979)
George Hassell
  BECKY SHARP(1935); CAPTAIN BLOOD(1935); DRESSED TO THRILL(1935); NIGHT LIFE OF THE GODS(1935); GIRLS' DORMITORY(1936); KING STEPS OUT, THE(1936); PETTICOAT FEVER(1936); WHITE HUNTER(1936); THINK FAST, MR. MOTO(1937); WEE WILLIE WINKIE(1937); WOMAN-WISE(1937)
Misc. Silents
  LA BOHEME(1926)
Susan Hassell
  MELODY(1971, Brit.)
Werner Hasselman
  HORNET'S NEST(1970); VALDEZ IS COMING(1971); PULP(1972, Brit.)
Jenny Hasselquist
Silents
  ONE ARABIAN NIGHT(1921, Ger.)
Misc. Silents
  LOVE'S CRUCIBLE(1922, Swed.); HELL SHIP, THE(1923, Swed.); LEGEND OF GOSTA BERLING(1928, Swed.)
Jamiel Hassen
  BEHIND THAT CURTAIN(1929)
Tom Hassen
  TRUCK STOP WOMEN(1974), art d
Oliver Hassencamp
  GIRL FROM HONG KONG(1966, Ger.), w
Werner Hassenland
  ONE, TWO, THREE(1961)
Marlin Hasset
  HEROES OF THE ALAMO(1938)
Marilyn Hassett
  THEY SHOOT HORSES, DON'T THEY?(1969); OTHER SIDE OF THE MOUNTAIN, THE(1975); SHADOW OF THE HAWK(1976, Can.); TWO-MINUTE WARNING(1976); OTHER SIDE OF THE MOUNTAIN–PART 2, THE(1978); BELL JAR, THE(1979)
1984
  MASSIVE RETALIATION(1984)
Ray Hassett
  SPY WHO LOVED ME, THE(1977, Brit.); SUPERMAN(1978); YANKS(1979); EMPIRE STRIKES BACK, THE(1980); GREEN ICE(1981, Brit.), w; RAGTIME(1981)
1984
  BODY DOUBLE(1984); THIEF OF HEARTS(1984)
Alex Hassilev
  RUSSIANS ARE COMING, THE RUSSIANS ARE COMING, THE(1966)
Reijo Hassinen
  MAKE LIKE A THIEF(1966, Fin.), ph
Jim Hassinger
  OCTAGON, THE(1980), set d
Bud Hassink
  LAST MOVIE, THE(1971)
Hugo Hasslo
  FANNY AND ALEXANDER(1983, Swed./Fr./Ger.)
Mark Hassman
1984
  DRIFTING(1984, Israel)
Signe Hasso
  JOURNEY FOR MARGARET(1942); ASSIGNMENT IN BRITTANY(1943); HEAVEN CAN WAIT(1943); SEVENTH CROSS, THE(1944); STORY OF DR. WASSELL, THE(1944); DANGEROUS PARTNERS(1945); HOUSE ON 92ND STREET, THE(1945); JOHNNY ANGEL(1945); SCANDAL IN PARIS, A(1946); STRANGE TRIANGLE(1946); DOUBLE LIFE, A(1947); WHERE THERE'S LIFE(1947); TO THE ENDS OF THE EARTH(1948); CRISIS(1950); OUTSIDE THE WALL(1950); TRUE AND THE FALSE, THE(1955, Swed.), a, p; PICTURE MOMMY DEAD(1966); REFLECTION OF FEAR, A(1973); BLACK BIRD, THE(1975); I NEVER PROMISED YOU A ROSE GARDEN(1977)
Jamiel Hasson
  UNDER TWO FLAGS(1936); STAMBOUL QUEST(1934); STUDENT TOUR(1934); LIVES OF A BENGAL LANCER(1935); SHEIK STEPS OUT, THE(1937); GUNGA DIN(1939); RAINS CAME, THE(1939); HONOLULU LU(1941); OUTLAWS OF THE DESERT(1941); RAIDERS OF THE DESERT(1941); ARABIAN NIGHTS(1942); ACTION IN ARABIA(1944); OUT OF THIS WORLD(1945); SPANISH MAIN, THE(1945); THRILL OF BRAZIL, THE(1946); SINBAD THE SAILOR(1947)
Thomas Hasson
  IN LIKE FLINT(1967)
Tommy Hasson
  BOOTLEGGERS(1974), art d
Alma Hasta
Misc. Silents
  GUARDSMAN, THE(1927, Aust.)
Jack Haste
  UNDER CAPRICORN(1949), ph
Chuck Hasting
  NO RETURN ADDRESS(1961)

Henry Hasting
NIGHT AND DAY(1946)

Bob Hastings
MOON PILOT(1962); MC HALE'S NAVY(1964); MC HALE'S NAVY JOINS THE AIR FORCE(1965); BAMBOO SAUCER, THE(1968); DID YOU HEAR THE ONE ABOUT THE TRAVELING SALESLADY?(1968); ANGEL IN MY POCKET(1969); LOVE GOD?, THE(1969); BOATNIKS, THE(1970); HOW TO FRAME A FIGG(1971); MARRIAGE OF A YOUNG STOCKBROKER, THE(1971); POSEIDON ADVENTURE, THE(1972); ALL-AMERICAN BOY, THE(1973); CHARLEY AND THE ANGEL(1973); NO DEPOSIT, NO RETURN(1976); HARPER VALLEY, P.T.A.(1978); SEPARATE WAYS(1981)

Carey Hastings
Misc. Silents
HER NEW YORK(1917); IT HAPPENED TO ADELE(1917); MAN WITHOUT A COUNTRY, THE(1917); STREET OF SEVEN STARS, THE(1918)

Carey L. Hastings
Misc. Silents
NAIDRA, THE DREAM WOMAN(1914, Ger.)

Chad Hastings
CATTLE ANNIE AND LITTLE BRITCHES(1981)

Charlotte Hastings
THUNDER ON THE HILL(1951), w; STRANGE AFFECTION(1959, Brit.), w, d&w

Chuck Hastings
VAN, THE(1977)

Doug Hastings
SCARECROW, THE(1982, New Zealand)

Guy Hastings
ANTS IN HIS PANTS(1940, Aus.)

Harold Hastings
TOP BANANA(1954), md; SOMETHING FOR EVERYONE(1970), md

Harry Hastings
FURY AND THE WOMAN(1937)

Henry Hastings
WITHOUT RESERVATIONS(1946); GALLANT LADY(1942); MR. CELEBRITY(1942); PRISON GIRL(1942); COLONEL EFFINGHAM'S RAID(1945); TOMORROW IS FOREVER(1946); WHITE WITCH DOCTOR(1953)

Hugh Hastings
GLORY AT SEA(1952, Brit.), a, w; IT STARTED IN PARADISE(1952, Brit.), w; CREST OF THE WAVE(1954, Brit.), w

Ian Hastings
ALL THINGS BRIGHT AND BEAUTIFUL(1979, Brit.)
1984
GIVE MY REGARDS TO BROAD STREET(1984, Brit.)

June Hastings
Silents
MADCAP BETTY(1915)

Lynn Hastings
Misc. Talkies
CHERRY HILL HIGH(1977)

Maire Hastings
ULYSSES(1967, U.S./Brit.)

Michael Hastings
ADVENTURERS, THE(1970), w; NIGHT COMERS, THE(1971, Brit.), w

Patrick Hastings
BLIND GODDESS, THE(1948, Brit.), w
Silents
NOTORIOUS LADY, THE(1927), w

Phyllis Hastings
RAPTURE(1965), w

Seymour Hastings
Silents
INNOCENT MAGDALENE, AN(1916)

Stephanie Hastings
Misc. Talkies
CHEERLEADERS BEACH PARTY(1978)

Walter Hastings
PHFFFT!(1954)

Wells Hastings
Silents
LITTLE MISS REBELLION(1920), w; SLEEPWALKER, THE(1922), w

John Eugene Hasty
THERE'S A GIRL IN MY HEART(1949), w

Susanne Hasty
TOUGH ENOUGH(1983)

Yoshio Hasuike
MAN FROM THE EAST, THE(1961, Jap.), w

Ara Haswell
I TAKE THIS WOMAN(1931); CRUSADER, THE(1932); DISGRACED(1933); SECOND HAND WIFE(1933)

Lou Haszillo
JOHNNY RENO(1966), makeup

Louis Haszillo
GREAT LOCOMOTIVE CHASE, THE(1956), makeup; TAFFY AND THE JUNGLE HUNTER(1965), makeup

Kenichi Hata
NONE BUT THE BRAVE(1965, U.S./Jap.)

Mac Hata
LAND OF FURY(1955 Brit.)

Eddie Earl Hatch
WARRIORS, THE(1979)

Eric Hatch
SIDEWALKS OF NEW YORK(1931), w; MY MAN GODFREY(1936), w; SPEND-THRIFT(1936), w; TOPPER(1937), w; ROAD SHOW(1941), w; UNEXPECTED UN-CLE(1941), w; MY MAN GODFREY(1957), w; HORSE IN THE GRAY FLANNEL SUIT, THE(1968), w

Helen Hatch
BOOMERANG(1947); MISTER 880(1950); HALLS OF MONTEZUMA(1951); DREAM-BOAT(1952)

Ike Hatch
DARK SANDS(1938, Brit.)

Michael Hatch
HARDCORE(1979)

Olive Hatch
VALIANT IS THE WORD FOR CARRIE(1936); HELLZAPOPPIN'(1941)

Richard Hatch
BEST FRIENDS(1975); BATTLESTAR GALACTICA(1979); MISSION GALACTICA: THE CYLON ATTACK(1979); CHARLIE CHAN AND THE CURSE OF THE DRAGON QUEEN(1981)
Misc. Talkies
BEST FRIENDS(1975)

Riley Hatch
Silents
LAW OF THE LAND, THE(1917); OTHER MEN'S DAUGHTERS(1918); PECK'S BAD GIRL(1918); LITTLE MISS REBELLION(1920); IDOL OF THE NORTH, THE(1921); NOBODY(1921); WHAT WOMEN WILL DO(1921); MISSING MILLIONS(1922); AMERICA(1924); NIGHT LIFE OF NEW YORK(1925)
Misc. Silents
CASE AT LAW, A(1917); DOUBLE CROSSED(1917); SHELTERED DAUGHT-ERS(1921); YOU FIND IT EVERYWHERE(1921)

Tony Hatch
STORK TALK(1964, Brit.), m; TRAVELS WITH MY AUNT(1972, Brit.), m; SWEENEY 2(1978, Brit.), m

Wilbur Hatch
MARK OF THE WHISTLER, THE(1944), m; WHISTLER, THE(1944), m; MYSTERI-OUS INTRUDER(1946), m; 13TH HOUR, THE(1947), m; SCARFACE MOB, THE(1962), m

William Riley Hatch
Silents
PIERRE OF THE PLAINS(1914); PRINCE OF INDIA, A(1914); PLUNDERER, THE(1915); EVE'S DAUGHTER(1918)
Misc. Silents
PAID IN FULL(1914); SHORE ACRES(1914); LITTLE GYPSY, THE(1915); CITY, THE(1916); HAZEL KIRKE(1916); BLIND MAN'S LUCK(1917); INNER VOICE, THE(1920); MATRIMONIAL WEB, THE(1921)

Iraz Hatche
TARGET: HARRY(1980)

Clifford Hatcher
Misc. Talkies
IN THE RAPTURE(1976)

Harley Hatcher
KILLERS THREE(1968), m; SATAN'S SADISTS(1969), m; WILD WHEELS(1969), m; BULLET FOR PRETTY BOY, A(1970), m; HARD RIDE, THE(1971), m&md

Mary Hatcher
OUR HEARTS WERE GROWING UP(1946); TILL THE CLOUDS ROLL BY(1946); VARIETY GIRL(1947); ISN'T IT ROMANTIC?(1948); BIG WHEEL, THE(1949); HOLI-DAY IN HAVANA(1949); TALES OF ROBIN HOOD(1951)

Frank Hatchett
KING OF MARVIN GARDENS, THE(1972)

Lt. Eunice Hatchitt
SO PROUDLY WE HAIL(1943), tech adv

Lt. Eunice C. Hatchitt
UP IN ARMS(1944), tech adv

John Hateley
1984
STREETS OF FIRE(1984)

John Hately
ROCK 'N' ROLL HIGH SCHOOL(1979)

Sarah Hater
RECKONING, THE(1971, Brit.)

Rev. Byron Ulric Hatfield
RAMPARTS WE WATCH, THE(1940)

Hal Hatfield
IT'S A BIG COUNTRY(1951)

Hurd Hatfield
DRAGON SEED(1944); PICTURE OF DORIAN GRAY, THE(1945); DIARY OF A CHAMBERMAID(1946); BEGINNING OR THE END, THE(1947); UNSUSPECTED, THE(1947); CHECKERED COAT, THE(1948); JOAN OF ARC(1948); CHINATOWN AT MIDNIGHT(1949); DESTINATION MURDER(1950); TARZAN AND THE SLAVE GIRL(1950); LEFT-HANDED GUN, THE(1958); EL CID(1961, U.S./Ital.); KING OF KINGS(1961); DOUBLE-BARRELLED DETECTIVE STORY, THE(1965); HAR-LOW(1965); MICKEY ONE(1965); THE BOSTON STRANGLER, THE(1968); VON RICHTHOFEN AND BROWN(1970)
Misc. Talkies
HOUSE AND THE BRAIN, THE(1973)

Jack Hatfield
RENDEZVOUS(1935); IT HAD TO HAPPEN(1936); PRINCESS COMES ACROSS, THE(1936); SMALL TOWN GIRL(1936); THEODORA GOES WILD(1936); THERE'S THAT WOMAN AGAIN(1938); HEADLEYS AT HOME, THE(1939); STRONGER THAN DESIRE(1939); GHOST BREAKERS, THE(1940)

John Hatfield
FOUL PLAY(1978)
Silents
RAIDERS, THE(1921)

Kristen Hatfield
PRIME OF MISS JEAN BRODIE, THE(1969, Brit.)

Kristin Hatfield
DULCIMA(1971, Brit.)

Michael Hatfield
TOGETHER FOR DAYS(1972)

Mike Hatfield
Misc. Talkies
WILLIE AND SCRATCH(1975)

Philip Hatfield
TEN MINUTE ALIBI(1935, Brit.)

Sharon Hatfield
PERSONAL BEST(1982)

Christine Hatfull
LIQUID SKY(1982)
Baby Hathaway
Silents
KID, THE(1921)
Bob Hathaway
CURSE OF THE PINK PANTHER(1983), ed
David Hathaway
GANDHI(1982), spec eff
Donny Hathaway
COME BACK CHARLESTON BLUE(1972), m
Henry Hathaway
WILD HORSE MESA(1932), d; HERITAGE OF THE DESERT(1933), d; MAN OF THE FOREST(1933), d; SUNSET PASS(1933), d; TO THE LAST MAN(1933), d; UNDER THE TONTO RIM(1933), d; COME ON, MARINES(1934), d; LAST ROUND-UP, THE(1934), d; NOW AND FOREVER(1934), d; THUNDERING HERD, THE(1934), d; WITCHING HOUR, THE(1934), d; LIVES OF A BENGAL LANCER(1935), d; PETER IBBETSON(1935), d; GO WEST, YOUNG MAN(1936), d; TRAIL OF THE LONESOME PINE, THE(1936), d; SOULS AT SEA(1937), p, d; SPAWN OF THE NORTH(1938), d; REAL GLORY, THE(1939), d; BRIGHAM YOUNG–FRONTIERSMAN(1940), d; JOHNNY APOLLO(1940), d; SHEPHERD OF THE HILLS, THE(1941), d; SUNDOWN(1941), d; CHINA GIRL(1942), d; TEN GENTLEMEN FROM WEST POINT(1942), d; HOME IN INDIANA(1944), d; WING AND A PRAYER(1944), d; HOUSE ON 92ND STREET, THE(1945), d; NOB HILL(1945), d; DARK CORNER, THE(1946), d; 13 RUE MADELEINE(1946), d; KISS OF DEATH(1947), d; CALL NORTHSIDE 777(1948), d; DOWN TO THE SEA IN SHIPS(1949), d; BLACK ROSE, THE(1950), d; DESERT FOX, THE(1951), d; FOURTEEN HOURS(1951), d; RAWHIDE(1951), d; YOU'RE IN THE NAVY NOW(1951), d; DIPLOMATIC COURIER(1952), d; O. HENRY'S FULL HOUSE(1952), d; NIAGARA(1953), d; WHITE WITCH DOCTOR(1953), d; GARDEN OF EVIL(1954), d; PRINCE VALIANT(1954), d; RACERS, THE(1955), d; BOTTOM OF THE BOTTLE, THE(1956), d; 23 PACES TO BAKER STREET(1956), d; LEGEND OF THE LOST(1957, U.S./Panama/Ital.), p&d; FROM HELL TO TEXAS(1958), d; WOMAN OBSESSED(1959), d; NORTH TO ALASKA(1960), p&d; SEVEN THIEVES(1960), d; HOW THE WEST WAS WON(1962), d; CIRCUS WORLD(1964), d; OF HUMAN BONDAGE(1964, Brit.), d; SONS OF KATIE ELDER, THE(1965), d; NEVADA SMITH(1966), p&d; LAST SAFARI, THE(1967, Brit.), p&d; FIVE CARD STUD(1968), d; TRUE GRIT(1969), d; AIRPORT(1970), d; RAID ON ROMMEL(1971), d; SHOOT OUT(1971), d; HANGUP(1974), d
Jean Hathaway
Silents
CRAVING, THE(1918)
Misc. Silents
BOBBIE OF THE BALLET(1916); COME THROUGH(1917); DIVORCEE, THE(1917); GIRL WHO COULDN'T GROW UP, THE(1917); LOYALTY(1918); WISHING RING MAN, THE(1919); SHORT SKIRTS(1921); BOY CRAZY(1922)
Lillian Hathaway
Silents
SERPENT, THE(1916)
Louise Hathaway
Silents
KID, THE(1921)
Maggie Hathaway
MANCHURIAN CANDIDATE, THE(1962)
Margaret Hathaway
TO HAVE AND HAVE NOT(1944)
Nancy Hathaway
Silents
OUT OF THE SHADOW(1919)
Noah Hathaway
IT'S MY TURN(1980); SEPARATE WAYS(1981); BEST FRIENDS(1982)
1984
NEVERENDING STORY, THE(1984, Ger.)
Noah Hathaway, Jr.
BATTLESTAR GALACTICA(1979)
Peggy Hathaway
Silents
POTTER'S CLAY(1922, Brit.); REPENTANCE(1922, Brit.)
Misc. Silents
HOW KITCHENER WAS BETRAYED(1921, Brit.); MARRIED LIFE(1921, Brit.); ROMANY, THE(1923, Brit.)
Rhody Hathaway
LIFE BEGINS AT 40(1935)
Silents
INTO THE NIGHT(1928); OLD CODE, THE(1928)
Misc. Silents
NOT A DRUM WAS HEARD(1924)
Sue Hathaway
NAME FOR EVIL, A(1970)
Terence Hathaway
Misc. Talkies
FULLER REPORT, THE(1966), d; TIFFANY MEMORANDUM(1966), d
Terence Hathaway [Sergio Grieco]
MISSION BLOODY MARY(1967, Fr./Ital./Span.), d
Jerry Hathcock
PETER PAN(1953), anim; LADY AND THE TRAMP(1955), anim; HEY THERE, IT'S YOGI BEAR(1964), anim; MAN CALLED FLINTSTONE, THE(1966), anim
Frank Hatherley
GREAT WALL OF CHINA, THE(1970, Brit.)
Vince Hatherly
MR. PATMAN(1980, Can.), ed
Heidemarie Hatheyer
AFFAIRS OF DR. HOLL(1954, Ger.); RATS, THE(1955, Ger.)
Pedro Paulo Hatheyer
GIRL IN ROOM 13(1961, U.S./Braz.)
Carl Hathwell
STORY OF ADELE H., THE(1975, Fr.)
Philip Hatkin
Silents
IRON RING, THE(1917), p; MAN WHO FORGOT, THE(1917), ph; JUST SYLVIA(1918), ph; COST, THE(1920), ph; GUILTY OF LOVE(1920), ph

Marvin Hatley
PACK UP YOUR TROUBLES(1932), a, m; OUR RELATIONS(1936); GENERAL SPANKY(1937), m; PICK A STAR(1937), m, md; TOPPER(1937), md; WAY OUT WEST(1937), m, md; MERRILY WE LIVE(1938), md; SWISS MISS(1938), md; THERE GOES MY HEART(1938), m, md; ZENOBIA(1939), m; CHUMP AT OXFORD, A(1940), m; SAPS AT SEA(1940), m; BROADWAY LIMITED(1941), md
Peri Hatman
ISTANBUL(1957)
Reiko Hatsune
MUDDY RIVER(1982, Jap.)
D.R.O. Hatswell
ONE HYSTERICAL NIGHT(1930)
Don Hatswell
QUIET MAN, THE(1952)
Donald Hatswell
Silents
MADNESS OF YOUTH(1923); MEDDLER, THE(1925)
Tom Hattan
SECRET OF NIMH, THE(1982)
Rohini Hattangady
GANDHI(1982)
1984
MOHAN JOSHI HAAZIR HO(1984, India)
Bradford Hatten
CONVICTED(1950)
Charles Hatten
Silents
STELLA DALLAS(1925)
Tom Hatten
SWEET CHARITY(1969)
Yankton Hatten
1984
PLACES IN THE HEART(1984)
Richard Hatteras
Silents
JOHN GLAYDE'S HONOR(1915)
Misc. Silents
OUTCAST(1917); FEAR MARKET, THE(1920)
Hattie
HARD TO GET(1938)
Hilo Hattie
SONG OF THE ISLANDS(1942); FOLLOW THE BAND(1943); TAHITI NIGHTS(1945); MISS TATLOCK'S MILLIONS(1948); CITY BENEATH THE SEA(1953); MA AND PA KETTLE AT WAIKIKI(1955); SUICIDE BATTALION(1958)
Ryno Hattinga
WILD GEESE, THE(1978, Brit.)
Barbara Hatton
RECKLESS MOMENTS, THE(1949)
Brad Hatton
FATHER OF THE BRIDE(1950); MYSTERY STREET(1950)
Bradford Hatton
UNKNOWN MAN, THE(1951); GREATEST SHOW ON EARTH, THE(1952); WALK EAST ON BEACON(1952); TOP BANANA(1954)
Branford Hatton
SAN FRANCISCO DOCKS(1941)
Charles Hatton
Silents
PECK'S BAD BOY(1921); LORNA DOONE(1927)
Claire Hatton
Misc. Silents
DESERT SCORPION, THE(1920)
Clare Hatton
Misc. Silents
RIDERS OF THE RANGE(1923)
David Hatton
PIRATES OF PENZANCE, THE(1983)
Dick Hatton
Silents
PLAYING DOUBLE(1923); WESTERN FATE(1924); HE-MAN'S COUNTRY, A(1926), a, d; ACTION CRAVER, THE(1927); WESTERN COURAGE(1927)
Misc. Silents
FEARLESS DICK(1922); FOUR HEARTS(1922); HELLHOUNDS OF THE WEST(1922); BLOOD TEST(1923); GOLDEN FLAME, THE(1923); RIDIN' THRU(1923); COME ON COWBOYS!(1924); SELL 'EM COWBOY(1924); TWO FISTED JUSTICE(1924), a, d; CACTUS CURE, THE(1925); MY PAL(1925); RANGE JUSTICE(1925); RIDIN' EASY(1925); RIP SNORTER, THE(1925); SECRET OF BLACK CANYON, THE(1925); WESTERN ENGAGEMENT, A(1925); WHERE ROMANCE RIDES(1925); IN BRONCHO LAND(1926); ROARING BILL ATWOOD(1926); TEMPORARY SHERIFF(1926), a, d; SADDLE JUMPERS(1927); SPEEDING HOOFS(1927)
Fanny Hatton
BACHELOR GIRL, THE(1929), w; FALL OF EVE, THE(1929), w; FATHER AND SON(1929), w; MIDSTREAM(1929), w; MISTER ANTONIO(1929), w; MOLLY AND ME(1929), w; NEW ORLEANS(1929), w; PAINTED FACES(1929), w; TWO MEN AND A MAID(1929), w; DAMAGED LOVE(1931), w; GREAT LOVER, THE(1931), w; TONIGHT OR NEVER(1931), w
Silents
PEACOCK ALLEY(1922), t; SOUTH SEA LOVE(1923), w; JUST OFF BROADWAY(1924), w; MARRIED FLIRTS(1924), t; KISS BARRIER, THE(1925), w; AUCTION BLOCK, THE(1926), w; WANING SEX, THE(1926), w; RUSH HOUR, THE(1927), w; ALBANY NIGHT BOAT, THE(1928), t; BEAUTIFUL BUT DUMB(1928), t; MAN IN HOBBLES, THE(1928), t; TRAGEDY OF YOUTH, THE(1928), t
Frances Hatton
Silents
ROWDY, THE(1921); JAVA HEAD(1923)
Misc. Silents
LOVETIME(1921); STRAIGHT FROM THE SHOULDER(1921)
Fred Hatton
FALL OF EVE, THE(1929), w; MOLLY AND ME(1929), w; NEW ORLEANS(1929), w

Frederic Hatton

BACHELOR GIRL, THE(1929), w; FATHER AND SON(1929), w; PAINTED FACES(1929), w; TWO MEN AND A MAID(1929), w; DAMAGED LOVE(1931), w; TONIGHT OR NEVER(1931), w

Silents

PEACOCK ALLEY(1922), t; JUST OFF BROADWAY(1924), w; MARRIED FLIRTS(1924), t; AUCTION BLOCK, THE(1926), w; LOVELORN, THE(1927), t; RUSH HOUR, THE(1927), w

Frederick Hatton

MIDSTREAM(1929), w; MISTER ANTONIO(1929), w; GREAT LOVER, THE(1931), w

Silents

SOUTH SEA LOVE(1923), w; KISS BARRIER, THE(1925), w; ALBANY NIGHT BOAT, THE(1928), t; BEAUTIFUL BUT DUMB(1928), t; KIT CARSON(1928), t; MAN IN HOBBLES, THE(1928), t; TRAGEDY OF YOUTH, THE(1928), t; DEVIL'S APPLE TREE(1929), t

Jean Hatton

MR. CHEDWORTH STEPS OUT(1939, Aus.); ANTS IN HIS PANTS(1940, Aus.)

John Hatton

Silents

CROSSING TRAILS(1921)

Joseph Hatton

Silents

JOHN NEEDHAM'S DOUBLE(1916), w

Leslie Hatton

KENTUCKY MINSTRELS(1934, Brit.); FLOOD TIDE(1935, Brit.)

Maurice Hatton

PRAISE MARX AND PASS THE AMMUNITION(1970, Brit.), p,d&w; LONG SHOT(1981, Brit.), p&d, w, ph; NELLY'S VERSION(1983, Brit.), d&w

Mercy Hatton

Silents

GIRL WHO TOOK THE WRONG TURNING, THE(1915, Brit.); TATTERLY(1919, Brit.); MASTER OF CRAFT, A(1922, Brit.)

Misc. Silents

HARBOUR LIGHTS, THE(1914, Brit.); INCOMPARABLE MISTRESS BELLAIRS, THE(1914, Brit.); BEAU BROCADE(1916, Brit.); MAN WITH THE GLASS EYE, THE(1916, Brit.); WHEN WOMAN HATES(1916, Brit.); LAUGHING CAVALIER, THE(1917, Brit.); QUICKSANDS(1917); SANDS OF TIME(1919, Brit.); CASE OF LADY CAMBER, THE(1920, Brit.); HER SON(1920, Brit.); CHRISTIE JOHNSTONE(1921, Brit.); SPORTSMAN'S WIFE, A(1921, Brit.)

Raymond Hatton

MIGHTY, THE(1929); OFFICE SCANDAL, THE(1929); HELL'S HEROES(1930); MIDNIGHT MYSTERY(1930); MURDER ON THE ROOF(1930); ROAD TO PARADISE(1930); ROGUE OF THE RIO GRANDE(1930); SILVER HORDE, THE(1930); HONEYMOON LANE(1931); LION AND THE LAMB(1931); SQUAW MAN, THE(1931); WOMAN HUNGRY(1931); ALIAS MARY SMITH(1932); CORNERED(1932); CROOKED CIRCLE(1932); DRIFTING(1932); EXPOSED(1932); LAW AND ORDER(1932); POLLY OF THE CIRCUS(1932); STRANGER IN TOWN(1932); UPTOWN NEW YORK(1932); VANISHING FRONTIER, THE(1932); VANITY STREET(1932); ALICE IN WONDERLAND(1933); BIG CAGE, THE(1933); DAY OF RECKONING(1933); FOURTH HORSEMAN, THE(1933); HIDDEN GOLD(1933); LADY KILLER(1933); MADE ON BROADWAY(1933); MALAY NIGHTS(1933); PENTHOUSE(1933); STATE TROOPER(1933); TERROR TRAIL(1933); UNDER THE TONTO RIM(1933); DEFENSE HESTS, THE(1934); FIFTEEN WIVES(1934); LAZY RIVER(1934); ONCE TO EVERY BACHELOR(1934); STRAIGHT IS THE WAY(1934); THUNDERING HERD, THE(1934); WAGON WHEELS(1934); WOMEN IN HIS LIFE, THE(1934); CALM YOURSELF(1935); DARING YOUNG MAN, THE(1935); G-MEN(1935); MURDER IN THE FLEET(1935); RED MORNING(1935); STEAMBOAT ROUND THE BEND(1935); TIMES SQUARE LADY(1935); WANDERER OF THE WASTELAND(1935); ARIZONA RAIDERS, THE(1936); DESERT GOLD(1936); EXCLUSIVE STORY(1936); FURY(1936); LAUGHING IRISH EYES(1936); MAD HOLIDAY(1936); NEVADA(1936); TIMOTHY'S QUEST(1936); WOMEN ARE TROUBLE(1936); YELLOWSTONE(1936); ADVENTUROUS BLONDE(1937); DEVIL'S SADDLE LEGION, THE(1937); FLY-AWAY BABY(1937); LOVE IS ON THE AIR(1937); MARKED WOMAN(1937); MISSING WITNESSES(1937); OVER THE GOAL(1937); PUBLIC WEDDING(1937); ROARING TIMBER(1937); SAN QUENTIN(1937); HE COULDN'T SAY NO(1938); LOVE FINDS ANDY HARDY(1938); OVER THE WALL(1938); TEXANS, THE(1938); TOUCHDOWN, ARMY(1938); AMBUSH(1939); CAREER(1939); COME ON RANGERS(1939); COWBOYS FROM TEXAS(1939); FRONTIER PONY EXPRESS(1939); I'M FROM MISSOURI(1939); KANSAS TERRORS, THE(1939); NEW FRONTIER(1939); PARIS HONEYMOON(1939); ROUGH RIDERS' ROUNDUP(1939); TOM SAWYER, DETECTIVE(1939); UNDERCOVER DOCTOR(1939); WALL STREET COWBOY(1939); WYOMING OUTLAW(1939); 6000 ENEMIES(1939); COVERED WAGON DAYS(1940); HEROES OF THE SADDLE(1940); HI-YO SILVER(1940); KIT CARSON(1940); OKLAHOMA RENEGADES(1940); PIONEERS OF THE WEST(1940); QUEEN OF THE MOB(1940); ROCKY MOUNTAIN RANGERS(1940); ARIZONA BOUND(1941); FORBIDDEN TRAILS(1941); GUN MAN FROM BODIE, THE(1941); TEXAS(1941); BELOW THE BORDER(1942); DAWN ON THE GREAT DIVIDE(1942); DOWN TEXAS WAY(1942); GHOST TOWN LAW(1942); GIRL FROM ALASKA(1942); REAP THE WILD WIND(1942); RIDERS OF THE WEST(1942); WEST OF THE LAW(1942); OUTLAWS OF STAMPEDE PASS(1943); SIX GUN GOSPEL(1943); STRANGER FROM PECOS, THE(1943); GHOST GUNS(1944); LAND OF THE OUTLAWS(1944); LAW MEN(1944); LAW OF THE VALLEY(1944); PARTNERS OF THE TRAIL(1944); RAIDERS OF THE BORDER(1944); RANGE LAW(1944); TALL IN THE SADDLE(1944); TEXAS KID, THE(1944); FLAME OF THE WEST(1945); FRONTIER FEUD(1945); LOST TRAIL, THE(1945); NAVAJO TRAIL, THE(1945); NORTHWEST TRAIL(1945); SUNBONNET SUE(1945); BORDER BANDITS(1946); DRIFTING ALONG(1946); GENTLEMAN FROM TEXAS(1946); UNDER ARIZONA SKIES(1946); BLACK GOLD(1947); CODE OF THE SADDLE(1947); FLASHING GUNS(1947); LAND OF THE LAWLESS(1947); PRAIRIE EXPRESS(1947); RAIDERS OF THE SOUTH(1947); UNCONQUERED(1947); BLACK TRAIL(1948); CROSSED TRAILS(1948); FIGHTING RANGER, THE(1948); FRONTIER AGENT(1948); GUNNING FOR JUSTICE(1948); HIDDEN DANGER(1949); COLORADO RANGER(1950); COUNTY FAIR(1950); CROOKED RIVER(1950); DALTON'S WOMEN, THE(1950); FAST ON THE DRAW(1950); HOSTILE COUNTRY(1950); MARSHAL OF HELDORADO(1950); OPERATION HAYLIFT(1950); WEST OF THE BRAZOS(1950); KENTUCKY JUBILEE(1951); SKIPALONG ROSENBLOOM(1951); GOLDEN HAWK, THE(1952); COW COUNTRY(1953); THUNDER PASS(1954); TREASURE OF RUBY HILLS(1955); TWINKLE IN GOD'S EYE, THE(1955); DAY THE WORLD ENDED, THE(1956); DIG THAT URANIUM(1956); GIRLS IN PRISON(1956); FLESH AND THE SPUR(1957); INVASION OF THE SAUCER MEN(1957); MOTORCYCLE GANG(1957); PAWNEE(1957); SHAKE, RATTLE, AND ROCK!(1957); ALASKA PASSAGE(1959); QUICK GUN, THE(1964); REQUIEM FOR A GUNFIGHTER(1965); IN COLD BLOOD(1967)

Misc. Talkies

DRIFTING SOULS(1932); CADETS ON PARADE(1942); GHOST RIDER, THE(1943); WEST OF THE RIO GRANDE(1944); GUN SMOKE(1945); RHYTHM ROUNDUP(1945); STRANGER FROM SANTA FE(1945); HAUNTED MINE, THE(1946); SHADOWS ON THE RANGE(1946); SILVER RANGE(1946); TRIGGER FINGERS(1946); LAW COMES TO GUNSIGHT, THE(1947); TRAILING DANGER(1947); VALLEY OF FEAR(1947); OVERLAND TRAILS(1948); SHERIFF OF MEDICINE BOW, THE(1948); TRIGGERMAN(1948); TRAIL OF THE ARROW(1952)

Silents

CIRCUS MAN, THE(1914); ARAB, THE(1915); ARMSTRONG'S WIFE(1915); CHIMMIE FADDEN(1915); CHIMMIE FADDEN OUT WEST(1915); GIRL OF THE GOLDEN WEST, THE(1915); GOLDEN CHANCE, THE(1915); IMMIGRANT, THE(1915); KINDLING(1915); TEMPTATION(1915); WARRENS OF VIRGINIA, THE(1915); WILD GOOSE CHASE, THE(1915); WOMAN, THE(1915); JOAN THE WOMAN(1916); OLIVER TWIST(1916); TENNESSEE'S PARDNER(1916); AMERICAN CONSUL, THE(1917); NAN OF MUSIC MOUNTAIN(1917); ROMANCE OF THE REDWOODS, A(1917); SECRET GAME, THE(1917); ARIZONA(1918); JULES OF THE STRONG HEART(1918); ONE MORE AMERICAN(1918); JOHNNY GET YOUR GUN(1919); MALE AND FEMALE(1919); STOP THIEF(1920); ACE OF HEARTS, THE(1921); AFFAIRS OF ANATOL, THE(1921); ALL'S FAIR IN LOVE(1921); BUNTY PULLS THE STRINGS(1921); DOUBLING FOR ROMEO(1921); PECK'S BAD BOY(1921); SALVAGE(1921); EBB TIDE(1922); TO HAVE AND TO HOLD(1922); ENEMIES OF CHILDREN(1923); HUNCHBACK OF NOTRE DAME, THE(1923); JAVA HEAD(1923); THREE WISE FOOLS(1923); TIE THAT BINDS, THE(1923); VIRGINIAN, THE(1923); FIGHTING AMERICAN, THE(1924); ADVENTURE(1925); DEVIL'S CARGO, THE(1925); IN THE NAME OF LOVE(1925); LORD JIM(1925); BEHIND THE FRONT(1926); WANING SEX, THE(1926), w; FIREMAN, SAVE MY CHILD(1927); NOW WE'RE IN THE AIR(1927); PARTNERS IN CRIME(1928); WIFE SAVERS(1928)

Misc. Silents

MAKING OF BOBBY BURNIT, THE(1914); HONORABLE FRIEND, THE(1916); TEMPTATION(1916); HASHIMURA TOGO(1917); LITTLE AMERICAN, THE(1917); WOMAN GOD FORGOT, THE(1917); CRUISE OF THE MAKE-BELIEVES, THE(1918); FIREFLY OF FRANCE, THE(1918); LESS THAN KIN(1918); WHISPERING CHORUS, THE(1918); DAUGHTER OF THE WOLF, A(1919); LOVE BURGLAR, THE(1919); WILD GOOSE CHASE(1919); DANCIN' FOOL, THE(1920); JES' CALL ME JIM(1920); SEA WOLF, THE(1920); CONCERT, THE(1921); HEAD OVER HEELS(1922); HIS BACK AGAINST THE WALL(1922); PINK GODS(1922); BIG BROTHER(1923); MAN OF ACTION, THE(1923); CORNERED(1924); HALF-A-DOLLAR BILL(1924); MINE WITH THE IRON DOOR, THE(1924); CONTRABAND(1925); SON OF HIS FATHER, A(1925); THUNDERING HERD, THE(1925); TOMORROW'S LOVE(1925); BORN TO THE WEST(1926); FORLORN RIVER(1926); SILENCE(1926); WE'RE IN THE NAVY NOW(1926); FASHIONS FOR WOMEN(1927); BIG KILLING, THE(1928); TRENT'S LAST CASE(1929)

Richard Hatton

Silents

SEVENTH SHERIFF, THE(1923), a, d&w; STING OF THE SCORPION, THE(1923), d

Misc. Silents

IN THE WEST(1923); UNBLAZED TRAIL(1923), a, d; HORSE SENSE(1924); SAGEBRUSH GOSPEL(1924), a, d; TROUBLE TRAIL(1924); WHIRLWIND RANGER, THE(1924), a, d

Robert Hatton

Misc. Silents

MISSING LINKS, THE(1916)

Ronald Hatton

WOMAN OF STRAW(1964, Brit.)

Rondo Hatton

HELL HARBOR(1930); IN OLD CHICAGO(1938); HUNCHBACK OF NOTRE DAME, THE(1939); CHAD HANNA(1940); OX-BOW INCIDENT, THE(1943); SLEEPY LAGOON(1943); JOHNNY DOESN'T LIVE HERE ANY MORE(1944); PEARL OF DEATH, THE(1944); PRINCESS AND THE PIRATE, THE(1944); JUNGLE CAPTIVE(1945); BRUTE MAN, THE(1946); SPIDER WOMAN STRIKES BACK, THE(1946)

Temple Hatton

I PASSED FOR WHITE(1960)

William Hatton

2,000 WOMEN(1944, Brit.)

Hatton & Manners

DODGING THE DOLE(1936, Brit.)

Mako Hattori

HOUSE WHERE EVIL DWELLS, THE(1982)

Lili Hatvany

TONIGHT OR NEVER(1931), w

Lilli Hatvany

MY KINGDOM FOR A COOK(1943), w

Helen Hatziagyri

YOU CAME TOO LATE(1962, Gr.)

Lawrence Hauben

POINT BLANK(1967); ONE FLEW OVER THE CUCKOO'S NEST(1975), w

Karl Haubenreiber

FOUR COMPANIONS, THE(1938, Ger.)

William Hauber

MIDNIGHT TAXI, THE(1928)

Gunter Haubold

PINOCCHIO(1969, E. Ger.), ph

Gisele Hauchecorne

MY LIFE TO LIVE(1963, Fr.); IMMORAL MOMENT, THE(1967, Fr.)

Didier Haudepin

MODERATO CANTABILE(1964, Fr./Ital.); THIS SPECIAL FRIENDSHIP(1967, Fr.); UNINHIBITED, THE(1968, Fr./Ital./Span.); HELLO—GOODBYE(1970); PROMISE AT DAWN(1970, U.S./Fr.); INNOCENT, THE(1979, Ital.); JUDGE AND THE ASSASSIN, THE(1979, Fr.)

Sabine Haudepin

JULES AND JIM(1962, Fr.); SOFT SKIN, THE(1964, Fr.); LAST METRO, THE(1981, Fr.)

Michael Hausserman
Misc. Talkies
SLAUGHTERDAY(1981)
Mischa Hausserman
1984
EVIL THAT MEN DO, THE(1984)
Michael Haussermann
SALZBURG CONNECTION, THE(1972)
Martin Haussler
MARRIAGE OF MARIA BRAUN, THE(1979, Ger.)
Richard Haussler
WOZZECK(1962, E. Ger.); MOONWOLF(1966, Fin./Ger.); U-47 LT. COMMANDER PRIEN(1967, Ger.)
Margit Haut
1984
BODY ROCK(1984)
Matthew Hautau
CHU CHU AND THE PHILLY FLASH(1981)
Grandfather Semu Haute
OUT(1982)
L. Hautecocur
CHRISTINE(1959, Fr.), ed
Louisette Hautecoeur
STORMY WATERS(1946, Fr.), ed; LES BELLES-DE-NUIT(1952, Fr.), ed; KNOCK(1955, Fr.), ed; GRAND MANEUVER, THE(1956, Fr.), ed; LE CIEL EST A VOUS(1957, Fr.), ed; GATES OF PARIS(1958, Fr./Ital.), ed; LOVE AND THE FRENCHWOMAN(1961, Fr.), ed; MAIDEN, THE(1961, Fr.), ed; DOUBLE DECEPTION(1963, Fr.), ed; MAGNIFICENT SINNER(1963, Fr.), ed; SCHEHERAZADE(1965, Fr./Ital./Span.), ed; THIS SPECIAL FRIENDSHIP(1967, Fr.), ed; MILKY WAY, THE(1969, Fr./Ital.), ed; PIAF–THE EARLY YEARS(1982, U.S./Fr.), ed
Louisette Hautecoeur-Taverna
DIARY OF A CHAMBERMAID(1964, Fr./Ital.), ed
Harvey Hautin
TARZAN THE MAGNIFICENT(1960, Brit.), p
Josef Hauvic
STOLEN DIRIGIBLE, THE(1966, Czech.)
Dafydd Havard
MR. H. C. ANDERSEN(1950, Brit.); CRUEL SEA, THE(1953); EVIL EYE(1964 Ital.); ZULU(1964, Brit.); WHERE'S JACK?(1969, Brit.); MOUSE AND THE WOMAN, THE(1981, Brit.)
Davydd Havard
UNDER MILK WOOD(1973, Brit.)
Elven Havard
TORA! TORA! TORA!(1970, U.S./Jap.)
Rene Havard
BABETTE GOES TO WAR(1960, Fr.); COW AND I, THE(1961, Fr., Ital., Ger.); NIGHTS OF SHAME(1961, Fr.); PLEASURES AND VICES(1962, Fr.); TAXI FOR TOBRUK(1965, Fr./Span./Ger.), w; LOST COMMAND, THE(1966)
Gene Havelick
SONG OF LOVE, THE(1929), ed; DECEIVER, THE(1931), ed; ATTORNEY FOR THE DEFENSE(1932), ed; HOLLYWOOD SPEAKS(1932), ed; LAST POSSE, THE(1953), ed
Svata Havelka
MATTER OF DAYS, A(1969, Fr./Czech.), m
Svatopluk Havelka
DIVINE EMMA, THE(1983, Czech,), m
Vaclav Havelka
LEMONADE JOE(1966, Czech.)
Anthony Havelock-Allan
CHECKMATE(1935, Brit.), p; CROSS CURRENTS(1935, Brit.), p; EXPERT'S OPINION(1935, Brit.), p; GENTLEMAN'S AGREEMENT(1935, Brit.), p; JUBILEE WINDOW(1935, Brit.), p; KEY TO HARMONY(1935, Brit.), p; LUCKY DAYS(1935, Brit.), p; MAD HATTERS, THE(1935, Brit.), p; ONCE A THIEF(1935, Brit.), p; PRICE OF WISDOM, THE(1935, Brit.), p; SCHOOL FOR STARS(1935, Brit.), p; VILLAGE SQUIRE, THE(1935, Brit.), p; BELLES OF ST. CLEMENTS, THE(1936, Brit.), p; GRAND FINALE(1936, Brit.), p; HOUSE BROKEN(1936, Brit.), p; LOVE AT SEA(1936, Brit.), p; MURDER BY ROPE(1936, Brit.), p; PAY BOX ADVENTURE(1936, Brit.), p; SCARAB MURDER CASE, THE(1936, Brit.), p; SECRET VOICE, THE(1936, Brit.), p; SHOW FLAT(1936, Brit.), p; TICKET OF LEAVE(1936, Brit.), p; TWO ON A DOORSTEP(1936, Brit.), p; WEDNESDAY'S LUCK(1936, Brit.), p; CAVALIER OF THE STREETS, THE(1937, Brit.), p; CROSS MY HEART(1937, Brit.), p; FATAL HOUR, THE(1937, Brit.), p; HOLIDAY'S END(1937, Brit.), p; INCIDENT IN SHANGHAI(1937, Brit.), p; LANCASHIRE LUCK(1937, Brit.), p; MISSING, BELIEVED MARRIED(1937, Brit.), p; MR. SMITH CARRIES ON(1937, Brit.), p; MUSEUM MYSTERY(1937, Brit.), p; NIGHT RIDE(1937, Brit.), p; LIGHTNING CONDUCTOR(1938, Brit.), p; SPOT OF BOTHER, A(1938, Brit.), p; CONTINENTAL EXPRESS(1939, Brit.), p; STOLEN LIFE(1939, Brit.), p; THIS MAN IN PARIS(1939, Brit.), p; THIS MAN IS NEWS(1939, Brit.), p; LAMBETH WALK, THE(1940, Brit.), p; UNPUBLISHED STORY(1942, Brit.), p, w; THIS HAPPY BREED(1944, Brit.), p, w; BLITHE SPIRIT(1945, Brit.), w; BRIEF ENCOUNTER(1945, Brit.), w; GREAT EXPECTATIONS(1946, Brit.), w; BLANCHE FURY(1948, Brit.), p; HIDEOUT(1948, Brit.), p; TAKE MY LIFE(1948, Brit.), p; INTERRUPTED JOURNEY, THE(1949, Brit.), p; OLIVER TWIST(1951, Brit.), p; NEVER TAKE NO FOR AN ANSWER(1952, Brit./Ital.), p; TONIGHT AT 8:30(1953, Brit.), p; SHADOW OF THE EAGLE(1955, Brit.), p; ORDERS TO KILL(1958, Brit.), p; QUARE FELLOW, THE(1962, Brit.), p; OTHELLO(1965, Brit.), p; MIKADO, THE(1967, Brit.), p; ROMEO AND JULIET(1968, Brit./Ital.), p; UP THE JUNCTION(1968, Brit.), p; RYAN'S DAUGHTER(1970, Brit.), p
Anthony Havelock-Brown
LAST CURTAIN, THE(1937, Brit.), p
Alexander D. Havemann
UNTAMED(1955)
Annette Haven
Misc. Talkies
DRACULA SUCKS(1979)
Karen Haven
HAVING WONDERFUL CRIME(1945)
Nina Haven
SPECTER OF THE ROSE(1946)

Ruth Haven
END OF THE ROAD, THE(1936, Brit.); IF I WERE RICH(1936); JOURNEY AHEAD(1947, Brit.)
Shirle Haven
GANG WAR(1958); SHOWDOWN AT BOOT HILL(1958); LONE TEXAN(1959)
Terri Haven
WOMAN INSIDE, THE(1981)
Misc. Talkies
HEAVY TRAFFIC(1974)
Terry Haven
HEY, GOOD LOOKIN'(1982)
Joseph Havener
BROTHERS(1977)
William Albert Havenmeyer
GREAT WALTZ, THE(1972), art d
Geno Havens
1984
HIGHWAY TO HELL(1984); RUNNING HOT(1984)
George Havens
KID'S LAST RIDE, THE(1941)
James C. Havens
CREATURE FROM THE BLACK LAGOON(1954), ph
James Havens
CHINA SEAS(1935), art d; LITTLE OLD NEW YORK(1940), art d; HOT RODS TO HELL(1967), d
Mildred Havens
Silents
SINS OF SOCIETY(1915); FRUITS OF DESIRE, THE(1916)
Misc. Silents
COURAGE OF THE COMMONPLACE(1917); UNDER THE GREENWOOD TREE(1918)
Richie Havens
CIAO MANHATTAN(1973), m; CATCH MY SOUL(1974); GREASED LIGHTNING(1977); BOSS'S SON, THE(1978)
Friedrich Havenstein
FREDDY UNTER FREMDEN STERNEN(1962, Ger.), makeup
Klaus Havenstein
PLAYGIRLS AND THE BELLBOY, THE(1962,Ger.); UNWILLING AGENT(1968, Ger.); SOMETHING FOR EVERYONE(1970)
June Haver
GANG'S ALL HERE, THE(1943); HOME IN INDIANA(1944); IRISH EYES ARE SMILING(1944); DOLLY SISTERS, THE(1945); WHERE DO WE GO FROM HERE?(1945); THREE LITTLE GIRLS IN BLUE(1946); WAKE UP AND DREAM(1946); I WONDER WHO'S KISSING HER NOW(1947); SCUDDA-HOO! SCUDDA-HAY!(1948); LOOK FOR THE SILVER LINING(1949); OH, YOU BEAUTIFUL DOLL!(1949); DAUGHTER OF ROSIE O'GRADY, THE(1950); I'LL GET BY(1950); LOVE NEST(1951); GIRL NEXT DOOR, THE(1953)
Phylis Haver
Silents
AFTER BUSINESS HOURS(1925)
Phyllis Haver
OFFICE SCANDAL, THE(1929); SAL OF SINGAPORE(1929); SHADY LADY, THE(1929); DOWN MEMORY LANE(1949)
Silents
SMALL TOWN IDOL, A(1921); COMMON LAW, THE(1923); FIGHTING COWARD, THE(1924); MIDNIGHT EXPRESS, THE(1924); SINGER JIM MCKEE(1924); SNOB, THE(1924); SO BIG(1924); NEW BROOMS(1925); RUGGED WATER(1925); CAVEMAN, THE(1926); DON JUAN(1926); NERVOUS WRECK, THE(1926); WHAT PRICE GLORY(1926); NO CONTROL(1927); NOBODY'S WIDOW(1927); WAY OF ALL FLESH, THE(1927); YOUR WIFE AND MINE(1927); BATTLE OF THE SEXES, THE(1928); CHICAGO(1928); THUNDER(1929)
Misc. Silents
BOLTED DOOR, THE(1923); CHRISTIAN, THE(1923); FOOLISH VIRGIN, THE(1924); ONE GLORIOUS NIGHT(1924); PERFECT FLAPPER, THE(1924); SINGLE WIVES(1924); FIGHT TO THE FINISH, A(1925); GOLDEN PRINCESS, THE(1925); I WANT MY MAN(1925); FIG LEAVES(1926); OTHER WOMEN'S HUSBANDS(1926); UP IN MABEL'S ROOM(1926); FIGHTING EAGLE, THE(1927); LITTLE ADVENTURESS, THE(1927); REJUVINATION OF AUNT MARY, THE(1927); WISE WIFE, THE(1927); TENTH AVENUE(1928)
Haver & Lee
RADIO FOLLIES(1935, Brit.); DON'T RUSH ME(1936, Brit.)
Haver and Lee
STUDENT'S ROMANCE, THE(1936, Brit.); WEEKEND MILLIONAIRE(1937, Brit.)
Ned Haverly
YES SIR, MR. BONES(1951)
Nigel Havers
POPE JOAN(1972, Brit.); CHARRIOTS OF FIRE(1981, Brit.)
1984
PASSAGE TO INDIA, A(1984, Brit.)
Sidney Havers
WHITE CORRIDORS(1952, Brit.), ed
A. Haverstock
FIDDLER ON THE ROOF(1971)
Hope Haves
GOING BERSERK(1983)
Tony Haves
CASE OF THE 44'S, THE(1964 Brit./Den.)
Bernard Havet
1984
LE DERNIER COMBAT(1984, Fr.)
Martine Havet
GREEN MARE, THE(1961, Fr./Ital.)
Ebba Havey
HORSEPLAY(1933), w; POOR RICH, THE(1934), w
Jean Havez
Silents
SAILOR-MADE MAN, A(1921), w; DOCTOR JACK(1922), w; GRANDMA'S BOY(1922), w; OUR HOSPITALITY(1923), w&t; THREE AGES, THE(1923), w; NAVIGATOR, THE(1924), w&t; SHERLOCK, JR.(1924), w; FRESHMAN, THE(1925), w; SEVEN CHANCES(1925)

Alex Havier
 ISLE OF MISSING MEN(1942); WE'VE NEVER BEEN LICKED(1943); WINGS OVER THE PACIFIC(1943); HERE COME THE WAVES(1944); THEY WERE EXPENDABLE(1945); NOBODY LIVES FOREVER(1946)
J. Alex Havier
 BATAAN(1943); TIGER FANGS(1943); CALL OF THE JUNGLE(1944); DRAGON SEED(1944); TWO-MAN SUBMARINE(1944); BACK TO BATAAN(1945)
Augusta Haviland
Misc. Silents
 PASSING OF THE THIRD FLOOR BACK, THE(1918, Brit.)
David Haviland
 COLLECTOR, THE(1965); KING RAT(1965)
Katharine Haviland-Taylor
 MAN TO REMEMBER, A(1938), w
Maurice Leon Havis
 COOLEY HIGH(1975)
Emil Haviv
 RICHARD(1972), ed
Ronit Haviv
 I SPIT ON YOUR GRAVE(1983)
Yuri Haviv
 I SPIT ON YOUR GRAVE(1983), ph
Alan Havlick
 SING WHILE YOU DANCE(1946), ed
Gene Havlick
 FALL OF EVE, THE(1929), ed; BROTHERS(1930), ed; MADONNA OF THE STREETS(1930), ed; SISTERS(1930), ed; FIFTY FATHOMS DEEP(1931), ed; LOVER COME BACK(1931), ed; SKY RAIDERS(1931), ed; LAST MAN(1932), ed; MENACE, THE(1932), ed; SHOPWORN(1932), ed; WAR CORRESPONDENT(1932), ed; BRIEF MOMENT(1933), ed; LADY FOR A DAY(1933), ed; MASTER OF MEN(1933), ed; WOMAN I STOLE, THE(1933), ed; BROADWAY BILL(1934), ed; IT HAPPENED ONE NIGHT(1934), ed; TWENTIETH CENTURY(1934), ed; EIGHT BELLS(1935), ed; SHE COULDN'T TAKE IT(1935), ed; UNKNOWN WOMAN(1935), ed; MR. DEEDS GOES TO TOWN(1936), ed; DANGEROUS ADVENTURE, A(1937), ed; IT'S ALL YOURS(1937), ed; LOST HORIZON(1937), ed; BLONDIE(1938), ed; EXTORTION(1938), ed; LAW OF THE PLAINS(1938), ed; START CHEERING(1938), ed; YOU CAN'T TAKE IT WITH YOU(1938), ed; BLONDIE MEETS THE BOSS(1939), ed; MISSING DAUGHTERS(1939), ed; MR. SMITH GOES TO WASHINGTON(1939), ed; MY SON IS A CRIMINAL(1939), ed; ANGELS OVER BROADWAY(1940), ed; BLONDIE HAS SERVANT TROUBLE(1940), ed; BLONDIE ON A BUDGET(1940), ed; HIS GIRL FRIDAY(1940), ed; BLONDIE GOES LATIN(1941), ed; GO WEST, YOUNG LADY(1941), ed; OUR WIFE(1941), ed; SHE KNEW ALL THE ANSWERS(1941), ed; COUNTER-ESPIONAGE(1942), ed; SHUT MY BIG MOUTH(1942), ed; WIFE TAKES A FLYER, THE(1942), ed; DESTROYER(1943), ed; KANSAS CITY KITTY(1944), ed; ONCE UPON A TIME(1944), ed; UNWRITTEN CODE, THE(1944), ed; THOUSAND AND ONE NIGHTS, A(1945), ed; YOUTH ON TRIAL(1945), ed; GENTLEMAN MISBEHAVES, THE(1946), ed; WALLS CAME TUMBLING DOWN, THE(1946), ed; DEAD RECKONING(1947), ed; IT HAD TO BE YOU(1947), ed; RELENTLESS(1948), ed; RETURN OF OCTOBER, THE(1948), ed; LUST FOR GOLD(1949), ed; RECKLESS MOMENTS, THE(1949), ed; RUSTY SAVES A LIFE(1949), ed; SHOCKPROOF(1949), ed; BETWEEN MIDNIGHT AND DAWN(1950), ed; FORTUNES OF CAPTAIN BLOOD(1950), ed; ROGUES OF SHERWOOD FOREST(1950), ed; LADY AND THE BANDIT, THE(1951), ed; SANTA FE(1951), ed; SON OF DR. JEKYLL, THE(1951), ed; CAPTAIN PIRATE(1952), ed; HANGMAN'S KNOT(1952), ed; MY SIX CONVICTS(1952), ed; VOODOO TIGER(1952), ed; KILLER APE(1953), ed; SERPENT OF THE NILE(1953), ed; STRANGER WORE A GUN, THE(1953), ed; VALLEY OF THE HEADHUNTERS(1953), ed; IRON GLOVE, THE(1954), ed; JUNGLE MAN-EATERS(1954), ed; SARACEN BLADE, THE(1954), ed; THREE HOURS TO KILL(1954), ed; INSIDE DETROIT(1955), ed; LAWLESS STREET, A(1955), ed; NEW ORLEANS UNCENSORED(1955), ed; TEN WANTED MEN(1955), ed; SEVENTH CAVALRY(1956), ed; DOMINO KID(1957), ed; SCREAMING MIMI(1958), ed
Silents
 BEAUTY AND BULLETS(1928), ed; GRIT WINS(1929), ed
June Havoc
 FOUR JACKS AND A JILL(1941); MY SISTER EILEEN(1942); POWDER TOWN(1942); SING YOUR WORRIES AWAY(1942); HELLO, FRISCO, HELLO(1943); HI DIDDLE DIDDLE(1943); NO TIME FOR LOVE(1943); CASANOVA IN BURLESQUE(1944); TIMBER QUEEN(1944); BREWSTER'S MILLIONS(1945); GENTLEMAN'S AGREEMENT(1947); INTRIGUE(1947); IRON CURTAIN, THE(1948); WHEN MY BABY SMILES AT ME(1948); CHICAGO DEADLINE(1949); RED, HOT AND BLUE(1949); STORY OF MOLLY X, THE(1949); MOTHER DIDN'T TELL ME(1949); ONCE A THIEF(1950); FOLLOW THE SUN(1951); LADY POSSESSED(1952); THREE FOR JAMIE DAWN(1956); PRIVATE FILES OF J. EDGAR HOOVER, THE(1978); CAN'T STOP THE MUSIC(1980)
Alois Havrilla
 SWEET SURRENDER(1935)
Gene Havtick
 LAST PARADE, THE(1931), ed
Ken Haward
 IDOL, THE(1966, Brit.)
Robin Hawdon
 DAY THE EARTH CAUGHT FIRE, THE(1961, Brit.); MIND BENDERS, THE(1963, Brit.); BEDAZZLED(1967, Brit.); ATTACK ON THE IRON COAST(1968, U.S./Brit.); WHEN DINOSAURS RULED THE EARTH(1971, Brit.); I WANT WHAT I WANT(1972, Brit.)
Misc. Talkies
 ZETA ONE(1969)
Bill Hawes
 FILE ON THELMA JORDAN, THE(1950)
Bob Hawes
 MAYTIME IN MAYFAIR(1952, Brit.)
Mary Hawes
Silents
 SOUL MATES(1925); SCARLET LETTER, THE(1926)
Michael Hawes
 ONE DARK NIGHT(1983), w
Robert Hawes
 THEY ALL LAUGHED(1981)

Tony Hawes
 UNSTOPPABLE MAN, THE(1961, Brit.); HAIR OF THE DOG(1962, Brit.), a, w; STRICTLY FOR THE BIRDS(1963, Brit.), a, w
William Hawes
 GREAT SINNER, THE(1949); SLATTERY'S HURRICANE(1949); HALLS OF MONTEZUMA(1951)
Anthony Sparrow Hawk
 RIO LOBO(1970)
Black Hawk
Silents
 SUZANNA(1922); PAINTED PONIES(1927)
Camilla Hawk
1984
 GRANDVIEW, U.S.A.(1984)
Jay Hawk
 TEENAGE ZOMBIES(1960)
Jeremy Hawk
 GOOSE STEPS OUT, THE(1942, Brit.); PETERVILLE DIAMOND, THE(1942, Brit.); UNHOLY FOUR, THE(1954, Brit.); RACE FOR LIFE, A(1955, Brit.); WHO DONE IT?(1956, Brit.); LUCKY JIM(1957, Brit.); DENTIST IN THE CHAIR(1960, Brit.); GET ON WITH IT(1963, Brit.); MYSTERY SUBMARINE(1963, Brit.); PANIC(1966, Brit.); TRYGON FACTOR, THE(1969, Brit.); RETURN OF THE PINK PANTHER, THE(1975, Brit.)
Jeremy Hawke
 LEFT, RIGHT AND CENTRE(1959)
Jonathan Hawke
 VALLEY OF THE DOLLS(1967)
John Hawker
 LOST IN THE STARS(1974); SPARKLE(1976); CALIFORNIA SUITE(1978); 10(1979)
Graham Hawkes
 FOR YOUR EYES ONLY(1981)
J. Kirby Hawkes
 GUILTY GENERATION, THE(1931), w
Stan Hawkes
 RISE AND RISE OF MICHAEL RIMMER, THE(1970, Brit.), ed
Stanley Hawkes
 SPANIARD'S CURSE, THE(1958, Brit.), ed; BOBBIKINS(1959, Brit.), ed
Steve Hawkes
Misc. Talkies
 STEVIE, SAMSON AND DELILAH(1975), d
Steven Hawkes, Jr.
Misc. Talkies
 STEVIE, SAMSON AND DELILAH(1975)
John Hawkesworth
 FALLEN IDOL, THE(1949, Brit.), prod d; THIRD MAN, THE(1950, Brit.), prod d; PANDORA AND THE FLYING DUTCHMAN(1951, Brit.), set d; BREAKING THE SOUND BARRIER(1952), art d; SAADIA(1953), art d; PRISONER, THE(1955, Brit.), art d; TIGER BAY(1959, Brit.), p, w
Rock Hawkey
 FLYING FISTS, THE(1938), w
Rock Hawkey [Robert Hill]
 WEST OF NEVADA(1936), w
Ricky Hawkeye
 WOLFEN(1981)
Alex Hawkins
 GATOR(1976)
Andrew Hawkins
 CHARRIOTS OF FIRE(1981, Brit.)
1984
 TOP SECRET!(1984)
Anthony Hawkins
 DAMIEN—OMEN II(1978); KITTY AND THE BAGMAN(1983, Aus.)
1984
 PHAR LAP(1984, Aus.); STRIKEBOUND(1984, Aus.)
Ben Hawkins
 RACING FEVER(1964)
Carol Hawkins
 CONFESSIONS OF A POP PERFORMER(1975, Brit.)
Carol-Anne Hawkins
 WHEN DINOSAURS RULED THE EARTH(1971, Brit.)
Charles Hawkins
 DUKE IS THE TOPS, THE(1938); GANG WAR(1940)
Charlotte Hawkins
 NIGHT OF THE QUARTER MOON(1959)
Coleman Hawkins
 CRIMSON CANARY(1945)
David Hawkins
 GOLDEN COACH, THE(1953, Fr./Ital.), ed; SAVAGE GUNS, THE(1962, U.S./Span.), ed
Dennis Hawkins
 FORBIDDEN(1949, Brit.)
Dolores Hawkins
 ADVENTURES OF HUCKLEBERRY FINN, THE(1960)
Don Hawkins
 VIRGIN SOLDIERS, THE(1970, Brit.); NATIONAL HEALTH, OR NURSE NORTON'S AFFAIR, THE(1973, Brit.)
Edward H. Hawkins
 SASQUATCH(1978), w
Emory Hawkins
 RAGGEDY ANN AND ANDY(1977), anim
Flow Hawkins
Misc. Talkies
 THAT MAN OF MINE(1947)
Frank Hawkins
 BLACK MEMORY(1947, Brit.); MYSTERIOUS MR. NICHOLSON, THE(1947, Brit.); GUNMAN HAS ESCAPED, A(1948, Brit.); OPERATION DIAMOND(1948, Brit.); TRIAL OF MADAM X, THE(1948, Brit.); HA' PENNY BREEZE(1951, Brit.); CHEER THE BRAVE(1951, Brit.); KING OF THE UNDERWORLD(1952, Brit.); STOLEN FACE(1952, Brit.); FLOATING DUTCHMAN, THE(1953, Brit.); SKID KIDS(1953, Brit.); HIDEOUT, THE(1956, Brit.); PRIVATE'S PROGRESS(1956, Brit.); CROOKED SKY, THE(1957,

Brit.); OPERATION MURDER(1957, Brit.); VIOLENT STRANGER(1957, Brit.); DIPLOMATIC CORPSE, THE(1958, Brit.); INDISCREET(1958); KILL HER GENTLY(1958, Brit.); MOONRAKER, THE(1958, Brit.); HIDDEN HOMICIDE(1959, Brit.); SHAKEDOWN, THE(1960, Brit.); SHOOT TO KILL(1961, Brit.); INFORMATION RECEIVED(1962, Brit.); MY WIFE'S FAMILY(1962, Brit.); YOUNG, WILLING AND EAGER(1962, Brit.)

Geoffrey Hawkins
TOWN LIKE ALICE, A(1958, Brit.)

George Hawkins
WINSTANLEY(1979, Brit.)

Georgia Hawkins
LIGHT OF WESTERN STARS, THE(1940); DOOMED CARAVAN(1941); PENNY SERENADE(1941)

Ira Hawkins
Misc. Talkies
PYRAMID, THE(1976)

Jack Hawkins
PERFECT ALIBI, THE(1931, Brit.); GOOD COMPANIONS(1933, Brit.); I LIVED WITH YOU(1933, Brit.); JEWEL, THE(1933, Brit.); SHOT IN THE DARK, A(1933, Brit.); AUTUMN CROCUS(1934, Brit.); DEATH AT A BROADCAST(1934, Brit.); PHANTOM FIEND, THE(1935, Brit.); PEG OF OLD DRURY(1936, Brit.); BEAUTY AND THE BARGE(1937, Brit.); FROG, THE(1937, Brit.); LOST CHORD, THE(1937, Brit.); ROYAL DIVORCE, A(1938, Brit.); WHO GOES NEXT?(1938, Brit.); MURDER WILL OUT(1939, Brit.); FLYING SQUAD, THE(1940, Brit.); NEXT OF KIN(1942, Brit.); BONNIE PRINCE CHARLIE(1948, Brit.); FALLEN IDOL, THE(1949, Brit.); HOUR OF GLORY(1949, Brit.); NO HIGHWAY IN THE SKY(1951, Brit.); BLACK ROSE, THE(1950); FIGHTING PIMPERNEL, THE(1950, Brit.); ADVENTURERS, THE(1951, Brit.); GREAT MANHUNT, THE(1951, Brit.); CRASH OF SILENCE(1952, Brit.); OUTPOST IN MALAYA(1952, Brit.); CRUEL SEA, THE(1953); MURDER ON MONDAY(1953, Brit.); TWICE UPON A TIME(1953, Brit.); ANGELS ONE FIVE(1954, Brit.); FRONT PAGE STORY(1954, Brit.); MALTA STORY(1954, Brit.); INTRUDER, THE(1955, Brit.); LAND OF FURY(1955 Brit.); LAND OF THE PHARAOHS(1955); LIGHT TOUCH, THE(1955, Brit.); PRISONER, THE(1955, Brit.); BRIDGE ON THE RIVER KWAI, THE(1957); DECISION AGAINST TIME(1957, Brit.); SHE PLAYED WITH FIRE(1957, Brit.); THIRD KEY, THE(1957, Brit.); BEN HUR(1959); GIDEON OF SCOTLAND YARD(1959, Brit.); TWO-HEADED SPY, THE(1959, Brit.); LEAGUE OF GENTLEMEN, THE(1961, Brit.); TWO LOVES(1961); FIVE FINGER EXERCISE(1962); LAWRENCE OF ARABIA(1962, Brit.); LAFAYETTE(1963, Fr.); RAMPAGE(1963); GUNS AT BATASI(1964, Brit.); THIRD SECRET, THE(1964, Brit.); ZULU(1964, Brit.); JUDITH(1965); LORD JIM(1965, Brit.); MASQUERADE(1965, Brit.); POPPY IS ALSO A FLOWER, THE(1966); GREAT CATHERINE(1968, Brit.); SHALAKO(1968, Brit.); OH! WHAT A LOVELY WAR(1969, Brit.); THOSE DARING YOUNG MEN IN THEIR JAUNTY JALOPIES(1969, Fr./Brit./ Ital.); NICHOLAS AND ALEXANDRA(1971, Brit.); ADVENTURES OF GERARD, THE(1970, Brit.); WATERLOO(1970, Ital./USSR); JANE EYRE(1971, Brit.); KIDNAPPED(1971, Brit.); LOLA(1971, Brit./Ital.); WHEN EIGHT BELLS TOLL(1971, Brit.); ESCAPE TO THE SUN(1972, Fr./Ger./Israel); RULING CLASS, THE(1972, Brit.), p; YOUNG WINSTON(1972, Brit.); TALES THAT WITNESS MADNESS(1973, Brit.); THEATRE OF BLOOD(1973, Brit.)
Misc. Talkies
BELOVED, THE(1972)

Jim Hawkins
CAUGHT(1949); HOLIDAY AFFAIR(1949); NEVER A DULL MOMENT(1950)

Jimmie Hawkins
SEA OF GRASS, THE(1947); MOONRISE(1948); LOVE THAT BRUTE(1950); WOMAN THEY ALMOST LYNCHED, THE(1953)

Jimmy Hawkins
IT'S A WONDERFUL LIFE(1946); THAT FORSYTE WOMAN(1949); MR. SCOUTMASTER; SAVAGE FRONTIER(1953); PRIVATE HELL 36(1954); COUNT THREE AND PRAY(1955); ZOTZ!(1962); GIRL HAPPY(1965); SPINOUT(1966)

John Hawkins
SECRET COMMAND(1944), w; CRIME WAVE(1954), w; KILLER IS LOOSE, THE(1956), w; SHADOW ON THE WINDOW, THE(1957), w; FLOODS OF FEAR(1958, Brit.), w; TO KILL A CLOWN(1972), m

John Ward Hawkins
HIDDEN FEAR(1957), w

Kai Hawkins
1984
VIGIL(1984, New Zealand), prod d

Kal Hawkins
GOODBYE PORK PIE(1981, New Zealand), art d

Kay Hawkins
BEYOND REASONABLE DOUBT(1980, New Zeal.), art d

Linda Hawkins
TALISMAN, THE(1966)

Loye Hawkins
Misc. Talkies
GUY FROM HARLEM, THE(1977)

Mark Hawkins
HELL BOATS(1970, Brit.); MY LOVER, MY SON(1970, Brit.)

Mary Ann Hawkins
LAST TIME I SAW PARIS, THE(1954)

Mary Hawkins
1984
LISTEN TO THE CITY(1984, Can.)

Michael Hawkins
HOUND OF THE BASKERVILLES, THE(1959, Brit.); DENTIST IN THE CHAIR(1960, Brit.); TERROR OF THE TONGS, THE(1961, Brit.); THEY CAME FROM BEYOND SPACE(1967, Brit.); TORTURE GARDEN(1968, Brit.); DECLINE AND FALL... OF A BIRD WATCHER(1969, Brit.)
Misc. Talkies
TRUCKIN' MAN(1975)

Mr. Hawkins
GALLOPING MAJOR, THE(1951, Brit.)

Odie Hawkins
MONKEY HUSTLE, THE(1976), w

Patricia Hawkins
OH! CALCUTTA!(1972); MAN ON A SWING(1974)

Richard Hawkins
FRANCES(1982)

Robert Hawkins
HARD PART BEGINS, THE(1973, Can.); AGE OF INNOCENCE(1977, Can.)

Ronnie Hawkins
RENALDO AND CLARA(1978); HEAVEN'S GATE(1980)

Screamin' Jay Hawkins
AMERICAN HOT WAX(1978)

Tim Hawkins
SHOW-OFF, THE(1946); THAT FORSYTE WOMAN(1949); WINCHESTER '73(1950); MA AND PA KETTLE AT WAIKIKI(1955)

Timmie Hawkins
MOONRISE(1948); MISTER 880(1950)

Timmy Hawkins
WINGED VICTORY(1944); CRISS CROSS(1949); SUN COMES UP, THE(1949)

Timothy Hawkins
EYES OF A STRANGER(1980); ABSENCE OF MALICE(1981); SMOKEY AND THE BANDIT–PART 3(1983)

Tommy Hawkins
SNIPER, THE(1952)

Tony Hawkins
LOOKIN' TO GET OUT(1982)

Trish Hawkins
HAPPY HOOKER, THE(1975)

Valerie Hawkins
STING OF DEATH(1966)

Virginia Hawkins
CYCLE SAVAGES(1969)

Ward Hawkins
SECRET COMMAND(1944), w; CRIME WAVE(1954), w; KILLER IS LOOSE, THE(1956), w; SHADOW ON THE WINDOW, THE(1957), w; FLOODS OF FEAR(1958, Brit.), w

Willis Hawkins
WORM EATERS, THE(1981), ph

Yvette Hawkins
NIGHTHAWKS(1981)

John Hawkner
WOMAN UNDER THE INFLUENCE, A(1974)

Barbara Hawks
BIG SKY, THE(1952)

F. G. Hawks
CHARLATAN, THE(1929), w

Capt. Frank Hawks
KLONDIKE(1932)

Howard Hawks
AIR CIRCUS, THE(1928), d; DAWN PATROL, THE(1930), d, w; CRIMINAL CODE(1931), d; CROWD ROARS, THE(1932), d&w; SCARFACE(1932), a, p, d; TIGER SHARK(1932), d; TODAY WE LIVE(1933), p&d; TWENTIETH CENTURY(1934), d; VIVA VILLA!(1934), d; BARBARY COAST(1935), d; CEILNG ZERO(1935), d; COME AND GET IT(1936), d; ROAD TO GLORY, THE(1936), d; BRINGING UP BABY(1938), p&d; TEST PILOT(1938), w; ONLY ANGELS HAVE WINGS(1939), p&d, w; HIS GIRL FRIDAY(1940), p&d; BALL OF FIRE(1941), d; AIR FORCE(1943), d; CORVETTE K-225(1943), p; OUTLAW, THE(1943), d; TO HAVE AND HAVE NOT(1944), p&d; BIG SLEEP, THE(1946), p&d; RED RIVER(1948), p&d; SONG IS BORN, A(1948), d; I WAS A MALE WAR BRIDE(1949), d; THING, THE(1951), p, d; BIG SKY, THE(1952), p&d; MONKEY BUSINESS(1952), d; O. HENRY'S FULL HOUSE(1952), d; GENTLEMEN PREFER BLONDES(1953), d; LAND OF THE PHARAOHS(1955), p&d; RIO BRAVO(1959), p&d; HATARI!(1962), p&d; MAN'S FAVORITE SPORT [?](1964), p&d; RED LINE 7000(1965), p&d, w; EL DORADO(1967), p&d; RIO LOBO(1970), p&d
Silents
GIRL IN EVERY PORT, A(1928), d, w
Misc. Silents
FIG LEAVES(1926), d; ROAD TO GLORY, THE(1926), d; CRADLE SNATCHERS, THE(1927), d; PAID TO LOVE(1927), d; FAZIL(1928), d; TRENT'S LAST CASE(1929), d

J. G. Hawks
DRAKE CASE, THE(1929), w; MELODY LANE(1929), w
Silents
DESPOILER, THE(1915), w; FORBIDDEN ADVENTURE, THE(1915), w; LIEUT. DANNY, U.S.A.(1916), w; PRIMAL LURE, THE(1916), w; CHICKEN CASEY(1917), w; DARK ROAD, THE(1917), w; DEVIL DODGER, THE(1917), w; PAWS OF THE BEAR(1917), w; TAR HEEL WARRIOR, THE(1917), w; TRUTHFUL TULLIVER(1917), w; WOODEN SHOES(1917), w; KAISER'S SHADOW, THE(1918), w; QUICKSANDS(1918), w; BREED OF MEN(1919), w; MICKEY(1919), w; BRANDING IRON, THE(1920), w; BUNTY PULLS THE STRINGS(1921), w; SNOWBLIND(1921), w; BLIND BARGAIN, A(1922), w; DANGEROUS AGE, THE(1922), w; STORM, THE(1922), w; ETERNAL STRUGGLE, THE(1923), w; WANTERS, THE(1923), w; INEZ FROM HOLLYWOOD(1924), w; SINGER JIM MCKEE(1924), w; ONE YEAR TO LIVE(1925), w; SPLENDID ROAD, THE(1925), w; CLANCY'S KOSHER WEDDING(1927), w; COWARD, THE(1927), w; SONORA KID, THE(1927), w; FREEDOM OF THE PRESS(1928), w; MICHIGAN KID, THE(1928), w; SILKS AND SADDLES(1929), w

John Kay Hawks
TAZA, SON OF COCHISE(1954)

Kenneth Hawks
BIG TIME(1929), d; SUCH MEN ARE DANGEROUS(1930), d
Silents
ANKLES PREFERRED(1927), w; EXALTED FLAPPER, THE(1929), sup; FUGITIVES(1929), sup; MASKED EMOTIONS(1929), d; NEW YEAR'S EVE(1929), sup

Patricia Hawks
SHE'S WORKING HER WAY THROUGH COLLEGE(1952)

William Hawks
INDIANAPOLIS SPEEDWAY(1939), w; IMITATION GENERAL(1958), p; LAW AND JAKE WADE, THE(1958), p

William B. Hawks
TALL MEN, THE(1955), p; LAST WAGON, THE(1956), p

Alan Hawkshaw
I AM A GROUPIE(1970, Brit.), m

Jean Hawkshaw
WILD WOMEN OF WONGO, THE(1959)

Tony Hawkson
LOOKIN' TO GET OUT(1982)

John Hawksworth
NAKED WORLD OF HARRISON MARKS, THE(1967, Brit.), m, md; PENTHOUSE, THE(1967, Brit.), m

John Hawkwood
HIRED KILLER, THE(1967, Fr./Ital.); YOUNG, THE EVIL AND THE SAVAGE, THE(1968, Ital.)

Cameron Hawley
EXECUTIVE SUITE(1954), w; CASH McCALL(1960), w

Deborah Hawley
RUNNERS(1983, Brit.)

Dudley Hawley
Silents
AMERICAN WIDOW, AN(1917)
Misc. Silents
HOW COULD YOU, CAROLINE?(1918)

H. Dudley Hawley
YOUNG MAN OF MANHATTAN(1930); SECRETS OF A SECRETARY(1931)

Helen Hawley
LAUGHING LADY, THE(1930); BIRTH OF A BABY(1938)
Misc. Silents
TWO-GUN BETTY(1918)

Helene Hawley
DELINQUENTS, THE(1957)

James Hawley
SUNSET BOULEVARD(1950)

Lowell S. Hawley
SIGN OF ZORRO, THE(1960), w; SWISS FAMILY ROBINSON(1960), w; BABES IN TOYLAND(1961), w; IN SEARCH OF THE CASTAWAYS(1962, Brit.), w; TIGER WALKS, A(1964), w; ADVENTURES OF BULLWHIP GRIFFIN, THE(1967), w; ONE AND ONLY GENUINE ORIGINAL FAMILY BAND, THE(1968), w

lp: Monte Hawley
Misc. Talkies
DOUBLE DEAL(1939)

Max Hawley
Silents
AIR MAIL PILOT, THE(1928)

Monte Hawley
DUKE IS THE TOPS, THE(1938); ONE DARK NIGHT(1939); REFORM SCHOOL(1939); AM I GUILTY?(1940); GANG WAR(1940); TAKE MY LIFE(1942); LOOK OUT SISTER(1948); MIRACLE IN HARLEM(1948); 2001: A SPACE ODYSSEY(1968, U.S./Brit.)
Misc. Talkies
GUN MOLL(1938); LIFE GOES ON(1938); MR. SMITH GOES GHOST(1940); MYSTERY IN SWING(1940); TALL, TAN AND TERRIFIC(1946)

Monty Hawley
MR. WASHINGTON GOES TO TOWN(1941)

Neil Hawley
STOP THE WORLD-I WANT TO GET OFF(1966, Brit.)

Ormi Hawley
Silents
NATION'S PERIL, THE(1915); ANTICS OF ANN, THE(1917); HER GREAT CHANCE(1918)
Misc. Silents
RAGGED EARL, THE(1914); THROUGH FIRE TO FORTUNE OR THE SUNKEN VILLAGE(1914); DESTINY'S SKEIN(1915); PATH TO THE RAINBOW, THE(1915); REGENERATING LOVE, THE(1915); ROMANCE OF THE NAVY, A(1915); HER AMERICAN PRINCE(1916); RACE SUICIDE(1916); SOCIAL HIGHWAYMAN, THE(1916); WEAKNESS OF STRENGTH, THE(1916); WHERE LOVE LEADS(1916); ORDEAL OF ROSETTA, THE(1918); SPLENDID ROMANCE, THE(1918); GREATER SINNER, THE(1919); ROAD CALLED STRAIGHT, THE(1919); UNWRITTEN CODE, THE(1919)

Pat Hawley
SILENCERS, THE(; CHOPPERS, THE(1961); PAINT YOUR WAGON(1969)

Rock Hawley
COWBOY HOLIDAY(1934), w

Rock Hawley [Bob Hill]
DANGER TRAILS(1935), w; LAW AND LEAD(1937), w

Rock Hawley [Robert Hill]
TOO MUCH BEEF(1936), w

Tom Hawley
Silents
GOLD RUSH, THE(1925)

Wanda Hawley
Misc. Talkies
PUEBLO TERROR(1931); TRAILS OF THE GOLDEN WEST(1931); CROOKED ROAD(1932)
Silents
MR. FIX-IT(1918); OLD WIVES FOR NEW(1918); PAIR OF SILK STOCKINGS, A(1918); FOOD FOR SCANDAL(1920); MISS HOBBS(1920); AFFAIRS OF ANATOL, THE(1921); KISS IN TIME, A(1921); LOVE CHARM, THE(1921); OUTSIDE WOMAN, THE(1921); BURNING SANDS(1922); THIRTY DAYS(1922); WOMAN WHO WALKED ALONE, THE(1922); FIRES OF FATE(1923, Brit.); NOBODY'S MONEY(1923); RECKLESS ROMANCE(1924); LAST ALARM, THE(1926); MIDNIGHT MESSAGE, THE(1926); PIRATES OF THE SKY(1927)
Misc. Silents
BORDER WIRELESS, THE(1918); GYPSY TRAIL, THE(1918); WAY OF A MAN WITH A MAID, THE(1918); WE CAN'T HAVE EVERYTHING(1918); EVERYWOMAN(1919); GREASED LIGHTING(1919); LOTTERY MAN, THE(1919); PEG O' MY HEART(1919); POOR BOOB(1919); SECRET SERVICE(1919); TOLD IN THE HILLS(1919); VIRTOUS SINNERS(1919); YOU'RE FIRED(1919); DOUBLE SPEED(1920); HELD BY THE ENEMY(1920); HER BELOVED VILLIAN(1920); HER FIRST ELOPEMENT(1920); MRS. TEMPLE'S TELEGRAM(1920); SIX BEST CELLARS, THE(1920); TREE OF KNOWLEDGE, THE(1920); HER FACE VALUE(1921); HER STURDY OAK(1921); HOUSE THAT JAZZ BUILT, THE(1921); SNOB, THE(1921); BOBBED HAIR(1922); TOO MUCH WIFE(1922); TRUTHFUL LIAR, THE(1922); YOUNG RAHAH, THE(1922); BRASS COMMANDMENTS(1923); MAN FROM BROD-

NEY'S, THE(1923); MASTERS OF MEN(1923); BREAD(1924); DESERT SHEIK, THE(1924); AMERICAN PLUCK(1925); BARRIERS BURNED AWAY(1925); FLYING FOOL(1925); LET WOMEN ALONE(1925); STOP FLIRTING(1925); UNNAMED WOMAN, THE(1925); COMBAT, THE(1926); DESPERATE MOMENT, A(1926); HEARTS AND SPANGLES(1926); MEN OF THE NIGHT(1926); MIDNIGHT LIMITED(1926); SMOKE EATERS, THE(1926); WHOM SHALL I MARRY(1926); EYES OF THE TOTEM(1927)

William Hawley
TOMORROW(1972)

Goldie Hawn
$(DOLLARS)**1/2 (1971); CACTUS FLOWER(1969); THERE'S A GIRL IN MY SOUP(1970, Brit.); BUTTERFLIES ARE FREE(1972); GIRL FROM PETROVKA, THE(1974); SUGARLAND EXPRESS, THE(1974); SHAMPOO(1975); DUCHESS AND THE DIRTWATER FOX, THE(1976); FOUL PLAY(1978); PRIVATE BENJAMIN(1980); SEEMS LIKE OLD TIMES(1980); LOVERS AND LIARS(1981, Ital.); BEST FRIENDS(1982)
1984
PROTOCOL(1984), a, ex p; SWING SHIFT(1984)

Goldy Jeanne Hawn
ONE AND ONLY GENUINE ORIGINAL FAMILY BAND, THE(1968)

Laura Hawn
1984
SWING SHIFT(1984)

Edward Haworth
INVASION OF THE BODY SNATCHERS(1956), art d; GODDESS, THE(1958), art d; I WANT TO LIVE!(1958), art d; WHO WAS THAT LADY?(1960), art d

Edward S. Haworth
SOUTHSIDE 1-1000(1950), prod d; I CONFESS(1953), art d, set d; KENTUCKIAN, THE(1955), prod d; MARTY(1955), art d; FRIENDLY PERSUASION(1956), art d; MIDDLE OF THE NIGHT(1959), art d; OUTSIDER, THE(1962), art d; RIDE THE WILD SURF(1964), art d; WILD AND WONDERFUL(1964), art d; GLORY GUYS, THE(1965), prod d; MAYA(1966), art d; PROFESSIONALS, THE(1966); JUNIOR BONNER(1972), art d

Ethyl Haworth
STORY OF VERNON AND IRENE CASTLE, THE(1939)

Gail Haworth
GODDESS, THE(1958)

Jill Haworth
EXODUS(1960); CARDINAL, THE(1963); YOUR SHADOW IS MINE(1963, Fr./Ital.); IN HARM'S WAY(1965); IT!(1967, Brit.); HORROR HOUSE(1970, Brit.); MUTATIONS, THE(1974, Brit.); BEYOND THE FOG(1981, Brit.)

Joe Haworth
WITHOUT RESERVATIONS(1946); I'LL BE SEEING YOU(1944); BORN TO SPEED(1947); STREET WITH NO NAME, THE(1948); THAT LADY IN ERMINE(1948); THAT WONDERFUL URGE(1948); FATHER WAS A FULLBACK(1949); I WAS A MALE WAR BRIDE(1949); THIEVES' HIGHWAY(1949); YOU'RE MY EVERYTHING(1949); MEET ME AFTER THE SHOW(1951); MY SIX CONVICTS(1952); OUTCASTS OF POKER FLAT, THE(1952); GUN BELT(1953); CAINE MUTINY, THE(1954); RUN FOR COVER(1955); WONDERFUL COUNTRY, THE(1959); SPARTACUS(1960); FIVE GUNS TO TOMBSTONE(1961); FLIGHT THAT DISAPPEARED, THE(1961); SHOWDOWN(1963)

Joseph Haworth
SOUTH OF DIXIE(1944); WING AND A PRAYER(1944); FRONTIER GAL(1945); SALOME, WHERE SHE DANCED(1945); WHERE DO WE GO FROM HERE?(1945); SLAVE GIRL(1947)

Peter Haworth
1984
FINDERS KEEPERS(1984)

Ted Haworth
WHEN YOU COMIN' BACK, RED RYDER?(1979), prod d; STRANGERS ON A TRAIN(1951), art d; NAKED STREET, THE(1955), art d; FOUR GIRLS IN TOWN(1956), art d; SAYONARA(1957), art d; NAKED AND THE DEAD, THE(1958), art d; SOME LIKE IT HOT(1959), art d; PEPE(1960), art d; LONGEST DAY, THE(1962), art d; WHAT A WAY TO GO(1964), art d; SECONDS(1966), art d; HALF A SIXPENCE(1967, Brit.), prod d; WAY WEST, THE(1967), art d; VILLA RIDES(1968), prod d; THOSE DARING YOUNG MEN IN THEIR JAUNTY JALOPIES(1969, Fr./Brit./Ital.), prod d; KREMLIN LETTER, THE(1970), prod d; GETAWAY, THE(1972), art d; JEREMIAH JOHNSON(1972), art d; PAT GARRETT AND BILLY THE KID(1973), art d; CLAUDINE(1974), set d; HARRY AND TONTO(1974), prod d; KILLER ELITE, THE(1975), prod d; SAILOR WHO FELL FROM GRACE WITH THE SEA, THE(1976, Brit.), prod d; TELEFON(1977), prod d; SOMEBODY KILLED HER HUSBAND(1978), prod d; BLOODLINE(1979), prod d; ROUGH CUT(1980, Brit.), prod d; DEATH HUNT(1981), prod d; JINXED!(1982), prod d
1984
BLAME IT ON THE NIGHT(1984), prod d

Vinton Haworth
NIGHT WAITRESS(1936); WITHOUT ORDERS(1936); CHINA PASSAGE(1937); RIDING ON AIR(1937); THAT GIRL FROM PARIS(1937); WE'RE ON THE JURY(1937); YOU CAN'T BUY LUCK(1937); MAD MISS MANTON, THE(1938); DAY THE BOOKIES WEPT, THE(1939); THAT'S RIGHT-YOU'RE WRONG(1939); WHEN TOMORROW COMES(1939); MEXICAN SPITFIRE OUT WEST(1940); LUCKY DEVILS(1941); MEXICAN SPITFIRE'S BABY(1941); PLAYMATES(1941); SAINT IN PALM SPRINGS, THE(1941); TWO-FACED WOMAN(1941); LADIES' DAY(1943); SPARTACUS(1960); POLICE DOG STORY, THE(1961)

Joseph Hawroth
NORTHERN PURSUIT(1943)

Beverly Hawthorne
LIVE WIRES(1946); SUSPENSE(1946)

David Hawthorne
BED AND BREAKFAST(1930, Brit.); ESCAPE(1930, Brit.); GLAMOUR(1931, Brit.); LIMPING MAN, THE(1931, Brit.); OTHER WOMAN, THE(1931, Brit.); PERFECT ALIBI, THE(1931, Brit.); MAN WHO WON, THE(1933, Brit.); LAD, THE(1935, Brit.); DREAMS COME TRUE(1936, Brit.); LABURNUM GROVE(1936, Brit.)
Silents
AUTUMN OF PRIDE, THE(1921, Brit.); IN HIS GRIP(1921, Brit.); OPEN COUNTRY(1922, Brit.); ROB ROY(1922, Brit.); SILENT EVIDENCE(1922, Brit.); MATING OF MARCUS, THE(1924, Brit.); PRESUMPTION OF STANLEY HAY, MP, THE(1925, Brit.); HIS HOUSE IN ORDER(1928, Brit.); BARNES MURDER CASE, THE(1930, Brit.)

Ryoji Hayama
TEMPTRESS AND THE MONK, THE(1963, Jap.); HOUSE OF STRANGE LOVES, THE(1969, Jap.)

Toshio Hayano
GIRL I ABANDONED, THE(1970, Jap.)

Fumio Hayasaka
DRUNKEN ANGEL(1948, Jap.), m; RASHOMON(1951, Jap.), m; UGETSU(1954, Jap.), m; SEVEN SAMURAI, THE(1956, Jap.), m; IKIRU(1960, Jap.), m; IDIOT, THE(1963, Jap.), m; STRAY DOG(1963, Jap.), m; SCANDAL(1964, Jap.), m; I LIVE IN FEAR(1967, Jap.), m; SANSHO THE BAILIFF(1969, Jap.), m

Kumi Hayase
HOTSPRINGS HOLIDAY(1970, Jap.); TOPSY-TURVY JOURNEY(1970, Jap.)

Chizu Hayashi
SHOWDOWN FOR ZATOICHI(1968, Jap.)

Fumiko Hayashi
LONELY LANE(1963, Jap.), w

Hikaru Hayashi
HAPPINESS OF US ALONE(1962, Jap.), m; ISLAND, THE(1962, Jap.), m; TILL TOMORROW COMES(1962, Jap.), m; MY HOBO(1963, Jap.), m; LOVE UNDER THE CRUCIFIX(1965, Jap.), m; ONIBABA(1965, Jap.), m; THIN LINE, THE(1967, Jap.), m; KUROENKO(1968, Jap.), m; LOST SEX(1968, Jap.), m; THOUSAND CRANES(1969, Jap.), m; PLAY IT COOL(1970, Jap.), m; VIXEN(1970, Jap.), m; AFFAIR AT AKIT-SU(1980, Jap.), m

Joichi Hayashi
KWAIDAN(1965, Jap.)

Kanji Hayashi
KARATE, THE HAND OF DEATH(1961)

Marc Hayashi
CHAN IS MISSING(1982)
1984
ANGEL(1984)

Miki Hayashi
HOUSE OF STRANGE LOVES, THE(1969, Jap.)

Teru Hayashi
1984
PREY, THE(1984), ph

Yoichi Hayashi
PERFORMERS, THE(1970, Jap.)

Ytaka Hayashi
GODZILLA VS. MEGALON(1976, Jap.)

Shigeo Hayashida
LOVE AT TWENTY(1963, Fr./Ital./Jap./Pol./Ger.), ph

Ernest Haycox
STAGECOACH(1939), w; UNION PACIFIC(1939), w; APACHE TRAIL(1942), w; SUNDOWN JIM(1942), w; ABILENE TOWN(1946), w; CANYON PASSAGE(1946), w; HEAVEN ONLY KNOWS(1947), w; MONTANA(1950), w; MAN IN THE SAD-DLE(1951), w; APACHE WAR SMOKE(1952), w; BUGLES IN THE AFTER-NOON(1952), w; STAGECOACH(1966), w

Kenneth Haycraft
MAYBE IT'S LOVE(1930)

Marcia Haydee
TURNING POINT, THE(1977)

Richard Haydel
HENRY ALDRICH, BOY SCOUT(1944); NATIONAL VELVET(1944)

Andrew Hayden
SWEET HUNTERS(1969, Panama)

Barbara Hayden
LOVES OF CARMEN, THE(1948); PERILOUS JOURNEY, A(1953); CRIMSON KIMO-NO, THE(1959)

Bob Hayden
WEST POINT STORY, THE(1950)

Christopher Hayden
CHANGES(1969)

Crystal Hayden
NUNZIO(1978)

Denis Hayden
MEN OF YESTERDAY(1936, Brit.)

Don Hayden
IN THE MEANTIME, DARLING(1944); RECKLESS AGE(1944); MARGIE(1946); MISS GRANT TAKES RICHMOND(1949); I WANT YOU(1951); TOO MUCH, TOO SOON(1958)

Eddie Hayden
HEARTBEAT(1946)

Frank Hayden
ONE WISH TOO MANY(1956, Brit.); ONE MILLION YEARS B.C.(1967, Brit./U.S.); PREHISTORIC WOMEN(1967, Brit.); LOST CONTINENT, THE(1968, Brit.); MC KEN-ZIE BREAK, THE(1970); UNDERGROUND(1970, Brit.); CREATURES THE WORLD FORGOT(1971, Brit.), a, stunts

Harry Hayden
TRUE TO LIFE(1943); UNCLE HARRY(1945); WITHOUT RESERVATIONS(1946); CASE OF THE BLACK CAT, THE(1936); COLLEGE HOLIDAY(1936); FURY(1936); I MARRIED A DOCTOR(1936); KILLER AT LARGE(1936); MAN I MARRY, THE(1936); PRINCESS COMES ACROSS, THE(1936); PUBLIC ENEMY'S WIFE(1936); THREE MEN ON A HORSE(1936); TWO AGAINST THE WORLD(1936); BLACK LEGION, THE(1937); EVER SINCE EVE(1937); EXCLUSIVE(1937); GOD'S COUNTRY AND THE WOMAN(1937); JOHN MEADE'S WOMAN(1937); LOVE IS NEWS(1937); LOVE IS ON THE AIR(1937); MAYTIME(1937); MELODY FOR TWO(1937); ANGELS WITH DIRTY FACES(1938); DELINQUENT PARENTS(1938); DOUBLE DANGER(1938); FOUR MEN AND A PRAYER(1938); I'LL GIVE A MILLION(1938); IN OLD CHICAGO(1938); KENTUCKY(1938); LITTLE TOUGH GUY(1938); SALESLADY(1938); SKY GIANT(1938); BARRICADE(1939); CISCO KID AND THE LADY, THE(1939); FIVE LITTLE PEPPERS AND HOW THEY GREW(1939); FLIGHT AT MIDNIGHT(1939); FRONTIER MARSHAL(1939); HERE I AM A STRANGER(1939); HONEYMOON'S OVER, THE(1939); HOUSE OF FEAR, THE(1939); INVITATION TO HAP-PINESS(1939); RAINS CAME, THE(1939); ROSE OF WASHINGTON SQUARE(1939); SOCIETY SMUGGLERS(1939); SWANEE RIVER(1939); WIFE, HUSBAND AND FRIEND(1939); CHRISTMAS IN JULY(1940); GREAT McGINTY, THE(1940); HE MARRIED HIS WIFE(1940); I LOVE YOU AGAIN(1940); KNUTE ROCKNE–ALL AMERICAN(1940); LILLIAN RUSSELL(1940); SAPS AT SEA(1940); WE WHO ARE YOUNG(1940); YESTERDAY'S HEROES(1940); YOU'RE NOT SO TOUGH(1940);

FOOTSTEPS IN THE DARK(1941); HIGH SIERRA(1941); HOLD THAT GHOST(1941); LAST OF THE DUANES(1941); MAD DOCTOR, THE(1941); MAN BETRAYED, A(1941); MOUNTAIN MOONLIGHT(1941); NIGHT OF JANUARY 16TH(1941); PAR-SON OF PANAMINT, THE(1941); REMEMBER THE DAY(1941); SLEEPERS WEST(1941); WEEKEND IN HAVANA(1941); GET HEP TO LOVE(1942); HENRY ALDRICH GETS GLAMOUR(1942); JOAN OF OZARK(1942); LONE STAR RAN-GER(1942); MAGNIFICENT DOPE, THE(1942); PALM BEACH STORY, THE(1942); RINGS ON HER FINGERS(1942); SPRINGTIME IN THE ROCKIES(1942); TALES OF MANHATTAN(1942); THIS GUN FOR HIRE(1942); VALLEY OF THE SUN(1942); WE WERE DANCING(1942); WHISPERING GHOSTS(1942); YANKEE DOODLE DAN-DY(1942); YOKEL BOY(1942); YOU CAN'T ESCAPE FOREVER(1942); YOU'RE TELL-ING ME(1942); DU BARRY WAS A LADY(1943); HELLO, FRISCO, HELLO(1943); MEANEST MAN IN THE WORLD, THE(1943); SHE HAS WHAT IT TAKES(1943); SLIGHTLY DANGEROUS(1943); UNKNOWN GUEST, THE(1943); YOU'RE A LUCKY FELLOW, MR. SMITH(1943); YOUTH ON PARADE(1943); BARBARY COAST GENT(1944); BIG NOISE, THE(1944); GREAT MOMENT, THE(1944); HAIL THE CONQUERING HERO(1944); HENRY ALDRICH PLAYS CUPID(1944); LADY AND THE MONSTER, THE(1944); SINCE YOU WENT AWAY(1944); THIN MAN GOES HOME, THE(1944); THIRTY SECONDS OVER TOKYO(1944); UP IN ARMS(1944); UP IN MABEL'S ROOM(1944); WEIRD WOMAN(1944); BOSTON BLACKIE'S RENDEZ-VOUS(1945); COLONEL EFFINGHAM'S RAID(1945); DANGEROUS PART-NERS(1945); INCENDIARY BLONDE(1945); MEDAL FOR BENNY, A(1945); WOMAN IN THE WINDOW, THE(1945); ZIEGFELD FOLLIES(1945); BLUE DAHLIA, THE(1946); HOODLUM SAINT, THE(1946); IF I'M LUCKY(1946); KILLERS, THE(1946); MY BROTHER TALKS TO HORSES(1946); NOTORIOUS(1946); SECRET HEART, THE(1946); TILL THE CLOUDS ROLL BY(1946); TILL THE END OF TIME(1946); TWO SISTERS FROM BOSTON(1946); EASY COME, EASY GO(1947); FOR THE LOVE OF RUSTY(1947); KEY WITNESS(1947); MERTON OF THE MO-VIES(1947); MILLIE'S DAUGHTER(1947); OUT OF THE PAST(1947); PERILS OF PAULINE, THE(1947); UNFINISHED DANCE,THE(1947); VARIETY GIRL(1947); DOCKS OF NEW ORLEANS(1948); DUDE GOES WEST, THE(1948); EVERY GIRL SHOULD BE MARRIED(1948); FAMILY HONEYMOON(1948); FIGHTING FATHER DUNNE(1948); GOOD SAM(1948); OUT OF THE STORM(1948); RUSTY LEADS THE WAY(1948); SILVER RIVER(1948); VELVET TOUCH, THE(1948); ABBOTT AND COSTELLO MEET THE KILLER, BORIS KARLOFF(1949); BEAUTIFUL BLONDE FROM BASHFUL BEND, THE(1949); GUN CRAZY(1949); INTRUDER IN THE DUST(1949); JOE PALOOKA IN THE BIG FIGHT(1949); JUDGE STEPS OUT, THE(1949); LONE WOLF AND HIS LADY, THE(1949); PRISON WARDEN(1949); TRAVELING SALESWOMAN(1950); UNION STATION(1950); DOUBLE DYNAMI-TE(1951); PIER 23(1951); STREET BANDITS(1951); ARMY BOUND(1952); CAR-RIE(1952); O. HENRY'S FULL HOUSE(1952); LAST POSSE, THE(1953); MONEY FROM HOME(1953)

Helen Hayden
TWO TICKETS TO BROADWAY(1951)

Helene Hayden
GREAT JESSE JAMES RAID, THE(1953); VICKI(1953); FRENCH LINE, THE(1954); SON OF SINBAD(1955)

Henry Hayden
HIDDEN POWER(1939)

J. Charles Hayden
Silents
SEA-WOLF, THE(1913)

James Hayden
NESTING, THE(1981)
1984
ONCE UPON A TIME IN AMERICA(1984)

James P. Hayden
Misc. Talkies
DON'T GO INTO THE WOODS(1980)

Jane Hayden
CONFESSIONS OF A POP PERFORMER(1975, Brit.); EMILY(1976, Brit.)

Jeff Hayden
THAT CERTAIN FEELING(1956)

Jeffrey Hayden
VINTAGE, THE(1957), d

John Hayden
SAP FROM SYRACUSE, THE(1930), w

Jon Hayden
SIX PACK(1982)

Kathleen Hayden
CLUE OF THE NEW PIN, THE(1929, Brit.), w
Silents
MAN WHO CHANGED HIS NAME, THE(1928, Brit.), w

Kirsten Hayden
RUMBLE FISH(1983)

Larry Hayden
MOVIE MOVIE(1978)

Linda Hayden
BABY LOVE(1969, Brit.); BLOOD ON SATAN'S CLAW, THE(1970, Brit.); TASTE THE BLOOD OF DRACULA(1970, Brit.); SOMETHING TO HIDE(1972, Brit.); NIGHT WATCH(1973, Brit.); CONFESSIONS OF A WINDOW CLEANER(1974, Brit.); MAD-HOUSE(1974, Brit.); OLD DRACULA(1975, Brit.); CONFESSIONS FROM A HOLIDAY CAMP(1977, Brit.); BOYS FROM BRAZIL, THE(1978)
Misc. Talkies
HOUSE ON STRAW HILL, THE(1976)

Melissa Hayden
LIMELIGHT(1952), a, ch

Nora Hayden
SCARLET WEEKEND, A(1932); PLUNDER ROAD(1957); ALASKA PASSAGE(1959); ANGRY RED PLANET, THE(1959); OPERATION CAMEL(1961, Den.)
Silents
OTHER PERSON, THE(1921, Brit.); WATCH YOUR WIFE(1926)
Misc. Silents
LIGHTS OF HOME, THE(1920, Brit.)

Peter Hayden
BEYOND REASONABLE DOUBT(1980, New Zeal.); PICTURES(1982, New Zealand)

Robert Hayden
NUNZIO(1978)

Ron Hayden
FORCE: FIVE(1981)
Russ Hayden
COLORADO RANGER(1950); CROOKED RIVER(1950); FAST ON THE DRAW(1950); MARSHAL OF HELDORADO(1950); WEST OF THE BRAZOS(1950); TEXANS NEVER CRY(1951)
Russ "Lucky" Hayden
EVERYBODY'S DANCIN'(1950)
Russell Hayden
HILLS OF OLD WYOMING(1937); HOPALONG RIDES AGAIN(1937); NORTH OF THE RIO GRANDE(1937); RUSTLER'S VALLEY(1937); TEXAS TRAIL(1937); BAR 20 JUSTICE(1938); CASSIDY OF BAR 20(1938); FRONTIERSMAN, THE(1938); HEART OF ARIZONA(1938); IN OLD MEXICO(1938); MYSTERIOUS RIDER, THE(1938); PARTNERS OF THE PLAINS(1938); PRIDE OF THE WEST(1938); SUNSET TRAIL(1938); HERITAGE OF THE DESERT(1939); LAW OF THE PAMPAS(1939); RANGE WAR(1939); RENEGADE TRAIL(1939); SILVER ON THE SAGE(1939); HIDDEN GOLD(1940); KNIGHTS OF THE RANGE(1940); LIGHT OF WESTERN STARS, THE(1940); SANTA FE MARSHAL(1940); SHOWDOWN, THE(1940); STAGECOACH WAR(1940); THREE MEN FROM TEXAS(1940); BORDER VIGILANTES(1941); DOOMED CARAVAN(1941); IN OLD COLORADO(1941), a, w; PIRATES ON HORSEBACK(1941); RIDERS OF THE BADLANDS(1941); ROYAL MOUNTED PATROL, THE(1941); TWO IN A TAXI(1941); WIDE OPEN TOWN(1941); BAD MEN OF THE HILLS(1942); DOWN RIO GRANDE WAY(1942); LAWLESS PLAINSMEN(1942); LONE PRAIRIE, THE(1942); LUCKY LEGS(1942); RIDERS OF THE NORTHLAND(1942); WEST OF TOMBSTONE(1942); FRONTIER LAW(1943); MINESWEEPER(1943); RIDERS OF THE NORTHWEST MOUNTED(1943); SILVER CITY RAIDERS(1943); GAMBLER'S CHOICE(1944); LAST HORSEMAN, THE(1944); MARSHAL OF GUNSMOKE(1944); SEVEN WERE SAVED(1947); ALBUQUERQUE(1948); SONS OF ADVENTURE(1948); APACHE CHIEF(1949); DEPUTY MARSHAL(1949); HOSTILE COUNTRY(1950); VALLEY OF FIRE(1951); WHEN THE GIRLS TAKE OVER(1962), p&d
Misc. Talkies
OVERLAND TO DEADWOOD(1942); TORNADO IN THE SADDLE, A(1942); SADDLES AND SAGEBRUSH(1943); VIGILANTES RIDE, THE(1944); WYOMING HURRICANE(1944); ROLLING HOME(1948)
Schuyler Hayden
RAT FINK(1965); RIOT ON SUNSET STRIP(1967)
Sean Hayden
SOMEWHERE IN TIME(1980)
Sterling Hayden
BAHAMA PASSAGE(1941); VIRGINIA(1941); BLAZE OF NOON(1947); VARIETY GIRL(1947); EL PASO(1949); MANHANDLED(1949); ASPHALT JUNGLE, THE(1950); FLAMING FEATHER(1951); JOURNEY INTO LIGHT(1951); DENVER AND RIO GRANDE(1952); FLAT TOP(1952); GOLDEN HAWK, THE(1952); HELLGATE(1952); FIGHTER ATTACK(1953); KANSAS PACIFIC(1953); SO BIG(1953); STAR, THE(1953); TAKE ME TO TOWN(1953); ARROW IN THE DUST(1954); CRIME WAVE(1954); JOHNNY GUITAR(1954); NAKED ALIBI(1954); PRINCE VALIANT(1954); SUDDENLY(1954); BATTLE TAXI(1955); ETERNAL SEA, THE(1955); LAST COMMAND, THE(1955); SHOTGUN(1955); TIMBERJACK(1955); TOP GUN(1955); COME ON, THE(1956); KILLING, THE(1956); CRIME OF PASSION(1957); FIVE STEPS TO DANGER(1957); GUN BATTLE AT MONTEREY(1957); IRON SHERIFF, THE(1957); VALERIE(1957); ZERO HOUR!(1957); TEN DAYS TO TULARA(1958); TERROR IN A TEXAS TOWN(1958); DR. STRANGELOVE: OR HOW I LEARNED TO STOP WORRYING AND LOVE THE BOMB(1964); HARD CONTRACT(1969); SWEET HUNTERS(1969, Panama); LOVING(1970); GODFATHER, THE(1972); LONG GOODBYE, THE(1973); DEADLY STRANGERS(1974, Brit.); LAST DAYS OF MAN ON EARTH, THE(1975, Brit.); 1900(1976, Ital.); KING OF THE GYPSIES(1978); WINTER KILLS(1979); NINE TO FIVE(1980); OUTSIDER, THE(1980); GAS(1981, Can.); VENOM(1982, Brit.)
Ted Hayden
WILD RIDERS(1971)
1984
PREY, THE(1984)
Vernon Hayden
BLUES FOR LOVERS(1966, Brit.); LOCK UP YOUR DAUGHTERS(1969, Brit.); WHERE'S JACK?(1969, Brit.); MC KENZIE BREAK, THE(1970); VON RICHTHOFEN AND BROWN(1970); WEDDING NIGHT(1970, Ireland)
William Hayden
VAMPIRE'S COFFIN, THE(1958, Mex.), art d
Richard Haydin
TONIGHT AND EVERY NIGHT(1945)
Franz Joseph Haydn
NEST, THE(1982, Span.), m
1984
BASILEUS QUARTET(1984, Ital.), m
Lili Haydn
MAKING LOVE(1982); EASY MONEY(1983)
Richard Haydn
BALL OF FIRE(1941); CHARLEY'S AUNT(1941); ARE HUSBANDS NECESSARY?(1942); THUNDER BIRDS(1942); FOREVER AND A DAY(1943); NO TIME FOR LOVE(1943); ADVENTURE(1945); AND THEN THERE WERE NONE(1945); CLUNY BROWN(1946); GREEN YEARS, THE(1946); BEGINNING OR THE END, THE(1947); FOREVER AMBER(1947); FOXES OF HARROW, THE(1947); LATE GEORGE APLEY, THE(1947); SINGAPORE(1947); EMPEROR WALTZ, THE(1948); MISS TATLOCK'S MILLIONS(1948); SITTING PRETTY(1948); DEAR WIFE(1949); MR. MUSIC(1950), d; ALICE IN WONDERLAND(1951); MERRY WIDOW, THE(1952); MONEY FROM HOME(1953); NEVER LET ME GO(1953, U.S./Brit.); HER TWELVE MEN(1954); TOY TIGER(1956); TWILIGHT FOR THE GODS(1958); LOST WORLD, THE(1960); PLEASE DON'T EAT THE DAISIES(1960); FIVE WEEKS IN A BALLOON(1962); MUTINY ON THE BOUNTY(1962); CLARENCE, THE CROSS-EYED LION(1965); SOUND OF MUSIC, THE(1965); ADVENTURES OF BULLWHIP GRIFFIN, THE(1967); YOUNG FRANKENSTEIN(1974)
Ron Haydock
LEMON GROVE KIDS MEET THE MONSTERS, THE(1966), w
Misc. Talkies
BLOOD MONSTER(1972)
Ronald Haydock
RAT PFINK AND BOO BOO(1966), w

C. Charles Haydon
Silents
LAST EGYPTIAN, THE(1914)
Charles J. Haydon
Misc. Silents
HEARTS OF LOVE(1918), d
Dick Haydon
ATTACK ON THE IRON COAST(1968, U.S./Brit.)
Don Haydon
Misc. Talkies
SIX-GUN DECISION(1953)
J. Charles Haydon
Silents
ALSTER CASE, THE(1915), d; NIGHT WORKERS, THE(1917), d
Misc. Silents
PHANTOM BUCCANEER, THE(1916), d; STING OF VICTORY, THE(1916), d; SATAN'S PRIVATE DOOR(1917), d
Julie Haydon
BEAST OF THE CITY, THE(1932); BILL OF DIVORCEMENT, A(1932); COME ON DANGER!(1932); CONQUERORS, THE(1932); SYMPHONY OF SIX MILLION(1932); THIRTEEN WOMEN(1932); WESTWARD PASSAGE(1932); GOLDEN HARVEST(1933); LUCKY DEVILS(1933); SCARLET RIVER(1933); SON OF THE BORDER(1933); SONG OF THE EAGLE(1933); AGE OF INNOCENCE(1934); THEIR BIG MOMENT(1934); WHEN STRANGERS MEET(1934); SCOUNDREL, THE(1935); LONGEST NIGHT, THE(1936); SON COMES HOME, A(1936); FAMILY AFFAIR, A(1937); CITIZEN SAINT(1947)
Helen Haye
ATLANTIC(1929 Brit.); BEYOND THE CITIES(1930, Brit.); BRAT, THE(1930, Brit.); KNOWING MEN(1930, Brit.); BROWN SUGAR(1931, Brit.); OFFICER'S MESS, THE(1931, Brit.); SKIN GAME, THE(1931, Brit.); CONGRESS DANCES(1932, Ger.); HER FIRST AFFAIRE(1932, Brit.); THIS WEEK OF GRACE(1933, Brit.); CRAZY PEOPLE(1934, Brit.); IT'S A BOY(1934, Brit.); MONEY MAD(1934, Brit.); DICTATOR, THE(1935, Brit./Ger.); DRAKE THE PIRATE(1935, Brit.); 39 STEPS, THE(1935, Brit.); EVERYBODY DANCE(1936, Brit.); INTERRUPTED HONEYMOON, THE(1936, Brit.); WOLF'S CLOTHING(1936, Brit.); COTTON QUEEN(1937, Brit.); GIRL IN THE TAXI(1937, Brit.); RIDING HIGH(1937, Brit.); WINGS OF THE MORNING(1937, Brit.); LOVES OF MADAME DUBARRY, THE(1938, Brit.); U-BOAT 29(1939, Brit.); CASE OF THE FRIGHTENED LADY, THE(1940. Brit.); SIDEWALKS OF LONDON(1940, Brit.); GIRL MUST LIVE, A(1941, Brit.); REMARKABLE MR. KIPPS(1942, Brit.); MAN IN GREY, THE(1943, Brit.); PLACE OF ONE'S OWN, A(1945, Brit.); RANDOLPH FAMILY, THE(1945, Brit.); MAN OF EVIL(1948, Brit.); MINE OWN EXECUTIONER(1948, Brit.); CONSPIRATOR(1949, Brit.); MRS. FITZHERBERT(1950, Brit.); THIRD TIME LUCKY(1950, Brit.); FRONT PAGE STORY(1954, Brit.); HOBSON'S CHOICE(1954, Brit.); LET'S MAKE UP(1955, Brit.); RICHARD III(1956, Brit.); ACTION OF THE TIGER(1957); GYPSY AND THE GENTLEMAN, THE(1958, Brit.); TEENAGE BAD GIRL(1959, Brit.)
Misc. Silents
SKIN GAME, THE(1920, Brit.); TILLY OF BLOOMSBURY(1921, Brit.)
Nicholas Hayer
DOUBLE CRIME IN THE MAGINOT LINE(1939, Fr.), ph; PANIQUE(1947, Fr.), ph; ORPHEUS(1950, Fr.), ph; EGYPT BY THREE(1953), ph; FIDELIO(1961, Aust.), ph
Nicolas Hayer
RAVEN, THE(1948, Fr.), ph; THEY ARE NOT ANGELS(1948, Fr.), ph; LEVIATHAN(1961, Fr.), ph; FINGERMAN, THE(1963, Fr.), ph; DOULOS-THE FINGER MAN(1964, Fr./Ital.), ph; CLOPORTES(1966, Fr., Ital.), ph
Sid Hayers
PRELUDE TO FAME(1950, Brit.), ed
Sidney Hayers
STOP PRESS GIRL(1949, Brit.), ed; WARNING TO WANTONS, A(1949, Brit.), ed; SOMETHING MONEY CAN'T BUY(1952, Brit.), ed; HIGH TIDE AT NOON(1957, Brit.), ed; TRIPLE DECEPTION(1957, Brit.), ed; NIGHT TO REMEMBER, A(1958, Brit.), ed; ONE THAT GOT AWAY, THE(1958, Brit.), ed; TOWN LIKE ALICE, A(1958, Brit.), ed; TIGER BAY(1959, Brit.), ed; WHITE TRAP, THE(1959, Brit.), d; CIRCUS OF HORRORS(1960, Brit.), d; ECHO OF BARBARA(1961, Brit.), d; BURN WITCH BURN(1962), d; PAYROLL(1962, Brit.), d; THIS IS MY STREET(1964, Brit.), d; THREE HATS FOR LISA(1965, Brit.), d; FINDERS KEEPERS(1966, Brit.), d; VIOLENT MOMENT(1966, Brit.), d, ed; MALPAS MYSTERY, THE(1967, Brit.), d; TRAP, THE(1967, Can./Brit.), d; SOUTHERN STAR, THE(1969, Fr./Brit.), d; FIRECHASERS, THE(1970, Brit.), d; ASSAULT(1971, Brit.), d; TERROR FROM UNDER THE HOUSE(1971, Brit.), d; DEADLY STRANGERS(1974, Brit.), d; DIAGNOSIS: MURDER(1974, Brit.), d; WHAT CHANGED CHARLEY FARTHING?(1976, Brit.), p, d; CONQUEST OF THE EARTH(1980), d
Misc. Talkies
ALL COPPERS ARE...(1972, Brit.), d
Sydney Hayers
NEVER TAKE NO FOR AN ANSWER(1952, Brit./Ital.), ed; ROMEO AND JULIET(1954, Brit.), ed
Adrienne Hayes
CASE OF PATTY SMITH, THE(1962); ELECTRA GLIDE IN BLUE(1973)
Alan Hayes
1984
FRIDAY THE 13TH-THE FINAL CHAPTER(1984); SAM'S SON(1984)
Alfred Hayes
TERESA(1951), w; CLASH BY NIGHT(1952), w; ACT OF LOVE(1953), w; HUMAN DESIRE(1954), w; LEFT HAND OF GOD, THE(1955), w; HATFUL OF RAIN, A(1957), w; ISLAND IN THE SUN(1957), w; THESE THOUSAND HILLS(1959), w; MOUNTAIN ROAD, THE(1960), w; JOY IN THE MORNING(1965), w; DOUBLE MAN, THE(1967), w; LOST IN THE STARS(1974), w; BLUE BIRD, THE(1976), w
Alice Hayes
Misc. Silents
TALE OF TWO NATIONS, A(1917)
Alick Hayes
NASTY HABITS(1976, Brit.)
Allison Hayes
FRANCIS JOINS THE WACS(1954); SIGN OF THE PAGAN(1954); SO THIS IS PARIS(1954); CHICAGO SYNDICATE(1955); COUNT THREE AND PRAY(1955); DOUBLE JEOPARDY(1955); PURPLE MASK, THE(1955); GUNSLINGER(1956); MOHAWK(1956); STEEL JUNGLE, THE(1956); DISEMBODIED, THE(1957); UNDEAD, THE(1957); UNEARTHLY, THE(1957); ZOMBIES OF MORA TAU(1957); ATTACK OF THE 50 FOOT WOMAN(1958); HONG KONG CONFIDENTIAL(1958); WOLF

DOG(1958, Can.); COUNTERPLOT(1959); PIER 5, HAVANA(1959); HIGH-POWERED RIFLE, THE(1960); THE HYPNOTIC EYE(1960); CRAWLING HAND, THE(1963); WHO'S BEEN SLEEPING IN MY BED?(1963); TICKLE ME(1965); RUBY(1977)

Misc. Talkies
LUST TO KILL(1960)

Anne Hayes
PAUL TEMPLE'S TRIUMPH(1951, Brit.)

Annelle Hayes
GEORGE WHITE'S SCANDALS(1945); DEADLINE AT DAWN(1946); TWO RODE TOGETHER(1961)

Annie Hayes
1984
FLESHBURN(1984), cos

Anthony Hayes
GHOST SHIP(1953, Brit.); RIDE THE WILD SURF(1964); WINTER A GO-GO(1965)

Barton Hayes
BOY WHO CRIED WEREWOLF, THE(1973), ed

Bernadene Hayes
FOLIES DERGERE(1935); LOVE IN BLOOM(1935); SHE GETS HER MAN(1935); ABSOLUTE QUIET(1936); ACCUSING FINGER, THE(1936); GREAT GUY(1936); PAROLE(1936); ALONG CAME LOVE(1937); EMPEROR'S CANDLESTICKS, THE(1937); GIRL LOVES BOY(1937); NORTH OF THE RIO GRANDE(1937); SWEETHEART OF THE NAVY(1937); THAT'S MY STORY(1937); TROUBLE AT MIDNIGHT(1937); MY OLD KENTUCKY HOME(1938); PRISON NURSE(1938); YOU AND ME(1938); DAY THE BOOKIES WEPT, THE(1939); HEROES IN BLUE(1939); IDIOT'S DELIGHT(1939); KING OF CHINATOWN(1939); LUCKY NIGHT(1939); PANAMA LADY(1939); SOME LIKE IT HOT(1939); SAILOR'S LADY(1940); SANTA FE MARSHAL(1940); DEADLY GAME, THE(1941); GAY VAGABOND, THE(1941); SING FOR YOUR SUPPER(1941); I LIVE ON DANGER(1942); NAZI AGENT(1942); THIS GUN FOR HIRE(1942); DON'T GAMBLE WITH STRANGERS(1946); CRIMSON KEY, THE(1947); DICK TRACY'S DILEMMA(1947); WOMEN IN THE NIGHT(1948); CAUGHT(1949); BUNCO SQUAD(1950); WICKED WOMAN(1953)

Misc. Talkies
TRIGGER TOM(1935)

Bernadine Hayes
RUSTLER'S VALLEY(1937); MR. WINKLE GOES TO WAR(1944); LIVING IN A BIG WAY(1947)

Misc. Talkies
JUDGMENT BOOK, THE(1935)

Bernardene Hayes
13TH HOUR, THE(1947)

Bernardine Hayes
HUMAN SIDE, THE(1934)

Bettina Hayes
HOTEL SAHARA(1951, Brit.)

Bill Hayes
STOP, YOU'RE KILLING ME(1952); CARDINAL, THE(1963); GEORGE(1973, U.S./Switz.), animal t

Billie Hayes
LI'L ABNER(1959); PUFNSTUF(1970)

Billy Hayes
MIDNIGHT EXPRESS(1978, Brit.), w

Bruce Hayes
DISC JOCKEY(1951)

Burton E. Hayes
JESSE JAMES' WOMEN(1954), ed

Cathy Lind Hayes
MOMMIE DEAREST(1981)

Charles Hayes
THOSE WERE THE DAYS(1934, Brit.); SONG OF THE FORGE(1937, Brit.); IN THE MEANTIME, DARLING(1944); TWO GIRLS AND A SAILOR(1944); SAFARI(1956); TOUGHEST GUN IN TOMBSTONE(1958); AFRICA–TEXAS STYLE!(1967 U.S./Brit.); LIVING FREE(1972, Brit.)

Chester A. Hayes
LAST OF THE SECRET AGENTS?, THE(1966)

Chester Hayes
VEILS OF BAGDAD, THE(1953); FROM HELL IT CAME(1957); WONDERFUL COUNTRY, THE(1959); ROUSTABOUT(1964); GREAT RACE, THE(1965)

Cliff Hayes
MAD MAX(1979, Aus.), ed

Clifford Hayes
WE OF THE NEVER NEVER(1983, Aus.), ed

Dallas Edward Hayes
TRICK BABY(1973); EYES OF LAURA MARS(1978)

Danny Hayes
Silents
WIDE-OPEN TOWN, A(1922); NEW KLONDIKE, THE(1926)

Daryl Hayes
1984
RUNAWAY(1984)

David Winnie Hayes
CRUISING(1980)

Debra S. Hayes
FRIDAY THE 13TH(1980)

Denise Hayes
UP FROM THE DEPTHS(1979, Phil.); DR. HECKYL AND MR. HYPE(1980)

Dennis Hayes
THRESHOLD(1983, Can.)

Diana Hayes
SMITHEREENS(1982)
1984
MUPPETS TAKE MANHATTAN, THE(1984)

Don Hayes
DUDE RANGER, THE(1934), ed; MEET THE MAYOR(1938), ed; HOLLYWOOD AND VINE(1945), ed; DETROIT 9000(1973)

Donn Hayes
RIVER WOMAN, THE(1928), ed; TIMES SQUARE(1929), ed; BAD ONE, THE(1930), ed; JAZZ CINDERELLA(1930), ed; LOST ZEPPELIN(1930), ed; PECK'S BAD BOY(1934), ed; COWBOY MILLIONAIRE(1935), ed

Silents
NEVER THE TWAIN SHALL MEET(1925), ed; CARNIVAL GIRL, THE(1926), ed; RUSH HOUR, THE(1927), ed; HEAD OF THE FAMILY, THE(1928), ed

Douglas Hayes
SCOTLAND YARD DRAGNET(1957, Brit.); COMEDY MAN, THE(1964), w

Edgar Hayes
WIFE WANTED(1946)

Eileen Hayes
GHASTLY ONES, THE(1968)

Elton Hayes
DATE WITH A DREAM, A(1948, Brit.); BLACK KNIGHT, THE(1954); ISABEL(1968, Can.); JOURNEY(1977, Can.)

Ernesto Hayes
RETURN OF SABATA(1972, Ital./Fr./Ger.)

Essie Hayes
RENEGADE GIRLS(1974)

Evie Hayes
ANTS IN HIS PANTS(1940, Aus.)

Fanny Hayes
Misc. Silents
WOLF OF DEBT, THE(1915)

Flora Hayes
HURRICANE, THE(1937); BLUE HAWAII(1961)

Frank Hayes
Silents
WHEN DO WE EAT?(1918); KILLER, THE(1921); GREED(1925)
Misc. Silents
AFTER HIS OWN HEART(1919); CUPID FORECLOSES(1919)

Gene Hayes
RIVALS(1972)

Geoffrey Hayes
GREAT PONY RAID, THE(1968, Brit.), w

George "Gabby" Hayes
SMILING IRISH EYES(1929); BOILING POINT, THE(1932); KLONDIKE(1932); LOVE ME TONIGHT(1932); TEXAS BUDDIES(1932); WILD HORSE MESA(1932); WITHOUT HONORS(1932); BREED OF THE BORDER(1933); FUGITIVE, THE(1933); PHANTOM BROADCAST, THE(1933); RETURN OF CASEY JONES(1933); RIDERS OF DESTINY(1933); SKYWAY(1933); SPHINX, THE(1933); BLUE STEEL(1934); HOUSE OF MYSTERY(1934); LUCKY TEXAN, THE(1934); MYSTERY LINER(1934); STAR PACKER, THE(1934); WEST OF THE DIVIDE(1934); DEATH FLIES EAST(1935); LAWLESS FRONTIER, THE(1935); SMOKEY SMITH(1935); THROWBACK, THE(1935); THUNDER MOUNTAIN(1935); TOMBSTONE TERROR(1935); TUMBLING TUMBLEWEEDS(1935); $1,000 A MINUTE(1935); LAWLESS NINETIES, THE(1936); MR. DEEDS GOES TO TOWN(1936); SWIFTY(1936); TEXAS RANGERS, THE(1936); THREE ON THE TRAIL(1936); TRAIL DUST(1936); VALIANT IS THE WORD FOR CARRIE(1936); HEART OF THE WEST(1937); MOUNTAIN MUSIC(1937); PLAINSMAN, THE(1937); RUSTLER'S VALLEY(1937); TEXAS TRAIL(1937); FRONTIERSMAN, THE(1938); GOLD IS WHERE YOU FIND IT(1938); HEART OF ARIZONA(1938); SUNSET TRAIL(1938); ARIZONA KID, THE(1939); DAYS OF JESSE JAMES(1939); LET FREEDOM RING(1939); RENEGADE TRAIL(1939); SAGA OF DEATH VALLEY(1939); SILVER ON THE SAGE(1939); SOUTHWARD HO!(1939); WALL STREET COWBOY(1939); BORDER LEGION, THE(1940); CARSON CITY KID(1940); COLORADO(1940); DARK COMMAND, THE(1940); MELODY RANCH(1940); RANGER AND THE LADY, THE(1940); WAGONS WESTWARD(1940); YOUNG BILL HICKOK(1940); YOUNG BUFFALO BILL(1940); BAD MAN OF DEADWOOD(1941); IN OLD CHEYENNE(1941); JESSE JAMES AT BAY(1941); RED RIVER VALLEY(1941); ROBIN HOOD OF THE PECOS(1941); SHERIFF OF TOMBSTONE(1941); HEART OF THE GOLDEN WEST(1942); MAN FROM CHEYENNE(1942); RIDIN' DOWN THE CANYON(1942); ROMANCE ON THE RANGE(1942); SONS OF THE PIONEERS(1942); SOUTH OF SANTA FE(1942); SUNSET ON THE DESERT(1942); SUNSET SERENADE(1942); BORDERTOWN GUNFIGHTERS(1943); DEATH VALLEY MANHUNT(1943); IN OLD OKLAHOMA(1943); MAN FROM THUNDER RIVER, THE(1943); OVERLAND MAIL ROBBERY(1943); WAGON TRACKS WEST(1943); BIG BONANZA, THE(1944); LIGHTS OF OLD SANTA FE(1944); MOJAVE FIREBRAND(1944); TALL IN THE SADDLE(1944); TUCSON RAIDERS(1944); ALONG THE NAVAJO TRAIL(1945); BELLS OF ROSARITA(1945); DON'T FENCE ME IN(1945); MAN FROM OKLAHOMA, THE(1945); SUNSET IN EL DORADO(1945); UTAH(1945); BADMAN'S TERRITORY(1946); HELLDORADO(1946); HOME IN OKLAHOMA(1946); MY PAL TRIGGER(1946); RAINBOW OVER TEXAS(1946); ROLL ON TEXAS MOON(1946); SONG OF ARIZONA(1946); UNDER NEVADA SKIES(1946); TRAIL STREET(1947); WYOMING(1947); ALBUQUERQUE(1948); RETURN OF THE BADMEN(1948); UNTAMED BREED, THE(1948); EL PASO(1949); CARIBOO TRAIL, THE(1950)

Misc. Talkies
BRAND OF HATE(1934)

George Hayes
BIG NEWS(1929); RAINBOW MAN(1929); FOR THE DEFENSE(1930); CAVALIER OF THE WEST(1931); GOD'S COUNTRY AND THE MAN(1931); BORDER DEVILS(1932); BROADWAY TO CHEYENNE(1932); DRAGNET PATROL(1932); HIDDEN VALLEY(1932); MAN FROM HELL'S EDGES(1932); NIGHT RIDER, THE(1932); RIDERS OF THE DESERT(1932); WINNER TAKE ALL(1932); CRASHING BROADWAY(1933); DEVIL'S MATE(1933); FIGHTING CHAMP(1933); FIGHTING TEXANS(1933); GALLANT FOOL, THE(1933); GALLOPING ROMEO(1933); MY MOTHER(1933); RANGER'S CODE, THE(1933); BEGGARS IN ERMINE(1934); MAN FROM HELL, THE(1934); MAN FROM UTAH, THE(1934); MONTE CARLO NIGHTS(1934); 'NEATH THE ARIZONA SKIES(1934); RANDY RIDES ALONE(1934); HOOSIER SCHOOLMASTER(1935); HOPALONG CASSIDY(1935); IN OLD SANTA FE(1935); INSIDE THE ROOM(1935, Brit.); JUSTICE OF THE RANGE(1935); LADIES CRAVE EXCITEMENT(1935); OLD ROSES(1935, Brit.); RAINBOW VALLEY(1935); TEXAS TERROR(1935); BAR 20 RIDES AGAIN(1936); CALL OF THE PRAIRIE(1936); EAGLE'S BROOD, THE(1936); FORBIDDEN MUSIC(1936, Brit.); HEARTS IN BONDAGE(1936); HITCH HIKE LADY(1936); HONEYMOON LIMITED(1936); HOPALONG CASSIDY RETURNS(1936); I MARRIED A DOCTOR(1936); MISTER HOBO(1936, Brit.); SILVER SPURS(1936); SONG OF THE TRAIL(1936); VALLEY OF THE LAWLESS(1936); WOLF'S CLOTHING(1936, Brit.); BORDERLAND(1937); DEATH CROONS THE BLUES(1937, Brit.); HILLS OF OLD WYOMING(1937); HOPALONG RIDES AGAIN(1937); NORTH OF THE RIO GRANDE(1937); BAR 20 JUSTICE(1938); BREAK THE NEWS(1938, Brit.); EMIL(1938, Brit.); IN OLD MEXICO(1938); NO PARKING(1938, Brit.); PRIDE OF THE WEST(1938); RETURN OF THE FROG, THE(1938, Brit.); STRANGE BOARDERS(1938, Brit.); COME ON GEORGE(1939, Brit.);

FIGHTING THOROUGHBREDS(1939); IN OLD CALIENTE(1939); IN OLD MONTEREY(1939); MAN OF CONQUEST(1939); SPY FOR A DAY(1939, Brit.); AMONG HUMAN WOLVES(1940 Brit.); MYSTERIOUS MR. REEDER, THE(1940, Brit.); NEVADA CITY(1941); STRANGLER, THE(1941, Brit.); VOICE IN THE NIGHT, A(1941, Brit.); CALLING WILD BILL ELLIOTT(1943); HIDDEN VALLEY OUTLAWS(1944); MARSHAL OF RENO(1944); GREAT EXPECTATIONS(1946, Brit.); ESTHER WATERS(1948, Brit.); FOR THEM THAT TRESPASS(1949, Brit.)
Misc. Talkies
NEVADA BUCKAROO, THE(1931); TRAILING NORTH(1933); OUTLAW TAMER, THE(1934)

Georgia Hayes
GLOBAL AFFAIR, A(1964)

Gillian Hayes
LITTLE ONES, THE(1965, Brit.); WUTHERING HEIGHTS(1970, Brit.)

Gordon Hayes
CORREGIDOR(1943); BLACK RODEO(1972)

Grace Hayes
RAINBOW OVER BROADWAY(1933); MYRT AND MARGE(1934); BABES IN ARMS(1939); ZIS BOOM BAH(1941); COLLEGE SWEETHEARTS(1942); ALWAYS LEAVE THEM LAUGHING(1949); CAGED(1950)

Hazel Hayes
KISS AND MAKE UP(1934); YOUNG AND BEAUTIFUL(1934)

Helen Hayes
ARROWSMITH(1931); SIN OF MADELON CLAUDET, THE(1931); FAREWELL TO ARMS, A(1932); SON-DAUGHTER, THE(1932); ANOTHER LANGUAGE(1933); NIGHT FLIGHT(1933); WHITE SISTER, THE(1933); CRIME WITHOUT PASSION(1934); WHAT EVERY WOMAN KNOWS(1934); VANESSA, HER LOVE STORY(1935); STAGE DOOR CANTEEN(1943); ANNA KARENINA(1948, Brit.); MY SON, JOHN(1952); MAIN STREET TO BROADWAY(1953); ANASTASIA(1956); THIRD MAN ON THE MOUNTAIN(1959); AIRPORT(1970); HERBIE RIDES AGAIN(1974); ONE OF OUR DINOSAURS IS MISSING(1975, Brit.); CANDLESHOE(1978)
Misc. Silents
LOVE AND AMBITION(1917); WEAVERS OF LIFE(1917); RODEO MIXUP, A(1924)

Herbert Hayes
IT AIN'T HAY(1943); MR. WINKLE GOES TO WAR(1944)
Silents
FINAL CURTAIN, THE(1916)
Misc. Silents
DON'T WRITE LETTERS(1922); I CAN EXPLAIN(1922)

Pfc. Ira H. Hayes
SANDS OF IWO JIMA(1949)

Isaac Hayes
MAIDSTONE(1970), m; SHAFT(1971), m; THREE TOUGH GUYS(1974, U.S./Ital.), a, m; TRUCK TURNER(1974), a, m; IT SEEMED LIKE A GOOD IDEA AT THE TIME(1975, Can.); ESCAPE FROM NEW YORK(1981)

Ivan Hayes
STORY OF THREE LOVES, THE(1953); TITANIC(1953); PRINCE OF PLAYERS(1955); SCARLET COAT, THE(1955)

Jack Hayes
MR. LEMON OF ORANGE(1931), w; MONSTER FROM THE OCEAN FLOOR, THE(1954); CRIMSON KIMONO, THE(1959), md

Jaysen Hayes
PRISONER OF ZENDA, THE(1979)

Jean Hayes
LIVING FREE(1972, Brit.)

Jerri Hayes
EMMA MAE(1976)

Jim Hayes
PEGGY(1950); LEPKE(1975, U.S./Israel)

Jimmy Hayes
UNTIL THEY SAIL(1957); TEA AND SYMPATHY(1956); THESE WILDER YEARS(1956); VERY SPECIAL FAVOR, A(1965)

Joan Hayes
TITANIC(1953)

John Anthony Hayes
STRAIT-JACKET(1964)

John Hayes
ROTTEN APPLE, THE(1963), d; SHELL SHOCK(1964), d, w; FARMER'S OTHER DAUGHTER, THE(1965), d; FANDANGO(1970), d&w; KINFOLK(1970), d&w; SWEET TRASH(1970), p, d&w; GARDEN OF THE DEAD(1972), d; TOMB OF THE UNDEAD(1972), d&w; SHAGGY D.A., THE(1976); END OF THE WORLD(1977), d
Misc. Talkies
HANG-UP, THE(1969), d; MAMA'S DIRTY GIRLS(1974), d

John J. Hayes
Misc. Silents
FATAL 30, THE(1921), a, d

John Maxwell Hayes
SONG OF BERNADETTE, THE(1943); DESIRE ME(1947)

John Michael Hayes
RED BALL EXPRESS(1952), w; THUNDER BAY(1953), w; TORCH SONG(1953), w; WAR ARROW(1953), w; REAR WINDOW(1954), w; BAR SINISTER, THE(1955), w; TO CATCH A THIEF(1955), w; TROUBLE WITH HARRY, THE(1955), w; MAN WHO KNEW TOO MUCH, THE(1956), w; PEYTON PLACE(1957), w; MATCHMAKER, THE(1958), w; BUT NOT FOR ME(1959), w; BUTTERFIELD 8(1960), w; CHILDREN'S HOUR, THE(1961), w; IMPERIAL VENUS(1963, Ital./Fr.), w; CARPETBAGGERS, THE(1964), w; CHALK GARDEN, THE(1964, Brit.), w; WHERE LOVE HAS GONE(1964), w; JUDITH(1965), w; NEVADA SMITH(1966), w

John Patrick Hayes
GRASS EATER, THE(1961), d, w; WALK THE ANGRY BEACH(1961), p,d&w; GRAVE OF THE VAMPIRE(1972), d, w

Joseph Hayes
DESPERATE HOURS, THE(1955), w; YOUNG DOCTORS, THE(1961), w; BON VOYAGE(1962), w; STOLEN HOURS(1963), w; THIRD DAY, THE(1965), w

Kaai Hayes
KONA COAST(1968)

Ken Hayes
NAKED WORLD OF HARRISON MARKS, THE(1967, Brit.)

Leonard Hayes
HOUND OF THE BASKERVILLES(1932, Brit.)

Lind Hayes
DANGER ON THE AIR(1938)

Linda Hayes
OUTSIDE OF PARADISE(1938); CONSPIRACY(1939); GIRL FROM MEXICO, THE(1939); MEXICAN SPITFIRE(1939); SPELLBINDER, THE(1939); I'M STILL ALIVE(1940); MEXICAN SPITFIRE OUT WEST(1940); MILLIONAIRE PLAYBOY(1940); MILLIONAIRES IN PRISON(1940); SUED FOR LIBEL(1940); CITADEL OF CRIME(1941); ELLERY QUEEN AND THE PERFECT CRIME(1941); MEN OF THE TIMBERLAND(1941); RAIDERS OF THE DESERT(1941); SAINT IN PALM SPRINGS, THE(1941); RIDIN' DOWN THE CANYON(1942); ROMANCE ON THE RANGE(1942); SOUTH OF SANTA FE(1942)

Lora Hayes
BLACK LIKE ME(1964), ed

Lorraine Hayes [Laraine Day]
DOOMED AT SUNDOWN(1937); TOUGH TO HANDLE(1937); LAW COMMANDS, THE(1938)

Lynn Hayes
RAVAGER, THE(1970)

Maggie Hayes
CASE AGAINST BROOKLYN, THE(1958); DAMN CITIZEN(1958); FRAULEIN(1958); GIRL IN THE WOODS(1958); GOOD DAY FOR A HANGING(1958); BEAT GENERATION, THE(1959); GIRLS' TOWN(1959)

Malcolm Hayes
MEETINGS WITH REMARKABLE MEN(1979, Brit.)

Manning H. Hayes
LOVE'S OLD SWEET SONG(1933, Brit.), d

Manning Hayes
SMITH'S WIVES(1935, Brit.), d
Misc. Silents
STELLA(1921); SAM'S BOY(1922, Brit.), d; WILL AND A WAY, A(1922, Brit.), d

Margaret Hayes
CITY, FOR CONQUEST(1941); IN OLD COLORADO(1941); LOUISIANA PURCHASE(1941); NIGHT OF JANUARY 16TH(1941); SKYLARK(1941); SULLIVAN'S TRAVELS(1941); GLASS KEY, THE(1942); LADY HAS PLANS, THE(1942); SABOTEUR(1942); SCATTERGOOD SURVIVES A MURDER(1942); TAKE A LETTER, DARLING(1942); ONE DANGEROUS NIGHT(1943); THEY GOT ME COVERED(1943); BLACKBOARD JUNGLE, THE(1955); VIOLENT SATURDAY(1955); BOTTOM OF THE BOTTLE, THE(1956); OMAR KHAYYAM(1957); HOUSE OF WOMEN(1962); THIRTEEN WEST STREET(1962)
Misc. Talkies
FROM THE DESK OF MARGARET TYDING(1958)

Marrijane Hayes
BON VOYAGE(1962), w

Marvin Hayes
CARMEN JONES(1954)

Mary Adams Hayes
IRISH EYES ARE SMILING(1944)

Mary Hayes
ROARING SIX GUNS(1937)

Maxwell Hayes
CLIMAX, THE(1944); YOUTH RUNS WILD(1944)

Melvyn Hayes
ADVENTURE IN THE HOPFIELDS(1954, Brit.); MAN WHO LOVED REDHEADS, THE(1955, Brit.); CURSE OF FRANKENSTEIN, THE(1957, Brit.); GOOD COMPANIONS, THE(1957, Brit.); WOMEN IN A DRESSING GOWN(1957, Brit.); BOTTOMS UP(1960, Brit.); OPERATION AMSTERDAM(1960, Brit.); MANIA(1961, Brit.); SILENT INVASION, THE(1962, Brit.); WONDERFUL TO BE YOUNG!(1962, Brit.); SUMMER HOLIDAY(1963, Brit.); CROOKS IN CLOISTERS(1964, Brit.); NO TREE IN THE STREET(1964, Brit.); SWINGER'S PARADISE(1965, Brit.); WALK WITH LOVE AND DEATH, A(1969); CARRY ON ENGLAND(1976, Brit.)

Michael Hayes
THUNDER BAY(1953), w; HARLOW(1965), w; PROMISE, THE(1969, Brit.), d&w

Nelson Hayes
BAHAMA PASSAGE(1941), w

Paddy Hayes
DUBLIN NIGHTMARE(1958, Brit.)

Pamela Hayes
SECOND FIDDLE TO A STEEL GUITAR(1965)

Pat Hayes
Misc. Talkies
AND THE WALL CAME TUMBLING DOWN(1984)

Patricia Hayes
DUMMY TALKS, THE(1943, Brit.); WHEN WE ARE MARRIED(1943, Brit.); 48 HOURS(1944, Brit.); GREAT DAY(1945, Brit.); HOTEL RESERVE(1946, Brit.); NICHOLAS NICKLEBY(1947, Brit.); SKIMPY IN THE NAVY(1949, Brit.); ENFORCER, THE(1951); LOVE MATCH, THE(1955, Brit.); BATTLE OF THE SEXES, THE(1960, Brit.); KILL OR CURE(1962, Brit.); SATURDAY NIGHT OUT(1964, Brit.); SICILIANS, THE(1964, Brit.); TERRORNAUTS, THE(1967, Brit.); CARRY ON AGAIN, DOCTOR(1969, Brit.); GOODBYE MR. CHIPS(1969, U.S./Brit.); FRAGMENT OF FEAR(1971, Brit.)
1984
NEVERENDING STORY, THE(1984, Ger.)
Misc. Talkies
GHOST OF A CHANCE, A(1968, Brit.); MAFIA JUNCTION(1977)

Peter Hayes
ALL WOMEN HAVE SECRETS(1939); DANCING ON A DIME(1940)

Peter Lind Hayes
MILLION DOLLAR LEGS(1939); NAUGHTY BUT NICE(1939); THESE GLAMOUR GIRLS(1939); SEVENTEEN(1940); PLAYMATES(1941); ZIS BOOM BAH(1941); COLLEGE SWEETHEARTS(1942); SEVEN DAYS LEAVE(1942); WINGED VICTORY(1944); SENATOR WAS INDISCREET, THE(1947); 5,000 FINGERS OF DR. T. THE(1953); ONCE YOU KISS A STRANGER(1969); LOOKIN' TO GET OUT(1982)

Raphael Hayes
REPRISAL(1956), w; NO TIME TO BE YOUNG(1957), w; HAVE ROCKET, WILL TRAVEL(1959), w; HEY BOY! HEY GIRL!(1959), w; ONE POTATO, TWO POTATO(1964), w

Rich Hayes
CARNIVAL LADY(1933)
Richard Hayes
ON THE YARD(1978)
Rita Hayes
ERRAND BOY, THE(1961)
Rob Hayes
ISABEL(1968, Can.)
Robert Hayes
EMPLOYEE'S ENTRANCE(1933), art d
Ron Hayes
FACE OF A FUGITIVE(1959); GUNMEN FROM LAREDO(1959); AROUND THE WORLD UNDER THE SEA(1966)
Misc. Talkies
FOUR AGAINST THE DESERT(1979)
Rosalind Hayes
CARIBBEAN(1952); MISS ROBIN CRUSOE(1954); RAINTREE COUNTY(1957)
Roz Hayes
LYDIA BAILEY(1952)
Sadie Hayes
CHASTITY(1969), cos
Sam Hayes
CROWD ROARS, THE(1932); KID MILLIONS(1934); ONE NIGHT OF LOVE(1934); STAND UP AND CHEER(1934 80m FOX bw); TWENTY MILLION SWEET-HEARTS(1934); LIVING ON VELVET(1935); EX-MRS. BRADFORD, THE(1936); FURY(1936); MILKY WAY, THE(1936); PIGSKIN PARADE(1936); ALI BABA GOES TO TOWN(1937); EXCLUSIVE(1937); GIRL WITH IDEAS, A(1937); SHALL WE DANCE(1937); COWBOY FROM BROOKLYN(1938); LETTER OF INTRODUC-TION(1938); REBECCA OF SUNNYBROOK FARM(1938); GOLDEN BOY(1939); IN-DIANAPOLIS SPEEDWAY(1939); TAIL SPIN(1939); THEY MADE ME A CRIMINAL(1939); HIGH SIERRA(1941); MAN WHO CAME TO DINNER, THE(1942); CHECKERED COAT, THE(1948); WHIPLASH(1948); FIGHTING FOOLS(1949); IT HAPPENS EVERY SPRING(1949); JOE PALOOKA IN THE COUNTERPUNCH(1949); HITCH-HIKER, THE(1953)
Sherman Hayes
DEATH CURSE OF TARTU(1967)
Sonny Boy Hayes
SCARECROW IN A GARDEN OF CUCUMBERS(1972)
Stanley Hayes
EVERYTHING IS RHYTHM(1940, Brit.), w
Steve Hayes
TIME AFTER TIME(1979, Brit.), w
Steven Hayes
ESCORT WEST(1959), w
Suzanne B. Hayes
1984
REVENGE OF THE NERDS(1984)
Sylvia Hayes
EVEL KNIEVEL(1971); YOUR THREE MINUTES ARE UP(1973); PIPE DREAMS(1976)
Teddy Hayes
MADISON SQUARE GARDEN(1932)
Terry Hayes
ROAD WARRIOR, THE(1982, Aus.), w
Theresa Hayes
VALLEY GIRL(1983)
Tom Hayes
1984
ANNE DEVLIN(1984, Ireland), p
Tony Hayes
UNDER YOUR HAT(1940, Brit.)
Troas Hayes
LITTLE DARLINGS(1980)
Tubby Hayes
SCHOONER GANG, THE(1937, Brit.); ALL NIGHT LONG(1961, Brit.)
Turina Hayes
LONNIE(1963)
Vickie Hayes
PROJECT X(1949)
W. Donn Hayes
EVERY NIGHT AT EIGHT(1935), ed; TARZAN ESCAPES(1936), ed; BETWEEN TWO WOMEN(1937), ed; ESCAPE BY NIGHT(1937), ed; ESPIONAGE(1937), ed; THIRTEENTH CHAIR, THE(1937), ed; GIRL OF THE GOLDEN WEST, THE(1938), ed; SHOPWORN ANGEL(1938), ed; STABLEMATES(1938), ed; DANCING CO-ED(1939), ed; ICE FOLLIES OF 1939(1939), ed; STRONGER THAN DESIRE(1939), ed; TELL NO TALES(1939), ed; SOUTH TO KARANGA(1940), ed; WHEN THE LIGHTS GO ON AGAIN(1944), ed; MAN WHO WALKED ALONE, THE(1945), ed; MISSING CORPSE, THE(1945), ed; DOWN MISSOURI WAY(1946), ed; BORN TO SPEED(1947), ed; BURY ME DEAD(1947), ed; GAS HOUSE KIDS IN HOLLYWOOD(1947), ed; PHILO VANCE'S GAMBLE(1947), ed; PHILO VANCE'S SECRET MISSION(1947), ed; ASSIGNED TO DANGER(1948), ed; INVASION U.S.A.(1952), ed; PARIS MO-DEL(1953), ed; SWORD OF VENUS(1953), ed; TORPEDO ALLEY(1953), ed
Ward Hayes
Misc. Silents
COME ON COWBOYS!(1924), d; HORSE SENSE(1924), d; SELL 'EM COWBOY(1924), d; CACTUS CURE, THE(1925), d; MY PAL(1925), d; RANGE JUSTICE(1925), d; RIDIN' EASY(1925), d; RIP SNORTER, THE(1925), d; SECRET OF BLACK CANYON, THE(1925), d; STRANGE RIDER, THE(1925), d; WHERE ROMANCE RIDES(1925), d; WOLVES OF THE ROAD(1925), d
Wesley Hayes
CIAO MANHATTAN(1973)
William Edward Hayes
BLACK DOLL, THE(1938), w
William Hayes
Silents
AMERICAN BUDS(1918); WINNING STROKE, THE(1919); ACE OF ACTION(1926)
Misc. Silents
AWAKENING OF RUTH, THE(1917); HOLLYWOOD REPORTER, THE(1926)

William T. Hayes
Silents
OUT OF THE SHADOW(1919)
Misc. Silents
PICCADILLY JIM(1920)
Hayes Football Clubs
SMALL TOWN STORY(1953, Brit.)
Rodolfo Hayes, Jr.
GLOBAL AFFAIR, A(1964)
Jimmy Hayeson
SHAFT'S BIG SCORE(1972)
Pat Hayess
REACH FOR GLORY(1963, Brit.)
Anthony Haygarth
PERCY(1971, Brit.); UNMAN, WITTERING AND ZIGO(1971, Brit.)
Cyd Haygarth
HUMAN FACTOR, THE(1979, Brit.)
Tony Haygarth
DRACULA(1979); HUMAN FACTOR, THE(1979, Brit.); MC VICAR(1982, Brit.)
Sid Haylan
CADDIE(1976, Aus.)
Grace Hayle
TRUE TO LIFE(1943); EVENINGS FOR SALE(1932); DESIGN FOR LIVING(1933); GOLD DIGGERS OF 1933(1933); HARD TO HANDLE(1933); MARY STEVENS, M.D.(1933); PROFESSIONAL SWEETHEART(1933); CHAINED(1934); MUSIC IN THE AIR(1934); NOW AND FOREVER(1934); SING AND LIKE IT(1934); TWENTY MIL-LION SWEETHEARTS(1934); WONDER BAR(1934); CASINO MURDER CASE, THE(1935); FRONT PAGE WOMAN(1935); LIVING ON VELVET(1935); MARY BURNS, FUGITIVE(1935); ROBERTA(1935); SHE MARRIED HER BOSS(1935); GREAT ZIEGFELD, THE(1936); MOON'S OUR HOME, THE(1936); REUNION(1936); SMALL TOWN GIRL(1936); THEODORA GOES WILD(1936); WINTERSET(1936); MAYTIME(1937); MUSIC FOR MADAME(1937); SINGING MARINE, THE(1937); TOVARICH(1937); MAN-PROOF(1938); NEXT TIME I MARRY(1938); SHINING HOUR, THE(1938); SHOPWORN ANGEL(1938); SWEETHEARTS(1938); THREE LOVES HAS NANCY(1938); YOUNG DR. KILDARE(1938); BOY TROUBLE(1939); FORGOTTEN WOMAN, THE(1939); OUR NEIGHBORS–THE CARTERS(1939); STAR MAKER, THE(1939); WOMEN, THE(1939); FARMER'S DAUGHTER, THE(1940); GHOST BREAKERS, THE(1940); GREAT DICTATOR, THE(1940); MA, HE'S MAKING EYES AT ME(1940); MARYLAND(1940); ROAD TO SINGAPORE(1940); SHOP AROUND THE CORNER, THE(1940); THIRD FINGER, LEFT HAND(1940); 'TIL WE MEET AGAIN(1940); HIT THE ROAD(1941); KNOCKOUT(1941); NEW YORK TOWN(1941); TWO-FACED WOMAN(1941); UNFINISHED BUSINESS(1941); WAG-ONS ROLL AT NIGHT, THE(1941); WEST POINT WIDOW(1941); CROSSROADS(1942); I MARRIED AN ANGEL(1942); MADAME SPY(1942); FOOTLIGHT GLAMOUR(1943); LET'S FACE IT(1943); SHE'S FOR ME(1943); SLIGHTLY DANGEROUS(1943); BEAUTIFUL BUT BROKE(1944); COVER GIRL(1944); MRS. PARKINGTON(1944); TOO YOUNG TO KISS(1951); DON'T BOTHER TO KNOCK(1952); FLESH AND FURY(1952); TURNING POINT, THE(1952); HOUDINI(1953); MONEY FROM HO-ME(1953); DANGEROUS MISSION(1954); FOXFIRE(1955); LOVING YOU(1957)
Brian Hayles
NOTHING BUT THE NIGHT(1975, Brit.), w; WARLORDS OF ATLANTIS(1978, Brit.), w; ARABIAN ADVENTURE(1979, Brit.), w
Kenneth Hayles
COMPANIONS IN CRIME(1954, Brit.), w
Kenneth R. Hayles
FINAL APPOINTMENT(1954, Brit.), w; NO SMOKING(1955, Brit.), w; SECRET VENTURE(1955, Brit.), w; STOLEN ASSIGNMENT(1955, Brit.), w; FIND THE LA-DY(1956, Brit.), w; HIDEOUT, THE(1956, Brit.), w; MURDER ON APPROVAL(1956, Brit.), w; PASSPORT TO TREASON(1956, Brit.), w; TRACK THE MAN DOWN(1956, Brit.), w; SUSPENDED ALIBI(1957, Brit.), w; BLIND SPOT(1958, Brit.), w
Alida Hayman
Misc. Silents
SAINTLY SINNER, THE(1917)
Cyd Hayman
PERCY(1971, Brit.); GODSEND, THE(1980, Can.)
Damaris Hayman
BUNNY LAKE IS MISSING(1965); MISSIONARY, THE(1982)
David Hayman
EYE OF THE NEEDLE(1981)
Joe Hayman
LUCKY NUMBER, THE(1933, Brit.); BORROWED CLOTHES(1934, Brit.); WITHOUT YOU(1934, Brit.); KISS ME GOODBYE(1935, Brit.); TERROR ON TIPTOE(1936, Brit.); ON VELVET(1938, Brit.)
Lillian Hayman
NIGHT THEY RAIDED MINSKY'S, THE(1968); MANDINGO(1975); DRUM(1976)
R. I. P. Hayman
1984
NIGHTSONGS(1984), m
John Haymer
EVEL KNIEVEL(1971); FOUR DEUCES, THE(1976)
Johnny Haymer
TEEN-AGE STRANGLER(1967); SECRET WAR OF HARRY FRIGG, THE(1968); ORGANIZATION, THE(1971); ANNIE HALL(1977); HERBIE GOES TO MONTE CARLO(1977); REAL LIFE(1979)
Bob Haymes
IS EVERYBODY HAPPY?(1943); SWING OUT THE BLUES(1943); TWO SENORITAS FROM CHICAGO(1943); BEAUTIFUL BUT BROKE(1944); MR. WINKLE GOES TO WAR(1944); SAILOR'S HOLIDAY(1944)
Dick Haymes
DRAMATIC SCHOOL(1938); DU BARRY WAS A LADY(1943); FOUR JILLS IN A JEEP(1944); IRISH EYES ARE SMILING(1944); DIAMOND HORSESHOE(1945); STATE FAIR(1945); DO YOU LOVE ME?(1946); CARNIVAL IN COSTA RICA(1947); SHOCKING MISS PILGRIM, THE(1947); ONE TOUCH OF VENUS(1948); UP IN CENTRAL PARK(1948); ST. BENNY THE DIP(1951); ALL ASHORE(1953); CRUISIN' DOWN THE RIVER(1953); WON TON TON, THE DOG WHO SAVED HOL-LYWOOD(1976)
Roy Haymond
Silents
REPENTANCE(1922, Brit.)

Raymond Haymstorf
Misc. Talkies
SEAWOLF(1974)
Ben Hayne
DON JUAN QUILLIGAN(1945), art d; DOWN TO THE SEA IN SHIPS(1949), art d; HIGH NOON(1952), art d; MONSTER FROM THE OCEAN FLOOR, THE(1954), prod d
Donald Hayne
CARDINAL, THE(1963)
Murray Hayne
DEATH TRAP(1962, Brit.); RIVALS, THE(1963, Brit.); VULTURE, THE(1967, U.S./Brit./Can.)
Anita Haynes
CARNY(1980); NIGHT THE LIGHTS WENT OUT IN GEORGIA, THE(1981)
Arthur Haynes
STRANGE BEDFELLOWS(1965); CARNABY, M.D.(1967, Brit.)
Betty Haynes
ACROSS 110TH STREET(1972)
Misc. Talkies
THAT MAN OF MINE(1947)
Bradley Haynes
LEAP OF FAITH(1931, Brit.), m
Cal Haynes
COMMITMENT, THE(1976)
Misc. Talkies
FYRE(1979)
Clarence Haynes
CHANGE OF MIND(1969)
Connie Haynes
SHIP AHOY(1942)
Cynthia Murtagh Haynes
LAST POST, THE(1929, Brit.)
Daniel Haynes
ESCAPE FROM DEVIL'S ISLAND(1935); MARY BURNS, FUGITIVE(1935); SO RED THE ROSE(1935); FURY(1936)
Silents
JOHN SMITH(1922)
Daniel L. Haynes
HALLELUJAH(1929); LAST MILE, THE(1932)
David N. Haynes
BABYLON(1980, Brit.)
Dick Haynes
FUZZY PINK NIGHTGOWN, THE(1957); PHANTOM PLANET, THE(1961); SILENT WITNESS, THE(1962); TIME TO SING, A(1968); REAL LIFE(1979)
Donald Haynes
MANHATTAN MELODRAMA(1934)
Eli Haynes
Misc. Talkies
CANDY TANGERINE MAN, THE(1975)
Ernie Haynes
RECKLESS(1935)
H. Manning Haynes
Silents
AVE MARIA(1918, Brit.)
Misc. Silents
LADY AUDLEY'S SECRET(1920, Brit.)
Harry Haynes
SATURDAY NIGHT OUT(1964, Brit.), cos
Hilda Haynes
TAXI(1953); STAGE STRUCK(1958); HOME FROM THE HILL(1960); GONE ARE THE DAYS(1963); DIARY OF A MAD HOUSEWIFE(1970); RIVER NIGER, THE(1976); TIME AFTER TIME(1979, Brit.)
Jackson Haynes
GREASER'S PALACE(1972)
Jerry Haynes
1984
PLACES IN THE HEART(1984)
Linda Haynes
LATITUDE ZERO(1969, U.S./Jap.); COFFY(1973); NICKEL RIDE, THE(1974); DROWNING POOL, THE(1975); ROLLING THUNDER(1977); BRUBAKER(1980); HUMAN EXPERIMENTS(1980)
Lloyd Haynes
MAD ROOM, THE(1969); TARZAN'S JUNGLE REBELLION(1970); GREATEST, THE(1977, U.S./Brit.); GOOD GUYS WEAR BLACK(1978)
Manning H. Haynes
TOMORROW WE LIVE(1936, Brit.), d&w
Manning Haynes
THOSE WHO LOVE(1929, Brit.), d; OFFICER'S MESS, THE(1931, Brit.), d; SHOULD A DOCTOR TELL?(1931, Brit.), d; TO OBLIGE A LADY(1931, Brit.), d; OLD MAN, THE(1932, Brit.), d; PERFECT FLAW, THE(1934, Brit.), p&d; HIGHLAND FLING(1936, Brit.), d; PEARLS BRING TEARS(1937, Brit.), d; CLAYDON TREASURE MYSTERY, THE(1938, Brit.), d; COMING OF AGE(1938, Brit.), d
Silents
LOST CHORD, THE(1917, Brit.); LEAD, KINDLY LIGHT(1918, Brit.); JACK, SAM AND PETE(1919, Brit.); FOUR MEN IN A VAN(1921, Brit.); MONTY WORKS THE WIRES(1921, Brit.), a, d, w; HEAD OF THE FAMILY, THE(1922, Brit.), d; SKIPPER'S WOOING, THE(1922, Brit.), d; MONKEY'S PAW, THE(1923, Brit.), d; PASSION ISLAND(1927, Brit.), d
Misc. Silents
THREE MEN IN A BOAT(1920, Brit.); WARE CASE, THE(1928, Brit.), d
Marie Haynes
Silents
SALVATION NELL(1921)
Marques Haynes
HARLEM GLOBETROTTERS, THE(1951)
Michael Haynes
MAROC 7(1967, Brit.); BULLET FOR PRETTY BOY, A(1970); DUNWICH HORROR, THE(1970); CHROME AND HOT LEATHER(1971), a, w

Nathaniel [Butch] Haynes
PROPERTY(1979)
Paul Haynes
ONE MAN(1979, Can.)
Percy Haynes
MEET THE NAVY(1946, Brit.)
Robert Haynes
Misc. Talkies
ASSIGNMENT ABROAD(1955)
Roberta Haynes
KNOCK ON ANY DOOR(1949); WE WERE STRANGERS(1949); FIGHTER, THE(1952); GUN FURY(1953); NEBRASKAN, THE(1953); RETURN TO PARADISE(1953); HELL SHIP MUTINY(1957); POINT BLANK(1967); ADVENTURERS, THE(1970); VALDEZ IS COMING(1971)
Robin Haynes
TO BE OR NOT TO BE(1983)
1984
HOT DOG...THE MOVIE(1984)
Sam Haynes
MUSIC FOR MADAME(1937)
Stanley Haynes
MAN BEHIND THE MASK, THE(1936, Brit.), w; CARNIVAL(1946, Brit.), d, w; ONE WOMAN'S STORY(1949, Brit.), w; MADELEINE(1950, Brit.), p, w; OLIVER TWIST(1951, Brit.), w; BLUE PARROT, THE(1953, Brit.), p; DANGEROUS CARGO(1954, Brit.), p, w
Tiger Haynes
TIMES SQUARE(1980)
1984
MOSCOW ON THE HUDSON(1984)
"Tommy" Haynes
GLEN OR GLENDA(1953)
Walter Haynes
COUNTRY BOY(1966)
William Haynes
DOCKS OF SAN FRANCISCO(1932)
Misc. Silents
DESERT OUTLAW, THE(1924)
Jim Haynie
ESCAPE FROM ALCATRAZ(1979); TIME AFTER TIME(1979, Brit.); FOG, THE(1980); CHU CHU AND THE PHILLY FLASH(1981); OUT(1982); 48 HOURS(1982); RIGHT STUFF, THE(1983)
1984
COUNTRY(1984)
Robert Haynos
MOUSE ON THE MOON, THE(1963, Brit.)
Leroy Hayns
LEGEND OF FRENCHIE KING, THE(1971, Fr./Ital./Span./Brit.)
Patricia Hayos
KNUTE ROCKNE–ALL AMERICAN(1940)
Barry Hays
HEROES OF THE HILLS(1938); ONE MAN'S LAW(1940); TRAIL BLAZERS, THE(1940)
Sir Bertran Hays
Silents
ROAD TO LONDON, THE(1921, Brit.)
Daniel W. Hays
HITLER(1962), spec eff; RUSSIANS ARE COMING, THE RUSSIANS ARE COMING, THE(1966), spec eff
Danny Hays
WAY WEST, THE(1967), spec eff
Douglas Hays
VIOLENT STRANGER(1957, Brit.)
Geoffrey Hays
SYNDICATE, THE(1968, Brit.), w
Kathryn Hays
LADYBUG, LADYBUG(1963); RIDE BEYOND VENGEANCE(1966); COUNTERPOINT(1967); THIS SAVAGE LAND(1969)
Kent Hays
YOUNG FURY(1965); THING, THE(1982)
Lee Hays
ALICE'S RESTAURANT(1969)
Leonara Hays
DOUBLE-BARRELLED DETECTIVE STORY, THE(1965), ch
Mildred Hays
STORM CENTER(1956)
Robert Hays
AIRPLANE!(1980); FALL OF THE HOUSE OF USHER, THE(1980); TAKE THIS JOB AND SHOVE IT(1981); AIRPLANE II: THE SEQUEL(1982); TOUCHED(1983); TRENCHCOAT(1983); UTILITIES(1983, Can.)
1984
SCANDALOUS(1984)
Ron Hays
DEMON SEED(1977), anim
Will H. Hays, Jr.
YOU'RE MY EVERYTHING(1949), w
Youda Hays
MEXICAN SPITFIRE OUT WEST(1940)
A. R. Haysel
FUGITIVE LADY(1934); HELL CAT, THE(1934)
Lisa Hayslip
1984
CRIMES OF PASSION(1984)
Harold Haysom
LOOK BEFORE YOU LOVE(1948, Brit.), ph
Mercy Haystead
WHAT THE BUTLER SAW(1950, Brit.); CHELSEA STORY(1951, Brit.); SMART ALEC(1951, Brit.); PRIVATE INFORMATION(1952, Brit.); SING ALONG WITH ME(1952, Brit.); ADMIRABLE CRICHTON, THE(1957, Brit.); GIRLS AT SEA(1958, Brit.); DEATH TRAP(1962, Brit.); GET ON WITH IT(1963, Brit.)

James Hayter
HELL, HEAVEN OR HOBOKEN(1958, Brit.); SENSATION(1936, Brit.); BIG FELLA(1937, Brit.); MARIGOLD(1938, Brit.); COME ON GEORGE(1939, Brit.); MURDER IN THE NIGHT(1940, Brit.); THREE COCKEYED SAILORS(1940, Brit.); END OF THE RIVER, THE(1947, Brit.); GHOSTS OF BERKELEY SQUARE(1947, Brit.); NICHOLAS NICKLEBY(1947, Brit.); BONNIE PRINCE CHARLIE(1948, Brit.); MARK OF CAIN, THE(1948, Brit.); OCTOBER MAN, THE(1948, Brit.); SONG FOR TOMORROW, A(1948, Brit.); VICE VERSA(1948, Brit.); ALL OVER THE TOWN(1949, Brit.); BLUE LAGOON, THE(1949, Brit.); DEAR MR. PROHACK(1949, Brit.); DON'T EVER LEAVE ME(1949, Brit.); FALLEN IDOL, THE(1949, Brit.); FOR THEM THAT TRESPASS(1949, Brit.); MY BROTHER JONATHAN(1949, Brit.); PASSPORT TO PIMLICO(1949, Brit.); SILENT DUST(1949, Brit.); EYE WITNESS(1950, Brit.); LAUGHING LADY, THE(1950, Brit.); NIGHT AND THE CITY(1950, Brit.); NO ROOM AT THE INN(1950, Brit.); TRIO(1950, Brit.); CALLING BULLDOG DRUMMOND(1951, Brit.); FLESH AND BLOOD(1951, Brit.); HER PANELLED DOOR(1951, Brit.); MANIACS ON WHEELS(1951, Brit.); OPERATION DISASTER(1951, Brit.); TOM BROWN'S SCHOOLDAYS(1951, Brit.); CRIMSON PIRATE, THE(1952); I'M A STRANGER(1952, Brit.); PICKWICK PAPERS, THE(1952, Brit.); SPIDER AND THE FLY, THE(1952, Brit.); STORY OF ROBIN HOOD, THE(1952, Brit.); WATERFRONT WOMEN(1952, Brit.); DAY TO REMEMBER, A(1953, Brit.); FOUR SIDED TRIANGLE(1953, Brit.); GREAT GAME, THE(1953, Brit.); ALWAYS A BRIDE(1954, Brit.); BEAU BRUMMELL(1954); FOR BETTER FOR WORSE(1954, Brit.); LAND OF THE PHARAOHS(1955); LIGHT TOUCH, THE(1955, Brit.); SEE HOW THEY RUN(1955, Brit.); WILL ANY GENTLEMAN?(1955, Brit.); IT'S A WONDERFUL WORLD(1956, Brit.); KEEP IT CLEAN(1956, Brit.); PORT AFRIQUE(1956, Brit.); ABANDON SHIP(1957, Brit.); HEART WITHIN, THE(1957, Brit.); SAIL INTO DANGER(1957, Brit.); KEY, THE(1958, Brit.); BOY AND THE BRIDGE, THE(1959, Brit.); GIDEON OF SCOTLAND YARD(1959, Brit.); CAPTAIN'S TABLE, THE(1960, Brit.); THIRTY NINE STEPS, THE(1960, Brit.); BIG MONEY, THE(1962, Brit.); GO TO BLAZES(1962, Brit.); OUT OF THE FOG(1962, Brit.); COP-OUT(1967, Brit.); CHALLENGE FOR ROBIN HOOD, A(1968, Brit.); OLIVER!(1968, Brit.); BLOOD ON SATAN'S CLAW, THE(1970, Brit.); DAVID COPPERFIELD(1970, Brit.); FIRECHASERS, THE(1970, Brit.); SCRAMBLE(1970, Brit.); SONG OF NORWAY(1970); BAWDY ADVENTURES OF TOM JONES, THE(1976, Brit.)

John Hayter
RIDE THE HIGH WIND(1967, South Africa); SEVEN AGAINST THE SUN(1968, South Africa); MY WAY(1974, South Africa)

Robin Hayter
PARTY PARTY(1983, Brit.)

Elton Haytes
STORY OF ROBIN HOOD, THE(1952, Brit.)

Harry Haythorne
HALF A SIXPENCE(1967, Brit.)

Joan Haythorne
COMING-OUT PARTY, A(; SCHOOL FOR SECRETS(1946, Brit.); WHEN THE BOUGH BREAKS(1947, Brit.); JASSY(1948, Brit.); HIGHLY DANGEROUS(1950, Brit.); WEAK AND THE WICKED, THE(1954, Brit.); ONE JUST MAN(1955, Brit.); SVENGALI(1955, Brit.); DRY ROT(1956, Brit.); GENTLE TOUCH, THE(1956, Brit.); THREE MEN IN A BOAT(1958, Brit.); SHAKEDOWN, THE(1960, Brit.); FRIGHTENED CITY, THE(1961, Brit.); SO EVIL SO YOUNG(1961, Brit.); BATTLEAXE, THE(1962, Brit.); DECLINE AND FALL... OF A BIRD WATCHER(1969, Brit.)

Lennie Hayton
GOING HOLLYWOOD(1933, a, md; H.M. PULHAM, ESQ.(1941, md; MARRIED BACHELOR(1941, m; VANISHING VIRGINIAN, THE(1941, m; BORN TO SING(1942, m; MAISIE GETS HER MAN(1942, m; PIERRE OF THE PLAINS(1942, m; STAND BY FOR ACTION(1942, m; ASSIGNMENT IN BRITTANY(1943, m; BEST FOOT FORWARD(1943, m; PILOT NO. 5(1943, m; SALUTE TO THE MARINES(1943, m; SWING SHIFT MAISIE(1943, m; MEET THE PEOPLE(1944, m; YOLANDA AND THE THIEF(1945, md; HARVEY GIRLS, THE(1946, md; TILL THE CLOUDS ROLL BY(1946, m, md; GOOD NEWS(1947, md; HUCKSTERS, THE(1947, m; LIVING IN A BIG WAY(1947, m; PIRATE, THE(1948, m; SUMMER HOLIDAY(1948, md; ANY NUMBER CAN PLAY(1949, m; BATTLEGROUND(1949, m; ON THE TOWN(1949, md; SIDE STREET(1950, m; INSIDE STRAIGHT(1951, m; IT'S A BIG COUNTRY(1951, m; STRICTLY DISHONORABLE(1951, m; LOVE IS BETTER THAN EVER(1952, m, md; SINGIN' IN THE RAIN(1952, md; BATTLE CIRCUS(1953, m; EASY TO LOVE(1953, md; STAR!(1968, md

Lenny Hayton
ZIEGFELD FOLLIES(1945, md; BARKLEYS OF BROADWAY, THE(1949, m; HELLO, DOLLY!(1969, m, md

Lillian Hayton
LEAP OF FAITH(1931, Brit.), set d

Harvey Hayutin
TARZAN'S GREATEST ADVENTURE(1959, Brit.), p

John Haywald
HIGH TIDE AT NOON(1957, Brit.)

Betty Hayward
I MARRIED AN ANGEL(1942); WE WERE DANCING(1942)

Brooke Hayward
MAD DOG COLL(1961); DAY OF THE DOLPHIN, THE(1973)

Carol Hayward
FEEDBACK(1979), ed

Chard Hayward
LADY, STAY DEAD(1982, Aus.)
1984
BROTHERS(1984, Aus.)

Charles Hayward
MAN WHO SHOT LIBERTY VALANCE, THE(1962)

Chris Hayward
REMOVALISTS, THE(1975, Aus.); DEATHCHEATERS(1976, Aus.); IN SEARCH OF ANNA(1978, Aus.); NEWSFRONT(1979, Aus.); DEAD MAN'S FLOAT(1980, Aus.)

Chuck Hayward
WAGONMASTER(1950); FAIR WIND TO JAVA(1953); JUBILEE TRAIL(1954); SEARCHERS, THE(1956); FORTY GUNS(1957); RUN OF THE ARROW(1957); BIG COUNTRY, THE(1958); ESCORT WEST(1959); HORSE SOLDIERS, THE(1959); PORK CHOP HILL(1959); SERGEANT RUTLEDGE(1960); SPARTACUS(1960); DEADLY COMPANIONS, THE(1961), a, stunts; TWO RODE TOGETHER(1961); MERRILL'S MARAUDERS(1962); TARAS BULBA(1962); GREAT RACE, THE(1965); FIVE CARD STUD(1968); RIO LOBO(1970); HORSEMEN, THE(1971), stunts; JOE KIDD(1972); NIGHT OF THE LEPUS(1972); LONGEST YARD, THE(1974); HUSTLE(1975); ROOSTER COGBURN(1975); MARCH OR DIE(1977, Brit.), Stunts; SWARM, THE(1978); LEGEND OF THE LONE RANGER, THE(1981)

David Hayward
NASHVILLE(1975); HAZING, THE(1978); VAN NUYS BLVD.(1979); LEGEND OF THE LONE RANGER, THE(1981)
1984
HOUSE WHERE DEATH LIVES, THE(1984); SLAYGROUND(1984, Brit.)
Misc. Talkies
HOUSE WHERE DEATH LIVES, THE(1982)

Davy Hayward
RIVER HOUSE MYSTERY, THE(1935, Brit.)

Doreen Hayward
ROYAL WEDDING(1951)

Douglas Hayward
MODESTY BLAISE(1966, Brit.), cos; RECKONING, THE(1971, Brit.), cos

Eldon Hayward
HIGHWAY TO BATTLE(1961, Brit.), w

Elma Hayward
EARLY BIRD, THE(1936, Brit.)

Frederick Hayward
LEND ME YOUR HUSBAND(1935, Brit.), d; ELDER BROTHER, THE(1937, Brit.), d; CRIMES AT THE DARK HOUSE(1940, Brit.), w

Fredrick Hayward
DEMON BARBER OF FLEET STREET, THE(1939, Brit.), w

Harry Hayward
WOMAN TO WOMAN(1946, Brit.), makeup; GREEN FINGERS(1947), makeup; MY BROTHER JONATHAN(1949, Brit.), makeup

Helen Hayward
SHOW BOAT(1936)
Silents
GOLD RUSH, THE(1925)
Misc. Silents
WRONG DOOR, THE(1916)

Henry Hayward
UNEASY TERMS(1948, Brit.), makeup; MRS. FITZHERBERT(1950, Brit.), makeup
Silents
CHASER, THE(1928)

Herbert Hayward
LIFE BEGINS AT 40(1935)

James Hayward
MYSTERY STREET(1950); VENGEANCE VALLEY(1951); PONY SOLDIER(1952); LUCKY ME(1954); MAN WITHOUT A STAR(1955)

Jane Hayward
HOUSE OF WHIPCORD(1974, Brit.); CONFESSIONAL, THE(1977, Brit.)

Jim Hayward
FRANCIS(1949); DOUBLE DEAL(1950); FATHER OF THE BRIDE(1950); EXCUSE MY DUST(1951); LET'S MAKE IT LEGAL(1951); RED BADGE OF COURAGE, THE(1951); RHUBARB(1951); CARRIE(1952); ARENA(1953); DEVIL'S CANYON(1953); SOUTH SEA WOMAN(1953); ALASKA SEAS(1954); BITTER CREEK(1954); SCARLET COAT, THE(1955); FIRST TRAVELING SALESLADY, THE(1956); HILDA CRANE(1956); KETTLES IN THE OZARKS, THE(1956); MOUNTAIN, THE(1956); NAKED GUN, THE(1956); NAKED HILLS, THE(1956); WHEN GANGLAND STRIKES(1956); BAND OF ANGELS(1957); NO DOWN PAYMENT(1957); STORM RIDER, THE(1957); TERROR AT BLACK FALLS(1962)

Joan Hayward
SWAPPERS, THE(1970, Brit.)

John Nugent Hayward
OVERLANDERS, THE(1946, Brit./Aus.)

Judy Hayward
CANDIDATE, THE(1972)

Kevin Hayward
1984
CONSTANCE(1984, New Zealand), ph; PALLET ON THE FLOOR(1984, New Zealand), ph

Leland Hayward
MISTER ROBERTS(1955), p; SPIRIT OF ST. LOUIS, THE(1957), p; OLD MAN AND THE SEA, THE(1958), p
Silents
WHIP WOMAN, THE(1928), w

Lillian Hayward
MAN HUNTER, THE(1930), w; MISS PINKERTON(1932), w; BEDSIDE(1934), w; ALOMA OF THE SOUTH SEAS(1941), w
Silents
BIG TREMAINE(1916); JANICE MEREDITH(1924), w
Misc. Silents
DEVIL, THE SERVANT AND THE MAN, THE(1916); UNTO THOSE WHO SIN(1916); RAINBOW GIRL, THE(1917); WILD WINSHIP'S WIDOW(1917)

Lillie Hayward
BIG CITY BLUES(1932), w; THEY CALL IT SIN(1932), w; FRISCO JENNY(1933), w; LADY KILLER(1933), w; BIG HEARTED HERBERT(1934), w; HOUSEWIFE(1934), w; REGISTERED NURSE(1934), w; FRONT PAGE WOMAN(1935), w; PERSONAL MAID'S SECRET(1935), w; WHITE COCKATOO(1935), w; WALKING DEAD, THE(1936), w; BLONDE TROUBLE(1937), w; EVER SINCE EVE(1937), w; EXPENSIVE HUSBANDS(1937), w; HER HUSBAND'S SECRETARY(1937), w; PENROD AND SAM(1937), w; THAT MAN'S HERE AGAIN(1937), w; HER JUNGLE LOVE(1938), w; SONS OF THE LEGION(1938), w; KING OF CHINATOWN(1939), w; TELEVISION SPY(1939), w; UNMARRIED(1939), w; BISCUIT EATER, THE(1940), w; HEART OF THE RIO GRANDE(1942), w; ON THE SUNNY SIDE(1942), w; UNDYING MONSTER, THE(1942), w; MARGIN FOR ERROR(1943), w; MY FRIEND FLICKA(1943), w; MY PAL, WOLF(1944), w; TAHITI NIGHTS(1945), w; BLACK BEAUTY(1946), w; CHILD OF DIVORCE(1946), p, w; SMOKY(1946), w; BANJO(1947), p, w; NORTHWEST STAMPEDE(1948), w; FOLLOW ME QUIETLY(1949), w; STRANGE BARGAIN(1949), w; CATTLE DRIVE(1951), w; BRONCO BUSTER(1952), w; RAIDERS, THE(1952), w; SANTA FE PASSAGE(1955), w; TARZAN AND THE LOST SAFARI(1957, Brit.), w; PROUD REBEL, THE(1958), w; TONKA(1958), w; SHAGGY DOG, THE(1959), w; BOY AND THE PIRATES, THE(1960), w; TOBY TYLER(1960), w; LAD: A DOG(1962), w; SMOKY(1966), w
Silents
EVERY MAN'S WIFE(1925), w; AMATEUR GENTLEMAN, THE(1926), w; RANSON'S FOLLY(1926), w; RUNAWAY GIRLS(1928), w

Louis Hayward
SELF-MADE LADY(1932, Brit.); CHELSEA LIFE(1933, Brit.); I'LL STICK TO YOU(1933, Brit.); MAN OUTSIDE, THE(1933, Brit.); THIRTEENTH CANDLE, THE(1933, Brit.); SORRELL AND SON(1934, Brit.); FEATHER IN HER HAT, A(1935); FLAME WITHIN, THE(1935); LOVE TEST, THE(1935, Brit.); ABSOLUTE QUIET(1936); ANTHONY ADVERSE(1936); LUCKIEST GIRL IN THE WORLD, THE(1936); TROUBLE FOR TWO(1936); WOMAN I LOVE, THE(1937); CONDEMNED WOMEN(1938); DUKE OF WEST POINT, THE(1938); MIDNIGHT INTRUDER(1938); RAGE OF PARIS, THE(1938); SAINT IN NEW YORK, THE(1938); MAN IN THE IRON MASK, THE(1939); DANCE, GIRL, DANCE(1940); MY SON, MY SON!(1940); SON OF MONTE CRISTO(1940); LADIES IN RETIREMENT(1941); MAGNIFICENT AMBERSONS, THE(1942); AND THEN THERE WERE NONE(1945); RETURN OF MONTE CRISTO, THE(1946); STRANGE WOMAN, THE(1946); YOUNG WIDOW(1946); REPEAT PERFORMANCE(1947); BLACK ARROW(1948); RUTHLESS(1948); WALK A CROOKED MILE(1948); PIRATES OF CAPRI, THE(1949); FORTUNES OF CAPTAIN BLOOD(1950); HOUSE BY THE RIVER(1950); LADY AND THE BANDIT, THE(1951); SON OF DR. JEKYLL, THE(1951); CAPTAIN PIRATE(1952); LADY IN THE IRON MASK(1952); ROYAL AFRICAN RIFLES, THE(1953); DUFFY OF SAN QUENTIN(1954); SAINT'S GIRL FRIDAY, THE(1954, Brit.); SEARCH FOR BRIDEY MURPHY, THE(1956); CHUKA(1967); CHRISTMAS KID, THE(1968, U.S., Span.); PHYNX, THE(1970); TERROR IN THE WAX MUSEUM(1973)

Louis M. Hayward
GLASS SPHINX, THE(1968, Egypt/Ital./Span.), w

Lydia Hayward
LAST POST, THE(1929, Brit.), w; THOSE WHO LOVE(1929, Brit.), w; LOVE'S OLD SWEET SONG(1933, Brit.), w; MRS. DANE'S DEFENCE(1933, Brit.), w; SORRELL AND SON(1934, Brit.), w; MISSING PEOPLE, THE(1940, Brit.), w; HARD STEEL(1941, Brit.), w; YOU WILL REMEMBER(1941, Brit.), w
Silents
MONTY WORKS THE WIRES(1921, Brit.), w; HEAD OF THE FAMILY, THE(1922, Brit.), w; SKIPPER'S WOOING, THE(1922, Brit.), w; MONKEY'S PAW, THE(1923, Brit.), w; NOT FOR SALE(1924, Brit.), w; EVERY MOTHER'S SON(1926, Brit.), w; PASSION ISLAND(1927, Brit.), w; SOMEHOW GOOD(1927, Brit.), w; ZERO(1928, Brit.), w; PEEP BEHIND THE SCENES, A(1929, Brit.), w

Milton Hayward
PACK UP YOUR TROUBLES(1940, Brit.), w

Richard Hayward
FLAME IN THE HEATHER(1935, Brit.); EARLY BIRD, THE(1936, Brit.); SHIPMATES O' MINE(1936, Brit.); LUCK OF THE IRISH, THE(1937, Ireland), a, p; DEVIL'S ROCK(1938, Brit.), a, w; IRISH AND PROUD OF IT(1938, Ireland); NIGHT TO REMEMBER, A(1958, Brit.)

Sheila Hayward
NOW, VOYAGER(1942)
Silents
ADORABLE DECEIVER, THE(1926)

Shirley Hayward
PICKUP ON 101(1972)

Susan Hayward
THEY WON'T BELIEVE ME(1947); HOLLYWOOD HOTEL(1937); COMET OVER BROADWAY(1938); GIRLS ON PROBATION(1938); SISTERS, THE(1938); BEAU GESTE(1939); OUR LEADING CITIZEN(1939); $1,000 A TOUCHDOWN(1939); ADAM HAD FOUR SONS(1941); AMONG THE LIVING(1941); SIS HOPKINS(1941); FOREST RANGERS, THE(1942); I MARRIED A WITCH(1942); REAP THE WILD WIND(1942); STAR SPANGLED RHYTHM(1942); HIT PARADE of 1943(1943); JACK LONDON(1943); YOUNG AND WILLING(1943); AND NOW TOMORROW(1944); FIGHTING SEABEES, THE(1944); CANYON PASSAGE(1946); DEADLINE AT DAWN(1946); LOST MOMENT, THE(1947); SMASH-UP, THE STORY OF A WOMAN(1947); SAXON CHARM, THE(1948); TAP ROOTS(1948); HOUSE OF STRANGERS(1949); MY FOOLISH HEART(1949); TULSA(1949); DAVID AND BATHSHEBA(1951); I CAN GET IT FOR YOU WHOLESALE(1951); I'D CLIMB THE HIGHEST MOUNTAIN(1951); RAWHIDE(1951); LUSTY MEN, THE(1952); SNOWS OF KILIMANJARO, THE(1952); WITH A SONG IN MY HEART(1952); PRESIDENT'S LADY, THE(1953); WHITE WITCH DOCTOR(1953); GARDEN OF EVIL(1954); I'LL CRY TOMORROW(1955); SOLDIER OF FORTUNE(1955); UNTAMED(1955); CONQUEROR, THE(1956); TOP SECRET AFFAIR(1957); I WANT TO LIVE!(1958); THUNDER IN THE SUN(1959); WOMAN OBSESSED(1959); MARRIAGE-GO-ROUND, THE(1960); ADA(1961); BACK STREET(1961); I THANK A FOOL(1962, Brit.); STOLEN HOURS(1963); WHERE LOVE HAS GONE(1964); HONEY POT, THE(1967, Brit.); VALLEY OF THE DOLLS(1967); REVENGERS, THE(1972, U.S./Mex.)

Tracy Hayward
FRATERNITY ROW(1977)

William Hayward
HIRED HAND, THE(1971), p; IDAHO TRANSFER(1975), p

Willie Hayward
BLOOD ON THE MOON(1948), w

Alan Haywood
CASH ON DEMAND(1962, Brit.)

Billie Haywood
ANGEL COMES TO BROOKLYN, AN(1945)

Chris Haywood
GREAT MACARTHY, THE(1975, Aus.); TRESPASSERS, THE(1976, Aus.); CLINIC, THE(1983, Aus.); HEATWAVE(1983, Aus.); LONELY HEARTS(1983, Aus.); MAN FROM SNOWY RIVER, THE(1983, Aus.)
1984
MAN OF FLOWERS(1984, Aus.); RAZORBACK(1984, Aus.); STRIKEBOUND(1984, Aus.)

Drexle Bobbie Haywood
SOUTHERN YANKEE, A(1948)

George Haywood
KNUTE ROCKNE–ALL AMERICAN(1940); MAN WHO TALKED TOO MUCH, THE(1940); SANTA FE TRAIL(1940); THEY DRIVE BY NIGHT(1940); GAY SISTERS, THE(1942)

Herbert Haywood
ARIZONA RAIDERS, THE(1936); RACKET BUSTERS(1938); KING OF THE LUMBERJACKS(1940); ALMOST MARRIED(1942); IDEA GIRL(1946); ALL MY SONS(1948)

Hilda Haywood
TELL NO TALES(1939)

Michael Haywood
1984
STRANGERS KISS(1984)

Mike Haywood
1984
SECRET PLACES(1984, Brit.)

Roy Haywood
BRONCO BULLFROG(1972, Brit.); LOOKS AND SMILES(1982, Brit.)

Lillie Hayword
DISBARRED(1939), w

Susan Hayword
HAIRY APE, THE(1944); DEMETRIUS AND THE GLADIATORS(1954)

Carmen Hayworth
BOSS NIGGER(1974)

Gilda Hayworth
GUN RUNNER(1969)

Joe Hayworth
GUNG HO!(1943)

Rita Hayworth
CRIMINALS OF THE AIR(1937); GAME THAT KILLS, THE(1937); GIRLS CAN PLAY(1937); PAID TO DANCE(1937); SHADOW, THE(1937); CONVICTED(1938); JUVENILE COURT(1938); RENEGADE RANGER(1938); THERE'S ALWAYS A WOMAN(1938); WHO KILLED GAIL PRESTON?(1938); HOMICIDE BUREAU(1939); LONE WOLF SPY HUNT, THE(1939); ONLY ANGELS HAVE WINGS(1939); SPECIAL INSPECTOR(1939); ANGELS OVER BROADWAY(1940); BLONDIE ON A BUDGET(1940); LADY IN QUESTION, THE(1940); MUSIC IN MY HEART(1940); SUSAN AND GOD(1940); AFFECTIONATELY YOURS(1941); BLOOD AND SAND(1941); STRAWBERRY BLONDE, THE(1941); YOU'LL NEVER GET RICH(1941); MY GAL SAL(1942); TALES OF MANHATTAN(1942); YOU WERE NEVER LOVELIER(1942); COVER GIRL(1944); TONIGHT AND EVERY NIGHT(1945); GILDA(1946); DOWN TO EARTH(1947); LADY FROM SHANGHAI, THE(1948); LOVES OF CARMEN, THE(1948); AFFAIR IN TRINIDAD(1952); MISS SADIE THOMPSON(1953); SALOME(1953); FIRE DOWN BELOW(1957, U.S./Brit.); PAL JOEY(1957); SEPARATE TABLES(1958); STORY ON PAGE ONE, THE(1959); THEY CAME TO CORDURA(1959); HAPPY THIEVES, THE(1962), a, p; CIRCUS WORLD(1964); MONEY TRAP, THE(1966); POPPY IS ALSO A FLOWER, THE(1966); ROVER, THE(1967, Ital.); SONS OF SATAN(1969, Ital./Fr./Ger.); NAKED ZOO, THE(1970); ROAD TO SALINA(1971, Fr./Ital.); WRATH OF GOD, THE(1972)

Vinton Hayworth
NEW YORK TOWN(1941); GIRL HE LEFT BEHIND, THE(1956); GREAT MAN, THE(1957); QUICK, LET'S GET MARRIED(1965); CHAMBER OF HORRORS(1966)

Michio Hazama
BEACH RED(1967)

Jack Hazan
RUDE BOY(1980, Brit.), p&d, w, ph
1984
BIGGER SPLASH, A(1984), p&d, w, ph

Dick Hazard
RADAR SECRET SERVICE(1950), m

Edwina Hazard
SON OF SINBAD(1955)

Jayne Hazard
MONSTER AND THE GIRL, THE(1941); POWERS GIRL, THE(1942); UNDERGROUND AGENT(1942); LET'S FACE IT(1943); SHE HAS WHAT IT TAKES(1943); CRAZY KNIGHTS(1944); LOST WEEKEND, THE(1945); STRANGE ILLUSION(1945); BLACK MARKET BABIES(1946); DAREDEVILS OF THE CLOUDS(1948); I CAN GET IT FOR YOU WHOLESALE(1951)

John Hazard
FIST OF FEAR, TOUCH OF DEATH(1980), ph

John W. Hazard
YOU'RE IN THE NAVY NOW(1951), w

Lawrence Hazard
FROM HELL TO HEAVEN(1933), w; HELLO, EVERYBODY(1933), w; MAN'S CASTLE, A(1933), w; FEATHER IN HER HAT, A(1935), w; HOORAY FOR LOVE(1935), w; I'LL LOVE YOU ALWAYS(1935), w; MAYBE IT'S LOVE(1935), w; MANNEQUIN(1937), w; THOROUGHBREDS DON'T CRY(1937), w; SPORTING BLOOD(1940), w; STRANGE CARGO(1940), w; DESTINATION UNKNOWN(1942), w; JACKASS MAIL(1942), w; SPOILERS, THE(1942), w; FOREVER AND A DAY(1943), w; GENTLE ANNIE(1944), w; DAKOTA(1945), w; SHE WENT TO THE RACES(1945), w; FABULOUS TEXAN, THE(1947), w; WYOMING(1947), w

Richard Hazard
CALYPSO JOE(1957), m; COMPANY OF KILLERS(1970), m; SOME CALL IT LOVING(1973), m, md; NICKELODEON(1976), m; HEROES(1977), m; ALL NIGHT LONG(1981), m

Hollie Haze
DON'T MAKE WAVES(1967)

Jonathan Haze
APACHE WOMAN(1955); FIVE GUNS WEST(1955); DAY THE WORLD ENDED, THE(1956); GUNSLINGER(1956); IT CONQUERED THE WORLD(1956); OKLAHOMA WOMAN, THE(1956); BAYOU(1957); SWAMP WOMEN(1956); CARNIVAL ROCK(1957); NAKED PARADISE(1957); NOT OF THIS EARTH(1957); ROCK ALL NIGHT(1957); SAGA OF THE VIKING WOMEN AND THEIR VOYAGE TO THE WATERS OF THE GREAT SEA SERPENT, THE(1957); GHOST OF THE CHINA SEA(1958); STAKEOUT ON DOPE STREET(1958); TEENAGE CAVEMAN(1958); FORBIDDEN ISLAND(1959); LITTLE SHOP OF HORRORS(1961); INVASION OF THE STAR CREATURES(1962), w; "X"–THE MAN WITH THE X-RAY EYES(1963); TERROR, THE(1963); VICE SQUAD(1982)

Stan Haze
FROM NOON TO THREE(1976); DON'T ANSWER THE PHONE(1980)

Hazel
GUIDE, THE(1965, U.S./India)

William Hazel
PRISONER OF ZENDA, THE(1952)

James Hazeldine
NICHOLAS AND ALEXANDRA(1971, Brit.); RULING CLASS, THE(1972, Brit.); NATIONAL HEALTH, OR NURSE NORTON'S AFFAIR, THE(1973, Brit.); STARDUST(1974, Brit.); MEDUSA TOUCH, THE(1978, Brit.); PINK FLOYD–THE WALL(1982, Brit.)

Jean Hazelewood
SECRET WAYS, THE(1961), w

Noni Hazelhurst
FATTY FINN(1980, Aus.); MONKEY GRIP(1983, Aus.)

Wayne Hazelhurst
UP IN SMOKE(1978)

William Hazelitt
DRUMS OF DESTINY(1937)

Derna Hazell
MY LEARNED FRIEND(1943, Brit.)

Hy Hazell
MEET ME AT DAWN(1947, Brit.); JUST WILLIAM'S LUCK(1948, Brit.); CELIA(1949, Brit.); PAPER ORCHID(1949, Brit.); BODY SAID NO!, THE(1950, Brit.); DANCE HALL(1950, Brit.); LADY CRAVED EXCITEMENT, THE(1950, Brit.); FRANCHISE AFFAIR, THE(1952, Brit.); NIGHT WON'T TALK, THE(1952, Brit.); FORCES' SWEETHEART(1953, Brit.); YELLOW BALLOON, THE(1953, Brit.); STOLEN ASSIGNMENT(1955, Brit.); ANASTASIA(1956); KEY MAN, THE(1957, Brit.); LIGHT FINGERS(1957, Brit.); UP IN THE WORLD(1957, Brit.); WHOLE TRUTH, THE(1958, Brit.); FIVE GOLDEN HOURS(1961, Brit.); WHAT EVERY WOMAN WANTS(1962, Brit.); IN TROUBLE WITH EVE(1964, Brit.); THINK DIRTY(1970, Brit.)

Leslie Hazell
JUST WILLIAM'S LUCK(1948, Brit.)

Horace Hazeltine [Charles Stokes Wayne]
Silents
SABLE LORCHA, THE(1915), w; APPEARANCE OF EVIL(1918), w

Nancy Hazeltine
CARNY(1980)

Phyllis Hazeltine
Silents
FRUITS OF DESIRE, THE(1916)

Beth Hazelton
MAGNIFICENT OBSESSION(1935); STRAIGHT FROM THE HEART(1935)

George C. Hazelton, Jr.
Silents
MISTRESS NELL(1915), w

Horace Hazelton [Charles Stokes Wayne]
Silents
IRON RING, THE(1917), w

Joseph Hazelton
Silents
IF ONLY JIM(1921); OLIVER TWIST(1922)

Philip Hazelton
EYE OF THE CAT(1969), p

Phillip Hazelton
COLD WIND IN AUGUST(1961), p; PSYCHE 59(1964, Brit.), p; SHUTTERED ROOM, THE(1968, Brit.), p

Robert Hazelton
Silents
SILVER WINGS(1922)

John Hazelwood
1984
NIGHT PATROL(1984)

Joseph H. Hazen
GIRL NAMED TAMIRO, A(1962), p

Jean-Pierre Hazi
LIFE LOVE DEATH(1969, Fr./Ital.)

Fabian Haziza
Misc. Silents
POIL DE CAROTTE(1926, Fr.)

George Hazle
CIRCLE CANYON(1934)

Bill Hazlet
GO WEST, YOUNG LADY(1941)

Bill Hazlett
OUTLAW EXPRESS(1938); SADDLEMATES(1941); GIRL CRAZY(1943)

Marlene Hazlett
TELEFON(1977)

Lee Hazlewood
MOONSHINE WAR, THE(1970)

Edith Hazley
RED, WHITE AND BLACK, THE(1970)

Frederick Hazlitt
WORDS AND MUSIC(1929), w

Jane Hazzard
RACKET, THE(1951)

Eugeniusz Hczkiewicz
1984
SUCCESS IS THE BEST REVENGE(1984, Brit.)

T.S. He
FIGHT TO THE LAST(1938, Chi.)

Gary R. Heacock
DR. TERROR'S GALLERY OF HORRORS(1967), w

Linnea Heacock
TAKING OFF(1971)

Anne Head
MINE OWN EXECUTIONER(1948, Brit.), set d

Anthony Head
LADY CHATTERLEY'S LOVER(1981, Fr./Brit.)

Betty Lou Head
DECOY(1946); WEST OF THE ALAMO(1946)

Bob Head
MUDLARK, THE(1950, Brit.); TREASURE ISLAND(1950, Brit.); NIGHT CREATURES(1962, Brit.)

Dino Head
FRENCH QUARTER(1978)

Edith Head
ROMA RIVUOLE CESARE(, cos; MAN'S FAVORITE SPORT(?) (1964), cos; LOVE ME TONIGHT(1932), cos; SHE DONE HIM WRONG(1933), cos; SHE LOVES ME NOT(1934), cos; YOU BELONG TO ME(1934), cos; MURDER WITH PICTURES(1936), cos; POPPY(1936), cos; RHYTHM ON THE RANGE(1936), cos; BIG BROADCAST OF

1938, THE(1937), cos; EBB TIDE(1937), cos; SOPHIE LANG GOES WEST(1937), cos; SOULS AT SEA(1937), cos; THIS WAY PLEASE(1937), cos; WAIKIKI WEDDING(1937), cos; ARTISTS AND MODELS ABROAD(1938), cos; HER JUNGLE LOVE(1938), cos; IF I WERE KING(1938), cos; TROPIC HOLIDAY(1938), cos; MAN OF CONQUEST(1939), cos; NEVER SAY DIE(1939), cos; STAR MAKER, THE(1939), cos; SUDDEN MONEY(1939), cos; GREAT McGINTY, THE(1940), cos; REMEMBER THE NIGHT(1940), cos; RHYTHM ON THE RIVER(1940), cos; BIRTH OF THE BLUES(1941), cos; HERE COMES MR. JORDAN(1941), cos; HOLD BACK THE DAWN(1941), cos; LADY EVE, THE(1941), cos; NEW YORK TOWN(1941), cos; ROAD TO ZANZIBAR(1941), cos; SULLIVAN'S TRAVELS(1941), cos; YOU BELONG TO ME(1941), cos; GAY SISTERS, THE(1942), cos; GREAT MAN'S LADY, THE(1942), cos; HOLIDAY INN(1942), cos; I MARRIED A WITCH(1942), cos; MAJOR AND THE MINOR, THE(1942), cos; ROAD TO MOROCCO(1942), cos; STAR SPANGLED RHYTHM(1942), cos; FIVE GRAVES TO CAIRO(1943), cos; FLESH AND FANTASY(1943), cos; LADY OF BURLESQUE(1943), cos; NO TIME FOR LOVE(1943), cos; TENDER COMRADE(1943), cos; YOUNG AND WILLING(1943), cos; DOUBLE INDEMNITY(1944), cos; GOING MY WAY(1944), cos; LADY IN THE DARK(1944), cos; MIRACLE OF MORGAN'S CREEK, THE(1944), cos; RAINBOW ISLAND(1944), cos; BELLS OF ST. MARY'S, THE(1945), cos; CHRISTMAS IN CONNECTICUT(1945), cos; LOST WEEKEND, THE(1945), cos; OUT OF THIS WORLD(1945), cos; ROAD TO UTOPIA(1945), cos; YOU CAME ALONG(1945), cos; BLUE DAHLIA, THE(1946), cos; BRIDE WORE BOOTS, THE(1946), cos; CALIFORNIA(1946), cos; MY REPUTATION(1946), cos; NOTORIOUS(1946), cos; PERFECT MARRIAGE, THE(1946), cos; STRANGE LOVE OF MARTHA IVERS, THE(1946), cos; TO EACH HIS OWN(1946), cos; CRY WOLF(1947), cos; DESERT FURY(1947), cos; DREAM GIRL(1947), cos; MY FAVORITE BRUNETTE(1947), cos; OTHER LOVE, THE(1947), cos; ROAD TO RIO(1947), cos; TROUBLE WITH WOMEN, THE(1947), cos; TWO MRS. CARROLLS, THE(1947), cos; VARIETY GIRL(1947), cos; WELCOME STRANGER(1947), cos; WHERE THERE'S LIFE(1947), cos; BIG CLOCK, THE(1948), cos; EMPEROR WALTZ, THE(1948), cos; FOREIGN AFFAIR, A(1948), cos; JUNE BRIDE(1948), cos; MISS TATLOCK'S MILLIONS(1948), cos; MY OWN TRUE LOVE(1948), cos; NIGHT HAS A THOUSAND EYES(1948), cos; RACHEL AND THE STRANGER(1948), cos; SAIGON(1948), cos; SO EVIL MY LOVE(1948, Brit.), cos; SORRY, WRONG NUMBER(1948), cos; ACCUSED, THE(1949), cos; BEYOND THE FOREST(1949), cos; CONNECTICUT YANKEE IN KING ARTHUR'S COURT, A(1949), cos; GREAT GATSBY, THE(1949), cos; HEIRESS, THE(1949), cos; MANHANDLED(1949), cos; MY FOOLISH HEART(1949), cos; MY FRIEND IRMA(1949), cos; RED, HOT AND BLUE(1949), cos; SAMSON AND DELILAH(1949), cos; ALL ABOUT EVE(1950), cos; DARK CITY(1950), cos; FILE ON THELMA JORDAN, THE(1950), cos; FURIES, THE(1950), cos; NO MAN OF HER OWN(1950), cos; RIDING HIGH(1950), cos; SUNSET BOULEVARD(1950), cos; DETECTIVE STORY(1951), cos; HERE COMES THE GROOM(1951), cos; MY FAVORITE SPY(1951), cos; PAYMENT ON DEMAND(1951), cos; PLACE IN THE SUN, A(1951), cos; THAT'S MY BOY(1951), cos; WHEN WORLDS COLLIDE(1951), cos; GREATEST SHOW ON EARTH, THE(1952), cos; JUST FOR YOU(1952), cos; RED SNOW(1952), cos; ROAD TO BALI(1952), cos; SOMETHING TO LIVE FOR(1952), cos; TURNING POINT, THE(1952), cos; FOREVER FEMALE(1953), cos; HOUDINI(1953), cos; LITTLE BOY LOST(1953), cos; NAKED JUNGLE, THE(1953), cos; SANGAREE(1953), cos; SAVAGE, THE(1953), cos; SCARED STIFF(1953), cos; SHANE(1953), cos; STARS ARE SINGING, THE(1953), cos; TROPIC ZONE(1953), cos; VANQUISHED, THE(1953), cos; WAR OF THE WORLDS, THE(1953), cos; BRIDGES AT TOKO-RI, THE(1954), cos; COUNTRY GIRL, THE(1954), cos; ELEPHANT WALK(1954), cos; REAR WINDOW(1954), cos; SABRINA(1954), cos; THEM!(1954), cos; THREE RING CIRCUS(1954), cos; WHITE CHRISTMAS(1954), cos; ARTISTS AND MODELS(1955), cos; DESPERATE HOURS, THE(1955), cos; FAR HORIZONS, THE(1955), cos; GIRL RUSH, THE(1955), cos; HELL'S ISLAND(1955), cos; LUCY GALLANT(1955), a, cos; ROSE TATTOO, THE(1955), cos; RUN FOR COVER(1955), cos; SEVEN LITTLE FOYS, THE(1955), cos; STRATEGIC AIR COMMAND(1955), cos; TO CATCH A THIEF(1955), cos; TROUBLE WITH HARRY, THE(1955), cos; YOU'RE NEVER TOO YOUNG(1955), cos; COURT JESTER, THE(1956), cos; MAN WHO KNEW TOO MUCH, THE(1956), cos; MOUNTAIN, THE(1956), cos; PARDNERS(1956), cos; PROUD AND THE PROFANE, THE(1956), cos; RAINMAKER, THE(1956), cos; SCARLET HOUR, THE(1956), cos; SEARCH FOR BRIDEY MURPHY, THE(1956), cos; TEN COMMANDMENTS, THE(1956), cos; THAT CERTAIN FEELING(1956), cos; THREE VIOLENT PEOPLE(1956), cos; DELICATE DELINQUENT, THE(1957), cos; DEVIL'S HAIRPIN, THE(1957), cos; FEAR STRIKES OUT(1957), c; FUNNY FACE(1957), cos; GUNFIGHT AT THE O.K. CORRAL(1957), cos; HEAR ME GOOD(1957), cos; JOKER IS WILD, THE(1957), cos; LOVING YOU(1957), cos; SAD SACK, THE(1957), cos; SHORT CUT TO HELL(1957), cos; TIN STAR, THE(1957), cos; WITNESS FOR THE PROSECUTION(1957), cos; GEISHA BOY, THE(1958), cos; HOUSEBOAT(1958), cos; KING CREOLE(1958), cos; MARACAIBO(1958), cos; MATCHMAKER, THE(1958), cos; ROCK-A-BYE BABY(1958), cos; SEPARATE TABLES(1958), cos; ST. LOUIS BLUES(1958), cos; TEACHER'S PET(1958), cos; VERTIGO(1958), cos; ALIAS JESSE JAMES(1959), cos; CAREER(1959), cos; HOLE IN THE HEAD, A(1959), cos; JAYHAWKERS, THE(1959), cos; THAT KIND OF WOMAN(1959), cos; CINDERFELLA(1960), cos; FACTS OF LIFE, THE(1960), cos; HELLER IN PINK TIGHTS(1960), cos; PEPE(1960), cos; RAT RACE, THE(1960), cos; TOUCH OF LARCENY, A(1960, Brit.), cos; VISIT TO A SMALL PLANET(1960), cos; BREAKFAST AT TIFFANY'S(1961), cos; ERRAND BOY, THE(1961), cos; LADIES MAN, THE(1961), cos; LOVE IN A GOLDFISH BOWL(1961), cos; MAN-TRAP(1961), cos; ON THE DOUBLE(1961), cos; PLEASURE OF HIS COMPANY, THE(1961), a, cos; POCKETFUL OF MIRACLES(1961), cos; SUMMER AND SMOKE(1961), cos; COUNTERFEIT TRAITOR, THE(1962), cos; GIRL NAMED TAMIRO, A(1962), cos; GIRLS! GIRLS! GIRLS!(1962), cos; HATARI!(1962), cos; IT'S ONLY MONEY(1962), cos; MAN WHO SHOT LIBERTY VALANCE, THE(1962), cos; MY GEISHA(1962), cos; TOO LATE BLUES(1962), cos; WHO'S GOT THE ACTION?(1962), cos; BIRDS, THE(1963), cos; COME BLOW YOUR HORN(1963), cos; CRITIC'S CHOICE(1963), cos; FUN IN ACAPULCO(1963), cos; HUD(1963), cos; I COULD GO ON SINGING(1963), cos; LOVE WITH THE PROPER STRANGER(1963), cos; MY SIX LOVES(1963), cos; NEW KIND OF LOVE, A(1963), cos; NUTTY PROFESSOR, THE(1963), cos; PAPA'S DELICATE CONDITION(1963), cos; WHO'S BEEN SLEEPING IN MY BED?(1963), cos; WHO'S MINDING THE STORE?(1963), cos; WIVES AND LOVERS(1963), cos; CARPETBAGGERS, THE(1964), cos; DISORDERLY ORDERLY, THE(1964), cos; HOUSE IS NOT A HOME, A(1964), cos; JOHN GOLDFARB, PLEASE COME HOME(1964), cos; MARNIE(1964), cos; PATSY, THE(1964), cos; ROUSTABOUT(1964), cos; SEX AND THE SINGLE GIRL(1964), cos; WHAT A WAY TO GO(1964), cos; WHERE LOVE HAS GONE(1964), cos; BIRDS AND THE BEES, THE(1965), cos; BOEING BOEING(1965), cos; FAMILY JEWELS, THE(1965), cos; GREAT RACE, THE(1965), cos; HALLELUJAH TRAIL, THE(1965), cos; INSIDE DAISY CLOVER(1965), cos; LOVE HAS MANY FACES(1965), cos; RED LINE 7000(1965), cos; SLENDER THREAD, THE(1965), cos; SONS OF KATIE ELDER,

THE(1965), cos; SYLVIA(1965), cos; YELLOW ROLLS-ROYCE, THE(1965, Brit.), cos; 36 HOURS(1965), cos; ASSAULT ON A QUEEN(1966), cos; LAST OF THE SECRET AGENTS?, THE(1966), cos; NOT WITH MY WIFE, YOU DON'T!(1966), cos; OSCAR, THE(1966), a, cos; PARADISE, HAWAIIAN STYLE(1966), cos; PENELOPE(1966), cos; SWINGER, THE(1966), cos; THIS PROPERTY IS CONDEMNED(1966), cos; TORN CURTAIN(1966), cos; WACO(1966), cos; BAREFOOT IN THE PARK(1967), cos; CAPER OF THE GOLDEN BULLS, THE(1967), cos; CHUKA(1967), cos; EL DORADO(1967), cos; HOTEL(1967), cos; WARNING SHOT(1967), cos; HELLFIGHTERS(1968), cos; IN ENEMY COUNTRY(1968), cos; PINK JUNGLE, THE(1968), cos; SECRET WAR OF HARRY FRIGG, THE(1968), cos; WHAT'S SO BAD ABOUT FEELING GOOD?(1968), cos; BUTCH CASSIDY AND THE SUNDANCE KID(1969), cos; EYE OF THE CAT(1969), cos; HOUSE OF CARDS(1969), cos; LOST MAN, THE(1969), cos; SWEET CHARITY(1969), cos; TELL THEM WILLIE BOY IS HERE(1969), cos; TOPAZ(1969, Brit.), cos; WINNING(1969), cos; AIRPORT(1970), cos; SKULLDUGGERY(1970), cos; STORY OF A WOMAN(1970, U.S./Ital.), cos; RED SKY AT MORNING(1971), cos; SOMETIMES A GREAT NOTION(1971), cos; HAMMERSMITH IS OUT(1972), cos; LIFE AND TIMES OF JUDGE ROY BEAN, THE(1972), cos; PETE 'N' TILLIE(1972), cos; DOLL'S HOUSE, A(1973, Brit.), cos; DON IS DEAD, THE(1973), cos; SHOWDOWN(1973), cos; STING, THE(1973), cos; AIRPORT 1975(1974), cos; GREAT GATSBY, THE(1974), cos; GREAT WALDO PEPPER, THE(1975), cos; MAN WHO WOULD BE KING, THE(1975, Brit.), cos; ROOSTER COGBURN(1975), cos; FAMILY PLOT(1976), cos; W.C. FIELDS AND ME(1976), cos; AIRPORT '77(1977), cos; BIG FIX, THE(1978), cos; OLLY, OLLY, OXEN FREE(1978), cos; SEXTETTE(1978), cos; LAST MARRIED COUPLE IN AMERICA, THE(1980), cos; DEAD MEN DON'T WEAR PLAID(1982), cos
Silents
WINGS(1927), cos
Gracie Head
SLAP SHOT(1977)
J. Manley Head
TEXANS, THE(1938)
Jack Big Head
JIM THORPE–ALL AMERICAN(1951)
John Head
1984
NOTHING LASTS FOREVER(1984), p
June Head
REMBRANDT(1936, Brit.), w
Marilyn Head
PRIVATE LIFE OF SHERLOCK HOLMES, THE(1970, Brit.)
Murray Head
FAMILY WAY, THE(1966, Brit.); TWO WEEKS IN SEPTEMBER(1967, Fr./Brit.); ROMEO AND JULIET(1968, Brit./Ital.); SUNDAY BLOODY SUNDAY(1971, Brit.); GAWAIN AND THE GREEN KNIGHT(1973, Brit.)
Ruby Head
UP THE JUNCTION(1968, Brit.)
Head East
J-MEN FOREVER(1980), m
Josephine Headley
Silents
LITTLE BROTHER, THE(1917)
Misc. Silents
SAWDUST RING, THE(1917)
Lou Headley
COAL MINER'S DAUGHTER(1980)
Glenne Headly
DOCTOR DETROIT(1983)
Master Richard Headrick
Silents
TOLL GATE, THE(1920)
Richard Headrick
Silents
SHOULD A WOMAN TELL?(1920); TESTING BLOCK, THE(1920); PLAYTHINGS OF DESTINY(1921); ENVIRONMENT(1922); RICH MEN'S WIVES(1922); SONG OF LIFE, THE(1922); MIRACLE MAKERS, THE(1923); SPIDER AND THE ROSE, THE(1923)
Misc. Silents
SAGE HEN, THE(1921); HEARTS AFLAME(1923); SILENT STRANGER, THE(1924)
Joan Heal
FLESH AND BLOOD(1951, Brit.); HAPPY GO LOVELY(1951, Brit.); PICKWICK PAPERS, THE(1952, Brit.); WEDDING OF LILLI MARLENE(1953, Brit.); GOOD DIE YOUNG, THE(1954, Brit.); SVENGALI(1955, Brit.); CROSS-UP(1958); DEAD LUCKY(1960, Brit.); MAKE MINE MINK(1960, Brit.); PRICE OF SILENCE, THE(1960, Brit.); FOLLOW THAT MAN(1961, Brit.); LIVE NOW–PAY LATER(1962, Brit.); HEAVENS ABOVE!(1963, Brit.); IN THE DOGHOUSE(1964, Brit.)
Anthony Heald
SILKWOOD(1983)
1984
TEACHERS(1984)
Margaret Heald
TO SIR, WITH LOVE(1967, Brit.); MAN AT THE TOP(1973, Brit.); CONFESSIONS OF A POP PERFORMER(1975, Brit.)
Patricia Heald
1984
ALLEY CAT(1984)
Tania Heald
LONG DARK HALL, THE(1951, Brit.)
Patrick K. Heale
ROMANY LOVE(1931, Brit.), p&w; FLAW, THE(1933, Brit.), p
Patrick Keenan Heale
MEN OF IRELAND(1938, Ireland), w
Ben Healey
TASTE OF EXCITEMENT(1969, Brit.), w
Chryss Healey
1984
LASSITER(1984)
Dan Healey
GLORIFYING THE AMERICAN GIRL(1930)

Jim Healey
RESURRECTION OF ZACHARY WHEELER, THE(1971)
Larry Healey
TOO YOUNG, TOO IMMORAL!(1962)
Mark Healey
STRANGE HOLIDAY(1969, Aus.)
Mary Healey
POPE JOAN(1972, Brit.)
Myron Healey
IRON MAJOR, THE(1943); SALUTE TO THE MARINES(1943); THOUSANDS CHEER(1943); MEET THE PEOPLE(1944); SEE HERE, PRIVATE HARGROVE(1944); TIME OF THEIR LIVES, THE(1946); DOWN TO EARTH(1947); IT HAD TO BE YOU(1947); I, JANE DOE(1948); LADIES OF THE CHORUS(1948); MAN FROM COLORADO, THE(1948); YOU GOTTA STAY HAPPY(1948); ACROSS THE RIO GRANDE(1949); BRAND OF FEAR(1949); GUN LAW JUSTICE(1949); HIDDEN DANGER(1949); KNOCK ON ANY DOOR(1949); LARAMIE(1949); LAWLESS CODE(1949); RIDERS OF THE DUSK(1949); RUSTY'S BIRTHDAY(1949); SLIGHTLY FRENCH(1949); SOUTH OF RIO(1949); TRAIL'S END(1949); WAKE OF THE RED WITCH(1949); WESTERN RENEGADES(1949); EMERGENCY WEDDING(1950); FENCE RIDERS(1950); FULLER BRUSH GIRL, THE(1950); HOT ROD(1950); I KILLED GERONIMO(1950); IN A LONELY PLACE(1950); LAW OF THE PANHANDLE(1950); MY BLUE HEAVEN(1950); OUTLAW GOLD(1950); OVER THE BORDER(1950); PIONEER MARSHAL(1950); SALT LAKE RAIDERS(1950); SHORT GRASS(1950); WEST OF WYOMING(1950); WOMAN OF DISTINCTION, A(1950); BIG NIGHT, THE(1951); BONANZA TOWN(1951); COLORADO AMBUSH(1951), a, w; ELEPHANT STAMPEDE(1951); JOURNEY INTO LIGHT(1951); LONGHORN, THE(1951); LORNA DOONE(1951); MONTANA DESPERADO(1951); NIGHT RIDERS OF MONTANA(1951); SLAUGHTER TRAIL(1951); TEXAS LAWMEN(1951), w; TEXAS RANGERS, THE(1951); APACHE WAR SMOKE(1952); DESPERADOES OUTPOST(1952); FARGO(1952); FORT OSAGE(1952); KID FROM BROKEN GUN, THE(1952); MAVERICK, THE(1952); MONTANA TERRITORY(1952); RODEO(1952); STORM OVER TIBET(1952); WILD BLUE YONDER, THE(1952); COMBAT SQUAD(1953); FIGHTING LAWMAN, THE(1953); KANSAS PACIFIC(1953); MONSOON(1953); MOONLIGHTER, THE(1953); PRIVATE EYES(1953); SAGINAW TRAIL(1953); SON OF BELLE STARR(1953); TEXAS BAD MAN(1953); VIGILANTE TERROR(1953); WHITE LIGHTNING(1953); CATTLE QUEEN OF MONTANA(1954); RAILS INTO LARAMIE(1954); SILVER LODE(1954); AFRICAN MANHUNT(1955); COUNT THREE AND PRAY(1955); GANG BUSTERS(1955); JUNGLE MOON MEN(1955); MA AND PA KETTLE AT WAIKIKI(1955); MAN FROM BITTER RIDGE, THE(1955); MAN WITHOUT A STAR(1955); RAGE AT DAWN(1955); TENNESSEE'S PARTNER(1955); THUNDER OVER SANGOLAND(1955); CALLING HOMICIDE(1956); DIG THAT URANIUM(1956); MAGNIFICENT ROUGHNECKS(1956); WHITE SQUAW, THE(1956); YOUNG GUNS, THE(1956); HARD MAN, THE(1957); HELL'S CROSSROADS(1957); RESTLESS BREED, THE(1957); SHOOT-OUT AT MEDICINE BEND(1957); UNDERSEA GIRL(1957); UNEARTHLY, THE(1957); APACHE TERRITORY(1958); COLE YOUNGER, GUNFIGHTER(1958); ESCAPE FROM RED ROCK(1958); QUANTRILL'S RAIDERS(1958); RIO BRAVO(1959); CONVICTS FOUR(1962); VARAN THE UNBELIEVABLE(1962, U.S./Jap.); CAVALRY COMMAND(1963, U.S./Phil.); HE RIDES TALL(1964); JOURNEY TO SHILOH(1968); TRUE GRIT(1969); CHEYENNE SOCIAL CLUB, THE(1970); SMOKE IN THE WIND(1975); INCREDIBLE MELTING MAN, THE(1978); OTHER SIDE OF THE MOUNTAIN–PART 2, THE(1978)
Misc. Talkies
TRAIL OF THE RUSTLERS(1950); CLAW MONSTERS, THE(1966); CLAWS(1977)
Myron O. Healey
SILVER CITY(1951)
Patricia Healey
O LUCKY MAN!(1973, Brit.)
Richard Healey
CLINIC, THE(1983, Aus.)
Betty Healy
OUR RELATIONS(1936)
Bill Healy
FOLLOW THE BOYS(1944)
Dan Healy
LAUGHING LADY, THE(1930)
David Healy
BE MY GUEST(1965, Brit.); DOUBLE MAN, THE(1967); ASSIGNMENT K(1968, Brit.); ISADORA(1968, Brit.); ONLY WHEN I LARF(1968, Brit.); PATTON(1970); DIAMONDS ARE FOREVER(1971, Brit.); LUST FOR A VAMPIRE(1971, Brit.); EMBASSY(1972, Brit.); TOUCH OF CLASS, A(1973, Brit.); SCOTT JOPLIN(1977); TWILIGHT'S LAST GLEAMING(1977, U.S./Ger.); SIGN OF FOUR, THE(1983, Brit.)
1984
SUPERGIRL(1984)
Eunice Healy
FOLLOW YOUR HEART(1936)
Gerard Healy
NO RESTING PLACE(1952, Brit.), w
Harold Healy
ENEMIES OF THE LAW(1931); SIGN OF THE CROSS, THE(1932); LADIES THEY TALK ABOUT(1933); PARACHUTE JUMPER(1933); GAMBLING(1934)
Jim Healy
SLIM CARTER(1957); RESURRECTION OF ZACHARY WHEELER, THE(1971); HEAVEN CAN WAIT(1978); WHERE THE BUFFALO ROAM(1980); ROCKY III(1982)
John Healy
TWELVE HOURS TO KILL(1960), p
Katherine Healy
SIX WEEKS(1982)
Kevin Healy
SIDECAR RACERS(1975, Aus.)
Mary Healy
JOSETTE(1938); SECOND FIDDLE(1939); 20,000 MEN A YEAR(1939); HE MARRIED HIS WIFE(1940); STAR DUST(1940); HARD GUY(1941); RIDE, KELLY, RIDE(1941); ZIS BOOM BAH(1941); COLLEGE SWEETHEARTS(1942); STRICTLY IN THE GROOVE(1942); YANKS ARE COMING, THE(1942); 5,000 FINGERS OF DR. T. THE(1953); LOOKIN' TO GET OUT(1982)
Michael C. Healy
DIRT GANG, THE(1972), w

Michael Healy
YOU CAN'T FOOL AN IRISHMAN(1950, Ireland), p, w
1984
VAMPING(1984), w
Myron Healy
CORPSE CAME C.O.D., THE(; CRIME DOCTOR'S MAN HUNT(1946); BLONDIE'S REWARD(1948); RANGE JUSTICE(1949); HOT NEWS(1953); RUNNING TARGET(1956); GUNFIGHT AT DODGE CITY, THE(1959)
Pat Healy
TEXAS TORNADO(1934)
Robert Healy
FROM HERE TO ETERNITY(1953)
Seamus Healy
NEVER PUT IT IN WRITING(1964)
Steve Healy
LOUISIANA(1947), w
Ted Healy
SOUP TO NUTS(1930); BOMBSHELL(1933); DANCING LADY(1933); MEET THE BARON(1933); STAGE MOTHER(1933); BAND PLAYS ON, THE(1934); DEATH OF THE DIAMOND(1934); FUGITIVE LOVERS(1934); HOLLYWOOD PARTY(1934); LAZY RIVER(1934); MYRT AND MARGE(1934); OPERATOR 13(1934); PARIS INTERLUDE(1934); CASINO MURDER CASE, THE(1935); HERE COMES THE BAND(1935); IT'S IN THE AIR(1935); MAD LOVE(1935); MURDER IN THE FLEET(1935); RECKLESS(1935); WINNING TICKET, THE(1935); LONGEST NIGHT, THE(1936); MAD HOLIDAY(1936); SAN FRANCISCO(1936); SING, BABY, SING(1936); SPEED(1936); GOOD OLD SOAR, THE(1937); HOLLYWOOD HOTEL(1937); MAN OF THE PEOPLE(1937); VARSITY SHOW(1937); LOVE IS A HEADACHE(1938)
John Heaner
1984
LAST NIGHT AT THE ALAMO(1984)
Kathleen Heaney
SAVAGE WEEKEND(1983)
Alan Heaps
LORD OF THE FLIES(1963, Brit.)
Jonathan Heaps
LORD OF THE FLIES(1963, Brit.)
H. Fowler Hear
HIGH TREASON(1937, Brit.), w
Charles Heard
MILLION DOLLAR MERMAID(1952); ELEPHANT WALK(1954); PHFFFT!(1954); HIDDEN GUNS(1956); BAND OF ANGELS(1957); DESK SET(1957); YOUNG LAND, THE(1959); LIKE FATHER LIKE SON(1961); YOUNG SINNER, THE(1965)
Cliff Heard
KNOCK ON ANY DOOR(1949)
Cordis Heard
CADDY SHACK(1980); I'M DANCING AS FAST AS I CAN(1982)
1984
C.H.U.D.(1984)
Daphne Heard
GOODBYE GEMINI(1970, Brit.); TRIPLE ECHO, THE(1973, Brit.); THREE SISTERS(1974, Brit.)
H. F. Heard
DEADLY BEES,THE(1967, Brit.), w
Jim Heard
SPOOK WHO SAT BY THE DOOR, THE(1973)
John Heard
BETWEEN THE LINES(1977); FIRST LOVE(1977); ON THE YARD(1978); HEART BEAT(1979); CUTTER AND BONE(1981); CAT PEOPLE(1982); CHILLY SCENES OF WINTER(1982)
1984
C.H.U.D.(1984)
Nathan C. Heard
GORDON'S WAR(1973)
Paul F. Heard
CITY STORY(1954), p; HONG KONG AFFAIR(1958), p, d, w
Roxanne Heard
LIKE FATHER LIKE SON(1961); YOUNG SINNER, THE(1965)
Susan Heard
Misc. Talkies
BODY BENEATH, THE(1970)
Chick Hearn
LOVED ONE, THE(1965); LOVE BUG, THE(1968); GAMBLER, THE(1974)
1984
FLETCH(1984)
E. Guy Hearn
PORT SINISTER(1953)
Ed Hearn
THIN MAN, THE(1934); SANTA FE TRAIL(1940)
Misc. Talkies
HOT OFF THE PRESS(1935)
Eddie Hearn
DRAKE CASE, THE(1929); EX-BAD BOY(1931); LADY BY CHOICE(1934); ANYTHING FOR A THRILL(1937); JUVENILE COURT(1938); LONE WOLF SPY HUNT, THE(1939); TEXAS STAMPEDE(1939); STORM WARNING(1950); STRANGERS ON A TRAIN(1951)
Misc. Silents
COAST OF OPPORTUNITY, THE(1920)
Eddie [Edward] Hearn
WEST OF SANTA FE(1938)
Edna Hearn
Silents
FREE LIPS(1928)
Edward Hearn
BACHELOR GIRL, THE(1929); DONOVAN AFFAIR, THE(1929); HIDE-OUT, THE(1930); RENO(1930); SPOILERS, THE(1930); AVENGER, THE(1931); CLEARING THE RANGE(1931); LADIES' MAN(1931); PAINTED DESERT, THE(1931); SMART MONEY(1931); SON OF THE PLAINS(1931); CHEYENNE CYCLONE, THE(1932); LOCAL BAD MAN(1932); RAINBOW TRAIL(1932); I'M NO ANGEL(1933); BELLE OF THE NINETIES(1934); CAT'S PAW, THE(1934); FIGHTING HERO(1934); TEXAS TORNADO(1934); YOUNG AND BEAUTIFUL(1934); IN OLD SANTA FE(1935);

NAUGHTY MARIETTA(1935); PAGE MISS GLORY(1935); RED SALUTE(1935); TALE OF TWO CITIES, A(1935); TUMBLING TUMBLEWEEDS(1935); CATTLE THIEF, THE(1936); KING OF THE PECOS(1936); LAWLESS NINETIES, THE(1936); RED RIVER VALLEY(1936); SAN FRANCISCO(1936); THREE WISE GUYS, THE(1936); UNKNOWN RANGER, THE(1936); DEVIL'S PLAYGROUND(1937); EXCLUSIVE(1937); OLD WYOMING TRAIL, THE(1937); PAID TO DANCE(1937); SHADOW, THE(1937); SOMETHING TO SING ABOUT(1937); SPRINGTIME IN THE ROCKIES(1937); TROUBLE AT MIDNIGHT(1937); FAST COMPANY(1938); PROFESSOR BEWARE(1938); YOU CAN'T TAKE IT WITH YOU(1938); YOUNG FUGITIVES(1938); ANOTHER THIN MAN(1939); ST. LOUIS BLUES(1939); STAND UP AND FIGHT(1939); DARK COMMAND, THE(1940); I LOVE YOU AGAIN(1940); MAN FROM DAKOTA, THE(1940); MY LITTLE CHICKADEE(1940); NEW MOON(1940); MEET JOHN DOE(1941); SHADOW OF THE THIN MAN(1941); SULLIVAN'S TRAVELS(1941); MY FAVORITE BLONDE(1942); NAZI AGENT(1942); SABOTAGE SQUAD(1942); TALK OF THE TOWN(1942); AIR RAID WARDENS(1943); DOUBLE INDEMNITY(1944); LOST ANGEL(1944); SUGARFOOT(1951); MAN BEHIND THE GUN, THE(1952)
Misc. Talkies
FIGHTING THROUGH(1934)
Silents
FAITH(1920); ALL DOLLED UP(1921); KEEPING UP WITH LIZZIE(1921); FLIRT, THE(1922); QUESTION OF HONOR, A(1922); DAUGHTERS OF TODAY(1924); LAWFUL CHEATERS(1925); ONE OF THE BRAVEST(1925); HOOK AND LADDER NO. 9(1927); SPUDS(1927); NED MCCOBB'S DAUGHTER(1929)
Misc. Silents
HEART'S CRUCIBLE, A(1916); HER BITTER CUP(1916); SEEKERS, THE(1916); DOUBLE-ROOM MYSTERY, THE(1917); HER SOUL'S INSPIRATION(1917); LAWLESS LOVE(1918); LURE OF LUXURY, THE(1918); DOWN HOME(1920); FACE OF THE WORLD(1921); THINGS MEN DO(1921); COLLEEN OF THE PINES(1922); FIRE BRIDE, THE(1922); HER NIGHT OF NIGHTS(1922); TRUTHFUL LIAR, THE(1922); MIRACLE BABY, THE(1923); DANGEROUS BLONDE, THE(1924); TURMOIL, THE(1924); WINNER TAKE ALL(1924); MAN WITHOUT A COUNTRY, THE(1925); PERIL OF THE RAIL(1926); SIGN OF THE CLAW, THE(1926); HEART OF THE YUKON, THE(1927); HERO ON HORSEBACK, A(1927); PALS IN PERIL(1927); DOG JUSTICE(1928)
Edwin Hearn
Silents
KING OF KINGS, THE(1927)
Fred Hearn
BONNIE PRINCE CHARLIE(1948, Brit.)
Silents
MY FOUR YEARS IN GERMANY(1918)
Guy E. Hearn
SPRINGFIELD RIFLE(1952); THREE SAILORS AND A GIRL(1953)
Guy Edward Hearn
PAINTED DESERT, THE(1931); PISTOL HARVEST(1951); ROAD AGENT(1952); CONQUEST OF COCHISE(1953); THIS ISLAND EARTH(1955)
Guy Hearn
TALL MAN RIDING(1955)
Harry Hearn
HANGMAN'S WHARF(1950, Brit.)
Lafcadio Hearn
KWAIDAN(1965, Jap.), w
Lew Hearn
ROYAL BOX, THE(1930); SEE AMERICA THIRST(1930); INTERNATIONAL CRIME(1938); FOLLIES GIRL(1943); I WONDER WHO'S KISSING HER NOW(1947); INSPECTOR GENERAL, THE(1949); GO, MAN, GO!(1954)
Lou Hearn
SPECTER OF THE ROSE(1946)
Mary Ann Hearn
RETURN TO MACON COUNTY(1975)
Misc. Talkies
DEATH DRIVER(1977)
Mary Hearn
Silents
CONQUERING POWER, THE(1921)
Maryann Hearn
GRIZZLY(1976)
Peter Hearn
TIKI TIKI(1971, Can.), ed
Ruby Dale Hearn
WABASH AVENUE(1950)
Sam Hearn
FLORIDA SPECIAL(1936); INSPECTOR GENERAL, THE(1949); I DON'T CARE GIRL, THE(1952); PAT AND MIKE(1952); BAND WAGON, THE(1953); ONCE UPON A HORSE(1958)
Catherine Hearne
HAWMPS!(1976)
Edna Hearne
Silents
OLD AGE HANDICAP(1928)
Edward Hearne
Silents
LOVE LETTER, THE(1923); MIND OVER MOTOR(1923); TOWN SCANDAL, THE(1923); EXCITEMENT(1924); OUTLAW'S DAUGHTER, THE(1925); DESERT PIRATE, THE(1928); ONE MAN DOG, THE(1929)
Misc. Silents
DARING DAYS(1925)
Erwin Hearne
BENJI(1974)
Fred Hearne
BIRDS OF A FEATHER(1935, Brit.); OVER SHE GOES(1937, Brit.)
Misc. Silents
AFTERGLOW(1923, Brit.)
Harrison Hearne
TRAIL OF THE YUKON(1949); WITHOUT HONOR(1949)
Jow Hearne
HELL SQUAD(1958)

Katie Hearne
BENJI(1974)

Reginald Hearne
DEVIL'S HARBOR(1954, Brit.); BLONDE BLACKMAILER(1955, Brit.); LOVE MATCH, THE(1955, Brit.); STRANGER'S MEETING(1957, Brit.); THERE'S ALWAYS A THURSDAY(1957, Brit.); THUNDER OVER TANGIER(1957, Brit.); MURDER REPORTED(1958, Brit.); ORDERS ARE ORDERS(1959, Brit.); HAND, THE(1960, Brit.); SENTENCED FOR LIFE(1960, Brit.); VIRGIN ISLAND(1960, Brit.); SWORD OF SHERWOOD FOREST(1961, Brit.); SERENA(1962, Brit.), w; ECHO OF DIANA(1963, Brit.), w; SICILIANS, THE(1964, Brit.), w; HALF A SIXPENCE(1967, Brit.)

Richard Hearne
DANCE BAND(1935, Brit.); NO MONKEY BUSINESS(1935, Brit.); GIVE HER A RING(1936, Brit.); MILLIONS(1936, Brit.); SPLINTERS IN THE AIR(1937, Brit.); MISS LONDON LTD.(1943, Brit.); ONE NIGHT WITH YOU(1948, Brit); HELTER SKELTER(1949, Brit.); WOMAN HATER(1949, Brit.); SOMETHING IN THE CITY(1950, Brit.); CAPTAIN HORATIO HORNBLOWER(1951, Brit.); MADAME LOUISE(1951, Brit.); MISS ROBIN HOOD(1952, Brit.); TIME OF HIS LIFE, THE(1955, Brit.), a, w; TONS OF TROUBLE(1956, Brit.), a, p, w

Yvonne Hearne
TIME OF HIS LIFE, THE(1955, Brit.); TONS OF TROUBLE(1956, Brit.)

Jean Hearsholt
Misc. Silents
SERVANT IN THE HOUSE, THE(1920)

Kevin Hearst
IDAHO TRANSFER(1975)

Heart
SGT. PEPPER'S LONELY HEARTS CLUB BAND(1978)

John X. Heart
SUDDEN IMPACT(1983)

Pearl Heart
ROSE, THE(1979)

Bob Heasley
CLOWN, THE(1953)

Jack Heasley
CLOWN, THE(1953)

John Heasley
5,000 FINGERS OF DR. T. THE(1953)

Robert Heasley
5,000 FINGERS OF DR. T. THE(1953)

The Heat Waves
FOLLIES GIRL(1943)

Claude Heater
BEN HUR(1959)

Elizabeth Heater
DON'T GET PERSONAL(1936)

A.B. Heath
MELODY OF LOVE, THE(1928), d, w

Arch Heath
MODERN LOVE(1929), d

Ariel Heath
HITLER'S CHILDREN(1942); BLACK HILLS EXPRESS(1943); LADIES' DAY(1943); LADY TAKES A CHANCE, A(1943); LEOPARD MAN, THE(1943); MR. LUCKY(1943); CAREER GIRL(1944); MACHINE GUN MAMA(1944)

Brendan Heath
MAD MAX(1979, Aus.)

Bruce Heath
DOCTOR DETROIT(1983)

Dave Heath
DEMON FROM DEVIL'S LAKE, THE(1964)

Dodie Heath
FORTUNE COOKIE, THE(1966)

Dody Heath
BRIGADOON(1954); ASK ANY GIRL(1959); DIARY OF ANNE FRANK, THE(1959); DOG EAT DOG(1963, U.S./Ger./Ital.); SECONDS(1966); TENDER FLESH(1976)

Earlene Heath
RECKLESS(1935); CAUGHT IN THE DRAFT(1941)

Ed Heath
HOUSE ON SORORITY ROW, THE(1983)

Edward Harris Heath
ANY NUMBER CAN PLAY(1949), w

Eira Heath
GANG WAR(1962, Brit.); MAN FOR ALL SEASONS, A(1966, Brit.)

Eric Heath
LIST OF ADRIAN MESSENGER, THE(1963); MY FAIR LADY(1964); WAVELENGTH(1983)

Evelyn Heath
Silents
SAVING THE FAMILY NAME(1916), w

Frank Heath
THIS IS THE ARMY(1943), md
Misc. Silents
DEFEAT OF THE CITY, THE(1917)

George Heath
THOROUGHBRED(1936, Aus.), ph; IT ISN'T DONE(1937, Aus.), ph; ORPHAN OF THE WILDERNESS(1937, Aus.), ph; TALL TIMBERS(1937, Aus.), ph; WILD INNOCENCE(1937, Aus.), ph; BROKEN MELODY(1938, Aus.), ph; DAD AND DAVE COME TO TOWN(1938, Aus.), ph; LOVERS AND LUGGERS(1938, Aus.), ph; GONE TO THE DOGS(1939, Aus.), ph; MR. CHEDWORTH STEPS OUT(1939, Aus.), ph; ANTS IN HIS PANTS(1940, Aus.), ph; VENGEANCE OF THE DEEP(1940, Aus.), ph; FORTY THOUSAND HORSEMEN(1941, Aus.), ph; SMITHY(1946, Aus.), ph; BUSH CHRISTMAS(1947, Aus.), ph; PACIFIC ADVENTURE(1947, Aus.), ph; MASSACRE HILL(1949, Brit.), ph; BITTER SPRINGS(1950, Aus.), ph; RATS OF TOBRUK(1951, Aus.), w, ph; PHANTOM STOCKMAN, THE(1953, Aus.), ph; WHEREVER SHE GOES(1953, Aus.), ph

Gordon Heath
ANIMAL FARM(1955, Brit.); PASSIONATE SUMMER(1959, Brit.); SAPPHIRE(1959, Brit.); MR. ARKADIN(1962, Brit./Fr./Span.); MY BABY IS BLACK!(1965, Fr.); LOST COMMAND, THE(1966); MADWOMAN OF CHAILLOT, THE(1969); STAIRCASE(1969 U.S./Brit./Fr.)

H. Heath
ILLEGAL(1932, Brit.)

Harold Heath
SPLINTERS IN THE NAVY(1931, Brit.)

Hy Heath
STALLION CANYON(1949), w

James Heath
SLAVES(1969)

John Heath
TONIGHT AND EVERY NIGHT(1945)

Kathleen Heath
UNEASY TERMS(1948, Brit.); MY BROTHER JONATHAN(1949, Brit.)

Larry Heath
PUSSYCAT, PUSSYCAT, I LOVE YOU(1970), ed; BILLY JACK(1971), ed

Len Heath
ROTTEN TO THE CORE(1956, Brit.), w; FURTHER UP THE CREEK!(1958, Brit.), w; UP THE CREEK(1958, Brit.), w; TWO-WAY STRETCH(1961, Brit.), w; LIFE IS A CIRCUS(1962, Brit.), w; OPERATION SNATCH(1962, Brit.), w; WRONG ARM OF THE LAW, THE(1963, Brit.), w

Louise Heath
PUTNEY SWOPE(1969)

Mark Heath
MR. BROWN COMES DOWN THE HILL(1966, Brit.); LOST CONTINENT, THE(1968, Brit.)

Michael Heath
SCARECROW, THE(1982, New Zealand), w; NEXT OF KIN(1983, Aus.), w

Percy Heath
CLOSE HARMONY(1929), w; MAN I LOVE, THE(1929), w; BORDER LEGION, THE(1930), w; L'ENIGMATIQUE MONSIEUR PARKES(1930), w; LET'S GO NATIVE(1930), w; ONLY SAPS WORK(1930), w; PLAYBOY OF PARIS(1930), w; SAFETY IN NUMBERS(1930), w; SLIGHTLY SCARLET(1930), w; DUDE RANCH(1931), w; GANG BUSTER, THE(1931), w; DR. JEKYLL AND MR. HYDE(1932), w; NO ONE MAN(1932), w; FROM HELL TO HEAVEN(1933), w
Silents
CHORUS GIRL'S ROMANCE, A(1920), w; LOVE CHARM, THE(1921), w; ONE WILD WEEK(1921), w; HER GILDED CAGE(1922), w; IMPOSSIBLE MRS. BELLEW, THE(1922), w; HUNTRESS, THE(1923), w; ROLLED STOCKINGS(1927), w; SONORA KID, THE(1927), w; TWO FLAMING YOUTHS(1927), w; HALF A BRIDE(1928), w; RED HAIR(1928), w

Rosalie Heath
Silents
GLORIOUS ADVENTURE, THE(1922, U.S./Brit.)

Ted Heath
THEATRE ROYAL(1943, Brit.); IT'S A WONDERFUL WORLD(1956, Brit.), a, m

William L. Heath
VIOLENT SATURDAY(1955), w

Heathcliff the Cat
LIGHT TOUCH, THE(1955, Brit.)

Thomas Heathcoate
SWORD AND THE ROSE, THE(1953); DOCTOR AT SEA(1955, Brit.)

Joe Heathcock
LAST PICTURE SHOW, THE(1971)

Douglas Heathcote
Silents
MARCH HARE, THE(1919, Brit.); JOYOUS ADVENTURES OF ARISTIDE PUJOL, THE(1920, Brit.)

Humphrey Heathcote
ADVENTURESS, THE(1946, Brit.); FURY AT SMUGGLERS BAY(1963, Brit.)

Roger Heathcote
ISLAND OF TERROR(1967, Brit.)

Thomas Heathcote
CLOUDBURST(1952, Brit.); LARGE ROPE, THE(1953, Brit.); MALTA STORY(1954, Brit.); PARATROOPER(1954, Brit.); LAND OF FURY(1955 Brit.); ABOVE US THE WAVES(1956, Brit.); BATTLE HELL(1956, Brit.); EYEWITNESS(1956, Brit.); LAST MAN TO HANG, THE(1956, Brit.); TIGER IN THE SMOKE(1956, Brit.); NIGHT TO REMEMBER, A(1958, Brit.); TREAD SOFTLY STRANGER(1959, Brit.); VILLAGE OF THE DAMNED(1960, Brit.); OPERATION SNAFU(1965, Brit.); MAN FOR ALL SEASONS, A(1966, Brit.); FIVE MILLION YEARS TO EARTH(1968, Brit.); FIXER, THE(1968); JULIUS CAESAR(1970, Brit.); ISLAND OF THE BURNING DAMNED(1971, Brit.); LUTHER(1974); DIRTY KNIGHT'S WORK(1976, Brit.)
1984
SWORD OF THE VALIANT(1984, Brit.)

Enid Heather
Silents
JACK, SAM AND PETE(1919, Brit.)

Jean Heather
DOUBLE INDEMNITY(1944); GOING MY WAY(1944); NATIONAL BARN DANCE(1944); OUR HEARTS WERE YOUNG AND GAY(1944); DUFFY'S TAVERN(1945); MURDER, HE SAYS(1945); WELL-GROOMED BRIDE, THE(1946); LAST ROUND-UP, THE(1947); RED STALLION IN THE ROCKIES(1949)

Roy Heather
EXPERIENCE PREFERRED... BUT NOT ESSENTIAL(1983, Brit.)

Ann Heatherington
PURE S(1976, Aus.)

Clifford Heatherley
HIGH TREASON(1929, Brit.); TESHA(1929, Brit.); COMPULSORY HUSBAND, THE(1930, Brit.); SYMPHONY IN TWO FLATS(1930, Brit.); "W" PLAN, THE(1931, Brit.); GLAMOUR(1931, Brit.); LOVE HABIT, THE(1931, Brit.); AFTER THE BALL(1932, Brit.); BROTHER ALFRED(1932, Brit.); FIRES OF FATE(1932, Brit.); HAPPY EVER AFTER(1932, Ger./Brit.); HELP YOURSELF(1932, Brit.); INDISCRETIONS OF EVE(1932, Brit.); MAGIC NIGHT(1932, Brit.); DISCORD(1933, Brit.); I ADORE YOU(1933, Brit.); LITTLE DAMOZEL, THE(1933, Brit.); SMITHY(1933, Brit.); YES, MR. BROWN(1933, Brit.); ADVENTURE LIMITED(1934, Brit.); CATHERINE THE GREAT(1934, Brit.); CHURCH MOUSE, THE(1934, Brit.); FOR LOVE OR MONEY(1934, Brit.); GET YOUR MAN(1934, Brit.); PRIVATE LIFE OF DON JUAN, THE(1934, Brit.); ABDUL THE DAMNED(1935, Brit.); LITTLE BIT OF BLUFF, A(1935, Brit.); NO MONKEY BUSINESS(1935, Brit.); RUNAWAY QUEEN, THE(1935, Brit.); CAFE MASCOT(1936, Brit.); IF I WERE RICH(1936); OLD SPANISH CUSTOM, AN(1936, Brit.); REASONABLE DOUBT(1936, Brit.); SHOW FLAT(1936, Brit.); DON'T GET ME WRONG(1937, Brit.); FEATHER YOUR NEST(1937, Brit.); IT'S NOT CRICK-

Eileen Heckart
BAD SEED, THE(1956); BUS STOP(1956); MIRACLE IN THE RAIN(1956); SOME-BODY UP THERE LIKES ME(1956); HOT SPELL(1958); HELLER IN PINK TIGHTS(1960); MY SIX LOVES(1963); UP THE DOWN STAIRCASE(1967); NO WAY TO TREAT A LADY(1968); TREE, THE(1969); BUTTERFLIES ARE FREE(1972); ZANDY'S BRIDE(1974); HIDING PLACE, THE(1975); BURNT OFFERINGS(1976)

James Heckart
COOL ONES THE(1967), ed

Amy Heckerling
FAST TIMES AT RIDGEMONT HIGH(1982), d
1984
JOHNNY DANGEROUSLY(1984), d

James Heckert
SWEET NOVEMBER(1968), ed; GENERATION(1969), ed

James T. Heckert
SWINGIN' SUMMER, A(1965), ed; TAKE THE MONEY AND RUN(1969), ed; VALDEZ IS COMING(1971), ed; EVERYTHING YOU ALWAYS WANTED TO KNOW ABOUT SEX, BUT WE'RE AFRAID TO ASK(1972), ed

Jim Heckert
TRAIN RIDE TO HOLLYWOOD(1975), ed

Charles Hecklemann
DEPUTY MARSHAL(1949), w

Charles N. Hecklemann
FRONTIER FEUD(1945), w

Darlyn Heckley
ZAZA(1939)

Else Heckman
STEPPENWOLF(1974), cos

Hein Heckroth
STAIRWAY TO HEAVEN(1946, Brit.), cos; RED SHOES, THE(1948, Brit.), art d, cos; HOUR OF GLORY(1949, Brit.), prod d; FIGHTING PIMPERNEL, THE(1950, Brit.), prod d; TALES OF HOFFMANN, THE(1951, Brit.), art d; WILD HEART, THE(1952, Brit.), prod d; GREAT GILBERT AND SULLIVAN, THE(1953, Brit.), prod d; PURSUIT OF THE GRAF SPEE(1957, Brit.), art d; THREE PENNY OPERA(1963, Fr./Ger.), set d, cos; GIRL AND THE LEGEND, THE(1966, Ger.), art d, set d; TORN CUR-TAIN(1966), prod d

Emily Hector
CAYMAN TRIANGLE, THE(1977)

Frank Hector
Silents
MESSAGE FROM MARS, A(1913, Brit.)

Kim Hector
SANCTUARY(1961); TO KILL A MOCKINGBIRD(1962)

Louis Hector
NORTHWEST PASSAGE(1940)

Hector and His Pals--Carmi Tryon
EASTER PARADE(1948)

Vladimir Hedar
FLAMING FRONTIER(1968, Ger./Yugo.)

Dan Hedaya
SEDUCTION OF JOE TYNAN, THE(1979); NIGHT OF THE JUGGLER(1980); ENDANGERED SPECIES(1982); I'M DANCING AS FAST AS I CAN(1982); HUNGER, THE(1983)
1984
ADVENTURES OF BUCKAROO BANZAI: ACROSS THE 8TH DIMENSION, THE(1984); BLOOD SIMPLE(1984); RECKLESS(1984); TIGHTROPE(1984)

Daniel Hedaya
PASSOVER PLOT, THE(1976, Israel)

Bink Hedberg
TWO YEARS BEFORE THE MAST(1946)

John Hedberg
DON'T GO IN THE HOUSE(1980)

Kerstin Hedeby
DREAMS(1960, Swed.)

June Heden
WAY OF ALL FLESH, THE(1940)

Sonya Hedenbratt
FANNY AND ALEXANDER(1983, Swed./Fr./Ger.)

Solveig Hedengran
CHILDREN, THE(1949, Swed.)

Bo Hederstrom
LOVING COUPLES(1966, Swed.)

Dan Hedeya
TRUE CONFESSIONS(1981)

Ray Hedge
MYRT AND MARGE(1934)

William J. Hedge
CREATURE WASN'T NICE,THE(1981), spec eff

Linda Hedger
LOOKING GLASS WAR, THE(1970, Brit.)

Ken Hedges
COMEDY MAN, THE(1964), ph

Robert Hedges
PROJECTED MAN, THE(1967, Brit.), spec eff

June Hedin
I REMEMBER MAMA(1948); IT'S A BIG COUNTRY(1951); MODEL AND THE MARRIAGE BROKER, THE(1951); THIRTEENTH LETTER, THE(1951); BELLES ON THEIR TOES(1952); MEMBER OF THE WEDDING, THE(1952)

Serene Hedin
WINDWALKER(1980)
1984
SACRED GROUND(1984)

Wolfgang Hedinger
JONATHAN(1973, Ger.), ed

Al Hedison
ENEMY BELOW, THE(1957); SON OF ROBIN HOOD(1959, Brit.)

Al "David" Hedison
FLY, THE(1958)

David Hedison
LOST WORLD, THE(1960); MARINES, LET'S GO(1961); GREATEST STORY EVER TOLD, THE(1965); LIVE AND LET DIE(1973, Brit.); FFOLKES(1980, Brit.)
1984
NAKED FACE, THE(1984)

Franciszka Hedland
VIDEODROME(1983, Can.)

Jack Hedley
BEHIND THE MASK(1958, Brit.); LEFT, RIGHT AND CENTRE(1959); MAKE MINE MINK(1960, Brit.); TROUBLE IN THE SKY(1961, Brit.); LONGEST DAY, THE(1962); IN THE FRENCH STYLE(1963, U.S./Fr.); NINE HOURS TO RAMA(1963, U.S./Brit.); VERY EDGE, THE(1963, Brit.); CRIMSON BLADE, THE(1964, Brit.); OF HUMAN BONDAGE(1964, Brit.); WITCHCRAFT(1964, Brit.); SECRET OF BLOOD ISLAND, THE(1965, Brit.); HOW I WON THE WAR(1967, Brit.); NEVER BACK LOSERS(1967, Brit.); ANNIVERSARY, THE(1968, Brit.); GOODBYE MR. CHIPS(1969, U.S./Brit.); FOR YOUR EYES ONLY(1981)

Maurice Hedley
STRANGLER'S WEB(1966, Brit.)

Thomas Hedley
CIRCLE OF TWO(1980, Can.), w; MR. PATMAN(1980, Can.), w

Thomas Hedley, Jr.
DOUBLE NEGATIVE(1980, Can.), w

Tom Hedley
DEATH VENGEANCE(1982), w; FLASHDANCE(1983), w
1984
HARD TO HOLD(1984), w

John Hedloe
FIREBALL, THE(1950); MY BLUE HEAVEN(1950); TEA FOR TWO(1950); WEST POINT STORY, THE(1950); GOODBYE, MY FANCY(1951); MISSING WOMEN(1951); ROYAL WEDDING(1951); STARLIFT(1951); MY WIFE'S BEST FRIEND(1952); WIN-NING TEAM, THE(1952); ABOVE AND BEYOND(1953); DRAGONFLY SQUAD-RON(1953); PROJECT MOONBASE(1953); EXECUTIVE SUITE(1954); RIDERS TO THE STARS(1954)

Guy Hedlund
LAST OF THE REDMEN(1947)

Laurie Hedlund
1984
HARDBODIES(1984)

Roland Hedlund
ADALEN 31(1969, Swed.)

Martha Hedman
Silents
CUB, THE(1915)

Harry Hednoff
WALPURGIS NIGHT(1941, Swed.)

Tippi Hedren
PETTY GIRL, THE(1950); BIRDS, THE(1963); MARNIE(1964); COUNTESS FROM HONG KONG, A(1967, Brit.); TIGER BY THE TAIL(1970); HARRAD EXPERIMENT, THE(1973); ROAR(1981)
Misc. Talkies
SATAN'S HARVEST(1970); MR. KINGSTREET'S WAR(1973)

Earl Hedrick
TRUE TO LIFE(1943), art d; WILD HORSE MESA(1932), art d; MAN OF THE FOREST(1933), art d; SUNSET PASS(1933), art d; TO THE LAST MAN(1933), art d; UNDER THE TONTO RIM(1933), art d; COME ON, MARINES(1934), art d; LAST ROUND-UP, THE(1934), art d; THUNDERING HERD, THE(1934), art d; WAGON WHEELS(1934), art d; WITCHING HOUR, THE(1934), art d; LAST OUTPOST, THE(1935), art d; F MAN(1936), art d; HOLLYWOOD BOULEVARD(1936), art d; PREVIEW MURDER MYSTERY(1936), art d; WEDDING PRESENT(1936), art d; NIGHT CLUB SCANDAL(1937), art d; BULLDOG DRUMMOND IN AFRICA(1938), art d; GIVE ME A SAILOR(1938), art d; HER JUNGLE LOVE(1938), art d; KING OF ALCATRAZ(1938), art d; GRACIE ALLEN MURDER CASE(1939), art d; OUR NEIGH-BORS–THE CARTERS(1939), art d; WHAT A LIFE(1939), art d; GREAT McGINTY, THE(1940), art d; OPENED BY MISTAKE(1940), art d; TEXAS RANGERS RIDE AGAIN(1940), art d; LAS VEGAS NIGHTS(1941), art d; SULLIVAN'S TRA-VELS(1941), art d; THERE'S MAGIC IN MUSIC(1941), art d; BEYOND THE BLUE HORIZON(1942), art d; DR. BROADWAY(1942), art d; FOREST RANGERS, THE(1942), art d; GREAT MAN'S LADY, THE(1942), art d; HENRY ALDRICH GETS GLAMOUR(1942), art d; WAKE ISLAND(1942), art d; LET'S FACE IT(1943), art d; SO PROUDLY WE HAIL(1943), art d; HOUR BEFORE THE DAWN, THE(1944), art d; I LOVE A SOLDIER(1944), art d; OUR HEARTS WERE YOUNG AND GAY(1944), art d; STANDING ROOM ONLY(1944), art d; LOST WEEKEND, THE(1945), spec eff; MISS SUSIE SLAGLE'S(1945), art d; STORK CLUB(1945), art d; UNSEEN, THE(1945), art d; MONSIEUR BEAUCAIRE(1946), art d; WELL-GROOMED BRIDE, THE(1946), art d; DEAR RUTH(1947), art d; MY FAVORITE BRUNETTE(1947), art d; ROAD TO RIO(1947), art d; TROUBLE WITH WOMEN, THE(1947), art d; WHERE THERE'S LIFE(1947), art d; PALEFACE, THE(1948), art d; SORRY, WRONG NUM-BER(1948), art d; ACCUSED, THE(1949), art d; DEAR WIFE(1949), art d; GREAT LOVER, THE(1949), art d; FANCY PANTS(1950), art d; FILE ON THELMA JORDAN, THE(1950), art d; MR. MUSIC(1950), art d; PAID IN FULL(1950), art d; UNION STATION(1950), art d; BIG CARNIVAL, THE(1951), art d; DETECTIVE STORY(1951), art d; HERE COMES THE GROOM(1951), art d; SOMEBODY LOVES ME(1952), art d; JAMAICA RUN(1953), art d; SANGAREE(1953), art d; TROPIC ZONE(1953), art d; VANQUISHED, THE(1953), art d; JIVARO(1954), art d; FAR HORIZONS, THE(1955), art d; STRATEGIC AIR COMMAND(1955), art d; YOU'RE NEVER TOO YOUNG(1955), art d; PROUD AND THE PROFANE, THE(1956), art d; THREE VIOLENT PEO-PLE(1956), art d; DELICATE DELINQUENT, THE(1957), art d; TEACHER'S PET(1958), art d; JORY(1972), prod d

Earle Hedrick
PRISON FARM(1938), art d

Earl Hedricks
DR. CYCLOPS(1940), art d

Pat Hedruck
BABY MAKER, THE(1970)

Tina Hedstrom
GUILT(1967, Swed.); TOPAZ(1969, Brit.); GEORGIA, GEORGIA(1972)

Deborah Hedwall
ALONE IN THE DARK(1982)

Helen Hedy
1984
FOURTH MAN, THE(1984, Neth.)

T. Hee [Walt Disney]
FANTASIA(1940), d; PINOCCHIO(1940), d; MAKE MINE MUSIC(1946), w

Thornton Hee
VARIETY GIRL(1947), Puppeteer

K. Heeley-Ray
ESCAPE(1948, Brit.), ed

Kenneth Heeley-Ray
TOM BROWN'S SCHOOLDAYS(1951, Brit.), ed

Barry Heenan
FOREVER AND A DAY(1943)

Joan Heeny
ONE MAN(1979, Can.)

Johanna Heer
FOREIGNER, THE(1978), ed; SUBWAY RIDERS(1981), P, ph, ed

Edith Heerdegen
SERPENT'S EGG, THE(1977, Ger./U.S.)

Astrid Heeren
THOMAS CROWN AFFAIR, THE(1968); CASTLE KEEP(1969); SILENT NIGHT, BLOODY NIGHT(1974)

Victor Heerman
ANIMAL CRACKERS(1930), d; PERSONALITY(1930), d, w; SEA LEGS(1930), d; LITTLE WOMEN(1933), w; AGE OF INNOCENCE(1934), w; LITTLE MINISTER, THE(1934), w; BREAK OF HEARTS(1935), w; MAGNIFICENT OBSESSION(1935), w; STELLA DALLAS(1937), w; GOLDEN BOY(1939), w; LITTLE WOMEN(1949), w; MAGNIFICENT OBSESSION(1954), w
Silents
JOHN SMITH(1922), d, w; LOVE IS AN AWFUL THING(1922), d&w; MY BOY(1922), d; OLD HOME WEEK(1925), d; LADIES MUST DRESS(1927), d, w
Misc. Silents
DON'T EVER MARRY(1920), d; POOR SIMP, THE(1920), d; CHICKEN IN THE CASE, THE(1921), d; DANGEROUS MAID, THE(1923), d; MODERN MATRIMONY(1923), d; CONFIDENCE MAN, THE(1924), d; IRISH LUCK(1925), d; FOR WIVES ONLY(1926), d; RUBBER HEELS(1927), d; LOVE HUNGRY(1928), d

Dick Heermance
SUSPENSE(1946), ed; CHEROKEE UPRISING(1950), ed; NEVADA BADMEN(1951), ed

Richard Heermance
ABROAD WITH TWO YANKS(1944), ed; BREWSTER'S MILLIONS(1945), ed; PARDON MY PAST(1945), ed; ABILENE TOWN(1946), ed; IT HAPPENED ON 5TH AVENUE(1947), ed; SONG OF MY HEART(1947), ed; BABE RUTH STORY, THE(1948), ed; DUDE GOES WEST, THE(1948), ed; HUNTED, THE(1948), ed; PANHANDLE(1948), ed; BAD MEN OF TOMBSTONE(1949), ed; BOMBA ON PANTHER ISLAND(1949), ed; RED LIGHT(1949), ed; STAMPEDE(1949), ed; ARIZONA TERRITORY(1950), ed; COUNTY FAIR(1950), ed; LOST VOLCANO, THE(1950), ed; OUTLAWS OF TEXAS(1950), ed; SILVER RAIDERS(1950), ed; WHIPPED, THE(1950), ed; ABILENE TRAIL(1951), ed; CAVALRY SCOUT(1951), ed; DRUMS IN THE DEEP SOUTH(1951), ed; FLIGHT TO MARS(1951), ed; LONGHORN, THE(1951), ed; FORT OSAGE(1952), ed; KANSAS TERRITORY(1952), ed; ROSE BOWL STORY, THE(1952), p; MAZE, THE(1953), p; ROAR OF THE CROWD(1953), p; ROYAL AFRICAN RIFLES, THE(1953), p; WICHITA(1955), p; CANYON RIVER(1956), p; WORLD WITHOUT END(1956), p; YOUNG GUNS, THE(1956), p; DEATH IN SMALL DOSES(1957), p; UP IN SMOKE(1957), ed; FORT MASSACRE(1958), ed; IN THE MONEY(1958), p; MAN OF THE WEST(1958), ed; MAN IN THE NET, THE(1959), ed; KENNER(1969), ed

Richard V. Heermance
GUNFIGHT AT DODGE CITY, THE(1959), ed; MAYA(1966), ed

Johannes Heesters
COURT CONCERT, THE(1936, Ger.); SCHLAGER-PARADE(1953); WHITE HORSE INN, THE(1959, Ger.)

Nicole Heesters
KAMIKAZE '89(1983, Ger.)

Heetu
WHEN A STRANGER CALLS(1979)

Robert Heeyes
Misc. Talkies
JUST TELL ME YOU LOVE ME(1979)

Haim Hefer
KAZABLAN(1974, Israel), w

Ralph Heff
MAN WHO KNEW TOO MUCH, THE(1956)

Dennis Heffend
BLOODEATERS(1980)

Richard Heffer
DOCTOR FAUSTUS(1967, Brit.); WOMEN IN LOVE(1969, Brit.); WATERLOO(1970, Ital./USSR)
Misc. Talkies
CZECH MATE(1984, Brit.)

Paul Hefferan
LOVIN' MOLLY(1974), set d; TEMPEST(1982), set d

Ann Hefferman
MADNESS OF THE HEART(1949, Brit.)

Eddie Hefferman
Silents
RACING HEARTS(1923)

Ann Heffernan
LAVENDER HILL MOB, THE(1951, Brit.); CAPTAIN'S PARADISE, THE(1953, Brit.); COURT MARTIAL(1954, Brit.); THERE WAS A CROOKED MAN(1962, Brit.)

Honor Heffernan
ANGEL(1982, Irish)

John Heffernan
TIME OF THE HEATHEN(1962); PUZZLE OF A DOWNFALL CHILD(1970); STING, THE(1973); 92 IN THE SHADE(1975, U.S./Brit.); GOD TOLD ME TO(1976)

Robert Heffernan
MINNIE AND MOSKOWITZ(1971), ed

Terence Heffernan
GREAT BIG THING, A(1968, U.S./Can.), w; HEARTACHES(1981, Can.), w

Wayne Heffley
BATTLE CRY(1959); CRIME AND PUNISHMENT, U.S.A.(1959); SUBMARINE SEAHAWK(1959); OUTSIDER, THE(1962); GUNN(1967); MARYJANE(1968); JOHNNY GOT HIS GUN(1971); KING KONG(1976); ORCA(1977); TESTAMENT(1983)

Kyle T. Heffner
YOUNG DOCTORS IN LOVE(1982); FLASHDANCE(1983)
1984
WOMAN IN RED, THE(1984)

Richard Heffron
GREAT ST. LOUIS BANK ROBBERY, THE(1959), w; NEWMAN'S LAW(1974), d

Richard T. Heffron
FUTUREWORLD(1976), d; TRACKDOWN(1976), d; OUTLAW BLUES(1977), d; FOOLIN' AROUND(1980), d; I, THE JURY(1982), d

T.N. Heffron
Misc. Silents
BLACK SHEEP, A(1915), d; HOUSE OF A THOUSAND CANDLES, THE(1915), d; INTO THE PRIMITIVE(1916), d; PECK O' PICKLES(1916), d; VALIANTS OF VIRGINIA, THE(1916), d

Thomas Heffron
Silents
THOU ART THE MAN(1920), d
Misc. Silents
ARISTOCRACY(1914), d; GRETNA GREEN(1915), d; MOUNTAIN DEW(1917), d; PLANTER, THE(1917), d; STAINLESS BARRIER, THE(1917), d; DEUCE DUNCAN(1918), d; BEST MAN, THE(1919), d

Thomas N. Heffron
Silents
ONE OF OUR GIRLS(1914), d; ONLY SON, THE(1914), d; SCALES OF JUSTICE, THE(1914), d; ARE YOU A MASON?(1915), d; KISS IN TIME, A(1921), d; LITTLE CLOWN, THE(1921), d; LOVE CHARM, THE(1921), d; SHAM(1921), d
Misc. Silents
MAN FROM MEXICO, THE(1914), d; LONESOME TOWN(1916), d; SUDDEN GENTLEMAN, THE(1917), d; HOPPER, THE(1918), d; LONELY WOMAN, THE(1918), d; MADAME SPHINX(1918), d; MASK, THE(1918), d; OLD HARTWELL'S CUB(1918), d; PAINTED LILY, THE(1918), d; PRICE OF APPLAUSE, THE(1918), d; SEA PANTHER, THE(1918), d; TONY AMERICA(1918), d; WHO KILLED WALTON?(1918), d; LIFE'S A FUNNY PROPOSITION(1919), d; PRODIGAL LIAR, THE(1919), d; CITY OF MASKS, THE(1920), d; FIREBRAND TREVISON(1920), d; SUNSET SPRAGUE(1920), d; HER FACE VALUE(1921), d; HER STURDY OAK(1921), d; TRUANT HUSBAND, THE(1921), d; BOBBED HAIR(1922), d; TOO MUCH WIFE(1922), d; TRUTHFUL LIAR, THE(1922), d; WIFE'S ROMANCE, A(1923), d

Frances Heflin
MOLLY MAGUIRES, THE(1970); MR. BILLION(1977)

Kate Heflin
KILLER ELITE, THE(1975); MR. BILLION(1977)

Mady Heflin
SENTINEL, THE(1977)

Marta Heflin
STAR IS BORN, A(1976); WEDDING, A(1978); PERFECT COUPLE, A(1979); COME BACK TO THE 5 & DIME, JIMMY DEAN, JIMMY DEAN(1982); KING OF COMEDY, THE(1983)

Nora Heflin
FANTASTIC PLANET(1973, Fr./Czech.); STUDENT TEACHERS, THE(1973); OUR TIME(1974); TELL ME A RIDDLE(1980); CHILLY SCENES OF WINTER(1982); HEART LIKE A WHEEL(1983)

Van Heflin
3:10 TO YUMA(1957); WOMAN REBELS, A(1936); ANNAPOLIS SALUTE(1937); FLIGHT FROM GLORY(1937); OUTCASTS OF POKER FLAT, THE(1937); SATURDAY'S HEROES(1937); SANTA FE TRAIL(1940); FEMININE TOUCH, THE(1941); H.M. PULHAM, ESQ.(1941); GRAND CENTRAL MURDER(1942); JOHNNY EAGER(1942); KID GLOVE KILLER(1942); SEVEN SWEETHEARTS(1942); TENNESSEE JOHNSON(1942); PRESENTING LILY MARS(1943); STRANGE LOVE OF MARTHA IVERS, THE(1946); TILL THE CLOUDS ROLL BY(1946); GREEN DOLPHIN STREET(1947); POSSESSED(1947); B. F.'S DAUGHTER(1948); TAP ROOTS(1948); THREE MUSKETEERS, THE(1948); ACT OF VIOLENCE(1949); EAST SIDE, WEST SIDE(1949); MADAME BOVARY(1949); PROWLER, THE(1951); TOMAHAWK(1951); WEEKEND WITH FATHER(1951); MY SON, JOHN(1952); SHANE(1953); WINGS OF THE HAWK(1953); BLACK WIDOW(1954); GOLDEN MASK, THE(1954, Brit.); RAID, THE(1954); TANGANYIKA(1954); WOMAN'S WORLD(1954); BATTLE FLAME(1955); COUNT THREE AND PRAY(1955); PATTERNS(1956); GUNMAN'S WALK(1958); TEMPEST(1958, Ital./Yugo./Fr.); THEY CAME TO CORDURA(1959); FIVE BRANDED WOMEN(1960); UNDER TEN FLAGS(1960, U.S./Ital.); CRY OF BATTLE(1963); WASTREL, THE(1963, Ital.); GREATEST STORY EVER TOLD, THE(1965); ONCE A THIEF(1965); STAGECOACH(1966); MAN OUTSIDE, THE(1968, Brit.); BIG BOUNCE, THE(1969); RUTHLESS FOUR, THE(1969, Ital./Ger.); AIRPORT(1970)

Avram Hefner
SINAI COMMANDOS: THE STORY OF THE SIX DAY WAR(1968, Israel/Ger.)

Hugh Hefner
HISTORY OF THE WORLD, PART 1(1981); COMEBACK TRAIL, THE(1982)

Keith Hefner
STAR 80(1983)

Neal Hefti
SEX AND THE SINGLE GIRL(1964), m, md; BOEING BOEING(1965), m; HARLOW(1965), m; HOW TO MURDER YOUR WIFE(1965), m; SYNANON(1965), m; DUEL AT DIABLO(1966), m; LORD LOVE A DUCK(1966), m; BAREFOOT IN THE PARK(1967), m; OH DAD, POOR DAD, MAMA'S HUNG YOU IN THE CLOSET AND I'M FEELIN' SO SAD(1967), m; ODD COUPLE, THE(1968), m; P.J.(1968), m; LAST OF THE RED HOT LOVERS(1972), m; WON TON TON, THE DOG WHO SAVED HOLLYWOOD(1976), m

Neil Hefti
JAMBOREE(1957), m

Jim Hegan
KID FROM CLEVELAND, THE(1949)

Alexander Hegarth
JACK OF DIAMONDS(1967, U.S./Ger.)

Hazel Hegarty
YOUNG FURY(1965), cos
Georgina Hegedos
1984
BIG MEAT EATER(1984, Can.)
Rosalie Hegedus
HUMAN CARGO(1936)
Alice Hegeman
LAUGHING LADY, THE(1930); LOVE KISS, THE(1930)
Emil Hegetschweiler
HEIDI AND PETER(1955, Switz.)
Lou Hegge
HOLIDAY RHYTHM(1950), ed
Logan Heggen
MISTER ROBERTS(1955), w
Thomas Heggen
MISTER ROBERTS(1955), w; ENSIGN PULVER(1964), w
James Heggie
MOONSHINE COUNTY EXPRESS(1977), set d
O.P. Heggie
LETTER, THE(1929); MIGHTY, THE(1929); MYSTERIOUS DR. FU MANCHU, THE(1929); WHEEL OF LIFE, THE(1929); BAD MAN, THE(1930); ONE ROMANTIC NIGHT(1930); PLAYBOY OF PARIS(1930); RETURN OF DR. FU MANCHU, THE(1930); SUNNY(1930); VAGABOND KING, THE(1930); DEVOTION(1931); EAST LYNNE(1931); TOO YOUNG TO MARRY(1931); WOMAN BETWEEN(1931); SMILIN' THROUGH(1932); KING'S VACATION, THE(1933); ZOO IN BUDAPEST(1933); ANNE OF GREEN GABLES(1934); COUNT OF MONTE CRISTO, THE(1934); MID-NIGHT(1934); PECK'S BAD BOY(1934); CHASING YESTERDAY(1935); DOG OF FLANDERS, A(1935); GINGER(1935); PRISONER OF SHARK ISLAND, THE(1936)
Silents
ACTRESS, THE(1928)
Anne Hegiba
Misc. Talkies
PITY ME NOT(1960)
Kathleen Hegierski
FOUL PLAY(1978)
Ann Hegira
LOVE WITH THE PROPER STRANGER(1963)
Anne Hegira
ON THE WATERFRONT(1954); ARRANGEMENT, THE(1969)
Knud Heglund
WHILE THE ATTORNEY IS ASLEEP(1945, Den.)
Monique Heguy
HOT SPUR(1968)
Robert Hegyes
Misc. Talkies
UNDERGROUND ACES(1981)
Peter Hehir
LAST OF THE KNUCKLEMEN, THE(1981, Aus.); HEATWAVE(1983, Aus.)
Addison F. Hehr
THEY CALL ME MISTER TIBBS(1970), art d
Addison Hehr
DAY THE EARTH STOOD STILL, THE(1951), art d; NIGHT WITHOUT SLEEP(1952), art d; O. HENRY'S FULL HOUSE(1952), art d; PRIDE OF ST. LOUIS, THE(1952), art d; DESERT RATS, THE(1953), art d; KID FROM LEFT FIELD, THE(1953), art d; RIVER OF NO RETURN(1954), art d; HOUSE OF BAMBOO(1955), art d; RAINS OF RANCHIPUR, THE(1955), art d; UNTAMED(1955), art d; KISS BEFORE DYING, A(1956), art d; TRUE STORY OF JESSE JAMES, THE(1957), art d; WAY TO THE GOLD, THE(1957), art d; YOUNG LIONS, THE(1958), art d; 10 NORTH FREDERICK(1958), art d; NEVER SO FEW(1959), art d; CIMARRON(1960), art d; HOW THE WEST WAS WON(1962), art d; DRUMS OF AFRICA(1963), art d; WHEEL-ER DEALERS, THE(1963), art d; GET YOURSELF A COLLEGE GIRL(1964), art d; GUNS OF DIABLO(1964), art d; GIRL HAPPY(1965), art d; ZEBRA IN THE KITCH-EN(1965), art d; BALLAD OF JOSIE(1968), art d; ICE STATION ZEBRA(1968), art d; MARLOWE(1969), art d; HALLS OF ANGER(1970), art d; WILD ROVERS(1971), art d
Michael Hehr
NINE TO FIVE(1980)
Dale Heibein
HOUNDS... OF NOTRE DAME, THE(1980, Can.)
Birgit Heiberg
CITY OF FEAR(1965, Brit.)
Else Heiberg
HUNGER(1968, Den./Norway/Swed.)
Marco Heiblim
PUTNEY SWOPE(1969)
William Heick
TROIKA(1969), ph
Graham Heid
BAMBI(1942), d
Inger Heidal
TERRORISTS, THE(1975, Brit.)
Leonard Heideman
CANYON CROSSROADS(1955), w; VALERIE(1957), w
Leonard Heidemann
WALK EAST ON BEACON(1952), w
Paul Heidemann
Misc. Silents
LITTLE NAPOLEON, THE(1923, Ger.); LEAP INTO LIFE(1924, Ger.)
Renier Heidemann
LITTLE ARK, THE(1972)
Eddie Dale Heiden
LITTLE MEN(1935)
Janice Heiden
99 AND 44/100% DEAD(1974); DOC SAVAGE... THE MAN OF BRONZE(1975); WILD McCULLOCHS, THE(1975); STUDENT BODY, THE(1976)
June Heiden
FOREIGN CORRESPONDENT(1940)

Pat Heider
Misc. Talkies
BLOOD OF THE IRON MAIDEN(1969)
Patti Heider
IS THIS TRIP REALLY NECESSARY?(1970); MACHISMO–40 GRAVES FOR 40 GUNS(1970)
1984
INITIATION, THE(1984)
William Heidloff
Misc. Silents
WAIF, THE(1915)
Thomas Heidt
SNIPER, THE(1952)
Josef Heidts
IN THE NAME OF LIFE(1947, USSR), w
Jascha Heifeiz
CARNEGIE HALL(1947)
Jascha Heifetz
THEY SHALL HAVE MUSIC(1939)
Joseph Heifetz
BALTIC DEPUTY(1937, USSR), d, w
L.E. Heifetz
SHADOWS OF THE ORIENT(1937), w
L.S. Heifetz
RECKLESS ROADS(1935), w
Lou Heifetz
I HAVE LIVED(1933), w; INTERNATIONAL HOUSE(1933), w; LOVE IS A HEAD-ACHE(1938), w
Louis Heifetz
DEFENDERS OF THE LAW(1931), w
Vladimir Heifetz
GREEN FIELDS(1937), m
Henry Heifitz
IN THE COUNTRY(1967)
Josef Heifitz
LAST HILL, THE(1945, USSR), d, w; IN THE NAME OF LIFE(1947, USSR), d
Helen Heigh
MONSIEUR VERDOUX(1947)
Helene Heigh
MURDER IS MY BUSINESS(1946); UNDERCOVER WOMAN, THE(1946); EASTER PARADE(1948); YOUNG MAN WITH A HORN(1950); FEMALE ON THE BEACH(1955); PLUNDER ROAD(1957); TEENAGE THUNDER(1957); WHAT'S THE MATTER WITH HELEN?(1971); NINE TO FIVE(1980)
1984
MASS APPEAL(1984)
Elsa Heiis
HOTEL BERLIN(1945)
Arthur Heil
BLONDE NIGHTINGALE(1931, Ger.)
Janet Marie Heil
1984
NINJA III–THE DOMINATION(1984)
Raymond Heil
LAS RATAS NO DUERMEN DE NOCHE(1974, Span./Fr.), ph
Ted Heil
SOMETHING WEIRD(1967)
Adelaide Heilbron
LITTLE JOHNNY JONES(1930), w; HIS WOMAN(1931), w; MY SIN(1931), w; PER-SONAL MAID(1931), w; MISLEADING LADY, THE(1932), w; IT'S ALL YOURS(1937), w; CHEERS FOR MISS BISHOP(1941), w; FRIENDLY ENEMIES(1942), w
Silents
DANGER POINT, THE(1922), t; GIRL OF THE GOLDEN WEST, THE(1923), w; SO BIG(1924), w; EVE'S SECRET(1925), w; NEW LIVES FOR OLD(1925), w; SYNCOPAT-ING SUE(1926), w; FRENCH DRESSING(1927), w; LADY BE GOOD(1928), w
Lorna Heilbron
CREEPING FLESH,THE(1973, Brit.); SYMPTOMS(1976, Brit.)
Vivien Heilbron
KIDNAPPED(1971, Brit.)
Marianne Heilig
ONCE(1974), p
Morton Heilig
ONCE(1974), p, d,w&ph
Morton L. Heilig
YEAR OF THE HORSE, THE(1966), ph
Heinrich Heilinger
RASPUTIN(1932, Ger.)
Claude Heilman
THIS EARTH IS MINE(1959), p
Ron Heilman
PERSONAL BEST(1982), cos
1984
RHINESTONE(1984), cos
Van Campel Heilner
Misc. Talkies
ANGRY GOD, THE(1948), d
Elayne Heilveil
PAYDAY(1972)
David Heilweil
FACE OF A FUGITIVE(1959), p
David Heilwell
3:10 TO YUMA(1957), p; INTIMACY(1966), p
Alan Heim
SEA GULL, THE(1968), ed; TWELVE CHAIRS, THE(1970), ed; DOC(1971), ed; GOD-SPELL(1973), ed; LENNY(1974), ed; NETWORK(1976), ed; ALL THAT JAZZ(1979), a, ed; FAN, THE(1981), ed; SO FINE(1981), ed; STAR 80(1983), ed
Carl Heim
PARTNERS OF THE TRAIL(1944), ed

Ed Heim
TOAST OF NEW YORK, THE(1937)
Eddie Heim
HISTORY OF THE WORLD, PART 1(1981)
Edward Heim
PENNIES FROM HEAVEN(1981)
Misc. Silents
LONE RIDER, THE(1922); LIGHTING BILL(1926)
Edward J. Heim
TO BE OR NOT TO BE(1983)
Francis Heim
WALK WITH LOVE AND DEATH, A(1969)
Jacques Heim
HOUSE OF THE SEVEN HAWKS, THE(1959), cos; CHEATERS, THE(1961, Fr.), cos
Ted Heim [Ted Garrotte]
MISS JESSICA IS PREGNANT(1970)
Wilhelm Heim
MONEY ON THE STREET(1930, Aust.)
Nachum Heiman
NEITHER THE SEA NOR THE SAND(1974, Brit.), m
Betsy Heimann
SKATETOWN, U.S.A.(1979), cos; HIGH ROAD TO CHINA(1983), cos
Peter Heimann
DOLLY GETS AHEAD(1931, Ger.), w
Richard G. Heimann
GODSPELL(1973), ph
Robert Heimann
DOLLY GETS AHEAD(1931, Ger.), ph
Rudolf Heimann
DECISION BEFORE DAWN(1951)
Otto Heimel
KLONDIKE ANNIE(1936); MY LITTLE CHICKADEE(1940)
Elsa Heims
GREAT SINNER, THE(1949)
Jo Heims
GIRL IN LOVER'S LANE, THE(1960), w; THREAT, THE(1960), w; DEVIL'S HAND, THE(1961), w; GUN HAWK, THE(1963), w; NAVAJO RUN(1966), w; DOUBLE TROUBLE(1967), w; TELL ME IN THE SUNLIGHT(1967), w; FIRST TIME, THE(1969), w; PLAY MISTY FOR ME(1971), w; YOU'LL LIKE MY MOTHER(1972), w; BREEZY(1973), w
Florence Hein
Silents
GOLDEN GIFT, THE(1922), w; SCARLET LILY, THE(1923), w
Keith Hein
LADY IN RED, THE(1979), set d; OSTERMAN WEEKEND, THE(1983), set d
Ray Heindorf
BIG CITY BLUES(1932), m; CAPTAIN BLOOD(1935), md; SAN QUENTIN(1937), md; FOUR'S A CROWD(1938), m; ROARING TWENTIES, THE(1939), m; KNUTE ROCKNE—ALL AMERICAN(1940), m; CITY, FOR CONQUEST(1941), m; THIS IS THE ARMY(1943), md; HOLLYWOOD CANTEEN(1944), m; UP IN ARMS(1944), m; WONDER MAN(1945), m; APRIL SHOWERS(1948), m; FIGHTER SQUADRON(1948), md; FLAMINGO ROAD(1949), md; IT'S A GREAT FEELING(1949), md; LOOK FOR THE SILVER LINING(1949), m, md; MY DREAM IS YOURS(1949), md; BACKFIRE(1950), m; BREAKING POINT, THE(1950), m; DAMNED DON'T CRY, THE(1950), md; STORM WARNING(1950), md; TEA FOR TWO(1950), md; WEST POINT STORY, THE(1950), md; YOUNG MAN WITH A HORN(1950), md; COME FILL THE CUP(1951), md; GOODBYE, MY FANCY(1951), m; I'LL SEE YOU IN MY DREAMS(1951), md; LULLABY OF BROADWAY, THE(1951), md; ON MOONLIGHT BAY(1951), md; PAINTING THE CLOUDS WITH SUNSHINE(1951), md; STARLIFT(1951), md; STRANGERS ON A TRAIN(1951), md; STREETCAR NAMED DESIRE, A(1951), md; TOMORROW IS ANOTHER DAY(1951), md; OPERATION SECRET(1952), md; SHE'S WORKING HER WAY THROUGH COLLEGE(1952), md; STOP, YOU'RE KILLING ME(1952), md; BY THE LIGHT OF THE SILVERY MOON(1953), md; CALAMITY JANE(1953), md; DESERT SONG, THE(1953), md; EDDIE CANTOR STORY, THE(1953), md; I CONFESS(1953), md; SO THIS IS LOVE(1953), md; THREE SAILORS AND A GIRL(1953), md; COMMAND, THE(1954), md; LUCKY ME(1954), md; STAR IS BORN, A(1954), md; THEM!(1954), md; PETE KELLY'S BLUES(1955), m; YOUNG AT HEART(1955), md; AUNTIE MAME(1958), md; HOME BEFORE DARK(1958), m, md; MARJORIE MORNINGSTAR(1958), md; NO TIME FOR SERGEANTS(1958), m, md; ONIONHEAD(1958), md; –30–(1959), m; MIRACLE, THE(1959), md; UP PERISCOPE(1959), m; YOUNG PHILADELPHIANS, THE(1959), md; MUSIC MAN, THE(1962), md; FINIAN'S RAINBOW(1968), md; 1776(1972), md
Leigh Heine
YOUR THREE MINUTES ARE UP(1973)
Laurie Heineman
SAVE THE TIGER(1973); FOREPLAY(1975); LADY IN RED, THE(1979)
Eda Heinemann
KISS OF DEATH(1947)
Pastor Peter Heinemann
MARTIN LUTHER(1953), cons
Thomasine Heiner
TWILIGHT'S LAST GLEAMING(1977, U.S./Ger.)
Jan Heininger
MANITOU, THE(1978)
Robert A. Heinlein
DESTINATION MOON(1950), w; PROJECT MOONBASE(1953), w
Hubert Heinrich
Silents
KRIEMHILD'S REVENGE(1924, Ger.); SIEGFRIED(1924, Ger.)
Mimi Heinrich
JOURNEY TO THE SEVENTH PLANET(1962, U.S./Swed.); REPTILICUS(1962, U.S./Den.); CHRISTINE KEELER AFFAIR, THE(1964, Brit.)
Susanne Heinrich
ERIC SOYA'S "17"(1967, Den.)
Willi Heinrich
CROSS OF IRON(1977, Brit., Ger.), w

Daniel Heintschel, Jr.
URBAN COWBOY(1980)
Albert Heintzelman
1984
SLAPSTICK OF ANOTHER KIND(1984), set d
Heinz
FAREWELL PERFORMANCE(1963, Brit.)
Albert Heinz
PAISAN(1948, Ital.)
Astrid Heinz
FLOWERS FOR THE MAN IN THE MOON(1975, Ger.)
Gerald Heinz
BROKEN JOURNEY(1948, Brit.); AFFAIRS OF A ROGUE, THE(1949, Brit.); HER MAN GILBEY(1949, Brit.); CLOUDED YELLOW, THE(1950, Brit.)
Gerard Heinz
CARAVAN(1946, Brit.); GIRL IN THE PAINTING, THE(1948, Brit.); FALLEN IDOL, THE(1949, Brit.); SLEEPING CAR TO TRIESTE(1949, Brit.); IF THIS BE SIN(1950, Brit.); LOST PEOPLE, THE(1950, Brit.); GREAT MANHUNT, THE(1951, Brit.); TRAVELLER'S JOY(1951, Brit.); HIS EXCELLENCY(1952, Brit.); PRIVATE INFORMATION(1952, Brit.); WHITE CORRIDORS(1952, Brit.); CRUEL SEA, THE(1953); DESPERATE MOMENT(1953, Brit.); MR. POTTS GOES TO MOSCOW(1953, Brit.); PRISONER, THE(1955, Brit.); YOU PAY YOUR MONEY(1957, Brit.); MAN INSIDE, THE(1958, Brit.); MARK OF THE HAWK, THE(1958); HOUSE OF THE SEVEN HAWKS, THE(1959); I AIM AT THE STARS(1960); HIGHWAY TO BATTLE(1961, Brit.); OFFBEAT(1961, Brit.); OPERATION SNATCH(1962, Brit.); MYSTERY SUBMARINE(1963, Brit.); DEVILS OF DARKNESS, THE(1965, Brit.); HEROES OF TELEMARK, THE(1965, Brit.); WHERE THE BULLETS FLY(1966, Brit.); PROJECTED MAN, THE(1967, Brit.)
Ray Heinz
Misc. Talkies
BLAZING GUNS(1935), d; BORDER VENGEANCE(1935), d
Richard Heinz
QUEEN OF SHEBA(1953, Ital.), w
Russell Ray Heinz
Misc. Talkies
JUST MY LUCK(1936), d
Wolfgang Heinz
Silents
NOSFERATU, THE VAMPIRE(1922, Ger.)
William Heinz
M(1970), w
Gertrud Heinz-Werner
GIRL FROM HONG KONG(1966, Ger.), makeup
Detlev Heinze
TINDER BOX, THE(1968, E. Ger.)
Peter Heinze
BIBLE...IN THE BEGINNING, THE(1966)
Rosemarie Heinze
1984
WOMAN IN FLAMES, A(1984, Ger.)
Bill Heinzman
NIGHT OF THE LIVING DEAD(1968)
Joyce Heiser
VALLEY GIRL(1983)
Hedi Heisig
EIGHT GIRLS IN A BOAT(1932, Ger.)
Teppo Heiskanen
TELEFON(1977)
Helmut Heisler
LAST ESCAPE, THE(1970, Brit.)
Stuart Heisler
BARKER, THE(1928), ed; CONDEMNED(1929), ed; RAFFLES(1930), ed; WHOOPEE(1930), ed; ONE HEAVENLY NIGHT(1931), ed; GREEKS HAD A WORD FOR THEM(1932), ed; KID FROM SPAIN, THE(1932), ed; MASQUERADER, THE(1933), ed; ROMAN SCANDALS(1933), ed; KID MILLIONS(1934), ed; WE'RE NOT DRESSING(1934), ed; MEN WITHOUT NAMES(1935), ed; PETER IBBETSON(1935), ed; WEDDING NIGHT, THE(1935), ed; BIG BROADCAST OF 1937, THE(1936), ed; KLONDIKE ANNIE(1936), ed; POPPY(1936), ed; STRAIGHT FROM THE SHOULDER(1936), d; HURRICANE, THE(1937), d; BISCUIT EATER, THE(1940), d; AMONG THE LIVING(1941), d; MONSTER AND THE GIRL, THE(1941), d; GLASS KEY, THE(1942), d; REMARKABLE ANDREW, THE(1942), d; ALONG CAME JONES(1945), d; BLUE SKIES(1946), d; SMASH-UP, THE STORY OF A WOMAN(1947), d; TOKYO JOE(1949), d; TULSA(1949), d; CHAIN LIGHTNING(1950), d; DALLAS(1950), d; STORM WARNING(1950), d; VENDETTA(1950), d; JOURNEY INTO LIGHT(1951), d; ISLAND OF DESIRE(1952, Brit.), d; STAR, THE(1953), d; BEACHHEAD(1954), d; THIS IS MY LOVE(1954), d; I DIED A THOUSAND TIMES(1955), d; LONE RANGER, THE(1955), d; BURNING HILLS, THE(1956), d; HITLER(1962), d
Silents
CYTHEREA(1924), ed; IN HOLLYWOOD WITH POTASH AND PERLMUTTER(1924), ed; STELLA DALLAS(1925), ed; DO YOUR DUTY(1928), ed; LADY BE GOOD(1928), ed
Carol Heiss
SNOW WHITE AND THE THREE STOOGES(1961)
Betty Heistand
MUSIC IN THE AIR(1934)
John Heistand
PERFECT SPECIMEN, THE(1937); KENTUCKY MOONSHINE(1938); RIDING HIGH(1943)
Michael Heit
PARADES(1972); BARE KNUCKLES(1978); LINE, THE(1982)
Misc. Talkies
BARE KNUCKLES(1977)
Sally Jane Heit
SO FINE(1981)
Sally-Jane Heit
TATTOO(1981)

Heinrich Heitfeld
  GHOUL, THE(1934, Brit.), makeup
Otto Hejdusek
  HIPPODROME(1961, Aust./Ger.)
Grethe Hejil
  SNOW TREASURE(1968), art d
Ruzena Hejskova
  VOYAGE TO THE END OF THE UNIVERSE(1963, Czech.), ed
Frank Hekinson
Silents
  HONEYMOON FLATS(1928), ed
Martin Hel
  SERPENT, THE(1973, Fr./Ital./Ger.)
Jane Helay
  BLOODTHIRSTY BUTCHERS(1970)
Sandy Helberg
  SHEILA LEVINE IS DEAD AND LIVING IN NEW YORK(1975); HOLLYWOOD KNIGHTS, THE(1980); HISTORY OF THE WORLD, PART 1(1981); MODERN PROBLEMS(1981)
1984
  THIS IS SPINAL TAP(1984); UP THE CREEK(1984)
Herbie Helbig
  CROWD INSIDE, THE(1971, Can.), m
Jeanne Helbling
  FIRE IN THE STRAW(1943)
Lance Helcomb
  GHOST STORY(1981)
Anna Held
Misc. Silents
  MADAME LA PRESIDENTE(1916)
Gigi Held
  PLAYGIRLS AND THE BELLBOY, THE(1962,Ger.)
John Held, Jr.
Silents
  SO'S YOUR OLD MAN(1926), art d
Karl Held
  READY FOR THE PEOPLE(1964); THAT DARN CAT(1965); 36 HOURS(1965); GNOME-MOBILE, THE(1967); DIAMONDS ARE FOREVER(1971, Brit.); EMBASSY(1972, Brit.)
Martin Held
  CANARIS(1955, Ger.); CAPTAIN FROM KOEPENICK, THE(1956, Ger.); ROSES FOR THE PROSECUTOR(1961, Ger.); VOR SONNENUNTERGANG(1961, Ger); END OF MRS. CHENEY(1963, Ger.); AND SO TO BED(1965, Ger.); TERROR AFTER MIDNIGHT(1965, Ger.); OLDEST PROFESSION, THE(1968, Fr./Ital./Ger.); DISORDER AND EARLY TORMENT(1977, Ger.)
Tom Held
  MEN OF THE NORTH(1930), ed; THEY LEARNED ABOUT WOMEN(1930), ed; DAYBREAK(1931), ed; SIN OF MADELON CLAUDET, THE(1931), ed; BUT THE FLESH IS WEAK(1932), ed; RASPUTIN AND THE EMPRESS(1932), ed; SKYSCRAPER SOULS(1932), ed; TARZAN, THE APE MAN(1932), ed; BARBARIAN, THE(1933), ed; GIRL FROM MISSOURI, THE(1934), ed; TARZAN AND HIS MATE(1934), ed; AFTER OFFICE HOURS(1935), ed; ESCAPADE(1935), ed; FORSAKING ALL OTHERS(1935), ed; I LIVE MY LIFE(1935), ed; ONE NEW YORK NIGHT(1935), ed; THREE LIVE GHOSTS(1935), ed; DEVIL IS A SISSY, THE(1936), ed; SAN FRANCISCO(1936), ed; CONQUEST(1937), ed; GREAT WALTZ, THE(1938), ed; TEST PILOT(1938), ed
John Heldabrand
  ON THE WATERFRONT(1954); WRONG MAN, THE(1956)
James Helder
  HARDCORE(1979)
Susan Heldfond
  WHY WOULD I LIE(1980); LOVE AND MONEY(1982)
Marjorie Helen
  OPPOSITE SEX, THE(1956)
Sascha Helen
  NIGHT OF THE ASKARI(1978, Ger./South African)
Dennis Helfand
  GROOVE TUBE, THE(1974)
Dennis Helfend
  LADY LIBERTY(1972, Ital./Fr.)
Britt Helfer
  YOUNG WARRIORS(1983)
1984
  ALLEY CAT(1984)
Ralph Helfer
  LION, THE(1962, Brit.), animal d; GENTLE GIANT(1967), cons; SAVAGE HARVEST(1981), p, w
Tana Helfer
  SAVAGE HARVEST(1981)
Cynthia Helferstay
1984
  ALLEY CAT(1984)
Dave Helfert
  OUTLAW BLUES(1977)
Henry Helfman
  KISS BEFORE DYING, A(1956), cos
Roger Helfond
  THAT TENDER TOUCH(1969)
Mark Helfrich
  REVENGE OF THE NINJA(1983), ed
Richard Helfritz
  NOBODY'S PERFEKT(1981), set d; PORKY'S II: THE NEXT DAY(1983), set d
Helga & Jo
  ON VELVET(1938, Brit.)
Mats Helge
Misc. Talkies
  NINJA MISSION(1984), d

Jeanne Helia
  MARRIAGE CAME TUMBLING DOWN, THE(1968, Fr.)
Jenny Helia
  LA BETE HUMAINE(1938, Fr.); RULES OF THE GAME, THE(1939, Fr.); TONI(1968, Fr.)
Simone Heliard
  TOPAZE(1935, Fr.)
Pierre-Jakez Helias
  HORSE OF PRIDE(1980, Fr.), w
Michael Allan Helie
  HARDCORE(1979)
John Helier
  JOHNNY, YOU'RE WANTED(1956, Brit.); ROGUE'S YARN(1956, Brit.); HARRY BLACK AND THE TIGER(1958, Brit.)
Agda Helin
  HOUR OF THE WOLF, THE(1968, Swed.); SHAME(1968, Swed.)
Inga-Lil Helin
  MAKE LIKE A THIEF(1966, Fin.)
Helmut Helisg
  CITY OF TORMENT(1950, Ger.)
Reino Helkesalo
  MAKE LIKE A THIEF(1966, Fin.), art d
Erik Hell
  BREAD OF LOVE, THE(1954, Swed.); PORT OF CALL(1963, Swed.); DEAR JOHN(1966, Swed.); PASSION OF ANNA, THE(1970, Swed.); RITUAL, THE(1970, Swed.)
Mathias Hell
  MARCH OR DIE(1977, Brit.)
Rene Hell
  COUNTERFEITERS OF PARIS, THE(1962, Fr., Ital.); MADEMOISELLE(1966, Fr./Brit.)
Richard Hell
  SMITHEREENS(1982); GEEK MAGGOT BINGO(1983)
Members of the Hell's Angels of Venice, California
  WILD ANGELS, THE(1966)
Jeanna Hella
  LA MARSEILLAISE(1938, Fr.)
Lisa Hella
1984
  WINDY CITY(1984)
Eric Helland
  DIFFERENT STORY, A(1978)
Suellen Helland
  WHERE ANGELS GO...TROUBLE FOLLOWS(1968)
Udo Helland
1984
  FLIGHT TO BERLIN(1984, Ger./Brit.)
Frank Hellard
  GRENDEL GRENDEL GRENDEL(1981, Aus.), anim d, anim
Kerstin Hellberg
  MEPHISTO(1981, Ger.)
Margrid Hellberg
  MEPHISTO(1981, Ger.)
Martin Hellberg
  PINOCCHIO(1969, E. Ger.)
Professor Martin Hellberg
  MEPHISTO(1981, Ger.)
Ruth Hellberg
  BROKEN LOVE(1946, Ital.)
Thomas Hellberg
Misc. Talkies
  ASSIGNMENT, THE(1978)
Olle Hellbom
  PIPPI IN THE SOUTH SEAS(1974, Swed./Ger.), d; PIPPI ON THE RUN(1977), d
Folke Helleberg
  INTERMEZZO(1937, Swed.); ONLY ONE NIGHT(1942, Swed.)
Marjorie Hellen
  GIRL IN THE RED VELVET SWING, THE(1955); TANK BATTALION(1958); MISSILE TO THE MOON(1959)
Marjorie Hellen [Leslie Parrish]
  VIRGIN QUEEN, THE(1955)
Fred Hellenburgh
  WHERE EAGLES DARE(1968, Brit.), spec eff
Abbey Heller
  HONEYMOON OF HORROR(1964)
Adolf Heller
  STRANGE FASCINATION(1952), md; THY NEIGHBOR'S WIFE(1953), md
Andre Heller
  OUR HITLER, A FILM FROM GERMANY(1980, Ger.)
Ariane Heller
  UP THE SANDBOX(1972)
Arianne Heller
  MIXED COMPANY(1974)
Barbara Heller
  HEY BOY! HEY GIRL!(1959); LONE TEXAN(1959); COMIC, THE(1969)
Chip Heller
1984
  BEVERLY HILLS COP(1984); RHINESTONE(1984)
Cindy Heller
  SINGING IN THE DARK(1956)
Clara Heller
Misc. Silents
  WHISPERING WOMEN(1921)
Dan Heller
  ATOMIC SUBMARINE, THE(1960), art d
Daniel Heller
  TIME FOR KILLING, A(1967), art d

Frank Heller
HAPPY DAYS(1930)
Ginny Heller
GOING HOME(1971)
Gloria Heller
Silents
CROSS BREED(1927)
Misc. Silents
GALLOPING JINX(1925)
Gregory K. Heller
1984
ALPHABET CITY(1984), w
Henry Heller
GALLANT ONE, THE(1964, U.S./Peru)
Herman Heller
GIRL ON THE FRONT PAGE, THE(1936), m; TWO IN A CROWD(1936), md
Herman S. Heller
SEA SPOILERS, THE(1936), md
Jack Heller
FLORIDA SPECIAL(1936)
1984
BEVERLY HILLS COP(1984)
Jackie Heller
REVERSE BE MY LOT, THE(1938, Brit.); DON'T WORRY, WE'LL THINK OF A TITLE(1966)
Jayne Heller
DEATHTRAP(1982)
John G. Heller
OPERATION CONSPIRACY(1957, Brit.); HAUNTED STRANGLER, THE(1958, Brit.); MISSILE FROM HELL(1960, Brit.); GREAT ARMORED CAR SWINDLE, THE(1964); DARLING(1965, Brit.); DOUBLE MAN, THE(1967); GIRL ON A MOTORCYCLE, THE(1968, Fr./Brit.); KELLY'S HEROES(1970, U.S./Yugo.)
Joseph Heller
SEX AND THE SINGLE GIRL(1964), w; CATCH-22(1970), w; DIRTY DINGUS MAGEE(1970), w
Leon Heller
END OF AUGUST, THE(1982), w
Little Jackie Heller
YANKS ARE COMING, THE(1942)
Lukas Heller
SAPPHIRE(1959, Brit.), w; WHATEVER HAPPENED TO BABY JANE?(1962), w; AGENT 8 3/4(1963, Brit.), w; HUSH... HUSH, SWEET CHARLOTTE(1964), w; FLIGHT OF THE PHOENIX, THE(1965), w; CANDIDATE FOR MURDER(1966, Brit.), w; DIRTY DOZEN, THE(1967, Brit.), w; NEVER BACK LOSERS(1967, Brit.), w; MONTE WALSH(1970), w; TOO LATE THE HERO(1970), w; DEADLY TRACKERS(1973), w; DAMNATION ALLEY(1977), w
Otto Heller
DREAMS COME TRUE(1936, Brit.), ph; ROMANCE AND RICHES(1937, Brit.), ph; HIGH COMMAND(1938, Brit.), ph; I MARRIED A SPY(1938), ph; SKELETON ON HORSEBACK(1940, Czech.), ph; THEY MET ON SKIS(1940, Fr.), ph; TWO WOMEN(1940, Fr.), ph; AT DAWN WE DIE(1943, Brit.), ph; DARK TOWER, THE(1943, Brit.), ph; NIGHT INVADER, THE(1943, Brit.), ph; UNDER SECRET ORDERS(1943, Brit.), ph; CANDLELIGHT IN ALGERIA(1944, Brit.), ph; FLIGHT FROM FOLLY(1945, Brit.), ph; MR. EMMANUEL(1945, Brit.), ph; THEY MET IN THE DARK(1945, Brit.), ph; NIGHT BOAT TO DUBLIN(1946, Brit.), ph; YANK IN LONDON, A(1946, Brit.), ph; YOU CAN'T DO WITHOUT LOVE(1946, Brit.), ph; I BECAME A CRIMINAL(1947), ph; BOND STREET(1948, Brit.), ph; QUEEN OF SPADES(1948, Brit.), ph; SHOWTIME(1948, Brit.), ph; LAST DAYS OF DOLWYN, THE(1949, Brit.), ph; NOW BARABBAS WAS A ROBBER(1949, Brit.), ph; TEMPTATION HARBOR(1949, Brit.), ph; FLESH AND BLOOD(1951, Brit.), ph; HER PANELLED DOOR(1951, Brit.), ph; LUCKY NICK CAIN(1951), ph; CRIMSON PIRATE, THE(1952), ph; NEVER TAKE NO FOR AN ANSWER(1952, Brit./Ital.), ph; HIS MAJESTY O'KEEFE(1953), ph; PARIS EXPRESS, THE(1953, Brit.), ph; RAINBOW JACKET, THE(1954, Brit.), ph; DIVIDED HEART, THE(1955, Brit.), ph; SQUARE RING, THE(1955, Brit.), ph; CHILD IN THE HOUSE(1956, Brit.), ph; LADYKILLERS, THE(1956, Brit.), ph; RICHARD III(1956, Brit.), ph; WHO DONE IT?(1956, Brit.), ph; NOVEL AFFAIR, A(1957, Brit.), ph; STOWAWAY GIRL(1957, Brit.), ph; DUKE WORE JEANS, THE(1958, Brit.), ph; HELLO LONDON(1958, Brit.), ph; SHERIFF OF FRACTURED JAW, THE(1958, Brit.), ph; TRUTH ABOUT WOMEN, THE(1958, Brit.), ph; DOG OF FLANDERS, A(1959), ph; FERRY TO HONG KONG(1959, Brit.), ph; SILENT ENEMY, THE(1959, Brit.), ph; PEEPING TOM(1960, Brit.), ph; BIG SHOW, THE(1961), ph; PORTRAIT OF A SINNER(1961, Brit.), ph; SINGER NOT THE SONG, THE(1961, Brit.), ph; TOO HOT TO HANDLE(1961, Brit.), ph; VICTIM(1961, Brit.), ph; CIRCUS FRIENDS(1962, Brit.), ph; LIGHT IN THE PIAZZA(1962), ph; TIARA TAHITI(1962, Brit.), ph; WE JOINED THE NAVY(1962, Brit.), ph; WEST 11(1963, Brit.), ph; WHAT A CRAZY WORLD(1963, Brit.), ph; WOMAN OF STRAW(1964, Brit.), ph; CURSE OF THE MUMMY'S TOMB, THE(1965, Brit.), ph; IPCRESS FILE, THE(1965, Brit.), ph; MASQUERADE(1965, Brit.), ph; ALFIE(1966, Brit.), ph; FUNERAL IN BERLIN(1966, Brit.), ph; WALK IN THE SHADOW(1966, Brit.), ph; I'LL NEVER FORGET WHAT'S 'IS NAME(1967, Brit.), ph; NAKED RUNNER, THE(1967, Brit.), ph; DON'T RAISE THE BRIDGE, LOWER THE RIVER(1968, Brit.), ph; DUFFY(1968, Brit.), ph; THAT RIVIERA TOUCH(1968, Brit.), ph; IN SEARCH OF GREGORY(1970, Brit./Ital.), ph; BLOOMFIELD(1971, Brit./Israel), ph
Paul Heller
HAPPY ANNIVERSARY(1959), prod d; COME SPY WITH ME(1967), p; ENTER THE DRAGON(1973), p; BLACK BELT JONES(1974), p; GOLDEN NEEDLES(1974), p; ULTIMATE WARRIOR, THE(1975), p; DIRTY KNIGHT'S WORK(1976, Brit.), p, w; HOT POTATO(1976), p; PACK, THE(1977), p; CHECKERED FLAG OR CRASH(1978), p; PROMISE, THE(1979), p, w; FIRST MONDAY IN OCTOBER(1981), p
Paul M. Heller
DAVID AND LISA(1962), p, art d; THE EAVESDROPPER(1966, U.S./Arg.), p; TRUCK TURNER(1974), p
Peter Heller
FEAR(1956, Ger.), ph
Randee Heller
FAST BREAK(1979)
1984
KARATE KID, THE(1984)

Rhodelle Heller
WRONG MAN, THE(1956)
Stewart Heller
TIME OF THE HEATHEN(1962)
Fred Hellerman
LOVIN' MOLLY(1974), m
John Hellerman
NAKED APE, THE(1973)
John Helles
HELL, HEAVEN OR HOBOKEN(1958, Brit.)
Jack Hellier
LAST WALTZ, THE(1936, Brit.); MERRY COMES TO STAY(1937, Brit.)
Silents
MY LORD THE CHAUFFEUR(1927, Brit.), a, w
Mark Hellinger
NIGHT COURT(1932), w; BROADWAY BILL(1934), w; COMET OVER BROADWAY(1938), w; WALKING DOWN BROADWAY(1938), w; ADVENTURES OF JANE ARDEN(1939), p; HELL'S KITCHEN(1939), p; ROARING TWENTIES, THE(1939), w; WOMEN IN THE WIND(1939), p; BROTHER ORCHID(1940), p; IT ALL CAME TRUE(1940), p; THEY DRIVE BY NIGHT(1940), p; TORRID ZONE(1940), p; AFFECTIONATELY YOURS(1941), p; HIGH SIERRA(1941), p; MANPOWER(1941), p; RISE AND SHINE(1941), p; MOONTIDE(1942), p; YOU CAN'T ESCAPE FOREVER(1942), p; HUNDRED POUND WINDOW, THE(1943, Brit.), w; THANK YOUR LUCKY STARS(1943), a, p; BETWEEN TWO WORLDS(1944), p; DOUGHGIRLS, THE(1944), p; HORN BLOWS AT MIDNIGHT, THE(1945), p; KILLERS, THE(1946), p; SWELL GUY(1946), p; BRUTE FORCE(1947), p; TWO MRS. CARROLLS, THE(1947), p; NAKED CITY, THE(1948), a, p; RIDING HIGH(1950), w
Max Hellinger
NORTH TO ALASKA(1960)
William Hellinger
EVERYTHING'S DUCKY(1961)
Bonnie Hellman
1984
FRIDAY THE 13TH-THE FINAL CHAPTER(1984)
George S. Hellman
NIGHT IN PARADISE, A(1946), w
Gloria Hellman
HELL NIGHT(1981)
Jaclyn Hellman
CHRISTIAN LICORICE STORE, THE(1971); TWO-LANE BLACKTOP(1971)
Jacqueline Hellman
FLIGHT TO FURY(1966, U.S./Phil.)
Jerome Hellman
WORLD OF HENRY ORIENT, THE(1964), p; FINE MADNESS, A(1966), p; MIDNIGHT COWBOY(1969), p; DAY OF THE LOCUST, THE(1975), p; COMING HOME(1978), p; PROMISES IN THE DARK(1979), p&d
Les Hellman
ENCHANTED ISLAND(1958)
Lillian Hellman
TOYS IN THE ATTIC(1963), w; DARK ANGEL, THE(1935), w; THESE THREE(1936), w; LITTLE FOXES, THE(1941), w; NORTH STAR, THE(1943), w; WATCH ON THE RHINE(1943), w; SEARCHING WIND, THE(1946), w; ANOTHER PART OF THE FOREST(1948), w; CHILDREN'S HOUR, THE(1961), w; CHASE, THE(1966), w; JULIA(1977), w
Marcel Hellman
ACCUSED(1936, Brit.), p; AMATEUR GENTLEMAN(1936, Brit.), p; CRIME OVER LONDON(1936, Brit.), p; WHEN THIEF MEETS THIEF(1937, Brit.), p; GIRL IN DISTRESS(1941, Brit.), p; TALK ABOUT JACQUELINE(1942, Brit.), p; SECRET MISSION(1944, Brit.), a, p; THEY MET IN THE DARK(1945, Brit.), p; WANTED FOR MURDER(1946, Brit.), p; MEET ME AT DAWN(1947, Brit.), p; THIS WAS A WOMAN(1949, Brit.), p; HAPPY GO LOVELY(1951, Brit.), p; DUEL IN THE JUNGLE(1954, Brit.), p; LET'S BE HAPPY(1957, Brit.), p; FLAME OVER INDIA(1960, Brit.), p; AMOROUS ADVENTURES OF MOLL FLANDERS, THE(1965), p
Marcoreta Hellman
WOMAN IN RED, THE(1935), tech adv; GIRL RUSH, THE(1955)
Marcoretta Hellman
WOMAN IN RED, THE(1935)
Marcorita Hellman
ROOM FOR ONE MORE(1952)
Melissa Hellman
TWO-LANE BLACKTOP(1971)
Miriam Hellman
HAPPY DAYS(1930)
Monte Hellman
BEAST FROM THE HAUNTED CAVE(1960), d; TERROR, THE(1963), p&d; BACK DOOR TO HELL(1964), d; FLIGHT TO FURY(1966, U.S./Phil.), d, w; RIDE IN THE WHIRLWIND(1966), p, d, ed; WILD ANGELS, THE(1966), ed; CHRISTIAN LICORICE STORE, THE(1971); SHOOTING, THE(1971), p, d, ed; TWO-LANE BLACKTOP(1971), d, ed; BORN TO KILL(1975), d; KILLER ELITE, THE(1975), ed; CHINA 9, LIBERTY 37(1978, Ital.), d; TARGET: HARRY(1980), ed
Oliver Hellman
BEYOND THE DOOR(1975, Ital./U.S.), d
Oliver Hellman [Olvidio Assonitis]
TENTACLES(1977, Ital.), d
Peter Hellman
VON RYAN'S EXPRESS(1965)
Richard Hellman
THE DIRTY GAME(1966, Fr./Ital./Ger.), p
Sam Hellman
GOOD DAME(1934), w; LITTLE MISS MARKER(1934), w; MURDER AT THE VANITIES(1934), w; SEARCH FOR BEAUTY(1934), w; THIRTY-DAY PRINCESS(1934), w; CAPTAIN JANUARY(1935), w; COUNTY CHAIRMAN, THE(1935), w; DARING YOUNG MAN, THE(1935), w; IN OLD KENTUCKY(1935), w; LOTTERY LOVER(1935), w; TWO FISTED(1935), w; MESSAGE TO GARCIA, A(1936), w; POOR LITTLE RICH GIRL(1936), w; REUNION(1936), w; SLAVE SHIP(1937), w; BARONESS AND THE BUTLER, THE(1938), w; WE'RE GOING TO BE RICH(1938, Brit.), w; FRONTIER MARSHAL(1939), w; HERE I AM A STRANGER(1939), w; STANLEY AND LIVINGSTONE(1939), w; THREE MUSKETEERS, THE(1939), w; HE MARRIED HIS WIFE(1940), w; RETURN OF FRANK JAMES, THE(1940), w; DOUGHGIRLS, THE(1944), w; SHINE ON, HARVEST MOON(1944), w; HORN BLOWS AT MID-

NIGHT, THE(1945), w; DARK HORSE, THE(1946), w; MY DARLING CLEMEN-
TINE(1946), w; RUNAROUND, THE(1946), w; PIRATES OF MONTEREY(1947), w;
SORROWFUL JONES(1949), w
Silents
   CASEY AT THE BAT(1927), t
Samuel Hellman
   IT'S A SMALL WORLD(1935), w
Peter Hellmann
   ANIMALS, THE(1971)
Karl Hellmer
   MARRIAGE IN THE SHADOWS(1948, Ger.); CASTLE, THE(1969, Ger.)
Fred Hellmich
   ARISTOCATS, THE(1970), anim; ROBIN HOOD(1973), anim
Kalus Hellmold
   BRIDGE, THE(1961, Ger.)
Gunnar Hellstrom
   RETURN TO PEYTON PLACE(1961); JUST ONCE MORE(1963, Swed.), d; NAME OF
THE GAME IS KILL, THE(1968), d
Klaus Hellwig
   PROVIDENCE(1977, Fr.), p
George Hellyer, Jr.
   RIVERRUN(1968)
Anne Helm
   DESIRE IN THE DUST(1960); COUCH, THE(1962); FOLLOW THAT DREAM(1962);
INTERNS, THE(1962); MAGIC SWORD, THE(1962); SWINGIN' MAIDEN, THE(1963,
Brit.); HONEYMOON HOTEL(1964); READY FOR THE PEOPLE(1964); MOTHER
GOOSE A GO-GO(1966); NIGHTMARE IN WAX(1969); HIDE IN PLAIN SIGHT(1980)
Misc. Talkies
   UNKISSED BRIDE(1966)
Brigitte Helm
   DAUGHTER OF EVIL(1930, Ger.); BLUE DANUBE(1932, Brit.); MISTRESS OF
ATLANTIS, THE(1932, Ger.); GOLD(1934, Ger.)
Silents
   METROPOLIS(1927, Ger.)
Misc. Silents
   AT THE EDGE OF THE WORLD(1929, Ger.); L'ARGENT(1929, Fr.)
Carina Helm
   FLIGHT FROM VIENNA(1956, Brit.)
Fay Helm
   GIRL WITH IDEAS, A(1937); MERRY-GO-ROUND OF 1938(1937); SONG OF THE
CITY(1937); BLONDIE(1938); I AM THE LAW(1938); MIDNIGHT INTRUDER(1938);
PECK'S BAD BOY WITH THE CIRCUS(1938); RACKET BUSTERS(1938); BLONDIE
BRINGS UP BABY(1939); DARK VICTORY(1939); LIGHT THAT FAILED, THE(1939);
OUR LEADING CITIZEN(1939); ABE LINCOLN IN ILLINOIS(1940); BLONDIE HAS
SERVANT TROUBLE(1940); BLONDIE ON A BUDGET(1940); CHILD IS BORN,
A(1940); DANCING ON A DIME(1940); DR. KILDARE'S STRANGE CASE(1940);
KITTY FOYLE(1940); LITTLE ORVIE(1940); UNTAMED(1940); WOMEN WITHOUT
NAMES(1940); MILLION DOLLAR BABY(1941); THERE'S MAGIC IN MUSIC(1941);
TWO IN A TAXI(1941); WAGONS ROLL AT NIGHT, THE(1941); WOLF MAN,
THE(1941); GIVE OUT, SISTERS(1942); HALF WAY TO SHANGHAI(1942); LIFE
BEGINS AT 8:30(1942); NIGHT MONSTER(1942); WINGS FOR THE EAGLE(1942);
YOU CAN'T ESCAPE FOREVER(1942); CALLING DR. DEATH(1943); CAPTIVE WILD
WOMAN(1943); HERS TO HOLD(1943); HONEYMOON LODGE(1943); MOONLIGHT
IN VERMONT(1943); YOUNG AND WILLING(1943); LADIES COURAGEOUS(1944);
LADY IN THE DARK(1944); MADEMOISELLE FIFI(1944); ONE BODY TOO MA-
NY(1944); PHANTOM LADY(1944); DANGEROUS INTRUDER(1945); SON OF LAS-
SIE(1945); SONG TO REMEMBER, A(1945); LOCKET, THE(1946); SISTER
KENNY(1946); THAT BRENNAN GIRL(1946)
Faye Helm
   FALCON IN SAN FRANCISCO, THE(1945)
Frances Helm
   NEVER WAVE AT A WAC(1952); REVOLT AT FORT LARAMIE(1957); UGLY
AMERICAN, THE(1963); LITTLE SEX, A(1982)
Harry Helm
   ALRAUNE(1952, Ger.)
Kathleen Helm
   OTLEY(1969, Brit.)
Levon Helm
   COAL MINER'S DAUGHTER(1980); RIGHT STUFF, THE(1983)
Lucy Helm
   SEEDS OF FREEDOM(1943, USSR)
Norie Helm
   PURPLE HAZE(1982)
Peter Helm
   LONGEST DAY, THE(1962); INSIDE DAISY CLOVER(1965)
Ryan Helm
   TAPS(1981)
Tiffany Helm
1984
   HARD TO HOLD(1984)
Tom Helm
   AMONG HUMAN WOLVES(1940 Brit.)
Andy Helman
Misc. Talkies
   FRIDAY ON MY MIND(1970)
Geoffrey Helman
   LAST SAFARI, THE(1967, Brit.), prod d
Henri Helman
1984
   WHERE IS PARSIFAL?(1984, Brit.), d
Kathleen Helme
   OH! WHAT A LOVELY WAR(1969, Brit.)
Heidi Helmen
   PURPLE HAZE(1982)
Karl Helmer
   LONGEST DAY, THE(1962), spec eff
R.L. Helmer
   SILENT RUNNING(1972), spec eff

Rich Helmer
   TOURIST TRAP, THE(1979), spec eff
Richard Helmer
   RACE WITH THE DEVIL(1975), spec eff; RIVER NIGER, THE(1976), spec eff;
ROLLING THUNDER(1977), spec eff; HIGH-BALLIN'(1978), spec eff
Richard O. Helmer
   SILENT RUNNING(1972), spec eff
Rick Helmer
   SWEET JESUS, PREACHER MAN(1973), spec eff
Peter Helmers
   DAYS OF GLORY(1944); MASK OF DIMITRIOS, THE(1944); TAMPICO(1944); 'TILL
WE MEET AGAIN(1944); SON OF LASSIE(1945)
Frans Helmerson
   FANNY AND ALEXANDER(1983, Swed./Fr./Ger.), m
Emad Helmey
   FRANCES(1982), set d
Katerina Helmi
   RED LANTERNS(1965, Gr.)
Paul H. Helmick
   CULPEPPER CATTLE COMPANY, THE(1972), p
Paul Helmick
   TEENAGE THUNDER(1957), d; THUNDER IN CAROLINA(1960), d
Florence Helminger
Silents
   PLEASURE GARDEN, THE(1925, Brit./Ger.)
Bill Helmintoller
1984
   NINJA III–THE DOMINATION(1984)
E. Helmke-Dassel
   JAZZBAND FIVE, THE(1932, Ger,)
Katherine Helmond
   BELIEVE IN ME(1971); HOSPITAL, THE(1971); HINDENBURG, THE(1975); BABY
BLUE MARINE(1976); FAMILY PLOT(1976); TIME BANDITS(1981, Brit.)
Arthur Helmore
Silents
   JOYOUS ADVENTURES OF ARISTIDE PUJOL, THE(1920, Brit.); KIPPS(1921, Brit.)
Tom Helmore
   RAISE THE ROOF(1930), m; WHITE CARGO(1930, Brit.); HOUSE OF UNREST,
THE(1931, Brit.); BARTON MYSTERY, THE(1932, Brit.); MY WIFE'S FAMILY(1932,
Brit.); KING'S CUP, THE(1933, Brit.); UP FOR THE DERBY(1933, Brit.); FEATHERED
SERPENT, THE(1934, Brit.); SCOOP, THE(1934, Brit.); SONG AT EVENTIDE(1934,
Brit.); VIRGINIA'S HUSBAND(1934, Brit.); RIGHT AGE TO MARRY, THE(1935, Brit.);
RIVERSIDE MURDER(1935, Brit.); LUCK OF THE TURF(1936, Brit.); SECRET
AGENT, THE(1936, Brit.); MERRY COMES TO STAY(1937, Brit.); EASY RICHES(1938,
Brit.); PAID IN ERROR(1938, Brit.); SHADOWED EYES(1939, Brit.); TREACHERY ON
THE HIGH SEAS(1939, Brit.); THREE DARING DAUGHTERS(1948); SCENE OF THE
CRIME(1949); SHADOW ON THE WALL(1950); LET'S DO IT AGAIN(1953); TROUBLE
ALONG THE WAY(1953); LUCY GALLANT(1955); TENDER TRAP, THE(1955); DE-
SIGNING WOMAN(1957); THIS COULD BE THE NIGHT(1957); VERTIGO(1958);
COUNT YOUR BLESSINGS(1959); MAN IN THE NET, THE(1959); TIME MACHINE,
THE(1960, Brit./U.S.); ADVISE AND CONSENT(1962); FLIPPER'S NEW ADVEN-
TURE(1964)
Bobby Helms
   CASE AGAINST BROOKLYN, THE(1958)
Jim Helms
   NIGHT CREATURE(1979), m
Lyne Helms
   20TH CENTURY OZ(1977, Aus.), p
Tim Helms
   HOW DO I LOVE THEE?(1970), md
Joyce D. Helmus
   STRIPES(1981)
Osvald Helmuth
   HUNGER(1968, Den./Norway/Swed.)
Emad Helmy
   ON GOLDEN POND(1981), set d; STRANGE INVADERS(1983), art d
Victor Helou
   HOT STUFF(1979)
Joe Helper
   JOHNNY O'CLOCK(1947)
Todd Helper
   FALLING IN LOVE AGAIN(1980)
David Helpern, Jr.
   SOMETHING SHORT OF PARADISE(1979), d
David M. Helpern, Jr.
   BETWEEN THE LINES(1977), w
Robert Helpmann
   ONE OF OUR AIRCRAFT IS MISSING(1942, Brit.); CARAVAN(1946, Brit.); HENRY
V(1946, Brit.); RED SHOES, THE(1948, Brit.), a, ch; TALES OF HOFFMANN,
THE(1951, Brit.); IRON PETTICOAT, THE(1956, Brit.); BIG MONEY, THE(1962, Brit.);
55 DAYS AT PEKING(1963); SOLDIER'S TALE, THE(1964, Brit.); QUILLER MEMO-
RANDUM, THE(1966, Brit.); CHITTY CHITTY BANG BANG(1968, Brit.); ALICE'S
ADVENTURES IN WONDERLAND(1972, Brit.); DON QUIXOTE(1973, Aus.), a, d;
PATRICK(1979, Aus.); MANGO TREE, THE(1981, Aus.)
1984
   SECOND TIME LUCKY(1984, Aus./New Zealand)
Sheila Helpmann
   GETTING OF WISDOM, THE(1977, Aus.)
Misc. Talkies
   IMAGE OF DEATH(1977, Brit.)
M. Helprin
   FORCED LANDING(1935), w
Henry E. Helseth
   STATE PENITENTIARY(1950), w
Henry Edward Helseth
   CRY OF THE CITY(1948), w; OUTSIDE THE WALL(1950), d&w
Rita Helsham
   MURDER ON THE SET(1936, Brit.)

Helmut Helsig
OUR DAILY BREAD(1950, Ger.)
Bob Helson
Misc. Talkies
SORCERESS(1983)
Eugene Heltai
LADY ESCAPES, THE(1937), w
J. R. Helton
WAY OUT(1966)
Jo Helton
YELLOW CANARY, THE(1963); YOUNG SWINGERS, THE(1963); READY FOR THE
PEOPLE(1964); SLENDER THREAD, THE(1965)
Percy Helton
MIRACLE ON 34TH STREET, THE(1947); CALL NORTHSIDE 777(1948); CHICKEN
EVERY SUNDAY(1948); HAZARD(1948); LARCENY(1948); LET'S LIVE AGAIN(1948);
THAT WONDERFUL URGE(1948); ABBOTT AND COSTELLO MEET THE KILLER,
BORIS KARLOFF(1949); CRISS CROSS(1949); CROOKED WAY, THE(1949); FREE
FOR ALL(1949); LUST FOR GOLD(1949); MY FRIEND IRMA(1949); RED, HOT AND
BLUE(1949); SET-UP, THE(1949); THIEVES' HIGHWAY(1949); COPPER CA-
NYON(1950); CYRANO DE BERGERAC(1950); FANCY PANTS(1950); HARBOR OF
MISSING MEN(1950); LIFE OF HER OWN, A(1950); SECRET FURY, THE(1950); SUN
SETS AT DAWN, THE(1950); UNDER MEXICALI STARS(1950); WABASH AVE-
NUE(1950); BAREFOOT MAILMAN, THE(1951); CHAIN OF CIRCUMSTANCE(1951);
DARLING, HOW COULD YOU!(1951); NIGHT INTO MORNING(1951); THREE GUYS
NAMED MIKE(1951); BELLE OF NEW YORK, THE(1952); GIRL IN EVERY PORT,
A(1952); I DREAM OF JEANIE(1952); AMBUSH AT TOMAHAWK GAP(1953); CALL
ME MADAM(1953); DOWN LAREDO WAY(1953); HOW TO MARRY A MIL-
LIONAIRE(1953); RIDE, VAQUERO!(1953); ROBE, THE(1953); SHE'S BACK ON
BROADWAY(1953); WICKED WOMAN(1953); ABOUT MRS. LESLIE(1954); LUCKY
ME(1954); STAR IS BORN, A(1954); WHITE CHRISTMAS(1954); 20,000 LEAGUES
UNDER THE SEA(1954); CRASHOUT(1955); DIANE(1955); JAIL BUSTERS(1955);
KISS ME DEADLY(1955); NO MAN'S WOMAN(1955); TRIAL(1955); FURY AT GUN-
SIGHT PASS(1956); TERROR AT MIDNIGHT(1956); JAILHOUSE ROCK(1957); LOOK-
ING FOR DANGER(1957); PHANTOM STAGECOACH, THE(1957); SHAKE, RATTLE,
AND ROCK!(1957); SPOOK CHASERS(1957); THIS COULD BE THE NIGHT(1957);
RALLY 'ROUND THE FLAG, BOYS!(1958); MUSIC MAN, THE(1962); RIDE THE
HIGH COUNTRY(1962); FOUR FOR TEXAS(1963); WHEELER DEALERS, THE(1963);
HUSH... HUSH, SWEET CHARLOTTE(1964); SONS OF KATIE ELDER, THE(1965);
ZEBRA IN THE KITCHEN(1965); DON'T WORRY, WE'LL THINK OF A TITLE(1966);
HEAD(1968)
Silents
SILVER WINGS(1922); OFFENDERS, THE(1924)
Misc. Silents
FLOWER OF FAITH, THE(1916)
Carol Helvey
CHINA SYNDROME, THE(1979)
James Helvick
BEAT THE DEVIL(1953), w
Lisa Helwig
LA HABANERA(1937, Ger.); INTERLUDE(1957); TIME TO LOVE AND A TIME TO
DIE, A(1958)
Annesley Hely
Misc. Silents
WINDING ROAD, THE(1920)
Gerald Hely
SPYLARKS(1965, Brit.)
Gerard Hely
MOHAMMAD, MESSENGER OF GOD(1976, Lebanon/Brit.)
Richard Helzberg
CARDIAC ARREST(1980), p
Narie Hem
DRAGON SKY(1964, Fr.)
Roman Hemala
FIFTH HORSEMAN IS FEAR, THE(1968, Czech.)
Oscar Hemberg
ON THE SUNNYSIDE(1936, Swed.), w
Victor Hembrow
GUNMAN HAS ESCAPED, A(1948, Brit.), art d
Carola Hembus
GERMAN SISTERS, THE(1982, Ger.)
Joe Hembus
NOT RECONCILED, OR "ONLY VIOLENCE HELPS WHERE IT RULES"(1969, Ger.)
John Hemel
INVISIBLE AVENGER, THE(1958), ed; NEW ORLEANS AFTER DARK(1958), ed
Roger Hemen
FOOTLIGHT SERENADE(1942), art d
Alfred Heming
Misc. Silents
MY COUNTRY FIRST(1916); SOCIETY WOLVES(1916)
Jack Heming
SCOOP, THE(1934, Brit.), w
Richard Heming
HELL CAT, THE(1934)
Violet Heming
ALMOST MARRIED(1932); MAN WHO PLAYED GOD, THE(1932)
Silents
RUNNING FIGHT, THE(1915); COST, THE(1920)
Misc. Silents
DANGER TRAIL, THE(1917); JUDGEMENT HOUSE, THE(1917); TURN OF THE
WHEEL, THE(1918); EVERYWOMAN(1919); WHEN THE DESERT CALLS(1922)
Louis Heminger
PONY SOLDIER(1952); TREASURE OF THE GOLDEN CONDOR(1953)
Barbara Hemingway
ROUSTABOUT(1964)
Carl Hemingway
YOICKS!(1932, Brit.)
Carole Hemingway
MANITOU, THE(1978); METEOR(1979); ROMANTIC COMEDY(1983)

Ernest Hemingway
FAREWELL TO ARMS, A(1932), w; FOR WHOM THE BELL TOLLS(1943), w; TO
HAVE AND HAVE NOT(1944), w; KILLERS, THE(1946), w; MACOMBER AFFAIR,
THE(1947), w; BREAKING POINT, THE(1950), w; UNDER MY SKIN(1950), w; FARE-
WELL TO ARMS, A(1957), w; SUN ALSO RISES, THE(1957), w; GUN RUNNERS,
THE(1958), w; OLD MAN AND THE SEA, THE(1958), w; ADVENTURES OF A
YOUNG MAN(1962), w; KILLERS, THE(1964), w; ISLANDS IN THE STREAM(1977),
w
Frank Hemingway
PRAIRIE, THE(1948); FIVE FINGERS(1952)
Gayle Hemingway
Misc. Talkies
NIGHTMARE COUNTY(1977)
Helen Hemingway
PATRICK(1979, Aus.)
Joan Hemingway
ROSEBUD(1975), w
Leigh Hemingway
JUD(1971)
Margaux Hemingway
LIPSTICK(1976); KILLER FISH(1979, Ital./Braz.); THEY CALL ME BRUCE(1982)
1984
OVER THE BROOKLYN BRIDGE(1984)
Marie Hemingway
Misc. Silents
SECOND MRS. TANQUERAY, THE(1916, Brit.); MASTER OF MEN, A(1917, Brit.)
Mariel Hemingway
LIPSTICK(1976); MANHATTAN(1979); PERSONAL BEST(1982); STAR 80(1983)
Pat Hemingway
MY BLOODY VALENTINE(1981, Can.)
Richard Hemingway
SOCIETY FEVER(1935); WIFE VERSUS SECRETARY(1936)
Misc. Talkies
WOMAN CONDEMNED(1934)
Hemlock
SWAP MEET(1979), m
Edouard Hemme
HANDS OF ORLAC, THE(1964, Brit./Fr.)
Martin Hemme
DAS BOOT(1982)
Edward L. Hemmer
Misc. Silents
ORPHAN SALLY(1922), d; SUNSHINE HARBOR(1922), d
Andre Hemmers
WALK, DON'T RUN(1966)
Alfred Hemming
Misc. Silents
CHIMES, THE(1914); MYSTERY OF EDWIN DROOD, THE(1914); FLAME OF
PASSION, THE(1915); SONG OF SIXPENCE, A(1917)
Lindy Hemming
1984
COMFORT AND JOY(1984, Brit.), cos
Percy Hemming
MOZART(1940, Brit.)
David Hemmings
RAINBOW JACKET, THE(1954, Brit.); HEART WITHIN, THE(1957, Brit.); SAINT
JOAN(1957); IN THE WAKE OF A STRANGER(1960, Brit.); WIND OF CHANGE,
THE(1961, Brit.); MURDER CAN BE DEADLY(1963, Brit.); NO TREE IN THE
STREET(1964, Brit.); SING AND SWING(1964, Brit.); SOME PEOPLE(1964, Brit.); BE
MY GUEST(1965, Brit.); TWO LEFT FEET(1965, Brit.); BLOW-UP(1966, Brit.); GIRL
GETTERS, THE(1966, Brit.); CAMELOT(1967); EYE OF THE DEVIL(1967, Brit.);
BARBARELLA(1968, Fr./Ital.); CHARGE OF THE LIGHT BRIGADE, THE(1968, Brit.);
LONG DAY'S DYING, THE(1968, Brit.); ONLY WHEN I LARF(1968, Brit.); ALFRED
THE GREAT(1969, Brit.); BEST HOUSE IN LONDON, THE(1969, Brit.); WALKING
STICK, THE(1970, Brit.); FRAGMENT OF FEAR(1971, Brit.); LOVE MACHINE,
THE(1971); UNMAN, WITTERING AND ZIGO(1971, Brit.); RUNNING SCARED(1972,
Brit.), d, w; FOURTEEN, THE(1973, Brit.), d; VOICES(1973, Brit.); JUGGER-
NAUT(1974, Brit.); MR. QUILP(1975, Brit.); DEEP RED(1976, Ital.); ISLANDS IN THE
STREAM(1977); SQUEEZE, THE(1977, Brit.); BLOOD RELATIVES(1978, Fr./Can.);
CROSSED SWORDS(1978); POWER PLAY(1978, Brit./Can.); JUST A GIGOLO(1979,
Ger.), a, d; MURDER BY DECREE(1979, Brit.); THIRST(1979, Aus.); BEYOND REA-
SONABLE DOUBT(1980, New Zeal.); HARLEQUIN(1980, Aus.); SURVIVOR(1980,
Aus.), d; DISAPPEARANCE, THE(1981, Brit./Can.), a, p; MAN, WOMAN AND
CHILD(1983)
1984
TREASURE OF THE YANKEE ZEPHYR(1984), p, d
Myra D. Hemmings
Misc. Talkies
GO DOWN DEATH(1944)
Louis Hemon
LOVERS, HAPPY LOVERS!(1955, Brit.), w; NAKED HEART, THE(1955, Brit.), w
Hempel
M(1933, Ger.)
Anoushka Hempel
ON HER MAJESTY'S SECRET SERVICE(1969, Brit.); SCARS OF DRACULA,
THE(1970, Brit.)
Anouska Hempel
SWEET SUZY(1973); TIFFANY JONES(1976)
Misc. Talkies
BLACKSNAKE(1973)
Elizabeth Hempel
Misc. Silents
CHAMBER OF HORRORS(1929, Brit.)
Frank Hemphill
CIRCUS KID, THE(1928); TOAST OF NEW YORK, THE(1937); MISSION TO
MOSCOW(1943)
Silents
YELLOW STAIN, THE(1922); NON-STOP FLIGHT, THE(1926)

Ray Hemphill
THIS PROPERTY IS CONDEMNED(1966); BABY MAKER, THE(1970); 9/30/55(1977)
Simpson Hemphill
ODE TO BILLY JOE(1976)
Peter Hempson
MRS. GIBBONS' BOYS(1962, Brit.)
David Hempstead
FINISHING SCHOOL(1934), w; VILLAGE TALE(1935), p; STRAIGHT, PLACE AND SHOW(1938), p; IT COULD HAPPEN TO YOU(1939), p; KITTY FOYLE(1940), p; JOAN OF PARIS(1942), p; FLIGHT FOR FREEDOM(1943), p; MR. LUCKY(1943), p; SKY'S THE LIMIT, THE(1943), p; TENDER COMRADE(1943), p; NONE BUT THE LONELY HEART(1944), p; HELL AND HIGH WATER(1954), w; KING AND FOUR QUEENS, THE(1956), p
David Hempstead, Jr.
MANHATTAN TOWER(1932), w
Hannah Hempstead
LITTLE DRAGONS, THE(1980), p; LOSIN' IT(1983), p
Guy Hemric
MUSCLE BEACH PARTY(1964); PAJAMA PARTY(1964); HOW TO STUFF A WILD BIKINI(1965); DEVIL'S ANGELS(1967), m/l Mike Curb; FIVE THE HARD WAY(1969), m; SKI FEVER(1969, U.S./Aust./Czech.), m
Arthur Hemsley
GLENROWAN AFFAIR, THE(1951, Aus.)
Estelle Hemsley
EDGE OF THE CITY(1957); GREEN MANSIONS(1959); TAKE A GIANT STEP(1959); LEECH WOMAN, THE(1960); AMERICA, AMERICA(1963); BABY, THE RAIN MUST FALL(1965)
Sherman Hemsley
LOVE AT FIRST BITE(1979)
Joyce Hemson
20,000 POUNDS KISS, THE(1964, Brit.); LEATHER BOYS, THE(1965, Brit.); DRACULA-PRINCE OF DARKNESS(1966, Brit.); ISLAND OF TERROR(1967, Brit.)
Percy Hemus
Silents
RENO(1923)
Joseph E. Henaberry
RED HOT SPEED ½(1929), d
Joseph E. Henabery
RIVER WOMAN, THE(1928), d; CLEAR THE DECKS(1929), d; LEATHER BURNERS, THE(1943), d
Misc. Silents
HELLSHIP BRONSON(1928), d; SAILORS' WIVES(1928), d; CLEAR THE DECKS(1929), d
Joseph Henabery
LIGHT FINGERS(1929), d; LOVE TRADER(1930), p, d
Silents
BIRTH OF A NATION, THE(1915); INTOLERANCE(1916); MAN FROM PAINTED POST, THE(1917), d; SAY! YOUNG FELLOW(1918), d&w; HIS MAJESTY THE AMERICAN(1919), d&w; INFERIOR SEX, THE(1920), d; BREWSTER'S MILLIONS(1921), d; DON'T CALL ME LITTLE GIRL(1921), d; HER WINNING WAY(1921), d; MAKING A MAN(1922), d; MISSING MILLIONS(1922), d; NORTH OF THE RIO GRANDE(1922), d; WHILE SATAN SLEEPS(1922), d; GENTLEMAN OF LEISURE, A(1923), d; SIXTY CENTS AN HOUR(1923), d; STEPHEN STEPS OUT(1923), d; TIGER'S CLAW, THE(1923), d; SAINTED DEVIL, A(1924), d; STRANGER, THE(1924), d; COBRA(1925), d; PLAY SAFE(1927), d
Misc. Silents
CHILDREN OF THE FEUD(1916), d; HER OFFICAL FATHERS(1917), d; FOURTEENTH MAN, THE(1920), d; LIFE OF THE PARTY, THE(1920), d; LOVE MADNESS(1920), d; CALL OF THE NORTH, THE(1921), d; MOONLIGHT AND HONEYSUCKLE(1921), d; TRAVELING SALESMAN, THE(1921), d; HER OWN MONEY(1922), d; MAN UNCONQUERABLE, THE(1922), d; GUILTY ONE, THE(1924), d; TONGUES OF FLAME(1924), d; PINCH HITTER, THE(1925), d; BROADWAY BOOB, THE(1926), d; MEET THE PRINCE(1926), d; SHIPWRECKED(1926), d; LONESOME LADIES(1927), d; SEE YOU IN JAIL(1927), d; UNITED STATES SMITH(1928), d; QUITTER, THE(1929), d; RIVER WOMAN(1929), d
Ralph Henabery
SPEED DEVILS(1935), d
James Henaghan
CHRISTMAS KID, THE(1968, U.S., Span.), w; MADIGAN'S MILLIONS(1970, Span./Ital), w
Jim Henaghan
STOP TRAIN 349(1964, Fr./Ital./Ger.), w; FICKLE FINGER OF FATE, THE(1967, Span./U.S.), w; TALL WOMEN, THE(1967, Aust./Ital./Span.), w
Gaspar Henaine
LOS ASTRONAUTAS(1960, Mex.); LOS INVISIBLES(1961, Mex.)
George Henare
1984
SILENT ONE, THE(1984, New Zealand)
Joe Henaway
Silents
ALL WOMAN(1918)
John Hench
MAKE MINE MUSIC(1946), art d; 20,000 LEAGUES UNDER THE SEA(1954), spec eff
Richard Hench
SCALPS(1983)
Misc. Talkies
BIO-HAZARD(1984)
John Henchley
WAY OF A GAUCHO(1952)
Jean-Marc Henchoz
1984
L'ARGENT(1984, Fr./Switz.), p
Paul Henckels
HIS MAJESTY, KING BALLYHOO(1931, Ger.); RASPUTIN(1932, Ger.); INHERITANCE IN PRETORIA(1936, Ger.); TESTAMENT OF DR. MABUSE, THE(1943, Ger.); CONFESSIONS OF FELIX KRULL, THE(1957, Ger.); DANCING HEART, THE(1959, Ger.)

Hubert Hend
THANK YOUR LUCKY STARS(1943)
Kenneth Hendel
DIE SCREAMING, MARIANNE(1970, Brit.); MAN OF VIOLENCE(1970, Brit.); RECKONING, THE(1971, Brit.)
Nehama Hendel
PILLAR OF FIRE, THE(1963, Israel)
Paolo Hendel
NIGHT OF THE SHOOTING STARS, THE(1982, Ital.)
Linda Hendelman
DARK SIDE OF TOMORROW, THE(1970)
Frederique Hender
CHLOE IN THE AFTERNOON(1972, Fr.)
Ed Hendershot
FOURTH HORSEMAN, THE(1933)
Enid Hendershot
STRAIGHT TIME(1978)
Eric Hendershot
TAKE DOWN(1979), w
A.C. Henderson
ARIZONA GUNFIGHTER(1937)
Abbi Henderson
UNHOLY ROLLERS(1972)
Al Henderson
SERPICO(1973)
Al C. Henderson
SCARLET LETTER, THE(1934)
Albert Henderson
COOGAN'S BLUFF(1968); MADIGAN(1968); WHAT'S SO BAD ABOUT FEELING GOOD?(1968); PURSUIT OF HAPPINESS, THE(1971); GREASER'S PALACE(1972); SUPER COPS, THE(1974); MODERN ROMANCE(1981); POSTMAN ALWAYS RINGS TWICE, THE(1981)
Anne Henderson
TERROR TRAIN(1980, Can.), ed
Betty Henderson
GORBALS STORY, THE(1950, Brit.); HOME TO DANGER(1951, Brit.); TWILIGHT WOMEN(1953, Brit.); HIGH AND DRY(1954, Brit.); THIRTY NINE STEPS, THE(1960, Brit.); UPSTAIRS AND DOWNSTAIRS(1961, Brit.)
Bill Henderson
UNCLE HARRY(1945); MOONLIGHT IN VERMONT(1943); ATTACK ON THE IRON COAST(1968, U.S./Brit.); TROUBLE MAN(1972); CORNBREAD, EARL AND ME(1975); MOTHER, JUGS & SPEED(1976); FIRE SALE(1977); INSIDE MOVES(1980); CONTINENTAL DIVIDE(1981); GET CRAZY(1983)
1984
ADVENTURES OF BUCKAROO BANZAI: ACROSS THE 8TH DIMENSION, THE(1984); FEAR CITY(1984); FLETCH(1984)
Billy Henderson
THAT HAGEN GIRL(1947)
Brenda Henderson
MY SON, MY SON!(1940); INTERNATIONAL SQUADRON(1941)
C. Henderson
FOLLOW THE LEADER(1930)
Catherine Henderson
BALL OF FIRE(1941); VERY YOUNG LADY, A(1941)
Charles Henderson
FOOTLIGHT SERENADE(1942), md; GANG'S ALL HERE, THE(1943), md; HELLO, FRISCO, HELLO(1943), md; SEEDS OF FREEDOM(1943, USSR); SWEET ROSIE O'GRADY(1943), md; WINTERTIME(1943), md; FOUR JILLS IN A JEEP(1944), md; GREENWICH VILLAGE(1944), m; IRISH EYES ARE SMILING(1944), md; PIN UP GIRL(1944), md; SOMETHING FOR THE BOYS(1944), md; SWEET AND LOWDOWN(1944), md; DIAMOND HORSESHOE(1945), md; DOLL FACE(1945), md; DOLLY SISTERS, THE(1945), m, md; NOB HILL(1945), md; STATE FAIR(1945), md; WHERE DO WE GO FROM HERE?(1945), md; DO YOU LOVE ME?(1946), md; BISHOP'S WIFE, THE(1947), art d; MOTHER WORE TIGHTS(1947), md; SHOCKING MISS PILGRIM, THE(1947), md; I'LL CRY TOMORROW(1955), md
Chuck Henderson
OPERATION DAMES(1959)
Dave Henderson
Misc. Talkies
BYE-BYE BUDDY(1929)
Del Henderson
EASIEST WAY, THE(1931); BOLERO(1934); BOTTOMS UP(1934); LEMON DROP KID, THE(1934); LONE COWBOY(1934); MRS. WIGGS OF THE CABBAGE PATCH(1934); NOTORIOUS SOPHIE LANG, THE(1934); SEARCH FOR BEAUTY(1934); YOU'RE TELLING ME(1934); DARING YOUNG MAN, THE(1935); DIAMOND JIM(1935); MYSTERY MAN, THE(1935); STEAMBOAT ROUND THE BEND(1935); THIS IS THE LIFE(1935); OUR RELATIONS(1936); POPPY(1936); LOVE IN A BUNGALOW(1937); ARSENE LUPIN RETURNS(1938); GOODBYE BROADWAY(1938); FRONTIER MARSHAL(1939); IF I HAD MY WAY(1940); LITTLE ORVIE(1940); YOU CAN'T FOOL YOUR WIFE(1940); YOUNG PEOPLE(1940); ONCE UPON A HONEYMOON(1942); WILSON(1944); STATE OF THE UNION(1948); NEPTUNE'S DAUGHTER(1949); ONCE MORE, MY DARLING(1949)
Silents
KENNEDY SQUARE(1916), d; KISS, THE(1916), d; IMPOSTER, THE(1918), d; SURE FIRE FLINT(1922), d; ONE LAW FOR THE WOMAN(1924), d; POWER OF THE PRESS, THE(1928); RILEY THE COP(1928)
Misc. Silents
REJUVINATION OF AUNT MARY, THE(1914); DIVORCONS(1915); ROLLING STONES(1916), d; GIRL LIKE THAT, A(1917), d; BELOVED BLACKMAILER, THE(1918), d; PLUNGER, THE(1920), d; DYNAMITE ALLEN(1921), d; BROKEN SILENCE, THE(1922), d; RAMBLING RANGER, THE(1927), d
Dell Henderson
HIT THE DECK(1930); SINS OF THE CHILDREN(1930); NEWLY RICH(1931); FROM HELL TO HEAVEN(1933); I HAVE LIVED(1933); RAINBOW OVER BROADWAY(1933); TOO MUCH HARMONY(1933); MARINES ARE COMING, THE(1935); RUGGLES OF RED GAP(1935); HITCH HIKE LADY(1936); MESSAGE TO GARCIA, A(1936); TEXAS RANGERS, THE(1936); ARTISTS AND MODELS(1937); HIGH, WIDE AND HANDSOME(1937); MAKE WAY FOR TOMORROW(1937); MEN WITH WINGS(1938); REBELLIOUS DAUGHTERS(1938); FIFTH AVENUE GIRL(1939); LOVE AFFAIR(1939); STRANGER ON THE THIRD FLOOR(1940); LOOK WHO'S

LAUGHING(1941); MAJOR AND THE MINOR, THE(1942); DIXIE(1943); DU BARRY WAS A LADY(1943); LOUISA(1950)

Silents
LOVE IN A HURRY(1919), d; JACQUELINE, OR BLAZING BARRIERS(1923), d; GAMBLING WIVES(1924), d; CROWD, THE(1928); SHOW PEOPLE(1928)

Misc. Silents
CONEY ISLAND PRINCESS, A(1916), d; BEAUTIFUL ADVENTURE, THE(1917), d; OUTCAST(1917), d; PLEASE HELP EMILY(1917), d; RUNAWAY, THE(1917), d; BY HOOK OR CROOK(1918), d; HER SECOND HUSBAND(1918), d; HITTING THE TRAIL(1918), d; MY WIFE(1918), d; ROAD TO FRANCE, THE(1918), d; WHO LOVED HIM BEST?(1918), d; COURAGE FOR TWO(1919), d; HIT OR MISS(1919), d; SOCIAL PIRATE, THE(1919), d; THREE GREEN EYES(1919), d; DEAD LINE, THE(1920), d; SERVANT QUESTION, THE(1920), d; SHARK, THE(1920), d; DEAD OR ALIVE(1921), d; GIRL FROM PORCUPINE, THE(1921), d; LOVE BANDIT, THE(1924), d; ACCUSED(1925), d; BAD LANDS, THE(1925), d; DEFEND YOURSELF(1925), d; PURSUED(1925), d; QUICK CHANGE(1925), d; ROUGH STUFF(1925), d; PAY OFF, THE(1926), d; PATSY, THE(1928)

Dick Henderson
GOLDEN DAWN(1930); JUST FOR A SONG(1930, Brit.); MAN FROM BLANKLEY'S, THE(1930); THINGS ARE LOOKING UP(1934, Brit.); MEN OF YESTERDAY(1936, Brit.)

Dick Henderson, Jr.
CAVALCADE(1933); THINGS ARE LOOKING UP(1934, Brit.)

Dickie Henderson
MAKE MINE A MILLION(1965, Brit.)

Dickie Henderson, Jr.
TIME WITHOUT PITY(1957, Brit.)

Don Henderson
LIKE FATHER LIKE SON(1961), ed; WEEKEND WITH THE BABYSITTER(1970), d, w; TOUCH OF SATAN, THE(1971), d; BRANNIGAN(1975, Brit.); GHOUL, THE(1975, Brit.); MARY, MARY, BLOODY MARY(1975, U.S./Mex.), w; LITTLEST HORSE THIEVES, THE(1977); STAR WARS(1977); BIG SLEEP, THE½(1978, Brit.); ISLAND, THE(1980)

Misc. Talkies
BABYSITTER, THE(1969), d; TOUCH OF SATAN, THE(1974), d

Donald Henderson
SLIME PEOPLE, THE(1963), ed; YOUNG SINNER, THE(1965), ed; BORN LOSERS(1967), p

Doug Henderson
OVER 21(1945); CAGE OF EVIL(1960); SANDPIPER, THE(1965); FIREBALL 590(1966)

Douglas Henderson
FLYING LEATHERNECKS(1951); EIGHT IRON MEN(1952); FROM HERE TO ETERNITY(1953); WAR OF THE WORLDS, THE(1953); KING DINOSAUR(1955); DALTON GIRLS, THE(1957); INVASION OF THE SAUCER MEN(1957); NO PLACE TO LAND(1958); SNIPER'S RIDGE(1961); MANCHURIAN CANDIDATE, THE(1962); BLACK ZOO(1963); JOHNNY COOL(1963); AMERICANIZATION OF EMILY, THE(1964); DON'T MAKE WAVES(1967); STAY AWAY, JOE(1968); PENDULUM(1969); ZIGZAG(1970)

Eddie Henderson
Misc. Talkies
ARNOLD'S WRECKING CO.(1973)

Edward Henderson
Silents
NINE AND THREE-FIFTHS SECONDS(1925), ph

Elmore Henderson
PAJAMA GAME, THE(1957)

Florence Henderson
SONG OF NORWAY(1970)

Frances Henderson
CAGED(1950)

Francine Henderson
WHOSE LIFE IS IT ANYWAY?(1981)

Frank Henderson
13 MEN AND A GUN(1938, Brit.); NEUTRAL PORT(1941, Brit.); MASTER OF BANKDAM, THE(1947, Brit.); MEET MR. CALLAGHAN(1954, Brit.); PROFILE(1954, Brit.); TERROR SHIP(1954, Brit.); LINKS OF JUSTICE(1958)

Grace Henderson
Silents
FAMILY CUPBOARD, THE(1915)

Harry Henderson
Misc. Silents
PRINCE OF HIS RACE, THE(1926); TEN NIGHTS IN A BARROOM(1926); SCAR OF SHAME, THE(1927); CHILDREN OF FATE(1928)

Iva Henderson
BULLDOG DRUMMOND COMES BACK(1937)

Ivo Henderson
ROGUES' TAVERN, THE(1936); TOWER OF LONDON(1939); MRS. PARKINGTON(1944)

Jack E. Henderson
WESTBOUND(1959)

Jack Henderson
HEADIN' NORTH(1930); LIFE BEGINS AT 40(1935); TALL MAN RIDING(1955); SUNRISE AT CAMPOBELLO(1960)
Silents
CAPTAIN'S COURAGE, A(1926)
Misc. Silents
LIGHTING BILL(1926); THUNDERBOLT'S TRACKS(1927)

Jane Henderson
BELLES OF ST. TRINIAN'S, THE(1954, Brit.); GREEN SCARF, THE(1954, Brit.); HEART OF THE MATTER, THE(1954, Brit.)

Jessie E. Henderson
Silents
AMATEUR DEVIL, AN(1921), w

Jim Henderson
ROSE BOWL(1936)

Jo Henderson
LIANNA(1983)

Jocko Henderson
JAMBOREE(1957)

Joe Henderson
SOUL OF NIGGER CHARLEY, THE(1973)

John Henderson
PRAIRIE LAW(1940)

John M. Henderson
LUCK OF THE IRISH, THE(1937, Ireland)

Kay Henderson
LITTLE BALLERINA, THE(1951, Brit.)

Lars Henderson
LAST TRAIN FROM GUN HILL(1959)

Laurence Henderson
SITTING TARGET(1972, Brit.), w

Leslie Henderson
STRIPES(1981)

Lil Henderson
CLAUDINE(1974)

Lorna Henderson
BELLES OF ST. TRINIAN'S, THE(1954, Brit.)

Lucius Henderson
Silents
NEW COMMANDMENT, THE(1925)
Misc. Silents
UNDER SOUTHERN SKIES(1915), d; WOMAN WHO LIED, THE(1915), p; HUNTRESS OF MEN, THE(1916), d; STRENGTH OF THE WEAK, THE(1916), d; THROWN TO THE LIONS(1916), d

Luther Henderson
RECESS(1967), m; SLAMS, THE(1973), m

Mame Henderson
HOLIDAY AFFAIR(1949)

Marcia Henderson
ALL I DESIRE(1953); BACK TO GOD'S COUNTRY(1953); GLASS WEB, THE(1953); THUNDER BAY(1953); NAKED ALIBI(1954); CANYON RIVER(1956); NAKED HILLS, THE(1956); WAYWARD GIRL, THE(1957); RIOT IN JUVENILE PRISON(1959); TIMBUKTU(1959); DOG'S BEST FRIEND, A(1960); NATCHEZ TRACE(1960); THE HYPNOTIC EYE(1960); DEADLY DUO(1962)

Marjorie Henderson
KING AND FOUR QUEENS, THE(1956), cos

Mary Henderson
HUSH... HUSH, SWEET CHARLOTTE(1964)

Maye Henderson
MANCHURIAN CANDIDATE, THE(1962); LIVING BETWEEN TWO WORLDS(1963); HALLS OF ANGER(1970); BROTHER JOHN(1971)

Melanie Henderson
DIE LAUGHING(1980)

Miles W. Henderson
GOD IS MY WITNESS(1931), set d

Neal Henderson
TRADER HORNEE(1970)

Patrick W. Henderson, Jr.
GREAT WALDO PEPPER, THE(1975)

Peggy Henderson
HASTY HEART, THE(1949), cos

Ray Henderson
SUNNY SIDE UP(1929), w, m; FOLLOW THE LEADER(1930), w; FOLLOW THRU(1930), w; GOOD NEWS(1930), w; HOLD EVERYTHING(1930), m; JUST IMAGINE(1930), p, w; INDISCREET(1931), p, w; CURLY TOP(1935), m; RIDERS FROM NOWHERE(1940); BILLY THE KID TRAPPED(1942); GOOD NEWS(1947), w

Richard Henderson
LAST WAVE, THE(1978, Aus.)

Robert G. Henderson
SUPERMAN III(1983)

Robert Henderson
NEVER LET ME GO(1953, U.S./Brit.); PENNY PRINCESS(1953, Brit.); TERROR STREET(1953); ORDERS TO KILL(1958, Brit.); TOO YOUNG TO LOVE(1960, Brit.); MIDAS RUN(1969); PHASE IV(1974); FUNNY MONEY(1983, Brit.)

Russ Henderson
DR. TERROR'S HOUSE OF HORRORS(1965, Brit.)

Simon Henderson
IT'S A 2"6" ABOVE THE GROUND WORLD(1972, Brit.)

Skitch Henderson
ON OUR MERRY WAY(1948), md; ACT ONE(1964), m; WHO SAYS I CAN'T RIDE A RAINBOW!(1971)

Spencer Henderson
HISTORY OF THE WORLD, PART 1(1981); TO BE OR NOT TO BE(1983)

Steffi Henderson
PICTURE MOMMY DEAD(1966)

Theodore Henderson
Misc. Silents
BEYOND ALL ODDS(1926)

Ty Henderson
COMPETITION, THE(1980)

V. T. Henderson
Silents
NANCY'S BIRTHRIGHT(1916)

William Henderson
REMEMBER THE DAY(1941); JUNIOR MISS(1945)

Wilt Henderson
1984
ANGEL(1984), ed

R. Henderson-Bland
Silents
FROM THE MANGER TO THE CROSS(1913)

Charles Hendle, Jr.
BOMBS OVER BURMA(1942), ed

Tony Hendra
1984
THIS IS SPINAL TAP(1984)

Dutch Hendrian [Oscar G. Hendrian]
THAT'S MY BOY(1932); VANITY STREET(1932); AIR HOSTESS(1933); SON OF KONG(1933); JEALOUSY(1934); MEN OF THE NIGHT(1934); MOST PRECIOUS THING IN LIFE(1934); HANDS ACROSS THE TABLE(1935); SHE GETS HER MAN(1935); SPECIAL AGENT(1935); FURY(1936); NEVADA(1936); NEXT TIME WE LOVE(1936); EXCLUSIVE(1937); FORLORN RIVER(1937); PARTNERS IN CRIME(1937); ANGELS WITH DIRTY FACES(1938); BROTHER RAT(1938); TEXANS, THE(1938); TIP-OFF GIRLS(1938); YOU AND ME(1938); YOU CAN'T TAKE IT WITH YOU(1938); COWBOY QUARTERBACK(1939); LADY'S FROM KENTUCKY, THE(1939); OUR LEADING CITIZEN(1939); SMASHING THE MONEY RING(1939); UNION PACIFIC(1939); FLIGHT ANGELS(1940); KNUTE ROCKNE–ALL AMERICAN(1940); LITTLE OLD NEW YORK(1940); THEY DRIVE BY NIGHT(1940); PHANTOM SUBMARINE, THE(1941); SEA WOLF, THE(1941); LARCENY, INC.(1942); TALK OF THE TOWN(1942); UNDERGROUND AGENT(1942); NO TIME FOR LOVE(1943); PRINCESS AND THE PIRATE, THE(1944); TAMPICO(1944)

Johannes Hendrich
MOONWOLF(1966, Fin./Ger.), w

Josef Hendrichs
ETERNAL WALTZ, THE(1959, Ger.); $100 A NIGHT(1968, Ger.)

Earl Hendrick
WINGS IN THE DARK(1935), art d; GERONIMO(1939), art d

Arch Hendricks
FLYING CADETS(1941); SHADOW OF THE THIN MAN(1941)

Baroness Yvonne Hendricks
MISSION TO MOSCOW(1943)

Bea Hendricks
ONE THIRD OF A NATION(1939)

Ben F. Hendricks
WE'RE NOT DRESSING(1934); DON'T BET ON BLONDES(1935); FRONT PAGE WOMAN(1935); MAN WHO RECLAIMED HIS HEAD, THE(1935); THEODORA GOES WILD(1936)

Ben Hendricks
BLACK WATERS(1929); FAST LIFE(1932); RAIN(1932); JIMMY THE GENT(1934); ST. LOUIS KID, THE(1934); DR. SOCRATES(1935); MISS PACIFIC FLEET(1935); O'SHAUGHNESSY'S BOY(1935); IT HAD TO HAPPEN(1936); ROAD GANG(1936); DRAEGERMAN COURAGE(1937); GO-GETTER, THE(1937); HOLY TERROR, THE(1937); MUSIC FOR MADAME(1937); NORTH OF NOME(1937); ROARING TIMBER(1937); SLIM(1937); WINDJAMMER(1937); ANGELS WITH DIRTY FACES(1938); HARD TO GET(1938); MARIE ANTOINETTE(1938); SERGEANT MURPHY(1938); SLIGHT CASE OF MURDER, A(1938); THREE BLIND MICE(1938)
Silents
JOHN GLAYDE'S HONOR(1915); NOTHING BUT THE TRUTH(1920)
Misc. Silents
BIRTH OF A RACE(1919); TEMPERAMENTAL WIFE, A(1919); BIG DAN(1923); GREATER THAN A CROWN(1925); TIDES OF PASSION(1925); WELCOME HOME(1925)

Ben Hendricks, Jr.
WILD PARTY, THE(1929); FOOTLIGHTS AND FOOLS(1929); TWIN BEDS(1929); FURIES, THE(1930); GIRL OF THE GOLDEN WEST(1930); GREAT DIVIDE, THE(1930); LADIES LOVE BRUTES(1930); MEN WITHOUT WOMEN(1930); ROAD TO PARADISE(1930); LITTLE CAESAR(1931); PUBLIC ENEMY, THE(1931); FIREMAN, SAVE MY CHILD(1932); KID FROM SPAIN, THE(1932); PACK UP YOUR TROUBLES(1932); WOMAN FROM MONTE CARLO, THE(1932); AFTER TONIGHT(1933); IMPORTANT WITNESS, THE(1933); REFORM GIRL(1933); GREEN EYES(1934); HIS FIGHTING BLOOD(1935); LAW BEYOND THE RANGE(1935); NORTHERN FRONTIER(1935); RED BLOOD OF COURAGE(1935); GREAT GUY(1936); OREGON TRAIL, THE(1936); STAGE DOOR(1937); BORN TO BE WILD(1938)
Misc. Talkies
DARK ENDEAVOUR(1933)
Silents
AGAINST ALL ODDS(1924); JUST OFF BROADWAY(1924); ONE MINUTE TO PLAY(1926); ROLLING HOME(1926); SKINNER'S DRESS SUIT(1926); TAKE IT FROM ME(1926); WHAT HAPPENED TO JONES(1926); BARBED WIRE(1927); OUT ALL NIGHT(1927); RACING ROMEO(1927)
Misc. Silents
LAND OF HOPE, THE(1921); HEADLESS HORSEMAN, THE(1922); BROAD ROAD, THE(1923); MAN WHO PLAYED SQUARE, THE(1924); BIRDS OF PREY(1927); MY FRIEND FROM INDIA(1927)

Ben Hendricks, Sr.
Silents
PERFECT LADY, A(1918)

Ben Hendricks III
PUBLIC ENEMY, THE(1931)

Bill Hendricks
CALIFORNIA MAIL, THE(1937)

Darlene Hendricks
NARCOTICS STORY, THE(1958); X-15(1961)

Dudley Hendricks
Misc. Silents
TERROR, THE(1926)

Evelyn Hendricks
NIGHT OF BLOODY HORROR zero(1969); WOMEN AND BLOODY TERROR(1970)

Jack Hendricks
CARYL OF THE MOUNTAINS(1936); FRONTIER FUGITIVES(1945); CODE OF THE SADDLE(1947); PRAIRIE EXPRESS(1947); SIX GUN SERENADE(1947); FRONTIER REVENGE(1948); MARK OF THE LASH(1948); TORNADO RANGE(1948); MARSHAL OF HELDORADO(1950)

Jan Hendricks
LOVE FEAST, THE(1966, Ger.)

John Hendricks
Silents
RED WIDOW, THE(1916)

Laurie Hendricks
FAST TIMES AT RIDGEMONT HIGH(1982)

Noah Hendricks
LAND OF MISSING MEN, THE(1930); AT THE RIDGE(1931)

Sebie Hendricks
IMITATION OF LIFE(1934)

Lance Hendricksen
CLOSE ENCOUNTERS OF THE THIRD KIND(1977)

Alton Hendrickson
SONG IS BORN, A(1948)

Ben Hendrickson, Jr.
SUNNY(1930)

Calista Hendrickson
MUPPET MOVIE, THE(1979), cos; GREAT MUPPET CAPER, THE(1981), cos

Evelyn Hendrickson
BAYOU(1957); MANDINGO(1975)

Nancy Hendrickson
MOTHER'S DAY(1980)

Robert Hendrickson
Misc. Talkies
CLOSE SHAVE(1981), d

Stephen Hendrickson
LIVE AND LET DIE(1973, Brit.), art d; SUPER COPS, THE(1974), art d; GOING IN STYLE(1979), prod d; ARTHUR(1981), prod d; LITTLE SEX, A(1982), prod d
1984
MUPPETS TAKE MANHATTAN, THE(1984), prod d

Alex Hendrie
1984
STRANGERS KISS(1984)

Chris Hendrie
PSYCHO II(1983)

Ernest Hendrie
Misc. Silents
WILL AND A WAY, A(1922, Brit.)

Jan Hendriks
MAGIC FIRE(1956); THREE MOVES TO FREEDOM(1960, Ger.); BRAINWASHED(1961, Ger.); DEVIL'S DAFFODIL, THE(1961, Brit./Ger.); ARMS AND THE MAN(1962, Ger.); BUFFALO BILL, HERO OF THE FAR WEST(1962, Ital.); SEVEN DARING GIRLS(1962, Ger.); ISLE OF SIN(1963, Ger.); JUDGE AND THE SINNER, THE(1964, Ger.)

Hugh Hendrikson
PAN-AMERICANA(1945)

Anders Hendriksson
WALPURGIS NIGHT(1941, Swed.)

Darlene Hendrix
STUDS LONIGAN(1960)

Gary Hendrix
CALIFORNIA SUITE(1978)

N. E. Hendrix
Silents
WALLOPING WALLACE(1924)

Napoleon Hendrix
UNCOMMON VALOR(1983)

Shorty Hendrix
OKLAHOMA CYCLONE(1930)
Silents
GALLOPING GALLAGHER(1924)

Wanda Hendrix
CONFIDENTIAL AGENT(1945); NORA PRENTISS(1947); RIDE THE PINK HORSE(1947); VARIETY GIRL(1947); MISS TATLOCK'S MILLIONS(1948); MY OWN TRUE LOVE(1948); PRINCE OF FOXES(1949); SONG OF SURRENDER(1949); ADMIRAL WAS A LADY, THE(1950); CAPTAIN CAREY, U.S.A(1950); SIERRA(1950); HIGHWAYMAN, THE(1951); MY BROTHER, THE OUTLAW(1951); MONTANA TERRITORY(1952); LAST POSSE, THE(1953); SEA OF LOST SHIPS(1953); BLACK DAKOTAS, THE(1954); GOLDEN MASK, THE(1954, Brit.); HIGHWAY DRAGNET(1954); BOY WHO CAUGHT A CROOK(1961); JOHNNY COOL(1963)

Wandra Hendrix
SADDLE TRAMP(1950)

Heather Hendrixson
MOTEL HELL(1980)

Shaylin Hendrixson
MOTEL HELL(1980)

Gloria Hendry
BLACK CAESAR(1973); HELL UP IN HARLEM(1973); LIVE AND LET DIE(1973, Brit.); SLAUGHTER'S BIG RIP-OFF(1973); BLACK BELT JONES(1974); SAVAGE SISTERS(1974); BARE KNUCKLES(1978)
Misc. Talkies
BLACK BELT JONES(1974); BARE KNUCKLES(1977)

Ian Hendry
ROOM AT THE TOP(1959, Brit.); IN THE NICK(1960, Brit.); LIVE NOW–PAY LATER(1962, Brit.); CHILDREN OF THE DAMNED(1963, Brit.); MODEL MURDER CASE, THE(1964, Brit.); THIS IS MY STREET(1964, Brit.); HILL, THE(1965, Brit.); REPULSION(1965, Brit.); BEAUTY JUNGLE, THE(1966, Brit.); SANDWICH MAN, THE(1966, Brit.); CRY WOLF(1968, Brit.); JOURNEY TO THE FAR SIDE OF THE SUN(1969, Brit.); SOUTHERN STAR, THE(1969, Fr./Brit.); MC KENZIE BREAK, THE(1970); GET CARTER(1971, Brit.); JERUSALEM FILE, THE(1972, U.S./Israel); TALES FROM THE CRYPT(1972, Brit.); ASSASSIN(1973, Brit.); THEATRE OF BLOOD(1973, Brit.); CAPTAIN KRONOS: VAMPIRE HUNTER(1974, Brit.); INTERNECINE PROJECT, THE(1974, Brit.); PASSENGER, THE(1975, Ital.); MC VICAR(1982, Brit.)
Misc. Talkies
ALL COPPERS ARE...(1972, Brit.); BITCH, THE(1979)

Len Hendry
HAIL THE CONQUERING HERO(1944); PRACTICALLY YOURS(1944); DUFFY'S TAVERN(1945); DARK HORSE, THE(1946); O.S.S.(1946); CALCUTTA(1947); SUDDENLY IT'S SPRING(1947); VARIETY GIRL(1947); WHERE THERE'S LIFE(1947); NIGHT HAS A THOUSAND EYES(1948); DEAR WIFE(1949); LADY TAKES A SAILOR, THE(1949); COPPER CANYON(1950); STORM WARNING(1950); SUNSET BOULEVARD(1950); HIS KIND OF WOMAN(1951); PLACE IN THE SUN, A(1951); CARRIE(1952); OPERATION SECRET(1952); PONY EXPRESS(1953); REAR WINDOW(1954); GIRL RUSH, THE(1955); STRATEGIC AIR COMMAND(1955); COURT JESTER, THE(1956); PARDNERS(1956); GUNFIGHT AT THE O.K. CORRAL(1957); OMAR KHAYYAM(1957); HOT SPELL(1958); LAST TRAIN FROM GUN HILL(1959); NORTH BY NORTHWEST(1959); WHO'S GOT THE ACTION?(1962); FASTEST GUITAR ALIVE, THE(1967)

Marsh Hendry
GERONIMO(1962), ed; MONKEYS, GO HOME!(1967), ed; NEVER A DULL MOMENT(1968), ed; WHERE THE RED FERN GROWS(1974), ed; AGAINST A CROOKED SKY(1975), ed; PONY EXPRESS RIDER(1976), ed

Miriam Hendry
MAN WITH A CLOAK, THE(1951)

Richard Hendry
JUDGE AND THE ASSASSIN, THE(1979, Fr.)

Zoe Hendry
TO THE DEVIL A DAUGHTER(1976, Brit./Ger.)

Wayland M. Hendrys
SINCE YOU WENT AWAY(1944), ed

Nona Hendryx
SGT. PEPPER'S LONELY HEARTS CLUB BAND(1978)

Shirl Hendryx
RUNNING BRAVE(1983, Can.), w

Gloria Hendy
LA DOLCE VITA(1961, Ital./Fr.)

James Heneghan, Jr.
SHENANDOAH(1965)

Patricia Heneghan
CROSSROADS TO CRIME(1960, Brit.); WHISTLE DOWN THE WIND(1961, Brit.)

David Heneker
HOUSE OF FRIGHT(1961), m

Hobart Henely
Misc. Silents
EXCHANGE OF WIVES(1925), d

Bruce Henenlotter
BASKET CASE(1982), ed

Frank Henenlotter
BASKET CASE(1982), d&w

George Henery
Silents
AMERICAN MAID(1917)

David Henesy
HOUSE OF DARK SHADOWS(1970)

Sharon Henesy
PLASTIC DOME OF NORMA JEAN, THE(1966); DETECTIVE, THE(1968); FOR LOVE OF IVY(1968); WHO FEARS THE DEVIL(1972)

Joan Heney
1984
HOTEL NEW HAMPSHIRE, THE(1984)

Janet Henfrey
DREAM MAKER, THE(1963, Brit.)

Janet Henfry
TAMARIND SEED, THE(1974, Brit.)

Butch Hengen
DARK AT THE TOP OF THE STAIRS, THE(1960)

Paul Hengge
24 HOURS IN A WOMAN'S LIFE(1968, Fr./Ger.), w; DUCK RINGS AT HALF PAST SEVEN, THE(1969, Ger./Ital.), w

Lutz Hengst
KING, QUEEN, KNAVE(1972, Ger./U.S.), p

Marilyn Hengst
BANANAS(1971)

Sonja Henie
ONE IN A MILLION(1936); THIN ICE(1937); HAPPY LANDING(1938); MY LUCKY STAR(1938); EVERYTHING HAPPENS AT NIGHT(1939); SECOND FIDDLE(1939); SUN VALLEY SERENADE(1941); ICELAND(1942); WINTERTIME(1943); IT'S A PLEASURE(1945); COUNTESS OF MONTE CRISTO, THE(1948); HELLO LONDON(1958, Brit.)

Dov Henig
MY MARGO(1969, Israel), ed; OPERATION THUNDERBOLT(1978, ISRAEL), ed; MAGICIAN OF LUBLIN, THE(1979, Israel/Ger.), ed

Rodulf Henig
DREAMER, THE(1970, Israel)

Emanuel Henigman
MADRON(1970, U.S./Israel), p

Henry Henigson
PORT OF SEVEN SEAS(1938), p

Rene Henil
Misc. Silents
MIDINETTE(1917 Fr.), d

Georges Henin
Silents
NAPOLEON(1927, Fr.)

Bonnie Henjum
THIS LOVE OF OURS(1945)

Charles Henkel
MEN OF THE PLAINS(1936), ed; STORMY TRAILS(1936), ed; CHEYENNE RIDES AGAIN(1937), ed; IDAHO KID, THE(1937), ed; LAW AND LEAD(1937), ph; SHADOW STRIKES, THE(1937), ed; TWO MINUTES TO PLAY(1937), ed; INTERNATIONAL CRIME(1938), ed; SIX SHOOTIN' SHERIFF(1938), ed; LIGHTNING STRIKES WEST(1940), ed; HARD GUY(1941), ed; SWAMP WOMAN(1941), ed; THEY RAID BY NIGHT(1942), ed; CORREGIDOR(1943), ed; WILDFIRE(1945), ed

Charles Henkel, Jr.
HERE'S FLASH CASEY(1937), ed; RANGERS TAKE OVER, THE(1942), ed; SECRETS OF A CO-ED(1942), ed; BAD MEN OF THUNDER GAP(1943), ed; BORDER BUCKAROOS(1943), ed; BOSS OF BIG TOWN(1943), ed; GHOST AND THE GUEST(1943), ed; GIRLS IN CHAINS(1943), ed; ISLE OF FORGOTTEN SINS(1943), ed; LADY FROM CHUNGKING(1943), ed; MY SON, THE HERO(1943), ed; PAYOFF, THE(1943), ed; UNDERDOG, THE(1943), ed; WEST OF TEXAS(1943), ed; BOSS OF THE RAWHIDE(1944), ed; BRAND OF THE DEVIL(1944), ph; GUNS OF THE LAW(1944), ed; GUNSMOKE MESA(1944), ed; MEN ON HER MIND(1944), ed; PINTO BANDIT, THE(1944), ed; SPOOK TOWN(1944), ed; TRAIL OF TERROR(1944), ed; I ACCUSE MY PARENTS(1945), ed

Charles V. Henkel, Jr.
LURE OF THE WASTELAND(1939), ed

Kim Henkel
TEXAS CHAIN SAW MASSACRE, THE(1974), w
1984
LAST NIGHT AT THE ALAMO(1984), a, p, w

Noel Henkel
FAR FROM THE MADDING CROWD(1967, Brit.)

Peter Henkel
WILD SEASON(1968, South Africa), ed; MY WAY(1974, South Africa), ed
Misc. Talkies
THREE BULLETS FOR A LONG GUN(1973), d

Paul Henkels
TALES OF THE UNCANNY(1932, Ger.); WOZZECK(1962, E. Ger.)

Charles Henker
PHANTOM OF THE RANGE, THE(1938), ed

Hilary Henkin
HEADIN' FOR BROADWAY(1980), w

Charles Henkle, Jr.
SEVEN DOORS TO DEATH(1944), ed; WATERFRONT(1944), ed

Herschel Henlere
CRAZY PEOPLE(1934, Brit.); WOMAN IN COMMAND, THE(1934 Brit.)

Althea Henley
UP THE RIVER(1930); PHANTOM BROADCAST, THE(1933); FIND THE LADY(1936, Brit.)

Beth Henley
1984
SWING SHIFT(1984)

Caro Henley
1984
SAHARA(1984)

David Henley
CROOKED ROAD, THE(, p; DEVIL'S PASS, THE(1957, Brit.), p; MAKE MINE A DOUBLE(1962, Brit.), p; STRANGLEHOLD(1962, Brit.), p; BLAZE OF GLORY(1963, Brit.), p; YELLOW HAT, THE(1966, Brit.), p

Don Henley
CRY BLOOD, APACHE(1970)

Drewe Henley
HEAVENS ABOVE!(1963, Brit.); NOTHING BUT THE BEST(1964, Brit.); SQUADRON 633(1964, U.S./Brit.); 633 SQUADRON(1964); 25TH HOUR, THE(1967, Fr./Ital./Yugo.); MRS. BROWN, YOU'VE GOT A LOVELY DAUGHTER(1968, Brit.); HELL BOATS(1970, Brit.); PUPPET ON A CHAIN(1971, Brit.); WHEN DINOSAURS RULED THE EARTH(1971, Brit.); STAR WARS(1977)

Dusty Henley
FINDERS KEEPERS(1951); TAKE ME TO TOWN(1953)

Hobart Henley
LADY OF CHANCE, A(1928), d; LADY LIES, THE(1929), d; BIG POND, THE(1930), d; FREE LOVE(1930), d; MOTHERS CRY(1930), d; ROADHOUSE NIGHTS(1930), d; BAD SISTER(1931), d; CAPTAIN APPLEJACK(1931), d; EXPENSIVE WOMEN(1931), d; NIGHT WORLD(1932), d; UNKNOWN BLONDE(1934), d
Silents
ALL WOMAN(1918), d; MRS. SLACKER(1918), d; SIN THAT WAS HIS, THE(1920), d; CHEATED HEARTS(1921), d; SOCIETY SNOBS(1921), d; STARDUST(1921), d; FLIRT, THE(1922), d; SCRAPPER, THE(1922), d; ABYSMAL BRUTE, THE(1923), d; MARRIED FLIRTS(1924); HIS SECRETARY(1925), d; AUCTION BLOCK, THE(1926), d; TILLIE THE TOILER(1927), d
Misc. Silents
COURT-MARTIALED(1915); LITTLE BROTHER OF THE RICH, A(1915); WHITE TERROR, THE(1915); CHILD OF MYSTERY, A(1916), a, d; EVIL WOMEN DO, THE(1916); SIGN OF THE POPPY, THE(1916); TEMPTATION AND THE MAN(1916); DOUBLE-ROOM MYSTERY, THE(1917), d; FACE IN THE DARK, THE(1918), d; GLORIOUS ADVENTURE, THE(1918), d; LAUGHING BILL HYDE(1918), d; MONEY MAD(1918), d; PARENTAGE(1918), a, d; TOO FAT TO FIGHT(1918), d; GAY OLD DOG, THE(1919), d; ONE WEEK OF LIFE(1919), d; PEACE OF ROARING RIVER, THE(1919), d; WOMAN ON THE INDEX, THE(1919), d; MIRACLE OF MONEY, THE(1920), d; HER NIGHT OF NIGHTS(1922), d; FLAME OF LIFE, THE(1923), d; LADY OF QUALITY, A(1924), d; SINNERS IN SILK(1924), d; SO THIS IS MARRIAGE(1924), d; TURMOIL, THE(1924), d; DENIAL, THE(1925), d; SLAVE OF FASHION, A(1925), d; CERTAIN YOUNG MAN, A(1928), d; HIS TIGER LADY(1928), d; WICKEDNESS PREFERRED(1928), d

Jack Henley
THREEPENNY OPERA, THE(1931, Ger./U.S.); HOOTS MON!(1939, Brit.), w; THAT'S THE TICKET(1940, Brit.), w; SPOOKS RUN WILD(1941), w; ZIS BOOM BAH(1941), w; COLLEGE SWEETHEARTS(1942), w; MR. WISE GUY(1942), w; NIGHT TO REMEMBER, A(1942), w; SNUFFY SMITH, YARD BIRD(1942), w; TWO YANKS IN TRINIDAD(1942), w; DANGEROUS BLONDES(1943), w; MY KINGDOM FOR A COOK(1943), w; REVEILLE WITH BEVERLY(1943), w; THOUSAND AND ONE NIGHTS, A(1945), w; IT'S GREAT TO BE YOUNG(1946), w; MEET ME ON BROADWAY(1946), w; ONE WAY TO LOVE(1946), w; BLONDIE IN THE DOUGH(1947), w; BLONDIE'S ANNIVERSARY(1947), w; BLONDIE'S SECRET(1948), w; BLONDIE HITS THE JACKPOT(1949), w; BEWARE OF BLONDIE(1950), w; BLONDIE'S HERO(1950), w; GIRLS' SCHOOL(1950), w; KATIE DID IT(1951), w; MA AND PA KETTLE BACK ON THE FARM(1951), w; BONZO GOES TO COLLEGE(1952), w; MA AND PA KETTLE AT THE FAIR(1952), w; MA AND PA KETTLE ON VACATION(1953), w; ROCKET MAN, THE(1954), w; MA AND PA KETTLE AT WAIKIKI(1955), w

Joan Henley
PURSE STRINGS(1933, Brit.); RELUCTANT HEROES(1951, Brit.); RECKONING, THE(1971, Brit.); PUBLIC EYE, THE(1972, Brit.); THIRTY NINE STEPS, THE(1978, Brit.)

John Henley
HE'S A COCKEYED WONDER(1950), w

Lucile Watson Henley
BLONDIE'S BIG DEAL(1949), w

Paul Henley
HIDING PLACE, THE(1975); MEETINGS WITH REMARKABLE MEN(1979, Brit.)

Rosina Henley
Silents
ADVENTURES OF CAROL, THE(1917); GUILTY OF LOVE(1920), w
Misc. Silents
(; GATES OF GLADNESS(1918)

Ted Henley
ROWDYMAN, THE(1973, Can.)
Althea Henly
OH, FOR A MAN!(1930)
Ray Henman
LADY, STAY DEAD(1982, Aus.), ph
1984
BROTHERS(1984, Aus.), ph
Elizabeth Henn
MALATESTA'S CARNIVAL(1973)
Henry Henna
PENAL CODE, THE(1933)
Mary Pat Hennagir
TAKE THIS JOB AND SHOVE IT(1981)
Dan Hennah
NATE AND HAYES(1983, U.S./New Zealand), art d
Clarence Hennecke
MURDER BY TELEVISION(1935), w; MAYOR OF 44TH STREET, THE(1942); DIXIE DUGAN(1943); NEPTUNE'S DAUGHTER(1949); PREJUDICE(1949); HUMPHREY TAKES A CHANCE(1950); MILLION DOLLAR MERMAID(1952)
Silents
CHASER, THE(1928), w; HEART TROUBLE(1928), w
Dermot Hennelly
DESERTERS(1983, Can.)
Paul Hennen
MACBETH(1971, Brit.); PIED PIPER, THE(1972, Brit.)
Maurice Hennequin
HERCULES' PILLS(1960, Ital.), w
Marilu Henner
BETWEEN THE LINES(1977); BLOODBROTHERS(1978); HAMMETT(1982); MAN WHO LOVED WOMEN, THE(1983)
1984
CANNONBALL RUN II(1984); JOHNNY DANGEROUSLY(1984)
Hennery
LIGHT ACROSSS THE STREET, THE(1957, Fr.)
Brian Hennessey
DO NOT THROW CUSHIONS INTO THE RING(1970)
Katherine Hennessey
Silents
LITTLE ANNIE ROONEY(1925), w
Michael Hennessey
GIRL WITH GREEN EYES(1964, Brit.)
Peggy Hennessey
RAT, THE(1938, Brit.), ed
Peter Hennessey
SUSPENDED ALIBI(1957, Brit.), ph
Robert Hennessey
NO RESTING PLACE(1952, Brit.)
Anthony Hennessy
FRIGHTMARE(1974, Brit.)
April Hennessy
SEVEN HILLS OF ROME, THE(1958); LA DOLCE VITA(1961, Ital./Fr.); FACTS OF MURDER, THE(1965, Ital.); LOVE AND MARRIAGE(1966, Ital.)
Dale Hennessy
CHRISTIAN LICORICE STORE, THE(1971), art d; SLITHER(1973), art d
Dan Hennessy
SUDDEN FURY(1975, Can.)
Emmett Hennessy
Misc. Talkies
CYNTHIA'S SISTER(1975)
Frank Hennessy
DINER(1982)
Hugh Hennessy
FANTASIA(1940), art d
Michael Hennessy
HOME IS THE HERO(1959, Ireland)
Monique Hennessy
FINGERMAN, THE(1963, Fr.); DOULOS–THE FINGER MAN(1964, Fr./Ital.)
Peggy Hennessy
MYSTERIOUS MR. REEDER, THE(1940, Brit.), ed
Peter Hennessy
ROCK AROUND THE WORLD(1957, Brit.), ph; CHAIN OF EVENTS(1958, Brit.), ph; HEART OF A CHILD(1958, Brit.), ph; SOLITARY CHILD, THE(1958, Brit.), ph; CARRY ON SERGEANT(1959, Brit.), ph; TIME LOCK(1959, Brit.), ph; SAVAGE INNOCENTS, THE(1960, Brit.), ph; QUARE FELLOW, THE(1962, Brit.), ph; EYES OF ANNIE JONES, THE(1963, Brit.), ph; LIFE IN DANGER(1964, Brit.), ph
Petter Hennessy
MODEL FOR MURDER(1960, Brit.), ph
Robert Hennessy
WHY RUSSIANS ARE REVOLTING(1970)
Sara Hennessy
PURPLE HAZE(1982)
Tom Hennessy
COMANCHEROS, THE(1961); SQUARES(1972)
Dale Hennesy
UNDER THE YUM-YUM TREE(1963), prod d; GOOD NEIGHBOR SAM(1964), prod d; JOHN GOLDFARB, PLEASE COME HOME(1964), art d; IN LIKE FLINT(1967), art d; COVER ME BABE(1970), art d; DIRTY HARRY(1971), art d; SIMON, KING OF THE WITCHES(1971), art d; EVERYTHING YOU ALWAYS WANTED TO KNOW ABOUT SEX, BUT WE'RE AFRAID TO ASK(1972), prod d; SLEEPER(1973), prod d; YOUNG FRANKENSTEIN(1974), artd; KING KONG(1976), prod d; LOGAN'S RUN(1976), prod d; COMPETITION, THE(1980), prod d; ISLAND, THE(1980), prod d; WHOLLY MOSES(1980), prod d; ANNIE(1982), prod d
Hugh Hennesy
SNOW WHITE AND THE SEVEN DWARFS(1937), art d; PINOCCHIO(1940), art d; RELUCTANT DRAGON, THE(1941), anim d
Tom Hennesy
IT SHOULD HAPPEN TO YOU(1954); LONG GRAY LINE, THE(1955); BIG JAKE(1971)

Del Henney
STRAW DOGS(1971, Brit.); VILLAIN(1971, Brit.); WHEN EIGHT BELLS TOLL(1971, Brit.); BRANNIGAN(1975, Brit.); SOLDIER OF ORANGE(1979, Dutch)
Heinz Hennig
CHRONICLE OF ANNA MAGDALENA BACH(1968, Ital., Ger.), md
Winifred Hennig
SISTERS, OR THE BALANCE OF HAPPINESS(1982, Ger.), art d, set d
William K. Hennigar
WICKED DIE SLOW, THE(1968), d
Henry Hennigson
GOOD FAIRY, THE(1935), p
Ann Henning
ORPHANS OF THE NORTH(1940)
Bunny Henning
GNOME-MOBILE, THE(1967)
Buzz Henning
HONKERS, THE(1972)
Carlos Henning
RUN FOR THE SUN(1956)
Eva Henning
DEVIL'S WANTON, THE(1962, Swed.)
Pat Henning
SHINE ON, HARVEST MOON(1938); RIDE 'EM COWGIRL(1939); MAN ON A TIGHTROPE(1953); ON THE WATERFRONT(1954); WIND ACROSS THE EVERGLADES(1958); CARDINAL, THE(1963); HELLO DOWN THERE(1969)
Paul Henning
LOVER COME BACK(1961), w; BEDTIME STORY(1964), w
Shelley Henning
1984
PRODIGAL, THE(1984)
Susan Henning
GNOME-MOBILE, THE(1967); LIVE A LITTLE, LOVE A LITTLE(1968)
Ted Henning
LINCOLN CONSPIRACY, THE(1977)
1984
FIRST TURN-ON!, THE(1984)
Tim Henning
PERFECT SPECIMEN, THE(1937); THAT CERTAIN WOMAN(1937); DAWN PATROL, THE(1938)
Uno Henning
ESCAPED FROM DARTMOOR(1930, Brit.)
Misc. Silents
LOVE OF JEANNE NEY, THE(1927, Ger.); THREE LOVES(1931, Ger.)
Winfried Henning
GERMANY IN AUTUMN(1978, Ger.), set d
Astrid Henning-Jensen
SHORT IS THE SUMMER(1968, Swed.), w; LURE OF THE JUNGLE, THE(1970, Den.), d&w
Bjarne Henning-Jensen
SHORT IS THE SUMMER(1968, Swed.), d, w; LURE OF THE JUNGLE, THE(1970, Den.), w
Albrecht Hennings
STOP TRAIN 349(1964, Fr./Ital./Ger.), set d
Elizabeth Hennings
HAMLET(1948, Brit.), cos
Fred Hennings
DON JUAN(1956, Aust.)
Lise Henningsen
CHRISTINE KEELER AFFAIR, THE(1964, Brit.)
Ten Henningsen
EVEL KNIEVEL(1971)
Ron Henon
JUMBO(1962)
Monika Henr
MY FAIR LADY(1964)
Monica Henreid
GIRLS ON THE LOOSE(1958)
Monika Henreid
DEAD RINGER(1964); BLUES FOR LOVERS(1966, Brit.); DIAMOND STUD(1970); OMEGA MAN, THE(1971)
Misc. Talkies
DIAMOND STUD(1970)
Paul Henreid
GOODBYE MR. CHIPS(1939, Brit.); CASABLANCA(1942); JOAN OF PARIS(1942); NOW, VOYAGER(1942); BETWEEN TWO WORLDS(1944); CONSPIRATORS, THE(1944); HOLLYWOOD CANTEEN(1944); IN OUR TIME(1944); SPANISH MAIN, THE(1945); DECEPTION(1946); DEVOTION(1946); OF HUMAN BONDAGE(1946); SONG OF LOVE(1947); HOLLOW TRIUMPH(1948), a, p; ROPE OF SAND(1949); LAST OF THE BUCCANEERS(1950); SO YOUNG, SO BAD(1950); PARDON MY FRENCH(1951, U.S./Fr.); FOR MEN ONLY(1952), a, p&d; STOLEN FACE(1952, Brit.); THIEF OF DAMASCUS(1952); SIREN OF BAGDAD(1953); WOMAN IN HIDING(1953, Brit.); DEEP IN MY HEART(1954); PIRATES OF TRIPOLI(1955); MEET ME IN LAS VEGAS(1956); WOMAN'S DEVOTION, A(1956), a, d; TEN THOUSAND BEDROOMS(1957); GIRLS ON THE LOOSE(1958), d; LIVE FAST, DIE YOUNG(1958), d; HOLIDAY FOR LOVERS(1959); NEVER SO FEW(1959); FOUR HORSEMEN OF THE APOCALYPSE, THE(1962); DEAD RINGER(1964), d; OPERATION CROSSBOW(1965, U.S./Ital.); BLUES FOR LOVERS(1966, Brit.), d, w; MADWOMAN OF CHAILLOT, THE(1969); EXORCIST II: THE HERETIC(1977)
Bobby Henrey
FALLEN IDOL, THE(1949, Brit.); WONDER BOY(1951, Brit./Aust.)
Marie Henriau
LUMIERE(1976, Fr.); LOVE ON THE RUN(1980, Fr.)
Linda Henrich
STATE FAIR(1962)
Diann Henrichsen
STRAWBERRY STATEMENT, THE(1970); DIRTY HARRY(1971)
Jacques Henrici
PARADISIO(1962, Brit.), p, w

John Henrick
DR. EHRLICH'S MAGIC BULLET(1940)
Lance Henricksen
PRINCE OF THE CITY(1981)
Bert Henrickson
JAIL BUSTERS(1955), cos; DINO(1957), cos
Calista Henrickson
1984
MUPPETS TAKE MANHATTAN, THE(1984), cos
Henricsson
VICTOR FRANKENSTEIN(1975, Swed./Ireland)
Monika Henried
BAD COMPANY(1972)
Jens Oliver Henriksen
WEEKEND(1964, Den.)
Lance Henriksen
IT AIN'T EASY(1972); DOG DAY AFTERNOON(1975); MANSION OF THE
DOOMED(1976); DAMIEN–OMEN II(1978); VISITOR, THE(1980, Ital./U.S.); DARK
END OF THE STREET, THE(1981); PIRANHA II: THE SPAWNING(1981, Neth.);
RIGHT STUFF, THE(1983)
1984
SAVAGE DAWN(1984); TERMINATOR, THE(1984)
Lena Henriksen
Z.P.G.(1972), makeup
Anders Henrikson
INTERMEZZO(1937, Swed.); WOMAN'S FACE, A(1939, Swed.); WHALERS,
THE(1942, Swed.), d; DEVIL'S WANTON, THE(1962, Swed.)
Bert Henrikson
BOBBY WARE IS MISSING(1955), cos; HIGH SOCIETY(1955), cos; CRASHING LAS
VEGAS(1956), cos; FRIENDLY PERSUASION(1956), cos; FOOTSTEPS IN THE
NIGHT(1957), cos; LOOKING FOR DANGER(1957), cos; HELL'S FIVE HOURS(1958),
cos; GREAT ESCAPE, THE(1963), cos
Linda Henrikson
PERSONAL BEST(1982), cos
Linda M. Henrikson
1984
RHINESTONE(1984), cos
Matthias Henrikson
OBSESSION(1968, Swed.)
Merriana Henrique
WHITE SISTER(1973, Ital./Span./Fr.)
Ron Henrique
HICKEY AND BOGGS(1972)
Darryl Henriques
RIGHT STUFF, THE(1983)
1984
BEST DEFENSE(1984); CRACKERS(1984)
Ed Henriques
DEEP, THE(1977), makeup; UNDER FIRE(1983), makeup
Edouard Henriques III
1984
ULTIMATE SOLUTION OF GRACE QUIGLEY, THE(1984), makeup
Marya Henriques
COOGAN'S BLUFF(1968)
Paula Henriques
HEART WITHIN, THE(1957, Brit.)
Ron Henriques
MAIN EVENT, THE(1979)
Sylvana Henriques
DOCTOR IN TROUBLE(1970, Brit.)
Sylvanna Henriques
ON HER MAJESTY'S SECRET SERVICE(1969, Brit.)
Ron Henriquez
WILLIE DYNAMITE(1973)
Bette Henritze
HOSPITAL, THE(1971); HAPPINESS CAGE, THE(1972); RAGE(1972); WORLD AC-
CORDING TO GARP, The(1982)
Agnes G. Henry
CHEAP DETECTIVE, THE(1978), cos
Agnes Henry
NORWOOD(1970), cos
Athol Henry
LITTLE CONVICT, THE(1980, Aus.), art d; DOT AND THE BUNNY(1983, Aus.), anim
d
Ben Henry
SOUTH AMERICAN GEORGE(1941, Brit.), p; MUCH TOO SHY(1942, Brit.), p;
WE'LL MEET AGAIN(1942, Brit.), p; BELL-BOTTOM GEORGE(1943, Brit.), p; GET
CRACKING(1943, Brit.), p; RHYTHM SERENADE(1943, Brit.), p; HE SNOOPS TO
CONQUER(1944, Brit.), p; I DIDN'T DO IT(1945, Brit.), p; GEORGE IN CIVVY
STREET(1946, Brit.), p; YOU CAN'T DO WITHOUT LOVE(1946, Brit.), p
Bill Henry
HARMON OF MICHIGAN(1941); GENTLEMAN AFTER DARK, A(1942); KLON-
DIKE FURY(1942); PARDON MY STRIPES(1942); RUBBER RACKETEERS(1942);
STARDUST ON THE SAGE(1942); ALASKA HIGHWAY(1943); FALSE FACES(1943);
I ESCAPED FROM THE GESTAPO(1943); JOHNNY COME LATELY(1943); NEARLY
EIGHTEEN(1943); SARONG GIRL(1943); TORNADO(1943); GOING MY WAY(1944);
NAVY WAY, THE(1944); FABULOUS SUZANNE, THE(1946); HOLIDAY AF-
FAIR(1949); MOTOR PATROL(1950); THUNDERING CARAVANS(1952); WHAT
PRICE GLORY?(1952); MARSHAL OF CEDAR ROCK(1953); MOVIE STUNT-
MEN(1953); SAVAGE FRONTIER(1953); TORPEDO ALLEY(1953); BULLET FOR
JOEY, A(1955); JUNGLE MOON MEN(1955); ACCUSED OF MURDER(1956); THREE
OUTLAWS, THE(1956); URANIUM BOOM(1956); SPOOK CHASERS(1957); WINGS OF
EAGLES, THE(1957); GUNSMOKE IN TUCSON(1958); LAST HURRAH, THE(1958);
LONE RANGER AND THE LOST CITY OF GOLD, THE(1958); HORSE SOLDIERS,
THE(1959); ALAMO, THE(1960); SERGEANT RUTLEDGE(1960); TWO RODE
TOGETHER(1961); HOW THE WEST WAS WON(1962); MAN WHO SHOT LIBERTY
VALANCE, THE(1962); TAGGART(1964)
Misc. Talkies
HOLLYWOOD THRILL-MAKERS(1954)

Billie Henry
GAL YOUNG UN(1979)
Buck Henry
TROUBLEMAKER, THE(1964), a, w; GRADUATE, THE(1967), a, w; CANDY(1968,
Ital./Fr.), w; SECRET WAR OF HARRY FRIGG, THE(1968); CATCH-22(1970), a, w;
OWL AND THE PUSSYCAT, THE(1970), a, w; TAKING OFF(1971); WHAT'S UP,
DOC?(1972), w; DAY OF THE DOLPHIN, THE(1973), w; MAN WHO FELL TO
EARTH, THE(1976, Brit.); HEAVEN CAN WAIT(1978), a, d; OLD BOY-
FRIENDS(1979); FIRST FAMILY(1980), a, d&w; GLORIA(1980); EATING
RAOUL(1982)
1984
PROTOCOL(1984), w
Misc. Talkies
IS THERE SEX AFTER DEATH(1971)
Buzz Henry
MR. CELEBRITY(1942); TRAIL TO GUNSIGHT(1944); TRIGGER TRAIL(1944); HER
LUCKY NIGHT(1945); KING OF THE WILD HORSES(1947); LAST OF THE RED-
MEN(1947); MOONRISE(1948); ROCKY MOUNTAIN(1950); HOMESTEADERS,
THE(1953); LAST OF THE PONY RIDERS(1953); HELL'S OUTPOST(1955); INDIAN
FIGHTER, THE(1955); ROAD TO DENVER, THE(1955); LAWLESS EIGHTIES,
THE(1957); COWBOY(1958); SHEEPMAN, THE(1958); FACE OF A FUGITIVE(1959);
RISE AND FALL OF LEGS DIAMOND, THE(1960); SPENCER'S MOUNTAIN(1963);
ROUNDERS, THE(1965), stunts; SHENANDOAH(1965); VON RYAN'S EX-
PRESS(1965); EL DORADO(1967); IN LIKE FLINT(1967); TONY ROME(1967); WATER-
HOLE NO. 3(1967); MACKENNA'S GOLD(1969), stunts
Misc. Talkies
BUZZY RIDES THE RANGE(1940); BUZZY AND THE PHANTOM PINTO(1941);
LAW OF THE CANYON(1947)
"Buzzy" Dee Henry
CALLING WILD BILL ELLIOTT(1943)
Miss C. Henry
Silents
SILENT VOICE, THE(1915)
Carol Ann Henry
1984
GHOSTBUSTERS(1984)
Carol Henry
STRANGER FROM PECOS, THE(1943); SANTA FE SADDLEMATES(1945); SHE-
RIFF OF CIMARRON(1945); COURTIN' TROUBLE(1948); COWBOY CAVA-
LIER(1948); GUN TALK(1948); GUNNING FOR JUSTICE(1948); RANGERS RIDE,
THE(1948); ACROSS THE RIO GRANDE(1949); GUN LAW JUSTICE(1949); GUN
RUNNER(1949); HIDDEN DANGER(1949); RANGE LAND(1949); ROLL, THUNDER,
ROLL(1949); SHADOWS OF THE WEST(1949); STAMPEDE(1949); TRAIL'S
END(1949); ARIZONA TERRITORY(1950); GUNSLINGERS(1950); LAW OF THE
PANHANDLE(1950); OUTLAW GOLD(1950); OVER THE BORDER(1950); WINCHES-
TER '73(1950); LONGHORN, THE(1951); THREE DESPERATE MEN(1951); CANYON
AMBUSH(1952); NIGHT RAIDERS(1952); DEERSLAYER, THE(1957); SHOOT-OUT
AT MEDICINE BEND(1957); MANIAC(1980)
Carroll Henry
HALLELUJAH TRAIL, THE(1965)
Catherine Henry
Silents
PARADISE GARDEN(1917); ROUGH LOVER, THE(1918); PRISONERS OF LO-
VE(1921), w
Cheryl Henry
I, THE JURY(1982)
Christopher Henry
SILENT SCREAM(1980), prod d
1984
LIES(1984, Brit.), prod d
Chuck Henry
NORTH AVENUE IRREGULARS, THE(1979)
Cynthia Henry
EYES THAT KILL(1947, Brit.), ed
Cynthia R. Henry
GUNMAN HAS ESCAPED, A(1948, Brit.), ed
D. Henry
DARING CABALLERO, THE(1949), w
Daryl Henry
CRAZY WORLD OF JULIUS VROODER, THE(1974), w
David Henry
1984
KILLING FIELDS, THE(1984, Brit.)
David Lee Henry
HARRY TRACY–DESPERADO(1982, Can.), w
1984
EVIL THAT MEN DO, THE(1984), w
Dee "Buzzy" Henry
RIDIN' DOWN THE CANYON(1942)
DeLaura Henry
TRIAL OF BILLY JACK, THE(1974)
Dennis Henry
TOGETHER FOR DAYS(1972)
Diane Henry
OVERLAND MAIL ROBBERY(1943)
Don Henry
WATCHER IN THE WOODS, THE(1980, Brit.), spec eff
Donte I. Henry
YOUNG GIANTS(1983)
Ella Henry
FLOWER THIEF, THE(1962)
Emmaline Henry
LUCKY ME(1954); TOP BANANA(1954); DIVORCE AMERICAN STYLE(1967);
ROSEMARY'S BABY(1968); HARRAD SUMMER, THE(1974)
F Patrick Henry
CARRIE(1952)
Frank Henry
MR. LUCKY(1943); HOPPY'S HOLIDAY(1947); SADDLE PALS(1947); HA-
ZARD(1948)

Frank Pat Henry
PERFECT STRANGERS(1950)
Frederic Henry
STAR SPANGLED RHYTHM(1942); NO TIME FOR LOVE(1943); SALUTE FOR THREE(1943)
Gale Henry
DARKENED ROOMS(1929); LOVE DOCTOR, THE(1929)
Silents
HUNCH, THE(1921); NIGHT LIFE IN HOLLYWOOD(1922); HELD TO AN-SWER(1923); ALONG CAME RUTH(1924); MERTON OF THE MOVIES(1924); OPEN ALL NIGHT(1924); NEW LIVES FOR OLD(1925); STRANDED(1927)
Misc. Silents
WILD WEST SHOW, THE(1928)
George Henry
Silents
ARE CHILDREN TO BLAME?(1922)
Misc. Silents
COME-BACK, THE(1916); WHERE IS MY FATHER?(1916); BERLIN VIA AMERI-CA(1918)
Gloria Henry
KEEPER OF THE BEES(1947); SPORT OF KINGS(1947); ADVENTURES IN SIL-VERADO(1948); PORT SAID(1948); RACING LUCK(1948); STRAWBERRY ROAN, THE(1948); TRIPLE THREAT(1948); AIR HOSTESS(1949); JOHNNY ALLEGRO(1949); LAW OF THE BARBARY COAST(1949); MISS GRANT TAKES RICHMOND(1949); RIDERS IN THE SKY(1949); RUSTY SAVES A LIFE(1949); KILL THE UMPIRE(1950); LIGHTNING GUNS(1950); ROOKIE FIREMAN(1950); TOUGHER THEY COME, THE(1950); AL JENNINGS OF OKLAHOMA(1951); YELLOW FIN(1951); RANCHO NOTORIOUS(1952); HOT NEWS(1953); GANG WAR(1958); FOR LOVE OF IVY(1968); LANDLORD, THE(1970)
Misc. Talkies
BULLDOG DRUMMOND STRIKES BACK(1947); FEUDIN' RHYTHM(1949)
Gregg Henry
MEAN DOG BLUES(1978); JUST BEFORE DAWN(1980); FUNNY MONEY(1983, Brit.)
1984
BODY DOUBLE(1984)
Gustav Henry
OUR MOTHER'S HOUSE(1967, Brit.)
Guy Henry
THUNDER IN THE BLOOD(1962, Fr.)
1984
ANOTHER COUNTRY(1984, Brit.)
Hank Henry
THIS IS THE ARMY(1943); JUNIOR PROM(1946); JOKER IS WILD, THE(1957); PAL JOEY(1957); OCEAN'S ELEVEN(1960); PEPE(1960); SERGEANTS 3(1962); JOHNNY COOL(1963); ROBIN AND THE SEVEN HOODS(1964); ONLY GAME IN TOWN, THE(1970)
Misc. Talkies
NOT TONIGHT HENRY(1961)
Harriet Henry
BOUGHT(1931), w; LADY WITH A PAST(1932), w
Herb Henry
BANG THE DRUM SLOWLY(1973)
J.D. Henry
GAL YOUNG UN(1979)
Jack Henry
FLANNELFOOT(1953, Brit.), w; PLAY IT COOL(1963, Brit.), w
Silents
TESS OF THE STORM COUNTRY(1914)
Jacques Henry
LIFE LOVE DEATH(1969, Fr./Ital.)
Jay Henry
WE'RE NOT DRESSING(1934)
Jean Henry
Silents
NAPOLEON(1927, Fr.)
Jeffrey D. Henry
HALLOWEEN III: SEASON OF THE WITCH(1982)
Joan Henry
WEAK AND THE WICKED, THE(1954, Brit.), w; BLONDE SINNER(1956, Brit.), w; PASSIONATE SUMMER(1959, Brit.), w
John Henry
MOVIE MOVIE(1978)
Silents
POISON(1924)
Julian Henry
VIPER, THE(1938, Brit.); FOOL AND THE PRINCESS, THE(1948, Brit.)
Julien Henry
UNEASY TERMS(1948, Brit.)
Justin Henry
KRAMER VS. KRAMER(1979)
1984
SIXTEEN CANDLES(1984)
Katherine Henry
Misc. Silents
YOUR GIRL AND MINE(1914)
Kenneth Henry
OLD MOTHER RILEY MP(1939, Brit.); FACING THE MUSIC(1941, Brit.); SOME-THING IN THE CITY(1950, Brit.); FORCES' SWEETHEART(1953, Brit.); END OF THE ROAD, THE(1954, Brit.); TERROR SHIP(1954, Brit.)
Lee Henry
POLICE NURSE(1963)
Len Henry
CAUGHT IN THE DRAFT(1941); WHERE DANGER LIVES(1950)
Leonard Henry
PUBLIC LIFE OF HENRY THE NINTH, THE(1934, Brit.); REGAL CAVAL-CADE(1935, Brit.); SUNSHINE AHEAD(1936, Brit.); MOUNTAINS O'MOURNE(1938, Brit.); FACE AT THE WINDOW, THE(1939, Brit.)

Louise Henry
HIDE-OUT(1934); PARIS INTERLUDE(1934); CASINO MURDER CASE, THE(1935); IN OLD KENTUCKY(1935); KING SOLOMON OF BROADWAY(1935); MURDER MAN(1935); ONE NEW YORK NIGHT(1935); RECKLESS(1935); REMEMBER LAST NIGHT(1935), a, a, w; SOCIETY DOCTOR(1935); END OF THE TRAIL(1936); EXCLU-SIVE STORY(1936); CHARLIE CHAN ON BROADWAY(1937); HIT PARADE, THE(1937); THERE GOES THE GROOM(1937); 45 FATHERS(1937); CHARLIE CHAN IN RENO(1939); PHANTOM STRIKES, THE(1939, Brit.)
Marguerite Henry
MISTY(1961), w; BRIGHTY OF THE GRAND CANYON(1967), d&w
Marie-Dominique Henry
LAST METRO, THE(1981, Fr.)
Marion Henry
Silents
TWO-EDGED SWORD, THE(1916)
Mary Henry
YENTL(1983)
Maxine Henry
GAMEKEEPER, THE(1980, Brit.), cos
Mike Henry
SPENCER'S MOUNTAIN(1963); TARZAN AND THE VALLEY OF GOLD(1966 U.S./Switz.); TARZAN AND THE GREAT RIVER(1967, U.S./Switz.); GREEN BERETS, THE(1968); MORE DEAD THAN ALIVE(1968); TARZAN AND THE JUNGLE BOY(1968, US/Switz.); NUMBER ONE(1969); RIO LOBO(1970); SKYJACKED(1972); SOYLENT GREEN(1973); ABBY(1974), p; LONGEST YARD, THE(1974); ADIOS AMIGO(1975); MEAN JOHNNY BARROWS(1976); SMOKEY AND THE BAN-DIT(1977); SMOKEY AND THE BANDIT II(1980); SMOKEY AND THE BANDIT-PART 3(1983)
Noelle Henry
SO LITTLE TIME(1953, Brit.), w
Norman Henry
10 RILLINGTON PLACE(1971, Brit.)
O. Henry
IN OLD ARIZONA(1929), w; TEXAN, THE(1930), w; DR. RHYTHM(1938), w; RE-TURN OF THE CISCO KID(1939), w; GAY CABALLERO, THE(1940), w; LLANO KID, THE(1940), w; RIDE ON VAQUERO(1941), w; ROMANCE OF THE RIO GRAN-DE(1941), w; BLACK EAGLE(1948), w; VALIANT HOMBRE, THE(1948), w; GAY AMIGO, THE(1949), w; SATAN'S CRADLE(1949), w; GIRL FROM SAN LORENZO, THE(1950), w; O. HENRY'S FULL HOUSE(1952), w; BIG CHIEF, THE(1960, Fr.), w
Silents
AMERICAN LIVE WIRE, AN(1918), w; EVERYBODY'S GIRL(1918), w; ALIAS JIMMY VALENTINE(1920), w
Oriole Henry
TUSK(1980, Fr.)
Pam Henry
PROM NIGHT(1980)
Pat Henry
SEA OF GRASS, THE(1947); STARLIFT(1951); DETECTIVE, THE(1968); LADY IN CEMENT(1968); HAPPY HOOKER, THE(1975)
Patrick Henry
TALL MAN RIDING(1955)
Peter Henry
BODY STEALERS, THE(1969), ph
Phyllis Henry
SUSPENSE(1946)
Pierre Henry
WHERE THE TRUTH LIES(1962, Fr.), m
R. J. Henry
Silents
EAGLE'S MATE, THE(1914)
Randolph Henry
GEORGIA, GEORGIA(1972)
Ric Henry
HELL'S ANGELS '69(1969)
Robert Buzz Henry
TEXAS ACROSS THE RIVER(1966), stunts
Robert "Buzz" Henry
UNKNOWN RANGER, THE(1936); RANGER COURAGE(1937); GREAT MIKE, THE(1944); DANNY BOY(1946); WILD BEAUTY(1946); WILD WEST(1946); PRAIRIE OUTLAWS(1948); BLUE GRASS OF KENTUCKY(1950); HEART OF THE ROCK-IES(1951); JUBILEE TRAIL(1954); OUTCAST, THE(1954); JUBAL(1956); TONKA(1958)
Robert Henry
WESTERN FRONTIER(1935); RIO GRANDE RANGER(1937)
Roy Henry
MONITORS, THE(1969), art d
Thomas B. Henry
MARRYING KIND, THE(1952); MAN ALONE, A(1955); CALLING HOMICIDE(1956); D-DAY, THE SIXTH OF JUNE(1956); FIGHTING TROUBLE(1956); LEATHER SAINT, THE(1956); BEGINNING OF THE END(1957); BLOOD OF DRACULA(1957); CHICAGO CONFIDENTIAL(1957); MY MAN GODFREY(1957); 20 MILLION MILES TO EARTH(1957); BRAIN FROM THE PLANET AROUS, THE(1958); CASE AGAINST BROOKLYN, THE(1958); HOW TO MAKE A MONSTER(1958); QUANTRILL'S RAID-ERS(1958); SAY ONE FOR ME(1959)
Thomas Brown Henry
MY BLUE HEAVEN(1950)
Thomas Browne Henry
JOHNNY ALLEGRO(1949); POST OFFICE INVESTIGATOR(1949); TULSA(1949); ASPHALT JUNGLE, THE(1950); FATHER OF THE BRIDE(1950); NO MAN OF HER OWN(1950); GUY WHO CAME BACK, THE(1951); MR. BELVEDERE RINGS THE BELL(1951); DEADLINE-U.S.A.(1952); HOODLUM EMPIRE(1952); O. HENRY'S FULL HOUSE(1952); JULIUS CAESAR(1953); LADY WANTS MINK, THE(1953); ROBE, THE(1953); VEILS OF BAGDAD, THE(1953); TOUGHEST MAN ALIVE(1955); STRANGE ADVENTURE, A(1956); SHOWDOWN AT BOOT HILL(1958); SPACE MASTER X-7(1958); I PASSED FOR WHITE(1960)
Tim Henry
EYE OF THE CAT(1969); HOMER(1970); 125 ROOMS OF COMFORT(1974, Can.); SUNDAY IN THE COUNTRY(1975, Can.); AGE OF INNOCENCE(1977, Can.); IMPROP-ER CHANNELS(1981, Can.)

Tom Browne Henry
BEHIND LOCKED DOORS(1948); HE WALKED BY NIGHT(1948); JOAN OF ARC(1948); DOUBLE DEAL(1950); IT'S A SMALL WORLD(1950); OPERATION SECRET(1952); PRISONER OF ZENDA, THE(1952); SCARLET ANGEL(1952); STARS AND STRIPES FOREVER(1952); WINNING TEAM, THE(1952); LAW AND ORDER(1953); SITTING BULL(1954); VIOLENT MEN, THE(1955); EARTH VS. THE FLYING SAUCERS(1956); POWER AND THE PRIZE, THE(1956); NO TIME FOR SERGEANTS(1958); WINK OF AN EYE(1958); GUNFIGHT AT COMANCHE CREEK(1964)

Tom Henry
HOLLOW TRIUMPH(1948); IMPACT(1949)

Victor Henry
PRIVILEGE(1967, Brit.); SORCERERS, THE(1967, Brit.); ALL NEAT IN BLACK STOCKINGS(1969, Brit.)

Will Henry
PILLARS OF THE SKY(1956), w; JOURNEY TO SHILOH(1968), w; MACKENNA'S GOLD(1969), w; YOUNG BILLY YOUNG(1969), w

William Henry
YELLOW JACK(1938); OPERATOR 13(1934); THIN MAN, THE(1934); WICKED WOMAN, A(1934); CHINA SEAS(1935); SOCIETY DOCTOR(1935); EXCLUSIVE STORY(1936); TARZAN ESCAPES(1936); DOUBLE OR NOTHING(1937); MADAME X(1937); ARIZONA WILDCAT(1938); CAMPUS CONFESSIONS(1938); FOUR MEN AND A PRAYER(1938); MAMA RUNS WILD(1938); MAN TO REMEMBER, A(1938); AMBUSH(1939); GERONIMO(1939); I'M FROM MISSOURI(1939); PERSONS IN HIDING(1939); TELEVISION SPY(1939); CHEROKEE STRIP(1940); EMERGENCY SQUAD(1940); PAROLE FIXER(1940); QUEEN OF THE MOB(1940); WAY OF ALL FLESH, THE(1940); BLOSSOMS IN THE DUST(1941); DANCE HALL(1941); JENNIE(1941); SCATTERGOOD MEETS BROADWAY(1941); SWEATER GIRL(1942); ADVENTURES OF MARK TWAIN, THE(1944); CALL OF THE SOUTH SEAS(1944); LADY AND THE MONSTER, THE(1944); SILENT PARTNER(1944); G.I. WAR BRIDES(1946); INVISIBLE INFORMER(1946); MYSTERIOUS MR. VALENTINE, THE(1946); TRAIL TO SAN ANTONE(1947); DENVER KID, THE(1948); KING OF THE GAMBLERS(1948); RENEGADES OF SONORA(1948); WOMEN IN THE NIGHT(1948); FEDERAL MAN(1950); OLD FRONTIER, THE(1950); FURY OF THE CONGO(1951); SECRET OF THE INCAS(1954); COURT-MARTIAL OF BILLY MITCHELL, THE(1955); FRESH FROM PARIS(1955); MISTER ROBERTS(1955); NEW ORLEANS UNCENSORED(1955); PARIS FOLLIES OF 1956(1955); TOWARD THE UNKNOWN(1956); CHEYENNE AUTUMN(1964); DEAR BRIGETTE(1965)

William A. Henry
DEATH VALLEY GUNFIGHTER(1949); STREETS OF SAN FRANCISCO(1949); MASTERSON OF KANSAS(1954)

William Albert Henry
EL DORADO(1967)

Henry King and Orchestra
SUNSET MURDER CASE(1941)

Willie Henry, Jr.
FAME(1980)

Katherine Henryk
FIERCEST HEART, THE(1961)
Misc. Talkies
BLOOD THIRST(1965 Phil./U.S.)

Robert Henryson
DEATH IS A NUMBER(1951, Brit.), p&d

Ron Henschel
BATTLE BEYOND THE STARS(1980)

David Hensen
Misc. Talkies
METAL MESSIAH(1978)

Lars Hensen
CHAMP, THE(1979)

Leslie Hensen
Silents
ALF'S BUTTON(1920, Brit.)

Roger Hensen
1984
NATURAL, THE(1984), spec eff

Bobbie "Uke" Henshaw
VARIETY(1935, Brit.)

Bobby Henshaw
SET-UP, THE(1949)

Eric Henshaw
PIRANHA(1978); WHOLE SHOOTIN' MATCH, THE(1979)

George H. Henshaw
PAD, THE(AND HOW TO USE IT)* (1966, Brit.), set d

lp: Jim Henshaw
Misc. Talkies
LIONS FOR BREAKFAST(1977)

Marjorie Henshaw
HERE COME THE WAVES(1944)

Judy Henske
HOOTENANNY HOOT(1963)

Paul Hensler
MORE AMERICAN GRAFFITI(1979); DON'T CRY, IT'S ONLY THUNDER(1982), a, w

Gail Hensley
HAPPY ENDING, THE(1969)

Pamela Hensley
THERE WAS A CROOKED MAN(1970); MAKING IT(1971); SELF-PORTRAIT(1973, U.S./Chile); DOC SAVAGE... THE MAN OF BRONZE(1975); ROLLERBALL(1975); BUCK ROGERS IN THE 25TH CENTURY(1979); NUDE BOMB, THE(1980); DOUBLE EXPOSURE(1982)

Ron Hensley
COAL MINER'S DAUGHTER(1980)

Tana Hensley
SILKWOOD(1983)

Lt. Col. F.D. Henslowe
DRUMS(1938, Brit.), tech adv

Basil Henson
DOUBLE, THE(1963, Brit.); CHANGE PARTNERS(1965, Brit.); DARLING(1965, Brit.); FROZEN DEAD, THE(1967, Brit.); CROMWELL(1970, Brit.); WALKING STICK, THE(1970, Brit.); LAST DAYS OF MAN ON EARTH, THE(1975, Brit.)

Bobbie Jean Henson
PAL JOEY(1957)

Brian Henson
GREAT MUPPET CAPER, THE(1981)

Chuck Henson
HONKERS, THE(1972)

Elizabeth Henson
GIRL WHO COULDN'T QUITE, THE(1949, Brit.); ALICE IN WONDERLAND(1951, Fr.)

Frank Henson
THOSE DARING YOUNG MEN IN THEIR JAUNTY JALOPIES(1969, Fr./Brit./Ital.); BLACK WINDMILL, THE(1974, Brit.); DRACULA(1979)

Gladys Henson
FRIEDA(1947, Brit.); CAPTIVE HEART, THE(1948, Brit.); COUNTER BLAST(1948, Brit.); DEVIL'S PLOT, THE(1948, Brit.); DULCIMER STREET(1948, Brit.); HISTORY OF MR. POLLY, THE(1949, Brit.); IT ALWAYS RAINS ON SUNDAY(1949, Brit.); TEMPTATION HARBOR(1949, Brit.); WEAKER SEX, THE(1949, Brit.); CAGE OF GOLD(1950, Brit.); CURE FOR LOVE, THE(1950, Brit.); DANCE HALL(1950, Brit.); HAPPIEST DAYS OF YOUR LIFE(1950, Brit.); HIGHLY DANGEROUS(1950, Brit.); MAGNET, THE(1950, Brit.); HAPPY GO LOVELY(1951, Brit.); FOUR AGAINST FATE(1952, Brit.); THOSE PEOPLE NEXT DOOR(1952, Brit.); TRAIN OF EVENTS(1952, Brit.); I BELIEVE IN YOU(1953, Brit.); MEET MR. LUCIFER(1953, Brit.); COCKLESHELL HEROES, THE(1955); LADY GODIVA RIDES AGAIN(1955, Brit.); DOCTOR AT LARGE(1957, Brit.); PRINCE AND THE SHOWGIRL, THE(1957, Brit.); DAVY(1958, Brit.); MAN WITH THE GREEN CARNATION, THE(1960, Brit.); DANGEROUS AFTERNOON(1961, Brit.); DOUBLE BUNK(1961, Brit.); NO LOVE FOR JOHNNIE(1961, Brit.); DEATH TRAP(1962, Brit.); FIRST MEN IN THE MOON(1964, Brit.); GO KART GO(1964, Brit.); STORK TALK(1964, Brit.); LEATHER BOYS, THE(1965, Brit.); CLUE OF THE TWISTED CANDLE(1968, Brit.); BAWDY ADVENTURES OF TOM JONES, THE(1976, Brit.)

Jim Henson
MUPPET MOVIE, THE(1979), a, p; GREAT MUPPET CAPER, THE(1981), a, d; DARK CRYSTAL, THE(1982, Brit.), a, p, d, w
1984
MUPPETS TAKE MANHATTAN, THE(1984)

John Henson
1984
SECRET PLACES(1984, Brit.)

Joseph Henson
RED RUNS THE RIVER(1963)

Laurence Henson
FLASH THE SHEEPDOG(1967, Brit.), d&w; BIG CATCH, THE(1968, Brit.), p, d

Leslie Henson
WARM CORNER, A(1930, Brit.); SPORT OF KINGS, THE(1931, Brit.); IT'S A BOY(1934, Brit.); OH DADDY!(1935, Brit.); GIRL FROM MAXIM'S, THE(1936, Brit.); ADVENTURE FOR TWO(1945, Brit.); HOME AND AWAY(1956, Brit.)
Misc. Silents
WANTED - A WIDOW(1916, Brit.); TONS OF MONEY(1924, Brit.)

Lin Henson
DOCTOR DEATH: SEEKER OF SOULS(1973); WESTWORLD(1973)

Nicky Henson
FATHER CAME TOO(1964, Brit.); CARNABY, M.D.(1967, Brit.); JOKERS, THE(1967, Brit.); CONQUEROR WORM, THE(1968, Brit.); HERE WE GO ROUND THE MULBERRY BUSH(1968, Brit.); 30 IS A DANGEROUS AGE, CYNTHIA(1968, Brit.); MOSQUITO SQUADRON(1970, Brit.); SOPHIE'S PLACE(1970); THERE'S A GIRL IN MY SOUP(1970, Brit.); PSYCHOMANIA(1974, Brit.); OLD DRACULA(1975, Brit.); BAWDY ADVENTURES OF TOM JONES, THE(1976, Brit.)
Misc. Talkies
ALL COPPERS ARE...(1972, Brit.)

Bruce Henstell
HARD TIMES(1975), w

Alex Henteloff
SLITHER(1973); LAST WORD, THE(1979); HARDLY WORKING(1981)

Ernest Henthaler
DON JUAN(1956, Aust.), w

Torsten Henties
DAVID(1979, Ger.)

David Hentschel
OPERATION DAYBREAK(1976, U.S./Brit./Czech.), m; SEVEN NIGHTS IN JAPAN(1976, Brit./Fr.), m; SQUEEZE, THE(1977, Brit.), m; EDUCATING RITA(1983), m

Michael Hentz
1984
BAD MANNERS(1984)

Pierre Hentz
CATHERINE & CO.(1976, Fr.)

Sandra Lee Henville
EAST SIDE OF HEAVEN(1939); LITTLE ACCIDENT(1939)

Dora Henwood
Misc. Silents
ISLAND OF ROMANCE, THE(1922, Brit.)

Peter Henwood
DEVIL'S WIDOW, THE(1972, Brit.)

Hans-Werner Henze
MURIEL(1963, Fr./Ital.), m; YOUNG TORLESS(1968, Fr./Ger.), m; YOUNG LORD, THE(1970, Ger.), w, m; LOST HONOR OF KATHARINA BLUM, THE(1975, Ger.), m
1984
SWANN IN LOVE(1984, Fr.Ger.), m

Jurgen Henze
MERCENARY, THE(1970, Ital./Span.), cos; DON'T TURN THE OTHER CHEEK(1974, Ital./Ger./Span.), cos; FRIENDS AND HUSBANDS(1983, Ger.), art d
1984
LOVE IN GERMANY, A(1984, Fr./Ger.), art d

Perry Henzell
HARDER THEY COME, THE(1973, Jamaica), p&d, w

ISLAND, THE(1953), d, w; MOON IS BLUE, THE(1953), p, w; LITTLE HUT, THE(1957), p, w; THIS HAPPY FEELING(1958), w, d&w
Silents
WANING SEX, THE(1926), w; ADAM AND EVIL(1927), w; ON ZE BOULE-VARD(1927), w; TEA FOR THREE(1927), w; BABY MINE(1928), w; SINGLE MAN, A(1929), w

F.H. Herbert
PENAL CODE, THE(1933), w

Frank Herbert
1984
DUNE(1984), w

Frederick Herbert
CITY BENEATH THE SEA(1953), m; RAILS INTO LARAMIE(1954), m

George Herbert
PIGSKIN PARADE(1936); CAFE METROPOLE(1937); CRAWLING EYE, THE(1958, Brit.); FURTHER UP THE CREEK!(1958, Brit.); SECRETS OF SEX(1970, Brit.); TALES FROM THE CRYPT(1972, Brit.)
Misc. Silents
SILENT PARTNER, THE(1917)

Gwynne Herbert
Silents
FIRM OF GIRDLESTONE, THE(1915, Brit.); GREATER NEED, THE(1916, Brit.); PRINCESS OF HAPPY CHANCE, THE(1916, Brit.); GREATEST WISH IN THE WORLD, THE(1918, Brit.); HANGING JUDGE, THE(1918, Brit.); NATURE OF THE BEAST, THE(1919, Brit.); POSSESSION(1919, Brit.); ALF'S BUTTON(1920, Brit.); ANNA THE ADVENTURESS(1920, Brit.); AYLWIN(1920, Brit.); ONCE ABOARD THE LUGGER(1920, Brit.); TEMPORARY VAGABOND, A(1920, Brit.); MR. JUSTICE RAFFLES(1921, Brit.); NARROW VALLEY, THE(1921, Brit.)
Misc. Silents
AS THE SUN WENT DOWN(1915, Brit.); ASHES OF REVENGE, THE(1915, Brit.); WHOSO DIGGETH A PIT(1915, Brit.); ANNIE LAURIE(1916, Brit.); HIS DAUGHT-ER'S DILEMMA(1916, Brit.); HOMEMAKER, THE(1919, Brit.); TOILERS, THE(1919, Brit.); DOLLARS IN SURREY(1921, Brit.); LUNATIC AT LARGE, THE(1921, Brit.); TIT FOR TAT(1922, Brit.)

H. E. Herbert
Silents
DOLL'S HOUSE, A(1918)
Misc. Silents
HIS WIFE(1915); HER LIFE AND HIS(1917); DIVORCEE, THE(1919)

H. J. Herbert
Silents
FIRES OF CONSCIENCE(1916); DAUGHTERS OF TODAY(1924)
Misc. Silents
MAN WITHOUT A COUNTRY, THE(1917); SUSPICIOUS WIVES(1921); WEEK END HUSBANDS(1924)

Hans Herbert
MEET THE WILDCAT(1940); GREAT IMPERSONATION, THE(1942); MAD GHOUL, THE(1943); PHANTOM OF THE OPERA(1943); HOUSE OF FRANKENSTEIN(1944); LAKE PLACID SERENADE(1944); SUDAN(1945); NIGHT AND DAY(1946); NIGHT IN PARADISE, A(1946); DESPERATE(1947); IMPACT(1949); UNDER MY SKIN(1950); LULLABY OF BROADWAY, THE(1951); FIRST TRAVELING SALESLADY, THE(1956)

Harry Herbert
SISTER TO ASSIST'ER, A(1938, Brit.); GARRISON FOLLIES(1940, Brit.); DANNY BOY(1941, Brit.); GERT AND DAISY CLEAN UP(1942, Brit.); WE'LL SMILE AGAIN(1942, Brit.); DUMMY TALKS, THE(1943, Brit.); LOYAL HEART(1946, Brit.); OLD MOTHER RILEY, HEADMISTRESS(1950, Brit.); TIME GENTLEMEN PLEA-SE!(1953, Brit.); SQUARE RING, THE(1955, Brit.); WILL ANY GENTLEMAN?(1955, Brit.)

Henry Herbert
THEIR OWN DESIRE(1929); PRESIDENT VANISHES, THE(1934); EASY MO-NEY(1936); IT COULDN'T HAVE HAPPENED--BUT IT DID(1936); HEAVENLY DAYS(1944); LADY LUCK(1946); MALACHI'S COVE(1973, Brit.), d&w; EMILY(1976, Brit.), d
Silents
CYCLONE, THE(1920); LITTLE WILDCAT(1922); SO BIG(1924); BLUE STREAK, THE(1926); ENCHANTED HILL, THE(1926); CROSS BREED(1927); GIRL FROM RIO, THE(1927); ONE CHANCE IN A MILLION(1927); LADDIE BE GOOD(1928)
Misc. Silents
WHEN DANGER SMILES(1922); STOLEN SECRETS(1924); CLEAN-UP MAN, THE(1928)

Henry J. Herbert
Silents
WILD HONEY(1919); HER ELEPHANT MAN(1920)

Holmes Herbert
ON TRIAL(1928); TERROR, THE(1928); CAREERS(1929); CARELESS AGE(1929); CHARLATAN, THE(1929); HER PRIVATE LIFE(1929); MADAME X(1929); SAY IT WITH SONGS(1929); UNTAMED(1929); SHIP FROM SHANGHAI, THE(1930); THIR-TEENTH CHAIR, THE(1930); BROADMINDED(1931); CHANCES(1931); DAUGHTER OF THE DRAGON(1931); HOT HEIRESS(1931); SINGLE SIN(1931); CENTRAL PARK(1932); DR. JEKYLL AND MR. HYDE(1932); MISS PINKERTON(1932); SHOP ANGEL(1932); INVISIBLE MAN, THE(1933); MYSTERY OF THE WAX MUSEUM, THE(1933); BELOVED(1934); COUNT OF MONTE CRISTO, THE(1934); HOUSE OF ROTHSCHILD, THE(1934); PURSUIT OF HAPPINESS, THE(1934); ACCENT ON YOUTH(1935); CAPTAIN BLOOD(1935); CURTAIN FALLS, THE(1935); DARK AN-GEL, THE(1935); MARK OF THE VAMPIRE(1935); SONS OF STEEL(1935); BRIL-LIANT MARRIAGE(1936); CHARGE OF THE LIGHT BRIGADE, THE(1936); COUNTRY BEYOND, THE(1936); FIFTEEN MAIDEN LANE(1936); GENTLEMAN FROM LOUISIANA(1936); LLOYDS OF LONDON(1936); WIFE VERSUS SECRE-TARY(1936); GIRL SAID NO, THE(1937); HERE'S FLASH CASEY(1937); HOUSE OF SECRETS, THE(1937); LANCER SPY(1937); LIFE OF EMILE ZOLA, THE(1937); LOVE UNDER FIRE(1937); PRINCE AND THE PAUPER, THE(1937); SLAVE SHIP(1937); THIRTEENTH CHAIR, THE(1937); ADVENTURES OF ROBIN HOOD, THE(1938); BLACK DOLL, THE(1938); BUCCANEER, THE(1938); KIDNAPPED(1938); MARIE ANTOINETTE(1938); SAY IT IN FRENCH(1938); ADVENTURES OF SHERLOCK HOLMES, THE(1939); BAD BOY(1939); EVERYTHING HAPPENS AT NIGHT(1939); HIDDEN POWER(1939); JUAREZ(1939); LITTLE PRINCESS, THE(1939); MR. MOTO'S LAST WARNING(1939); MYSTERY OF MR. WONG, THE(1939); MYSTERY OF THE WHITE ROOM(1939); STANLEY AND LIVINGSTONE(1939); TOWER OF LON-DON(1939); TRAPPED IN THE SKY(1939); WE ARE NOT ALONE(1939); WOLF

CALL(1939); BRITISH INTELLIGENCE(1940); DISPATCH FROM REUTERS, A(1940); EARL OF CHICAGO, THE(1940); FOREIGN CORRESPONDENT(1940); LETTER, THE(1940); SOUTH OF SUEZ(1940); WOMEN IN WAR(1940); INTERNATIONAL SQUADRON(1941); MAN HUNT(1941); RAGE IN HEAVEN(1941); SCOTLAND YARD(1941); DANGER IN THE PACIFIC(1942); GHOST OF FRANKENSTEIN, THE(1942); INVISIBLE AGENT(1942); LADY IN A JAM(1942); SHERLOCK HOLMES AND THE SECRET WEAPON(1942); STRICTLY IN THE GROOVE(1942); THIS ABOVE ALL(1942); UNDYING MONSTER, THE(1942); CALLING DR. DEATH(1943); CORVETTE K-225(1943); SHERLOCK HOLMES FACES DEATH(1943); SHERLOCK HOLMES IN WASHINGTON(1943); TWO TICKETS TO LONDON(1943); ENTER ARSENE LUPIN(1944); MUMMY'S CURSE, THE(1944); OUR HEARTS WERE YOUNG AND GAY(1944); PEARL OF DEATH, THE(1944); UNINVITED, THE(1944); CONFIDENTIAL AGENT(1945); GEORGE WHITE'S SCANDALS(1945); HOUSE OF FEAR, THE(1945); JEALOUSY(1945); UNCLE HARRY(1945); BANDIT OF SHER-WOOD FOREST, THE(1946); CLOAK AND DAGGER(1946); LOVE LAUGHS AT ANDY HARDY(1946); THREE STRANGERS(1946); VERDICT, THE(1946); IVY(1947); SIN-GAPORE(1947); SWORDSMAN, THE(1947); THIS TIME FOR KEEPS(1947); FAMILY HONEYMOON(1948); JOHNNY BELINDA(1948); JUNGLE JIM(1948); BARBARY PIRATE(1949); POST OFFICE INVESTIGATOR(1949); STRATTON STORY, THE(1949); IROQUOIS TRAIL, THE(1950); MAGNIFICENT YANKEE, THE(1950); TO PLEASE A LADY(1950); ANNE OF THE INDIES(1951); AT SWORD'S POINT(1951); DAVID AND BATHSHEBA(1951); LAW AND THE LADY, THE(1951); SON OF DR. JEKYLL, THE(1951); UNKNOWN MAN, THE(1951); BRIGAND, THE(1952); WILD NORTH, THE(1952)
Misc. Talkies
SISTER TO JUDAS(1933); BULLDOG DRUMMOND AT BAY(1947)
Silents
INNER CHAMBER, THE(1921); WILD GOOSE, THE(1921); ANY WIFE(1922); MOON-SHINE VALLEY(1922); ANOTHER SCANDAL(1924); ENCHANTED COTTAGE, THE(1924); HER OWN FREE WILL(1924); LOVE'S WILDERNESS(1924); SINNERS IN HEAVEN(1924); JOSSELYN'S WIFE(1926); GAY RETREAT, THE(1927); MR. WU(1927); NEST, THE(1927); SILVER SLAVE, THE(1927); SLAVES OF BEAU-TY(1927); GENTLEMEN PREFER BLONDES(1928); KISS, THE(1929)
Misc. Silents
DEATH DANCE, THE(1918); WHIRLPOOL, THE(1918); ABC OF LOVE, THE(1919); MARKET OF SOULS, THE(1919); OTHER MEN'S WIVES(1919); WHITE HEATHER, THE(1919); BLACK IS WHITE(1920); DEAD MEN TELL NO TALES(1920); HIS HOUSE IN ORDER(1920); LADY ROSE'S DAUGHTER(1920); MY LADY'S GARTER(1920); RIGHT TO LOVE, THE(1920); TRUTH ABOUT HUSBANDS, THE(1920); FAMILY CLOSET, THE(1921); HEEDLESS MOTHS(1921); HER LORD AND MASTER(1921); DIVORCE COUPONS(1922); EVIDENCE(1922); STAGE ROMANCE, A(1922); WO-MAN'S WOMAN, A(1922); SWORDS AND THE WOMAN(1923, Brit.); TOILERS OF THE SEA(1923 US/Ital.); UP THE LADDER(1925); WILDFIRE(1925); WOMAN OF THE WORLD, A(1925); WRECKAGE(1925); FIRE BRIGADE, THE(1926); HONEY-MOON EXPRESS, THE(1926); HEART OF SALOME, THE(1927); ONE INCREASING PURPOSE(1927); SPORTING AGE, THE(1928); THROUGH THE BREAKERS(1928)

Holmes Herbert, Sr.
ONE IN A MILLION(1935)

Hugh Herbert
AIR CIRCUS, THE(1928), w; CAUGHT IN THE FOG(1928); LIGHTS OF NEW YORK(1928), w; GREAT GABBO, THE(1929), w; DANGER LIGHTS(1930), a, s; HE KNEW WOMEN(1930), d, w; HOOK, LINE AND SINKER(1930); SECOND WI-FE(1930), w; FRIENDS AND LOVERS(1931); LAUGH AND GET RICH(1931); SIN SHIP(1931), a, w; TRAVELING HUSBANDS(1931); FAITHLESS(1932); LOST SQUA-DRON, THE(1932); MILLION DOLLAR LEGS(1932); BUREAU OF MISSING PER-SONS(1933); COLLEGE COACH(1933); CONVENTION CITY(1933); DIPLOMANIACS(1933); FOOTLIGHT PARADE(1933); FROM HEADQUAR-TERS(1933); GOODBYE AGAIN(1933); SHE HAD TO SAY YES(1933); STRICTLY PERSONAL(1933); DAMES(1934); EASY TO LOVE(1934); FASHIONS OF 1934(1934); FOG OVER FRISCO(1934); HAROLD TEEN(1934); KANSAS CITY PRINCESS(1934); MERRY FRINKS, THE(1934); MERRY WIVES OF RENO, THE(1934); WONDER BAR(1934); GOLD DIGGERS OF 1935(1935); MIDSUMMER'S NIGHT'S DREAM, A(1935); MISS PACIFIC FLEET(1935); SWEET ADELINE(1935); TO BEAT THE BAND(1935); TRAVELING SALESLADY, THE(1935); WE'RE IN THE MONEY(1935); COLLEEN(1936); LOVE BEGINS AT TWENTY(1936); ONE RAINY AFTER-NOON(1936); SING ME A LOVE SONG(1936); WE WENT TO COLLEGE(1936); HOLLYWOOD HOTEL(1937); MARRY THE GIRL(1937); PERFECT SPECIMEN, THE(1937); SH! THE OCTOPUS(1937); SINGING MARINE, THE(1937); THAT MAN'S HERE AGAIN(1937); TOP OF THE TOWN(1937); FOUR'S A CROWD(1938); GOLD DIGGERS IN PARIS(1938); GREAT WALTZ, THE(1938); MEN ARE SUCH FOOLS(1938); ETERNALLY YOURS(1939); FAMILY NEXT DOOR, THE(1939); LADY'S FROM KENTUCKY, THE(1939); LITTLE ACCIDENT(1939); HIT PARADE OF 1941(1940); LA CONGA NIGHTS(1940); LITTLE BIT OF HEAVEN, A(1940); PRIVATE AFFAIRS(1940); SLIGHTLY TEMPTED(1940); VILLAIN STILL PURSUED HER, THE(1940); BADLANDS OF DAKOTA(1941); BLACK CAT, THE(1941); DON'T GET PERSONAL(1941); HELLO SUCKER(1941); HELLZAPOPPIN'(1941); MEET THE CHUMP(1941); MRS. WIGGS OF THE CABBAGE PATCH(1942); THERE'S ONE BORN EVERY MINUTE(1942); YOU'RE TELLING ME(1942); IT'S A GREAT LIFE(1943); STAGE DOOR CANTEEN(1943); EVER SINCE VENUS(1944); KISMET(1944); MUSIC FOR MILLIONS(1944); ONE WAY TO LOVE(1946); BLONDIE IN THE DOUGH(1947); GIRL FROM MANHATTAN(1948); ON OUR MERRY WAY(1948); ONE TOUCH OF VENUS(1948); SO THIS IS NEW YORK(1948); SONG IS BORN, A(1948); BEAUTIFUL BLONDE FROM BASHFUL BEND, THE(1949); HAVANA ROSE(1951)
Silents
HUSBANDS FOR RENT(1927)
Misc. Silents
THERE YOU ARE!(1926), d

Ivor Herbert
GREAT ST. TRINIAN'S TRAIN ROBBERY, THE(1966, Brit.), w

Jack Herbert
Silents
EXCUSE MY DUST(1920); TOO MUCH SPEED(1921); WHITE AND UNMAR-RIED(1921); ACROSS THE CONTINENT(1922); SIX DAYS(1923); STEPHEN STEPS OUT(1923)

James Herbert
DEADLY EYES(1982), w

Jean Herbert
COUSIN, COUSINE(1976, Fr.)

Ronald Herdman
MC VICAR(1982, Brit.)
Virginia Herdman
MYSTERY RANCH(1932)
Georges Hereaux
UNDER SECRET ORDERS(1943, Brit.), w
Joseph Heredia
HELL'S ISLAND(1955)
Lisa Heredia
AVIATOR'S WIFE, THE(1981, Fr.); LE BEAU MARIAGE(1982, Fr.), ed
Luis Heredia
VIRIDIANA(1962, Mex./Span.)
Kathryn Hereford
KEY WITNESS(1960), p
Jean Heremans
SCARAMOUCHE(1952), ch; LAST TIME I SAW PARIS, THE(1954)
Frederick Herendeen
ALL THE KING'S HORSES(1935), w
Ken Hergenroeder
COACH(1978), art d
Kenneth H. Hergenroeder
VAN NUYS BLVD.(1979), art d
Aukie Herger
POSSESSION OF JOEL DELANEY, THE(1972)
Paul Hergermann
NEPTUNE FACTOR, THE(1973, Can.), ph
Jessica Hergert
DOZENS, THE(1981)
Joseph Hergesheimer
TOL'ABLE DAVID(1930), w; WOMAN I STOLE, THE(1933), w. Jo Swerling; JAVA
HEAD(1935, Brit.), w
Silents
TOL'ABLE DAVID(1921), w; JAVA HEAD(1923), w; CYTHEREA(1924), w
Ann Hergira
WITHOUT EACH OTHER(1962)
Robert J. Herguth
SLAUGHTER IN SAN FRANCISCO(1981)
Joel Herholdt
DIAMOND SAFARI(1958)
B.J. Herholz
RIDE IN THE WHIRLWIND(1966)
Philippe Heriat
ROTHSCHILD(1938, Fr.); ROSIE!(1967), w
Silents
NAPOLEON(1927, Fr.)
Misc. Silents
ELDORADO(1921, Fr.); DON JUAN ET FAUST(1923, Fr.); LA MARCHAND DE
PLAISIR(1923, Fr.); L'INHUMAINE(1923, Fr.); LA GALERIE DES MONSTRES(1924,
Fr.); L'INONDATION(1924, Fr.)
Rene Heribel
Misc. Silents
CAGLIOSTRO(1928, Fr.)
Renee Heribel
Misc. Silents
MINUIT...PLACE PIGALLE(1928, Fr.); APPASSIONATA(1929, Fr.)
Jutta Hering
DESPERADO TRAIL, THE(1965, Ger./Yugo.), ed
Diana Heringova
SHOP ON MAIN STREET, THE(1966, Czech.), ed
Katherine Herington
TO ALL A GOODNIGHT(1980)
Ursula Herion
SNOW WHITE AND ROSE RED(1966, Ger.)
Clarence Heritage
Silents
MAN WORTH WHILE, THE(1921)
Misc. Silents
LIGHT WITHIN, THE(1918); BROMLEY CASE, THE(1920)
Dora Heritage
Misc. Silents
DRIFTWOOD(1916)
Leslie Heritage
CRAWLING EYE, THE(1958, Brit.)
Catherine Heriza
TAKING OFF(1971)
H. Herkan
WHITE ZOMBIE(1932), m
Ursula Herking
FOUR COMPANIONS, THE(1938, Ger.); SPECIAL DELIVERY(1955, Ger.)
Richard A. Herland
MINI-AFFAIR, THE(1968, Brit.), p
Richard Herland
STEPPENWOLF(1974), p
Eileen Herlie
HUNGRY HILL(1947, Brit.); HAMLET(1948, Brit.); ANGEL WITH THE TRUMPET,
THE(1950, Brit.); GREAT GILBERT AND SULLIVAN, THE(1953, Brit.); ISN'T LIFE
WONDERFUL(1953, Brit.); FOR BETTER FOR WORSE(1954, Brit.); FREUD(1962);
SHE DIDN'T SAY NO!(1962, Brit.); HAMLET(1964); SEA GULL, THE(1968)
Ed Herlihy
KING OF COMEDY, THE(1983); ZELIG(1983)
James Leo Herlihy
BLUE DENIM(1959), w; ALL FALL DOWN(1962), w; IN THE FRENCH STYLE(1963,
U.S./Fr.); MIDNIGHT COWBOY(1969), w; FOUR FRIENDS(1981)
Josie Herlihy
1984
VIGIL(1984, New Zealand)
George Herliman
RACING LUCK(1935), p

Jacques Herlin
GOLIATH AND THE SINS OF BABYLON(1964, Ital.); WHAT!(1965, Fr./Brit./Ital.);
WHITE VOICES(1965, Fr./Ital.); SECRET AGENT SUPER DRAGON(1966, Fr./Ital./
Ger./Monaco); GIRL AND THE GENERAL, THE(1967, Fr./Ital.); MATCHLESS(1967,
Ital.); STRANGER, THE(1967, Algeria/Fr./Ital.); TIGER AND THE PUSSYCAT,
THE(1967, U.S., Ital.); CATCH AS CATCH CAN(1968, Ital.); SHAFT IN AFRICA(1973);
THREE TOUGH GUYS(1974, U.S./Ital.); MOON IN THE GUTTER, THE(1983, Fr./Ital.);
SALAMANDER, THE(1983, U.S./Ital./Brit.)
Carl Herlinger
SHOW BOAT(1929)
Silents
INSIDE THE LINES(1918)
Karl H. Herlinger
MIRACLE OF THE BELLS, THE(1948), makeup
Roberto Herlitzka
SEVEN BEAUTIES(1976, Ital.)
1984
JOKE OF DESTINY LYING IN WAIT AROUND THE CORNER LIKE A STREET-
BANDIT, A(1984, Ital.)
Kurt Herlth
MERRY WIVES OF WINDSOR, THE(1952, Ger.), ph; SPESSART INN, THE(1961,
Ger.), art d
Robert Herlth
EMPRESS AND I, THE(1933, Ger.), set d; MAGIC FIRE(1956), art d; SPESSART INN,
THE(1961, Ger.), art d; TRAPP FAMILY, THE(1961, Ger.), set d; DEVIL IN SILK(1968,
Ger.), art d
Silents
LAST LAUGH, THE(1924, Ger.), art d; FAUST(1926, Ger.), art d; TARTUFFE(1927,
Ger.), set d
Herman
GAZEBO, THE(1959)
Herman the Hermit
SQUARE DANCE JUBILEE(1949)
Herman the Lion
REFORMER AND THE REDHEAD, THE(1950)
Herman the Rabbit
ETERNALLY YOURS(1939)
Herman the Wonder Dog
FIREBALL JUNGLE(1968)
Ace Herman
SHANGHAI COBRA, THE(1945), ed; BEHIND THE MASK(1946), ed; BELOW THE
DEADLINE(1946), ed; DARK ALIBI(1946), ed; FEAR(1946), ed; FREDDIE STEPS
OUT(1946), ed; HIGH SCHOOL HERO(1946), ed; MISSING LADY, THE(1946), ed;
RED DRAGON, THE(1946), ed; SHADOW RETURNS, THE(1946), ed; WIFE WANT-
ED(1946), ed; CHINESE RING, THE(1947), ed; GINGER(1947), ed; LOUISIANA(1947),
ed; TRAP, THE(1947), ed; VACATION DAYS(1947), ed; DOCKS OF NEW OR-
LEANS(1948), ed; FEATHERED SERPENT, THE(1948), ed; FRENCH LEAVE(1948),
ed; INCIDENT(1948), ed; JIGGS AND MAGGIE IN SOCIETY(1948), ed; MYSTERY OF
THE GOLDEN EYE, THE(1948), ed; SHANGHAI CHEST, THE(1948), ed; BLACK
MIDNIGHT(1949), ed; MISSISSIPPI RHYTHM(1949), ed; TRAIL OF THE YU-
KON(1949), ed; WOLF HUNTERS, THE(1949), ed; CALL OF THE KLONDIKE(1950),
ed; SIDESHOW(1950), ed; SNOW DOG(1950), ed; SQUARE DANCE KATY(1950), ed;
CASA MANANA(1951), ed; RHYTHM INN(1951), ed; YELLOW FIN(1951), ed; YU-
KON MANHUNT(1951), ed; SEA TIGER(1952), ed; STEEL FIST, THE(1952), ed;
MURDER WITHOUT TEARS(1953), ed; HIGHWAY DRAGNET(1954), ed; LOO-
PHOLE(1954), ed; OUTLAW'S DAUGHTER, THE(1954), ed; RACING BLOOD(1954),
ed; SECURITY RISK(1954), ed; BETRAYED WOMEN(1955), ed; NIGHT
FREIGHT(1955), p; PORT OF HELL(1955), ed; TREASURE OF RUBY HILLS(1955),
ed; WAR IS HELL(1964), ed; THAT TENNESSEE BEAT(1966), ed
Adrian Herman
DIRTY MARY, CRAZY LARRY(1974)
Afred Herman
CROSSFIRE(1947), art d
Al Herman
BIG CHANCE, THE(1933), d; EMERGENCY CALL(1933), set d; KING KONG(1933),
art d; SON OF KONG(1933), art d; COWBOY AND THE BANDIT, THE(1935), d;
HARMONY LANE(1935); SHE(1935), art d; WESTERN FRONTIER(1935), art d; BARS OF
HATE(1936), d; BRIDE WALKS OUT, THE(1936), art d; FURY(1936); RIFF-
RAFF(1936); ADVENTUROUS BLONDE(1937); EVER SINCE EVE(1937); HEADIN'
EAST(1937); HOLLYWOOD COWBOY(1937); MANHATTAN MERRY-GO-
ROUND(1937); MR. DODD TAKES THE AIR(1937); PAID TO DANCE(1937); PERFECT
SPECIMEN, THE(1937); RENFREW OF THE ROYAL MOUNTED(1937), p&d; TAL-
ENT SCOUT(1937); ACCIDENTS WILL HAPPEN(1938); JUVENILE COURT(1938);
LONE WOLF IN PARIS, THE(1938); ON THE GREAT WHITE TRAIL(1938), p&d;
ROLLIN' PLAINS(1938), d; ROOM SERVICE(1938), art d; STARLIGHT OVER TEX-
AS(1938), d; UTAH TRAIL(1938), d; WHERE THE BUFFALO ROAM(1938), d; DOWN
THE WYOMING TRAIL(1939), d; LET US LIVE(1939); MAN FROM TEXAS,
THE(1939), d; ROLL, WAGONS, ROLL(1939), d; ROLLIN' WESTWARD(1939), d;
SMASHING THE MONEY RING(1939); SONG OF THE BUCKAROO(1939), d; SUN-
DOWN ON THE PRAIRIE(1939), d; SWANEE RIVER(1939); ARIZONA FRON-
TIER(1940), d; GOLDEN TRAIL, THE(1940), d; LITTLE MEN(1940), art d;
OKLAHOMA RENEGADES(1940); PALS OF THE SILVER SAGE(1940), d; RAINBOW
OVER THE RANGE(1940), d; RHYTHM OF THE RIO GRANDE(1940), d; SPEED
LIMITED(1940), d; DATE WITH THE FALCON, A(1941), art d; GENTLEMAN FROM
DIXIE(1941), d; MANPOWER(1941); PIONEERS, THE(1941), d; ROLLIN' HOME TO
TEXAS(1941), d; WAGONS ROLL AT NIGHT, THE(1941); BOSTON BLACKIE GOES
HOLLYWOOD(1942); ONCE UPON A HONEYMOON(1942), art d; SABOTAGE
SQUAD(1942); SYNCOPATION(1942), art d; BAD MEN OF THUNDER GAP(1943), d;
GANGWAY FOR TOMORROW(1943), art d; ROOKIES IN BURMA(1943), art d;
MUSIC IN MANHATTAN(1944), art d; HAVING WONDERFUL CRIME(1945), art d;
MAN ALIVE(1945), art d; SING YOUR WAY HOME(1945), art d; NIGHTMARE
ALLEY(1947); DANGEROUS PROFESSION, A(1949), art d; THEY LIVE BY
NIGHT(1949), art d; DREAMBOAT(1952); REDHEAD FROM MANHATTAN(1954)
Misc. Talkies
BIG BOY RIDES AGAIN(1935), d; HOT OFF THE PRESS(1935), d; TRAIL'S
END(1935), d; TWISTED RAILS(1935), d; BLAZING JUSTICE(1936), d; OUTLAWS
OF THE RANGE(1936), d; VALLEY OF TERROR(1937), d; TAKE ME BACK TO
OKLAHOMA(1940), d

Misc. Silents
BEYOND THE TRAIL(1926), d
Alan Herman
DEADLY HERO(1976), art d
Albert Herman
SPORTING CHANCE(1931), p&d; EXPOSED(1932), d; WHAT PRICE CRIME?(1935), d; GUN PLAY(1936), d; DAWN EXPRESS, THE(1942), d; MISS V FROM MOSCOW(1942), d; RANGERS TAKE OVER, THE(1942), d; YANK IN LIBYA, A(1942), d; DELINQUENT DAUGHTERS(1944), p, d; SHAKE HANDS WITH MURDER(1944), d; MISSING CORPSE, THE(1945), d; PHANTOM OF 42ND STREET, THE(1945), p, d; ROGUES GALLERY(1945), p, d
Misc. Talkies
THUNDERGAP OUTLAWS(1947), d
Alfred H. Herman
FROM THIS DAY FORWARD(1946), art d
Alfred Herman
LADY TAKES A CHANCE, A(1943), art d; LOCKET, THE(1946), art d; BERLIN EXPRESS(1948), art d; EASY LIVING(1949), art d; GAMBLING HOUSE(1950), art d; WALK SOFTLY, STRANGER(1950), art d; MY FORBIDDEN PAST(1951), art d; LUSTY MEN, THE(1952), art d
Bill Herman
MURDER, INC.(1960), makeup; MAD DOG COLL(1961), makeup; LILITH(1964), makeup; PAWNBROKER, THE(1965), makeup
Eleanor Herman
NIGHTBEAST(1982)
1984
ALIEN FACTOR, THE(1984)
Freddie Herman
WORLD IN MY CORNER(1956)
Gary Herman
CONAN THE BARBARIAN(1982)
George Herman
DIXIANA(1930)
Georgio Herman
CASANOVA '70(1965, Ital.), set d
Gerald Herman
JORY(1972), w
Gil Herman
I WAS A MALE WAR BRIDE(1949); SANDS OF IWO JIMA(1949); MY FRIEND IRMA GOES WEST(1950); WHEN WILLIE COMES MARCHING HOME(1950); WOMAN FROM HEADQUARTERS(1950); DAY THE EARTH STOOD STILL, THE(1951); FOLLOW THE SUN(1951); I WAS AN AMERICAN SPY(1951); HOODLUM EMPIRE(1952); WILD BLUE YONDER, THE(1952); CITY THAT NEVER SLEEPS(1953); OLD OVERLAND TRAIL(1953)
Giorgio Herman
HUNCHBACK OF ROME, THE(1963, Ital.), set d
Hal Herman
AROUND THE WORLD(1943), art d
Helena Herman
STREET ANGEL(1928)
Irm Herman
FOX AND HIS FRIENDS(1976, Ger.)
Jack Herman
BEYOND THE TIME BARRIER(1960)
Jean Herman
FAREWELL, FRIEND(1968, Fr./Ital.), d; POPSY POP(1971, Fr.), d, w; INQUISITOR, THE(1982, Fr.), w
1984
DOG DAY(1984, Fr.), w
Jeffrey Herman
DOCTOR DEATH: SEEKER OF SOULS(1973)
Jerry Herman
MAME(1974), w
Kate Herman
NICE GIRL LIKE ME, A(1969, Brit.)
Ken Herman
TREASURE OF THE GOLDEN CONDOR(1953)
Kid Herman
HOLD'EM YALE(1935); SATAN MET A LADY(1936)
Leonard Herman
BIG TIMBER(1950), ed; KILLER SHARK(1950), ed; ARCTIC FLIGHT(1952), ed; DESERT PURSUIT(1952), ed
Leonard W. Herman
KIDNAPPED(1948), ed; TUNA CLIPPER(1949), ed; SIERRA PASSAGE(1951), ed; JACK SLADE(1953), ed; MEXICAN MANHUNT(1953), ed; NORTHERN PATROL(1953), ed; TANGIER INCIDENT(1953), ed; CREATION OF THE HUMANOIDS(1962), ed
Lewis Herman
STRANGE IMPERSONATION(1946), w
Lewis Helmer Herman
PERSONALITY KID(1946), w
Lila Herman
BREATHLESS(1959, Fr.), ed; WOMAN IS A WOMAN, A(1961, Fr./Ital.), ed; LE PETIT SOLDAT(1965, Fr.), ed
Lisa Herman
AMERICAN GRAFFITI(1973)
Muriel Herman
MARY HAD A LITTLE(1961, Brit.), w
Nora Herman
SOMEWHERE IN FRANCE(1943, Brit.)
Norman Herman
HOT ROD GIRL(1956), p
Norman T. Herman
HOT ROD RUMBLE(1957), p; SIERRA STRANGER(1957), p; UNDERSEA GIRL(1957), p; TOKYO AFTER DARK(1959), p, d, w; LEGEND OF HELL HOUSE, THE(1973, Brit.), p; DIRTY MARY, CRAZY LARRY(1974), p; ROLLING THUNDER(1977), p

Paul Herman
DEAR MR. WONDERFUL(1983, Ger.)
1984
COTTON CLUB, THE(1984); FALLING IN LOVE(1984); ONCE UPON A TIME IN AMERICA(1984); POPE OF GREENWICH VILLAGE, THE(1984)
Pete Herman
NEW ORLEANS UNCENSORED(1955)
Randy Herman
OUR WINNING SEASON(1978); DEFIANCE(1980); LITTLE MISS MARKER(1980)
Tommy Herman
HARDER THEY FALL, THE(1956)
Victor Herman
Silents
RUPERT OF HENTZAU(1923), d
William Herman
WITHOUT EACH OTHER(1962), w
Woody Herman
NEW ORLEANS(1947)
Herman Darewski and His Blackpool Tower Band
NO LADY(1931, Brit.)
Herman's Hermits
WHEN THE BOYS MEET THE GIRLS(1965)
Herman's Mountaineers
HEART OF THE ROCKIES(1937)
Hans Hermann
OPERATION EICHMANN(1961)
Ingo Hermann
ITALIAN CONNECTION, THE(1973, U.S./Ital./Ger.), w
Irm Hermann
AMERICAN SOLDIER, THE(1970 Ger.); BITTER TEARS OF PETRA VON KANT, THE(1972, Ger.); EFFI BRIEST(1974, Ger.); FEAR EATS THE SOUL(1974, Ger.); MOTHER KUSTERS GOES TO HEAVEN(1976, Ger.); JAIL BAIT(1977, Ger.); WHY DOES HERR R. RUN AMOK?(1977, Ger.)
Kai Hermann
CIRCLE OF DECEIT(1982, Fr./Ger.), w
Nori Elisabeth Hermann
BRIDGE TO THE SUN(1961)
Peter Hermann
JOURNEY TO THE BEGINNING OF TIME(1966, Czech)
Shelley Hermann
1984
LIES(1984, Brit.), p
Sylvia Hermann
TOXI(1952, Ger.)
Henry Hermann-Cattani
MORITURI(1965)
Jan Hermannsson
OUTLAW: THE SAGE OF GISLI(1982, Iceland), p
Joe Hermano
PENGUIN POOL MURDER, THE(1932)
Peris Hermanos
MYSTERIOUS ISLAND OF CAPTAIN NEMO, THE(1973, Fr./Ital. 87m Span./Cameroon), cos
Mogens Hermansen
LURE OF THE JUNGLE, THE(1970, Den.)
Abel Hermant
ENTENTE CORDIALE(1939, Fr.), w
Raymond Hermantier
COUP DE TORCHON(1981, Fr.)
Leonard Hermes
STRYKER(1983, Phil.), w
Brigitte Hermetz
QUARTET(1981, Brit./Fr.)
Pepi Hermine
PUTNEY SWOPE(1969)
Ruth Hermine
PUTNEY SWOPE(1969)
Hermine's Midgets
COURT JESTER, THE(1956)
M.P. Roy Hermitage, Jr.
NICHOLAS NICKLEBY(1947, Brit.)
Shlomo Hermon
CAST A GIANT SHADOW(1966)
James A. Hermstad
TOMAHAWK(1951)
Guus Hermus
SOLDIER OF ORANGE(1979, Dutch)
Art Hern
SIMON, KING OF THE WITCHES(1971)
Bernie Hern
MAN WITH TWO BRAINS, THE(1983); TABLE FOR FIVE(1983)
Edward Hern
GO CHASE YOURSELF(1938)
June Hern
KIMBERLEY JIM(1965, South Africa)
Pepe Hern
ANGELS IN DISGUISE(1949); KNOCK ON ANY DOOR(1949); BANDIT QUEEN(1950); BORDERLINE(1950); CRISIS(1950); FURIES, THE(1950); HEART OF THE ROCKIES(1951); MY FAVORITE SPY(1951); RING, THE(1952); THUNDERBIRDS(1952); JUBILEE TRAIL(1954); MAKE HASTE TO LIVE(1954); BAMBOO PRISON, THE(1955); HELL'S ISLAND(1955); JAGUAR(1956); SUMMER AND SMOKE(1961); THIRTEEN WEST STREET(1962); MADIGAN(1968); JOE KIDD(1972)
Gyula Hernadi
RED AND THE WHITE, THE(1969, Hung./USSR), w; ROUND UP, THE(1969, Hung.), w; WINTER WIND(1970, Fr./Hung.), w; FORTRESS, THE(1979, Hung.), w; ANNA(1981, Fr./Hung.), w
Judit Hernadi
MEPHISTO(1981, Ger.)

Aida Hernandez
ONE MILLION B.C.(1940)
Andy "Sugarcoated" Hernandez
1984
MIXED BLOOD(1984), m
Anna Hernandez
Silents
AMATEUR DEVIL, AN(1921); MOLLY O'(1921); ROWDY, THE(1921); KENTUCKY DERBY, THE(1922); EXTRA GIRL, THE(1923); TOWN SCANDAL, THE(1923); LAW FORBIDS, THE(1924)
Misc. Silents
LEAVE IT TO SUSAN(1919)
Bell Hernandez
LOSIN' IT(1983)
Cornelio Hernandez
LOSIN' IT(1983)
Dolores Hernandez
FORT APACHE, THE BRONX(1981)
Elodia Hernandez
EXTERMINATING ANGEL, THE(1967, Mex.)
Enrique Hernandez
UNDER FIRE(1983)
Ernesto Hernandez
WHICH WAY IS UP?(1977)
Frank Hernandez
Misc. Talkies
TREASURE OF TAYOPA(1974)
Freddie Hernandez
SCANDALOUS JOHN(1971)
George Hernandez
Silents
GREATER LAW, THE(1917); JUST OUT OF COLLEGE(1921); BILLY JIM(1922)
Misc. Silents
BLUEBEARD, JR.(; END OF THE RAINBOW, THE(1916); IT HAPPENED IN HONOLULU(1916); ROMANCE OF BILLY GOAT HILL, A(1916); SECRET OF THE SWAMP, THE(1916); BROADWAY ARIZONA(1917); GOD'S CRUCIBLE(1917); MR. OPP(1917); MUTINY(1917); SHOW-DOWN, THE(1917); SOUTHERN JUSTICE(1917); UP OR DOWN(1917); HOPPER, THE(1918); BE A LITTLE SPORT(1919); COURAGEOUS COWARD, THE(1919); LOST PRINCESS, THE(1919); MISS ADVENTURE(1919); REBELLIOUS BRIDE, THE(1919); SILVER GIRL, THE(1919); TIN PAN ALLEY(1920); AFTER YOUR OWN HEART(1921); INNOCENT CHEAT, THE(1921); ROAD DEMON, THE(1921); ARABIA(1922); FLAMING HEARTS(1922); MAN UNDER COVER, THE(1922)
Mrs. George Hernandez
Silents
PRIDE OF PALOMAR, THE(1922); RIDE FOR YOUR LIFE(1924)
Gerard Hernandez
BOBBY DEERFIELD(1977); COUP DE TORCHON(1981, Fr.)
Guillermano Hernandez
RAGE(1966, U.S./Mex.), w
Guillermo Hernandez
AZTEC MUMMY, THE(1957, Mex.); CURSE OF THE AZTEC MUMMY, THE(1965, Mex.); ROBOT VS. THE AZTEC MUMMY, THE(1965, Mex.); GUNS FOR SAN SEBASTIAN(1968, U.S./Fr./Mex./Ital.); WRATH OF GOD, THE(1972)
Jesus Hernandez
SHARKFIGHTERS, THE(1956)
Joaquin Romero Hernandez
KILL THEM ALL AND COME BACK ALONE(1970, Ital./Span.), w
Joe Hernandez
WHEN YOU COMIN' BACK, RED RYDER?(1979); LONG SHOT, THE(1939); GENTLEMAN FROM DIXIE(1941); BLACK GOLD(1947); THAT'S MY MAN(1947)
Juano Hernandez
INTRUDER IN THE DUST(1949); BREAKING POINT, THE(1950); STARS IN MY CROWN(1950); YOUNG MAN WITH A HORN(1950); KISS ME DEADLY(1955); TRIAL(1955); RANSOM(1956); SOMETHING OF VALUE(1957); MACHETE(1958); MARK OF THE HAWK, THE(1958); ST. LOUIS BLUES(1958); SERGEANT RUTLEDGE(1960); SINS OF RACHEL CADE, THE(1960); TWO LOVES(1961); ADVENTURES OF A YOUNG MAN(1962); PAWNBROKER, THE(1965); EXTRAORDINARY SEAMAN, THE(1969); REIVERS, THE(1969); THEY CALL ME MISTER TIBBS(1970)
Kai Hernandez
MACK, THE(1973)
Luis Hernandez
INVASION OF THE VAMPIRES, THE(1961, Mex.), m
Paul Hernandez
TO BE FREE(1972)
Pete Hernandez
HOMBRE(1967)
Rafael Hernandez
MURDERS IN THE RUE MORGUE(1971)
Ramon Hernandez
SUN ALSO RISES, THE(1957), md
Raul "Pin" Hernandez
SCALPHUNTERS, THE(1968)
Robert Hernandez
WAR OF THE COLOSSAL BEAST(1958); THIRD VOICE, THE(1960); JAWS II(1978), ed
Rogelio Hernandez
BIG BOODLE, THE(1957)
Sosimo Hernandez
NORMAN...IS THAT YOU?(1976); LOSIN' IT(1983)
Tessie Hernandez
CURSE OF THE VAMPIRES(1970, Phil., U.S.)
Tom Hernandez
SALOME(1953); SOMBRERO(1953); PARTY GIRL(1958); THIRD VOICE, THE(1960); TENDER IS THE NIGHT(1961); FUN IN ACAPULCO(1963)
Tony Hernandez
ROCKY III(1982)

Wilfredo Hernandez
MARATHON MAN(1976); OLIVER'S STORY(1978)
Willie Hernandez
SHORT EYES(1977)
Walter Scott Herndan
HERO AIN'T NOTHIN' BUT A SANDWICH, A(1977), prod d
Bill Herndon
SIDELONG GLANCES OF A PIGEON KICKER, THE(1970); RIVALS(1972)
Cleo Herndon
DARK MANHATTAN(1937)
Irene Herndon
TAMING OF THE WEST, THE(1939)
Pauline Herndon
BOOK OF NUMBERS(1973)
Venable Herndon
ALICE'S RESTAURANT(1969), w
Walter Herndon
BLACULA(1972), art d; SOUNDER(1972), prod d
Walter S. Herndon
HOOPER(1978), w
Walter Scott Herndon
LOVING(1970), prod d; PUFNSTUF(1970), art d; LAST PICTURE SHOW, THE(1971), art d; CORKY(1972), art d; CONRACK(1974), prod d; BABY BLUE MARINE(1976), prod d; BIRCH INTERVAL(1976), prod d; MOTHER, JUGS & SPEED(1976), prod d; SOUNDER, PART 2(1976), prod d; SEMI-TOUGH(1977), prod d; BAD NEWS BEARS GO TO JAPAN, THE(1978), prod d; MANITOU, THE(1978), prod d; NORMA RAE(1979), prod d; PROMISES IN THE DARK(1979), prod d; THOSE LIPS, THOSE EYES(1980), prod d; BACK ROADS(1981), prod d; SHARKY'S MACHINE(1982), prod d; CROSS CREEK(1983), prod d
1984
SOLDIER'S STORY, A(1984), prod d
Clancy Herne
YOUNG AND DANGEROUS(1957)
James A. Herne
Silents
HEARTS OF OAK(1924), w
Julie Herne
Silents
HEART RAIDER, THE(1923), w; BREAKING POINT, THE(1924), w; SIDESHOW OF LIFE, THE(1924), w
Mary Herne
KILLING OF A CHINESE BOOKIE, THE(1976), cos
Jocelyn Hernfield
SMILEY(1957, Brit.)
Pat Hernon
ABDUCTION(1975)
Stephen Hero
THREE DARING DAUGHTERS(1948)
Teresa Hero
HOLIDAY IN MEXICO(1946)
Tonia Hero
HOLIDAY IN MEXICO(1946)
Bernie Herold
ZELIG(1983)
Frank Herold
OH! CALCUTTA!(1972), ed
John Herold
PURSUIT OF D.B. COOPER, THE(1981)
Bobby Heron
WESTBOUND(1959)
Frank Heron
SINS OF THE FATHERS(1948, Can.)
Joyce Heron
WOMEN AREN'T ANGELS(1942, Brit.); TWILIGHT HOUR(1944, Brit.); DON CHICAGO(1945, Brit.); AGITATOR, THE(1949); SHE SHALL HAVE MURDER(1950, Brit.); THREE CORNERED FATE(1954, Brit.); WEAK AND THE WICKED, THE(1954, Brit.); BEYOND THIS PLACE(1959, Brit.)
Julia Heron
INFORMER, THE(1935), set d; COME AND GET IT(1936), set d; HURRICANE, THE(1937), set d; ADVENTURES OF MARCO POLO, THE(1938), set d; REAL GLORY, THE(1939), set d; WUTHERING HEIGHTS(1939), set d; LONG VOYAGE HOME, THE(1940), set d; WESTERNER, THE(1940), set d; THAT HAMILTON WOMAN(1941), set d; JUNGLE BOOK(1942), set d; TO BE OR NOT TO BE(1942), set d; EDGE OF DARKNESS(1943), set d; JOHNNY COME LATELY(1943), set d; WATCH ON THE RHINE(1943), set d; CASANOVA BROWN(1944), set d; ALONG CAME JONES(1945), set d; WOMAN IN THE WINDOW, THE(1945), set d; BEST YEARS OF OUR LIVES, THE(1946), set d; ENCHANTMENT(1948), set d; MY FOOLISH HEART(1949), set d; EDGE OF DOOM(1950), set d; GROOM WORE SPURS, THE(1951), set d; LADY PAYS OFF, THE(1951), set d; STRANGE DOOR, THE(1951), set d; IT GROWS ON TREES(1952), set d; MEET DANNY WILSON(1952), set d; ALL I DESIRE(1953), set d; MISSISSIPPI GAMBLER, THE(1953), set d; TAKE ME TO TOWN(1953), set d; ALL THAT HEAVEN ALLOWS(1955), set d; THIS ISLAND EARTH(1955), set d; THERE'S ALWAYS TOMORROW(1956), set d; WRITTEN ON THE WIND(1956), set d; ISTANBUL(1957), set d; IMITATION OF LIFE(1959), set d; GREAT IMPOSTOR, THE(1960), set d; PORTRAIT IN BLACK(1960), set d; SPARTACUS(1960), set d; NIGHT WALKER, THE(1964), set d; DARK INTRUDER(1965), set d; LOVE AND KISSES(1965), set d; SWORD OF ALI BABA, THE(1965), set d; THAT FUNNY FEELING(1965), set d; LET'S KILL UNCLE(1966), set d; PERILS OF PAULINE, THE(1967), set d
Julie Heron
DEAD END(1937), set d; COWBOY AND THE LADY, THE(1938), set d; RAFFLES(1939), set d; HOUSE ACROSS THE BAY(1940), set d; BALL OF FIRE(1941), set d; LYDIA(1941), set d; HANGMEN ALSO DIE(1943), cos; BISHOP'S WIFE, THE(1947), set d; MUNSTER, GO HOME(1966), set d
Pierre Heros
LIGHT YEARS AWAY(1982, Fr./Switz.), p
The Heros
PARIS OOH-LA-LA!(1963, U.S./Fr.)

Claude Heroux
JE T'AIME(1974, Can.), p; BREAKING POINT(1976), p; ANGELA(1977, Can.), p; UNCANNY, THE(1977, Brit./Can.), p; IN PRAISE OF OLDER WOMEN(1978, Can.), p; BROOD, THE(1979, Can.), p; CITY ON FIRE(1979 Can.), p; HOG WILD(1980, Can.), p; DIRTY TRICKS(1981, Can.), p; GAS(1981, Can.), p; SCANNERS(1981, Can.), p; FUNNY FARM, THE(1982, Can.), p; VISITING HOURS(1982, Can.), p; GOING BERSERK(1983), p; OF UNKNOWN ORIGIN(1983, Can.), p; VIDEODROME(1983, Can.), p
1984
COVERGIRL(1984, Can.), p
Denis Heroux
JACQUES BREL IS ALIVE AND WELL AND LIVING IN PARIS(1975), d; UNCANNY, THE(1977, Brit./Can.), d; ATLANTIC CITY(1981, U.S./Can.), p; QUEST FOR FIRE(1982, Fr./Can.), p
1984
BAY BOY(1984, Can.), p; LOUISIANE(1984, Fr./Can.), p
Bianca Herr
Misc. Talkies
SWINGING COEDS, THE(1976)
Michael Herr
APOCALYPSE NOW(1979)
Gonzalo Herralde
JETLAG(1981, U.S./Span.), d&w, w
Marcel Herrand
CHILDREN OF PARADISE(1945, Fr.); DEVIL'S ENVOYS, THE(1947, Fr.); ROOM UPSTAIRS, THE(1948, Fr.); RUY BLAS(1948, Fr.); FANFAN THE TULIP(1952, Fr.)
D. Herrara
POCKET MONEY(1972)
Joe Herrara
SECOND CHANCE(1953)
The Herrara Sisters
DOWN MEXICO WAY(1941)
Brandy Herred
AROUSERS, THE(1973)
Anthony Herrera
NUDE BOMB, THE(1980)
Bernardo Herrera
PROUD AND THE DAMNED, THE(1972)
Daniel Chino Herrera
LOS INVISIBLES(1961, Mex.); CHIQUTTO PERO PICOSO(1967, Mex.)
Dave Herrera
USED CARS(1980)
Joe Herrera
NORTHERN PURSUIT(1943); JOE PALOOKA IN THE COUNTERPUNCH(1949); GREEN FIRE(1955); HARDER THEY FALL, THE(1956)
Jorge Herrera
ALSINO AND THE CONDOR(1983, Nicaragua), ph
Joseph Herrera
1984
DUBEAT-E-O(1984)
Juan Manuel Herrera
POLITICAL ASYLUM(1975, Mex./Guatemalan), ph
Norma Herrera
BIG CUBE, THE(1969)
Sam Herrera
CRISIS(1950); CALLAWAY WENT THATAWAY(1951)
Victor Herrera
DOCTOR CRIMEN(1953, Mex.), ph; CASTLE OF THE MONSTERS(1958, Mex.), ph; VAMPIRE'S COFFIN, THE(1958, Mex.), ph; LIVING COFFIN, THE(1965, Mex.), ph
Anthony Herrero
NIGHT OF BLOODY HORROR zero(1969)
Jose Herrero
UGLY ONES, THE(1968, Ital./Span.), ph
Ricardo Herrero
BLACK MAMA, WHITE MAMA(1973)
Subas Herrero
ENTER THE NINJA(1982)
Regino Herrerra
RETURN OF A MAN CALLED HORSE, THE(1976)
Hugo Herrestrup
WEEKEND(1964, Den.); CRAZY PARADISE(1965, Den.); ERIC SOYA'S "17"(1967, Den.)
Eileen Herric
KISMET(1944)
Anthony Herrick
BARRY LYNDON(1975, Brit.)
F. Herrick
PISTOL HARVEST(1951)
F. Herrick Herrick
GHOST TOWN GOLD(1937)
Misc. Talkies
OBEAH(1935), d
Fred Herrick
STREET OF SINNERS(1957); GODDESS, THE(1958); TERROR FROM THE YEAR 5,000(1958); ODDS AGAINST TOMORROW(1959)
Herrick Herrick
MY FAVORITE SPY(1951)
Hubert Herrick
Silents
ALL THE SAD WORLD NEEDS(1918, Brit.), d
Jack Herrick
ARIZONA KID, THE(1930); PARDON US(1931); BOWERY, THE(1933); STOLEN HARMONY(1935); STREET WITH NO NAME, THE(1948)
Silents
ABYSMAL BRUTE, THE(1923); IN FAST COMPANY(1924); DICK TURPIN(1925); GOLD RUSH, THE(1925); BROADWAY BILLY(1926); ONE PUNCH O'DAY(1926); IS ZAT SO?(1927); WHEEL OF DESTINY, THE(1927)
Joseph Herrick
WHITE FANG(1936)

Kimball Herrick
TROUBLE AT MIDNIGHT(1937), w
Robert Herrick
HEALER, THE(1935), w; NO TIME FOR LOVE(1943)
Roy Herrick
PRIEST OF LOVE(1981, Brit.)
Samuel Herrick
TALL TEXAN, THE(1953)
Virginia Herrick
I KILLED GERONIMO(1950); SILVER RAIDERS(1950); VIGILANTE HIDEOUT(1950); MONTANA DESPERADO(1951); FRONTIER PHANTOM, THE(1952)
Robert Herridge
URBAN COWBOY(1980)
Jacques Herrien
PLEASURES AND VICES(1962, Fr.)
Mark Herrier
PORKY'S(1982); PORKY'S II: THE NEXT DAY(1983)
1984
TANK(1984)
Bill Herrin
TAMMY, TELL ME TRUE(1961)
John Herrin
PHANTOM PLANET, THE(1961)
Kym Herrin
1984
GHOSTBUSTERS(1984); ROMANCING THE STONE(1984)
William Herrin
FLAMING STAR(1960)
Aggie Herring
DARK STREETS(1929); SMILING IRISH EYES(1929); CLANCY IN WALL STREET(1930); IN THE NEXT ROOM(1930); KATHLEEN MAVOURNEEN(1930); MILLIE(1931); TEN CENTS A DANCE(1931); TAXI!(1932); SHE DONE HIM WRONG(1933); SIN OF NORA MORAN(1933); GREEN EYES(1934); KEY, THE(1934); QUITTERS, THE(1934); STAND UP AND CHEER(1934 80m FOX bw); STOLEN SWEETS(1934); CURTAIN FALLS, THE(1935); DANIEL BOONE(1936); DARK HOUR, THE(1936); DON'T TELL THE WIFE(1937); MAN IN BLUE, THE(1937); ISLAND IN THE SKY(1938)
Silents
CORNER IN COLLEENS, A(1916); EYE OF THE NIGHT, THE(1916); HOME(1916); FEMALE OF THE SPECIES(1917); MORE TROUBLE(1918); HOODLUM THE(1919); LORD LOVES THE IRISH, THE(1919); MAN IN THE OPEN, A(1919); HAIRPINS(1920); PARIS GREEN(1920); QUEENIE(1921); ROOKIE'S RETURN(1921); BLIND BARGAIN, A(1922); NINETY AND NINE, THE(1922); OLIVER TWIST(1922); RAGGED HEIRESS, THE(1922); ISLE OF LOST SHIPS, THE(1923); ANY WOMAN(1925); WATCH YOUR WIFE(1926); FINNEGAN'S BALL(1927); PRINCESS FROM HOBOKEN, THE(1927); DO YOUR DUTY(1928); HEAD OF THE FAMILY, THE(1928); LADY BE GOOD(1928)
Misc. Silents
MADCAP MADGE(1917); SNARL, THE(1917); WITHIN THE CUP(1918); TODD OF THE TIMES(1919); YANKEE PRINCESS, A(1919); DOWN HOME(1920); GIRL NAMED MARY, A(1920); NINE POINTS OF THE LAW(1922); LOCO LUCK(1927); THAT CERTAIN THING(1928)
John Herring
EYES OF FATE(1933, Brit.)
Moree Herring
DEAD MAN'S GOLD(1948), w
Paul Herring
NATIONAL LAMPOON'S VACATION(1983), ed
Pem Herring
1984
JOHNNY DANGEROUSLY(1984), ed
Pembroke J. Herring
TORA! TORA! TORA!(1970, U.S./Jap.), ed; BUCK AND THE PREACHER(1972), ed; WARM DECEMBER, A(1973, Brit.), ed; UPTOWN SATURDAY NIGHT(1974), ed; LET'S DO IT AGAIN(1975), ed; BOUND FOR GLORY(1976), ed; PIECE OF THE ACTION, A(1977), ed; FOUL PLAY(1978), ed; THE RUNNER STUMBLES(1979), ed; LITTLE DARLINGS(1980), ed; NINE TO FIVE(1980), ed; BEST LITTLE WHOREHOUSE IN TEXAS, THE(1982), ed
George Herrington
RUNNING TARGET(1956), cos
John Herrington
SHOT IN THE DARK, A(1964); IT HAPPENED HERE(1966, Brit.); BOFORS GUN, THE(1968, Brit.)
Ramsey Herrington
COMPELLED(1960, Brit.), d
Tabitha Herrington
MR. PATMAN(1980, Can.); STAR 80(1983)
James Herriot
ALL CREATURES GREAT AND SMALL(1975, Brit.), w; ALL THINGS BRIGHT AND BEAUTIFUL(1979, Brit.), w
Mary Herriot
THREE RUSSIAN GIRLS(1943); MISS SUSIE SLAGLE'S(1945)
Max Herriquez
SATURDAY NIGHT FEVER(1977), makeup
Daniel Herris
STUCK ON YOU(1983)
Eugene Herly
ELUSIVE CORPORAL, THE(1963, Fr.), set d
Jeanine Herly
FRIENDS(1971, Brit.), cos
Bernard Herrman
MAN IN THE GREY FLANNEL SUIT, THE(1956), m; WRONG MAN, THE(1956), m
Karl Herrman
ONE FROM THE HEART(1982)
Bernard Herrmann
CITIZEN KANE(1941), m; DEVIL AND DANIEL WEBSTER, THE(1941), m; GHOST AND MRS. MUIR, THE(1942), m; MAGNIFICENT AMBERSONS, THE(1942), m; JANE EYRE(1944), m; HANGOVER SQUARE(1945), m; DAY THE EARTH STOOD STILL, THE(1951), m; ON DANGEROUS GROUND(1951), m; FIVE FINGERS(1952), m; BENEATH THE 12-MILE REEF(1953), m; KING OF THE KHYBER RIFLES(1953),

m; WHITE WITCH DOCTOR(1953), m; EGYPTIAN. THE(1954), m; GARDEN OF EVIL(1954), m; KENTUCKIAN, THE(1955), m; PRINCE OF PLAYERS(1955), m; TROUBLE WITH HARRY, THE(1955), m; MAN WHO KNEW TOO MUCH, THE(1956), m, md; HATFUL OF RAIN, A(1957), m; NAKED AND THE DEAD, THE(1958), m, md; SEVENTH VOYAGE OF SINBAD, THE(1958), m; VERTIGO(1958), m; BLUE DENIM(1959), m; JOURNEY TO THE CENTER OF THE EARTH(1959), m; NORTH BY NORTHWEST(1959), m; PSYCHO(1960), m; THREE WORLDS OF GULLIVER, THE(1960, Brit.), m, md; MYSTERIOUS ISLAND(1961, U.S./Brit.), m, md; TENDER IS THE NIGHT(1961), m; CAPE FEAR(1962), m; BIRDS, THE(1963), m; JASON AND THE ARGONAUTS(1963, Brit.), m, md; MARNIE(1964), m; JOY IN THE MORNING(1965), m; FAHRENHEIT 451(1966, Brit.), m; BRIDE WORE BLACK, THE(1968, Fr./Ital.), m; TWISTED NERVE(1969, Brit.), m; ENDLESS NIGHT(1971, Brit.), m; NIGHT DIGGER, THE(1971, Brit.), m; SISTERS(1973), m; IT'S ALIVE(1974), m; OBSESSION(1976), m; TAXI DRIVER(1976), m, md; IT LIVES AGAIN(1978), m

Edward Herrmann
LADY LIBERTY(1972, Ital./Fr.); DAY OF THE DOLPHIN, THE(1973); PAPER CHASE, THE(1973); GREAT GATSBY, THE(1974); GREAT WALDO PEPPER, THE(1975); BETSY, THE(1978); BRASS TARGET(1978); NORTH AVENUE IRREGULARS, THE(1979); TAKE DOWN(1979); HARRY'S WAR(1981); REDS(1981); ANNIE(1982); DEATH VALLEY(1982); LITTLE SEX, A(1982)
1984
MRS. SOFFEL(1984)

Julius E. Herrmann
BEAUTIFUL ADVENTURE(1932, Ger.)

Karl-Ernst Herrmann
1984
CLASS ENEMY(1984, Ger.), prod d

Lucille Fletcher Herrmann
ONCE UPON A TIME(1944), w

W.A. Herrmann
SHOT AT DAWN, A(1934, Ger.), art d

Kurt Herrnfeld
OPERATION DELILAH(1966, U.S./Span.), ed

Grant Herrocks
INBREAKER, THE(1974, Can.), m

Julie Herrod
WAIT UNTIL DARK(1967)

Alastair Herron
ACCEPTABLE LEVELS(1983, Brit.), w, art d

Bob Herron
FAR HORIZONS, THE(1955); OKLAHOMA CRUDE(1973); DOMINO PRINCIPLE, THE(1977); MR. BILLION(1977); LOCAL COLOR(1978)
1984
CITY HEAT(1984)

J. Barry Herron
YOUNG GRADUATES, THE(1971), ph; MUSTANG COUNTRY(1976), ph

Joel Herron
MARCO POLO JUNIOR(1973, Aus.), md, m/l

Mark Herron
8 ½(1963, Ital.); GIRL IN GOLD BOOTS(1968); EYE OF THE CAT(1969)

Red Herron
HOLLYWOOD BARN DANCE(1947)

Robert Herron
$(DOLLARS)**1/2 (1971); GUN FURY(1953); FOUR GUNS TO THE BORDER(1954); RISE AND FALL OF LEGS DIAMOND, THE(1960); MOVIE MOVIE(1978)

Robert D. Herron
SASKATCHEWAN(1954)

Zdenka Hersak
EVENT, AN(1970, Yugo.); HIGH ROAD TO CHINA(1983)

Herschel
THANK YOU, JEEVES(1936), cos; THIRTY SIX HOURS TO KILL(1936), cos; UNDER YOUR SPELL(1936), cos; STEP LIVELY, JEEVES(1937), cos; THANK YOU, MR. MOTO(1937), cos; THAT I MAY LIVE(1937), cos; THINK FAST, MR. MOTO(1937), cos; WOMAN-WISE(1937), cos; MR. MOTO TAKES A CHANCE(1938), cos; MR. MOTO TAKES A VACATION(1938), cos; ROAD DEMON(1938), cos; FRONTIER MARSHAL(1939), cos; HOLLYWOOD CAVALCADE(1939), cos; MR. MOTO IN DANGER ISLAND(1939), cos; STREET OF MEMORIES(1940), cos; GREAT GUNS(1941), cos; MURDER AMONG FRIENDS(1941), cos; ROMANCE OF THE RIO GRANDE(1941), cos; SMALL TOWN DEB(1941), cos; WE GO FAST(1941), cos; MY FRIEND FLICKA(1943), cos; TULSA(1949), cos

Bernard Herschensen
SATAN IN HIGH HEELS(1962), ph

Lou Herscher
ENLIGHTEN THY DAUGHTER(1934), m

Stuart Herschman
LIMIT, THE(1972)

Charles Hersee
TILLY OF BLOOMSBURY(1940, Brit.); ECHO MURDERS, THE(1945, Brit.)

Samuel Hersenhoren
SINS OF THE FATHERS(1948, Can.), md

Philippe Hersent
END OF THE WORLD, THE(1930, Fr.); HOUSE OF INTRIGUE, THE(1959, Ital.); GIANT OF MARATHON, THE(1960, Ital.); GUNS OF THE BLACK WITCH(1961, Fr./Ital.); MIGHTY CRUSADERS, THE(1961, Ital.); HUNS, THE(1962, Fr./Ital.); WAR OF THE ZOMBIES, THE(1965 Ital.); MISSION BLOODY MARY(1967, Fr./Ital./Span.); MURDER CLINIC, THE(1967, Ital./Fr.)

Phillipe Hersent
GOLIATH AND THE DRAGON(1961, Ital./Fr.)

John Hersey
BELL FOR ADANO, A(1945), w; WAR LOVER, THE(1962, U.S./Brit.), w

Ben Hersh
SO THIS IS WASHINGTON(1943), p; TWO WEEKS TO LIVE(1943), p; PARTNERS IN TIME(1946), p; GROOM WORE SPURS, THE(1951), prod d

Sam Hersh
GOD IS MY PARTNER(1957), p; LURE OF THE SWAMP(1957), p; I'LL GIVE MY LIFE(1959), p

Michael Hershewe
BIG FIX, THE(1978); BLOODBROTHERS(1978); CASEY'S SHADOW(1978)

Barbara Hershey
HEAVEN WITH A GUN(1969); LAST SUMMER(1969); BABY MAKER, THE(1970); LIBERATION OF L.B. JONES, THE(1970); DEALING: OR THE BERKELEY-TO-BOSTON FORTY-BRICK LOST-BAG BLUES(1971); PURSUIT OF HAPPINESS, THE(1971); BOXCAR BERTHA(1972); DIRTY KNIGHT'S WORK(1976, Brit.); LAST HARD MEN, THE(1976); STUNT MAN, THE(1980); AMERICANA(1981); TAKE THIS JOB AND SHOVE IT(1981); ENTITY, THE(1982); RIGHT STUFF, THE(1983)
1984
NATURAL, THE(1984)

Barbara Hershey [Seagull]
WITH SIX YOU GET EGGROLL(1968)

Burnett Hershey
SEA GHOST, THE(1931), w; SAVAGE GOLD(1933), w; INSIDE INFORMATION(1939), w
Silents
NEWS PARADE, THE(1928), w

Christopher Hershey
PROPERTY(1979)

June Hershey
MOONLIGHT ON THE RANGE(1937), m; DEEP IN THE HEART OF TEXAS(1942), m/l Johnny Bond

Ben Hershfield
Silents
GIRLS WHO DARE(1929), w

Ludwig Hershfield
YES, MR. BROWN(1933, Brit.), w

Alan Hersholt
SKY LINER(1949)

Jean Hersholt
ABIE'S IRISH ROSE(1928); GIRL ON THE BARGE, THE(1929); GIVE AND TAKE(1929); MODERN LOVE(1929); YOUNGER GENERATION(1929); CASE OF SERGEANT GRISCHA, THE(1930); CAT CREEPS, THE(1930); CLIMAX, THE(1930); EAST IS WEST(1930); HELL HARBOR(1930); MAMBA(1930); THIRD ALARM, THE(1930); VIENNESE NIGHTS(1930); DAYBREAK(1931); PHANTOM OF PARIS, THE(1931); PRIVATE LIVES(1931); SIN OF MADELON CLAUDET, THE(1931); SOLDIER'S PLAYTHING, A(1931); SUSAN LENOX–HER FALL AND RISE(1931); TRANSATLANTIC(1931); ARE YOU LISTENING?(1932); BEAST OF THE CITY, THE(1932); EMMA(1932); FLESH(1932); GRAND HOTEL(1932); HEARTS OF HUMANITY(1932); MASK OF FU MANCHU, THE(1932); NEW MORALS FOR OLD(1932); NIGHT COURT(1932); SKYSCRAPER SOULS(1932); UNASHAMED(1932); CHRISTOPHER BEAN(1933); CRIME OF THE CENTURY, THE(1933); DINNER AT EIGHT(1933); SONG OF THE EAGLE(1933); CAT AND THE FIDDLE(1934); FOUNTAIN, THE(1934); MEN IN WHITE(1934); PAINTED VEIL, THE(1934); BREAK OF HEARTS(1935); MARK OF THE VAMPIRE(1935); MURDER IN THE FLEET(1935); COUNTRY DOCTOR, THE(1936); HIS BROTHER'S WIFE(1936); ONE IN A MILLION(1936); REUNION(1936); SINS OF MAN(1936); TOUGH GUY(1936); HEIDI(1937); SEVENTH HEAVEN(1937); ALEXANDER'S RAGTIME BAND(1938); FIVE OF A KIND(1938); HAPPY LANDING(1938); I'LL GIVE A MILLION(1938); MEET DR. CHRISTIAN(1939); MR. MOTO IN DANGER ISLAND(1939); COURAGEOUS DR. CHRISTIAN, THE(1940); DR. CHRISTIAN MEETS THE WOMEN(1940); MELODY FOR THREE(1941); REMEDY FOR RICHES(1941); THEY MEET AGAIN(1941); STAGE DOOR CANTEEN(1943); DANCING IN THE DARK(1949); RUN FOR COVER(1955)
Silents
APOSTLE OF VENGEANCE, THE(1916); HELL'S HINGES(1916); KINKAID, GAMBLER(1916); FIGHTING FOR LOVE(1917); GREATER LAW, THE(1917); LOVE AFLAME(1917); ANSWER, THE(1918); MADAME SPY(1918); RED LANE, THE(1920); FOUR HORSEMEN OF THE APOCALYPSE, THE(1921), a, makeup; STRANGER'S BANQUET(1922); TESS OF THE STORM COUNTRY(1922); JAZZMANIA(1923); RED LIGHTS(1923); GOLDFISH, THE(1924); SO BIG(1924); TORMENT(1924); DON Q, SON OF ZORRO(1925); GREED(1925); STELLA DALLAS(1925); IT MUST BE LOVE(1926); OLD SOAK, THE(1926); ALIAS THE DEACON(1928); BATTLE OF THE SEXES, THE(1928); JAZZ MAD(1928); SECRET HOUR, THE(1928); 13 WASHINGTON SQUARE(1928)
Misc. Silents
SOUTHERN JUSTICE(1917); STORMY KNIGHT, A(1917); DECEIVER, THE(1920), a, d; GOLDEN TRAIL, THE(1920), a, d; CERTAIN RICH MAN, A(1921); MAN OF THE FOREST, THE(1921); GRAY DAWN, THE(1922), d; WHEN ROMANCE RIDES(1922); HER NIGHT OF ROMANCE(1924); SINNERS IN SILK(1924); DANGEROUS INNOCENCE(1925); IF MARRIAGE FAILS(1925); WOMAN'S FAITH, A(1925); FLAMES(1926); MY OLD DUTCH(1926); STUDENT PRINCE IN OLD HEIDELBERG, THE(1927); WRONG MR. WRIGHT, THE(1927)

Jean Hersholt, Jr.
FORGOTTEN(1933)

Anne Hershon
WILD SCENE, THE(1970)

Robert Hershorn
TAKE IT ALL(1966, Can.), p

Siegfried Hersig
BREWSTER'S MILLIONS(1945), w

Janos Hersko
DIALOGUE(1967, Hung.), a, d&w; FATHER(1967, Hung.), w
1984
ELEMENT OF CRIME, THE(1984, Den.)

Pat Herskovic
DEADLY BLESSING(1981), p

Bernard Herstrum
COURAGEOUS DR. CHRISTIAN, THE(1940), art d

Hanna Hertalanda
JESUS TRIP, THE(1971)

Gunter Hertel
RUMPELSTILTSKIN(1965, Ger.); GOOSE GIRL, THE(1967, Ger.)

Richard Hertel
MAGIC FOUNTAIN, THE(1961), ed

John Hertelandy
C'MON, LET'S LIVE A LITTLE(1967), p

Hanna Hertelendy
GIRL FROM PETROVKA, THE(1974)
1984
MICKI AND MAUDE(1984)

Francis Herter
Misc. Silents
PRINCE AND THE PAUPER, THE(1929, Aust./Czech.)

Gerard Herter
CALTIKI, THE IMMORTAL MONSTER(1959, Ital.); FIVE BRANDED WO-
MEN(1960); GREAT WAR, THE(1961, Fr., Ital.); THEN THERE WERE THREE(1961);
WHITE WARRIOR, THE(1961, Ital./Yugo.); TWO COLONELS, THE(1963, Ital.); ANY
GUN CAN PLAY(1968, Ital./Span.); FRAULEIN DOKTOR(1969, Ital./Yugo.); LAST
DAY OF THE WAR, THE(1969, U.S./Ital./Span.); BOUNTY HUNTERS, THE(1970,
Ital.); HORNET'S NEST(1970); ADIOS SABATA(1971, Ital./Span.)

Gerhard Herter
LUDWIG(1973, Ital./Ger./Fr.)

James Herter
Silents
MRS. BLACK IS BACK(1914)

Franz Herterich
BURG THEATRE(1936, Ger.)
Misc. Silents
SAMSON AND DELILAH(1922, Aust.)

Will Hertford
Misc. Silents
SADDLE CYCLONE(1925)

Margaret Hertlein
1984
FINDERS KEEPERS(1984)

Walter Hertner
WOODEN HORSE, THE(1951)

B. Russell Herts
GRAND SLAM(1933), w

Kenneth Herts
DEVIL'S MESSENGER, THE(1962 U.S./Swed.), p, art d

Marc Hertsens
DIRTY HARRY(1971)

Alfred Hertz
Silents
JAZZ MAD(1928)

David Hertz
WOMAN CHASES MAN(1937), w; I MET MY LOVE AGAIN(1938), w; THREE
LOVES HAS NANCY(1938), w; BLACKMAIL(1939), w; LOVE CRAZY(1941), w;
JOURNEY FOR MARGARET(1942), w; PILOT NO. 5(1943), w; MARRIAGE IS A
PRIVATE AFFAIR(1944), w; DAISY KENYON(1947), w

Hathan Hertz
CROOKED WEB, THE(1955), d

James Hertz
LAST DANCE, THE(1930)

Jim Hertz
I CONQUER THE SEA(1936)

Lone Hertz
CRAZY PARADISE(1965, Den.)

Nathan Hertz
ATTACK OF THE 50 FOOT WOMAN(1958), d; BRAIN FROM THE PLANET AROUS,
THE(1958), d

Ralph Hertz
SLEEPING CITY, THE(1950)
Misc. Talkies
ALICE IN WONDERLAND(1931)

Roland Hertz
FEMALE TROUBLE(1975)

Dagfinn Hertzberg
DOLL'S HOUSE, A(1973, Brit.)

Michael Hertzberg
TWELVE CHAIRS, THE(1970), p; BLAZING SADDLES(1974), p; SILENT MO-
VIE(1976), p
1984
JOHNNY DANGEROUSLY(1984), p

Seymour Hertzberg [Eugene Archer]
LA COLLECTIONNEUSE(1971, Fr.)

Bernard Hertzbrun
FINDERS KEEPERS(1951), art d

Charles Hertzinger
Misc. Talkies
TANGLED FORTUNES(1932)

Lawrence Hertzog
WHY SHOOT THE TEACHER(1977, Can.), p; FINAL ASSIGNMENT(1980, Can.), p

Harry Hertzsch
TURKISH CUCUMBER, THE(1963, Ger.)

Michel Herubel
TRIAL OF JOAN OF ARC(1965, Fr.)

Lucienne Herval
SONG OF SOHO(1930, Brit.)

Jean Herve
Misc. Silents
LA TERRE(1921, Fr.)

Pitt Hervert
HARPER VALLEY, P.T.A.(1978)

Grizelda Hervey
UP TO THE NECK(1933, Brit.); BIG NOISE, THE(1936, Brit.); GIRLS IN THE
STREET(1937, Brit.); GIRL IN THE STREET(1938, Brit.); YELLOW CANARY,
THE(1944, Brit.); KISS THE BLOOD OFF MY HANDS(1948); TROUBLE IN THE
GLEN(1954, Brit.); TEENAGE BAD GIRL(1959, Brit.)

Harry Hervey
CHEAT, THE(1931), w; DEVIL AND THE DEEP(1932), w; PASSPORT TO
HELL(1932), w; PRESTIGE(1932), w; SHANGHAI EXPRESS(1932), w; WISER SEX,
THE(1932), w; DEVIL'S IN LOVE, THE(1933), w; HIS GREATEST GAMBLE(1934), w;
SON COMES HOME, A(1936), w; UNDER SUSPICION(1937); ROAD TO SIN-
GAPORE(1940), w; MEET THE MOB(1942), w; PEKING EXPRESS(1951), w

Irene Hervey
STRANGER'S RETURN(1933); COUNT OF MONTE CRISTO, THE(1934); DUDE
RANGER, THE(1934); HOLLYWOOD PARTY(1934); LET'S TRY AGAIN(1934); THREE
ON A HONEYMOON(1934); WOMEN IN HIS LIFE, THE(1934); CHARLIE CHAN IN
SHANGHAI(1935); HARD ROCK HARRIGAN(1935); HIS NIGHT OUT(1935); MOTIVE
FOR REVENGE(1935); WHITE LIES(1935); WINNING TICKET, THE(1935); ABSO-
LUTE QUIET(1936); HONEYMOON LIMITED(1936); THREE GODFATHERS(1936);
ALONG CAME LOVE(1937); GIRL SAID NO, THE(1937); LADY FIGHTS BACK(1937);
LEAGUE OF FRIGHTENED MEN(1937); WOMAN IN DISTRESS(1937); SAY IT IN
FRENCH(1938); DESTRY RIDES AGAIN(1939); EAST SIDE OF HEAVEN(1939);
HOUSE OF FEAR, THE(1939); MISSING EVIDENCE(1939); SOCIETY SMUG-
GLERS(1939); BOYS FROM SYRACUSE(1940); CROOKED ROAD, THE(1940); THREE
CHEERS FOR THE IRISH(1940); MR. DYNAMITE(1941); SAN FRANCISCO
DOCKS(1941); BOMBAY CLIPPER(1942); DESTINATION UNKNOWN(1942); FRISCO
LILL(1942); HALF WAY TO SHANGHAI(1942); NIGHT MONSTER(1942); UNSEEN
ENEMY(1942); HE'S MY GUY(1943); MICKEY(1948); MR. PEABODY AND THE
MERMAID(1948); CHICAGO DEADLINE(1949); LUCKY STIFF, THE(1949); MAN-
HANDLED(1949); CRY IN THE NIGHT, A(1956); TEENAGE REBEL(1956); CRASH
LANDING(1958); GOING STEADY(1958); CACTUS FLOWER(1969); PLAY MISTY
FOR ME(1971)

Jason Hervey
1984
BUDDY SYSTEM, THE(1984); MEATBALLS PART II(1984)

Paul Hervey
HAT, COAT AND GLOVE(1934)

Richard Hervey
IT! THE TERROR FROM BEYOND SPACE(1958)

Jeanne Herviale
LITTLE ROMANCE, A(1979, U.S./Fr.)
1984
HERE COMES SANTA CLAUS(1984)

Luz Gloria Hervias
THIRTEEN FRIGHTENED GIRLS(1963)

Juliette Hervieu
VICE AND VIRTUE(1965, Fr./Ital.)

Rene Hervil
AZAIS(1931, Fr.), d
Misc. Silents
SUZANNE(1916, Fr.), d; LA P'TITE DU SIXIEME(1917, Fr.), d; LE TABLIER
BLANC(1917, Fr.), d; MERES FRANCAISES(1917, Fr.), d; OH! CE BAISER(1917,
Fr.), d; BOUCLETTE(1918, Fr.), d; LE TORRENT(1918, Fr.), d; UN ROMAN D'AMOUR
ET D'AVENTURES(1918, Fr.), d; SIMPLETTE(1919, Fr.), d; SON ADVENTURE(1919,
Fr.), d; L'AMI FRITZ(1920, Fr.), d; BLANCHETTE(1921, Fr.), d; LE CRIME DE LORD
ARTHUR SAVILLE(1922, Fr.), d; AUX JARDINS DE MURCIE(1923, Fr.), d; LE
SECRET DE POLICHINELLE(1923, Fr.), d; SARATI-LE-TERRIBLE(1923, Fr.), d; PA-
RIS(1924, Fr.), d; LA FLAMME(1925, Fr.), d; KNOCK(1926, Fr.), d; LA PETITE
CHOCOLATIERE(1927, Fr.), d; LE PRINCE JEAN(1928, Fr.), d; MINUIT...PLACE
PIGALLE(1928, Fr.), d; LA MEILLEURE MAITRESSE(1929, Fr.), d

Renee Hervil
MYSTERY OF THE PINK VILLA, THE(1930, Fr.), w

Marian Herwood
NO MINOR VICES(1948), cos

Claude Herz
IT SEEMED LIKE A GOOD IDEA AT THE TIME(1975, Can.), w

Juraj Herz
TRANSPORT FROM PARADISE(1967, Czech.); CREMATOR, THE(1973, Czech.), d;
NINTH HEART, THE(1980, Czech.), d&w

Michael Herz
SQUEEZE PLAY(1981), p; WAITRESS(1982), p, d; STUCK ON YOU(1983), p, d, w
1984
FIRST TURN-ON!, THE(1984), p, d, w; STUCK ON YOU(1984), p, w

Ralph Herz
Misc. Silents
PURPLE LADY, THE(1916); MYSTERY OF NO. 47, THE(1917)

Tamara Herz
PARSIFAL(1983, Fr.)

Miguel Herz-Kestranek
WAGNER(1983, Brit./Hung./Aust.)

Arnold Herzatein
CALIFORNIA SPLIT(1974)

Bernard Herzbaum
ONE WAY STREET(1950), art d

Alexander Herzberg
1984
JOHNNY DANGEROUSLY(1984)

Elmer Herzberg
TEXAN MEETS CALAMITY JANE, THE(1950)

Bernard Herzbrun
SEVEN DAYS LEAVE(1930), art d; TOM SAWYER(1930), art d; DEVIL AND THE
DEEP(1932), art d; I'M NO ANGEL(1933), art d; BELLE OF THE NINETIES(1934), art
d; MISSISSIPPI(1935), art d; STOLEN HARMONY(1935), art d; MILKY WAY,
THE(1936), art d; POPPY(1936), art d; TEXAS RANGERS, THE(1936), art d; ALI
BABA GOES TO TOWN(1937), art d; LOVE AND HISSES(1937), art d; MAID OF
SALEM(1937), art d; MAKE WAY FOR TOMORROW(1937), art d; ONE MILE FROM
HEAVEN(1937), art d; SECOND HONEYMOON(1937), art d; THANK YOU, MR.
MOTO(1937), art d; ALEXANDER'S RAGTIME BAND(1938), art d; ALWAYS GOOD-
BYE(1938), art d; BARONESS AND THE BUTLER, THE(1938), art d; DOWN ON THE
FARM(1938), art d; FIVE OF A KIND(1938), art d; FOUR MEN AND A PRAYER(1938),
art d; GATEWAY(1938), art d; HOLD THAT CO-ED(1938), art d; I'LL GIVE A
MILLION(1938), art d; INTERNATIONAL SETTLEMENT(1938), art d; ISLAND IN
THE SKY(1938), art d; JOSETTE(1938), art d; JUST AROUND THE CORNER(1938),
art d; KENTUCKY(1938), art d; KENTUCKY MOONSHINE(1938), art d; LOVE ON A
BUDGET(1938), art d; MR. MOTO'S GAMBLE(1938), art d; MYSTERIOUS MR.
MOTO(1938), art d; ONE WILD NIGHT(1938), art d; REBECCA OF SUNNYBROOK
FARM(1938), art d; SALLY, IRENE AND MARY(1938), art d; SPEED TO BURN(1938),
art d; STRAIGHT, PLACE AND SHOW(1938), art d; SUEZ(1938), art d; THANKS FOR
EVERYTHING(1938), art d; UP THE RIVER(1938), art d; WALKING DOWN BROAD-
WAY(1938), art d; BARRICADE(1939), art d; INSIDE STORY(1939), art d; LITTLE
PRINCESS, THE(1939), art d; MEET DR. CHRISTIAN(1939), art d; TAIL SPIN(1939),
art d; DREAMING OUT LOUD(1940), art d; MELODY FOR THREE(1941), art d;
REMEDY FOR RICHES(1941), art d; SCATTERGOOD PULLS THE STRINGS(1941),
art d; SCATTERGOOD SURVIVES A MURDER(1942), art d; JACK LONDON(1943),
art d; LADY OF BURLESQUE(1943), art d; SONG OF THE OPEN ROAD(1944), art d;
PARDON MY PAST(1945), prod d; STRANGE HOLIDAY(1945), art d; ANGEL ON MY

SHOULDER(1946), art d; TEMPTATION(1946), art d; BRUTE FORCE(1947), art d; BUCK PRIVATES COME HOME(1947), art d; DOUBLE LIFE, A(1947), art d; EGG AND I, THE(1947), prod d; EXILE, THE(1947), art d; RIDE THE PINK HORSE(1947), art d; SENATOR WAS INDISCREET, THE(1947), art d; SINGAPORE(1947), art d; TIME OUT OF MIND(1947), art d; WEB, THE(1947), art d; WISTFUL WIDOW OF WAGON GAP, THE(1947), art d; WOMAN'S VENGEANCE, A(1947), art d; ALL MY SONS(1948), art d; FAMILY HONEYMOON(1948), art d; FEUDIN', FUSSIN' AND A-FIGHTIN'(1948), art d; KISS THE BLOOD OFF MY HANDS(1948), art d; LARCENY(1948), art d; MEXICAN HAYRIDE(1948), art d; MR. PEABODY AND THE MERMAID(1948), art d; ONE TOUCH OF VENUS(1948), art d; RIVER LADY(1948), art d; ABANDONED(1949), art d; CALAMITY JANE AND SAM BASS(1949), art d; CITY ACROSS THE RIVER(1949), art d; CRISS CROSS(1949), art d; FIGHTING O'FLYNN, THE(1949), art d; FRANCIS(1949), art d; FREE FOR ALL(1949), art d; GAL WHO TOOK THE WEST, THE(1949), art d; ILLEGAL ENTRY(1949), art d; JOHNNY STOOL PIGEON(1949), art d; LIFE OF RILEY, THE(1949), art d; MA AND PA KETTLE(1949), art d; ONCE MORE, MY DARLING(1949), art d; RED CANYON(1949), art d; STORY OF MOLLY X, THE(1949), art d; SWORD IN THE DESERT(1949), art d; TAKE ONE FALSE STEP(1949), art d; UNDERTOW(1949), art d; WOMAN IN HIDING(1949), art d; YES SIR, THAT'S MY BABY(1949), art d; BUCCANEER'S GIRL(1950), art d; DEPORTED(1950), art d; DESERT HAWK, THE(1950), art d; DOUBLE CROSSBONES(1950), art d; HARVEY(1950), art d; KANSAS RAIDERS(1950), art d; KID FROM TEXAS, THE(1950), art d; LOUISA(1950), art d; MA AND PA KETTLE GO TO TOWN(1950), art d; MILKMAN, THE(1950), art d; MYSTERY SUBMARINE(1950), art d; PEGGY(1950), art d; SADDLE TRAMP(1950), art d; SHAKEDOWN(1950), art d; SIERRA(1950), art d; SLEEPING CITY, THE(1950), art d; SOUTH SEA SINNER(1950), art d; SPY HUNT(1950), art d; UNDERCOVER GIRL(1950), art d; WINCHESTER '73(1950), art d; WYOMING MAIL(1950), art d; AIR CADET(1951), art d; BRIGHT VICTORY(1951), art d; FAT MAN, THE(1951), art d; FLAME OF ARABY(1951), art d; GOLDEN HORDE, THE(1951), art d; HOLLYWOOD STORY(1951), art d; IRON MAN, THE(1951), art d; LADY FROM TEXAS, THE(1951), art d; LADY PAYS OFF, THE(1951), art d; LITTLE EGYPT(1951), art d; MA AND PA KETTLE BACK ON THE FARM(1951), art d; MARK OF THE RENEGADE(1951), art d; PRINCE WHO WAS A THIEF, THE(1951), art d; RAGING TIDE, THE(1951), art d; REUNION IN RENO(1951), art d; STRANGE DOOR, THE(1951), art d; TARGET UNKNOWN(1951), art d; THUNDER ON THE HILL(1951), art d; TOMAHAWK(1951), art d; UNDER THE GUN(1951), art d; UP FRONT(1951), art d; WEEKEND WITH FATHER(1951), art d; YOU NEVER CAN TELL(1951), art d; AGAINST ALL FLAGS(1952), art d; BEND OF THE RIVER(1952), art d; DUEL AT SILVER CREEK, THE(1952), art d; FLESH AND FURY(1952), art d; FRANCIS GOES TO WEST POINT(1952), art d; HAS ANYBODY SEEN MY GAL?(1952), art d; HERE COME THE NELSONS(1952), art d; HORIZONS WEST(1952), art d; IT GROWS ON TREES(1952), art d; JUST ACROSS THE STREET(1952), art d; LAWLESS BREED, THE(1952), art d; LOST IN ALASKA(1952), art d; MA AND PA KETTLE AT THE FAIR(1952), art d; MEET DANNY WILSON(1952), art d; MEET ME AT THE FAIR(1952), art d; NO ROOM FOR THE GROOM(1952), art d; RAIDERS, THE(1952), art d; RED BALL EXPRESS(1952), art d; SALLY AND SAINT ANNE(1952), art d; SAN FRANCISCO STORY, THE(1952), art d; SCARLET ANGEL(1952), art d; SON OF ALI BABA(1952), art d; STEEL TOWN(1952), art d; TREASURE OF LOST CANYON, THE(1952), art d; UNTAMED FRONTIER(1952), art d; WORLD IN HIS ARMS, THE(1952), art d; YANKEE BUCCANEER(1952), art d; ALL I DESIRE(1953), art d; EAST OF SUMATRA(1953), art d; FORBIDDEN(1953), art d; FRANCIS COVERS THE BIG TOWN(1953), art d; GLASS WEB, THE(1953), art d; GOLDEN BLADE, THE(1953), art d; IT CAME FROM OUTER SPACE(1953), art d; IT HAPPENS EVERY THURSDAY(1953), art d; MA AND PA KETTLE ON VACATION(1953), art d; REDHEAD FROM WYOMING, THE(1953), art d; STAND AT APACHE RIVER, THE(1953), art d; TAKE ME TO TOWN(1953), art d; TUMBLEWEED(1953), art d; WALKING MY BABY BACK HOME(1953), art d; WAR ARROW(1953), art d; WINGS OF THE HAWK(1953), art d; ABBOTT AND COSTELLO MEET DR. JEKYLL AND MR. HYDE(1954), art d; JOHNNY DARK(1954), art d; MA AND PA KETTLE AT HOME(1954), art d; MAGNIFICENT OBSESSION(1954), art d; SASKATCHEWAN(1954), art d; TAZA, SON OF COCHISE(1954), art d; MA AND PA KETTLE AT WAIKIKI(1955), art d

David Herzbrun
SMUGGLER'S ISLAND(1951), art d

Bernard Herzburn
ROAD DEMON(1938), art d; KATIE DID IT(1951), art d

Kenneth Herzenroder
BEACH GIRLS(1982), art d

Guido Herzfeld
Silents
NOSFERATU, THE VAMPIRE(1922, Ger.)

John Herzfeld
CANNONBALL(1976, U.S./Hong Kong); VOICES(1979), w; TWO OF A KIND(1983), d&w

Bernard Herzgrup
KLONDIKE ANNIE(1936), art d

Sid Herzig
MOONLIGHT AND PRETZELS(1933), w; ROMANCE IN THE RAIN(1934), w; OLD MAN RHYTHM(1935), w; FOUR'S A CROWD(1938), w; THEY MADE ME A CRIMINAL(1939), w

Siegfried Herzig
THREE ON A SPREE(1961, Brit.), w

Siegried M. Herzig
LOTTERY LOVER(1935), w

Sig Herzig
LONE WOLF'S DAUGHTER, THE(1929), w; BROADWAY GONDOLIER(1935), w; MILLIONS IN THE AIR(1935), w; COLLEEN(1936), w; SING ME A LOVE SONG(1936), w; ARTISTS AND MODELS(1937), w; MARRY THE GIRL(1937), w; READY, WILLING AND ABLE(1937), w; VARSITY SHOW(1937), w; GOING PLACES(1939), w; INDIANAPOLIS SPEEDWAY(1939), w; ON YOUR TOES(1939), w; MY FAVORITE SPY(1942), w; FOREVER AND A DAY(1943), w; I DOOD IT(1943), w; WHERE DO WE GO FROM HERE?(1945), w; BECAUSE OF HIM(1946), w
Silents
OBJECT-ALIMONY(1929), w

Sigfried Herzig
MY HEART GOES CRAZY(1953, Brit.), w

Carl Herzinger
LUM AND ABNER ABROAD(1956), w

Charles Herzinger
DEVIL AND DANIEL WEBSTER, THE(1941)
Silents
BAT, THE(1926)

Charles W. Herzinger
PLAINSMAN, THE(1937)

Paolo Herzl
STRANGER, THE(1967, Algeria/Fr./Ital.)

Herzog
DREYFUS CASE, THE(1931, Brit.), w

Arthur Herzog
SWARM, THE(1978), w

Col. Dean Hess
BATTLE HYMN(1957), w

F. Herzog
Silents
GANGSTERS OF NEW YORK, THE(1914)

Fred Herzog
Silents
RED LANE, THE(1920); SCARLET LETTER, THE(1926)
Misc. Silents
BIG ADVENTURE, THE(1921)

Frederick Herzog
Silents
FAITH(1920); KING SPRUCE(1920)

Sid Herzog
I WANTED WINGS(1941), w

Sig Herzog
SUNNY(1941), w

Stanton Herzog
WHITE HEAT(1949)

Suzynn Herzog
1984
CANNONBALL RUN II(1984)

Werner Herzog
EVERY MAN FOR HIMSELF AND GOD AGAINST ALL(1975, Ger.), p,d&w; AGUIRRE, THE WRATH OF GOD(1977, W. Ger.), p,d&w; NOSFERATU, THE VAMPIRE(1979, Fr./Ger.), p,d&w; SIGNS OF LIFE(1981, Ger.), p,d&w; FITZCARRALDO(1982), p, d&w
1984
MAN OF FLOWERS(1984, Aus.)

Bohumil Hes
ECSTASY(1940, Czech.), art d

Pamela Hesbitt
DUMMY TALKS, THE(1943, Brit.)

Gottlieb Hesch
Silents
PANDORA'S BOX(1929, Ger.), cos

Albert Heschong
HAIL, HERO!(1969), art d

Alfred Hese
Silents
PURSUING VENGEANCE, THE(1916)

Simon Hesera
DAY AT THE BEACH, A(1970), d

Karin Heske
SEVEN DARING GIRLS(1962, Ger.)

Sharon Hesky
BLADE RUNNER(1982)

Tom Heslewood
PEG OF OLD DRURY(1936, Brit.)
Silents
GLORIOUS ADVENTURE, THE(1922, U.S./Brit.)

Paul Heslin
JUD(1971)

Charles Heslop
THIS IS THE LIFE(1933, Brit.); STRAUSS' GREAT WALTZ(1934, Brit.); CHARING CROSS ROAD(1935, Brit.); MAN WITH 100 FACES, THE(1938, Brit.); LAMBETH WALK, THE(1940, Brit.); FLYING FORTRESS(1942, Brit.); PETERVILLE DIAMOND, THE(1942, Brit.); DON'T SAY DIE(1950, Brit.); SECOND MATE, THE(1950, Brit.); OBSESSED(1951, Brit.); HELLO LONDON(1958, Brit.); FOLLOW A STAR(1959, Brit.); NOTHING BARRED(1961, Brit.); PAIR OF BRIEFS, A(1963, Brit.)

Arnold Hess, Jr.
EASY RIDER(1969)

Betty Jane Hess
COVER GIRL(1944)

David Hess
LAST HOUSE ON THE LEFT(1972), a, m; SWISS CONSPIRACY, THE(1976, U.S./Ger.); AVALANCHE EXPRESS(1979); TO ALL A GOODNIGHT(1980), d; SWAMP THING(1982)

Eloise Hess
Silents
SWORD OF VALOR, THE(1924)

Frances Hess
Silents
AT THE STAGE DOOR(1921)

Harry Hess
FOUR IN A JEEP(1951, Switz.)

James Hess
WAVELENGTH(1983)

Jim Hess
STUNT MAN, THE(1980)

Joachim Hess
DER FREISCHUTZ(1970, Ger.), d; FIDELIO(1970, Ger.), d; MARRIAGE OF FIGARO, THE(1970, Ger.), d

John D. Hess
MATTER OF MORALS, A(1961, U.S./Swed.), p, w

Joseph Hess
1984
HARRY AND SON(1984)
Karl Heinz Hess
GREAT BRITISH TRAIN ROBBERY, THE(1967, Ger.)
Laura Hess
STRAIT-JACKET(1964)
Louis Hess
HI-DE-HO(1947), ed
Urs Hess
GIRL AND THE LEGEND, THE(1966, Ger.)
Walter Hess
BLACK SPIDER, THE(1983, Swit.)
William Hess
MELODY OF THE PLAINS(1937), ed
Adam Hesse
PREACHERMAN(1971)
Baron Hesse
PURSUIT OF HAPPINESS, THE(1934); MARK OF THE VAMPIRE(1935); STORY OF LOUIS PASTEUR, THE(1936)
Barron Hesse
WE LIVE AGAIN(1934)
Charles Hesse
ALBERT, R.N.(1953, Brit.), ed
Gerhard Hesse
MALOU(1983)
Helen Hesse
STEPPENWOLF(1974)
Hermann Hesse
SIDDHARTHA(1972), w; STEPPENWOLF(1974), d&w
Julia Hesse
Silents
ABRAHAM LINCOLN(1924)
Lew Hesse
DOWN THE STRETCH(1936), ed
Lou Hesse
EXPENSIVE HUSBANDS(1937), ed; FOOTLOOSE HEIRESS, THE(1937), ed; PATIENT IN ROOM 18, THE(1938), ed
Louis Hesse
HERE COMES CARTER(1936), ed; HEART OF THE NORTH(1938), ed; NANCY DREW AND THE HIDDEN STAIRCASE(1939), ed; WATERFRONT(1939), ed
Howard Hesseman
KID BLUE(1973); STEELYARD BLUES(1973); SHAMPOO(1975); SUNSHINE BOYS, THE(1975); WHIFFS(1975); BIG BUS, THE(1976); JACKSON COUNTY JAIL(1976); SILENT MOVIE(1976); TUNNELVISION(1976); OTHER SIDE OF MIDNIGHT, THE(1977); AMERICATHON(1979); LOOSE SHOES(1980); HONKY TONK FREEWAY(1981); PRIVATE LESSONS(1981); DOCTOR DETROIT(1983)
1984
THIS IS SPINAL TAP(1984)
Misc. Talkies
PRISONERS(1975)
Werner Hessenland
MAN WHO WALKED THROUGH THE WALL, THE(1964, Ger.)
Edwin Bower Hesser
Silents
NOT GUILTY(1921), w
Misc. Silents
TRIUMPH OF VENUS, THE(1918), d
Audrey Hessey
TIME IS MY ENEMY(1957, Brit.)
Russ Hessey
INVASION OF THE BODY SNATCHERS(1978), spec eff
Walter Hessig
ASSAULT ON AGATHON(1976, Brit./Gr.)
Chris Hession
PIRATE MOVIE, THE(1982, Aus.)
1984
RAZORBACK(1984, Aus.)
Horst Hesslein
$(DOLLARS) (1971)
Gordon Hessler
WOMAN WHO WOULDN'T DIE, THE(1965, Brit.), d; LAST SHOT YOU HEAR, THE(1969, Brit.), d; OBLONG BOX, THE(1969, Brit.), p&d; CRY OF THE BANSHEE(1970, Brit.), p&d; SCREAM AND SCREAM AGAIN(1970, Brit.), d; MURDERS IN THE RUE MORGUE(1971), d; EMBASSY(1972, Brit.), d; GOLDEN VOYAGE OF SINBAD, THE(1974, Brit.), d
Misc. Talkies
ESCAPE FROM EL DIABLO(1983, U.S./Brit./Span.), d
Tom Hesslewood
VICTORIA THE GREAT(1937, Brit.)
Catherine Hessling
FROM TOP TO BOTTOM(1933, Fr.); CRIME AND PUNISHMENT(1935, Fr.)
Misc. Silents
CATHERINE(1924, Fr.); LA FILLE DE L'EAU(1924, Fr.); NANA(1926, Fr.); EN RADE(1927, Fr.)
Christia Hester
SECRET AGENT SUPER DRAGON(1966, Fr./Ital./Ger./Monaco)
Harvey Hester
GREAT LOCOMOTIVE CHASE, THE(1956)
Penelope Hester
HARD KNOCKS(1980, Aus.), cos
Starr Hester
GONG SHOW MOVIE, THE(1980)
Andrea Hesterasy
FINE PAIR, A(1969, Ital.)
Trude Hesterberg
DIE MANNER UM LUCIE(1931); TEMPEST(1932, Ger.)
Misc. Silents
MADAME WANTS NO CHILDREN(1927, Ger.)

Alan Heston
PEER GYNT(1965)
Charleton Heston
SAVAGE, THE(1953)
Charlton Heston
DARK CITY(1950); GREATEST SHOW ON EARTH, THE(1952); JULIUS CAESAR(1952); RUBY GENTRY(1952); ARROWHEAD(1953); NAKED JUNGLE, THE(1953); PONY EXPRESS(1953); PRESIDENT'S LADY, THE(1953); BAD FOR EACH OTHER(1954); SECRET OF THE INCAS(1954); FAR HORIZONS, THE(1955); LUCY GALLANT(1955); PRIVATE WAR OF MAJOR BENSON, THE(1955); TEN COMMANDMENTS, THE(1956); THREE VIOLENT PEOPLE(1956); BIG COUNTRY, THE(1958); BUCCANEER, THE(1958); TOUCH OF EVIL(1958); BEN HUR(1959); WRECK OF THE MARY DEAR, THE(1959); EL CID(1961, U.S./Ital.); DIAMOND HEAD(1962); PIGEON THAT TOOK ROME, THE(1962); 55 DAYS AT PEKING(1963); AGONY AND THE ECSTASY, THE(1965); GREATEST STORY EVER TOLD, THE(1965); MAJOR DUNDEE(1965); PEER GYNT(1965); WAR LORD, THE(1965); KHARTOUM(1966, Brit.); COUNTERPOINT(1967); PLANET OF THE APES(1968); WILL PENNY(1968); NUMBER ONE(1969); BENEATH THE PLANET OF THE APES(1970); HAWAIIANS, THE(1970); JULIUS CAESAR(1970, Brit.); OMEGA MAN, THE(1971); CALL OF THE WILD(1972, Ger./ Span./Ital./Fr.); SKYJACKED(1972); ANTONY AND CLEOPATRA(1973, Brit.), a, d&w; SOYLENT GREEN(1973); AIRPORT 1975(1974); EARTHQUAKE(1974); THREE MUSKETEERS, THE(1974, Panama); FOUR MUSKETEERS, THE(1975); LAST HARD MEN, THE(1976); MIDWAY(1976); TWO-MINUTE WARNING(1976); CROSSED SWORDS(1978); GRAY LADY DOWN(1978); AWAKENING, THE(1980); MOUNTAIN MEN, THE(1980); MOTHER LODE(1982), a, d
Fraser Clarke Heston
MOUNTAIN MEN, THE(1980), w; MOTHER LODE(1982), p, w
Fraser Heston
TEN COMMANDMENTS, THE(1956)
John Heston
Misc. Talkies
OLD TESTAMENT(1963, Ital.)
Terese Heston
HOT STUFF(1979)
Joan Hestor
Silents
MANCHESTER MAN, THE(1920, Brit.)
Hanna Hetelendy
TWO-MINUTE WARNING(1976)
Pal Hetenyi
FATHER(1967, Hung.)
Gary Hetherington
FIRST BLOOD(1982)
John Hetherington
HAMLET(1964)
Keith Hetherington
HE RAN ALL THE WAY(1951)
Stuart Hetherington
PORTRAIT OF THE ARTIST AS A YOUNG MAN, A(1979, Ireland), ph
Jenni Hetrick
SQUEEZE PLAY(1981)
Heinz Hetter
I LOVE YOU, I KILL YOU(1972, Ger.), m
Hetty Schneider Quartet
POPDOWN(1968, Brit.)
Herb Hetzer
ONE DOWN TWO TO GO(1982), m
Edmund Heuberger
Misc. Silents
ASIAN SUN, THE(1921, Ger.), d
Jeanne Heuclin
MATTER OF DAYS, A(1969, Fr./Czech.)
Raymonde Heudeline
1984
LE BAL(1984, Fr./Ital./Algeria)
Andrea Heuer
LOLA(1982, Ger.)
Charon Heuer
1984
ALLEY CAT(1984)
John Heuer
TWO VOICES(1966)
Oliver Heuffer
HIS LORDSHIP(1932, Brit.), w
William Heughan
PRIVATE LIFE OF HENRY VIII, THE(1933); PRIVATE LIFE OF DON JUAN, THE(1934, Brit.)
William Heughen
TALKING FEET(1937, Brit.)
Karl Heuglin
WRONG IS RIGHT(1982), art d
Archie Heugly
MACBETH(1948)
Reuben Heura
BLACK RODEO(1972)
Paolo Heusch
DAY THE SKY EXPLODED, THE(1958, Fr./Ital.), d
Andre Heuse
DIARY OF A CHAMBERMAID(1946), w
Ted Heusel
Misc. Talkies
METAMORPHOSIS(1951)
Herman Heuser
MY FATHER'S HOUSE(1947, Palestine)
Jurt Heuser
TRIAL, THE(1948, Aust.), w

Kurt Heuser
FINAL CHORD, THE(1936, Ger.), w; LIFE BEGINS ANEW(1938, Ger.), w; DIE FASTNACHTSBEICHTE(1962, Ger.), w; GIRL FROM HONG KONG(1966, Ger.), w

Loni Heuser
DECISION BEFORE DAWN(1951); SCHLAGER-PARADE(1953); BIMBO THE GREAT(1961, Ger.)

Nahid Heusser
GUNS AND THE FURY, THE(1983), art d

Reed Heustis
Silents
KNIGHT OF THE WEST, A(1921), t

Russell Heustis
I AM THE LAW(1938); THERE'S THAT WOMAN AGAIN(1938)

Alfred Heuston
Silents
WEB OF THE LAW, THE(1923); SPLITTING THE BREEZE(1927); SKY RIDER, THE(1928)
Misc. Silents
MASQUERADE BANDIT, THE(1926)

Eleanore Heutschy
1984
AMERICAN DREAMER(1984)

Vic Heutschy
MAIN EVENT, THE(1979)
1984
AMERICAN DREAMER(1984)

Andre Heuze
Misc. Silents
POIL DE CAROTTE(1926, Fr.)

Bob Hevelone
DEAD MEN DON'T WEAR PLAID(1982)

Jerold Hevener
Silents
ALL FOR A GIRL(1915)

Martha Heveran
VOGUES OF 1938(1937)

John Hewer
ASSASSIN FOR HIRE(1951, Brit.); DARK MAN, THE(1951, Brit.); COLONEL MARCH INVESTIGATES(1952,Brit.); LAW AND DISORDER(1958, Brit.); STRIP TEASE MURDER(1961, Brit.); THREE SPARE WIVES(1962, Brit.); MISTER TEN PERCENT(1967, Brit.)
Misc. Talkies
OPERATION STOGIE(1960, Brit.)

Bentley Hewett
FIREFLY, THE(1937)

Bill Hewett
LOVE IS A CAROUSEL(1970)

Christopher Hewett
LAVENDER HILL MOB, THE(1951, Brit.); PRODUCERS, THE(1967)

Dorothy Hewett
JOURNEY AMONG WOMEN(1977, Aus.), w

Robert Hewett
END PLAY(1975, Aus.)

Sean Hewett
Misc. Talkies
BIG ZAPPER(1974)

Wyndham Hewett
WHO GOES NEXT?(1938, Brit.)

Enid Hewit
SPELL OF AMY NUGENT, THE(1945, Brit.)

Eric Hewitson
TOO YOUNG TO LOVE(1960, Brit.)

Harry Hewitson
SECRETS OF CHINATOWN(1935)

Ian Hewitson
HOUND OF THE BASKERVILLES, THE(1959, Brit.); MAN WHO COULD CHEAT DEATH, THE(1959, Brit.)

Michael Hewitson
I WANNA HOLD YOUR HAND(1978)

Walford Hewitson
WAITING FOR CAROLINE(1969, Can.), p

Alan Hewitt
PRIVATE'S AFFAIR, A(1959); ABSENT-MINDED PROFESSOR, THE(1961); BACHELOR IN PARADISE(1961); DAYS OF WINE AND ROSES(1962); FOLLOW THAT DREAM(1962); THAT TOUCH OF MINK(1962); SON OF FLUBBER(1963); MISADVENTURES OF MERLIN JONES, THE(1964); HOW TO MURDER YOUR WIFE(1965); MONKEY'S UNCLE, THE(1965); BROTHERHOOD, THE(1968); HORSE IN THE GRAY FLANNEL SUIT, THE(1968); SWEET CHARITY(1969); COMPUTER WORE TENNIS SHOES, THE(1970); R.P.M.(1970); BAREFOOT EXECUTIVE, THE(1971); NOW YOU SEE HIM, NOW YOU DON'T(1972); SENIORS, THE(1978)

Albert Hewitt
Silents
KENTUCKIANS, THE(1921)

Allan Hewitt
CAREER(1959)

Barbara Hewitt
EQUINOX(1970)

Beverly Hewitt
1984
WINTER FLIGHT(1984, Brit.)

Celia Hewitt
PLEASE TURN OVER(1960, Brit.); LIFE IN DANGER(1964, Brit.); SHUTTERED ROOM, THE(1968, Brit.); SATAN'S SLAVE(1976, Brit.)

Christopher Hewitt
POOL OF LONDON(1951, Brit.)

David Hewitt
TIME TRAVELERS, THE(1964), d&w, spec eff; DEVONSVILLE TERROR, THE(1983), spec eff

David L. Hewitt
WIZARD OF MARS(1964), p,d&w; GIRLS FROM THUNDER STRIP, THE(1966), p, d; DR. TERROR'S GALLERY OF HORRORS(1967), p, d; JOURNEY TO THE CENTER OF TIME(1967), p, d; HELL'S CHOSEN FEW(1968), p&d; MIGHTY GORGA, THE(1969), p, d; HORROR OF THE BLOOD MONSTERS(1970, U.S./Phil.), spec eff
Misc. Talkies
LUCIFER COMPLEX, THE(1978), d

Enid Hewitt
WHILE I LIVE(1947, Brit.); OLD MOTHER RILEY, HEADMISTRESS(1950, Brit.); EIGHT O'CLOCK WALK(1954, Brit.); SOLUTION BY PHONE(1954, Brit.); HAPPY IS THE BRIDE(1958, Brit.)

G. Fletcher Hewitt
Misc. Silents
POTTERY GIRL'S ROMANCE, A(1918, Brit.), d

Heather Hewitt
MISSION MARS(1968); I EAT YOUR SKIN(1971)

Henry Hewitt
SCHOOL FOR SCANDAL, THE(1930, Brit.); MADAME GUILLOTINE(1931, Brit.); STAMBOUL(1931, Brit.); WRITTEN LAW, THE(1931, Brit.); BETRAYAL(1932, Brit.); FIRST MRS. FRASER, THE(1932, Brit.); POWER(1934, Brit.); ADMIRALS ALL(1935, Brit.); REMBRANDT(1936, Brit.); HIGH COMMAND(1938, Brit.); OLD IRON(1938, Brit.); JUST LIKE A WOMAN(1939, Brit.); THREE COCKEYED SAILORS(1940, Brit.); BLACK SHEEP OF WHITEHALL, THE(1941 Brit.); AVENGERS, THE(1942, Brit.); YOUNG MR. PITT, THE(1942, Brit.); GIVE US THE MOON(1944, Brit.); DULCIMER STREET(1948, Brit.); CHRISTMAS CAROL, A(1951, Brit.); HAPPY GO LOVELY(1951, Brit.); TRAIN OF EVENTS(1952, Brit.); WHERE'S CHARLEY?(1952, Brit.); HUNDRED HOUR HUNT(1953, Brit.); ISN'T LIFE WONDERFUL!(1953, Brit.); MR. POTTS GOES TO MOSCOW(1953, Brit.); JOHN WESLEY(1954, Brit.); ROB ROY, THE HIGHLAND ROGUE(1954, Brit.); NOW AND FOREVER(1956, Brit.); YOUR PAST IS SHOWING(1958, Brit.)

Irene Hewitt
DIMBOOLA(1979, Aus.); LONELY HEARTS(1983, Aus.); NEXT OF KIN(1983, Aus.)

Jean Hewitt
BLOOD OF DRACULA'S CASTLE(1967), d; MIGHTY GORGA, THE(1969), w; HORROR OF THE BLOOD MONSTERS(1970, U.S./Phil.), makeup

Jerry Hewitt
WARRIORS, THE(1979); NESTING, THE(1981); ROLLOVER(1981); TEMPEST(1982)
1984
PREPPIES(1984), stunts

Jery Hewitt
WANDERERS, THE(1979); WOLFEN(1981); SOLDIER, THE(1982)
1984
ALPHABET CITY(1984); FIRSTBORN(1984)

John Hewitt
FIGHTING PIMPERNEL, THE(1950, Brit.)

Lee J. Hewitt
KENTUCKY RIFLE(1956), w

Lew Hewitt
GOLDEN MISTRESS, THE(1954), w

Martin Hewitt
ENDLESS LOVE(1981); YELLOWBEARD(1983)

Master Russel Hewitt
Silents
ANNE OF GREEN GABLES(1919)

Raymond Hewitt
Silents
FLAPPER, THE(1920)

Robert Hewitt
PETERSEN(1974, Aus.); HIGH ROLLING(1977, Aus.)

Sanford Hewitt
Silents
HOLD 'EM YALE!(1928), w; MARKED MONEY(1928), w

Sean Hewitt
MADE(1972, Brit.); HANK WILLIAMS: THE SHOW HE NEVER GAVE(1982, Can.); SENDER, THE(1982, Brit.)

Virginia Hewitt
MY DEAR SECRETARY(1948); FLYING SAUCER, THE(1950); BOWERY BATTALION(1951); PEOPLE AGAINST O'HARA, THE(1951)

Brian Hewitt-Jones
QUARE FELLOW, THE(1962, Brit.)

Philip Hewland
BLOCKADE(1928, Brit.); ALF'S CARPET(1929, Brit.); HARMONY HEAVEN(1930, Brit.); GLAMOUR(1931, Brit.); MANY WATERS(1931, Brit.); SHERLOCK HOLMES' FATAL HOUR(1931, Brit.); TONS OF MONEY(1931, Brit.); MISSING REMBRANDT, THE(1932, Brit.); MAROONED(1933, Brit.); PASSING SHADOWS(1934, Brit.); MURDER BY ROPE(1936, Brit.)
Silents
ALTAR CHAINS(1916, Brit.); ARSENE LUPIN(1916, Brit.); GREATER NEED, THE(1916, Brit.); MARCH HARE, THE(1919, Brit.); NOT GUILTY(1919, Brit.); KISSING CUP'S RACE(1920, Brit.); MONEY HABIT, THE(1924, Brit.)
Misc. Silents
ASHES OF REVENGE, THE(1915, Brit.); HIS VINDICATION(1915, Brit.); MAN IN THE ATTIC, THE(1915, Brit.); HIS DAUGHTER'S DILEMMA(1916, Brit.); SECRET OF THE MOOR, THE(1919, Brit.); LADY TETLEY'S DEGREE(1920, Brit.); SCARLET KISS, THE(1920, Brit.); HER PENALTY(1921, Brit.); IN FULL CRY(1921, Brit.); COUPLE OF DOWN AND OUTS, A(1923, Brit.)

Phillip Hewland
Silents
DOUBLE LIFE OF MR. ALFRED BURTON, THE(1919, Brit.)
Misc. Silents
MAN IN MOTLEY, THE(1916, Brit.)

Arthur Hewlett
DELAYED ACTION(1954, Brit.); EIGHT O'CLOCK WALK(1954, Brit.); TIME OF HIS LIFE, THE(1955, Brit.); WAR LOVER, THE(1962, U.S./Brit.); REACH FOR GLORY(1963, Brit.); THREE BITES OF THE APPLE(1967); CHALLENGE FOR ROBIN HOOD, A(1968, Brit.); DANDY IN ASPIC, A(1968, Brit.); NIGHT VISITOR, THE(1970, Swed./U.S.); PIED PIPER, THE(1972, Brit.)

Ben Hewlett
NOT QUITE DECENT(1929); ON THE LEVEL(1930); SPEED WINGS(1934)
Silents
ENVIRONMENT(1922); JILT, THE(1922)
Bentley Hewlett
MRS. WIGGS OF THE CABBAGE PATCH(1934); WHITE COCKATOO(1935); SECOND WIFE(1936); TOAST OF NEW YORK, THE(1937); BORN TO BE WILD(1938); WESTERN JAMBOREE(1938); WOMAN IS THE JUDGE, A(1939)
Bob Hewlett
NORSEMAN, THE(1978)
Brian Hewlett
MASQUE OF THE RED DEATH, THE(1964, U.S./Brit.)
Donald Hewlett
ORDERS ARE ORDERS(1959, Brit.); BOTTOMS UP(1960, Brit.); TOUCH OF CLASS, A(1973, Brit.); MOMENTS(1974, Brit.); GREAT TRAIN ROBBERY, THE(1979, Brit.)
Maurice Hewlett
Silents
OPEN COUNTRY(1922, Brit.), w
Ben Hewlitt
Silents
PROTECTION(1929)
David Hewson
1984
DARK ENEMY(1984, Brit.), m
J.A. Hewson
Misc. Silents
WOODPIGEON PATROL, THE(1930, Brit.)
Lindsay Hewson
KILLING OF ANGEL STREET, THE(1983, Aus.), art d
Richard Hewson
MELODY(1971, Brit.), m
Sherrie Hewson
SLIPPER AND THE ROSE, THE(1976, Brit.); HANOVER STREET(1979, Brit.)
Alfred Hewston
WEST OF THE ROCKIES(1929); FIREBRAND JORDAN(1930)
Silents
ON THE GO(1925); OUT OF THE WEST(1926)
Misc. Silents
BLIND CIRCUMSTANCES(1922); DIAMOND CARLISLE(1922); HATE TRAIL, THE(1922); CYCLONE BUDDY(1924); TEARIN' LOOSE(1925); ARIZONA STREAK, THE(1926); MAN FROM NEVADA, THE(1929); BREEZY BILL(1930)
George Hewston
Misc. Silents
BREEZY BILL(1930)
Jon-Erik Hexum
1984
BEAR, THE(1984)
Christopher Hey
INNOCENT SINNERS(1958, Brit.)
Virginia Hey
NORMAN LOVES ROSE(1982, Aus.); ROAD WARRIOR, THE(1982, Aus.)
Weldon Heyburn
CALL HER SAVAGE(1932); CARELESS LADY(1932); CHANDU THE MAGICIAN(1932); GAY CABALLERO, THE(1932); SILENT WITNESS, THE(1932); WEST OF SINGAPORE(1933); HIRED WIFE(1934); CONVENTION GIRL(1935); SPEED(1936); ATLANTIC FLIGHT(1937); GIT ALONG, LITTLE DOGIES(1937); SEA RACKETEERS(1937); THIRTEENTH MAN, THE(1937); CRIME SCHOOL(1938); DYNAMITE DELANEY(1938); EVERY DAY'S A HOLIDAY(1938); MYSTERIOUS RIDER, THE(1938); SALESLADY(1938); FUGITIVE AT LARGE(1939); PANAMA PATROL(1939); SHOULD A GIRL MARRY?(1939); EMERGENCY SQUAD(1940); NORTHWEST MOUNTED POLICE(1940); TRAIL BLAZERS, THE(1940); CAUGHT IN THE DRAFT(1941); CRIMINALS WITHIN(1941); FLIGHT FROM DESTINY(1941); IN OLD COLORADO(1941); JUNGLE MAN(1941); REDHEAD(1941); ROUNDUP, THE(1941); STICK TO YOUR GUNS(1941); YOU'RE IN THE ARMY NOW(1941); CODE OF THE OUTLAW(1942); ROCK RIVER RENEGADES(1942); THEY DIED WITH THEIR BOOTS ON(1942); DEATH VALLEY MANHUNT(1943); OVERLAND MAIL ROBBERY(1943); CHINESE CAT, THE(1944); CODE OF THE PRAIRIE(1944); DEATH VALLEY RANGERS(1944); HERE COME THE WAVES(1944); MAN FROM FRISCO(1944); PRINCESS AND THE PIRATE, THE(1944); WESTWARD BOUND(1944); WHEN STRANGERS MARRY(1944); YELLOW ROSE OF TEXAS, THE(1944); SOUTHERN YANKEE, A(1948); PERFECT STRANGERS(1950)
Misc. Talkies
BORDERTOWN TRAIL(1944); FRONTIER GUNLAW(1946)
Dean Heyde
DEAD RUN(1961, Fr./Ital./Ger.); CORRUPT ONES, THE(1967, Ger.); COUNTERFEIT KILLER, THE(1968)
Eva Heyde
SEARCHING WIND, THE(1946)
Ben Heydenrych
ELEPHANT GUN(1959, Brit.)
Louis Jean Heydt
BEFORE MORNING(1933); MAKE WAY FOR TOMORROW(1937); I AM THE LAW(1938); TEST PILOT(1938); CHARLIE CHAN AT TREASURE ISLAND(1939); EACH DAWN I DIE(1939); GONE WITH THE WIND(1939); JOE AND ETHEL TURP CALL ON THE PRESIDENT(1939); LET FREEDOM RING(1939); RENO(1939); THEY MADE HER A SPY(1939); THEY MADE ME A CRIMINAL(1939); ABE LINCOLN IN ILLINOIS(1940); CHILD IS BORN, A(1940); DR. EHRLICH'S MAGIC BULLET(1940); GREAT McGINTY, THE(1940); IRENE(1940); JOHNNY APOLLO(1940); LET'S MAKE MUSIC(1940); MAN WHO TALKED TOO MUCH, THE(1940); PIER 13(1940); SANTA FE TRAIL(1940); DIVE BOMBER(1941); HIGH SIERRA(1941); MIDNIGHT ANGEL(1941); POWER DIVE(1941); SLEEPERS WEST(1941); CAPTAINS OF THE CLOUDS(1942); COMMANDOS STRIKE AT DAWN, THE(1942); MANILA CALLING(1942); PACIFIC BLACKOUT(1942); TEN GENTLEMEN FROM WEST POINT(1942); TORTILLA FLAT(1942); FIRST COMES COURAGE(1943); GUNG HO!(1943); IRON MAJOR, THE(1943); MISSION TO MOSCOW(1943); ONE DANGEROUS NIGHT(1943); GREAT MOMENT, THE(1944); HER PRIMITIVE MAN(1944); SEE HERE, PRIVATE HARGROVE(1944); THIRTY SECONDS OVER TOKYO(1944); BETRAYAL FROM THE EAST(1945); OUR VINES HAVE TENDER GRAPES(1945); THEY WERE EXPENDABLE(1945); YOU CAME ALONG(1945); ZOMBIES ON BROADWAY(1945); BIG SLEEP, THE(1946); HOODLUM SAINT, THE(1946); I COVER

BIG TOWN(1947); SINBAD THE SAILOR(1947); SPOILERS OF THE NORTH(1947); BAD MEN OF TOMBSTONE(1949); COME TO THE STABLE(1949); KID FROM CLEVELAND, THE(1949); MAKE BELIEVE BALLROOM(1949); FURIES, THE(1950); GREAT MISSOURI RAID, THE(1950); PAID IN FULL(1950); AL JENNINGS OF OKLAHOMA(1951); CLOSE TO MY HEART(1951); CRIMINAL LAWYER(1951); DRUMS IN THE DEEP SOUTH(1951); RATON PASS(1951); RAWHIDE(1951); ROADBLOCK(1951); SAILOR BEWARE(1951); TWO OF A KIND(1951); WARPATH(1951); FLESH AND FURY(1952); MODELS, INC.(1952); MUTINY(1952); OLD WEST, THE(1952); ISLAND IN THE SKY(1953); VANQUISHED, THE(1953); BOY FROM OKLAHOMA, THE(1954); STAR IS BORN, A(1954); ETERNAL SEA, THE(1955); NO MAN'S WOMAN(1955); TEN WANTED MEN(1955); STRANGER AT MY DOOR(1956); BADGE OF MARSHAL BRENNAN, THE(1957); RAIDERS OF OLD CALIFORNIA(1957); WINGS OF EAGLES, THE(1957); MAN WHO DIED TWICE, THE(1958); INSIDE THE MAFIA(1959)
Nancy Heye
LOST BOUNDARIES(1949)
Georgette Heyer
RELUCTANT WIDOW, THE(1951, Brit.), w
Martha Heyer
GUN SMUGGLERS(1948)
Ursula Heyer
DIE FASTNACHTSBEICHTE(1962, Ger.); JUST A GIGOLO(1979, Ger.)
Uschi Heyer
FUNERAL IN BERLIN(1966, Brit.)
Douglas Heyes
BATTLE OF ROGUE RIVER(1954), w; DRUMS OF TAHITI(1954), w; IRON GLOVE, THE(1954), w; MASTERSON OF KANSAS(1954), w; KITTEN WITH A WHIP(1964), d&w; BEAU GESTE(1966), d&w; ICE STATION ZEBRA(1968), w
Herbert Heyes
DESTINATION UNKNOWN(1942); BOMBARDIER(1943); CALLING WILD BILL ELLIOTT(1943); CAMPUS RHYTHM(1943); CHATTERBOX(1943); DEATH VALLEY MANHUNT(1943); IS EVERYBODY HAPPY?(1943); MISSION TO MOSCOW(1943); DETECTIVE KITTY O'DAY(1944); MILLION DOLLAR KID(1944); OUTLAWS OF SANTA FE(1944); STANDING ROOM ONLY(1944); MIRACLE ON 34TH STREET, THE(1947); T-MEN(1947); BEHIND LOCKED DOORS(1948); COBRA STRIKES, THE(1948); KISS TOMORROW GOODBYE(1950); TRIPOLI(1950); UNION STATION(1950); BEDTIME FOR BONZO(1951); ONLY THE VALIANT(1951); PLACE IN THE SUN, A(1951); THREE GUYS NAMED MIKE(1951); CARBINE WILLIAMS(1952); PARK ROW(1952); RUBY GENTRY(1952); SOMETHING TO LIVE FOR(1952); LET'S DO IT AGAIN(1953); MAN OF CONFLICT(1953); COURT-MARTIAL OF BILLY MITCHELL, THE(1955); FAR HORIZONS, THE(1955); LOVE IS A MANY-SPLENDORED THING(1955); NEW YORK CONFIDENTIAL(1955); SEVEN LITTLE FOYS, THE(1955); SINCERELY YOURS(1955)
Silents
DARLING OF PARIS, THE(1917); TIGER WOMAN, THE(1917); GAMBLING IN SOULS(1919); BLUSHING BRIDE, THE(1921); DR. JIM(1921); QUEEN OF SHEBA, THE(1921); ONE STOLEN NIGHT(1923); IT IS THE LAW(1924)
Misc. Silents
JEALOUSY(1916); STRAIGHT WAY, THE(1916); UNDER TWO FLAGS(1916); VICTIM, THE(1916); VIXEN, THE(1916); WILD OATS(1916); LESSON, THE(1917); OUTSIDER, THE(1917); BIRD OF PREY, THE(1918); FALLEN ANGEL, THE(1918); HEART OF RACHAEL, THE(1918); HEART OF THE SUNSET(1918); CHILDREN OF BANISHMENT(1919); MORE DEADLY THAN THE MALE(1919); LAND OF JAZZ, THE(1920); EVER SINCE EVE(1921); WOLVES OF THE NORTH(1921); SHATTERED DREAMS(1922)
Norman Heyes
KIND OF LOVING, A(1962, Brit.)
John Heygate
HEART SONG(1933, Brit.), w; BLACK ROSES(1936, Ger.), w
Werner Heyking
DOWNHILL RACER(1969)
Werner J. Heyking
WILLY WONKA AND THE CHOCOLATE FACTORY(1971)
Carl Jules Heyl
MISSION TO MOSCOW(1943), art d
John Heyl
SEPARATE PEACE, A(1972)
Kaiser Heyl
CRUISER EMDEN(1932, Ger.)
Nancy Heyl
WALK EAST ON BEACON(1952)
Syd Heylen
STIR(1980, Aus.); ROAD WARRIOR, THE(1982, Aus.)
Alice Heyliger
TESTAMENT OF ORPHEUS, THE(1962, Fr.)
Francis Heym
NEW LIFE STYLE, THE(1970, Ger.)
Stefan Heym
HOSTAGES(1943), w
Albert Heyman
DANGER AHEAD(1935), d
Barton Heyman
NAKED FLAME, THE(1970, Can.); LET'S SCARE JESSICA TO DEATH(1971); VALDEZ IS COMING(1971); TRIAL OF THE CATONSVILLE NINE, THE(1972); BANG THE DRUM SLOWLY(1973); SUPER COPS, THE(1974); HAPPY HOOKER, THE(1975); BABY BLUE MARINE(1976); CRUISING(1980); NIGHT OF THE JUGGLER(1980)
Claude Heyman
RECORD 413(1936, Fr.), ph
Edward Heyman
CURLY TOP(1935), m; FIRST BABY(1936), m
John Heyman
PRIVILEGE(1967, Brit.), p; BOOM!(1968), p; SECRET CEREMONY(1968, Brit.), p; BLOOMFIELD(1971, Brit./Israel), p; GO-BETWEEN, THE(1971, Brit.), p; BLACK GUNN(1972), p; JESUS(1979), p
Norma Heyman
BEYOND THE LIMIT(1983), p
Werner Heyman
HE STAYED FOR BREAKFAST(1940), m; TO BE OR NOT TO BE(1942), md; LOST HONEYMOON(1947), m

Claude Heymann
AMERICAN LOVE(1932, Fr.), d; CROSSROADS OF PASSION(1951, Fr.), d; SHOOT THE PIANO PLAYER(1962, Fr.)
Gotz Heymann
1984
LOVE IN GERMANY, A(1984, Fr./Ger.), art d
Werner Heymann
THAT UNCERTAIN FEELING(1941), m; CONGRESS DANCES(1932, Ger.), m; THIS THING CALLED LOVE(1940), m; MY LIFE WITH CAROLINE(1941), m; HAIL THE CONQUERING HERO(1944), m; MADEMOISELLE FIFI(1944), m; OUR HEARTS WERE YOUNG AND GAY(1944), m; HOLD THAT BLONDE(1945), m; IT'S IN THE BAG(1945), m; ALWAYS TOGETHER(1947), m; LET'S LIVE A LITTLE(1948), m; ALRAUNE(1952, Ger.), m
Werner R. Heymann
LOVE WALTZ, THE(1930, Ger.), m; BOMBARDMENT OF MONTE CARLO, THE(1931, Ger.), m; NINOTCHKA(1939), m; EARL OF CHICAGO, THE(1940), m; ONE MILLION B.C.(1940), m; PRIMROSE PATH(1940), m; SHOP AROUND THE CORNER, THE(1940), m; FLIGHT LIEUTENANT(1942), m; NIGHT TO REMEMBER, A(1942), m; THEY ALL KISSED THE BRIDE(1942), m; WIFE TAKES A FLYER, THE(1942), m; KNICKERBOCKER HOLIDAY(1944), m; MY PAL, WOLF(1944), m; TOGETHER AGAIN(1944), m; 3 IS A FAMILY(1944), m; KISS AND TELL(1945), m; MATING OF MILLIE, THE(1948), m; KISS FOR CORLISS, A(1949), m; TELL IT TO THE JUDGE(1949), m; EMERGENCY WEDDING(1950), m; WOMAN OF DISTINCTION, A(1950), m
Silents
SPIES(1929, Ger.), m
Werner Richard Heymann
ADORABLE(1933), m; MAD WEDNESDAY(1950), m; CONGRESS DANCES(1957, Ger.), m
Max Heymans
SPY IN THE SKY(1958), cos
Albert Heyn
COURT MARTIAL(1962, Ger.)
Wilfried-Jan Heyn
KING IN SHADOW(1961, Ger.)
Arnd Heyne
HIPPODROME(1961, Aust./Ger.), ed; DIE FLEDERMAUS(1964, Aust.), ed; HEIDI(1968, Aust.), ed
Arndt Heyne
AS THE SEA RAGES(1960 Ger.), ed
Laurent Heynemann
QUESTION, THE(1977, Fr.), d, w
Kurt Heynicke
MOSCOW SHANGHAI(1936, Ger.), w
Michele Heyraud
SMALL CHANGE(1976, Fr.)
Paul Heyraud
SMALL CHANGE(1976, Fr.)
Dilart Heyson
DETROIT 9000(1973)
Dorothy Heyward
PORGY AND BESS(1959), w
DuBose Heyward
EMPEROR JONES, THE(1933), w
Louis M. Heyward
PAJAMA PARTY(1964), w; CITY UNDER THE SEA(1965, Brit.), w; PLANET OF THE VAMPIRES(1965, U.S./Ital./Span.), w; SERGEANT DEADHEAD(1965), w; DR. GOLDFOOT AND THE GIRL BOMBS(1966, Ital.), p, w; GHOST IN THE INVISIBLE BIKINI(1966), w; CONQUEROR WORM, THE(1968, Brit.), w; CRIMSON CULT, THE(1970, Brit.), p; ABOMINABLE DR. PHIBES, THE(1971, Brit.), p; MURDERS IN THE RUE MORGUE(1971), p; DOCTOR PHIBES RISES AGAIN(1972, Brit.), p
Orien Heyward
SHE ASKED FOR IT(1937)
Richard Heyward
FOURTEEN, THE(1973, Brit.)
Alan Heywood
DOOMSDAY AT ELEVEN(1963 Brit.)
Anne Heywood
FIND THE LADY(1956, Brit.); CHECKPOINT(1957, Brit.); DEPRAVED, THE(1957, Brit.); DOCTOR AT LARGE(1957, Brit.); DANGEROUS EXILE(1958, Brit.); FLOODS OF FEAR(1958, Brit.); VIOLENT PLAYGROUND(1958, Brit.); HEART OF A MAN, THE(1959, Brit.); NIGHT FIGHTERS, THE(1960); CARTHAGE IN FLAMES(1961, Fr./Ital.); PETTICOAT PIRATES(1961, Brit.); UPSTAIRS AND DOWNSTAIRS(1961, Brit.); VERY EDGE, THE(1963, Brit.); STORK TALK(1964, Brit.); BRAIN, THE(1965, Ger./Brit.); 90 DEGREES IN THE SHADE(1966, Czech./Brit.); FOX, THE(1967); CHAIRMAN, THE(1969); MIDAS RUN(1969); LADY OF MONZA, THE(1970, Ital.); I WANT WHAT I WANT(1972, Brit.); TRADER HORN(1973); GOOD LUCK, MISS WYCKOFF(1979)
Misc. Talkies
LOVE UNDER THE ELMS(1973)
Baby Eastman Heywood
Misc. Silents
JAN OF THE BIG SNOWS(1922)
Chris Heywood
CARS THAT ATE PARIS, THE(1974, Aus.)
Donald Heywood
BLACK KING(1932), w
Herb Heywood
IRISH IN US, THE(1935); THREE BLIND MICE(1938)
Herbert Heywood
THEY WON'T BELIEVE ME(1947); MUSIC IN THE AIR(1934); ESCAPE FROM DEVIL'S ISLAND(1935); LADIES CRAVE EXCITEMENT(1935); IT HAD TO HAPPEN(1936); KING OF THE PECOS(1936); MOONLIGHT ON THE PRAIRIE(1936); ROAD GANG(1936); STORY OF LOUIS PASTEUR, THE(1936); CRIMINALS OF THE AIR(1937); DRAEGERMAN COURAGE(1937); MOUNTAIN JUSTICE(1937); SLAVE SHIP(1937); SLIM(1937); BORN TO BE WILD(1938); SWING, SISTER, SWING(1938); LET US LIVE(1939); YOUNG MR. LINCOLN(1939); GRAPES OF WRATH(1940); LEGION OF THE LAWLESS(1940); LITTLE OLD NEW YORK(1940); NO TIME FOR COMEDY(1940); GREAT AMERICAN BROADCAST, THE(1941); MANPOWER(1941); ONE FOOT IN HEAVEN(1941); STRAWBERRY BLONDE, THE(1941); IN THIS OUR

LIFE(1942); KING'S ROW(1942); THEY DIED WITH THEIR BOOTS ON(1942); HONEYMOON LODGE(1943); NORTHERN PURSUIT(1943); NONE BUT THE LONELY HEART(1944); SWINGTIME JOHNNY(1944); ALONG CAME JONES(1945); COLONEL EFFINGHAM'S RAID(1945); SCARLET STREET(1945); THIS LOVE OF OURS(1945); SMOKY(1946); TILL THE CLOUDS ROLL BY(1946); BRUTE FORCE(1947); EGG AND I, THE(1947); I WONDER WHO'S KISSING HER NOW(1947); THIS TIME FOR KEEPS(1947); FAMILY HONEYMOON(1948); FEUDIN', FUSSIN' AND A-FIGHTIN'(1948); GREEN GRASS OF WYOMING(1948); SCUDDA-HOO! SCUDDA-HAY!(1948); WALLS OF JERICHO(1948); TAKE ONE FALSE STEP(1949); MALAYA(1950); PETTY GIRL, THE(1950); TICKET TO TOMAHAWK(1950)
John Heywood
VISITOR, THE(1973, Can.); DEAD MAN'S FLOAT(1980, Aus.)
Pat Heywood
ROMEO AND JULIET(1968, Brit./Ital.); STAIRCASE(1969 U.S./Brit./Fr.); ALL THE WAY UP(1970, Brit.); MUMSY, NANNY, SONNY, AND GIRLY(1970, Brit.); WHO SLEW AUNTIE ROO?(1971, U.S./Brit.); 10 RILLINGTON PLACE(1971, Brit.); YOUNG WINSTON(1972, Brit.); NELSON AFFAIR, THE(1973, Brit.)
Robbie Heywood
MINX, THE(1969)
W. Heywood
Silents
SON OF THE WOLF, THE(1922), w
W. L. Heywood
Silents
SWAMP, THE(1921), art d; CRIMSON RUNNER, THE(1925), art d
Malcolm B. Heyworth
BLACK BEAUTY(1971, Brit./Ger./Span.), p
Malcolm Heyworth
BLOOD ON SATAN'S CLAW, THE(1970, Brit.), p
Mimi Heyworth
THREE CAME HOME(1950)
Avner Hezkiyahu
IMPOSSIBLE ON SATURDAY(1966, Fr./Israel)
Hi, Lo, Jack and a Dame
HEY, ROOKIE(1944)
The Hi-Hatters
RIDE 'EM COWBOY(1942)
The Hi-Lo's
CALYPSO HEAT WAVE(1957); GOOD NEIGHBOR SAM(1964)
Joe Hiakawa
RIP ROARING RILEY(1935)
Michael Hiat
GETTING OVER(1981)
Albert Hiatt
Misc. Silents
COMBAT(1927), d
Frederick Hiatt
Misc. Silents
MONTMARTE ROSE(1929), d
Philippa Hiatt
BELLS GO DOWN, THE(1943, Brit.); HALF-WAY HOUSE, THE(1945, Brit.); GEORGE IN CIVVY STREET(1946, Brit.)
Ruth Hiatt
HER MAN(1930); NIGHT WORK(1930); SUNSET TRAIL(1932); DOUBLE TROUBLE(1941)
Misc. Talkies
RIDIN' THRU(1935)
Misc. Silents
HIS FIRST FLAME(1927); MISSING LINK, THE(1927); SHANGHAI ROSE(1929)
Suzzanne Hiatt
CANDIDATE, THE(1964)
Edna Hibbard
Misc. Silents
APACHES OF PARIS, THE(1915)
Enid Hibbard
Silents
EVERY MAN'S WIFE(1925), w; COWARD, THE(1927), w; DRIVEN FROM HOME(1927), w; CHICAGO AFTER MIDNIGHT(1928), w; SALLY OF THE SCANDALS(1928), w; HARDBOILED(1929), w
Gary Hibbard
NATIONAL LAMPOON'S CLASS REUNION(1982)
Jim Hibbard
BY DESIGN(1982)
Jimmy Hibbard
CYBORG 2087(1966)
Robert Hibbard
SPLIT IMAGE(1982)
Jack Hibberd
DIMBOOLA(1979, Aus.), w
Rod Hibberd
1984
FANTASY MAN(1984, Aus.), ed
Stuart Hibberd
REGAL CAVALCADE(1935, Brit.); DEVIL GIRL FROM MARS(1954, Brit.)
Dora Hibbert
LEAVE IT TO ME(1937, Brit.)
Geoffrey Hibbert
HELL, HEAVEN OR HOBOKEN(1958, Brit.); COMMON TOUCH, THE(1941, Brit.); IN WHICH WE SERVE(1942, Brit.); NEXT OF KIN(1942, Brit.); SHIPBUILDERS, THE(1943, Brit.); LOVE ON THE DOLE(1945, Brit.); SECRET PEOPLE(1952, Brit.); ALBERT, R.N.(1953, Brit.); HUNDRED HOUR HUNT(1953, Brit.); FOR BETTER FOR WORSE(1954, Brit.); LINKS OF JUSTICE(1958); ORDERS TO KILL(1958, Brit.); CRASH DRIVE(1959, Brit.); END OF THE LINE, THE(1959, Brit.); GAOLBREAK(1962, Brit.); LIVE NOW—PAY LATER(1962, Brit.); GREAT VAN ROBBERY, THE(1963, Brit.); HEAVENS ABOVE!(1963, Brit.)
Jimmy Hibbert
BLOODY KIDS(1983, Brit.)

Norman Hibbert
WRONG BOX, THE(1966, Brit.)
Bobby Hibbitts
TENDER MERCIES(1982)
Gene Hibbs
ROSE BOWL(1936); INVADERS FROM MARS(1953), makeup; TWICE TOLD TALES(1963), makeup; HOUSE IS NOT A HOME, A(1964), make-up; HUSH... HUSH, SWEET CHARLOTTE(1964), makeup; LADY IN A CAGE(1964), makeup; WHERE LOVE HAS GONE(1964), makeup
Jesse Hibbs
TOUCHDOWN!(1931); WINCHESTER '73(1950), m; ALL-AMERICAN, THE(1953), d; BLACK HORSE CANYON(1954), d; RAILS INTO LARAMIE(1954), d; RIDE CLEAR OF DIABLO(1954), d; YELLOW MOUNTAIN, THE(1954), d; SPOILERS, THE(1955), d; TO HELL AND BACK(1955), d; WALK THE PROUD LAND(1956), d; WORLD IN MY CORNER(1956), d; JOE BUTTERFLY(1957), d; RIDE A CROOKED TRAIL(1958), d
Winston Hibler
MELODY TIME(1948), w; ADVENTURES OF ICHABOD AND MR. TOAD(1949), w; CINDERELLA(1950), w; ALICE IN WONDERLAND(1951), w; PETER PAN(1953), w; NIKKI, WILD DOG OF THE NORTH(1961, U.S./Can.), p, w; BIG RED(1962), p; THOSE CALLOWAYS(1964), p; UGLY DACHSHUND, THE(1966), p; CHARLIE, THE LONESOME COUGAR(1967), p, w; HORSE IN THE GRAY FLANNEL SUIT, THE(1968), p; ARISTOCATS, THE(1970), p; KING OF THE GRIZZLIES(1970), a, p; NAPOLEON AND SAMANTHA(1972), p; ONE LITTLE INDIAN(1973), p; BEARS AND I, THE(1974), p; CASTAWAY COWBOY, THE(1974), p; ISLAND AT THE TOP OF THE WORLD, THE(1974), p
Ed Hice
SOUL OF NIGGER CHARLEY, THE(1973)
Eddie Hice
YOUNG FURY(1965); HELL'S BELLES(1969); WALK PROUD(1979)
1984
HARD TO HOLD(1984)
Fred Hice
DOGS(1976); TWO-MINUTE WARNING(1976); NATIONAL LAMPOON'S ANIMAL HOUSE(1978)
Robert Hichens
BELLA DONNA(1934, Brit.), w; GARDEN OF ALLAH, THE(1936), w; TEMPTA-TION(1946), w; PARADINE CASE, THE(1947), w; CALL OF THE BLOOD(1948, Brit.), w
Silents
FLAMES(1917, Brit.), w; AFTER THE VERDICT(1929, Brit.), w
Bob Hick
Silents
EVERYBODY'S SWEETHEART(1920)
Howard Hickam
ALIAS JIMMY VALENTINE(1928)
Bernie R. Hickban
REVENGE OF THE PINK PANTHER(1978)
Ian Hickenbotham
SENDER, THE(1982, Brit.), cos
Ernest Hickerson
MR. MUGGS STEPS OUT(1943), set d; FOLLOW THE LEADER(1944), set d; MIL-LION DOLLAR KID(1944), art d
Bill Hickey
NUNZIO(1978)
Dennis Hickey
Misc. Talkies
BLAST-OFF GIRLS(1967)
Donna Lee Hickey
DREAMBOAT(1952); FARMER TAKES A WIFE, THE(1953); GIRL NEXT DOOR, THE(1953)
Joe Hickey
HERE COMES MR. JORDAN(1941); LOOK WHO'S LAUGHING(1941)
Kieran Hickey
CRIMINAL CONVERSATION(1980, Ireland), d, w
Lynn Hickey
ONLY WAY HOME, THE(1972)
Marilyn Hickey
NIGHT THE LIGHTS WENT OUT IN GEORGIA, THE(1981)
Michael Hickey
1984
SILENT NIGHT, DEADLY NIGHT(1984), w
Paul Hickey
1984
DADDY'S DEADLY DARLING(1984)
Thomas Hickey
FLIGHT OF THE DOVES(1971)
Tim Hickey
MAIDSTONE(1970)
Tom Hickey
1984
CAL(1984, Ireland)
William Hickey
HATFUL OF RAIN, A(1957); SOMETHING WILD(1961); INVITATION TO A GUN-FIGHTER(1964); PRODUCERS, THE(1967); THE BOSTON STRANGLER, THE(1968); LITTLE BIG MAN(1970); HAPPY BIRTHDAY, WANDA JUNE(1971); 92 IN THE SHADE(1975, U.S./Brit.); MIKEY AND NICKY(1976); SENTINEL, THE(1977)
Misc. Talkies
TELEPHONE BOOK, THE(1971)
Larry Hickie
TOMBOY AND THE CHAMP(1961)
Lee Hickin
GAMEKEEPER, THE(1980, Brit.)
Les Hickin
LOOKS AND SMILES(1982, Brit.)
Catherine Hickland
LAST MARRIED COUPLE IN AMERICA, THE(1980)
Ronald D. Hicklin
YOUNG GIRLS OF ROCHEFORT, THE(1968, Fr.)

Al Hickman
Silents
ON THE QUIET(1918)
Alfred Hickman
LAST OF THE LONE WOLF(1930); PHANTOM OF PARIS, THE(1931); WOMAN OF EXPERIENCE, A(1931)
Silents
ARE YOU A MASON?(1915); LITTLE MISS HOOVER(1918); ERSTWHILE SU-SAN(1919); ENCHANTED COTTAGE, THE(1924); RESCUE, THE(1929)
Misc. Silents
WOMAN'S PAST, A(1915); CHAIN INVISIBLE, THE(1916); FOURTH ESTATE, THE(1916); IRON WOMAN, THE(1916); WITCH, THE(1916); FALL OF THE ROMAN-OFFS, THE(1917); FINAL PAYMENT, THE(1917); LONE WOLF, THE(1917); FEDO-RA(1918); VENUS MODEL, THE(1918); LOVE CHEAT, THE(1919); CIVILIAN CLOTHES(1920); SHADOW OF ROSALIE BYRNES, THE(1920)
Beau Hickman
GUN HAWK, THE(1963), makeup
Bill Hickman
TO PLEASE A LADY(1950); FIXED BAYONETS(1951); JOKER IS WILD, THE(1957); HOUSEBOAT(1958); POINT BLANK(1967); BULLITT(1968); LOVE BUG, THE(1968); PATTON(1970); FRENCH CONNECTION, THE(1971), a, stunts; HICKEY AND BOGGS(1972); WHAT'S UP, DOC?(1972); SEVEN UPS, THE(1973), a, stunts
Bob Hickman
HELL IS FOR HEROES(1962), makeup
Charles Hickman
COMPROMISED!(1931, Brit.); JOSSER ON THE RIVER(1932, Brit.); MAYFAIR GIRL(1933, Brit.); SMITHY(1933, Brit.); JIMMY THE GENT(1934); SWEET ADELI-NE(1935); TEN MINUTE ALIBI(1935, Brit.); CONQUEST OF THE AIR(1940); PHONY AMERICAN, THE(1964, Ger.); STOP TRAIN 349(1964, Fr./Ital./Ger.); JACK OF DIAMONDS(1967, U.S./Ger.)
Silents
THREE WISE FOOLS(1923); ONE SPLENDID HOUR(1929)
Charles H. Hickman
Misc. Silents
YAQUI, THE(1916)
Cordell Hickman
BISCUIT EATER, THE(1940); TARZAN'S SECRET TREASURE(1941); WEST OF CIMARRON(1941); ARABIAN NIGHTS(1942); MOKEY(1942); TALES OF MANHAT-TAN(1942); BIG BONANZA, THE(1944)
Darryl Hickman
EMERGENCY SQUAD(1940); FARMER'S DAUGHTER, THE(1940); GRAPES OF WRATH(1940); UNTAMED(1940); WAY OF ALL FLESH(1940); YOUNG PEO-PLE(1940); GLAMOUR BOY(1941); MEN OF BOYS TOWN(1941); MOB TOWN(1941); SIGN OF THE WOLF(1941); JACKASS MAIL(1942); JOE SMITH, AMERICAN(1942); KEEPER OF THE FLAME(1942); NORTHWEST RANGERS(1942); YOUNG AMERI-CA(1942); ASSIGNMENT IN BRITTANY(1943); HUMAN COMEDY, THE(1943); SONG OF RUSSIA(1943); HENRY ALDRICH, BOY SCOUT(1944); MEET ME IN ST. LOUIS(1944); CAPTAIN EDDIE(1945); KISS AND TELL(1945); RHAPSODY IN BLUE(1945); SALTY O'ROURKE(1945); BOYS' RANCH(1946); LEAVE HER TO HEAV-EN(1946); STRANGE LOVE OF MARTHA IVERS, THE(1946); TWO YEARS BEFORE THE MAST(1946); BLACK GOLD(1947); DANGEROUS YEARS(1947); DEVIL ON WHEELS, THE(1947); BIG TOWN SCANDAL(1948); FIGHTING FATHER DUN-NE(1948); SAINTED SISTERS, THE(1948); ALIAS NICK BEAL(1949); ANY NUMBER CAN PLAY(1949); KISS FOR CORLISS, A(1949); SET-UP, THE(1949); HAPPY YEARS, THE(1950); CRIMINAL LAWYER(1951); LIGHTNING STRIKES TWICE(1951); SUB-MARINE COMMAND(1951); DESTINATION GOBI(1953); ISLAND IN THE SKY(1953); SEA OF LOST SHIPS(1953); PRISONER OF WAR(1954); RICOCHET ROMANCE(1954); SOUTHWEST PASSAGE(1954); TEA AND SYMPATHY(1956); IRON SHERIFF, THE(1957); PERSUADER, THE(1957); TINGLER, THE(1959); NETWORK(1976); LOOKER(1981); SHARKY'S MACHINE(1982)
Dwayne Hickman
CAPTAIN EDDIE(1945); HOODLUM SAINT, THE(1946); SECRET HEART, THE(1946); FOR THE LOVE OF RUSTY(1947); HER HUSBAND'S AFFAIRS(1947); MY DOG RUSTY(1948); RUSTY LEADS THE WAY(1948); BOY WITH THE GREEN HAIR, THE(1949); RUSTY SAVES A LIFE(1949); RUSTY'S BIRTHDAY(1949); SUN COMES UP, THE(1949); RALLY 'ROUND THE FLAG, BOYS!(1958); 1001 ARABIAN NIGHTS(1959); CAT BALLOU(1965); DR. GOLDFOOT AND THE BIKINI MA-CHINE(1965); HOW TO STUFF A WILD BIKINI(1965); SKI PARTY(1965); DOCTOR, YOU'VE GOT TO BE KIDDING(1967)
Frank Hickman
Silents
CIRCUS MAN, THE(1914)
Gail Morgan Hickman
BIG SCORE, THE(1983), w
George Hickman
MORE THAN A SECRETARY(1936); I'LL TAKE ROMANCE(1937); SHADOW, THE(1937); BOY MEETS GIRL(1938); COWBOY FROM BROOKLYN(1938); HOLI-DAY(1938); SAY IT IN FRENCH(1938); SHE KNEW ALL THE ANSWERS(1941); THREE GIRLS ABOUT TOWN(1941); I WAKE UP SCREAMING(1942); MY FAVOR-ITE BLONDE(1942); TALK OF THE TOWN(1942); BRINGING UP FATHER(1946); UNFAITHFUL, THE(1947); KNOCK ON ANY DOOR(1949); KETTLES ON OLD MACDONALD'S FARM, THE(1957)
George B. Hickman
ROMANCE IN THE DARK(1938); JOHN LOVES MARY(1949)
Herman Hickman
ALL-AMERICAN, THE(1953)
Howard Hickman
BROADWAY HOOFER, THE(1929); HIS FIRST COMMAND(1929); BRO-THERS(1930); HELLO SISTER(1930); RIGHT TO ROMANCE(1933); EVELYN PREN-TICE(1934); FUGITIVE LADY(1934); GEORGE WHITE'S SCANDALS(1934); GIRL FROM MISSOURI, THE(1934); HERE COMES THE NAVY(1934); JIMMY THE GENT(1934); LOST LADY, A(1934); MAN WITH TWO FACES, THE(1934); MYSTERY LINER(1934); PERSONALITY KID(1934); RETURN OF THE TERROR(1934); SISTERS UNDER THE SKIN(1934); TWENTIETH CENTURY(1934); UPPER WORLD(1934); I LIVE MY LIFE(1935); IT'S IN THE AIR(1935); RED HOT TIRES(1935); RENDEZVOUS(1935); AUGUST WEEK-END(1936, Brit.); CAREER WOMAN(1936); HELL-SHIP MORGAN(1936); LIBELED LADY(1936); SWING TIME(1936); TWO AGAINST THE WORLD(1936); WHIPSAW(1936); WILD BRIAN KENT(1936); ART-ISTS AND MODELS(1937); BORROWING TROUBLE(1937); CHARLIE CHAN AT THE OLYMPICS(1937); HAPPY-GO-LUCKY(1937); JIM HANVEY, DETECTIVE(1937);

JOIN THE MARINES(1937); LADY ESCAPES, THE(1937); MAN WHO CRIED WOLF, THE(1937); MAYTIME(1937); ONE MILE FROM HEAVEN(1937); VENUS MAKES TROUBLE(1937); WE WHO ARE ABOUT TO DIE(1937); WESTERN GOLD(1937); 100 MEN AND A GIRL(1937); COME ON, LEATHERNECKS(1938); FLIGHT INTO NO-WHERE(1938); HOLIDAY(1938); I STAND ACCUSED(1938); JUVENILE COURT(1938); KING OF THE NEWSBOYS(1938); RASCALS(1938); START CHEER-ING(1938); YOUNG DR. KILDARE(1938); CONVICT'S CODE(1939); ESPIONAGE AGENT(1939); EVERYBODY'S BABY(1939); GOOD GIRLS GO TO PARIS(1939); KANSAS TERRORS, THE(1939); LITTLE ACCIDENT(1939); OFF THE RECORD(1939); RETURN OF DR. X, THE(1939); THUNDER AFLOAT(1939); TROUBLE IN SUN-DOWN(1939); WHEN TOMORROW COMES(1939); WIFE, HUSBAND AND FRIEND(1939); WINGS OF THE NAVY(1939); BOWERY BOY(1940); BULLET CO-DE(1940); DARK COMMAND, THE(1940); GANGS OF CHICAGO(1940); GIRLS OF THE ROAD(1940); ISLAND OF DOOMED MEN(1940); IT ALL CAME TRUE(1940); LITTLE MEN(1940); MY SON IS GUILTY(1940); SECRET SEVEN, THE(1940); SLIGHTLY HONORABLE(1940); STRIKE UP THE BAND(1940); THEY DRIVE BY NIGHT(1940); VIRGINIA CITY(1940); BELLE STARR(1941); CHEERS FOR MISS BISHOP(1941); CITY, FOR CONQUEST(1941); DIVE BOMBER(1941); DOCTORS DON'T TELL(1941); HOLD THAT GHOST(1941); NINE LIVES ARE NOT ENOUGH(1941); PARIS CALLING(1941); ROBBERS OF THE RANGE(1941); SCAT-TERGOOD PULLS THE STRINGS(1941); TUXEDO JUNCTION(1941); WASHINGTON MELODRAMA(1941); YOU BELONG TO ME(1941); ANDY HARDY'S DOUBLE LI-FE(1942); HURRICANE SMITH(1942); I WAS FRAMED(1942); TARZAN'S NEW YORK ADVENTURE(1942); TISH(1942); HEAVENLY BODY, THE(1943); THREE HEARTS FOR JULIA(1943); WATCH ON THE RHINE(1943); FOLLOW THE BOYS(1944); GYPSY WILDCAT(1944); MRS. PARKINGTON(1944)

Silents

READY MONEY(1914); CIVILIZATION(1916); JUNGLE CHILD, THE(1916); CHICK-EN CASEY(1917); FEMALE OF THE SPECIES(1917); WOODEN SHOES(1917); ALL OF A SUDDEN NORMA(1919), d; KILLER, THE(1921), d; NOBODY'S KID(1921), d, w

Misc. Silents

MAN FROM OREGON, THE(1915); MATRIMONY(1915); HONORABLE ALGY, THE(1916); MORAL FABRIC(1916); SOMEWHERE IN FRANCE(1916); WOLF WOMAN, THE(1916); BLOOD WILL TELL(1917); MADAM WHO?(1917); SNARL, THE(1917); HEART OF RACHAEL, THE(1918), d; ROSE O' PARADISE(1918); SOCIAL AMBITION(1918); THOSE WHO PAY(1918); TWO-GUN BETTY(1918), d; HEARTS ASLEEP(1919), d; HER PURCHASE PRICE(1919), d; JOSSELYN'S WIFE(1919), d; KITTY KELLY, M.D.(1919), d; TRICK OF FATE, A(1919), d; BECKONING ROADS(1920), d; JUST A WIFE(1920), d; CERTAIN RICH MAN, A(1921), d; LURE OF EGYPT, THE(1921), d

Howard C. Hickman

STRAIGHT FROM THE HEART(1935); FURY(1936); LOVE LETTERS OF A STAR(1936); MURDER WITH PICTURES(1936); TOO MANY PARENTS(1936); CRACK-UP, THE(1937); CRIME NOBOBY SAW, THE(1937); CRIMINALS OF THE AIR(1937)

James Hickman

CARDINAL, THE(1963)

Jason Hickman

ZAPPED!(1982)

Joe Hickman

SAFE AT HOME(1962)

Mark Hickman

TRUE STORY OF JESSE JAMES, THE(1957); THIRTEEN FIGHTING MEN(1960)

Roberta Hickman

Silents

MADCAP BETTY(1915); NEARLY A LADY(1915)

Robin Hickman

HOW TO BEAT THE HIGH COST OF LIVING(1980)

Tom Hickman

MR. MAJESTYK(1974)

William Hickman

WAR BETWEEN MEN AND WOMEN, THE(1972)

Rodney Hickok

Silents

RAWHIDE KID, THE(1928), ed

Sid Hickok

BEDSIDE(1934), ph

Anthony Hickox

ADVENTURERS, THE(1970)

Douglas Hickox

BEHEMOTH, THE SEA MONSTER(1959, Brit.), d; IT'S ALL OVER TOWN(1963, Brit.), d; ENTERTAINING MR. SLOANE(1970, Brit.), d; SITTING TARGET(1972, Brit.), d; THEATRE OF BLOOD(1973, Brit.), d; BRANNIGAN(1975, Brit.), d; SKY RIDERS(1976, U.S./Gr.), d; ZULU DAWN(1980, Brit.), d; HOUND OF THE BASKER-VILLES, THE(1983, Brit.), d

Harry Hickox

SCARLET HOUR, THE(1956); MUSIC MAN, THE(1962); GHOST AND MR. CHICK-EN, THE(1966); HOLD ON(1966); HOTEL(1967); ROSIE!(1967); SPEEDWAY(1968); SPLIT, THE(1968); WHERE WERE YOU WHEN THE LIGHTS WENT OUT?(1968)

Sid Hickox

HOT STUFF(1929), ph; LOVE RACKET, THE(1929), ph; SMILING IRISH EYES(1929), ph; TWO WEEKS OFF(1929), ph; FLIRTING WIDOW, THE(1930), ph; STRICTLY MODERN(1930), ph; SWEET MAMA(1930), ph; THOSE WHO DAN-CE(1930), ph; TOP SPEED(1930), ph; BLONDE CRAZY(1931), ph; BROADMIN-DED(1931), ph; GORILLA, THE(1931), ph; LAST FLIGHT, THE(1931), ph; NAUGHTY FLIRT, THE(1931), ph; PARTY HUSBAND(1931), ph; SAFE IN HELL(1931), ph; TOO YOUNG TO MARRY(1931), ph; BILL OF DIVORCEMENT, A(1932), ph; CENTRAL PARK(1932), ph; CROWD ROARS, THE(1932), ph; HATCHET MAN, THE(1932), ph; LOVE IS A RACKET(1932), ph; PURCHASE PRICE, THE(1932), ph; SO BIG(1932), ph; UNDER EIGHTEEN(1932), ph; AVENGER, THE(1933), ph; CENTRAL AIR-PORT(1933), ph; FEMALE(1933), ph; FRISCO JENNY(1933), ph; GRAND SLAM(1933), ph; LILY TURNER(1933), ph; LITTLE GIANT, THE(1933), ph; MARY STEVENS, M.D.(1933), ph; BIG SHAKEDOWN, THE(1934), ph; CIRCUS CLOWN(1934), ph; DAMES(1934), ph; HEAT LIGHTNING(1934), ph; I SELL ANY-THING(1934), ph; LOST LADY, A(1934), ph; REGISTERED NURSE(1934), ph; SEN-SATION HUNTERS(1934), ph; ST. LOUIS KID, THE(1934), ph; TWENTY MILLION SWEETHEARTS(1934), ph; BRIGHT LIGHTS(1935), ph; GOOSE AND THE GANDER, THE(1935), ph; I AM A THIEF(1935), ph; I FOUND STELLA PARISH(1935), ph; LIVING ON VELVET(1935), ph; RIGHT TO LIVE, THE(1935), ph; SPECIAL AGENT(1935), ph; STRANDED(1935), ph; BRIDES ARE LIKE THAT(1936), ph; CASE

OF THE VELVET CLAWS, THE(1936), ph; FRESHMAN LOVE(1936), ph; GIVE ME YOUR HEART(1936), ph; LAW IN HER HANDS, THE(1936), ph; TWO AGAINST THE WORLD(1936), ph; CONFESSION(1937), ph; FIRST LADY(1937), ph; MISSING WIT-NESSES(1937), ph; SAN QUENTIN(1937), ph; SINGING MARINE, THE(1937), ph; SLIM(1937), ph; STOLEN HOLIDAY(1937), ph; MEN ARE SUCH FOOLS(1938), ph; MY BILL(1938), ph; SECRETS OF AN ACTRESS(1938), ph; SLIGHT CASE OF MURDER, A(1938), ph; WOMEN ARE LIKE THAT(1938), ph; BLACKWELL'S IS-LAND(1939), ph; EVERYBODY'S HOBBY(1939), ph; INDIANAPOLIS SPEED-WAY(1939), ph; KID FROM KOKOMO, THE(1939), ph; KING OF THE UNDERWORLD(1939), ph; RETURN OF DR. X, THE(1939), ph; WOMEN IN THE WIND(1939), ph; BRITISH INTELLIGENCE(1940), ph; DOCTOR TAKES A WI-FE(1940), ph; EAST OF THE RIVER(1940), ph; FLOWING GOLD(1940), ph; KING OF THE LUMBERJACKS(1940), ph; MAN WHO TALKED TOO MUCH, THE(1940), ph; TEAR GAS SQUAD(1940), ph; LAW OF THE TROPICS(1941), ph; THIEVES FALL OUT(1941), ph; UNDERGROUND(1941), ph; WAGONS ROLL AT NIGHT, THE(1941), ph; ALL THROUGH THE NIGHT(1942), ph; ALWAYS IN MY HEART(1942), ph; BIG SHOT, THE(1942), ph; GENTLEMAN JIM(1942), ph; EDGE OF DARKNESS(1943), ph; NORTHERN PURSUIT(1943), ph; UNCERTAIN GLORY(1944), ph; GOD IS MY CO-PILOT(1945), ph; HORN BLOWS AT MIDNIGHT, THE(1945), ph; MAN I LOVE, THE(1946), ph; CHEYENNE(1947), ph; DARK PASSAGE(1947), ph; FIGHTER SQUA-DRON(1948), ph; ONE SUNDAY AFTERNOON(1948), ph; SILVER RIVER(1948), ph; COLORADO TERRITORY(1949), ph; WHITE HEAT(1949), ph; GREAT JEWEL ROB-BER, THE(1950), ph; THREE SECRETS(1950), ph; WEST POINT STORY, THE(1950), ph; ALONG THE GREAT DIVIDE(1951), ph; DISTANT DRUMS(1951), ph; FORT WORTH(1951), ph; LIGHTNING STRIKES TWICE(1951), ph; WINNING TEAM, THE(1952), ph; BLOWING WILD(1953), ph; THEM!(1954), ph; BATTLE FLAME(1955), ph

Silents

OH, KAY(1928), ph

Sidney Hickox

FOOTLIGHTS AND FOOLS(1929), ph; CONVICTED(1931), ph; SEA GHOST, THE(1931), ph; PLEASURE(1933), ph; TRAILIN' WEST(1936), ph; TO HAVE AND HAVE NOT(1944), ph; BIG SLEEP, THE(1946), ph

Silents

SCHOOL DAYS(1921), ph; LILAC TIME(1928), ph; WHY BE GOOD?(1929), ph

Alan Hicks

TO FIND A MAN(1972), set d; DEER HUNTER, THE(1978), set d; KRAMER VS. KRAMER(1979), set d; SEDUCTION OF JOE TYNAN, THE(1979), set d; ENDLESS LOVE(1981), set d; RICH AND FAMOUS(1981), set d; AUTHOR! AUTHOR!(1982), set d; WITHOUT A TRACE(1983), set

1984

FIRSTBORN(1984), set d

Alfie Hicks

LEOPARD IN THE SNOW(1979, Brit./Can.), ph

Alfred Hicks

TROUBLESOME DOUBLE, THE(1971, Brit.), ph

Andrew Hicks

Silents

IS MONEY EVERYTHING?(1923)

Barbara Hicks

HELL, HEAVEN OR HOBOKEN(1958, Brit.); FUSS OVER FEATHERS(1954, Brit.); PANIC IN THE PARLOUR(1957, Brit.); HAND IN HAND(1960, Brit.); HIS AND HERS(1961, Brit.); MURDER SHE SAID(1961, Brit.); PETTICOAT PIRATES(1961, Brit.); MATTER OF WHO, A(1962, Brit.); OPERATION BULLSHINE(1963, Brit.); THIRD SECRET, THE(1964, Brit.); CHARGE OF THE LIGHT BRIGADE, THE(1968, Brit.); MEMOIRS OF A SURVIVOR(1981, Brit.); BRITTANIA HOSPITAL(1982, Brit.); EVIL UNDER THE SUN(1982, Brit.)

Bert Hicks

THREE HEARTS FOR JULIA(1943); SENTIMENTAL JOURNEY(1946); ONCE MORE, MY DARLING(1949); O. HENRY'S FULL HOUSE(1952)

Beryl Hicks

ELEPHANT MAN, THE(1980, Brit.)

Betty Hicks

GLAMOUR(1931, Brit.); PAT AND MIKE(1952)

Bill Hicks

CHEYENNE SOCIAL CLUB, THE(1970)

Carolyn Hicks

RENEGADE GIRLS(1974), ed

Catherine Hicks

DEATH VALLEY(1982); BETTER LATE THAN NEVER(1983)

1984

GARBO TALKS(1984); RAZOR'S EDGE, THE(1984)

Charles Hicks

ICE PALACE(1960); DIRTY HARRY(1971)

Chuck Hicks

SILENCERS, THE(; GUNFIRE AT INDIAN GAP(1957); MERRILL'S MARAU-DERS(1962); SHOCK CORRIDOR(1963); JOHNNY RENO(1966); COOL HAND LU-KE(1967); POINT BLANK(1967); SOMETHING BIG(1971); SLAUGHTER'S BIG RIP-OFF(1973); HARD TIMES(1975); NIGHT MOVES(1975); MOVIE MOVIE(1978); BRONCO BILLY(1980); CHEAPER TO KEEP HER(1980); HIDE IN PLAIN SIGHT(1980); IN GOD WE TRUST(1980)

1984

CITY HEAT(1984); JOHNNY DANGEROUSLY(1984); STAR TREK III: THE SEARCH FOR SPOCK(1984)

Don Hicks

FATHER WAS A FULLBACK(1949); IT HAPPENS EVERY SPRING(1949); SLAT-TERY'S HURRICANE(1949); TWELVE O'CLOCK HIGH(1949); I'LL GET BY(1950); MY BLUE HEAVEN(1950); FATHER TAKES THE AIR(1951); HALLS OF MON-TEZUMA(1951)

Edwin P. Hicks

HOT SUMMER NIGHT(1957), w

George Hicks

Misc. Talkies

BLOW BUGLES BLOW(1936)

Grant Hicks

NELLY'S VERSION(1983, Brit.), prod d

1984

1984(1984, Brit.), art d

Henry Hicks
Silents
  THOU ART THE MAN(1920)
Hilly Hicks
  NEW CENTURIONS, THE(1972); GO TELL THE SPARTANS(1978); GRAY LADY DOWN(1978); RAISE THE TITANIC(1980, Brit.)
Joanne Hicks
  MAKING LOVE(1982)
Misc. Talkies
  REUNION, THE(1977)
Jodi Hicks
  SECRET OF NIMH, THE(1982)
John Alan Hicks
  JENNY(1969), set d
John Allen Hicks
  LOVERS AND OTHER STRANGERS(1970), set d
John Hicks
  FREE, WHITE AND 21(1963); UNDER AGE(1964)
Johnny Hicks
  JUMP(1971)
Julie Anna Hicks
  MORE AMERICAN GRAFFITI(1979)
Leonard Hicks
  GUNS OF THE TREES(1964); SANTA CLAUS CONQUERS THE MARTIANS(1964)
Lew Hicks
  FOLIES DERGERE(1935)
Lou Hicks
  WE'RE IN THE LEGION NOW(1937); SAN FRANCISCO DOCKS(1941)
Maxine Elliott Hicks
  OLD-FASHIONED WAY, THE(1934); ONE HOUR LATE(1935); LADIES IN LOVE(1936); LIVE, LOVE AND LEARN(1937)
Silents
  CRIMSON DOVE, THE(1917); NEIGHBORS(1918); GILDED DREAM, THE(1920); NOBODY'S KID(1921); EAST SIDE-WEST SIDE(1923); RENO(1923); BABBITT(1924); LOVER'S LANE(1924)
Maxine Hicks
  TOAST OF NEW YORK, THE(1937)
Silents
  POOR LITTLE RICH GIRL, A(1917)
Munson Hicks
  GOODBYE GIRL, THE(1977)
Neill Hicks
  ESCAPE 2000(1983, Aus.), w; FINAL TERROR, THE(1983), w
Lt.Comdr. Norman Hicks
  TOWERING INFERNO, THE(1974)
Oliver Hicks
1984
  DARK ENEMY(1984, Brit.)
Parris Hicks
  BOYS IN COMPANY C, THE(1978, U.S./Hong Kong); DEER HUNTER, THE(1978)
Pat Hicks
  ROOT OF ALL EVIL, THE(1947, Brit.); HAND, THE(1960, Brit.)
Patricia Hicks
  DARK ROAD, THE(1948, Brit.)
Peter Hicks
  PHOBIA(1980, Can.)
Russel Hicks
  HOTEL FOR WOMEN(1939); SANTA FE TRAIL(1940)
Russell Hicks
  SERGEANT YORK(; BEFORE MORNING(1933); BABBITT(1934); CASE OF THE HOWLING DOG, THE(1934); ENLIGHTEN THY DAUGHTER(1934); FIREBIRD, THE(1934); GENTLEMEN ARE BORN(1934); HAPPINESS AHEAD(1934); MURDER IN THE CLOUDS(1934); ST. LOUIS KID, THE(1934); CARDINAL RICHELIEU(1935); CHARLIE CHAN IN SHANGHAI(1935); DANTE'S INFERNO(1935); DEVIL DOGS OF THE AIR(1935); GRAND EXIT(1935); LADIES CRAVE EXCITEMENT(1935); LADIES LOVE DANGER(1935); LADY TUBBS(1935); LIVING ON VELVET(1935); MILLIONS IN THE AIR(1935); SECRET BRIDE, THE(1935); SWEET MUSIC(1935); THANKS A MILLION(1935); THUNDER IN THE NIGHT(1935); WHILE THE PATIENT SLEPT(1935); WOMAN IN RED, THE(1935); $1,000 A MINUTE(1935); BUNKER BEAN(1936); FATAL LADY(1936); FIFTEEN MAIDEN LANE(1936); FOLLOW THE FLEET(1936); GRAND JURY(1936); HEARTS IN BONDAGE(1936); HONEYMOON LIMITED(1936); LAUGHING IRISH EYES(1936); MR. DEEDS GOES TO TOWN(1936); ROSE MARIE(1936); SEA SPOILERS, THE(1936); SPECIAL INVESTIGATOR(1936); SPENDTHRIFT(1936); TICKET TO PARADISE(1936); TWO IN THE DARK(1936); BIG BROADCAST OF 1938, THE(1937); BIG SHOT, THE(1937); CRIMINALS OF THE AIR(1937); DANGEROUS ADVENTURE, A(1937); DODGE CITY TRAIL(1937); ESPIONAGE(1937); FIFTY ROADS TO TOWN(1937); FIT FOR A KING(1937); GIRL OVERBOARD(1937); KING OF GAMBLERS(1937); LAUGHING AT TROUBLE(1937); MAN WHO CRIED WOLF, THE(1937); MAYTIME(1937); MIDNIGHT TAXI(1937); ON AGAIN-OFF AGAIN(1937); PARTNERS IN CRIME(1937); PICK A STAR(1937); SECRET VALLEY(1937); TOAST OF NEW YORK, THE(1937); WESTLAND CASE, THE(1937); WILDCATTER, THE(1937); 23 ½ HOURS LEAVE(1937); FUGITIVES FOR A NIGHT(1938); GATEWAY(1938); HOLD THAT CO-ED(1938); IN OLD CHICAGO(1938); KENTUCKY(1938); KIDNAPPED(1938); LITTLE MISS BROADWAY(1938); MEN WITH WINGS(1938); THAT CERTAIN AGE(1938); YOU CAN'T TAKE IT WITH YOU(1938); BIG GUY, THE(1939); BOY TROUBLE(1939); EAST SIDE OF HEAVEN(1939); HOLLYWOOD CAVALCADE(1939); HONEYMOON'S OVER, THE(1939); HOTEL IMPERIAL(1939); I WAS A CONVICT(1939); JOE AND ETHEL TURP CALL ON THE PRESIDENT(1939); NORTH OF SHANGHAI(1939); OUR LEADING CITIZEN(1939); REAL GLORY, THE(1939); STANLEY AND LIVINGSTONE(1939); STORY OF ALEXANDER GRAHAM BELL, THE(1939); STORY OF VERNON AND IRENE CASTLE, THE(1939); SWANEE RIVER(1939); THREE MUSKETEERS, THE(1939); UNION PACIFIC(1939); BANK DICK, THE(1940); EARTHBOUND(1940); EAST OF THE RIVER(1940); ENEMY AGENT(1940); JOHNNY APOLLO(1940); LADY WITH RED HAIR(1940); LOVE THY NEIGHBOR(1940); MORTAL STORM, THE(1940); NIGHT AT EARL CARROLL'S, A(1940); NO, NO NANETTE(1940); NOBODY'S CHILDREN(1940); PAROLE FIXER(1940); QUEEN OF THE MOB(1940); RETURN OF FRANK JAMES, THE(1940); SEVEN SINNERS(1940); SPORTING BLOOD(1940); VIRGINIA CITY(1940); ARKANSAS JUDGE(1941); BLOOD AND SAND(1941); BUY ME THAT TOWN(1941); DIVE BOMBER(1941); DOCTORS DON'T TELL(1941); EL-

LERY QUEEN'S PENTHOUSE MYSTERY(1941); GREAT GUNS(1941); GREAT LIE, THE(1941); HERE COMES HAPPINESS(1941); HOLD THAT GHOST(1941); HONKY TONK(1941); LITTLE FOXES, THE(1941); MAN BETRAYED, A(1941); MAN MADE MONSTER(1941); MAN WHO LOST HIMSELF, THE(1941); MIDNIGHT ANGEL(1941); PARSON OF PANAMINT, THE(1941); PUBLIC ENEMIES(1941); SEALED LIPS(1941); STRAWBERRY BLONDE, THE(1941); UNEXPECTED UNCLE(1941); WESTERN UNION(1941); BEHIND THE EIGHT BALL(1942); BUTCH MINDS THE BABY(1942); FINGERS AT THE WINDOW(1942); HITLER-DEAD OR ALIVE(1942); JOE SMITH, AMERICAN(1942); LADY IN A JAM(1942); PACIFIC RENDEZVOUS(1942); RIDE 'EM COWBOY(1942); SHIP AHOY(1942); STRICTLY IN THE GROOVE(1942); TARZAN'S NEW YORK ADVENTURE(1942); TENNESSEE JOHNSON(1942); THEY DIED WITH THEIR BOOTS ON(1942); TO THE SHORES OF TRIPOLI(1942); WE WERE DANCING(1942); AIR RAID WARDENS(1943); FOLLOW THE BAND(1943); HARRIGAN'S KID(1943); HIS BUTLER'S SISTER(1943); KING OF THE COWBOYS(1943); NORTHERN PURSUIT(1943); SOMEONE TO REMEMBER(1943); THREE HEARTS FOR JULIA(1943); WOMAN OF THE TOWN, THE(1943); HAT CHECK HONEY(1944); JANIE(1944); LOUISIANA HAYRIDE(1944); PORT OF 40 THIEVES, THE(1944); APOLOGY FOR MURDER(1945); FIRST YANK INTO TOKYO(1945); FLAME OF THE BARBARY COAST(1945); GAME OF DEATH, A(1945); GUY, A GAL AND A PAL, A(1945); HIDDEN EYE, THE(1945); NOB HILL(1945); SCARLET STREET(1945); SHE GETS HER MAN(1945); VALLEY OF DECISION, THE(1945); WEEKEND AT THE WALDORF(1945); BACHELOR'S DAUGHTERS, THE(1946); BANDIT OF SHERWOOD FOREST, THE(1946); CLOSE CALL FOR BOSTON BLACKIE, A(1946); DARK ALIBI(1946); GAY BLADES(1946); G.I. WAR BRIDES(1946); HOODLUM SAINT, THE(1946); PLAINSMAN AND THE LADY(1946); SHOW-OFF, THE(1946); SWING PARADE OF 1946(1946); TILL THE CLOUDS ROLL BY(1946); EXPOSED(1947); LOUISIANA(1947); PILGRIM LADY, THE(1947); SEA OF GRASS, THE(1947); VARIETY GIRL(1947); WEB OF DANGER, THE(1947); BLACK ARROW(1948); GALLANT LEGION, THE(1948); HUNTED, THE(1948); MANHATTAN ANGEL(1948); MY DEAR SECRETARY(1948); NOOSE HANGS HIGH, THE(1948); PLUNDERERS, THE(1948); RACE STREET(1948); RETURN OF OCTOBER, THE(1948); SHANGHAI CHEST, THE(1948); SILVER RIVER(1948); VELVET TOUCH, THE(1948); BARBARY PIRATE(1949); I CHEATED THE LAW(1949); SAMSON AND DELILAH(1949); BIG HANGOVER, THE(1950); BLUE GRASS OF KENTUCKY(1950); FLYING SAUCER, THE(1950); PETTY GIRL, THE(1950); SQUARE DANCE KATY(1950); UNMASKED(1950); AS YOU WERE(1951); BOWERY BATTALION(1951); FOURTEEN HOURS(1951); KENTUCKY JUBILEE(1951); OVERLAND TELEGRAPH(1951); MAVERICK, THE(1952); MR. WALKIE TALKIE(1952); OLD OKLAHOMA PLAINS(1952); MAN OF CONFLICT(1953); SEVENTH CAVALRY(1956); FUN ON A WEEKEND(1979)
Misc. Talkies
  BLIND FOOLS(1940, Brit.)
Seymour Hicks
  MATRIMONIAL BED, THE(1930), w; SLEEPING PARTNERS(1930, Brit.), a, d&w; GLAMOUR(1931, Brit.), a, p, d, w; LOVE HABIT, THE(1934, Brit.), a, w; MONEY FOR NOTHING(1932, Brit.), a, p, w; SECRET OF THE LOCH, THE(1934, Brit.); MR. WHAT'S-HIS-NAME(1935, Brit.), a, w; REGAL CAVALCADE(1935, Brit.); SCROOGE(1935, Brit.), a, w; VINTAGE WINE(1935, Brit.), a, w; ELIZA COMES TO STAY(1936, Brit.); IT'S YOU I WANT(1936, Brit.); CHANGE FOR A SOVEREIGN(1937, Brit.), a, w; BUSMAN'S HONEYMOON(1940, Brit.); LAMBETH WALK, THE(1940, Brit.); PASTOR HALL(1940, Brit.); KISSES FOR BREAKFAST(1941, Brit.), w; YOUNG MAN'S FANCY(1943, Brit.); FAME IS THE SPUR(1947, Brit.); SILENT DUST(1949, Brit.)
Stephen Sherrard Hicks
1984
  MUPPETS TAKE MANHATTAN, THE(1984)
Thomas Hicks
  EDUCATION OF SONNY CARSON, THE(1974)
Tommie Hicks
Misc. Talkies
  JOE'S BED-STUY BARBERSHOP: WE CUT HEADS(1983)
Tommy Hicks
  SWEATER GIRL(1942)
Tony Hicks
  POPDOWN(1968, Brit.)
William T. Hicks
  CHALLENGE(1974); MIDNIGHT MAN, THE(1974); LIVING LEGEND(1980)
E.R. Hickson
  NEAR THE RAINBOW'S END(1930), set d; HOUSE OF MYSTERY(1934), art d; MYSTERY LINER(1934), set d; TRAIL BEYOND, THE(1934), art d; MYSTERIOUS MR. WONG(1935), set d; I COVER THE WAR(1937), art d; STREETS OF NEW YORK(1939), art d; WOLF CALL(1939), art d; APE, THE(1940), art d; KLONDIKE FURY(1942), art d; DETECTIVE KITTY O'DAY(1944), art d; HOT RHYTHM(1944), art d; FLAME OF THE WEST(1945), art d; THERE GOES KELLY(1945), art d; BLACK GOLD(1947), art d
Ernest Hickson
  STAMPEDE(1949), art d
Ernest R. Hickson
  SUNBONNET SUE(1945), art d; SWING PARADE OF 1946(1946), art d
Ernie Hickson
  STRANGER FROM PECOS, THE(1943), art d
Jamie Hickson
  WILD REBELS, THE(1967)
Joan Hickson
  WIDOW'S MIGHT(1934, Brit.); LOVE FROM A STRANGER(1937, Brit.); MAN WHO COULD WORK MIRACLES, THE(1937, Brit.); CRIME OF PETER FRAME, THE(1938, Brit.); LILAC DOMINO(1940, Brit.); DON'T TAKE IT TO HEART(1944, Brit.); TROJAN BROTHERS, THE(1946); JUST WILLIAM'S LUCK(1948, Brit.); CELIA(1949, Brit.); OUTSIDER, THE(1949, Brit.); THIS WAS A WOMAN(1949, Brit.); MAGNET, THE(1950, Brit.); SEVEN DAYS TO NOON(1950, Brit.); HELL IS SOLD OUT(1951, Brit.); HIGH TREASON(1951, Brit.); CURTAIN UP(1952, Brit.); FRIGHTENED BRIDE, THE(1952, Brit.); HOLIDAY WEEK(1952, Brit.); MAGIC BOX, THE(1952, Brit.); NO HAUNT FOR A GENTLEMAN(1952, Brit.); PROMOTER, THE(1952, Brit.); DEADLY NIGHTSHADE(1953, Brit.); SHOOT FIRST(1953, Brit.); DANCE LITTLE LADY(1954, Brit.); DOCTOR IN THE HOUSE(1954, Brit.); HEATWAVE(1954, Brit.); MAD ABOUT MEN(1954, Brit.); MAN WITH A MILLION(1954, Brit.); WHAT EVERY WOMAN WANTS(1954, Brit.); DOCTOR AT SEA(1955, Brit.); PORT OF ESCAPE(1955, Brit.); TIME TO KILL, A(1955, Brit.); WOMAN FOR JOE, THE(1955, Brit.); CHILD IN THE HOUSE(1956, Brit.); EXTRA DAY, THE(1956, Brit.); JUMPING FOR JOY(1956, Brit.); LAST MAN TO HANG, THE(1956, Brit.); MAN WHO NEVER WAS, THE(1956, Brit.); SIMON AND LAURA(1956, Brit.); AS LONG AS THEY'RE HAPPY(1957, Brit.); CARRY

ON ADMIRAL(1957, Brit.); NO TIME FOR TEARS(1957, Brit.); SEA WIFE(1957, Brit.); TEARS FOR SIMON(1957, Brit.); VALUE FOR MONEY(1957, Brit.); ALL AT SEA(1958, Brit.); CHAIN OF EVENTS(1958, Brit.); HAPPY IS THE BRIDE(1958, Brit.); LAW AND DISORDER(1958, Brit.); CARRY ON NURSE(1959, Brit.); CARRY ON CONSTABLE(1960, Brit.); PLEASE TURN OVER(1960, Brit.); THIRTY NINE STEPS, THE(1960, Brit.); BEWARE OF CHILDREN(1961, Brit.); CARRY ON REGARDLESS(1961, Brit.); HIS AND HERS(1961, Brit.); MURDER SHE SAID(1961, Brit.); UPSTAIRS AND DOWNSTAIRS(1961, Brit.); I THANK A FOOL(1962, Brit.); ROOMMATES(1962, Brit.); HEAVENS ABOVE!(1963, Brit.); IN THE DOGHOUSE(1964, Brit.); NURSE ON WHEELS(1964, Brit.); SECRET OF MY SUCCESS, THE(1965, Brit.); MRS. BROWN, YOU'VE GOT A LOVELY DAUGHTER(1968, Brit.); CARRY ON LOVING(1970, Brit.); DAY IN THE DEATH OF JOE EGG, A(1972, Brit.); THEATRE OF BLOOD(1973, Brit.); CONFESSIONS OF A WINDOW CLEANER(1974, Brit.); YANKS(1979); WICKED LADY, THE(1983, Brit.)

John Hickson
ONE WAY TRAIL, THE(1931), ph; CRIMSON TRAIL, THE(1935), ph; BOSS OF LONELY VALLEY(1937), ph; LAW FOR TOMBSTONE(1937), ph

Louis Hickus
BORDER LAW(1931)

Sid Hicox
BLACKWELL'S ISLAND(1939), ph

Ayako Hidaka
ESCAPADE IN JAPAN(1957)

Shigeaki Hidaka
FINAL WAR, THE(1960, Jap.), d

Sugeaki Hidaka
GIGANTIS(1959, Jap./U.S.), w

Maribel Hidalgo
TOWN CALLED HELL, A(1971, Span./Brit.)

Juan Hidalgo-Gato
DEVIL'S SISTERS, THE(1966), p; STING OF DEATH(1966), p

Raymundo Hidalgo-Gato
Misc. Talkies
EL SUPER(1979)

Bokuzen Hidari
SEVEN SAMURAI, THE(1956, Jap.); IKIRU(1960, Jap.); LOWER DEPTHS, THE(1962, Jap.); IDIOT, THE(1963, Jap.); HUMAN VAPOR, THE(1964, Jap.); SCANDAL(1964, Jap.)

Sachiko Hidari
INSECT WOMAN, THE(1964, Jap.); THIS MADDING CROWD(1964, Jap.); SCARLET CAMELLIA, THE(1965, Jap.); SHE AND HE(1967, Jap.)

Tokie Hidari
DOUBLE SUICIDE(1970, Jap.)

Tompei Hidari
1984
BALLAD OF NARAYAMA, THE(1984, Jap.)

Tonpei Hidari
HOTSPRINGS HOLIDAY(1970, Jap.)

Tosen Hidari
HOTSPRINGS HOLIDAY(1970, Jap.)

Sean Hide
FOURTEEN, THE(1973, Brit.)

Bernard Hides
ODD ANGRY SHOT, THE(1979, Aus.), prod d; ESCAPE 2000(1983, Aus.), prod d
1984
TREASURE OF THE YANKEE ZEPHYR(1984), prod d

Jean Hidey
SAVAGE EYE, THE(1960)

Val Hidey
STUDS LONIGAN(1960)

Levente Hidvegi
WINTER WIND(1970, Fr./Hung.)

Hiecke
ELLERY QUEEN AND THE MURDER RING(1941), art d

Keve Hielm
Misc. Talkies
BROTHER CARL(1972)

Margot Hielscher
SCHLAGER-PARADE(1953)

Jan Hieronimko
VAMPYR(1932, Fr./Ger.)

Richard Hieronymous
ANGELS DIE HARD(1970), m; ANGELS HARD AS THEY COME(1971), m; LOVE BUTCHER, THE(1982), m
1984
INVISIBLE STRANGLER(1984), m

Richard Hieronymus
BURY ME AN ANGEL(1972), m; FOREST, THE(1983), m

Walter Hiers
DANCERS IN THE DARK(1932); PRIVATE SCANDAL, A(1932); 70,000 WITNESSES(1932)
Silents
LIFE'S WHIRLPOOL(1917); OUR LITTLE WIFE(1918); MISS HOBBS(1920); OH, LADY, LADY(1920); KISS IN TIME, A(1921); SHAM(1921); SPEED GIRL, THE(1921); HER GILDED CAGE(1922); MR. BILLINGS SPENDS HIS DIME(1923); SIXTY CENTS AN HOUR(1923); ALONG CAME RUTH(1924); NIGHT LIFE(1927); RACING ROMEO(1927); SPEEDY(1928)
Misc. Silents
END OF THE TOUR, THE(1917); LESSON, THE(1917); MYSTERIOUS MISS TERRY, THE(1917); OVER THERE(1917); NYMPH OF THE FOOTHILLS, A(1918); WAIFS(1918); EXPERIMENTAL MARRIAGE(1919); FEAR WOMAN, THE(1919); IT PAYS TO ADVERTISE(1919); WHAT'S YOUR HUSBAND DOING?(1919); WHEN DOCTORS DISAGREE(1919); CITY SPARROW, THE(1920); FOURTEENTH MAN, THE(1920); MRS. TEMPLE'S TELEGRAM(1920); SO LONG LETTY(1920); HER STURDY OAK(1921); SNOB, THE(1921); BOUGHT AND PAID FOR(1922); GHOST BREAKER, THE(1922); IS MATRIMONY A FAILURE?(1922); FAIR WEEK(1924); HOLD YOUR BREATH(1924); TRIFLERS, THE(1924); EXCUSE ME(1925); HOLD THAT LION(1926); BEWARE OF WINDOWS(1927); BLONDES BY CHOICE(1927); NAUGHTY(1927)

John Hiestand
TRUE TO LIFE(1943); LOVE AND HISSES(1937); NAVY BLUE AND GOLD(1937); SLIGHT CASE OF MURDER, A(1938); SWING, SISTER, SWING(1938); SECOND FIDDLE(1939); MAN I MARRIED, THE(1940); GREAT AMERICAN BROADCAST, THE(1941); I WANTED WINGS(1941); REMEMBER THE DAY(1941); RISE AND SHINE(1941); HUCKSTERS, THE(1947); YOU'RE MY EVERYTHING(1949); MISTER 880(1950); GLASS WEB, THE(1953); GOOD MORNING, MISS DOVE(1955); MAN FROM BUTTON WILLOW, THE(1965); STEAGLE, THE(1971)

Kathleen Hietala
FIRST NUDIE MUSICAL, THE(1976)

Joseph Hieu
TWILIGHT ZONE–THE MOVIE(1983)

Reiko Higa
JOE BUTTERFLY(1957)

Teruyuki Higa
FIST OF FEAR, TOUCH OF DEATH(1980)

Emiko Higashi
INSECT WOMAN, THE(1964, Jap.)

Eijiro Higashino
SEVEN SAMURAI, THE(1956, Jap.)

Chieko Higashiyama
IDIOT, THE(1963, Jap.)

Chiyeko Higashiyama
TOKYO STORY(1972, Jap.)

Wilbur Higbee
Silents
BY PROXY(1918); FLAMES OF CHANCE, THE(1918)

Mrs. Higby
Silents
NINA, THE FLOWER GIRL(1917)

Mary Jane Higby
HONEYMOON KILLERS, THE(1969)

Walter Higby
Silents
TRUE HEART SUSIE(1919)

Wilbur Higby
HAT, COAT AND GLOVE(1934)
Silents
FLIRTING WITH FATE(1916); MATRIMANIAC, THE(1916); OLD FOLKS AT HOME, THE(1916); REGGIE MIXES IN(1916); TAR HEEL WARRIOR, THE(1917); ANSWER, THE(1918); BROKEN BLOSSOMS(1919); I'LL GET HIM YET(1919); NUGGET NELL(1919); JAILBIRD, THE(1920); DESERT BLOSSOMS(1921); GIRLS DON'T GAMBLE(1921); LIVE WIRES(1921); DO AND DARE(1922); MY DAD(1922)
Misc. Silents
HOODOO ANN(1916); MIXED BLOOD(1916); SIGN OF THE POPPY, THE(1916); MIGHT AND THE MAN(1917); WILD SUMAC(1917); UNTIL THEY GET ME(1918); VORTEX, THE(1918); LADDER JINX, THE(1922); BORDER WHIRLWIND, THE(1926)

Wilbur J. Higby
Misc. Silents
MAINSPRING, THE(1916)

William Higby
Silents
LONE HAND, THE(1920)

Don Higdon
NIGHT THEY ROBBED BIG BERTHA'S, THE(1975); RETURN TO MACON COUNTY(1975)

George V. Higgens
FRIENDS OF EDDIE COYLE, THE(1973), w

John C. Higgens
CHECKERED COAT, THE(1948), w

Vi Higgenson
THAT'S THE WAY OF THE WORLD(1975)

Howard Higgin
LEATHERNECK, THE(1929), d; SAL OF SINGAPORE(1929), d, w; HER MAN(1930), w; FINAL EDITION(1932), d; HELL'S HOUSE(1932), d, w; LAST MAN(1932), d; CARNIVAL LADY(1933), d; LINEUP, THE(1934), d; MARRIAGE ON APPROVAL(1934), d, w; REVOLT OF THE ZOMBIES(1936), w; THE INVISIBLE RAY(1936), w; GOLD RACKET, THE(1937), w; CAFE HOSTESS(1940), w
Silents
IN THE NAME OF LOVE(1925), d; NEW COMMANDMENT, THE(1925), d, w; RECKLESS LADY, THE(1926), d; WILDERNESS WOMAN, THE(1926), d
Misc. Silents
RENT FREE(1922), d; GREAT DECEPTION, THE(1926), d; PERFECT SAP, THE(1927), d; POWER(1928), d; SKYSCRAPER(1928), d

Russel Higginbotham
SILENT RAGE(1982)

John C. Higgings
T-MEN(1947), w

Higgins
BENJI(1974); FOR THE LOVE OF BENJI(1977)

Anthony Higgins
QUARTET(1981, Brit./Fr.); RAIDERS OF THE LOST ARK(1981); DRAUGHTSMAN'S CONTRACT, THE(1983, Brit.)

Arthur Higgins
HIS ROYAL HIGHNESS(1932, Aus.), ph; HARMONY ROW(1933, Aus.), ph; WHITE DEATH(1936, Aus.), ph

Audelle Higgins
Silents
EVIDENCE(1918)

Barry Higgins
HAROLD AND MAUDE(1971)

Clare Higgins
1984
1919(1984, Brit.)

Clark Higgins
ONE FROM THE HEART(1982)

Colin Higgins
HAROLD AND MAUDE(1971), p, w; SILVER STREAK(1976), w; FOUL PLAY(1978), d&w; NINE TO FIVE(1980), d, w; BEST LITTLE WHOREHOUSE IN TEXAS, THE(1982), d, w

David Higgins
Silents
HIS LAST DOLLAR(1914), a, w; ROUGH AND READY(1918)
Misc. Silents
LITTLE GIANT, THE(1926)
Dianne Higgins
LADYBUG, LADYBUG(1963)
Dirk Higgins
1984
SACRED HEARTS(1984, Brit.), m
Doug Higgins
DOG DAY AFTERNOON(1975), art d; DIFFERENT STORY, A(1978)
Douglas Higgins
SERPICO(1973), art d; KIDNAPPING OF THE PRESIDENT, THE(1980, Can.), art d; MOTHER LODE(1982), prod d; GOLDEN SEAL, THE(1983), prod d
1984
RUNAWAY(1984), prod d
Ed Higgins
TERROR EYES(1981)
Edward Higgins
WOMAN EATER, THE(1959, Brit.); ALL THE RIGHT NOISES(1973, Brit.)
Fran Higgins
SQUIRM(1976)
George Higgins
GOLDEN COACH, THE(1953, Fr./Ital.); ROMAN HOLIDAY(1953)
George Higgins III
RED-DRAGON(1967, Ital./Ger./US), w
Howard Higgins
HIGH VOLTAGE(1929), d; RACKETEER, THE(1929), d; PAINTED DESERT, THE(1931), d, w; BATTLE OF GREED(1934), d; KING KELLY OF THE U.S.A(1934), w; I CONQUER THE SEA(1936), w
Jack Higgins
EAGLE HAS LANDED, THE(1976, Brit.), w
James Higgins
1984
WOMAN IN RED, THE(1984)
Joe Higgins
GERONIMO(1962); FLIPPER(1963); FLIPPER'S NEW ADVENTURE(1964); NAMU, THE KILLER WHALE(1966); PERILS OF PAULINE, THE(1967); SIX PACK ANNIE(1975); RECORD CITY(1978)
John Higgins
MY WAY(1974, South Africa)
Misc. Talkies
SUPER-JOCKS, THE(1980)
John C. Higgins
MURDER MAN(1935), w; THEY ALL COME OUT(1939), w; KID GLOVE KILLER(1942), w; ADVENTURES OF TARTU(1943, Brit.), w; MAIN STREET AFTER DARK(1944), w; RAILROADED(1947), w; HE WALKED BY NIGHT(1948), w; RAW DEAL(1948), w; BORDER INCIDENT(1949), w; PONY SOLDIER(1952), w; DIAMOND WIZARD, THE(1954, Brit.), w; SHIELD FOR MURDER(1954), w; BIG HOUSE, U.S.-A.(1955), w; SEVEN CITIES OF GOLD(1955), w; BLACK SLEEP, THE(1956), w; BROKEN STAR, THE(1956), w; HOLD BACK THE NIGHT(1956), w; QUINCANNON, FRONTIER SCOUT(1956), w; UNTAMED YOUTH(1957), w; ROBINSON CRUSOE ON MARS(1964), w; FILE OF THE GOLDEN GOOSE, THE(1969, Brit.), w; IMPASS-E(1969), w; DAUGHTERS OF SATAN(1972), w
John Q. Higgins
PENALTY, THE(1941), w
Ken Higgins
FRENCH DRESSING(1964, Brit.), ph; DARLING(1965, Brit.), ph; SWINGER'S PARADISE(1965, Brit.), ph; UP JUMPED A SWAGMAN(1965, Brit.), ph; GEORGY GIRL(1966, Brit.), ph; IDOL, THE(1966, Brit.), ph; SPY WITH A COLD NOSE, THE(1966, Brit.), ph; COP-OUT(1967, Brit.), ph; HOT MILLIONS(1968, Brit.), ph; SALT & PEPPER(1968, Brit.), ph; MIDAS RUN(1969), ph; ON HER MAJESTY'S SECRET SERVICE(1969, Brit.), ph; JULIUS CAESAR(1970, Brit.), ph; VIRGIN SOLDIERS, THE(1970, Brit.), ph; GAMES THAT LOVERS PLAY(1971, Brit.), ph; GOLDEN RENDEZVOUS(1977), ph
Kenneth Higgins
ALL-AMERICAN CO-ED(1941), w; STRICTLY IN THE GROOVE(1942), w; GHOSTS ON THE LOOSE(1943), w; HE'S MY GUY(1943), w; UNKNOWN TERROR, THE(1957), w; YOU CAN'T WIN 'EM ALL(1970, Brit.), ph
Larry Higgins
GROUND ZERO(1973)
Michael Higgins
EDGE OF FURY(1958); PIE IN THE SKY(1964); ARRANGEMENT, THE(1969); DESPERATE CHARACTERS(1971); WANDA(1971); CONVERSATION, THE(1974); STEPFORD WIVES, THE(1975); DEATH PLAY(1976); ENEMY OF THE PEOPLE, AN(1978); KING OF THE GYPSIES(1978); BLACK STALLION, THE(1979); SEDUCTION OF JOE TYNAN, THE(1979); FORT APACHE, THE BRONX(1981); MIDSUMMER NIGHT'S SEX COMEDY, A(1982); RUMBLE FISH(1983)
Monk Higgins
SHEBA BABY(1975), m
Patrick Higgins
ACCEPTABLE LEVELS(1983, Brit.)
Peter Higgins
PAINTED ANGEL, THE(1929)
Robert Higgins
FINO A FARTI MALE(1969, Fr./Ital.)
Rose Higgins
GIRL CRAZY(1943); LEOPARD MAN, THE(1943); NORTHERN PURSUIT(1943); RAMROD(1947); UNCONQUERED(1947); MY FRIEND IRMA GOES WEST(1950)
Ross Higgins
FATTY FINN(1980, Aus.); DOT AND THE BUNNY(1983, Aus.)
Sharon Higgins
ODD ANGRY SHOT, THE(1979, Aus.)
Tasman Higgins
IN THE WAKE OF THE BOUNTY(1933, Aus.), ph; HERITAGE(1935, Aus.), ph; UNCIVILISED(1937, Aus.), ph

Terry Higgins
NUTTY PROFESSOR, THE(1963); WINSTANLEY(1979, Brit.)
Wilbur Higgins
Misc. Silents
ONCE IN A LIFETIME(1925)
Ed Higginson
1984
ISAAC LITTLEFEATHERS(1984, Can.), ph
John Higginson
HIGH ROAD TO CHINA(1983)
Tex Higginson
ONLY ANGELS HAVE WINGS(1939)
"Blind Blake" Higgs
ISLAND WOMEN(1958)
Richard Higgs
LILITH(1964); TAXI DRIVER(1976)
High Priest Of Lake Bosomtwe
1984
WHITE ELEPHANT(1984, Brit.)
Mark High
1984
MIKE'S MURDER(1984)
Pauline High
PARIS INTERLUDE(1934)
High Country
SILENCE(1974), m
Danny Higham
IMPROPER CHANNELS(1981, Can.)
Mary Jane Highbee
Silents
WHERE THE TRAIL DIVIDES(1914)
Ron Highfield
BATTLETRUCK(1982), art d; MONKEY GRIP(1983, Aus.), art d
1984
UTU(1984, New Zealand), prod d
Allen Highfill
HEAVEN'S GATE(1980), cos
J. Allen Highfill
THREE WOMEN(1977), cons; REMEMBER MY NAME(1978), cos; BREATH-LESS(1983), cos
Danny Highham
DEATH SHIP(1980, Can.)
Patricia Highsmith
STRANGERS ON A TRAIN(1951), w; PURPLE NOON(1961, Fr./Ital.), w; ENOUGH ROPE(1966, Fr./Ital./Ger.), w; ONCE YOU KISS A STRANGER(1969), w; AMERICAN FRIEND, THE(1977, Ger.), w
Brian "Slim" Hightower
MAN WHO SHOT LIBERTY VALANCE, THE(1962)
Bryan Hightower
DAKOTA LIL(1950); FLAMING FEATHER(1951)
Harold Hightower
Silents
FOUR FEATHERS(1929)
Linda Hightower
PERSONAL BEST(1982)
Red Hightower
SUDDEN BILL DORN(1938)
Rosella Hightower
NEOPOLITAN CAROUSEL(1961, Ital.); MERRY WIVES OF WINDSOR, THE(1966, Aust.), a, ch
Slim Hightower
THUNDER TRAIL(1937); TEXANS, THE(1938); SUNSET PASS(1946); FORT DEFIANCE(1951); SEARCHERS, THE(1956)
Raimondo Higino
DONA FLOR AND HER TWO HUSBANDS(1977, Braz.), ed
Philo Higley
REMEMBER THE DAY(1941), w
H.R. Hignett
TILLY OF BLOOMSBURY(1931, Brit.); BREAK THE NEWS(1938, Brit.); YANK IN LONDON, A(1946, Brit.); SPRING IN PARK LANE(1949, Brit.); FOUR AGAINST FATE(1952, Brit.)
Silents
SILENT EVIDENCE(1922, Brit.)
Mary Hignett
PREHISTORIC WOMEN(1967, Brit.); CRUCIBLE OF HORROR(1971, Brit.)
Kazumi Higuchi
LAKE, THE(1970, Jap.)
Kiyoshi Higuchi
FIGHT FOR THE GLORY(1970, Jap.), p
Toshiko Higuchi
HIDDEN FORTRESS, THE(1959, Jap.); PLEASURES OF THE FLESH, THE(1965)
Tomoe Hiiro
TUNNEL TO THE SUN(1968, Jap.)
Bob Hike
BLUES FOR LOVERS(1966, Brit.), ph
Barbara Hiken
FUNNYMAN(1967)
Gerald Hiken
GODDESS, THE(1958); UNCLE VANYA(1958); INVITATION TO A GUNFIGHTER(1964); FUNNYMAN(1967); COMPANY OF KILLERS(1970); CANDIDATE, THE(1972); FUZZ(1972); THREE SISTERS, THE(1977); REDS(1981)
Nat Hiken
LOVE GOD?, THE(1969), d&w
Yoshio Hikida
SECRET DOOR, THE(1964)
Lida Hikox
Misc. Silents
SOCIETY WOLVES(1916)

Crisanto Hilario
YANK IN VIET-NAM, A(1964), spec eff
Santos Hilario
LOST BATTALION(1961, U.S./Phil.), spec eff; MORO WITCH DOCTOR(1964, U.S./Phil.), spec eff; MISSION BATANGAS(1968), spec eff
Teofilo Hilario
BEAST OF BLOOD(1970, U.S./Phil.), spec eff; DANCE OF THE DWARFS(1983, U.S., Phil.), spec eff
Captain George Hill
ZIEGFELD FOLLIES(1945)
Hilario Brothers
CRY OF BATTLE(1963), art d
A. Hilarius
HEAVEN IS ROUND THE CORNER(1944, Brit.), w
Jennifer Hilary
BECKET(1964, Brit.); HEROES OF TELEMARK, THE(1965, Brit.); IDOL, THE(1966, Brit.); JOURNEY INTO DARKNESS(1968, Brit.); ONE BRIEF SUMMER(1971, Brit.); FFOLKES(1980, Brit.); FIVE DAYS ONE SUMMER(1982)
Emil Hilb
FIGHTING CARAVANS(1931), m
Emile Hilb
NIGHT AND DAY(1946)
Fernando Hilbeck
PYRO(1964, U.S./Span.); KID RODELO(1966, U.S./Span.); SON OF A GUNFIGHTER(1966, U.S./Span.); CHIMES AT MIDNIGHT(1967, Span.,Switz.); FICKLE FINGER OF FATE, THE(1967, Span./U.S.); TALL WOMEN, THE(1967, Aust./Ital./Span.); CHRISTMAS KID, THE(1968, U.S., Span.); DESPERATE ONES(1968 U.S./Span.); YOUNG REBEL, THE(1969, Fr./Ital./Span.); MADIGAN'S MILLIONS(1970, Span./Ital); MAN CALLED NOON, THE(1973, Brit.); DON'T OPEN THE WINDOW(1974, Ital.)
Phillipa Hilbere
LOVE AND HISSES(1937); SECOND HONEYMOON(1937)
Lise Hilboldt
SUPERMAN(1978); HUNGER, THE(1983)
Ben Hilbun
INTRUDER IN THE DUST(1949)
Betty Hilburn
Silents
SINNERS IN HEAVEN(1924)
Misc. Silents
GIRL OF THE SEA(1920); HEART STRINGS(1920); CONCEIT(1921); CHILDREN OF FATE(1926); BROADWAY MADNESS(1927)
Jewel Hilburn
Silents
LITTLE MISS BROWN(1915)
Percy Hilburn
HIS GLORIOUS NIGHT(1929), ph; MYSTERIOUS ISLAND(1929), ph; CHILDREN OF PLEASURE(1930), ph; GOOD NEWS(1930), ph; REDEMPTION(1930), ph; ROGUE SONG, THE(1930), ph; UNHOLY THREE, THE(1930), ph; WAY FOR A SAILOR(1930), ph; IRON MAN, THE(1931), ph
Silents
NARROW PATH, THE(1918), ph; PEST, THE(1919), ph; BRANDING IRON, THE(1920), ph; BUNTY PULLS THE STRINGS(1921), ph; POVERTY OF RICHES, THE(1921), ph; SNOWBLIND(1921), ph; STORM, THE(1922), ph; ETERNAL STRUGGLE, THE(1923), ph; BEN-HUR(1925), ph; TOWER OF LIES, THE(1925), ph; BEVERLY OF GRAUSTARK(1926), ph; BLACK BIRD, THE(1926), ph; MEMORY LANE(1926), ph; AFTER MIDNIGHT(1927), ph; WEST OF ZANZIBAR(1928), ph
Bert Hilckman
LAST GUNFIGHTER, THE(1961, Can.)
Harry Hilcox
HOT RODS TO HELL(1967)
Irene Hilda
TWO FOR THE ROAD(1967, Brit.)
Luis Hildago
Silents
PAGES OF LIFE(1922, Brit.)
Oscar Hildago
LONE WOLF McQUADE(1983)
Juan Hildalgo-Gato
DEATH CURSE OF TARTU(1967), p
Caroline Hildebrand
IDAHO TRANSFER(1975)
Helmut Hildebrand
JOURNEY TO THE LOST CITY(1960, Ger./Fr./Ital.)
Hilde Hildebrand
BEAUTIFUL ADVENTURE(1932, Ger.); CASE VAN GELDERN(1932, Ger.); PRIVATE LIFE OF LOUIS XIV(1936, Ger.); DAY AFTER THE DIVORCE, THE(1940, Ger.)
Istvan Hildebrand
GOLDEN HEAD, THE(1965, Hung., U.S.), ph
Rodney Hildebrand
BLACK CAT, THE(1934); HARMONY LANE(1935); LIFE BEGINS AT 40(1935); STONE OF SILVER CREEK(1935); LONELY TRAIL, THE(1936)
Weyler Hildebrand
COUNT OF THE MONK'S BRIDGE, THE(1934, Swed.); WHALERS, THE(1942, Swed.), w; OCEAN BREAKERS(1949, Swed.)
Astrid Hildebrandt
SCREWBALLS(1983)
Charles George Hildebrandt
DEADLY SPAWN, THE(1983)
Dieter Hildebrandt
PLAYGIRLS AND THE BELLBOY, THE(1962,Ger.), w
Gudrun Hildebrandt
DIE FLEDERMAUS(1964, Aust.), cos
H. Hildebrandt
MANULESCU(1933, Ger.)
Hilde Hildebrandt
DIE FASTNACHTSBEICHTE(1962, Ger.); THREE PENNY OPERA(1963, Fr./Ger.)
Hildegarde
MUSIC HATH CHARMS(1935, Brit.)

Anthony Hilder
EXILES, THE(1966), m
Kim Hilder
NEWSFRONT(1979, Aus.), spec eff; STARSTRUCK(1982, Aus.), art d
Rodney Hilderbrand
Silents
EARLY TO WED(1926)
Olle Hilding
FANNY AND ALEXANDER(1983, Swed./Fr./Ger.)
Bob Hilditch
MAD DOG MORGAN(1976,Aus.), art d; EARTHLING, THE(1980), prod d
Robert Hilditch
RIDE A WILD PONY(1976, U.S./Aus.), art d
Rick Hildreth
TOWN THAT DREADED SUNDOWN, THE(1977)
Michel Hildsheim
Z.P.G.(1972)
Jack Hildyard
FRENCH WITHOUT TEARS(1939, Brit.), ph; PIMPERNEL SMITH(1942, Brit.), ph; LAMP STILL BURNS, THE(1943, Brit.), ph; CAESAR AND CLEOPATRA(1946, Brit.), ph; HENRY V(1946, Brit.), ph; SCHOOL FOR SECRETS(1946, Brit.), ph; VICE VERSA(1948, Brit.), ph; AFFAIRS OF A ROGUE, THE(1949, Brit.), ph; AMAZING MR. BEECHAM, THE(1949, Brit.), ph; CARDBOARD CAVALIER, THE(1949, Brit.), ph; SLEEPING CAR TO TRIESTE(1949, Brit.), ph; PERFECT WOMAN, THE(1950, Brit.), ph; WHILE THE SUN SHINES(1950, Brit.), ph; RELUCTANT WIDOW, THE(1951, Brit.), ph; TONY DRAWS A HORSE(1951, Brit.), ph; BREAKING THE SOUND BARRIER(1952), ph; YOU CAN'T BEAT THE IRISH(1952, Brit.), ph; FOLLY TO BE WISE(1953), ph; MURDER ON MONDAY(1953, Brit.), ph; GREEN SCARF, THE(1954, Brit.), ph; HEART OF THE MATTER, THE(1954, Brit.), ph; HOBSON'S CHOICE(1954, Brit.), ph; DEEP BLUE SEA, THE(1955, Brit.), ph; SUMMERTIME(1955), ph; TECKMAN MYSTERY, THE(1955, Brit), ph; ANASTASIA(1956), ph; CHARLEY MOON(1956, Brit.), ph; MARCH HARE, THE(1956, Brit.), ph; BRIDGE ON THE RIVER KWAI, THE(1957), ph; LIVING IDOL, THE(1957), ph; ANOTHER TIME, ANOTHER PLACE(1958), ph; GYPSY AND THE GENTLEMAN, THE(1958, Brit.), ph; DEVIL'S DISCIPLE, THE(1959), ph; JOURNEY, THE(1959, U.S./Aust.), ph; SUDDENLY, LAST SUMMER(1959, Brit.), ph; MILLIONAIRESS, THE(1960, Brit.), ph; SUNDOWNERS, THE(1960), ph; JET STORM(1961, Brit.), ph; LIVE NOW–PAY LATER(1962, Brit.), ph; ROAD TO HONG KONG, THE(1962, U.S./Brit.), ph; V.I.P.s, THE(1963, Brit.), ph; 55 DAYS AT PEKING(1963), ph; CIRCUS WORLD(1964), ph; BATTLE OF THE BULGE(1965), ph; YELLOW ROLLS-ROYCE, THE(1965, Brit.), ph; MODESTY BLAISE(1966, Brit.), ph; CASINO ROYALE(1967, Brit.), ph; LONG DUEL, THE(1967, Brit.), ph; MRS. BROWN, YOU'VE GOT A LOVELY DAUGHTER(1968, Brit.), ph; VILLA RIDES(1968), ph; HARD CONTRACT(1969), ph; TOPAZ(1969, Brit.), ph; PUPPET ON A CHAIN(1971, Brit.), ph; BEAST MUST DIE, THE(1974, Brit.), p; EMILY(1976, Brit.), ph; MOHAMMAD, MESSENGER OF GOD(1976, Lebanon/Brit.), ph; WILD GEESE, THE(1978, Brit.), ph; LION OF THE DESERT(1981, Libya/Brit.), ph
Moshe Hilel
KAZABLAN(1974, Israel)
Hilero
PORTRAIT OF INNOCENCE(1948, Fr.), w
Paul Hiley
PERSECUTION AND ASSASSINATION OF JEAN-PAUL MARAT AS PERFORMED BY THE INMATES OF THE ASYLUM OF CHARENTON UNDER THE DIRECTION OF THE MARQUIS DE SADE, THE(1967, Brit.)
Shirley Hilf
SOCIETY FEVER(1935)
Karen Hilger
BOYS IN COMPANY C, THE(1978, U.S./Hong Kong)
Richard Hilgert
NAKED AMONG THE WOLVES(1967, Ger.)
Patty Lee Hilka
MUSIC MAN, THE(1962)
Michael Hilkene
JACKSON COUNTY JAIL(1976)
Al Hill
ALIBI(1929); RACKETEER, THE(1929); SIDE STREET(1929); DOORWAY TO HELL(1930); TOP SPEED(1930); WIDOW FROM CHICAGO, THE(1930); RULING VOICE, THE(1931); TEN CENTS A DANCE(1931); LAST MILE, THE(1932); MAID TO ORDER(1932); NIGHT AFTER NIGHT(1932); DEATH KISS, THE(1933); I COVER THE WATERFRONT(1933); LADY KILLER(1933); PICK-UP(1933); PRIVATE JONES(1933); SHE DONE HIM WRONG(1933); AGAINST THE LAW(1934); LEMON DROP KID, THE(1934); MEN OF THE NIGHT(1934); MURDER IN THE MUSEUM(1934); NAME THE WOMAN(1934); PALOOKA(1934); PERSONALITY KID, THE(1934); PICTURE BRIDES(1934); SHE LEARNED ABOUT SAILORS(1934); TAKE THE STAND(1934); WHARF ANGEL(1934); AIR HAWKS(1935); CAR 99(1935); DR. SOCRATES(1935); G-MEN(1935); PAYOFF, THE(1935); VIRGINIA JUDGE, THE(1935); WE'RE IN THE MONEY(1935); WHOLE TOWN'S TALKING, THE(1935); BIG NOISE, THE(1936); BORDER PATROLMAN, THE(1936); BULLETS OR BALLOTS(1936); CALL OF THE PRAIRIE(1936); CRASH DONOVAN(1936); NEXT TIME WE LOVE(1936); RIFFRAFF(1936); SWORN ENEMY(1936); THREE ON THE TRAIL(1936); WINTERSET(1936); BIG SHOT, THE(1937); HOLLYWOOD COWBOY(1937); I'LL TAKE ROMANCE(1937); MOTOR MADNESS(1937); PAROLE RACKET(1937); SAN QUENTIN(1937); SMART BLONDE(1937); STAGE DOOR(1937); LADY IN THE MORGUE(1938); MEN WITH WINGS(1938); PARTNERS OF THE PLAINS(1938); RAWHIDE(1938); SHE'S GOT EVERYTHING(1938); CAFE SOCIETY(1939); EACH DAWN I DIE(1939); ETERNALLY YOURS(1939); GAMBLING SHIP(1939); I STOLE A MILLION(1939); KID FROM KOKOMO, THE(1939); ROARING TWENTIES, THE(1939); WINTER CARNIVAL(1939); BANK DICK, THE(1940); INVISIBLE STRIPES(1940); ISLAND OF DOOMED MEN(1940); LUCKY PARTNERS(1940); MAN FROM TUMBLEWEEDS, THE(1940); THEY DRIVE BY NIGHT(1940); CONFESSIONS OF BOSTON BLACKIE(1941); FACE BEHIND THE MASK, THE(1941); HONKY TONK(1941); HONOLULU LU(1941); PENALTY, THE(1941); UNHOLY PARTNERS(1941); WHISTLING IN THE DARK(1941); ZIEGFELD GIRL(1941); GLASS KEY, THE(1942); HARVARD, HERE I COME(1942); LADY BODYGUARD(1942); LUCKY LEGS(1942); MAN'S WORLD, A(1942); MY FAVORITE SPY(1942); SABOTAGE SQUAD(1942); TRAMP, TRAMP, TRAMP(1942); TWO YANKS IN TRINIDAD(1942); AFTER MIDNIGHT WITH BOSTON BLACKIE(1943); DESTROYER(1943); GOVERNMENT GIRL(1943); DRAGON SEED(1944); LOST ANGEL(1944); MRS. PARKINGTON(1944); PRINCESS AND THE PIRATE, THE(1944); RATIONING(1944); SHINE ON, HARVEST MOON(1944); EVE KNEW HER APPLES(1945); ROAD TO UTO-

PIA(1945); SAN ANTONIO(1945); CRACK-UP(1946); KID FROM BOOKLYN, THE(1946); KILLERS, THE(1946); MAGNIFICENT DOLL(1946); NOCTURNE(1946); OUR HEARTS WERE GROWING UP(1946); PERILOUS HOLIDAY(1946); BRUTE FORCE(1947); CHRISTMAS EVE(1947); HIGH WALL(1947); IT HAPPENED IN BROOKLYN(1947); JOHNNY O'CLOCK(1947); MY FAVORITE BRUNETTE(1947); SMASH-UP, THE STORY OF A WOMAN(1947); FURY AT FURNACE CREEK(1948); RIVER LADY(1948); STATION WEST(1948); KNOCK ON ANY DOOR(1949); SLIGHTLY FRENCH(1949); TO PLEASE A LADY(1950); GIRL ON THE BRIDGE, THE(1951); MILLIONAIRE FOR CHRISTY, A(1951); SEALED CARGO(1951); SMUGGLER'S GOLD(1951); STRANGERS ON A TRAIN(1951); KANSAS CITY CONFIDENTIAL(1952); SNIPER, THE(1952); BAND WAGON, THE(1953); CLOWN, THE(1953); MONEY FROM HOME(1953); SOUTH SEA WOMAN(1953); STRANGER WORE A GUN, THE(1953); THREE SAILORS AND A GIRL(1953); VICKI(1953); SILVER LODE(1954); THREE RING CIRCUS(1954)

Al Hill, Jr.
OFF THE RECORD(1939); INVISIBLE STRIPES(1940)

Al M. Hill
MONSTER AND THE GIRL, THE(1941); LUCKY JORDAN(1942); PALEFACE, THE(1948)

Albert Hill, Jr.
BOY'S REFORMATORY(1939)

Rev. Albert Fay Hill
NORTH AVENUE IRREGULARS, THE(1979), w

Alex Hill
RACING LADY(1937)

Alfred Hill
BROKEN MELODY(1938, Aus.), m

Alice Hill
ONE PLUS ONE(1961, Can.)

All Hill
DANCERS IN THE DARK(1932); ONE YEAR LATER(1933); LAST GANGSTER, THE(1937)

Angela Hill
1984
TIGHTROPE(1984)

Arthur Hill
MADAME RACKETEER(1932); BODY SAID NO!, THE(1950, Brit.); MISS PILGRIM'S PROGRESS(1950, Brit.); SCARLET THREAD(1951, Brit.); PAUL TEMPLE RETURNS(1952, Brit.); SALUTE THE TOFF(1952, Brit.); DAY TO REMEMBER, A(1953, Brit.); FAMILY AFFAIR(1954, Brit.); DEEP BLUE SEA, THE(1955, Brit.); RAISING A RIOT(1957, Brit.); YOUNG DOCTORS, THE(1961); IN THE COOL OF THE DAY(1963); UGLY AMERICAN, THE(1963); HARPER(1966); MOMENT TO MOMENT(1966); PETULIA(1968, U.S./Brit.); CHAIRMAN, THE(1969); DON'T LET THE ANGELS FALL(1969, Can.); RABBIT, RUN(1970); ANDROMEDA STRAIN, THE(1971); PURSUIT OF HAPPINESS, THE(1971); KILLER ELITE, THE(1975); FUTUREWORLD(1976); BRIDGE TOO FAR, A(1977, U.S./Brit.); BUTCH AND SUNDANCE: THE EARLY DAYS(1979); CHAMP, THE(1979); LITTLE ROMANCE, A(1979, U.S./Fr.); DIRTY TRICKS(1981, Can.); AMATEUR, THE(1982); MAKING LOVE(1982); SOMETHING WICKED THIS WAY COMES(1983)

Arthur Raymond Hill
LONE WOLF RETURNS, THE(1936)

Barbara Hill
LOVE NOW...PAY LATER(1966, Ital.)

Barry Hill
GRENDEL GRENDEL GRENDEL(1981, Aus.)

Ben Hill
Misc. Silents
BORDER RAIDERS, THE(1921); ON THE HIGH CARD(1921)

Benny Hill
WHO DONE IT?(1956, Brit.); LIGHT UP THE SKY(1960, Brit.); THOSE MAGNIFICENT MEN IN THEIR FLYING MACHINES; OR HOW I FLEWFROM LONDON TO PARIS IN 25 HOURS AND 11 MINUTES(1965, Brit.); CHITTY CHITTY BANG BANG(1968, Brit.); ITALIAN JOB, THE(1969, Brit.)

Bernard Hill
DIRTY KNIGHT'S WORK(1976, Brit.); SAILOR'S RETURN, THE(1978, Brit.)
1984
BOUNTY, THE(1984)

Betty Hill
LADY FOR A NIGHT(1941); EVE KNEW HER APPLES(1945); NIGHT EDITOR(1946); NOCTURNE(1946); STRANGE LOVE OF MARTHA IVERS, THE(1946); RIFFRAFF(1947); TRAIL STREET(1947); UNFAITHFUL, THE(1947); JOLSON SINGS AGAIN(1949); KISS IN THE DARK, A(1949)

Billie Hill
NORMAN CONQUEST(1953, Brit.)

Bob Hill
COWBOY HOLIDAY(1934), d; FRONTIER DAYS(1934), d; CYCLONE RANGER(1935), d; DANGER TRAILS(1935), d; FACE IN THE FOG, A(1936), d; PUT ON THE SPOT(1936), d; ROGUES' TAVERN, THE(1936), d; CHEYENNE RIDES AGAIN(1937), d; LAW AND LEAD(1937), d; MYSTERY RANGE(1937), d; TAMING THE WILD(1937), d; $1,000,000 RACKET(1937), d; FLYING FISTS(1938), d; PHANTOM OF THE RANGE, THE(1938), d; WHIRLWIND HORSEMAN(1938), d; FLYING WILD(1941); GIRLS IN CHAINS(1943); KEEP 'EM SLUGGING(1943); WOLVES OF THE RANGE(1943); SPOOK WHO SAT BY THE DOOR, THE(1973); LADY, STAY DEAD(1982, Aus.), art d
Misc. Talkies
OUTLAWS' HIGHWAY(1934), d; TEXAS RAMBLER, THE(1935), d

Bonnie Hill
Misc. Talkies
FOLLOW ME(1969)
Silents
BRAT, THE(1919); DARK STAIRWAYS(1924)
Misc. Silents
MICROBE, THE(1919)

C. Ramsay Hill
UNSINKABLE MOLLY BROWN, THE(1964)

C. Ramsey Hill
LETTER FROM AN UNKNOWN WOMAN(1948)

Carl Hill
STROKER ACE(1983)

Carol Hill
ROBIN AND THE SEVEN HOODS(1964); ROMEO AND JULIET(1966, Brit.)

Casey Robinson Gus Hill
MC FADDEN'S FLATS(1935), w

Cecil Burtis Hill
Silents
LITTLE WILD GIRL, THE(1928), w; OLD AGE HANDICAP(1928), w; GIRLS WHO DARE(1929), w

Cecil Hill
1984
STRANGERS KISS(1984)

Charles Hill
RAINBOW'S END(1935); LUCKY TERROR(1936); VIOLENT STRANGER(1957, Brit.); MILLIONAIRESS, THE(1960, Brit.); CHARLIE BUBBLES(1968, Brit.)
Misc. Silents
EAGLE'S WINGS, THE(1916); FAKER, THE(1929)

Claudio Guerin Hill
Misc. Talkies
BELL OF HELL, THE(1973), d

Craig Hill
ALL ABOUT EVE(1950); CHEAPER BY THE DOZEN(1950); DETECTIVE STORY(1951); FIXED BAYONETS(1951); I DON'T CARE GIRL, THE(1952); OUTCASTS OF POKER FLAT, THE(1952); WHAT PRICE GLORY?(1952); BLACK SHIELD OF FALWORTH, THE(1954); SIEGE AT RED RIVER, THE(1954); TAMMY AND THE BACHELOR(1957); FLIGHT THAT DISAPPEARED, THE(1961); DEADLY DUO(1962); FOLLOW ME, BOYS!(1966); SWINGER, THE(1966); ASSIGNMENT TERROR(1970, Ger./Span./Ital.); DRUMMER OF VENGEANCE(1974, Brit.)

Dana Hill
SHOOT THE MOON(1982); CROSS CREEK(1983)

Dave Hill
NOW YOU SEE HIM, NOW YOU DON'T(1972); FLAME(1975, Brit.); REMEMBRANCE(1982, Brit.); DRAUGHTSMAN'S CONTRACT, THE(1983, Brit.)

David Hill
KARATE, THE HAND OF DEATH(1961), w

Debbie Hill
TRIAL OF BILLY JACK, THE(1974)

Debra Hill
HALLOWEEN(1978), p, w; FOG, THE(1980), p, w; ESCAPE FROM NEW YORK(1981), p; HALLOWEEN 11(1981), p&w; HALLOWEEN III: SEASON OF THE WITCH(1982), p; DEAD ZONE, THE(1983), p

Del Hill
THEY WERE EXPENDABLE(1945)

Dennis Hill
NASHVILLE(1975), ed; BUFFALO BILL AND THE INDIANS, OR SITTING BULL'S HISTORY LESSON(1976), ed; THREE WOMEN(1977), ed; LOVE AND MONEY(1982), ed
1984
LIES(1984, Brit.), ed

Dennis M. Hill
QUINTET(1979), ed; HEALTH(1980), ed

Derek Hill
WHAT'S NEXT?(1975, Brit.), w; SILKWOOD(1983), set d
1984
PLACES IN THE HEART(1984), set d

Diane Hill
1941(1979); USED CARS(1980)

Doris Hill
DARKENED ROOMS(1929); HIS GLORIOUS NIGHT(1929); STUDIO MURDER MYSTERY, THE(1929); CODE OF HONOR(1930); MEN ARE LIKE THAT(1930); SONG OF THE CABELLERO(1930); SONS OF THE SADDLE(1930); MONTANA KID, THE(1931); ONE WAY TRAIL, THE(1931); BATTLING BUCKAROO(1932); SOUTH OF THE RIO GRANDE(1932); SPIRIT OF THE WEST(1932); TANGLED DESTINIES(1932); CRASHING BROADWAY(1933); GALLOPING ROMEO(1933); RANGER'S CODE, THE(1933); VIA PONY EXPRESS(1933); TEXAS TORNADO(1934)
Misc. Talkies
TRAILING NORTH(1933)
Silents
BETTER 'OLE, THE(1926); IS THAT NICE?(1926); TOM AND HIS PALS(1926); CASEY AT THE BAT(1927); ROUGH HOUSE ROSIE(1927); AVALANCHE(1928); TAKE ME HOME(1928); TILLIE'S PUNCTURED ROMANCE(1928)
Misc. Silents
TIMID TERROR, THE(1926); BEAUTY SHOPPERS(1927); FIGURES DON'T LIE(1927); TELL IT TO SWEENEY(1927); COURT-MARTIAL(1928); THIEF IN THE DARK, A(1928)

Ed Hill
DEVONSVILLE TERROR, THE(1983), m

Eddie Hill
FORTY ACRE FEUD(1965); GOLD GUITAR, THE(1966)

Elaine Welton Hill
COMPETITION, THE(1980)

Elizabeth Hill
OUR DAILY BREAD(1934), w; CITADEL, THE(1938), w; H.M. PULHAM, ESQ.(1941), w; STREETS OF LAREDO(1949), w; TWELVE CHAIRS, THE(1970), d&w

Emma Hill
BIG POND, THE(1930), ed; YOUNG MAN OF MANHATTAN(1930), ed; MY SIN(1931), ed; NIGHT ANGEL, THE(1931), ed; STOLEN HEAVEN(1931), ed

Ethel Hill
SCARLET BRAND(1932), w; VIRTUE(1932), w; SHIP OF WANTED MEN(1933), w; BLIND DATE(1934), w; FOG(1934), w; FURY OF THE JUNGLE(1934), w; I'LL FIX IT(1934), w; MOST PRECIOUS THING IN LIFE(1934), w; WHIRLPOOL(1934), w; EIGHT BELLS(1935), w; PARTY WIRE(1935), w; PUBLIC MENACE(1935), w; MORE THAN A SECRETARY(1936), w; IT HAPPENED IN HOLLYWOOD(1937), w; LET'S GET MARRIED(1937), w; WHEN YOU'RE IN LOVE(1937), w; JUST AROUND THE CORNER(1938), w; LITTLE PRINCESS, THE(1939), w; MARYLAND(1940), w; DANCE HALL(1941), w; FOR BEAUTY'S SAKE(1941), w; SMALL TOWN DEB(1941), w; MAISIE GETS HER MAN(1942), w; IN OLD OKLAHOMA(1943), w; MAN FROM FRISCO(1944), w; TWICE BLESSED(1945), w; TWO SMART PEOPLE(1946), w

Silents

EAGLE, THE(1918), w; EVERY MAN'S WIFE(1925), w; DRIVEN FROM HOME(1927), w; FANGS OF THE WILD(1928), w; YOUNG WHIRLWIND(1928), w

Frank E. Hill

HERE COMES THE BAND(1935), ed; LORD JEFF(1938), ed

Frank Hill

ARIZONA(1940); INVISIBLE MAN RETURNS, THE(1940)

Frank O. Hill

STROKER ACE(1983)

1984

CANNONBALL RUN II(1984)

Frankie Hill

WARGAMES(1983)

1984

FRIDAY THE 13TH–THE FINAL CHAPTER(1984)

George Hill

BIG HOUSE, THE(1930), d; MIN AND BILL(1930), d; SECRET SIX, THE(1931), d; STOLEN HEAVEN(1931), w; HELL DIVERS(1932), d; CLEAR ALL WIRES(1933), d; PHFFFT!(1954); STORK TALK(1964, Brit.); LAST MOVIE, THE(1971)

Silents

FLYING TORPEDO, THE(1916), ph; ZANDER THE GREAT(1925), d; BARRIER, THE(1926), d; TELL IT TO THE MARINES(1926); CALLAHANS AND THE MURPHYS, THE(1927), d; FLYING FEET, THE(1929), d

Misc. Silents

HILL BILLY, THE(1924), d; THROUGH THE DARK(1924), d; LIMITED MAIL, THE(1925), d; BUTTONS(1927), d; COSSACKS, THE(1928), d

George Roy Hill

TOYS IN THE ATTIC(1963), d; THOROUGHLY MODERN MILLIE(1967), d; WALK EAST ON BEACON(1952); PERIOD OF ADJUSTMENT(1962), d; WORLD OF HENRY ORIENT, THE(1964), d; HAWAII(1966), d; BUTCH CASSIDY AND THE SUNDANCE KID(1969), d; SLAUGHTERHOUSE-FIVE(1972), d; STING, THE(1973), d; GREAT WALDO PEPPER, THE(1975), p&d, w; SLAP SHOT(1977), d; LITTLE ROMANCE, A(1979, U.S./Fr.), d; WORLD ACCORDING TO GARP, The(1982), p, d

1984

LITTLE DRUMMER GIRL, THE(1984), d

George W. Hill

Silents

POLLY OF THE CIRCUS(1917), ph; GET YOUR MAN(1921), d; MIDNIGHT EXPRESS, THE(1924), d&w

Misc. Silents

WHILE THE DEVIL LAUGHS(1921), d; FOOLISH VIRGIN, THE(1924), d

Gilbert R. Hill

1984

BEVERLY HILLS COP(1984)

Gladys Hill

NIGHT OF THE IGUANA, THE(1964); REFLECTIONS IN A GOLDEN EYE(1967), w; KREMLIN LETTER, THE(1970), w; MAN WHO WOULD BE KING, THE(1975, Brit.), w; WINTER KILLS(1979)

Gloria Hill

WEEKEND WITH THE BABYSITTER(1970); JUD(1971)

Grady Hill

MOLLY AND LAWLESS JOHN(1972)

Graham Hill

FAST LADY, THE(1963, Brit.); GRAND PRIX(1966); CARAVAN TO VACCARES(1974, Brit./Fr)

Graig Hill

YOU HAVE TO RUN FAST(1961)

Gundy Hill

PACIFIC ADVENTURE(1947, Aus.)

Hallene Hill

ONE HOUR LATE(1935); REMEDY FOR RICHES(1941); TRAMP, TRAMP, TRAMP(1942); WIFE TAKES A FLYER, THE(1942); GANG'S ALL HERE, THE(1943); LAUGH YOUR BLUES AWAY(1943); COLONEL EFFINGHAM'S RAID(1945); LIFE WITH FATHER(1947); FIGHTER SQUADRON(1948); LADY TAKES A SAILOR, THE(1949); MA AND PA KETTLE AT THE FAIR(1952); SEARCH FOR BRIDEY MURPHY, THE(1956); KETTLES ON OLD MACDONALD'S FARM, THE(1957); VAMPIRE, THE(1957); SPARTACUS(1960); FORTY POUNDS OF TROUBLE(1962); CAT BALLOU(1965)

Harold William Hill

SAL OF SINGAPORE(1929)

Harry Hill

RABID(1976, Can.); OH, HEAVENLY DOG!(1980)

Hattie Hill

OPERATOR 13(1934)

Helen Hill

FOR YOU ALONE(1945, Brit.); HOME SWEET HOME(1945, Brit.); MR. H. C. ANDERSEN(1950, Brit.)

Silents

WOMAN, THE(1915)

Herbert Hill

SHADOWED EYES(1939, Brit.), w

Howard Hill

SINGING BUCKAROO, THE(1937); ADVENTURES OF ROBIN HOOD, THE(1938); SAN ANTONIO(1945)

J.L. Hill

WAY OUT WEST(1937), m

Jack Hill

PARDON US(1931); PACK UP YOUR TROUBLES(1932); DEVIL'S BROTHER, THE(1933); TREASURE ISLAND(1934); MILLIONS IN THE AIR(1935); STOLEN HARMONY(1935); OUR RELATIONS(1936); PICK A STAR(1937); WAY OUT WEST(1937); SWISS MISS(1938); LONE WOLF SPY HUNT, THE(1939); SAPS AT SEA(1940); GUNPLAY(1951); VANQUISHED, THE(1953); FEMALE JUNGLE, THE(1955); BRAIN EATERS, THE(1958); TONIGHT FOR SURE(1961), ph; TERROR, THE(1963), p&d, w; PORTRAIT IN TERROR(1965), d; BLOOD BATH(1966), p, d&w; FEAR CHAMBER, THE(1968, US/Mex.), d, w; HOUSE OF EVIL(1968, U.S./Mex.), d, w; SNAKE PEOPLE, THE(1968, Mex./U.S.), d, w; SPIDER BABY(1968), d&w; PIT STOP(1969), d&w, ed; BIG DOLL HOUSE, THE(1971), d; INCREDIBLE INVASION, THE(1971, Mex./U.S.), d; BIG BIRD CAGE, THE(1972), d&w; COFFY(1973), d, w; FOXY DROWN(1974), d&w; SWITCHBLADE SISTERS(1975), d; CITY ON FIRE(1979 Can.), d; LONELY HEARTS(1983, Aus.); SORCERESS(1983), p

Misc. Talkies

BIG DOLL HOUSE, THE(1971), d; SWINGING CHEERLEADERS, THE(1974), d

Silents

SPEEDY(1928)

Jacqueline Hill

BLUE PARROT, THE(1953, Brit.)

James Hill

HOODLUM SAINT, THE(1946), w; CLUE OF THE MISSING APE, THE(1953, Brit.), d&w; HIS MAJESTY O'KEEFE(1953), w; VERA CRUZ(1954), p; PERIL FOR THE GUY(1956, Brit.), d&w; TRAPEZE(1956), p; SWEET SMELL OF SUCCESS(1957), p; THUNDER IN THE SUN(1959), w; UNFORGIVEN, THE(1960), p; KITCHEN, THE(1961, Brit.), d; HAPPY THIEVES, THE(1962), p; LUNCH HOUR(1962, Brit.), d; STOLEN PLANS, THE(1962, Brit.), d&w; TRIAL AND ERROR(1962, Brit.), d; SEASIDE SWINGERS(1965, Brit.), d, w; BORN FREE(1966), d; STUDY IN TERROR, A(1966, Brit./Ger.), d; CORRUPT ONES, THE(1967, Ger.), d; JOURNEY INTO DARKNESS(1968, Brit.), d; CAPTAIN NEMO AND THE UNDERWATER CITY(1969, Brit.), d; ELEPHANT CALLED SLOWLY, AN(1970, Brit.), p&w, d; BLACK BEAUTY(1971, Brit./Ger./Span.), d; BELSTONE FOX, THE(1976, 1976), d; CHRISTIAN THE LION(1976, Brit.), p,d&w

Misc. Talkies

MAN FROM NOWHERE, THE(1976, Brit.), d

Silents

IMPOSSIBLE CATHERINE(1919)

Misc. Silents

FATHER TOM(1921)

James A. Hill

MAN FROM O.R.G.Y., THE(1970), d

James H. Hill

KEEPING COMPANY(1941), w

Jane Hill

OLGA'S GIRLS(1964)

Janine Hill

COUNTESS FROM HONG KONG, A(1967, Brit.)

Jean Hill

POLYESTER(1981)

Jennifer Hill

GIRO CITY(1982, Brit.)

Jenny Hill

FIRST LOVE(1977)

Jerome Hill

SAND CASTLE, THE(1961), p,d&w, art d; HALLELUJAH THE HILLS(1963); OPEN THE DOOR AND SEE ALL THE PEOPLE(1964), p,d&w

Jim Hill

POLYESTER(1981); ROCKY III(1982)

Johanna Hill

OPEN THE DOOR AND SEE ALL THE PEOPLE(1964)

John Hill

SILENT WITNESS, THE(1962); SEVEN-PER-CENT SOLUTION, THE(1977, Brit.); HEARTBEEPS(1981), w

John Stephen Hill

HUNGER, THE(1983); NEVER SAY NEVER AGAIN(1983)

1984

BLOODBATH AT THE HOUSE OF DEATH(1984, Brit.)

Jon Hill

WHERE ANGELS GO...TROUBLE FOLLOWS(1968); MODEL SHOP, THE(1969); STRAWBERRY STATEMENT, THE(1970); PEACE KILLERS, THE(1971)

Josephine Hill

KID FROM ARIZONA, THE(1931); WEST OF CHEYENNE(1931); WILD WEST WHOOPEE(1931); LONE TRAIL, THE(1932)

Misc. Talkies

POTLUCK PARDS(1934)

Silents

NIGHT LIFE IN HOLLYWOOD(1922); KING'S CREEK LAW(1923); LOSER'S END, THE(1924); ACROSS THE DEADLINE(1925); DON X(1925); JOSSELYN'S WIFE(1926); SKY RIDER, THE(1928)

Misc. Silents

(; LOVE AND THE LAW(1919); BURNT WINGS(1920); MAN TRACKERS, THE(1921); LONE FIGHTER(1923); LONE HORSEMAN, THE(1923); WESTERN JUSTICE(1923); HUNTIN' TROUBLE(1924); LIGHTNIN' JACK(1924); NOT BUILT FOR RUNNIN'(1924); PAYABLE ON DEMAND(1924); RIDING DOUBLE(1924); BLOOD BOND, THE(1925); FLASH O'LIGHTING(1925); LUCK AND SAND(1925); RANCHERS AND RASCALS(1925); SHIELD OF SILENCE, THE(1925); SILENT SHELDON(1925); TROUBLE BUSTER, THE(1925); WIN, LOSE OR DRAW(1925); WINNING A WOMAN(1925); BLIND TRAIL(1926); HI-JACKING RUSTLERS(1926); HIGH HAND, THE(1926); LAWLESS TRAILS(1926); WITHOUT ORDERS(1926); DEVIL'S TWIN, THE(1927); TWO-GUN OF THE TUMBLEWEED(1927); SILENT SENTINEL(1929)

Josephine Hill

Misc. Silents

HEADIN' THROUGH(1924)

Katherine Hill

ON THE BEACH(1959)

Kathryn Hill

Silents

YANKEE SENOR, THE(1926)

Misc. Silents

WHEN LOVE GROWS COLD(1925)

Kathy Hill

1984

BLIND DATE(1984)

Ken Hill

1984

PROTOCOL(1984)

Kenneth Hill

Silents

TRUTH, THE(1920)

Misc. Silents

LIVING LIES(1922)

Lee Hill
Silents
CHALLENGE OF CHANCE, THE(1919); MASTER STROKE, A(1920); CYTHEREA(1924)
Misc. Silents
WHEN BABY FORGOT(1917); FALSE AMBITION(1918); GOOD LOSER, THE(1918); LONELY WOMAN, THE(1918); OLD LOVES FOR NEW(1918); STATION CONTENT(1918); GIRLS(1919); DECEIVER, THE(1920)
Linda Lee Hill
Misc. Talkies
STAIRWAY FOR A STAR(1947)
Lucienne Hill
IT STARTED IN PARADISE(1952, Brit.); MASTER PLAN, THE(1955, Brit.)
Mallene Hill
GREAT MAN, THE(1957)
Mariana Hill
EL CONDOR(1970); THUMB TRIPPING(1972); BABY, THE(1973); HIGH PLAINS DRIFTER(1973); SCHIZOID(1980); BLOOD BEACH(1981)
1984
INVISIBLE STRANGLER(1984)
Marianna Hill
MARRIED TOO YOUNG(1962); BLACK ZOO(1963); NEW INTERNS, THE(1964); ROUSTABOUT(1964); RED LINE 7000(1965); PARADISE, HAWAIIAN STYLE(1966); MEDIUM COOL(1969); TRAVELING EXECUTIONER, THE(1970); DEAD PEOPLE(1974); GODFATHER, THE, PART II(1974); LAST PORNO FLICK, THE(1974)
Marla Hill
SORCERESS(1983)
Mary Hill
MODELS, INC.(1952); BEAST FROM 20,000 FATHOMS, THE(1953); MESA OF LOST WOMEN, THE(1956)
Maud Hill
Silents
WHISPERS(1920)
Misc. Silents
SISTER AGAINST SISTER(1917); SACRED FLAME, THE(1919)
Maude Hill
Silents
NO MOTHER TO GUIDE HER(1923)
Misc. Silents
DANGEROUS AFFAIR, A(1919); PURITAN PASSIONS(1923); SIX CYLINDER LOVE(1923)
Maurice J. Hill
TRACK OF THUNDER(1967), w
Maury Hill
TOBOR THE GREAT(1954); BENGAZI(1955); LIEUTENANT WORE SKIRTS, THE(1956); GLASS HOUSES(1972)
Michael Hill
1984
SPLASH(1984), ed
Michael Elliott Hill
D.C. CAB(1983)
Mike Hill
NIGHT SHIFT(1982), ed
Morgan Hill
23 ½ HOURS LEAVE(1937)
Nellid Hill
Misc. Talkies
MURDER WITH MUSIC(1941)
Nicholas Hill
YELLOW ROBE, THE(1954, Brit.)
Norman Hill
BURN(1970)
Olive Hill
TEN CENTS A DANCE(1931)
Patricia Hill
SHE KNEW ALL THE ANSWERS(1941)
Paul Hill
BUFFALO BILL RIDES AGAIN(1947)
Paula Hill
HELLFIRE(1949); HOT CARS(1956); JOKER IS WILD, THE(1957)
Peter Murray Hill
JANE STEPS OUT(1938, Brit.); OUTSIDER, THE(1940, Brit.); GHOST TRAIN, THE(1941, Brit.); HOUSE OF MYSTERY(1941, Brit.); MYSTERY OF ROOM 13(1941, Brit.); POISON PEN(1941, Brit.); BELL-BOTTOM GEORGE(1943, Brit.); RHYTHM SERENADE(1943, Brit.); MADONNA OF THE SEVEN MOONS(1945, Brit.); THEY WERE SISTERS(1945, Brit.)
Phil Hill
RACERS, THE(1955), tech adv; GRAND PRIX(1966), a, tech adv
Phyllis Hill
JOAN OF ARC(1948); WHIRLPOOL(1949); SINGING IN THE DARK(1956); PENDULUM(1969)
R. Lance Hill
1984
EVIL THAT MEN DO, THE(1984), w
R. Lee Hill
Misc. Silents
PALS OF THE WEST(1922)
Ralston Hill
1776(1972)
Ramsay Hill
MAN WHO BROKE THE BANK AT MONTE CARLO, THE(1935); EMPEROR'S CANDLESTICKS, THE(1937); MARIE ANTOINETTE(1938); WHEN WORLDS COLLIDE(1951); BWANA DEVIL(1953); BENGAL BRIGADE(1954); TEN COMMANDMENTS, THE(1956); ONE HUNDRED AND ONE DALMATIANS(1961); THREE STOOGES GO AROUND THE WORLD IN A DAZE, THE(1963)
Ramsey Hill
DOWN TO THEIR LAST YACHT(1934); RIP TIDE(1934); CRUSADES, THE(1935); LAST OUTPOST, THE(1935); EVERYBODY'S OLD MAN(1936); FIREFLY, THE(1937); HOUSE OF SECRETS, THE(1937); LIVE, LOVE AND LEARN(1937); OLD LOUISIANA(1938); BATTLES OF CHIEF PONTIAC(1952); CARIBBEAN(1952); IRON MIS-

TRESS, THE(1952); ROGUE'S MARCH(1952); KING OF THE KHYBER RIFLES(1953)
Ray Hill
1984
MAKING THE GRADE(1984)
Ray Hill,Jr.
MEGAFORCE(1982)
Raymond G. Hill
Silents
GREEN FLAME, THE(1920), w
Richard Hill
TO KILL A CLOWN(1972), m; DEATHSTALKER(1983, Arg./U.S.)
1984
DEATHSTALKER, THE(1984)
Richy Hill
FINNEY(1969)
Riley Hill
WHEN YOU COMIN' BACK, RED RYDER?(1979); BOMBAY CLIPPER(1942); GHOST GUNS(1944); FLAME OF THE WEST(1945); LOST TRAIL, THE(1945); NAVAJO TRAIL, THE(1945); SHERIFF OF CIMARRON(1945); BORDER BANDITS(1946); DESERT HORSEMAN, THE(1946); UNDER ARIZONA SKIES(1946); CODE OF THE SADDLE(1947); FRONTIER AGENT(1948); RANGE RENEGADES(1948); RANGERS RIDE, THE(1948); ACROSS THE RIO GRANDE(1949); LAW OF THE WEST(1949); LAWLESS CODE(1949); RANGE JUSTICE(1949); SHADOWS OF THE WEST(1949); WESTERN RENEGADES(1949); FENCE RIDERS(1950); GUNSLINGERS(1950); JIGGS AND MAGGIE OUT WEST(1950); LAW OF THE PANHANDLE(1950); RADAR SECRET SERVICE(1950); SHORT GRASS(1950); SILVER RAIDERS(1950); CANYON RAIDERS(1951); I WAS AN AMERICAN SPY(1951); NAVY BOUND(1951); NEVADA BADMEN(1951); VALLEY OF FIRE(1951); VANISHING OUTPOST, THE(1951); LUSTY MEN, THE(1952); NIGHT STAGE TO GALVESTON(1952); RAIDERS, THE(1952); TARGET(1952); WAGONS WEST(1952); WHITE LIGHTNING(1953); RIO BRAVO(1959); MA BARKER'S KILLER BROOD(1960); DEADLY COMPANIONS, THE(1961); OUTSIDER, THE(1962); EL DORADO(1967); TRIAL OF BILLY JACK, THE(1974); WANDA NEVADA(1979)
Misc. Talkies
GUN SMOKE(1945); HAUNTED MINE, THE(1946); TRIGGER FINGERS(1946); JIGGS AND MAGGIE IN COURT(1948)
Rob Hill
INSIDE INFORMATION(1934)
Robert Hill
SUNDOWN TRAIL(1931), d&w; COME ON DANGER!(1932), d; LOVE BOUND(1932), d; CHEYENNE KID, THE(1933), d; TARZAN THE FEARLESS(1933), d; DEMON FOR TROUBLE, A(1934), d; KELLY OF THE SECRET SERVICE(1936), d; MEN OF THE PLAINS(1936), d; PRISON SHADOWS(1936), d; RIO GRANDE ROMANCE(1936), d; RIP ROARIN' BUCKAROO(1936), d; TOO MUCH BEEF(1936), d; WEST OF NEVADA(1936), d; IDAHO KID, THE(1937), d; ROAMING COWBOY, THE(1937), d; TWO MINUTES TO PLAY(1937), d; FEUD OF THE TRAIL(1938), d; MAN'S COUNTRY(1938), d; PAINTED TRAIL, THE(1938), d; DRIFTING WESTWARD(1939), d; OVERLAND MAIL(1939), d; WILD HORSE CANYON(1939), d; WANDERERS OF THE WEST(1941), d; BOSS OF THE RAWHIDE(1944); FUZZY SETTLES DOWN(1944); TRAIL OF TERROR(1944); COMIN' THRU' THE RYE(1947, Brit.), ed; ARCTIC FLIGHT(1952), w; STOLEN IDENTITY(1953), w; REDHEAD FROM MANHATTAN(1954); FEMALE ON THE BEACH(1955), w; BEAST OF HOLLOW MOUNTAIN, THE(1956), w; FUN AT ST. FANNY'S(1956, Brit.), ed; RAW EDGE(1956), w; WOMAN'S DEVOTION, A(1956), w; GIRL IN THE KREMLIN, THE(1957), w; FEMALE ANIMAL, THE(1958), w; SHE-GODS OF SHARK REEF(1958), w; DESERT DESPERADOES(1959), w; TARZAN, THE APE MAN(1959), w; HAND, THE(1960, Brit.), ed; SEX KITTENS GO TO COLLEGE(1960), w; PRIVATE LIVES OF ADAM AND EVE, THE(1961), w; CONFESSIONS OF AN OPIUM EATER(1962), w; MURDER IN EDEN(1962, Brit.), ed; DOG EAT DOG(1963, U.S./Ger./Ital.), w; MAN WHO COULDN'T WALK, THE(1964, Brit.), ed; FANNY HILL: MEMOIRS OF A WOMAN OF PLEASURE zero(1965), w; NOBODY WAVED GOODBYE(1965, Can.); TOGETHER FOR DAYS(1972)
Misc. Talkies
SIX GUN JUSTICE(1935), d; VANISHING RIDERS(1935), d; SILKS AND SADDLES(1938), d
Robert E. Hill
INSIDE INFORMATION(1934), d
Silents
BABBLING TONGUES(1917)
Robert F. Hill
LAST WARNING, THE(1929), w; MELODY LANE(1929), d, w; FIGHTING PLAYBOY(1937), d; EAST SIDE KIDS(1940), d; LITTLE JOE, THE WRANGLER(1942); GHOSTS ON THE LOOSE(1943); MORE THE MERRIER, THE(1943); COVER GIRL(1944)
Silents
NANCY COMES HOME(1918), w; RECKONING DAY, THE(1918), w; JUBILO(1919), w; CROOKED ALLEY(1923), d, w; DARK STAIRWAYS(1924), d; EXCITEMENT(1924), d; JACK O' CLUBS(1924), d; BLAZING DAYS(1927), w; CAT AND THE CANARY, THE(1927), w; MILLION FOR LOVE, A(1928), d; SILKS AND SADDLES(1929), d
Misc. Silents
TEMPTATION AND THE MAN(1916), d; RAGGEDY QUEEN, THE(1917); CROOKED ALLEY(1923), d; HIS MYSTERY'S GIRL(1923), d; SHADOWS OF THE NORTH(1923), d; BREATHLESS MOMENT, THE(1924), d; DANGEROUS BLONDE, THE(1924), d; YOUNG IDEAS(1924), d; BAR-C MYSTERY, THE(1926), d; LIFE'S MOCKERY(1928), d
Robert Jordan Hill
MELODY IN THE DARK(1948, Brit.), p&d; BLESS 'EM ALL(1949, Brit.), p&d; HIGH JINKS IN SOCIETY(1949, Brit.), p,d&w; PAPER GALLOWS(1950, Brit.), p, ed; HAPPINESS OF THREE WOMEN, THE(1954, Brit.), ed; WHAT EVERY WOMAN WANTS(1954, Brit.), ed; STARS IN YOUR EYES(1956, Brit.), ed
Robert Lee Hill
Misc. Silents
MAN AND HIS ANGEL(1916)
Roger Hill
EDUCATION OF SONNY CARSON, THE(1974); WARRIORS, THE(1979)
Rollo Lee Hill
Misc. Silents
IDOLATORS(1917)

Ronald Hill
HE LOVED AN ACTRESS(1938, Brit.); RED RUNS THE RIVER(1963); ZULU(1964, Brit.)
Rose Hill
BANK RAIDERS, THE(1958, Brit.); HOUSE OF WHIPCORD(1974, Brit.)
Rosemary Hill
Silents
WARRENS OF VIRGINIA, THE(1924)
Rowland Hill
Silents
KILTIES THREE(1918, Brit.)
Misc. Silents
HOW COULD YOU UNCLE?(1918, Brit.)
Roy Hill
WHO SAYS I CAN'T RIDE A RAINBOW!(1971)
Seymour Hill
HOUSE OF UNREST, THE(1931, Brit.), p
Shirley Hill
MOON OVER HER SHOULDER(1941)
Sinclair Hill
CRIMSON CIRCLE, THE(1930, Brit.), d; DARK RED ROSES(1930, Brit.), d; LATIN LOVE(1930, Brit.), d; SUCH IS THE LAW(1930, Brit.), d; GENTLEMAN OF PARIS, A(1931), d; GREAT GAY ROAD, THE(1931, Brit.), p&d; OTHER PEOPLE'S SINS(1931, Brit.), p&d; FIRST MRS. FRASER, THE(1932, Brit.), d; BRITANNIA OF BILLINGS-GATE(1933, Brit.), d; MAN FROM TORONTO, THE(1933, Brit.), d; MY OLD DUTCH(1934, Brit.), d; HYDE PARK CORNER(1935, Brit.), d; CARDINAL, THE(1936, Brit.), d; GAY ADVENTURE, THE(1936, Brit.), d; BOMBS OVER LONDON(1937, Brit.), d; COMMAND PERFORMANCE(1937, Brit.), d, w; TAKE A CHANCE(1937, Brit.), d; FOLLOW YOUR STAR(1938, Brit.), d, w
Silents
AMATEUR GENTLEMAN, THE(1920, Brit.); AT THE VILLA ROSE(1920, Brit.), w; QUESTION OF TRUST, A(1920, Brit.), w; MYSTERY OF MR. BERNARD BROWN(1921, Brit.), d; PLACE OF HONOUR, THE(1921, Brit.), d; EXPERIMENT, THE(1922, Brit.), d; HALF A TRUTH(1922, Brit.), d; NONENTITY, THE(1922, Brit.), d&w; OPEN COUNTRY(1922, Brit.), d&w; DON QUIXOTE(1923, Brit.), w; INDIAN LOVE LYRICS, THE(1923, Brit.), d&w; PREHISTORIC MAN, THE(1924, Brit.), w; PRESUMPTION OF STANLEY HAY, MP, THE(1925, Brit.), d; QUALIFIED ADVEN-TURER, THE(1925, Brit.), d&w; CHINESE BUNGALOW, THE(1926, Brit.), d; BARNES MURDER CASE, THE(1930, Brit.), d&w
Misc. Silents
TIDAL WAVE, THE(1920, Brit.), d; EXPIATION(1922, Brit.), d; LONELY LADY OF GROSVENOR, THE(1922, Brit.), d; TRUANTS, THE(1922, Brit.), d; ONE ARABIAN NIGHT(1923, Brit.), d; PORT OF LOST SOULS(1924, Brit.), d; BEYOND THE VEIL(1925, Brit.), d; SQUIRE OF LONG HADLEY, THE(1925, Brit.), d; BOADI-CEA(1926, Brit.), d; CHINESE BUNGALOW, THE(1926, Brit.), d; SAHARA LO-VE(1926, Brit.), d; KING'S HIGHWAY, THE(1927, Brit.), d; WOMAN REDEEMED, A(1927, Brit.), d; GUNS OF LOOS, THE(1928, Brit.), d; PRICE OF DIVORCE, THE(1928, Brit.), d
Stephanie Hill
ALVAREZ KELLY(1966); DEAD HEAT ON A MERRY-GO-ROUND(1966); WHAT AM I BID?(1967)
Steve Hill
GODDESS, THE(1958)
Steven Hill
LADY WITHOUT PASSPORT, A(1950); STORM FEAR(1956); CHILD IS WAITING, A(1963); SLENDER THREAD, THE(1965); IT'S MY TURN(1980); EYEWITNESS(1981); RICH AND FAMOUS(1981); YENTL(1983)
1984
GARBO TALKS(1984); TEACHERS(1984)
Misc. Talkies
KISS HER GOODBYE(1959)
Sydney Hill
TURNERS OF PROSPECT ROAD, THE(1947, Brit.), makeup
Teddy Hill
TWO WORLD(1930, Brit.)
Terence Hill
REVENGE AT EL PASO(1968, Ital.); ACE HIGH(1969, Ital.); BOOT HILL(1969, Ital.); GOD FORGIVES–I DON'T!(1969, Ital./Span.); THEY CALL ME TRINITY(1971, Ital.); TRINITY IS STILL MY NAME(1971, Ital.); ALL THE WAY, BOYS(1973, Ital.); MAN FROM THE EAST, A(1974, Ital./Fr.); MY NAME IS NOBODY(1974, Ital./Fr./Ger.); GENIUS, THE(1976, Ital./Fr./Ger.); MARCH OR DIE(1977, Brit.); MR. BILLION(1977); TWO SUPER COPS(1978, Ital.); SUPER FUZZ(1981)
Thelma Hill
MIRACLE WOMAN, THE(1931)
Silents
FAIR CO-ED, THE(1927); PLAY GIRL, THE(1928)
Misc. Silents
CHORUS KID, THE(1928); CROOKS CAN'T WIN(1928); HEARTS OF MEN(1928)
Thomas Hill
SLENDER THREAD, THE(1965); HIDE IN PLAIN SIGHT(1980); NUDE BOMB, THE(1980); FIREFOX(1982); I'M DANCING AS FAST AS I CAN(1982)
1984
NEVERENDING STORY, THE(1984, Ger.)
Toby Hill
JAILBREAKERS, THE(1960)
Tom Hill
MC CABE AND MRS. MILLER(1971); QUINTET(1979); POSTMAN ALWAYS RINGS TWICE, THE(1981); TRUE CONFESSIONS(1981)
Tommy Hill
THAT TENNESSEE BEAT(1966), md
Travers Hill
CLOUD DANCER(1980), ph
Trevening Hill
SCHOOL FOR SECRETS(1946, Brit.)
Trevor Hill
MISS PILGRIM'S PROGRESS(1950, Brit.); SECRET CAVE, THE(1953, Brit.); VIL-LAGE, THE(1953, Brit./Switz.)

Valedia Hill
GIRL, THE BODY, AND THE PILL, THE(1967)
Walt Hill
SUMMER CAMP(1979)
Walter Hill
GETAWAY, THE(1972), w; HICKEY AND BOGGS(1972), w; MACKINTOSH MAN, THE(1973, Brit.), w; THIEF WHO CAME TO DINNER, THE(1973), w; DROWNING POOL, THE(1975), w; HARD TIMES(1975), d, w; DRIVER, THE(1978), d&w; ALIEN(1979), p; WARRIORS, THE(1979), d, w; LONG RIDERS, THE(1980), d; SOUTHERN COMFORT(1981), d, w; 48 HOURS(1982), d, w
1984
STREETS OF FIRE(1984), d, w
Silents
LITTLE MISS REBELLION(1920), ph
Weldon Hill
ONIONHEAD(1958), w
Winfrey Hester Hill
Misc. Talkies
PREMONITION(1972)
William Hill-Rowan
BIG FRAME, THE(1953, Brit.), m
Marcel Hillaire
SABRINA(1954); NORTH TO ALASKA(1960); SEVEN THIEVES(1960); HONEY-MOON MACHINE, THE(1961); BON VOYAGE(1962); FOUR HORSEMEN OF THE APOCALYPSE, THE(1962); TAKE HER, SHE'S MINE(1963); WHEELER DEALERS, THE(1963); MC HALE'S NAVY(1964); WHAT A WAY TO GO(1964); WILD AND WONDERFUL(1964); ART OF LOVE, THE(1965); VERY SPECIAL FAVOR, A(1965); MADE IN PARIS(1966); MURDERERS' ROW(1966); MONKEYS, GO HOME!(1967); TAKE THE MONEY AND RUN(1969)
Katherine Hillaker
Silents
PASSION(1920, Ger.), t
Ernest Hillard
REVEILLE WITH BEVERLY(1943)
Misc. Silents
LADY RAFFLES(1928)
Jane Hillary
ACCIDENT(1967, Brit.)
Richard Hillary
FOR THOSE IN PERIL(1944, Brit.), w
Linnea Hillberg
WALPURGIS NIGHT(1941, Swed.)
Torsten Hillberg
WALPURGIS NIGHT(1941, Swed.)
Colorado Hillbillies
LAND OF FIGHTING MEN(1938)
The Hillbillies
SATURDAY NIGHT REVUE(1937, Brit.)
Percy Hillburn
CLEAR ALL WIRES(1933), ph
Ellen Hille
ETERNAL WALTZ, THE(1959, Ger.)
Fred Hillebrand
HOUSE ON 92ND STREET, THE(1945); HOUSE OF STRANGERS(1949)
Angela Hillebrecht
DEGREE OF MURDER, A(1969, Ger.); DUCK RINGS AT HALF PAST SEVEN, THE(1969, Ger./Ital.)
Clarissa Hillel
TWO FOR THE ROAD(1967, Brit.)
Arthur Hiller
CARELESS YEARS, THE(1957), d; MIRACLE OF THE WHITE STALLIONS(1963), d; WHEELER DEALERS, THE(1963), d; AMERICANIZATION OF EMILY, THE(1964), d; PENELOPE(1966), d; PROMISE HER ANYTHING(1966, Brit.), d; TOBRUK(1966), d; TIGER MAKES OUT, THE(1967), d; POPI(1969), d; LOVE STORY(1970), d; OUT OF TOWNERS, THE(1970), d; HOSPITAL, THE(1971), d; PLAZA SUITE(1971), d; MAN OF LA MANCHA(1972), p&d; CRAZY WORLD OF JULIUS VROODER, THE(1974), p, d; MAN IN THE GLASS BOOTH, THE(1975), d; SILVER STREAK(1976), d; W.C. FIELDS AND ME(1976), d; IN-LAWS, THE(1979), p, d; NIGHTWING(1979), d; AU-THOR! AUTHOR!(1982), d; MAKING LOVE(1982), d; ROMANTIC COMEDY(1983), d
1984
LONELY GUY, THE(1984), p&d; TEACHERS(1984), d
Bernardo Hiller
LORDS OF FLATBUSH, THE(1974)
Charles Hiller
MAN WITH 100 FACES, THE(1938, Brit.)
Erica Hiller
MAKING LOVE(1982); ROMANTIC COMEDY(1983)
1984
LONELY GUY, THE(1984)
Erwin Hiller
I KNOW WHERE I'M GOING(1947, Brit.), ph; WOMAN'S ANGLE, THE(1954, Brit.), ph; CHASE A CROOKED SHADOW(1958, Brit.), ph
Gunda Hiller
DON'T TURN THE OTHER CHEEK(1974, Ital./Ger./Span.)
Kurt Hiller
Silents
LAST LAUGH, THE(1924, Ger.)
Lambert Hiller
PARENTS ON TRIAL(1939), w
Wendy Hiller
TOYS IN THE ATTIC(1963); LANCASHIRE LUCK(1937, Brit.); PYGMALION(1938, Brit.); MAJOR BARBARA(1941, Brit.); I KNOW WHERE I'M GOING(1947, Brit.); SAILOR OF THE KING(1953, Brit.); HOW TO MURDER A RICH UNCLE(1957); SOMETHING OF VALUE(1957); SEPARATE TABLES(1958); SONS AND LO-VERS(1960, Brit.); MAN FOR ALL SEASONS, A(1966, Brit.); DAVID COPPER-FIELD(1970, Brit.); MURDER ON THE ORIENT EXPRESS(1974, Brit.); VOYAGE OF THE DAMNED(1976, Brit.); CAT AND THE CANARY, THE(1979, Brit.); ELEPHANT MAN, THE(1980, Brit.); MAKING LOVE(1982)

Misc. Talkies
KINGFISHER, THE(1982)
John Hillerman
LAST PICTURE SHOW, THE(1971); LAWMAN(1971); CAREY TREATMENT, THE(1972); SKYJACKED(1972); WHAT'S UP, DOC?(1972); HIGH PLAINS DRIFTER(1973); OUTSIDE MAN, THE(1973, U.S./FR.); PAPER MOON(1973); THIEF WHO CAME TO DINNER, THE(1973); BLAZING SADDLES(1974); CHINATOWN(1974); NICKEL RIDE, THE(1974); AT LONG LAST LOVE(1975); DAY OF THE LOCUST, THE(1975); LUCKY LADY(1975); AUDREY ROSE(1977); SUNBURN(1979); HISTORY OF THE WORLD, PART 1(1981)
1984
UP THE CREEK(1984)
Hillevi
LADY VANISHES, THE(1980, Brit.)
Vivien Hillgrove
SILENCE(1974), ed
Brenda Hillhouse
CANNERY ROW(1982)
Bob Hilliard
LIVING IT UP(1954), w
Ernest Hilliard
BROADWAY HOOFER, THE(1929); WALL STREET(1929); DYNAMITE(1930); RED HOT RHYTHM(1930); DRUMS OF JEOPARDY(1931); MOTHER AND SON(1931); SECOND HONEYMOON(1931); FLIRTING WITH DANGER(1935); RACING LUCK(1935); SMART GIRL(1935); BOSS RIDER OF GUN CREEK(1936); SEA SPOILERS, THE(1936); SHOW BOAT(1936); JOAN OF OZARK(1942); LUCKY LEGS(1942); MAKE YOUR OWN BED(1944); MR. WINKLE GOES TO WAR(1944); SOUL OF A MONSTER, THE(1944); MASQUERADE IN MEXICO(1945); DEADLINE FOR MURDER(1946); GILDA(1946); UNDERCURRENT(1946); CHRISTMAS EVE(1947); DOWN TO EARTH(1947); RIDE THE PINK HORSE(1947)
Silents
ANNABEL LEE(1921); RULING PASSION, THE(1922); SILVER WINGS(1922); MODERN MARRIAGE(1923); RECOIL, THE(1924); BOWERY CINDERELLA(1927); MIDNIGHT WATCH, THE(1927); SMILE, BROTHER, SMILE(1927); WHEEL OF DESTINY, THE(1927); DEVIL DOGS(1928); MATINEE IDOL, THE(1928); NOOSE, THE(1928); OUT WITH THE TIDE(1928); RED WINE(1928); SINNERS IN LOVE(1928)
Misc. Silents
MARRIED PEOPLE(1922); WHO ARE MY PARENTS?(1922); FOREST HAVOC(1926); FRONTIER TRAIL, THE(1926); WHITE MICE(1926); MODERN DAUGHTERS(1927); RACING FOOL, THE(1927); SCORCHER, THE(1927); SILENT HERO, THE(1927); WIDE OPEN(1927); BIG HOP, THE(1928); BURNING UP BROADWAY(1928); DIVINE SINNER(1928); DUGAN OF THE DUGOUTS(1928); MIDNIGHT ADVENTURE, THE(1928); SECOND HONEYMOON(1930)
Evangeline Hilliard
Misc. Silents
WILL, THE(1921, Brit.)
Frank Hilliard
LADY IN QUESTION, THE(1940)
Harriet Hilliard
FOLLOW THE FLEET(1936); LIFE OF THE PARTY, THE(1937); NEW FACES OF 1937(1937); COCOANUT GROVE(1938); CONFESSIONS OF BOSTON BLACKIE(1941); SWEETHEART OF THE CAMPUS(1941); CANAL ZONE(1942); JUKE BOX JENNY(1942); FALCON STRIKES BACK, THE(1943); GALS, INCORPORATED(1943); HI, BUDDY(1943); HONEYMOON LODGE(1943); HI, GOOD-LOOKIN'(1944); SWINGTIME JOHNNY(1944); TAKE IT BIG(1944)
Harry Hilliard
ADVENTURES OF MARK TWAIN, THE(1944)
Silents
ROMEO AND JULIET(1916); NEW YORK PEACOCK, THE(1917)
Misc. Silents
GOLD AND THE WOMAN(1916); LITTLE MISS HAPPINESS(1916); MERELY MARY ANN(1916); MODERN THELMA, A(1916); RAGGED PRINCESS, THE(1916); STRENGTH OF THE WEAK, THE(1916); EVERY GIRL'S DREAM(1917); HEART AND SOUL(1917); HER GREATEST LOVE(1917); PATSY(1917); SET FREE(1918); SUCCESSFUL ADVENTURE, THE(1918); CHEATING HERSELF(1919); LITTLE ROWDY, THE(1919); LITTLE WHITE SAVAGE, THE(1919); DANGEROUS TALENT, THE(1920); GIRL IN NUMBER 29, THE(1920)
Harry S. Hilliard
Silents
CAPRICE OF THE MOUNTAINS(1916)
Henry Hilliard
WE'LL SMILE AGAIN(1942, Brit.)
Jacqueline Dalya Hilliard
MYSTERY SUBMARINE(1950)
Mabel Hilliard
Silents
SALOMY JANE(1914)
Patricia Hilliard
GIRL IN THE CROWD, THE(1934, Brit.); PRIVATE LIFE OF DON JUAN, THE(1934, Brit.); FULL CIRCLE(1935, Brit.); GHOST GOES WEST, THE(1936); LIMPING MAN, THE(1936, Brit.); THINGS TO COME(1936, Brit.); NIGHT JOURNEY(1938, Brit.); TROOPSHIP(1938, Brit.); GENTLEMAN'S GENTLEMAN, A(1939, Brit.); SHADOWED EYES(1939, Brit.); MISSING MILLION, THE(1942, Brit.)
Richard Hilliard
WILD IS MY LOVE(1963), p&d, w; PLAYGROUND, THE(1965), p&d
Richard L. Hilliard
CURSE OF THE LIVING CORPSE, THE(1964), ph; HORROR OF PARTY BEACH, THE(1964), w, ph; PSYCHOMANIA(1964), d, w
Ruth Hilliard
MURDER AT THE VANITIES(1934); ALL-AMERICAN SWEETHEART(1937); CRIMINALS OF THE AIR(1937); GIRLS CAN PLAY(1937); PAID TO DANCE(1937); EXTORTION(1938); WHO KILLED GAIL PRESTON?(1938); TROCADERO(1944)
Ryan Hilliard
NIGHT OF THE ZOMBIES(1981)
Stafford Hilliard
LOYALTIES(1934, Brit.); PATH OF GLORY, THE(1934, Brit.); SECRET OF THE LOCH, THE(1934, Brit.); HANDLE WITH CARE(1935, Brit.); WANDERING JEW, THE(1935, Brit.); MAN IN THE MIRROR, THE(1936, Brit.); COMMAND PERFORMANCE(1937, Brit.); TALK OF THE DEVIL(1937, Brit.); REBEL SON, THE ½(1939, Brit.); SPY OF NAPOLEON(1939, Brit.); SPELL OF AMY NUGENT, THE(1945, Brit.)

Vera Hilliard
QUEEN OF HEARTS(1936, Brit.)
Ernest Hilliarp
Silents
LET IT RAIN(1927)
Peg Hillias
STREETCAR NAMED DESIRE, A(1951); PEYTON PLACE(1957); WAYWARD GIRL, THE(1957)
Verna D. Hillie
SIX OF A KIND(1934)
Verna Hillie
DUCK SOUP(1933); FROM HELL TO HEAVEN(1933); MAN OF THE FOREST(1933); UNDER THE TONTO RIM(1933); HOUSE OF MYSTERY(1934); SEARCH FOR BEAUTY(1934); STAR PACKER, THE(1934); TRAIL BEYOND, THE(1934); I'VE BEEN AROUND(1935); MR. DYNAMITE(1935); PRINCESS O'HARA(1935); RESCUE SQUAD(1935); REBELLIOUS DAUGHTERS(1938)
Claire Hillier
Silents
SONG OF THE WAGE SLAVE, THE(1915)
Cyril Hillier
FATAL HOUR, THE(1937, Brit.)
Edwin Hillier
ISN'T LIFE WONDERFUL!(1953, Brit.), ph; DAM BUSTERS, THE(1955, Brit.), ph; SHADOW OF THE EAGLE(1955, Brit.), ph; MARK OF THE HAWK, THE(1958), ph; SCHOOL FOR SCOUNDRELS(1960, Brit.), ph; LONG AND THE SHORT AND THE TALL, THE(1961, Brit.), ph; POT CARRIERS, THE(1962, Brit.), ph; QUILLER MEMORANDUM, THE(1966, Brit.), ph
Erwin Hillier
LADY FROM LISBON(1942, Brit.), ph; BUTLER'S DILEMMA, THE(1943, Brit.), ph; RHYTHM SERENADE(1943, Brit.), ph; CANTERBURY TALE, A(1944, Brit.), ph; WELCOME, MR. WASHINGTON(1944, Brit.), ph; GREAT DAY(1945, Brit.), ph; SILVER FLEET, THE(1945, Brit.), ph; THEY KNEW MR. KNIGHT(1945, Brit.), ph; HIGH FURY(1947, Brit.), ph; MARK OF CAIN, THE(1948, Brit.), ph; MR. PERRIN AND MR. TRAILL(1948, Brit.), ph; OCTOBER MAN, THE(1948, Brit.), ph; INTERRUPTED JOURNEY, THE(1949, Brit.), ph; PRIVATE ANGELO(1949, Brit.), ph; WEAKER SEX, THE(1949, Brit.), ph; HAPPY GO LOVELY(1951, Brit.), ph; CASTLE IN THE AIR(1952, Brit.), ph; FATHER'S DOING FINE(1952, Brit.), ph; WHERE'S CHARLEY?(1952, Brit.), ph; HOUSE OF THE ARROW, THE(1953, Brit.), ph; MY HEART GOES CRAZY(1953, Brit.), ph; YOUNG WIVES' TALE(1954, Brit.), ph; WILL ANY GENTLEMAN?(1955, Brit.), ph; NOW AND FOREVER(1956, Brit.), ph; LET'S BE HAPPY(1957, Brit.), ph; GIRLS AT SEA(1958, Brit.), ph; NAKED EARTH, THE(1958, Brit.), ph; SHAKE HANDS WITH THE DEVIL(1959, Ireland), ph; NAKED EDGE, THE(1961), ph; GO TO BLAZES(1962, Brit.), ph; MATTER OF WHO, A(1962, Brit.), ph; BOY TEN FEET TALL, A(1965, Brit.), ph; OPERATION CROSSBOW(1965, U.S./Ital.), ph; SANDS OF THE KALAHARI(1965, Brit.), ph; EYE OF THE DEVIL(1967, Brit.), ph; SHOES OF THE FISHERMAN, THE(1968), ph; VALLEY OF GWANGI, THE(1969), ph
Florette Hillier
HOUSE OF FEAR, THE(1945)
Rose Hillier
KNACK ... AND HOW TO GET IT, THE(1965, Brit.); POOR COW(1968, Brit.)
Stuart Hillier
HIGH JUMP(1959, Brit.); WEEKEND WITH LULU, A(1961, Brit.)
Candace Hilligoss
CARNIVAL OF SOULS(1962); CURSE OF THE LIVING CORPSE, THE(1964)
Katherine Hilliker
CHRISTINA(1929), w, ed; LUCKY STAR(1929), ed; CITY GIRL(1930), ed
Silents
LOVE'S PENALTY(1921), t&ed; WELCOME STRANGER(1924), t; BEN-HUR(1925), t; PRAIRIE WIFE, THE(1925), t, ed; TORRENT, THE(1926), t; SEVENTH HEAVEN(1927), t, ed; SUNRISE–A SONG OF TWO HUMANS(1927), t, ed; AWAKENING, THE(1928), t, ed; FOUR SONS(1928), t; GATEWAY OF THE MOON, THE(1928), t; NO OTHER WOMAN(1928), t; ETERNAL LOVE(1929), t; RESCUE, THE(1929), t, ed
Jacques Hilling
BEDEVILLED(1955); FRENCH CANCAN(1956, Fr.); GERVAISE(1956, Fr.); HUNCHBACK OF NOTRE DAME, THE(1957, Fr.); PARIS DOES STRANGE THINGS(1957, Fr./Ital.); MAIGRET LAYS A TRAP(1958, Fr.); TRUTH, THE(1961, Fr./Ital.); CARTOUCHE(1962, Fr./Ital.)
John Hilling
IN THE DOGHOUSE(1964, Brit.), cos; FROM BEYOND THE GRAVE(1974, Brit.), cos; INTERNATIONAL VELVET(1978, Brit.), cos
Wolf Hillinger
REQUIEM FOR A SECRET AGENT(1966, Ital.); SAILOR FROM GIBRALTAR, THE(1967, Brit.); ANZIO(1968, Ital.)
Wolfgang Hillinger
MODESTY BLAISE(1966, Brit.); DANGER: DIABOLIK(1968, Ital./Fr.); FELLINI SATYRICON(1969, Fr./Ital.); NARCO MEN, THE(1969, Span./Ital.)
Alfred Hillman
BLOB, THE(1958), ed
Bernard M. Hillman
NOBODY'S PERFECT(1968), tech adv
Bill Hillman
ICE STATION ZEBRA(1968)
Carl Hillman
THUNDER IN DIXIE(1965), art d
Dwayne Hillman
STARSTRUCK(1982, Aus.)
George Hillman
LAST EMBRACE(1979)
Gertrude Hillman
Misc. Silents
MARIE, LTD.(1919); SOMETHING DIFFERENT(1920); RADIO-MANIA(1923)
Gordon Malherbe Hillman
GREAT MAN VOTES, THE(1939), w; HERE I AM A STRANGER(1939), w
June Hillman
RIVER, THE(1951); LES MISERABLES(1952)
Les Hillman
WHEN EIGHT BELLS TOLL(1971, Brit.), spec eff; BILLY TWO HATS(1973, Brit.), spec eff

Leslie Hillman
DIAMONDS ARE FOREVER(1971, Brit.), spec eff
Mary Hillman
MIDNIGHT EXPRESS(1978, Brit.), makeup
Philip Hillman
GIVE ME THE STARS(1944, Brit.)
Tom Hillman
OUTSIDERS, THE(1983)
William Byron Hillman
DOUBLE EXPOSURE(1982), p,d&w
William Hillman
1984
LOVELINES(1984), w
Beverly Hills
BREAKFAST AT TIFFANY'S(1961); COMEDY OF TERRORS, THE(1964); I'LL TAKE SWEDEN(1965); LOVED ONE, THE(1965); YOUNG DILLINGER(1965); LAST CHALLENGE, THE(1967); BRIDES OF BLOOD(1968, US/Phil.); SPEEDWAY(1968); SPLIT, THE(1968)
David Hills
Misc. Talkies
ATOR: THE FIGHTING EAGLE(1983), d; ATOR, THE INVINCIBLE(1984), d
Denis Hills
AMIN–THE RISE AND FALL(1982, Kenya)
Frank Hills
THREE RUSSIAN GIRLS(1943), spec eff
Gillian Hills
LES LIAISONS DANGEREUSES(1961, Fr./Ital.); TALES OF PARIS(1962, Fr./Ital.); BLOW-UP(1966, Brit.); INADMISSIBLE EVIDENCE(1968, Brit.); THREE(1969, Brit.); CLOCKWORK ORANGE, A(1971, Brit.); DEMONS OF THE MIND(1972, Brit.)
H. F. Hills
WHITE CORRIDORS(1952, Brit.)
H.S. Hills
NEVER LOOK BACK(1952, Brit.)
Joan Hills
Misc. Talkies
BLANCHEVILLE MONSTER(1963)
R.M. Hills
SPYLARKS(1965, Brit.), w; MAGNIFICENT TWO, THE(1967, Brit.), w
Reginald Hills
BROTHER SUN, SISTER MOON(1973, Brit./Ital.), ed
Richard Hills
CARRY ON CABBIE(1963, Brit.), w
Richard M. Hills
THAT RIVIERA TOUCH(1968, Brit.), w
George Hillsden
WRONG BOX, THE(1966, Brit.)
Harvey Hillyer
PARTY PARTY(1983, Brit.)
Lambert Hillyer
BEAU BANDIT(1930), d; HIDE-OUT, THE(1930), w; DEADLINE, THE(1932), d&w; FIGHTING FOOL, THE(1932), d; HELLO TROUBLE(1932), d&w; ONE-MAN LAW(1932), d&w; SOUTH OF THE RIO GRANDE(1932), d; WHITE EAGLE(1932), d; CALIFORNIA TRAIL, THE(1933), d; MASTER OF MEN(1933), d; POLICE CAR 17(1933), d&w; STATE TROOPER(1933), w; SUNDOWN RIDER, THE(1933), d, w; UNKNOWN VALLEY(1933), d&w; AGAINST THE LAW(1934), d; BEFORE MIDNIGHT(1934), d; DEFENSE HESTS, THE(1934), d; FIGHTING CODE, THE(1934), d&w; MAN TRAILER, THE(1934), d&w; MEN OF THE NIGHT(1934), d&w; MOST PRECIOUS THING IN LIFE(1934), d; ONCE TO EVERY WOMAN(1934), d; ONE IS GUILTY(1934), d; STRAIGHTAWAY(1934), w; AWAKENING OF JIM BURKE(1935), d; BEHIND THE EVIDENCE(1935), d; GUARD THAT GIRL(1935), d&w; IN SPITE OF DANGER(1935), d; LAW BEYOND THE RANGE(1935), w; MEN OF THE HOUR(1935), d; SUPERSPEED(1935), d; DANGEROUS WATERS(1936), d; DRACULA'S DAUGHTER(1936), d; FORBIDDEN TRAIL(1936), d; THE INVISIBLE RAY(1936), d; ALL-AMERICAN SWEETHEART(1937), d; GIRLS CAN PLAY(1937), d, w; SPEED TO SPARE(1937), d, w; EXTORTION(1938), d; GANG BULLETS(1938), d; HIGHWAY PATROL(1938), w; MY OLD KENTUCKY HOME(1938), d; WOMEN IN PRISON(1938), d; CONVICT'S CODE(1939), d; GIRL FROM RIO, THE(1939), d; SHOULD A GIRL MARRY?(1939), d; DURANGO KID, THE(1940), d; BEYOND THE SACRAMENTO(1941), d; KING OF DODGE CITY(1941), d; MEDICO OF PAINTED SPRINGS, THE(1941), d; NORTH FROM LONE STAR(1941), d; OFFICER AND THE LADY, THE(1941), d; PINTO KID, THE(1941), d; PRAIRIE STRANGER(1941), d; RETURN OF DANIEL BOONE, THE(1941), d; ROYAL MOUNTED PATROL(1941), d; SON OF DAVY CROCKETT, THE(1941), d&w; THUNDER OVER THE PRAIRIE(1941), d; WILDCAT OF TUCSON(1941), d; DEVIL'S TRAIL, THE(1942), d; FIGHTING FRONTIER(1943), d; SIX GUN GOSPEL(1943), d; SMART GUY(1943), d; STRANGER FROM PECOS, THE(1943), d; GHOST GUNS(1944), d; LAND OF THE OUTLAWS(1944), d; LAW MEN(1944), d; PARTNERS OF THE TRAIL(1944), d; RANGE LAW(1944), d; TEXAS KID, THE(1944), d; BEYOND THE PECOS(1945), d; FLAME OF THE WEST(1945), d; FRONTIER FEUD(1945), d; LOST TRAIL, THE(1945), d; SOUTH OF THE RIO GRANDE(1945), d; BORDER BANDITS(1946), d; GENTLEMAN FROM TEXAS(1946), w; UNDER ARIZONA SKIES(1946), d; FLASHING GUNS(1947), d; LAND OF THE LAWLESS(1947), d; PRAIRIE EXPRESS(1947), d; RAIDERS OF THE SOUTH(1947), d; CROSSED TRAILS(1948), d; FIGHTING RANGER, THE(1948), d; FRONTIER AGENT(1948), d; GUN TALK(1948), d; OKLAHOMA BLUES(1948), d; OUTLAW BRAND(1948), d; PARTNERS OF THE SUNSET(1948), d; RANGE RENEGADES(1948), d; SONG OF THE DRIFTER(1948), d; SUNDOWN RIDERS(1948), d; GUN LAW JUSTICE(1949), d; GUN RUNNER(1949), d; RANGE LAND(1949), d; RIDERS OF THE DUSK(1949), d; TRAIL'S END(1949), d
Misc. Talkies
SUNDOWN RIDER(1933), d; MAN TRAILER, THE(1934), d; HANDS ACROSS THE ROCKIES(1941), d; ROARING FRONTIERS(1941), d; NORTH OF THE ROCKIES(1942), d; PRAIRIE GUNSMOKE(1942), d; VENGEANCE OF THE WEST(1942), d; WEST OF THE RIO GRANDE(1944), d; STRANGER FROM SANTA FE(1945), d; SHADOWS ON THE RANGE(1946), d; SILVER RANGE(1946), d; TRIGGER FINGERS(1946), d; LAW COMES TO GUNSIGHT, THE(1947), d; TRAILING DANGER(1947), d; VALLEY OF FEAR(1947), d; OVERLAND TRAILS(1948), d; SHERIFF OF MEDICINE BOW, THE(1948), d; HAUNTED TRAILS(1949), d
Silents
LITTLE BROTHER, THE(1917), w; ONE SHOT ROSS(1917), w; BRANDING BROADWAY(1918), d; BREED OF MEN(1919), d; MONEY CORRAL, THE(1919), d&w; POP-

PY GIRL'S HUSBAND, THE(1919), d; SAND(1920), d, w; TESTING BLOCK, THE(1920), d&w; TOLL GATE, THE(1920), d, w; O'MALLEY OF THE MOUNTED(1921), d; WHITE OAK(1921), d; ALTAR STAIRS, THE(1922), d; SUPER-SEX, THE(1922), d&w; TRAVELIN' ON(1922), d&w; WHITE HANDS(1922), d&w; SCARS OF JEALOUSY(1923), d&w; SHOCK, THE(1923), d; TEMPORARY MARRIAGE(1923), d, w; KNOCKOUT, THE(1925), d; UNGUARDED HOUR, THE(1925), d; MISS NOBODY(1926), d; WAR HORSE, THE(1927), d&w
Misc. Silents
EVEN BREAK, AN(1917), d; NARROW TRAIL, THE(1917), d; RIDDLE GAWNE(1918), d; JOHN PETTICOATS(1919), d; WAGON TRACKS(1919), d; CRADLE OF COURAGE, THE(1920), d; TOLL GATE, THE(1920), d; THREE WORD BRAND(1921), d; WHISTLE, THE(1921), d; CAUGHT BLUFFING(1922), d; SKIN DEEP(1922), d; EYES OF THE FOREST(1923), d; LONE STAR RANGER, THE(1923), d; MILE-A-MINUTE ROMEO(1923), d; SPOILERS, THE(1923), d; BARBARA FRIETCHIE(1924), d; IDLE TONGUES(1924), d; THOSE WHO DANCE(1924), d; I WANT MY MAN(1925), d; MAKING OF O'MALLEY, THE(1925), d; CHAIN LIGHTING(1927), d; HILLS OF PERIL(1927), d; BRANDED SOMBRERO, THE(1928), d; FLEETWING(1928), d
Sharon Hillyer
KARATE KILLERS, THE(1967)
Sharyn Hillyer
HUD(1963); GUIDE FOR THE MARRIED MAN, A(1967)
Heinz Hilpert
GOLDEN PLAGUE, THE(1963, Ger.)
George Hilsden
FIENDISH PLOT OF DR. FU MANCHU, THE(1980)
George Hilsdon
SKULL, THE(1965, Brit.); MADWOMAN OF CHAILLOT, THE(1969); LONG AGO, TOMORROW(1971, Brit.)
George Hilson
DULCIMA(1971, Brit.)
Rondi Hilstrom-Davis
1984
NOT FOR PUBLICATION(1984), cos
Robert Hilt
MONSTER OF HIGHGATE PONDS, THE(1961, Brit.), ed
Anthony Hilton
SHE SHALL HAVE MURDER(1950, Brit.)
Arthur Hilton
UNCLE HARRY(1945), ed; CAPTAIN THUNDER(1931), ed; VIRTUOUS HUSBAND(1931), ad; NIGHT OF TERROR(1933), ed; WHAT PRICE INNOCENCE?(1933), ed; THAT'S GRATITUDE(1934), ed; HIGH SCHOOL GIRL(1935), ed; SWELLHEAD(1935), ed; TOGETHER WE LIVE(1935), ed; UNWELCOME STRANGER(1935), ed; MINE WITH THE IRON DOOR, THE(1936), ed; O'MALLEY OF THE MOUNTED(1936), ed; CALIFORNIAN, THE(1937), ed; MAKE A WISH(1937), ed; THUNDER IN THE CITY(1937, Brit.), ed; BREAKING THE ICE(1938), ed; HAWAII CALLS(1938), ed; PECK'S BAD BOY WITH THE CIRCUS(1938), ed; ROLL ALONG, COWBOY(1938), ed; ESCAPE TO PARADISE(1939), ed; EVERYTHING'S ON ICE(1939), ed; FISHERMAN'S WHARF(1939), ed; WAY DOWN SOUTH(1939), ed; BANK DICK, THE(1940), ed; LEATHER-PUSHERS, THE(1940), ed; MEET THE WILDCAT(1940), ed; VILLAIN STILL PURSUED HER, THE(1940), ed; KEEP 'EM FLYING(1941), ed; KID FROM KANSAS, THE(1941), ed; MAN MADE MONSTER(1941), ed; MOB TOWN(1941), ed; MODEL WIFE(1941), ed; MOONLIGHT IN HAWAII(1941), ed; NEVER GIVE A SUCKER AN EVEN BREAK(1941), ed; SEALED LIPS(1941), ed; SING ANOTHER CHORUS(1941), ed; MISSISSIPPI GAMBLER(1942), ed; PARDON MY SARONG(1942), ed; WHAT'S COOKIN'?(1942), ed; WHO DONE IT?(1942), ed; CRAZY HOUSE(1943), ed; FLESH AND FANTASY(1943), ed; GALS, INCORPORATED(1943), ed; BOWERY TO BROADWAY(1944), ed; GHOST CATCHERS(1944), ed; PHANTOM LADY(1944), ed; SUSPECT, THE(1944), ed; HERE COME THE CO-EDS(1945), ed; NAUGHTY NINETIES, THE(1945), ed; SCARLET STREET(1945), ed; UNDER WESTERN SKIES(1945), ed; KILLERS, THE(1946), ed; LET'S LIVE A LITTLE(1948), ed; SECRET BEYOND THE DOOR, THE(1948), ed; I CHEATED THE LAW(1949), ed; BARON OF ARIZONA, THE(1950), ed; BLONDE BANDIT, THE(1950), ed; THREE FOR BEDROOM C(1952), ed; CAT WOMEN OF THE MOON(1953), d; BIG CHASE, THE(1954), d; GUN BROTHERS(1956), ed; POLICE DOG STORY, THE(1961), ed
Arthur D. Hilton
HOUSE BY THE RIVER(1950), ed
Arthur David Hilton
RETURN OF JESSE JAMES, THE(1950), d
Arthur L. Hilton
HARRY IN YOUR POCKET(1973), ed
Collins Hilton
ON THE BEACH(1959)
Constance Hilton
ON THE LOOSE(1951)
Daisy Hilton
CHAINED FOR LIFE(1950)
David Hilton
ROSE BOWL STORY, THE(1952), art d
Edward Hilton
DAVID AND GOLIATH(1961, Ital.)
Francesca Hilton
SAFE PLACE, A(1971)
Frank Hilton
Silents
ON THE QUIET(1918)
Misc. Silents
IN SEARCH OF A HUSBAND(1915, Brit.)
George Hilton
ANY GUN CAN PLAY(1968, Ital./Span.); BRUTE AND THE BEAST, THE(1968, Ital.); RUTHLESS FOUR, THE(1969, Ital./Ger.); SWEET BODY OF DEBORAH, THE(1969, Ital./Fr.); VENGEANCE IS MINE(1969, Ital./Span.); BULLET FOR SANDOVAL, A(1970, Ital./Span.); NEXT!(1971, Ital./Span.)
Misc. Talkies
BATTLE OF EL ALAMEIN(1971); NEXT VICTIM(1971); SALT IN THE WOUND(1972); THEY CALL ME HALLELUJAH(1973); DEMONS OF THE DEAD(1976, Brit.); THEY'RE COMING TO GET YOU(1976); DEVIL HAS SEVEN FACES, THE(1977)

Harlan Hilton
Silents
LILAC TIME(1928)
Helen Hilton
Silents
HOW MOLLY MADE GOOD(1915)
James Hilton
CAMILLE(1937), w; KNIGHT WITHOUT ARMOR(1937, Brit.), w; LOST HORI-
ZON(1937), w; GOODBYE MR. CHIPS(1939, Brit.), w; WE ARE NOT ALONE(1939), w;
FOREIGN CORRESPONDENT(1940), w; RAGE IN HEAVEN(1941), w; MRS. MINI-
VER(1942), w; RANDOM HARVEST(1942), w; TUTTLES OF TAHITI(1942), w;
FOREVER AND A DAY(1943), w; MADAME CURIE(1943); STORY OF DR. WASSELL,
THE(1944), w; SO WELL REMEMBERED(1947, Brit.), a, w; GOODBYE MR.
CHIPS(1969, U.S./Brit.), w; LOST HORIZON(1973), w
Jasmina Hilton
VAULT OF HORROR, THE(1973, Brit.)
John Hilton
SOUTHERN YANKEE, A(1948); WATERFRONT AT MIDNIGHT(1948); SPECIAL
AGENT(1949)
Kathy Hilton
Misc. Talkies
COCKTAIL HOSTESSES, THE(1976)
LaSesne Hilton
DEATHMASTER, THE(1972)
Les Hilton
SMOKY(1966), anim t
Paul Hilton
MURDER, MY SWEET(1945); STRANGE HOLIDAY(1945)
Robert Hilton
COW TOWN(1950); INDIAN TERRITORY(1950); MULE TRAIN(1950); GENE AUTRY
AND THE MOUNTIES(1951); OLD WEST, THE(1952)
Robyn Hilton
LAST PORNO FLICK, THE(1974); DOC SAVAGE... THE MAN OF BRONZE(1975)
Rovamel Hilton
IN SOCIETY(1944)
Roxanne Hilton
TANGIER(1946)
Tony Hilton
NORMAN CONQUEST(1953, Brit.); HAND, THE(1960, Brit.), a, w; NIGHT WE GOT
THE BIRD, THE(1961, Brit.), w; WHAT A CARVE UP!(1962, Brit.), w
Violet Hilton
FREAKS(1932); CHAINED FOR LIFE(1950)
Lawrence Hilton-Jacobs
CLAUDINE(1974)
Roxanne Hiltron
ROYAL SCANDAL, A(1945)
Jim Hiltz
YELLOW SUBMARINE(1958, Brit.), animation; SHINBONE ALLEY(1971), anim
Robert Hiltzik
SLEEPAWAY CAMP(1983), d&w
Helene Hily
1984
AMERICAN DREAMER(1984)
Dene Hilyard
VENGEANCE(1964), d
Christopher Himaras
NAKED BRIGADE, THE(1965, U.S./Gr.)
Karin Himbold
TALE OF FIVE WOMEN, A(1951, Brit.)
Masahisa Himeda
INSECT WOMAN, THE(1964, Jap.), ph; UNHOLY DESIRE(1964, Jap.), ph; EAST
CHINA SEA(1969, Jap.), ph
Shinsaku Himeda
TORA! TORA! TORA!(1970, U.S./Jap.), ph; VENGEANCE IS MINE(1980, Jap.), ph
Howard Himelstein
MAX DUGAN RETURNS(1983)
Chester Himes
COTTON COMES TO HARLEM(1970), w; COME BACK CIHARLESTON
BLUE(1972), w
John Himes
NIGHT OF EVIL(1962); LAWYER, THE(1969); DEATHSPORT(1978)
John W. Himes
CHRISTINE JORGENSEN STORY, THE(1970)
Madelyn Himes
LOVE AND KISSES(1965)
Masahisa Himi
YOG-MONSTER FROM SPACE(1970, Jap.), ed
Carl Himm
WELCOME DANGER(1929), ed; FOURTH ALARM, THE(1930), ed; LOTUS LA-
DY(1930), ed; UNDER MONTANA SKIES(1930), ed; WORLDLY GOODS(1930), ed; IN
OLD CHEYENNE(1931), ed; RIDERS OF THE NORTH(1931), ph; WEST OF
CHEYENNE(1931), ed; TARZAN THE FEARLESS(1933), ed; FEUD OF THE
WEST(1936), ed; RIDING AVENGER, THE(1936), ed; SPEED REPORTER(1936), ed;
SWIFTY(1936), ed; SANTA FE BOUND(1937), ed; DANGEROUS LADY(1941), ed;
LAW OF THE TIMBER(1941), ed; TOO MANY WOMEN(1942), ed; WHAT A
MAN!(1944), ed
Silents
KING OF THE WILD HORSES, THE(1924), w
Michael Himm
GUN FEVER(1958)
Otto Himm
CODE OF HONOR(1930), ph; UNDER TEXAS SKIES(1931), ph; TEX TAKES A
HOLIDAY(1932), ph
Scott Himm
LAST DANCE, THE(1930), ed
Shinichi Himori
IKIRU(1960, Jap.)

William Hinant
FOUR BOYS AND A GUN(1957)
Michael Hinchcliffe
GAMEKEEPER, THE(1980, Brit.)
Tamara Hinchco
PRIVATE RIGHT, THE(1967, Brit.)
Pippa Hinchley
1984
SECRET PLACES(1984, Brit.)
Bert Hinchman
STINGRAY(1978); DREAMER(1979); SECOND THOUGHTS(1983)
Warren Hinckle
BREAKOUT(1975), w
Alfred Hinckley
LADY LIBERTY(1972, Ital./Fr.)
William Hinckley
Silents
MARTHA'S VINDICATION(1916); AMAZONS, THE(1917); BAB'S BURGLAR(1917)
Misc. Silents
WOLF-MAN, THE(1915); CHILDREN IN THE HOUSE, THE(1916); REPUTA-
TION(1917); SECRET OF EVE, THE(1917)
C. J. Hincks
NIGHT MOVES(1975)
Reginald Hincks
SECRETS OF CHINATOWN(1935); SECRET PATROL(1936); STAMPEDE(1936);
FIGHTING PLAYBOY(1937); FURY AND THE WOMAN(1937); WHAT PRICE VEN-
GEANCE?(1937); WOMAN AGAINST THE WORLD(1938); DEATH GOES
NORTH(1939); MANHATTAN SHAKEDOWN(1939)
Charles Hincus
Silents
ALI BABA AND THE FORTY THIEVES(1918)
Bill Hind
NIGHT AND DAY(1946)
Madeline Hinde
INCENSE FOR THE DAMNED(1970, Brit.); LAST VALLEY, THE(1971, Brit.);
CHARLEY-ONE-EYE(1973, Brit.); SCHOOL FOR UNCLAIMED GIRLS(1973, Brit.)
Misc. Talkies
BEWARE MY BRETHREN(1972, Brit.); HELL HOUSE GIRLS(1975, Brit.)
Harry Hindemith
SOMEWHERE IN BERLIN(1949, E. Ger.); OUR DAILY BREAD(1950, Ger.)
Art Hindle
BLACK CHRISTMAS(1974, Can.); SMALL TOWN IN TEXAS, A(1976); INVASION OF
THE BODY SNATCHERS(1978); BROOD, THE(1979, Can.); OCTAGON, THE(1980);
PORKY'S(1982); MAN WHO WASN'T THERE, THE(1983); PORKY'S II: THE NEXT
DAY(1983)
1984
RAW COURAGE(1984); SURROGATE, THE(1984, Can.)
Misc. Talkies
WINTER COMES EARLY(1972)
Colin Hindley
PROSTITUTE(1980, Brit.)
Richard Hindley
ON THE RUN(1983, Aus.), ed
Bill Hindman
ABSENCE OF MALICE(1981); PORKY'S(1982); NIGHT IN HEAVEN, A(1983)
Earl Hindman
TAKING OF PELHAM ONE, TWO, THREE, THE(1974); WHO KILLED MARY
WHAT'SER NAME?(1971); PARALLAX VIEW, THE(1974); SHOOT IT: BLACK,
SHOOT IT: BLUE(1974); GREASED LIGHTNING(1977); BRINK'S JOB, THE(1978);
TAPS(1981)
William Hindman
PORKY'S II: THE NEXT DAY(1983)
Heinz Hindrich
ROMAN HOLIDAY(1953)
Alf Hinds
GOOD DIE YOUNG, THE(1954, Brit.)
Anthony Hinds
ADVENTURES OF PC 49, THE(1949, Brit.), p; CELIA(1949, Brit.), p; DICK BARTON
STRIKES BACK(1949, Brit.), p; DR. MORELLE-THE CASE OF THE MISSING
HEIRESS(1949, Brit.), p; MEET SIMON CHERRY(1949, Brit.), p; ROOM TO LET(1949,
Brit.), p; LADY CRAVED EXCITEMENT, THE(1950, Brit.), p; MAN IN BLACK,
THE(1950, Brit.), p; ROSSITER CASE, THE(1950, Brit.), p; SOMEONE AT THE
DOOR(1950, Brit.), p; WHAT THE BUTLER SAW(1950, Brit.), p; BLACK WI-
DOW(1951, Brit.), p; CASE FOR PC 49, A(1951, Brit.), p; TO HAVE AND TO
HOLD(1951, Brit.), p; CLOUDBURST(1952, Brit.), p; DEAD ON COURSE(1952, Brit.),
p; DEATH OF AN ANGEL(1952, Brit.), p; GAMBLER AND THE LADY, THE(1952,
Brit.), p; MAN BAIT(1952, Brit.), p; SCOTLAND YARD INSPECTOR(1952, Brit.), p;
STOLEN FACE(1952, Brit.), p; WHISPERING SMITH VERSUS SCOTLAND
YARD(1952, Brit.), p; BAD BLONDE(1953, Brit.), p; TERROR STREET(1953, Brit.),
p; HEATWAVE(1954, Brit.), p; PAID TO KILL(1954, Brit.), p; SAINT'S GIRL FRIDAY,
THE(1954, Brit.), p; GLASS TOMB, THE(1955, Brit.), p; BLONDE BAIT(1956, U.S./
Brit.), p; THE CREEPING UNKNOWN(1956, Brit.), p; CURSE OF FRANKENSTEIN,
THE(1957, Brit.), p; ENEMY FROM SPACE(1957, Brit.), p; X THE UNKNOWN(1957,
Brit.), p; CAMP ON BLOOD ISLAND, THE(1958, Brit.), p; HORROR OF DRACULA,
THE(1958, Brit.), p; I ONLY ASKED!(1958, Brit.), p; REVENGE OF FRANKENSTEIN,
THE(1958, Brit.), p; HOUND OF THE BASKERVILLES, THE(1959, Brit.), p; BRIDES
OF DRACULA, THE(1960, Brit.), p; STRANGLERS OF BOMBAY, THE(1960, Brit.), p;
CURSE OF THE WEREWOLF, THE(1961), p; NEVER TAKE CANDY FROM A
STRANGER(1961, Brit.), p; NIGHT CREATURES(1962, Brit.), w; PHANTOM OF THE
OPERA, THE(1962, Brit.), p; KISS OF EVIL(1963, Brit.), p; OLD DARK HOUSE,
THE(1963, Brit.), p; PARANOIAC(1963, Brit.), p; EVIL OF FRANKENSTEIN,
THE(1964, Brit.), p; DIE, DIE, MY DARLING(1965, Brit.), p; THESE ARE THE
DAMNED(1965, Brit.), p
Ciarin Hinds
EXCALIBUR(1981)
Cindy Hinds
BROOD, THE(1979, Can.)
Misc. Talkies
DEADLINE(1984)

Errol Hinds
CLAIRVOYANT, THE(1935, Brit.), ph; RANGLE RIVER(1939, Aus.), ph
Joe Hinds
GOOD SAM(1948)
Nandu Hinds
CHINATOWN(1974)
Samuel Hinds
BED OF ROSES(1933); DAY OF RECKONING(1933); DELUGE(1933); GABRIEL OVER THE WHITE HOUSE(1933); HOLD THE PRESS(1933); FOG(1934); HAT, COAT AND GLOVE(1934); BEHIND THE EVIDENCE(1935); DR. SOCRATES(1935); FATAL LADY(1936)
Samuel S. Hinds
IF I HAD A MILLION(1932); BERKELEY SQUARE(1933); CRIME OF THE CENTURY, THE(1933); LITTLE WOMEN(1933); NUISANCE, THE(1933); ONE MAN'S JOURNEY(1933); SON OF A SAILOR(1933); THIS DAY AND AGE(1933); BIG SHAKEDOWN, THE(1934); CAT'S PAW, THE(1934); CRIME DOCTOR, THE(1934); EVELYN PRENTICE(1934); HAVE A HEART(1934); HE WAS HER MAN(1934); LOST LADY, A(1934); MANHATTAN MELODRAMA(1934); MASSACRE(1934); MEN IN WHITE(1934); NINTH GUEST, THE(1934); NO GREATER GLORY(1934); SEQUOIA(1934); SISTERS UNDER THE SKIN(1934); STRAIGHTAWAY(1934); WOMEN IN HIS LIFE, THE(1934); ACCENT ON YOUTH(1935); ANNAPOLIS FAREWELL(1935); BIG BROADCAST OF 1936, THE(1935); BORDERTOWN(1935); COLLEGE SCANDAL(1935); DEVIL DOGS OF THE AIR(1935); IN PERSON(1935); LIVING ON VELVET(1935); MILLIONS(1935); MILLS OF THE GODS(1935); OIL FOR THE LAMPS OF CHINA(1935); PRIVATE WORLDS(1935); RAVEN, THE(1935); RENDEZVOUS(1935); RUMBA(1935); SECRET BRIDE, THE(1935); SHADOW OF A DOUBT(1935); SHE(1935); STRANGERS ALL(1935); TWO FISTED(1935); WEST OF THE PECOS(1935); WINGS IN THE DARK(1935); BORDER FLIGHT(1936); GORGEOUS HUSSY, THE(1936); HIS BROTHER'S WIFE(1936); LONGEST NIGHT, THE(1936); LOVE LETTERS OF A STAR(1936); RHYTHM ON THE RANGE(1936); SWORN ENEMY(1936); TIMOTHY'S QUEST(1936); TRAIL OF THE LONESOME PINE, THE(1936); WOMAN TRAP(1936); BLACK LEGION, THE(1937); DOUBLE OR NOTHING(1937); GIRL WITH IDEAS, A(1937); MIGHTY TREVE, THE(1937); NAVY BLUE AND GOLD(1937); NIGHT KEY(1937); PRESCRIPTION FOR ROMANCE(1937); ROAD BACK,THE(1937); SHE'S DANGEROUS(1937); STAGE DOOR(1937); TOP OF THE TOWN(1937); WINGS OVER HONOLULU(1937); DEVIL'S PARTY, THE(1938); DOUBLE DANGER(1938); FORBIDDEN VALLEY(1938); JURY'S SECRET, THE(1938); PERSONAL SECRETARY(1938); RAGE OF PARIS, THE(1938); ROAD TO RENO, THE(1938); SECRETS OF A NURSE(1938); STORM, THE(1938); SWING THAT CHEER(1938); TEST PILOT(1938); WIVES UNDER SUSPICION(1938); YOU CAN'T TAKE IT WITH YOU(1938); YOUNG DR. KILDARE(1938); CALLING DR. KILDARE(1939); CAREER(1939); CHARLIE MC CARTHY, DETECTIVE(1939); DESTRY RIDES AGAIN(1939); EX-CHAMP(1939); FIRST LOVE(1939); HAWAIIAN NIGHTS(1939); HERO FOR A DAY(1939); NEWSBOY'S HOME(1939); ONE HOUR TO LIVE(1939); PIRATES OF THE SKIES(1939); RIO(1939); SECRET OF DR. KILDARE, THE(1939); TROPIC FURY(1939); UNDER-PUP, THE(1939); WITHIN THE LAW(1939); BOYS FROM SYRACUSE(1940); DR. KILDARE GOES HOME(1940); DR. KILDARE'S STRANGE CASE(1940); I'M NOBODY'S SWEETHEART NOW(1940); IT'S A DATE(1940); SEVEN SINNERS(1940); SKI PATROL(1940); SPRING PARADE(1940); TRAIL OF THE VIGILANTES(1940); ZANZIBAR(1940); ADVENTURE IN WASHINGTON(1941); BACK STREET(1941); BADLANDS OF DAKOTA(1941); BLOSSOMS IN THE DUST(1941); BUCK PRIVATES(1941); DR. KILDARE'S WEDDING DAY(1941); LADY FROM CHEYENNE(1941); MAN MADE MONSTER(1941); MOB TOWN(1941); ROAD AGENT(1941); SHEPHERD OF THE HILLS, THE(1941); TIGHT SHOES(1941); UNFINISHED BUSINESS(1941); FRISCO LILL(1942); GRAND CENTRAL MURDER(1942); JAIL HOUSE BLUES(1942); KID GLOVE KILLER(1942); LADY IN A JAM(1942); PARDON MY SARONG(1942); PITTSBURGH(1942); RIDE 'EM COWBOY(1942); SABOTEUR(1942); SPOILERS, THE(1942); STRANGE CASE OF DR. RX, THE(1942); FIRED WIFE(1943); FOLLOW THE BAND(1943); GOOD MORNING, JUDGE(1943); HERS TO HOLD(1943); HE'S MY GUY(1943); IT AIN'T HAY(1943); KEEP 'EM SLUGGING(1943); LARCENY WITH MUSIC(1943); MR. BIG(1943); SING A JINGLE(1943); SON OF DRACULA(1943); TOP MAN(1943); CHIP OFF THE OLD BLOCK(1944); COBRA WOMAN(1944); FOLLOW THE BOYS(1944); JUNGLE WOMAN(1944); LADIES COURAGEOUS(1944); SINGING SHERIFF, THE(1944); SOUTH OF DIXIE(1944); ESCAPE IN THE DESERT(1945); FRISCO SAL(1945); I'LL REMEMBER APRIL(1945); LADY ON A TRAIN(1945); MEN IN HER DIARY(1945); SCARLET STREET(1945); SWING OUT, SISTER(1945); UNCLE HARRY(1945); WEEKEND AT THE WALDORF(1945); BLONDE ALIBI(1946); DANGER WOMAN(1946); INSIDE JOB(1946); IT'S A WONDERFUL LIFE(1946); LITTLE MISS BIG(1946); RUNAROUND, THE(1946); STRANGE CONQUEST(1946); WHITE TIE AND TAILS(1946); EGG AND I, THE(1947); TIME OUT OF MIND(1947); PERILOUS WATERS(1948); RETURN OF OCTOBER, THE(1948); BOY WITH THE GREEN HAIR, THE(1949); BRIBE, THE(1949)
Misc. Talkies
IN SELF DEFENSE(1947)
Walter Hinds
HUMAN FACTOR, THE(1979, Brit.)
The Hindustans
OLD MOTHER RILEY'S CIRCUS(1941, Brit.)
Joseph Hindy
LOVERS AND OTHER STRANGERS(1970)
1984
CRACKERS(1984)
Al Hine
LORD LOVE A DUCK(1966), w
Kelly Hine
BLADE RUNNER(1982)
Rupert Hine
SHOUT, THE(1978, Brit.), m
Phil Hiner
HIDEOUS SUN DEMON, THE(1959), w
Alf Hines
SQUARE RING, THE(1955, Brit.)
Barbara Hines
WHO WAS THAT LADY?(1960); DAYS OF WINE AND ROSES(1962); THREE STOOGES MEET HERCULES, THE(1962); WALK ON THE WILD SIDE(1962); ISLAND OF LOVE(1963); ON HER BED OF ROSES(1966)
Barry Hines
KES(1970, Brit.), w; GAMEKEEPER, THE(1980, Brit.), w; LOOKS AND SMILES(1982, Brit.), w

Blanche Hines
Misc. Silents
BLUE-EYED MARY(1918)
Charles Hines
WINGS IN THE DARK(1935)
Silents
ARGYLE CASE, THE(1917); EARLY BIRD, THE(1925), d; STEPPING ALONG(1926), d; ALL ABOARD(1927), d; WHITE PANTS WILLIE(1927), d
Misc. Silents
CONDUCTOR 1492(1924), d; SPEED SPOOK, THE(1924), d; CRACKERJACK, THE(1925), d; LIVE WIRE, THE(1925), d; BROWN DERBY, THE(1926), d; RAINBOW RILEY(1926), d; HOME MADE(1927), d; CHINATOWN CHARLIE(1928), d; WRIGHT IDEA, THE(1928), d
Charley Hines
WINGS IN THE DARK(1935)
Cindy Hines
DEAD ZONE, THE(1983)
Connie Hines
THUNDER IN CAROLINA(1960)
Damon Hines
1984
ADVENTURES OF BUCKAROO BANZAI: ACROSS THE 8TH DIMENSION, THE(1984)
David Hines
2001: A SPACE ODYSSEY(1968, U.S./Brit.)
Dennis Hines
BUCK AND THE PREACHER(1972)
Eleanor Hines
DRUMS O' VOODOO(1934)
Frank Hines
TOGETHER FOR DAYS(1972)
Fraser Hines
STOCK CAR(1955, Brit.); WEAPON, THE(1957, Brit.); X THE UNKNOWN(1957, Brit.); SALVAGE GANG, THE(1958, Brit.)
Frazer Hines
PERIL FOR THE GUY(1956, Brit.); WITNESS IN THE DARK(1959, Brit.); WOMAN'S TEMPTATION, A(1959, Brit.); GO KART GO(1964, Brit.); LAST VALLEY, THE(1971, Brit.); ZEPPELIN(1971, Brit.)
Frazier Hines
Misc. Talkies
YOUNG JACOBITES(1959)
Gordon Hines
Misc. Silents
TRAIL DUST(1924), d
Grainger Hines
DAY OF THE LOCUST, THE(1975); SUMMER SCHOOL TEACHERS(1977)
1984
PROTOCOL(1984)
Gregory Hines
HISTORY OF THE WORLD, PART 1(1981); WOLFEN(1981); DEAL OF THE CENTURY(1983)
1984
COTTON CLUB, THE(1984), a, ch; MUPPETS TAKE MANHATTAN, THE(1984)
Harry Hines
HARVEY(1950); JACKPOT, THE(1950); ONE TOO MANY(1950); FATHER'S LITTLE DIVIDEND(1951); I CAN GET IT FOR YOU WHOLESALE(1951); MR. BELVEDERE RINGS THE BELL(1951); STRANGERS ON A TRAIN(1951); UNKNOWN MAN, THE(1951); BOOTS MALONE(1952); CARRIE(1952); KANSAS CITY CONFIDENTIAL(1952); MILLION DOLLAR MERMAID(1952); SCANDAL SHEET(1952); TALK ABOUT A STRANGER(1952); TURNING POINT, THE(1952); CITY OF BAD MEN(1953); HOUDINI(1953); LAST OF THE PONY RIDERS(1953); POWDER RIVER(1953); RAID, THE(1954); RIDING SHOTGUN(1954); FRIENDLY PERSUASION(1956); KETTLES IN THE OZARKS, THE(1956); JAILHOUSE ROCK(1957); THIS COULD BE THE NIGHT(1957); PARTY GIRL(1958); INTERNS, THE(1962)
Janear Hines
HIT(1973); DIRTY MARY, CRAZY LARRY(1974)
John Hines
MAGNIFICENT DOLL(1946)
Silents
AS YE SOW(1914); ARRIVAL OF PERPETUA, THE(1915); FAMILY CUPBOARD, THE(1915); LITTLE MISS BROWN(1915); PRICE FOR FOLLY, A(1915); JUST SYLVIA(1918)
Misc. Silents
ALIAS JIMMY VALENTINE(1915); SUNSHINE NAN(1918); HEART OF GOLD(1919); LITTLE INTRUDER, THE(1919); WHAT LOVE FORGIVES(1919)
Johnny Hines
RUNAROUND, THE(1931); GIRL IN 419(1933); HER BODYGUARD(1933); WHISTLING IN THE DARK(1933); SOCIETY DOCTOR(1935); RHYTHM RACKETEER(1937, Brit.); TOO HOT TO HANDLE(1938)
Silents
WISHING RING, THE(1914); CUB, THE(1915); ALL MAN(1916); DANCER'S PERIL, THE(1917); GIRL'S FOLLY, A(1917); TILLIE WAKES UP(1917); NEIGHBORS(1918); BURN 'EM UP BARNES(1921), a, d; SURE FIRE FLINT(1922); LUCK(1923); EARLY BIRD, THE(1925); STEPPING ALONG(1926); ALL ABOARD(1927); WHITE PANTS WILLIE(1927)
Misc. Silents
YANKEE PLUCK(1917); YOUTH(1917); STUDIO GIRL, THE(1918); EASTWARD HO!(1919); LITTLE JOHNNY JONES(1923); CONDUCTOR 1492(1924); SPEED SPOOK, THE(1924); CRACKERJACK, THE(1925); LIVE WIRE, THE(1925); BROWN DERBY, THE(1926); RAINBOW RILEY(1926); HOME MADE(1927); CHINATOWN CHARLIE(1928); WRIGHT IDEA, THE(1928)
Leonard J. Hines
GHOUL, THE(1934, Brit.), w
Maurice Hines
1984
COTTON CLUB, THE(1984)
Mimi Hines
SATURDAY NIGHT IN APPLE VALLEY(1965)

Patrick Hines
1776(1972); BRINK'S JOB, THE(1978)
1984
AMADEUS(1984)
Randy Hines
LADY LIBERTY(1972, Ital./Fr.)
Ronald Hines
DUNKIRK(1958, Brit.); TWO-HEADED SPY, THE(1959, Brit.); ECHO OF BARBARA(1961, Brit.); WHISTLE DOWN THE WIND(1961, Brit.); SEANCE ON A WET AFTERNOON(1964 Brit.); UNDERWORLD INFORMERS(1965, Brit.); YOUNG WINSTON(1972, Brit.); ROUGH CUT(1980, Brit.)
Roy Hines
CARRY ON TEACHER(1962, Brit.)
Samuel Hines
Silents
SHORE LEAVE(1925)
Samuel E. Hines
GILDED LILY, THE(1935)
Samuel S. Hines
WE'VE NEVER BEEN LICKED(1943)
W.E. Hines
HAUNTED(1976), ph
William Hines
JUMBO(1962); MARINE BATTLEGROUND(1966, U.S/S.K.), ph
Wilmer Hines
THEY WON'T FORGET(1937)
Bill Hiney
CALIFORNIA DREAMING(1979), art d
William Hiney
STAR IS BORN, A(1976), art d; LITTLE DARLINGS(1980), prod d; DEATH WISH II(1982), prod d
William M. Hiney
SCOTT JOPLIN(1977), art d; ALMOST SUMMER(1978), art d
1984
UP THE CREEK(1984), prod d
Dora Hing
AGE OF CONSENT(1969, Austral.)
Tom Hing
Misc. Silents
WAR OF THE TONGS, THE(1917)
Pat Hingle
WHEN YOU COMIN' BACK, RED RYDER?(1979); ON THE WATERFRONT(1954); NO DOWN PAYMENT(1957); STRANGE ONE, THE(1957); SPLENDOR IN THE GRASS(1961); ALL THE WAY HOME(1963); UGLY AMERICAN, THE(1963); INVITATION TO A GUNFIGHTER(1964); NEVADA SMITH(1966); HANG'EM HIGH(1968); JIGSAW(1968); SOL MADRID(1968); BLOODY MAMA(1970); NORWOOD(1970); WUSA(1970); CAREY TREATMENT, THE(1972); HAPPY AS THE GRASS WAS GREEN(1973); NIGHTMARE HONEYMOON(1973); ONE LITTLE INDIAN(1973); RUNNING WILD(1973); SUPER COPS, THE(1974); GAUNTLET, THE(1977); HAZEL'S PEOPLE(1978); NORMA RAE(1979); GOING BERSERK(1983); RUNNING BRAVE(1983, Can.); SUDDEN IMPACT(1983)
1984
ACT, THE(1984)
Misc. Talkies
DEADLY HONEYMOON(1974); DELIVER US FROM EVIL(1975); RUNNING SCARED(1980)
Charles Hinkle, Jr.
FIGHTING VALLEY(1943), ed; GANGSTERS OF THE FRONTIER(1944), ed
Ed Hinkle
FLESH AND FURY(1952); SCARLET ANGEL(1952); TREASURE OF LOST CANYON, THE(1952); DEMENTIA(1955)
Melody Hinkle
GUNS OF A STRANGER(1973)
Robert Hinkle
FIRST TRAVELING SALESLADY, THE(1956); OKLAHOMAN, THE(1957); UNDER FIRE(1957); HUD(1963); YOUNG GUNS OF TEXAS(1963); GUNS OF A STRANGER(1973), p&d
Misc. Talkies
OLE REX(1961), d; COUNTRY MUSIC(1972), d
Tim Hinkle
DR. TERROR'S GALLERY OF HORRORS(1967), ed
Del Hinkley
SURVIVORS, THE(1983)
William Hinkley
Silents
LILY AND THE ROSE, THE(1915)
Joan Hinkson
FRIENDS(1971, Brit.)
Michael Hinn
HALLIDAY BRAND, THE(1957); DEVIL'S MESSENGER, THE(1962 U.S./Swed.); VALDEZ IS COMING(1971); MECHANIC, THE(1972)
Bill Hinnant
NICE GIRL LIKE ME, A(1969, Brit.)
Skip Hinnant
PLASTIC DOME OF NORMA JEAN, THE(1966)
Misc. Talkies
NINE LIVES OF FRITZ THE CAT, THE(1974)
George Hinners
JULIUS CAESAR(1952); LOVE ISLAND(1952), ph
George F. Hinners
TWO SISTERS(1938), ph
Giovanni Hinrich
WANDERING JEW, THE(1948, Ital.); CROSSROADS OF PASSION(1951, Fr.)
Hans Hinrich
WANDERING JEW, THE(1948, Ital.)
Hartmuth Hinrichs
FOUNTAIN OF LOVE, THE(1968, Aust.)

Niels Hinrichsen
HAGBARD AND SIGNE(1968, Den./Iceland/Swed.); ISLAND AT THE TOP OF THE WORLD, THE(1974)
Harriet Hinsdale
Silents
APACHE, THE(1928), w; NO BABIES WANTED(1928), w
Milas C. Hinshaw
1984
MYSTERY MANSION(1984), ph
William Hinshaw
MA BARKER'S KILLER BROOD(1960), md
Humphrey Hinshelwood
CAMILLE 2000(1969), ed
William S. Hinshelwood
Silents
FLOWING GOLD(1924), art d
Geoff Hinsliff
O LUCKY MAN!(1973, Brit.)
Bonnie Hinson
MOONSHINE MOUNTAIN(1964)
Brian Hinson
SPLIT IMAGE(1982)
Carlo Hinterman
ATTILA(1958, Ital.); FIVE BRANDED WOMEN(1960)
Carlo Hintermann
FAREWELL TO ARMS, A(1957); BREATH OF SCANDAL, A(1960); STOP TRAIN 349(1964, Fr./Ital./Ger.); CONQUERED CITY(1966, Ital.); SECRET AGENT SUPER DRAGON(1966, Fr./Ital./Ger./Monaco); BLACK VEIL FOR LISA, A(1969 Ital./Ger.)
Darby Hinton
HERO'S ISLAND(1962); SON OF FLUBBER(1963); MR. SYCAMORE(1975); BLACK OAK CONSPIRACY(1977); GOODBYE FRANKLIN HIGH(1978); HI-RIDERS(1978); WITHOUT WARNING(1980); FIRECRACKER(1981)
Daryn Hinton
SHOOT-OUT AT MEDICINE BEND(1957); ERRAND BOY, THE(1961)
Ed Hinton
SAMSON AND DELILAH(1949); JOURNEY INTO LIGHT(1951); RED BADGE OF COURAGE, THE(1951); FLESH AND FURY(1952); HELLGATE(1952); LEADVILLE GUNSLINGER(1952); LION AND THE HORSE, THE(1952); FARMER TAKES A WIFE, THE(1953); HITCH-HIKER, THE(1953); THREE SAILORS AND A GIRL(1953); LAST TIME I SAW PARIS, THE(1954); RIVER OF NO RETURN(1954); DEVIL GODDESS(1955); GANG BUSTERS(1955); JUNGLE MOON MEN(1955); SEMINOLE UPRISING(1955); TIGHT SPOT(1955); JULIE(1956); TEN COMMANDMENTS, THE(1956); WALK THE PROUD LAND(1956); DALTON GIRLS, THE(1957); UNDER FIRE(1957); 27TH DAY, THE(1957); CRY TERROR(1958); DECKS RAN RED, THE(1958); ESCAPE FROM RED ROCK(1958); FORT BOWIE(1958); GOOD DAY FOR A HANGING(1958); GIDGET(1959)
Edgar Hinton
HARPOON(1948)
Edward Hinton
WHILE THE CITY SLEEPS(1956); SHOOT-OUT AT MEDICINE BEND(1957)
James David Hinton
GALAXINA(1980)
James E. Hinton
GANJA AND HESS(1973), ph
Jane Hinton
GOD'S GIFT TO WOMEN(1931), w; KISS AND MAKE UP(1934), w; I'LL BE YOURS(1947), w
Mary Hinton
ONCE IN A NEW MOON(1935, Brit.); GASLIGHT(1940); POISON PEN(1941, Brit.); WOMEN AREN'T ANGELS(1942, Brit.); BROKEN JOURNEY(1948, Brit.); HATTER'S CASTLE(1948, Brit.); GAY LADY, THE(1949, Brit.); IT'S NOT CRICKET(1949, Brit.); QUARTET(1949, Brit.); TAMING OF DOROTHY, THE(1950, Brit.); WINSLOW BOY, THE(1950); SECOND MRS. TANQUERAY, THE(1952, Brit.); SOMETHING MONEY CAN'T BUY(1952, Brit.); WHITE CORRIDORS(1952, Brit.); VILLAGE, THE(1953, Brit./Switz.)
Phillip Hinton
CADDIE(1976, Aus.); MANGANINNIE(1982, Aus.)
Robert Hinton
SNOW CREATURE, THE,(1954)
S.E. Hinton
TEX(1982), a, w; OUTSIDERS, THE(1983), w; RUMBLE FISH(1983), a, w
Sam Hinton
LAST DAYS OF DOLWYN, THE(1949, Brit.)
Sean Hinton
CADDIE(1976, Aus.)
Simon Hinton
CADDIE(1976, Aus.)
Barbara Hintz
GERMANY, YEAR ZERO(1949, Ger.)
Anny Hintze
Silents
METROPOLIS(1927, Ger.)
Ingetraut Hintze
GERMANY, YEAR ZERO(1949, Ger.)
Naomi A. Hintze
YOU'LL LIKE MY MOTHER(1972), w
Carl Hinun
DEATH IN THE SKY(1937), ed
Peter Hinwood
ROCKY HORROR PICTURE SHOW, THE(1975, Brit.)
Adelheid Hinz
MONSTER OF LONDON CITY, THE(1967, Ger.)
Don Hinz
JACKSON COUNTY JAIL(1976)
Edgar Hinz
1984
CHINESE BOXES(1984, Ger./Brit.), a, art d

Michael Hinz
BRIDGE, THE(1961, Ger.); LONGEST DAY, THE(1962); PHONY AMERICAN, THE(1964, Ger.); LAST ESCAPE, THE(1970, Brit.); TOUCH ME NOT(1974, Brit.); DEATH OF MARIO RICCI, THE(1983, Ital.)

Terry Hinz
TWO-MINUTE WARNING(1976)

Theo Hinz
GERMANY IN AUTUMN(1978, Ger.), p; WAR AND PEACE(1983, Ger.), p

Werner Hinz
GIRL OF THE MOORS, THE(1961, Ger.); LONGEST DAY, THE(1962); RESTLESS NIGHT, THE(1964, Ger.); TONIO KROGER(1968, Fr./Ger.)

Gerhard Hinze [Gerard Heinz]
THUNDER ROCK(1944, Brit.); FRIEDA(1947, Brit.)

Bill Hinzman
THERE'S ALWAYS VANILLA(1972); HUNGRY WIVES(1973), a, ph

S. William Hinzman
THE CRAZIES(1973), ph

Sam Hiona
HOT POTATO(1976); EYE FOR AN EYE, AN(1981)

Steve Hiott
IF EVER I SEE YOU AGAIN(1978)

B.H. Hipkins
SILENT BARRIERS(1937, Brit.), ed

Ricardo Hipolito
MAD DOCTOR OF BLOOD ISLAND, THE(1969, Phil./U.S.)

Paul E. Hipp
SWEET JESUS, PREACHER MAN(1973), ph

Paul Hipp
FARMER'S OTHER DAUGHTER, THE(1965), ph; FANDANGO(1970), p, ph; KINFOLK(1970), ph; SWEET TRASH(1970), ph; TRADER HORNEE(1970), ph; BLOOD AND LACE(1971), ph; INCREDIBLE TWO-HEADED TRANSPLANT, THE(1971), ph; WILD RIDERS(1971), ph; GRAVE OF THE VAMPIRE(1972), ph; SUPERCHICK(1973), ph; HANGAR 18(1980), ph; IN SEARCH OF HISTORIC JESUS(1980), ph; BOOGENS, THE(1982), ph; PSYCHO FROM TEXAS(1982), ph

Young Hipp
Silents
DINTY(1920)

Laura Hippe
LOGAN'S RUN(1976); SWINGING BARMAIDS, THE(1976); MAUSOLEUM(1983)

Lewis Hippe
Silents
MOLLYCODDLE, THE(1920)

Lou Hippe
20,000 LEAGUES UNDER THE SEA(1954), makeup; LORD LOVE A DUCK(1966), makeup

E. Hippelainen
DAY THE EARTH FROZE, THE(1959, Fin./USSR)

Eric Hipple
1984
BEAR, THE(1984)

Louis Hipple
KID FROM CLEVELAND, THE(1949), makeup

The Hippodrome Chorus
CLUE OF THE NEW PIN, THE(1929, Brit.)

Hippy the Dog
Silents
SCHOOL DAYS(1921)

Philippe Hiquilly
SIX IN PARIS(1968, Fr.)

Mikijiro Hira
FACE OF ANOTHER, THE(1967, Jap.); RIVER OF FOREVER(1967, Jap.); THOUSAND CRANES(1969, Jap.)

Kiyoko Hirai
MYSTERIOUS SATELLITE, THE(1956, Jap.)

Shoichi Hirai
JUDO SHOWDOWN(1966, Jap.)

Sei Hiraizumi
FALCON FIGHTERS, THE(1970, Jap.)

Joe Hirakawa
KARATE, THE HAND OF DEATH(1961)

Totetsu Hirakawa
THREE WEEKS OF LOVE(1965), art d; LIVE YOUR OWN WAY(1970, Jap.), art d

Hiralai
JUNGLE, THE(1952), ch

Hiralil
GUIDE, THE(1965, U.S./India), ch

Shanti Hiranand
SIDDHARTHA(1972)

Robert Hirano
GEISHA BOY, THE(1958)

Yoshimi Hirano
LIFE OF OHARU(1964, Jap.), ph

Shizuo Hirase
GIRARA(1967, Jap.), ph; GOKE, BODYSNATCHER FROM HELL(1968, Jap.), ph

Akihiko Hirata
SAMURAI(PART II)** (1967, Jap.); SECRET SCROLLS(PART I)**1/2 (1968, Jap.); SAMURAI(1955, Jap.); GODZILLA, RING OF THE MONSTERS(1956, Jap.); RODAN(1958, Jap.); H-MAN, THE(1959, Jap.); MYSTERIANS, THE(1959, Jap.); MAN AGAINST MAN(1961, Jap.); SECRET OF THE TELEGIAN, THE(1961, Jap.); WESTWARD DESPERADO(1961, Jap.); MOTHRA(1962, Jap.); SANJURO(1962, Jap.); VARAN THE UNBELIEVABLE(1962, U.S./Jap.); KING KONG VERSUS GODZILLA(1963, Jap.); GORATH(1964, Jap.); SAGA OF THE VAGABONDS(1964, Jap.); ATRAGON(1965, Jap.); GHIDRAH, THE THREE-HEADED MONSTER(1965, Jap.); SON OF GODZILLA(1967, Jap.); EMPEROR AND A GENERAL, THE(1968, Jap.); DAREDEVIL IN THE CASTLE(1969, Jap.); LATITUDE ZERO(1969, U.S./Jap.); GODZILLA VERSUS THE COSMIC MONSTER(1974, Jap.); MONSTERS FROM THE UNKNOWN PLANET(1975, Jap.)

Daizaburo Hirata
INSECT WOMAN, THE(1964, Jap.)

Mamoru Hirata
PLEASURES OF THE FLESH, THE(1965)

Hirataka
RIFIFI IN TOKYO(1963, Fr./Ital.), art d

Kazue Hirataka
ROAD TO ETERNITY(1962, Jap.), art d; SOLDIER'S PRAYER, A(1970, Jap.), art d

Kazve Hirataka
HUMAN CONDITION, THE(1959, Jap.), art d

Dick Hirbe
DOUGHGIRLS, THE(1944); LADY ON A TRAIN(1945); WEEKEND AT THE WALDORF(1945); WHAT NEXT, CORPORAL HARGROVE?(1945)

Richard Hirbe
SHE GETS HER MAN(1945)

Robert Hird
Misc. Talkies
MR. HORATIO KNIBBLES(1971), d

Thora Hird
BLACK SHEEP OF WHITEHALL, THE(1941 Brit.); NEXT OF KIN(1942, Brit.); SOMEWHERE IN FRANCE(1943, Brit.); 2,000 WOMEN(1944, Brit.); 48 HOURS(1944, Brit.); COURTNEY AFFAIR, THE(1947, Brit.); CORRIDOR OF MIRRORS(1948, Brit.); GIRL IN THE PAINTING, THE(1948, Brit.); BOY, A GIRL AND A BIKE, A(1949 Brit.); BOYS IN BROWN(1949, Brit.); CONSPIRATOR(1949, Brit.); FOOLS RUSH IN(1949, Brit.); MADNESS OF THE HEART(1949, Brit.); MY BROTHER JONATHAN(1949, Brit.); WEAKER SEX, THE(1949, Brit.); CURE FOR LOVE, THE(1950, Brit.); MAGNET, THE(1950, Brit.); GALLOPING MAJOR, THE(1951, Brit.); MANIACS ON WHEELS(1951, Brit.); FRIGHTENED MAN, THE(1952, Brit.); MAGIC BOX, THE(1952, Brit.); MAYTIME IN MAYFAIR(1952, Brit.); ONCE A SINNER(1952, Brit.); BACKGROUND(1953, Brit.); BIG FRAME, THE(1953, Brit.); BOTH SIDES OF THE LAW(1953, Brit.); DAY TO REMEMBER, A(1953, Brit.); GREAT GAME, THE(1953, Brit.); HUNDRED HOUR HUNT(1953, Brit.); LONG MEMORY, THE(1953, Brit.); TIME GENTLEMEN PLEASE!(1953, Brit.); CROWDED DAY, THE(1954, Brit.); DON'T BLAME THE STORK(1954, Brit.); FOR BETTER FOR WORSE(1954, Brit.); PERSONAL AFFAIR(1954, Brit.); TURN THE KEY SOFTLY(1954, Brit.); LOVE MATCH, THE(1955, Brit.); ONE GOOD TURN(1955, Brit.); BLONDE BAIT(1956, U.S./Brit.); HOME AND AWAY(1956, Brit.); SIMON AND LAURA(1956, Brit.); THE CREEPING UNKNOWN(1956, Brit.); GOOD COMPANIONS, THE(1957, Brit.); PANIC IN THE PARLOUR(1957, Brit.); TEARS FOR SIMON(1957, Brit.); CROSS-UP(1958); DANGEROUS YOUTH(1958, Brit.); FURTHER UP THE CREEK(1958, Brit.); ENTERTAINER, THE(1960, Brit.); OVER THE ODDS(1961, Brit.); KIND OF LOVING, A(1962, Brit.); TERM OF TRIAL(1962, Brit.); BITTER HARVEST(1963, Brit.); RATTLE OF A SIMPLE MAN(1964, Brit.); SOME WILL, SOME WON'T(1970, Brit.); NIGHT COMERS, THE(1971, Brit.)

Ingvar Hirdwall
RAVEN'S END(1970, Swed.)

Gail Hire
RED LINE 7000(1965)

Hugh Hires
GHOST STORY(1981)

Walter Hires
Silents
FLAMING BARRIERS(1924); HUSBAND HUNTERS(1927)

Lacarnist Hiriams
1984
SOLDIER'S STORY, A(1984)

Dilip Hiro
PRIVATE ENTERPRISE, A(1975, Brit.), w

John S. Hirohata
IRON ANGEL(1964)

David Hirokane
CHARLIE CHAN AND THE CURSE OF THE DRAGON QUEEN(1981)

Sakae Hirosawa
SONG FROM MY HEART, THE(1970, Jap.), w; RED LION(1971, Jap.), w

George Hirose
GAMERA THE INVINCIBLE(1966, Jap.)

Kenjiro Hirose
SNOW IN THE SOUTH SEAS(1963, Jap.), m; LET'S GO, YOUNG GUY!(1967, Jap.), m; YOUNG GUY GRADUATES(1969, Jap.), m; YOUNG GUY ON MT. COOK(1969, Jap.), m; DUEL AT EZO(1970, Jap.), m

Minoru Hirose
PORTRAIT OF CHIEKO(1968, Jap.), w

Yuzuru Hirose
THROUGH DAYS AND MONTHS(1969 Jap.), w

Kimiko Hiroshige
HONKY TONK FREEWAY(1981)

Kimiro Hiroshige
BLADE RUNNER(1982)

Kimiko Hiroshigi
NAVY WIFE(1956)

Mikiko Hirota
FIGHT FOR THE GLORY(1970, Jap.)

Reona Hirota
ALL RIGHT, MY FRIEND(1983, Japan)

Charles Hirsch
HI, MOM!(1970), p, w, d&w

Daniel Hirsch
Misc. Talkies
BLOWN SKY HIGH(1984)

Elroy "Crazylegs" Hirsch
CRAZYLEGS, ALL AMERICAN(1953); ZERO HOUR!(1957)

Emi Florence Hirsch
BRIDGE TO THE SUN(1961)

George Hirsch
STARTING OVER(1979)

Judd Hirsch
KING OF THE GYPSIES(1978); ORDINARY PEOPLE(1980); WITHOUT A TRACE(1983)

1984
GOODBYE PEOPLE, THE(1984); TEACHERS(1984)
Klaus Hirsch
WONDER BOY(1951, Brit./Aust.)
Linda Hirsch
MY BREAKFAST WITH BLASSIE(1983)
Lou Hirsch
LONELY LADY, THE(1983); SUPERMAN III(1983)
Marjorie Hirsch
FEMALE RESPONSE, THE(1972)
Max Hirsch
ONE THIRD OF A NATION(1939)
Michael Hirsch
1984
MUPPETS TAKE MANHATTAN, THE(1984)
Paul Hirsch
HI, MOM!(1970), ed; SISTERS(1973), ed; PHANTOM OF THE PARADISE(1974), ed; MONEY, THE(1975), ed; CARRIE(1976), ed; OBSESSION(1976), ed; STAR WARS(1977), ed; FURY, THE(1978), ed; KING OF THE GYPSIES(1978), ed; EMPIRE STRIKES BACK, THE(1980), ed; BLOW OUT(1981), ed; CREEPSHOW(1982), ed; BLACK STALLION RETURNS, THE(1983), ed
1984
FOOTLOOSE(1984), ed; PROTOCOL(1984), ed
Ray Hirsch
HER FIRST ROMANCE(1940); FORCE OF EVIL(1948); I, JANE DOE(1948)
Robert Hirsch
HUNCHBACK OF NOTRE DAME, THE(1957, Fr.); PLEASE! MR. BALZAC(1957, Fr.); IMPOSSIBLE ON SATURDAY(1966, Fr./Israel); SHOCK TREATMENT(1973, Fr.)
Steven Hirsch
CHU CHU AND THE PHILLY FLASH(1981); TWO OF A KIND(1983)
1984
UNFAITHFULLY YOURS(1984)
Tina Hirsch
BIG BAD MAMA(1974), ed; MACON COUNTY LINE(1974), ed; DEATH RACE 2000(1975), ed; DRIVER, THE(1978), ed; MORE AMERICAN GRAFFITI(1979), ed; HEARTBEEPS(1981), ed; TWILIGHT ZONE–THE MOVIE(1983), ed
1984
GREMLINS(1984), ed
Walter Hirsch
HUGS AND KISSES(1968, Swed.), art d
Win Hirsch
CRAZYLEGS, ALL AMERICAN(1953)
Peretz Hirschbein
GREEN FIELDS(1937), w
Bernie Hirschenson
Misc. Talkies
PICK-UP(1975), d
Alec Hirschfeld
LOVE LETTERS(1983), ph; SPACE RAIDERS(1983), ph
Bob Hirschfeld
PROMISE, THE(1979)
Gerald Hirschfeld
GUILTY BYSTANDER(1950), ph; FAIL SAFE(1964), ph; INCIDENT, THE(1967), ph; GOODBYE COLUMBUS(1969), ph; LAST SUMMER(1969), ph; SOME KIND OF A NUT(1969), ph; DOC(1971), ph; T.R. BASKIN(1971), ph; CHILD'S PLAY(1972), ph; SUMMER WISHES, WINTER DREAMS(1973), ph; TWO PEOPLE(1973), ph; ULTIMATE WARRIOR, THE(1975), ph; ONE SUMMER LOVE(1976), ph; TWO-MINUTE WARNING(1976), ph; WORLD'S GREATEST LOVER, THE(1977), ph; COMA(1978), ph; AMERICATHON(1979), ph; WHY WOULD I LIE(1980), ph; NEIGHBORS(1981), ph; MY FAVORITE YEAR(1982), ph; TO BE OR NOT TO BE(1983), ph
1984
HOUSE OF GOD, THE(1984), ph
Jerry Hirschfeld
GRAVY TRAIN, THE(1974), ph; W(1974), ph
Robert Hirschfeld
ESCAPE FROM ALCATRAZ(1979)
Gerald Hirschfield
C-MAN(1949), ph; MR. UNIVERSE(1951), ph; TWO GALS AND A GUY(1951), ph; COTTON COMES TO HARLEM(1970), ph; DIARY OF A MAD HOUSEWIFE(1970), ph; YOUNG FRANKENSTEIN(1974), ph; CAR, THE(1977), ph; BELL JAR, THE(1979), ph
Robert E. Hirschfield
MORE AMERICAN GRAFFITI(1979)
Jerry Hirschfield
SUNDAY LOVERS(1980, Ital./Fr.), ph
Leonard Hirschfield
DAVID AND LISA(1962), ph
Kurt Hirschler
RUNNING(1979, Can.), ed
Herbert Hirschman
HALLS OF ANGER(1970), p; THEY CALL ME MISTER TIBBS(1970), p
Stuart Z. Hirschman
RED, WHITE AND BLACK, THE(1970), a, p
Alfred Hirschmeier
NAKED AMONG THE WOLVES(1967, Ger.), w, art d
Hans Hirschmuller
ALICE IN THE CITIES(1974, W. Ger.)
Murdine Hirsh
OUT OF THE BLUE(1982)
Nurit Hirsh
WORLDS APART(1980, U.S., Israel), m
Tina Hirsh
EAT MY DUST!(1976), ed
Peretz Hirshbein
HITLER'S MADMAN(1943), w
Albert S. Hirshberg
FEAR STRIKES OUT(1957), w
Ludwig Hirshfeld
MAD MARTINDALES, THE(1942), w

Leonard Hirshfield
LADYBUG, LADYBUG(1963), ph
Fred Hirshhorn
PUTNEY SWOPE(1969)
Joel Hirshhorn
FAT SPY(1966), m
Kurt Hirshler
ENTER THE DRAGON(1973), ed
Steve Hirshon
BUDDY BUDDY(1981)
Alice Hirson
GANG THAT COULDN'T SHOOT STRAIGHT, THE(1971); BEING THERE(1979); NIGHTWING(1979)
1984
MASS APPEAL(1984); REVENGE OF THE NERDS(1984)
Roger Hirson
BRIDGE AT REMAGEN, THE(1969), w
Roger O. Hirson
PIECES OF DREAMS(1970), w; DEMON SEED(1977), w
Audrey Hirst
GIRDLE OF GOLD(1952, Brit.), p
Denise Hirst
STORK TALK(1964, Brit.)
Mabel Hirst
Misc. Silents
THEN YOU'LL REMEMBER ME(1918, Brit.)
Robert Hirst
NO SAFETY AHEAD(1959, Brit.), w
Stephen Hirst
BLACK JACK(1979, Brit.)
Ursula Hirst
IT'S IN THE BAG(1936, Brit.); PLEASE TURN OVER(1960, Brit.); THIS IS MY STREET(1964, Brit.)
George Hirste
MILLIONS LIKE US(1943, Brit.); GIVE US THE MOON(1944, Brit.); JOHNNY FRENCHMAN(1946, Brit.); NIGHT BOAT TO DUBLIN(1946, Brit.); INSPECTOR CALLS, AN(1954, Brit.); LOVE MATCH, THE(1955, Brit.); HAUNTED STRANGLER, THE(1958, Brit.)
Al Hirt
ROME ADVENTURE(1962); WHAT AM I BID?(1967); NUMBER ONE(1969)
Corinne Hirt
BLACK SPIDER, THE(1983, Swit.)
Eleonore Hirt
VERY PRIVATE AFFAIR, A(1962, Fr./Ital.); WHAT'S NEW, PUSSYCAT?(1965, U.S./Fr.); NIGHT OF THE GENERALS, THE(1967, Brit./Fr.); KILLING GAME, THE(1968, Fr.); SEVEN NIGHTS IN JAPAN(1976, Brit./Fr.); GET OUT YOUR HANDKERCHIEFS(1978, Fr.); LA NUIT DE VARENNES(1983, Fr./Ital.)
Martin Hirthe
JUST A GIGOLO(1979, Ger.)
Dagmar Hirtz
CASTLE, THE(1969, Ger.), ed; FIRST LOVE(1970, Ger./Switz.), ed; PEDESTRIAN, THE(1974, Ger.), a, ed; END OF THE GAME(1976, Ger./Ital.), ed; GERMAN SISTERS, THE(1982, Ger.), ed; FRIENDS AND HUSBANDS(1983, Ger.), ed; MALOU(1983), ed; WAR AND PEACE(1983, Ger.), ed
Jukka Hirvikangas
GORKY PARK(1983)
Yushitake Hisa
TRAITORS(1957, Jap.), w
Eijiro Hisaita
HIGH AND LOW(1963, Jap.), w; IDIOT, THE(1963, Jap.), w
M. Hisaka
YAKUZA, THE(1975, U.S./Jap.)
Mikio Hisamatsu
Misc. Silents
SOULS ON THE ROAD(1921, Jap.)
Seiji Hisamatsu
WOMEN IN PRISON(1957, Jap.), d; WAYSIDE PEBBLE, THE(1962, Jap.), d; SNOW IN THE SOUTH SEAS(1963, Jap.), d
Sharon Hisamoto
WHAT'S THE MATTER WITH HELEN?(1971)
Hiroshi Hisamune
VARAN THE UNBELIEVABLE(1962, U.S./Jap.)
Elizabeth Hiscott
SEVENTH SURVIVOR, THE(1941, Brit.), p; LADY FROM LISBON(1942, Brit.), p; SABOTAGE AT SEA(1942, Brit.), p; BUTLER'S DILEMMA, THE(1943, Brit.), p; WELCOME, MR. WASHINGTON(1944, Brit.), p; TIME OF HIS LIFE, THE(1955, Brit.), p; TONS OF TROUBLE(1956, Brit.), p
Leslie H. Hiscott
SHE SHALL HAVE MUSIC(1935, Brit.), d
Leslie Hiscott
FEATHER, THE(1929, Brit.), d&w; TO WHAT RED HELL(1929, Brit.), w; CALL OF THE SEA, THE(1930, Brit.), d; HOUSE OF THE ARROW, THE(1930, Brit.), d; MYSTERY AT THE VILLA ROSE(1930, Brit.), d; MYSTERY OF THE PINK VILLA, THE(1930, Fr.), d; BLACK COFFEE(1931, Brit.), d; BROWN SUGAR(1931, Brit.), d; NIGHT IN MONTMARTE, A(1931, Brit.), d; CROOKED LADY, THE(1932, Brit.), d; FACE AT THE WINDOW, THE(1932, Brit.), d; MISSING REMBRANDT, THE(1932, Brit.), d; MURDER AT COVENT GARDEN(1932, Brit.), d; WHEN LONDON SLEEPS(1932, Brit.), d; CLEANING UP(1933, Brit.), d; GREAT STUFF(1933, Brit.), d; I'LL STICK TO YOU(1933, Brit.), d; IRON STAIR, THE(1933, Brit.), d; MAROONED(1933, Brit.), d; MELODY MAKER, THE(1933, Brit.), d; OUT OF THE PAST(1933, Brit.), d; STRIKE IT RICH(1933, Brit.), d; THAT'S MY WIFE(1933, Brit.), d; CRAZY PEOPLE(1934, Brit.), d; KEEP IT QUIET(1934, Brit.), d; MAN I WANT, THE(1934, Brit.), d; PASSING SHADOWS(1934, Brit.), d; ANNIE, LEAVE THE ROOM(1935, Brit.), d; BIG SPLASH, THE(1935, Brit.), d; DEPARTMENT STORE(1935, Brit.), d; FIRE HAS BEEN ARRANGED, A(1935, Brit.), d; INSIDE THE ROOM(1935, Brit.), d; THREE WITNESSES(1935, Brit.), d; TRIUMPH OF SHERLOCK HOLMES, THE(1935, Brit.), d; FAME(1936, Brit.), d; GAY LOVE(1936, Brit.), d; INTERRUPTED HONEYMOON, THE(1936, Brit.), d; MILLIONS(1936, Brit.), d; FINE FEATHERS(1937, Brit.), d; TILLY OF BLOOMSBURY(1940, Brit.), d; SEVENTH SURVIVOR, THE(1941, Brit.), d; LADY FROM LISBON(1942, Brit.), d; SABOTAGE AT SEA(1942, Brit.), d;

BUTLER'S DILEMMA, THE(1943, Brit.), d; WELCOME, MR. WASHINGTON(1944, Brit.), d; TIME OF HIS LIFE, THE(1955, Brit.), d, w; TONS OF TROUBLE(1956, Brit.), d, w
Silents
SQUIBS, MP(1923, Brit.), w; THIS MARRIAGE BUSINESS(1927, Brit.), d&w; PASSING OF MR. QUIN, THE(1928, Brit.), d&w
Misc. Silents
S.O.S.(1928, Brit.), d; RINGING THE CHANGES(1929, Brit.), d

Leslie S. Hiscott
ALIBI(1931, Brit.), d; SHERLOCK HOLMES' FATAL HOUR(1931, Brit.), d, w; MURDER ON THE SET(1936, Brit.), d

Richard Hiscott
1984
LASSITER(1984), ed

David Hiscox
OUT OF THE BLUE(1982), art d

Joe Hiser
EGG AND I, THE(1947); DEADLINE(1948); KID FROM GOWER GULCH, THE(1949)

Yuriko Hishimi
WAR OF THE MONSTERS(1972, Jap.)

Chiang Hising-lung
DRACULA AND THE SEVEN GOLDEN VAMPIRES(1978, Brit./Chi.), ed

Betsey Ann Hisle
SINS OF THE CHILDREN(1930)

Betsy Ann Hisle
Silents
NELLIE, THE BEAUTIFUL CLOAK MODEL(1924)

Betty Ann Hisle
JENNIE GERHARDT(1933)

Geraldine Hislop
FAME(1936, Brit.); SPLINTERS IN THE AIR(1937, Brit.); RAT, THE(1938, Brit.); SUICIDE LEGION(1940, Brit.)

Isaac Hislop
GREY FOX, THE(1983, Can.)

Joseph Hislop
LOVES OF ROBERT BURNS, THE(1930, Brit.)

Nicole Hiss
DESTROY, SHE SAID(1969, Fr.)

Hiroshi Hissamuni
GREAT BANK ROBBERY, THE(1969)

George Histman
COBRA, THE(1968)

N. L. Hitch
THEY LIVE BY NIGHT(1949)

Alex Hitchcock
GREASER'S PALACE(1972)

Alfred Hitchcock
BLACKMAIL(1929, Brit.), d, w; JUNO AND THE PAYCOCK(1930, Brit.), d, w; MURDER(1930, Brit.), d, w; SKIN GAME, THE(1931, Brit.), d, w; LORD CAMBER'S LADIES(1932, Brit.), p; NUMBER SEVENTEEN(1932, Brit.), d, w; RICH AND STRANGE(1932, Brit.), d, w; STRAUSS' GREAT WALTZ(1934, Brit.), d; MAN WHO KNEW TOO MUCH, THE(1935, Brit.), d; 39 STEPS, THE(1935, Brit.), d; SECRET AGENT, THE(1936, Brit.), d; SABOTAGE(1937, Brit.), d; LADY VANISHES, THE(1938, Brit.), d; YOUNG AND INNOCENT(1938, Brit.), a, d; JAMAICA INN(1939, Brit.), d; FOREIGN CORRESPONDENT(1940), a, d; REBECCA(1940), d; MR. AND MRS. SMITH(1941), d; SUSPICION(1941), d; SABOTEUR(1942), a, d, w; SHADOW OF A DOUBT(1943), d; LIFEBOAT(1944), a, d; SPELLBOUND(1945), a, d; NOTORIOUS(1946), p&d; PARADINE CASE, THE(1947), d; ROPE(1948), p, d; UNDER CAPRICORN(1949), p, d; STAGE FRIGHT(1950, Brit.), a, p&d; STRANGERS ON A TRAIN(1951), a, p&d; I CONFESS(1953), p&d; DIAL M FOR MURDER(1954), a, p&d; REAR WINDOW(1954), a, p&d; TO CATCH A THIEF(1955), a, p&d; TROUBLE WITH HARRY, THE(1955), p&d; MAN WHO KNEW TOO MUCH, THE(1956), p&d; WRONG MAN, THE(1956), p&d; VERTIGO(1958), p&d; NORTH BY NORTHWEST(1959), a, p&d; PSYCHO(1960), a, p&d; BIRDS, THE(1963), a, p&d; MARNIE(1964), p&d; TORN CURTAIN(1966), a, p&d; TOPAZ(1969, Brit.), a, p&d; FRENZY(1972, Brit.), p&d; FAMILY PLOT(1976), a, p&d
Silents
PASSIONATE ADVENTURE, THE(1924, Brit.), w; PRUDES FALL, THE(1924, Brit.), w; PLEASURE GARDEN, THE(1925, Brit./Ger.), d; FEAR O' GOD(1926, Brit./Ger.), d; LODGER, THE(1926, Brit.), d, w; EASY VIRTUE(1927, Brit.), d; RING, THE(1927, Brit.), d, w; CHAMPAGNE(1928, Brit.), d, w; FARMER'S WIFE, THE(1928, Brit.), d&w; WHEN BOYS LEAVE HOME(1928, Brit.); MANXMAN, THE(1929, Brit.), d
Misc. Silents
FEAR O'GOD(1926, Brit.), d

Edward Hitchcock
ROMA RIVUOLE CESARE(; NEVER TAKE NO FOR AN ANSWER(1952, Brit./Ital.)

Jane Hitchcock
NICKELODEON(1976)

Jane Stanton Hitchcock
FIRST LOVE(1977), w

Keith Hitchcock
RAFFLES(1939); HUDSON'S BAY(1940); LITTLE OLD NEW YORK(1940); SUSAN AND GOD(1940); MAN HUNT(1941); ONE NIGHT IN LISBON(1941); BLACK SWAN, THE(1942); LONDON BLACKOUT MURDERS(1942); NIGHTMARE(1942); FRENCHMAN'S CREEK(1944); NONE BUT THE LONELY HEART(1944); SECRETS OF SCOTLAND YARD(1944); WHITE CLIFFS OF DOVER, THE(1944); TONIGHT AND EVERY NIGHT(1945); DRAGONWYCH(1946); LOCKET, THE(1946); THREE STRANGERS(1946); EXILE, THE(1947); HOMESTRETCH, THE(1947); LOVE FROM A STRANGER(1947); KISS THE BLOOD OFF MY HANDS(1948); SON OF DR. JEKYLL, THE(1951); ABBOTT AND COSTELLO MEET DR. JEKYLL AND MR. HYDE(1954); DRAGON'S GOLD(1954)

Mike Hitchcock
NIGHTMARE IN BLOOD(1978)

Pat Hitchcock
SKATEBOARD(1978)

Patricia Hitchcock
MUDLARK, THE(1950, Brit.); STAGE FRIGHT(1950, Brit.); STRANGERS ON A TRAIN(1951); PSYCHO(1960)

Raymond Hitchcock
PERCY(1971, Brit.), w
Silents
BROADWAY AFTER DARK(1924); REDHEADS PREFERRED(1926); MONKEY TALKS, THE(1927)
Misc. Silents
RINGTAILED RHINOCEROS, THE(1915); BEAUTY SHOP, THE(1922); TIRED BUSINESS MAN, THE(1927)

Rex Hitchcock
Silents
EVE'S DAUGHTER(1918)

Walter Hitchcock
Silents
CLIMBERS, THE(1915); AUCTION BLOCK, THE(1917)
Misc. Silents
WALLS OF JERICHO, THE(1914); GIRL I LEFT BEHIND ME, THE(1915); HOUSE OF TEARS, THE(1915); SOUL OF A WOMAN, THE(1915); MORAL CODE, THE(1917)

Dolores Hitchens
BAND OF OUTSIDERS(1966, Fr.), w

Glenys Hitchins
SCARECROW, THE(1982, New Zealand), cos

Henry Hite [Height]
MONSTER A GO-GO(1965)

Hite and Stanley
NEW FACES OF 1937(1937)

Velimir Hitil
TREASURE OF SILVER LAKE(1965, Fr./Ger./Yugo.); LAST OF THE RENEGADES(1966, Fr./Ital./Ger./Yugo.)

Adolf Hitler
EXTRAORDINARY SEAMAN, THE(1969)

Reiko Hitomi
SOLDIER'S PRAYER, A(1970, Jap.)

Laurence Hitt
Silents
WINGS(1927), art d

Lawrence Hitt
Silents
SAINTED DEVIL, A(1924), art d

Robert Hitt
PLEASANTVILLE(1976); ALL THAT JAZZ(1979); SOMETHING SHORT OF PARADISE(1979); FOUR SEASONS, THE(1981); RAGTIME(1981); TATTOO(1981); MISSING(1982)

Carl K. Hittelman
LAST OF THE WILD HORSES(1948), p

Carl Hittleman
BUCKSKIN LADY, THE(1957), p&d, w; BILLY THE KID VS. DRACULA(1966), w

Carl K. Hittleman
RETURN OF WILDFIRE, THE(1948), p, w; GRAND CANYON(1949), p, w; I SHOT JESSE JAMES(1949), p; TOUGH ASSIGNMENT(1949), p, w; BARON OF ARIZONA, THE(1950), p; RETURN OF JESSE JAMES, THE(1950), p, w,Jack Natteford; LITTLE BIG HORN(1951), p; KENTUCKY RIFLE(1956), p&d, w; GUN BATTLE AT MONTEREY(1957), p, d; 36 HOURS(1965), d&w; JESSE JAMES MEETS FRANKENSTEIN'S DAUGHTER(1966), w; BIG DADDY(1969), p,d&w

Paul Hittscher
FITZCARRALDO(1982)

Hitu
Silents
TABU(1931)

Zita Hitz
SNOW WHITE(1965, Ger.)

Rubert Hitzig
HAPPY BIRTHDAY, GEMINI(1980), p

Rupert Hitzig
ELECTRA GLIDE IN BLUE(1973), w; CATTLE ANNIE AND LITTLE BRITCHES(1981), p; WOLFEN(1981), p; JAWS 3-D(1983), p

Majabalo Hiubi
KING SOLOMON'S MINES(1937, Brit.)

Amatsia Hiuni
NOT MINE TO LOVE(1969, Israel), p, w

Ron Hiveley
DEMON LOVER, THE(1977)

Geo. Hively
FARMER IN THE DELL, THE(1936), ed

George C. Hively
Silents
LOOKING FOR TROUBLE(1926), w; WESTERN ROVER, THE(1927), w

George Hively
CAUGHT SHORT(1930), ed; CHASING RAINBOWS(1930), ed; OUR BLUSHING BRIDES(1930), ed; THOSE THREE FRENCH GIRLS(1930), ed; DANCE, FOOLS, DANCE(1931), ed; LAUGHING SINNERS(1931), ed; TAILOR MADE MAN, A(1931), ed; WEST OF BROADWAY(1931), ed; AS YOU DESIRE ME(1932), ed; BLONDIE OF THE FOLLIES(1932), ed; POLLY OF THE CIRCUS(1932), ed; ROCKABYE(1932), ed; ACE OF ACES(1933), ed; NO MARRIAGE TIES(1933), ed; AGE OF INNOCENCE(1934), ed; LIFE OF VERGIE WINTERS, THE(1934), ed; SUCCESS AT ANY PRICE(1934), ed; WEDNESDAY'S CHILD(1934), ed; WHERE SINNERS MEET(1934), ed; ANOTHER FACE(1935), ed; CAPTAIN HURRICANE(1935), ed; ENCHANTED APRIL(1935), ed; INFORMER, THE(1935), ed; THREE MUSKETEERS, THE(1935), ed; LAST OUTLAW, THE(1936), ed; PLOUGH AND THE STARS, THE(1936), ed; SPECIAL INVESTIGATOR(1936), ed; WALKING ON AIR(1936), ed; BREAKFAST FOR TWO(1937), ed; TOAST OF NEW YORK, THE(1937), ed; BRINGING UP BABY(1938), ed; MAD MISS MANTON, THE(1938), ed; MOTHER CAREY'S CHICKENS(1938), ed; BAD LANDS(1939), ed; CONSPIRACY(1939), ed; LOVE AFFAIR(1939), ed; ANNE OF WINDY POPLARS(1940), ed; LADDIE(1940), ed; LITTLE MEN(1940), ed; FATHER TAKES A WIFE(1941), ed; FOUR JACKS AND A JILL(1941), ed; HURRY, CHARLIE, HURRY(1941), ed; SAINT IN PALM SPRINGS, THE(1941), ed; ABOVE SUSPICION(1943), ed; SONG OF RUSSIA(1943), ed; BLONDE FEVER(1944), ed; LOST IN A HAREM(1944), ed; THREE MEN IN WHITE(1944), ed; HIDDEN EYE, THE(1945), ed; LONGEST YARD, THE(1974), ed; LUCKY LADY(1975), ed; MOVIE MOVIE(1978), ed; FRIDAY THE 13TH PART III(1982), ed; OFF THE WALL(1983), ed

1984
BLAME IT ON RIO(1984), ed
Silents
ALTAR STAIRS, THE(1922), w; LOADED DOOR, THE(1922), w; MAN OF NERVE, A(1925), w; ALTARS OF DESIRE(1927), w; ON ZE BOULEVARD(1927), ed; TAXI DANCER, THE(1927), ed; EXCESS BAGGAGE(1928), ed; DUKE STEPS OUT, THE(1929), ed; MAN'S MAN, A(1929), ed; TRAIL OF '98, THE(1929), ed

Jack Hively
MAN OF TWO WORLDS(1934), ed; ANNIE OAKLEY(1935), ed; ARIZONIAN, THE(1935), ed; ROMANCE IN MANHATTAN(1935), ed; STRANGERS ALL(1935), ed; BUNKER BEAN(1936), ed; GRAND JURY(1936), ed; MURDER ON A BRIDLE PATH(1936), ed; MUSS 'EM UP(1936), ed; SMARTEST GIRL IN TOWN(1936), ed; BIG SHOT, THE(1937), ed; BORDER CAFE(1937), ed; CRIMINAL LAWYER(1937), ed; DON'T TELL THE WIFE(1937), ed; LIFE OF THE PARTY, THE(1937), ed; MAN WHO FOUND HIMSELF, THE(1937), ed; THERE GOES THE GROOM(1937), ed; WISE GIRL(1937), ed; YOU CAN'T BUY LUCK(1937), ed; JOY OF LIVING(1938), ed; MAN TO REMEMBER, A(1938), ed; NEXT TIME I MARRY(1938), ed; GREAT MAN VOTES, THE(1939), ed; PANAMA LADY(1939), d; SAINT STRIKES BACK, THE(1939), d; SPELLBINDER, THE(1939), d; THEY MADE HER A SPY(1939), d; THREE SONS(1939), d; TWO THOROUGHBREDS(1939), d; ANNE OF WINDY POPLARS(1940), d; LADDIE(1940), d; SAINT TAKES OVER, THE(1940), d; SAINT'S DOUBLE TROUBLE, THE(1940), d; FATHER TAKES A WIFE(1941), d; FOUR JACKS AND A JILL(1941), d; SAINT IN PALM SPRINGS, THE(1941), d; THEY MET IN ARGENTINA(1941), d; STREET OF CHANCE(1942), d; ARE YOU WITH IT?(1948), d
Misc. Talkies
ADVENTURES OF STAR BIRD(1978), d

Jack B. Hively
Misc. Talkies
LASSIE, THE VOYAGER(1966), d; STARBIRD AND SWEET WILLIAM(1975), d

Norman Hiwell
COWBOYS, THE(1972)

Don Hix
DIARY OF A HIGH SCHOOL BRIDE(1959)

Oliver Hix
MUSIC MAN, THE(1962)

Butler Hixon
STRANGERS ON A HONEYMOON(1937, Brit.)

Donald Hixon
LONGEST YARD, THE(1974)

John Hixon
STORMY(1935), ph

John P. Hixon
LEGEND OF BOGGY CREEK, THE(1973)

Ken Hixon
KNIGHTRIDERS(1981)
1984
GRANDVIEW, U.S.A.(1984), w; LONELY GUY, THE(1984)

Sky Hixon
THIRD OF A MAN(1962)

Butler Hixson
EDDY DUCHIN STORY, THE(1956)

Albert Hizkia
IMPOSSIBLE ON SATURDAY(1966, Fr./Israel)

Avner Hizkyahu
MY MARGO(1969, Israel)

Hakon Hjelde
Misc. Silents
SYV DAGER FOR ELISABETH(1927, Swed.)

Keve Hjelm
RAILROAD WORKERS(1948, Swed.); NIGHT GAMES(1966, Swed.); RAVEN'S END(1970, Swed.)

Rune Hjelm
SEA GULL, THE(1968), set d

Ingmarie Hjort
WINTER LIGHT, THE(1963, Swed.)

Sonja Hjort
LOVING COUPLES(1966, Swed.)

Arne Hjorth
DAKOTA LIL(1950)

Ragnhild Hjorthoy
PASSIONATE DEMONS, THE(1962, Norway)

William Hjortsberg
THUNDER AND LIGHTNING(1977), w

Lenn Hjortzberg
DEVIL'S EYE, THE(1960, Swed.); HOUR OF THE WOLF, THE(1968, Swed.)

Doreen Hlantie
ELEPHANT GUN(1959, Brit.)

Marek Hlasko
EIGHTH DAY OF THE WEEK, THE(1959, Pol./Ger.), w

Suzanne Hlavacek
LITTLE DARLINGS(1980)

Fr. Hlavaty
INSPECTOR GENERAL, THE(1937, Czech.)

Vladimir Hlavaty
MAN FROM THE FIRST CENTURY, THE(1961, Czech.)

Josef Hlinomatz
MAN FROM THE FIRST CENTURY, THE(1961, Czech.)

Josef Hlinomaz
DEVIL'S TRAP, THE(1964, Czech.); LEMONADE JOE(1966, Czech.); DEATH OF TARZAN, THE(1968, Czech); HAPPY END(1968, Czech.); WISHING MACHINE(1971, Czech.)

Jiri Hlupy
ROCKET TO NOWHERE(1962, Czech.), spec eff; VOYAGE TO THE END OF THE UNIVERSE(1963, Czech.), spec eff; LAST ACT OF MARTIN WESTON, THE(1970, Can./Czech.), art d; ON THE COMET(1970, Czech.), art d

Mario Hmaya
LOVE HUNGER(1965, Arg.)

A. Kitman Ho
LOVELESS, THE(1982), p

Andy Ho
OUTPOST IN MALAYA(1952, Brit.); LAUGHING ANNE(1954, Brit./U.S.); LADY OF VENGEANCE(1957, Brit); STOWAWAY GIRL(1957, Brit.); MARK OF THE HAWK, THE(1958); SAVAGE INNOCENTS, THE(1960, Brit.); SWISS FAMILY ROBINSON(1960); WORLD OF SUZIE WONG, THE(1960); SATAN NEVER SLEEPS(1962); 55 DAYS AT PEKING(1963); FERRY ACROSS THE MERSEY(1964, Brit.); KISS THE GIRLS AND MAKE THEM DIE(1967, U.S./Ital.); MATCHLESS(1967, Ital.); S(1974)

Cheng Chang Ho
FIVE FINGERS OF DEATH(1973, Hong Kong), d

Douglas Ho
OPEN THE DOOR AND SEE ALL THE PEOPLE(1964)

F.K. Ho
FIGHT TO THE LAST(1938, Chi.)

Hugh Ho
BLOOD ON THE SUN(1945)

John Ho
Misc. Silents
ILLUSION OF LOVE(1929)

Leonard K.C. Ho
S.T.A.B.(1976, Hong Kong/Thailand), p&d; SLAUGHTER IN SAN FRANCISCO(1981), p

Linda Ho
CONFESSIONS OF AN OPIUM EATER(1962); NUN AND THE SERGEANT, THE(1962); DIMENSION 5(1966); HILLBILLYS IN A HAUNTED HOUSE(1967)

Lou Ho
MILESTONES(1975)

Peter Chen Ho
SONS OF GOOD EARTH(1967, Hong Kong)

Marshall Ho'o
OSTERMAN WEEKEND, THE(1983)

C. B. Hoadley
Silents
ONCE A PLUMBER(1920), w; SHOCKING NIGHT, A(1921), w

Hal Hoadley
Silents
HER FIVE-FOOT HIGHNESS(1920), w

Christopher Hoag
CHILD'S PLAY(1972)

Doane Hoag
HIDEOUS SUN DEMON, THE(1959), w

Doan R. Hoag
COUNT THE HOURS(1953), w

Grant Hoag
SQUARES(1972), ed

Mitzi Hoag
TAMMY AND THE DOCTOR(1963); DEVIL'S ANGELS(1967); TRIP, THE(1967); COVER ME BABE(1970); PIECES OF DREAMS(1970); PLAY IT AS IT LAYS(1972); HOMETOWN U.S.A.(1979); WHY WOULD I LIE(1980); ALL NIGHT LONG(1981); HEART LIKE A WHEEL(1983)

Robert Hoag
ROLLIN' HOME TO TEXAS(1941); ATLANTIS, THE LOST CONTINENT(1961), spec eff

Robert R. Hoag
TWO WEEKS IN ANOTHER TOWN(1962), spec eff; GREEN MANSIONS(1959), spec eff; NEVER SO FEW(1959), spec eff; TARZAN, THE APE MAN(1959), spec eff; CIMARRON(1960), spec eff; GO NAKED IN THE WORLD(1961), spec eff; HONEYMOON MACHINE, THE(1961), spec eff; TWO LOVES(1961), spec eff; FOUR HORSEMEN OF THE APOCALYPSE, THE(1962), spec eff; HOW THE WEST WAS WON(1962), spec eff; JUMBO(1962), spec eff; MUTINY ON THE BOUNTY(1962), spec eff; WONDERFUL WORLD OF THE BROTHERS ERIMM, THE(1962), spec eff; COURTSHIP OF EDDY'S FATHER, THE(1963), spec eff; DRUMS OF AFRICA(1963), spec eff; OUTRAGE, THE(1964), spec eff; SEVEN FACES OF DR. LAO(1964), spec eff; UNSINKABLE MOLLY BROWN, THE(1964), spec eff; GREATEST STORY EVER TOLD, THE(1965), spec eff; SOYLENT GREEN(1973), spec eff

Edward Hoagland
ALICE IN WONDERLAND(1933), ed

Elisworth Hoagland
GOLDBERGS, THE(1950), ed

Ellsworth Hoagland
ONE SUNDAY AFTERNOON(1933), ed; NOW AND FOREVER(1934), ed; TRUMPET BLOWS, THE(1934), ed; LIVES OF A BENGAL LANCER(1935), ed; MILLIONS IN THE AIR(1935), ed; GIVE US THIS NIGHT(1936), ed; JUNGLE PRINCESS, THE(1936), ed; RHYTHM ON THE RANGE(1936), ed; DAUGHTER OF SHANGHAI(1937), ed; SOULS AT SEA(1937), ed; SPAWN OF THE NORTH(1938), ed; TIP-OFF GIRLS(1938), ed; ISLAND OF LOST MEN(1939), ed; SUDDEN MONEY(1939), ed; TOM SAWYER, DETECTIVE(1939), ed; CHRISTMAS IN JULY(1940), ed; DR. CYCLOPS(1940), ed; GHOST BREAKERS, THE(1940), ed; NIGHT OF JANUARY 16TH(1941), ed; SHEPHERD OF THE HILLS, THE(1941), ed; HOLIDAY INN(1942), ed; NIGHT IN NEW ORLEANS, A(1942), ed; NIGHT PLANE FROM CHUNGKING(1942), ed; HAPPY GO LUCKY(1943), ed; SO PROUDLY WE HAIL(1943), ed; HERE COME THE WAVES(1944), ed; I LOVE A SOLDIER(1944), ed; BRIDE WORE BOOTS, THE(1946), ed; PERFECT MARRIAGE, THE(1946), ed; MY FAVORITE BRUNETTE(1947), ed; ROAD TO RIO(1947), ed; PALEFACE, THE(1948), ed; GREAT GATSBY, THE(1949), ed; GREAT LOVER, THE(1949), ed; LET'S DANCE(1950), ed; UNION STATION(1950), ed; HERE COMES THE GROOM(1951), ed; GIRLS OF PLEASURE ISLAND, THE(1953), ed; CASANOVA'S BIG NIGHT(1954), ed; COUNTRY GIRL, THE(1954), ed; SEVEN LITTLE FOYS, THE(1955), ed; GREAT LOCOMOTIVE CHASE, THE(1956), ed; GUNSIGHT RIDGE(1957), ed; PRIDE AND THE PASSION, THE(1957), ed; PARIS HOLIDAY(1958), ed; GREAT GATSBY, THE(1974), ed

George Hoagland
SMART GIRLS DON'T TALK(1948); PEGGY(1950); LAS VEGAS STORY, THE(1952)

H. Ellsworth Hoagland
TONKA(1958), ed

Harlan Hoagland
GAL WHO TOOK THE WEST, THE(1949); SHE'S BACK ON BROADWAY(1953)

Jim Hoagland
1984
FLESHBURN(1984), spec eff
Ellsworth Hoaglund
CROSS MY HEART(1946), ed
Peter Hoar
OLIVER!(1968, Brit.)
Frank A. Hoare
SECRET CAVE, THE(1953, Brit.), p; JOHN OF THE FAIR(1962, Brit.), p
Frank Hoare
CIRCUS BOY(1947, Brit.), p; FOOL AND THE PRINCESS, THE(1948, Brit.), p; TRAPPED BY THE TERROR(1949, Brit.), p
John Hoare
RED PLANET MARS(1952), w
Lionel Hoare
THE BLACK HAND GANG(1930, Brit.); DARK JOURNEY(1937, Brit.), ed; REBELSON, THE ½(1939, Brit.), ed; GREAT PONY RAID, THE(1968, Brit.), p
Marjorie Hoare
Silents
UNREST(1920, Brit.)
Richard Hoare
MERRY CHRISTMAS MR. LAWRENCE(1983, Jap./Brit.)
Douglas Hoare
DOUBLE EVENT, THE(1934, Brit.), w
Ray Hoback
WAY DOWN EAST(1935)
Gordon Hoban
1984
MIKE'S MURDER(1984)
Robert Hoban
MR. RICCO(1975), w
Russell Hoban
MOUSE AND HIS CHILD, THE(1977), w
Stella Hoban
Misc. Silents
LURING LIGHTS(1915)
Alice Tisdale Hobart
OIL FOR THE LAMPS OF CHINA(1935), w; LAW OF THE TROPICS(1941), w; THIS EARTH IS MINE(1959), w
C. Doty Hobart
Silents
KINGDOM OF LOVE, THE(1918), w
Doty Hobart
Silents
BABY MINE(1917), w; WOMAN GOD CHANGED, THE(1921), w; LUCK(1923), w
Doug Hobart
STING OF DEATH(1966); DEATH CURSE OF TARTU(1967); FIREBALL JUNGLE(1968), sp eff; SCREAM, BABY, SCREAM(1969), makeup; FLESH FEAST(1970), spec eff
Henry Hobart
PAY OFF, THE(1930), p; SHE'S MY WEAKNESS(1930), p; HIGH STAKES(1931), p; WHITE SHOULDERS(1931), p
Silents
CRYSTAL CUP, THE(1927), p; NOOSE, THE(1928), p
Lyndon Hobart
Silents
RIDGEWAY OF MONTANA(1924)
Rose Hobart
LADY SURRENDERS, A(1930); LILIOM(1930); CHANCES(1931); COMPROMISED(1931); EAST OF BORNEO(1931); DR. JEKYLL AND MR. HYDE(1932); SCANDAL FOR SALE(1932); CONVENTION GIRL(1935); TOWER OF LONDON(1939); NIGHT AT EARL CARROLL'S, A(1940); SUSAN AND GOD(1940); WOLF OF NEW YORK(1940); I'LL SELL MY LIFE(1941); LADY BE GOOD(1941); MR. AND MRS. NORTH(1941); NO HANDS ON THE CLOCK(1941); NOTHING BUT THE TRUTH(1941); SINGAPORE WOMAN(1941); ZIEGFELD GIRL(1941); DR. GILLESPIE'S NEW ASSISTANT(1942); GALLANT LADY(1942); GENTLEMAN AT HEART, A(1942); PRISON GIRL(1942); AIR RAID WARDENS(1943); CRIME DOCTOR'S STRANGEST CASE(1943); MAD GHOUL, THE(1943); SALUTE TO THE MARINES(1943); SWING SHIFT MAISIE(1943); SONG OF THE OPEN ROAD(1944); SOUL OF A MONSTER, THE(1944); BRIGHTON STRANGLER, THE(1945); CONFLICT(1945); CANYON PASSAGE(1946); CAT CREEPS, THE(1946); CLAUDIA AND DAVID(1946); CASS TIMBERLANE(1947); FARMER'S DAUGHTER, THE(1947); TROUBLE WITH WOMEN, THE(1947); MICKEY(1948); BRIDE OF VENGEANCE(1949)
Misc. Talkies
SHADOW LAUGHS(1933)
Vera Hobart
RING AROUND THE MOON(1936), w
Halliwell Hobbes
JEALOUSY(1929); LUCKY IN LOVE(1929); CHARLEY'S AUNT(1930); GRUMPY(1930); SCOTLAND YARD(1930); BACHELOR FATHER(1931); FIVE AND TEN(1931); PLATINUM BLONDE(1931); RIGHT OF WAY, THE(1931); SIN OF MADELON CLAUDET, THE(1931); WOMAN BETWEEN(1931); DEVIL'S LOTTERY(1932); DR. JEKYLL AND MR. HYDE(1932); FORBIDDEN(1932); LOVE AFFAIR(1932); LOVERS COURAGEOUS(1932); MAN ABOUT TOWN(1932); MENACE, THE(1932); PAYMENT DEFERRED(1932); SIX HOURS TO LIVE(1932); WEEK-ENDS ONLY(1932); IF I WERE FREE(1933); LADY FOR A DAY(1933); LOOKING FORWARD(1933); MASQUERADER(1933); MIDNIGHT MARY(1933); SHOULD LADIES BEHAVE?(1933); STUDY IN SCARLET, A(1933); ALL MEN ARE ENEMIES(1934); BRITISH AGENT(1934); BULLDOG DRUMMOND STRIKES BACK(1934); DOUBLE DOOR(1934); I AM SUZANNE(1934); KEY, THE(1934); MADAME DU BARRY(1934); MANDALAY(1934); MENACE(1934); RIP TIDE(1934); WE LIVE AGAIN(1934); CAPTAIN BLOOD(1935); CARDINAL RICHELIEU(1935); CHARLIE CHAN IN SHANGHAI(1935); FATHER BROWN, DETECTIVE(1935); FOLIES DERGERE(1935); JALNA(1935); MILLIONS IN THE AIR(1935); RIGHT TO LIVE, THE(1935); DRACULA'S DAUGHTER(1936); GIVE ME YOUR HEART(1936); HEARTS DIVIDED(1936); HERE COMES TROUBLE(1936); LOVE LETTERS OF A STAR(1936); ROSE MARIE(1936); SPENDTHRIFT(1936); STORY OF LOUIS PASTEUR, THE(1936); WHIPSAW(1936); WHITE ANGEL, THE(1936); FIT FOR A KING(1937); MAID OF SALEM(1937); PARNELL(1937); PRINCE AND THE PAUPER, THE(1937); VARSITY SHOW(1937); BULLDOG DRUMMOND'S PERIL(1938); CHRISTMAS CAROL, A(1938);

JURY'S SECRET, THE(1938); KIDNAPPED(1938); SERVICE DE LUXE(1938); STORM OVER BENGAL(1938); YOU CAN'T TAKE IT WITH YOU(1938); HARDYS RIDE HIGH, THE(1939); LIGHT THAT FAILED, THE(1939); NAUGHTY BUT NICE(1939); NURSE EDITH CAVELL(1939); PACIFIC LINER(1939); REMEMBER?(1939); TELL NO TALES(1939); EARL OF CHICAGO, THE(1940); LADY WITH RED HAIR(1940); SEA HAWK, THE(1940); THIRD FINGER, LEFT HAND(1940); WATERLOO BRIDGE(1940); HERE COMES MR. JORDAN(1941); THAT HAMILTON WOMAN(1941); JOURNEY FOR MARGARET(1942); SON OF FURY(1942); TO BE OR NOT TO BE(1942); UNDYING MONSTER, THE(1942); WAR AGAINST MRS. HADLEY, THE(1942); FOREVER AND A DAY(1943); MR. MUGGS STEPS OUT(1943); SHERLOCK HOLMES FACES DEATH(1943); CASANOVA BROWN(1944); INVISIBLE MAN'S REVENGE(1944); MR. SKEFFINGTON(1944); CANYON PASSAGE(1946); IF WINTER COMES(1947); YOU GOTTA STAY HAPPY(1948); MIRACLE IN THE RAIN(1956)
Peter Hobbes
BARRETTS OF WIMPOLE STREET, THE(1934); TOP HAT(1935); WITHOUT REGRET(1935); SYLVIA SCARLETT(1936); IDEAL HUSBAND, AN(1948, Brit.); KISS THE BLOOD OFF MY HANDS(1948); MY BROTHER JONATHAN(1949, Brit.); LADY WITH A LAMP, THE(1951, Brit.); GLORY AT SEA(1952, Brit.); VIOLENT STRANGER(1957, Brit.); CURSE OF THE DEMON(1958)
Peter Halliwell Hobbes
MAXWELL ARCHER, DETECTIVE(1942, Brit.)
Duke Hobbie
CAT BALLOU(1965); WINTER A GO-GO(1965); ALVAREZ KELLY(1966); IN COLD BLOOD(1967); TIME FOR KILLING, A(1967); FOR SINGLES ONLY(1968); MACKENNA'S GOLD(1969); MAROONED(1969); MODEL SHOP, THE(1969)
Carleton Hobbs
PERFECT FRIDAY(1970, Brit.); DARK PLACES(1974, Brit.)
Carol Hobbs
PUTNEY SWOPE(1969)
Cecily Hobbs
FRENCH LIEUTENANT'S WOMAN, THE(1981)
1984
PLOUGHMAN'S LUNCH, THE(1984, Brit.)
Christopher Hobbs
JUBILEE(1978, Brit.), d&w, prod d
David Hobbs
STROKER ACE(1983)
Frank Hobbs
J.W. COOP(1971)
Frederic Hobbs
TROIKA(1969), d, w, set d
Fredric Hobbs
TROIKA(1969)
Misc. Talkies
ALABAMA'S GHOST(1972), d
Hayford Hobbs
DEVIL'S MAZE, THE(1929, Brit.); HIGH TREASON(1929, Brit.)
Silents
FIRM OF GIRDLESTONE, THE(1915, Brit.); KING'S DAUGHTER, THE(1916, Brit.); PRINCESS OF HAPPY CHANCE, THE(1916, Brit.); ASTHORE(1917, Brit.); GAY LORD QUEX, THE(1917, Brit.); GRIT OF A JEW(1917, Brit.); MAN AND THE MOMENT, THE(1918, Brit.); NOT GUILTY(1919, Brit.); POLAR STAR, THE(1919, Brit.); MANCHESTER MAN, THE(1920, Brit.); STRANGER'S BANQUET(1922); PRISONER, THE(1923); FLAG LIEUTENANT, THE(1926, Brit.); RINGER, THE(1928, Brit.); SMASHING THROUGH(1928, Brit.)
Misc. Silents
HEART OF A CHILD, THE(1915, Brit.); HEART OF SISTER ANN, THE(1915, Brit.); SONS OF SATAN, THE(1915, Brit.); THIRD GENERATION, THE(1915, Brit.); 1914(1915, Brit.); MAN IN MOTLEY, THE(1916, Brit.); WHEN KNIGHTS WERE BOLD(1916, Brit.); DOMBEY AND SON(1917, Brit.); HINDLE WAKES(1918, Brit.); RUGGED PATH, THE(1918, Brit.); SLAVE, THE(1918, Brit.); TOP DOG, THE(1918, Brit.); WAGES OF SIN, THE(1918, Brit.); FETTERED(1919, Brit.); SPLENDID FOLLY(1919, Brit.); WHEN IT WAS DARK(1919, Brit.); WHOSOEVER SHALL OFFEND(1919, Brit.); BACHELOR HUSBAND, THE(1920 Brit.); BREED OF THE TRESHAMS(1920, Brit.); CASTLES IN SPAIN(1920, Brit.); GLAD EYE, THE(1920, Brit.); IN THE NIGHT(1920, Brit.); THAT MAN JACK!(1925); LUCK OF THE NAVY, THE(1927, Brit.); REMEMBRANCE(1927, Brit.); THIRD EYE, THE(1929, Brit.)
Jack Hobbs
DR. JOSSER KC(1931, Brit.); LOVE LIES(1931, Brit.); LOVE RACE, THE(1931, Brit.); MISCHIEF(1931, Brit.); NEVER TROUBLE TROUBLE(1931, Brit.); HIS WIFE'S MOTHER(1932, Brit.); JOSSER IN THE ARMY(1932, Brit.); JOSSER JOINS THE NAVY(1932, Brit.); LAST COUPON, THE(1932, Brit.); TOO MANY WIVES(1933, Brit.); OH NO DOCTOR!(1934, Brit.); CAR OF DREAMS(1935, Brit.); HANDLE WITH CARE(1935, Brit.); NO LIMIT(1935, Brit.); ALL THAT GLITTERS(1936, Brit.); INTERRUPTED HONEYMOON, THE(1936, Brit.); MILLIONS(1936, Brit.); FINE FEATHERS(1937, Brit.); INTIMATE RELATIONS(1937, Brit.); LEAVE IT TO ME(1937, Brit.); SHOW GOES ON, THE(1937, Brit.); WHEN THE DEVIL WAS WELL(1937, Brit.); WHY PICK ON ME?(1937, Brit.); MAKE IT THREE(1938, Brit.); MIRACLES DO HAPPEN(1938, Brit.); IT'S IN THE AIR(1940, Brit.)
Silents
CALL OF YOUTH, THE(1920, Brit.); FACE AT THE WINDOW, THE(1920, Brit.); CRIMSON CIRCLE, THE(1922, Brit.); ELEVENTH COMMANDMENT, THE(1924, Brit.)
Misc. Silents
TOM BROWN'S SCHOOLDAYS(1916, Brit.); LADY CLARE, THE(1919, Brit.); INHERITANCE(1920, Brit.); SHUTTLE OF LIFE, THE(1920, Brit.); CALL OF YOUTH, THE(1921, Brit.); LONELY LADY OF GROSVENOR, THE(1922, Brit.); HAPPY ENDING, THE(1925, Brit.)
Jessica Hobbs
GYPSY GIRL(1966, Brit.)
Nick Hobbs
OCTOPUSSY(1983, Brit.), stunts
Peter Hobbs
YANK IN LONDON, A(1946, Brit.); LOST BOUNDARIES(1949); GOOD NEIGHBOR SAM(1964); KILLERS, THE(1964); NEW INTERNS, THE(1964); STAR SPANGLED GIRL(1971); STEAGLE(1971); SLEEPER(1973); WIZARDS(1977); LADY IN RED, THE(1979); LOVING COUPLES(1980); NINE TO FIVE(1980); NEXT ONE, THE(1982, U.S./Gr.); MAN WITH TWO BRAINS, THE(1983)

Ralph Hobbs
ON THE YARD(1978)
Robert Hobbs
BUSMAN'S HOLIDAY(1936, Brit.); DR. SIN FANG(1937, Brit.); RACING ROMAN-CE(1937, Brit.); CHINATOWN NIGHTS(1938, Brit.); FATHER O'FLYNN(1938, Irish)
Ron Hobbs
MAIDSTONE(1970); DOMINO PRINCIPLE, THE(1977), art d; DEER HUNTER, THE(1978), art d; JUST YOU AND ME, KID(1979), prod d; HUNTER, THE(1980), prod d; TOM HORN(1980), art d; PERSONAL BEST(1982), prod d; SMOKEY AND THE BANDIT–PART 3(1983), art d
1984
COUNTRY(1984), prod d; FOOTLOOSE(1984), prod d
Ronald E. Hobbs
RAVAGERS, THE(1979), prod d
Ronald Hobbs
LORD SHANGO(1975), p
Valerie Hobbs
MAGIC CHRISTMAS TREE(1964)
Virginia Hobbs
Silents
IS YOUR DAUGHTER SAFE?(1927)
William Hobbs
OTHELLO(1965, Brit.); MACBETH(1971, Brit.); THREE MUSKETEERS, THE(1974, Panama); ROBIN AND MARIAN(1976, Brit.), stunts; JOSEPH ANDREWS(1977, Brit.), stunts
Patrick Hobby
HOLLYWOOD BOULEVARD(1976), w
Les Hobeaux
INBETWEEN AGE, THE(1958, Brit.)
Gordon Hobel
BORN LOSERS(1967)
Mara Hobel
HAND, THE(1981); MOMMIE DEAREST(1981)
Mary-Ann Hobel
TENDER MERCIES(1982), p
Philip S. Hobel
TENDER MERCIES(1982), p
Barry Hober
ABSENCE OF MALICE(1981); SPRING BREAK(1983)
Hildor Hoberg
Misc. Silents
PRINCESS OF PATCHES, THE(1917)
Halliwell Hobes
GASLIGHT(1944)
Eugene Hobgood
MIKEY AND NICKY(1976)
Adam Hobhouse
REMEMBER LAST NIGHT(1935), w
Henry Hobhouse
FILES FROM SCOTLAND YARD(1951, Brit.), p
Pavel Hobl
LOST FACE, THE(1965, Czech.), d, w; DO YOU KEEP A LION AT HOME?(1966, Czech.), a, d, w
Macdonald Hobley
NO PLACE FOR JENNIFER(1950, Brit.); MEET MR. LUCIFER(1953, Brit.); MAN OF THE MOMENT(1955, Brit.)
McDonald Hobley
CHECKPOINT(1957, Brit.); ENTERTAINER, THE(1960, Brit.)
The Hobnobbers
YES SIR, MR. BONES(1951)
Hobo
TORTILLA FLAT(1942); NORTH TO ALASKA(1960)
Hobo the Dog
UNDERDOG, THE(1943); PLEASE DON'T EAT THE DAISIES(1960)
Al Hobson
STARHOPS(1978)
Gene Hobson
STUDENT BODIES(1981), m
Hubert Hobson
DANGEROUS PARTNERS(1945), art d; LITTLE MISTER JIM(1946), art d; MIGHTY MCGURK, THE(1946), art d
Hubert B. Hobson
MARRIAGE IS A PRIVATE AFFAIR(1944), art d; SON OF LASSIE(1945), art d
I.M. Hobson
ANNIE(1982)
Laura Z. Hobson
GENTLEMAN'S AGREEMENT(1947), w; HER TWELVE MEN(1954), w
Noah Hobson
RED, WHITE AND BLACK, THE(1970)
Valerie Hobson
EYES OF FATE(1933, Brit.); BADGER'S GREEN(1934, Brit.); PATH OF GLORY, THE(1934, Brit.); TWO HEARTS IN WALTZ TIME(1934, Brit.); CHINATOWN SQUAD(1935); GREAT IMPERSONATION, THE(1935); MAN WHO RECLAIMED HIS HEAD, THE(1935); MYSTERY OF EDWIN DROOD, THE(1935); OH, WHAT A NIGHT(1935); RENDEZVOUS AT MIDNIGHT(1935); STRANGE WIVES(1935); WERE-WOLF OF LONDON, THE(1935); AUGUST WEEK-END(1936, Brit.); NO ESCAPE(1936, Brit.); SECRET OF STAMBOUL, THE(1936, Brit.); WHEN THIEF MEETS THIEF(1937, Brit.); DRUMS(1938, Brit.); CLOUDS OVER EUROPE(1939, Brit.); CONTINENTAL EXPRESS(1939, Brit.); LIFE RETURNS(1939); THIS MAN IN PARIS(1939, Brit.); THIS MAN IS NEWS(1939, Brit.); U-BOAT 29(1939, Brit.); BLACKOUT(1940, Brit.); ATLAN-TIC FERRY(1941, Brit.); UNPUBLISHED STORY(1942, Brit.); ADVENTURES OF TARTU(1943, Brit.); GREAT EXPECTATIONS(1946, Brit.); YEARS BETWEEN, THE(1947, Brit.); BLANCHE FURY(1948, Brit.); HIDEOUT(1948, Brit.); INTERRUPT-ED JOURNEY, THE(1949, Brit.); KIND HEARTS AND CORONETS(1949, Brit.); ROCKING HORSE WINNER, THE(1950, Brit.); PASSIONATE SENTRY, THE(1952, Brit.); PROMOTER, THE(1952, Brit.); TRAIN OF EVENTS(1952, Brit.); BACK-GROUND(1953, Brit.); MURDER WILL OUT(1953, Brit.); TONIGHT AT 8:30(1953, Brit.); LOVERS, HAPPY LOVERS!(1955, Brit.)

Misc. Talkies
TUGBOAT PRINCESS(1936)
William Hobson
WILD PACK, THE(1972)
Takanobu Hobuzi
SHE AND HE(1967, Jap.)
Dew Hocevar
CHRISTMAS STORY, A(1983)
Edward D. Hoch
IT TAKES ALL KINDS(1969, U.S./Aus.), w
Emil Hoch
CHAMPAGNE WALTZ(1937)
Silents
PURSUING VENGEANCE, THE(1916); ROMANCE OF THE AIR, A(1919); AMERI-CA(1924)
Emile Hoch
Silents
EARL OF PAWTUCKET, THE(1915)
Winton Hoch
MELODY TIME(1948), ph; TULSA(1949), ph; RETURN TO PARADISE(1953), ph; BIG CIRCUS, THE(1959), ph; LOST WORLD, THE(1960), ph; FIVE WEEKS IN A BALLOON(1962), ph; NECROMANCY(1972), ph
Winton C. Hoch
DR. CYCLOPS(1940), ph; DIVE BOMBER(1941), ph; RELUCTANT DRAGON, THE(1941), ph; TAP ROOTS(1948), ph; THREE GODFATHERS, THE(1948), ph; SHE WORE A YELLOW RIBBON(1949), ph; SO DEAR TO MY HEART(1949), ph; SUN-DOWNERS, THE(1950), ph; BIRD OF PARADISE(1951), ph; HALLS OF MON-TEZUMA(1951), ph; QUIET MAN, THE(1952), ph; REDHEAD FROM WYOMING, THE(1953), ph; MISTER ROBERTS(1955), ph; SEARCHERS, THE(1956), ph; JET PILOT(1957), ph, ph; MISSOURI TRAVELER, THE(1958), ph; DARBY O'GILL AND THE LITTLE PEOPLE(1959), ph; THIS EARTH IS MINE(1959), ph; YOUNG LAND, THE(1959), ph; VOYAGE TO THE BOTTOM OF THE SEA(1961), ph; SERGEANTS 3(1962), ph; ROBINSON CRUSOE ON MARS(1964), ph; GREEN BERETS, THE(1968), ph
Werner Hochbaum
ETERNAL MASK, THE(1937, Swiss), d
Charles Hochberg
SIDEWALKS OF NEW YORK(1931), ed
Trudi Hochfilzer
ASSIGNMENT K(1968, Brit.)
Rolf Hochhuth
1984
LOVE IN GERMANY, A(1984, Fr./Ger.), w
Larry Hochman
1984
BIRDY(1984)
Rosemary Hochschild
KING BLANK(1983), a, w
Gerda Hochst
SERGEANT BERRY(1938, Ger.)
Joseph Hochstein
LIGHT FANTASTIC(1964), w
John Hock
CATTLE ANNIE AND LITTLE BRITCHES(1981)
Peter Hock
LADY IN CEMENT(1968); GOD TOLD ME TO(1976); Q(1982); TRADING PLA-CES(1983)
Charles Hockberg
UNTAMED(1929), ed
David Hockenberry
HARDCORE(1979)
Hocker
M(1933, Ger.)
Harry Hocker
PASSION HOLIDAY(1963)
Oskar Hocker
THREEPENNY OPERA, THE(1931, Ger./U.S.)
Paul Oskar Hocker
TESTAMENT OF DR. MABUSE, THE(1943, Ger.)
Alan Hockey
GET CARTER(1971, Brit.)
Anne Hocking
SURGEON'S KNIFE, THE(1957, Brit.), w
Dorothy Hocking
LADY GODIVA RIDES AGAIN(1955, Brit.)
Joseph Hocking
Silents
ALL MEN ARE LIARS(1919, Brit.), w
Ned Hockman
STARK FEAR(1963), p, d
Albert Hockmeister
MC MASTERS, THE(1970)
David Hockney
1984
BIGGER SPLASH, A(1984)
Edmund Hockridge
FOR BETTER FOR WORSE(1954, Brit.); KING'S RHAPSODY(1955, Brit.)
Harry Hocky
Silents
NEW YORK IDEA, THE(1920)
Harriet Hoctor
SHALL WE DANCE(1937)
Harriett Hoctor
GREAT ZIEGFELD, THE(1936)
Gregory Hodal
1984
IRRECONCILABLE DIFFERENCES(1984)

Gregory L. Hodal
PARTNERS(1982)
Kane Hodder
1984
HARDBODIES(1984)
Alun Hoddinott
SWORD OF SHERWOOD FOREST(1961, Brit.), m
Barbara Hoddinott
MY BODYGUARD(1980)
Bert Hoddinott
MY BODYGUARD(1980)
Steve Hoddy
Misc. Talkies
THEIR ONLY CHANCE(1978)
Andre Hodeir
LA PARISIENNE(1958, Fr./Ital.), m; COME DANCE WITH ME(1960, Fr.), m; TIME BOMB(1961, Fr./Ital.), m; DE L'AMOUR(1968, Fr./Ital.), m; CHECKERBOARD(1969, Fr.), m
Mike Hodel
PUNISHMENT PARK(1971)
Terry Hodel
PUNISHMENT PARK(1971), ed
Roberta O. Hodes
LAD: A DOG(1962), w
Stuart Hodes
VOICES(1979), ch
John Philip Hodgdon
VISIT TO A CHIEF'S SON(1974)
William Hodgdon
ESCAPED FROM DARTMOOR(1930, Brit.), m
Al Hodge
LOVER COME BACK(1961); OUTSIDER, THE(1962)
Bill Hodge
DANGEROUS ASSIGNMENT(1950, Brit.)
Bob Hodge
Misc. Talkies
FUN AND GAMES(1973)
Christopher Hodge
HOME TO DANGER(1951, Brit.)
Edward Hodge
SONG OF THE FORGE(1937, Brit.); BRIEF ENCOUNTER(1945, Brit.); HIDEOUT(1948, Brit.)
Harold Hodge
LAW FOR TOMBSTONE(1937); SANDFLOW(1937); SUDDEN BILL DORN(1938)
Jim Hodge
1984
OH GOD! YOU DEVIL(1984)
Jonathan Hodge
VILLAIN(1971, Brit.), m; EMBASSY(1972, Brit.), m; Z.P.G.(1972), m
Mary Jane Hodge
FOLIES DERGERE(1935)
Patricia Hodge
ELEPHANT MAN, THE(1980, Brit.)
Raymond Hodge
WOMAN'S TEMPTATION, A(1959, Brit.)
Robert Hodge
WINDOWS(1980)
Steven Hodge
Misc. Talkies
COUNTRY CUZZINS(1972)
Vicky Hodge
TOMCAT, THE(1968, Brit.)
W. E. Hodge
SILK NOOSE, THE(1950, Brit.)
W. Edward Hodge
DOUBLE OR QUITS(1938, Brit.)
W. T. Hodge
MEN WITHOUT HONOUR(1939, Brit.)
William Hodge
NO SAFETY AHEAD(1959, Brit.); TOP FLOOR GIRL(1959, Brit.)
Ted Hodgeman
MONEY MOVERS(1978, Aus.)
Bob Hodges
STORMY TRAILS(1936)
Clay Hodges
MOVIE MOVIE(1978); CHINA SYNDROME, THE(1979)
Douglas Hodges
THE INVISIBLE RAY(1936), w
Earl Hodges
ROARING SIX GUNS(1937)
Eddie Hodges
HOLE IN THE HEAD, A(1959); ADVENTURES OF HUCKLEBERRY FINN, THE(1960); ADVISE AND CONSENT(1962); SUMMER MAGIC(1963); C'MON, LET'S LIVE A LITTLE(1967); HAPPIEST MILLIONAIRE, THE(1967); LIVE A LITTLE, LOVE A LITTLE(1968)
Eric Hodges
JOHN OF THE FAIR(1962, Brit.), ed
Greg Hodges
THE DOUBLE McGUFFIN(1979)
Hal Hodges
FROGS(1972)
Hollis Hodges
WHY WOULD I LIE(1980), w
Horace Hodges
ESCAPE(1930, Brit.); GRUMPY(1930), w; NIGHT IN MONTMARTE, A(1931, Brit.); OTHER PEOPLE'S SINS(1931, Brit.); SUMMER LIGHTNING(1933, Brit.); ROLLING IN MONEY(1934, Brit.); BIRDS OF A FEATHER(1935, Brit.); OLD FAITHFUL(1935, Brit.); OLD ROSES(1935, Brit.); GIRLS IN THE STREET(1937, Brit.); SHOW GOES ON, THE(1937, Brit.); FOLLOW YOUR STAR(1938, Brit.); GIRL IN THE STREET(1938, Brit.); SHOW GOES ON, THE(1938, Brit.); JAMAICA INN(1939, Brit.)

Jack Hodges
SHIPMATES O' MINE(1936, Brit.); IT'S A WONDERFUL DAY(1949, Brit.)
Joy Hodges
OLD MAN RHYTHM(1935); TO BEAT THE BAND(1935); FOLLOW THE FLEET(1936); MERRY-GO-ROUND OF 1938(1937); SPECIAL AGENT K-7(1937); PERSONAL SECRETARY(1938); SERVICE DE LUXE(1938); FAMILY NEXT DOOR, THE(1939); LITTLE ACCIDENT(1939); THEY ASKED FOR IT(1939); UNEXPECTED FATHER(1939); LAUGHING AT DANGER(1940); MARGIE(1940)
Ken Hodges
FACES IN THE DARK(1960, Brit.), ph; SWORD OF SHERWOOD FOREST(1961, Brit.), ph; WEEKEND WITH LULU, A(1961, Brit.), ph; DEAD MAN'S EVIDENCE(1962, Brit.), ph; DREAM MAKER, THE(1963, Brit.), ph; ASSIGNMENT K(1968, Brit.), ph; FILE OF THE GOLDEN GOOSE, THE(1969, Brit.), ph; DAVID COPPERFIELD(1970, Brit.), ph; THINK DIRTY(1970, Brit.), ph; ASSAULT(1971, Brit.), ph; TERROR FROM UNDER THE HOUSE(1971, Brit.), ph; DAY IN THE DEATH OF JOE EGG, A(1972, Brit.), ph; RULING CLASS, THE(1972, Brit.), ph; SPIRAL STAIRCASE, THE(1975, Brit.), ph; CONFESSIONS FROM A HOLIDAY CAMP(1977, Brit.), ph; STAND UP VIRGIN SOLDIERS(1977, Brit.), ph; ODD JOB, THE(1978, Brit.), ph; NO SEX PLEASE–WE'RE BRITISH(1979, Brit.), ph
Kenneth Hodges
DESERT MICE(1960, Brit.), ph; GREAT ST. TRINIAN'S TRAIN ROBBERY, THE(1966, Brit.), ph; JOKERS, THE(1967, Brit.), ph; INADMISSIBLE EVIDENCE(1968, Brit.), ph; SHUTTERED ROOM, THE(1968, Brit.), ph
Maxine Hodges
Silents
JUNGLE, THE(1914)
Michael Hodges
PULP(1972, Brit.), d&w; DAMIEN–OMEN II(1978), w
Mike Hodges
GET CARTER(1971, Brit.), d&w; TERMINAL MAN, THE(1974), p,d&w; FLASH GORDON(1980), d
Pat Hodges
HEAVEN'S GATE(1980)
Ralph Hodges
NEARLY EIGHTEEN(1943); HEADING FOR HEAVEN(1947); MANHATTAN ANGEL(1948); NO WAY OUT(1950); MILLIONAIRE FOR CHRISTY, A(1951); TWO DOLLAR BETTOR(1951); TWO TICKETS TO BROADWAY(1951); YANK IN KOREA, A(1951)
Misc. Talkies
SWEET GENEVIEVE(1947)
Ron Hodges
YOICKS!(1932, Brit.)
Runa Hodges
Silents
FOOL THERE WAS, A(1915)
Misc. Silents
SHOULD A MOTHER TELL?(1915)
Barry Hodgin
BLOOD WATERS OF DOCTOR Z(1982), m
Earl Hodgins
CYCLONE RANGER(1935); HARMONY LANE(1935); ACES AND EIGHTS(1936); BORDER CABALLERO(1936); GUNS AND GUITARS(1936); I COVER THE WAR(1937); NATION AFLAME(1937); OH, SUSANNA(1937); LAST STAND, THE(1938); ALMOST A GENTLEMAN(1939); HOME ON THE PRAIRIE(1939); CAPTAIN IS A LADY, THE(1940); INSIDE THE LAW(1942); AVENGING RIDER, THE(1943); COLT COMRADES(1943); HI'YA, CHUM(1943); BEDSIDE MANNER(1945); G.I. HONEYMOON(1945); SONG OF THE THIN MAN(1947); RETURN OF THE BADMEN(1948); COPPER CANYON(1950); CAUSE FOR ALARM(1951); GREAT JESSE JAMES RAID, THE(1953); BITTER CREEK(1954); FIRST TRAVELING SALESLADY, THE(1956)
Earle Hodgins
CIRCUS CLOWN(1934); PARADISE CANYON(1935); SINGING COWBOY, THE(1936); TICKET TO PARADISE(1936); ALL OVER TOWN(1937); GHOST TOWN GOLD(1937); HEADIN' EAST(1937); HILLS OF OLD WYOMING(1937); LAW FOR TOMBSTONE(1937); LAWMAN IS BORN, A(1937); MOUNTAIN JUSTICE(1937); RANGE DEFENDERS(1937); ROUNDUP TIME IN TEXAS(1937); SMOKE TREE RANGE(1937); TEXAS TRAIL(1937); TRAIL OF VENGEANCE(1937); BAREFOOT BOY(1938); CALL THE MESQUITEERS(1938); HEROES OF THE ALAMO(1938); LAWLESS VALLEY(1938); OLD BARN DANCE, THE(1938); OUTLAWS OF THE PRAIRIE(1938); PARTNERS OF THE PLAINS(1938); PRIDE OF THE WEST(1938); PURPLE VIGILANTES, THE(1938); RANGER'S ROUNDUP, THE(1938); LONG SHOT, THE(1939); PANAMA LADY(1939); RANGE WAR(1939); FLORIAN(1940); LAW AND ORDER(1940); MEN AGAINST THE SKY(1940); MY FAVORITE WIFE(1940); RANGE BUSTERS, THE(1940); SAGEBRUSH FAMILY TRAILS WEST, THE(1940); SANTA FE MARSHAL(1940); STRIKE UP THE BAND(1940); TRAIL OF THE VIGILANTES(1940); UNDER TEXAS SKIES(1940); BOSS OF BULLION CITY(1941); KEEP 'EM FLYING(1941); SCATTERGOOD PULLS THE STRINGS(1941); SIERRA SUE(1941); SING FOR YOUR SUPPER(1941); BASHFUL BACHELOR, THE(1942); DEEP IN THE HEART OF TEXAS(1942); FIGHTING BILL FARGO(1942); MY FAVORITE SPY(1942); RIDING THE WIND(1942); SCATTERGOOD SURVIVES A MURDER(1942); SHUT MY BIG MOUTH(1942); SILVER QUEEN(1942); UNDERCOVER MAN(1942); BAR 20(1943); CHATTERBOX(1943); FALSE COLORS(1943); FRONTIER BADMEN(1943); FRONTIER LAW(1943); GANGWAY FOR TOMORROW(1943); GILDERSLEEVE'S BAD DAY(1943); HOPPY SERVES A WRIT(1943); LADIES' DAY(1943); LAUGH YOUR BLUES AWAY(1943); LONE STAR TRAIL, THE(1943); MAN FROM THE RIO GRANDE, THE(1943); OLD CHISHOLM TRAIL(1943); RAIDERS OF SAN JOAQUIN(1943); RED RIVER ROBIN HOOD(1943); RIDERS OF THE DEADLINE(1943); TENTING TONIGHT ON THE OLD CAMP GROUND(1943); FIREBRANDS OF ARIZONA(1944); HIDDEN VALLEY OUTLAWS(1944); LUMBERJACK(1944); PRACTICALLY YOURS(1944); RIDERS OF THE SANTA FE(1944); SAN ANTONIO KID, THE(1944); SENSATIONS OF 1945(1944); OREGON TRAIL(1945); PHANTOM OF THE PLAINS(1945); SOUTHERNER, THE(1945); TOPEKA TERROR, THE(1945); UNDER WESTERN SKIES(1945); ACCOMPLICE(1946); BACHELOR'S DAUGHTERS, THE(1946); DEADLINE AT DAWN(1946); DEVIL'S PLAYGROUND(1946); FOOL'S GOLD(1946); GUN TOWN(1946); LIVE WIRES(1946); RUSTLER'S ROUNDUP(1946); UNEXPECTED GUEST(1946); VALLEY OF THE ZOMBIES(1946); DESIRE ME(1947); HOLLYWOOD BARN DANCE(1947); MARAUDERS, THE(1947); OREGON TRAIL SCOUTS(1947); RETURN OF RIN TIN TIN, THE(1947); SEA OF GRASS, THE(1947); VIGILANTES OF BOOMTOWN(1947); BIG CLOCK, THE(1948); HAZARD(1948); IF

YOU KNEW SUSIE(1948); LET'S LIVE AGAIN(1948); OKLAHOMA BAD-LANDS(1948); OLD LOS ANGELES(1948); PALEFACE, THE(1948); SILENT CONFLICT(1948); HENRY, THE RAINMAKER(1949); SHERIFF OF WICHITA(1949); SLIGHTLY FRENCH(1949); PETTY GIRL, THE(1950); SAVAGE HORDE, THE(1950); SQUARE DANCE KATY(1950); WHERE DANGER LIVES(1950); SHOW BOAT(1951); STRIP, THE(1951); TEXAS CARNIVAL(1951); BOOTS MALONE(1952); LONE STAR(1952); GIRL WHO HAD EVERYTHING, THE(1953); THUNDER OVER THE PLAINS(1953); FORTYNINERS, THE(1954); GUYS AND DOLLS(1955); FASTEST GUN ALIVE(1956); FRIENDLY PERSUASION(1956); D.I., THE(1957); OKLAHOMAN, THE(1957); UP IN SMOKE(1957); IN THE MONEY(1958); MARDI GRAS(1958); MISSOURI TRAVELER, THE(1958); MAN WHO SHOT LIBERTY VALANCE, THE(1962); SAINTLY SINNERS(1962)
Misc. Talkies
TEXAS RAMBLER, THE(1935); AND NOW TOMORROW(1952)
Eric Hodgins
MR. BLANDINGS BUILDS HIS DREAM HOUSE(1948), w
George Hodgins
DRAGSTRIP RIOT(1958), w
Brian Hodgson
LEGEND OF HELL HOUSE, THE(1973, Brit.), m
Charles Hodgson
PERCY(1971, Brit.)
Gaynor Hodgson
SCROOGE(1970, Brit.)
J.L. Hodgson
GOOD COMPANIONS, THE(1957, Brit.), w
Leland Hodgson
HUMAN SIDE, THE(1934); ADVENTUROUS BLONDE(1937); MY SON, MY SON!(1940); SHANGHAI GESTURE, THE(1941); JOHNNY ANGEL(1945); BEDLAM(1946); JOAN OF ARC(1948); KISS THE BLOOD OFF MY HANDS(1948)
Leyland Hodgson
CASE OF SERGEANT GRISCHA, THE(1930); HIGH STAKES(1931); LADIES OF THE JURY(1932); ONCE IN A LIFETIME(1932); UNDER-COVER MAN(1932); EAGLE AND THE HAWK, THE(1933); FEATHER IN HER HAT, A(1935); BELOVED ENEMY(1936); TROUBLE FOR TWO(1936); CALL IT A DAY(1937); GREAT GARRICK, THE(1937); PERSONAL PROPERTY(1937); PRINCE AND THE PAUPER, THE(1937); WHEN YOU'RE IN LOVE(1937); FOOLS FOR SCANDAL(1938); MR. MOTO TAKES A VACATION(1938); DARK VICTORY(1939); ETERNALLY YOURS(1939); LOVE AFFAIR(1939); MR. MOTO'S LAST WARNING(1939); RAFFLES(1939); RAINS CAME, THE(1939); SECOND FIDDLE(1939); SUSANNAH OF THE MOUNTIES(1939); THEY MADE ME A CRIMINAL(1939); WE ARE NOT ALONE(1939); WITNESS VANISHES, THE(1939); YOU CAN'T CHEAT AN HONEST MAN(1939); ARISE, MY LOVE(1940); HE MARRIED HIS WIFE(1940); INVISIBLE MAN RETURNS, THE(1940); LILLIAN RUSSELL(1940); MAN I MARRIED, THE(1940); MURDER OVER NEW YORK(1940); REBECCA(1940); SEA HAWK, THE(1940); SON OF MONTE CRISTO(1940); SOUTH OF SUEZ(1940); CASE OF THE BLACK PARROT, THE(1941); INTERNATIONAL LADY(1941); INTERNATIONAL SQUADRON(1941); KID FROM KANSAS, THE(1941); MOON OVER MIAMI(1941); RAGE IN HEAVEN(1941); SCOTLAND YARD(1941); WOLF MAN, THE(1941); ESCAPE FROM HONG KONG(1942); GHOST OF FRANKENSTEIN, THE(1942); JOURNEY FOR MARGARET(1942); JUST OFF BROADWAY(1942); MY FAVORITE BLONDE(1942); SECRET AGENT OF JAPAN(1942); SHERLOCK HOLMES AND THE SECRET WEAPON(1942); SHERLOCK HOLMES AND THE VOICE OF TERROR(1942); STRANGE CASE OF DR. RX, THE(1942); TO BE OR NOT TO BE(1942); FLESH AND FANTASY(1943); GANG'S ALL HERE, THE(1943); HAPPY GO LUCKY(1943); HOLY MATRIMONY(1943); ENTER ARSENE LUPIN(1944); FOLLOW THE BOYS(1944); FRENCHMAN'S CREEK(1944); INVISIBLE MAN'S REVENGE(1944); MAN IN HALF-MOON STREET, THE(1944); NATIONAL VELVET(1944); NONE BUT THE LONELY HEART(1944); PEARL OF DEATH, THE(1944); UNINVITED, THE(1944); HANGOVER SQUARE(1945); MOLLY AND ME(1945); MY NAME IS JULIA ROSS(1945); BLACK BEAUTY(1946); RENDEZVOUS 24(1946); TERROR BY NIGHT(1946); THREE STRANGERS(1946); TO EACH HIS OWN(1946); UNDER NEVADA SKIES(1946); CALCUTTA(1947); IMPERFECT LADY, THE(1947); SINGAPORE(1947); TWO MRS. CARROLLS, THE(1947); WOMAN'S VENGEANCE, A(1947); CHALLENGE, THE(1948); MY OWN TRUE LOVE(1948); THAT FORSYTE WOMAN(1949)
Phoebe Hodgson
PANDORA AND THE FLYING DUTCHMAN(1951, Brit.); LADYKILLERS, THE(1956, Brit.)
John Hodiak
I DOOD IT(1943); SONG OF RUSSIA(1943); STRANGER IN TOWN, A(1943); SWING SHIFT MAISIE(1943); LIFEBOAT(1944); MAISIE GOES TO RENO(1944); MARRIAGE IS A PRIVATE AFFAIR(1944); SUNDAY DINNER FOR A SOLDIER(1944); BELL FOR ADANO, A(1945); HARVEY GIRLS, THE(1946); SOMEWHERE IN THE NIGHT(1946); TWO SMART PEOPLE(1946); ARNELO AFFAIR, THE(1947); DESERT FURY(1947); LOVE FROM A STRANGER(1947); COMMAND DECISION(1948); HOMECOMING(1948); BATTLEGROUND(1949); BRIBE, THE(1949); AMBUSH(1950); LADY WITHOUT PASSPORT, A(1950); MALAYA(1950); MINIVER STORY, THE(1950, Brit./U.S.); ACROSS THE WIDE MISSOURI(1951); NIGHT INTO MORNING(1951); PEOPLE AGAINST O'HARA, THE(1951); SELLOUT, THE(1951); BATTLE ZONE(1953); AMBUSH AT TOMAHAWK GAP(1953); CONQUEST OF COCHISE(1953); DRAGONFLY SQUADRON(1953); MISSION OVER KOREA(1953); TRIAL(1955); ON THE THRESHOLD OF SPACE(1956)
Katrina Hodiak
JANE AUSTEN IN MANHATTAN(1980)
Keith Hodiak
REVENGE OF THE PINK PANTHER(1978)
Yanko Hodjis
DEATH OF MARIO RICCI, THE(1983, Ital.), prod d
Burt Hodkins
Silents
MAN WORTH WHILE, THE(1921)
David Hodo
CAN'T STOP THE MUSIC(1980)
Zdenek Hodr
FIFTH HORSEMAN IS FEAR, THE(1968, Czech.)
J.L. Hodson
UNDER THE RED ROBE(1937, Brit.), w

James Lansdale Hodson
SOMETHING MONEY CAN'T BUY(1952, Brit.), w
Albert Hoeberg
DAY OF WRATH(1948, Den.)
Hans Hoebus
SEARCHING WIND, THE(1946)
Ernst Hoechstaetter
DECISION BEFORE DAWN(1951)
Marilyn Hoeck
HERE COME THE CO-EDS(1945)
Petros Hoedas
RECONSTRUCTION OF A CRIME(1970, Ger.)
Ursula Hoef
ALL-AROUND REDUCED PERSONALITY–OUTTAKES, THE(1978, Ger.), ed
Anita Hoefer
I, TOO, AM ONLY A WOMAN(1963, Ger.); SITUATION HOPELESS–BUT NOT SERIOUS(1965)
Jack Hoefer
Silents
GOLD RUSH, THE(1925)
Carl Hoeffle
SONG OF OLD WYOMING(1945), md
Carl Hoefle
CARAVAN TRAIL, THE(1946), m; DEATH VALLEY(1946), m; FLIGHT TO NOWHERE(1946), m; ROMANCE OF THE WEST(1946), md; SCARED TO DEATH(1947), m
Jocky Hoefli
Silents
SILVER VALLEY(1927)
Lucie Hoeflich
CASE VAN GELDERN(1932, Ger.); 1914(1932, Ger.)
Eleanor Wessel Hoeft
BOULDER DAM(1936)
Eric Hoeg
SPRINGFIELD RIFLE(1952)
Karel Hoeger
KRAKATIT(1948, Czech.)
Gunnar Hoeglund
WHALERS, THE(1942, Swed.)
Carola Hoehn
ROYAL WALTZ, THE(1936); ETERNAL LOVE(1960, Ger.)
George Hoellering
MURDER IN THE CATHEDRAL(1952, Brit.), p,d&w
Heinz Hoelscher
I, TOO, AM ONLY A WOMAN(1963, Ger.), ph
Anna Hoeltering
TRIAL, THE(1948, Aust.), ed
Rodney Hoeltzel
KING'S PIRATE(1967)
Hans Hoemburg
VICTOR/VICTORIA(1982), w
George Hoemier
BEGINNING OR THE END, THE(1947), ed
Jeremy Hoenack
HITCHHIKERS, THE(1972), ed
Misc. Talkies
KILLER'S DELIGHT(1978), d
Dov Hoenig
SOPHIE'S WAYS(1970, Fr.), ed; KAZABLAN(1974, Israel), ed; DIAMONDS(1975, U.S./Israel), ed; LEPKE(1975, U.S./Israel), ed; PASSOVER PLOT, THE(1976, Israel), ed; STONY ISLAND(1978), ed; THIEF(1981), ed; KEEP, THE(1983), ed
1984
BEAT STREET(1984), ed
Dov Hoening
YOUNG DOCTORS IN LOVE(1982), ed
Winfield Hoeny
NIAGARA(1953)
Paul Hoer
WALK WITH LOVE AND DEATH, A(1969)
Paolo Hoerbiger
LAUGH PAGLIACCI(1948, Ital.)
Paul Hoerbiger
ROYAL WALTZ, THE(1936); LITTLE MELODY FROM VIENNA(1948, Aust.); MOZART STORY, THE(1948, Aust.); OPERETTA(1949, Ger.); THIRD MAN, THE(1950, Brit.); ONE APRIL 2000(1952, Aust.); APRIL 1, 2000(1953, Aust.); DANCING HEART, THE(1959, Ger.)
Arthur Hoerl
BRIDE OF THE DESERT(1929), w; HANDCUFFED(1929), w; IN OLD CALIFORNIA(1929), w; PHANTOM IN THE HOUSE, THE(1929), w; SHOULD A GIRL MARRY?(1929), w; AIR POLICE(1931), w; GRIEF STREET(1931), w; HELL BENT FOR 'FRISCO(1931), w; LAWLESS WOMAN(1931), w; MIDNIGHT SPECIAL(1931), w; ARM OF THE LAW(1932), w; BIG TOWN(1932), d&w; CROSS-EXAMINATION(1932), w; DEVIL PAYS, THE(1932), w; LAST RIDE, THE(1932), w; MIDNIGHT PATROL, THE(1932), w; PROBATION(1932), w; STRANGE ADVENTURE(1932), w; THEY NEVER COME BACK(1932), w; THIRTEENTH GUEST, THE(1932), w; BEFORE MORNING(1933), d; HOTEL VARIETY(1933), p, w; DRUMS O' VOODOO(1934), d; ENLIGHTEN THY DAUGHTER(1934), w; LADY IN SCARLET, THE(1935), w; REEFER MADNESS(1936), w; FIGHTING PLAYBOY(1937), w; SPIRIT OF YOUTH(1937), w; CALIFORNIA FRONTIER(1938), w; CIPHER BUREAU(1938), w; LAW OF THE TEXAN(1938), w; PANAMA PATROL(1939), w; RIDE 'EM COWGIRL(1939), w; SINGING COWGIRL, THE(1939), w; WATER RUSTLERS(1939), w; ISLE OF DESTINY(1940), w; KILLERS OF THE WILD(1940), w; CRIMINALS WITHIN(1941), w; REG'LAR FELLERS(1941), w; SUNSET MURDER CASE(1941), w; ARIZONA STAGECOACH(1942), w; TEXAS TO BATAAN(1942), w; BOSS OF BIG TOWN(1943), w; GIRL FROM MONTEREY, THE(1943), w; HAUNTED RANCH, THE(1943), w; MYSTERY OF THE 13TH GUEST, THE(1943), w; SARONG GIRL(1943), w; ALASKA PATROL(1949), w; LOST TRIBE, THE(1949), w; SHAMROCK HILL(1949), w; THERE'S A GIRL IN MY HEART(1949), w; BORDER OUTLAWS(1950), w; KILLER APE(1953), w; AFRICAN MANHUNT(1955), w; DRUMS OF AFRICA(1963), w; TAFFY AND THE JUNGLE HUNTER(1965), w; YOUNG DILLIN-

GER(1965), w; FOR SINGLES ONLY(1968), w
Misc. Talkies
SHADOW LAUGHS(1933), d
Silents
LOVER'S ISLAND(1925), w; PRIDE OF THE FORCE, THE(1925), w; LIGHT IN THE WINDOW, THE(1927), w; ADORABLE CHEAT, THE(1928), w; GYPSY OF THE NORTH(1928), w; MAN FROM HEADQUARTERS(1928), w; MY HOME TOWN(1928), w; OBEY YOUR HUSBAND(1928), w; SWEET SIXTEEN(1928), w; ANNE AGAINST THE WORLD(1929), w; CAMPUS KNIGHTS(1929), w; DEVIL'S CHAPLAIN(1929), w; JUST OFF BROADWAY(1929), w, t; PEACOCK FAN(1929), w

Hoermann
M(1933, Ger.)
Jean Claude Hoerner
NEST, THE(1982, Span.), art d
Marjorie Hoerner
SWEETHEART OF SIGMA CHI(1946)
Albert Hoerrmann
GREAT BRITISH TRAIN ROBBERY, THE(1967, Ger.)
John Hoesli
ZARDOZ, set d; HOUR OF GLORY(1949, Brit.), set d; LONG HAUL, THE(1957, Brit.), art d; LION, THE(1962, Brit.), art d; SATAN NEVER SLEEPS(1962), art d; I COULD GO ON SINGING(1963), set d; STOLEN HOURS(1963), set d; LONG SHIPS, THE(1964, Brit./Yugo.), art d; HIGH WIND IN JAMAICA, A(1965), art d; 2001: A SPACE ODYSSEY(1968, U.S./Brit.), art d; ADVENTURERS, THE(1970), art d; SEE NO EVIL(1971, Brit.), art d; WILBY CONSPIRACY, THE(1975, Brit.), art d; EYE OF THE NEEDLE(1981), art d
1984
SAHARA(1984), art d
Julius Hoest
WHO'S YOUR LADY FRIEND?(1937, Brit.), w
James Wong Hoew
HANGMEN ALSO DIE(1943), ph
Bud Hoey
HELLO DOWN THERE(1969)
Dennis Hoey
BATTLE OF GALLIPOLI(1931, Brit.); LOVE LIES(1931, Brit.); MAN FROM CHICAGO, THE(1931, Brit.); NEVER TROUBLE TROUBLE(1931, Brit.); LIFE GOES ON(1932, Brit.); MAID OF THE MOUNTAINS, THE(1932, Brit.); FACING THE MUSIC(1933, Brit.); GOOD COMPANIONS(1933, Brit.); I SPY(1933, Brit.); LOVE IN MOROCCO(1933, Fr.); MAID HAPPY(1933, Brit.); MY OLD DUCHESS(1933, Brit.); BRIDE OF THE LAKE(1934, Brit.); CHU CHIN CHOW(1934, Brit.); POWER(1934, Brit.); BREWSTER'S MILLIONS(1935, Brit.); HONEYMOON FOR THREE(1935, Brit.); IMMORTAL GENTLEMAN(1935, Brit.); WANDERING JEW, THE(1935, Brit.); BLACK ROSES(1936, Ger.); MURDER IN THE OLD RED BARN(1936, Brit.); PHANTOM SHIP(1937, Brit.); UNCIVILISED(1937, Aus.); CONFIRM OR DENY(1941); YANK IN THE R.A.F., A(1941); CAIRO(1942); SHERLOCK HOLMES AND THE SECRET WEAPON(1942); SON OF FURY(1942); THIS ABOVE ALL(1942); WE WERE DANCING(1942); BOMBER'S MOON(1943); FRANKENSTEIN MEETS THE WOLF MAN(1943); SHERLOCK HOLMES FACES DEATH(1943); THEY CAME TO BLOW UP AMERICA(1943); KEYS OF THE KINGDOM, THE(1944); NATIONAL VELVET(1944); PEARL OF DEATH, THE(1944); SHERLOCK HOLMES AND THE SPIDER WOMAN(1944); UNCERTAIN GLORY(1944); HOUSE OF FEAR, THE(1945); KITTY(1945); THOUSAND AND ONE NIGHTS, A(1945); ANNA AND THE KING OF SIAM(1946); ROLL ON TEXAS MOON(1946); SHE-WOLF OF LONDON(1946); STRANGE WOMAN, THE(1946); TARZAN AND THE LEOPARD WOMAN(1946); TERROR BY NIGHT(1946); CHRISTMAS EVE(1947); CRIMSON KEY, THE(1947); FOXES OF HARROW, THE(1947); GOLDEN EARRINGS(1947); IF WINTER COMES(1947); SECOND CHANCE(1947); WHERE THERE'S LIFE(1947); JOAN OF ARC(1948); RUTHLESS(1948); BAD MEN OF TOMBSTONE(1949); SECRET GARDEN, THE(1949); WAKE OF THE RED WITCH(1949); KID FROM TEXAS, THE(1950); DAVID AND BATHSHEBA(1951); CARIBBEAN(1952); PLYMOUTH ADVENTURE(1952)
Misc. Talkies
ALI BABA NIGHTS(1953)
Iris Hoey
HER REPUTATION(1931, Brit.); THOSE WERE THE DAYS(1934, Brit.); REGAL CAVALCADE(1935, Brit.); LIMPING MAN, THE(1936, Brit.); LIVING DANGEROUSLY(1936, Brit.); STAR FELL FROM HEAVEN, A(1936, Brit.); LET'S MAKE A NIGHT OF IT(1937, Brit.); PERFECT CRIME, THE(1937, Brit.); TENTH MAN, THE(1937, Brit.); WEEKEND MILLIONAIRE(1937, Brit.); JANE STEPS OUT(1938, Brit.); PYGMALION(1938, Brit.); JUST WILLIAM(1939, Brit.); MIDAS TOUCH, THE(1940, Brit.); TERROR, THE(1941, Brit.); GIRL WHO COULDN'T QUITE, THE(1949, Brit.); POET'S PUB(1949, Brit.)
Jack Hoey
Misc. Silents
TRACY THE OUTLAW(1928)
John Hoey
PROFESSOR TIM(1957, Ireland); HOME IS THE HERO(1959, Ireland); POACHER'S DAUGHTER, THE(1960, Brit.); SWORD OF SHERWOOD FOREST(1961, Brit.); QUACKSER FORTUNE HAS A COUSIN IN THE BRONX(1970)
Johnny Hoey
BLACK BEAUTY(1971, Brit./Ger./Span.)
Michael A. Hoey
PALM SPRINGS WEEKEND(1963), p; LIVE A LITTLE, LOVE A LITTLE(1968), w; STAY AWAY, JOE(1968), w; CANCEL MY RESERVATION(1972), ed; CLASS OF '44(1973), a, ed
Uti Hof
FRANCIS OF ASSISI(1961)
Ernest Hofbauer
RED-DRAGON(1967, Ital./Ger./US), d
Ernst Hofbauer
FOUNTAIN OF LOVE, THE(1968, Aust.), d; OFFICE GIRLS(1974), d
R. Hofbauer
TRUNKS OF MR. O.F., THE(1932, Ger.)
Maria Hofen
PILLARS OF SOCIETY(1936, Ger.)
Anita Hofer
ONLY A WOMAN(1966, Ger.)

Botho Hofer
HOUSE OF LIFE(1953, Ger.), set d
Chris Hofer
HOUSE OF INTRIGUE, THE(1959, Ital.)
Christopher Hofer
WAR AND PEACE(1956, Ital./U.S.)
Hilla Hofer
JUDGE AND THE SINNER, THE(1964, Ger.)
Johanna Hofer
ABOVE SUSPICION(1943); HITLER'S MADMAN(1943); HOTEL BERLIN(1945); LOST ONE, THE(1951, Ger.); FAREWELL TO ARMS, A(1957); VOR SONNENUNTERGANG(1961, Ger); PEDESTRIAN, THE(1974, Ger.); POSSESSION(1981, Fr./Ger.); VERONIKA VOSS(1982, Ger.)
Lambert Hofer
WILD DUCK, THE(1977, Ger./Aust.), cos
Sigi Hofer
HIS MAJESTY, KING BALLYHOO(1931, Ger.); VIENNA, CITY OF SONGS(1931, Ger.)
Lambert Hofer, Jr.
SALZBURG CONNECTION, THE(1972), cos
Cecil Hoff
TOUCHDOWN!(1931)
Halvard Hoff
Misc. Silents
PRESIDENT, THE(1918, Den.); LEAVES FROM SATAN'S BOOK(1921, Den.)
Harold Hoff
I STOLE A MILLION(1939); IN NAME ONLY(1939)
Margarate Hoff
HIGH FURY(1947, Brit.)
Morton Hoff
1984
ZAPPA(1984, Den.)
Robin Hoff
PRIVATE BENJAMIN(1980); CHARLIE CHAN AND THE CURSE OF THE DRAGON QUEEN(1981); PENNIES FROM HEAVEN(1981)
Nat Hoffberg
CARMELA(1949, Ital.), titles
Barbara Hoffe
WOMAN DECIDES, THE(1932, Brit.)
Misc. Silents
MARRIAGE LINES, THE(1921, Brit.); BELONGING(1922, Brit.); EUGENE ARAM(1924, Brit.)
Monckton Hoffe
STREET ANGEL(1928), w; HIGH SEAS(1929, Brit.), w; PLEASURE CRAZED(1929), w; FLAME OF LOVE, THE(1930, Brit.), w; HATE SHIP, THE(1930, Brit.), w; MANY WATERS(1931, Brit.), a, w; FAITHFUL HEART(1933, Brit.), w; LITTLE DAMOZEL, THE(1933, Brit.), w; MYSTERY OF MR. X, THE(1934), w; WHAT EVERY WOMAN KNOWS(1934), w; RUNAWAY QUEEN, THE(1935, Brit.), w; CLOWN MUST LAUGH, A(1936, Brit.), w; EMPEROR'S CANDLESTICKS, THE(1937), w; GIRLS IN THE STREET(1937, Brit.), w; LAST OF MRS. CHEYNEY, THE(1937), w; GIRL IN THE STREET(1938, Brit.), w; BUSMAN'S HONEYMOON(1940, Brit.), w; LADY EVE, THE(1941), w; JULIA MISBEHAVES(1948), w; FOUR DAYS(1951, Brit.), w; LADY WITH A LAMP, THE(1951, Brit.), w; FOUR AGAINST FATE(1952, Brit.), w; BIRDS AND THE BEES, THE(1965), w
Silents
MAN WITHOUT DESIRE, THE(1923, Brit.), w
Monkton Hoffe
UNDER THE GREENWOOD TREE(1930, Brit.), w
Jeffrey Hoffeld
STILL OF THE NIGHT(1982)
Mason Hoffenberg
CANDY(1968, Ital./Fr.), w
Samuel Hoffenstein
AMERICAN TRAGEDY, AN(1931), w; ONCE A LADY(1931), w; DR. JEKYLL AND MR. HYDE(1932), w; LOVE ME TONIGHT(1932), w; MIRACLE MAN, THE(1932), w; SINNERS IN THE SUN(1932), w; SONG OF SONGS(1933), w; WHITE WOMAN(1933), w; ALL MEN ARE ENEMIES(1934), w; CHANGE OF HEART(1934), w; FOUNTAIN, THE(1934), w; WHARF ANGEL(1934), w; ENCHANTED APRIL(1935), w; PARIS IN SPRING(1935), w; DESIRE(1936), w; VOICE OF BUGLE ANN(1936), w; CONQUEST(1937), w; GREAT WALTZ, THE(1938), w; BRIDAL SUITE(1939), w; LYDIA(1941), w; THAT NIGHT IN RIO(1941), w; LOVES OF EDGAR ALLAN POE, THE(1942), w; TALES OF MANHATTAN(1942), w; FLESH AND FANTASY(1943), w; HIS BUTLER'S SISTER(1943), w; PHANTOM OF THE OPERA(1943), w; LAURA(1944), w; CLUNY BROWN(1946), w; SENTIMENTAL JOURNEY(1946), w; CARNIVAL IN COSTA RICA(1947), w; GIVE MY REGARDS TO BROADWAY(1948), w
William Hoffer
STAGECOACH(1939); MIDNIGHT EXPRESS(1978, Brit.), w
Brenda Hoffert
WILD HORSE HANK(1979, Can.), m; FIREBIRD 2015 AD(1981), m
Paul Hoffert
OFFERING, THE(1966, Can.), m; WINTER KEPT US WARM(1968, Can.), m; DR. FRANKENSTEIN ON CAMPUS(1970, Can.), m; PROUD RIDER, THE(1971, Can.), m; GROUNDSTAR CONSPIRACY, THE(1972, Can.), m; SUNDAY IN THE COUNTRY(1975, Can.), m; OUTRAGEOUS!(1977, Can.), m; HIGH-BALLIN'(1978), m; THIRD WALKER, THE(1978, Can.), m; WILD HORSE HANK(1979, Can.), m; CIRCLE OF TWO(1980, Can.), m; DOUBLE NEGATIVE(1980, Can.), m; MR. PATMAN(1980, Can.), m; FIREBIRD 2015 AD(1981), m; PARADISE(1982), m
1984
BEDROOM EYES(1984, Can.), m
Hoffman
SUICIDE LEGION(1940, Brit.), m
Aaron Hoffman
COHENS AND KELLYS IN ATLANTIC CITY, THE(1929), w; GIVE AND TAKE(1929), w; FRIENDLY ENEMIES(1942), w
Silents
TIGRESS, THE(1914), w; SONG OF THE WAGE SLAVE, THE(1915), w; WELCOME STRANGER(1924), w; COHENS AND KELLYS, THE(1926), w

Abbie Hoffman
PROLOGUE(1970, Can.)
Misc. Talkies
BRAND X(1970)
Alan Hoffman
ROOMMATES, THE(1973), cos
Alfred Hoffman
THAT LUCKY TOUCH(1975, Brit.)
Alice Hoffman
INDEPENDENCE DAY(1983), w
Aneta Hoffman
TWO SISTERS(1938)
Anne Byrne Hoffman
PAPILLON(1973)
Basil Hoffman
LADY LIBERTY(1972, Ital./Fr.); COMES A HORSEMAN(1978); ELECTRIC HORSE-MAN, THE(1979); LOVE AT FIRST BITE(1979); ORDINARY PEOPLE(1980); MY FAVORITE YEAR(1982); NIGHT SHIFT(1982)
1984
ALL OF ME(1984)
Benno Hoffman
REVOLT OF THE SLAVES, THE(1961, Ital./Span./Ger.)
Bern Hoffman
ON THE TOWN(1949); LI'L ABNER(1959); MAN WHO UNDERSTOOD WOMEN, THE(1959); BRAMBLE BUSH, THE(1960); SCARFACE MOB, THE(1962); KISS ME, STUPID(1964); DON'T JUST STAND THERE(1968); OUTFIT, THE(1973)
Bernard Hoffman
NOCTURNE(1946); NAKED CITY, THE(1948)
Bert Hoffman
WALK THE WALK(1970)
Bob Hoffman
LUCKY CISCO KID(1940); MOONRISE(1948); UNION STATION(1950)
Bud Hoffman
TORN CURTAIN(1966), ed; HELLCATS, THE(1968), ed; BIG FOOT(1973), ed
Carl Hoffman
TEMPORARY WIDOW, THE(1930, Ger./Brit.), ph; IMMORTAL VAGABOND(1931, Ger.), ph
Silents
FAUST(1926, Ger.), ph
Carla Hoffman
AS YOUNG AS WE ARE(1958)
Cary Hoffman
TUNNELVISION(1976); ISLAND, THE(1980); HARDLY WORKING(1981)
Charles Hoffman
AFFAIRS OF ANNABEL(1938), w; ANNABEL TAKES A TOUR(1938), w; IT COULD HAPPEN TO YOU(1939), w; REUNION IN FRANCE(1942), w; SOMEWHERE I'LL FIND YOU(1942), w; JANIE(1944), w; PILLOW TO POST(1945), w; CINDERELLA JONES(1946), w; HER KIND OF MAN(1946), w; NIGHT AND DAY(1946), w; ONE MORE TOMORROW(1946), w; THAT HAGEN GIRL(1947), w; THAT WAY WITH WOMEN(1947), p; UNSUSPECTED, THE(1947), p; VOICE OF THE TURTLE, THE(1947), p, w; WEST POINT STORY, THE(1950), w; WOMAN OF DISTINCTION, A(1950), w; BLUE GARDENIA, THE(1953), w; SO THIS IS PARIS(1954), w; SECOND GREATEST SEX, THE(1955), w; SPOILERS, THE(1955), w; NEVER SAY GOOD-BYE(1956), w; MIRACLE OF THE HILLS, THE(1959), w; SAD HORSE, THE(1959), w
Silents
CHALLENGE ACCEPTED, THE(1918), ph
Dark Hoffman
1984
BODY ROCK(1984)
David Hoffman
UNDERGROUND(1941); DANGER IN THE PACIFIC(1942); FLESH AND FAN-TASY(1943); MISSION TO MOSCOW(1943); CONSPIRATORS, THE(1944); MASK OF DIMITRIOS, THE(1944); BEAST WITH FIVE FINGERS, THE(1946); DESIRE ME(1947); CREEPER, THE(1948); TROUBLE MAKERS(1948); ROPE OF SAND(1949); BACKFIRE(1950); TITANIC(1953); WOMAN'S WORLD(1954); BEST OF EVERY-THING, THE(1959); KING, MURRAY(1969), a, d, ph; BLADE(1973), ph
Dustin Hoffman
GRADUATE, THE(1967); TIGER MAKES OUT, THE(1967); JOHN AND MARY(1969); MIDNIGHT COWBOY(1969); LITTLE BIG MAN(1970); MADIGAN'S MILLIONS(1970, Span./Ital.); STRAW DOGS(1971, Brit.); WHO IS HARRY KELLERMAN AND WHY IS HE SAYING THOSE TERRIBLE THINGS ABOUT ME?(1971); ALFREDO, AL-FREDO(1973, Ital.); PAPILLON(1973); LENNY(1974); ALL THE PRESIDENT'S MEN(1976); MARATHON MAN(1976); STRAIGHT TIME(1978), a, d; AGATHA(1979, Brit.); KRAMER VS. KRAMER(1979); TOOTSIE(1982)
E. T. A. Hoffman
NUTCRACKER FANTASY(1979), w
Elizabeth Hoffman
FEAR NO EVIL(1981)
Ellen Hoffman
JESUS CHRIST, SUPERSTAR(1973)
Eugene Hoffman
MY FAIR LADY(1964)
Ferdie Hoffman
ALL THE WAY HOME(1963)
Fred Hoffman
PAPER LION(1968), ph
George Hoffman
SONG OF THE EAGLE(1933)
Gerard Hoffman
MY LIFE TO LIVE(1963, Fr.)
Gertrude Hoffman
HELL AND HIGH WATER(1933); GENTLEMAN FROM LOUISIANA(1936); MOUN-TAIN JUSTICE(1937); APE, THE(1940); FOREIGN CORRESPONDENT(1940); SUSPI-CION(1941); GUY NAMED JOE, A(1943); WHAT A WOMAN!(1943); CALIFORNIA(1946); WELCOME STRANGER(1947); CAGED(1950); WAR OF THE WORLDS, THE(1953)
Gertrude V. Hoffman
ROSEANNA McCOY(1949)

Gertrude W. Hoffman
BEFORE DAWN(1933); SON COMES HOME, A(1936); CASSIDY OF BAR 20(1938); LAUGH IT OFF(1939); UNTAMED(1940); I MARRIED AN ANGEL(1942); WIFE TAKES A FLYER, THE(1942); HEAVENLY BODY, THE(1943); FILE ON THELMA JORDAN, THE(1950)
Guenther Hoffman
BRIDGE, THE(1961, Ger.)
Guy Hoffman
VIOLETTE(1978, Fr.)
H. F. Hoffman
Silents
EAST LYNNE(1916)
H.H. Hoffman
ONE YEAR LATER(1933), p
Harold Hoffman
TRIAL OF LEE HARVEY OSWALD, THE(1964), p; UNDER AGE(1964), p, w; BLACK CAT, THE(1966), d&w; IN THE YEAR 2889(1966), w
Harry Hoffman
MOONSHINE MOUNTAIN(1964)
Herb Hoffman
LOST, LONELY AND VICIOUS(1958), ed
Herbert R. Hoffman
LEGION OF THE DOOMED(1958), ed; ARSON FOR HIRE(1959), ed
Herman Hoffman
GREAT AMERICAN PASTIME, THE(1956), d; INVISIBLE BOY, THE(1957), d; ATTACK ON THE IRON COAST(1968, U.S./Brit.), w; GUNS OF THE MAGNIFICENT SEVEN(1969), w; LAST ESCAPE, THE(1970, Brit.), w
Hermann Hoffman
BAR SINISTER, THE(1955), d
Holli Hoffman
RUNNERS(1983, Brit.)
Howard Hoffman
I DIED A THOUSAND TIMES(1955); HOUSE ON HAUNTED HILL(1958); LITTLEST HOBO, THE(1958); MACABRE(1958); SUMMER PLACE, A(1959); STRAIT-JACK-ET(1964)
Hugh Hoffman
Silents
LOVE LETTER, THE(1923), w; NEAR LADY, THE(1923), w; TOWN SCANDAL, THE(1923), w; EXCITEMENT(1924), w
Ivan J. Hoffman
ANGRY RED PLANET, THE(1959), ed
J. Hoffman
MAN HUNTERS OF THE CARIBBEAN(1938), w
Jac Hoffman
LIFE BEGINS AT 40(1935)
Jane Hoffman
LADYBUG, LADYBUG(1963); WHERE'S POPPA?(1970); THEY MIGHT BE GIANTS(1971); UP THE SANDBOX(1972); DAY OF THE LOCUST, THE(1975); SENTI-NEL, THE(1977); TATTOO(1981)
Jerry Hoffman
ROAD DEMON(1938), p; SPEED TO BURN(1938), p; WINNER TAKE ALL(1939), p; FIRST NUDIE MUSICAL, THE(1976)
Joan Hoffman
OUT OF THE BLUE(1982)
Joe Hoffman
1984
FRIDAY THE 13TH–THE FINAL CHAPTER(1984), art d
John Hoffman
ONE NIGHT OF LOVE(1934), spec eff; BETWEEN TWO WOMEN(1937), spec eff; NAVY BLUE AND GOLD(1937), spec eff; MAN-PROOF(1938), spe eff; CRIMSON CANARY(1945), d; STRANGE CONFESSION(1945), d; FABULOUS SUZANNE, THE(1946), ed; LONE WOLF AND HIS LADY, THE(1949), d; I KILLED GERONI-MO(1950), d; FIVE(1951), ed; STORM OVER TIBET(1952), ed; BWANA DEVIL(1953), ed; NUN AND THE SERGEANT, THE(1962), ed; WAR HUNT(1962), ed
Misc. Talkies
WRECK OF THE HESPERUS(1948), d
Joseph Hoffman
YOUR UNCLE DUDLEY(1935), w; CHARLIE CHAN'S SECRET(1936), w; JAIL-BREAK(1936), w; THANK YOU, JEEVES(1936), w; COUNTRY GENTLEMEN(1937), w; DAMAGED GOODS(1937), w; HEADIN' EAST(1937), w; UNDER SUSPI-CION(1937), w; HOLLYWOOD ROUNDUP(1938), w; SAFETY IN NUMBERS(1938), w; SHADOWS OVER SHANGHAI(1938), w; SHE'S GOT EVERYTHING(1938), w; BOY FRIEND(1939), w; JONES FAMILY IN HOLLYWOOD, THE(1939), w; PRIDE OF THE NAVY(1939), w; QUICK MILLIONS(1939), w; YOUNG AS YOU FEEL(1940), w; OF-FICER AND THE LADY, THE(1941), w; RETURN OF DANIEL BOONE, THE(1941), w; CITY OF SILENT MEN(1942), w; LIVING GHOST, THE(1942), w; MAN WITH TWO LIVES, THE(1942), w; ONE THRILLING NIGHT(1942), w; HIGH EXPLOSIVE(1943), w; MY KINGDOM FOR A COOK(1943), w; SWING FEVER(1943), w; CAROLINA BLUES(1944), w; GIRL IN THE CASE(1944), w; GOODNIGHT SWEETHEART(1944), w; CHINA SKY(1945), w; ONE WAY TO LOVE(1946), w; THAT'S MY GAL(1947), w; DON'T TRUST YOUR HUSBAND(1948), w; AND BABY MAKES THREE(1949), w; BUCCANEER'S GIRL(1950), w; AT SWORD'S POINT(1951), w; WEEKEND WITH FATHER(1951), w; AGAINST ALL FLAGS(1952), w; DUEL AT SILVER CREEK, THE(1952), w; HAS ANYBODY SEEN MY GAL?(1952), w; NO ROOM FOR THE GROOM(1952), w; LONE HAND(1953), w; RAILS INTO LARAMIE(1954), w; REDHEAD FROM MANHATTAN(1954), w; YANKEE PASHA(1954), w; CHICAGO SYNDICATE(1955), w; TALL MAN RIDING(1955), w; PIER 5, HAVANA(1959), w; SEX AND THE SINGLE GIRL(1964), w; KING'S PIRATE(1967), w
Julian Hoffman
BLOODY BROOD, THE(1959, Can.), p&d
Karl Hoffman
Misc. Silents
MYSTIC MIRROR, THE(1928, Ger.), d
Kiva Hoffman
CRY DANGER(1951), makeup
Kristian Hoffman
FIRST MEN IN THE MOON(1964, Brit.); OFFENDERS, THE(1980)

Lee Hoffman
CHINO(1976, Ital., Span., Fr.), w

M.H. Hoffman, Jr.
HARD HOMBRE(1931), p; GAY BUCKAROO, THE(1932), p; INTRUDER, THE(1932), p; SPIRIT OF THE WEST(1932), p; FIGHTING PARSON, THE(1933), ph; PENT-HOUSE PARTY(1936), p

Leonard Hoffman
HEAVEN WITH A BARBED WIRE FENCE(1939), w; HONEYMOON'S OVER, THE(1939), w; CALL NORTHSIDE 777(1948), w

Leslie Hoffman
I WANNA HOLD YOUR HAND(1978)
1984
NIGHTMARE ON ELM STREET, A(1984)

Lou Hoffman
So SAD ABOUT GLORIA(1973)

M.H. Hoffman
MAD PARADE, THE(1931), p; BOILING POINT, THE(1932), p; LOCAL BAD MAN(1932), p; THIRTEENTH GUEST, THE(1932), p; UNHOLY LOVE(1932), p; VANITY FAIR(1932), p; SHRIEK IN THE NIGHT, A(1933), p; ONCE TO EVERY BACHELOR(1934), p; PICTURE BRIDES(1934), p; TAKE THE STAND(1934), p; TWO HEADS ON A PILLOW(1934), p; BORN TO GAMBLE(1935), p; FORCED LANDING(1935), p; OLD HOMESTEAD, THE(1935), p; SCHOOL FOR GIRLS(1935), p; SPANISH CAPE MYSTERY(1935), p; SWEEPSTAKE ANNIE(1935), p; DIZZY DAMES(1936), p; BOOTS OF DESTINY(1937), p

M.K. Hoffman
TRAILING TROUBLE(1937), p

M.S. Hoffman
FILE 113(1932), p

Margaret Hoffman
SONG OF BERNADETTE, THE(1943); TANGIER(1946); MONSIEUR VER-DOUX(1947)

Maury Hoffman
OKLAHOMA CRUDE(1973), set d

Max Hoffman
KID GALAHAD(1937); WINGS OF THE NAVY(1939); STRANGER ON THE THIRD FLOOR(1940); MEET JOHN DOE(1941)

Michael Hoffman
PRIVILEGED(1982, Brit.), a, d, w

Michael W. Hoffman
FINAL CHAPTER–WALKING TALL zero(1977), cos

Mike Hoffman
COMING HOME(1978), cos

Morrie Hoffman
CRIME OF PASSION(1957), set d; STAND UP AND BE COUNTED(1972), d; GUM-BALL RALLY, THE(1976), set d

Morris Hoffman
INSIDE THE MAFIA(1959), set d; FLIGHT THAT DISAPPEARED, THE(1961), set d; SECRET OF DEEP HARBOR(1961), set d; SEVEN WOMEN FROM HELL(1961), set d; TWIST AROUND THE CLOCK(1961), set d; ONE MAN'S WAY(1964), set d; IN HARM'S WAY(1965), set d; WINTER A GO-GO(1965), set d; FRANKIE AND JOHN-NY(1966), set d; WHO'S MINDING THE MINT?(1967), set d; DEVIL'S BRIGADE, THE(1968), set d; COMIC, THE(1969), set d; PENDULUM(1969), set d; TELL ME THAT YOU LOVE ME, JUNIE MOON(1970), set d; FAT CITY(1972), set d; TROUBLE MAN(1972), set d

Nancy Hoffman
Misc. Talkies
ONE PAGE OF LOVE(1979)

Olive Hoffman
THERE'S A GIRL IN MY HEART(1949), ed

Otto Hoffman
NOAH'S ARK(1928); TERROR, THE(1928); ACQUITTED(1929); DESERT SONG, THE(1929); HOTTENTOT, THE(1929); IS EVERYBODY HAPPY?(1929); MADONNA OF AVENUE A(1929); ON WITH THE SHOW(1929); ABRAHAM LINCOLN(1930); KISMET(1930); OTHER TOMORROW, THE(1930); SINNER'S HOLIDAY(1930); AVENGER, THE(1931); CAPTAIN APPLEJACK(1931); CIMARRON(1931); CRIMINAL CODE(1931); SIDE SHOW(1931); SIN OF MADELON CLAUDET, THE(1931); COUNTY FAIR, THE(1932); DOWNSTAIRS(1932); HAUNTED GOLD(1932); HELLO TROU-BLE(1932); TWO SECONDS(1932); CHEYENNE KID, THE(1933); IRON MASTER, THE(1933); MAN OF SENTIMENT, A(1933); DEATH TAKES A HOLIDAY(1934); KID MILLIONS(1934); MARRYING WIDOWS(1934); MURDER AT THE VANITIES(1934); BARBARY COAST(1935); BEHOLD MY WIFE(1935); CAPTAIN HURRICANE(1935); FIGHTING SHADOWS(1935); SHOW THEM NO MERCY(1935); SMART GIRL(1935); CAREER WOMAN(1936); CASE AGAINST MRS. AMES, THE(1936); STORY OF LOUIS PASTEUR, THE(1936); WEDDING PRESENT(1936); WINTERSET(1936); ALL OVER TOWN(1937); GIRL LOVES BOY(1937); HIDEAWAY(1937); LAST TRAIN FROM MADRID, THE(1937); TOAST OF NEW YORK, THE(1937); MR. BOGGS STEPS OUT(1938); ROMANCE IN THE DARK(1938); OUR LEADING CITIZEN(1939); STORY OF ALEXANDER GRAHAM BELL, THE(1939); WHEN TOMORROW COMES(1939); YOU CAN'T CHEAT AN HONEST MAN(1939); FOREIGN CORRESPONDENT(1940); LUCKY CISCO KID(1940); LUCKY PARTNERS(1940); STRANGER ON THE THIRD FLOOR(1940); GHOST OF FRANKENSTEIN, THE(1942); I MARRIED AN AN-GEL(1942); MAD MARTINDALES, THE(1942); RED RIVER ROBIN HOOD(1943); SAGEBRUSH LAW(1943); THIS LAND IS MINE(1943); THIS IS THE LIFE(1944); ONE MORE TOMORROW(1946)
Silents
FAMILY SKELETON, THE(1918); KAISER'S SHADOW, THE(1918); NINE O'CLOCK TOWN, A(1918); JAILBIRD, THE(1920); PARIS GREEN(1920); STOP THIEF(1920); BRONZE BELL, THE(1921); BUNTY PULLS THE STRINGS(1921); JUST OUT OF COLLEGE(1921); WHATEVER SHE WANTS(1921); NEW TEACHER, THE(1922); PARDON MY NERVE!(1922); RIDIN' WILD(1922); ONE STOLEN NIGHT(1923); STRANGERS OF THE NIGHT(1923); BROADWAY AFTER DARK(1924); EAGLE, THE(1925); PAINTED PONIES(1927); STOLEN BRIDE, THE(1927); GRAIN OF DUST, THE(1928)
Misc. Silents
SECRET OF BLACK MOUNTAIN, THE(1917), d; HIS OWN HOME TOWN(1918); CITY OF COMRADES, THE(1919); HOMER COMES HOME(1920); PASSING THRU(1921); DANGEROUS GAME, A(1922); FIVE DOLLAR BABY, THE(1922); GAS, OIL AND WATER(1922); VERY TRULY YOURS(1922); HIGH SPEED(1924)

Otto F. Hoffman
MY LITTLE CHICKADEE(1940)

Pam Hoffman
T.R. BASKIN(1971)

Pamela Hoffman
LOOSE SHOES(1980)

Pat Hoffman
WOMEN OF DESIRE(1968), cos

Paul Hoffman
FEDERAL MAN(1950); MYSTERY SUBMARINE(1950); TIMBER FURY(1950); AS-SIGNMENT-PARIS(1952); MY SIX CONVICTS(1952); VOODOO TIGER(1952); DONO-VAN'S BRAIN(1953); SALOME(1953); ROGUE COP(1954); TENNESSEE CHAMP(1954); CREATURE WITH THE ATOM BRAIN(1955); ODDS AGAINST TO-MORROW(1959)

Renaud Hoffman
BLAZE O' GLORY(1930), d, w; CLIMAX, THE(1930), d; WANTED BY THE POLI-CE(1938), w; OUR NEIGHBORS–THE CARTERS(1939), w
Silents
LEGEND OF HOLLYWOOD, THE(1924), d; HIS MASTER'S VOICE(1925), d; ONE OF THE BRAVEST(1925), sup; OVERLAND LIMITED, THE(1925), sup; SILENT POWER, THE(1926), sup
Misc. Silents
WHICH SHALL IT BE?(1924), d; ON THE THRESHOLD(1925), d; PRIVATE AF-FAIRS(1925), d; UNKNOWN SOLDIER, THE(1926), d; HARP IN HOCK, A(1927), d; STOOL PIGEON(1928), d

Robert Hoffman
FBI CODE 98(1964), ph; GRAND SLAM(1968, Ital., Span., Ger.); BLACK VEIL FOR LISA, A(1969 Ital./Ger.); RIDE A NORTHBOUND HORSE(1969), ph; CERTAIN, VERY CERTAIN, AS A MATTER OF FACT... PROBABLE(1970, Ital,)
Misc. Talkies
EYES BEHIND THE STARS(1972); SPASMO(1976)

Robert W. Hoffman
JOE PANTHER(1976)

Roseline Hoffman
JE T'AIME(1974, Can.)

Roy Hoffman
1984
SKYLINE(1984, Spain)

Ruby Hoffman
Silents
DANGER SIGNAL, THE(1915); KEEP MOVING(1915); MISTRESS NELL(1915)
Misc. Silents
CHILDREN OF THE GHETTO, THE(1915); HELLO BILL!(1915); POLITICIANS, THE(1915); DEVIL'S PRAYER-BOOK, THE(1916); SUMMER GIRL, THE(1916); SLAVE MARKET, THE(1917); UPSIDE DOWN(1919)

Stan Hoffman
SINGING IN THE DARK(1956)

Thom Hoffman
1984
FOURTH MAN, THE(1984, Neth.)

Todd Hoffman
MEATBALLS(1979, Can.)
1984
ANGEL(1984)

Valley Hoffman
RENEGADE GIRLS(1974)

Walt Hoffman
LASSIE'S GREAT ADVENTURE(1963), cos; WILD, WILD WINTER(1966), cos

Walter Hoffman
WAR OF THE WORLDS, THE(1953), spec eff

Willi Hoffman
$100 A NIGHT(1968, Ger.), m

William Hoffman
TERROR FROM THE YEAR 5,000(1958), set d

Max Hoffman, Jr.
SAILOR BE GOOD(1933); POLO JOE(1936); DEVIL'S SADDLE LEGION, THE(1937); GAME THAT KILLS, THE(1937); GO-GETTER, THE(1937); ROOTIN' TOOTIN' RHYTHM(1937); ACCIDENTS WILL HAPPEN(1938); DAREDEVIL DRIVERS(1938); SERGEANT MURPHY(1938); SKY GIANT(1938); ANGELS WASH THEIR FA-CES(1939); COWBOY QUARTERBACK(1939); EACH DAWN I DIE(1939); HELL'S KITCHEN(1939); KID NIGHTINGALE(1939); SMASHING THE MONEY RING(1939); GRANNY GET YOUR GUN(1940); HOUSE ACROSS THE BAY, THE(1940); INVISI-BLE STRIPES(1940); DIVE BOMBER(1941); STRAWBERRY BLONDE, THE(1941); BLACK DRAGONS(1942); FRECKLES COMES HOME(1942); MAN FROM HEAD-QUARTERS(1942); THEY DIED WITH THEIR BOOTS ON(1942); WIFE TAKES A FLYER, THE(1942)

Dr. Hoffman-Harnisch
PRIVATE LIFE OF LOUIS XIV(1936, Ger.), w

Benno Hoffmann
COW AND I, THE(1961, Fr., Ital., Ger.); TOMORROW IS MY TURN(1962, Fr./Ital./Ger.); CASTLE, THE(1969, Ger.)

Carl Hoffmann
CONGRESS DANCES(1932, Ger.), ph; WHITE DEMON, THE(1932, Ger.), ph
Silents
KRIEMHILD'S REVENGE(1924, Ger.), ph; SIEGFRIED(1924, Ger.), ph

Frank Hoffmann
ACE OF ACES(1982, Fr./Ger.)

Gert Gunter Hoffmann
ORDERED TO LOVE(1963, Ger.)

Gertrude Hoffmann
TISH(1942)

Guy Hoffmann
TAKE IT ALL(1966, Can.)

Klaus Hoffmann
SERPENT'S EGG, THE(1977, Ger./U.S.)

Kurt Hoffmann
CONFESSIONS OF FELIX KRULL, THE(1957, Ger.), d; ARENT WE WONDER-FUL?(1959, Ger.), p&d; SPESSART INN, THE(1961, Ger.), d

Brit.); JUDGMENT DEFERRED(1952, Brit.); WHISPERING SMITH VERSUS SCOT-
LAND YARD(1952, Brit.)

David Hogarty
QUACKSER FORTUNE HAS A COUSIN IN THE BRONX(1970)

Michael Hogben
POSSESSION(1981, Fr./Ger.)

Axel Hogel
DOLLAR(1938, Swed.); RAILROAD WORKERS(1948, Swed.)

Hannelore Hoger
LOST HONOR OF KATHARINA BLUM, THE(1975, Ger.); GERMANY IN AU-
TUMN(1978, Ger.)

Ian Hogg
PERSECUTION AND ASSASSINATION OF JEAN-PAUL MARAT AS PERFORMED
BY THE INMATES OF THE ASYLUM OF CHARENTON UNDER THE DIRECTION
OF THE MARQUIS DE SADE, THE(1967, Brit.); TELL ME LIES(1968, Brit.); KING
LEAR(1971, Brit./Den.); LAST VALLEY, THE(1971, Brit.); MACBETH(1971, Brit.);
HIRELING, THE(1973, Brit.); HENNESSY(1975, Brit.); LITTLEST HORSE THIEVES,
THE(1977); LEGACY, THE(1979, Brit.); MEETINGS WITH REMARKABLE MEN(1979,
Brit.); RED MONARCH(1983, Brit.)

Justin Hogg
1984
PARIS, TEXAS(1984, Ger./Fr.)

Steve Hogg
TOM SAWYER(1973)

Michael Hoggan
1984
HOLLYWOOD HOT TUBS(1984), ed

Nigel Hogge
Misc. Talkies
ONE ARMED EXECUTIONER(1980)

Robert Hogins
MORE AMERICAN GRAFFITI(1979)

Claudine Hogleenel
PARIS OOH-LA-LA!(1963, U.S./Fr.)

Gunnar Hoglund
OBSESSION(1968, Swed.), d, w

Albert Hogsett
LIFE BEGINS AT 40(1935), art d; STEAMBOAT ROUND THE BEND(1935), set d;
LANCER SPY(1937), art d; THANK YOU, MR. MOTO(1937), art d; GATEWAY(1938),
art d; INTERNATIONAL SETTLEMENT(1938), art d; INSIDE STORY(1939), art d;
PACK UP YOUR TROUBLES(1939), art d; FOUR SONS(1940), art d; GREAT AMERI-
CAN BROADCAST, THE(1941), art d; GREAT GUNS(1941), art d; PERFECT SNOB,
THE(1941), art d; MAN IN THE TRUNK, THE(1942), art d; RINGS ON HER FIN-
GERS(1942), art d; MEANEST MAN IN THE WORLD, THE(1943), art d; FOUR JILLS
IN A JEEP(1944), art d; SOMETHING FOR THE BOYS(1944), art d; TAMPICO(1944),
art d; COLONEL EFFINGHAM'S RAID(1945), art d; MOLLY AND ME(1945), art d;
SENTIMENTAL JOURNEY(1946), art d; STRANGE TRIANGLE(1946), art d; CRY OF
THE CITY(1948), art d; FURY AT FURNACE CREEK(1948), art d; SCUDDA-HOO!
SCUDDA-HAY!(1948), art d; YELLOW SKY(1948), art d; I WAS A MALE WAR
BRIDE(1949), art d; SLATTERY'S HURRICANE(1949), art d; FROGMEN, THE(1951),
art d; LET'S MAKE IT LEGAL(1951), art d; MY PAL GUS(1952), art d; MR. SCOUT-
MASTER(1953), art d; TREASURE OF THE GOLDEN CONDOR(1953), art d; HILDA
CRANE(1956), art d; ENEMY BELOW, THE(1957), art d

Arthur Hogsett
BROKEN ARROW(1950), art d

Albert Hogstett
HALLS OF MONTEZUMA(1951), art d

Billy Hogue
J.W. COOP(1971)

Eades Hogue
BABY DOLL(1956)

Robert R. Hogue
HOME FROM THE HILL(1960), spec eff

Roland Hogue
HIS DOUBLE LIFE(1933)

Luli Hohenberg
MY FRIEND THE KING(1931, Brit.)

Joey Hohenfels
PETERSEN(1974, Aus.)

Alex Hohenlohe
DECISION BEFORE DAWN(1951)

Nina Hohenlohe
LA DOLCE VITA(1961, Ital./Fr.)

Frank Hohimer
THIEF(1981), w

Arthur Hohl
CHEAT, THE(1931); NIGHT OF JUNE 13(1932); SIGN OF THE CROSS, THE(1932);
BABY FACE(1933); BRIEF MOMENT(1933); CAPTURED(1933); FOOTLIGHT
PARADE(1933); INFERNAL MACHINE(1933); ISLAND OF LOST SOULS(1933); KEN-
NEL MURDER CASE, THE(1933); LIFE OF JIMMY DOLAN, THE(1933); MAN'S
CASTLE, A(1933); NARROW CORNER, THE(1933); PRIVATE DETECTIVE 62(1933);
SILK EXPRESS, THE(1933); WILD BOYS OF THE ROAD(1933); WORLD CHANGES,
THE(1933); AGAINST THE LAW(1934); AMONG THE MISSING(1934); AS THE
EARTH TURNS(1934); BULLDOG DRUMMOND STRIKES BACK(1934); CLEOPA-
TRA(1934); DEFENSE HESTS, THE(1934); GIRL IN DANGER(1934); JEALOU-
SY(1934); JIMMY THE GENT(1934); LADY BY CHOICE(1934); MASSACRE(1934);
MODERN HERO, A(1934); AFTER THE DANCE(1935); ATLANTIC ADVEN-
TURE(1935); CASE OF THE MISSING MAN, THE(1935); EIGHT BELLS(1935);
GUARD THAT GIRL(1935); I'LL LOVE YOU ALWAYS(1935); IN SPITE OF DAN-
GER(1935); ONE FRIGHTENED NIGHT(1935); ROMANCE IN MANHATTAN(1935);
SUPERSPEED(1935); UNKNOWN WOMAN(1935); VILLAGE TALE(1935); WHOLE
TOWN'S TALKING, THE(1935); DEVIL DOLL, THE(1936); FORGOTTEN FA-
CES(1936); IT HAD TO HAPPEN(1936); LLOYDS OF LONDON(1936); SHOW
BOAT(1936); WE'RE ONLY HUMAN(1936); HOT WATER(1937); MOUNTAIN MU-
SIC(1937); ROAD BACK, THE(1937); SLAVE SHIP(1937); TRAPPED BY G-MEN(1937);
BAD MAN OF BRIMSTONE(1938); BOY SLAVES(1938); CRIME TAKES A HOLI-
DAY(1938); KIDNAPPED(1938); PENITENTIARY(1938); STABLEMATES(1938); AD-
VENTURES OF SHERLOCK HOLMES, THE(1939); BLACKMAIL(1939); FUGITIVE
AT LARGE(1939); HUNCHBACK OF NOTRE DAME, THE(1939); THEY SHALL HAVE
MUSIC(1939); TWO THOROUGHBREDS(1939); YOU CAN'T CHEAT AN HONEST

MAN(1939); BLONDIE HAS SERVANT TROUBLE(1940); TWENTY MULE
TEAM(1940); MEN OF BOYS TOWN(1941); RIDE ON VAQUERO(1941); WE GO
FAST(1941); MOONTIDE(1942); SON OF FURY(1942); WHISPERING GHOSTS(1942);
IDAHO(1943); PAYOFF, THE(1943), w; SONG OF BERNADETTE, THE(1943); WOM-
AN OF THE TOWN, THE(1943); EVE OF ST. MARK, THE(1944); IRISH EYES ARE
SMILING(1944); SCARLET CLAW, THE(1944); SHERLOCK HOLMES AND THE
SPIDER WOMAN(1944); THIN MAN GOES HOME, THE(1944); FROZEN GHOST,
THE(1945); LOVE LETTERS(1945); OUR VINES HAVE TENDER GRAPES(1945);
SALOME, WHERE SHE DANCED(1945); YEARLING, THE(1946); IT HAPPENED ON
5TH AVENUE(1947); MONSIEUR VERDOUX(1947); VIGILANTES RETURN,
THE(1947); THREE MUSKETEERS, THE(1948); YOU GOTTA STAY HAPPY(1948);
DOWN TO THE SEA IN SHIPS(1949)
Silents
IT IS THE LAW(1924)

Salty Hohmes
ARIZONA DAYS(1937)

Carola Hohn
LIFE BEGINS ANEW(1938, Ger.); TOXI(1952, Ger.); NIGHT CROSSING(1982)

Gustav Hohn
KING STEPS OUT, THE(1936), w

Elmer Hohnber
VELVET TRAP, THE(1966), ph

Harvey Hohnecker
WEST SIDE STORY(1961)

Harvey Hohneckey
GIRL MOST LIKELY, THE(1957)

Peter Hohnen
Z.P.G.(1972)

Christian Hohoff
FOX AND HIS FRIENDS(1976, Ger.), p, w; MOTHER KUSTERS GOES TO HEAV-
EN(1976, Ger.), p

Grethe Hoholdt
LURE OF THE JUNGLE, THE(1970, Den.)

Peter Hoimark
EMIGRANTS, THE(1972, Swed.)
1984
ELEMENT OF CRIME, THE(1984, Den.), prod d

Tom Hoirer
SLEEPING CITY, THE(1950)

Dr. Max Hoisboer
S.O.S. ICEBERG(1933)

Ronald F. Hoiseck
1984
SPLASH(1984)

Ronald Hoiseck
TABLE FOR FIVE(1983)

Solbjorg Hojfeldt
1984
ZAPPA(1984, Den.)

Else Hojgaard
HAGBARD AND SIGNE(1968, Den./Iceland/Swed.)

Peter Hojmark
Z.P.G.(1972), art d

Hideji Hojo
SAMURAI(1955, Jap.), w

Mary Alan Hokanson
STORM WARNING(1950); CRIMINAL LAWYER(1951); FAMILY SECRET,
THE(1951); MISSING WOMEN(1951); MOB, THE(1951); STRANGERS ON A
TRAIN(1951); THIS WOMAN IS DANGEROUS(1952); LADY WANTS MINK,
THE(1953); MR. SCOUTMASTER(1953); CRIME WAVE(1954); DEEP IN MY
HEART(1954); EXECUTIVE SUITE(1954); CULT OF THE COBRA(1955); GUYS AND
DOLLS(1955); PRIVATE WAR OF MAJOR BENSON, THE(1955); RANSOM(1956); TEA
AND SYMPATHY(1956); THESE WILDER YEARS(1956); SPOILERS OF THE FOR-
EST(1957); LONELYHEARTS(1958); SOMEBODY KILLED HER HUSBAND(1978);
ARTHUR(1981)
1984
UNFAITHFULLY YOURS(1984)

Mary Ann Hokanson
THEM!(1954)

Mary Ellen Hokanson
DESPERATE CHARACTERS(1971)

Mary Hokanson
I WAS A COMMUNIST FOR THE F.B.I.(1951)

Dennis Holahan
HALLOWEEN II(1981); SCARFACE(1983)

William Holand
VIOLATED(1953), p

Lawrence Holben
HIDING PLACE, THE(1975), w; NO LONGER ALONE(1978), w

Nathalie Holberg
1984
LIFE IS A BED OF ROSES(1984, Fr.)

Fred Holbert
Misc. Talkies
SCREAM BLOODY MURDER(1973)

Robinson Holbert
LADIES' MAN(1947), w

Jackie Holborough
1984
SCRUBBERS(1984, Brit.)

Allen Holbrook
FIGHTING COWBOY(1933); CIRCLE CANYON(1934); RIDING SPEED(1934)
Misc. Talkies
TRAILS OF ADVENTURE(1935)

David Holbrook
1984
GIRLS NIGHT OUT(1984)

Fern Holbrook
HARD ROAD, THE(1970)
Gerald Holbrook
GETTING TOGETHER(1976), art d
Hal Holbrook
GROUP, THE(1966); WILD IN THE STREETS(1968); GREAT WHITE HOPE, THE(1970); PEOPLE NEXT DOOR, THE(1970); THEY ONLY KILL THEIR MASTERS(1972); JONATHAN LIVINGSTON SEAGULL(1973); MAGNUM FORCE(1973); GIRL FROM PETROVKA, THE(1974); ALL THE PRESIDENT'S MEN(1976); MIDWAY(1976); JULIA(1977); CAPRICORN ONE(1978); NATURAL ENEMIES(1979); CREEPER, THE(1980, Can.); FOG, THE(1980); KIDNAPPING OF THE PRESIDENT, THE(1980, Can.); CREEPSHOW(1982); STAR CHAMBER, THE(1983)
1984
GIRLS NIGHT OUT(1984)
J.K. Holbrook
Misc. Silents
PROFITEER, THE(1919), d
John Holbrook
SHADOW OF THE HAWK(1976, Can.), ph
John K. Holbrook
Silents
ROMANCE OF THE AIR, A(1919), ph
Ruby Holbrook
GOODBYE GIRL, THE(1977)
Stan Holbrook
STARLIFT(1951)
Stann Holbrook
WILD BLUE YONDER, THE(1952)
Tami Holbrook
1984
HOT MOVES(1984)
Vic Holbrook
VEILS OF BAGDAD, THE(1953)
Walter Holbrook
CHARGE OF THE LIGHT BRIGADE, THE(1936)
Allen Holbubar
Misc. Silents
FIELD OF HONOR, THE(1917)
Kristin Holby
TRADING PLACES(1983)
Victor Holchak
Misc. Talkies
HUGHES AND HARLOW: ANGELS IN HELL(1978)
Grant Holcomb
X-15(1961)
Herb Holcomb
LADY IN THE DARK(1944)
Homer Holcomb
STICK TO YOUR GUNS(1941)
Kathryn Holcomb
OUR TIME(1974)
Lance Holcomb
VENOM(1982, Brit.)
Sandra Holcomb
SHE FREAK(1967)
Sarah Holcomb
NATIONAL LAMPOON'S ANIMAL HOUSE(1978); WALK PROUD(1979); CADDYSHACK(1980); HAPPY BIRTHDAY, GEMINI(1980)
Harry Holcombe
SILENCERS, THE(; YOUNG SAVAGES, THE(1961); COUCH, THE(1962); FOLLOW THAT DREAM(1962); MANCHURIAN CANDIDATE, THE(1962); KING KONG VERSUS GODZILLA(1963, Jap.); SUMMER MAGIC(1963); UNSINKABLE MOLLY BROWN, THE(1964); HARLOW(1965); MONKEY'S UNCLE, THE(1965); FORTUNE COOKIE, THE(1966); GRADUATE, THE(1967); GAILY, GAILY(1969); GETTING STRAIGHT(1970); HAWAIIANS, THE(1970); FOXY DROWN(1974); ESCAPE TO WITCH MOUNTAIN(1975); PSYCHIC KILLER(1975); EMPIRE OF THE ANTS(1977); FUN WITH DICK AND JANE(1977)
Harry Holcombe, Jr.
PORTRAIT OF A MOBSTER(1961)
Herb Holcombe
SIX SHOOTIN' SHERIFF(1938)
Herbert Holcombe
MADAME SPY(1934); PHANTOM RANGER(1938); WEST POINT WIDOW(1941); KISS OF DEATH(1947); PROJECT X(1949)
Jean Holcombe
HOW TO BE VERY, VERY, POPULAR(1955)
Misc. Talkies
HOLLYWOOD THRILL-MAKERS(1954)
Joan Holcombe
MOVIE STUNTMEN(1953)
W.L. Holcombe
PSYCHOMANIA(1964), m
Wilford Holcombe
WILD IS MY LOVE(1963), m, md
John Hold [Mario Bava]
KNIVES OF THE AVENGER(1967, Ital.), d
Siegfried Hold
MONSTER OF LONDON CITY, THE(1967, Ger.), ph; OLD SHATTERHAND(1968, Ger./Yugo./Fr./Ital.), ph
Jim Holdaway
MODESTY BLAISE(1966, Brit.), w
Julien Holdaway
BOYS OF PAUL STREET, THE(1969, Hung./US)
Anton Holden
Misc. Talkies
AROUSED(1968), d
David Holden
WARRIORS, THE(1979), ed; LONG RIDERS, THE(1980), ed; BUSTIN' LOOSE(1981), ed

1984
IMPULSE(1984), ed
Diana Holden
ICE CASTLES(1978)
Diane Holden
GRAVE OF THE VAMPIRE(1972)
Misc. Talkies
BLACK STARLET(1974)
Eddie Holden
FIGHTING DEPUTY, THE(1937); BATTLE OF BROADWAY(1938); TORTURE SHIP(1939); MAD MONSTER, THE(1942)
Fay Holden
POLO JOE(1936); WIVES NEVER KNOW(1936); BULLDOG DRUMMOND ESCAPES(1937); DOUBLE OR NOTHING(1937); EXCLUSIVE(1937); INTERNES CAN'T TAKE MONEY(1937); KING OF GAMBLERS(1937); SOULS AT SEA(1937); HOLD THAT KISS(1938); JUDGE HARDY'S CHILDREN(1938); LOVE FINDS ANDY HARDY(1938); LOVE IS A HEADACHE(1938); OUT WEST WITH THE HARDYS(1938); SWEETHEARTS(1938); TEST PILOT(1938); YOU'RE ONLY YOUNG ONCE(1938); ANDY HARDY GETS SPRING FEVER(1939); HARDYS RIDE HIGH, THE(1939); JUDGE HARDY AND SON(1939); SERGEANT MADDEN(1939); ANDY HARDY MEETS DEBUTANTE(1940); BITTER SWEET(1940); ANDY HARDY'S PRIVATE SECRETARY(1941); BLOSSOMS IN THE DUST(1941); DR. KILDARE'S WEDDING DAY(1941); H.M. PULHAM, ESQ.(1941); I'LL WAIT FOR YOU(1941); LIFE BEGINS FOR ANDY HARDY(1941); WASHINGTON MELODRAMA(1941); ZIEGFELD GIRL(1941); ANDY HARDY'S DOUBLE LIFE(1942); COURTSHIP OF ANDY HARDY, THE(1942); ANDY HARDY'S BLONDE TROUBLE(1944); CANYON PASSAGE(1946); LITTLE MISS BIG(1946); LOVE LAUGHS AT ANDY HARDY(1946); WHISPERING SMITH(1948); SAMSON AND DELILAH(1949); BIG HANGOVER, THE(1950); ANDY HARDY COMES HOME(1958)
Frankie J. Holden
ODD ANGRY SHOT, THE(1979, Aus.)
Georgia Holden
RIGHT HAND OF THE DEVIL, THE(1963)
Gloria Holden
DRACULA'S DAUGHTER(1936); WIFE VERSUS SECRETARY(1936); LIFE OF EMILE ZOLA, THE(1937); GIRLS' SCHOOL(1938); HAWAII CALLS(1938); TEST PILOT(1938); DODGE CITY(1939); MIRACLES FOR SALE(1939); CHILD IS BORN, A(1940); THIS THING CALLED LOVE(1940); CORSICAN BROTHERS, THE(1941); PASSAGE FROM HONG KONG(1941); APACHE TRAIL(1942); GENTLEMAN AFTER DARK, A(1942); MISS ANNIE ROONEY(1942); BEHIND THE RISING SUN(1943); ADVENTURES OF RUSTY(1945); GIRL OF THE LIMBERLOST, THE(1945); HIT THE HAY(1945); STRANGE HOLIDAY(1945); SISTER KENNY(1946); HUCKSTERS, THE(1947); KILLER McCOY(1947); UNDERCOVER MAISIE(1947); PERILOUS WATERS(1948); KISS FOR CORLISS, A(1949); HAS ANYBODY SEEN MY GAL?(1952); SEEDS OF DESTRUCTION(1952); DREAM WIFE(1953); EDDY DUCHIN STORY, THE(1956); THIS HAPPY FEELING(1958)
Misc. Talkies
IN SELF DEFENSE(1947)
Grant Holden
GIRL HUNTERS, THE(1963, Brit.)
Harry Holden
SHOW BOAT(1929); CODE OF HONOR(1930); SHOCK(1934)
Silents
KAISER, BEAST OF BERLIN, THE(1918); NEW LOVE FOR OLD(1918); TREASURE ISLAND(1920); YANKEE CLIPPER, THE(1927)
Misc. Silents
CRICKET, THE(1917); GIRL AND THE CRISIS, THE(1917); SILENT LADY, THE(1917); MIDNIGHT MADNESS(1918); RICH MAN'S DAUGHTER, A(1918); FOUR FLUSHER, THE(1919); GAME'S UP, THE(1919); VIRTOUS SINNERS(1919); WINDS OF THE PAMPAS(1927)
Jack Holden
I SELL ANYTHING(1934), art d; MURDER IN THE CLOUDS(1934), art d; DEVOTION(1946), spec eff; HORROR HOUSE(1970, Brit.), set d
Silents
HUSBANDS AND LOVERS(1924), art d
James Holden
FIGHTER SQUADRON(1948); HOUSE ACROSS THE STREET, THE(1949); IT'S A GREAT FEELING(1949); SANDS OF IWO JIMA(1949); TASK FORCE(1949); FLIGHT NURSE(1953)
Jan Holden
HORNET'S NEST, THE(1955, Brit.); FIRE MAIDENS FROM OUTER SPACE(1956, Brit.); ENEMY FROM SPACE(1957, Brit.); HIGH FLIGHT(1957, Brit.); LINKS OF JUSTICE(1958); WHOLE TRUTH, THE(1958, Brit.); WOMAN POSSESSED, A(1958, Brit.); PASSIONATE SUMMER(1959, Brit.); TOP FLOOR GIRL(1959, Brit.); ESCORT FOR HIRE(1960, Brit.); STRANGLERS OF BOMBAY, THE(1960, Brit.); MILLION DOLLAR MANHUNT(1962, Brit.); PRIMITIVES, THE(1962, Brit.); WORK IS A FOUR LETTER WORD(1968, Brit.); BEST HOUSE IN LONDON, THE(1969, Brit.); HORROR HOUSE(1970, Brit.); ONE BRIEF SUMMER(1971, Brit.)
Jane Holden
Misc. Talkies
PLOTTERS, THE(1966)
Jennifer Holden
JAILHOUSE ROCK(1957); BUCHANAN RIDES ALONE(1958); GANG WAR(1958)
John Holden
THEY DRIVE BY NIGHT(1940), spec eff; FIGHTER SQUADRON(1948), spec eff; FOUNTAINHEAD, THE(1949), spec eff; ONCE MORE, MY DARLING(1949), makeup; RED CANYON(1949), makeup; WOMAN IN HIDING(1949), makeup; TROOPER HOOK(1957), makeup
Silents
MARRIAGE OF WILLIAM ASHE, THE(1921), art d
Joyce Holden
MA AND PA KETTLE GO TO TOWN(1950); MILKMAN, THE(1950); IRON MAN, THE(1951); TARGET UNKNOWN(1951); YOU NEVER CAN TELL(1951); BRONCO BUSTER(1952); GIRLS IN THE NIGHT(1953); MURDER WITHOUT TEARS(1953); PRIVATE EYES(1953); WEREWOLF, THE(1956); TERROR FROM THE YEAR 5,-000(1958)
June Holden
LORNA DOONE(1935, Brit.); HATTER'S CASTLE(1948, Brit.); IDOL OF PARIS(1948, Brit.)

Katerina Holden
STOP THE WORLD–I WANT TO GET OFF(1966, Brit.)
Katrina Holden
UNCANNY, THE(1977, Brit./Can.)
Lansing C. Holden
SHE(1935), d
Mark Holden
NEWSFRONT(1979, Aus.)
Maxine Holden
LOLITA(1962)
Michael Holden
FERRY ACROSS THE MERSEY(1964, Brit.), p
Norman Holden
LUPE(1967)
Peter Holden
GREAT MAN VOTES, THE(1939)
Richard Holden
TERROR FROM UNDER THE HOUSE(1971, Brit.)
Ruth Holden
JUST TELL ME WHAT YOU WANT(1980)
Scott Holden
REVENGERS, THE(1972, U.S./Mex.); BREEZY(1973)
Tommy Holden
GET OUTTA TOWN(1960); MAGIC SPECTACLES(1961); WHAT'S UP FRONT(1964)
Virginia Holden
WALK ON THE WILD SIDE(1962)
William Holden
FAST LIFE(1929); HIS CAPTIVE WOMAN(1929); TRESPASSER, THE(1929); WEARY RIVER(1929); DYNAMITE(1930); FRAMED(1930); HOLIDAY(1930); NOT SO DUMB(1930); NUMBERED MEN(1930); THREE FACES EAST(1930); WHAT A WIDOW(1930); CHARLIE CHAN CARRIES ON(1931); DANCE, FOOLS, DANCE(1931); MAN WHO CAME BACK, THE(1931); SIX CYLINDER LOVE(1931); PRISON FARM(1938); GOLDEN BOY(1939); MILLION DOLLAR LEGS(1939); ARIZONA(1940); INVISIBLE STRIPES(1940); OUR TOWN(1940); THOSE WERE THE DAYS(1940); I WANTED WINGS(1941); TEXAS(1941); FLEET'S IN, THE(1942); MEET THE STEWARTS(1942); REMARKABLE ANDREW, THE(1942); YOUNG AND WILLING(1943); BLAZE OF NOON(1947); DEAR RUTH(1947); VARIETY GIRL(1947); APARTMENT FOR PEGGY(1948); DARK PAST, THE(1948); MAN FROM COLORADO, THE(1948); RACHEL AND THE STRANGER(1948); DEAR WIFE(1949); MISS GRANT TAKES RICHMOND(1949); STREETS OF LAREDO(1949); FATHER IS A BACHELOR(1950); SUNSET BOULEVARD(1950); UNION STATION(1950); BORN YESTERDAY(1951); FORCE OF ARMS(1951); SUBMARINE COMMAND(1951); BOOTS MALONE(1952); TURNING POINT, THE(1952); ESCAPE FROM FORT BRAVO(1953); FOREVER FEMALE(1953); MOON IS BLUE, THE(1953); STALAG 17(1953); BRIDGES AT TOKO-RI, THE(1954); COUNTRY GIRL, THE(1954); EXECUTIVE SUITE(1954); SABRINA(1954); LOVE IS A MANY-SPLENDORED THING(1955); PICNIC(1955); SAMURAI(1955, Jap.), a, ed; PROUD AND THE PROFANE, THE(1956); TOWARD THE UNKNOWN(1956); BRIDGE ON THE RIVER KWAI, THE(1957); KEY, THE(1958, Brit.); HORSE SOLDIERS, THE(1959); WORLD OF SUZIE WONG, THE(1960); COUNTERFEIT TRAITOR, THE(1962); LION, THE(1962, Brit.); SATAN NEVER SLEEPS(1962); PARIS WHEN IT SIZZLES(1964); SEVENTH DAWN, THE(1964); ALVAREZ KELLY(1966); CASINO ROYALE(1967, Brit.); DEVIL'S BRIGADE, THE(1968); CHRISTMAS TREE, THE(1969, Fr.); WILD BUNCH, THE(1969); WILD ROVERS(1971); REVENGERS, THE(1972, U.S./Mex.); BREEZY(1973); OPEN SEASON(1974, U.S./Span.); TOWERING INFERNO, THE(1974); NETWORK(1976); DAMIEN–OMEN II(1978); FEDORA(1978, Ger./Fr.); ASHANTI(1979); EARTHLING, THE(1980); WHEN TIME RAN OUT(1980); S.O.B.(1981)
William [Stage] Holden
Silents
BAB'S CANDIDATE(1920)
Pierre Holdener
JONAH–WHO WILL BE 25 IN THE YEAR 2000(1976, Switz.)
Boscoe Holder
LOVE LOTTERY, THE(1954, Brit.); ROUND TRIP(1967); HAND OF NIGHT, THE(1968, Brit.), ch
Christian Holder
HAIR(1979)
Geoffrey Holder
ALL NIGHT LONG(1961, Brit.); DOCTOR DOLITTLE(1967); KRAKATOA, EAST OF JAVA(1969); EVERYTHING YOU ALWAYS WANTED TO KNOW ABOUT SEX, BUT WE'RE AFRAID TO ASK(1972); LIVE AND LET DIE(1973, Brit.), a, ch; SWASHBUCKLER(1976), a, ch; ANNIE(1982)
Noddy Holder
FLAME(1975, Brit.), a, m
Owen Holder
WILD HEART, THE(1952, Brit.); HIGH FLIGHT(1957, Brit.)
Peter Holder
BUGSY MALONE(1976, Brit.)
Philip Holder
SCARECROW, THE(1982, New Zealand)
Phin Holder
MAN FROM COLORADO, THE(1948)
Ram John Holder
TWO GENTLEMEN SHARING(1969, Brit.); LEO THE LAST(1970, Brit.); EDUCATION OF SONNY CARSON, THE(1974); BRITTANIA HOSPITAL(1982, Brit.)
Ramjohn Holder
PRESSURE(1976, Brit.)
Roland Holder
EXILE, THE(1931)
Roscoe Holder
PASSIONATE SUMMER(1959, Brit.)
Roy Holder
WHISTLE DOWN THE WIND(1961, Brit.); TERM OF TRIAL(1962, Brit.); MURDER AHOY(1964, Brit.); OTHELLO(1965, Brit.); TAMING OF THE SHREW, THE(1967, U.S./Ital.); HERE WE GO ROUND THE MULBERRY BUSH(1968, Brit.); ROMEO AND JULIET(1968, Brit./Ital.); VIRGIN AND THE GYPSY, THE(1970, Brit.); VIRGIN SOLDIERS, THE(1970, Brit.); LOOT(1971, Brit.); PSYCHOMANIA(1974, Brit.); LAND THAT TIME FORGOT, THE(1975, Brit.); DIRTY KNIGHT'S WORK(1976, Brit.)

Wilbert Holder
Misc. Talkies
BIM(1976)
Fay Holderness
LONESOME(1928); HONKY TONK(1941)
Silents
HEARTS OF THE WORLD(1918); DICK TURPIN(1925); SALVATION JANE(1927)
Faye Holderness
Silents
BLIND HUSBANDS(1919)
Susan Holderness
THAT'LL BE THE DAY(1974, Brit.)
Noble Lee Holderread, Jr.
BOB AND CAROL AND TED AND ALICE(1969)
Derek Holding
KONGA(1961, Brit.), spec eff; DEATH TRAP(1962, Brit.), ed; WE SHALL SEE(1964, Brit.), ed; 20,000 POUNDS KISS, THE(1964, Brit.), ed; ACT OF MURDER(1965, Brit.), ed; SINISTER MAN, THE(1965, Brit.), ed; INCIDENT AT MIDNIGHT(1966, Brit.), ed; MAIN CHANCE, THE(1966, Brit.), ed; PARTNER, THE(1966, Brit.), ed; RICOCHET(1966, Brit.), ed; SOLO FOR SPARROW(1966, Brit.), ed; NEVER BACK LOSERS(1967, Brit.), ed; ON THE RUN(1967, Brit.), ed; PROJECTED MAN, THE(1967, Brit.), ed
Elisabeth S. Holding
RECKLESS MOMENTS, THE(1949), w
Elizabeth Sanxay Holding
BRIDE COMES HOME(1936), w
Thomas Holding
Silents
ETERNAL CITY, THE(1915); SOLD(1915); SPIDER, THE(1916); HER FIGHTING CHANCE(1917); THREE MUSKETEERS, THE(1921); STRANGER'S BANQUET(1922); COURTSHIP OF MILES STANDISH, THE(1923); RUGGLES OF RED GAP(1923); NECESSARY EVIL, THE(1925); PACE THAT THRILLS, THE(1925); NEST, THE(1927)
Misc. Silents
BELLA DONNA(1915); LYDIA GILMORE(1916); MOMENT BEFORE, THE(1916); SILKS AND SATINS(1916); DAUGHTER OF DESTINY(1917); GREAT WHITE TRAIL, THE(1917); MAGDA(1917); REDEEMING LOVE, THE(1917); WAX MODEL, THE(1917); DANGER ZONE, THE(1918); DREAM LADY, THE(1918); LIFE MASK, THE(1918); LIGHT WITHIN, THE(1918); TEMPERED STEEL(1918); VANITY POOL, THE(1918); LADY OF RED BUTTE, THE(1919); LONE WOLF'S DAUGHTER, THE(1919); ONE WEEK OF LIFE(1919); PEACE OF ROARING RIVER, THE(1919); HONEY BEE, THE(1920); WOMAN IN HIS HOUSE, THE(1920); WOMAN WHO UNDERSTOOD, A(1920); LURE OF JADE, THE(1921); SACRED AND PROFANE LOVE(1921); WITHOUT BENEFIT OF CLERGY(1921); ROSE O' THE SEA(1922); TROUPER, THE(1922); WHITE MONKEY, THE(1925); SATAN AND THE WOMAN(1928)
Protea Holdings
HOUSE OF THE LIVING DEAD(1973, S. Afr.), spec eff
Judd Holdren
ALL THE KING'S MEN(1949); FRANCIS(1949); ROCKETSHIP X-M(1950); LADY PAYS OFF, THE(1951); PURPLE HEART DIARY(1951); GOLD FEVER(1952); LADY IN THE IRON MASK(1952); THIS IS MY LOVE(1954); JEANNE EAGELS(1957); SPOILERS OF THE FOREST(1957); SATAN'S SATELLITES(1958); SPACE MASTER X-7(1958); ICE PALACE(1960); RISE AND FALL OF LEGS DIAMOND, THE(1960)
Misc. Talkies
COMMANDO CODY(1953)
Cheryl Holdridge
SUMMER PLACE, A(1959)
Desmond Holdridge
END OF THE RIVER, THE(1947, Brit.), w
Lee Holdridge
SIDELONG GLANCES OF A PIGEON KICKER, THE(1970), m; JEREMY(1973), m; JONATHAN LIVINGSTON SEAGULL(1973), m; MAHOGANY(1975), md; FOREVER YOUNG, FOREVER FREE(1976, South Afr.), m; GOIN' HOME(1976), m; MUSTANG COUNTRY(1976), m; WINTERHAWK(1976), m; PACK, THE(1977), m; MOMENT BY MOMENT(1978), m; OLIVER'S STORY(1978), m; OTHER SIDE OF THE MOUNTAIN–PART 2, THE(1978), m; FRENCH POSTCARDS(1979), m; TILT(1979), m; AMERICAN POP(1981), m; BEASTMASTER, THE(1982), m; MR. MOM(1983), m
1984
MICKI AND MAUDE(1984), m; SPLASH(1984), m
Rex Holdsworth
1984
ORDEAL BY INNOCENCE(1984, Brit.)
Edward V. Hole
CARETAKERS DAUGHTER, THE(1952, Brit.), w
Fred Hole
RETURN OF THE JEDI(1983), art d
Jonathan Hole
KID FROM LEFT FIELD, THE(1953); WOMAN'S WORLD(1954); MAN CALLED PETER, THE(1955); THREE BRAVE MEN(1957); CRY TERROR(1958); DECKS RAN RED, THE(1958); I'D RATHER BE RICH(1964); GRADUATE, THE(1967); SPLIT, THE(1968); SOME KIND OF A NUT(1969)
William Hole
SPRINGTIME IN THE ROCKIES(1937)
William Hole, Jr.
GHOST OF DRAGSTRIP HOLLOW(1959), d; SPEED CRAZY(1959), d
William J. Hole, Jr.
HELL BOUND(1957), d; FOUR FAST GUNS(1959), p&d; DEVIL'S HAND, THE(1961), d; TWIST ALL NIGHT(1961), d
Walter Holeby
Misc. Silents
GIANT OF HIS RACE, A(1921); SHOT IN THE NIGHT, A(1923)
Adam Holender
MIDNIGHT COWBOY(1969), ph; PUZZLE OF A DOWNFALL CHILD(1970), ph; PANIC IN NEEDLE PARK(1971), ph; EFFECT OF GAMMA RAYS ON MAN-IN-THE-MOON MARIGOLDS, THE(1972), ph; MAN ON A SWING(1974), ph; IF EVER I SEE YOU AGAIN(1978), ph; PROMISES IN THE DARK(1979), ph; SEDUCTION OF JOE TYNAN, THE(1979), ph; IDOLMAKER, THE(1980), ph; SIMON(1980), ph

Thomas Holer
BIG TOWN(1932)
Diane Holgate
WHISTLE DOWN THE WIND(1961, Brit.)
Ronald Holgate
1776(1972)
Helmut Holger
CORPSE OF BEVERLY HILLS, THE(1965, Ger.), cos
Pamela Holhouse
PARIS OOH-LA-LA!(1963, U.S./Fr.)
Heidi Holicker
PINK MOTEL(1983); VALLEY GIRL(1983)
1984
JOY OF SEX(1984)
Billie Holiday
NEW ORLEANS(1947); LADY SINGS THE BLUES(1972), w
Billy Holiday
NUMBER ONE(1969)
Billy Holiday
Misc. Talkies
TERROR IN THE SWAMP(1984)
Bishop Holiday
TIN MAN(1983), w, m
1984
JOY OF SEX(1984), m
Chase Holiday
1984
CHOOSE ME(1984)
David Holiday
PROJECTIONIST, THE(1970)
Hope Holiday
APARTMENT, THE(1960); LADIES MAN, THE(1961); IRMA LA DOUCE(1963); ROUNDERS, THE(1965); HOW TO SEDUCE A WOMAN(1974); RAW FORCE(1982)
1984
KILLPOINT(1984)
Jason Holiday
Misc. Talkies
PORTRAIT OF JASON(1967)
Marly Holiday
YOUNG GRADUATES, THE(1971)
Polly Holiday
DISTANCE(1975)
1984
GREMLINS(1984)
Ron Holiday
Misc. Talkies
LEGEND OF ALFRED PACKER, THE(1979)
Stacy Holiday
STARTING OVER(1979)
Kees Holierhoek
SOLDIER OF ORANGE(1979, Dutch), w; OUTSIDER IN AMSTERDAM(1983, Neth.), w
Raphael Holinshed
CHIMES AT MIDNIGHT(1967, Span.,Switz.), w
Blazena Holisova
DEATH IS CALLED ENGELCHEN(1963, Czech.)
Steve Holister
Misc. Talkies
AROUSED(1968)
Wendy Holker
GREAT MUPPET CAPER, THE(1981)
Jurg Holl
5 SINNERS(1961, Ger.)
Milo Holl [Miroslav Holub]
FABULOUS WORLD OF JULES VERNE, THE(1961, Czech.)
Hollaender
Silents
VARIETY(1925, Ger.), w
Friedrich Hollaender
HEART SONG(1933, Brit.), d
Adelaide Holland
Misc. Silents
HATE(1917)
Agnieszka Holland
DANTON(1983), w
1984
LOVE IN GERMANY, A(1984, Fr./Ger.), w
Anita Holland
LITTLE BALLERINA, THE(1951, Brit.)
Anne Holland
GREAT EXPECTATIONS(1946, Brit.); WOMAN HATER(1949, Brit.)
Anthony Holland
KING'S RHAPSODY(1955, Brit.), cos; GOLDSTEIN(1964); FEARLESS FRANK(1967); BYE BYE BRAVERMAN(1968); VIRGIN PRESIDENT, THE(1968); MIDNIGHT COWBOY(1969); POPI(1969); LOVERS AND OTHER STRANGERS(1970); OUT OF TOWNERS, THE(1970); ANDERSON TAPES, THE(1971); KLUTE(1971); MC CABE AND MRS. MILLER(1971); HAMMERSMITH IS OUT(1972); PARADES(1972); LUCKY LADY(1975); SENTINEL, THE(1977); HOUSE CALLS(1978); ALL THAT JAZZ(1979); OH GOD! BOOK II(1980); TEMPEST(1982); GREY FOX, THE(1983, Can.); LONELY LADY, THE(1983)
Arthur Holland
KISS OF DEATH(1947)
Bert Holland
TARANTULA(1955); THERE'S ALWAYS TOMORROW(1956); WRITTEN ON THE WIND(1956); LINEUP, THE(1958)
Betty Lou Holland
GODDESS, THE(1958); MAN IN THE NET, THE(1959)

Bill Holland
SUCH IS LIFE(1936, Brit.); CAESAR AND CLEOPATRA(1946, Brit.); SUBURBAN WIVES(1973, Brit.), ph
Billy Holland
BYPASS TO HAPPINESS(1934, Brit.); BREAKERS AHEAD(1935, Brit.); MAN WITHOUT A FACE, THE(1935, Brit.); REAL BLOKE, A(1935, Brit.); WHITE LILAC(1935, Brit.); GAY OLD DOG(1936, Brit.); RIDING HIGH(1937, Brit.); WANTED(1937, Brit.); FATHER O'FLYNN(1938, Irish); WIFE OF GENERAL LING, THE(1938, Brit.); DEMON BARBER OF FLEET STREET, THE(1939, Brit.); THIS WAS PARIS(1942, Brit.); YOUNG MR. PITT, THE(1942, Brit.); FRENZY(1946, Brit.)
Buck Holland
SWINGIN' SUMMER, A(1965); WINTER A GO-GO(1965); WILD, WILD WINTER(1966); SIMON, KING OF THE WITCHES(1971)
Byrd Holland
STAKEOUT ON DOPE STREET(1958); VENGEANCE(1964); BLACK KLANSMAN, THE(1966); LAST MOMENT, THE(1966); MADAME X(1966); MONEY JUNGLE, THE(1968); TERROR IN THE JUNGLE(1968); WILD WHEELS(1969); RED, WHITE AND BLACK, THE(1970); JOURNEY THROUGH ROSEBUD(1972), makeup; RABID(1976, Can.), makeup
Carol Holland
EDEN CRIED(1967)
Carole Holland
TOOTSIE(1982)
Cecil Holland
FIGHTING KENTUCKIAN, THE(1949), makeup
Silents
CITY OF PURPLE DREAMS, THE(1918); BURNING SANDS(1922); MORAN OF THE LADY LETTY(1922); PENROD(1922); WOMAN WHO WALKED ALONE, THE(1922); GIRL OF THE GOLDEN WEST, THE(1923); RENDEZVOUS, THE(1923)
Misc. Silents
BISHOP OF THE OZARKS, THE(1923)
Charles Holland
HULLABALOO(1940); YOUTH WILL BE SERVED(1940)
Charlotte Holland
PROMISE HER ANYTHING(1966, Brit.)
Clifford Holland
REFORM SCHOOL(1939); MY GAL LOVES MUSIC(1944)
Silents
SUMMER BACHELORS(1926)
Misc. Silents
RICH BUT HONEST(1927); SECRET STUDIO, THE(1927)
Danny Holland
WHERE'S JACK?(1969, Brit.)
Dick Holland
LAST GANGSTER, THE(1937)
Dorothy Holland
SUMMERSPELL(1983)
Dutch Holland
WILD REBELS, THE(1967)
E. Holland
Misc. Silents
THOUGHTLESS WOMEN(1920)
Edna Holland
BACHELOR MOTHER(1939); JUDGE HARDY AND SON(1939); THIRD FINGER, LEFT HAND(1940); LOOK WHO'S LAUGHING(1941); TOM, DICK AND HARRY(1941); ALLERGIC TO LOVE(1943); LAUGH YOUR BLUES AWAY(1943); KISS AND TELL(1945); SUNBONNET SUE(1945); CENTENNIAL SUMMER(1946); DARK ALIBI(1946); INTRIGUE(1947); MAGIC TOWN(1947); BIG CLOCK, THE(1948); HUNTED, THE(1948); PRAIRIE, THE(1948); RUTHLESS(1948); HENRY, THE RAINMAKER(1949); LOVABLE CHEAT, THE(1949); MY FOOLISH HEART(1949); SHEP COMES HOME(1949); SKY DRAGON(1949); SON OF A BADMAN(1949); NEVER A DULL MOMENT(1950); NO MAN OF HER OWN(1950); LOVE NEST(1951); STRANGERS ON A TRAIN(1951); HAS ANYBODY SEEN MY GAL?(1952); MEET ME AT THE FAIR(1952); PAULA(1952); SCANDAL SHEET(1952); ROAR OF THE CROWD(1953); TREASURE OF THE GOLDEN CONDOR(1953); COURT-MARTIAL OF BILLY MITCHELL, THE(1955); TEN WANTED MEN(1955); TO HELL AND BACK(1955); WOMEN'S PRISON(1955); THESE WILDER YEARS(1956); THIS COULD BE THE NIGHT(1957); TOP SECRET AFFAIR(1957); INSIDE DAISY CLOVER(1965)
Edna M. Holland
CRISS CROSS(1949); ONCE MORE, MY DARLING(1949); OVER-EXPOSED(1956)
Misc. Silents
ALWAYS IN THE WAY(1915)
Edwin Holland
Silents
AMERICA(1924)
Erik Holland
PRIZE, THE(1963); GLORY GUYS, THE(1965); TORN CURTAIN(1966); CHILDISH THINGS(1969); TELL THEM WILLIE BOY IS HERE(1969); GREAT NORTHFIELD, MINNESOTA RAID, THE(1972); TRADER HORN(1973); MORE AMERICAN GRAFFITI(1979); TABLE FOR FIVE(1983)
1984
DADDY'S DEADLY DARLING(1984); LONELY GUY, THE(1984)
Eugene Holland
ADVENTURES OF MARK TWAIN, THE(1944)
Frank Holland
Silents
LOLA(1914); SPRINGTIME(1915); TIDES OF FATE(1917); BLAZING TRAIL, THE(1921)
Misc. Silents
MORGAN'S RAIDERS(1918); TRAVELING SALESMAN, THE(1921)
Gene Holland
SONG OF THE SOUTH(1946); FAR COUNTRY, THE(1955)
George Holland
DON'T TELL THE WIFE(1937), w
Gerry Holland
JAWS OF SATAN(1980), w
Gilbert Holland
ESCAPADE(1955, Brit.), w

Gladys Holland
LIGHT TOUCH, THE(1951); LYDIA BAILEY(1952); RACERS, THE(1955); TO CATCH A THIEF(1955); MAN WHO KNEW TOO MUCH, THE(1956); CARPETBAGGERS, THE(1964); DON'T JUST STAND THERE!(1968); ULZANA'S RAID(1972)

Gretchen Holland
THIRTEENTH CHAIR, THE(1930)

Harold Holland
Silents
MIDNIGHT PATROL, THE(1918); WHERE LIGHTS ARE LOW(1921); COME ON OVER(1922)

Henry Holland
Misc. Silents
MAINSPRING, THE(1916)

Hilary Holland
MAN WHO FELL TO EARTH, THE(1976, Brit.)

J. H. Holland
Silents
JACK AND JILL(1917)

Jack Holland
DANCE BAND(1935, Brit.); PEACEMAKER, THE(1956); MY GUN IS QUICK(1957); FEAR NO EVIL(1981)

Jerry Holland
TAKING OF PELHAM ONE, TWO, THREE, THE(1974); MAC ARTHUR(1977); AMERICAN POP(1981)

Joan Holland
GREAT ZIEGFELD, THE(1936)

Joe Holland
HAPPY DAYS(1930)

Jogi Holland
REVENGE OF THE NINJA(1983)

John Holland
COLLEGE COQUETTE, THE(1929); SHE GOES TO WAR(1929); EYES OF THE WORLD, THE(1930); GUILTY?(1930); HELL HARBOR(1930); LADIES MUST PLAY(1930); DEFENDERS OF THE LAW(1931); GRIEF STREET(1931); LADIES' MAN(1931); LADY FROM NOWHERE(1931); MORALS FOR WOMEN(1931); SILVER LINING(1932); CIRCUS GIRL(1937); JOIN THE MARINES(1937); PARADISE EX-PRESS(1937); UP IN THE AIR(1940); DANGEROUS LADY(1941); GENTLEMAN FROM DIXIE(1941); HOLD BACK THE DAWN(1941); PALS OF THE PECOS(1941); ROAR OF THE PRESS(1941); CALL OF THE CANYON(1942); HOUSE OF ER-RORS(1942); INVISIBLE AGENT(1942); LUCKY LEGS(1942); PALM BEACH STORY, THE(1942); SHE'S IN THE ARMY(1942); TAKE A LETTER, DARLING(1942); WE WERE DANCING(1942); VOICE OF THE TURTLE, THE(1947); KING OF THE GAMBLERS(1948); ROMANCE ON THE HIGH SEAS(1948); SONS OF ADVEN-TURE(1948); THREE MUSKETEERS, THE(1948); BLONDE ICE(1949); LAW OF THE GOLDEN WEST(1949); MASSACRE RIVER(1949); STATE DEPARTMENT-FILE 649(1949); RIO GRANDE PATROL(1950); ROCK ISLAND TRAIL(1950); MAN OF CONFLICT(1953); JUBILEE TRAIL(1954); GIRL IN BLACK STOCKINGS(1957); STREET OF SINNERS(1957); HIGH-POWERED RIFLE, THE(1960); LITTLE SHE-PHERD OF KINGDOM COME(1961); AIR PATROL(1962); GATHERING OF EAGLES, A(1963); POLICE NURSE(1963); PRIZE, THE(1963); MY FAIR LADY(1964); OPEN THE DOOR AND SEE ALL THE PEOPLE(1964); THEY SAVED HITLER'S BRAIN(1964); MY BLOOD RUNS COLD(1965); NAKED BRIGADE, THE(1965, U.S./Gr.); OSCAR, THE(1966); 1776(1972); CHINATOWN(1974); LOST IN THE STARS(1974); HOW TO SUCCEED IN BUSINESS WITHOUT REALLY TRYING(1976)
Misc. Silents
BLACK MAGIC(1929)

Joseph Holland
RALLY 'ROUND THE FLAG, BOYS!(1958)

Joseph W. Holland
HIGH WALL, THE(1947), set d; NEW YORK CONFIDENTIAL(1955), set d

Katherine Holland
TALK ABOUT JACQUELINE(1942, Brit.), w; DOG OF FLANDERS, A(1959)

Kristina Holland
STRAWBERRY STATEMENT, THE(1970); DOCTORS' WIVES(1971); WIN, PLACE, OR STEAL(1975)

Lee Holland
SHANTY TRAMP(1967)

Leslie Holland
Misc. Silents
CHAMBER OF HORRORS(1929, Brit.)

Leza Holland
DESPERATE(1947)

Mamie Holland
KISS ME, SERGEANT(1930, Brit.); OLD SOLDIERS NEVER DIE(1931, Brit.)

Marty Holland
FALLEN ANGEL(1945), w; FILE ON THELMA JORDAN, THE(1950), w

Mary Holland
TOMMY(1975, Brit.)

P. Holland
COMANCHE STATION(1960)

Pamela Holland
DORM THAT DRIPPED BLOOD, THE(1983)
Misc. Talkies
PRANKS(1982)

Paula Holland
PATERNITY(1981)

Randy Holland
WHEN A STRANGER CALLS(1979)

Ray Holland
GREATEST, THE(1977, U.S./Brit.); SUMMER CAMP(1979)
Misc. Talkies
HOT T-SHIRTS(1980)

Rita Holland
MASK OF DIMITRIOS, THE(1944)

Rodney Holland
1984
SCRUBBERS(1984, Brit.), ed

Simon Holland
BARTLEBY(1970, Brit.), art d; BOY FRIEND, THE(1971, Brit.), art d; ROSE-BUD(1975), art d; "EQUUS"(1977), art d; SWALLOWS AND AMAZONS(1977, Brit.), art d; SHOUT, THE(1978, Brit.), art d; AGATHA(1979, Brit.), art d; QUADRO-PHENIA(1979, Brit.), prod d; REDS(1981), art d
1984
GREYSTOKE: THE LEGEND OF TARZAN, LORD OF THE APES(1984), art d

Steve Holland
COURT-MARTIAL OF BILLY MITCHELL, THE(1955)

Sylvia Holland
MAKE MINE MUSIC(1946), w

Terence Holland
ROOMMATES(1962, Brit.)

Tom Holland
UNWRITTEN CODE, THE(1944); JUDGE, THE(1949); BEAST WITHIN, THE(1982), w; CLASS OF 1984(1982, Can.), w; PSYCHO II(1983), a, w
1984
CLOAK AND DAGGER(1984), w; SCREAM FOR HELP(1984), w

W. T. Holland
OLD MOTHER RILEY'S CIRCUS(1941, Brit.)

William Holland
VANDERGILT DIAMOND MYSTERY, THE(1936)

Wim Holland
VIOLATED(1953)

Zeke Holland
DRIFTWOOD(1947)

Giles Holland-Martin
GALLIPOLI(1981, Aus.)

Holland's Magyar Band
MURDER AT THE CABARET(1936, Brit.)

Adam Hollander
J.W. COOP(1971), ph; HALLOWEEN(1978)

David Hollander
SCAVENGER HUNT(1979); SMALL CIRCLE OF FRIENDS, A(1980); AMY(1981)
1984
MEATBALLS PART II(1984)
Misc. Talkies
ONE LAST RIDE(1980)

Eli Hollander
OUT(1982), p&d, w, ed

Frederick Hollander
DESIRE(1936), m; ANGEL(1937), m; JOHN MEADE'S WOMAN(1937), m; TRUE CONFESSION(1937), m; DISPUTED PASSAGE(1939), m; INVITATION TO HAPPI-NESS(1939), m; ZAZA(1939), m; FARMER'S DAUGHTER, THE(1940), m/l Frank Loesser; GREAT McGINTY, THE(1940), m; RANGERS OF FORTUNE(1940), m; REMEMBER THE NIGHT(1940), m; SAFARI(1940), m; TOO MANY HUS-BANDS(1940), m; TYPHOON(1940), m; VICTORY(1940), m; ALOMA OF THE SOUTH SEAS(1941), m/l Frank Loesser; FOOTSTEPS IN THE DARK(1941), m; HERE COMES MR. JORDAN(1941), md; MILLION DOLLAR BABY(1941), m; YOU BELONG TO ME(1941), m; MAN WHO CAME TO DINNER, THE(1942), m; TALK OF THE TOWN(1942), m; WINGS FOR THE EAGLE(1942), m; BACKGROUND TO DAN-GER(1943), m; PRINCESS O'ROURKE(1943), m; ONCE UPON A TIME(1944), m; CHRISTMAS IN CONNECTICUT(1945), m; CONFLICT(1945), m; PILLOW TO POST(1945), m; BRIDE WORE BOOTS, THE(1946), m; CINDERELLA JONES(1946), m; JANIE GETS MARRIED(1946), m; NEVER SAY GOODBYE(1946), m; PERFECT MARRIAGE, THE(1946), m; VERDICT, THE(1946), m; RED STALLION, THE(1947), m; STALLION ROAD(1947), m; THAT WAY WITH WOMEN(1947), m; BERLIN EXPRESS(1948), m; FOREIGN AFFAIR, A(1948), m, md; WALLFLOWER(1948), m; ADVENTURE IN BALTIMORE(1949), m; CAUGHT(1949), m; DANGEROUS PROFES-SION, A(1949), m; WOMAN'S SECRET, A(1949), m; NEVER A DULL MOMENT(1950), m; WALK SOFTLY, STRANGER(1950), m; BORN YESTERDAY(1951), m; DARLING, HOW COULD YOU!(1951), m; MY FORBIDDEN PAST(1951), m; ANDROCLES AND THE LION(1952), m; FIRST TIME, THE(1952), m; 5,000 FINGERS OF DR. T, THE(1953), m; IT SHOULD HAPPEN TO YOU(1954), m; PHFFFT!(1954), m; SA-BRINA(1954), m; WE'RE NO ANGELS(1955), m

Friedrich "Frederick" Hollander
BLUE ANGEL, THE(1930, Ger.), m; TEMPEST(1932, Ger.), m; EMPRESS AND I, THE(1933, Ger.), d

Hanna Hollander
Misc. Talkies
I WANT TO BE A MOTHER(1937)

Howard Hollander
TEENAGE MILLIONAIRE(1961), art d; COVENANT WITH DEATH, A(1966), art d; CHUBASCO(1968), art d; FIRECREEK(1968), art d; 80 STEPS TO JONAH(1969), art d; WILLARD(1971), art d

Jack Hollander
MIRACLE WORKER, THE(1962); JENNIFER ON MY MIND(1971); BANG THE DRUM SLOWLY(1973); DEATH PLAY(1976); ROCKY(1976); FOR PETE'S SAKE(1977); ...AND JUSTICE FOR ALL(1979); ROSE, THE(1979)

John Hollander
FAST TIMES AT RIDGEMONT HIGH(1982)

Owen Hollander
HAPPY HOOKER, THE(1975); FIREPOWER(1979, Brit.)

Providence Hollander
THOSE LIPS, THOSE EYES(1980)

Steve Hollander
1984
FIRST TURN-ON!, THE(1984)

Steven Hollander
FAME(1980)

Victor Hollander
Silents
ONE ARABIAN NIGHT(1921, Ger.), w, m

Xaviera Hollander
HAPPY HOOKER, THE(1975), w
Misc. Talkies
MY PLEASURE IS MY BUSINESS(1974, Can.)

John Hollands
1984
MELVIN, SON OF ALVIN(1984, Aus.), ed
Lloyd Hollar
THE CRAZIES(1973)
Allan Holleb
Misc. Talkies
CANDY STRIPE NURSES(1974), d
Chicken Holleman
BOXCAR BERTHA(1972)
Saskia Holleman
WHO'S THAT KNOCKING AT MY DOOR?(1968)
Harry Hollenberger
ARIZONA(1940), ph
Anna Hollering
DEVIL IN SILK(1968, Ger.), ed
Franz Hollering
MAEDCHEN IN UNIFORM(1965, Ger./Fr.), w
Anthony Holles
BRITANNIA OF BILLINGSGATE(1933, Brit.); LOYALTIES(1934, Brit.); THINGS TO COME(1936, Brit.); DARK JOURNEY(1937, Brit.); BLIND FOLLY(1939, Brit.); MISSING PEOPLE, THE(1940, Brit.); LARCENY STREET(1941, Brit.); NEUTRAL PORT(1941, Brit.); FRONT LINE KIDS(1942, Brit.); BATTLE FOR MUSIC(1943, Brit.); IT'S IN THE BAG(1943, Brit.); CAESAR AND CLEOPATRA(1946, Brit.); CARNIVAL(1946, Brit.); BONNIE PRINCE CHARLIE(1948, Brit.)
Antony Holles
HOTEL SPLENDIDE(1932, Brit.); LIFE GOES ON(1932, Brit.); MIDSHIPMAID GOB(1932, Brit.); REUNION(1932, Brit.); WATCH BEVERLY(1932, Brit.); SHE WAS ONLY A VILLAGE MAIDEN(1933, Brit.); THAT'S A GOOD GIRL(1933, Brit.); BORROWED CLOTHES(1934, Brit.); FOR LOVE OR MONEY(1934, Brit.); GREEN PACK, THE(1934, Brit.); BREWSTER'S MILLIONS(1935, Brit.); GENTLEMAN'S AGREEMENT(1935, Brit.); PHANTOM FIEND, THE(1935, Brit.); DOMMED CARGO(1936, Brit.); GAY ADVENTURE, THE(1936, Brit.); MILLIONS(1936, Brit.); PUBLIC NUISANCE NO. 1(1936, Brit.); SENSATION(1936, Brit.); BACKSTAGE(1937, Brit.); GLAMOROUS NIGHT(1937, Brit.); LET'S MAKE A NIGHT OF IT(1937, Brit.); SKY'S THE LIMIT, THE(1937, Brit.); TENTH MAN, THE(1937, Brit.); DANGEROUS MEDICINE(1938, Brit.); GAIETY GIRLS, THE(1938, Brit.); HIS LORDSHIP REGRETS(1938, Brit.); MIRACLES DO HAPPEN(1938, Brit.); ROMANCE A LA CARTE(1938, Brit.); THEY DRIVE BY NIGHT(1938, Brit.); THIS'LL MAKE YOU WHISTLE(1938, Brit.); WEDDINGS ARE WONDERFUL(1938, Brit.); DOWN OUR ALLEY(1939, Brit.); SPIDER, THE(1940, Brit.); MISSING TEN DAYS(1941, Brit.); LADY FROM LISBON(1942, Brit.); TALK ABOUT JACQUELINE(1942, Brit.); OLD MOTHER RILEY OVERSEAS(1943, Brit.); THURSDAY'S CHILD(1943, Brit.); UNDER SECRET ORDERS(1943, Brit.); UP WITH THE LARK(1943, Brit.); WARN THAT MAN(1943, Brit.); GIVE ME THE STARS(1944, Brit.); UNCENSORED(1944, Brit.); THEY KNEW MR. KNIGHT(1945, Brit.); FORTUNE LANE(1947, Brit.); MAGIC BOW, THE(1947, Brit.); DARK ROAD, THE(1948, Brit.); SHOWTIME(1948, Brit.); HER MAN GILBEY(1949, Brit.); ROCKING HORSE WINNER, THE(1950, Brit.)
H. Holles
Silents
IVANHOE(1913)
Philip Holles
GRAND FINALE(1936, Brit.); SEXTON BLAKE AND THE HOODED TERROR(1938, Brit.)
Robert Holles
GUNS AT BATASI(1964, Brit.), w
Bernard Holley
TRAVELS WITH MY AUNT(1972, Brit.); DEADLY FEMALES, THE(1976, Brit.)
Gibson Holley
D.I., THE(1957), art d; –30–(1959), art d; FEAR NO MORE(1961), art d
Richard Holley
SORCERER(1977)
Rick Holley
1984
BIRDY(1984)
Ruth Holley
Silents
SHERLOCK, JR.(1924)
Ted Holley
MR. WINKLE GOES TO WAR(1944)
Timothy Holley
CRAZY JOE(1974)
Art Holliday
MAN WITH TWO BRAINS, THE(1983)
Bill Holliday
TOY, THE(1982)
1984
TIGHTROPE(1984)
Charlie Holliday
1984
CHATTANOOGA CHOO CHOO(1984)
Don Holliday
NIGHT OF THE LEPUS(1972), w
Donald Holliday
CINDERELLA(1950), ed
Doreen Holliday
DEVIL'S HARBOR(1954, Brit.)
Frank Holliday
PARDON US(1931); IT HAPPENED ONE NIGHT(1934)
Fred Holliday
PRIZE, THE(1963); GUIDE FOR THE MARRIED MAN, A(1967)
J. Frank Holliday
Silents
TRAMP, TRAMP, TRAMP(1926), w
Judy Holliday
SOMETHING FOR THE BOYS(1944); WINGED VICTORY(1944); ADAM'S RIB(1949); ON THE TOWN(1949); BORN YESTERDAY(1951); MARRYING KIND, THE(1952); IT SHOULD HAPPEN TO YOU(1954); PHFFFT!(1954); SOLID GOLD CADILLAC, THE(1956); BELLS ARE RINGING(1960)

Kene Holliday
1984
NO SMALL AFFAIR(1984); PHILADELPHIA EXPERIMENT, THE(1984)
Marjorie Holliday
HOUSE OF STRANGERS(1949); JACKPOT, THE(1950); O. HENRY'S FULL HOUSE(1952); SHE COULDN'T SAY NO(1954); SON OF SINBAD(1955)
Martha Holliday
GEORGE WHITE'S SCANDALS(1945); FLAME, THE(1948); I, JANE DOE(1948); LULU BELLE(1948)
Michael Holliday
LIFE IS A CIRCUS(1962, Brit.)
Nan Holliday
LAND OF THE OUTLAWS(1944)
Polly Holliday
CATAMOUNT KILLING, THE(1975, Ger.); ALL THE PRESIDENT'S MEN(1976); ONE AND ONLY, THE(1978)
Raylene Holliday
DIRTY HARRY(1971)
Richard Holliday
Misc. Talkies
ASSAULT WITH A DEADLY WEAPON(1983)
Sasha Holliday
PRETTY BABY(1978)
Sheilagh Holliday
MY WAY(1974, South Africa)
Ted Holliday
STRANGER IN BETWEEN, THE(1952, Brit.), ed
Sgt. Ted Holliday
SOLDIER, SAILOR(1944, Brit.)
Emery Hollier
CAT PEOPLE(1982)
The Hollies
IT'S ALL OVER TOWN(1963, Brit.)
Peter Holliger
BLACK SPIDER, THE(1983, Swit.)
John Holligsworth
MUMMY, THE(1959, Brit.), md
Earl Holliman
DESTINATION GOBI(1953); DEVIL'S CANYON(1953); EAST OF SUMATRA(1953); ALASKA SEAS(1954); BRIDGES AT TOKO-RI, THE(1954); BROKEN LANCE(1954); TENNESSEE CHAMP(1954); BIG COMBO, THE(1955); I DIED A THOUSAND TIMES(1955); BURNING HILLS, THE(1956); FORBIDDEN PLANET(1956); GIANT(1956); RAINMAKER, THE(1956); GUNFIGHT AT THE O.K. CORRAL(1957); TROOPER HOOK(1957); HOT SPELL(1958); LAST TRAIN FROM GUN HILL(1959); TRAP, THE(1959); VISIT TO A SMALL PLANET(1960); ARMORED COMMAND(1961); SUMMER AND SMOKE(1961); SONS OF KATIE ELDER, THE(1965); COVENANT WITH DEATH, A(1968); ANZIO(1968, Ital.); POWER, THE(1968); TRIBES(1970); BISCUIT EATER, THE(1972); DON'T GO NEAR THE WATER(1975); GOOD LUCK, MISS WYCKOFF(1979); SHARKY'S MACHINE(1982)
Harry Hollingshead
SECRET SERVICE OF THE AIR(1939)
Alfred Hollingsworth
Silents
HELL'S HINGES(1916); FAIR ENOUGH(1918); JOYOUS LIAR, THE(1919); WHITE YOUTH(1920); INFAMOUS MISS REVELL, THE(1921); SAPHEAD, THE(1921); MARRY IN HASTE(1924)
Misc. Talkies
PURITY(1916); RIGHT DIRECTION, THE(1916); LEAVE IT TO SUSAN(1919); SNEAK, THE(1919); UPLIFTERS, THE(1919); LEOPARD WOMAN, THE(1920); TRIMMED(1922)
Darcey Hollingsworth
Misc. Talkies
BLUE SUMMER(1973)
Harry Hollingsworth
LONE WOLF RETURNS, THE(1936); POLO JOE(1936); SING ME A LOVE SONG(1936); PERFECT SPECIMEN, THE(1937); THEY WON'T FORGET(1937); PENITENTIARY(1938); YOU CAN'T TAKE IT WITH YOU(1938); TORCHY PLAYS WITH DYNAMITE(1939); CONFESSIONS OF BOSTON BLACKIE(1941); MY FAVORITE BLONDE(1942)
Jill Hollingsworth
COMBAT SQUAD(1953)
John Hollingsworth
I BECAME A CRIMINAL(1947), md; SILVER DARLINGS, THE(1947, Brit.), md; WHEN THE BOUGH BREAKS(1947, Brit.), md; HAMLET(1948, Brit.), md; MARK OF CAIN, THE(1948, Brit.); INVITATION TO THE DANCE(1956), md; X THE UNKNOWN(1957, Brit.), md; HORROR OF DRACULA, THE(1958, Brit.), md; SNORKEL, THE(1958, Brit.), md; STEEL BAYONET, THE(1958, Brit.), md; ELEPHANT GUN(1959, Brit.), md; HOUND OF THE BASKERVILLES, THE(1959, Brit.), md; MAN WHO COULD CHEAT DEATH, THE(1959, Brit.), md; HOUSE OF FRIGHT(1961), md; MARK, THE(1961, Brit.), md; NEVER TAKE CANDY FROM A STRANGER(1961, Brit.), md; SCREAM OF FEAR(1961, Brit.), md; CASH ON DEMAND(1962, Brit.), md; PIRATES OF BLOOD RIVER, THE(1962, Brit.), md; HEAVENS ABOVE!(1963, Brit.), md; MYSTERY SUBMARINE(1963, Brit.), md; WRONG ARM OF THE LAW, THE(1963, Brit.), md; CRIMSON BLADE, THE(1964, Brit.), md; WHY BOTHER TO KNOCK(1964, Brit.), md; THESE ARE THE DAMNED(1965, Brit.), md
Laura Hollingsworth
Misc. Talkies
PIT, THE(1984)
Perry Hollingsworth
HELL'S ANGELS(1930), ed
Ray D. Hollingsworth
HONEYSUCKLE ROSE(1980)
Alan Hollis
Silents
VORTEX, THE(1927, Brit.)
Ann Hollis
DRACULA(THE DIRTY OLD MAN) (1969); RAVAGER, THE(1970)

Anthony Hollis
MISSING REMBRANDT, THE(1932, Brit.)
Carey Hollis, Jr.
RAGGEDY MAN(1981)
Glen Hollis
NORSEMAN, THE(1978)
J. B. Hollis
Silents
POLLY OF THE CIRCUS(1917)
Jack B. Hollis
Silents
ANNE OF GREEN GABLES(1919)
Jeff Hollis
YOUNGBLOOD(1978)
John Hollis
ON THE RUN(1969, Brit.); SUPERMAN(1978); EMPIRE STRIKES BACK, THE(1980); FLASH GORDON(1980); SUPERMAN II(1980)
Ralph Hollis
Silents
IT'S HAPPINESS THAT COUNTS(1918, Brit.)
Roy Hollis
CUTTER AND BONE(1981)
Tommy Hollis
1984
GHOSTBUSTERS(1984)
Sarah Hollis-Andrews
Misc. Talkies
MAN FROM NOWHERE, THE(1976, Brit.)
Alice Hollister
Silents
FROM THE MANGER TO THE CROSS(1913); CELEBRATED CASE, A(1914); KNIFE, THE(1918); VOICE IN THE DARK(1921); WISE FOOL, A(1921); MARRIED FLIRTS(1924)
Misc. Silents
DON CAESAR DE BAZAN(1915); LOTUS WOMAN, THE(1916); HER BETTER SELF(1917); GREAT LOVER, THE(1920); MILESTONES(1920)
Boyd Hollister
CLONUS HORROR, THE(1979)
Flora Hollister
Misc. Silents
FIGHTING STRANGER, THE(1921)
George Hollister
Silents
ARIZONA KID, THE(1929)
George K. Hollister
Silents
FROM THE MANGER TO THE CROSS(1913), ph; GREAT ADVENTURE, THE(1918), ph
Len D. Hollister
GOLD DUST GERTIE(1931), w
Steve Hollister
STRANGE LOVERS(1963); LOVE HUNGER(1965, Arg.)
Bridget Hollman
SLUMBER PARTY '57(1977)
Winnie Hollman
EYES OF LAURA MARS(1978)
Werner Hollmann
KARAMAZOV(1931, Ger.); RASPUTIN(1932, Ger.)
Joan Hollmark
INDIAN PAINT(1965)
Chuck Hollom
WHAT'S UP, DOC?(1972)
Andrew Scott Hollon
TENDER MERCIES(1982)
Stacy Hollow
WHAT'S THE MATTER WITH HELEN?(1971)
Ann Holloway
STOP THE WORLD–I WANT TO GET OFF(1966, Brit.); TWO A PENNY(1968, Brit.)
Baliol Holloway
UNDER THE RED ROBE(1937, Brit.)
Carol Holloway
ONE HOUR LATE(1935); STOLEN HARMONY(1935); LADY'S FROM KENTUCKY, THE(1939)
Silents
SAPHEAD, THE(1921); SEA LION, THE(1921); RICH MEN'S WIVES(1922)
Misc. Silents
SECRETARY OF FRIVOLOUS AFFAIRS, THE(1915); WAIFS, THE(1916); DEAD-SHOT BAKER(1917); TENDERFOOT, THE(1917); DECEIVER, THE(1920); TWO MOONS(1920); UP AND GOING(1922)
Dorothy Holloway
SONG OF FREEDOM(1938, Brit.), w
Freda Holloway
JAMBOREE(1957)
Gordon Holloway
Silents
NARROW VALLEY, THE(1921, Brit.)
Jean Holloway
TILL THE CLOUDS ROLL BY(1946), w; MADAME X(1966), w; MAGIC OF LASSIE, THE(1978), w
Joan Holloway
DIARY OF A BACHELOR(1964)
John Holloway
Misc. Silents
ACROSS THE DIVIDE(1921), d
Julian Holloway
HAVING A WILD WEEKEND(1965, Brit.); KNACK ... AND HOW TO GET IT, THE(1965, Brit.); FOLLOW THAT CAMEL(1967, Brit.); JOKERS, THE(1967, Brit.); CARRY ON DOCTOR(1968, Brit.); CARRY ON, UP THE KHYBER(1968, Brit.); CARRY ON CAMPING(1969, Brit.); LAST SHOT YOU HEAR, THE(1969, Brit.); CARRY ON HENRY VIII(1970, Brit.); CARRY ON LOVING(1970, Brit.); SCREAM AND SCREAM

AGAIN(1970, Brit.); YOUNG WINSTON(1972, Brit.); CARRY ON ENGLAND(1976, Brit.); DOING TIME(1979, Brit.); ROUGH CUT(1980, Brit.); LOOPHOLE(1981, Brit.), p
Liddy Holloway
CLINIC, THE(1983, Aus.)
Mary Lou Holloway
HOUSE OF WAX(1953); STRANGER WORE A GUN, THE(1953); BOUNTY HUNTER, THE(1954); RIDING SHOTGUN(1954)
Merritt Holloway
DEATH VALLEY(1982)
Nancy Holloway
PARIS OOH-LA-LA!(1963, U.S./Fr.); MAN FROM COCODY(1966, Fr./Ital.); KILLING GAME, THE(1968, Fr.)
Stanley Holloway
SLEEPING CAR(1933, Brit.); BRIDE OF THE LAKE(1934, Brit.); ROAD HOUSE(1934, Brit.); SING AS WE GO(1934, Brit.); PLAY UP THE BAND(1935, Brit.); SQUIBS(1935, Brit.); COTTON QUEEN(1937, Brit.); SAM SMALL LEAVES TOWN(1937, Brit.); SONG OF THE FORGE(1937, Brit.); VICAR OF BRAY, THE(1937, Brit.); GIRL THIEF, THE(1938); CAPTAIN MOONLIGHT(1940, Brit.); MAJOR BARBARA(1941, Brit.); SALUTE JOHN CITIZEN(1942, Brit.); CHAMPAGNE CHARLIE(1944, Brit.); THIS HAPPY BREED(1944, Brit.); BRIEF ENCOUNTER(1945, Brit.); JOHNNY IN THE CLOUDS(1945, Brit.); WAY AHEAD, THE(1945, Brit.); CAESAR AND CLEOPA-TRA(1946, Brit.); CARNIVAL(1946, Brit.); WANTED FOR MURDER(1946, Brit.); MEET ME AT DAWN(1947, Brit.); NICHOLAS NICKLEBY(1947, Brit.); ANOTHER SHO-RE(1948, Brit.); HAMLET(1948, Brit.); ONE NIGHT WITH YOU(1948, Brit); PASSPORT TO PIMLICO(1949, Brit.); SNOWBOUND(1949, Brit.); PERFECT WOMAN, THE(1950, Brit.); SILK NOOSE, THE(1950, Brit.); WINSLOW BOY, THE(1950); LAVENDER HILL MOB, THE(1951, Brit.); MIDNIGHT EPISODE(1951, Brit.); ONE WILD OAT(1951, Brit.); MAGIC BOX, THE(1952, Brit.); MR. LORD SAYS NO(1952, Brit.); BEGGAR'S OPERA, THE(1953); DAY TO REMEMBER, A(1953, Brit.); MEET MR. LUCIFER(1953, Brit.); TITFIELD THUNDERBOLT, THE(1953, Brit.); TONIGHT AT 8:30(1953, Brit.); FAST AND LOOSE(1954, Brit.); LADY GODIVA RIDES AGAIN(1955, Brit.); JUMPING FOR JOY(1956, Brit.); ALLIGATOR NAMED DAISY, AN(1957, Brit.); HELLO LON-DON(1958, Brit.); NO LOVE FOR JOHNNIE(1961, Brit.); ALIVE AND KICKING(1962, Brit.); MY FAIR LADY(1964); NO TREE IN THE STREET(1964, Brit.); IN HARM'S WAY(1965); OPERATION SNAFU(1965, Brit.); TEN LITTLE INDIANS(1965, Brit.); SANDWICH MAN, THE(1966, Brit.); MRS. BROWN, YOU'VE GOT A LOVELY DAUGHTER(1968, Brit.); PRIVATE LIFE OF SHERLOCK HOLMES, THE(1970, Brit.); FLIGHT OF THE DOVES(1971); UP THE FRONT(1972, Brit.); JOURNEY INTO FEAR(1976, Can); TARGET: HARRY(1980)
Sterling Holloway
BLONDE VENUS(1932); FAITHLESS(1932); ROCKABYE(1932); ADVICE TO THE LOVELORN(1933); ALICE IN WONDERLAND(1933); BLONDIE JOHNSON(1933); DANCING LADY(1933); ELMER THE GREAT(1933); FAST WORKERS(1933); FEMALE(1933); GOLD DIGGERS OF 1933(1933); HARD TO HANDLE(1933); HELL BELOW(1933); INTERNATIONAL HOUSE(1933); LAWYER MAN(1933); PICTURE SNATCHER(1933); PROFESSIONAL SWEETHEART(1933); WILD BOYS OF THE ROAD(1933); DOWN TO THEIR LAST YACHT(1934); GIFT OF GAB(1934); MERRY WIDOW, THE(1934); OPERATOR 13(1934); STRICTLY DYNAMITE(1934); WICKED WOMAN, A(1934); DOUBTING THOMAS(1935); GIRL O' MY DREAMS(1935); I LIVE MY LIFE(1935); LIFE BEGINS AT 40(1935); LOTTERY LOVER(1935); RENDEZ-VOUS(1935); $1,000 A MINUTE(1935); CAREER WOMAN(1936); GIRL FROM MAX-IM'S, THE(1936, Brit.); PALM SPRINGS(1936); BEHIND THE MIKE(1937); JOIN THE MARINES(1937); MAID OF SALEM(1937); VARSITY SHOW(1937); WHEN LOVE IS YOUNG(1937); WOMAN I LOVE, THE(1937); DR. RHYTHM(1938); OF HUMAN HEARTS(1938); PROFESSOR BEWARE(1938); SPRING MADNESS(1938); NICK CARTER, MASTER DETECTIVE(1939); ST. LOUIS BLUES(1939); BLUE BIRD, THE(1940); HIT PARADE OF 1941(1940); LITTLE MEN(1940); REMEMBER THE NIGHT(1940); STREET OF MEMORIES(1940); CHEERS FOR MISS BISHOP(1941); DON'T GET PERSONAL(1941); DUMBO(1941); LOOK WHO'S LAUGHING(1941); MEET JOHN DOE(1941); NEW WINE(1941); TOP SERGEANT MULLIGAN(1941); BAMBI(1942); ICELAND(1942); LADY IS WILLING, THE(1942); STAR SPANGLED RHYTHM(1942); THREE CABALLEROS, THE(1944); WALK IN THE SUN, A(1945); WILDFIRE(1945); DEATH VALLEY(1946); MAKE MINE MUSIC(1946); SIOUX CITY SUE(1946); ROBIN OF TEXAS(1947); SADDLE PALS(1947); TRAIL TO SAN AN-TONE(1947); TWILIGHT ON THE RIO GRANDE(1947); BEAUTIFUL BLONDE FROM BASHFUL BEND, THE(1949); ALICE IN WONDERLAND(1951); KENTUCKY RI-FLE(1956); SHAKE, RATTLE, AND ROCK!(1957); ADVENTURES OF HUCKLEBER-RY FINN, THE(1960); ALAKAZAM THE GREAT!(1961, Jap.); IT'S A MAD, MAD, MAD, MAD WORLD(1963); MY SIX LOVES(1963); JUNGLE BOOK, THE(1967); LIVE A LITTLE, LOVE A LITTLE(1968); ARISTOCATS, THE(1970); WON TON TON, THE DOG WHO SAVED HOLLYWOOD(1976); THUNDER AND LIGHTNING(1977)
Misc. Talkies
BACK PAGE(1934); TOMORROW'S CHILDREN(1934); SUPER SEAL(1976)
Silents
CASEY AT THE BAT(1927)
Susan Holloway
SILENCERS, THE(; WHEN THE BOYS MEET THE GIRLS(1965); POINT BLANK(1967); ANGELS FROM HELL(1968)
W.E. Holloway
RIVER HOUSE MYSTERY, THE(1935, Brit.); JURY'S EVIDENCE(1936, Brit.); ELEPHANT BOY(1937, Brit.); MEMBER OF THE JURY(1937, Brit.); JOHN HALIFAX-GENTLEMAN(1938, Brit.); YOUNG MR. PITT, THE(1942, Brit.); SARABAND(1949, Brit.); SHADOW OF THE PAST(1950, Brit.); STRANGER AT MY DOOR(1950, Brit.); HONEYMOON DEFERRED(1951, Brit.); CRASH OF SILENCE(1952, Brit.)
William Holloway
MILL ON THE FLOSS(1939, Brit.)
Ellen Holly
TAKE A GIANT STEP(1959); COPS AND ROBBERS(1973)
Helen Holly
Silents
WHITE OAK(1921); NANCY FROM NOWHERE(1922)
Martin Holly
SHOP ON MAIN STREET, THE(1966, Czech.)
Mary Holly
SNIPER, THE(1952)
Rick Holly
1984
THIEF OF HEARTS(1984)

Ruth Holly
FRIENDLY ENEMIES(1942)
Theo Holly
SHE MARRIED HER BOSS(1935)
Jack Hollyday
Misc. Silents
MASKED LOVER, THE(1928)
Judy Hollyday
FULL OF LIFE(1956)
Burnes Hollyman
LORD OF THE FLIES(1963, Brit.)
Tom Hollyman
LORD OF THE FLIES(1963, Brit.), ph
Edwin L. Hollywood
Silents
POLLY OF THE CIRCUS(1917), d; CHALLENGE ACCEPTED, THE(1918), d; NO TRESPASSING(1922), d; JAMESTOWN(1923), d
Misc. Silents
ONE HOUR(1917), d; BIRTH OF A SOUL, THE(1920), d; FLAMING CLUE, THE(1920), d; GAUNTLET, THE(1920), d; SEA RIDER, THE(1920), d; FRENCH HEELS(1922), d; COLUMBUS(1923), d
Jimmie Hollywood
EVERY NIGHT AT EIGHT(1935)
Jimmy Hollywood
HATS OFF(1937); SQUADRON OF HONOR(1938); SPOTLIGHT SCANDALS(1943)
Paul Hollywood
RADIO ON(1980, Brit./Ger.)
Peter Hollywood
SILVER DREAM RACER(1982, Brit.), ed
1984
RIDDLE OF THE SANDS, THE(1984, Brit.), ed; WHERE IS PARSIFAL?(1984, Brit.), ed
The Hollywood American Legion Post
SONS OF THE DESERT(1933)
The Hollywood Blondes
IT AIN'T HAY(1943)
The Hollywood Bowl Symphony Orchestra
Silents
JAZZ MAD(1928)
The Hollywood Canteen Kids
SONG OF THE OPEN ROAD(1944)
Hollywood Chamber Jazz Group
STAKEOUT ON DOPE STREET(1958)
The Hollywood Lovelies
MERRY MONAHANS, THE(1944)
The Hollywood Press Corps
COLLEGE CONFIDENTIAL(1960)
The Hollywood Rock and Rollers
UNTAMED YOUTH(1957)
Arwen Holm
FINAL CONFLICT, THE(1981); EXPERIENCE PREFERRED... BUT NOT ESSENTIAL(1983, Brit.)
Astrid Holm
Misc. Silents
PHANTOM CARRIAGE, THE(1921, Swed.); MASTER OF THE HOUSE(1925, Den.)
Barnaby Holm
FINAL CONFLICT, THE(1981)
Bert Holm
JOHNNY ANGEL(1945)
Celeste Holm
THREE LITTLE GIRLS IN BLUE(1946); CARNIVAL IN COSTA RICA(1947); GENTLEMAN'S AGREEMENT(1947); CHICKEN EVERY SUNDAY(1948); LETTER TO THREE WIVES, A(1948); ROAD HOUSE(1948); SNAKE PIT, THE(1948); COME TO THE STABLE(1949); EVERYBODY DOES IT(1949); ALL ABOUT EVE(1950); CHAMPAGNE FOR CAESAR(1950); TENDER TRAP, THE(1955); HIGH SOCIETY(1956); BACHELOR FLAT(1962); DOCTOR, YOU'VE GOT TO BE KIDDING(1967); TOM SAWYER(1973); BITTERSWEET LOVE(1976); PRIVATE FILES OF J. EDGAR HOOVER, THE(1978)
Claus Holm
MARRIAGE IN THE SHADOWS(1948, Ger.); MERRY WIVES OF WINDSOR, THE(1952, Ger.); DEVIL STRIKES AT NIGHT, THE(1959, Ger.); ETERNAL LOVE(1960, Ger.); JOURNEY TO THE LOST CITY(1960, Ger./Fr./Ital.); BIMBO THE GREAT(1961, Ger.); GIRL OF THE MOORS, THE(1961, Ger.); IS PARIS BURNING?(1966, U.S./Fr.); MARRIAGE OF MARIA BRAUN, THE(1979, Ger.)
Darry Holm
JOHNNY STEALS EUROPE(1932, Ger.)
Eleanor Holm
TARZAN'S REVENGE(1938)
Ellen Holm
DOLL'S HOUSE, A(1973, Brit.)
Elsie Holm
MONTENEGRO(1981, Brit./Swed.)
Eske Holm
PEOPLE MEET AND SWEET MUSIC FILLS THE HEART(1969, Den./Swed.), a, ch
Hanya Holm
VAGABOND KING, THE(1956), ch
Ian Holm
BOFORS GUN, THE(1968, Brit.); FIXER, THE(1968); MIDSUMMER NIGHT'S DREAM, A(1969, Brit.); OH! WHAT A LOVELY WAR(1969, Brit.); NICHOLAS AND ALEXANDRA(1971, Brit.); MARY, QUEEN OF SCOTS(1971, Brit.); SEVERED HEAD, A(1971, Brit.); YOUNG WINSTON(1972, Brit.); HOMECOMING, THE(1973); JUGGERNAUT(1974, Brit.); ROBIN AND MARIAN(1976, Brit.); SHOUT AT THE DEVIL(1976, Brit.); MARCH OR DIE(1977, Brit.); ALIEN(1979); CHARIOTS OF FIRE(1981, Brit.); TIME BANDITS(1981, Brit.); RETURN OF THE SOLDIER, THE(1983, Brit.)
1984
GREYSTOKE: THE LEGEND OF TARZAN, LORD OF THE APES(1984); LAUGHTER HOUSE(1984, Brit.)

Jan Holm
BOY MEETS GIRL(1938); BROADWAY MUSKETEERS(1938); GIRLS ON PROBATION(1938); MY BILL(1938); RACKET BUSTERS(1938)
John Cecil Holm
THREE MEN ON A HORSE(1936), w; BLONDE INSPIRATION(1941), w; IT HAPPENED TO JANE(1959)
Jorg Holm
KAMIKAZE '89(1983, Ger.)
Kai Holm
COUNTERFEIT TRAITOR, THE(1962); CRAZY PARADISE(1965, Den.)
Kwabena Holm
1984
WHITE ELEPHANT(1984, Brit.)
Magda Holm
Misc. Silents
SYV DAGER FOR ELISABETH(1927, Swed.)
Michael Holm
MARK OF THE DEVIL(1970, Ger./Brit.), m
Renate Holm
SCHLAGER-PARADE(1953)
Richard Holm
FIDELIO(1961, Aust.)
Sonia Holm
LOVES OF JOANNA GODDEN, THE(1947, Brit.); WHEN THE BOUGH BREAKS(1947, Brit.); BROKEN JOURNEY(1948, Brit.); CALENDAR, THE(1948, Brit.); BAD LORD BYRON, THE(1949, Brit.); MIRANDA(1949, Brit.); STOP PRESS GIRL(1949, Brit.); WARNING TO WANTONS, A(1949, Brit.); 13 EAST STREET(1952, Brit.); CROWDED DAY, THE(1954, Brit.); RADIO CAB MURDER(1954, Brit.)
Valso Holm
CRAZY PARADISE(1965, Den.); GERTRUD(1966, Den.); ERIC SOYA'S "17"(1967, Den.); OPERATION LOVEBIRDS(1968, Den.); TONIO KROGER(1968, Fr./Ger.)
Bill Holman
GET OUTTA TOWN(1960), m
Bryce Holman
SMALL HOURS, THE(1962)
Edna Holman
Misc. Silents
FACE TO FACE(1920)
Harry Holman
WITHOUT RESERVATIONS(1946); HER MAJESTY LOVE(1931); SPORTING BLOOD(1931); CENTRAL PARK(1932); CONQUERORS, THE(1932); DARK HORSE, THE(1932); DOCTOR X(1932); FORBIDDEN(1932); SILVER DOLLAR(1932); SO BIG(1932); WEEK-END MARRIAGE(1932); BACHELOR MOTHER(1933); CIRCUS QUEEN MURDER, THE(1933); DEVIL'S MATE(1933); EAST OF FIFTH AVE.(1933); HARD TO HANDLE(1933); LADY KILLER(1933); LUCKY DOG(1933); MY WOMAN(1933); OLIVER TWIST(1933); ONE YEAR LATER(1933); PHANTOM THUNDERBOLT, THE(1933); ROMAN SCANDALS(1933); SOLITAIRE MAN, THE(1933); STATE FAIR(1933); WOMAN ACCUSED(1933); DAMES(1934); FUGITIVE LADY(1934); FUGITIVE ROAD(1934); I'LL FIX IT(1934); IT HAPPENED ONE NIGHT(1934); JEALOUSY(1934); JIMMY THE GENT(1934); LOST JUNGLE(1934); MEANEST GAL IN TOWN, THE(1934); MEN OF THE NIGHT(1934); OUR DAILY BREAD(1934); BARBARY COAST(1935); DANTE'S INFERNO(1935); EVERY NIGHT AT EIGHT(1935); FOLIES DERGERE(1935); HERE COMES COOKIE(1935); IN CALIENTE(1935); LIVING ON VELVET(1935); NIGHT ALARM(1935); TRAVELING SALESLADY, THE(1935); WELCOME HOME(1935); CHEERS OF THE CROWD(1936); GENTLE JULIA(1936); GORGEOUS HUSSY, THE(1936); HITCH HIKE TO HEAVEN(1936); LONE WOLF RETURNS, THE(1936); MURDER AT GLEN ATHOL(1936); NATION AFLAME(1937); WHEN YOU'RE IN LOVE(1937); I DEMAND PAYMENT(1938); JOSETTE(1938); PROFESSOR BEWARE(1938); WESTERN JAMBOREE(1938); HOTEL IMPERIAL(1939); LET US LIVE(1939); SLIGHTLY TEMPTED(1940); BRIDE CAME C.O.D., THE(1941); MANPOWER(1941); MEET JOHN DOE(1941); PUBLIC ENEMIES(1941); I KILLED THAT MAN(1942); INSIDE THE LAW(1942); MEXICAN SPITFIRE AT SEA(1942); SEVEN DAYS LEAVE(1942); SHADOWS ON THE SAGE(1942); SILVER BULLET, THE(1942); TOO MANY WOMEN(1942); HERS TO HOLD(1943); HIGHER AND HIGHER(1943); KEEP 'EM SLUGGING(1943); SWING HOSTESS(1944); WHAT A MAN!(1944); WHERE DO WE GO FROM HERE?(1945); BADMAN'S TERRITORY(1946); IT'S A WONDERFUL LIFE(1946); MAGIC TOWN(1947)
Misc. Talkies
CALLING ALL CARS(1935)
Henry Holman
TWO'S COMPANY(1939, Brit.)
Joel Holman
NIGHTMARES(1983)
Rex Holman
THIRTEEN FIGHTING MEN(1960); YOUNG JESSE JAMES(1960); CHOPPERS, THE(1961); 20,000 EYES(1961); PANIC IN YEAR ZERO!(1962); QUICK GUN, THE(1964); YOUR CHEATIN' HEART(1964); OUTLAWS IS COMING, THE(1965); SANDPIPER, THE(1965); WRECKING CREW, THE(1968); NAPOLEON AND SAMANTHA(1972); WHEN THE LEGENDS DIE(1972); ESCAPE TO WITCH MOUNTAIN(1975); HINDENBURG, THE(1975); APPLE DUMPLING GANG RIDES AGAIN, THE(1979)
Vincent Holman
THESE CHARMING PEOPLE(1931, Brit.); JEWEL, THE(1933, Brit.); DEATH AT A BROADCAST(1934, Brit.); FEATHERED SERPENT, THE(1934, Brit.); RIGHT AGE TO MARRY, THE(1935, Brit.); SEXTON BLAKE AND THE MADEMOISELLE(1935, Brit.); SHADOW OF MIKE EMERALD, THE(1935, Brit.); SILENT PASSENGER, THE(1935, Brit.); GAOL BREAK(1936, Brit.); PRISON BREAKER(1936, Brit.); TO CATCH A THIEF(1936, Brit.); TOUCH OF THE MOON, A(1936, Brit.); KATE PLUS TEN(1938, Brit.); SHOW GOES ON, THE(1938, Brit.); SPECIAL EDITION(1938, Brit.); TORSO MURDER MYSTERY, THE(1940, Brit.); FRONT LINE KIDS(1942, Brit.); KING ARTHUR WAS A GENTLEMAN(1942, Brit.); HE SNOOPS TO CONQUER(1944, Brit.); TIME FLIES(1944, Brit.); COLONEL BLIMP(1945, Brit.); ECHO MURDERS, THE(1945, Brit.); HOME SWEET HOME(1945, Brit.); I DIDN'T DO IT(1945, Brit.); VACATION FROM MARRIAGE(1945, Brit.); JOHNNY FRENCHMAN(1946, Brit.); TROJAN BROTHERS, THE(1946); LADY SURRENDERS, A(1947, Brit.); CARDBOARD CAVALIER, THE(1949, Brit.); BREAKING THE SOUND BARRIER(1952); JOHN WESLEY(1954, Brit.); STORM OVER THE NILE(1955, Brit.); YOU PAY YOUR MONEY(1957, Brit.)

Willie Holman
RICHARD'S THINGS(1981, Brit.)
Willis "Bill" Holman
SWAMP WOMEN(1956), m
Winnie Holman
POOR COW(1968, Brit.)
Henric Holmberg
FLIGHT OF THE EAGLE(1983, Swed.)
Holly Beth Holmberg
TERMS OF ENDEARMENT(1983)
Kalle Holmberg
TIME OF ROSES(1970, Fin.)
Thea Holme
LORNA DOONE(1935, Brit.); TOMORROW WE LIVE(1936, Brit.)
Jorg Holmer
YOUNG GO WILD, THE(1962, Ger.)
Ben Holmes
EXPERT, THE(1932); MELODY CRUISE(1933), w; COCKEYED CAVALIERS(1934), w; LIGHTNING STRIKES TWICE(1935), d; TOP HAT(1935); FARMER IN THE DELL, THE(1936), d; PLOT THICKENS, THE(1936), d; THERE GOES MY GIRL(1937), d; TOO MANY WIVES(1937), d; WE'RE ON THE JURY(1937), d; I'M FROM THE CITY(1938), d, w; LITTLE ORPHAN ANNIE(1938), d; MAID'S NIGHT OUT(1938), d; SAINT IN NEW YORK, THE(1938), d; ONE CROWDED NIGHT(1940), w; SAINT'S DOUBLE TROUBLE, THE(1940), w; PETTICOAT LARCENY(1943), d
Bill Holmes
ILLICIT(1931), ed; MANHATTAN PARADE(1931), ed; LOVE IS A RACKET(1932), ed; BUSHWHACKERS, THE(1952); CURSE OF THE LIVING CORPSE, THE(1964), m; HORROR OF PARTY BEACH, THE(1964), md
Brown Holmes
MALTESE FALCON, THE(1931), w; I AM A FUGITIVE FROM A CHAIN GANG(1932), w; PLAY GIRL(1932), w; STRANGE LOVE OF MOLLY LOUVAIN, THE(1932), w; STREET OF WOMEN(1932), w; AVENGER, THE(1933), w; LADIES THEY TALK ABOUT(1933), w; STRANGER'S RETURN(1933), w; 20,000 YEARS IN SING SING(1933), w; DARK HAZARD(1934), w; HEAT LIGHTNING(1934), w; I SELL ANYTHING(1934), w; CASE OF THE CURIOUS BRIDE, THE(1935), w; CASE OF THE LUCKY LEGS, THE(1935), w; FLORENTINE DAGGER, THE(1935), w; WE'RE IN THE MONEY(1935), w; FLYING HOSTESS(1936), w; SATAN MET A LADY(1936), w; SNOWED UNDER(1936), w; LADY FIGHTS BACK(1937), w; LIFE BEGINS WITH LOVE(1937), w; OH DOCTOR(1937), w; TOP OF THE TOWN(1937), w; CRIME OF DR. HALLET(1938), w; THREE BLIND MICE(1938), w; HOLLYWOOD CAVALCADE(1939), w; CASTLE ON THE HUDSON(1940), w; MOON OVER MIAMI(1941), w; THREE LITTLE GIRLS IN BLUE(1946), w; LEATHER GLOVES(1948), w; SHED NO TEARS(1948), w; MY TRUE STORY(1951), w
Cecil Holmes
THREE IN ONE(1956, Aus.), d; KILLING OF ANGEL STREET, THE(1983, Aus.), w
Chris Holmes
DIRTY MARY, CRAZY LARRY(1974), ed
Christopher Holmes
DUNWICH HORROR, THE(1970), ed; FIVE EASY PIECES(1970), ed; PADDY(1970, Irish), ed; DRIVE, HE SAID(1971), ed; ALL-AMERICAN BOY, THE(1973), ed; SLAUGHTER'S BIG RIP-OFF(1973), ed; COOLEY HIGH(1975), ed; CARWASH(1976), ed; GREASED LIGHTNING(1977), ed; SGT. PEPPER'S LONELY HEARTS CLUB BAND(1978), ed; SCAVENGER HUNT(1979), ed; NIGHTHAWKS(1981), ed
1984
COVERGIRL(1984, Can.), ed
Cpl. Darby Holmes
Silents
WANTED FOR MURDER(1919)
David Holmes
LITTLE ONES, THE(1965, Brit.), ph; WHERE THE BULLETS FLY(1966, Brit.), ph; LAST SHOT YOU HEAR, THE(1969, Brit.), ph; SUDDEN TERROR(1970, Brit.), ph
Denis Holmes
ATTEMPT TO KILL(1961, Brit.); FLIGHT FROM SINGAPORE(1962, Brit.); CRIMSON BLADE, THE(1964, Brit.); SECOND BEST SECRET AGENT IN THE WHOLE WIDE WORLD, THE(1965, Brit.); PARTNER, THE(1966, Brit.); MOONLIGHTING(1982, Brit.)
Dennis Holmes
PAUL TEMPLE RETURNS(1952, Brit.); HOUND-DOG MAN(1959); WOMAN OBSESSED(1959); KEY WITNESS(1960); FIERCEST HEART, THE(1961); MIRACLE OF SANTA'S WHITE REINDEER, THE(1963); RETURN OF MR. MOTO, THE(1965, Brit.)
Douglas Holmes
STRANGERS WHEN WE MEET(1960)
Earl Holmes
THIRTEEN FIGHTING MEN(1960); SWINGIN' ALONG(1962)
Ed Holmes
WOLF DOG(1958, Can.); LAST GUNFIGHTER, THE(1961, Can.); GROUP, THE(1966)
Edna Holmes
Silents
IT'S A BEAR(1919)
Edna Phillips Holmes
Silents
PAIR OF SIXES, A(1918)
Misc. Silents
REGULAR FELLOW, A(1919)
Edward Holmes
I'D RATHER BE RICH(1964)
Elizabeth Holmes
PAT AND MIKE(1952); WHITE CHRISTMAS(1954)
Elsie Holmes
RHUBARB(1951); MARRYING KIND, THE(1952); FRANCIS JOINS THE WACS(1954)
Fenwicke L. Holmes
Silents
OFFENDERS, THE(1924), d
Franklin Holmes
RAW WEEKEND(1964), ph
Fred Holmes
IF I HAD A MILLION(1932); OUR RELATIONS(1936); COURAGEOUS DR. CHRISTIAN, THE(1940)

Silents
LIGHTNING LARIATS(1927)
Misc. Silents
GAMBLING FOOL, THE(1925)
Garret Holmes
TROCADERO(1944), w
Geoffrey Holmes
HOT CARGO(1946), w; ROADBLOCK(1951), w
George Holmes
FOOTLIGHT SERENADE(1942); IT HAPPENED IN FLATBUSH(1942); LIFE BEGINS AT 8:30(1942); MAN IN THE TRUNK, THE(1942); TEN GENTLEMEN FROM WEST POINT(1942); THRU DIFFERENT EYES(1942); CRASH DIVE(1943); GUADALCANAL DIARY(1943); ROGER TOUHY, GANGSTER!(1944); FALCON IN SAN FRANCISCO, THE(1945); THOSE ENDEARING YOUNG CHARMS(1945); DARK ALIBI(1946); FALCON'S ALIBI, THE(1946); LITTLE GIANT(1946); SONG OF SCHEHERAZADE(1947)
Gerda Holmes
Silents
ALL MAN(1916); FRIDAY THE 13TH(1916); GILDED CAGE, THE(1916); IRON RING, THE(1917); MAN WHO FORGOT, THE(1917)
Misc. Silents
MOTHS(1913); ROBIN HOOD(1913); VICTORY OF VIRTUE, THE(1915); CHAIN INVISIBLE, THE(1916); HER GREAT HOUR(1916); HUSBAND AND WIFE(1916); SUDDEN RICHES(1916); AS MAN MADE HER(1917); BRAND OF SATAN, THE(1917); HUNGRY HEART, A(1917); WANTED - A MOTHER(1918)
Gerry Holmes
PAPER CHASE, THE(1973), set d; "EQUUS"(1977), set d; LOST AND FOUND(1979), set d
Gilbert Holmes
MAN FROM HELL'S EDGES(1932); ROBBERS' ROOST(1933)
Misc. Silents
BIG TOWN ROUND-UP(1921); BUSTER, THE(1923); BORDER SHERIFF, THE(1926)
Gilbert "Pee Wee" Holmes
SPURS(1930); RUSTLERS' ROUNDUP(1933)
Silents
ONE GLORIOUS SCRAP(1927)
Harold Holmes
CONTINENTAL DIVIDE(1981)
Helen Holmes
DUDE COWBOY(1941); MORE THE MERRIER, THE(1943)
Silents
JUDITH OF THE CUMBERLANDS(1916); HILLS OF MISSING MEN(1922); ONE MILLION IN JEWELS(1923); STORMY SEAS(1923); BARRIERS OF THE LAW(1925); OUTWITTED(1925)
Misc. Silents
DIAMOND RUNNERS, THE(1916); MANAGER OF THE B&A, THE(1916); MEDICINE BEND(1916); WHISPERING SMITH(1916); CROOK'S ROMANCE, A(1921); GHOST CITY(1921); LONE HAND, THE(1922); FIGHTING FURY(1924); 40-HORSE HAWKINS(1924); BLOOD AND STEEL(1925); DUPED(1925); SIGN OF THE CACTUS, THE(1925); TRAIN WRECKERS, THE(1925); WEBS OF STEEL(1925); CROSSED SIGNALS(1926); LOST EXPRESS, THE(1926); MISTAKEN ORDERS(1926); OPEN SWITCH, THE(1926); PERIL OF THE RAIL(1926)
Hollye Holmes
ADVENTURES OF THE WILDERNESS FAMILY, THE(1975)
Ione Holmes
JAZZ AGE, THE(1929)
Silents
CONVOY(1927)
J. Merrill Holmes
THIRTY-DAY PRINCESS(1934); SHE COULDN'T TAKE IT(1935); BANDIT TRAIL, THE(1941); LAND OF THE OPEN RANGE(1941); PRAIRIE PALS(1942); RIDERS OF THE WEST(1942); ROLLING DOWN THE GREAT DIVIDE(1942)
J. Ward Holmes
LAND OF FURY(1955 Brit.)
Jack Holmes
SADDLE MOUNTAIN ROUNDUP(1941); TUMBLEDOWN RANCH IN ARIZONA(1941); WRANGLER'S ROOST(1941); LONE RIDER IN CHEYENNE, THE(1942); WOLVES OF THE RANGE(1943)
1984
FEAR CITY(1984), ed
Jack H. Holmes
THUNDER RIVER FEUD(1942)
Jack M. Holmes
LAST ROUND-UP, THE(1934)
Jack N. Holmes
SPOILERS, THE(1930)
Jack W. Holmes
BLUE ANGEL, THE(1959), ed; JOURNEY TO THE CENTER OF THE EARTH(1959), ed; WARLOCK(1959), ed; MARRIAGE-GO-ROUND, THE(1960), ed; STORY OF RUTH, THE(1960), ed; SNOW WHITE AND THE THREE STOOGES(1961), ed
Jennifer Holmes
DEMON, THE(1981, S. Africa); RAW FORCE(1982)
Jerry Holmes
HOW THE WEST WAS WON(1962)
Jessie Holmes
MY BROTHER'S WEDDING(1983)
John Holmes
DANGER ON WHEELS(1940); SHADOW OF THE CAT, THE(1961, Brit.), animal t; KILL OR CURE(1962, Brit.), animal t; PIED PIPER, THE(1972, Brit.), animal
John Holmes
FANTASM(1976, Aus.); RUNNERS(1983, Brit.)
Misc. Talkies
FRIEND OR FOE(1982, Brit.)
John Holmes
CHUBASCO(1968), ed
Misc. Talkies
AMAZING LOVE SECRET(1975)

John W. Holmes
GOODBYE CHARLIE(1964), ed; ONLY GAME IN TOWN, THE(1970), ed; AN-DROMEDA STRAIN, THE(1971), ed; SHOWDOWN(1973), ed; JUST YOU AND ME, KID(1979), ed

Joi Holmes
PAJAMA PARTY(1964)

Karil Holmes
PLEASURE PLANTATION(1970)

Katherine Holmes
Silents
OFFENDERS, THE(1924), w

Kelda Holmes
UNSUITABLE JOB FOR A WOMAN, AN(1982, Brit.)

Lee Holmes
Misc. Silents
HARD FISTS(1927)

Leon Holmes
I LOVE THAT MAN(1933); UNDER SECRET ORDERS(1933); GUILTY PA-RENTS(1934)
Silents
MAN OF NERVE, A(1925); APRIL FOOL(1926); KING OF KINGS, THE(1927)
Misc. Silents
FRISCO SALLY LEVY(1927)

Leroy Holmes
SMILE(1975), m

Leslie Holmes
WHEN YOU COME HOME(1947, Brit.)

Lois Holmes
EDGE OF FURY(1958)

Luree Holmes
MUSCLE BEACH PARTY(1964); PAJAMA PARTY(1964); DR. GOLDFOOT AND THE BIKINI MACHINE(1965); HOW TO STUFF A WILD BIKINI(1965); SERGEANT DEADHEAD(1965); SKI PARTY(1965); GHOST IN THE INVISIBLE BIKINI(1966)

Lynne Holmes
TOGETHER BROTHERS(1974)

Mabel Holmes
Misc. Silents
GIANT OF HIS RACE, A(1921)

Madeleine Holmes
FLIGHT TO TANGIER(1953); LONG ROPE, THE(1961)

Madeleine Taylor Holmes
MACKENNA'S GOLD(1969); GREAT NORTHFIELD, MINNESOTA RAID, THE(1972)

Margaret Holmes
END OF THE AFFAIR, THE(1955, Brit.)

Marian Holmes
MIRACLE IN THE RAIN(1956)

Mark Holmes
TIME BANDITS(1981, Brit.); MONTY PYTHON'S THE MEANING OF LIFE(1983, Brit.)

Mary J. Holmes
LENA RIVERS(1932), w

Maynard Holmes
DANCING LADY(1933); MADAME DU BARRY(1934); STOLEN SWEETS(1934); SHE COULDN'T TAKE IT(1935); AUGUST WEEK-END(1936, Brit.); GO WEST, YOUNG MAN(1936); LEATHERNECKS HAVE LANDED, THE(1936); SATAN MET A LA-DY(1936); HERE'S FLASH CASEY(1937); WINGS OVER HONOLULU(1937); MON-STER AND THE GIRL, THE(1941); NEW WINE(1941); NEW YORK TOWN(1941); TOP SERGEANT MULLIGAN(1941); MAGNIFICENT AMBERSONS, THE(1942); MAN FROM HEADQUARTERS(1942); REMEMBER PEARL HARBOR(1942); STAR SPAN-GLED RHYTHM(1942); TALK OF THE TOWN(1942); SOMEWHERE IN THE NIGHT(1946); DEAD RECKONING(1947); GOLDEN EARRINGS(1947); CAS-BAH(1948); LADY FROM SHANGHAI, THE(1948); TROUBLE MAKERS(1948); LEAVE IT TO HENRY(1949); MY DREAM IS YOURS(1949); TRAIL OF THE YUKON(1949); HERE COME THE NELSONS(1952)

Michael Holmes
SLAYER, THE(1982); SUMMERSPELL(1983)

Milton Holmes
GODLESS GIRL, THE(1929); MR. LUCKY(1943), w; SALTY O'ROURKE(1945), w; JOHNNY O'CLOCK(1947), w; MR. SOFT TOUCH(1949), p, w; BOOTS MALONE(1952), p&w; NAKED EARTH, THE(1958, Brit.), w; MATTER OF WHO, A(1962, Brit.), p, w
Misc. Talkies
SPY, THE(1931)
Misc. Silents
SHIP COMES IN, A(1928)

Neil Holmes
SEPARATION(1968, Brit.)

Pam Holmes
RUBBER GUN, THE(1977, Can.)

Patrick Holmes
STRANGE FASCINATION(1952)

Pee Wee Holmes
MOUNTAIN JUSTICE(1930); SAGEBRUSH POLITICS(1930); DESERT VEN-GEANCE(1931); MAN FROM HELL'S EDGES(1932); FLAMING GUNS(1933)
Misc. Talkies
LIGHTNIN' SMITH RETURNS(1931)
Silents
LADIES TO BOARD(1924); ARIZONA CYCLONE(1928); SKY SKIDDER, THE(1929); SUNSET PASS(1929)
Misc. Silents
FEARLESS RIDER, THE(1928); PUT 'EM UP(1928); TRAIL RIDERS(1928)

Philips Holmes
CONFESSIONS OF A CO-ED(1931)

Phillips Holmes
WILD PARTY, THE(1929); DANCERS, THE(1930); DEVIL'S HOLIDAY, THE(1930); GRUMPY(1930); HER MAN(1930); ONLY THE BRAVE(1930); POINTED HEELS(1930); AMERICAN TRAGEDY, AN(1931); MAN TO MAN(1931); STOLEN HEAVEN(1931); BROKEN LULLABY(1932); MAKE ME A STAR(1932); NIGHT COURT(1932); TWO KINDS OF WOMEN(1932); 70,000 WITNESSES(1932); BEAUTY FOR SALE(1933); BIG BRAIN, THE(1933); DINNER AT EIGHT(1933); LOOKING FORWARD(1933); MEN MUST FIGHT(1933); PENTHOUSE(1933); SECRET OF MADAME BLANCHE, THE(1933); STAGE MOTHER(1933); STORM AT DAYBREAK(1933); CARAVAN(1934); GREAT EXPECTATIONS(1934); MILLION DOLLAR RANSOM(1934); NANA(1934); PRIVATE SCANDAL(1934); DIVINE SPARK, THE(1935, Brit./Ital.); NO RAN-SOM(1935); TEN MINUTE ALIBI(1935, Brit.); CHATTERBOX(1936); HOUSE OF A THOUSAND CANDLES, THE(1936); RETURN OF SHERLOCK HOLMES(1936); DOMINANT SEX, THE(1937, Brit.); GENERAL SPANKY(1937); HOUSEMAS-TER(1938, Brit.)

Phillips R. Holmes
VARSITY(1928)
Silents
STAIRS OF SAND(1929)

Phillis Holmes
CRIMINAL CODE(1931)

Rapley Holmes
Misc. Silents
VICTORY OF VIRTUE, THE(1915); NOTHING BUT LIES(1920)

Rich Holmes
Misc. Talkies
TOUGH(1974)

Richard Holmes
RITZ, THE(1976)

Robert Holmes
MY FRIEND THE KING(1931, Brit.); ROSARY, THE(1931, Brit.); HYDE PARK CORNER(1935, Brit.); GAY ADVENTURE, THE(1936, Brit.); INVASION(1965, Brit.), w; STATE OF SIEGE(1973, Fr./U.S./Ital./Ger.)

Rubberneck Holmes
DUKE IS THE TOPS, THE(1938)

Rupert Holmes
DEATH PLAY(1976), m
1984
NO SMALL AFFAIR(1984), a, m

Salty Holmes
BANJO ON MY KNEE(1936)

Samuel Holmes
MY FAIR LADY(1964)

Shirley Holmes
FLAMING TEEN-AGE, THE(1956)

Start Holmes
CARRIE(1952)

Stuart Holmes
CAVALIER, THE(1928); CAPTAIN OF THE GUARD(1930); MY PAL, THE KING(1932); SITTING PRETTY(1933); ARE WE CIVILIZED?(1934); BELLE OF THE NINETIES(1934); CASE OF THE VELVET CLAWS, THE(1936); EARTHWORM TRAC-TORS(1936); MURDER BY AN ARISTOCRAT(1936); POLO JOE(1936); PUBLIC ENE-MY'S WIFE(1936); SATAN MET A LADY(1936); SNOWED UNDER(1936); TRAILIN' WEST(1936); HER HUSBAND'S SECRETARY(1937); ACCIDENTS WILL HAP-PEN(1938); COWBOY FROM BROOKLYN(1938); MYSTERY HOUSE(1938); SISTERS, THE(1938); CODE OF THE SECRET SERVICE(1939); DARK VICTORY(1939); EACH DAWN I DIE(1939); ESPIONAGE AGENT(1939); KING OF THE UNDER-WORLD(1939); NAUGHTY BUT NICE(1939); OKLAHOMA KID, THE(1939); ON TRIAL(1939); ROARING TWENTIES, THE(1939); THEY MADE ME A CRIMI-NAL(1939); BRITISH INTELLIGENCE(1940); DEVIL'S ISLAND(1940); DR. EHR-LICH'S MAGIC BULLET(1940); MONEY AND THE WOMAN(1940); BODY DISAPPEARS, THE(1941); MEET JOHN DOE(1941); MILLION DOLLAR BABY(1941); GHOST AND MRS. MUIR, THE(1942); SECRET ENEMIES(1942); LAST RIDE, THE(1944); LODGER, THE(1944); HER LUCKY NIGHT(1945); SHADY LADY(1945); THRILL OF A ROMANCE(1945); MIGHTY MCGURK, THE(1946); SMOOTH AS SILK(1946); MOSS ROSE(1947); JOAN OF ARC(1948); LETTER TO THREE WIVES, A(1948); NIGHT HAS A THOUSAND EYES(1948); STREET CORNER(1948); UP IN CENTRAL PARK(1948); ALIAS NICK BEAL(1949); KISS IN THE DARK, A(1949); MADAME BOVARY(1949); SUN COMES UP, THE(1949); COPPER CANYON(1950); FATHER OF THE BRIDE(1950); WHERE DANGER LIVES(1950); HIS KIND OF WOMAN(1951); LAW AND THE LADY, THE(1951); PEOPLE WILL TALK(1951); RHUBARB(1951); SWORD OF MONTE CRISTO, THE(1951); SINGIN' IN THE RAIN(1952); REMAINS TO BE SEEN(1953); STAR IS BORN, A(1954); COBWEB, THE(1955); GIRL IN THE RED VELVET SWING, THE(1955); KETTLES IN THE OZARKS, THE(1956); WINGS OF EAGLES, THE(1957); HORSE SOLDIERS, THE(1959); MAN WHO SHOT LIBERTY VALANCE, THE(1962)
Silents
IN THE STRETCH(1914); THOU SHALT NOT(1914); CLEMENCEAU CASE, THE(1915); EAST LYNNE(1916); DUST OF DESIRE(1919); NEW MOON, THE(1919); OTHER MAN'S WIFE, THE(1919); ROMANCE OF THE AIR, A(1919); WAY OF A WOMAN(1919); LIFTING SHADOWS(1920); ALL'S FAIR IN LOVE(1921); FOUR HORSEMEN OF THE APOCALYPSE, THE(1921); NO WOMAN KNOWS(1921); PAID BACK(1922); PRISONER OF ZENDA, THE(1922); STRANGER'S BANQUET(1922); RIP-TIDE, THE(1923); SCARLET LILY, THE(1923); TEMPORARY MARRIAGE(1923); TIPPED OFF(1923); IN EVERY WOMAN'S LIFE(1924); ON TIME(1924); TESS OF THE D'URBERVILLES(1924); FIGHTING CUB, THE(1925); SALVATION HUNTERS, THE(1925); BROKEN HEARTS OF HOLLYWOOD(1926); GOOD AND NAUGHT-Y(1926); HURRICANE, THE(1926); MIDNIGHT MESSAGE, THE(1926); MAN WHO LAUGHS, THE(1927); YOUR WIFE AND MINE(1927); DEVIL DOGS(1928); HEROIC LOVER, THE(1929)
Misc. Silents
LIFE'S SHOP WINDOW(1914); THROUGH DANTE'S FLAMES(1914); WALLS OF JERICHO, THE(1914); BLINDNESS OF DEVOTION(1915); DR. RAMEAU(1915); GAL-LEY SLAVE, THE(1915); GIRL I LEFT BEHIND ME, THE(1915); SHOULD A MOTHER TELL?(1915); UNFAITHFUL WIFE, THE(1915); DAUGHTER OF THE GODS, A(1916); GREEN-EYED MONSTER, THE(1916); HER DOUBLE LIFE(1916); LOVE AND HA-TE(1916); SINS OF MEN(1916); TORTURED HEART, A(1916); UNDER TWO FLAGS(1916); WIFE'S SACRIFICE, A(1916); BROADWAY SPORT, THE(1917); DERE-LICT, THE(1917); LOVE'S LAW(1917); SCARLET LETTER, THE(1917); TANGLED LIVES(1917); TEST OF WOMANHOOD, THE(1917); WILD GIRL, THE(1917); GHOSTS OF YESTERDAY(1918); POOR RICH MAN, THE(1918); SINS OF THE CHIL-DREN(1918); TREASON(1918); DANGEROUS AFFAIR, A(1919); LOVE, HONOR AND ?(1919); BODY AND SOUL(1920); MAN'S PLAYTHING(1920); PASSION FRUIT(1921); HER HUSBAND'S TRADEMARK(1922); UNDER TWO FLAGS(1922); UNKNOWN PURPLE, THE(1923); BELOVED BRUTE, THE(1924); SIREN OF SEVILLE, THE(1924); VANITY'S PRICE(1924); FOOL AND HIS MONEY, A(1925); NORTH STAR(1925); PAINT AND POWDER(1925); PRIMROSE PATH, THE(1925); STELLE OF THE

ROYAL MOUNTED(1925); SHADOW OF THE LAW, THE(1926); DANGER TRAIL(1928)

Taylor Holmes
BEFORE MORNING(1933); CRIME OF DR. FORBES(1936); FIRST BABY(1936); MAKE WAY FOR A LADY(1936); BOOMERANG(1947); EGG AND I, THE(1947); KISS OF DEATH(1947); NIGHTMARE ALLEY(1947); TIME OUT OF MIND(1947); ACT OF MURDER, AN(1948); HAZARD(1948); JOAN OF ARC(1948); LET'S LIVE AGAIN(1948); PLUNDERERS, THE(1948); SMART WOMAN(1948); THAT WONDERFUL UR-GE(1948); ACT OF VIOLENCE(1949); JOE PALOOKA IN THE BIG FIGHT(1949); MR. BELVEDERE GOES TO COLLEGE(1949); ONCE MORE, MY DARLING(1949); WOM-AN IN HIDING(1949); BRIGHT LEAF(1950); CAGED(1950); COPPER CANYON(1950); DOUBLE DEAL(1950); FATHER OF THE BRIDE(1950); QUICKSAND(1950); DRUMS IN THE DEEP SOUTH(1951); FIRST LEGION, THE(1951); RHUBARB(1951); TWO TICKETS TO BROADWAY(1951); BEWARE, MY LOVELY(1952); HOLD THAT LI-NE(1952); HOODLUM EMPIRE(1952); RIDE THE MAN DOWN(1952); WOMAN OF THE NORTH COUNTRY(1952); GENTLEMEN PREFER BLONDES(1953); SHE'S BACK ON BROADWAY(1953); OUTCAST, THE(1954); TOBOR THE GREAT(1954); UNTAMED HEIRESS(1954); FIGHTING CHANCE, THE(1955); HELL'S OUT-POST(1955); MAVERICK QUEEN, THE(1956); PEACEMAKER, THE(1956); WINK OF AN EYE(1958); SLEEPING BEAUTY(1959)

Silents
EFFICIENCY EDGAR'S COURTSHIP(1917); PAIR OF SIXES, A(1918); IT'S A BEAR(1919); NOTHING BUT THE TRUTH(1920); BORROWED FINERY(1925); CRIM-SON RUNNER, THE(1925); ONE HOUR OF LOVE(1927)

Misc. Silents
FOOLS FOR LUCK(1917); SMALL TOWN GUY, THE(1917); TWO-BITS SEATS(1917); RUGGLES OF RED GAP(1918); UNEASY MONEY(1918); REGULAR FELLOW, A(1919); TAXI(1919); UPSIDE DOWN(1919); NOTHING BUT LIES(1920); VERY IDEA, THE(1920); $20 A WEEK(1924)

Thor Holmes
LAW AND ORDER(1953)

Tracey Holmes
MY FRIEND THE KING(1931, Brit.); JURY'S EVIDENCE(1936, Brit.)

Tracy Holmes
HIGH SOCIETY(1932, Brit.); LUCKY LADIES(1932, Brit.); GHOST TRAIN, THE(1933, Brit.); GOING STRAIGHT(1933, Brit.)

W.J. Holmes
TERROR TRAIL(1933)

Wendell Holmes
LOST BOUNDARIES(1949); GOOD DAY FOR A HANGING(1958); I WANT TO LIVE!(1958); YOUNG AND WILD(1958); BUT NOT FOR ME(1959); EDGE OF ETERNI-TY(1959); BECAUSE THEY'RE YOUNG(1960); ELMER GANTRY(1960); ABSENT-MINDED PROFESSOR, THE(1961)

William Holmes
AVIATOR, THE(1929), ed; HARDBOILED ROSE(1929), ed; MILLION DOLLAR COL-LAR, THE(1929), ed; HOLD EVERYTHING(1930), ed; LIFE OF THE PARTY, THE(1930), ed; THREE FACES EAST(1930), ed; ROAD TO SINGAPORE(1931), ed; SVENGALI(1931), ed; ALIAS THE DOCTOR(1932), ed; I AM A FUGITIVE FROM A CHAIN GANG(1932), ed; MAN WHO PLAYED GOD, THE(1932), ed; PURCHASE PRICE, THE(1932), ed; SO BIG(1932), ed; FEAR SHIP, THE(1933, Brit.); HARD TO HANDLE(1933), ed; PICTURE SNATCHER(1933), ed; WORLD CHANGES, THE(1933), ed; FLIRTATION WALK(1934), ed; MAN WITH TWO FACES, THE(1934), ed; VERY HONORABLE GUY, A(1934), ed; CEILNG ZERO(1935), ed; FRISCO KID(1935); LIVING ON VELVET(1935), ed; SHIPMATES FOREVER(1935), ed; STRANDED(1935), ed; CAIN AND MABEL(1936), ed; HEARTS DIVIDED(1936), ed; EVER SINCE EVE(1937), ed; GO-GETTER, THE(1937), ed; SAN QUENTIN(1937), ed; SUBMARINE D-1(1937), ed; BOY MEETS GIRL(1938), ed; BROTHER RAT(1938), ed; FOOLS FOR SCANDAL(1938), ed; DARK VICTORY(1939), ed; INDIANAPOLIS SPEEDWAY(1939), ed; WINGS OF THE NAVY(1939), ed; BROTHER ORCHID(1940), ed; THREE CHEERS FOR THE IRISH(1940), ed; CITY, FOR CONQUEST(1941), ed; STRAWBERRY BLONDE, THE(1941), ed; IN THIS OUR LIFE(1942), ed; THEY DIED WITH THEIR BOOTS ON(1942), ed; WOMAN OF THE YEAR(1942); WOMAN IN THE WINDOW, THE(1945); SEA OF GRASS, THE(1947); IN OLD AMARILLO(1951); UTAH WAGON TRAIN(1951); DAUGHTER OF THE SUN GOD(1962)

Silents
OBEY YOUR HUSBAND(1928), ed

William J. Holmes
ONCE A GENTLEMAN(1930); LIFE BEGINS FOR ANDY HARDY(1941); NOTHING BUT TROUBLE(1944)

William S. Holmes
PRESIDENT VANISHES, THE(1934)

Arthur Holmes-Gore
Silents
PRISONER OF ZENDA, THE(1915, Brit.)

Dorothy Holmes-Gore
MEN OF THE SEA(1951, Brit.)
Silents
MIRAGE, THE(1920, Brit.)

Holmes-Paul
COUNSEL'S OPINION(1933, Brit.), prod d

R. Holmes-Paul
DUAL ALIBI(1947, Brit.), art d; FINAL TEST, THE(1953, Brit.), art d

Erick Holmey
CONAN THE BARBARIAN(1982)

Anders Holmquist
LUMIERE(1976, Fr.)

Sigrid Holmquist
Silents
JUST AROUND THE CORNER(1921); GENTLEMAN OF LEISURE, A(1923); YOUTH FOR SALE(1924); EARLY BIRD, THE(1925)
Misc. Silents
MY OLD KENTUCKY HOME(1922); PROPHET'S PARADISE, THE(1922); LIGHT THAT FAILED, THE(1923); MEDDLING WOMEN(1924); TWO SHALL BE BORN(1924); CRACKERJACK, THE(1925)

Billy Holms
LAST MARRIED COUPLE IN AMERICA, THE(1980)

Lyvingston Holms
PROPHECY(1979)

Egil Holmsen
TIME OF DESIRE, THE(1957, Swed.), d&w

Karl-Arne Holmsten
SECRETS OF WOMEN(1961, Swed.)

Hap Holmwood
THEY SAVED HITLER'S BRAIN(1964)

Harold Holness
TARZAN AND THE LOST SAFARI(1957, Brit.), ch; HOT MILLIONS(1968, Brit.)

Arnold Holop
NIGHT OF EVIL(1962), m

Rosie Holotick
ENCOUNTER WITH THE UNKNOWN(1973)

Rosie Holotik
DON'T LOOK IN THE BASEMENT(1973); HORROR HIGH(1974)

Gustaw Holoubek
PARTINGS(1962, Pol.); YELLOW SLIPPERS, THE(1965, Pol.); SALTO(1966, Pol.); SARAGOSSA MANUSCRIPT, THE(1972, Pol.)

Carol Holoway
SIGN OF THE CROSS, THE(1932)

Norton Holper
MANTIS IN LACE(1968)

Frank Holquist
YANK IN VIET-NAM, A(1964), art d

Ronald Holroyd
DON'T PANIC CHAPS!(1959, Brit.), w

Max Holsboer
CHALLENGE, THE(1939, Brit.)

Heinz Holscher
FANNY HILL: MEMOIRS OF A WOMAN OF PLEASURE zero(1965), ph; ONLY A WOMAN(1966, Ger.), ph; RAMPAGE AT APACHE WELLS(1966, Ger./Yugo.), ph; UNCLE TOM'S CABIN(1969, Fr./Ital./Ger./Yugo.), ph

Walter Holscher
HEAT'S ON, THE(1943), ait d; LOUISIANA HAYRIDE(1944), art d; RACKET MAN, THE(1944), art d; STARS ON PARADE(1944), art d; STRANGE AFFAIR(1944), art d; FIGHTING GUARDSMAN, THE(1945), art d; ROUGH, TOUGH AND READY(1945), art d; SNAFU(1945), art d; JOLSON STORY, THE(1946), art d; MEET ME ON BROADWAY(1946), art d; RENEGADES(1946), art d; GUILT OF JANET AMES, THE(1947), art d; MATING OF MILLIE, THE(1948), art d; RELENTLESS(1948), art d; THUNDERHOOF(1948), art d; WOMAN FROM TANGIER, THE(1948), art d; JOLSON SINGS AGAIN(1949), art d; MISS GRANT TAKES RICHMOND(1949), art d; UNDER-COVER MAN, THE(1949), art d; GOOD HUMOR MAN, THE(1950), art d; HARRIET CRAIG(1950), art d; KILLER THAT STALKED NEW YORK, THE(1950), art d; PETTY GIRL, THE(1950), art d; INDIAN UPRISING(1951), art d; SANTA FE(1951), art d; SON OF DR. JEKYLL, THE(1951), art d; SUNNY SIDE OF THE STREET(1951), art d; TWO OF A KIND(1951), art d; AFFAIR IN TRINIDAD(1952), art d; SNIPER, THE(1952), art d; LET'S DO IT AGAIN(1953), art d; WILD ONE, THE(1953), art d; DRIVE A CROOKED ROAD(1954), art d; PUSHOVER(1954), art d; MY SISTER EILEEN(1955), art d; THREE FOR THE SHOW(1955), art d; EDDY DUCHIN STORY, THE(1956), art d; HE LAUGHED LAST(1956), art d; REPRISAL(1956), art d; ES-CAPADE IN JAPAN(1957), art d; PAL JOEY(1957), art d; ME AND THE COLO-NEL(1958), art d; SONG WITHOUT END(1960), art d; CRY FOR HAPPY(1961), art d; GIDGET GOES HAWAIIAN(1961), art d; THIRTEEN WEST STREET(1962), art d; CATTLE KING(1963), art d; WINTER A GO-GO(1965), art d

Glen Holse
MAN CALLED DAGGER, A(1967), art d

Ivy Holsen
WHITE SLAVE SHIP(1962, Fr./Ital.)

Ernest Holser
GOODBYE GEMINI(1970, Brit.), ed

Ted Holsopple
INDESTRUCTIBLE MAN, THE(1956), art d; CASE OF PATTY SMITH, THE(1962), art d

Theobold Holsopple
ROCKETSHIP X-M(1950), art d; STEEL HELMET, THE(1951), art d; PARK ROW(1952), art d; RING, THE(1952), art d; DAUGHTER OF DR. JEKYLL(1957), art d; DEERSLAYER, THE(1957), art d; KRONOS(1957), prod d, art d; SHE DEVIL(1957), art d; FLY, THE(1958), art d; WIZARD OF BAGHDAD, THE(1960), art d; THREE BLONDES IN HIS LIFE(1961), art d; HANDS OF A STRANGER(1962), art d; CALI-FORNIA(1963), art d; FOR PETE'S SAKE!(1966), art d; BAMBOO SAUCER, THE(1968), art d

Ernie Holst
FOLLIES GIRL(1943), md

Maria Holst
OPERETTA(1949, Ger.); TRAPP FAMILY, THE(1961, Ger.)

Svea Holst
RAILROAD WORKERS(1948, Swed.); SMILES OF A SUMMER NIGHT(1957, Swed.); PASSION OF ANNA, THE(1970, Swed.); FANNY AND ALEXANDER(1983, Swed./Fr./Ger.)

Nils Holstius
TILLY OF BLOOMSBURY(1940, Brit.), w

Rand Holston
FM(1978), p

Gary Holstrom
Misc. Talkies
DEAFULA(1975)

Abbe Holt
YOICKS!(1932, Brit.), w

Andrew Holt
STRANGE VOYAGE(1945), w; AVALANCHE(1946), w

Arva Holt
VOICES(1979)

Betsy Holt
THUNDER ROAD(1958)

Betty Holt
WITHOUT REGRET(1935)

Bob Holt
ABBY(1974); DAY OF THE LOCUST, THE(1975); MOUSE AND HIS CHILD, THE(1977); WIZARDS(1977)

Misc. Talkies
NINE LIVES OF FRITZ THE CAT, THE(1974)
Bobby Holt
Misc. Talkies
STRAIGHT JACKET(1980)
Calvin Holt
LOVING(1970)
Charlene Holt
DAYS OF WINE AND ROSES(1962); IF A MAN ANSWERS(1962); ISLAND OF LOVE(1963); MAN'S FAVORITE SPORT[?](1964); RED LINE 7000(1965); EL DORADO(1967); ZIGZAG(1970); MELVIN AND HOWARD(1980)
Charles Holt
Silents
NIGHT OF LOVE, THE(1927)
Craig Holt
STAR IS BORN, A(1954), ed
David Holt
YOU BELONG TO ME(1934); BIG BROADCAST OF 1936, THE(1935); LAST DAYS OF POMPEII, THE(1935); MEN WITHOUT NAMES(1935); BIG BROADCAST OF 1937, THE(1936); IT'S A GREAT LIFE(1936); STRAIGHT FROM THE SHOULDER(1936); TROUBLE FOR TWO(1936); ADVENTURES OF TOM SAWYER, THE(1938); BEAU GESTE(1939); HERO FOR A DAY(1939); MILITARY ACADEMY(1940); REMEMBER THE DAY(1941); PRIDE OF THE YANKEES, THE(1942); HUMAN COMEDY, THE(1943); TOP MAN(1943); HENRY ALDRICH, BOY SCOUT(1944); RECKLESS AGE(1944); CHEATERS(1945); AFFAIRS OF GERALDINE(1946); BLUE SIERRA(1946); COURAGE OF LASSIE(1946); HOT CARGO(1946); SWEETHEART OF SIGMA CHI(1946); SKY LINER(1949); WILD WEED(1949); COMBAT SQUAD(1953)
Misc. Talkies
SECOND CHANCE(1950)
David Jack Holt
CAT'S PAW, THE(1934); SHOCK(1934); AGE OF INDISCRETION(1935)
Denis Holt
STOLEN HOURS(1963), p
Dennis Holt
PLAY IT COOL(1963, Brit.), p
Edward Holt
Silents
TIGER WOMAN, THE(1917)
Edwin Holt
Silents
PRETENDERS, THE(1916); ROMEO AND JULIET(1916)
Misc. Silents
WHEEL OF THE LAW, THE(1916)
Evelyn Holt
Misc. Silents
THREE KINGS, THE(1929, Brit.)
Felix Holt
KENTUCKIAN, THE(1955), w
Fonda Holt
Misc. Silents
DEVIL'S BOWL, THE(1923)
George Holt
Silents
ALADDIN FROM BROADWAY(1917); WESTERN FATE(1924), d; GOLD RUSH, THE(1925)
Misc. Silents
CAPTAIN ALVAREZ(1914); CHALICE OF COURAGE, THE(1915); GOD'S COUNTRY AND THE WOMAN(1916); THROUGH THE WALL(1916); WHITE MASKS, THE(1921), d; IN THE WEST(1923), d; TROUBLE TRAIL(1924), d
Gudron Holt
SOME OF MY BEST FRIENDS ARE...(1971), makeup
Hans Holt
MOZART STORY, THE(1948, Aust.); EMBEZZLED HEAVEN(1959,Ger.); TRAPP FAMILY, THE(1961, Ger.); ALMOST ANGELS(1962)
Harry Holt
HEY THERE, IT'S YOGI BEAR(1964), anim
Hazel Holt
Misc. Silents
FIGHTING SHERIFF, THE(1925)
Henry Holt
SPIDER, THE(1940, Brit.), w
Jack Holt
DONOVAN AFFAIR, THE(1929); FATHER AND SON(1929); FLIGHT(1929); BORDER LEGION, THE(1930); HELL'S ISLAND(1930); SQUEALER, THE(1930); VENGEANCE(1930); DANGEROUS AFFAIR, A(1931); DIRIGIBLE(1931); FIFTY FATHOMS DEEP(1931); LAST PARADE, THE(1931); MAKER OF MEN(1931); SUBWAY EXPRESS(1931); WHITE SHOULDERS(1931); BEHIND THE MASK(1932); MAN AGAINST WOMAN(1932); THIS SPORTING AGE(1932); WAR CORRESPONDENT(1932); MASTER OF MEN(1933); WHEN STRANGERS MARRY(1933); WOMAN I STOLE, THE(1933); WRECKER, THE(1933); BLACK MOON(1934); DEFENSE HESTS, THE(1934); I'LL FIX IT(1934); WHIRLPOOL(1934); AWAKENING OF JIM BURKE(1935); BEST MAN WINS, THE(1935); LITTLEST REBEL, THE(1935); STORM OVER THE ANDES(1935); UNWELCOME STRANGER(1935); CRASH DONOVAN(1936); DANGEROUS WATERS(1936); END OF THE TRAIL(1936); SAN FRANCISCO(1936); NORTH OF NOME(1937); OUTLAWS OF THE ORIENT(1937); ROARING TIMBER(1937); TRAPPED BY G-MEN(1937); TROUBLE IN MOROCCO(1937); UNDER SUSPICION(1937); CRIME TAKES A HOLIDAY(1938); FLIGHT INTO NOWHERE(1938); MAKING THE HEADLINES(1938); REFORMATORY(1938); FUGITIVE AT LARGE(1939); HIDDEN POWER(1939); STRANGE CASE OF DR. MEADE(1939); TRAPPED IN THE SKY(1939); WHISPERING ENEMIES(1939); FUGITIVE FROM A PRISON CAMP(1940); GREAT PLANE ROBBERY, THE(1940); OUTSIDE THE 3-MILE LIMIT(1940); PASSPORT TO ALCATRAZ(1940); GREAT SWINDLE, THE(1941); CAT PEOPLE(1942); NORTHWEST RANGERS(1942); THUNDER BIRDS(1942); THEY WERE EXPENDABLE(1945); CHASE, THE(1946); FLIGHT TO NOWHERE(1946); MY PAL TRIGGER(1946); RENEGADE GIRL(1946); WILD FRONTIER, THE(1947); ARIZONA RANGER, THE(1948); GALLANT LEGION, THE(1948); LOADED PISTOLS(1948); STRAWBERRY ROAN(1948); TREASURE OF THE SIERRA MADRE, THE(1948); BRIMSTONE(1949); LAST BANDIT, THE(1949); RED DESERT(1949); TASK FORCE(1949); DALTON'S WOMEN, THE(1950); KING OF THE BULLWHIP(1950); RETURN OF THE FRONTIERSMAN(1950); TRAIL OF

ROBIN HOOD(1950); ACROSS THE WIDE MISSOURI(1951)
Silents
SALOMY JANE(1914); CAMPBELLS ARE COMING, THE(1915); NAKED HEARTS(1916); SAVING THE FAMILY NAME(1916); SECRET GAME, THE(1917); HEADIN' SOUTH(1918); ONE MORE AMERICAN(1918); MIDNIGHT ROMANCE, A(1919); CROOKED STREETS(1920); MIDSUMMER MADNESS(1920); SINS OF ROZANNE(1920); AFTER THE SHOW(1921); ALL SOULS EVE(1921); DUCKS AND DRAKES(1921); MASK, THE(1921); MAKING A MAN(1922); NORTH OF THE RIO GRANDE(1922); ON THE HIGH SEAS(1922); WHILE SATAN SLEEPS(1922); GENTLEMAN OF LEISURE, A(1923); NOBODY'S MONEY(1923); TIGER'S CLAW, THE(1923); EMPTY HANDS(1924); NORTH OF 36(1924); ANCIENT HIGHWAY, THE(1925); EVE'S SECRET(1925); BLIND GODDESS, THE(1926); ENCHANTED HILL, THE(1926); SEA HORSES(1926); WARNING, THE(1927); AVALANCHE(1928); SMART SET, THE(1928); SUNSET PASS(1929)
Misc. Silents
BLACK SHEEP OF THE FAMILY, THE(1916); CALL OF THE EAST, THE(1917); GIVING BECKY A CHANCE(1917); INNER SHRINE, THE(1917); LITTLE AMERICAN, THE(1917); SACRIFICE(1917); DESERT WOOING, A(1918); GREEN EYES(1918); HONOR OF HIS HOUSE, THE(1918); LOVE ME(1918); MARRIAGE RING, THE(1918); ROAD THROUGH THE DARK, THE(1918); WHITE MAN'S LAW, THE(1918); CHEATING CHEATERS(1919); KITTY KELLY, M.D.(1919); LIFE LINE, THE(1919); SPORTING CHANCE, A(1919); VICTORY(1919); WOMAN MICHAEL MARRIED, THE(1919); WOMAN THOU GAVEST ME, THE(1919); BEST OF LUCK, THE(1920); HELD BY THE ENEMY(1920); CALL OF THE NORTH, THE(1921); GRIM COMEDIAN, THE(1921); LOST ROMANCE, THE(1921); BOUGHT AND PAID FOR(1922); MAN UNCONQUERABLE, THE(1922); CHEAT, THE(1923); MARRIAGE MAKER, THE(1923); DON'T CALL IT LOVE(1924); LONE WOLF, THE(1924); WANDERER OF THE WASTELAND(1924); LIGHT OF THE WESTERN STARS, THE(1925); THUNDERING HERD, THE(1925); WILD HORSE MESA(1925); BORN TO THE WEST(1926); FORLORN RIVER(1926); MAN OF THE FOREST(1926); MYSTERIOUS RIDER, THE(1927); TIGRESS, THE(1927); COURT-MARTIAL(1928); SUBMARINE(1928); VANISHING PIONEER, THE(1928); WATER HOLE, THE(1928); SUNSET PASS(1929)
Jacqueline Holt
STICK TO YOUR GUNS(1941)
Jany Holt
COURRIER SUD(1937, Fr.); LIFE AND LOVES OF BEETHOVEN, THE(1937, Fr.); LOWER DEPTHS, THE(1937, Fr.); ALIBI, THE(1939, Fr.); RASPUTIN(1939, Fr.); DOCTEUR LAENNEC(1949, Fr.); ANGELS OF THE STREETS(1950, Fr.); GREEN GLOVE, THE(1952); GERVAISE(1956, Fr.); LEFT-HANDED WOMAN, THE(1980, Ger.)
Jennifer Holt
DEEP IN THE HEART OF TEXAS(1942); LITTLE JOE, THE WRANGLER(1942); PRIVATE BUCKAROO(1942); SILVER BULLET, THE(1942); CHEYENNE ROUNDUP(1943); COWBOY IN MANHATTAN(1943); FRONTIER LAW(1943); GET GOING(1943); HERS TO HOLD(1943); HI, BUDDY(1943); LONE STAR TRAIL, THE(1943); OLD CHISHOLM TRAIL(1943); RAIDERS OF SAN JOAQUIN(1943); RAIDERS OF SUNSET PASS(1943); TENTING TONIGHT ON THE OLD CAMP GROUND(1943); MARSHAL OF GUNSMOKE(1944); OKLAHOMA RAIDERS(1944); OUTLAW TRAIL(1944); RIDERS OF THE SANTA FE(1944); BEYOND THE PECOS(1945); LOST TRAIL, THE(1945); NAVAJO TRAIL, THE(1945); RENEGADES OF THE RIO GRANDE(1945); SONG OF OLD WYOMING(1945); UNDER WESTERN SKIES(1945); BUFFALO BILL RIDES AGAIN(1947); FIGHTING VIGILANTES, THE(1947); GHOST TOWN RENEGADES(1947); PIONEER JUSTICE(1947); SHADOW VALLEY(1947); STAGE TO MESA CITY(1947); HAWK OF POWDER RIVER, THE(1948); RANGE RENEGADES(1948); TIOGA KID, THE(1948); TORNADO RANGE(1948)
Misc. Talkies
GUN SMOKE(1945); MOON OVER MONTANA(1946); TRIGGER FINGERS(1946); OVER THE SANTA FE TRAIL(1947)
Jenny Holt
GOLEM, THE(1937, Czech./Fr.)
Joel Holt
KARATE, THE HAND OF DEATH(1961), a, p&d; PRIMITIVE LOVE(1966, Ital.), p
John Holt
Silents
DUMB GIRL OF PORTICI(1916)
Jonathan Holt
BLOODTHIRSTY BUTCHERS(1970)
Kealoha Holt
HONOLULU(1939)
Larry Holt
ROLLERCOASTER(1977); PRISONER OF ZENDA, THE(1979); THING, THE(1982)
Liam Holt
1984
FOREVER YOUNG(1984, Brit.)
Michael Holt
SWORD AND THE SORCERER, THE(1982)
Mike Holt
KIMBERLEY JIM(1965, South Africa)
Nat Holt
GEORGE WHITE'S SCANDALS(1945), p; BADMAN'S TERRITORY(1946), p; RIVERBOAT RHYTHM(1946), p; RIFFRAFF(1947), p; TRAIL STREET(1947), p; RACE STREET(1948), p; RETURN OF THE BADMEN(1948), p; CANADIAN PACIFIC(1949), p; FIGHTING MAN OF THE PLAINS(1949), p; CARIBOO TRAIL, THE(1950), p; GREAT MISSOURI RAID, THE(1950), p; FLAMING FEATHER(1951), p; SILVER CITY(1951), p; WARPATH(1951), p; DENVER AND RIO GRANDE(1952), p; HURRICANE SMITH(1952), p; ARROWHEAD(1953), p; FLIGHT TO TANGIER(1953), p; PONY EXPRESS(1953), p; RAGE AT DAWN(1955), p; TEXAS LADY(1955), p; CATTLE KING(1963), p
Nick Holt
Misc. Talkies
INVASION FROM INNER EARTH(1977)
Nicki Holt
ODDO(1967)
Olimpio Holt
VOICE IN YOUR HEART, A(1952, Ital.)
Patrick Holt
GENGHIS KHAN(U.S./Brit./Ger./Yugo); FRIEDA(1947, Brit.); MASTER OF BANKDAM, THE(1947, Brit.); WHEN THE BOUGH BREAKS(1947, Brit.); FLY AWAY PETER(1948, Brit.); GIRL IN THE PAINTING, THE(1948, Brit.); MARK OF CAIN, THE(1948, Brit.); MY SISTER AND I(1948, Brit.); OCTOBER MAN, THE(1948, Brit.);

BOY, A GIRL AND A BIKE, A(1949 Brit.); BOYS IN BROWN(1949, Brit.); MARRY ME!(1949, Brit.); GUILT IS MY SHADOW(1950, Brit.); COME BACK PETER(1952, Brit.); IVANHOE(1952, Brit.); MAGIC BOX, THE(1952, Brit.); 13 EAST STREET(1952, Brit.); CIRCUMSTANIAL EVIDENCE(1954, Brit.); GOLDEN LINK, THE(1954, Brit.); JOHN WESLEY(1954, Brit.); UNHOLY FOUR, THE(1954, Brit.); COUNT OF TWELVE(1955, Brit.); MISS TULIP STAYS THE NIGHT(1955, Brit.); STOLEN ASSIGNMENT(1955, Brit.); WARRIORS, THE(1955); ALIAS JOHN PRESTON(1956); DYNAMITERS, THE(1956, Brit.); GIRL IN THE PICTURE, THE(1956, Brit.); MEN OF SHERWOOD FOREST(1957, Brit.); OPERATION MURDER(1957, Brit.); SHE PLAYED WITH FIRE(1957, Brit.); SUSPENDED ALIBI(1957, Brit.); THERE'S ALWAYS A THURSDAY(1957, Brit.); FURTHER UP THE CREEK!(1958, Brit.); MURDER REPORTED(1958, Brit.); IT TAKES A THIEF(1960, Brit.); FRIGHTENED CITY, THE(1961, Brit.); TOO HOT TO HANDLE(1961, Brit.); FLIGHT FROM SINGAPORE(1962, Brit.); NIGHT OF THE PROWLER(1962, Brit.); SERENA(1962, Brit.); GET ON WITH IT(1963, Brit.); GUNS AT BATASI(1964, Brit.); MODEL MURDER CASE, THE(1964, Brit.); FIGHTING PRINCE OF DONEGAL, THE(1966, Brit.); VULTURE, THE(1967, U.S./ Brit./Can.); HAMMERHEAD(1968); DESPERADOS, THE(1969); CROMWELL(1970, Brit.); MAGIC CHRISTIAN, THE(1970, Brit.); NO BLADE OF GRASS(1970); WHEN DINOSAURS RULED THE EARTH(1971, Brit.); YOUNG WINSTON(1972, Brit.); PSYCHOMANIA(1974, Brit.); PRIEST OF LOVE(1981, Brit.); SEA WOLVES, THE(1981, Brit.)

Paul Holt
BAD LORD BYRON, THE(1949, Brit.), w

Ralph Holt
FORWARD PASS, THE(1929, ed; TWO WEEKS OFF(1929), ed; RIVER'S END(1931), ed

Rex Holt
SAN DEMETRIO, LONDON(1947, Brit.)

Richard Holt
Silents
EASY GOING GORDON(1925); GOING THE LIMIT(1925); CAPTAIN'S COURAGE, A(1926)
Misc. Silents
CANVAS KISSER, THE(1925); ONCE IN A LIFETIME(1925); TEN DAYS(1925); TOO MUCH YOUTH(1925); BOASTER, THE(1926); IN SEARCH OF A HERO(1926); RECKLESS MOLLYCODDLE, THE(1927)

Robert Holt
JULIUS CAESAR(1952); BEDKNOBS AND BROOMSTICKS(1971); CHARLOTTE'S WEB(1973)

Robert I. Holt
RAMPAGE(1963), w; WEDDING NIGHT(1970, Ireland), w

Seth Holt
DANCE HALL(1950, Brit.), ed; LAVENDER HILL MOB, THE(1951, Brit.), ed; CRASH OF SILENCE(1952, Brit.), ed; HIS EXCELLENCY(1952, Brit.), ed; SPIDER AND THE FLY, THE(1952, Brit.), ed; TITFIELD THUNDERBOLT, THE(1953, Brit.), ed; LOVE LOTTERY, THE(1954, Brit.), ed; LIGHT TOUCH, THE(1955, Brit.), p; LADYKILLERS, THE(1956, Brit.), p; DECISION AGAINST TIME(1957, Brit.), p; NOWHERE TO GO(1959, Brit.), d; SATURDAY NIGHT AND SUNDAY MORNING(1961, Brit.), ed; SCREAM OF FEAR(1961, Brit.), d; STATION SIX-SAHARA(1964, Brit./Ger.), d; NANNY, THE(1965, Brit.), d; DANGER ROUTE(1968, Brit.), d; BLOOD FROM THE MUMMY'S TOMB(1972, Brit.), d

Sheila Holt
CRACKSMAN, THE(1963, Brit.)

Steven Holt
1984
PREPPIES(1984)

Thelma Holt
DOUBLE, THE(1963, Brit)

Tim Holt
STELLA DALLAS(1937); GOLD IS WHERE YOU FIND IT(1938); I MET MY LOVE AGAIN(1938); LAW WEST OF TOMBSTONE, THE(1938); RENEGADE RANGER(1938); SONS OF THE LEGION(1938); FIFTH AVENUE GIRL(1939); GIRL AND THE GAMBLER, THE(1939); ROOKIE COP, THE(1939); SPIRIT OF CULVER, THE(1939); STAGECOACH(1939); LADDIE(1940); SWISS FAMILY ROBINSON(1940); WAGON TRAIN(1940); ALONG THE RIO GRANDE(1941); BACK STREET(1941); BANDIT TRAIL, THE(1941); CYCLONE ON HORSEBACK(1941); DUDE COWBOY(1941); FARGO KID, THE(1941); LAND OF THE OPEN RANGE(1941); ROBBERS OF THE RANGE(1941); SIX GUN GOLD(1941); THUNDERING HOOFS(1941); BANDIT RANGER(1942); COME ON DANGER(1942); HITLER'S CHILDREN(1942); MAGNIFICENT AMBERSONS, THE(1942); PIRATES OF THE PRAIRIE(1942); RIDING THE WIND(1942); AVENGING RIDER, THE(1943); FIGHTING FRONTIER(1943); RED RIVER ROBIN HOOD(1943); SAGEBRUSH LAW(1943); MY DARLING CLEMENTINE(1946); THUNDER MOUNTAIN(1947); UNDER THE TONTO RIM(1947); WILD HORSE MESA(1947); ARIZONA RANGER, THE(1948); GUN SMUGGLERS(1948); GUNS OF HATE(1948); INDIAN AGENT(1948); TREASURE OF THE SIERRA MADRE, THE(1948); WESTERN HERITAGE(1948); BROTHERS IN THE SADDLE(1949); MASKED RAIDERS(1949); MYSTERIOUS DESPERADO, THE(1949); RIDERS OF THE RANGE(1949); RUSTLERS(1949); STAGECOACH KID(1949); BORDER TREASURE(1950); DYNAMITE PASS(1950); LAW OF THE BADLANDS(1950); RIDER FROM TUCSON(1950); RIO GRANDE PATROL(1950); STORM OVER WYOMING(1950); GUNPLAY(1951); HIS KIND OF WOMAN(1951); HOT LEAD(1951); OVERLAND TELEGRAPH(1951); PISTOL HARVEST(1951); SADDLE LEGION(1951); DESERT PASSAGE(1952); ROAD AGENT(1952); TARGET(1952); TRAIL GUIDE(1952); MONSTER THAT CHALLENGED THE WORLD, THE(1957); THIS STUFF'LL KILL YA!(1971)

Toni Holt
BLACK GUNN(1972); EVERYTHING YOU ALWAYS WANTED TO KNOW ABOUT SEX, BUT WE'RE AFRAID TO ASK(1972)

Ula Holt
NEW ADVENTURES OF TARZAN(1935); TARZAN AND THE GREEN GODDESS(1938)

W. Holt
NOWHERE TO GO(1959, Brit.), d

Will Holt
ZELIG(1983)

Willy Holt
TRAIN, THE(1965, Fr./Ital./U.S.), prod d; UP FROM THE BEACH(1965), art d; IS PARIS BURNING?(1966, U.S./Fr.), art d; TWO FOR THE ROAD(1967), art d; SERGEANT, THE(1968), prod d; STAIRCASE(1969 U.S./Brit./Fr.), art d; LADY IN THE CAR WITH GLASSES AND A GUN, THE(1970, U.S./Fr.), art d; DAY OF THE

JACKAL, THE(1973, Brit./Fr.), art d; DESTRUCTORS, THE(1974, Brit.), art s; LOVE AND DEATH(1975), art d; JULIA(1977), prod d; ALMOST PERFECT AFFAIR, AN(1979), art d

Winifred Holtby
SOUTH RIDING(1938, Brit.), w

Helen Holte
Silents
SAPHEAD, THE(1921)

Bo Holten
1984
ELEMENT OF CRIME, THE(1984, Den.), m; ZAPPA(1984, Den.), m

Gerd Holtenau
1984
LOVE IN GERMANY, A(1984, Fr./Ger.)

Chris Holter
WESTWORLD(1973)

Christine Holter
DR. COPPELIUS(1968, U.S./Span.)

Karl Holter
WHALERS, THE(1942, Swed.)

Gary Holton
BREAKING GLASS(1980, Brit.); BLOODY KIDS(1983, Brit.)

Michael Holton
HAPPY BIRTHDAY, GEMINI(1980)

Percy Holton
Misc. Silents
INSINUATION(1922)

Robert Holton
YOUNG WIDOW(1946); MONKEY ON MY BACK(1957)

Rod Holton
WEST OF THE ALAMO(1946)

Annamarie Holtz
FILM WITHOUT A NAME(1950, Ger.)

Gary Holtz
DEATH CURSE OF TARTU(1967)

George Holtz
OUTLAW DEPUTY, THE(1935)
1984
RENO AND THE DOC(1984, Can.)

Lou Holtz
FOLLOW THE LEADER(1930); ZIEGFELD FOLLIES(1945), w

Marvin Holtz
SATAN'S BED(1965)

Nicola Holtz
JACK OF DIAMONDS(1967, U.S./Ger.), cos

T. Holtz
HOUSE OF HORROR(1929)

Tenen Holtz
KIBITZER, THE(1929); THREE LIVE GHOSTS(1929); LILIES OF THE FIELD(1930); MELODY MAN(1930); WOMAN RACKET, THE(1930); GENTLEMAN'S FATE(1931); WHISTLING IN THE DARK(1933); BRITISH AGENT(1934); MONEY MEANS NOTHING(1934); LIVE, LOVE AND LEARN(1937); CIPHER BUREAU(1938); INTERNATIONAL CRIME(1938); LET FREEDOM RING(1939)
Silents
EXIT SMILING(1926); LATEST FROM PARIS, THE(1928); LAW OF THE RANGE, THE(1928); SHOW PEOPLE(1928); DUKE STEPS OUT, THE(1929); TRAIL OF '98, THE(1929)
Misc. Silents
UPSTAGE(1926); DEMI-BRIDE, THE(1927); FRISCO SALLY LEVY(1927); DETECTIVES(1928)

Allan Holtzman
BATTLE BEYOND THE STARS(1980), ed

Glenn Holtzman
URBAN COWBOY(1980)

Iris Holtzman
UNSTRAP ME(1968)

Thomas Holtzmann
TRIAL, THE(1963, Fr./Ital./Ger.); FUNERAL IN BERLIN(1966, Brit.)

Miloslav Holub
WISHING MACHINE(1971, Czech.)

Al Holubar
Misc. Silents
COURT-MARTIALED(1915)

Allen Holubar
Silents
20,000 LEAGUES UNDER THE SEA(1916); SLANDER THE WOMAN(1923), d
Misc. Silents
CONSCIENCE(1915); WHITE TERROR, THE(1915); FEAR NOT(1917), d; FIELD OF HONOR, THE(1917), d; HEART STRINGS(1917), a, d; REED CASE, THE(1917), a, d; SIRENS OF THE SEA(1917); TREASON(1917), a, d; MORTGAGED WIFE, THE(1918), d; SOUL FOR SALE, A(1918), d; TALK OF THE TOWN(1918), d; HEART OF HUMANITY, THE(1919), d; PAID IN ADVANCE(1919), d; RIGHT TO HAPPINESS, THE(1919), d; ONCE TO EVERY WOMAN(1920), d; MAN–WOMAN–MARRIAGE(1921), d; BROKEN CHAINS(1922), d; HURRICANE'S GAL(1922), d

Allen J. Holubar
Misc. Silents
HEARTSTRINGS(1917), d

Gwen Holubar
PARACHUTE NURSE(1942)

Stanis lav Holubec
FIREMAN'S BALL, THE(1968, Czech.)

Jose Holupi
PISTOL FOR RINGO, A(1966, Ital./Span.)

Kermit Holven
HIGH HAT(1937)

Michael Holy
NOT RECONCILED, OR "ONLY VIOLENCE HELPS WHERE IT RULES"(1969, Ger.)

Arno Holz
DREAMER, THE(1936, Ger.), w
Tenen Holz
HOLLYWOOD MYSTERY(1934)
Dirk Holzapfel
1984
MISUNDERSTOOD(1984)
Gunther Holzapfel
IN A YEAR OF THIRTEEN MOONS(1980, Ger.)
Gustav Holzapfel
MOTHER KUSTERS GOES TO HEAVEN(1976, Ger.)
Roger Holzberg
1984
PREY, THE(1984), art d
Max Holzboer
BLUE LIGHT, THE(1932, Ger.)
Gus Holzer
GAL YOUNG UN(1979)
Hans Holzer
AMITYVILLE II: THE POSSESSION(1982), w
Ivy Holzer
PLAYGIRLS AND THE VAMPIRE(1964, Ital.)
Jenny Holzer
TRAP DOOR, THE(1980)
Susan Holzer
GAL YOUNG UN(1979), a, cos
J. Holzleitner
FREUD(1962)
Allan Holzman
CRAZY MAMA(1975), ed; AMSTERDAM KILL, THE(1978, Hong Kong), ed; FORBIDDEN WORLD(1982), d, ed
Daniel Holzman
IT'S ALIVE(1974)
Ernest Holzman
GETTING EVEN(1981), ph
Kenneth Holzman
TELL THEM WILLIE BOY IS HERE(1969)
Judith Holzmeister
ONE APRIL 2000(1952, Aust.); APRIL 1, 2000(1953, Aust.)
Bob Homans
FOR THE DEFENSE(1930); DESTINY(1944); RIVER GANG(1945); GIRL ON THE SPOT(1946)
Robert Homans
CONCENTRATIN' KID, THE(1930); ALIAS THE BAD MAN(1931); BLACK CAMEL, THE(1931); CITY STREETS(1931); CLEARING THE RANGE(1931); DRUMS OF JEOPARDY(1931); LADY KILLER(1933); JIMMY THE GENT(1934); WOMAN IN RED, THE(1935); EASY MONEY(1936); HERE COMES TROUBLE(1936); CARNIVAL QUEEN(1937); DANCE, CHARLIE, DANCE(1937); EASY LIVING(1937); EVER SINCE EVE(1937); FORLORN RIVER(1937); HOLLYWOOD HOTEL(1937); AMAZING DR. CLITTERHOUSE, THE(1938); ANGELS WITH DIRTY FACES(1938); CRASHIN' THRU DANGER(1938); GOLD IS WHERE YOU FIND IT(1938); GOLD MINE IN THE SKY(1938); HEART OF THE NORTH(1938); HOLLYWOOD STADIUM MYSTERY(1938); SISTERS, THE(1938); DODGE CITY(1939); EACH DAWN I DIE(1939); HELL'S KITCHEN(1939); OKLAHOMA KID, THE(1939); UNION PACIFIC(1939); YOUNG MR. LINCOLN(1939); BARNYARD FOLLIES(1940); BEYOND TOMORROW(1940); CAPTAIN IS A LADY, THE(1940); CASTLE ON THE HUDSON(1940); EAST OF THE RIVER(1940); ENEMY AGENT(1940); GRAPES OF WRATH(1940); LILLIAN RUSSELL(1940); 'TIL WE MEET AGAIN(1940); DOUBLE CROSS(1941); GANG'S ALL HERE(1941); FINGERS AT THE WINDOW(1942); FOREST RANGERS, THE(1942); LADY IN A JAM(1942); SPOILERS, THE(1942); FRONTIER BADMEN(1943); JACK LONDON(1943); MAN FROM THE RIO GRANDE, THE(1943); COVER GIRL(1944); BEYOND THE PECOS(1945); COME OUT FIGHTING(1945); THEY WERE EXPENDABLE(1945); EARL CARROLL SKETCHBOOK(1946)
Silents
LEGALLY DEAD(1923); COLLEGE DAYS(1926); GALLOPING GOBS, THE(1927); PRINCESS FROM HOBOKEN, THE(1927); MASKED ANGEL(1928); OBEY YOUR HUSBAND(1928)
Misc. Silents
BORDER JUSTICE(1925); PALS IN PERIL(1927); RIDE 'EM HIGH(1927); FURY OF THE WILD(1929)
Robert E. Homans, Sr.
SOMBRERO KID, THE(1942)
Robert E. L. Homans
MEDAL FOR BENNY, A(1945)
Robert Emmett Homans
IF I HAD A MILLION(1932); PACK UP YOUR TROUBLES(1932)
Robert H. Homans
MARY OF SCOTLAND(1936)
Robert Homas
MALTESE FALCON, THE(1941)
Hans Homberg
TRUNKS OF MR. O.F., THE(1932, Ger.), w
Concha Hombria
VALDEZ IS COMING(1971)
Patrick Kirwan Home
AMAZING MR. BEECHAM, THE(1949, Brit.), w
William Douglas Home
AMAZING MR. BEECHAM, THE(1949, Brit.), w; FOR THEM THAT TRESPASS(1949, Brit.), w; NOW BARABBAS WAS A ROBBER(1949, Brit.), w; SLEEPING CAR TO TRIESTE(1949, Brit.), w; EYE WITNESS(1950, Brit.), w; MADE IN HEAVEN(1952, Brit.), w; RELUCTANT DEBUTANTE, THE(1958), w; FOLLOW THAT HORSE!(1960, Brit.), w; DUCH IN ORANGE SAUCE(1976, Ital.), w
William Home
MEDICINE MAN, THE(1933, Brit.)
Skip Homeier
ARTHUR TAKES OVER(1948); BIG CAT, THE(1949); GUNFIGHTER, THE(1950); FIXED BAYONETS(1951); HALLS OF MONTEZUMA(1951); SEALED CARGO(1951); HAS ANYBODY SEEN MY GAL?(1952); LAST POSSE, THE(1953); BEACHHEAD(1954); BLACK WIDOW(1954); CRY VENGEANCE(1954); DAWN AT SOCORRO(1954); LONE GUN, THE(1954); AT GUNPOINT(1955); ROAD TO DENVER,

THE(1955); TEN WANTED MEN(1955); BETWEEN HEAVEN AND HELL(1956); BURNING HILLS, THE(1956); DAKOTA INCIDENT(1956); STRANGER AT MY DOOR(1956); THUNDER OVER ARIZONA(1956); LURE OF THE SWAMP(1957); NO ROAD BACK(1957, Brit.); TALL T, THE(1957); DAY OF THE BAD MAN(1958); PLUNDERERS OF PAINTED FLATS(1959); COMANCHE STATION(1960); SHOWDOWN(1963); STARK FEAR(1963); BULLET FOR A BADMAN(1964); GHOST AND MR. CHICKEN, THE(1966); TIGER BY THE TAIL(1970); GREATEST, THE(1977, U.S./Brit.)
Misc. Talkies
STARBIRD AND SWEET WILLIAM(1975); ADVENTURES OF STAR BIRD(1978)
Skippy Homeier
TOMORROW THE WORLD(1944); BOYS' RANCH(1946); MICKEY(1948)
Bob Homel
NEVER A DULL MOMENT(1968); BOY WHO CRIED WEREWOLF, THE(1973), a, w
Robert Homel
SAMURAI(1955, Jap.), ed; HOW SWEET IT IS(1968)
Skip Homeler
SAILOR BEWARE(1951)
Homer
ULYSSES(1955, Ital.), w
Homer and Jethro
SECOND FIDDLE TO A STEEL GUITAR(1965)
Paul Homer
HELL BELOW ZERO(1954, Brit.); BLACK TENT, THE(1956, Brit.); MANOLIS(1962, Brit.)
Pete Homer, Sr.
IN MACARTHUR PARK(1977)
Peter Homer, Sr.
OUTSIDER, THE(1962)
Geoffrey Homes [Daniel Mainwaring]
NO HANDS ON THE CLOCK(1941), w; SECRETS OF THE UNDERGROUND(1943), w; CRIME BY NIGHT(1944), w; DANGEROUS PASSAGE(1944), w; SCARED STIFF(1945), w; TOKYO ROSE(1945), w; SWAMP FIRE(1946), w; THEY MADE ME A KILLER(1946), w; BIG TOWN(1947), w; OUT OF THE PAST(1947), w; BIG STEAL, THE(1949), w; ROUGHSHOD(1949), w; EAGLE AND THE HAWK, THE(1950), w; LAWLESS, THE(1950), w; LAST OUTPOST, THE(1951), w; TALL TARGET, THE(1951), w; BUGLES IN THE AFTERNOON(1952), w; THIS WOMAN IS DANGEROUS(1952), w; POWDER RIVER(1953), w; THOSE REDHEADS FROM SEATTLE(1953), w; ALASKA SEAS(1954), w; BLACK HORSE CANYON(1954), w; DESPERADO, THE(1954), w; SOUTHWEST PASSAGE(1954), w; ANNAPOLIS STORY, AN(1955), w; BULLET FOR JOEY, A(1955), w
Leon Homes
Silents
REDHEADS PREFERRED(1926)
Margaret Homes
VIOLENT STRANGER(1957, Brit.)
Stuart Homes
MISS PACIFIC FLEET(1935)
Brigitte Homey
GLASS TOWER, THE(1959, Ger.)
Peter Homfield
MISTRESS OF THE WORLD(1959, Ital./Fr./Ger.), ph
Don Homfray
WEATHER IN THE STREETS, THE(1983, Brit.), art d
Louise Homfray
LIBIDO(1973, Aus.)
Fumiko Homma
RASHOMON(1951, Jap.); SEVEN SAMURAI, THE(1956, Jap.)
Hope Hommersand
T.R. BASKIN(1971)
Robert Hommet
ROYAL AFFAIRS IN VERSAILLES(1957, Fr.)
Miroslav Homola
DEATH OF TARZAN, THE(1968, Czech)
Miroslav Homolka
KRAKATIT(1948, Czech.)
Oscar Homolka
1914(1932, Ger.); INVISIBLE OPPONENT(1933, Ger.); EVERYTHING IS THUNDER(1936, Brit.); RHODES(1936, Brit.); EBB TIDE(1937); SABOTAGE(1937, Brit.); COMRADE X(1940); DREYFUS CASE, THE(1940, Ger.); SEVEN SINNERS(1940); BALL OF FIRE(1941); INVISIBLE WOMAN, THE(1941); RAGE IN HEAVEN(1941); HOSTAGES(1943); MISSION TO MOSCOW(1943); CODE OF SCOTLAND YARD)(1948); I REMEMBER MAMA(1948); ANNA LUCASTA(1949); WHITE TOWER, THE(1950); HOUSE OF THE ARROW, THE(1953, Brit.); MR. POTTS GOES TO MOSCOW(1953, Brit.); PRISONER OF WAR(1954); SEVEN YEAR ITCH, THE(1955); WAR AND PEACE(1956, Ital./U.S.); FAREWELL TO ARMS, A(1957); KEY, THE(1958, Brit.); TEMPEST(1958, Ital./Yugo./Fr.); MR. SARDONICUS(1961); BOYS' NIGHT OUT(1962); WONDERFUL WORLD OF THE BROTHERS ERIMM, THE(1962); LONG SHIPS, THE(1964, Brit./Yugo.); JOY IN THE MORNING(1965); FUNERAL IN BERLIN(1966, Brit.); BILLION DOLLAR BRAIN(1967, Brit.); HAPPENING, THE(1967); ASSIGNMENT TO KILL(1968); MADWOMAN OF CHAILLOT, THE(1969); EXECUTIONER, THE(1970, Brit.); SONG OF NORWAY(1970); TAMARIND SEED, THE(1974, Brit.)
Tom Hompertz
LONESOME COWBOYS(1968)
Sigrid Homquist
Misc. Silents
SCHOOL FOR WIVES(1925)
Louis Homyak
STUCK ON YOU(1983)
1984
STUCK ON YOU(1984)
Mary L. Honaker
GRAVY TRAIN, THE(1974)
Stephen Honanie
MIXED COMPANY(1974)
Mimi Honce
TOGETHER FOR DAYS(1972); LINCOLN CONSPIRACY, THE(1977)

Frank Honda
Silents
DAWN OF THE EAST(1921)
Inoshiro Honda
HALF HUMAN(1955, Jap.), d; RODAN(1958, Jap.), d; H-MAN, THE(1959, Jap.), d; MYSTERIANS, THE(1959, Jap.), d; BATTLE IN OUTER SPACE(1960), d; MOTHRA(1962, Jap.), d; VARAN THE UNBELIEVABLE(1962, U.S./Jap.), d; KING KONG VERSUS GODZILLA(1963, Jap.), d; ATTACK OF THE MUSHROOM PEOPLE(1964, Jap.), d; DAGORA THE SPACE MONSTER(1964, Jap.), d; FRANKENSTEIN CONQUERS THE WORLD(1964, Jap./US), d; GODZILLA VS. THE THING(1964, Jap.), d; GORATH(1964, Jap.), d; HUMAN VAPOR, THE(1964, Jap.), d; ATRAGON(1965, Jap.), d; GHIDRAH, THE THREE-HEADED MONSTER(1965, Jap.), d; KING KONG ESCAPES(1968, Jap.), d; GODZILLA'S REVENGE(1969), d; LATITUDE ZERO(1969, U.S./Jap.), d; MONSTER ZERO(1970, Jap.), d; SPACE AMOEBA, THE(1970, Jap.), d; WAR OF THE GARGANTUAS, THE(1970, Jap.), d, w; MONSTERS FROM THE UNKNOWN PLANET(1975, Jap.), d
Ishiro Honda
GODZILLA, RING OF THE MONSTERS(1956, Jap.), d, w; DESTROY ALL MONSTERS(1969, Jap.), d, w; YOG-MONSTER FROM SPACE(1970, Jap.), d
Shozo Honda
JUDO SHOWDOWN(1966, Jap.), ph; ZATOICHI(1968, Jap.), ph; ZATOICHI'S CONSPIRACY(1974, Jap.), ph
Yoshibumi Honda
YOUNG GUY GRADUATES(1969, Jap.), art d
The Hondells
SKI PARTY(1965)
Med Hondo
SHOCK TROOPS(1968, Ital./Fr.); ZITA(1968, Fr.); WALK WITH LOVE AND DEATH, A(1969)
Emily Hone
EVIL UNDER THE SUN(1982, Brit.); BIDDY(1983, Brit.)
Joe Hone
RISING OF THE MOON, THE(1957, Ireland)
Arthur Honegger
CRIME AND PUNISHMENT(1935, Fr.), m; MAYERLING(1937, Fr.), m; PYGMALION(1938, Brit.), m; FRIEND WILL COME TONIGHT, A(1948, Fr.), m; STORM OVER TIBET(1952), m; JOAN AT THE STAKE(1954, Ital./Fr.), w
Silents
NAPOLEON(1927, Fr.), m
Martin Honer
SOLDIER, THE(1982)
Peter Honess
HELL UP IN HARLEM(1973), ed; IT'S ALIVE(1974), ed
1984
CHAMPIONS(1984), ed; ELECTRIC DREAMS(1984), ed; MEMED MY HAWK(1984, Brit.), ed
Fiffi Honeth
CHILDREN, THE(1949, Swed.)
Honey
BORN IN FLAMES(1983)
Bert Honey
HANDS OF A STRANGER(1962), ed; MERMAIDS OF TIBURON, THE(1962), ed; CALIFORNIA(1963), ed
John Honey
MANGANINNIE(1982, Aus.), d
Jyana Honey
1984
HOTEL NEW HAMPSHIRE, THE(1984)
Varnum Honey
1984
REPO MAN(1984)
Ike Honeyball
SEVEN AGAINST THE SUN(1968, South Africa), spec eff
Jack Honeyborne
PIRATES OF PENZANCE, THE(1983)
Honeycomb
CAT ATE THE PARAKEET, THE(1972)
Gordon Honeycombe
NEITHER THE SEA NOR THE SAND(1974, Brit.), w; MEDUSA TOUCH, THE(1978, Brit.)
Robin Honeywell
MY TUTOR(1983)
Alison Hong
CHARLIE CHAN AND THE CURSE OF THE DRAGON QUEEN(1981); HAMMETT(1982); JEKYLL AND HYDE...TOGETHER AGAIN(1982)
Elliot Hong
THEY CALL ME BRUCE(1982), p&d, w
1984
HOT AND DEADLY(1984), p, d
Misc. Talkies
KILL THE GOLDEN GOOSE(1979), d
James Hong
LOVE IS A MANY-SPLENDORED THING(1955); CHINA GATE(1957); BLOOD AND STEEL(1959); FLOWER DRUM SONG(1961); SATAN BUG, THE(1965); DESTINATION INNER SPACE(1966); ONE SPY TOO MANY(1966); SAND PEBBLES, THE(1966); BAMBOO SAUCER, THE(1968); COLOSSUS: THE FORBIN PROJECT(1969); HAWAIIANS, THE(1970); CAREY TREATMENT, THE(1972); CHINATOWN(1974); WORLD'S GREATEST LOVER, THE(1977); GO TELL THE SPARTANS(1978); IN-LAWS, THE(1979); AIRPLANE!(1980); SO FINE(1981); TRUE CONFESSIONS(1981); BLADE RUNNER(1982); YES, GIORGIO(1982); BREATHLESS(1983)
1984
MISSING IN ACTION(1984); NINJA III–THE DOMINATION(1984)
Misc. Talkies
DYNAMITE BROTHERS, THE(1974); GIRLS NEXT DOOR, THE(1979), d
Sungchil Hong
MARINE BATTLEGROUND(1966, U.S/S.K.), art d
Wilson S. Hong
BIG FOOT(1973), ph

Kojiro Hongo
BUDDHA(1965, Jap.); GREAT WALL, THE(1965, Jap.); GAMERA VERSUS BARUGON(1966, Jap./U.S.); GAMERA VERSUS GAOS(1967, Jap.); GAMERA VERSUS VIRAS(1968, Jap); HIKEN YABURI(1969, Jap.); FALCON FIGHTERS, THE(1970, Jap.); GATEWAY TO GLORY(1970, Jap.); MAGOICHI SAGA, THE(1970, Jap.)
Peter Honiball
ROCKERS(1980)
Heinz Honig
DAS BOOT(1982)
Howard Honig
GLOVE, THE(1980)
Irving Honigman
CANTOR'S SON, THE(1937)
Mari Honjo
DEATH MACHINES(1976)
Yohei Honma
1984
FAMILY GAME, THE(1984, Jap.), d&w
Yuji Honma
MERRY CHRISTMAS MR. LAWRENCE(1983, Jap./Brit.)
Wellington Honn
SPENCER'S MOUNTAIN(1963), spec eff
Arthur Honneger
LES MISERABLES(1936, Fr.), m; WOMAN I LOVE, THE(1937), m; HARVEST(1939, Fr.), m
Gail Honney
WRITTEN ON THE WIND(1956)
Nancy Honnold
MAD BOMBER, THE(1973)
Kayoko Honoo
YOUTH IN FURY(1961, Jap.)
Robert Honorat
DEVIL PROBABLY, THE(1977, FR.)
Roger Honorat
TRIAL OF JOAN OF ARC(1965, Fr.)
Marzio C. Honorato
CAFE EXPRESS(1980, Ital.)
Andre Honore
SLUMBER PARTY MASSACRE, THE(1982)
Jean-Pierre Honore
JOY HOUSE(1964, Fr.); HERCULES AGAINST THE MOON MEN(1965, Fr./Ital.); VICE AND VIRTUE(1965, Fr./Ital.); IS PARIS BURNING?(1966, U.S./Fr.)
Anthony Honour
SPACEFLIGHT IC-1(1965, Brit.); CHRISTMAS TREE, THE(1966, Brit.)
Mary Honri
SCHOONER GANG, THE(1937, Brit.)
Percy Honri
SAY IT WITH FLOWERS(1934, Brit.); SCHOONER GANG, THE(1937, Brit.)
Peter Honri
MATTER OF INNOCENCE, A(1968, Brit.)
Ron Honthaner
FALLGUY(1962), ed; HOSTAGE, THE(1966), ed; HOUSE ON SKULL MOUNTAIN, THE(1974), d; HOT LEAD AND COLD FEET(1978)
Maria Hontzas
SPRING FEVER(1983, Can.)
Eugene Hoo
ADVENTURES OF MARCO POLO, THE(1938)
Geri Hoo
CONFESSIONS OF AN OPIUM EATER(1962)
Hayward Soo Hoo
INTRIGUE(1947); TENSION(1949); YANK IN INDO-CHINA, A(1952); SOME KIND OF HERO(1982)
Howard Soo Hoo
BIG BONANZA, THE(1944); LOVE IS A MANY-SPLENDORED THING(1955)
Hugh Hoo
BETRAYAL FROM THE EAST(1945)
Roland Soo Hoo
MY FAVORITE BRUNETTE(1947)
Walter Soo Hoo
LADY FROM CHUNGKING(1943); HEAVENLY DAYS(1944); LEFT HAND OF GOD, THE(1955); LOVE IS A MANY-SPLENDORED THING(1955); CHINA GATE(1957); MAN WHO LOVED WOMEN, THE(1983)
William Soo Hoo
CHINA GATE(1957)
Luther Hoobyar
NIGHT AT THE OPERA, A(1935)
A. J. Hood
CALIFORNIA SPLIT(1974)
Alan Hood
NOW THAT APRIL'S HERE(1958, Can.)
Ann Hood
SINGING IN THE DARK(1956), w
Misc. Talkies
RUDDIGORE(1967, Brit.)
Barbara Hood
Misc. Silents
BELLS OF ST. MARY'S, THE(1928, Brit.)
Darla Hood
BOHEMIAN GIRL, THE(1936); ICE FOLLIES OF 1939(1939); BORN TO SING(1942); HAPPY LAND(1943); CALYPSO HEAT WAVE(1957); BAT, THE(1959)
Misc. Talkies
NEIGHBORHOOD HOUSE(1936)
Don Hood
OBSESSION(1976); FRENCH QUARTER(1978); PRETTY BABY(1978); ABSENCE OF MALICE(1981); CAT PEOPLE(1982); TOY, THE(1982)
1984
RIVER, THE(1984)

Dusty Hood
MYSTERY SUBMARINE(1963, Brit.)
Ed Hood
CHELSEA GIRLS, THE(1967)
Forester Hood
LOVE IS A FUNNY THING(1970, Fr./Ital.)
Foster Hood
COMANCHE STATION(1960); PROFESSIONALS, THE(1966)
George F. Hood .
Misc. Talkies
STARK RAVING MAD(1983), d
Gerald Hood
SORCERESS(1983)
Gordon Hood
DINGAKA(1965, South Africa)
Harry Hood
DEVIL AND DANIEL WEBSTER, THE(1941)
Janice Hood
JET PILOT(1957)
Jim Hood
NAVAJO TRAIL, THE(1945)
Jock Hood
Misc. Silents
REDEMPTION OF HIS NAME, THE(1918, Brit.)
Miki Hood
GUEST OF HONOR(1934, Brit.); LEAVE IT TO BLANCHE(1934, Brit.); TRUST THE NAVY(1935, Brit.); FAME(1936, Brit.); GIRLS IN THE STREET(1937, Brit.); GIRL IN THE STREET(1938, Brit.); SHOW GOES ON, THE(1938, Brit.); THIS'LL MAKE YOU WHISTLE(1938, Brit.); INSPECTOR HORNLEIGH(1939, Brit.); THIEF OF BAGHDAD, THE(1940, Brit.); WALKING ON AIR(1946, Brit.)
Morag Hood
WUTHERING HEIGHTS(1970, Brit.)
Ned Hood
TRACK THE MAN DOWN(1956, Brit.)
Noel Hood
CROOKS TOUR(1940, Brit.); CONSTANT HUSBAND, THE(1955, Brit.); CURSE OF FRANKENSTEIN, THE(1957, Brit.); HIGH FLIGHT(1957, Brit.); HOW TO MURDER A RICH UNCLE(1957, Brit.); SURGEON'S KNIFE, THE(1957, Brit.); DUKE WORE JEANS, THE(1958, Brit.); INN OF THE SIXTH HAPPINESS, THE(1958); RX MURDER(1958, Brit.); BOBBIKINS(1959, Brit.); DEVIL'S BAIT(1959, Brit.); SON OF ROBIN HOOD(1959, Brit.); TWO-WAY STRETCH(1961, Brit.); SATAN NEVER SLEEPS(1962); TAMAHINE(1964, Brit.); 20,000 POUNDS KISS, THE(1964, Brit.)
Randall Hood
TWO LITTLE BEARS, THE(1961), d
Misc. Talkies
DIE SISTER, DIE(1978), d
Robin Hood
Silents
TIGER'S CLAW, THE(1923)
Wally Hood
Silents
WARMING UP(1928)
Wilson Hood
RED SKIES OF MONTANA(1952)
Carla Hoogeveen
INN OF THE DAMNED(1974, Aus.)
Misc. Talkies
ALTERNATIVE(1976)
Debra Hook
HOPSCOTCH(1980)
Pope Hook
TALES OF A SALESMAN(1965)
Trevor Hook
CHARLIE CHAN AND THE CURSE OF THE DRAGON QUEEN(1981)
Nina Warner Hooke
GYPSY AND THE GENTLEMAN, THE(1958, Brit.), w; DEADLY RECORD(1959, Brit.), w
Buddy Joe Hooken
TAKE A HARD RIDE(1975, U.S./Ital.)
Bill Hooker
NATIONAL LAMPOON'S ANIMAL HOUSE(1978)
Brian Hooker
VAGABOND KING, THE(1930), w; CORONADO(1935), w; ROSE OF THE RANCHO(1936), w; VAGABOND KING, THE(1956), w
Bud Hooker
LOVABLE CHEAT, THE(1949); FAST ON THE DRAW(1950)
Buddy Joe Hooker
WHITE LIGHTNING(1973); CASTAWAY COWBOY, THE(1974); GUS(1976), stunts; HOT LEAD AND COLD FEET(1978), stunts; HERBIE GOES BANANAS(1980); SERIAL(1980); KING OF THE MOUNTAIN(1981); SEARCH AND DESTROY(1981), stunts; OSTERMAN WEEKEND, THE(1983)
1984
AGAINST ALL ODDS(1984)
Hank Bill Hooker
KING OF THE MOUNTAIN(1981)
Hank Hooker
SKATETOWN, U.S.A.(1979), stunts
Hugh Hooker
DEAD RECKONING(1947); BANDIT QUEEN(1950); KING OF THE BULLWHIP(1950); TEXAN MEETS CALAMITY JANE, THE(1950); GOLD RAIDERS, THE(1952); EMPIRE OF THE ANTS(1977)
Hugh M. Hooker
DEVIL'S PARTNER, THE(1958), p; LITTLEST HOBO, THE(1958), p
Joe Buddy Hooker
VIGILANTE FORCE(1976), stunts
Joe Hooker
HELL'S ANGELS '69(1969); HAROLD AND MAUDE(1971); MELINDA(1972); WHITE LINE FEVER(1975, Can.), stunt

Misc. Talkies
NOT MY DAUGHTER(1975)
John J. Hooker
REDS(1981)
John Lee Hooker
MISTER BROWN(1972), m
Ken Hooker
DARK INTRUDER(1965)
Misc. Talkies
BABYSITTER, THE(1969)
Kenneth Hooker
LONELY MAN, THE(1957)
Mark Hooker
EMPIRE OF THE ANTS(1977)
Son Hooker
INCREDIBLY STRANGE CREATURES WHO STOPPED LIVING AND BECAME CRAZY MIXED-UP ZOMBIES, THE(1965); J.W. COOP(1971)
Richard Hooker [Dr. H. Richard Hornberger]
M(1970), w
Ted Hooker
CRUCIBLE OF TERROR(1971, Brit.), d, w
Bebe Drake Hooks
REPORT TO THE COMMISSIONER(1975)
David Hooks
DARK ODYSSEY(1961); HOSPITAL, THE(1971); CLONUS HORROR, THE(1979)
Eric Hooks
SOUNDER(1972)
Jim Hooks
1984
FLASH OF GREEN, A(1984)
Kevin Hooks
SOUNDER(1972); AARON LOVES ANGELA(1975); HERO AIN'T NOTHIN' BUT A SANDWICH, A(1977); TAKE DOWN(1979)
Linda Hooks
CARRY ON ENGLAND(1976, Brit.)
Robert Hooks
HURRY SUNDOWN(1967); SWEET LOVE, BITTER(1967); TROUBLE MAN(1972); AARON LOVES ANGELA(1975); AIRPORT '77(1977); FAST-WALKING(1982)
1984
STAR TREK III: THE SEARCH FOR SPOCK(1984)
Constanza Hool
1984
EVIL THAT MEN DO, THE(1984)
Lance Hool
DOGS(1976); SURVIVAL RUN(1980), p; CABOBLANCO(1981), p; 10 TO MIDNIGHT(1983), p
1984
MISSING IN ACTION(1984), w
Bill Hoolahahn
DIAMOND JIM(1935)
Raymond Hoole
CAPTAIN'S PARADISE, THE(1953, Brit.)
E. Mason Hooper
MIDNIGHT MORALS(1932), d
Misc. Talkies
TEMPTATION(1930), d; SISTER TO JUDAS(1933), d
Misc. Silents
RED WOMAN, THE(1917), d; REGENERATES, THE(1917), d; WAX MODEL, THE(1917), d; LOVE'S PAY DAY(1918), d; WIFE OR COUNTRY(1919), d; GLORIOUS FOOL, THE(1922), d
Eddie Hooper
SHE SHALL HAVE MUSIC(1935, Brit.)
Elric Hooper
1984
CONSTANCE(1984, New Zealand)
Ewan Hooper
HOW I WON THE WAR(1967, Brit.); DRACULA HAS RISEN FROM HIS GRAVE(1968, Brit.); JULIUS CAESAR(1970, Brit.)
Geoffrey Hooper
NO BLADE OF GRASS(1970, Brit.)
Hal Hooper
BEAU GESTE(1966)
Hedda Hooper
Misc. Silents
VIRTUOUS WIVES(1919); BLACK TEARS(1927)
Helen Hooper
1984
RAZORBACK(1984, Aus.), cos
Jack Hooper
WIZARDS(1977), ph
Jane Hooper
1984
KINGS AND DESPERATE MEN(1984, Brit.)
John Hooper
WEATHER IN THE STREETS, THE(1983, Brit.), ph
Keith Hooper
FAR FROM THE MADDING CROWD(1967, Brit.)
Les Hooper
FINNEY(1969), m
Lewis Hooper
Silents
NEPTUNE'S DAUGHTER(1914)
Lindsay Hooper
FLOATING DUTCHMAN, THE(1953, Brit.); WRONG BOX, THE(1966, Brit.)
Peter Hooper
DEATHSPORT(1978)
Prue Hooper
RECESS(1967), cos

R.B. Hooper
RIDERS OF THE CACTUS(1931), ph
Roy Hooper
SKY RIDERS(1976, U.S./Gr.)
Terry Hooper
HARD DAY'S NIGHT, A(1964, Brit.)
Tobe Hooper
WINDSPLITTER, THE(1971); TEXAS CHAIN SAW MASSACRE, THE(1974), p&d,
w, m; EATEN ALIVE(1976), d; FUNHOUSE, THE(1981), d; POLTERGEIST(1982), d
Wally Hooper, Jr.
TERROR EYES(1981)
Ralph Hoopers
Misc. Talkies
RIDERS OF THE SAGE(1939)
Julie Hoopman
HONKYTONK MAN(1982)
Arthur Hoops
Silents
STRAIGHT ROAD, THE(1914); SUCH A LITTLE QUEEN(1914); DANGER SIGNAL,
THE(1915); ESMERALDA(1915); MISTRESS NELL(1915); SONG OF HATE, THE(1915);
FINAL CURTAIN, THE(1916)
Misc. Silents
ARISTOCRACY(1914); GRETNA GREEN(1915); MUMMY AND THE HUMMING-
BIRD, THE(1915); DEVIL'S PRAYER-BOOK, THE(1916); ETERNAL QUESTION,
THE(1916); EXTRAVAGANCE(1916); LURE OF HEART'S DESIRE, THE(1916); PLAY-
ING WITH FIRE(1916); SCARLET WOMAN, THE(1916); SOUL MARKET, THE(1916);
BRIDGES BURNED(1917); SECRET OF EVE, THE(1917)
Fritz Hoopts
GIRL FROM THE MARSH CROFT, THE(1935, Ger.)
Van Hoorebeke
SECRET DOCUMENT – VIENNA(1954, Fr.), m
Fred Hoose
ROGUE OF THE RANGE(1937); EAST SIDE KIDS(1940); DRIFTIN' KID, THE(1941);
DYNAMITE CANYON(1941); RIDING THE SUNSET TRAIL(1941); SILVER STAL-
LION(1941); THERE'S MAGIC IN MUSIC(1941); WANDERERS OF THE WEST(1941);
LONE STAR LAW MEN(1942); LAW RIDES AGAIN, THE(1943); DOUBLE LIFE,
A(1947); MEXICAN HAYRIDE(1948); EAST SIDE, WEST SIDE(1949); SURREN-
DER(1950); PROWLER, THE(1951); OKLAHOMA ANNIE(1952)
Frederick Hoose
MR. SMITH GOES TO WASHINGTON(1939)
J. Michael Hoose
NO LONGER ALONE(1978), ed
The Hoosier Hotshots
HOOSIER HOLIDAY(1943); ROCKIN' IN THE ROCKIES(1945); COWBOY
BLUES(1946); SONG OF IDAHO(1948)
Misc. Talkies
RHYTHM ROUND-UP(1945); SINGING ON THE TRAIL(1946); THAT TEXAS JAM-
BOREE(1946); OVER THE SANTA FE TRAIL(1947); SMOKY RIVER SERENA-
DE(1947); SWING THE WESTERN WAY(1947); SINGING SPURS(1948)
Al Hoosman
TOXI(1952, Ger.); PHONY AMERICAN, THE(1964, Ger.); JACK OF DIA-
MONDS(1967, U.S./Ger.)
The Hoot Gibson Cowboys
GAY BUCKAROO, THE(1932)
Peter Hooten
TRIBES(1970); STUDENT BODY, THE(1976); ORCA(1977); COUNTERFEIT COM-
MANDOS(1981, Ital.); FANTASIES(1981); SOLDIER, THE(1982)
Misc. Talkies
PRISONERS(1975); SUNBURST(1975); WOMAN FOR ALL MEN, A(1975)
Bill Hootkins
TWILIGHT'S LAST GLEAMING(1977, U.S./Ger.)
William Hootkins
VALENTINO(1977, Brit.); HANOVER STREET(1979, Brit.); FLASH GORDON(1980);
RAIDERS OF THE LOST ARK(1981); SPHINX(1981); TRAIL OF THE PINK PAN-
THER, THE(1982); CURSE OF THE PINK PANTHER(1983)
Clara Hoover
ILLIAC PASSION, THE(1968)
Elva Mai Hoover
"EQUUS"(1977)
Elva May Hoover
SUPERMAN II(1980)
Hy Hoover
TICKET TO CRIME(1934)
Hyram A. Hoover
MAN WHO RECLAIMED HIS HEAD, THE(1935)
Hyram Hoover
HAPPY LANDING(1934)
J. Edgar Hoover
PERSONS IN HIDING(1939), w; UNDERCOVER DOCTOR(1939), w; PAROLE FIX-
ER(1940), w; QUEEN OF THE MOB(1940), w; NEXT OF KIN(1942, Brit.); HOUSE ON
92ND STREET, THE(1945); WALK EAST ON BEACON(1952), w
Joe Hoover
BLACK SPURS(1965)
Joseph Hoover
HELL IS FOR HEROES(1962); MAN WHO SHOT LIBERTY VALANCE, THE(1962);
FATE IS THE HUNTER(1964); STAGECOACH(1966); ASTRO-ZOMBIES, THE(1969)
Laura Hoover
SHE DANCES ALONE(1981, Aust./U.S.)
Michael Hoover
CRATER LAKE MONSTER, THE(1977)
Mike Hoover
EQUINOX(1970), ph
Phil Hoover
HARD TRAIL(1969); THING WITH TWO HEADS, THE(1972); SUPERCHICK(1973);
SWEET JESUS, PREACHER MAN(1973); POLICEWOMAN(1974); BLACK GESTAPO,
THE(1975); RACE WITH THE DEVIL(1975); BAKER'S HAWK(1976); ACAPULCO
GOLD(1978)

Putnam Hoover
Silents
LITTLE WILD GIRL, THE(1928), w; OLD AGE HANDICAP(1928), t
Robert Hoover
NAVY BLUE AND GOLD(1937); OVER THE GOAL(1937); GALLANT JOUR-
NEY(1946)
Robynne Hoover
EQUINOX(1970), makeup
Arthur Hopcraft
AGATHA(1979, Brit.), w
Ann Hope
ALONG CAME SALLY(1934, Brit.)
Anna Hope
BOWERY AT MIDNIGHT(1942); VERBOTEN!(1959)
Anthony Hope
PRISONER OF ZENDA, THE(1952), w; PRISONER OF ZENDA, THE(1979), w
Silents
RUPERT OF HENTZAU(1915, Brit.), w; ADVENTURE IN HEARTS, AN(1919), w;
PRISONER OF ZENDA, THE(1922), w; RUPERT OF HENTZAU(1923), w
Anthony J. Hope
PRISONER OF ZENDA, THE(1937), w
Avis Hope
EIGHT ON THE LAM(1967)
Bob Hope
BIG BROADCAST OF 1938, THE(1937); COLLEGE SWING(1938); GIVE ME A
SAILOR(1938); THANKS FOR THE MEMORY(1938); CAT AND THE CANARY,
THE(1939); NEVER SAY DIE(1939); SOME LIKE IT HOT(1939); GHOST BREAKERS,
THE(1940); ROAD TO SINGAPORE(1940); CAUGHT IN THE DRAFT(1941); LOUISIA-
NA PURCHASE(1941); NOTHING BUT THE TRUTH(1941); ROAD TO ZAN-
ZIBAR(1941); MY FAVORITE BLONDE(1942); ROAD TO MOROCCO(1942); STAR
SPANGLED RHYTHM(1942); LET'S FACE IT(1943); THEY GOT ME COVERED(1943);
PRINCESS AND THE PIRATE, THE(1944); ROAD TO UTOPIA(1945); MONSIEUR
BEAUCAIRE(1946); MY FAVORITE BRUNETTE(1947); ROAD TO RIO(1947); VARIE-
TY GIRL(1947); WHERE THERE'S LIFE(1947); PALEFACE, THE(1948); GREAT
LOVER, THE(1949); SORROWFUL JONES(1949); FANCY PANTS(1950); LEMON
DROP KID, THE(1951); MY FAVORITE SPY(1951); GREATEST SHOW ON EARTH,
THE(1952); ROAD TO BALI(1952); SON OF PALEFACE(1952); HERE COME THE
GIRLS(1953); OFF LIMITS(1953); SCARED STIFF(1953); CASANOVA'S BIG
NIGHT(1954); SEVEN LITTLE FOYS, THE(1955); IRON PETTICOAT, THE(1956, Brit.);
THAT CERTAIN FEELING(1956); BEAU JAMES(1957); PARIS HOLIDAY(1958);
ALIAS JESSE JAMES(1959); FACTS OF LIFE, THE(1960); BACHELOR IN PARA-
DISE(1961); ROAD TO HONG KONG, THE(1962, U.S./Brit.); CALL ME BWANA(1963,
Brit.); CRITIC'S CHOICE(1963); GLOBAL AFFAIR, A(1964); I'LL TAKE SWE-
DEN(1965); BOY, DID I GET A WRONG NUMBER!(1966); OSCAR, THE(1966); EIGHT
ON THE LAM(1967); PRIVATE NAVY OF SGT. O'FARRELL, THE(1968); HOW TO
COMMIT MARRIAGE(1969); CANCEL MY RESERVATION(1972); MUPPET MOVIE,
THE(1979)
Carlos Noriega Hope
SANTA(1932, Mex.), w
Courtney Hope
MEET SIMON CHERRY(1949, Brit.); MAN IN BLACK, THE(1950, Brit.); DEAD ON
COURSE(1952, Brit.)
Dallas Hope
Silents
ABRAHAM LINCOLN(1924)
David Hope
EBB TIDE(1937)
Dawn Hope
MELODY(1971, Brit.); BLACK JOY(1977, Brit.); RICHARD'S THINGS(1981, Brit.)
Diana Hope
MAN FROM BLANKLEY'S, THE(1930); WOMAN HATER(1949, Brit.); RUN FOR
YOUR MONEY, A(1950, Brit.); SILK NOOSE, THE(1950, Brit.); HOLIDAY WEEK(1952,
Brit.); WILL ANY GENTLEMAN?(1955, Brit.)
Dorothy Hope
NO FUNNY BUSINESS(1934, Brit.), w; WIFE OF GENERAL LING, THE(1938,
Brit.), w; AT DAWN WE DIE(1943, Brit.), w; CANDLELIGHT IN ALGERIA(1944,
Brit.), w
Edward Hope
SHE LOVES ME NOT(1934), w; CALM YOURSELF(1935), w; MARRY THE
GIRL(1937), w; TRUE TO THE ARMY(1942), w; DOWN AMONG THE SHELTERING
PALMS(1953), w; HOW TO BE VERY, VERY, POPULAR(1955), w; LONG GRAY
LINE, THE(1955), w; THREE FOR THE SHOW(1955), w
Evelyn Hope
Silents
IVANHOE(1913)
Misc. Silents
IVANHOE(1913, Brit.); SINGLE LIFE(1921, Brit.)
Faith Hope
Misc. Silents
SON OF THE DESERT, A(1928)
Fred Hope
DINNER AT EIGHT(1933), set d
Frederic Hope
STRANGER'S RETURN(1933), art d; MERRY WIDOW, THE(1934), art d; SWORN
ENEMY(1936), art d; WE WENT TO COLLEGE(1936), art d; MAYTIME(1937), art d
Silents
EXIT SMILING(1926), set d; ON ZE BOULEVARD(1927), art d; BABY MINE(1928),
set d
Frederick Hope
Silents
FLESH AND THE DEVIL(1926), set d
Fredric Hope
HOLLYWOOD PARTY(1934), art d; RIP TIDE(1934), art d; TALE OF TWO CITIES,
A(1935), art d
Garry Hope
CLEGG(1969, Brit.)
Gary Hope
DAY OF THE TRIFFIDS, THE(1963); JUST FOR FUN(1963, Brit.); SECOND BEST
SECRET AGENT IN THE WHOLE WIDE WORLD, THE(1965, Brit.)

Misc. Talkies
BIG ZAPPER(1974)
Gillian Hope
SOLO(1978, New Zealand/Aus.)
Gloria Hope
TWICE BLESSED(1945); HARVEY GIRLS, THE(1946)
Silents
GREAT LOVE, THE(1918); NAUGHTY, NAUGHTY!(1918); OUTCASTS OF POKER FLAT, THE(1919); COURAGE(1921); TESS OF THE STORM COUNTRY(1922); TROUBLE(1922); SANDY(1926)
Misc. Silents
TIME LOCKS AND DIAMONDS(1917); GUILTY MAN, THE(1918); LAW OF THE NORTH, THE(1918); $5,000 REWARD(1918); BILL APPERSON'S BOY(1919); BURGLAR BY PROXY(1919); DESPERATE HERO, THE(1920); GAY LORD QUEX, THE(1920); PRAIRIE TRAILS(1920); SEEDS OF VENGEANCE(1920); TEXAN, THE(1920); THIRD WOMAN, THE(1920); COLORADO(1921); GRIM COMEDIAN, THE(1921)
Harry Hope
SUNSET COVE(1978), p
Henry Hope
MY FAVORITE SPY(1951)
J. Hope
Misc. Silents
YOUTH OF FORTUNE, A(1916)
Jack Hope
STAR SPANGLED RHYTHM(1942); ALIAS JESSE JAMES(1959), p
James Hope
WHEN THE LIGHTS GO ON AGAIN(1944); ICE PALACE(1960)
Jean Hope
Silents
GIMMIE(1923)
Jim Hope
SPOTLIGHT SCANDALS(1943)
John Hope
OTHER PEOPLE'S SINS(1931, Brit.)
Kathryn Ruth Hope
STUDENT BODIES(1981), ed
Laurence Hope
Silents
INDIAN LOVE LYRICS, THE(1923, Brit.), w
Leslie Hope
1984
LOVE STREAMS(1984)
Misc. Talkies
UPS AND DOWNS(1981)
Maidie Hope
MARRY THE GIRL(1935, Brit.); MUSIC HATH CHARMS(1935, Brit.); HAPPY FAMILY, THE(1936, Brit.); THEY DIDN'T KNOW(1936, Brit.); THIS'LL MAKE YOU WHISTLE(1938, Brit.)
Silents
ALL THE WINNERS(1920, Brit.)
Margaret Hope
Silents
HALF A TRUTH(1922, Brit.); GAMBLE WITH HEARTS, A(1923, Brit.); BARNES MURDER CASE, THE(1930, Brit.)
Misc. Silents
IT'S NEVER TOO LATE TO MEND(1917, Brit.); ISLAND OF WISDOM, THE(1920, Brit.)
Margot Hope
MOTEL HELL(1980)
Michaela Hope
FEMALE RESPONSE, THE(1972)
Mike Hope
PROJECTED MAN, THE(1967, Brit.), spec eff
Richard Hope
FRENCH LIEUTENANT'S WOMAN, THE(1981); BLOODY KIDS(1983, Brit.)
1984
LAUGHTER HOUSE(1984, Brit.); SCANDALOUS(1984)
Robert Hope
PARIS HOLIDAY(1958), p, w; EIGHT ON THE LAM(1967); POWERFORCE(1983), ph
Ruth Hope
STARSHIP INVASIONS(1978, Can.), ed
Teri Hope
FORCE OF IMPULSE(1961); FUN IN ACAPULCO(1963); PAJAMA PARTY(1964); ROUSTABOUT(1964)
Terry Hope
GYPSY(1962)
Vida Hope
JOHNNY IN THE CLOUDS(1945, Brit.); SCHOOL FOR SECRETS(1946, Brit.); I BECAME A CRIMINAL(1947); NICHOLAS NICKLEBY(1947, Brit.); MARK OF CAIN, THE(1948, Brit.); VICE VERSA(1948, Brit.); FOR THEM THAT TRESPASS(1949, Brit.); HER MAN GILBEY(1949, Brit.); INTERRUPTED JOURNEY, THE(1949, Brit.); IT ALWAYS RAINS ON SUNDAY(1949, Brit.); PAPER ORCHID(1949, Brit.); WOMAN HATER(1949, Brit.); FIVE ANGLES ON MURDER(1950, Brit.); WHILE THE SUN SHINES(1950, Brit.); CHEER THE BRAVE(1951, Brit.); GREEN GROW THE RUSHES(1951, Brit.); MAN IN THE WHITE SUIT, THE(1952); BROKEN HORSESHOE, THE(1953, Brit.); DOUBLE CONFESSION(1953, Brit.); HUNDRED HOUR HUNT(1953, Brit.); LONG MEMORY, THE(1953, Brit.); MARILYN(1953, Brit.); TWILIGHT WOMEN(1953, Brit.); ANGELS ONE FIVE(1954, Brit.); FAST AND LOOSE(1954, Brit.); LEASE OF LIFE(1954, Brit.); RX MURDER(1958, Brit.); IN THE DOGHOUSE(1964, Brit.)
Williams Hope
LORDS OF DISCIPLINE, THE(1983)
Norman Hope-Bell
LOVE UP THE POLE(1936, Brit.), p; OLD MOTHER RILEY(1937, Brit.), p; SONG OF THE FORGE(1937, Brit.), p; ROSE OF TRALEE(1938, Ireland), p

Tim Hopewell-Ash
PANDORA AND THE FLYING DUTCHMAN(1951, Brit.), art d
Hans Hopf
GREAT SINNER, THE(1949)
Heinz Hopf
LOVING COUPLES(1966, Swed.); WOMAN OF DARKNESS(1968, Swed.); THEY CALL HER ONE EYE(1974, Swed.); FANNY AND ALEXANDER(1983, Swed./Fr./Ger.)
Alan Hopgood
ALVIN PURPLE(1974, Aus.), w; ALVIN RIDES AGAIN(1974, Aus.), w; TRUE STORY OF ESKIMO NELL, THE(1975, Aus.), w; BLUE LAGOON, THE(1980); MY BRILLIANT CAREER(1980, Aus.); ROAD GAMES(1981, Aus.)
Fincina Hopgood
WE OF THE NEVER NEVER(1983, Aus.)
David Hopi
PERFECT SNOB, THE(1941)
George James Hopkind
BREAKING POINT, THE(1950), set d
Alan Hopkins
TOO LATE BLUES(1962); SAND PEBBLES, THE(1966)
Allan Hopkins
BALTIMORE BULLET, THE(1980)
Anthony Hopkins
VICE VERSA(1948, Brit.), m; IT'S HARD TO BE GOOD(1950, Brit.), m; PICKWICK PAPERS, THE(1952, Brit.), m, md; DECAMERON NIGHTS(1953, Brit.), m; ANGEL WHO PAWNED HER HARP, THE(1956, Brit.), m; CAST A DARK SHADOW(1958, Brit.), m; BEASTS OF MARSEILLES, THE(1959, Brit.), m; NAVY HEROES(1959, Brit.), m; BILLY BUDD(1962), m
Anthony Hopkins
LION IN WINTER, THE(1968, Brit.); HAMLET(1969, Brit.); LOOKING GLASS WAR, THE(1970, Brit.); WHEN EIGHT BELLS TOLL(1971, Brit.); YOUNG WINSTON(1972, Brit.); DOLL'S HOUSE, A(1973); GIRL FROM PETROVKA, THE(1974); JUGGERNAUT(1974, Brit.); ALL CREATURES GREAT AND SMALL(1975, Brit.); AUDREY ROSE(1977); BRIDGE TOO FAR, A(1977, Brit.); INTERNATIONAL VELVET(1978, Brit.); MAGIC(1978); CHANGE OF SEASONS, A(1980); ELEPHANT MAN, THE(1980, Brit.)
1984
BOUNTY, THE(1984)
Arthur Hopkins
DANCE OF LIFE, THE(1929), w; PARIS BOUND(1929), p; HIS DOUBLE LIFE(1933), d, w; SWING HIGH, SWING LOW(1937), w; WHEN MY BABY SMILES AT ME(1948), w; CAPTURE THAT CAPSULE(1961), m
Silents
ETERNAL MAGDALENE, THE(1919), d
Barry Hopkins
PRIME TIME, THE(1960)
Benjamin Hopkins
Misc. Silents
SOLDIER'S SONS(1916)
Bernard Hopkins
1984
COVERGIRL(1984, Can.)
Bert Hopkins
UNHOLY QUEST, THE(1934, Brit.), p
Betty Hopkins
FLIGHT LIEUTENANT(1942), w
Bo Hopkins
BRIDGE AT REMAGEN, THE(1969); WILD BUNCH, THE(1969); 1,000 PLANE RAID, THE(1969); MACHO CALLAHAN(1970); MONTE WALSH(1970); MOONSHINE WAR, THE(1970); CULPEPPER CATTLE COMPANY, THE(1972); GETAWAY, THE(1972); ONLY WAY HOME, THE(1972); AMERICAN GRAFFITI(1973); MAN WHO LOVED CAT DANCING, THE(1973); WHITE LIGHTNING(1973); NICKEL RIDE, THE(1974); DAY OF THE LOCUST, THE(1975); KILLER ELITE, THE(1975); POSSE(1975); SMALL TOWN IN TEXAS, A(1976); TENTACLES(1977, Ital.); MIDNIGHT EXPRESS(1978, Brit.); MORE AMERICAN GRAFFITI(1979); FIFTH FLOOR, THE(1980); SWEET SIXTEEN(1983)
1984
NIGHT SHADOWS(1984)
Bob Hopkins
ON STAGE EVERYBODY(1945); LUCKY STIFF, THE(1949); KID FROM LEFT FIELD, THE(1953); LET'S DO IT AGAIN(1953); SHE COULDN'T SAY NO(1954); I'LL CRY TOMORROW(1955); SON OF SINBAD(1955); TIGHT SPOT(1955); AUTUMN LEAVES(1956); CRASHING LAS VEGAS(1956); FLIGHT TO HONG KONG(1956); OPPOSITE SEX, THE(1956); GARMENT JUNGLE, THE(1957); JEANNE EAGELS(1957); NARCOTICS STORY, THE(1958); ERRAND BOY, THE(1961); UNDERWORLD U.S.A.(1961); SAINTLY SINNERS(1962)
Charles Hopkins
1984
REPO MAN(1984)
Chris Hopkins
1984
POWER, THE(1984), prod d
Clyde Hopkins
Silents
HELL-TO-PAY AUSTIN(1916); INTOLERANCE(1916); MATRIMANIAC, THE(1916)
Misc. Silents
GIRL OF THE TIMBER CLAIMS, THE(1917)
Elizabeth Hopkins
SIGN OF THE WOLF(1941), w
Ellen Hopkins
EFFECTS(1980), art d
George Hopkins
TELL ME IN THE SUNLIGHT(1967); CHEYENNE SOCIAL CLUB, THE(1970), set d; LOVE MACHINE, THE(1971), set d; DIRTY LITTLE BILLY(1972), set d; FORTY CARATS(1973), set d; DAY OF THE LOCUST, THE(1975), set d
Silents
INFERIOR SEX, THE(1920), art d; TOP OF NEW YORK, THE(1925), w
George James Hopkins
CASABLANCA(1942), set d; PRINCESS O'ROURKE(1943), set d; PASSAGE TO MARSEILLE(1944), set d; MILDRED PIERCE(1945), set d; ROUGHLY SPEAKING(1945), set d; MY REPUTATION(1946), set d; ONE MORE TOMORROW(1946),

set d; SUSPENSE(1946), set d; LIFE WITH FATHER(1947), set d; TASK FORCE(1949),
set d; DALLAS(1950), set d; PERFECT STRANGERS(1950), set d; I'LL SEE YOU IN
MY DREAMS(1951), set d; STRANGERS ON A TRAIN(1951), set d; STREETCAR
NAMED DESIRE, A(1951), set d; IRON MISTRESS, THE(1952), set d; I CON-
FESS(1953), art d, set d; DIAL M FOR MURDER(1954), art d; STAR IS BORN,
A(1954), set d; EAST OF EDEN(1955), set d; SINCERELY YOURS(1955), set d;
AUNTIE MAME(1958), set d; TOO MUCH, TOO SOON(1958), set d; FEVER IN THE
BLOOD, A(1961), set d; PORTRAIT OF A MOBSTER(1961), set d; DAYS OF WINE
AND ROSES(1962), set d; MUSIC MAN, THE(1962), set d; ISLAND OF LOVE(1963),
set d; PALM SPRINGS WEEKEND(1963), set d; RAMPAGE(1963), set d; MY FAIR
LADY(1964), set d; GREAT RACE, THE(1965), set d; INSIDE DAISY CLOVER(1965),
set d; NONE BUT THE BRAVE(1965, U.S./Jap.), set d; NOT WITH MY WIFE, YOU
DON'T!(1966), set d; WHO'S AFRAID OF VIRGINIA WOOLF?(1966), set d; HO-
TEL(1967), set d; WAIT UNTIL DARK(1967), set d; HELLO, DOLLY!(1969), set d;
R.P.M.(1970), set d; 1776(1972), set d

Georgia Hopkins
Misc. Silents
BACHELOR APARTMENTS(1920)
Harold Hopkins
MR. MOTO TAKES A VACATION(1938); SHINING VICTORY(1941); TWO-FACED
WOMAN(1941); AGE OF CONSENT(1969, Austral.); DEMONSTRATOR(1971, Aus.);
ADAM'S WOMAN(1972, Austral.); DON'S PARTY(1976, Aus.); CLUB, THE(1980, Aus.);
PICTURE SHOW MAN, THE(1980, Aus.); GALLIPOLI(1981, Aus.); BUDDIES(1983,
Aus.); MONKEY GRIP(1983, Aus.)
1984
FANTASY MAN(1984, Aus.)
Jack Hopkins
Silents
ADVENTURES OF KITTY COBB, THE(1914); IN THE STRETCH(1914); LIFE
WITHOUT SOUL(1916); OPEN YOUR EYES(1919); SCARAB RING, THE(1921)
Misc. Silents
BITTER TRUTH(1917); BROKEN SILENCE, THE(1922); MOTHER MACHREE(1922)
Jim Hopkins
SPASMS(1983, Can.), makeup
Joan Hopkins
WE DIVE AT DAWN(1943, Brit.); AFFAIRS OF A ROGUE, THE(1949, Brit.); MAN ON
THE RUN(1949, Brit.); TEMPTATION HARBOR(1949, Brit.); WEAKER SEX,
THE(1949, Brit.); DOUBLE CONFESSION(1953, Brit.)
John Hopkins
THUNDERBALL(1965, Brit.), w; TWO LEFT FEET(1965, Brit.), w; ASTRO-ZOM-
BIES, THE(1969); NED KELLY(1970, Brit.); VIRGIN SOLDIERS, THE(1970, Brit.), w;
OFFENSE, THE(1973, Brit.), w; MURDER BY DECREE(1979, Brit.), w
1984
POWER, THE(1984), w
Silents
AMERICAN MAID(1917); CHALLENGE ACCEPTED, THE(1918); WILD HO-
NEY(1919); LOYAL LIVES(1923)
Misc. Silents
MY COUNTRY FIRST(1916)
Julia Hopkins
FALCON AND THE CO-EDS, THE(1943)
Julie Hopkins
OPERATION BULLSHINE(1963, Brit.); LIFE IN DANGER(1964, Brit.)
Karen Lee Hopkins
GOING BERSERK(1983)
Karen Leigh Hopkins
1984
CLOAK AND DAGGER(1984)
Katherine Hopkins
Misc. Talkies
CAPTURE OF BIGFOOT, THE(1979)
Kenneth Hopkins
PHANTOM LADY(1944), cos
Kenyon Hopkins
BABY DOLL(1956), m; STRANGE ONE, THE(1957), m, md; 12 ANGRY MEN(1957),
m; FUGITIVE KIND, THE(1960), m; WILD RIVER(1960), m; HUSTLER, THE(1961),
m; WILD IN THE COUNTRY(1961), m; YELLOW CANARY, THE(1963), m; LI-
LITH(1964), m, md; MISTER BUDDWING(1966), m; THIS PROPERTY IS CON-
DEMNED(1966), m; DOCTOR, YOU'VE GOT TO BE KIDDING(1967), m; LOVELY
WAY TO DIE, A(1968), m; DOWNHILL RACER(1969), m; FIRST TIME, THE(1969), m;
TREE, THE(1969), m
Leah Marie Hopkins
SILENCE OF THE NORTH(1981, Can.)
Lightnin' Hopkins
COME BACK BABY(1968), m
Linda Hopkins
EDUCATION OF SONNY CARSON, THE(1974); HONKYTONK MAN(1982)
1984
GO TELL IT ON THE MOUNTAIN(1984)
Mary Hopkins
GETTING OVER(1981)
May Hopkins
Silents
EVERYBODY'S GIRL(1918); DIANE OF STAR HOLLOW(1921); NIGHT HORSE-
MAN, THE(1921)
Miriam Hopkins
FAST AND LOOSE(1930); SMILING LIEUTENANT, THE(1931); 24 HOURS(1931);
DANCERS IN THE DARK(1932); DR. JEKYLL AND MR. HYDE(1932); TROUBLE IN
PARADISE(1932); TWO KINDS OF WOMEN(1932); WORLD AND THE FLESH,
THE(1932); DESIGN FOR LIVING(1933); STORY OF TEMPLE DRAKE, THE(1933);
STRANGER'S RETURN(1933); ALL OF ME(1934); RICHEST GIRL IN THE WORLD,
THE(1934); SHE LOVES ME NOT(1934); BARBARY COAST(1935); BECKY
SHARP(1935); SPLENDOR(1935); THESE THREE(1936); MEN ARE NOT GODS(1937,
Brit.); WISE GIRL(1937); WOMAN CHASES MAN(1937); WOMAN I LOVE, THE(1937);
OLD MAID, THE(1939); LADY WITH RED HAIR(1940); VIRGINIA CITY(1940);
GENTLEMAN AFTER DARK, A(1942); OLD ACQUAINTANCE(1943); HEIRESS,
THE(1949); MATING SEASON, THE(1951); CARRIE(1952); OUTCASTS OF POKER
FLAT, THE(1952); CHILDREN'S HOUR, THE(1961); FANNY HILL: MEMOIRS OF A
WOMAN OF PLEASURE zero(1965); CHASE, THE(1966)

Muriel Hopkins
SET, THE(1970, Aus.)
Nan Hopkins
THERE AIN'T NO JUSTICE(1939, Brit.)
Paul Hopkins
PROMOTER, THE(1952, Brit.)
Peggy Hopkins
Silents
DIMPLES(1916)
Misc. Silents
WOMAN AND THE LAW(1918)
R.E. Hopkins
FLYING HIGH(1931), w
Rhoda Leigh Hopkins
Misc. Talkies
COVER GIRL MODELS(1975)
Rhonda Leigh Hopkins
TIDAL WAVE(1975, U.S./Jap.); SUMMER SCHOOL TEACHERS(1977)
Robert Hopkins
CAUGHT SHORT(1930), w; FLORODORA GIRL, THE(1930), w; CHIEF, THE(1933),
w; SAN FRANCISCO(1936), w; SARATOGA(1937), w; NO WAY BACK(1976), ph
Silents
OLD CLOTHES(1925), t; ONE YEAR TO LIVE(1925), t; BETTER 'OLE, THE(1926), t;
CARNIVAL GIRL, THE(1926), t; AMERICAN BEAUTY(1927), t; LAW OF THE
RANGE, THE(1928), t; SHADOWS OF THE NIGHT(1928), t; SMART SET, THE(1928),
t; HONEYMOON(1929), t; SPITE MARRIAGE(1929), t
Robert E. Hopkins
LOVE IN THE ROUGH(1930), w; PARLOR, BEDROOM AND BATH(1931), w; POLIT-
ICS(1931), w; REDUCING(1931), w; SIDEWALKS OF NEW YORK(1931), w; WHAT!
NO BEER?(1933), w
Shirley Knight Hopkins
SECRETS(1971)
Speed Hopkins
MIDSUMMER NIGHT'S SEX COMEDY, A(1982), art d; ZELIG(1983), art d
1984
FALLING IN LOVE(1984), art d; NATURAL, THE(1984), art d
Steve Hopkins
JOE HILL(1971, Swed./U.S.), w
Steven Hopkins
MATTER OF MORALS, A(1961, U.S./Swed.), p
Tom J. Hopkins
Silents
LURE OF THE WILD, THE(1925), w; TAXI MYSTERY, THE(1926), w
Trinidad Hopkins
TRIAL OF BILLY JACK, THE(1974)
Una Hopkins
Silents
DUCKS AND DRAKES(1921), art d
Una Nixon Hopkins
Silents
OH, LADY, LADY(1920), art d
Joey Hopkinson
MELODY AND ROMANCE(1937, Brit.); DOWN OUR ALLEY(1939, Brit.)
Gordon Hopkirk
Silents
FOUR MEN IN A VAN(1921, Brit.); SKIPPER'S WOOING, THE(1922, Brit.); NOTORI-
OUS MRS. CARRICK, THE(1924, Brit.)
Misc. Silents
PORT OF LOST SOULS(1924, Brit.); ISLAND OF DESPAIR, THE(1926, Brit.);
SAHARA LOVE(1926, Brit.)
Hubert Gordon Hopkirk
Silents
ERNEST MALTRAVERS(1920, Brit.)
Misc. Silents
ERNEST MALTRAVERS(1920, Brit.); SYBIL(1921, Brit.)
Mark Hopley
SPOTS ON MY LEOPARD, THE(1974, S. Africa)
Gerald Hopman
DEVIL'S RAIN, THE(1975, U.S./Mex.), w
Ulrich Hopmann
NOT RECONCILED, OR "ONLY VIOLENCE HELPS WHERE IT RULES"(1969, Ger.)
Denis Hoppe
WRONG IS RIGHT(1982)
Eva Maria Hoppe
DECISION BEFORE DAWN(1951)
Fritz Hoppe
YOUNG LORD, THE(1970, Ger.)
Marianne Hoppe
TEN LITTLE INDIANS(1965, Brit.); TREASURE OF SILVER LAKE(1965, Fr./Ger./
Yugo.)
Michael Hoppe
1984
MISUNDERSTOOD(1984), m
Rolf Hoppe
MEPHISTO(1981, Ger.)
Gynthia Hoppenfeld
WHY WOULD I LIE(1980)
Hopper
LAST MOVIE, THE(1971), ed
B.J. Hopper
TOY, THE(1982)
Bill Hopper
CASTLE ON THE HUDSON(1940); MALTESE FALCON, THE(1941); ACROSS THE
PACIFIC(1942); SECRET ENEMIES(1942); SITTING BULL(1954)
De Wolf Hopper [William Hopper]
MURDER WITH PICTURES(1936); LARCENY ON THE AIR(1937); COWBOY QUAR-
TERBACK(1939); NANCY DREW AND THE HIDDEN STAIRCASE(1939); OLD MAID,
THE(1939); PRIDE OF THE BLUEGRASS(1939); RETURN OF DR. X, THE(1939);
FLIGHT ANGELS(1940); LADIES MUST LIVE(1940); TEAR GAS SQUAD(1940);
VIRGINIA CITY(1940); AFFECTIONATELY YOURS(1941); BODY DISAPPEARS,

THE(1941); BULLETS FOR O'HARA(1941); DIVE BOMBER(1941); FLIGHT FROM DESTINY(1941); HERE COMES HAPPINESS(1941); KNOCKOUT(1941); MANPOWER(1941); LADY GANGSTER(1942); LARCENY, INC.(1942); MURDER ON THE WATERFRONT(1943); MYSTERIOUS DOCTOR, THE(1943); HIGH AND THE MIGHTY, THE(1954)

Misc. Silents
CASEY AT THE BAT(1916); DON QUIXOTE(1916); MR. GOODE, THE SAMARITAN(1916); STRANDED(1916); SUNSHINE DAD(1916)

Deborah Hopper
ALL THE RIGHT MOVES(1983), cos
1984
REVENGE OF THE NERDS(1984), cos; TIGHTROPE(1984), cos

Dennis Hopper
I DIED A THOUSAND TIMES(1955); REBEL WITHOUT A CAUSE(1955); GIANT(1956); GUNFIGHT AT THE O.K. CORRAL(1957); STORY OF MANKIND, THE(1957); FROM HELL TO TEXAS(1958); YOUNG LAND, THE(1959); KEY WITNESS(1960); NIGHT TIDE(1963); SONS OF KATIE ELDER, THE(1965); QUEEN OF BLOOD(1966); COOL HAND LUKE(1967); GLORY STOMPERS, THE(1967); TRIP, THE(1967); HANG'EM HIGH(1968); PANIC IN THE CITY(1968); EASY RIDER(1969), a, d, w; TRUE GRIT(1969); LAST MOVIE, THE(1971), a, d, w; KID BLUE(1973); MAD DOG MORGAN(1976,Aus.); AMERICAN FRIEND, THE(1977, Ger.); TRACKS(1977); APOCALYPSE NOW(1979); KING OF THE MOUNTAIN(1981); HUMAN HIGHWAY(1982); OUT OF THE BLUE(1982), a, d; OSTERMAN WEEKEND, THE(1983); RUMBLE FISH(1983)
Misc. Talkies
REBORN(1978)

E. Mason Hopper
CARNATION KID(1929), d; SQUARE SHOULDERS(1929), d; THEIR OWN DESIRE(1929), d; WISE GIRLS(1930), d; ALIAS MARY SMITH(1932), d; HER MAD NIGHT(1932), d; NO LIVING WITNESS(1932), d; SHOP ANGEL(1932), d; MALAY NIGHTS(1933), d; ONE YEAR LATER(1933), d; CURTAIN AT EIGHT(1934), d; HONG KONG NIGHTS(1935), d; SUNSET BOULEVARD(1950)

Silents
AS MEN LOVE(1917), d; TAR HEEL WARRIOR, THE(1917), d; ANSWER, THE(1918), d; AS THE SUN WENT DOWN(1919), d; ALL'S FAIR IN LOVE(1921), d; FROM THE GROUND UP(1921), d; HUNGRY HEARTS(1922), d; DADDY(1923), d; JANICE MEREDITH(1924), d; ALMOST A LADY(1926), d; NIGHT BRIDE, THE(1927), d; RUSH HOUR, THE(1927), d

Misc. Silents
LABYRINTH, THE(1915), d; BIRTH OF CHARACTER, THE(1916), d; GLORIANA(1916), d; RIGHT DIRECTION, THE(1916), d; SELFISH WOMAN, THE(1916), d; FIREFLY OF TOUGH LUCK, THE(1917), d; HIDDEN SPRING, THE(1917), d; PRISON WITHOUT WALLS, THE(1917), d; SPIRIT OF ROMANCE, THE(1917), d; BOSTON BLACKIE'S LITTLE PAL(1918), d; HER AMERICAN HUSBAND(1918), d; MYSTIC FACES(1918), d; UNEXPECTED PLACES(1918), d; WITHOUT HONOR(1918), d; COME AGAIN SMITH(1919), d; IT'S A GREAT LIFE(1920), d; DANGEROUS CURVE AHEAD(1921), d; HOLD YOUR HORSES(1921), d; BROTHERS UNDER THE SKIN(1922), d; LOVE PIKER, THE(1923), d; GREAT WHITE WAY, THE(1924), d; CROWED HOUR, THE(1925), d; PARIS AT MIDNIGHT(1926), d; UP IN MABEL'S ROOM(1926), d; GETTING GERTIE'S GARTER(1927), d; MY FRIEND FROM INDIA(1927), d; WISE WIFE, THE(1927), d; BLONDE FOR A NIGHT, A(1928), d

Edna Wallace Hopper
Silents
BY WHOSE HAND?(1916)
Misc. Silents
PERILS OF DIVORCE(1916)

Frank Hopper
Silents
ROUGH RIDERS, THE(1927)

Guillan Hopper
EXPERT'S OPINION(1935, Brit.), w

Hal Hopper
KITTEN WITH A WHIP(1964); MOTOR PSYCHO(1965), w; ROPE OF FLESH(1965); SHALAKO(1968, Brit.), w

Harold Hopper
LUXURY LINER(1948)

Heather Hopper
FEAR STRIKES OUT(1957); FUNNY FACE(1957)

Hedda Hopper
HALF-MARRIAGE(1929); LAST OF MRS. CHEYNEY, THE(1929); RACKETEER, THE(1929); SONG OF KENTUCKY(1929); BLUSHING BRIDES(1930); HIGH SOCIETY BLUES(1930); HOLIDAY(1930); LET US BE GAY(1930); MURDER WILL OUT(1930); OUR BLUSHING BRIDES(1930); SUCH MEN ARE DANGEROUS(1930); WAR NURSE(1930); COMMON LAW, THE(1931); EASIEST WAY, THE(1931); FLYING HIGH(1931); GOOD SPORT(1931); MEN CALL IT LOVE(1931); MYSTERY TRAIN(1931); PRODIGAL, THE(1931); REBOUND(1931); SHIPMATES(1931); TAILOR MADE MAN, A(1931); WEST OF BROADWAY(1931); AS YOU DESIRE ME(1932); DOWNSTAIRS(1932); MAN WHO PLAYED GOD, THE(1932); NIGHT WORLD(1932); SKYSCRAPER SOULS(1932); SPEAK EASILY(1932); UNWRITTEN LAW, THE(1932); BARBARIAN, THE(1933); BEAUTY FOR SALE(1933); MEN MUST FIGHT(1933); PILGRIMAGE(1933); BOMBAY MAIL(1934); LET'S BE RITZY(1934); LITTLE MAN, WHAT NOW?(1934); ALICE ADAMS(1935); I LIVE MY LIFE(1935); LADY TUBBS(1935); NO RANSOM(1935); ONE FRIGHTENED NIGHT(1935); SOCIETY FEVER(1935); THREE KIDS AND A QUEEN(1935); BUNKER BEAN(1936); DARK HOUR, THE(1936); DOUGHNUTS AND SOCIETY(1936); DRACULA'S DAUGHTER(1936); ARTISTS AND MODELS(1937); DANGEROUS HOLIDAY(1937); NOTHING SACRED(1937); TOPPER(1937); VOGUES OF 1938(1937); YOU CAN'T BUY LUCK(1937); DANGEROUS TO KNOW(1938); MAID'S NIGHT OUT(1938); TARZAN'S REVENGE(1938); THANKS FOR THE MEMORY(1938); LAUGH IT OFF(1939); MIDNIGHT(1939); THAT'S RIGHT-YOU'RE WRONG(1939); WHAT A LIFE(1939); WOMEN, THE(1939); CROSS COUNTRY ROMANCE(1940); QUEEN OF THE MOB(1940); I WANTED WINGS(1941); LIFE WITH HENRY(1941); REAP THE WILD WIND(1942); BREAKFAST IN HOLLYWOOD(1946); SUNSET BOULEVARD(1950); PEPE(1960); PATSY, THE(1964); OSCAR, THE(1966)
Silents
ISLE OF CONQUEST(1919); NEW YORK IDEA, THE(1920); SHERLOCK HOLMES(1922); HAS THE WORLD GONE MAD!(1923); RENO(1923); ANOTHER SCANDAL(1924); GAMBLING WIVES(1924); SNOB, THE(1924); BORROWED FINERY(1925); RAFFLES THE AMATEUR CRACKSMAN(1925); ZANDER THE GREAT(1925); CAVEMAN, THE(1926); DON JUAN(1926); PLEASURES OF THE

RICH(1926); SKINNER'S DRESS SUIT(1926); ADAM AND EVIL(1927); CHILDREN OF DIVORCE(1927); DROPKICK, THE(1927); MATINEE LADIES(1927); ONE WOMAN TO ANOTHER(1927); WINGS(1927); HAROLD TEEN(1928); LOVE AND LEARN(1928); RUNAWAY GIRLS(1928); WHIP WOMAN, THE(1928); GIRLS GONE WILD(1929)

Misc. Silents
BELOVED TRAITOR, THE(1918); THIRD DEGREE, THE(1919); MAN WHO LOST HIMSELF, THE(1920); CONCEIT(1921); HEEDLESS MOTHS(1921); WOMEN MEN MARRY(1922); HAPPINESS(1924); MIAMI(1924); HER MARKET VALUE(1925); TEASER, THE(1925); DANCE MADNESS(1926); LEW TYLER'S WIVES(1926); OBEY THE LAW(1926); RENO DIVORCE, A(1927); CHORUS KID, THE(1928); GREEN GRASS WIDOWS(1928); PORT OF MISSING GIRLS, THE(1928); UNDRESSED(1928)

Jerry Hopper
ATOMIC CITY, THE(1952), d; HURRICANE SMITH(1952), d; PONY EXPRESS(1953), d; ALASKA SEAS(1954), d; NAKED ALIBI(1954), d; SECRET OF THE INCAS(1954), d; ONE DESIRE(1955), d; PRIVATE WAR OF MAJOR BENSON, THE(1955), d; SMOKE SIGNAL(1955), d; SQUARE JUNGLE, THE(1955), d; EVERYTHING BUT THE TRUTH(1956), d; NEVER SAY GOODBYE(1956), d; SHARKFIGHTERS, THE(1956), d; TOY TIGER(1956), d; MISSOURI TRAVELER, THE(1958), d; BLUEPRINT FOR ROBBERY(1961), d; MADRON(1970, U.S./Israel), d

Mrs. De Wolf Hopper
Silents
INNER CHAMBER, THE(1921)

Victoria Hopper
CONSTANT NYMPH, THE(1933, Brit.); LORNA DOONE(1935, Brit.); LABURNUM GROVE(1936, Brit.); SCOTLAND YARD COMMANDS(1937, Brit.); MILL ON THE FLOSS(1939, Brit.); MOZART(1940, Brit.)

Wes Hopper
LUXURY LINER(1948); MILKMAN, THE(1950); SEALED CARGO(1951)

Wesley Hopper
DEVIL'S PLAYGROUND(1937); KISS THE BLOOD OFF MY HANDS(1948); KNOCK ON ANY DOOR(1949); SURRENDER(1950)

William Hopper [De Wolf Hopper]
ADVENTUROUS BLONDE(1937); FOOTLOOSE HEIRESS, THE(1937); LOVE IS ON THE AIR(1937); MR. DODD TAKES THE AIR(1937); OVER THE GOAL(1937); PUBLIC WEDDING(1937); DAREDEVIL DRIVERS(1938); MYSTERY HOUSE(1938); PATIENT IN ROOM 18, THE(1938); ESPIONAGE AGENT(1939); FIGHTING 69TH, THE(1940); INVISIBLE STRIPES(1940); KNUTE ROCKNE-ALL AMERICAN(1940); LADY WITH RED HAIR(1940); MAN WHO TALKED TOO MUCH, THE(1940); SANTA FE TRAIL(1940); 'TIL WE MEET AGAIN(1940); BRIDE CAME C.O.D., THE(1941); FOOTSTEPS IN THE DARK(1941); HIGH SIERRA(1941); INTERNATIONAL SQUADRON(1941); MANPOWER(1941); NAVY BLUES(1941); DESPERATE JOURNEY(1942); GENTLEMAN JIM(1942); JUKE GIRL(1942); MALE ANIMAL, THE(1942); THEY DIED WITH THEIR BOOTS ON(1942); YANKEE DOODLE DANDY(1942); AIR FORCE(1943); THIS IS MY LOVE(1954); TRACK OF THE CAT(1954); CONQUEST OF SPACE(1955); ONE DESIRE(1955); REBEL WITHOUT A CAUSE(1955); ROBBER'S ROOST(1955); BAD SEED, THE(1956); FIRST TEXAN, THE(1956); GOODBYE, MY LADY(1956); DEADLY MANTIS, THE(1957); SLIM CARTER(1957); 20 MILLION MILES TO EARTH(1957)

Marie Hopps
FAR FROM THE MADDING CROWD(1967, Brit.)

Stewart Hopps
WICKER MAN, THE(1974, Brit.), ch

Walter Hopsburgh
ONE MORE TIME(1970, Brit.)

Al Hopson
HIRED HAND, THE(1971); LAST MOVIE, THE(1971); SILENT MOVIE(1976); HIGH ANXIETY(1977)
1984
RACING WITH THE MOON(1984)

Nicholas Hopson
Misc. Silents
IN THE GLOAMING(1919, Brit.)

Violet Hopson
SELF-MADE LADY(1932, Brit.); ONE PRECIOUS YEAR(1933, Brit.)
Silents
HER BOY(1915, Brit.); MOLLY BAWN(1916, Brit.); MUNITION GIRL'S ROMANCE, A(1917, Brit.); RAGGED MESSENGER, THE(1917, Brit.); WARE CASE, THE(1917, Brit.); MISSING THE TIDE(1918, Brit.); SNARE, THE(1918, Brit.); KISSING CUP'S RACE(1920, Brit.); WHEN GREEK MEETS GREEK(1922, Brit.); BEAUTIFUL KITTY(1923, Brit.); DAUGHTER OF LOVE, A(1925, Brit.)
Misc. Silents
VICAR OF WAKEFIELD, THE(1913, Brit.); GREAT POISON MYSTERY, THE(1914, Brit.); HEART OF MIDLOTHIAN, THE(1914, Brit.); BARNABY RUDGE(1915); MAN WHO STAYED AT HOME, THE(1915, Brit.); NIGHTBIRDS OF LONDON, THE(1915, Brit.); WHITE HOPE, THE(1915, Brit.); BUNCH OF VIOLETS, A(1916, Brit.); MARRIAGE OF WILLIAM ASHE, THE(1916, Brit.); SOWING THE WIND(1916, Brit.); TRELAWNEY OF THE WELLS(1916, Brit.); COBWEB, THE(1917, Brit.); ETERNAL TRIANGLE, THE(1917, Brit.); GAMBLE FOR LOVE, A(1917, Brit.); HER MARRIAGE LINES(1917, Brit.); HOUSE OPPOSITE, THE(1917, Brit.); FORTUNE AT STAKE, A(1918, Brit.); TURF CONSPIRACY, A(1918, Brit.); DAUGHTER OF EVE, A(1919, Brit.); HEARTS AND SADDLES(1919, Brit.); IN THE GLOAMING(1919, Brit.); IRRESISTIBLE FLAPPER, THE(1919, Brit.); SNOW IN THE DESERT(1919, Brit.); SOUL'S CRUCIFIXION, A(1919, Brit.); CASE OF LADY CAMBER, THE(1920, Brit.); HER SON(1920, Brit.); KISSING CUP'S RACE(1920, Brit.); IMPERFECT LOVER, THE(1921, Brit.); SPORTSMAN'S WIFE, A(1921, Brit.); VI OF SMITH'S ALLEY(1921, Brit.); SCARLET LADY, THE(1922, Brit.); SON OF KISSING CUP(1922, Brit.); WHITE HOPE, THE(1922, Brit.); LADY OWNER, THE(1923, Brit.); WHAT PRICE LOVING CUP?(1923, Brit.); GREAT TURF MYSTERY, THE(1924, Brit.); STIRRUP CUP SENSATION, THE(1924, Brit.); WIDECOMBE FAIR(1928, Brit.)

Nancy Hopton
SILKWOOD(1983)

Russell Hopton
CALL OF THE FLESH(1930); COLLEGE LOVERS(1930); MIN AND BILL(1930); REMOTE CONTROL(1930); ARROWSMITH(1931); BLONDE CRAZY(1931); DANCE, FOOLS, DANCE(1931); MIRACLE WOMAN, THE(1931); RECKLESS LIVING(1931); STAR WITNESS(1931); STREET SCENE(1931); AIR MAIL(1932); DISCARDED LOVERS(1932); DRIFTER, THE(1932); FAMOUS FERGUSON CASE, THE(1932); LAW AND ORDER(1932); MAN WHO PLAYED GOD, THE(1932); NIGHT WORLD(1932); ONCE IN A LIFETIME(1932); RADIO PATROL(1932); TOM BROWN OF CUL-

VER(1932); DESTINATION UNKNOWN(1933); ELMER THE GREAT(1933); I'M NO ANGEL(1933); LADY KILLER(1933); LAUGHTER IN HELL(1933), w; LITTLE GIANT, THE(1933); ONE YEAR LATER(1933); SECRET OF THE BLUE ROOM(1933); BORN TO BE BAD(1934); CURTAIN AT EIGHT(1934); DESIRABLE(1934); GIRL FROM MISSOURI, THE(1934); GOOD DAME(1934); HALF A SINNER(1934); HE WAS HER MAN(1934); I SELL ANYTHING(1934); MEN IN WHITE(1934); SUCCESSFUL FAILURE, A(1934); TAKE THE STAND(1934); CAR 99(1935); FALSE PRETENSES(1935); FRISCO WATERFRONT(1935); G-MEN(1935); HEADLINE WOMAN, THE(1935); NORTHERN FRONTIER(1935); SCHOOL FOR GIRLS(1935); STAR OF MIDNIGHT(1935); TIMES SQUARE LADY(1935); WINGS IN THE DARK(1935); WORLD ACCUSES, THE(1935); BELOW THE DEADLINE(1936); CHEERS OF THE CROWD(1936); DEATH FROM A DISTANCE(1936); LAST OUTLAW, THE(1936); ROSE OF THE RANCHO(1936); SONG OF THE TRAIL(1936), d; ANGEL'S HOLIDAY(1937); BEWARE OF LADIES(1937); HIGH, WIDE AND HANDSOME(1937); IDOL OF THE CROWDS(1937); ONE MILE FROM HEAVEN(1937); WE WHO ARE ABOUT TO DIE(1937); WITH LOVE AND KISSES(1937); CRIME TAKES A HOLIDAY(1938); LETTER OF INTRODUCTION(1938); MADE FOR EACH OTHER(1939); MUTINY IN THE BIG HOUSE(1939); RENEGADE TRAIL(1939); SAINT STRIKES BACK, THE(1939); TORTURE SHIP(1939); NEVADA(1944); NIGHT OF ADVENTURE, A(1944); TALL IN THE SADDLE(1944); YOUTH RUNS WILD(1944); JOHNNY ANGEL(1945); WEST OF THE PECOS(1945); ZOMBIES ON BROADWAY(1945)

Misc. Talkies

BACK PAGE(1934); CIRCUS SHADOWS(1935); VALLEY OF WANTED MEN(1935)

Silents

ELLA CINDERS(1926)

Avery Hopwood

GOLD DIGGERS OF BROADWAY(1929), w; BAT WHISPERS, THE(1930), w; FAST AND LOOSE(1930), w; HER WEDDING NIGHT(1930), w; THIS IS THE NIGHT(1932), w; GOLD DIGGERS OF 1933(1933), w; NIGHT OF THE GARTER(1933, Brit.), w; GETTING GERTIE'S GARTER(1945), w; PAINTING THE CLOUDS WITH SUNSHINE(1951), w; BAT, THE(1959), w

Silents

JUDY FORGOT(1915), w; OUR LITTLE WIFE(1918), w; GUILTY OF LOVE(1920), w; LITTLE CLOWN, THE(1921), w; GOLD DIGGERS, THE(1923), w; MISS BLUEBEARD(1925), w; NOBODY'S WIDOW(1927), w

Keith Hopwood

HOLD ON(1966); MRS. BROWN, YOU'VE GOT A LOVELY DAUGHTER(1968, Brit.)

Robin Hopwood

MELODY(1971, Brit.)

Anthony Hora

FABULOUS WORLD OF JULES VERNE, THE(1961, Czech.), ph

John Hora

MAURIE(1973), ph; FURTHER ADVENTURES OF THE WILDERNESS FAMILY–PART TWO(1978), ph; HOWLING, THE(1981), ph; LIAR'S MOON(1982), ph; TWILIGHT ZONE–THE MOVIE(1983), ph

1984

GREMLINS(1984), ph

Johnny Horace

STORMY WEATHER(1943)

Horace Heidt and His Orchestra

POT O' GOLD(1941)

Horace Sheldon and his Orchestra

LIEUTENANT DARING, RN(1935, Brit.); VARIETY(1935, Brit.); SHIPMATES O' MINE(1936, Brit.)

Horace Sheldon's Orchestra

KING OF HEARTS(1936, Brit.); MELODY OF MY HEART(1936, Brit.)

Galli Horacio

1984

DELIVERY BOYS(1984)

Antonin Horak

JOURNEY TO THE BEGINNING OF TIME(1966, Czech), ph

Edwin Horak

BLACK SPIDER, THE(1983, Swit.), ph

Barbra Horan

MY FAVORITE YEAR(1982)

Bonnie Horan

WAITRESS(1982)

Charles Horan

Silents

SPLENDID LIE, THE(1922), d&w; NO MOTHER TO GUIDE HER(1923), d; ATTA BOY!(1926), w; PLAY SAFE(1927), w; SPIDER WEBS(1927), w

Misc. Silents

TABLES TURNED(1915), d; BLINDNESS OF LOVE, THE(1916), d; QUITTER, THE(1916), d; ROSE OF THE ALLEY(1916), d; UPHEAVAL, THE(1916), d; LOVE, HATE AND A WOMAN(1921), d; YOU FIND IT EVERYWHERE(1921), d; DOES IT PAY?(1923), d

Charles T. Horan

Misc. Silents

MAN'S PLAYTHING(1920), d

Charles Thomas Horan

Silents

POLLY OF THE CIRCUS(1917), d

Hillary Horan

SATAN'S CHEERLEADERS(1977); SEED OF INNOCENCE(1980); YOUNG DOCTORS IN LOVE(1982)

James Horan

CLOWN, THE(1953)

1984

CHATTANOOGA CHOO CHOO(1984)

James W. Horan

FAR COUNTRY, THE(1955)

Joe Horan

MAKE A FACE(1971)

John Horan

RISING OF THE MOON, THE(1957, Ireland)

Kathy Horan

GREEN SLIME, THE(1969)

Barbara Horawianka

ECHO, THE(1964, Pol.); PASSENGER, THE(1970, Pol.)

Attila Horbiger

AFFAIRS OF MAUPASSANT(1938, Aust.)

Paul Horbiger

TREMENDOUSLY RICH MAN, A(1932, Ger.); STORY OF VICKIE, THE(1958, Aust.); CITY OF SECRETS(1963, Ger.)

Silents

SPIES(1929, Ger.)

Michael Hordern

HELL, HEAVEN OR HOBOKEN(1958, Brit.); GENGHIS KHAN(U.S./Brit./Ger./Yugo); GIRL MUST LIVE, A(1941, Brit.); GIRL IN A MILLION, A(1946, Brit.); SCHOOL FOR SECRETS(1946, Brit.); YEARS BETWEEN, THE(1947, Brit.); GIRL IN THE PAINTING, THE(1948, Brit.); HIDEOUT(1948, Brit.); MINE OWN EXECUTIONER(1948, Brit.); NIGHT BEAT(1948, Brit.); PASSPORT TO PIMLICO(1949, Brit.); ASTONISHED HEART, THE(1950, Brit.); GOOD TIME GIRL(1950, Brit.); HIGHLY DANGEROUS(1950, Brit.); THIRD TIME LUCKY(1950, Brit.); TRIO(1950, Brit.); CHRISTMAS CAROL, A(1951, Brit.); FLESH AND BLOOD(1951, Brit.); TOM BROWN'S SCHOOLDAYS(1951, Brit.); HOUR OF THIRTEEN, THE(1952); MAGIC BOX, THE(1952, Brit.); PROMOTER, THE(1952, Brit.); STORY OF ROBIN HOOD, THE(1952, Brit.); TRAIN OF EVENTS(1952, Brit.); BOTH SIDES OF THE LAW(1953, Brit.); FORBIDDEN CARGO(1954, Brit.); HEART OF THE MATTER, THE(1954, Brit.); PERSONAL AFFAIR(1954, Brit.); YOU KNOW WHAT SAILORS ARE(1954, Brit.); CONSTANT HUSBAND, THE(1955, Brit.); NIGHT MY NUMBER CAME UP, THE(1955, Brit.); STORM OVER THE NILE(1955, Brit.); THE BEACHCOMBER(1955, Brit.); WARRIORS, THE(1955); WICKED WIFE(1955, Brit.); ALEXANDER THE GREAT(1956); MAN WHO NEVER WAS, THE(1956, Brit.); PACIFIC DESTINY(1956, Brit.); BABY AND THE BATTLESHIP, THE(1957, Brit.); SPANISH GARDENER, THE(1957, Span.); GIRLS AT SEA(1958, Brit.); I ACCUSE(1958, Brit.); SPANIARD'S CURSE, THE(1958, Brit.); WINDOM'S WAY(1958, Brit.); SINK THE BISMARCK!(1960, Brit.); EL CID(1961, U.S./Ital.); MAN IN THE MOON(1961, Brit.); MALAGA(1962, Brit.); CLEOPATRA(1963); MACBETH(1963); V.I.P.s, THE(1963, Brit.); SPY WHO CAME IN FROM THE COLD, THE(1965, Brit.); YELLOW ROLLS-ROYCE, THE(1965, Brit.); CAST A GIANT SHADOW(1966); FUNNY THING HAPPENED ON THE WAY TO THE FORUM, A(1966); KHARTOUM(1966, Brit.); HOW I WON THE WAR(1967, Brit.); I'LL NEVER FORGET WHAT'S 'IS NAME(1967, Brit.); JOKERS, THE(1967, Brit.); TAMING OF THE SHREW, THE(1967, U.S./Ital.); WHERE EAGLES DARE(1968, Brit.); ANNE OF THE THOUSAND DAYS(1969, Brit.); BED SITTING ROOM, THE(1969, Brit.); SOME WILL, SOME WON'T(1970, Brit.); GIRL STROKE BOY(1971, Brit.); UP POMPEII(1971, Brit.); DEMONS OF THE MIND(1972, Brit.); PIED PIPER, THE(1972, Brit.); POSSESSION OF JOEL DELANEY, THE(1972); ENGLAND MADE ME(1973, Brit.); MACKINTOSH MAN, THE(1973, Brit.); THEATRE OF BLOOD(1973, Brit.); BARRY LYNDON(1975, Brit.); DR. SYN, ALIAS THE SCARECROW(1975); LUCKY LADY(1975); MR. QUILP(1975, Brit.); ROYAL FLASH(1975, Brit.); SLIPPER AND THE ROSE, THE(1976, Brit.); JOSEPH ANDREWS(1977, Brit.); MEDUSA TOUCH, THE(1978, Brit.); WATERSHIP DOWN(1978, Brit.); WILDCATS OF ST. TRINIAN'S, THE(1980, Brit.); GANDHI(1982); MISSIONARY, THE(1982); YELLOWBEARD(1983)

Bill Te Hore

PICTURES(1982, New Zealand)

Jitka Horejsi

END OF AUGUST AT THE HOTEL OZONE, THE(1967, Czech.)

Stephen Horelick

MADMAN(1982), m

Jay Horenstein

1984

AMERICAN TABOO(1984), a, w

Laszlo Horesnyi

FORBIDDEN RELATIONS(1983, Hung.)

Erzsebet Horeszku

FATHER(1967, Hung.)

Paul Horgan

DISTANT TRUMPET, A(1964), w

Patrick Horgan

EVIL OF FRANKENSTEIN, THE(1964, Brit.); THOMAS CROWN AFFAIR, THE(1968)

Jack Horger

DR. BLACK AND MR. HYDE(1976), ed; FRISCO KID, THE(1979), ed

John C. Horger

COLD TURKEY(1971), ed; BATTLE FOR THE PLANET OF THE APES(1973), ed; SEVEN UPS, THE(1973), ed; THIEF WHO CAME TO DINNER, THE(1973), ed; SMALL TOWN IN TEXAS, A(1976), ed

John Horger

GRAVY TRAIN, THE(1974), ed

Kenichi Horie

ALONE ON THE PACIFIC(1964, Jap.), w

Shiro Horie

PRODIGAL SON, THE(1964, Jap.), p

Hiromichi Horikawa

ETERNITY OF LOVE(1961, Jap.), d, w; NAKED GENERAL, THE(1964, Jap.), d; PRESSURE OF GUILT(1964, Jap.), d; PRODIGAL SON, THE(1964, Jap.), d; BEAUTIFUL SWINDLERS, THE(1967, Fr./Ital./Jap./Neth.), d; GOODBYE, MOSCOW(1968, Jap.), d; SUN ABOVE, DEATH BELOW(1969, Jap.), d

Masanori Horimoto

ISLAND, THE(1962, Jap.)

Miss A. Horine

Silents

GANGSTERS OF NEW YORK, THE(1914)

Tad Horino

DIMENSION 5(1966); GO TELL THE SPARTANS(1978); GALAXINA(1980); UNCOMMON VALOR(1983)

Kaida Horiuchi

SAVAGE INNOCENTS, THE(1960, Brit.)

Vladimir Horka

ROCKET TO NOWHERE(1962, Czech.)

H.D. Horkheimer

Misc. Silents

POWER OF EVIL, THE(1916), d

H.M. & E.D. Horkheimer
Misc. Silents
SPELLBOUND(1916), d
H.M. Horkheimer
Misc. Silents
POWER OF EVIL, THE(1916), d
Franz Horky
ECSTASY(1940, Czech.), p, w
Cathy Horlan
GOKE, BODYSNATCHER FROM HELL(1968, Jap.)
Sidney Horler
TWO'S COMPANY(1939, Brit.), w
Sydney Horler
HOUSE OF SECRETS(1929), w; HOUSE OF SECRETS, THE(1937), w
Joanna Horlock
CAUGHT IN THE NET(1960, Brit.)
Arthur Horman
MEANEST GAL IN TOWN, THE(1934), w; THIS IS THE LIFE(1935), w; WELCOME HOME(1935), w; DARK WATERS(1944), w
Arthur T Horman
CALL A MESSENGER(1939), w
Arthur T. Horman
GRAND OLD GIRL(1935), w; BRIDGE OF SIGHS(1936), w; CRIME PATROL, THE(1936), w; EASY MONEY(1936), w; IT COULDN'T HAVE HAPPENED–BUT IT DID(1936), w; TANGO(1936), w; THREE OF A KIND(1936), w; BIG SHOT, THE(1937), w; SHADOW, THE(1937), w; YOU CAN'T BUY LUCK(1937), w; DOUBLE DANGER(1938), w; LONE WOLF IN PARIS, THE(1938), w; QUICK MONEY(1938), w; WHEN G-MEN STEP IN(1938), w; BEHIND PRISON GATES(1939), w; CODE OF THE STREETS(1939), w; FOR LOVE OR MONEY(1939), w; LIFE RETURNS(1939), w; MISSING EVIDENCE(1939), w; MY SON IS A CRIMINAL(1939), w; SMASHING THE SPY RING(1939), w; SOCIETY SMUGGLERS(1939), w; THEY ASKED FOR IT(1939), w; ARGENTINE NIGHTS(1940), w; GIVE US WINGS(1940), w; I CAN'T GIVE YOU ANYTHING BUT LOVE, BABY(1940), w; OH JOHNNY, HOW YOU CAN LOVE!(1940), w; SLIGHTLY TEMPTED(1940), w; YOU'RE NOT SO TOUGH(1940), w; BANDIT TRAIL, THE(1941), w; BUCK PRIVATES(1941), w; HELLO SUCKER(1941), w; IN THE NAVY(1941), w; NAVY BLUES(1941), w; OBLIGING YOUNG LADY(1941), w; CAPTAINS OF THE CLOUDS(1942), w; DESPERATE JOURNEY(1942), w; BOWERY TO BROADWAY(1944), w; SUSPECT, THE(1944), w; CONFLICT(1945), w; HERE COME THE CO-EDS(1945), w; RUNAROUND, THE(1946), w; UNDERTOW(1949), w; GOBS AND GALS(1952), w; TROPICAL HEAT WAVE(1952), w; WAC FROM WALLA WALLA, THE(1952), w; DAY OF TRIUMPH(1954), w; JUVENILE JUNGLE(1958), w; YOUNG AND WILD(1958), w
Nicholas Hormann
KRAMER VS. KRAMER(1979); HAND, THE(1981); INCREDIBLE SHRINKING WOMAN, THE(1981)
Geordie Hormel
INTIMACY(1966), m
Gregory Hormel
1984
MIKE'S MURDER(1984)
Alfred Aloysius Horn
TRADER HORN(1931), w
Billy Horn
FOREIGN CORRESPONDENT(1940)
Camilla Horn
GREAT YEARNING, THE(1930, Ger.); ROYAL BOX, THE(1930); RETURN OF RAFFLES, THE(1932, Brit.); LOVE NEST, THE(1933, Brit.); MATINEE IDOL(1933, Brit.); LUCK OF A SAILOR, THE(1934, Brit.); BROKEN LOVE(1946, Ital.)
Silents
FAUST(1926, Ger.); TEMPEST(1928); ETERNAL LOVE(1929)
Christiane B. Horn
1984
WOMAN IN FLAMES, A(1984, Ger.)
Denis Horn
TOGETHER(1956, Brit.), w
Dick Horn
YELLOW SUBMARINE(1958, Brit.), animation
Dimitri Horn
WE HAVE ONLY ONE LIFE(1963, Gr.)
Editha Horn
SISTERS, OR THE BALANCE OF HAPPINESS(1982, Ger.)
Edward Horn
Silents
AS IN A LOOKING GLASS(1916), ph; DUST OF DESIRE(1919), ph
Harald Horn
PINOCCHIO(1969, E. Ger.), set d
Herta Horn
BURGLAR, THE(1956), ed
Holloway Horn
EYES OF FATE(1933, Brit.), w
Isabelle Horn
PIPE DREAMS(1976)
James Horn
GLASS MENAGERIE, THE(1950)
Jim Horn
LAST DETAIL, THE(1973)
John F. Horn
VIRGIN SACRIFICE(1959), p
John Horn
W.I.A.(WOUNDED IN ACTION)*1/2 (1966); FIRE SALE(1977); STAR 80(1983)
Joyce Horn
SINCE YOU WENT AWAY(1944)
June Horn
PALM SPRINGS(1936)
Ken Horn
RETURN, THE(1980), makeup; HELL NIGHT(1981), makeup
Lanny Horn
HOMEWORK(1982)

Leonard Horn
MAGIC GARDEN OF STANLEY SWEETHART, THE(1970), d; CORKY(1972), d
Misc. Talkies
ROGUE'S GALLERY(1968), d
Lew Horn
MARIGOLD MAN(1970)
1984
BUDDY SYSTEM, THE(1984)
Linda Horn
GREAT MUPPET CAPER, THE(1981)
Lou Horn
PASSION HOLIDAY(1963)
Marion Horn
NICHOLAS NICKLEBY(1947, Brit.), cos
Mary Horn
UNEASY TERMS(1948, Brit.)
Mildred Horn
MOM AND DAD(1948), w
Mildred A. Horn
LAWTON STORY, THE(1949), w; PRINCE OF PEACE, THE(1951), w
P.T. Horn
JAWS 3-D(1983)
Pat Horn
SO THIS IS PARIS(1954)
Paul Horn
WILD AND WONDERFUL(1964)
Robert Horn
PERSONAL BEST(1982)
Tom Horn
TOM HORN(1980), w
Tyler Horn
HERO AT LARGE(1980)
Van Horn
Silents
SCARAMOUCHE(1923), cos
Virginia Horn
PASSION HOLIDAY(1963)
Wayne Van Horn
RARE BREED, THE(1966)
Mario Horna
NO EXIT(1962, U.S./Arg.)
Jeffery Hornaday
D.C. CAB(1983), ch; FLASHDANCE(1983), ch
1984
STREETS OF FIRE(1984), ch
Jeffery D. Hornaday
1984
ROMANCING THE STONE(1984), ch
Lucy Hornak
MOONLIGHTING(1982, Brit.); NEVER SAY NEVER AGAIN(1983); WICKED LADY, THE(1983, Brit.)
William Hornbeck
MIDNIGHT DADDIES(1929), ed; HYPNOTIZED(1933), ed; SCARLET PIMPERNEL, THE(1935, Brit.), ed; REMBRANDT(1936, Brit.), ed; DARK JOURNEY(1937, Brit.), ed; ELEPHANT BOY(1937, Brit.), ed; KNIGHT WITHOUT ARMOR(1937, Brit.), ed; MAN WHO COULD WORK MIRACLES, THE(1937, Brit.), ed; MEN ARE NOT GODS(1937, Brit.), ed; DIVORCE OF LADY X. THE(1938, Brit.), ed; DRUMS(1938, Brit.), ed; FOUR FEATHERS, THE(1939, Brit.), ed; REBEL SON, THE ½(1939, Brit.), ed; U-BOAT 29(1939, Brit.), ed; THIEF OF BAGHDAD, THE(1940, Brit.), ed; TWENTY-ONE DAYS TOGETHER(1940, Brit.), ed; LYDIA(1941), ed; THAT HAMILTON WOMAN(1941), ed; JUNGLE BOOK(1942), ed; IT'S A WONDERFUL LIFE(1946), ed; SINGAPORE(1947), ed; STATE OF THE UNION(1948), ed; HEIRESS, THE(1949), ed; RIDING HIGH(1950), ed; PLACE IN THE SUN, A(1951), ed; SOMETHING TO LIVE FOR(1952), ed; ACT OF LOVE(1953), ed; SHANE(1953), ed; BAREFOOT CONTESSA, THE(1954), ed; GIRL RUSH, THE(1955), ed; GIANT(1956), ed; I WANT TO LIVE!(1958), ed; QUIET AMERICAN, THE(1958), ed; HOLE IN THE HEAD, A(1959), ed
Silents
GOOD-BYE KISS, THE(1928), ed
William W. Hornbeck
SUDDENLY, LAST SUMMER(1959, Brit.), ed
Dieter Hornberg
NOT RECONCILED, OR "ONLY VIOLENCE HELPS WHERE IT RULES"(1969, Ger.)
Arthur Hornblow
Silents
KINDLING(1915), w; ISLE OF CONQUEST(1919), w; MASK, THE(1921), w
Arthur Hornblow, Jr.
PURSUIT OF HAPPINESS, THE(1934), p; FOUR HOURS TO KILL(1935), p; MISSISSIPPI(1935), p; RUGGLES OF RED GAP(1935), p; WINGS IN THE DARK(1935), p; PRINCESS COMES ACROSS, THE(1936), p; THREE MARRIED MEN(1936), p; EASY LIVING(1937), p; HIGH, WIDE AND HANDSOME(1937), p; SWING HIGH, SWING LOW(1937), p; WAIKIKI WEDDING(1937), p; ARTISTS AND MODELS ABROAD(1938), p; TROPIC HOLIDAY(1938), p; CAT AND THE CANARY, THE(1939), p; MAN ABOUT TOWN(1939), p; MIDNIGHT(1939), p; ARISE, MY LOVE(1940), p; GHOST BREAKERS, THE(1940), p; HOLD BACK THE DAWN(1941), p; I WANTED WINGS(1941), p; NOTHING BUT THE TRUTH(1941), p; MAJOR AND THE MINOR, THE(1942), p; HEAVENLY BODY, THE(1943), p; GASLIGHT(1944), p; WEEKEND AT THE WALDORF(1945), p; CASS TIMBERLANE(1947), p; DESIRE ME(1947), p; HUCKSTERS, THE(1947), p; CONSPIRATOR(1949, Brit.), p; ASPHALT JUNGLE, THE(1950), p; MILLION DOLLAR MERMAID(1952), p; REMAINS TO BE SEEN(1953), p; OKLAHOMA(1955), p; WITNESS FOR THE PROSECUTION(1957), p; WAR LOVER, THE(1962, U.S./Brit.), p
Eugene Hornbostel
Silents
TWELVE MILES OUT(1927), set d
Gene Hornbostel
INTRUDER, THE(1932), art d; THIRTEENTH GUEST, THE(1932), art d; COWBOY COUNSELOR(1933), artr d; IRON MASTER, THE(1933), art d; OFFICER 13(1933), art d; SHRIEK IN THE NIGHT, A(1933), art d

Eugene Hornbostle
Silents
  GREAT SHADOW, THE(1920)
Benjamin Hornbuckle
  DAVY CROCKETT, KING OF THE WILD FRONTIER(1955)
Jean Hornbustal
  VANITY FAIR(1932), art d
Jean Hornbustel
  SPIRIT OF THE WEST(1932), set d
Fred Hornby
Misc. Silents
  CALL OF THE HILLS, THE(1923), d
Andrew Horne
  LORD OF THE FLIES(1963, Brit.)
David Horne
  GENERAL JOHN REGAN(1933, Brit.); LORD OF THE MANOR(1933, Brit.); BADGER'S GREEN(1934, Brit.); CASE FOR THE CROWN, THE(1934, Brit.); GENTLEMAN'S AGREEMENT(1935, Brit.); LATE EXTRA(1935, Brit.); REGAL CAVALCADE(1935, Brit.), p; THAT'S MY UNCLE(1935, Brit.); VILLAGE SQUIRE, THE(1935, Brit.); CARDINAL, THE(1936, Brit.); DEBT OF HONOR(1936, Brit.); DOMMED CARGO(1936, Brit.); HOUSE OF THE SPANIARD, THE(1936, Brit.); INTERRUPTED HONEYMOON, THE(1936, Brit.); IT'S LOVE AGAIN(1936, Brit.); TOUCH OF THE MOON, A(1936, Brit.); UNDER PROOF(1936, Brit.); TROOPSHIP(1938, Brit.); BLIND FOLLY(1939, Brit.); MILL ON THE FLOSS(1939, Brit.); CONQUEST OF THE AIR(1940); CRIMES AT THE DARK HOUSE(1940, Brit.); NIGHT TRAIN(1940, Brit.); RETURN TO YESTERDAY(1940, Brit.); TWENTY-ONE DAYS TOGETHER(1940, Brit.); CHAMBER OF HORRORS(1941, Brit.); MAIL TRAIN(1941, Brit.); AVENGERS, THE(1942, Brit.); WINGS AND THE WOMAN(1942, Brit.); ADVENTURE IN BLACKMAIL(1943, Brit.); HUNDRED POUND WINDOW, THE(1943, Brit.); SPITFIRE(1943, Brit.); DON'T TAKE IT TO HEART(1944, Brit.); YELLOW CANARY, THE(1944, Brit.); NOTORIOUS GENTLEMAN(1945, Brit.); THEY WERE SISTERS(1945, Brit.); CARAVAN(1946, Brit.); MAN FROM MOROCCO, THE(1946, Brit.); SEVENTH VEIL, THE(1946, Brit.); WICKED LADY, THE(1946, Brit.); YANK IN LONDON, A(1946, Brit.); MAGIC BOW, THE(1947, Brit.); SAN DEMETRIO, LONDON(1947, Brit.); EASY MONEY(1948, Brit.); SHOWTIME(1948, Brit.); SMUGGLERS, THE(1948, Brit.); SPRINGTIME(1948, Brit.); HISTORY OF MR. POLLY, THE(1949, Brit.); ONCE UPON A DREAM(1949, Brit.); SARABAND(1949, Brit.); IT'S HARD TO BE GOOD(1950, Brit.); ISLAND RESCUE(1952, Brit.); KISENGA, MAN OF AFRICA(1952, Brit.); BOTH SIDES OF THE LAW(1953, Brit.); MARTIN LUTHER(1953); SPACEWAYS(1953, Brit.); BEAU BRUMMELL(1954); TALE OF THREE WOMEN, A(1954, Brit.); INTRUDER, THE(1955, Brit.); THREE CASES OF MURDER(1955, Brit.); LAST MAN TO HANG, THE(1956, Brit.); LUST FOR LIFE(1956); PRINCE AND THE SHOWGIRL, THE(1957, Brit.); SAFECRACKER, THE(1958, Brit.); SHERIFF OF FRACTURED JAW, THE(1958, Brit.); DEVIL'S DISCIPLE, THE(1959); CLUE OF THE NEW PIN, THE(1961, Brit.); GOODBYE AGAIN(1961); GET ON WITH IT(1963, Brit.); NURSE ON WHEELS(1964, Brit.); BIG JOB, THE(1965, Brit.); DIAMONDS FOR BREAKFAST(1968, Brit.); FLEA IN HER EAR, A(1968, Fr.)
David D. Horne
  MOTHRA(1962, Jap.), p
Derek Horne
  ALICE'S ADVENTURES IN WONDERLAND(1972, Brit.), p; CALLAN(1975, Brit.), p; GULLIVER'S TRAVELS(1977, Brit., Bel.), p
Geoffrey Horne
  BRIDGE ON THE RIVER KWAI, THE(1957); STRANGE ONE, THE(1957); BONJOUR TRISTESSE(1958); TEMPEST(1958, Ital./Yugo./Fr.); STORY OF JOSEPH AND HIS BRETHREN THE(1962, Ital.); TWO PEOPLE(1973)
James Horne
  ALL OVER TOWN(1937), d; BACK TRAIL(1948); MAGNIFICENT YANKEE, THE(1950); GIRL WHO HAD EVERYTHING, THE(1953)
Misc. Silents
  KOSHER KITTY KELLY(1926), d
James W. Horne
  BONNIE SCOTLAND(1935), d; BOHEMIAN GIRL, THE(1936), d; WAY OUT WEST(1937), d; GOLDEN EARRINGS(1947); PLACE IN THE SUN, A(1951)
Silents
  OCCASIONALLY YOURS(1920), d; BRONZE BELL, THE(1921), d; SUNSHINE TRAIL, THE(1923), d; ALIMONY(1924), d; AMERICAN MANNERS(1924), d; IN FAST COMPANY(1924), d; LAUGHING AT DANGER(1924), d; COLLEGE(1927), d
Misc. Silents
  BARNSTORMERS, THE(1915), d; PITFALL, THE(1915), d; DANGEROUS PASTIME(1922), d; DON'T DOUBT YOUR WIFE(1922), d; FORGOTTEN LAW(1922), d; HOTTENTOT, THE(1922), d; BLOW YOUR OWN HORN(1923), d; CAN A WOMAN LOVE TWICE?(1923), d; ITCHING PALMS(1923), d; MAN OF ACTION, THE(1923), d; HAIL THE HERO(1924), d; STEPPING LIVELY(1924), d; YANKEE CONSUL, THE(1924), d; YOUTH AND ADVENTURE(1925), d; CRUISE OF THE JASPER B, THE(1926), d; BIG HOP, THE(1928), d; BLACK BUTTERFLIES(1928), d
Jimmy Horne
  OTHER LOVE, THE(1947); EAST SIDE, WEST SIDE(1949)
John Horne
  ROMAN HOLIDAY(1953); BAREFOOT CONTESSA, THE(1954); WAR AND PEACE(1956, Ital./U.S.)
Joyce Horne
  MOONLIGHT IN HAVANA(1942); YANKEE DOODLE DANDY(1942)
June Horne
  VIVACIOUS LADY(1938); BALL OF FIRE(1941); VERY YOUNG LADY, A(1941)
Ken Horne
  BED SITTING ROOM, THE(1969, Brit.), m
Kenneth Horne
  ALMOST A HONEYMOON(1938, Brit.), w; JANE STEPS OUT(1938, Brit.), w; FLYING FIFTY-FIVE(1939, Brit.), w; SPIDER, THE(1940, Brit.), w; MINE OWN EXECUTIONER(1948, Brit.), prod d; FOOLS RUSH IN(1949, Brit.), w; AUNT CLARA(1954, Brit.), w; LADY MISLAID, A(1958, Brit.), w
Lena Horne
  WIZ, THE(1978); DUKE IS THE TOPS, THE(1938); PANAMA HATTIE(1942); CABIN IN THE SKY(1943); I DOOD IT(1943); STORMY WEATHER(1943); SWING FEVER(1943); THOUSANDS CHEER(1943); BROADWAY RHYTHM(1944); TWO GIRLS AND A SAILOR(1944); ZIEGFELD FOLLIES(1945); TILL THE CLOUDS ROLL BY(1946); DUCHESS OF IDAHO, THE(1950); DEATH OF A GUNFIGHTER(1969)

Lotte Horne
  PEOPLE MEET AND SWEET MUSIC FILLS THE HEART(1969, Den./Swed.)
Marilynn Horne
  CARMEN JONES(1954)
Michael Geoffrey Horne
  BABY MAKER, THE(1970)
Pliny Horne
Silents
  SPINDLE OF LIFE, THE(1917), ph; FLAMES OF CHANCE, THE(1918), ph; MAN ABOVE THE LAW(1918), ph
Richard Horne
  LORD OF THE FLIES(1963, Brit.)
Sandy Horne
1984
  LISTEN TO THE CITY(1984, Can.)
Suzi Horne
1984
  JUNGLE WARRIORS(1984, U.S./Ger./Mex.)
Timothy Horne
  LORD OF THE FLIES(1963, Brit.)
Victoria Horne
  GHOST AND MRS. MUIR, THE(1942); MURDER IN THE BLUE ROOM(1944); SAN DIEGO, I LOVE YOU(1944); SCARLET CLAW, THE(1944); LOVE, HONOR AND GOODBYE(1945); PILLOW TO POST(1945); THAT'S THE SPIRIT(1945); UNSEEN, THE(1945); BLUE SKIES(1946); IN OLD SACRAMENTO(1946); SHE WROTE THE BOOK(1946); TO EACH HIS OWN(1946); CRIMSON KEY, THE(1947); DAISY KENYON(1947); FOREVER AMBER(1947); GUILT OF JANET AMES(1947); KEY WITNESS(1947); SUDDENLY IT'S SPRING(1947); GENTLEMAN FROM NOWHERE, THE(1948); RETURN OF OCTOBER, THE(1948); SNAKE PIT, THE(1948); ABBOTT AND COSTELLO MEET THE KILLER, BORIS KARLOFF(1949); LIFE OF RILEY, THE(1949); MARY RYAN, DETECTIVE(1949); GOOD HUMOR MAN, THE(1950); HARVEY(1950); HUMPHREY TAKES A CHANCE(1950); NEVER A DULL MOMENT(1950); CUBAN FIREBALL(1951); DREAMBOAT(1952); SCANDAL SHEET(1952); AFFAIR WITH A STRANGER(1953)
William Horne
Silents
  WESTERN FIREBRANDS(1921); PUTTING IT OVER(1922)
Misc. Silents
  STAR REPORTER, THE(1921)
James Horne, Jr.
  KEEP 'EM FLYING(1941)
Sigrid Horne-Rasmussen
  HUNGER(1968, Den./Norway/Swed.)
Anna Marie Hornemann
  HOUSE ON 92ND STREET, THE(1945)
Adele Horner
  STREET OF MEMORIES(1940); THERE'S MAGIC IN MUSIC(1941)
Chris Horner
  MOVIE MOVIE(1978), set d; FORBIDDEN WORLD(1982), prod d; JAWS 3-D(1983), art d
Christopher Horner
  JAZZ SINGER, THE(1980), set d
Harry Horner
  OUR TOWN(1940), prod d; STAGE DOOR CANTEEN(1943), prod d; DOUBLE LIFE, A(1947), prod d; HEIRESS, THE(1949), art d; HE RAN ALL THE WAY(1951), art d; BEWARE, MY LOVELY(1952), d; RED PLANET MARS(1952), d; VICKI(1953), d; NEW FACES(1954), d; LIFE IN THE BALANCE, A(1955), d; MAN FROM DEL RIO(1956), d; WILD PARTY, THE(1956), d; SEPARATE TABLES(1958), prod d; WONDERFUL COUNTRY, THE(1959), art d; HUSTLER, THE(1961), prod d, art d; LUCK OF GINGER COFFEY, THE(1964, U.S./Can.), prod d; THEY SHOOT HORSES, DON'T THEY?(1969), prod d; WHO IS HARRY KELLERMAN AND WHY IS HE SAYING THOSE TERRIBLE THINGS ABOUT ME?(1971), prod d; UP THE SANDBOX(1972), prod d; HARRY AND WALTER GO TO NEW YORK(1976), prod d; AUDREY ROSE(1977), prod d; DRIVER, THE(1978), prod d; MOMENT BY MOMENT(1978), prod d; JAZZ SINGER, THE(1980), prod d
Jackie Horner
  SAPS AT SEA(1940); SMILIN' THROUGH(1941); PANAMA HATTIE(1942)
James Horner
  LADY IN RED, THE(1979), m; BATTLE BEYOND THE STARS(1980), m; HUMANOIDS FROM THE DEEP(1980), m; DEADLY BLESSING(1981), m; HAND, THE(1981), m; PURSUIT OF D.B. COOPER, THE(1981), m; WOLFEN(1981), m; STAR TREK II: THE WRATH OF KHAN(1982), m; 48 HOURS(1982), m; BRAINSTORM(1983), m; DRESSER, THE(1983), m; GORKY PARK(1983), m; KRULL(1983), m; SOMETHING WICKED THIS WAY COMES(1983), m; SPACE RAIDERS(1983), m; TESTAMENT(1983), m; UNCOMMON VALOR(1983), m
1984
  STAR TREK III: THE SEARCH FOR SPOCK(1984), m; STONE BOY, THE(1984), m
Lottie Horner
  WASHINGTON MELODRAMA(1941), ch
Silents
  ACCORDING TO HOYLE(1922), w
Mitchell Horner
  MEETINGS WITH REMARKABLE MEN(1979, Brit.)
Penelope Horner
  NUN'S STORY, THE(1959); ANGRY SILENCE, THE(1960, Brit.); DEVIL'S DAFFODIL, THE(1961, Brit./Ger.); HOT MONEY GIRL(1962, Brit./Ger.); LOCKER 69(1962, Brit.); HALF A SIXPENCE(1967, Brit.); MAN WHO HAD POWER OVER WOMEN, THE(1970, Brit.)
Richard Horner
  RAGGEDY ANN AND ANDY(1977), p
Robert Horner
Misc. Talkies
  WHIRLWIND RIDER, THE(1935), d
Robert J. Horner
  KID FROM ARIZONA, THE(1931), p&d; w; WILD WEST WHOOPEE(1931), p,d&w
Misc. Talkies
  DEFYING THE LAW(1935), d; PHANTOM COWBOY, THE(1935), d; WESTERN RACKETEERS(1935), d

Silents
PONY EXPRESS RIDER(1926), d
Misc. Silents
DEFYING THE LAW(1922), d; VIRGINIAN OUTCAST(1924), d; COWBOY COURAGE(1925), d; HIS GREATEST BATTLE(1925), d; MILLIONAIRE ORPHAN, THE(1926), d; TWIN SIX O'BRIEN(1926), d; WALLOPING KID(1926), d; ACROSS THE PLAINS(1928), d; ARIZONA SPEED(1928), d; CHEYENNE TRAILS(1928), d; FORBIDDEN TRAILS(1928), d; MYSTERY RIDER(1928), d; RANGER'S OATH(1928), d; RIDERS OF VENGEANCE(1928), d; RIP ROARING LOGAN(1928), d; SECRETS OF THE RANGE(1928), d; TEXAS FLASH(1928), d; THRILL CHASER, THE(1928), d; THROWING LEAD(1928), d; TRAILS OF TREACHERY(1928), d; TWO GUN O'BRIEN(1928), d; WHERE THE WEST BEGINS(1928), d; FAR WESTERN TRAILS(1929), d; MIDNIGHT ON THE BARBARY COAST(1929), d; WHITE OUTLAW, THE(1929), d
Rosalie Horner
MY LOVER, MY SON(1970, Brit.)
Shelley Horner
Misc. Talkies
MAG WHEELS(1978)
Victoria Horner
PILLOW OF DEATH(1945)
Violet Horner
Silents
RING AND THE MAN, THE(1914)
Misc. Silents
GARDEN OF LIES, THE(1915); MARBLE HEART, THE(1916); FOLKS FROM WAY DOWN EAST(1924)
Yvonne Horner
ONE MILLION YEARS B.C.(1967, Brit./U.S.); PREHISTORIC WOMEN(1967, Brit.)
Brigitte Horney
RASPUTIN(1932, Ger.); HOUSE OF THE SPANIARD, THE(1936, Brit.); DEAD MELODY(1938, Ger.); I MARRIED A SPY(1938); AS LONG AS YOU'RE NEAR ME(1956, Ger.); MIRACLE OF THE WHITE STALLIONS(1963); TRYGON FACTOR, THE(1969, Brit.); VERONIKA VOSS(1982, Ger.); BELLA DONNA(1983, Ger.)
Andre Hornez
WHIRLWIND OF PARIS(1946, Fr.), w
Jane Hornick
COME BACK BABY(1968)
Ray Horniman
PARISIAN, THE(1931, Fr.), w
Roy Horniman
BEDTIME STORY, A(1933), w; KIND HEARTS AND CORONETS(1949, Brit.), w
Silents
EDUCATION OF ELIZABETH, THE(1921), w
Benjamin Horning
Silents
NAKED HEARTS(1916)
William Horning
AH, WILDERNESS!(1935), art d; WHIPSAW(1936), art d; GIGI(1958), art d; HIGH COST OF LOVING, THE(1958), art d; MERRY ANDREW(1958), art d; BEN HUR(1959), art d
William A. Horning
UNTIL THEY SAIL(1957), art d; FURY(1936), art d; MARIE ANTOINETTE(1938), art d; GREAT AMERICAN PASTIME, THE(1956), art d; POWER AND THE PRIZE, THE(1956), art d; SLANDER(1956), art d; TEA AND SYMPATHY(1956), art d; TEAHOUSE OF THE AUGUST MOON, THE(1956), art d; GUN GLORY(1957), art d; HIRED GUN, THE(1957), art d; HOT SUMMER NIGHT(1957), art d; JAILHOUSE ROCK(1957), art d; LES GIRLS(1957), art d; MAN ON FIRE(1957), art d; RAINTREE COUNTY(1957), art d; SEVENTH SIN, THE(1957), art d; SILK STOCKINGS(1957), art d; SOMETHING OF VALUE(1957), art d; TEN THOUSAND BEDROOMS(1957), art d; TIP ON A DEAD JOCKEY(1957), art d; WINGS OF EAGLES, THE(1957), art d; CAT ON A HOT TIN ROOF(1958), art d; HANDLE WITH CARE(1958), art d; HIGH SCHOOL CONFIDENTIAL(1958), art d; IMITATION GENERAL(1958), art d; LAW AND JAKE WADE, THE(1958), art d; PARTY GIRL(1958), art d; SADDLE THE WIND(1958), art d; SHEEPMAN, THE(1958), art d; TORPEDO RUN(1958), art d; TUNNEL OF LOVE, THE(1958), art d; COUNT YOUR BLESSINGS(1959), art d; GREEN MANSIONS(1959), art d; MATING GAME, THE(1959), art d; NIGHT OF THE QUARTER MOON(1959), art d; NORTH BY NORTHWEST(1959), art d; SOME CAME RUNNING(1959), art d; WATUSI(1959), art d; WORLD, THE FLESH, AND THE DEVIL, THE(1959), art d; DON'T GO NEAR THE WATER(1975), art d
William C. Horning
1984
REVENGE OF THE NERDS(1984)
Harry Hornisch
MIRACLE OF THE WHITE STALLIONS(1963)
Rudy Hornish
P.O.W., THE(1973)
Christina Hornisher
Misc. Talkies
HOLLYWOOD 90028(1973), d
Joseph R. Hornok
WHITE DOG(1982)
Charles Hornsby
DEATHMASTER, THE(1972)
Peter Hornsby
THUNDER ROAD(1958)
Richard Hornsby
1984
BREAKOUT(1984, Brit.), art d; ORDEAL BY INNOCENCE(1984, Brit.), art d
Martin Hornstein
TIKI TIKI(1971, Can.), w; ONE ON ONE(1977), p
E.W. Hornung
RETURN OF RAFFLES, THE(1932, Brit.), w; STINGAREE(1934), w; RAFFLES(1939), w
Silents
MR. JUSTICE RAFFLES(1921, Brit.), w
Ernest William Hornung
RAFFLES(1930), w
Silents
OUT OF THE SHADOW(1919), w; RAFFLES, THE AMATEUR CRACKSMAN(1925), w

Paul Hornung
DEVIL'S BRIGADE, THE(1968); SEMI-TOUGH(1977)
William A. Hornung
LIBELED LADY(1936), art d
George Horold
HOME FROM HOME(1939, Brit.)
Philip Horomato
MADAME BUTTERFLY(1932)
Marian Horosko
ROYAL WEDDING(1951)
David Horovitch
UNSUITABLE JOB FOR A WOMAN, AN(1982, Brit.)
Israel Horovitz
STRAWBERRY STATEMENT, THE(1970), a, w; BELIEVE IN ME(1971), w; AUTHOR! AUTHOR!(1982), w
Joseph Horovitz
TARZAN'S THREE CHALLENGES(1963), m
Gideon Horowitz
VORTEX(1982)
Helen Horowitz
NAKED APE, THE(1973)
Howie Horowitz
MONEY, WOMEN AND GUNS(1958), p
Irving Horowitz
HOT TIMES(1974)
M. G. Horowitz
PROPERTY(1979)
Margaret Horowitz [Margherita Orowitz]
UP THE MACGREGORS(1967, Ital./Span.); SEVEN GUNS FOR THE MACGREGORS(1968, Ital./Span.)
Margherita Horowitz
SUSPIRIA(1977, Ital.)
Mark Horowitz
1984
ALMOST YOU(1984), w
Craig Horrall
1984
DELIVERY BOYS(1984), a, p; PREPPIES(1984)
Misc. Talkies
PLACE WITHOUT PARENTS, A(1974); TRUCKIN'(1975)
Reinhard Horras
BATTLE OF BRITAIN, THE(1969, Brit.)
Billy Horrigan
RAIDERS OF THE LOST ARK(1981)
Cyril Horrocks
STOLEN LIFE(1939, Brit.)
Roger Horrocks
SKIN DEEP(1978, New Zealand), w
Tamara Horrocks
M(1970)
Anthony Mendleson, Horrockses Fashions
IT ALWAYS RAINS ON SUNDAY(1949, Brit.), cos
Walter Horsborough
23 PACES TO BAKER STREET(1956)
Walter Horsbrugh
NAUGHTY ARLETTE(1951, Brit.); FLOATING DUTCHMAN, THE(1953, Brit.); MR. POTTS GOES TO MOSCOW(1953, Brit.); SCOTCH ON THE ROCKS(1954, Brit.); INNOCENTS IN PARIS(1955, Brit.); YOU CAN'T ESCAPE(1955, Brit.); MOMENT OF INDISCRETION(1958, Brit.); INNOCENT MEETING(1959, Brit.); LADY IS A SQUARE, THE(1959, Brit.); KNACK ... AND HOW TO GET IT, THE(1965, Brit.); ONE WAY PENDULUM(1965, Brit.); SHARE OUT, THE(1966, Brit.); ABOMINABLE DR. PHIBES, THE(1971, Brit.)
Mike Horsburgh
DIRTY KNIGHT'S WORK(1976, Brit.)
Walter Horsburgh
GREEN SCARF, THE(1954, Brit.); SUSPENDED ALIBI(1957, Brit.); NO SAFETY AHEAD(1959, Brit.); WALKING STICK, THE(1970, Brit.)
Katy Horsch
PURPLE HAZE(1982)
Buffalo Horse
TRIAL OF BILLY JACK, THE(1974)
Champion, Jr. the Horse
SAGINAW TRAIL(1953)
George American Horse
SERIAL(1980)
Michael Horse
LEGEND OF THE LONE RANGER, THE(1981)
Yellow Horse
ROMANCE IN THE RAIN(1934)
John Horsely
NIGHT PEOPLE(1954)
George C. Horsetzky
Silents
PANDORA'S BOX(1929, Ger.), p
Martin Horsey
PRESIDENT'S ANALYST, THE(1967); SINGLE ROOM FURNISHED(1968); TOO LATE THE HERO(1970)
Bernard Horsfall
HIGH FLIGHT(1957, Brit.); STEEL BAYONET, THE(1958, Brit.); MAN IN THE MOON(1961, Brit.); GUNS AT BATASI(1964, Brit.); ON HER MAJESTY'S SECRET SERVICE(1969, Brit.); GOLD(1974, Brit.); SHOUT AT THE DEVIL(1976, Brit.); GANDHI(1982)
Bob Horsfall
TRUE STORY OF ESKIMO NELL, THE(1975, Aus.)
Anna Maria Horsford
ALMOST PERFECT AFFAIR, AN(1979); TIMES SQUARE(1980); FAN, THE(1981); LOVE CHILD(1982); CLASS(1983)
1984
CRACKERS(1984)

Dianne Horsham
ROMEO AND JULIET(1966, Brit.)
Bill Horsley
RING OF BRIGHT WATER(1969, Brit.)
D.S. Horsley
CANYON PASSAGE(1946), spec eff; KILLERS, THE(1946), spec eff
David Alison Horsley
THREE LOVES HAS NANCY(1938)
David Horsley
NO MORE LADIES(1935); ROUGH RIDING RANGER(1935); LONE WOLF RE-TURNS, THE(1936); MY MAN GODFREY(1936); ROSE BOWL(1936); EXILE, THE(1947), spec eff; SINGAPORE(1947); ONE TOUCH OF VENUS(1948), spec eff; JOLSON SINGS AGAIN(1949)
David S. Horsley
SWELL GUY(1946), ph; BRUTE FORCE(1947), spec eff; DOUBLE LIFE, A(1947), ph; SENATOR WAS INDISCREET, THE(1947), spec eff; ABBOTT AND COSTELLO MEET FRANKENSTEIN(1948), spec eff; CASBAH(1948), spec eff; FAMILY HONEY-MOON(1948), spec eff; KISS THE BLOOD OFF MY HANDS(1948), spec eff; MR. PEABODY AND THE MERMAID(1948), ph; SAXON CHARM, THE(1948), spec eff; UP IN CENTRAL PARK(1948), spec eff; YOU GOTTA STAY HAPPY(1948), spec eff; ABBOTT AND COSTELLO MEET THE KILLER, BORIS KARLOFF(1949), spec eff; CITY ACROSS THE RIVER(1949), spec eff; CRISS CROSS(1949), spec eff; FIGHTING O'FLYNN, THE(1949), spec eff; ILLEGAL ENTRY(1949), spec eff; JOHNNY STOOL PIGEON(1949), spec eff; ONCE MORE, MY DARLING(1949), spec eff; UNDER-TOW(1949), spec eff; WOMAN IN HIDING(1949), spec eff; BUCCANEER'S GIRL(1950), spec eff; COMMANCHE TERRITORY(1950), spec eff; MYSTERY SUB-MARINE(1950), spec eff; SPY HUNT(1950), spec eff; STRANGE DOOR, THE(1951), spec eff; MEET DANNY WILSON(1952), spec eff; CITY BENEATH THE SEA(1953), spec eff; IT CAME FROM OUTER SPACE(1953), spec eff; ABBOTT AND COSTELLO MEET DR. JEKYLL AND MR. HYDE(1954), spec eff; TARANTULA(1955), spec eff; JACK THE GIANT KILLER(1962), ph
E. Horsley
CALIFORNIA STRAIGHT AHEAD(1937), ed
Erma Horsley
Silents
DEVIL'S TOWER(1929), ed
John David Horsley
70,000 WITNESSES(1932); FLAMING SIGNAL(1933); FINISHING SCHOOL(1934)
John Horsley
HIGHLY DANGEROUS(1950, Brit.); ENCORE(1951, Brit.); QUIET WOMAN, THE(1951, Brit.); FRIGHTENED MAN, THE(1952, Brit.); ISLAND RESCUE(1952, Brit.); DEADLY NIGHTSHADE(1953, Brit.); LONG MEMORY, THE(1953, Brit.); RECOIL(1953); SAILOR OF THE KING(1953, Brit.); TERROR ON A TRAIN(1953); WHEEL OF FATE(1953, Brit.); DELAYED ACTION(1954, Brit.); DESTINATION MILAN(1954, Brit.); DETECTIVE, THE(1954, Qit.); DOUBLE EXPOSURE(1954, Brit.); MAD ABOUT MEN(1954, Brit.); MEET MR. MALCOLM(1954, Brit.); RUNAWAY BUS, THE(1954, Brit.); BRAIN MACHINE, THE(1955, Brit.); CASE OF THE RED MON-KEY(1955, Brit.); TIME TO KILL, A(1955, Brit.); BOND OF FEAR(1956, Brit.); BREAKAWAY(1956, Brit.); MURDER ON APPROVAL(1956, Brit.); STRANGER IN TOWN(1957, Brit.); VIOLENT STRANGER(1957, Brit.); WEAPON, THE(1957, Brit.); DUNKIRK(1958, Brit.); HELL DRIVERS(1958, Brit.); STORMY CROSSING(1958, Brit.); BEN HUR(1959); CARRY ON NURSE(1959, Brit.); WRONG NUMBER(1959, Brit.); OPERATION AMSTERDAM(1960, Brit.); SINK THE BISMARCK!(1960, Brit.); SECRET WAYS, THE(1961); CIRCUS FRIENDS(1962, Brit.); NIGHT OF THE PROWLER(1962, Brit.); SERENA(1962, Brit.); RETURN TO SENDER(1963, Brit.); JIG SAW(1965, Brit.); SINISTER MAN, THE(1965, Brit.); PANIC(1966, Brit.); WHERE THE BULLETS FLY(1966, Brit.); LIMBO LINE, THE(1969, Brit.)
1984
SECRETS(1984, Brit.)
Lee Horsley
SWORD AND THE SORCERER, THE(1982)
Stanley Horsley
THIS ISLAND EARTH(1955), spec eff
Jack Horsman
NINE MEN(1943, Brit.)
Michael R. Horst
JOE KIDD(1972)
Harold Horsten
SPY IN THE SKY(1958)
Joseph Horstmann
HANSEL AND GRETEL(1954), anim d
Bert Horswell
CONQUEST OF CHEYENNE(1946), w; BONANZA TOWN(1951), w
Sam Horta
GAY PURR-EE(1962), ed; MAN FROM BUTTON WILLOW, THE(1965), ed; MR. MAGOO'S HOLIDAY FESTIVAL(1970), ed
Rena Horten
ROPE OF FLESH(1965); MURDERERS' ROW(1966); OUT OF SIGHT(1966)
Walter Hortner
THIRD MAN, THE(1950, Brit.)
Aida Horton
Silents
DESIRED WOMAN, THE(1918)
Misc. Silents
BLIND MAN'S HOLIDAY(1917); HEART OF A GYPSY, THE(1919)
Alton E. Horton
OUT OF THE BLUE(1947)
Clara Horton
GIRLS ON PROBATION(1938)
Silents
HUCK AND TOM(1918); ALMOST A HUSBAND(1919); NINETEEN AND PHYL-LIS(1920); PRISONERS OF LOVE(1921); PENROD(1922); MIND OVER MOTOR(1923); FORTUNE HUNTER, THE(1927); SAILOR IZZY MURPHY(1927)
Misc. Silents
PLOW WOMAN, THE(1917); YELLOW DOG, THE(1918); GIRL FROM THE OUT-SIDE, THE(1919); IN WRONG(1919); HEART OF A WOMAN, THE(1920); IT'S A GREAT LIFE(1920); LITTLE SHEPARD OF KINGDOM COME, THE(1920); SERVANT IN THE HOUSE, THE(1920); LIGHT IN THE CLEARING, THE(1921); WRONGS RIGHTED(1924); MAKERS OF MEN(1925); SPEED MADNESS(1925); BROADWAY GALLANT, THE(1926); WINNING THE FUTURITY(1926); FIGHTIN' COMEBACK,

THE(1927)
Claud Horton
UNDER SECRET ORDERS(1943, Brit.)
Claude Horton
GLIMPSE OF PARADISE, A(1934, Brit.); INSIDE THE ROOM(1935, Brit.); ELDER BROTHER, THE(1937, Brit.); LEAVE IT TO ME(1937, Brit.)
Clem Horton
CATTLE RAIDERS(1938); WEST OF SANTA FE(1938); MAN FROM SUNDOWN, THE(1939); RIDERS OF BLACK RIVER(1939); THUNDERING WEST, THE(1939)
Dave Horton
MAN CALLED FLINTSTONE, THE(1966), ed
Edward Everett Horton
TERROR, THE(1928); AVIATOR, THE(1929); HOTTENTOT, THE(1929); SAP, THE(1929); SONNY BOY(1929); HOLIDAY(1930); ONCE A GENTLEMAN(1930); TAKE THE HEIR(1930); WIDE OPEN(1930); AGE FOR LOVE, THE(1931); FRONT PAGE, THE(1931); KISS ME AGAIN(1931); LONELY WIVES(1931); REACHING FOR THE MOON(1931); SIX CYLINDER LOVE(1931); SMART WOMAN(1931); BUT THE FLESH IS WEAK(1932); ROAR OF THE DRAGON(1932); TROUBLE IN PARADISE(1932); ALICE IN WONDERLAND(1933); BEDTIME STORY, A(1933); DESIGN FOR LI-VING(1933); WAY TO LOVE, THE(1933); EASY TO LOVE(1934); GAY DIVORCEE, THE(1934); IT'S A BOY(1934, Brit.); KISS AND MAKE UP(1934); LADIES SHOULD LISTEN(1934); MERRY WIDOW, THE(1934); POOR RICH, THE(1934); SING AND LIKE IT(1934); SMARTY(1934); SUCCESS AT ANY PRICE(1934); UNCERTAIN LA-DY(1934); WOMAN IN COMMAND, THE(1934 Brit.); ALL THE KING'S HORSES(1935); BIOGRAPHY OF A BACHELOR GIRL(1935); DEVIL IS A WOMAN, THE(1935); GOING HIGHBROW(1935); HIS NIGHT OUT(1935); IN CALIENTE(1935); LITTLE BIG SHOT(1935); NIGHT IS YOUNG, THE(1935); PRIVATE SECRETARY, THE(1935, Brit.); TOP HAT(1935); YOUR UNCLE DUDLEY(1935); $10 RAISE(1935); HEARTS DIVIDED(1936); HIS MASTER'S VOICE(1936); MAN IN THE MIRROR, THE(1936, Brit.); NOBODY'S FOOL(1936); SINGING KID, THE(1936); ANGEL(1937); DANGER–LOVE AT WORK(1937); GREAT GARRICK, THE(1937); HITTING A NEW HIGH(1937); KING AND THE CHORUS GIRL, THE(1937); LET'S MAKE A MIL-LION(1937); LOST HORIZON(1937); OH DOCTOR(1937); PERFECT SPECIMEN, THE(1937); SHALL WE DANCE(1937); WILD MONEY(1937); BLUEBEARD'S EIGHTH WIFE(1938); COLLEGE SWING(1938); HOLIDAY(1938); LITTLE TOUGH GUYS IN SOCIETY(1938); PARIS HONEYMOON(1939); THAT'S RIGHT-YOU'RE WRONG(1939); BACHELOR DADDY(1941); BODY DISAPPEARS, THE(1941); HERE COMES MR. JORDAN(1941); SUNNY(1941); WEEKEND FOR THREE(1941); YOU'RE THE ONE(1941); ZIEGFELD GIRL(1941); I MARRIED AN ANGEL(1942); MAGNIFI-CENT DOPE, THE(1942); SPRINGTIME IN THE ROCKIES(1942); AMAZING MR. FORREST, THE(1943, Brit.); FOREVER AND A DAY(1943); GANG'S ALL HERE, THE(1943); THANK YOUR LUCKY STARS(1943); ARSENIC AND OLD LACE(1944); BRAZIL(1944); HER PRIMITIVE MAN(1944); SAN DIEGO, I LOVE YOU(1944); SUMMER STORM(1944); LADY ON A TRAIN(1945); STEPPIN' IN SOCIETY(1945); TOWN WENT WILD, THE(1945); CINDERELLA JONES(1946); EARL CARROLL SKETCHBOOK(1946); FAITHFUL IN MY FASHION(1946); DOWN TO EARTH(1947); GHOST GOES WILD, THE(1947); HER HUSBAND'S AFFAIRS(1947); STORY OF MANKIND, THE(1957); POCKETFUL OF MIRACLES(1961); IT'S A MAD, MAD, MAD, MAD WORLD(1963); SEX AND THE SINGLE GIRL(1964); PERILS OF PAULINE, THE(1967); 2000 YEARS LATER(1969); COLD TURKEY(1971)
Misc. Talkies
TWO THOUSAND YEARS LATER(1969)
Silents
FRONT PAGE STORY, A(1922); TOO MUCH BUSINESS(1922); RUGGLES OF RED GAP(1923); HELEN'S BABIES(1924); BEGGAR ON HORSEBACK(1925); NUT-CRACK-ER, THE(1926); TAXI! TAXI!(1927)
Misc. Silents
LADDER JINX, THE(1922); TO THE LADIES(1923); FLAPPER WIVES(1924); MAN WHO FIGHTS ALONE, THE(1924); TRY AND GET IT(1924); BUSINESS OF LOVE, THE(1925); MARRY ME(1925); POKER FACES(1926); WHOLE TOWN'S TALKING, THE(1926); TAKE THE HEIR(1930)
Gail L. Horton
BREAKING AWAY(1979)
Helen Horton
VILLAGE, THE(1953, Brit./Switz.); LET'S BE HAPPY(1957, Brit.); MARK OF THE HAWK, THE(1958); NEVER TAKE CANDY FROM A STRANGER(1961, Brit.); CHAIR-MAN, THE(1969); LAST SHOT YOU HEAR, THE(1969, Brit.); PHASE IV(1974); WIDOWS' NEST(1977, U.S./Span.); SUPERMAN III(1983)
1984
RAZOR'S EDGE, THE(1984)
Herbert Horton
Misc. Silents
SANDY BURKE OF THE U-BAR-U(1919)
Jack Horton
SMOKE IN THE WIND(1975)
Jamie Horton
1984
LOVE STREAMS(1984)
Jeanette Horton
Misc. Silents
LURE OF HEART'S DESIRE, THE(1916)
John E. Horton
WILD HERITAGE(1958), p
John Horton
GUNS IN THE HEATHER(1968, Brit.); DEATHLINE(1973, Brit.), spec eff
Judy Horton
DOWN AMONG THE Z MEN(1952, Brit.)
Ladye Horton
MEDICINE MAN, THE(1930), w
Leslie Horton
THAT NIGHT WITH YOU(1945), ch
Lester Horton
GYPSY WILDCAT(1944), ch; FRISCO SAL(1945), ch; SALOME, WHERE SHE DANCED(1945), ch; SHADY LADY(1945), ch; TANGIER(1946), ch; TARZAN AND THE LEOPARD WOMAN(1946), ch; SIREN OF ATLANTIS(1948), ch; SOUTH SEA WOMAN(1953), ch
Louisa Horton
ALL MY SONS(1948); WALK EAST ON BEACON(1952); SWASHBUCKLER(1976); ALICE, SWEET ALICE(1978)

Marion Horton
STOP THE WORLD–I WANT TO GET OFF(1966, Brit.)
Michael Horton
MIDDLE AGE SPREAD(1979, New Zealand), ed; BEYOND REASONABLE DOUBT(1980, New Zeal.), ed; LORDS OF DISCIPLINE, THE(1983)
1984
HEART OF THE STAG(1984, New Zealand), ed; UTU(1984, New Zealand), ed
Mike Horton
GOODBYE PORK PIE(1981, New Zealand), ed; SMASH PALACE(1982, New Zealand), ed
Nigel Horton
SECRETS OF SCOTLAND YARD(1944); TONIGHT AND EVERY NIGHT(1945)
Peter Horton
FADE TO BLACK(1980); SERIAL(1980); SPLIT IMAGE(1982)
1984
CHILDREN OF THE CORN(1984)
Robert Horton
BIRDS OF A FEATHER(1931, Brit.); LIFE GOES ON(1932, Brit.); BLARNEY KISS(1933, Brit.); ONE PRECIOUS YEAR(1933, Brit.); GREAT DEFENDER, THE(1934, Brit.); INSIDE THE ROOM(1935, Brit.); JUBILEE WINDOW(1935, Brit.); MURDER AT THE BASKERVILLES(1941, Brit.); WHEN KNIGHTS WERE BOLD(1942, Brit.); APACHE WAR SMOKE(1952); PONY SOLDIER(1952); RETURN OF THE TEXAN(1952); ARENA(1953); BRIGHT ROAD(1953); CODE TWO(1953); STORY OF THREE LOVES, THE(1953); MEN OF THE FIGHTING LADY(1954); PRISONER OF WAR(1954); MAN IS ARMED, THE(1956); GREEN SLIME, THE(1969)
Robert J. Horton
Silents
SINGING RIVER(1921), w
Russell Horton
GIRL ON THE SPOT(1946); PARADES(1972); ANNIE HALL(1977); GIRLFRIENDS(1978); STARTING OVER(1979); WINDOWS(1980); LINE, THE(1982)
Suzanne Horton
VIGILANTE FORCE(1976)
Tommy Horton
SILENCERS, THE(
Tony Horton
HOLLOW TRIUMPH(1948)
Walter Horton
Silents
HIS FATHER'S SON(1917); BAB'S CANDIDATE(1920)
Misc. Silents
SLEEPING MEMORY, A(1917); BLACK CIRCLE, THE(1919); GAUNTLET, THE(1920)
Horton Dance Group
MOONLIGHT IN HAVANA(1942)
Alexandre Horvath
TRAIN ROBBERY CONFIDENTIAL(1965, Braz.), art d; LOLLIPOP(1966, Braz.), set d
Charles Frank Horvath
MONEY FROM HOME(1953)
Emil Horvath, Jr.
ON THE COMET(1970, Czech.)
John Horvath
FICKLE FINGER OF FATE, THE(1967, Span./U.S.), ed; TREASURE OF MAKUBA, THE(1967, U.S./Span.), ed; WITCH WITHOUT A BROOM, A(1967, U.S./Span.), ed; CHRISTMAS KID, THE(1968, U.S., Span.), ed
Jozsef Horvath
ROUND UP, THE(1969, Hung.); FORBIDDEN RELATIONS(1983, Hung.)
Laszlo Horvath
ROUND UP, THE(1969, Hung.); WINTER WIND(1970, Fr./Hung.); ANGI VERA(1980, Hung.); FORBIDDEN RELATIONS(1983, Hung.); WAGNER(1983, Brit./Hung./Aust.)
1984
BRADY'S ESCAPE(1984, U.S./Hung.)
Leif Horvath
MICROWAVE MASSACRE(1983), m
Louis Horvath
TOM(1973), ph; DEAD KIDS(1981 Aus./New Zealand), ph; STRANGE INVADERS(1983), ph
Stefan Horvath
STEPS TO THE MOON(1963, Rum.), ph; FANTASTIC COMEDY, A(1975, Rum.), ph
Andy Horvitch
ANDROID(1982), ed
Ralph E. Horwedel
SUGARLAND EXPRESS, THE(1974)
Craig Horwich
SMOKEY AND THE BANDIT–PART 3(1983)
C. Jerome Horwin
SEE AMERICA THIRST(1930), w
Jerry Horwin
SPORT PARADE, THE(1932), w; TWO AGAINST THE WORLD(1932), w; GOLD DIGGERS IN PARIS(1938), w; ROSE OF WASHINGTON SQUARE(1939), w; SUN NEVER SETS, THE(1939), w; STORMY WEATHER(1943), w; HITCHHIKE TO HAPPINESS(1945), w
Dominique Horwitz
DAVID(1979, Ger.)
Harry Horwitz
I MARRIED AN ANGEL(1942)
Howie Horwitz
SLIM CARTER(1957), p; APPOINTMENT WITH A SHADOW(1958), p
Julius Horwitz
NATURAL ENEMIES(1979), w
Kurt Horwitz
WHAT WOMEN DREAM(1933, Ger.)
Lewis M. Horwitz
MAN CALLED DAGGER, A(1967), p
Murray Horwitz
NIGHT OF THE JUGGLER(1980)

C. Jerome Horwn
VIRTUOUS HUSBAND(1931), w
Robert Hosai
HOUSE OF BAMBOO(1955)
Hosch
ECSTASY(1940, Czech.), set d
Klaus Hoser
1984
WOMAN IN FLAMES, A(1984, Ger.)
Athena Hosey
NEW LIFE STYLE, THE(1970, Ger.), m
Mary Hosford
MISSOURI TRAVELER, THE(1958)
Maud Hosford
Silents
MARRIAGE PRICE(1919)
Mike Hosford
LAST PICTURE SHOW, THE(1971)
Chikako Hoshawa
CHILDREN OF HIROSHIMA(1952, Jap.)
Marjorie Hoshelle
FIND THE BLACKMAILER(1943); OLD ACQUAINTANCE(1943); THANK YOUR LUCKY STARS(1943); MAKE YOUR OWN BED(1944); MASK OF DIMITRIOS, THE(1944); CONFLICT(1945); STRANGE MR. GREGORY, THE(1945); BEHIND THE MASK(1946); BLACK MARKET BABIES(1946); BLONDE FOR A DAY(1946); CLOAK AND DAGGER(1946); MY REPUTATION(1946); ONE MORE TOMORROW(1946); RED DRAGON, THE(1946); BUNGALOW 13(1948); LADIES OF THE CHORUS(1948); RIDING HIGH(1950); I CAN GET IT FOR YOU WHOLESALE(1951); DANGEROUS CROSSING(1953)
Hikaru Hoshi
FIRES ON THE PLAIN(1962, Jap.)
Masaru Hoshi
ALMOST TRANSPARENT BLUE(1980, Jap.), m
Michiko Hoshi
FINAL WAR, THE(1960, Jap.)
Yuriko Hoshi
DANGEROUS KISS, THE(1961, Jap.); MAN AGAINST MAN(1961, Jap.); MAN FROM THE EAST, THE(1961, Jap.); LAST WAR, THE(1962, Jap.); TILL TOMORROW COMES(1962, Jap.); WISER AGE(1962, Jap.); CHUSHINGURA(1963, Jap.); HONOLULU-TOKYO-HONG KONG(1963, Hong Kong/Jap.); WARRING CLANS(1963, Jap.); GODZILLA VS. THE THING(1964, Jap.); OPERATION ENEMY FORT(1964, Jap.); GHIDRAH, THE THREE-HEADED MONSTER(1965, Jap.); RABBLE, THE(1965, Jap.); IT STARTED IN THE ALPS(1966, Jap.); NIGHT IN BANGKOK(1966, Jap.); RISE AGAINST THE SWORD(1966, Jap.); DAPHNE, THE(1967); KOJIRO(1967, Jap.); LET'S GO, YOUNG GUY!(1967, Jap.); RIVER OF FOREVER(1967, Jap.); KILL(1968, Jap.); WHIRLWIND(1968, Jap.); DAREDEVIL IN THE CASTLE(1969, Jap.)
Ichiro Hoshijima
GEISHA GIRL(1952), ph; MAN IN THE MOONLIGHT MASK, THE(1958, Jap.), ph
Yuriko Hoshio
WOMAN'S LIFE, A(1964, Jap.)
Peter Hosking
1984
SQUIZZY TAYLOR(1984, Aus.)
Alan Hoskins
KRAKATOA, EAST OF JAVA(1969)
Basil Hoskins
IT STARTED IN PARADISE(1952, Brit.); DESERT ATTACK(1958, Brit.); FLAME OVER INDIA(1960, Brit.); MILLIONAIRESS, THE(1960, Brit.)
Bob Hoskins
NATIONAL HEALTH, OR NURSE NORTON'S AFFAIR, THE(1973, Brit.); ZULU DAWN(1980, Brit.); LONG GOOD FRIDAY, THE(1982, Brit.); PINK FLOYD–THE WALL(1982, Brit.); BEYOND THE LIMIT(1983)
1984
COTTON CLUB, THE(1984); LASSITER(1984)
Hazel Hoskins
STATUE, THE(1971, Brit.)
John Hoskins
MONEY FOR SPEED(1933, Brit.)
Mary Rae Hoskins
SEMI-TOUGH(1977)
Percy Hoskins
BLUE PARROT, THE(1953, Brit.), w; BURNT EVIDENCE(1954, Brit.), w; DANGEROUS CARGO(1954, Brit.), w
Raymond Hoskins
SCROOGE(1970, Brit.)
Shawn Hoskins
1984
HOT AND DEADLY(1984)
Troy Hoskins
SENIORS, THE(1978)
Troy K. Hoskins
BULLET FOR PRETTY BOY, A(1970)
Winfield Hoskins
GULLIVER'S TRAVELS(1939), anim d
Ernest Hosler
MIX ME A PERSON(1962, Brit.), ed; EAST OF SUDAN(1964, Brit.), ed; I'VE GOTTA HORSE(1965, Brit.), ed; FAMILY WAY, THE(1966, Brit.), ed; ATTACK ON THE IRON COAST(1968, U.S./Brit.), ed; HIGH COMMISSIONER, THE(1968, U.S./Brit.), ed; SOME GIRLS DO(1969, Brit.), ed; LAST GRENADE, THE(1970, Brit.), ed; STATUE, THE(1971, Brit.), ed
Toshiyuki Hosokaw
ZATOICHI MEETS YOJIMBO(1970, Jap.)
Chikako Hosokawa
ETERNITY OF LOVE(1961, Jap.); KURAGEJIMA–LEGENDS FROM A SOUTHERN ISLAND(1970, Jap.)
Toshio Hosokawa
TORA! TORA! TORA!(1970, U.S./Jap.)

Yoshiyuki Hosokawa
FIGHT FOR THE GLORY(1970, Jap.)
Nabih Aboul Hoson
HONEYBABY, HONEYBABY(1974)
Tatsuo Hosoya
HAHAKIRI(1963, Jap.), p
Americo Hoss
MASTER OF HORROR(1965, Arg.), ph
Andre Hoss
WITHOUT APPARENT MOTIVE(1972, Fr.), prod d
Traute Hoss
LILI MARLEEN(1981, Ger.)
Andre Hossein
LIARS, THE(1964, Fr.), m; SCHEHERAZADE(1965, Fr./Ital./Span.), m
Robert Hossein
RIFIFI(1956, Fr.); NUDE IN A WHITE CAR(1960, Fr.), a, d&w; GAME OF TRUTH, THE(1961, Fr.), a, d; WICKED GO TO HELL, THE(1961, Fr.), a, d; RIFF RAFF GIRLS(1962, Fr./Ital.); ROAD TO SHAME, THE(1962, Fr.); LOVE ON A PILLOW(1963, Fr./Ital.); MADAME(1963, Fr./Ital./Span.); NIGHT ENCOUNTER(1963, Fr./Ital.), a, d, w; PARIS PICK-UP(1963, Fr./Ital.); OF FLESH AND BLOOD(1964, Fr./Ital.); VICE AND VIRTUE(1965, Fr./Ital.); ENOUGH ROPE(1966, Fr./Ital./Ger.); MARCO THE MAGNIFICENT(1966, Ital./Fr./Yugo./Egypt/Afghanistan); THE DIRTY GAME(1966, Fr./Ital./Ger.); SHADOW OF EVIL(1967, Fr./Ital.); NO ROSES FOR OSS 117(1968, Fr.); LIFE LOVE DEATH(1969, Fr./Ital.); TIME OF THE WOLVES(1970, Fr.); BURGLARS, THE(1972, Fr./Ital.); HEIST, THE(1979, Ital.); BOLERO(1982, Fr.); LES MISERABLES(1982, Fr.), d, w
Roberto Hossein
HIGHWAY PICKUP(1965, Fr./Ital.)
Auyar Hosseini
ZARAK(1956, Brit.), m
Jack Hossey
MOM AND DAD(1948), p
Eve Hossner
DEVIL'S MESSENGER, THE(1962 U.S./Swed.)
Barry Hostetler
WORM EATERS, THE(1981)
1984
MYSTERY MANSION(1984)
Ginny Hostetler
FOUR FOR THE MORGUE(1962)
Paul Hostetler
PANIC IN THE STREETS(1950); MALATESTA'S CARNIVAL(1973)
Paul S. Hostetler
DAMN CITIZEN(1958)
Curtis Hostetter
HE KNOWS YOU'RE ALONE(1980)
John Hostetter
HEART BEAT(1979); IN-LAWS, THE(1979); KNIGHTRIDERS(1981)
John Hostettner
1984
BEST DEFENSE(1984)
Pierre Hot
Misc. Silents
FALL OF THE HOUSE OF USHER, THE(1928, Fr.)
Hot Gossip
WORLD IS FULL OF MARRIED MEN, THE(1980, Brit.)
The Hot Shots
THUMBS UP(1943)
The Hot Soup
WANDERLOVE(1970)
Arthur Hotaling
Silents
KING OF THE HERD(1927); LITTLE WILD GIRL, THE(1928); OLD AGE HANDICAP(1928); GIRLS WHO DARE(1929), t
Misc. Silents
GENTLEMAN PREFFERED, A(1928), d
Frank Hotaling
3:10 TO YUMA(1957), art d; FACES IN THE FOG(1944), art d; FIREBRANDS OF ARIZONA(1944), art d; LIGHTS OF OLD SANTA FE(1944), art d; EARL CARROLL'S VANITIES(1945), art d; ROUGH RIDERS OF CHEYENNE(1945), art d; SANTA FE SADDLEMATES(1945), art d; SCOTLAND YARD INVESTIGATOR(1945, Brit.), art d; SUNSET IN EL DORADO(1945), art d; TIGER WOMAN, THE(1945), art d; HOME IN OKLAHOMA(1946), art d; MAGNIFICENT ROGUE, THE(1946), art d; ONE EXCITING WEEK(1946), art d; HIT PARADE OF 1947(1947), art d; MAIN STREET KID, THE(1947), art d; ON THE OLD SPANISH TRAIL(1947), art d; TRESPASSER, THE(1947), art d; TWILIGHT ON THE RIO GRANDE(1947), art d; UNDER COLORADO SKIES(1947), art d; WYOMING(1947), art d; DAREDEVILS OF THE CLOUDS(1948), art d; DESPERADOES OF DODGE CITY(1948), art d; EYES OF TEXAS(1948), art d; GAY RANCHERO, THE(1948), art d; GRAND CANYON TRAIL(1948), art d; HOMICIDE FOR THREE(1948), art d; NIGHT TIME IN NEVADA(1948), art d; SUNDOWN IN SANTA FE(1948), art d; TIMBER TRAIL, THE(1948), art d; UNDER CALIFORNIA STARS(1948), art d; DEATH VALLEY GUNFIGHTER(1949), art d; DOWN DAKOTA WAY(1949), art d; FAR FRONTIER, THE(1949), art d; FLAME OF YOUTH(1949), art d; FLAMING FURY(1949), art d; FRONTIER INVESTIGATOR(1949), art d; GOLDEN STALLION, THE(1949), art d; HIDEOUT(1949), art d; I SHOT JESSE JAMES(1949), art d; LAW OF THE GOLDEN WEST(1949), art d; POWDER RIVER RUSTLERS(1949), art d; RANGER OF CHEROKEE STRIP(1949), art d; ROSE OF THE YUKON(1949), art d; SAN ANTONE AMBUSH(1949), art d; SOUTH OF RIO(1949), art d; STREETS OF SAN FRANCISCO(1949), art d; SUSANNA PASS(1949), art d; DESTINATION BIG HOUSE(1950), art d; PIONEER MARSHAL(1950), art d; RIO GRANDE(1950), art d; SUNSET IN THE WEST(1950), art d; TRIAL WITHOUT JURY(1950), art d; TWILIGHT IN THE SIERRAS(1950), ed; UNMASKED(1950), art d; HAVANA ROSE(1951), art d; HEART OF THE ROCKIES(1951), art d; HONEYCHILE(1951), art d; IN OLD AMARILLO(1951), art d; INSURANCE INVESTIGATOR(1951), art d; MILLION DOLLAR PURSUIT(1951), art d; MISSING WOMEN(1951), art d; NIGHT RIDERS OF MONTANA(1951), art d; PRIDE OF MARYLAND(1951), art d; ROUGH RIDERS OF DURANGO(1951), art d; SILVER CITY BONANZA(1951), art d; SOUTH OF CALIENTE(1951), art d; THUNDER IN GOD'S COUNTRY(1951), art d; WELLS FARGO GUNMASTER(1951), art d; DESPERADOES OUTPOST(1952), art d; I DREAM OF

JEANIE(1952), art d; PALS OF THE GOLDEN WEST(1952), art d; QUIET MAN, THE(1952), art d; SOUTH PACIFIC TRAIL(1952), art d; THUNDERBIRDS(1952), art d; THUNDERING CARAVANS(1952), art d; TOUGHEST MAN IN ARIZONA(1952), art d; WOMAN IN THE DARK(1952), art d; GERALDINE(1953), art d; MARSHAL OF CEDAR ROCK(1953), art d; RED RIVER SHORE(1953), art d; SHADOWS OF TOMBSTONE(1953), art d; SUN SHINES BRIGHT, THE(1953), art d; CAROLINA CANNONBALL(1955), art d; ETERNAL SEA, THE(1955), art d; SEARCHERS, THE(1956), art d; WAGON WHEELS WESTWARD(1956), art d; MONKEY ON MY BACK(1957), art d; HORSE SOLDIERS, THE(1959), art d; SERGEANTS 3(1962), art d
Fred Hotaling
OLD OKLAHOMA PLAINS(1952), art d
J. Frank Hotaling
MY BUDDY(1944), art d
Davis Hotard
TOY, THE(1982)
Yukitaro Hotaru
GAMERA VERSUS GAOS(1967, Jap.)
Tracy Hotchiner
LADY LIBERTY(1972, Ital./Fr.)
Joan Hotchkis
LATE LIZ, THE(1971); BREEZY(1973); LEGACY(1976), a, w; ODE TO BILLY JOE(1976); OLD BOYFRIENDS(1979)
John Hotchkis
CRUCIBLE OF HORROR(1971, Brit.), m; WEDDING, A(1978), m
Frank Hotchkiss
CISCO PIKE(1971)
Vic Hotchkiss
MONSTER OF HIGHGATE PONDS, THE(1961, Brit.), anim
A.E. Hotchner
ADVENTURES OF A YOUNG MAN(1962), w
Tracy Hotchner
LITTLE BIG MAN(1970); MOMMIE DEAREST(1981), w
May Hotely
Silents
GIRLS WHO DARE(1929)
L. Hotivari
DRAGONFLY, THE(1955 USSR), w
Yoshie Hotta
MOTHRA(1962, Jap.), w
Donald Hotten
WHAT'S SO BAD ABOUT FEELING GOOD?(1968)
Donald Hotton
UP IN SMOKE(1978); CHINA SYNDROME, THE(1979); NIGHTWING(1979); HEARSE, THE(1980); ONE DARK NIGHT(1983)
Clegg Hoty
FIGHTING TROUBLE(1956)
Dee Hoty
HARRY AND WALTER GO TO NEW YORK(1976)
Tony Hoty
SQUEEZE PLAY(1981)
Sandra Hotz
1984
PASSAGE TO INDIA, A(1984, Brit.)
Edward Hou
AIR CADET(1951), art d
Mouchy Houblinne
MAMMA DRACULA(1980, Bel./Fr.), cos
Doris Houch
Misc. Talkies
HEADING WEST(1946)
J.N. Houch, Jr.
BOOTLEGGERS(1974)
Ken Houchins
LIGHTNING GUNS(1950)
Byron Houck
Silents
NAVIGATOR, THE(1924), ph; SHERLOCK, JR.(1924), ph; SEVEN CHANCES(1925), ph
Clyde Houck
KENTUCKY RIFLE(1956)
Doris Houck
SHE WOULDN'T SAY YES(1945); CLOSE CALL FOR BOSTON BLACKIE, A(1946); LANDRUSH(1946); MAN WHO DARED, THE(1946); SHADOWED(1946); THRILL OF BRAZIL, THE(1946); DOWN TO EARTH(1947); WHEN A GIRL'S BEAUTIFUL(1947)
Misc. Talkies
TWO-FISTED STRANGER(1946)
Jay Houck
GIRL IN TROUBLE(1963)
Leo Houck
Silents
JACK AND JILL(1917)
Willis Houck
KING OF THE BULLWHIP(1950)
Joy Houck, Jr.
CREATURE FROM BLACK LAKE, THE(1976), d; WISHBONE CUTTER(1978)
Joy N. Houck, Jr.
SHEPHERD OF THE HILLS, THE(1964); NIGHT OF BLOODY HORROR zero(1969), p&d, w; WOMEN AND BLOODY TERROR(1970), d, w; NIGHT OF THE STRANGLER(1975), d; SOGGY BOTTOM U.S.A.(1982), w
1984
TIGHTROPE(1984)
Misc. Talkies
BRAIN MACHINE, THE(1972), d
Joy N. Houck, Sr.
WOMEN AND BLOODY TERROR(1970), w
Harry Houdini
Silents
GRIM GAME, THE(1919); MAN FROM BEYOND, THE(1922), a, w; HALDANE OF THE SECRET SERVICE(1923), a, d

Misc. Silents
TERROR ISLAND(1920); SOUL OF BRONZE, THE(1921)
Mme. Harry Houdini
MYSTIC CIRCLE MURDER(1939)
Erica Houen
OVER THE ODDS(1961, Brit.)
Donald Hough
DUDES ARE PRETTY PEOPLE(1942), w
E. Morton Hough
BORN TO GAMBLE(1935), w; CHAMPAGNE FOR BREAKFAST(1935), w; BOOTS OF DESTINY(1937), w
Silents
NAMELESS MEN(1928), w
Emerson Hough
CONQUERING HORDE, THE(1931), w; TEXANS, THE(1938), w
Silents
CAMPBELLS ARE COMING, THE(1915), w; COVERED WAGON, THE(1923), w; NORTH OF 36(1924), w; ONE HOUR OF LOVE(1927), w
Frank Hough
EXCUSE MY GLOVE(1936, Brit.)
Gillian Hough
HALF A SIXPENCE(1967, Brit.)
John Hough
SUDDEN TERROR(1970, Brit.), d; TWINS OF EVIL(1971, Brit.), d; TREASURE ISLAND(1972, Brit./Span./Fr./Ger.), d; LEGEND OF HELL HOUSE, THE(1973, Brit.), d; DIRTY MARY, CRAZY LARRY(1974), d; ESCAPE TO WITCH MOUNTAIN(1975), d; BRASS TARGET(1978), d; RETURN FROM WITCH MOUNTAIN(1978), d; WATCHER IN THE WOODS, THE(1980, Brit.), d; INCUBUS, THE(1982, Can.), d; TRIUMPHS OF A MAN CALLED HORSE(1983, US/Mex.), d
Misc. Talkies
BLACK CARRION(1984), d; CZECH MATE(1984, Brit.), d
Julian Hough
JABBERWOCKY(1977, Brit.); SHOUT, THE(1978, Brit.)
Paul Hough
IN COLD BLOOD(1967)
R. Lee Hough
Misc. Silents
GIRL-SHY COWBOY, THE(1928), d; WILD WEST ROMANCE(1928), d
R.L. Hough
SILENT WITNESS, THE(1932), d
Richard Hough
1984
BOUNTY, THE(1984), w
Stan Hough
EMPEROR OF THE NORTH POLE(1973), p; SCOTT JOPLIN(1977), p; VIVA KNIEVEL!(1977), p
Stanley L. Hough
BANDOLERO!(1968), w; UNDEFEATED, THE(1969), w
Will Hough
TIME, THE PLACE AND THE GIRL, THE(1929), w
Arnold Houghland
PANIC IN YEAR ZERO!(1962), p
Regan Houghston
Misc. Silents
HER EXCELLENCY, THE GOVERNOR(1917)
Barrie Houghton
SEE NO EVIL(1971, Brit.); FLAME(1975, Brit.); FIREFOX(1982)
1984
LASSITER(1984)
Barry Houghton
HORROR PLANET(1982, Brit.)
Buck Houghton
I DEAL IN DANGER(1966), p; ESCAPE ARTIST, THE(1982), p
Don Houghton
DRACULA A.D. 1972(1972, Brit.), w; CALL HIM MR. SHATTER(1976, Hong Kong), w; COUNT DRACULA AND HIS VAMPIRE BRIDE(1978, Brit.), w; DRACULA AND THE SEVEN GOLDEN VAMPIRES(1978, Brit./Chi.), w
Eddie Houghton
WHERE THERE'S A WILL(1936, Brit)
James Houghton
SWEET SUGAR(1972); I WANNA HOLD YOUR HAND(1978); MORE AMERICAN GRAFFITI(1979)
Katharine Houghton
GUESS WHO'S COMING TO DINNER(1967); SEEDS OF EVIL(1981); EYES OF THE AMARYLLIS, THE(1982)
Lawson Houghton
O.S.S.(1946)
Margaret Houghton
VANDERGILT DIAMOND MYSTERY, THE(1936), w; SCRUFFY(1938, Brit.), w
Shep Houghton
SEND ME NO FLOWERS(1964)
Shephard Houghton
OBJECTIVE, BURMA!(1945); JOAN OF ARC(1948)
Stanley Houghton
HINDLE WAKES(1931, Brit.), w; HOLIDAY WEEK(1952, Brit.), w
Ralph Houk
SAFE AT HOME(1962)
Ra Hould
BELOVED ENEMY(1936); BOOTS AND SADDLES(1937); DANGEROUS HOLIDAY(1937); DOCTOR'S DIARY, A(1937)
Norman Houle
EVEL KNIEVEL(1971), art d; TOP OF THE HEAP(1972), art d; BIG FOOT(1973), art d
Ray Houle
TWO(1975)
Carolyn Houlihan
BURNING, THE(1981); LITTLE SEX, A(1982)

Dale Houlihan
SPRING FEVER(1983, Can.)
James Houlihan
HIDE AND SEEK(1964, Brit.)
Keri Houlihan
TESTAMENT(1983)
Honor Hound
WHO FEARS THE DEVIL(1972)
"Hour of Charm" All-Girl Orchestra
WHEN JOHNNY COMES MARCHING HOME(1943)
James Hourigan
CAPTAIN MILKSHAKE(1970)
Henri Houry
Misc. Silents
CLUTCH OF CIRCUMSTANCE, THE(1918), d; LOVE WATCHES(1918), d
Henry Houry
Misc. Silents
MISS AMBITION(1918), d; DARING HEARTS(1919), d
Allan House
MEANEST MAN IN THE WORLD, THE(1943), w
Ashley House
SEVEN-PER-CENT SOLUTION, THE(1977, Brit.)
Billy House
GOD'S GIFT TO WOMEN(1931); SMART MONEY(1931); TALE OF TWO CITIES, A(1935); MERRY-GO-ROUND OF 1938(1937); THRILL OF A ROMANCE(1945); BEDLAM(1946); STRANGER THE(1946); EGG AND I, THE(1947); TRAIL STREET(1947); INNER SANCTUM(1948); ROGUES OF SHERWOOD FOREST(1950); WHERE DANGER LIVES(1950); PEOPLE WILL TALK(1951); SANTA FE(1951); SILVER CITY(1951); ALADDIN AND HIS LAMP(1952); OUTLAW WOMEN(1952); NAKED GUN, THE(1956); IMITATION OF LIFE(1959)
Misc. Talkies
JOE PALOOKA IN THE KNOCKOUT(1947)
Chandler House
MISSISSIPPI(1935), ed; ACCUSING FINGER, THE(1936), ed; ARIZONA RAIDERS, THE(1936), ed; BORDER FLIGHT(1936), ed; DESERT GOLD(1936), ed; BIG BROADCAST OF 1938, THE(1937), ed; SOPHIE LANG GOES WEST(1937), ed; HOTEL IMPERIAL(1939), ed; $1,000 A TOUCHDOWN(1939), ed; MOURNING BECOMES ELECTRA(1947), ed; VELVET TOUCH, THE(1948), ed; MAN OF CONFLICT(1953), ed; BETRAYED WOMEN(1955), ed; BIG TIP OFF, THE(1955), ed; LAS VEGAS SHAKEDOWN(1955), ed; NIGHT FREIGHT(1955), ed; TOUGHEST MAN ALIVE(1955), ed
Chuck House
ROOMMATES, THE(1973), makeup
Dale House
FIRST MONDAY IN OCTOBER(1981)
1984
NIGHT OF THE COMET(1984)
Dana House
CHECKERED FLAG OR CRASH(1978); GREAT SMOKEY ROADBLOCK, THE(1978)
Derina House
SUMMER HOLIDAY(1963, Brit.); STOP THE WORLD–I WANT TO GET OFF(1966, Brit.)
Don House
BURY ME NOT ON THE LONE PRAIRIE(1941); WHERE DANGER LIVES(1950); KANSAS CITY CONFIDENTIAL(1952); ABBOTT AND COSTELLO MEET THE KEYSTONE KOPS(1955); PARDNERS(1956); PROUD AND THE PROFANE, THE(1956)
Donald House
OX-BOW INCIDENT, THE(1943)
Silents
MICHIGAN KID, THE(1928)
Eric House
OEDIPUS REX(1957, Can.); ACT OF THE HEART(1970, Can.); STRANGE BREW(1983)
1984
HIGHPOINT(1984, Can.)
Jack House
Misc. Silents
SMOKING TRAIL, THE(1924); FIGHTIN' ODDS(1925)
Jane House
FUNNYMAN(1967); UP THE SANDBOX(1972); FRIENDS OF EDDIE COYLE, THE(1973); WEREWOLF OF WASHINGTON(1973); FRIDAY THE 13TH... THE ORPHAN(1979)
Jimmie House
WHITE EAGLE(1932)
Marguerite House
Silents
WARRENS OF VIRGINIA, THE(1915)
Max House
WILD RACERS, THE(1968), w
Newton House
GIRL OF THE GOLDEN WEST(1930); WE LIVE AGAIN(1934); DEVIL DOGS OF THE AIR(1935)
Peter R. House
GALLIPOLI(1981, Aus.)
Ron House
MODERN PROBLEMS(1981); BULLSHOT(1983), a, w
Ronald E. House
GOING BERSERK(1983)
Stephen House
ROMAN HOLIDAY(1953)
William House
EXPENSIVE WOMEN(1931); RECKLESS HOUR, THE(1931)
Geoffrey Household
MAN HUNT(1941), w; BRANDY FOR THE PARSON(1952, Brit.), w; SHOOT FIRST(1953, Brit.), w; DANCE OF THE DWARFS(1983, U.S., Phil.), w
Housekeeper
OBSESSED(1951, Brit.)

Houseman
WEDDING, A(1978)

Arthur Houseman
HER BODYGUARD(1933); DIAMOND JIM(1935); FIRETRAP, THE(1935); THEY MADE ME A CRIMINAL(1939); GO WEST(1940)
Silents
CLAY DOLLARS(1921); SHADOWS OF THE SEA(1922); UNDER THE RED ROBE(1923); NELLIE, THE BEAUTIFUL CLOAK MODEL(1924); BAT, THE(1926); DESERT'S PRICE, THE(1926); ANKLES PREFERRED(1927)
Misc. Silents
SNITCHING HOUR, THE(1922)

John Houseman
TWO WEEKS IN ANOTHER TOWN(1962), p; JANE EYRE(1944), w; MISS SUSIE SLAGLE'S(1945), p; UNSEEN, THE(1945), p; BLUE DAHLIA, THE(1946), p; LETTER FROM AN UNKNOWN WOMAN(1948), p; THEY LIVE BY NIGHT(1949), p; COMPANY SHE KEEPS, THE(1950), p; ON DANGEROUS GROUND(1951), p; BAD AND THE BEAUTIFUL, THE(1952), p; HOLIDAY FOR SINNERS(1952), p; JULIUS CAESAR(1953), p; EXECUTIVE SUITE(1954), p; HER TWELVE MEN(1954), p; COBWEB, THE(1955), p; MOONFLEET(1955), p; LUST FOR LIFE(1956), p; NIGHT AMBUSH(1958, Brit.); ALL FALL DOWN(1962), p; IN THE COOL OF THE DAY(1963), p; SEVEN DAYS IN MAY(1964); THIS PROPERTY IS CONDEMNED(1966), p; PAPER CHASE, THE(1973); ROLLERBALL(1975); THREE DAYS OF THE CONDOR(1975); ST. IVES(1976); CHEAP DETECTIVE, THE(1978); OLD BOYFRIENDS(1979); FOG, THE(1980); MY BODYGUARD(1980); WHOLLY MOSES(1980); BELLS(1981, Can.); GHOST STORY(1981)

Phyllis Houseman
NIGHT AMBUSH(1958, Brit.)

Vanaghan S. Housepian
THINGS ARE TOUGH ALL OVER(1982)

Bud Houser
Silents
COLLEGE(1927)

Gretchen Houser
HOLLYWOOD OR BUST(1956); LADIES MAN, THE(1961)

Jerry Houser
SUMMER OF '42(1971); BAD COMPANY(1972); CLASS OF '44(1973); SLAP SHOT(1977); MAGIC(1978)

Kelly Houser
COWARDS(1970)

Lionel Houser
GRAND EXIT(1935), w; PUBLIC MENACE(1935), w; DEVIL'S SQUADRON(1936), w; LONE WOLF RETURNS, THE(1936), w; BORDER CAFE(1937), w; I PROMISE TO PAY(1937), w; LET THEM LIVE(1937), w; BLIND ALIBI(1938), w; CONDEMNED WOMEN(1938), w; NIGHT SPOT(1938), w; SKY GIANT(1938), w; SMASHING THE RACKETS(1938), w; FIRST LOVE(1939), w; FORGOTTEN WOMAN, THE(1939), w; GIRL FROM MEXICO, THE(1939), w; SABOTAGE(1939), w; TELL NO TALES(1939), w; THEY MADE HER A SPY(1939), w; THIRD FINGER, LEFT HAND(1940), w; DESIGN FOR SCANDAL(1941), w; YANK AT ETON, A(1942), w; THREE HEARTS FOR JULIA(1943), w; CHRISTMAS IN CONNECTICUT(1945), w; BLUE SIERRA(1946), w; COURAGE OF LASSIE(1946), w; FAITHFUL IN MY FASHION(1946), p, w; ADVENTURE IN BALTIMORE(1949), w; CARGO TO CAPETOWN(1950), p&w; SECRET FURY, THE(1950), w

Lionel Mervin Houser
LOVE TAKES FLIGHT(1937), w

Marvin J. Houser
PARDNERS(1956), w

Mervin J. Houser
RHYTHM ON THE RANGE(1936), w

Patrick Houser
ENDANGERED SPECIES(1982)
1984
HOT DOG...THE MOVIE(1984)

Robert Houser
HANGUP(1974), ph

Arthur Housman
SINGING FOOL, THE(1928); SINS OF THE FATHERS(1928); BROADWAY(1929); FAST COMPANY(1929); QUEEN OF THE NIGHTCLUBS(1929); SIDE STREET(1929); SONG OF LOVE, THE(1929); TIMES SQUARE(1929); FEET FIRST(1930); GIRL OF THE GOLDEN WEST(1930); OFFICER O'BRIEN(1930); SQUEALER(1930); ANYBODY'S BLONDE(1931); FIVE AND TEN(1931); NIGHT LIFE IN RENO(1931); HAT CHECK GIRL(1932); INTRUDER(1932); MOVIE CRAZY(1932); NO MORE ORCHIDS(1933); SHE DONE HIM WRONG(1933); SING SINNER, SING(1933); WAY TO LOVE, THE(1933); HERE IS MY HEART(1934); KANSAS CITY PRINCESS(1934); MERRY WIDOW, THE(1934); MRS. WIGGS OF THE CABBAGE PATCH(1934); 365 NIGHTS IN HOLLYWOOD(1934); HOLD'EM YALE(1935); PARIS IN SPRING(1935); TWO FOR TONIGHT(1935); OUR RELATIONS(1936); RIFF-RAFF(1936); SHOW BOAT(1936); DOUBLE OR NOTHING(1937); STEP LIVELY, JEEVES(1937); WITH LOVE AND KISSES(1937); HARD TO GET(1938); RACING BLOOD(1938); WHERE THE WEST BEGINS(1938); NAVY SECRETS(1939); NO TIME FOR COMEDY(1940); PUBLIC ENEMIES(1941)
Silents
PERSUASIVE PEGGY(1917); ALL WOMAN(1918); FLAPPER, THE(1920); FIGHTER, THE(1921); WAY OF A MAID, THE(1921); DESTINY'S ISLE(1922); NECESSARY EVIL, THE(1925); NIGHT LIFE OF NEW YORK(1925); EARLY TO WED(1926); BERTHA, THE SEWING MACHINE GIRL(1927); LOVE MAKES 'EM WILD(1927); ROUGH HOUSE ROSIE(1927); SUNRISE–A SONG OF TWO HUMANS(1927); PARTNERS IN CRIME(1928)
Misc. Silents
APACHES OF PARIS, THE(1915); HER GOOD NAME(1917); MOTHER'S ORDEAL, A(1917); BACK TO THE WOODS(1918); BONDAGE OF BARBARA, THE(1919); TOBY'S BOW(1919); BLOOMING ANGEL, THE(1920); FOOL AND HIS MONEY, A(1920); ROAD OF AMBITION, THE(1920); IS LIFE WORTH LIVING?(1921); ROOM AND BOARD(1921); MAN WANTED(1922); PROPHET'S PARADISE, THE(1922); WHY ANNOUNCE YOUR MARRIAGE?(1922); MALE WANTED(1923); WIFE IN NAME ONLY(1923); BRAVEHEART(1925)

Laurence Housman
VICTORIA THE GREAT(1937, Brit.), w
Silents
PRUNELLA(1918), w

Jerry Housner
NEVER FEAR(1950); BIGAMIST,THE(1953)

Alfred Houston
NEAR THE RAINBOW'S END(1930)

Anthony Houston
MARS NEEDS WOMEN(1966); ZONTAR, THE THING FROM VENUS(1966)

Bill Houston
IN-LAWS, THE(1979)

Billie Houston
HAPPY DAYS ARE HERE AGAIN(1936, Brit.)

Bob Houston
1941(1979)

Bobby Houston
1984
BAD MANNERS(1984), a, d, w

Brett Houston
BLAZING FOREST, THE(1952); COW COUNTRY(1953); JUBILEE TRAIL(1954)

Charles Houston
ROOM TO LET(1949, Brit.); PANIC IN THE PARLOUR(1957, Brit.); MAN UPSTAIRS, THE(1959, Brit.); HELL IS A CITY(1960, Brit.); NEVER LET GO(1960, Brit.); PRIVATE POOLEY(1962, Brit./E. Ger.); VALIANT, THE(1962, Brit./Ital.); THAT KIND OF GIRL(1963, Brit.); CRIMSON BLADE, THE(1964, Brit.); DEVIL-SHIP PIRATES, THE(1964, Brit.); BLACK TORMENT, THE(1965, Brit.); JIG SAW(1965, Brit.); PANIC(1966, Brit.); WHERE THE BULLETS FLY(1966, Brit.); LOST CONTINENT, THE(1968, Brit.)

Clyde Houston
Misc. Talkies
FOX STYLE(1973), d

Danny Houston
HUMAN FACTOR, THE(1975)

David Houston
CARNIVAL ROCK(1957); COTTONPICKIN' CHICKENPICKERS(1967)

Donald Houston
BLUE LAGOON, THE(1949, Brit.); DANCE HALL(1950, Brit.); RUN FOR YOUR MONEY, A(1950, Brit.); CROW HOLLOW(1952, Brit.); MY DEATH IS A MOCKERY(1952, Brit.); LARGE ROPE, THE(1953, Brit.); SMALL TOWN STORY(1953, Brit.); DEVIL'S HARBOR(1954, Brit.); DOCTOR IN THE HOUSE(1954, Brit.); HAPPINESS OF THREE WOMEN, THE(1954, Brit.); PARATROOPER(1954, Brit.); FLAW, THE(1955, Brit.); BATTLE HELL(1956, Brit.); DOUBLE CROSS(1956, Brit.); FIND THE LADY(1956, Brit.); GIRL IN THE PICTURE, THE(1956, Brit.); SURGEON'S KNIFE, THE(1957, Brit.); MAN UPSTAIRS, THE(1959, Brit.); QUESTION OF ADULTERY, A(1959, Brit.); ROOM AT THE TOP(1959, Brit.); BREAKOUT(1960, Brit.); MARK, THE(1961, Brit.); LONGEST DAY, THE(1962); TWICE AROUND THE DAFFODILS(1962, Brit.); 300 SPARTANS, THE(1962); CARRY ON JACK(1963, Brit.); DOCTOR IN DISTRESS(1963, Brit.); MANIAC(1963, Brit.); SQUADRON 633(1964, U.S./Brit.); 633 SQUADRON(1964); STUDY IN TERROR, A(1966, Brit./Ger.); VIKING QUEEN, THE(1967, Brit.); WHERE EAGLES DARE(1968, Brit.); BUSHBABY, THE(1970); MY LOVER, MY SON(1970, Brit.); TALES THAT WITNESS MADNESS(1973, Brit.); CLASH OF THE TITANS(1981); SEA WOLVES, THE(1981, Brit.)

Eddy L. Houston
Misc. Talkies
GO DOWN DEATH(1944)

George Houston
MELODY LINGERS ON, THE(1935); CAPTAIN CALAMITY(1936); LET'S SING AGAIN(1936); CONQUEST(1937); WALLABY JIM OF THE ISLANDS(1937); BLOCKADE(1938); GREAT WALTZ, THE(1938); MARIE ANTOINETTE(1938); FRONTIER SCOUT(1939); HOWARDS OF VIRGINIA, THE(1940); LAUGHING AT DANGER(1940); LONE RIDER AMBUSHED, THE(1941); LONE RIDER CROSSES THE RIO, THE(1941); LONE RIDER FIGHTS BACK, THE(1941); LONE RIDER IN GHOST TOWN, THE(1941); LONE RIDER AND THE BANDIT, THE(1942); LONE RIDER IN CHEYENNE, THE(1942)
Misc. Talkies
LONE RIDER IN FRONTIER FURY, THE(1941); LONE RIDER RIDES ON, THE(1941); BORDER ROUNDUP(1942); OUTLAWS OF BOULDER PASS(1942); TEXAS JUSTICE(1942)

Glyn Houston
TRIO(1950, Brit.); HOME TO DANGER(1951, Brit.); GIRDLE OF GOLD(1952, Brit.); GLORY AT SEA(1952, Brit.); WIDE BOY(1952, Brit.); CRUEL SEA, THE(1953); GREAT GAME, THE(1953, Brit.); HAPPINESS OF THREE WOMEN, THE(1954, Brit.); HELL BELOW ZERO(1954, Brit.); RAINBOW JACKET, THE(1954, Brit.); RIVER BEAT(1954); SLEEPING TIGER, THE(1954, Brit.); TURN THE KEY SOFTLY(1954, Brit.); PASSAGE HOME(1955, Brit.); SEA SHALL NOT HAVE THEM, THE(1955, Brit.); PRIVATE'S PROGRESS(1956, Brit.); HIGH FLIGHT(1957, Brit.); TEARS FOR SIMON(1957, Brit.); THIRD KEY, THE(1957, Brit.); ONE THAT GOT AWAY, THE(1958, Brit.); CRY FROM THE STREET, A(1959, Brit.); BULLDOG BREED, THE(1960, Brit.); CIRCUS OF HORRORS(1960, Brit.); FLAME IN THE STREETS(1961, Brit.); GREEN HELMET, THE(1961, Brit.); JET STORM(1961, Brit.); WIND OF CHANGE, THE(1961, Brit.); EMERGENCY(1962, Brit.); MIX ME A PERSON(1962, Brit.); PAYROLL(1962, Brit.); BRIGAND OF KANDAHAR, THE(1965, Brit.); INVASION(1965, Brit.); ONE WAY PENDULUM(1965, Brit.); SECRET OF BLOOD ISLAND, THE(1965, Brit.); PANIC(1966, Brit.); SOLO FOR SPARROW(1966, Brit.); STITCH IN TIME, A(1967, Brit.); HEADLINE HUNTERS(1968, Brit.); SEA WOLVES, THE(1981, Brit.)

Grace Houston
SENATOR WAS INDISCREET, THE(1947), cos; MR. PEABODY AND THE MERMAID(1948), cos; NAKED CITY, THE(1948), cos; CRIME OF PASSION(1957), cos

James Houston
DUNGEONS OF HARROW(1964), ph; NO MAN'S LAND(1964), ph; WHITE DAWN, THE(1974), w

Jean Houston
I KNOW WHERE I'M GOING(1947, Brit.)

Josephine Houston
ON WITH THE SHOW(1929)

Julian Houston
STRANGERS ON A HONEYMOON(1937, Brit.), w

Karen Houston
RETURN OF COUNT YORGA, THE(1971)

Melvin Houston
Silents
BOWERY CINDERELLA(1927), w

Brit.); FOOTSTEPS IN THE FOG(1955, Brit.); GLASS TOMB, THE(1955, Brit.); INTRUDER, THE(1955, Brit.); LADY GODIVA RIDES AGAIN(1955, Brit.); LIGHT TOUCH, THE(1955, Brit.); LOVERS, HAPPY LOVERS!(1955, Brit.); ONE WAY OUT(1955, Brit.); WICKED WIFE(1955, Brit.); WILL ANY GENTLEMAN?(1955, Brit.); ONE WISH TOO MANY(1956, Brit.); OUT OF THE CLOUDS(1957, Brit.); I ACCUSE(1958, Brit.); I ONLY ASKED!(1958, Brit.); LAW AND DISORDER(1958, Brit.); MAD LITTLE ISLAND(1958, Brit.); LIBEL(1959, Brit.); NOWHERE TO GO(1959, Brit.); BOTTOMS UP(1960, Brit.); WATCH IT, SAILOR!(1961, Brit.); KILL OR CURE(1962, Brit.); PARADISIO(1962, Brit.); FRIENDS AND NEIGHBORS(1963, Brit.); JOY HOUSE(1964, Fr.); LADIES WHO DO(1964, Brit.); LADY L(1965, Fr./Ital.); GRAND PRIX(1966); SHOES OF THE FISHERMAN, THE(1968); BEST HOUSE IN LONDON, THE(1969, Brit.); HOVERBUG(1970, Brit.); MY LOVER, MY SON(1970, Brit.); STEPTOE AND SON(1972, Brit.); BAWDY ADVENTURES OF TOM JONES, THE(1976, Brit.); MOONRAKER(1979, Brit.); PRISONER OF ZENDA, THE(1979); MISSIONARY, THE(1982); TRAIL OF THE PINK PANTHER, THE(1982); CURSE OF THE PINK PANTHER(1983)
1984
ANOTHER COUNTRY(1984, Brit.)
Silents
BROKEN BLOSSOMS(1919)
Misc. Silents
PERIWINKLE(1917)

Barbara Howard
1984
FRIDAY THE 13TH–THE FINAL CHAPTER(1984); RACING WITH THE MOON(1984)

Ben Howard
OH! WHAT A LOVELY WAR(1969, Brit.); VILLAIN(1971, Brit.); ZEPPELIN(1971, Brit.); FROM BEYOND THE GRAVE(1974, Brit.); LAND THAT TIME FORGOT, THE(1975, Brit.)

Bert Howard
BOY MEETS GIRL(1938); LADY SCARFACE(1941); IT HAPPENED ON 5TH AVENUE(1947)

Betsy Howard
SINCE YOU WENT AWAY(1944)

Bette Howard
SUCH GOOD FRIENDS(1971)

Betty-Joy Howard
KID MILLIONS(1934)

Bill Howard
MISSISSIPPI(1935)

Billy Howard
MEET SEXTON BLAKE(1944, Brit.); ECHO MURDERS, THE(1945, Brit.); NO ROOM AT THE INN(1950, Brit.); HOT ICE(1952, Brit.)
Misc. Talkies
MURDER WITH MUSIC(1941)

Bob Howard
Misc. Talkies
JUNCTION 88(1940)

Boothe Howard
TEXAS BAD MAN(1932); HOT PEPPER(1933); MY WOMAN(1933); TRICK FOR TRICK(1933); GAY BRIDE, THE(1934); MIDNIGHT ALIBI(1934); MYSTERY LINER(1934); EVERY NIGHT AT EIGHT(1935); MARY BURNS, FUGITIVE(1935); SHOW THEM NO MERCY(1935); SMART GIRL(1935); CHARLIE CHAN AT THE CIRCUS(1936); GREAT ZIEGFELD, THE(1936); RED RIVER VALLEY(1936); ROBIN HOOD OF EL DORADO(1936); OH, SUSANNA(1937)

Breena Howard
NAKED KISS, THE(1964)

Brenna Howard
BILLIE(1965)

Brie Howard
ANDROID(1982)

Bronson Howard
Silents
ONE OF OUR GIRLS(1914), w; SAPHEAD, THE(1921), w

Bruce Howard
KING KONG VERSUS GODZILLA(1963, Jap.), w

Buddy Howard
DATE WITH JUDY, A(1948)

Cal Howard
MR. BUG GOES TO TOWN(1941), w; ZIEGFELD FOLLIES(1945), w

Candice Howard
HOPSCOTCH(1980)

Catherine Howard
NO ROOM FOR THE GROOM(1952); GOOD MORNING, MISS DOVE(1955); HARD ROAD, THE(1970)

Cathy Howard
SCHOOL FOR SEX(1969, Brit.); SECRETS OF SEX(1970, Brit.)

Charles Howard
NIGHT ANGEL, THE(1931); STRANGE EXPERIMENT(1937, Brit.); GABLES MYSTERY, THE(1938, Brit.)
Silents
IN FOLLY'S TRAIL(1920); HOME STRUCK(1927)

Charles Gordon Howard
DEVIL MAKES THREE, THE(1952)

Cheryl Howard
1984
SPLASH(1984)

Chris Howard
GIRL IN GOLD BOOTS(1968)

Christine Howard
ZAZIE(1961, Fr.)

Christopher Howard
LADYBUG, LADYBUG(1963)

Clarence Howard
GREEN SLIME, THE(1969)

Clifford Howard
Silents
LADY ROBINHOOD(1925), w; KING OF KINGS, THE(1927), ed

Clint Howard
EYE FOR AN EYE, AN(1966); GENTLE GIANT(1967); JUNGLE BOOK, THE(1967); WILD COUNTRY, THE(1971); SALTY(1975); EAT MY DUST!(1976); GRAND THEFT AUTO(1977); HARPER VALLEY, P.T.A.(1978); ROCK 'N' ROLL HIGH SCHOOL(1979); EVILSPEAK(1982); NIGHT SHIFT(1982)
1984
SPLASH(1984)

Connie Howard
SPLENDOR(1935)

Constance Howard
WEDDING NIGHT, THE(1935)
Silents
WHITE BLACK SHEEP, THE(1926); NIGHT BRIDE, THE(1927); SMART SET, THE(1928)
Misc. Silents
HOLD THAT LION(1926); POOR MILLIONAIRE, THE(1930)

Curly Howard
HOLLYWOOD PARTY(1934); MYRT AND MARGE(1934)

Cy Howard
MY FRIEND IRMA(1949), w; MY FRIEND IRMA GOES WEST(1950), w; THAT'S MY BOY(1951), w; MARRIAGE ON THE ROCKS(1965), w; LOVERS AND OTHER STRANGERS(1970), d; EVERY LITTLE CROOK AND NANNY(1972), d, w; WON TON TON, THE DOG WHO SAVED HOLLYWOOD(1976), w

Daffyd Howard
LAST DAYS OF DOLWYN, THE(1949, Brit.)

Dan Howard
EIGER SANCTION, THE(1975); HOLLYWOOD HIGH(1977)

Dave Howard
LOST JUNGLE, THE(1934), d; DEMON LOVER, THE(1977)

David Howard
GOLDEN WEST, THE(1932), d; MYSTERY RANCH(1932), d; RAINBOW TRAIL(1932), d; QUANDO EL AMOR RIE(1933), d; CRIMSON ROMANCE(1934), d; LOST JUNGLE, THE(1934), w; HARD ROCK HARRIGAN(1935), d; IN OLD SANTA FE(1935), d; MARINES ARE COMING, THE(1935), d; THUNDER MOUNTAIN(1935), d; WHISPERING SMITH SPEAKS(1935), d; BORDER PATROLMAN, THE(1936), d; DANIEL BOONE(1936), d; MINE WITH THE IRON DOOR, THE(1936), d; O'MALLEY OF THE MOUNTED(1936), d; CONFLICT(1937), d; PARK AVENUE LOGGER(1937), d; WINDJAMMER(1937), p; BORDER G-MAN(1938), d; GUN LAW(1938), d; HOLLYWOOD STADIUM MYSTERY(1938), d; LAWLESS VALLEY(1938), d; PAINTED DESERT, THE(1938), d; RENEGADE RANGER(1938), d; ARIZONA LEGION(1939), d; FIGHTING GRINGO, THE(1939), d; MARSHAL OF MESA CITY, THE(1939), d; ROOKIE COP, THE(1939), d; TIMBER STAMPEDE(1939), d; TROUBLE IN SUNDOWN(1939), d; BULLET CODE(1940), d; LEGION OF THE LAWLESS(1940), d; PRAIRIE LAW(1940), d; TRIPLE JUSTICE(1940), d; DUDE COWBOY(1941), d; SIX GUN GOLD(1941), d
Misc. Talkies
SMOKE LIGHTNING(1933), d
Silents
ANN'S FINISH(1918)
Misc. Silents
BIT OF JADE, A(1918); JILTED JANET(1918)

Dennis Howard
GO TELL THE SPARTANS(1978); MAKING LOVE(1982)

Dick Howard
CAPTAINS COURAGEOUS(1937)
Silents
CYCLONE OF THE RANGE(1927)

Don Howard
MAHOGANY(1975)

Douglas Howard
DESPERATE WOMEN, THE(?)

Duke Howard
SOMETHING WILD(1961); MURDERERS' ROW(1966)

Ed Howard
MAGNIFICENT AMBERSONS, THE(1942)

Edward Howard
STORY OF DR. WASSELL, THE(1944); TUCSON RAIDERS(1944); CODE OF THE LAWLESS(1945); LADY CONFESSES(1945); THREE IN THE SADDLE(1945); NAVAJO KID, THE(1946); THUNDER TOWN(1946)

Edward M. Howard
FRONTIER GAL(1945)

Eldon Howard
WOMAN OF MYSTERY, A(1957, Brit.), w; BETRAYAL, THE(1958, Brit.), w; LINKS OF JUSTICE(1958), w; MOMENT OF INDISCRETION(1958, Brit.), w; ON THE RUN(1958, Brit.), w; THREE CROOKED MEN(1958, Brit.), w; WOMAN POSSESSED, A(1958, Brit.), w; CHILD AND THE KILLER, THE(1959, Brit.), w; CRASH DRIVE(1959, Brit.), w; HIGH JUMP(1959, Brit.), w; HONOURABLE MURDER, AN(1959, Brit.), w; INNOCENT MEETING(1959, Brit.), w; TOP FLOOR GIRL(1959, Brit.), w; WEB OF SUSPICION(1959, Brit.), w; WOMAN'S TEMPTATION, A(1959, Brit.), w; SENTENCED FOR LIFE(1960, Brit.), w; SPIDER'S WEB, THE(1960, Brit.), w; TWO WIVES AT ONE WEDDING(1961, Brit.), w; DURANT AFFAIR, THE(1962, Brit.), w; TELL-TALE HEART, THE(1962, Brit.), w; THREE SPARE WIVES(1962, Brit.), w; GREAT VAN ROBBERY, THE(1963, Brit.), w

Elizabeth Howard
GIRL IN ROOM 13(1961, U.S./Braz.)

Elizabeth Jane Howard
VERY EDGE, THE(1963, Brit.), w

Eric Howard
LYONS MAIL, THE(1931, Brit.)

Ernest Howard
Silents
TRAFFIC COP, THE(1916)
Misc. Silents
FIVE FAULTS OF FLO, THE(1916); WOMAN IN POLITICS, THE(1916); FIRES OF YOUTH(1917)

Esther Howard
TRUE TO LIFE(1943); WITHOUT RESERVATIONS(1946); VICE SQUAD, THE(1931); COHENS, AND KELLYS IN HOLLYWOOD, THE(1932); LADIES OF THE BIG HOUSE(1932); MERRILY WE GO TO HELL(1932); RACKETY RAX(1932); WINNER TAKE ALL(1932); BELOW THE SEA(1933); IRON MASTER, THE(1933); SECOND

HAND WIFE(1933); READY FOR LOVE(1934); FARMER TAKES A WIFE, THE(1935); MARY BURNS, FUGITIVE(1935); STARS OVER BROADWAY(1935); STRAIGHT FROM THE HEART(1935); KLONDIKE ANNIE(1936); M'LISS(1936); DEAD END(1937); PARTNERS IN CRIME(1937); RHYTHM IN THE CLOUDS(1937); SWING HIGH, SWING LOW(1937); MARIE ANTOINETTE(1938); MEET THE MAYOR(1938); SCANDAL STREET(1938); SWING, SISTER, SWING(1938); TEXANS, THE(1938); BROADWAY SERENADE(1939); GREAT McGINTY, THE(1940); LADY FROM CHEYENNE(1941); SAN FRANCISCO DOCKS(1941); SULLIVAN'S TRAVELS(1941); JACKASS MAIL(1942); MY FAVORITE BLONDE(1942); PALM BEACH STORY, THE(1942); TALES OF MANHATTAN(1942); BIG NOISE, THE(1944); HAIL THE CONQUERING HERO(1944); MIRACLE OF MORGAN'S CREEK, THE(1944); ONCE UPON A TIME(1944); SAN DIEGO, I LOVE YOU(1944); ADVENTURE(1945); DE-TOUR(1945); FALCON IN SAN FRANCISCO, THE(1945); GREAT FLAMARION, THE(1945); LETTER FOR EVIE, A(1945); MURDER, MY SWEET(1945); DICK TRACY VS. CUEBALL(1946); FALCON'S ALIBI, THE(1946); BORN TO KILL(1947); SONG OF THE THIN MAN(1947); TROUBLE WITH WOMEN, THE(1947); JUNE BRIDE(1948); VELVET TOUCH, THE(1948); BEAUTIFUL BLONDE FROM BASHFUL BEND, THE(1949); HELLFIRE(1949); HOMICIDE(1949); LADY GAMBLES, THE(1949); LOOK FOR THE SILVER LINING(1949); CAGED(1950); NO MAN OF HER OWN(1950)

Ethlyn Howard
GEORGE WHITE'S SCANDALS(1934)

F. Ruth Howard
DANGEROUS INTRUDER(1945), w

Flora Howard
Silents
KID, THE(1921)

Florence Howard
HIGH BARBAREE(1947)

Frances Howard
Misc. Silents
SHOCK PUNCH, THE(1925); SWAN, THE(1925); TOO MANY KISSES(1925)

Frank Howard
IT GROWS ON TREES(1952)
1984
SIXTEEN CANDLES(1984)
Misc. Silents
TEXAS TORNADO, THE(1928), d

Frankie Howard
RUNAWAY BUS, THE(1954, Brit.); LADYKILLERS, THE(1956, Brit.); GREAT ST. TRINIAN'S TRAIN ROBBERY, THE(1966, Brit.)

Fred Howard
FRONT PAGE, THE(1931); MAN WHO PLAYED GOD, THE(1932); RICHEST GIRL IN THE WORLD, THE(1934); ONCE UPON A TIME(1944); TOGETHER AGAIN(1944); VAMPIRE'S GHOST, THE(1945); TILL THE END OF TIME(1946); DOWN TO EARTH(1947); GUILT OF JANET AMES, THE(1947); HER HUSBAND'S AF-FAIRS(1947); SLIGHTLY FRENCH(1949)

Frederic Howard
RAIN(1932)

Frederick Howard
FOOTLIGHTS AND FOOLS(1929); NUMBERED MEN(1930); GUILTY GENERA-TION, THE(1931); DESTRY RIDES AGAIN(1932); TWO SECONDS(1932); FOURTH HORSEMAN, THE(1933); GREAT STAGECOACH ROBBERY(1945)

Fredrick Howard
GOODBYE, MY FANCY(1951)

Garth Howard
MALIBU HIGH(1979); STACY'S KNIGHTS(1983)

Gene Howard
CODE OF THE FEARLESS(1939); IN OLD MONTANA(1939); TWO-GUN TROUBA-DOR(1939)

George Howard
TOY, THE(1982)
Misc. Silents
DARKEST HOUR, THE(1920); THIEF, THE(1920); WHAT'S YOUR REPUTATION WORTH?(1921)

George Bronson Howard
Silents
BORROWED FINERY(1925), w; MAN FROM HEADQUARTERS(1928), w

George Bronston Howard
Silents
SNOBS(1915), w

Gertrude Howard
HEARTS IN DIXIE(1929); HIS CAPTIVE WOMAN(1929); SHOW BOAT(1929); CON-SPIRACY(1930); GUILTY?(1930); FATHER'S SON(1931); PRODIGAL, THE(1931); SE-CRET SERVICE(1931); STRANGERS IN LOVE(1932); WET PARADE, THE(1932); I'M NO ANGEL(1933); FIGHTING CODE, THE(1934); PECK'S BAD BOY(1934); FORBID-DEN TRAIL(1936)
Silents
EASY PICKINGS(1927)

Gordon Howard
THEY WERE SO YOUNG(1955); BATTLE STATIONS(1956)
Misc. Talkies
BLACK FOREST, THE(1954)

Harold Howard
DARK ANGEL, THE(1935); MAID OF SALEM(1937); EARL OF CHICAGO, THE(1940); ONE MILLION B.C.(1940); MRS. MINIVER(1942)
Silents
TAILOR MADE MAN, A(1922)
Misc. Silents
OFFICER 666(1914); STOP THIEF(1915)

Harry Howard
SUCH GOOD FRIENDS(1971), ed; SHAFT'S BIG SCORE(1972), ed; EDUCATION OF SONNY CARSON, THE(1974), ph; SUPER COPS, THE(1974), ed; LEADBELLY(1976), ed

Hartley Howard
ASSIGNMENT K(1968, Brit.), w

Hash Howard
OUT OF TOWNERS, THE(1970)

Hazel Howard
GIRLS ABOUT TOWN(1931)

Helen Howard
VARIETY HOUR(1937, Brit.); TOY, THE(1982)
Silents
DESERTED AT THE ALTAR(1922)
Misc. Silents
GHOST OF ROSY TAYLOR, THE(1918); BRASS BUTTONS(1919); MY WILD IRISH ROSE(1922)

Henry Howard
LOVE WITH THE PROPER STRANGER(1963)
Misc. Talkies
BRIG, THE(1965)

Irving Howard
THESE CHARMING PEOPLE(1931, Brit.), w

Jack Howard
BLUE GRASS OF KENTUCKY(1950); MAN IN THE WHITE SUIT, THE(1952); CRUEL SEA, THE(1953)
Silents
LOVES OF RICARDO, THE(1926)

James Howard
ESCAPE ARTIST, THE(1982)

Jane Howard
FRANCIS IN THE NAVY(1955); TARANTULA(1955); I'VE LIVED BEFORE(1956); THERE'S ALWAYS TOMORROW(1956); WRITTEN ON THE WIND(1956); GUN FOR A COWARD(1957); NIGHT RUNNER, THE(1957); BIG SWITCH, THE(1970, Brit.)

Jean Howard
BROADWAY TO HOLLYWOOD(1933); PRIZEFIGHTER AND THE LADY, THE(1933); WOMEN IN HIS LIFE, THE(1934); BREAK OF HEARTS(1935); WE'RE ON THE JURY(1937); CLAUDIA(1943); BERMUDA MYSTERY(1944)

Jeff Howard
UP THE DOWN STAIRCASE(1967); PRIVATE BENJAMIN(1980), art d; TRUE CONFESSIONS(1981)

Jennifer Howard
GENTLEMAN'S AGREEMENT(1935, Brit.), w; RETURN TO PEYTON PLACE(1961); ALL FALL DOWN(1962); CHAPMAN REPORT, THE(1962); HOUSE OF WO-MEN(1962); Q(1982)

Jenny Howard
DODGING THE DOLE(1936, Brit.)

Jerry Howard
DANCING LADY(1933); MEET THE BARON(1933); FUGITIVE LOVERS(1934)

Jerry "Curly" Howard
ROCKIN' IN THE ROCKIES(1945)

Joan Howard
REUNION(1936); LOVE IN A BUNGALOW(1937); SWING YOUR LADY(1938); WOMAN DOCTOR(1939); WHAT'S UP FRONT(1964); INCREDIBLY STRANGE CREA-TURES WHO STOPPED LIVING AND BECAME CRAZY MIXED-UP ZOMBIES, THE(1965); MC MASTERS, THE(1970)

John Howard
ANNAPOLIS FAREWELL(1935); CAR 99(1935); FOUR HOURS TO KILL(1935); MILLIONS IN THE AIR(1935); BORDER FLIGHT(1936); EASY TO TAKE(1936); SOAK THE RICH(1936); THIRTEEN HOURS BY AIR(1936); VALIANT IS THE WORD FOR CARRIE(1936); BULLDOG DRUMMOND COMES BACK(1937); BULLDOG DRUM-MOND'S REVENGE(1937); HITTING A NEW HIGH(1937); HOLD'EM NAVY!(1937); LET THEM LIVE(1937); LOST HORIZON(1937); MOUNTAIN MUSIC(1937); BULL-DOG DRUMMOND IN AFRICA(1938); BULLDOG DRUMMOND'S PERIL(1938); PENITENTIARY(1938); PRISON FARM(1938); TOUCHDOWN, ARMY(1938); ARREST BULLDOG DRUMMOND(1939, Brit.); BULLDOG DRUMMOND'S BRIDE(1939); BULLDOG DRUMMOND'S SECRET POLICE(1939); DISPUTED PASSAGE(1939); GRAND JURY SECRETS(1939); WHAT A LIFE(1939); GREEN HELL(1940); MAN FROM DAKOTA, THE(1940); PHILADELPHIA STORY, THE(1940); TEXAS RANG-ERS RIDE AGAIN(1940); FATHER TAKES A WIFE(1941); INVISIBLE WOMAN, THE(1941); MAD DOCTOR, THE(1941); THREE GIRLS ABOUT TOWN(1941); TIGHT SHOES(1941); ISLE OF MISSING MEN(1942); MAN WHO RETURNED TO LIFE, THE(1942); SUBMARINE RAIDER(1942); TRAGEDY AT MIDNIGHT, A(1942); UNDY-ING MONSTER, THE(1942); LAMP STILL BURNS, THE(1943, Brit.); TWILIGHT HOUR(1944, Brit.); JOHNNY IN THE CLOUDS(1945, Brit.); WALTZ TIME(1946, Brit.); LOVE FROM A STRANGER(1947); I, JANE DOE(1948); QUEEN OF SPADES(1948, Brit.); THEY ARE NOT ANGELS(1948, Fr.); FIGHTING KENTUCKIAN, THE(1949); EXPERIMENT ALCATRAZ(1950); RADAR SECRET SERVICE(1950); MODELS, INC.(1952); HIGH AND THE MIGHTY, THE(1954); MAKE HASTE TO LIVE(1954); UNKNOWN TERROR, THE(1957); DESTINATION INNER SPACE(1966); SKY BIKE, THE(1967, Brit.); DESTRUCTORS, THE(1968); BUCK AND THE PREACHER(1972); SCALAWAG(1973, Yugo.), ed; YOUNG FRANKENSTEIN(1974), ed; DROWNING POOL, THE(1975), ed; CLUB, THE(1980, Aus.); HISTORY OF THE WORLD, PART 1(1981), ed; BUSH CHRISTMAS(1983, Aus.)
1984
RAZORBACK(1984, Aus.)

John C. Howard
BUTCH CASSIDY AND THE SUNDANCE KID(1969), ed; BELIEVE IN ME(1971), ed; SEPARATE PEACE, A(1972), ed; BLAZING SADDLES(1974), ed; SILENT MO-VIE(1976), ed; W.C. FIELDS AND ME(1976), ed; HIGH ANXIETY(1977), ed; MARCH OR DIE(1977, Brit.), ed; AMERICATHON(1979), ed; NIGHTWING(1979), ed; WHY WOULD I LIE(1980), ed; ROMANTIC COMEDY(1983), ed

Joseph E. Howard
TIME, THE PLACE AND THE GIRL, THE(1929), w
Silents
SHOULD A WIFE FORGIVE?(1915), w

Josie Howard
Silents
GOLD RUSH, THE(1925)

Joyce Howard
COMMON TOUCH, THE(1941, Brit.); VOICE IN THE NIGHT, A(1941, Brit.); BACK ROOM BOY(1942, Brit.); TALK ABOUT JACQUELINE(1942, Brit.); TERROR HOUSE(1942, Brit.); GENTLE SEX, THE(1943, Brit.); APPOINTMENT WITH CRI-ME(1945, Brit.); LOVE ON THE DOLE(1945, Brit.); THEY KNEW MR. KNIGHT(1945, Brit.); THEY MET IN THE DARK(1945, Brit.); WOMAN TO WOMAN(1946, Brit.); MRS. FITZHERBERT(1950, Brit.); SHADOW OF THE PAST(1950, Brit.)

Judy Howard
GHOST OF DRAGSTRIP HOLLOW(1959); STUDS LONIGAN(1960); ANATOMY OF A PSYCHO(1961); ERRAND BOY, THE(1961)

Kate Howard
GREAT MUPPET CAPER, THE(1981)

Kathleen Howard
DEATH TAKES A HOLIDAY(1934); IT'S A GIFT(1934); ONCE TO EVERY BACHE-LOR(1934); ONE MORE RIVER(1934); YOU'RE TELLING ME(1934); MAN ON THE FLYING TRAPEZE, THE(1935); STOLEN HOLIDAY(1937); LETTER OF INTRODUC-TION(1938); FIRST LOVE(1939); LITTLE ACCIDENT(1939); FIVE LITTLE PEPPERS IN TROUBLE(1940); MYSTERY SEA RAIDER(1940); ONE NIGHT IN THE TRO-PICS(1940); YOUNG PEOPLE(1940); BALL OF FIRE(1941); BLOSSOMS IN THE DUST(1941); GIRL, A GUY AND A GOB, A(1941); SWEETHEART OF THE CAM-PUS(1941); LADY IN A JAM(1942); MAD MARTINDALES, THE(1942); TAKE A LETTER, DARLING(1942); YOU WERE NEVER LOVELIER(1942); CRASH DI-VE(1943); MY KINGDOM FOR A COOK(1943); SWING OUT THE BLUES(1943); LAURA(1944); RECKLESS AGE(1944); EADIE WAS A LADY(1945); MISS SUSIE SLAGLE'S(1945); SHADY LADY(1945); SNAFU(1945); CENTENNIAL SUM-MER(1946); CROSS MY HEART(1946); DANGER WOMAN(1946); MYSTERIOUS INTRUDER(1946); CYNTHIA(1947); LATE GEORGE APLEY, THE(1947); BRIDE GOES WILD, THE(1948); CRY OF THE CITY(1948); BORN TO BE BAD(1950); PETTY GIRL, THE(1950)

Kathryn Howard
CIRCUS GIRL(1937)

Keble Howard
LORD BABS(1932, Brit.), w; FAST LADY, THE(1963, Brit.), w
Silents
GOD IN THE GARDEN, THE(1921, Brit.), w; KING OF THE CASTLE(1925, Brit.), w

Ken Howard
TELL ME THAT YOU LOVE ME, JUNIE MOON(1970); SUCH GOOD FRIENDS(1971); STRANGE VENEGEANCE OF ROSALIE, THE(1972); 1776(1972); SECOND THOUGHTS(1983)
Misc. Talkies
MANHUNT IN SPACE(1954)

Kevyn Howard
SERIAL(1980)

Kevyn Major Howard
DEATH WISH II(1982); SUDDEN IMPACT(1983)
1984
ROADHOUSE 66(1984)

Langley Howard
SHE SHALL HAVE MUSIC(1935, Brit.); LOVE UP THE POLE(1936, Brit.); FALSE EVIDENCE(1937, Brit.); TALK OF THE DEVIL(1937, Brit.); MOUNTAINS O'MOURNE(1938, Brit.); FLAW, THE(1955, Brit.)

Laura Howard
Misc. Silents
BLAZING ARROWS(1922)

Lee Howard
SQUIRM(1976), spec eff

Leigh Howard
CHANCE MEETING(1960, Brit.), w

Leslie Howard
OUTWARD BOUND(1930); DEVOTION(1931); FIVE AND TEN(1931); FREE SOUL, A(1931); NEVER THE TWAIN SHALL MEET(1931); ANIMAL KINGDOM, THE(1932); RESERVED FOR LADIES(1932, Brit.); SMILIN' THROUGH(1932); BERKELEY SQUARE(1933); CAPTURED(1933); SECRETS(1933); BRITISH AGENT(1934); LADY IS WILLING, THE(1934, Brit.); OF HUMAN BONDAGE(1934); SCARLET PIMPERNEL, THE(1935, Brit.); PETRIFIED FOREST, THE(1936); ROMEO AND JULIET(1936); IT'S LOVE I'M AFTER(1937); STAND-IN(1937); PYGMALION(1938, Brit.), a, d; GONE WITH THE WIND(1939); INTERMEZZO: A LOVE STORY(1939); INVADERS, THE,(1941); PIMPERNEL SMITH(1942, Brit.), a, p&d; GENTLE SEX, THE(1943, Brit.), a, p, d; LAMP STILL BURNS, THE(1943, Brit.), p; SPITFIRE(1943, Brit.), a, p, d
Misc. Silents
LACKEY AND THE LADY, THE(1919, Brit.)

Lewis Howard
FIRST LOVE(1939); I'M NOBODY'S SWEETHEART NOW(1940); IT'S A DATE(1940); HELLO SUCKER(1941); HELLZAPOPPIN'(1941); HORROR ISLAND(1941); MEET THE CHUMP(1941); RAIDERS OF THE DESERT(1941); SAN FRANCISCO DOCKS(1941); SWING IT SOLDIER(1941); SEVEN SWEETHEARTS(1942); I'VE AL-WAYS LOVED YOU(1946); UP GOES MAISIE(1946); SONG OF MY HEART(1947); IN A LONELY PLACE(1950); THAT MAN IN ISTANBUL(1966, Fr./Ital./Span.), w

Lillie Howard
NIGHT CLUB SCANDAL(1937), w

Linda Howard
1984
SECRET DIARY OF SIGMUND FREUD, THE(1984), w

Lionelle Howard
Silents
HER BOY(1915, Brit.); MOLLY BAWN(1916, Brit.); AUNT RACHEL(1920, Brit.); NO. 5 JOHN STREET(1921, Brit.); DEBT OF HONOR(1922, Brit.); FLYING FIFTY-FIVE, THE(1924, Brit.); NOT FOR SALE(1924, Brit.)
Misc. Silents
DEAD HEART, THE(1914, Brit.); AS THE SUN WENT DOWN(1915, Brit.); MAN WHO STAYED AT HOME, THE(1915, Brit.); NIGHTBIRDS OF LONDON, THE(1915, Brit.); WHEN LONDON BURNED(1915, Brit.); WHITE HOPE, THE(1915, Brit.); ANNIE LAURIE(1916, Brit.); BUNCH OF VIOLETS, A(1916, Brit.); GRAND BABYLON HOTEL, THE(1916, Brit.); TRELAWNEY OF THE WELLS(1916, Brit.); CARROTS(1917, Brit.); DICK CARSON WINS THROUGH(1917, Brit.); ETERNAL TRIANGLE, THE(1917, Brit.); HER MARRIAGE LINES(1917, Brit.); MAN BEHIND "THE TIMES", THE(1917, Brit.); MERELY MRS. STUBBS(1917, Brit.); FOREST ON THE HILL, THE(1919, Brit); SHEBA(1919, Brit.); CHANNINGS, THE(1920, Brit.); THREE MEN IN A BOAT(1920, Brit.); CHERRY RIPE(1921, Brit.); DOUBLE EVENT, THE(1921, Brit.); STREET OF ADVENTURE, THE(1921, Brit.); WONDERFUL YEAR, THE(1921, Brit.); EXPIATION(1922, Brit.); PETTICOAT LOOSE(1922, Brit.); ONE ARABIAN NIGHT(1923, Brit.)

Lisa Howard
MAN WHO CHEATED HIMSELF, THE(1951); HINDU, THE(1953, Brit.); RUN-NERS(1983, Brit.)

Lisa K. Howard
DONOVAN'S BRAIN(1953)

Lois Howard
Misc. Silents
THROUGH DANTE'S FLAMES(1914)

Marianne Howard
CADDIE(1976, Aus.)

Marvin C. Howard
CREMATORS, THE(1972)

Mary Howard
MY WEAKNESS(1933); GREAT ZIEGFELD, THE(1936); ALL OVER TOWN(1937); FAST COMPANY(1938); LOVE FINDS ANDY HARDY(1938); MAN-PROOF(1938); MARIE ANTOINETTE(1938); SHOPWORN ANGEL(1938); SWEETHEARTS(1938); TEST PILOT(1938); FOUR GIRLS IN WHITE(1939); NURSE EDITH CAVELL(1939); ABE LINCOLN IN ILLINOIS(1940); BILLY THE KID(1941); RIDERS OF THE PURPLE SAGE(1941); SWAMP WATER(1941); WILD MAN OF BORNEO, THE(1941); LOVES OF EDGAR ALLAN POE, THE(1942); THRU DIFFERENT EYES(1942); WHO IS HOPE SCHUYLER?(1942); SPIRIT OF WEST POINT, THE(1947), w

Matthew Howard
GROUNDSTAR CONSPIRACY, THE(1972, Can.), w

Mel Howard
QUACKSER FORTUNE HAS A COUSIN IN THE BRONX(1970), p; HESTER STREET(1975); RENALDO AND CLARA(1978), p

Meredith Howard
KENTUCKY(1938); THEY MEET AGAIN(1941)

Michael Howard
ADVENTURESS, THE(1946, Brit.); SISTER TO ASSIST'ER, A(1948, Brit.); IT AL-WAYS RAINS ON SUNDAY(1949, Brit.); FRONT PAGE STORY(1954, Brit.); BABY AND THE BATTLESHIP, THE(1957, Brit.); OUT OF THE CLOUDS(1957, Brit.)

Mike Howard
JUST TELL ME WHAT YOU WANT(1980)

Milford W. Howard
Misc. Silents
BISHOP OF THE OZARKS, THE(1923)

Moe Howard
DANCING LADY(1933); MEET THE BARON(1933); FUGITIVE LOVERS(1934); HOLLYWOOD PARTY(1934); MYRT AND MARGE(1934); ROCKIN' IN THE ROCK-IES(1945); GOLD RAIDERS, THE(1952); SPACE MASTER X-7(1958); HAVE ROCKET, WILL TRAVEL(1959); THREE STOOGES IN ORBIT, THE(1962); THREE STOOGES MEET HERCULES, THE(1962); THREE STOOGES GO AROUND THE WORLD IN A DAZE, THE(1963); OUTLAWS IS COMING, THE(1965); DON'T WORRY, WE'LL THINK OF A TITLE(1966); DOCTOR DEATH: SEEKER OF SOULS(1973)

Nancy Howard
HICKEY AND BOGGS(1972)

Noel Howard
55 DAYS AT PEKING(1963), d; MARCO THE MAGNIFICENT(1966, Ital./Fr./Yugo./ Egypt/Afghanistan), d

Norah Howard
"W" PLAN, THE(1931, Brit.); CONDEMNED TO DEATH(1932, Brit.); LOVE, LIFE AND LAUGHTER(1934, Brit.); CAR OF DREAMS(1935, Brit.); FIGHTING STOCK(1935, Brit.); BIG NOISE, THE(1936, Brit.); LAST ADVENTURERS, THE(1937, Brit); I'VE GOT A HORSE(1938, Brit.); SAINT IN LONDON, THE(1939, Brit.); HIDDEN MENACE, THE(1940, Brit.); LAMBETH WALK, THE(1940, Brit.); MAD MEN OF EUROPE(1940, Brit.); TWO LOVES(1961)

Norman Howard
Misc. Silents
AVIATOR SPY, THE(1914, Brit.); FIENDS OF HELL(1914, Brit.)

Olin [Howlin] Howard
WIFE, DOCTOR AND NURSE(1937)

Oliver Howard
TERROR IN THE JUNGLE(1968)

Pamela Howard
GNOME-MOBILE, THE(1967)

Patricia Howard
NEW KIND OF LOVE, A(1963)

Paul Howard
CHARRIOTS OF FIRE(1981, Brit.)

Peggy Howard
HER MAN(1930)

Peter Howard
THREE NUTS IN SEARCH OF A BOLT(1964); VOICE OF THE HURRICANE(1964), w; MR. BROWN COMES DOWN THE HILL(1966, Brit.), w; GIVE A DOG A BO-NE(1967, Brit.), w; HAPPY DEATHDAY(1969, Brit.), d&w

Philip Howard
BOYD'S SHOP(1960, Brit.), w

Rachel Howard
FRIDAY THE 13TH PART III(1982)

Ralph Howard
ONCE IN A NEW MOON(1935, Brit.)

Rance Howard
MUSIC MAN, THE(1962); DESERT RAVEN, THE(1965); EYE FOR AN EYE, AN(1966); COOL HAND LUKE(1967); GENTLE GIANT(1967); WILD COUNTRY, THE(1971); CHINATOWN(1974); WHERE THE LILIES BLOOM(1974); EAT MY DUST!(1976); GRAND THEFT AUTO(1977), a, w; LOVE LETTERS(1983)
1984
LONELY GUY, THE(1984); SPLASH(1984)
Misc. Talkies
FRONTIER WOMAN(1956)

Ray Howard
Silents
NEIGHBORS(1918); COURAGE(1921); LEECH, THE(1921)

Richard Howard
TWO IN THE DARK(1936); OH! WHAT A LOVELY WAR(1969, Brit.)

Rita Howard
RAGMAN'S DAUGHTER, THE(1974, Brit.)

Robert E. Howard
CONAN THE BARBARIAN(1982), w
1984
CONAN THE DESTROYER(1984), w

Robert Howard
LASSIE'S GREAT ADVENTURE(1963); WAR IS HELL(1964)

Robert S. Howard
WINNER'S CIRCLE, THE(1948)

Romald Howard
I ACCUSE(1958, Brit.)

Ron Howard
HAPPY MOTHER'S DAY... LOVE, GEORGE(1973); SPIKES GANG, THE(1974); EAT MY DUST!(1976); SHOOTIST, THE(1976); GRAND THEFT AUTO(1977), a, d, w; MORE AMERICAN GRAFFITI(1979); NIGHT SHIFT(1982), d
1984
SPLASH(1984), d

Ronald Howard
PIMPERNEL SMITH(1942, Brit.); BOND STREET(1948, Brit.); NIGHT BEAT(1948, Brit.); QUEEN OF SPADES(1948, Brit.); MY BROTHER JONATHAN(1949, Brit.); NOW BARABBAS WAS A ROBBER(1949, Brit.); WHILE THE SUN SHINES(1950, Brit.); ASSASSIN FOR HIRE(1951, Brit.); BROWNING VERSION, THE(1951, Brit.); FLESH AND BLOOD(1951, Brit.); NIGHT WAS OUR FRIEND(1951, Brit.); PORTRAIT OF CLARE(1951, Brit.); WIDE BOY(1952, Brit.); BOTH SIDES OF THE LAW(1953, Brit.); DOUBLE CONFESSION(1953, Brit.); FLANNELFOOT(1953, Brit.); GLAD TIDINGS(1953, Brit.); NOOSE FOR A LADY(1953, Brit.); HIDEOUT, THE(1956, Brit.); DRANGO(1957); HOUSE IN THE WOODS, THE(1957, Brit.); LIGHT FINGERS(1957, Brit.); MOMENT OF INDISCRETION(1958, Brit.); GIDEON OF SCOTLAND YARD(1959, Brit.); MAN ACCUSED(1959); BABETTE GOES TO WAR(1960, Fr.); COMPELLED(1960, Brit.); SPIDER'S WEB(1960, Brit.); BOMB IN THE HIGH STREET(1961, Brit.); COME SEPTEMBER(1961); MONSTER OF HIGHGATE PONDS, THE(1961, Brit.); MURDER SHE SAID(1961, Brit.); NAKED EDGE, THE(1961); FATE TAKES A HAND(1962, Brit.); LIVE NOW–PAY LATER(1962, Brit.); SPANISH SWORD, THE(1962, Brit.); BAY OF SAINT MICHEL, THE(1963, Brit.); SIEGE OF THE SAXONS(1963, Brit.); NO TREE IN THE STREET(1964, Brit.); NURSE ON WHEELS(1964, Brit.); CURSE OF THE MUMMY'S TOMB, THE(1965, Brit.); SKIN GAME, THE(1965, Brit.); YOU MUST BE JOKING!(1965, Brit.); WEEKEND AT DUNKIRK(1966, Fr./Ital.); AFRICA–TEXAS STYLE!(1967 U.S./Brit.); MALPAS MYSTERY, THE(1967, Brit.); PERSECUTION(1974, Brit.); TAKE A HARD RIDE(1975, U.S./Ital.); HUNTING PARTY, THE(1977, Brit.)
Misc. Talkies
BLACK ORCHID(1952); THIRTEENTH GREEN(1954, Brit.)

Ronny Howard [Ron Howard]
JOURNEY, THE(1959, U.S./Aust.); FIVE MINUTES TO LIVE(1961); MUSIC MAN, THE(1962); COURTSHIP OF EDDY'S FATHER, THE(1963); VILLAGE OF THE GIANTS(1965); WILD COUNTRY, THE(1971); AMERICAN GRAFFITI(1973)

Rose M. Howard
PRECIOUS JEWELS(1969)

Rosemary Howard
DELINQUENTS, THE(1957)

Rosie Howard
POLITICAL PARTY, A(1933, Brit.); PRIDE OF THE FORCE, THE(1933, Brit.)

Sandy Howard
DIARY OF A BACHELOR(1964), p&d; CITY OF FEAR(1965, Brit.), p; JACK OF DIAMONDS(1967, U.S./Ger.), p; ONE STEP TO HELL(1969, U.S./Ital./Span.), p&d, w; MAN CALLED HORSE, A(1970), p; CIRCLE OF IRON(1979, Brit.), p; SAVAGE HARVEST(1981), p; VICE SQUAD(1982), w; DEADLY FORCE(1983), p
1984
HAMBONE AND HILLIE(1984), p

Sanford Howard
MAN IN THE WILDERNESS(1971, U.S./Span.), p; NEPTUNE FACTOR, THE(1973, Can.), p

Scott Howard
KING OF MARVIN GARDENS, THE(1972)

Sheila Howard
MY THIRD WIFE GEORGE(1968)

Shemp Howard
CONVENTION GIRL(1935); HEADIN' EAST(1937); HOLLYWOOD ROUNDUP(1938); ANOTHER THIN MAN(1939); BANK DICK, THE(1940); GIVE US WINGS(1940); LEATHER-PUSHERS, THE(1940); MILLIONAIRES IN PRISON(1940); BUCK PRIVATES(1941); CRACKED NUTS(1941); FLAME OF NEW ORLEANS, THE(1941); HELLZAPOPPIN'(1941); HIT THE ROAD(1941); HOLD THAT GHOST(1941); IN THE NAVY(1941); INVISIBLE WOMAN, THE(1941); MEET THE CHUMP(1941); MR. DYNAMITE(1941); SAN ANTONIO ROSE(1941); SIX LESSONS FROM MADAME LA ZONGA(1941); TIGHT SHOES(1941); TOO MANY BLONDES(1941); ARABIAN NIGHTS(1942); BUTCH MINDS THE BABY(1942); MISSISSIPPI GAMBLER(1942); PITTSBURGH(1942); PRIVATE BUCKAROO(1942); STRANGE CASE OF DR. RX, THE(1942); STRICTLY IN THE GROOVE(1942); WHO DONE IT?(1942); CRAZY HOUSE(1943); HOW'S ABOUT IT?(1943); IT AIN'T HAY(1943); KEEP 'EM SLUGGING(1943); CRAZY KNIGHTS(1944); MOONLIGHT AND CACTUS(1944); STRANGE AFFAIR(1944); BLONDIE KNOWS BEST(1946); DANGEROUS BUSINESS(1946); GENTLEMAN MISBEHAVES, THE(1946); ONE EXCITING WEEK(1946); AFRICA SCREAMS(1949); GOLD RAIDERS, THE(1952)
Misc. Talkies
THREE OF A KIND(1944); TROUBLE CHASERS(1945)

Shingzie Howard
Misc. Silents
DUNGEON, THE(1922); UNCLE JASPAR'S WILL(1922); VIRGIN OF SEMINOLE, THE(1923); HOUSE BEHIND THE CEDARS, THE(1927); CHILDREN OF FATE(1928)

Shirlee Howard
ZIEGFELD FOLLIES(1945)

Sidney Howard
YELLOW JACK(1938), w; BULLDOG DRUMMOND(1929), w; CONDEMNED(1929), w; FREE LOVE(1930), w; LADY TO LOVE, A(1930), w; RAFFLES(1930), w; ARROWSMITH(1931), w; ONE HEAVENLY NIGHT(1931), w; GREEKS HAD A WORD FOR THEM(1932), w; CHRISTOPHER BEAN(1933), w; SILVER CORD(1933), w; DODSWORTH(1936), w; GONE WITH THE WIND(1939), w; RAFFLES(1939), w; HE STAYED FOR BREAKFAST(1940), w; THEY KNEW WHAT THEY WANTED(1940), w; BREATH OF SCANDAL, A(1960), w
Silents
WE'RE ALL GAMBLERS(1927), w; SECRET HOUR, THE(1928), d&w; NED MCCOBB'S DAUGHTER(1929), w

Stan Howard
MID-DAY MISTRESS(1968)

Susan Howard
MOONSHINE COUNTY EXPRESS(1977); SIDEWINDER ONE(1977)

Sydney Howard
SPLINTERS(1929, Brit.); ALMOST A DIVORCE(1931, Brit.); FRENCH LEAVE(1931, Brit.); SPLINTERS IN THE NAVY(1931, Brit.); TILLY OF BLOOMSBURY(1931, Brit.); UP FOR THE CUP(1931, Brit.); MAYOR'S NEST, THE(1932, Brit.); IT'S A KING(1933, Brit.); NIGHT OF THE GARTER(1933, Brit.); TROUBLE(1933, Brit.); UP FOR THE DERBY(1933, Brit.); GIRLS PLEASE!(1934, Brit.); TRANSATLANTIC MERRY-GO-ROUND(1934); HOPE OF HIS SIDE(1935, Brit.); CHICK(1936, Brit.); FAME(1936, Brit.); SPLINTERS IN THE AIR(1937, Brit.); WHAT A MAN!(1937, Brit.); SHIPYARD SALLY(1940, Brit.); TILLY OF BLOOMSBURY(1940, Brit.); ONCE A CROOK(1941, Brit.); WHEN WE ARE MARRIED(1943, Brit.); FLIGHT FROM FOLLY(1945, Brit.)

Ted Howard
MOBY DICK(1956, Brit.)

Thomas Howard
1984
SOLDIER'S STORY, A(1984)

Tom Howard
RAIN OR SHINE(1930); THIEF OF BAGHDAD, THE(1940, Brit.), spec eff; IDOL OF PARIS(1948, Brit.), spec eff; CONSPIRATOR(1949, Brit.), spec eff; EDWARD, MY SON(1949, U.S./Brit.), spec eff; MINIVER STORY, THE(1950, Brit./U.S.), spec eff; IVANHOE(1952, Brit.), spec eff; INVITATION TO THE DANCE(1956), spec eff; LIBEL(1959, Brit.), spec eff; SUDDENLY, LAST SUMMER(1959, Brit.), spec eff; VILLAGE OF THE DAMNED(1960, Brit.), spec eff; GORGO(1961, Brit.), spec eff; GREEN HELMET, THE(1961, Brit.), spec eff; MURDER SHE SAID(1961, Brit.), spec eff; THIEF OF BAGHDAD, THE(1961, Ital./Fr.), spec eff; I THANK A FOOL(1962, Brit.), spec eff; KILL OR CURE(1962, Brit.), spec eff; LIGHT IN THE PIAZZA(1962), spec eff; MATTER OF WHO, A(1962, Brit.), spec eff; CAPTAIN SINDBAD(1963), spec eff; HAUNTING, THE(1963), spec eff; MURDER AT THE GALLOP(1963, Brit.), spec eff; V.I.P.s, THE(1963, Brit.), spec eff; SQUADRON 633(1964, U.S./Brit.), spec eff; 633 SQUADRON(1964), spec eff; OPERATION CROSSBOW(1965, U.S./Ital.), spec eff; YELLOW ROLLS-ROYCE, THE(1965), spec eff; 2001: A SPACE ODYSSEY(1968, U.S./Brit.), spec eff; YOUNG WINSTON(1972, Brit.), spec eff; THIEF(1981)

Tommy Howard
MAN WHO HAUNTED HIMSELF, THE(1970, Brit.), spec eff

Trevor Howard
BRIEF ENCOUNTER(1945, Brit.); JOHNNY IN THE CLOUDS(1945, Brit.); ADVENTURESS, THE(1946, Brit.); GREEN FOR DANGER(1946, Brit.); I BECAME A CRIMINAL(1947); SO WELL REMEMBERED(1947, Brit.); ONE WOMAN'S STORY(1949, Brit.); CLOUDED YELLOW, THE(1950, Brit.); GOLDEN SALAMANDER(1950, Brit.); THIRD MAN, THE(1950, Brit.); ODETTE(1951, Brit.); GLORY AT SEA(1952, Brit.); OUTCAST OF THE ISLANDS(1952, Brit.); HEART OF THE MATTER, THE(1954, Brit.); COCKLESHELL HEROES, THE(1955); LADY GODIVA RIDES AGAIN(1955, Brit.); STRANGER'S HAND, THE(1955, Brit.); AROUND THE WORLD IN 80 DAYS(1956); RUN FOR THE SUN(1956); LOVER'S NET(1957, Fr.); PICKUP ALLEY(1957, Brit.); STOWAWAY GIRL(1957, Brit.); KEY, THE(1958, Brit.); ROOTS OF HEAVEN, THE(1958); SONS AND LOVERS(1960, Brit.); LION, THE(1962, Brit.); MALAGA(1962, Brit.); MUTINY ON THE BOUNTY(1962); FATHER GOOSE(1964); MAN IN THE MIDDLE(1964, U.S./Brit.); MORITURI(1965); OPERATION CROSSBOW(1965, U.S./Ital.); VON RYAN'S EXPRESS(1965); LIQUIDATOR, THE(1966, Brit.); POPPY IS ALSO A FLOWER, THE(1966); LONG DUEL, THE(1967, Brit.); TRIPLE CROSS(1967, Fr./Brit.); CHARGE OF THE LIGHT BRIGADE, THE(1968, Brit.); MATTER OF INNOCENCE, A(1968, Brit.); BATTLE OF BRITAIN(1969, Brit.); NIGHT VISITOR, THE(1970, Swed./U.S.); RYAN'S DAUGHTER(1970, Brit.); CATCH ME A SPY(1971, Brit./Fr.); KIDNAPPED(1971, Brit.); LOLA(1971, Brit./Ital.); MARY, QUEEN OF SCOTS(1971, Brit.); POPE JOAN(1972, Brit.); DOLL'S HOUSE, A(1973, Brit.); LUDWIG(1973, Ital./Ger./Fr.); OFFENSE, THE(1973, Brit.); CRAZE(1974, Brit.); PERSECUTION(1974, Brit.); 11 HARROWHOUSE(1974, Brit.); CONDUCT UNBECOMING(1975, Brit.); HENNESSY(1975, Brit.); WHO?(1975, Brit./Ger.); BAWDY ADVENTURES OF TOM JONES, THE(1976, Brit.); COUNT OF MONTE CRISTO(1976, Brit.); ELIZA FRASER(1976, Aus.); ACES HIGH(1977, Brit.); LAST REMAKE OF BEAU GESTE, THE(1977); SLAVERS(1977, Ger.); NIGHT OF THE ASKARI(1978, Ger./South African); STEVIE(1978, Brit.); SUPERMAN(1978); HURRICANE(1979); METEOR(1979); SHILLINGBURY BLOWERS, THE(1980, Brit.); SIR HENRY AT RAWLINSON END(1980, Brit.); WINDWALKER(1980); SEA WOLVES, THE(1981, Brit.); GANDHI(1982); LIGHT YEARS AWAY(1982, Fr./Switz.); MISSIONARY, THE(1982)
1984
SWORD OF THE VALIANT(1984, Brit.)
Misc. Talkies
ALBINO(1980); DEADLY GAMES(1982)

V. Howard
Misc. Silents
SUNLIGHT'S LAST RAID(1917)

Vanessa Howard
BLOOD BEAST TERROR, THE(1967, Brit.); CORRUPTION(1968, Brit.); HERE WE GO ROUND THE MULBERRY BUSH(1968, Brit.); LOCK UP YOUR DAUGHTERS(1969, Brit.); SOME GIRLS DO(1969, Brit.); ALL THE WAY UP(1970, Brit.); MUMSY, NANNY, SONNY, AND GIRLY(1970, Brit.); RISE AND RISE OF MICHAEL RIMMER, THE(1970, Brit.); THIS, THAT AND THE OTHER(1970, Brit.); WHAT BECAME OF JACK AND JILL?(1972, Brit.)

Veronica Howard
TASTE OF HONEY, A(1962, Brit.)

Vince Howard
I LOVE YOU, ALICE B. TOKLAS!(1968); WHERE IT'S AT(1969); COMPANY OF KILLERS(1970); SUPPOSE THEY GAVE A WAR AND NOBODY CAME?(1970); BAREFOOT EXECUTIVE, THE(1971); FUZZ(1972); MAN, THE(1972); TROUBLE MAN(1972)

Violet Howard
DREYFUS CASE, THE(1931, Brit.); CHALLENGE, THE(1939, Brit.)

Walter Howard
Silents
PRINCE AND THE BEGGARMAID, THE(1921, Brit.), w

Warda Howard
Misc. Silents
RAVEN, THE(1915); THAT SORT(1916)

Wendy Howard
PHFFFT!(1954)

Wendy Smith Howard
SEDUCTION, THE(1982)

William Howard
J-MEN FOREVER(1980), p

William K. Howard
CHRISTINA(1929), d; LOVE, LIVE AND LAUGH(1929), d; VALIANT, THE(1929), d; GOOD INTENTIONS(1930), d, w; SCOTLAND YARD(1930), d; DON'T BET ON WOMEN(1931), d; SURRENDER(1931), d; TRANSATLANTIC(1931), d; FIRST YEAR, THE(1932), d; SHERLOCK HOLMES(1932), d; TRIAL OF VIVIENNE WARE, THE(1932), d; POWER AND THE GLORY, THE(1933), d; CAT AND THE FIDDLE(1934), d; EVELYN PRENTICE(1934), d; THIS SIDE OF HEAVEN(1934), d; MARY BURNS, FUGITIVE(1935), d; RENDEZVOUS(1935), d; VANESSA, HER LOVE STORY(1935), d; PRINCESS COMES ACROSS, THE(1936), d; FIRE OVER ENGLAND(1937, Brit.), d; MURDER ON DIAMOND ROW(1937, Brit.), d; BACK DOOR TO HEAVEN(1939), p&d, w; MONEY AND THE WOMAN(1940), d; OVER THE MOON(1940, Brit.), d; BULLETS FOR O'HARA(1941), d; KLONDIKE FURY(1942), d; JOHNNY COME LATELY(1943), d; WHEN THE LIGHTS GO ON AGAIN(1944), d; GUY COULD CHANGE, A(1946), p&d; GREEN COCKATOO, THE(1947, Brit.), p, d
Silents
GET YOUR MAN(1921), d; DESERTED AT THE ALTAR(1922), d; EAST OF BROADWAY(1924), d; RED DICE(1926), d; VOLCANO(1926), d; WHITE GOLD(1927), d
Misc. Silents
PLAY SQUARE(1921), d; WHAT LOVE WILL DO(1921), d; CAPTAIN FLY-BY-NIGHT(1922), d; EXTRA! EXTRA!(1922), d; LUCKY DAN(1922), d; DANGER AHEAD(1923), d; FOURTH MUSKETEER, THE(1923), d; LET'S GO(1923), d; BORDER LEGION, THE(1924), d; CODE OF THE WEST(1925), d; LIGHT OF THE WESTERN STARS(1925), d; THUNDERING HERD, THE(1925), d; BACHELOR BRIDES(1926), d; GIGOLO(1926), d; MAIN EVENT, THE(1927), d; SHIP COMES IN, A(1928), d

Willie Howard
MILLIONS IN THE AIR(1935); ROSE OF THE RANCHO(1936); BROADWAY MELODY OF '38(1937)

Howard A. Anderson Co.
KING DINOSAUR(1955), spec eff; SHOOT OUT AT BIG SAG(1962), cos; ESCAPE FROM THE PLANET OF THE APES(1971), spec eff; SEVEN MINUTES, THE(1971), cos; NIGHT OF THE LEPUS(1972), set d

Alan Howarth
HALLOWEEN II(1981), m; HALLOWEEN III: SEASON OF THE WITCH(1982), m; STAR TREK II: THE WRATH OF KHAN(1982), spec eff; CHRISTINE(1983), m

Betty Jane Howarth
GREAT SINNER, THE(1949); PROWLER, THE(1951); STRIP, THE(1951); ONE DESIRE(1955); PURPLE MASK, THE(1955); STRAIGHT TIME(1978)

David Howarth
SUICIDE MISSION(1956, Brit.), w

Humphrey Howarth
WHITE CORRIDORS(1952, Brit.)

Ian Howarth
LOOPHOLE(1981, Brit.)

Jack Howarth
CURE FOR LOVE, THE(1950, Brit.); SCOTLAND YARD INSPECTOR(1952, Brit.); HOBSON'S CHOICE(1954, Brit.); PROFESSOR TIM(1957, Ireland); SPRING AND PORT WINE(1970, Brit.)

Jocelyn Howarth
SQUATTER'S DAUGHTER(1933, Aus.); SILENCE OF DEAN MAITLAND, THE(1934, Aus.)

Kristine Howarth
DRACULA(1979); HANOVER STREET(1979, Brit.)

Michael Howarth
SPY WHO LOVED ME, THE(1977, Brit.)
1984
LASSITER(1984)

Clark Howat
CUSTOMS AGENT(1950); IT GROWS ON TREES(1952); PAULA(1952); SNIPER, THE(1952); GLASS WEB, THE(1953); HITCH-HIKER, THE(1953); EARTH VS. THE FLYING SAUCERS(1956); GIANT CLAW, THE(1957); HIGH-POWERED RIFLE, THE(1960); AIRPORT(1970); BILLY JACK(1971)
1984
HIGHWAY TO HELL(1984); RUNNING HOT(1984)

Milan Howath
MERRY WIVES OF WINDSOR, THE(1966, Aust.), md

Clark Howatt
KISS TOMORROW GOODBYE(1950); CITY THAT NEVER SLEEPS(1953); SUDDENLY(1954); ILLEGAL(1955)

Nina Howatt
MYSTERIOUS MR. WONG(1935), w

Robert Howay
SWEET SUBSTITUTE(1964, Can.); WAITING FOR CAROLINE(1969, Can.); NAKED FLAME, THE(1970, Can.)

Mike Howden
HOT LEAD AND COLD FEET(1978)

Clyde Howdy
PT 109(1963); MY FAIR LADY(1964); BONNIE AND CLYDE(1967)

Arther Howe
STRAIGHT FROM THE HEART(1935)

Betty Howe
Misc. Silents
ALIBI, THE(1916); FOR FRANCE(1917); BLIND ADVENTURE, THE(1918); LIE, THE(1918); TO HELL WITH THE KAISER(1918); AS A MAN THINKS(1919); MAN OF STONE, THE(1921)

Bob Howe
HALF A SIXPENCE(1967, Brit.); YOUNG GIRLS OF ROCHEFORT, THE(1968, Fr.)

Caroline Howe
Misc. Talkies
GHOSTS THAT STILL WALK(1977)

Darrell Howe
ANATOMY OF A PSYCHO(1961)

David Howe
MALACHI'S COVE(1973, Brit.)

Dorothy Howe
BIG BROADCAST OF 1938, THE(1937); NIGHT CLUB SCANDAL(1937); COCOANUT GROVE(1938); HER JUNGLE LOVE(1938); KING OF ALCATRAZ(1938); PERSONS IN HIDING(1939); UNMARRIED(1939)

Eilean Howe
COMBAT SQUAD(1953)

Eileen Howe
DESERT HAWK, THE(1950); PETTY GIRL, THE(1950); MAGIC CARPET, THE(1951)

Eliot Howe
Misc. Silents
SILVER GIRL, THE(1919), d; TODD OF THE TIMES(1919), d; GRAY DAWN, THE(1922), d; WHEN ROMANCE RIDES(1922), d

Frank Howe, Jr.
Silents
TILLIE(1922), w

George Howe
DECISION BEFORE DAWN(1951), w; MAN WHO KNEW TOO MUCH, THE(1956); GREAT WALTZ, THE(1972); WHAT BECAME OF JACK AND JILL?(1972, Brit.), m

Hilda Howe
WIFE VERSUS SECRETARY(1936)

Irving Howe
ZELIG(1983)

J. A. Howe
Silents
KID BROTHER, THE(1927), d

James Wong Howe
PERFECT CRIME, THE(1928), ph; TODAY(1930), ph; CRIMINAL CODE(1931), ph; SPIDER, THE(1931), ph; SURRENDER(1931), ph; TRANSATLANTIC(1931), ph; YELLOW TICKET, THE(1931), ph; AFTER TOMORROW(1932), ph; AMATEUR DADDY(1932), ph; CHANDU THE MAGICIAN(1932), ph; DANCE TEAM(1932), ph; MAN ABOUT TOWN(1932), ph; BEAUTY FOR SALE(1933), ph; HELLO SISTER!(1933), ph; POWER AND THE GLORY, THE(1933), ph; HAVE A HEART(1934), ph; HOLLYWOOD PARTY(1934), ph; MANHATTAN MELODRAMA(1934), ph; SHOW-OFF, THE(1934), ph; STAMBOUL QUEST(1934), ph; THIN MAN, THE(1934), ph; VIVA VILLA!(1934), ph; BIOGRAPHY OF A BACHELOR GIRL(1935), ph; FLAME WITHIN, THE(1935), ph; MARK OF THE VAMPIRE(1935), ph; NIGHT IS YOUNG, THE(1935), ph; O'SHAUGHNESSY'S BOY(1935), ph; THREE LIVE GHOSTS(1935), ph; WHIPSAW(1936), ph; FIRE OVER ENGLAND(1937, Brit.), ph; PRISONER OF ZENDA, THE(1937), ph; UNDER THE RED ROBE(1937, Brit.), ph; ADVENTURES OF TOM SAWYER, THE(1938), ph; ALGIERS(1938), ph; COMET OVER BROADWAY(1938), ph; TROOPSHIP(1938, Brit.), ph; DAUGHTERS COURAGEOUS(1939), ph; DUST BE MY DESTINY(1939), ph; OKLAHOMA KID, THE(1939), ph; ON YOUR TOES(1939), ph; THEY MADE ME A CRIMINAL(1939), ph; ABE LINCOLN IN ILLINOIS(1940), ph; DISPATCH FROM REUTERS, A(1940), ph; DR. EHRLICH'S MAGIC BULLET(1940), ph; SATURDAY'S CHILDREN(1940), ph; TORRID ZONE(1940), ph; CITY, FOR CONQUEST(1941), ph; NAVY BLUES(1941), ph; OUT OF THE FOG(1941), ph; SHINING VICTORY(1941), ph; STRAWBERRY BLONDE, THE(1941), ph; HARD WAY, THE(1942), ph; KING'S ROW(1942), ph; YANKEE DOODLE DANDY(1942), ph; AIR FORCE(1943), ph; NORTH STAR, THE(1943), ph; PASSAGE TO MARSEILLE(1944), ph; CONFIDENTIAL AGENT(1945), ph; COUNTER-ATTACK(1945), ph; DANGER SIGNAL(1945), ph; OBJECTIVE, BURMA!(1945), ph; MY REPUTATION(1946), ph; BODY AND SOUL(1947), ph; NORA PRENTISS(1947), ph; PURSUED(1947), ph; MR. BLANDINGS BUILDS HIS DREAM HOUSE(1948), ph; TIME OF YOUR LIFE, THE(1948), ph; BARON OF ARIZONA, THE(1950), ph; EAGLE AND THE HAWK, THE(1950), ph; TRIPOLI(1950), ph; BEHAVE YOURSELF(1951), ph; BRAVE BULLS, THE(1951), ph; HE RAN ALL THE WAY(1951), ph; LADY SAYS NO, THE(1951), ph; COME BACK LITTLE SHEBA(1952), ph; FIGHTER, THE(1952), ph; JENNIFER(1953), ph; MAIN STREET TO BROADWAY(1953), ph; GO, MAN, GO!(1954), d; PICNIC(1955), ph; ROSE TATTOO, THE(1955), ph; DEATH OF A SCOUNDREL(1956), ph; DRANGO(1957), ph; SWEET SMELL OF SUCCESS(1957), ph; BELL, BOOK AND CANDLE(1958), ph; INVISIBLE AVENGER, THE(1958), d; OLD MAN AND THE SEA, THE(1958), ph; LAST ANGRY MAN, THE(1959), ph; STORY ON PAGE ONE, THE(1959), ph; SONG WITHOUT END(1960), ph; TESS OF THE STORM COUNTRY(1961), ph; HUD(1963), ph; OUTRAGE, THE(1964), ph; GLORY GUYS, THE(1965), ph; SECONDS(1966), ph; THIS PROPERTY IS CONDEMNED(1966), ph; HOMBRE(1967), ph; HEART IS A LONELY HUNTER, THE(1968), ph; MOLLY MAGUIRES, THE(1970), ph; FUNNY LADY(1975), ph; PERFECT COUPLE, A(1979), ph
Silents
TO THE LAST MAN(1923), ph; BREAKING POINT, THE(1924), ph; PETER PAN(1924), ph; SIDESHOW OF LIFE, THE(1924), ph; NOT SO LONG AGO(1925), ph; SEA HORSES(1926), ph; ROUGH RIDERS(1927), ph; FOUR WALLS(1928), ph; LAUGH, CLOWN, LAUGH(1928), ph

Janet Howe
SARABAND(1949, Brit.)

Jay Howe
Silents
SPEEDY(1928), w

John Howe
WHY ROCK THE BOAT?(1974, Can.), d, m

La Verne "Sonny" Howe
PLACE IN THE SUN, A(1951)

Larry Howe
METALSTORM: THE DESTRUCTION OF JARED-SYN(1983)

Linda Howe
COVER ME BABE(1970)

Michael Howe
UNMAN, WITTERING AND ZIGO(1971, Brit.); HUNGER, THE(1983)
1984
BLIND DATE(1984)

Monica Howe
PROSTITUTE(1980, Brit.), cos
1984
SACRED HEARTS(1984, Brit.), cos

Phillip Howe
1984
CONSTANCE(1984, New Zealand), ed

Simon Howe
CLASS OF MISS MAC MICHAEL, THE(1978, Brit./U.S.); PIRATES OF PENZANCE, THE(1983)
Sonny Howe
TOMORROW IS FOREVER(1946); PEGGY(1950)
Wallace Howe
MOVIE CRAZY(1932)
Silents
GRANDMA'S BOY(1922); WHY WORRY(1923)
Wallie Howe
OPERATOR 13(1934)
Wally Howe
LAWLESS RANGE(1935); MILKY WAY, THE(1936); TUNDRA(1936); ADVENTURE'S END(1937)
Walter Howe
Misc. Silents
$20 A WEEK(1924)
Alice Howell
Silents
TILLIE'S PUNCTURED ROMANCE(1914); LOVE IS AN AWFUL THING(1922)
Arthur Howell
JAZZ CINDERELLA(1930), w; WHIRLPOOL(1959, Brit.)
C. Thomas Howell
OUTSIDERS, THE(1983)
1984
GRANDVIEW, U.S.A.(1984); RED DAWN(1984); TANK(1984)
Cheri Howell
SOYLENT GREEN(1973)
Misc. Talkies
SISTERS OF DEATH(1976)
Chris Howell
HONKERS, THE(1972); DEATHSPORT(1978); NIGHT OF THE JUGGLER(1980), stunts; CUTTER AND BONE(1981); SMOKEY BITES THE DUST(1981), stunts; ENTITY, THE(1982)
Cliff Howell
TOUGH KID(1939)
Dorothy Howell
DONOVAN AFFAIR, THE(1929), w; SONG OF LOVE, THE(1929), w; FOR THE LOVE O'LIL(1930), w; GUILTY?(1930), w; LADIES MUST PLAY(1930), w; MEN WITHOUT LAW(1930), w; RAIN OR SHINE(1930), w; SOLDIERS AND WOMEN(1930), w; SQUEALER, THE(1930), w; DIRIGIBLE(1931), w; FIFTY FATHOMS DEEP(1931), w; LAST PARADE, THE(1931), w; LOVER COME BACK(1931), w; MEN ARE LIKE THAT(1931), w; MEN IN HER LIFE(1931), w; MIRACLE WOMAN, THE(1931), w; PLATINUM BLONDE(1931), w; TEN CENTS A DANCE(1931), w; FINAL EDITION(1932), w; LOVE AFFAIR(1932), w; MENACE, THE(1932), w; I'LL FIX IT(1934), w; WHIRLPOOL(1934), w
Silents
NEW CHAMPION(1925), w; SPEED MAD(1925), w; CLOWN, THE(1927), w; KID SISTER, THE(1927), w; SALLY IN OUR ALLEY(1927), w; STAGE KISSES(1927), w; WANDERING GIRLS(1927), w; RANSOM(1928), w; RUNAWAY GIRLS(1928), w
E. G. Howell
UNCIVILISED(1937, Aus.)
Edward Howell
CARS THAT ATE PARIS, THE(1974, Aus,)
1984
CAREFUL, HE MIGHT HEAR YOU(1984, Aus.)
Elizabeth Howell
DAMN YANKEES(1958)
Erik Howell
DARK, THE(1979)
George Howell
PLEASE TURN OVER(1960, Brit.); CARRY ON TEACHER(1962, Brit.)
Silents
NEW YORK IDEA, THE(1920)
Hazel Howell
MURDER ON THE ROOF(1930); GOD'S GIFT TO WOMEN(1931); ILLICIT(1931)
Silents
BROADWAY BILLY(1926); LAST ALARM, THE(1926); LAW OF THE SNOW COUNTRY, THE(1926); SENSATION SEEKERS(1927); SPUDS(1927); WHAT EVERY GIRL SHOULD KNOW(1927)
Misc. Silents
FIXED BY GEORGE(1920); FULL HOUSE, A(1920); OLD DAD(1920); 45 MINUTES FROM BROADWAY(1920); SCANDAL PROOF(1925)
Helen Howell
DOWN RIVER(1931, Brit.); MADAME DU BARRY(1934); MERRY FRINKS, THE(1934); MICHAEL O'HALLORAN(1937)
Herman Howell
GEORGIA, GEORGIA(1972), ch
Hoke Howell
SHENANDOAH(1965); LAST OF THE SECRET AGENTS?, THE(1966); FIVE THE HARD WAY(1969); MARLOWE(1969); BAD CHARLESTON CHARLIE(1973); SLAUGHTER'S BIG RIP-OFF(1973); KLANSMAN, THE(1974); FRAMED(1975); FROM NOON TO THREE(1976); GRAND THEFT AUTO(1977); HUMANOIDS FROM THE DEEP(1980)
Jean Howell
FAST AND THE FURIOUS, THE(1954), a, w; APACHE WOMAN(1955); CRIME OF PASSION(1957); HELL'S CROSSROADS(1957); VAN, THE(1977)
1984
LIES(1984, Brit.)
John Howell
IT PAYS TO ADVERTISE(1931); JOURNEY TOGETHER(1946, Brit.), prod d; FAME IS THE SPUR(1947, Brit.), art d; OUTSIDER, THE(1949, Brit.), art d; PRIVATE ANGELO(1949, Brit.), art d; HAPPY GO LOVELY(1951, Brit.), art d; ISLAND OF DESIRE(1952, Brit.), art d; PROJECT M7(1953, Brit.), art d; FORBIDDEN CARGO(1954, Brit.), art d; SIMBA(1955, Brit.), art d; STOWAWAY GIRL(1957, Brit.), art d; ORDERS TO KILL(1958, Brit.), art d; THREE MEN IN A BOAT(1958, Brit.), art d; ELEPHANT GUN(1959, Brit.), art d; THIRD MAN ON THE MOUNTAIN(1959), prod d; SWISS FAMILY ROBINSON(1960), prod d, art d; WEEKEND WITH LULU, A(1961, Brit.), art d; GUNS OF DARKNESS(1962, Brit.), art d; WE JOINED THE NAVY(1962, Brit.), art d; WONDERFUL TO BE YOUNG!(1962, Brit.), art d; MOUSE ON THE

MOON, THE(1963, Brit.), prod d; MAN IN THE MIDDLE(1964, U.S./Brit.), art d; HIGH WIND IN JAMAICA, A(1965), art d; WHERE THE SPIES ARE(1965, Brit.), art d; KHARTOUM(1966, Brit.), art d; CASINO ROYALE(1967, Brit.), art d; DEADLY AFFAIR, THE(1967, Brit.), art d; DON'T RAISE THE BRIDGE, LOWER THE RIVER(1968, Brit.), art d; HAMMERHEAD(1968), art d; PRIME OF MISS JEAN BRODIE, THE(1969, Brit.), prod d; HELLO–GOODBYE(1970), prod d; THERE'S A GIRL IN MY SOUP(1970, Brit.), art d; WALKING STICK, THE(1970, Brit.), prod d; PETER RABBIT AND TALES OF BEATRIX POTTER(1971, Brit.), art d; EMBASSY(1972, Brit.), prod d; UNDERCOVERS HERO(1975, Brit.), art d
Katherine Howell
SCARECROW IN A GARDEN OF CUCUMBERS(1972)
Ken Howell
DOWN ON THE FARM(1938); SAFETY IN NUMBERS(1938); TRIP TO PARIS, A(1938); EVERYBODY'S BABY(1939); JONES FAMILY IN HOLLYWOOD, THE(1939); QUICK MILLIONS(1939); TOO BUSY TO WORK(1939); ON THEIR OWN(1940); IN OLD AMARILLO(1951)
Kenneth Howell
EAGLE AND THE HAWK, THE(1933); I GIVE MY LOVE(1934); EDUCATING FATHER(1936); EVERY SATURDAY NIGHT(1936); FOUR DAYS WONDER(1936); LITTLE RED SCHOOLHOUSE(1936); BIG BUSINESS(1937); BORROWING TROUBLE(1937); HOT WATER(1937); OFF TO THE RACES(1937); STAR IS BORN, A(1937); GIRLS' SCHOOL(1938); LOVE ON A BUDGET(1938); YOUNG AS YOU FEEL(1940); BALL OF FIRE(1941); HENRY ALDRICH FOR PRESIDENT(1941); HER FIRST BEAU(1941); HURRY, CHARLIE, HURRY(1941); PRIDE OF THE BOWERY(1941); GIRLS' TOWN(1942); SCATTERGOOD RIDES HIGH(1942); SWEATER GIRL(1942)
Lottice Howell
IN GAY MADRID(1930)
Margaret Howell
1984
TIGHTROPE(1984)
Margret Howell
SCARECROW IN A GARDEN OF CUCUMBERS(1972)
Maude Howell
OLD ENGLISH(1930), w; ALEXANDER HAMILTON(1931), w; EXPERT, THE(1932), w; MAN WHO PLAYED GOD, THE(1932), w; SUCCESSFUL CALAMITY, A(1932), w; CARDINAL RICHELIEU(1935), w; EAST MEETS WEST(1936, Brit.), w; MISTER HOBO(1936, Brit.), w
Maude T. Howell
KING'S VACATION, THE(1933), w; VOLTAIRE(1933), w; WORKING MAN, THE(1933), w; MAN OF AFFAIRS(1937, Brit.), w
Norman Howell
1984
FOOTLOOSE(1984)
Peter Howell
TARZAN THE MAGNIFICENT(1960, Brit.); WATCH YOUR STERN(1961, Brit.); ROOMMATES(1962, Brit.); TWO LETTER ALIBI(1962); HELLFIRE CLUB, THE(1963, Brit.); DEVIL-SHIP PIRATES, THE(1964, Brit.); INCIDENT AT MIDNIGHT(1966, Brit.); SCUM(1979, Brit.)
Philly Howell
CRY OF THE BANSHEE(1970, Brit.)
Ray Howell
SHADOW, THE(1937), cos; ANGELS OVER BROADWAY(1940), cos; BLONDIE ON A BUDGET(1940), cos; LADY IN QUESTION, THE(1940), cos
Reg Howell
DEADFALL(1968, Brit.)
Russ Howell
FREEWHEELIN'(1976); SEVEN(1979)
Tom Howell
E.T. THE EXTRA-TERRESTRIAL(1982)
Virgina Howell
GIRLS' SCHOOL(1938)
Virginia Howell
OKAY AMERICA(1932); EVER IN MY HEART(1933); OUR BETTERS(1933); THEY JUST HAD TO GET MARRIED(1933); TOMORROW AT SEVEN(1933); DOUBLE DOOR(1934); SCARLET LETTER, THE(1934); SPITFIRE(1934); ALICE ADAMS(1935); HIS NIGHT OUT(1935); TANGO(1936); GIRL OF THE GOLDEN WEST, THE(1938); GOODBYE BROADWAY(1938); LITTLE ADVENTURESS, THE(1938); ST. LOUIS BLUES(1939); STAR REPORTER(1939); WOMEN, THE(1939)
W.A. Howell
FIGHTING MARSHAL, THE(1932)
Yvonne Howell
Silents
GREAT MAIL ROBBERY, THE(1927); SOMEWHERE IN SONORA(1927); TAKE ME HOME(1928)
Norman Howell, Jr.
COWBOYS, THE(1972)
Barnie Howells
WAITING FOR CAROLINE(1969, Can.), ed
Colin Howells
TERROR(1979, Brit.)
Jack Howells
SKID KIDS(1953, Brit.), w; FRONT PAGE STORY(1954, Brit.), w
Ursula Howells
FLESH AND BLOOD(1951, Brit.); HORSE'S MOUTH, THE(1953, Brit.); I BELIEVE IN YOU(1953, Brit.); GILDED CAGE, THE(1954, Brit.); WEAK AND THE WICKED, THE(1954, Brit.); CONSTANT HUSBAND, THE(1955, Brit.); HANDCUFFS, LONDON(1955, Brit.); THEY CAN'T HANG ME(1955, Brit.); KEEP IT CLEAN(1956, Brit.); TRACK THE MAN DOWN(1956, Brit.); ACCOUNT RENDERED(1957, Brit.); FIGHTING WILDCATS, THE(1957, Brit.); THIRD KEY, THE(1957, Brit.); TWO LETTER ALIBI(1962); 80,000 SUSPECTS(1963, Brit.); SICILIANS, THE(1964, Brit.); DR. TERROR'S HOUSE OF HORRORS(1965, Brit.); ASSIGNMENT K(1968, Brit.); TORTURE GARDEN(1968, Brit.); CROSSPLOT(1969, Brit.); MUMSY, NANNY, SONNY, AND GIRLY(1970, Brit.)
Frankie Howerd
JUMPING FOR JOY(1956, Brit.); TOUCH OF THE SUN, A(1956, Brit.); FURTHER UP THE CREEK!(1958, Brit.); WATCH IT, SAILOR!(1961, Brit.); COOL MIKADO, THE(1963, Brit.); FAST LADY, THE(1963, Brit.); MOUSE ON THE MOON, THE(1963, Brit.); FAST LADY, THE(1963, Brit.); MOUSE ON THE MOON, THE(1963, Brit.); CARRY ON DOCTOR(1968, Brit.); CARRY ON UP THE JUNGLE(1970, Brit.); UP POMPEII(1971, Brit.); UP THE CHASTITY BELT(1971, Brit.); UP THE FRONT(1972, Brit.); SGT. PEPPER'S LONELY HEARTS CLUB BAND(1978)

Candace Howerton
YOUR THREE MINUTES ARE UP(1973)
Charles Howerton
BLACK GESTAPO, THE(1975); EAT MY DUST!(1976); UP FROM THE DEPTHS(1979, Phil.); DR. HECKYL AND MR. HYPE(1980); WOLFEN(1981)
Basil Howes
NEW HOTEL, THE(1932, Brit.)
Bobby Howes
THIRD TIME LUCKY(1931, Brit.); LORD BABS(1932, Brit.); FOR THE LOVE OF MIKE(1933, Brit.); OVER THE GARDEN WALL(1934, Brit.); PLEASE TEACHER(1937, Brit.); SWEET DEVIL(1937, Brit.); YES, MADAM?(1938, Brit.); TROJAN BROTHERS, THE(1946); HAPPY GO LOVELY(1951, Brit.); GOOD COMPANIONS, THE(1957, Brit.); WATCH IT, SAILOR!(1961, Brit.)
Misc. Silents
GUNS OF LOOS, THE(1928, Brit.)
Hans Howes
FIRE AND ICE(1983)
Oliver Howes
THREE TO GO(1971, Aus.), d&w; LET THE BALLOON GO(1977, Aus.), d, w
Peter Howes
OUTSIDER, THE(1949, Brit.)
Reed Howes
SINGING FOOL, THE(1928); TERROR, THE(1928); COME ACROSS(1929); STOLEN KISSES(1929); CLANCY IN WALL STREET(1930); ANYBODY'S BLONDE(1931); GORILLA SHIP, THE(1932); HELL DIVERS(1932); 70,000 WITNESSES(1932); TRAIL BEYOND, THE(1934); DAWN RIDER(1935); PARADISE CANYON(1935); FEUD OF THE WEST(1936); DEATH IN THE SKY(1937); SWEETHEART OF THE NAVY(1937); TAMING THE WILD(1937); TOAST OF NEW YORK, THE(1937); FLIGHT TO FAME(1938); GHOST TOWN RIDERS(1938); MILLION TO ONE, A(1938); WEST OF RAINBOW'S END(1938); FIGHTING RENEGADE(1939); FLAMING LEAD(1939); HONOR OF THE WEST(1939); PHANTOM STAGE, THE(1939); PORT OF HATE(1939); ROLL, WAGONS, ROLL(1939); SIX-GUN RHYTHM(1939); SOUTH OF THE BORDER(1939); TEXAS WILDCATS(1939); TRIGGER SMITH(1939); CHEYENNE KID, THE(1940); COVERED WAGON DAYS(1940); FRONTIER CRUSADER(1940); HEROES OF THE SADDLE(1940); LIGHTNING STRIKES WEST(1940); MYSTERY SEA RAIDER(1940); PHANTOM RANCHER(1940); STRAIGHT SHOOTER(1940); TEXAS TERRORS(1940); VIRGINIA CITY(1940); WESTBOUND STAGE(1940); DEATH VALLEY OUTLAWS(1941); DOWN MEXICO WAY(1941); FUGITIVE VALLEY(1941); KANSAS CYCLONE(1941); LONE RIDER IN GHOST TOWN, THE(1941); SUNSET IN WYOMING(1941); TONTO BASIN OUTLAWS(1941); DAWN ON THE GREAT DIVIDE(1942); LONE STAR LAW MEN(1942); PIRATES OF THE PRAIRIE(1942); RAIDERS OF THE RANGE(1942); CARSON CITY CYCLONE(1943); RED RIVER ROBIN HOOD(1943); SANTA FE SCOUTS(1943); TENTING TONIGHT ON THE OLD CAMP GROUND(1943); THUNDERING TRAILS(1943); WILD HORSE STAMPEDE(1943); BRAND OF THE DEVIL(1944); DEAD OR ALIVE(1944); LAW OF THE SADDLE(1944); RAIDERS OF RED GAP(1944); STORK CLUB, THE(1945); TILL THE CLOUDS ROLL BY(1946); UNDER ARIZONA SKIES(1946); LOADED PISTOLS(1948); MEXICAN HAYRIDE(1948); RIVER LADY(1948); UNTAMED BREED, THE(1948); RANGE LAND(1949); TASK FORCE(1949); WALKING HILLS, THE(1949); GUNSLINGERS(1950); SAVAGE HORDE, THE(1950); SILVER RAIDERS(1950); STAGE TO TUCSON(1950); SANTA FE(1951); THUNDERING TRAIL, THE(1951); HANGMAN'S KNOT(1952); IRON MISTRESS, THE(1952); MAN BEHIND THE GUN, THE(1952); STRANGER WORE A GUN, THE(1953); THREE HOURS TO KILL(1954); LAWLESS STREET, A(1955); TEN WANTED MEN(1955); RUNAWAY DAUGHTERS(1957); SEVEN GUNS TO MESA(1958); SIERRA BARON(1958); ARSON FOR HIRE(1959); DALTON THAT GOT AWAY(1960); GUNFIGHTERS OF ABILENE(1960); SINISTER URGE, THE(1961)
Misc. Talkies
WHITE RENEGADE(1931); DEVIL ON DECK(1932); DARK ENDEAVOUR(1933); MILLION DOLLAR HAUL(1935); DEATH IN THE AIR(1937); SADDLE LEATHER LAW(1944)
Silents
GEARED TO GO(1924); LIGHTNING ROMANCE(1924); BASHFUL BUCCANEER(1925); KENTUCKY HANDICAP(1926); NIGHT OWL, THE(1926); RACING ROMANCE(1926); WINGS OF THE STORM(1926); LOST LIMITED, THE(1927); ROUGH HOUSE ROSIE(1927); MILLION FOR LOVE, A(1928)
Misc. Silents
HIGH SPEED LEE(1923); CYCLONE RIDER, THE(1924); COURAGEOUS FOOL(1925); CRACK O'DAWN(1925); CYCLONE CAVALIER(1925); SNOB BUSTER, THE(1925); SUPER SPEED(1925); YOUTH'S GAMBLE(1925); DANGER QUEST(1926); DANGEROUS DUDE, THE(1926); GENTLE CYCLONE, THE(1926); HIGH FLYER, THE(1926); MORAN OF THE MOUNTED(1926); SELF STARTER, THE(1926); RACING FOOL, THE(1927); ROMANTIC ROGUE(1927); ROYAL AMERICAN, THE(1927); SCORCHER, THE(1927); FASHION MADNESS(1928); HELLSHIP BRONSON(1928); SAWDUST PARADISE, THE(1928)
Sally Ann Howes
THURSDAY'S CHILD(1943, Brit.); HALF-WAY HOUSE, THE(1945, Brit.); DEAD OF NIGHT(1946, Brit.); NICHOLAS NICKLEBY(1947, Brit.); ANNA KARENINA(1948, Brit.); MY SISTER AND I(1948, Brit.); FOOLS RUSH IN(1949, Brit.); HISTORY OF MR. POLLY, THE(1949, Brit.); STOP PRESS GIRL(1949, Brit.); PINK STRING AND SEALING WAX(1950, Brit.); HONEYMOON DEFERRED(1951, Brit.); ADMIRABLE CRICHTON, THE(1957, Brit.); CHITTY CHITTY BANG BANG(1968, Brit.); DEATH SHIP(1980, Can.)
David Howey
FLESH AND BLOOD SHOW, THE(1974, Brit.); ROUGH CUT(1980, Brit.)
1984
NUMBER ONE(1984, Brit.)
John Howitt
1984
FANTASY MAN(1984, Aus.)
Louise Howitt
LADY, STAY DEAD(1982, Aus.)
Peter Howitt
MIKADO, THE(1967, Brit.), art d; ANNE OF THE THOUSAND DAYS(1969, Brit.), set d; CARRY ON LOVING(1970, Brit.), set d; MARY, QUEEN OF SCOTS(1971, Brit.), set d; PUBLIC EYE, THE(1972, Brit.), set d; TOUCH OF CLASS, A(1973, Brit.), set d; INCREDIBLE SARAH, THE(1976, Brit.), set d; MOONRAKER(1979, Brit.), set d; CLASH OF THE TITANS(1981), art d; LORDS OF DISCIPLINE, THE(1983), set d; NEVER SAY NEVER AGAIN(1983), set d; PIRATES OF PENZANCE, THE(1983), set d

1984
INDIANA JONES AND THE TEMPLE OF DOOM(1984), set d
Peter James Howitt
ASSAULT(1971, Brit.), set d
Bronson Howitzer
SHOWDOWN(1963), w
Bob Howland
PUFNSTUF(1970)
Chris Howland
JAMBOREE(1957); APACHE GOLD(1965, Ger.); FANNY HILL: MEMOIRS OF A WOMAN OF PLEASURE zero(1965); MAD EXECUTIONERS, THE(1965, Ger.)
Jobyna Howland
CUCKOOS, THE(1930); DIXIANA(1930); HONEY(1930); HOOK, LINE AND SINKER(1930); LADY'S MORALS, A(1930); VIRTUOUS SIN, THE(1930); BIG CITY BLUES(1932); ONCE IN A LIFETIME(1932); ROCKABYE(1932); SILVER DOLLAR(1932); STEPPING SISTERS(1932); COHENS AND KELLYS IN TROUBLE, THE(1933); STORY OF TEMPLE DRAKE, THE(1933); TOPAZE(1933)
Silents
WAY OF A WOMAN(1919); SECOND YOUTH(1924)
Lucille Howland
DEMENTIA(1955)
Robert Howland
DON'T CRY, IT'S ONLY THUNDER(1982)
1984
SWORDKILL(1984), prod d
Todd Howland
S.O.B.(1981)
Tom Howland
GOOD MORNING... AND GOODBYE(1967)
Joan Howlett
INVITATION TO MURDER(1962, Brit.)
John Howlett
DISTANT TRUMPET(1952, Brit.); IF ...(1968, Brit.), w
May Howlett
1984
STRIKEBOUND(1984, Aus.)
Noel Howlett
MEN ARE NOT GODS(1937, Brit.); YANK AT OXFORD, A(1938); GEORGE AND MARGARET(1940, Brit.); PROUD VALLEY, THE(1941, Brit.); WHEN THE BOUGH BREAKS(1947, Brit.); CALENDAR, THE(1948, Brit.); CORRIDOR OF MIRRORS(1948, Brit.); MARK OF CAIN, THE(1948, Brit.); ONCE UPON A DREAM(1949, Brit.); SARABAND(1949, Brit.); SCOTT OF THE ANTARCTIC(1949, Brit.); THIS WAS A WOMAN(1949, Brit.); EYE WITNESS(1950, Brit.); GOOD TIME GIRL(1950, Brit.); PERFECT WOMAN, THE(1950, Brit.); WINSLOW BOY, THE(1950); CHRISTMAS CAROL, A(1951, Brit.); LAUGHTER IN PARADISE(1951, Brit.); RELUCTANT WIDOW, THE(1951, Brit.); CLOUDBURST(1952, Brit.); DETECTIVE, THE(1954, Brit.); HANDCUFFS, LONDON(1955, Brit.); LUST FOR LIFE(1956); NOWHERE TO GO(1959, Brit.); SCAPEGOAT, THE(1959, Brit.); BATTLE OF THE SEXES, THE(1960, Brit.); MARY HAD A LITTLE(1961, Brit.); VICTIM(1961, Brit.); IMMORAL CHARGE(1962, Brit.); KISS OF EVIL(1963, Brit.); MURDER AT THE GALLOP(1963, Brit.); TOMORROW AT TEN(1964, Brit.); AMOROUS ADVENTURES OF MOLL FLANDERS, THE(1965); FIVE MILLION YEARS TO EARTH(1968, Brit.); BUSHBABY, THE(1970); PLEASE SIR(1971, Brit.)
Rose Howlett
MARK OF CAIN, THE(1948, Brit.); MONKEY'S PAW, THE(1948, Brit.); GIRL WHO COULDN'T QUITE, THE(1949, Brit.); CHEER THE BRAVE(1951, Brit.); I'LL NEVER FORGET YOU(1951); ONCE A SINNER(1952, Brit.); ONE JUMP AHEAD(1955, Brit.)
Irene Howley
Silents
MOTH AND THE FLAME, THE(1915); HIS FATHER'S SON(1917); IS LOVE EVERYTHING?(1924)
Misc. Silents
YELLOW STREAK, A(1915); LIFE'S SHADOWS(1916); PURPLE LADY, THE(1916); HER FATHER'S KEEPER(1917)
Olin Howlin [Olin Howland]
OVER THE HILL(1931); CHEATERS AT PLAY(1932); SO BIG(1932); BLONDIE JOHNSON(1933); LITTLE WOMEN(1933); TREASURE ISLAND(1934); WAGON WHEELS(1934); BEHOLD MY WIFE(1935); CASE OF THE CURIOUS BRIDE, THE(1935); CASE OF THE LUCKY LEGS, THE(1935); DR. SOCRATES(1935); FOLIES DERGERE(1935); BIG NOISE, THE(1936); BOULDER DAM(1936); CASE OF THE VELVET CLAWS, THE(1936); EARTHWORM TRACTORS(1936); GOLD DIGGERS OF 1937(1936); I MARRIED A DOCTOR(1936); LONGEST NIGHT, THE(1936); LOVE LETTERS OF A STAR(1936); MAN HUNT(1936); ROAD GANG(1936); SATAN MET A LADY(1936); SNOWED UNDER(1936); WIDOW FROM MONTE CARLO, THE(1936); COUNTRY GENTLEMEN(1937); MARRY THE GIRL(1937); MEN IN EXILE(1937); MOUNTAIN MUSIC(1937); NOTHING SACRED(1937); ADVENTURES OF TOM SAWYER, THE(1938); BROTHER RAT(1938); GIRL OF THE GOLDEN WEST, THE(1938); KENTUCKY MOONSHINE(1938); LITTLE TOUGH GUY(1938); MAD MISS MANTON, THE(1938); MR. MOTO'S GAMBLE(1938); SWEETHEARTS(1938); SWING YOUR LADY(1938); BLONDIE BRINGS UP BABY(1939); DAYS OF JESSE JAMES(1939); GONE WITH THE WIND(1939); KID FROM KOKOMO, THE(1939); MADE FOR EACH OTHER(1939); NANCY DREW–REPORTER(1939); ONE HOUR TO LIVE(1939); RETURN OF DR. X, THE(1939); ZENOBIA(1939); CHAD HANNA(1940); COMIN' ROUND THE MOUNTAIN(1940); DOCTOR TAKES A WIFE(1940); LUCKY PARTNERS(1940); YOUNG PEOPLE(1940); BELLE STARR(1941); BUY ME THAT TOWN(1941); ELLERY QUEEN AND THE MURDER RING(1941); GREAT LIE, THE(1941); ONE FOOT IN HEAVEN(1941); SHEPHERD OF THE HILLS, THE(1941); ALMOST MARRIED(1942); DR. BROADWAY(1942); HENRY AND DIZZY(1942); HOME IN WYOMIN'(1942); IN OLD CALIFORNIA(1942); JOAN OF OZARK(1942); LADY BODYGUARD(1942); MAN WHO WOULDN'T DIE, THE(1942); MRS. WIGGS OF THE CABBAGE PATCH(1942); RIDIN' DOWN THE CANYON(1942); THIS GUN FOR HIRE(1942); ALLERGIC TO LOVE(1943); FALCON AND THE CO-EDS, THE(1943); GOOD FELLOWS, THE(1943); JACK LONDON(1943); SECRETS OF THE UNDERGROUND(1943); SKY'S THE LIMIT, THE(1943); STRANGER IN TOWN, A(1943); WHEN JOHNNY COMES MARCHING HOME(1943); CAN'T HELP SINGING(1944); GOODNIGHT SWEETHEART(1944); I'LL BE SEEING YOU(1944); IN THE MEANTIME, DARLING(1944); MAN FROM FRISCO(1944); SING, NEIGHBOR, SING(1944); TWILIGHT ON THE PRAIRIE(1944); CAPTAIN EDDIE(1945); COLONEL EFFINGHAM'S RAID(1945); DAKOTA(1945); FALLEN ANGEL(1945); HER LUCKY NIGHT(1945); SANTA FE SADDLEMATES(1945); SENORITA FROM THE WEST(1945); SHE GETS HER

MAN(1945); SHERIFF OF CIMARRON(1945); TOWN WENT WILD, THE(1945); CRIME DOCTOR'S MAN HUNT(1946); HOME SWEET HOMICIDE(1946); SHE WROTE THE BOOK(1946); STRANGE LOVE OF MARTHA IVERS, THE(1946); ANGEL AND THE BADMAN(1947); APACHE ROSE(1947); EASY COME, EASY GO(1947); FABULOUS TEXAN, THE(1947); FOR THE LOVE OF RUSTY(1947); WYOMING(1947); DUDE GOES WEST, THE(1948); I WALK ALONE(1948); ISN'T IT ROMANTIC?(1948); LAST OF THE WILD HORSES(1948); MY DOG RUSTY(1948); PALEFACE, THE(1948); RETURN OF THE WHISTLER, THE(1948); STATION WEST(1948); BAD MEN OF TOMBSTONE(1949); GRAND CANYON(1949); LEAVE IT TO HENRY(1949); LITTLE WOMEN(1949); SMOKY MOUNTAIN MELODY(1949); FATHER MAKES GOOD(1950); NEVADAN, THE(1950); NEVER A DULL MOMENT(1950); ROCK ISLAND TRAIL(1950); STAGE TO TUCSON(1950); TICKET TO TOMAHAWK(1950); FIGHTING COAST GUARD(1951); SANTA FE(1951); FABULOUS SENORITA, THE(1952); STAR IS BORN, A(1954); THEM!(1954); STORM RIDER, THE(1957); BLOB, THE(1958)
Silents
JANICE MEREDITH(1924); ZANDER THE GREAT(1925)
Olin Howlin [Howland]
YOUNG AND WILLING(1943); SPIRIT OF ST. LOUIS, THE(1957)
David Howman
MONTY PYTHON'S LIFE OF BRIAN(1979, Brit.), m
Karl Howman
STARDUST(1974, Brit.); THAT'LL BE THE DAY(1974, Brit.); BABYLON(1980, Brit.); PARTY PARTY(1983, Brit.)
Alan Howorth
ESCAPE FROM NEW YORK(1981), m
Ted Howorth
CARBON COPY(1981), art d
Frank Allen Howren
YOUNG GIRLS OF ROCHEFORT, THE(1968, Fr.)
Janet Howse
SPARROWS CAN'T SING(1963, Brit.)
A. Howson
GREYHOUND LIMITED, THE(1929), w
Albert Howson
Misc. Silents
MY MADONNA(1916)
Albert S. Howson
Silents
MATINEE LADIES(1927), w
Misc. Silents
DEVIL'S PRIZE, THE(1916)
Denzil Howson
1984
STRIKEBOUND(1984, Aus.)
John-Michael Howson
1984
SECOND TIME LUCKY(1984, Aus./New Zealand)
Leslie Howson
RINGER, THE(1932, Brit.), ph
Al Hoxie
Misc. Silents
ACE OF CLUBS, THE(1926); BATTLING KID(1926); BLUE STREAK O'NEIL(1926); BURIED GOLD(1926); FIGHTING RANGER(1926); LOST TRAIL, THE(1926); RED BLOOD(1926); RIDING ROMANCE(1926); ROAD AGENT(1926); SON OF A GUN(1926); TEXAS TERROR, THE(1926); UNSEEN ENEMIES(1926); OUTLAW'S PARADISE(1927); RANGE RAIDER, THE(1927); RIDER OF THE LAW(1927); SMOKING GUNS(1927); BATTLING BURKE(1928); DEADSHOT CASEY(1928); HIS LAST BULLET(1928); RANGER'S OATH(1928); RIP ROARING LOGAN(1928); RUSTLER'S END, THE(1928); THROWING LEAD(1928); TWO GUN MURPHY(1928); FIGHTING COWBOY(1930); ROARING GUNS(1930)
Hart Hoxie
Silents
SCARLET SIN, THE(1915); DUMB GIRL OF PORTICI(1916); JACK AND JILL(1917); NOBODY'S WIFE(1918)
Misc. Silents
FATHERHOOD(1915); BLUE BLAZES RAWDEN(1918); WOLF AND HIS MATE, THE(1918); LOVE CALL, THE(1919)
Jack Hoxie
GOLD(1932); LAW AND LAWLESS(1932); GUN LAW(1933); OUTLAW JUSTICE(1933); VIA PONY EXPRESS(1933)
Misc. Talkies
TROUBLE BUSTERS(1933)
Silents
BACK FIRE(1922); MARSHAL OF MONEYMINT, THE(1922); GALLOPING THRU(1923); BACK TRAIL, THE(1924); DARING CHANCES(1924); GALLOPING ACE, THE(1924); MAN FROM WYOMING, THE(1924); RIDGEWAY OF MONTANA(1924); WHITE OUTLAW, THE(1925); LOOKING FOR TROUBLE(1926); WESTERN WHIRLWIND, THE(1927)
Misc. Silents
MAN FROM NOWHERE, A(1920); BROKEN SPUR, THE(1921); CUPID'S BRAND(1921); CYCLONE BLISS(1921); DEAD OR ALIVE(1921); DEVIL DOG DAWSON(1921); DOUBLE O, THE(1921); HILLS OF HATE(1921); SHERIFF OF HOPE ETERNAL, THE(1921); SPARKS OF FLINT(1921); BARB WIRE(1922); CROW'S NEST, THE(1922); DESERT BRIDEGROOM, A(1922); DESERT'S CRUCIBLE, THE(1922); RIDERS OF THE LAW(1922); TWO-FISTED JEFFERSON(1922); DESERT RIDER(1923); DON QUICKSHOT OF THE RIO GRANDE(1923); FORBIDDEN TRAIL, THE(1923); MEN IN THE RAW(1923); RED WARNING, THE(1923); WHERE IS THIS WEST?(1923); WOLF'S TRACKS(1923); FIGHTING FURY(1924); PHANTOM HORSEMAN, THE(1924); WESTERN WALLOP, THE(1924); BUSTIN' THRU(1925); DON DARE DEVIL(1925); FLYING HOOFS(1925); HIDDEN LOOT(1925); RED RIDER, THE(1925); RIDIN' THUNDER(1925); ROARING ADVENTURE, A(1925); SIGN OF THE CACTUS, THE(1925); TWO-FISTED JONES(1925); BORDER SHERIFF, THE(1926); DEMON, THE(1926); FIGHTING PEACEMAKER, THE(1926); LAST FRONTIER, THE(1926); RED HOT LEATHER(1926); SIX SHOOTIN' ROMANCE, A(1926); WILD HORSE STAMPEDE, THE(1926); FIGHTING THREE, THE(1927); GRINNING GUNS(1927); MEN OF DARING(1927); RAMBLING RANGER, THE(1927); ROUGH AND READY(1927)

Hart Hoxie [Jack Hoxie]
Silents
NAN OF MUSIC MOUNTAIN(1917)
Richmond Hoxie
STILL OF THE NIGHT(1982); WITHOUT A TRACE(1983)
Bob Hoy
SCREAM BLACULA SCREAM(1973); DUCHESS AND THE DIRTWATER FOX, THE(1976)
Bobbie Hoy
LAWLESS BREED, THE(1952)
Bobby Hoy
BRONCO BILLY(1980)
Danny Hoy
Silents
NO WOMAN KNOWS(1921); TESS OF THE STORM COUNTRY(1922); ABRAHAM LINCOLN(1924); WEDDING MARCH, THE(1927)
Misc. Silents
SAVAGES OF THE SEA(1925); PHANTOM OF THE TURF(1928); WHEN DREAMS COME TRUE(1929)
Dru Hoy
HARD TRAIL(1969)
Drucilla Hoy
CORPSE GRINDERS, THE(1972)
John Hoy
LAST CHANCE, THE(1945, Switz.)
Maysie Hoy
MC CABE AND MRS. MILLER(1971); THREE WOMEN(1977); WEDDING, A(1978)
Renate Hoy
MISSISSIPPI GAMBLER, THE(1953); CERTAIN SMILE, A(1958); MISSILE TO THE MOON(1959)
Rheta Hoy
WHITE PARADE, THE(1934)
Robert Hoy
FOUR GUNS TO THE BORDER(1954); TAZA, SON OF COCHISE(1954); ONE DESIRE(1955); FOUR GIRLS IN TOWN(1956); RAW EDGE(1956); GUN FOR A COWARD(1957); TWILIGHT FOR THE GODS(1958); OPERATION PETTICOAT(1959); SLENDER THREAD, THE(1965); TICKLE ME(1965); TOBRUK(1966); FIVE CARD STUD(1968); LOVE BUG, THE(1968); BITE THE BULLET(1975); LEGEND OF THE LONE RANGER, THE(1981)
Rodolfo Hoyas
FIRST TEXAN, THE(1956)
Arthur Hoydt
FURY(1936)
Cherron Hoye
DANCE OF THE DWARFS(1983, U.S., Phil.)
Gloria Hoye
JOE(1970)
Nicholas Hoye
UNMAN, WITTERING AND ZIGO(1971, Brit.)
Stephen Hoye
SILVER DREAM RACER(1982, Brit.)
Ole Hoyer
ERIC SOYA'S "17"(1967, Den.), m
Chuck Hoyes
EFFECTS(1980)
William Hoyland
ASSAULT(1971, Brit.); FOR YOUR EYES ONLY(1981)
Arthur T. Hoyle
DISCARDED LOVERS(1932), w
Geoff Hoyle
POPEYE(1980); CHU CHU AND THE PHILLY FLASH(1981)
Lester C. Hoyle
PRISONER OF WAR(1954)
Mickey Hoyle
CHOPPERS, THE(1961)
Myles Hoyle
BATTLE OF BRITAIN, THE(1969, Brit.)
Christina Hoyos
BLOOD WEDDING(1981, Sp.)
1984
BIZET'S CARMEN(1984, Fr./Ital.)
Nelly Hoyos
ROLLOVER(1981)
Pablo Hoyos
TO BEGIN AGAIN(1982, Span.)
Rodolfo Hoyos
NIGHT AT THE OPERA, A(1935); GILDA(1946); WE WERE STRANGERS(1949); SECRET OF THE INCAS(1954); BRAVE ONE, THE(1956); SECRET OF TREASURE MOUNTAIN(1956); STAGECOACH TO FURY(1956); THREE OUTLAWS, THE(1956); TIMETABLE(1956); CRASH LANDING(1958); TEN DAYS TO TULARA(1958); TOUGHEST GUN IN TOMBSTONE(1958); VILLA!(1958); LITTLE SAVAGE, THE(1959); OPERATION EICHMANN(1961); CALIFORNIA(1963); GUN HAWK, THE(1963); SEVEN DAYS IN MAY(1964); MADAME X(1966); EL DORADO(1967); CHANGE OF HABIT(1969); LOVE AND MONEY(1982)
Rodolfo Hoyos, Jr.
CRISIS(1950); RATON PASS(1951); FIGHTER, THE(1952); SECOND CHANCE(1953); GYPSY COLT(1954); JUBILEE TRAIL(1954); AMERICANO, THE(1955); FIGHTING CHANCE, THE(1955); GREEN FIRE(1955); GHOST DIVER(1957)
Rodolpho Hoyos, Sr.
HONEYMOON(1947)
Terry Hoyos
1984
CRIMES OF PASSION(1984)
Albert Hoysett
RETURN OF THE TEXAN(1952), art d
Hoyt
Silents
I WANT TO FORGET(1918), w

Arthur Hoyt
MY MAN(1928); STOLEN KISSES(1929); WHEEL OF LIFE, THE(1929); DUMB-BELLS IN ERMINE(1930); EXTRAVAGANCE(1930); HER PRIVATE AFFAIR(1930); LIFE OF THE PARTY, THE(1930); NIGHT WORK(1930); ON YOUR BACK(1930); PEACOCK ALLEY(1930); SEVEN DAYS LEAVE(1930); ALONG CAME YOUTH(1931); CRIMINAL CODE(1931); FLOOD, THE(1931); GANG BUSTER, THE(1931); GOING WILD(1931); GOLD DUST GERTIE(1931); INSPIRATION(1931); PEACH O' RE-NO(1931); AMERICAN MADNESS(1932); BEAST OF THE CITY, THE(1932); CALL HER SAVAGE(1932); CRUSADER, THE(1932); DEVIL AND THE DEEP(1932); DYNA-MITE RANCH(1932); IMPATIENT MAIDEN(1932); MADAME RACKETEER(1932); MAKE ME A STAR(1932); RED-HAIRED ALIBI, THE(1932); VANITY STREET(1932); WASHINGTON MERRY-GO-ROUND(1932); ANN VICKERS(1933); DANGEROUSLY YOURS(1933); DARING DAUGHTERS(1933); EASY MILLIONS(1933); ELEVENTH COMMANDMENT(1933); EMERGENCY CALL(1933); GOLDIE GETS ALONG(1933); HIS PRIVATE SECRETARY(1933); ONLY YESTERDAY(1933); PLEASURE CRUI-SE(1933); PRIZEFIGHTER AND THE LADY, THE(1933); SHANGHAI MAD-NESS(1933); SHRIEK IN THE NIGHT, A(1933); SING SINNER, SING(1933); 20,000 YEARS IN SING SING(1933); CAT'S PAW, THE(1934); CROSBY CASE, THE(1934); I SELL ANYTHING(1934); IN THE MONEY(1934); IT HAPPENED ONE NIGHT(1934); JEALOUSY(1934); KANSAS CITY PRINCESS(1934); LET'S TRY AGAIN(1934); MAR-RYING WIDOWS(1934); MEANEST GAL IN TOWN, THE(1934); NOTORIOUS SOPHIE LANG, THE(1934); SPRINGTIME FOR HENRY(1934); STUDENT TOUR(1934); UN-CERTAIN LADY(1934); UNKNOWN BLONDE(1934); WAKE UP AND DREAM(1934); WHEN STRANGERS MEET(1934); CHINATOWN SQUAD(1935); MAGNIFICENT OBSESSION(1935); MURDER ON A HONEYMOON(1935); NIGHT AT THE RITZ, A(1935); NO RANSOM(1935); ONE HOUR LATE(1935); RAVEN, THE(1935); VAGA-BOND LADY(1935); WELCOME HOME(1935); $1,000 A MINUTE(1935); DON'T TURN-'EM LOOSE(1936); EARLY TO BED(1936); GREAT GUY(1936); LADY LUCK(1936); M'LISS(1936); MR. DEEDS GOES TO TOWN(1936); POOR LITTLE RICH GIRL(1936); WALKING ON AIR(1936); EASY LIVING(1937); EVER SINCE EVE(1937); IT'S ALL YOURS(1937); JOIN THE MARINES(1937); LET'S GET MARRIED(1937); LOVE IN A BUNGALOW(1937); LOVE TAKES FLIGHT(1937); PARADISE EXPRESS(1937); PART-NERS IN CRIME(1937); SHE'S NO LADY(1937); STAR IS BORN, A(1937); WESTLAND CASE, THE(1937); WHEN YOU'RE IN LOVE(1937); WRONG ROAD, THE(1937); COWBOY AND THE LADY, THE(1938); DEVIL'S PARTY, THE(1938); GIRLS ON PROBATION(1938); HARD TO GET(1938); SISTERS, THE(1938); START CHEE-RING(1938); YOU AND ME(1938); EAST SIDE OF HEAVEN(1939); MADE FOR EACH OTHER(1939); SHOULD HUSBANDS WORK?(1939); CHRISTMAS IN JULY(1940); GREAT McGINTY, THE(1940); I LOVE YOU AGAIN(1940); LADY EVE, THE(1941); SULLIVAN'S TRAVELS(1941); THEY MEET AGAIN(1941); PALM BEACH STORY, THE(1942); KEEP 'EM SLUGGING(1943); HAIL THE CONQUERING HERO(1944); MIRACLE OF MORGAN'S CREEK, THE(1944); MAD WEDNESDAY(1950)
Misc. Talkies
LOVE IN HIGH GEAR(1932)
Silents
GRIM GAME, THE(1919); NURSE MARJORIE(1920); FOUR HORSEMEN OF THE APOCALYPSE, THE(1921); KISSED(1922); LITTLE WILDCAT(1922); LOVE IS AN AWFUL THING(1922); STRANGER'S BANQUET(1922); SOULS FOR SALE(1923); WHITE FLOWER, THE(1923); BLUFF(1924); DARING YOUTH(1924); ANY WO-MAN(1925); COMING OF AMOS, THE(1925); EVE'S LOVER(1925); LOST WORLD, THE(1925); TOP OF NEW YORK, THE(1925); GILDED BUTTERFLY, THE(1926); AFFAIR OF THE FOLLIES, AN(1927); HUSBANDS FOR RENT(1927); TEXAS STEER, A(1927); TILLIE THE TOILER(1927); JUST MARRIED(1928); PROTECTION(1929)
Misc. Silents
BRINGING HOME FATHER(1917); MR. OPP(1917); SHOW-DOWN, THE(1917); HIGH STAKES(1918), d; STATION CONTENT(1918), d; YELLOW DOG, THE(1918); COWARDICE COURT(1919); CAMILLE(1921); FOOLISH AGE, THE(1921); RESTLESS SOULS(1922); TOO MUCH WIFE(1922); DANGEROUS BLONDE, THE(1924); DO IT NOW(1924); SUNDOWN(1924); HEAD WINDS(1925); DANGEROUS FRIENDS(1926); FOOTLOOSE WIDOWS(1926); FOR WIVES ONLY(1926)

Charles Hale Hoyt
Silents
TEXAS STEER, A(1927), w

Clegg Hoyt
SANTIAGO(1956); RESTLESS BREED, THE(1957); ROCK ALL NIGHT(1957); TRUE STORY OF JESSE JAMES, THE(1957); DAMN CITIZEN(1958); GUN FEVER(1958); YOUNG SAVAGES, THE(1961); INCIDENT IN AN ALLEY(1962); PARADISE AL-LEY(1962); PRESSURE POINT(1962); THAT TOUCH OF MINK(1962); THIRTEEN WEST STREET(1962); ADVANCE TO THE REAR(1964); SEVEN DAYS IN MAY(1964); GREAT RACE, THE(1965); IN THE HEAT OF THE NIGHT(1967)

Edward N. Hoyt
Silents
CRIMSON DOVE, THE(1917)

Eric Hoyt
KEEPER, THE(1976, Can.), m

Fannie Hoyt
Misc. Silents
MILL ON THE FLOSS, THE(1915)

Frank Hoyt
WE'RE IN THE LEGION NOW(1937)

Harry Hoyt
MAN FROM NEW MEXICO, THE(1932), w; FIGHTING RANGER, THE(1934), w

Harry O. Hoyt
DARKENED SKIES(1930), d; RAMPANT AGE, THE(1930), w; SECOND HONEY-MOON(1931), w; JUNGLE BRIDE(1933), d; THRILL HUNTER, THE(1933), w; HEAD-LINE CRASHER(1937), w; LEGION OF MISSING MEN(1937), w; RUSTLER'S VALLEY(1937), w; SINGING OUTLAW(1937), w; LAST STAND, THE(1938), w; AVENGING RIDER, THE(1943), w; LOST CANYON(1943), w; LADY IN THE DEATH HOUSE(1944), w; MISSING CORPSE, THE(1945), w
Silents
DIMPLES(1916), w; JUST SYLVIA(1918), w; NEIGHBORS(1918), w; CURSE OF DRINK, THE(1922), d&w; LOST WORLD, THE(1925), d; ADORABLE DECEIVER, THE(1926), w; CLOWN, THE(1927), w; KID SISTER, THE(1927), w; PAINTING THE TOWN(1927), w; WANDERING GIRLS(1927), w; STOP THAT MAN(1928), w; 13 WASHINGTON SQUARE(1928), w
Misc. Silents
BROADWAY SAINT, A(1919), d; FOREST RIVALS(1919), d; HAND INVISIBLE, THE(1919), d; THROUGH THE TOILS(1919), d; RIDER OF THE KING LOG, THE(1921), d; THAT WOMAN(1922), d; FANGS OF THE WOLF(1924), d; FATAL PLUNGE, THE(1924), d; LAW DEMANDS, THE(1924), d; RADIO FLYER, THE(1924),

d; WOMAN ON THE JURY, THE(1924), d; PRIMROSE PATH, THE(1925), d; UN-NAMED WOMAN, THE(1925), d; WHEN LOVE GROWS COLD(1925), d; BELLE OF BROADWAY, THE(1926), d; BITTER APPLES(1927), d; RETURN OF BOSTON BLACKIE, THE(1927), d; PASSION SONG, THE(1928), d

John Hoyt
O.S.S.(1946); BRUTE FORCE(1947); MY FAVORITE BRUNETTE(1947); UNFAITH-FUL, THE(1947); DECISION OF CHRISTOPHER BLAKE, THE(1948); SEALED VER-DICT(1948); TO THE ENDS OF THE EARTH(1948); WINTER MEETING(1948); BRIBE, THE(1949); EVERYBODY DOES IT(1949); GREAT DAN PATCH, THE(1949); LADY GAMBLES, THE(1949); TRAPPED(1949); COMPANY SHE KEEPS, THE(1950); LAW-LESS, THE(1950); OUTSIDE THE WALL(1950); DESERT FOX, THE(1951); INSIDE STRAIGHT(1951); LOST CONTINENT(1951); NEW MEXICO(1951); QUEBEC(1951); WHEN WORLDS COLLIDE(1951); ANDROCLES AND THE LION(1952); BLACK CASTLE, THE(1952); LOAN SHARK(1952); JULIUS CAESAR(1953); SINS OF JEZE-BEL(1953); CASANOVA'S BIG NIGHT(1954); DESIREE(1954); STUDENT PRINCE, THE(1954); BIG COMBO, THE(1955); BLACKBOARD JUNGLE, THE(1955); GIRL IN THE RED VELVET SWING, THE(1955); MOONFLEET(1955); PURPLE MASK, THE(1955); TRIAL(1955); COME ON, THE(1956); CONQUEROR, THE(1956); DEATH OF A SCOUNDREL(1956); FOREVER DARLING(1956); MOHAWK(1956); BABY FACE NELSON(1957); GOD IS MY PARTNER(1957); SIERRA STRANGER(1957); ATTACK OF THE PUPPET PEOPLE(1958); BEAST OF BUDAPEST(1958); CURSE OF THE UNDEAD(1959); NEVER SO FEW(1959); RIOT IN JUVENILE PRISON(1959); SPAR-TACUS(1960); MERRILL'S MARAUDERS(1962); "X"-THE MAN WITH THE X-RAY EYES(1963); CLEOPATRA(1963); GLASS CAGE, THE(1964), a, p, w; TIME TRAVEL-ERS, THE(1964); OPERATION CIA(1965); TWO ON A GUILLOTINE(1965); YOUNG DILLINGER(1965); DUEL AT DIABLO(1966); GUNPOINT(1966); PANIC IN THE CITY(1968); IN SEARCH OF HISTORIC JESUS(1980)

Marlene Hoyt
LIFE OF HER OWN, A(1950)

Reata Hoyt
Misc. Silents
LILY, THE(1926)

Richard Hoyt
SUPPORT YOUR LOCAL SHERIFF(1969)

Robert Hoyt
Misc. Talkies
RACKETEER ROUND-UP(1934), d

Russell Hoyt
LUCKY JORDAN(1942); SECRETS OF A CO-ED(1942); SEVEN DAYS LEAVE(1942); GANG'S ALL HERE, THE(1943); GUADALCANAL DIARY(1943); LADIES' DAY(1943); THIS LAND IS MINE(1943); SINCE YOU WENT AWAY(1944)

Vance Joseph Hoyt
SEQUOIA(1934), w

Wendell Hoyt
THEY CAME TO CORDURA(1959)

Clyde Hoyte
MANFISH(1956)

Julia Hoyte
Misc. Silents
WONDERFUL THING, THE(1921)

Tiffany Hoyveld
ACE HIGH(1969, Ital.)

Takanobu Hozumi
EAST CHINA SEA(1969, Jap.); SNOW COUNTRY(1969, Jap.)

Bohumil Hrabal
CLOSELY WATCHED TRAINS(1967, Czech.), w

Buddie Hrabal
TENDER MERCIES(1982)

Vladimir Hrabanek
TRANSPORT FROM PARADISE(1967, Czech.)

Eva Hrabetova
ROCKET TO NOWHERE(1962, Czech.)

Dora Hrach
VIENNA, CITY OF SONGS(1931, Ger.)

Charles Hradilac
36 HOURS(1965)

Agnes Hranitsky
ANNA(1981, Fr./Hung.), ed

Doro Vlado Hreljanovic
JUST BEFORE DAWN(1980), p

Zoran Hristic
HOROSCOPE(1950, Yugo.), m

Vera Hruba [Ralston]
ICE-CAPADES(1941); ICE-CAPADES REVUE(1942)

Anna Hruby
CATHY'S CHILD(1979, Aus.)

Frank Hruby
THOSE LIPS, THOSE EYES(1980)

Jiri Hruby
LOVES OF A BLONDE(1966, Czech.)

Joy Hruby
CADDIE(1976, Aus.); WINTER OF OUR DREAMS(1982, Aus.)
Misc. Talkies
LOVELETTERS FROM TERALBA ROAD(1977)

Jan Hrusinsky
DAY THAT SHOOK THE WORLD, THE(1977, Yugo./Czech.)

Rudolf Hrusinsky
90 DEGREES IN THE SHADE(1966, Czech./Brit.); CAPRICIOUS SUMMER(1968, Czech.); DEATH OF TARZAN, THE(1968, Czech); MURDER CZECH STYLE(1968, Czech.); CREMATOR, THE(1973, Czech.); ADELE HASN'T HAD HER SUPPER YET(1978, Czech.)

Rudolph Hrusinsky
BLACK SUN, THE(1979, Czech.)

Quentin J. Hruska
KRAMER VS. KRAMER(1979)

Jiri Hrzan
SIR, YOU ARE A WIDOWER(1971, Czech.)

Radoslav Hrzobohary
BLACK SUN, THE(1979, Czech.)
Calvin Hsai
WORLD OF SUZIE WONG, THE(1960)
Suzanne Hsaio
GENGHIS KHAN(U.S./Brit./Ger./Yugo)
Nancy Hseuh
CHEYENNE AUTUMN(1964)
Chu Sheng Hsi
RETURN OF THE DRAGON(1974, Chin.), cos
Chou Hsi-fan
Misc. Silents
BLUE EXPRESS(1929, USSR)
Julia Hsia
SONS OF GOOD EARTH(1967, Hong Kong)
Li Hsiang-chun
MAGNIFICENT CONCUBINE, THE(1964, Hong Kong)
Chi Hsiang-tang
ENCHANTING SHADOW, THE(1965, Hong Kong), m
Ke Hsiangting
DEADLY CHINA DOLL(1973, Hong Kong)
Susanne Hsiao
FANNY HILL: MEMOIRS OF A WOMAN OF PLEASURE zero(1965)
Ko Hsiao-Pao
DRAGON INN(1968, Chi.)
Wang Hsieh
INFRA-MAN(1975, Hong Kong)
Warren Hsieh
EDDY DUCHIN STORY, THE(1956); CHINA GATE(1957); SOUTH PACIFIC(1958); DEVIL AT FOUR O'CLOCK, THE(1961); EXPERIMENT IN TERROR(1962); FOLLOW ME, BOYS!(1966)
Li Hsiu Hsien
BRUCE LEE AND I(1976, Chi.)
Ch'ieng Hsin
RETURN OF THE DRAGON(1974, Chin.), art d
Chen Hsing
TRIPLE IRONS(1973, Hong Kong)
Chiang Hsing-ling
MAGNIFICENT CONCUBINE, THE(1964, Hong Kong), ed
Chiang Hsing-lung
LAST WOMAN OF SHANG, THE(1964, Hong Kong), ed; GRAND SUBSTITUTION, THE(1965, Hong Kong), ed; SHEPHERD GIRL, THE(1965, Hong Kong), ed; MERMAID, THE(1966, Hong Kong), ed; SACRED KNIVES OF VENGEANCE, THE(1974, Hong Kong), ed
Ching Hsing-lung
VERMILION DOOR(1969, Hong Kong), ed
Siao Hsinmei
DEADLY CHINA DOLL(1973, Hong Kong), makeup
Miao Ke Hsiu
FISTS OF FURY(1973, Chi.)
Li Hsiu-Hsien
INFRA-MAN(1975, Hong Kong); GOLIATHON(1979, Hong Kong)
Chao Hsiung
FIVE FINGERS OF DEATH(1973, Hong Kong)
Kao Hsiung
CALL HIM MR. SHATTER(1976, Hong Kong)
S. I. Hsiung
MAJOR BARBARA(1941, Brit.)
Nancy Hsueh
INTRIGUE(1947); LT. ROBIN CRUSOE, U.S.N.(1966); SPY WITH MY FACE, THE(1966); TARGETS(1968); HOUSE CALLS(1978)
Wei F. Hsueh
DRAGON SEED(1944), tech adv; INTRIGUE(1947)
Wei Fan HSueh
PEKING EXPRESS(1951)
Huang Chung Hsun
RETURN OF THE DRAGON(1974, Chin.)
Nan-Kung Hsun
FIVE FINGERS OF DEATH(1973, Hong Kong)
An Tsan Hu
CHECKMATE(1973)
Robert Hu
TARZAN'S THREE CHALLENGES(1963)
Li Li Hua
CHINA DOLL(1958)
Liu Loke Hua
CLEOPATRA JONES AND THE CASINO OF GOLD(1975 U. S. Hong Kong)
Sian Hua
GRAND SUBSTITUTION, THE(1965, Hong Kong), m
Tsung Hua
SACRED KNIVES OF VENGEANCE, THE(1974, Hong Kong)
Yueh Hua
MERMAID, THE(1966, Hong Kong); THREE STOOGES VS. THE WONDER WOMEN(1975, Ital./Chi.)
Hua-Shan
INFRA-MAN(1975, Hong Kong), d
Carter Huang
DEADLY CHINA DOLL(1973, Hong Kong)
Essie Huang
MILLION EYES OF SU-MURU, THE(1967, Brit.)
Gerard Antoine Huart
JOY(1983, Fr./Can.)
Mario Huarte
RAGE(1966, U.S./Mex.), cos
Mikulas Huba
SEVENTH CONTINENT, THE(1968, Czech./Yugo.)
Crody Hubach
HONEYSUCKLE ROSE(1980)

Edy Hubacher
END OF THE GAME(1976, Ger./Ital.)
Eileen Huban
Misc. Silents
FIND THE WOMAN(1922)
Adam Hubbard
TEX(1982)
Allan Hubbard
TENDER MERCIES(1982)
Beulah Hubbard
SAINTED SISTERS, THE(1948)
Bruce Hubbard
1984
COTTON CLUB, THE(1984)
Charles Hubbard
ROB ROY, THE HIGHLAND ROGUE(1954, Brit.)
David Hubbard
SCOTT JOPLIN(1977); GETTING OVER(1981)
Doug Hubbard
GUARDIAN OF THE WILDERNESS(1977), spec eff; BEYOND AND BACK(1978), spec eff
Eddie Hubbard
DISC JOCKEY(1951)
Elbert Hubbard
MESSAGE TO GARCIA, A(1936), w
Elizabeth Hubbard
I NEVER SANG FOR MY FATHER(1970); BELL JAR, THE(1979); ORDINARY PEOPLE(1980); COLD RIVER(1982)
Esme Hubbard
DISCORD(1933, Brit.)
Silents
GREAT ADVENTURE, THE(1915, Brit.)
Misc. Silents
HIS DEAREST POSSESSION(1919, Brit.); LINKED BY FATE(1919, Brit.); MIST IN THE VALLEY(1923, Brit.)
Geoff Hubbard
IT'S MY TURN(1980), set d; FIRST MONDAY IN OCTOBER(1981), set d; WHITE DOG(1982), set d; SCARFACE(1983), set d
George Hubbard
Silents
LOVE GAMBLER, THE(1922), w
Gerald E. Hubbard, Jr.
1984
PURPLE RAIN(1984)
Gordon Hubbard
WOMAN FROM TANGIER, THE(1948), makeup; NEVER A DULL MOMENT(1968), makeup; ONE AND ONLY GENUINE ORIGINAL FAMILY BAND, THE(1968), makeup
Hazel Hubbard
Misc. Silents
DESTINY'S SKEIN(1915)
Jack Hubbard
HOLD'EM NAVY!(1937); BUCCANEER, THE(1938); COCOANUT GROVE(1938); MEN WITH WINGS(1938); PRISON FARM(1938); YOU AND ME(1938)
Jim Hubbard
GYPSY(1962); VIRGIN PRESIDENT, THE(1968), p
Joe Hubbard
JERK, THE(1979), set d; ONION FIELD, THE(1979), set d
John Hubbard
COLLEGE SWING(1938); HOUSEKEEPER'S DAUGHTER(1939); ONE MILLION B.C.(1940); TURNABOUT(1940); WHO KILLED AUNT MAGGIE?(1940); MURDER AMONG FRIENDS(1941); OUR WIFE(1941); ROAD SHOW(1941); SHE KNEW ALL THE ANSWERS(1941); YOU'LL NEVER GET RICH(1941); CANAL ZONE(1942); MUMMY'S TOMB, THE(1942); CHATTERBOX(1943); DANGEROUS BLONDES(1943); SECRETS OF THE UNDERGROUND(1943); THERE'S SOMETHING ABOUT A SOLDIER(1943); WHAT'S BUZZIN COUSIN?(1943); WHISPERING FOOTSTEPS(1943); YOUTH ON PARADE(1943); BEAUTIFUL BUT BROKE(1944); COWBOY AND THE SENORITA(1944); UP IN MABEL'S ROOM(1944); LINDA BE GOOD(1947); FIGHTING MAD(1948); MEXICAN HAYRIDE(1948); OLD-FASHIONED GIRL, AN(1948); BULLFIGHTER AND THE LADY(1951); CIMARRON KID, THE(1951); BIG JIM McLAIN(1952); HORIZONS WEST(1952); BLADES OF THE MUSKETEERS(1953); WALKING MY BABY BACK HOME(1953); PAL JOEY(1957); TALL T, THE(1957); ESCORT WEST(1959); SOLDIER IN THE RAIN(1963); FATE IS THE HUNTER(1964); GUNFIGHT AT COMANCHE CREEK(1964); FAMILY JEWELS, THE(1965); DUEL AT DIABLO(1966); LOVE GOD?, THE(1969)
Misc. Talkies
SECOND CHANCE(1950)
Joseph E. Hubbard
TO BE OR NOT TO BE(1983), set d
Kevin Hubbard
TO SIR, WITH LOVE(1967, Brit.)
Lorna Hubbard
MUSIC HATH CHARMS(1935, Brit.); GAOL BREAK(1936, Brit.); LOVE UP THE POLE(1936, Brit.)
Lucien Hubbard
MYSTERIOUS ISLAND(1929), d, w; ISLE OF ESCAPE(1930), w; PAID(1930), w; MALTESE FALCON, THE(1931), w; SMART MONEY(1931), w; SQUAW MAN, THE(1931), w; STAR WITNESS(1931), w; CROONER(1932), p; STRANGER IN TOWN(1932), p; SUCCESSFUL CALAMITY, A(1932), p; THREE ON A MATCH(1932), w; TWO AGAINST THE WORLD(1932), p; EMPLOYEE'S ENTRANCE(1933), p; EX-LADY(1933), p; KING'S VACATION, THE(1933), p; MADE ON BROADWAY(1933), p; MAYOR OF HELL, THE(1933), p; MIDNIGHT MARY(1933), p; STORM AT DAYBREAK(1933), p; DEATH OF THE DIAMOND(1934), p; LAZY RIVER(1934), p, w; OPERATOR 13(1934), p; PARIS INTERLUDE(1934), p; SHOW-OFF, THE(1934), p; STRAIGHT IS THE WAY(1934), p; WOMEN IN HIS LIFE, THE(1934), p; CALM YOURSELF(1935), p; CASINO MURDER CASE, THE(1935), p; HERE COMES THE BAND(1935), p; KIND LADY(1935), p; MURDER IN THE FLEET(1935), p; PUBLIC HERO NO. 1(1935), p; PURSUIT(1935), p; SHADOW OF A DOUBT(1935), p; SOCIETY DOCTOR(1935), p; TIMES SQUARE LADY(1935), p; ALL-AMERICAN CHUMP(1936), p; EXCLUSIVE STORY(1936), p; GARDEN MURDER CASE, THE(1936), p; LONG-

EST NIGHT, THE(1936), p; MOONLIGHT MURDER(1936), p; SINNER TAKE ALL(1936), p; SPEED(1936), p; SWORN ENEMY(1936), p; WOMEN ARE TROUBLE(1936), p; EBB TIDE(1937), p; FAMILY AFFAIR, A(1937), p; MAN OF THE PEOPLE(1937), p; SONG OF THE CITY(1937), p; UNDER COVER OF NIGHT(1937), p; TEXANS, THE(1938), p; I AM NOT AFRAID(1939), w; MAN WHO DARED, THE(1939), w; NICK CARTER, MASTER DETECTIVE(1939), w; 6000 ENEMIES(1939), p; BRIDE WORE CRUTCHES, THE(1940), p; STREET OF MEMORIES(1940), p; YOUTH WILL BE SERVED(1940), p; FOR BEAUTY'S SAKE(1941), p; STORY OF G.I. JOE, THE(1945)

Silents

BAB'S CANDIDATE(1920), w; MASTER STROKE, A(1920), w; BLAZING TRAIL, THE(1921), w; OUTSIDE THE LAW(1921), w; RAGE OF PARIS, THE(1921), w; REPUTATION(1921), w; WILD HONEY(1922), w; DAUGHTERS OF TODAY(1924), w; WE'RE ALL GAMBLERS(1927), sup; WINGS(1927), p, ed

Misc. Silents

ROSE-MARIE(1928), d

Paul Hubbard

JULIE DARLING(1982, Can./Ger.); CHRISTMAS STORY, A(1983); RUNNING BRAVE(1983, Can.)

Philip Hubbard

Silents

EAST IS EAST(1916, Brit.), w; BLOT, THE(1921)

Ralph Hubbard

WITHOUT RESERVATIONS(1946)

Thomas C. Hubbard

RAIDERS OF OLD CALIFORNIA(1957), w

Thomas G. Hubbard

BADGE OF MARSHAL BRENNAN, THE(1957), w

Tina-Bess Hubbard

1984

LAST NIGHT AT THE ALAMO(1984)

Tom Hubbard

WITHOUT RESERVATIONS(1946); TWO LOST WORLDS(1950), a, w; HOODLUM, THE(1951); BUFFALO BILL IN TOMAHAWK TERRITORY(1952); RED SNOW(1952), w; MURDER WITHOUT TEARS(1953); HIGHWAY DRAGNET(1954), a, w; THUNDER PASS(1954), a, w; PORT OF HELL(1955), a, w; TREASURE OF RUBY HILLS(1955), w; HIDDEN GUNS(1956); SECRET OF TREASURE MOUNTAIN(1956); DANIEL BOONE, TRAIL BLAZER(1957), w; HELL CANYON OUTLAWS(1957); RAIDERS OF OLD CALIFORNIA(1957); LEGION OF THE DOOMED(1958), a, w; ARSON FOR HIRE(1959), a, w

Misc. Talkies

LUST TO KILL(1960)

Carl Hubbell

BIG LEAGUER(1953)

Chris Hubbell

NATIONAL LAMPOON'S CLASS REUNION(1982)

Lorraine Hubbell

MIRACLE WOMAN, THE(1931)

Raymond Hubbell

Silents

SONNY(1922), w

Cork Hubbert

WHERE THE BUFFALO ROAM(1980); CAVEMAN(1981); UNDER THE RAINBOW(1981)

1984

NOT FOR PUBLICATION(1984)

Corky Hubbert

PROPERTY(1979)

Gil Hubbs

HELLCATS, THE(1968), ph; WRESTLER, THE(1974), ph; THIS IS ELVIS(1982), ph

Gilbert Hubbs

ENTER THE DRAGON(1973), ph; GOLDEN NEEDLES(1974), ph

Gill Hubbs

FORCE: FIVE(1981), ph

Svatava Hubenakova

VOYAGE TO THE END OF THE UNIVERSE(1963, Czech.)

Alex Huber

SEXTON BLAKE AND THE HOODED TERROR(1938, Brit.)

Benjamin Huber

WINDWALKER(1980)

Billie Huber

DANTE'S INFERNO(1935)

Chad Huber

Silents

PRETTY LADIES(1925)

Chieko Huber

GENGHIS KHAN(U.S./Brit./Ger./Yugo)

David Huber

WINDWALKER(1980)

Gottlieb Huber

NEXT TIME WE LOVE(1936)

Grischa Huber

SERPENT'S EGG, THE(1977, Ger./U.S.); MALOU(1983)

Gusti Huber

DIARY OF ANNE FRANK, THE(1959)

Harold Huber

CENTRAL PARK(1932); MATCH KING, THE(1932); BOWERY, THE(1933); FRISCO JENNY(1933); GIRL MISSING(1933); LADIES THEY TALK ABOUT(1933); LIFE OF JIMMY DOLAN, THE(1933); MARY STEVENS, M.D.(1933); MAYOR OF HELL, THE(1933); MIDNIGHT MARY(1933); PARACHUTE JUMPER(1933); POLICE CAR 17(1933); SILK EXPRESS, THE(1933); 20,000 YEARS IN SING SING(1933); CHEATING CHEATERS(1934); CROSBY CASE, THE(1934); DEFENSE HESTS, THE(1934); FURY OF THE JUNGLE(1934); HE WAS HER MAN(1934); HI, NELLIE!(1934); HIDEOUT(1934); LINEUP, THE(1934); MERRY FRINKS, THE(1934); NO MORE WOMEN(1934); THIN MAN, THE(1934); VERY HONORABLE GUY, A(1934); G-MEN(1935); MAD LOVE(1935); NAUGHTY MARIETTA(1935); ONE NEW YORK NIGHT(1935); PORT OF LOST DREAMS(1935); PURSUIT(1935); RECKLESS(1935); WORLD ACCUSES, THE(1935); DEVIL IS A SISSY, THE(1936); GAY DESPERADO, THE(1936); KELLY THE SECOND(1936); KLONDIKE ANNIE(1936); MUSS 'EM UP(1936); SAN FRANCISCO(1936); WE'RE ONLY HUMAN(1936); WOMEN ARE

TROUBLE(1936); ANGEL'S HOLIDAY(1937); CHARLIE CHAN AT MONTE CARLO(1937); CHARLIE CHAN ON BROADWAY(1937); GOOD EARTH, THE(1937); LOVE UNDER FIRE(1937); MIDNIGHT TAXI(1937); OUTLAWS OF THE ORIENT(1937); TROUBLE IN MOROCCO(1937); YOU CAN'T BEAT LOVE(1937); ADVENTURES OF MARCO POLO, THE(1938); GANGS OF NEW YORK(1938); INTERNATIONAL SETTLEMENT(1938); LITTLE TOUGH GUYS IN SOCIETY(1938); MR. MOTO'S GAMBLE(1938); MYSTERIOUS MR. MOTO(1938); PASSPORT HUSBAND(1938); SLIGHT CASE OF MURDER, A(1938); TRIP TO PARIS, A(1938); WHILE NEW YORK SLEEPS(1938); BEAU GESTE(1939); CHARLIE CHAN IN THE CITY OF DARKNESS(1939); CHARLIE MC CARTHY, DETECTIVE(1939); CHASING DANGER(1939); GOING PLACES(1939); KING OF THE TURF(1939); LADY AND THE MOB, THE(1939); MAIN STREET LAWYER(1939); YOU CAN'T GET AWAY WITH MURDER(1939); 6000 ENEMIES(1939); DANCE, GIRL, DANCE(1940); GHOST COMES HOME, THE(1940); KIT CARSON(1940); CHARLIE CHAN IN RIO(1941); COUNTRY FAIR(1941); DOWN MEXICO WAY(1941); MAN BETRAYED, A(1941); GENTLEMAN AFTER DARK, A(1942); ICE-CAPADES REVUE(1942); LITTLE TOKYO, U.S.A.(1942); MANILA CALLING(1942); PARDON MY STRIPES(1942); SLEEPYTIME GAL(1942); CRIME DOCTOR(1943); LADY FROM CHUNGKING(1943); LET'S DANCE(1950); MY FRIEND IRMA GOES WEST(1950); JOKER IS WILD, THE(1957)

Max Huber

SHELL SHOCK(1964)

Noreen Huber

HAPPY AS THE GRASS WAS GREEN(1973); HAZEL'S PEOPLE(1978)

Patrick Huber

SMUGGLERS, THE(1969, Fr.)

Peter Huber

LE MANS(1971)

Brian Huberman

1984

LAST NIGHT AT THE ALAMO(1984), ph

Ali Hubert

PATRIOT, THE(1928), cos; MERRY WIDOW, THE(1934), cos; LIFE OF EMILE ZOLA, THE(1937), cos; PRIVATE LIVES OF ELIZABETH AND ESSEX, THE(1939), tech adv

Silents

PASSION(1920, Ger.), cos; ONE ARABIAN NIGHT(1921, Ger.), cos

Axel Hubert

BORN AGAIN(1978), ed

Dolores Hubert

FOREVER MY LOVE(1962)

F. Hugh Hubert

TOGETHER AGAIN(1944), w

Frank Hubert

STARS ON PARADE(1944)

George Hubert

FOREIGN INTRIGUE(1956)

Harold Hubert

Silents

BATTLE CRY OF PEACE, THE(1915)

Irene Hubert

WINGS OF THE MORNING(1937, Brit.), cos; DIVORCE OF LADY X. THE(1938, Brit.), cos

Jacques Hubert

SHADOW OF THE HAWK(1976, Can.)

Jean Hubert

STARS ON PARADE(1944)

Lucien Hubert

FORBIDDEN GAMES(1953, Fr.); GERVAISE(1956, Fr.); LIGHT ACROSSS THE STREET, THE(1957, Fr.); HORROR CHAMBER OF DR. FAUSTUS, THE(1962, Fr./Ital.)

Lyn Hubert

GOODBYE, NORMA JEAN(1976), w

Myra Hubert

EYES OF THE WORLD, THE(1930)

Rene Hubert

TEMPORARY WIDOW, THE(1930, Ger./Brit.); THOSE THREE FRENCH GIRLS(1930), cos; WAR NURSE(1930), cos; WHAT A WIDOW(1930), cos; EASIEST WAY, THE(1931), cos; MUSIC IN THE AIR(1934), cos; SERVANTS' ENTRANCE(1934), cos; UNDER THE PAMPAS MOON(1935), cos; GHOST GOES WEST, THE(1936), cos; THINGS TO COME(1936, Brit.), cos; DARK JOURNEY(1937, Brit.), cos; DINNER AT THE RITZ(1937, Brit.), cos; FIRE OVER ENGLAND(1937, Brit.), cos; MEN ARE NOT GODS(1937, Brit.), cos; UNDER THE RED ROBE(1937, Brit.), cos; GAIETY GIRLS, THE(1938, Brit.), cos; RETURN OF THE SCARLET PIMPERNEL(1938, Brit.), cos; FOUR FEATHERS, THE(1939, Brit.), cos; OVER THE MOON(1940, Brit.), cos; FLAME OF NEW ORLEANS, THE(1941), cos; NEW WINE(1941), cos; THAT HAMILTON WOMAN(1941), cos; PRIDE OF THE YANKEES, THE(1942), cos; TWIN BEDS(1942), cos; HEAVEN CAN WAIT(1943), cos; SKY'S THE LIMIT, THE(1943), cos; SONG OF BERNADETTE, THE(1943), cos; WINTERTIME(1943), cos; JANE EYRE(1944), cos; PIN UP GIRL(1944), cos; WILSON(1944), cos; ROYAL SCANDAL, A(1945), cos; DRAGONWYCH(1946), cos; MY DARLING CLEMENTINE(1946), cos; 13 RUE MADELEINE(1946), cos; FOREVER AMBER(1947), cos; LATE GEORGE APLEY, THE(1947), cos; FURY AT FURNACE CREEK(1948), cos; THAT LADY IN ERMINE(1948), cos; FAN, THE(1949), cos; ANASTASIA(1956), cos; JOURNEY, THE(1959, U.S./Aust.), cos; FOUR HORSEMEN OF THE APOCALYPSE, THE(1962), cos; VISIT, THE(1964, Ger./Fr./Ital./U.S.), cos

Silents

FOREIGN DEVILS(1927), cos; TWELVE MILES OUT(1927), cos

Roger Hubert

END OF THE WORLD, THE(1930, Fr.), ph; BATTLE, THE(1934, Fr.), ph; J'ACCUSE(1939, Fr.), ph; MAN OF THE HOUR, THE(1940, Fr.), ph; ETERNAL RETURN, THE(1943, Fr.), ph; CHILDREN OF PARADISE(1945, Fr.), ph; DEVIL'S ENVOYS, THE(1947, Fr.), ph; BLIND DESIRE(1948, Fr.), ph; FANNY(1948, Fr.), ph; ROOM UPSTAIRS, THE(1948, Fr.), ph; HENRIETTE'S HOLIDAY(1953, Fr.), ph; SEVEN DEADLY SINS, THE(1953, Fr./Ital.), ph; HOLIDAY FOR HENRIETTA(1955, Fr.), ph; PARIS HOLIDAY(1958), ph; FEMALE, THE(1960, Fr.), ph; COW AND I, THE(1961, Fr., Ital., Ger.), ph; DYNAMITE JACK(1961, Fr.), ph; LAFAYETTE(1963, Fr.), ph; LA BONNE SOUPE(1964, Fr./Ital.), ph; MY WIFE'S HUSBAND(1965, Fr./Ital.), ph

Roger Huberts

BIG CHIEF, THE(1960, Fr.), ph

Henry Hubinet
DAISY MILLER(1974)
Richard G. Hubler
BUNGALOW 13(1948), w; I CHEATED THE LAW(1949), w; GREAT PLANE ROBBERY(1950), w; BEACHHEAD(1954), w
Richard Q. Hubler
MAN-EATER OF KUMAON(1948), w
Faith Hubley
OF STARS AND MEN(1961), p, w, ed; YEAR OF THE HORSE, THE(1966), w
Hamp Hubley
OF STARS AND MEN(1961)
John Hubley
FANTASIA(1940), art d; PINOCCHIO(1940), art d; OF STARS AND MEN(1961), p, d, w; YEAR OF THE HORSE, THE(1966), anim
K.S. Hubley
JEALOUSY(1934)
Mark Hubley
OF STARS AND MEN(1961); YEAR OF THE HORSE, THE(1966)
Season Hubley
LOLLY-MADONNA XXX(1973); CATCH MY SOUL(1974); HARDCORE(1979); ESCAPE FROM NEW YORK(1981); VICE SQUAD(1982)
Misc. Talkies
BLACK CARRION(1984)
Brigitte Hubner
BENJAMIN(1973, Ger.), ed
Herbert Hubner
COURT CONCERT, THE(1936, Ger.); LIFE BEGINS ANEW(1938, Ger.); SERGEANT BERRY(1938, Ger.)
Ronald M. Hubner
1984
INITIATION, THE(1984)
Bernard Hubrenne
DIARY OF A COUNTRY PRIEST(1954, Fr.)
Edi Hubschmid
YOL(1982, Turkey), p
Paul Hubschmid [Paul Christian]
AFFAIRS OF JULIE, THE(1958, Ger.); DAY THE SKY EXPLODED, THE(1958, Fr./Ital.); HELDINNEN(1962, Ger.); I, TOO, AM ONLY A WOMAN(1963, Ger.); AND SO TO BED(1965, Ger.); FUNERAL IN BERLIN(1966, Brit.); MOZAMBIQUE(1966, Brit.); ONLY A WOMAN(1966, Ger.); IN ENEMY COUNTRY(1968); MANON 70(1968, Fr.); THAT WOMAN(1968, Ger.); TASTE OF EXCITEMENT(1969, Brit.); SKULLDUGGERY(1970)
Hubert Hubson
LETTER FOR EVIE, A(1945), art d
Roberta Huby
CASE OF CHARLES PEACE, THE(1949, Brit.); TAKE ME TO PARIS(1951, Brit.); WALLET, THE(1952, Brit.); ELECTRONIC MONSTER. THE(1960, Brit.)
Pierre Huchet
CRIME OF MONSIEUR LANGE, THE(1936, Fr.)
Cooper Huckabee
POM POM GIRLS, THE(1976); FOUL PLAY(1978); JONI(1980); URBAN COWBOY(1980); FUNHOUSE, THE(1981); PURSUIT OF D.B. COOPER, THE(1981)
Misc. Talkies
GETTING WASTED(1980)
Pete Huckabee
COCAINE COWBOYS(1979)
Tom Huckabee
TAKING TIGER MOUNTAIN(1983, U.S./Welsh), d, w
Annie Huckle
1984
MIDSUMMER NIGHT'S DREAM, A(1984, Brit./Span.)
Gary Huckstep
SUDDEN FURY(1975, Can.)
David Huckvale
1984
MRS. SOFFEL(1984)
Douglas Huckvale
1984
MRS. SOFFEL(1984)
Coni Hudak
DAVID AND LISA(1962)
Pamela Hudak
1984
WINDY CITY(1984)
Roy Hudd
BLOOD BEAST TERROR, THE(1967, Brit.); MAGNIFICENT SEVEN DEADLY SINS, THE(1971, Brit.); UP POMPEII(1971, Brit.); UP THE CHASTITY BELT(1971, Brit.)
Walter Hudd
I STAND CONDEMNED(1936, Brit.); REMBRANDT(1936, Brit.); ELEPHANT BOY(1937, Brit.); BLACK LIMELIGHT(1938, Brit.); HOUSEMASTER(1938, Brit.); DEAD MAN'S SHOES(1939, Brit.); DR. O'DOWD(1940, Brit.); OUTSIDER, THE(1940, Brit.); MAJOR BARBARA(1941, Brit.); UNCENSORED(1944, Brit.); YANK IN LONDON, A(1946, Brit.); I KNOW WHERE I'M GOING(1947, Brit.); LADY SURRENDERS, A(1947, Brit.); ESCAPE(1948, Brit.); PAPER ORCHID(1949, Brit.); IMPORTANCE OF BEING EARNEST, THE(1952, Brit.); LANDFALL(1953, Brit.); SLASHER, THE(1953, Brit.); GOOD DIE YOUNG, THE(1954, Brit.); LAST MAN TO HANG, THE(1956, Brit.); LOSER TAKES ALL(1956, Brit.); SATELLITE IN THE SKY(1956); CAST A DARK SHADOW(1958, Brit.); FURTHER UP THE CREEK!(1958, Brit.); LOOK BACK IN ANGER(1959); MAN UPSTAIRS, THE(1959, Brit.); NAVY LARK, THE(1959, Brit.); TWO-HEADED SPY, THE(1959, Brit.); SINK THE BISMARCK!(1960, Brit.); TWO-WAY STRETCH(1961, Brit.); DREAM MAKER, THE(1963, Brit.); PUNCH AND JUDY MAN, THE(1963, Brit.); WALK IN THE SHADOW(1966, Brit.)
Suzanne Huddart
ABDICATION, THE(1974, Brit.)
Elizabeth Huddle
PILGRIM, FAREWELL(1980)
David Huddleston
SLAVES(1969); NORWOOD(1970); RIO LOBO(1970); WUSA(1970); FOOLS' PARADE(1971); SOMETHING BIG(1971); BAD COMPANY(1972); BILLY TWO HATS(1973, Brit.); BLAZING SADDLES(1974); KLANSMAN, THE(1974); MC Q(1974); BREAK-

HEART PASS(1976); GREATEST, THE(1977, U.S./Brit.); WORLD'S GREATEST LOVER, THE(1977); CAPRICORN ONE(1978); GORP(1980); SMOKEY AND THE BANDIT II(1980)
1984
ACT, THE(1984)
Misc. Talkies
COUNTRY BLUE(1975)
Michaekl Huddleston
WORLD'S GREATEST LOVER, THE(1977)
Michael Huddleston
FOUR FRIENDS(1981)
1984
WOMAN IN RED, THE(1984)
Erica Huddy
HARDLY WORKING(1981)
Donald Hudgins
RED RUNS THE RIVER(1963)
Donald H. Hudgins
TOGETHER FOR DAYS(1972), ph
Joe Hudgins
PUNISHMENT PARK(1971)
Ken Hudgins
STATE FAIR(1962)
Kenneth Hudgins
SUGARLAND EXPRESS, THE(1974)
Sarah Louise Hudgins
1984
LAST NIGHT AT THE ALAMO(1984)
Wayne Hudgins
CINDERELLA LIBERTY(1973)
Norman Hudis
BOND OF FEAR(1956, Brit.), w; BREAKAWAY(1956, Brit.), w; PASSPORT TO TREASON(1956, Brit.), w; CROOKED SKY, THE(1957, Brit.), w; FIGHTING WILDCATS, THE(1957, Brit.), w; HIGH TERRACE(1957, Brit.), w; HOUR OF DECISION(1957, Brit.), w; MAILBAG ROBBERY(1957, Brit.), w; ROCK AROUND THE WORLD(1957, Brit.), w; STRANGER IN TOWN(1957, Brit.), w; DEATH OVER MY SHOULDER(1958, Brit.), w; DUKE WORE JEANS, THE(1958, Brit.), w; MARK OF THE PHOENIX(1958, Brit.), w; MENACE IN THE NIGHT(1958, Brit.), w; 6.5 SPECIAL(1958, Brit.), w; CARRY ON NURSE(1959, Brit.), w; CARRY ON SERGEANT(1959, Brit.), w; CARRY ON CONSTABLE(1960, Brit.), w; PLEASE TURN OVER(1960, Brit.), w; BEWARE OF CHILDREN(1961, Brit.), w; CARRY ON REGARDLESS(1961, Brit.), w; CARRY ON CRUISING(1962, Brit.), w; CARRY ON TEACHER(1962, Brit.), w; TWICE AROUND THE DAFFODILS(1962, Brit.), w; NURSE ON WHEELS(1964, Brit.), w; KARATE KILLERS, THE(1967), w; MISTER TEN PERCENT(1967, Brit.), w
Stephen Hudis
COWBOYS, THE(1972)
Bear Hudkins
DOMINO PRINCIPLE, THE(1977), a, stunts
Clyde Hudkins, Jr.
COLT .45(1950)
D. Hudkins
POCKET MONEY(1972)
Dick Hudkins
COLT .45(1950); OCEAN'S ELEVEN(1960); STAGECOACH(1966), stunts; GREAT BANK ROBBERY, THE(1969); SOMETIMES A GREAT NOTION(1971)
John "Bear" Hudkins
MONTE WALSH(1970)
John Hudkins
WESTBOUND(1959); HERO'S ISLAND(1962); GUESS WHO'S COMING TO DINNER(1967); TELL THEM WILLIE BOY IS HERE(1969); DIRTY HARRY(1971); LIFE AND TIMES OF JUDGE ROY BEAN, THE(1972); OKLAHOMA CRUDE(1973), a, stunts; FIRE SALE(1977); MOVIE MOVIE(1978); PRISONER OF ZENDA, THE(1979); TWO OF A KIND(1983)
Wes Hudman
SATAN'S CRADLE(1949); GIRL FROM SAN LORENZO, THE(1950); BATTLE OF ROGUE RIVER(1954); BLACKJACK KETCHUM, DESPERADO(1956)
Wesley Hudman
I KILLED GERONIMO(1950); INDIAN TERRITORY(1950); FORT DEFIANCE(1951); FORT DODGE STAMPEDE(1951); BLACK HILLS AMBUSH(1952); LEADVILLE GUNSLINGER(1952); PACK TRAIN(1953); MASTERSON OF KANSAS(1954); SCARLET COAT, THE(1955); LONELY MAN, THE(1957)
Richard Hudolin
HOUNDS... OF NOTRE DAME, THE(1980, Can.), art d; FIREBIRD 2015 AD(1981), art d
1984
ISAAC LITTLEFEATHERS(1984, Can.), art d
Arch Hudson
MALE SERVICE(1966), d
Barbara Hudson
WIRETAPPERS(1956)
Barry Hudson
ILLEGAL(1955)
Beverly Hudson
TRUE TO LIFE(1943); BORN TO SING(1942); HENRY ALDRICH SWINGS IT(1943); SWEET AND LOWDOWN(1944)
Bill Hudson
AIR STRIKE(1955); HEADLINE SHOOTER(1933); LOVER COME BACK(1946); STARLIFT(1951); STEEL TRAP, THE(1952); SHE-CREATURE, THE(1956); WRONG MAN, THE(1956); MY SIX LOVES(1963)
Brett Hudson
HYSTERICAL(1983), a, w
Brooke Hudson
WAVELENGTH(1983)
Christopher Hudson
OVERLORD(1975, Brit.), w
Daral Hudson
CARIBBEAN MYSTERY, THE(1945); CANYON PASSAGE(1946)

Dawn Hudson
ROSEANNA McCOY(1949)
Derek Hudson
THREE SISTERS(1974, Brit.), m
Earl Hudson
Silents
SO BIG(1924), sup, w; AS MAN DESIRES(1925), sup, w; IF I MARRY AGAIN(1925), sup; KNOCKOUT, THE(1925), sup; LOST WORLD, THE(1925), sup
Eddy Hudson
JUNIOR MISS(1945)
Edgar Hudson
Silents
WHISPERS(1920)
Elise Hudson
MELVIN AND HOWARD(1980)
Ernie Hudson
MAIN EVENT, THE(1979); JONI(1980); PENITENTIARY II(1982); GOING BER-SERK(1983); SPACEHUNTER: ADVENTURES IN THE FORBIDDEN ZONE(1983); TWO OF A KIND(1983)
1984
GHOSTBUSTERS(1984); JOY OF SEX(1984)
Ethel Hudson
RAMPARTS WE WATCH, THE(1940)
Eva Hudson
WHO'S YOUR FATHER?(1935, Brit.); END OF THE RIVER, THE(1947, Brit.)
Fred Hudson
EDUCATION OF SONNY CARSON, THE(1974), w
Gary Hudson
SKATETOWN, U.S.A.(1979); KING OF THE MOUNTAIN(1981)
Gary Hudson [Gianni Garko]
10,000 DOLLARS BLOOD MONEY(1966, Ital.)
Hal Hudson
OPENED BY MISTAKE(1940), w; MEET THE CHUMP(1941), w; TRAGEDY AT MIDNIGHT, A(1942), w
Hugh Hudson
CHARRIOTS OF FIRE(1981, Brit.), d
1984
GREYSTOKE: THE LEGEND OF TARZAN, LORD OF THE APES(1984), p, d
James Hudson
HONG KONG AFFAIR(1958)
Jarvais Hudson
MOMENT BY MOMENT(1978)
Jim Hudson
MODERN PROBLEMS(1981)
John Hudson
DESTINATION TOKYO(1944); ONE WOMAN'S STORY(1949, Brit.); HUE AND CRY(1950); CIMARRON KID, THE(1951); BATTLE AT APACHE PASS, THE(1952); RED BALL EXPRESS(1952); RETURN TO PARADISE(1953); SEA OF LOST SHIPS(1953); SILVER LODE(1954); FORT YUMA(1955); MANY RIVERS TO CROSS(1955); MARAUDERS, THE(1955); RACERS, THE(1955); MOHAWK(1956); WHEN GANGLAND STRIKES(1956); GUNFIGHT AT THE O.K. CORRAL(1957); VALLEY OF THE REDWOODS(1960); ALL IN A NIGHT'S WORK(1961); SINAI COMMANDOS: THE STORY OF THE SIX DAY WAR(1968, Israel/Ger.); PRIEST OF LOVE(1981, Brit.)
John Hudson [William Hudson]
SCREAMING SKULL, THE(1958)
John Paul Hudson
GREASER'S PALACE(1972)
Jeffrey Hudson [Michael Crichton]
CAREY TREATMENT, THE(1972), w
Kim Hudson
MANIAC(1980)
Larry Hudson
STRIP, THE(1951); SMOKY CANYON(1952); HITCH-HIKER, THE(1953); REDHEAD FROM WYOMING, THE(1953); DOWN THREE DARK STREETS(1954); I DIED A THOUSAND TIMES(1955); CREATURE WALKS AMONG US, THE(1956); JU-BAL(1956); SOLID GOLD CADILLAC, THE(1956); TANK COMMANDOS(1959)
Lee Hudson
SCREAM AND SCREAM AGAIN(1970, Brit.)
Leslie Ann Hudson
THREE WOMEN(1977)
Lord Tim Hudson
ARISTOCATS, THE(1970)
Mark Hudson
HYSTERICAL(1983), a, w
Maxine Hudson
UNDERCURRENT(1946)
Patricia Ann Hudson
THREE WOMEN(1977)
Patty Lou Hudson
BEST THINGS IN LIFE ARE FREE, THE(1956)
Phyllis Hudson
MEET THE NAVY(1946, Brit.)
Renee Hudson
I CONFESS(1953)
Rochelle Hudson
ARE THESE OUR CHILDREN?(1931); FANNY FOLEY HERSELF(1931); BEYOND THE ROCKIES(1932); HELL'S HIGHWAY(1932); PENGUIN POOL MURDER, THE(1932); SAVAGE GIRL, THE(1932); SECRETS OF THE FRENCH POLICE(1932); DR. BULL(1933); LOVE IS LIKE THAT(1933); MR. SKITCH(1933); PAST OF MARY HOLMES, THE(1933); SCARLET RIVER(1933); SHE DONE HIM WRONG(1933); WALLS OF GOLD(1933); WILD BOYS OF THE ROAD(1933); BACHELOR BAIT(1934); HAROLD TEEN(1934); IMITATION OF LIFE(1934); JUDGE PRIEST(1934); MIGHTY BARNUM, THE(1934); NOTORIOUS BUT NICE(1934); SUCH WOMEN ARE DANGER-OUS(1934); CURLY TOP(1935); I'VE BEEN AROUND(1935); LES MISERABLES(1935); LIFE BEGINS AT 40(1935); SHOW THEM NO MERCY(1935); WAY DOWN EAST(1935); COUNTRY BEYOND, THE(1936); EVERYBODY'S OLD MAN(1936); MUSIC GOES ROUND, THE(1936); POPPY(1936); REUNION(1936); BORN RECK-LESS(1937); SHE HAD TO EAT(1937); THAT I MAY LIVE(1937); WOMAN-WISE(1937); MR. MOTO TAKES A CHANCE(1938); RASCALS(1938); STORM OVER BEN-

GAL(1938); KONGA, THE WILD STALLION(1939); MISSING DAUGHTERS(1939); PIRATES OF THE SKIES(1939); PRIDE OF THE NAVY(1939); SMUGGLED CAR-GO(1939); WOMAN IS THE JUDGE, A(1939); BABIES FOR SALE(1940); CONVICTED WOMAN(1940); GIRLS UNDER TWENTY-ONE(1940); ISLAND OF DOOMED MEN(1940); MEN WITHOUT SOULS(1940); MEET BOSTON BLACKIE(1941); OFFIC-ER AND THE LADY, THE(1941); STORK PAYS OFF, THE(1941); QUEEN OF BROADWAY(1942); RUBBER RACKETEERS(1942); DEVIL'S CARGO, THE(1948); SKY LINER(1949); REBEL WITHOUT A CAUSE(1955); NIGHT WALKER, THE(1964); STRAIT-JACKET(1964)
Misc. Talkies
BUSH PILOT(1947)
Rock Hudson
FIGHTER SQUADRON(1948); DESERT HAWK, THE(1950); I WAS A SHOPLIF-TER(1950); ONE WAY STREET(1950); PEGGY(1950); WINCHESTER '73(1950); AIR CADET(1951); BRIGHT VICTORY(1951); FAT MAN, THE(1951); IRON MAN, THE(1951); TOMAHAWK(1951); BEND OF THE RIVER(1952); HAS ANYBODY SEEN MY GAL?(1952); HERE COME THE NELSONS(1952); HORIZONS WEST(1952); LAW-LESS BREED, THE(1952); SCARLET ANGEL(1952); BACK TO GOD'S COUN-TRY(1953); GOLDEN BLADE, THE(1953); GUN FURY(1953); SEA DEVILS(1953); SEMINOLE(1953); BENGAL BRIGADE(1954); MAGNIFICENT OBSESSION(1954); TAZA, SON OF COCHISE(1954); ALL THAT HEAVEN ALLOWS(1955); CAPTAIN LIGHTFOOT(1955); ONE DESIRE(1955); FOUR GIRLS IN TOWN(1956); GIANT(1956); NEVER SAY GOODBYE(1956); WRITTEN ON THE WIND(1956); BATTLE HYMN(1957); FAREWELL TO ARMS, A(1957); SOMETHING OF VALUE(1957); TARNISHED ANGELS, THE(1957); TWILIGHT FOR THE GODS(1958); PILLOW TALK(1959); THIS EARTH IS MINE(1959); COME SEPTEMBER(1961); LAST SUN-SET, THE(1961); LOVER COME BACK(1961); SPIRAL ROAD, THE(1962); GATHER-ING OF EAGLES, A(1963); MAN'S FAVORITE SPORT(1964); SEND ME NO FLOWERS(1964); STRANGE BEDFELLOWS(1965); VERY SPECIAL FAVOR, A(1965); BLINDFOLD(1966); SECONDS(1966); TOBRUK(1966); ICE STATION ZEBRA(1968); FINE PAIR, A(1969, Ital.); UNDEFEATED, THE(1969); DARLING LILI(1970); HOR-NET'S NEST(1970); PRETTY MAIDS ALL IN A ROW(1971); SHOWDOWN(1973); EMBRYO(1976); AVALANCHE(1978); MIRROR CRACK'D, THE(1980, Brit.)
1984
AMBASSADOR, THE(1984)
Tim Hudson
JUNGLE BOOK, THE(1967)
Tina Hudson
OCTOPUSSY(1983, Brit.)
Toni Hudson
CROSS CREEK(1983)
1984
PLACES IN THE HEART(1984)
Valerie Hudson
SUBTERFUGE(1969, US/Brit.)
Vanda Hudson
INNOCENT SINNERS(1958, Brit.); LIBEL(1959, Brit.); BOTTOMS UP(1960, Brit.); CIRCUS OF HORRORS(1960, Brit.); TICKET TO PARADISE(1961, Brit.); JUNGLE STREET GIRLS(1963, Brit.); FATHER CAME TOO(1964, Brit.); THIS, THAT AND THE OTHER(1970, Brit.)
Virginia Tyler Hudson
Silents
CABARET, THE(1918), w; OLDEST LAW, THE(1918), w
Wanda Hudson
STRIP TEASE MURDER(1961, Brit.)
Wilbur Hudson
Misc. Silents
AMERICAN GENTLEMAN, AN(1915)
William Henry Hudson
GREEN MANSIONS(1959), w
William Hudson
DESTINATION TOKYO(1944); WEIRD WOMAN(1944); OBJECTIVE, BURMA!(1945); OVER 21(1945); LADY GAMBLES, THE(1949); TASK FORCE(1949); FATHER MAKES GOOD(1950); HARD, FAST, AND BEAUTIFUL(1951); LET'S GO NAVY(1951); MISTER ROBERTS(1955); STRATEGIC AIR COMMAND(1955); AMAZING COLOSSAL MAN, THE(1957); BATTLE HYMN(1957); MAN WHO TURNED TO STONE, THE(1957); MY MAN GODFREY(1957); ATTACK OF THE 50 FOOT WOMAN(1958); MOON PI-LOT(1962); HYSTERICAL(1983), a, w
The Hudson Wonders
SEE MY LAWYER(1945)
Tomasz Hudziec
1984
SHIVERS(1984, Pol.)
Huguette Hue
DEADLY DECOYS, THE(1962, Fr.)
Edward Huebach
CIGARETTE GIRL(1947), w
Klaus Huebel
BLACK AND WHITE IN COLOR(1976, Fr.)
Craig Huebing
COMIC, THE(1969); MAROONED(1969)
Herbert Huebner
STORM IN A WATER GLASS(1931, Aust.); DREAMER, THE(1936, Ger.); DAY WILL COME, A(1960, Ger.); ETERNAL LOVE(1960, Ger.); SPESSART INN, THE(1961, Ger.)
Karin Huebner
ENDLESS NIGHT, THE(1963, Ger.)
Mark Huebner
TEX(1982)
Zygmunt Huebner
TIN DRUM, THE(1979, Ger./Fr./Yugo./Pol.)
Edward Huebsch
MILLIE'S DAUGHTER(1947), w; SPORT OF KINGS(1947), w; BLACK EAGLE(1948), w; TWILIGHT'S LAST GLEAMING(1977, U.S./Ger.), w
Reginald Huegenin
BROKEN ENGLISH(1981)
Willy Huegli
END OF THE GAME(1976, Ger./Ital.)

Dick Huemer
DUMBO(1941), w; MAKE MINE MUSIC(1946), w; ALICE IN WONDERLAND(1951), w

Ernst Rune Huemer
CHILDREN OF GOD'S EARTH(1983, Norwegian)

Niki Huen
LITTLE JUNGLE BOY(1969, Aus.)

George Huerrera
MANDALAY(1934)

Chris Huerta
BANDIDOS(1967, Ital.); MORE THAN A MIRACLE(1967, Ital./Fr.); NAVAJO JOE(1967, Ital./Span.)

Cris Huerta
DESPERATE ONES, THE(1968 U.S./Span.); SEVEN GUNS FOR THE MACGREGORS(1968, Ital./Span.)

Kris Huerta
SECRET SEVEN, THE(1966, Ital./Span.)

Rosa Huerta
TERROR IN THE WAX MUSEUM(1973)

Ernest Huerta, Jr.
1984
LAST NIGHT AT THE ALAMO(1984)

Chris Huertas
TOWN CALLED HELL, A(1971, Span./Brit.)

Russell Huestes
GOVERNMENT GIRL(1943)

Russell Huestis
RINGS ON HER FINGERS(1942)

Fred Hueston
WOMAN IN THE WINDOW, THE(1945); CRACK-UP(1946); TILL THE CLOUDS ROLL BY(1946)

Woody Hueston
BREAKING AWAY(1979)

Henri-Jacques Huet
BREATHLESS(1959, Fr.); LE PETIT SOLDAT(1965, Fr.); SELLERS OF GIRLS(1967, Fr.); DIANE'S BODY(1969, Fr./Czech.); SLOGAN(1970, Fr.); CESAR AND ROSALIE(1972, Fr.); VIOLETTE(1978, Fr.); BEAU PERE(1981, Fr.)

Otto Huett
AMBUSH AT TOMAHAWK GAP(1953)

John Huettner
FOUR HOURS TO KILL(1935); THIRTEEN HOURS BY AIR(1936)

Francisco Hueva
1984
IT'S NEVER TOO LATE(1984, Span.), p

Garrick Huey
CHARLIE CHAN AND THE CURSE OF THE DRAGON QUEEN(1981)

Alvin Huff
GREASED LIGHTNING(1977)

Brent Huff
COACH(1978)
1984
PERILS OF GWENDOLINE, THE(1984, Fr.)

Carrie Huff
DRUMS O' VOODOO(1934)

Charles Huff
WORDS AND MUSIC(1929)

George Huff
Silents
KAISER, BEAST OF BERLIN, THE(1918)

Jack Huff
Silents
KEEP SMILING(1925)

Justina Huff
Misc. Silents
COURAGE AND THE MAN(1915); ON BITTER CREEK(1915); REGENERATING LOVE, THE(1915); MAN INSIDE, THE(1916)

Louise Huff
Silents
RANSOM, THE(1916); GREAT EXPECTATIONS(1917); JACK AND JILL(1917); SEVENTH DAY, THE(1922)
Misc. Silents
FOR FIVE THOUSAND DOLLARS A YEAR(1915); MARSE COVINGTON(1915); BLAZING LOVE(1916); DESTINY'S TOY(1916); OLD HOMESTEAD, THE(1916); REWARD OF PATIENCE, THE(1916); SEVENTEEN(1916); FRECKLES(1917); GHOST HOUSE, THE(1917); LONESOME CHAP, THE(1917); VARMINT, THE(1917); WHAT MONEY CAN'T BUY(1917); HIS MAJESTY BUNKER BEAN(1918); MILE-A-MINUTE KENDALL(1918); SANDY(1918); SEA WAIF, THE(1918); T'OTHER DEAR CHARMER(1918); WILD YOUTH(1918); CROOK OF DREAMS(1919); HEART OF GOLD(1919); LITTLE INTRUDER, THE(1919); OH, YOU WOMEN!(1919); DANGEROUS PARADISE, THE(1920); WHAT WOMEN WANT(1920)

Master Jack Huff
Silents
ZANDER THE GREAT(1925)

Philip Huff
DEATHSPORT(1978), spec eff

Richard L. Huff
GIANT SPIDER INVASION, THE(1975), p, w

Thomas Huff
JOYRIDE(1977), stunts

Tom Huff
DIRTY O'NEIL(1974); TWO-MINUTE WARNING(1976); WARRIORS, THE(1979)
1984
WOMAN IN RED, THE(1984), stunts

Clair Huffaker
FLAMING STAR(1960), w; SEVEN WAYS FROM SUNDOWN(1960), w; COMANCHEROS, THE(1961), w; POSSE FROM HELL(1961), w; RIO CONCHOS(1964), w; TARZAN AND THE VALLEY OF GOLD(1966 U.S./Switz.), w; WAR WAGON, THE(1967), w; HELLFIGHTERS(1968), w; 100 RIFLES(1969), w; FLAP(1970), w; DESERTER, THE(1971 Ital./Yugo.), w

Samantha Huffaker
FUNNY LADY(1975)

Ray Huffine
THREE CABALLEROS, THE(1944), art d; FUN AND FANCY FREE(1947), art d; LADY AND THE TRAMP(1955), art d

David Huffman
F.I.S.T.(1978); ICE CASTLES(1978); ONION FIELD, THE(1979); LEO AND LOREE(1980); BLOOD BEACH(1981); ST. HELENS(1981); FIREFOX(1982)
Misc. Talkies
LAST PLANE OUT(1983)

Linda Huffman
ONLY THING YOU KNOW, THE(1971, Can.)

Arthur Huffsmith
CARNATION KID(1929), w; BLAZE O' GLORY(1930), ed; SUBWAY EXPRESS(1931), ed; TEN CENTS A DANCE(1931), ed
Silents
TILLIE'S PUNCTURED ROMANCE(1928), ed

Billy Hufsey
OFF THE WALL(1983)

Steven Hufsteter
1984
REPO MAN(1984), m

Armand Hug
Misc. Talkies
STORYVILLE(1974)

Franz Hug
SWISS MISS(1938)

Scotty Hugenberg
PURSUED(1947)

Mike Hugg
UP THE JUNCTION(1968, Brit.), m; VENUS IN FURS(1970, Ital./Brit./Ger.), m; LIKELY LADS, THE(1976, Brit.), m

Jonathan Hugger
1984
REPO MAN(1984)

David Huggett
MONKEY GRIP(1983, Aus.), ed

Richard Huggett
DEADLIEST SIN, THE(1956, Brit.)

Annabelle Huggins
BACK DOOR TO HELL(1964)

Bob Huggins
Misc. Silents
TELLTALE STEP, THE(1917)

Jere Huggins
BIG BIRD CAGE, THE(1972), ed; PERSONAL BEST(1982), ed; DEAL OF THE CENTURY(1983), ed

R.C. Huggins
HANGMAN'S WHARF(1950, Brit.)

Roy Huggins
I LOVE TROUBLE(1947), w; FULLER BRUSH MAN(1948), w; LADY GAMBLES, THE(1949), w; TOO LATE FOR TEARS(1949), w; WOMAN IN HIDING(1949), w; GOOD HUMOR MAN, THE(1950), w; GREAT MANHUNT, THE(1951, Brit.), w; SEALED CARGO(1951), w; HANGMAN'S KNOT(1952), d&w; GUN FURY(1953), w; PUSHOVER(1954), w; THREE HOURS TO KILL(1954), w; FEVER IN THE BLOOD, A(1961), p, w

Fred Hugh
10 RILLINGTON PLACE(1971, Brit.)

John Hugh
NAKED IN THE SUN(1957), w; LISETTE(1961), p,d&w; JOHNNY TIGER(1966), w; CHARLIE CHAN AND THE CURSE OF THE DRAGON QUEEN(1981)

R. John Hugh
YELLOWNECK(1955), d, w; NAKED IN THE SUN(1957), p&d; TOUCH OF FLESH, THE(1960), p&d; JOHNNY TIGER(1966), p; MEAL, THE(1975), p,d&w
Misc. Talkies
DEADLY ENCOUNTER(1979), d

Soto Joe Hugh
KILLING OF A CHINESE BOOKIE, THE(1976)

Daniel Hugh-Kelly
CUJO(1983)

Adelaide Hughes
Silents
GIMMIE(1923), w

Adrian Hughes
SIX-GUN RHYTHM(1939)

Albert Hughes
HUE AND CRY(1950, Brit.)

Alison Hughes
WICKER MAN, THE(1974, Brit.)

Andrew Hughes
LAST VOYAGE, THE(1960); FLIGHT FROM ASHIYA(1964, U.S./Jap.); TERROR BENEATH THE SEA(1966, Jap.); DESTROY ALL MONSTERS(1969, Jap.)

Ann Hughes
JEALOUSY(1934)

Anna Ruth Hughes
REG'LAR FELLERS(1941)

Anthony Hughes
CALL OF THE YUKON(1938); LADIES IN DISTRESS(1938); WIVES UNDER SUSPICION(1938); COURT-MARTIAL OF BILLY MITCHELL, THE(1955)

Arnold Hughes
CITY BENEATH THE SEA(1953), m; RAILS INTO LARAMIE(1954), m

Arthur Hughes
PLASTIC DOME OF NORMA JEAN, THE(1966); BANANAS(1971); GREAT GATSBY, THE(1974)

B.B. Hughes
HERE COME THE JETS(1959)

Barnard Hughes
YOUNG DOCTORS, THE(1961); HAMLET(1964); MIDNIGHT COWBOY(1969); WHERE'S POPPA?(1970); COLD TURKEY(1971); HOSPITAL, THE(1971); PURSUIT OF HAPPINESS, THE(1971); RAGE(1972); SISTERS(1973); OH, GOD!(1977); FIRST

MONDAY IN OCTOBER(1981); BEST FRIENDS(1982); DEADHEAD MILES(1982); TRON(1982)

Beulah Hughes
HANDS OF ORLAC, THE(1964, Brit./Fr.); HANDS OF THE RIPPER(1971, Brit.); GREEK TYCOON, THE(1978)
1984
SUPERGIRL(1984)

Bill Hughes
THREE BRAVE MEN(1957); GERONIMO(1962); SMOKE IN THE WIND(1975), p

Billy Hughes
STAKEOUT!(1962); MY SIX LOVES(1963)
Misc. Talkies
OLE REX(1961)

Billy Hughes, Jr.
SMOKE IN THE WIND(1975)

Bob Hughes
CATHY'S CHILD(1979, Aus.); MAN, A WOMAN, AND A BANK, A(1979, Can.)

Brendon Hughes
OUTLAND(1981)

C. Anthony Hughes
PEOPLE AGAINST O'HARA, THE(1951)

Carol Hughes
CEILNG ZERO(1935); CASE OF THE VELVET CLAWS, THE(1936); EARTHWORM TRACTORS(1936); POLO JOE(1936); STAGE STRUCK(1936); THREE MEN ON A HORSE(1936); EVER SINCE EVE(1937); MARRY THE GIRL(1937); MEET THE BOY FRIEND(1937); READY, WILLING AND ABLE(1937); RENFREW OF THE ROYAL MOUNTED(1937); WESTLAND CASE, THE(1937); GOLD MINE IN THE SKY(1938); MAN FROM MUSIC MOUNTAIN(1938); UNDER WESTERN STARS(1938); DAY THE BOOKIES WEPT, THE(1939); LOVE AFFAIR(1939); WOMEN, THE(1939); BORDER LEGION, THE(1940); FLIGHT ANGELS(1940); MARRIED AND IN LOVE(1940); DESPERATE CARGO(1941); EMERGENCY LANDING(1941); GIRL, A GUY AND A GOB, A(1941); I'LL WAIT FOR YOU(1941); SCATTERGOOD BAINES(1941); TOP SERGEANT MULLIGAN(1941); UNDER FIESTA STARS(1941); I MARRIED AN ANGEL(1942); LUCKY JORDAN(1942); MIRACLE KID(1942); SHIP AHOY(1942); MY SON, THE HERO(1943); SHE'S FOR ME(1943); WHAT'S BUZZIN COUSIN?(1943); WEEKEND PASS(1944); NAUGHTY NINETIES, THE(1945); PILLOW TO POST(1945); BEAUTIFUL CHEAT, THE(1946); BLONDIE KNOWS BEST(1946); HOME IN OKLAHOMA(1946); JOE PALOOKA, CHAMP(1946); RED DRAGON, THE(1946); BACHELOR AND THE BOBBY-SOXER, THE(1947); EVERY GIRL SHOULD BE MARRIED(1948); SLIGHTLY FRENCH(1949); STAGECOACH KID(1949); SCARAMOUCHE(1952)

Carole Hughes
GIRL ON THE SPOT(1946)

Carolyn Hughes
BONNIE PARKER STORY, THE(1958); PARATROOP COMMAND(1959); LOLLIPOP COVER, THE(1965)

Cary Hughes
HIDE AND SEEK(1964, Brit.), m

Catherine Hughes
TROUBLE AT MIDNIGHT(1937)

Charles A. Hughes
I WANTED WINGS(1941); PRACTICALLY YOURS(1944); MASQUERADE IN MEXICO(1945); BLUE DAHLIA, THE(1946)

Charles Anthony Hughes
FRONTIERSMAN, THE(1938); WOMEN IN THE WIND(1939); ROUGHLY SPEAKING(1945); ON OUR MERRY WAY(1948); DADDY LONG LEGS(1955)

Charles Hughes
WINTERHAWK(1976), art d; MAN WHO WASN'T THERE, THE(1983), art d
Misc. Talkies
CALL OF THE FOREST(1949)

Charlie Hughes
FIGHTING RANGER, THE(1948); FARMER, THE(1977), art d
1984
STARMAN(1984)

Chris Hughes
SAFE AT HOME(1962); ROBIN AND THE SEVEN HOODS(1964); REQUIEM FOR A GUNFIGHTER(1965)

Colin Hughes
OUTBACK(1971, Aus.)

Cooper Hughes
1984
C.H.U.D.(1984), m

David H. Hughes
QUIET MAN, THE(1952)

David Hillary Hughes
NOTORIOUS LANDLADY, THE(1962)

David Hughes
GRAPES OF WRATH(1940); LONG VOYAGE HOME, THE(1940); GOVERNMENT GIRL(1943); CORN IS GREEN, THE(1945); PRISON SHIP(1945); SHIELD FOR MURDER(1954); BRAIN EATERS, THE(1958); LOVING COUPLES(1966, Swed.), w; NIGHT GAMES(1966, Swed.), w; GIRLS, THE(1972, Swed.), w; SUNDAY IN THE COUNTRY(1975, Can.)

Derek Hughes
ROAD HUSTLERS, THE(1968)

Diana Hughes
WOMEN IN THE WIND(1939); BLONDE COMET(1941)

Doreen Hughes
MR. H. C. ANDERSEN(1950, Brit.)

Dorothy B. Hughes
FALLEN SPARROW, THE(1943), w; RIDE THE PINK HORSE(1947), w; IN A LONELY PLACE(1950), w

Dorothy Hughes
Silents
POVERTY OF RICHES, THE(1921); SORROWS OF SATAN(1926)

Doug Hughes
CAPTURE THAT CAPSULE(1961)

Earl Hughes
WORDS AND MUSIC(1929)

Edward P. Hughes
HANG YOUR HAT ON THE WIND(1969), ph

Elizabeth Hughes
HOT MILLIONS(1968, Brit.)

Eric Hughes
RAISE THE TITANIC(1980, Brit.), w
1984
AGAINST ALL ODDS(1984), w

Finola Hughes
NUTCRACKER(1982, Brit.); STAYING ALIVE(1983)
Misc. Talkies
NUTCRACKER(1984)

Frank Hughes
OX-BOW INCIDENT, THE(1943), set d

Frank E. Hughes
SONG OF BERNADETTE, THE(1943), set d; SWEET ROSIE O'GRADY(1943), set d; KEYS OF THE KINGDOM, THE(1944), set d; DON JUAN QUILLIGAN(1945), set d; TREE GROWS IN BROOKLYN, A(1945), set d; ANNA AND THE KING OF SIAM(1946), set d; BRASHER DOUBLOON, THE(1947), set d

Frederick Hughes
STACY'S KNIGHTS(1983)

Gareth Hughes
MISTER ANTONIO(1929); SCAREHEADS(1931)
Misc. Talkies
BROKEN HEARTED(1929)
Silents
ISLE OF CONQUEST(1919); CHORUS GIRL'S ROMANCE, A(1920); HUNCH, THE(1921); LIFE'S DARN FUNNY(1921); LURE OF YOUTH, THE(1921); KICK IN(1922); LITTLE EVA ASCENDS(1922); ENEMIES OF WOMEN(1923); PENROD AND SAM(1923); AUCTIONEER, THE(1927); OLD AGE HANDICAP(1928); SKY RIDER, THE(1928)
Misc. Silents
GINGER(1919); RED VIPER, THE(1919); WOMAN UNDER OATH, THE(1919); WOMAN! WOMAN!(1919); GARMENTS OF YOUTH(1921); INDISCRETION(1921); SENTIMENTAL TOMMY(1921); DON'T WRITE LETTERS(1922); FORGET-ME-NOT(1922); I CAN EXPLAIN(1922); CHRISTIAN, THE(1923); SUNSET TRAIL, THE(1924); MIDNIGHT GIRL, THE(1925); MEN OF THE NIGHT(1926); BETTER DAYS(1927); BROADWAY AFTER MIDNIGHT(1927); EYES OF THE TOTEM(1927); HEROES IN BLUE(1927); COMRADES(1928); TOP SERGEANT MULLIGAN(1928); SILENT SENTINEL(1929)

Gary Hughes
PIRATES OF BLOOD RIVER, THE(1962, Brit.), m; CRIMSON BLADE, THE(1964, Brit.), m; DEVIL-SHIP PIRATES, THE(1964, Brit.), m; VIKING QUEEN, THE(1967, Brit.), m; CHALLENGE FOR ROBIN HOOD, A(1968, Brit.), m; THREE SISTERS(1974, Brit.), m

Geoffrey Hughes
YELLOW SUBMARINE(1958, Brit.); SMASHING TIME(1967 Brit.); BOFORS GUN, THE(1968, Brit.); VIRGIN SOLDIERS, THE(1970, Brit.); TERROR FROM UNDER THE HOUSE(1971, Brit.); ADOLF HITLER—MY PART IN HIS DOWNFALL(1973, Brit.); NIJINSKY(1980, Brit.)

George Hughes
TWELVE GOOD MEN(1936, Brit.); PERFECT CRIME, THE(1937, Brit.)
Misc. Silents
SOME WAITER!(1916, Brit.)

Glenn Hughes
DIARY OF A HIGH SCHOOL BRIDE(1959); CAN'T STOP THE MUSIC(1980)

Gwyneth Hughes
CORN IS GREEN, THE(1945)

Harold Hughes
MONKEY'S PAW, THE(1933); BORN AGAIN(1978)

Harry Hughes
GABLES MYSTERY, THE(1931, Brit.), d, w; GLAMOUR(1931, Brit.), d; BACHELOR'S BABY(1932, Brit.), d&w; HIS WIFE'S MOTHER(1932, Brit.), d&w; FACING THE MUSIC(1933, Brit.), d; SOUTHERN MAID, A(1933, Brit.), d; THEIR NIGHT OUT(1933, Brit.), p,d&w; BROKEN ROSARY, THE(1934, Brit.), d; SONG AT EVENTIDE(1934, Brit.), d; WOMANHOOD(1934, Brit.), d; BARNACLE BILL(1935, Brit.), d; JOY RIDE(1935, Brit.), d; PLAY UP THE BAND(1935, Brit.), d; IMPROPER DUCHESS, THE(1936, Brit.), d, w; TROPICAL TROUBLE(1936, Brit.), w; LAST CHANCE, THE(1937, Brit.), w; GABLES MYSTERY, THE(1938, Brit.), d, w; MOUNTAINS O'-MOURNE(1938, Brit.), p&d; DEAD MEN ARE DANGEROUS(1939, Brit.), w; KIMBERLEY JIM(1965, South Africa), ed
Silents
ROGUE IN LOVE, A(1922, Brit.), w; DAUGHTER IN REVOLT, A(1927, Brit.), d&w; VIRGINIA'S HUSBAND(1928, Brit.), d
Misc. Silents
HELLCAT, THE(1928, Brit.), d; TROUBLESOME WIVES(1928, Brit.), d; LITTLE MISS LONDON(1929, Brit.), d

Hazel Hughes
IRELAND'S BORDER LINE(1939, Ireland); LUNCH HOUR(1962, Brit.); LADY L(1965, Fr./Ital.); SEASIDE SWINGERS(1965, Brit.); STITCH IN TIME, A(1967, Brit.); CLUE QF THE TWISTED CANDLE(1968, Brit.)

Heather Hughes
FLESH FEAST(1970)

Helen Hughes
OUTRAGEOUS!(1977, Can.); LUCKY STAR, THE(1980, Can.); MIDDLE AGE CRAZY(1980, Can.); SUZANNE(1980, Can.); INCUBUS, THE(1982, Can.); VISITING HOURS(1982, Can.)
Misc. Talkies
TOPA TOPA(1938)

Herbert Hughes
NORAH O'NEALE(1934, Brit.), m

Howard Hughes
HELL'S ANGELS(1930), p, d; AGE FOR LOVE, THE(1931), p; FRONT PAGE, THE(1931), p; COCK OF THE AIR(1932), p; SCARFACE(1932), p; SKY DEVILS(1932), p; OUTLAW, THE(1943), p, d; VENDETTA(1950), p, d; TWO TICKETS TO BROADWAY(1951), p; MAN, A WOMAN, AND A BANK, A(1979, Can.)
Silents
RACKET, THE(1928), p

Ian Hughes
TOO YOUNG TO LOVE(1960, Brit.); VICTORS, THE(1963)
J. Anthony Hughes
COUNTRY DOCTOR, THE(1936); EDUCATING FATHER(1936); IT HAD TO HAP-
PEN(1936); WHIPSAW(1936); IN OLD CHICAGO(1938); CISCO KID AND THE LADY,
THE(1939); I STOLE A MILLION(1939); TAIL SPIN(1939); BEYOND TOMOR-
ROW(1940); DIAMOND FRONTIER(1940); FIGHTING 69TH, THE(1940); HOWARDS
OF VIRGINIA, THE(1940); INVISIBLE STRIPES(1940); THEY DRIVE BY
NIGHT(1940); TWO GIRLS ON BROADWAY(1940); BUCK PRIVATES(1941); LAST OF
THE DUANES(1941); MEN OF SAN QUENTIN(1942); PACIFIC RENDEZVOUS(1942);
KEYS OF THE KINGDOM, THE(1944); GUY WHO CAME BACK, THE(1951); SNIPER,
THE(1952); DADDY LONG LEGS(1955); WARLOCK(1959)
J. J. Hughes
Silents
JUNE MADNESS(1922), art d; YOUTH TO YOUTH(1922), art d
Jackie Hughes
GENTLE JULIA(1936)
Jake Hughes
WINTER KILLS(1979)
Janice Hughes
HEART WITHIN, THE(1957, Brit.)
Jimmy Hughes
BUSTIN' LOOSE(1981)
John B. Hughes
MEET JOHN DOE(1941); RHAPSODY IN BLUE(1945)
John H. Hughes
GIRL IN THE GLASS CAGE, THE(1929), art d
John Hughes
HOT STUFF(1929), art d; SHERLOCK HOLMES(1932), art d; BABBITT(1934), art d;
CASE OF THE HOWLING DOG, THE(1934), art d; DESIRABLE(1934), art d; HAROLD
TEEN(1934), art d; JOURNAL OF A CRIME(1934), art d; KANSAS CITY PRIN-
CESS(1934), art d; MAN WITH TWO FACES, THE(1934), art d; MASSACRE(1934), art
d; PERSONALITY KID, THE(1934), art d; RETURN OF THE TERROR(1934), art d;
SMARTY(1934), art d; CEILNG ZERO(1935), art d; DINKY(1935), art d; FRISCO
KID(1935), art d; FRONT PAGE WOMAN(1935), art d; GIRL FROM TENTH AVENUE,
THE(1935), art d; MAYBE IT'S LOVE(1935), art d; WHITE COCKATOO(1935), art d;
CHARGE OF THE LIGHT BRIGADE, THE(1936), art d; PETRIFIED FOREST,
THE(1936), art d; DAWN PATROL, THE(1938), art d; FOUR DAUGHTERS(1938), art
d; WHITE BANNERS(1938), art d; FOUR WIVES(1939), art d; SANTA FE
TRAIL(1940), art d; THEY DRIVE BY NIGHT(1940), art d; BIG SHOT, THE(1942), art
d; LARCENY, INC.(1942), art d; THEY DIED WITH THEIR BOOTS ON(1942), art d;
OLD ACQUAINTANCE(1943), art d; THIS IS THE ARMY(1943), art d; ESCAPE IN
THE DESERT(1945), art d; GOD IS MY CO-PILOT(1945), art d; HOTEL BERLIN(1945),
art d; RHAPSODY IN BLUE(1945), art d; NIGHT AND DAY(1946), art d; TREASURE
OF THE SIERRA MADRE, THE(1948), art d; LOOK FOR THE SILVER LINING(1949),
art d; ONE LAST FLING(1949), art d
John Hughes
GREAT GILBERT AND SULLIVAN, THE(1953, Brit.); KIDNAPPED(1971, Brit.);
THAT SINKING FEELING(1979, Brit.)
John Hughes
NATIONAL LAMPOON'S CLASS REUNION(1982), w; MR. MOM(1983), w; NATE
AND HAYES(1983, U.S./New Zealand), w; NATIONAL LAMPOON'S VACA-
TION(1983), w
1984
SIXTEEN CANDLES(1984), d&w; 1984(1984, Brit.)
Silents
YANKEE CLIPPER, THE(1927), art d
John J. Hughes
DRAG(1929), art d; WEARY RIVER(1929), art d; HAPPINESS AHEAD(1934), art d;
RAFTER ROMANCE(1934), art d; G-MEN(1935), art d; THING, THE(1951), art d
Silents
REVELATION(1924), art d
Judy Hughes
RAT FINK(1965)
Kathleen Hughes
MOTHER IS A FRESHMAN(1949); MR. BELVEDERE GOES TO COLLEGE(1949);
I'LL GET BY(1950); MISTER 880(1950); WHERE THE SIDEWALK ENDS(1950); TAKE
CARE OF MY LITTLE GIRL(1951); FOR MEN ONLY(1952); SALLY AND SAINT
ANNE(1952); GLASS WEB, THE(1953); GOLDEN BLADE, THE(1953); IT CAME FROM
OUTER SPACE(1953); THY NEIGHBOR'S WIFE(1953); DAWN AT SOCORRO(1954);
CULT OF THE COBRA(1955); THREE BAD SISTERS(1956); UNWED MOTHER(1958);
PRESIDENT'S ANALYST, THE(1967)
Kay Hughes
GEORGE WHITE'S 1935 SCANDALS(1935); EVERY SATURDAY NIGHT(1936);
RIDE, RANGER, RIDE(1936); ROBIN HOOD OF EL DORADO(1936); SINGING KID,
THE(1936); SNOWED UNDER(1936); THREE MESQUITEERS, THE(1936); BIG SHOW,
THE(1937); GHOST TOWN GOLD(1937); MAN BETRAYED, A(1937); MANDARIN
MYSTERY, THE(1937); HONOLULU LU(1941); RIDERS OF THE BADLANDS(1941);
ENEMY OF THE LAW(1945); FIGHTING BILL CARSON(1945); LAST OF THE
SECRET AGENTS?, THE(1966)
Ken Hughes
WIDE BOY(1952, Brit.), d; BLACK 13(1954, Brit.), d; HEATWAVE(1954, Brit.), d&w;
ATOMIC MAN, THE(1955, Brit.), d, w; BRAIN MACHINE(1955, Brit.), d&w;
CASE OF THE RED MONKEY(1955, Brit.), d, w; FLYING EYE, THE(1955, Brit.), d,
w; JOE MACBETH(1955), d; DEADLIEST SIN, THE(1956, Brit.), d, w; POSTMARK FOR
DANGER(1956, Brit.), w; LONG HAUL, THE(1957, Brit.), d&w; PORTRAIT IN
SMOKE(1957, Brit.), d, w; TOWN ON TRIAL(1957, Brit.), w; IN THE NICK(1960,
Brit.), d&w; JAZZ BOAT(1960, Brit.), d, w; MAN WITH THE GREEN CARNATION,
THE(1960, Brit.), d&w; SMALL WORLD OF SAMMY LEE, THE(1963, Brit.), d&w; OF
HUMAN BONDAGE(1964, Brit.), d; ARRIVEDERCI, BABY!(1966, Brit.), p,d&w; CHIT-
TY CHITTY BANG BANG(1968, Brit.), d, w; CROMWELL(1970, Brit.), d, w; IN-
TERNECINE PROJECT, THE(1974, Brit.), d; ALFIE DARLING(1975, Brit.), d&w;
SEXTETTE(1978), d
Misc. Talkies
PLAY IT COOLER(1961), d
Kenneth Hughes
HIGH FLIGHT(1957, Brit.), w; CASINO ROYALE(1967, Brit.), d; PAPER
MOON(1973); NIGHT SCHOOL(1981), d

Kenneth "Ken" Hughes
TERROR EYES(1981), d
Kevin Hughes
TIMERIDER(1983), set d
Langston Hughes
WAY DOWN SOUTH(1939), w
Lawrence Hughes
Silents
ALTAR STAIRS, THE(1922)
Leonora Hughes
Silents
REJECTED WOMAN, THE(1924)
Llewellyn Hughes
SKY HAWK(1929), w; TEMPLE TOWER(1930), w; HEARTBREAK(1931), w; FALSE
FACES(1932), w; UNDER THE BIG TOP(1938), w
Llewelyn Hughes
SECRET OF THE CHATEAU(1935), w
Lloyd Hughes
ACQUITTED(1929); MYSTERIOUS ISLAND(1929); BIG BOY(1930); EXTRAVA-
GANCE(1930); HELLO SISTER(1930); LOVE COMES ALONG(1930); MOBY
DICK(1930); RUNAWAY BRIDE(1930); SWEETHEARTS ON PARADE(1930); DECEIV-
ER, THE(1931); DRUMS OF JEOPARDY(1931); HELL BOUND(1931); SHIPS OF
HATE(1931); SKY RAIDERS(1931); AIR EAGLES(1932); HEART PUNCH(1932); MIRA-
CLE MAN, THE(1932); PRIVATE SCANDAL, A(1932); HARMONY LANE(1935); MAN
WHO RECLAIMED HIS HEAD, THE(1935); RECKLESS ROADS(1935); RIP ROARING
RILEY(1935); SOCIETY FEVER(1935); FACE IN THE FOG, A(1936); HONEYMOON
LIMITED(1936); KELLY OF THE SECRET SERVICE(1936); LITTLE RED SCHOOL-
HOUSE(1936); NIGHT CARGO(1936); MAN BETRAYED, A(1937); BROKEN MELO-
DY(1938, Aus.); CLIPPED WINGS(1938); I DEMAND PAYMENT(1938); LOVERS AND
LUGGERS(1938, Aus.); ROMANCE OF THE REDWOODS(1939); VENGEANCE OF
THE DEEP(1940, Aus.)
Misc. Talkies
MIDNIGHT PHANTOM, THE(1935); SKYBOUND(1935); NUMBERED WO-
MAN(1938)
Silents
BEAU REVEL(1921); TESS OF THE STORM COUNTRY(1922); ARE YOU A FAIL-
URE?(1923); HUNTRESS, THE(1923); SCARS OF JEALOUSY(1923); IN EVERY
WOMAN'S LIFE(1924); JUDGMENT OF THE STORM(1924); WELCOME STRAN-
GER(1924); DESERT FLOWER, THE(1925); IF I MARRY AGAIN(1925); LOST WORLD,
THE(1925); SALLY(1925); ELLA CINDERS(1926); FOREVER AFTER(1926); IRE-
NE(1926); LADIES AT PLAY(1926); AFFAIR OF THE FOLLIES, AN(1927); AMERI-
CAN BEAUTY(1927); STOLEN BRIDE, THE(1927); WHERE EAST IS EAST(1929)
Misc. Silents
IMPOSSIBLE SUSAN(1918); HAUNTED BEDROOM, THE(1919); INNOCENT AD-
VENTURESS, AN(1919); SATAN JUNIOR(1919); TURN IN THE ROAD, THE(1919);
VIRTUOUS THIEF, THE(1919); BELOW THE SURFACE(1920); DANGEROUS
HOURS(1920); FALSE ROAD, THE(1920); HOMESPUN FOLKS(1920); HAIL THE
WOMAN(1921); LOVE NEVER DIES(1921); MOTHER O' MINE(1921); HER REPUTA-
TION(1923); OLD FOOL, THE(1923); HERITAGE OF THE DESERT, THE(1924); SEA
HAWK, THE(1924); UNTAMED YOUTH(1924); WHIPPING BOSS, THE(1924); DE-
CLASSE(1925); DIXIE HANDICAP, THE(1925); HALF-WAY GIRL, THE(1925); SCAR-
LET SAINT(1925); HIGH STEPPERS(1926); PALS FIRST(1926); VALENCIA(1926); NO
PLACE TO GO(1927); TOO MANY CROOKS(1927); HEART TO HEART(1928); SAIL-
ORS' WIVES(1928); THREE-RING MARRIAGE(1928)
Louise Hughes
Silents
MERRY WIDOW, THE(1925)
Marion Hughes
DRUMS O' VOODOO(1934)
Mark Hughes
FOURTEEN, THE(1973, Brit.)
Mary Beth Hughes
COVERED TRAILER, THE(1939); DANCING CO-ED(1939); FAST AND FURI-
OUS(1939); THESE GLAMOUR GIRLS(1939); WOMEN, THE(1939); FOUR SONS(1940);
FREE, BLONDE AND 21(1940); GREAT PROFILE, THE(1940); LUCKY CISCO
KID(1940); STAR DUST(1940); CHARLIE CHAN IN RIO(1941); COWBOY AND THE
BLONDE, THE(1941); DESIGN FOR SCANDAL(1941); DRESSED TO KILL(1941);
GREAT AMERICAN BROADCAST, THE(1941); RIDE ON VAQUERO(1941); SLEEP-
ERS WEST(1941); NIGHT BEFORE THE DIVORCE, THE(1942); ORCHESTRA WI-
VES(1942); OVER MY DEAD BODY(1942); FOLLOW THE BAND(1943); GOOD
MORNING, JUDGE(1943); MELODY PARADE(1943); NEVER A DULL MO-
MENT(1943); OX-BOW INCIDENT, THE(1943); MEN ON HER MIND(1944); TAKE IT
BIG(1944); TIMBER QUEEN(1944); GREAT FLAMARION, THE(1945); I ACCUSE MY
PARENTS(1945); LADY CONFESSES, THE(1945); ROCKIN' IN THE ROCKIES(1945);
CAGED FURY(1948); INNER SANCTUM(1948); JOE PALOOKA IN WINNER TAKE
ALL(1948); LAST OF THE WILD HORSES(1948); RETURN OF WILDFIRE, THE(1948);
WATERFRONT AT MIDNIGHT(1948); DEVIL'S HENCHMEN, THE(1949); EL PA-
SO(1949); GRAND CANYON(1949); RIDERS IN THE SKY(1949); RIMFIRE(1949);
SQUARE DANCE JUBILEE(1950); HOLIDAY RHYTHM(1950); YOUNG MAN WITH
A HORN(1950); CLOSE TO MY HEART(1951); PASSAGE WEST(1951); HIGHWAY
DRAGNET(1954); LOOPHOLE(1954); LAS VEGAS SHAKEDOWN(1955); DIG THAT
URANIUM(1956); GUN BATTLE AT MONTEREY(1957); WORKING GIRLS,
THE(1973)
Mary Hughes
MUSCLE BEACH PARTY(1964); PAJAMA PARTY(1964); DR. GOLDFOOT AND THE
BIKINI MACHINE(1965); HOW TO STUFF A WILD BIKINI(1965); SERGEANT
DEADHEAD(1965); SKI PARTY(1965); FIREBALL 590(1966); GHOST IN THE INVISI-
BLE BIKINI(1966); MURDERERS' ROW(1966)
Melanie Hughes
FUNNY MONEY(1983, Brit.)
Michael Hughes
SIOUX CITY SUE(1946); GHOST GOES WILD, THE(1947)
Mildred Hughes
FUNHOUSE, THE(1981)
Morris Hughes
Silents
MOLLYCODDLE, THE(1920); NUT, THE(1921)

John Huglies
AIR FORCE(1943), art d
Laurence Hugo
YOU'RE IN THE NAVY NOW(1951); THREE HOURS TO KILL(1954)
Mauritz Hugo
WANTED BY THE POLICE(1938); MISSION TO MOSCOW(1943); OUTLAWS OF STAMPEDE PASS(1943); REVENGE OF THE ZOMBIES(1943); MARKED TRAILS(1944); JEALOUSY(1945); BANDIT OF SHERWOOD FOREST, THE(1946); BLONDE FOR A DAY(1946); DARK HORSE, THE(1946); MASK OF DIIJON, THE(1946); RUSTLER'S ROUNDUP(1946); SECRETS OF A SORORITY GIRL(1946); DAISY KENYON(1947); GENTLEMAN'S AGREEMENT(1947); HOMESTEADERS OF PARADISE VALLEY(1947); FURY AT FURNACE CREEK(1947); IRON CURTAIN, THE(1948); RENEGADES OF SONORA(1948); SAXON CHARM, THE(1948); WHEN MY BABY SMILES AT ME(1948); DEATH VALLEY GUNFIGHTER(1949); SEARCH FOR DANGER(1949); WHIRLPOOL(1949); FRISCO TORNADO(1950); LOVE THAT BRUTE(1950); TICKET TO TOMAHAWK(1950); DAKOTA KID, THE(1951); GUN-PLAY(1951); NO QUESTIONS ASKED(1951); PISTOL HARVEST(1951); SADDLE LEGION(1951); BLUE CANADIAN ROCKIES(1952); CAPTIVE OF BILLY THE KID(1952); KID FROM BROKEN GUN, THE(1952); ROAD AGENT(1952); TRAIL GUIDE(1952); YUKON GOLD(1952); RUN FOR THE HILLS(1953); DRAGON'S GOLD(1954); LOVE ME OR LEAVE ME(1955); CRIME AGAINST JOE(1956); FIRST TRAVELING SALESLADY, THE(1956); SCANDAL INCORPORATED(1956); GUN BATTLE AT MONTEREY(1957); TALL STRANGER, THE(1957); VAMPIRE, THE(1957); WAR DRUMS(1957); OLD MAN AND THE SEA, THE(1958); SEVEN GUNS TO MESA(1958); GUNFIGHT AT DODGE CITY, THE(1959); PURPLE GANG, THE(1960); THIRTEEN FIGHTING MEN(1960); STAGECOACH TO DANCER'S PARK(1962); PRIZE, THE(1963); ALVAREZ KELLY(1966); MAROONED(1969)
Merlin Hugo
PAISAN(1948, Ital.)
Michael Hugo
GORP(1980), ph; MOUNTAIN MEN, THE(1980), ph
Michel Hugo
HEAD(1968), ph; APRIL FOOLS, THE(1969), ph; MODEL SHOP, THE(1969), ph; NUMBER ONE(1969), ph; COVER ME BABE(1970), ph; FOOLS(1970), ph; PHYNX, THE(1970), ph; R.P.M.(1970), ph; BLESS THE BEASTS AND CHILDREN(1971), ph; ONE IS A LONELY NUMBER(1972), ph; THEY ONLY KILL THEIR MASTERS(1972), ph; TROUBLE MAN(1972), ph; SPOOK WHO SAT BY THE DOOR, THE(1973), ph; MURPH THE SURF(1974), ph; ODE TO BILLY JOE(1976), ph; MANI-TOU, THE(1978), ph; OCTAGON, THE(1980), ph; PANDEMONIUM(1982), ph
Ron Hugo
1984
SUBURBIA(1984)
Sven Hugo
LAW OF THE TIMBER(1941)
Victor Hugo
LES MISERABLES(1935), w; LES MISERABLES(1936, Fr.), w; TOILERS OF THE SEA(1936, Brit.), w; HUNCHBACK OF NOTRE DAME, THE(1939), w; RUY BLAS(1948, Fr.), w; LES MISERABLES(1952), w; SEA DEVILS(1953), w; HUNCH-BACK OF NOTRE DAME, THE(1957, Fr.), w; LES MISERABLES(1982, Fr.), w
Silents
DARLING OF PARIS, THE(1917), w; ETERNAL SIN(1917), w; LES MISERA-BLES(1918), w; HUNCHBACK OF NOTRE DAME, THE(1923), w; MAN WHO LAUGHS, THE(1927), w
Robert Hugo [Ugo Guerra]
WHAT!(1965, Fr./Brit./Ital.), w
Sven Hugo-Borg
INVISIBLE AGENT(1942)
Andre Hugon
MOULIN ROUGE(1944, Fr.), p
Misc. Silents
BEAUTE FATALE(1916, Fr.), d; CHIGNON D'OR(1916, Fr.), d; FLEUR DE PA-RIS(1916, Fr.), d; L'EMPREINTE(1916, Fr.), d; SOUS LA MENACE(1916, Fr.), d; ANGOISSE(1917, Fr.), d; LE VERTIGE(1917, Fr.), d; MARIAGE D'AMOUR(1917, Fr.), d; MYSTERE D'UNE VIE(1917, Fr.), d; REQUINS(1917, Fr.), d; CHACALS(1918, Fr.), d; JOHANNES, FILS DE JOHANNES(1918, Fr.), d; LA FUGITIVE(1918, Fr.), d; JACQUES LANDAUZE(1919, Fr.), d; UN CRIME A ETE COMMIS(1919, Fr.), d; LES CHERES IMAGES(1920, Fr.), d; FILLE DE RIEN(1921, Fr.), d; LA PREUVE(1921, Fr.), d; LE ROI DE CAMARGUE(1921, Fr.), d; DIAMANT NOIR(1922, Fr.), d; NOTRE DAME D'AMOUR(1922, Fr.), d; LA RUE DU PAVE D'AMOUR(1923, Fr.), d; LE PETIT CHOSE(1923, Fr.), d; GITANELLA(1924, Fr.), d; L'ARRIVISTE(1924, Fr.), d; LA PRIN-CESSE AUX CLOWNS(1925, Fr.), d; L'HOMME DES BALEARES(1925, Fr.), d; YAS-MINA(1926, Fr.), d; A L'OMBRE DES TOMBEAUX(1927, Fr.), d; LA VESTALE DU GANGE(1927, Fr.), d; LA GRANDE PASSION(1928, Fr.), d; LA MARCHE NUP-TIALE(1929, Fr.), d
Jean-Michael Hugon
1984
PAR OU T'ES RENTRE? ON T'A PAS VUE SORTIR(1984, Fr./Tunisia), art d
Jean-Rene Huguenin
YOUR SHADOW IS MINE(1963, Fr./Ital.), w
Suzanne Huguenin
MOUCHETTE(1970, Fr.)
Sharon Hugueny
MAJORITY OF ONE, A(1961); PARRISH(1961); CARETAKERS, THE(1963); YOUNG LOVERS, THE(1964)
Albert Hugues
SUNDAYS AND CYBELE(1962, Fr.)
Marthe Huguet
LA MARSEILLAISE(1938, Fr.), ed
Austin O. Huhn
Misc. Silents
CLOUDED NAME, A(1923), d
Ann Hui
SECRET, THE(1979, Hong Kong), d
Chrinstina Hui
MOONRAKER(1979, Brit.)
KuChia Hui
RETURN OF THE DRAGON(1974, Chin.), m

Mary Hui
YEAR OF THE HORSE, THE(1966)
Michael Hui
CANNONBALL RUN, THE(1981)
Tsao Hui-chi
FLYING GUILLOTINE, THE(1975, Chi.), ph
Hua Hui-ying
DRAGON INN(1968, Chi.), ph
Gook Te Huia
1984
UTU(1984, New Zealand)
Donald Huie
DULCY(1940)
William Bradford Huie
REVOLT OF MAMIE STOVER, THE(1956), w; WILD RIVER(1960), w; OUTSIDER, THE(1962), w; AMERICANIZATION OF EMILY, THE(1964), w; KLANSMAN, THE(1974), w
Huillet
NOT RECONCILED, OR "ONLY VIOLENCE HELPS WHERE IT RULES"(1969, Ger.), w
Daniele Huillet
CHRONICLE OF ANNA MAGDALENA BACH(1968, Ital., Ger.), w, ed, prod d; MOSES AND AARON(1975, Ger./Fr./Ital.), d&w, ed
Danielle Huillet
NOT RECONCILED, OR "ONLY VIOLENCE HELPS WHERE IT RULES"(1969, Ger.), p, ed
Gaspard Huit
BRIDE IS MUCH TOO BEAUTIFUL, THE(1958, Fr.), p
Tadeusz Huk
DANTON(1983)
Bob Huke
WAR LOVER, THE(1962, U.S./Brit.), ph; REACH FOR GLORY(1963, Brit.), ph; VERY EDGE, THE(1963, Brit.), ph; BRAIN, THE(1965, Ger./Brit.), ph; BATTLE OF BRITAIN(1969, Brit.), ph; VIRGIN AND THE GYPSY, THE(1970, Brit.), ph; LOVERS, THE(1972, Brit.), ph; UNDER MILK WOOD(1973, Brit.), ph; CONDUCT UNBECOMING(1975, Brit.), ph; DOING TIME(1979, Brit.), ph; POWERFORCE(1983), ph
Nigel C. Huke
ALL OVER THE TOWN(1949, Brit.), ph
Nigel Huke
DEAR MR. PROHACK(1949, Brit.), ph; INHERITANCE, THE(1951, Brit.), ph
Ludek Hulan
90 DEGREES IN THE SHADE(1966, Czech./Brit.), m; MURDER CZECH STY-LE(1968, Czech.), md
Claude Hulbert
FACE AT THE WINDOW, THE(1932, Brit.); LET ME EXPLAIN, DEAR(1932); MAYOR'S NEST, THE(1932, Brit.); NIGHT LIKE THIS, A(1932, Brit.); THARK(1932, Brit.); FALLING FOR YOU(1933, Brit.), w; IT'S A KING(1933, Brit.), w; THEIR NIGHT OUT(1933, Brit.); BIG BUSINESS(1934, Brit.), w; CUP OF KINDNESS, A(1934, Brit.); GIRL IN POSSESSION(1934, Brit.); LILIES OF THE FIELD(1934, Brit.); SONG YOU GAVE ME, THE(1934, Brit.); ALIAS BULLDOG DRUMMOND(1935, Brit.); HELLO SWEETHEART(1935, Brit.); MAN OF THE MOMENT(1935, Brit.); HAIL AND FARE-WELL(1936, Brit.); INTERRUPTED HONEYMOON, THE(1936, Brit.); WHERE'S SAL-LY?(1936, Brit.); WOLF'S CLOTHING(1936, Brit.); IT'S NOT CRICKET(1937, Brit.); TAKE A CHANCE(1937, Brit.); VULTURE, THE(1937, Brit.); YOU LIVE AND LEARN(1937, Brit.); GIRL THIEF, THE(1938); HIS LORDSHIP REGRETS(1938, Brit.); IT'S IN THE BLOOD(1938, Brit.); MANY TANKS MR. ATKINS(1938, Brit.); SIMPLY TERRIFIC(1938, Brit.); VIPER, THE(1938, Brit.); ANYTHING TO DECLARE?(1939, Brit.); HONEYMOON MERRY-GO-ROUND(1939, Brit.); THREE COCKEYED SAIL-ORS(1940, Brit.); GHOST OF ST. MICHAEL'S. THE(1941, Brit.); DUMMY TALKS, THE(1943, Brit.); MY LEARNED FRIEND(1943, Brit.); GHOSTS OF BERKELEY SQUARE(1947, Brit.); CARDBOARD CAVALIER, THE(1949, Brit.); MY HEART GOES CRAZY(1953, Brit.); FUN AT ST. FANNY'S(1956, Brit.); NOT A HOPE IN HELL(1960, Brit.)
Silents
CHAMPAGNE(1928, Brit.)
Don Hulbert
PENROD AND SAM(1937); SINGIN' IN THE RAIN(1952)
Donald Hulbert
PENROD AND HIS TWIN BROTHER(1938)
Jack Hulbert
HAPPY EVER AFTER(1932, Ger./Brit.), a, w; LOVE ON WHEELS(1932, Brit.); OFFICE GIRL, THE(1932, Brit.); FALLING FOR YOU(1933, Brit.), a, d; GHOST TRAIN, THE(1933, Brit.); NIGHT AND DAY(1933, Brit.), a, w; CAMELS ARE COM-ING, THE(1934, Brit.), a, w; WOMAN IN COMMAND, THE(1934 Brit.), w; ALIAS BULLDOG DRUMMOND(1935, Brit.); JACK AHOY!(1935, Brit.), a, w; TAKE MY TIP(1937, Brit.), a, w; GAIETY GIRLS, THE(1938, Brit.); KATE PLUS TEN(1938, Brit.), a, w; TWO OF US, THE(1938, Brit.), a, d, w; UNDER YOUR HAT(1940, Brit.), a, p, w; MAN IN THE DINGHY, THE(1951, Brit.); MAGIC BOX, THE(1952, Brit.); MISS TULIP STAYS THE NIGHT(1955, Brit.), a, w; SPIDER'S WEB, THE(1960, Brit.)
Bud Hulburd
WILD BUNCH, THE(1969), spec eff; GETAWAY, THE(1972), spec eff
Horace L. Hulburd
DAYS OF WINE AND ROSES(1962), spec eff
Thomas Hulce
9/30/55(1977); NATIONAL LAMPOON'S ANIMAL HOUSE(1978); THOSE LIPS, THOSE EYES(1980)
Tom Hulce
1984
AMADEUS(1984)
Mark Hulcher
ROLLERCOASTER(1977)
Jack Hulcup
Misc. Silents
KISSING CUP(1913, Brit.), d; BY THE SHORTEST OF HEADS(1915, Brit.)
Hilde Huldebrand
BARCAROLE(1935, Ger.)

Paul Huldschinsky
GASLIGHT(1944), set d; MEET ME IN ST. LOUIS(1944), set d; COURAGE OF LASSIE(1946), set d; EMPEROR WALTZ, THE(1948), set d

Otto Hulett
ONE THIRD OF A NATION(1939); HER FIRST ROMANCE(1951); MOB, THE(1951); SATURDAY'S HERO(1951); CARBINE WILLIAMS(1952); FRANCIS GOES TO WEST POINT(1952); PAULA(1952); SALLY AND SAINT ANNE(1952); YOU FOR ME(1952); CITY THAT NEVER SLEEPS(1953); PHENIX CITY STORY, THE(1955); REPRISAL(1956); FOUR BOYS AND A GUN(1957)

Ralph Hulett
FUN AND FANCY FREE(1947), art d; LADY AND THE TRAMP(1955), art d; SLEEPING BEAUTY(1959), art d; ONE HUNDRED AND ONE DALMATIANS(1961), art d; SWORD IN THE STONE, THE(1963), art d; ARISTOCATS, THE(1970), anim

Steve Hulett
FOX AND THE HOUND, THE(1981), w

Don Hulette
BREAKER! BREAKER!(1977), p&d, m

Donald Hulette
Misc. Talkies
GREAT RIDE, THE(1978), d

Gladys Hulette
HER RESALE VALUE(1933); GIRL FROM MISSOURI, THE(1934); ONE HOUR LATE(1935)
Silents
EUGENE ARAM(1915); TRAFFIC COP, THE(1916); ANNEXING BILL(1918); MRS. SLACKER(1918); TOL'ABLE DAVID(1921); REFEREE, THE(1922); SECRETS OF PARIS, THE(1922); AS A MAN LIVES(1923); ENEMIES OF WOMEN, THE(1923); FAMILY SECRET, THE(1924); IRON HORSE, THE(1924); PRIDE OF THE FORCE, THE(1925); JACK O'HEARTS(1926); NIGHT OWL, THE(1926); SKYROCKET, THE(1926); BOWERY CINDERELLA(1927); MAKING THE VARSITY(1928)
Misc. Silents
FLIGHT OF THE DUCHESS, THE(1916); OTHER PEOPLE'S MONEY(1916); PRUDENCE THE PIRATE(1916); SHINE GIRL, THE(1916); CANDY GIRL, THE(1917); CIGARETTE GIRL, THE(1917); CROOKED ROMANCE, A(1917); HER NEW YORK(1917); LAST OF THE CARNABYS, THE(1917); MISS NOBODY(1917); OVER THE HILL(1917); POTS AND PANS PEGGIE(1917); STREETS OF ILLUSION, THE(1917); FOR SALE(1918); WAIFS(1918); HIGH SPEED(1920); SILENT BARRIER, THE(1920); FAIR LADY(1922); HOW WOMEN LOVE(1922); HOODMAN BLIND(1923); WHISPERING PALMS(1923); NIGHT MESSAGE, THE(1924); RIDIN' KID FROM POWDER RIVER, THE(1924); SLANDERERS, THE(1924); LENA RIVERS(1925); ON THE THRESHOLD(1925); PRIVATE AFFAIRS(1925); THOROUGHBRED, THE(1925); UNKNOWN TREASURES(1926); WARNING SIGNAL, THE(1926); COMBAT(1927); FAITHLESS LOVER(1928); LIFE'S CROSSROADS(1928)

Dominique Hulin
1984
HERE COMES SANTA CLAUS(1984)

Lorraine Huling
Silents
ARE YOU A MASON?(1915); KING LEAR(1916)
Misc. Silents
UNWELCOME MRS. HATCH, THE(1914); BACHELOR'S ROMANCE, THE(1915); DANCING GIRL, THE(1915); HIS WIFE(1915); FALL OF A NATION, THE(1916)

Malcolm Hulke
MAN IN THE BACK SEAT, THE(1961, Brit.), w; LIFE IN DANGER(1964, Brit.), w

Alexander Hull
PAINTED HILLS, THE(1951), w

Alisa Ann Hull
1984
HOLLYWOOD HIGH PART II(1984)

Archie Hull
KANGAROO(1952)

Arthur Hull
GLASS KEY, THE(1942)
Silents
PRINCE THERE WAS, A(1921); IMPOSSIBLE MRS. BELLEW, THE(1922); THORNS AND ORANGE BLOSSOMS(1922)
Misc. Silents
LOVE BRAND, THE(1923)

Arthur S. Hull
HUMAN SIDE, THE(1934); HOLD'EM YALE(1935)
Misc. Silents
MIDNIGHT(1922)

Arthur Stuart Hull
BOUGHT(1931); RACING YOUTH(1932); ONE NIGHT OF LOVE(1934); SISTERS UNDER THE SKIN(1934); STAND UP AND CHEER(1934 80m FOX bw); I LIVE MY LIFE(1935); MAN WHO BROKE THE BANK AT MONTE CARLO, THE(1935); SHE COULDN'T TAKE IT(1935); SHE MARRIED HER BOSS(1935); LONE WOLF RETURNS, THE(1936); MEET NERO WOLFE(1936); YOURS FOR THE ASKING(1936); LIVE, LOVE AND LEARN(1937); MAYTIME(1937); PAID TO DANCE(1937); PERSONAL PROPERTY(1937); SECOND HONEYMOON(1937); WHEN YOU'RE IN LOVE(1937); TEST PILOT(1938); LADY EVE, THE(1941); RAGE IN HEAVEN(1941); PALM BEACH STORY, THE(1942); THEY ALL KISSED THE BRIDE(1942)
Silents
NEW DISCIPLE, THE(1921); PAID BACK(1922); QUESTION OF HONOR, A(1922); SONG OF LIFE, THE(1922); JAVA HEAD(1923)
Misc. Silents
WHAT'S WORTH WHILE?(1921); GOING UP(1923); YANKEE CONSUL, THE(1924)

Charles Hull
IN SOCIETY(1944)

Cynthia Hull
EYE CREATURES, THE(1965); FOR PETE'S SAKE!(1966); YOUNG RUNAWAYS, THE(1968); STERILE CUCKOO, THE(1969)

Dave Hull
FREE GRASS(1969)

David Hull
SOMEWHERE IN TIME(1980)

Dennis Hull
KING OF THE MOUNTAIN(1981)

Diane Hull
HOT SUMMER WEEK(1973, Can.); ONION FIELD, THE(1979)

Dianne Hull
ARRANGEMENT, THE(1969); MAGIC GARDEN OF STANLEY SWEETHART, THE(1970); MAN ON A SWING(1974); ALOHA, BOBBY AND ROSE(1975); FIFTH FLOOR, THE(1980); YOU BETTER WATCH OUT(1980)

Edith Maude Hull
Silents
SHEIK, THE(1921), w; OLD LOVES AND NEW(1926), w; SON OF THE SHEIK(1926), w

Edward Hull
BOY, A GIRL, AND A DOG, A(1946), ph

Frank E. Hull
AWFUL TRUTH, THE(1929), ed; BORN RECKLESS(1930), ed; ON YOUR BACK(1930), ed; UP THE RIVER(1930), ed; MERELY MARY ANN(1931), ed; OVER THE HILL(1931), ed; SEAS BENEATH, THE(1931), ed; DISORDERLY CONDUCT(1932), ed; HELLO SISTER!(1933), ed; I LOVED YOU WEDNESDAY(1933), ed; STAGE MOTHER(1933), ed; CAT AND THE FIDDLE(1934), ed; EVELYN PRENTICE(1934), ed; STUDENT TOUR(1934), ed; THIS SIDE OF HEAVEN(1934), ed; AH, WILDERNESS!(1935), ed; NO MORE LADIES(1935), ed; VANESSA, HER LOVE STORY(1935), ed; SWORN ENEMY(1936), ed; THREE WISE GUYS, THE(1936), ed; UNGUARDED HOUR, THE(1936), ed; WIFE VERSUS SECRETARY(1936), ed; DAY AT THE RACES, A(1937), ed; MADAME X(1937), ed; OF HUMAN HEARTS(1938), ed; RICH MAN, POOR GIRL(1938), ed; SHINING HOUR, THE(1938), ed; BRIDAL SUITE(1939), ed; HUCKLEBERRY FINN(1939), ed; SECRET OF DR. KILDARE, THE(1939), ed; THUNDER AFLOAT(1939), ed; CAPTAIN IS A LADY, THE(1940), ed; DULCY(1940), ed; FLORIAN(1940), ed; BARNACLE BILL(1941), ed; COME LIVE WITH ME(1941), ed; DR. KILDARE'S VICTORY(1941), ed; FREE AND EASY(1941), ed; WHISTLING IN THE DARK(1941), ed; NAZI AGENT(1942), ed; NORTHWEST RANGERS(1942), ed; SOMEWHERE I'LL FIND YOU(1942), ed; SLIGHTLY DANGEROUS(1943), ed; MAISIE GOES TO RENO(1944), ed; SEE HERE, PRIVATE HARGROVE(1944), ed; KEEP YOUR POWDER DRY(1945), ed; THEY WERE EXPENDABLE(1945), ed; LITTLE MISTER JIM(1946), ed; MERTON OF THE MOVIES(1947), ed
Silents
MARRIED FLIRTS(1924), ed; GREED(1925), ed; MERRY WIDOW, THE(1925), ed; BEVERLY OF GRAUSTARK(1926), ed; WEDDING MARCH, THE(1927), ed

George Hull
TANNED LEGS(1929), ph; SON OF OKLAHOMA(1932), w
Silents
WHITE YOUTH(1920), w; OUT OF THE SILENT NORTH(1922), w; PHANTOM OF THE NORTH(1929), w

George C. Hull
Silents
LIGHT OF VICTORY(1919), w; CONFLICT, THE(1921), w; SHARK MASTER, THE(1921), w; WALLOP, THE(1921), w; ACROSS THE DEAD-LINE(1922), w; KENTUCKY DERBY, THE(1922), w; MAN TO MAN(1922), w; TRAP, THE(1922), w; OUT OF LUCK(1923), w; LORD JIM(1925), w; OVERLAND TELEGRAPH, THE(1929), w; SIOUX BLOOD(1929), w

Henry Hull
YELLOW JACK(1938); GREAT EXPECTATIONS(1934); MIDNIGHT(1934); TRANSIENT LADY(1935); WEREWOLF OF LONDON, THE(1935); MURDER AT GLEN ATHOL(1936); BOYS TOWN(1938); GREAT WALTZ, THE(1938); PARADISE FOR THREE(1938); THREE COMRADES(1938); BABES IN ARMS(1939); BAD LITTLE ANGEL(1939); JESSE JAMES(1939); JUDGE HARDY AND SON(1939); MIRACLES FOR SALE(1939); NICK CARTER, MASTER DETECTIVE(1939); RETURN OF THE CISCO KID(1939); SPIRIT OF CULVER, THE(1939); STANLEY AND LIVINGSTONE(1939); MY SON, MY SON!(1940); RETURN OF FRANK JAMES, THE(1940); HIGH SIERRA(1941); SEEDS OF FREEDOM(1943, USSR); WEST SIDE KID(1943); WOMAN OF THE TOWN, THE(1943); GOODNIGHT SWEETHEART(1944); LIFEBOAT(1944); WHAT A MAN!(1944); OBJECTIVE, BURMA!(1945); DEEP VALLEY(1947); HIGH BARBAREE(1947); MOURNING BECOMES ELECTRA(1947); FIGHTER SQUADRON(1948); SCUDDA-HOO! SCUDDA-HAY!(1948); WALLS OF JERICHO(1948); COLORADO TERRITORY(1949); EL PASO(1949); FOUNTAINHEAD, THE(1949); GREAT DAN PATCH, THE(1949); GREAT GATSBY, THE(1949); PORTRAIT OF JENNIE(1949); RIMFIRE(1949); SONG OF SURRENDER(1949); RETURN OF JESSE JAMES, THE(1950); HOLLYWOOD STORY(1951); TREASURE OF LOST CANYON, THE(1952); INFERNO(1953); LAST POSSE, THE(1953); THUNDER OVER THE PLAINS(1953); MAN WITH THE GUN(1955); KENTUCKY RIFLE(1956); BUCKSKIN LADY, THE(1957); BUCCANEER, THE(1958); PROUD REBEL, THE(1958); SHERIFF OF FRACTURED JAW, THE(1958, Brit.); OREGON TRAIL, THE(1959); MASTER OF THE WORLD(1961); FOOL KILLER, THE(1965); CHASE, THE(1966)
Silents
ONE EXCITING NIGHT(1922); BRIDE FOR A NIGHT, A(1923); EAST SIDE–WEST SIDE(1923), w; ROULETTE(1924); WASTED LIVES(1925)
Misc. Silents
FAMILY HONOR, THE(1917); RASPUTIN, THE BLACK MONK(1917); SQUARE DEAL, A(1917); VOLUNTEER, THE(1918); LAST MOMENT, THE(1923); HOOSIER SCHOOLMASTER, THE(1924); WRONG DOERS, THE(1925)

Howard E. Hull
MERTON OF THE MOVIES(1947), art d

Jack Hull
Silents
ALI BABA AND THE FORTY THIEVES(1918); ALL NIGHT(1918); SINGING RIVER(1921)

Jacob Hull
ARCTIC FURY(1949), ph

John Hull
WEREWOLVES ON WHEELS(1971)

Josephine Hull
AFTER TOMORROW(1932); CARELESS LADY(1932); ARSENIC AND OLD LACE(1944); HARVEY(1950); LADY FROM TEXAS, THE(1951)

Mary Hull
SWAMP WOMAN(1941)

Shelly Hull
Misc. Silents
SAPPHO(1913)

Syd Hull
EXCUSE MY GLOVE(1936, Brit.)
Warren Hull
MISS PACIFIC FLEET(1935); PERSONAL MAID'S SECRET(1935); ANY MAN'S WIFE(1936); BENGAL TIGER(1936); BIG NOISE, THE(1936); FRESHMAN LOVE(1936); LAW IN HER HANDS, THE(1936); LOVE BEGINS AT TWENTY(1936); WALKING DEAD, THE(1936); BRIDE FOR HENRY, A(1937); FUGITIVE IN THE SKY(1937); HER HUSBAND'S SECRETARY(1937); MICHAEL O'HALLORAN(1937); NIGHT KEY(1937); PARADISE ISLE(1937); RHYTHM IN THE CLOUDS(1937); HAWAII CALLS(1938); CRASHING THRU(1939); GIRL FROM RIO, THE(1939); SHOULD A GIRL MARRY?(1939); SMASHING THE SPY RING(1939); STAR REPORTER(1939); HIDDEN ENEMY(1940); LONE WOLF MEETS A LADY, THE(1940); MARKED MEN(1940); RIDE, TENDERFOOT, RIDE(1940); WAGONS WESTWARD(1940); YUKON FLIGHT(1940); BOWERY BLITZKRIEG(1941); REMEDY FOR RICHES(1941)
Misc. Talkies
LAST ALARM, THE(1940)
Wayne Hull
WAGONS WESTWARD(1940)
William C. Hull
Silents
IF ONLY JIM(1921), w
Winter Hull
IF I WERE KING(1938)
Jean Hulley
CAESAR AND CLEOPATRA(1946, Brit.)
Martha Hully
GENTLE PEOPLE AND THE QUIET LAND, THE(1972)
Tony Hulman
WINNING(1969)
Anthony Hulme
YANK AT OXFORD, A(1938); FROZEN LIMITS, THE(1939, Brit.); FOR FREEDOM(1940, Brit.); LAUGH IT OFF(1940, Brit.); THEY CAME BY NIGHT(1940, Brit.); UP WITH THE LARK(1943, Brit.); SEND FOR PAUL TEMPLE(1946, Brit.); MYSTERIOUS MR. NICHOLSON, THE(1947, Brit.); THREE WEIRD SISTERS, THE(1948, Brit.); CARDBOARD CAVALIER, THE(1949, Brit.); IT'S A GRAND LIFE(1953, Brit.)
Dennis Hulme
GRAND PRIX(1966)
Kathryn C. Hulme
NUN'S STORY, THE(1959), w
Wendell Hulott
FOREVER AND A DAY(1943)
George Hulse
FEMALE TROUBLE(1975); POLYESTER(1981)
D James G. Hulsey
FUN WITH DICK AND JANE(1977), prod
James G. Hulsey
MAN, THE(1972), art d
James Hulsey
VIVA MAX!(1969), prod d
Patrick Hulsey
ROCKERS(1980), p
Robert Hulsh
RUN FOR YOUR WIFE(1966, Fr./Ital.)
Mart Hulswit
COME SPY WITH ME(1967); LOVING(1970); DOC(1971)
Paul Hultberg
EDGE, THE(1968)
Ken Hultgren
SLEEPING BEAUTY(1959), anim; 1001 ARABIAN NIGHTS(1959), anim
Rune Hultman
CODE OF THE LAWLESS(1945); NIGHT AND DAY(1946)
Sgt. Rune Hultman
WINGED VICTORY(1944)
Sylvaine Humair
DIARY OF A BAD GIRL(1958, Fr.)
William Human
Misc. Silents
FORFEIT, THE(1919); UNBROKEN PROMISE, THE(1919)
Helena Humann
LAST PICTURE SHOW, THE(1971); TENDER MERCIES(1982); DEEP IN THE HEART(1983)
Yamilli Humar
MAN COULD GET KILLED, A(1966)
George Humbart
CALIFORNIA TRAIL, THE(1933)
Eve Humber
OUT OF THE BLUE(1982)
George Humber
ESCAPE ME NEVER(1947)
Arthur Humberstone
YELLOW SUBMARINE(1958, Brit.), animation
Bruce Humberstone
TO THE SHORES OF TRIPOLI(1942), d; WONDER MAN(1945), d; SOUTH SEA SINNER(1950), d; HAPPY GO LOVELY(1951, Brit.), d; DESERT SONG, THE(1953), d; TEN WANTED MEN(1955), d; TARZAN AND THE LOST SAFARI(1957, Brit.), d; TARZAN'S FIGHT FOR LIFE(1958), d
H. Bruce Humberstone
CROOKED CIRCLE(1932), d; IF I HAD A MILLION(1932), d; KING OF THE JUNGLE(1933), d; DRAGON MURDER CASE, THE(1934), d; GOODBYE LOVE(1934), d; MERRY WIVES OF RENO, THE(1934), d; LADIES LOVE DANGER(1935), d; SILK HAT KID(1935), d; THREE LIVE GHOSTS(1935), d; CHARLIE CHAN AT THE OPERA(1936), d; CHARLIE CHAN AT THE RACE TRACK(1936), d; CHARLIE CHAN AT THE OLYMPICS(1937), d; CHECKERS(1937), d; CHARLIE CHAN IN HONOLULU(1938), d; RASCALS(1938), d; TIME OUT FOR MURDER(1938), d; WHILE NEW YORK SLEEPS(1938), d; PACK UP YOUR TROUBLES(1939), d; PARDON OUR NERVE(1939), d; LUCKY CISCO KID(1940), d; QUARTERBACK, THE(1940), d; SUN VALLEY SERENADE(1941), d; TALL, DARK AND HANDSOME(1941), d; I WAKE UP SCREAMING(1942), d; ICELAND(1942), d; HELLO, FRISCO, HELLO(1943), d; PIN UP GIRL(1944), d; WITHIN THESE WALLS(1945), d; THREE LITTLE GIRLS IN BLUE(1946), d; HOMESTRETCH, THE(1947), d; FURY AT FURNACE CREEK(1948),

d; SHE'S WORKING HER WAY THROUGH COLLEGE(1952), d; PURPLE MASK, THE(1955), d
H. Bruce "Lucky" Humberstone
STRANGERS OF THE EVENING(1932), d
George Humbert
STREET SCENE(1931); FAREWELL TO ARMS, A(1932); HEARTS OF HUMANITY(1932); LADIES OF THE JURY(1932); LOVE ME TONIGHT(1932); NIGHT CLUB LADY(1932); TROUBLE IN PARADISE(1932); I COVER THE WATERFRONT(1933); KEYHOLE, THE(1933); LAUGHING AT LIFE(1933); MAYOR OF HELL, THE(1933); OFFICER 13(1933); CHAINED(1934); DESIRABLE(1934); FASHIONS OF 1934(1934); FUGITIVE ROAD(1934); HI, NELLIE!(1934); NAME THE WOMAN(1934); RED HEAD(1934); REGISTERED NURSE(1934); RETURN OF THE TERROR(1934); TWENTY MILLION SWEETHEARTS(1934); WHOM THE GODS DESTROY(1934); CASE OF THE CURIOUS BRIDE, THE(1935); DANTE'S INFERNO(1935); HARD ROCK HARRIGAN(1935); IN CALIENTE(1935); PAYOFF, THE(1935); BANJO ON MY KNEE(1936); PEPPER(1936); SEA SPOILERS, THE(1936); WINTERSET(1936); DEAD END(1937); EXPENSIVE HUSBANDS(1937); GIRL WITH IDEAS, A(1937); HEIDI(1937); KID GALAHAD(1937); LOVE AND HISSES(1937); LOVE IS NEWS(1937); LOVE UNDER FIRE(1937); NANCY STEELE IS MISSING(1937); ROSALIE(1937); TROUBLE AT MIDNIGHT(1937); YOU CAN'T HAVE EVERYTHING(1937); BRINGING UP BABY(1938); CITY STREETS(1938); FLIRTING WITH FATE(1938); ISLAND IN THE SKY(1938); LETTER OF INTRODUCTION(1938); NO TIME TO MARRY(1938); PORT OF SEVEN SEAS(1938); PROFESSOR BEWARE(1938); TOY WIFE, THE(1938); DAUGHTERS COURAGEOUS(1939); FISHERMAN'S WHARF(1939); FORGOTTEN WOMAN, THE(1939); FULL CONFESSION(1939); ROARING TWENTIES, THE(1939); TOPPER TAKES A TRIP(1939); WHEN TOMORROW COMES(1939); BOYS OF THE CITY(1940); GIRL FROM AVENUE A(1940); HIRED WIFE(1940); I TAKE THIS WOMAN(1940); MIRACLE ON MAIN STREET, A(1940); MUSIC IN MY HEART(1940); TORRID ZONE(1940); YUKON FLIGHT(1940); BOSS OF BULLION CITY(1941); LAW OF THE TIMBER(1941); MILLION DOLLAR BABY(1941); MOON OVER MIAMI(1941); SIX LESSONS FROM MADAME LA ZONGA(1941); STRAWBERRY BLONDE, THE(1941); I MARRIED AN ANGEL(1942); LUCKY JORDAN(1942); TISH(1942); TRUCK BUSTERS(1943); JOHNNY DOESN'T LIVE HERE ANY MORE(1944); MY BUDDY(1944); SENSATIONS OF 1945(1944); STORM OVER LISBON(1944); WINGED VICTORY(1944); LOVE LETTERS(1945); SARATOGA TRUNK(1945); GILDA(1946); LOCKET, THE(1946); TEMPTATION(1946); MY FRIEND IRMA GOES WEST(1950); SEPTEMBER AFFAIR(1950); ROSE TATTOO, THE(1955)
Silents
STARDUST(1921)
Misc. Silents
WOMAN AND THE LAW(1918)
Henri Humbert
DIABOLIQUE(1955, Fr.)
Humberto Herpera and His Orchestra
TOO MANY BLONDES(1941)
Gwen Humble
CHEAPER TO KEEP HER(1980)
Concha Humbria
YOUNG REBEL, THE(1969, Fr./Ital./Span.)
Alan Hume
BEWARE OF CHILDREN(1961, Brit.), ph; CARRY ON REGARDLESS(1961, Brit.), ph; CARRY ON CRUISING(1962, Brit.), ph; ROOMMATES(1962, Brit.), ph; TWICE AROUND THE DAFFODILS(1962, Brit.), ph; CARRY ON CABBIE(1963, Brit.), ph; CARRY ON JACK(1963, Brit.), ph; KISS OF EVIL(1963, Brit.), ph; SWINGIN' MAIDEN, THE(1963, Brit.), ph; CARRY ON CLEO(1964, Brit.), ph; CARRY ON SPYING(1964, Brit.), ph; IN THE DOGHOUSE(1964, Brit.), ph; NURSE ON WHEELS(1964, Brit.), ph; THIS IS MY STREET(1964, Brit.), ph; DR. TERROR'S HOUSE OF HORRORS(1965, Brit.), ph; THREE HATS FOR LISA(1965, Brit.), ph; CARRY ON COWBOY(1966, Brit.), ph; CARRY ON SCREAMING(1966, Brit.), ph; FINDERS KEEPERS(1966, Brit.), ph; DON'T LOSE YOUR HEAD(1967, Brit.), ph; FOLLOW THAT CAMEL(1967, Brit.), ph; BOFORS GUN, THE(1968, Brit.), ph; CARRY ON DOCTOR(1968, Brit.), ph; CAPTAIN NEMO AND THE UNDERWATER CITY(1969, Brit.), ph; CARRY ON HENRY VIII(1970, Brit.), ph; LAST GRENADE, THE(1970, Brit.), ph; PERFECT FRIDAY(1970, Brit.), ph; ZEPPELIN(1971, Brit.), ph; LEGEND OF HELL HOUSE, THE(1973, Brit.), ph; FROM BEYOND THE GRAVE(1974, Brit.), ph; CLEOPATRA JONES AND THE CASINO OF GOLD(1975 U. S. Hong Kong), ph; CONFESSIONS OF A POP PERFORMER(1975, Brit.), ph; LAND THAT TIME FORGOT, THE(1975, Brit.), ph; AT THE EARTH'S CORE(1976, Brit.), ph; DIRTY KNIGHT'S WORK(1976, Brit.), ph; GULLIVER'S TRAVELS(1977, Brit.), ph; PEOPLE THAT TIME FORGOT, THE(1977, Brit.), ph; WOMBLING FREE(1977, Brit.), ph; AMSTERDAM KILL, THE(1978, Hong Kong), ph; CARRY ON EMANUELLE(1978, Brit.), ph; WARLORDS OF ATLANTIS(1978, Brit.), ph; ARABIAN ADVENTURE(1979, Brit.), ph; LEGACY, THE(1979, Brit.), ph; BEAR ISLAND(1980, Brit.-Can.), ph; WATCHER IN THE WOODS, THE(1980, Brit.), ph; CAVEMAN(1981), ph; EYE OF THE NEEDLE(1981), ph; FOR YOUR EYES ONLY(1981), ph; OCTOPUSSY(1983, Brit.), ph; RETURN OF THE JEDI(1983), ph
1984
SUPERGIRL(1984), ph
Austin Hume
Silents
CARDIGAN(1922)
Benita Hume
CLUE OF THE NEW PIN, THE(1929, Brit.); HIGH TREASON(1929, Brit.); HOUSE OF THE ARROW, THE(1930, Brit.); FLYING FOOL, THE(1931, Brit.); HAPPY ENDING, THE(1931, Brit.); BLAME THE WOMAN(1932, Brit.); FOOTSTEPS IN THE NIGHT(1932, Brit.); HELP YOURSELF(1932, Brit.); LORD CAMBER'S LADIES(1932, Brit.); MEN OF STEEL(1932, Brit.); RESERVED FOR LADIES(1932, Brit.); SALLY BISHOP(1932, Brit.); WOMEN WHO PLAY(1932, Brit.); CLEAR ALL WIRES(1933); DISCORD(1933, Brit.); GAMBLING SHIP(1933); LITTLE DAMOZEL, THE(1933, Brit.); LOOKING FORWARD(1933); ONLY YESTERDAY(1933); WORST WOMAN IN PARIS(1933); POWER(1934, Brit.); PRIVATE LIFE OF DON JUAN, THE(1934, Brit.); DIVINE SPARK, THE(1935, Brit./Ital.); GAY DECEPTION, THE(1935); 18 MINUTES(1935, Brit.); GARDEN MURDER CASE, THE(1936); MOONLIGHT MURDER(1936); RAINBOW ON THE RIVER(1936); SUZY(1936); TARZAN ESCAPES(1936); LAST OF MRS. CHEYNEY(1937); PECK'S BAD BOY WITH THE CIRCUS(1938)
Silents
EASY VIRTUE(1927, Brit.); LADY OF THE LAKE, THE(1928, Brit.)
Misc. Silents
SECOND TO NONE(1926, Brit.); DOLORES(1928, Brit.); JAWS OF HELL(1928, Brit.); SOUTH SEA BUBBLE, A(1928, Brit.); WRECKER, THE(1928, Brit.); CLUE OF THE

Misc. Silents
RETURN OF MAURICE DONNELLY, THE(1915), d; FATHERS OF MEN(1916), a, d; FOOTLIGHTS OF FATE, THE(1916), d; TWO MEN AND A WOMAN(1917), d; ATONEMENT(1920), d; FOOLISH MONTE CARLO(1922), d; ONE NIGHT IN ROME(1924); MIDNIGHT LIMITED(1926); LIFE'S CROSSROADS(1928)
William J. Humphrey
STRANGE ADVENTURE(1932)
Misc. Silents
BLACK SPIDER, THE(1920, Brit.), d; MIDNIGHT BRIDE, THE(1920), d
Humphrey Lyttelton's Band
ROCK AROUND THE WORLD(1957, Brit.)
A. Humphreys
HAMLET(1976, Brit.), ph
Alf Humphreys
GAS(1981, Can.); MY BLOODY VALENTINE(1981, Can.); FIRST BLOOD(1982); FUNERAL HOME(1982, Can.)
1984
FINDERS KEEPERS(1984)
Alfred Humphreys
IMPROPER CHANNELS(1981, Can.)
Anderson Humphreys
CAYMAN TRIANGLE, THE(1977), a, p/d, w
Basil Humphreys
MONEY MAD(1934, Brit.), p; BARNACLE BILL(1935, Brit.), p; JOY RIDE(1935, Brit.), p; PLAY UP THE BAND(1935, Brit.), p; EVERYTHING OKAY(1936, Brit.), p; YOU MUST GET MARRIED(1936, Brit.), p
Cecil Humphreys
77 PARK LANE(1931, Brit.); OLD MAN, THE(1932, Brit.); DICK TURPIN(1933, Brit.); IT'S A KING(1933, Brit.); ADVENTURE LIMITED(1934, Brit.); GUEST OF HONOR(1934, Brit.); OH NO DOCTOR!(1934, Brit.); SILVER SPOON, THE(1934, Brit.); KOENIGSMARK(1935, Fr.); ACCUSED(1936, Brit.); CHICK(1936, Brit.); FAIR EXCHANGE(1936, Brit.); REASONABLE DOUBT(1936, Brit.); WUTHERING HEIGHTS(1939); RAZOR'S EDGE, THE(1946); DESIRE ME(1947); WOMAN'S VENGEANCE, A(1947); UNFINISHED SYMPHONY, THE(1953, Aust./Brit.)
Silents
PLEYDELL MYSTERY, THE(1916, Brit.); PROFLIGATE, THE(1917, Brit.); VEILED WOMAN, THE(1917, Brit.); ELUSIVE PIMPERNEL, THE(1919, Brit.); AMATEUR GENTLEMAN, THE(1920, Brit.); HOUSE ON THE MARSH, THE(1920, Brit.); PRIDE OF THE NORTH, THE(1920, Brit.); FALSE EVIDENCE(1922, Brit.); GLORIOUS ADVENTURE, THE(1922, U.S./Brit.); BROKEN MELODY, THE(1929, Brit.)
Misc. Silents
SORROWS OF SATAN, THE(1917); ROMANCE OF LADY HAMILTON, THE(1919, Brit.); SWINDLER, THE(1919, Brit.); HOUR OF THE TRIAL, THE(1920, Brit.); TAVERN KNIGHT, THE(1920, Brit.); WINDING ROAD, THE(1920); FOUR JUST MEN, THE(1921, Brit.); GREATHEART(1921, Brit.); SHADOW OF EVIL(1921, Brit.); WHITE HEN, THE(1921, Brit.); DICK TURPIN'S RIDE TO YORK(1922, Brit.); GAYEST OF THE GAY, THE(1924, Brit.); IRISH LUCK(1925); WOMAN IN WHITE, THE(1929, Brit.)
Dick Humphreys
MOONLIGHT IN HAVANA(1942); HI, BUDDY(1943); IF YOU KNEW SUSIE(1948); SUMMER STOCK(1950)
Dickie Humphreys
MY REPUTATION(1946)
Griffith Humphreys
ONE EMBARRASSING NIGHT(1930, Brit.); WOLVES(1930, Brit.); CONDEMNED TO DEATH(1932, Brit.); FORTUNATE FOOL, THE(1933, Brit.); MAROONED(1933, Brit.); THREE MEN IN A BOAT(1933, Brit.); LOYALTIES(1934, Brit.)
Silents
DAWN(1928, Brit.)
Laraine Humphreys
SAY HELLO TO YESTERDAY(1971, Brit.); UP POMPEII(1971, Brit.)
Ned Humphreys
PERSONAL BEST(1982), ed; DEAL OF THE CENTURY(1983), ed
1984
JOY OF SEX(1984), ed
Nigel Humphreys
SCUM(1979, Brit.); BREAKING GLASS(1980, Brit.)
Peter Humphreys
FLAMING FRONTIER(1958, Can.)
Suzie Humphreys
DEEP IN THE HEART(1983)
William Humphreys
COWBOY COUNSELOR(1933)
Silents
BEAU BRUMMEL(1924); UNHOLY THREE, THE(1925); AFLAME IN THE SKY(1927)
Albert Humphries
SHAPE OF THINGS TO COME, THE(1979, Can.)
Barry Humphries
BEDAZZLED(1967, Brit.); ADVENTURES OF BARRY McKENZIE(1972, Austral.), a, w; BARRY MC KENZIE HOLDS HIS OWN(1975, Aus.), a, w; GREAT MACARTHY, THE(1975, Aus.); GETTING OF WISDOM, THE(1977, Aus.); SHOCK TREATMENT(1981)
Bee Humphries
SIDE STREET(1950)
Betty Humphries
LAST DAYS OF DOLWYN, THE(1949, Brit.)
Dave Humphries
FULL CIRCLE(1977, Brit./Can.), w; QUADROPHENIA(1979, Brit.), w; STUD, THE(1979, Brit.), w; HAUNTING OF JULIA, THE(1981, Brit./Can.), w
George Humphries
MASTER AND MAN(1934, Brit.)
Hamilton Humphries
CAESAR AND CLEOPATRA(1946, Brit.); MY HANDS ARE CLAY(1948, Irish)
Joe Humphries
Silents
REFEREE, THE(1922)
John Humphries
THREE WEIRD SISTERS, THE(1948, Brit.)

Nigel Humphries
FINAL OPTION, THE(1983, Brit.)
Peter Humphries
PRIVATE ANGELO(1949, Brit.)
Whitmore Humphries
MANNEQUIN(1933, Brit.); CASE FOR THE CROWN, THE(1934, Brit.); PRIMROSE PATH, THE(1934, Brit.); LUCKY DAYS(1935, Brit.)
William Humphries
MANHATTAN PARADE(1931); SECRET SINNERS(1933); ARE WE CIVILIZED?(1934); FALSE PRETENSES(1935); GET THAT MAN(1935); PLAINSMAN, THE(1937); THIS ENGLAND(1941, Brit.)
Eric Humphris
TAKE OFF THAT HAT(1938, Brit.), p&d
Gordon Humphris
COME DANCE WITH ME(1950, Brit.); MIRACLE IN SOHO(1957, Brit.)
John Humphry
MOHAMMAD, MESSENGER OF GOD(1976, Lebanon/Brit.)
Walter Humphry
SING SINNER, SING(1933)
Basil Humphrys
KING OF THE CASTLE(1936, Brit.), p; TROPICAL TROUBLE(1936, Brit.), p
Paul Humpoletz
BLACK WINDMILL, THE(1974, Brit.); NOTHING BUT THE NIGHT(1975, Brit.)
Torben Hundahl
Z.P.G.(1972)
Robert Hundar
DOLLARS FOR A FAST GUN(1969, Ital./Span.); LADY HAMILTON(1969, Ger./Ital./Fr.); NARCO MEN, THE(1969, Span./Ital.); SABATA(1969, Ital.); WEEKEND MURDERS, THE(1972, Ital.)
Misc. Talkies
RAMON(1972)
Wolfgang Hundhammer
DEGREE OF MURDER, A(1969, Ger.), art d
Branko Hundic
SEVENTH CONTINENT, THE(1968, Czech./Yugo.), art d; DAY THAT SHOOK THE WORLD, THE(1977, Yugo./Czech.), cos
Craig Hundley
TAMMY AND THE MILLIONAIRE(1967); ROADIE(1980), m; SCHIZOID(1980), m; AMERICANA(1981), m; BOOGEYMAN II(1983), m
John Hundley
MOONLIGHT AND PRETZELS(1933)
Rodney Hundley
MIXED COMPANY(1974)
Charles J. Hundt
SIN OF MONA KENT, THE(1961), p&d
Alan Hune
BIG JOB, THE(1965, Brit.), ph
Andre Hunebelle
SIMPLE CASE OF MONEY, A(1952, Fr.), p&d; CASINO DE PARIS(1957, Fr./Ger.), d; FANTOMAS STRIKES BACK(1965, Fr./Ital.), d; FANTOMAS(1966, Fr./Ital.), d; OSS 117-MISSION FOR A KILLER(1966, Fr./Ital.), d, w; SHADOW OF EVIL(1967, Fr./Ital.), d, w; NO ROSES FOR OSS 117(1968, Fr.), d; DEVIL'S NIGHTMARE, THE(1971 Bel./Ital.), w
John Huneck
END OF THE WORLD(1977), ph
Ming Hung
KENNER(1969)
Pat Ting Hung
LAST WOMAN OF SHANG, THE(1964, Hong Kong)
Roy Chiao Hung
FERRY TO HONG KONG(1959, Brit.)
The Hungarian Folk Dancers
GOLDEN HEAD, THE(1965, Hung., U.S.)
Hungarian Opera Ballet
GOLDEN HEAD, THE(1965, Hung., U.S.)
Anna Hunger
SECRET OF CONVICT LAKE, THE(1951), w; PEARL OF THE SOUTH PACIFIC(1955), w
Dewey Hungerford
STONE(1974, Aus.)
Marguerite Hungerford
Silents
JESSE JAMES AS THE OUTLAW(1921); JESSE JAMES UNDER THE BLACK FLAG(1921)
Mrs. Hungerford
Silents
MOLLY BAWN(1916, Brit.), w
Ty Hungerford
AS YOUNG AS WE ARE(1958); I MARRIED A MONSTER FROM OUTER SPACE(1958)
Hungry the Baby Elephant
TARZAN'S THREE CHALLENGES(1963)
Henryk Hunko
LOTNA(1966, Pol.); PORTRAIT OF LENIN(1967, Pol./USSR); SARAGOSSA MANUSCRIPT, THE(1972, Pol.)
Gary Hunley
CARNIVAL ROCK(1957); UNHOLY WIFE, THE(1957); LEGEND OF TOM DOOLEY, THE(1959)
Andre Hunnebelle
CADET-ROUSSELLE(1954, Fr.), d
Hamilton Hunneker
NOW, VOYAGER(1942)
Arthur Hunnicut
TWO FLAGS WEST(1950); SHE COULDN'T SAY NO(1954); APACHE UPRISING(1966); WINTERHAWK(1976)
Arthur Hunnicutt
PARDON MY GUN(1942); SILVER QUEEN(1942); WILDCAT(1942); CHANCE OF A LIFETIME, THE(1943); FIGHTING BUCKAROO, THE(1943); HAIL TO THE RANGERS(1943); JOHNNY COME LATELY(1943); LAW OF THE NORTHWEST(1943); ROBIN HOOD OF THE RANGE(1943); ABROAD WITH TWO YANKS(1944); RIDING

WEST(1944); BORDER INCIDENT(1949); GREAT DAN PATCH, THE(1949); LUST FOR GOLD(1949); PINKY(1949); BROKEN ARROW(1950); FURIES, THE(1950); STARS IN MY CROWN(1950); TICKET TO TOMAHAWK(1950); DISTANT DRUMS(1951); PASSAGE WEST(1951); RED BADGE OF COURAGE, THE(1951); SUGARFOOT(1951); BIG SKY, THE(1952); LUSTY MEN, THE(1952); DEVIL'S CANYON(1953); SPLIT SECOND(1953); FRENCH LINE(1954); LAST COMMAND, THE(1955); KETTLES IN THE OZARKS, THE(1956); TALL T, THE(1957); BORN RECKLESS(1959); CARDINAL, THE(1963); TIGER WALKS, A(1964); CAT BALLOU(1965); ADVENTURES OF BULLWHIP GRIFFIN, THE(1967); EL DORADO(1967); SHOOT OUT(1971); $1,000,000 DUCK(1971); REVENGERS, THE(1972, U.S./Mex.); HARRY AND TONTO(1974); SPIKES GANG, THE(1974); MOONRUNNERS(1975)
Misc. Talkies
RIDING THROUGH NEVADA(1942)
Brooks Hunnicutt
PUFNSTUF(1970)
Donnis Hunnicutt
FRENCH QUARTER(1978), ch
Gayle Hunnicutt
WILD ANGELS, THE(1966); P.J.(1968); EYE OF THE CAT(1969); MARLOWE(1969); FRAGMENT OF FEAR(1971, Brit.); LOVE MACHINE, THE,(1971); RUNNING SCARED(1972, Brit.); LEGEND OF HELL HOUSE, THE(1973, Brit.); SCORPIO(1973); VOICES(1973, Brit.); SHADOWMAN(1974, Fr./Ital.); SPIRAL STAIRCASE, THE(1975, Brit.); SELL OUT, THE(1976); STRANGE SHADOWS IN AN EMPTY ROOM(1977, Can./Ital.); ONCE IN PARIS(1978)
Misc. Talkies
BLAZING MAGNUM(1976); SAINT AND THE BRAVE GOOSE, THE(1981, Brit.)
Jean Hunnisett
JOSEPH ANDREWS(1977, Brit.), cos
Rainer Hunold
JUST A GIGOLO(1979, Ger.)
Earl Hunsaker
THANK YOUR LUCKY STARS(1943)
John Hunsaker
JUST BEFORE DAWN(1980)
Vic Hunsberger
CHARLIE CHAN AND THE CURSE OF THE DRAGON QUEEN(1981)
Richard Hunsinger
LOVE CHILD(1982)
Rudolf Hunsperger
END OF THE GAME(1976, Ger./Ital.)
Adam Hunt
MUPPET MOVIE, THE(1979)
Allan Hunt
DIFFERENT STORY, A(1978); HERBIE GOES BANANAS(1980)
Amanda Hunt
PETERSEN(1974, Aus.)
Bill Hunt
SHADY LADY(1945)
Bob Hunt
BOOGENS, THE(1982), w
Bobbie Hunt
IT ISN'T DONE(1937, Aus.)
Brock Hunt
WITHOUT RESERVATIONS(1946)
Brooks Hunt
NOB HILL(1945)
C. J. Hunt
BUDDY BUDDY(1981)
Caroline Hunt
FAHRENHEIT 451(1966, Brit.)
Cecil Hunt
GIANT GILA MONSTER, THE(1959)
Charles Hunt
JUST LIKE HEAVEN(1930), ed; RIDERS OF THE NORTH(1931), ed; SECOND HONEYMOON(1931), ed; DISCARDED LOVERS(1932), ed; FAME STREET(1932), ed; TRAIL BEYOND, THE(1934), ed; RACING LUCK(1935), ed; FEDERAL AGENT(1936), ed; CALIFORNIA FRONTIER(1938), ed; LAW OF THE TEXAN(1938), ed; ORPHANS OF THE NORTH(1940), ed; SHARK WOMAN, THE(1941), p
Silents
AS MAN DESIRES(1925), ed; MIDNIGHT WATCH, THE(1927), d; SMOKE BELLEW(1929), ed
Misc. Silents
SMOKE EATERS, THE(1926), d; WARNING SIGNAL, THE(1926), d
Charles J. Hunt
NEAR THE RAINBOW'S END(1930), ed
Silents
IN EVERY WOMAN'S LIFE(1924), ed; JUST A WOMAN(1925), ed; LURE OF THE WILD, THE(1925), ed; ONE YEAR TO LIVE(1925), ed; SPEED MAD(1925), ed; DIXIE FLYER, THE(1926), d; SHOW GIRL, THE(1927), ed; OBEY YOUR HUSBAND(1928), d
Misc. Silents
BOY OF THE STREETS, A(1927), d; CASEY JONES(1927), d; MILLION DOLLAR MYSTERY(1927), d; MODERN DAUGHTERS(1927), d; ON THE STROKE OF TWELVE(1927), d; QUEEN OF THE CHORUS(1928), d; THUNDERGOD(1928), d; YOU CAN'T BEAT THE LAW(1928), d
Christopher Hunt
CLEOPATRA JONES AND THE CASINO OF GOLD(1975 U. S. Hong Kong)
Clara Hunt
CIMARRON(1931)
David Hunt
WAITRESS(1982)
Dennis Hunt
YELLOW SUBMARINE(1958, Brit.), animation; STIR(1980, Aus.)
1984
TREASURE OF THE YANKEE ZEPHYR(1984)
Dolly Hunt
CHASTITY(1969)
Ed Hunt
DIAMOND STUD(1970), ed; PLAGUE(1978, Can.), p&w, d; STARSHIP INVASIONS(1978, Can.), p, d&w

Misc. Talkies
BLOODY BIRTHDAY(1980), d; M3: THE GEMINI STRAIN(1980), d
Silents
KID, THE(1921)
Edward Hunt
Misc. Talkies
ALIEN ENCOUNTER(1979), d
Silents
INVISIBLE FEAR, THE(1921)
Eleanor Hunt
WHOOPEE(1930); GOLDIE(1931); GOOD SPORT(1931); TESS OF THE STORM COUNTRY(1932); BLUE STEEL(1934); MERRY WIDOW, THE(1934); NORTHERN FRONTIER(1935); YELLOW CARGO(1936); BANK ALARM(1937); GOLD RACKET, THE(1937); NAVY SPY(1937); WE'RE IN THE LEGION NOW(1937)
Misc. Talkies
GO-GET-'EM HAINES(1936); STOLEN PARADISE(1941)
Elizabeth Hunt
GERT AND DAISY'S WEEKEND(1941, Brit.); GERT AND DAISY CLEAN UP(1942, Brit.); VOTE FOR HUGGETT(1948, Brit.)
Florence Hunt
BLACK TULIP, THE(1937, Brit.)
Frances Hunt
YOU'RE A SWEETHEART(1937)
Gareth Hunt
WORLD IS FULL OF MARRIED MEN, THE(1980, Brit.); FUNNY MONEY(1983, Brit.)
1984
BLOODBATH AT THE HOUSE OF DEATH(1984, Brit.)
Misc. Talkies
LICENSED TO LOVE AND KILL(1979, Brit.)
Gordon Hunt
YOUNG CAPTIVES, THE(1959), w
1984
CRIMES OF PASSION(1984)
Grady Hunt
MUNSTER, GO HOME(1966), cos; PERILS OF PAULINE, THE(1967), cos; JIGSAW(1968), cos; SHAKIEST GUN IN THE WEST, THE(1968), cos; ONE MORE TRAIN TO ROB(1971), cos; OTHER SIDE OF THE MOUNTAIN, THE(1975), cos
Harry Hunt
CRAZY QUILT, THE(1966)
Heidy Hunt
TOBRUK(1966)
Helen Hunt
WORDS AND MUSIC(1929); WAGON WHEELS(1934); ROLLERCOASTER(1977)
Helene Hunt
OCTOPUSSY(1983, Brit.)
Henry Hunt
Misc. Silents
OLD FOOL, THE(1923)
Hugh Hunt
PANAMA HATTIE(1942), set d; SOMEWHERE I'LL FIND YOU(1942), set d; MADAME CURIE(1943), set d; DRAGON SEED(1944), set d; PICTURE OF DORIAN GRAY, THE(1945), set d; DARK MIRROR, THE(1946), set d; TEMPTATION(1946), set d; THREE WISE FOOLS(1946), set d; BRIBE, THE(1949), set d; SUN COMES UP, THE(1949), set d; KIM(1950), set d; STRICTLY DISHONORABLE(1951), set d; PAT AND MIKE(1952), set d; PLYMOUTH ADVENTURE(1952), set d; YOUNG MAN WITH IDEAS(1952), set d; JULIUS CAESAR(1953), art d; RHAPSODY(1954), set d; SEVEN BRIDES FOR SEVEN BROTHERS(1954), set d; I'LL CRY TOMORROW(1955), set d; IT'S ALWAYS FAIR WEATHER(1955), set d; FORBIDDEN PLANET(1956), set d; RAINTREE COUNTY(1957), set d; SILK STOCKINGS(1957), set d; SHEEPMAN, THE(1958), set d; WRECK OF THE MARY DEAR, THE(1959), set d; SUBTERRANEANS, THE(1960), set d; TWO LOVES(1961), set d; JUMBO(1962), set d; MUTINY ON THE BOUNTY(1962), set d; SWEET BIRD OF YOUTH(1962), set d; IT HAPPENED AT THE WORLD'S FAIR(1963), set d; TWILIGHT OF HONOR(1963), set d; QUICK, BEFORE IT MELTS(1964), set d; SEVEN FACES OF DR. LAO(1964), set d; UNSINKABLE MOLLY BROWN, THE(1964), set d; CINCINNATI KID, THE(1965), set d; GIRL HAPPY(1965), set d; GLASS BOTTOM BOAT, THE(1966), set d; MISTER BUDDWING(1966), set d; SPINOUT(1966), set d; DOUBLE TROUBLE(1967), set d; VENETIAN AFFAIR, THE(1967), set d; IMPOSSIBLE YEARS, THE(1968), set d; SOL MADRID(1968), set d; EXTRAORDINARY SEAMAN, THE(1969), set d; MARLOWE(1969), set d; SUPPORT YOUR LOCAL SHERIFF(1969), set d; MOONSHINE WAR, THE(1970), set d
Mrs. J. Hunt
Silents
BRIDE OF HATE, THE(1917)
J. Roy Hunt
INTERFERENCE(1928), ph; CLOSE HARMONY(1929), ph; DANCE OF LIFE, THE(1929), ph; DOCTOR'S SECRET(1929), ph; DUMMY(1929), ph; MIGHTY, THE(1929), ph; VIRGINIAN, THE(1929), ph; ALIAS FRENCH GERTIE(1930), ph; LEATHERNECKING(1930), ph; LOVE COMES ALONG(1930), ph; PAY OFF, THE(1930), ph; BEAU IDEAL(1931), ph; CONSOLATION MARRIAGE(1931), ph; WOMAN BETWEEN(1931), ph; AGE OF CONSENT(1932), ph; ROADHOUSE MURDER, THE(1932), ph; SPORT PARADE, THE(1932), ph; WAY BACK HOME(1932), ph; AGGIE APPLEBY, MAKER OF MEN(1933), ph; FLYING DOWN TO RIO(1933), ph; LUCKY DEVILS(1933), ph; MEN OF AMERICA(1933), ph; OLIVER TWIST(1933), ph; FINISHING SCHOOL(1934), ph; HAT, COAT AND GLOVE(1934), ph; LET'S TRY AGAIN(1934), ph; MEANEST GAL IN TOWN, THE(1934), ph; ANNIE OAKLEY(1935), ph; DANGEROUS CORNER(1935), ph; DOG OF FLANDERS, A(1935), ph; SHE(1935), ph; STAR OF MIDNIGHT(1935), ph; BRIDE WALKS OUT, THE(1936), ph; EX-MRS. BRADFORD, THE(1936), ph; LADY CONSENTS, THE(1936), ph; MUSS 'EM UP(1936), ph; SMARTEST GIRL IN TOWN(1936), ph; WALKING ON AIR(1936), ph; WE'RE ONLY HUMAN(1936), ph; WITHOUT ORDERS(1936), ph; BREAKFAST FOR TWO(1937), ph; HITTING A NEW HIGH(1937), ph; LIFE OF THE PARTY, THE(1937), ph; MAN WHO FOUND HIMSELF, THE(1937), ph; NEW FACES OF 1937(1937), ph; SEA DEVILS(1937), ph; THAT GIRL FROM PARIS(1937), w; YOU CAN'T BUY LUCK(1937), ph; BOY SLAVES(1938), ph; LAW WEST OF TOMBSTONE, THE(1938), ph; MAN TO REMEMBER, A(1938), ph; MOTHER CAREY'S CHICKENS(1938), ph; RADIO CITY REVELS(1938), ph; ROOM SERVICE(1938), ph; ALMOST A GENTLEMAN(1939), ph; FIXER DUGAN(1939), ph; FLYING IRISHMAN, THE(1939), ph; FULL CONFESSION(1939), ph; IN NAME ONLY(1939), ph; PANAMA LADY(1939), ph; RENO(1939), ph; CROSS COUNTRY ROMANCE(1940), ph; I'M STILL ALI-

VE(1940), ph; MARRIED AND IN LOVE(1940), ph; ONE CROWDED NIGHT(1940), ph; PRAIRIE LAW(1940), ph; SAINT'S DOUBLE TROUBLE, THE(1940), ph; STAGE TO CHINO(1940), ph; TRIPLE JUSTICE(1940), ph; YOU CAN'T FOOL YOUR WIFE(1940), ph; PARACHUTE BATTALION(1941), ph; THEY MET IN ARGENTINA(1941), ph; THUNDERING HOOFS(1941), ph; CALL OUT THE MARINES(1942), ph; SYNCOPATION(1942), ph; AVENGING RIDER, THE(1943), ph; I WALKED WITH A ZOMBIE(1943), ph; BRIGHTON STRANGLER, THE(1945), ph; GAME OF DEATH, A(1945), ph; WHAT A BLONDE(1945), ph; CROSSFIRE(1947), ph; DEVIL THUMBS A RIDE, THE(1947), ph; TRAIL STREET(1947), ph; UNDER THE TONTO RIM(1947), ph; ARIZONA RANGER, THE(1948), ph; GUN SMUGGLERS(1948), ph; INDIAN AGENT(1948), ph; RACE STREET(1948), ph; RETURN OF THE BADMEN(1948), ph; BROTHERS IN THE SADDLE(1949), ph; MIGHTY JOE YOUNG(1949), ph; RIDERS OF THE RANGE(1949), ph; RUSTLERS(1949), ph; BORDER TREASURE(1950), ph; KILL OR BE KILLED(1950), ph; RIO GRANDE PATROL(1950), ph; STORM OVER WYOMING(1950), ph; GUNPLAY(1951), ph; OVERLAND TELEGRAPH(1951), ph; PISTOL HARVEST(1951), ph; SADDLE LEGION(1951), ph; DESERT PASSAGE(1952), ph; ROAD AGENT(1952), ph; TARGET(1952), ph

Silents

ETERNAL SIN, THE(1917), ph; BRANDED WOMAN, THE(1920), ph; TRUTH, THE(1920), ph; LOVE'S REDEMPTION(1921), ph; WHAT WOMEN WILL DO(1921), ph; WOMAN'S PLACE(1921), ph; SHERLOCK HOLMES(1922), ph; HER OWN FREE WILL(1924), ph; SECOND YOUTH(1924), ph; MISS BLUEBEARD(1925), ph; ACE OF CADS, THE(1926), ph; AMERICAN VENUS, THE(1926), ph; BEAU GESTE(1926), ph; DANCING MOTHERS(1926), ph; KISS FOR CINDERELLA, A(1926), ph; NEW YORK(1927), ph; SHE'S A SHEIK(1927), ph; FIFTY-FIFTY GIRL, THE(1928), ph; TAKE ME HOME(1928), ph

James Hunt
HIGH BARBAREE(1947)

Jane Hunt
SPRINGTIME IN THE ROCKIES(1937)

1984
MUPPETS TAKE MANHATTAN, THE(1984)

Jay Hunt
IN OLD CHEYENNE(1931); SKY SPIDER, THE(1931); CHEYENNE CYCLONE, THE(1932)

Silents
CIVILIZATION(1916), d; HUNCHBACK OF NOTRE DAME, THE(1923); AFTER A MILLION(1924); MAN FOUR-SQUARE, A(1926); ONE MINUTE TO PLAY(1926); CAPTAIN SALVATION(1927)

Misc. Silents
BLACK SHEEP OF THE FAMILY, THE(1916), d; WHAT LOVE CAN DO(1916), d; PROMISE, THE(1917), d; YANKEE SPEED(1924); COUNSEL FOR THE DEFENSE(1925); LIGHTNIN'(1925); GOLDEN WEB, THE(1926); HARVESTER, THE(1927)

Jean Hunt
NOBODY'S CHILDREN(1940)

Jerry Hunt
IT HAD TO BE YOU(1947)

Jewel Hunt
Misc. Silents
KITTY MACKAY(1917)

Jimmie Hunt
SONG OF LOVE(1947)

Jimmy Hunt
FAMILY HONEYMOON(1948); FULLER BRUSH MAN(1948); MATING OF MILLIE, THE(1948); PITFALL(1948); SAINTED SISTERS, THE(1948); SORRY, WRONG NUMBER(1948); RUSTY'S BIRTHDAY(1949); SPECIAL AGENT(1949); TOP O' THE MORNING(1949); CAPTURE, THE(1950); CHEAPER BY THE DOZEN(1950); LOUISA(1950); ROCK ISLAND TRAIL(1950); SADDLE TRAMP(1950); SHADOW ON THE WALL(1950); HER FIRST ROMANCE(1951); KATIE DID IT(1951); MATING SEASON, THE(1951); WEEKEND WITH FATHER(1951); BELLES ON THEIR TOES(1952); ALL-AMERICAN, THE(1953); INVADERS FROM MARS(1953); LONE HAND, THE(1953); SHE COULDN'T SAY NO(1954)

John Hunt
KEEPERS OF YOUTH(1931, Brit.); TRAPPED IN A SUBMARINE(1931, Brit.); WHITE ENSIGN(1934, Brit.), d&w; FULL SPEED AHEAD(1939, Brit.), p&d

Juliet Hunt
NIGHT TRAIN TO PARIS(1964, Brit.)

Leslie Hunt
HOUSTON STORY, THE(1956)

Silents
LIFE'S WHIRLPOOL(1917); PECK'S BAD GIRL(1918); ERSTWHILE SUSAN(1919); INNER MAN, THE(1922); STEADFAST HEART, THE(1923); OLD HOME WEEK(1925)

Misc. Silents
WILD OATS(1919)

Linda Hunt
POPEYE(1980); YEAR OF LIVING DANGEROUSLY, THE(1982, Aus.)

1984
BOSTONIANS, THE(1984); DUNE(1984)

Lois Kelsa Hunt
HOUSE ON SORORITY ROW, THE(1983)

Lola Hunt
NEVER TROUBLE TROUBLE(1931, Brit.); NO LADY(1931, Brit.); MAN IN GREY, THE(1943, Brit.)

Madge Hunt
Silents
BLAZING TRAIL, THE(1921); LAMPLIGHTER, THE(1921); REPUTATION(1921); ABRAHAM LINCOLN(1924); HEART TROUBLE(1928); QUEEN KELLY(1929)

Marsha Hunt
VIRGINIA JUDGE, THE(1935); ACCUSING FINGER, THE(1936); ARIZONA RAIDERS, THE(1936); COLLEGE HOLIDAY(1936); DESERT GOLD(1936); EASY TO TAKE(1936); GENTLE JULIA(1936); HOLLYWOOD BOULEVARD(1936); ANNAPOLIS SALUTE(1937); BORN TO THE WEST(1937); EASY LIVING(1937); MURDER GOES TO COLLEGE(1937); THUNDER TRAIL(1937); COME ON, LEATHERNECKS(1938); HARDYS RIDE HIGH, THE(1939); JOE AND ETHEL TURP CALL ON THE PRESIDENT(1939); LONG SHOT, THE(1939); STAR REPORTER(1939); THESE GLAMOUR GIRLS(1939); WINTER CARNIVAL(1939); ELLERY QUEEN. MASTER DETECTIVE(1940); FLIGHT COMMAND(1940); IRENE(1940); PRIDE AND PREJUDICE(1940); BLOSSOMS IN THE DUST(1941); CHEERS FOR MISS BISHOP(1941); I'LL WAIT FOR YOU(1941); PENALTY, THE(1941); TRIAL OF MARY DUGAN, THE(1941);

UNHOLY PARTNERS(1941); AFFAIRS OF MARTHA, THE(1942); JOE SMITH, AMERICAN(1942); KID GLOVE KILLER(1942); PANAMA HATTIE(1942); SEVEN SWEETHEARTS(1942); CRY HAVOC(1943); HUMAN COMEDY, THE(1943); PILOT NO. 5(1943); THOUSANDS CHEER(1943); BRIDE BY MISTAKE(1944); LOST ANGEL(1944); MUSIC FOR MILLIONS(1944); NONE SHALL ESCAPE(1944); LETTER FOR EVIE, A(1945); VALLEY OF DECISION, THE(1945); CARNEGIE HALL(1947); SMASH-UP, THE STORY OF A WOMAN(1947); INSIDE STORY, THE(1948); RAW DEAL(1948); JIGSAW(1949); MARY RYAN, DETECTIVE(1949); TAKE ONE FALSE STEP(1949); ACTORS AND SIN(1952); HAPPY TIME, THE(1952); DIPLOMATIC PASSPORT(1954, Brit.); NO PLACE TO HIDE(1956); BACK FROM THE DEAD(1957); BOMBERS B-52(1957); BLUE DENIM(1959); PLUNDERERS, THE(1960); JOHNNY GOT HIS GUN(1971); DRACULA A.D. 1972(1972, Brit.); RICH AND FAMOUS(1981); BRITTANIA HOSPITAL(1982, Brit.); SENDER, THE(1982, Brit.)

Martita Hunt
LOVE ON WHEELS(1932, Brit.); RESERVED FOR LADIES(1932, Brit.); FRIDAY THE 13TH(1934, Brit.); I WAS A SPY(1934, Brit.); TOO MANY MILLIONS(1934, Brit.); CASE OF GABRIEL PERRY, THE(1935, Brit.); FIRST A GIRL(1935, Brit.); MR. WHAT'S-HIS-NAME(1935, Brit.); INTERRUPTED HONEYMOON, THE(1936, Brit.); LADY JANE GREY(1936, Brit.); POT LUCK(1936, Brit.); SABOTAGE(1937, Brit.); SECOND BEST BED(1937, Brit.); WHERE THERE'S A WILL(1937, Brit.); EVERYTHING HAPPENS TO ME(1938, Brit.); STRANGE BOARDERS(1938, Brit.); TROOPSHIP(1938, Brit.); GOOD OLD DAYS, THE(1939, Brit.); MIDDLE WATCH, THE(1939, Brit.); MILL ON THE FLOSS(1939, Brit.); NURSEMAID WHO DISAPPEARED, THE(1939, Brit.); OLD MOTHER RILEY JOINS UP(1939, Brit.); PRISON WITHOUT BARS(1939, Brit.); TROUBLE BREWING(1939, Brit.); TILLY OF BLOOMSBURY(1940, Brit.); GIRL MUST LIVE, A(1941, Brit.); HOUSE OF MYSTERY(1941, Brit.); QUIET WEDDING(1941, Brit.); SEVENTH SURVIVOR, THE(1941, Brit.); STRANGLER, THE(1941, Brit.); VOICE IN THE NIGHT, A(1941, Brit.); LADY FROM LISBON(1942, Brit.); SABOTAGE AT SEA(1942, Brit.); TALK ABOUT JACQUELINE(1942, Brit.); WHEN KNIGHTS WERE BOLD(1942, Brit.); WINGS AND THE WOMAN(1942, Brit.); MAN IN GREY, THE(1943, Brit.); YOUNG MAN'S FANCY(1943, Brit.); WELCOME, MR. WASHINGTON(1944, Brit.); GREAT EXPECTATIONS(1946, Brit.); WICKED LADY, THE(1946, Brit.); GHOSTS OF BERKELEY SQUARE(1947, Brit.); ANNA KARENINA(1948, Brit.); MY SISTER AND I(1948, Brit.); SO EVIL MY LOVE(1948, Brit.); FAN, THE(1949); LITTLE BALLERINA, THE(1951, Brit.); IT STARTED IN PARADISE(1952, Brit.); STORY OF ROBIN HOOD, THE(1952, Brit.); TREASURE HUNT(1952, Brit.); FOLLY TO BE WISE(1953, Brit.); MELBA(1953, Brit.); TONIGHT AT 8:30(1953, Brit.); KING'S RHAPSODY(1955, Brit.); ANASTASIA(1956); MARCH HARE, THE(1956, Brit.); ADMIRABLE CRICHTON, THE(1957, Brit.); BONJOUR TRISTESSE(1958); DANGEROUS EXILE(1958, Brit.); ME AND THE COLONEL(1958); THREE MEN IN A BOAT(1958, Brit.); BOTTOMS UP(1960, Brit.); BRIDES OF DRACULA, THE(1960, Brit.); SONG WITHOUT END(1960); I LIKE MONEY(1962, Brit.); WONDERFUL WORLD OF THE BROTHERS ERIMM, THE(1962); BECKET(1964, Brit.); UNSINKABLE MOLLY BROWN, THE(1964); BUNNY LAKE IS MISSING(1965); BEST HOUSE IN LONDON, THE(1969, Brit.)

Silents
RANK OUTSIDER(1920, Brit.)

Mary Hunt
Silents
MOLLY O'(1921), w

Maurice Hunt
NIGHT THEY ROBBED BIG BERTHA'S, THE(1975); RETURN TO MACON COUNTY(1975); LINCOLN CONSPIRACY, THE(1977)

Misc. Talkies
BRASS RING, THE(1975)

Michael Hunt
GREAT MR. HANDEL, THE(1942, Brit.); AMOROUS MR. PRAWN, THE(1965, Brit.)

Neil Hunt
FIREFOX(1982); JEKYLL AND HYDE...TOGETHER AGAIN(1982)

Paul Hunt
HAREM BUNCH; OR WAR AND PIECE, THE(1969), d; SCAVENGERS, THE(1969); MACHISMO-40 GRAVES FOR 40 GUNS(1970), d, w, ed; CLONES, THE(1973), p, d; GREAT GUNDOWN, THE(1977), d

Misc. Talkies
WOMAN IN THE RAIN(1976), d

Pee Wee Hunt
MAKE BELIEVE BALLROOM(1949)

Peter Hunt
LIGHT TOUCH, THE(1955, Brit.); HELL IN KOREA(1956, Brit.), ed; ADMIRABLE CRICHTON, THE(1957, Brit.), ed; CRY FROM THE STREET, A(1959, Brit.), ed; FERRY TO HONG KONG(1959, Brit.), ed; NEXT TO NO TIME(1960, Brit.), ed; SINK THE BISMARCK!(1960, Brit.), ed; LOSS OF INNOCENCE(1961, Brit.), ed; DAMN THE DEFIANT!(1962, Brit.), ed; DR. NO(1962, Brit.), ed; THERE WAS A CROOKED MAN(1962, Brit.), ed; CALL ME BWANA(1963, Brit.), ed; FROM RUSSIA WITH LOVE(1963, Brit.), ed; GOLDFINGER(1964, Brit.), ed; HANDS OF ORLAC, THE(1964, Brit./Fr.); IPCRESS FILE, THE(1965, Brit.), ed; OPERATION SNAFU(1965, Brit.), ed; THUNDERBALL(1965, Brit.), ed; YOU ONLY LIVE TWICE(1967, Brit.), ed; ON HER MAJESTY'S SECRET SERVICE(1969, Brit.), d; GOLD(1974, Brit.), d; SHOUT AT THE DEVIL(1976, Brit.), d; GULLIVER'S TRAVELS(1977, Brit., Bel.), d; NIGHT GAMES(1980), ed; DEATH HUNT(1981), d

Misc. Talkies
MYSTERIOUS STRANGER(1982), d

Peter Austin Hunt
GAMES THAT LOVERS PLAY(1971, Brit.), ed

Peter H. Hunt
1776(1972), d

Misc. Talkies
BULLY(1978), d

Phil Hunt
1984
FLASH OF GREEN, A(1984)

Philip Hunt
Silents
DANCER'S PERIL, THE(1917)

Phoebe Hunt
Misc. Silents
GRIM COMEDIAN, THE(1921)

Ralph S. Hunt
PHYNX, THE(1970), set d
Ray Hunt
LAST DAYS OF POMPEII, THE(1935), ph
Richard Hunt
MUPPET MOVIE, THE(1979); GREAT MUPPET CAPER, THE(1981); TRADING PLACES(1983)
1984
MUPPETS TAKE MANHATTAN, THE(1984); OXFORD BLUES(1984)
Robert B. Hunt
THERE'S ONE BORN EVERY MINUTE(1942), w
Robert E. Hunt
BOOGIE MAN WILL GET YOU, THE(1942), w
Roger Hunt
THEY MADE HER A SPY(1939)
Ronald Leigh Hunt
COMING-OUT PARTY, A(; COLONEL MARCH INVESTIGATES(1952,Brit.); PAUL TEMPLE RETURNS(1952, Brit.); BROKEN HORSESHOE, THE(1953, Brit.); SHADOW OF A MAN(1955, Brit.); HAND, THE(1960, Brit.); PICCADILLY THIRD STOP(1960, Brit.); CURSE OF THE VOODOO(1965, Brit.); CLEGG(1969, Brit.)
Roy Hunt
CASE OF SERGEANT GRISCHA, THE(1930), ph; DIXIANA(1930), ph; LAWFUL LARCENY(1930), ph; FRIENDS AND LOVERS(1931), ph; HIGH STAKES(1931), ph; GIRL CRAZY(1932), ph; EMERGENCY CALL(1933), ph; SILVER STREAK, THE(1935), ph; LITTLE ORVIE(1940), ph; FALCON AND THE CO-EDS, THE(1943), ph; ACTION IN ARABIA(1944), ph; HEAVENLY DAYS(1944), ph; BLACK BEAUTY(1946), ph; LIKELY STORY, A(1947), ph; LAWLESS, THE(1950), ph; EIGHT IRON MEN(1952), ph; JUGGLER, THE(1953), ph
Silents
ARGENTINE LOVE(1924), ph; REJECTED WOMAN, THE(1924), ph; SPIDER WEBS(1927), ph
Russel C. Hunt
Misc. Silents
SKY-EYE(1920)
Ruth Hunt
GHOST STORY(1981)
Susan Hunt
CLONES, THE(1973)
Susan Kay Hunt
NEW YORK, NEW YORK(1977)
Suzanne Hunt
BEST HOUSE IN LONDON, THE(1969, Brit.)
Teresa Wilkerson Hunt
OUTSIDERS, THE(1983)
Tony Hunt
LONG WEEKEND(1978, Aus.), set d
Virginia Hunt
TAKE CARE OF MY LITTLE GIRL(1951)
Gov. W.P. Hunt
Misc. Silents
WESTERN GOVERNOR'S HUMANITY, A(1915)
William Hunt
STARLIFT(1951)
Marsha Hunte
WELCOME TO THE CLUB(1971)
Muriel Hunte
POOR COW(1968, Brit.)
Otto Hunte
BLUE ANGEL, THE(1930, Ger.), set d
Silents
KRIEMHILD'S REVENGE(1924, Ger.), art d; SIEGFRIED(1924, Ger.), art d; METROPOLIS(1927, Ger.), art d; SPIES(1929, Ger.), art d; WOMAN ON THE MOON, THE(1929, Ger.), art d
A.C. Hunter
Misc. Silents
DECEPTION(1918, Brit.), d
Alastair Hunter
OPERATION DIAMOND(1948, Brit.); FLOODTIDE(1949, Brit.); OPERATION DISASTER(1951, Brit.); SCOTLAND YARD INSPECTOR(1952, Brit.); MARTIN LUTHER(1953, Brit.); DIAMOND WIZARD(1954, Brit.); WHITE FIRE(1953, Brit.); EMBEZZLER, THE(1954, Brit.); TIME TO KILL, A(1955, Brit.); WARRIORS, THE(1955); WINDFALL(1955 Brit.); SATELLITE IN THE SKY(1956); OPERATION MURDER(1957, Brit.); PORTRAIT IN SMOKE(1957, Brit.); TIME IS MY ENEMY(1957, Brit.); GIDEON OF SCOTLAND YARD(1959, Brit.); MAN WHO LIKED FUNERALS, THE(1959, Brit.); SON OF ROBIN HOOD(1959, Brit.); NIGHT TRAIN FOR INVERNESS(1960, Brit.); CALAMITY THE COW(1967, Brit.)
Alberta Hunter
RADIO FOLLIES(1935, Brit.); REMEMBER MY NAME(1978), m
Alec Hunter
SISTER TO ASSIST'ER, A(1930, Brit.); INQUEST(1931, Brit.)
Silents
ROB ROY(1922, Brit.)
Alistair Hunter
TIGHT LITTLE ISLAND(1949, Brit.); CHANCE OF A LIFETIME(1950, Brit.); HOLIDAY WEEK(1952, Brit.); SPIDER AND THE FLY, THE(1952, Brit.); YOU'RE ONLY YOUNG TWICE(1952, Brit.); THREE STEPS IN THE DARK(1953, Brit.); RUNAWAY BUS, THE(1954, Brit.); TROUBLE IN THE GLEN(1954, Brit.); HALF A SIXPENCE(1967, Brit.); ASSIGNMENT K(1968, Brit.); ITALIAN JOB, THE(1969, Brit.); NICE GIRL LIKE ME, A(1969, Brit.)
Ann Hunter
HI DIDDLE DIDDLE(1943); ONE DANGEROUS NIGHT(1943); ROYAL SCANDAL, A(1945)
Anne Hunter
GAY FALCON, THE(1941); DISTANT TRUMPET(1952, Brit.)
Arlene Hunter
SON OF SINBAD(1955); REVOLT IN THE BIG HOUSE(1958); SEX KITTENS GO TO COLLEGE(1960)

Arline Hunter
MADISON AVENUE(1962); DON'T WORRY, WE'LL THINK OF A TITLE(1966); WHITE LIGHTNIN' ROAD(1967); BIG DADDY(1969)
Arthur Hunter
Silents
TRAFFIC IN SOULS(1913)
Barbara Hunter
GERALDINE(1929), ed; SQUARE SHOULDERS(1929), ed; TROUBLE WITH ANGELS, THE(1966); WHERE ANGELS GO...TROUBLE FOLLOWS(1968)
Silents
DRESS PARADE(1927), ed; VANITY(1927), ed
Bernard Hunter
ROCK AROUND THE WORLD(1957, Brit.); GIRLS OF LATIN QUARTER(1960, Brit.), a, w; INVASION QUARTET(1961, Brit.); OPERATION SNATCH(1962, Brit.); ROOMMATES(1962, Brit.); HELLFIRE CLUB, THE(1963, Brit.)
Bill Hunter
TOUGH TO HANDLE(1937); SPY TRAIN(1943); DESTINATION TOKYO(1944); JANIE(1944); MYSTERY MAN(1944); PRINCESS AND THE PIRATE, THE(1944); TEXAS MASQUERADE(1944); THIN MAN GOES HOME, THE(1944); UP IN ARMS(1944); CAGED(1950); LUCY GALLANT(1955); NED KELLY(1970, Brit.); STONE(1974, Aus.); 27A(1974, Aus.); MAN FROM HONG KONG(1975); ELIZA FRASER(1976, Aus.); MAD DOG MORGAN(1976,Aus.); IN SEARCH OF ANNA(1978, Aus.); WEEKEND OF SHADOWS(1978, Aus.); NEWSFRONT(1979, Aus.); DEAD MAN'S FLOAT(1980, Aus.); HARD KNOCKS(1980, Aus.); GALLIPOLI(1981, Aus.); HEATWAVE(1983, Aus.); RETURN OF CAPTAIN INVINCIBLE, THE(1983, Aus./U.S.)
Brian Hunter
GEORGY GIRL(1966, Brit.), m
Bruce Hunter
BATTLE BEYOND THE SUN(1963)
Buddy Hunter
MOUNTED STRANGER, THE(1930); SPURS(1930); SUNSET TRAIL(1932)
Charles Hunter
STORMY(1935)
Charlotte Hunter
KEEP YOUR POWDER DRY(1945); MAN WITH A CLOAK, THE(1951); MY FAVORITE SPY(1951); ROYAL WEDDING(1951)
Colin Hunter
LODGER, THE(1944); IMPERFECT LADY, THE(1947); PARADINE CASE, THE(1947)
Connie Hunter
1984
PREY, THE(1984)
Coralie Hunter
TEX(1982)
Craig Hunter
CLOCKWORK ORANGE, A(1971, Brit.)
Dennis M. Hunter
DON'T GO IN THE HOUSE(1980)
Diane Hunter
MILLIONAIRE PLAYBOY(1940); SUBSTITUTION(1970)
Dick Hunter
FATAL HOUR, THE(1937, Brit.); LAWLESS VALLEY(1938); RACKETEERS OF THE RANGE(1939)
E.M. Inman Hunter
OVERLANDERS, THE(1946, Brit./Aus.), ed
Edna Hunter
Silents
COMMON LAW, THE(1916); PRINCE IN A PAWNSHOP, A(1916); NAULAHKA, THE(1918)
Misc. Silents
HALF A ROGUE(1916); TWO LITTLE IMPS(1917)
Evan Hunter
BLACKBOARD JUNGLE, THE(1955), d&w; STRANGERS WHEN WE MEET(1960), w; YOUNG SAVAGES, THE(1961), w; BIRDS, THE(1963), w; MISTER BUDDWING(1966), w; LAST SUMMER(1969), w; FUZZ(1972), w; WALK PROUD(1979), w
Fern Hunter
Misc. Talkies
KILLING GROUND, THE(1972)
Fran Hunter
LADY CHATTERLEY'S LOVER(1981, Fr./Brit.)
G. R. Hunter
MIDDLETON FAMILY AT THE N.Y. WORLD'S FAIR(1939), w
Glen Hunter
Misc. Silents
PINCH HITTER, THE(1925)
Glenn Hunter
FOR BEAUTY'S SAKE(1941)
Silents
CRADLE BUSTER, THE(1922); SECOND FIDDLE(1923); GRIT(1924); MERTON OF THE MOVIES(1924)
Misc. Silents
CASE OF BECKY, THE(1921); COUNTRY FLAPPER, THE(1922); PURITAN PASSIONS(1923); YOUTHFUL CHEATERS(1923); SILENT WATCHER, THE(1924); WEST OF THE WATER TOWER(1924); HIS BUDDY'S WIFE(1925); BROADWAY BOOB, THE(1926); LITTLE GIANT, THE(1926); ROMANCE OF A MILLION DOLLARS, THE(1926)
Hall Hunter
BENGAL BRIGADE(1954), w
Hans Hunter
FAT SPY(1966), m
Harrison Hunter
Misc. Silents
STRONGEST, THE(1920)
Harvey Hunter
Misc. Talkies
ASTROLOGER, THE(1975)
Henry Hunter
LOVE LETTERS OF A STAR(1936); NOBODY'S FOOL(1936); PAROLE(1936); POSTAL INSPECTOR(1936); YELLOWSTONE(1936); GIRL WITH IDEAS, A(1937); PRESCRIPTION FOR ROMANCE(1937); ROAD BACK,THE(1937); TROUBLE AT MIDNIGHT(1937); WESTBOUND LIMITED(1937); FORBIDDEN VALLEY(1938);

CALLING DR. KILDARE(1939); GOOD GIRLS GO TO PARIS(1939); THUNDER AFLOAT(1939); BOY WHO CAUGHT A CROOK(1961); SON OF FLUBBER(1963); MARYJANE(1968)

Holly Hunter
1984
SWING SHIFT(1984)

Honey Hunter
Misc. Talkies
CAREER BED(1972)

Horace Hunter
Silents
UNDER SUSPICION(1919, Brit.), a, w

Ian Hunter
SYNCOPATION(1929); ESCAPE(1930, Brit.); LOVE STORM, THE(1931, Brit.); SALLY IN OUR ALLEY(1931, Brit.); MARRY ME(1932, Brit.); SIGN OF FOUR, THE(1932, Brit.); WATER GYPSIES, THE(1932, Brit.); MAN FROM TORONTO, THE(1933, Brit.); CHURCH MOUSE, THE(1934, Brit.); DEATH AT A BROADCAST(1934, Brit.); NIGHT OF THE PARTY, THE(1934, Brit.); NO ESCAPE(1934, Brit.); ORDERS IS ORDERS(1934, Brit.); SILVER SPOON, THE(1934, Brit.); SOMETHING ALWAYS HAPPENS(1934, Brit.); GIRL FROM TENTH AVENUE, THE(1935); I FOUND STELLA PARISH(1935); JALNA(1935); LAZYBONES(1935); MIDSUMMER'S NIGHT'S DREAM, A(1935); PHANTOM LIGHT, THE(1935, Brit.); DEVIL IS A SISSY, THE(1936); MORALS OF MARCUS, THE(1936, Brit.); TO MARY–WITH LOVE(1936); WHITE ANGEL, THE(1936); ANOTHER DAWN(1937); CALL IT A DAY(1937); CONFESSION(1937); STOLEN HOLIDAY(1937); THAT CERTAIN WOMAN(1937); 52ND STREET(1937); ADVENTURES OF ROBIN HOOD, THE(1938); ALWAYS GOODBYE(1938); COMET OVER BROADWAY(1938); SECRETS OF AN ACTRESS(1938); SISTERS, THE(1938); BAD LITTLE ANGEL(1939); BROADWAY SERENADE(1939); LITTLE PRINCESS, THE(1939); MAISIE(1939); TARZAN FINDS A SON!(1939); TOWER OF LONDON(1939); YES, MY DARLING DAUGHTER(1939); BITTER SWEET(1940); BROADWAY MELODY OF 1940(1940); DULCY(1940); GALLANT SONS(1940); LONG VOYAGE HOME, THE(1940); STRANGE CARGO(1940); ANDY HARDY'S PRIVATE SECRETARY(1941); ARKANSAS JUDGE(1941), w; BILLY THE KID(1941); COME LIVE WITH ME(1941); DR. JEKYLL AND MR. HYDE(1941); SMILIN' THROUGH(1941); ZIEGFELD GIRL(1941); YANK AT ETON, A(1942); FOREVER AND A DAY(1943); IT COMES UP LOVE(1943); BEDELIA(1946, Brit.); BAD SISTER(1947, Brit.); HIGH FURY(1947, Brit.); EDWARD, MY SON(1949, U.S./Brit.); IT STARTED IN PARADISE(1952, Brit.); STRANGER IN BETWEEN, THE(1952, Brit.); APPOINTMENT IN LONDON(1953, Brit.); DON'T BLAME THE STORK(1954, Brit.); EIGHT O'CLOCK WALK(1954, Brit.); HIGH FLIGHT(1957, Brit.); SHE PLAYED WITH FIRE(1957, Brit.); MAD LITTLE ISLAND(1958, Brit.); BULLDOG BREED, THE(1960, Brit.); FLAME OVER INDIA(1960, Brit.); DR. BLOOD'S COFFIN(1961); SECRET OF MONTE CRISTO, THE(1961, Brit.); GUNS OF DARKNESS(1962, Brit.); DREAM OF KINGS, A(1969), w
Silents
NOT FOR SALE(1924, Brit.); GIRL OF LONDON, A(1925, Brit.); EASY VIRTUE(1927, Brit.); RING, THE(1927, Brit.); HIS HOUSE IN ORDER(1928, Brit.); PHYSICIAN, THE(1928, Brit.); WHEN BOYS LEAVE HOME(1928, Brit.)
Misc. Silents
CONFESSIONS(1925, Brit.); THOROUGHBRED, THE(1928, Brit.); VALLEY OF THE GHOSTS(1928, Brit.)

Ian McLellan Hunter
ROMA RIVUOLE CESARE(, w; FISHERMAN'S WHARF(1939), w; MEET DR. CHRISTIAN(1939), w; COURAGEOUS DR. CHRISTIAN, THE(1940), w; FOOTLIGHT FEVER(1941), w; SLIGHTLY DANGEROUS(1943), w; YOUNG IDEAS(1943), w; MR. DISTRICT ATTORNEY(1946), w; SPIRITUALIST, THE(1948), w; EYE WITNESS(1950, Brit.), w; WOMAN OF DISTINCTION, A(1950), w; OUTSIDE MAN, THE(1973, U.S./FR.), w

Inman Hunter
CASE OF THE RED MONKEY(1955, Brit.), ed; FOUR DESPERATE MEN(1960, Brit.), w

J. Evans Hunter
Misc. Silents
VARSITY(1930, Brit.)

J. Michael Hunter
ROLLERCOASTER(1977)

J.A. Hunter
KILLERS OF KILIMANJARO(1960, Brit.), w

J.E. Hunter
FARMER'S WIFE, THE(1941, Brit.), w

Jack Hunter
MACK, THE(1973)

Jack D. Hunter
BLUE MAX, THE(1966), w

Jackie Hunter
GIVE ME THE STARS(1944, Brit.); DON CHICAGO(1945, Brit.)

James Hunter
KING AND COUNTRY(1964, Brit.); WINDFLOWERS(1968)

Jeff Hunter
BRAINSTORM(1965)

Jeffrey Hunter
CALL ME MISTER(1951); FOURTEEN HOURS(1951); FROGMEN, THE(1951); TAKE CARE OF MY LITTLE GIRL(1951); BELLES ON THEIR TOES(1952); DREAMBOAT(1952); LURE OF THE WILDERNESS(1952); RED SKIES OF MONTANA(1952); SAILOR OF THE KING(1953, Brit.); PRINCESS OF THE NILE(1954); THREE YOUNG TEXANS(1954); SEVEN ANGRY MEN(1955); SEVEN CITIES OF GOLD(1955); WHITE FEATHER(1955); GREAT LOCOMOTIVE CHASE, THE(1956); KISS BEFORE DYING, A(1956); PROUD ONES, THE(1956); SEARCHERS, THE(1956); GUN FOR A COWARD(1957); NO DOWN PAYMENT(1957); TRUE STORY OF JESSE JAMES, THE(1957); WAY TO THE GOLD, THE(1957); COUNT FIVE AND DIE(1958, Brit.); IN LOVE AND WAR(1958); LAST HURRAH, THE(1958); MARDI GRAS(1958); HELL TO ETERNITY(1960); KEY WITNESS(1960); SERGEANT RUTLEDGE(1960); KING OF KINGS(1961); MAN-TRAP(1961); LONGEST DAY, THE(1962); NO MAN IS AN ISLAND(1962); GOLD FOR THE CAESARS(1964); MAN FROM GALVESTON, THE(1964); MURIETA(1965, Span.); DIMENSION 5(1966); GUIDE FOR THE MARRIED MAN, A(1967); WITCH WITHOUT A BROOM, A(1967, U.S./Span.); CHRISTMAS KID, THE(1968, U.S., Span.); CUSTER OF THE WEST(1968, U.S., Span.); PRIVATE NAVY OF SGT. O'FARRELL, THE(1968)

Jerry Hunter
BOY, A GIRL, AND A DOG, A(1946); DATE WITH JUDY, A(1948); GREAT LOVER, THE(1949); RENEGADES OF THE SAGE(1949); IT'S A BIG COUNTRY(1951); TREASURE OF THE GOLDEN CONDOR(1953)

Jesse Lee Hunter
1984
KILLPOINT(1984)

Jim Hunter
CHRISTMAS STORY, A(1983)

John Hunter
GREEN PACK, THE(1934, Brit.), w; LUCK OF THE TURF(1936, Brit.), w; RACING ROMANCE(1937, Brit.), w; EASY RICHES(1938, Brit.), w; MERELY MR. HAWKINS(1938, Brit.), w; BLIND FOLLY(1939, Brit.), w; GLASS MOUNTAIN, THE(1950, Brit), w; HONEYMOON DEFERRED(1951, Brit.), w; ODETTE(1951, Brit.); NEVER LOOK BACK(1952, Brit.), w; COURT MARTIAL(1954, Brit.), w; INTRUDER, THE(1955, Brit.), w; BEHIND THE MASK(1958, Brit.), w; NEVER TAKE CANDY FROM A STRANGER(1961, Brit.), w; PIRATES OF BLOOD RIVER, THE(1962, Brit.), w; LAFAYETTE(1963, Fr.), titles; BLOOD AND GUTS(1978, Can.), w; GREY FOX, THE(1983, Can.), w
Silents
ONE YEAR TO LIVE(1925), w; SMASHING THROUGH(1928, Brit.), w

John Clifton Hunter
HARD PART BEGINS, THE(1973, Can.), p, w

Julee Hunter
HOW SWEET IT IS(1968)

Kaki Hunter
ROADIE(1980); WILLIE AND PHIL(1980); WHOSE LIFE IS IT ANYWAY?(1981); PORKY'S(1982); PORKY'S II: THE NEXT DAY(1983)
1984
JUST THE WAY YOU ARE(1984)

Kelly Hunter
1984
SUPERGIRL(1984)

Kenneth Hunter
ANOTHER DAWN(1937); LANCER SPY(1937); LEAGUE OF FRIGHTENED MEN(1937); ADVENTURES OF ROBIN HOOD, THE(1938); KIDNAPPED(1938); LITTLE PRINCESS, THE(1939); DISPATCH FROM REUTERS, A(1940); EARL OF CHICAGO, THE(1940); SUSPICION(1941); MOON AND SIXPENCE, THE(1942); FRENCHMAN'S CREEK(1944); LODGER, THE(1944); HOLD THAT BLONDE(1945); DECEPTION(1946); RED DANUBE, THE(1949); KNOCK ON WOOD(1954)
Silents
AMBITION(1916); RANSOM, THE(1916)
Misc. Silents
DAREDEVIL KATE(1916)

Kim Hunter
SEVENTH VICTIM, THE(1943); TENDER COMRADE(1943); WHEN STRANGERS MARRY(1944); YOU CAME ALONG(1945); STAIRWAY TO HEAVEN(1946, Brit.); STREETCAR NAMED DESIRE, A(1951); ANYTHING CAN HAPPEN(1952); DEADLINE–U.S.A.(1952); BERMUDA AFFAIR(1956, Brit.); STORM CENTER(1956); YOUNG STRANGER, THE(1957); MONEY, WOMEN AND GUNS(1958); LILITH(1964); PLANET OF THE APES(1968); SWIMMER, THE(1968); BENEATH THE PLANET OF THE APES(1970); ESCAPE FROM THE PLANET OF THE APES(1971)
Misc. Talkies
DARK AUGUST(1975)

Kristin Hunter
LANDLORD, THE(1970), w

Larry Hunter
COWARDS(1970)
Misc. Talkies
AMAZING TRANSPLANT, THE(1970)

Lynne Hunter
LADY PAYS OFF, THE(1951); NO ROOM FOR THE GROOM(1952)

Margaret Hunter
LIFE AND TIMES OF CHESTER-ANGUS RAMSGOOD, THE(1971, Can.)

Margot Hunter
KING ARTHUR WAS A GENTLEMAN(1942, Brit.)

Marvin Hunter
DINER(1982)

N.C. Hunter
POISON PEN(1941, Brit.), w

Nita Hunter
SUSIE STEPS OUT(1946); WHITE TIE AND TAILS(1946); ROCKY(1948); SMART WOMAN(1948); MEN, THE(1950)

Oliver Hunter
BEGGAR'S OPERA, THE(1953)

Philip Hunter
COTTONPICKIN' CHICKENPICKERS(1967)

Ray Hunter
KID FOR TWO FARTHINGS, A(1956, Brit.)

Raymond Hunter
WAY BACK HOME(1932)

Rene Hunter
IT'S IN THE BAG(1936, Brit.)

Richard Hunter
MARSHAL OF MESA CITY, THE(1939); ELEPHANT MAN, THE(1980, Brit.); HOUSE OF LONG SHADOWS, THE(1983, Brit.)

Rick Hunter
MOONRUNNERS(1975)

Robert Hunter
GOLDEN HORDE, THE(1951); BIG SKY, THE(1952); FORTY-NINTH MAN, THE(1953); PURPLE MASK, THE(1955); MEN OF SHERWOOD FOREST(1957, Brit.); WOMAN OF MYSTERY, A(1957, Brit.); TRAITOR'S GATE(1966, Brit./Ger.); TERROR IN THE JUNGLE(1968), makeup
Misc. Silents
WESTERN BLOOD(1923), d

Robin Hunter
SPANISH SWORD, THE(1962, Brit.); THREE SPARE WIVES(1962, Brit.); MODESTY BLAISE(1966, Brit.); CARNABY, M.D.(1967, Brit.); MELODY(1971, Brit.); VAMPIRE CIRCUS(1972, Brit.)

Ronald Hunter
SEDUCTION OF JOE TYNAN, THE(1979)
1984
TEACHERS(1984)
Ross Hunter
THOROUGHLY MODERN MILLIE(1967), p; PAD, THE(AND HOW TO USE IT)*
(1966, Brit.), p; EVER SINCE VENUS(1944); LOUISIANA HAYRIDE(1944); SHE'S A
SWEETHEART(1944); GUY, A GAL AND A PAL, A(1945); HIT THE HAY(1945);
BANDIT OF SHERWOOD FOREST, THE(1946); OUT OF THE DEPTHS(1946); SWEET-
HEART OF SIGMA CHI(1946); GROOM WORE SPURS, THE(1951); ALL I DESI-
RE(1953), p; TAKE ME TO TOWN(1953), p; TUMBLEWEED(1953), p; MAGNIFICENT
OBSESSION(1954), p; TAZA, SON OF COCHISE(1954), p; YELLOW MOUNTAIN,
THE(1954), p; ALL THAT HEAVEN ALLOWS(1955), p; CAP-
TAIN LIGHTFOOT(1955), p; ONE DESIRE(1955), p; SPOILERS, THE(1955), p;
THERE'S ALWAYS TOMORROW(1956), a, p; BATTLE HYMN(1957), p; INTER-
LUDE(1957), p; MY MAN GODFREY(1957), p; TAMMY AND THE BACHELOR(1957),
p; RESTLESS YEARS, THE(1958), p; THIS HAPPY FEELING(1958), p; IMITATION
OF LIFE(1959), p; PILLOW TALK(1959), p; STRANGER IN MY ARMS(1959), p;
MIDNIGHT LACE(1960), p; PORTRAIT IN BLACK(1960), p; BACK STREET(1961), p;
FLOWER DRUM SONG(1961), p; TAMMY, TELL ME TRUE(1961), p; IF A MAN
ANSWERS(1962), p; TAMMY AND THE DOCTOR(1963), p; THRILL OF IT ALL,
THE(1963), p; CHALK GARDEN, THE(1964, Brit.), p; I'D RATHER BE RICH(1964), p;
ART OF LOVE, THE(1965), p; MADAME X(1966), p; AIRPORT(1970), p; LOST HORI-
ZON(1973), p
Rudolph Hunter
YOU'LL NEVER GET RICH(1941)
Russell Hunter
GORBALS STORY, THE(1950, Brit.); LILLI MARLENE(1951, Brit.); TASTE THE
BLOOD OF DRACULA(1970, Brit.); CALLAN(1975, Brit.); CHANGELING, THE(1980,
Can.), w
Sheena Hunter
PRIVATE LIFE OF SHERLOCK HOLMES, THE(1970, Brit.)
Shirley Hunter
SUDAN(1945); KILLER DILL(1947)
Stephen John Hunter
1984
BLAME IT ON THE NIGHT(1984)
T. H. Hunter
CALENDAR, THE(1931, Brit.), d
T. Hayes Hunter
CRIMINAL AT LARGE(1932, Brit.), d; SALLY BISHOP(1932, Brit.), d; MAN THEY
COULDN'T ARREST, THE(1933, Brit.), d, w; WHITE FACE(1933, Brit.), d; GHOUL,
THE(1934, Brit.), d; GREEN PACK, THE(1934, Brit.), d; JOSSER ON THE FARM(1934,
Brit.), p&d; WARN LONDON!(1934, Brit.), d
Silents
FIRE AND SWORD(1914), d; SEATS OF THE MIGHTY, THE(1914), d; JUDY
FORGOT(1915), d; RECOIL, THE(1924), d; ONE OF THE BEST(1927, Brit.), d
Misc. Silents
COMRADE JOHN(1915), d; DESERT GOLD(1919), d; CUP OF FURY, THE(1920), d;
EARTHBOUND(1920), d; LIGHT IN THE CLEARING, THE(1921), d; DAMAGED
HEARTS(1924), d; TROUPING WITH ELLEN(1924), d; SKY RAIDER, THE(1925), d;
WILDFIRE(1925), d; SCARLET DAREDEVIL, THE(1928, Brit.), d; SOUTH SEA BUB-
BLE, A(1928, Brit.), d; SILVER KING, THE(1929, Brit.), d
Tab Hunter
LAWLESS, THE(1950); ISLAND OF DESIRE(1952, Brit.); GUN BELT(1953); STEEL
LADY, THE(1953); RETURN TO TREASURE ISLAND(1954); TRACK OF THE
CAT(1954); BATTLE FLAME(1955); SEA CHASE, THE(1955); BURNING HILLS,
THE(1956); GIRL HE LEFT BEHIND, THE(1956); DAMN YANKEES(1958); GUN-
MAN'S WALK(1958); LAFAYETTE ESCADRILLE(1958); THAT KIND OF WO-
MAN(1959); THEY CAME TO CORDURA(1959); PLEASURE OF HIS COMPANY,
THE(1961); OPERATION BIKINI(1963); GOLDEN ARROW, THE(1964, Ital.); RIDE
THE WILD SURF(1964); CITY UNDER THE SEA(1965, Brit.); LOVED ONE,
THE(1965); BIRDS DO IT(1966); FICKLE FINGER OF FATE, THE(1967, Span./U.S.);
HOSTILE GUNS(1967); LIFE AND TIMES OF JUDGE ROY BEAN, THE(1972);
AROUSERS, THE(1973); WON TON TON, THE DOG WHO SAVED HOL-
LYWOOD(1976); POLYESTER(1981); GREASE 2(1982); PANDEMONIUM(1982)
Misc. Talkies
TROUBLED WATERS(1964, Brit.); TIMBER TRAMPS(1975)
Tanna Hunter
INVASION OF THE BLOOD FARMERS(1972)
Thomas Hunter
WHAT DID YOU DO IN THE WAR, DADDY?(1966); HILLS RUN RED, THE(1967,
Ital.); ANZIO(1968, Ital.); FINAL COUNTDOWN, THE(1980), w
Tich Hunter
ROYAL DEMAND, A(1933, Brit.)
Tim Hunter
SALLY'S HOUNDS(1968); OVER THE EDGE(1979), w; TEX(1982), d, w
Tom Hunter
HUMAN FACTOR, THE(1975), a, w
1984
ACT, THE(1984)
Tony Hunter
NAKED IN THE SUN(1957)
Vic Hunter
HOT STUFF(1979)
Virginia Hunter
HARVEY GIRLS, THE(1946); NOTORIOUS LONE WOLF, THE(1946); DOWN TO
EARTH(1947); HER HUSBAND'S AFFAIRS(1947); IT HAD TO BE YOU(1947); LAST
DAYS OF BOOT HILL(1947); HE WALKED BY NIGHT(1948); MATING OF MILLIE,
THE(1948); PHANTOM VALLEY(1948); RECKLESS MOMENTS, THE(1949); DESERT
HAWK, THE(1950); FILE ON THELMA JORDAN, THE(1950)
Misc. Talkies
RIDERS OF THE LONE STAR(1947); SMOKY RIVER SERENADE(1947); STRAN-
GER FROM PONCA CITY, THE(1947)
William Hunter
GREAT GAME, THE(1930), w; COUNTY FAIR(1937); NO PLACE FOR A LA-
DY(1943); TO EACH HIS OWN(1946); MOONLIGHTER, THE(1953); HOT ROD HUL-
LABALOO(1966)

Silents
SHEER BLUFF(1921)
William Hunter III
CONRACK(1974)
Willie Hunter, Jr.
CHIEF CRAZY HORSE(1955)
Ian Hunters
QUEEN'S GUARDS, THE(1963, Brit.)
Gardner Hunting
Silents
CLEVER MRS. CARFAX, THE(1917), w; JACK AND JILL(1917), w; JOHNNY GET
YOUR GUN(1919), w
Lawrence Huntingdon
ROMANCE IN RHYTHM(1934, Brit.), p,d&w; IMPULSE(1955, Brit.), w; OBLONG
BOX, THE(1969, Brit.), w
Terry Huntingdon
GIDGET GOES HAWAIIAN(1961); SAIL A CROOKED SHIP(1961)
Helen Huntington
EASY LIVING(1937)
Helene Huntington
JOURNEY INTO LIGHT(1951)
Joan Huntington
YOUNG FURY(1965); HELL RAIDERS(1968); GAILY, GAILY(1969); WHAT EVER
HAPPENED TO AUNT ALICE?(1969); HONKERS, THE(1972)
Lawerence Huntington
SANDERS(1963, Brit.), w
Lawrence Huntington
LIEUTENANT DARING, RN(1935, Brit.), p; BANK MESSENGER MYSTERY,
THE(1936, Brit.), d&w; CAFE MASCOT(1936, Brit.), d; FULL SPEED AHEAD(1936,
Brit.), p&d, w; STRANGE CARGO(1936, Brit.), p&d; TWO ON A DOORSTEP(1936,
Brit.), d; PASSENGER TO LONDON(1937, Brit.), p&d; TWIN FACES(1937, Brit.), d;
BAD BOY(1938, Brit.), d&w; WHO IS GUILTY?(1940, Brit.), w; TOWER OF TERROR,
THE(1942, Brit.), d; WOMEN AREN'T ANGELS(1942, Brit.), d, w; SUSPECTED PER-
SON(1943, Brit.), d&w; WARN THAT MAN(1943, Brit.), d, w; NIGHT BOAT TO
DUBLIN(1946, Brit.), d, w; WANTED FOR MURDER(1946, Brit.), d; PATIENT
VANISHES, THE(1947, Brit.), d; UPTURNED GLASS, THE(1947, Brit.), d; WHEN
THE BOUGH BREAKS(1947, Brit.), d; MR. PERRIN AND MR. TRAILL(1948, Brit.), d;
MAN ON THE RUN(1949, Brit.), p,d&w; ONE WILD OAT(1951, Brit.), w; FRAN-
CHISE AFFAIR, THE(1952, Brit.), d, w; DEADLY NIGHTSHADE(1953, Brit.), w;
GENIE, THE(1953, Brit.), d; THERE WAS A YOUNG LADY(1953, Brit.), d&w; DESTI-
NATION MILAN(1954, Brit.), w, w; RED DRESS, THE(1954, Brit.), d; CONTRABAND
SPAIN(1955, Brit.), d&w; DEADLY RECORD(1959, Brit.), d, w; QUESTION OF SUS-
PENSE, A(1961, Brit.), w; TRUNK, THE(1961, Brit.), p; FUR COLLAR, THE(1962,
Brit.), p,d&w; STRANGLEHOLD(1962, Brit.), d; SANDERS(1963, Brit.), d; VULTURE,
THE(1967, U.S./Brit./Can.), p,d&w
Misc. Talkies
ACCUSED, THE(1953), d
Silents
AFTER MANY YEARS(1930, Brit.), d&w
Louise Huntington
FAIR WARNING(1931); THREE ROGUES(1931); VIKING, THE(1931)
Pam Huntington
FORCE: FIVE(1981); THEY CALL ME BRUCE(1982)
Sheila Huntington
NOTORIOUS GENTLEMAN(1945, Brit.); UPTURNED GLASS, THE(1947, Brit.);
WHEN THE BOUGH BREAKS(1947, Brit.); MR. PERRIN AND MR. TRAILL(1948,
Brit.); IT'S NOT CRICKET(1949, Brit.)
Terry Huntington
FIVE FINGER EXERCISE(1962); THREE STOOGES MEET HERCULES, THE(1962)
William Huntington
Misc. Silents
LOVE'S CROSS ROADS(1916)
Anne Huntley
1984
HARDBODIES(1984), set d; NIGHTMARE ON ELM STREET, A(1984), set d
Chet Huntley
GUNG HO!(1943); ARCTIC MANHUNT(1949); I CHEATED THE LAW(1949); PORT
OF NEW YORK(1949); PRIDE OF ST. LOUIS, THE(1952); EXECUTIVE SUITE(1954);
CRY TERROR(1958)
Darrell Huntley
STORK CLUB, THE(1945); JET PILOT(1957)
Eleanor Huntley
STRIKE ME PINK(1936); TICKET TO PARADISE(1936)
Fred Huntley
Silents
CARPET FROM BAGDAD, THE(1915); FIRES OF CONSCIENCE(1916); DADDY
LONG LEGS(1919); JOHNNY GET YOUR GUN(1919); EXCUSE MY DUST(1920);
ROUND UP, THE(1920); SOUL OF YOUTH, THE(1920); AFFAIRS OF ANATOL,
THE(1921); BREWSTER'S MILLIONS(1921); BRONZE BELL, THE(1921); GASOLINE
GUS(1921); PRINCE THERE WAS, A(1921); WISE FOOL, A(1921); CRIMSON CHAL-
LENGE, THE(1922); NORTH OF THE RIO GRANDE(1922); TO HAVE AND TO
HOLD(1922); WHILE SATAN SLEEPS(1922); LAW OF THE LAWLESS, THE(1923); TO
THE LAST MAN(1923); KING OF KINGS, THE(1927)
Misc. Silents
MAN OF SORROW, A(1916); JOHANNA ENLISTS(1918); ONLY ROAD, THE(1918);
SEA FLOWER, THE(1918); HEART OF WETONA, THE(1919); BORDERLAND(1922);
AGE OF INNOCENCE, THE(1924); THUNDERING HOOFS(1924)
G.P. Huntley
MERELY MARY ANN(1931); AS HUSBANDS GO(1934); DEATH TAKES A HOLI-
DAY(1934); IMITATION OF LIFE(1934); LITTLE MAN, WHAT NOW?(1934); NOW I'LL
TELL(1934); SERVANTS' ENTRANCE(1934); BECKY SHARP(1935); DRESSED TO
THRILL(1935); I'VE BEEN AROUND(1935); MAN WHO RECLAIMED HIS HEAD,
THE(1935); ONE EXCITING ADVENTURE(1935); TWO FISTED(1935); ANY MAN'S
WIFE(1936); AUGUST WEEK-END(1936, Brit.); CHARGE OF THE LIGHT BRIGADE,
THE(1936); CHARLIE CHAN AT THE RACE TRACK(1936); GO WEST, YOUNG
MAN(1936); GOLDEN ARROW, THE(1936); SONS O' GUNS(1936); ANOTHER
DAWN(1937); MICHAEL O'HALLORAN(1937); ARTISTS AND MODELS
ABROAD(1938); BEAU GESTE(1939); TOWER OF LONDON(1939); PRIVATE AF-
FAIRS(1940); YANK IN THE R.A.F., A(1941); JOURNEY FOR MARGARET(1942);
THEY DIED WITH THEIR BOOTS ON(1942)

George Huntley
I WANT A DIVORCE(1940)
George P. Huntley
SAY IT IN FRENCH(1938); I'M FROM MISSOURI(1939); CROSS COUNTRY RO-MANCE(1940); PLAY GIRL(1940); GREAT MAN'S LADY, THE(1942)
Hugh Huntley
BAT WHISPERS, THE(1930); EYES OF THE WORLD, THE(1930); SECOND WI-FE(1930); DOUBLE HARNESS(1933); WHOM THE GODS DESTROY(1934); I FOUND STELLA PARISH(1935); LLOYDS OF LONDON(1936); SUZY(1936); FOOLS FOR SCANDAL(1938); MARIE ANTOINETTE(1938); PIRATES OF THE SKIES(1939); IN-TERNATIONAL SQUADRON(1941); LUCKY DEVILS(1941)
Silents
CLIMBERS, THE(1919); STEADFAST HEART, THE(1923); SECOND YOUTH(1924); SOCIAL CELEBRITY, A(1926)
Misc. Silents
YOUTHFUL FOLLY(1920)
Jean Huntley
Silents
GOLD RUSH, THE(1925)
Laura Huntley
Silents
TRAFFIC IN SOULS(1913)
Luray Huntley
Silents
INTOLERANCE(1916); LITTLE SCHOOL MA'AM, THE(1916)
Raymond Huntley
WHAT HAPPENED THEN?(1934, Brit.); CAN YOU HEAR ME MOTHER?(1935, Brit.); REMBRANDT(1936, Brit.); DINNER AT THE RITZ(1937, Brit.); KNIGHT WITHOUT ARMOR(1937, Brit.); NIGHT TRAIN(1940, Brit.); GHOST OF ST. MICHA-EL'S. THE(1941, Brit.); GHOST TRAIN, THE(1941, Brit.); MAIL TRAIN(1941, Brit.); ONCE A CROOK(1941, Brit.); VOICE IN THE NIGHT, A(1941, Brit.); PIMPERNEL SMITH(1942, Brit.); WHEN WE ARE MARRIED(1943, Brit.); THEY CAME TO A CITY(1944, Brit.); WAY AHEAD, THE(1945, Brit.); ADVENTURESS, THE(1946, Brit.); SCHOOL FOR SECRETS(1946, Brit.); BROKEN JOURNEY(1948, Brit.); MR. PERRIN AND MR. TRAILL(1948, Brit.); SO EVIL MY LOVE(1948, Brit.); PASSPORT TO PIMLICO(1949, Brit.); IT'S HARD TO BE GOOD(1950, Brit.); TRIO(1950, Brit.); I'LL NEVER FORGET YOU(1951); LONG DARK HALL, THE(1951, Brit.); MAN BAIT(1952, Brit.); GLAD TIDINGS(1953, Brit.); MEET MR. LUCIFER(1953, Brit.); MR. DENNING DRIVES NORTH(1953, Brit.); AUNT CLARA(1954, Brit.); HOBSON'S CHOICE(1954, Brit.); SCOTCH ON THE ROCKS(1954, Brit.); CONSTANT HUSBAND, THE(1955, Brit.); DAM BUSTERS, THE(1955, Brit.); DOCTOR AT SEA(1955, Brit.); PRISONER, THE(1955, Brit.); TECKMAN MYSTERY, THE(1955, Brit); LAST MAN TO HANG, THE(1956, Brit.); ROTTEN TO THE CORE(1956, Brit.); WEE GEORDIE(1956, Brit.); BROTHERS IN LAW(1957, Brit.); GREEN MAN, THE(1957, Brit.); TOWN ON TRIAL(1957, Brit.); I'M ALL RIGHT, JACK(1959, Brit.); INNOCENT MEETING(1959, Brit.); MUMMY, THE(1959, Brit.); ORDERS ARE ORDERS(1959, Brit.); ROOM AT THE TOP(1959, Brit.); BOTTOMS UP(1960, Brit.); FOLLOW THAT HORSE!(1960, Brit.); FRENCH MISTRESS(1960, Brit.); MAKE MINE MINK(1960, Brit.); MAN IN A COCKED HAT(1960, Bri.); NEXT TO NO TIME(1960, Brit.); OUR MAN IN HAVA-NA(1960, Brit.); SANDS OF THE DESERT(1960, Brit.); PURE HELL OF ST. TRI-NIAN'S, THE(1961, Brit.); RISK, THE(1961, Brit.); ON THE BEAT(1962, Brit.); ONLY TWO CAN PLAY(1962, Brit.); WALTZ OF THE TOREADORS(1962, Brit.); CROOKS ANONYMOUS(1963, Brit.); FATHER CAME TOO(1964, Brit.); GUTTER GIRLS(1964, Brit.); NURSE ON WHEELS(1964, Brit.); BLACK TORMENT, THE(1965, Brit.); GREAT ST. TRINIAN'S TRAIN ROBBERY, THE(1966, Brit.); HOSTILE WITNESS(1968, Brit.); HOT MILLIONS(1968, Brit.); ADDING MACHINE, THE(1969); YOUNG WIN-STON(1972, Brit.); SYMPTOMS(1976, Brit.)
Misc. Talkies
THAT'S YOUR FUNERAL(1974, Brit.)
Tim Huntley
FOREVER AMBER(1947); GALLANT BLADE, THE(1948); SWORD OF THE AVENG-ER(1948); ADVENTURES OF DON JUAN(1949); COME TO THE STABLE(1949); ROGUES OF SHERWOOD FOREST(1950); MONSTER FROM THE GREEN HELL(1958)
Betty Huntley-Wright
COMMISSIONAIRE(1933, Brit.); MEET SEXTON BLAKE(1944, Brit.); AFFAIRS OF A ROGUE, THE(1949, Brit.)
Fred Huntly
Silents
NE'ER-DO-WELL, THE(1916); WHAT EVERY WOMAN KNOWS(1921)
Misc. Silents
CHIP OF THE FLYING U(1914)
Helen Hunton
Silents
LOVES OF RICARDO, THE(1926)
William Huntre
Silents
OTHER PERSON, THE(1921, Brit.)
Mary Huntress
Silents
IT CAN BE DONE(1921); MILLIONAIRE, THE(1921); ELOPE IF YOU MUST(1922)
Charles Huntsberry
1984
PURPLE RAIN(1984)
Sandor Hunyady
STORM AT DAYBREAK(1933), w; GIRL DOWNSTAIRS, THE(1938), w
Alexander Hunzinger
LOST ONE, THE(1951, Ger.); UNWILLING AGENT(1968, Ger.)
Juliette Huot
LUCK OF GINGER COFFEY, THE(1964, U.S./Can.)
Ludovic Huot
PASSION HOLIDAY(1963)
Herman Hupfeld
TAKE A CHANCE(1933), m
George Hupp
Silents
NAKED HEARTS(1916); PARADISE GARDEN(1917)

Jack Hupp
WAR DRUMS(1957)
Master Georgie Hupp
Silents
KAISER, BEAST OF BERLIN, THE(1918)
Arnold Huppert
RANCHO DELUXE(1975)
Isabelle Huppert
CESAR AND ROSALIE(1972, Fr.); GOING PLACES(1974, Fr.); ROSEBUD(1975); LACEMAKER, THE(1977, Fr.); NO TIME FOR BREAKFAST(1978, Fr.); VIOLET-TE(1978, Fr.); BRONTE SISTERS, THE(1979, Fr.); JUDGE AND THE ASSASSIN, THE(1979, Fr.); EVERY MAN FOR HIMSELF(1980, Fr.); HEAVEN'S GATE(1980); LOULOU(1980, Fr.); COUP DE TORCHON(1981, Fr.); TROUT, THE(1982, Fr.); ENTRE NOUS(1983, Fr.); PASSION(1983, Fr./Switz.)
1984
MY BEST FRIEND'S GIRL(1984, Fr.)
Earl Hurd
SNOW WHITE AND THE SEVEN DWARFS(1937), w; FANTASIA(1940), art d, anim
Gale Ann Hurd
1984
TERMINATOR, THE(1984), w
Gale Anne Hurd
1984
TERMINATOR, THE(1984), p
Gale Hurd
SMOKEY BITES THE DUST(1981), p
Hugh Hurd
CRISIS(1950), set d; SHADOWS(1960); FOR LOVE OF IVY(1968); BLADE(1973); WOMAN UNDER THE INFLUENCE, A(1974)
Michael Hurd
GIRLS, THE(1972, Swed.), m
1984
SCRUBBERS(1984, Brit.), m
Mitzi Hurd
SWEET SUBSTITUTE(1964, Can.)
Ruth Hurd
RUBY(1971)
Georg Hurdalek
DEVIL'S GENERAL, THE(1957, Ger.), w; TOWN WITHOUT PITY(1961, Ger./Switz./U.S.), w
George Hurdalek
ROSES FOR THE PROSECUTOR(1961, Ger.), w; TRAPP FAMILY, THE(1961, Ger.), w
James Hurde
LOST AND FOUND(1979)
James Hurdle
"EQUUS"(1977)
Wesley Hurdman
FARMER TAKES A WIFE, THE(1953)
Philip Hurdwood
EDUCATING RITA(1983)
Peter Hurkos
BOXOFFICE(1982)
Isobel Hurl
1984
GIVE MY REGARDS TO BROAD STREET(1984, Brit.)
William Hurlbert
CAT CREEPS, THE(1930), w
Carolyn Hurlburt
BELL JAR, THE(1979)
Gladys Hurlbut
BY YOUR LEAVE(1935), w; LOVE ON THE RUN(1936), w; HIGHER AND HIGH-ER(1943), w; MATING SEASON, THE(1951); SHADOW IN THE SKY(1951); CAPTIVE CITY(1952); SOMETHING FOR THE BIRDS(1952); PRESIDENT'S LADY, THE(1953); LONG, LONG TRAILER, THE(1954); LUCKY ME(1954); MAN CALLED PETER, THE(1955); RAINS OF RANCHIPUR, THE(1955)
William Hurlbut
LILIES OF THE FIELD(1930), w; GOOD SPORT(1931), w; LADIES MUST LO-VE(1933), w; ONLY YESTERDAY(1933), w; SECRET OF THE BLUE ROOM(1933), w; IMITATION OF LIFE(1934), w; MADAME SPY(1934), w; BRIDE OF FRANKEN-STEIN, THE(1935), w; DARING YOUNG MAN, THE(1935), w; ONE EXCITING ADVENTURE(1935), w; ORCHIDS TO YOU(1935), w; WAY DOWN EAST(1935), w; RAINBOW ON THE RIVER(1936), w; MAKE A WISH(1937), w
Silents
NEW YORK(1916), w; MADE IN HEAVEN(1921), w
William J. Hurlbut
Silents
ROMANCE AND ARABELLA(1919), w
William Hurlbutt
ADAM HAD FOUR SONS(1941), w
Alec Hurley
BLOCKADE(1928, Brit.); FLYING SCOTSMAN, THE(1929, Brit.)
Arthur Hurley
ROYAL BOX, THE(1930), w
Capt. Frank Hurley
SQUATTER'S DAUGHTER(1933, Aus.), ph; TALL TIMBERS(1937, Aus.), w
Cheryl Hurley
WINTER A GO-GO(1965)
Frank Hurley
SILENCE OF DEAN MAITLAND, THE(1934, Aus.), ph; GRANDAD RUDD(1935, Aus.), ph; LOVERS AND LUGGERS(1938, Aus.), ph
Silents
JUNGLE WOMAN, THE(1926, Brit.), p,d&w; PEARL OF THE SOUTH SEAS(1927, Brit.), p,d&w
Gene Hurley
PROJECT X(1949), w
Harold Hurley
WILD HORSE MESA(1932), p; HERITAGE OF THE DESERT(1933), p; MAN OF THE FOREST(1933), p; MYSTERIOUS RIDER, THE(1933), p; TO THE LAST MAN(1933), p; LAST ROUND-UP, THE(1934), p; THUNDERING HERD, THE(1934), p; WAGON

WHEELS(1934), p; HOME ON THE RANGE(1935), p; MILLIONS IN THE AIR(1935), p; ROCKY MOUNTAIN MYSTERY(1935), p; SHIP CAFE(1935), p; TWO FISTED(1935), p; WANDERER OF THE WASTELAND(1935), p; DESERT GOLD(1936), p; DRIFT FENCE(1936), p; IT'S A GREAT LIFE(1936), p; NEVADA(1936), p; PREVIEW MURDER MYSTERY(1936), p; SKY PARADE(1936), p; TIMOTHY'S QUEST(1936), p; WOMAN TRAP(1936), p; DAUGHTER OF SHANGHAI(1937), p; FORLORN RIVER(1937), p; LET'S MAKE A MILLION(1937), p; PARTNERS IN CRIME(1937), p; BULLDOG DRUMMOND IN AFRICA(1938), p; HUNTED MEN(1938), p; KING OF CHINATOWN(1939), p

James F. Hurley
VELVET TRAP, THE(1966); SOMETHING WEIRD(1967), p, w; SOMETHING FOR EVERYONE(1970)

Jim Hurley
SQUAD CAR(1961)

Joan Hurley
YOUR PAST IS SHOWING(1958, Brit.); SUNDAY IN THE COUNTRY(1975, Can.)

Joseph Hurley
PSYCHO(1960), prod d

Julia Hurley
Silents
COST, THE(1920); EASY TO GET(1920); GUILTY OF LOVE(1920); NEW YORK IDEA, THE(1920); WOMAN'S MAN(1920); JANE EYRE(1921); ARGENTINE LOVE(1924)
Misc. Silents
BEWARE(1919); MARRIED?(1926)

Julia R. Hurley
Silents
JUNGLE, THE(1914)

Lu Hurley
CANDIDATE, THE(1972)

Maureen Hurley
SCARLET HOUR, THE(1956)

Maurice Hurley
FIREBIRD 2015 AD(1981), w

Maury Hurley
IT AIN'T EASY(1972), d

Mrs. Hurley
Misc. Silents
BELOVED IMPOSTER, THE(1918)

Ronald Hurley
1984
HOT DOG...THE MOVIE(1984)

Russell Hurley
INSIDE LOOKING OUT(1977, Aus.), ed

Dolores Hurlic
JEZEBEL(1938)

Lucky Hurlic
HELLDORADO(1935)

Philip Hurlic
PENROD AND SAM(1937); PENROD AND HIS TWIN BROTHER(1938); PENROD'S DOUBLE TROUBLE(1938)

Phillip Hurlic
SCATTERGOOD RIDES HIGH(1942)

Phillip [Lucky] Hurlic
HEARTS DIVIDED(1936); WINGS OVER HONOLULU(1937); JEZEBEL(1938)

Phillip Hurlick
GOLDEN HOOFS(1941)

Philip Hurlie
ADVENTURES OF TOM SAWYER, THE(1938)

Phillip Hurlie
ZENOBIA(1939); FATHER'S SON(1941); TALES OF MANHATTAN(1942)

Silvia Hurlimann
PEDESTRIAN, THE(1974, Ger.)

H. Hurlock
Silents
LEAD, KINDLY LIGHT(1918, Brit.), w

Douglas Hurn
WOMAN FOR JOE, THE(1955, Brit.)

Philip D. Hurn
WINGS IN THE DARK(1935), w

Philip Hurn
Silents
PINK TIGHTS(1920), w; TORRENT, THE(1921), w; HANDLE WITH CARE(1922), ph; ROAD HOUSE(1928), w
Misc. Silents
FRAMING FRAMERS(1918), d

Phillip Hurn
Silents
SIREN CALL, THE(1922), w

Richard Hurndall
HOSTILE WITNESS(1968, Brit.); JOANNA(1968, Brit.); SOME GIRLS DO(1969, Brit.); I, MONSTER(1971, Brit.); ZEPPELIN(1971, Brit.); LADY CAROLINE LAMB(1972, Brit./Ital.); GAWAIN AND THE GREEN KNIGHT(1973, Brit.)

William Hurndell
FOLLOW THAT CAMEL(1967, Brit.)

Arthur Hurni
ANGEL(1937); I MET HIM IN PARIS(1937)

Yoshitami Huroiwa
BUSHIDO BLADE, THE(1982 Brit./U.S.), ed

Sol Hurok
TONIGHT WE SING(1953), w

Tom Huron
NOTORIOUS CLEOPATRA, THE(1970)

Kristina Hurrell
GOODBYE GIRL, THE(1977)

Bonnie Hurren
THAT LUCKY TOUCH(1975, Brit.)

Sherry Hursey
ALMOST SUMMER(1978)

Edmond Hurshell
MERRY WIVES OF WINDSOR, THE(1966, Aust.)

D. S. Hursley
SLIGHTLY SCANDALOUS(1946), spec eff

D.S. Hursley
TIME OF THEIR LIVES, THE(1946), spec eff

Brandon Hurst
INTERFERENCE(1928); GREENE MURDER CASE, THE(1929); HER PRIVATE LIFE(1929); WOLF OF WALL STREET, THE(1929); EYES OF THE WORLD, THE(1930); HIGH SOCIETY BLUES(1930); CONNECTICUT YANKEE, A(1931); MURDER AT MIDNIGHT(1931); RIGHT OF WAY, THE(1931); DOWN TO EARTH(1932); MIDNIGHT LADY(1932); MURDERS IN THE RUE MORGUE(1932); SHERLOCK HOLMES(1932); WHITE ZOMBIE(1932); BRIGHT EYES(1934); HOUSE OF MYSTERY(1934); LOST PATROL, THE,(1934); VIVA VILLA!(1934); GREAT IMPERSONATION, THE(1935); RED MORNING(1935); WHILE THE PATIENT SLEPT(1935); WOMAN IN RED, THE(1935); CHARGE OF THE LIGHT BRIGADE, THE(1936); MARY OF SCOTLAND(1936); MOON'S OUR HOME, THE(1936); PLOUGH AND THE STARS, THE(1936); FIREFLY, THE(1937); MAID OF SALEM(1937); MAYTIME(1937); WEE WILLIE WINKIE(1937); FOUR MEN AND A PRAYER(1938); KIDNAPPED(1938); PROFESSOR BEWARE(1938); SUEZ(1938); EAST SIDE OF HEAVEN(1939); STANLEY AND LIVINGSTONE(1939); TELL NO TALES(1939); HOWARDS OF VIRGINIA, THE(1940); IF I HAD MY WAY(1940); RHYTHM ON THE RIVER(1940); SIGN OF THE WOLF(1941); GHOST OF FRANKENSTEIN, THE(1942); MAD MARTINDALES, THE(1942); PIED PIPER, THE(1942); REMARKABLE ANDREW, THE(1942); ROAD TO HAPPINESS(1942); ROAD TO MOROCCO(1942); TENNESSEE JOHNSON(1942); DIXIE(1943); LEOPARD MAN, THE(1943); THANK YOUR LUCKY STARS(1943); ADVENTURES OF MARK TWAIN, THE(1944); HOUSE OF FRANKENSTEIN(1944); JANE EYRE(1944); MAN IN HALF-MOON STREET, THE(1944); MRS. PARKINGTON(1944); PRINCESS AND THE PIRATE, THE(1944); SHINE ON, HARVEST MOON(1944); CORN IS GREEN, THE(1945); ROAD TO UTOPIA(1945); SAN ANTONIO(1945); SPANISH MAIN, THE(1945); DEVOTION(1946); MAGNIFICENT DOLL(1946); MONSIEUR BEAUCAIRE(1946); MY FAVORITE BRUNETTE(1947); MY WILD IRISH ROSE(1947); ROAD TO RIO(1947); WELCOME STRANGER(1947); WHERE THERE'S LIFE(1947)
Silents
DR. JEKYLL AND MR. HYDE(1920); HUNCHBACK OF NOTRE DAME, THE(1923); LEGALLY DEAD(1923); CYTHEREA(1924); HE WHO GETS SLAPPED(1924); THIEF OF BAGDAD, THE(1924); AMATEUR GENTLEMAN, THE(1926); ENCHANTED HILL, THE(1926); GRAND DUCHESS AND THE WAITER, THE(1926); RAINMAKER, THE(1926); VOLCANO(1926); ANNIE LAURIE(1927); KING OF KINGS, THE(1927); LOVE(1927); MAN WHO LAUGHS, THE(1927); SEVENTH HEAVEN(1927); NEWS PARADE, THE(1928)
Misc. Silents
VIA WIRELESS(1915); DARK LANTERN, A(1920); LADY, THE(1925)

Brent Hurst
ACE ELI AND RODGER OF THE SKIES(1973)

Brian Desmond Hurst
BUCKET OF BLOOD(1934, Brit.), d; NORAH O'NEALE(1934, Brit.), d&w; SENSATION(1936, Brit.), d; GLAMOROUS NIGHT(1937, Brit.), d; TENTH MAN, THE(1937, Brit.), d; PRISON WITHOUT BARS(1939, Brit.), d; FUGITIVE, THE(1940, Brit.), d, w; LION HAS WINGS, THE(1940, Brit.), d; SUICIDE SQUADRON(1942, Brit.), d, w; ALIBI, THE(1943, Brit.), d; HUNDRED POUND WINDOW, THE(1943, Brit.), d; HUNGRY HILL(1947, Brit.), d; MARK OF CAIN, THE(1948, Brit.), d; GAY LADY, THE(1949, Brit.), d; CHRISTMAS CAROL, A(1951, Brit.), d; TOM BROWN'S SCHOOLDAYS(1951, Brit.), p; MALTA STORY(1954, Brit.), d; SIMBA(1955, Brit.), d; BLACK TENT, THE(1956, Brit.), d; BEHIND THE MASK(1958, Brit.), d; DANGEROUS EXILE(1958, Brit.), d; HIS AND HERS(1961, Brit.), d; PLAYBOY OF THE WESTERN WORLD, THE(1963, Ireland), d&w

David Hurst
PERFECT WOMAN, THE(1950, Brit.); TONY DRAWS A HORSE(1951, Brit.); MR. POTTS GOES TO MOSCOW(1953, Brit.); SHOOT FIRST(1953, Brit.); SO LITTLE TIME(1953, Brit.); ALWAYS A BRIDE(1954, Brit.); MAD ABOUT MEN(1954, Brit.); RIVER BEAT(1954); ONE GOOD TURN(1955, Brit.); ALL FOR MARY(1956, Brit.); AFTER THE BALL(1957, Brit.); AS LONG AS THEY'RE HAPPY(1957, Brit.); MY SON, THE VAMPIRE(1963, Brit.); QUICK, LET'S GET MARRIED(1965); HELLO, DOLLY!(1969); MALTESE BIPPY, THE(1969); KELLY'S HEROES(1970, U.S./Yugo.); BOYS FROM BRAZIL, THE(1978)

Denise Hurst
MR. H. C. ANDERSEN(1950, Brit.)

Fannie Hurst
PAINTED ANGEL, THE(1929), w; YOUNGER GENERATION(1929), w; BACK PAY(1930), w; LUMMOX(1930), w; FIVE AND TEN(1931), w; BACK STREET(1932), w; SYMPHONY OF SIX MILLION(1932), w; IMITATION OF LIFE(1934), w; FOUR DAUGHTERS(1938), w; FOUR WIVES(1939), w; SKELETON ON HORSEBACK(1940, Czech.), ed, titles; BACK STREET(1941), w; FOUR MOTHERS(1941), w; HUMORESQUE(1946), w; IMITATION OF LIFE(1959), w; BACK STREET(1961), w
Silents
HER GREAT CHANCE(1918), w; PETAL ON THE CURRENT, THE(1919), w; JUST AROUND THE CORNER(1921), w; STARDUST(1921), w; NTH COMMANDMENT, THE(1923), w; UNTAMED LADY, THE(1926), w

Fanny Hurst
HELLO, EVERYBODY(1933), w; YOUNG AT HEART(1955), w

George Hurst
FOLLY TO BE WISE(1953); KID FOR TWO FARTHINGS, A(1956, Brit.)

Gordon Hurst
LAST PICTURE SHOW, THE(1971); SUGARLAND EXPRESS, THE(1974); DRIVE-IN(1976); NICKELODEON(1976); SILVER STREAK(1976)

Hawthorne Hurst
GOLDIE GETS ALONG(1933), w

Hillary Hurst
BORN IN FLAMES(1983)

Margaret Hurst
MEET THE NAVY(1946, Brit.)

Patrick Hurst
WHIRLWIND RAIDERS(1948)

Paul Hurst
HIS FIRST COMMAND(1929); OH, YEAH!(1929); RACKETEER, THE(1929); SAILORS' HOLIDAY(1929); BORROWED WIVES(1930); HOT CURVES(1930); LOTTERY BRIDE, THE(1930); MOUNTAIN JUSTICE(1930); OFFICER O'BRIEN(1930); PARADISE ISLAND(1930); RUNAWAY BRIDE(1930); SHADOW OF THE LAW(1930);

SWELLHEAD, THE(1930); THIRD ALARM, THE(1930); BAD COMPANY(1931); KICK IN(1931); PUBLIC DEFENDER, THE(1931); SECRET SIX, THE(1931); SECRET WITNESS, THE(1931); SINGLE SIN(1931); SWEEPSTAKES(1931); BIG STAMPEDE, THE(1932); HOLD'EM JAIL(1932); MY PAL, THE KING(1932); PANAMA FLO(1932); PHANTOM PRESIDENT, THE(1932); THIRTEENTH GUEST, THE(1932); DAY OF RECKONING(1933); HOLD YOUR MAN(1933); ISLAND OF LOST SOULS(1933); MEN ARE SUCH FOOLS(1933); OUT ALL NIGHT(1933); QUEEN CHRISTINA(1933); SATURDAY'S MILLIONS(1933); SPHINX, THE(1933); TERROR ABOARD(1933); TUGBOAT ANNIE(1933); AMONG THE MISSING(1934); BIG RACE, THE(1934); LINEUP, THE(1934); MIDNIGHT ALIBI(1934); SEQUOIA(1934); TAKE THE STAND(1934); WOMEN IN HIS LIFE, THE(1934); CALM YOURSELF(1935); CASE OF THE CURIOUS BRIDE, THE(1935); GAY DECEPTION, THE(1935); MISSISSIPPI(1935); PUBLIC HERO NO. 1(1935); SHADOW OF A DOUBT(1935); STAR OF MIDNIGHT(1935); TOMORROW'S YOUTH(1935); WILDERNESS MAIL(1935); BLACKMAILER(1936); GAY DESPERADO, THE(1936); I'D GIVE MY LIFE(1936); IT HAD TO HAPPEN(1936); MR. DEEDS GOES TO TOWN(1936); RIFF-RAFF(1936); ROBIN HOOD OF EL DORADO(1936); TO MARY–WITH LOVE(1936); ALI BABA GOES TO TOWN(1937); ANGEL'S HOLIDAY(1937); DANGER–LOVE AT WORK(1937); FIFTY ROADS TO TOWN(1937); LADY FIGHTS BACK(1937); LEGION OF MISSING MEN(1937); NORTH OF NOME(1937); SECOND HONEYMOON(1937); SHE'S NO LADY(1937); SLAVE SHIP(1937); SMALL TOWN BOY(1937); SUPER SLEUTH(1937); THIS IS MY AFFAIR(1937); TROUBLE IN MOROCCO(1937); WAKE UP AND LIVE(1937); WE WHO ARE ABOUT TO DIE(1937); WIFE, DOCTOR AND NURSE(1937); YOU CAN'T BEAT LOVE(1937); YOU CAN'T HAVE EVERYTHING(1937); ALEXANDER'S RAGTIME BAND(1938); HOLD THAT CO-ED(1938); IN OLD CHICAGO(1938); ISLAND IN THE SKY(1938); JOSETTE(1938); LAST EXPRESS, THE(1938); MY LUCKY STAR(1938); NO TIME TO MARRY(1938); PRISON BREAK(1938); REBECCA OF SUNNYBROOK FARM(1938); SECRETS OF A NURSE(1938); THANKS FOR EVERYTHING(1938); BAD LANDS(1939); BROADWAY SERENADE(1939); CAFE SOCIETY(1939); EACH DAWN I DIE(1939); IT COULD HAPPEN TO YOU(1939); KID FROM KOKOMO, THE(1939); ON YOUR TOES(1939); QUICK MILLIONS(1939); REMEMBER?(1939); TOPPER TAKES A TRIP(1939); BOWERY BOY(1940); EDISON, THE MAN(1940); SOUTH TO KARANGA(1940); STAR DUST(1940); THEY DRIVE BY NIGHT(1940); TORRID ZONE(1940); TUGBOAT ANNIE SAILS AGAIN(1940); WESTERNER, THE(1940); CAUGHT IN THE DRAFT(1941); ELLERY QUEEN AND THE MURDER RING(1941); GREAT MR. NOBODY, THE(1941); PARSON OF PANAMINT, THE(1941); PETTICOAT POLITICS(1941); TALL, DARK AND HANDSOME(1941); THIS WOMAN IS MINE(1941); VIRGINIA(1941); DUDES ARE PRETTY PEOPLE(1942); NIGHT IN NEW ORLEANS, A(1942); PARDON MY STRIPES(1942); SUNDOWN JIM(1942); CONEY ISLAND(1943); HI'YA, CHUM(1943); JACK LONDON(1943); OX-BOW INCIDENT, THE(1943); SKY'S THE LIMIT, THE(1943); YOUNG AND WILLING(1943); BARBARY COAST GENT(1944); GHOST THAT WALKS ALONE, THE(1944); GIRL RUSH(1944); GREENWICH VILLAGE(1944); SOMETHING FOR THE BOYS(1944); SUMMER STORM(1944); BIG SHOW-OFF, THE(1945); DAKOTA(1945); DOLLY SISTERS, THE(1945); HER LUCKY NIGHT(1945); ONE EXCITING NIGHT(1945); PENTHOUSE RHYTHM(1945); SCARED STIFF(1945); STEPPIN' IN SOCIETY(1945); IN OLD SACRAMENTO(1946); MURDER IN THE MUSIC HALL(1946); PLAINSMAN AND THE LADY(1946); ANGEL AND THE BADMAN(1947); UNDER COLORADO SKIES(1947); ARIZONA RANGER, THE(1948); CALIFORNIA FIREBRAND(1948); GUN SMUGGLERS(1948); HEART OF VIRGINIA(1948); MADONNA OF THE DESERT(1948); SON OF GOD'S COUNTRY(1948); YELLOW SKY(1948); LAW OF THE GOLDEN WEST(1949); OUTCASTS OF THE TRAIL(1949); PRINCE OF THE PLAINS(1949); RANGER OF CHEROKEE STRIP(1949); SAN ANTONE AMBUSH(1949); SOUTH OF RIO(1949); MISSOURIANS, THE(1950); OLD FRONTIER, THE(1950); PIONEER MARSHAL(1950); VANISHING WESTERNER, THE(1950); MILLION DOLLAR PURSUIT(1951); BIG JIM McLAIN(1952); TOUGHEST MAN IN ARIZONA(1952); SUN SHINES BRIGHT, THE(1953)

Silents

KINGFISHER'S ROOST, THE(1922), d&w; BRANDED A BANDIT(1924), d; FIGHTING CUB, THE(1925), d; HAUNTED RANGE, THE(1926), d; LAW OF THE SNOW COUNTRY, THE(1926), d; MIDNIGHT MESSAGE, THE(1926), d; MAN FROM HARDPAN, THE(1927); LAWLESS LEGION, THE(1929)

Misc. Silents

INVISIBLE POWER, THE(1914), Cleo Ridgely; RIMROCK JONES(1918); BLACK SHEEP(1921), d; SHADOWS OF THE WEST(1921), d; CROW'S NEST, THE(1922), d; HEART OF A TEXAN, THE(1922), d; TABLE TOP RANCH(1922), d; GOLDEN SILENCE(1923), d; COURAGEOUS COWARD, THE(1924), d; PASSING OF WOLF MacLEAN, THE(1924), d; BATTLING BUNYON(1925), d; DEMON RIDER, THE(1925), d; GOLD HUNTERS, THE(1925), d; RATTLER, THE(1925), d; SON OF SONTAG, THE(1925), d; WESTERN ENGAGEMENT, A(1925), d; BATTLING KID(1926), d; BLUE STREAK O'NEIL(1926), d; FIGHTING RANGER(1926), d; HIGH HAND, THE(1926); ROARING ROAD(1926), d; SHADOWS OF CHINATOWN(1926), d; SON OF A GUN(1926), d; BUTTONS(1927); RANGE RAIDER, THE(1927), d; RED RAIDERS, THE(1927); RIDER OF THE LAW(1927); CALIFORNIA MAIL, THE(1929)

Paul C. Hurst

Silents

JUDITH OF THE CUMBERLANDS(1916)

Misc. Silents

DIAMOND RUNNERS, THE(1916); MANAGER OF THE B&A, THE(1916); MEDICINE BEND(1916); WHISPERING SMITH(1916)

Paul Causey Hurst

ON OUR MERRY WAY(1948)

Peter Hurst

GHOST STORY(1974, Brit.), ph

1984

SWORD OF THE VALIANT(1984, Brit.), ph

Ralph Hurst

GUY NAMED JOE, A(1943), set d; SEE HERE, PRIVATE HARGROVE(1944), set d; DESPERATE SEARCH(1952), set d; SKY FULL OF MOON(1952), set d; ABOVE AND BEYOND(1953), set d; ESCAPE FROM FORT BRAVO(1953), set d; TRACK OF THE CAT(1954), set d; GREEN FIRE(1955), set d; GIANT(1956), prod d; LAFAYETTE ESCADRILLE(1958), set d; OLD MAN AND THE SEA, THE(1958), set d; PLAY MISTY FOR ME(1971), set d

Ralph C. Hurst

MAN WHO LOVED CAT DANCING, THE(1973), set d

Ralph S. Hurst

THIRTY SECONDS OVER TOKYO(1944), set d; KEEP YOUR POWDER DRY(1945), set d; THEY WERE EXPENDABLE(1945), set d; SHOW-OFF, THE(1946), set d; HIGH BARBAREE(1947), set d; INTRUDER IN THE DUST(1949), set d; STRATTON STORY, THE(1949), set d; MYSTERY STREET(1950), set d; TO PLEASE A LADY(1950), set d;

WESTWARD THE WOMEN(1951), set d; FBI STORY, THE(1959), set d; RIO BRAVO(1959), set d; SINS OF RACHEL CADE, THE(1960), set d; MAJORITY OF ONE, A(1961), set d; GYPSY(1962), set d; MARY, MARY(1963), set d; SPENCER'S MOUNTAIN(1963), set d; MY BLOOD RUNS COLD(1965), set d; NEVER TOO LATE(1965), set d; THIRD DAY, THE(1965), set d; YOUNG FURY(1965), set d; COVENANT WITH DEATH, A(1966), set d; COOL ONES THE(1967), set d; COUNTDOWN(1968), set d; SWEET NOVEMBER(1968), set d; GOOD GUYS AND THE BAD GUYS, THE(1969), set d; WHERE IT'S AT(1969), set d; FLAP(1970), set d; WILLARD(1971), set d

Richard Hurst

EXECUTIVE ACTION(1973)

Misc. Talkies

TO HELL YOU PREACH(1972)

Richard D. Hurst

W. W. AND THE DIXIE DANCEKINGS(1975)

Rick Hurst

UNHOLY ROLLERS(1972); TUNNELVISION(1976); CAT FROM OUTER SPACE, THE(1978); GOING APE!(1981)

Roy Hurst

SAVAGE(1962)

Veronica Hurst

LAUGHTER IN PARADISE(1951, Brit.); GIRL ON THE PIER, THE(1953, Brit.); MAZE, THE(1953); ROYAL AFRICAN RIFLES, THE(1953); YELLOW BALLOON, THE(1953, Brit.); ANGELS ONE FIVE(1954, Brit.); BANG! YOU'RE DEAD(1954, Brit.); DON'T BLAME THE STORK(1954, Brit.); GILDED CAGE, THE(1954, Brit.); WILL ANY GENTLEMAN?(1955, Brit.); PEEPING TOM(1960, Brit.); DEAD MAN'S EVIDENCE(1962, Brit.); SING AND SWING(1964, Brit.); SECOND BEST SECRET AGENT IN THE WHOLE WIDE WORLD, THE(1965, Brit.); BOY CRIED MURDER, THE(1966, Ger./Brit./Yugo.)

Vida Hurst

BLIND DATE(1934), w; HONEYMOON LIMITED(1936), w; TANGO(1936), w

Gareth Hurt

Misc. Talkies

AND THE WALL CAME TUMBLING DOWN(1984)

Isabel Hurt

MYTH, THE(1965, Ital.)

J. D. Hurt

ALAMBRISTA!(1977)

James Hurt

1984

RIVER RAT, THE(1984)

John Hurt

THIS IS MY STREET(1964, Brit.); YOUNG AND WILLING(1964, Brit.); MAN FOR ALL SEASONS, A(1966, Brit.); SAILOR FROM GIBRALTAR, THE(1967, Brit.); BEFORE WINTER COMES(1969, Brit.); SINFUL DAVEY(1969, Brit.); IN SEARCH OF GREGORY(1970, Brit./Ital.); 10 RILLINGTON PLACE(1971, Brit.); CRY OF THE PENGUINS(1972, Brit.); PIED PIPER, THE(1972, Brit.); LITTLE MALCOLM(1974, Brit.); GHOUL, THE(1975, Brit.); EAST OF ELEPHANT ROCK(1976, Brit.); MIDNIGHT EXPRESS(1978, Brit.); SHOUT, THE(1978, Brit.); WATERSHIP DOWN(1978, Brit.); ALIEN(1979); ELEPHANT MAN, THE(1980, Brit.); HEAVEN'S GATE(1980); DISAPPEARANCE, THE(1981, Brit./Can.); HISTORY OF THE WORLD, PART 1(1981); NIGHT CROSSING(1982); PARTNERS(1982); OSTERMAN WEEKEND, THE(1983)

1984

CHAMPIONS(1984); PLAGUE DOGS, THE(1984, U.S./Brit.); SUCCESS IS THE BEST REVENGE(1984, Brit.); 1984(1984, Brit.)

Mary Beth Hurt

CHILLY SCENES OF WINTER(1982); WORLD ACCORDING TO GARP, The(1982)

Marybeth Hurt

INTERIORS(1978); CHANGE OF SEASONS, A(1980)

Morrigan Hurt

DEVONSVILLE TERROR, THE(1983)

Wesley Ivan Hurt

POPEYE(1980)

William Hurt

ALTERED STATES(1980); BODY HEAT(1981); EYEWITNESS(1981); BIG CHILL, THE(1983); GORKY PARK(1983)

Carlos Hurtado

TEXICAN, THE(1966, U.S./Span.)

Juan Jose Hurtado

SEVEN CITIES OF GOLD(1955)

Luis Hurtado

SPIRIT AND THE FLESH, THE(1948, Ital.)

Teresa Hurtado

HOUSE THAT SCREAMED, THE(1970, Span.)

Albert Hurter

PINOCCHIO(1940), art d

Hettie Lynne Hurtes

1984

TERMINATOR, THE(1984)

Angelika Hurwicz

OUR DAILY BREAD(1950, Ger.)

Alvin Hurwitz

JULIUS CAESAR(1953)

Harry Hurwitz

PROJECTIONIST, THE(1970), a, p,d,w&ed; RICHARD(1972), d, w; UNDER THE RAINBOW(1981), w; COMEBACK TRAIL, THE(1982), p,d&w, ed; SAFARI 3000(1982), d

1984

ROSEBUD BEACH HOTEL(1984), p, d

Steve Hurwitz

1984

LONELY GUY, THE(1984)

Tom D. Hurwitz

1984

WHITE ELEPHANT(1984, Brit.), ph

Tom Hurwitz

1984

HARD CHOICES(1984), ph

Victor Hurwitz
LAST HOUSE ON THE LEFT(1972), ph
Edward Husbach
BEST MAN WINS(1948), w
Bergliot Husberg
Misc. Silents
MAN THERE WAS, A(1917, Swed.)
Rolf Husberg
COUNT OF THE MONK'S BRIDGE, THE(1934, Swed.), ed; CHILDREN, THE(1949, Swed.), d, w; MAKE WAY FOR LILA(1962, Swed./Ger.), d, w
Knut Husebo
FLIGHT OF THE EAGLE(1983, Swed.)
Theis Ib Husfelt
Z.P.G.(1972)
Lisabeth Hush
THOROUGHLY MODERN MILLIE(1967); THREAT, THE(1960); X-15(1961); BUS RILEY'S BACK IN TOWN(1965); STONE KILLER, THE(1973)
Tom Hush
SECRET OF NIMH, THE(1982), spec eff
Ted Husing
TO PLEASE A LADY(1950)
Ferlin Husky
MISTER ROCK AND ROLL(1957); COUNTRY MUSIC HOLIDAY(1958); FORTY ACRE FEUD(1965); LAS VEGAS HILLBILLYS(1966); HILLBILLYS IN A HAUNTED HOUSE(1967)
Ron Husmann
LOVE HAS MANY FACES(1965)
Paul Huson
RICHARD III(1956, Brit.)
Jon Huss
Misc. Talkies
PREMONITION(1972)
Talat Hussain
PRIVATES ON PARADE(1982)
1984
PRIVATES ON PARADE(1984, Brit.)
Zakir Hussain
HEAT AND DUST(1983, Brit.)
Zafir Hussaini
ISLAND OF ALLAH(1956)
Sanny Bin Hussan
WINDOM'S WAY(1958, Brit.)
Aisha Hussein
LION OF THE DESERT(1981, Libya/Brit.)
Anwar Hussein
GUIDE, THE(1965, U.S./India)
Sanny Bin Hussein
TOWN LIKE ALICE, A(1958, Brit.)
Waris Hussein
THANK YOU ALL VERY MUCH(1969, Brit.), d; QUACKSER FORTUNE HAS A COUSIN IN THE BRONX(1970), d; MELODY(1971, Brit.), d; HENRY VIII AND HIS SIX WIVES(1972, Brit.), d; POSSESSION OF JOEL DELANEY, THE(1972), d
Hassan Husseiny
CIRCLE OF DECEIT(1982, Fr./Ger.)
Isaaf Husseiny
CIRCLE OF DECEIT(1982, Fr./Ger.)
Oliver Hussenot
AMAZING MONSIEUR FABRE, THE(1952, Fr.); VOYAGE TO AMERICA(1952, Fr.); SECRET DOCUMENT – VIENNA(1954, Fr.); BEDEVILLED(1955)
Olivia Hussenot
UTOPIA(1952, Fr./Ital.)
Olivier Hussenot
FANFAN THE TULIP(1952, Fr.); OBSESSION(1954, Fr./Ital.); MAIGRET LAYS A TRAP(1958, Fr.); ROOTS OF HEAVEN, THE(1958); GUNMEN OF THE RIO GRANDE(1965, Fr./Ital./Span.); FLEA IN HER EAR, A(1968, Fr.)
Olivier Hussenote
GRAND MANEUVER, THE(1956, Fr.)
John A. Hussey
STERILE CUCKOO, THE(1969)
John Hussey
PERSECUTION AND ASSASSINATION OF JEAN-PAUL MARAT AS PERFORMED BY THE INMATES OF THE ASYLUM OF CHARENTON UNDER THE DIRECTION OF THE MARQUIS DE SADE, THE(1967, Brit.); TELL ME LIES(1968, Brit.); OH! WHAT A LOVELY WAR(1969, Brit.); GET CARTER(1971, Brit.); RECKONING, THE(1971, Brit.); GOLD(1974, Brit.)
Olivia Hussey
BATTLE OF THE VILLA FIORITA, THE(1965, Brit.); ROMEO AND JULIET(1968, Brit./Ital.); ALL THE RIGHT NOISES(1973, Brit.); LOST HORIZON(1973); SUMMERTIME KILLER(1973); BLACK CHRISTMAS(1974, Can.); DEATH ON THE NILE(1978, Brit.); CAT AND THE CANARY, THE(1979, Brit.); MAN WITH BOGART'S FACE, THE(1980); VIRUS(1980, Jap.); ESCAPE 2000(1983, Aus.)
Ruth Hussey
MADAME X(1937); HOLD THAT KISS(1938); JUDGE HARDY'S CHILDREN(1938); MAN-PROOF(1938); MARIE ANTOINETTE(1938); RICH MAN, POOR GIRL(1938); SPRING MADNESS(1938); TIME OUT FOR MURDER(1938); ANOTHER THIN MAN(1939); BLACKMAIL(1939); FAST AND FURIOUS(1939); HONOLULU(1939); MAISIE(1939); WITHIN THE LAW(1939); WOMEN, THE(1939); FLIGHT COMMAND(1940); NORTHWEST PASSAGE(1940); PHILADELPHIA STORY, THE(1940); SUSAN AND GOD(1940); FREE AND EASY(1941); H.M. PULHAM, ESQ.(1941); MARRIED BACHELOR(1941); OUR WIFE(1941); PIERRE OF THE PLAINS(1942); TENNESSEE JOHNSON(1942); TENDER COMRADE(1943); MARINE RAIDERS(1944); UNINVITED, THE(1944); BEDSIDE MANNER(1945); I, JANE DOE(1948); GREAT GATSBY, THE(1949); LOUISA(1950); MR. MUSIC(1950); THAT'S MY BOY(1951); STARS AND STRIPES FOREVER(1952); WOMAN OF THE NORTH COUNTRY(1952); LADY WANTS MINK, THE(1953); FACTS OF LIFE, THE(1960)
Misc. Talkies
THAT I MAY SEE(1953)

Sue Hussey
THUNDERING TRAIL, THE(1951); VANISHING OUTPOST, THE(1951)
Will Hussing
MAN CALLED ADAM, A(1966); LOOKING UP(1977)
Albert Husson
WE'RE NO ANGELS(1955), w; WHERE THE TRUTH LIES(1962, Fr.), w; TRAIN, THE(1965, Fr./Ital./U.S.), w
Will Hussong
ZELIG(1983)
Will Hussung
LEGEND OF NIGGER CHARLEY, THE(1972)
1984
ALMOST YOU(1984)
J. Roy Hust
WHY BRING THAT UP?(1929), ph
Zdenek Hustak
JOURNEY TO THE BEGINNING OF TIME(1966, Czech)
Charles Husted
Misc. Silents
HIGH SPEED(1920)
Francis Huster
LUMIERE(1976, Fr.); ANOTHER MAN, ANOTHER CHANCE(1977 Fr/US); ADOLESCENT, THE(1978, Fr./W.Ger.); BOLERO(1982, Fr.)
1984
EDITH AND MARCEL(1984, Fr.)
Al Hustin
WOMAN OBSESSED(1959)
Pat Hustis
HEROES(1977)
1984
STONE BOY, THE(1984)
Anjelica Huston
HAMLET(1969, Brit.); WALK WITH LOVE AND DEATH, A(1969); LAST TYCOON, THE(1976); SWASHBUCKLER(1976); POSTMAN ALWAYS RINGS TWICE, THE(1981)
1984
ICE PIRATES, THE(1984); THIS IS SPINAL TAP(1984)
Anthony Huston
JOURNEY TO THE BEGINNING OF TIME(1966, Czech), ph
Brick Huston
WRECKING CREW, THE(1968)
Craig Huston
FIRST BLOOD(1982)
Dulcie Huston
1984
SUPERGIRL(1984)
Fred Huston
Silents
MAN FROM HEADQUARTERS(1928)
J. Wesley Huston
48 HOURS(1982)
Jimmy Huston
SEABO(1978), d, ed; FINAL EXAM(1981), d&w
Misc. Talkies
DEATH DRIVER(1977), d; DARK SUNDAY(1978), d
John Huston
HOUSE DIVIDED, A(1932), w; LAW AND ORDER(1932), w; MURDERS IN THE RUE MORGUE(1932), w; DEATH DRIVES THROUGH(1935, Brit.), w; IT HAPPENED IN PARIS(1935, Brit.), w; AMAZING DR. CLITTERHOUSE, THE(1938), w; JEZEBEL(1938), w; JUAREZ(1939), w; DR. EHRLICH'S MAGIC BULLET(1940), w; HIGH SIERRA(1941), w; MALTESE FALCON, THE(1941), d, w; ACROSS THE PACIFIC(1942), d; IN THIS OUR LIFE(1942), d, w; KILLERS, THE(1946), w; STRANGER THE(1946), w; THREE STRANGERS(1946), w; KEY LARGO(1948), d; TREASURE OF THE SIERRA MADRE, THE(1948), d, w; WE WERE STRANGERS(1949), w; ASPHALT JUNGLE, THE(1950), d, w; AFRICAN QUEEN, THE(1951, U.S./Brit.), d, w; RED BADGE OF COURAGE, THE(1951), d&w; MOULIN ROUGE(1952), p&d, w; BEAT THE DEVIL(1953), d, w; MOBY DICK(1956, Brit.), p, d, w; HEAVEN KNOWS, MR. ALLISON(1957), d, w; BARBARIAN AND THE GEISHA, THE(1958), d; ROOTS OF HEAVEN, THE(1958), d; UNFORGIVEN, THE(1960), d; MISFITS, THE(1961), d; FREUD(1962), d; CARDINAL, THE(1963), a; LIST OF ADRIAN MESSENGER, THE(1963), a, d; NIGHT OF THE IGUANA, THE(1964), d, w; BIBLE...IN THE BEGINNING, THE(1966), a, d; CASINO ROYALE(1967, Brit.), a, d; REFLECTIONS IN A GOLDEN EYE(1967), d; CANDY(1968, Ital./Fr.), a; DE SADE(1969); SINFUL DAVEY(1969, Brit.), d; WALK WITH LOVE AND DEATH, A(1969), a, d; KREMLIN LETTER, THE(1970), a, d, w; DESERTER, THE(1971 Ital./Yugo.); MAN IN THE WILDERNESS(1971, U.S./Span.); FAT CITY(1972), d; LIFE AND TIMES OF JUDGE ROY BEAN, THE(1972), a, d; BATTLE FOR THE PLANET OF THE APES(1973); MACKINTOSH MAN, THE(1973, Brit.), d; CHINATOWN(1974); BREAKOUT(1975); MAN WHO WOULD BE KING, THE(1975, Brit.), d, w; WIND AND THE LION, THE(1975); ANGELA(1977, Can.); TENTACLES(1977, Ital.); DELIRIUM(1979), ph; JAGUAR LIVES(1979); WINTER KILLS(1979); WISE BLOOD(1979, U.S./Ger.), a, d; PHOBIA(1980, Can.), d; VISITOR, THE(1980, Ital./U.S.); HEAD ON(1981, Can.); VICTORY(1981), d; ANNIE(1982), d; CANNERY ROW(1982); LOVESICK(1983); YOUNG GIANTS(1983)
1984
UNDER THE VOLCANO(1984), d
Misc. Talkies
BRIDGE IN THE JUNGLE, THE(1971)
Silents
ACQUITTAL, THE(1923), w
Karen Huston
VON RICHTHOFEN AND BROWN(1970)
Marty Huston
Misc. Talkies
CALLIOPE(1971)
Michael Huston
LADY CHATTERLEY'S LOVER(1981, Fr./Brit.)
Patricia Huston
PARATROOP COMMAND(1959); EXPERIMENT IN TERROR(1962); HOUSE OF WOMEN(1962); FANNY HILL: MEMOIRS OF A WOMAN OF PLEASURE zero(1965)

Patt Huston
BONNIE PARKER STORY, THE(1958)
Paul Huston
DEVIL'S PIPELINE, THE(1940), w; SKI PATROL(1940), w; MUTINY IN THE ARCTIC(1941), w; DRUMS OF THE CONGO(1942), w
Phil Huston
CLOSE-UP(1948)
Philip Huston
BEHIND THE HEADLINES(1937); MAN WHO FOUND HIMSELF, THE(1937); WE'RE ON THE JURY(1937)
Roy Huston
MOONSHINER'S WOMAN(1968)
Tony Huston
CURSE OF THE SWAMP CREATURE(1966), w; FIVE THE HARD WAY(1969), w
Virginia Huston
NOCTURNE(1946); OUT OF THE PAST(1947); DOOLINS OF OKLAHOMA, THE(1949); FLAMINGO ROAD(1949); WOMAN FROM HEADQUARTERS(1950); FLIGHT TO MARS(1951); RACKET, THE(1951); TARZAN'S PERIL(1951); NIGHT STAGE TO GALVESTON(1952); SUDDEN FEAR(1952); KNOCK ON WOOD(1954)
Walter Anthony Huston
LIST OF ADRIAN MESSENGER, THE(1963)
Walter Huston
GENTLEMEN OF THE PRESS(1929); LADY LIES, THE(1929); VIRGINIAN, THE(1929); ABRAHAM LINCOLN(1930); BAD MAN, THE(1930); VIRTUOUS SIN, THE(1930); CRIMINAL CODE(1931); RULING VOICE, THE(1931); STAR WITNESS(1931); AMERICAN MADNESS(1932); BEAST OF THE CITY, THE(1932); HOUSE DIVIDED, A(1932); KONGO(1932); LAW AND ORDER(1932); NIGHT COURT(1932); RAIN(1932); WET PARADE, THE(1932); WOMAN FROM MONTE CARLO, THE(1932); ANN VICKERS(1933); GABRIEL OVER THE WHITE HOUSE(1933); HELL BELOW(1933); PRIZEFIGHTER AND THE LADY, THE(1933); STORM AT DAYBREAK(1933); KEEP 'EM ROLLING(1934); TRANSATLANTIC TUNNEL(1935, Brit.); DODSWORTH(1936); RHODES(1936, Brit.); OF HUMAN HEARTS(1938); LIGHT THAT FAILED, THE(1939); DEVIL AND DANIEL WEBSTER, THE(1941); MALTESE FALCON, THE(1941); SHANGHAI GESTURE, THE(1941); SWAMP WATER(1941); ALWAYS IN MY HEART(1942); IN THIS OUR LIFE(1942); YANKEE DOODLE DANDY(1942); EDGE OF DARKNESS(1943); MISSION TO MOSCOW(1943); NORTH STAR, THE(1943); OUTLAW, THE(1943); DRAGON SEED(1944); AND THEN THERE WERE NONE(1945); DRAGONWYCH(1946); DUEL IN THE SUN(1946); SUMMER HOLIDAY(1948); TREASURE OF THE SIERRA MADRE, THE(1948); GREAT SINNER, THE(1949); FURIES, THE(1950)
Alfred Hustwick
Silents
AFRAID TO LOVE(1927), t; ARIZONA BOUND(1927), t
Frank Huszar
TEENAGE THUNDER(1957), stunts
Karl Huszar-Puffy
BLUE ANGEL, THE(1930, Ger.); DIE MANNER UM LUCIE(1931)
Peter Huszti
FATHER(1967, Hung.)
Hutch
HOT MONEY GIRL(1962, Brit./Ger.)
Willie Hutch
MACK, THE(1973), m; FOXY DROWN(1974), m
Roy Hutchcroft
GAY PURR-EE(1962), ph
David Hutchenson
CONVOY(1940)
Bobby Hutcherson
THEY SHOOT HORSES, DON'T THEY?(1969)
LeVern Hutcherson
CARMEN JONES(1954)
David Hutcheson
FAST AND LOOSE(1930); ROMANCE IN RHYTHM(1934, Brit.); LOVE TEST, THE(1935, Brit.); WRATH OF JEALOUSY(1936, Brit.); SKY'S THE LIMIT, THE(1937, Brit.); THIS'LL MAKE YOU WHISTLE(1938, Brit.); GENTLEMAN'S GENTLEMAN, A(1939, Brit.); LUCKY TO ME(1939, Brit.); MIDDLE WATCH, THE(1939, Brit.); SHE COULDN'T SAY NO(1939, Brit.); BULLDOG SEES IT THROUGH(1940, Brit.); NEXT OF KIN(1942, Brit.); HUNDRED POUND WINDOW, THE(1943, Brit.); COLONEL BLIMP(1945, Brit.); SCHOOL FOR SECRETS(1946, Brit.); TROJAN BROTHERS, THE(1946); VICE VERSA(1948, Brit.); HOUR OF GLORY(1949, Brit.); MADNESS OF THE HEART(1949, Brit.); SLEEPING CAR TO TRIESTE(1949, Brit.); WOMAN HATER(1949, Brit.); NO HIGHWAY IN THE SKY(1951, Brit.); FIGHTING PIMPERNEL, THE(1950, Brit.); CIRCLE OF DANGER(1951, Brit.); ENCORE(1951, Brit.); OPERATION X(1951, Brit.); SOMETHING MONEY CAN'T BUY(1952, Brit.); LAW AND DISORDER(1958, Brit.); EVIL OF FRANKENSTEIN, THE(1964, Brit.); AMOROUS ADVENTURES OF MOLL FLANDERS, THE(1965); MAGIC CHRISTIAN, THE(1970, Brit.); ABOMINABLE DR. PHIBES, THE(1971, Brit.); PUBLIC EYE, THE(1972, Brit.); NATIONAL HEALTH, OR NURSE NORTON'S AFFAIR, THE(1973, Brit.)
David [Dave] Hutcheson
SABOTAGE AT SEA(1942, Brit.)
Jack Hutcheson
WHITE HUNTER(1965)
Sarah Hutcheson
EYES OF A STRANGER(1980)
Debbie Hutchings
MEMOIRS OF A SURVIVOR(1981, Brit.)
Fred Hutchings
SHOW GOES ON, THE(1937, Brit.)
Linda Hutchings
BEST OF EVERYTHING, THE(1959)
Bill Hutchins
GAMES THAT LOVERS PLAY(1971, Brit.), art d
Bobby "Wheezer" Hutchins
EXPOSED(1932)
Charles Hutchins
WRONG IS RIGHT(1982)
Linda Hutchins
LITTLE SHEPHERD OF KINGDOM COME(1961); MARINES, LET'S GO(1961); TENDER IS THE NIGHT(1961)

Miriam Hutchins
Silents
GOD'S HALF ACRE(1916)
Peter Hutchins
SALT & PEPPER(1968, Brit.); WORK IS A FOUR LETTER WORD(1968, Brit.); PUPPET ON A CHAIN(1971, Brit.)
Will Hutchins
LAFAYETTE ESCADRILLE(1958); NO TIME FOR SERGEANTS(1958); CLAUDELLE INGLISH(1961); MERRILL'S MARAUDERS(1962); SPINOUT(1966); CLAMBAKE(1967); SHOOTING, THE(1971); SLUMBER PARTY '57(1977)
A.S.M. Hutchinson
IF WINTER COMES(1947), w
Silents
ONCE ABOARD THE LUGGER(1920, Brit.), w
Belle Hutchinson
Misc. Silents
WHISPERING SMITH(1916)
Betty Hutchinson
Silents
DUST OF DESIRE(1919)
Bill Hutchinson
EXODUS(1960), art d; TRUNK, THE(1961, Brit.), art d; MAIN ATTRACTION, THE(1962, Brit.), art d; ROAD TO HONG KONG, THE(1962, U.S./Brit.), art d; LORD JIM(1965, Brit.), art d; BATTLE BENEATH THE EARTH(1968, Brit.); GREAT CATHERINE(1968, Brit.), art d; ADDING MACHINE, THE(1969); DIAMONDS ARE FOREVER(1971, Brit.); ALVIN RIDES AGAIN(1974, Aus.), art d; PETERSEN(1974, Aus.), art d; THREE SISTERS(1974, Brit.), art d; END PLAY(1975, Aus.), art d; SCOBIE MALONE(1975, Aus.), art d
Brenda I. Hutchinson
LIQUID SKY(1982), m
Bruce Hutchinson
PARK AVENUE LOGGER(1937), w; KANSAS CITY BOMBER(1972), makeup
Charles Hutchinson
WOMEN MEN MARRY(1931), d; OUT OF SINGAPORE(1932), d; PRIVATE SCANDAL, A(1932), d; FOUND ALIVE(1934), d; HOUSE OF DANGER(1934), d; NIGHT CARGO(1936), d; PHANTOM PATROL(1936), d; BORN TO FIGHT(1938), d; KILLERS OF THE WILD(1940), d
Misc. Talkies
CIRCUS SHADOWS(1935), d; JUDGMENT BOOK, THE(1935), d; TOPA TOPA(1938), d
Silents
DESIRED WOMAN, THE(1918); AFTER DARK(1924); ON PROBATION(1924), d; FAIR PLAY(1925), sup; WAS IT BIGAMY?(1925), d
Misc. Silents
DIVORCED(1915); WAR BRIDES(1916); GOD OF LITTLE CHILDREN(1917); GOLDEN GOD, THE(1917); MYSTIC HOUR, THE(1917); FATAL PLUNGE, THE(1924); HURRICANE HUTCH IN MANY ADVENTURES(1924, Brit.), a, d; HUTCH OF THE U.S.A.(1924); LAW DEMANDS, THE(1924); RADIO FLYER, THE(1924); FLYING HIGH(1926), d; WINNING WALLOP, THE(1926), d; HIDDEN ACES(1927); LITTLE FIREBRAND, THE(1927), d; TRUNK MYSTERY, THE(1927); DANGER MAN, THE(1930)
Chuck Hutchinson
HARD ROAD, THE(1970)
Dale Hutchinson
BATTLE TAXI(1955)
David Hutchinson
THINK DIRTY(1970, Brit.)
Enrique Hutchinson
WOMEN IN THE NIGHT(1948), makeup
Harry Hutchinson
LIMPING MAN, THE(1936, Brit.); LAST CHANCE, THE(1937, Brit.); RIVER OF UNREST(1937, Brit.); CHAMBER OF HORRORS(1941, Brit.); ADVENTURESS, THE(1946, Brit.); SAINTS AND SINNERS(1949, Brit.); LAST HOLIDAY(1950, Brit.); STRANGER AT MY DOOR(1950, Brit.); TONIGHT'S THE NIGHT(1954, Brit.); STORY OF ESTHER COSTELLO, THE(1957, Brit.); DUBLIN NIGHTMARE(1958, Brit.); DENTIST IN THE CHAIR(1960, Brit.); SHE DIDN'T SAY NO!(1962, Brit.); BLOW-UP(1966, Brit.); MAN OUTSIDE, THE(1968, Brit.); SALT & PEPPER(1968, Brit.); UP THE JUNCTION(1968, Brit.); GUMSHOE(1972, Brit.); WEEKEND MURDERS, THE(1972, Ital.)
J. Hutchinson
UP THE ACADEMY(1980)
James C. Hutchinson
Misc. Silents
RED BLOOD AND BLUE(1925), d
James Hutchinson, Jr.
CASEY'S SHADOW(1978)
Jeanette Hutchinson
SUSPENDED ALIBI(1957, Brit.)
Jerry Hutchinson
TWO IN REVOLT(1936), w
Jiver Hutchinson
THEATRE ROYAL(1943, Brit.)
Joanne Hutchinson
ROCKY(1976), cos
Jody Hutchinson
SEMINOLE(1953)
Joie Hutchinson
DEMON SEED(1977), cos
Josephine Hutchinson
HAPPINESS AHEAD(1934); MELODY LINGERS ON, THE(1935); OIL FOR THE LAMPS OF CHINA(1935); RIGHT TO LIVE, THE(1935); I MARRIED A DOCTOR(1936); STORY OF LOUIS PASTEUR, THE(1936); MOUNTAIN JUSTICE(1937); WOMEN MEN MARRY, THE(1937); CRIME OF DR. HALLET(1938); SON OF FRANKENSTEIN(1939); MY SON, MY SON!(1940); TOM BROWN'S SCHOOL DAYS(1940); HER FIRST BEAU(1941); SOMEWHERE IN THE NIGHT(1946); CASS TIMBERLANE(1947); TENDER YEARS, THE(1947); ADVENTURE IN BALTIMORE(1949); LOVE IS BETTER THAN EVER(1952); RUBY GENTRY(1952); MANY RIVERS TO CROSS(1955); MIRACLE IN THE RAIN(1956); GUN FOR A COWARD(1957); SING, BOY, SING(1958); STEP DOWN TO TERROR(1958); NORTH BY NORTHWEST(1959); ADVENTURES OF HUCKLEBERRY FINN, THE(1960); WALK LIKE A DRAGON(1960); BABY, THE

RAIN MUST FALL(1965); NEVADA SMITH(1966); RABBIT, RUN(1970)

Ken Hutchinson
JULIUS CAESAR(1970, Brit.); WRATH OF GOD, THE(1972)

Leo Hutchinson
GROUND ZERO(1973)

Leslie "Hutch" Hutchinson
COCK O' THE NORTH(1935, Brit.); BELOVED IMPOSTER(1936, Brit.); HAPPI-DROME(1943, Brit.); LUCKY MASCOT, THE(1951, Brit.)

Lois Hutchinson
Silents
GIRL WHO WOULDN'T WORK, THE(1925), w

Lt. Hutchinson
WAY WE LIVE, THE(1946, Brit.)

Muriel Hutchinson
ANOTHER THIN MAN(1939); JOE AND ETHEL TURP CALL ON THE PRESI-DENT(1939)

Murray Hutchinson
PICTURES(1982, New Zealand)

Nigel Hutchinson
GOODBYE PORK PIE(1981, New Zealand), p

Peter Hutchinson
KIDNAPPING OF THE PRESIDENT, THE(1980, Can.), spec eff; EXCALIBUR(1981), spec eff; PRIVATES ON PARADE(1982); LORDS OF DISCIPLINE, THE(1983)
1984
PRIVATES ON PARADE(1984, Brit.), spec eff; SHEENA(1984), spec eff

Robert Hutchinson
OUTSIDE IN(1972), w
Misc. Talkies
DOWN TO THE SEA(1975)

Ross Hutchinson
RUNAWAY, THE(1964, Brit.)

Thomas Hutchinson
BLADE RUNNER(1982)

Tim Hutchinson
EAGLE'S WING(1979, Brit.), cos; THAT SUMMER(1979, Brit.), art d; ROUGH CUT(1980, Brit.), art d; EXCALIBUR(1981), art d; TRAIL OF THE PINK PANTHER, THE(1982), art d; VICTOR/VICTORIA(1982), art d; CURSE OF THE PINK PAN-THER(1983), art d; YELLOWBEARD(1983), set d

Tom Hutchinson
TAPS(1981)
Silents
GOLD RUSH, THE(1925)

Urban P. Hutchinson
IDEAL HUSBAND, AN(1948, Brit.), makeup

Vanessa Hutchinson
1984
MIRRORS(1984)

W. E. Hutchinson
HELL, HEAVEN OR HOBOKEN(1958, Brit.), art d

W. G. D. Hutchinson
HOUSE OF TRENT, THE(1933, Brit.), p

W. R. Hutchinson
MR. H. C. ANDERSEN(1950, Brit.), ph

W.E. Hutchinson
RINGER, THE(1953, Brit.), prod d; DIRTY DOZEN, THE(1967, Brit.), art d

Wendy Hutchinson
VILLAIN(1971, Brit.)

William Hutchinson
DEVIL'S DAFFODIL, THE(1961, Brit./Ger.), art d; INFORMATION RECEI-VED(1962, Brit.), art d; MAGUS, THE(1968, Brit.), art d; BATTLE OF BRITAIN, THE(1969, Brit.), art d; YOUNG WINSTON(1972, Brit.), art d; DON QUIXOTE(1973, Aus.), art d

Charles Hutchison
BACHELOR MOTHER(1933), d; MYSTIC HOUR, THE(1934); ON PROBATION(1935), a, d; DESERT GUNS(1936), d
Misc. Talkies
RIDDLE RANCH(1936), d
Silents
HUTCH STIRS 'EM UP(1923, Brit.); POISON(1924), a, w; SURGING SEAS(1924); CATCH AS CATCH CAN(1927), d; DOWN GRADE, THE(1927), d; PIRATES OF THE SKY(1927); OUT WITH THE TIDE(1928), d
Misc. Silents
FANGS OF THE WOLF(1924); SILENT WIRES(1924); TURNED UP(1924); HIDDEN MENACE, THE(1925), a, d; WHEN DANGER CALLS(1927), d; BITTER SWEETS(1928), d

Janelle Hutchison
CURTAINS(1983, Can.)

Ken Hutchison
STRAW DOGS(1971, Brit.); DEADLY STRANGERS(1974, Brit.); SWEENEY 2(1978, Brit.)

Muriel Hutchison
PARTNERS IN CRIME(1937); ONE THIRD OF A NATION(1939); WOMEN, THE(1939)

Robert Hutchison
FROGS(1972), w

Terry Hutchison
WHEN THE LEGENDS DIE(1972)

Angela Huth
PAUL AND MICHELLE(1974, Fr./Brit.), w

Bett Huth
LANCASHIRE LUCK(1937, Brit.)

Harold Huth
CITY OF PLAY(1929, Brit.); GUILT(1930, Brit.); HOURS OF LONELINESS(1930, Brit.); BRACELETS(1931, Brit.); DOWN RIVER(1931, Brit.); MADAME GUIL-LOTINE(1931, Brit.), w; ARENT WE ALL?(1932, Brit.); FIRST MRS. FRASER, THE(1932, Brit.); FLYING SQUAD, THE(1932, Brit.); FOOTSTEPS IN THE NIGHT(1932, Brit.); SALLY BISHOP(1932, Brit.); WORLD, THE FLESH, AND THE DEVIL, THE(1932, Brit.); DISCORD(1933, Brit.); MY LUCKY STAR(1933, Brit.); OUTSIDER, THE(1933, Brit.); ROME EXPRESS(1933, Brit.); CAMELS ARE COMING, THE(1934, Brit.); GHOUL, THE(1934, Brit.); TAKE MY TIP(1937, Brit.); DANGEROUS

CARGO(1939, Brit.), d; BULLDOG SEES IT THROUGH(1940, Brit.), d; STRANGLER, THE(1941, Brit.), d; THIS WAS PARIS(1942, Brit.); ADVENTURE IN BLACK-MAIL(1943, Brit.), d; THEY WERE SISTERS(1945, Brit.), p; CARAVAN(1946, Brit.), p; BAD SISTER(1947, Brit.), p; LADY SURRENDERS, A(1947, Brit.), p; ROOT OF ALL EVIL, THE(1947, Brit.), p; LOOK BEFORE YOU LOVE(1948, Brit.), p; MY SISTER AND I(1948, Brit.), p, d; NIGHT BEAT(1948, Brit.), p&d; BLACKMAILED(1951, Brit.), a, p; SING ALONG WITH ME(1952, Brit.), a, p; POLICE DOG(1955, Brit.), p; HOS-TAGE, THE(1956, Brit.), d; MAN INSIDE, THE(1958, Brit.), p; IDOL ON PARA-DE(1959, Brit.), p; IN THE NICK(1960, Brit.), p; JAZZ BOAT(1960, Brit.), p; MAN WITH THE GREEN CARNATION, THE(1960, Brit.), p; HELLIONS, THE(1962, Brit.), p, w
Silents
ONE OF THE BEST(1927, Brit.)
Misc. Silents
DOWNSTREAM(1929, Brit.)

Jochen Huth
BURG THEATRE(1936, Ger.), w; FOUR COMPANIONS, THE(1938, Ger.), w; RATS, THE(1955, Ger.), w; AS LONG AS YOU'RE NEAR ME(1956, Ger.), w; VOR SON-NENUNTERGANG(1961, Ger.), w

Jon Hutman
1984
HOTEL NEW HAMPSHIRE, THE(1984)

Cozette Hutner
ISLAND OF LOVE(1963)

Edward Everett Hutshing
ANDY HARDY COMES HOME(1958), w

Eric Hutson
WAY OUT(1966)

Mimi Hutson
MAN CALLED PETER, THE(1955)

Sandy Hutson
CLASS OF MISS MAC MICHAEL, THE(1978, Brit./U.S.), w

Robert Hutt
YAQUI DRUMS(1956)

William Hutt
OEDIPUS REX(1957, Can.); THERE WAS A CROOKED MAN(1962, Brit.); MACBETH(1963); FIXER, THE(1968); SHAPE OF THINGS TO COME, THE(1979, Can.)
1984
COVERGIRL(1984, Can.)

Renate Hutte
FANNY HILL: MEMOIRS OF A WOMAN OF PLEASURE zero(1965)

Bill Hutten
SANTA AND THE THREE BEARS(1970), anim

Christina Hutter
SECOND THOUGHTS(1983)

Hans Hutter
$(DOLLARS)**1/2 (1971); BLACK VEIL FOR LISA, A(1969 Ital./Ger.), art d

Mark Hutter
ON THE RIGHT TRACK(1981)

R. Hutter
LILAC DOMINO, THE(1940, Brit.), w

Richard Hutter
STUDENT'S ROMANCE, THE(1936, Brit.), w

Burt Huttinger
HOOKED GENERATION, THE(1969)

Betty Hutton
FLEET'S IN, THE(1942); STAR SPANGLED RHYTHM(1942); HAPPY GO LUCK-Y(1943); LET'S FACE IT(1943); AND THE ANGELS SING(1944); HERE COME THE WAVES(1944); MIRACLE OF MORGAN'S CREEK, THE(1944); DUFFY'S TA-VERN(1945); INCENDIARY BLONDE(1945); STORK CLUB, THE(1945); CROSS MY HEART(1946); DREAM GIRL(1947); PERILS OF PAULINE, THE(1947); RED, HOT AND BLUE(1949); ANNIE GET YOUR GUN(1950); LET'S DANCE(1950); SAILOR BEWARE(1951); GREATEST SHOW ON EARTH, THE(1952); SOMEBODY LOVES ME(1952); SPRING REUNION(1957)

Beulah Hutton
FUGITIVE LADY(1934)

Bob Hutton
DESTINATION TOKYO(1944)

Brian G. Hutton
PAD, THE(AND HOW TO USE IT)* (1966, Brit.), d; INTERNS, THE(1962); WILD SEED(1965), d; SOL MADRID(1968), d; WHERE EAGLES DARE(1968, Brit.), d; KEL-LY'S HEROES(1970, U.S./Yugo.), d; X Y & ZEE(1972, Brit.), d; NIGHT WATCH(1973, Brit.), d; FIRST DEADLY SIN, THE(1980), d; HIGH ROAD TO CHINA(1983), d

Brian Hutton
CARNIVAL ROCK(1957); FEAR STRIKES OUT(1957); GUNFIGHT AT THE O.K. CORRAL(1957); CASE AGAINST BROOKLYN, THE(1958); KING CREOLE(1958); BIG FISHERMAN, THE(1959); LAST TRAIN FROM GUN HILL(1959)

Bullus Hutton
WOLFPEN PRINCIPLE, THE(1974, Can.)

Clayton Hutton
FASCINATION(1931, Brit.), p; VERDICT OF THE SEA(1932, Brit.), p; TOMORROW WE LIVE(1936, Brit.), p; INTIMATE RELATIONS(1937, Brit.), d

David Hutton
MONSTER ISLAND(1981, Span./U.S.)

Dana J. Hutton [Jim Hutton]
TIME TO LOVE AND A TIME TO DIE, A(1958)

Ina Ray Hutton
EVER SINCE VENUS(1944)

James Hutton
NIGHT IN PARADISE, A(1946)

Jim Hutton
SUBTERRANEANS, THE(1960); WHERE THE BOYS ARE(1960); BACHELOR IN PARADISE(1961); HONEYMOON MACHINE, THE(1961); HORIZONTAL LIEUTEN-ANT, THE(1962); PERIOD OF ADJUSTMENT(1962); LOOKING FOR LOVE(1964); HALLELUJAH TRAIL, THE(1965); MAJOR DUNDEE(1965); NEVER TOO LA-TE(1965); TROUBLE WITH ANGELS, THE(1966); WALK, DON'T RUN(1966); WHO'S MINDING THE MINT?(1967); GREEN BERETS, THE(1968); HELLFIGHTERS(1968); PSYCHIC KILLER(1975)

John Phillips Hutton
FRATERNITY ROW(1977), m
Joseph Hutton
1984
SWING SHIFT(1984)
June Hutton
LUXURY LINER(1948)
Lauren Hutton
PAPER LION(1968); LITTLE FAUSS AND BIG HALSY(1970); PIECES OF DREAMS(1970); GAMBLER, THE(1974); ROCCO PAPALEO(1974, Ital./Fr.); GATOR(1976); WELCOME TO L.A.(1976); VIVA KNIEVEL!(1977); WEDDING, A(1978); AMERICAN GIGOLO(1980); PATERNITY(1981); ZORRO, THE GAY BLADE(1981)
1984
LASSITER(1984)
Len Hutton
FINAL TEST, THE(1953, Brit.)
Leona Hutton
Silents
TYPHOON, THE(1914); MARKET OF VAIN DESIRE, THE(1916)
Misc. Silents
MAN WHO WOULD NOT DIE, THE(1916); SOUL MATES(1916)
Linda Hutton
MAN WHO FELL TO EARTH, THE(1976, Brit.)
Lucille Hutton
Silents
MIRACLE MAN, THE(1919); EAST SIDE–WEST SIDE(1923); ANY WOMAN(1925); DICK TURPIN(1925)
Misc. Silents
PAINTED LADY, THE(1924); SUNSET TRAIL, THE(1924); WINNER, THE(1926)
Mal Hutton
HARD TRAIL(1969)
Malcolm Hutton
REG'LAR FELLERS(1941)
Marion Hutton
ORCHESTRA WIVES(1942); CRAZY HOUSE(1943); BABES ON SWING STREET(1944); IN SOCIETY(1944); LOVE HAPPY(1949)
Michael Clayton Hutton
MR. LORD SAYS NO(1952, Brit.), w
Peter Hutton
GAMBLER AND THE LADY, THE(1952, Brit.)
Raymond Hutton
GUN TALK(1948)
Ric Hutton
GUNS AT BATASI(1964, Brit.); IPCRESS FILE, THE(1965, Brit.)
Robert Hutton
NORTHERN PURSUIT(1943); HOLLYWOOD CANTEEN(1944); JANIE(1944); ROUGHLY SPEAKING(1945); TOO YOUNG TO KNOW(1945); JANIE GETS MARRIED(1946); ONE MORE TOMORROW(1946); ALWAYS TOGETHER(1947); LOVE AND LEARN(1947); TIME OUT OF MIND(1947); SMART GIRLS DON'T TALK(1948); WALLFLOWER(1948); AND BABY MAKES THREE(1949); MAN ON THE EIFFEL TOWER, THE(1949); YOUNGER BROTHERS, THE(1949); BEAUTY ON PARADE(1950); NEW MEXICO(1951); RACKET, THE(1951); SLAUGHTER TRAIL(1951); STEEL HELMET, THE(1951); GOBS AND GALS(1952); TROPICAL HEAT WAVE(1952); PARIS MODEL(1953); CASANOVA'S BIG NIGHT(1954); BIG BLUFF, THE(1955); SCANDAL INCORPORATED(1956); MAN WITHOUT A BODY, THE(1957, Brit.); THUNDER OVER TANGIER(1957, Brit.); COLOSSUS OF NEW YORK, THE(1958); OUTCASTS OF THE CITY(1958); SHOWDOWN AT BOOT HILL(1958); INVISIBLE INVADERS(1959); CINDERFELLA(1960); JAILBREAKERS, THE(1960); WILD YOUTH(1961); SLIME PEOPLE, THE(1963), a, d; SECRET DOOR, THE(1964); SICILIANS, THE(1964, Brit.); FINDERS KEEPERS(1966, Brit.); CARNABY, M.D.(1967, Brit.); THEY CAME FROM BEYOND SPACE(1967, Brit.); VULTURE, THE(1967, U.S./Brit./Can.); YOU ONLY LIVE TWICE(1967, Brit.); TORTURE GARDEN(1968, Brit.); CRY OF THE BANSHEE(1970, Brit.); TROG(1970, Brit.); TALES FROM THE CRYPT(1972, Brit.)
Robert B. Hutton
PERSECUTION(1974, Brit.), w
Stuart Hutton
Misc. Talkies
VOICE OVER(1983)
Timothy Hutton
ORDINARY PEOPLE(1980); TAPS(1981); DANIEL(1983)
1984
ICEMAN(1984)
Tom Hutton
DEMON LOVER, THE(1977)
Robin Hutton-Potts
DOWNHILL RACER(1969)
Gerhard Huttula
SLEEPING BEAUTY(1965, Ger.), ph; GOOSE GIRL, THE(1967, Ger.), ph
Kendrick Huxham
UNTIL THEY SAIL(1957); PIRATES OF TORTUGA(1961); VOYAGE TO THE BOTTOM OF THE SEA(1961); MY FAIR LADY(1964); GAMES(1967)
Aldous Huxley
PRIDE AND PREJUDICE(1940), w; JANE EYRE(1944), w; WOMAN'S VENGEANCE, A(1947), w; PRELUDE TO FAME(1950, Brit.), w
Amos Huxley [Albert T. Viola]
PREACHERMAN(1971)
Rick Huxley
HAVING A WILD WEEKEND(1965, Brit.)
Shirley Huxley
Misc. Silents
HOUSE DIVIDED, A(1919)
Sophie Huxley
SARATOGA TRUNK(1945)
Judy Huxtable
SECOND BEST SECRET AGENT IN THE WHOLE WIDE WORLD, THE(1965, Brit.); PSYCHOPATH, THE(1966, Brit.); DIE SCREAMING, MARIANNE(1970, Brit.); SCREAM AND SCREAM AGAIN(1970, Brit.); THINK DIRTY(1970, Brit.)

Misc. Talkies
TOUCHABLES, THE(1968, Brit.)
Victoria Huxtable
SERIAL(1980)
Patsy Huxter
INADMISSIBLE EVIDENCE(1968, Brit.)
Renata Huy
SEA CHASE, THE(1955)
Renate Huy
GOLDEN BLADE, THE(1953)
Willard Huyck
AMERICAN GRAFFITI(1973), w; DEAD PEOPLE(1974), d, w; LUCKY LADY(1975), w; FRENCH POSTCARDS(1979), d, w; MORE AMERICAN GRAFFITI(1979), w
1984
BEST DEFENSE(1984), d, w; INDIANA JONES AND THE TEMPLE OF DOOM(1984), w
William Huyck
DEVIL'S 8, THE(1969), w
Rigmor Hvidtfeldt
LURE OF THE JUNGLE, THE(1970, Den.)
Carl Johan Hviid
WEEKEND(1964, Den.)
Lier Hwang
WORLD OF SUZIE WONG, THE(1960); ROAD TO HONG KONG, THE(1962, U.S./Brit.)
Loretta Han-Yi Hwong
OUT OF THE TIGER'S MOUTH(1962)
Fran Dinh Hy
LOSERS, THE(1970)
Alan Hyams
BIG DADDY(1969), m
Burt Hyams
NIGHT OF MAGIC, A(1944, Brit.), p
Danna Hyams
STAR CHAMBER, THE(1983)
Edward Hyams
YOU KNOW WHAT SAILORS ARE(1954, Brit.), w
Joe Hyams
LOST MISSILE, THE(1958, U.S./Can.); TEACHER'S PET(1958); PEPE(1960); LOVE IN A GOLDFISH BOWL(1961)
John Hyams
BROADWAY SCANDALS(1929); CAMEO KIRBY(1930); WOMEN WON'T TELL(1933); BIG SHAKEDOWN, THE(1934); EVELYN PRENTICE(1934); MIGHTY BARNUM, THE(1934); IN CALIENTE(1935); MASQUERADE(1935); WONDER OF WOMEN(1929); BIG HOUSE, THE(1930); BISHOP MURDER CASE, THE(1930); FLIRTING WIDOW, THE(1930); GIRL SAID NO, THE(1930); PART TIME WIFE(1930); SINS OF THE CHILDREN(1930); SWEETHEARTS AND WIVES(1930); THIRTEENTH CHAIR, THE(1930); WAY FOR A SAILOR(1930); WAY OUT WEST(1930); GENTLEMAN'S FATE(1931); MEN CALL IT LOVE(1931); NEW ADVENTURES OF GET-RICH-QUICK WALLINGFORD, THE(1931); PHANTOM OF PARIS, THE(1931); SURRENDER(1931); BIG BROADCAST, THE(1932); FREAKS(1932); RED HEADED WOMAN(1932); HORSEPLAY(1933); ISLAND OF LOST SOULS(1933); SATURDAY'S MILLIONS(1933); SING SINNER, SING(1933); AFFAIRS OF A GENTLEMAN(1934); POOR RICH, THE(1934); NO RANSOM(1935); PEOPLE WILL TALK(1935); RUGGLES OF RED GAP(1935); $1,000 A MINUTE(1935); YELLOW DUST(1936)
Misc. Talkies
STEPPING OUT(1931); CONSTANT WOMAN, THE(1933)
Silents
KICK-OFF, THE(1926); SUMMER BACHELORS(1926); BRUTE, THE(1927); ONE-ROUND HOGAN(1927); WHITE PANTS WILLIE(1927); CRIMSON CITY, THE(1928); GIRL IN EVERY PORT, A(1928); FAR CALL, THE(1929); SPITE MARRIAGE(1929)
Misc. Silents
SANDRA(1924); BUSH LEAGUER, THE(1927); WIZARD, THE(1927); BRANDED SOMBRERO, THE(1928); HONOR BOUND(1928)
Nicholas Hyams
GOOD TIMES(1967), w
Norman J. Hyams
INN FOR TROUBLE(1960, Brit.), p
Peter Hyams
T.R. BASKIN(1971), p, w; BUSTING(1974), d&w; OUR TIME(1974), d; PEEPER(1975), d; TELEFON(1977), w; CAPRICORN ONE(1978), d&w; HANOVER STREET(1979, Brit.), d&w; HUNTER, THE(1980), w; OUTLAND(1981), d&w; STAR CHAMBER, THE(1983), d, w
1984
2010(1984), p,d&w, ph
Hans Hyan
CASE VAN GELDERN(1932, Ger.), w
Ed Hyans
SUDAN(1945)
Eddie Hyans
MASK OF DIMITRIOS, THE(1944)
Edward Hyans
BELL FOR ADANO, A(1945); TEN CENTS A DANCE(1945)
Edward M. Hyans, Jr.
JUNGLE WOMAN(1944)
Vincent Hyapa
THEY WERE FIVE(1938, Fr.)
Hyatt
IT'S A BIG COUNTRY(1951), d

Bobby Hyatt
STAGECOACH TO DENVER(1946); HIGH WALL, THE(1947); DARK PAST, THE(1948); MR. PEABODY AND THE MERMAID(1948); NO MINOR VICES(1948); RECKLESS MOMENTS, THE(1949); EVERYBODY'S DANCIN'(1950); BASKETBALL FIX, THE(1951); HE RAN ALL THE WAY(1951); IT'S A BIG COUNTRY(1951); TOMORROW IS ANOTHER DAY(1951); WHEN I GROW UP(1951); CARBINE WILLIAMS(1952); LES MISERABLES(1952); TOUGHEST MAN IN ARIZONA(1952); FARMER TAKES A WIFE, THE(1953); SMALL TOWN GIRL(1953); GYPSY COLT(1954); CARELESS YEARS, THE(1957)

Charles Hyatt
HIGH WIND IN JAMAICA, A(1965); BUSHBABY, THE(1970)

Daniel Hyatt
REVOLT IN THE BIG HOUSE(1958), w; GORGO(1961, Brit.), w

Gail Hyatt
TIME AFTER TIME(1979, Brit.)

Robert Hyatt
MIRACLE ON 34TH STREET, THE(1947)

Barbara Hyde
GRAVEYARD OF HORROR(1971, Span.), art d

Cyprian Hyde
Silents
ALL THE SAD WORLD NEEDS(1918, Brit.)

David Hyde
SKATEBOARD(1978)

Donald Hyde
RED PLANET MARS(1952), p; PLEASE MURDER ME(1956), p, w

Dora Hyde
PRELUDE TO FAME(1950, Brit.)

Eva Hyde
BABIES FOR SALE(1940); PURPLE V, THE(1943); SALOME(1953)

George Hyde
INVISIBLE MAN RETURNS, THE(1940)

Glenn Hyde
HOUND OF THE BASKERVILLES, THE(1980, Brit.), ed

Mrs. Herbert Hyde
PEER GYNT(1965)

Ivan Hyde
JUST WILLIAM'S LUCK(1948, Brit.)

Jack Hyde
REDHEAD FROM WYOMING, THE(1953)

Jacquelyn Hyde
TAKE THE MONEY AND RUN(1969); THEY SHOOT HORSES, DON'T THEY?(1969); DARK, THE(1979); HOPSCOTCH(1980); LITTLE MISS MARKER(1980); GOING APE!(1981)

Jemma Hyde
IN THE WAKE OF A STRANGER(1960, Brit.); HEROES OF TELEMARK, THE(1965, Brit.)

John W. Hyde
RAVAGERS, THE(1979), p

Kenneth Hyde
AGAINST THE WIND(1948, Brit.); BAIT(1950, Brit.); ROSSITER CASE, THE(1950, Brit.), w; SPANIARD'S CURSE, THE(1958, Brit.), w

Kimberly Hyde
LAST PICTURE SHOW, THE(1971); YOUNG NURSES, THE(1973)
Misc. Talkies
CANDY STRIPE NURSES(1974)

Leroy Hyde
MOON OVER THE ALLEY(1980, Brit.)

Mary Ann Hyde
THAT NIGHT IN RIO(1941); FLESH AND FANTASY(1943); UP IN ARMS(1944)

Matt Hyde
YOU LIGHT UP MY LIFE(1977)

Montgomery Hyde
MAN WITH THE GREEN CARNATION, THE(1960, Brit.), w

Roy Hyde
RASPUTIN-THE MAD MONK(1966, Brit.), ed; REPTILE, THE(1966, Brit.), ed; PREHISTORIC WOMEN(1967, Brit.), ed

Sally Hyde
PEER GYNT(1965), cos

Tracy Hyde
MELODY(1971, Brit.)

Wilfrid Hyde-White
ADMIRALS ALL(1935, Brit.); NIGHT MAIL(1935, Brit.); SMITH'S WIVES(1935, Brit.); MURDER BY ROPE(1936, Brit.); SCARAB MURDER CASE, THE(1936, Brit.); CHANGE FOR A SOVEREIGN(1937, Brit.); ELEPHANT BOY(1937, Brit.); I'VE GOT A HORSE(1938, Brit.); MEET MR. PENNY(1938, Brit.); LAMBETH WALK, THE(1940, Brit.); TURNED OUT NICE AGAIN(1941, Brit.); ASKING FOR TROUBLE(1942, Brit.); LADY FROM LISBON(1942, Brit.); ADVENTURE FOR TWO(1945, Brit.); NIGHT BOAT TO DUBLIN(1946, Brit.); WANTED FOR MURDER(1946, Brit.); GHOSTS OF BERKELEY SQUARE(1947, Brit.); MEET ME AT DAWN(1947, Brit.); AFFAIRS OF ADELAIDE(1949, U. S./Brit); BAD LORD BYRON, THE(1949, Brit.); CONSPIRATOR(1949, Brit.); HELTER SKELTER(1949, Brit.); MAN ON THE EIFFEL TOWER, THE(1949); MY BROTHER JONATHAN(1949, Brit.); MY BROTHER'S KEEPER(1949, Brit.); ONE WOMAN'S STORY(1949, Brit.); QUARTET(1949, Brit.); NO HIGHWAY IN THE SKY(1951, Brit.); ADAM AND EVELYNE(1950, Brit.); ANGEL WITH THE TRUMPET, THE(1950, Brit.); GOLDEN SALAMANDER(1950, Brit.); HIGHLY DANGEROUS(1950, Brit.); IF THIS BE SIN(1950, Brit.); LAST HOLIDAY(1950, Brit.); MUDLARK, THE(1950, Brit.); THIRD MAN, THE(1950, Brit.); TRIO(1950, Brit.); WHILE THE SUN SHINES(1950, Brit.); WINSLOW BOY, THE(1950, Brit.); BLACKMAILED(1951, Brit.); BROWNING VERSION, THE(1951, Brit.); MIDNIGHT EPISODE(1951, Brit.); MR. DRAKE'S DUCK(1951, Brit.); OUTCAST OF THE ISLANDS(1952, Brit.); PROMOTER, THE(1952, Brit.); GREAT GILBERT AND SULLIVAN, THE(1953, Brit.); MR. DENNING DRIVES NORTH(1953, Brit.); MR. POTTS GOES TO MOSCOW(1953, Brit.); BETRAYED(1954); MAN WITH A MILLION(1954, Brit.); RAINBOW JACKET, THE(1954, Brit.); SEE HOW THEY RUN(1955, Brit.); CASH ON DELIVERY(1956, Brit.); MARCH HARE, THE(1956, Brit.); CITY AFTER MIDNIGHT(1957, Brit.); JOHN AND JULIE(1957, Brit.); TARZAN AND THE LOST SAFARI(1957, Brit.); TRUTH ABOUT WOMEN, THE(1958, Brit.); UP THE CREEK(1958, Brit.); WONDERFUL THINGS!(1958, Brit.); CARRY ON NURSE(1959, Brit.); CIRCLE, THE(1959, Brit.); LADY IS A SQUARE, THE(1959, Brit.); LIBEL(1959, Brit.); LIFE IN EMERGENCY

WARD 10(1959, Brit.); TEENAGE BAD GIRL(1959, Brit.); LET'S MAKE LOVE(1960); ADA(1961); HIS AND HERS(1961, Brit.); ON THE DOUBLE(1961); TWO-WAY STRETCH(1961, Brit.); IN SEARCH OF THE CASTAWAYS(1962, Brit.); CROOKS ANONYMOUS(1963, Brit.); JOHN GOLDFARB, PLEASE COME HOME(1964); MY FAIR LADY(1964); OPERATION SNAFU(1965, Brit.); TEN LITTLE INDIANS(1965, Brit.); YOU MUST BE JOKING!(1965, Brit.); BANG, BANG, YOU'RE DEAD(1966); CHAMBER OF HORRORS(1966); LIQUIDATOR, THE(1966, Brit.); SANDWICH MAN, THE(1966, Brit.); MILLION EYES OF SU-MURU(1967, Brit.); P.J.(1968); GAILY, GAILY(1969); MAGIC CHRISTIAN, THE(1970, Brit.); SKULLDUGGERY(1970); FRAGMENT OF FEAR(1971, Brit.); KING SOLOMON'S TREASURE(1978, Can.); NO LONGER ALONE(1978); BATTLESTAR GALACTICA(1979); CAT AND THE CANARY, THE(1979, Brit.); IN GOD WE TRUST(1980); OH GOD! BOOK II(1980); TARZAN, THE APE MAN(1981); TOY, THE(1982)
Misc. Talkies
ALIKI-MY LOVE(1963, U.S./Gr.)

[Wilfrid] Hyde-White
JOSSER ON THE FARM(1934, Brit.)

James Hyden
CRUISING(1980)

John Hyden
TOUGH ENOUGH(1983)

Walford Hyden
CAFE COLETTE(1937, Brit.), w; CARAVAN(1946, Brit.), md; GREAT EXPECTATIONS(1946, Brit.); LADY GODIVA RIDES AGAIN(1955, Brit.)

David Hydes
RED DANUBE, THE(1949)

Jim Hydes
INVASION QUARTET(1961, Brit.), makeup; GUNS OF DARKNESS(1962, Brit.), makeup; MALAGA(1962, Brit.), makeup; IN TROUBLE WITH EVE(1964, Brit.), makeup; PUSSYCAT ALLEY(1965, Brit.), makeup; JOKERS, THE(1967, Brit.), makeup

Jill Hyem
GENTLE TERROR, THE(1962, Brit.); LEOPARD IN THE SNOW(1979, Brit./Can.), w

Bill Hyer
CARYL OF THE MOUNTAINS(1936), ph; FACE IN THE FOG, A(1936), ph; PUT ON THE SPOT(1936), ph; ROGUES' TAVERN, THE(1936), ph; AMATEUR CROOK(1937), ph; CHEYENNE RIDES AGAIN(1937), ph; LOST RANCH(1937), ph; ROAMING COWBOY, THE(1937), ph; TAMING THE WILD(1937), ph; BROTHERS OF THE WEST(1938), ph; FEUD OF THE TRAIL(1938), ph; FLYING FISTS, THE(1938), ph; ORPHAN OF THE PECOS(1938), ph; PHANTOM OF THE RANGE, THE(1938), ph; TRIGGER FINGERS ½(1939), ph

Billy Hyer
BARS OF HATE(1936), ph

Frank Hyer
T-MEN(1947); GOODBYE, MY FANCY(1951)

Martha Hyer
LOCKET, THE(1946); THUNDER MOUNTAIN(1947); VELVET TOUCH, THE(1948); CLAY PIGEON, THE(1949); JUDGE STEPS OUT(1949); ROUGHSHOD(1949); RUSTLERS(1949); FRISCO TORNADO(1950); KANGAROO KID, THE(1950, Aus./U.S.); LAWLESS, THE(1950); OUTCAST OF BLACK MESA(1950); SALT LAKE RAIDERS(1950); GEISHA GIRL(1952); WILD STALLION(1952); YUKON GOLD(1952); ABBOTT AND COSTELLO GO TO MARS(1953); SO BIG(1953); BATTLE OF ROGUE RIVER(1954); CRY VENGEANCE(1954); DOWN THREE DARK STREETS(1954); LUCKY ME(1954); RIDERS TO THE STARS(1954); SABRINA(1954); SCARLET SPEAR, THE(1954, Brit.); FRANCIS IN THE NAVY(1955); FRESH FROM PARIS(1955); KISS OF FIRE(1955); PARIS FOLLIES OF 1956(1955); WYOMING RENEGADES(1955); RED SUNDOWN(1956); SHOWDOWN AT ABILENE(1956); BATTLE HYMN(1957); DELICATE DELINQUENT, THE(1957); KELLY AND ME(1957); MISTER CORY(1957); MY MAN GODFREY(1957); HOUSEBOAT(1958); ONCE UPON A HORSE(1958); PARIS HOLIDAY(1958); BEST OF EVERYTHING, THE(1959); BIG FISHERMAN, THE(1959); MISTRESS OF THE WORLD(1959, Ital./Fr./Ger.); SOME CAME RUNNING(1959); DESIRE IN THE DUST(1960); ICE PALACE(1960); LAST TIME I SAW ARCHIE, THE(1961); RIGHT APPROACH, THE(1961); GIRL NAMED TAMIKO, A(1962); MAN FROM THE DINERS' CLUB, THE(1963); WIVES AND LOVERS(1963); BIKINI BEACH(1964); BLOOD ON THE ARROW(1964); CARPETBAGGERS, THE(1964); FIRST MEN IN THE MOON(1964, Brit.); PYRO(1964, U.S./Span.); SONS OF KATIE ELDER, THE(1965); CHASE, THE(1966); NIGHT OF THE GRIZZLY, THE(1966); PICTURE MOMMY DEAD(1966); HAPPENING, THE(1967); HOUSE OF 1,000 DOLLS(1967, Ger./Span./Brit.); SOME MAY LIVE(1967, Brit.); WAR ITALIAN STYLE(1967, Ital.); CATCH AS CATCH CAN(1968, Ital.); CROSSPLOT(1969, Brit.); ONCE YOU KISS A STRANGER(1969); DAY OF THE WOLVES(1973)
Misc. Talkies
TYRANT, THE(1972, Can.)

William Hyer
DISCARDED LOVERS(1932), ph; SHOP ANGEL(1932), ph; DANGER AHEAD(1935), ph; KID COURAGEOUS(1935), ph; RAINBOW VALLEY(1935), ph; GUN PLAY(1936), ph; KELLY OF THE SECRET SERVICE(1936), ph; MILLIONAIRE KID(1936), ph; PRISON SHADOWS(1936), ph; RIO GRANDE ROMANCE(1936), ph; SPEED REPORTER(1936), ph; PINTO RUSTLERS(1937), ph; SANTA FE BOUND(1937), ph; TWO MINUTES TO PLAY(1937), ph; $1,000,000 RACKET(1937), ph; HARLEM ON THE PRAIRIE(1938), ph; RACING BLOOD(1938), ph; RANGER'S ROUNDUP, THE(1938), ph; SIX SHOOTIN' SHERIFF(1938), ph; KID FROM SANTA FE, THE(1940), ph; LAND OF THE SIX GUNS(1940), ph; RIDERS FROM NOWHERE(1940), ph; SPEED LIMITED(1940), ph
Silents
CODE OF THE RANGE(1927), ph; LAFFIN' FOOL, THE(1927), ph

Frank Hyers
FIGHTING MAD(1948); AT WAR WITH THE ARMY(1950); FATHER OF THE BRIDE(1950); TO PLEASE A LADY(1950); PLACE IN THE SUN, A(1951); STRIP, THE(1951); LOVE IS BETTER THAN EVER(1952)

Frankie Hyers
PEOPLE AGAINST O'HARA, THE(1951)

Martha Hyers
WOMAN ON THE BEACH, THE(1947)

William Hyers
REFORM SCHOOL(1939), ph; PHANTOM RANCHER(1940), ph

Lois Hyett
FRAGMENT OF FEAR(1971, Brit.)

Ray Hyke
FORCE OF EVIL(1948); FORT APACHE(1948); MAN FROM COLORADO, THE(1948); RED RIVER(1948); THAT LADY IN ERMINE(1948); CAPTAIN CHINA(1949); RO-SEANNA McCOY(1949); SHE WORE A YELLOW RIBBON(1949); TWELVE O'CLOCK HIGH(1949); CARIBOO TRAIL, THE(1950); LAWLESS, THE(1950); NO WAY OUT(1950); TRIPOLI(1950); WHEN WILLIE COMES MARCHING HOME(1950); FROGMEN, THE(1951); SILVER CITY(1951); RED SKIES OF MONTANA(1952); WHAT PRICE GLORY?(1952); WILD BLUE YONDER, THE(1952); BEAST FROM 20,000 FATHOMS, THE(1953); BLUEPRINT FOR MURDER, A(1953); DOWN AMONG THE SHELTERING PALMS(1953)

Catherine Hyland
1984
VAMPING(1984)

Diana Hyland
ONE MAN'S WAY(1964); CHASE, THE(1966); SMOKY(1966); JIGSAW(1968)
Misc. Talkies
HERCULES AND THE PRINCESS OF TROY(1966)

Dick Hyland
WAVE, A WAC AND A MARINE, A(1944), w

Dick I. Hyland
NIGHT CLUB GIRL(1944), w

Dick Irving Hyland
HI BEAUTIFUL(1944), p, w; HER PRIMITIVE MAN(1944), w; LAKE PLACID SERENADE(1944), w; LOVE, HONOR AND GOODBYE(1945), w; I RING DOOR-BELLS(1946), w; KILROY WAS HERE(1947), p, w; NEW ORLEANS(1947), w; NIGHT SONG(1947), w; THREAT, THE(1949), w; PRICE OF FEAR, THE(1956), w

Edward Hyland
ONE THIRD OF A NATION(1939), ph

Frances Hyland
MARRIAGE BY CONTRACT(1928), w; PAINTED FACES(1929), w; TWO MEN AND A MAID(1929), w; EXTRAVAGANCE(1930), w; KATHLEEN MAVOURNEEN(1930), w; LOST ZEPPELIN(1930), w; PEACOCK ALLEY(1930), w; THIRD ALARM, THE(1930), w; CAUGHT CHEATING(1931), w; MORALS FOR WOMEN(1931), w; SINGLE SIN(1931), w; INTRUDER, THE(1932), w; THIRTEENTH GUEST, THE(1932), w; UNHOLY LOVE(1932), w; OFFICER 13(1933), w; SHRIEK IN THE NIGHT, A(1933), w; SIN OF NORA MORAN(1933), w; MONEY MEANS NOTHING(1934), w; HELLDORADO(1935), w; SMART GIRL(1935), w; THUNDER IN THE NIGHT(1935), w; CRIME OF DR. FORBES(1936), w; MY MARRIAGE(1936), w; STAR FOR A NIGHT(1936), w; UNDER YOUR SPELL(1936), w; STEP LIVELY, JEEVES(1937), w; 45 FATHERS(1937), w; ARIZONA WILDCAT(1938), w; CHANGE OF HEART(1938), w; CITY GIRL(1938), w; ISLAND IN THE SKY(1938), w; KEEP SMILING(1938), w; WHILE NEW YORK SLEEPS(1938), w; CHARLIE CHAN IN RENO(1939), w; CISCO KID AND THE LADY, THE(1939), w; EVERYBODY'S BABY(1939), w; WINNER TAKE ALL(1939), w; FREE, BLONDE AND 21(1940), w; GIRL FROM AVENUE A(1940), w; IN OLD CALIFORNIA(1942), w; YOU'RE TELLING ME(1942), w; SOME-ONE TO REMEMBER(1943), w; CHEATERS, THE(1945), w; MURDER IN THE MUSIC HALL(1946), w; THAT'S MY GAL(1947), w; DRYLANDERS(1963, Can.); CHANGELING, THE(1980, Can.); HOUNDS... OF NOTRE DAME, THE(1980, Can.); HAPPY BIRTHDAY TO ME(1981)
Silents
GRAIN OF DUST, THE(1928), w

George Hyland
CASBAH(1948)

James Hyland
IT SHOULD HAPPEN TO YOU(1954); MIDNIGHT STORY, THE(1957)

James J. Hyland
TARANTULA(1955)

Jane Hyland
1984
SQUIZZY TAYLOR(1984, Aus.), cos

Jim Hyland
BEHIND THE HIGH WALL(1956); CRIME AND PUNISHMENT, U.S.A.(1959); NO NAME ON THE BULLET(1959); MIDNIGHT LACE(1960)

Peggy Hyland
Silents
JOHN HALIFAX, GENTLEMAN(1915, Brit.); PERSUASIVE PEGGY(1917); OTHER MEN'S DAUGHTERS(1918); PEG OF THE PIRATES(1918); FAITH(1920); PRICE OF SILENCE, THE(1920, Brit.); FORBIDDEN CARGOES(1925, Brit.)
Misc. Silents
INFELICE(1915, Brit.); CHATTEL, THE(1916); ENEMY, THE(1916); PAIR OF SPEC-TACLES, A(1916, Brit.); ROSE OF THE SOUTH(1916); SAINTS AND SINNERS(1916); SALLY BISHOP(1916, Brit.); BABETTE(1917); CASTLE(1917, Brit.); HER RIGHT TO LIVE(1917); INTRIGUE(1917); SIXTEENTH WIFE, THE(1917); BONNIE ANNIE LAURIE(1918); CAUGHT IN THE ACT(1918); DEBT OF HONOR, THE(1918); MAR-RIAGES ARE MADE(1918); OTHER WOMAN, THE(1918); CHEATING HER-SELF(1919); COWARDICE COURT(1919); GIRL IN BOHEMIA, A(1919); GIRL WITH NO REGRETS, THE(1919); MERRY-GO ROUND, THE(1919); MISS ADVEN-TURE(1919); REBELLIOUS BRIDE, THE(1919); WEB OF CHANCE, THE(1919); BLACK SHADOWS(1920); HONEYPOT, THE(1920, Brit.); LOVE MAGGY(1921, Brit.); MR. PIM PASSES BY(1921, Brit.); SHIFTING SANDS(1922, Brit.)

Richard Irving Hyland
LINDA BE GOOD(1947), w

Ricky Hyland
EMIL(1938, Brit.)

Wendy Hyland
1984
SECRET DIARY OF SIGMUND FREUD, THE(1984), p

Scott Hylands
DADDY'S GONE A-HUNTING(1969); FOOLS(1970); VISITOR, THE(1973, Can.); EARTHQUAKE(1974); SLIPSTREAM(1974, Can.); BITTERSWEET LOVE(1976); BOYS IN COMPANY C, THE(1978, U.S./Hong Kong); DEATH HUNT(1981)
1984
ISAAC LITTLEFEATHERS(1984, Can.); OASIS, THE(1984)
Misc. Talkies
OPERATION SNAFU(1970, Ital./Yugo.)

Joe Hyler
1984
SAVAGE STREETS(1984)

Tammy Hyler
1984
CLOAK AND DAGGER(1984)

Walter Hyler
NATIONAL BARN DANCE(1944), art d

Richard Hylland
GREEN SLIME, THE(1969)

Ragnar Hylten-Cavallius
NIGHT IN JUNE, A(1940, Swed.), w

Andy Hylton
1984
STARMAN(1984), cos

Edgar W. Hylton
Misc. Silents
SECRET OF THE MOOR, THE(1919, Brit.)

Jack Hylton
BAND WAGGON(1940, Brit.); BATTLE FOR MUSIC(1943, Brit.)

Jane Hylton
DEAR MURDERER(1947, Brit.); HOLIDAY CAMP(1947, Brit.); UPTURNED GLASS, THE(1947, Brit.); WHEN THE BOUGH BREAKS(1947, Brit.); DAYDREAK(1948, Brit.); HERE COME THE HUGGETTS(1948, Brit.); MY SISTER AND I(1948, Brit.); IT ALWAYS RAINS ON SUNDAY(1949, Brit.); MY BROTHER'S KEEPER(1949, Brit.); PASSPORT TO PIMLICO(1949, Brit.); DANCE HALL(1950, Brit.); GOOD TIME GIRL(1950, Brit.); QUIET WOMAN, THE(1951, Brit.); FRIGHTENED BRIDE, THE(1952, Brit.); IT STARTED IN PARADISE(1952, Brit.); LAUGHING IN THE SUNSHINE(1953, Brit./Swed.); BURNT EVIDENCE(1954, Brit.); WEAK AND THE WICKED, THE(1954, Brit.); SECRET VENTURE(1955, Brit.); YOU PAY YOUR MONEY(1957, Brit.); DEADLY RECORD(1959, Brit.); DEVIL'S BAIT(1959, Brit.); CIRCUS OF HORRORS(1960, Brit.); NIGHT TRAIN FOR INVERNESS(1960, Brit.); HOUSE OF MYSTERY(1961, Brit.); MANSTER, THE(1962, Jap.); VIOLENT MO-MENT(1966, Brit.); WILD GEESE, THE(1978, Brit.)

Richard Hylton
LOST BOUNDARIES(1949); FIXED BAYONETS(1951); HALLS OF MON-TEZUMA(1951); SECRET OF CONVICT LAKE, THE(1951); O. HENRY'S FULL HOUSE(1952); PRIDE OF ST. LOUIS, THE(1952)

A. Hyman
TROUBLE AHEAD(1936, Brit.), w

Arthur S. Hyman
HUDDLE(1932), w

B. Hyman
Silents
SCARAMOUCHE(1923); SON OF THE SHEIK(1926); NIGHT OF LOVE, THE(1927); WHEEL OF DESTINY, THE(1927)

Bernard H. Hyman
GIRL FROM MISSOURI, THE(1934), p; TARZAN AND HIS MATE(1934), p; AFTER OFFICE HOURS(1935), p; ESCAPADE(1935), p; FORSAKING ALL OTHERS(1935), p; I LIVE MY LIFE(1935), p; ONE NEW YORK NIGHT(1935), p; SAN FRANCIS-CO(1936), p; CONQUEST(1937), p; SARATOGA(1937), p; I TAKE THIS WO-MAN(1940), p

Bernard Hyman
RASPUTIN AND THE EMPRESS(1932), p; CAT AND THE FIDDLE(1934), p; GREAT WALTZ, THE(1938), p
Misc. Silents
MORALS FOR MEN(1925), d

Bob Hyman
CRATER LAKE MONSTER, THE(1977)

Dick Hyman
FRENCH QUARTER(1978), m; ZELIG(1983), m

Earl Hyman
POSSESSION OF JOEL DELANEY, THE(1972)

Earle Hyman
BAMBOO PRISON, THE(1955)

Ed Hyman
CASEY'S SHADOW(1978)

Jerry Hyman
1984
BEST DEFENSE(1984)

Kenneth Hyman
TERROR OF THE TONGS, THE(1961, Brit.), p; GIGOT(1962), p; HILL, THE(1965, Brit.), p; DIRTY DOZEN, THE(1967, Brit.), p

Louis Hyman
Silents
BROKEN HEARTS(1926)

Mac Hyman
NO TIME FOR SERGEANTS(1958), w

Matt Hyman
WIRE SERVICE(1942)

Prudence Hyman
DESIGN FOR LOVING(1962, Brit.); GORGON, THE(1964, Brit.)

Richard Hyman
SCOTT JOPLIN(1977), m

Walter Hyman
WHO IS HARRY KELLERMAN AND WHY IS HE SAYING THOSE TERRIBLE THINGS ABOUT ME?(1971)

Walter Hyman, Jr.
WHO IS HARRY KELLERMAN AND WHY IS HE SAYING THOSE TERRIBLE THINGS ABOUT ME?(1971)

John B. Hymer
FAST LIFE(1929), w; LOVE, LIVE AND LAUGH(1929), w; EAST IS WEST(1930), w; SCARLET PAGES(1930), w; HALF A SINNER(1934), w; LAW OF THE UNDER-WORLD(1938), w
Silents
EAST IS WEST(1922), w; ALOMA OF THE SOUTH SEAS(1926), w; ALIAS THE DEACON(1928), w
Misc. Silents
PATH FORBIDDEN, THE(1914)

John H. Hymer
ALIAS THE DEACON(1940), w

John Hymer
PAY OFF, THE(1930), w
Warren B. Hymer
SAN FRANCISCO(1936)
Warren Hymer
COCK-EYED WORLD, THE(1929); FOX MOVIETONE FOLLIES(1929); FROZEN JUSTICE(1929); GIRL FROM HAVANA, THE(1929); SPEAKEASY(1929); BORN RECKLESS(1930); LONE STAR RANGER, THE(1930); MEN WITHOUT WOMEN(1930); OH, FOR A MAN!(1930); SINNER'S HOLIDAY(1930); UP THE RIVER(1930); CHARLIE CHAN CARRIES ON(1931); GOLDIE(1931); MEN ON CALL(1931); SEAS BENEATH, THE(1931); SPIDER, THE(1931); UNHOLY GARDEN, THE(1931); BILLION DOLLAR SCANDAL(1932); HOLD'EM JAIL(1932); LOVE IS A RACKET(1932); MADISON SQUARE GARDEN(1932); NIGHT MAYOR, THE(1932); ONE WAY PASSAGE(1932); HER FIRST MATE(1933); I LOVE THAT MAN(1933); KING FOR A NIGHT(1933); LADY'S PROFESSION, A(1933); MIDNIGHT MARY(1933); MY WOMAN(1933); MYSTERIOUS RIDER, THE(1933); 20,000 YEARS IN SING SING(1933); BELLE OF THE NINETIES(1934); CAT'S PAW, THE(1934); CROSBY CASE, THE(1934); GEORGE WHITE'S SCANDALS(1934); IN THE MONEY(1934); KID MILLIONS(1934); LITTLE MISS MARKER(1934); ONE IS GUILTY(1934); SHE LOVES ME NOT(1934); WOMAN UNAFRAID(1934); YOUNG AND BEAUTIFUL(1934); CASE OF THE CURIOUS BRIDE, THE(1935); CONFIDENTIAL(1935); DANTE'S INFERNO(1935); DARING YOUNG MAN, THE(1935); GILDED LILY, THE(1935); HOLD'EM YALE(1935); HONG KONG NIGHTS(1935); OUR LITTLE GIRL(1935); SHE GETS HER MAN(1935); SHOW THEM NO MERCY(1935); SILK HAT KID(1935); DESERT JUSTICE(1936); EVERYBODY'S OLD MAN(1936); HITCH HIKE LADY(1936); LAUGHING IRISH EYES(1936); LEAVENWORTH CASE, THE(1936); LOVE LETTERS OF A STAR(1936); MESSAGE TO GARCIA, A(1936); MR. DEEDS GOES TO TOWN(1936); NAVY WIFE(1936); NOBODY'S FOOL(1936); RHYTHM ON THE RANGE(1936); TANGO(1936); THIRTY SIX HOURS TO KILL(1936); WIDOW FROM MONTE CARLO, THE(1936); ALI BABA GOES TO TOWN(1937); BAD GUY(1937); JOIN THE MARINES(1937); LADY BEHAVE(1937); MARRIED BEFORE BREAKFAST(1937); MEET THE BOY FRIEND(1937); NAVY BLUES(1937); SEA RACKETEERS(1937); SHE'S DANGEROUS(1937); WAKE UP AND LIVE(1937); WE HAVE OUR MOMENTS(1937); YOU ONLY LIVE ONCE(1937); ARSON GANG BUSTERS(1938); GATEWAY(1938); JOY OF LIVING(1938); SUBMARINE PATROL(1938); TELEPHONE OPERATOR(1938); THANKS FOR EVERYTHING(1938); YOU AND ME(1938); BOY FRIEND(1939); CALLING ALL MARINES(1939); CHARLIE MC CARTHY, DETECTIVE(1939); COAST GUARD(1939); DESTRY RIDES AGAIN(1939); LADY AND THE MOB, THE(1939); MR. MOTO IN DANGER ISLAND(1939); I CAN'T GIVE YOU ANYTHING BUT LOVE, BABY(1940); LOVE, HONOR AND OH, BABY(1940); BIRTH OF THE BLUES(1941); BUY ME THAT TOWN(1941); MEET JOHN DOE(1941); REACHING FOR THE SUN(1941); SKYLARK(1941); BABY FACE MORGAN(1942); DR. BROADWAY(1942); GIRLS' TOWN(1942); HENRY AND DIZZY(1942); HITLER–DEAD OR ALIVE(1942); JAIL HOUSE BLUES(1942); LURE OF THE ISLANDS(1942); MEET THE MOB(1942); MR. WISE GUY(1942); ONE THRILLING NIGHT(1942); PHANTOM KILLER(1942); POLICE BULLETS(1942); SHE'S IN THE ARMY(1942); DANGER! WOMEN AT WORK(1943); GANGWAY FOR TOMORROW(1943); GOVERNMENT GIRL(1943); SPY TRAIN(1943); SINCE YOU WENT AWAY(1944); 3 IS A FAMILY(1944)
Misc. Talkies
BEAUTY'S DAUGHTER(1935)
Silents
FAR CALL, THE(1929)
Hymer-Clemens
ALOMA OF THE SOUTH SEAS(1941), w
Allen Hymson
MACABRE(1958), w
Alan Hynd
BETRAYAL FROM THE EAST(1945), w
Noel Hynd
AGENCY(1981, Can.), w
Ronald Hynd
ROMEO AND JULIET(1966, Brit.)
Karen Hynes
HAPPY BIRTHDAY TO ME(1981)
Neal Hynes
INCIDENT, THE(1967)
Patrick Hynes
MEATBALLS(1979, Can.)
Richard Hynes
HOLLYWOOD HIGH(1977)
Joel Hynick
ZELIG(1983), spec eff
David Hyry
NORTHVILLE CEMETERY MASSACRE, THE(1976)
Joyce Hyser
THEY ALL LAUGHED(1981); STAYING ALIVE(1983)
1984
THIS IS SPINAL TAP(1984)
Jeffrey Hyslop
JESUS CHRIST, SUPERSTAR(1973)
Ricky Hyslop
WHY SHOOT THE TEACHER(1977, Can.), m
Carl Hyson
Silents
SILVER LINING, THE(1921)
Dorothy Hyson
THAT'S A GOOD GIRL(1933, Brit.); TURKEY TIME(1933, Brit.); CUP OF KINDNESS, A(1934, Brit.); GHOUL, THE(1934, Brit.); HAPPY(1934, Brit.); SING AS WE GO(1934, Brit.); WOMAN IN COMMAND, THE(1934 Brit.); SPARE A COPPER(1940, Brit.); YOU WILL REMEMBER(1941, Brit.)
Roberta Hyson
Misc. Talkies
GEORGIA ROSE(1930)
Vincent Hyspa
A NOUS LA LIBERTE(1931, Fr.)
Kress Hytes
HOLLYWOOD HIGH(1977)

Olaf Hytten
CITY OF PLAY(1929, Brit.); KITTY(1929, Brit.); GRUMPY(1930); PLAYBOY OF PARIS(1930); PLATINUM BLONDE(1931); BERKELEY SQUARE(1933); DESIGN FOR LIVING(1933); EAGLE AND THE HAWK, THE(1933); LADY KILLER(1933); STUDY IN SCARLET, A(1933); BRITISH AGENT(1934); GLAMOUR(1934); JIMMY THE GENT(1934); JOURNAL OF A CRIME(1934); KEY, THE(1934); MANDALAY(1934); MONEY MEANS NOTHING(1934); MOONSTONE, THE(1934); MYSTERY LINER(1934); MYSTERY OF MR. X, THE(1934); ONE NIGHT OF LOVE(1934); PAINTED VEIL, THE(1934); RICHEST GIRL IN THE WORLD, THE(1934); SHOCK(1934); BECKY SHARP(1935); CLIVE OF INDIA(1935); DARK ANGEL, THE(1935); FEATHER IN HER HAT, A(1935); GOING HIGHBROW(1935); I FOUND STELLA PARISH(1935); JANE EYRE(1935); LAST OUTPOST, THE(1935); LIVING ON VELVET(1935); RED MORNING(1935); SECRET OF THE CHATEAU(1935); SHE COULDN'T TAKE IT(1935); SPANISH CAPE MYSTERY(1935); STRANGE WIVES(1935); TWO SINNERS(1935); AND SO THEY WERE MARRIED(1936); DOUGHNUTS AND SOCIETY(1936); HOUSE OF A THOUSAND CANDLES, THE(1936); LAST OF THE MOHICANS, THE(1936); LIBELED LADY(1936); LLOYDS OF LONDON(1936); LONE WOLF RETURNS, THE(1936); SONS O' GUNS(1936); SYLVIA SCARLETT(1936); TROUBLE FOR TWO(1936); WHITE HUNTER(1936); WIDOW FROM MONTE CARLO, THE(1936); ANGEL(1937); CALIFORNIA STRAIGHT AHEAD(1937); DANGEROUS HOLIDAY(1937); DOUBLE OR NOTHING(1937); EASY LIVING(1937); EBB TIDE(1937); EMPEROR'S CANDLESTICKS, THE(1937); FIRST LADY(1937); GOOD EARTH, THE(1937); GREAT GARRICK, THE(1937); I COVER THE WAR(1937); LANCER SPY(1937); SOULS AT SEA(1937); WE HAVE OUR MOMENTS(1937); WITH LOVE AND KISSES(1937); BLOND CHEAT(1938); LONE WOLF IN PARIS, THE(1938); MARIE ANTOINETTE(1938); YOUTH TAKES A FLING(1938); ALLEGHENY UPRISING(1939); LITTLE ACCIDENT(1939); LITTLE PRINCESS, THE(1939); OUR LEADING CITIZEN(1939); OUR NEIGHBORS–THE CARTERS(1939); RAFFLES(1939); RULERS OF THE SEA(1939); TELEVISION SPY(1939); WE ARE NOT ALONE(1939); ZAZA(1939); ARISE, MY LOVE(1940); CAPTAIN CAUTION(1940); EARL OF CHICAGO, THE(1940); ESCAPE TO GLORY(1940); GAUCHO SERENADE(1940); HOWARDS OF VIRGINIA, THE(1940); NO TIME FOR COMEDY(1940); PAROLE FIXER(1940); FOOTSTEPS IN THE DARK(1941); FOR BEAUTY'S SAKE(1941); GREAT COMMANDMENT, THE(1941); MAN HUNT(1941); NINE LIVES ARE NOT ENOUGH(1941); RAGE IN HEAVEN(1941); THAT HAMILTON WOMAN(1941); WASHINGTON MELODRAMA(1941); WHEN LADIES MEET(1941); WOLF MAN, THE(1941); BEDTIME STORY(1942); BLACK SWAN, THE(1942); CASABLANCA(1942); DESTINATION UNKNOWN(1942); EAGLE SQUADRON(1942); GHOST OF FRANKENSTEIN, THE(1942); GREAT IMPERSONATION, THE(1942); JOURNEY FOR MARGARET(1942); LUCKY JORDAN(1942); SHERLOCK HOLMES AND THE VOICE OF TERROR(1942); SON OF FURY(1942); SPY SHIP(1942); THIS ABOVE ALL(1942); TO BE OR NOT TO BE(1942); YOU'RE TELLING ME(1942); DRUMS OF FU MANCHU(1943); FLESH AND FANTASY(1943); HAPPY GO LUCKY(1943); MISSION TO MOSCOW(1943); SHERLOCK HOLMES FACES DEATH(1943); DETECTIVE KITTY O'DAY(1944); HOUSE OF FRANKENSTEIN(1944); LEAVE IT TO THE IRISH(1944); LODGER, THE(1944); NATIONAL VELVET(1944); OH, WHAT A NIGHT(1944); OUR HEARTS WERE YOUNG AND GAY(1944); SCARLET CLAW, THE(1944); BRIGHTON STRANGLER, THE(1945); CHRISTMAS IN CONNECTICUT(1945); HOLD THAT BLONDE(1945); MINISTRY OF FEAR(1945); MY NAME IS JULIA ROSS(1945); PURSUIT TO ALGIERS(1945); WOMAN IN GREEN, THE(1945); BLACK BEAUTY(1946); MAGNIFICENT DOLL(1946); NOTORIOUS LONE WOLF, THE(1946); THREE STRANGERS(1946); BELLS OF SAN ANGELO(1947); IMPERFECT LADY(1947); PRIVATE AFFAIRS OF BEL AMI, THE(1947); THAT WAY WITH WOMEN(1947); UNCONQUERED(1947); KIDNAPPED(1948); SHANGHAI CHEST, THE(1948); THAT FORSYTE WOMAN(1949); FANCY PANTS(1950); KIM(1950); ROGUES OF SHERWOOD FOREST(1950); ANNE OF THE INDIES(1951); SON OF DR. JEKYLL, THE(1951); AGAINST ALL FLAGS(1952); LES MISERABLES(1952); SCARLET COAT, THE(1955)
Misc. Talkies
ALIAS MR. TWILIGHT(1946)
Silents
CRIMSON CIRCLE, THE(1922, Brit.); TRAPPED BY THE MORMONS(1922, Brit.); GAMBLE WITH HEARTS, A(1923, Brit.); LITTLE DOOR INTO THE WORLD, THE(1923, Brit.); OUT TO WIN(1923, Brit.); IT IS THE LAW(1924); SALVATION HUNTERS, THE(1925); OLD AGE HANDICAP(1928)
Misc. Silents
KNAVE OF DIAMONDS, THE(1921, Brit.); SONIA(1921, Brit.); HIS WIFE'S HUSBAND(1922, Brit.); KNIGHT ERRANT, THE(1922, Brit.)
Maud Hyttenberg-Bartoletti
FANNY AND ALEXANDER(1983, Swed./Fr./Ger.)
Lena Hyun
JOURNEYS FROM BERLIN–1971(1980)
Peter Lee Hyun
WHITE HEAT(1934)
Dafydd Hywel
MOUSE AND THE WOMAN, THE(1981, Brit.)
1984
YR ALCOHOLIG LION(1984, Brit.)

Feng I
LADY GENERAL, THE(1965, Hong Kong)
Feng I
MERMAID, THE(1966, Hong Kong)
Yen I-feng
DEADLY CHINA DOLL(1973, Hong Kong)
Peter Iacangelo
BLOODBROTHERS(1978); HERO AT LARGE(1980); TIMES SQUARE(1980); TATTOO(1981)
Loumi Iacobesco
LACOMBE, LUCIEN(1974)
Georges Iaconelli
UP FROM THE BEACH(1965), spec eff; SHOCK TROOPS(1968, Ital./Fr.), spec eff; DAY OF THE JACKAL(1973, Brit./Fr.), spec eff; MAGNIFICENT ONE, THE(1974, Fr./Ital.), spec eff
Lucy Iacono
1984
BROADWAY DANNY ROSE(1984)
Nilo Iacoponi
SONS OF SATAN(1969, Ital./Fr./Ger.), makeup
Ian Dalrymple
DEAR MR. PROHACK(1949, Brit.), w
Ronnie Ianderweer
LAST BLITZKRIEG, THE(1958)
Giuseppe Ianigro
AMARCORD(1974, Ital.)
Enzo Iannacci
SEVEN BEAUTIES(1976, Ital.), m
Perry Iannaconi
LIQUID SKY(1982)
Richard Ianni
DELTA FACTOR, THE(1970)
Bruno Iannone
1984
ONCE UPON A TIME IN AMERICA(1984)
Patricia Iannone
WAR OF THE WORLDS, THE(1953); PRODIGAL, THE(1955)
Raul Iavista
MUSHROOM EATER, THE(1976, Mex.), m
Helene Iawkoff
LOLA MONTES(1955, Fr./Ger.)
Alicia Ibanez
DIANE(1955)
Alicia Ibanez "Miss Uruguay"
YANKEE PASHA(1954)
Bonaventure Ibanez
Silents
ROMOLA(1925)
Jhon Ibanez
HOUSE OF EVIL(1968, U.S./Mex.), p
Juan Ibanez
FEAR CHAMBER, THE(1968, US/Mex.), d; SNAKE PEOPLE, THE(1968, Mex./U.S.), p, d; INCREDIBLE INVASION, THE(1971, Mex./U.S.), d
Maria Fernanda Ibanez
DEVIL'S GODMOTHER, THE(1938, Mex.)
Roger Ibanez
ZITA(1968, Fr.)
Roman Ibanez
Silents
WHITE SISTER, THE(1923)
Vicente Blasco Ibanez
FOUR HORSEMEN OF THE APOCALYPSE, THE(1962), w
Vincent Ibanez
Silents
ARGENTINE LOVE(1924), w
Vincente Blasco Ibanez
BLOOD AND SAND(1941), w
Saikaku Ibara
LIFE OF OHARU(1964, Jap.), w
Angel Ibarra
NARCO MEN, THE(1969, Span./Ital.), p
Martin Ibbertson
MERRY CHRISTMAS MR. LAWRENCE(1983, Jap./Brit.)
Arthur Ibbetson
BLUE LAGOON, THE(1949, Brit.), ph; FLOODTIDE(1949, Brit.), ph; POET'S PUB(1949, Brit.), ph; STOP PRESS GIRL(1949, Brit.), ph; ISLAND OF DESIRE(1952, Brit.), ph; MELBA(1953, Brit.), ph; HORSE'S MOUTH, THE(1958, Brit.), ph; KEY, THE(1958, Brit.), spec eff; BRIDAL PATH, THE(1959, Brit.), ph; ANGRY SILENCE, THE(1960, Brit.), ph; TUNES OF GLORY(1960, Brit.), ph; CANADIANS, THE(1961, Brit.), ph; LEAGUE OF GENTLEMEN, THE(1961, Brit.), ph; WHISTLE DOWN THE WIND(1961, Brit.), ph; LISA(1962, Brit.), ph; THERE WAS A CROOKED MAN(1962, Brit.), ph; I COULD GO ON SINGING(1963), ph; MURDER AT THE GALLOP(1963, Brit.), ph; NINE HOURS TO RAMA(1963, U.S./Brit.), ph; CHALK GARDEN, THE(1964, Brit.), ph; DIE, DIE, MY DARLING(1965, Brit.), ph; FIGHTING PRINCE OF DONEGAL, THE(1966, Brit.), ph; GYPSY GIRL(1966, Brit.), ph; WILD AFFAIR, THE(1966, Brit.), ph; COUNTESS FROM HONG KONG, A(1967, Brit.), ph; INSPECTOR CLOUSEAU(1968, Brit.), ph; MATTER OF INNOCENCE, A(1968, Brit.), ph; WHERE EAGLES DARE(1968, Brit.), ph; ANNE OF THE THOUSAND DAYS(1969, Brit.), ph; WALKING STICK, THE(1970, Brit.), ph; RAILWAY CHILDREN, THE(1971, Brit.), ph; WHEN EIGHT BELLS TOLL(1971, Brit.), ph; WILLY WONKA AND THE CHOCOLATE FACTORY(1971), ph; 11 HARROWHOUSE(1974, Brit.), ph; OUT OF SEASON(1975, Brit.), ph; SELL OUT, THE(1976), ph; LITTLE NIGHT MUSIC, A(1977, Aust./U.S./Ger.), ph; MEDUSA TOUCH, THE(1978, Brit.), ph; ALL THINGS BRIGHT AND BEAUTIFUL(1979, Brit.), ph; PRISONER OF ZENDA, THE(1979), ph; HOP-

SCOTCH(1980), ph; NOTHING PERSONAL(1980, Can.), ph
1984
BOUNTY, THE(1984), ph
Ronald Ibbs
BLUE MURDER AT ST. TRINIAN'S(1958, Brit.); YOUNG CASSIDY(1965, U.S./Brit.)
Harumi Ibe
WAY OUT, WAY IN(1970, Jap.), m
Claude Iberia
BEAUTY AND THE BEAST(1947, Fr.), ed
Jacques Ibert
DON QUIXOTE(1935, Fr.), m; GOLGOTHA(1937, Fr.), m; PANIQUE(1947, Fr.), m; MACBETH(1948), m; INVITATION TO THE DANCE(1956), m
Henry Ibling
THANK YOUR LUCKY STARS(1943)
Henry Iblings
GIRL FROM JONES BEACH, THE(1949)
John Iboko
WHITE WITCH DOCTOR(1953)
Abdel Moneim Ibrihim
GOLDEN ARROW, THE(1964, Ital.)
Henrik Ibsen
PILLARS OF SOCIETY(1936, Ger.), w; PEER GYNT(1965), w; DOLL'S HOUSE, A(1973), w, w; HEDDA(1975, Brit.), w; WILD DUCK, THE(1977, Ger./Aust.), w; ENEMY OF THE PEOPLE, AN(1978), w; WILD DUCK, THE(1983, Aus.), w
Silents
DOLL'S HOUSE, A(1918), w
Tancred Ibsen
WHALERS, THE(1942, Swed.), w
Toru Ibuki
OPERATION ENEMY FORT(1964, Jap.); NONE BUT THE BRAVE(1965, U.S./Jap.); SIEGE OF FORT BISMARK(1968, Jap.)
Rafael Icardo
PORTRAIT OF MARIA(1946, Mex.)
Icarus
LOVE IS A CAROUSEL(1970)
Moya Iceton
GETTING OF WISDOM, THE(1977, Aus.), w
Leon Ichaso
Misc. Talkies
EL SUPER(1979), d
Kon Ichekawa
HARP OF BURMA(1967, Jap.), d
Hiromi Ichida
BUDDHA(1965, Jap.)
Isamu Ichida
ONIMASA(1983, Jap.), ed
Kiichi Ichida
LATITUDE ZERO(1969, U.S./Jap.), cos
Raizo Ichigawa
ENJO(1959, Jap.)
Kiyohiko Ichiha
WOMAN IN THE DUNES(1964, Jap.)
Etsuko Ichihara
FACE OF ANOTHER, THE(1967, Jap.); REBELLION(1967, Jap.)
Chusha Ichikawa
CHUSHINGURA(1963, Jap.); SAMURAI ASSASSIN(1965, Jap.)
Danko Ichikawa
BALLAD OF NARAYAMA(1961, Jap.); DAREDEVIL IN THE CASTLE(1969, Jap.)
Haruo Ichikawa
LIFE OF OHARU(1964, Jap.)
Hiroshi Ichikawa
WAR OF THE MONSTERS(1972, Jap.)
K. Ichikawa
LAKE, THE(1970, Jap.)
Kazuko Ichikawa
TORA! TORA! TORA!(1970, U.S./Jap.)
Kiichi Ichikawa
WOMAN IN THE DUNES(1964, Jap.), p
Kodaya Ichikawa
BARBARIAN AND THE GEISHA, THE(1958)
Kon Ichikawa
ENJO(1959, Jap.), d; ODD OBSESSION(1961, Jap.), d, w, ed; FIRES ON THE PLAIN(1962, Jap.), d, ed; ACTOR'S REVENGE, AN(1963, Jap.), d; ALONE ON THE PACIFIC(1964, Jap.), d; HINOTORI(1980, Jap.), d
Raizo Ichikawa
BUDDHA(1965, Jap.); GREAT WALL, THE(1965, Jap.)
Somegoro Ichikawa
YOUNG SWORDSMAN(1964, Jap.); RABBLE, THE(1965, Jap.); WHIRLWIND(1968, Jap.)
Suisen Ichikawa
SCANDALOUS ADVENTURES OF BURAIKAN, THE(1970, Jap.)
Utaemon Ichikawa
TRAITORS(1957, Jap.)
Hirokazu Ichimura
FIGHT FOR THE GLORY(1970, Jap.), d; HOTSPRINGS HOLIDAY(1970, Jap.), d
Mia Ichioaka
WEST OF SHANGHAI(1937)
Mia Ichioka
WONDER BAR(1934); LOVE BEFORE BREAKFAST(1936)
Zaizu Ichiro
FIGHT FOR THE GLORY(1970, Jap.); TOPSY-TURVY JOURNEY(1970, Jap.)
Mario Icido
SUSPENSE(1946)
G. Icini
RING AROUND THE CLOCK(1953, Ital.), m
Rudolf Icsey
RAPTURE(1950, Ital.), ph; CURUCU, BEAST OF THE AMAZON(1956), ph

D. Iczenko
BORDER STREET(1950, Pol.)
Tan Ida
HOUSE OF STRANGE LOVES, THE(1969, Jap.), d
Fatma Idam
Misc. Silents
STAMPEDE(1930, Sudan)
Matthew Iddings
PROWLER, THE(1981)
Leonard Ide
SECRET BRIDE, THE(1935), w
Masato Ide
TATSU(1962, Jap.), w; BANDITS ON THE WIND(1964, Jap.), w; RABBLE, THE(1965, Jap.), w; SCARLET CAMELLIA, THE(1965, Jap.), w; OUTPOST OF HELL(1966, Jap.), w; RED BEARD(1966, Jap.), w; RISE AGAINST THE SWORD(1966, Jap.), w; TUNNEL TO THE SUN(1968, Jap.), w; KAGEMUSHA(1980, Jap.), p, w
Toshiro Ide
ETERNITY OF LOVE(1961, Jap.), w; NIGHT IN HONG KONG, A(1961, Jap.), w; WISER AGE(1962, Jap.), w; LONELY LANE(1963, Jap.), w; YOUTH AND HIS AMULET, THE(1963, Jap.), w; SCHOOL FOR SEX(1966, Jap.), w; THIN LINE, THE(1967, Jap.), w
Albert E. Idell
CENTENNIAL SUMMER(1946), w
Mindi Iden
1984
DREAMSCAPE(1984)
Mindy Iden
1984
JUNGLE WARRIORS(1984, U.S./Ger./Mex.)
Eric Idle
AND NOW FOR SOMETHING COMPLETELY DIFFERENT(1972, Brit.), a, w; MONTY PYTHON AND THE HOLY GRAIL(1975, Brit.), a, w; MONTY PYTHON'S LIFE OF BRIAN(1979, Brit.), a, w, m; MONTY PYTHON'S THE MEANING OF LIFE(1983, Brit.), a, w, m; YELLOWBEARD(1983)
Cinnamon Idles
1984
KIDCO(1984); SIXTEEN CANDLES(1984)
Gerri Idol
LAST AMERICAN VIRGIN, THE(1982)
Roy Idom
SHEPHERD OF THE HILLS, THE(1964)
John Idrisano
TWO WEEKS IN ANOTHER TOWN(1962)
Ramez Idriss
HIDDEN GUNS(1956), m; MAN OR GUN(1958), m; BUFFALO GUN(1961), m
Slawomir Idziak
CONSTANT FACTOR, THE(1980, Pol.), ph; CONDUCTOR, THE(1981, Pol.), ph; CONTRACT, THE(1982, Pol.), ph
Edgar Ievins
BASKET CASE(1982), p
Frank Ifield
UP JUMPED A SWAGMAN(1965, Brit.)
Eva Ifkovitch
STONE(1974, Aus.)
John Ifkovitch
STONE(1974, Aus.)
Claire Ifrane
MADEMOISELLE(1966, Fr./Brit.)
Iftikhar
GUIDE, THE(1965, U.S./India)
A. Ifukube
ANATAHAN(1953, Jap.), m
Akaira Ifukube
MYSTERIANS, THE(1959, Jap.), m; DESTROY ALL MONSTERS(1969, Jap.), m
Akira Ifukube
SECRET SCROLLS(PART I)**1/2 (1968, Jap.), m, m; CHILDREN OF HIROSHIMA(1952, Jap.), m; GODZILLA, KING OF THE MONSTERS(1956, Jap.), m; RODAN(1958, Jap.), m; BATTLE IN OUTER SPACE(1960), m; DIFFERENT SONS(1962, Jap.), m; VARAN THE UNBELIEVABLE(1962, U.S./Jap.), m; CHUSHINGURA(1963, Jap.), m; KING KONG VERSUS GODZILLA(1963, Jap.), m; FRANKENSTEIN CONQUERS THE WORLD(1964, Jap./US), m; GODZILLA VS. THE THING(1964, Jap.), m; ATRAGON(1965, Jap.), m; BUDDHA(1965, Jap.), m; GREAT WALL, THE(1965, Jap.), m; HARP OF BURMA(1967, Jap.), m; KING KONG ESCAPES(1968, Jap.), m; MAJIN(1968, Jap.), m; SHOWDOWN FOR ZATOICHI(1968, Jap.), m; ZATOICHI(1968, Jap.), m; DEVIL'S TEMPLE(1969, Jap.), m; LATITUDE ZERO(1969, U.S./Jap.), m; MONSTER ZERO(1970, Jap.), m; WAR OF THE GARGANTUAS, THE(1970, Jap.), m; YOG-MONSTER FROM SPACE(1970, Jap.), m; ZATOICHI CHALLENGED(1970, Jap.), m; ZATOICHI MEETS YOJIMBO(1970, Jap.), m; ZATOICHI'S CONSPIRACY(1974, Jap.), m
Ikira Ifukube
GHIDRAH, THE THREE-HEADED MONSTER(1965, Jap.), m
Stanislaw Igar
SARAGOSSA MANUSCRIPT, THE(1972, Pol.)
Mariko Igarashi
SHE AND HE(1967, Jap.)
Hisashi Igawa
HAHAKIRI(1963, Jap.); PRESSURE OF GUILT(1964, Jap.); FACE OF ANOTHER, THE(1967, Jap.); DEMON POND(1980, Jap.)
Hishashi Igawa
SUMMER SOLDIERS(1972, Jap.)
Togo Igawa
ALMOST TRANSPARENT BLUE(1980, Jap.)
Peter Igelhoff
SCHLAGER-PARADE(1953)
Julie Iger
HILDUR AND THE MAGICIAN(1969), a, m
Igin-Khorlo
SON OF MONGOLIA(1936, USSR)

James Iglehart
ANGELS HARD AS THEY COME(1971); SEVEN MINUTES, THE(1971)
Misc. Talkies
BAMBOO GODS AND IRON MEN(1974); DEATH FORCE(1978)
Robert Iglesia
ZELIG(1983)
Iglesias
SWORD OF EL CID, THE(1965, Span./Ital.), w
Alfonso Pompin Iglesias
CHIQUTTO PERO PICOSO(1967, Mex.)
Amalia Iglesias
THUNDERSTORM(1956)
Eugene Iglesias
BRAVE BULLS, THE(1951); INDIAN UPRISING(1951); MASK OF THE AVENGER(1951); CALIFORNIA CONQUEST(1952); DUEL AT SILVER CREEK, THE(1952); EAST OF SUMATRA(1953); JACK MCCALL, DESPERADO(1953); TUMBLEWEED(1953); TAZA, SON OF COCHISE(1954); THEY RODE WEST(1954); NAKED DAWN, THE(1955); UNDERWATER!(1955); WALK THE PROUD LAND(1956); DOMINO KID(1957); COWBOY(1958); RIO BRAVO(1959); FRONTIER UPRISING(1961); SAFE AT HOME(1962); MONEY TRAP, THE(1966)
Gene Iglesias
HIAWATHA(1952)
Lonnie Iglesias
RED RUNS THE RIVER(1963)
Losardo Iglesias
VALDEZ IS COMING(1971)
Miguel Iglesias
SWORD OF EL CID, THE(1965, Span./Ital.), d&w
Paulita Iglesias
POSSESSION OF JOEL DELANEY, THE(1972)
Ron Iglesias
DARK, THE(1979)
Michael Ignatieff
1984
1919(1984, Brit.), w
Kyunna Ignatova
STORM PLANET(1962, USSR)
A. Ignatyev
HOUSE ON THE FRONT LINE, THE(1963, USSR)
G. Ignatyeva
FAREWELL, DOVES(1962, USSR)
Ignatz the Mouse
Silents
RED MILL, THE(1927)
Pasquale Igneri
NUNZIO(1978)
Vincent Igneri
NUNZIO(1978)
Helena Ignez
TRAIN ROBBERY CONFIDENTIAL(1965, Braz.)
Robin Ignico
ANNIE(1982)
Gui Ignon
NURSE EDITH CAVELL(1939)
Igor
COUP DE GRACE(1978, Ger./Fr.), ph
Luciano Igozzi
TWO WOMEN(1961, Ital./Fr.)
Alan Igpon
SCUM(1979, Brit.)
Lloyd Igraham
ENEMY AGENT(1940)
Rex Igram
WATUSI(1959)
Francisco Igual
PANDORA AND THE FLYING DUTCHMAN(1951, Brit.)
Yoneo Iguchi
GREEN MANSIONS(1959); VARAN THE UNBELIEVABLE(1962, U.S./Jap.); GREAT BANK ROBBERY, THE(1969)
Darrow Igus
CARWASH(1976); FUN WITH DICK AND JANE(1977); NORTH AVENUE IRREGULARS, THE(1979); FOG, THE(1980)
Wiard Ihman
GALLANT HOURS, THE(1960), art d
Steve Ihnat
DRAGSTRIP RIOT(1958); PASSION STREET, U.S.A.(1964); CHASE, THE(1966); HOUR OF THE GUN(1967); COUNTDOWN(1968); KONA COAST(1968); MADIGAN(1968); DO NOT THROW CUSHIONS INTO THE RING(1970), a, p,d,w&ed; ZIGZAG(1970); FUZZ(1972); HONKERS, THE(1972), d, w
B. Ihnen
RETURN OF THE CISCO KID(1939), art d
Beverly Ihnen
FRATERNITY ROW(1977), cos
W.B. Ihnen
ONE SUNDAY AFTERNOON(1933), art d
Wiard B. Ihnen
HOLLYWOOD CAVALCADE(1939), art d; STAGECOACH(1939), set d; HUDSON'S BAY(1940), art d; JOHNNY APOLLO(1940), art d; RETURN OF FRANK JAMES, THE(1940), art d; MAN HUNT(1941), art d; WESTERN UNION(1941), art d; ICELAND(1942), art d; MAGNIFICENT DOPE, THE(1942), art d; ROXIE HART(1942), art d; JANE EYRE(1944), art d; ALONG CAME JONES(1945), prod d; TOMORROW IS FOREVER(1946), art d
Wiard Ihnen
TIME OF YOUR LIFE, THE(1948), art d; BLONDE VENUS(1932), art d; LOVE ON TOAST(1937), art d; MIDNIGHT MADONNA(1937), art d; EVERY DAY'S A HOLIDAY(1938), art d; MARYLAND(1940), art d; CRASH DIVE(1943), art d; WILSON(1944), art d; BLOOD ON THE SUN(1945), art d; KISS TOMORROW GOODBYE(1950), prod d, art d; ONLY THE VALIANT(1951), prod d; RANCHO NOTORIOUS(1952), prod d; I, THE JURY(1953), art d; LION IS IN THE STREETS, A(1953), prod d; CRASHOUT(1955), art d; INDIAN FIGHTER, THE(1955), art d; TOP

OF THE WORLD(1955), art d; KING AND FOUR QUEENS, THE(1956), art d
Willard Ihnen
DUCK SOUP(1933), art d
Willian Ihnen
DANCING PIRATE(1936), art d
Seiji Iho
HAHAKIRI(1963, Jap.), stunts
Choko Iida
RICKSHAW MAN, THE(1960, Jap.); IT STARTED IN THE ALPS(1966, Jap.); LET'S GO, YOUNG GUY!(1967, Jap.); YOUNG GUY GRADUATES(1969, Jap.); YOUNG GUY ON MT. COOK(1969, Jap.)
Kenjim Iida
SAMURAI(PART II)** (1967, Jap.)
Yumiko Iida
TWO IN THE SHADOW(1968, Jap.)
Ayako Iijima
Misc. Silents
CRAZY PAGE, A(1926, Jap.)
Daisuke Iijima
MERRY CHRISTMAS MR. LAWRENCE(1983, Jap./Brit.)
Tadashi Iimura
SECRET SCROLLS(PART I)**1/2 (1968, Jap.), ph, ph; DON'T CALL ME A CON MAN(1966, Jap.), ph; IT STARTED IN THE ALPS(1966, Jap.), ph
Iiodor
Misc. Silents
FALL OF THE ROMANOFFS, THE(1917)
Seikichi Iizumi
BANISHED(1978, Jap.), p
Kei Ijisato
ALMOST TRANSPARENT BLUE(1980, Jap.), p
Ikada
TOWN LIKE ALICE, A(1958, Brit.)
Chosuke Ikariya
HOTSPRINGS HOLIDAY(1970, Jap.)
Baby Ike
WORLD IN MY CORNER(1956)
Ike Carpenter Orchestra
HOLIDAY RHYTHM(1950)
Ryo Ikebe
BATTLE IN OUTER SPACE(1960); MAN AGAINST MAN(1961, Jap.); GORATH(1964, Jap.); TWILIGHT PATH(1965, Jap.); SIEGE OF FORT BISMARCK(1968, Jap.); WAR OF THE PLANETS(1977, Jap.)
Shim'ichiro Ikebe
1984
BALLAD OF NARAYAMA, THE(1984, Jap.), m
Shinichiro Ikebe
KAGEMUSHA(1980, Jap.), m; VENGEANCE IS MINE(1980, Jap.), m
Hiroshi Ikeda
GIRARA(1967, Jap.), spec eff
Ichiro Ikeda
MAN AGAINST MAN(1961, Jap.), w; VIXEN(1970, Jap.), w
Junko Ikeda
1984
WARRIORS OF THE WIND(1984, Jap.), anim
Kazue Ikeda
HOUSE OF BAMBOO(1955)
Otokichi Ikeda
SEA WIFE(1957, Brit.)
Ryoko Ikeda
LADY OSCAR(1979, Fr./Jap.), w
Susan Ikeda
WALK, DON'T RUN(1966); M(1970)
Tadashi Ikeda
WIND CANNOT READ, THE(1958, Brit.)
Tadeo Ikeda
FLOATING WEEDS(1970, Jap.), w
Thomas Ikeda
1984
MOSCOW ON THE HUDSON(1984); RHINESTONE(1984)
Tomio Ikeda
NAKED YOUTH(1961, Jap.), p
Kaneo Ikegami
GANGSTER VIP, THE(1968, Jap.), w
Kimiko Ikegami
MAN WHO STOLE THE SUN, THE(1980, Jap.)
Kazuo Ikehiro
HIKEN YABURI(1969, Jap.), d
Sei Ikeno
LAKE, THE(1970, Jap.), m
Shigeru Ikeno
SCHOOL FOR SEX(1966, Jap.), m; FOX WITH NINE TAILS, THE(1969, Jap.), m
Tokujiro Iketaniuchi
BARBARIAN AND THE GEISHA, THE(1958)
Junko Ikeuchi
TATSU(1962, Jap.); TILL TOMORROW COMES(1962, Jap.); THIS MADDING CROWD(1964, Jap.); YOUNG SWORDSMAN(1964, Jap.); ILLUSION OF BLOOD(1966, Jap.)
Alexander Ikonikoff
MAN WHO PLAYED GOD, THE(1932)
Gen. Ikonnikoff
LIVES OF A BENGAL LANCER(1935)
Alexander Ikonnikov
Silents
LAST COMMAND, THE(1928)
Juichi Ikuno
YOUNG GUY ON MT. COOK(1969, Jap.), art d
Etsuko Ikuta
FIGHT FOR THE GLORY(1970, Jap.); HOTSPRINGS HOLIDAY(1970, Jap.)

Nico Il Grande
LOVES AND TIMES OF SCARAMOUCHE, THE(1976, Ital.)
Jay Ilagan
MORO WITCH DOCTOR(1964, U.S./Phil.)
Ilak the Wolf Dog
Silents
JUSTICE OF THE FAR NORTH(1925)
Joseph Ilardi
SO FINE(1981)
Mohamed Ilbagi
DREAM WIFE(1953)
Danilo Ilchenko
AND QUIET FLOWS THE DON(1960 USSR)
Frances Iles [Anthony Berkeley Cox]
SUSPICION(1941), w
Gerald Iles
OH, HEAVENLY DOG!(1980)
Joe Iles
FLASH GORDON(1980)
Moya Iles
CAESAR AND CLEOPATRA(1946, Brit.)
Elie Ilf
KEEP YOUR SEATS PLEASE(1936, Brit.), w
Ilya Arnoldovich Ilf
TWELVE CHAIRS, THE(1970), d&w
Benito Ilforte
SEVEN TASKS OF ALI BABA, THE(1963, Ital.), w
Dragan Ilic
MONTENEGRO(1981, Brit./Swed.)
Ilija Ilijevski
STRANGE BREW(1983)
Strong Ilimaiti
GREEN SLIME, THE(1969)
A. Ilin
SPRINGTIME ON THE VOLGA(1961, USSR), md
Sasha Ilin
VIOLIN AND ROLLER(1962, USSR)
Peter Iling
CHILDREN OF CHANCE(1949, Brit.); WRECK OF THE MARY DEAR, THE(1959)
Igor Ilinski
Misc. Silents
AELITA(1929, USSR)
Igor Ilinsky
Misc. Silents
CIGARETTE GIRL FROM MOSSELPROM(1924, USSR); MISS MEND(1926, USSR)
Dinos Iliopoulos
GROUCH, THE(1961, Gr.)
David Ilku
LIQUID SKY(1982)
Jorge Illa
THAT MAN IN ISTANBUL(1966, Fr./Ital./Span.), w; THEY CAME TO ROB LAS VEGAS(1969, Fr./Ital./Span./Ger.), w
Ladislav Illavsky
MOSES AND AARON(1975, Ger./Fr./Ital.)
Robert Iller
MAN ON A STRING(1960)
Pola Illery
UNDER THE ROOFS OF PARIS(1930, Fr.)
Gyorgy Illes
DIALOGUE(1967, Hung.), ph; BOYS OF PAUL STREET, THE(1969, Hung./US), ph
Charles Illescas
DR. TARR'S TORTURE DUNGEON(1972, Mex.), w
Giuliano Illiani
DIARY OF AN ITALIAN(1972, Ital.), m
Lugi Illica
LA BOHEME(1965, Ital.), w
Paul Illidge
HEAD ON(1981, Can.), w
Josef Illig
WATER FOR CANITOGA(1939, Ger.), ph; HOUSE OF LIFE(1953, Ger.), ph
Rolf Illig
CELESTE(1982, Ger.)
Peter Illimg
I ACCUSE(1958, Brit.)
Evzen Illin
LOVES OF A BLONDE(1966, Czech.), m; DEATH OF TARZAN, THE(1968, Czech), m
Peter Illing
END OF THE RIVER, THE(1947, Brit.); SILVER DARLINGS, THE(1947, Brit.); AGAINST THE WIND(1948, Brit.); FLOODTIDE(1949, Brit.); HUGGETTS ABROAD, THE(1949, Brit.); MADNESS OF THE HEART(1949, Brit.); MASSACRE HILL(1949, Brit.); TAMING OF DOROTHY, THE(1950, Brit.); GREAT MANHUNT, THE(1951, Brit.); LUCKY NICK CAIN(1951); OPERATION X(1951, Brit.); TRAVELLER'S JOY(1951, Brit.); OUTCAST OF THE ISLANDS(1952, Brit.); AFFAIR IN MONTE CARLO(1953, Brit.); NEVER LET ME GO(1953, U.S./Brit.); CHANCE MEETING(1954, Brit.); FLAME AND THE FLESH(1954); HEATWAVE(1954, Brit.); WEST OF ZANZI-BAR(1954, Brit.); WOMAN'S ANGLE, THE(1954, Brit.); INNOCENTS IN PARIS(1955, Brit.); RACE FOR LIFE, A(1955, Brit.); SVENGALI(1955, Brit.); THAT LADY(1955, Brit.); BHOWANI JUNCTION(1956); LOSER TAKES ALL(1956, Brit.); PASSPORT TO TREASON(1956, Brit.); ZARAK(1956, Brit.); AS LONG AS THEY'RE HAPPY(1957, Brit.); CAMPBELL'S KINGDOM(1957, Brit.); FAREWELL TO ARMS, A(1957, Brit.); FIRE DOWN BELOW(1957, U.S./Brit.); MIRACLE IN SOHO(1957, Brit.); PICKUP AL-LEY(1957, Brit.); PURSUIT OF THE GRAF SPEE(1957, Brit.); STOWAWAY GIRL(1957, Brit.); VIOLENT STRANGER(1957, Brit.); IT'S NEVER TOO LATE(1958, Brit.); ANGRY HILLS, THE(1959, Brit.); WHIRLPOOL(1959, Brit.); BLUEBEARD'S TEN HONEY-MOONS(1960, Brit.); ELECTRONIC MONSTER. THE(1960, Brit.); SANDS OF THE DESERT(1960, Brit.); DEVIL'S DAFFODIL, THE(1961, Brit./Ger.); JET STORM(1961, Brit.); MIDDLE COURSE, THE(1961, Brit.); SECRET PARTNER, THE(1961, Brit.); HAPPY THIEVES, THE(1962); MALAGA(1962, Brit.); VILLAGE OF DAUGHT-ERS(1962, Brit.); ECHO OF DIANA(1963, Brit.); FRIENDS AND NEIGHBORS(1963, Brit.); NINE HOURS TO RAMA(1963, U.S./Brit.); V.I.P.s, THE(1963, Brit.); SECRET

DOOR, THE(1964); DEVILS OF DARKNESS, THE(1965, Brit.); MAN COULD GET KILLED, A(1966)
Misc. Talkies
BORN FOR TROUBLE(1955); OPERATION STOGIE(1960, Brit.)

John Illingsworth
WALKABOUT(1971, Aus./U.S.)

Neil Illingsworth
1984
HEART OF THE STAG(1984, New Zealand), w

Louise Illington
JOLSON SINGS AGAIN(1949)

Margaret Illington
Misc. Silents
INNER SHRINE, THE(1917); SACRIFICE(1917)

Marie Illington
Silents
FIRES OF INNOCENCE(1922, Brit.)
Misc. Silents
VICAR OF WAKEFIELD, THE(1916, Brit.); HEADMASTER, THE(1921, Brit.)

Commodore Sir Gordon Illingworth/ret.
TITANIC(1953), tech adv

Maurine Illouz
DEAR DETECTIVE(1978, Fr.)

Stanley Illsley
SIEGE OF SIDNEY STREET, THE(1960, Brit.)

Edward Ilou
HE WALKED BY NIGHT(1948), art d; HOLLOW TRIUMPH(1948), art d; MAN FROM TEXAS, THE(1948), art d; BLACK BOOK, THE(1949), art d; PORT OF NEW YORK(1949), art d; IROQUOIS TRAIL, THE(1950), art d; FACE TO FACE(1952), art d; MY SIX CONVICTS(1952), art d

Edward L. Ilou
BEHIND LOCKED DOORS(1948), art d; IN THIS CORNER(1948), art d; LET'S LIVE A LITTLE(1948), art d; NOOSE HANGS HIGH, THE(1948), art d; NORTHWEST STAMPEDE(1948), art d; RAW DEAL(1948), art d; UNDER THE GUN(1951), art d; KANSAS CITY CONFIDENTIAL(1952), art d; GUN BELT(1953), art d; RAIDERS OF THE SEVEN SEAS(1953), art d; EL ALAMEIN(1954), art d; BOY AND THE PIRATES, THE(1960), art d; WICKED DREAMS OF PAULA SCHULTZ, THE(1968), art d

N. Ilushin
SKY CALLS, THE(1959, USSR), spec eff

B. Ilyasov
HAMLET(1966, USSR)

V. Ilyenko
FAREWELL, DOVES(1962, USSR), ph; KIEV COMEDY, A(1963, USSR), ph; SHADOWS OF FORGOTTEN ANCESTORS(1967, USSR), ph

Igor Ilyinsky
BALLAD OF A HUSSAR(1963, USSR)

L. Ilyukhin
LAST GAME, THE(1964, USSR)

Chiaki Imada
GALAXY EXPRESS(1982, Jap.), p

Jeff Imada
GOING BERSERK(1983)

Masao Imafuku
GODZILLA VERSUS THE COSMIC MONSTER(1974, Jap.)

Jean Image
JOHNNY THE GIANT KILLER(1953, Fr.), p, d

Kinetic Image
NIGHTBEAST(1982), spec eff

Image 3
SPACEHUNTER: ADVENTURES IN THE FORBIDDEN ZONE(1983), spec eff

Hiroshi Imai
BUDDHA(1965, Jap.), ph

Kentaro Imai
PERFORMERS, THE(1970, Jap.)

Hideo Imamura
VARAN THE UNBELIEVABLE(1962, U.S./Jap.); WOMAN HUNT(1962)

Shohei Imamura
INSECT WOMAN, THE(1964, Jap.), d, w; UNHOLY DESIRE(1964, Jap.), d, w; EAST CHINA SEA(1969, Jap.), w; KURAGEJIMA–LEGENDS FROM A SOUTHERN ISLAND(1970, Jap.), d, w; VENGEANCE IS MINE(1980, Jap.), d
1984
BALLAD OF NARAYAMA, THE(1984, Jap.), d&w

Iman
HUMAN FACTOR, THE(1979, Brit.)

Eddie Imazu
MURDER MAN(1935), art d; THREE WISE GUYS, THE(1936), art d; BOOM TOWN(1940), art d; NEW MOON(1940), art d; HONKY TONK(1941), art d; KILLER McCOY(1947), art d; ROMANCE OF ROSY RIDGE, THE(1947), art d; SECOND CHANCE(1947), art d; HILLS OF HOME(1948), art d; CHALLENGE TO LASSIE(1949), art d; MISS MINK OF 1949(1949), art d; TROUBLE PREFERRED(1949), art d; SHADOW ON THE WALL(1950), art d; SKIPPER SURPRISED HIS WIFE, THE(1950), art d; WATCH THE BIRDIE(1950), art d; CALLAWAY WENT THATAWAY(1951), art d; GO FOR BROKE(1951), art d; IT'S A BIG COUNTRY(1951), art d; TALL TARGET, THE(1951), art d; CARBINE WILLIAMS(1952), art d; DESPERATE SEARCH(1952), art d; TALK ABOUT A STRANGER(1952), art d; YOU FOR ME(1952), art d; I LOVE MELVIN(1953), art d; MARAUDERS, THE(1955), art d; TEAHOUSE OF THE AUGUST MOON, THE(1956), art d; STOPOVER TOKYO(1957), art d; HOLE IN THE HEAD, A(1959), art d; CROWDED SKY, THE(1960), art d; SERGEANT RUTLEDGE(1960), art d; ESCAPE FROM ZAHRAIN(1962), art d; MAN WHO SHOT LIBERTY VALANCE, THE(1962), art d; DONOVAN'S REEF(1963), art d; MC LINTOCK!(1963), art d; ADVANCE TO THE REAR(1964), art d; KISSIN' COUSINS(1964), art d; WHEN THE BOYS MEET THE GIRLS(1965), art d; HOLD ON(1966), art d; NAMU, THE KILLER WHALE(1966), art d; SEVEN WOMEN(1966), art d
Silents
CALIFORNIA(1927), set d

Eddieu Imazu
YELLOW CAB MAN, THE(1950), art d

Edward Imazu
THREE WISE FOOLS(1946), art d; CLARENCE, THE CROSS-EYED LION(1965), art d

Fernando Imbert
TIN GIRL, THE(1970, Ital.), w

David Imboden
Silents
GIMMIE(1923); SOULS FOR SALE(1923); KING OF KINGS, THE(1927)

A.B. Imeson
LAST POST, THE(1929, Brit.); RIVER HOUSE MYSTERY, THE(1935, Brit.)
Silents
PICTURE OF DORIAN GRAY, THE(1916, Brit.); WHAT EVERY WOMAN KNOWS(1917, Brit.); AVE MARIA(1918, Brit.); MONKEY'S PAW, THE(1923, Brit.); OUT TO WIN(1923, Brit.); NOTORIOUS MRS. CARRICK, THE(1924, Brit.)
Misc. Silents
DIANA OF DOBSON'S(1917, Brit.); WHAT WOULD A GENTLEMAN DO?(1918, Brit.); RUSSIA - LAND OF TOMORROW(1919, Brit.); BREED OF THE TRESHAMS, THE(1920, Brit.); FAITHFUL HEART, THE(1922, Brit.); HOUSE OF PERIL, THE(1922, Brit.); BONNIE PRINCE CHARLIE(1923, Brit.); CLAUDE DUVAL(1924, Brit.); WHITE SHADOWS(1924, Brit.)

Gary Imhof
Misc. Talkies
SENIORS, THE(1978)

Marcelle Imhof
JIGGS AND MAGGIE IN SOCIETY(1948); ACCORDING TO MRS. HOYLE(1951)

Roger Imhof
ME AND MY GAL(1932); CHARLIE CHAN'S GREATEST CASE(1933); HOO-PLA(1933); PADDY, THE NEXT BEST THING(1933); DAVID HARUM(1934); EVER SINCE EVE(1934); GRAND CANARY(1934); HANDY ANDY(1934); JUDGE PRIEST(1934); LOVE TIME(1934); MUSIC IN THE AIR(1934); SLEEPERS EAST(1934); WILD GOLD(1934); FARMER TAKES A WIFE, THE(1935); GEORGE WHITE'S 1935 SCANDALS(1935); LIFE BEGINS AT 40(1935); ONE MORE SPRING(1935); STEAMBOAT ROUND THE BEND(1935); UNDER PRESSURE(1935); IN HIS STEPS(1936); RIFF-RAFF(1936); ROAMING LADY(1936); SAN FRANCISCO(1936); SON COMES HOME, A(1936); THREE GODFATHERS(1936); GIRL LOVES BOY(1937); HIGH, WIDE AND HANDSOME(1937); NORTH OF NOME(1937); RED LIGHTS AHEAD(1937); SWEETHEART OF THE NAVY(1937); THERE GOES THE GROOM(1937); EVERY DAY'S A HOLIDAY(1938); DRUMS ALONG THE MOHAWK(1939); EVERYTHING HAPPENS AT NIGHT(1939); NANCY DREW, TROUBLE SHOOTER(1939); TELL NO TALES(1939); THEY SHALL HAVE MUSIC(1939); ABE LINCOLN IN ILLINOIS(1940); GRAPES OF WRATH(1940); I WAS AN ADVENTURESS(1940); LITTLE OLD NEW YORK(1940); WAY OF ALL FLESH, THE(1940); LADY FROM CHEYENNE(1941); MAN HUNT(1941); MYSTERY SHIP(1941); IT HAPPENED IN FLATBUSH(1942); THIS GUN FOR HIRE(1942); CASANOVA IN BURLESQUE(1944); HOME IN INDIANA(1944)

Fred Imhoff
MOZART STORY, THE(1948, Aust.)

Fritz Imhoff
LITTLE MELODY FROM VIENNA(1948, Aust.); VIENNA WALTZES(1961, Aust.); GOOD SOLDIER SCHWEIK, THE(1963, Ger.); YOU ARE THE WORLD FOR ME(1964, Aust.)

Gary Imhoff
SENIORS, THE(1978); NUDE BOMB, THE(1980)

Anthony Imi
INADMISSIBLE EVIDENCE(1968, Brit.), ph

Tomy Imi
NATE AND HAYES(1983, U.S./New Zealand), ph

Tony Imi
JUNKET 89(1970, Brit.), ph; DULCIMA(1971, Brit.), ph; LONG AGO, TOMORROW(1971, Brit.), ph; UNIVERSAL SOLDIER(1971, Brit.), ph; IT'S A 2"6" ABOVE THE GROUND WORLD(1972, Brit.), ph; LIKELY LADS, THE(1976, Brit.), ph; SLIPPER AND THE ROSE, THE(1976, Brit.), ph; BRASS TARGET(1978), ph; BREAKTHROUGH(1978, Ger.), ph; INTERNATIONAL VELVET(1978, Brit.), ph; IT'S NOT THE SIZE THAT COUNTS(1979, Brit.), ph; FFOLKES(1980, Brit.), ph; SEA WOLVES, THE(1981, Brit.), ph; NIGHT CROSSING(1982), ph

Anton Imkamp
MY HEART IS CALLING(1935, Brit.)

Agnes Imlay
ADMIRAL'S SECRET, THE(1934, Brit.); ELIZA COMES TO STAY(1936, Brit.); MORALS OF MARCUS, THE(1936, Brit.); HIGH TREASON(1937, Brit.)

Jerrold Immel
HOUSE ON SKULL MOUNTAIN, THE(1974), m; SOURDOUGH(1977), m; DEATH HUNT(1981), m; MEGAFORCE(1982), m

Frederich Immler
Silents
PASSION(1920, Ger.)

Nino Imparato
NAVAJO JOE(1967, Ital./Span.)

Toni Impekoven
COURT CONCERT, THE(1936, Ger.), w

Leo Impellizzeri
1984
STRANGERS KISS(1984)

Rino Imperio
'TIS A PITY SHE'S A WHORE(1973, Ital.)

Rosario Imperio
ON THE RIVERA(1951); MA AND PA KETTLE ON VACATION(1953)

Margie Impert
HOWLING, THE(1981); STAR CHAMBER, THE(1983)

Ernie Impett
FURY AND THE WOMAN(1937)

Betty Impey
NAUGHTY ARLETTE(1951, Brit.); RELUCTANT HEROES(1951, Brit.); ENEMY FROM SPACE(1957, Brit.); STRANGER IN TOWN(1957, Brit.)

Craig Impleman
FAST BREAK(1979)

John Impolito
G-MEN(1935); TOP HAT(1935); SONG IS BORN, A(1948)

Celia Imrie
HOUSE OF WHIPCORD(1974, Brit.); WICKED LADY, THE(1983, Brit.)
Kathy Imrie
SHAFT'S BIG SCORE(1972)
Richard Imrie
OPERATION CROSSBOW(1965, U.S./Ital.), w; THEY'RE A WEIRD MOB(1966, Aus.), w
A.B. Imseon
RIVER HOUSE MYSTERY, THE(1935, Brit.), p
Henry Imus
WINGS OF THE MORNING(1937, Brit.), ph
Kanta Ina
WAR OF THE MONSTERS(1972, Jap.)
Ina Ray Hutton's band
BIG BROADCAST OF 1936, THE(1935)
Sayo Inaba
1984
KILLING FIELDS, THE(1984, Brit.)
Misc. Talkies
SPACE RIDERS(1984)
Yoshio Inaba
SEVEN SAMURAI, THE(1956, Jap.); HAHAKIRI(1963, Jap.); CHALLENGE, THE(1982)
Inagaki
RABBLE, THE(1965, Jap.), w
Hiroshi Inagaki
SAMURAI(PART III)** (1967, Jap.), d, w, d, w; SECRET SCROLLS(PART I)**1/2 (1968, Jap.), d, w, d, w; SAMURAI(1955, Jap.), d, w; RICKSHAW MAN, THE(1960, Jap.), d, w; LIFE OF A COUNTRY DOCTOR(1961, Jap.), d; TATSU(1962, Jap.), d; CHUSHINGURA(1963, Jap.), d; YOUTH AND HIS AMULET, THE(1963, Jap.), p&d; BANDITS ON THE WIND(1964, Jap.), d; YOUNG SWORDSMAN(1964, Jap.), d, w; RABBLE, THE(1965, Jap.), p, d; RISE AGAINST THE SWORD(1966, Jap.), d, w; KOJIRO(1967, Jap.), d, w; WHIRLWIND(1968, Jap.), d, w; DAREDEVIL IN THE CASTLE(1969, Jap.), d; UNDER THE BANNER OF SAMURAI(1969, Jap.), d
Koichi Inagaki
INHERITANCE, THE(1964, Jap.), w; SOLDIER'S PRAYER, A(1970, Jap.), w
Shun Inagaki
GLOWING AUTUMN(1981, Jap.), w
Takashi Inagaki
TILL TOMORROW COMES(1962, Jap.); NONE BUT THE BRAVE(1965, U.S./Jap.); TIGER FLIGHT(1965, Jap.)
Takeshi Kimura Inagaki
DAREDEVIL IN THE CASTLE(1969, Jap.), w
Vinay Inambar
ELEPHANT CALLED SLOWLY, AN(1970, Brit.)
Hideo Inamura
MARINES, LET'S GO(1961)
Kuzako Inano
WHIRLPOOL OF WOMAN(1966, Jap.)
Inansi
LIQUID SKY(1982)
Ada Ince
FIGHTING ROOKIE, THE(1934); FRONTIER DAYS(1934); RAINBOW'S END(1935); STOLEN HARMONY(1935)
E.S. Ince
FLIGHT FROM ASHIYA(1964, U.S./Jap.)
James Ince
SHOOT(1976, Can.)
John Ince
ALIAS FRENCH GERTIE(1930); HOT CURVES(1930); MOBY DICK(1930); OKLAHOMA CYCLONE(1930); HEADIN' FOR TROUBLE(1931); MOUNTED FURY(1931); WILD WEST WHOOPEE(1931); DESTRY RIDES AGAIN(1932); HONOR OF THE PRESS(1932); HUMAN TARGETS(1932); NO LIVING WITNESS(1932); THIRTEENTH GUEST, THE(1932); BOWERY, THE(1933); KISS BEFORE THE MIRROR, THE(1933); ONE YEAR LATER(1933); PENAL CODE, THE(1933); PICTURE SNATCHER(1933); ROMAN SCANDALS(1933); THRILL HUNTER, THE(1933); CAT'S PAW, THE(1934); WE LIVE AGAIN(1934); CHINA SEAS(1935); CIRCLE OF DEATH(1935); FOLIES DERGERE(1935); IN OLD KENTUCKY(1935); LIFE BEGINS AT 40(1935); MAN WHO RECLAIMED HIS HEAD, THE(1935); SHE COULDN'T TAKE IT(1935); SHE MARRIED HER BOSS(1935); STAR OF MIDNIGHT(1935); TEXAS TERROR(1935); COMIN' ROUND THE MOUNTAIN(1936); DON'T TURN'EM LOOSE(1936); NIGHT CARGO(1936); SPEED REPORTER(1936); SAN QUENTIN(1937); TENDERFOOT GOES WEST, A(1937); WAY OUT WEST(1937); GO CHASE YOURSELF(1938); YOU CAN'T TAKE IT WITH YOU(1938); RETURN OF WILD BILL, THE(1940); THIRD FINGER, LEFT HAND(1940); BILLY THE KID'S RANGE WAR(1941); HERE COMES MR. JORDAN(1941); MEET JOHN DOE(1941); CODE OF THE OUTLAW(1942); FRECKLES COMES HOME(1942); GALLANT LADY(1942); MEN OF SAN QUENTIN(1942); MIRACLE KID(1942); PANTHER'S CLAW, THE(1942); PRISON GIRL(1942); MAN OF COURAGE(1943); SCREAM IN THE NIGHT(1943); HEAVENLY DAYS(1944); WHAT A MAN!(1944); WILSON(1944); LOST TRAIL, THE(1945); CRACK-UP(1946); DEADLINE AT DAWN(1946); LAST FRONTIER UPRISING(1947); MAGIC TOWN(1947); WELCOME STRANGER(1947)
Misc. Talkies
GUNS FOR HIRE(1932)
Silents
SEALED LIPS(1915), d
Misc. Silents
BATTLE OF SHILOH, THE(1914), d; ONLY WAY OUT, THE(1915); CRUCIAL TEST, THE(1916), d; HER MATERNAL RIGHT(1916), d; STRUGGLE, THE(1916), d; SECRET STRINGS(1918), d; BLACKIE'S REDEMPTION(1919), d; BLIND MAN'S EYES(1919), d; FAVOR TO A FRIEND, A(1919), d; ONE-THING-AT-A-TIME O'DAY(1919), d; PLEASE GET MARRIED(1919), d; HELD IN TRUST(1920), d; OLD LADY 31(1920), d; FATE(1921); LOVE TRAP, THE(1923), d; CHEAP KISSES(1924), d; GIRL OF GOLD, THE(1925), d; GREAT JEWEL ROBBERY, THE(1925), d; IF MARRIAGE FAILS(1925), d; HER BIG ADVENTURE(1926), d; WAGES OF CONSCIENCE(1927), a, d
John E. Ince
MR. CELEBRITY(1942)

Silents
SHOULD A WOMAN TELL?(1920), d
Misc. Silents
SOMEONE IN THE HOUSE(1920), d; PASSION FRUIT(1921), d; HOUR OF RECKONING, THE(1927), a, d; BLACK FEATHER(1928), d
Ralph Ince
HURRICANE(1929), d; WALL STREET(1929); NUMBERED MEN(1930); BIG GAMBLE, THE(1931); GENTLEMAN'S FATE(1931); LITTLE CAESAR(1931); STAR WITNESS(1931); COUNTY FAIR, THE(1932); GIRL OF THE RIO(1932); GORILLA SHIP, THE(1932); GUILTY AS HELL(1932); HATCHET MAN, THE(1932); LAW AND ORDER(1932); LAW OF THE SEA(1932); LOST SQUADRON, THE(1932); MEN OF CHANCE(1932); MOUTHPIECE, THE(1932); PRIDE OF THE LEGION, THE(1932); STATE'S ATTORNEY(1932); TENDERFOOT, THE(1932); BIG PAYOFF, THE(1933); HAVANA WIDOWS(1933); LUCKY DEVILS(1933), d; MALAY NIGHTS(1933); MEN OF AMERICA(1933), a, d; FLAMING GOLD(1934), d; GLIMPSE OF PARADISE, A(1934, Brit.), d; NO ESCAPE(1934, Brit.), a, d; BLACK MASK(1935, Brit.), d; BLUE SMOKE(1935, Brit.), a, d; CRIME UNLIMITED(1935, Brit.), d; MR. WHAT'S-HIS-NAME(1935, Brit.), d; MURDER AT MONTE CARLO(1935, Brit.), d; ROLLING HOME(1935, Brit.), a, d; SO YOU WON'T TALK?(1935, Brit.); FAIR EXCHANGE(1936, Brit.), d; GAOL BREAK(1936, Brit.), a, d; HAIL AND FAREWELL(1936, Brit.), d; IT'S YOU I WANT(1936, Brit.), d; JURY'S EVIDENCE(1936, Brit.), d; TWELVE GOOD MEN(1936, Brit.), d; IT'S NOT CRICKET(1937, Brit.), d; MAN WHO MADE DIAMONDS, THE(1937, Brit.), d; PERFECT CRIME, THE(1937, Brit.), a, d; SIDE STREET ANGEL(1937, Brit.), d; VULTURE, THE(1937, Brit.), d; GIRL THIEF, THE(1938)
Misc. Talkies
HIT OF THE SNOW(1928), d; BIG FIGHT, THE(1930)
Silents
JUGGERNAUT, THE(1915), d, w; SINS OF THE MOTHERS(1915), d; ARGYLE CASE, THE(1917), d, w; TODAY(1917), d; OUR MRS. McCHESNEY(1918), d; PERFECT LOVER, THE(1919), d; OUT YONDER(1919), d; AFTER MIDNIGHT(1921), d; MAN'S HOME, A(1921), d; WET GOLD(1921), a, d; RECKLESS YOUTH(1922), d; REFEREE, THE(1922), d; WIDE-OPEN TOWN, A(1922), d; SUCCESS(1923), d; HOUSE OF YOUTH, THE(1924), d; LADY ROBINHOOD(1925), d; YELLOW FINGERS(1926); HOME STRUCK(1927), d; WANDERING GIRLS(1927), d; CHICAGO AFTER MIDNIGHT(1928), a, d; HARDBOILED(1929), d&t
Misc. Silents
MILLION BID, A(1914), d; COMBAT, THE(1916), d; CONFLICT, THE(1916), d; DESTROYERS, THE(1916), d; MY LADY'S SLIPPER(1916), d; CO-RESPONDENT, THE(1917), d; FIELDS OF HONOR(1918), d; FIVE THOUSAND AN HOUR(1918), d; HER MAN(1918), d; TEMPERED STEEL(1918), d; WOMAN ETERNAL, THE(1918), d; FROM HEADQUARTERS(1919), d; PAINTED WORLD, THE(1919), d; PANTHER WOMAN, THE(1919), d; SEALED HEARTS(1919), d; SHADOWS OF THE PAST(1919), d; STITCH IN TIME, A(1919), d; TOO MANY CROOKS(1919), d; TWO WOMEN(1919), d; VIRTUOUS MEN(1919), d; WRECK, THE(1919), d; HIS WIFE'S MONEY(1920), d; OUT OF THE SHOWS(1920), a, d; RED FOAM(1920), d; HIGHEST LAW, THE(1921), a, d; REMORSELESS LOVE(1921), d; TROPICAL LOVE(1921), d; CHANNING OF THE NORTHWEST(1922), d; COUNTERFEIT LOVE(1923), d; HOMEWARD BOUND(1923), d; CHORUS LADY, THE(1924), d; DYNAMITE SMITH(1924), d; MORAL SINNER, THE(1924), d; UNINVITED GUEST, THE(1924), d; ALIAS MARY FLYNN(1925), d; PLAYING WITH SOULS(1925), d; SMOOTH AS SATIN(1925), d; BETTER WAY, THE(1926), a, d; BIGGER THAN BARNUM'S(1926), a, d; BREED OF THE SEA(1926), a, d; LONE WOLF RETURNS, THE(1926), d; SEA WOLF, THE(1926), a, d; MOULDERS OF MEN(1927), d; NOT FOR PUBLICATION(1927), d; SHANGHAIED(1927), a, d; SOUTH SEA LOVE(1927), d; CONEY ISLAND(1928), d; DANGER STREET(1928), d; HIT OF THE SHOW(1928), d; SINGAPORE MUTINY, THE(1928), a, d
Ralph W. Ince
Misc. Silents
NINETY AND NINE, THE(1916), d
Thomas Ince
Silents
JIM GRIMSBY'S BOY(1916), sup; ASHES OF HOPE(1917), w
Thomas H. Ince
Silents
BATTLE OF GETTYSBURG(1914), d; TYPHOON, THE(1914), sup; WRATH OF THE GODS, THE or THE DESTRUCTION OF SAKURA JIMA(1914), sup; ALIEN, THE(1915), d; DESPOILER, THE(1915), d, w; EDGE OF THE ABYSS, THE(1915), sup; ITALIAN, THE(1915), sup, w; REWARD, THE(1915), w; CAPTIVE GOD, THE(1916), p; CIVILIZATION, THE(1917), p, d; PRICE MARK, THE(1917), sup; TRUTHFUL TULLIVER(1917), sup; BRANDING BROADWAY(1918), sup; FAMILY SKELETON, THE(1918), sup; KAISER'S SHADOW, THE(1918), sup; MIDNIGHT PATROL, THE(1918), sup; NAUGHTY, NAUGHTY!(1918), sup; NINE O'CLOCK TOWN, A(1918), sup; PLAYING THE GAME(1918), sup; QUICKSANDS(1918), sup; WHEN DO WE EAT?(1918), sup; BREED OF MEN(1919), sup; EXTRAVAGANCE(1919), sup; FALSE FACES(1919), sup; POPPY GIRL'S HUSBAND, THE(1919), sup; ALARM CLOCK ANDY(1920), sup; DARK MIRROR, THE(1920), sup; JAILBIRD, THE(1920), sup; OLD FASHIONED BOY, AN(1920), sup; PARIS GREEN(1920), sup; RED HOT DOLLARS(1920), sup; BEAU REVEL(1921), sup; BRONZE BELL, THE(1921), sup; CHICKENS(1921), sup; LYING LIPS(1921), sup; ONE A MINUTE(1921), sup; ROOKIE'S RETURN, THE(1921), sup; ANNA CHRISTIE(1923), p
Misc. Silents
CUSTER'S LAST FIGHT(1925), p
Thomas H. Ince, Jr.
MAN FROM GUN TOWN, THE(1936), w
Bonnie Inch
THERE IS NO 13(1977)
Kemal Inci
DRY SUMMER(1967, Turkey), w
Manuel Inclan
PORTRAIT OF MARIA(1946, Mex.)
Miguel Inclan
FUGITIVE, THE(1947); FORT APACHE(1948); LOS OLVIDADOS(1950, Mex.); INDIAN UPRISING(1951); SEVEN CITIES OF GOLD(1955); BANDIDO(1956)
S. Federico Inclan
POLITICAL ASYLUM(1975, Mex./Guatemalan), w
Annabella Incontrera
GOLIATH AND THE VAMPIRES(1964, Ital.); LOVE NOW...PAY LATER(1966, Ital.); DEVIL IN LOVE, THE(1968, Ital.); ASSASSINATION BUREAU, THE(1969, Brit.); VENGEANCE IS MINE(1969, Ital./Span.); BLACK BELLY OF THE TARANTULA, THE(1972, Ital.); RETURN OF SABATA(1972, Ital./Fr./Ger.); VOYAGE, THE(1974,

Ital.)

The Incredible Orlando [Jack Birkett]
1984
MIDSUMMER NIGHT'S DREAM, A(1984, Brit./Span.)

Agenore Incrocci
SIGN OF VENUS, THE(1955, Ital.), w; PASSIONATE THIEF, THE(1963, Ital.), w; CASANOVA '70(1965, Ital.), w; TIGER AND THE PUSSYCAT, THE(1967, U.S., Ital.), w; WITCHES, THE(1969, Fr./Ital.), w
1984
CRACKERS(1984), w

Alberto Incrocci
PASSION OF LOVE(1982, Ital./Fr.)

Estela Inda
LOS OLVIDADOS(1950, Mex.)

Stella Inda
CAPTAIN FROM CASTILE(1947)

Indian Actors Workshop of Hollywood
SMITH(1969)

Indian Dancers from the Taos Pueblo
PRIEST OF LOVE(1981, Brit.)

Gary Indiana
TRAP DOOR, THE(1980)

800 Pawnee, Sioux, Cheyenne Indians
Silents
IRON HORSE, THE(1924)

Franco Indovina
THREE FACES OF A WOMAN(1965, Ital.), d, w; CATCH AS CATCH CAN(1968, Ital.), d, w; OLDEST PROFESSION, THE(1968, Fr./Ital./Ger.), d

Mary Indovino
8 ½(1963, Ital.)

Ratanaporn Indrakamhaeng
1 2 3 MONSTER EXPRESS(1977, Thai.)

Seeta Indrani
NUTCRACKER(1982, Brit.)

John Indresano
MR. HEX(1946)

John Indriasano
MILLIONAIRE FOR CHRISTY, A(1951)

John Indrisano
TWO FISTED(1935); GO WEST, YOUNG MAN(1936); LAUGHING IRISH EYES(1936); MURDER GOES TO COLLEGE(1937); EVERY DAY'S A HOLIDAY(1938); RINGSIDE MAISIE(1941); DUFFY'S TAVERN(1945); GREAT JOHN L. THE(1945), stunts; MURDER, MY SWEET(1945); NAUGHTY NINETIES, THE(1945); IN FAST COMPANY(1946); KID FROM BOOKLYN, THE(1946); LIVE WIRES(1946); OUR HEARTS WERE GROWING UP(1946); CHRISTMAS EVE(1947); FORCE OF EVIL(1948); LULU BELLE(1948); TROUBLE MAKERS(1948); FIGHTING FOOLS(1949); JOE PALOOKA IN THE BIG FIGHT(1949), a, staging; JOE PALOOKA IN THE COUNTERPUNCH(1949); KNOCK ON ANY DOOR(1949); LADY GAMBLES, THE(1949); SET-UP, THE(1949), tech adv; TENSION(1949); YELLOW CAB MAN, THE(1950); IRON MAN, THE(1951); GLORY ALLEY(1952); MEET DANNY WILSON(1952); NO HOLDS BARRED(1952); SOMETHING TO LIVE FOR(1952); GUYS AND DOLLS(1955); SEA CHASE, THE(1955); DEVIL'S HAIRPIN, THE(1957); JAILHOUSE ROCK(1957); HOT SPELL(1958); 10 NORTH FREDERICK(1958); SOME LIKE IT HOT(1959); OCEAN'S ELEVEN(1960); PURPLE GANG, THE(1960); WHO'S GOT THE ACTION?(1962); FOR LOVE OR MONEY(1963); FOUR FOR TEXAS(1963), stunts; HUD(1963); UNDER THE YUM-YUM TREE(1963); HOUSE IS NOT A HOME, A(1964); HUMAN DUPLICATORS, THE(1965); LEGEND OF LYLAH CLARE, THE(1968), stunts

Johnny Indrisano
SHE GETS HER MAN(1935); WINNING TICKET, THE(1935); JOHNNY ANGEL(1945); CRACK-UP(1946); FIGHTING MAD(1948); IN THIS CORNER(1948); CALLAWAY WENT THATAWAY(1951); PIER 23(1951); ISLAND IN THE SKY(1953); TENNESSEE CHAMP(1954); CHICAGO CONFIDENTIAL(1957); BLUEPRINT FOR ROBBERY(1961); MANCHURIAN CANDIDATE, THE(1962)

Rame Indriss
BADGE OF MARSHAL BRENNAN, THE(1957), m

Luis Induni
SHAME OF THE SABINE WOMEN, THE(1962, Mex.); UNSATISFIED, THE(1964, Span.); SWORD OF EL CID, THE(1965, Span./Ital.); TEXICAN, THE(1966, U.S./Span.); THAT MAN IN ISTANBUL(1966, Fr./Ital./Span.); FEW BULLETS MORE, A(1968, Ital./Span.); CAPTAIN APACHE(1971, Brit.)

Industrial Light & Magic
DRAGONSLAYER(1981), spec off; E.T. THE EXTRA-TERRESTRIAL(1982), spec eff
1984
HERE COMES SANTA CLAUS(1984), spec eff

Elaine Inescort
ROLLING IN MONEY(1934, Brit.)

Freida Inescort
SHADOWS ON THE STAIRS(1941); JUKE BOX RHYTHM(1959)

Frieda Inescort
DARK ANGEL, THE(1935); GARDEN MURDER CASE, THE(1936); GIVE ME YOUR HEART(1936); HOLLYWOOD BOULEVARD(1936); IF YOU COULD ONLY COOK(1936); KING STEPS OUT, THE(1936); MARY OF SCOTLAND(1936); ANOTHER DAWN(1937); CALL IT A DAY(1937); GREAT O'MALLEY, THE(1937); PORTIA ON TRIAL(1937); TARZAN FINDS A SON!(1939); WOMAN DOCTOR(1939); WOMAN IS THE JUDGE, A(1939); ZERO HOUR, THE(1939); CONVICTED WOMAN(1940); LETTER, THE(1940); PRIDE AND PREJUDICE(1940); FATHER'S SON(1941); REMEMBER THE DAY(1941); SUNNY(1941); TRIAL OF MARY DUGAN, THE(1941); YOU'LL NEVER GET RICH(1941); COURTSHIP OF ANDY HARDY, THE(1942); STREET OF CHANCE(1942); SWEATER GIRL(1942); IT COMES UP LOVE(1943); MISSION TO MOSCOW(1943); HEAVENLY DAYS(1944); RETURN OF THE VAMPIRE, THE(1944); JUDGE STEPS OUT, THE(1949); WHIPPED, THE(1950); PLACE IN THE SUN, A(1951); NEVER WAVE AT A WAC(1952); CASANOVA'S BIG NIGHT(1954); FLAME OF THE ISLANDS(1955); FOXFIRE(1955); SHE-CREATURE, THE(1956); DARBY'S RANGERS(1958); SENIOR PROM(1958); ALLIGATOR PEOPLE, THE(1959)

Irene Inescort
DEMONSTRATOR(1971, Aus.); LONELY HEARTS(1983, Aus.)

Frieda Inescourt
BEAUTY FOR THE ASKING(1939); AMAZING MRS. HOLLIDAY(1943); EDDY DUCHIN STORY, THE(1956); CROWDED SKY, THE(1960)

Inesita
HERE COME THE GIRLS(1953)

Sim Iness
SIGN OF THE PAGAN(1954); LADY GODIVA(1955)

Angelo Infante
VALACHI PAPERS, THE(1972, Ital./Fr.); COUNT OF MONTE CRISTO(1976, Brit.)

Eddie Infante
AMERICAN GUERRILLA IN THE PHILIPPINES, AN(1950); NO PLACE TO HIDE(1956); NO MAN IS AN ISLAND(1962); CAVALRY COMMAND(1963, U.S./Phil.); WARKILL(1968, U.S./Phil.)
Misc. Talkies
BLOOD THIRST(1965 Phil./U.S.)

Frank Infante
ROADIE(1980)

Sonia Infante
MACARIO(1961, Mex.); DOCTOR OF DOOM(1962, Mex.)

Angelo Infanti
FRAGMENT OF FEAR(1971, Brit.); LE MANS(1971); GODFATHER, THE(1972); AND NOW MY LOVE(1975, Fr.); SQUEEZE, THE(1980, Ital.)

Luigi Infantino
THREE BROTHERS(1982, Ital.)

Carlo Infascelli
STRANGER IN TOWN, A(1968, U.S./Ital.), p

Roberto Infascelli
SHOOT FIRST, LAUGH LAST(1967, Ital./Ger./U.S.), p; STRANGER RETURNS, THE(1968, U.S./Ital./Ger./Span.), p

Carlo Infescelli
GRAN VARIETA(1955, Ital.), p

Manuel Infiesta
UNSATISFIED, THE(1964, Span.), art d

Information International, Inc.
LOOKER(1981), anim

Ted Infuhr
MADAME BOVARY(1949)

Teddy Infuhr
GHOST OF FRANKENSTEIN, THE(1942); PARDON MY SARONG(1942); TUTTLES OF TAHITI(1942); AMAZING MRS. HOLLIDAY(1943); HERS TO HOLD(1943); MADAME CURIE(1943); NORTH STAR, THE(1943); SHE'S FOR ME(1943); HEAVENLY DAYS(1944); SAN DIEGO, I LOVE YOU(1944); SHERLOCK HOLMES AND THE SPIDER WOMAN(1944); UNWRITTEN CODE, THE(1944); DANGEROUS PARTNERS(1945); SPELLBOUND(1945); THAT NIGHT WITH YOU(1945); TREE GROWS IN BROOKLYN, A(1945); LITTLE MISS BIG(1946); TILL THE END OF TIME(1946); DESPERATE(1947); DRIFTWOOD(1947); EGG AND I, THE(1947); FOR THE LOVE OF RUSTY(1947); HER HUSBAND'S AFFAIRS(1947); CAMPUS HONEYMOON(1948); MY DOG RUSTY(1948); PHANTOM VALLEY(1948); RUSTY LEADS THE WAY(1948); BOY WITH THE GREEN HAIR, THE(1948); FIGHTING FOOLS(1949); MA AND PA KETTLE(1949); RUSTY'S BIRTHDAY(1949); SUN COMES UP, THE(1949); THEY LIVE BY NIGHT(1949); WEST OF EL DORADO(1949); BLONDIE'S HERO(1950); MA AND PA KETTLE GO TO TOWN(1950); SUMMER STOCK(1950); TRAVELING SALESWOMAN(1950); DAVID AND BATHSHEBA(1951); GENE AUTRY AND THE MOUNTIES(1951); TOO YOUNG TO KISS(1951); VALLEY OF FIRE(1951); MA AND PA KETTLE AT THE FAIR(1952); TALK ABOUT A STRANGER(1952); MR. SCOUTMASTER(1953); MEN OF THE FIGHTING LADY(1954)

Alvin Ing
FINAL COUNTDOWN, THE(1980); STIR CRAZY(1980)

Ronald Ing
PASSPORT TO CHINA(1961, Brit.)

Wang Ing
STAR OF HONG KONG(1962, Jap.); HONOLULU-TOKYO-HONG KONG(1963, Hong Kong/Jap.)

Dee Ingalls
ICE CASTLES(1978)

Don Ingalls
AIRPORT 1975(1974), w

Joyce Ingalls
MAN WHO WOULD NOT DIE, THE(1975); PARADISE ALLEY(1978); DEADLY FORCE(1983)

Bob Ingarao
MOST WANTED MAN, THE(1962, Fr./Ital.); CHECKERBOARD(1969, Fr.)

Mandy Ingber
MR. MOM(1983)

Yvonne Ingdal
SUDDENLY, A WOMAN!(1967, Den.)

Joe Inge
LIMELIGHT(1952), ed

William Inge
COME BACK LITTLE SHEBA(1952), w; PICNIC(1955), w; BUS STOP(1956), w; DARK AT THE TOP OF THE STAIRS, THE(1960), w; SPLENDOR IN THE GRASS(1961), a, w; ALL FALL DOWN(1962), w; STRIPPER, THE(1963), w; BUS RILEY'S BACK IN TOWN(1965), w; GOOD LUCK, MISS WYCKOFF(1979), w

Jean Marie Ingels
Misc. Talkies
SINGLE GIRLS(1973)

Marty Ingels
ARMORED COMMAND(1961); LADIES MAN, THE(1961); HORIZONTAL LIEUTENANT, THE(1962); BUSYBODY(1967); GUIDE FOR THE MARRIED MAN, A(1967); FOR SINGLES ONLY(1968); IF IT'S TUESDAY, THIS MUST BE BELGIUM(1969); HOW TO SEDUCE A WOMAN(1974)

Mary Ingels
WILD AND WONDERFUL(1964)

Sylvia Ingemarsson
FANNY AND ALEXANDER(1983, Swed./Fr./Ger.), ed
1984
AFTER THE REHEARSAL(1984, Swed.), ed

Manfred Inger
MAGIC FACE, THE(1951, Aust.); NO TIME FOR FLOWERS(1952); STOLEN IDENTITY(1953); ARMS AND THE MAN(1962, Ger.)

Sylvia Ingermarsson
MONTENEGRO(1981, Brit./Swed.), ed

Amy Ingersoll
KNIGHTRIDERS(1981)

1984
SPLASH(1984)

Bob Ingersoll
SEA OF GRASS, THE(1947)

Felice Ingersoll
HE WALKED BY NIGHT(1948); HOLLOW TRIUMPH(1948); RANGE JUSTICE(1949)

James Ingersoll
MIDWAY(1976); IN SEARCH OF HISTORIC JESUS(1980)

Thomas Ingersoll
CRY OF THE CITY(1948); NO WAY OUT(1950)

Tom Ingersoll
GREAT SINNER, THE(1949)

William Ingersoll
MARY BURNS, FUGITIVE(1935); HALF ANGEL(1936); WHIPSAW(1936)
Silents
PARTNERS OF THE NIGHT(1920)

Barrie Ingham
DR. WHO AND THE DALEKS(1965, Brit.); INVASION(1965, Brit.); CHALLENGE FOR ROBIN HOOD, A(1968, Brit.); DAY OF THE JACKAL, THE(1973, Brit./Fr.)

Geoffrey Ingham
LAKE PLACID SERENADE(1944); ALONG CAME JONES(1945)

Jill Ingham
SUPERMAN(1978)

Robert Ingham
DAMIEN–OMEN II(1978)

Travis Ingham
MOST PRECIOUS THING IN LIFE(1934), w

Frank L. Inghram
Silents
ON THE GO(1925), w; COMING AN' GOING(1926), w; GALLOPING GOBS, THE(1927), w
Misc. Silents
BIFF BANG BUDDY(1924), d

Joyce Ingle
SILENT RAGE(1982)

James Inglehart
Misc. Talkies
SAVAGE!(1973)

Madeleine Inglehearn
WICKED LADY, THE(1983, Brit.), ch

Rufino Ingles
GOLIATH AGAINST THE GIANTS(1963, Ital./Span.); MURIETA(1965, Span.); GOD FORGIVES–I DON'T!(1969, Ital./Span.)

E. M. Ingleton
Silents
IVORY SNUFF BOX, THE(1915), w; ETERNAL LOVE(1917), w

Mrs. E. M. Ingleton
Silents
BROKEN CHAINS(1916), w

E. Magnus Ingleton
Silents
ALIAS MARY BROWN(1918), w; ANSWER, THE(1918), w; DARK MIRROR, THE(1920), w; SECRET OF THE HILLS, THE(1921), w; ON THE HIGH SEAS(1922), w; ALIMONY(1924), w; KISS BARRIER, THE(1925), w
Misc. Silents
BIRTH OF PATRIOTISM, THE(1917), d

George Ingleton
Silents
SINS OF SOCIETY(1915)

I. M. Ingleton
Silents
TRILBY(1915), w

Michael Ingleton
FIDDLER ON THE ROOF(1971)

Sue Ingleton
DIMBOOLA(1979, Aus.)

Brand Inglis
WHITE CORRIDORS(1952, Brit.)

Elizabeth Inglis
BORROWED CLOTHES(1934, Brit.); LANDSLIDE(1937, Brit.); MUSEUM MYSTERY(1937, Brit.); THUNDER IN THE CITY(1937, Brit.)

Hamilton G. Inglis
NIGHT BOAT TO DUBLIN(1946, Brit.), p; NO PLACE FOR JENNIFER(1950, Brit.), p; WILL ANY GENTLEMAN?(1955, Brit.), p; GOOD COMPANIONS, THE(1957, Brit.), p; MOONRAKER, THE(1958, Brit.), p; MY WIFE'S FAMILY(1962, Brit.), p

Margaret Inglis
HOUSE OF THE LIVING DEAD(1973, S. Afr.)

Sarah Inglis
1984
FIRSTBORN(1984)

Tony Inglis
MURDER IN EDEN(1962, Brit.); GIRL HUNTERS, THE(1963, Brit.), art d; CURSE OF THE VOODOO(1965, Brit.), art d; JOHNNY NOBODY(1965, Brit.), art d; YOUR MONEY OR YOUR WIFE(1965, Brit.), art d; TRAITOR'S GATE(1966, Brit./Ger.), art d; PRIVATE LIFE OF SHERLOCK HOLMES, THE(1970, Brit.), art d; MAN WHO WOULD BE KING, THE(1975, Brit.), art d, set d

Elizabeth Inglise
TONIGHT AND EVERY NIGHT(1945)

Sylvia Ingmarsdotter
AUTUMN SONATA(1978, Swed.), ed

Robin Ingnico
1984
WOMAN IN RED, THE(1984)

Leonard B. Ingoldest
MY FRIEND IRMA(1949)

Leonard Ingoldsby
GOOD MORNING, MISS DOVE(1955)

David Ingolf
ERIC SOYA'S "17"(1967, Den.)

J. M. Ingraffia
MONGREL(1982)

Amo Ingraham
PALMY DAYS(1931); NIGHT WORLD(1932); GOLD DIGGERS OF 1933(1933); WOMAN ACCUSED(1933); WONDER BAR(1934); TAKE A LETTER, DARLING(1942)

Doris Ingraham
DETROIT 9000(1973)

Geoffrey Ingraham
KILLERS, THE(1946)

Harrish Ingraham
Silents
MILLION DOLLAR ROBBERY, THE(1914); CHILD OF M'SIEU(1919), a, d
Misc. Silents
TOLL OF LOVE, THE(1914); BLOOD OF HIS FATHERS(1917), d; EYE OF ENVY, THE(1917), d; PAINTED LIE, THE(1917); SINGLE CODE, THE(1917)

Jack Ingraham
GANG'S ALL HERE(1941); MAN WITH TWO LIVES, THE(1942); BORDER BUCKAROOS(1943); SUNDOWN RIDERS(1948); BATTLE AT APACHE PASS, THE(1952)

Lloyd Ingraham
NIGHT PARADE(1929, Brit.); RAINBOW MAN(1929); SO LONG LETTY(1929); UNTAMED(1929); LAST OF THE DUANES(1930); MONTANA MOON(1930); SPOILERS, THE(1930); TAKE THE HEIR(1930), d; WIDE OPEN(1930); LADY WHO DARED, THE(1931); CORNERED(1932); CRUSADER, THE(1932); HOUSE DIVIDED, A(1932); MIDNIGHT WARNING, THE(1932); SINISTER HANDS(1932); TEXAS GUN FIGHTER(1932); THIRTEEN WOMEN(1932); WIDOW IN SCARLET(1932); MARY STEVENS, M.D.(1933); OFFICER 13(1933); REVENGE AT MONTE CARLO(1933); SLIGHTLY MARRIED(1933); WORLD GONE MAD, THE(1933); BATTLE OF GREED(1934); DUDE RANGER, THE(1934); LOST JUNGLE, THE(1934); PECK'S BAD BOY(1934); SIXTEEN FATHOMS DEEP(1934); BETWEEN MEN(1935); BRANDED A COWARD(1935); COWBOY MILLIONAIRE(1935); GHOST RIDER, THE(1935); NORTHERN FRONTIER(1935); ON PROBATION(1935); RAINBOW VALLEY(1935); RIDER OF THE LAW, THE(1935); SONS OF STEEL(1935); TEXAS TERROR(1935); TRAIL OF TERROR(1935); WORLD ACCUSES, THE(1935); BURNING GOLD(1936); CAPTAIN CALAMITY(1936); EVERYMAN'S LAW(1936); FRONTIER JUSTICE(1936); GHOST PATROL(1936); GUN SMOKE(1936); HEARTS IN BONDAGE(1936); LAWLESS NINETIES, THE(1936); LONELY TRAIL, THE(1936); MILKY WAY, THE(1936); MODERN TIMES(1936); RED RIVER VALLEY(1936); STORMY TRAILS(1936); TIMBER WAR(1936); TOO MUCH BEEF(1936); UNDERCOVER MAN(1936); WINDS OF THE WASTELAND(1936); CAPTAINS COURAGEOUS(1937); EMPTY SADDLES(1937); GUN LORDS OF STIRRUP BASIN(1937); LAW AND LEAD(1937); LIGHTNIN' CRANDALL(1937); OH DOCTOR(1937); PARK AVENUE LOGGER(1937); RIDERS OF THE DAWN(1937); ROGUE OF THE RANGE(1937); TOAST OF NEW YORK, THE(1937); FEUD MAKER(1938); GUN LAW(1938); GUN PACKER(1938); MAN FROM MUSIC MOUNTAIN(1938); PAINTED DESERT, THE(1938); REFORMATORY(1938); SWING, SISTER, SWING(1938); VIVACIOUS LADY(1938); DAY THE BOOKIES WEPT, THE(1939); DESTRY RIDES AGAIN(1939); EAST SIDE OF HEAVEN(1939); ESPIONAGE AGENT(1939); IN NAME ONLY(1939); LOVE AFFAIR(1939); MARSHAL OF MESA CITY, THE(1939); OKLAHOMA FRONTIER(1939); RIDE 'EM COWGIRL(1939); SINGING COWGIRL, THE(1939); WATER RUSTLERS(1939); YOU CAN'T CHEAT AN HONEST MAN(1939); BAD MAN FROM RED BUTTE(1940); COLORADO(1940); LEGION OF THE LAWLESS(1940); LUCKY PARTNERS(1940); MELODY RANCH(1940); MY LITTLE CHICKADEE(1940); PONY POST(1940); SON OF ROARING DAN(1940); TWENTY MULE TEAM(1940); DUDE COWBOY(1941); JESSE JAMES AT BAY(1941); PRIDE OF THE BOWERY(1941); ROBBERS OF THE RANGE(1941); THUNDERING HOOFS(1941); BANDIT RANGER(1942); MEXICAN SPITFIRE'S ELEPHANT(1942); PHANTOM PLAINSMEN, THE(1942); SILVER BULLET, THE(1942); SPOILERS, THE(1942); STAGECOACH BUCKAROO(1942); STRICTLY IN THE GROOVE(1942); VALLEY OF THE SUN(1942); BLAZING GUNS(1943); BOMBARDIER(1943); BOSS OF BIG TOWN(1943); FIRST COMES COURAGE(1943); MR. LUCKY(1943); MYSTERY OF THE 13TH GUEST, THE(1943); SEVENTH VICTIM, THE(1943); THIS LAND IS MINE(1943); HEAVENLY DAYS(1944); HOT RHYTHM(1944); MERRY MONAHANS, THE(1944); PARTNERS OF THE TRAIL(1944); RANGE LAW(1944); FRONTIER FEUD(1945); FRONTIER GAL(1945); MAN WHO WALKED ALONE, THE(1945); SUDAN(1945); CARAVAN TRAIL, THE(1946); LAWLESS EMPIRE(1946); LOVER COME BACK(1946); SISTER KENNY(1946); SLAVE GIRL(1947); WEST OF SONORA(1948); SAVAGE HORDE, THE(1950)
Misc. Talkies
GO-GET-'EM HAINES(1936); WEST OF THE RIO GRANDE(1944)
Silents
SABLE LORCHA, THE(1915), d; AMERICAN ARISTOCRACY(1916), d; INTOLERANCE(1916); LITTLE LIAR, THE(1916), d; NINA, THE FLOWER GIRL(1917), d; EYES OF JULIA DEEP, THE(1918), d; AMAZING IMPOSTER, THE(1919), d; JAILBIRD, THE(1920), d; TWIN BEDS(1920), d; KEEPING UP WITH LIZZIE(1921), d; LAVENDER AND OLD LACE(1921), d; DANGER POINT, THE(1922), d; FRONT PAGE STORY, A(1922), d; SECOND HAND ROSE(1922), d; SCARAMOUCHE(1923); NO MORE WOMEN(1924), d; HEARTS AND FISTS(1926), d; NUT-CRACKER, THE(1926), d; OH, WHAT A NIGHT!(1926), d; DON MIKE(1927), d; JESSE JAMES(1927), d; SILVER COMES THROUGH(1927), d&w; KIT CARSON(1928), d; PIONEER SCOUT, THE(1928), d; SUNSET LEGION, THE(1928), d
Misc. Silents
CASEY AT THE BAT(1916), d; CHILD OF THE PARIS STREETS, A(1916), d; CHILDREN PAY, THE(1916), d; HOODOO ANN(1916), d; MISSING LINKS, THE(1916), d; STRANDED(1916), d; CHARITY CASTLE(1917), d; HER COUNTRY'S CALL(1917), d; MISS JACKIE OF THE ARMY(1917), d; PEGGY LEADS THE WAY(1917), d; IMPOSSIBLE SUSAN(1918), d; JILTED JANET(1918), d; MOLLY, GO GET 'EM(1918), d; PRIMITIVE WOMAN, THE(1918), d; ROSEMARY CLIMBS THE HEIGHTS(1918), d; SQUARE DEAL, A(1918), d; INTRUSION OF ISABEL, THE(1919), d; MAN'S DESIRE(1919), d; WHAT'S YOUR HUSBAND DOING?(1919), d; WIVES AND OTHER WIVES(1919), d; LET'S BE FASHIONABLE(1920), d; MARY'S ANKLE(1920), d; OLD DAD(1920), d; GIRL IN THE TAXI, THE(1921), d; MARRY THE

POOR GIRL(1921), d; MY LADY FRIENDS(1921), d; AT THE SIGN OF THE JACK O'LANTERN(1922), d; VEILED WOMAN, THE(1922), d; GOING UP(1923), d; LIGHTING RIDER, THE(1924), d; WISE VIRGIN, THE(1924), d; MIDNIGHT MOLLY(1925), d; SOFT SHOES(1925), d; ARIZONA NIGHTS(1927), d; TAKE THE HEIR(1930), d

Lois Ingraham
Silents
HEARTS AND FISTS(1926)

Mitchell Ingraham
MEN OF THE NIGHT(1934); GIVE ME YOUR HEART(1936); HOTEL HAYWIRE(1937); LAST GANGSTER, THE(1937); COMET OVER BROADWAY(1938); HUNTED MEN(1938); TEST PILOT(1938); DESIGN FOR SCANDAL(1941); NO TIME FOR LOVE(1943)

Rex Ingraham
Misc. Silents
REWARD OF THE FAITHLESS, THE(1917), d

Roy Ingraham
SILVER SKATES(1943), m

Sunny Ingraham
WHITE PARADE, THE(1934)

Vi Ingraham
PATHFINDER, THE(1952); OPERATION PETTICOAT(1959)

Zella Ingraham
Silents
LAVENDER AND OLD LACE(1921)

Lloyd Ingrahm
Silents
ANN'S FINISH(1918), d

Abel Ingram
SO IT'S SUNDAY(1932), w

Amo Ingram
WILD PARTY, THE(1929)

Clifford Ingram
HEARTS IN DIXIE(1929)

Donna Patrice Ingram
WIZ, THE(1978)

Edward Ingram
THIS ISLAND EARTH(1955); GUNFIGHT AT THE O.K. CORRAL(1957)

Elisa Ingram
JUDY'S LITTLE NO-NO(1969)
Misc. Talkies
REVENGE IS MY DESTINY(1971)

Jack Ingram
LONELY TRAIL, THE(1936); WINDS OF THE WASTELAND(1936); DOOMED AT SUNDOWN(1937); GUNSMOKE RANCH(1937); HEADLINE CRASHER(1937); OLD CORRAL, THE(1937); PUBLIC COWBOY NO. 1(1937); RANGERS STEP IN, THE(1937); RIO GRANDE RANGER(1937); TOUGH TO HANDLE(1937); WHISTLING BULLETS(1937); YODELIN' KID FROM PINE RIDGE(1937); DESERT PATROL(1938); DURANGO VALLEY RAIDERS(1938); GUNSMOKE TRAIL(1938); IN EARLY ARIZONA(1938); OUTLAW EXPRESS(1938); OUTLAWS OF SONORA(1938); PHANTOM GOLD(1938); REBELLION(1938); RIDERS OF THE BLACK HILLS(1938); STAGECOACH DAYS(1938); TWO-GUN JUSTICE(1938); UNDER WESTERN STARS(1938); WESTERN JAMBOREE(1938); WESTERN TRAILS(1938); WILD HORSE RODEO(1938); BLUE MONTANA SKIES(1939); COLORADO SUNSET(1939); DAYS OF JESSE JAMES(1939); DOWN THE WYOMING TRAIL(1939); FEUD OF THE RANGE(1939); FRONTIER SCOUT(1939); FRONTIERS OF '49(1939); HOME ON THE PRAIRIE(1939); LAW COMES TO TEXAS, THE(1939); LONE STAR PIONEERS(1939); MEXICALI ROSE(1939); MOUNTAIN RHYTHM(1939); NEW FRONTIER(1939); NIGHT RIDERS, THE(1939); PAL FROM TEXAS, THE(1939); ROVIN' TUMBLEWEEDS(1939); SAGA OF DEATH VALLEY(1939); SOUTHWARD HO!(1939); TWO-GUN TROUBADOR(1939); WALL STREET COWBOY(1939); WYOMING OUTLAW(1939); CARSON CITY KID(1940); GHOST VALLEY RAIDERS(1940); MELODY RANCH(1940); ONE MAN'S LAW(1940); RANCHO GRANDE(1940); STRAIGHT SHOOTER(1940); UNDER TEXAS SKIES(1940); YOUNG BILL HICKOK(1940); KING OF DODGE CITY(1941); LONE RIDER AMBUSHED, THE(1941); LONE RIDER IN GHOST TOWN, THE(1941); NEVADA CITY(1941); PRAIRIE PIONEERS(1941); SHERIFF OF TOMBSTONE(1941); SON OF DAVY CROCKETT(1941); SOUTH OF PANAMA(1941); TEXAS(1941); ARIZONA ROUNDUP(1942); ARIZONA STAGECOACH(1942); BILLY THE KID TRAPPED(1942); CODE OF THE OUTLAW(1942); LONE RIDER AND THE BANDIT, THE(1942); LONE RIDER IN CHEYENNE, THE(1942); LONE STAR LAW MEN(1942); MAN FROM CHEYENNE(1942); MYSTERIOUS RIDER, THE(1942); RAIDERS OF THE RANGE(1942); ROLLING DOWN THE GREAT DIVIDE(1942); SOUTH OF SANTA FE(1942); SUNDOWN KID, THE(1942); SUNSET SERENADE(1942); TOMORROW WE LIVE(1942); ARIZONA TRAIL(1943); BAD MEN OF THUNDER GAP(1943); DANGER! WOMEN AT WORK(1943); FRONTIER LAW(1943); IDAHO(1943); LONE STAR TRAIL, THE(1943); MAN FROM THUNDER RIVER(1943); RAIDERS OF SAN JOAQUIN(1943); RAIDERS OF SUNSET PASS(1943); RIDERS OF THE NORTHWEST MOUNTED(1943); RIDERS OF THE RIO GRANDE(1943); SANTA FE SCOUTS(1943); SILVER CITY RAIDERS(1943); WAGON TRACKS WEST(1943); WEST OF TEXAS(1943); WOLVES OF THE RANGE(1943); BOSS OF THE RAWHIDE(1944); DEVIL RIDERS(1944); DRIFTER, THE(1944); FRONTIER OUTLAWS(1944); GHOST GUNS(1944); GUNS OF THE LAW(1944); GUNSMOKE MESA(1944); MOJAVE FIREBRAND(1944); MY BUDDY(1944); OKLAHOMA RAIDERS(1944); PARTNERS OF THE TRAIL(1944); PINTO BANDIT, THE(1944); RANGE LAW(1944); SUNDOWN VALLEY(1944); THUNDERING GUN SLINGERS(1944); TRAIL OF TERROR(1944); TRIGGER TRAIL(1944); VALLEY OF VENGEANCE(1944); BANDITS OF THE BADLANDS(1945); BEYOND THE PECOS(1945); ENEMY OF THE LAW(1945); FLAME OF THE WEST(1945); FRONTIER FEUD(1945); FRONTIER FUGITIVES(1945); FRONTIER GAL(1945); JADE MASK, THE(1945); MARKED FOR MURDER(1945); SHERIFF OF CIMARRON(1945); UNDER WESTERN SKIES(1945); MAGNIFICENT DOLL(1946); WEST OF THE ALAMO(1946); FABULOUS TEXAN, THE(1947); GHOST TOWN RENEGADES(1947); PIONEER JUSTICE(1947); SLAVE GIRL(1947); GALLANT LEGION, THE(1948); RACING LUCK(1948); STRAWBERRY ROAN, THE(1948); WHIRLWIND RAIDERS(1948); DESERT VIGILANTE(1949); GAL WHO TOOK THE WEST, THE(1949); LAW OF THE WEST(1949); ROARING WESTWARD(1949); SON OF A BADMAN(1949); BANDIT QUEEN(1950); MA AND PA KETTLE GO TO TOWN(1950); SHORT GRASS(1950); SIDESHOW(1950); SIERRA(1950); STREETS OF GHOST TOWN(1950); TEXAN MEETS CALAMITY JANE, THE(1950); FORT DODGE STAMPEDE(1951); FARGO(1952); LOST IN ALASKA(1952); COW COUNTRY(1953); GREAT SIOUX UPRISING, THE(1953); LAW AND OR-

DER(1953); SON OF THE RENEGADE(1953); FIVE GUNS WEST(1955); MAN WITHOUT A STAR(1955); UTAH BLAINE(1957)

Misc. Silents
VALLEY OF TERROR(1937); ADVENTURES OF THE MASKED PHANTOM, THE(1939); RIDIN' THE TRAIL(1940); LAW OF THE WILD(1941); BOSS OF BOOMTOWN(1944); OATH OF VENGEANCE(1944); OUTLAW ROUNDUP(1944); ROUGH RIDIN' JUSTICE(1945); SADDLE SERENADE(1945); STRANGER FROM SANTA FE(1945); MOON OVER MONTANA(1946); THUNDERGAP OUTLAWS(1947)

Jay Ingram
PEACEMAKER, THE(1956), w

Jean Ingram
THREE CAME TO KILL(1960); TICKLE ME(1965)

Joan Ingram
2,000 WOMEN(1944, Brit.); MIRANDA(1949, Brit.); ONE GOOD TURN(1955, Brit.); TROUBLE IN STORE(1955, Brit.); JUST MY LUCK(1957, Brit.); MAN INSIDE, THE(1958, Brit.); GIDEON OF SCOTLAND YARD(1959, Brit.); L-SHAPED ROOM, THE(1962, Brit.); GET CHARLIE TULLY(1976, Brit.)

John Ingram
KING IN NEW YORK, A(1957, Brit.); BATTLEAXE, THE(1962, Brit.), p; DESIGN FOR LOVING(1962, Brit.), p; SHE ALWAYS GETS THEIR MAN(1962, Brit.), p

Josephine Ingram
WEAKER SEX, THE(1949, Brit.); MAYTIME IN MAYFAIR(1952, Brit.)

Kate Ingram
1984
SCRUBBERS(1984, Brit.)

Lindsay Ingram
BUTLEY(1974, Brit.)

Lloyd Ingram
GET THAT GIRL(1932)

Malcolm Ingram
FRAULEIN DOKTOR(1969, Ital./Yugo.)

Ralph Ingram
STRIP TEASE MURDER(1961, Brit.), p

Rex Ingram
LOVE IN MOROCCO(1933, Fr.), a, p, d, w; GREEN PASTURES(1936); HUCKLEBERRY FINN(1939); THIEF OF BAGHDAD, THE(1940, Brit.); TALK OF THE TOWN(1942); CABIN IN THE SKY(1943); FIRED WIFE(1943); SAHARA(1943); DARK WATERS(1944); THOUSAND AND ONE NIGHTS, A(1945); MOONRISE(1948); TARZAN'S HIDDEN JUNGLE(1955); CONGO CROSSING(1956); HELL ON DEVIL'S ISLAND(1957); ANNA LUCASTA(1958); GOD'S LITTLE ACRE(1958); ESCORT WEST(1959); DESIRE IN THE DUST(1960); ELMER GANTRY(1960); YOUR CHEATIN' HEART(1964); HURRY SUNDOWN(1967); JOURNEY TO SHILOH(1968)
Silents
SONG OF HATE, THE(1915), w; HIS ROBE OF HONOR(1918), d; TARZAN OF THE APES(1918); CONQUERING POWER, THE(1921), p&d; FOUR HORSEMEN OF THE APOCALYPSE, THE(1921), d; PRISONER OF ZENDA, THE(1922), p&d; SCARAMOUCHE(1923), d⊃ ARAB, THE(1924), d&w; MARE NOSTRUM(1926), p&d
Misc. Silents
BROKEN FETTERS(1916), d; CHALICE OF SORROW, THE(1916), d; BLACK ORCHIDS(1917), d; FLOWER OF DOOM, THE(1917), d; LITTLE TERROR, THE(1917), d; PULSE OF LIFE, THE(1917), d; HUMDRUM BROWN(1918), d; DAY SHE PAID, THE(1919), d; HEARTS ARE TRUMPS(1920), d; SHORE ACRES(1920), d; UNDER CRIMSON SKIES(1920), d; TRIFLING WOMEN(1922), d; TURN TO THE RIGHT(1922), d; WHERE THE PAVEMENT ENDS(1923), d; MAGICIAN, THE(1926), d; GARDEN OF ALLAH, THE(1927), d; THREE PASSIONS, THE(1928, Brit.), d

Shelly Ingram
STAR 80(1983)

Rev. J.H. Ingraham
TEN COMMANDMENTS, THE(1956), w

William Ingram
NAVY HEROES(1959, Brit.)

Willie Ingram
MUTATIONS, THE(1974, Brit.)

Donna Ingram-Young
1984
MOSCOW ON THE HUDSON(1984)

Jonathan Ingrams
HEADLINE HUNTERS(1968, Brit.), d, w
Misc. Talkies
BOY WITH TWO HEADS, THE(1974, Brit.), d

Michael Ingrams
TERROR SHIP(1954, Brit.); SQUARE RING, THE(1955, Brit.)

William Ingrams
GIRO CITY(1982, Brit.)

Ciccio Ingrassia
00-2 MOST SECRET AGENTS(1965, Ital.); DR. GOLDFOOT AND THE GIRL BOMBS(1966, Ital.); PRIMITIVE LOVE(1966, Ital.); DOS COSMONAUTAS A LA FUERZA(1967, Span./*Ital.); WAR ITALIAN STYLE(1967, Ital.); AMARCORD(1974, Ital.)

Lloyd Ingrham
Misc. Silents
BEAUTY PRIZE, THE(1924), d

Rex Ingrham
Misc. Silents
GREAT PROBLEM, THE(1916), d

Eduard Ingris
GALLANT ONE, THE(1964, U.S./Peru), m

Diana Ingro
GAMES MEN PLAY, THE(1968, Arg.)

Boris Ingster
LAST DAYS OF POMPEII, THE(1935), w; DANCING PIRATE(1936), w; THIN ICE(1937), w; HAPPY LANDING(1938), w; I'LL GIVE A MILLION(1938), w; MIRACLE ON MAIN STREET, A(1940), w; STRANGER ON THE THIRD FLOOR(1940), d; AMAZING MRS. HOLLIDAY(1943), w; HEAT'S ON, THE(1943), w; PARIS UNDERGROUND(1945), w; CALIFORNIA(1946), w; CLOAK AND DAGGER(1946), w; JUDGE STEPS OUT, THE(1949), d, w; SOUTHSIDE 1-1000(1950), d, w; SOMETHING FOR THE BIRDS(1952), w; ABDULLAH'S HAREM(1956, Brit./Egypt.), w; GUNS OF DIABLO(1964), p; ONE OF OUR SPIES IS MISSING(1966), p; SPY IN THE GREEN HAT, THE(1966), p; KARATE KILLERS, THE(1967), p, w

Inhabitants of Fouke, Arkansas
LEGEND OF BOGGY CREEK, THE(1973)
the Inhabitants of St. Severe-Sur-Indre
JOUR DE FETE(1952, Fr.)
Steve Inhat
IN LIKE FLINT(1967)
Wiard B. Inhen
MOON OVER MIAMI(1941), art d
Enrique Inigo
SIERRA BARON(1958)
G. Iniutina
MEN OF THE SEA(1938, USSR)
V. Inkijinoff
BATTLE, THE(1934, Fr.); SHANGHAI DRAMA, THE(1945, Fr.); MICHAEL STROG-OFF(1960, Fr./Ital./Yugo.)
Valery Inkijinoff
WIFE OF GENERAL LING, THE(1938, Brit.); JOURNEY TO THE LOST CITY(1960, Ger./Fr./Ital.); SAMSON AND THE SEVEN MIRACLES OF THE WORLD(1963, Fr./Ital.); UP TO HIS EARS(1966, Fr./Ital.); MATCHLESS(1967, Ital.)
Valery Inkijnoff
BLONDE FROM PEKING, THE(1968, Fr.); LEGEND OF FRENCHIE KING, THE(1971, Fr./Ital./Span./Brit.)
V. Inkizhinov
Silents
STORM OVER ASIA(1929, USSR)
Valeri Inkizhinov
Misc. Silents
HEIR TO JENGHIS-KHAN, THE(1928, USSR)
V. Inkyinoff
MATA HARI'S DAUGHTER(1954, Fr./Ital)
A. B. Inlson
Silents
AFTER THE VERDICT(1929, Brit.)
James Inman
DETECTIVE, THE(1968)
John Inman
Misc. Talkies
ARE YOU BEING SERVED?(1977)
Walter Inman
JIM, THE WORLD'S GREATEST(1976)
William Inman
HENRY ALDRICH HAUNTS A HOUSE(1943)
Frank Inn
HAWMPS!(1976); FOR THE LOVE OF BENJI(1977), animal t
Juanita Inn
FOR THE LOVE OF BENJI(1977), animal t; OH, HEAVENLY DOG!(1980), animal t
Won Inn
NIGHT IN HONG KONG, A(1961, Jap.)
Albert Innaurato
HAPPY BIRTHDAY, GEMINI(1980), w
Chairman Innes
BAND OF THIEVES(1962, Brit.)
Charmain Innes
FLAMINGO AFFAIR, THE(1948, Brit.)
Charmian Innes
DARK INTERVAL(1950, Brit.); UP FOR THE CUP(1950, Brit.)
Edward Innes
ANGRY RED PLANET, THE(1959)
George Innes
BILLY LIAR(1963, Brit.); CHARLIE BUBBLES(1968, Brit.); BEFORE WINTER COMES(1969, Brit.); ITALIAN JOB, THE(1969, Brit.); LAST VALLEY, THE(1971, Brit.); GUMSHOE(1972, Brit.); POPE JOAN(1972, Brit.); MEDUSA TOUCH, THE(1978, Brit.); ODD JOB, THE(1978, Brit.); SWEENEY 2(1978, Brit.)
1984
ORDEAL BY INNOCENCE(1984, Brit.)
Hammond Innes
SNOWBOUND(1949, Brit.), w; HELL BELOW ZERO(1954, Brit.), w; CAMPBELL'S KINGDOM(1957, Brit.), w; WRECK OF THE MARY DEAR, THE(1959), w
Ian Innes
RATS ARE COMING! THE WEREWOLVES ARE HERE!, THE(1972)
Jean Innes
EDGE OF DOOM(1950); GOOD MORNING, MISS DOVE(1955); GREEN-EYED BLONDE, THE(1957); GUN FEVER(1958)
John Innes
1984
MRS. SOFFEL(1984)
Michael Innes
CANDLESHOE(1978), w
Neil Innes
MONTY PYTHON AND THE HOLY GRAIL(1975, Brit.), a, m; JABBERWOCK-Y(1977, Brit.); MONTY PYTHON'S LIFE OF BRIAN(1979, Brit.); MISSIONARY, THE(1982)
Phillip Innes
WARKILL(1968, U.S./Phil.), ed; PROUD AND THE DAMNED, THE(1972), ed
Elaine Innescourt
Silents
ABABIAN KNIGHT, AN(1920)
Marcus Innesley
MR. H. C. ANDERSEN(1950, Brit.)
Jean Inness
REVEILLE WITH BEVERLY(1943); MRS. MIKE(1949); PINKY(1949); GUNFIGHT-ER, THE(1950); I'D CLIMB THE HIGHEST MOUNTAIN(1951); MAN WITH A CLOAK, THE(1951); FRIENDLY PERSUASION(1956); NIGHT RUNNER(1957); STORY OF RUTH, THE(1960); ROSEMARY'S BABY(1968)
Harold Innocent
NOTORIOUS LANDLADY, THE(1962); LOOT(1971, Brit.)
Carlo Innocenzi
DAVID AND GOLIATH(1961, Ital.), m; SAMSON(1961, Ital.), m; TEACHER AND THE MIRACLE, THE(1961, Ital./Span.), m; CENTURION, THE(1962, Fr./Ital.), m; PRISONER OF THE IRON MASK(1962, Fr./Ital./Yugo.), m; ATLAS AGAINST THE CYCLOPS(1963, Ital.), m; GOLIATH AGAINST THE GIANTS(1963, Ital./Span.), m; LADY DOCTOR, THE(1963, Fr./Ital./Span.), m; MILL OF THE STONE WOMEN(1963, Fr./Ital.), m; SEVEN REVENGES, THE(1967, Ital.), m; GUILT IS NOT MINE(1968, Ital.), m

Benny Inocencio
REAL GLORY, THE(1939); ROAD TO SINGAPORE(1940); SOMEWHERE I'LL FIND YOU(1942)
Takashi Inomata
GOKE, BODYSNATCHER FROM HELL(1968, Jap.), p
Dan Inosanto
SHARKY'S MACHINE(1982)
Danny Inosanto
GAME OF DEATH, THE(1979)
Daisuke Inoue
IDIOT, THE(1963, Jap.)
Kazuo Inoue
VENGEANCE IS MINE(1980, Jap.), p
Kinji Inoue
KARATE, THE HAND OF DEATH(1961)
Masao Inoue
Misc. Silents
CRAZY PAGE, A(1926, Jap.)
Taiko Inoue
GODZILLA VERSUS THE SMOG MONSTER(1972, Jap.), art d
Takayuki Inoue
MAN WHO STOLE THE SUN, THE(1980, Jap.), m
Umeji Inoue
MAN FROM THE EAST, THE(1961, Jap.), d; PERFORMERS, THE(1970, Jap.), d&w
Yasushi Inoue
UNDER THE BANNER OF SAMURAI(1969, Jap.), w
Yasuyuki Inoue
YOG-MONSTER FROM SPACE(1970, Jap.), set d
Luis Inouni
UNINHIBITED, THE(1968, Fr./Ital./Span.)
Yasushi Inouye
MADAME AKI(1963, Jap.), w
Artyom Inozemstsev
KATERINA IZMAILOVA(1969, USSR)
the Ins and Outs
TURN ON TO LOVE(1969), m
Stephanie Insall
JOURNEY FOR MARGARET(1942); THIS ABOVE ALL(1942)
Gino Insana
CRACKING UP(1977)
Tino Insana
NEIGHBORS(1981); GOING BERSERK(1983)
Albert Insinnia
CORVETTE SUMMER(1978); ROLLER BOOGIE(1979)
David Insley
POLYESTER(1981), ph
the Edison Institute
EDISON, THE MAN(1940), tech adv
Albert Insua
HUNCHBACK OF THE MORGUE, THE(1972, Span.), w
Stephani Insull
FOOLS FOR SCANDAL(1938)
Franco Interlenghi
SHOE SHINE(1947, Ital.); TERESA(1951); LITTLE WORLD OF DON CAMILLO, THE(1953, Fr./Ital.); BAREFOOT CONTESSA, THE(1954); CENTO ANNI D'AMO-RE(1954, Ital.); ULYSSES(1955, Ital.); VITELLONI(1956, Ital./Fr.); FAREWELL TO ARMS, A(1957); YOUNG HUSBANDS(1958, Ital./Fr.); LOVE IS MY PROFES-SION(1959, Fr.); LA NOTTE BRAVA(1962, Fr./Ital.)
International Cine Ballet
DR. COPPELIUS(1968, U.S./Span.)
International Velvet
MIDNIGHT COWBOY(1969)
John Intlekofer
HAND OF DEATH(1962), cos
Jerald Intrator
SATAN IN HIGH HEELS(1962), d
Hiroshi Inuzuka
COMPUTER FREE-FOR-ALL(1969, Jap.); HOTSPRINGS HOLIDAY(1970, Jap.)
Minoru Inuzuka
ZATOICHI(1968, Jap.), w
Boyd Irvin
CRUSADES, THE(1935); CHARGE OF THE LIGHT BRIGADE, THE(1936)
Coulter Irvin
CRIME DOCTOR'S WARNING(1945)
Alice Inward
Misc. Silents
DUNGEON OF DEATH, THE(1915, Brit.); LIFE OF AN ACTRESS, THE(1915, Brit.); PORT OF MISSING WOMEN, THE(1915, Brit.); VICE AND VIRTUE; OR, THE TEMPTERS OF LONDON(1915, Brit.)
Steve Inwood
HURRY UP OR I'LL BE 30(1973); CRUISING(1980); FAME(1980); PRINCE OF THE CITY(1981); STAYING ALIVE(1983)
John Inzerella
LAST OF THE RED HOT LOVERS(1972), makeup
Rina Ioannou
THREE TO GO(1971, Aus.)
Kim Iocouvozzi
SQUIRM(1976)
Edward Ioganson
Misc. Silents
SON OF THE LAND(1931, USSR), d
Ione
SOMETHING WEIRD(1967)

Lillian Irene
ESCAPADE(1935)
Lilyan Irene
VANITY FAIR(1932); FARMER TAKES A WIFE, THE(1935); MAN WHO RE-CLAIMED HIS HEAD, THE(1935); LOVE ON THE RUN(1936); SYLVIA SCAR-LETT(1936); PARADISE FOR THREE(1938); NEW YORK TOWN(1941); SCOTLAND YARD(1941); THEY MET IN BOMBAY(1941); JOURNEY FOR MARGARET(1942); SWEET ROSIE O'GRADY(1943); WHAT A WOMAN!(1943); TILL THE CLOUDS ROLL BY(1946)
Richard Ireson
DARWIN ADVENTURE, THE(1972, Brit.)
1984
SCANDALOUS(1984)
Carol Irey
"X"–THE MAN WITH THE X-RAY EYES(1963)
Marie-Louise Iribe
Misc. Silents
L'ATLANTIDE(1921, Fr.); MARQUITTA(1927, Fr.)
Paul Iribe
Silents
TEN COMMANDMENTS, THE(1923), art d; FORTY WINKS(1925), d; NIGHT CLUB, THE(1925), d
Misc. Silents
GREAT MEN AMONG US(1915); CHANGING HUSBANDS(1924), d
Miki Irie
FACE OF ANOTHER, THE(1967, Jap.)
Takako Irie
SANJURO(1962, Jap.)
Misc. Silents
METROPOLITAN SYMPHONY(1929, Jap.)
Iris
BELLISSIMA(1952, Ital.)
Lily Iris
Misc. Silents
LOST LEADER, A(1922, Brit.)
Iris and Pierre
CLUB HAVANA(1946)
Iris Kirkwhite Dancers
HERE COMES THE SUN(1945, Brit.)
Kitty Irish
THAT'S MY MAN(1947)
Nancy Irish
OVER THE HILL(1931)
R. E. Irish
Silents
JUDGE NOT OR THE WOMAN OF MONA DIGGINGS(1915), ph
Roy E. Irish
Silents
RECKONING DAY, THE(1918), ph
Tom Irish
FATHER OF THE BRIDE(1950); FATHER'S LITTLE DIVIDEND(1951); SHOW BOAT(1951); ONE MINUTE TO ZERO(1952); CITY THAT NEVER SLEEPS(1953); HONDO(1953); ISLAND IN THE SKY(1953); SABRE JET(1953); SEVEN ANGRY MEN(1955); FRIENDLY PERSUASION(1956); STREET IS MY BEAT, THE(1966)
William Irish
HOUSE OF HORROR(1929), w; OBSESSION(1954, Fr./Ital.), w; BRIDE WORE BLACK, THE(1968, Fr./Ital.), w
William Irish [Cornell Woolrich]
PHANTOM LADY(1944), w; DEADLINE AT DAWN(1946), w; FEAR IN THE NIGHT(1947), d; NO MAN OF HER OWN(1950), w; NIGHTMARE(1956), d&w; MIS-SISSIPPI MERMAID(1970, Fr./Ital.), w
The Irish Abbey Players
PLOUGH AND THE STARS, THE(1936)
Tina Irissari
DEVIL PROBABLY, THE(1977, FR.)
Frank Irizarry
NOCTURNA(1979)
Gloria Irizarry
OLIVER'S STORY(1978); FORT APACHE, THE BRONX(1981)
1984
LONELY GUY, THE(1984)
Guillermo Irizarry
HAPPY HOOKER, THE(1975)
Nikolas Irizuing
WILLIE AND PHIL(1980)
Frank Irizzary
NIGHT OF THE JUGGLER(1980)
Hans Irle
FAUST(1963, Ger.)
Vladimir Irman
TARAS BULBA(1962)
Vjaceslav Irmanov
MURDER CZECH STYLE(1968, Czech.)
Judy Irola
NORTHERN LIGHTS(1978), ph
Iron Butterfly
MUSICAL MUTINY(1970)
Jeremy Irons
NIJINSKY(1980, Brit.); FRENCH LIEUTENANT'S WOMAN, THE(1981); MOON-LIGHTING(1982, Brit.); BETRAYAL(1983, Brit.); WILD DUCK, THE(1983, Aus.)
1984
SWANN IN LOVE(1984, Fr.Ger.)
Stanley Irons
SMILE ORANGE(1976, Jamaican)
Tommy Irons
PSYCHOTRONIC MAN, THE(1980), m
Michael Ironside
I, MAUREEN(1978, Can.); SUZANNE(1980, Can.); SCANNERS(1981, Can.); VISITING HOURS(1982, Can.); CROSS COUNTRY(1983, Can.); SPACEHUNTER: ADVENTURES IN THE FORBIDDEN ZONE(1983)

1984
AMERICAN NIGHTMARE(1984); SURROGATE, THE(1984, Can.)
Misc. Talkies
AMERICAN NIGHTMARE(1981, Can.)
Mike Ironside
OUTRAGEOUS!(1977, Can.)
Tatjana Irrah
Misc. Silents
UNCANNY ROOM, THE(1915, Ger.)
Gloria Irrizzary
I'M DANCING AS FAST AS I CAN(1982)
Umberto Irsini
DIARY OF A CLOISTERED NUN(1973, Ital./Fr./Ger.)
Billy Irvin
LOUDSPEAKER, THE(1934)
Charles Irvin
CHINA SEAS(1935); SEA HAWK, THE(1940); CADDY, THE(1953)
Christopher Irvin
DRESSER, THE(1983)
Emily Irvin
RETURN OF THE SOLDIER, THE(1983, Brit.)
Frances Irvin
HOLD THAT BABY!(1949)
Gregory Irvin
FEAR NO MORE(1961)
John Irvin
DOGS OF WAR, THE(1980, Brit.), d; GHOST STORY(1981), d
1984
CHAMPIONS(1984), d
Sam Irvin
FIRST TIME, THE(1983), p
Victor Irvin
CAVALIER, THE(1928), w
Silents
SIREN CALL, THE(1922), w
Irvin-Talbot
UNDERCOVER MAN(1942), md
Andrew Irvine
TALE OF FIVE WOMEN, A(1951, Brit.); ROOM AT THE TOP(1959, Brit.)
Beth Irvine
Misc. Silents
QUEEN OF THE SEA(1918)
Blanaid Irvine
BROTH OF A BOY(1959, Brit.), w; THIS OTHER EDEN(1959, Brit.), w; OF HUMAN BONDAGE(1964, Brit.)
Frank Irvine
GREY FOX, THE(1983, Can.), ed
1984
MY KIND OF TOWN(1984, Can.), a, ed
Jennifer Irvine
PRIME OF MISS JEAN BRODIE, THE(1969, Brit.)
Rich Irvine
SECRET OF NIMH, THE(1982), p
Richard Irvine
HOUSE ACROSS THE BAY, THE(1940), art d; SNUFFY SMITH, YARD BIRD(1942), art d; NO PLACE FOR A LADY(1943), art d; SPIDER, THE(1945), art d; WITHIN THESE WALLS(1945), art d; BRASHER DOUBLOON, THE(1947), art d; MIRACLE ON 34TH STREET, THE(1947), art d; APARTMENT FOR PEGGY(1948), art d; YOU WERE MEANT FOR ME(1948), art d; EVERYBODY DOES IT(1949), art d; MR. BELVEDERE GOES TO COLLEGE(1949), art d; FOR HEAVEN'S SAKE(1950), art d; GUNFIGHTER, THE(1950), art d; LOVE THAT BRUTE(1950), art d; MOTHER DIDN'T TELL ME(1950), art d; ELOPEMENT(1951), art d; FOLLOW THE SUN(1951), art d; SECRET OF CONVICT LAKE, THE(1951), art d; DON'T BOTHER TO KNOCK(1952), art d; I DON'T CARE GIRL, THE(1952), art d; O. HENRY'S FULL HOUSE(1952), art d; TAXI(1953), art d; VICKI(1953), art d
Richard F. Irvine
THREE CABALLEROS, THE(1944), art d
Robert Irvine
ESCAPE FROM ALCATRAZ(1979)
Robin Irvine
KNIGHT IN LONDON, A(1930, Brit./Ger.); KEEPERS OF YOUTH(1931, Brit.)
Silents
EASY VIRTUE(1927, Brit.); LAND OF HOPE AND GLORY(1927, Brit.); PALAIS DE DANSE(1928, Brit.); WHEN BOYS LEAVE HOME(1928, Brit.)
Misc. Silents
CONFETTI(1927, Brit.); RISING GENERATION, THE(1928, Brit.); SHIP OF LOST MEN, THE(1929, Ger.); YOUNG WOODLEY(1929, Brit.)
St. John Irvine
FIRST MRS. FRASER, THE(1932, Brit.), w; MAN WITHOUT A FACE, THE(1935, Brit.), w
Terry Irvine
REUNION(1932, Brit.)
Amanda Irving
SQUEEZE A FLOWER(1970, Aus.)
Amy Irving
CARRIE(1976); FURY, THE(1978); VOICES(1979); COMPETITION, THE(1980); HONEYSUCKLE ROSE(1980); YENTL(1983)
1984
MICKI AND MAUDE(1984)
Bill Irving
ALL QUIET ON THE WESTERN FRONT(1930); MANHATTAN PARADE(1931); AIR HAWKS(1935); PAID TO DANCE(1937); SHADOW, THE(1937); CONVICTED(1938); WHO KILLED GAIL PRESTON?(1938); GOOD GIRLS GO TO PARIS(1939); SPECIAL INSPECTOR(1939)
Buster Irving
Silents
BREED OF MEN(1919)
Misc. Silents
HEART OF YOUTH, THE(1920)

Carolyn Irving
STOP THE WORLD–I WANT TO GET OFF(1966, Brit.)
Charles Irving
FACE IN THE CROWD, A(1957); THREE NUTS IN SEARCH OF A BOLT(1964); COUNTDOWN(1968); HEAD(1968); PROJECT X(1968)
Colin Irving
1984
HOTEL NEW HAMPSHIRE, THE(1984)
David Irving
GREAT TEXAS DYNAMITE CHASE, THE(1976), p
Misc. Talkies
GOODBYE CRUEL WORLD(1983), d
Ellia Irving
HOUSE OF THE SEVEN GABLES, THE(1940)
Ellis Irving
BERMONDSEY KID, THE(1933, Brit.); NINE FORTY-FIVE(1934, Brit.); BLACK MASK(1935, Brit.); MURDER AT MONTE CARLO(1935, Brit.); MEMBER OF THE JURY(1937, Brit.); DISPATCH FROM REUTERS, A(1940); EARL OF CHICAGO, THE(1940); FLORIAN(1940); INVISIBLE MAN RETURNS, THE(1940); SEA HAWK, THE(1940); STRAWBERRY ROAN(1945, Brit.); VARIETY JUBILEE(1945, Brit.); I'LL TURN TO YOU(1946, Brit.); MURDER IN REVERSE(1946, Brit.); GREEN FINGERS(1947, Brit.); SHOOT FIRST(1953, Brit.); STRICTLY CONFIDENTIAL(1959, Brit.)
Elsie Irving
FLAW, THE(1933, Brit.); BADGER'S GREEN(1934, Brit.); SEEING IS BELIEVING(1934, Brit.); CAN YOU HEAR ME MOTHER?(1935, Brit.); LUCKY DAYS(1935, Brit.)
Ernest Irving
GREAT, MEADOW, THE(1931), md; JAVA HEAD(1935, Brit.), m; HIGH COMMAND(1938, Brit.), m; THERE AIN'T NO JUSTICE(1939, Brit.), m; TROUBLE BREWING(1939, Brit.), md; WARE CASE, THE(1939, Brit.), m; LET GEORGE DO IT(1940, Brit.), md; RETURN TO YESTERDAY(1940, Brit.), m; SALOON BAR(1940, Brit.), m; SECRET FOUR, THE(1940, Brit.), m; THREE COCKEYED SAILORS(1940, Brit.), md; TURNED OUT NICE AGAIN(1941, Brit.), m; GREAT MR. HANDEL, THE(1942, Brit.), md; NEXT OF KIN(1942, Brit.), md; MY LEARNED FRIEND(1943, Brit.), m; YOUNG MAN'S FANCY(1943, Brit.), m; CHAMPAGNE CHARLIE(1944, Brit.), md; 48 HOURS(1944, Brit.), md; DEAD OF NIGHT(1946, Brit.), md; FRIEDA(1947, Brit.), md; LOVES OF JOANNA GODDEN, THE(1947, Brit.), md; NICHOLAS NICKLEBY(1947, Brit.), md; SAN DEMETRIO, LONDON(1947, Brit.), md; IT ALWAYS RAINS ON SUNDAY(1949, Brit.), md; SARABAND(1949, Brit.), md; SCOTT OF THE ANTARCTIC(1949, Brit.), md; TIGHT LITTLE ISLAND(1949, Brit.), m; BLUE LAMP, THE(1950, Brit.), m; HUE AND CRY(1950, Brit.), md; MAGNET, THE(1950, Brit.), md; RUN FOR YOUR MONEY, A(1950, Brit.), m; LAVENDER HILL MOB, THE(1951, Brit.), md; MEN OF THE SEA(1951, Brit.), md; HIS EXCELLENCY(1952, Brit.), m, md; IVORY HUNTER(1952, Brit.), md; MAN IN THE WHITE SUIT, THE(1952), md; I BELIEVE IN YOU(1953, Brit.), m; WHEREVER SHE GOES(1953, Aus.), md
Ethel Irving
CALL ME MAME(1933, Brit.)
Silents
PEEP BEHIND THE SCENES, A(1929, Brit.)
Ethelyn Irving
Misc. Silents
MICHAEL O'HALLORAN(1923)
George Irving
SERGEANT YORK(; COQUETTE(1929); DANCE OF LIFE, THE(1929); GODLESS GIRL, THE(1929); LAST PERFORMANCE, THE(1929); THUNDERBOLT(1929); DIVORCEE, THE(1930); FREE LOVE(1930); MAYBE IT'S LOVE(1930); ONLY SAPS WORK(1930); PUTTIN' ON THE RITZ(1930); SHADOW OF THE LAW(1930); SON OF THE GODS(1930); SPOILERS, THE(1930); YOUNG DESIRE(1930); YOUNG EAGLES(1930); CISCO KID(1931); CONFESSIONS OF A CO-ED(1931); DISHONORED(1931); FIVE AND TEN(1931); FREE SOUL, A(1931); GIRLS DEMAND EXCITEMENT(1931); GRAFT(1931); HOT HEIRESS(1931); HUSH MONEY(1931); NAUGHTY FLIRT, THE(1931); RESURRECTION(1931); SHIPMATES(1931); STAR WITNESS(1931); TOUCHDOWN!(1931); LADY WITH A PAST(1932); MERRILY WE GO TO HELL(1932); THRILL OF YOUTH(1932); VANISHING FRONTIER, THE(1932); HUMANITY(1933); ISLAND OF LOST SOULS(1933); ONE YEAR LATER(1933); SON OF A SAILOR(1933); WORST WOMAN IN PARIS(1933); 42ND STREET(1933); BORN TO BE BAD(1934); BRIGHT EYES(1934); GEORGE WHITE'S SCANDALS(1934); HERE COMES THE NAVY(1934); MANHATTAN MELODRAMA(1934); ONCE TO EVERY BACHELOR(1934); PURSUED(1934); WONDER BAR(1934); WORLD MOVES ON, THE(1934); YOU'RE TELLING ME(1934); CAPTAIN JANUARY(1935); CHARLIE CHAN IN EGYPT(1935); DANTE'S INFERNO(1935); DEATH FLIES EAST(1935); NIGHT AT THE OPERA, A(1935); OIL FOR THE LAMPS OF CHINA(1935); SOCIETY FEVER(1935); UNDER THE PAMPAS MOON(1935); CHARLIE CHAN AT THE RACE TRACK(1936); DANGEROUS(1936); HEARTS DIVIDED(1936); HEARTS IN BONDAGE(1936); IT HAD TO HAPPEN(1936); MESSAGE TO GARCIA, A(1936); NAVY BORN(1936); NAVY WIFE(1936); PRIVATE NUMBER(1936); SEA SPOILERS, THE(1936); SUTTER'S GOLD(1936); BIG SHOT, THE(1937); BORDER CAFE(1937); BREAKFAST FOR TWO(1937); CHINA PASSAGE(1937); CRASHING HOLLYWOOD(1937); DAMAGED LIVES(1937); HATS OFF(1937); HIGH FLYERS(1937); LIFE OF THE PARTY, THE(1937); MAN WHO FOUND HIMSELF, THE(1937); MANDARIN MYSTERY, THE(1937); MEET THE MISSUS(1937); OUTCASTS OF POKER FLAT, THE(1937); SATURDAY'S HEROES(1937); THERE GOES THE GROOM(1937); TOAST OF NEW YORK, THE(1937); TOO MANY WIVES(1937); WE'RE ON THE JURY(1937); YOU CAN'T BUY LUCK(1937); BRINGING UP BABY(1938); CONDEMNED WOMEN(1938); CRIME RING(1938); GO CHASE YOURSELF(1938); LAW WEST OF TOMBSTONE, THE(1938); MAID'S NIGHT OUT(1938); MOTHER CAREY'S CHICKENS(1938); MR. DOODLE KICKS OFF(1938); SAINT IN NEW YORK, THE(1938); SHE'S GOT EVERYTHING(1938); SMASHING THE RACKETS(1938); THIS MARRIAGE BUSINESS(1938); DUST BE MY DESTINY(1939); ESPIONAGE AGENT(1939); HARDYS RIDE HIGH, THE(1939); HELL'S KITCHEN(1939); SERGEANT MADDEN(1939); STORY OF VERNON AND IRENE CASTLE, THE(1939); STREETS OF NEW YORK(1939); WIFE, HUSBAND AND FRIEND(1939); CALLING PHILO VANCE(1940); CHILD IS BORN, A(1940); FLORIAN(1940); JOHNNY APOLLO(1940); KNUTE ROCKNE–ALL AMERICAN(1940); NEW MOON(1940); YESTERDAY'S HEROES(1940); GOLDEN HOOFS(1941); LOVE CRAZY(1941); SHE COULDN'T SAY NO(1941); GREAT MAN'S LADY, THE(1942); ONCE UPON A HONEYMOON(1942); SPY SHIP(1942); HANGMEN ALSO DIE(1943); SON OF DRACULA(1943); IMPOSTER, THE(1944); LADY IN THE DEATH HOUSE(1944); I'LL TELL THE WORLD(1945); MAGIC TOWN(1947); UP THE SANDBOX(1972)

GUILTY OR NOT GUILTY(1932)
Silents
JUNGLE, THE(1914); BALLET GIRL, THE(1916), d; NORTH OF 36(1924); AIR MAIL, THE(1925); FANGS OF JUSTICE(1926); HIS JAZZ BRIDE(1926); KING OF THE TURF, THE(1926); BRONCHO TWISTER(1927); HOME STRUCK(1927); TWO FLAMING YOUTHS(1927); WINGS(1927); CRAIG'S WIFE(1928); PARTNERS IN CRIME(1928); RUNAWAY GIRLS(1928)
Misc. Silents
FAIRY AND THE WAIF, THE(1915), d; JAFFERY(1915), d; THEN I'LL COME BACK TO YOU(1916), d; WHAT HAPPENED AT 22(1916), d; WITCHING HOUR, THE(1916), d; WOMAN IN 47, THE(1916), d; DAUGHTER OF DESTINY(1917), d; GOD'S MAN(1917), d; RAFFLES, THE AMATEUR CRACKSMAN(1917), d; BACK TO THE WOODS(1918), d; HER BOY(1918), d; HIDDEN FIRES(1918), d; LANDLOPER, THE(1918), d; TO HELL WITH THE KAISER(1918), d; AS A MAN THINKS(1919), d; GLORIOUS LADY, THE(1919), d; SILVER KING, THE(1919), d; VOLCANO, THE(1919), d; BLUE PEARL, THE(1920), d; CAPITOL, THE(1920), d; CHILDREN OF DESTINY(1920), d; MISLEADING LADY, THE(1920), d; JUST OUTSIDE THE DOOR(1921), d; WAKEFIELD CASE, THE(1921), d; HER MAJESTY(1922), d; LOST IN A BIG CITY(1923), d; FLOODGATES(1924), d; WANDERER OF THE WASTELAND(1924), d; GOOSE HANGS HIGH, THE(1925); CITY, THE(1926); MIDNIGHT KISS, THE(1926); SHANGHAI BOUND(1927); FEEL MY PULSE(1928); POOR MILLIONAIRE, THE(1930)
George Irving, Sr.
PARIS BOUND(1929)
George S. Irving
FOREPLAY(1975); CHILD IS A WILD THING, A(1976); DEADLY HERO(1976); RAGGEDY ANN AND ANDY(1977)
Gregg Irving
JUST BEFORE DAWN(1980), w
H. B. Irving
LADIES IN RETIREMENT(1941), w
H.B. Irving
Misc. Silents
MASKS AND FACES(1917, Brit.)
Henry Irving
I SAILED TO TAHITI WITH AN ALL GIRL CREW(1969), w
Henry George Irving
Silents
JOHN GLAYDE'S HONOR(1915), d&w
Henry R. Irving
BLACK FURY(1935), w
Hollis Irving
CROWDED SKY, THE(1960); FACTS OF LIFE, THE(1960)
Holly Irving
FROGS(1972); GLASS HOUSES(1972); TWO-MINUTE WARNING(1976)
I.W. Irving
Misc. Silents
SKY'S THE LIMIT(1925), d
Jane Irving
Silents
NIGHT LIFE(1927)
Jerry Irving
I PASSED FOR WHITE(1960), m
Joe Irving
MURDER MAN(1935)
John Irving
WORLD ACCORDING TO GARP, The(1982), a, w
1984
HOTEL NEW HAMPSHIRE, THE(1984), d&w
Johnny Irving
1984
COMFORT AND JOY(1984, Brit.)
Judy Irving
OFF THE WALL(1977), ph
Jules Irving
IT CAME FROM BENEATH THE SEA(1955)
Katherine Irving
WORDS AND MUSIC(1929); MADAME SATAN(1930)
Laurence Irving
TAMING OF THE SHREW, THE(1929), art d; PYGMALION(1938, Brit.), art d; INHERITANCE, THE(1951, Brit.), p
Lori Irving
FEDERAL MAN(1950); SON OF THE RENEGADE(1953)
Margaret Irving
ANIMAL CRACKERS(1930); THANKS A MILLION(1935); CAPTAIN CALAMITY(1936); CHARLIE CHAN AT THE OPERA(1936); EXCLUSIVE STORY(1936); FOLLOW YOUR HEART(1936); FOUR DAYS WONDER(1936); I MARRIED A DOCTOR(1936); SAN FRANCISCO(1936); THREE MEN ON A HORSE(1936); WIFE VERSUS SECRETARY(1936); WOMEN ARE TROUBLE(1936); MEN IN EXILE(1937); OUTCASTS OF POKER FLAT, THE(1937); SH! THE OCTOPUS(1937); UNDER SUSPICION(1937); WIFE, DOCTOR AND NURSE(1937); BARONESS AND THE BUTLER, THE(1938); KENTUCKY(1938); LITTLE MISS ROUGHNECK(1938); LOVE, HONOR AND BEHAVE(1938); SWEETHEARTS(1938); TOY WIFE, THE(1938); MR. MOTO'S LAST WARNING(1939); IN SOCIETY(1944); BEAUTIFUL CHEAT, THE(1946)
Misc. Talkies
NEIGHBORHOOD HOUSE(1936)
Misc. Silents
RADIO-MANIA(1923)
Marjorie Irving
GALLIPOLI(1981, Aus.)
Mary Jane Irving
GODLESS GIRL, THE(1929); FLORODORA GIRL, THE(1930); TOM SAWYER(1930); ARSENE LUPIN(1932); PROBATION(1932); WITHOUT HONORS(1932); STUDENT TOUR(1934); HAVING WONDERFUL TIME(1938)
Silents
ALIEN ENEMY, AN(1918); BROKEN DOLL, A(1921), a, w; CRADLE, THE(1922); TRAVELIN' ON(1922); LITTLE CHURCH AROUND THE CORNER(1923); STRANGER, THE(1924); SPLENDID ROAD, THE(1925); TOP OF NEW YORK, THE(1925)

Michael Irving-

Misc. Silents
SQUARE DEAL MAN, THE(1917); WILL YOU BE STAYING FOR SUPPER?(1919); LOST AND FOUND ON A SOUTH SEA ISLAND(1923); OLD SWEETHEART OF MINE, AN(1923); GOOD BAD BOY(1924)

Michael Irving
HANGAR 18(1980)

Paul Irving
COUNT OF MONTE CRISTO, THE(1934); MISS PACIFIC FLEET(1935); AUGUST WEEK-END(1936, Brit.); GOLD DIGGERS OF 1937(1936); GREAT ZIEGFELD, THE(1936); HOLLYWOOD HOTEL(1937); IT'S LOVE I'M AFTER(1937); LIFE OF EMILE ZOLA, THE(1937); ON THE AVENUE(1937); BATTLE OF BROADWAY(1938); YOU CAN'T TAKE IT WITH YOU(1938); BALALAIKA(1939); DISPATCH FROM REUTERS, A(1940); FOREIGN CORRESPONDENT(1940); NO, NO NANETTE(1940); YOU'LL NEVER GET RICH(1941); NORTHERN PURSUIT(1943)

Misc. Silents
LOVE'S CROSS ROADS(1916)

Penny Irving
HOUSE OF WHIPCORD(1974, Brit.); OLD DRACULA(1975, Brit.)

Raf Irving
SLEEPING DOGS(1977, New Zealand)

Richard Irving
THIS IS THE ARMY(1943); MIRACLE ON 34TH STREET, THE(1947); VIOLENCE(1947); CANON CITY(1948); JIGGS AND MAGGIE IN SOCIETY(1948); SONS OF ADVENTURE(1948); TRAIN TO ALCATRAZ(1948); SCENE OF THE CRIME(1949); TOO LATE FOR TEARS(1949); BLONDE BANDIT, THE(1950); BORDERLINE(1950); MOB, THE(1951); ON DANGEROUS GROUND(1951); ROADBLOCK(1951); WOMAN IN THE DARK(1952); THREE GUNS FOR TEXAS(1968), p; NEWMAN'S LAW(1974), p; SIDECAR RACERS(1975, Aus.), p

Robert Irving
JORY(1972), w

Roy Irving
ODD MAN OUT(1947, Brit.)

Sandy Irving
DANGEROUS SEAS(1931, Brit.)

Stanley Irving
FOREVER YOURS(1937, Brit.), d

Washington Irving
ADVENTURES OF ICHABOD AND MR. TOAD(1949), w

Silents
RIP VAN WINKLE(1914), w; RIP VAN WINKLE(1921), w

William Irving
FROM HEADQUARTERS(1929); HEARTS IN EXILE(1929); LIFE OF THE PARTY, THE(1930); ROUGH WATERS(1930); SONG OF THE CABELLERO(1930); HER MAJESTY LOVE(1931); DIPLOMANIACS(1933); TILLIE AND GUS(1933); CAT'S PAW, THE(1934); JEALOUSY(1934); LADY BY CHOICE(1934); MANHATTAN MELODRAMA(1934); ORIENT EXPRESS(1934); AND SO THEY WERE MARRIED(1936); DOWN ON THE FARM(1938); IDIOT'S DELIGHT(1939); NINOTCHKA(1939); MORTAL STORM, THE(1940); MY FAVORITE BLONDE(1942); HARD, FAST, AND BEAUTIFUL(1951)

Silents
GENTLE JULIA(1923); BEAUTIFUL BUT DUMB(1928); CAMERAMAN, THE(1928); NOTHING TO WEAR(1928); RED HAIR(1928)

William J. Irving
MELODY IN SPRING(1934)

Silents
TWIN BEDS(1920); HAM AND EGGS AT THE FRONT(1927)

Misc. Silents
BILLIONS(1920)

Perry Irvins
RED RIVER RANGE(1938)

Avanell Irwin
SIMON, KING OF THE WITCHES(1971)

Bill Irwin
POPEYE(1980)

Boyd Irwin
MADAME SATAN(1930); MAN FROM YESTERDAY, THE(1932); PURSUIT OF HAPPINESS, THE(1934); WHAT EVERY WOMAN KNOWS(1934); MAN WHO RECLAIMED HIS HEAD, THE(1935); DEVIL'S SQUADRON(1936); KILLER AT LARGE(1936); UNDER YOUR SPELL(1936); LOST HORIZON(1937); PRISONER OF ZENDA, THE(1937); SERGEANT MURPHY(1938); YOU CAN'T TAKE IT WITH YOU(1938); I AM NOT AFRAID(1939); MAN IN THE IRON MASK, THE(1939); SKY PATROL(1939); WE ARE NOT ALONE(1939); WITNESS VANISHES, THE(1939); DRUMS OF THE DESERT(1940); EARL OF CHICAGO, THE(1940); INVISIBLE KILLER, THE(1940); CITY OF MISSING GIRLS(1941); CRIMINALS WITHIN(1941); GREAT SWINDLE, THE(1941); PASSAGE FROM HONG KONG(1941); SECRET EVIDENCE(1941); UNFINISHED BUSINESS(1941); MAJOR AND THE MINOR, THE(1942); THEY ALL KISSED THE BRIDE(1942); THANK YOUR LUCKY STARS(1943); YOUTH ON PARADE(1943); DOUBLE INDEMNITY(1944); FRENCHMAN'S CREEK(1944); LODGER, THE(1944); MINISTRY OF FEAR(1945); MOLLY AND ME(1945); SCARLET STREET(1945); DECEPTION(1946); DRAGONWYCH(1946); GIRL ON THE SPOT(1946); IN OLD SACRAMENTO(1946); MAGNIFICENT DOLL(1946); NIGHT AND DAY(1946); RENDEZVOUS 24(1946); TIME OF THEIR LIVES, THE(1946); TOMORROW IS FOREVER(1946); DOUBLE LIFE, A(1947); DOWN TO EARTH(1947); FOREVER AMBER(1947); IMPERFECT LADY, THE(1947); MONSIEUR VERDOUX(1947); THAT HAGEN GIRL(1947); CAMPUS HONEYMOON(1948); DOCKS OF NEW ORLEANS(1948); I, JANE DOE(1948); KING OF THE BANDITS(1948)

Silents
GILDED DREAM, THE(1920); LADY IN LOVE, A(1920); THREE MUSKETEERS, THE(1921); LONG CHANCE, THE(1922); ASHES OF VENGEANCE(1923); ENEMIES OF CHILDREN(1923)

Misc. Silents
LUCK OF GERALDINE LAIRD, THE(1920)

Boyd Irwin, Sr.
TALE OF TWO CITIES, A(1935); BLACKMAILER(1936); DANGEROUS INTRIGUE(1936); MEET NERO WOLFE(1936); WIDOW FROM MONTE CARLO, THE(1936); LANCER SPY(1937); MARRIED BEFORE BREAKFAST(1937)

Bruce Irwin
THESE WILDER YEARS(1956)

Carl Irwin
MODERN PROBLEMS(1981)

Carolyn Irwin
Misc. Silents
YOUNG MOTHER HUBBARD(1917)

Charles Irwin
BLIND ADVENTURE(1933); HELL BELOW(1933); LOOKING FORWARD(1933); BULLDOG DRUMMOND STRIKES BACK(1934); KEY, THE(1934); LONG LOST FATHER(1934); MOONSTONE, THE(1934); MYSTERY OF MR. X, THE(1934); TREASURE ISLAND(1934); GILDED LILY, THE(1935); MUTINY ON THE BOUNTY(1935); PAGE MISS GLORY(1935); AND SO THEY WERE MARRIED(1936); GO WEST, YOUNG MAN(1936); LIBELED LADY(1936); LOVE ON THE RUN(1936); MORE THAN A SECRETARY(1936); SPENDTHRIFT(1936); WHIPSAW(1936); WHITE ANGEL, THE(1936); WIFE VERSUS SECRETARY(1936); ANOTHER DAWN(1937); DOUBLE OR NOTHING(1937); LEAGUE OF FRIGHTENED MEN(1937); LET'S GET MARRIED(1937); LIVE, LOVE AND LEARN(1937); SHALL WE DANCE(1937); WINGS OVER HONOLULU(1937); KIDNAPPED(1938); LORD JEFF(1938); I STOLE A MILLION(1939); LIGHT THAT FAILED, THE(1939); LITTLE ACCIDENT(1939); RAFFLES(1939); SUSANNAH OF THE MOUNTIES(1939); SWEEPSTAKES WINNER(1939); WE ARE NOT ALONE(1939); WOLF CALL(1939); ADVENTURE IN DIAMONDS(1940); LETTER, THE(1940); MAN I MARRIED, THE(1940); RANGERS OF FORTUNE(1940); SOUTH OF SUEZ(1940); DEVIL AND MISS JONES, THE(1941); GIRL, A GUY AND A GOB, A(1941); SHADOWS ON THE STAIRS(1941); YANK IN THE R.A.F., A(1941); BLACK SWAN, THE(1942); DESPERATE JOURNEY(1942); EAGLE SQUADRON(1942); GORILLA MAN(1942); GREAT IMPERSONATION, THE(1942); JOURNEY FOR MARGARET(1942); MRS. MINIVER(1942); SON OF FURY(1942); TO BE OR NOT TO BE(1942); BACKGROUND TO DANGER(1943); CRYSTAL BALL, THE(1943); FIRST COMES COURAGE(1943); FOREVER AND A DAY(1943); IMMORTAL SERGEANT, THE(1943); JOHNNY COME LATELY(1943); LASSIE, COME HOME(1943); NO TIME FOR LOVE(1943); THANK YOUR LUCKY STARS(1943); THUMBS UP(1943); WINTERTIME(1943); JANE EYRE(1944); NONE BUT THE LONELY HEART(1944); PRACTICALLY YOURS(1944); SING, NEIGHBOR, SING(1944); WHITE CLIFFS OF DOVER, THE(1944); HANGOVER SQUARE(1945); KITTY(1945); WONDER MAN(1945); FOXES OF HARROW, THE(1947); MY WILD IRISH ROSE(1947); LUCK OF THE IRISH(1948); BOMBA ON PANTHER ISLAND(1949); BOMBA THE JUNGLE BOY(1949); CHALLENGE TO LASSIE(1949); FORTUNES OF CAPTAIN BLOOD(1950); MONTANA(1950); MYSTERY JUNCTION(1951, Brit.); TALE OF FIVE WOMEN, A(1951, Brit.); CAPTAIN PIRATE(1952); CHARGE OF THE LANCERS(1953); FORT VENGEANCE(1953); IRON GLOVE, THE(1954); COURT JESTER, THE(1956); KING AND I, THE(1956); SHERIFF OF FRACTURED JAW, THE(1958, Brit.)

Charles W. Irwin
HE RIDES TALL(1964), w

Coulter Irwin
UNCLE HARRY(1945); PRISON SHIP(1945); COWBOY BLUES(1946); JOLSON STORY, THE(1946); NIGHT EDITOR(1946); OUT OF THE DEPTHS(1946)

Don Irwin
ULYSSES(1967, U.S./Brit.)

Edward Irwin
Silents
GIRL OF LONDON, A(1925, Brit.)

Frances Irwin
GUN CRAZY(1949)

Jack Irwin
Misc. Talkies
LIGHTNIN' SMITH RETURNS(1931), d; WHITE RENEGADE(1931), d

Jacques Irwin
LES JEUX SONT FAITS(1947, Fr.)

Joe Irwin [Vjaceslav Irmanov]
VOYAGE TO THE END OF THE UNIVERSE(1963, Czech.)

John Irwin
CONVICT'S CODE(1930); BOLERO(1934); WE'RE NOT DRESSING(1934); ROAD GANG(1936); SOMEONE AT THE DOOR(1936, Brit.); INVISIBLE STRIPES(1940); BADGER'S GREEN(1949, Brit.), d

Karen Irwin
PROPERTY(1979)

Lew Irwin
X-15(1961)

Margaret Irwin
YOUNG BESS(1953), w

Mark Irwin
BLOOD AND GUTS(1978, Can.), ph; STARSHIP INVASIONS(1978, Can.), ph; BROOD, THE(1979, Can.), ph; NIGHT SCHOOL(1981), ph; SCANNERS(1981, Can.), ph; TANYA'S ISLAND(1981, Can.), ph; TERROR EYES(1981), ph; FUNERAL HOME(1982, Can.), ph; DEAD ZONE, THE(1983), ph; SPASMS(1983, Can.), ph; VIDEODROME(1983, Can.), ph

May Irwin
Silents
MRS. BLACK IS BACK(1914)

Nate Irwin
THING, THE(1982)

Ray Irwin
Misc. Silents
TAME CAT, THE(1921)

Robert Irwin
MOUNTAINS O'MOURNE(1938, Brit.)

Roxanne Irwin
MADELEINE IS(1971, Can.)

Ted Irwin
STREET OF SINNERS(1957)

Theodore D. Irwin
UNKNOWN BLONDE(1934), w

Tom Irwin
QUARE FELLOW, THE(1962, Brit.); YOUNG CASSIDY(1965, U.S./Brit.); LOCK UP YOUR DAUGHTERS(1969, Brit.); FLIGHT OF THE DOVES(1971)

Trudy Irwin
MY FAVORITE SPY(1942); SWING FEVER(1943)
Virginia Lee Irwin
SOMETHING TO SING ABOUT(1937)
Wallace Irwin
WOMAN IN RED, THE(1935), w
Silents
MAKING THE GRADE(1921), w; AMERICAN BEAUTY(1927), w
Will Irwin
Silents
EXALTED FLAPPER, THE(1929), w
Wynn Irwin
DIRTYMOUTH(1970); WILLIE DYNAMITE(1973); HUNTER, THE(1980); LITTLE MISS MARKER(1980)
Alberto Isaac
PRETTY MAIDS ALL IN A ROW(1971); SOME KIND OF HERO(1982)
Leon Isaac
HAMMER(1972)
Misc. Talkies
DEATH FORCE(1978)
Luceoro Isaac
MISSING(1982), art d
Lucero Isaac
FOXTROT(1977, Mex./Swiss), art d
Vincent Isaac
1984
ANGEL(1984)
Vincent J. Isaac
KISS ME GOODBYE(1982); VICE SQUAD(1982); DOCTOR DETROIT(1983); TWILIGHT ZONE–THE MOVIE(1983)
Anthony Rufus Isaacs
BLOCKHOUSE, THE(1974, Brit.), p
Bob Isaacs
SAFARI(1956)
Bud Isaacs
BREAKOUT(1975), ed
Bud S. Isaacs
1984
CHATTANOOGA CHOO CHOO(1984), ed; INVISIBLE STRANGLER(1984), ed
Charles Isaacs
SQUEEZE A FLOWER(1970, Aus.), w
F. H. Isaacs
METALSTORM: THE DESTRUCTION OF JARED-SYN(1983), makeup
Gregory Isaacs
ROCKERS(1980)
Ike Isaacs
THEY SHOOT HORSES, DON'T THEY?(1969)
Jack Isaacs
ONLY WAY HOME, THE(1972)
Karyn Isaacs
1984
CHOOSE ME(1984)
M.A. Isaacs
GURU, THE MAD MONK(1971), w
Troy Isaacs
SCARFACE(1983)
Vincent J. Isaacs
FIREFOX(1982)
Charles D. Isaacson
Silents
WISE HUSBANDS(
Joan Isaacson
1984
LOUISIANE(1984, Fr./Can.), makeup
Todd Isaacson
SO FINE(1981)
Isabel and Emma
OLD MOTHER RILEY'S CIRCUS(1941, Brit.)
Isabelita
THAT'S MY BABY(1944); GAY SENORITA, THE(1945); PAN-AMERICANA(1945); CLUB HAVANA(1946); DON RICARDO RETURNS(1946); HIGH SCHOOL HERO(1946); SLIGHTLY SCANDALOUS(1946); THAT'S MY GAL(1947)
Henry Isabell
WILD HORSE RODEO(1938)
Isabella
CIRCLE OF DECEIT(1982, Fr./Ger.)
Ray Isabelle
OUT OF THE BLUE(1982)
Pete Isacksen
EAT MY DUST!(1976); GRAND THEFT AUTO(1977)
Peter Isacksen
FISH THAT SAVED PITTSBURGH, THE(1979); EARTHBOUND(1981); UNDER THE RAINBOW(1981)
1984
SURF II(1984)
Misc. Talkies
REUNION, THE(1977)
Mara Isaja
1984
MEMED MY HAWK(1984, Brit.)
Valeriy Isakov
SHE-WOLF, THE(1963, USSR)
Antonije Isakovic
THREE(1967, Yugo.), w
Ulla Isaksson
BRINK OF LIFE(1960, Swed.), d&w; VIRGIN SPRING, THE(1960, Swed.), w
Boris Isarov
HUMAN FACTOR, THE(1979, Brit.)

Antonio Isasi [Isamendi]
ADVENTURES OF SCARAMOUCHE, THE(1964, Fr.), d, w; THAT MAN IN ISTANBUL(1966, Fr./Ital./Span.), p&d, w; THEY CAME TO ROB LAS VEGAS(1969, Fr./Ital./Span./Ger.), d; SUMMERTIME KILLER(1973), p&d
Iwao Isayama
TIME SLIP(1981, Jap.), ph
Edwin "Frog" Isbell
SUGARLAND EXPRESS, THE(1974)
Jack Isbell
DRIVE-IN(1976)
Jane Isbell
SERGEANT YORK(; YOUNGEST PROFESSION, THE(1943); NATIONAL VELVET(1944)
John C. Isbell
CAT PEOPLE(1982)
Merrill C. Isbell
HOMBRE(1967)
Jose Isbert
MAN WHO WAGGED HIS TAIL, THE(1961, Ital./Span.); NOT ON YOUR LIFE(1965, Ital./Span.); OPERATION DELILAH(1966, U.S./Span.)
Maruda Isbert
VIRIDIANA(1962, Mex./Span.)
Maruja Isbert
NOT ON YOUR LIFE(1965, Ital./Span.)
Tony Isbert
SAGA OF DRACULA, THE(1975, Span.)
Claire Isbister
KITCHEN, THE(1961, Brit.)
Feodor Ischenko
LAST HILL, THE(1945, USSR)
Rob Iscove
JESUS CHRIST, SUPERSTAR(1973), ch; SILENT MOVIE(1976), ch
Tor Isedal
VIRGIN SPRING, THE(1960, Swed.); DOLL, THE(1964, Swed.); SWEDISH WEDDING NIGHT(1965, Swed.); PIPPI IN THE SOUTH SEAS(1974, Swed./Ger.)
Michel Isella
WAR OF THE BUTTONS(1963 Fr.)
John Isenbarger
BLACK SIX, THE(1974)
Lenny Isenberg
CHEAPER TO KEEP HER(1980), p
Robert Isenberg
EASY COME, EASY GO(1967)
Isenta
M(1933, Ger.)
Michiko Iseri
KING AND I, THE(1956)
Bjorn Isfalt
GRASS IS SINGING, THE(1982, Brit./Swed.), m
1984
KILLING HEAT(1984), m
Frederic Stewart Isham
THREE LIVE GHOSTS(1929), w
Frederick S. Isham
THREE LIVE GHOSTS(1935), w; NOTHING BUT THE TRUTH(1941), w
Silents
NOTHING BUT THE TRUTH(1920), w
Frederick Stewart Isham
Silents
ALADDIN FROM BROADWAY(1917), w; NUT-CRACKER, THE(1926), w
Gyles Isham
ANNE ONE HUNDRED(1933, Brit.); PURSE STRINGS(1933, Brit.); ANNA KARENINA(1935); IRON DUKE, THE(1935, Brit.); REGAL CAVALCADE(1935, Brit.); HOUSE OF THE SPANIARD, THE(1936, Brit.); I MARRIED A SPY(1938); UNDER SECRET ORDERS(1943, Brit.)
Mark Isham
NEVER CRY WOLF(1983), m
1984
MRS. SOFFEL(1984), m
Isham Jones and His Orchestra
CONVENTION GIRL(1935)
Christopher Isherwood
LITTLE FRIEND(1934, Brit.), w; RAGE IN HEAVEN(1941), w; FOREVER AND A DAY(1943), w; ADVENTURE IN BALTIMORE(1949), w; GREAT SINNER, THE(1949), w; DIANE(1955), w; I AM A CAMERA(1955, Brit.), w; LOVED ONE, THE(1965), w; SAILOR FROM GIBRALTAR, THE(1967, Brit.), w; RICH AND FAMOUS(1981)
Mark P. Isherwood
MONDO TRASHO(1970)
Tomiko Ishi
GATE OF FLESH(1964, Jap.)
Eitaro Ishibashi
COMPUTER FREE-FOR-ALL(1969, Jap.)
Ayumi Ishida
RIVER OF FOREVER(1967, Jap.); TIDAL WAVE(1975, U.S./Jap.)
Moriyoshi Ishida
GIRARA(1967, Jap.), w
Yoshiyuki Ishida
CHALLENGE, THE(1982), prod d
Toshiro Ishido
1984
ANTARCTICA(1984, Jap.), w
Noboru Ishiguro
SPACE CRUISER(1977 Jap.), anim
Tatsuya Ishiguro
GATE OF HELL(1954, Jap.)
Akira Ishihama
HUMAN CONDITION, THE(1959, Jap.); HAHAKIRI(1963, Jap.)

Hatsune Ishihara
BAD NEWS BEARS GO TO JAPAN, THE(1978)
May Ishihara
WILD IN THE STREETS(1968)
Sankichi Ishihara
ANGRY ISLAND(1960, Jap.)
Shintaro Ishihara
DANGEROUS KISS, THE(1961, Jap.); LOVE AT TWENTY(1963, Fr./Ital./Jap./Pol./Ger.), d&w
Yuiro Ishihara
ALONE ON THE PACIFIC(1964, Jap.)
Yujiro Ishihara
THOSE MAGNIFICENT MEN IN THEIR FLYING MACHINES; OR HOW I FLEW FROM LONDON TO PARIS IN 25 HOURS AND 11 MINUTES(1965, Brit.); TUNNEL TO THE SUN(1968, Jap.), a, p; UNDER THE BANNER OF SAMURAI(1969, Jap.); TENCHU!(1970, Jap.)
Arnold Ishii
EVERYTHING BUT THE TRUTH(1956); NAVY WIFE(1956)
Iwao Ishii
TORA-SAN PART 2(1970, Jap.), ed
Kan Ishii
TATSU(1962, Jap.), m; BANDITS ON THE WIND(1964, Jap.), m
Mitsuharu Ishii
INCHON(1981), p
Ryuichi Ishii
BUDDHA(1965, Jap.)
Teruo Ishii
DEATH ON THE MOUNTAIN(1961, Jap.), w; FRIENDLY KILLER, THE(1970, Jap.), d&w
Komel Ishikawa
ALAKAZAM THE GREAT!(1961, Jap.), ph
Mitsuaki Ishikawa
MAGIC BOY(1960, Jap.), ph
Tamio Ishikura
MERRY CHRISTMAS MR. LAWRENCE(1983, Jap./Brit.)
Kan Ishil
GORATH(1964, Jap.), m
Yoshihiro Ishimatsu
CREATURE CALLED MAN, THE(1970, Jap.), w; GATEWAY TO GLORY(1970, Jap.), w
Shiro Ishimori
FIGHT FOR THE GLORY(1970, Jap.), w; GALAXY EXPRESS(1982, Jap.), w
Ishimoto
WALK, DON'T RUN(1966)
Dale Ishimoto
BATTLE AT BLOODY BEACH(1961); MAJORITY OF ONE, A(1961); OPERATION BOTTLENECK(1961); NUN AND THE SERGEANT, THE(1962); MC HALE'S NAVY(1964); MORO WITCH DOCTOR(1964, U.S./Phil.); KING RAT(1965); BEACH RED(1967); GAMES, THE(1970); M(1970); SUPERCHICK(1973); SHARK'S TREASURE(1975); MIDWAY(1976); ENTER THE NINJA(1982)
1984
CANNONBALL RUN II(1984); NINJA III–THE DOMINATION(1984)
Shotaro Ishinori
MESSAGE FROM SPACE(1978, Jap.), spec eff
Tetsuo Ishitachi
LONGING FOR LOVE(1966, Jap.)
Kenjiro Ishiyama
HIGH AND LOW(1963, Jap.); WHITE ROSE OF HONG KONG(1965, Jap.); KOJIRO(1967, Jap.); EMPEROR AND A GENERAL, THE(1968, Jap.)
Koji Ishizaka
THROUGH DAYS AND MONTHS(1969 Jap.)
Ole Ishoj
CHRISTINE KEELER AFFAIR, THE(1964, Brit.)
Yoshio Isihido
LAKE, THE(1970, Jap.), w
Vincent Isla
THEY WERE EXPENDABLE(1945)
Nancy Island
MASK, THE(1961, Can.)
Balanec & d'Ouessant Islanders
Misc. Silents
FINNIS TERRAE(1929, Fr.)
Francisco Islas
TREASURE OF THE SIERRA MADRE, THE(1948)
V. Islavin
WAR AND PEACE(1968, USSR)
Evans Isle
NEW HOUSE ON THE LEFT, THE(1978, Brit.), p&d
Misc. Talkies
LAST STOP ON THE NIGHT TRAIN(1976), d
Lucille Isle
WIFE TAKES A FLYER, THE(1942)
Loreto Isleta
IGOROTA, THE LEGEND OF THE TREE OF LIFE(1970, Phil.), ph
Jack Isley
TRUE CONFESSION(1937)
Phyllis Isley [Jennifer Jones]
NEW FRONTIER(1939)
Islington
Silents
LODGER, THE(1926, Brit.), set d; EASY VIRTUE(1927, Brit.), set d; WHEN BOYS LEAVE HOME(1928, Brit.), set d
Zoreen Ismael
NOT A HOPE IN HELL(1960, Brit.); SHOOT TO KILL(1961, Brit.)
Zoreen Ismail
PASSPORT TO CHINA(1961, Brit.)
P. Ismatov
VOW, THE(1947, USSR.)

Ali Ismir
THERE IS STILL ROOM IN HELL(1963, Ger.), ph
Isnard
CROISIERES SIDERALES(1941, Fr.), ph
Jean Isnard
GUTS IN THE SUN(1959, Fr.), ph; PLEASURES AND VICES(1962, Fr.), ph; STORY OF THE COUNT OF MONTE CRISTO, THE(1962, Fr./Ital.), ph; FIRE IN THE FLESH(1964, Fr.), ph; CHECKERBOARD(1969, Fr.), ph
Marie Isnard
KINGS GO FORTH(1958)
Monique Isnardon
BRIDGE TO THE SUN(1961), ed; PASSION OF SLOW FIRE, THE(1962, Fr.), ed; SWORDSMAN OF SIENA, THE(1962, Fr./Ital.), ed; WHERE THE TRUTH LIES(1962, Fr.), ed; HOW NOT TO ROB A DEPARTMENT STORE(1965, Fr./Ital.), ed; PLAYMATES(1969, Fr./Ital.), ed; TO COMMIT A MURDER(1970, Fr./Ital./Ger.), ed; LA CAGE AUX FOLLES(1979, Fr./Ital.), ed
Raymond Isnardon
UTOPIA(1952, Fr./Ital.), ed
Robert Isnardon
BRIDGE TO THE SUN(1961), ed; NUDE IN HIS POCKET(1962, Fr.), ed; PASSION OF SLOW FIRE, THE(1962, Fr.), ed; SWORDSMAN OF SIENA, THE(1962, Fr./Ital.), ed; WHERE THE TRUTH LIES(1962, Fr.), ed; MISTRESS FOR THE SUMMER, A(1964, Fr./Ital.), ed; HOW NOT TO ROB A DEPARTMENT STORE(1965, Fr./Ital.), ed; MURDER AT 45 R.P.M.(1965, Fr.), ed; RAVISHING IDIOT, A(1966, Ital./Fr.), ed; DRACULA AND SON(1976, Fr.), ed; LA CAGE AUX FOLLES(1979, Fr./Ital.), ed; SUNDAY LOVERS(1980, Ital./Fr.), ed; LA CAGE AUX FOLLES II(1981, Ital./Fr.), ed
Kurnaoshuke Isoda
TORA! TORA! TORA!(1970, U.S./Jap.), tech adv
Christian Isodore
DON'T GO IN THE HOUSE(1980)
Lyle Isom
HUMANOIDS FROM THE DEEP(1980)
Tadahiko Isomi
EAST CHINA SEA(1969, Jap.), d, w
Nancy Ison
Misc. Talkies
CINDY AND DONNA(1971)
Al Israel
SOLDIER, THE(1982); SCARFACE(1983)
1984
BODY DOUBLE(1984); OLD ENOUGH(1984)
Ben Israel
PUTNEY SWOPE(1969)
Charles E. Israel
KLONDIKE FEVER(1980), w
Charles Israel
MARK, THE(1961, Brit.), w; ANGELA(1977, Can.), w; ANGRY MAN, THE(1979 Fr./Can.), w
Chuck Israel
1984
LOUISIANE(1984, Fr./Can.), w
Frank Israel
NIGHT GAMES(1980), art d
Irving Israel
NIGHTMARE IN BLOOD(1978)
Judy Israel
GURU, THE MAD MONK(1971)
Lillian Israel
CRISIS(1950)
Meir Israel
JESUS CHRIST, SUPERSTAR(1973)
Michel Israel
MAMMA DRACULA(1980, Bel./Fr.)
Mohamed Ibn Israel
GODDESS, THE(1962, India)
Neal Israel
1984
JOHNNY DANGEROUSLY(1984); POLICE ACADEMY(1984), w
Neil Israel
TUNNELVISION(1976), a, d, w; CRACKING UP(1977); AMERICATHON(1979), d, w
Ricky Israel
NEW YEAR'S EVIL(1980)
Tovia Israel
Misc. Talkies
ONE PAGE OF LOVE(1979)
Victor Israel
PLACE CALLED GLORY, A(1966, Span./Ger.); TEXICAN, THE(1966, U.S./Span.); UP THE MACGREGORS(1967, Ital./Span.); NARCO MEN, THE(1969, Span./Ital.); HOUSE THAT SCREAMED, THE(1970, Span.); GRAVEYARD OF HORROR(1971, Span.); LIGHT AT THE EDGE OF THE WORLD, THE(1971, U.S./Span./Lichtenstein); DON'T TURN THE OTHER CHEEK(1974, Ital./Ger./Span.); LAS RATAS NO DUERMEN DE NOCHE(1974, Span./Fr.); NIGHT OF THE ZOMBIES(1983, Span./Ital.)
Misc. Talkies
SWEET SOUND OF DEATH(1965, U.S./Span.)
Walter J. Israel
Silents
OLIVER TWIST(1922), cos
Shimon Israeli
CLOUDS OVER ISRAEL(1966, Israel)
The Israelite Spiritual Church Choir of New Orleans
PETE KELLY'S BLUES(1955)
Paul Issa
PIRANHA II: THE SPAWNING(1981, Neth.)
Vincent Issac
SAVAGE HARVEST(1981)

Marian Issacks
1984
CANNONBALL RUN II(1984)
Bud S. Issacs
SHOOT OUT AT BIG SAG(1962), p, ed; MUNSTER, GO HOME(1966), ed
A. Issaverdens
MAN WHO LAUGHS, THE(1966, Ital.), w
Members of Istanbul Theater of Performing Arts
DRY SUMMER(1967, Turkey)
Agustin Isunza
LEGEND OF A BANDIT, THE(1945, Mex.); EL TOPO(1971, Mex.); ILLUSION TRAVELS BY STREETCAR, THE(1977, Mex.)
Yunosuke Ita
SCARLET CAMELLIA, THE(1965, Jap.)
The Itah Sisters
DESTROY ALL MONSTERS(1969, Jap.)
Italian State Radio Orchestra of Rome
NEOPOLITAN CAROUSEL(1961, Ital.)
Icchizo Itami
55 DAYS AT PEKING(1963)
Ichizo Itami
LORD JIM(1965, Brit.)
Juzo Itami
1984
FAMILY GAME, THE(1984, Jap.)
Mansaku Itami
RICKSHAW MAN, THE(1960, Jap.), w
Mansaku Itani
NEW EARTH, THE(1937, Jap./Ger.), d
Takeo Itch
CHILDREN OF HIROSHIMA(1952, Jap.), ph
Al Iteman
BAD COMPANY(1931)
Dion Itheradge
DR. RHYTHM(1938), w
Paul Henry Itken
BLACK MARBLE, THE(1980)
Sylvain Itkine
CRIME OF MONSIEUR LANGE, THE(1936, Fr.); GRAND ILLUSION(1938, Fr.); LA CHIENNE(1975, Fr.)
Daisuke Ito
ACTOR'S REVENGE, AN(1963, Jap.), w; SHOWDOWN FOR ZATOICHI(1968, Jap.), w; HIKEN YABURI(1969, Jap.), w
Eimi Ito
GODZILLA VS. THE THING(1964, Jap.)
Emi Ito
MOTHRA(1962, Jap.); GHIDRAH, THE THREE-HEADED MONSTER(1965, Jap.)
Fujio Ito
KARATE, THE HAND OF DEATH(1961)
H. Ito
WHEN A WOMAN ASCENDS THE STAIRS(1963, Jap.), ed
Hiroko Ito
WOMAN IN THE DUNES(1964, Jap.)
Hisaya Ito
MYSTERIANS, THE(1959, Jap.); DEATH ON THE MOUNTAIN(1961, Jap.); GHIDRAH, THE THREE-HEADED MONSTER(1965, Jap.); DESTROY ALL MONSTERS(1969, Jap.)
Jerry Ito
MANSTER, THE(1962, Jap.); MOTHRA(1962, Jap.); WALL-EYED NIPPON(1963, Jap.)
Kazunori Ito
1984
WARRIORS OF THE WIND(1984, Jap.), w
Keiichi Ito
NO GREATER LOVE THAN THIS(1969, Jap.), w
Kinuko Ito "Miss Japan"
YANKEE PASHA(1954)
Kinuko Ann Ito
HOUSE OF BAMBOO(1955)
Kisaku Ito
SAMURAI(PART III)** (1967, Jap.), art d; UGETSU(1954, Jap.), art d; CHUSHINGURA(1963, Jap.), art d; SANSHO THE BAILIFF(1969, Jap.), art d
Kisaya Ito
BATTLE IN OUTER SPACE(1960)
Kisuka Ito
BALLAD OF NARAYAMA(1961, Jap.), art d
Michio Ito
BOOLOO(1938); SPAWN OF THE NORTH(1938)
Robert Ito
DIMENSION 5(1966); WOMEN OF THE PREHISTORIC PLANET(1966); SOME KIND OF A NUT(1969); NAKED APE, THE(1973); TERMINAL MAN, THE(1974); PEEPER(1975); ROLLERBALL(1975); MIDWAY(1976); SPECIAL DELIVERY(1976)
1984
ADVENTURES OF BUCKAROO BANZAI: ACROSS THE 8TH DIMENSION, THE(1984)
Roger Ito
MODERN ROMANCE(1981)
Takao Ito
VIXEN(1970, Jap.)
Takeo Ito
DRUNKEN ANGEL(1948, Jap.), ph
Teiji Ito
MAEVA(1961), m; VIRGIN PRESIDENT, THE(1968), m
Toshiya Ito
Misc. Talkies
SPACE RIDERS(1984)
Yonosuke Ito
MAN WHO STOLE THE SUN, THE(1980, Jap.)

Yumi Ito
MOTHRA(1962, Jap.); GODZILLA VS. THE THING(1964, Jap.); GHIDRAH, THE THREE-HEADED MONSTER(1965, Jap.)
Yunosuke Ito
IKIRU(1960, Jap.); BALLAD OF NARAYAMA(1961, Jap.); YOUTH IN FURY(1961, Jap.); SANJURO(1962, Jap.); JUDO SAGA(1965, Jap.); SAMURAI ASSASSIN(1965, Jap.); FORT GRAVEYARD(1966, Jap.); HARP OF BURMA(1967, Jap.); EMPEROR AND A GENERAL, THE(1968, Jap.); DAY THE SUN ROSE, THE(1969, Jap.); RED LION(1971, Jap.)
Haruo Itoga
UNHOLY DESIRE(1964, Jap.)
Shinobu Itomi
FACE OF ANOTHER, THE(1967, Jap.)
Michio Itow
Silents
DAWN OF THE EAST(1921)
Kaethe Itter
ETERNAL LOVE(1960, Ger.)
Martha Ittimangnaq
NEVER CRY WOLF(1983)
Zachary Ittimangnaq
NEVER CRY WOLF(1983)
Augustin Ituarte
SUNBURN(1979), art d; HIGH RISK(1981), prod d
1984
ROMANCING THE STONE(1984), art d
Amparo Iturbi
HOLIDAY IN MEXICO(1946); THREE DARING DAUGHTERS(1948); THAT MIDNIGHT KISS(1949)
Jose Iturbi
THOUSANDS CHEER(1943); MUSIC FOR MILLIONS(1944); TWO GIRLS AND A SAILOR(1944); ANCHORS AWEIGH(1945); SONG TO REMEMBER, A(1945), m; HOLIDAY IN MEXICO(1946); THREE DARING DAUGHTERS(1948); THAT MIDNIGHT KISS(1949)
Misc. Talkies
ADVENTURE IN MUSIC(1944)
Rea Iturbi
FURY IN PARADISE(1955, U.S./Mex.)
Rebecca Iturbi
SUN ALSO RISES, THE(1957)
Rebeca Iturbide
LAST REBEL, THE(1961, Mex.)
Rebecca Iturbide
JET OVER THE ATLANTIC(1960); OF LOVE AND DESIRE(1963)
Javier Iturralde
1984
DEMONS IN THE GARDEN(1984, Span.), m
Mabel Itzcovich
THE EAVESDROPPER(1966, U.S./Arg.), w
Gregory Itzen
1984
HARD TO HOLD(1984)
Sam Itzkovitch
THOSE DARING YOUNG MEN IN THEIR JAUNTY JALOPIES(1969, Fr./Brit./Ital.), d
Howard Itzkowitz
STAR TREK: THE MOTION PICTURE(1979)
Rate Iurlan
HUNS, THE(1962, Fr./Ital.), w
Dan Ivan
SLAUGHTER IN SAN FRANCISCO(1981)
Doug Ivan
ENTER THE NINJA(1982)
Erze Ivan
CRUISIN' DOWN THE RIVER(1953)
John Ivan
YELLOW CARGO(1936)
Rosalind Ivan
GARDEN MURDER CASE, THE(1936); PARIS CALLING(1941); NONE BUT THE LONELY HEART(1944); SUSPECT, THE(1944); CORN IS GREEN, THE(1945); PILLOW OF DEATH(1945); PURSUIT TO ALGIERS(1945); SCARLET STREET(1945); THAT BRENNAN GIRL(1946); THREE STRANGERS(1946); VERDICT, THE(1946); IVY(1947); JOHNNY BELINDA(1948); ROBE, THE(1953); ELEPHANT WALK(1954)
Misc. Talkies
ALIAS MR. TWILIGHT(1946)
Silents
ARMS AND THE WOMAN(1916)
Michele Ivan-Zadeh
GREAT MUPPET CAPER, THE(1981)
Zeljko Ivanck
SOLDIER, THE(1982)
Paul Ivanechevitch
RUN FOR THE HILLS(1953), ph
Zeljko Ivanek
SENDER, THE(1982, Brit.); TEX(1982)
1984
MASS APPEAL(1984)
Paul Ivanho
BREAKDOWN(1953), ph
Boris Ivanitski
Misc. Silents
SON OF THE LAND(1931, USSR)
Paul Ivano
UNCLE HARRY(1945), ph; BATTLE OF GREED(1934), ph; CAVALCADE OF THE WEST(1936), ph; RIDING AVENGER, THE(1936), ph; ATLANTIC FLIGHT(1937), ph; BLAZING BARRIERS(1937), ph; HOOSIER SCHOOLBOY(1937), ph; LUCK OF ROARING CAMP, THE(1937), ph; THIRTEENTH MAN, THE(1937), ph; FURY BELOW(1938), ph; GIRL FROM RIO, THE(1939), ph; I AM A CRIMINAL(1939), ph; SHOULD A GIRL MARRY?(1939), ph; SHANGHAI GESTURE, THE(1941), ph; ABOUT FACE(1942), ph; BASHFUL BACHELOR, THE(1942), ph; HITLER–DEAD OR

ALIVE(1942), ph; ISLE OF MISSING MEN(1942), ph; ALL BY MYSELF(1943), ph; FIRED WIFE(1943), ph; FLESH AND FANTASY(1943), ph; HONEYMOON LODGE(1943), ph; LARCENY WITH MUSIC(1943), ph; SHE'S FOR ME(1943), ph; YOU'RE A LUCKY FELLOW, MR. SMITH(1943), ph; DEAD MAN'S EYES(1944), ph; DESTINY(1944), ph; HI BEAUTIFUL(1944), ph; IMPOSTER, THE(1944), ph; PARDON MY RHYTHM(1944), ph; SLIGHTLY TERRIFIC(1944), ph; SUSPECT, THE(1944), ph; FROZEN GHOST, THE(1945), ph; HONEYMOON AHEAD(1945), ph; I'LL TELL THE WORLD(1945), ph; MEN IN HER DIARY(1945), ph; PURSUIT TO ALGIERS(1945), ph; SENORITA FROM THE WEST(1945), ph; SWING OUT, SISTER(1945), ph; BLACK ANGEL(1946), ph; DARK HORSE, THE(1946), ph; LITTLE MISS BIG(1946), ph; SPIDER WOMAN STRIKES BACK, THE(1946), ph; GANGSTER, THE(1947), ph; MILLION DOLLAR WEEKEND(1948), ph; LOVABLE CHEAT, THE(1949), ph; SEARCH FOR DANGER(1949), ph; CHAMPAGNE FOR CAESAR(1950), ph; SECOND FACE, THE(1950), ph; GIRL ON THE BRIDGE, THE(1951), ph; HELLO GOD(1951, U.S./Ital.), ph; PICKUP(1951), ph; CAPTIVE WOMEN(1952), ph; FOR MEN ONLY(1952), ph; GOLD RAIDERS, THE(1952), ph; RED SNOW(1952), ph; STRANGE FASCINATION(1952), ph; ONE GIRL'S CONFESSION(1953), ph; THY NEIGHBOR'S WIFE(1953), ph; FANGS OF THE WILD(1954), ph; HOLD BACK TOMORROW(1955), ph; LIZZIE(1957), ph; NUN AND THE SERGEANT, THE(1962), ph; CHUBASCO(1968), ph; NAKED FLAME, THE(1970, Can.), ph; FUN ON A WEEKEND(1979), ph
Silents
YELLOW FINGERS(1926), ph; NO OTHER WOMAN(1928), ph; QUEEN KELLY(1929), ph

Alexander Ivanoff
Misc. Silents
TRANSPORT OF FIRE(1931, USSR), d

V. Ivanoff
END OF THE WORLD, THE(1930, Fr.), p

Victor Ivanoff
AFTER YOU, COMRADE(1967, S. Afr.)

A. Ivanov
WHEN THE TREES WERE TALL(1965, USSR), makeup

Boris Ivanov
LAD FROM OUR TOWN(1941, USSR), d

D. Ivanov
THEY WANTED PEACE(1940, USSR)

G. Ivanov
BRIDE WITH A DOWRY(1954, USSR); WAR AND PEACE(1968, USSR)

Lev Ivanov
THREE SISTERS, THE(1969, USSR); TURNING POINT, THE(1977), ch

M. Ivanov
LADY WITH THE DOG, THE(1962, USSR)

Nicolai Ivanov
RED TENT, THE(1971, Ital./USSR)

S. Ivanov
GORDEYEV FAMILY, THE(1961, U.S.S.R.), spec eff

Tamara Ivanov
1984
HARDBODIES(1984)

V. Ivanov
DESTINY OF A MAN(1961, USSR); SHE-WOLF, THE(1963, USSR)

Victor Ivanov
KIEV COMEDY, A(1963, USSR), d&w

Vladimir Ivanov
HORSEMEN, THE(1971), ph

Yevgeni Ivanov-Barkov
Misc. Silents
DELUGE, THE(1925, USSR), d; MABUL(1927, USSR), d

A. Ivanov-Gai
Misc. Silents
TSAR IVAN VASILYEVICH GROZNY(1915, USSR), d

Alexander Ivanov-Gai
Misc. Silents
HE WHO GETS SLAPPED(1916, USSR), d

Ivan Ivanov-vano
Misc. Talkies
MAGIC PONY(1979), d

F. Ivanova
KIEV COMEDY, A(1963, USSR)

L. Ivanova
IDIOT, THE(1960, USSR); RESURRECTION(1963, USSR)

M. Ivanova
TRAIN GOES TO KIEV, THE(1961, USSR)

Maria Ivanova
WITH LOVE AND TENDERNESS(1978, Bulgaria), art d

Nina Ivanova
ONCE THERE WAS A GIRL(1945, USSR)

Alexander Ivanovksy
Misc. Silents
PALACE AND FORTRESS(1924, USSR), d

A.V. Ivanovsky
HOUSE OF GREED(1934, USSR), d&w

Alexander Ivanovsky
TIGER GIRL(1955, USSR), d
Misc. Silents
STEPAN KHALTURIN(1925, USSR), d; DECEMBRISTS(1927, USSR), d

Elaine Ivans
Silents
JOHN GLAYDE'S HONOR(1915)

Perry Ivans
GIRL WITHOUT A ROOM(1933); GILDED LILY, THE(1935); MADE FOR EACH OTHER(1939); FORCE OF EVIL(1948); SUN SETS AT DAWN, THE(1950)

Jozsef Ivanyi
WITNESS, THE(1982, Hung.)

Ivargwema
KING SOLOMON'S MINES(1950)

Ike Ivarsen
PRIZE, THE(1963)

Dana Ivarson
JACKALS, THE(1967, South Africa)

Diana Ivarson
JESUS TRIP, THE(1971)

Gerald Ivas
Misc. Silents
WHERE AMBITION LEADS(1919, Brit.)

V.S. Ivasbeva
ALEXANDER NEVSKY(1939)

A. Ivashchenko
NIGHT BEFORE CHRISTMAS, A(1963, USSR), set d

Vera Ivasheva
RAINBOW, THE(1944, USSR)

Vladimir Ivashov
BALLAD OF A SOLDIER(1960, USSR); TEST OF PILOT PIRX, THE(1978, Pol./USSR); STAR INSPECTOR, THE(1980, USSR)

Branko Ivatovic
ONE-EYED SOLDIERS(1967, U.S./Brit./Yugo.), ph

K. Ivayev
SECRET MISSION(1949, USSR), w

Viktor Ivchenko
SONG OF THE FOREST(1963, USSR), d&w

John Iven
LOVE IN A BUNGALOW(1937)

Olaf Ivens
$(DOLLARS)**1/2 (1971), art d

Perry Ivens
HIGH WALL, THE(1947)

Jeanne Iver
Silents
ONE DAY(1916)

Miki Iveria
ORDERS TO KILL(1958, Brit.); TOO YOUNG TO LOVE(1960, Brit.); ARRIVEDERCI, BABY!(1966, Brit.); BERSERK(1967); FIDDLER ON THE ROOF(1971)

Daniel Ivernal
COUNT OF MONTE-CRISTO(1955, Fr., Ital.); FEMALE, THE(1960, Fr.); PARIS IN THE MONTH OF AUGUST(1968, Fr.)

Daniel Ivernel
MANON(1950, Fr.); HENRIETTE'S HOLIDAY(1953, Fr.); DAUGHTERS OF DESTINY(1954, Fr./Ital.); MADAME DU BARRY(1954 Fr./Ital.); HOLIDAY FOR HENRIETTA(1955, Fr.); ULYSSES(1955, Ital.); SUNDAYS AND CYBELE(1962, Fr.); DIARY OF A CHAMBERMAID(1964, Fr./Ital.); THAT MAN GEORGE!(1967, Fr./Ital./Span.); BORSALINO(1970, Fr.); DOCTEUR POPAUL(1972, Fr.); FRENCH CONSPIRACY, THE(1973, Fr.); BORSALINO AND CO.(1974, Fr.)

Bob Ivers
PATSY, THE(1964)

Julia Crawford Ivers
Silents
PARSON OF PANAMINT, THE(1916), w; GOOD NIGHT, PAUL(1918), w; HUCK AND TOM(1918), w; EASY TO GET(1920), w; HUCKLEBERRY FINN(1920), w; JENNY BE GOOD(1920), w; NURSE MARJORIE(1920), w; SOUL OF YOUTH, THE(1920), w; BEYOND(1921), w; MORALS(1921), w; WEALTH(1921), w; WITCHING HOUR, THE(1921), w; WHITE FLOWER, THE(1923), d&w; MARRIED FLIRTS(1924), w
Misc. Silents
MAJESTY OF THE LAW, THE(1915), d; SON OF ERIN, A(1916), d

Peter Ivers
GRAND THEFT AUTO(1977), m

Robert Ivers
DELICATE DELINQUENT, THE(1957); SHORT CUT TO HELL(1957); I MARRIED A MONSTER FROM OUTER SPACE(1958); G.I. BLUES(1960); ERRAND BOY, THE(1961); CATTLE KING(1963); YOUNG AND THE BRAVE, THE(1963); TOWN TAMER(1965)

Jon Iversen
Misc. Silents
HVEM ER HUN?(1914, Den.)

Diana Iverson
MACHO CALLAHAN(1970)

John Iverson
SONG OF THE LOON(1970)

Anne Ives
REINCARNATION OF PETER PROUD, THE(1975)

Burl Ives
SMOKY(1946); GREEN GRASS OF WYOMING(1948); STATION WEST(1948); SO DEAR TO MY HEART(1949); SIERRA(1950); EAST OF EDEN(1955); POWER AND THE PRIZE, THE(1956); BIG COUNTRY, THE(1958); CAT ON A HOT TIN ROOF(1958); DESIRE UNDER THE ELMS(1958); WIND ACROSS THE EVERGLADES(1958); DAY OF THE OUTLAW(1959); LET NO MAN WRITE MY EPITAPH(1960); OUR MAN IN HAVANA(1960, Brit.); SPIRAL ROAD, THE(1962); SUMMER MAGIC(1963); BRASS BOTTLE, THE(1964); ENSIGN PULVER(1964); DAYDREAMER, THE(1966); THOSE FANTASTIC FLYING FOOLS(1967, Brit); OTHER SIDE OF BONNIE AND CLYDE, THE(1968); MC MASTERS, THE(1970); BAKER'S HAWK(1976); HUGO THE HIPPO(1976, Hung./U.S.); JUST YOU AND ME, KID(1979); EARTHBOUND(1981); WHITE DOG(1982)
Misc. Talkies
ONLY WAY OUT IS DEAD, THE(1970)

Charles Ives
GOOD DISSONANCE LIKE A MAN, A(1977), w

Charlotte Ives
Silents
PRINCE IN A PAWNSHOP, A(1916)
Misc. Silents
MAN OF MYSTERY, THE(1917); WARFARE OF THE FLESH, THE(1917); SPLENDID ROMANCE, THE(1918)

Douglas Ives
CHEER THE BRAVE(1951, Brit.); DOCTOR IN THE HOUSE(1954, Brit.); GAY DOG, THE(1954, Brit.); MAD ABOUT MEN(1954, Brit.); WHAT EVERY WOMAN WANTS(1954, Brit.); INNOCENTS IN PARIS(1955, Brit.); ROOM IN THE HOUSE(1955, Brit.); BIG CHANCE, THE(1957, Brit.); MIRACLE IN SOHO(1957, Brit.); VIOLENT STRANGER(1957, Brit.); LEFT, RIGHT AND CENTRE(1959); LIFE IN EMERGENCY WARD 10(1959, Brit.); TWO WIVES AT ONE WEDDING(1961, Brit.); ROOM-

MATES(1962, Brit.); JUST FOR FUN(1963, Brit.); SWINGIN' MAIDEN, THE(1963, Brit.); SING AND SWING(1964, Brit.); BE MY GUEST(1965, Brit.); TWO LEFT FEET(1965, Brit.)

Frederick Ives
SYNDICATE, THE(1968, Brit.), ed

Fredrick Ives
LOVE IS A WOMAN(1967, Brit.), ed; HAND OF NIGHT, THE(1968, Brit.), ed

George Ives
NIAGARA(1953); HOT RODS TO HELL(1967); SECRET WAR OF HARRY FRIGG, THE(1968); GET TO KNOW YOUR RABBIT(1972)

Kenneth Ives
DEADLY AFFAIR, THE(1967, Brit.); LION IN WINTER, THE(1968, Brit.)

Norman Ives
Silents
LOVES OF RICARDO, THE(1926)

Terry Ives
FOURTEEN, THE(1973, Brit.)

Elaine Ives-Cameron
TERROR(1979, Brit.)
1984
SUPERGIRL(1984)

Bob Iveson
TITLE SHOT(1982, Can.), p

Don Ivey
GENTLE GIANT(1967), set d; HAPPENING, THE(1967), set d; HELLO DOWN THERE(1969), set d; DARKER THAN AMBER(1970), set d; STANLEY(1973), art d, set d; HARDLY WORKING(1981), art d; ISLAND CLAWS(1981), art d; LOVE CHILD(1982), art d; BLUE SKIES AGAIN(1983), art d

Don K. Ivey
NOBODY'S PERFEKT(1981), art d; SMOKEY AND THE BANDIT-PART 3(1983), set d
1984
HARRY AND SON(1984), set d; WHERE THE BOYS ARE '84(1984), set d

Edith Ivey
NORMA RAE(1979); LITTLE DARLINGS(1980)

Judith Ivey
1984
HARRY AND SON(1984); LONELY GUY, THE(1984); WOMAN IN RED, THE(1984)

Lewis Ivey
GAL YOUNG UN(1979)

Ilija Ivezic
APACHE GOLD(1965, Ger.); DESPERADO TRAIL, THE(1965, Ger./Yugo.); TREASURE OF SILVER LAKE(1965, Fr./Ger./Yugo.); LAST OF THE RENEGADES(1966, Fr./Ital./Ger./Yugo.); RAMPAGE AT APACHE WELLS(1966, Ger./Yugo.); RAT SAVIOUR, THE(1977, Yugo.)

Beth Ivins
Silents
DOING THEIR BIT(1918); IN FOLLY'S TRAIL(1920)
Misc. Silents
SCARLET TRAIL, THE(1919)

Perry Ivins
LOVE PARADE, THE(1929), d; BENSON MURDER CASE, THE(1930); NO LIMIT(1931); RECKLESS LIVING(1931); TROUBLE IN PARADISE(1932); SILVER CORD(1933); CHARLIE CHAN IN LONDON(1934); EVELYN PRENTICE(1934); MERRY WIDOW, THE(1934); MUSIC IN THE AIR(1934); NOTORIOUS SOPHIE LANG, THE(1934); ORIENT EXPRESS(1934); STAMBOUL QUEST(1934); CHARLIE CHAN IN PARIS(1935); FOLIES DERGERE(1935); G-MEN(1935); LADY TUBBS(1935); LES MISERABLES(1935); SMART GIRL(1935); WINGS IN THE DARK(1935); ARSENE LUPIN RETURNS(1938); PENITENTIARY(1938); SON OF FRANKENSTEIN(1939); THEY SHALL HAVE MUSIC(1939); I WONDER WHO'S KISSING HER NOW(1947); CALL NORTHSIDE 777(1948); SAIGON(1948); THAT WONDERFUL URGE(1948); GREAT SINNER, THE(1949); STREETS OF LAREDO(1949); TOO LATE FOR TEARS(1949); WHITE HEAT(1949); MISSOURIANS, THE(1950); MYSTERY STREET(1950); REDHEAD AND THE COWBOY, THE(1950)

Tom Ivo
GHOST OF DRAGSTRIP HOLLOW(1959)

Tommy Ivo
EARL CARROLL'S VANITIES(1945); SONG OF ARIZONA(1946); CARNIVAL IN COSTA RICA(1947); STEPCHILD(1947); FIGHTING BACK(1948); I REMEMBER MAMA(1948); MOONRISE(1948); SECRET SERVICE INVESTIGATOR(1948); SONG OF IDAHO(1948); LARAMIE(1949); OUTCASTS OF THE TRAIL(1949); PREJUDICE(1949); SMOKY MOUNTAIN MELODY(1949); TAKE ONE FALSE STEP(1949); FATHER IS A BACHELOR(1950); HORSEMEN OF THE SIERRAS(1950); KILLER THAT STALKED NEW YORK, THE(1950); LOST VOLCANO, THE(1950); OPERATION HAYLIFT(1950); SUNSET BOULEVARD(1950); SNAKE RIVER DESPERADOES(1951); WHIRLWIND(1951); BELLES ON THEIR TOES(1952); PLYMOUTH ADVENTURE(1952); ROUGH, TOUGH WEST, THE(1952); TREASURE OF LOST CANYON, THE(1952); YOU'RE NEVER TOO YOUNG(1955); DRAGSTRIP GIRL(1957); BEAST OF BUDAPEST, THE(1958); LIFE BEGINS AT 17(1958); CAT BURGLAR, THE(1961)
Misc. Talkies
TRAIL TO LAREDO(1948); FEUDIN' RHYTHM(1949); TRAIL OF THE RUSTLERS(1950)

A. Ivonin
Misc. Silents
NIKOLAI STAVROGIN(1915, USSR); TSAR NIKOLAI II(1917, USSR), d

Julia Crawford Ivors
Silents
NEARLY A LADY(1915), w

James Ivory
HOUSEHOLDER, THE(1963, US/India), d; SHAKESPEARE WALLAH(1966, India), d, w; GURU, THE(1969, U.S./India), d, w; BOMBAY TALKIE(1970, India), d, w; SAVAGES(1972), d, w; WILD PARTY, THE(1975), d; ROSELAND(1977), d; EUROPEANS, THE(1979, Brit.), d; HULLABALOO OVER GEORGIE AND BONNIE'S PICTURES(1979, Brit.), d; JANE AUSTEN IN MANHATTAN(1980), d; QUARTET(1981, Brit./Fr.), d, w; HEAT AND DUST(1983, Brit.), d
1984
BOSTONIANS, THE(1984), d

Claude Ivry
SEPTEMBER STORM(1960); COUNTERFEITERS OF PARIS, THE(1962, Fr., Ital.)

Don Ivy
LIMBO(1972), set d

Ivy Benson's All Ladies Orchestra
DUMMY TALKS, THE(1943, Brit.)

Hidemitsu Iwahashi
HOUSE OF STRANGE LOVES, THE(1969, Jap.), ph

Hanshiro Iwai
SECRET SCROLLS(PART I)**1/2 (1968, Jap.); DAREDEVIL IN THE CASTLE(1969, Jap.)

Tomomi Iwai
HIKEN YABURI(1969, Jap.)

Hiroshi Iwamoto
GODZILLA VS. THE THING(1964, Jap.)

Amy Iwanabe
WILD BLUE YONDER, THE(1952)

Frank Iwanaga
I WAS AN AMERICAN SPY(1951); GODZILLA, RING OF THE MONSTERS(1956, Jap.)

Natalie Iwanow
1984
MOSCOW ON THE HUDSON(1984)

Hisaya Iwasa
SILENCE HAS NO WINGS(1971, Jap.), w

Fusako Iwasaki
1984
BALLAD OF NARAYAMA, THE(1984, Jap.)

Kaneko Iwasaki
ROAD TO ETERNITY(1962, Jap.); SHOWDOWN FOR ZATOICHI(1968, Jap.); SNOW COUNTRY(1969, Jap.)

Taka Iwashaiki
THREE CAME HOME(1950)

Hiroichi Iwashita
MYSTERIANS, THE(1959, Jap.), ed

Kiyoshi Iwashita
BANISHED(1978, Jap.), p

Shima Iwashita
YOUTH IN FURY(1961, Jap.); HAHAKIRI(1963, Jap.); SAMURAI FROM NOWHERE(1964, Jap.); TWIN SISTERS OF KYOTO(1964, Jap.); SCARLET CAMELLIA, THE(1965, Jap.); TWILIGHT PATH(1965, Jap.); PORTRAIT OF CHIEKO(1968, Jap.); DAY THE SUN ROSE, THE(1969, Jap.); SNOW COUNTRY(1969, Jap.); THROUGH DAYS AND MONTHS(1969 Jap.); DOUBLE SUICIDE(1970, Jap.); SCANDALOUS ADVENTURES OF BURAIKAN, THE(1970, Jap.); SONG FROM MY HEART, THE(1970, Jap.); RED LION(1971, Jap.); BANISHED(1978, Jap.); ONIMASA(1983, Jap.)

Jaroslav Iwaszkiewcz
JOAN OF THE ANGELS(1962, Pol.), w

Jaroslav Iwaszkiewicz
YOUNG GIRLS OF WILKO, THE(1979, Pol./Fr.), w

Katsumi Iwauchi
LET'S GO, YOUNG GUY!(1967, Jap.), d; NIGHT OF THE SEAGULL, THE(1970, Jap.), d, w

Ub Iwerks
RELUCTANT DRAGON, THE(1941), spec eff; POLLYANNA(1960), spec eff; TEN WHO DARED(1960), spec eff; TOBY TYLER(1960), spec eff; PARENT TRAP, THE(1961), spec eff; BIRDS, THE(1963), spec eff; THREE LIVES OF THOMASINA, THE(1963, U.S./Brit.), spec eff

Up Iwerks
SONG OF THE SOUTH(1946), spec eff

Pat Iyotte
JOURNEY THROUGH ROSEBUD(1972)

Juan Luis Izaguirre
SUPERSONIC MAN(1979, Span.), m

R. Izakson
QUEEN OF SPADES(1961, USSR), ed

Forrest Izard
GOLGOTHA(1937, Fr.), w; SACRIFICE OF HONOR(1938, Fr.), ed; FABIOLA(1951, Ital.), w

Winifred Izard
EVERYTHING HAPPENS TO ME(1938, Brit.); QUIET PLEASE(1938, Brit.)
Silents
BARNES MURDER CASE, THE(1930, Brit.)

Victor Izay
W.I.A.(WOUNDED IN ACTION)*1/2 (1966); EDEN CRIED(1967); GIRL IN GOLD BOOTS(1968); ASTRO-ZOMBIES, THE(1969); BILLY JACK(1971); TRIAL OF BILLY JACK, THE(1974)
Misc. Talkies
PREMONITION(1972)

Teresa Izewska
KANAL(1961, Pol.)

Olya Izgorodina
SONS AND MOTHERS(1967, USSR)

Irina Izicarova
END OF AUGUST AT THE HOTEL OZONE, THE(1967, Czech.)

Elena Izmailova
SECRET MISSION(1949, USSR)

Ye. Izmaylova
LULLABY(1961, USSR)

Eduard Izotov
JACK FROST(1966, USSR)

Vilmos Izsof
WINTER WIND(1970, Fr./Hung.)

K. Izumi
DEMON POND(1980, Jap.), w

Kyoka Izumi
TEMPTRESS AND THE MONK, THE(1963, Jap.), w

Naoki Izumi
SONG FROM MY HEART, THE(1970, Jap.)

Taku Izumi
TOPSY-TURVY JOURNEY(1970, Jap.), m; YOSAKOI JOURNEY(1970, Jap.), m
I. Izvitskaya
PEACE TO HIM WHO ENTERS(1963, USSR)
Isolda Izvitskaya
FATHERS AND SONS(1960, USSR)
Izvolsky
Misc. Silents
DEAD MAN, THE(1914, USSR)
Francesco Izzarelli
MELODY OF LOVE(1954, Ital.), ph; FURY OF HERCULES, THE(1961, Ital.), ph;
SAMSON(1961, Ital.), ph
Renato Izzo
TIGER OF THE SEVEN SEAS(1964, Fr./Ital.)
Renato Izzo
SABATA(1969, Ital.), w; BOUNTY HUNTERS, THE(1970, Ital.), w; ADIOS SABA-
TA(1971, Ital./Span.), w; RETURN OF SABATA(1972, Ital./Fr./Ger.), w

J

GORGON, THE(1964, Brit.), w

J.L. Frank's "Golden West Cowboys"
GOLD MINE IN THE SKY(1938)

Nelan Jaap
GREAT POWER, THE(1929)

Paul Jabara
MIDNIGHT COWBOY(1969); OUT OF TOWNERS, THE(1970); LORDS OF FLAT-BUSH, THE(1974), a, m; DAY OF THE LOCUST, THE(1975); THANK GOD IT'S FRIDAY(1978), a, m; CHANEL SOLITAIRE(1981), m; HONKY TONK FREE-WAY(1981)

Gabriel Jabbour
GOHA(1958, Tunisia); DOLL, THE(1962, Fr.); MARRY ME! MARRY ME!(1969, Fr.); Z(1969, Fr./Algeria); MADAME ROSA(1977, Fr.)

Jabely
LOVE AND THE FRENCHWOMAN(1961, Fr.), anim

Juliusz Jablczynski
SARAGOSSA MANUSCRIPT, THE(1972, Pol.)

Rachel Jablonski
SATIN MUSHROOM, THE(1969)

Joachim Jablouski
NAKED AMONG THE WOLVES(1967, Ger.)

Michael Jablow
MODERN PROBLEMS(1981), ed; GET CRAZY(1983), ed
1984
WILD LIFE, THE(1984), ed

Arnaldo Jabor
ALL NUDITY SHALL BE PUNISHED(1974, Brazil), d, w

Paul Jabor
MEDEA(1971, Ital./Fr./Ger.)

Vladimir Jabotinsky
SAMSON AND DELILAH(1949), w

Arch Jaboulian
Misc. Talkies
MEATEATER(1979)

Shonagh Jabour
FUNERAL HOME(1982, Can.), makeup

Ceila Jaccard
RIO GRANDE RANGER(1937), w

Jacques Jaccard
CHEYENNE KID, THE(1930), d, w; DESERT GUNS(1936), w; PHANTOM OF SAN-TA FE(1937), d; RIO GRANDE RANGER(1937), w
Misc. Talkies
SENOR JIM(1936), d
Silents
KNIGHT OF THE RANGE, A(1916), d; IF ONLY JIM(1921), d; RIDING WITH DEATH(1921), d, w; GALLOPING ACE, THE(1924), w; RIDIN' MAD(1924), d&w; LARIAT KID, THE(1929), w; ONE SPLENDID HOUR(1929), w; ROYAL RIDER, THE(1929), w
Misc. Silents
DESERT LOVE(1920), d; GREAT AIR ROBBERY, THE(1920), d; HONOR BOUND(1920), d; TERROR, THE(1920), d; UNDER NORTHERN LIGHTS(1920), d; GREAT ALONE, THE(1922), d; CALIFORNIA IN '49(1924), d; HIS MAJESTY THE OUTLAW(1924), d; UNSEEN HANDS(1924), d; SAND BLIND(1925), d; VIC DYSON PAYS(1925), d; DESERT GREED(1926), d

Joan Jaccard
CHEYENNE KID, THE(1930)

Silvana Jachino
JULIET OF THE SPIRITS(1965, Fr./Ital./W.Ger.)

Alaska Jack
Silents
SMOKE BELLEW(1929)

"Black Jack"
CARSON CITY RAIDERS(1948); DENVER KID, THE(1948); DESPERADOES OF DODGE CITY(1948); BANDIT KING OF TEXAS(1949); SHERIFF OF WICHITA(1949); CODE OF THE SILVER SAGE(1950); SALT LAKE RAIDERS(1950); DESERT OF LOST MEN(1951); NIGHT RIDERS OF MONTANA(1951); DESPERADOES OUTPOST(1952); EL PASO STAMPEDE(1953)
Silents
LONE HORSEMAN, THE(1929)

Collette Jack
NIGHT HAIR CHILD(1971, Brit.)

Crystal Jack
TWO THOROUGHBREDS(1939)

Del Jack
SAMMY STOPS THE WORLD zero(1978), p

George Jack
WHAT AM I BID?(1967), ch

Max Jack
1984
AMBASSADOR, THE(1984), w

Richard Jack
THAT CERTAIN WOMAN(1937)

Roland Jack
TULSA(1949)

Stephen Jack
ROYAL DIVORCE, A(1938, Brit.); TREASURE ISLAND(1950, Brit.); HIGH TREA-SON(1951, Brit.); ROOM AT THE TOP(1959, Brit.); NELSON AFFAIR, THE(1973, Brit.); GULLIVER'S TRAVELS(1977, Brit., Bel.)

Universal Jack
CHEYENNE WILDCAT(1944)

Wolfman Jack
SEVEN MINUTES, THE(1971); AMERICAN GRAFFITI(1973); MORE AMERICAN GRAFFITI(1979); MOTEL HELL(1980)

Jack and Max
AROUND THE WORLD(1943)

Jack Cole & Co
MOON OVER MIAMI(1941)

Jack Costanzo and Orchestra
BERNARDINE(1957)

Jack Denny's Orchestra
MOONLIGHT AND PRETZELS(1933)

Jack Harris and His Band
TWO HEARTS IN HARMONY(1935, Brit.); LET'S MAKE A NIGHT OF IT(1937, Brit.)

Jack Hart and His Band
CAPTAIN'S ORDERS(1937, Brit.)

Jack Hylton and His Band
SHE SHALL HAVE MUSIC(1935, Brit.)

Jack Hylton's Band
BAND WAGGON(1940, Brit.)

Jack Jackson and His Band
LET'S MAKE A NIGHT OF IT(1937, Brit.)

Jack Jenny and Their Orchestras
MANHATTAN MERRY-GO-ROUND(1937)

Jack McVea Orchestra
SARGE GOES TO COLLEGE(1947)

Jack Payne and His Band
SUNSHINE AHEAD(1936, Brit.)

Jack Payne and the BBC Dance Band
SYMPHONY IN TWO FLATS(1930, Brit.)

Jack Simpson and His Sextet
STRAWBERRY ROAN(1945, Brit.); NOTHING VENTURE(1948, Brit.)

Jack Teagarden and His Orchestra
HI, GOOD-LOOKIN'(1944); TWILIGHT ON THE PRAIRIE(1944)

Jack Teagarden Orchestra
SO'S YOUR UNCLE(1943)

Charmain Jacka
PETERSEN(1974, Aus.)

James Jackel
COLOR ME BLOOD RED(1965)

Bill Jackie
DON'T TELL THE WIFE(1937)

Linda Jackson Jackie
BLACK ANGELS, THE(1970)

William Jackie
TWO GUN MAN, THE(1931)

Jackie and Gayle
WILD ON THE BEACH(1965); WILD, WILD WINTER(1966)

Jackie the Lion
MAD WEDNESDAY(1950)

Jackie Jackler
CUBAN REBEL GIRLS(1960)

Jolyon Jackley
BREAKING THE SOUND BARRIER(1952); VIRGIN SOLDIERS, THE(1970, Brit.)

Nat Jackley
DEMOBBED(1944, Brit.); HONEYMOON HOTEL(1946, Brit.); STARS IN YOUR EYES(1956, Brit.); MRS. BROWN, YOU'VE GOT A LOVELY DAUGHTER(1968, Brit.)
1984
PLOUGHMAN'S LUNCH, THE(1984, Brit.)

Ross Jacklin
THINGS TO COME(1936, Brit.), spec eff

Clyde Jackman
FIVE GRAVES TO CAIRO(1943)

Floyd Jackman
Silents
CALL FROM THE WILD, THE(1921), ph; CALL OF THE WILD, THE(1923), ph; KING OF THE WILD HORSES, THE(1924), ph; BLACK CYCLONE(1925), ph; NO MAN'S LAW(1927), ph

Frank Jackman
CENTRAL AIRPORT(1933), spec eff

Fred H. Jackman
STRAWBERRY ROAN, THE(1948), ph; GET YOURSELF A COLLEGE GIRL(1964), ph; HARUM SCARUM(1965), ph

Fred Jackman
NOAH'S ARK(1928), spec eff; DAWN PATROL, THE(1930), spec eff; CAPTAIN BLOOD(1935), spec eff; CASE OF THE CURIOUS BRIDE, THE(1935), spec eff; CEILNG ZERO(1935), spec eff; MIDSUMMER'S NIGHT'S DREAM, A(1935), spec eff; CHARGE OF THE LIGHT BRIGADE, THE(1936), spec eff; CHINA CLIPPER(1936), spec eff; ISLE OF FURY(1936), spec eff; PETRIFIED FOREST, THE(1936), spec eff; FUGITIVE IN THE SKY(1937), ph; ON SUCH A NIGHT(1937), spec eff; PARADISE ISLE(1937), spec eff; RIDING ON AIR(1937), spec eff; STOLEN HOLIDAY(1937), spec eff; MYSTERY PLANE(1939), spec eff; GAMBLER'S CHOICE(1944), ph; ADVEN-TURES OF DON COYOTE(1947), ph; BIG TOWN(1947), ph; SLAUGHTER ON TENTH AVENUE(1957), ph; CASE AGAINST BROOKLYN, THE(1958), ph; LIFE BEGINS AT 17(1958), ph; SENIOR PROM(1958), ph; FLYING FONTAINES, THE(1959), ph; JUKE BOX RHYTHM(1959), ph; GOING HOME(1971), ph; VIVA KNIEVEL!(1977), ph
Silents
MOLLY O'(1921), ph; SMALL TOWN IDOL, A(1921), ph; CALL OF THE WILD, THE(1923), d&w; KING OF THE WILD HORSES, THE(1924), d; BLACK CY-CLONE(1925), d; NO MAN'S LAW(1927), d
Misc. Silents
DEVIL HORSE, THE(1926), d

Fred Jackman, Jr
CASE OF THE CURIOUS BRIDE, THE(1935), spec eff; BULLETS OR BAL-LOTS(1936), spec eff; MOONLIGHT ON THE PRAIRIE(1936), ph; TWO AGAINST THE WORLD(1936), spec eff; GREAT O'MALLEY, THE(1937), spec eff; GREEN LIGHT(1937), spec eff; DANGER FLIGHT(1939), ph; SKY PATROL(1939), ph; WOLF CALL(1939), ph; DRUMS OF THE DESERT(1940), ph; LAUGHING AT DAN-GER(1940), ph; PHANTOM OF CHINATOWN(1940), ph; UP IN THE AIR(1940), ph; FLYING BLIND(1941), ph; FLYING WILD(1941), ph; FORCED LANDING(1941), Spec eff; NO HANDS ON THE CLOCK(1941), ph; SIGN OF THE WOLF(1941), ph;

YOU'RE OUT OF LUCK(1941), ph; I LIVE ON DANGER(1942), ph; TORPEDO BOAT(1942), ph; WILDCAT(1942), ph; WRECKING CREW(1942), ph; AERIAL GUNNER(1943), ph; ALASKA HIGHWAY(1943), ph; HIGH EXPLOSIVE(1943), ph; MINESWEEPER(1943), ph; SUBMARINE ALERT(1943), ph; TORNADO(1943), ph; DANGEROUS PASSAGE(1944), ph; DARK MOUNTAIN(1944), ph; DOUBLE EXPOSURE(1944), ph; NAVY WAY, THE(1944), ph; TAKE IT BIG(1944), ph; TIMBER QUEEN(1944), ph; FOLLOW THAT WOMAN(1945), ph; HIGH POWERED(1945), ph; ONE EXCITING NIGHT(1945), ph; PEOPLE ARE FUNNY(1945), ph; SCARED STIFF(1945), ph; TOKYO ROSE(1945), ph; HOT CARGO(1946), ph; SWAMP FIRE(1946), ph; THEY MADE ME A KILLER(1946), ph; JUNGLE FLIGHT(1947), ph; ALBUQUERQUE(1948), ph; UNKNOWN ISLAND(1948); CANADIAN PACIFIC(1949), ph; FIGHTING MAN OF THE PLAINS(1949), ph; CARIBOO TRAIL, THE(1950), ph; MAN WITH MY FACE, THE(1951), ph; APACHE AMBUSH(1955), ph; CHICAGO SYNDICATE(1955), ph; CREATURE WITH THE ATOM BRAIN(1955), ph; NIGHT HOLDS TERROR, THE(1955), ph; BLACKJACK KETCHUM, DESPERADO(1956), ph; EARTH VS. THE FLYING SAUCERS(1956), ph; FURY AT GUNSIGHT PASS(1956), ph; URANIUM BOOM(1956), ph

Fred H. Jackman, Jr.
GUNFIGHTERS, THE(1947), ph; PRINCE OF THIEVES, THE(1948), ph

Fred W. Jackman
Silents
SUZANNA(1922), ph

Hope Jackman
BEYOND THIS PLACE(1959, Brit.); BARTLEBY(1970, Brit.)

Joe Jackman
AGAINST A CROOKED SKY(1975), ph

Lisa Jackman
OCTOPUSSY(1983, Brit.)

Tom Jackman
CAT FROM OUTER SPACE, THE(1978); APPLE DUMPLING GANG RIDES AGAIN, THE(1979); SWEET CREEK COUNTY WAR, THE(1979)

Fred B. Jackman, Jr.
STUNT PILOT(1939), ph

Glen Jackobson
WILD GYPSIES(1969)

Jeff Jacks
BLACK EYE(1974), w

Robert Jacks
KISS BEFORE DYING, A(1956), p

Robert J. Jacks
BANDOLERO!(1968), p

Robert L. Jacks
LURE OF THE WILDERNESS(1952), p; DESERT RATS, THE(1953), p; MAN IN THE ATTIC(1953), p; MAN ON A TIGHTROPE(1953), p; GORILLA AT LARGE(1954), p; PRINCE VALIANT(1954), p; PRINCESS OF THE NILE(1954), p; RAID, THE(1954), p; WHITE FEATHER(1955), p; BANDIDO(1956), p; KILLER IS LOOSE, THE(1956), p; MAN FROM DEL RIO(1956), p; PROUD ONES, THE(1956), p; UNDEFEATED, THE(1969), p

Adrian Jackson
Silents
DARLING OF PARIS, THE(1917), w

Al Jackson
BOY! WHAT A GIRL(1947); SLIGHT CASE OF LARCENY, A(1953)

Alex Jackson
HERE COME THE GIRLS(1953); GOG(1954)

Alfred Jackson
LEATHERNECKING(1930), w; KEPT HUSBANDS(1931), w; RUNAROUND, THE(1931), w

Andrew Jackson
SHAKIEST GUN IN THE WEST, THE(1968), ph; THREE GUNS FOR TEXAS(1968), ph; BACKTRACK(1969), ph; DEATH OF A GUNFIGHTER(1969), ph; CASTAWAY COWBOY, THE(1974), ph; SUPERDAD(1974), ph; STRONGEST MAN IN THE WORLD, THE(1975), ph; GLITTERBALL, THE(1977, Brit)

Anne Jackson
SO YOUNG, SO BAD(1950); JOURNEY, THE(1959, U.S./Aust.); TALL STORY(1960); TIGER MAKES OUT, THE(1967); HOW TO SAVE A MARRIAGE–AND RUIN YOUR LIFE(1968); SECRET LIFE OF AN AMERICAN WIFE, THE(1968); ANGEL LEVINE, THE(1970); DIRTY DINGUS MAGEE(1970); LOVERS AND OTHER STRANGERS(1970); ZIGZAG(1970); NASTY HABITS(1976, Brit.); BELL JAR, THE(1979); SHINING, THE(1980)
1984
SAM'S SON(1984)
Misc. Talkies
BLOOD DEBTS(1983)

Archie Jackson
TOO MANY HUSBANDS(1938, Brit.)

Arline Jackson
PENNY SERENADE(1941)

Avonne Jackson
LITTLE COLONEL, THE(1935)

Barbara Jackson
COCOANUT GROVE(1938); TIP-OFF GIRLS(1938); YOU AND ME(1938)

Barry Jackson
STRANGLER'S WEB(1966, Brit.); BOFORS GUN, THE(1968, Brit.); ALFRED THE GREAT(1969, Brit.); RYAN'S DAUGHTER(1970, Brit.); LONG AGO, TOMORROW(1971, Brit.); BARRY LYNDON(1975, Brit.); GLITTERBALL, THE(1977, Brit)
Silents
WEB OF THE LAW, THE(1923)

Ben Jackson
HIS DOUBLE LIFE(1933), p

Brad Jackson
IT CAME FROM OUTER SPACE(1953); WAR ARROW(1953); TAZA, SON OF COCHISE(1954); APRIL LOVE(1957); SAGA OF THE VIKING WOMEN AND THEIR VOYAGE TO THE WATERS OF THE GREAT SEA SERPENT, THE(1957)

Bradford Jackson
SEARCH FOR BRIDEY MURPHY, THE(1956); JEANNE EAGELS(1957)

Brian Jackson
HEROES OF TELEMARK, THE(1965, Brit.); DEADLY FEMALES, THE(1976, Brit.)

C.J. Montgomery Jackson
PACIFIC ADVENTURE(1947, Aus.)

Calvin Jackson
HER HIGHNESS AND THE BELLBOY(1945), md; BLOOD AND STEEL(1959), m; I PASSED FOR WHITE(1960); TORMENTED(1960), m; THREE WEEKS OF LOVE(1965), m

Carol Jackson
Silents
SHOULD A WOMAN TELL?(1920)

Carolyn Ann Jackson
BRIGHT ROAD(1953)

Carson Jackson
NORTHVILLE CEMETERY MASSACRE, THE(1976)

Ceri Jackson
MISSIONARY, THE(1982)
1984
CHAMPIONS(1984)

Charles C. Jackson
Silents
FLASHLIGHT, THE(1917)

Charles Jackson
MISTER BROWN(1972); MIDNIGHT(1983)
Misc. Silents
FOR HIS SAKE(1922)

Charles R. Jackson
LOST WEEKEND, THE(1945), w

Charlotte Jackson
Silents
MIDSUMMER MADNESS(1920); PRINCE THERE WAS, A(1921)

Chiquita Jackson
BOOK OF NUMBERS(1973)

Christopher Jackson
NATIONAL LAMPOON'S VACATION(1983)

Clim Jackson
PERSONAL BEST(1982)

Clinton Jackson
WIZ, THE(1978)

Colette Jackson
BEAST OF BUDAPEST, THE(1958); ALL FALL DOWN(1962); HOUSE OF WOMEN(1962); SEVEN DAYS IN MAY(1964)

Collette Jackson
TEENAGE DOLL(1957); UNWED MOTHER(1958)

Craig Jackson
HOW TO BEAT THE HIGH COST OF LIVING(1980)

Crane Jackson
LEPKE(1975, U.S./Israel)

Crispin Tyrone Jackson
HOT STUFF(1979)

Curtis Jackson
BOY WITH THE GREEN HAIR, THE(1949); CHAMP, THE(1979)

Curtis Loys Jackson, Jr.
GREAT LOVER, THE(1949)

Daisy Jackson
Silents
YE BANKS AND BRAES(1919, Brit.)

Dan Jackson
PAUL TEMPLE RETURNS(1952, Brit.); ODONGO(1956, Brit.); ACROSS THE BRIDGE(1957, Brit.); BEYOND MOMBASA(1957); HEART WITHIN, THE(1957, Brit.); ROOTS OF HEAVEN, THE(1958); FLAME IN THE STREETS(1961, Brit.); MYSTERIOUS ISLAND(1961, U.S./Brit.); HIGH WIND IN JAMAICA, A(1965); EXORCISM AT MIDNIGHT(1966, Brit. revised 1973, U.S.); ON THE RUN(1969, Brit.); MIND OF MR. SOAMES, THE(1970, Brit.)

Danny Jackson
MY LITTLE CHICKADEE(1940); KING'S ROW(1942); GILDERSLEEVE'S BAD DAY(1943); WE'VE NEVER BEEN LICKED(1943); I'M FROM ARKANSAS(1944); JANIE(1944); THEY LIVE IN FEAR(1944); ONE MORE TOMORROW(1946); BEAUTIFUL BLONDE FROM BASHFUL BEND, THE(1949); COME TO THE STABLE(1949); RECKLESS MOMENTS, THE(1949); MY SIX CONVICTS(1952)

David Jackson
UNMAN, WITTERING AND ZIGO(1971, Brit.); 10 RILLINGTON PLACE(1971, Brit.); BLOOD FROM THE MUMMY'S TOMB(1972, Brit.)
1984
BREAKOUT(1984, Brit.)
Misc. Talkies
KILLER'S MOON(1978)

David E. Jackson
GROUND ZERO(1973), ed; LEGEND OF COUGAR CANYON(1974), ph
1984
MYSTERY MANSION(1984), d, w; SACRED GROUND(1984), ed

David M. Jackson
MOMENTS(1974, Brit.), p

Dean Jackson
TOWN WITHOUT PITY(1961, Ger./Switz./U.S.)

Diane Jackson
YELLOW SUBMARINE(1958, Brit.), animation

Dickie Jackson
ETERNALLY YOURS(1939)

Don Jackson
DAYTONA BEACH WEEKEND(1965)

Donald Jackson
DEMON LOVER, THE(1977), p,d&w

Donniece Jackson
GETTING OVER(1981)

Dorothy Ann Jackson
HE'S MY GUY(1943)

Doug Jackson
FALLING IN LOVE AGAIN(1980), ed
1984
SLAPSTICK OF ANOTHER KIND(1984), ed

Douglas W. Jackson
DO NOT THROW CUSHIONS INTO THE RING(1970)
Earl Jackson
PORGY AND BESS(1959)
Ed Jackson
OUTSIDERS, THE(1983)
Eddie Jackson
ROADHOUSE NIGHTS(1930); TWO SISTERS FROM BOSTON(1946)
Edna Jackson
TREE GROWS IN BROOKLYN, A(1945)
Edward Jackson
NEW YEAR'S EVIL(1980)
Elinor Jackson
BIG SHAKEDOWN, THE(1934)
Elma V. Jackson
MAN WITH TWO BRAINS, THE(1983)
Ernest Jackson
BLAST OF SILENCE(1961)
Ernestina Jackson
HOMEWORK(1982)
Ernestine Jackson
AARON LOVES ANGELA(1975)
Ethel Jackson
Misc. Talkies
SIX GUN JUSTICE(1935); VANISHING RIDERS(1935)
Eugene Jackson
HEARTS IN DIXIE(1929); DIXIANA(1930); CIMARRON(1931); SECRET SER-VICE(1931); SPORTING BLOOD(1931); SPORTING CHANCE(1931); TUMBLING TUM-BLEWEEDS(1935); GUNS AND GUITARS(1936); HEARTS IN BONDAGE(1936); LONELY TRAIL, THE(1936); RED RIVER VALLEY(1936); WINE, WOMEN AND HORSES(1937); LADY'S FROM KENTUCKY, THE(1939); REFORM SCHOOL(1939); TELEVISION SPY(1939); SPORTING BLOOD(1940); UNFINISHED BUSINESS(1941); REAP THE WILD WIND(1942); TAKE MY LIFE(1942); REVEILLE WITH BEVER-LY(1943); WHAT'S BUZZIN COUSIN?(1943); SCUDDA-HOO! SCUDDA-HAY!(1948); JEANNE EAGELS(1957); LONG, HOT SUMMER, THE(1958)
1984
SWING SHIFT(1984)
Silents
PENROD AND SAM(1923); LITTLE ANNIE ROONEY(1925)
Eugene Jackson, Jr.
SHENANDOAH(1965)
Eugene W. Jackson
ESCAPE FROM ALCATRAZ(1979)
Felix Jackson
GIRL DOWNSTAIRS, THE(1938), w; MAD ABOUT MUSIC(1938), w; RAGE OF PARIS, THE(1938), w; BACHELOR MOTHER(1939), w; DESTRY RIDES AGAIN(1939), w; THREE SMART GIRLS GROW UP(1939), w; SPRING PARA-DE(1940), w; APPOINTMENT FOR LOVE(1941), w; BACK STREET(1941), w; BROAD-WAY(1942), w; HERS TO HOLD(1943), p; HIS BUTLER'S SISTER(1943), p; CAN'T HELP SINGING(1944), p; CHRISTMAS HOLIDAY(1944), p; LADY ON A TRAIN(1945), p; BECAUSE OF HIM(1946), p; I'LL BE YOURS(1947), p; DE-STRY(1954), w; BUNDLE OF JOY(1956), w
Flomanita Jackson
PICNIC(1955)
Frances Jackson
YANKEE DON(1931), w
Fred Jackson
HOLE IN THE WALL(1929), w; MY SIN(1931), w; CLUB HAVANA(1946), w; WATERLOO(1970, Ital./USSR)
Silents
MAN HUNT, THE(1918), w; ONE A MINUTE(1921), w; EXILES, THE(1923), w; ARIZONA EXPRESS, THE(1924), w
Fred Jackson, Jr.
BLACK LEGION, THE(1937), spec eff; ONE BODY TOO MANY(1944), ph; WILD WEST(1946), ph; CELL 2455, DEATH ROW(1955), ph; JULIE(1956), ph
Freda Jackson
MOUNTAINS O'MOURNE(1938, Brit.); CANTERBURY TALE, A(1944, Brit.); BEWARE OF PITY(1946, Brit.); GREAT EXPECTATIONS(1946, Brit.); HENRY V(1946, Brit.); NO ROOM AT THE INN(1950, Brit.); FLESH AND BLOOD(1951, Brit.); MR. DENNING DRIVES NORTH(1951, Brit.); TWILIGHT WOMEN(1953, Brit.); CROWDED DAY, THE(1954, Brit.); GOOD DIE YOUNG, THE(1954, Brit.); BHOWANI JUNC-TION(1956); LAST MAN TO HANG, THE(1956, Brit.); FLESH IS WEAK, THE(1957, Brit.); TALE OF TWO CITIES, A(1958, Brit.); BRIDES OF DRACULA, THE(1960, Brit.); ATTEMPT TO KILL(1961, Brit.); GREYFRIARS BOBBY(1961, Brit.); SHADOW OF THE CAT, THE(1961, Brit.); TOM JONES(1963, Brit.); WEST 11(1963, Brit.); THIRD SECRET, THE(1964, Brit.); DIE, MONSTER, DIE(1965, Brit.); JOKERS, THE(1967, Brit.); VALLEY OF GWANGI, THE(1969); CLASH OF THE TITANS(1981)
Freddie Jackson
REFORM SCHOOL(1939); IN THIS OUR LIFE(1942); TAKE MY LIFE(1942)
Misc. Talkies
DOUBLE DEAL(1939)
Frederick J. Jackson
Silents
DIAMONDS ADRIFT(1921), w; IT CAN BE DONE(1921), w
Frederick Jackson
PERFECT LADY, THE(1931, Brit.), p&d, w; BRIDEGROOM FOR TWO(1932, Brit.), w; HER FIRST AFFAIRE(1932, Brit.), w; BISHOP MISBEHAVES, THE(1933), w; WIDOW'S MIGHT(1934, Brit.), w; THAT'S MY UNCLE(1935, Brit.), w; GREAT GAM-BINI, THE(1937), w; SHE ASKED FOR IT(1937), w; WELLS FARGO(1937), w; SAY IT IN FRENCH(1938), w; STOLEN HEAVEN(1938), w; SCHOOL FOR HUSBANDS(1939, Brit.), w; HALF A SINNER(1940), w; MIRACLE ON MAIN STREET, A(1940), w; THERE'S MAGIC IN MUSIC(1941), w; THIS WOMAN IS MINE(1941), w; HI DIDDLE DIDDLE(1943), w; STORMY WEATHER(1943), w; SENSATIONS OF 1945(1944), w; BEDSIDE MANNER(1945), w
Gary Jackson
BLUE VEIL, THE(1951); YES SIR, MR. BONES(1951)
Gary Lee Jackson
MRS. MIKE(1949); MA AND PA KETTLE AT THE FAIR(1952); MA AND PA KETTLE ON VACATION(1953); SCANDAL AT SCOURIE(1953)

George Jackson
UNDER TWO FLAGS(1936); RAMPARTS WE WATCH, THE(1940); SHEPHERD OF THE HILLS, THE(1964); PLASTIC DOME OF NORMA JEAN, THE(1966); GOLD(1974, Brit.)
Capt. George Jackson
UNFAITHFUL(1931)
Gerald Jackson
GHASTLY ONES, THE(1968), ed
Ginny Jackson
EVERYBODY'S DANCIN'(1950)
Glenda Jackson
PERSECUTION AND ASSASSINATION OF JEAN-PAUL MARAT AS PERFORMED BY THE INMATES OF THE ASYLUM OF CHARENTON UNDER THE DIRECTION OF THE MARQUIS DE SADE, THE(1967, Brit.); NEGATIVES(1968, Brit.); TELL ME LIES(1968, Brit.); WOMEN IN LOVE(1969, Brit.); BOY FRIEND, THE(1971, Brit.); MARY, QUEEN OF SCOTS(1971, Brit.); MUSIC LOVERS, THE(1971, Brit.); SUNDAY BLOODY SUNDAY(1971, Brit.); NELSON AFFAIR, THE(1973, Brit.); TOUCH OF CLASS, A(1973, Brit.); TRIPLE ECHO, THE(1973, Brit.); TEMPTER, THE(1974, Ital./Brit.); DEVIL IS A WOMAN, THE(1975, Brit./Ital.); HEDDA(1975, Brit.); MAIDS, THE(1975, Brit.); ROMANTIC ENGLISHWOMAN, THE(1975, Brit./Fr.); INCREDIBLE SARAH, THE(1976, Brit.); NASTY HABITS(1976, Brit.); CLASS OF MISS MAC MICHAEL, THE(1978, Brit./U.S.); HOUSE CALLS(1978); STEVIE(1978, Brit.); LOST AND FOUND(1979); HEALTH(1980); HOPSCOTCH(1980); GIRO CITY(1982, Brit.); RETURN OF THE SOLDIER, THE(1983, Brit.)
Glenys Jackson
1984
VIGIL(1984, New Zealand), cos
Gordon Jackson
YESTERDAY'S ENEMY(1959, Brit.); MILLIONS LIKE US(1943, Brit.); NINE MEN(1943, Brit.); SOMEWHERE IN FRANCE(1943, Brit.); SAN DEMETRIO, LON-DON(1947, Brit.); AGAINST THE WIND(1948, Brit.); CAPTIVE HEART, THE(1948, Brit.); FLOODTIDE(1949, Brit.); MASSACRE HILL(1949, Brit.); STOP PRESS GIRL(1949, Brit.); TIGHT LITTLE ISLAND(1949, Brit.); BITTER SPRINGS(1950, Aus.); PINK STRING AND SEALING WAX(1950, Brit.); HAPPY GO LOVELY(1951, Brit.); LADY WITH A LAMP, THE(1951, Brit.); CASTLE IN THE AIR(1952, Brit.); DEATM GOES TO SCHOOL(1953, Brit.); MEET MR. LUCIFER(1953, Brit.); DELAVINE AF-FAIR, THE(1954, Brit.); LOVE LOTTERY, THE(1954, Brit.); PASSAGE HOME(1955, Brit.); WINDFALL(1955 Brit.); BLONDE BAIT(1956, U.S./Brit.); PACIFIC DES-TINY(1956, Brit.); THE CREEPING UNKNOWN(1956, Brit.); ABANDON SHIP(1957, Brit.); BABY AND THE BATTLESHIP, THE(1957, Brit.); BLACK ICE, THE(1957, Brit.); LET'S BE HAPPY(1957, Brit.); PANIC IN THE PARLOUR(1957, Brit.); VIOLENT STRANGER(1957, Brit.); BLIND SPOT(1958, Brit.); HELL DRIVERS(1958, Brit.); MAD LITTLE ISLAND(1958, Brit.); THREE CROOKED MEN(1958, Brit.); BRIDAL PATH, THE(1959, Brit.); DEVIL'S BAIT(1959, Brit.); NAVY LARK, THE(1959, Brit.); CHANCE MEETING(1960, Brit.); PRICE OF SILENCE, THE(1960, Brit.); SNOWBALL(1960, Brit.); TUNES OF GLORY(1960, Brit.); GREYFRIARS BOBBY(1961, Brit.); TROUBLE IN THE SKY(1961, Brit.); TWO WIVES AT ONE WEDDING(1961, Brit.); MUTINY ON THE BOUNTY(1962); GREAT ESCAPE, THE(1963); DAYLIGHT ROBBERY(1964, Brit.); LONG SHIPS, THE(1964, Brit./Yugo.); IPCRESS FILE, THE(1965, Brit.); THOSE MAGNIFICENT MEN IN THEIR FLYING MACHINES; OR HOW I FLEW FROM LONDON TO PARIS IN 25 HOURS AND 11 MINUTES(1965, Brit.); CAST A GIANT SHADOW(1966); FIGHTING PRINCE OF DONEGAL, THE(1966, Brit.); NIGHT OF THE GENERALS, THE(1967, Brit./Fr.); DANGER ROUTE(1968, Brit.); HAMLET(1969, Brit.); ON THE RUN(1969, Brit.); PRIME OF MISS JEAN BRODIE, THE(1969, Brit.); RUN WILD, RUN FREE(1969, Brit.); SCROOGE(1970, Brit.); KIDNAPPED(1971, Brit.); RUSSIAN ROULETTE(1975); GOLDEN RENDEZVOUS(1977); MEDUSA TOUCH, THE(1978, Brit.)
H. Landers Jackson
Silents
SHADOWS OF CONSCIENCE(1921), t; MIND OVER MOTOR(1923), w, t
Harold Jackson
1984
SWING SHIFT(1984)
Harry Jackson
BROADWAY SCANDALS(1929), ph; LUCKY BOY(1929), ph; NEW ORLEANS(1929), ph; TWO MEN AND A MAID(1929), ph; WHISPERING WINDS(1929), ph; BLAZE O' GLORY(1930), ph; CLANCY IN WALL STREET(1930), ph; COSTELLO CASE, THE(1930), ph; KATHLEEN MAVOURNEEN(1930), ph; RENO(1930), ph; PART-NERS(1932), ph; JUNGLE BRIDE(1933), ph; BABES IN TOYLAND(1934), md; SHE LEARNED ABOUT SAILORS(1934), ph; 365 NIGHTS IN HOLLYWOOD(1934), ph; LIFE BEGINS AT 40(1935), ph; YOUR UNCLE DUDLEY(1935), ph; $10 RAISE(1935), ph; CHARLIE CHAN AT THE RACE TRACK(1936), ph; HERE COMES TROU-BLE(1936), ph; IN HIS STEPS(1936), ph; WHITE LEGION, THE(1936), ph; CHARLIE CHAN ON BROADWAY(1937), ph; GREAT HOSPITAL MYSTERY, THE(1937), ph; THINK FAST, MR. MOTO(1937), ph; WILD AND WOOLLY(1937), ph; 45 FA-THERS(1937), ph; CITY GIRL(1938), ph; WE GO FAST(1941), ph; TO THE SHORES OF TRIPOLI(1942), ph; GREENWICH VILLAGE(1944), ph; IRISH EYES ARE SMIL-ING(1944), ph; CIRCUMSTANTIAL EVIDENCE(1945), ph; JOHNNY COMES FLY-ING HOME(1946), ph; STRANGE TRIANGLE(1946), ph; WAKE UP AND DREAM(1946), ph; CARNIVAL IN COSTA RICA(1947), ph; MOTHER WORE TIGHTS(1947), ph; APARTMENT FOR PEGGY(1948), ph; CHICKEN EVERY SUN-DAY(1948), ph; CUP-TIE HONEYMOON(1948, Brit.), w; FURY AT FURNACE CREEK(1948), ph; GIVE MY REGARDS TO BROADWAY(1948), ph; HOLIDAYS WITH PAY(1948, Brit.), w; WHEN MY BABY SMILES AT ME(1948), ph; BEAUTIFUL BLONDE FROM BASHFUL BEND, THE(1949), ph; DANCING IN THE DARK(1949), ph; OH, YOU BEAUTIFUL DOLL(1949), ph; SOMEWHERE IN POLITICS(1949, Brit.), w; AMERICAN GUERRILLA IN THE PHILIPPINES, AN(1950), ph; THREE LITTLE WORDS(1950), ph; TICKET TO TOMAHAWK(1950), ph; HALLS OF MON-TEZUMA(1951), ph; TAKE CARE OF MY LITTLE GIRL(1951), ph; LYDIA BAI-LEY(1952), ph; PONY SOLDIER(1952), ph; WAY OF A GAUCHO(1952), ph; BAND WAGON, THE(1953), ph; KID FROM LEFT FIELD, THE(1953), ph; MONOLITH MONSTERS, THE(1957); NIGHT RUNNER, THE(1957); PANAMA SAL(1957); GUN FEVER(1958), p; TRUE STORY OF LYNN STUART, THE(1958); STRANGERS WHEN WE MEET(1960)
Silents
FLOATING COLLEGE, THE(1928), ph; GUN RUNNER, THE(1928), ph; MAN IN HOBBLES, THE(1928), ph
Misc. Silents
YORK STATE FOLKS(1915), d

Helen Hunt Jackson
RAMONA(1936), w
Silents
RAMONA(1916), w; RAMONA(1928), w
Henry Jackson
UNDER THE PAMPAS MOON(1935), w
Horace Jackson
AWFUL TRUTH, THE(1929), w, ed; PARIS BOUND(1929), w; STRANGE CAR-
GO(1929), w; THIS THING CALLED LOVE(1929), w; HOLIDAY(1930), w; LOTTERY
BRIDE, THE(1930), w; SIN TAKES A HOLIDAY(1930), w; BEYOND VICTORY(1931),
w; COMMON LAW, THE(1931), w; DEVOTION(1931), w; REBOUND(1931), w; ANI-
MAL KINGDOM, THE(1932), w; LADY WITH A PAST(1932), w; WOMAN COM-
MANDS, A(1932), w; DANGEROUSLY YOURS(1933), w; I LOVED YOU
WEDNESDAY(1933), w; BOLERO(1934), w; WE'RE NOT DRESSING(1934), w; BIOG-
RAPHY OF A BACHELOR GIRL(1935), w; NO MORE LADIES(1935), w; SUZY(1936),
w; MEN ARE SUCH FOOLS(1938), w; WOMEN ARE LIKE THAT(1938), w; MODEL
WIFE(1941), w; LIVING BETWEEN TWO WORLDS(1963), a, p, w; BUS IS COMING,
THE(1971), p, w
Misc. Talkies
TOUGH(1974), d
Horace B. Jackson
Misc. Talkies
JOEY(1977), d
Howard Jackson
BROADWAY(1929), m; HEARTS IN DIXIE(1929), m; SUNNY SIDE UP(1929), md;
SITTING PRETTY(1933), md; THIS DAY AND AGE(1933), m; BELOVED(1934), m;
OLD HOMESTEAD, THE(1935), m; AND SO THEY WERE MARRIED(1936), m;
DIZZY DAMES(1936), m; ISLE OF FURY(1936), m; LONE WOLF RETURNS,
THE(1936), md; MEET NERO WOLFE(1936), md; MR. DEEDS GOES TO TOWN(1936),
md; MUSIC GOES ROUND, THE(1936), md; COWBOY QUARTERBACK(1939), m;
LAW OF THE TROPICS(1941), m; BULLET SCARS(1942), m; WILD BILL HICKOK
RIDES(1942), m; CLUB HAVANA(1946), m; HOW DO YOU DO?(1946), md; MILLION
DOLLAR WEEKEND(1948), m; TOBOR THE GREAT(1954), m; RUN FOR CO-
VER(1955), m, md; WAKAMBA!(1955), m; CRY TERROR(1958), m; MANHUNT IN
THE JUNGLE(1958), m; YELLOWSTONE KELLY(1959), md; SERGEANT RUT-
LEDGE(1960), m; CLAUDELLE INGLISH(1961), m; GOLD OF THE SEVEN
SAINTS(1961), m; HOUSE OF WOMEN(1962), m; MERRILL'S MARAUDERS(1962),
m; WHEN THE GIRLS TAKE OVER(1962), md; BLACK GOLD(1963), m; HUMAN
TORNADO, THE(1976)
Inigo Jackson
SATURDAY NIGHT OUT(1964, Brit.); BRIGAND OF KANDAHAR, THE(1965, Brit.);
DOCTOR ZHIVAGO(1965); FIGHTING PRINCE OF DONEGAL, THE(1966, Brit.); HE
WHO RIDES A TIGER(1966, Brit.); TRYGON FACTOR, THE(1969, Brit.); HELL
BOATS(1970, Brit.); TWINS OF EVIL(1971, Brit.)
Inman Jackson
HARLEM GLOBETROTTERS, THE(1951)
Ivor Jackson
GOIN' DOWN THE ROAD(1970, Can.)
J. J. Jackson
BADGE 373(1973), m; CARWASH(1976); SUMMER SCHOOL TEACHERS(1977), m;
RETURN OF THE JEDI(1983)
Jack Jackson
NONE BUT THE LONELY HEART(1944); NEVER A DULL MOMENT(1950); STARS
IN YOUR EYES(1956, Brit.); JAMBOREE(1957)
Silents
ARIZONA CYCLONE(1928), ed; OLD CODE, THE(1928), ph
Jackie Jackson
WOMAN ON THE BEACH, THE(1947); EASY LIVING(1949); GREAT LOVER,
THE(1949); RED PONY, THE(1949); TAKE ME OUT TO THE BALL GAME(1949); MA
AND PA KETTLE GO TO TOWN(1950); MA AND PA KETTLE AT THE FAIR(1952);
MA AND PA KETTLE ON VACATION(1953); MA AND PA KETTLE AT WAIKI-
KI(1955)
Jacko Jackson
OUTBACK(1971, Aus.)
James Jackson
TOM JONES(1963, Brit.)
Jamie Smith Jackson
BREEZY(1973); BUG(1975)
Jeanine Jackson
ZELIG(1983)
Jenie Jackson
RIDE THE HIGH COUNTRY(1962); HOW SWEET IT IS(1968); TO BE FREE(1972)
Misc. Talkies
IMAGO(1970)
Jerome Jackson
CASTE(1930, Brit.), p; MY FRIEND THE KING(1931, Brit.), p; BORN LUCKY(1932,
Brit.), p; C.O.D.(1932, Brit.), p; HIS LORDSHIP(1932, Brit.), p; HOTEL SPLEN-
DIDE(1932, Brit.), p; FIRE RAISERS, THE(1933, Brit.), p, w; NIGHT OF THE PARTY,
THE(1934, Brit.), p; STRIKE!(1934, Brit.), p, w; HEAT WAVE(1935, Brit.), p, w; MY
SONG FOR YOU(1935, Brit.), p; PHANTOM LIGHT, THE(1935, Brit.), p; DANGER-
OUS MEDICINE(1938, Brit.), p; EVERYTHING HAPPENS TO ME(1938, Brit.), p;
MANY TANKS MR. ATKINS(1938, Brit.), p; RETURN OF CAROL DEANE, THE(1938,
Brit.), p; THEY DRIVE BY NIGHT(1938, Brit.), p; ANYTHING TO DECLARE?(1939,
Brit.), p; GENTLEMAN'S GENTLEMAN, A(1939, Brit.), p; GOOD OLD DAYS,
THE(1939, Brit.), p; NURSEMAID WHO DISAPPEARED, THE(1939, Brit.), p; TOO
DANGEROUS TO LIVE(1939, Brit.), p
Jessie Jackson
COMET OVER BROADWAY(1938)
Jessie Mae Jackson
ENEMY AGENT(1940)
Jessie May Jackson
SING FOR YOUR SUPPER(1941)
Jill Jackson
TAMMY AND THE DOCTOR(1963); I'D RATHER BE RICH(1964); MADAME X(1966)
Jim Jackson
1984
TANK(1984)

Jimmy Jackson
SHOW BOAT(1936)
Jocella Jackson
LILITH(1964)
Jocelyn Jackson
BIRTHDAY PRESENT, THE(1957, Brit.), ed; 6.5 SPECIAL(1958, Brit.), ed
Joe Jackson
BARKER, THE(1928), w; MY MAN(1928), w; NO DEFENSE(1929), titles; LONGEST
YARD, THE(1974)
1984
MIKE'S MURDER(1984), m
Misc. Silents
MODERN ENOCH ARDEN, A(1916)
Joe Jackson, Jr.
ICE-CAPADES REVUE(1942)
Joey Jackson
ROBIN AND THE SEVEN HOODS(1964)
John Jackson
STORMY(1935); MEDIUM COOL(1969); BACK ROADS(1981); LOCAL HERO(1983,
Brit.)
John S. Jackson
LIBERATION OF L.B. JONES, THE(1970)
Johnnie Jackson
J.W. COOP(1971)
Jonathan Jackson
BENEATH THE 12-MILE REEF(1953)
Jose Jackson
CAT GIRL(1957), ed
Joseph Jackson
LAND OF THE SILVER FOX(1928), w; MIDNIGHT TAXI, THE(1928), w; SINGING
FOOL, THE(1928), w; TENDERLOIN(1928), w; TERROR, THE(1928), w; GREY-
HOUND LIMITED, THE(1929), w; IN THE HEADLINES(1929), w; IS EVERYBODY
HAPPY?(1929), w; REDEEMING SIN, THE(1929), w; SAY IT WITH SONGS(1929), w;
BE YOURSELF(1930), w; DANCING SWEETIES(1930), w; MAMMY(1930), w; MAN
FROM BLANKLEY'S, THE(1930), w; MAYBE IT'S LOVE(1930), w; OH! SAILOR,
BEHAVE!(1930), w; SECOND CHOICE(1930), w; SECOND FLOOR MYSTERY,
THE(1930), w; THOSE WHO DANCE(1930), w; FIFTY MILLION FRENCHMEN(1931),
w; GOD'S GIFT TO WOMEN(1931), w; HER MAJESTY LOVE(1931), w; MAN TO
MAN(1931), w; SAFE IN HELL(1931), w; SMART MONEY(1931), w; BEAUTY AND
THE BOSS(1932), w; DARK HORSE, THE(1932), w; HIGH PRESSURE(1932), w;
MOUTHPIECE, THE(1932), w; ONE WAY PASSAGE(1932), w
Silents
AFRAID TO LOVE(1927), w; HUSBANDS FOR RENT(1927), t; IF I WERE SIN-
GLE(1927), t; ON TO RENO(1928), w; POWDER MY BACK(1928), w
Joy Jackson
BRIGHT ROAD(1953)
Julia Jackson
Misc. Silents
EYE OF ENVY, THE(1917); WIFE ON TRAIL, A(1917); HIGH TIDE(1918)
Julie Jackson
WHISTLE DOWN THE WIND(1961, Brit.)
Kate Jackson
NIGHT OF DARK SHADOWS(1971); LIMBO(1972); THUNDER AND LIGHT-
NING(1977); DIRTY TRICKS(1981, Can.); MAKING LOVE(1982)
Kathryn Jackson
DIFFERENT STORY, A(1978)
Misc. Talkies
BLACK HOOKER(1974)
Keith Jackson
FORTUNE COOKIE, THE(1966)
Kendall Jackson
HAUNTS(1977)
Kenny Jackson
EXPERIMENT IN TERROR(1962)
Kyle Scott Jackson
WINDOWS(1980)
Kyle-Scott Jackson
GLORIA(1980)
Lamar Jackson
SMOKEY AND THE BANDIT(1977); SHARKY'S MACHINE(1982)
Lamont Jackson
Misc. Talkies
ASSAULT WITH A DEADLY WEAPON(1983)
Larry Jackson
ICE FOLLIES OF 1939(1939); BUGS BUNNY, SUPERSTAR(1975), d
Larry E. Jackson
LAS VEGAS HILLBILLYS(1966), p; COTTONPICKIN' CHICKENPICKERS(1967),
p&d, w; DESTRUCTORS, THE(1968), w; ROAD HUSTLERS, THE(1968), d
Lary E. Jackson
LAS VEGAS HILLBILLYS(1966), w
Lee Jackson
SUMMER WISHES, WINTER DREAMS(1973)
Leonard Jackson
TOGETHER FOR DAYS(1972); FIVE ON THE BLACK HAND SIDE(1973); GANJA
AND HESS(1973); SUPER SPOOK(1975), a, w; CARWASH(1976); KING OF THE
GYPSIES(1978)
1984
BROTHER FROM ANOTHER PLANET, THE(1984)
Misc. Talkies
BLOOD COUPLE(1974)
Lewis Jackson
YOU BETTER WATCH OUT(1980), d&w
Lois H. Jackson
UNEASY TERMS(1948, Brit.), p
Lois Jackson
Silents
WHAT EVERY GIRL SHOULD KNOW(1927), w

Lou Jackson
SWEET JESUS, PREACHER MAN(1973)
Louis H. Jackson
MEET SEXTON BLAKE(1944, Brit.), p; TWILIGHT HOUR(1944, Brit.), p; WORLD OWES ME A LIVING, THE(1944, Brit.), p; APPOINTMENT WITH CRIME(1945, Brit.), p; DON CHICAGO(1945, Brit.), p; ECHO MURDERS, THE(1945, Brit.), p; OLD MOTHER RILEY AT HOME(1945, Brit.), p; STRAWBERRY ROAN(1945, Brit.), p; GAY INTRUDERS, THE(1946, Brit.), p; LISBON STORY, THE(1946, Brit.), p; LOYAL HEART(1946, Brit.), p; MEET THE NAVY(1946, Brit.), p; MURDER IN REVERSE(1946, Brit.), p; TROJAN BROTHERS, THE(1946), p; WALTZ TIME(1946, Brit.), p; WOMAN TO WOMAN(1946, Brit.), p; DUAL ALIBI(1947, Brit.), p; GHOSTS OF BERKELEY SQUARE(1947, Brit.), p; GREEN FINGERS(1947), p; COUNTER BLAST(1948, Brit.), p; DEVIL'S PLOT, THE(1948, Brit.), p; SPRINGTIME(1948, Brit.), p; THREE WEIRD SISTERS, THE(1948, Brit.), p; AGITATOR, THE(1949), p; LAUGHING LADY, THE(1950, Brit.), p; MRS. FITZHERBERT(1950, Brit.), p
Louis Jackson
FRENZY(1946, Brit.), p
Louise Jackson
Misc. Talkies
SOULS OF SIN(1949)
Lynne Jackson
ADIOS AMIGO(1975)
Mahalia Jackson
ST. LOUIS BLUES(1958); IMITATION OF LIFE(1959); BEST MAN, THE(1964)
Margaret Jackson
TWO SMART PEOPLE(1946)
Marion Jackson
WAGON MASTER, THE(1929), w; MIN AND BILL(1930), w; BIG STAMPEDE, THE(1932), w; CARNIVAL BOAT(1932), w; LAND BEYOND THE LAW(1937), w
Silents
GALLOPING GALLAGHER(1924), w; LIGHTNING ROMANCE(1924), w; NORTH OF NEVADA(1924), w; EASY MONEY(1925), w; RIDIN' THE WIND(1925), w; MIKE(1926), w; UNKNOWN CAVALIER, THE(1926), w; ARIZONA BOUND(1927), w; SOMEWHERE IN SONORA(1927), w
Marjorie Jackson
DO YOU LOVE ME?(1946); JULIA MISBEHAVES(1948); SONG IS BORN, A(1948); YOU FOR ME(1952)
Mark Jackson
EYES OF A STRANGER(1980), w
Mary Ann Jackson
MA AND PA KETTLE GO TO TOWN(1950)
Mary Jackson
FRIENDLY PERSUASION(1956); TARGETS(1968); AIRPORT(1970); WILD ROVERS(1971); TERROR HOUSE(1972); TRIAL OF THE CATONSVILLE NINE, THE(1972); KID BLUE(1973); OUR TIME(1974); AUDREY ROSE(1977); FUN WITH DICK AND JANE(1977); COMING HOME(1978); SOME KIND OF HERO(1982)
Maynard Jackson
GREASED LIGHTNING(1977)
Merrell Jackson
GODSPELL(1973)
Michael Jackson
WIZ, THE(1978); GOODBYE CHARLIE(1964); WAY...WAY OUT(1966); LOVE MACHINE, THE,(1971); BUGSY MALONE(1976, Brit.)
Michal Jackson
SWEENEY 2(1978, Brit.)
Mike Jackson
BLACK KING(1932)
O.C. Jackson
Misc. Silents
WHAT LOVE CAN DO(1916)
Pat Jackson
OVER 21(1945); ENCORE(1951, Brit.), d; SOMETHING MONEY CAN'T BUY(1952, Brit.), d, w; WHITE CORRIDORS(1952, Brit.), d, w; GENTLE TOUCH, THE(1956, Brit.), d; BIRTHDAY PRESENT, THE(1957, Brit.), d; SNOWBALL(1960, Brit.), d; VIRGIN ISLAND(1960, Brit.), d, w; DON'T TALK TO STRANGE MEN(1962, Brit.), d; SEVEN KEYS(1962, Brit.), d; WHAT A CARVE UP!(1962, Brit.), d; SEVENTY DEADLY PILLS(1964, Brit.), d&w; ON THE RUN(1969, Brit.), d&w
Patricia Jackson
EASTER PARADE(1948); PRODIGAL, THE(1955)
Patrick Jackson
SHADOW ON THE WALL(1950), d
Paul Jackson
CINDERELLA LIBERTY(1973)
Peaches Jackson
GODLESS GIRL, THE(1929)
Silents
GREATEST THING IN LIFE, THE(1918); I LOVE YOU(1918); CIRCUS DAYS(1923); ETERNAL THREE, THE(1923); CYTHEREA(1924)
Misc. Silents
LAHOMA(1920)
"Peaches" Jackson
Misc. Silents
ONE OF THE FINEST(1919)
Peggy Jackson
FATAL WITNESS, THE(1945)
Penny Jackson
MY WAY(1974, South Africa)
Phil Jackson
MUSIC BOX KID, THE(1960)
Philip Jackson
SCUM(1979, Brit.)
1984
GIVE MY REGARDS TO BROAD STREET(1984, Brit.)
Phillip Jackson
HAMMER(1972)
Pirty Lee Jackson
SMOKEY AND THE BANDIT–PART 3(1983)

Ray Jackson
FRIEDA(1947, Brit.); FINAL TEST, THE(1953, Brit.); CREST OF THE WAVE(1954, Brit.); TEARS FOR SIMON(1957, Brit.); DANGEROUS YOUTH(1958, Brit.); DUNKIRK(1958, Brit.)
Richard Jackson
Misc. Talkies
BIG BUST-OUT, THE(1973), d
Richardina Jackson
TRYGON FACTOR, THE(1969, Brit.)
Riley Jackson
I BOMBED PEARL HARBOR(1961, Jap.), w
Robert Jackson
DEATH PLAY(1976); FRIGHTMARE(1983), ed
Roland Jackson
ON THE YARD(1978)
Ron Jackson
EDDIE MACON'S RUN(1983); SPRING FEVER(1983, Can.)
1984
PLAGUE DOGS, THE(1984, U.S./Brit.), ph
Roosevelt Jackson
BLACKENSTEIN(1973)
Ruth Jackson
PUZZLE OF A DOWNFALL CHILD(1970)
Sally Jane Jackson
REMEMBRANCE(1982, Brit.)
Sam Jackson
TOGETHER FOR DAYS(1972)
Samadu Jackson
SOMETHING OF VALUE(1957)
Sammy Jackson
NO TIME FOR SERGEANTS(1958); NONE BUT THE BRAVE(1965, U.S./Jap.); NIGHT OF THE GRIZZLY, THE(1966); FASTEST GUITAR ALIVE, THE(1967); BOATNIKS, THE(1970); NORWOOD(1970); $1,000,000 DUCK(1971)
Misc. Talkies
COUNTRY MUSIC(1972)
Samuel L. Jackson
RAGTIME(1981)
Sara Jackson
CINDERELLA LIBERTY(1973)
Selmar Jackson
BRIGHAM YOUNG–FRONTIERSMAN(1940)
Selmer Jackson
SERGEANT YORK(; WHY BRING THAT UP?(1929); LOVIN' THE LADIES(1930); DIRIGIBLE(1931); LEFTOVER LADIES(1931); SECRET CALL, THE(1931); SUBWAY EXPRESS(1931); BIG CITY BLUES(1932) 65m WB bw; MOUTHPIECE, THE(1932); THREE ON A MATCH(1932); WINNER TAKE ALL(1932); YOU SAID A MOUTHFUL(1932); FORGOTTEN(1933); HELL AND HIGH WATER(1933); LITTLE GIANT, THE(1933); PICTURE SNATCHER(1933); WORKING MAN, THE(1933); FOG OVER FRISCO(1934); I'LL FIX IT(1934); I'VE GOT YOUR NUMBER(1934); JEALOUSY(1934); LET'S FALL IN LOVE(1934); NOW I'LL TELL(1934); RICHEST GIRL IN THE WORLD, THE(1934); SISTERS UNDER THE SKIN(1934); STAND UP AND CHEER(1934 80m FOX bw); WITCHING HOUR, THE(1934); ALIBI IKE(1935); BROADWAY GONDOLIER(1935); DEVIL DOGS OF THE AIR(1935); DON'T BET ON BLONDES(1935); FRONT PAGE WOMAN(1935); GRAND EXIT(1935); LIVING ON VELVET(1935); NIGHT AT THE OPERA, A(1935); PADDY O'DAY(1935); PAGE MISS GLORY(1935); PUBLIC HERO NO. 1(1935); RED SALUTE(1935); SECRET BRIDE, THE(1935); SHE MARRIED HER BOSS(1935); THIS IS THE LIFE(1935); TRAVELING SALESLADY, THE(1935); CHARLIE CHAN AT THE OPERA(1936); EASY MONEY(1936); GREAT ZIEGFELD, THE(1936); IT HAD TO HAPPEN(1936); LIBELED LADY(1936); MAGNIFICENT BRUTE, THE(1936); MY MAN GODFREY(1936); NEXT TIME WE LOVE(1936); PAROLE(1936); PUBLIC ENEMY'S WIFE(1936); REVOLT OF THE ZOMBIES(1936); SHOW BOAT(1936); CASE OF THE STUTTERING BISHOP, THE(1937); CHARLIE CHAN AT THE OLYMPICS(1937); DUKE COMES BACK, THE(1937); FAMILY AFFAIR, A(1937); FEDERAL BULLETS(1937); HOT WATER(1937); MAN IN BLUE, THE(1937); MAN WHO CRIED WOLF, THE(1937); MANHATTAN MERRY-GO-ROUND(1937); MEET THE BOY FRIEND(1937); THIRTEENTH MAN, THE(1937); THREE SMART GIRLS(1937); TWO WISE MAIDS(1937); WEST OF SHANGHAI(1937); WESTLAND CASE, THE(1937); WRONG ROAD, THE(1937); ALEXANDER'S RAGTIME BAND(1938); ARSON GANG BUSTERS(1938); CHASER, THE(1938); DOWN IN ARKANSAW(1938); FLIGHT TO FAME(1938); FOUR MEN AND A PRAYER(1938); GANGSTER'S BOY(1938); LITTLE TOUGH GUY(1938); MIDNIGHT INTRUDER(1938); MISSING GUEST, THE(1938); PERSONAL SECRETARY(1938); PRISON NURSE(1938); SECRETS OF AN ACTRESS(1938); YOU'RE ONLY YOUNG ONCE(1938); CALLING ALL MARINES(1939); CONFESSIONS OF A NAZI SPY(1939); DEAD END KIDS ON DRESS PARADE(1939); EACH DAWN I DIE(1939); ESPIONAGE AGENT(1939); FORGOTTEN WOMAN, THE(1939); GAMBLING SHIP(1939); INSIDE INFORMATION(1939); NAUGHTY BUT NICE(1939); OFF THE RECORD(1939); OUTSIDE THESE WALLS(1939); PRIVATE DETECTIVE(1939); SOCIETY LAWYER(1939); SORORITY HOUSE(1939); SOUTH OF THE BORDER(1939); STAND UP AND FIGHT(1939); STAR MAKER, THE(1939); TWO THOROUGHBREDS(1939); UNDERCOVER AGENT(1939); UNION PACIFIC(1939); WINGS OF THE NAVY(1939); 6000 ENEMIES(1939); BABIES FOR SALE(1940); BOWERY BOY(1940); GRAPES OF WRATH(1940); HIRED WIFE(1940); INVISIBLE STRIPES(1940); JOHNNY APOLLO(1940); LADY WITH RED HAIR(1940); MEN AGAINST THE SKY(1940); MILLIONAIRES IN PRISON(1940); MURDER IN THE AIR(1940); NO TIME FOR COMEDY(1940); PLAY GIRL(1940); PUBLIC DEB NO. 1(1940); QUEEN OF THE MOB(1940); SAILOR'S LADY(1940); SANTA FE TRAIL(1940); SCANDAL SHEET(1940); SON OF THE NAVY(1940); WAGONS WESTWARD(1940); BUCK PRIVATES(1941); CITY, FOR CONQUEST(1941); HERE COMES MR. JORDAN(1941); INTERNATIONAL LADY(1941); INTERNATIONAL SQUADRON(1941); LOVE CRAZY(1941); MAN WHO LOST HIMSELF, THE(1941); MEET JOHN DOE(1941); NAVY BLUES(1941); PAPER BULLETS(1941); PARACHUTE BATTALION(1941); REMEMBER THE DAY(1941); SHE KNEW ALL THE ANSWERS(1941); SHEPHERD OF THE HILLS, THE(1941); TIGHT SHOES(1941); FALCON TAKES OVER, THE(1942); JOE SMITH, AMERICAN(1942); MADAME SPY(1942); MISS ANNIE ROONEY(1942); MY FAVORITE SPY(1942); ROAD TO HAPPINESS(1942); SABOTEUR(1942); SECRET AGENT OF JAPAN(1942); TEN GENTLEMEN FROM WEST POINT(1942); THEY DIED WITH THEIR BOOTS ON(1942); THRU DIFFERENT EYES(1942); THUNDER BIRDS(1942); TRUE TO THE ARMY(1942); AROUND THE WORLD(1943); GUADALCANAL DIARY(1943); HARRIGAN'S KID(1943); HONEY-

MOON LODGE(1943); IT AIN'T HAY(1943); MARGIN FOR ERROR(1943); SOMEONE TO REMEMBER(1943); WHAT A WOMAN!(1943); BIG NOISE, THE(1944); DESTINY(1944); HEAVENLY DAYS(1944); HEY, ROOKIE(1944); ROGER TOUHY, GANGSTER!(1944); SHERIFF OF LAS VEGAS(1944); STARS ON PARADE(1944); SULLIVANS, THE(1944); WING AND A PRAYER(1944); ALLOTMENT WIVES, INC.(1945); CIRCUMSTANTIAL EVIDENCE(1945); DAKOTA(1945); FIRST YANK INTO TOKYO(1945); FOREVER YOURS(1945); OUT OF THIS WORLD(1945); SPORTING CHANCE, A(1945); THIS LOVE OF OURS(1945); THRILL OF A ROMANCE(1945); BLACK MARKET BABIES(1946); BOSTON BLACKIE AND THE LAW(1946); CHILD OF DIVORCE(1946); DANGEROUS MONEY(1946); FRENCH KEY, THE(1946); GIRL ON THE SPOT(1946); GLASS ALIBI, THE(1946); JOHNNY COMES FLYING HOME(1946); SHE WROTE THE BOOK(1946); SHOCK(1946); TIME OF THEIR LIVES, THE(1946); WIFE WANTED(1946); DREAM GIRL(1947); FABULOUS TEXAN, THE(1947); HEADING FOR HEAVEN(1947); HER HUSBAND'S AFFAIRS(1947); HIGH WALL, THE(1947); KEY WITNESS(1947); MAGIC TOWN(1947); PRETENDER, THE(1947); SARGE GOES TO COLLEGE(1947); STEPCHILD(1947); 13TH HOUR, THE(1947); EVERY GIRL SHOULD BE MARRIED(1948); FULLER BRUSH MAN(1948); GIRL FROM MANHATTAN(1948); KING OF THE GAMBLERS(1948); PITFALL(1948); SEALED VERDICT(1948); STAGE STRUCK(1948); ALASKA PATROL(1949); CRIME DOCTOR'S DIARY, THE(1949); FORGOTTEN WOMEN(1949); FOUNTAINHEAD, THE(1949); MIGHTY JOE YOUNG(1949); RENEGADES OF THE SAGE(1949); SORROWFUL JONES(1949); TULSA(1949); GUNMEN OF ABILENE(1950); LUCKY LOSERS(1950); MAGNIFICENT YANKEE, THE(1950); MARK OF THE GORILLA(1950); NO MAN OF HER OWN(1950); BOWERY BATTALION(1951); BUCKAROO SHERIFF OF TEXAS(1951); ELOPEMENT(1951); PURPLE HEART DIARY(1951); THAT'S MY BOY(1951); DEADLINE–U.S.A.(1952); WE'RE NOT MARRIED(1952); YOUNG MAN WITH IDEAS(1952); JACK MCCALL, DESPERADO(1953); PRESIDENT'S LADY, THE(1953); SKY COMMANDO(1953); DEMETRIUS AND THE GLADIATORS(1954); DEVIL GODDESS(1955); AUTUMN LEAVES(1956); HELLCATS OF THE NAVY(1957); THREE BRAVE MEN(1957); LOST MISSILE, THE(1958, U.S./Can.); ATOMIC SUBMARINE, THE(1960); GALLANT HOURS, THE(1960)

Sherry Jackson
YOU'RE MY EVERYTHING(1949); BREAKING POINT, THE(1950); COVERED WAGON RAID(1950); LOUISA(1950); MA AND PA KETTLE GO TO TOWN(1950); WHERE DANGER LIVES(1950); GREAT CARUSO, THE(1951); HELLO GOD(1951, U.S./Ital.); LORNA DOONE(1951); WHEN I GROW UP(1951); LION AND THE HORSE, THE(1952); MA AND PA KETTLE AT THE FAIR(1952); MIRACLE OF OUR LADY OF FATIMA, THE(1952); SOMETHING TO LIVE FOR(1952); THIS WOMAN IS DANGEROUS(1952); MA AND PA KETTLE ON VACATION(1953); TROUBLE ALONG THE WAY(1953); COME NEXT SPRING(1956); ADVENTURES OF HUCKLEBERRY FINN, THE(1960); MODERN MARRIAGE, A(1962); WILD ON THE BEACH(1965); GUNN(1967); MINI-SKIRT MOB, THE(1968); MONITORS, THE(1969); BARE KNUCKLES(1978); STINGRAY(1978)
Misc. Talkies
COTTER(1972); CURSE OF THE MOON CHILD(1972); BARE KNUCKLES(1977)

Shirley Jackson
LIZZIE(1957), w; HAUNTING, THE(1963), w

Spence Jackson
MEDIUM COOL(1969)

Stanley Jackson
MAN WHO WOULDN'T TALK, THE(1958, Brit.), w

Stoney Jackson
ROLLER BOOGIE(1979)
1984
STREETS OF FIRE(1984)

T. E. Jackson
NEAR THE RAINBOW'S END(1930), ph

Theron Jackson
BANJO(1947); ZAMBA(1949); GLORY(1955); FIRST TRAVELING SALESLADY, THE(1956); SCARLET HOUR, THE(1956)

Thomas Jackson
DOORWAY TO HELL(1930); DOUBLE CROSS ROADS(1930); FOR THE DEFENSE(1930); GOOD NEWS(1930); LAWLESS WOMAN, THE(1931); LITTLE CAESAR(1931); RECKLESS LIVING(1931); WOMEN GO ON FOREVER(1931); BIG CITY BLUES(1932) 65m WB bw; DEVIL PAYS, THE(1932); DOCTOR X(1932); ESCAPADE(1932); AVENGER, THE(1933); FROM HELL TO HEAVEN(1933); TERROR ABOARD(1933); GEORGE WHITE'S SCANDALS(1934); MANHATTAN MELODRAMA(1934); MELODY IN SPRING(1934); NAME THE WOMAN(1934); THIN MAN, THE(1934); CARNIVAL(1935); CASE OF THE CURIOUS BRIDE, THE(1935); GEORGE WHITE'S 1935 SCANDALS(1935); IRISH IN US, THE(1935); SHE COULDN'T TAKE IT(1935); BELOW THE DEADLINE(1936); HOLLYWOOD BOULEVARD(1936); IT HAD TO HAPPEN(1936); LITTLE MISS NOBODY(1936); PREVIEW MURDER MYSTERY(1936); SON COMES HOME, A(1936); DEAD END(1937); THEY WON'T FORGET(1937); WESTLAND CASE, THE(1937); AMAZING DR. CLITTERHOUSE, THE(1938); CRIME TAKES A HOLIDAY(1938); INTERNATIONAL CRIME(1938); LADY IN THE MORGUE(1938); ANOTHER THIN MAN(1939); BEAU GESTE(1939); NANCY DREW–REPORTER(1939); STRONGER THAN DESIRE(1939); TELL NO TALES(1939); FREE, BLONDE AND 21(1940); FUGITIVE FROM JUSTICE, A(1940); GIRL FROM GOD'S COUNTRY(1940); LADY WITH RED HAIR(1940); OH JOHNNY, HOW YOU CAN LOVE!(1940); LAW OF THE TROPICS(1941); YANKEE DOODLE DANDY(1942); CRIME DOCTOR'S STRANGEST CASE(1943); NO PLACE FOR A LADY(1943); ROGER TOUHY, GANGSTER!(1944); CIRCUMSTANTIAL EVIDENCE(1945); HIDDEN EYE, THE(1945); SCARLET STREET(1945); SHADY LADY(1945); WHY GIRLS LEAVE HOME(1945); BIG SLEEP, THE(1946); DEADLINE FOR MURDER(1946); DEVIL'S MASK, THE(1946); HOW DO YOU DO?(1946); JUST BEFORE DAWN(1946); MYSTERIOUS MR. VALENTINE, THE(1946); VALLEY OF THE ZOMBIES(1946); GUILT OF JANET AMES, THE(1947); GUILTY, THE(1947); HERE COMES TROUBLE(1948); HUNTED, THE(1948); UP IN CENTRAL PARK(1948); PHONE CALL FROM A STRANGER(1952)
Misc. Silents
RULER OF THE ROAD(1918)

Thomas E. Jackson
BROADWAY(1929); 24 HOURS(1931); STRANGE JUSTICE(1932); STRANGE LOVE OF MOLLY LOUVAIN, THE(1932); MYSTERY OF THE WAX MUSEUM, THE(1933); PARACHUTE JUMPER(1933); STRICTLY PERSONAL(1933); MYRT AND MARGE(1933); PERSONALITY KID, THE(1934); SECRET BRIDE, THE(1935); SPECIAL AGENT(1935); DANGEROUS HOLIDAY(1937); MAN BETRAYED, A(1937); BLONDES AT WORK(1938); I STAND ACCUSED(1938); GOLDEN GLOVES(1940); MILLIONAIRES IN PRISON(1940); WOMEN WITHOUT NAMES(1940); WOMAN IN THE WINDOW, THE(1945); FACE OF MARBLE, THE(1946); UNION STATION(1950);

MEET ME AT THE FAIR(1952); STARS AND STRIPES FOREVER(1952)

Tom Jackson
FALL GUY, THE(1930); SWEEPSTAKES(1931); AFRAID TO TALK(1932); I'D GIVE MY LIFE(1936); MAGNIFICENT BRUTE, THE(1936); FUGITIVE IN THE SKY(1937); LOVE, HONOR AND OH, BABY!(1940); GREAT JOHN L. THE(1945); LAWLESS BREED, THE(1952)

Tommy Jackson
CALL OF THE WILD(1935); OUTCAST(1937); ANGELS WITH DIRTY FACES(1938); TORCHY GETS HER MAN(1938); MYSTERY OF THE WHITE ROOM(1939); CRIME WAVE(1954); LAST HURRAH, THE(1958)

Tommy "Thomas" Jackson
UNASHAMED(1932)

Tony Jackson
2001: A SPACE ODYSSEY(1968, U.S./Brit.)

Travis Jackson
MOUNTAIN, THE(1935, Brit.), p,d&w

Tyrone Jackson
ASHANTI(1979)

Valerie Jackson
GOLDEN BLADE, THE(1953); LAW AND ORDER(1953); TAKE ME TO TOWN(1953)

Virginia Jackson
RED ROCK OUTLAW(1950); SILVER BANDIT, THE(1950)

Walter Jackson
USED CARS(1980)

Warren Jackson
CALL THE MESQUITEERS(1938); HOLLYWOOD ROUNDUP(1938); STORY OF ALEXANDER GRAHAM BELL, THE(1939); MEXICAN SPITFIRE OUT WEST(1940); GUN MAN FROM BODIE, THE(1941); SOUTH OF PANAMA(1941); MEXICAN SPITFIRE AT SEA(1942); MIRACLE KID(1942); DIXIE(1943); GILDERSLEEVE'S BAD DAY(1943); HIGHER AND HIGHER(1943); SO'S YOUR UNCLE(1943); CORNERED(1945); HER LUCKY NIGHT(1945); ON STAGE EVERYBODY(1945); UNDER WESTERN SKIES(1945); NOTORIOUS(1946); TRAIL STREET(1947); CORONER CREEK(1948); RETURN OF THE BADMEN(1948); OH, YOU BEAUTIFUL DOLL(1949); MONTANA(1950); SQUARE DANCE KATY(1950)

Wilfred Jackson
SNOW WHITE AND THE SEVEN DWARFS(1937), d; FANTASIA(1940), d; PINOCCHIO(1940), d; DUMBO(1941), d; MELODY TIME(1948), d; CINDERELLA(1950), d; PETER PAN(1953), d; LADY AND THE TRAMP(1955), d

William Jackson
Misc. Silents
VENGEANCE IS MINE!(1916)

Jackson and Lynam
ICE-CAPADES(1941); ICE-CAPADES REVUE(1942); SONG OF THE SOUTH(1946), d

The Jacksons
GUMSHOE(1972, Brit.)

Tom Jacksop
RECKONING, THE(1932)

Elli Jacno
1984
FULL MOON IN PARIS(1984, Fr.), m

Cindy Jaco
STUDENT BODY, THE(1976)

Dennis Jacob
TERROR, THE(1963), p&d; WILD RACERS, THE(1968), ed

Don Jacob
D.C. CAB(1983)

Donald Jacob
BEING THERE(1979)

Gordon Jacob
JOURNEY TOGETHER(1946, Brit.), m; ESTHER WATERS(1948, Brit.), m

Harrison Jacob
HOPALONG CASSIDY(1935), w

Jasper Jacob
PRIVATES ON PARADE(1982)

Naomi Jacob
GLAMOUR(1931, Brit.)

Peter Jacob
IS PARIS BURNING?(1966, U.S./Fr.); DON'T LOOK NOW(1969, Brit./Fr.)
Misc. Talkies
MISS MELODY JONES(1973)

Walter Jacob
DAS LETZTE GEHEIMNIS(1959, Ger.)

Franco Jacobbi
MEDEA(1971, Ital./Fr./Ger.)

Ruggero Jacobbi
PRISONER OF THE IRON MASK(1962, Fr./Ital.), w; WHITE SLAVE SHIP(1962, Fr./Ital.), w

Remedos Jacobe
I WAS AN AMERICAN SPY(1951)

Marie Jacobeni
Misc. Silents
STRANGE CASE OF DISTRICT ATTORNEY M.(1930)

Derek Jacobi
OTHELLO(1965, Brit.); INTERLUDE(1968, Brit.); BLUE BLOOD(1973, Brit.); DAY OF THE JACKAL, THE(1973, Brit./Fr.); ODESSA FILE, THE(1974, Brit./Ger.); THREE SISTERS(1974, Brit.); MEDUSA TOUCH, THE(1978, Brit.); HUMAN FACTOR, THE(1979, Brit.); SECRET OF NIMH, THE(1982); ENIGMA(1983)

Ernst Jacobi
TIN DRUM, THE(1979, Ger./Fr./Yugo./Pol.)
1984
GERMANY PALE MOTHER(1984, Ger.)

Georg Jacobi
Misc. Silents
ROMANCE OF A RUSSIAN BALLERINA(1913, USSR), d

Hans Jacobi
CIRCUS OF LOVE(1958, Ger.), w

Lou Jacobi
GOOD BEGINNING, THE(1953, Brit.); IS YOUR HONEYMOON REALLY NECESSARY?(1953, Brit.); CHARLEY MOON(1956, Brit.); KID FOR TWO FARTHINGS, A(1956, Brit.); DIARY OF ANNE FRANK, THE(1959); SONG WITHOUT END(1960);

IRMA LA DOUCE(1963); LAST OF THE SECRET AGENTS?, THE(1966); PENELO-
PE(1966); COTTON COMES TO HARLEM(1970); LITTLE MURDERS(1971); EVERY-
THING YOU ALWAYS WANTED TO KNOW ABOUT SEX, BUT WE'RE AFRAID TO
ASK(1972); NEXT STOP, GREENWICH VILLAGE(1976); ROSELAND(1977); MAGI-
CIAN OF LUBLIN, THE(1979, Israel/Ger.); LUCKY STAR, THE(1980, Can.); AR-
THUR(1981); CHU CHU AND THE PHILLY FLASH(1981); MY FAVORITE
YEAR(1982)
1984
ISAAC LITTLEFEATHERS(1984, Can.)
Misc. Talkies
OFF YOUR ROCKER(1980)
Marianne Jacobi
MONTENEGRO(1981, Brit./Swed.)
Maria Jacobini
Misc. Silents
MAMAN COLIBRI(1929, Fr.); LIVING CORPSE, A(1931, USSR)
Jacobo
NEST, THE(1982, Span.)
Al Jacobs
DEVIL'S SISTERS, THE(1966), m; STING OF DEATH(1966), m; WILD REBELS,
THE(1967), m
Alan Jacobs
BUG(1975), ed
1984
JOY OF SEX(1984), ed
Alexander Jacobs
POINT BLANK(1967), w; HELL IN THE PACIFIC(1968), w; SITTING TARGET(1972,
Brit.), w; SEVEN UPS, THE(1973), w; FRENCH CONNECTION 11(1975), w; ENEMY
OF THE PEOPLE, AN(1978), w
Allan Jacobs
MOONSHINE WAR, THE(1970), ed; MAKING IT(1971), ed; BLACULA(1972), ed;
CLEOPATRA JONES(1973), ed; LONGEST YARD, THE(1974), ed; RACE WITH THE
DEVIL(1975), ed; HOW TO SUCCEED IN BUSINESS WITHOUT REALLY
TRYING(1976), ed; LOVE AT FIRST BITE(1979), ed; DEATH HUNT(1981), ed; PUR-
SUIT OF D.B. COOPER, THE(1981), ed
Allan A. Jacobs
MATILDA(1978), ed
Angela Jacobs
COUNSELLOR-AT-LAW(1933)
Anthony Jacobs
KILLERS OF KILIMANJARO(1960, Brit.); WINGS OF MYSTERY(1963, Brit.); FILE
OF THE GOLDEN GOOSE, THE(1969, Brit.)
Art Jacobs
DIRT GANG, THE(1972), p
Arthur A. Jacobs
SHE DEMONS(1958), p
Arthur P. Jacobs
GIANT FROM THE UNKNOWN(1958), p; WHAT A WAY TO GO(1964), p; DOCTOR
DOLITTLE(1967), p; PLANET OF THE APES(1968), p; GOODBYE MR. CHIPS(1969,
U.S./Brit.), p; BENEATH THE PLANET OF THE APES(1970), p; ESCAPE FROM THE
PLANET OF THE APES(1971), p; PLAY IT AGAIN, SAM(1972), p; BATTLE FOR THE
PLANET OF THE APES(1973), p; TOM SAWYER(1973), p; HUCKLEBERRY
FINN(1974), p
Barry Jacobs
I AM A GROUPIE(1970, Brit.), p
Betty Jacobs
TWO SISTERS(1938)
Billy Jacobs
Misc. Silents
CLOWN, THE(1916); HOUSE OF THE GOLDEN WINDOWS, THE(1916); PRIMROSE
RING, THE(1917)
Carl Jacobs
STUDENT BODIES(1981)
Corelli Jacobs
SIN OF MONA KENT, THE(1961), m; WACKY WORLD OF DR. MORGUS,
THE(1962), m
David Jacobs
INBETWEEN AGE, THE(1958, Brit.); RING-A-DING RHYTHM(1962, Brit. 73m
Amicus/COL bw (G.B: IT'S TRAD, DAD!); JUST FOR FUN(1963, Brit.); YOU MUST BE
JOKING!(1965, Brit.)
Debbie Jacobs
INADMISSIBLE EVIDENCE(1968, Brit.)
Deborah Jacobs
LIQUID SKY(1982)
Earl Jacobs
SINCE YOU WENT AWAY(1944)
Edward Jacobs
JUDY'S LITTLE NO-NO(1969), p
Emma Jacobs
STUD, THE(1979, Brit.)
Frank Jacobs
Silents
NEVER SAY QUIT(1919)
Harrison Jacobs
AFTER THE DANCE(1935), w; LITTLE BIG SHOT(1935), w; EAGLE'S BROOD,
THE(1936), w; HOPALONG CASSIDY RETURNS(1936), w; BARRIER, THE(1937), w;
BORDERLAND(1937), w; TEXAS TRAIL(1937), w; BAR 20 JUSTICE(1938), w; FRON-
TIERSMAN, THE(1938), w; IN OLD MEXICO(1938), w; PARTNERS OF THE
PLAINS(1938), w; HERITAGE OF THE DESERT(1939), w; I AM A CRIMINAL(1939),
w; LAW OF THE PAMPAS(1939), w; RENEGADE TRAIL(1939), w; COLORADO(1940),
w; SANTA FE MARSHAL(1940), w; WAGONS WESTWARD(1940), w; YOUNG BUF-
FALO BILL(1940), w; JESSE JAMES AT BAY(1941), w; WIDE OPEN TOWN(1941), w;
SMART GUY(1943), w; FALSE PARADISE(1948), w
Silents
LAZY LIGHTNING(1926), w; RUSTLER'S RANCH(1926), w; WESTERN WHIRL-
WIND, THE(1927), w
Henry Jacobs
THX 1138(1971)

Herb Jacobs
PROJECT MOONBASE(1953); STEEL CAGE, THE(1954)
"Indian" Jack Jacobs
TRIPLE THREAT(1948)
Jack Jacobs
MAN ON FIRE(1957), w; SINAI COMMANDOS: THE STORY OF THE SIX DAY
WAR(1968, Israel/Ger.), w; IN SEARCH OF HISTORIC JESUS(1980), w
Jacqueline Jacobs
VAN, THE(1977); MALIBU BEACH(1978); VAN NUYS BLVD.(1979); BEACH
GIRLS(1982); MY TUTOR(1983)
1984
WEEKEND PASS(1984)
James Jacobs
MEDIUM COOL(1969)
James H. Jacobs
LOVE IN A TAXI(1980)
Jim Jacobs
GREASE(1978), w
Joan Jacobs
DEVIL'S SISTERS, THE(1966)
Joan Browning Jacobs
STUDENT BODIES(1981)
Joe Jacobs
BUSTIN' LOOSE(1981)
Joe D. Jacobs
WALK PROUD(1979)
Joey Jacobs
Misc. Silents
MATERNAL SPARK, THE(1917); BOSTON BLACKIE'S LITTLE PAL(1918)
Jon Jacobs
1984
GIVE MY REGARDS TO BROAD STREET(1984, Brit.)
John Ian Jacobs
LEPKE(1975, U.S./Israel)
Jon Ian Jacobs
UP IN SMOKE(1978); COMMITMENT, THE(1976); BALTIMORE BULLET, THE(1980)
Larry Jacobs
Misc. Talkies
HOW TO SCORE WITH GIRLS(1980)
Lawrence-Hilton Jacobs
COOLEY HIGH(1975); YOUNGBLOOD(1978)
Lee Jacobs
EVERY SPARROW MUST FALL(1964), ed
Lewis Jacobs
SWEET LOVE, BITTER(1967), p, w
Little Billy Jacobs
Silents
THOSE WITHOUT SIN(1917)
Lou Jacobs
GREATEST SHOW ON EARTH, THE(1952)
Manny Jacobs
1984
OLD ENOUGH(1984)
Marianne Jacobs
FANNY AND ALEXANDER(1983, Swed./Fr./Ger.), m
Martyn Jacobs
FINAL OPTION, THE(1983, Brit.)
Morton Jacobs
SHRIEK OF THE MUTILATED(1974)
Newton P. Jacobs
FIRST SPACESHIP ON VENUS(1960, Ger./Pol.), p
Olu Jacobs
DOGS OF WAR, THE(1980, Brit.)
Paul Jacobs
RETURN TO CAMPUS(1975)
Paula Jacobs
AMERICAN WEREWOLF IN LONDON, AN(1981)
Raymond Jacobs
MINX, THE(1969), p, d, w, spec eff
Richard Jacobs
FINAL TERROR, THE(1983)
Robert Jacobs
SOUTH PACIFIC(1958)
Ronald Jacobs
ON THE RIGHT TRACK(1981), p; JIMMY THE KID(1982), p
Rusty Jacobs
TAPS(1981)
1984
ONCE UPON A TIME IN AMERICA(1984)
Sally Jacobs
HAVING A WILD WEEKEND(1965, Brit.), cos; PERSECUTION AND ASSASSINA-
TION OF JEAN-PAUL MARAT AS PERFORMED BY THE INMATES OF THE
ASYLUM OF CHARENTON UNDER THE DIRECTION OF THE MARQUIS DE SADE,
THE(1967, Brit.), prod d; TELL ME LIES(1968, Brit.), prod d
Seaman Jacobs
IT HAPPENED AT THE WORLD'S FAIR(1963), w; OH GOD! BOOK II(1980), w
Shirley Jacobs
SECRET TENT, THE(1956, Brit.)
Suzanne Jacobs
TENDER MERCIES(1982)
T.C.H. Jacobs
TORSO MURDER MYSTERY, THE(1940, Brit.), w
Tammy Jacobs
BLOODY KIDS(1983, Brit.)
Tom Jacobs
METALSTORM: THE DESTRUCTION OF JARED-SYN(1983)
W.W. Jacobs
THIRD STRING, THE(1932, Brit.), w; MONKEY'S PAW, THE(1933), w; BEAUTY
AND THE BARGE(1937, Brit.), w; SAILOR'S DON'T CARE(1940, Brit.), w; MON-
KEY'S PAW, THE(1948, Brit.), w; FOOTSTEPS IN THE FOG(1955, Brit.), w; SPIRIT-

ISM(1965, Mex.), w

Silents

HEAD OF THE FAMILY, THE(1922, Brit.), w; MASTER OF CRAFT, A(1922, Brit.), w; SKIPPER'S WOOING, THE(1922, Brit.), w; MONKEY'S PAW, THE(1923, Brit.), w; PASSION ISLAND(1927, Brit.), w

Werner Jacobs

BEGGAR STUDENT, THE(1958, Ger.), d; HEIDI(1968, Aust.), d

William Jacobs

NIGHT OF TERROR(1933), w; SWELL-HEAD(1935), w; UNWELCOME STRANGER(1935), w; BIG NOISE, THE(1936), w; DOWN THE STRETCH(1936), w; HOT MONEY(1936), w; ISLE OF FURY(1936), w; MOONLIGHT ON THE PRAIRIE(1936), w; SONG OF THE SADDLE(1936), w; TREACHERY RIDES THE RANGE(1936), w; DANCE, CHARLIE, DANCE(1937), w; OVER THE GOAL(1937), w; TALENT SCOUT(1937), w; PENROD AND HIS TWIN BROTHER(1938), w; SERGEANT MURPHY(1938), w; CALLING ALL HUSBANDS(1940), p; FLOWING GOLD(1940), p; RIVER'S END(1940), p; SOUTH OF SUEZ(1940), p; CASE OF THE BLACK PARROT, THE(1941), p; GREAT MR. NOBODY, THE(1941), p; HERE COMES HAPPINESS(1941), p; NINE LIVES ARE NOT ENOUGH(1941), p; NURSE'S SECRET, THE(1941), p; PASSAGE FROM HONG KONG(1941), p; SHADOWS ON THE STAIRS(1941), p; SHE COULDN'T SAY NO(1941), p; SHOT IN THE DARK, THE(1941), p; THREE SONS O'GUNS(1941), p; ALWAYS IN MY HEART(1942), p; ESCAPE FROM CRIME(1942), p; HIDDEN HAND, THE(1942), p; MURDER IN THE BIG HOUSE(1942), p; SECRET ENEMIES(1942), p; ADVENTURES IN IRAQ(1943), p; FIND THE BLACKMAILER(1943), p; MURDER ON THE WATERFRONT(1943), p; MYSTERIOUS DOCTOR, THE(1943), p; TRUCK BUSTERS(1943), p; CRIME BY NIGHT(1944), p; SHINE ON, HARVEST MOON(1944), p; CHRISTMAS IN CONNECTICUT(1945), p; CONFLICT(1945), p; DANGER SIGNAL(1945), p; TOO YOUNG TO KNOW(1945), p; BEAST WITH FIVE FINGERS, THE(1946), p; NEVER SAY GOODBYE(1946), p; SHADOW OF A WOMAN(1946), p; VERDICT, THE(1946), p; LOVE AND LEARN(1947), p; MY WILD IRISH ROSE(1947), p; NORA PRENTISS(1947), p; APRIL SHOWERS(1948), p; WHIPLASH(1948), p; LOOK FOR THE SILVER LINING(1949), p; STORY OF SEABISCUIT, THE(1949), p; DAUGHTER OF ROSIE O'GRADY, THE(1950), p; MONTANA(1950), p; ROCKY MOUNTAIN(1950), p; TEA FOR TWO(1950), p; CLOSE TO MY HEART(1951), p; LULLABY OF BROADWAY, THE(1951), p; ON MOONLIGHT BAY(1951), p; PAINTING THE CLOUDS WITH SUNSHINE(1951), p; ABOUT FACE(1952), p; SHE'S WORKING HER WAY THROUGH COLLEGE(1952), p; APRIL IN PARIS(1953), p; BY THE LIGHT OF THE SILVERY MOON(1953), p; CALAMITY JANE(1953), p

William Wymark Jacobs

OUR RELATIONS(1936), w

Wilma Jacobs

VIEW FROM POMPEY'S HEAD, THE(1955)

Henrik Jacobsen

SLEEPING CAR TO TRIESTE(1949, Brit.); GREEN GROW THE RUSHES(1951, Brit.); HOTEL SAHARA(1951, Brit.); ISLAND RESCUE(1952, Brit.)

Irving Jacobsen

ART OF LOVE, THE(1965)

Jock Jacobsen

MAN AT THE TOP(1973, Brit.), p

Johan Jacobsen

WHILE THE ATTORNEY IS ASLEEP(1945, Den.), d; STRANGER KNOCKS, A(1963, Den.), p, d

Kjeld Jacobsen

HIDDEN FEAR(1957)

Sven Erik Jacobsen

FANNY AND ALEXANDER(1983, Swed./Fr./Ger.)

Ulla Jacobsen

FOX AND HIS FRIENDS(1976, Ger.)

Willy Jacobsen

1984

ZAPPA(1984, Den.)

Arthur Jacobson

HOME ON THE RANGE(1935), d

Egon Jacobson

M(1933, Ger.), w; M(1951), w

Frank R. Jacobson

FOR PETE'S SAKE!(1966), p; TWO A PENNY(1968, Brit.), p; HIDING PLACE, THE(1975), p; NO LONGER ALONE(1978), p

Gela Jacobson

1984

BODY DOUBLE(1984)

George Jacobson

HEY, LET'S TWIST!(1961), ph; ONE PLUS ONE(1961, Can.), ph

Gil Jacobson

1984

PURPLE RAIN(1984)

Glenn Jacobson

OPERATION PETTICOAT(1959)

1984

LAST HORROR FILM, THE(1984)

Harvey Jacobson

GIRLS ON THE BEACH(1965), p

Henrietta Jacobson

CATSKILL HONEYMOON(1950); HERO AT LARGE(1980)

Henrik Jacobson

GREAT MANHUNT, THE(1951, Brit.)

Hy Jacobson

CATSKILL HONEYMOON(1950), m

Irving Jacobson

ELI ELI(1940)

Misc. Talkies

GREATER ADVISOR, THE(1940)

Jill Jacobson

NURSE SHERRI(1978)

Joanne Jacobson

1984

DESIREE(1984, Neth.)

Jock Jacobson

SPARE THE ROD(1961, Brit.), p

Joel Jacobson

CATSKILL HONEYMOON(1950), w

Johan Jacobson

STRANGER KNOCKS, A(1963, Den.), ph

Leigh Jacobson

Silents

ONE GLORIOUS SCRAP(1927), w; SHIELD OF HONOR, THE(1927), w

Leopold Jacobson

MARRIED IN HOLLYWOOD(1929), w; SMILING LIEUTENANT, THE(1931), w

Mark David Jacobson

WILD PARTY, THE(1975)

Nate Jacobson

TAKE THE MONEY AND RUN(1969)

Norman Jacobson

Silents

IT'S A BEAR(1919), w

Paul L. Jacobson

SANTA CLAUS CONQUERS THE MARTIANS(1964), p, w

Sherrie Sanet Jacobson

JAWS II(1978), ed

Steven Jacobson

Misc. Talkies

TEAM-MATES(1978), d

Sylvia Jacobson

SHEBA BABY(1975)

Warren Jacobson

END OF AUGUST, THE(1982), p, prod d

Nils Jacobsson

NIGHT IN JUNE, A(1940, Swed.)

Ulla Jacobsson

SMILES OF A SUMMER NIGHT(1957, Swed.); LOVE IS A BALL(1963); RESTLESS NIGHT, THE(1964, Ger.); ZULU(1964, Brit.); HEROES OF TELEMARK, THE(1965, Brit.); MY FATHER'S MISTRESS(1970, Swed.)

Nicky Jacobstahl

SWEET SUGAR(1972)

Jay Jacobus

MORE AMERICAN GRAFFITI(1979)

Jim Jacobus

FOG, THE(1980)

Annalee Whitmore Jacoby

TISH(1942), w

Bill Jacoby

1984

RECKLESS(1984)

Billy Jacoby

BACK ROADS(1981); BEASTMASTER, THE(1982); HOSPITAL MASSACRE(1982); CUJO(1983); MAN, WOMAN AND CHILD(1983); NIGHTMARES(1983)

Billy J. Jacoby

THE RUNNER STUMBLES(1979)

Carl Jacoby

Silents

RIDDLE: WOMAN, THE(1920), w

Elsa Jacoby

SET, THE(1970, Aus.)

Georg Jacoby

MONEY ON THE STREET(1930, Aust.), d; STORM IN A WATER GLASS(1931, Aust.), d

Misc. Silents

LITTLE NAPOLEON, THE(1923, Ger.), d

George Jacoby

Silents

FAKE, THE(1927, Brit.), d; PHYSICIAN, THE(1928, Brit.), d

Misc. Silents

LAST PAYMENT(1921, Ger.), d

Gert Jacoby

BLUE LAGOON, THE(1980)

Hans Jacoby

MONEY ON THE STREET(1930, Aust.), art d; SCANDALS OF PARIS(1935, Brit.), w; ETERNAL MASK, THE(1937, Swiss), art d; I WAS AN ADVENTURESS(1940), w; TARZAN AND THE AMAZONS(1945), w; CHAMPAGNE FOR CAESAR(1950), w; TARZAN AND THE SLAVE GIRL(1950), w; REUNION IN RENO(1951), w; SIROCCO(1951), w; TARZAN'S SAVAGE FURY(1952), w; TAXI(1953), w; CARNIVAL STORY(1954), w; STRANGER FROM VENUS, THE(1954, Brit.), w; IT HAPPENED IN BROAD DAYLIGHT(1960, Ger./Switz.), w; GOOD SOLDIER SCHWEIK, THE(1963, Ger.), w; JUDGE AND THE SINNER, THE(1964, Ger.), w; MAN WHO WALKED THROUGH THE WALL, THE(1964, Ger.), w

Irving Jacoby

SNOW TREASURE(1968), p&d, w

John Jacoby

AMAZING MRS. HOLLIDAY(1943), w; HAPPY GO LUCKY(1943), w; PHANTOM OF THE OPERA(1943), w; SHE WOULDN'T SAY YES(1945), w; TARS AND SPARS(1946), w

Joseph Jacoby

SHAME, SHAME, EVERYBODY KNOWS HER NAME(1969), p&d, w; HURRY UP OR I'LL BE 30(1973), p&d, w; GREAT BANK HOAX, THE(1977), d&w

Laura Jacoby

VALLEY GIRL(1983)

M. Jacoby

HERE COMES CARTER(1936), w

Michael Jacoby

SMUGGLED CARGO(1939), w; DOOMED TO DIE(1940), w; NO GREATER SIN(1941), w; FRISCO LILL(1942), w; MYSTERY OF MARIE ROGET, THE(1942), w; UNDYING MONSTER, THE(1942), w; THEY CAME TO BLOW UP AMERICA(1943), w; FACE OF MARBLE, THE(1946), w

Michel Jacoby

CHARGE OF THE LIGHT BRIGADE, THE(1936), w; TWO AGAINST THE WORLD(1936), w; WHITE ANGEL, THE(1936), w; LOVE, HONOR AND BEHAVE(1938), w; ARE THESE OUR PARENTS?(1944), w; YOUTH ON TRIAL(1945), w;

SWEETHEART OF SIGMA CHI(1946), w

Mme. Jacoby
NOTORIOUS SOPHIE LANG, THE(1934)

Sam Jacoby
WILD SCENE, THE(1970), p

Samuel J. Jacoby
IRON GLOVE, THE(1954), w

Scott Jacoby
ANDERSON TAPES, THE(1971); RIVALS(1972); BAXTER(1973, Brit.); LITTLE GIRL WHO LIVES DOWN THE LANE, THE(1977, Can.); LOVE AND THE MIDNIGHT AUTO SUPPLY(1978); OUR WINNING SEASON(1978)

Shari Jacoby
FOG, THE(1980)

Richard Jacome
NIGHT OF THE LEPUS(1972)

Georges Jaconelli
TIN DRUM, THE(1979, Ger./Fr./Yugo./Pol.), spec eff

Antonio Jacono
LA DOLCE VITA(1961, Ital./Fr.)

Nilo Jacoponi
GIRL AND THE GENERAL, THE(1967, Fr./Ital.), makeup; MADE IN ITALY(1967, Fr./Ital.), makeup; MAIDEN FOR A PRINCE, A(1967, Fr./Ital.), makeup

Michael Jacot
LAST ACT OF MARTIN WESTON, THE(1970, Can./Czech.), p,d&w

Jacouty
Silents
NAPOLEON(1927, Fr.), art d

Felix Jacoves
EMBRACEABLE YOU(1948), d; HOMICIDE(1949), d

Jack Jacovides
ANNA OF RHODES(1950, Gr.), m

Lelos Jacovides
ANNA OF RHODES(1950, Gr.)

Alessandro Jacovoni
LA NOTTE BRAVA(1962, Fr./Ital.), p; DUEL OF THE TITANS(1963, Ital.), p

Ciela Jacquard
ROLLIN' PLAINS(1938), w

Jacques Jacquard
ROLLIN' PLAINS(1938), w

Jacqueline
GOOD NEIGHBOR SAM(1964), cos

Andre Jacquemin
MONTY PYTHON'S LIFE OF BRIAN(1979, Brit.), m

Maurice Jacquemont
CONFESSION, THE(1970, Fr.); STATE OF SIEGE(1973, Fr./U.S./Ital./Ger.); JUDGE AND THE ASSASSIN, THE(1979, Fr.); RETURN OF MARTIN GUERRE, THE(1983, Fr.)

Jacques
ESCAPE FROM YESTERDAY(1939, Fr.), art d

A. Rene-St. Norbert Jacques
TESTAMENT OF DR. MABUSE, THE(1943, Ger.), w

Hattie Jacques
GREEN FOR DANGER(1946, Brit.); NICHOLAS NICKLEBY(1947, Brit.); GAY LADY, THE(1949, Brit.); CHANCE OF A LIFETIME(1950, Brit.); CHRISTMAS CAROL, A(1951, Brit.); OLIVER TWIST(1951, Brit.); NO HAUNT FOR A GENTLEMAN(1952, Brit.); PICKWICK PAPERS, THE(1952, Brit.); SPIDER AND THE FLY, THE(1952, Brit.); WATERFRONT WOMEN(1952, Brit.); LOVE LOTTERY, THE(1954, Brit.); UP TO HIS NECK(1954, Brit.); ADVENTURES OF SADIE, THE(1955, Brit.); AS LONG AS THEY'RE HAPPY(1957, Brit.); SQUARE PEG, THE(1958, Brit.); CARRY ON NURSE(1959, Brit.); CARRY ON SERGEANT(1959, Brit.); FOLLOW A STAR(1959, Brit.); LEFT, RIGHT AND CENTRE(1959); NAVY LARK, THE(1959, Brit.); CARRY ON CONSTABLE(1960, Brit.); MAKE MINE MINK(1960, Brit.); SCHOOL FOR SCOUNDRELS(1960, Brit.); CARRY ON REGARDLESS(1961, Brit.); WATCH YOUR STERN(1961, Brit.); CARRY ON TEACHER(1962, Brit.); MAKE MINE A DOUBLE(1962, Brit.); CARRY ON CABBIE(1963, Brit.); MAID FOR MURDER(1963, Brit.); MY SON, THE VAMPIRE(1963, Brit.); PUNCH AND JUDY MAN, THE(1963, Brit.); IN THE DOGHOUSE(1964, Brit.); BOBO, THE(1967, Brit.); PLANK, THE(1967, Brit.); CARRY ON DOCTOR(1968, Brit.); CARRY ON AGAIN, DOCTOR(1969, Brit.); CARRY ON CAMPING(1969, Brit.); THOSE DARING YOUNG MEN IN THEIR JAUNTY JALOPIES(1969, Fr./Brit./ Ital.); CARRY ON LOVING(1970, Brit.); MAGIC CHRISTIAN, THE(1970, Brit.); SOPHIE'S PLACE(1970)
Misc. Talkies
CARRY ON MATRON(1973, Brit.)

Henry Jacques
MICHELLE(1970, Fr.), d, w

Lucile Jacques
WORDS AND MUSIC(1929)

Norbert Jacques
THOUSAND EYES OF DR. MABUSE, THE(1960, Fr./Ital./Ger.), w

Ted Jacques
NO TIME FOR LOVE(1943); DESTINATION TOKYO(1944); POWDER RIVER RUSTLERS(1949); BLONDE BANDIT, THE(1950); WESTERN PACIFIC AGENT(1950); BLACK PATCH(1957); GUN RUNNERS(1958); EDGE OF ETERNITY(1959); FLAMING STAR(1960); WALK ON THE WILD SIDE(1962); MOVE OVER, DARLING(1963); KILLERS, THE(1964); BEAU GESTE(1966)

Ted E. Jacques
MISSION TO MOSCOW(1943)

William Jacques
CONFESSION, THE(1970, Fr.)

Jacques III the Dog
Silents
LITTLE 'FRAID LADY, THE(1920)

Dany Jacquet
L'ETOILE DU NORD(1983, Fr.)

Frank Jacquet
WAR IS A RACKET(1934); SHINE ON, HARVEST MOON(1938); MISBEHAVING HUSBANDS(1941); CITY OF SILENT MEN(1942); IN OLD CALIFORNIA(1942); RAIDERS OF THE RANGE(1942); MISSION TO MOSCOW(1943); BENEATH WESTERN SKIES(1944); SILVER CITY KID(1944); BEYOND THE PECOS(1945); CHEROKEE FLASH, THE(1945); COLORADO PIONEERS(1945); IN OLD NEW

MEXICO(1945); MR. MUGGS RIDES AGAIN(1945); TOPEKA TERROR, THE(1945); GREAT SINNER, THE(1949); HOUSE OF STRANGERS(1949); KING OF THE BULLWHIP(1950); MOTOR PATROL(1950); MULE TRAIN(1950); OUTLAW GOLD(1950); JUNGLE JIM IN THE FORBIDDEN LAND(1952); JUPITER'S DARLING(1955)
Misc. Talkies
CALL OF THE ROCKIES(1944)

Gaston Jacquet
DAVID GOLDER(1932, Fr.); GOLEM, THE(1937, Czech./Fr.)

Guy Jacquet
RETURN OF MARTIN GUERRE, THE(1983, Fr.)

H. Maurice Jacquet
WHITE ZOMBIE(1932), m

Jeffrey Jacquet
RETURN FROM WITCH MOUNTAIN(1978); WHOLLY MOSES(1980)

Roger Jacquet
WISE GUYS(1969, Fr./Ital.)

Marc Jacquier
TRIAL OF JOAN OF ARC(1965, Fr.)

Abel Jacquin
ANNE-MARIE(1936, Fr.); BETRAYAL(1939, Fr.); ULTIMATUM(1940, Fr.); IT HAPPENED IN GIBRALTAR(1943, Fr.); NIGHTS OF SHAME(1961, Fr.)

Gisele Jacquin
WOMAN OF SIN(1961, Fr.), makeup; SELLERS OF GIRLS(1967, Fr.), makeup

Maurice Jacquin
LAFAYETTE(1963, Fr.), p, w; UPPER HAND, THE(1967, Fr./Ital./Ger.), p

Maurice Jacquin, Jr.
UPPER HAND, THE(1967, Fr./Ital./Ger.)

Jack Jacquine
LA CAGE(1975, Fr.), w

Tony Jacquot
END OF A DAY, THE(1939, Fr.)

George Jadarku
WE OF THE NEVER NEVER(1983, Aus.)

Claude Jade
STOLEN KISSES(1969, Fr.); TOPAZ(1969, Brit.); BED AND BOARD(1971, Fr.); LOVE ON THE RUN(1980, Fr.)

Jimmy Jade
ON THE AIR(1934, Brit.)

Callen Jader
TOO MANY PARENTS(1936)

Chabon Jadi
MOHAWK(1956)

Chebon Jadi
FOXFIRE(1955)

Jadine Wong and Li Sun
AROUND THE WORLD(1943)

Marie Jadoul
GREEN ROOM, THE(1979, Fr.)

Richard Jaeckel
3:10 TO YUMA(1957); GUADALCANAL DIARY(1943); WING AND A PRAYER(1944); JUNGLE PATROL(1948); BATTLEGROUND(1949); CITY ACROSS THE RIVER(1949); SANDS OF IWO JIMA(1949); GUNFIGHTER, THE(1950); WYOMING MAIL(1950); FIGHTING COAST GUARD(1951); SEA HORNET, THE(1951); COME BACK LITTLE SHEBA(1952); HOODLUM EMPIRE(1952); MY SON, JOHN(1952); BIG LEAGUER(1953); SEA OF LOST SHIPS(1953); SHANGHAI STORY, THE(1954); APACHE AMBUSH(1955); VIOLENT MEN, THE(1955); ATTACK!(1956); COWBOY(1958); GUN RUNNERS, THE(1958); LINEUP, THE(1958); NAKED AND THE DEAD, THE(1958); WHEN HELL BROKE LOOSE(1958); FLAMING STAR(1960); GALLANT HOURS, THE(1960); PLATINUM HIGH SCHOOL(1960); TOWN WITHOUT PITY(1961, Ger./Switz./U.S.); FOUR FOR TEXAS(1963); YOUNG AND THE BRAVE, THE(1963); NIGHTMARE IN THE SUN(1964); TOWN TAMER(1965); DIRTY DOZEN, THE(1967, Brit.); ONCE BEFORE I DIE(1967, U.S./Phil.); DEVIL'S BRIGADE, THE(1968); GREEN SLIME, THE(1969); LATITUDE ZERO(1969, U.S./Jap.); CHISUM(1970); SOMETIMES A GREAT NOTION(1971); ULZANA'S RAID(1972); OUTFIT, THE(1973); PAT GARRETT AND BILLY THE KID(1973); CHOSEN SURVIVORS(1974 U.S.-Mex.); DROWNING POOL, THE(1975); WALKING TALL, PART II(1975); GRIZZLY(1976); MAKO: THE JAWS OF DEATH(1976); DAY OF THE ANIMALS(1977); TWILIGHT'S LAST GLEAMING(1977, U.S./Ger.); SPEEDTRAP(1978); DARK, THE(1979); DELTA FOX(1979); HERBIE GOES BANANAS(1980); ...ALL THE MARBLES(1981); AIRPLANE II: THE SEQUEL(1982); COLD RIVER(1982)
1984
STARMAN(1984)
Misc. Talkies
KILL, THE(1973); DEADLY GAME, THE(1974); SURABAYA CONSPIRACY(1975); BLOOD SONG(1982)

Just Jaeckin
LADY CHATTERLEY'S LOVER(1981, Fr./Brit.), d, w
1984
PERILS OF GWENDOLINE, THE(1984, Fr.), d&w

C. K. Jaeger
NAKED HEART, THE(1955, Brit.), w

Cass Jaeger
SHOW BOAT(1951); MY SIX LOVES(1963)

Claude Jaeger
DEVIL AND THE TEN COMMANDMENTS, THE(1962, Fr.), p; DIARY OF A CHAMBERMAID(1964, Fr./Ital.); MALE HUNT(1965, Fr./Ital.), p

Denny Jaeger
HUNGER, THE(1983), m

Ernst Jaeger
DEVIL BAT'S DAUGHTER, THE(1946), w

Frederick Jaeger
BLACK TENT, THE(1956, Brit.); DESERT ATTACK(1958, Brit.); ONE THAT GOT AWAY, THE(1958, Brit.); FAREWELL PERFORMANCE(1963, Brit.); MYSTERY SUBMARINE(1963, Brit.); LIMBO LINE, THE(1969, Brit.); LOOKING GLASS WAR, THE(1970, Brit.); SONG OF NORWAY(1970); SCORPIO(1973); SEVEN-PER-CENT SOLUTION, THE(1977, Brit.); PASSAGE, THE(1979, Brit.); NIJINSKY(1980, Brit.)
Misc. Talkies
SLAUGHTERDAY(1981)

H. Jack Jaeger
HIDE IN PLAIN SIGHT(1980)
Hilde Jaeger
NO TIME FOR FLOWERS(1952)
Inge Jaeger
CABARET(1972)
Kobi Jaeger
SALTY(1975), p
Sigrum Jaeger
BELLA DONNA(1983, Ger.), ed
Susan Jaeger
JUST A GIGOLO(1979, Ger.), ed
Otto Jaegersberg
DIE HAMBURGER KRANKHEIT(1979, Ger./Fr.), w
Tawin Jaengsawang
1 2 3 MONSTER EXPRESS(1977, Thai.)
Kate Jaenicke
ESCAPE FROM EAST BERLIN(1962); TIN DRUM, THE(1979, Ger./Fr./Yugo./Pol.)
Julius Jaenzon
OCEAN BREAKERS(1949, Swed.), ph
Amir Jafari
INVINCIBLE SIX, THE(1970, U.S./Iran)
Parviz Jafari
CARAVANS(1978, U.S./Iranian)
Henry Jaffa
HOLLYWOOD CAVALCADE(1939), cons
Melissa Jaffa
CARS THAT ATE PARIS, THE(1974, Aus,)
Allen Jaffe
FIREBRAND, THE(1962); WAR LORD, THE(1965); PAPILLON(1973)
Carl Jaffe
SECOND BEST BED(1937, Brit.); SAINT IN LONDON, THE(1939, Brit.); GAS-BAGS(1940, Brit.); LAW AND DISORDER(1940, Brit.); LION HAS WINGS, THE(1940, Brit.); MAD MEN OF EUROPE(1940, Brit.); OVER THE MOON(1940, Brit.); NIGHT INVADER, THE(1943, Brit); SQUADRON LEADER X(1943, Brit.); WARN THAT MAN(1943, Brit.); UNCENSORED(1944, Brit.); 2,000 WOMEN(1944, Brit.); COLONEL BLIMP(1945, Brit.); I DIDN'T DO IT(1945, Brit.); MAN FROM MOROCCO, THE(1946, Brit.); BLIND GODDESS, THE(1948, Brit.); SHOWTIME(1948, Brit.); I WAS A MALE WAR BRIDE(1949); DANCING YEARS, THE(1950, Brit.); GREAT MANHUNT, THE(1951, Brit.); LILLI MARLENE(1951, Brit.); TALE OF FIVE WOMEN, A(1951, Brit.); IVANHOE(1952, Brit.); APPOINTMENT IN LONDON(1953, Brit.); DESPERATE MOMENT(1953, Brit.); NORMAN CONQUEST(1953, Brit.); CHILD'S PLAY(1954, Brit.); ATOMIC MAN, THE(1955, Brit.); CROSS CHANNEL(1955, Brit.); PORT OF ESCAPE(1955, Brit.); HOSTAGE, THE(1956, Brit.); SATELLITE IN THE SKY(1956); TRIPLE DECEPTION(1957, Brit.); ACCURSED, THE(1958, Brit.); I ACCUSE(1958, Brit.); MAD LITTLE ISLAND(1958, Brit.); FIRST MAN INTO SPACE(1959, Brit.); SUBWAY IN THE SKY(1959, Brit.); ELECTRONIC MONSTER. THE(1960, Brit.); MAN ON A STRING(1960); MISSILE FROM HELL(1960, Brit.); ROMAN SPRING OF MRS. STONE, THE(1961, U.S./Brit.); DOOMSDAY AT ELEVEN(1963 Brit.); UP JUMPED A SWAGMAN(1965, Brit.); DOUBLE MAN, THE(1967); BATTLE BENEATH THE EARTH(1968, Brit.); FIDDLER ON THE ROOF(1971)
Carol Jaffe
SOPHIE'S CHOICE(1982), set d
Chapelle Jaffe
WHO HAS SEEN THE WIND(1980, Can.); AMATEUR, THE(1982); DEAD ZONE, THE(1983)
Chappelle Jaffe
KIDNAPPING OF THE PRESIDENT, THE(1980, Can.); SILENCE OF THE NORTH(1981, Can.)
Gib Jaffe
1984
BREAKIN'(1984), ed
Herb Jaffe
WIND AND THE LION, THE(1975), p; DEMON SEED(1977), p; WHO'LL STOP THE RAIN?(1978), p; TIME AFTER TIME(1979, Brit.), p; JINXED!(1982), p; LORDS OF DISCIPLINE, THE(1983), p
Howard Jaffe
LAST BLITZKRIEG, THE(1958)
Howard B. Jaffe
REFLECTION OF FEAR, A(1973), p; TAPS(1981), p
Howard P. Jaffe
MAN ON A SWING(1974), p
Jewel Jaffe
TROUBLE WITH ANGELS, THE(1966)
Joan Jaffe
NIGHT THEY ROBBED BIG BERTHA'S, THE(1975)
Karl Jaffe
COUNTER BLAST(1948, Brit.); DEVIL'S PLOT, THE(1948, Brit.)
Mortimer Jaffe
Silents
AMERICAN METHODS(1917)
Nicole Jaffe
TROUBLE WITH GIRLS(AND HOW TO GET INTO IT), THE*1/2 (1969); LOVE BUG, THE(1968); MARLOWE(1969)
Patricia Jaffe
LAST MILE, THE(1959), ed; FOR LOVE OF IVY(1968), ed; TRUMAN CAPOTE'S TRILOGY(1969), ed
Patricia Lewis Jaffe
FRIENDS OF EDDIE COYLE, THE(1973), ed
Robert Jaffe
FUZZ(1972); MAGNIFICENT SEVEN RIDE, THE(1972); DEMON SEED(1977), w; MOTEL HELL(1980), p, w; SCARAB(1982, U.S./Span.), w
Rona Jaffe
BEST OF EVERYTHING, THE(1959), w
Sam Jaffe
VANISHING FRONTIER, THE(1932), p; ACE OF ACES(1933), p; EMERGENCY CALL(1933), p; SCARLET EMPRESS, THE(1934); WE LIVE AGAIN(1934); LOST HORIZON(1937); GUNGA DIN(1939); STAGE DOOR CANTEEN(1943); SULLIVANS, THE(1944), p; 13 RUE MADELEINE(1946); GENTLEMAN'S AGREEMENT(1947); ACCUSED, THE(1949); ROPE OF SAND(1949); ASPHALT JUNGLE, THE(1950); DAY

THE EARTH STOOD STILL, THE(1951); I CAN GET IT FOR YOU WHOLESALE(1951); UNDER THE GUN(1951); BARBARIAN AND THE GEISHA, THE(1958); BEN HUR(1959); DAMON AND PYTHIAS(1962), p; BORN FREE(1966), p; GUIDE FOR THE MARRIED MAN, A(1967); GUNS FOR SAN SEBASTIAN(1968, U.S./Fr./Mex./Ital.); GREAT BANK ROBBERY, THE(1969); DUNWICH HORROR, THE(1970); TARZAN'S JUNGLE REBELLION(1970); BEDKNOBS AND BROOMSTICKS(1971); BATTLE BEYOND THE STARS(1980)
1984
NOTHING LASTS FOREVER(1984); ON THE LINE(1984, Span.)
Shirley Jaffe
TASTE THE BLOOD OF DRACULA(1970, Brit.); CLOCKWORK ORANGE, A(1971, Brit.)
Stanley Jaffe
I START COUNTING(1970, Brit.), p
Stanley R. Jaffe
GOODBYE COLUMBUS(1969), p; BAD COMPANY(1972), p; BAD NEWS BEARS, THE(1976), p; KRAMER VS. KRAMER(1979), p; TAPS(1981), p; WITHOUT A TRACE(1983), p&d
Steven-Charles Jaffe
MOTEL HELL(1980), p, w; THOSE LIPS, THOSE EYES(1980), p; SCARAB(1982, U.S./Span.), d, w
Taliesin Jaffe
MR. MOM(1983)
1984
2010(1984)
Carl Jaffee
CONTINENTAL EXPRESS(1939, Brit.)
Melissa Jaffer
CADDIE(1976, Aus.); RIDE A WILD PONY(1976, U.S./Aus.); WEEKEND OF SHADOWS(1978, Aus.); STARSTRUCK(1982, Aus.)
Herbert Jaffey
MINX, THE(1969), p, w
Madhur Jaffrey
SHAKESPEARE WALLAH(1966, India); GURU, THE(1969, U.S./India); HEAT AND DUST(1983, Brit.)
Saeed Jaffrey
GURU, THE(1969, U.S./India); HORSEMEN, THE(1971); MAN WHO WOULD BE KING, THE(1975, Brit.); WILBY CONSPIRACY, THE(1975, Brit.); CHESS PLAYERS, THE(1978, India); HULLABALOO OVER GEORGIE AND BONNIE'S PICTURES(1979, Brit.); SPHINX(1981); GANDHI(1982)
1984
PASSAGE TO INDIA, A(1984, Brit.); RAZOR'S EDGE, THE(1984)
William Jaffrey
WOMAN CHASES MAN(1937)
Christina Jagaeus
CHILDREN, THE(1949, Swed.)
Paula Jagaeus
CHILDREN, THE(1949, Swed.)
Sime Jagarinac
DESPERADO TRAIL, THE(1965, Ger./Yugo.)
Sime Jagarinas
HIGH ROAD TO CHINA(1983)
Jagdev
NINE HOURS TO RAMA(1963, U.S./Brit.)
Hanns Ernst Jager
CASTLE, THE(1969, Ger.)
Kurt Jager
MIRACLE OF THE WHITE STALLIONS(1963)
Lisa Jager
LAST VALLEY, THE(1971, Brit.)
Lucien Jager
BLOOD OF A POET, THE(1930, Fr.)
Bianca Jagger
AMERICAN SUCCESS COMPANY, THE(1980); CANNONBALL RUN, THE(1981)
Dean Jagger
HANDCUFFED(1929); WHOOPEE(1930); COLLEGE RHYTHM(1934); YOU BELONG TO ME(1934); BEHOLD MY WIFE(1935); CAR 99(1935); HOME ON THE RANGE(1935); MEN WITHOUT NAMES(1935); PEOPLE WILL TALK(1935); WANDERER OF THE WASTELAND(1935); WINGS IN THE DARK(1935); IT'S A GREAT LIFE(1936); PEPPER(1936); REVOLT OF THE ZOMBIES(1936); STAR FOR A NIGHT(1936); THIRTEEN HOURS BY AIR(1936); WOMAN TRAP(1936); DANGEROUS NUMBER(1937); ESCAPE BY NIGHT(1937); EXILED TO SHANGHAI(1937); UNDER COVER OF NIGHT(1937); WOMAN IN DISTRESS(1937); HAVING WONDERFUL TIME(1938); BRIGHAM YOUNG–FRONTIERSMAN(1940); MEN IN HER LIFE, THE(1941); WESTERN UNION(1941); OMAHA TRAIL, THE(1942); VALLEY OF THE SUN(1942); I ESCAPED FROM THE GESTAPO(1943); NORTH STAR, THE(1943); ALASKA(1944); WHEN STRANGERS MARRY(1944); SISTER KENNY(1946); YANK IN LONDON, A(1946, Brit.); DRIFTWOOD(1947); PURSUED(1947); C-MAN(1949); TWELVE O'CLOCK HIGH(1949); DARK CITY(1950); SIERRA(1950); RAWHIDE(1951); WARPATH(1951); DENVER AND RIO GRANDE(1952); IT GROWS ON TREES(1952); MY SON, JOHN(1952); ROBE, THE(1953); EXECUTIVE SUITE(1954); PRIVATE HELL 36(1954); WHITE CHRISTMAS(1954); BAD DAY AT BLACK ROCK(1955); BAR SINISTER, THE(1955); ETERNAL SEA, THE(1955); ON THE THRESHOLD OF SPACE(1956); RED SUNDOWN(1956); BERNARDINE(1957); FORTY GUNS(1957); GREAT MAN, THE(1957); THREE BRAVE MEN(1957); X THE UNKNOWN(1957, Brit.); KING CREOLE(1958); PROUD REBEL, THE(1958); NUN'S STORY, THE(1959); CASH McCALL(1960); ELMER GANTRY(1960); HONEYMOON MACHINE, THE(1961); PARRISH(1961); JUMBO(1962); FIRST TO FIGHT(1967); DAY OF THE EVIL GUN(1968); FIRECREEK(1968); SMITH(1969); KREMLIN LETTER, THE(1970); TIGER BY THE TAIL(1970); VANISHING POINT(1971); SO SAD ABOUT GLORIA(1973); END OF THE WORLD(1977); GAME OF DEATH, THE(1979); ALLIGATOR(1980)
Misc. Talkies
GREAT LESTER BOGGS, THE(1975); GOD BLESS DR. SHAGETZ(1977)
Misc. Silents
WOMAN FROM HELL, THE(1929)
Mick Jagger
NED KELLY(1970, Brit.)

Misc. Talkies
PERFORMANCE(1970, Brit.)

Alan Jaggs
MAXWELL ARCHER, DETECTIVE(1942, Brit.), ed; SUICIDE SQUADRON(1942, Brit.), ed; WINGS AND THE WOMAN(1942, Brit.), spec eff; ALIBI, THE(1943, Brit.), ed; MR. EMMANUEL(1945, Brit.), ed; OCTOBER MAN, THE(1948, Brit.), ed; HER MAN GILBEY(1949, Brit.), ed; CONQUEST OF THE PLANET OF THE APES(1972), ed

Alan L. Jaggs
HUNGRY HILL(1947, Brit.), ed; ESCAPE(1948, Brit.), ed; CARDBOARD CAVALIER, THE(1949, Brit.), ed; TREASURE ISLAND(1950, Brit.), ed; BATTLE FOR THE PLANET OF THE APES(1973), ed

Jagirdar
GUIDE, THE(1965, U.S./India)

Henry Jaglom
PSYCH-OUT(1968); 1,000 PLANE RAID, THE(1969); DRIVE, HE SAID(1971); LAST MOVIE, THE(1971); SAFE PLACE, A(1971), d&w, ed; TRACKS(1977), d&w; SITTING DUCKS(1979), a, d&w; CAN SHE BAKE A CHERRY PIE?(1983), d&w

Jo Jago
GRAND ESCAPADE, THE(1946, Brit.), ph; FORTUNE LANE(1947, Brit.), ph; LAST LOAD, THE(1948, Brit.), ph; MELODY IN THE DARK(1948, Brit.), ph; MERRY-GO-ROUND(1948, Brit.), ph; NOTHING VENTURE(1948, Brit.), ph; BLUE SCAR(1949, Brit.), ph; YOU'RE ONLY YOUNG TWICE(1952, Brit.), ph; SMALL TOWN STORY(1953, Brit.), ph; BURNT EVIDENCE(1954, Brit.), ph; ADVENTURES OF HAL 5, THE(1958, Brit.), ph; BLOW YOUR OWN TRUMPET(1958, Brit.), ph; STOLEN AIRLINER, THE(1962, Brit.), ph

June Jago
CAPTAIN'S TABLE, THE(1960, Brit.); PLEASE TURN OVER(1960, Brit.); BEWARE OF CHILDREN(1961, Brit.); CARRY ON REGARDLESS(1961, Brit.); CARRY ON DOCTOR(1968, Brit.); GAMES, THE(1970); MELODY(1971, Brit.); MAN FROM SNOWY RIVER, THE(1983, Aus.)

Penelope Jago
HOT MILLIONS(1968, Brit.)

Syme Jago
INCREDIBLE JOURNEY, THE(1963)

Marine Jahan
FLASHDANCE(1983)
1984
STREETS OF FIRE(1984)

Jahman
COUNTRYMAN(1982, Jamaica)

Margot Jahn
STOP TRAIN 349(1964, Fr./Ital./Ger.), ed

Stephen Jahn
SAND PEBBLES, THE(1966)

Hakan Jahnberg
SILENCE, THE(1964, Swed.); HAGBARD AND SIGNE(1968, Den./Iceland/Swed.)

Robert Jahne
WINDS OF THE WASTELAND(1936), ed

Margaret Jahnen
QUESTION 7(1961, U.S./Ger.); CAPTAIN SINDBAD(1963); STOP TRAIN 349(1964, Fr./Ital./Ger.)

Edward Jahnke
WARGAMES(1983)

Robert Jahns
CHARLATAN, THE(1929), ed; LAST PERFORMANCE, THE(1929), ed; MURDER ON THE ROOF(1930), ed; LEATHERNECKS HAVE LANDED, THE(1936), ed; BIG SHOW, THE(1937), ed; GOLD RACKET, THE(1937), ed; HARLEM ON THE PRAIRIE(1938), ed; KNIGHT OF THE PLAINS(1939), ed; THAT'S MY BABY(1944), ed, ed; ACCOMPLICE(1946), ed; FRENCH KEY, THE(1946), ed; LIGHTHOUSE(1947), ed; WINTER WONDERLAND(1947), ed; MOVIE STUNTMEN(1953), ed
Silents
STOP THAT MAN(1928), ed

Mieczyslaw Jahoda
KNIGHTS OF THE TEUTONIC ORDER, THE(1962, Pol.), ph; PARTINGS(1962, Pol.), ph; SARAGOSSA MANUSCRIPT, THE(1972, Pol.), ph

Wieczyslaw Jahoda
GATES TO PARADISE(1968, Brit./Ger.), ph

Adolf Jahr
LAUGHING IN THE SUNSHINE(1953, Brit./Swed.)

Don Jahraus
STAND BY FOR ACTION(1942), spec eff; PILOT NO. 5(1943), spec eff

Donald Jahraus
TEST PILOT(1938), spec eff; GUY NAMED JOE, A(1943), spec eff; THIRTY SECONDS OVER TOKYO(1944), spec eff; THIS MAN'S NAVY(1945), spec eff; GREEN YEARS, THE(1946), spec eff

Charles Jahrblum
COUNSEL FOR ROMANCE(1938, Fr.), titles; ROTHSCHILD(1938, Fr.), titles

Howard Jahre
P.O.W., THE(1973)

Jack Jahries
MR. BLANDINGS BUILDS HIS DREAM HOUSE(1948); KNOCK ON ANY DOOR(1949); IN A LONELY PLACE(1950); DOUBLE DYNAMITE(1951)

Jai
TARZAN GOES TO INDIA(1962, U.S./Brit./Switz.)

Ildiko Jaid
NIGHT SHIFT(1982)
1984
IRRECONCILABLE DIFFERENCES(1984)

Panchal Jaikishan
TARZAN GOES TO INDIA(1962, U.S./Brit./Switz.), m

Jaime
NEST, THE(1982, Span.)

Sam Jaimes
BON VOYAGE, CHARLIE BROWN(AND DON'T COME BACK)*** (1980), anim; RACE FOR YOUR LIFE, CHARLIE BROWN(1977), anim

William Jaimison
Silents
CHASER, THE(1928)

Jairaj
NINE HOURS TO RAMA(1963, U.S./Brit.); MAYA(1966)

Nazirali Jairazbnoy
BOOM!(1968), m

Yoshifumi Jajima
GODZILLA VS. THE THING(1964, Jap.)

Lisa Jak
HAMMERSMITH IS OUT(1972)

Gaborne Jakab
WINTER WIND(1970, Fr./Hung.)

Jake
ONCE UPON A COFFEE HOUSE(1965)
1984
UP THE CREEK(1984)

Inge Jaklyn
IN LIKE FLINT(1967)

Pal Jako
WITNESS, THE(1982, Hung.)

Dennis Jakob
PSYCHOPATH, THE(1973), ed

Jost Jakob
ORCA(1977), cos

Rudolf H. Jakob
HAMLET(1962, Ger.), ph

Greti Jakob-Gugger
BLACK SPIDER, THE(1983, Swit.)

August Jakobson
SILVER DUST(1953, USSR), w

Maggie Jakobson
SOUP FOR ONE(1982)

Don Jakoby
BLUE THUNDER(1983), w
1984
PHILADELPHIA EXPERIMENT, THE(1984), w

O. Jakov
SEVEN BRAVE MEN(1936, USSR); CONCENTRATION CAMP(1939, USSR)

M. Jakowitsch
THREE DAYS OF VIKTOR TSCHERNIKOFF(1968, USSR), ph

W. Jakubinska
PORTRAIT OF LENIN(1967, Pol./USSR)

Juro Jakubisko
DESERTER AND THE NOMADS, THE(1969, Czech./Ital.), d, w, ph

Alain Jakubowicz
APPLE, THE(1980 U.S./Ger.), ed; WORLDS APART(1980, U.S., Israel), ed

Wanda Jakubowska
LAST STOP, THE(1949, Pol.), p&d, w; GREAT BIG WORLD AND LITTLE CHILDREN, THE(1962, Pol.), p

Adrienne Jalbert
MINX, THE(1969); SOMETHING SHORT OF PARADISE(1979)
Misc. Talkies
BLUE SEXTET(1972)

Joe Jay Jalbert
DOWNHILL RACER(1969)

Pierre Jalbert
CONCORDE, THE–AIRPORT '79(; SKI BUM, THE(1971); VAN, THE(1977), ed
Misc. Talkies
PETTY STORY, THE(1974)

Renato Jalenti
CHINA IS NEAR(1968, Ital.)

Jabeen Jalil
HOUSEHOLDER, THE(1963, US/India)

Johnnie Jallings
NO WAY OUT(1950)

Romiro Jaloma
HELL'S ISLAND(1955)

Vasa Jalovec
ECSTACY OF YOUNG LOVE(1936, Czech.)

Ahmed A. Jamal
1984
MAJDHAR(1984, Brit.), d&w

Mahmood Jamal
1984
MAJDHAR(1984, Brit.), p

Salah Jamal
TARZAN'S THREE CHALLENGES(1963)

Jamalia
FLASH GORDON(1980)

Francisco Jambrino
LOS OLVIDADOS(1950, Mex.)

Peter Jamerson
BETWEEN US GIRLS(1942)

Thomas Jamerson
FOUL PLAY(1978)

Adrian James
GOD TOLD ME TO(1976)

Alan James
COME ON TARZAN(1933), d&w; DRUM TAPS(1933), w; FARGO EXPRESS(1933), d, w; KING OF THE ARENA(1933), d, w; LONE AVENGER, THE(1933), d, w; PHANTOM THUNDERBOLT, THE(1933), d; STRAWBERRY ROAN(1933), d; GUN JUSTICE(1934), d; HONOR OF THE RANGE(1934), d; SMOKING GUNS(1934), d; TRAIL DRIVE, THE(1934), d&w; WHEN A MAN SEES RED(1934), d&w; ARIZONA TRAILS(1935), d; DESERT MESA(1935), d; LUCKY TERROR(1936), d, w; SWIFTY(1936), d; WILD HORSE ROUND-UP(1937), d; LAND OF FIGHTING MEN(1938), d; TWO-GUN JUSTICE(1938), d; WEST OF RAINBOW'S END(1938), d; TRIGGER SMITH(1939), d; LAW RIDES AGAIN, THE(1943), d; WILD HORSE STAMPEDE(1943), d; MULE TRAIN(1950), w; SILVER CANYON(1951), w
Misc. Talkies
MEN OF ACTION(1935), d; VALLEY OF WANTED MEN(1935), d

Alan James [Alvin J. Neitz]
TOMBSTONE CANYON(1932), d
Albert James
HAREM BUNCH; OR WAR AND PIECE, THE(1969)
Alf James
MADAME RACKETEER(1932); THRILL HUNTER, THE(1933); UNKNOWN VALLEY(1933); FIGHTING CODE, THE(1934); O'SHAUGHNESSY'S BOY(1935)
Alf P. James
HEAVEN ON EARTH(1931); COCKEYED CAVALIERS(1934); ELMER AND ELSIE(1934); ROCKY RHODES(1934)
Alfred P. James
EVERYTHING'S ROSIE(1931); SIX OF A KIND(1934); WONDER BAR(1934); DR. SOCRATES(1935); GREAT ZIEGFELD, THE(1936); NEXT TIME WE LOVE(1936); SINGING COWBOY, THE(1936)
Allan James
TEX TAKES A HOLIDAY(1932), w; WHEELS OF DESTINY(1934), d; CALL OF THE ROCKIES(1938), d
Alphie James
Misc. Silents
SILENT WITNESS, THE(1917)
Anne James
BARBED WIRE(1952); SOUND OFF(1952)
Anneke James
NICKEL QUEEN, THE(1971, Aus.), w
Anthony James
LAST DAYS OF DOLWYN, THE(1949, Brit.); TRAITOR'S GATE(1966, Brit./Ger.); IN THE HEAT OF THE NIGHT(1967); SAM WHISKEY(1969); COMPANY OF KILLERS(1970); ...TICK...TICK...TICK...(1970); VANISHING POINT(1971); CULPEPPER CATTLE COMPANY, THE(1972); HIGH PLAINS DRIFTER(1973); TEACHER, THE(1974); HEARTS OF THE WEST(1975); BURNT OFFERINGS(1976); RETURN FROM WITCH MOUNTAIN(1978); RAVAGERS, THE(1979); NIGHTMARES(1983); WACKO(1983)
Ashton James
CHILDREN OF BABYLON(1980, Jamaica)
Barbara James
PATIENT VANISHES, THE(1947, Brit.); DEMETRIUS AND THE GLADIATORS(1954); TO HELL AND BACK(1955); CAT ATE THE PARAKEET, THE(1972)
Barry James
DANCE OF DEATH, THE(1971, Brit.)
Barton K. James
1984
FOOTLOOSE(1984), cos
Beatrice James
DRUMS O' VOODOO(1934)
Silents
SALAMANDER, THE(1915)
Benedict James
KISSING CUP'S RACE(1930, Brit.), w
Silents
GREAT ADVENTURE, THE(1915, Brit.), w; NEW CLOWN, THE(1916, Brit.), w; UNDER SUSPICION(1919, Brit.), w; KISSING CUP'S RACE(1920, Brit.), w; OTHER PERSON, THE(1921, Brit.), w; SHEER BLUFF(1921), w
Betty James
IMPOSTORS(1979)
Billy James
STREET OF SINNERS(1957); CHRISTIAN LICORICE STORE, THE(1971)
1984
LONELY GUY, THE(1984)
Bob James
SERPICO(1973), md; DANIEL(1983), m
Brian James
ON THE BEACH(1959); ADULTEROUS AFFAIR(1966)
Brion James
HARRY AND WALTER GO TO NEW YORK(1976); NICKELODEON(1976); CORVETTE SUMMER(1978); WHOLLY MOSES(1980); POSTMAN ALWAYS RINGS TWICE, THE(1981); SOUTHERN COMFORT(1981); BLADE RUNNER(1982); 48 HOURS(1982); BALLAD OF GREGORIO CORTEZ, THE(1983)
1984
BREED APART, A(1984)
Carol James
YOUNG WIVES' TALE(1954, Brit.); IT HAPPENED HERE(1966, Brit.); CONVOY(1978), cos
Charity James
GET CRAZY(1983)
Charles James
FOUR FOR TEXAS(1963), cos; YELLOW CANARY, THE(1963), cos
Charles E. James
APOCALYPSE NOW(1979), cos
Chick James
4D MAN(1959)
Christopher James
WINGS OF EAGLES, THE(1957)
Claire James
BLONDIE ON A BUDGET(1940); ROAD TO SINGAPORE(1940); THEY DRIVE BY NIGHT(1940); NAVY BLUES(1941); ZIEGFELD GIRL(1941); VOODOO MAN(1944); ROAD TO UTOPIA(1945); FREDDIE STEPS OUT(1946); VACATION DAYS(1947); ONE TOO MANY(1950); REVOLT OF MAMIE STOVER, THE(1956)
Clare James
SCOTLAND YARD INSPECTOR(1952, Brit.); TWILIGHT WOMEN(1953, Brit.)
Cliff James
LAUGHING POLICEMAN, THE(1973)
Clifton James
STRANGE ONE, THE(1957); LAST MILE, THE(1959); SOMETHING WILD(1961); DAVID AND LISA(1962); EXPERIMENT IN TERROR(1962); BLACK LIKE ME(1964); INVITATION TO A GUNFIGHTER(1964); CHASE, THE(1966); CAPER OF THE GOLDEN BULLS, THE(1967); COOL HAND LUKE(1967); HAPPENING, THE(1967); WILL PENNY(1968); REIVERS, THE(1969); ...TICK...TICK...(1970); WUSA(1970); BISCUIT EATER, THE(1972); NEW CENTURIONS, THE(1972); ICEMAN COMETH, THE(1973); KID BLUE(1973); LAST DETAIL, THE(1973); LIVE AND LET DIE(1973, Brit.); WEREWOLF OF WASHINGTON(1973); BANK SHOT(1974); JUG-

GERNAUT(1974, Brit.); MAN WITH THE GOLDEN GUN, THE(1974, Brit.); RANCHO DELUXE(1975); SILVER STREAK(1976); BAD NEWS BEARS IN BREAKING TRAINING, THE(1977); SUPERMAN II(1980)
Misc. Talkies
BUSTER AND BILLIE(1974)
Dan James
THREE RUSSIAN GIRLS(1943), w
David James
LADY IS WILLING, THE(1942); TAKE A LETTER, DARLING(1942); FRENCHMAN'S CREEK(1944)
Misc. Silents
MADAME BEHAVE(1925)
Delores James
SHEPHERD OF THE HILLS, THE(1964)
Dennis James
MR. UNIVERSE(1951); ONE AND ONLY, THE(1978); ROCKY III(1982)
Diane James
SON OF SINBAD(1955)
Diann James
YOU FOR ME(1952)
Donald James
JOURNEY TO THE FAR SIDE OF THE SUN(1969, Brit.), w; LIMBO LINE, THE(1969, Brit.), w
Dorothy James
CROSS AND THE SWITCHBLADE, THE(1970); BOBBY DEERFIELD(1977); INCHON(1981)
Dudley James
STUDENT TOUR(1934); HAZARD(1948)
E. K. James
Silents
ACCORDING TO LAW(1916)
Eddie James
WAY OUT(1966)
Silents
CHALLENGE OF CHANCE, THE(1919), ph; WILD OATS LANE(1926)
Edward James
YOUNG FUGITIVES(1938), w; LADY FROM LOUISIANA(1941), w; OVER MY DEAD BODY(1942), w; PRIVATE BUCKAROO(1942), w; ADVENTURES OF A ROOKIE(1943), w; HOOSIER HOLIDAY(1943), w; ROOKIES IN BURMA(1943), w; SO THIS IS WASHINGTON(1943), w
Elizabeth James
PEARLS BRING TEARS(1937, Brit.); BORN LOSERS(1967); DIRTY MARY, CRAZY LARRY(1974)
Emrys James
DRAGONSLAYER(1981); GIRO CITY(1982, Brit.); EUREKA(1983, Brit.)
Enid James
MOZART(1940, Brit.); SANCTUARY(1961)
Etta James
SGT. PEPPER'S LONELY HEARTS CLUB BAND(1978)
Forrest James
Misc. Silents
STARK LOVE(1927)
Francis James
MRS. DANE'S DEFENCE(1933, Brit.); LINE ENGAGED(1935, Brit.); LABURNUM GROVE(1936, Brit.); WHO GOES NEXT?(1938, Brit.)
Frank James
NOTORIOUS CLEOPATRA, THE(1970)
Frankie James
Silents
CALL FROM THE WILD, THE(1921)
Franklin James
LIEUTENANT WORE SKIRTS, THE(1956)
Freddie James
SKI BUM, THE(1971)
Frederick James
HUMANOIDS FROM THE DEEP(1980), w
Gardner James
STUDIO MURDER MYSTERY, THE(1929); DAWN PATROL, THE(1930); DANTE'S INFERNO(1935); CRASH DONOVAN(1936)
Silents
AMATEUR GENTLEMAN, THE(1926); GILDED HIGHWAY, THE(1926); NIGHT PATROL, THE(1926); EAGER LIPS(1927); LADIES AT EASE(1927); SOULS AFLAME(1928); FLYING FEET, THE(1929)
Misc. Silents
SILENT SANDERSON(1925); UNRESTRAINED YOUTH(1925); FLAMING FOREST, THE(1926); HELL-BENT FOR HEAVEN(1926); PASSIONATE QUEST, THE(1926); SINGAPORE MUTINY, THE(1928)
Gavin James
MR. BILLION(1977); NIGHT CROSSING(1982)
Gennie James
1984
PLACES IN THE HEART(1984)
Gerald James
MAN WITH THE GOLDEN GUN, THE(1974, Brit.)
Geraldine James
SWEET WILLIAM(1980, Brit.); GANDHI(1982)
Gertie James
CHEATING BLONDES(1933), w
Ginger James
LOOKING UP(1977)
Gladden James
HIS CAPTIVE WOMAN(1929); WEARY RIVER(1929); PARADISE ISLAND(1930); LUCKY DEVILS(1933); JEALOUSY(1934); MAGNIFICENT OBSESSION(1935); PUBLIC HERO NO. 1(1935); IT HAD TO HAPPEN(1936); PRINCESS COMES ACROSS, THE(1936); CAPTAINS COURAGEOUS(1937); LOVE IS NEWS(1937); THREE SMART GIRLS(1937); TOAST OF NEW YORK, THE(1937); WRONG ROAD, THE(1937); TEST PILOT(1938); MADE FOR EACH OTHER(1939); PIRATES OF THE SKIES(1939); TELL NO TALES(1939); EARL OF CHICAGO, THE(1940); MARYLAND(1940); STRANGER ON THE THIRD FLOOR(1940); LIFE BEGINS FOR ANDY HARDY(1941); STREET OF CHANCE(1942); HENRY ALDRICH PLAYS CUPID(1944); WILSON(1944); WEEKEND

AT THE WALDORF(1945); NIGHT AND DAY(1946); STRANGE LOVE OF MARTHA IVERS, THE(1946)

Silents

WISE HUSBANDS(?); SYLVIA GRAY(1914); AS IN A LOOKING GLASS(1916); SOCIAL SECRETARY, THE(1916); BABBLING TONGUES(1917); SILVER LINING, THE(1921); MARRY IN HASTE(1924); WEDDING SONG, THE(1925); ADORABLE CHEAT, THE(1928); DRIFTIN' SANDS(1928); SWEET SIXTEEN(1928); PEACOCK FAN(1929)

Misc. Silents

DECOY, THE(1916); FATHER AND SON(1916); WHAT HAPPENED AT 22(1916); QUESTION, THE(1917); TENTH CASE, THE(1917); HEARTS OF LOVE(1918); SAFETY CURTAIN, THE(1918); HEART OF WETONA, THE(1919); IN HONOR'S WEB(1919); THIRD DEGREE, THE(1919); THOU SHALT NOT(1919); KEEP TO THE RIGHT(1920); MIDNIGHT BRIDE, THE(1920); YES OR NO?(1920); BUCKING THE TIGER(1921); FOOTFALLS(1921); CHANNING OF THE NORTHWEST(1922); FAITHLESS SEX, THE(1922); CLOUDED NAME, A(1923); ALIAS MARY FLYNN(1925); TEX(1926); GIRL HE DIDN'T BUY, THE(1928); HOUND OF THE SILVER CREEK, THE(1928)

Gladden M. James

I WANTED WINGS(1941)

Godfrey James

SEANCE ON A WET AFTERNOON(1964 Brit.); AMOROUS MR. PRAWN, THE(1965, Brit.); CONQUEROR WORM, THE(1968, Brit.); OBLONG BOX, THE(1969, Brit.); CRY OF THE BANSHEE(1970, Brit.); PRIVATE LIFE OF SHERLOCK HOLMES, THE(1970, Brit.); VILLAIN(1971, Brit.); LAND THAT TIME FORGOT, THE(1975, Brit.); AT THE EARTH'S CORE(1976, Brit.)

Gordon James

TONS OF MONEY(1931, Brit.); THARK(1932, Brit.); CUCKOO IN THE NEST, THE(1933, Brit.); SUMMER LIGHTNING(1933, Brit.); CUP OF KINDNESS, A(1934, Brit.); DIRTY WORK(1934, Brit.); FOREIGN AFFAIRES(1935, Brit.); STORMY WEATHER(1935, Brit.); CLOWN MUST LAUGH, A(1936, Brit.); POT LUCK(1936, Brit.); FOR VALOR(1937, Brit.); SECOND BEST BED(1937, Brit.); SPOT OF BOTHER, A(1938, Brit.); SALOON BAR(1940, Brit.); YOUNG MR. PITT, THE(1942, Brit.)

Graham James

HORROR OF FRANKENSTEIN, THE(1970, Brit.); VAMPIRE LOVERS, THE(1970, Brit.); BLOOD FROM THE MUMMY'S TOMB(1972, Brit.)

Harrison James

ABDUCTION(1975), w

Harry James

PRIVATE BUCKAROO(1942), md; SYNCOPATION(1942); DO YOU LOVE ME?(1946); IF I'M LUCKY(1946); CARNEGIE HALL(1947); ON OUR MERRY WAY(1948); I'LL GET BY(1950); BENNY GOODMAN STORY, THE(1956); OPPOSITE SEX, THE(1956); LADIES MAN(1961); STING II, THE(1983)

Misc. Talkies

OUTLAW QUEEN(1957)

William H. James

DESERTER, THE(1971 Ital./Yugo.), w

Henry James

LOST MOMENT, THE(1947), w; HEIRESS, THE(1949), w; INNOCENTS, THE(1961, U.S./Brit.), w; NIGHT COMERS, THE(1971, Brit.), w; DAISY MILLER(1974), w; EUROPEANS, THE(1979, Brit.), w; GREEN ROOM, THE(1979, Fr.), w

1984

BOSTONIANS, THE(1984), w

Silents

RAMSHACKLE HOUSE(1924)

Henry C. James

SPITFIRE(1943, Brit.), w; LATE AT NIGHT(1946, Brit.), w; SWISS HONEY-MOON(1947, Brit.), d; NICKEL QUEEN, THE(1971, Aus.), w

Horace James

GUNS AT BATASI(1964, Brit.); LOST CONTINENT, THE(1968, Brit.)

Silents

ADAM AND EVA(1923)

Hugh James

Misc. Talkies

NIGHT CARGOES(1963)

Ida James

POCOMANIA(1939); TROCADERO(1944); HI-DE-HO(1947)

Idell James

HUSH... HUSH, SWEET CHARLOTTE(1964); RED LINE 7000(1965)

Inez James

PENTHOUSE RHYTHM(1945), m

Irene James

KING AND I, THE(1956); NATCHEZ TRACE(1960)

Iris James

SITTING PRETTY(1948)

Ivor James

YOUNG MAN WITH A HORN(1950)

J. Frank James

SWEET CREEK COUNTY WAR, THE(1979), p, d&w

J. Randolph James

Silents

RED PEARLS(1930, Brit.), w

J. Wharton James

Silents

POLLYANNA(1920); MYSTERIOUS WITNESS, THE(1923)

Jack James

BLUE SCAR(1949, Brit.)

Jackie James

1984

OVER THE BROOKLYN BRIDGE(1984)

Jason James

DEVIL'S CARGO, THE(1948), w; FURY AT SHOWDOWN(1957), w; VAMPIRE CIRCUS(1972, Brit.)

Jean James

Misc. Talkies

RED ROSES OF PASSION(1967)

Jeri Lou James

GLASS WEB, THE(1953)

Jerry James

DIXIE(1943); LET'S FACE IT(1943); PRACTICALLY YOURS(1944); AFFAIRS OF SUSAN(1945); LOST WEEKEND, THE(1945); MISS SUSIE SLAGLE'S(1945); BLUE DAHLIA, THE(1946); O.S.S.(1946); DREAM GIRL(1947); TROUBLE WITH WOMEN, THE(1947); VARIETY GIRL(1947); NIGHT HAS A THOUSAND EYES(1948); CHICAGO DEADLINE(1949); FILE ON THELMA JORDAN, THE(1950); UNION STATION(1950); WHERE DANGER LIVES(1950); HIS KIND OF WOMAN(1951); MY FAVORITE SPY(1951); SUBMARINE COMMAND(1951); CARRIE(1952); TURNING POINT, THE(1952); PONY EXPRESS(1953); WAR OF THE WORLDS, THE(1953); FLIGHT THAT DISAPPEARED, THE(1961); HOUSE IS NOT A HOME, A(1964); ROUSTABOUT(1964); PSYCHIC KILLER(1975)

Jessica James

HEAVEN WITH A GUN(1969); SO FINE(1981); DINER(1982); I, THE JURY(1982); SOUP FOR ONE(1982); EASY MONEY(1983); SPRING BREAK(1983)

Jim James

MANHATTAN MELODRAMA(1934)

Jimmy James

OVER THE GARDEN WALL(1950, Brit.); THOSE PEOPLE NEXT DOOR(1952, Brit.); CONQUEROR WORM, THE(1968, Brit.), set d

Jo Frances James

JESSE JAMES(1939), w

Joe James

DEMONSTRATOR(1971, Aus.); SCOBIE MALONE(1975, Aus.)

John James

MURDER BY INVITATION(1941); OUTLAWS OF THE CHEROKEE TRAIL(1941); WEST OF CIMARRON(1941); CYCLONE KID, THE(1942); FLYING TIGERS(1942); MY FAVORITE SPY(1942); SOMBRERO KID, THE(1942); WESTWARD HO(1942); GUNG HO!(1943); MAN FROM THUNDER RIVER, THE(1943); RIDERS OF THE RIO GRANDE(1943); SANTA FE SCOUTS(1943); THIS IS THE ARMY(1943); THUNDERING TRAILS(1943); WE'VE NEVER BEEN LICKED(1943); HIDDEN VALLEY OUTLAWS(1944); I'LL BE SEEING YOU(1944); LARAMIE TRAIL, THE(1944); PRACTICALLY YOURS(1944); ANCHORS AWEIGH(1945); BEDSIDE MANNER(1945); GREAT STAGECOACH ROBBERY(1945); OVER 21(1945); RENEGADES OF THE RIO GRANDE(1945); RIDERS OF THE DAWN(1945); DEVIL BAT'S DAUGHTER, THE(1946); PARTNERS IN TIME(1946); HOMESTEADERS OF PARADISE VALLEY(1947); RIDIN' DOWN THE TRAIL(1947); SONG OF THE WASTELAND(1947); WILD FRONTIER, THE(1947); COUNTESS OF MONTE CRISTO, THE(1948); OUTLAW BRAND(1948); RANGE RENEGADES(1948); TAP ROOTS(1948); VALIANT HOMBRE, THE(1948); GAL WHO TOOK THE WEST, THE(1949); GUN LAW JUSTICE(1949); SON OF BILLY THE KID(1949); TOPEKA(1953); VIGILANTE TERROR(1953)

Misc. Talkies

LONESOME TRAIL(1945); SADDLE SERENADE(1945)

John A. James

SINCE YOU WENT AWAY(1944)

Joseph James

PRIEST OF LOVE(1981, Brit.), m

Josephine James

PLEASE, NOT NOW!(1963, Fr./Ital.); WRECKING CREW, THE(1968)

Joycelyn James

BEGGAR'S OPERA, THE(1953)

Juliette James

TIME BANDITS(1981, Brit.)

Keith James

DUTCHMAN(1966, Brit.); OPERATION DAYBREAK(1976, U.S./Brit./Czech.)

Ken James

LAST GUNFIGHTER, THE(1961, Can.); CROWD INSIDE, THE(1971, Can.); WHY ROCK THE BOAT?(1974, Can.); BREAKING POINT(1976); "EQUUS"(1977); BLOOD AND GUTS(1978, Can.); CITY ON FIRE(1979 Can.); SUMMER'S CHILDREN(1979, Can.); CREEPER, THE(1980, Can.); PLUMBER, THE(1980, Aus.), art d; SILENCE OF THE NORTH(1981, Can.); THRESHOLD(1983, Can.)

1984

HIGHPOINT(1984, Can.)

Kent James

LONG GOODBYE, THE(1973), cos

Kyle James

DUEL AT SILVER CREEK, THE(1952); HELLGATE(1952); ARROWHEAD(1953); DONOVAN'S BRAIN(1953)

Laura James

LOSIN' IT(1983)

Lawrence James

MIX ME A PERSON(1962, Brit.); PSYCHO-CIRCUS(1967, Brit.)

Lee James

RED, WHITE AND BLACK, THE(1970); JUD(1971)

Misc. Talkies

FROZEN SCREAM(1980)

Lefty James

Silents

BIG TOWN IDEAS(1921); LIVE WIRES(1921)

Leon James

CABIN IN THE SKY(1943)

Linda James

1984

ADERYN PAPUR(1984, Brit.), p

Lisa James

TWO TICKETS TO PARIS(1962); NECROMANCY(1972); DIFFERENT STORY, A(1978)

Lois James

STRIKE UP THE BAND(1940)

Loren James

SONS OF KATIE ELDER, THE(1965)

Luther James

WHO'S MINDING THE MINT?(1967)

M. E. Clifton James

HELL, HEAVEN OR HOBOKEN(1958, Brit.), a, w

Marie James

Misc. Silents

HEART OF TARA, THE(1916)

Marijo James
MALE ANIMAL, THE(1942); YANKEE DOODLE DANDY(1942)
Melinda James
YOICKS!(1932, Brit.), set d
Mike James
WARRIORS, THE(1979)
Montague R. James
CURSE OF THE DEMON(1958), w
Olga James
CARMEN JONES(1954); VAMPIRE LOVERS, THE(1970, Brit.)
Oscar James
GUMSHOE(1972, Brit.); PRESSURE(1976, Brit.); BLACK JOY(1977, Brit.); JAGUAR LIVES(1979); STUDENT BODIES(1981)
1984
LAST NIGHT AT THE ALAMO(1984)
P.D. James
UNSUITABLE JOB FOR A WOMAN, AN(1982, Brit.), w
Penton James
JONIKO AND THE KUSH TA KA(1969)
Peter James
INNOCENTS, THE(1961, U.S./Brit.), set d; RISK, THE(1961, Brit.), set d; LOLITA(1962), set d; TERM OF TRIAL(1962, Brit.), set d; MODEL MURDER CASE, THE(1964, Brit.), set d; PUMPKIN EATER, THE(1964, Brit.), set d; SEANCE ON A WET AFTERNOON(1964 Brit.), set d; PLEASURE GIRLS, THE(1966, Brit.), set d; WRONG BOX, THE(1966, Brit.), set d; FAR FROM THE MADDING CROWD(1967, Brit.), set d; WHISPERERS, THE(1967, Brit.), set d; LION IN WINTER, THE(1968, Brit.), set d; OH! WHAT A LOVELY WAR(1969, Brit.), set d; DULCIMA(1971, Brit.), set d; RECKONING, THE(1971, Brit.), set d; STRAW DOGS(1971, Brit.), set d; YOUNG WINSTON(1972, Brit.), set d; MACKINTOSH MAN, THE(1973, Brit.), set d; NIGHT WATCH(1973, Brit.), set d; CADDIE(1976, Aus.), ph; EAGLE HAS LANDED, THE(1976, Brit.), set d; SEVEN-PER-CENT SOLUTION, THE(1977, Brit.), set d; CARAVANS(1978, U.S./Iranian), art d; IRISHMAN(1978, Aus.), ph; ROUGH CUT(1980, Brit.), set d; KILLING OF ANGEL STREET, THE(1983, Aus.), ph; WILD DUCK, THE(1983, Aus.), ph; YELLOWBEARD(1983), set d
Peter S. James
FLASH GORDON(1980)
Polly James
MRS. PARKINGTON(1944), w; RAIDERS, THE(1952), w; REDHEAD FROM WYOMING, THE(1953), w; QUANTRILL'S RAIDERS(1958), w
Rachel Nicholas James
NIGHTHAWKS(1978, Brit.)
Ralph James
FRASIER, THE SENSUOUS LION(1973); BIG BAD MAMA(1974); CRAZY MAMA(1975); TIDAL WAVE(1975, U.S./Jap.); FAST CHARLIE... THE MOONBEAM RIDER(1979)
Misc. Talkies
LOONEY, LOONEY, LOONEY BUGS BUNNY MOVIE, THE(1981)
Raymond James
GIRL ON THE PIER, THE(1953, Brit.)
Rian James
CROONER(1932), w; HAT CHECK GIRL(1932), w; LOVE IS A RACKET(1932), w; BEST OF ENEMIES(1933), d; CENTRAL AIRPORT(1933), w; LAWYER MAN(1933), w; MARY STEVENS, M.D.(1933), w; PARACHUTE JUMPER(1933), w; PRIVATE DETECTIVE 62(1933), w; SHE HAD TO SAY YES(1933), w; 42ND STREET(1933), w; BEDSIDE(1934), w; BIG SHAKEDOWN, THE(1934), w; DRAGON MURDER CASE, THE(1934), w; GIFT OF GAB(1934), a, w; WHITE PARADE, THE(1934), w; IT HAPPENED IN NEW YORK(1935), w; REDHEADS ON PARADE(1935), w; TO BEAT THE BAND(1935), w; WE'RE ONLY HUMAN(1936), w; WITNESS CHAIR, THE(1936), w; EXCLUSIVE(1937), w; INTERNES CAN'T TAKE MONEY(1937), w; SUBMARINE PATROL(1938), w; GORILLA, THE(1939), w; HOUSEKEEPER'S DAUGHTER(1939), w; DOWN ARGENTINE WAY(1940), w; TURNABOUT(1940), w; BROADWAY LIMITED(1941), w; PARACHUTE NURSE(1942), w; THIS TIME FOR KEEPS(1942), w; EVE KNEW HER APPLES(1945), w; WHISPERING CITY(1947, Can.), w; DEAD RINGER(1964), w
Richard James
RAW EDGE(1956); ONE MILLION YEARS B.C.(1967, Brit./U.S.); LOCAL HERO(1983, Brit.), art d; SILKWOOD(1983), art d
Robert James
BRIDAL PATH, THE(1959, Brit.); TWO-WAY STRETCH(1961, Brit.); LOVE BUG, THE(1968); SPEEDWAY(1968); MARY, QUEEN OF SCOTS(1971, Brit.)
Misc. Talkies
MAN OUTSIDE(1965)
Rodney James
RAGTIME(1981)
Roger James
GAMEKEEPER, THE(1980, Brit.), ed
Ron James
BOOGEY MAN, THE(1980); BOOGEYMAN II(1983); STRANGE BREW(1983)
Rosamond James
MAN FROM OKLAHOMA, THE(1945)
Rosemonde James
SECRETS OF A SORORITY GIRL(1946)
Roy James
THERE GOES MY GIRL(1937); WE'RE ON THE JURY(1937); OVERLAND STAGE RAIDERS(1938)
Sally James
RAILWAY CHILDREN, THE(1971, Brit.)
Samuel H. James
Misc. Talkies
GO DOWN DEATH(1944)
Sandra James
SECRET INVASION, THE(1964), makeup
Sheila James
SEVEN BRIDES FOR SEVEN BROTHERS(1954); TEENAGE REBEL(1956)
Shirley James
LIAR'S DICE(1980)
Sidney James
HELL, HEAVEN OR HOBOKEN(1958, Brit.); BLACK MEMORY(1947, Brit.); NIGHT BEAT(1948, Brit.); NO ORCHIDS FOR MISS BLANDISH(1948, Brit.); HOUR OF GLORY(1949, Brit.); PAPER ORCHID(1949, Brit.); SALT TO THE DEVIL(1949, Brit.);

LADY CRAVED EXCITEMENT, THE(1950, Brit.); LAST HOLIDAY(1950, Brit.); MAN IN BLACK, THE(1950, Brit.); GALLOPING MAJOR, THE(1951, Brit.); LAVENDER HILL MOB, THE(1951, Brit.); MANIACS ON WHEELS(1951, Brit.); FATHER'S DOING FINE(1952, Brit.); GLORY AT SEA(1952, Brit.); MAGIC BOX, THE(1952, Brit.); MISS ROBIN HOOD(1952, Brit.); YOU CAN'T BEAT THE IRISH(1952, Brit.); ASSASSIN, THE(1953, Brit.); BAD BLONDE(1953, Brit.); HUNDRED HOUR HUNT(1953, Brit.); I BELIEVE IN YOU(1953, Brit.); IS YOUR HONEYMOON REALLY NECESSARY?(1953, Brit.); NORMAN CONQUEST(1953, Brit.); SLASHER, THE(1953, Brit.); TIME GENTLEMEN PLEASE!(1953, Brit.); TITFIELD THUNDERBOLT, THE(1953, Brit.); WEDDING OF LILLI MARLENE, THE(1953, Brit.); AUNT CLARA(1954, Brit.); CREST OF THE WAVE(1954, Brit.); CROWDED DAY, THE(1954, Brit.); DETECTIVE, THE(1954, Qit.); ESCAPE BY NIGHT(1954, Brit.); FOR BETTER FOR WORSE(1954, Brit.); HEATWAVE(1954, Brit.); RAINBOW JACKET, THE(1954, Brit.); WEAK AND THE WICKED, THE(1954, Brit.); DEEP BLUE SEA, THE(1955, Brit.); GLASS TOMB, THE(1955, Brit.); JOE MACBETH(1955); LADY GODIVA RIDES AGAIN(1955, Brit.); SQUARE RING, THE(1955, Brit.); WILL ANY GENTLEMAN?(1955, Brit.); YANK IN ERMINE, A(1955, Brit.); DRY ROT(1956, Brit.); EXTRA DAY, THE(1956, Brit.); IRON PETTICOAT, THE(1956, Brit.); IT'S A GREAT DAY(1956, Brit.); KID FOR TWO FARTHINGS, A(1956, Brit.); RAMSBOTTOM RIDES AGAIN(1956, Brit.); TRAPEZE(1956); CAMPBELL'S KINGDOM(1957, Brit.); JOHN AND JULIE(1957, Brit.); KING IN NEW YORK, A(1957, Brit.); OUT OF THE CLOUDS(1957, Brit.); PICKUP ALLEY(1957, Brit.); PORTRAIT IN SMOKE(1957, Brit.); SHIRALEE, THE(1957, Brit.); SMALLEST SHOW ON EARTH, THE(1957, Brit.); STORY OF ESTHER COSTELLO, THE(1957, Brit.); ANOTHER TIME, ANOTHER PLACE(1958); HELL DRIVERS(1958, Brit.); MAN INSIDE, THE(1958, Brit.); SHERIFF OF FRACTURED JAW, THE(1958, Brit.); IDOL ON PARADE(1959, Brit.); ORDERS ARE ORDERS(1959, Brit.); SILENT ENEMY, THE(1959, Brit.); TOO MANY CROOKS(1959, Brit.); AND THE SAME TO YOU(1960, Brit.); CARRY ON CONSTABLE(1960, Brit.); DESERT MICE(1960, Brit.); NEXT TO NO TIME(1960, Brit.); THIRTY NINE STEPS, THE(1960, Brit.); TOMMY THE TOREADOR(1960, Brit.); CARRY ON REGARDLESS(1961, Brit.); DOUBLE BUNK(1961, Brit.); GREEN HELMET, THE(1961, Brit.); PURE HELL OF ST. TRINIAN'S, THE(1961, Brit.); UPSTAIRS AND DOWNSTAIRS(1961, Brit.); WATCH YOUR STERN(1961, Brit.); WEEKEND WITH LULU, A(1961, Brit.); WHAT A WHOPPER(1961, Brit.); CARRY ON CRUISING(1962, Brit.); ROOMMATES(1962, Brit.); WE JOINED THE NAVY(1962, Brit.); WHAT A CARVE UP!(1962, Brit.); CARRY ON CABBIE(1963, Brit.); CARRY ON CLEO(1964, Brit.); BIG JOB, THE(1965); MAKE MINE A MILLION(1965, Brit.); THREE HATS FOR LISA(1965, Brit.); CARRY ON COWBOY(1966, Brit.); WHERE THE BULLETS FLY(1966, Brit.); DON'T LOSE YOUR HEAD(1967, Brit.); CARRY ON DOCTOR(1968, Brit.); CARRY ON, UP THE KHYBER(1968, Brit.); CARRY ON AGAIN, DOCTOR(1969, Brit.); CARRY ON CAMPING(1969, Brit.); CARRY ON HENRY VIII(1970, Brit.); CARRY ON LOVING(1970, Brit.); CARRY ON UP THE JUNGLE(1970, Brit.)
Misc. Talkies
BLESS THIS HOUSE(1972, Brit.); CARRY ON 'ROUND THE BEND(1972, Brit.); CARRY ON MATRON(1973, Brit.); TOKOLOSHE(1973); CARRY ON ABROAD(1974, Brit.); CARRY ON GIRLS(1974, Brit.); CARRY ON BEHIND(1975, Brit.); CARRY ON DICK(1975, Brit.)
Sonny James
SECOND FIDDLE TO A STEEL GUITAR(1965); LAS VEGAS HILLBILLYS(1966); NASHVILLE REBEL(1966); HILLBILLYS IN A HAUNTED HOUSE(1967)
Stanley James
RAINBOW BOYS, THE(1973, Can.)
Steve James
LAND THAT TIME FORGOT, THE(1975, Brit.); EXTERMINATOR, THE(1980); MOUSE AND THE WOMAN, THE(1981, Brit.); SOLDIER, THE(1982)
1984
BROTHER FROM ANOTHER PLANET, THE(1984)
Steve W. James
HE KNOWS YOU'RE ALONE(1980); TIMES SQUARE(1980)
Steven James
WARRIORS, THE(1979)
Stewart James
SMILIN' THROUGH(1932), w
Stuart James
COME SPY WITH ME(1967), w
Misc. Talkies
TEXAS RAMBLER, THE(1935)
Susan Saint James
JIGSAW(1968); OUTLAW BLUES(1977)
Sydney James
FRIGHTENED BRIDE, THE(1952, Brit.); YELLOW BALLOON, THE(1953, Brit.); ENEMY FROM SPACE(1957, Brit.)
Synthia James
EMMA MAE(1976)
Terry James
ECHOES OF A SUMMER(1976), m
Tiffany James
WOMEN OF DESIRE(1968)
Tim James
WANDA NEVADA(1979)
Tina James
Misc. Talkies
ABAR-THE FIRST BLACK SUPERMAN(1977)
Valerie James
DOCTOR FAUSTUS(1967, Brit.)
Van A. James
Silents
WASTED LIVES(1925), w
Vera James
Misc. Silents
MCGUIRE OF THE MOUNTED(1923)
Victoria James
MOMMIE DEAREST(1981)
Walter James
HELL'S HEROES(1930); SHADOW OF THE LAW(1930); SCAREHEADS(1931); STREET SCENE(1931); MODERN TIMES(1936); OH, SUSANNA(1937); THIS IS MY AFFAIR(1937); CONVICTS AT LARGE(1938), w; PROFESSOR BEWARE(1938); ETERNALLY YOURS(1939); INVISIBLE STRIPES(1940); PANTHER'S CLAW, THE(1942)

Silents
IDOL DANCER, THE(1920); SECRETS OF PARIS, THE(1922); LITTLE ANNIE ROONEY(1925); MONSTER, THE(1925); BATTLING BUTLER(1926); IRRESISTIBLE LOVER, THE(1927); KID BROTHER, THE(1927)

Misc. Silents
GLENISTER OF THE MOUNTED(1926); BLOOD SHIP, THE(1927); WRIGHT IDEA, THE(1928)

Warren James
SCAVENGERS, THE(1969)

Wharton James
Silents
ALMOST MARRIED(1919); CALL FROM THE WILD, THE(1921), a, p,d&w

Will James
SMOKY(1933), a, w; LONE COWBOY(1934), w; SMOKY(1946), w; SAND(1949), w; SMOKY(1966), w; SHOOT OUT(1971), w

William James
Silents
LOVE FLOWER, THE(1920)

James Brown and the Famous Flames
SKI PARTY(1965)

The James Gang
ZACHARIAH(1971)

James Haake and Scamp
TO BE OR NOT TO BE(1983)

James Never Miss A Shot
MAN CALLED HORSE, A(1970)

James White and the Blacks
UNDERGROUND U.S.A.(1980), m

Cyndi James-Reese
VICE SQUAD(1982)

Barry Jamesby
1984
ALLEY CAT(1984)

Adair Jameson
DEAR BRIGETTE(1965); SMOKE IN THE WIND(1975)

Ann Jameson
BOY FRIEND, THE(1971, Brit.); SEVERED HEAD, A(1971, Brit.)

Bud Jameson
GRAND PARADE, THE(1930)

Buster Jameson
COUNTRYMAN(1982, Jamaica)

Conrad Jameson
PINOCCHIO IN OUTER SPACE(1965, U.S./Bel.); PLAYGROUND, THE(1965)

House Jameson
NAKED CITY, THE(1948); PARRISH(1961); MIRAGE(1965); SWIMMER, THE(1968)

Jack Jameson
MRS. PYM OF SCOTLAND YARD(1939, Brit.)

Jerry Jameson
DIRT GANG, THE(1972), d; BAT PEOPLE, THE(1974), d; AIRPORT '77(1977), d; RAISE THE TITANIC(1980, Brit.), d
Misc. Talkies
BRUTE CORPS(1972), d

Joyce Jameson
SHOW BOAT(1951); SON OF DR. JEKYLL, THE(1951); STRIP, THE(1951); PROBLEM GIRLS(1953); PHFFFT!(1954); GANG BUSTERS(1955); CRIME AGAINST JOE(1956); TIP ON A DEAD JOCKEY(1957); APARTMENT, THE(1960); TALES OF TERROR(1962); BALCONY, THE(1963); COMEDY OF TERRORS, THE(1964); GOOD NEIGHBOR SAM(1964); BOY, DID I GET A WRONG NUMBER!(1966); SPLIT, THE(1968); COMPANY OF KILLERS(1970); OUTLAW JOSEY WALES, THE(1976); SCORCHY(1976)
1984
HARDBODIES(1984)

Jesse James, Jr.
Silents
JESSE JAMES AS THE OUTLAW(1921); JESSE JAMES UNDER THE BLACK FLAG(1921); JESSE JAMES(1927), w

Leslie Jameson
TRACK OF THUNDER(1967)

Michael Jameson
FIVE WILD GIRLS(1966, Fr.)

Pauline Jameson
QUEEN OF SPADES(1948, Brit.); MANIACS ON WHEELS(1951, Brit.); BLACK KNIGHT, THE(1954); MILLIONAIRESS, THE(1960, Brit.); CROOKS ANONYMOUS(1963, Brit.); DOCTOR IN DISTRESS(1963, Brit.); I COULD GO ON SINGING(1963); PUNCH AND JUDY MAN, THE(1963, Brit.); MURDER MOST FOUL(1964, Brit.); TWO LIVING, ONE DEAD(1964, Brit./Swed.); GYPSY GIRL(1966, Brit.); NIGHT WATCH(1973, Brit.); FULL CIRCLE(1977, Brit./Can.); HAUNTING OF JULIA, THE(1981, Brit./Can.)

Susan Jameson
I, MONSTER(1971, Brit.)

Frederique Jamet
MAN WHO LOVED WOMEN, THE(1977, Fr.)

Nicole Jamet
POURQUOI PAS!(1979, Fr.)
1984
HEAT OF DESIRE(1984, Fr.)

The Jamez
PICKUP ON 101(1972), ed

Jamie Hilliard & the Countrymen
WHEN YOU COMIN' BACK, RED RYDER?(1979)

Bud Jamieson
MELODY OF THE PLAINS(1937)
Silents
PLAY SAFE(1927); TEXAS STEER, A(1927); HEART TROUBLE(1928)

Harold Jamieson
TREASURE ISLAND(1950, Brit.); CRUEL SEA, THE(1953); LISBON(1956)

Hazel Jamieson
DANGEROUS WATERS(1936), w; REFORM SCHOOL(1939), w

Silents
DREAM MELODY, THE(1929), w

Ian Jamieson
MAN FROM HONG KONG(1975); MONEY MOVERS(1978, Aus.), spec eff

John Jamieson
SECRET OF THE LOCH, THE(1934, Brit.)

Lachlan Jamieson
STONE(1974, Aus.)

Malcolm Jamieson
VICTOR/VICTORIA(1982)

Peter Jamieson
CRYSTAL BALL, THE(1943)

Richard Jamieson
ON THE YARD(1978); CRUISING(1980)

Rev. Robert H. Jamieson
DAMN CITIZEN(1958)

Joudi Mohammed Jamil
THIEF OF BAGHDAD, THE(1961, Ital./Fr.)

Georges Jamin
DAUGHTERS OF DARKNESS(1971, Bel./ Fr./ Ger./ Ital.); JE T'AIME, JE T'AIME(1972, Fr./Swed.)

Milt Jamin
WRONG IS RIGHT(1982); TO BE OR NOT TO BE(1983)

Adair Jamison
CAIN'S WAY(1969)

Bill Jamison
STARDUST ON THE SAGE(1942)

Brad Jamison
1984
REPO MAN(1984)

Bud Jamison
TRUE TO LIFE(1943); MAKE ME A STAR(1932); WONDER BAR(1934); IN PERSON(1935); FUGITIVE SHERIFF, THE(1936); HEROES OF THE RANGE(1936); LAWLESS RIDERS(1936); TICKET TO PARADISE(1936); PAID TO DANCE(1937); SHADOW, THE(1937); I AM THE LAW(1938); THERE'S ALWAYS A WOMAN(1938); LONE WOLF SPY HUNT, THE(1939); CAPTAIN CAUTION(1940); LI'L ABNER(1940); LITTLE MEN(1940); SLIGHTLY HONORABLE(1940); MONSTER AND THE GIRL, THE(1941); JOAN OF OZARK(1942); TRAMP, TRAMP, TRAMP(1942); YOUTH ON PARADE(1943); LOUISIANA HAYRIDE(1944); MRS. PARKINGTON(1944)
Silents
DANTE'S INFERNO(1924); JAKE THE PLUMBER(1927)

Mrs. C.V. Jamison
RAINBOW ON THE RIVER(1936), w

Cheri Jamison
SOUP FOR ONE(1982)

Chuck Jamison
Misc. Talkies
STRAIGHT JACKET(1980)

Earl Jamison
ROSE BOWL(1936)

Francine Jamison
1984
FLETCH(1984), cos

Joyce Jamison
1984
LOVELINES(1984)

Mikki Jamison
BEACH BALL(1965); SKI PARTY(1965)

Peter Jamison
BIG BAD MAMA(1974), art d; PHANTOM OF THE PARADISE(1974), cos; CRAZY MAMA(1975), art d; DARKTOWN STRUTTERS(1976), art d; EAT MY DUST!(1976), art d; MOONSHINE COUNTY EXPRESS(1977), art d; EVIL, THE(1978), art d; I WANNA HOLD YOUR HAND(1978), art d; OLD BOYFRIENDS(1979), art d; ALL NIGHT LONG(1981), prod d; CONTINENTAL DIVIDE(1981), prod d; CHILLY SCENES OF WINTER(1982), prod d; HALLOWEEN III: SEASON OF THE WITCH(1982), prod d; MISSING(1982), prod d
1984
BEST DEFENSE(1984), prod d; MIKE'S MURDER(1984), prod d; SWING SHIFT(1984), prod d

Peter M. Jamison
USED CARS(1980), prod d

Richard Jamison
DUCHESS AND THE DIRTWATER FOX, THE(1976); OVER THE EDGE(1979)

Mikki Jamison-Olsen
SEA GYPSIES, THE(1978)

Armand Jammot
TOMORROW IS MY TURN(1962, Fr./Ital./Ger.), w

Franco Jamonte
SWORD OF THE CONQUEROR(1962, Ital.)

Joe Jamrog
YOU BETTER WATCH OUT(1980)
1984
MUPPETS TAKE MANHATTAN, THE(1984)

Leos Jan
DON'S PARTY(1976, Aus.), m

Paulette Jan
ANTOINE ET ANTOINETTE(1947 Fr.)

Jan & Kelly
IT'S ALL OVER TOWN(1963, Brit.)

Jan Garber and His Band
HERE COMES ELMER(1943)

Jan Garber Orchestra
SO'S YOUR UNCLE(1943); JAM SESSION(1944); SWEETHEARTS OF THE U.S.A.(1944)

Jan Savitt and His Top Hatters
THAT'S MY GAL(1947)

Jan Savitt Orchestra Featuring Isabelita
HIGH SCHOOL HERO(1946)

Jaromir Janacek
SHOP ON MAIN STREET, THE(1966, Czech.), ed
Leos Janacek
HAUNTING OF M, THE(1979), m
Christian Janakiev
WATERLOO(1970, Ital./USSR)
Helmut Janatsch
NO TIME FOR FLOWERS(1952); ELUSIVE CORPORAL, THE(1963, Fr.); MIRACLE OF THE WHITE STALLIONS(1963); GREAT WALTZ, THE(1972)
Helmuth Janatsch
SECRET WAYS, THE(1961)
Richard Janaver
ONE PLUS ONE(1961, Can.)
Camille Janclaire
THREE STRIPES IN THE SUN(1955)
Miklos Jancso
BOYS OF PAUL STREET, THE(1969, Hung./US); RED AND THE WHITE, THE(1969, Hung./USSR), d, w; ROUND UP, THE(1969, Hung.), d; WINTER WIND(1970, Fr./Hung.), d, w; ROME WANTS ANOTHER CAESAR(1974, Ital.), d, w
Miklos Jancso, Jr.
1984
DIARY FOR MY CHILDREN(1984, Hung.), ph
Andrew Janczak
NO RETURN ADDRESS(1961), ph; UNDERTAKER AND HIS PALS, THE(1966), ph
Krzysztof Janczar
MAN OF IRON(1981, Pol.)
Tadeusz Janczar
KANAL(1961, Pol.); PARTINGS(1962, Pol.)
Krystana Janda
BELLA DONNA(1983, Ger.)
Krystyna Janda
MAN OF MARBLE(1979, Pol.); GOLEM(1980, Pol.); CONDUCTOR, THE(1981, Pol.); MAN OF IRON(1981, Pol.); MEPHISTO(1981, Ger.); WAR OF THE WORLDS–NEXT CENTURY, THE(1981, Pol.)
Vitezslav Jandek
OPERATION DAYBREAK(1976, U.S./Brit./Czech.)
Ivan Jandl
SEARCH, THE(1948)
Bucky Jandrich
LOOSE ENDS(1975)
Jane
SUBWAY RIDERS(1981)
Baby Jane
ALIAS MARY DOW(1935); PORKY'S II: THE NEXT DAY(1983)
Margot Jane
YOURS, MINE AND OURS(1968)
Mary Jane
MALAY NIGHTS(1933)
Peggy Jane
Silents
PENROD(1922)
Sybil Jane
HOUND OF THE BASKERVILLES(1932, Brit.); LUCKY SWEEP, A(1932, Brit.)
Topsy Jane
LONELINESS OF THE LONG DISTANCE RUNNER, THE(1962, Brit.); MIX ME A PERSON(1962, Brit.)
Jane and Dotty
SING WHILE YOU'RE ABLE(1937)
Alan Janes
1984
WINTER FLIGHT(1984, Brit.), w
Elizabeth Janes
Silents
SOUL OF YOUTH, THE(1920)
Misc. Silents
LURE OF LUXURY, THE(1918)
Ellen Janes
HARRY AND WALTER GO TO NEW YORK(1976)
H. Hurford Janes
REVENGE OF FRANKENSTEIN, THE(1958, Brit.), w
Harold Janes
Silents
CONFLICT, THE(1921), ph; REPUTATION(1921), ph
Loren Janes
SAND PEBBLES, THE(1966); WILD, WILD WINTER(1966); KING'S PIRATE(1967); WHAT'S UP, DOC?(1972); GOIN' SOUTH(1978); FORCE: FIVE(1981)
Keith Janess
UNMAN, WITTERING AND ZIGO(1971, Brit.)
Janine Janet
TESTAMENT OF ORPHEUS, THE(1962, Fr.), cos
Pierre Janet
GHOST GUNS(1944), ed; LAW OF THE VALLEY(1944), ed; RETURN TO CAMPUS(1975), ph
Elizabeth Janeway
DAISY KENYON(1947), w
Alain Janey
HERBIE GOES TO MONTE CARLO(1977)
1984
AMERICAN DREAMER(1984)
Kook-jin Jang
MARINE BATTLEGROUND(1966, U.S/S.K.), w
Jerry Janger
RUMBLE ON THE DOCKS(1956); 27TH DAY, THE(1957)
Jani-Z
OCTOPUSSY(1983, Brit.)
Jean-Pierre Janic
OSS 117–MISSION FOR A KILLER(1966, Fr./Ital.); CONFESSION, THE(1970, Fr.)

Nikola Janic
MONTENEGRO(1981, Brit./Swed.)
Dusan Janicijevic
RAMPAGE AT APACHE WELLS(1966, Ger./Yugo.); FLAMING FRONTIER(1968, Ger./Yugo.)
Joelle Janin
NUDE IN HIS POCKET(1962, Fr.)
Janina
SAVE THE TIGER(1973)
Bob Janis
SIERRA BARON(1958)
Conrad Janis
SNAFU(1945); MARGIE(1946); BRASHER DOUBLOON, THE(1947); THAT HAGEN GIRL(1947); BEYOND GLORY(1948); LET'S ROCK(1958); AIRPORT 1975(1974); HAPPY HOOKER, THE(1975); DUCHESS AND THE DIRTWATER FOX, THE(1976); ROSELAND(1977); BUDDY HOLLY STORY, THE(1978); OH GOD! BOOK II(1980)
Dorothy Janis
PAGAN, THE(1929); LUMMOX(1930)
Silents
KIT CARSON(1928); OVERLAND TELEGRAPH, THE(1929)
Misc. Silents
FLEETWING(1928); PAGAN, THE(1929)
Edward Janis
BEACH GIRLS AND THE MONSTER, THE(1965), p
Elsie Janis
CLOSE HARMONY(1929), w; MADAME SATAN(1930), w; REACHING FOR THE MOON(1931), w; SQUAW MAN, THE(1931), w; WOMEN IN WAR(1940)
Silents
CAPRICES OF KITTY, THE(1915), a, w; MADCAP BETTY(1915), a, w; NEARLY A LADY(1915), a, w; OH, KAY(1928), w
Misc. Silents
TWAS EVER THUS(1915); REGULAR GIRL, A(1919); IMP, THE(1920)
Gail Janis
TASTE OF BLOOD, A(1967)
Ursula Janis
HOUSE OF 1,000 DOLLS(1967, Ger./Span./Brit.)
Vivi Janis
PHANTOM FROM 10,000 LEAGUES, THE(1956)
Michael Janisch
MIRACLE OF THE WHITE STALLIONS(1963); GIRL FROM PETROVKA, THE(1974)
Vivi Janiss
KANSAS CITY CONFIDENTIAL(1952); SPRING REUNION(1957)
Chas Jankel
UNSUITABLE JOB FOR A WOMAN, AN(1982, Brit.), m
James Jankins
BRIDGES AT TOKO-RI, THE(1954)
Linda LeRoy Janklow
STILL OF THE NIGHT(1982)
Stole Jankovic
Misc. Talkies
HELL RIVER(1977), d
Gustav Jankovsky
LEMONADE JOE(1966, Czech.)
Rotislav Jankowski
WATERLOO(1970, Ital./USSR)
Si Janks
REVEILLE WITH BEVERLY(1943)
Walter Jankulm
BECAUSE I LOVED YOU(1930, Ger.)
Francisco Janmandreu
FRANKENSTEIN'S BLOODY TERROR(1968, Span.), ed
Gerald Jann
CONFESSIONS OF AN OPIUM EATER(1962); DIMENSION 5(1966); RED TOMAHAWK(1967); LOVE BUG, THE(1968)
1984
BEST DEFENSE(1984)
Enzo Jannacci
LA NUIT DE VARENNES(1983, Fr./Ital.)
1984
JOKE OF DESTINY LYING IN WAIT AROUND THE CORNER LIKE A STREETBANDIT, A(1984, Ital.)
Angelo Jannarelli
MONTE CASSINO(1948, Ital.), ph
Julie Janney
POPEYE(1980)
Leon Janney
COURAGE(1930); DOORWAY TO HELL(1930); OLD ENGLISH(1930); FATHER'S SON(1931); PENROD AND SAM(1931); FAME STREET(1932); LAST MILE, THE(1959); CHARLY(1968)
Misc. Talkies
STOLEN PARADISE(1941)
Russell Janney
MIRACLE OF THE BELLS, THE(1948), w
Sam Janney
LOOSE ANKLES(1930), w
Silents
LADIES AT PLAY(1926), w
William Janney
COQUETTE(1929); MEXICALI ROSE(1929); SALUTE(1929); DAWN PATROL, THE(1930); GIRL SAID NO, THE(1930); PAY OFF, THE(1930); SHOOTING STRAIGHT(1930); THOSE WHO DANCE(1930); YOUNG DESIRE(1930); CIMARRON(1931); GIRLS DEMAND EXCITEMENT(1931); MEET THE WIFE(1931); RIGHT OF WAY, THE(1931); CROONER(1932); MAN WHO PLAYED GOD, THE(1932); MOUTHPIECE, THE(1932); SUCCESSFUL CALAMITY, A(1932); TWO SECONDS(1932); UNDER-COVER MAN(1932); CRIME OF THE CENTURY, THE(1933); IRON MASTER, THE(1933); SECRET OF THE BLUE ROOM(1933); SHOULD LADIES BEHAVE?(1933); TERROR ABOARD(1933); WORLD CHANGES, THE(1933); AS THE EARTH TURNS(1934); KING OF THE WILD HORSES, THE(1934); MODERN HERO, A(1934); SUCCESSFUL FAILURE, A(1934); BONNIE SCOTLAND(1935); BORN TO GAMBLE(1935); GREAT HOTEL MURDER(1935); SWEEPSTAKE ANNIE(1935);

HOPALONG CASSIDY RETURNS(1936); PENTHOUSE PARTY(1936); SITTING ON THE MOON(1936); SUTTER'S GOLD(1936); CLIPPED WINGS(1938)

Joseph Janni
GLASS MOUNTAIN, THE(1950, Brit), p, w; HONEYMOON DEFERRED(1951, Brit.), p; SOMETHING MONEY CAN'T BUY(1952, Brit.), p; WHITE CORRIDORS(1952, Brit.), p; ROMEO AND JULIET(1954, Brit.), p; ROBBERY UNDER ARMS(1958, Brit.), p; TOWN LIKE ALICE, A(1958, Brit.), p; CAPTAIN'S TABLE, THE(1960, Brit.), p; SAVAGE INNOCENTS, THE(1960, Brit.), p; KIND OF LOVING, A(1962, Brit.), p; BILLY LIAR(1963, Brit.), p; DARLING(1965, Brit.), p, w; MODESTY BLAISE(1966, Brit.), p; FAR FROM THE MADDING CROWD(1967, Brit.), p; POOR COW(1968, Brit.), p; IN SEARCH OF GREGORY(1970, Brit./Ital.), p; SUNDAY BLOODY SUNDAY(1971, Brit.), p; MADE(1972, Brit.), p; DEAF SMITH AND JOHNNY EARS(1973, Ital.), p; YANKS(1979), p

Pierre Jannic
1984
CHEECH AND CHONG'S THE CORSICAN BROTHERS(1984), set d

Hans Jannig
REBEL, THE(1933, Ger.)

Carrie Jannings
CYNTHIA(1947)

Emil Jannings
PATRIOT, THE(1928); SINS OF THE FATHERS(1928); BLUE ANGEL, THE(1930, Ger.); TEMPEST(1932, Ger.); DREAMER, THE(1936, Ger.)
Silents
PASSION(1920, Ger.); LAST LAUGH, THE(1924, Ger.); VARIETY(1925, Ger.); FAUST(1926, Ger.); TARTUFFE(1927, Ger.); WAY OF ALL FLESH, THE(1927); LAST COMMAND, THE(1928); STREET OF SIN, THE(1928)
Misc. Silents
ALGOL(1920, Ger.); ALL FOR A WOMAN(1921, Ger.); VENDETTA(1921, Ger.); OTHELLO(1922, Ger.); WIFE OF THE PHARAOH, THE(1922, Ger.); PETER THE GREAT(1923, Ger.); TRAGEDY OF LOVE(1923, Ger.); QUO VADIS?(1925, Ital.); SINS OF THE FATHER(1928); BETRAYAL(1929)

Gordon Jannings
ROPE OF SAND(1949), spec eff

Orin Jannings
MR. SOFT TOUCH(1949), w; FORCE OF ARMS(1951), w; SHE'S BACK ON BROADWAY(1953), w; TIME TO LOVE AND A TIME TO DIE, A(1958), w; GENE KRUPA STORY, THE(1959), w

Vivi Jannis
MAN ON THE PROWL(1957)

Vittorio Jannitti
FAREWELL TO ARMS, A(1957)

Toni Jannotta
SCARED TO DEATH(1981)

Else Jannsen
DILLINGER(1945)

Werner Jannssen
UNCLE VANYA(1958), m

Lano Jannuzzi
RE: LUCKY LUCIANO(1974, Fr./Ital.), w

Vaszary Janos
I MARRIED AN ANGEL(1942), w

Victor Janos
LAST HOUSE ON DEAD END STREET(1977), d
Misc. Talkies
FUN HOUSE, THE(1977), d

Veronique Janot
FRENCH POSTCARDS(1979)

Ellen Janov
HORSE IN THE GRAY FLANNEL SUIT, THE(1968)

Michael Janover
HARDLY WORKING(1981), w
1984
PHILADELPHIA EXPERIMENT, THE(1984), w

Walter Janovitz
BILLY THE KID VS. DRACULA(1966)

Hans Janowitz
Silents
CABINET OF DR. CALIGARI, THE(1921, Ger.), w

Walter Janowitz
36 HOURS(1965); FRISCO KID, THE(1979); JAZZ SINGER, THE(1980); JEKYLL AND HYDE...TOGETHER AGAIN(1982)

Alice Jans
GOLD DIGGERS OF 1933(1933); LITTLE GIANT, THE(1933); PICTURE SNATCHER(1933); 42ND STREET(1933)

Harry Jans
CHARLIE CHAN AT THE RACE TRACK(1936); DON'T TURN'EM LOOSE(1936); GRAND JURY(1936); LAST OUTLAW, THE(1936); MURDER ON A BRIDLE PATH(1936); SMARTEST GIRL IN TOWN(1936); SPECIAL INVESTIGATOR(1936); TWO IN REVOLT(1936); RACING LADY(1937); THAT GIRL FROM PARIS(1937)

Jansen
SEVEN CAPITAL SINS(1962, Fr./Ital.), m

Adolf Jansen
ARIANE(1931, Ger.), ph; M(1933, Ger.), w; M(1951), w

Allan Jansen
WOMEN OF DESIRE(1968), ph

Corinne Jansen
FRENCH CANCAN(1956, Fr.); PARIS DOES STRANGE THINGS(1957, Fr./Ital.)

Harry A. Jansen
A-HAUNTING WE WILL GO(1942)

Janus Billeskov Jansen
1984
ZAPPA(1984, Den.), ed

Jim Jansen
SO FINE(1981); TOOTSIE(1982)
1984
BEST DEFENSE(1984)

Noortje Jansen
1984
QUESTION OF SILENCE(1984, Neth.)

Nora Jansen
Silents
MODERN SALOME, A(1920), w

Paul Jansen
TRUE STORY OF ESKIMO NELL, THE(1975, Aus.)

Per Jansen
1984
KAMILLA(1984, Norway)

Pierre Jansen
LANDRU(1963, Fr./Ital), m; THIRD LOVER, THE(1963, Fr./Ital.), m; OPHELIA(1964, Fr.), m; BEAUTIFUL SWINDLERS, THE(1967, Fr./Ital./Jap./Neth.), m; CHAMPAGNE MURDERS, THE(1968, Fr.), m; LES BICHES(1968, Fr.), m; LA FEMME INFIDELE(1969, Fr./Ital.), m; THIS MAN MUST DIE(1970, Fr./Ital.), m; WHO'S GOT THE BLACK BOX?(1970, Fr./Gr./Ital.), m; LE BOUCHER(1971, Fr./Ital.), m; DOCTEUR POPAUL(1972, Fr.), m; TEN DAYS' WONDER(1972, Fr.), m; JUST BEFORE NIGHTFALL(1975, Fr./Ital.), m; DIRTY HANDS(1976, Fr/Ital./Ger.), m; ALICE, OR THE LAST ESCAPADE(1977, Fr.), m; LACEMAKER, THE(1977, Fr.), m; VIOLETTE(1978, Fr.), m; HORSE OF PRIDE(1980, Fr.), m

Victor Jansen
Misc. Silents
THOU SHALT NOT STEAL(1929, Ger.), d

Wolfgang Jansen
SECRET OF SANTA VITTORIA, THE(1969)

Michael Jansich
GOOD SOLDIER SCHWEIK, THE(1963, Ger.)

Ladislav Jansky
DIAMONDS OF THE NIGHT(1968, Czech.); MATTER OF DAYS, A(1969, Fr./Czech.)

Frank Janson
CHILD, THE(1977)

Horst Janson
ESCAPE FROM EAST BERLIN(1962); GLASS OF WATER, A(1962, Cgr.); MOONWOLF(1966, Fin./Ger.); MC KENZIE BREAK, THE(1970); YOU CAN'T WIN 'EM ALL(1970, Brit.); MURPHY'S WAR(1971, Brit.); CAPTAIN KRONOS: VAMPIRE HUNTER(1974, Brit.); SHOUT AT THE DEVIL(1976, Brit.)

Victor Janson
Misc. Silents
OYSTER PRINCESS, THE(1919, Ger.)

Alexandre Janssen
LOVE ON THE RUN(1980, Fr.)

David Janssen
SWAMP FIRE(1946); BONZO GOES TO COLLEGE(1952); FRANCIS GOES TO WEST POINT(1952); NO ROOM FOR THE GROOM(1952); YANKEE BUCCANEER(1952); CHIEF CRAZY HORSE(1955); CULT OF THE COBRA(1955); FRANCIS IN THE NAVY(1955); PRIVATE WAR OF MAJOR BENSON, THE(1955); SQUARE JUNGLE, THE(1955); TO HELL AND BACK(1955); FRANCIS IN THE HAUNTED HOUSE(1956); GIRL HE LEFT BEHIND, THE(1956); NEVER SAY GOODBYE(1956); SHOWDOWN AT ABILENE(1956); TOY TIGER(1956); LAFAYETTE ESCADRILLE(1958); HELL TO ETERNITY(1960); DONDI(1961); KING OF THE ROARING TWENTIES–THE STORY OF ARNOLD ROTHSTEIN(1961); MAN-TRAP(1961); RING OF FIRE(1961); TWENTY PLUS TWO(1961); MY SIX LOVES(1963); WARNING SHOT(1967); GREEN BERETS, THE(1968); SHOES OF THE FISHERMAN, THE(1968); GENERATION(1969); MAROONED(1969); WHERE IT'S AT(1969); MACHO CALLAHAN(1970); ONCE IS NOT ENOUGH(1975); SWISS CONSPIRACY, THE(1976, U.S./Ger.); TWO-MINUTE WARNING(1976); GOLDEN RENDEZVOUS(1977); COVERT ACTION(1980, Ital.); INCHON(1981)
Misc. Talkies
BELLE SOMMERS(1962); WARHEAD(1974)

Eileen Janssen
RENEGADES(1946); ON OUR MERRY WAY(1948); BUCKAROO SHERIFF OF TEXAS(1951); ABOUT MRS. LESLIE(1954)

Eilene Janssen
SINCE YOU WENT AWAY(1944); 'TILL WE MEET AGAIN(1944); TWO GIRLS AND A SAILOR(1944); GREEN YEARS, THE(1946); RENDEZVOUS 24(1946); SONG OF LOVE(1947); WHO KILLED "DOC" ROBBIN?(1948); BOY WITH THE GREEN HAIR, THE(1949); ARIZONA MANHUNT(1951); DAKOTA KID, THE(1951); WILD HORSE AMBUSH(1952); SEARCH FOR BRIDEY MURPHY, THE(1956); ESCAPE FROM RED ROCK(1958); BLACK ZOO(1963); PANIC IN THE CITY(1968)

Elois Janssen
MAN WHO CHEATED HIMSELF, THE(1951), cos

Eloise Janssen
DIPLOMATIC COURIER(1952), cos

Elsa Janssen
JOURNAL OF A CRIME(1934); WEDNESDAY'S CHILD(1934); DRACULA'S DAUGHTER(1936); IT COULD HAPPEN TO YOU(1937); PRESCRIPTION FOR ROMANCE(1937); THIN ICE(1937); COMMANDOS STRIKE AT DAWN, THE(1942); HITLER'S CHILDREN(1942); PRIDE OF THE YANKEES, THE(1942); CLAUDIA(1943); HIS BUTLER'S SISTER(1943); SO PROUDLY WE HAIL(1943); THEY CAME TO BLOW UP AMERICA(1943); 3 IS A FAMILY(1944); CLAUDIA AND DAVID(1946)

Else Janssen
GREAT LOVER, THE(1931); GORGEOUS HUSSY, THE(1936); SONG OF LOVE(1947)

Janken Janssen
1984
GERMANY PALE MOTHER(1984, Ger.), cos

Jean-Paul Janssen
TIGHT SKIRTS, LOOSE PLEASURES(1966, Fr.)

Jean-Pierre Janssen
TIGHT SKIRTS, LOOSE PLEASURES(1966, Fr.)

Jill Janssen
SO BIG(1953); NEVER SAY GOODBYE(1956)

Kathryn Janssen
1984
GHOSTBUSTERS(1984)

Kitty Janssen
Misc. Talkies
LOVE COMES QUIETLY(1974)

Rex Janssen
HAWMPS!(1976)
Teri Janssen
KING OF THE ROARING TWENTIES–THE STORY OF ARNOLD ROTH-STEIN(1961); TWENTY PLUS TWO(1961)
Walter Janssen
MASTER OF THE WORLD(1935, Ger.); DECISION BEFORE DAWN(1951); HANSEL AND GRETEL(1965, Ger.), d; SOMETHING FOR EVERYONE(1970)
Misc. Silents
BEYOND THE RIVER(1922, Ger.); PETER THE GREAT(1923, Ger.)
Walther Janssen
Misc. Silents
DESTINY(1921, Ger.)
Werner Janssen
GENERAL DIED AT DAWN, THE(1936), m; BLOCKADE(1938), m; ETERNALLY YOURS(1939), m; WINTER CARNIVAL(1939), m&md; HOUSE ACROSS THE BAY, THE(1940), m, md; SLIGHTLY HONORABLE(1940), m; GUEST IN THE HOUSE(1944), m; SOUTHERNER, THE(1945), m; NIGHT IN CASABLANCA, A(1946), m; RUTHLESS(1948), m
William Janssen
FOLLOW THE SUN(1951); SEMINOLE(1953)
William A. Janssen
HOODLUM SAINT, THE(1946)
Gun Jansson
BRINK OF LIFE(1960, Swed.)
Walther Jansson
MOZART STORY, THE(1948, Aust.)
Azemat Janti
27TH DAY, THE(1957)
David Janti
MR. SARDONICUS(1961)
Mark Jantzen
1984
JOHNNY DANGEROUSLY(1984)
Maureen Jantzen
SEND ME NO FLOWERS(1964)
Paul Jantzen
DARK OF THE SUN(1968, Brit.)
January
MISSISSIPPI(1935)
Lois January
BY CANDLELIGHT(1934); EMBARRASSING MOMENTS(1934); HUMAN SIDE, THE(1934); LET'S BE RITZY(1934); ARIZONA BADMAN(1935); SOCIETY FE-VER(1935); SPLENDOR(1935); STOLEN HARMONY(1935); BORDER CABAL-LERO(1936); LIGHTNING BILL CARSON(1936); ONE RAINY AFTERNOON(1936); BAR Z BAD MEN(1937); COURAGE OF THE WEST(1937); LIGHTNIN' CRAN-DALL(1937); MOONLIGHT ON THE RANGE(1937); RED ROPE, THE(1937); ROAM-ING COWBOY, THE(1937); ROGUE OF THE RANGE(1937); TRUSTED OUTLAW, THE(1937); SKULL AND CROWN(1938); LIFE RETURNS(1939); LITTLE SHEPHERD OF KINGDOM COME(1961)
Misc. Talkies
COCAINE FIENDS(1937)
Bengt Janus
OPERATION LOVEBIRDS(1968, Den.), w
Phyllis Janus
STRANGER IN HOLLYWOOD(1968)
Joseph Janusaitis
DON QUIXOTE(1973, Aus.)
Lala Janvier
PALACE OF NUDES(1961, Fr./Ital.), makeup
Joelle Jany
LE PLAISIR(1954, Fr.)
Andy Janzack
TERROR IN THE JUNGLE(1968), ph
Iva Janzurova
FIFTH HORSEMAN IS FEAR, THE(1968, Czech.); CASTLE, THE(1969, Ger.); I KILLED EINSTEIN, GENTLEMEN(1970, Czech.); SIR, YOU ARE A WIDOWER(1971, Czech.)
Michael Japher
DOMINIQUE(1978, Brit.)
Japp the Dog
REUNION(1932, Brit.)
Sebastian Japrisot
FAREWELL, FRIEND(1968, Fr./Ital.), w; RIDER ON THE RAIN(1970, Fr./Ital.), w
Sebastien Japrisot
SLEEPING CAR MURDER THE(1966, Fr.), w; LADY IN THE CAR WITH GLASSES AND A GUN, THE(1970, U.S./Fr.), w; AND HOPE TO DIE(1972 Fr/US), w
1984
ONE DEADLY SUMMER(1984, Fr.), w
Roland Jaquarello
1984
GIVE MY REGARDS TO BROAD STREET(1984, Brit.)
Christian Jaque
PEARLS OF THE CROWN(1938, Fr.), d; CARMEN(1946, Ital.), d; DAUGHTERS OF DESTINY(1954, Fr./Ital.), d; BABETTE GOES TO WAR(1960, Fr.), d
Christian Jaques
BELLMAN, THE(1947, Fr.), d
Sandra Jaques
LITTLE AUSTRALIANS(1940, Aus.)
David Jaquest
PHOBIA(1980, Can.), art d
Frank Jaquet
UNCLE HARRY(1945); MANNEQUIN(1937); CRIME SCHOOL(1938); MARIE AN-TOINETTE(1938); MY LUCKY STAR(1938); STRANGE FACES(1938); TEST PI-LOT(1938); WHEN WERE YOU BORN?(1938); DUST BE MY DESTINY(1939); ETERNALLY YOURS(1939); MR. SMITH GOES TO WASHINGTON(1939); STANLEY AND LIVINGSTONE(1939); THEY SHALL HAVE MUSIC(1939); DISPATCH FROM REUTERS, A(1940); DOUBLE TROUBLE(1941); FATHER TAKES A WIFE(1941); MEET JOHN DOE(1941); NO GREATER SIN(1941); REDHEAD(1941); ICE-CAPADES REVUE(1942); MAGNIFICENT DOPE, THE(1942); TALES OF MANHATTAN(1942);

TENNESSEE JOHNSON(1942); CORREGIDOR(1943); SOMEONE TO REMEM-BER(1943); BOWERY CHAMPS(1944); CALL OF THE SOUTH SEAS(1944); CHARLIE CHAN IN BLACK MAGIC(1944); NONE SHALL ESCAPE(1944); THIN MAN GOES HOME, THE(1944); BELL FOR ADANO, A(1945); EVE KNEW HER APPLES(1945); GRISSLY'S MILLIONS(1945); OREGON TRAIL(1945); SANTA FE SAD-DLEMATES(1945); TRAIL TO VENGEANCE(1945); VAMPIRE'S GHOST, THE(1945); BARBARY PIRATE(1949); DARING CABALLERO, THE(1949); MUTINEERS, THE(1949); RIDERS IN THE SKY(1949); SHOCKPROOF(1949); NO WAY OUT(1950); OVER THE BORDER(1950); ACCORDING TO MRS. HOYLE(1951); BIG CARNIVAL, THE(1951); SCARF, THE(1951); O. HENRY'S FULL HOUSE(1952); OPERATION SECRET(1952); HOUDINI(1953); WINNING OF THE WEST(1953)
Gaston Jaquet
BARRANCO(1932, Fr.)
Nicole Jaquet
EVERY MAN FOR HIMSELF(1980, Fr.)
Morris Jar
CONQUEROR WORM, THE(1968, Brit.)
Maurice Jara
CRISIS(1950); LAWLESS, THE(1950); FLYING LEATHERNECKS(1951); PALS OF THE GOLDEN WEST(1952); FIGHTER ATTACK(1953); NEBRASKAN, THE(1953); SECOND CHANCE(1953); TAKE THE HIGH GROUND(1953); TROPIC ZONE(1953); JUBILEE TRAIL(1954); THEY RODE WEST(1954); GIANT(1956); WALK THE PROUD LAND(1956); LONE RANGER AND THE LOST CITY OF GOLD, THE(1958); THEY CAME TO CORDURA(1959)
Sergio Jara
1984
ERENDIRA(1984, Mex./Fr./Ger.), spec eff
Anna Jaraczowna
PASSENGER, THE(1970, Pol.)
Han Jaray
AFFAIRS OF MAUPASSANT(1938, Aust.)
Hans Jaray
FEDORA(1978, Ger./Fr.)
Bruce Jarchow
MY BODYGUARD(1980); CONTINENTAL DIVIDE(1981)
Herbert Jarczk
CAVE OF THE LIVING DEAD(1966, Yugo./Ger.), m
Herbert Jarczyk
PHONY AMERICAN, THE(1964, Ger.), m
Alan Jardin
GIRLS ON THE BEACH(1965)
Pascal Jardin
DEAD RUN(1961, Fr./Ital./Ger.), w; DEVIL AND THE TEN COMMANDMENTS, THE(1962, Fr.), w; MIDNIGHT FOLLY(1962, Fr.), w; ADORABLE JULIA(1964, Fr./Aust.), w; JOY HOUSE(1964, Fr.), w; MONSIEUR(1964, Fr.), w; TWO WEEKS IN SEPTEMBER(1967, Fr./Brit.), w; POSTMAN GOES TO WAR, THE(1968, Fr.), w; MADLY(1970, Fr.), w; ROAD TO SALINA(1971, Fr./Ital.), w; BORSALINO AND CO.(1974, Fr.), w; CAT, THE(1975, Fr.), w; LA CAGE(1975, Fr.), w
Betty Jardine
ALMOST A HONEYMOON(1938, Brit.); GHOST TRAIN, THE(1941, Brit.); GIRL IN THE NEWS, THE(1941, Brit.); MAIL TRAIN(1941, Brit.); REMARKABLE MR. KIPPS(1942, Brit.); WE'LL MEET AGAIN(1942, Brit.); RHYTHM SERENADE(1943, Brit.); CANTERBURY TALE, A(1944, Brit.); 2,000 WOMEN(1944, Brit.)
Paully Jardine
SUMMER'S CHILDREN(1979, Can.)
Dr. Jardini
FAREWELL TO ARMS, A(1932), tech adv
Edward Jardon
ALIBI(1929)
Don Jarel
CLOSE ENCOUNTERS OF THE THIRD KIND(1977), ph
Charles Jarell
MR. PEEK-A-BOO(1951, Fr.)
"Brother" Frank Jares
NO HOLDS BARRED(1952)
Jill Jaress
RESURRECTION OF ZACHARY WHEELER, THE(1971); JAZZ SINGER, THE(1980); S.O.B.(1981); STING II, THE(1983)
Bella Jarett
JANE AUSTEN IN MANHATTAN(1980)
Ondrej Jariabek
END OF AUGUST AT THE HOTEL OZONE, THE(1967, Czech.)
Ike Jarlego, Jr.
NO PLACE TO HIDE(1956)
Gerard Jarlot
LONG ABSENCE, THE(1962, Fr./Ital.), w; MODERATO CANTABILE(1964, Fr./Ital.), w
Derek Jarman
JUBILEE(1978, Brit.), d&w
Misc. Talkies
TEMPEST, THE(1980, Brit.), d
Claude Jarman, Jr.
YEARLING, THE(1946); HIGH BARBAREE(1947); INTRUDER IN THE DUST(1949); ROUGHSHOD(1949); SUN COMES UP, THE(1949); OUTRIDERS, THE(1950); RIO GRANDE(1950); INSIDE STRAIGHT(1951); HANGMAN'S KNOT(1952); FAIR WIND TO JAVA(1953); GREAT LOCOMOTIVE CHASE, THE(1956)
Misc. Talkies
OUTRIDERS, THE(1950)
Geraldine Jarman
LOVER COME BACK(1946)
Jack Jarman
MELODY OF MY HEART(1936, Brit.)
Silents
UNDER SUSPICION(1919, Brit.)
Misc. Silents
(; AT THE TORRENT'S MERCY(1915, Brit.); JADE HEART, THE(1915, Brit.); ON THE STEPS OF THE ALTAR(1916, Brit.); IN THE GLOAMING(1919, Brit.); WINDING ROAD, THE(1920)

Michelle Jarman
SUMMERFIELD(1977, Aus.)
Reginald Jarman
ZARDOZ(; CHALLENGE, THE(1939, Brit.)
Jim Jarmusch
PERMANENT VACATION(1982), p,d&w, m, ed
1984
STRANGER THAN PARADISE(1984, U.S./Ger.), d&w, ed
Jack Jarmuth
JAZZ SINGER, THE(1927), w
Silents
OLD SAN FRANCISCO(1927), t; SLIGHTLY USED(1927), t; POWDER MY BACK(1928), t
Jil Jarmyn
LAY THAT RIFLE DOWN(1955); NO MAN'S WOMAN(1955); TWINKLE IN GOD'S EYE, THE(1955); SWAMP WOMEN(1956); WAR DRUMS(1957); MAN OR GUN(1958)
Jill Jarmyn
TARZAN'S FIGHT FOR LIFE(1958); SPARTACUS(1960)
Dorothy Jarnac
HERE COME THE WAVES(1944); LILI(1953), a, ch
James Jarnigan
GREAT BRAIN, THE(1978); SWORD AND THE SORCERER, THE(1982)
Bengt Jarnmark
ILLICIT INTERLUDE(1954, Swed.), ph
M.I. Jaroff
THUNDERSTORM(1934, USSR)
Janus Jaron
FIRST START(1953, Pol.)
Doreen Jaros
WHERE THE BUFFALO ROAM(1980)
Frank Jaros
OPERATION HAYLIFT(1950)
Ruth Jaroslow
HARVEY MIDDLEMAN, FIREMAN(1965); LAST OF THE RED HOT LOVERS(1972)
Zofia Jaroszewska
YOUNG GIRLS OF WILKO, THE(1979, Pol./Fr.)
Magda Jaroszowna
CONTRACT, THE(1982, Pol.)
Janice Jarratt
KID MILLIONS(1934)
John Jarratt
GREAT MACARTHY, THE(1975, Aus.); PICNIC AT HANGING ROCK(1975, Aus.); BLUE FIN(1978, Aus.); ODD ANGRY SHOT, THE(1979, Aus.); NEXT OF KIN(1983, Aus.); WE OF THE NEVER NEVER(1983, Aus.)
Maurice Jarre
CRACK IN THE MIRROR(1960), m; BIG GAMBLE, THE(1961), m; HORROR CHAMBER OF DR. FAUSTUS, THE(1962, Fr./Ital.), m; LAWRENCE OF ARABIA(1962, Brit.), m; LONGEST DAY, THE(1962), m; LOVERS ON A TIGHTROPE(1962, Fr.), m; SUNDAYS AND CYBELE(1962, Fr.), m; THERESE(1963, Fr.), m; THREE FACES OF SIN(1963, Fr./Ital.), m; YOUR SHADOW IS MINE(1963, Fr./Ital.), m&md; BEHOLD A PALE HORSE(1964), m; DRAGON SKY(1964, Fr.), m; COLLECTOR, THE(1965), m; DOCTOR ZHIVAGO(1965), m; TRAIN, THE(1965, Fr./Ital./U.S.), m, md; GAMBIT(1966), m; GRAND PRIX(1966), m&md; IS PARIS BURNING?(1966, U.S./Fr.), m; JUDEX(1966, Fr./Ital.), m; PROFESSIONALS, THE(1966), m, md; WEEKEND AT DUNKIRK(1966, Fr./Ital.), m, md; NIGHT OF THE GENERALS, THE(1967, Brit./Fr.), m, md; OLIVE TREES OF JUSTICE, THE(1967, Fr.), m; FIVE CARD STUD(1968), m; FIXER, THE(1968), m; ISADORA(1968, Brit.), md; VILLA RIDES(1968), m, md; EXTRAORDINARY SEAMAN, THE(1969), m; TOPAZ(1969, Brit.), m, md; EL CONDOR(1970), m; ONLY GAME IN TOWN, THE(1970), m, md; RYAN'S DAUGHTER(1970, Brit.), m, md; PLAZA SUITE(1971), m, md; EFFECT OF GAMMA RAYS ON MAN-IN-THE-MOON MARIGOLDS, THE(1972), m; LIFE AND TIMES OF JUDGE ROY BEAN, THE(1972), m, md; POPE JOAN(1972, Brit.), m, md; RED SUN(1972, Fr./Ital./Span.), m, md; ASH WEDNESDAY(1973), m; MACKINTOSH MAN, THE(1973, Brit.), m; ISLAND AT THE TOP OF THE WORLD, THE(1974), m; GREAT EXPECTATIONS(1975, Brit.), m; MAN WHO WOULD BE KING, THE(1975, Brit.), m; MANDINGO(1975), m; MR. SYCAMORE(1975), m; POSSE(1975), m; LAST TYCOON, THE(1976), m; MOHAMMAD, MESSENGER OF GOD(1976, Lebanon/Brit.), m, md; SHOUT AT THE DEVIL(1976), m, md; MARCH OR DIE(1977), m, md; CROSSED SWORDS(1978), m; TWO SOLITUDES(1978, Can.), m; MAGICIAN OF LUBLIN, THE(1979, Israel/Ger.), m; TIN DRUM, THE(1979, Ger./Fr./Yugo./Pol.), m; WINTER KILLS(1979), m; AMERICAN SUCCESS COMPANY, THE(1980), m; BLACK MARBLE, THE(1980), m; LAST FLIGHT OF NOAH'S ARK, THE(1980), m; RESURRECTION(1980), m; LION OF THE DESERT(1981, Libya/Brit.), m; TAPS(1981), m; CIRCLE OF DECEIT(1982, Fr./Ger.), m; DON'T CRY, IT'S ONLY THUNDER(1982), m; FIREFOX(1982), m; YEAR OF LIVING DANGEROUSLY, THE(1982, Aus.), m; YOUNG DOCTORS IN LOVE(1982), m
1984
DREAMSCAPE(1984), m; PASSAGE TO INDIA, A(1984, Brit.), m; TOP SECRET!(1984), m
Janine Jarreau
RAPTURE(1965), makeup; YOUNG GIRLS OF ROCHEFORT, THE(1968, Fr.), makeup
Susan Player Jarreau
MALIBU BEACH(1978)
Randall Jarrel
THREE SISTERS, THE(1977), w
Stig Jarrel
WALPURGIS NIGHT(1941, Swed.); TORMENT(1947, Swed.); AFFAIRS OF A MODEL(1952, Swed.); DEVIL'S EYE, THE(1960, Swed.)
Andrew Jarrell
LIMBO(1972)
Andy Jarrell
LADY IN CEMENT(1968); HELLO DOWN THERE(1969); WELCOME TO THE CLUB(1971); BANG THE DRUM SLOWLY(1973)
Emanual Jarrell
SOUNDER, PART 2(1976)
Yvonne Jarrell
SOUNDER(1972)

Jerry Jarret
KILLER'S KISS(1955)
Art Jarrett
ACE OF ACES(1933); DANCING LADY(1933); SITTING PRETTY(1933); GAY DIVORCEE, THE(1934); TRIGGER PALS(1939); FOLLIES GIRL(1943), w
Arthur Jarrett
MOONLIGHT AND PRETZELS(1933), w; HOLLYWOOD PARTY(1934); LET'S FALL IN LOVE(1934); RIP TIDE(1934); BIRTH OF A BABY(1938), w; TATTOOED STRANGER, THE(1950)
Arthur Jarrett, Jr.
MY LUCKY STAR(1938)
Bertie Jarrett
WALKING ON AIR(1946, Brit.)
Catherine Jarrett
1984
BASILEUS QUARTET(1984, Ital.)
Charles Jarrett
TIME TO REMEMBER(1962, Brit.), d
Curtis Jarrett
TREASURE OF MONTE CRISTO(1949); RACKET, THE(1951)
Dan Jarrett
HER FIRST MATE(1933), w; COWBOY MILLIONAIRE(1935), a, w; HARD ROCK HARRIGAN(1935), w; THUNDER MOUNTAIN(1935), w; WHEN A MAN'S A MAN(1935), w; WHISPERING SMITH SPEAKS(1935), w; BORDER PATROLMAN, THE(1936), w; DAN MATTHEWS(1936), w; LET'S SING AGAIN(1936), w; O'MALLEY OF THE MOUNTED(1936), w; HOLLYWOOD COWBOY(1937), w; PARK AVENUE LOGGER(1937), w; SECRET VALLEY(1937), w; WINDJAMMER(1937), w; FLIRTING WITH FATE(1938), w; HAWAIIAN BUCKAROO(1938), w; RAWHIDE(1938), w; ROLL ALONG, COWBOY(1938), w
Silents
KENNEDY SQUARE(1916)
Daniel Jarrett
DANIEL BOONE(1936), w; MINE WITH THE IRON DOOR, THE(1936), w; TOMAHAWK(1951), w
Silents
SCALES OF JUSTICE, THE(1914); GOD'S HALF ACRE(1916)
Misc. Silents
WAGER, THE(1916); SLACKER, THE(1917)
Jerry Jarrette
SING, NEIGHBOR, SING(1944), ch; VAMPIRE'S GHOST, THE(1945), ch
Paul Jarrico
LITTLE ADVENTURESS, THE(1938), w; NO TIME TO MARRY(1938), w; FACE BEHIND THE MASK, THE(1941), w; MEN OF THE TIMBERLAND(1941), w; TOM, DICK AND HARRY(1941), w; SONG OF RUSSIA(1943), w; THOUSANDS CHEER(1943), w; LITTLE GIANT(1946), w; SEARCH, THE(1948), w; NOT WANTED(1949), w; WHITE TOWER, THE(1950), w; SALT OF THE EARTH(1954), p; GIRL MOST LIKELY, THE(1957), w; DAY THE HOTLINE GOT HOT, THE(1968, Fr./Span.), w; DAY THAT SHOOK THE WORLD, THE(1977, Yugo./Czech.), w
Bernard La Jarrige
TRAIN, THE(1965, Fr./Ital./U.S.)
Charles Jarrot
CONDORMAN(1981), d
Charles Jarrott
ANNE OF THE THOUSAND DAYS(1969, Brit.), d; MARY, QUEEN OF SCOTS(1971, Brit.), d; LOST HORIZON(1973), d; DOVE, THE(1974, Brit.), d; LITTLEST HORSE THIEVES, THE(1977), d; OTHER SIDE OF MIDNIGHT, THE(1977), d; LAST FLIGHT OF NOAH'S ARK, THE(1980), d; AMATEUR, THE(1982), d
John Jarrott
Silents
SCARLET ROAD, THE(1916)
Ashton Jarry
UNCIVILISED(1937, Aus.)
Gro Jarto
EDVARD MUNCH(1976, Norway/Swed.)
Ary Jartul
STRANGE WORLD(1952)
Tom Jarus
WARRIORS, THE(1979)
Risto Jarva
TIME OF ROSES(1970, Fin.), p&d, w
Al Jarvis
MAKE BELIEVE BALLROOM(1949), a, w; TWONKY, THE(1953); PHANTOM PLANET, THE(1961)
Bill Jarvis
HAMLET(1969, Brit.); THIS, THAT AND THE OTHER(1970, Brit.)
Bob Jarvis
STRAIGHT TIME(1978); NEW YEAR'S EVIL(1980)
Bobby Jarvis
GOLD DIGGERS OF 1937(1936)
Dick Jarvis
FORBIDDEN JOURNEY(1950, Can.), p,d&w
Dolly Jarvis
STOP, YOU'RE KILLING ME(1952)
E. Jarvis
YOUNG WIVES' TALE(1954, Brit.), ed; POCKET MONEY(1972)
E.B. Jarvis
YELLOW MASK, THE(1930, Brit.), ed; LOVE HABIT, THE(1931, Brit.), ed; SECRET AGENT(1933, Brit.), ed; SOUTHERN MAID, A(1933, Brit.), ed; RADIO FOLLIES(1935, Brit.), ed; GIVE HER A RING(1936, Brit.), ed; DARK SANDS(1938, Brit.), ed; GAIETY GIRLS, THE(1938, Brit.), ed; CHALLENGE, THE(1939, Brit.), ed; CASTLE OF CRIMES(1940, Brit.), ed; MURDER IN THE NIGHT(1940, Brit.), ed; AMAZING MR. FORREST, THE(1943, Brit.), ed; SECRET MISSION(1944, Brit.), ed; VACATION FROM MARRIAGE(1945, Brit.), ed; WANTED FOR MURDER(1946, Brit.), ed; MEET ME AT DAWN(1947, Brit.), ed; HASTY HEART, THE(1949), ed; THIS WAS A WOMAN(1949, Brit.), ed; MURDER WITHOUT CRIME(1951, Brit.), ed; CASTLE IN THE AIR(1952, Brit.), ed; ISN'T LIFE WONDERFUL!(1953, Brit.), ed; DUEL IN THE JUNGLE(1954, Brit.), ed; WARRIORS, THE(1955), ed; LET'S BE HAPPY(1957, Brit.), ed; GIRLS AT SEA(1958, Brit.), ed; WORLD IN MY POCKET, THE(1962, Fr./Ital./Ger.), ed; OPERATION BULLSHINE(1963, Brit.), ed

E.H. Jarvis
YOU CAN'T BEAT THE IRISH(1952, Brit.), ed
Edward Jarvis
STAGE FRIGHT(1950, Brit.), ed; MARK OF THE HAWK, THE(1958), ed; ATTEMPT TO KILL(1961, Brit.), ed; DOUBLE, THE(1963, Brit), ed
Edward B. Jarvis
GIRL IN DISTRESS(1941, Brit.), ed
Francesca Jarvis
LILIES OF THE FIELD(1963); LIFE AND TIMES OF JUDGE ROY BEAN, THE(1972); NIGHT OF THE LEPUS(1972)
Frank Jarvis
ROTTEN TO THE CORE(1956, Brit.); MIX ME A PERSON(1962, Brit.); THAT KIND OF GIRL(1963, Brit.); ITALIAN JOB, THE(1969, Brit.)
Graham Jarvis
ALICE'S RESTAURANT(1969); MOVE(1970); OUT OF TOWNERS, THE(1970); R.P.M.(1970); TRAVELING EXECUTIONER, THE(1970); COLD TURKEY(1971); NEW LEAF, A(1971); ORGANIZATION, THE(1971); WHAT'S UP, DOC?(1972); RUSSIAN ROULETTE(1975); PROPHECY(1979); MIDDLE AGE CRAZY(1980, Can.); AMATEUR, THE(1982); DEAL OF THE CENTURY(1983); MR. MOM(1983); SILKWOOD(1983)
Graham P. Jarvis
HOT ROCK, THE(1972)
Greg Jarvis
SLENDER THREAD, THE(1965)
Howard Jarvis
AIRPLANE!(1980)
Jeff Jarvis
EXORCIST II: THE HERETIC(1977), spec eff; BLUE THUNDER(1983), spec eff
1984
FIRESTARTER(1984), spec eff
John Jarvis
ROMAN SPRING OF MRS. STONE, THE(1961, U.S./Brit.), set d; LISA(1962, Brit.), set d; HAUNTING, THE(1963), set d; NINE HOURS TO RAMA(1963, U.S./Brit.), set d; CHALK GARDEN, THE(1964, Brit.), set d; YELLOW ROLLS-ROYCE, THE(1965, Brit.), set d; PRUDENCE AND THE PILL(1968, Brit.), set d; SLEUTH(1972, Brit.), set d; LAST OF SHEILA, THE(1973), set d
Joyce Jarvis
PROBLEM GIRLS(1953)
Martin Jarvis
SECRETS OF A WINDMILL GIRL(1966, Brit.); LAST ESCAPE, THE(1970, Brit.); TASTE THE BLOOD OF DRACULA(1970, Brit.)
May Jarvis
CANNIBAL GIRLS(1973)
Mike Jarvis
STICK UP, THE(1978, Brit.), cos
Nina Jarvis
DEAD MAN'S SHOES(1939, Brit.), w; IT HAPPENED TO ONE MAN(1941, Brit.), w
Peter Jarvis
TALES OF ORDINARY MADNESS(1983, Ital.)
Richard Jarvis
Silents
LILAC TIME(1928)
Richard J. Jarvis
SINS OF THE FATHERS(1948, Can.), d, ed
Robert Lee Jarvis
PENNIES FROM HEAVEN(1981)
Sam Jarvis
BUG(1975)
Sidney Jarvis
FOOTLIGHTS AND FOOLS(1929); UNHOLY NIGHT, THE(1929); KISMET(1930); MAYTIME(1937); PLAINSMAN, THE(1937)
Misc. Silents
CIRCUS ROOKIES(1928); UPLAND RIDER, THE(1928)
Sydney Jarvis
MOVIE CRAZY(1932)
Silents
CASEY AT THE BAT(1927)
Michael Jary
SCHLAGER-PARADE(1953); THEY WERE SO YOUNG(1955), m, md; CITY OF SECRETS(1963, Ger.), m
Viram Jasani
BOOM!(1968), m
Ejissu Jasantua
1984
WHITE ELEPHANT(1984, Brit.)
Jose Jasd
MACHISMO-40 GRAVES FOR 40 GUNS(1970)
Adib Jashan
1984
LITTLE DRUMMER GIRL, THE(1984)
Jay Jasin
HILLBILLYS IN A HAUNTED HOUSE(1967)
F. Jasinski
YOUNG GIRLS OF WILKO, THE(1979, Pol./Fr.)
Stanislav Jasiukiewicz
JOAN OF THE ANGELS(1962, Pol.)
Stanislow Jasiukiewicz
KNIGHTS OF THE TEUTONIC ORDER, THE(1962, Pol.)
Paul Jasiukonis
SOME CALL IT LOVING(1973), ed
Kenneth J. Jaskolski
FINAL COUNTDOWN, THE(1980)
Paul Jasmin
RIOT IN JUVENILE PRISON(1959); MIDNIGHT COWBOY(1969); LOOKER(1981)
Arthur Jasmine
Silents
NINETY AND NINE, THE(1922); SALOME(1922); SON OF THE WOLF, THE(1922); SCARAMOUCHE(1923); LURE OF THE YUKON(1924); AFTER MARRIAGE(1925); JUSTICE OF THE FAR NORTH(1925)

Misc. Silents
THUNDER ISLAND(1921)
Milutin Jasnik
TEMPEST(1958, Ital./Yugo./Fr.)
Ryszard Jasny
BEADS OF ONE ROSARY, THE(1982, Pol.)
Jason
SMART POLITICS(1948), m/1
Basil Jason
WALTZ TIME(1946, Brit.)
David Jason
UNDER MILK WOOD(1973, Brit.); ODD JOB, THE(1978, Brit.)
Harvey Jason
LILITH(1964); STAR!(1968); GAILY, GAILY(1969); TOO LATE THE HERO(1970); COLD TURKEY(1971); NECROMANCY(1972); OKLAHOMA CRUDE(1973); SAVE THE TIGER(1973); LOST IN THE STARS(1974); DR. MINX(1975); SPECIALIST, THE(1975); GUMBALL RALLY, THE(1976)
Hy Jason
FEAR(1946)
Jack Jason
CHUKA(1967), p
Leigh Jason
HIGH GEAR(1933), p&d, w; BRIDE WALKS OUT, THE(1936), d; LOVE ON A BET(1936), d; NEW FACES OF 1937(1937), d; THAT GIRL FROM PARIS(1937), d; WISE GIRL(1937), d; MAD MISS MANTON, THE(1938), d; CAREER(1939), d; FLYING IRISHMAN, THE(1939), d; LADY FOR A NIGHT(1941), d; MODEL WIFE(1941), p&d, w; THREE GIRLS ABOUT TOWN(1941), d; DANGEROUS BLONDES(1943), d; CAROLINA BLUES(1944), d; NINE GIRLS(1944), d; MEET ME ON BROADWAY(1946), d; LOST HONEYMOON(1947), d; OUT OF THE BLUE(1947), d; MAN FROM TEXAS, THE(1948), d; OKINAWA(1952); CHOPPERS, THE(1961), d
Silents
EYES OF THE UNDERWORLD(1929), d, w
Misc. Silents
PRICE OF FEAR, THE(1928), d; BODY PUNCH, THE(1929), d; TIP-OFF, THE(1929), d; WOLVES OF THE CITY(1929), d
Mitchell Jason
HEARTBREAK KID, THE(1972); NETWORK(1976); SOUP FOR ONE(1982)
Neville Jason
FROM RUSSIA WITH LOVE(1963, Brit.); AMOROUS ADVENTURES OF MOLL FLANDERS, THE(1965); MOHAMMAD, MESSENGER OF GOD(1976, Lebanon/Brit.); PASSAGE, THE(1979, Brit.)
Peter Jason
RIO LOBO(1970); DRIVER, THE(1978); LONG RIDERS, THE(1980); TEXAS LIGHTNING(1981); BUTTERFLY(1982); SOME KIND OF HERO(1982); TRICK OR TREATS(1982); 48 HOURS(1982)
1984
ANGEL(1984); DREAMSCAPE(1984); IMPULSE(1984); KARATE KID, THE(1984); OXFORD BLUES(1984); STREETS OF FIRE(1984)
Rick Jason
SOMBRERO(1953); SARACEN BLADE, THE(1954); THIS IS MY LOVE(1954); LIEUTENANT WORE SKIRTS, THE(1956); WAYWARD BUS, THE(1957); RX MURDER(1958, Brit.); SIERRA BARON(1958); COLOR ME DEAD(1969, Aus.); DAY OF THE WOLVES(1973); PARTNERS(1982)
Misc. Talkies
TIME FOR LOVE, A(1974); WITCH WHO CAME FROM THE SEA, THE(1976)
Sheri Jason
HOMETOWN U.S.A.(1979)
Sybil Jason
BARNACLE BILL(1935, Brit.); I FOUND STELLA PARISH(1935); LITTLE BIG SHOT(1935); SINGING KID, THE(1936); CAPTAIN'S KID(1937); COMET OVER BROADWAY(1938); LITTLE PRINCESS, THE(1939); WOMAN DOCTOR(1939)
Sybill Jason
GREAT O'MALLEY, THE(1937)
Will Jason
SOUL OF A MONSTER, THE(1944), d; EVE KNEW HER APPLES(1945), d; TAHITI NIGHTS(1945), d; TEN CENTS A DANCE(1945), d; BLONDE ALIBI(1946), d; DARK HORSE, THE(1946), d; IDEA GIRL(1946), d; SLIGHTLY SCANDALOUS(1946), d; SARGE GOES TO COLLEGE(1947), p&d; CAMPUS SLEUTH(1948), p&d, m; MUSIC MAN(1948), p&d; RUSTY LEADS THE WAY(1948), d; SMART POLITICS(1948), p&d; KAZAN(1949), d; EVERYBODY'S DANCIN'(1950), d; CHAIN OF CIRCUMSTANCE(1951), d; DISC JOCKEY(1951), d; HARLEM GLOBETROTTERS, THE(1951), d; THIEF OF DAMASCUS(1952), d
Jose Jasp
SAVAGE PAMPAS(1967, Span./Arg.)
Jose Jaspe
GREAT HOPE, THE(1954, Ital.); QUEEN OF THE PIRATES(1961, Ital./Ger.); CENTURION, THE(1962, Fr./Ital.); RAGE OF THE BUCCANEERS(1963, Ital.); GOLDEN ARROW, THE(1964, Ital.); HOUSE OF 1,000 DOLLS(1967, Ger./Span./Brit.); MISSION STARDUST(1968, Ital./Span./Ger.); SAUL AND DAVID(1968, Ital./Span.); YOUNG REBEL, THE(1969, Fr./Ital./Span.); MAN CALLED NOON, THE(1973, Brit.)
Pete Jasper
ONE FROM THE HEART(1982)
Thena Jasper
Silents
OUTSIDE WOMAN, THE(1921)
Zina Jasper
DEATH PLAY(1976)
Bella Jaspers
YOUNG LORD, THE(1970, Ger.)
Jose Jaspes
DON'T TURN THE OTHER CHEEK(1974, Ital./Ger./Span.)
Jose Jasso
FRANKENSTEIN, THE VAMPIRE AND CO.(1961, Mex.); LOS INVISIBLES(1961, Mex.); MIGHTY JUNGLE, THE(1965, U.S./Mex.); CHIQUTTO PERO PICOSO(1967, Mex.)
Nicholas Jasso
HIGH RISK(1981)

Peter Jassop
HARDER THEY COME, THE(1973, Jamaica), ph

Terry Jastrow
FM(1978); SEVEN(1979); LOVE AND MONEY(1982); WALTZ ACROSS TEXAS(1982), a, w

Marian Jastrzebski
GUESTS ARE COMING(1965, Pol.)

Peter Jasuai
SPETTERS(1983, Holland), art d

Igor Jasulovic
WATERLOO(1970, Ital./USSR)

Iara Jati
XICA(1982, Braz.)

Maurice Jaubert
LE DENIER MILLIARDAIRE(1934, Fr.), m; PORT OF SHADOWS(1938, Fr.), m; UN CARNET DE BAL(1938, Fr.), m; END OF A DAY, THE(1939, Fr.), m; DAY-BREAK(1940, Fr.), m; STORY OF ADELE H., THE(1975, Fr.), m; SMALL CHANGE(1976, Fr.), m; MAN WHO LOVED WOMEN, THE(1977, Fr.), m; GREEN ROOM, THE(1979, Fr.), m

Thierry Jault
MAIS OU ET DONC ORNICAR(1979, Fr.), ph

Elena Jaumandreu
THEY CAME TO ROB LAS VEGAS(1969, Fr./Ital./Span./Ger.), ed

Georg Jaun
RESTLESS NIGHT, THE(1964, Ger.), ed

Ed Jauregi
RANGERS STEP IN, THE(1937)

Edward Jauregui
CATTLE EMPIRE(1958)

Edward Jaurequi
YOUNG LAND, THE(1959)

Mike Edward Jaurequi
MAN WHO SHOT LIBERTY VALANCE, THE(1962)

Georg Jauss
SPESSART INN, THE(1961, Ger.), makeup

Lady Java
HUMAN TORNADO, THE(1976)

Java's Tzigane Band
KING OF HEARTS(1936, Brit.)

Bertrand Javal
TIME OUT FOR LOVE(1963, Ital./Fr.), p; CLOPORTES(1966, Fr., Ital.), p; CONFESSION, THE(1970, Fr.), p; COUSIN, COUSINE(1976, Fr.), p

Francoise Javet
PURPLE NOON(1961, Fr./Ital.), ed; VIEW FROM THE BRIDGE, A(1962, Fr./Ital.), ed; THAT MAN FROM RIO(1964, Fr./Ital.), ed; MALE COMPANION(1965, Fr./Ital.), ed; UP TO HIS EARS(1966, Fr./Ital.), ed; COMEDIANS, THE(1967), ed; KING OF HEARTS(1967, Fr./Ital.), ed; DEVIL BY THE TAIL, THE(1969, Fr./Ital.), ed; RIDER ON THE RAIN(1970, Fr./Ital.), ed; DEADLY TRAP, THE(1972, Fr./Ital.), ed; TWO MEN IN TOWN(1973, Fr.), ed; DEAR DETECTIVE(1978, Fr.), ed; LA BALANCE(1983, Fr.), ed

Susanna Javicoli
SUSPIRIA(1977, Ital.)

Maria Delia Javier
DR. HECKYL AND MR. HYPE(1980), set d

Mary Delia Javier
VALLEY GIRL(1983), prod d

Sam Javis
MORITURI(1965); PIECES OF DREAMS(1970); PSYCHOPATH, THE(1973)

Marion Javits
WHO WAS THAT LADY?(1960)

Romana Javitz
FINNEGANS WAKE(1965), w

Pal Javor
MISS PRESIDENT(1935, Hung.); CARMELA(1949, Ital.)

Paul Javor
BLUE IDOL, THE(1931, Hung.); HIPPOLYT, THE LACKEY(1932, Hung.); GREAT CARUSO, THE(1951); IRON MAN, THE(1951); ASSIGNMENT–PARIS(1952)

Ed Javregi
OLD WYOMING TRAIL, THE(1937)

Samir Jawad
GERMAN SISTERS, THE(1982, Ger.)

Alex Jawdokimov
SAVAGE MESSIAH(1972, Brit.); NEXT MAN, THE(1976)

Alexei Jawdokimov
TAMARIND SEED, THE(1974, Brit.); EAGLE HAS LANDED, THE(1976, Brit.); FIREFOX(1982)

Alex Jawdokinov
MUSIC LOVERS, THE(1971, Brit.)

Louis Jawitz
MANIAC(1980)

Jax
SOME CALL IT LOVING(1973), cos

Budd Jaxon
KID MONK BARONI(1952)

Cepheus Jaxon
PENITENTIARY II(1982)

David Jaxon
HARD DAY'S NIGHT, A(1964, Brit.)

Wilfred Jaxon
ALICE IN WONDERLAND(1951), d

Alan Jay
UNCLE SCAM(1981)

Angela Jay
DEADLY FEMALES, THE(1976, Brit.)

Bill Jay
SUPER SPOOK(1975), a, w; SHAPE OF THINGS TO COME, THE(1979, Can.)

Don Jay
TATTOO(1981)

Dorothy Jay
Silents
IS YOUR DAUGHTER SAFE?(1927)

Earnest Jay
FRANCHISE AFFAIR, THE(1952, Brit.)

Ed Jay
YUKON MANHUNT(1951), md

Eddie Jay
NO LADY(1931, Brit.)

Edward J. Jay
YOUNG DANIEL BOONE(1950), m

Ernest Jay
MY LUCKY STAR(1933, Brit.); TIGER BAY(1933, Brit.); CHECKMATE(1935, Brit,); BROKEN BLOSSOMS(1936, Brit.); MEN OF YESTERDAY(1936, Brit.); SONG OF THE ROAD(1937, Brit.); YOU'RE IN THE ARMY NOW(1937, Brit.); I SEE ICE(1938); DON'T TAKE IT TO HEART(1944, Brit.); SCHOOL FOR SECRETS(1946, Brit.); BLANCHE FURY(1948, Brit.); VICE VERSA(1948, Brit.); EDWARD, MY SON(1949, U.S./Brit.); HISTORY OF MR. POLLY, THE(1949, Brit.); RELUCTANT WIDOW, THE(1951, Brit.); GAY ADVENTURE, THE(1953, Brit.); I BELIEVE IN YOU(1953, Brit.); MR. POTTS GOES TO MOSCOW(1953, Brit.); SWORD AND THE ROSE, THE(1953); WICKED WIFE(1955, Brit.); WHO DONE IT?(1956, Brit.); CURSE OF FRANKENSTEIN, THE(1957, Brit.); DOCTOR AT LARGE(1957, Brit.); TWO GROOMS FOR A BRIDE(1957)

Griffin Jay
AIR HAWKS(1935), w; KID FROM KANSAS, THE(1941), w; MEN OF THE TIMBERLAND(1941), w; TIMBER(1942), w; TOP SERGEANT(1942), w; CAPTIVE WILD WOMAN(1943), w; CRY OF THE WEREWOLF(1944), w; RETURN OF THE VAMPIRE, THE(1944), w; TWO-MAN SUBMARINE(1944), w; DEVIL BAT'S DAUGHTER, THE(1946), w; MASK OF DIIJON, THE(1946), w; MUMMY, THE(1959, Brit.), w

Griffith Jay
MUMMY'S HAND, THE(1940), w; MUMMY'S TOMB, THE(1942), w; MUMMY'S GHOST, THE(1944), w

Harriet Jay
Silents
ALONE IN LONDON(1915, Brit.), w

Helen Jay
FRONTIER GAMBLER(1956); NAKED GUN, THE(1956); BADLANDS OF MONTANA(1957); CHICAGO CONFIDENTIAL(1957); CRIME OF PASSION(1957); DEADLY MANTIS, THE(1957); SHE DEVIL(1957); GANG WAR(1958); SPACE MASTER X-7(1958); OCEAN'S ELEVEN(1960); EXPERIMENT IN TERROR(1962); SIMON, KING OF THE WITCHES(1971)

Ivor Jay
WRONG ARM OF THE LAW, THE(1963, Brit.), w

J. Griffin Jay
TOO TOUGH TO KILL(1935), w; BANK ALARM(1937), w

Jean Jay
SCHOOL FOR SCANDAL, THE(1930, Brit.), w
Silents
EVERY MOTHER'S SON(1926, Brit.); ONLY WAY, THE(1926, Brit.); AFTERWARDS(1928, Brit.); PALAIS DE DANSE(1928, Brit.), w
Misc. Silents
SILVER KING, THE(1929, Brit.)

Larry Jay
GIVE ME THE STARS(1944, Brit.)

Marjory Jay
LAST PICTURE SHOW, THE(1971)

Stanley Jay
HANGMAN WAITS, THE(1947, Brit.); SILVER DARLINGS, THE(1947, Brit.)

Tony Jay
MY WAY(1974, South Africa); LOVE AND DEATH(1975); GREEK TYCOON, THE(1978); TIME BANDITS(1981, Brit.)

Jay and The Americans
WILD, WILD WINTER(1966)

Jay Whidden and His Orchestra
HIS BROTHER'S WIFE(1936)

Jay Wilbur and His Band
HI, GANG!(1941, Brit.)

Jayant
SIMON(1980)

The Jaybees
WAITING FOR CAROLINE(1969, Can.), m

Errol Jaye
UPTIGHT(1968)

Ron Jaye
THERE'S ALWAYS VANILLA(1972)

Sidney Jaye
TASTE OF BLOOD, A(1967)

George Jayne
TO BE OR NOT TO BE(1983)

Jennifer Jayne
BLACK WIDOW(1951, Brit.); MANIACS ON WHEELS(1951, Brit.); IT'S A GRAND LIFE(1953, Brit.); YANK IN ERMINE, A(1955, Brit.); WOMAN OF MYSTERY, A(1957, Brit.); CRAWLING EYE, THE(1958, Brit.); MAN WHO WOULDN'T TALK, THE(1958, Brit.); MARK OF THE PHOENIX(1958, Brit.); END OF THE LINE, THE(1959, Brit.); BAND OF THIEVES(1962, Brit.); ON THE BEAT(1962, Brit.); ROOMMATES(1962, Brit.); DR. TERROR'S HOUSE OF HORRORS(1965, Brit.); ESCAPE BY NIGHT(1965, Brit.); HYSTERIA(1965, Brit.); LIQUIDATOR, THE(1966, Brit.); THEY CAME FROM BEYOND SPACE(1967, Brit.); MEDUSA TOUCH, THE(1978, Brit.)

Keith Jayne
GLITTERBALL, THE(1977, Brit)

Mitchell Jayne
FISH HAWK(1981, Can.), w

Rob Jayne
MERRY CHRISTMAS MR. LAWRENCE(1983, Jap./Brit.)

Valerie Jayne
LITTLE ONES, THE(1965, Brit.)

Betty Jaynes
SWEETHEARTS(1938); BABES IN ARMS(1939); AIR RAID WARDENS(1943); HITLER'S MADMAN(1943); PILOT NO. 5(1943); SWING SHIFT MAISIE(1943); THOUSANDS CHEER(1943); MEET THE PEOPLE(1944)

Clare Jaynes
MY REPUTATION(1946), w
Enid Jaynes
GERONIMO(1962)
Roderick Jaynes
1984
BLOOD SIMPLE(1984), ed
Basil Jayson
CAESAR AND CLEOPATRA(1946, Brit.)
Jay Jayson
CAPRICE(1967), w
Pamela Jayson
BUSTER KEATON STORY, THE(1957)
Michael Jayston
MIDSUMMER NIGHT'S DREAM, A(1969, Brit.); CROMWELL(1970, Brit.); NI-
CHOLAS AND ALEXANDRA(1971, Brit.); ALICE'S ADVENTURES IN WONDER-
LAND(1972, Brit.); PUBLIC EYE, THE(1972, Brit.); HOMECOMING, THE(1973);
NELSON AFFAIR, THE(1973, Brit.); TALES THAT WITNESS MADNESS(1973, Brit.);
CRAZE(1974, Brit.); INTERNECINE PROJECT, THE(1974, Brit.); DOMINIQUE(1978,
Brit.); ZULU DAWN(1980, Brit.)
The Jazz Messengers
ROAD TO SHAME, THE(1962, Fr.), m
Jdanov
ROMEO AND JULIET(1955, USSR)
Frederick Jeages
HELL, HEAVEN OR HOBOKEN(1958, Brit.)
A.E. Jeakins
SOLDIER, SAILOR(1944, Brit.), ph
Adrian Jeakins
ONE WISH TOO MANY(1956, Brit.), ph
Dorothy Jeakins
WAY WE WERE, THE(1973), cos; JOAN OF ARC(1948), cos; SAMSON AND DELI-
LAH(1949), cos; GREATEST SHOW ON EARTH, THE(1952), cos; MY COUSIN RACH-
EL(1952), cos; OUTCASTS OF POKER FLAT, THE(1952), cos; NIAGARA(1953), cos;
TITANIC(1953), cos; TREASURE OF THE GOLDEN CONDOR(1953), cos; WHITE
WITCH DOCTOR(1953), cos; THREE COINS IN THE FOUNTAIN(1954), cos; FRIEND-
LY PERSUASION(1956), cos; TEN COMMANDMENTS, THE(1956), cos; SOUTH
PACIFIC(1958), cos; GREEN MANSIONS(1959), cos; CHILDREN'S HOUR, THE(1961),
cos; ALL FALL DOWN(1962), cos; BEST MAN, THE(1964), cos; ENSIGN PUL-
VER(1964), cos; NIGHT OF THE IGUANA, THE(1964), cos; FOOL KILLER,
THE(1965), cos; SOUND OF MUSIC, THE(1965), cos; ANY WEDNESDAY(1966), cos;
HAWAII(1966), a, cos; FLIM-FLAM MAN, THE(1967), cos; REFLECTIONS IN A
GOLDEN EYE(1967), cos; FINIAN'S RAINBOW(1968), cos; STALKING MOON,
THE(1969), cos; TRUE GRIT(1969), cos; LITTLE BIG MAN(1970), cos; MOLLY MA-
GUIRES, THE(1970), cos; FAT CITY(1972), cos; FUZZ(1972), cos; ICEMAN COMETH,
THE(1973), cos; YOUNG FRANKENSTEIN(1974), cos; HINDENBURG, THE(1975),
cos; YAKUZA, THE(1975, U.S./Jap.), cos; AUDREY ROSE(1977), cos; BETSY,
THE(1978), cos; LOVE AND BULLETS(1979, Brit.), cos; NORTH DALLAS FOR-
TY(1979), cos; ON GOLDEN POND(1981), cos; POSTMAN ALWAYS RINGS TWICE,
THE(1981), cos
Dorothy Jeakinsch
LET'S MAKE LOVE(1960), cos
Jean
Silents
TABU(1931)
Jean the Dog
Silents
RAMONA(1928)
Billie Jean
Silents
LURE OF THE WILD, THE(1925)
Christine Jean
LES MISERABLES(1982, Fr.)
Dorothy Jean
WONDER MAN(1945)
Gloria Jean
AIR STRIKE(1955); UNDER-PUP, THE(1939); IF I HAD MY WAY(1940); LITTLE BIT
OF HEAVEN, A(1940); NEVER GIVE A SUCKER AN EVEN BREAK(1941); GET HEP
TO LOVE(1942); WHAT'S COOKIN'?(1942); IT COMES UP LOVE(1943); MOONLIGHT
IN VERMONT(1943); MR. BIG(1943); WHEN JOHNNY COMES MARCHING HO-
ME(1943); DESTINY(1944); FOLLOW THE BOYS(1944); GHOST CATCHERS(1944);
PARDON MY RHYTHM(1944); RECKLESS AGE(1944); EASY TO LOOK AT(1945);
I'LL REMEMBER APRIL(1945); RIVER GANG(1945); COPACABANA(1947); I SUR-
RENDER DEAR(1948); MANHATTAN ANGEL(1948); OLD-FASHIONED GIRL,
AN(1948); THERE'S A GIRL IN MY HEART(1949); LADIES MAN, THE(1961)
Isabel Jean
Silents
EASY VIRTUE(1927, Brit.)
Rozaa Jean
LEADBELLY(1976)
Susan Jean
LAST OF THE SECRET AGENTS?, THE(1966)
Victoria Jean
CARPETBAGGERS, THE(1964)
Jean Bachelet et Ribault
PASTEUR(1936, Fr.), ph
Jean Louis
RECKLESS MOMENTS, THE(1949), cos; LONG GRAY LINE, THE(1955), cos; MY
SISTER EILEEN(1955), cos
Nicaise Jean-Louis
MOONRAKER(1979, Brit.)
Jean-Max
SECOND BUREAU(1936, Fr.)
Yvon Jeanclaude
SUCKER, THE(1966, Fr./Ital.)
Gertrude Jeanette
NOTHING BUT A MAN(1964); LEGEND OF NIGGER CHARLEY, THE(1972)

Joe Jeanette
Misc. Silents
SQUARE JOE(1921)
Jeanine
LOVE NOW...PAY LATER(1966, Ital.)
Sonja Jeanine
Misc. Talkies
BOD SQUAD, THE(1976)
Jeanmaire
ANYTHING GOES(1956)
[Renee] Jeanmaire
HANS CHRISTIAN ANDERSEN(1952)
Zizi Jeanmaire
FOLIES BERGERE(1958, Fr.); GUINGUETTE(1959, Fr.); BLACK TIGHTS(1962, Fr.)
Jeanne
LOVE FINDS ANDY HARDY(1938), cos; KISS OF FIRE, THE(1940, Fr.); CIRCLE OF
DECEIT(1982, Fr./Ger.)
Sophie Jeanne
TWO ENGLISH GIRLS(1972, Fr.)
Gertrude Jeannette
SHAFT(1971)
Yannis Jeannino
YOUNG APHRODITES(1966, Gr.)
Clarence Greene Jeans
HAPPY MOTHER'S DAY... LOVE, GEORGE(1973)
Desmond Jeans
BLAME THE WOMAN(1932, Brit.); BLUE DANUBE(1932, Brit.); COLONEL
BLOOD(1934, Brit.); HIS MAJESTY AND CO(1935, Brit.); GIRL FROM MAXIM'S,
THE(1936, Brit.); SIX MEN, THE(1951, Brit.)
Gladys Jeans
BEAU GESTE(1939)
Isabel Jeans
RETURN OF THE RAT, THE(1929, Brit.); SALLY BISHOP(1932, Brit.); ROLLING IN
MONEY(1934, Brit.); DICTATOR, THE(1935, Brit./Ger.); CROUCHING BEAST,
THE(1936, U. S./Brit.); TOVARICH(1937); FOOLS FOR SCANDAL(1938); GARDEN OF
THE MOON(1938); HARD TO GET(1938); SECRETS OF AN ACTRESS(1938); YOUTH
TAKES A FLING(1938); GOOD GIRLS GO TO PARIS(1939); MAN ABOUT
TOWN(1939); BANANA RIDGE(1941, Brit.); SUSPICION(1941); GREAT DAY(1945,
Brit.); ELIZABETH OF LADYMEAD(1949, Brit.); GIGI(1958); IT HAPPENED IN
ROME(1959, Ital.); BREATH OF SCANDAL, A(1960); HEAVENS ABOVE!(1963, Brit.);
MAGIC CHRISTIAN, THE(1970, Brit.)
Silents
PROFLIGATE, THE(1917, Brit.); FURTHER ADVENTURES OF THE FLAG LIEU-
TENANT(1927, Brit.); WHEN BOYS LEAVE HOME(1928, Brit.); POWER OVER
MEN(1929, Brit.)
Misc. Silents
TRIUMPH OF THE RAT, THE(1926, Brit.)
Isobel Jeans
Silents
RAT, THE(1925, Brit.)
Marjorie Jeans
RIVER OF UNREST(1937, Brit.), w
Ronald Jeans
YOUNG WIVES' TALE(1954, Brit.), w; YOUR MONEY OR YOUR WIFE(1965,
Brit.), w
Ursula Jeans
LOVE HABIT, THE(1931, Brit.); BARTON MYSTERY, THE(1932, Brit.); CROOKED
LADY, THE(1932, Brit.); CAVALCADE(1933); I LIVED WITH YOU(1933, Brit.); ON
THIN ICE(1933, Brit.); FRIDAY THE 13TH(1934, Brit.); MAN IN THE MIRROR,
THE(1936, Brit.); DARK JOURNEY(1937, Brit.); STORM IN A TEACUP(1937, Brit.);
OVER THE MOON(1940, Brit.); COLONEL BLIMP(1945, Brit.); MR. EMMANUEL(1945,
Brit.); SHOWTIME(1948, Brit.); WEAKER SEX, THE(1949, Brit.); WOMAN IN THE
HALL, THE(1949, Brit.); DAM BUSTERS, THE(1955, Brit.); NIGHT MY NUMBER
CAME UP, THE(1955, Brit.); FLAME OVER INDIA(1960, Brit.); GREEN HELMET,
THE(1961, Brit.); QUEEN'S GUARDS, THE(1963, Brit.); BATTLE OF THE VILLA
FIORITA, THE(1965, Brit.)
Silents
FAKE, THE(1927, Brit.); PASSING OF MR. QUIN, THE(1928, Brit.)
Misc. Silents
S.O.S.(1928, Brit.)
Blandine Jeanson
LA CHINOISE(1967, Fr.); WEEKEND(1968, Fr./Ital.); TWO OR THREE THINGS I
KNOW ABOUT HER(1970, Fr.)
Francis Jeanson
LA CHINOISE(1967, Fr.)
Henri Jeanson
PEPE LE MOKO(1937, Fr.), w; UN CARNET DE BAL(1938, Fr.), w; CURTAIN RISES,
THE(1939, Fr.), w; COMPLIMENTS OF MR. FLOW(1941, Fr.), w; ANGEL AND
SINNER(1947, Fr.), w; CONFESSIONS OF A ROGUE(1948, Fr.), w; FANFAN THE
TULIP(1952, Fr.), w; HENRIETTE'S HOLIDAY(1953, Fr.), w; DAUGHTERS OF DES-
TINY(1954, Fr./Ital.), w; MADAME DU BARRY(1954 Fr./Ital.), w; HOLIDAY FOR
HENRIETTA(1955, Fr.), w; NANA(1957, Fr./Ital.), w; GUINGUETTE(1959, Fr.), w;
NATHALIE, AGENT SECRET(1960, Fr.), w; COW AND I, THE(1961, Fr., Ital., Ger.), w;
CRIME DOES NOT PAY(1962, Fr.), w; DEVIL AND THE TEN COMMANDMENTS,
THE(1962, Fr.), w; MAXIME(1962, Fr.), w; MADAME(1963, Fr./Ital./Span.), w;
THREE FACES OF SIN(1963, Fr./Ital.), w; DON'T TEMPT THE DEVIL(1964, Fr./Ital.),
w; PARIS WHEN IT SIZZLES(1964), w; TWO ARE GUILTY(1964, Fr.), w; PARIS IN
THE MONTH OF AUGUST(1968, Fr.), w
Laure Jeanson
EGLANTINE(1972, Fr.)
Karine Jeantet
STOLEN KISSES(1969, Fr.); THINGS OF LIFE, THE(1970, Fr./Ital./Switz.)
Patrick Jeantet
YOUNG GIRLS OF ROCHEFORT, THE(1968, Fr.)
Henry Jeason
HIS LAST TWELVE HOURS(1953, Ital.), w
Allan Jeaves
CAMELS ARE COMING, THE(1934, Brit.)

Colin Jeavons
DEVIL'S DAFFODIL, THE(1961, Brit./Ger.); FRANKENSTEIN CREATED WOMAN(1965, Brit.); OBLONG BOX, THE(1969, Brit.); BARTLEBY(1970, Brit.); GAMES, THE(1970); DIAGNOSIS: MURDER(1974, Brit.); SCHIZO(1977, Brit.); ISLAND, THE(1980); FRENCH LIEUTENANT'S WOMAN, THE(1981)

Allan Jeayes
HATE SHIP, THE(1930, Brit.); STRANGLEHOLD(1931, Brit.); WOMAN IN CHAINS(1932, Brit.); ANNE ONE HUNDRED(1933, Brit.); ASK BECCLES(1933, Brit.); COUNTY FAIR(1933, Brit.); EYES OF FATE(1933, Brit.); GHOST TRAIN, THE(1933, Brit.); PARIS PLANE(1933, Brit.); PURSE STRINGS(1933, Brit.); CATHERINE THE GREAT(1934, Brit.); COLONEL BLOOD(1934, Brit.); STRIKE!(1934, Brit.); DRAKE THE PIRATE(1935, Brit.); KOENIGSMARK(1935, Fr.); SANDERS OF THE RIVER(1935, Brit.); SCARLET PIMPERNEL, THE(1935, Brit.); CROWN VS STEVENS(1936); DOMMED CARGO(1936, Brit.); HOUSE OF THE SPANIARD, THE(1936, Brit.); KING OF THE DAMNED(1936, Brit.); REMBRANDT(1936, Brit.); THINGS TO COME(1936, Brit.); ACTION FOR SLANDER(1937, Brit.); ELEPHANT BOY(1937, Brit.); FOREVER YOURS(1937, Brit.); KNIGHT WITHOUT ARMOR(1937, Brit.); MAN OF AFFAIRS(1937, Brit.); MURDER ON DIAMOND ROW(1937, Brit.); DANGEROUS MEDICINE(1938, Brit.); EVERYTHING HAPPENS TO ME(1938, Brit.); ROYAL DIVORCE, A(1938, Brit.); THEY DRIVE BY NIGHT(1938, Brit.); 13 MEN AND A GUN(1938, Brit.); FOUR FEATHERS, THE(1939, Brit.); GOOD OLD DAYS, THE(1939, Brit.); SPY FOR A DAY(1939, Brit.); CONVOY(1940); OLD BILL AND SON(1940, Brit.); STARS LOOK DOWN, THE(1940, Brit.); THIEF OF BAGHDAD, THE(1940, Brit.); THREE COCK-EYED SAILORS(1940, Brit.); PROUD VALLEY, THE(1941, Brit.); YOU WILL REMEMBER(1941, Brit.); PIMPERNEL SMITH(1942, Brit.); AT DAWN WE DIE(1943, Brit.); SHIPBUILDERS, THE(1943, Brit.); UNCENSORED(1944, Brit.); VACATION FROM MARRIAGE(1945, Brit.); DEAD OF NIGHT(1946, Brit.); LISBON STORY, THE(1946, Brit.); GREEN COCKATOO, THE(1947, Brit.); BLANCHE FURY(1948, Brit.); SMUGGLERS, THE(1948, Brit.); HIDDEN ROOM, THE(1949, Brit.); SARABAND(1949, Brit.); RELUCTANT WIDOW, THE(1951, Brit.); WATERFRONT WOMEN(1952, Brit.); REACH FOR GLORY(1963, Brit.)
Silents
NELSON(1918, Brit.)

Allen Jeayes
HIGH COMMAND(1938, Brit.); RETURN OF THE SCARLET PIMPERNEL(1938, Brit.); SPIDER, THE(1940, Brit.)

Ruth Jecklin
MADDEST CAR IN THE WORLD, THE(1974, Ger.)

Helmut Jedele
JACK OF DIAMONDS(1967, U.S./Ger.), p; DEEP END(1970 Ger./U.S.), p

Joanna Jedlewska
WALKOVER(1969, Pol.)

Antonin Jedlicka
LEMONADE JOE(1966, Czech.)

Jedlinska
FRENCH CANCAN(1956, Fr.)

Kalina Jedrusik
JOVITA(1970, Pol.)

Joanna Jedryka
SARAGOSSA MANUSCRIPT, THE(1972, Pol.)

Victoria Jee
ADIOS AMIGO(1975)

Jeebee
MARRY THE BOSS' DAUGHTER(1941)

Robin Jeep
PHANTOM OF THE PARADISE(1974)

Michael Jeeter
ZELIG(1983)

Mahatma Kane Jeeves "Fields"
BANK DICK, THE(1940), w

O.W. Jeeves [Orson Wells]
TREASURE ISLAND(1972, Brit./Span./Fr./Ger.), w

Patricia Jeffares
EDUCATING RITA(1983)

Nigel Jeffcoat
FLASH GORDON(1980)

Douglas Jefferies
FRIEDA(1947, Brit.); LOVES OF JOANNA GODDEN, THE(1947, Brit.)

Phil Jefferies
TRAIN RIDE TO HOLLYWOOD(1975), art d

Philip Jefferies
SYNANON(1965), art d; BUTCH CASSIDY AND THE SUNDANCE KID(1969), art d; MOVE(1970), art d; SOMETIMES A GREAT NOTION(1971), art d; EVERY LITTLE CROOK AND NANNY(1972), prod d; ODE TO BILLY JOE(1976), art d

Philip M. Jefferies
WHEN TIME RAN OUT(1980), prod d; FIRST MONDAY IN OCTOBER(1981), prod d; KISS ME GOODBYE(1982), prod d

Phillip Jefferies
TOM SAWYER(1973), prod d; GREASE(1978), prod d

Roy Jefferies
OPERATION CUPID(1960, Brit.)

Stanton Jefferies
REGAL CAVALCADE(1935, Brit.)

Wes Jefferies
DESERT SANDS(1955), cos; ORGANIZATION, THE(1971), cos

Wesley V. Jefferies
CRIME AGAINST JOE(1956), cos; EMERGENCY HOSPITAL(1956), cos; GHOST TOWN(1956), cos; HOT CARS(1956), cos; THREE BAD SISTERS(1956), cos; SERGEANTS 3(1962), cos

Arnold Jeffers
WHITE LINE FEVER(1975, Can.)

Chris Jeffers
Misc. Talkies
THEIR ONLY CHANCE(1978)

Megan Jeffers
ALTERED STATES(1980)

Michael Jeffers
PARADISE ALLEY(1978)

Mike Jeffers
RUSTLERS(1949)

Ray Jeffers
LOST IN ALASKA(1952), set d; JOE DAKOTA(1957), set d; NIGHT RUNNER, THE(1957), set d

Ray L. Jeffers
RENEGADES OF THE RIO GRANDE(1945), set d

Bob Jefferson
SHAFT'S BIG SCORE(1972)

Herb Jefferson, Jr.
BATTLESTAR GALACTICA(1979)

Herbert Jefferson, Jr.
BLACK GUNN(1972); PRIVATE DUTY NURSES(1972); DETROIT 9000(1973); HANG-UP(1974); MISSION GALACTICA: THE CYLON ATTACK(1979)

I. J. Jefferson
HEAD(1968); PSYCH-OUT(1968); DRIVE, HE SAID(1971)

Joseph Jefferson
ONCE A THIEF(1950)
Silents
RIP VAN WINKLE(1914), w; RIP VAN WINKLE(1921), w

Kevin Jefferson
TOM SAWYER(1973)

L.V. Jefferson
REDEEMING SIN, THE(1929), w; FIGHTING COWBOY(1933), w; LIGHTNING RANGE(1934), w; LION'S DEN, THE(1936), w
Silents
OVERALLS(1916), w; RIDERS OF THE DAWN(1920), w; CROSSING TRAILS(1921), w; NO MAN'S WOMAN(1921), w; PARTNERS OF THE TIDE(1921), d; REDEEMING SIN, THE(1925), w; VANISHING HOOFS(1926), w; CATCH AS CATCH CAN(1927), w; ONE CHANCE IN A MILLION(1927), w; LADDIE BE GOOD(1928), w

Laurie Brooks Jefferson
BAT PEOPLE, THE(1974)

Marc Jefferson
MAX DUGAN RETURNS(1983)

Robert Jefferson
STATION WEST(1948); LIGHT TOUCH, THE(1951)

Roy Jefferson
Misc. Talkies
BROTHERHOOD OF DEATH(1976)

Thomas Jefferson
ON WITH THE SHOW(1929); DOUBLE CROSS ROADS(1930); JUST LIKE HEAVEN(1930); LIGHTNIN'(1930); TEN NIGHTS IN A BARROOM(1931); FORBIDDEN(1932)
Silents
CLASSMATES(1914); RIP VAN WINKLE(1914); SEATS OF THE MIGHTY, THE(1914); SABLE LORCHA, THE(1915); ROMANCE OF TARZAN, THE(1918); TARZAN OF THE APES(1918); GRIM GAME, THE(1919); HELP WANTED–MALE!(1920); WHITE YOUTH(1920); IDLE RICH, THE(1921); RIP VAN WINKLE(1921); SON OF THE WOLF, THE(1922); TAILOR MADE MAN, A(1922); FORTUNE HUNTER, THE(1927)
Misc. Silents
DORA THORNE(1915); CHILD OF MYSTERY, A(1916); MISSING LINKS, THE(1916); POLLY PUT THE KETTLE ON(1917); HOOSIER ROMANCE, A(1918); SIS HOPKINS(1919); SPENDER, THE(1919); FORGED BRIDE, THE(1920); GOOD MEN AND TRUE(1922); PAID TO LOVE(1927)

Thomas Jefferson, Jr.
Misc. Silents
GIRL IN THE WEB, THE(1920)

William Jefferson
Silents
HABIT OF HAPPINESS, THE(1916)
Misc. Silents
WILD OATS(1919)

William W. Jefferson
Misc. Silents
MARRYING MONEY(1915)

William Winter Jefferson
Misc. Silents
OUT OF THE WRECK(1917)

June Jeffery
SEALED VERDICT(1948)

Richard Jeffies
BLOOD TIDE(1982), w

Barbara Jefford
MIDSUMMERS NIGHT'S DREAM, A(1961, Czech.); ULYSSES(1967, U.S./Brit.); BOFORS GUN, THE(1968, Brit.); SHOES OF THE FISHERMAN, THE(1968); MIDSUMMER NIGHT'S DREAM, A(1969, Brit.); LUST FOR A VAMPIRE(1971, Brit.); HITLER: THE LAST TEN DAYS(1973, Brit./Ital.); AND THE SHIP SAILS ON(1983, Ital./Fr.); NELLY'S VERSION(1983, Brit.)

Alan Jeffory
VELVET TRAP, THE(1966)

Dawn Jeffory
TOURIST TRAP, THE(1979); AMY(1981); MOMMIE DEAREST(1981)

Jeffrey
BASHFUL ELEPHANT, THE(1962, Aust.)

Alan Jeffrey
WAY TO THE GOLD, THE(1957)

Cheryl Jeffrey
UP IN SMOKE(1978)

Howard Jeffrey
ON A CLEAR DAY YOU CAN SEE FOREVER(1970), ch; WILLY WONKA AND THE CHOCOLATE FACTORY(1971), ch; BLACK BIRD, THE(1975); CHAPTER TWO(1979); LOOKER(1981), p

Hugh Jeffrey
Silents
PRETENDERS, THE(1916); POWER OF DECISION, THE(1917)
Misc. Silents
WAGER, THE(1916); UNDER SUSPICION(1918)

Jan Jeffrey
JOE PALOOKA IN THE SQUARED CIRCLE(1950), w; JOE PALOOKA IN TRIPLE CROSS(1951), w
John Jeffrey
NIGHT INTO MORNING(1951)
Mark Jeffrey
STAKEOUT ON DOPE STREET(1958), ph
Michael Jeffrey
DANGEROUS HOLIDAY(1937); MAN IN THE GREY FLANNEL SUIT, THE(1956); BLACK CAESAR(1973); WARRIORS, THE(1979)
Omer Jeffrey
BLACK CAESAR(1973)
Paul Jeffrey
Silents
YOUTH TO YOUTH(1922)
Peter Jeffrey
BECKET(1964, Brit.); EARLY BIRD, THE(1965, Brit.); FIGHTING PRINCE OF DONEGAL, THE(1966, Brit.); FIXER, THE(1968); IF ...(1968, Brit.); THAT RIVIERA TOUCH(1968, Brit.); ANNE OF THE THOUSAND DAYS(1969, Brit.); RING OF BRIGHT WATER(1969, Brit.); GOODBYE GEMINI(1970, Brit.); ABOMINABLE DR. PHIBES, THE(1971, Brit.); HORSEMEN, THE(1971); KIDNAPPED(1971, Brit.); COUNTESS DRACULA(1972, Brit.); DOCTOR PHIBES RISES AGAIN(1972, Brit.); WHAT BECAME OF JACK AND JILL?(1972, Brit.); O LUCKY MAN!(1973, Brit.); DEADLY STRANGERS(1974, Brit.); ODESSA FILE, THE(1974, Brit./Ger.); RETURN OF THE PINK PANTHER, THE(1975, Brit.); MIDNIGHT EXPRESS(1978, Brit.); BRITTANIA HOSPITAL(1982, Brit.)
R. E. Jeffrey
MURDER(1930, Brit.)
R.E. Jeffrey
SKIN GAME, THE(1931, Brit.)
Tom Jeffrey
REMOVALISTS, THE(1975, Aus.), d; WEEKEND OF SHADOWS(1978, Aus.), p, d; ODD ANGRY SHOT, THE(1979, Aus.), p, d; FIGHTING BACK(1983, Brit.), p, w
William Jeffrey
EYES OF THE WORLD, THE(1930); MY WOMAN(1933); UPPER WORLD(1934); GOING HIGHBROW(1935); ONE HOUR LATE(1935); SHE MARRIED HER BOSS(1935); ROSE BOWL(1936); TOAST OF NEW YORK, THE(1937)
Anne Jeffreys
BILLY THE KID TRAPPED(1942); I MARRIED AN ANGEL(1942); JOAN OF OZARK(1942); OLD HOMESTEAD, THE(1942); TARZAN'S NEW YORK ADVENTURE(1942); X MARKS THE SPOT(1942); YOKEL BOY(1942); BORDERTOWN GUNFIGHTERS(1943); CALLING WILD BILL ELLIOTT(1943); CHATTERBOX(1943); DEATH VALLEY MANHUNT(1943); MAN FROM THUNDER RIVER, THE(1943); OVERLAND MAIL ROBBERY(1943); WAGON TRACKS WEST(1943); HIDDEN VALLEY OUTLAWS(1944); MOJAVE FIREBRAND(1944); NEVADA(1944); STEP LIVELY(1944); DICK TRACY(1945); DILLINGER(1945); SING YOUR WAY HOME(1945); THOSE ENDEARING YOUNG CHARMS(1945); ZOMBIES ON BROADWAY(1945); DICK TRACY VS. CUEBALL(1946); DING DONG WILLIAMS(1946); GENIUS AT WORK(1946); STEP BY STEP(1946); VACATION IN RENO(1946); RIFFRAFF(1947); TRAIL STREET(1947); RETURN OF THE BADMEN(1948); BOYS' NIGHT OUT(1962); PANIC IN THE CITY(1968)
Misc. Talkies
SOUTHERN DOUBLE CROSS(1973)
Arthur Jeffreys
DEMENTED(1980), p, d
Ellis Jeffreys
RAISE THE ROOF(1930); PERFECT ALIBI, THE(1931, Brit.); TILLY OF BLOOMSBURY(1931, Brit.); BARTON MYSTERY, THE(1932, Brit.); LEAP YEAR(1932, Brit.); WHERE IS THIS LADY?(1932, Brit.); WIVES BEWARE(1933, Brit.); LILIES OF THE FIELD(1934, Brit.); WHILE PARENTS SLEEP(1935, Brit.); ELIZA COMES TO STAY(1936, Brit.); BACKSTAGE(1937, Brit.); SWEET DEVIL(1937, Brit.); FACE BEHIND THE SCAR(1940, Brit.)
Herman Jeffreys
1984
KILLPOINT(1984), m
Lionel Jeffreys
FURTHER UP THE CREEK!(1958, Brit.)
Mark Jeffreys
PURSUIT OF D.B. COOPER, THE(1981)
Jayson Jeffried
1984
PURPLE RAIN(1984), makeup
Betty Jeffries
INVISIBLE AVENGER, THE(1958), w
Carol Jeffries
MAN HUNTERS OF THE CARIBBEAN(1938)
Dean Jeffries
WHAT'S UP, DOC?(1972); DAMNATION ALLEY(1977), stunts
1984
FLETCH(1984), stunts
Dick Jeffries
THIRTEEN FIGHTING MEN(1960)
Douglas Jeffries
SAFE AFFAIR, A(1931, Brit.); CHANNEL CROSSING(1934, Brit.); WHAT HAPPENED TO HARKNESS(1934, Brit.); CARDINAL, THE(1936, Brit.); LONG DARK HALL, THE(1951, Brit.)
Fran Jeffries
BUCCANEER, THE(1958); PINK PANTHER, THE(1964); SEX AND THE SINGLE GIRL(1964); HARUM SCARUM(1965)
Herb Jeffries
DISC JOCKEY(1951); WICKED WOMAN(1953); CALYPSO JOE(1957); CHROME AND HOT LEATHER(1971)
Misc. Talkies
FLAMINGO(1947)
Herbert Jeffries
HARLEM ON THE PRAIRIE(1938); BRONZE BUCKAROO, THE(1939)
James Jeffries
MR. CELEBRITY(1942)

James J. Jeffries
FIGHTING GENTLEMAN, THE(1932); THEY NEVER COME BACK(1932); JEALOUSY(1934); BIG CITY(1937)
Silents
ONE-ROUND HOGAN(1927)
Jan Jeffries
G.I. JANE(1951), w; HIGHWAYMAN, THE(1951), w
Jim Jeffries
MIDNIGHT PATROL, THE(1932); PRIZEFIGHTER AND THE LADY, THE(1933); BARNYARD FOLLIES(1940)
Silents
PENNINGTON'S CHOICE(1915)
Lang Jeffries
REVOLT OF THE SLAVES, THE(1961, Ital./Span./Ger.); DON'T KNOCK THE TWIST(1962); MISSION STARDUST(1968, Ital./Span./Ger.); FIGHT FOR ROME(1969, Ger./Rum.); JUNKMAN, THE(1982)
Misc. Talkies
SOLDIER NAMED JOE, A(1970)
Lionel Jeffries
BLACK RIDER, THE(1954, Brit.); COLDITZ STORY, THE(1955, Brit.); NO SMOKING(1955, Brit.); WILL ANY GENTLEMAN?(1955, Brit.); WINDFALL(1955 Brit.); ALL FOR MARY(1956, Brit.); BHOWANI JUNCTION(1956); EYEWITNESS(1956, Brit.); JUMPING FOR JOY(1956, Brit.); LUST FOR LIFE(1956); THE CREEPING UNKNOWN(1956, Brit.); BABY AND THE BATTLESHIP, THE(1957, Brit.); DECISION AGAINST TIME(1957, Brit.); DOCTOR AT LARGE(1957, Brit.); HIGH TERRACE(1957, Brit.); HOUR OF DECISION(1957, Brit.); UP IN THE WORLD(1957, Brit.); BEHIND THE MASK(1958, Brit.); BLUE MURDER AT ST. TRINIAN'S(1958, Brit.); DUNKIRK(1958, Brit.); GIRLS AT SEA(1958, Brit.); LAW AND DISORDER(1958, Brit.); ORDERS TO KILL(1958, Brit.); REVENGE OF FRANKENSTEIN, THE(1958, Brit.); UP THE CREEK(1958, Brit.); BOBBIKINS(1959, Brit.); CIRCLE, THE(1959, Brit.); IDOL ON PARADE(1959, Brit.); NOWHERE TO GO(1959, Brit.); NUN'S STORY, THE(1959); JAZZ BOAT(1960, Brit.); LET'S GET MARRIED(1960, Brit.); MAN WITH THE GREEN CARNATION, THE(1960, Brit.); PLEASE TURN OVER(1960, Brit.); TARZAN THE MAGNIFICENT(1960, Brit.); FANNY(1961); TWO-WAY STRETCH(1961, Brit.); HELLIONS, THE(1962, Brit.); KILL OR CURE(1962, Brit.); LIFE IS A CIRCUS(1962, Brit.); MRS. GIBBONS' BOYS(1962, Brit.); NOTORIOUS LANDLADY, THE(1962); OPERATION SNATCH(1962, Brit.); CALL ME BWANA(1963, Brit.); WRONG ARM OF THE LAW, THE(1963, Brit.); CRIMSON BLADE, THE(1964, Brit.); FIRST MEN IN THE MOON(1964, Brit.); LONG SHIPS, THE(1964, Brit./Yugo.); MURDER AHOY(1964, Brit.); SECRET OF MY SUCCESS, THE(1965, Brit.); TRUTH ABOUT SPRING, THE(1965, Brit.); YOU MUST BE JOKING!(1965, Brit.); ARRIVEDERCI, BABY!(1966, Brit.); SPY WITH A COLD NOSE, THE(1966, Brit.); CAMELOT(1967); OH DAD, POOR DAD, MAMA'S HUNG YOU IN THE CLOSET AND I'M FEELIN' SO SAD(1967); THOSE FANTASTIC FLYING FOOLS(1967, Brit); CHITTY CHITTY BANG BANG(1968, Brit.); SUDDEN TERROR(1970, Brit.); LOLA(1971, Brit./Ital.); RAILWAY CHILDREN, THE(1971, Brit.), d&w; WHO SLEW AUNTIE ROO?(1971, U.S./Brit.); AMAZING MR. BLUNDEN, THE(1973, Brit.), d&w; BAXTER(1973, Brit.), d; ROYAL FLASH(1975, Brit.); WHAT CHANGED CHARLEY FARTHING?(1976, Brit.); WOMBLING FREE(1977, Brit.), d&w; PRISONER OF ZENDA, THE(1979); WATER BABIES, THE(1979, Brit.), d; BETTER LATE THAN NEVER(1983)
Mike Jeffries
TOAST OF NEW YORK, THE(1937); MR. BOGGS STEPS OUT(1938)
Oliver Jeffries
DRACULA'S DAUGHTER(1936), w
Oliver Jeffries [David O. Selznick]
RECKLESS(1935), w
Phil Jeffries
MANCHURIAN CANDIDATE, THE(1962), art d; THIS PROPERTY IS CONDEMNED(1966), art d; OH DAD, POOR DAD, MAMA'S HUNG YOU IN THE CLOSET AND I'M FEELIN' SO SAD(1967), art d; ST. VALENTINE'S DAY MASSACRE, THE(1967), art d; WALKING TALL, PART II(1975), art d
Philip Jeffries
WUSA(1970), art d; CONQUEST OF THE PLANET OF THE APES(1972), art d; COWBOYS, THE(1972), prod d; HUCKLEBERRY FINN(1974), prod d; ISLAND OF DR. MOREAU, THE(1977), prod d
1984
MASS APPEAL(1984), prod d
Philip M. Jeffries
ST. IVES(1976), prod d; DAMIEN–OMEN II(1978), prod d; OFFICER AND A GENTLEMAN, AN(1982), prod d
Ray Jeffries
LOCAL HERO(1983, Brit.)
1984
ANOTHER TIME, ANOTHER PLACE(1984, Brit.); COMFORT AND JOY(1984, Brit.)
Richard Jeffries
SNIPER'S RIDGE(1961); RAT FINK(1965); BLOOD TIDE(1982), d
W.A. Jeffries
Misc. Silents
FAITH AND ENDURIN'(1918)
Wes Jeffries
WAGONMASTER(1950), cos; SATAN BUG, THE(1965), cos
Wesley V. Jeffries
BLACK SLEEP, THE(1956), cos
Will Jeffries
REFUGE(1981)
Misc. Silents
LAW OF THE GREAT NORTHWEST, THE(1918)
William Jeffries
NOTORIOUS SOPHIE LANG, THE(1934)
Misc. Silents
SOULS OF MEN(1921); FIRE PATROL, THE(1924)
Fred Jeffs
Misc. Silents
CASEY'S MILLIONS(1922, Brit.); CRUISKEEN LAWN(1922, Brit.)
Jo Jeggo
O LUCKY MAN!(1973, Brit.)
A. Jeggs
RETURN OF THE FROG, THE(1938, Brit.), ed

Daniel Jegou
BIRD WATCH, THE(1983, Fr.)
Edith Jehanne
Misc. Silents
LOVE OF JEANNE NEY, THE(1927, Ger.)
Edithe Jehanne
Misc. Silents
CHESS PLAYER, THE(1930, Fr.)
Otto Jehle
SWISS MISS(1938)
Otto Jehly
I MET HIM IN PARIS(1937)
Gregory Jein
CLOSE ENCOUNTERS OF THE THIRD KIND(1977), spec eff
Anna Jekielek
1984
SHIVERS(1984, Pol.), prod d
Eric Jelde
HANNIBAL BROOKS(1969, Brit.)
Erich Jelde
DECISION BEFORE DAWN(1951)
Erik Jelde
MAGIC FOUNTAIN, THE(1961); QUESTION 7(1961, U.S./Ger.); SOMETHING FOR EVERYONE(1970)
Bibi Jelinek
UNCLE TOM'S CABIN(1969, Fr./Ital./Ger./Yugo.)
Henriette Jelinek
ADOLESCENT, THE(1978, Fr./W.Ger.), w
Jiri Jelinek
LEMONADE JOE(1966, Czech.)
Rudolf Jelinek
BARON MUNCHAUSEN(1962, Czech.); BRIDGE AT REMAGEN, THE(1969); SIGN OF THE VIRGIN(1969, Czech.)
Zdenek Jelinek
TRANSPORT FROM PARADISE(1967, Czech.)
Vlasta Jelinkova
90 DEGREES IN THE SHADE(1966, Czech./Brit.)
Val Jellay
DIMBOOLA(1979, Aus.)
Jack Jellet
Silents
INTO THE NIGHT(1928), ph
Ann Jellicoe
KNACK ... AND HOW TO GET IT, THE(1965, Brit.), w
Earl Jellicoe
BLOCKADE(1928, Brit.)
Bill Jelliffe
SERIAL(1980)
Roy Jelliffe
FOOLS(1970)
Tristam Jellineck
1984
GREYSTOKE: THE LEGEND OF TARZAN, LORD OF THE APES(1984)
Oskar Jellinek
THY NEIGHBOR'S WIFE(1953), w
Tristram Jellinek
KILL OR CURE(1962, Brit.); TRIAL AND ERROR(1962, Brit.)
1984
ANOTHER COUNTRY(1984, Brit.); LASSITER(1984); SUCCESS IS THE BEST REVENGE(1984, Brit.); TOP SECRET!(1984)
Bob Jellison
JUDGE, THE(1949); LOVE NEST(1951); TOO YOUNG TO KISS(1951); STAR IS BORN, A(1954); GREAT AMERICAN PASTIME, THE(1956)
John Jellison
1984
COLD FEET(1984)
Karel Jellnek
BOHEMIAN RAPTURE(1948, Czech)
Carlotta Jelm
MEET JOHN DOE(1941); ONE FOOT IN HEAVEN(1941); MAJOR AND THE MINOR, THE(1942); HERE COME THE WAVES(1944); INCENDIARY BLONDE(1945)
Anna Jemison
SMASH PALACE(1982, New Zealand); HEATWAVE(1983, Aus.)
Jean-Louis Jemma
WOULD-BE GENTLEMAN, THE(1960, Fr.)
M. Jemma
LUCIANO(1963, Ital.), w
Ottavio Jemma
SAUL AND DAVID(1968, Ital./Span.), w; SHE AND HE(1969, Ital.), w; WHEN WOMEN HAD TAILS(1970, Ital.), w; SACCO AND VANZETTI(1971, Ital./Fr.), w; MALICIOUS(1974, Ital.), w; GIRL FROM TRIESTE, THE(1983, Ital.), w
C. Jen
FIGHT TO THE LAST(1938, Chi.)
Ho Jen
DEADLY CHINA DOLL(1973, Hong Kong), w
B. Jenbach
LILAC DOMINO, THE(1940, Brit.), w
Oesterreicher Jenbach
WHO'S YOUR LADY FRIEND?(1937, Brit.), w
Joe Jenckes
IRON ANGEL(1964); MOONLIGHTING WIVES(1966)
Clinton Jencks
SALT OF THE EARTH(1954)
Nancy Jencks
ONE FROM THE HEART(1982)
Virginia Jencks
SALT OF THE EARTH(1954)

Roger Jendely
INVITATION, THE(1975, Fr./Switz.)
Roger Jendly
JONAH–WHO WILL BE 25 IN THE YEAR 2000(1976, Switz.); EVERY MAN FOR HIMSELF(1980, Fr.); DEATH OF MARIO RICCI, THE(1983, Ital.)
Hans Dieter Jendreyko
JONATHAN(1973, Ger.)
Istvan Jeney
1984
BRADY'S ESCAPE(1984, U.S./Hung.)
Olivia Jeng
POWERFORCE(1983)
Len Jenkin
1984
BLAME IT ON THE NIGHT(1984), w
Albin Jenkins
BUGSY MALONE(1976, Brit.)
Allan Jenkins
CRAZY OVER HORSES(1951)
Allen Jenkins
GIRL HABIT(1931); BLESSED EVENT(1932); I AM A FUGITIVE FROM A CHAIN GANG(1932); RACKETY RAX(1932); THREE ON A MATCH(1932); BLONDIE JOHNSON(1933); BUREAU OF MISSING PERSONS(1933); EMPLOYEE'S ENTRANCE(1933); HARD TO HANDLE(1933); HAVANA WIDOWS(1933); KEYHOLE, THE(1933); LAWYER MAN(1933); MAYOR OF HELL, THE(1933); MIND READER, THE(1933); PROFESSIONAL SWEETHEART(1933); SILK EXPRESS, THE(1933); TOMORROW AT SEVEN(1933); 42ND STREET(1933); BEDSIDE(1934); BIG SHAKEDOWN, THE(1934); CASE OF THE HOWLING DOG, THE(1934); HAPPINESS AHEAD(1934); I'VE GOT YOUR NUMBER(1934); JIMMY THE GENT(1934); MERRY FRINKS, THE(1934); ST. LOUIS KID, THE(1934); TWENTY MILLION SWEETHEARTS(1934); WHIRLPOOL(1934); BROADWAY HOSTESS(1935); CASE OF THE CURIOUS BRIDE, THE(1935); CASE OF THE LUCKY LEGS, THE(1935); I LIVE FOR LOVE(1935); IRISH IN US, THE(1935); MISS PACIFIC FLEET(1935); NIGHT AT THE RITZ, A(1935); PAGE MISS GLORY(1935); SWEET MUSIC(1935); WHILE THE PATIENT SLEPT(1935); CAIN AND MABEL(1936); SING ME A LOVE SONG(1936); SINGING KID, THE(1936); SINS OF MAN(1936); THREE MEN ON A HORSE(1936); DANCE, CHARLIE, DANCE(1937); DEAD END(1937); MARKED WOMAN(1937); MARRY THE GIRL(1937); PERFECT SPECIMEN, THE(1937); READY, WILLING AND ABLE(1937); SH! THE OCTOPUS(1937); SINGING MARINE, THE(1937); AMAZING DR. CLITTERHOUSE, THE(1938); FOOLS FOR SCANDAL(1938); GOLD DIGGERS IN PARIS(1938); HARD TO GET(1938); HEART OF THE NORTH(1938); RACKET BUSTERS(1938); SLIGHT CASE OF MURDER, A(1938); SWING YOUR LADY(1938); DESTRY RIDES AGAIN(1939); FIVE CAME BACK(1939); GOING PLACES(1939); NAUGHTY BUT NICE(1939); SWEEPSTAKES WINNER(1939); TORCHY PLAYS WITH DYNAMITE(1939); BROTHER ORCHID(1940); MARGIE(1940); MEET THE WILDCAT(1940); OH JOHNNY, HOW YOU CAN LOVE!(1940); TIN PAN ALLEY(1940); BALL OF FIRE(1941); DATE WITH THE FALCON, A(1941); DIVE BOMBER(1941); FOOTSTEPS IN THE DARK(1941); GAY FALCON, THE(1941); GO WEST, YOUNG LADY(1941); TIME OUT FOR RHYTHM(1941); EYES IN THE NIGHT(1942); FALCON TAKES OVER, THE(1942); MAISIE GETS HER MAN(1942); THEY ALL KISSED THE BRIDE(1942); TORTILLA FLAT(1942); STAGE DOOR CANTEEN(1943); LADY ON A TRAIN(1945); WONDER MAN(1945); DARK HORSE, THE(1946); MEET ME ON BROADWAY(1946); SINGIN' IN THE CORN(1946); EASY COME, EASY GO(1947); SENATOR WAS INDISCREET, THE(1947); WILD HARVEST(1947); INSIDE STORY, THE(1948); BIG WHEEL, THE(1949); BODYHOLD(1950); CHAINED FOR LIFE(1950); BEHAVE YOURSELF(1951); LET'S GO NAVY(1951); OKLAHOMA ANNIE(1952); WAC FROM WALLA WALLA, THE(1952); PILLOW TALK(1959); IT'S A MAD, MAD, MAD, MAD WORLD(1963); FOR THOSE WHO THINK YOUNG(1964); I'D RATHER BE RICH(1964); ROBIN AND THE SEVEN HOODS(1964); SPY IN THE GREEN HAT, THE(1966); DOCTOR, YOU'VE GOT TO BE KIDDING(1967); FRONT PAGE, THE(1974); FUN ON A WEEKEND(1979)
Arlene Jenkins
ALIAS NICK BEAL(1949); RED, HOT AND BLUE(1949); PAID IN FULL(1950)
Bobby Jenkins
LOOSE ENDS(1975)
Burke Jenkins
Silents
BASHFUL BUCCANEER(1925), w; LADY ROBINHOOD(1925), w
Butch Jenkins
ABBOTT AND COSTELLO IN HOLLYWOOD(1945); BIG CITY(1948); BRIDE GOES WILD, THE(1948)
"Butch" Jenkins
MY BROTHER TALKS TO HORSES(1946)
Charles Jenkins
YELLOW SUBMARINE(1958, Brit.), spec eff
Charles B. Jenkins
POSTMAN ALWAYS RINGS TWICE, THE(1981)
Cliff Jenkins
1984
MIKE'S MURDER(1984)
Cynthia Jenkins
PUNISHMENT PARK(1971)
Cyril Jenkins
1984
MUPPETS TAKE MANHATTAN, THE(1984)
Dal Jenkins
INVITATION TO A GUNFIGHTER(1964); GREATEST STORY EVER TOLD, THE(1965); WAR LORD, THE(1965); YOUNG FURY(1965); ZEBRA IN THE KITCHEN(1965); WILL PENNY(1968); BAD CHARLESTON CHARLIE(1973)
Dan Jenkins
SEMI-TOUGH(1977), w
David Jenkins
I'M DANCING AS FAST AS I CAN(1982), prod d
Dorothy Jenkins
ELMER GANTRY(1960), cos
Ed Jenkins
MR. WINKLE GOES TO WAR(1944)

Eric Jenkins
HEART BEAT(1979), ed; ALTERED STATES(1980), ed; FAST TIMES AT RIDGE-MONT HIGH(1982), ed; PANDEMONIUM(1982), ed
Fred Jenkins
Silents
COUNTERFEIT(1919)
Geoffrey Jenkins
TWIST OF SAND, A(1968, Brit.), w
George Jenkins
BEST YEARS OF OUR LIVES, THE(1946), art d; SECRET LIFE OF WALTER MITTY, THE(1947), art d; ENCHANTMENT(1948), art d; SONG IS BORN, A(1948), art d; ROSEANNA McCOY(1949), art d; SAN FRANCISCO STORY, THE(1952), prod d; MIRACLE WORKER, THE(1962), art d; MICKEY ONE(1965), prod d; UP THE DOWN STAIRCASE(1967), art d; WAIT UNTIL DARK(1967), art d; NO WAY TO TREAT A LADY(1968), art d, set d; SUBJECT WAS ROSES, THE(1968), art d; ME, NATA-LIE(1969), art d; ANGEL LEVINE, THE(1970), art d; KLUTE(1971), art d; PURSUIT OF HAPPINESS, THE(1971), art d; 1776(1972), art d; PAPER CHASE, THE(1973), art d; PARALLAX VIEW, THE(1974), prod d, art d; FUNNY LADY(1975), prod d; NIGHT MOVES(1975), prod d; ALL THE PRESIDENT'S MEN(1976), prod d; COMES A HORSEMAN(1978), prod d; CHINA SYNDROME, THE(1979), art d; STARTING OVER(1979), prod d; POSTMAN ALWAYS RINGS TWICE, THE(1981), prod d; ROL-LOVER(1981), prod d; SOPHIE'S CHOICE(1982), prod d
Gordon Jenkins
STRANGE HOLIDAY(1945), m; BWANA DEVIL(1953), m; FIRST DEADLY SIN, THE(1980), m
Harry Jenkins
SHOT AT DAWN, A(1934, Ger.), w
Herbert Jenkins
Silents
PATRICIA BRENT, SPINSTER(1919, Brit.), w
J. W. Jenkins
Silents
SILENT COMMAND, THE(1923)
Jackie "Butch" Jenkins
HUMAN COMEDY, THE(1943); NATIONAL VELVET(1944); OUR VINES HAVE TENDER GRAPES(1945); BOYS' RANCH(1946); LITTLE MISTER JIM(1946); SUM-MER HOLIDAY(1948)
Janice Jenkins
CLARENCE AND ANGEL(1981)
Joe Jenkins
ON THE BEACH(1959); HUMAN FACTOR, THE(1975)
John Jenkins
LOOSE ENDS(1975)
Joseph Jenkins
CAPE FEAR(1962)
Julian Jenkins
STATUE, THE(1971, Brit.)
Larry "Flash" Jenkins
1984
BODY DOUBLE(1984); FLETCH(1984)
LeRoy Jenkins
CHILDISH THINGS(1969)
Linda Jenkins
LOOSE ENDS(1975)
Lloyd Jenkins
STORM WARNING(1950)
Louis Jenkins
LILITH(1964)
Margaret Jenkins
DAY OF THE LOCUST, THE(1975)
Margo Jenkins
EXPERIENCE PREFERRED... BUT NOT ESSENTIAL(1983, Brit.)
Mark Jenkins
RIVERRUN(1968); DOCTORS' WIVES(1971)
Megs Jenkins
CONTINENTAL EXPRESS(1939, Brit.); POISON PEN(1941, Brit.); IT'S IN THE BAG(1943, Brit.); MILLIONS LIKE US(1943, Brit.); GREEN FOR DANGER(1946, Brit.); GIRL ON THE CANAL, THE(1947, Brit.); BROTHERS, THE(1948, Brit.); MONKEY'S PAW, THE(1948, Brit.); BOY, A GIRL AND A BIKE, A(1949 Brit.); FACTS OF LOVE(1949, Brit.); HISTORY OF MR. POLLY, THE(1949, Brit.); SARABAND(1949, Brit.); NO PLACE FOR JENNIFER(1950, Brit.); IVANHOE(1952, Brit.); SECRET PEOPLE(1952, Brit.); WHITE CORRIDORS(1952, Brit.); CRUEL SEA, THE(1953); SHOOT FIRST(1953, Brit.); GAY DOG, THE(1954, Brit.); PERSONAL AFFAIR(1954, Brit.); TROUBLE IN STORE(1955, Brit.); DECISION AGAINST TIME(1957, Brit.); JOHN AND JULIE(1957, Brit.); NOVEL AFFAIR, A(1957, Brit.); OUT OF THE CLOUDS(1957, Brit.); STORY OF ESTHER COSTELLO, THE(1957, Brit.); INDIS-CREET(1958); TIGER BAY(1959, Brit.); CONSPIRACY OF HEARTS(1960, Brit.); GREEN HELMET, THE(1961, Brit.); INNOCENTS, THE(1961, U.S./Brit.); JET STORM(1961, Brit.); BARBER OF STAMFORD HILL, THE(1963, Brit.); FRIENDS AND NEIGHBORS(1963, Brit.); MACBETH(1963); MURDER MOST FOUL(1964, Brit.); YOUNG AND WILLING(1964, Brit.); BUNNY LAKE IS MISSING(1965); WALK IN THE SHADOW(1966, Brit.); COP-OUT(1967, Brit.); OLIVER!(1968, Brit.); DAVID COPPERFIELD(1970, Brit.); ASYLUM(1972, Brit.); SCHOOL FOR UNCLAIMED GIRLS(1973, Brit.)
Michael Jenkins
1984
CAREFUL, HE MIGHT HEAR YOU(1984, Aus.), w
Pat Jenkins
GAMBLER AND THE LADY, THE(1952, Brit.), d
Patrick Jenkins
LEASE OF LIFE(1954, Brit.), w
Paul Jenkins
ORGANIZATION, THE(1971); ONE IS A LONELY NUMBER(1972); CHINA-TOWN(1974); NETWORK(1976); NIGHT GAMES(1980)
1984
HARD TO HOLD(1984)
Ralph Jenkins
Misc. Talkies
AFFAIRS OF ROBIN HOOD, THE(1981)

Shirley Jenkins
TEARS FOR SIMON(1957, Brit.)
Terry Jenkins
BANDIDOS(1967, Ital.); PAINT YOUR WAGON(1969)
Teryn Jenkins
NEW YORK, NEW YORK(1977); PROMISES IN THE DARK(1979)
Timothy Jenkins
HAPPY BIRTHDAY, GEMINI(1980); MIDSUMMER NIGHT'S SEX COMEDY, A(1982)
Uncle Tom Jenkins
Silents
WHITE ROSE, THE(1923)
Warren Jenkins
ABDUL THE DAMNED(1935, Brit.); IT HAPPENED IN PARIS(1935, Brit.); RADIO PIRATES(1935, Brit.); IT'S LOVE AGAIN(1936, Brit.); GANGWAY(1937, Brit.); LITTLE DOLLY DAYDREAM(1938, Brit.); LAUGH IT OFF(1940, Brit.)
Warren C. Jenkins
SINGING THROUGH(1935, Brit.)
Wes Jenkins
Silents
BAB'S CANDIDATE(1920)
Wesley Jenkins
Silents
KENTUCKIANS, THE(1921)
Will Jenkins
MURDER WILL OUT(1930), w
Will F. Jenkins
TORCHY BLANE IN CHINATOWN(1938), w
Silents
PURPLE CIPHER, THE(1920), w
William Jenkins
TWO HEARTS IN WALTZ TIME(1934, Brit.)
Chris Jenkinson
EYE OF THE NEEDLE(1981)
Harry Jenkinson
Misc. Silents
KIDDER & KO.(1918)
Mike Jenkinson
BAY OF SAINT MICHEL, THE(1963, Brit.)
Bob Jenkis
1984
BREAKIN' 2: ELECTRIC BOOGALOO(1984), ed
David Jenks
TOM BROWN'S SCHOOLDAYS(1951, Brit.)
Frank Jenks
DON'T TURN'EM LOOSE(1936); FARMER IN THE DELL, THE(1936); FOLLOW THE FLEET(1936); LAST OUTLAW, THE(1936); OLD HUTCH(1936); SMARTEST GIRL IN TOWN(1936); SWING TIME(1936); WALKING ON AIR(1936); WITNESS CHAIR, THE(1936); ANGEL'S HOLIDAY(1937); LADY FIGHTS BACK(1937); PRESCRIPTION FOR ROMANCE(1937); SATURDAY'S HEROES(1937); THAT GIRL FROM PA-RIS(1937); THERE GOES MY GIRL(1937); WE WHO ARE ABOUT TO DIE(1937); WESTLAND CASE, THE(1937); WHEN'S YOUR BIRTHDAY?(1937); YOU'RE A SWEETHEART(1937); 100 MEN AND A GIRL(1937); DEVIL'S PARTY, THE(1938); GOODBYE BROADWAY(1938); LADY IN THE MORGUE(1938); LAST WARNING, THE(1938); LETTER OF INTRODUCTION(1938); LOVE IS A HEADACHE(1938); RECKLESS LIVING(1938); STORM, THE(1938); STRANGE FACES(1938); YOUTH TAKES A FLING(1938); BIG TOWN CZAR(1939); FIRST LOVE(1939); GOLDEN BOY(1939); SOCIETY SMUGGLERS(1939); S.O.S. TIDAL WAVE(1939); UNDER-PUP, THE(1939); YOU CAN'T CHEAT AN HONEST MAN(1939); DANCING ON A DI-ME(1940); HIS GIRL FRIDAY(1940); LITTLE BIT OF HEAVEN, A(1940); MELODY AND MOONLIGHT(1940); THREE CHEERS FOR THE IRISH(1940); BACK STREET(1941); FLAME OF NEW ORLEANS, THE(1941); SCATTERGOOD MEETS BROADWAY(1941); TALL, DARK AND HANDSOME(1941); WHERE DID YOU GET THAT GIRL?(1941); MAISIE GETS HER MAN(1942); NAVY COMES THROUGH, THE(1942); SEVEN MILES FROM ALCATRAZ(1942); SYNCOPATION(1942); TWO YANKS IN TRINIDAD(1942); CORREGIDOR(1943); GILDERSLEEVE'S BAD DAY(1943); HI' YA, SAILOR(1943); HIS BUTLER'S SISTER(1943); HUMAN COMEDY, THE(1943); SHANTYTOWN(1943); SO'S YOUR UNCLE(1943); THOUSANDS CHEER(1943); FALCON IN HOLLYWOOD, THE(1944); FOLLOW THE BOYS(1944); IMPATIENT YEARS, THE(1944); LADIES COURAGEOUS(1944); ROGER TOUHY, GANGSTER!(1944); ROSIE THE RIVETER(1944); SHAKE HANDS WITH MUR-DER(1944); STRANGE AFFAIR(1944); TAKE IT OR LEAVE IT(1944); THIS IS THE LIFE(1944); THREE LITTLE SISTERS(1944); TWO GIRLS AND A SAILOR(1944); BEDSIDE MANNER(1945); CHRISTMAS IN CONNECTICUT(1945); DIXIE JAM-BOREE(1945); G.I. HONEYMOON(1945); KID SISTER, THE(1945); MISSING CORPSE, THE(1945); PHANTOM OF 42ND STREET, THE(1945); ROGUES GALLERY(1945); STEPPIN' IN SOCIETY(1945); ZOMBIES ON BROADWAY(1945); BLONDIE'S LUCKY DAY(1946); ONE WAY TO LOVE(1946); THAT BRENNAN GIRL(1946); WHITE TIE AND TAILS(1946); BLONDE SAVAGE(1947); HIGH WALL, THE(1947); KILROY WAS HERE(1947); PHILO VANCE'S GAMBLE(1947); PHILO VANCE'S SECRET MIS-SION(1947); THAT'S MY GAL(1947); BLONDIE'S REWARD(1948); FAMILY HONEY-MOON(1948); JOE PALOOKA IN WINNER TAKE ALL(1948); MARY LOU(1948); YOU GOTTA STAY HAPPY(1948); SHEP COMES HOME(1949); BLONDIE'S HERO(1950); JOE PALOOKA IN THE SQUARED CIRCLE(1950); LUCKY LOSERS(1950); MOTHER DIDN'T TELL ME(1950); MOTOR PATROL(1950); PETTY GIRL, THE(1950); TO PLEASE A LADY(1950); WOMAN ON THE RUN(1950); BOWERY BATTALION(1951); I WAS AN AMERICAN SPY(1951); LET'S GO NAVY(1951); PECOS RIVER(1951); SCARF, THE(1951); SILVER CITY BONANZA(1951); UTAH WAGON TRAIN(1951); MR. WALKIE TALKIE(1952); WHITE LIGHTNING(1953); HIGHWAY DRAG-NET(1954); OUTLAW TREASURE(1955); SUDDEN DANGER(1955); DIG THAT URANIUM(1956); FRIENDLY PERSUASION(1956); HOUSTON STORY, THE(1956); SHE-CREATURE, THE(1956); AMAZING COLOSSAL MAN, THE(1957); SHAKE, RATTLE, AND ROCK!(1957)
George Elwood Jenks
Silents
END OF THE GAME, THE(1919), w; MAN WHO TURNED WHITE, THE(1919), w; CUB REPORTER, THE(1922), w

Harry Jenks
SANTA'S CHRISTMAS CIRCUS(1966), m
Jasmin Jenks
THRILL OF BRAZIL, THE(1946)
L. Jenks
Silents
KID, THE(1921)
S. Jenks
RIDERS OF DESTINY(1933)
Si Jenks
SERGEANT YORK(; MAN FROM DEATH VALLEY, THE(1931); NEAR THE
TRAIL'S END(1931); OKLAHOMA JIM(1931); TWO-FISTED JUSTICE(1931); GAL-
LOPING THRU(1932); MY MOTHER(1933); CHARLIE CHAN'S COURAGE(1934);
DUDE RANGER, THE(1934); LIGHTNING RANGE(1934); MURDER IN THE MU-
SEUM(1934); OPERATOR 13(1934); SIXTEEN FATHOMS DEEP(1934); STAND UP
AND CHEER(1934 80m FOX bw); CAPTAIN JANUARY(1935); FIGHTING SHA-
DOWS(1935); LAW BEYOND THE RANGE(1935); MUSIC IS MAGIC(1935); OUTLAW
DEPUTY, THE(1935); RIDER OF THE LAW, THE(1935); STEAMBOAT ROUND THE
BEND(1935); COWBOY STAR, THE(1936); FOLLOW YOUR HEART(1936); FU-
RY(1936); GO WEST, YOUNG MAN(1936); GUN PLAY(1936); MESSAGE TO GARCIA,
A(1936); PIGSKIN PARADE(1936); PRESIDENT'S MYSTERY, THE(1936); SPECIAL
INVESTIGATOR(1936); DAY AT THE RACES, A(1937); DODGE CITY TRAIL(1937);
DON'T TELL THE WIFE(1937); LADY FIGHTS BACK(1937); MARRIED BEFORE
BREAKFAST(1937); OLD WYOMING TRAIL, THE(1937); OUTCASTS OF POKER
FLAT, THE(1937); PICK A STAR(1937); SARATOGA(1937); TENDERFOOT GOES
WEST, A(1937); THRILL OF A LIFETIME(1937); TOPPER(1937); WITH LOVE AND
KISSES(1937); YOU CAN'T HAVE EVERYTHING(1937); KENTUCKY MOON-
SHINE(1938); RAWHIDE(1938); BURN 'EM UP O'CONNER(1939); DRUMS ALONG
THE MOHAWK(1939); FRONTIER MARSHAL(1939); GONE WITH THE WIND(1939);
MILLION DOLLAR LEGS(1939); STAGECOACH(1939); TOM SAWYER, DETEC-
TIVE(1939); UNION PACIFIC(1939); YOU CAN'T CHEAT AN HONEST MAN(1939);
CHAD HANNA(1940); FARMER'S DAUGHTER(1940); GIRL FROM GOD'S
COUNTRY(1940); MY LITTLE CHICKADEE(1940); RANGER AND THE LADY,
THE(1940); RIDE, TENDERFOOT, RIDE(1940); TRAIL BLAZERS, THE(1940); BUY
ME THAT TOWN(1941); COME LIVE WITH ME(1941); GREAT TRAIN ROBBERY,
THE(1941); OLD SWIMMIN' HOLE, THE(1941); COWBOY SERENADE(1942); ICE-
CAPADES REVUE(1942); IT'S A GREAT LIFE(1943); WILD HORSE STAM-
PEDE(1943); LOUISIANA HAYRIDE(1943); SONG OF NEVADA(1944); STORY OF DR.
WASSELL, THE(1944); BANDITS OF THE BADLANDS(1945); EVE KNEW HER
APPLES(1945); MAN FROM OKLAHOMA, THE(1945); MURDER, HE SAYS(1945);
OREGON TRAIL(1945); SAN ANTONIO(1945); DARK HORSE, THE(1946); DUEL IN
THE SUN(1946); GOD'S COUNTRY(1946); SINGIN' IN THE CORN(1946); UNCON-
QUERED(1947); DUDE GOES WEST, THE(1948); FURY AT FURNACE CREEK(1948);
TAKE ME OUT TO THE BALL GAME(1949); KENTUCKY JUBILEE(1951); RAW-
HIDE(1951); OKLAHOMA ANNIE(1952)
Misc. Talkies
LAWLESS VALLEY(1932); RAWHIDE ROMANCE(1934)
Sy Jenks
ANOTHER FACE(1935); TRAIL STREET(1947)
Michael Jenn
1984
ANOTHER COUNTRY(1984, Brit.)
Stephen Jenn
1984
CHAMPIONS(1984)
Ann Jenner
ROMEO AND JULIET(1966, Brit.)
Barry Jenner
LOOKER(1981)
Bert Jenner
CHILDREN OF THE FOG(1935, Brit.)
Bruce Jenner
CAN'T STOP THE MUSIC(1980)
Jennett
ON PROBATION(1935), set d
Adam Jennette
ROMAN HOLIDAY(1953)
Jack Jenney
SYNCOPATION(1942)
Al Jennings
LAND OF MISSING MEN, THE(1930); AT THE RIDGE(1931); SONG OF THE
GRINGO(1936), a, w; WHITE CLIFFS OF DOVER, THE(1944), ed
Silents
CAPTAIN OF THE GRAY HORSE TROOP, THE(1917)
Misc. Silents
LADY OF THE DUGOUT(1918); RIDIN' RASCAL, THE(1926)
Anna Jennings
Silents
GHOST TRAIN, THE(1927, Brit.)
Misc. Silents
GHOST TRAIN, THE(1927, Brit.)
Bob Jennings
COUNTRY BOY(1966)
Brent Jennings
BRUBAKER(1980)
1984
FEAR CITY(1984)
Claudia Jennings
JUD(1971); LOVE MACHINE, THE,(1971); UNHOLY ROLLERS(1972); FORTY
CARATS(1973); GATOR BAIT(1974); TRUCK STOP WOMEN(1974); GREAT TEXAS
DYNAMITE CHASE, THE(1976); MOONSHINE COUNTY EXPRESS(1977); DEATH-
SPORT(1978)
Misc. Talkies
GROUP MARRIAGE(1972); SINGLE GIRLS(1973); STEPMOTHER, THE(1973); WIL-
LIE AND SCRATCH(1975); SISTERS OF DEATH(1976); FAST COMPANY(1979)
De Witt Jennings
FOX MOVIETONE FOLLIES(1929); SEVEN FOOTPRINTS TO SATAN(1929); BIG
HOUSE, THE(1930); SEVEN KEYS TO BALDPATE(1930); ARROWSMITH(1931);
DANGEROUS AFFAIR, A(1931); MIDNIGHT MORALS(1932); SILVER DOL-
LAR(1932); TESS OF THE STORM COUNTRY(1932); GRAND SLAM(1933); REFORM

GIRL(1933); MUTINY ON THE BOUNTY(1935); ACCUSING FINGER, THE(1936);
FIFTY ROADS TO TOWN(1937)
Silents
FROM THE GROUND UP(1921); INVISIBLE POWER, THE(1921); POVERTY OF
RICHES, THE(1921); SHERLOCK BROWN(1921); RIGHT THAT
FAILED, THE(1922); CIRCUS DAYS(1923); OUT OF LUCK(1923); ENEMY SEX,
THE(1924); MERTON OF THE MOVIES(1924); SPLENDID ROAD, THE(1925); EXIT
SMILING(1926); ICE FLOOD, THE(1926); GREAT MAIL ROBBERY, THE(1927);
MARRY THE GIRL(1928)
Misc. Silents
GREATER CLAIM, THE(1921); THERE ARE NO VILLAINS(1921); FLESH AND
BLOOD(1922); BLINKY(1923); HOME MADE(1927)
De Witt C. Jennings
OPERATOR 13(1934)
Dean Jennings
SECRET SEVEN, THE(1940), w; DUFFY OF SAN QUENTIN(1954), d&w
Dev Jennings
SALLY(1929), ph; SAP, THE(1929), ph; BRIDE OF THE REGIMENT(1930), ph;
DUMBBELLS IN ERMINE(1930), ph; GOLDEN DAWN(1930), ph; HOLD EVERY-
THING(1930), ph; LIFE OF THE PARTY, THE(1930), ph; MATRIMONIAL BED,
THE(1930), ph; OH! SAILOR, BEHAVE!(1930), ph; SONG OF THE WEST(1930), ph;
DIVORCE AMONG FRIENDS(1931), ph; FIFTY MILLION FRENCHMEN(1931), ph;
FINN AND HATTIE(1931), ph; MANHATTAN PARADE(1931), ph; PUBLIC ENEMY,
THE(1931), ph; SIDE SHOW(1931), ph; FAMOUS FERGUSON CASE, THE(1932), ph;
STRANGER IN TOWN(1932), ph
Silents
STING OF THE LASH(1921), ph; EAGLE, THE(1925), ph; BATTLING BUT-
LER(1926), ph; FLYING ROMEOS(1928), ph; HEART TROUBLE(1928), ph; STEAM-
BOAT BILL, JR.(1928), ph; VAMPING VENUS(1928), ph
Devereaux Jennings
SAMSON AND DELILAH(1949), spec eff; GREATEST SHOW ON EARTH,
THE(1952), spec eff
Devereux Jennings
BLAZE OF NOON(1947), spec eff; UNCONQUERED(1947), spec eff
DeWitt C. Jennings
CAT'S PAW, THE(1934); CHARLIE CHAN'S COURAGE(1934); FRONT PAGE WOM-
AN(1935); KELLY THE SECOND(1936)
Silents
BEATING THE GAME(1921)
DeWitt Jennings
ALIBI(1929); RED HOT SPEED ½(1929); THRU DIFFERENT EYES(1929); TRIAL OF
MARY DUGAN, THE(1929); VALIANT, THE(1929); BAT WHISPERS, THE(1930); BIG
TRAIL, THE(1930); IN THE NEXT ROOM(1930); MIN AND BILL(1930); NIGHT
RIDE(1930); OUTSIDE THE LAW(1930); SCARLET PAGES(1930); THOSE WHO
DANCE(1930); CAUGHT PLASTERED(1931); CRIMINAL CODE(1931); DECEIVER,
THE(1931); SALVATION NELL(1931); SECRET SIX, THE(1931); SQUAW MAN,
THE(1931); CENTRAL PARK(1932); DANCERS IN THE DARK(1932); MATCH KING,
THE(1932); MOVIE CRAZY(1932); LADIES THEY TALK ABOUT(1933); LADY'S
PROFESSION, A(1933); MYSTERY OF THE WAX MUSEUM, THE(1933); ONE YEAR
LATER(1933); POLICE CAR 17(1933); STRICTLY PERSONAL(1933); DEATH OF THE
DIAMOND(1934); FIGHTING ROOKIE, THE(1934); LITTLE MAN, WHAT
NOW?(1934); MAN'S GAME, A(1934); MASSACRE(1934); PRESIDENT VANISHES,
THE(1934); TAKE THE STAND(1934); WICKED WOMAN, A(1934); DARING YOUNG
MAN, THE(1935); DOG OF FLANDERS, A(1935); FARMER TAKES A WIFE,
THE(1935); MARY JANE'S PA(1935); MURDER ON A HONEYMOON(1935); SECRET
OF THE CHATEAU(1935); VILLAGE TALE(1935); CRIME OF DR. FORBES(1936);
SINS OF MAN(1936); NANCY STEELE IS MISSING(1937); SLAVE SHIP(1937); THAT
I MAY LIVE(1937); WE WHO ARE ABOUT TO DIE(1937)
Silents
WARRENS OF VIRGINIA, THE(1915); NINETEEN AND PHYLLIS(1920); ALONG
CAME RUTH(1924); AIR MAIL PILOT, THE(1928); NIGHT FLYER, THE(1928)
Misc. Silents
SPORTING BLOOD(1916); DESERT OUTLAW, THE(1924)
Edward Jennings
ALIBI(1929)
Elizabeth Jennings
GUNSIGHT RIDGE(1957), w
Ernest C. Jennings
TALES FROM THE CRYPT(1972, Brit.)
Ernest Jennings
RECKONING, THE(1971, Brit.)
Evelyn Jennings
Silents
OVERLAND LIMITED, THE(1925)
Fabian Jennings
RECOMMENDATION FOR MERCY(1975, Can.), w
Frank Jennings
Misc. Silents
LADY OF THE DUGOUT(1918)
Gladys Jennings
SHOULD A DOCTOR TELL?(1931, Brit.); TO OBLIGE A LADY(1931, Brit.); I'M AN
EXPLOSIVE(1933, Brit.); LILIES OF THE FIELD(1934, Brit.); SOMETIMES
GOOD(1934, Brit.); ALIBI INN(1935, Brit.)
Silents
FACE AT THE WINDOW, THE(1920, Brit.); ROB ROY(1922, Brit.); PRUDES FALL,
THE(1924, Brit.)
Misc. Silents
SHUTTLE OF LIFE, THE(1920, Brit.); PREY OF THE DRAGON, THE(1921, Brit.);
LAMP IN THE DESERT(1922, Brit.); BECKET(1923, Brit.); LITTLE MISS NOBO-
DY(1923, Brit.); YOUNG LOCHINVAR(1923, Brit.); HENRY, KING OF NAVAR-
RE(1924, Brit.); LOVES OF COLLEEN BAWN, THE(1924, Brit.); WOMAN IN PAWN,
A(1927, Brit.)
Gordon Jennings
ALICE IN WONDERLAND(1933), spec eff; ISLAND OF LOST SOULS(1933), spec eff;
SCARLET EMPRESS, THE(1934), spec eff; CRUSADES, THE(1935), spec eff; PETER
IBBETSON(1935), spec eff; GENERAL DIED AT DAWN, THE(1936), spec eff; GIVE US
THIS NIGHT(1936), ph; THIRTEEN HOURS BY AIR(1936), spec eff; BIG BROAD-
CAST OF 1938, THE(1937), spec eff; EBB TIDE(1937), spec eff; HIGH, WIDE AND
HANDSOME(1937), spec eff; MAKE WAY FOR TOMORROW(1937), spec. eff.;
PLAINSMAN, THE(1937), spec eff; SOULS AT SEA(1937), spec eff; IF I WERE

KING(1938), spec eff; SPAWN OF THE NORTH(1938), spec eff; RULERS OF THE SEA(1939), spec eff; UNION PACIFIC(1939), spec eff; NORTHWEST MOUNTED POLICE(1940), spec eff; TYPHOON(1940), spec eff; ALOMA OF THE SOUTH SEAS(1941), spec eff; I WANTED WINGS(1941), spec eff; GREAT MAN'S LADY, THE(1942), spec eff; I MARRIED A WITCH(1942), spec eff; REAP THE WILD WIND(1942), spec eff; CHINA(1943), spec eff; DIXIE(1943), spec eff; FOR WHOM THE BELL TOLLS(1943), spec eff; NO TIME FOR LOVE(1943), spec eff; SO PROUDLY WE HAIL(1943), spec eff; FRENCHMAN'S CREEK(1944), spec eff; GOING MY WAY(1944), spec eff; HERE COME THE WAVES(1944), spec eff; HOUR BEFORE THE DAWN, THE(1944), spec eff; LADY IN THE DARK(1944), spec eff; OUR HEARTS WERE YOUNG AND GAY(1944), spec eff; PRACTICALLY YOURS(1944), spec eff; RAINBOW ISLAND(1944), spec eff; STORY OF DR. WASSELL, THE(1944), spec eff; 'TILL WE MEET AGAIN(1944), spec eff; DUFFY'S TAVERN(1945), spec eff; HOLD THAT BLONDE(1945), spec eff; KITTY(1945), spec eff; LOST WEEKEND, THE(1945), spec eff; LOVE LETTERS(1945), spec eff; MASQUERADE IN MEXICO(1945), spec eff; MEDAL FOR BENNY, A(1945), spec eff; MURDER, HE SAYS(1945), spec eff; BLUE SKIES(1946), spec eff; CALIFORNIA(1946), spec eff; MONSIEUR BEAUCAIRE(1946), spec eff; O.S.S.(1946), spec eff; TO EACH HIS OWN(1946), spec eff; TWO YEARS BEFORE THE MAST(1946), spec eff; VIRGINIAN, THE(1946), spec eff; WELL-GROOMED BRIDE, THE(1946), spec eff; BLAZE OF NOON(1947), spec eff; CALCUTTA(1947), spec eff; DESERT FURY(1947), spec eff; DREAM GIRL(1947), spec eff; GOLDEN EARRINGS(1947), spec eff; MY FAVORITE BRUNETTE(1947), spec eff; ROAD TO RIO(1947), spec eff; UNCONQUERED(1947), spec eff; VARIETY GIRL(1947), spec eff; WHERE THERE'S LIFE(1947), spec eff; BIG CLOCK, THE(1948), spec eff; EMPEROR WALTZ, THE(1948), spec eff; FOREIGN AFFAIR, A(1948), spec eff; MISS TATLOCK'S MILLIONS(1948), spec eff; MY OWN TRUE LOVE(1948), spec eff; PALEFACE, THE(1948), spec eff; SAIGON(1948), spec eff; SEALED VERDICT(1948), spec eff; SORRY, WRONG NUMBER(1948), spec eff; WHISPERING SMITH(1948), spec eff; ACCUSED, THE(1949), spec eff; HEIRESS, THE(1949), spec eff; SAMSON AND DELILAH(1949), spec eff; SORROWFUL JONES(1949), spec eff; FILE ON THELMA JORDAN, THE(1950), spec eff; FURIES, THE(1950), spec eff; NO MAN OF HER OWN(1950), spec eff; SUNSET BOULEVARD(1950), spec eff; PLACE IN THE SUN, A(1951), spec eff; WHEN WORLDS COLLIDE(1951), spec eff; GREATEST SHOW ON EARTH, THE(1952), spec eff; SON OF PALEFACE(1952), spec eff; STOOGE, THE(1952), spec eff; TURNING POINT, THE(1952), spec eff; FOREVER FEMALE(1953), spec eff; SCARED STIFF(1953), spec eff; SHANE(1953), spec eff; STALAG 17(1953), spec eff; WAR OF THE WORLDS, THE(1953), spec eff

Silents
BLOT, THE(1921), ph; OUR HOSPITALITY(1923), ph

Gunter W. Jennings
1984
WINDY CITY(1984), spec eff

Hazel Jennings
NEVER TAKE CANDY FROM A STRANGER(1961, Brit.)

Irene Jennings
Silents
KID, THE(1921)

J.D. Jennings
BORN TO THE WEST(1937), ph; TWO YEARS BEFORE THE MAST(1946), spec eff
Silents
CIVILIZATION(1916), ph; FAME AND FORTUNE(1918), ph; MISTRESS OF SHENSTONE, THE(1921), ph; SALVAGE(1921), ph; COBRA(1925), ph

J. Devereaux Jennings
PRACTICALLY YOURS(1944), spec eff; DARK MIRROR, THE(1946), spec eff
Silents
COLLEGE(1927), ph; GENERAL, THE(1927), ph

Jane Jennings
Silents
I WANT TO FORGET(1918); CLIMBERS, THE(1919); COST, THE(1920); HEART OF MARYLAND, THE(1921); INNER CHAMBER, THE(1921); WHAT WOMEN WILL DO(1921); DARLING OF THE RICH, THE(1923); HALDANE OF THE SECRET SERVICE(1923); ENEMIES OF YOUTH(1925); KICK-OFF, THE(1926)
Misc. Silents
EMBLEMS OF LOVE(1924); BROKEN HOMES(1926); ROMANCE OF A MILLION DOLLARS, THE(1926); FAITHLESS LOVER(1928)

Jean Jennings
THERE IS NO 13(1977)

Joe Jennings
STAR TREK: THE MOTION PICTURE(1979), art d

John Jennings
WHERE THERE'S LIFE(1947); TOGETHER BROTHERS(1974)

Joseph R. Jennings
KANSAS CITY BOMBER(1972), art d; STAR TREK II: THE WRATH OF KHAN(1982), prod d; YELLOWBEARD(1983), prod d
1984
JOHNNY DANGEROUSLY(1984), prod d

Julia Jennings
1984
TEACHERS(1984)

Junero Jennings
CURIOUS FEMALE, THE(1969); MACK, THE(1973); SUPERCHICK(1973); THREE THE HARD WAY(1974); TRACKDOWN(1976)

Louis Jennings
CHUBASCO(1968), ph

Louise Birt Gertrude Jennings
GIRL WHO FORGOT, THE(1939, Brit.), w

Margaret Jennings
SLEEP, MY LOVE(1948), cos

Marjorie Jennings
HOURS OF LONELINESS(1930, Brit.)

Maxine Jennings
OLD MAN RHYTHM(1935); ROBERTA(1935); DON'T TURN 'EM LOOSE(1936); FARMER IN THE DELL, THE(1936); FOLLOW THE FLEET(1936); LAST OUTLAW, THE(1936); MAKE WAY FOR A LADY(1936); MUSS 'EM UP(1936); WALKING ON AIR(1936); WITNESS CHAIR, THE(1936); BIG SHOT, THE(1937); ON AGAIN-OFF AGAIN(1937); THERE GOES MY GIRL(1937); WE'RE ON THE JURY(1937); YOU CAN'T BUY LUCK(1937); MR. WONG, DETECTIVE(1938); G.I. WAR BRIDES(1946)

Mrs. Jennings
Silents
BROADWAY ROSE(1922)

S.E. Jennings
BAT WHISPERS, THE(1930)
Misc. Silents
DEAD-SHOT BAKER(1917); LUCKY DAN(1922); SUNSET TRAIL, THE(1924)

Sidney Jennings
PERFECT FRIDAY(1970, Brit.)

Sonia Jennings
YOUNG DOCTORS IN LOVE(1982)

Sonya Jennings
SOMETHING SHORT OF PARADISE(1979); SQUEEZE PLAY(1981)

Talbot Jennings
MUTINY ON THE BOUNTY(1935), w; ROMEO AND JULIET(1936), w; GOOD EARTH, THE(1937), w; SPAWN OF THE NORTH(1938), w; RULERS OF THE SEA(1939), w; EDISON, THE MAN(1940), w; NORTHWEST PASSAGE(1940), w; SO ENDS OUR NIGHT(1941), w; FRENCHMAN'S CREEK(1944), w; ANNA AND THE KING OF SIAM(1946), w; BLACK ROSE, THE(1950), w; ACROSS THE WIDE MISSOURI(1951), w; KNIGHTS OF THE ROUND TABLE(1953), w; LANDFALL(1953, Brit.), w; ESCAPE TO BURMA(1955), w; PEARL OF THE SOUTH PACIFIC(1955), w; UNTAMED(1955), w; GUNSIGHT RIDGE(1957), w; NAKED MAJA, THE(1959, Ital./U.S.), w; SONS OF KATIE ELDER, THE(1965), w

Virginia Jennings
TEXANS, THE(1938)

Waylon Jennings
NASHVILLE REBEL(1966); MOONRUNNERS(1975)

William Dale Jennings
COWBOYS, THE(1972), w

Jane Jennis
Misc. Silents
FOR HIS SAKE(1922)

Elizabeth Jenns
FORTUNATE FOOL, THE(1933, Brit.); LEAVE IT TO BLANCHE(1934, Brit.); LOVE, LIFE AND LAUGHTER(1934, Brit.); FULL CIRCLE(1935, Brit.); JIMMY BOY(1935, Brit.); STAR IS BORN, A(1937)

Andy Jenny
TUSK(1980, Fr.)

Art Jenoff
NOW THAT APRIL'S HERE(1958, Can.); LAST GUNFIGHTER, THE(1961, Can.); NAKED ANGELS(1969)

Rita Jenrette
Misc. Talkies
ZOMBIE ISLAND MASSACRE(1984)

Arnette Jens
BALCONY, THE(1963)

Blanche Jens
LUM AND ABNER ABROAD(1956), ed

Salome Jens
TERROR FROM THE YEAR 5,000(1958); ANGEL BABY(1961); FOOL KILLER, THE(1965); SECONDS(1966); ME, NATALIE(1969); SAVAGES(1972); CLOUD DANCER(1980); HARRY'S WAR(1981)

Arthur Jensen
CRAZY PARADISE(1965, Den.); ERIC SOYA'S "17"(1967, Den.); OPERATION LOVEBIRDS(1968, Den.); LURE OF THE JUNGLE, THE(1970, Den.)

Astrid Henning Jensen
1984
ELEMENT OF CRIME, THE(1984, Den.)
Misc. Talkies
BOY OF TWO WORLDS(1970), d

Beate Jensen
1984
CHINESE BOXES(1984, Ger./Brit.)

Bing Jensen
KEEPER, THE(1976, Can.)

Birger Jensen
EPILOGUE(1967, Den.)

Cleo Jensen
ELVIRA MADIGAN(1967, Swed.)

Deborah Jensen
STAYING ALIVE(1983)

Dick Jensen
LONE WOLF SPY HUNT, THE(1939); HONOLULU LU(1941); RIDERS OF THE NORTHLAND(1942); TALK OF THE TOWN(1942)

Egil Hjort Jensen
HUNGER(1968, Den./Norway/Swed.)

Eugen Jensen
DIE MANNER UM LUCIE(1931)

Eulalie Jensen
SHE GOES TO WAR(1929); CONFESSIONS OF A CO-ED(1931); SMART MONEY(1931); UP POPS THE DEVIL(1931); HAT CHECK GIRL(1932); MISS PINKERTON(1932); SO BIG(1932); TWO AGAINST THE WORLD(1932); UNION DEPOT(1932); LOST LADY, A(1934)
Silents
JUGGERNAUT, THE(1915); WHEELS OF JUSTICE(1915); KID, THE(1916); DESIRED WOMAN, THE(1918); EVE'S DAUGHTER(1918); CAPTAIN'S CAPTAIN, THE(1919); MAN AND HIS WOMAN(1920); ANY WIFE(1922); DESERTED AT THE ALTAR(1922); RAGS TO RICHES(1922); HUNCHBACK OF NOTRE DAME, THE(1923); SLAVE OF DESIRE(1923); RANGER OF THE BIG PINES(1925); FOREVER AFTER(1926); VOLCANO(1926); KING OF KINGS, THE(1927); STRONG BOY(1929)
Misc. Silents
TARANTULA, THE(1916); CLOVER'S REBELLION(1917); LITTLE MISS NO-ACCOUNT(1918); TRIUMPH OF THE WEAK, THE(1918); WILD PRIMROSE(1918); HUMAN DESIRE, THE(1919); SPARK DIVINE, THE(1919); TEMPERAMENTAL WIFE, A(1919); WHISPER MARKET, THE(1920); CRIMSON CROSS, THE(1921); PASSION FLOWER, THE(1921); WHEN HUSBANDS DECEIVE(1922); HAVOC(1925); BACHELOR BRIDES(1926); FRECKLES(1928); GOD OF MANKIND(1928)

Eulalie Jensen
NEVER THE TWAIN SHALL MEET(1931)

Frederick Jensen
Silents
HER SECRET(1919, Brit.)

Frederick S. Jensen
Silents
HER SECRET(1919, Brit.), d&w

George Jensen
RED RUNS THE RIVER(1963), ed

Hans Ejner Jensen
OPERATION LOVEBIRDS(1968, Den.)

Hardy Jensen
REPTILICUS(1962, U.S./Den.)

Howard Jensen
MURDERERS' ROW(1966), spec eff; LOVE BUG, THE(1968), spec eff; BIG JA-KE(1971), spec eff; TRAIN ROBBERS, THE(1973), spec eff; MC Q(1974), spec eff; SPECIAL DELIVERY(1976), spec eff; SWARM, THE(1978), spec eff

Inger Jensen
GIRL FROM PETROVKA, THE(1974)

Irja Jensen
OPERATION MANHUNT(1954)

Jeff Jensen
1984
STAR TREK III: THE SEARCH FOR SPOCK(1984)

Jens Jensen
ERIC SOYA'S "17"(1967, Den.)

Jeri Jensen
MICKEY ONE(1965)

Jerry Jensen
REAL LIFE(1979)

Jesper Jensen
WEEKEND(1964, Den.)

Johannes Vilhelm Jensen
SUDDENLY, A WOMAN!(1967, Den.), w

John Jensen
TEN COMMANDMENTS, THE(1956), cos

Johnny Jensen
WAR LORD, THE(1965); FOR PETE'S SAKE!(1966)

Karen Jensen
OUT OF SIGHT(1966); SULLIVAN'S EMPIRE(1967); BALLAD OF JOSIE(1968); SALZBURG CONNECTION, THE(1972)

Keith Jensen
FM(1978)

Kim Jensen
1984
FOOTLOOSE(1984)

Kimberly Jensen
SCHIZOID(1980)

Linda Jensen
1984
REPO MAN(1984)

Lola Jensen
THRILL OF A LIFETIME(1937); THERE'S THAT WOMAN AGAIN(1938); YOU AND ME(1938); LONE WOLF SPY HUNT, THE(1939); DANCE, GIRL, DANCE(1940); MAYOR OF 44TH STREET, THE(1942)

Lucy Jensen
SORCERESS(1983)

Maren Jensen
BATTLESTAR GALACTICA(1979); BEYOND THE REEF(1981); DEADLY BLESS-ING(1981)

Merrill Jensen
WINDWALKER(1980), m

Nick Jensen
BROTHERS AND SISTERS(1980, Brit.)

Paul Jensen
BLOOD RELATIVES(1978, Fr./Can.), m

Peter Jensen
SHADOW OF THE HAWK(1976, Can.), w
Misc. Talkies
HILARY'S BLUES(1983), d

Randee Jensen
CURIOUS FEMALE, THE(1969); WILD WHEELS(1969); EVEL KNIEVEL(1971)

Rayland D. Jensen
LINCOLN CONSPIRACY, THE(1977), p

Rene Jensen
TRADER HORNEE(1970), ch

Roy Jensen
BUCHANAN RIDES ALONE(1958); MISSOURI TRAVELER, THE(1958); NORTH TO ALASKA(1960); HOW THE WEST WAS WON(1962); HARPER(1966); COUNT YOUR BULLETS(1972); GETAWAY, THE(1972); OUTFIT, THE(1973); BUSTIN' LOOSE(1981)

Roy C. Jensen
FOOLS(1970)

Sanford Jensen
1984
BEST DEFENSE(1984)

Soren Elung Jensen
KING LEAR(1971, Brit./Den.)

Victor Jensen
1914(1932, Ger.)

Roy Jenseon
HALLS OF ANGER(1970)

Al Jenson
LOVE IS NEWS(1937)

Angela Jenson
SCREWBALLS(1983)

Carl Jenson
Silents
GOLD RUSH, THE(1925)

Eulalie Jenson
EYES OF THE WORLD, THE(1930)

Jeremy Jenson
CURTAINS(1983, Can.)

Jerry Jenson
Misc. Talkies
GHOSTS THAT STILL WALK(1977)

John Jenson
Silents
YE BANKS AND BRAES(1919, Brit.)

John R. Jenson
SPACEHUNTER: ADVENTURES IN THE FORBIDDEN ZONE(1983), art d

Linda Jenson
Misc. Talkies
CHEERLEADERS BEACH PARTY(1978)

Merrill B. Jenson
TAKE DOWN(1979), m; HARRY'S WAR(1981), m

Roy Cameron Jenson
DEMONOID(1981)

Roy Jenson
WAY WE WERE, THE(1973); OPERATION SECRET(1952); HELL ON DEVIL'S ISLAND(1957); RIDE LONESOME(1959); LET NO MAN WRITE MY EPITAPH(1960); RISE AND FALL OF LEGS DIAMOND, THE(1960); LAW OF THE LAWLESS(1964); STAGE TO THUNDER ROCK(1964); MORITURI(1965); 36 HOURS(1965); AMBUSH-ERS, THE(1967); HOSTILE GUNS(1967); RED TOMAHAWK(1967); WATERHOLE NO. 3(1967); FIVE CARD STUD(1968); JIGSAW(1968); WILL PENNY(1968); NUMBER ONE(1969); PAINT YOUR WAGON(1969); SOMETIMES A GREAT NOTION(1971); JOURNEY THROUGH ROSEBUD(1972); LIFE AND TIMES OF JUDGE ROY BEAN, THE(1972); DILLINGER(1973); NIGHTMARE HONEYMOON(1973); SOYLENT GREEN(1973); CHINATOWN(1974); THUNDERBOLT AND LIGHTFOOT(1974); 99 AND 44/100% DEAD(1974); BREAKOUT(1975); FRAMED(1975); WIND AND THE LION, THE(1975); BREAKHEART PASS(1976); DUCHESS AND THE DIRTWATER FOX, THE(1976); CAR, THE(1977); GAUNTLET, THE(1977); TELEFON(1977); ANY WHICH WAY YOU CAN(1980); FOOLIN' AROUND(1980); TOM HORN(1980); HON-KYTONK MAN(1982)
1984
RED DAWN(1984)

Elois Jenssen
DISHONORED LADY(1947), cos; LET'S LIVE A LITTLE(1948), cos; SO THIS IS NEW YORK(1948), cos; SAMSON AND DELILAH(1949), cos; CRY DANGER(1951), cos; PHONE CALL FROM A STRANGER(1952), cos; WE'RE NOT MARRIED(1952), cos; FOREVER DARLING(1956), cos; TRON(1982), cos

Eloise Jenssen
KISS FOR CORLISS, A(1949), cos; DEADLINE–U.S.A.(1952), cos

Wiers Jenssens
DAY OF WRATH(1948, Den.), w

Eloise Jensson
GROOM WORE SPURS, THE(1951), cos

Jacie Jensson
GROOM WORE SPURS, THE(1951), cos

Whitey Jent
WORLD'S GREATEST SINNER, THE(1962)

Heber Jentzsch
1776(1972)

Zoltan Jeny
1984
REVOLT OF JOB, THE(1984, Hung./Ger.), m

Arthur Jeph
WRONG IS RIGHT(1982), set d

Dominic Jephcott
HORROR PLANET(1982, Brit.)

Samuel Jephcott
MERRY WIVES OF TOBIAS ROUKE, THE(1972, Can.)

Jorn Jeppesen
EPILOGUE(1967, Den.)

Klaus Jepsen
FUNERAL IN BERLIN(1966, Brit.)

Edgar Jepson
Silents
HER WINNING WAY(1921), w

Helen Jepson
GOLDWYN FOLLIES, THE(1938)

Selwyn Jepson
FOR LOVE OF YOU(1933, Brit.), w; MONEY MAD(1934, Brit.), w; DARK WORLD(1935, Brit.), w; HYDE PARK CORNER(1935, Brit.), w; KISS ME GOOD-BYE(1935, Brit.), w; LOVE TEST, THE(1935, Brit.), w; RIVERSIDE MURDER, THE(1935, Brit.), w; SCARAB MURDER CASE, THE(1936, Brit.), w; TOILERS OF THE SEA(1936, Brit.), d, w; WELL DONE, HENRY(1936, Brit.), w; WRATH OF JEAL-OUSY(1936, Brit.), w; SAILING ALONG(1938, Brit.), w; STAGE FRIGHT(1950, Brit.), w; FOREVER MY HEART(1954, Brit.), w; LAST MOMENT, THE(1954, Brit.), w; RED DRESS, THE(1954, Brit.), w
Silents
QUALIFIED ADVENTURER, THE(1925, Brit.), w; LADY NOGGS-PEERESS(1929, Brit.), w

Marblum Jequier
DEATH OF MARIO RICCI, THE(1983, Ital.)

Susi Jera
IDEAL LODGER, THE(1957, Ger.)

Kenneth Augustus Jeremy
IVORY HUNTER(1952, Brit.)

Ron Jeremy
Misc. Talkies
BLONDE GODDESS(1982)

Jose Luis Jerez
ADIOS GRINGO(1967, Ital./Fr./Span.), w; MAGNIFICENT BANDITS, THE(1969, Ital./Span.), w

Adele Jergens
CORPSE CAME C.O.D., THE(; JANE EYRE(1944); TOGETHER AGAIN(1944); SHE WOULDN'T SAY YES(1945); THOUSAND AND ONE NIGHTS, A(1945); TONIGHT AND EVERY NIGHT(1945); BLONDIE'S ANNIVERSARY(1947); DOWN TO

EARTH(1947); I LOVE TROUBLE(1947); WHEN A GIRL'S BEAUTIFUL(1947); DARK PAST, THE(1948); FULLER BRUSH MAN(1948); LADIES OF THE CHORUS(1948); PRINCE OF THIEVES, THE(1948); WOMAN FROM TANGIER, THE(1948); CRIME DOCTOR'S DIARY, THE(1949); LAW OF THE BARBARY COAST(1949); MAKE BELIEVE BALLROOM(1949); MUTINEERS, THE(1949); SLIGHTLY FRENCH(1949); TREASURE OF MONTE CRISTO(1949); ARMORED CAR ROBBERY(1950); BEWARE OF BLONDIE(1950); BLONDE DYNAMITE(1950); BLUES BUSTERS(1950); EDGE OF DOOM(1950); EVERYBODY'S DANCIN'(1950); RADAR SECRET SERVICE(1950); SIDE STREET(1950); SOUND OF FURY, THE(1950); TRAVELING SALES-WOMAN(1950); ABBOTT AND COSTELLO MEET THE INVISIBLE MAN(1951); SHOW BOAT(1951); SUGARFOOT(1951); AARON SLICK FROM PUNKIN CRICK(1952); SOMEBODY LOVES ME(1952); BIG CHASE, THE(1954); FIREMAN SAVE MY CHILD(1954); MIAMI STORY, THE(1954); OVERLAND PACIFIC(1954); COBWEB, THE(1955); LONESOME TRAIL, THE(1955); OUTLAW TREASURE(1955); STRANGE LADY IN TOWN(1955); DAY THE WORLD ENDED, THE(1956); FIGHT-ING TROUBLE(1956); GIRLS IN PRISON(1956); RUNAWAY DAUGHTERS(1957)

Curt Jergens
LONGEST DAY, THE(1962); MIRACLE OF THE WHITE STALLIONS(1963); VAULT OF HORROR, THE(1973, Brit.)

Diane Jergens
BOB MATHIAS STORY, THE(1954); FRIENDLY PERSUASION(1956); TEENAGE REBEL(1956); DESK SET(1957); THREE BRAVE MEN(1957); HIGH SCHOOL CONFI-DENTIAL(1958); SING, BOY, SING(1958); FBI STORY, THE(1959); ISLAND OF LOST WOMEN(1959); LOST BATTALION(1961, U.S./Phil.); TEENAGE MILLIONAIRE(1961)

Burr Jerger
NO SURVIVORS, PLEASE(1963, Ger.); GENERAL MASSACRE(1973, U.S./Bel.), a, p&d, w

Dusko Jericevic
TREASURE OF SILVER LAKE(1965, Fr./Ger./Yugo.), art d; RAMPAGE AT AP-ACHE WELLS(1966, Ger./Yugo.), art d&set d

Vida Jerman
ROMANCE OF A HORSE THIEF(1971); SOPHIE'S CHOICE(1982)

Paula Jermunson
RANCHO DELUXE(1975)

Peter Jermyn
SIEGE(1983, Can.), m

Bertil Jernberg
INVASION OF THE ANIMAL PEOPLE(1962, U.S./Swed.), p

Peter Jerndorff
Misc. Silents
ONCE UPON A TIME(1922, Den.)

Rebecca Jernigan
ODE TO BILLY JOE(1976)

Mary Jerold
JAMAICA INN(1939, Brit.)
Misc. Silents
DISRAELI(1916, Brit.); MIDNIGHT GAMBOLS(1919, Brit.)

Adele Jerome
STOLEN HARMONY(1935)

Edwin Jerome
HOUSE ON 92ND STREET, THE(1945); NAKED CITY, THE(1948); PEYTON PLA-CE(1957); TATTERED DRESS, THE(1957); THREE FACES OF EVE, THE(1957); GIGI(1958); MAN WHO UNDERSTOOD WOMEN, THE(1959)

Elmer Jerome
INTERNES CAN'T TAKE MONEY(1937); TRUE CONFESSION(1937); ICE-CAPADES REVUE(1942); MAGNIFICENT AMBERSONS, THE(1942); FALSE COLORS(1943); SWING YOUR PARTNER(1943); YOUTH ON PARADE(1943); DOUGHGIRLS, THE(1944); HEAVENLY DAYS(1944); THAT'S MY GAL(1947)

Helen Jerome
CONQUEST(1937), w; PRIDE AND PREJUDICE(1940), w

Helga Jerome
Misc. Silents
DAWN OF THE TRUTH, THE(1920, Brit.)

Jerome J. Jerome
SKY RAIDERS(1931)

Jerome K. Jerome
THREE MEN IN A BOAT(1933, Brit.), w; PASSING OF THE THIRD FLOOR BACK, THE(1936, Brit.), w; THREE MEN IN A BOAT(1958, Brit.), w
Silents
MISS HOBBS(1920), w; ALL ROADS LEAD TO CALVARY(1921, Brit.), w

Jerry Jerome
FLIGHT(1929); TILLIE AND GUS(1933); CHARLIE CHAN'S COURAGE(1934); MADAME SPY(1934); CEILNG ZERO(1935); LAST GANGSTER, THE(1937); SUNSET TRAIL(1938); ANGELS OVER BROADWAY(1940); CAUGHT IN THE DRAFT(1941); I'LL WAIT FOR YOU(1941); PUBLIC ENEMIES(1941); SHADOW OF THE THIN MAN(1941); HILLBILLY BLITZKRIEG(1942); STARDUST ON THE SAGE(1942); ARSON SQUAD(1945); SHE GETS HER MAN(1945); CAT CREEPS, THE(1946); MAGNIFICENT DOLL(1946); ROMANCE OF THE WEST(1946); T-MEN(1947); WIST-FUL WIDOW OF WAGON GAP, THE(1947); HOMECOMING(1948); KEY LAR-GO(1948); LIGHTNIN' IN THE FOREST(1948); PHANTOM VALLEY(1948); RIVER LADY(1948); SILVER RIVER(1948); MISS GRANT TAKES RICHMOND(1949)

Joey Jerome
I AM THE CHEESE(1983)

M.K. Jerome
FRESHMAN LOVE(1936), m; MARKED WOMAN(1937), m/l

Mark Jerome
INVITATION TO HAPPINESS(1939), w

Patti Jerome
RANCHO DELUXE(1975); SGT. PEPPER'S LONELY HEARTS CLUB BAND(1978); BUDDY BUDDY(1981)

Suzanne Jerome
OCTOPUSSY(1983, Brit.)

Vincent Jerosa
ZELIG(1983)
1984
COTTON CLUB, THE(1984)

Jeanne Jerrems
DARK ODYSSEY(1961)

Paul Jerricho
THIRTY NINE STEPS, THE(1978, Brit.)

Joe Jerrick
BOWERY, THE(1933)

Paul Jerrico
BEAUTY FOR THE ASKING(1939), w

Mary Jerrold
"W" PLAN, THE(1931, Brit.); ALIBI(1931, Brit.); SPORT OF KINGS, THE(1931, Brit.); BLIND SPOT(1932, Brit.); LAST COUPON, THE(1932, Brit.); SHADOW BETWEEN, THE(1932, Brit.); PERFECT UNDERSTANDING(1933, Brit.); DOCTOR'S OR-DERS(1934, Brit.); FRIDAY THE 13TH(1934, Brit.); GREAT DEFENDER, THE(1934, Brit.); LASH, THE(1934, Brit.); SPRING IN THE AIR(1934, Brit.); FIGHTING STOCK(1935, Brit.); PRICE OF WISDOM, THE(1935, Brit.); SATURDAY NIGHT REVUE(1937, Brit.); TWO OF US, THE(1938, Brit.); RETURN TO YESTERDAY(1940, Brit.); TALK ABOUT JACQUELINE(1942, Brit.); FLEMISH FARM, THE(1943, Brit.); GENTLE SEX, THE(1943, Brit.); WAY AHEAD, THE(1945, Brit.); GHOSTS OF BERKELEY SQUARE(1947, Brit.); MAGIC BOW, THE(1947, Brit.); BOND STREET(1948, Brit.); COLONEL BOGEY(1948, Brit.); MR. PERRIN AND MR. TRAILL(1948, Brit.); QUEEN OF SPADES(1948, Brit.); MARRY ME!(1949, Brit.); WOMAN HATER(1949, Brit.); SHE SHALL HAVE MURDER(1950, Brit.); TONIGHT AT 8:30(1953, Brit.); TOP OF THE FORM(1953, Brit.)

Jerry the Giant
Silents
GAY RETREAT, THE(1927); LAST TRAIL, THE(1927)

Jerry Wald and His Orchestra
LITTLE MISS BROADWAY(1947)

Gerhard Jersch
DOCTOR ZHIVAGO(1965)

Oskar Jerschke
DREAMER, THE(1936, Ger.), w

Bill Jersey
FLAMING TEEN-AGE, THE(1956), art d

William Jersey
MANHUNT IN THE JUNGLE(1958), art d; 4D MAN(1959), art d

Jorgen Jersild
GERTRUD(1966, Den.), m

Members of Jerusalem Theater Arts Players
DRY SUMMER(1967, Turkey)

Jack Jerve
BARNACLE BILL(1941), w

Alan Jervis
SKIN DEEP(1978, New Zealand)

Kenyon Jervis
MR. H. C. ANDERSEN(1950, Brit.)

Eulalie Jesen
Misc. Silents
MARY JANE'S PA(1917)

Joerg Jeshel
YOUNG MONK, THE(1978, Ger.), ph

George Jeske
MIDNIGHT PATROL, THE(1932), w; FLAMING SIGNAL(1933), d; DAY THE BOOK-IES WEPT, THE(1939), w; MOON OVER LAS VEGAS(1944), w

Jespah
LIVING FREE(1972, Brit.)

Dan Jesse
PROTECTORS, BOOK 1, THE(1981)

Dewayne Jesse
HALLS OF ANGER(1970); DARKTOWN STRUTTERS(1975)

F. Tennyson Jesse
HALF ANGEL(1936), w; SAN DEMETRIO, LONDON(1947, Brit.), w
Silents
'MARRIAGE LICENSE?'(1926), w

Vera Jesse
SLAVERS(1977, Ger.)

Jesse and James
SHOW BUSINESS(1944)

Jesse Stafford and His Orchestra
CLOSE HARMONY(1929)

Don Jessee
STREET WITH NO NAME, THE(1948)

George Jessel
LOVE, LIVE AND LAUGH(1929), a, w; LUCKY BOY(1929), a, w; HAPPY DAYS(1930); STAGE DOOR CANTEEN(1943); FOUR JILLS IN A JEEP(1944); SHOW BUSINESS(1944); DOLLY SISTERS, THE(1945), p; DO YOU LOVE ME?(1946), p; I WONDER WHO'S KISSING HER NOW(1947), p; NIGHTMARE ALLEY(1947), p; WHEN MY BABY SMILES AT ME(1948), p; DANCING IN THE DARK(1949), p; OH, YOU BEAUTIFUL DOLL(1949), p; YOU'RE MY EVERYTHING(1949), w; ANNE OF THE INDIES(1951), p; GOLDEN GIRL(1951), p; MEET ME AFTER THE SHOW(1951), p; BLOODHOUNDS OF BROADWAY(1952), p; I DON'T CARE GIRL, THE(1952), a, p; WAIT 'TIL THE SUN SHINES, NELLIE(1952), p; TONIGHT WE SING(1953), p; BEAU JAMES(1957); JUKE BOX RHYTHM(1959); BUSYBODY, THE(1967); VALLEY OF THE DOLLS(1967); PHYNX, THE(1970); WON TON TON, THE DOG WHO SAVED HOLLYWOOD(1976); REDS(1981)
Misc. Talkies
CAN HIERONYMUS MERKIN EVER FORGET MERCY HUMPPE AND FIND TRUE HAPPINESS?(1969)
Silents
OTHER MAN'S WIFE, THE(1919); PRIVATE IZZY MURPHY(1926); GINSBERG THE GREAT(1927); SAILOR IZZY MURPHY(1927)
Misc. Silents
GEORGE WASHINGTON COHEN(1928)

John Jessel
SHE DEVIL(1957), w

Patricia Jessel
FLESH IS WEAK, THE(1957, Brit.); MAN UPSTAIRS, THE(1959, Brit.); HORROR HOTEL(1960, Brit.); MODEL FOR MURDER(1960, Brit.); BEWARE OF CHIL-DREN(1961, Brit.); JOLLY BAD FELLOW, A(1964, Brit.); FUNNY THING HAPPENED ON THE WAY TO THE FORUM, A(1966)

Ford Jessen
Silents
OLD AGE HANDICAP(1928)
De Wayne Jessie
SCOTT JOPLIN(1977)
DeWayne Jessie
CRAZY WORLD OF JULIUS VROODER, THE(1974); BINGO LONG TRAVELING ALL-STARS AND MOTOR KINGS, THE(1976); CARWASH(1976); SPARKLE(1976); FUN WITH DICK AND JANE(1977); WHICH WAY IS UP?(1977); NATIONAL LAMPOON'S ANIMAL HOUSE(1978); THANK GOD IT'S FRIDAY(1978); WHERE THE BUFFALO ROAM(1980); D.C. CAB(1983); STAR CHAMBER, THE(1983)
Leopold Jessner
CHILDREN OF THE FOG(1935, Brit.), d
Misc. Silents
BACKSTAIRS(1921, Ger.), d
Gene Jesso
JUD(1971)
Gwendoline Jesson
Silents
ONE SUMMER'S DAY(1917, Brit.)
Marguerita Jesson
Silents
IRON JUSTICE(1915, Brit.)
Paul Jesson
ACCEPTABLE LEVELS(1983, Brit.)
1984
PLOUGHMAN'S LUNCH, THE(1984, Brit.)
Peter Jesson
CARRY ON CABBIE(1963, Brit.); SWINGIN' MAIDEN, THE(1963, Brit.)
Clytie Jessop
INNOCENTS, THE(1961, U.S./Brit.); NIGHTMARE(1963, Brit.); TORTURE GARDEN(1968, Brit.)
Jack Jessop
1984
MRS. SOFFEL(1984)
Peter Jessop
COOL IT, CAROL!(1970, Brit.), ph; FRIGHTMARE(1974, Brit.), ph; CONFESSIONAL, THE(1977, Brit.), ph; SCHIZO(1977, Brit.), ph; COMEBACK, THE(1982, Brit.), ph; NUTCRACKER(1982, Brit.), ph
1984
REAL LIFE(1984, Brit.), ph
Alain Jessua
LIFE UPSIDE DOWN(1965, Fr.), d&w; KILLING GAME, THE(1968, Fr.), d&w; SHOCK TREATMENT(1973, Fr.), d&w; PARADISE POUR TOUS(1982, Fr.), p&d, w
Aaron Jessup
PATERNITY(1981)
Bob Jessup
SUGAR HILL(1974), ph; SMALL TOWN IN TEXAS, A(1976), ph
Carrie Jessup
DRIVE-IN(1976)
Harley Jessup
TWICE UPON A TIME(1983), art d
Ian Jessup
LIONHEART(1968, Brit.)
Peter Jessup
1984
GIVE MY REGARDS TO BROAD STREET(1984, Brit.)
Richard Jessup
YOUNG DON'T CRY, THE(1957), w; DEADLY DUO(1962), w; CINCINNATI KID, THE(1965), w; CHUKA(1967), w
Robert Jessup
RACE WITH THE DEVIL(1975), ph; DRIVE-IN(1976), ph; SENIORS, THE(1978), ph; BIG BRAWL, THE(1980), ph; DEADLY BLESSING(1981), ph; SILENT RAGE(1982), ph; SPLIT IMAGE(1982), ph
Robert C. Jessup
7TH COMMANDMENT, THE(1961), ph; IN THE YEAR 2889(1966), ph; MARS NEEDS WOMEN(1966), ph
Frank Jessy
SILENT WITNESS, THE(1962), w
Eva Jessye
SLAVES(1969)
Ralph Jester
TEN COMMANDMENTS, THE(1956), cos; OMAR KHAYYAM(1957), cos
Jester Hairston Singers
YES SIR, MR. BONES(1951)
The Jesters
COWBOY IN THE CLOUDS(1943)
Diamond Jet
SMOKY(1966)
Jet Motion Pictures
PLEASURE PLANTATION(1970), ed
Irma Jeter
MOONLIGHT IN VERMONT(1943)
James Jeter
SAND PEBBLES, THE(1966); COOL HAND LUKE(1967); CHRISTIAN LICORICE STORE, THE(1971); OKLAHOMA CRUDE(1973); BIG BUS, THE(1976); BLACK SUNDAY(1977); FUN WITH DICK AND JANE(1977); FAST BREAK(1979); CHANGE OF SEASONS, A(1980); HOLLYWOOD KNIGHTS, THE(1980); BORDER, THE(1982)
Michael Jeter
HAIR(1979); RAGTIME(1981); SOUP FOR ONE(1982)
Trilak Jetley
RIVER, THE(1951)
Jetsam
CHU CHIN CHOW(1934, Brit.)
Mr. Jetsam
CRIMES OF STEPHEN HAWKE, THE(1936, Brit.)
Joan Jett
1984
DUBEAT-E-O(1984)

Roger Jett
SMITHEREENS(1982)
Seldon Jett
MACAO(1952)
Sheldon Jett
GOIN' TO TOWN(1935); PALM BEACH STORY, THE(1942); HEAVENLY DAYS(1944); TWO GIRLS AND A SAILOR(1944); WOMAN IN THE WINDOW, THE(1945); EXILE, THE(1947); ANNE OF THE INDIES(1951); LADY AND THE BANDIT, THE(1951); LULLABY OF BROADWAY, THE(1951)
Sue Jett
IF EVER I SEE YOU AGAIN(1978)
Claude Jetter
MILKY WAY, THE(1969, Fr./Ital.)
Gloria Jetter
DIXIE JAMBOREE(1945); CRACK-UP(1946)
Edward Jeuesbury
SACCO AND VANZETTI(1971, Ital./Fr.)
Jack Jeume
WONDER MAN(1945), w
Lindy Jeune
NEW HOTEL, THE(1932, Brit.)
Jack Jevne
HONEYMOON LANE(1931), w; EASY MILLIONS(1933), w; I COVER THE WATERFRONT(1933), w; PALOOKA(1934), w; COWBOY AND THE BANDIT, THE(1935), w; KELLY THE SECOND(1936), w; MISTER CINDERELLA(1936), w; OUR RELATIONS(1936), w; TOPPER(1937), w; WAY OUT WEST(1937), w; MERRILY WE LIVE(1938), w; THERE GOES MY HEART(1938), w; CAPTAIN FURY(1939), w; TOPPER TAKES A TRIP(1939), w; WYOMING(1940), w; AIR RAID WARDENS(1943), w; WINTERTIME(1943), w; AUTUMN LEAVES(1956), w
Austin Jewel
Silents
GREED(1925)
Betty Jewel
Silents
SILENT COMMAND, THE(1923); NECESSARY EVIL, THE(1925); NEW COMMANDMENT, THE(1925); PARTNERS AGAIN(1926); ARIZONA BOUND(1927)
Misc. Silents
MILE-A-MINUTE ROMEO(1923); LAST OUTLAW, THE(1927); MYSTERIOUS RIDER, THE(1927)
Ed C. Jewel
MEN ARE SUCH FOOLS(1933), art d
Isabel Jewel
CROWD ROARS, THE(1938)
Izetta Jewel
VICKI(1953)
Jimmy Jewel
RHYTHM SERENADE(1943, Brit.); STICK 'EM UP(1950, Brit.); MAN WHO HAD POWER OVER WOMEN, THE(1970, Brit.)
Ward Jewel
CRACKING UP(1977), m
Wendy Jewel
PHOBIA(1980, Can.)
Austen Jewell
HOLD THAT HYPNOTIST(1957), d; LOOKING FOR DANGER(1957), d
Edward Jewell
RICH PEOPLE(1929), art d; THIS THING CALLED LOVE(1929), art d; BROTHERS(1930), art d; MADONNA OF THE STREETS(1930), art d; MEN WITHOUT LAW(1930), art d; NIGHT WORK(1930), art d; OFFICER O'BRIEN(1930), art d; SHADOW RANCH(1930), art d; SQUEALER, THE(1930), art d; TOL'ABLE DAVID(1930), art d; TEN CENTS A DANCE(1931), art d; TOMORROW AT SEVEN(1933), art d; GREEN EYES(1934), art d; MURDER ON THE CAMPUS(1934), art d; GHOST WALKS, THE(1935), art d; GREAT COMMANDMENT, THE(1941), art d; COMMANDOS STRIKE AT DAWN, THE(1942), art d; ONCE UPON A TIME(1944), art d; SECRET COMMAND(1944), art d; COUNTER-ATTACK(1945), art d; SERGEANT MIKE(1945), art d; MASK OF DIIJON, THE(1946), art d; QUEEN OF BURLESQUE(1946), art d; SECRETS OF A SORORITY GIRL(1946), art d; OUT OF THE BLUE(1947), art d; LADY AT MIDNIGHT(1948), art d; STRANGE MRS. CRANE, THE(1948), art d; DARING CABALLERO, THE(1949), art d; STATE DEPARTMENT–FILE 649(1949), art d; GUNFIGHT AT COMANCHE CREEK(1964), art d; ONE MAN'S WAY(1964), art d
Silents
ANNAPOLIS(1928), art d; CRAIG'S WIFE(1928), art d; MARKED MONEY(1928), art d; NED MCCOBB'S DAUGHTER(1929), art d
Edward C. Jewell
SECRETS OF WU SIN(1932), art d; STRANGE PEOPLE(1933), art d; SHOT IN THE DARK, A(1935), art d; DARK HOUR, THE(1936), art d; DEATH FROM A DISTANCE(1936), art d; IT COULDN'T HAVE HAPPENED–BUT IT DID(1936), art d; OLD LOUISIANA(1938), art d; REBELLION(1938), art d; DETOUR(1945), art d; SHADOW OF TERROR(1945), art d; SONG OF OLD WYOMING(1945), art d; STRANGLER OF THE SWAMP(1945), art d; WHITE PONGO(1945), art d; WHY GIRLS LEAVE HOME(1945), art d; DANNY BOY(1946), art d; DOWN MISSOURI WAY(1946), art d; DRIFTIN' RIVER(1946), art d; FLYING SERPENT, THE(1946), art d; HER SISTER'S SECRET(1946), art d; HOW DO YOU DO?(1946), art d; JOE PALOOKA, CHAMP(1946), art d; LARCENY IN HER HEART(1946), art d; MURDER IS MY BUSINESS(1946), art d; ROMANCE OF THE WEST(1946), art d; STARS OVER TEXAS(1946), art d; WIFE OF MONTE CRISTO, THE(1946), art d; WILD WEST(1946), art d; HEARTACHES(1947), art d; IT'S A JOKE, SON!(1947), art d; LOST HONEYMOON(1947), art d; REPEAT PERFORMANCE(1947), art d; T-MEN(1947), art d
Edward G. Jewell
DEVIL BAT'S DAUGHTER, THE(1946), art d
Edward S. Jewell
FIFTEEN WIVES(1934), art d
Estelle Jewell
SHADOW OF A DOUBT(1943)
Hollis Jewell
ROMANCE OF THE LIMBERLOST(1938); STRANGE CASE OF DR. MEADE(1939); GRAPES OF WRATH(1940); LIFE BEGINS FOR ANDY HARDY(1941); NIGHTMARE ALLEY(1947); LUCK OF THE IRISH(1948)

Isabel Jewell
BLESSED EVENT(1932); ADVICE TO THE LOVELORN(1933); BOMBSHELL(1933); BONDAGE(1933); COUNSELLOR-AT-LAW(1933); DAY OF RECKONING(1933); DESIGN FOR LIVING(1933); EVELYN PRENTICE(1934); HERE COMES THE GROOM(1934); LET'S BE RITZY(1934); MANHATTAN MELODRAMA(1934); SHE HAD TO CHOOSE(1934); WOMEN IN HIS LIFE, THE(1934); CASINO MURDER CASE, THE(1935); I'VE BEEN AROUND(1935); MAD LOVE(1935); SHADOW OF A DOUBT(1935); TALE OF TWO CITIES, A(1935); TIMES SQUARE LADY(1935); BIG BROWN EYES(1936); CAREER WOMAN(1936); DANCING FEET(1936); GO WEST, YOUNG MAN(1936); LEATHERNECKS HAVE LANDED, THE(1936); MAN WHO LIVED TWICE(1936); SMALL TOWN GIRL(1936); THIRTY SIX HOURS TO KILL(1936); VALIANT IS THE WORD FOR CARRIE(1936); LOST HORIZON(1937); LOVE ON TOAST(1937); MARKED WOMAN(1937); SWING IT SAILOR(1937); GONE WITH THE WIND(1939); MISSING DAUGHTERS(1939); THEY ASKED FOR IT(1939); BABIES FOR SALE(1940); IRENE(1940); LITTLE MEN(1940); MARKED MEN(1940); NORTHWEST PASSAGE(1940); OH JOHNNY, HOW YOU CAN LOVE!(1940); SCATTERBRAIN(1940); FOR BEAUTY'S SAKE(1941); HIGH SIERRA(1941); DANGER! WOMEN AT WORK(1943); FALCON AND THE CO-EDS, THE(1943); LEOPARD MAN, THE(1943); SEVENTH VICTIM, THE(1943); MERRY MONAHANS, THE(1944); SENSATION HUNTERS(1945); STEPPIN' IN SOCIETY(1945); BADMAN'S TERRITORY(1946); BELLE STARR'S DAUGHTER(1947); MICHAEL O'HALLORAN(1948); SNAKE PIT, THE(1948); UNFAITHFULLY YOURS(1948); STORY OF MOLLY X, THE(1949); MAN IN THE ATTIC(1953); DRUM BEAT(1954); BERNARDINE(1957); AROUSERS, THE(1973); CIAO MANHATTAN(1973)

Isabell Jewell
CEILNG ZERO(1935); BORN TO KILL(1947)

Isobel Jewell
BEAUTY FOR SALE(1933)

Jefferson Jewell
BRONCO BILLY(1980)

Jimmy Jewell
WHAT A CARRY ON!(1949, Brit.)

Ray Jewell
NIKKI, WILD DOG OF THE NORTH(1961, U.S./Can.), ph

Robert Jewell
DALEKS–INVASION EARTH 2155 A.D.(1966, Brit.); TERRORNAUTS, THE(1967, Brit.)

Ray Jewers
SPY WHO LOVED ME, THE(1977, Brit.); TWILIGHT'S LAST GLEAMING(1977, U.S./Ger.); JAGUAR LIVES(1979)

Edward Jewesbury
JOHN WESLEY(1954, Brit.)

Brad Jewett
STUDENT TEACHERS, THE(1973)

Ethel Jewett
Silents
NET, THE(1916)

Joe Jewett
ROAD TO MOROCCO(1942)

Martha Jewett
ROYAL SCANDAL, A(1945)

Tom Jewett
1984
CENSUS TAKER, THE(1984), ph

Norman Jewison
FORTY POUNDS OF TROUBLE(1962), d; THRILL OF IT ALL, THE(1963), d; SEND ME NO FLOWERS(1964), d; ART OF LOVE, THE(1965), d; CINCINNATI KID, THE(1965), d; RUSSIANS ARE COMING, THE RUSSIANS ARE COMING, THE(1966), p&d; IN THE HEAT OF THE NIGHT(1967), d; THOMAS CROWN AFFAIR, THE(1968), p&d; GAILY, GAILY(1969), p&d; LANDLORD, THE(1970), p; FIDDLER ON THE ROOF(1971), p&d; BILLY TWO HATS(1973, Brit.), p; JESUS CHRIST, SUPERSTAR(1973), p, d, w; ROLLERBALL(1975), p&d; F.I.S.T.(1978), p&d; ...AND JUSTICE FOR ALL(1979), p, d; BEST FRIENDS(1982), p, d
1984
ICEMAN(1984), p; SOLDIER'S STORY, A(1984), p, d

Ricky Jewitt
1984
SUBURBIA(1984)

Delos Jewkes
NAUGHTY MARIETTA(1935); ROSE MARIE(1936); MY GAL SAL(1942); GIRL ON THE SPOT(1946); STARS AND STRIPES FOREVER(1952)

J. Delos Jewkes
MUSIC MAN, THE(1962)

Richard Jewkes
1984
PHILADELPHIA EXPERIMENT, THE(1984)

Bob Jewson
STIR(1980, Aus.), w

Jazzer Jeyes
WILD GEESE, THE(1978, Brit.); OCTOPUSSY(1983, Brit.), stunts

Michael Jeyes
CHARRIOTS OF FIRE(1981, Brit.)

"Jezebel"
WILD IS MY LOVE(1963)

Charles Jezequel
JOHNNY FRENCHMAN(1946, Brit.)

Julie Jezequel
NORTH STAR, THE(1982, Fr.); L'ETOILE DU NORD(1983, Fr.)

E. Jezewska
PORTRAIT OF LENIN(1967, Pol./USSR)

Richard Jeziorny
1984
CONSTANCE(1984, New Zealand), prod d

Marie Jezkova
FIREMAN'S BALL, THE(1968, Czech.)

Milada Jezkova
LOVES OF A BLONDE(1966, Czech.); MOST BEAUTIFUL AGE, THE(1970, Czech.)

Ruth Prawer Jhabuala
GURU, THE(1969, U.S./India), w

Ruth Prawer Jhabvala
HOUSEHOLDER, THE(1963, US/India), w; SHAKESPEARE WALLAH(1966, India), w; BOMBAY TALKIE(1970, India), w; ROSELAND(1977), w; EUROPEANS, THE(1979, Brit.), w; JANE AUSTEN IN MANHATTAN(1980), w; QUARTET(1981, Brit./Fr.), w; HEAT AND DUST(1983, Brit.), w
1984
BOSTONIANS, THE(1984), w

Ruth Prawer Jhabwala
HULLABALOO OVER GEORGIE AND BONNIE'S PICTURES(1979, Brit.), w

Mahendra Jhaveri
KENNER(1969)

Jho Jhenkins
ARENA, THE(1973); SHAFT IN AFRICA(1973)

Karel Jicinsky
SKELETON ON HORSEBACK(1940, Czech.)

Williard Jielson
WHEN THE LIGHTS GO ON AGAIN(1944)

Jiggs
HER JUNGLE LOVE(1938); BRIGHTY OF THE GRAND CANYON(1967)

Jiggs The Dog
LOVE PARADE, THE(1929)

Jiggs the Monkey
TARZAN AND THE GREEN GODDESS(1938)

Lisa Jill
FORTUNE COOKIE, THE(1966)

Ann Jillian
BABES IN TOYLAND(1961); MR. MOM(1983)

Ann Jilliann
GYPSY(1962)

Joyce Jillson
SUPERCHICK(1973); SLUMBER PARTY '57(1977)

Willard Jillson
ABROAD WITH TWO YANKS(1944); HARPOON(1948)

William Jillson
SINCE YOU WENT AWAY(1944)

Cyril Jilly
PRIVATE POOLEY(1962, Brit./E. Ger.), w

Jaroslav Jilovec
LEMONADE JOE(1966, Czech.), p

Jim
ONCE UPON A COFFEE HOUSE(1965)

Jim Jr
RAVEN, THE(1963)

"Jim" the Crow
ENCHANTED FOREST, THE(1945)

Marion Jim
KING AND I, THE(1956)

Sonny Jim
FIVE ON THE BLACK HAND SIDE(1973)

The Jim Wakely Trio
CHEYENNE ROUNDUP(1943)

Agustin Jimenez
CRIMINAL LIFE OF ARCHIBALDO DE LA CRUZ, THE(1962, Mex.), ph

Augustin Jimenez
BRUTE, THE(1952, Mex.), ph
1984
YELLOW HAIR AND THE FORTRESS OF GOLD(1984), cos

George Jimenez
OUR RELATIONS(1936)

George W. Jimenez
SWING HIGH, SWING LOW(1937)

Guillermina Jimenez
IMPORTANT MAN, THE(1961, Mex.)

Jose Luis Jimenez
MACARIO(1961, Mex.); EMPTY STAR, THE(1962, Mex.); SANTO EN EL MUSEO DE CERA(1963, Mex.); VAMPIRE, THE(1968, Mex.)

Juan Antonio Jimenez
BLOOD WEDDING(1981, Sp.); CARMEN(1983, Span.)
1984
BIZET'S CARMEN(1984, Fr./Ital.)

Juan Ramon Jimenez
I HATE MY BODY(1975, Span./Switz.), p

Luis Jimenez
SWEET SUGAR(1972)

Soledad Jimenez
IN CALIENTE(1935); RUMBA(1935); ROBIN HOOD OF EL DORADO(1936); LIVE, LOVE AND LEARN(1937); WHEN YOU'RE IN LOVE(1937); REAL GLORY, THE(1939); RETURN OF THE CISCO KID(1939); CHRISTMAS EVE(1947); FIESTA(1947); BLACK BART(1948); CRISIS(1950); SEMINOLE(1953)

Orlando Jimenez-Leal
Misc. Talkies
EL SUPER(1979), d

Antonio Jimeno
WEREWOLF VS. THE VAMPIRE WOMAN, THE(1970, Span./Ger.), ed

C. Jimerson
SHAME OF THE SABINE WOMEN, THE(1962, Mex.)

Carlos Jiminez
1984
DELIVERY BOYS(1984)

David Jiminez
GIANT(1956)

Edwardo Jiminez
PALS OF THE GOLDEN WEST(1952)

Felisa Jiminez
RETURN OF THE SEVEN(1966, Span.)

Jaime Jiminez
MYSTERY IN MEXICO(1948)
Jose Luis Jiminez
SPIRITISM(1965, Mex.)
Mrs. Jiminez
ARIZONA KID, THE(1930)
Sharyn Jiminez
WAY OUT(1966)
Soledad Jiminez
IN OLD ARIZONA(1929); ROMANCE OF THE RIO GRANDE(1929); DEVIL WITH WOMEN, A(1930); TEXAN, THE(1930); BROKEN WING, THE(1932); BORDERTOWN(1935); CYCLONE RANGER(1935); UNDER THE PAMPAS MOON(1935); TRAITOR, THE(1936); KID GALAHAD(1937); LAW AND LEAD(1937); MAN OF THE PEOPLE(1937); CALIFORNIA FRONTIER(1938); FORBIDDEN VALLEY(1938); PHANTOM OF THE RANGE, THE(1938); GIRL FROM RIO, THE(1939); OKLAHOMA KID, THE(1939); NORTHWEST MOUNTED POLICE(1940); HOLD BACK THE DAWN(1941); FOR WHOM THE BELL TOLLS(1943); SOUTH OF THE RIO GRANDE(1945); CARNIVAL IN COSTA RICA(1947); RED LIGHT(1949); DAKOTA LIL(1950); LAW AND THE LADY, THE(1951); TURNING POINT, THE(1952)
Solidad Jiminez
COCK-EYED WORLD, THE(1929)
Yadira Jiminez
CASA MANANA(1951)
Yadiro Jiminez
STRONGHOLD(1952, Mex.)
Jimmie Davis and His Sunshine Band
SQUARE DANCE KATY(1950)
Jimmie Grier's Orchestra
NOBODY'S BABY(1937)
Jimmie Lewis and his Texas Cowboys
CAROLINA MOON(1940)
Jimmy
MONTE CARLO STORY, THE(1957, Ital.)
"Petit" Jimmy
Misc. Silents
PEAU DE PECHE(1929, Fr.)
Jimmy the Crow
MIRACULOUS JOURNEY(1948)
Jimmy Bryant and the Night Jumpers
SKYDIVERS, THE(1963)
Jimmy Cavallo House Rockers
ROCK, ROCK, ROCK!(1956)
Jimmy Daley's Ding-A-Lings
SUMMER LOVE(1958)
Jimmy Dean and His Trail Riders
I'LL TELL THE WORLD(1945)
Jimmy Dorsey and his Band
FLEET'S IN, THE(1942); FOUR JILLS IN A JEEP(1944); HOLLYWOOD CANTEEN(1944)
Jimmy Dorsey and his Orchestra
LOST IN A HAREM(1944)
Jimmy Dorsey and Orchestra
I DOOD IT(1943)
Jimmy Dorsey's Orchestra
FABULOUS DORSEYS, THE(1947)
The Jimmy Grier Orchestra
TRANSATLANTIC MERRY-GO-ROUND(1934)
Jimmy LeFieur's Saddle Pals
FRONTIER TOWN(1938)
Jimmy LeFuer's Saddle Pals
SPRINGTIME IN THE ROCKIES(1937)
Jimmy Nervo & Teddy Knox
FROZEN LIMITS, THE(1939, Brit.)
The Jimmy Smith Trio
GET YOURSELF A COLLEGE GIRL(1964)
Jimmy Wakely and His Oklahoma Cowboys
SWING IN THE SADDLE(1944)
Jimmy Wakely and his Rough Riders
PONY POST(1940); TEXAS TERRORS(1940); TRAILING DOUBLE TROUBLE(1940); TULSA KID, THE(1940)
Jimmy Wakely and his Saddle Pals
COWBOY CANTEEN(1944); CYCLONE PRAIRIE RANGERS(1944); SUNDOWN VALLEY(1944)
Jimmy Wakely Trio
TWILIGHT ON THE TRAIL(1941); DEEP IN THE HEART OF TEXAS(1942); HEART OF THE RIO GRANDE(1942); LITTLE JOE, THE WRANGLER(1942); STRICTLY IN THE GROOVE(1942); LONE STAR TRAIL, THE(1943); RAIDERS OF SAN JOAQUIN(1943); ROBIN HOOD OF THE RANGE(1943); TENTING TONIGHT ON THE OLD CAMP GROUND(1943)
Jimmy Wakely's Rough Riders
BURY ME NOT ON THE LONE PRAIRIE(1941)
Siresh Jinda
CHESS PLAYERS, THE(1978, India), p
E.R. Jinedas
FOUR FRIGHTENED PEOPLE(1934)
Mickey Jines
ORGY OF THE DEAD(1965); PRECIOUS JEWELS(1969)
Kien Jing
REVENGE OF THE PINK PANTHER(1978)
Johnny Jingles
MISTER BROWN(1972)
Miyoshi Jingu
NAVY WIFE(1956); TEAHOUSE OF THE AUGUST MOON, THE(1956); MANCHURIAN CANDIDATE, THE(1962); WALK, DON'T RUN(1966); DREAMS OF GLASS(1969)
Mari Jinishian
THOUSAND AND ONE NIGHTS, A(1945)
Bob Jiras
HUSTLER, THE(1961), makeup; NEXT STOP, GREENWICH VILLAGE(1976), makeup; JAWS II(1978), makeup

John Jiras
ONLY GAME IN TOWN, THE(1970), makeup
Robert Jiras
GODDESS, THE(1958), makeup; LAST MILE, THE(1959), makeup; ODDS AGAINST TOMORROW(1959), makeup; SPLENDOR IN THE GRASS(1961), makeup; TWO TICKETS TO PARIS(1962), makeup; LILITH(1964), makeup; MICKEY ONE(1965), makeup; PRETTY POISON(1968), makeup; MC CABE AND MRS. MILLER(1971), makeup; I AM THE CHEESE(1983), d, w
Jirina Jiraskova
90 DEGREES IN THE SHADE(1966, Czech./Brit.)
O. Jisneva
Misc. Silents
GHOST THAT NEVER RETURNS, THE(1930, USSR)
Jitney
Silents
SIGNAL TOWER, THE(1924)
Emily Jiuliano
SECRET OF NIMH, THE(1982), anim
Joe Jiuliano
SECRET OF NIMH, THE(1982), ph
The Jivaro Indians of Ecuador
SAVAGE GOLD(1933)
Jivin' Jacks and Jills
GIVE OUT, SISTERS(1942)
The Jivin' Jacks and Jills
PRIVATE BUCKAROO(1942); WHAT'S COOKIN'?(1942); ALWAYS A BRIDESMAID(1943)
Jo Jo
Misc. Talkies
BRIDGES TO HEAVEN(1975)
Jo Bouillon and Willie Lewis Bands
CINDERELLA(1937, Fr.)
Marguerite Tong Jo-ching
ENCHANTING SHADOW, THE(1965, Hong Kong)
Anthony Joachim
DRAGON'S GOLD(1954)
Irene Joachim
LA MARSEILLAISE(1938, Fr.)
Thomas Joachim
NUTCRACKER FANTASY(1979), w
Tony Joachim
GUNFIGHT AT THE O.K. CORRAL(1957)
Hans Joachim-Beyer
OUR DAILY BREAD(1950, Ger.), w
Felix Joachimson
AFFAIRS OF MAUPASSANT(1938, Aust.), w
Oolipika Joamie
WHITE DAWN, THE(1974)
Joan
ONCE UPON A COFFEE HOUSE(1965)
Joan Davis Dancers
LAUGH IT OFF(1940, Brit.)
Joan Davis' Eight Rose Petals
GARRISON FOLLIES(1940, Brit.)
Joann the Wonder Hen
NORWOOD(1970)
Vangelis Joannides
YOUNG APHRODITES(1966, Gr.)
Leo Joannon
DANGEROUS CARGO(1939, Brit.), w; CONFESSIONS OF A NEWLYWED(1941, Fr.), p&d; UTOPIA(1952, Fr./Ital.), d, w
Leon Joannon
CHILDREN OF CHAOS(1950, Fr.), d
Clotilde Joano
AMELIE OR THE TIME TO LOVE(1961, Fr.); YOUR SHADOW IS MINE(1963, Fr./Ital.); DEVIL BY THE TAIL, THE(1969, Fr./Ital.); Z(1969, Fr./Algeria)
Adelaide Joao
1984
THREE CROWNS OF THE SAILOR(1984, Fr.)
Lily Joaquino
MISSION BATANGAS(1968), makeup
Enrico Job
END OF THE WORLD(in Our Usual Bed In a Night Full of Rain), THE*1/2 (1978, Ital.), art d; SHOOT LOUD, LOUDER... I DON'T UNDERSTAND(1966, Ital.), cos; LOVE AND ANARCHY(1974, Ital.), set d&cos; SWEPT AWAY...BY AN UNUSUAL DESTINY IN THE BLUE SEA OF AUGUST(1975, Ital.), set d&cos; ALL SCREWED UP(1976, Ital.), set d&cos; SEVEN BEAUTIES(1976, Ital.), art d
1984
BIZET'S CARMEN(1984, Fr./Ital.), prod d, set d, cos; JOKE OF DESTINY LYING IN WAIT AROUND THE CORNER LIKE A STREETBANDIT, A(1984, Ital.), art d
Thomas Job
UNCLE HARRY(1945), w; ESCAPE IN THE DESERT(1945), w; TWO MRS. CARROLLS, THE(1947), w; SIREN OF ATLANTIS(1948), w
William Job
PRIVILEGE(1967, Brit.); HOUSE OF CARDS(1969); RISE AND RISE OF MICHAEL RIMMER, THE(1970, Brit.)
Bill Jobe
W.C. FIELDS AND ME(1976), cos; MR. BILLION(1977), cos; JAWS II(1978), cos; DEAD AND BURIED(1981), cos
Marlene Jobert
MASCULINE FEMININE(1966, Fr./Swed.); THIEF OF PARIS, THE(1967, Fr./Ital.); VERY HAPPY ALEXANDER(1969, Fr.); RIDER ON THE RAIN(1970, Fr./Ital.); CATCH ME A SPY(1971, Brit./Fr.); TEN DAYS' WONDER(1972, Fr.)
Stephane Jobert
DANTON(1983)
Marigray Jobes
LAST AFFAIR, THE(1976)

Antonio Carlos Jobim
BLACK ORPHEUS(1959 Fr./Ital./Braz.), m; ADVENTURERS, THE(1970), m
1984
GABRIELA(1984, Braz.), m
Benoit Jobin
OPERATION MANHUNT(1954), ph
Louise Jobin
STRANGE SHADOWS IN AN EMPTY ROOM(1977, Can./Ital.), cos; SUZANNE(1980, Can.), cos
Peter Jobin
HAPPY BIRTHDAY TO ME(1981), w; GREY FOX, THE(1983, Can.)
Katja Jobs
DECISION BEFORE DAWN(1951)
Lisskulla Jobs
CRIME AND PUNISHMENT(1948, Swed.)
Dickie Jobson
COUNTRYMAN(1982, Jamaica), d, w
Edward Jobson
Silents
AMAZING IMPOSTER, THE(1919); CHORUS GIRL'S ROMANCE, A(1920); OFF-SHORE PIRATE, THE(1921); SAPHEAD, THE(1921); KISSES(1922); SCRAPPER, THE(1922); STEPPING FAST(1923)
Misc. Silents
CLEAN GUN, THE(1917); MISS MISCHIEF MAKER(1918); NO CHILDREN WANT-ED(1918); WHICH WOMAN?(1918); MERRY-GO ROUND, THE(1919); MINTS OF HELL, THE(1919); CITY OF MASKS, THE(1920); FRIVOLOUS WIVES(1920); PIN-TO(1920); MATCH-BREAKER, THE(1921)
Edwin Jobson
Silents
EVIDENCE(1918)
Misc. Silents
MATERNAL SPARK, THE(1917)
Jack Jobson
CHAFED ELBOWS(1967)
Gerty Jobstmann
LONE CLIMBER, THE(1950, Brit./Aust.)
Hans Joby
HELL'S ANGELS(1930); SUICIDE FLEET(1931); PANAMA FLO(1932); CAP-TURED(1933); ONE NIGHT OF LOVE(1934); STAMBOUL QUEST(1934); SONS O' GUNS(1936); BORDER PHANTOM(1937); I MET HIM IN PARIS(1937); LANCER SPY(1937); MAYTIME(1937); BEASTS OF BERLIN(1939); THUNDER AFLOAT(1939); MAN HUNT(1941); LADY HAS PLANS, THE(1942)
Andre Jocelyn
WEB OF PASSION(1961, Fr.); SEVEN CAPITAL SINS(1962, Fr./Ital.); OPHELIA(1964, Fr.)
Gordon Jocelyn
DEAD ZONE, THE(1983); THRESHOLD(1983, Can.)
June Jocelyn
AMAZING COLOSSAL MAN, THE(1957); FEAR STRIKES OUT(1957); ROCKABIL-LY BABY(1957); ATTACK OF THE PUPPET PEOPLE(1958); SPIDER, THE(1958); TEENAGE CAVEMAN(1958); VERTIGO(1958); WAR OF THE COLOSSAL BEAST(1958); RUNAWAY GIRL(1966)
Beverly Jocher
GOG(1954)
Anthony Jochim
HE WALKED BY NIGHT(1948); SAXON CHARM, THE(1948); FIGHTING MAN OF THE PLAINS(1949); DAVID HARDING, COUNTERSPY(1950); MALAYA(1950); WESTERN PACIFIC AGENT(1950); THREE DESPERATE MEN(1951); STRANGE FASCINATION(1952); CITY OF BAD MEN(1953); DANGEROUS CROSSING(1953); ONE GIRL'S CONFESSION(1953); PROBLEM GIRLS(1953); ROBE, THE(1953); I'LL CRY TOMORROW(1955); STAR IN THE DUST(1956); DRANGO(1957); JOE DAKO-TA(1957); HOT SPELL(1958); LEGEND OF TOM DOOLEY, THE(1959); SOME CAME RUNNING(1959); STORY OF RUTH, THE(1960)
Tony Jochim
GIRL ON THE BRIDGE, THE(1951); THY NEIGHBOR'S WIFE(1953); TENDER HEARTS(1955); EDGE OF HELL(1956); BORN TO BE LOVED(1959); DREAM OF KINGS, A(1969)
Max Jocson
JAGUAR(1980, Phil.), m
Garry Jode
1984
LE DERNIER COMBAT(1984, Fr.)
Anita Jodelsohn
CHANGE OF SEASONS, A(1980)
Alexandro Jodorowsky
EL TOPO(1971, Mex.), a, d&w&m; HOLY MOUNTAIN, THE(1973, U.S./Mex.), a, d&w, m; TUSK(1980, Fr.), d, w
Brontis Jodorowsky
EL TOPO(1971, Mex.)
Cousin Jody
NASHVILLE REBEL(1966)
Joe
YOU GOTTA STAY HAPPY(1948)
Joe, the Raven
AVALANCHE(1946)
Bradley Joe
YEAR OF THE HORSE, THE(1966)
Honest Joe
MY DOG, BUDDY(1960)
Jeanne Joe
FIRST MONDAY IN OCTOBER(1981)
Joe and Eddie
HOOTENANNY HOOT(1963)
Joe Aston & Renee
WEAPON, THE(1957, Brit.)
Joe Brown and the Breakaways
JUST FOR FUN(1963, Brit.)

Joe Loss and His Band
LET'S MAKE A NIGHT OF IT(1937, Brit.)
Joe Venuti and his Swing Cats
GARDEN OF THE MOON(1938)
Aviva Joel
1984
LITTLE DRUMMER GIRL, THE(1984)
Clara Joel
Misc. Silents
VIRTUOUS MEN(1919)
Dennis Joel
TOBY TYLER(1960)
Robert Joel
VERY NATURAL THING, A(1974)
Thelma Joel
MY FAVORITE WIFE(1940); MEET THE PEOPLE(1944); ONCE UPON A TIME(1944)
Joel Feig Double Choir
Misc. Talkies
KOL NIDRE(1939)
Wilhelm Joerres
RIVERRUN(1968)
Joey Joey
Silents
RAMSHACKLE HOUSE(1924)
Joey the Mule
PROMOTER, THE(1952, Brit.)
A. E. Joffe
MARRIAGE BY CONTRACT(1928), m/l
Alex Joffe
DEVIL'S DAUGHTER(1949, Fr.), w; SIMPLE CASE OF MONEY, A(1952, Fr.), w; MONTE CARLO BABY(1953, Fr.), w; TAXI(1953), w; RIFF RAFF GIRLS(1962, Fr./Ital.), d, w; SHOOT THE PIANO PLAYER(1962, Fr.); IMPOSSIBLE ON SATUR-DAY(1966, Fr./Israel), d
Charles H. Joffe
DON'T DRINK THE WATER(1969), p; TAKE THE MONEY AND RUN(1969), p; BANANAS(1971), p; EVERYTHING YOU ALWAYS WANTED TO KNOW ABOUT SEX, BUT WE'RE AFRAID TO ASK(1972), p; LOVE AND DEATH(1975), p; ANNIE HALL(1977), p; INTERIORS(1978), p; MANHATTAN(1979), p
1984
HOUSE OF GOD, THE(1984), p
Roland Joffe
1984
KILLING FIELDS, THE(1984, Brit.), d
Lou Jofferd
HITCHHIKERS, THE(1972)
Joffre
END OF A DAY, THE(1939, Fr.)
Joffre Swales Quartet
MOUSE AND THE WOMAN, THE(1981, Brit.)
Lou Joffred
MACHISMO—40 GRAVES FOR 40 GUNS(1970)
Marissa Joffrey
WHO'S THAT KNOCKING AT MY DOOR?(1968)
Alessandro Jogan
HORNET'S NEST(1970)
Louise Johan
1984
RUNAWAY(1984)
Linda Johanesen
WILD RIDERS(1971)
Albert Johann
MURDERERS AMONG US(1948, Ger.)
Zita Johann
STRUGGLE, THE(1931); MUMMY, THE(1932); TIGER SHARK(1932); LUXURY LINER(1933); MAN WHO DARED, THE(1933); SIN OF NORA MORAN(1933); GRAND CANARY(1934)
Johanne
TAKE IT ALL(1966, Can.), a, w
Phyllis Johannes
RAINS OF RANCHIPUR, THE(1955)
Ola B. Johannesen
HUNGER(1968, Den./Norway/Swed.)
Fritz Johannet
IN OLD KENTUCKY(1935)
Allan Johannson
INVASION OF THE ANIMAL PEOPLE(1962, U.S./Swed.), m
Aud Johansen
LILLI MARLENE(1951, Brit.); COME BACK PETER(1952, Brit.); FUN AT ST. FANNY'S(1956, Brit.); SECOND FIDDLE(1957, Brit.); MACBETH(1971, Brit.)
Kenneth Johansen
1984
KAMILLA(1984, Norway)
Svend Johansen
OPERATION CAMEL(1961, Den.); REPTILICUS(1962, U.S./Den.)
Virgil Johansen
PHFFFT!(1954)
Eduard Johanson
Misc. Silents
CHILDREN OF STORM(1926, USSR), d; KATKA'S REINETTE APPLES(1926, USSR), d
Johannas Johanson
WOODEN HORSE, THE(1951)
Ron Johanson
FINAL CUT, THE(1980, Aus.), ph
Sharon Johanson
YOUR THREE MINUTES ARE UP(1973)
Ulf Johanson
HOUR OF THE WOLF, THE(1968, Swed.)

Virgil Johanson
TAMPICO(1944)
Erik Johansson
EMIGRANTS, THE(1972, Swed.)
Ingemar Johansson
ALL THE YOUNG MEN(1960); 48 HOURS TO LIVE(1960, Brit./Swed.)
Ivar Johansson
OCEAN BREAKERS(1949, Swed.), d&w
Jan Johansson
NIGHT GAMES(1966, Swed.), m; TOUCH, THE(1971, U.S./Swed.), m
Tina Johansson
PERSONA(1967, Swed.), makeup; SEA GULL, THE(1968), makeup
Ulf Johansson
SEVENTH SEAL, THE(1958, Swed.); LOVING COUPLES(1966, Swed.); SHAME(1968, Swed.); FACE TO FACE(1976, Swed.)
Ullabella Johansson
SCANDAL IN DENMARK(1970, Den.)
I.S. Johar
HARRY BLACK AND THE TIGER(1958, Brit.); FLAME OVER INDIA(1960, Brit.); LAWRENCE OF ARABIA(1962, Brit.); MAYA(1966); DEATH ON THE NILE(1978, Brit.)
Azizi Johari
DREAMER(1979); SEED OF INNOCENCE(1980)
Zizi Johari
KILLING OF A CHINESE BOOKIE, THE(1976)
Al "Fuzzy" St. John
MYSTERIOUS RIDER, THE(1942)
Al St. John
APACHE KID, THE(1941)
Alexander John
DIRTY KNIGHT'S WORK(1976, Brit.); FIVE DAYS ONE SUMMER(1982)
Alice John
THESE THIRTY YEARS(1934)
Caroline John
1984
RAZOR'S EDGE, THE(1984)
lp: Carl John
Misc. Talkies
REFLECTIONS FROM A BRASS BED(1976)
D'Oyley John
ESCAPE TO DANGER(1943, Brit.)
David John
CHARRIOTS OF FIRE(1981, Brit.); SHOCK TREATMENT(1981); REMEMBRANCE(1982, Brit.)
Doyley John
THEY KNEW MR. KNIGHT(1945, Brit.)
Elton John
FRIENDS(1971, Brit.), m; TOMMY(1975, Brit.)
Emerson John
WINDWALKER(1980)
Erica John
S.O.B.(1981)
Errol John
HEART OF THE MATTER, THE(1954, Brit.); SIMBA(1955, Brit.); ODONGO(1956, Brit.); NUN'S STORY, THE(1959); SINS OF RACHEL CADE, THE(1960); PT 109(1963); GUNS AT BATASI(1964, Brit.); MAN IN THE MIDDLE(1964, U.S./Brit.); ASSAULT ON A QUEEN(1966); BUCK AND THE PREACHER(1972)
1984
SHEENA(1984)
Evan John
LAST CURTAIN, THE(1937, Brit.)
Georg John
DANTON(1931, Ger.); F.P. 1 DOESN'T ANSWER(1933, Ger.); M(1933, Ger.); TESTAMENT OF DR. MABUSE, THE(1943, Ger.)
Silents
KRIEMHILD'S REVENGE(1924, Ger.); LAST LAUGH, THE(1924, Ger.); SIEGFRIED(1924, Ger.); METROPOLIS(1927, Ger.); SPIES(1929, Ger.)
Misc. Silents
HILDE WARREN AND DEATH(1916, Ger.); FIVE SINISTER STORIES(1919, Ger.); HARAKIRI(1919, Ger.); STONE RIDER, THE(1923, Ger.)
Gottfried John
MOTHER KUSTERS GOES TO HEAVEN(1976, Ger.); DESPAIR(1978, Ger.); FEDORA(1978, Ger./Fr.); MARRIAGE OF MARIA BRAUN, THE(1979, Ger.); IN A YEAR OF THIRTEEN MOONS(1980, Ger.); LILI MARLEEN(1981, Ger.)
1984
CHINESE BOXES(1984, Ger./Brit.)
Graham John
DEVOTION(1931), w; MONKEY'S PAW, THE(1933), w
Guinevere John
WICKED LADY, THE(1983, Brit.)
H.W. John
I AIM AT THE STARS(1960), w
Ian John
SLEEPING DOGS(1977, New Zealand), ed; SCARECROW, THE(1982, New Zealand), ed
1984
UTU(1984, New Zealand), ed
Karl John
LOST ONE, THE(1951, Ger.); MAN BETWEEN, THE(1953, Brit.); DEVIL'S GENERAL, THE(1957, Ger.); LONGEST DAY, THE(1962); SORCERER(1977)
Lucien John
WALKABOUT(1971, Aus./U.S.)
Michael John
FRONT LINE KIDS(1942, Brit.)
Monika John
DEVIL STRIKES AT NIGHT, THE(1959, Ger.); JUDGE AND THE SINNER, THE(1964, Ger.)

Nicholas John
FRIGHTMARE(1974, Brit.)
Peter John
TOWN LIKE ALICE, A(1958, Brit.); OTHELLO(1965, Brit.)
Robert John
CREATURES THE WORLD FORGOT(1971, Brit.); EL TOPO(1971, Mex.)
Rosamund John
GENTLE SEX, THE(1943, Brit.); LAMP STILL BURNS, THE(1943, Brit.); SPITFIRE(1943, Brit.); SOLDIER, SAILOR(1944, Brit.); JOHNNY IN THE CLOUDS(1945, Brit.); GREEN FOR DANGER(1946, Brit.); FAME IS THE SPUR(1947, Brit.); TAWNY PIPIT(1947, Brit.); UPTURNED GLASS, THE(1947, Brit.); WHEN THE BOUGH BREAKS(1947, Brit.); NO PLACE FOR JENNIFER(1950, Brit.); SHE SHALL HAVE MURDER(1950, Brit.); NEVER LOOK BACK(1952, Brit.); BOTH SIDES OF THE LAW(1953, Brit.); OPERATION MURDER(1957, Brit.)
Rupert John
MOULIN ROUGE(1952)
Stephen John
MARY HAD A LITTLE(1961, Brit.)
Tom H. John
THANK GOD IT'S FRIDAY(1978), prod d; ZOOT SUIT(1981), prod d
Tom John
GANJA AND HESS(1973), prod d
The John Barry Seven
COOL MIKADO, THE(1963, Brit.)
John Gary Williams and the Newcomers
DARKTOWN STRUTTERS(1975)
King John III
BLACK ANGELS, THE(1970)
John Kirby's Band
SEPIA CINDERELLA(1947)
John LaSalle Jazz Combo
COURTSHIP OF EDDY'S FATHER, THE(1963)
John Payne's Negro Choir
LILY OF LAGUNA(1938, Brit.)
John Reynders and His Band
OUT OF THE BLUE(1931, Brit.)
John Reynders and The BBC Orchestra
SATURDAY NIGHT REVUE(1937, Brit.)
John-Alderman
SEVEN(1979)
Virgil Johnansen
DOUBLE DYNAMITE(1951)
JohnBradbury
PINOCCHIO(1940), anim
Brian Johncock
TASTE THE BLOOD OF DRACULA(1970, Brit.), spec eff; WHEN DINOSAURS RULED THE EARTH(1971, Brit.), spec eff
Madison Johnes
I WALK THE LINE(1970), w
Tom Johnigarn
SWEET JESUS, PREACHER MAN(1973); TOM(1973)
Misc. Talkies
BAD BUNCH, THE(1976)
Harald Johnke
DANCING HEART, THE(1959, Ger.)
Arkansas Johnny
WHEELS OF DESTINY(1934); WESTERN COURAGE(1935)
Glenn Langan Johnny
ONE GIRL'S CONFESSION(1953)
Talib Johnny
OCTOPUSSY(1983, Brit.)
Johnny & The Tornados
GAS-S-S-S!(1970)
Johnny Bond and his Red River Valley Boys
ARIZONA TRAIL(1943); FRONTIER LAW(1943); MARSHAL OF GUNSMOKE(1944); OKLAHOMA RAIDERS(1944)
Johnny Burnette Trio
ROCK, ROCK, ROCK!(1956)
Johnny Claes and His Claepigeons
GEORGE IN CIVVY STREET(1946, Brit.)
Johnny Conrad and Dancers
JACK AND THE BEANSTALK(1952)
Johnny Green and His Orchestra
START CHEERING(1938)
Johnny Long and Band
FOLLIES GIRL(1943)
Johnny Long and His Orchestra
IRENE(1940)
Johnny Luther's Cowboy Band
ROUGH RIDING RANGER(1935)
Johnny Luther's Ranch Boys
FIGHTING BUCKAROO, THE(1943)
Johnny Olenn and His Group
BORN RECKLESS(1959)
The Johnny Otis Show
PLAY MISTY FOR ME(1971)
Anne Johns
DEATH COLLECTOR(1976)
Misc. Talkies
FAMILY ENFORCER(1978)
Bertram Johns
THIRTEENTH CHAIR, THE(1930)
Silents
BLUSHING BRIDE, THE(1921); KISS IN TIME, A(1921); STEPHEN STEPS OUT(1923); TAKE IT FROM ME(1926)
Bob Johns
PORT OF HATE(1939), ed

Brooke Johns
Misc. Silents
THAT OLD GANG OF MINE(1925)
Cathryn Johns
WILD MUSTANG(1935)
Chet Johns
PROJECT X(1968), spec eff
Clay Johns
GROUP, THE(1966)
Edith Johns
MY THIRD WIFE GEORGE(1968), makeup
Edwin Johns
JAZZ CINDERELLA(1930), w
Ehren Johns
MIDNIGHT SPECIAL(1931), w
Ernest Johns
LOOKS AND SMILES(1982, Brit.)
Esme Johns
I AM A GROUPIE(1970, Brit.)
Florence Johns
REGISTERED NURSE(1934), w
Silents
OUT OF THE DRIFTS(1916); AUCTION BLOCK, THE(1917)
Glynis Johns
MURDER IN THE FAMILY(1938, Brit.); SOUTH RIDING(1938, Brit.); PRISON WITHOUT BARS(1939, Brit.); BRIGGS FAMILY, THE(1940, Brit.); FUGITIVE, THE(1940, Brit.); UNDER YOUR HAT(1940, Brit.); INVADERS, THE(1941); PRIME MINISTER, THE(1941, Brit.); ADVENTURES OF TARTU(1943, Brit.); HALF-WAY HOUSE, THE(1945, Brit.); VACATION FROM MARRIAGE(1945, Brit.); THIS MAN IS MINE(1946 Brit.); FRIEDA(1947, Brit.); IDEAL HUSBAND, AN(1948, Brit.); DEAR MR. PROHACK(1949, Brit.); HELTER SKELTER(1949, Brit.); MIRANDA(1949, Brit.); THIRD TIME LUCKY(1950, Brit.); FLESH AND BLOOD(1951, Brit.); GREAT MAN-HUNT, THE(1951, Brit.); NO HIGHWAY IN THE SKY(1951, Brit.); ISLAND RESCUE(1952, Brit.); MAGIC BOX, THE(1952, Brit.); PROMOTER, THE(1952, Brit.); SWORD AND THE ROSE, THE(1953); MAD ABOUT MEN(1954, Brit.); PERSONAL AFFAIR(1954, Brit.); ROB ROY, THE HIGHLAND ROGUE(1954, Brit.); WEAK AND THE WICKED, THE(1954, Brit.); JOSEPHINE AND MEN(1955); LAND OF FURY(1955 Brit.); THE BEACHCOMBER(1955, Brit.); AROUND THE WORLD IN 80 DAYS(1956); COURT JESTER, THE(1956); LOSER TAKES ALL(1956, Brit.); ALL MINE TO GIVE(1957); ANOTHER TIME, ANOTHER PLACE(1958); SHAKE HANDS WITH THE DEVIL(1959, Ireland); SPIDER'S WEB, THE(1960, Brit.); SUNDOWNERS, THE(1960); CABINET OF CALIGARI, THE(1962); CHAPMAN REPORT, THE(1962); PAPA'S DELICATE CONDITION(1963); MARY POPPINS(1964); DEAR BRIGETTE(1965); DON'T JUST STAND THERE!(1968); LOCK UP YOUR DAUGHTERS(1969, Brit.); UNDER MILK WOOD(1973, Brit.); VAULT OF HORROR, THE(1973, Brit.)
Harriette Johns
IDEAL HUSBAND, AN(1948, Brit.); EDWARD, MY SON(1949, U.S./Brit.); MEET MR. CALLAGHAN(1954, Brit.); NIGHT TO REMEMBER, A(1958, Brit.); TWO-HEADED SPY, THE(1959, Brit.); DATE AT MIDNIGHT(1960, Brit.); GUTTER GIRLS(1964, Brit.); HAPPY DEATHDAY(1969, Brit.)
I. R. Johns
MAD YOUTH(1940), ed
Jane Johns
IDOL OF THE CROWDS(1937)
John P. Johns
RETURN OF CASEY JONES(1933), w
Judith Johns
1984
RUNAWAY(1984)
Larry Johns
BELLE STARR'S DAUGHTER(1947); DAKOTA LIL(1950); LAW OF THE BAD-LANDS(1950); RIO GRANDE PATROL(1950); QUEEN FOR A DAY(1951); SEALED CARGO(1951); PROJECT MOONBASE(1953)
Lorin Johns
SHARKFIGHTERS, THE(1956)
Malcolm Johns
PERFECT FRIDAY(1970, Brit.)
Margo Johns
MEET SEXTON BLAKE(1944, Brit.); MYSTERY AT THE BURLESQUE(1950, Brit.); KONGA(1961, Brit.); THIS IS MY STREET(1964, Brit.)
Margot Johns
MYSTERY AT THE BURLESQUE(1950, Brit.)
Marion Johns
SMILEY(1957, Brit.); SHIRLEY THOMPSON VERSUS THE ALIENS(1968, Aus.)
Misc. Talkies
GONE TO GROUND(1976)
Mervyn Johns, Jr.
ONCE MORE, WITH FEELING(1960)
Mervyn Johns
LADY IN DANGER(1934, Brit.); DISHONOR BRIGHT(1936, Brit.); IN THE SOUP(1936, Brit.); MISTER HOBO(1936, Brit.); SONG OF THE FORGE(1937, Brit.); ALMOST A GENTLEMAN(1938, Brit.); JAMAICA INN(1939, Brit.); MIDAS TOUCH, THE(1940, Brit.); SALOON BAR(1940, Brit.); GIRL IN THE NEWS, THE(1941, Brit.); NEXT OF KIN(1942, Brit.); BELLS GO DOWN, THE(1943, Brit.); MY LEARNED FRIEND(1943, Brit.); SOMEWHERE IN FRANCE(1943, Brit.); TWILIGHT HOUR(1944, Brit.); 48 HOURS(1944, Brit.); HALF-WAY HOUSE, THE(1945, Brit.); THEY KNEW MR. KNIGHT(1945, Brit.); DEAD OF NIGHT(1946, Brit.); CAPTAIN BOYCOTT(1947, Brit.); SAN DEMETRIO, LONDON(1947, Brit.); CAPTIVE HEART, THE(1948, Brit.); COUNTER BLAST(1948, Brit.); DEVIL'S PLOT, THE(1948, Brit.); EASY MONEY(1948, Brit.); DIAMOND CITY(1949, Brit.); EDWARD, MY SON(1949, U.S./Brit.); HELTER SKELTER(1949, Brit.); QUARTET(1949, Brit.); PINK STRING AND SEALING WAX(1950, Brit.); TONY DRAWS A HORSE(1951, Brit.); FRIGHTENED BRIDE, THE(1952, Brit.); MAGIC BOX, THE(1952, Brit.); HORSE'S MOUTH, THE(1953, Brit.); MASTER OF BALLANTRAE, THE(1953, U.S./Brit.); MEN ARE CHILDREN TWICE(1953, Brit.); ROMEO AND JULIET(1954, Brit.); FIND THE LADY(1956, Brit.); FINGER OF GUILT(1956, Brit.); MOBY DICK(1956, Brit.); 1984(1956, Brit.); COUNTERFEIT PLAN, THE(1957, Brit.); DOCTOR AT LARGE(1957, Brit.); SURGEON'S KNIFE, THE(1957, Brit.); GYPSY AND THE GENTLEMAN, THE(1958, Brit.); CIRCLE, THE(1959, Brit.); DEVIL'S DISCIPLE, THE(1959, Brit.); NAVY HEROES(1959, Brit.); NEVER LET GO(1960, Brit.); SUNDOWNERS, THE(1960, Brit.); CALL ME GENIUS(1961, Brit.);

ECHO OF BARBARA(1961, Brit.); FRANCIS OF ASSISI(1961); DAY OF THE TRIF-FIDS, THE(1963); OLD DARK HOUSE, THE(1963, Brit.); VICTORS, THE(1963); 55 DAYS AT PEKING(1963); 80,000 SUSPECTS(1963, Brit.); JOLLY BAD FELLOW, A(1964, Brit.); HEROES OF TELEMARK, THE(1965, Brit.); WHO KILLED THE CAT?(1966, Brit.); NATIONAL HEALTH, OR NURSE NORTON'S AFFAIR, THE(1973, Brit.); CONFESSIONAL, THE(1977, Brit.); KILL AND KILL AGAIN(1981)
Michael Johns
TOTO AND THE POACHERS(1958, Brit.), w; SEPARATION(1968, Brit.), ed
Milton Johns
EMPIRE STRIKES BACK, THE(1980)
Norman Johns
HARRY BLACK AND THE TIGER(1958, Brit.); MIX ME A PERSON(1962, Brit.); MYSTERY SUBMARINE(1963, Brit.)
Richard Johns
SECRET INVASION, THE(1964)
Robert Johns
OUTLAW DEPUTY, THE(1935), ed; MAN FROM GUN TOWN, THE(1936), ed; RANGER'S ROUNDUP, THE(1938), ed; SONGS AND BULLETS(1938), ed
Roy Thomas Johns
ONE FROM THE HEART(1982)
Shirley Johns
CYNTHIA(1947); LUXURY LINER(1948); SUMMER HOLIDAY(1948)
Stan Johns
BOYS IN COMPANY C, THE(1978, U.S./Hong Kong)
Stratford Johns
NIGHT MY NUMBER CAME UP, THE(1955, Brit.); LADYKILLERS, THE(1956, Brit.); SHIP THAT DIED OF SHAME, THE(1956, Brit.); TIGER IN THE SMOKE(1956, Brit.); WHO DONE IT?(1956, Brit.); THIRD KEY, THE(1957, Brit.); ONE THAT GOT AWAY, THE(1958, Brit.); HAND IN HAND(1960, Brit.); PROFESSIONALS, THE(1960, Brit.); TWO LETTER ALIBI(1962); GREAT ST. TRINIAN'S TRAIN ROBBERY, THE(1966, Brit.); PLANK, THE(1967, Brit.); THOSE FANTASTIC FLYING FOOLS(1967, Brit); CROMWELL(1970, Brit.); FIENDISH PLOT OF DR. FU MANCHU, THE(1980); GEORGE AND MILDRED(1980, Brit.)
Misc. Talkies
SAINT AND THE BRAVE GOOSE, THE(1981, Brit.)
Val Johns
BIG CUBE, THE(1969), m
Vere Johns
MANFISH(1956)
Vernon Johns
RIDERS IN THE SKY(1949)
Andre Johnsen
DANTE'S INFERNO(1935)
Sande Johnsen
1,000 SHAPES OF A FEMALE(1963); OLGA'S GIRLS(1964), set d; TEENAGE GANG DEBS(1966), d
Sande N. Johnsen
1,000 SHAPES OF A FEMALE(1963), w, art d; VIXENS, THE(1969), p
A.E. Johnson
MILL ON THE FLOSS(1939, Brit.)
Adele Cook Johnson
GREATEST SHOW ON EARTH, THE(1952)
Adrian Johnson
JAZZ CINDERELLA(1930), w; LADY FROM NOWHERE(1931), w; FOUND ALIVE(1934), w
Silents
BATTLE OF LIFE, THE(1916), w; ROMEO AND JULIET(1916), w; TIGER WOMAN, THE(1917), w; JUNGLE TRAIL, THE(1919), w; CROOKED ALLEY(1923), w; BOWERY CINDERELLA(1927), w
Agnes C. Johnson
THREE WISE GIRLS(1932), w; HARDYS RIDE HIGH, THE(1939), w
Agnes Christine Johnson
MOVIE CRAZY(1932), w; HEADLINE SHOOTER(1933), w; LUCKY DEVILS(1933), w; WHEN A MAN'S A MAN(1935), w; ALL WOMEN HAVE SECRETS(1939), w; ANDY HARDY'S DOUBLE LIFE(1942), w; COURTSHIP OF ANDY HARDY, THE(1942), w; ANDY HARDY'S BLONDE TROUBLE(1944), w; BLACK GOLD(1947), w; STAGE STRUCK(1948), w
Silents
ALTARS OF DESIRE(1927), w; SHOW PEOPLE(1928), w
Alan Johnson
PRODUCERS, THE(1967), ch; BLAZING SADDLES(1974), ch; ADVENTURES OF SHERLOCK HOLMES' SMARTER BROTHER, THE(1975, Brit.), ch; HISTORY OF THE WORLD, PART 1(1981), ch; TO BE OR NOT TO BE(1983), d
Albert Johnson
SCOUNDREL, THE(1935), set d; PLAY IT AS IT LAYS(1972)
Alex Johnson
RUN FOR YOUR WIFE(1966, Fr./Ital.); CHILLY SCENES OF WINTER(1982)
Alexandra Johnson
PROMISES IN THE DARK(1979); S.O.B.(1981)
Andrew Johnson
1984
MAJDHAR(1984, Brit.)
Angeline Johnson
BREWSTER McCLOUD(1970)
Anna Hill Johnson
BYE BYE BRAVERMAN(1968), cos
Anna Lee Johnson
VIRGINIA JUDGE, THE(1935)
Annette Johnson
NAKED WORLD OF HARRISON MARKS, THE(1967, Brit.)
April Johnson
Misc. Talkies
ALL THE YOUNG WIVES(1975)
Arch Johnson
NIAGARA(1953); SOMEBODY UP THERE LIKES ME(1956); GUN GLORY(1957); G.I. BLUES(1960); EXPLOSIVE GENERATION, THE(1961); TWILIGHT OF HONOR(1963); SULLIVAN'S EMPIRE(1967); CHEYENNE SOCIAL CLUB, THE(1970); LIBERATION OF L.B. JONES, THE(1970); NAPOLEON AND SAMANTHA(1972); STING, THE(1973); WALKING TALL(1973); BUDDY HOLLY STORY, THE(1978); EASY MONEY(1983)

Arch W. Johnson
GARDEN OF EDEN(1954)
Arno Johnson
ONE NIGHT OF LOVE(1934)
Arnold Johnson
PUTNEY SWOPE(1969); SHAFT(1971); PIPE DREAMS(1976); HERO AIN'T NOTHIN' BUT A SANDWICH, A(1977); ON THE NICKEL(1980); CHU CHU AND THE PHILLY FLASH(1981); HONKY TONK FREEWAY(1981)
1984
OH GOD! YOU DEVIL(1984); RACING WITH THE MOON(1984)
Art Johnson
LAST REBEL, THE(1971)
Arte Johnson
MIRACLE IN THE RAIN(1956); SUBTERRANEANS, THE(1960); THAT FUNNY FEELING(1965); THIRD DAY, THE(1965); PRESIDENT'S ANALYST, THE(1967); P.J.(1968); CHARGE OF THE MODEL-T'S(1979); LOVE AT FIRST BITE(1979)
1984
CANNONBALL RUN II(1984)
Arthur Johnson
BITTER TEA OF GENERAL YEN, THE(1933); PENNIES FROM HEAVEN(1936), m; SIDEWALKS OF LONDON(1940, Brit.), m
Avis Johnson
FLIRTATION WALK(1934)
Bari Johnson
CALL ME BWANA(1963, Brit.); PREHISTORIC WOMEN(1967, Brit.); GIRL ON A MOTORCYCLE, THE(1968, Fr./Brit.); ON THE RUN(1969, Brit.)
Ben Johnson
NAUGHTY NINETIES, THE(1945); THREE GODFATHERS, THE(1948); MIGHTY JOE YOUNG(1949); SHE WORE A YELLOW RIBBON(1949); RIO GRANDE(1950); WAGONMASTER(1950); FORT DEFIANCE(1951); WILD STALLION(1952); SHANE(1953); OKLAHOMA(1955); SIMBA(1955, Brit.); REBEL IN TOWN(1956); SLIM CARTER(1957); WAR DRUMS(1957); FORT BOWIE(1958); TEN WHO DARED(1960); ONE-EYED JACKS(1961); TOMBOY AND THE CHAMP(1961); CHEYENNE AUTUMN(1964); MAJOR DUNDEE(1965); RARE BREED(1966); HONEY POT, THE(1967, Brit.), w; HANG'EM HIGH(1968); WILL PENNY(1968); RIDE A NORTHBOUND HORSE(1969); UNDEFEATED, THE(1969); WILD BUNCH, THE(1969); CHISUM(1970); LAST PICTURE SHOW, THE(1971); SOMETHING BIG(1971); CORKY(1972); GETAWAY, THE(1972); JUNIOR BONNER(1972); DILLINGER(1973); KID BLUE(1973); TRAIN ROBBERS, THE(1973); SUGARLAND EXPRESS, THE(1974); BITE THE BULLET(1975); HUSTLE(1975); BREAKHEART PASS(1976); GRAYEAGLE(1977); GREATEST, THE(1977, U.S./Brit.); TOWN THAT DREADED SUNDOWN, THE(1977); SWARM, THE(1978); HUNTER, THE(1980); TERROR TRAIN(1980, Can.); RUCKUS(1981); SOGGY BOTTOM U.S.A.(1982); TEX(1982)
1984
CHAMPIONS(1984); RED DAWN(1984)
Silents
OAKDALE AFFAIR, THE(1919)
Misc. Silents
BRINGING UP BETTY(1919)
Bernard Johnson
CLAUDINE(1974), cos; BINGO LONG TRAVELING ALL-STARS AND MOTOR KINGS, THE(1976), cos; SCOTT JOPLIN(1977), cos; HANKY-PANKY(1982), cos
1984
BEAT STREET(1984), cos; GO TELL IT ON THE MOUNTAIN(1984), cos
Bertil Johnson
DEVIL'S MESSENGER, THE(1962 U.S./Swed.)
Bertina Johnson
DREAM ON(1981)
Bettie Johnson
PARALLAX VIEW, THE(1974)
Bettina Johnson
GIRL IN TROUBLE(1963)
Betty Johnson
NEW FACES OF 1937(1937)
Misc. Silents
GHOST BREAKER(1914), d
Beverly Johnson
ASHANTI(1979); SATAN'S MISTRESS(1982), p, w
Bill Johnson
IT'S A PLEASURE(1945); KEEP YOUR POWDER DRY(1945); SLEEPING DOGS(1977, New Zealand); SKIN DEEP(1978, New Zealand); NATE AND HAYES(1983, U.S./New Zealand)
Billy Johnson
LINCOLN CONSPIRACY, THE(1977)
Bob Johnson
WHY SAILORS LEAVE HOME(1930, Brit.); MY FRIEND IRMA GOES WEST(1950)
Bobbie Johnson
NARROW MARGIN, THE(1952)
Bobby Johnson
TWO SMART PEOPLE(1946); EMERGENCY WEDDING(1950); GIRL WHO HAD EVERYTHING, THE(1953); RACING BLOOD(1954); CAT ON A HOT TIN ROOF(1958); NORTH BY NORTHWEST(1959); LIVING BETWEEN TWO WORLDS(1963), d; PATSY, THE(1964); BUCK AND THE PREACHER(1972)
Brad Johnson
BEDTIME FOR BONZO(1951); GREATEST SHOW ON EARTH, THE(1952); OUTLAW WOMEN(1952); LADY WANTS MINK, THE(1953); MARKSMAN, THE(1953); MAGNIFICENT OBSESSION(1954)
Bradley Johnson
MISS GRANT TAKES RICHMOND(1949)
Brett Johnson
UNCOMMON VALOR(1983)
Brian Johnson
ASSASSIN(1973, Brit.), ph; GLITTERBALL, THE(1977, Brit), spec eff; REVENGE OF THE PINK PANTHER(1978), spec eff; EMPIRE STRIKES BACK, THE(1980), spec eff; DRAGONSLAYER(1981), spec off
1984
NEVERENDING STORY, THE(1984, Ger.), spec eff

Bruce Johnson
WARM IN THE BUD(1970)
Bryan Johnson
SMASH PALACE(1982, New Zealand)
Bubber Johnson
RED BALL EXPRESS(1952)
Cammilla Johnson
Silents
SPARROWS(1926)
Candy Johnson
BEACH PARTY(1963); BIKINI BEACH(1964); MUSCLE BEACH PARTY(1964); PAJAMA PARTY(1964)
Carlene King Johnson
WRITTEN ON THE WIND(1956)
Carlton Johnson
WIZ, THE(1978); SWEET CHARITY(1969); DOCTOR DETROIT(1983), a, ch
Carmen Johnson
HENRY ALDRICH FOR PRESIDENT(1941)
Carmencita Johnson
WIND, THE(1928); WONDER OF WOMEN(1929); FORBIDDEN(1932); WILD GIRL(1932); KID MILLIONS(1934); MISS FANE'S BABY IS STOLEN(1934); MRS. WIGGS OF THE CABBAGE PATCH(1934); THESE THREE(1936); QUALITY STREET(1937); TRUE CONFESSION(1937); BELOVED BRAT(1938); KEEP SMILING(1938); YOUNG AMERICA(1942); HOLLOW TRIUMPH(1948); PLACE IN THE SUN, A(1951)
Silents
WAY OF ALL FLESH, THE(1927)
Casey Johnson
FIVE CAME BACK(1939); BOOM TOWN(1940); LITTLE MEN(1940); ONE CROWDED NIGHT(1940); ONE FOOT IN HEAVEN(1941); HURRICANE SMITH(1942); THIS LAND IS MINE(1943); PEOPLE ARE FUNNY(1945)
Celene Johnson
Misc. Silents
DIVINE SACRIFICE, THE(1918)
Celia Johnson
IN WHICH WE SERVE(1942, Brit.); THIS HAPPY BREED(1944, Brit.); BRIEF ENCOUNTER(1945, Brit.); RANDOLPH FAMILY, THE(1945, Brit.); ASTONISHED HEART, THE(1950, Brit.); CAPTAIN'S PARADISE, THE(1953, Brit.); I BELIEVE IN YOU(1953, Brit.); HOLLY AND THE IVY, THE(1954, Brit.); KID FOR TWO FARTHINGS, A(1956, Brit.); GOOD COMPANIONS, THE(1957, Brit.); PRIME OF MISS JEAN BRODIE, THE(1969, Brit.)
Charles Johnson
THUNDER AFLOAT(1939); HAMMER(1972), w; BEYOND ATLANTIS(1973, Phil.), w; SLAUGHTER'S BIG RIP-OFF(1973), w; THAT MAN BOLT(1973), w; MONKEY HUSTLE, THE(1976), w
Chic Johnson
GOLD DUST GERTIE(1931); ALL OVER TOWN(1937); COUNTRY GENTLEMEN(1937); HELLZAPOPPIN'(1941); CRAZY HOUSE(1943); GHOST CATCHERS(1944); SEE MY LAWYER(1945)
Chick Johnson
OH! SAILOR, BEHAVE!(1930)
Chip Johnson
BATTLESTAR GALACTICA(1979)
Chubby Johnson
ROCKY MOUNTAIN(1950); FORT DODGE STAMPEDE(1951); FORT WORTH(1951); NIGHT RIDERS OF MONTANA(1951); RAGING TIDE, THE(1951); SCARF, THE(1951); WELLS FARGO GUNMASTER(1951); BEND OF THE RIVER(1952); HERE COME THE NELSONS(1952); LAST OF THE COMANCHES(1952); TREASURE OF LOST CANYON, THE(1952); BACK TO GOD'S COUNTRY(1953); CALAMITY JANE(1953); GUNSMOKE(1953); LAW AND ORDER(1953); CATTLE QUEEN OF MONTANA(1954); HUMAN JUNGLE, THE(1954); OVERLAND PACIFIC(1954); FAR COUNTRY, THE(1955); HEADLINE HUNTERS(1955); RAGE AT DAWN(1955); TENNESSEE'S PARTNER(1955); FASTEST GUN ALIVE(1956); FIRST TEXAN, THE(1956); RAWHIDE YEARS, THE(1956); TRIBUTE TO A BADMAN(1956); YOUNG GUNS, THE(1956); DRANGO(1957); GUNFIRE AT INDIAN GAP(1957); RIVER'S EDGE, THE(1957); TRUE STORY OF JESSE JAMES, THE(1957); FIREBRAND, THE(1962); TWILIGHT OF HONOR(1963); SEVEN FACES OF DR. LAO(1964); CYBORG 2087(1966); SAM WHISKEY(1969)
Clark Johnson
CAT ATE THE PARAKEET, THE(1972), p
Claude Johnson
HOW THE WEST WAS WON(1962); PAPA'S DELICATE CONDITION(1963); MOONSHINE WAR, THE(1970); NAPOLEON AND SAMANTHA(1972)
Clint Johnson
BLACK MIDNIGHT(1949), w; DAVID HARDING, COUNTERSPY(1950), w; YELLOW FIN(1951), w
Colin Keith Johnson
ROGUES OF SHERWOOD FOREST(1950)
Constance Johnson
Silents
LITTLE PAL(1915); SNOBS(1915)
Misc. Silents
SQUARE DEAL, A(1918)
Coslough Johnson
BUNNY O'HARE(1971), w
Criss Johnson
STONY ISLAND(1978)
Cullen Johnson
TO THE LAST MAN(1933); HOUSE OF ROTHSCHILD, THE(1934); MISS FANE'S BABY IS STOLEN(1934); BLOOD AND SAND(1941); WOLFEN(1981)
Cynthia Johnson
PICKUP ON 101(1972)
D. Johnson
MR. AND MRS. SMITH(1941)
D.G. Johnson
1984
CHILDREN OF THE CORN(1984)

Dale Johnson
DID YOU HEAR THE ONE ABOUT THE TRAVELING SALESLADY?(1968), ed
Dani Johnson
VORTEX(1982)
Dany Johnson
TRAP DOOR, THE(1980)
Dariel Johnson
MOONLIGHT IN VERMONT(1943)
Darlene Johnson
SHOCK TREATMENT(1981)
Dave Johnson
SOMEBODY KILLED HER HUSBAND(1978)
Dawn Johnson
LUGGAGE OF THE GODS(1983), cos
Deeann Johnson
RUN FOR THE HILLS(1953)
Denis Johnson
COMEBACK, THE(1982, Brit.), prod d
Dennis Johnson
SHAME, SHAME, EVERYBODY KNOWS HER NAME(1969); STUNTS(1977), w
Misc. Talkies
BROTHERHOOD OF DEATH(1976)
Diane Johnson
MAGIC CHRISTMAS TREE(1964), p; HOT STUFF(1979); SHINING, THE(1980), w
Dick Johnson
KING RAT(1965); TRUE GRIT(1969), spec eff
Silents
ABRAHAM LINCOLN(1924)
Dick Winslow Johnson
LOVE, LIVE AND LAUGH(1929)
Dolores Johnson
GODLESS GIRL, THE(1929); THRU DIFFERENT EYES(1929)
Silents
RED WINE(1928); STRONG BOY(1929)
Misc. Silents
WHAT PRICE BEAUTY(1928)
Don Johnson
GOOD MORNING... AND GOODBYE(1967); MAGIC GARDEN OF STANLEY SWEE-THART, THE(1970); ZACHARIAH(1971); HARRAD EXPERIMENT, THE(1973); BOY AND HIS DOG, A(1975); RETURN TO MACON COUNTY(1975); MELANIE(1982, Can.); SOGGY BOTTOM U.S.A.(1982)
Doretta Johnson
DOUBLE LIFE, A(1947); LETTER FROM AN UNKNOWN WOMAN(1948); SHAKE-DOWN(1950); MAGIC CARPET, THE(1951)
Dorothy Johnson
VIVACIOUS LADY(1938); LIFE BEGINS AT 17(1958); LITTLEST HOBO, THE(1958); FLYING FONTAINES, THE(1959)
Dorothy M. Johnson
HANGING TREE, THE(1959), w; MAN WHO SHOT LIBERTY VALANCE, THE(1962), w; MAN CALLED HORSE, A(1970), w; RETURN OF A MAN CALLED HORSE, THE(1976), w; TRIUMPHS OF A MAN CALLED HORSE(1983, US/Mex.), w
Dots Johnson
NO WAY OUT(1950)
Dots M. Johnson
PAISAN(1948, Ital.)
Dotts Johnson
JOE LOUIS STORY, THE(1953); GRISSOM GANG, THE(1971)
Misc. Talkies
TALL, TAN AND TERRIFIC(1946)
Doug Johnson
LOST MAN, THE(1969); BUCK AND THE PREACHER(1972); SPOOK WHO SAT BY THE DOOR, THE(1973); LET'S DO IT AGAIN(1975); HEARTLAND(1980); MAKING LOVE(1982)
Douglas Johnson
FIVE ON THE BLACK HAND SIDE(1973)
Douglas G. Johnson
TAKE DOWN(1979), art d; HARRY'S WAR(1981), prod d
Duane F. Johnson
WHOSE LIFE IS IT ANYWAY?(1981)
Duke Johnson
SHINE ON, HARVEST MOON(1944); SUDAN(1945); YOUTH AFLAME(1945); SONG OF SCHEHERAZADE(1947); VARIETY GIRL(1947); MAN WITH A CLOAK, THE(1951); TEXAS CARNIVAL(1951); SALOME(1953); TOBY TYLER(1960)
Dyke Johnson
RIDE LONESOME(1959); COMANCHE STATION(1960); RISE AND FALL OF LEGS DIAMOND, THE(1960)
E. Lamont Johnson
SUNNYSIDE(1979); FOXES(1980); DEATH WISH II(1982)
Earl Johnson
TWO IN REVOLT(1936), w; ROOKIE COP, THE(1939), w; ENCHANTED VALLEY, THE(1948), animalt
Earl W. Johnson
I'LL BE SEEING YOU(1944)
Ed Johnson
BEYOND MOMBASA(1957)
Eddie Johnson
SWISS MISS(1938); STAR SPANGLED RHYTHM(1942); STRICTLY IN THE GROOVE(1942); TRAITOR WITHIN, THE(1942); MY FAVORITE BRUNETTE(1947); SUDDENLY IT'S SPRING(1947); ISN'T IT ROMANTIC?(1948)
Edith Johnson
Silents
STEELHEART(1921); WHERE MEN ARE MEN(1921); SILENT VOW, THE(1922); PLAYING IT WILD(1923)
Misc. Silents
CIRCULAR STAIRCASE, THE(1915); SWEET ALYSSUM(1915); BEHIND THE LINES(1916); CYCLE OF FATE, THE(1916); FIGHTING GRIN, THE(1918); SCARLET CAR, THE(1918); SHUTTLE, THE(1918); NO DEFENSE(1921); FIGHTING GUIDE, THE(1922); WHEN DANGER SMILES(1922); SMASHING BARRIERS(1923)

Edna Johnson
LIVING GHOST, THE(1942)
Edward Johnson
MEN AGAINST THE SUN(1953, Brit.); WEST OF ZANZIBAR(1954, Brit.); MATTER OF INNOCENCE, A(1968, Brit.); TARZAN AND THE JUNGLE BOY(1968, US/Switz.)
Edwin Johnson
GEORGE WHITE'S SCANDALS(1945)
Elinor Johnson
DANTE'S INFERNO(1935)
Ellen Johnson
SECRETS(1933); TOO MANY GIRLS(1940); LET'S FACE IT(1943)
Emilie Johnson
THIRD ALARM, THE(1930), w
Silents
SEA LION, THE(1921), w; THIRD ALARM, THE(1922), w; MAILMAN, THE(1923), w; LAST EDITION, THE(1925), w; NON-STOP FLIGHT, THE(1926), w; LONE EAGLE, THE(1927), w; SHIELD OF HONOR, THE(1927), w
Emille Johnson
Silents
BLIND HEARTS(1921), w
Emory Johnson
THIRD ALARM, THE(1930), d; PHANTOM EXPRESS, THE(1932), d, w; I WANTED WINGS(1941)
Silents
KENTUCKY CINDERELLA, A(1917); NEW LOVE FOR OLD(1918); ALIAS MIKE MORAN(1919); POLLY OF THE STORM COUNTRY(1920); PRISONERS OF LO-VE(1921); SEA LION, THE(1921); ALWAYS THE WOMAN(1922); THIRD ALARM, THE(1922), p&d; MAILMAN, THE(1923), d; LAST EDITION, THE(1925), p&d; NON-STOP FLIGHT, THE(1926), d; LONE EAGLE, THE(1927), d; SHIELD OF HONOR, THE(1927), d
Misc. Silents
BARRIERS OF SOCIETY(1916); BLACK FRIDAY(1916); DEVIL'S BOND WOMAN, THE(1916); DR. NEIGHBOR(1916); MIRACLE OF LOVE, A(1916); MORALS OF HILDA, THE(1916); TWO MEN OF SANDY BAR(1916); UNATTAINABLE, THE(1916); WAY OF THE WORLD, THE(1916); YOKE OF GOLD, A(1916); CIRCUS OF LIFE, THE(1917); GIFT GIRL, THE(1917); MY LITTLE BOY(1917); BEAUTY IN CHAINS(1918); GREEN EYES(1918); JOHANNA ENLISTS(1918); LADY'S NAME, A(1918); MOTHER'S SECRET, A(1918); CHARGE IT TO ME(1919); HELLION, THE(1919); PUT UP YOUR HANDS!(1919); TIGER LILY, THE(1919); TRIXIE FROM BROADWAY(1919); VICKY VAN(1919); HUSBAND HUNTER, THE(1920); WALK-OFFS, THE(1920); SHE COULDN'T HELP IT(1921); DON'T DOUBT YOUR WIFE(1922); IN THE NAME OF THE LAW(1922), d; WESTBOUND LIMITED, THE(1923), d; LIFE'S GREATEST GAME(1924), d; SPIRIT OF THE U.S.A., THE(1924), d; FOURTH COMMANDMENT, THE(1927), d
Ercelle Johnson
DOCTOR DETROIT(1983); GOING BERSERK(1983)
Eric Johnson
DRIVE, HE SAID(1971); MONTENEGRO(1981, Brit./Swed.), set d
Ernest W. Johnson
Silents
STREET OF SIN, THE(1928)
Erskine Johnson
THAT'S RIGHT–YOU'RE WRONG(1939); NIGHT FOR CRIME, A(1942); MAN OF COURAGE(1943); TROCADERO(1944); TEACHER'S PET(1958); UNDER THE YUM-YUM TREE(1963)
Eyvind Johnson
HERE'S YOUR LIFE(1968, Swed.), w
Femi Johnson
KONGI'S HARVEST(1971, U.S./Nigeria)
Florence Johnson
I ACCUSE MY PARENTS(1945)
Frank Johnson
TO HAVE AND HAVE NOT(1944); DON JUAN QUILLIGAN(1945); TWO SMART PEOPLE(1946); GOLDEN EARRINGS(1947); HOLIDAY AFFAIR(1949); RAW FOR-CE(1982), p, ph
Fred Johnson
NATIVE LAND(1942); KNICKERBOCKER HOLIDAY(1944); NORA PREN-TISS(1947); MARK OF CAIN, THE(1948, Brit.); ADAM AND EVELYNE(1950, Brit.); DANCE HALL(1950, Brit.); CHRISTMAS CAROL, A(1951, Brit.); FLESH AND BLOOD(1951, Brit.); TREASURE HUNT(1952, Brit.); YOU CAN'T BEAT THE IRISH(1952, Brit.); LONG MEMORY, THE(1953, Brit.); MARTIN LUTHER(1953); BLACK GLOVE(1954, Brit.); SAINT'S GIRL FRIDAY, THE(1954, Brit.); TONIGHT'S THE NIGHT(1954, Brit.); LAND OF FURY(1955 Brit.); NAKED HEART, THE(1955, Brit.); THEY CAN'T HANG ME(1955, Brit.); LUST FOR LIFE(1956); MARCH HARE, THE(1956, Brit.); BREAK IN THE CIRCLE, THE(1957, Brit.); CURSE OF FRANKEN-STEIN, THE(1957, Brit.); MIRACLE IN SOHO(1957, Brit.); WEAPON, THE(1957, Brit.); SEA FURY(1959, Brit.); BRIDES OF DRACULA, THE(1960, Brit.); HORROR HO-TEL(1960, Brit.); DR. BLOOD'S COFFIN(1961); LOSS OF INNOCENCE(1961, Brit.); SCREAM OF FEAR(1961, Brit.); LIFE IS A CIRCUS(1962, Brit.); YOUNG CAS-SIDY(1965, U.S./Brit.); EDEN CRIED(1967), d&w; WHERE'S JACK?(1969, Brit.); VON RICHTHOFEN AND BROWN(1970)
Misc. Silents
DICK CARSON WINS THROUGH(1917, Brit.)
Frederick Johnson
HI-DE-HO(1947); NO RESTING PLACE(1952, Brit.)
Gary Johnson
PUNISHMENT PARK(1971)
Gene Johnson
JAWS II(1978), art d
Georgann Johnson
SHORT CUT TO HELL(1957); MIDNIGHT COWBOY(1969); FROM THE MIXED-UP FILES OF MRS. BASIL E. FRANKWEILER(1973); FRONT, THE(1976); LOO-KER(1981); SHOOT THE MOON(1982)
George Clayton Johnson
OCEAN BREAKERS(1949, Swed.), w; OCEAN'S ELEVEN(1960), w; INTRUDER, THE(1962); LOGAN'S RUN(1976), w; TWILIGHT ZONE–THE MOVIE(1983), w
George Johnson
SALLY FIELDGOOD & CO.(1975, Can.), ed; KEEPER, THE(1976, Can.), ed; 9/30/55(1977)

1984
WOMAN IN RED, THE(1984)
George M. Johnson
SHADOW RANCH(1930), w
Silents
TERROR OF BAR X, THE(1927), w
Geraldine Johnson
Silents
IS YOUR DAUGHTER SAFE?(1927)
Gerry Johnson
MY DOG, BUDDY(1960); MAN CALLED FLINTSTONE, THE(1966)
Gladys Johnson
Silents
GOLD RUSH, THE(1925)
Gladys E. Johnson
Silents
LIGHTS OF THE DESERT(1922), w; THUMBS DOWN(1927), w
Glen Johnson
CANNONBALL(1976, U.S./Hong Kong)
Glenn Johnson
SHAFT(1971)
Gloria Johnson
NOBODY IN TOYLAND(1958, Brit.)
Grace Johnson
WONDER MAN(1945)
Misc. Silents
WANTED - A HOME(1916); LAST TIDE, THE(1931, Brit.)
Gray Johnson
HIRED HAND, THE(1971); LAST MOVIE, THE(1971); WEREWOLVES ON WHEELS(1971); ULTIMATE WARRIOR, THE(1975)
Gus Johnson
FRIENDS OF EDDIE COYLE, THE(1973)
Gustave Johnson
GANG THAT COULDN'T SHOOT STRAIGHT, THE(1971); DARK END OF THE STREET, THE(1981)
Gwen Johnson
SEA GYPSIES, THE(1978), animal t
Hackberry Johnson
HONEYSUCKLE ROSE(1980)
Hall Johnson
GREEN PASTURES(1936), m
Hap Johnson
JAZZ BABIES(1932)
Harold Johnson
SPOOK WHO SAT BY THE DOOR, THE(1973)
Harold W. Johnson
PEACE FOR A GUNFIGHTER(1967), p
Harry Johnson
RICHEST MAN IN TOWN(1941); KNICKERBOCKER HOLIDAY(1944); TOBY TYLER(1960)
Harry C. Johnson
ARTISTS AND MODELS(1937); ROAD TO ZANZIBAR(1941)
Harry C. Johnson, Jr.
ROAD TO ZANZIBAR(1941)
Harry Charles Johnson
SHINE ON, HARVEST MOON(1944)
Harry "Duke" Johnson
CAROUSEL(1956); WOMAN OBSESSED(1959)
Harvey Johnson
JUST AROUND THE CORNER(1938), ed; LADY'S FROM KENTUCKY, THE(1939), ed
Helen Johnson
CHILDREN OF PLEASURE(1930); DIVORCEE, THE(1930); SIN TAKES A HOLIDAY(1930); SOLDIERS AND WOMEN(1930); IT PAYS TO ADVERTISE(1931); WOMEN LOVE ONCE(1931)
Helen Johnson [Judith Wood]
VICE SQUAD, THE(1931)
Henry Johnson
ARIZONA TO BROADWAY(1933), w; MAD GAME, THE(1933), w; EVER SINCE EVE(1934), w; HANDY ANDY(1934), w; LOVE TIME(1934), w; OLSEN'S BIG MOMENT(1934), w; SHE LEARNED ABOUT SAILORS(1934), w; WILD GOLD(1934), w; 365 NIGHTS IN HOLLYWOOD(1934), w; FIGHTING YOUTH(1935), w; IN OLD KENTUCKY(1935), w; VIRGINIA JUDGE, THE(1935), w; $10 RAISE(1935), w; F MAN(1936), w; GREAT GUY(1936), w; ARTISTS AND MODELS(1937)
Silents
CRAZY TO MARRY(1921); TOO MUCH SPEED(1921)
Henry M. Johnson
DEVIL WITH WOMEN, A(1930), w
Hillary Johnson
1984
SWORD OF THE VALIANT(1984, Brit.)
Howard E. Johnson
INCIDENT AT PHANTOM HILL(1966), art d; TAMMY AND THE MILLIONAIRE(1967), art d; VALLEY OF MYSTERY(1967), art d; JIGSAW(1968), art d; BACKTRACK(1969), art d; DEATH OF A GUNFIGHTER(1969), art d
Howard Johnson
PRODIGAL, THE(1931), m; VOICE IN THE WIND(1944); BOY, A GIRL, AND A DOG, A(1946)
Isabelle Johnson
Silents
HER ELEPHANT MAN(1920), w
J. J. Johnson
MAN AND BOY(1972), m; TOP OF THE HEAP(1972), m; CLEOPATRA JONES(1973), m
J. Lewis Johnson
MISS SUSIE SLAGLE'S(1945); SARATOGA TRUNK(1945)
J. Louis Johnson
WITHOUT RESERVATIONS(1946); MAGNIFICENT AMBERSONS, THE(1942); GOVERNMENT GIRL(1943); MY PAL, WOLF(1944); UNKNOWN, THE(1946); HOMECOMING(1948); THEY LIVE BY NIGHT(1949); NO WAY OUT(1950); SURRENDER(1950);

STRANGERS ON A TRAIN(1951)
J. MacMillan Johnson
JUNGLE BOOK(1942), set d; LI'L ABNER(1959), art d; FACTS OF LIFE, THE(1960), art d
J. McMillan Johnson
DUEL IN THE SUN(1946), prod d; PARADINE CASE, THE(1947), prod d; PORTRAIT OF JENNIE(1949), prod d, spec eff; HIS KIND OF WOMAN(1951), prod d; ONE-EYED JACKS(1961), art d; JUMBO(1962), spec eff; MUTINY ON THE BOUNTY(1962), art d; PRIZE, THE(1963), spec eff; TICKLISH AFFAIR, A(1963), spec eff; OUTRAGE, THE(1964), spec eff; SIGNPOST TO MURDER(1964), spec eff; UNSINKABLE MOLLY BROWN, THE(1964), spec eff; GREATEST STORY EVER TOLD, THE(1965), spec eff; JOY IN THE MORNING(1965), spec eff; WHEN THE BOYS MEET THE GIRLS(1965), spec eff; GLASS BOTTOM BOAT, THE(1966), spec eff; HOLD ON(1966), spec eff; SEVEN WOMEN(1966), spec eff; SPINOUT(1966), spec eff; DOUBLE TROUBLE(1967), spec eff; HOT RODS TO HELL(1967), spec eff; POINT BLANK(1967), spec eff; GUNS FOR SAN SEBASTIAN(1968, U.S./Fr./Mex./Ital.), spec eff; POWER, THE(1968), spec eff; WHERE WERE YOU WHEN THE LIGHTS WENT OUT?(1968), spec eff; EXTRAORDINARY SEAMAN, THE(1969), spec eff; DIRTY DINGUS MAGEE(1970), art d
J.D. Johnson
Misc. Talkies
LONE STAR COUNTRY(1983)
J.J. Johnson
ACROSS 110TH STREET(1972), m; WILLIE DYNAMITE(1973), m
J.S. Johnson
GAILY, GAILY(1969); MC CABE AND MRS. MILLER(1971); FUZZ(1972); LEPKE(1975, U.S./Israel); WILD PARTY, THE(1975)
J.W. Johnson
LADY LUCK(1946)
Silents
SEALED VALLEY, THE(1915)
Misc. Silents
FIFTY-FIFTY(1916)
Jack Johnson
MADISON SQUARE GARDEN(1932); PASSION HOLIDAY(1963), spec eff; HONEYMOON OF HORROR(1964), spec eff; GENTLE GIANT(1967), spec eff
Misc. Silents
AS THE WORLD ROLLS ON(1921); BLACK THUNDERBOLT, THE(1922); FOR HIS MOTHER'S SAKE(1922)
Jack W. Johnson
Silents
OUT OF THE SHADOW(1919)
Misc. Silents
COST OF HATRED, THE(1917); AT THE MERCY OF MEN(1918)
James Johnson
RING OF FIRE(1961); ON THE YARD(1978); PURPLE HAZE(1982), art d
James Burr Johnson
FOOLS(1970)
Janet Johnson
EVERYBODY DANCE(1936, Brit.); BLONDES FOR DANGER(1938, Brit.); MRS. PYM OF SCOTLAND YARD(1939, Brit.); PROUD VALLEY, THE(1941, Brit.)
Janine Johnson
MR. SYCAMORE(1975)
Jason Johnson
ABDUCTORS, THE(1957); INVASION OF THE SAUCER MEN(1957); PERSUADER, THE(1957); I WANT TO LIVE!(1958); ARSON FOR HIRE(1959); LEGEND OF TOM DOOLEY, THE(1959); CAPE CANAVERAL MONSTERS(1960); IF HE HOLLERS, LET HIM GO(1968)
Jed Johnson
L'AMOUR(1973), ph, ed
Jelly Bean Johnson
1984
PURPLE RAIN(1984)
Jerry Johnson
IMAGES(1972, Ireland), spec eff; KILL SQUAD(1982)
Jesse Johnson
1984
PURPLE RAIN(1984)
Jessie Johnson
BETRAYAL, THE(1948)
Jill Johnson
ACCIDENT(1967, Brit.); MOONLIGHTING(1982, Brit.)
Jilly Johnson
HISTORY OF THE WORLD, PART 1(1981)
Jim Johnson
THUNDER IN DIXIE(1965), art d
Jimmie Johnson
DIAMOND STUD(1970)
Joe Johnson
SLUMBER PARTY MASSACRE, THE(1982)
Misc. Talkies
GRAD NIGHT(1980)
Joey Johnson
PATSY, THE(1964)
John L. Johnson
RADIO PATROL(1932)
John Lester Johnson
HELL'S HIGHWAY(1932); MIGHTY BARNUM, THE(1934); STEAMBOAT ROUND THE BEND(1935); KLONDIKE ANNIE(1936); GLORY TRAIL, THE(1937); THIS IS MY AFFAIR(1937); TARZAN'S REVENGE(1938); SCREAM IN THE NIGHT(1943)
Misc. Silents
SQUARE JOE(1921)
John Louis Johnson
DUCHESS OF IDAHO, THE(1950)
Johnnie Johnson
LADY IN THE DARK(1944); SPOOK WHO SAT BY THE DOOR, THE(1973)
Johnny Johnson
KNICKERBOCKER HOLIDAY(1944)

Joseph H. Johnson
CAUGHT SHORT(1930), w
Joseph Johnson
TENTACLES(1977, Ital.)
Harold C. Johnson
WEDDING, A(1978)
Joseph MacMillan Johnson
ELEPHANT WALK(1954), art d; DESPERATE HOURS, THE(1955), art d; TO CATCH A THIEF(1955), art d; HEAR ME GOOD(1957), art d; OMAR KHAYYAM(1957), art d; TIN STAR, THE(1957), art d; DESIRE UNDER THE ELMS(1958), art d; KING CREOLE(1958), art d; MARACAIBO(1958), art d
Joseph McMillan Johnson
ROAD TO BALI(1952), art d; TURNING POINT, THE(1952), art d; REAR WINDOW(1954), art d
Joshua Johnson
DEATH MACHINES(1976)
Josie Johnson
STIGMA(1972); NIGHT THEY ROBBED BIG BERTHA'S, THE zero(1975)
Joyce Johnson
FRENCH LINE, THE(1954); SON OF SINBAD(1955)
Jugo Johnson
Silents
SCARLET ROAD, THE(1916), ph
Julanne Johnson
Silents
PRUDES FALL, THE(1924, Brit.)
Julian Johnson
ABIE'S IRISH ROSE(1928), w; PATRIOT, THE(1928), w; WHEEL OF LIFE, THE(1929), w; RANGO(1931), ed; LUCKY CISCO KID(1940), w
Silents
SORROWS OF SATAN(1926), t, ed; SO'S YOUR OLD MAN(1926), t, ed; ROLLED STOCKINGS(1927), t, ed; WAY OF ALL FLESH, THE(1927), t; WINGS(1927), t; WOMAN ON TRIAL, THE(1927), t; BEAU SABREUR(1928), t HALF A BRIDE(1928), t; SECRET HOUR, THE(1928), t; STREET OF SIN, THE(1928), t; THREE SINNERS(1928), t; FOUR FEATHERS(1929), t
Julianne Johnson
Misc. Silents
CITY OF TEMPTATION(1929, Brit.)
Julie Johnson
MIDNIGHT MAN, THE(1974)
Julie Ann Johnson
KARATE KILLERS, THE(1967); DIRTY HARRY(1971); NICKELODEON(1976)
June Johnson
ROSE BOWL(1936); ANYTHING FOR A THRILL(1937); DOUBLE DANGER(1938); VIVACIOUS LADY(1938); LONE STAR RAIDERS(1940); GANGS OF SONORA(1941); PALS OF THE PECOS(1941)
Junior Johnson
CIMARRON(1931); THREE ON A MATCH(1932)
Karen Johnson
YOUNG NURSES, THE(1973), ed; FLASH GORDON(1980)
Karen Mae Johnson
BUNNY O'HARE(1971)
Karl Johnson
UP IN SMOKE(1978); MADAME BOVARY(1949); JUBILEE(1978, Brit.); VALLEY GIRL(1983)
1984
NIGHT OF THE COMET(1984)
Misc. Talkies
TEMPEST, THE(1980, Brit.)
Kathy Johnson
SIDESHOW(1950); OLD WEST, THE(1952); GIRL RUSH, THE(1955); STUDS LONIGAN(1960)
Kathy Jeanne Johnson
PURSUED(1947)
Katie Johnson
AFTER OFFICE HOURS(1932, Brit.); GLIMPSE OF PARADISE, A(1934, Brit.); LABURNUM GROVE(1936, Brit.); LAST ADVENTURERS, THE(1937, Brit); DARK STAIRWAY, THE(1938, Brit.); HIDEOUT IN THE ALPS(1938, Brit.); MARIGOLD(1938, Brit.); TWO FOR DANGER(1940, Brit.); BLACK SHEEP OF WHITEHALL, THE(1941 Brit.); GIRL IN DISTRESS(1941, Brit.); VOICE IN THE NIGHT, A(1941, Brit.); TALK ABOUT JACQUELINE(1942, Brit.); HE SNOOPS TO CONQUER(1944, Brit.); ADVENTURESS, THE(1946, Brit.); MEET ME AT DAWN(1947, Brit.); TAWNY PIPIT(1947, Brit.); YEARS BETWEEN, THE(1947, Brit.); DEATH OF AN ANGEL(1952, Brit.); SCOTLAND YARD INSPECTOR(1952, Brit.); I BELIEVE IN YOU(1953, Brit.); THREE STEPS IN THE DARK(1953, Brit.); DELAVINE AFFAIR, THE(1954, Brit.); RAINBOW JACKET, THE(1954, Brit.); LADYKILLERS, THE(1956, Brit.); HOW TO MURDER A RICH UNCLE(1957, Brit.); OUT OF THE CLOUDS(1957, Brit.); MALIBU HIGH(1979)
Kay Johnson
BILLY THE KID(1930); DYNAMITE(1930); MADAME SATAN(1930); PASSION FLOWER(1930); SHIP FROM SHANGHAI, THE(1930); SPOILERS, THE(1930); THIS MAD WORLD(1930); SINGLE SIN(1931); AMERICAN MADNESS(1932); THIRTEEN WOMEN(1932); EIGHT GIRLS IN A BOAT(1934); OF HUMAN BONDAGE(1934); THEIR BIG MOMENT(1934); THIS MAN IS MINE(1934); JALNA(1935); VILLAGE TALE(1935); WHITE BANNERS(1938); REAL GLORY, THE(1939); SON OF FURY(1942); ADVENTURES OF MARK TWAIN, THE(1944); JIVARO(1954)
Misc. Talkies
SPY, THE(1931)
Kay Cousins Johnson
JENNIFER(1978), w
Kelly Johnson
WHAT DID YOU DO IN THE WAR, DADDY?(1966); GOODBYE PORK PIE(1981, New Zealand)
1984
UTU(1984, New Zealand)
Ken Johnson
SET, THE(1970, Aus.); SIXTH AND MAIN(1977), ed; END, THE(1978)
1984
SLAPSTICK OF ANOTHER KIND(1984)

King Johnson
WACO(1966)
Silents
BASHFUL BUCCANEER(1925), w
Kirk Johnson
NIGHT THE LIGHTS WENT OUT IN GEORGIA, THE(1981)
Kitty Johnson
Silents
NEIGHBORS(1918)
Kurt Johnson
JANE AUSTEN IN MANHATTAN(1980); FAN, THE(1981); GHOST STORY(1981)
1984
SOLE SURVIVOR(1984)
Kyle Johnson
LIVING BETWEEN TWO WORLDS(1963); LEARNING TREE, THE(1969); PRETTY MAIDS ALL IN A ROW(1971)
Misc. Talkies
BOOTS TURNER(1973); BROTHER ON THE RUN(1973); WOMAN IN THE RAIN(1976)
L. A. Johnson
HUMAN HIGHWAY(1982), p
Lamont Johnson
SALLY AND SAINT ANNE(1952); GLORY BRIGADE, THE(1953); HUMAN JUNGLE, THE(1954); PLEASE MURDER ME(1956); BROTHERS RICO, THE(1957); COVENANT WITH DEATH, A(1966), d; KONA COAST(1968), p&d; MC KENZIE BREAK, THE(1970), d; GUNFIGHT, A(1971), d; GROUNDSTAR CONSPIRACY, THE(1972, Can.), d; YOU'LL LIKE MY MOTHER(1972), d; LAST AMERICAN HERO, THE(1973), d; VISIT TO A CHIEF'S SON(1974), d; HOW COME NOBODY'S ON OUR SIDE?(1975), m; LIPSTICK(1976), d; ONE ON ONE(1977), a, d; SOMEBODY KILLED HER HUSBAND(1978), d; CATTLE ANNIE AND LITTLE BRITCHES(1981), d; SPACEHUNTER: ADVENTURES IN THE FORBIDDEN ZONE(1983), d
Laraine Johnson
BORDER G-MAN(1938); ARIZONA LEGION(1939)
Johnson & Diehl
SCANDAL STREET(1938); MEET ME AT THE FAIR(1952)
Larry Johnson
CHRISTOPHER BEAN(1933), w; GIRL IN TROUBLE(1963); DANCE OF THE DWARFS(1983, U.S., Phil.), w
Larry D. Johnson
SUGAR HILL(1974)
Larry H. Johnson
LORD LOVE A DUCK(1966), w
Laura Johnson
OPENING NIGHT(1977)
Misc. Talkies
BEYOND REASON(1977)
Laurence Johnson
POLLY OF THE CIRCUS(1932), w
Laurence E. Johnson
BACHELOR FATHER(1931), w; IT'S A WISE CHILD(1931), w; PASSIONATE PLUMBER(1932), w; SPEAK EASILY(1932), w
Laurence G. Johnson
PASSION FLOWER(1930), w
Laurie Johnson
GIRLS AT SEA(1958, Brit.), m; MOONRAKER, THE(1958, Brit.), m; TIGER BAY(1959, Brit.), m; I AIM AT THE STARS(1960), m; SPARE THE ROD(1961, Brit.), m; WHAT A WHOPPER(1961, Brit.), m; BITTER HARVEST(1963, Brit.), m; OPERATION BULLSHINE(1963, Brit.), m; SIEGE OF THE SAXONS(1963, Brit.), m; DR. STRANGELOVE: OR HOW I LEARNED TO STOP WORRYING AND LOVE THE BOMB(1964), m; EAST OF SUDAN(1964, Brit.), m; FIRST MEN IN THE MOON(1964, Brit.), m; NO TREE IN THE STREET(1964, Brit.), m; YOU MUST BE JOKING!(1965, Brit.), m; BEAUTY JUNGLE, THE(1966, Brit.), m; HOT MILLIONS(1968, Brit.), m; LOCK UP YOUR DAUGHTERS(1969, Brit.), w; AND SOON THE DARKNESS(1970, Brit.), m; CAPTAIN KRONOS: VAMPIRE HUNTER(1974, Brit.), m; DIAGNOSIS: MURDER(1974, Brit.), m; HEDDA(1975, Brit.), m; MAIDS, THE(1975, Brit.), m; BELSTONE FOX, THE(1976, 1976), m; IT LIVES AGAIN(1978), m; ALL THINGS BRIGHT AND BEAUTIFUL(1979, Brit.), m
Lawrence Johnson
Silents
MAN WORTH WHILE, THE(1921); SALVATION NELL(1921); ANY WIFE(1922)
Misc. Silents
SILVER KING, THE(1919)
Leanne Johnson
ENTERTAINER, THE(1975)
Leonora Johnson
LADY IN THE DARK(1944)
Leroy Johnson
COLT .45(1950); HAWK OF WILD RIVER, THE(1952); SMOKY CANYON(1952); PONY EXPRESS(1953); FAR HORIZONS, THE(1955); TEXAS LADY(1955); MAGIC SWORD, THE(1962); SHENANDOAH(1965); RARE BREED, THE(1966); MONTE WALSH(1970); LIFE AND TIMES OF JUDGE ROY BEAN, THE(1972)
Les Johnson
GIRL HE LEFT BEHIND, THE(1956); TOWARD THE UNKNOWN(1956)
Lex Johnson
SHAME OF THE SABINE WOMEN, THE(1962, Mex.)
Linda Johnson
STRIKE UP THE BAND(1940); SUNDOWN KID, THE(1942); WILD HORSE RUSTLERS(1943); BANDITS OF DARK CANYON(1947); JUNGLE GODDESS(1948); IMPACT(1949); WHERE DANGER LIVES(1950)
Llewellyn Johnson
VANQUISHED, THE(1953)
Lois Johnson
COUNTRY BOY(1966)
Lorimer Johnson
MADAME SATAN(1930); EX-FLAME(1931); SON OF FRANKENSTEIN(1939)
Silents
STRANGER'S BANQUET(1922)
Misc. Silents
BREEZY JIM(1919), d; DEVIL MCCARE(1919), d

Louis Johnson
WIZ, THE(1978), ch
Louise Johnson
WHICH WAY IS UP?(1977)
Luke Johnson
PUNISHMENT PARK(1971); PORTRAIT OF THE ARTIST AS A YOUNG MAN, A(1979, Ireland)
Lydia Johnson
FRENCH CANCAN(1956, Fr.)
Lynn Holly Johnson
ICE CASTLES(1978); FOR YOUR EYES ONLY(1981)
Lynn-Holly Johnson
WATCHER IN THE WOODS, THE(1980, Brit.)
1984
WHERE THE BOYS ARE '84(1984)
Mabel Johnson
Misc. Silents
PLAIN JANE(1916)
Mae E. Johnson
STORMY WEATHER(1943)
Margaret Johnson
LOVERS, HAPPY LOVERS!(1955, Brit.)
Marilyn Johnson
JAM SESSION(1944); ONCE UPON A TIME(1944); SHE'S A SOLDIER TOO(1944); BOSTON BLACKIE'S RENDEZVOUS(1945); LEAVE IT TO BLONDIE(1945); MY NAME IS JULIA ROSS(1945); OVER 21(1945); SHE WOULDN'T SAY YES(1945); TEN CENTS A DANCE(1945); TONIGHT AND EVERY NIGHT(1945); SECRETS OF A SORORITY GIRL(1946); TWO TICKETS TO BROADWAY(1951)
Marion Page Johnson
G.I. HONEYMOON(1945), w
Marj Johnson
MISS JESSICA IS PREGNANT(1970)
Marjorie Johnson
WOMAN IN THE WINDOW, THE(1945), ed
Mark Johnson
THIN RED LINE, THE(1964); ROCKY HORROR PICTURE SHOW, THE(1975, Brit.)
1984
NATURAL, THE(1984), p
Martha Johnson
TURNING POINT, THE(1977)
Martin Johnson
BLACK JACK(1979, Brit.), prod d; GAMEKEEPER, THE(1980, Brit.), art d; PROSTITUTE(1980, Brit.), art d; LOOKS AND SMILES(1982, Brit.), art d; BLOODY KIDS(1983, Brit.), art d
1984
NUMBER ONE(1984, Brit.), prod d; REFLECTIONS(1984, Brit.), art d
Marv Johnson
TEENAGE MILLIONAIRE(1961)
Mary Johnson
Misc. Silents
GUNNAR HEDE'S SAGA(1922, Swed.)
Mary Ann Johnson
BELL JAR, THE(1979)
May Johnson
WITCH WITHOUT A BROOM, A(1967, U.S./Span.)
Melodie Johnson
RIDE TO HANGMAN'S TREE, THE(1967); COOGAN'S BLUFF(1968); GAILY, GAILY(1969); MOONSHINE WAR, THE(1970); RABBIT, RUN(1970)
Merle Johnson
Silents
STRIVING FOR FORTUNE(1926), w
Merrill C. Johnson
NIGHT OF EVIL(1962)
Michael Johnson
MUSIC BOX KID, THE(1960); ANNE OF THE THOUSAND DAYS(1969, Brit.); LUST FOR A VAMPIRE(1971, Brit.); HOMEBODIES(1974); SUDDEN IMPACT(1983)
Michele Johnson
PUNISHMENT PARK(1971)
Michelle Johnson
JOURNEY AMONG WOMEN(1977, Aus.)
1984
BLAME IT ON RIO(1984)
Mike Johnson
BED AND BREAKFAST(1930, Brit.); RAISE THE ROOF(1930); DON'T BE A DUMMY(1932, Brit.); MONEY FOR NOTHING(1932, Brit.); RIVER HOUSE GHOST, THE(1932, Brit.); TONIGHT'S THE NIGHT(1932, Brit.); GOOD COMPANIONS(1933, Brit.); LOST IN THE LEGION(1934, Brit.); LOYALTIES(1934, Brit.); KEEP YOUR SEATS PLEASE(1936, Brit.); QUEEN OF HEARTS(1936, Brit.); FEATHER YOUR NEST(1937, Brit.); SMILING ALONG(1938, Brit.); THERE AIN'T NO JUSTICE(1939, Brit.); QUIET WEDDING(1941, Brit.); PLAYBOY, THE(1942, Brit.); GET CRACKING(1943, Brit.); OLD MOTHER RILEY, DETECTIVE(1943, Brit.); GEORGE IN CIVVY STREET(1946, Brit.); HOTEL RESERVE(1946, Brit.); WATERLOO ROAD(1949, Brit.); SILENT RAGE(1982)
Silents
SMASHING THROUGH(1928, Brit.)
Mildred Johnson
BOILING POINT, THE(1932), ed; MAN'S LAND, A(1932), ed; COWBOY COUNSELOR(1933), ed
Silents
NIGHT FLYER, THE(1928), ed; ON TO RENO(1928), ed; RED MARK, THE(1928), ed
Miss Johnson
Silents
GOOSE GIRL, THE(1915)
Mitchell Johnson
PROJECT X(1949), w
Mitzie Johnson
TERROR IN THE JUNGLE(1968)

Moffat Johnson
MIDNIGHT(1934)
Mollie Johnson
Silents
PEARL OF THE SOUTH SEAS(1927, Brit.)
Molly Johnson
77 PARK LANE(1931, Brit.); CHELSEA LIFE(1933, Brit.); MIXED DOUBLES(1933, Brit.); WE DIVE AT DAWN(1943, Brit.)
Silents
MATING OF MARCUS, THE(1924, Brit.)
Misc. Silents
ROMANCE OF THE MAYFAIR, A(1925, Brit.)
Monica Johnson
AMERICATHON(1979), w; REAL LIFE(1979), w; MODERN ROMANCE(1981), w; JEKYLL AND HYDE...TOGETHER AGAIN(1982), w
Muriel Johnson
CROSS MY HEART(1937, Brit.)
Nancy Johnson
STRANGE INVADERS(1983)
Nancy Lee Johnson
SMOKEY AND THE BANDIT II(1980)
Narelle Johnson
FINAL CUT, THE(1980, Aus.)
Noble Johnson
NOAH'S ARK(1928); BLACK WATERS(1929); MYSTERIOUS DR. FU MANCHU, THE(1929); SAL OF SINGAPORE(1929); KISMET(1930); MAMBA(1930); MOBY DICK(1930); EAST OF BORNEO(1931); SAFE IN HELL(1931); MOST DANGEROUS GAME, THE(1932); MUMMY, THE(1932); MURDERS IN THE RUE MORGUE(1932); MYSTERY RANCH(1932); KING KONG(1933); NAGANA(1933); SON OF KONG(1933); WHITE WOMAN(1933); KID MILLIONS(1934); MURDER IN TRINIDAD(1934); DANTE'S INFERNO(1935); ESCAPE FROM DEVIL'S ISLAND(1935); LIVES OF A BENGAL LANCER(1935); SHE(1935); CONQUEST(1937); LOST HORIZON(1937); PLAINSMAN, THE(1937); WEE WILLIE WINKIE(1937); FOUR MEN AND A PRAYER(1938); DRUMS ALONG THE MOHAWK(1939); FRONTIER PONY EXPRESS(1939); JUAREZ(1939); TROPIC FURY(1939); UNION PACIFIC(1939); GHOST BREAKERS, THE(1940); GREEN HELL(1940); NORTHWEST MOUNTED POLICE(1940); RANGER AND THE LADY, THE(1940); ALOMA OF THE SOUTH SEAS(1941); HURRY, CHARLIE, HURRY(1941); ROAD TO ZANZIBAR(1941); JUNGLE BOOK(1942); MAD DOCTOR OF MARKET STREET, THE(1942); NIGHT IN NEW ORLEANS, A(1942); SHUT MY BIG MOUTH(1942); TEN GENTLEMEN FROM WEST POINT(1942); DESERT SONG, THE(1943); THANK YOUR LUCKY STARS(1943); GAME OF DEATH, A(1945); PLAINSMAN AND THE LADY(1946); DREAM GIRL(1947); HARD BOILED MAHONEY(1947); SLAVE GIRL(1947); UNCONQUERED(1947); GALLANT LEGION, THE(1948); SHE WORE A YELLOW RIBBON(1949); NORTH OF THE GREAT DIVIDE(1950)
Silents
KINKAID, GAMBLER(1916); FIGHTING FOR LOVE(1917); LOVE AFLAME(1917); BRONZE BELL, THE(1921); FOUR HORSEMEN OF THE APOCALYPSE, THE(1921); WALLOP, THE(1921); LOADED DOOR, THE(1922); TEN COMMANDMENTS, THE(1923); MIDNIGHT EXPRESS, THE(1924); NAVIGATOR, THE(1924); THIEF OF BAGDAD, THE(1924); HANDS UP(1926); LAW OF THE SNOW COUNTRY, THE(1926); KING OF KINGS, THE(1927); SOFT CUSHIONS(1927); VANITY(1927); GATEWAY OF THE MOON, THE(1928); MANHATTAN KNIGHTS(1928); FOUR FEATHERS(1929)
Misc. Silents
MR. DOLAN OF NEW YORK(1917); ADORABLE SAVAGE, THE(1920); LEOPARD WOMAN, THE(1920); MAN'S MATE, A(1924); TOPSY AND EVA(1927); YELLOW CONTRABAND(1928)
Noel Johnson
REFORM GIRL(1933); HIGHLY DANGEROUS(1950, Brit.); ISLAND RESCUE(1952, Brit.); CASE OF THE RED MONKEY(1955, Brit.); PARTNER, THE(1966, Brit.); FRIGHTMARE(1974, Brit.); GREAT TRAIN ROBBERY, THE(1979, Brit.); FOR YOUR EYES ONLY(1981)
Nora Johnson
WORLD OF HENRY ORIENT, THE(1964), w
Norman Johnson
MAN'S AFFAIR, A(1949, Brit.), ph
Norris Johnson
Silents
PARIS GREEN(1920); AMATEUR DEVIL, AN(1921); NEW DISCIPLE, THE(1921); SPEED GIRL, THE(1921); SCARLET CAR, THE(1923); LORNA DOONE(1927)
Nunnally Johnson
BEDTIME STORY, A(1933), w; MAMA LOVES PAPA(1933), w; BULLDOG DRUMMOND STRIKES BACK(1934), w; HOUSE OF ROTHSCHILD, THE(1934), w; KID MILLIONS(1934), w; MOULIN ROUGE(1934), w; MAN WHO BROKE THE BANK AT MONTE CARLO, THE(1935), p, w; THANKS A MILLION(1935), w; BANJO ON MY KNEE(1936), p, w; DIMPLES(1936), w; PRISONER OF SHARK ISLAND, THE(1936), w; CAFE METROPOLE(1937), w; LOVE UNDER FIRE(1937), p; NANCY STEELE IS MISSING(1937), p; JESSE JAMES(1939), p, w; ROSE OF WASHINGTON SQUARE(1939), w; WIFE, HUSBAND AND FRIEND(1939), p, w; CHAD HANNA(1940), p, w; GRAPES OF WRATH(1940), w; TOBACCO ROAD(1941), w; LIFE BEGINS AT 8:30(1942), p, w; PIED PIPER, THE(1942), p, w; ROXIE HART(1942), p, w; HOLY MATRIMONY(1943), p, w; MOON IS DOWN, THE(1943), p, w; CASANOVA BROWN(1944), p, w; KEYS OF THE KINGDOM, THE(1944), w; ALONG CAME JONES(1945), w; SOUTHERNER, THE(1945), w; WOMAN IN THE WINDOW, THE(1945), p, w; DARK MIRROR, THE(1946), p, w; SENATOR WAS INDISCREET, THE(1947), p; MR. PEABODY AND THE MERMAID(1948), p; EVERYBODY DOES IT(1949), p, w; GUNFIGHTER, THE(1950), p; MUDLARK, THE(1950, Brit.), p, w; THREE CAME HOME(1950), p, w; DESERT FOX, THE(1951), p&w, w; LONG DARK HALL, THE(1951, Brit.), w; MY COUSIN RACHEL(1952), p, w; O. HENRY'S FULL HOUSE(1952), w; PHONE CALL FROM A STRANGER(1952), p, w; WE'RE NOT MARRIED(1952), p, w; HOW TO MARRY A MILLIONAIRE(1953), p, w; BLACK WIDOW(1954), p&d, w; NIGHT PEOPLE(1954), p,d,&w; HOW TO BE VERY, VERY, POPULAR(1955), p,d&w; MAN IN THE GREY FLANNEL SUIT, THE(1956), d&w; OH, MEN! OH, WOMEN!(1957), p,d&w; THREE FACES OF EVE, THE(1957), p,d&w; TRUE STORY OF JESSE JAMES, THE(1957), w; MAN WHO UNDERSTOOD WOMEN, THE(1959), p,d&w; ANGEL WORE RED, THE(1960), d&w; FLAMING STAR(1960), w; MR. HOBBS TAKES A VACATION(1962), w; TAKE HER, SHE'S MINE(1963), w; WORLD OF HENRY ORIENT, THE(1964), w; DIRTY DOZEN, THE(1967, Brit.), w

Silents
ROUGH HOUSE ROSIE(1927), w
Olive Johnson
Silents
COMMANDING OFFICER, THE(1915)
Oliver Johnson
STOLEN LIFE(1939, Brit.)
Oliver Johnson, Jr.
JUNGLE BOOK, THE(1967), anim d
Orin Johnson
Silents
PENITENTES, THE(1915)
Misc. Silents
SATAN SANDERSON(1915); D'ARTAGNAN(1916); PRICE OF POWER, THE(1916); WHITHER THOU GOEST(1917)
Orrin Johnson
Silents
FIGHTING BOB(1915); LIGHT AT DUSK, THE(1916)
Owen Johnson
HAPPY YEARS, THE(1950), w
Silents
SALAMANDER, THE(1915), w; ENEMY SEX, THE(1924), w; CHILDREN OF DIVORCE(1927), w
P. Johnson
POCKET MONEY(1972)
P.J. Johnson
PAPER MOON(1973)
Page Johnson
FINNEGANS WAKE(1965)
Pat Johnson
GOLDEN NEEDLES(1974); ULTIMATE WARRIOR, THE(1975), a, stunts; FORCE OF ONE, A(1979), w; BIG BRAWL, THE(1980); LITTLE DRAGONS, THE(1980); FORCE: FIVE(1981), stunt
Pat E. Johnson
1984
KARATE KID, THE(1984), a, ch
Patricia Johnson
PINKY(1949)
Patty Johnson
CHRISTMAS STORY, A(1983)
Paul Johnson
DRUMS O' VOODOO(1934)
Paul Rubey Johnson
NO MERCY MAN, THE(1975), p
Pauline Johnson
FLYING SCOTSMAN, THE(1929, Brit.); WOULD YOU BELIEVE IT!(1930, Brit.); MAYTIME IN MAYFAIR(1952, Brit.)
Silents
LOVE AT THE WHEEL(1921, Brit.); MR. NOBODY(1927, Brit.); MY LORD THE CHAUFFEUR(1927, Brit.); ONE OF THE BEST(1927, Brit.)
Misc. Silents
GREAT GAY ROAD, THE(1920, Brit.); BLANCHETTE(1921, Fr.); CLASS AND NO CLASS(1921, Brit.); SAILOR TRAMP, A(1922, Brit.); HELLCAT, THE(1928, Brit.); WAIT AND SEE(1928, Brit.); WHAT NEXT?(1928, Brit.); LITTLE MISS LONDON(1929, Brit.)
Payne Johnson
WHEN TOMORROW COMES(1939)
Payne B. Johnson
STRANGE LOVE OF MARTHA IVERS, THE(1946)
Peaches Johnson
ONE DARK NIGHT(1983)
Peggy LeRoy Johnson
LOVESICK(1983)
Penny Johnson
1984
SWING SHIFT(1984)
Per G. Johnson
SUICIDE MISSION(1956, Brit.), ph
Peter Johnson
LONG ROPE, THE(1961), ed; 20,000 EYES(1961), ed
Peter C. Johnson
SECRET OF THE PURPLE REEF, THE(1960), ed
Peter Rolfe Johnson
JOE MACBETH(1955), ed; SPIN A DARK WEB(1956, Brit.), ed; WEAPON, THE(1957, Brit.), ed
Petronia Johnson
ANNIE HALL(1977)
Plas Johnson, Jr.
SUMMER LOVE(1958)
Plunkett Edward Johnson
Silents
AMAZING IMPOSTER, THE(1919)
R. H. Johnson
Silents
SOULS FOR SALE(1923)
Rafer Johnson
SINS OF RACHEL CADE, THE(1960); FIERCEST HEART, THE(1961); PIRATES OF TORTUGA(1961); WILD IN THE COUNTRY(1961); GLOBAL AFFAIR, A(1964); NONE BUT THE BRAVE(1965, U.S./Jap.); TARZAN AND THE GREAT RIVER(1967, U.S./Switz.); TARZAN AND THE JUNGLE BOY(1968, US/Switz.); GAMES, THE(1970); LAST GRENADE, THE(1970, Brit.); RED, WHITE AND BLACK, THE(1970)
Ralph Johnson
THREE THE HARD WAY(1974)
Misc. Silents
FROZEN WARNING, THE(1918)
Ralph K. Johnson
FREE, WHITE AND 21(1963), ph; EYE CREATURES, THE(1965), ph
Ray Johnson
MAGNIFICENT OBSESSION(1935); LOVE IS NEWS(1937); MEN AGAINST THE SKY(1940); MR. LUCKY(1943); KNOCK ON ANY DOOR(1949)

Ray Rainbow Johnson
EDUCATION OF SONNY CARSON, THE(1974)
Raymond Johnson
PINTO CANYON(1940), d; JUBILEE TRAIL(1954); DIRTY HARRY(1971)
Raymond K. Johnson
KENTUCKY BLUE STREAK(1935), d; SPECIAL AGENT K-7(1937), d; CODE OF THE FEARLESS(1939), d; DAUGHTER OF THE TONG(1939), d; IN OLD MONTANA(1939), d, w; TWO-GUN TROUBADOR(1939), d; CHEYENNE KID, THE(1940), d; COVERED WAGON TRAILS(1940), d; KID FROM SANTA FE, THE(1940), d; LAND OF THE SIX GUNS(1940), d; RIDERS FROM NOWHERE(1940), d
Misc. Talkies
SKYBOUND(1935), d; I'LL NAME THE MURDERER(1936), d; IN OLD MONTANA(1939), d; LAND OF SIX GUNS(1940), d; RIDIN' THE TRAIL(1940), d; WILD HORSE RANGE(1940), d; LAW OF THE WILD(1941), d
Rebecca Johnson
HIGH RISK(1981)
1984
SECRETS(1984, Brit.)
Red Johnson
PEACE FOR A GUNFIGHTER(1967), set d; SEVEN(1979)
Reed Johnson
PSYCHO FROM TEXAS(1982)
Reggie Vel Johnson
1984
GHOSTBUSTERS(1984)
Reginald Johnson
TIMERIDER(1983)
Richard Johnson
SCOTLAND YARD INSPECTOR(1952, Brit.); SAADIA(1953); NEVER SO FEW(1959); CAIRO(1963); HAUNTING, THE(1963); 80,000 SUSPECTS(1963, Brit.); PUMPKIN EATER, THE(1964, Brit.); AMOROUS ADVENTURES OF MOLL FLANDERS, THE(1965); KHARTOUM(1966, Brit.); DEADLIER THAN THE MALE(1967, Brit.); ROVER, THE(1967, Ital.); DANGER ROUTE(1968, Brit.); OEDIPUS THE KING(1968, Brit.); TWIST OF SAND, A(1968, Brit.); LADY HAMILTON(1969, Ger./Ital./Fr.); SOME GIRLS DO(1969, Brit.); WITCH, THE(1969, Ital.); JULIUS CAESAR(1970, Brit.); BEYOND THE DOOR(1975, Ital./U.S.); HENNESSY(1975, Brit.), a, w; NIGHT CHILD(1975, Brit./Ital.); ACES HIGH(1977, Brit.); SCREAMERS(1979, Ital.); TAKE ALL OF ME(1978, Ital.); OVER THE EDGE(1979), spec eff; GREAT ALLIGATOR(1980, Ital.); ZOMBIE(1980, Ital.); MONSTER CLUB, THE(1981, Brit.); COMEBACK, THE(1982, Brit.)
Misc. Talkies
BELOVED, THE(1972); TYRANT, THE(1972, Can.); AERODROME, THE(1983, Brit.)
Misc. Silents
HIS OLD-FASHIONED DAD(1917)
Richard E. Johnson
MARATHON MAN(1976), spec eff
1984
BEST DEFENSE(1984), spec eff
Richard L. Johnson
1984
KILLPOINT(1984)
Rick Johnson
EMIL AND THE DETECTIVES(1964)
Rifa Johnson
GOLDEN FLEECING, THE(1940)
Rita Johnson
THEY WON'T BELIEVE ME(1947); LONDON BY NIGHT(1937); MY DEAR MISS ALDRICH(1937); GIRL DOWNSTAIRS, THE(1938); LETTER OF INTRODUCTION(1938); MAN-PROOF(1938); RICH MAN, POOR GIRL(1938); SMASHING THE RACKETS(1938); BROADWAY SERENADE(1939); HONOLULU(1939); NICK CARTER, MASTER DETECTIVE(1939); STRONGER THAN DESIRE(1939); THEY ALL COME OUT(1939); WITHIN THE LAW(1939); 6000 ENEMIES(1939); CONGO MAISIE(1940); EDISON, THE MAN(1940); FORTY LITTLE MOTHERS(1940); APPOINTMENT FOR LOVE(1941); HERE COMES MR. JORDAN(1941); MAJOR AND THE MINOR, THE(1942); MY FRIEND FLICKA(1943); AFFAIRS OF SUSAN(1945); MINISTRY OF FEAR(1945); NAUGHTY NINETIES, THE(1945); PARDON MY PAST(1945); THUNDERHEAD-SON OF FLICKA(1945); PERFECT MARRIAGE, THE(1946); MICHIGAN KID, THE(1947); BIG CLOCK, THE(1948); DON'T TRUST YOUR HUSBAND(1948); FAMILY HONEYMOON(1948); SLEEP, MY LOVE(1948); SECOND FACE, THE(1950); SUSAN SLEPT HERE(1954); EMERGENCY HOSPITAL(1956); ALL MINE TO GIVE(1957)
Silents
AVE MARIA(1918, Brit.)
Robert Johnson
GANG WAR(1940); SINCE YOU WENT AWAY(1944); RHAPSODY IN BLUE(1945); HOUSE OF DARKNESS(1948, Brit.), ed; I WANT YOU(1951); VIEW FROM POMPEY'S HEAD, THE(1955); RIDE THE HIGH IRON(1956); BLOODY BROOD, THE(1959, Can.), ed; HERO'S ISLAND(1962); BLACK ANGELS, THE(1970); I WALK THE LINE(1970), md; ON THE YARD(1978)
Robert Lee Johnson
HUDDLE(1932), w; GENTLEMEN ARE BORN(1934), w; DOWN TO THE SEA(1936), w; HARVESTER, THE(1936), w; HOOSIER SCHOOLBOY(1937), w; TAMING OF THE WEST, THE(1939), w; GIRL FROM GOD'S COUNTRY(1940), w; GIVE US WINGS(1940), w; PRAIRIE SCHOONERS(1940), w; RETURN OF WILD BILL, THE(1940), w; HIT THE ROAD(1941), w; ATLANTIC CONVOY(1942), w; CANAL ZONE(1942), w; DEVIL'S TRAIL, THE(1942), w; SHE HAS WHAT IT TAKES(1943), w; ENCHANTED FOREST, THE(1945), w; MAN WHO WALKED ALONE, THE(1945), w; SERGEANT MIKE(1945), w; PACE THAT THRILLS, THE(1952), w
Roberta Johnson
LIFE OF HER OWN, A(1950)
Robin Johnson
TIMES SQUARE(1980); BABY, IT'S YOU(1983)
1984
SPLITZ(1984)
Ron Johnson
BRITANNIA OF BILLINGSGATE(1933, Brit.); EMIL AND THE DETECTIVES(1964); GRAVE OF THE VAMPIRE(1972), ed; WOMAN INSIDE, THE(1981), ph

Rondi Johnson
1984
ICEMAN(1984), cos
Ronnie Johnson
SEVENTY DEADLY PILLS(1964, Brit.); OLIVER!(1968, Brit.)
Rosamond Johnson
EMPEROR JONES, THE(1933), m
Rule Royce Johnson
RECESS(1967), d
Russell Johnson
BACK AT THE FRONT(1952); FOR MEN ONLY(1952); LOAN SHARK(1952); TURN-ING POINT, THE(1952); COLUMN SOUTH(1953); IT CAME FROM OUTER SPA-CE(1953); LAW AND ORDER(1953); SEMINOLE(1953); STAND AT APACHE RIVER, THE(1953); TUMBLEWEED(1953); JOHNNY DARK(1954); RIDE CLEAR OF DIA-BLO(1954); ROGUE COP(1954); BLACK TUESDAY(1955); MA AND PA KETTLE AT WAIKIKI(1955); MANY RIVERS TO CROSS(1955); STRANGE LADY IN TOWN(1955); THIS ISLAND EARTH(1955); ATTACK OF THE CRAB MONSTERS(1957); COURAGE OF BLACK BEAUTY(1957); ROCK ALL NIGHT(1957); BADMAN'S COUNTRY(1958); SAGA OF HEMP BROWN, THE(1958); SPACE CHILDREN, THE(1958); DISTANT TRUMPET, A(1964); GREATEST STORY EVER TOLD, THE(1965)
Misc. Talkies
HITCHHIKE TO HELL(1978)
Russell D. Johnson
MAC ARTHUR(1977)
Ruthellen Johnson
HOODLUM SAINT, THE(1946)
Sabel Johnson
Silents
DUDE COWBOY, THE(1926); JAZZ GIRL, THE(1926)
Sander Johnson
1984
ICE PIRATES, THE(1984)
Sandra Johnson
ASH WEDNESDAY(1973)
Sandy Johnson
TWO-MINUTE WARNING(1976); HALLOWEEN(1978); H.O.T.S.(1979)
Scott Johnson
1984
LASSITER(1984)
Seesel Ann Johnson
FORBIDDEN(1932)
Silents
RIDERS OF THE PURPLE SAGE(1925); SPARROWS(1926)
Seesel Anne Johnson
TRUE CONFESSION(1937)
Selmer Johnson
THRU DIFFERENT EYES(1929)
Sharon Johnson
SEX AND THE SINGLE GIRL(1964)
Shelley Johnson
WHOLLY MOSES(1980)
Shirley Johnson
HAVING WONDERFUL CRIME(1945)
Sidney Johnson
NICE GIRL LIKE ME, A(1969, Brit.); RUNNERS(1983, Brit.)
Sol Johnson
UNDERWORLD(1937)
Spunky-Funk Johnson
PUTNEY SWOPE(1969)
Stan Johnson
PRACTICALLY YOURS(1944); MASQUERADE IN MEXICO(1945); MISS SUSIE SLAGLE'S(1945); BLUE DAHLIA, THE(1946); TILL THE END OF TIME(1946); WELL-GROOMED BRIDE, THE(1946); SONG OF MY HEART(1947); TROUBLE WITH WOMEN, THE(1947); HE WALKED BY NIGHT(1948); DARK CITY(1950); FILE ON THELMA JORDAN, THE(1950); LOVE THAT BRUTE(1950); MY FRIEND IRMA GOES WEST(1950); NO MAN OF HER OWN(1950); NO WAY OUT(1950); SEPTEMBER AFFAIR(1950); SUNSET BOULEVARD(1950)
Stanley E. Johnson
ERRAND BOY, THE(1961), ed; FUN IN ACAPULCO(1963), ed; TOGETHER BROTH-ERS(1974), ed
Stanley I. Johnson
GIRLS! GIRLS! GIRLS!(1962), ed
Stephen Johnson
PROTECTORS, BOOK 1, THE(1981); S.O.B.(1981)
1984
MYSTERY MANSION(1984), ed
Misc. Talkies
ANGEL OF H.E.A.T.(1982)
Stephen L. Johnson
WINDWALKER(1980), ed
Steve Johnson
THE LADY DRACULA(1974)
Steven L. Johnson
1984
SACRED GROUND(1984), ed
Sunny Johnson
NATIONAL LAMPOON'S ANIMAL HOUSE(1978); DR. HECKYL AND MR. HY-PE(1980); WHERE THE BUFFALO ROAM(1980); NIGHT THE LIGHTS WENT OUT IN GEORGIA, THE(1981); FLASHDANCE(1983)
T. Earl Johnson
LOST, LONELY AND VICIOUS(1958)
Taborah Johnson
TITLE SHOT(1982, Can.)
Teddy Johnson
GIRLS AT SEA(1958, Brit.)
Tefft Johnson
Silents
NEW KLONDIKE, THE(1926); STRIVING FOR FORTUNE(1926)

Misc. Silents
C.O.D.(1915), d; TURN OF THE ROAD, THE(1915), d; WHO KILLED JOE MER-RION?(1915), d; SHE LEFT WITHOUT HER TRUNKS(1916), d; WRITING ON THE WALL, THE(1916), d; LOVE'S LAW(1917), d; LOVE NET, THE(1918), d; HOME WANTED(1919), d; LOVE AND THE WOMAN(1919), d; LOVE DEFENDER, THE(1919), a, d
Terrellyne Johnson
THIS LAND IS MINE(1943)
Terri Johnson
Misc. Talkies
COCKTAIL HOSTESSES, THE(1976)
Terry Johnson
1984
PRODIGAL, THE(1984)
Thomas Johnson
MAGNET, THE(1950, Brit.)
Tim Johnson
DADDY LONG LEGS(1955); GOOD MORNING, MISS DOVE(1955); WOMEN OF PITCAIRN ISLAND, THE(1957); PARADISE ALLEY(1962)
Tom Johnson
GULLIVER'S TRAVELS(1939), anim d
Toni Johnson
SCREAMING SKULL, THE(1958)
Tor Johnson
UNDER TWO FLAGS(1936); KID MILLIONS(1934); MAN ON THE FLYING TRA-PEZE, THE(1935); SHADOW OF THE THIN MAN(1941); SWING OUT THE BLUES(1943); GHOST CATCHERS(1944); LOST IN A HAREM(1944); SUDAN(1945); ROAD TO RIO(1947); STATE OF THE UNION(1948); ABBOTT AND COSTELLO IN THE FOREIGN LEGION(1950); LEMON DROP KID, THE(1951); SAN FRANCISCO STORY, THE(1952); HOUDINI(1953); BRIDE OF THE MONSTER(1955); BLACK SLEEP, THE(1956); CAROUSEL(1956); JOURNEY TO FREEDOM(1957); UNEARTH-LY, THE(1957); NIGHT OF THE GHOULS(1959); PLAN 9 FROM OUTER SPACE(1959); BEAST OF YUCCA FLATS, THE(1961)
Misc. Talkies
HUMAN GORILLA(1948)
Tyler Johnson
LI'L ABNER(1940), w
Tyrone Johnson
DARK END OF THE STREET, THE(1981), m
Van Johnson
DESERT MESA(1935), w; TOO MANY GIRLS(1940); DR. GILLESPIE'S NEW AS-SISTANT(1942); MURDER IN THE BIG HOUSE(1942); SOMEWHERE I'LL FIND YOU(1942); WAR AGAINST MRS. HADLEY, THE(1942); DR. GILLESPIE'S CRIMI-NAL CASE(1943); GUY NAMED JOE, A(1943); HUMAN COMEDY, THE(1943); MADAME CURIE(1943); PILOT NO. 5(1943); BETWEEN TWO WOMEN(1944); THIRTY SECONDS OVER TOKYO(1944); THREE MEN IN WHITE(1944); TWO GIRLS AND A SAILOR(1944); WHITE CLIFFS OF DOVER, THE(1944); THRILL OF A ROMANCE(1945); WEEKEND AT THE WALDORF(1945); EASY TO WED(1946); NO LEAVE, NO LOVE(1946); TILL THE CLOUDS ROLL BY(1946); HIGH BAR-BAREE(1947); ROMANCE OF ROSY RIDGE, THE(1947); BRIDE GOES WILD, THE(1948); COMMAND DECISION(1948); STATE OF THE UNION(1948); BATTLE-GROUND(1949); IN THE GOOD OLD SUMMERTIME(1949); MOTHER IS A FRESH-MAN(1949); SCENE OF THE CRIME(1949); BIG HANGOVER, THE(1950); DUCHESS OF IDAHO, THE(1950); GROUNDS FOR MARRIAGE(1950); GO FOR BROKE(1951); IT'S A BIG COUNTRY(1951); THREE GUYS NAMED MIKE(1951); TOO YOUNG TO KISS(1951); INVITATION(1952); PLYMOUTH ADVENTURE(1952); WASHINGTON STORY(1952); WHEN IN ROME(1952); CONFIDENTIAL CONNIE(1953); EASY TO LOVE(1953); REMAINS TO BE SEEN(1953); BRIGADOON(1954); CAINE MUTINY, THE(1954); LAST TIME I SAW PARIS, THE(1954); MEN OF THE FIGHTING LADY(1954); SIEGE AT RED RIVER, THE(1954); END OF THE AFFAIR, THE(1955, Brit.); BOTTOM OF THE BOTTLE, THE(1956); MIRACLE IN THE RAIN(1956); SLANDER(1956); 23 PACES TO BAKER STREET(1956); ACTION OF THE TI-GER(1957); KELLY AND ME(1957); LAST BLITZKRIEG, THE(1958); BEYOND THIS PLACE(1959, Brit.); SUBWAY IN THE SKY(1959, Brit.); ENEMY GENERAL, THE(1960); WIVES AND LOVERS(1963); DIVORCE AMERICAN STYLE(1967); WHERE ANGELS GO...TROUBLE FOLLOWS(1968); YOURS, MINE AND OURS(1968); PRICE OF POWER, THE(1969, Ital./Span.); COMPANY OF KILLERS(1970); EAGLE OVER LONDON(1973, Ital.); KIDNAPPING OF THE PRESIDENT, THE(1980, Can.)
Misc. Talkies
ABSURD–ANTROPOPHAGOUS 2(1982); SCORPION WITH TWO TAILS(1982)
Victor Johnson
YOUNG DON'T CRY, THE(1957)
Victoria Johnson
STARSHIP INVASIONS(1978, Can.)
Misc. Talkies
DAWN OF THE MUMMY(1981)
Vida Johnson
Misc. Silents
DESERT SCORPION, THE(1920); WOLVES OF THE STREET(1920)
Virgie Johnson
SPOOK WHO SAT BY THE DOOR, THE(1973)
Vivienne Johnson
CARRY ON ENGLAND(1976, Brit.)
W. Cameron Johnson
VOICE OF THE HURRICANE(1964), art d
W. Ray Johnson
FOURTH ALARM, THE(1930), p; SON OF THE PLAINS(1931), p; AIR EA-GLES(1931), p
Walter Johnson
BRIGHT EYES(1934); CHARLIE CHAN IN LONDON(1934); WHITE PARADE, THE(1934); GEORGE WHITE'S 1935 SCANDALS(1935); GINGER(1935); F MAN(1936); FRESHMAN LOVE(1936); LOVE ON A BET(1936); SMALL TOWN GIRL(1936); JAILHOUSE ROCK(1957)
Will B. Johnson
Silents
REPORTED MISSING(1922), t
William Johnson
FELLER NEEDS A FRIEND(1932), w; OTHER SIDE OF THE MOUNTAIN, THE(1975)

William R. Johnson
DEAR, DEAD DELILAH(1972), ph
Willie Johnson
Misc. Silents
COURAGE OF SILENCE, THE(1917)
Laraine Johnson [Day]
PAINTED DESERT, THE(1938)
Johnson Brothers
HEY, ROOKIE(1944); SENSATIONS OF 1945(1944)
Agnes C. Johnston
NOBODY'S FOOL(1936), w
Silents
MRS. SLACKER(1918), w
Agnes Christine Johnston
MAN AND THE MOMENT, THE(1929), w; OUT WEST WITH THE HARDYS(1938), w; SEVENTEEN(1940), w; DOUBLE DATE(1941), w; LIFE BEGINS FOR ANDY HARDY(1941), w; HENRY ALDRICH, BOY SCOUT(1944), w; JANIE(1944), w; BLACK BEAUTY(1946), w; JANIE GETS MARRIED(1946), w; TIME, THE PLACE AND THE GIRL, THE(1946), w; MICKEY(1948), w
Silents
GREAT ADVENTURE, THE(1918), w; DADDY LONG LEGS(1919), w; OLD MAID'S BABY, THE(1919), w; ALARM CLOCK ANDY(1920), w; OLD FASHIONED BOY, AN(1920), w; CHICKENS(1921), w; HOME STUFF(1921), w; RICH MEN'S WIVES(1922), w; MOTHERS-IN-LAW(1923), w; POOR MEN'S WIVES(1923), w; FORBIDDEN PARADISE(1924), w; PROUD FLESH(1925), w; TOWER OF LIES, THE(1925), w; BEVERLY OF GRAUSTARK(1926), w; ENEMY, THE(1927), w; TILLIE THE TOILER(1927), w; OUTCAST(1928), w
Agnes Johnston
SHANNONS OF BROADWAY, THE(1929), w
Alan Johnston
SCOBIE MALONE(1975, Aus.), m
Alena Johnston
FUNNY GIRL(1968)
Alva Johnston
END OF THE ROAD(1944), w
Amy Johnston
BUDDY HOLLY STORY, THE(1978); JENNIFER(1978)
Anne Johnston
WOMEN MUST DRESS(1935)
Annie Fellows Johnston
LITTLE COLONEL, THE(1935), w
Arthur Johnston
MURDER AT THE VANITIES(1934), m; YOU'RE TELLING ME(1934), m; GILDED LILY, THE(1935), m
Audrey Johnston
SOLDIER, THE(1982)
1984
CAL(1984, Ireland)
Barbara Johnston
HIT PARADE, THE(1937)
Barney Johnston
SIX PACK(1982)
Becky Johnston
BORN IN FLAMES(1983)
Bill Johnston
1984
ISAAC LITTLEFEATHERS(1984, Can.), p
Bob Johnston
HINDLE WAKES(1931, Brit.); CISCO PIKE(1971), md
Brian Johnston
FOUR AGAINST FATE(1952, Brit.); RETURN OF THE SECAUCUS SEVEN(1980)
Bruce Johnston
SGT. PEPPER'S LONELY HEARTS CLUB BAND(1978)
Calvin Johnston
Silents
WITHOUT LIMIT(1921), w
Carl Johnston
RAVAGER, THE(1970), ph
Cheri Johnston
TOWN THAT DREADED SUNDOWN, THE(1977), makeup
Clint Johnston
SKY DRAGON(1949), w; YOUNG DANIEL BOONE(1950), w; NAKED PREY, THE(1966, U.S./South Africa), w; BEACH RED(1967), w
Cullen Johnston
POWER AND THE GLORY, THE(1933)
Dee Ann Johnston
GYPSY(1962); HARDCORE(1979)
Dennis Johnston
RIVER OF UNREST(1937, Brit.), w
Denny Johnston
SKATETOWN, U.S.A.(1979)
Dorian Johnston
I'LL FIX IT(1934)
Elliott Johnston
1984
LASSITER(1984)
Ernestine Johnston
JOHNNY GOT HIS GUN(1971)
F.A. Johnston
Misc. Silents
SINGLE CODE, THE(1917)
Gerry Johnston
ZARDOZ(, spec eff
Gladys Johnston
WEST OF THE ROCKIES(1931)
Silents
HUNCHBACK OF NOTRE DAME, THE(1923)
Misc. Silents
NORTH OF NOME(1925)

Harvey Johnston
HOLLYWOOD BOULEVARD(1936), ed; ILLEGAL TRAFFIC(1938), ed; PAROLE FIXER(1940), ed
Isabel Johnston
Silents
NINETEEN AND PHYLLIS(1920), w
Isabel M. Johnston
Silents
CUPID BY PROXY(1918), w
J.J. Johnston
TOWING(1978); WHOSE LIFE IS IT ANYWAY?(1981)
J.W. Johnston
BUY ME THAT TOWN(1941); LADY EVE, THE(1941); WOMAN IN THE WINDOW, THE(1945); LOCKET, THE(1946)
Silents
ROSE OF THE RANCHO(1914); VIRGINIAN, THE(1914); GOD'S HALF ACRE(1916); OUT OF THE DRIFTS(1916); ADOPTED SON, THE(1917); AS MEN LOVE(1917); ON THE QUIET(1918); PRAISE AGENT, THE(1919); NEGLECTED WIVES(1920); KENTUCKIANS, THE(1921); RULING PASSION, THE(1922); VALLEY OF SILENT MEN, THE(1922); NEW KLONDIKE, THE(1926); TAKE ME HOME(1928)
Misc. Silents
DESTINY'S TOY(1916); MOMENT BEFORE, THE(1916); ETERNAL MOTHER, THE(1917); LAND OF PROMISE, THE(1917); UNCLE TOM'S CABIN(1918); WOMAN THE GERMANS SHOT(1918); TWIN PAWNS, THE(1919); MAN'S PLAYTHING(1920); PARTNERS OF THE SUNSET(1922); GREATEST LOVE OF ALL, THE(1925); DESERT VALLEY(1926); FLYING LUCK(1927); DRIFTWOOD(1928)
Jack Johnston
Silents
CARDIGAN(1922); OBEY YOUR HUSBAND(1928)
Jack W. Johnston
Silents
MAN FROM HOME, THE(1914); WHERE THE TRAIL DIVIDES(1914)
James Johnston
Misc. Talkies
BLOODRAGE(1979)
Jane A. Johnston
CORVETTE SUMMER(1978)
Jo Johnston
Misc. Talkies
SWINGING CHEERLEADERS, THE(1974)
Jody Johnston
OUTSIDER, THE(1962)
Joe Johnston
RETURN OF THE JEDI(1983), art d
1984
INDIANA JONES AND THE TEMPLE OF DOOM(1984), art d
John Dennis Johnston
ROSE, THE(1979); BACK ROADS(1981); BEAST WITHIN, THE(1982); JEKYLL AND HYDE...TOGETHER AGAIN(1982); 48 HOURS(1982); TWILIGHT ZONE–THE MOVIE(1983)
1984
BREED APART, A(1984); STREETS OF FIRE(1984)
John Johnston
TERROR IN THE JUNGLE(1968)
Johnnie Johnston
PRIORITIES ON PARADE(1942); STAR SPANGLED RHYTHM(1942); SWEATER GIRL(1942); YOU CAN'T RATION LOVE(1944); THIS TIME FOR KEEPS(1947); MAN FROM TEXAS, THE(1948); LADY GODIVA RIDES AGAIN(1955, Brit.)
Johnny Johnston
TILL THE CLOUDS ROLL BY(1946); UNCHAINED(1955); ROCK AROUND THE CLOCK(1956)
Julanne Johnston
GENERAL CRACK(1929); PRISONERS(1929); SMILING IRISH EYES(1929); YOUNGER GENERATION(1929); GOLDEN DAWN(1930); STRICTLY MODERN(1930); SCARLET EMPRESS, THE(1934)
Silents
FICKLE WOMEN(1920); MISS HOBBS(1920); MADNESS OF YOUTH(1923); THIEF OF BAGDAD, THE(1924); BIG PAL(1925); ALOMA OF THE SOUTH SEAS(1926); DAME CHANCE(1926); PLEASURES OF THE RICH(1926); TWINKLETOES(1926); NAME THE WOMAN(1928); OH, KAY(1928); OLYMPIC HERO, THE(1928); WHIP WOMAN, THE(1928)
Misc. Silents
VENUS OF VENICE(1927)
Julian Johnston
Silents
WEDDING MARCH, THE(1927), ed
Julianne Johnston
MADAME SATAN(1930)
Justine Johnston
ARTHUR(1981)
Misc. Silents
CRUCIBLE, THE(1914)
Katherine Johnston
Silents
IRON RING, THE(1917); DAMSEL IN DISTRESS, A(1919); FLAPPER, THE(1920)
Kevin Johnston
SUBSTITUTION(1970); HERBIE GOES TO MONTE CARLO(1977)
L. Johnston
Silents
APARTMENT 29(1917)
Lamar Johnston
Misc. Silents
CALENDER GIRL, THE(1917)
Lawrence Johnston
Silents
GUILTY OF LOVE(1920)
Lionel Johnston
EARTHQUAKE(1974)

Lorimer Johnston
FEATHER IN HER HAT, A(1935); SYLVIA SCARLETT(1936)
Silents
SAMSON(1914), d, w; SCARAMOUCHE(1923); DANTE'S INFERNO(1924)
Misc. Silents
ENVOY EXTRAORDINARY, THE(1914), d; CRICKET ON THE HEARTH, THE(1923), d; MIDNIGHT ROSE(1928)

Lyell Johnston
Misc. Silents
LUNATIC AT LARGE, THE(1921)

Margaret Johnston
NOTORIOUS GENTLEMAN(1945, Brit.); MAN ABOUT THE HOUSE, A(1947, Brit.); PORTRAIT OF CLARE(1951, Brit.); MAGIC BOX, THE(1952, Brit.); LIGHT TOUCH, THE(1955, Brit.); BURN WITCH BURN(1962); MODEL MURDER CASE, THE(1964, Brit.); LIFE AT THE TOP(1965, Brit.); PSYCHOPATH, THE(1966, Brit.); SEBASTIAN(1968, Brit.)

Mary Johnston
Silents
AUDREY(1916), w; TO HAVE AND TO HOLD(1922), w; JAMESTOWN(1923), w

Mildred Johnston
HARD HOMBRE(1931), ed; WILD HORSE(1931), ed; GAY BUCKAROO, THE(1932), ed; INTRUDER, THE(1932), ed; LOCAL BAD MAN(1932), ed; PARISIAN ROMANCE, A(1932), ed; SPIRIT OF THE WEST(1932), ed; UNHOLY LOVE(1932), ed; DUDE BANDIT, THE(1933), ed; ELEVENTH COMMANDMENT(1933), ed; IRON MASTER, THE(1933), ed; ONE YEAR LATER(1933), ed; ONCE TO EVERY BACHELOR(1934), ed; PICTURE BRIDES(1934), ed; TAKE THE STAND(1934), ed; TWO HEADS ON A PILLOW(1934), ed; WHEN STRANGERS MEET(1934), ed; NO RANSOM(1935), ed; OLD HOMESTEAD, THE(1935), ed; SCHOOL FOR GIRLS(1935), ed; SWEEPSTAKE ANNIE(1935), ed; PENTHOUSE PARTY(1936), ed

Muriel Johnston
YELLOW SANDS(1938, Brit.)

Narmon Johnston
Misc. Silents
DECEIT(1923)

Neil Johnston
CRY OF THE BANSHEE(1970, Brit.)

Oliver Johnston
KATE PLUS TEN(1938, Brit.); GOOD BEGINNING, THE(1953, Brit.); TALE OF THREE WOMEN, A(1954, Brit.); TERROR SHIP(1954, Brit.); ROOM IN THE HOUSE(1955, Brit.); YOU CAN'T ESCAPE(1955, Brit.); KING IN NEW YORK, A(1957, Brit.); SCOTLAND YARD DRAGNET(1957, Brit.); HELLO LONDON(1958, Brit.); INDISCREET(1958); BEYOND THIS PLACE(1959, Brit.); NOWHERE TO GO(1959, Brit.); SON OF ROBIN HOOD(1959, Brit.); KIDNAPPED(1960); TOUCH OF LARCENY, A(1960, Brit.); BACKFIRE!(1961, Brit.); FRANCIS OF ASSISI(1961); MAKE MINE A DOUBLE(1962, Brit.); ROOMMATES(1962, Brit.); FAST LADY, THE(1963, Brit.); THREE LIVES OF THOMASINA, THE(1963, U.S./Brit.); TOMB OF LIGEIA, THE(1965, Brit.); COUNTESS FROM HONG KONG, A(1967, Brit.); IT!(1967, Brit.)

Oliver Johnston, Jr.
PETER PAN(1953), anim; LADY AND THE TRAMP(1955), anim d; ONE HUNDRED AND ONE DALMATIANS(1961), anim; SWORD IN THE STONE, THE(1963), anim

Oliver M. Johnston
PINOCCHIO(1940), anim; ARISTOCATS, THE(1970), anim d

Oliver M. Johnston, Jr.
FANTASIA(1940), anim; BAMBI(1942), anim; THREE CABALLEROS, THE(1944), anim; MAKE MINE MUSIC(1946), anim; SONG OF THE SOUTH(1946), anim

Ollie Johnston
ALICE IN WONDERLAND(1951), anim d; MARY POPPINS(1964), anim; ROBIN HOOD(1973), anim d; RESCUERS, THE(1977), anim d; FOX AND THE HOUND, THE(1981), anim

Paddy Johnston
MAYTIME IN MAYFAIR(1952, Brit.)

Peter Johnston
DEVIL'S BAIT(1959, Brit.), w; FIDDLER ON THE ROOF(1971); MAN OF LA MANCHA(1972)

Philip Johnston
OUTLAND(1981)

Ray Johnston
Misc. Talkies
CALL OF THE ROCKIES(1931), d
Misc. Silents
CALL OF THE ROCKIES(1931), d

Raymond K. Johnston
Misc. Silents
NORTH OF NOME(1925), d

Robert Lee Johnston
TARZAN'S REVENGE(1938), w

Rosemary Johnston
LAST HUNT, THE(1956); GHOST OF DRAGSTRIP HOLLOW zero(1959)

Scott Johnston
1984
ANOTHER TIME, ANOTHER PLACE(1984, Brit.)

Sibyl Johnston
Silents
SWEET ADELINE(1926)

Stuart Johnston
IMITATION OF LIFE(1934)

Tee Jay Johnston
LOVE IS A CAROUSEL(1970), a, art d

Trace Johnston
HYSTERICAL(1983), w

W. Ray Johnston
UNDER TEXAS SKIES(1931), p
Silents
HEART OF A COWARD, THE(1926), p; MIDNIGHT WATCH, THE(1927), p; ISLE OF LOST MEN(1928), p
Misc. Silents
TENTACLES OF THE NORTH(1926), d

William A. Johnston
ALIAS MARY DOW(1935), w

William Allen Johnston
SILVER QUEEN(1942), w

Alan Johnstone
GIVE ME THE STARS(1944, Brit.)

Anna Hill Johnstone
TAKING OF PELHAM ONE, TWO, THREE, THE(1974), cos; PORTRAIT OF JENNIE(1949), cos; EAST OF EDEN(1955), cos; BABY DOLL(1956), cos; EDGE OF THE CITY(1957), cos; FACE IN THE CROWD, A(1957), cos; ODDS AGAINST TOMORROW(1959), cos; WILD RIVER(1960), cos; SPLENDOR IN THE GRASS(1961), cos; DAVID AND LISA(1962), cos; LADYBUG, LADYBUG(1963), cos; HARVEY MIDDLEMAN, FIREMAN(1965), cos; PAWNBROKER, THE(1965), cos; GROUP, THE(1966), cos; NIGHT THEY RAIDED MINSKY'S, THE(1968), cos; SUBJECT WAS ROSES, THE(1968), cos; SWIMMER, THE(1968), cos; TRUMAN CAPOTE'S TRILOGY(1969), cos; COTTON COMES TO HARLEM(1970), cos; THERE WAS A CROOKED MAN(1970), cos; WHO IS HARRY KELLERMAN AND WHY IS HE SAYING THOSE TERRIBLE THINGS ABOUT ME?(1971), cos; COME BACK CHARLESTON BLUE(1972), cos; EFFECT OF GAMMA RAYS ON MAN-IN-THE-MOON MARIGOLDS, THE(1972), cos; GODFATHER, THE(1972), cos; PLAY IT AGAIN, SAM(1972), cos; GORDON'S WAR(1973), cos; SERPICO(1973), cos; SUMMER WISHES, WINTER DREAMS(1973), cos; DOG DAY AFTERNOON(1975), cos; REPORT TO THE COMMISSIONER(1975), cos; LAST TYCOON, THE(1976), cos; NEXT MAN, THE(1976), cos; KING OF THE GYPSIES(1978), cos; GOING IN STYLE(1979), cos; PRINCE OF THE CITY(1981), cos; RAGTIME(1981), cos; VERDICT, THE(1982), cos; DANIEL(1983), cos; NIGHT IN HEAVEN, A(1983), cos
1984
GARBO TALKS(1984), cos

Babs Johnstone
AWFUL TRUTH, THE(1937), set d; LOST HORIZON(1937), set d; HOLIDAY(1938), set d; I AM THE LAW(1938), set d; THERE'S THAT WOMAN AGAIN(1938), set d

Belle Johnstone
NO MORE ORCHIDS(1933); YOU CAN'T TAKE IT WITH YOU(1938); WIFE TAKES A FLYER, THE(1942)

Belle Stoddard Johnstone
SCARLET EMPRESS, THE(1934)

Billy Johnstone
1984
COMFORT AND JOY(1984, Brit.)

Dick Johnstone
NIGHT UNTO NIGHT(1949); CHEYENNE SOCIAL CLUB, THE(1970)

Harold Johnstone
Silents
MIDNIGHT PATROL, THE(1918)

Harvey Johnstone
KING OF GAMBLERS(1937), ed

Isobel Johnstone
Silents
MONEY ISN'T EVERYTHING(1925, Brit.), w

J.W. Johnstone
NIGHT AND DAY(1946)

Jane Anne Johnstone
DIXIE DYNAMITE(1976)

Johnny Johnstone
ROCK AROUND THE CLOCK(1956)

Justine Johnstone
Silents
NEVER THE TWAIN SHALL MEET(1925)
Misc. Silents
BLACKBIRDS(1920); NOTHING BUT LIES(1920); HEART TO LET, A(1921); PLAYTHING OF BROADWAY, THE(1921); SHELTERED DAUGHTERS(1921)

Lamar Johnstone
Silents
NE'ER-DO-WELL, THE(1916); TONGUES OF MEN, THE(1916); MAN IN THE OPEN, A(1919)
Misc. Silents
BEN BLAIR(1916); GIRL OF MY DREAMS, THE(1918); THAT DEVIL, BATEESE(1918); DIANE OF THE GREEN VAN(1919)

Norman Johnstone
Misc. Silents
SCAR OF SHAME, THE(1927)

Oliver Johnstone
DR. CRIPPEN(1963, Brit.)

Paul Johnstone
MAD MAX(1979, Aus.)

Viola Johnstone
NAUGHTY ARLETTE(1951, Brit.)

W. B. Johnstone
MONKEY BUSINESS(1931), w

William B. Johnstone
Silents
TAKE IT FROM ME(1926), w

William Johnstone
ALL MY SONS(1948); ENCHANTMENT(1948); MAGNIFICENT YANKEE, THE(1950); MILITARY ACADEMY WITH THAT TENTH AVENUE GANG(1950); HALF ANGEL(1951); MY FAVORITE SPY(1951); TITANIC(1953); DOWN THREE DARK STREETS(1954); RIDING SHOTGUN(1954)

William Llewellyn Johnstone
BENEATH THE 12-MILE REEF(1953)

Robert Johnstreet
MISSING(1982)
1984
MIKE'S MURDER(1984)

Marilyn Joi
KENTUCKY FRIED MOVIE, THE(1977); NURSE SHERRI(1978)

Evelyn Joice
42ND STREET(1933)

Anne Joiliffe
GRENDEL GRENDEL GRENDEL(1981, Aus.), anim
Patricia Joiner
MEN, THE(1950); ENFORCER, THE(1951); MISSING WOMEN(1951)
Alf Joint
GOLDFINGER(1964, Brit.); HEROES OF TELEMARK, THE(1965, Brit.); SORCER-
ERS, THE(1967, Brit.); CONQUEROR WORM, THE(1968, Brit.); GREAT CATH-
ERINE(1968, Brit.); LOST CONTINENT, THE(1968, Brit.); KELLY'S HEROES(1970,
U.S./Yugo.), stunts; MACBETH(1971, Brit.); S(1974); PERMISSION TO KILL(1975,
U.S./Aust.); RUSSIAN ROULETTE(1975), stunts; MONEY MOVERS(1978, Aus.),
stunts
1984
SUPERGIRL(1984), stunts
Ludovico Dello Joio
YOR, THE HUNTER FROM THE FUTURE(1983, Ital.)
Lidija Jojic
KAYA, I'LL KILL YOU(1969, Yugo./Fr.), m
Louis Jojot
KING OF HEARTS(1967, Fr./Ital.)
Mons. Jojot
WEEKEND(1968, Fr./Ital.)
Lana Jokel
BEYOND THE LAW(1968), ed; MAIDSTONE(1970), ed; YOU'VE GOT TO WALK IT
LIKE YOU TALK IT OR YOU'LL LOSE THAT BEAT(1971), ed; L'AMOUR(1973), ed
Petra Jokisch
KAMIKAZE '89(1983, Ger.)
Edward Joleson
Misc. Silents
SUNNY JANE(1917)
Paul Jolicoeur
HIGH COUNTRY, THE(1981, Can.); GREY FOX, THE(1983, Can.)
1984
FINDERS KEEPERS(1984)
Jacqueline Jolivet
JOY(1983, Fr./Can.)
Pierre Jolivet
1984
LE DERNIER COMBAT(1984, Fr.), a, p, w
Rita Jolivet
Silents
ONE LAW FOR BOTH(1917)
Misc. Silents
UNAFRAID, THE(1915); INTERNATIONAL MARRIAGE, AN(1916); LEST WE FOR-
GET(1918); BRIDE'S CONFESSION, THE(1921)
Jason Jolivette
LILITH(1964)
Robert Jolivette
LILITH(1964)
Inge Jolles
CLOWN, THE(1953)
Pvt. Alfred C. Jolley, USA
BACK TO BATAAN(1945)
I. Stanford Jolley
GHOST TOWN GOLD(1937); KID GALAHAD(1937); THEY WON'T FORGET(1937);
LONE WOLF SPY HUNT, THE(1939); PRIVATE LIVES OF ELIZABETH AND ESSEX,
THE(1939); CHASING TROUBLE(1940); MIDNIGHT LIMITED(1940); CRIMINALS
WITHIN(1941); DESPERATE CARGO(1941); EMERGENCY LANDING(1941); GEN-
TLEMAN FROM DIXIE(1941); ROLLIN' HOME TO TEXAS(1941); TRAIL OF THE
SILVER SPURS(1941); BLACK DRAGONS(1942); DAWN ON THE GREAT DIVI-
DE(1942); PRAIRIE PALS(1942); RANGERS TAKE OVER, THE(1942); SOMBRERO
KID, THE(1942); BAD MEN OF THUNDER GAP(1943); BLACK RAVEN, THE(1943);
FRONTIER LAW(1943); KID RIDES AGAIN, THE(1943); MAN FROM MUSIC MOUN-
TAIN(1943); RETURN OF THE RANGERS, THE(1943); WILD HORSE STAM-
PEDE(1943); WOLVES OF THE RANGE(1943); BLAZING FRONTIER(1944); BRAND
OF THE DEVIL(1944); CALL OF THE JUNGLE(1944); CHINESE CAT, THE(1944);
CYCLONE PRAIRIE RANGERS(1944); DEATH RIDES THE PLAINS(1944); GANG-
STERS OF THE FRONTIER(1944); OKLAHOMA RAIDERS(1944); SHAKE HANDS
WITH MURDER(1944); TRAIL OF TERROR(1944); WHAT A MAN!(1944); WHISPER-
ING SKULL, THE(1944); FIGHTING BILL CARSON(1945); FLAMING BUL-
LETS(1945); FRONTIER FUGITIVES(1945); LIGHTNING RAIDERS(1945); MR.
MUGGS RIDES AGAIN(1945); OUTLAWS OF THE ROCKIES(1945); PRAIRIE RUS-
TLERS(1945); SCARLET CLUE, THE(1945); STAGECOACH OUTLAWS(1945); AM-
BUSH TRAIL(1946); CYCLOTRODE X(1946); SIX GUN MAN(1946); TERRORS ON
HORSEBACK(1946); LAND OF THE LAWLESS(1947); PRAIRIE EXPRESS(1947);
WILD COUNTRY(1947); CHECK YOUR GUNS(1948); FEUDIN', FUSSIN' AND A-
FIGHTIN'(1948); FIGHTING RANGER, THE(1948); GUNNING FOR JUSTICE(1948);
OKLAHOMA BLUES(1948); PRINCE OF THIEVES, THE(1948); WHIPLASH(1948);
BANDIT KING OF TEXAS(1949); DESERT VIGILANTE(1949); GUN LAW JUS-
TICE(1949); RIMFIRE(1949); ROLL, THUNDER, ROLL(1949); SANDS OF IWO JI-
MA(1949); SON OF BILLY THE KID(1949); STAMPEDE(1949); BARON OF ARIZONA,
THE(1950); COLORADO RANGER(1950); CURTAIN CALL AT CACTUS CREEK(1950);
FAST ON THE DRAW(1950); HOSTILE COUNTRY(1950); SIERRA(1950); TRIGGER,
JR.(1950); CANYON RAIDERS(1951); CATTLE QUEEN(1951); NEVADA BAD-
MEN(1951); OKLAHOMA JUSTICE(1951); STAGE TO BLUE RIVER(1951); TEXANS
NEVER CRY(1951); TEXAS LAWMEN(1951); DEAD MAN'S TRAIL(1952); FORT
OSAGE(1952); KANSAS TERRITORY(1952); LAWLESS BREED, THE(1952); LAW-
LESS COWBOYS(1952); LEADVILLE GUNSLINGER(1952); MAN FROM BLACK
HILLS, THE(1952); RANCHO NOTORIOUS(1952); RODEO(1952); WACO(1952); WAG-
ONS WEST(1952); WILD STALLION(1952); YUKON GOLD(1952); MARKSMAN,
THE(1953); REBEL CITY(1953); SON OF BELLE STARR(1953); TOPEKA(1953); TUM-
BLEWEED(1953); VIGILANTE TERROR(1953); DESPERADO, THE(1954); SILVER
LODE(1954); TWO GUNS AND A BADGE(1954); WHITE CHRISTMAS(1954); I
KILLED WILD BILL HICKOK(1956); KENTUCKY RIFLE(1956); PROUD ONES,
THE(1956); RAWHIDE YEARS, THE(1956); VIOLENT YEARS, THE(1956); WILD
DAKOTAS, THE(1956); YOUNG GUNS, THE(1956); GUN BATTLE AT MON-
TEREY(1957); GUNSIGHT RIDGE(1957); HALLIDAY BRAND, THE(1957); IRON
SHERIFF, THE(1957); OKLAHOMAN, THE(1957); LONG, HOT SUMMER, THE(1958);
GHOST OF ZORRO(1959); HERE COME THE JETS(1959); LONE TEXAN(1959);
MIRACLE OF THE HILLS, THE(1959); REBEL SET, THE(1959); ICE PALACE(1960);
THIRTEEN FIGHTING MEN(1960); TOBY TYLER(1960), art d; LITTLE SHEPHERD

OF KINGDOM COME(1961); VALLEY OF THE DRAGONS(1961); FIREBRAND,
THE(1962); TERROR AT BLACK FALLS(1962); HAUNTED PALACE, THE(1963);
BOUNTY KILLER, THE(1965); RESTLESS ONES, THE(1965); NIGHT OF THE
LEPUS(1972)
Misc. Talkies
OUTLAW ROUNDUP(1944); SWING, COWBOY, SWING(1944); SPRINGTIME IN
TEXAS(1945); SILVER RANGE(1946); HAUNTED TRAILS(1949); TROUBLE AT
MELODY MESA(1949); GUNMAN, THE(1952); HIRED GUN(1952); MAN FROM THE
BLACK HILLS(1952)
Norman Jolley
FLASHING GUNS(1947); PURSUED(1947); SILVER RIVER(1948); I'VE LIVED
BEFORE(1956), w; TWO-GUN LADY(1956), a, w; JOE DAKOTA(1957), w; MONO-
LITH MONSTERS, THE(1957), w; APPOINTMENT WITH A SHADOW(1958), w
Stan Jolley
CORREGIDOR(1943); JOAN OF ARC(1948); LONGHORN, THE(1951); MAIL ORDER
BRIDE(1964), art d; RESTLESS ONES, THE(1965), art d; RIDE BEYOND VEN-
GEANCE(1966), art d; GOOD GUYS AND THE BAD GUYS, THE(1969), prod d & art
d; YOUNG BILLY YOUNG(1969), art d; PHYNX, THE(1970), prod d; LAWMAN(1971),
prod d; NIGHT OF THE LEPUS(1972), prod d; WAR BETWEEN MEN AND WOMEN,
THE(1972), prod d; TERROR IN THE WAX MUSEUM(1973), prod d; WALKING
TALL(1973), prod d; GRAVY TRAIN, THE(1974), prod d; MIXED COMPANY(1974),
prod d; DRUM(1976), prod d; SWARM, THE(1978), prod d; CATTLE ANNIE AND
LITTLE BRITCHES(1981), prod d; TAPS(1981), art d
Stan [I. Stanford] Jolley
WHISTLING HILLS(1951); SEVEN BRIDES FOR SEVEN BROTHERS(1954)
Stanford Jolley
FATAL HOUR, THE(1940); RED BADGE OF COURAGE, THE(1951); FARGO(1952);
FORTYNINERS, THE(1954)
Sue Jolley
CRASH DIVE(1943)
Vic Jolley
STUDENT BODY, THE(1976)
Anne Jolliffe
YELLOW SUBMARINE(1958, Brit.), animation
Charles Jolliffe
1984
COVERGIRL(1984, Can.); MRS. SOFFEL(1984)
David Jolliffe
1984
LOVELINES(1984)
John Jolliffe
MURDER IN THE MUSIC HALL(1946)
Muriel Jolliffe
DAYS OF HEAVEN(1978)
E.B. Jolly
DEVIL'S BEDROOM, THE(1964)
Nick Jolly
Misc. Talkies
ASYLUM OF SATAN(1972)
Pete Jolly
I WANT TO LIVE!(1958)
Robert Jolly
YEAR OF THE YAHOO(1971)
Stan Jolly
FRAMED(1975), prod d; CADDY SHACK(1980), prod d
The Jolly Stompers
EDUCATION OF SONNY CARSON, THE(1974)
Friedrich Joloff
DESPERATE MOMENT(1953, Brit.); MAN ON A STRING(1960); JOHNNY BAN-
CO(1969, Fr./Ital./Ger.)
Al Jolson
JAZZ SINGER, THE(1927); SINGING FOOL, THE(1928); SAY IT WITH SONGS(1929);
SONNY BOY(1929); BIG BOY(1930); MAMMY(1930); HALLELUJAH, I'M A
BUM(1933); WONDER BAR(1934); GO INTO YOUR DANCE(1935); SINGING KID,
THE(1936); HOLLYWOOD CAVALCADE(1939); ROSE OF WASHINGTON SQUA-
RE(1939); SWANEE RIVER(1939); RHAPSODY IN BLUE(1945)
Dominque Joly
MY UNCLE ANTOINE(1971, Can.)
Gaston Joly
MURIEL(1963, Fr./Ital.); DAY FOR NIGHT(1973, Fr.)
Jocelyn Joly
CHILD UNDER A LEAF(1975, Can.), art d; FANTASTICA(1980, Can./Fr.), art d
Monique Joly
TAKE IT ALL(1966, Can.)
Paul Joly
SEVENTH JUROR, THE(1964, Fr.), p
Sylvie Joly
PAUL AND MICHELLE(1974, Fr./Brit.); GET OUT YOUR HANDKERCHIEFS(1978,
Fr.); WE'LL GROW THIN TOGETHER(1979, Fr.); PIAF-THE EARLY YEARS(1982,
U.S./Fr.)
Neil Jon
LOST HORIZON(1973)
Jon-Jon
RED, WHITE AND BLACK, THE(1970)
Dolly Jonah
HARRY AND TONTO(1974)
Willie Jonah
SHAFT IN AFRICA(1973)
Willy Jonah
BUSHBABY, THE(1970)
Julius Jonak
LAST TEN DAYS, THE(1956, Ger.)
Jonas
JONAH-WHO WILL BE 25 IN THE YEAR 2000(1976, Switz.)
Joanne Jonas
GODSPELL(1973)
Norman Jonas
LET'S SCARE JESSICA TO DEATH(1971), w

Gunnar Jonason
JUNGLE OF CHANG(1951), m
Jane Jonason
PARIS OOH-LA-LA!(1963, U.S./Fr.)
Frank Jonasson
COCK O' THE WALK(1930)
Silents
FIGHTING COWARD, THE(1924); MERTON OF THE MOVIES(1924); OLD IRON-SIDES(1926)
Misc. Silents
PITFALL, THE(1915); WHAT HAPPENED TO JONES(1920)
Jonathan
SUBSTITUTION(1970), m
Robert Jonay
CALCUTTA(1947), ch
Roberta Jonay
HERE COME THE WAVES(1944); DUFFY'S TAVERN(1945); MASQUERADE IN MEXICO(1945); STORK CLUB, THE(1945); BLUE DAHLIA, THE(1946); O.S.S.(1946); WELL-GROOMED BRIDE, THE(1946); GOLDEN EARRINGS(1947); LADIES' MAN(1947); SUDDENLY IT'S SPRING(1947); VARIETY GIRL(1947); EMPEROR WALTZ, THE(1948)
Francois Jone
MODIGLIANI OF MONTPARNASSE(1961, Fr./Ital.)
Akili Jones
TROUBLE MAN(1972)
Al Jones
SCREAM BLACULA SCREAM(1973); WARGAMES(1983), stunts
1984
ICE PIRATES, THE(1984); PURPLE RAIN(1984); SAVAGE STREETS(1984), stunts; STAR TREK III: THE SEARCH FOR SPOCK(1984)
Silents
YELLOW BACK, THE(1926), ph; BLAZING DAYS(1927), ph; PAINTING THE TOWN(1927), ph; GATE CRASHER, THE(1928), ph; EYES OF THE UNDER-WORLD(1929), ph; KID'S CLEVER, THE(1929), ph
Alan Jones
PINK PANTHER STRIKES AGAIN, THE(1976, Brit.), ed; REVENGE OF THE PINK PANTHER(1978), ed; DOING TIME(1979, Brit.), ed; THERE GOES THE BRIDE(1980, Brit.), ed; TRAIL OF THE PINK PANTHER, THE(1982), ed
Alfred Jones
LEARNING TREE, THE(1969)
Alida B. Jones
Silents
ROWDY, THE(1921); DON'T GET PERSONAL(1922)
Alida D. Jones
Silents
WHITE YOUTH(1920)
Alida Jones
Misc. Silents
HER MOMENT(1918)
Alister Jones
MONKEY GRIP(1983, Aus.)
Allan Jones
NIGHT AT THE OPERA, A(1935); RECKLESS(1935); ROSE MARIE(1936); SHOW BOAT(1936); DAY AT THE RACES, A(1937); FIREFLY, THE(1937); EVERYBODY SING(1938); GREAT VICTOR HERBERT, THE(1939); HONEYMOON IN BALI(1939); BOYS FROM SYRACUSE(1940); ONE NIGHT IN THE TROPICS(1940); THERE'S MAGIC IN MUSIC(1941); MOONLIGHT IN HAVANA(1942); TRUE TO THE AR-MY(1942); CRAZY HOUSE(1943); LARCENY WITH MUSIC(1943); RHYTHM OF THE ISLANDS(1943); SING A JINGLE(1943); WHEN JOHNNY COMES MARCHING HOME(1943); YOU'RE A LUCKY FELLOW, MR. SMITH(1943); HONEYMOON AHEAD(1945); SENORITA FROM THE WEST(1945); STAGE TO THUNDER ROCK(1964); SWINGIN' SUMMER, A(1965); MAN CALLED SLEDGE, A(1971, Ital.); BULLSHOT(1983), ed
Allen Jones
WEREWOLVES ON WHEELS(1971), art d
Allen H. Jones
SWEET CREEK COUNTY WAR, THE(1979), prod d; DEATH VALLEY(1982), art d
Allyn C. Jones
FOLLOW YOUR HEART(1936), ph
Amanda Jones
HUNCH, THE(1967, Brit.); WINTER KILLS(1979)
Misc. Talkies
ADVENTURES OF YOUNG ROBIN HOOD(1983)
Amy Jones
HOLLYWOOD BOULEVARD(1976), ed; CORVETTE SUMMER(1978), ed; SLUM-BER PARTY MASSACRE, THE(1982), p, d; LOVE LETTERS(1983), d&w
Amy Holden Jones
SECOND-HAND HEARTS(1981), ed
Angela Jones
NICE GIRL LIKE ME, A(1969, Brit.)
Anissa Jones
TROUBLE WITH GIRLS(AND HOW TO GET INTO IT), THE*1/2 (1969)
Annabelle Jones
THEY DIED WITH THEIR BOOTS ON(1942)
Anne Jones
ROAD WARRIOR, THE(1982, Aus.)
Anne Scott Jones
LOCAL HERO(1983, Brit.)
Annie Jones
1984
MIKE'S MURDER(1984)
Art Jones
SEVEN DAYS IN MAY(1964), makeup
Arthur A. Jones
SAVAGE(1962), p,d&w
Arthur V. Jones
KELLY THE SECOND(1936), w; PRAIRIE LAW(1940), w; STAGE TO CHINO(1940), w; TRIPLE JUSTICE(1940), w; ALONG THE RIO GRANDE(1941), w; FARGO KID, THE(1941), w; ROBBERS OF THE RANGE(1941), w; SWING IT SOLDIER(1941), w; FIGHTING BILL FARGO(1942), w; FRISCO LILL(1942), w; JUKE BOX JENNY(1942),

w; STAGECOACH EXPRESS(1942), w; FLIGHT TO NOWHERE(1946), w; UNDER-SEA GIRL(1957), w
Arthur Vernon Jones
MISTER CINDERELLA(1936), w; PICK A STAR(1937), w
B.J. Jones
1984
BODY DOUBLE(1984)
Barbara Jones
MEDIUM COOL(1969); TENDER MERCIES(1982)
Barbara O. Jones
DEMON SEED(1977)
Misc. Talkies
BLACK CHARIOT(1971)
Barry Jones
ARMS AND THE MAN(1932, Brit.); NUMBER SEVENTEEN(1932, Brit.); WOMEN WHO PLAY(1932, Brit.); GAY ADVENTURE, THE(1936, Brit.); MURDER IN THE FAMILY(1938, Brit.); SQUADRON LEADER X(1943, Brit.); DANCING WITH CRI-ME(1947, Brit.); FRIEDA(1947, Brit.); CALENDAR, THE(1948, Brit.); UNEASY TERMS(1948, Brit.); BAD LORD BYRON, THE(1949, Brit.); CLOUDED YELLOW, THE(1950, Brit.); IF THIS BE SIN(1950, Brit.); MADELEINE(1950, Brit.); SEVEN DAYS TO NOON(1950, Brit.); ISLAND RESCUE(1952, Brit.); MAGIC BOX, THE(1952, Brit.); PLYMOUTH ADVENTURE(1952); WHITE CORRIDORS(1952, Brit.); RETURN TO PARADISE(1953); BRIGADOON(1954); DEMETRIUS AND THE GLADIATORS(1954); PRINCE VALIANT(1954); GLASS SLIPPER, THE(1955); ALEXANDER THE GREAT(1956); WAR AND PEACE(1956, Ital./U.S.); SAINT JOAN(1957); SAFECRACK-ER, THE(1958, Brit.); THIRTY NINE STEPS, THE(1960, Brit.); HEROES OF TELE-MARK, THE(1965, Brit.); STUDY IN TERROR, A(1966, Brit./Ger.)
Ben Jones
TOGETHER FOR DAYS(1972); LINCOLN CONSPIRACY, THE(1977); THEY WENT THAT-A-WAY AND THAT-A-WAY(1978); DEEP IN THE HEART(1983)
Bertram Jones
Silents
NICE PEOPLE(1922)
Beti Jones
MOUSE AND THE WOMAN, THE(1981, Brit.)
Betsy Jones
THANK GOD IT'S FRIDAY(1978), cos
1984
HEARTBREAKERS(1984), cos
Beulah Hall Jones
CAMEO KIRBY(1930); JUDGE PRIEST(1934); PRISONER OF SHARK ISLAND, THE(1936); TOY WIFE, THE(1938); DRUMS ALONG THE MOHAWK(1939)
Bill Jones
BIGGER THAN LIFE(1956)
Billy Jones
GET THAT GIRL(1932); SANTA FE MARSHAL(1940); DUFFY'S TAVERN(1945); FULLER BRUSH MAN(1948); SHE WORE A YELLOW RIBBON(1949)
Billy "Red" Jones
Silents
SPARROWS(1926)
Misc. Silents
SLOW AS LIGHTING(1923); PHANTOM FLYER, THE(1928)
Bob Jones
WEST 11(1963, Brit.), art d; STEVIE(1978, Brit.), art d; ENTER THE NINJA(1982)
Bob Jones, Jr.
RED RUNS THE RIVER(1963)
Misc. Talkies
MACBETH(1950)
Bobby Jones
DREAMING(1944, Brit.)
Bonnie Jones
DIARY OF A BACHELOR(1964)
Booker T. Jones
UPTIGHT(1968), m; OPENING NIGHT(1977), md
1984
SONGWRITER(1984)
Brian Jones
DEGREE OF MURDER, A(1969, Ger.), m
Bryan Jones
1984
THIS IS SPINAL TAP(1984), prod d
Bryn Jones
UNDER MILK WOOD(1973, Brit.)
Misc. Talkies
CURSE OF KILIMANJARO(1978)
Buck Jones
LONE RIDER, THE(1930); MEN WITHOUT LAW(1930); SHADOW RANCH(1930); AVENGER, THE(1931); BORDER LAW(1931); BRANDED(1931); DAWN TRAIL, THE(1931); DESERT VENGEANCE(1931); FIGHTING SHERIFF, THE(1931); RANGE FEUD, THE(1931); TEXAS RANGER, THE(1931); DEADLINE(1932); HELLO TROUBLE(1932); HIGH SPEED(1932); MC KENNA OF THE MOUNTED(1932); ONE-MAN LAW(1932); SOUTH OF THE RIO GRANDE(1932); WHITE EAGLE(1932); CALIFORNIA TRAIL, THE(1933); SUNDOWN RIDER, THE(1933); THRILL HUNTER, THE(1933); FIGHTING CODE, THE(1934); FIGHTING RANGER, THE(1934); MAN TRAILER, THE(1934); ROCKY RHODES(1934), p; WHEN A MAN SEES RED(1934), a, p; BORDER BRIGANDS(1935); CRIMSON TRAIL, THE(1935), a, p; IVORY-HAN-DLED GUN(1935), a, p; OUTLAWED GUNS(1935), a, p; STONE OF SILVER CREEK(1935); THROWBACK, THE(1935), a, p; BOSS RIDER OF GUN CREEK(1936), a, p; COWBOY AND THE KID, THE(1936), a, p, w; FOR THE SERVICE(1936), a, p&d; FORBIDDEN TRAIL(1936); RIDE 'EM COWBOY(1936), a, p, w; SUNSET OF POWER(1936), a, p; BLACK ACES(1937), a, p&d; BOSS OF LONELY VALLEY(1937), a, p; EMPTY SADDLES(1937), a, p; HEADIN' EAST(1937); LAW FOR TOMB-STONE(1937), a, p, d; LEFT-HANDED LAW(1937), a, p; SANDFLOW(1937), a, p; SMOKE TREE RANGE(1937), a, p; CALIFORNIA FRONTIER(1938); HOLLYWOOD ROUNDUP(1938); LAW OF THE TEXAN(1938); OVERLAND EXPRESS, THE(1938); STRANGER FROM ARIZONA, THE(1938); SUDDEN BILL DORN(1938), a, p; UN-MARRIED(1939); WAGONS WESTWARD(1940); ARIZONA BOUND(1941); FORBID-DEN TRAILS(1941); GUN MAN FROM BODIE, THE(1941); BELOW THE BORDER(1942); DAWN ON THE GREAT DIVIDE(1942); DOWN TEXAS WAY(1942); GHOST TOWN LAW(1942); RIDERS OF THE WEST(1942); WEST OF THE LAW(1942)

Silents

LAST STRAW, THE(1920); BAR NOTHIN'(1921); BIG PUNCH, THE(1921); GET YOUR MAN(1921); ARIZONA ROMEO, THE(1925); GOLD AND THE GIRL(1925); DESERT'S PRICE, THE(1926); MAN FOUR-SQUARE, A(1926); WAR HORSE, THE(1927), a, w

Misc. Silents

FIREBRAND TREVISON(1920); FORBIDDEN TRAILS(1920); JUST PALS(1920); SQUARE SHOOTER, THE(1920); SUNSET SPRAGUE(1920); TWO MOONS(1920); ONE-MAN TRAIL, THE(1921); STRAIGHT FROM THE SHOULDER(1921); TO A FINISH(1921); DESERT OUTLAW, THE(1924); MAN WHO PLAYED SQUARE, THE(1924); WINNER TAKE ALL(1924); DURAND OF THE BAD LANDS(1925); HEARTS AND SPURS(1925); TIMBER WOLF(1925); TRAIL RIDER, THE(1925); COWBOY AND THE COUNTESS, THE(1926); DESERT VALLEY(1926); FIGHTING BUCKAROO, THE(1926); FLYING HORSEMAN, THE(1926); GENTLE CYCLONE, THE(1926); 30 BELOW ZERO(1926); BLACK JACK(1927); BLOOD WILL TELL(1927); CHAIN LIGHTING(1927); GOOD AS GOLD(1927); HILLS OF PERIL(1927); WHISPERING SAGE(1927); BIG HOP, THE(1928); BRANDED SOMBRERO, THE(1928)

Butch Jones

PRIVATE WAR OF MAJOR BENSON, THE(1955)

C. Allen Jones

DAMES AHOY(1930), ph

C. Allyn Jones

SEE AMERICA THIRST(1930), ph

C.R. Jones

ENEMIES OF THE LAW(1931), w

Carl Jones

MY GAL LOVES MUSIC(1944)

Carolyn Jones

ROAD TO BALI(1952); TURNING POINT, THE(1952); BIG HEAT, THE(1953); GERALDINE(1953); HOUSE OF WAX(1953); OFF LIMITS(1953); WAR OF THE WORLDS, THE(1953); DESIREE(1954); MAKE HASTE TO LIVE(1954); SARACEN BLADE, THE(1954); SHIELD FOR MURDER(1954); THREE HOURS TO KILL(1954); SEVEN YEAR ITCH, THE(1955); TENDER TRAP, THE(1955); INVASION OF THE BODY SNATCHERS(1956); MAN WHO KNEW TOO MUCH, THE(1956); OPPOSITE SEX, THE(1956); BABY FACE NELSON(1957); BACHELOR PARTY, THE(1957); JOHNNY TROUBLE(1957); KING CREOLE(1958); MARJORIE MORNINGSTAR(1958); CAREER(1959); HOLE IN THE HEAD, A(1959); LAST TRAIN FROM GUN HILL(1959); MAN IN THE NET, THE(1959); ICE PALACE(1960); SAIL A CROOKED SHIP(1961); HOW THE WEST WAS WON(1962); TICKLISH AFFAIR, A(1963); COLOR ME DEAD(1969, Aus.); HEAVEN WITH A GUN(1969); DANCE OF DEATH, THE(1971, Brit.); EATEN ALIVE(1976); GOOD LUCK, MISS WYCKOFF(1979)

Carrie Jones

RISING DAMP(1980, Brit.)

1984

OXFORD BLUES(1984)

Cathy Jones

TWO FOR THE ROAD(1967, Brit.)

Ceri Jones

DEATHLINE(1973, Brit.), w

Charlene Jones

CURIOUS FEMALE, THE(1969); UNHOLY ROLLERS(1972); WOMAN HUNT, THE(1975, U.S./Phil.)

1984

HARD TO HOLD(1984)

Charles Jones

CHILD OF MANHATTAN(1933)

Silents

PARDON MY NERVE!(1922); WEST OF CHICAGO(1922); ELEVENTH HOUR, THE(1923); SECOND HAND LOVE(1923); SKID PROOF(1923); WESTERN LUCK(1924); LAZYBONES(1925)

Misc. Silents

BELLS OF SAN JUAN(1922); BOSS OF CAMP 4, THE(1922); FAST MAIL, THE(1922); TROOPER O'NEIL(1922); WESTERN SPEED(1922); BIG DAN(1923); CUPID'S FIREMAN(1923); FOOTLIGHT RANGER, THE(1923); HELL'S HOLE(1923); CIRCUS COWBOY, THE(1924); NOT A DRUM WAS HEARD(1924); VAGABOND TRAIL, THE(1924)

Charles "Buck" Jones

RIDIN' FOR JUSTICE(1932); UNKNOWN VALLEY(1933); ROCKY RHODES(1934); SILVER SPURS(1936)

Silents

RIDING WITH DEATH(1921); AGAINST ALL ODDS(1924); ROUGH SHOD(1925)

Charles Reed Jones

KING MURDER, THE(1932), w

Charlie Jones

PERSONAL BEST(1982)

Charlotte Jones

FOOL KILLER, THE(1965); LOVERS AND OTHER STRANGERS(1970)

Chester Jones

THEY LIVE BY NIGHT(1949); YOU'RE MY EVERYTHING(1949); GAMBLING HOUSE(1950); STREETCAR NAMED DESIRE, A(1951); MY SIX CONVICTS(1952); DANGEROUS MISSION(1954); LEECH WOMAN, THE(1960); WALK ON THE WILD SIDE(1962); CLARENCE, THE CROSS-EYED LION(1965); DARK INTRUDER(1965); BUBBLE, THE(1967); WHO FEARS THE DEVIL(1972)

Christine Jones

COOLEY HIGH(1975); ANNIE HALL(1977)

Christopher Jones

CHUBASCO(1968); THREE IN THE ATTIC(1968); WILD IN THE STREETS(1968); LOOKING GLASS WAR, THE(1970, Brit.); RYAN'S DAUGHTER(1970, Brit.)

Chuck Jones

GAY PURR-EE(1962), w; PHANTOM TOLLBOOTH, THE(1970), p, d, w; GREAT AMERICAN BUGS BUNNY-ROAD RUNNER CHASE(1979), p&d, w

1984

GREMLINS(1984)

Claud Jones

HAUNTING, THE(1963)

Claude Jones

THUNDER AND LIGHTNING(1977)

Claude Earl Jones

I WANNA HOLD YOUR HAND(1978); USED CARS(1980); EVILSPEAK(1982)

1984

IMPULSE(1984)

Clifford Jones

MAN WHO DARED, THE(1933); TRICK FOR TRICK(1933); COMING OUT PARTY(1934); CRIME OF HELEN STANLEY(1934); PRINCESS O'HARA(1935); STRANGERS ALL(1935); TRANSIENT LADY(1935); DON'T GAMBLE WITH LOVE(1936); FOR THE SERVICE(1936); GIRL ON THE FRONT PAGE, THE(1936); HIS FAMILY TREE(1936)

1984

WINDY CITY(1984), ed

Clifford Jones, Jr.

POWER AND THE GLORY, THE(1933)

Clifton Jones

V.I.P.s, THE(1963, Brit.); JOANNA(1968, Brit.); ONLY WHEN I LARF(1968, Brit.); DECLINE AND FALL... OF A BIRD WATCHER(1969, Brit.); INNOCENT BYSTANDERS(1973, Brit.); GREAT MCGONAGALL, THE(1975, Brit.); WATERSHIP DOWN(1978, Brit.)

1984

SHEENA(1984)

Cline Jones

MISFITS, THE(1961), spec eff

Com. Herbert A. Jones

HERE COMES THE NAVY(1934), tech adv

Comdr. Herbert A. Jones

SUICIDE FLEET(1931), w

Constance Jones

LUCK OF THE IRISH(1948), w; MR. PEABODY AND THE MERMAID(1948), w

Cornelius Jones

MOVING FINGER, THE(1963)

Dan Jones

PURPLE HAZE(1982)

Daniel Jones

WITHOUT PITY(1949, Ital.)

Darby Jones

TARZAN THE FEARLESS(1933); VIRGINIA JUDGE, THE(1935); TARZAN ESCAPES(1936); SWING HIGH, SWING LOW(1937); MARYLAND(1940); SAFARI(1940); SUNDOWN(1941); VIRGINIA(1941); WHITE CARGO(1942); I WALKED WITH A ZOMBIE(1943); PASSPORT TO SUEZ(1943); ZOMBIES ON BROADWAY(1945); MACOMBER AFFAIR, THE(1947); ROPE OF SAND(1949); ZAMBA(1949); WHITE GODDESS(1953)

Dario O. Jones

STUDENT BODIES(1981)

Dave Jones

CASTLE KEEP(1969)

David Jones

SHADOWS(1960); DARK ODYSSEY(1961), set d; HEAD(1968); COLD JOURNEY(1975, Can.), w; BETRAYAL(1983, Brit.), d

David G. Jones

CHRISTINA(1974, Can.)

Deacon Jones

BLACK GUNN(1972); HEAVEN CAN WAIT(1978); NORSEMAN, THE(1978)

Dean Jones

UNTIL THEY SAIL(1957); GREAT AMERICAN PASTIME, THE(1956); OPPOSITE SEX, THE(1956); RACK, THE(1956); SOMEBODY UP THERE LIKES ME(1956); TEA AND SYMPATHY(1956); THESE WILDER YEARS(1956); JAILHOUSE ROCK(1957); TEN THOUSAND BEDROOMS(1957); HANDLE WITH CARE(1958); IMITATION GENERAL(1958); TORPEDO RUN(1958); NEVER SO FEW(1959); NIGHT OF THE QUARTER MOON(1959); UNDER THE YUM-YUM TREE(1963); NEW INTERNS, THE(1964); THAT DARN CAT(1965); TWO ON A GUILLOTINE(1965); ANY WEDNESDAY(1966); UGLY DACHSHUND, THE(1966); MONKEYS, GO HOME!(1967); BLACKBEARD'S GHOST(1968); HORSE IN THE GRAY FLANNEL SUIT, THE(1968); LOVE BUG, THE(1968); $1,000,000 DUCK(1971); SNOWBALL EXPRESS(1972); MR. SUPERINVISIBLE(1974, Ital./Span./Ger.); SHAGGY D.A., THE(1976); HERBIE GOES TO MONTE CARLO(1977); BORN AGAIN(1978)

Debbie Jones

Misc. Talkies

KAHUNA!(1981)

Deborah Jones

CONRACK(1974)

Dennis Jones

GIRLS ON THE BEACH(1965)

Derrick Jones

SPRING FEVER(1983, Can.)

Diana Jones

WILD RIDERS(1971)

Dick Jones

ANGEL ON THE AMAZON(1948); STRAWBERRY ROAN, THE(1948); SANDS OF IWO JIMA(1949); SONS OF NEW MEXICO(1949); MILITARY ACADEMY WITH THAT TENTH AVENUE GANG(1950); REDWOOD FOREST TRAIL(1950); ROCKY MOUNTAIN(1950); OLD WEST, THE(1952); WAGON TEAM(1952); LAST OF THE PONY RIDERS(1953); BAMBOO PRISON, THE(1955); WILD DAKOTAS, THE(1956); COOL AND THE CRAZY, THE(1958); DEVIL'S BEDROOM, THE(1964); HOW TO STUFF A WILD BIKINI(1965); REQUIEM FOR A GUNFIGHTER(1965)

1984

TREASURE OF THE YANKEE ZEPHYR(1984)

Dickie Jones

FIFTEEN WIVES(1934); LITTLE MEN(1935); STRANGE WIVES(1935); DANIEL BOONE(1936); MOONLIGHT ON THE PRAIRIE(1936); WESTWARD HO(1936); BLACK LEGION, THE(1937); KID COMES BACK, THE(1937); LOVE IS ON THE AIR(1937); READY, WILLING AND ABLE(1937); RENFREW OF THE ROYAL MOUNTED(1937); SMOKE TREE RANGE(1937); STELLA DALLAS(1937); WILD HORSE ROUND-UP(1937); BORDER WOLVES(1938); DEVIL'S PARTY, THE(1938); FLYING FISTS, THE(1938); FRONTIERSMAN, THE(1938); HOLLYWOOD ROUNDUP(1938); LAND OF FIGHTING MEN(1938); MAN TO REMEMBER, A(1938); DESTRY RIDES AGAIN(1939); I AM NOT AFRAID(1939); MAN WHO DARED, THE(1939); NANCY DREW-REPORTER(1939); SERGEANT MADDEN(1939); SKY PATROL(1939); WOMAN DOCTOR(1939); YOUNG MR. LINCOLN(1939); BRIGHAM YOUNG-FRONTIERSMAN(1940); HI-YO SILVER(1940); HOWARDS OF VIRGINIA, THE(1940); KNUTE ROCKNE-ALL AMERICAN(1940); MARYLAND(1940); PI-

NOCCHIO(1940); VIRGINIA CITY(1940); ADVENTURE IN WASHINGTON(1941); VANISHING VIRGINIAN, THE(1941); MAJOR AND THE MINOR, THE(1942); MOUNTAIN RHYTHM(1942); HEAVEN CAN WAIT(1943); OUTLAW, THE(1943); ADVENTURES OF MARK TWAIN, THE(1944)
Misc. Talkies
HAWK, THE(1935); TRAIL OF THE HAWK(1935)

Dinny Jones
OH! WHAT A LOVELY WAR(1969, Brit.)

Disley Jones
MIKADO, THE(1967, Brit.), set d, cos; LONG DAY'S DYING, THE(1968, Brit.), art d; ITALIAN JOB, THE(1969, Brit.), prod d; REVOLUTIONARY, THE(1970, Brit.), prod d; FRIGHT(1971, Brit.), prod d; MURPHY'S WAR(1971, Brit.), prod d; LEGACY, THE(1979, Brit.), prod d; BEYOND THE FOG(1981, Brit.), art d
1984
KILLING HEAT(1984), prod d

Don Jones
INSIDE AMY(1975), ph; FIRECRACKER(1981), ph; LOVE BUTCHER, THE(1982), d, w, ph; FOREST, THE(1983), a, p&d
Misc. Talkies
SWEATER GIRLS(1978), d

Donald Jones
OUTSIDER IN AMSTERDAM(1983, Neth.)

Doree Jones
1984
EXTERMINATOR 2(1984), set d

Dorothy Jones
THIN ICE(1937); GAY PURR-EE(1962), w

Dorothy L. Jones
KEEP 'EM FLYING(1941)

Duane Jones
NIGHT OF THE LIVING DEAD(1968); GANJA AND HESS(1973)
1984
BEAT STREET(1984)
Misc. Talkies
BLOOD COUPLE(1974); LOSING GROUND(1982)

Dudley Jones
LAST DAYS OF DOLWYN, THE(1949, Brit.); RUN FOR YOUR MONEY, A(1950, Brit.); MANIACS ON WHEELS(1951, Brit.); MEN ARE CHILDREN TWICE(1953, Brit.); ON HER MAJESTY'S SECRET SERVICE(1969, Brit.); VIRGIN SOLDIERS, THE(1970, Brit.); UNDER MILK WOOD(1973, Brit.)

Mrs. E. Jones
Silents
GREED(1925)

E. Rodney Jones
MAHOGANY(1975)

Ed Jones
BIG BROWN EYES(1936)
Misc. Silents
WOMAN'S FOOL, A(1918); SUNDOWN SLIM(1920)

Ed "Too Tall" Jones
THE DOUBLE McGUFFIN(1979)

Eddie Jones
BLOODBROTHERS(1978); ON THE YARD(1978); PRINCE OF THE CITY(1981); Q(1982); TRADING PLACES(1983)
1984
C.H.U.D.(1984)

Edgar Jones
Silents
DIMPLES(1916), d; GIRL WHO WOULDN'T QUIT, THE(1918), d; WILD HONEY(1919); BIG PUNCH, THE(1921)
Misc. Silents
NOTHING TO BE DONE(1914), d; COURAGE AND THE MAN(1915), a, d; ENEMY TO SOCIETY, AN(1915), d; ON BITTER CREEK(1915), a, d; WOMAN PAYS, THE(1915), d; HALF MILLION BRIBE, THE(1916), d; LOVELY MARY(1916), d; TURMOIL, THE(1916), d; GIRL ANGLE, THE(1917), d; LADY IN THE LIBRARY, THE(1917), d; MENTIONED IN CONFIDENCE(1917), d; RICH MAN'S DAUGHTER, A(1918), d; WILD WOMEN(1918); WHEN QUACKEL DID HYDE(1920); LONESOME CORNERS(1922), a, d

Edmund Jones
AFTER THE FOG(1930)

Edna Mae Jones
STUDENT TOUR(1934); GEORGE WHITE'S 1935 SCANDALS(1935); TEN GENTLEMEN FROM WEST POINT(1942); LADIES OF WASHINGTON(1944); NOB HILL(1945)

Edna May Jones
GEORGE WHITE'S SCANDALS(1934)

Edward Jones
SEMI-TOUGH(1977)
Misc. Silents
.45 CALIBRE WAR(1929)

Eleanor Jones
CURSE OF THE FLY(1965, Brit.), makeup

Eliot Jones
THANKS FOR LISTENING(1937)

Elizabeth Jones
LADY BY CHOICE(1934); YOUNG MR. LINCOLN(1939); QUIET MAN, THE(1952)

Elizabeth "Tiny" Jones
DRUMS ALONG THE MOHAWK(1939)

Eluned Jones
1984
YR ALCOHOLIG LION(1984, Brit.)

Elvin Jones
ZACHARIAH(1971)

Emma Jones
Misc. Talkies
BODY BENEATH, THE(1970)

Emrys Jones
ONE OF OUR AIRCRAFT IS MISSING(1942, Brit.); SHIPBUILDERS, THE(1943, Brit.); GIVE ME THE STARS(1944, Brit.); NOTORIOUS GENTLEMAN(1945, Brit.); WICKED LADY, THE(1946, Brit.); HOLIDAY CAMP(1947, Brit.); NICHOLAS NICKLEBY(1947, Brit.); BLUE SCAR(1949, Brit.); DARK SECRET(1949, Brit.); HOUR OF

GLORY(1949, Brit.); THIS WAS A WOMAN(1949, Brit.); MISS PILGRIM'S PROGRESS(1950, Brit.); DEADLY NIGHTSHADE(1953, Brit.); SHIELD OF FAITH, THE(1956, Brit.); MAN WITH THE GREEN CARNATION, THE(1960, Brit.); TICKET TO PARADISE(1961, Brit.); SERENA(1962, Brit.); ON THE RUN(1967, Brit.)

Eric Jones
CLAUDINE(1974)

Evan Jones
EVA(1962, Fr./Ital.), w; KING AND COUNTRY(1964, Brit.), w; THESE ARE THE DAMNED(1965, Brit.), w; FUNERAL IN BERLIN(1966, Brit.), w; MODESTY BLAISE(1966, Brit.), w; TWO GENTLEMEN SHARING(1969, Brit.), w; OUTBACK(1971, Aus.), w; NIGHT WATCH(1973, Brit.), w; VICTORY(1981), w; FOREST, THE(1983), w; KILLING OF ANGEL STREET, THE(1983, Aus.), w
1984
CHAMPIONS(1984), w

F. Richard Jones
BULLDOG DRUMMOND(1929), p, d
Silents
MICKEY(1919), d; FLYING PAT(1920), d; MOLLY O'(1921), d; SUZANNA(1922), d; EXTRA GIRL, THE(1923), d; NO MAN'S LAW(1927), w; GAUCHO, THE(1928), d
Misc. Silents
LOVE, HONOR AND BEHAVE(1920), d; GHOST IN THE GARRET, THE(1921), d; OH, JO!(1921), d; COUNTRY FLAPPER, THE(1922), d; CROSSROADS OF NEW YORK, THE(1922), d; SHRIEK OF ARABY, THE(1923), d; BIG KILLING, THE(1928), d; SOMEONE TO LOVE(1928), d; WATER HOLE, THE(1928), d

Fenton Jones
SQUARE DANCE KATY(1950); SLAUGHTER TRAIL(1951); ONE-EYED JACKS(1961)

Frank Jones
Misc. Talkies
LISA(1977)

Fred Jones
DONOVAN'S REEF(1963); ON THE YARD(1978)
Silents
GIRL WITHOUT A SOUL, THE(1917); HER FIGHTING CHANCE(1917); ABABIAN KNIGHT, AN(1920)
Misc. Silents
SUCCESSFUL ADVENTURE, THE(1918)

Fred C. Jones
Misc. Silents
GOD'S COUNTRY AND THE LAW(1921); MAN WHO PAID, THE(1922); UNCONQUERED WOMAN(1922); WHY NOT MARRY?(1922); DON QUICKSHOT OF THE RIO GRANDE(1923)

Fred F. Jones
Silents
INFIDELITY(1917)

Fred T. Jones
Misc. Silents
QUEEN OF THE MOULIN ROUGE(1922)

Freda Jones
TATTERED DRESS, THE(1957)

Freddie Jones
ACCIDENT(1967, Brit.); FAR FROM THE MADDING CROWD(1967, Brit.); PERSECUTION AND ASSASSINATION OF JEAN-PAUL MARAT AS PERFORMED BY THE INMATES OF THE ASYLUM OF CHARENTON UNDER THE DIRECTION OF THE MARQUIS DE SADE, THE(1967, Brit.); BLISS OF MRS. BLOSSOM, THE(1968, Brit.); FRANKENSTEIN MUST BE DESTROYED!(1969, Brit.); DOCTOR IN TROUBLE(1970, Brit.); GOODBYE GEMINI(1970, Brit.); MAN WHO HAUNTED HIMSELF, THE(1970, Brit.); ASSAULT(1971, Brit.); KIDNAPPED(1971, Brit.); SITTING TARGET(1972, Brit.); ANTONY AND CLEOPATRA(1973, Brit.); JUGGERNAUT(1974, Brit.); SON OF DRACULA(1974, Brit.); ALL CREATURES GREAT AND SMALL(1975, Brit.); OLD DRACULA(1975, Brit.); COUNT DRACULA AND HIS VAMPIRE BRIDE(1978, Brit.); ELEPHANT MAN, THE(1980, Brit.); ZULU DAWN(1980, Brit.); FIREFOX(1982); AND THE SHIP SAILS ON(1983, Ital./Fr.); KRULL(1983)
1984
DUNE(1984); FIRESTARTER(1984)

Freddy Jones
OTLEY(1969, Brit.)

Frederick Jones
Misc. Silents
LOVE'S LAW(1918)

G. Stanley Jones
HITLER(1962); CRAWLING HAND, THE(1963)

Garth Jones
CHARRIOTS OF FIRE(1981, Brit.)

Gary Jones
DRESSED TO KILL(1980), cos

Gemma Jones
Misc. Talkies
DEVILS, THE(1971)

Geoffrey Jones
RED AND THE BLACK, THE(1954, Fr./Ital.), titles

George Jones
FORTY ACRE FEUD(1965); FROM NASHVILLE WITH MUSIC(1969); LONGEST YARD, THE(1974)

George Washington Jones
Silents
STRUGGLE, THE(1921)

Gillian Jones
FIGHTING BACK(1983, Brit.); HEATWAVE(1983, Aus.)

Glenn-Michael Jones
STRIPES(1981)

Glenna Forster Jones
LEO THE LAST(1970, Brit.); FLASH GORDON(1980)

Gloria Jones
LA DOLCE VITA(1961, Ital./Fr.)

Glyn Jones
VERDICT, THE(1964, Brit.)

Glynn Jones
RETURN OF THE JEDI(1983)
Gomer Jones
BIG GAME, THE(1936)
Gordon Jones
MONKEY'S PAW, THE(1933); LET 'EM HAVE IT(1935); RED SALUTE(1935); DEVIL'S SQUADRON(1936); DON'T TURN'EM LOOSE(1936); NIGHT WAITRESS(1936); STRIKE ME PINK(1936); WALKING ON AIR(1936); BIG SHOT, THE(1937); CHINA PASSAGE(1937); FIGHT FOR YOUR LADY(1937); FORLORN RIVER(1937); SEA DEVILS(1937); THERE GOES MY GIRL(1937); THEY WANTED TO MARRY(1937); WE WHO ARE ABOUT TO DIE(1937); I STAND ACCUSED(1938); NIGHT SPOT(1938); OUT WEST WITH THE HARDYS(1938); QUICK MONEY(1938); RICH MAN, POOR GIRL(1938); DISPUTED PASSAGE(1939); HENRY GOES ARIZONA(1939); INVITATION TO HAPPINESS(1939); LONG SHOT, THE(1939); PRIDE OF THE NAVY(1939); WHEN TOMORROW COMES(1939); DOCTOR TAKES A WIFE(1940); GIRL FROM HAVANA(1940); I TAKE THIS OATH(1940); TEXAS RANGERS RIDE AGAIN(1940); UP IN THE AIR(1940); AMONG THE LIVING(1941); BLONDE FROM SINGAPORE, THE(1941); FEMININE TOUCH, THE(1941); YOU BELONG TO ME(1941); FLYING TIGERS(1942); HIGHWAYS BY NIGHT(1942); MY SISTER EILEEN(1942); THEY ALL KISSED THE BRIDE(1942); TO THE SHORES OF TRIPOLI(1942); TRUE TO THE ARMY(1942); YOUTH RUNS WILD(1944); SECRET LIFE OF WALTER MITTY, THE(1947); WISTFUL WIDOW OF WAGON GAP, THE(1947); BLACK EAGLE(1948); FOREIGN AFFAIR, A(1948); SONS OF ADVENTURE(1948); UNTAMED BREED, THE(1948); BLACK MIDNIGHT(1949); DEAR WIFE(1949); EASY LIVING(1949); MR. SOFT TOUCH(1949); TAKE ME OUT TO THE BALL GAME(1949); TOKYO JOE(1949); ARIZONA COWBOY, THE(1950); BELLE OF OLD MEXICO(1950); BIG TIMBER(1950); BODYHOLD(1950); NORTH OF THE GREAT DIVIDE(1950); PALOMINO, THE(1950); SUNSET IN THE WEST(1950); TRAIL OF ROBIN HOOD(1950); TRIGGER, JR.(1950); CORKY OF GASOLINE ALLEY(1951); HEART OF THE ROCKIES(1951); SPOILERS OF THE PLAINS(1951); YELLOW FIN(1951); GOBS AND GALS(1952); MARRYING KIND, THE(1952); SOUND OFF(1952); WAGON TEAM(1952); WINNING TEAM, THE(1952); ISLAND IN THE SKY(1953); WOMAN THEY ALMOST LYNCHED, THE(1953); OUTLAW STALLION, THE(1954); SMOKE SIGNAL(1955); TREASURE OF RUBY HILLS(1955); MONSTER THAT CHALLENGED THE WORLD, THE(1957); SHOOT-OUT AT MEDICINE BEND(1957); SPRING REUNION(1957); LIVE FAST, DIE YOUNG(1958); PERFECT FURLOUGH, THE(1958); BATTLE CRY(1959); SHAGGY DOG, THE(1959); RISE AND FALL OF LEGS DIAMOND, THE(1960); EVERYTHING'S DUCKY(1961); MC LINTOCK!(1963); SON OF FLUBBER(1963)
Grace Jones
GORDON'S WAR(1973)
1984
CONAN THE DESTROYER(1984)
Grandpa Jones
COUNTRY BOY(1966)
Gregory Jones
1984
CHAMPIONS(1984); FLASH OF GREEN, A(1984)
Griffith Jones
MONEY TALKS(1933, Brit.); CATHERINE THE GREAT(1934, Brit.); LEAVE IT TO BLANCHE(1934, Brit.); ESCAPE ME NEVER(1935, Brit.); FIRST A GIRL(1935, Brit.); WIFE OF GENERAL LING, THE(1938, Brit.); YANK AT OXFORD, A(1938); MILL ON THE FLOSS(1939, Brit.); FACE BEHIND THE SCAR(1940, Brit.); SECRET FOUR, THE(1940, Brit.); ATLANTIC FERRY(1941, Brit.); THIS WAS PARIS(1942, Brit.); YOUNG MAN'S FANCY(1943, Brit.); UNCENSORED(1944, Brit.); NOTORIOUS GENTLEMAN(1945, Brit.); HENRY V(1946, Brit.); WICKED LADY, THE(1946, Brit.); I BECAME A CRIMINAL(1947); LOOK BEFORE YOU LOVE(1948, Brit.); MIRANDA(1949, Brit.); ONCE UPON A DREAM(1949, Brit.); GOOD TIME GIRL(1950, Brit.); HONEYMOON DEFERRED(1951, Brit.); SCARLET WEB, THE(1954, Brit.); STAR OF MY NIGHT(1954, Brit.); SEA SHALL NOT HAVE THEM, THE(1955, Brit.); ACCOUNT RENDERED(1957, Brit.); NOT WANTED ON VOYAGE(1957, Brit.); KILL HER GENTLY(1958, Brit.); MENACE IN THE NIGHT(1958, Brit.); TRUTH ABOUT WOMEN, THE(1958, Brit.); CROWNING TOUCH, THE(1959, Brit.); HIDDEN HOMICIDE(1959, Brit.); STRANGLER'S WEB(1966, Brit.); DECLINE AND FALL... OF A BIRD WATCHER(1969, Brit.)
Grover Jones
MIGHTY, THE(1929), w; VIRGINIAN, THE(1929), w; BURNING UP(1930), w; DANGEROUS PARADISE(1930), w; DERELICT(1930), w; LIGHT OF WESTERN STARS, THE(1930), w; LOVE AMONG THE MILLIONAIRES(1930), w; TOM SAWYER(1930), w; YOUNG EAGLES(1930), w; CONQUERING HORDE, THE(1931), w; DUDE RANCH(1931), w; GUN SMOKE(1931), w; HUCKLEBERRY FINN(1931), w; RICH MAN'S FOLLY(1931), w; TOUCHDOWN!(1931), w; BROKEN WING, THE(1932), w; IF I HAD A MILLION(1932), w; LADY AND GENT(1932), w; SKY BRIDE(1932), w; STRANGERS IN LOVE(1932), w; TROUBLE IN PARADISE(1932), w; HELL AND HIGH WATER(1933), d, w; ONE SUNDAY AFTERNOON(1933), w; LIMEHOUSE BLUES(1934), w; YOU BELONG TO ME(1934), w; ANNAPOLIS FAREWELL(1935), w; BEHOLD MY WIFE(1935), w; LIVES OF A BENGAL LANCER(1935), w; ONE-WAY TICKET(1935), w; MILKY WAY, THE(1936), w; TRAIL OF THE LONESOME PINE, THE(1936), w; PLAINSMAN, THE(1937), w; SOULS AT SEA(1937), p, w; 52ND STREET(1937), w; CAPTAIN FURY(1939), w; LUCKY NIGHT(1939), w; UNDER-PUP, THE(1939), w; UNMARRIED(1939), w; CAPTAIN CAUTION(1940), w; DARK COMMAND, THE(1940), w; LITTLE BIT OF HEAVEN, A(1940), w; ONE MILLION B.C.(1940), w; SON OF THE NAVY(1940), w; GIRL, A GUY AND A GOB, A(1941), w; SHEPHERD OF THE HILLS, THE(1941), w; KID FROM BOOKLYN, THE(1946), w
Silents
UNKNOWN, THE(1921), d; PUTTING IT OVER(1922), d&w; TAKING CHANCES(1922), d; SPEED KING(1923), d; EASY GOING GORDON(1925), w; GOAT GETTER(1925), w; GOING THE LIMIT(1925), w; DOUBLING WITH DANGER(1926), w; SPEED COP(1926), w; SPEED CRAZED(1926), w; SHE'S A SHEIK(1927), w; WEDDING BILL$(1927), w; HOT NEWS(1928), w; PARTNERS IN CRIME(1928), w; WHAT A NIGHT!(1928), w; WIFE SAVERS(1928), w
Misc. Silents
SLOW AS LIGHTING(1923), d; GENTLEMAN ROUGHNECK, A(1925), d; HEIRLOONS(1925), d; THRILLING YOUTH(1926), d; UNKNOWN DANGERS(1926), d; GOD OF MANKIND(1928), d
Guy Jones
KATHLEEN(1938, Ireland), a, md; HUMAN MONSTER, THE(1940, Brit.), m; LUCK OF THE IRISH(1948), w; MR. PEABODY AND THE MERMAID(1948), w

1984
BIRDY(1984)
Gwendolyn Jones
PRINCE AND THE PAUPER, THE(1937)
Gwyneth Jones
WAGNER(1983, Brit./Hung./Aust.)
Hal Jones
SPLINTERS(1929, Brit.); SPLINTERS IN THE NAVY(1931, Brit.)
Hank Jones
VILLAGE OF THE GIANTS(1965); YOUNG WARRIORS, THE(1967); TORA! TORA! TORA!(1970, U.S./Jap.); $1,000,000 DUCK(1971); HERBIE RIDES AGAIN(1974); SHAGGY D.A., THE(1976); CAT FROM OUTER SPACE, THE(1978)
Hannah Jones
BLACKMAIL(1929, Brit.); THOSE WHO LOVE(1929, Brit.); MURDER(1930, Brit.); PICCADILLY(1932, Brit.); RICH AND STRANGE(1932, Brit.); COMMISSIONAIRE(1933, Brit.)
Silents
WHEN BOYS LEAVE HOME(1928, Brit.)
Harmon Jones
HOME IN INDIANA(1944), ed; IRISH EYES ARE SMILING(1944), ed; COLONEL EFFINGHAM'S RAID(1945), ed; HOUSE ON 92ND STREET, THE(1945), ed; NOB HILL(1945), ed; SHOCK(1946), ed; 13 RUE MADELEINE(1946), ed; BOOMERANG(1947), ed; GENTLEMAN'S AGREEMENT(1947), ed; CRY OF THE CITY(1948), ed; SCUDDA-HOO! SCUDDA-HAY!(1948), ed; SITTING PRETTY(1948), ed; YELLOW SKY(1948), ed; HOUSE OF STRANGERS(1949), ed; MR. BELVEDERE GOES TO COLLEGE(1949), ed; PINKY(1949), ed; MOTHER DIDN'T TELL ME(1950), ed; PANIC IN THE STREETS(1950), ed; STELLA(1950), ed; TICKET TO TOMAHAWK(1950), ed; AS YOUNG AS YOU FEEL(1951), d; BLOODHOUNDS OF BROADWAY(1952), d; PRIDE OF ST. LOUIS, THE(1952), d; CITY OF BAD MEN(1953), d; KID FROM LEFT FIELD, THE(1953), d; SILVER WHIP, THE(1953), d; GORILLA AT LARGE(1954), d; PRINCESS OF THE NILE(1954), d; TARGET ZERO(1955), d; CANYON RIVER(1956), d; DAY OF FURY, A(1956), d; BULLWHIP(1958), d; WOLF LARSEN(1958), d; DON'T WORRY, WE'LL THINK OF A TITLE(1966), d
Harmon C. Jones
BEAST OF BUDAPEST, THE(1958), d
Harold Jones
LEADBELLY(1976), stunts; I'M DANCING AS FAST AS I CAN(1982); UNDER FIRE(1983)
Harold Wayne Jones
THE CRAZIES(1973); KNIGHTRIDERS(1981)
Harry Jones
BROTHERLY LOVE(1970, Brit.); CLASH OF THE TITANS(1981); TRENCHCOAT(1983)
1984
SWORD OF THE VALIANT(1984, Brit.)
Silents
GOLD RUSH, THE(1925); SOFT CUSHIONS(1927)
Harry O. Jones
RETURN OF CASEY JONES(1933), w
Harry O. Jones [Harry Fraser]
FUGITIVE, THE(1933), d&w; GALLANT FOOL, THE(1933), w; GALLOPING ROMEO(1933), w; RAINBOW RANCH(1933), w; RANGER'S CODE, THE(1933), w
Hayden Jones
SOMEWHERE IN TIME(1980)
Haywood Jones
DOCKS OF NEW ORLEANS(1948)
Hazel Jones
MAMBA(1930); STRICTLY PERSONAL(1933)
Silents
IS YOUR DAUGHTER SAFE?(1927)
Henry Jones
3:10 TO YUMA(1957); THIS IS THE ARMY(1943); LADY SAYS NO, THE(1951); TAXI(1953); BAD SEED, THE(1956); GIRL CAN'T HELP IT, THE(1956); GIRL HE LEFT BEHIND, THE(1956); WILL SUCCESS SPOIL ROCK HUNTER?(1957); VERTIGO(1958); BRAMBLE BUSH, THE(1960); CASH McCALL(1960); ANGEL BABY(1961); NEVER TOO LATE(1965); CHAMPAGNE MURDERS, THE(1968, Fr.); PROJECT X(1968); STAY AWAY, JOE(1968); ANGEL IN MY POCKET(1969); BUTCH CASSIDY AND THE SUNDANCE KID(1969); RASCAL(1969); SUPPORT YOUR LOCAL SHERIFF(1969); COCKEYED COWBOYS OF CALICO COUNTY, THE(1970); DIRTY DINGUS MAGEE(1970); RABBIT, RUN(1970); SKIN GAME(1971); SUPPORT YOUR LOCAL GUNFIGHTER(1971); NAPOLEON AND SAMANTHA(1972); PETE 'N' TILLIE(1972); OUTFIT, THE(1973); TOM SAWYER(1973); NINE TO FIVE(1980); DEATHTRAP(1982)
Henry Arthur Jones
MRS. DANE'S DEFENCE(1933, Brit.), w
Silents
MASQUERADERS, THE(1915), w; CALL OF YOUTH, THE(1920, Brit.), w; BEYOND(1921), w; PHYSICIAN, THE(1928, Brit.), w
Herb Jones
IRMA LA DOUCE(1963); LEGEND OF BOGGY CREEK, THE(1973)
Herbert Jones
MAVERICK QUEEN, THE(1956)
Howard Jones
MAYBE IT'S LOVE(1930); TOUCHDOWN!(1931); KNUTE ROCKNE–ALL AMERICAN(1940)
Ian Jones
NED KELLY(1970, Brit.), w
Ike Jones
KID FROM LEFT FIELD, THE(1953); PRISONER OF WAR(1954); TARZAN'S HIDDEN JUNGLE(1955); SOMETHING OF VALUE(1957); THIS REBEL BREED(1960); WILD SEED(1965), w; MAN CALLED ADAM, A(1966), p
Iris Jones
UNDER MILK WOOD(1973, Brit.)
Isaac Jones
JOE LOUIS STORY, THE(1953); ABOUT MRS. LESLIE(1954)
Isaac L. Jones
RIVER NIGER, THE(1976), p

Isabelle Jones
LOST LAGOON(1958)
Issac Jones
ANNA LUCASTA(1958)
Ivy Jones
RIDE IN A PINK CAR(1974, Can.)
J.B. Jones
THUNDER AND LIGHTNING(1977), spec eff
J. Bill Jones
METALSTORM: THE DESTRUCTION OF JARED-SYN(1983)
J. Parke Jones
Silents
ARAB, THE(1915)
J. Parkes Jones
Silents
SALVATION JANE(1927)
J. Parks Jones
Silents
ALIEN SOULS(1916); OLD WIVES FOR NEW(1918); FAITH(1920)
Misc. Silents
EVIL EYE, THE(1917); INTRUSION OF ISABEL, THE(1919); LITTLE SHEPARD OF KINGDOM COME, THE(1920)
J. Paul Jones
BACHELOR MOTHER(1933); LUCKY DEVILS(1941)
J. W. Jones
Silents
WILD AND WOOLLY(1917)
Jack Jones
DAWN RIDER(1935); PROUD VALLEY, THE(1941, Brit.), a, w; HALF-WAY HOUSE, THE(1945, Brit.); JUKE BOX RHYTHM(1959); AIRPLANE II: THE SEQUEL(1982); COMEBACK, THE(1982, Brit.)
Jacqueline Jones
FOURTH SQUARE, THE(1961, Brit.); MATTER OF WHO, A(1962, Brit.); ROAD TO HONG KONG, THE(1962, U.S./Brit.); COOL MIKADO, THE(1963, Brit.); JUNGLE STREET GIRLS(1963, Brit.); IN THE DOGHOUSE(1964, Brit.); SPYLARKS(1965, Brit.); BEAUTY JUNGLE, THE(1966, Brit.); INCIDENT AT MIDNIGHT(1966, Brit.)
James Jones
ROSE BOWL(1936); FROM HERE TO ETERNITY(1953), a, w, m/l; SOME CAME RUNNING(1959), w; LONGEST DAY, THE(1962), w; THIN RED LINE, THE(1964), w; DESTRUCTORS, THE(1974, Brit.)
James B. Jones
Misc. Talkies
BLOOD OF JESUS(1941)
James Cellan Jones
NELSON AFFAIR, THE(1973, Brit.), d
James Earl Jones
DR. STRANGELOVE: OR HOW I LEARNED TO STOP WORRYING AND LOVE THE BOMB(1964); COMEDIANS, THE(1967); GREAT WHITE HOPE, THE(1970); MAN, THE(1972); CLAUDINE(1974); BINGO LONG TRAVELING ALL-STARS AND MOTOR KINGS, THE(1976); DEADLY HERO(1976); RIVER NIGER, THE(1976); SWASHBUCKLER(1976); EXORCIST II: THE HERETIC(1977); GREATEST, THE(1977, U.S./Brit.); LAST REMAKE OF BEAU GESTE, THE(1977); PIECE OF THE ACTION, A(1977); BLOOD TIDE(1982); BUSHIDO BLADE, THE(1982 Brit./U.S.); CONAN THE BARBARIAN(1982); RETURN OF THE JEDI(1983)
Jan Jones
Misc. Talkies
POLK COUNTY POT PLANE(1977)
Jane Jones
SLAVE SHIP(1937); ALEXANDER'S RAGTIME BAND(1938); PORT OF MISSING GIRLS(1938); EAST SIDE OF HEAVEN(1939); NOB HILL(1945); NIGHT SONG(1947); PRIZE FIGHTER, THE(1979), cos
Misc. Talkies
PORT OF MISSING GIRLS(1938)
Janet Jones
1984
FLAMINGO KID, THE(1984)
January Jones
DON'T WORRY, WE'LL THINK OF A TITLE(1966)
Jay D. Jones
WEDDING, A(1978)
Jeffrey Jones
WEDDING, A(1978); SOLDIER, THE(1982); EASY MONEY(1983)
1984
AMADEUS(1984)
Jennifer Jones
SONG OF BERNADETTE, THE(1943); SINCE YOU WENT AWAY(1944); LOVE LETTERS(1945); CLUNY BROWN(1946); DUEL IN THE SUN(1946); MADAME BOVARY(1949); PORTRAIT OF JENNIE(1949); WE WERE STRANGERS(1949); CARRIE(1952); RUBY GENTRY(1952); WILD HEART, THE(1952, Brit.); BEAT THE DEVIL(1953); INDISCRETION OF AN AMERICAN WIFE(1954, U.S./Ital.); GOOD MORNING, MISS DOVE(1955); LOVE IS A MANY-SPLENDORED THING(1955); MAN IN THE GREY FLANNEL SUIT, THE(1956); BARRETTS OF WIMPOLE STREET, THE(1957); FAREWELL TO ARMS, A(1957); TENDER IS THE NIGHT(1961); IDOL, THE(1966, Brit.); ANGEL, ANGEL, DOWN WE GO(1969); TOWERING INFERNO, THE(1974)
Jenny Jones
FRONT PAGE STORY(1954, Brit.); INSPECTOR CALLS, AN(1954, Brit.); DEVIL'S DISCIPLE, THE(1959)
Misc. Talkies
CARRINGTON SCHOOL MYSTERY, THE(1958, Brit.)
Jeremy Jones
QUACKSER FORTUNE HAS A COUSIN IN THE BRONX(1970); UNDERGROUND(1970, Brit.)
Jerry Jones
M(1970); TOP OF THE HEAP(1972); HIT(1973); LONG GOODBYE, THE(1973); DOLEMITE(1975), a, w; HUMAN TORNADO, THE(1976), a, w; TENDER MERCIES(1982)

Jill Jones
1984
PURPLE RAIN(1984)
Jim W. Jones
1984
BREAKIN' 2: ELECTRIC BOOGALOO(1984); LOVE STREAMS(1984)
Joanna Jones
NURSE ON WHEELS(1964, Brit.), w; TWO FOR THE ROAD(1967, Brit.)
Jocelyn Jones
OTHER SIDE OF THE MOUNTAIN, THE(1975); GREAT TEXAS DYNAMITE CHASE, THE(1976); TOURIST TRAP, THE(1979)
John Glyn Jones
CONVOY(1940); THEY CAME BY NIGHT(1940, Brit.); THREE COCKEYED SAILORS(1940, Brit.); MEN ARE CHILDREN TWICE(1953, Brit.); VALUE FOR MONEY(1957, Brit.); ADVENTURES OF HAL 5, THE(1958, Brit.); MAN IN A COCKED HAT(1960, Bri.); SMOKESCREEN(1964, Brit.); DARK PLACES(1974, Brit.)
John Glynn Jones
HEART OF A CHILD(1958, Brit.)
John Glynne Jones
GUTTER GIRLS(1964, Brit.); DECLINE AND FALL... OF A BIRD WATCHER(1969, Brit.)
John Jones
INBETWEEN AGE, THE(1958, Brit.), art d; HAVING A WILD WEEKEND(1965, Brit.); NIGHT OF THE WITCHES(1970); GARDEN OF THE DEAD(1972), w
1984
COUNTRY(1984)
John Paul Jones
PAROLE GIRL(1933)
1984
SCREAM FOR HELP(1984), m
John Pierce Jones
MOUSE AND THE WOMAN, THE(1981, Brit.); WICKED LADY, THE(1983, Brit.)
John R. Jones
ISLAND OF ALLAH(1956)
John Randolph Jones
ARRANGEMENT, THE(1969); THREE DAYS OF THE CONDOR(1975); EYES OF LAURA MARS(1978); TRADING PLACES(1983)
John Turner Jones II
1984
BRADY'S ESCAPE(1984, U.S./Hung.)
Johnny Jones
Silents
NIGHT LIFE IN HOLLYWOOD(1922)
Jon Jones
RED RUNS THE RIVER(1963)
Jona Jones
KEEP, THE(1983)
Jonah Jones
COLONEL MARCH INVESTIGATES(1952,Brit.), ph; LIMPING MAN, THE(1953, Brit.), ph; CHILDREN GALORE(1954, Brit.), ph; DELAVINE AFFAIR, THE(1954, Brit.), ph; EMBEZZLER, THE(1954, Brit.), ph; FINAL APPOINTMENT(1954, Brit.), ph; IMPULSE(1955, Brit.), ph; MASTER PLAN, THE(1955, Brit.), ph; NARROWING CIRCLE, THE(1956, Brit.), ph
Joy Jones
1984
INITIATION, THE(1984)
Juan Jones
SUMMERSKIN(1962, Arg.)
July Jones
Misc. Talkies
JUKE JOINT(1947)
Karen Jones
TOWN THAT DREADED SUNDOWN, THE(1977), cos
Kathleen Hazel Jones
Silents
MERCHANT OF VENICE, THE(1916, Brit.)
Kedren Jones
MAKING LOVE(1982)
Ken Jones
INDISCREET(1958), m; TOM THUMB(1958, Brit./U.S.), m; FERRY TO HONG KONG(1959, Brit.), m; ROOM 43(1959, Brit.), m; DENTIST IN THE CHAIR(1960, Brit.), m; FOXHOLE IN CAIRO(1960, Brit.), m; HORROR HOTEL(1960, Brit.), m; TARZAN THE MAGNIFICENT(1960, Brit.), m; GREEN HELMET, THE(1961, Brit.), m; OFFBEAT(1961, Brit.), m; PORTRAIT OF A SINNER(1961, Brit.), m; TWO-WAY STRETCH(1961, Brit.), m, md; NEARLY A NASTY ACCIDENT(1962, Brit.), m; OPERATION SNATCH(1962, Brit.), m, md; TARZAN GOES TO INDIA(1962, U.S./Brit./Switz.), m; GET ON WITH IT(1963, Brit.), m; BRAIN, THE(1965, Ger./Brit.), m; LITTLE ONES, THE(1965, Brit.); BATTLE BENEATH THE EARTH(1968, Brit.), m; UP THE JUNCTION(1968, Brit.), art d; FILE OF THE GOLDEN GOOSE, THE(1969, Brit.); WOMEN IN LOVE(1969, Brit.), art d; MELODY(1971, Brit.); SEVEN MINUTES, THE(1971); CANDIDATE, THE(1972); GUMSHOE(1972, Brit.); KENNY AND CO.(1976); HUMAN FACTOR, THE(1979, Brit.); MURDER BY DECREE(1979, Brit.); PHANTASM(1979); BATTLE BEYOND THE STARS(1980), spec eff; BEYOND THE FOG(1981, Brit.), m; STRANGE INVADERS(1983), spec eff
1984
LOOSE CONNECTIONS(1984, Brit.)
Kenneth Jones
SUMMER STORM(1944); DR. CRIPPEN(1963, Brit.), m, md; LEOPARD IN THE SNOW(1979, Brit./Can.), m
Kenneth B. Jones
BANDIT OF ZHOBE, THE(1959), m
Kenneth K.V. Jones
MAROC 7(1967, Brit.), m
Kenneth V. Jones
HIGH FLIGHT(1957, Brit.), m; HOW TO MURDER A RICH UNCLE(1957, Brit.), m; SEA WIFE(1957, Brit.), m; HORSE'S MOUTH, THE(1958, Brit.), m; INTENT TO KILL(1958, Brit.), m; TANK FORCE(1958, Brit.), m; TEN SECONDS TO HELL(1959), m; FOUR DESPERATE MEN(1960, Brit.), m; JAZZ BOAT(1960, Brit.), m; OSCAR WILDE(1960, Brit.), m; THERE WAS A CROOKED MAN(1962, Brit.), m; CAIRO(1963), m; PSYCHE 59(1964, Brit.), m, md; TOMB OF LIGEIA, THE(1965, Brit.), m, md;

PROJECTED MAN, THE(1967, Brit.), m; WHO SLEW AUNTIE ROO?(1971, U.S./Brit.), m

Kentucky Jones
Misc. Talkies
MANSON MASSACRE, THE(1976), d

Kirk Jones
DRYLANDERS(1963, Can.), ed; PAPERBACK HERO(1973, Can.), ed; I, MAUREEN(1978, Can.), ed; AGENCY(1981, Can.), ed; SPRING FEVER(1983, Can.), ed

Kitty Jones
SHAFT'S BIG SCORE(1972)

L.Q. Jones
ANNAPOLIS STORY, AN(1955); TARGET ZERO(1955); BETWEEN HEAVEN AND HELL(1956); LOVE ME TENDER(1956); SANTIAGO(1956); TOWARD THE UNKNOWN(1956); MEN IN WAR(1957); OPERATION MAD BALL(1957); BUCHANAN RIDES ALONE(1958); NAKED AND THE DEAD, THE(1958); TORPEDO RUN(1958); YOUNG LIONS, THE(1958); BATTLE OF THE CORAL SEA(1959); HOUND-DOG MAN(1959); WARLOCK(1959); CIMARRON(1960); FLAMING STAR(1960); TEN WHO DARED(1960); HELL IS FOR HEROES(1962); RIDE THE HIGH COUNTRY(1962); SHOWDOWN(1963); APACHE RIFLES(1964); DEVIL'S BEDROOM, THE(1964), d; IRON ANGEL(1964); MAJOR DUNDEE(1965); COUNTERFEIT KILLER, THE(1968); HANG'EM HIGH(1968); STAY AWAY, JOE(1968); WILD BUNCH, THE(1969); BALLAD OF CABLE HOGUE, THE(1970); MC MASTERS, THE(1970); BROTHERHOOD OF SATAN, THE(1971), a, p; PAT GARRETT AND BILLY THE KID(1973); BOY AND HIS DOG, A(1975), d&w; WHITE LINE FEVER(1975, Can.); MOTHER, JUGS & SPEED(1976); WINTERHAWK(1976); HUNTING PARTY, THE(1977, Brit.); FAST CHARLIE... THE MOONBEAM RIDER(1979); BEAST WITHIN, THE(1982); MELANIE(1982, Can.); LONE WOLF McQUADE(1983); TIMERIDER(1983)
1984
SACRED GROUND(1984)
Misc. Talkies
PETTY STORY, THE(1974)

Larry Jones
Misc. Talkies
BROTHERHOOD OF DEATH(1976); GREAT CALL OF THE WILD, THE(1976)

Lauren Jones
LIBERATION OF L.B. JONES, THE(1970); CARWASH(1976)

LaVerne Jones
MONSTER FROM THE GREEN HELL(1958)

Len Jones
SEVENTY DEADLY PILLS(1964, Brit.); GYPSY GIRL(1966, Brit.); SPRING AND PORT WINE(1970, Brit.); STRAW DOGS(1971, Brit.)

Lenore Jones
Misc. Silents
LURE OF A WOMAN, THE(1921)

Leon Jones
1984
LONELY GUY, THE(1984)

LeRoi Jones
DUTCHMAN(1966, Brit.), w; FABLE, A(1971), w

Leviticus Jones
Silents
20,000 LEAGUES UNDER THE SEA(1916)

Lewis Jones
OTHELLO(1965, Brit.)

Linda Jones
ADVANCE TO THE REAR(1964)

Linda "Texas" Jones
1984
DUBEAT-E-O(1984)
Misc. Talkies
SUNDOWN RIDER(1933); TREASON(1933); MAN TRAILER, THE(1934)

Lindsey Jones
YOU LIGHT UP MY LIFE(1977)

Lisa Jones
LIFE AND TIMES OF GRIZZLY ADAMS, THE(1974)

Liz Jones
1984
MISSION, THE(1984)

Llewelyn Jones
1984
ADERYN PAPUR(1984, Brit.)

Lloyd Jones
DANGEROUS AGE, A(1960, Can.); THIEVES LIKE US(1974)

Lois Jones
WILD WHEELS(1969)

Lu Anne Jones
WHEN MY BABY SMILES AT ME(1948)

Lucinda Jones
WILD DUCK, THE(1983, Aus.)

Luke Jones
TIMERIDER(1983)

Luther Jones
Misc. Silents
PAIR OF HELLIONS, A(1924)

Lyall Jones
WHO IS KILLING THE GREAT CHEFS OF EUROPE?(1978, US/Ger.)

Mack Jones
INDEPENDENCE DAY(1983)

Macon Jones
WHOM THE GODS DESTROY(1934)

Mal Jones
PORKY'S II: THE NEXT DAY(1983)
1984
WHERE THE BOYS ARE '84(1984)

Malcolm Jones
THUNDER AND LIGHTNING(1977)

Mallory Jones
TOOTSIE(1982)

Marc Edmund Jones
Silents
YOUR WIFE AND MINE(1927), t

Marcia Mae Jones
WAY WE WERE, THE(1973); CHAMP, THE(1931); NIGHT NURSE(1931); GARDEN OF ALLAH, THE(1936); THESE THREE(1936); HEIDI(1937); LADY BEHAVE(1937); LIFE OF EMILE ZOLA, THE(1937); MOUNTAIN JUSTICE(1937); TWO WISE MAIDS(1937); ADVENTURES OF TOM SAWYER, THE(1938); BAREFOOT BOY(1938); MAD ABOUT MUSIC(1938); FIRST LOVE(1939); LITTLE PRINCESS, THE(1939); MEET DR. CHRISTIAN(1939); DR. KILDARE'S STRANGE CASE(1940); HAUNTED HOUSE, THE(1940); TOMBOY(1940); GANG'S ALL HERE(1941); LET'S GO COLLEGIATE(1941); NICE GIRL?(1941); OLD SWIMMIN' HOLE, THE(1941); SECRETS OF A CO-ED(1942); NOBODY'S DARLING(1943); TOP MAN(1943); YOUNGEST PROFESSION, THE(1943); LADY IN THE DEATH HOUSE(1944); NINE GIRLS(1944); SNAFU(1945); STREET CORNER(1948); ARSON, INC.(1949); TROUBLE PREFERRED(1949); TUCSON(1949)
Misc. Talkies
YELLOW HAIRED KID, THE(1952)

Marcie Mae Jones
ANNE OF WINDY POPLARS(1940)

Margot Jones
HAROLD AND MAUDE(1971)

Marianne Jones
SHADOW OF THE HAWK(1976, Can.)

Maribel Jones
1984
SUCCESS IS THE BEST REVENGE(1984, Brit.)

Marilyn Jones
SUPPORT YOUR LOCAL SHERIFF(1969); SCENIC ROUTE, THE(1978); METEOR(1979)

Mark Edmund Jones
SKIN DEEP(1929), w

Mark Jones
MEET SEXTON BLAKE(1944, Brit.); PERSECUTION AND ASSASSINATION OF JEAN-PAUL MARAT AS PERFORMED BY THE INMATES OF THE ASYLUM OF CHARENTON UNDER THE DIRECTION OF THE MARQUIS DE SADE, THE(1967, Brit.); TELL ME LIES(1968, Brit.); CONNECTING ROOMS(1971, Brit.); UNDER MILK WOOD(1973, Brit.); GIRL FROM STARSHIP VENUS, THE(1975, Brit.); MEDUSA TOUCH, THE(1978, Brit.); EMPIRE STRIKES BACK, THE(1980)
1984
DON'T OPEN TILL CHRISTMAS(1984, Brit.)
Misc. Talkies
KEEP IT UP, JACK!(1975)
Silents
WHY WORRY(1923)

Marlin Jones
SILENT RUNNING(1972), spec eff

Marsha Jones
DAUGHTER OF ROSIE O'GRADY, THE(1950); HI-JACKED(1950); CHICAGO CALLING(1951)

Marsha Mae Jones
SPECTRE OF EDGAR ALLAN POE, THE(1974)

Marshall Jones
INDIAN PAINT(1965); CRY OF THE BANSHEE(1970, Brit.); SCREAM AND SCREAM AGAIN(1970, Brit.); MURDERS IN THE RUE MORGUE(1971)

Marvin Jones
MOTHERS CRY(1930); SWEETHEARTS(1938); VIVACIOUS LADY(1938); LET'S GO COLLEGIATE(1941); WAKE ISLAND(1942); WHERE DANGER LIVES(1950); PENITENTIARY II(1982)

Mary Jones
GAY LADY, THE(1949, Brit.); AMERICAN IN PARIS, AN(1951); STEEL KEY, THE(1953, Brit.); HAPPINESS OF THREE WOMEN, THE(1954, Brit.); ONE JUMP AHEAD(1955, Brit.); TIME TO KILL, A(1955, Brit.); NARROWING CIRCLE, THE(1956, Brit.); SCOTLAND YARD DRAGNET(1957, Brit.); PROMISE, THE(1969, Brit.); UNDER MILK WOOD(1973, Brit.)

Mary Kay Jones
OUR HEARTS WERE GROWING UP(1946)

Matthew Jones
THANK YOUR LUCKY STARS(1943)

Maurice Jones
MOUNTAIN, THE(1935, Brit.); MR. PERRIN AND MR. TRAILL(1948, Brit.); MY BROTHER JONATHAN(1949, Brit.); OLIVER TWIST(1951, Brit.)

Max Jones
GOIN' DOWN THE ROAD(1970, Can.)

Melissa Jones
GUARDIAN OF THE WILDERNESS(1977)

Melvin Jones
THING, THE(1982)
1984
SOLDIER'S STORY, A(1984), stunts

Mervyn Jones
CONVOY(1940); SHIELD OF FAITH, THE(1956, Brit.); NO LOVE FOR JOHNNIE(1961, Brit.); JOHN AND MARY(1969), w

Michael Jones
HELL'S BELLES(1969)
1984
NIGHT SHADOWS(1984), w

Michael Steve Jones
WHOSE LIFE IS IT ANYWAY?(1981)

Mick Jones
RUDE BOY(1980, Brit.), m; KING OF COMEDY, THE(1983)

Mickey Jones
TOM HORN(1980); MAKING LOVE(1982); WRONG IS RIGHT(1982); NATIONAL LAMPOON'S VACATION(1983)
1984
STARMAN(1984)

Mike Jones
METALSTORM: THE DESTRUCTION OF JARED-SYN(1983); SPACE RAIDERS(1983), makeup

JULIUS VROODER, THE(1974), ed; COMING HOME(1978), w; HEAVEN CAN WAIT(1978), ed; LOOKIN' TO GET OUT(1982), ed
Robert Earl Jones
WILD RIVER(1960); ONE POTATO, TWO POTATO(1964); PIE IN THE SKY(1964); MISSISSIPPI SUMMER(1971); STING, THE(1973); COLD RIVER(1982); SLEEPAWAY CAMP(1983); TRADING PLACES(1983)
1984
COTTON CLUB, THE(1984)
Robert Edmond Jones
BECKY SHARP(1935), prod d
Robert J. Jones, Jr.
DAMIEN-OMEN II(1978)
Robert Page Jones
THAT MAN GEORGE!(1967, Fr./Ital./Span.), w
Rev. Robert R. Jones
Misc. Silents
UNBEATABLE GAME, THE(1925)
Rod Jones
TEX(1982)
Roger Jones
DEADLY AFFAIR, THE(1967, Brit.)
Roland Jones
GLENN MILLER STORY, THE(1953)
Ronald Jones
UNHOLY ROLLERS(1972)
Rosamund Jones [Rosamund John]
SECRET OF THE LOCH, THE(1934, Brit.)
Roy Jones
SONG OF NORWAY(1970); MACBETH(1971, Brit.); MAN OF LA MANCHA(1972)
Russ Jones
DR. TERROR'S GALLERY OF HORRORS(1967), w
Sabra Jones
NIGHT FLOWERS(1979)
Thomas D. Jones
RAISIN IN THE SUN, A(1961)
"Sach" Jones
SPOOK CHASERS(1957)
Salina Jones
YELLOW HAT, THE(1966, Brit.)
Sam Jones
CALIFORNIA SPLIT(1974), set d; ENTERTAINER, THE(1975), set d; WHITE LINE FEVER(1975, Can.), set d; MR. BILLION(1977), set d; 10(1979)
Sam J. Jones
FLASH GORDON(1980)
Samantha Jones
WAIT UNTIL DARK(1967); WAY WE LIVE NOW, THE(1970); GET TO KNOW YOUR RABBIT(1972)
Samee Lee Jones
WHAT'S THE MATTER WITH HELEN?(1971)
Sebastian Graham Jones
1984
LITTLE DRUMMER GIRL, THE(1984)
Seth Jones
MADMAN(1982)
Shirley Jones
OKLAHOMA(1955); CAROUSEL(1956); APRIL LOVE(1957); BOBBIKINS(1959, Brit.); NEVER STEAL ANYTHING SMALL(1959); ELMER GANTRY(1960); PEPE(1960); TWO RODE TOGETHER(1961); MUSIC MAN, THE(1962); COURTSHIP OF EDDY'S FATHER, THE(1963); TICKLISH AFFAIR, A(1963); BEDTIME STORY(1964); DARK PURPOSE(1964); FLUFFY(1965); SECRET OF MY SUCCESS, THE(1965, Brit.); HAPPY ENDING, THE(1969); CHEYENNE SOCIAL CLUB, THE(1970); BEYOND THE POSEIDON ADVENTURE(1979)
1984
TANK(1984)
Simon Jones
GIRO CITY(1982, Brit.); PRIVATES ON PARADE(1982); MONTY PYTHON'S THE MEANING OF LIFE(1983, Brit.)
1984
PRIVATES ON PARADE(1984, Brit.)
Skip Jones
SECRET OF NIMH, THE(1982), anim
Sonny Jones
FROM NOON TO THREE(1976); SILENT RAGE(1982)
Stan Jones
RIO GRANDE(1950); WHIRLWIND(1951); LAST MUSKETEER, THE(1952); GREAT LOCOMOTIVE CHASE, THE(1956); RAINMAKER, THE(1956); HORSE SOLDIERS, THE(1959); TEN WHO DARED(1960)
Stephanie Jones
ORGY OF THE DEAD(1965)
Steve Jones
BUCK ROGERS IN THE 25TH CENTURY(1979); FOXES(1980); KING OF THE MOUNTAIN(1981); LADIES AND GENTLEMEN, THE FABULOUS STAINS(1982)
Stewart Jones
1984
ADERYN PAPUR(1984, Brit.)
Sue Jones
DEAD MAN'S FLOAT(1980, Aus.)
Susan Jones
JULIA(1977)
Susan Holly Jones
INSIDE LOOKING OUT(1977, Aus.), w
Sylvia Lewis Jones
NIGHT TRAIN TO PARIS(1964, Brit.)
T.C. Jones
PROMISES, PROMISES(1963); THREE NUTS IN SEARCH OF A BOLT(1964); MOVIE STAR, AMERICAN STYLE, OR, LSD I HATE YOU!(1966); HEAD(1968); NAME OF THE GAME IS KILL, THE(1968)

Tamara Jones
1984
NEW YORK NIGHTS(1984)
Terry Jones
AND NOW FOR SOMETHING COMPLETELY DIFFERENT(1972, Brit.), a, w; MONTY PYTHON AND THE HOLY GRAIL(1975, Brit.), a, d, w; JABBERWOCK-Y(1977, Brit.); MONTY PYTHON'S LIFE OF BRIAN(1979, Brit.), a, d, w; MONTY PYTHON'S THE MEANING OF LIFE(1983, Brit.), a, d, w
Terwyn Jones
UNDERGROUND GUERRILLAS(1944, Brit.)
Tex Jones
WAY OF THE WEST, THE(1934); TIMBER TERRORS(1935)
Thad Jones
TELL NO TALES(1939)
Thaddeus Jones
KENTUCKY(1938); LILLIAN RUSSELL(1940); MARYLAND(1940); BRIGHT VICTO-RY(1951)
Thomas Jones
CITY THAT NEVER SLEEPS(1953)
"Tia Juana" Matthew Jones
AM I GUILTY?(1940)
Tiffany Jones
Misc. Talkies
C.B. HUSTLERS(1978)
Tim Jones
GET CRAZY(1983)
1984
UP THE CREEK(1984)
Tiny Jones
MAN FROM BLANKLEY'S, THE(1930); DANTE'S INFERNO(1935); IN PER-SON(1935); STORY OF VERNON AND IRENE CASTLE, THE(1939); MELODY RANCH(1940); SEVENTH VICTIM, THE(1943); NONE BUT THE LONELY HEART(1944); CRACK-UP(1946); HUCKSTERS, THE(1947); NORA PRENTISS(1947); UNCONQUERED(1947); LADY FROM SHANGHAI, THE(1948); YOU GOTTA STAY HAPPY(1948); PROWLER, THE(1951)
Tom Jones
LAST DAYS OF DOLWYN, THE(1949, Brit.); RUN FOR YOUR MONEY, A(1950, Brit.); MOLLY MAGUIRES, THE(1970); HEX(1973)
Tom Lee Jones
LIFE STUDY(1973); ELIZA'S HOROSCOPE(1975, Can.)
Tom [Tommy] Lee Jones
LOVE STORY(1970)
Tommy Lee Jones
JACKSON COUNTY JAIL(1976); ROLLING THUNDER(1977); BETSY, THE(1978); EYES OF LAURA MARS(1978); COAL MINER'S DAUGHTER(1980); BACK ROADS(1981); NATE AND HAYES(1983, U.S./New Zealand)
1984
RIVER RAT, THE(1984)
Tony Jones
HOMEWORK(1982), m
Tony-Llewelyn Jones
PICNIC AT HANGING ROCK(1975, Aus.)
Trefor Jones
OLD ROSES(1935, Brit.); RUNAWAY QUEEN, THE(1935, Brit.); GLAMOROUS NIGHT(1937, Brit.); GREAT MR. HANDEL, THE(1942, Brit.); COMIN' THRU' THE RYE(1947, Brit.); HELLO LONDON(1958, Brit.)
Trevor Jones
ALL OVER THE TOWN(1949, Brit.); HERE WE GO ROUND THE MULBERRY BUSH(1968, Brit.); BROTHERS AND SISTERS(1980, Brit.), m; EXCALIBUR(1981), m; DARK CRYSTAL, THE(1982, Brit.), m; SENDER, THE(1982, Brit.), m; NATE AND HAYES(1983, U.S./New Zealand), m; RETURN OF THE JEDI(1983)
1984
ADERYN PAPUR(1984, Brit.), m; GIVE MY REGARDS TO BROAD STREET(1984, Brit.)
Vanda Jones
PASSENGER, THE(1970, Pol.)
Vernon Jones
Misc. Silents
BARTON MYSTERY, THE(1920, Brit.)
Victor Jones
HOLLOW TRIUMPH(1948)
Volus Jones
GAY PURR-EE(1962), anim; SANTA AND THE THREE BEARS(1970), anim
W.W. Jones
Misc. Silents
MAN FROM NEW YORK, THE(1923)
W. W. Jones
Silents
AMERICA(1924)
Waddy Jones
WOMEN AND BLOODY TERROR(1970)
Walt Jones
ONLY WAY HOME, THE(1972)
Walter Jones
PUTNEY SWOPE(1969); WORLD IS JUST A 'B' MOVIE, THE(1971)
Wharton Jones
Misc. Silents
WHEN A GIRL LOVES(1919)
Whitney Jones
GETAWAY, THE(1972)
Willard Jones
ONE MAN'S WAY(1964), md
Willie Jones
Misc. Talkies
GREAT LESTER BOGGS, THE(1975)
William H. Jones, Jr.
NOCTURNA(1979)

Winfield Jones
Silents
IS YOUR DAUGHTER SAFE?(1927)
Winston Jones
WINK OF AN EYE(1958), d, w, ph; METALSTORM: THE DESTRUCTION OF JARED-SYN(1983)
Z.X. Jones [Kennedy]
HANNIE CALDER(1971, Brit.), w
The Jones Boys
FROM NASHVILLE WITH MUSIC(1969)
Sue Jones-Davies
RADIO ON(1980, Brit./Ger.)
Sue Jones-Davis
MONTY PYTHON'S LIFE OF BRIAN(1979, Brit.)
Betsey Jones-Moreland
CREATURE FROM THE HAUNTED SEA(1961); LAST TYCOON, THE(1976)
Betsy Jones-Moreland
SAGA OF THE VIKING WOMEN AND THEIR VOYAGE TO THE WATERS OF THE GREAT SEA SERPENT, THE(1957); LAST WOMAN ON EARTH, THE(1960); HINDENBURG, THE(1975); JONI(1980)
Peter Jonfield
TIME BANDITS(1981, Brit.); MC VICAR(1982, Brit.); PINK FLOYD–THE WALL(1982, Brit.); REMEMBRANCE(1982, Brit.)
Slosson Bing Jong
CHILD, THE(1977)
Wik Jongsma
LITTLE ARK, THE(1972)
Jonilowicz
WITHOUT A HOME(1939, Pol.), ph
J. Jonilowicz
YIDDLE WITH HIS FIDDLE(1937, Pol.), ph
Yuki Jono
HARBOR LIGHT YOKOHAMA(1970, Jap.)
Beverly Jons
RIDIN' DOWN THE TRAIL(1947); CARSON CITY RAIDERS(1948); FEATHERED SERPENT, THE(1948); MICHAEL O'HALLORAN(1948); GAY AMIGO, THE(1949); GREAT PLANE ROBBERY(1950); WELL, THE(1951)
Fritz Jupther Jonsdorff
STOLEN IDENTITY(1953), art d
Edward Jonsenn
SLEEPING PARTNERS(1930, Brit.), ed
Ben Jonson
VOLPONE(1947, Fr.), w
Lisa Jonson
Misc. Talkies
PAWN, THE(1968)
Ted Jonson
NIGHT OF THE WITCHES(1970), art d
Tod Jonson
MARINE BATTLEGROUND(1966, U.S/S.K.), art d; WILD GYPSIES(1969), set d
Tom Jonson
BRAIN EATERS, THE(1958), m
Arnar Jonsson
OUTLAW: THE SAGE OF GISLI(1982, Iceland)
Bo Jonsson
MONTENEGRO(1981, Brit./Swed.), p, w
Nine-Christine Jonsson
PORT OF CALL(1963, Swed.)
Tage Jonsson
HERE'S YOUR LIFE(1968, Swed.)
Fritz Jonstorff
TALE OF FIVE WOMEN, A(1951, Brit.), art d
Chua Kah Joo
HIGH ROAD TO CHINA(1983)
1984
INDIANA JONES AND THE TEMPLE OF DOOM(1984)
Laszlo Joo
FORBIDDEN RELATIONS(1983, Hung.)
Dominique Joos
TWO FOR THE ROAD(1967, Brit.)
Kathryn Joosten
1984
GRANDVIEW, U.S.A.(1984)
Christine Jope-Slade
BRITANNIA OF BILLINGSGATE(1933, Brit.), w; MAD HATTERS, THE(1935, Brit.), w; FORBIDDEN HEAVEN(1936), w
Gareth Joplin
KING OF BURLESQUE(1936)
Scott Joplin
STING, THE(1973), m; SCOTT JOPLIN(1977), m
Benjamino Joppolo
LES CARABINIERS(1968, Fr./Ital.), w
Samson Jorah
NEVER CRY WOLF(1983)
Jim Jorahan
SATAN NEVER SLEEPS(1962), art d
Richard Jordahl
CAPTURE THAT CAPSULE(1961); STARFIGHTERS, THE(1964); TO THE SHORES OF HELL(1966)
Misc. Talkies
SPY SQUAD(1962)
Helge Jordal
1984
KAMILLA(1984, Norway)
Jordan
JUBILEE(1978, Brit.)
Albert Jordan
PANAMINT'S BAD MAN(1938), ed; ROLL ALONG, COWBOY(1938), ed

Albert A. Jordan
HAWAIIAN BUCKAROO(1938), ed
Angel Jordan
NARCO MEN, THE(1969, Span./Ital.)
Anne Jordan
LUCKIEST GIRL IN THE WORLD, THE(1936), w; NIGHT SPOT(1938), w
Armin Jordan
PARSIFAL(1983, Fr.), a, md
Bert Jordan
DEVIL'S BROTHER, THE(1933), ed; SONS OF THE DESERT(1933), ed; BABES IN TOYLAND(1934), ed; BONNIE SCOTLAND(1935), ed; BOHEMIAN GIRL, THE(1936), ed; OUR RELATIONS(1936), ed; WAY OUT WEST(1937), ed; BLOCKHEADS(1938), ed; SWISS MISS(1938), ed; OF MICE AND MEN(1939), ed; ZENOBIA(1939), ed; CHUMP AT OXFORD, A(1940), ed; TURNABOUT(1940), ed; ALL-AMERICAN CO-ED(1941), ed; BROADWAY LIMITED(1941), ed; ROAD SHOW(1941), ed; ABOUT FACE(1942), ed; DEVIL WITH HITLER, THE(1942), ed; DUDES ARE PRETTY PEOPLE(1942), ed; THAT NAZTY NUISANCE(1943), ed; GAY INTRUDERS, THE(1948), ed; JUNGLE PATROL(1948), ed; LET'S LIVE AGAIN(1948), ed; 711 OCEAN DRIVE(1950), ed
Betty Jordan
Misc. Talkies
HAWK, THE(1935); TRAIL OF THE HAWK(1935)
Bill Jordan
BUDDY HOLLY STORY, THE(1978)
Bob Jordan
MAN IS ARMED, THE(1956)
Bobbi Jordan
MAME(1974)
Bobbie Jordan
YOUNG TOM EDISON(1940)
Bobby Jordan
DEAD END(1937); ANGELS WITH DIRTY FACES(1938); CRIME SCHOOL(1938); MY BILL(1938); REFORMATORY(1938); SLIGHT CASE OF MURDER, A(1938); ANGELS WASH THEIR FACES(1939); DEAD END KIDS ON DRESS PARADE(1939); DUST BE MY DESTINY(1939); HELL'S KITCHEN(1939); OFF THE RECORD(1939); THEY MADE ME A CRIMINAL(1939); BOYS OF THE CITY(1940); GIVE US WINGS(1940); MILITARY ACADEMY(1940); THAT GANG OF MINE(1940); YOU'RE NOT SO TOUGH(1940); BOWERY BLITZKRIEG(1941); FLYING WILD(1941); PRIDE OF THE BOWERY(1941); SPOOKS RUN WILD(1941); LET'S GET TOUGH(1942); MR. WISE GUY(1942); 'NEATH BROOKLYN BRIDGE(1942); SMART ALECKS(1942); CLANCY STREET BOYS(1943); DESTROYER(1943); GHOSTS ON THE LOOSE(1943); JUNIOR ARMY(1943); KEEP 'EM SLUGGING(1943); KID DYNAMITE(1943); BOWERY CHAMPS(1944); BOWERY BOMBSHELL(1946); IN FAST COMPANY(1946); LIVE WIRES(1946); MR. HEX(1946); SPOOK BUSTERS(1946); BOWERY BUCK-AROOS(1947); HARD BOILED MAHONEY(1947); NEWS HOUNDS(1947)
Byers Jordan
SANTA'S CHRISTMAS CIRCUS(1966), p, d
Cecil Jordan
ON THE NICKEL(1980)
Cedric Jordan
MARRIED TOO YOUNG(1962)
Charles Jordan
PLATINUM BLONDE(1931); PENROD AND HIS TWIN BROTHER(1938); UNHOLY PARTNERS(1941); BROADWAY(1942); NATIVE LAND(1942); POLICE BULLETS(1942); CORREGIDOR(1943); HERE COMES KELLY(1943); HONEYMOON LODGE(1943); NEVER A DULL MOMENT(1943); OLD ACQUAINTANCE(1943); SA-RONG GIRL(1943); CHARLIE CHAN IN BLACK MAGIC(1944); EVER SINCE VENUS(1944); OH, WHAT A NIGHT(1944); ESCAPE IN THE FOG(1945); HER LUCKY NIGHT(1945); HOLLYWOOD AND VINE(1945); IDENTITY UNKNOWN(1945); MAN WHO WALKED ALONE, THE(1945); MILDRED PIERCE(1945); MISSING CORPSE, THE(1945); PILLOW TO POST(1945); SCARLET CLUE, THE(1945); CUBAN PE-TE(1946); JANIE GETS MARRIED(1946); JOLSON STORY, THE(1946); MY REPUTA-TION(1946); PARTNERS IN TIME(1946); DEAD RECKONING(1947); DOUBLE LIFE, A(1947); LITTLE MISS BROADWAY(1947); NORA PRENTISS(1947); ROAD TO THE BIG HOUSE(1947); UNFAITHFUL, THE(1947); WILD COUNTRY(1947); 13TH HOUR, THE(1947); MARY LOU(1948); GAL WHO TOOK THE WEST, THE(1949); MISSISSIPPI RHYTHM(1949); PAROLE, INC.(1949); RECKLESS MOMENTS, THE(1949); SHOCK-PROOF(1949); SLIGHTLY FRENCH(1949); WOMAN OF DISTINCTION, A(1950); 711 OCEAN DRIVE(1950); EDGE OF THE CITY(1957); PIE IN THE SKY(1964)
Charlie Jordan
SHADOWS OVER CHINATOWN(1946); SKY DRAGON(1949); STREET OF SIN-NERS(1957)
Chrystine Jordan
STORY OF RUTH, THE(1960)
Constance Jordan
MURDER AT THE VANITIES(1934)
Curtis Jordan
NORSEMAN, THE(1978)
Dennis Jordan
SUNSTRUCK(1973, Aus.)
Desmond Jordan
SILENT ENEMY, THE(1959, Brit.); SUMARINE X-1(1969, Brit.)
Donna Jordan
L'AMOUR(1973)
Doris Jordan
SORORITY HOUSE(1939)
Dorothy Jordan
DEVIL MAY CARE(1929); TAMING OF THE SHREW, THE(1929); WORDS AND MUSIC(1929); CALL OF THE FLESH(1930); IN GAY MADRID(1930); LOVE IN THE ROUGH(1930); MIN AND BILL(1930); BELOVED BACHELOR, THE(1931); SHIP-MATES(1931); TAILOR MADE MAN, A(1931); YOUNG SINNERS(1931); CABIN IN THE COTTON(1932); DOWN TO EARTH(1932); HELL DIVERS(1932); ROADHOUSE MURDER, THE(1932); THAT'S MY BOY(1932); WET PARADE, THE(1932); 70,000 WITNESSES(1932); BONDAGE(1933); ONE MAN'S JOURNEY(1933); STRICTLY PER-SONAL(1933); SUN SHINES BRIGHT, THE(1953); SEARCHERS, THE(1956); WINGS OF EAGLES, THE(1957)
Echoe Jordan
WILD HARVEST(1962)

Ed Jordan
SEVEN UPS, THE(1973)
Elizabeth Jordan
MAKE WAY FOR A LADY(1936), w
1984
STREETS OF FIRE(1984)
Emil Jordan
TRAMPLERS, THE(1966, Ital.)
Erik Jordan
LORD OF THE FLIES(1963, Brit.)
Faye Jordan
LAST PICTURE SHOW, THE(1971)
Frankie Jordan
ROMANTIC ENGLISHWOMAN, THE(1975, Brit./Fr.)
Geraldine Jordan
ROAD HOUSE(1948); FILE ON THELMA JORDAN, THE(1950)
Glenn Jordan
ONLY WHEN I LAUGH(1981), d
1984
BUDDY SYSTEM, THE(1984), d; MASS APPEAL(1984), d
Harlan Jordan
TENDER MERCIES(1982); LOCAL HERO(1983, Brit.)
Harry Jordan
MURDER WITH PICTURES(1936); HIDEAWAY GIRL(1937)
Henry Jordan
ONE MYSTERIOUS NIGHT(1944); JOHNNY STOOL PIGEON(1949), w
Jack Jordan
THRU DIFFERENT EYES(1929); THOSE WERE THE DAYS(1934, Brit.), w; BEST FOOT FORWARD(1943); ALF 'N' FAMILY(1968, Brit.); GEORGIA, GEORGIA(1972), p; HONEYBABY, HONEYBABY(1974), p
Silents
PICTURE OF DORIAN GRAY, THE(1916, Brit.)
Jackie Jordan
HOTEL VARIETY(1933); SECRET LIFE OF WALTER MITTY, THE(1947)
James Jordan
IRON MAJOR, THE(1943)
James Jordan, Jr.
SING YOUR WAY HOME(1945)
James B. Jordan
COURT JESTER, THE(1956)
James Carrol Jordan
SUPERCHICK(1973)
Jeraldine Jordan
CRISS CROSS(1949); GREAT SINNER, THE(1949); WHERE DANGER LIVES(1950)
Jeri Jordan
SNAKE PIT, THE(1948); HOUSE OF STRANGERS(1949)
Jerri Jordan
HIS KIND OF WOMAN(1951)
Jessica Jordan
THAT HAGEN GIRL(1947)
Jewel Jordan
CONFESSION(1937)
Jewell Jordan
NEW MOON(1940)
Jim Jordan
THIS WAY PLEASE(1937); LOOK WHO'S LAUGHING(1941); HERE WE GO AGAIN(1942); HEAVENLY DAYS(1944); RESCUERS, THE(1977)
Jimmy Jordan
FALCON IN HOLLYWOOD, THE(1944); DICK TRACY(1945); FIRST YANK INTO TOKYO(1945); HAVING WONDERFUL CRIME(1945); THOSE ENDEARING YOUNG CHARMS(1945)
Jo Jordan
RATTLERS(1976); MOMENT BY MOMENT(1978)
Joan Jordan
TWO TICKETS TO BROADWAY(1951); JET PILOT(1957)
Joanne Jordan
FARMER TAKES A WIFE, THE(1953); LOOPHOLE(1954); I COVER THE UNDERWORLD(1955); SON OF SINBAD(1955); WRITTEN ON THE WIND(1956)
Joanne Moore Jordan
FACES(1968); CAPTAIN MILKSHAKE(1970); DUNWICH HORROR, THE(1970); PIECES OF DREAMS(1970); BURY ME AN ANGEL(1972); I DISMEMBER MAMA(1974); WOMAN UNDER THE INFLUENCE, A(1974)
Joanne Morre Jordan
DIRTY HANDS(1976, Fr./Ital./Ger.)
Joe Jordan
HARLEM IS HEAVEN(1932), m
John Jordan
2001: A SPACE ODYSSEY(1968, U.S./Brit.); ON HER MAJESTY'S SECRET SERVICE(1969, Brit.), ph
Judi Jordan
RAINTREE COUNTY(1957)
Judith Jordan
Misc. Silents
BACK TO OLD VIRGINIA(1923)
Judy Jordan
BOATNIKS, THE(1970); GATLING GUN, THE(1972)
Kate Jordan
TRANSGRESSION(1931), w
Silents
TIDES OF FATE(1917), w; IN SEARCH OF A THRILL(1923), w
Kerry Jordan
MAILBAG ROBBERY(1957, Brit.); ZULU(1964, Brit.); MY WAY(1974, South Africa); SAFARI 3000(1982)
Larry Jordan
HILDUR AND THE MAGICIAN(1969), p,d, w, ph, ed
1984
TANK(1984)

Lorna Jordan
WHERE THERE'S LIFE(1947); JOAN OF ARC(1948); YOUNG MAN WITH A HORN(1950); GREATEST SHOW ON EARTH, THE(1952)
Lothrop W. Jordan
PLAY DEAD(1981), w
Louis Jordan
BEWARE(1946); SWING PARADE OF 1946(1946); LOOK OUT SISTER(1948)
Marian Jordan
THIS WAY PLEASE(1937); LOOK WHO'S LAUGHING(1941); HERE WE GO AGAIN(1942); HEAVENLY DAYS(1944)
Marsha Jordan
RAMRODDER, THE(1969); COUNT YORGA, VAMPIRE(1970); GOLDEN BOX, THE(1970); INSIDE AMY(1975)
Misc. Talkies
SWEET GEORGIA(1972)
Mathew M. Jordan
BILLIE(1965)
Matty Jordan
UNDER THE YUM-YUM TREE(1963); LAST OF THE SECRET AGENTS?, THE(1966)
Michael Jordan
SCENE OF THE CRIME(1949)
Mike Jordan
OCEAN'S ELEVEN(1960)
Miriam Jordan
SHERLOCK HOLMES(1932); SIX HOURS TO LIVE(1932); DANGEROUSLY YOURS(1933); I LOVED YOU WEDNESDAY(1933); LET'S FALL IN LOVE(1934); TWO HEADS ON A PILLOW(1934); MY OWN TRUE LOVE(1948)
Neil Jordan
ANGEL(1982, Irish), d&w
Nick Jordan [Aldo Canti]
FANTASTIC THREE, THE(1967, Ital./Ger./Fr./Yugo.); SABATA(1969, Ital.); RETURN OF SABATA(1972, Ital./Fr./Ger.); THREE STOOGES VS. THE WONDER WOMEN(1975, Ital./Chi.)
Nina Jordan
OLD BOYFRIENDS(1979)
Patricia Jordan
HILDUR AND THE MAGICIAN(1969), w
Patrick Jordan
COMPANIONS IN CRIME(1954, Brit.); EMBEZZLER, THE(1954, Brit.); GILDED CAGE, THE(1954, Brit.); PROFILE(1954, Brit.); RIVER BEAT(1954); IT'S A GREAT DAY(1956, Brit.); OPERATION CONSPIRACY(1957, Brit.); ANGRY HILLS, THE(1959, Brit.); MAN UPSTAIRS, THE(1959, Brit.); FRIGHTENED CITY, THE(1961, Brit.); YOUNG, WILLING AND EAGER(1962, Brit.); MARKED ONE, THE(1963, Brit.); VICTORS, THE(1963); WINGS OF MYSTERY(1963, Brit.); AMOROUS MR. PRAWN, THE(1965, Brit.); BUNNY LAKE IS MISSING(1965); HEROES OF TELEMARK, THE(1965, Brit.); WHERE THE BULLETS FLY(1966, Brit.); ROBBERY(1967, Brit.); PLAY DIRTY(1969, Brit.); LAST ESCAPE, THE(1970, Brit.); MAN OF VIOLENCE(1970, Brit.); PERFECT FRIDAY(1970, Brit.); TOO LATE THE HERO(1970); ASSAULT(1971, Brit.); SALZBURG CONNECTION, THE(1972); SLIPPER AND THE ROSE, THE(1976, Brit.)
Paul Jordan
BORDER RANGERS(1950); GUNFIRE(1950); MISSION MARS(1968), ed; TAKE THE MONEY AND RUN(1969), ed
Philip Jordan
UNKNOWN GUEST, THE(1943), w
Pierre Jordan
HEART OF A NATION, THE(1943, Fr.)
Porter Jordan
CHROME AND HOT LEATHER(1971), m
Richard Jordan
READY FOR THE PEOPLE(1964); LAWMAN(1971); VALDEZ IS COMING(1971); CHATO'S LAND(1972); TRIAL OF THE CATONSVILLE NINE, THE(1972); FRIENDS OF EDDIE COYLE, THE(1973, Can./Fr.); KAMOURASKA(1973, Can./Fr.); ROOSTER COGBURN(1975); YAKUZA, THE(1975, U.S./Jap.); LOGAN'S RUN(1976); ONE NIGHT STAND(1976, Fr.); INTERIORS(1978); OLD BOYFRIENDS(1979); RAISE THE TITANIC(1980, Brit.)
1984
DUNE(1984); FLASH OF GREEN, A(1984), a, p
Misc. Talkies
NIGHTINGALE SANG IN BERKELEY SQUARE, A(1979)
Robert Jordan
TREASURE OF MONTE CRISTO(1949); FAT MAN, THE(1951); LONE WOLF McQUADE(1983)
Robert Stone Jordan
Misc. Talkies
SECTOR 13(1982), d
Ruth Jordan
CRASH DIVE(1943)
Sally Jordan
CYCLE SAVAGES(1969), cos
Misc. Talkies
SAVAGE!(1973)
Sid Jordan
DUDE RANGER, THE(1934); HOLLYWOOD COWBOY(1937); MARSHAL OF MESA CITY, THE(1939); IRON MAJOR, THE(1943)
Silents
NIGHT HORSEMAN, THE(1921); CHASING THE MOON(1922); SKY HIGH(1922); JOHNSTOWN FLOOD, THE(1926)
Misc. Silents
FIGHTING FOR GOLD(1919); WILDERNESS TRAIL, THE(1919); TEXAN, THE(1920); FOR BIG STAKES(1922); EYES OF THE FOREST(1923); MEN IN THE RAW(1923); WHERE IS THIS WEST?(1923)
Steve Jordan
STILL OF THE NIGHT(1982), set d
Steven Jordan
1984
FALLING IN LOVE(1984), set d; MOSCOW ON THE HUDSON(1984), set d

Ted Jordan
SILENCERS, THE(; DRAGONWYCH(1946); MOTHER WORE TIGHTS(1947); WHEN MY BABY SMILES AT ME(1948); MISS GRANT TAKES RICHMOND(1949); SLATTERY'S HURRICANE(1949); THIEVES' HIGHWAY(1949); UNDERCOVER MAN, THE(1949); WHIRLPOOL(1949); COUNTERSPY MEETS SCOTLAND YARD(1950); EMERGENCY WEDDING(1950); ROOKIE FIREMAN(1950); SIERRA(1950); WOMAN OF DISTINCTION, A(1950); BONANZA TOWN(1951); LORNA DOONE(1951); BUSHWHACKERS, THE(1952); LAS VEGAS STORY, THE(1952); LURE OF THE WILDERNESS(1952); FARMER TAKES A WIFE, THE(1953); MARSHAL'S DAUGHTER, THE(1953); MISS SADIE THOMPSON(1953); $1,000,000 DUCK(1971); WALKING TALL(1973); APPLE DUMPLING GANG RIDES AGAIN, THE(1979)

Ted H. Jordan
WRECKING CREW, THE(1968)

Tom Jordan
OTHER SIDE OF THE MOUNTAIN–PART 2, THE(1978)

Victor Jordan
MASSACRE(1956)

Will Jordan
I WANNA HOLD YOUR HAND(1978)
1984
BROADWAY DANNY ROSE(1984)

William Jordan
NOTHING BUT A MAN(1964); LOVE IS A WOMAN(1967, Brit.), ph; HAND OF NIGHT, THE(1968, Brit.), ph; MAN CALLED HORSE, A(1970); DEATHMASTER, THE(1972); RAGE(1972); PARALLAX VIEW, THE(1974); GRAY LADY DOWN(1978)
1984
HAMBONE AND HILLIE(1984)

The Jordanaires
JAILHOUSE ROCK(1957); LOVING YOU(1957); COUNTRY MUSIC HOLIDAY(1958); FLAMING STAR(1960); G.I. BLUES(1960); BUFFALO GUN(1961); GIRLS! GIRLS! GIRLS!(1962); FROM NASHVILLE WITH MUSIC(1969)

Daniel Jordano
1984
ALPHABET CITY(1984)

Jan Jorden
LAST MARRIED COUPLE IN AMERICA, THE(1980)

Scott Jorden [William Henry]
THERE'S ONE BORN EVERY MINUTE(1942)

Marcelle Jordine
BARRY MC KENZIE HOLDS HIS OWN(1975, Aus.)

Merdel Jordine
Misc. Talkies
DEATH MAY BE YOUR SANTA CLAUS(1969)

Charles Jordon
CITY OF SILENT MEN(1942)

Charlie Jordon
THERE GOES KELLY(1945)

Dorothy Jordon
LOST SQUADRON, THE(1932)

Geraldine Jordon
APARTMENT FOR PEGGY(1948)

J. Rob Jordon
FUN WITH DICK AND JANE(1977)

Jennifer Jordon
Misc. Talkies
SEX DU JOUR(1976)

Lewis Jordon
MATCHLESS(1967, Ital.)

Lorna Jordon
FILE ON THELMA JORDAN, THE(1950)

Michael Jordon
NEPTUNE'S DAUGHTER(1949)

Mike Jordon
HOUSE OF USHER(1960)

Patricia Jordon
HILDUR AND THE MAGICIAN(1969)

Patrick Jordon
MAN DETAINED(1961, Brit.)

Sid Jordon
Misc. Silents
RIDIN' ROMEO, A(1921)

Henry Jorell
UNPUBLISHED STORY(1942, Brit.)

Judy Jorell
SON OF SINBAD(1955)

Jean-Louis Jorge
SERPENTS OF THE PIRATE MOON, THE(1973), p,d&w

Victor Jorge
LAST RITES(1980)

Alf Jorgensen
GYPSY FURY(1950, Fr.), p

Bill Jorgensen
NASTY HABITS(1976, Brit.)

Emilius Jorgensen
Silents
JOAN THE WOMAN(1916)

Erling Jorgensen
Z.P.G.(1972), set d

Kim Jorgensen
1984
BAD MANNERS(1984), p

William Jorgensen
KING OF COMEDY, THE(1983)

Connie Jorgenson
00-2 MOST SECRET AGENTS(1965, Ital.)

Emil Jorgenson
Silents
MORAN OF THE LADY LETTY(1922)

Hans Jorgseeberger
GREEN SLIME, THE(1969)

Fereidun G. Jorjani
Misc. Talkies
FOX AFFAIR, THE(1978), d

Mildred Jorman
CAMPUS SLEUTH(1948)

Ake Jornfalk
SHAME(1968, Swed.)

Corinne Jorry
1984
LES COMPERES(1984, Fr.), cos

Nicholas Jory
NEW WINE(1941), w

Victor Jory
RENEGADES(1930); HANDLE WITH CARE(1932); PRIDE OF THE LEGION, THE(1932); BIG PAYOFF, THE(1933); DEVIL'S IN LOVE, THE(1933); I LOVED YOU WEDNESDAY(1933); INFERNAL MACHINE(1933); MY WOMAN(1933); SAILOR'S LUCK(1933); SECOND HAND WIFE(1933); SMOKY(1933); STATE FAIR(1933); TRICK FOR TRICK(1933); HE WAS HER MAN(1934); I BELIEVED IN YOU(1934); MADAME DU BARRY(1934); MURDER IN TRINIDAD(1934); PURSUED(1934); ESCAPE FROM DEVIL'S ISLAND(1935); MIDSUMMER'S NIGHT'S DREAM, A(1935); MILLS OF THE GODS(1935); PARTY WIRE(1935); STREAMLINE EXPRESS(1935); TOO TOUGH TO KILL(1935); WHITE LIES(1935); HELL-SHIP MORGAN(1936); KING STEPS OUT, THE(1936); MEET NERO WOLFE(1936); BULLDOG DRUMMOND AT BAY(1937, Brit.); FIRST LADY(1937); GLAMOROUS NIGHT(1937, Brit.); ADVENTURES OF TOM SAWYER, THE(1938); BLACKWELL'S ISLAND(1939); CALL A MESSENGER(1939); DODGE CITY(1939); EACH DAWN I DIE(1939); GONE WITH THE WIND(1939); I STOLE A MILLION(1939); MAN OF CONQUEST(1939); RANGLE RIVER(1939, Aus.); SUSANNAH OF THE MOUNTIES(1939); WINGS OF THE NAVY(1939); WOMEN IN THE WIND(1939); GIRL FROM HAVANA(1940); GIVE US WINGS(1940); KNIGHTS OF THE RANGE(1940); LADY WITH RED HAIR(1940); LIGHT OF WESTERN STARS, THE(1940); LONE WOLF MEETS A LADY, THE(1940); RIVER'S END(1940); BAD MEN OF MISSOURI(1941); BORDER VIGILANTES(1941); CHARLIE CHAN IN RIO(1941); SECRETS OF THE LONE WOLF(1941); STORK PAYS OFF, THE(1941); WIDE OPEN TOWN(1941); SHUT MY BIG MOUTH(1942); TOMBSTONE, THE TOWN TOO TOUGH TO DIE(1942); BAR 20(1943); BUCKSKIN FRONTIER(1943); COLT COMRADES(1943); HOPPY SERVES A WRIT(1943); KANSAN, THE(1943); LEATHER BURNERS, THE(1943); POWER OF THE PRESS(1943); UNKNOWN GUEST, THE(1943); GALLANT BLADE, THE(1948); LOVES OF CARMEN, THE(1948); CANADIAN PACIFIC(1949); FIGHTING MAN OF THE PLAINS(1949); SOUTH OF ST. LOUIS(1949); WOMAN'S SECRET, A(1949); CAPTURE, THE(1950); CARIBOO TRAIL, THE(1950); CAVE OF OUTLAWS(1951); FLAMING FEATHER(1951); HIGHWAYMAN, THE(1951); SON OF ALI BABA(1952); TOUGHEST MAN IN ARIZONA(1952); CAT WOMEN OF THE MOON(1953); HINDU, THE(1953, Brit.); MAN FROM THE ALAMO, THE(1953); VALLEY OF THE KINGS(1954); BLACKJACK KETCHUM, DESPERADO(1956); DEATH OF A SCOUNDREL(1956); MANFISH(1956); LAST STAGECOACH WEST, THE(1957); MAN WHO TURNED TO STONE, THE(1957); FUGITIVE KIND, THE(1960); MIRACLE WORKER, THE(1962); CHEYENNE AUTUMN(1964); JIGSAW(1968); MACKENNA'S GOLD(1969); FLAP(1970); TIME FOR DYING, A(1971); FRASIER, THE SENSUOUS LION(1973); PAPILLON(1973); MOUNTAIN MEN, THE(1980)
Misc. Talkies
MAN WHO TALKS TO WHALES, THE(197?)

Lola Josane
Misc. Silents
PAWNS OF PASSION(1929, Fr./USSR)

Christina Josani
MY NAME IS PECOS(1966, Ital.)

Heidi Joschko
1984
LOVE IN GERMANY, A(1984, Fr./Ger.)

Cathy Jose
LOLA(1971, Brit./Ital.)

Edward Jose
Silents
STAIN, THE(1914); FOOL THERE WAS, A(1915); SIMON THE JESTER(1915), d; MY COUSIN(1918), d; PRIVATE PEAT(1918), d; ISLE OF CONQUEST(1919), d; RIDDLE: WOMAN, THE(1920), d; INNER CHAMBER, THE(1921), d; RAINBOW(1921), d; SCARAB RING, THE(1921), d; WHAT WOMEN WILL DO(1921), d
Misc. Silents
BELOVED VAGABOND, THE(1912), d; CORSAIR, THE(1914), d; CLOSING NET, THE(1915), d; NEDRA(1915), d; LIGHT THAT FAILED, THE(1916), d; HER SILENT SACRIFICE(1917), d; MAYBLOSSOM(1917), d; MOTH, THE(1917), d; POPPY(1917), d; DOCTOR AND THE BRICKLAYER, THE(1918), d; FEDORA(1918), d; LA TOSCA(1918), d; LOVE'S CONQUEST(1918), d; RESURRECTION(1918), d; SPLENDID ROMANCE, THE(1918), d; WOMAN AND WIFE(1918), d; WOMAN OF IMPULSE, A(1918), d; TWO BRIDES, THE(1919), d; FIGHTING SHEPHERDESS, THE(1920), d; MOTHERS OF MEN(1920), d; YELLOW TAIFUN, THE(1920), d; YELLOW TYPHOON, THE(1920), d; HER LORD AND MASTER(1921), d; MATRIMONIAL WEB, THE(1921), d; GIRL IN HIS ROOM, THE(1922), d; MAN FROM DOWNING STREET, THE(1922), d; PRODIGAL JUDGE, THE(1922), d; GOD'S PRODIGAL(1923, Brit.), d; TERREUR(1924, Fr.), d

Richard J. Jose
Silents
SILVER THREADS AMONG THE GOLD(1915)

The Jose Cansino Dancers
MASKED RIDER, THE(1941)

Jose Eslava's Orchestra
GAUCHO SERENADE(1940)

Ben Josef
FAITHFUL CITY(1952, Israel)

Zbigniew Josefowicz
GREAT BIG WORLD AND LITTLE CHILDREN, THE(1962, Pol.)

Milt Josefsberg
ICE-CAPADES(1941), w

A. Joseph
BE MINE TONIGHT(1933, Brit.), w

Aaron Joseph
TARZAN GOES TO INDIA(1962, U.S./Brit./Switz.)

Al Joseph
SCANDAL IN PARIS, A(1946), ed; LOVE HAPPY(1949), ed; SUPERMAN AND THE MOLE MEN(1951), ed; LOAN SHARK(1952), ed; GREAT MAN, THE(1957), ed; INCREDIBLE SHRINKING MAN, THE(1957), ed; NIGHT RUNNER, THE(1957), ed; DESERT HELL(1958), ed; RESTLESS YEARS, THE(1958), ed; EYES OF LAURA MARS(1978)

Albrecht Joseph
HITLER'S MADMAN(1943), w; STORY OF G.I. JOE, THE(1945), ed; PRIVATE AFFAIRS OF BEL AMI, THE(1947), ed

Allen Joseph
VERY SPECIAL FAVOR, A(1965); RETURN OF COUNT YORGA, THE(1971); MARATHON MAN(1976); ERASERHEAD(1978); CHILLY SCENES OF WINTER(1982); HEY, GOOD LOOKIN'(1982)

Arek Joseph
CAYMAN TRIANGLE, THE(1977)

David Joseph
PIRATE MOVIE, THE(1982, Aus.), p

Don Joseph
COLOR ME BLOOD RED(1965)

Eddy Joseph
PARTY PARTY(1983, Brit.), ed

Edmund Joseph
ROYAL BOX, THE(1930), w; WOMEN MUST DRESS(1935), w; HATS OFF(1937), w; EVERYBODY'S DOING IT(1938), w; WHO DONE IT?(1942), w; YANKEE DOODLE DANDY(1942), w; BOWERY TO BROADWAY(1944), w; MAKE YOUR OWN BED(1944), w; NAUGHTY NINETIES, THE(1945), w; SING YOUR WAY HOME(1945), w

Eric Joseph
THAT SINKING FEELING(1979, Brit.)

George Joseph
HORROR OF THE BLOOD MONSTERS(1970, U.S./Phil.), d

Jackie Joseph
SUICIDE BATTALION(1958); SPEED CRAZY(1959); LITTLE SHOP OF HORRORS(1961); GUIDE FOR THE MARRIED MAN, A(1967); WHO'S MINDING THE MINT?(1967); SPLIT, THE(1968); WITH SIX YOU GET EGGROLL(1968); CHEYENNE SOCIAL CLUB, THE(1970); GET CRAZY(1983)
1984
GREMLINS(1984)

James Joseph
SLITHER(1973)

Jeannette Joseph
1984
STRANGERS KISS(1984)

Joanna Joseph
FRENCH LIEUTENANT'S WOMAN, THE(1981)
Misc. Talkies
CHILD'S PLAY(1984, Brit.)

John Joseph
CHANGE OF HABIT(1969), w

Kenny Joseph
RUDE BOY(1980, Brit.)

Lou Joseph
METALSTORM: THE DESTRUCTION OF JARED-SYN(1983)

Masoud Joseph
DR. MINX(1975), ph; SPECIALIST, THE(1975), ph

Michael Joseph
EYE OF THE NEEDLE(1981)

Norma Joseph
RETURN TO CAMPUS(1975)

Paul A. Joseph
CABOBLANCO(1981), p

Peter Joseph
Misc. Silents
RICHTOFEN(1932, Ger.), d

Phillip Joseph
KEEP, THE(1983)

Robert Joseph
HITCH-HIKER, THE(1953), w; GUNSMOKE IN TUCSON(1958), w; FIVE MINUTES TO LIVE(1961), w; ENTERTAINER, THE(1975), m

Robert L. Joseph
THIRD SECRET, THE(1964, Brit.), p, w; JACK OF DIAMONDS(1967, U.S./Ger.), w; ONE STEP TO HELL(1969, U.S./Ital./Span.), w; SKI FEVER(1969, U.S./Aust./Czech.), w; STRATEGY OF TERROR(1969), w; ECHOES OF A SUMMER(1976), p, w

Robert R. Joseph
NO MAN IS AN ISLAND(1962), spec eff

Ron Joseph
1984
EL NORTE(1984)

Ronald Joseph
SCARFACE(1983)

Stevie Joseph
NO MAN IS AN ISLAND(1962)

Teddy Joseph
WHAT A WHOPPER(1961, Brit.), p

Teresanne Joseph
PLAINSONG(1982)

Wilfred Joseph
WEBSTER BOY, THE(1962, Brit.), m

Joseph Papp and The Shakespeare Theatre in the Park
SUCH GOOD FRIENDS(1971)

Josephine the Monkey
THIS GUN FOR HIRE(1942)

Josephine-Joseph
FREAKS(1932)

Ann Josephs
WORLD'S GREATEST SINNER, THE(1962)

Harrison Josephs
Silents
SOUTH SEA LOVE(1923), w

Wilfred Josephs
CASH ON DEMAND(1962, Brit.), m; TOUCH OF DEATH(1962, Brit.), w; DIE, DIE, MY DARLING(1965, Brit.), m; 24 HOURS TO KILL(1966, Brit.), m; DEADLY BEES, THE(1967, Brit.), m; MY SIDE OF THE MOUNTAIN(1969), m; DARK PLACES(1974, Brit.), m; ALL CREATURES GREAT AND SMALL(1975, Brit.), m; SWALLOWS AND AMAZONS(1977, Brit.), m; UNCANNY, THE(1977, Brit./Can.), m

Erland Josephsen
CRIES AND WHISPERS(1972, Swed.)

Bonnie Charyl Josephson
EL DORADO(1967)

Elva Josephson
BLUE LAGOON, THE(1980); LITTLE SEX, A(1982)

Erland Josephson
MAGICIAN, THE(1959, Swed.); BRINK OF LIFE(1960, Swed.); ALL THESE WOMEN(1964, Swed.), w; HOUR OF THE WOLF, THE(1968, Swed.); PASSION OF ANNA, THE(1970, Swed.); GIRLS, THE(1972, Swed.); SCENES FROM A MARRIAGE(1974, Swed.); FACE TO FACE(1976, Swed.); AUTUMN SONATA(1978, Swed.); MONTENEGRO(1981, Brit./Swed.); BELLA DONNA(1983, Ger.); FANNY AND ALEXANDER(1983, Swed./Fr./Ger.)
1984
AFTER THE REHEARSAL(1984, Swed.); BEYOND GOOD AND EVIL(1984, Ital./Fr./Ger.); NOSTALGHIA(1984, USSR/Ital.)

Gilbert Josephson
MURDER IN THE OLD RED BARN(1936, Brit.), p

Julian Josephson
CLIMAX, THE(1930), w; GREEN GODDESS, THE(1930), w; ALEXANDER HAMILTON(1931), w; HELL BOUND(1931), w; KISS ME AGAIN(1931), w; MISBEHAVING LADIES(1931), w; EXPERT, THE(1932), w; CHANCE AT HEAVEN(1933), w
Silents
IT MUST BE LOVE(1926), w; DO YOUR DUTY(1928), w

Julien Josephson
DISRAELI(1929), w; MILLIONAIRE, THE(1931), w; MAN WHO PLAYED GOD, THE(1932), w; SUCCESSFUL CALAMITY, A(1932), w; HEIDI(1937), w; WEE WILLIE WINKIE(1937), w; SUEZ(1938), w; RAINS CAME, THE(1939), w; STANLEY AND LIVINGSTONE(1939), w; GREAT GILDERSLEEVE, THE(1942), w; HAPPY LAND(1943), w
Silents
MIDNIGHT PATROL, THE(1918), w; PLAYING THE GAME(1918), w; JAILBIRD, THE(1920), w; PARIS GREEN(1920), w; RED HOT DOLLARS(1920), w; WATCH YOUR STEP(1922), w; ALL THE BROTHERS WERE VALIANT(1923), w; COUNTRY KID, THE(1923), w; NARROW STREET, THE(1924), w; LADY WINDERMERE'S FAN(1925), w; ROSE OF THE WORLD(1925), w; RED MARK, THE(1928), w

Les Josephson
NICKELODEON(1976); HEAVEN CAN WAIT(1978)

Matthew Josephson
TOAST OF NEW YORK, THE(1937), w

Rich Josephson
1984
SILENT NIGHT, DEADLY NIGHT(1984), spec eff

Alvin Josephy
OPERATION SECRET(1952), w

Alvin M. Josephy
SOMETHING FOR THE BIRDS(1952), w

Alvin M. Josephy, Jr.
CAPTIVE CITY(1952), w

Jennifer Josey
TERMS OF ENDEARMENT(1983)

June Josey
Misc. Talkies
STORYVILLE(1974)

Larry Joshua
BURNING, THE(1981); STILL OF THE NIGHT(1982)

Guido Josia
MINUTE TO PRAY, A SECOND TO DIE, A(1968, Ital.), set d; LAST REBEL, THE(1971), art d

Dagmar Josipovich
ROMEO AND JULIET(1954, Brit.)

Howard Joslin
TEXAS RANGERS, THE(1936); MISS TATLOCK'S MILLIONS(1948); HIGH LONESOME(1950); SUNSET BOULEVARD(1950); HERE COMES THE GROOM(1951); QUEBEC(1951); SILVER CITY(1951); SOMEBODY LOVES ME(1952); SON OF PALEFACE(1952); PONY EXPRESS(1953); VANQUISHED, THE(1953); COUNTRY GIRL, THE(1954); RUN FOR COVER(1955); ROUSTABOUT(1964)

Margaret Joslin
Silents
GIRLS DON'T GAMBLE(1921); DANGER POINT, THE(1922)

Warren Joslin
VARIETY GIRL(1947)

Allan Joslyn
NIGHTMARE IN THE SUN(1964)

Allyn Joslyn
YOU CAN'T RUN AWAY FROM IT(1956); EXPENSIVE HUSBANDS(1937); HOLLYWOOD HOTEL(1937); THEY WON'T FORGET(1937); SHINING HOUR, THE(1938); SWEETHEARTS(1938); CAFE SOCIETY(1939); FAST AND FURIOUS(1939); ONLY ANGELS HAVE WINGS(1939); GREAT McGINTY, THE(1940); IF I HAD MY WAY(1940); NO TIME FOR COMEDY(1940); SPRING PARADE(1940); THIS THING CALLED LOVE(1940); AFFAIRS OF MARTHA, THE(1942); BEDTIME STORY(1942); I WAKE UP SCREAMING(1942); MY SISTER EILEEN(1942); WIFE TAKES A FLYER, THE(1942); DANGEROUS BLONDES(1943); HEAVEN CAN WAIT(1943); IMMORTAL SERGEANT, THE(1943); YOUNG IDEAS(1943); BRIDE BY MISTAKE(1944); IMPOSTER, THE(1944); STRANGE AFFAIR(1944); SWEET AND LOWDOWN(1944); COLONEL EFFINGHAM'S RAID(1945); HORN BLOWS AT MIDNIGHT, THE(1945); JUNIOR MISS(1945); IT SHOULDN'T HAPPEN TO A DOG(1946); THRILL OF BRAZIL, THE(1946); SHOCKING MISS PILGRIM, THE(1947); IF YOU KNEW SUSIE(1948); MOONRISE(1948); LADY TAKES A SAILOR, THE(1949); HARRIET CRAIG(1950); AS YOUNG AS YOU FEEL(1951); I LOVE MELVIN(1953); ISLAND IN THE SKY(1953); JAZZ SINGER, THE(1953); TITANIC(1953); FASTEST GUN ALIVE(1956); PUBLIC

PIGEON NO. 1(1957); BROTHERS O'TOOLE, THE(1973)

Don Joslyn
HOODLUM PRIEST, THE(1961); CHILDISH THINGS(1969); UP YOUR TEDDY BEAR(1970), p,d&w

Donald Joslyn
HEROES DIE YOUNG(1960)

Howard Joslyn
DETECTIVE STORY(1951); RACKET, THE(1951)

Jim Joslyn
IT HAPPENED HERE(1966, Brit.)

Talbert Joslyn
NAVY BOUND(1951), w

W.H.D. Joss
RING OF BRIGHT WATER(1969, Brit.)

Willie Joss
BIG CATCH, THE(1968, Brit.); LOCAL HERO(1983, Brit.)
1984
EVERY PICTURE TELLS A STORY(1984, Brit.)

Josselin
CASE OF DR. LAURENT(1958, Fr.)

Talbert Josselyn
SMUGGLERS' COVE(1948), w

Edith Jost
HOUSE OF INTRIGUE, THE(1959, Ital.); RICE GIRL(1963, Fr./Ital.)

John Jost
CHAMELEON(1978), p&d, w, ph

Jon Jost
1984
SLOW MOVES(1984), p,d,w,ph,m&ed

Paul Jost
LAST RITES(1980), m

Peter Jost
MIRACLE OF THE WHITE STALLIONS(1963)

Darwin Jostin
RATTLERS(1976)

Darwin Joston
CAIN'S WAY(1969); ASSAULT ON PRECINCT 13(1976); COAST TO COAST(1980); FOG, THE(1980)

Jay Jostyn
HILDA CRANE(1956); REVOLT OF MAMIE STOVER, THE(1956); HUNTERS, THE(1958); LIVE FAST, DIE YOUNG(1958); TOO MUCH, TOO SOON(1958); NEVER STEAL ANYTHING SMALL(1959); WAKE ME WHEN IT'S OVER(1960)

Josyane
Misc. Silents
MORGANE, THE ENCHANTRESS(1929, Fr.)

Paul Jott
HOSPITAL, THE(1971)

Jacques Jou-Jerville
L'ENIGMATIQUE MONSIEUR PARKES(1930); EVENINGS FOR SALE(1932); EAGLE AND THE HAWK, THE(1933)

Jacques Jouanneau
FRENCH CANCAN(1956, Fr.)

Jacques Jouanneau
PARIS DOES STRANGE THINGS(1957, Fr./Ital.); PEEK-A-BOO(1961, Fr.); ELUSIVE CORPORAL, THE(1963, Fr.); FRIEND OF THE FAMILY(1965, Fr./Ital.); JUDEX(1966, Fr./Ital.); BED AND BOARD(1971, Fr.); LEGEND OF FRENCHIE KING, THE(1971, Fr./Ital./Span./Brit.)

Romauld Joube
Misc. Silents
MADEMOISELLE DE LA SEIGLIERE(1921, Fr.); MIRACLE OF WOLVES, THE(1925, Fr.)

Romuald Joube
Misc. Silents
J'ACCUSE(1919, Fr.); LE MANOIR DE LA PEUR(1927, Fr.); PASSION OF ST. FRANCIS(1932, Ital.)

Felix Joubert
Silents
FIELD OF HONOR, THE(1922, Brit.), a, w

Patricia Joudry
RESTLESS YEARS, THE(1958), w

Alain Jouffroy
LA COLLECTIONNEUSE(1971, Fr.)

Lucien Joulin
ALERT IN THE SOUTH(1954, Fr.), ph; THUNDER IN THE BLOOD(1962, Fr.), ph

Jouma
FURY AT SMUGGLERS BAY(1963, Brit.)

Hassan Joundi
MOHAMMAD, MESSENGER OF GOD(1976, Lebanon/Brit.)

Mrs. Joupert
Silents
OPEN YOUR EYES(1919)

Andre Jourdan
SHAMELESS OLD LADY, THE(1966, Fr.)

Catherine Jourdan
GIRL ON A MOTORCYCLE, THE(1968, Fr./Brit.); GODSON, THE(1972, Ital./Fr.)

Erven Jourdan
HALF PINT, THE(1960), p,d&w
Misc. Talkies
MONEY IN MY POCKET(1962), d

Louis Jourdan
HER FIRST AFFAIR(1947, Fr.); PARADINE CASE, THE(1947); LETTER FROM AN UNKNOWN WOMAN(1948); NO MINOR VICES(1948); MADAME BOVARY(1949); ANNE OF THE INDIES(1951); BIRD OF PARADISE(1951); HAPPY TIME, THE(1952); DECAMERON NIGHTS(1953, Brit.); THREE COINS IN THE FOUNTAIN(1954); JULIE(1956); SWAN, THE(1956); BRIDE IS MUCH TOO BEAUTIFUL, THE(1958, Fr.); DANGEROUS EXILE(1958, Brit.); GIGI(1958); BEST OF EVERYTHING, THE(1959); CAN-CAN(1960); LEVIATHAN(1961, Fr.); STORY OF THE COUNT OF MONTE CRISTO, THE(1962, Fr./Ital.); MATHIAS SANDORF(1963, Fr.); V.I.P.s, THE(1963, Brit.); DISORDER(1964, Fr./Ital.); MADE IN PARIS(1966); FLEA IN HER EAR, A(1968, Fr.); YOUNG REBEL, THE(1969, Fr./Ital./Span.); TO COMMIT A MURDER(1970,

Fr./Ital./Ger.); COUNT OF MONTE CRISTO(1976, Brit.); SILVER BEARS(1978); SWAMP THING(1982); OCTOPUSSY(1983, Brit.)
Misc. Talkies
TO DIE IN PARIS(1968)

Michel Jourdan
VICE AND VIRTUE(1965, Fr./Ital.)

Pierre Jourdan
RED AND THE BLACK, THE(1954, Fr./Ital.)

Raymond Jourdan
PICNIC ON THE GRASS(1960, Fr.); ELUSIVE CORPORAL, THE(1963, Fr.); RISE OF LOUIS XIV, THE(1970, Fr.)

Ted Jourdan
HOLD THAT LINE(1952)

Frank Jourdano
GANG THAT COULDN'T SHOOT STRAIGHT, THE(1971); WANDA(1971)

Lucienne Jourfier
BARBER OF SEVILLE(1949, Fr.)

Donald Journeau
MIDNIGHT LACE(1960)

Madge Journeay
STORY OF WILL ROGERS, THE(1952)

Journet
ROYAL AFFAIRS IN VERSAILLES(1957, Fr.)

Marcel Journet
CRIME DOCTOR'S GAMBLE(1947); FOXES OF HARROW, THE(1947); LETTER FROM AN UNKNOWN WOMAN(1948); SEALED VERDICT(1948); TO THE ENDS OF THE EARTH(1948); JOE PALOOKA IN THE COUNTERPUNCH(1949); POST OFFICE INVESTIGATOR(1949); GREAT PLANE ROBBERY(1950); DESPERATE DECISION(1954, Fr.)

Journey
TRON(1982), m/l

Reggie Jouvain
NAKED CITY, THE(1948)

Gary Jules Jouvenat
OUT OF THE BLUE(1982), w

Pierre Jouvenet
STOLEN LIFE(1939, Brit.)

Lisa Jouvet
COUNTERFEITERS OF PARIS, THE(1962, Fr., Ital.); LADY IN THE CAR WITH GLASSES AND A GUN, THE(1970, U.S./Fr.)

Louis Jouvet
TOPAZE(1935, Fr.); CARNIVAL IN FLANDERS(1936, Fr.); DR. KNOCK(1936, Fr.), a, d; LOWER DEPTHS, THE(1937, Fr.); LA MARSEILLAISE(1938, Fr.); UN CARNET DE BAL(1938, Fr.); ALIBI, THE(1939, Fr.); BIZARRE BIZARRE(1939, Fr.); CURTAIN RISES, THE(1939, Fr.); END OF A DAY, THE(1939, Fr.); COMPLIMENTS OF MR. FLOW(1941, Fr.); HEART OF A NATION, THE(1943, Fr.); SHANGHAI DRAMA, THE(1945, Fr.); VOLPONE(1947, Fr.); CONFESSIONS OF A ROGUE(1948, Fr.); JENNY LAMOUR(1948, Fr.); KNOCK(1955, Fr.)

Francois Joux
ANTOINE ET ANTOINETTE(1947 Fr.); ROYAL AFFAIR, A(1950); JULIETTA(1957, Fr.)

Slavitza Jovan
1984
BODY DOUBLE(1984); GHOSTBUSTERS(1984)

Gordana Jovanovic
I EVEN MET HAPPY GYPSIES(1968, Yugo.)

Jelena Jovanovic
FLAMING FRONTIER(1968, Ger./Yugo.)

Lyubisa Jovanovic
RAT(1960, Yugo.)

Milorad Jovanovic
I EVEN MET HAPPY GYPSIES(1968, Yugo.)

Vera Jovanovic
INNOCENCE UNPROTECTED(1971, Yugo.)

Zvonko Jovcic
GENGHIS KHAN(U.S./Brit./Ger./Yugo)

Ljubica Jovic
FURY OF THE PAGANS(1963, Ital.)

Nenad Jovicic
SCOTLAND YARD HUNTS DR. MABUSE(1963, Ger.), ph; OPERATION CROSS EAGLES(1969, U.S./Yugo.), ph

Ljubica Jovil
BLAZE OF GLORY(1963, Brit.)

Fabrizio Jovine
ROVER, THE(1967, Ital.)

Bob Jowe
GENERAL DIED AT DAWN, THE(1936)

John Jowett
THERE WAS A YOUNG LADY(1953, Brit.), w

Whitey Jowett
DESPERATE CARGO(1941), ed

Anthony Jowitt
SAN FRANCISCO(1936)
Misc. Silents
COAST OF FOLLY, THE(1925); SPLENDID CRIME, THE(1926)

Betty Joy
SOUTH OF SONORA(1930)

C.E. Joy
ONCE MORE, WITH FEELING(1960)

Charlie Joy
Misc. Silents
WHEN QUACKEL DID HYDE(1920)

Chris Joy
HALLS OF ANGER(1970)

Christopher Joy
UP IN SMOKE(1978); HIT MAN(1972); CLEOPATRA JONES(1973); DARKTOWN STRUTTERS(1975); SHEBA BABY(1975); SEVEN(1979)

Deanna Joy
DOCTOR DETROIT(1983)
Ernest Joy
Silents
AFTER FIVE(1915); ARMSTRONG'S WIFE(1915); CHIMMIE FADDEN(1915); CHIM-
MIE FADDEN OUT WEST(1915); GOLDEN CHANCE, THE(1915); GOOSE GIRL,
THE(1915); IMMIGRANT, THE(1915); SNOBS(1915); TEMPTATION(1915); WILD
GOOSE CHASE, THE(1915); WOMAN, THE(1915); DUPE, THE(1916); JOAN THE
WOMAN(1916); RACE, THE(1916); AMERICAN CONSUL, THE(1917); EACH TO HIS
KIND(1917); NAN OF MUSIC MOUNTAIN(1917); JULES OF THE STRONG
HEART(1918); ONE MORE AMERICAN(1918); JOHNNY GET YOUR GUN(1919);
LADY IN LOVE, A(1920); NOTORIOUS MISS LISLE, THE(1920); WHAT'S YOUR
HURRY?(1920)
Misc. Silents
BLACKLIST(1916); HEART OF NORA FLYNN, THE(1916); MARIA ROSA(1916);
SOWERS, THE(1916); UNPROTECTED(1916); VICTORIA CROSS, THE(1916); LITTLE
MISS OPTIMIST(1917); SILENT PARTNER, THE(1917); BELIEVE ME, XANTIP-
PE(1918)
Gail Joy
SUMMER RUN(1974)
Gloria Joy
Misc. Talkies
PASSPORT TO PARADISE(1932)
Silents
OLD FASHIONED BOY, AN(1920)
Misc. Silents
LITTLE MISS GROWN-UP(1918); LOCKED HEART, THE(1918); MIDNIGHT BUR-
GLAR, THE(1918); MISS MISCHIEF MAKER(1918); NO CHILDREN WANTED(1918);
WANTED - A BROTHER(1918); GIRL FROM ROCKY POINT, THE(1922); CIRCUS
JOYS(1923)
Karen Joy
DR. TERROR'S GALLERY OF HORRORS(1967)
Leatrice Joy
BELLAMY TRIAL, THE(1929); MOST IMMORAL LADY, A(1929); LOVE TRA-
DER(1930); FIRST LOVE(1939); OLD SWIMMIN' HOLE, THE(1941); AIR HOS-
TESS(1949); RED STALLION IN THE ROCKIES(1949); LOVE NEST(1951)
Misc. Talkies
BIG TIME(1977)
Silents
GIRL'S FOLLY, A(1917); PRIDE OF THE CLAN, THE(1917); ACE OF HEARTS,
THE(1921); BUNTY PULLS THE STRINGS(1921); POVERTY OF RICHES, THE(1921);
TALE OF TWO WORLDS, A(1921); MAN WHO SAW TOMORROW, THE(1922);
SATURDAY NIGHT(1922); JAVA HEAD(1923); SILENT PARTNER, THE(1923); TEN
COMMANDMENTS, THE(1923); WEDDING SONG, THE(1925); ANGEL OF BROAD-
WAY, THE(1927); NOBODY'S WIDOW(1927); VANITY(1927); MAN-MADE WO-
MEN(1928); SHOW PEOPLE(1928); STRONG BOY(1929)
Misc. Silents
HIS TURNING POINT(1915); CITY OF TEARS, THE(1918); WATER LILY,
THE(1919); BLIND YOUTH(1920); DOWN HOME(1920); INVISIBLE DIVORCE,
THE(1920); JUST A WIFE(1920); RIGHT OF WAY, THE(1920); LADIES MUST
LIVE(1921); NIGHT ROSE, THE(1921); SMILING ALL THE WAY(1921); BACHELOR
DADDY, THE(1922); MANSLAUGHTER(1922); MINNIE(1922); YOU CAN'T FOOL
YOUR WIFE(1923); CHANGING HUSBANDS(1924); MARRIAGE CHEAT(1924);
TRIUMPH(1924); DRESSMAKER FROM PARIS, THE(1925); HELL'S HIGH-
ROAD(1925); CLINGING VINE, THE(1926); EVE'S LEAVES(1926); FOR ALIMONY
ONLY(1926); MADE FOR LOVE(1926); BLUE DANUBE, THE(1928); TROPIC MAD-
NESS(1928)
Liya Joy [Joyzelle]
HOUSE OF MYSTERY(1934)
Nicholas Joy
SECRET HEART, THE(1946); DAISY KENYON(1947); DISHONORED LADY(1947);
GENTLEMAN'S AGREEMENT(1947); IF WINTER COMES(1947); FULLER BRUSH
MAN(1948); IRON CURTAIN, THE(1948); JOAN OF ARC(1948); LARCENY(1948);
NAKED CITY, THE(1948); ABBOTT AND COSTELLO MEET THE KILLER, BORIS
KARLOFF(1949); AND BABY MAKES THREE(1949); BRIDE OF VENGEANCE(1949);
GREAT GATSBY, THE(1949); SONG OF SURRENDER(1949); SUN COMES UP,
THE(1949); HERE COMES THE GROOM(1951); MAN WITH A CLOAK, THE(1951);
NATIVE SON(1951, U.S., Arg.); AFFAIR WITH A STRANGER(1953); DESK SET(1957)
Patricia Joy
RACE FOR YOUR LIFE, CHARLIE BROWN(1977), anim
Richard W. Joy
TO PLEASE A LADY(1950)
Robert Joy
ATLANTIC CITY(1981, U.S./Can.); RAGTIME(1981); TICKET TO HEAVEN(1981);
AMITYVILLE 3-D(1983); THRESHOLD(1983, Can.)
Ron Joy
ANIMALS, THE(1971), d
Shirley Joy
SHE DIDN'T SAY NO!(1962, Brit.); RESCUE SQUAD, THE(1963, Brit.)
Violet Joy
Silents
STRANGER'S BANQUET(1922)
Nathalie Joyaut
AU HASARD, BALTHAZAR(1970, Fr.)
Adrien Joyce [Carol Eastman]
MODEL SHOP, THE(1969), w; FIVE EASY PIECES(1970), w; PUZZLE OF A DOWN-
FALL CHILD(1970), w; SHOOTING, THE(1971), w; FORTUNE, THE(1975), w
Alice Joyce
SQUALL, THE(1929); GREEN GODDESS, THE(1930); HE KNEW WOMEN(1930);
SONG O' MY HEART(1930)
Silents
CELEBRATED CASE, A(1914); CHRISTIAN, THE(1914); EVERYBODY'S
GIRL(1918); CAPTAIN'S CAPTAIN, THE(1919); INNER CHAMBER, THE(1921); SCA-
RAB RING, THE(1921); PASSIONATE ADVENTURE, THE(1924, Brit.); STELLA
DALLAS(1925); ACE OF CADS, THE(1926); BEAU GESTE(1926); DANCING MOTH-
ERS(1926); SO'S YOUR OLD MAN(1926); NOOSE, THE(1928); 13 WASHINGTON
SQUARE(1928)
Misc. Silents
SCHOOL FOR SCANDAL, THE(1914); WHOM THE GODS DESTROY(1916); COUR-
AGE OF SILENCE, THE(1917); FETTERED WOMAN, THE(1917); HER SECRET(1917);

QUESTION, THE(1917); RICHARD THE BRAZEN(1917); WITHIN THE LAW(1917);
BUSINESS OF LIFE, THE(1918); FIND THE WOMAN(1918); SONG OF THE SOUL,
THE(1918); TO THE HIGHEST BIDDER(1918); TRIUMPH OF THE WEAK, THE(1918);
WOMAN BETWEEN FRIENDS, THE(1918); CAMBRIC MASK, THE(1919); LION AND
THE MOUSE, THE(1919); SPARK DIVINE, THE(1919); THIRD DEGREE, THE(1919);
VENGEANCE OF DURAND, THE(1919); WINCHESTER WOMAN, THE(1919); DOL-
LARS AND THE WOMAN(1920); PREY, THE(1920); SLAVES OF PRIDE(1920);
SPORTING DUCHESS, THE(1920); VICE OF FOOLS, THE(1920); COUSIN KA-
TE(1921); HER LORD AND MASTER(1921); GREEN GODDESS, THE(1923); WHITE
MAN(1924); DADDY'S GONE A-HUNTING(1925); HEADLINES(1925); HOME MAK-
ER, THE(1925); LITTLE FRENCH GIRL, THE(1925); MANNEQUIN(1926); RISING
GENERATION, THE(1928, Brit.)
Angela Joyce
BILL'S LEGACY(1931, Brit.)
Babe Joyce
OUANGA(1936, Brit.)
Barbara Joyce
KILLERS OF KILIMANJARO(1960, Brit.); HOTHEAD(1963); NIGHT OF THE IGUA-
NA, THE(1964)
Bill Joyce
TOP BANANA(1954); PARALLAX VIEW, THE(1974)
Brenda Joyce
HERE I AM A STRANGER(1939); RAINS CAME, THE(1939); LITTLE OLD NEW
YORK(1940); MARYLAND(1940); PUBLIC DEB NO. 1(1940); MARRY THE BOSS'
DAUGHTER(1941); PRIVATE NURSE(1941); LITTLE TOKYO, U.S.A.(1942); POST-
MAN DIDN'T RING, THE(1942); RIGHT TO THE HEART(1942); WHISPERING
GHOSTS(1942); THUMBS UP(1943); ENCHANTED FOREST, THE(1945); I'LL TELL
THE WORLD(1945); PILLOW OF DEATH(1945); STRANGE CONFESSION(1945);
TARZAN AND THE AMAZONS(1945); DANGER WOMAN(1946); LITTLE
GIANT(1946); SPIDER WOMAN STRIKES BACK, THE(1946); TARZAN AND THE
LEOPARD WOMAN(1946); STEPCHILD(1947); TARZAN AND THE HUN-
TRESS(1947); SHAGGY(1948); TARZAN AND THE MERMAIDS(1948); TARZAN'S
MAGIC FOUNTAIN(1949)
Debbie Joyce
PRIVATE'S AFFAIR, A(1959)
Ed Joyce
INGAGI(1931), ph
Eileen Joyce
GIRL IN A MILLION, A(1946, Brit.); WHEREVER SHE GOES(1953, Aus.)
1984
MAN OF FLOWERS(1984, Aus.)
Elaine Joyce
CHRISTINE JORGENSEN STORY, THE(1970); HOW TO FRAME A FIGG(1971);
SUCH GOOD FRIENDS(1971); MOTEL HELL(1980)
Frances Joyce
VOGUES OF 1938(1937)
Francine Joyce
PORKY'S II: THE NEXT DAY(1983)
Harold Joyce
SUNSET MURDER CASE(1941), w
Hester Joyce
1984
CONSTANCE(1984, New Zealand)
Jack Joyce
FLORIAN(1940)
Silents
NEW LIVES FOR OLD(1925)
James Joyce
TOO LATE BLUES(1962); FINNEGANS WAKE(1965), w; ULYSSES(1967, U.S./Brit.),
w; DIRTY HARRY(1971); WOMAN UNDER THE INFLUENCE, A(1974); PORTRAIT
OF THE ARTIST AS A YOUNG MAN, A(1979, Ireland), w
Jean Joyce
OUTLAWS OF SONORA(1938); ROMANCE ON THE RUN(1938); OVERLAND
MAIL(1939); RIDERS OF THE FRONTIER(1939); TOUGH KID(1939)
Jimmy Joyce
KILLERS, THE(1964); SWIMMER, THE(1968); MINNIE AND MOSKOWITZ(1971)
John Joyce
EQUINOX(1970), ed; UP YOUR TEDDY BEAR(1970), ed; ADVENTURES OF BAR-
RY McKENZIE(1972, Austral.)
Kathleen Joyce
RINGER, THE(1932, Brit.); SPOT OF BOTHER, A(1938, Brit.)
Kathy Joyce
STIGMA(1972)
Lind Joyce
MEET ME AT DAWN(1947, Brit.); CLOUDED CRYSTAL, THE(1948, Brit.); OH!
WHAT A LOVELY WAR(1969, Brit.)
Lyle Joyce
NADA GANG, THE(1974, Fr./Ital.)
1984
UNTIL SEPTEMBER(1984)
Marty Joyce
FIGHTING CABALLERO(1935)
Mary Joyce
ORPHANS OF THE NORTH(1940)
Michael Joyce
Silents
DO YOUR DUTY(1928), ph; HEAD MAN, THE(1928), ph
Michael P. Joyce
BOY WHO CRIED WEREWOLF, THE(1973), ph
Miles Joyce
INNOCENTS IN PARIS(1955, Brit.)
Natalie Joyce
MIDNIGHT DADDIES(1929); SAILORS' HOLIDAY(1929); TIMES SQUARE(1929);
COCK O' THE WALK(1930)
Silents
CIRCUS ACE, THE(1927); DAREDEVIL'S REWARD(1928); GIRL IN EVERY PORT,
A(1928); NAUGHTY BABY(1929); PALS OF THE PRAIRIE(1929)
Misc. Silents
WHISPERING SAGE(1927); THROUGH THE BREAKERS(1928); LAUGHING AT
DEATH(1929); LAW OF THE PLAINS(1929); MAN FROM NEVADA, THE(1929)

Paddy Joyce
GIRL IN THE PICTURE, THE(1956, Brit.); ONE WISH TOO MANY(1956, Brit.);
DUBLIN NIGHTMARE(1958, Brit.); STEEL BAYONET, THE(1958, Brit.); CAT GANG,
THE(1959, Brit.); UP JUMPED A SWAGMAN(1965, Brit.); POOR COW(1968, Brit.); OH!
WHAT A LOVELY WAR(1969, Brit.); LADY CAROLINE LAMB(1972, Brit./Ital.)

Pat Joyce
HAVE A NICE WEEKEND(1975)

Patricia Joyce
VISITORS, THE(1972); CATAMOUNT KILLING, THE(1975, Ger.)

Peggy Hopkins Joyce
INTERNATIONAL HOUSE(1933)
Silents
SKYROCKET, THE(1926)

Rosemary Joyce
SQUEEZE PLAY(1981)

Sean Joyce
MINNIE AND MOSKOWITZ(1971)

Stephen Joyce
STREET OF SINNERS(1957); IRISH WHISKEY REBELLION(1973); STRANGER IS
WATCHING, A(1982)

Susan Joyce
TOM SAWYER(1973)

Teddy Joyce
CROONER(1932)

Vern Joyce
FIRST NUDIE MUSICAL, THE(1976)

Virginia Joyce
HAPPY DAYS(1930)

William Joyce
BLIND ALIBI(1938), w; CANYON CROSSROADS(1955), p; I EAT YOUR SKIN(1971);
YOUNG NURSES, THE(1973)

William Ogden Joyce
THIS COULD BE THE NIGHT(1957)

Yootha Joyce
SPARROWS CAN'T SING(1963, Brit.); PUMPKIN EATER, THE(1964, Brit.); DIE,
DIE, MY DARLING(1965, Brit.); HAVING A WILD WEEKEND(1965, Brit.); KALEIDO-
SCOPE(1966, Brit.); MAN FOR ALL SEASONS, A(1966, Brit.); COP-OUT(1967, Brit.);
OUR MOTHER'S HOUSE(1967, Brit.); CHARLIE BUBBLES(1968, Brit.); FRAGMENT
OF FEAR(1971, Brit.); NIGHT DIGGER, THE(1971, Brit.); BURKE AND HARE(1972,
Brit.); ALL THE RIGHT NOISES(1973, Brit.); GEORGE AND MILDRED(1980, Brit.)
Misc. Talkies
MAN ABOUT THE HOUSE(1974, Brit.)

Odetta Joyeux
SYLVIA AND THE PHANTOM(1950, Fr.)

Odette Joyeux
CURTAIN RISES, THE(1939, Fr.); LOVE STORY(1949, Fr.); LA RONDE(1954, Fr.); IF
PARIS WERE TOLD TO US(1956, Fr.); BRIDE IS MUCH TOO BEAUTIFUL, THE(1958,
Fr.), w

Francis Joyner
Silents
AUCTION BLOCK, THE(1917)
Misc. Silents
HEARTACHES(1915); ONLY WAY OUT, THE(1915); RIGHTS OF MAN, THE(1915)

Frank Joyner
BENEATH THE 12-MILE REEF(1953)
Silents
NANETTE OF THE WILDS(1916); OUTWITTED(1917); OAKDALE AFFAIR,
THE(1919); KENTUCKIANS, THE(1921)
Misc. Silents
COPPERHEAD, THE(1920)

Henry Joyner
DAVY CROCKETT, KING OF THE WILD FRONTIER(1955)

Jackie Joyner
WILL ANY GENTLEMAN?(1955, Brit.)

Joyzelle Joyner
SIGN OF THE CROSS, THE(1932); WHISTLIN' DAN(1932)
Silents
OUT OF THE PAST(1927)

Paul Joynt
ECHOES(1983)

Joyzelle
BLACK WATCH, THE(1929); JUST IMAGINE(1930); LOTUS LADY(1930); ONE
HYSTERICAL NIGHT(1930); PRINCE OF DIAMONDS(1930); SONG OF THE CABEL-
LERO(1930); VANISHING FRONTIER, THE(1932); I BELIEVED IN YOU(1934)

Sofia Jozeffi
Misc. Silents
RED IMPS(1923, USSR)

Wang Ju-jen
VERMILION DOOR(1969, Hong Kong), m

Juan
NEST, THE(1982, Span.)

Olga San Juan
OUT OF THIS WORLD(1945); VARIETY GIRL(1947)

Juana
VIOLATED(1953); NIGHT OF THE WITCHES(1970)

San Juana
Silents
APACHE, THE(1925, Brit.)

Julio Molina Juanes
EL CONDOR(1970), art d

Juanita
OPERATION CIA(1965)

Juanita Hall Choir
MIRACLE IN HARLEM(1948)

Israel Juarbe
1984
BEVERLY HILLS COP(1984); HADLEY'S REBELLION(1984); KARATE KID,
THE(1984)

Lupe Juarez
RAGGEDY MAN(1981)

Roman Juarez
TARZAN AND THE VALLEY OF GOLD(1966 U.S./Switz.), makeup

The Jubalaires
DUCHESS OF IDAHO, THE(1950); HIT THE DECK(1955)

Alice Jubert
J.D.'S REVENGE(1976)

Jubilee Girls
VARIETY JUBILEE(1945, Brit.)

The Jubilee Singers
SHOW BOAT(1929)

Judd
PURSUIT OF THE GRAF SPEE(1957, Brit.)

Alan Judd
BONNIE PRINCE CHARLIE(1948, Brit.); 13 EAST STREET(1952, Brit.)

Bill Judd
HELL SHIP MUTINY(1957), ph

Carolyn Judd
Misc. Talkies
FIVE ANGRY WOMEN(1975)

Dino Judd
NICKELODEON(1976)

Edward Judd
HELL, HEAVEN OR HOBOKEN(1958, Brit.); HIDEOUT(1948, Brit.); OUTSIDER,
THE(1949, Brit.); MANIACS ON WHEELS(1951, Brit.); LARGE ROPE, THE(1953, Brit.);
ADVENTURE IN THE HOPFIELDS(1954, Brit.); GOOD DIE YOUNG, THE(1954, Brit.);
X THE UNKNOWN(1957, Brit.); MAN UPSTAIRS, THE(1959, Brit.); NO SAFETY
AHEAD(1959, Brit.); SUBWAY IN THE SKY(1959, Brit.); IT TAKES A THIEF(1960,
Brit.); SHAKEDOWN, THE(1960, Brit.); DAY THE EARTH CAUGHT FIRE, THE(1961,
Brit.); CONCRETE JUNGLE, THE(1962, Brit.); MYSTERY SUBMARINE(1963, Brit.);
STOLEN HOURS(1963); FIRST MEN IN THE MOON(1964, Brit.); LONG SHIPS,
THE(1964, Brit./Yugo.); INVASION(1965, Brit.); PUSSYCAT ALLEY(1965, Brit.);
STRANGE BEDFELLOWS(1965); ISLAND OF TERROR(1967, Brit.); VENGEANCE OF
SHE, THE(1968, Brit.); UNIVERSAL SOLDIER(1971, Brit.); LIVING FREE(1972, Brit.);
ASSASSIN(1973, Brit.); O LUCKY MAN!(1973, Brit.); VAULT OF HORROR, THE(1973,
Brit.); INCREDIBLE SARAH, THE(1976, Brit.); HOUND OF THE BASKERVILLES,
THE(1983, Brit.)
Misc. Talkies
WHOSE CHILD AM I?(1976)

Forrest Judd
BELOW THE DEADLINE(1946), w; SIXTEEN FATHOMS DEEP(1948), w; MON-
SOON(1953), p, w

Jack Judd
EMBALMER, THE(1966, Ital.)

John Judd
TEXAS TRAIL(1937); RIDERS OF PASCO BASIN(1940); TRIPLE JUSTICE(1940);
NORTH STAR, THE(1943); TEXAS KID, THE(1944); SCUM(1979, Brit.); THAT SUM-
MER(1979, Brit.)
Silents
KINGFISHER'S ROOST, THE(1922); OUT OF LUCK(1923)

Johnny Judd
COWBOY AND THE LADY, THE(1938)
Silents
HEADIN' SOUTH(1918)

Lesley Judd
HALF A SIXPENCE(1967, Brit.)

Naomi Judd
MORE AMERICAN GRAFFITI(1979)

Philip Judd
STARSTRUCK(1982, Aus.)

Robb Judd
RECOMMENDATION FOR MERCY(1975, Can.)

Robert Judd
FIGHT FOR YOUR LIFE(1977)

Lee James Jude
NIGHTMARES(1983)

Charles Judeis
CAPTAIN THUNDER(1931)

Charles Judel
HOODLUM SAINT, THE(1946)

Charles Judela
MOUNTAIN MUSIC(1937)

B.N. Judell
DELINQUENT PARENTS(1938), p; REBELLIOUS DAUGHTERS(1938), p; SLAN-
DER HOUSE(1938), p

Ben Judell
HITLER-DEAD OR ALIVE(1942), p

Charles Judels
MOTHER KNOWS BEST(1928), d; FROZEN JUSTICE(1929); BIG PARTY,
THE(1930); CHEER UP AND SMILE(1930); COLLEGE LOVERS(1930); DOORWAY TO
HELL(1930); HOT FOR PARIS(1930); LET'S GO PLACES(1930); LIFE OF THE PARTY,
THE(1930); OH! SAILOR, BEHAVE!(1930); EASIEST WAY, THE(1931); FIFTY MIL-
LION FRENCHMEN(1931); GOLD DUST GERTIE(1931); WOMEN OF ALL NA-
TIONS(1931); HIGH PRESSURE(1932); ONE HOUR WITH YOU(1932); MIGHTY
BARNUM, THE(1934); ENCHANTED APRIL(1935); FLORENTINE DAGGER,
THE(1935); NIGHT IS YOUNG, THE(1935); SYMPHONY OF LIVING(1935); GREAT
ZIEGFELD, THE(1936); I'D GIVE MY LIFE(1936); LOVE ON THE RUN(1936); ROSE
BOWL(1936); SAN FRANCISCO(1936); SUZY(1936); ALONG CAME LOVE(1937); BIG
SHOW, THE(1937); BRIDE WORE RED, THE(1937); EBB TIDE(1937); FIGHT FOR
YOUR LADY(1937); HIGH FLYERS(1937); IT CAN'T LAST FOREVER(1937); LIFE OF
THE PARTY, THE(1937); LIVE, LOVE AND LEARN(1937); LOVE AND HISSES(1937);
MARRY THE GIRL(1937); MAYTIME(1937); PLAINSMAN, THE(1937); RHYTHM IN
THE CLOUDS(1937); SONG OF THE CITY(1937); SWING HIGH, SWING LOW(1937);
WHEN'S YOUR BIRTHDAY?(1937); WIFE, DOCTOR AND NURSE(1937); FLIRTING
WITH FATE(1938); GIRL DOWNSTAIRS, THE(1938); MAD ABOUT MUSIC(1938);
RECKLESS LIVING(1938); STOLEN HEAVEN(1938); SWISS MISS(1938); YOU'RE
ONLY YOUNG ONCE(1938); ICE FOLLIES OF 1939(1939); IDIOT'S DELIGHT(1939);
NINOTCHKA(1939); THAT'S RIGHT-YOU'RE WRONG(1939); DOWN ARGENTINE
WAY(1940); FLORIAN(1940); GOLD RUSH MAISIE(1940); IT ALL CAME TRUE(1940);

ON THEIR OWN(1940); PINOCCHIO(1940); PUBLIC DEB NO. 1(1940); STRANGE CARGO(1940); STRANGER ON THE THIRD FLOOR(1940); VIVA CISCO KID(1940); CHEERS FOR MISS BISHOP(1941); CHOCOLATE SOLDIER, THE(1941); KATHLEEN(1941); LAW OF THE TROPICS(1941); SWEETHEART OF THE CAMPUS(1941); THIS WOMAN IS MINE(1941); BABY FACE MORGAN(1942); CLOSE CALL FOR ELLERY QUEEN, A(1942); HARD WAY, THE(1942); I MARRIED AN ANGEL(1942); TORTILLA FLAT(1942); DU BARRY WAS A LADY(1943); KID DYNAMITE(1943); SWING YOUR PARTNER(1943); CAREER GIRL(1944); KISMET(1944); KNICKERBOCKER HOLIDAY(1944); BELL FOR ADANO, A(1945); SUNBONNET SUE(1945); HER ADVENTUROUS NIGHT(1946); IN OLD SACRAMENTO(1946); MIGHTY MCGURK, THE(1946); PLAINSMAN AND THE LADY(1946); TANGIER(1946); WHISTLE STOP(1946); I WONDER WHO'S KISSING HER NOW(1947); PANHANDLE(1948); SAMSON AND DELILAH(1949)
Silents
UNDER THE RED ROBE(1923)
Misc. Silents
COMMUTORS, THE(1915)
R. Juden
Misc. Silents
WHEN LONDON BURNED(1915, Brit.)
Alfred Judge
HOUR OF THIRTEEN, THE(1952), art d
Arline Judge
AMERICAN TRAGEDY, AN(1931); ARE THESE OUR CHILDREN?(1931); AGE OF CONSENT(1932); GIRL CRAZY(1932); IS MY FACE RED?(1932); ROAR OF THE DRAGON(1932); YOUNG BRIDE(1932); FLYING DEVILS(1933); LOOKING FOR TROUBLE(1934); NAME THE WOMAN(1934); PARTY'S OVER, THE(1934); SENSATION HUNTERS(1934); SHOOT THE WORKS(1934); WHEN STRANGERS MEET(1934); BACHELOR OF ARTS(1935); COLLEGE SCANDAL(1935); GEORGE WHITE'S 1935 SCANDALS(1935); MILLION DOLLAR BABY(1935); MUSIC IS MAGIC(1935); MYSTERIOUS MR. WONG(1935); ONE HOUR LATE(1935); SHIP CAFE(1935); WELCOME HOME(1935); HERE COMES TROUBLE(1936); IT HAD TO HAPPEN(1936); KING OF BURLESQUE(1936); ONE IN A MILLION(1936); PIGSKIN PARADE(1936); STAR FOR A NIGHT(1936); VALIANT IS THE WORD FOR CARRIE(1936); HARVARD, HERE I COME(1942); LADY IS WILLING, THE(1942); LAW OF THE JUNGLE(1942); WILDCAT(1942); GIRLS IN CHAINS(1943); SONG OF TEXAS(1943); CONTENDER, THE(1944); TAKE IT BIG(1944); G.I. HONEYMOON(1945); FROM THIS DAY FORWARD(1946); MAD WEDNESDAY(1950); CRAWLING HAND, THE(1963); SWINGIN' AFFAIR, A(1963)
Chris Judge
RUNNING BRAVE(1983, Can.)
Elwell Judge
Silents
PAIR OF CUPIDS, A(1918)
Jack Judge
HOLD'EM YALE(1935); REGAL CAVALCADE(1935, Brit.); STOLEN HARMONY(1935)
James P. Judge
BABY, TAKE A BOW(1934), w
Jeremy Judge
JET STORM(1961, Brit.)
Joel Judge
GOLDEN MISTRESS, THE(1954), d, w
John Judge
Silents
PAIR OF CUPIDS, A(1918)
Michael T. Judge
1984
UP THE CREEK(1984)
Naomi Judge
TERROR TRAIL(1933); WATERFRONT LADY(1935); GOLD DIGGERS OF 1937(1936); SNOWED UNDER(1936)
Misc. Talkies
MAN FROM ARIZONA, THE(1932)
Neoma Judge
YOUNG BLOOD(1932); YOUNG AND BEAUTIFUL(1934)
Ghennadj Judin
WATERLOO(1970, Ital./USSR)
Gary Judis
WILD YOUTH(1961), w; INCIDENT IN AN ALLEY(1962); ZEBRA IN THE KITCHEN(1965)
Lester Judson
SAND CASTLE, THE(1961); OPEN THE DOOR AND SEE ALL THE PEOPLE(1964)
Stephen Judson
STUDENT NURSES, THE(1970), ed; VELVET VAMPIRE, THE(1971), ed
William Judson
COLD RIVER(1982), w
Judy
ESCAPE TO BURMA(1955)
Cindy Judy
TOUGH ENOUGH(1983)
Judy Clark and The Solid Senders
HEY, ROOKIE(1944)
Craig Jue
GREEN BERETS, THE(1968)
Derek Jue
DIRTY HARRY(1971)
Kirk Jue
RACE FOR YOUR LIFE, CHARLIE BROWN(1977)
Bente Juel
JOURNEY TO THE SEVENTH PLANET(1962, U.S./Swed.)
Inger Juel
DEVIL'S WANTON, THE(1962, Swed.)
Meinhard Juenger
TWO WORLD(1930, Brit.)
Curd Juergens [Curt Jurgens]
MOZART STORY, THE(1948, Aust.); APRIL 1, 2000(1953, Aust.)

Kurt Juergens [Curt Jurgens]
ROYAL WALTZ, THE(1936)
Philip Juergens
BLONDE COMET(1941), w
Edwin Juergensen
MOSCOW SHANGHAI(1936, Ger.)
Juergen Juerges
GERMANY IN AUTUMN(1978, Ger.), ph
Arno Juerging
Misc. Talkies
ANDY WARHOL'S DRACULA(1974)
Little Brown Jug
WHIRLWIND RAIDERS(1948); RED PONY, THE(1949); COWBOY AND THE PRIZE-FIGHTER(1950)
Rudolf Jugert
DAY WILL COME, A(1960, Ger.), d
Rudolph Jugert
FILM WITHOUT A NAME(1950, Ger.), d, w
Gerard Jugnot
TENANT, THE(1976, Fr.); HERBIE GOES TO MONTE CARLO(1977); JUDGE AND THE ASSASSIN, THE(1979, Fr.)
1984
JUST THE WAY YOU ARE(1984)
Jenny Jugo
JAZZBAND FIVE, THE(1932, Ger,)
Misc. Silents
ROYAL SCANDAL(1929, Ger.)
William J. Jugo
GAVILAN(1968), p,d&w
Evelyna Juhanova
DO YOU KEEP A LION AT HOME?(1966, Czech.)
Jacint Juhasz
RED AND THE WHITE, THE(1969, Hung./USSR); ROUND UP, THE(1969, Hung.)
Jerry Juhl
MUPPET MOVIE, THE(1979), w; GREAT MUPPET CAPER, THE(1981), w
Benny Juhlin
REPTILICUS(1962, U.S./Den.); PEOPLE MEET AND SWEET MUSIC FILLS THE HEART(1969, Den./Swed.)
Harald Juhnke
TERROR OF DR. MABUSE, THE(1965, Ger.); RED-DRAGON(1967, Ital./Ger./US); U-47 LT. COMMANDER PRIEN(1967, Ger.)
Ka Jui-fan
MADAME WHITE SNAKE(1963, Hong Kong), w
Ke Jui-feng
LADY GENERAL, THE(1965, Hong Kong), w
Lu Jui-ying
DREAM OF THE RED CHAMBER, THE(1966, Chi.)
Argus Spear Juillard
GUNS OF THE TREES(1964)
Jean Juillard
ROAD TO SHAME, THE(1962, Fr.)
Robert Juillard
GERMANY, YEAR ZERO(1949, Ger.), ph; LES BELLES-DE-NUIT(1952, Fr.), ph; FORBIDDEN GAMES(1953, Fr.), ph; COUNT OF MONTE-CRISTO(1955, Fr., Ital.), ph; GRAND MANEUVER, THE(1956, Fr.), ph; HAPPY ROAD, THE(1957), ph; ROAD TO SHAME, THE(1962, Fr.), ph
Charles Juin
NOUS IRONS A PARIS(1949, Fr.), ph
Kazafumi Jujii
GAMERA VERSUS VIRAS(1968, Jap), spec eff
Alain Jukabowicz
NEITHER BY DAY NOR BY NIGHT(1972, U.S./Israel), ed
Bernard Jukes
SAP FROM SYRACUSE, THE(1930); TORSO MURDER MYSTERY, THE(1940, Brit.)
Christen Jul
VAMPYR(1932, Fr./Ger.), w
Jules
Silents
TABU(1931)
Maurice Jules
VELVET VAMPIRE, THE(1971), w; SCREAM BLACULA SCREAM(1973), w
Raul Julia
ORGANIZATION, THE(1971); PANIC IN NEEDLE PARK(1971); GUMBALL RALLY, THE(1976); BEEN DOWN SO LONG IT LOOKS LIKE UP TO ME(1977); EYES OF LAURA MARS(1978); ESCAPE ARTIST, THE(1982); ONE FROM THE HEART(1982); TEMPEST(1982)
Julian
WRECK OF THE MARY DEAR, THE(1959), p
Albert Julian
SECRET AGENT, THE(1936, Brit.), set d
Alice Julian
Silents
UNHOLY THREE, THE(1925)
Arthur Julian
BEATNIKS, THE(1960), w; HOW TO STUFF A WILD BIKINI(1965); BOATNIKS, THE(1970), w
Chuck Julian
WAR LOVER, THE(1962, U.S./Brit.); SPACEFLIGHT IC-1(1965, Brit.); PROMISE HER ANYTHING(1966, Brit.); SUPERMAN(1978); TERROR(1979, Brit.)
1984
SCREAM FOR HELP(1984)
Janet Julian
SMOKEY BITES THE DUST(1981); HUMONGOUS(1982, Can.)
1984
FEAR CITY(1984); SWORDKILL(1984)
Jeffrey Julian
Misc. Silents
WOMAN AND OFFICER 26, THE(1920, Brit.)

Joe Julian
THAT NIGHT(1957); VIOLATORS, THE(1957)
Joseph Julian
DEAD TO THE WORLD(1961)
Marcel Julian
BRAIN, THE(1969, Fr./US), w; DON'T LOOK NOW(1969, Brit./Fr.), w; DELUSIONS OF GRANDEUR(1971 Fr.), w
Paul Julian
FOUR POSTER, THE(1952), anim; CHARLOTTE'S WEB(1973), art d; METAMORPHOSES(1978), prod d; HEIDI'S SONG(1982), art d
Ray Julian
GUILTY BYSTANDER(1950); GUERRILLA GIRL(1953)
Rupert Julian
PHANTOM OF THE OPERA, THE(1929), d; CAT CREEPS, THE(1930), d; LOVE COMES ALONG(1930), d
Silents
PRETTY SISTER OF JOSE(1915); SCANDAL(1915); DUMB GIRL OF PORTICI(1916); NAKED HEARTS(1916), a, d, w; KENTUCKY CINDERELLA, A(1917), a, d; KAISER, BEAST OF BERLIN, THE(1918), a, d, w; MERRY-GO-ROUND(1923), d; PHANTOM OF THE OPERA, THE(1925), d; YANKEE CLIPPER, THE(1927), d; LEOPARD LADY, THE(1928), d; WALKING BACK(1928), d
Misc. Silents
MERCHANT OF VENICE, THE(1914); JEWEL(1915); LONE STAR RUSH, THE(1915); BETTINA LOVED A SOLDIER(1916), a; BUGLER OF ALGIERS, THE(1916), a, d; EVIL WOMEN DO, THE(1916), a, d; CIRCUS OF LIFE, THE(1917), d; DESIRE OF THE MOTH, THE(1917), a, d; DOOR BETWEEN, THE(1917), d; GIFT GIRL, THE(1917), a, d; MOTHER O'MINE(1917), a, d; MYSTERIOUS MR. TILLER, THE(1917), a, d; RIGHT TO BE HAPPY, THE(1917), a, d; SAVAGE, THE(1917), d; FIRES OF YOUTH(1918), d; HANDS DOWN(1918), a, d; HUNGRY EYES(1918), a, d; MIDNIGHT MADNESS(1918), d; SCANDAL MONGERS(1918); CREAKING STAIRS(1919), d; MILLIONAIRE PIRATE, THE(1919), d; SLEEPING LION, THE(1919), d; HONEY BEE, THE(1920), d; GIRL WHO RAN WILD, THE(1922), d; LOVE AND GLORY(1924), d; HELL'S HIGHROAD(1925), d; SILENCE(1926), d; THREE FACES EAST(1926), d; COUNTRY DOCTOR, THE(1927), d
Sally Julian
HOMETOWN U.S.A.(1979)
Victor Julian
JUMBO(1962)
John Juliani
MADELEINE IS(1971, Can.); MARIE-ANN(1978, Can.); DIRTY TRICKS(1981, Can.)
Claire Julianne
YOUNG AND BEAUTIFUL(1934), cos
Jorge Juliao
PIXOTE(1981, Braz.)
Julias Ladies Choir
LAUGH IT OFF(1940, Brit.)
Julie
BEST FRIENDS(1975)
Lady Julie
Misc. Silents
LOVE MASTER, THE(1924)
A. M. Julien
CHILDREN OF CHAOS(1950, Fr.)
Andre Julien
1984
PERILS OF GWENDOLINE, THE(1984, Fr.)
Arthur Julien
HAPPY ROAD, THE(1957), w
Jacqueline Julien
RED LIPS(1964, Fr./Ital.)
Jay Julien
KING OF COMEDY, THE(1983); TALES OF ORDINARY MADNESS(1983, Ital.)
Martin Julien
ROOSTER COGBURN(1975), w
Max Julien
BLACK KLANSMAN, THE(1966); PSYCH-OUT(1968); SAVAGE SEVEN, THE(1968); UPTIGHT(1968); GETTING STRAIGHT(1970); CLEOPATRA JONES(1973), w; MACK, THE(1973); THOMASINE AND BUSHROD(1974), a, p, w
Pierre Julien
QUARTET(1981, Brit./Fr.)
Sandra Julien
Misc. Talkies
I AM FRIGID...WHY?(1973); STRANGE THINGS HAPPEN AT NIGHT(1979)
Serge Julien
FIENDISH PLOT OF DR. FU MANCHU, THE(1980)
Remy Julienne
BOBBY DEERFIELD(1977), stunts; OCTOPUSSY(1983, Brit.), stunts
Bill Juliff
GOODBYE PORK PIE(1981, New Zealand)
1984
UTU(1984, New Zealand)
Julika
PIED PIPER, THE(1942)
Montserrat Julio
ROBIN AND MARIAN(1976, Brit.)
Julissa
SNAKE PEOPLE, THE(1968, Mex./U.S.)
Ami Julius
1984
HOT DOG...THE MOVIE(1984)
H. Julius
DEAD OF NIGHT(1946, Brit.), ph
Harold Julius
BEDELIA(1946, Brit.), ph
Maxine Julius
JUST A GIGOLO(1979, Ger.), ed
R. Julius
PINK STRING AND SEALING WAX(1950, Brit.), ph

Jean Julliac
RETURN OF MARTIN GUERRE, THE(1983, Fr.)
Marcel Jullian
SUCKER, THE(1966, Fr./Ital.), w
Rene Julliard
GERVAISE(1956, Fr.), ph
Ivan Jullien
1984
WHERE IS PARSIFAL?(1984, Brit.), m
Bill Julliff
SLEEPING DOGS(1977, New Zealand)
Albert Jullion
39 STEPS, THE(1935, Brit.), prod d; SABOTAGE(1937, Brit.), set d; LADY VANISHES, THE(1938, Brit.), set d; IDOL OF PARIS(1948, Brit.), art d
Evelyn July
ANNA(1981, Fr./Hung.), p
Juma
WEST OF ZANZIBAR(1954, Brit.); ODONGO(1956, Brit.); SAFARI(1956)
Lenny Juma
1984
SHEENA(1984)
Frank Jumagai
HOUSE OF BAMBOO(1955)
Jumble
JUST WILLIAM'S LUCK(1948, Brit.)
Jumble the Dog
WILLIAM COMES TO TOWN(1948, Brit.)
Betty Jumel
DEMOBBED(1944, Brit.); HONEYMOON HOTEL(1946, Brit.); CUP-TIE HONEYMOON(1948, Brit.)
Lily Jumel
Silents
ITALIAN STRAW HAT, AN(1927, Fr.), art d
Gordon Jump
FLAREUP(1969); CONQUEST OF THE PLANET OF THE APES(1972); HOUSE CALLS(1978); SKATEBOARD(1978)
1984
MAKING THE GRADE(1984)
Misc. Talkies
EVIDENCE OF POWER(1979)
Betty Mae Jumper
PORKY'S II: THE NEXT DAY(1983)
Johnny Jumpup
SCARECROW IN A GARDEN OF CUCUMBERS(1972)
Arthur Junaluska
HOSPITAL, THE(1971)
Tito Junco
LEGEND OF A BANDIT, THE(1945, Mex.); REBELLION OF THE HANGED, THE(1954, Mex.); THUNDERSTORM(1956); JET OVER THE ATLANTIC(1960); GINA(1961, Fr./Mex.); INVASION OF THE VAMPIRES, THE(1961, Mex.); EMPTY STAR, THE(1962, Mex.); EXTERMINATING ANGEL, THE(1967, Mex.); DEATH IN THE GARDEN(1977, Fr./Mex.)
Victor Junco
REBELLION OF THE HANGED, THE(1954, Mex.); BANDIDO(1956); BLUE DEMON VERSUS THE INFERNAL BRAINS(1967, Mex.); MADAME DEATH(1968, Mex.); BIG CUBE, THE(1969); UNDEFEATED, THE(1969); VENGEANCE OF THE VAMPIRE WOMEN, THE(1969, Mex.)
Victor Juncos
SEVEN CITIES OF GOLD(1955)
June
Silents
LODGER, THE(1926, Brit.)
Miss June
Silents
AULD ROBIN GRAY(1917, Brit.)
Misc. Silents
AULD ROBIN GRAY(1917, Brit.)
Mildred June
Silents
RICH MEN'S WIVES(1922); CRINOLINE AND ROMANCE(1923); HOOK AND LADDER(1924); WHEN SECONDS COUNT(1927)
Misc. Silents
FASHIONABLE FAKERS(1923); TROUBLES OF A BRIDE(1924); SNARL OF HATE, THE(1927)
Ray June
RIVER WOMAN, THE(1928), ph; ALIBI(1929), ph; LOCKED DOOR, THE(1929), ph; NEW YORK NIGHTS(1929), ph; TIMES SQUARE(1929), ph; EYES OF THE WORLD, THE(1930), ph; LOTTERY BRIDE, THE(1930), ph; PUTTIN' ON THE RITZ(1930), ph; ARROWSMITH(1931), ph; BOUGHT(1931), ph; CORSAIR(1931), ph; INDISCREET(1931), ph; REACHING FOR THE MOON(1931), ph; CYNARA(1932), ph; DISORDERLY CONDUCT(1932), ph; HORSE FEATHERS(1932), ph; JAZZ BABIES(1932), ph; SINNERS IN THE SUN(1932), ph; ANOTHER LANGUAGE(1933), ph; I COVER THE WATERFRONT(1933), ph; SECRETS(1933), ph; WHEN LADIES MEET(1933), ph; GAY BRIDE, THE(1934), ph; GIRL FROM MISSOURI, THE(1934), ph; HIDE-OUT(1934), ph; KID MILLIONS(1934), ph; RIP TIDE(1934), ph; TREASURE ISLAND(1934), ph; WOMEN IN HIS LIFE, THE(1934), ph; BARBARY COAST(1935), ph; CHINA SEAS(1935), ph; VANESSA, HER LOVE STORY(1935), ph; BORN TO DANCE(1936), ph; GREAT ZIEGFELD, THE(1936), ph; RIFF-RAFF(1936), ph; SUZY(1936), ph; WIFE VERSUS SECRETARY(1936), ph; ESPIONAGE(1937), ph; LIVE, LOVE AND LEARN(1937), ph; NIGHT MUST FALL(1937), ph; SARATOGA(1937), ph; RICH MAN, POOR GIRL(1938), ph; TEST PILOT(1938), ph; VACATION FROM LOVE(1938), ph; WOMAN AGAINST WOMAN(1938), ph; BABES IN ARMS(1939), ph; FAST AND FURIOUS(1939), ph; HONOLULU(1939), ph; LUCKY NIGHT(1939), ph; AND ONE WAS BEAUTIFUL(1940), ph; EARL OF CHICAGO, THE(1940), ph; LITTLE NELLIE KELLY(1940), ph; MAN FROM DAKOTA, THE(1940), ph; STRIKE UP THE BAND(1940), ph; FEMININE TOUCH, THE(1941), ph; H.M. PULHAM, ESQ.(1941), ph; LOVE CRAZY(1941), ph; ZIEGFELD GIRL(1941), ph; CAIRO(1942), ph; CALLING DR. GILLESPIE(1942), ph; I MARRIED AN ANGEL(1942), ph; JOURNEY FOR MARGARET(1942), ph; I DOOD IT(1943), ph; MARRIAGE IS A PRIVATE AFFAIR(1944), ph; THREE MEN IN WHITE(1944), ph; KEEP YOUR POWDER

DRY(1945), ph; TWICE BLESSED(1945), ph; COCKEYED MIRACLE, THE(1946), ph; HOODLUM SAINT, THE(1946), ph; BEGINNING OR THE END, THE(1947), ph; ALIAS A GENTLEMAN(1948), ph; BRIDE GOES WILD, THE(1948), ph, ph; SOUTHERN YANKEE, A(1948), ph; THREE DARING DAUGHTERS(1948), ph; SECRET GARDEN, THE(1949), ph; SUN COMES UP, THE(1949), ph; CRISIS(1950), ph; MRS. O'MALLEY AND MR. MALONE(1950), ph; NANCY GOES TO RIO(1950), ph; REFORMER AND THE REDHEAD, THE(1950), ph; SHADOW ON THE WALL(1950), ph; CALLAWAY WENT THATAWAY(1951), ph; INSIDE STRAIGHT(1951), ph; IT'S A BIG COUNTRY(1951), ph; STRICTLY DISHONORABLE(1951), ph; INVITATION(1952), ph; JUST THIS ONCE(1952), ph; SKY FULL OF MOON(1952), ph; ABOVE AND BEYOND(1953), ph; CODE TWO(1953), ph; EASY TO LOVE(1953), ph; SLIGHT CASE OF LARCENY, A(1953), ph; SOMBRERO(1953), ph; DAY OF TRIUMPH(1944), ph; THIS IS MY LOVE(1954), ph; COURT JESTER, THE(1956), ph; HOT BLOOD(1956), ph; FUNNY FACE(1957), ph; SEVENTH SIN, THE(1957), ph; GIGI(1958), ph; HOUSEBOAT(1958), ph

Silents
PENROD(1922), ph; BOY OF MINE(1923), ph; PENROD AND SAM(1923), ph; NARROW STREET, THE(1924), ph; ONE OF THE BRAVEST(1925), ph; SILENT POWER, THE(1926), ph; CROSS BREED(1927), ph; GIRL FROM RIO, THE(1927), ph; WARNING, THE(1927), ph; WOMAN WHO DID NOT CARE, THE(1927), ph; MIDNIGHT LIFE(1928), ph; SO THIS IS LOVE(1928), ph

Allan Jung
MURDER BY TELEVISION(1935); BEHIND THE RISING SUN(1943)

Allen Jung
SHE LEARNED ABOUT SAILORS(1934); NIGHT PLANE FROM CHUNGKING(1942); SOMEWHERE I'LL FIND YOU(1942); GUADALCANAL DIARY(1943); MISSION TO MOSCOW(1943); WE'VE NEVER BEEN LICKED(1943); PURPLE HEART, THE(1944); BLOOD AND STEEL(1959); DIMENSION 5(1966); PARTY, THE(1968); STAR SPANGLED GIRL(1971)

Allen Durlin Jung
LAST OF THE SECRET AGENTS?, THE(1966)

Calvin Jung
FORMULA, THE(1980); CHALLENGE, THE(1982)

Friedrich Jung
CRUISER EMDEN(1932, Ger.), m

Jurgen Jung
JONATHAN(1973, Ger.)

Kurt A. Jung
WILLY(1963, U.S./Ger.)

Manfred Jung
WAGNER(1983, Brit./Hung./Aust.)

Paul Jung
GREATEST SHOW ON EARTH, THE(1952)

Shia Jung
CHARLIE CHAN AT THE CIRCUS(1936); PORT OF HATE(1939)

Taft Jung
GENERAL DIED AT DAWN, THE(1936)

Tsao Shao Jung
EXIT THE DRAGON, ENTER THE TIGER(1977, Hong Kong)

Kurt Jung-Alsen
PRIVATE POOLEY(1962, Brit./E. Ger.), d

Alfred Junge
TWO WORLD(1930, Brit.), art d; EIGHT GIRLS IN A BOAT(1932, Ger.), set d; PICCADILLY(1932, Brit.), art d; RESERVED FOR LADIES(1932, Brit.), prod d; MARIUS(1933, Fr.), prod d; STRAUSS' GREAT WALTZ(1934, Brit.), set d; STRIKE!(1934, Brit.), art d; MAN WHO KNEW TOO MUCH, THE(1935, Brit.), art d & set d; CITADEL, THE(1938), art d; YOUNG AND INNOCENT(1938, Brit.), art d; GOODBYE MR. CHIPS(1939, Brit.), art d; SILVER FLEET, THE(1945, Brit.), prod d; STAIRWAY TO HEAVEN(1946, Brit.), prod d; I KNOW WHERE I'M GOING(1947, Brit.), art d; CONSPIRATOR(1949, Brit.), art d; EDWARD, MY SON(1949, U.S./Brit.), art d; MINIVER STORY, THE(1950, Brit./U.S.), art d; IVANHOE(1952, Brit.), art d; KNIGHTS OF THE ROUND TABLE(1953), art d; MOGAMBO(1953), art d; NEVER LET ME GO(1953, U.S./Brit.), art d; TERROR ON A TRAIN(1953), art d; BEAU BRUMMELL(1954), art d; BETRAYED(1954), art d; FLAME AND THE FLESH(1954), art d; QUENTIN DURWARD(1955), art d; INVITATION TO THE DANCE(1956), art d; BARRETTS OF WIMPOLE STREET, THE(1957), art d

Karl Junge
HELP I'M INVISIBLE(1952, Ger.), p

Kellogg Junge, Jr.
TRUE STORY OF JESSE JAMES, THE(1957)

Kelly Junge, Jr.
WORLD WAS HIS JURY, THE(1958)

Alf Jungermann
BATTLE OF BRITAIN, THE(1969, Brit.)

Karl Junghans
Misc. Silents
SUCH IS LIFE(1929, Czech.), d

The Jungleland Elephants
TOBY TYLER(1960)

Jack Jungmeyer
SHOW FOLKS(1928), w; BIG NEWS(1929), w; HIS FIRST COMMAND(1929), w; OFFICE SCANDAL, THE(1929), w; SHADY LADY, THE(1929), w; MEN OF AMERICA(1933), w; SHOWDOWN, THE(1940), w; STREET CORNER(1948), w
Silents
CIRCUS ACE, THE(1927), w; TUMBLING RIVER(1927), w

Jack Jungmeyer, Jr.
HIGH SCHOOL(1940), w; MANHATTAN HEARTBEAT(1940), w; ON THEIR OWN(1940), w; THAT OTHER WOMAN(1942), w; TENDER YEARS, THE(1947), w; HIGHWAY DRAGNET(1954), p

Jack Jungmeyer, Sr.
WHEN THE DALTONS RODE(1940), w

Frieda Jungwirth
DIE FLEDERMAUS(1964, Aust.), makeup

Junia the Dog
KILL OR CURE(1962, Brit.)

Junior
ISLAND OF THE BLUE DOLPHINS(1964); NATIONAL LAMPOON'S ANIMAL HOUSE(1978)

Don Junior
TREASURE OF MONTE CRISTO(1949)

Fabio Junior
BYE-BYE BRASIL(1980, Braz.)

John Junior
Silents
MY BEST GIRL(1927)
Misc. Silents
DAUGHTER OF THE CITY, A(1915); CAPTAIN JINKS OF THE HORSE MARINES(1916); LITTLE SHEPHERD OF BARGIAN ROW, THE(1916)

John Junkens
CONFESSIONS FROM A HOLIDAY CAMP(1977, Brit.)

Hans Junkermann
LOVE WALTZ, THE(1930, Ger.); HIS MAJESTY, KING BALLYHOO(1931, Ger.); BARBERINA(1932, Ger.); DREAM OF SCHONBRUNN(1933, Aus.)
Misc. Silents
HAMLET(1921, Ger.)

Eberhard Junkersdorf
LOST HONOR OF KATHARINA BLUM, THE(1975, Ger.), p; COUP DE GRACE(1978, Ger./Fr.), p; GERMANY IN AUTUMN(1978, Ger.), p; GERMAN SISTERS, THE(1982, Ger.), p; SISTERS, OR THE BALANCE OF HAPPINESS(1982, Ger.), p; FRIENDS AND HUSBANDS(1983, Ger.), p

Eberhardt Junkersdorf
WAR AND PEACE(1983, Ger.), p

Harry W. Junkin
SLANDER(1956), w

John Junkin
AND THE SAME TO YOU(1960, Brit.), w; WRONG ARM OF THE LAW, THE(1963, Brit.); HARD DAY'S NIGHT, A(1964, Brit.); PUMPKIN EATER, THE(1964, Brit.); BRAIN, THE(1965, Ger./Brit.); KALEIDOSCOPE(1966, Brit.); WRONG BOX, THE(1966, Brit.); HOW I WON THE WAR(1967, Brit.); PLANK, THE(1967, Brit.); MAN AT THE TOP(1973, Brit.), w; THAT SUMMER(1979, Brit.)

Juno
MAKE ME AN OFFER(1954, Brit.)

Douglas Junor
WHO HAS SEEN THE WIND(1980, Can.)

Victor Junquera
POPI(1969)

Eric Jupp
TIM(1981, Aus.), m

Fritz Juptner-Jonstorff
DIE FLEDERMAUS(1964, Aust.), set d; YOU ARE THE WORLD FOR ME(1964, Aust.), set d; HEIDI(1968, Aust.), art d

Fritz Juptner-Joustorff
STORY OF VICKIE, THE(1958, Aust.), art d

Hans Jura
ENDLESS NIGHT, THE(1963, Ger.), ph; CARMEN, BABY(1967, Yugo./Ger.), ph; THERESE AND ISABELLE(1968, U.S./Ger.), ph; HANNIBAL BROOKS(1969, Brit.), ph; LITTLE MOTHER(1973, U.S./Yugo./Ger.), ph

Pavel Juracek
VOYAGE TO THE END OF THE UNIVERSE(1963, Czech.), w; END OF AUGUST AT THE HOTEL OZONE, THE(1967, Czech.), w

Arthur Jurado
MEN, THE(1950)

Carlos Jurado
REAL LIFE(1979)

Danny Jurado
SAMAR(1962)

Elena Jurado
Silents
WHAT PRICE GLORY(1926); GIRL IN EVERY PORT, A(1928)

Katy Jurado
BULLFIGHTER AND THE LADY(1951); BRUTE, THE(1952, Mex.); HIGH NOON(1952); ARROWHEAD(1953); SAN ANTONE(1953); BROKEN LANCE(1954); RACERS, THE(1955); TRIAL(1955); MAN FROM DEL RIO(1956); TRAPEZE(1956); DRAGON WELLS MASSACRE(1957); BADLANDERS, THE(1958); ONE-EYED JACKS(1961); BARABBAS(1962, Ital.); COVENANT WITH DEATH, A(1966); SMOKY(1966); STAY AWAY, JOE(1968); ONCE UPON A SCOUNDREL(1973); PAT GARRETT AND BILLY THE KID(1973); CHILDREN OF SANCHEZ, THE(1978, U. S./Mex.)
1984
UNDER THE VOLCANO(1984)
Misc. Talkies
BRIDGE IN THE JUNGLE, THE(1971)

Boris Juraga
CLEOPATRA(1963), art d; DOCTOR FAUSTUS(1967, Brit.), art d; HONEY POT, THE(1967, Brit.), art d; THOSE DARING YOUNG MEN IN THEIR JAUNTY JALOPIES(1969, Fr./Brit./ Ital.), art d; CHINO(1976, Ital., Span., Fr.), set d; ORCA(1977), art d

Vlasta Jurajdova
MIDSUMMERS NIGHT'S DREAM, A(1961, Czech), anim

Jerry Juran
DR. BLOOD'S COFFIN(1961), w

Nathan Juran
CHARLEY'S AUNT(1941), art d; HOW GREEN WAS MY VALLEY(1941), art d; DR. RENAULT'S SECRET(1942), art d; I WAKE UP SCREAMING(1942), art d; LOVES OF EDGAR ALLAN POE, THE(1942), art d; TEN GENTLEMEN FROM WEST POINT(1942), art d; THAT OTHER WOMAN(1942), art d; RAZOR'S EDGE, THE(1946), art d; BODY AND SOUL(1947), art d; OTHER LOVE, THE(1947), art d; KISS THE BLOOD OFF MY HANDS(1948), art d; FREE FOR ALL(1949), art d; TULSA(1949), art d; UNDERTOW(1949), art d; DEPORTED(1950), art d; WINCHESTER '73(1950), art d; BRIGHT VICTORY(1951), art d; REUNION IN RENO(1951), art d; THUNDER ON THE HILL(1951), art d; BEND OF THE RIVER(1952), art d; BLACK CASTLE, THE(1952), d; MEET DANNY WILSON(1952), art d; UNTAMED FRONTIER(1952), art d; GOLDEN BLADE, THE(1953), d; GUNSMOKE(1953), d; LAW AND ORDER(1953), d; TUMBLEWEED(1953), d; DRUMS ACROSS THE RIVER(1954), d; HIGHWAY DRAGNET(1954), d; DEADLY MANTIS, THE(1957), d; 20 MILLION MILES TO EARTH(1957), d; GOOD DAY FOR A HANGING(1958), d; SEVENTH VOYAGE OF SINBAD, THE(1958), d; BOY WHO CAUGHT A CROOK(1961), w; FLIGHT OF THE LOST BALLOON(1961), d&w; JACK THE GIANT KILLER(1962), d, w; SIEGE OF THE SAXONS(1963, Brit.), d; EAST OF SUDAN(1964, Brit.), p, d; FIRST

MEN IN THE MOON(1964, Brit.), d

Nathan Juran [Nathan Hertz]
HELLCATS OF THE NAVY(1957), d

Peter Jurasik
BORN AGAIN(1978); STRAIGHT TIME(1978); TRON(1982)

A. Jurczak
PORTRAIT OF LENIN(1967, Pol./USSR)

Andrei Jurenev
WATERLOO(1970, Ital./USSR)

Jan Jurewicz
CONSTANT FACTOR, THE(1980, Pol.); CONTRACT, THE(1982, Pol.)

Claus Jurgen
SAVAGES(1972)

Curd [Curt] Jurgens
LIFE BEGINS ANEW(1938, Ger.); OPERETTA(1949, Ger.); MICHAEL STRO-GOFF(1960, Fr./Ital./Yugo.); THREE PENNY OPERA(1963, Fr./Ger.)

Curt Jurgens
ONE APRIL 2000(1952, Aust.); RATS, THE(1955, Ger.); AND GOD CREATED WOMAN(1957, Fr.); DEVIL'S GENERAL, THE(1957, Ger.); ENEMY BELOW, THE(1957); BITTER VICTORY(1958, Fr.); CIRCUS OF LOVE(1958, Ger.); INN OF THE SIXTH HAPPINESS, THE(1958); ME AND THE COLONEL(1958); THIS HAPPY FEELING(1958); BLUE ANGEL, THE(1959); FERRY TO HONG KONG(1959, Brit.); HOUSE OF INTRIGUE, THE(1959, Ital.); TAMANGO(1959, Fr.); I AIM AT THE STARS(1960); THREE MOVES TO FREEDOM(1960, Ger.); BRAINWASHED(1961, Ger.); TIME BOMB(1961, Fr./Ital.); MAGNIFICENT SINNER(1963, Fr.); OF LOVE AND DESIRE(1963); DISORDER(1964, Fr./Ital.); ENCOUNTERS IN SALZBURG(1964, Ger.); HIDE AND SEEK(1964, Brit.); NUTTY, NAUGHTY CHATEAU(1964, Fr./Ital.); PSYCHE 59(1964, Brit.); LORD JIM(1965, Brit.); KARATE KILLERS, THE(1967); DEVIL IN SILK(1968, Ger.); NO ROSES FOR OSS 117(1968, Fr.); ASSASSINATION BUREAU, THE(1969, Brit.); BATTLE OF BRITAIN, THE(1969, Brit.); DOCTOR OF ST. PAUL, THE(1969, Ger.); CANNABIS(1970, Fr.); HELLO–GOODBYE(1970); INVINCIBLE SIX, THE(1970, U.S./Iran); PRIEST OF ST. PAULI(1970, Ger.); BATTLE OF THE NERETVA(1971, Yugo./Ital./Ger.); DIRTY HEROES(1971, Ital./Fr./Ger.); MEPHISTO WALTZ, THE(1971); NICHOLAS AND ALEXANDRA(1971, Brit.); KILL! KILL! KILL!(1972, Fr./Ger./Ital./Span.); CAGLIOSTRO(1975, Ital.); UNDERCOVERS HERO(1975, Brit.); TWIST, THE(1976, Fr.); SPY WHO LOVED ME, THE(1977, Brit.); BREAKTHROUGH(1978, Ger.); GOLDENGIRL(1979); JUST A GIGOLO(1979, Ger.)
Misc. Talkies
ORIENT EXPRESS(1952); SLAP IN THE FACE(1974); NURSES FOR SALE(1977); CRUISE MISSILE(1978)

Deana Jurgens
TIN MAN(1983)

Maximilian Jurgens
Misc. Silents
ONE OF MILLIONS(1914)

Albert Jurgensen
PURPLE TAXI, THE(1977, Fr./Ital./Ireland), ed

Edwin Jurgensen
COURT CONCERT, THE(1936, Ger.); LA HABANERA(1937, Ger.); LIFE BEGINS ANEW(1938, Ger.)

Randy Jurgensen
GOD TOLD ME TO(1976); SORCERER(1977); BRINK'S JOB, THE(1978); CRUISING(1980); MANIAC(1980)

William Jurgensen
TERROR IN THE WAX MUSEUM(1973), ph

Albert Jurgenson
CHEATERS, THE(1961, Fr.), ed; LA BELLE AMERICAINE(1961, Fr.), ed; TRUTH, THE(1961, Fr./Ital.), ed; EMPIRE OF NIGHT, THE(1963, Fr.), ed; PLEASE, NOT NOW!(1963, Fr./Ital.), ed; RIFIFI IN TOKYO(1963, Fr./Ital.), ed; MODERATO CANTABILE(1964, Fr./Ital.), ed; SECRET OF MAGIC ISLAND, THE(1964, Fr./Ital.), ed; COUNTERFEIT CONSTABLE, THE(1966, Fr.), ed; DEFECTOR, THE(1966, Ger./Fr.), ed; MARCO THE MAGNIFICENT(1966, Ital./Fr./Yugo./Egypt/Afghanistan), ed; SUCKER, THE(1966, Fr./Ital.), ed; BRAIN, THE(1969, Fr./US), ed; DON'T LOOK NOW(1969, Brit./Fr.), ed; SICILIAN CLAN, THE(1970, Fr.), ed; DELUSIONS OF GRANDEUR(1971 Fr.), ed; JE T'AIME, JE T'AIME(1972, Fr./Swed.), ed; ADVENTURES OF RABBI JACOB, THE(1973, Fr.), ed; IMPOSSIBLE OBJECT(1973, Fr.), ed; STAVISKY(1974, Fr.), ed; LUMIERE(1976, Fr.), ed; PROVIDENCE(1977, Fr.), ed; ADOLESCENT, THE(1978, Fr./W.Ger.), ed; MON ONCLE D'AMERIQUE(1980, Fr.), ed; INQUISITOR, THE(1982, Fr.), ed; BENVENUTA(1983, Fr.), ed
1984
DOG DAY(1984, Fr.), ed; LIFE IS A BED OF ROSES(1984, Fr.), ed

Aseneth Jurgenson
NATIONAL LAMPOON'S ANIMAL HOUSE(1978)

Randy Jurgenson
SUPERMAN(1978); FORT APACHE, THE BRONX(1981); STILL OF THE NIGHT(1982)

William Jurgenson
ARNOLD(1973), ph

Jurgen Jurges
FEAR EATS THE SOUL(1974, Ger.), ph
1984
GERMANY PALE MOTHER(1984, Ger.), ph; WOMAN IN FLAMES, A(1984, Ger.), ph

Julie Juristova
NINTH HEART, THE(1980, Czech.)

Franco Jurjek
CAVE OF THE LIVING DEAD(1966, Yugo./Ger.), set d

Walter Jurman
GREAT COMMANDMENT, THE(1941), m

Walter Jurmann
TRAPEZE(1932, Ger.), m; MAN STOLEN(1934, Fr.), m; ESCAPADE(1935), m; DAY AT THE RACES, A(1937), m; KILL OR BE KILLED(1950), p

Kara Juro
DIARY OF A SHINJUKU BURGLAR(1969, Jap.)

Albert Juross
LES CARABINIERS(1968, Fr./Ital.); SMUGGLERS, THE(1969, Fr.)

Erin Jo Jurow
END OF AUGUST, THE(1982), prod d

Martin Jurow
HANGING TREE, THE(1959), p; FUGITIVE KIND, THE(1960), p; BREAKFAST AT TIFFANY'S(1961), p; LOVE IN A GOLDFISH BOWL(1961), p; SOLDIER IN THE RAIN(1963), p; PINK PANTHER, THE(1964), p; GREAT RACE, THE(1965), p; WALTZ ACROSS TEXAS(1982), p; TERMS OF ENDEARMENT(1983), p

Georg Jurowski
Silents
SIEGFRIED(1924, Ger.)

Members of the Juruba Tribes
SANDERS OF THE RIVER(1935, Brit.)

Richard Jury
BROTHERS O'TOOLE, THE(1973); IN SEARCH OF HISTORIC JESUS(1980)

Maya Jusanova
FRENCH CANCAN(1956, Fr.)

Brigitte Juslin
PARIS BELONGS TO US(1962, Fr.); SUITOR, THE(1963, Fr.)

Galliano Juso
DESIRE, THE INTERIOR LIFE(1980, Ital,/Ger.), p

V. Jusov
MEXICO IN FLAMES(1982, USSR/Mex./Ital.), ph

Vadim Jusov
SOLARIS(1972, USSR), ph

Jussara
GRAND SLAM(1968, Ital., Span., Ger.)

Raggah Jussef
OPERATION CAMEL(1961, Den.)

Gerhard Just
UNWILLING AGENT(1968, Ger.)

Monique Just
I SPIT ON YOUR GRAVE(1962, Fr.); PSYCOSISSIMO(1962, Ital.); SIN ON THE BEACH(1964, Fr.)

Phillip Just [Filippano Sanjust]
CALTIKI, THE IMMORTAL MONSTER(1959, Ital.), w

Norton Juster
PHANTOM TOLLBOOTH, THE(1970), w

Paulo Justi
WHO'S GOT THE BLACK BOX?(1970, Fr./Gr./Ital.)

Roy Justi
Misc. Silents
HEART OF THE NORTH, THE(1921)

Barry Justice
KING AND COUNTRY(1964, Brit.); CARNABY, M.D.(1967, Brit.)

Bill Justice
FANTASIA(1940), anim; THREE CABALLEROS, THE(1944), anim; MAKE MINE MUSIC(1946), anim; ALICE IN WONDERLAND(1951), anim; PETER PAN(1953), anim

Edgar Justice
GOLDEN NEEDLES(1974)

James R. Justice
DOCTOR IN THE HOUSE(1954, Brit.)

James Robertson Justice
COMING-OUT PARTY, A(; CHAMPAGNE CHARLIE(1944, Brit.); FIDDLERS THREE(1944, Brit.); FOR THOSE IN PERIL(1944, Brit.); AGAINST THE WIND(1948, Brit.); VICE VERSA(1948, Brit.); CHRISTOPHER COLUMBUS(1949, Brit.); MY BROTHER JONATHAN(1949, Brit.); POET'S PUB(1949, Brit.); PRIVATE ANGELO(1949, Brit.); QUARTET(1949, Brit.); SCOTT OF THE ANTARCTIC(1949, Brit.); STOP PRESS GIRL(1949, Brit.); TIGHT LITTLE ISLAND(1949, Brit.); BLACK ROSE, THE(1950); PRELUDE TO FAME(1950, Brit.); ANNE OF THE INDIES(1951); BLACKMAILED(1951, Brit.); CAPTAIN HORATIO HORNBLOWER(1951, Brit.); DAVID AND BATHSHEBA(1951); LADY SAYS NO, THE(1951); OPERATION X(1951, Brit.); POOL OF LONDON(1951, Brit.); LES MISERABLES(1952); MISS ROBIN HOOD(1952, Brit.); STORY OF ROBIN HOOD, THE(1952, Brit.); MURDER WILL OUT(1953, Brit.); SWORD AND THE ROSE, THE(1953); ROB ROY, THE HIGHLAND ROGUE(1954, Brit.); DOCTOR AT SEA(1955, Brit.); LAND OF THE PHARAOHS(1955); STORM OVER THE NILE(1955, Brit.); ABOVE US THE WAVES(1956, Brit.); IRON PETTICOAT, THE(1956, Brit.); MOBY DICK(1956, Brit.); ALLIGATOR NAMED DAISY, AN(1957, Brit.); CAMPBELL'S KINGDOM(1957, Brit.); CHECKPOINT(1957, Brit.); DOCTOR AT LARGE(1957, Brit.); LIVING IDOL, THE(1957); OUT OF THE CLOUDS(1957, Brit.); ORDERS TO KILL(1958, Brit.); BEASTS OF MARSEILLES, THE(1959, Brit.); DOCTOR IN LOVE(1960, Brit.); FRENCH MISTRESS(1960, Brit.); GUNS OF NAVARONE, THE(1961); MURDER SHE SAID(1961, Brit.); UPSTAIRS AND DOWNSTAIRS(1961, Brit.); GUNS OF DARKNESS(1962, Brit.); ROOMMATES(1962, Brit.); DOCTOR IN DISTRESS(1963, Brit.); DR. CRIPPEN(1963, Brit.); FAST LADY, THE(1963, Brit.); LOVE ON A PILLOW(1963, Fr./Ital.); PAIR OF BRIEFS, A(1963, Brit.); FATHER CAME TOO(1964, Brit.); FACE OF FU MANCHU, THE(1965, Brit.); THOSE MAGNIFICENT MEN IN THEIR FLYING MACHINES; OR HOW I FLEWFROM LONDON TO PARIS IN 25 HOURS AND 11 MINUTES(1965, Brit.); UP FROM THE BEACH(1965); YOU MUST BE JOKING!(1965, Brit.); CARNABY, M.D.(1967, Brit.); HELL IS EMPTY(1967, Brit./Ital); TWO WEEKS IN SEPTEMBER(1967, Fr./Brit.); CHITTY CHITTY BANG BANG(1968, Brit.); DOCTOR IN TROUBLE(1970, Brit.); SOME WILL, SOME WON'T(1970, Brit.)
Misc. Talkies
ZETA ONE(1969)

Katherine Justice
WAY WEST, THE(1967); FIVE CARD STUD(1968); LIMBO(1972); FRASIER, THE SENSUOUS LION(1973); SEPARATE WAYS(1981)
Misc. Talkies
STEPMOTHER, THE(1973)

Maibelle Herkes Justice
Silents
END OF THE TRAIL, THE(1916), w

Martin Justice
Misc. Silents
BLIND MAN'S HOLIDAY(1917), d; INDIAN SUMMER OF DRY VALLEY JOHNSON, THE(1917), d; SKYLIGHT ROOM, THE(1917), d; SOAP GIRL, THE(1918), d

Susan Justice
WILD, WILD PLANET, THE(1967, Ital.)
Misc. Talkies
SWINGING COEDS, THE(1976)

George Justin
MIDDLE OF THE NIGHT(1959), p; SOMETHING WILD(1961), p; TIGER MAKES OUT, THE(1967), p; CHINATOWN(1974)
John Justin
THIEF OF BAGHDAD, THE(1940, Brit.); GENTLE SEX, THE(1943, Brit.); JOURNEY TOGETHER(1946, Brit.); CALL OF THE BLOOD(1948, Brit.); ANGEL WITH THE TRUMPET, THE(1950, Brit.); BREAKING THE SOUND BARRIER(1952); HOT ICE(1952, Brit.); KING OF THE KHYBER RIFLES(1953); MELBA(1953, Brit.); VILLAGE, THE(1953, Brit./Switz.); CREST OF THE WAVE(1954, Brit.); MAN WHO LOVED REDHEADS, THE(1955, Brit.); TECKMAN MYSTERY, THE(1955, Brit); UNTAMED(1955); GUILTY?(1956, Brit.); SAFARI(1956); ISLAND IN THE SUN(1957); SPIDER'S WEB, THE(1960, Brit.); CANDIDATE FOR MURDER(1966, Brit.); SAVAGE MESSIAH(1972, Brit.); LISZTOMANIA(1975, Brit.); VALENTINO(1977, Brit.); BIG SLEEP, THE½(1978, Brit.); TRENCHCOAT(1983)
Larry Justin
MEAT CLEAVER MASSACRE(1977)
Morgan Len Justin
FATE IS THE HUNTER(1964)
Nikki Justin
YOU FOR ME(1952)
Susan Justin
FORBIDDEN WORLD(1982), m; FINAL TERROR, THE(1983), m; STRYKER(1983, Phil.), m
William Justin
HIS KIND OF WOMAN(1951)
Frances Dee Justine
WELLS FARGO(1937)
Martin Justine
Misc. Silents
THEY SHALL PAY(1921), d
William Justine
GANG BUSTERS(1955); BRIDE AND THE BEAST, THE(1958); OCEAN'S ELEVEN(1960); TRAUMA(1962)
Carlo Justini
NOVEL AFFAIR, A(1957, Brit.); INTENT TO KILL(1958, Brit.); WHOLE TRUTH, THE(1958, Brit.); SILENT ENEMY, THE(1959, Brit.); FOUR DESPERATE MEN(1960, Brit.)
Bill Justis
DEAR, DEAD DELILAH(1972), m; SMOKEY AND THE BANDIT(1977), m; HOOPER(1978), m; VILLAIN, THE(1979), m; ISLAND CLAWS(1981), m
Joseph Justman
NEW MEXICO(1951), p; UNWED MOTHER(1958), p; SWEET SMELL OF LOVE(1966, Ital./Ger.), p
Paul Justman
1984
GIMME AN 'F'(1984), d
Rafael Justo
TRAIN ROBBERY CONFIDENTIAL(1965, Braz.), ed; LOLLIPOP(1966, Braz.), ed
Nikki Juston
LAW AND THE LADY, THE(1951)
Terry Juston
Misc. Talkies
MISS LESLIE'S DOLLS(1972)
Kevin Justrich
S.O.B.(1981)
Tracy Justrich
SGT. PEPPER'S LONELY HEARTS CLUB BAND(1978)
Hannalore Juterbock
ORDERED TO LOVE(1963, Ger.)
Claude Jutra
TAKE IT ALL(1966, Can.), a, p, d, w, ed; MY UNCLE ANTOINE(1971, Can.), a, d, w, ed; KAMOURASKA(1973, Can./Fr.), d, w; TWO SOLITUDES(1978, Can.); BY DESIGN(1982), d, w
Richard Jutras
1984
HOTEL NEW HAMPSHIRE, THE(1984)
Bob Jutson
RACE WITH THE DEVIL(1975)
William Jutte
HE KNEW WOMEN(1930), w
Herbert Juttke
SECRET AGENT(1933, Brit.), w; I WAS AN ADVENTURESS(1940), w
R. Juttke
ALIBI, THE(1939, Fr.), w; ALIBI, THE(1943, Brit.), w
Christian Juttner
I WANNA HOLD YOUR HAND(1978); RETURN FROM WITCH MOUNTAIN(1978); SWARM, THE(1978)
Shelly Juttner
FREAKY FRIDAY(1976)
William B. Jutto
CHINATOWN NIGHTS(1929), w
Phil Jutzl
BERLIN ALEXANDERPLATZ(1933, Ger.), d
Ole Juul
CRAZY PARADISE(1965, Den.), w
Vida Juvan
CAVE OF THE LIVING DEAD(1966, Yugo./Ger.)
Jeanne Juvelier
JOHNNY HOLIDAY(1949)
Pierre Juvenet
CALL, THE(1938, Fr.); DEVIL'S DAUGHTER(1949, Fr.)
Nathalie Juvent
1984
SWANN IN LOVE(1984, Fr.Ger.)
Philippe Juzau
TESTAMENT OF ORPHEUS, THE(1962, Fr.)
lana Jvandova
DAY THAT SHOOK THE WORLD, THE(1977, Yugo./Czech.)

Tsou Jyh-liang
DRAGON INN(1968, Chi.), art d
John Jympson
FRENCH MISTRESS(1960, Brit.), ed; RISK, THE(1961, Brit.), ed; SECRET OF MONTE CRISTO, THE(1961, Brit.), ed; PRIZE OF ARMS, A(1962, Brit.), ed; DREAM MAKER, THE(1963, Brit.), ed; HARD DAY'S NIGHT, A(1964, Brit.), ed; STORK TALK(1964, Brit.), ed; ZULU(1964, Brit.), ed; BEDFORD INCIDENT, THE(1965, Brit.), ed; DINGAKA(1965, South Africa), ed; SANDS OF THE KALAHARI(1965, Brit.), ed; KALEIDOSCOPE(1966, Brit.), ed; BOBO, THE(1967, Brit.), ed; MAN WHO FINALLY DIED, THE(1967, Brit.), ed; MAROC 7(1967, Brit.), ed; DEADFALL(1968, Brit.), ed; WHERE EAGLES DARE(1968, Brit.), ed; KELLY'S HEROES(1970, U.S./Yugo.), ed; WALKING STICK, THE(1970, Brit.), ed; FLIGHT OF THE DOVES(1971), ed; FRENZY(1972, Brit.), ed; NIGHT WATCH(1973, Brit.), ed; OPTIMISTS, THE(1973, Brit.), ed; DOVE, THE(1974, Brit.), ed; MR. QUILP(1975, Brit.), ed; CRIME AND PASSION(1976, U.S., Ger.), ed; INCREDIBLE SARAH, THE(1976, Brit.), ed; LITTLE NIGHT MUSIC, A(1977, Aust./U.S./Ger.), ed; MEETINGS WITH REMARKABLE MEN(1979, Brit.), ed; BEYOND THE REEF(1981), ed; GREEN ICE(1981, Brit.), ed; HIGH ROAD TO CHINA(1983), ed